KENKYUSHA'S
NEW COLLEGIATE
JAPANESE-ENGLISH DICTIONARY

新和英中辞典

第三版

早稲田大学教授
市川繁治郎

シェフィールド大学教授
R.M.V. Collick

武蔵大学教授
日南田一男

早稲田大学教授
牧 雅夫

KENKYUSHA

© 1983　株式会社　研究社 (Kenkyusha Ltd.)

新 和 英 中 辞 典

第 1 版 1933 年
第 2 版 1963 年
第 3 版 1983 年

はしがき

　この改訂第3版を作るに際しての私たちの目標は、英語の実態に即した辞書を提供することであった。そのためには、記載する訳語・訳文は、すべて、英米人が認める現代英語であること、そして、日本語の意味をよく伝えるものであること、を条件とし、この条件に合わないものは載せない、という方針を定めた。

　この方針を貫くために、たとえ我が国の学校で教えられてきた英語であっても、今日の英語の実態と合わない点があるときは、思い切って改めた。それは本辞典の英語の随所に盛られているが、このことを特に明らかにしたい場合は、さらに ★ や 用法 のマークを付けて、注・解説を施した。

　日本語に対しても、同様の方針を採り、各種の国語辞典を参考にはしたが、国語辞典の定義にとらわれず、現在、実際に使われている日本語の語義・慣用を尊重することとした。また、日本語の普通の表現で今までの辞書に洩れているものを、できるだけ広く収集採録することに努めた。

　和英辞典は英語を書くための辞書であるという考えで、これまでの和英辞典は作られてきたと言ってよいと思う。この考えは本書でも変わりはない。しかし、今日のように国際交流が盛んになってくると、口頭によるコミュニケーションにも大いに留意しなければ、真に役立つ現代の和英辞典にはならないであろう。また、今では口頭で使われる英語が書き言葉に盛んに使われるようになってきてもいる。この現実を重視して、この改訂版では日常英語を優先することにした。

　この改訂版で新たに目につくのは、《文》という表示が多用されていることであろう。日常英語ではあまり使われないやや堅い表現にこの表示を施したが、これは今回の新しい試みであり、本書の大きな特徴となっている。なお、《文》、《口語》、《俗》等の意味については、「この辞書の読み方」の中で詳しく解説してあるので、ぜひよく読んでいただきたい。これらの使用域表示は、主に Collick が担当した。

　私たちは、記載したすべての事項について、頻繁な編集会議、原稿及び校正刷りの航空便による往復、などによって、徹底的な討議をした。これによって、従来の和英辞典に見られた不自然な、または、古臭い表現は、まず完全に排除することができたと思う。《文》、《口語》、《俗》等の区別に

注意して下さりさえすれば、本書に記載した英語は、どれも、安心して使っていただけるものである。また、下欄にまとめた文例は、現代の生活感覚を持った新鮮な内容のものを多く掲載した。旧版同様、この部分だけを、軽い知的な読み物としても利用していただけると思う。

この改訂作業に当たって、編集部では、編集担当取締役 河野亨雄氏の下に、大橋 進氏が終始一貫、実務の推進に当たられ、編集の最終段階では窪田幸夫氏が参加して、ご尽力下さった。また、上下両欄に分かれた複雑な組版などで、栗林みつ子氏をはじめとする製版所の方々には多大なご面倒を煩わした。校正を担当された多くの方々のご努力も忘れることができない。これらすべての方々に心から感謝の意を表する。関係者各位のご協力によって、本書を、面目を一新した現代の辞書として世に送り出すことができることは、私たちの無上の喜びである。

この改訂には、全員、最善の努力を尽くしたが、まだ不備な点の見落としがあるやもしれない。そのような点については、ぜひ、ご指摘をいただきたい。読者の方々のご協力を得て、この辞書をさらによいものにしていきたいと念願している。

1983年7月　　　　　　　　　　　　　　　　　　　　編　者　識

刊行のことば

　この辞書の前身、岡倉由三郎編 *Kenkyusha's New School Dictionary (Japanese-English)*『新和英中辞典』——のちに『スクール和英新辞典』と改称——が出版されたのは 1933 年のことでありました。これは主として学生を対象とした和英学習辞典として好評を博し、英語学習の促進に貢献するところ多大でありました。戦後 1963 年に、増田 綱氏によって改訂が行なわれ、和名を再び『新和英中辞典』に戻して出版いたしました。以来 20 年にわたって多くの方々の支持を得て版を重ねて参りましたが、今回ようやく、全面的に稿を改めた改訂新版を刊行する運びとなりました。

　この第 3 版は高校生・大学生を対象とする学習辞典として、英語のタイトルを *Kenkyusha's New Collegiate Japanese-English Dictionary* と改めましたが、内容的には一般社会人の方々に充分に利用していただけるものを持っております。

　この改訂新版の執筆には、早稲田大学教授 市川繁治郎、英国シェフィールド大学日本研究所教授 R.M.V. Collick, 武蔵大学教授 日南田一男、早稲田大学教授 牧 雅夫の 4 氏が当たられ、内容を徹底的に書き改められました。

　市川繁治郎氏は、研究社『新和英大辞典』の編集主任として、また、本辞典の第 2 版を初めいくつかの和英辞典を手がけられ、その経験と貯えられた資料カードの量において、現在の日本における有数の和英辞典編纂者であり、日南田一男氏もまた、本辞典の第 2 版、さらに、『新和英大辞典』の執筆と編集協力の作業にたずさわり、和英辞典に長年の経験を有する方であります。今回新たに加わられた 牧 雅夫氏は、従来の和英辞典について一家言を持たれ、日頃関心を払っておられる英語の基本語彙の意味と用法の研究の成果を活かし、平易な日常英語の表現が多くなるように努められました。

　今回の改訂で特筆すべき点は、英国人の日本語学者として、Collick 博士が執筆陣に加わられたことであります。インフォーマントとして英米人に協力してもらうことは、既にいくつもの和英辞典で行なわれておりますが、それでは、どうしても不充分で、日本人の執筆者の気付かない不備の点が残るものであります。今回の改訂では、Collick 博士が、その驚くべき該博な日本語の知識を駆使されて、隅々まで、全面的に日本語と英語の

照合・勘案に当たられました。また米語についての疑問点については、多くのアメリカ人の助言を求めて解決されました。これによって、従来の和英辞典について言われた、古めかしい表現が残っているとか、いろいろの文体の例文が無差別に並べられている、というような批判に対して、この改訂版は充分な答となりうるものと確信いたします。

執筆者4氏は、それぞれの持ち味を出し合い、執筆に当たられましたが、同時に、突っ込んだ話し合いを行なって、それぞれの記述にメスを加えられました。企画の当初から校了にいたるまで、丸一日を費やした編集会議は合計121回に及び、特にCollick氏の2回にわたる長期の日本滞在中には集中的に編集会議が開かれました。こうした4氏の緊密なご協力によって、ここに、真に信頼できる、すべて生きた英語から成る和英辞典を刊行することができますことは、小社の誇りとするところでありますが、それにもましてご執筆の4氏の並々ならぬご努力に対する感謝は、ことばに尽くせぬものがあります。この画期的な新辞典が、できるだけ多くの方方に利用されますことを願ってやみません。

最後に、編集については、関係者一同ベストを尽くしましたが、誤植の見逃しなど不備な点につきましては、ご指摘・ご教示をいただきたく、お願い申し上げます。

1983年7月　　　　　　　　　　　　　　　　社長　植田虎雄

目　次

はしがき iii
刊行のことば v
この辞書の読み方 viii

新和英中辞典 1–1348

付　録

不規則動詞活用表 1351
米英の綴り字の違い 1354
英語句読法 1355
英語の手紙・名刺・履歴書 1362
年号対照表 1369
度量衡複式換算表 1370

この辞書の読み方

I 上下段の区分

各ページを上下に区切り、上段には見出し語とその訳、句例、連語を収め、下段には文例を示した。

II 見出し語

(1) かな見出しとし、五十音順に配列した。外来語、外国の地名・人名などはカタカナ書きとした。

(2) 同じかなの場合は、清音、濁音、半濁音の順にした。

　　例： てんけん 点検、でんげん 電源
　　　　 はんば 飯場、はんば 半端

(3) つまる音、拗音の表記に用いた小さい字(っ、ゃ、ゅ、ょ)は、大きい字のあとにした。

　　例： はつか 二十日、はっか¹ 発火、はっか² 〖植〗
　　　　 しや 視野、しゃ¹ 紗、しゃ² 斜

(4) 長音を「ー」で表記した場合、例えば**インターン、イースト、ウーマンリブ、ウエーブ、イコール**は、インタ<u>ア</u>ン、イ<u>イ</u>スト、ウ<u>ウ</u>マンリブ、ウエ<u>エ</u>ブ、イコ<u>オ</u>ルの位置に配列した。

(5) 同音語の順序は原則として次のようにする。 (a) カタカナ表記のものはひらがな表記のもののあとに、(b) 活用しない品詞(例えば名詞)を先に、活用する品詞(例えば動詞)をあとに配列した。固有名詞は普通名詞のあとにした。そして、(c) 漢字表記を伴うものを先にし、かな表記だけのものをあとにした。また、(d) 漢字表記を示したもので漢字の字数が同じものについては、1字目の画数の少ないものから多いものへと配列し、1字目の画数が同じときは、2字目の画数の順とした。

同音語については、他の見出し語との相互参照のため、下段の文例検索の便を考えて右肩に番号をつけた。

　　例： ぼたん 〖植〗、ボタン
　　　　 さる¹ 猿、さる² 去る、さる³ 然る
　　　　 その¹ 園、その²
　　　　 いし¹ 石、いし² 医師、いし³ 意志、いし⁴ 意思、いし⁵ 遺志

(6) 独立して使われない語(助詞・接頭辞・接尾辞など)を見出しに立てた場合は、ハイフンをつけて、単語の後に置いた。

　　例： で¹ 出、で² 〈それで〉…、-で 〈場所〉…
　　　　 まい 舞、まい- 毎…、-まい¹ 枚、-まい²

(7) 漢字の使用は、常用漢字の範囲にとどめるのを原則とするが、意味の別を明らかにするために、その範囲外のものを用いることもある。

III 訳 語

(1) 同一見出し語にいろいろの意味がある場合、またはいくつかの訳を与えることができる場合には、主要なもの、普通のものを先にした。その場合、〈 〉を使って意味の区別を示し、必要に応じて、さらに（ ）内に説明を加えた。

　　例： ところ 所, 処 〈場所〉 a place; a spot (狭い); a
　　　　 scene (現場); a seat (所在地); 〈所番地〉 an ad-
　　　　 dress; 〈地方〉 a locality; a district; an area;
　　　　 〈家〉 *one's* house [home]; 〈点〉 a point; 〈文章
　　　　 の中の〉 a passage; 〈部分〉 a part.

(2) 見出し語の訳のあとは ¶ で句切って、以下に句例、連語を示した。記載事項の多い項目では、検索の便を計って、句例は見出し語のあとの助詞によって、「が」「の」「を」「に」の順にした。き³ (気) の項参照。

　　連語は見出し語があとにつくものを先に、前につくものをそのあとに、だいたい五十音順に配列した。

　　例： ざいせい² 財政... ¶...国家[地方]財政...財政援
　　　　 助...財政学...財政状態...財政難におちいる

(3) 訳語・訳文のうちで、使用域の点で注意を要するものについては、《文》、《口語》、《俗》、《卑》、《戯言》、《小児語》などの表示をした。

　　《文》の表示は、日本語で言う「文語」よりももっと意味を広げて、日常会話で使うのには堅い感じであまり使われない英語にすべてつけてある。この表示は文脈によってきまる相対的なものであって、ある特定の語が常に《文》であるとは限らない。例えば、「手を伸ばす」を extend *one's* arm と表現するのは《文》であるが、一般的に物を「伸ばす」意味で使われた extend は《文》ではない。get [grow, 《文》 become] rich の場合は get, grow に対して become は相対的に堅い感じになるので《文》であるが、become clear, become extinct などの句では get, grow などは用いられず、become に堅い感じはないので《文》ではない。confess (to) *one's* crime [sin]; confess that *one* has committed a crime;《文》confess *oneself* guilty のように、使い方によって《文》となる例もある。また、かなりくだけた話の中でも、面白味をもたせるためにわざと《文》の語を使うことも珍しくない。要は、《文》であることを承知の上で使うことである。なお、準専門語と考えられる用語、例えば antibacterial (抗菌性の)、(the art of) mnemonics (記憶術) のような語については、特に《文》の表示はしない。

　　《口語》の表示のある語句や文は、日常会話で一般に使われているが、言葉使いに気をつけねばならないような場面ではあまり使われない、ややくだけた表現である。

　　《俗》はだいたい、英語の slang に当たる。学生・同僚など、親しい者同士の間だけで、その会話に生き生きとした感じを与えるためによく使われるが、文章に書く際はもちろん、一般の会話でも避けられる言葉にこの表示をつけた。この中には、性などに関するタブー語なども含まれているし、はやりすたりもあるので、その言葉のフィーリングがよくわからないときは、使わないほうが安全である。なおこれらの表示 (《文》、《口語》、《俗》、《米》、《英》など) は同一項目内の同じ事項については、繰返して付けないことを原則とした。

この辞書は、全般的に、現代英語で用いられる普通の表現を示すことを眼目としているので、例えば、depend on [upon] という表記は採らず、depend on だけとしてある。will [shall] となる可能性のある場合も will だけにとどめてある。文脈から考えて、upon, shall でなければ適切を欠くと思われる時に限って upon, shall を用いた。He is older than I. の形を採らずに、He is older than me. としたのも同じ趣旨である（より² 囲法 参照）。

(4) 訳語の名詞に不定冠詞をつけてあるのは可算名詞 (countable noun)、無冠詞のものは不可算名詞 (uncountable noun) であるが、不定冠詞が ( ) に入れてある場合は、可算・不可算の両様の用法があることを示す。用法上注意すべき点があるときは、必要に応じて注を加えてある（くだものの項参照）。また、可算名詞のうちで、複数形で使われることが特に多いものについては、

　　　しげん² 資源 a (natural) resource; (natural) resources

のような記載法を採った項目もある。複数で使うのが普通の場合には

　　　そうるい² 藻類【植】(the) algae 《*sing.* alga》; seaweeds; waterweeds

のように記載した。

複数形が不規則変化をするものについては《 》を用いて、

　　　ちそう 地層 a (geologic) stratum 《*pl.* -ta》

のように表示し、規則変化・不規則変化の両様の変化のあるものについては、

　　　だいち² 台地 ...a plateau 《*pl.* -s, -x》

のように表示した。

語尾が -o で終わる語についても、a photo 《*pl.* -s》 / a potato 《*pl.* -es》 / a mosquito 《*pl.* -(e)s》 という記載をした。この最後の例は mosquitoes, mosquitos の両様があることを示す。

(5) 動植物名には英名がないものや、たとえあっても専門的に過ぎて一般には通じないものもある。例えば、貝のあさりを a Japanese little neck と訳しても実用性がないので、この辞書では an *asari* clam とした。ひぐらしは a *higurashi* cicada とした。

(6) 日本の事物で相当する英語がない場合は、英米人にその事物を説明するのに役立つような簡略な定義を示した。

(7) 訳語のなかでイタリック体にしたものは、外来語でまだ完全には英語化していないものである。

　　例： まんねんゆき 万年雪 ...《ドイツ語》*firn* (snow); 《フランス語》*névé*.

日本語から英語に入ったものについても同じ扱いをしたものがあるが、その場合は単複同形とみなして、複数語尾の -s を付した形はないものとした。

　　例： きもの 着物 〈和服〉 a *kimono*
　　　　ぞうり 草履 ...(a pair of) *zori*

(8) *one, one's, oneself*; *sb* (=somebody), *sb's* (=somebody's); *sth* (=something) もイタリック体にしてあるが、これは、文脈によって、I, we, my, our, myself, ourselves, he, she, they, his, Mary's, a dog, a pen, water, etc. のように自由に変化することを示す。このうち、だいたいにおいて、one は動作主または自分、

sb は動作主とは別の人あるいは他人を表わすと考えてよい。sb, sth を受ける代名詞は he, it とした。また、すべての動詞を代表する表記として do を用いた。

IV 記号の用法

(1) 《 》 (*a*) 英米語の区別や他の外国語、使用域の表示 (⇨ 上記 **III** (3)):
　　《米》、《英》、《米口語》、《英俗》
　　登場人物《ラテン語》the *dramatis personae*.
(*b*) 訳語の補足、前置詞・複数形の表示:
　　先史時代《study》the prehistory《of Japan》/
　　先頭に立つ be at the head《of》; take the lead
　　《in》; ....

この《 》内に示したのは用例であって、必ずしも、それが絶対に必要であることを意味するものではない。例えば、wait《for》は He waited for her arrival. のような用法を示すが、単に He waited. という文も、もちろんあるし、incompatible《with》は That is incompatible with this. という構造を示したものであるが、They are incompatible. という文を排除するものではない (複数形については ⇨ 上記 **III** (4))。

(2) 〈 〉 語義の区別を示す。⇨ 上記 **III** (1).
(3) ( ) (*a*) 省略できる語・句・綴りを示す:
　　型紙 a (paper) pattern / 見掛けによらず despite appearances (to the contrary) / 級の首席を占めている be (at the) top of the class / つげ材 box(wood) / あみだ(くじ)をやる / 農具 a farm(ing) tool.
(*b*) 簡単な追加説明:
　　(選手が)調子を崩さないようにする keep in training / 停学《英》rustication (大学の).
(4) [ ] (*a*) その前の語句の言いかえ:
　　定額 a fixed amount [sum] / 入る come [go, get, step] in [into] / 仲裁人[者] an arbitrator.

なお、言いかえ部分の範囲がまぎらわしいときは、[ ] 内の初めの部分を一部重複させてある:
　　I hadn't thought that he was as foolish as that [《口語》he was that foolish].
(*b*) 2種または数種の語句を一括する:
　　学者[芸術家]かたぎの人 a man of scholarly type [an artistic temperament] / 一般に使用されている[されるようになる] be in [come into] general use.
(5) 〘 〙 専門語などの表示:
　　〘動〙〘植〙〘気象〙〘音楽〙〘諺〙〘掲示〙.
(6) < 語源を示す:
　　ゼッケン [<《ドイツ語》*Decken*].
(7) ¶ 句例・連語の初めを示す。
(8) / と |: / は句例・文例の境界を、| は文例を2つ以上列記した場合の境界を示す。

(9) ⇨　参照項目の指示。関連事項が他項目にある場合、⇨ によってその事を示し、この辞書を有機的・総合的に利用できるように配慮してある。

(10) 文例⇩　本文の項目末尾に付して、下段に関連した文例があることを示す。文例は左右に開いた見開きの両ページの中に収めてある。

(11) 囲説　⇨ 下記 V.

(12) ★　⇨ 下記 V.

V　参考事項の注

訳語・訳文などだけでは充分に説明できない事柄については、随所に注解を加えた。やや長い解説は項目の末尾に 囲説 で示し、短いものは関係箇所に ★ のマークをつけて入れた。

この ★ は、例えば、

　　でいり　出入り〈人の〉…;〈収支〉income and expenditure; receipts and expenditures ★ 日・英順序が逆になる点に注意

のように、前の記述全体に関するものは（ ）をつけずに入れ、

　　ところが　but; however; and yet; on the contrary; as it is [was] (★ 仮定法の文のあとに用いて、「ところが実際には」と直説法に切換える).

のように、直前の1つの語句だけ（この例では as it is [was]）に関するものは（ ）でくくった。

VI　スペリングその他

(1) スペリングは米国式とした：
　　honor; judgment; meter; offense; skillful; traveler.

ただし、《英》のスペリングが《米》と著しく異なる場合は《英》a gaol のように示した。また《英》独特の表現を示す場合のスペリングは英国式とした。

(2) ハイフンは - と - の2つを使用した。- はその語に本来必要なもの、またはその表現では省けないものを示し、- はその語を行末から次行にわたって印刷するために、たまたま分離したことを示す。

VII　文　例

(1) 文例は原則として、上段の本文で扱いにくい表現を、文脈の明らかになる完全な文の形で示すためのものであるが、中には本文で示した語句が文の中でどのように使われるかを示すためのものも含まれている。

本文の見出し語に肩番号のあるものについては、同じ番号を文例の見出しにもつけた。

完全な文の形になっていないもの、例えば、「私の説は…だ」In my opinion …;《文》I am of the opinion that… のようなものは、たとえ大文字で始まっていても本文で扱った。その他、文の形になっているものでも、ごく簡単で短いものは、小文字で本文扱いとしたものがある。

例: the sun rises / night falls.

文例については、煩を避けて、《文》、《口語》等の表示は特別に必要と思われるもの以外は省いてある。
(2) 諺については、日本語の諺に非常に近い英語の諺がある場合はそれを載せて、そのあとに〖諺〗の表示をつけた。日本語の諺にぴったりする諺がない場合が多いが、その場合には、使われなくなったものや、その趣旨にずれのあるものをあえて載せることはせず、日本語の諺の趣旨を伝える英語を載せた。その場合には〖諺〗の表示はつけない。

略 語 表

〖医〗 医 学	〖劇〗 演 劇	〖商〗 商 業	〖電〗 電 気
〖化〗 化 学	〖建〗 建 築	〖植〗 植 物	〖動〗 動 物
〖貝〗 貝 類	〖工〗 工 学	〖数〗 数 学	〖物〗 物理学
〖海〗 海 事	〖光〗 光 学	〖生化〗生化学	〖法〗 法 律
〖解〗 解剖学	〖鉱〗 鉱 物	〖鳥〗 鳥 類	〖紋〗 紋章学
〖機〗 機 械	〖昆〗 昆 虫	〖哲〗 哲 学	〖薬〗 薬 学
〖魚〗 魚 類	〖史〗 歴 史	〖天〗 天文学	〖論〗 論理学
sing. 単 数	*pl.* 複 数	*sb* =somebody	*sth* =something

上記のほか〖映画〗〖航空〗〖測量〗〖体操〗などなるべく自明のものを用いた。

あ

ああ[1] 〈あのように〉like that ¶ああいう男 a man like that [him] ; that sort of (a) man ; 《文》such a man (as he) / ああいうふうに (in) that way ; like that. 文例↓

ああ[2], 〈感動〉Ah! ; Oh! ; 〈肯定〉yes ; 〈呼び掛け〉O! ; Oh! ; I say! 文例↓

アーカンソー Arkansas (略: Ark.) ¶アーカンソー州の人 an Arkansan.

アークとう アーク灯 an arc lamp [light].

アーケード an arcade.

アース 【電】《米》(a) ground ; 《英》(an) earth ¶アースする ground ; earth / アース線 a ground [an earth] wire.

アーチ an arch ; 〈杉・檜(ひのき)などの葉で包んだ〉緑門》a green arch.

アーチェリー archery.

アート art ¶アートペーパー 《米》coated paper ; 《英》art paper.

アーメン Amen!

アーモンド an almond.

アール 〈面積の単位〉an are.

アールエイチ Rh [＜rhesus] ¶Rh因子 an Rh [a rhesus] factor / Rh式血液型 (blood types of) Rh groups / Rhプラス Rh positive (略: Rh＋) / Rhマイナス Rh negative (略: Rh－).

あーん 〈子供が〉あーん，あーんと泣く wail ; bawl. 文例↓

あい[1] 愛 love (for *sb*, of *sth*) ; affection (for, toward) ¶親の愛 parental love / 愛の告白をする declare *one*'s love (to) / 愛を誓い合う promise to love each other (for ever) ; 《文》exchange tender vows / 子の愛に溺(おぼ)れる dote on *one*'s child / 愛に報いる return [《文》requite] *sb*'s love ; love *sb* back.

あい[2] 藍 〈植物〉a Japanese indigo plant ; 〈色〉indigo (blue) ; deep blue (color) ¶あいに染める dye《a cloth》deep blue / あい色の indigo ; deep blue.

あいあいがさ 相合傘 ¶相合傘で under one umbrella.

アイアン 〖ゴルフ〗an iron.

あいいれない 相容れない be inconsistent [incompatible] , 《文》irreconcilable《with》; contradict ; run counter《to》.

あいいん 愛飲 ¶愛飲する drink《Scotch whisky》regularly ; be fond of drinking《a particular brand of *sake*》.

あいうち 相打ち ¶相打ちになる hit [kill] each other at the same time.

アイエムエフ ⇨こくさい[2] (国際通貨基金).

アイエルオーじょうやく アイエルオー条約 the ILO [International Labor Organization] Convention.

あいえんか 愛煙家 a regular [habitual] smoker.

アイオワ Iowa (略: Ia.) ¶アイオワ州の人 an Iowan.

あいか 哀歌 an elegy ; 《文》a threnody ⇨ばんか[1].

あいかぎ 合鍵 〈同じ鍵〉a duplicate key ; 〈どれにも合う鍵〉a master key ; a passkey ; a skeleton key.

あいかわらず 相変わらず as usual ; as always ; as before ¶相変わらず貧乏である be as poor as ever.

あいかん 哀歓 ¶人生の哀歓《文》the joys and sorrows of life.

あいがん 哀願《文》an entreaty ; an appeal ; a (humble) petition ; 《文》supplication ¶哀願する implore [《文》entreat]《*sb* to *do*》; make a (humble) petition《to *sb*》; 《文》supplicate《*sb* to *do*, *sb* for pardon》; appeal《to *sb* for mercy》/ 哀願するように imploringly.

あいがん 愛玩 ¶愛玩する pet《a dog》; fondle / 愛玩犬 a pet dog / 愛玩動物 a pet.

あいぎ 合着 a spring [an autumn] suit.

あいきどう 合気道 *aikido*, an art of self-defense derived from *judo*, in which the opponent's joints are used to advantage in executing holds and throws.

アイキュー an IQ [I.Q.] ; an intelligence quotient ¶IQが109ある have an IQ of 109.

あいきょう 愛嬌 (personal) charm ; attractiveness ¶愛嬌のある charming ; attractive / 愛嬌のある失敗 an amusing blunder / 愛嬌のない unattractive ; blunt ; curt / 愛嬌を振りまく try to please everybody ; make *oneself* pleasant (say nice things) to everybody / ご愛嬌に100円まける take 100 yen off the price for

---

ああ[1] 彼がああまで有名とは知らなかった. I did not know he was so [that] famous. | ああ言えばこう言うという男だ. He's always ready to talk [answer] back. | He always wants to have the last word. | あの男はいつもああだ. He's always like that. | ああでもないこうでもないと悩んでだいぶ時間を無駄にした. I wasted a good deal of time trying to decide between this, that, and the other. | さんざんああでもな

いこうでもないと言ったが, やっと我々と同行することを承知した. After a lot of shilly-shallying [《英》humming and hawing] he at last agreed to come with us. / 彼は我々のすることをああでもないこうでもないとけちをつけるのだ. He's forever finding fault with what we do.

ああ[2] ああ, 思い出した. Oh, yes, I remember it now. | ああうれしい. Oh, I am pleased [glad]! | ああそうですか. Oh, really? | Oh, is

that so? | ゆうべはよく眠れたかい.—ああ, 眠れた. Did you sleep well last night?—Yes, I did. | この映画は見たくないのか.—ああ, 見たくない. Don't you want to see this movie?—No, I don't.

あーん 口をあーんと開けてごらん. 〈医者が子供に〉Say 'aah', | 〈歯医者が〉Open your mouth wide.

あいかわらず 医者に止められても彼は相変わらずタバコを吸っている. He keeps on smoking in spite of his doctor's warning.

あいきょうしん 愛郷心 love of one's hometown [birthplace].

あいくち 合口〈短刀〉a dagger ¶合口を呑んでいる have a dagger concealed under one's clothes.

あいくるしい 愛くるしい lovely; charming; sweet;《米》cute.

あいけん 愛犬 one's pet dog ¶愛犬家 a lover of dogs; a dog lover [fancier].

あいこ[1] 愛顧《文》favor;《文》patronage; custom ¶愛顧を請う《文》solicit sb's patronage [custom]. 文例⇩

あいこ[2]〖あいこになる〈勝負が〉end in a tie;〈勝負で〉tie with sb.;〈仕返しなどの末〉get [be] even [quits] with sb. 文例⇩

あいご 愛護 kind treatment; protection ¶愛護する treat (an animal) kindly; be kind (to) / 動物愛護の精神 kindness to animals.

あいこう 愛好 ¶愛好する love; be a lover of; be fond of; have a liking for ¶愛好者 a lover;〈動植物の〉a fancier;〈芸術などの〉a devotee;〈スポーツなどの〉an enthusiast; a fan. 文例⇩

あいこうしん 愛校心 love of [for] one's school;〈母校に対する〉attachment to one's old school [《米》alma mater].

あいこく 愛国 love of [for] one's country; patriotism ¶愛国心 patriotism; patriotic spirit [《米》sentiment] / 愛国者 a patriot / 愛国的 patriotic.

あいことば 合言葉 a password ¶合言葉を言う give the password. 文例⇩

あいごま 合駒《将棋》a piece placed to intercept the opponent's check; a guard [guarding piece] (for the king).

あいさい 愛妻 one's (beloved) wife ¶愛妻家 a devoted [a doting,《文》an uxorious] husband.

あいさつ 挨拶〈会釈〉a greeting;《文》a salutation;〈返答〉a reply; an answer;〈通告〉notice ¶挨拶する greet;《文》salute; reply; answer / 朝晩の挨拶をする pass [bid sb] the time of day / 挨拶を交わす exchange greetings [courtesies] (with);〈頭を下げて〉exchange bows / 挨拶に行く call on sb to pay one's respects / 挨拶代わりに by way of a compliment / 挨拶状 a letter of greeting; a greeting(s) card;《通知状》a notice. 文例⇩

あいし 哀史 a sad [tragic, pathetic] story [history]《of factory girls》.

あいじ 愛児 one's dear [《文》beloved] child.

あいしゃ 愛車 one's own car; one's cherished car ¶愛車を駆って箱根へ行く go to Hakone by car.

あいしゃせいしん 愛社精神 loyalty [devotion] to one's company; company loyalty.

アイシャドー eye shadow ¶アイシャドーをつける put on [apply] eye shadow / アイシャドーをしている wear eye shadow / アイシャドーを濃く塗った女 a woman with heavily shadowed eyelids.

あいしゅう 哀愁 sadness; sorrow;《文》pathos ¶哀愁を感じる feel sad [《文》sorrowful].

あいしょう[1] 相性《文》affinity;《文》compatibility ¶相性のいい compatible (in temperament); well-suited (to each other) / 相性の悪い incompatible (in temperament); ill-suited; ill-matched. 文例⇩

あいしょう[2] 愛称 a pet name; a term of endearment.

あいしょう[3] 愛唱 ¶愛唱する love to sing《a song》/ 愛唱歌 a song one likes to sing; one's favorite song.

あいしょう[4] 愛誦 ¶愛誦する love to recite [read]《a poem》.

あいじょう 愛情 love;《文》affection ¶愛情のある affectionate; loving; warmhearted / 愛情のない coldhearted;《文》unfeeling / 愛情のこもった言葉 affectionate words / 愛情を抱く be fond (of); feel affection (toward) / 愛情をこめて affectionately; with love [affection].

あいしょか 愛書家 a book lover; a lover of books;《文》a bibliophile.

あいじん 愛人〈男〉one's lover;〈女〉one's mistress;《口語》one's woman ¶愛人同士 (a pair of) lovers.

アイス ice ¶アイスクリーム (an) ice cream / アイスクリームサンデー a sundae / アイスクリームソーダ《eat》an ice cream soda / アイスコーヒー iced coffee / アイスショー an ice show / アイススケート ice skating / アイスティー iced tea / アイスフォール《登山》an icefall / アイスホッケー ice hockey;《米》hockey ★単に hockey といえば普通《英》では

あいきょう なに，それもご愛嬌さ．〈失敗をした人に〉Don't worry. It's nothing serious.

あいこ[1] なお一層のご愛顧をお願い申し上げます．We hope you will continue to patronize us.

あいこ[2] これであいこだ．Now we're quits!

あいこう 我々は平和を愛好する国民だ．We are a peace-loving nation. / FM 放送は戦後音楽ファンに愛好されるようになった．FM broadcasts became popular with music lovers after World War II.

あいことば「自然を守ろう」というのが私たちのグループの合言葉です．'Let's protect nature' is the motto of our group.

あいさつ（会などで）一言ご挨拶申し上げます．Ladies and gentlemen, let me say a few words on this occasion. / 彼は挨拶もせずに帰ってしまった．He left without so much as saying good-bye. / おや，これはまたご挨拶だね．Well, you put it rather strong. / What a thing to hear from you! / 同じテーブルに座るなら一言挨拶があって然るべきだ と思った．I thought he should have asked my permission to share the table with me.

あいしょう[1] あの2人は相性がよくないようだ．Those two don't seem to be cut out for each other [to hit it off very well].

あいする 2人は愛し合っている．They are in love (with each other). / 彼は，自分は人に愛されず，孤独で，疎外されていると思っていた．He felt that he was unloved, lonely and alienated. / 彼女は「愛してる」「愛してない」と唱えながら花びらを1つ1つ

field hockey をさす ⇨ ホッケー.
あいず 合図 a signal; a sign; an alarm《変事の》 ¶合図する give a signal; make a sign《with one's eye》/ 合図の旗 a signal flag / 合図をして電車を止める flag down a train / 太郎の合図で at [on] a sign from Taro / 銃声を合図に at the signal of a gunshot / 合図に手を上げる raise one's hand as a signal 《to do》.
アイスバーン [<《ドイツ語》*Eisbahn*] a frozen ski slope.
アイスランド Iceland ¶アイスランドの Icelandic / アイスランド共和国 the Republic of Iceland / アイスランド語 Icelandic / アイスランド人 an Icelander.
あいする 愛する love; be fond of; be attached to; care for ¶深く愛する love sb deeply [dearly] / 愛するもの one's darling; one's dear [loved] one; one's pet / 愛するわが子 one's beloved child / 自然を愛する心 love of [for] nature / 愛し愛されたいという気持 a desire to love and be loved in return / 愛すべき lovable. 文例⇩
あいせき¹ 相席 ¶相席する share a table 《with sb》. 文例⇩
あいせき² 哀惜《文》lamentation ¶哀惜する mourn over [《文》lament] 《sb's death》.
あいせつ 哀切 ¶哀切な pathetic; plaintive; mournful; 《文》sorrowful; sad.
アイゼン [<《ドイツ語》*Steigeisen*] climbing irons; crampons; a clamper.
あいそう 愛想《如才なさ》friendliness;《文》affability;《文》amiability;《世辞》compliments;《歓待》hospitality ¶愛想のよい《性質・様子の》friendly(-seeming); amiable;《口先のうまい》smooth-tongued[-talking];《文》fair-spoken;《客扱いのよい》hospitable / 愛想よく in a friendly way; amiably; affably / 愛想のない unfriendly; cold; curt; inhospitable / 愛想がつきる[をつかす] be disgusted 《with, at》; despair 《of》/ 愛想をいう pay sb compliments; say nice things 《to》/ 愛想尽かしを言う say spiteful [unkind] things 《to》/ 愛想笑い a flattering [an ingratiating] smile. 文例⇩
あいぞう¹ 愛憎 love and hate [hatred] ¶愛憎のからみ合った関係 a love-hate relationship.
あいぞう² 愛蔵 ¶愛蔵する treasure;《文》cherish / 愛蔵の書物 a book one treasures.
アイソトープ【物】an isotope.
あいた 開いた《空,明いた》〈ひらいた〉open;〈からの〉empty; vacant;〈使わない〉unoccupied ¶空いた席 a vacant [an unoccupied] seat. 文例⇩
あいだ 間〈間隔〉an interval; a space;〈すきま〉an opening; a gap;〈距離〉(a) distance;〈時間〉time; an interval; a period ¶5年の間 for (the space of) five years / 数キロの距離 (a distance of) several kilometers / 長い間 for a long time / …の間 for; during《my stay there》; while《I was staying there》; as long as 《…する間は》/ 話がうまく行く get on [along] well 《with》/ 間を置いて at intervals; intermittently (間欠的に) / 間をさく《文》estrange 《A》from《B》; come between《A and B》/ 間を詰めて書く write close(ly) / 間に[で] between; among; amid (取巻かれて); halfway between (中間に) / 1週間の間に in the course [space] of a week / 過去10年の間に in the past [last] ten years / 食事と食事の間に between meals / その間に meanwhile; in the meantime / 間にはさまる[入る] get between《A and B》/ 私が生きている間は so [as] long as I live / 戦争の期間中 throughout [for the duration of] the war; while the war lasted. 文例⇩
用法 between は「2つのものの間に」, among は「3つ以上のものの間に」の意味で使われる: I sat between Tom and Jean. / They lived among the mountains. 位置でなく,関係を表わす場合も同様であるが,3者以上の場合でも,関係が個別的であるときは, among でなく between を用いる: the treaty between the three nations. また, between は繰り返される事柄の間を指すときにも用いる: have a drink between dances.
あいたいする 相対する face [confront] each other; stand opposite [facing] each other ¶相対してすわる《two people》 sit face to face; sit facing sb; sit opposite《each other, sb》.
あいだがら 間柄 ¶親子の間柄 the relation of [between] father and son / …と親しい間柄になる make friends with…; become a good [close] friend of…; 《文》achieve a close relationship with…; …と親しい間柄である be on good [friendly] terms with…. 文例⇩
あいだぐい 間食い ⇨ かんしょく².

取っていた. She was plucking the petals one by one, repeating, 'He loves me; he loves me not,' as she did so.
あいせき¹ ご相席でよろしいですか. Would you mind sharing a table?
あいそう 彼女はどの客に対してもにっこり笑ってお愛想を言うことも忘れなかった She always had a smile and a pleasant word for every customer who came in. / 自分ながら愛想が尽きた. I am angry with [mad at] myself. / 何のお愛想もございません. I am sorry that I have nothing better to offer you.
あいた びっくりして開いた口がふさがらなかった. I was dumbfounded [flabbergasted, completely taken aback] 《at the answer》. | I stood in open-mouthed amazement.
あいだ 僕がそこにいた間は好天気だった. It was fine while I was staying 《during my stay》 there. / 彼はその間中黙っていた. He kept silent all the while. / 間に人を入れずに[我々2人の間で]解決しよう. Let us settle the matter ourselves [between the two of us].
あいたいする 私はテーブルを中にして彼と相対した. I sat facing him across the table.
あいだがら あの人たちは師弟の間柄です. Their relationship is that [one] of master and disciple. | They are master and disciple. / 君とあの人とはどういう間柄なのですか. What relation is he to you? | How are you related to him? 伯父甥の間柄です. I am his nephew.

アイダホ Idaho (略: Id., Ida.) ¶アイダホ州の人 an Idahoan.

あいちゃく 愛着 love;《文》attachment; affection ¶深い愛着を感じる be deeply attached ((to)).

あいちょう 哀調 ¶哀調を帯びた mournful; plaintive.

あいちょうしゅうかん 愛鳥週間 Bird Week.

あいつ 〈男〉 that fellow [chap]; he; 〈女〉 that woman; she; 〈物〉 that one.

あいついで 相次いで one after another; in (rapid) succession. 文例⇩

あいづち 相槌 ¶相槌をうつ give responses (to make the conversation go smoothly) ★英語では時々相槌に uh-huh などと言うが、日本語の会話のように頻繁に相槌を打つことはしない。文例⇩

あいて 相手 〈仲間〉a companion; a partner; 〈勝負の〉 an opponent; a rival ¶相手にする [なる] deal with sb;〈競技の〉play ((at golf)); play ((against)) sb ((at))/相手にしない refuse to deal with sb; have nothing to do with sb; ignore; spurn /相手をする keep company ((with)); entertain ((one's guests)); keep ((a child)) occupied /相手方 the other party / (劇の)相手役を勤める play a part opposite ((an actor)). 文例⇩

アイデア an idea ¶アイデア商品 a novelty /アイデアマン an idea('s) man; a man of ideas.

あいてどる 相手取る take sb (on) as an [one's] opponent ¶…を相手取って訴訟を起こす sue sb; go to law with sb; take sb to court ((to make him pay for the damage)).

あいとう 哀悼《文》condolence; sympathy;《文》lamentation ¶哀悼する mourn [《文》lament, grieve] ((over, for))/哀悼の意を表する express one's regret ((over the death of…));〈遺族に〉offer one's condolences ((to sb on his bereavement)); express one's sympathy ((for sb on the death of his father)).

あいどく 愛読 ¶愛読する like to read; be fond of reading;〈雑誌を〉read ((a magazine)) regularly /愛読者 a reader ((of a book)); an admirer ((of an author)); a regular reader ((of a magazine)); a subscriber ((to a magazine)) /愛読書 one's favorite book. 文例⇩

アイドル an idol ((of college boys)).

あいなめ 〔魚〕a greenling.

あいにく 生憎 unfortunately; unluckily; I'm afraid (that)…; as ill luck would have it;〈気の毒ながら〉I am sorry, but… ¶あいにくの unfortunate; unlucky; ill-timed;《文》unseasonable. 文例⇩

アイヌ an Ainu ((pl. -(s)) ¶アイヌ語 Ainu.

あいのこ 合の子〈混血の人〉a person of mixed race; a half-breed (★軽蔑的意味の語として避けられることが多い)⇒こんけつ;〈動植物の〉a cross ((between)); a hybrid ((between)) ¶日本人とフランス人の合の子 a person who is half Japanese and half French (by birth); a person of mixed Japanese and French parentage /合の子の half-bred /あいの子をつくる cross ((one breed with another)).

あいのて 間の手〈間奏〉a short interlude ((of samisen music filling a break in the vocal part of traditional Japanese music));〈掛け声〉a call thrown in to enliven a song ((in traditional Japanese music)).

あいのり 相乗り ¶相乗りする ride together; ride [go ((to a place))] in the same car ((as sb));〈オートバイなどの)後に〉ride pillion ((behind sb))/タクシーに相乗りする share a taxi ((with)).

あいば 愛馬 one keeps with tender care;《文》one's cherished mount.

アイバンク an eye bank.

あいはんする 相反する be contrary ((to each other)); run counter ((to)); conflict ((with)) ¶相反する概念《文》antithetic(al) concepts; directly-opposed ideas.

あいびき¹ 合挽き beef and pork ground together.

あいびき² 逢引 a (secret) date;《文》a rendezvous;《文》an assignation ¶逢引する have a rendezvous ((with)); meet sb secretly.

あいぶ 愛撫 a caress;《口語》petting ¶愛撫する caress; fondle; pet (互いに).

あいふく 間服 ⇒あいぎ.

あいふだ 合札 a check; a tally.

───────────────

あいついで 事件が相次いで起こった。One incident followed on the heels of another. /両親は相次いでこの世を去った。My parents died within a short time of each other.

あいづち 彼はさかんに相槌を打ちながら彼女の話を聞いていた。He was expressing his agreement at frequent intervals as he listened to her.

あいて 新聞記者を相手にする時には気をつけた方だ。You need to be careful (when you're dealing) with newspapermen. /改心しなければどれも相手にしてくれないぞ。If you don't mend your ways, no one will have anything to do with you. /僕はとても君の相手になれない。I am no match for you. /あの男なら相手にとって不足はない。He is a worthy opponent for me. /相手が悪い。I hate dealing with him. /相手を見るものを言うがいい。Do you realize who you're talking to? | Is that the way you talk to me? /相手のないけんかはできない。It takes two to make a quarrel.

あいどく この本は高校生に愛読されている。This book is popular with [among] high school students. /氏の小説は愛読者が多い。His novels have a large circle of readers.

あいにく あいにく金の持ち合わせがない。Unfortunately I have no money with me. /お訪ねしたいのですが、あいにく悪い風邪にかかりまして。I'd like to call on you, only I've caught a bad cold. /それはあいにくだ。That's a pity. | That's too bad. /あいにく父は旅行中です。I'm afraid [I'm sorry to say that] my father is away on a trip.

あいまつ 性能のよさとデザインの優美さが両々相まって本機種の声価を高めてきた。The high performance and the elegant design of this model have combined to give it a high reputation.

あいもかわらぬ 朝食は相も変わらぬハムエッグスだった。For breakfast we were served the eternal ham and eggs.

あいべつりく 愛別離苦〘仏教〙the anguish of parting from *one's* loved ones.

あいべや 相部屋 ¶相部屋になる share a room 《with *sb* at an inn》.

あいぼう 相棒 《口語》 *one's* pal ; 《米口語》 *one's* buddy ; 《英口語》 *one's* mate ; *one's* partner ; *one's* comrade ; an accomplice (共犯者) ¶相棒になる become a partner 《of *sb*, in a job》 ; pal up 《with》.

あいま 合間 ¶合間に 〈間に〉 in the intervals 《between, of》 ; 〈余暇に〉 at *one's* leisure ; when *one* has time to spare / 仕事の合間に in spare moments from *one's* work / 合間合間に at intervals ; at odd moments.

あいまい 曖昧 vagueness ; 《文》 obscurity ; 《文》 ambiguity (語義の) ¶曖昧な vague 《expressions》 ; obscure 《vowels》 ; 《文》 indistinct 《pronunciation》 ; ambiguous 《wording》 ; 〈あやしげな〉 suspicious 《actions》 ; questionable 《characters》 / 曖昧な返事 〈漠然とした〉 a vague answer ; 〈言を左右にした〉 an evasive answer ; 〈言質をとられないような〉 a non-committal answer / 曖昧なことを言う make an ambiguous remark ; 《文》 equivocate / 曖昧な態度をとる do not commit *oneself* ; take a noncommittal [《文》 an equivocal] attitude.

あいまつ 相まつ go hand in hand 《with》 ; 《文》 be interdependent ¶…と相まって combined [coupled] with… ; 〈協力して〉 in cooperation with…. [文例⇩]

あいもかわらぬ 相も変わらぬ always the same ; no better than before ; conventional. [文例⇩]

あいよう 愛用 ¶愛用する use *sth* regularly [habitually] / 愛用の *one's* favorite 《fountain pen》 / 愛用者 a regular user 《of》 ; a person who favors 《the products of our company》.

あいよく 愛欲 《文》 sexual desire ; 《文》 lust ; passion.

あいらしい 愛らしい sweet ; charming ; lovely ; 《米口語》 cute ¶愛らしく charmingly.

アイルランド Ireland ¶アイルランド共和国 the Irish Republic ; the Republic of Ireland / アイルランド(人)の Irish / アイルランド語 Irish (Gaelic) / アイルランド人 an Irishman ; an Irishwoman (女) ; the Irish (総称).

あいろ 隘路 〈狭い道〉 a narrow path ; 〈障害〉 a bottleneck ¶隘路を打開する break (through) [《文》 resolve] a bottleneck.

アイロン an iron ¶アイロンをかける iron 《a shirt》 ; press 《the trousers》 / アイロンをかけてないワイシャツ an unpressed shirt / 蒸気[電気]アイロン a steam [an electric] iron / ノーアイロンの wash-and-wear 《fabrics》 ; drip-dry 《shirts》 / アイロン台 an ironing board.

あいわ 哀話 a sad story ; a tragic tale.

アインスタイニウム〘化〙einsteinium.

あう[1] 会う, 逢う, 遭う 〈面会する〉 see ; interview ; 〈出会う〉 meet (with) ; come across [upon] ; 《文》 encounter ; 〈風雨に〉 be caught 《in》 ; be overtaken 《by》 ¶会ったことのない人 a (complete) stranger / 逢いに行く go to [and] see *sb* / 事故に遭う meet with an accident / 危ない目に遭う be exposed to [get into] danger. [文例⇩]

あう[2] 合う 〈適合する〉 fit ; suit ; be suited 《to》 ; 〈似合う〉 become ; 〈調和する〉 harmonize 《with》 ; 《文》 accord [be in accord] 《with》 ; 〈合致する〉 agree 《with》 ; coincide 《with》 ; tally 《with》 ; 〈正しい〉 be right ; be correct ; 〈引合う〉 pay ¶ぴったり合う fit perfectly [neatly] ; be an excellent fit ; fit like a glove [to a T] / 身体によく合う[合わない]衣服 well-[ill-]fitting clothes / 口[趣味]に合う suit *one's* taste / (気候・食物が)性に合う[合わない] agree [disagree] with *one* / お互いに話[気]が合う agree [get on] with each other ; 《口語》 be on the same wavelength. [文例⇩]

アウト〘野球〙out ¶アウトになる be put out / 打ってアウトになる hit into an out / アウトにする put [get] 《a runner》 out ; retire 《a batter》 / 本塁に投球してアウトにする throw 《a runner》 out at the plate / 凡フライでスリーアウトになる knock a pop fly for the third out / アウトカウント the number of outs [batters out]. [文例⇩]

アウトコース 〈トラックの〉 an outside lane ¶(野球で)アウトコースへ直球を投げる deliver a straight ball over the far side of the

---

あう[1] ここへ来る途中で中島さんに会った. I met [《口語》 bumped into] Mr. Nakajima on my way here. / あの人には近頃少しも会わない. I have seen nothing of him lately. / 彼女はあまり人と会わない. She does not see many people. | She doesn't have much company. / 僕らは明朝7時に駅で会うことになっている. We are to meet at the station at seven tomorrow morning. / では来週お会いしましょう. See you next week. / こんな所でお会いするなんて. Fancy meeting you here! / 彼は不幸な目にあった. Something terrible happened to him. | 《文》 A misfortune befell him. / 火事にあって蔵書をおおかた焼いてしまった. He had the greater part of his library burned in the fire.

あう[2] この上着はよく合う[合わない]. This coat is a good [poor] fit. / この上着は僕には全然合わない. This coat does not fit me at all. / 袖丈が5センチほど長過ぎて体に合わない. The sleeves are about two inches too long for a proper fit. / 東京の気候は私の体に合わない. The climate of Tokyo does not agree with me. / このじゅうたんは壁紙と合わない. This carpet does not match [go well with] the wallpaper. / こういう絵は日本間には合わない. A painting like this doesn't fit into a Japanese room. / 君の時計は合っているか. Is your watch right? / この時計は合っていない. This clock is wrong. / 君の時計は僕のと合っている. Your watch agrees with mine. / この機械の値段はべらぼうに高くて国際的標準に全く合わない. The price of this machine is enormous and totally out of line with international standards. / 合計が100円合わない. The total is 100 yen out. / それは千ドル以下で売っては合わない. It wouldn't pay to sell it for less than 1,000 dollars.

アウト ヤンキースは2アウトでランナー二塁, 三塁だった. The Yankees had men on second and third with two gone [with two (men) out].

アウトプット　　　　　　　　　　　　　6　　　　　　　　　　　　　　　　　あおまめ

plate (from the batter).
アウトプット 【コンピューター】 (an) output.
あえぐ 喘ぐ pant; breathe hard [heavily]; gasp (for breath) ¶重い荷物を背負ってあえぐ pant under a heavy load / あえぎながら gasping; panting; out of breath / あえぎながら言う gasp out. 文例↓
あえて ¶あえて…する dare [《文》venture] to do / あえて辞さない be even ready to do; 《文》 do not shrink from doing / …といってもあえて過言でない We may safely say that…. 文例↓
あえない 〈悲しい〉 sad; tragic; miserable; 〈はかない〉 transient ¶あえない最期をとげる 《文》 come to [meet with] a sad [tragic] end; die a tragic death. 文例↓
あえもの 和え物 foods, such as fish, shellfish or vegetables, dressed with (various kinds of) sauce.
あえる dress (vegetables) with ((vinegar, miso, etc.)).
あえん 亜鉛 zinc ¶亜鉛引の galvanized; coated with zinc / 亜鉛板 a zinc plate [sheet] / 亜鉛華 flowers of zinc; zinc oxide / 亜鉛華軟膏 zinc (oxide) ointment.
あお 青 blue (緑) green; 〈馬〉 a (bluish) black horse ¶青々した fresh and green; 《文》 verdant 《hills》/ 青梅 a green ume / 青黒い blueblack. 文例↓
あおい¹ 【植】 a hollyhock.
あおい² 青い 〈青色の〉 blue; 《文》 azure; green (緑); 《文》 pallid; 《文》 pallid ¶青い鳥 〈メーテルリンクの劇〉 The Blue Bird / 顔が青い look pale / 青い物 green plants / 青いもののない工場街 an industrial district without a trace of greenery / 青いりんご a green apple / 青く染める dye 《a cloth》 blue / 青くなる become blue; 〈顔が〉 go [turn] pale / 青さ blueness; the blue (of the sky). 文例↓
あおいきといき 青息吐息 ¶青息吐息である 《口語》 be at one's last gasp; 《文》 be in great distress; have a hard time (of it).
あおいろしんこく 青色申告 (file) a blue return.
あおがえる 青蛙 a green frog; a tree frog.
あおかび 青かび blue mold.
あおき 青木 【植】 a Japanese laurel.
あおぎみる 仰ぎ見る 〈見上げる〉 look up at 《the stars》; 〈尊敬して〉 look up to sb 《as one's master》.

あおぎり 【植】 a Chinese parasol tree.
あおぐ¹ 仰ぐ 〈見上げる〉 look up 《at》; 〈尊敬する〉 respect; look up to; 〈…に求める〉 depend [rely] on 《sb for sth》; look [turn] to 《sb for advice》 ¶天を仰ぐ look up at the sky / 教えを仰ぐ ask for instruction / 援助を仰ぐ turn [look] to sb for assistance / 毒を仰ぐ take poison / 師と仰がれる be looked up to [《文》 be revered] as a teacher. 文例↓
あおぐ² 扇ぐ fan 《a fire, oneself》; use a fan. 文例↓
あおくさ 青草 green grass.
あおくさい 青臭い 〈においが〉 smelling of grass; 〈経験のない〉 green; inexperienced; immature; 《文》 callow; 《口語》 wet behind the ears.
あおさぎ 青さぎ 【鳥】 a (gray) heron.
あおざめる 青ざめる go [turn] pale [white] ¶青ざめた pale; 《文》 pallid / 青ざめている look pale.
あおじゃしん 青写真 a blueprint ¶青写真にとる make a blueprint of; blueprint 《a plan》.
あおじろい 青白い pale; 《文》 wan ¶青白い顔をした女 a pale-faced woman.
あおしんごう 青信号 a green light; a green (traffic) signal ¶青信号で道を渡る cross a street on the green signal. 文例↓
あおすじ 青筋 blue veins ¶青筋の見える手 a veiny hand / 青筋をたてて怒る go [turn] purple with rage. 文例↓
あおぞら 青空 a blue [《文》 an azure] sky ¶青空市場 [教室] an open-air market [class].
あおた 青田 a green paddy [rice] field ¶青田刈りをする start recruiting activities [sign employment contracts 《with college students》] earlier than the officially agreed date.
あおだいしょう 青大将 a blue-green snake.
あおだたみ 青畳 a new tatami.
あおてんじょう 青天井 a blue sky.
あおな 青菜 greens ¶青菜に塩である be crestfallen.
あおにさい 青二才 an immature [a green, 《文》 a callow] youth; a greenhorn. 文例↓
あおのり 青海苔 green laver.
あおば 青葉 green leaves [foliage] ¶青葉のころ the season of fresh greenery [《文》 verdure] / 青葉になる come into leaf.
あおびょうたん 青瓢箪 a pale-faced man; a ghost of a man.
あおまめ 青豆 green beans [peas].

あえぐ 同社は経営難にあえいでいる. The firm is having a hard time carrying on as a going concern.
あえて 私は自分が正しいと信じるのであえてこの手段を取る. I dare to take this step because I am sure that I am in the right. | あえて驚くに足りない. There is nothing particularly strange about it. | I don't see why you should be surprised at it.
あえない 期待に反して, 日本チームはあえなくも敗れてしまった. Contrary to expectations, the Japanese team was miserably defeated.
あお ひげを剃ったあとが青々としている. His chin is all blue where he has shaved.
あおい² 心臓病で青い顔をしていた. He had a gray face from heart trouble. / 彼はパスポートをなくして青くなった. He is white with shock at having lost his passport.

あおぐ¹ 日本は棉花の供給を米国に仰いでいる. Japan depends [relies] on America for her supply of raw cotton.
あおぐ² 彼は扇子を広げて, パタパタ扇いだ. He spread the fan and worked it briskly.
あおしんごう 計画を実施してよいという青信号が出された. We got [were given] the green light to go ahead with the project.
あおすじ 左のこめかみに青筋を立てていた. The veins on his left

あおみ 青味 blueness; greenness; a tinge of blue [green] ¶青味がかった bluish; greenish / 青味を帯びている be tinged with blue [green] / (料理に)青味を添える add a touch of green (to the dish with a sprig of parsley).

あおみどろ 《植》(one of the green algae forming) pond scum.

あおむく 仰向く look up [upward]; turn one's face up [upward].

あおむけ 仰向け ¶仰向けに寝る lie on one's back / 仰向けにする turn sth up [upward] / 仰向けになる〈寝返りをして〉turn on one's back; 〈ばたんと〉throw oneself down on one's back.

あおむし 青虫 a green caterpillar.

あおもの 青物 greens; (green) vegetables.

あおり 煽り〈風の〉a blast; a gust;〈余波〉repercussions; influence;〈側杖〉(get) a by-blow ¶あおりを食う suffer from the repercussions (of); be hit (by the recession) / あおり足《水泳》a scissors kick / (扉の)あおり止め a doorstop.

あおる¹ 呷る gulp down ¶うさ晴らしにウイスキーをあおる toss off glasses of whisky to drown one's sorrows.

あおる² 煽る〈風が〉flap; swing;〈あおぐ〉fan;〈扇動する〉stir [whip] up; incite ¶風にあおられる be hit [buffeted] by a gust of wind.

あおんそく 亜音速 (at) subsonic speed ¶亜音速の subsonic (airplanes). 文例⇩

あか¹ 赤〈色〉red; crimson (深紅); scarlet (緋);〈共産主義者〉a Red ¶赤の他人 a complete [an utter] stranger. 文例⇩

あか² 垢〈よごれ〉dirt; filth;〈新陳代謝した皮膚〉scurf ¶垢を落とす wash off the dirt / 垢だらけの dirty; filthy / 垢じみる get [《文》become] grimy; be stained with dirt / 垢じみた grimy; grubby; dirty. 文例⇩

あか³ 〈船底の〉bilge (water) ¶あかを汲み出す bail the water out.

あかあか 明々 ¶明々と 《burn》brightly.

あかい 赤い red; crimson (深紅); scarlet (緋) ¶赤くなる〈色が〉turn red [scarlet, crimson]; redden;〈思想が〉go [turn] Red [communistic]; 顔を赤くする[赤らめる] blush / 顔を赤くして[赤らめて] blushing(ly); with a blush / 興奮して赤くなる flush with excitement / 赤くなって怒る be red [flushed] with anger / 爪を赤く染めた女 a woman with her fingernails painted red.

あかいはね 赤い羽根 ¶赤い羽根をつけている wear a red feather (on one's coat lapel) / 赤い羽根募金運動 a 'Red Feather' campaign; a community chest drive.

あかえい 赤鱏《魚》a stingray.

あかがい 赤貝 an ark shell.

あかがえる 赤蛙 a true frog; a ranid.

あがき 足掻き ¶あがきがとれない stick [be stuck] in the mud; be stranded; be in a fix; be struggling helplessly.

あかぎれ 皹 a chap; a crack (in the skin) ¶あかぎれになる get chapped; chap.

あがく 足掻く struggle; flounder ¶足掛かりを得ようとしてあがく scrabble for a foothold / 困難から抜け出そうとあがく try hard to wriggle out of a difficult situation.

あかげ 赤毛 red [carroty] hair ¶赤毛の人 a red-haired[-headed] person; a redhead / 赤毛ざる《動》a rhesus monkey.

あかご 赤子 ⇨ あかんぼう. 文例⇩

あかし 証〈証拠〉(a) proof; evidence ¶あかしを立てる prove; give evidence 《for sth, that...》/ 身のあかしを立てる prove one's innocence;《文》vindicate oneself 《of》;《文》exonerate oneself 《from the charge of...》.

あかじ 赤字 a deficit; a loss ¶赤字になる show a loss; go [get, run] into the red / 赤字である be in the red / 赤字を埋める[なくす] make up the deficit / 赤字から脱け出す get out of the red / 赤字経営をする operate in the red [at a deficit] / 赤字公債 a deficit(-covering) bond / 赤字財政赤字 [unbalanced] financing [finances] / (鉄道の)赤字(路)線 a loss-making [deficit-ridden] railroad line. 文例⇩

アカシア《植》an acacia.

あかしお 赤潮 a red tide; red water.

あかしんごう 赤信号 a red (traffic) light; a red [danger] signal ¶赤信号を無視して突っ走る run through a red light / 赤信号を無視して通りを渡る cross a street against the (red) light / 赤信号で止まる stop at a red light.

あかす¹ 明かす〈過ごす〉pass; spend;〈打明ける〉tell;《文》reveal;《文》disclose ¶寝ずに夜を明かす stay [sit] up all night / 計画[意中]を明かす reveal [lay bare] a scheme [one's intentions] to sb / 名[身分]を明かす reveal [disclose] one's name [identity] / 手品の種を明かす show how the trick is done. 文例⇩

あかす² 飽かす cloy;《文》satiate;〈嫌などをせる〉bore;《文》weary ¶金に飽かして豪邸を建てる build a grand house sparing no

---

temple stood out [bulged].

あおにさい まだ青二才だ。He is still green.

あおる² くぐり戸が風にあおられている。The side door is flapping [slamming] in the wind. / 火は強風にあおられて四方に広がった。Fanned by the strong wind, the flames spread in all directions. / それが外国からの移民達に対する反感をあおりたてた。It stirred up ill feeling against foreign immigrants.

あか¹ 夕日が赤々と沈むところだった。The sun was setting with a deep red glow. / 日本の経済に赤ランプがついた。There are warning signs ahead [out] for the Japanese economy.

あか² 体をこすると垢がぼろぼろ出た。A lot of dirt rolled [came] off as he scrubbed himself.

あかご 赤子の手をねじるようなものだ。It's child's play for us. |

It's like taking candy from a baby.

あかじ 家計が赤字だ。We can't make both ends meet. / 国鉄は赤字に悩む30の地方線の廃止を決定した。J.N.R. decided to discontinue services on 30 deficit-ridden local lines.

あかす¹ この事はだれにも明かさずにおこう。I'll keep this [the matter] to myself.

あかだし　赤だし　red-*miso* soup.
あかちゃける　赤茶ける　turn reddish-brown；〈変色する〉be [get] discolored.
あかちゃん　赤ちゃん ⇨ あかんぼう　¶赤ちゃんコンクール a baby show.
あかチン　赤チン　[商標名] Mercurochrome；[薬] merbromin solution.
あかつき　暁　(at) dawn；(at) daybreak　¶…の暁には when…；in the event [in case] of…／勝利の暁には《文》when the day of victory dawns／成功の暁に《文》when success is *one's*；《文》when *one* has achieved success.
あがったり　上がったり
あかつち　赤土　red clay [earth].
アカデミー　an academy　¶アカデミー賞 [映画] the Academy Award；the Oscar.
アカデミック　アカデミックな academic.
あかでんわ　赤電話　a pay (tele)phone ⇨ こうしゅう[2]〈公衆電話〉.
あかとんぼ　赤とんぼ　a red dragonfly.
あがなう　贖う　〈罪を〉《文》atone 《for》；《文》expiate.
あかぬ　飽かぬ　¶飽かぬ眺めを a sight *one* never tires of (gazing at).
あかぬけ　垢抜け　¶あかぬけのした polished；refined；sophisticated；elegant／あかぬけのしない unsophisticated；unrefined；《文》inelegant；〈人が〉《文》gauche.
あかね　[植] a madder　¶あかね色 madder red.
あかはじ　赤恥　¶赤恥をかく be humiliated；be put to shame；be disgraced (in public)／赤恥をかかせる humiliate；put *sb* to shame (in public)；《口語》show *sb* up；《口語》put *sb* down.
あかはた　赤旗　a red flag；〈共産党・労組などの〉the Red Flag.
あかはだか　赤裸　¶赤裸の 〈まっぱだか〉stark-naked；stripped to the skin；〈鳥獣が〉with all *its* hair [feathers] plucked off／赤裸にされる be stripped of all *one's* clothes.
あかぼう　赤帽　a porter；《米》a redcap.
あかまつ　赤松　a Japanese red pine.
あかみ[1]　赤身　〈肉の〉lean meat；〈木材の〉heartwood　¶赤身の魚 a fish with red-colored flesh.
あかみ[2]　赤味　redness；a tinge of red　¶赤味がかった reddish；tinged with red／赤味を帯び

る take on a red tinge. [文例⇩]
あがめる　崇める　respect；have respect for；look up to；《文》revere；《文》honor；《文》hold *sb* in high honor；〈崇拝する〉worship　¶神とあがめられる be worshiped as a god；《文》be deified.
あからがお　赤ら顔　a red [ruddy] face　¶赤ら顔の人 a person with a red face；a ruddy-faced [《文》rubicund] person／赤ら顔をしている be red-faced；《文》be florid of face.
あからさま　あからさまな〈明白〉plain；〈卒直〉frank；candid；openhearted；honest；〈単刀直入〉blunt；direct；straightforward；forthright／あからさまに plainly；frankly；candidly；bluntly；honestly；directly；straightwardly；forthrightly／あからさまに事実を述べる state the facts as they are／あからさまに言えば to be frank [candid, honest](with you)；frankly [plainly] speaking；to put it bluntly [frankly, baldly]. [文例⇩]
あからむ　赤らむ ⇨ あかい（赤くなる）.
あからめる　赤らめる ⇨ あかい.
あかり　明かり　〈灯火〉a light；a lamp（灯油・ガスの）；〈光〉light　¶明かりをつける turn [put] the light on／明かりを消す turn [put] the light off／ろうそくの明かりで本を読む read a book by candlelight／明かり取り a light；〈天窓〉a skylight；〈ドアの上の〉a fanlight；〈窓の上の〉a transom (window). [文例⇩]
あがり　上がり　〈登り〉a rise；《文》an ascent；〈物価などの〉a rise；an advance；〈収入〉(an) income；proceeds；receipts；takings；〈収穫〉a crop；a yield　¶(すごろく・マージャンなどで)上がりになる ⇨ あがる／上がり下(お)りする go up and down；〈文〉ascend and descend／階段の上り下りに注意する watch *one's* step going up and down the stairs／上がり下がり rise and fall；ups and downs；〈相場の〉fluctuations；movement／上がり下がりがある rise and fall；go up and down；fluctuate／上がり口〈入口〉the entrance；〈玄関口〉the doorway；the porch／上がり目 almond eyes；inward slanting eyes／上がり湯 clean hot water used outside the bathtub.
-あがり　…上がり　¶雨上がりの道 a road (just) after rain／病気上がりの人 a person who has just recovered from an illness／役人上がりの実業家 a businessman who was once a Gov-

---

あがったり　商売は上がったりだ．Business is terrible [dreadful]. | If things go on this way I'll soon be bust [bankrupt].
あかみ　彼女の青白い頬にわずかに赤味がさした．A slight [faint] flush came into her pale cheeks.
あからさま　私はあからさまに自分の考えを述べた．I gave him my honest opinion.
あかり　明かりがついている．The light is on.／部屋に明かりがついている．A light is burning in the room.／明かりがついた．The light went on.／明かりが消えた．

The light has gone out [is out].
あがる　犬が縁側に上がった．The dog has got on to the verandah.／旗が上がっている．A flag is flying.／対流圏内で高度が100メートル上がるごとに気温はセ氏約0.6度下がる．Within the troposphere, air temperature drops about 0.6°C. with every 100 meters of elevation.／物価は上がるばかりだ．Prices go on rising.／僕はこんどの試験で10番以内に上がった．I went up [jumped] over ten places in the last exam.／今晩それを頂きにあがります．I will call

for it this evening.／建築費は5千万円ぐらいで上がるだろう．The cost of building the house will not go over [exceed] 50,000,-000 yen.／雨が上がった．It has stopped raining.／犯人はまだあがらない．The culprit is still at large.／証拠は充分あがった．Sufficient evidence has been secured.／(食べ物を出して)どうぞおあがり下さい．Help yourself, please.／ちょうど彼は風呂からあがったところです．He had just got out of the bath.／溺死した人の遺体はまだ上がらない．The

あがりこむ 上がり込む come [go] in [into]; 《文》enter 《a house》.

あがる 上[挙,揚]がる 〈登[昇]る〉go [come] up; rise; 《文》ascend; climb (up) / 〈名などが〉be raised; rise 《in reputation》; 〈物価などが〉rise; go up / 〈地位などが〉be promoted; get promotion / 〈進歩する〉make progress 《headway》; improve; 〈入る〉go (come) in; 《文》enter / 〈訪問する〉call 《on sb, at sb's house》 / 〈仕上がる〉be completed; be finished; 〈終わる〉be over; come to an end; be through with 《a task》; 〈マージャンなどで〉go out; complete one's hand; 〈すごろくなどで〉finish; 〈飲食する〉eat; 〈落着きを失う〉get nervous; 《文》lose one's composure; get [suffer from] stage fright (舞台などで); 〈蚕が〉begin spinning / 屋根に上がる go [climb] up on the roof / 2階に上がる go upstairs / 名が挙がる become famous [well known] / 値段が上がる go up [rise] in price / 俸給が上がる have one's salary raised / 《口語》get a raise [《英》rise] / 腕が上がる get better; one's skill (at tennis) improves / 学校へ上がる enter [be admitted to] a school. 文例⇩

あかるい 明るい bright; light; 〈通じている〉(be) familiar (with); 《文》(be) versed (in); 〈明朗な〉cheerful; sunny ¶ 明るい部屋 a well-lit room / 《家の中で》一番明るい部屋 the room with the most light / 明るい顔 a cheerful look / 明るい家庭 a happy home [family] / 明るい気持ち 《with》a happy [light] heart; (in) a cheerful mood / 明るい性格 a sunny disposition / 明るい政治 clean politics / 明るい所で in the light / 充分明るい所で in good light / 充分明るい所でなら if the light is good enough / 明るいうちに while it is light; before (it gets) dark / 昼間のように明るい be as bright as day / アメリカ文学に明るい be well read in American literature / 明るくなる brighten; grow light; 《文》dawn (夜明けの空が) / 明るくする light up; make sth brighter. 文例⇩

あかるみ 明るみ ¶ 明るみに[で] in the light / 明るみに出す bring 《a matter》to light [into the open, before the public] / 明るみに出る come [be brought] to light; become known. 文例⇩

あかんたい 亜寒帯 the subarctic [subantarctic] zone.

あかんべえ ¶ あかんべえをする pull down the lower lid of one of one's eyes as a gesture of rejection toward [contempt for] sb.

あかんぼう 赤ん坊 a baby; 《文》an infant ¶ 男[女]の赤ん坊 a baby boy [girl] / 赤ん坊のころに when one was a baby / 《文》in one's babyhood / 赤ん坊のような babyish; infantile / 赤ん坊扱いにする treat sb like [as if he were] a baby. 文例⇩

あき¹ 空[明]き 〈すきま〉a gap; an opening; 〈余白〉a space; 〈余地〉room; 〈欠員〉a vacancy; a vacant position; 〈空席〉a vacant [an unoccupied] seat ¶ 空きを埋める fill [stop] a gap; fill up a space / 空き缶[箱・瓶] an empty can [box, bottle] / 空き時間 spare time; unoccupied hours. 文例⇩

あき² 秋 autumn; 《米》(the) fall ¶ 秋の autumn; 《文》autumnal / 秋の夕暮 an autumn evening / 秋風 an autumn [《文》autumnal] breeze / 秋口 the beginning of autumn; early autumn [fall] / 秋晴れの日 a fine autumn day. 文例⇩

あき³ 飽き 〈つかれ〉weariness; tiresomeness; 〈飽きること〉satiety ¶ 飽きやすい ⇒ あきっぽい / 飽きが来る grow [get] tired 《of》; 《文》become weary 《of》; lose interest (in) / 飽き飽きする get sick and tired 《of》; be bored 《with》 / 《口語》be fed up [fed to the teeth] 《with》 / 飽き飽きする仕事 tedious [《文》wearisome] work.

あきさめ 秋雨 autumn rain ¶ 秋雨前線 an autumnal rain front.

あきすねらい 空巣狙い a thief who steals from a house in the absence of the occupiers. 文例⇩

あきたりない 飽き足りない 〈人が主語〉be not satisfied [《文》be dissatisfied] 《with》; 〈事が主語〉be unsatisfactory; be not good enough; leave something to be desired.

あきち 空き地 vacant land; 《米》a vacant [an empty] lot; 《英》an empty [a vacant] plot (of land).

あきっぽい 飽きっぽい be apt to get tired [《文》weary] 《of sth》soon; lack endurance.

あきない 商い ⇒しょうばい. 文例⇩

あきなう 商う deal (in); sell. 文例⇩

---

body of the drowned person has not yet been recovered. / じゃがいもがいい色に揚がった。 The potatoes have been fried to a beautiful brown.

あかるい この電灯は明るい。 This electric lamp gives a good [bright] light. / まだ外は明るい。 It is still light outside. / なんとなく気持ちが明るくなった。 Somehow my heart felt lighter. | Somehow I felt better (about things). / 氏はこの町の地理に明るい。 He knows his way around this town. / 氏は米国の事情に明るい。 He is well up in [《文》conversant with] American affairs.

あかるみ もはや事は明るみに出てしまった。 The cat is out of the bag now.

あかんぼう 赤ん坊が生まれた。 A child was born. / 僕は赤ん坊じゃないよ。 I wasn't born yesterday.

あき¹ 君の会社に空きはありませんか。 Isn't there a vacancy in your firm? / 僕は時間の空きがない。 I have no time to spare.

あき² 秋が来た。 Autumn has come. / お父さん, 小鳥たちは秋になったのがわかるの。 Daddy, do birds know that fall is here?

あき³ この音楽には飽き飽きした。 I'm sick and tired of this music.

あきすねらい 空巣狙いにやられた。 Our house was robbed while we were away.

あきっぽい 彼は飽きっぽいから何事にも成功しない。 He never makes a success of anything he does, because he cannot stick to it.

あきなう 彼は絹物を商っている。 He deals in silk(s). | He is a silk dealer [a dealer in silk].

あきま 空き間 a vacant [an unoccupied, an unused] room; a room for rent.
あきや 空き家 a vacant [an unoccupied] house. 文例⇩
あきらか 明らか ¶明らかな〈明瞭な〉clear; distinct; plain; evident; obvious / 明らかに clearly; plainly; evidently; obviously; 〈断然〉undoubtedly / 明らかな事実 an obvious fact / 明らかな区別 a clear distinction / 明らかになる become clear [plain]; 〈わかる〉be (made) known; come [be brought] to light / 明らかにする make (a matter) clear [plain]; throw [shed] light on *sth*; explain; 〈公にする〉bring (a matter) to light; disclose; reveal; 〈公表する〉make (a matter) public; announce / 態度を明らかにする make *one's* attitude clear / 立場を明らかにする define [clarify] *one's* position. 文例⇩
あきらめ 諦め 《文》resignation; 《文》acceptance; 《文》abandonment 〈放棄〉¶諦めのいい人 a man who knows how to accept the inevitable [《文》resign himself to his lot]. 文例⇩
あきらめる 諦める 〈断念する〉give up (an idea); abandon; 〈観念する〉《文》resign [reconcile] *oneself* ((to)); 《文》be resigned [reconciled] ((to)); accept the situation; make up *one's* mind ((to *sth*)) ¶渡米を諦める give up the idea of going to America / 死んだ[無くなった]ものと諦める give *sb* [*sth*] up for dead [lost] / 運命と諦める accept *one's* fate (philosophically); 《文》resign *oneself* to *one's* lot / 諦めた気持ちになる feel resigned. 文例⇩
あきる 飽きる get [grow] tired ((of)); tire ((of)); 《文》become weary ((of)); get sick ((of)); lose interest ((in)); 《文》be satiated ((with)) ¶飽きるほど to *one's* heart's content; 《文》to satiety / 飽きるほど食う eat *one's* fill / 飽きることを知らない be insatiable. 文例⇩
アキレスけん アキレス腱 【解】Achilles' tendon; 〈弱点〉*one's* Achilles(') heel; a vulnerable point.
あきれる 呆れる be amazed ((at)); 《口語》be staggered ((by, at)); be disgusted ((with, at)); be shocked ((at)); be appalled ((at)); be scandalized ((at)) ¶あきれた人間 a disgusting fellow / あきれた値段 an absurd [a staggering, an impossible] price / あきれた顔 an amazed look / あきれ返る be aghast ((at)) / あきれてものが言えない be thoroughly disgusted 《with, at》 / あきれて in disgust / あきれてものが言えない feel [be] utterly scandalized ((at)). 文例⇩
あく¹ 悪 《文》(an) evil; wickedness; (a) vice; badness ¶悪に走る take to crime; go wrong [to the bad] / 悪に耽(*ふけ*)る be given to evil ways / 悪にそまる 《文》be steeped in vice / 悪に報いるに善を以てする《文》return good for evil. 文例⇩
あく² 〈灰汁〉lye; 〈野菜などの〉harshness ¶あくの強い男 a man with rather too strong a personality / 《口語》a pushy fellow / あくを抜く remove harshness 《from vegetables》 / 煮物をしながら、浮いて来るあくをすくい取る skim off the scum that rises to the surface of the cooking water.
あく³ 開[空]く 〈開く〉open; 〈始まる〉begin; 〈場所・部屋などが〉become vacant [free]; 〈時間・手が〉be free; 〈済む〉have done with; finish ¶開いている be open / 空いている〈部屋などが〉be unoccupied; be vacant; be free / 〈道具などが〉be not in use; 〈時間が〉have time to spare / 空いている方の手 *one's* free hand; the hand *one* is not using ⇨ あいた. 文例⇩
アクアラング 《商標名》an Aqualung; a scuba ¶アクアラングをつけて潜水する人 an Aqualung [a scuba] diver.
あくい 悪意 ill will; 《文》malice ¶悪意のある《文》malicious; spiteful / 悪意で with malicious intent; out of malice / 悪意のない innocent / 悪意を抱く bear *sb* ill will; 《文》harbor malice ((to, toward)) / 悪意に解する take *sth* amiss. 文例⇩
あくうん 悪運 悪運が強い《文》thrive in spite of *one's* evil deeds; 《戯言》have the devil's (own) luck. 文例⇩
あくえいきょう 悪影響 a bad [harmful] influence; ill effects ¶悪影響を与える have [《文》exert] a bad influence ((on)) / 悪影響を受ける receive a bad influence ((from)); 《文》be adversely affected ((by)).

あきや あの家は半年前から空家になっています。That house has been empty [has not been lived in] for the last six months.

あきらか 彼が間違っているのは明らかだ。It is obvious that he is mistaken. | He is obviously wrong. / 出火の原因は今に不明らかでない。The cause of the fire is still unknown. / その金をどう使ったかは明らかでない。The money has not been accounted for.

あきらめ 何事も諦めがかんじんだ。You must learn not to cry over spilt milk. / この損はなかなか諦めがつきません。I cannot get over this loss easily. / 君はいつも諦めが早すぎる。You always give up too soon [easily] / 私の失敗が世間の人への警告になったと思えばいくらか諦めがつく。It is some consolation to know that my failure has served as a warning to the public.

あきらめる このパズルはどうしても解けない。もう諦めた。I've tried hard to solve this puzzle but I can't. I give up. / しょせん逃げられないと諦めた。I gave up all hope of escaping.

あきる この絵は何度見ても飽きない。I never get weary of looking at this picture. / この雨にはもう飽きた。I am sick of [fed up with] this rain. | We have had (more than) enough of this rain. ★ We have had enough rain. と言えば「もう充分の降雨があった」の意味になる。/ 彼は初めから終わりまで聴衆を飽きさせなかった。He carried the audience with him from beginning to end.

アキレスけん 彼は練習中にアキレス腱を切った。He tore his Achilles' tendon while training.

あきれる あきれました。Words fail me! | Well, I never! / 忘れっぽいのには自分ながらあきれる。I am disgusted with myself for my poor memory. / 彼のばかにはあきれて物が言えない。His stupidity really staggers me.

あくえき 悪疫 a plague; a pestilence; an epidemic ¶悪疫流行地 a plague spot; a pestilence-stricken district.

あくかんじょう 悪感情 ill feeling ¶悪感情を抱く have [((文)) harbor] bad [ill] feeling (toward); ((文)) be ill disposed (toward) / 悪感情を与える offend; ((文)) impress sb unfavorably.

あくさい 悪妻 a bad wife.

あくじ 悪事 〈悪行〉((文)) an evil [a wicked] deed; 〈罪悪〉a crime; ((文)) a sinful deed ¶悪事を働く do wrong [((文)) evil]; do sb harm; commit a crime / 悪事を重ねる commit one crime after another. 用例⇩

あくじき 悪食 ¶悪食をする人 ((文)) a gross feeder; a person who eats bizarre foods.

あくしつ 悪質 ¶悪質な wicked; ((文)) pernicious (propaganda); 〈悪性の〉malignant ((tumors)).

あくしゅ[1] 悪手 〈囲碁・将棋などの〉a bad move [play] ((at chess)).

あくしゅ[2] 握手 shaking hands; a handshake; 〈了解〉an understanding; 〈仲直り〉((口語)) making-up; ((文)) reconciliation ¶握手をする shake hands ((with)); 〈妥結する〉come to an understanding; 〈仲直りする〉((文)) be reconciled ((with)); 〈口語〉make up / 握手を求める offer sb one's hand / 握手を交わす shake hands with each other / 握手し合う shake each other's hands; shake each other by the hand / 全員と握手を交わす shake hands all around. 用例⇩

あくしゅう[1] 悪臭 a bad [nasty] smell; ((文)) an offensive odor; a stench; ((口語)) a stink ¶悪臭のある stinking; evil-smelling; ((文)) malodorous / 悪臭を放つ give off a bad smell; give off [emit] an evil smell [stench]; smell bad; stink. 用例⇩

あくしゅう[2] 悪習 a bad habit; evil ways; ((文)) a vice; 〈悪風〉a bad custom; ((文)) an evil practice; ((文)) an abuse ¶悪習がつく contract a bad habit.

あくしゅみ 悪趣味 bad [vulgar] taste. 用例⇩

あくじゅんかん 悪循環 ((form)) a vicious circle ¶賃金と物価の悪循環 a wage-price spiral.

あくしょ 悪書 a bad book; an [a morally] offensive book ¶悪書を追放する get rid of undesirable books.

あくじょうけん 悪条件 bad [((文)) unfavorable] conditions; a handicap ¶悪条件の下ですぐれた成果を上げる achieve excellent results under unfavorable conditions / 悪条件を克服する get over [((文)) surmount] a handicap.

アクション action ¶アクションドラマ an action drama / アクションペインティング action painting.

あくせい[1] 悪性 ¶悪性の malignant; virulent (diseases) / 悪性の感冒 a bad cold / 悪性のインフレ vicious inflation / 悪性腫瘍(しゅよう) a malignant tumor; a malignancy.

あくせい[2] 悪政 bad government; ((文)) misgovernment; ((文)) misrule ¶悪政を行なう misgovern (a country) / 悪政に苦しむ suffer under the misrule (of a tyrant).

あくぜい 悪税 a bad [an unreasonable] tax.

あくせく ¶あくせくと busily / あくせくする busy oneself ((about)); be busy ((about)); 〈心を煩わす〉worry (oneself) ((about)) / あくせく働く work hard (with almost no rest); toil and moil; slave away / 金もうけにあくせくする be bent on making money / 小さな事にあくせくする worry (oneself) about trifles. 用例⇩

アクセサリー 〈wear〉 accessories.

アクセル an accelerator ¶アクセルを踏む press [step on] the accelerator [((米口語)) gas pedal] / アクセルを踏む足をゆるめる ease [((口語)) let] up on the accelerator.

あくせん 悪銭 ill-gotten gains. 用例⇩

あくせんくとう 悪戦苦闘 ¶悪戦苦闘する fight desperately [against heavy odds]; struggle hard (against).

あくせんでん 悪宣伝 〈悪意な〉((文)) pernicious propaganda; 〈悪意のある〉malicious propaganda; 〈虚偽の〉false propaganda ¶悪宣伝をする make [spread] pernicious propaganda ((about)).

アクセント (an) accent; (a) stress ¶アクセントのある[ない] accented [unaccented]; stressed [unstressed] / アクセントをつける accent (a word on the second syllable); stress (the first syllable). 用例⇩

あく[1] パンドラが箱を開けると、あらゆる悪がそこから出て来て、それ以来世界を悩ますことになった. When Pandora opened the box, all kinds of evil came out of it and have plagued the world ever since.

あく[2] 行ってみたら戸が少し開いていた. I found the door ajar [slightly open]. / 雨戸が開かない. The shutters will not open. / その店は午前8時に開きます. The store opens at 8 a.m. / 席がたくさん空いている. There are a lot of empty seats. / この席は空いていますか. Is this seat free? / その新聞、空いたら回してください. Please give me the paper when you have done [are through] with it.

あくい 彼に悪意があって言ったわけではない. He meant no harm by it [when he said it]. / 彼の言葉には悪意は少しもなかった. There was no malice whatever in what he said.

あくうん 悪運尽きて彼はついに逮捕された. His luck finally ran out and he got himself [he was] arrested.

あくじ 悪事千里を走る. The evil that men do is quickly known.

あくしゅ[2] 2人は固い握手をして別れた. They parted after exchanging a firm handshake.

あくしゅう[1] 悪臭ふんぷんとして鼻をついた. An offensive smell greeted my nose. | It stank to high heaven.

あくしゅみ 彼はひどく悪趣味なネクタイをしていた. His tie was in very bad taste.

あくせく これは私があくせく働いて稼いだ金だ. I earned this money by the sweat of my brow.

あくせん 悪銭身に付かず. Easy come, easy go. 〈諺〉

あくせんくとう 彼は悪戦苦闘の末今日の地位を克ち得たのだ. He has attained his present status after a long and hard struggle against great difficulties.

アクセント この語は第2音節にアクセントがある. The word is

あ

あくたい 悪態 ¶悪態をつく abuse;《口語》fling [throw] dirt at *sb*; call *sb* names.

あくだま 悪玉《口語》a baddie;《米口語》a bad guy; a villain.

アクチニウム【化】actinium.

あくてんこう 悪天候 bad [《文》unfavorable, nasty] weather; 〈荒天〉rough [stormy] weather.

あくどい 〈けばけばしい〉gaudy; showy; loud《colors》; 〈意地の悪い〉vicious ¶あくどい化粧をしている wear heavy [too much] make-up; be too heavily made up / あくどいやり方で金もうけをする make money by hook or by crook [《文》by unscrupulous means].

あくとう[1] 悪投【野球】《make》a bad throw《to second base》.

あくとう[2] 悪党 a rascal; a villain; a scoundrel;《文》a blackguard.

あくどう 悪童 a bad [naughty] boy.

あくとく 悪徳 (a) vice ¶悪徳業者 a dishonest [《口語》crooked] businessman [trader].

あくにん 悪人 a wicked [bad] person;《文》a wrongdoer.

あぐねる ⇨あぐむ ¶考えあぐねる think and think《about *sth*》but get nowhere.

あくび a yawn ¶あくびする yawn; give a《big》yawn / あくびの出るような boring; dull; tedious / 手であくびを隠す hide a yawn behind *one's* hand / あくびをかみ殺す stifle [smother] a yawn. [文例⇩]

あくひつ 悪筆 bad [poor,《文》execrable] handwriting;《文》a poor [bad] hand ¶悪筆である have bad handwriting;《文》write a poor [bad] hand.

あくひょう 悪評《文》unfavorable criticism; 〈不評判〉a bad reputation;《文》ill fame [repute] ¶とかくの悪評のある人 a person with a bad [《文》of somewhat unsavory] reputation / 悪評を受ける〈批評〉《文》be criticized unfavorably;《口語》get a bad press (新聞などで); 〈評判〉be spoken ill of / 悪評を買う get a bad reputation.

あくびょうどう 悪平等《文》misapplied equality. [文例⇩]

あくふう 悪風 a bad custom; (a) vice ¶世間の悪風に染まる《文》be led astray [infected] with the vices of others [the vices practiced in the world around *one*].

あくぶん 悪文 a bad style.

あくへい 悪弊《文》an abuse;《文》an evil [a corrupt] practice ¶悪弊を一掃する stamp [wipe] out evils; uproot [extirpate] evil practices.

あくへき 悪癖 a bad habit; a vice ¶喫煙の悪癖を覚える get into the (bad) habit of smoking / 悪癖を直す〈人の〉cure *sb* of a bad habit; 〈自分の〉break *oneself* of [get over,《口語》kick] a bad habit.

あくほう 悪法 a bad law. [文例⇩]

あくま 悪魔 a devil; a demon;《文》a fiend; Satan (特にキリスト教の) ¶悪魔のような devilish; fiendish / 悪魔払い exorcism (of demons).

あくまで(も) 飽くまで(も) 〈最後まで〉to the last; to the (bitter) end; 〈頑強に〉persistently; stubbornly; 〈極力〉《文》to the utmost; to the best of *one's* ability ¶飽くまでもがんばる persist to the bitter end / 飽くまでも自説を曲げない stick to *one's* opinion / 飽くまでも戦う fight it out. [文例⇩]

あくむ 悪夢 a bad [an unpleasant, a terrible] dream; a nightmare ¶悪夢に襲われる have [be troubled by] a nightmare / 悪夢からさめる wake from a nightmare; 〈本心に立ち返る〉come to *one's* senses. [文例⇩]

あぐむ 倦む 〈飽きる〉《文》grow [get] weary《of》; get [be] tired《of》 ¶待ちあぐむ get tired of waiting / 攻めあぐむ be at a loss how to continue the offensive.

あくめい 悪名 a bad name [reputation];《文》notoriety ¶悪名高い notorious.

あくやく 悪役 (the role of) the villain ¶悪役を演じる play the villain《in a film》.

あくゆう 悪友 a bad friend [companion]; bad company (集合的) ¶悪友と交わる keep bad company. [文例⇩]

あくよう 悪用《文》(an) abuse; (a) misuse;《文》(an) improper use ¶悪用する make bad [wrong] use《of》; abuse; use *sth* for the wrong [《文》an evil] purpose;《文》put [turn] *sth* to evil ends.

あぐら ¶あぐらをかく sit cross-legged [tailor fashion]; sit with *one's* legs crossed / (過去の)名声の上にあぐらをかいている rest on *one's* laurels.

あくらつ 悪辣 ¶悪辣な crafty; wily; villainous;《文》knavish / 悪辣な事をする play a wily trick; 〈常習的に〉be given to sharp

---

accented on the second syllable. | In this word the accent [stress] is [falls] on the second syllable.

あくび あくびはうつる. Yawning is catching. / あの先生の講義はあくびが出る. His lectures are boring [as dull as ditchwater].

あくびょうどう この場合, それは悪平等というものだ. The principle of equality ought not to be applied in this case.

あくほう たとえ悪法でも法は法である. A law is a law, however undesirable it may be.

あくまで(も) 彼は飽くまでも反対した. He opposed it stubbornly. | He maintained his opposition to the bitter end. / 彼は飽くまで落胆しなかった. Come what might, he never allowed himself to be discouraged. | Nothing could make him lose heart.

あくむ 悪夢のような一日だった. It was a nightmarish day.

あくゆう (おどけて)いやー, 悪友にさそわれちゃってね, バーで一杯やって来たんだ. As a matter of fact, a friend of mine insisted that I join him. I just couldn't shake him off and went to a bar to have a drink with him.

あくろ 山頂からT温泉への道は非常な悪路であった. The trail that led from the top of the mountain to the T hot spring was in an extremely bad state of repair.

あげく ひどい目にあって, あげくの果てに首になった. To complete [add to] his misfortune, he was fired from his job. / 口論の

practices.
あくりょう 悪霊 an evil [a malevolent] spirit ¶悪霊を払う ward off evil spirits / 悪霊に取りつかれる be possessed by an evil spirit.
あくりょく 握力 grasping power; grip ¶握力が強い[弱い] have a strong [weak] grip / 右手の握力が約70キロある be able to exert a right-handed squeeze of 70 kilograms or so / 握力計 a (squeeze) dynamometer.
アクリル 《化》 ¶アクリル樹脂[繊維] (an) acrylic resin [fiber].
あくる- 明くる… ¶明くる日[年] the next [following] day [year] / 明くる3月10日に on the following day, the tenth of March.
あくれい 悪例 ¶悪例を作る[残す] set [leave] a bad [poor] example (for); set [establish, create] a bad precedent.
アグレマン 《フランス語》《give, ask for》 an agrément.
あくろ 悪路 a bad road. 文例⇩
アクロバット 〈人〉 an acrobat; 〈曲芸〉 acrobatics ¶アクロバットダンサー an acrobatic dancer; a contortionist (体をくにゃくにゃに曲げる) / アクロバットダンス an acrobatic dance.
-あけ… 明け ¶つゆ明け the end of the rainy season / 休会明けの国会 the first session of the Diet after the recess.
あげ[1] 上げ 〈着物の〉 a tuck ¶上げをする tuck (a dress); put [make] a tuck in (the skirt) / 上げを下ろす undo [let out] a tuck.
あげ[2] 揚げ 〈豆腐の〉 fried bean curd.
あげあし 揚げ足 ¶揚げ足を取る catch sb tripping; trip sb up / 揚げ足取りの好きな faultfinding (colleagues); 《文》 captious (critics).
あげおろし 上げ下ろし raising and lowering; 〈荷物の〉 loading and unloading.
あけがた 明け方 dawn; daybreak ¶明け方に at dawn [daybreak]; at (the) break of dawn; 〈明け方近くなって〉 toward daybreak.
あげく ¶あげく(の果てに) in the end; finally; on top of all that; to make matters worse (悪いことに) / さんざん捜したあげくに after all one's efforts to find (it) / 長く患ったあげくに after a long illness. 文例⇩
あけくれ 明け暮れ morning and evening; day and night; day in, day out; 〈常に〉 always; all the time.
あけくれる 明け暮れる ¶読書に明け暮れる spend all one's time reading; 《文》 devote all one's time to reading. 文例⇩
あげしお 上げ潮 the rising [incoming] tide; (a) flood tide; (at) high tide. 文例⇩
-あげで 文例⇩
あけすけ ¶あけすけに frankly; 《文》 unreservedly; straightforwardly.
あげぜん 上げ膳 ¶上げ膳下げ膳で暮らす do not need to lift a finger about the house.
あげぞこ 上げ底 a raised bottom.
あけたて 開け閉て ¶開けたてする open and shut (a door) / 戸の開けたてに注意する be careful in handling the doors.
あげだま 揚げ玉 bits of fried *tempura* batter.
あけっぱなし 開けっ放し ¶開けっ放しにする [しておく] leave [keep] (a door) open.
あけっぴろげ 開けっ広げ ¶開けっ広げな frank; open. 文例⇩
あげつらう take [bring] (a matter) up for discussion; discuss sth (with sb); comment on sth; 〈批判する〉 criticize.
あげて 挙げて all; 《文》 (in a body) ¶全財産を挙げて事業に投資する invest all one has in an enterprise. 文例⇩
あけてもくれても 明けても暮れても ⇨あけくれ.
あげはちょう 《昆》 a swallowtailed butterfly; a swallowtail.
あけはなし 明[開]け放し ⇨あけっぱなし. 文例⇩
あけはなす 明[開]け放す throw [fling] (a window) open.
あけぼの 曙 dawn; daybreak ⇨よあけ.
あげもの 揚げ物 (deep-)fried food.
あける[1] 明ける 〈始まる〉 begin; 〈終わる〉 end; be over ¶夜が明ける day breaks [《文》 dawns] / 明けゆく空 the dawning sky. 文例⇩
あける[2] 開[空]ける 〈開く〉 open; 〈穴を〉 bore; make (a hole); 〈中を〉 empty (a box); clear (a room); 〈注ぎ出す〉 pour out; 〈明け渡す〉 leave; 《文》 vacate (the house) ¶第30ページを開ける open the book at [to] page 30 / 包みを開ける open [undo] the wrapper / ビールを1ダース空ける put away a dozen bottles of beer / 鍋にミルクを空ける empty the milk into a pan / 席を空ける make room (for) / 家を空ける stay away from home / 戸をすこし開けておく keep [leave] the door ajar [slightly open] / 口を大きく開けて with one's mouth wide open. 文例⇩

あげくに殴り合いになった. The quarrel developed into a fistfight.
あけくれる 娘の急死に会って, 涙に明け暮れる毎日でした. We spent the days weeping over the sudden death of our daughter.
あげしお 今は上げ潮です. 〈潮が差して来る〉 The tide is rising [coming in]. 〈満潮である〉 The tide is in.
-あげず あの男は三日にあげずやって来る. He comes to see me virtually every other day.
あげぞこ この箱は上げ底になっている. This box has a raised bottom.
あけっぴろげ あの人はいつもあけっぴろげで腹蔵がない. He always wears his heart on his sleeve.
あげて 彼は一家を挙げて南米に移住した. He emigrated to South America with his whole family.
あけはなし ドアを開け放しにしないで下さい. 《掲示》 Please shut the door. | Keep this door closed.
あける[1] 夜が明けた. Day dawned./ もう2時間すると夜が明ける. It will be daylight in two hours. / すっかり夜が明けはなれた. It is broad daylight. | It is quite light now. / 3月3日. The sun rose on the morning of March 3. / 明けましておめでとう. A Happy New Year (to you)! / 梅雨が明けた. The rainy season is over. / 彼女は君でなければ夜も日も明けない. You are everything to her. | 《口語》 She thinks the sun shines out of your eyes.
あける[2] 裏口の戸を開けるとすぐ

あげる 上[揚, 挙]げる 〈上に〉raise;《文》elevate; lift (up); send up; hold up (かざす);〈昇進させる〉promote;〈吐く〉vomit;〈口語〉bring up (one's breakfast);〈俗〉throw up (★自動詞として使うのが普通);〈与える〉give;〈終える〉finish;〈式などを〉hold;〈示す〉mention;〈列挙する〉list;《文》enumerate;〈検挙する〉arrest; round up (一斉に);〈揚物を〉(deep-)fry ¶本をたなに上げる put a book on a shelf / 旗を揚げる raise [hoist] a flag; run a flag up (a pole) / 顔を上げる raise one's face; look up / (15+16のような計算で)下に1を書いて1を上に上げる put down one and carry one / 腕を上げる improve one's skill (in, at) / 100万円の純益をあげる make a net profit of one million yen; clear a million yen / 賃金を上げて もらう have [get] one's wages raised; get a raise《英》rise] (in salary) / 子供を学校に上げる send one's child to school / 実例を挙げる give an example;《文》cite an instance / 警察に挙げられる be arrested; be taken to the police station / 野菜をサラダ油で揚げる fry vegetables in salad oil. 文例⇩

-あげる 文例⇩

あけわたし 明け渡し evacuation; surrender ¶明け渡しを要求する ask (the tenant) to vacate (the house) / 明け渡しを通告する give (the tenant) notice to quit.

あけわたす 明け渡す vacate (a house); evacuate (a town); surrender (a castle).

あご 顎 the chin; the jaw ¶二重あごの double-chinned / あごを出す be exhausted; get tired out;《米俗》poop out / あごを引く draw in one's chin / 水にあごまで浸る be up to one's chin (be chin-deep) in water / あごで使う have sb at one's beck and call. 文例⇩

アコーデオン an accordion ¶アコーデオンドア an accordion door / アコーデオンプリーツ accordion pleats.

あこがれ 憧れ《文》(a) yearning《for》; (a) longing《for》.

あこがれる 憧れる《文》yearn for [after]; hanker for [wish] for;〈すばらしいと思う〉admire; adore ¶都会生活にあこがれる hanker after [be attracted by] city life.

あごひげ 顎鬚 a beard ¶あごひげを生やしている have [wear] a beard / あごひげを生やした人 a bearded man.

あごひも 顎紐 a chin strap ¶帽子のあごひもをかける have one's cap strapped to one's chin.

あこやがい〈貝〉a pearl oyster.

あさ¹ 麻〈繊維〉hemp;〈布〉hemp (cloth);〈植〉a hemp (plant) / 麻(製)の hemp(en) / 麻糸[ひも, なわ] hemp yarn [twine, rope].

あさ² 朝 morning ¶朝早く early in the morning / 朝から晩まで from morning till night; all day (long) / 朝まで until morning / 朝までには by (tomorrow) morning; before morning / 朝(のうち)に in the morning / 5日の朝に on the morning of the 5th / 日曜の朝に on Sunday morning / (毎週)火曜と木曜の朝に on Tuesday and Thursday mornings; every Tuesday and Thursday morning / ある夏の朝 one summer morning / 朝昼晩と3度食事をする have three meals a day, at morning, noon and evening / 朝型の人 a person who is at his best in the morning(s). 文例⇩

あざ¹ 字 a (village) section ¶中野村字吉田 Yoshida, Nakano Village.

あざ² 痣〈生まれつきの〉a birthmark;〈打撲傷〉a bruise ¶あざができるほどひどく打つ beat sb black and blue / なぐられて目の回りが黒いあざになっている have a black eye.

あさい 浅い shallow;〈浅薄な〉superficial;〈傷が〉slight;〈関係が〉slight; not close;〈色が〉light;〈皿〉pale ¶浅い眠り a light sleep / 浅い皿 a shallow dish / 浅い眠り a light sleep / 考えの浅い人 a shallow thinker / 経験が浅い do not have much experience (in) / 浅からぬ関係 a close relationship [connection];《文》intimacy (特に異性間の) / 椅子に浅く腰かけている sit forward in one's chair. 文例⇩

あさいち 朝市 a morning fair.

あさおき 朝起き ⇨はやおき. 文例⇩

あさがお 朝顔〈植〉a morning glory;〈ラッパ類の〉the bell《of a trombone》¶朝顔形の trumpet-[funnel-]shaped.

あさぎ¹ 浅黄 light [pale] yellow.

あさぎ² 浅葱 light [pale] blue.

狭い路地だ。The back door opens onto a narrow lane. / だれかが戸を開けようとした。Someone tried the door. / 2人でウィスキーを1本空けた。We killed a bottle of whisky between the two of us. / ちょっとの間お手があけられますか。Do you have a few moments to spare?

あげる 新聞から目を上げて窓の外を見た。He raised his eyes from his newspaper and looked out of the window. / この本を君に上げよう。You can have this book. / I'll give you this book. / 今は機械時代で, ほんの2,3の例を挙げれば, 自動車もテレビも衣服も書物もみな機械で作られたものである。We live in a machine age; motorcars, TV sets, clothes, and books, to name but a few (to mention only a few), are all machine-made products.

-あげる 手伝ってあげよう。I'll help you (with your work). / 切符を買ってあげよう。I'll buy [get] you a ticket. | I'll buy [get] a ticket for you. / そのおばあさんに手を貸してバスから降ろしてあげた。I helped the old woman down from the bus. / 年寄りには親切にしてあげましょう。Be kind to old people.

あご あごを引いて, 胸を張れ。Chin down, chest out! / あごがはずれた。I dislocated my jaw. | I got a dislocated jaw. / あごに1発がんと食らわせてやった。I let him have it right on (the point of) the chin. / もっといい商売を見つけないとあごが干上がってしまう。I'll starve if I can't find a better job.

あこがれ 彼はあこがれのナポリに着いた。He arrived in Naples that he had wanted to visit for so long. / スイス訪問が私の長年のあこがれであった。To visit Switzerland was my long-cherished desire.

あさ² 朝からずっと雨が降っている。It has been raining since morning. / あの人は朝が早い[遅い]。He is an early [a late] riser. /

あさぎり 朝霧 a morning mist.
あさぐろい 浅黒い darkish; swarthy ¶色が浅黒い have a dark complexion / 色の浅黒い男 a dark-complexioned man.
あざけり 嘲り ridicule;《文》scorn; a sneer ¶あざけりを受ける be sneered at;《文》be subjected to ridicule [scorn].
あざける 嘲る ridicule; sneer (at); scoff (at); jeer (at); mock (at); make fun of ¶あざけり笑う laugh at.
あさざけ 朝酒 a morning drink;《米》an eye-opener.
あさせ 浅瀬 shallows; a shoal; a ford (歩いて, 又は車で, 渡れる所) ¶浅瀬に乗り上げる run [go] aground.
あさつき〖植〗chives.
あさって 明後日 (the) day after tomorrow ¶あさっての朝[晩] the morning [evening] after next.
あさつゆ 朝露 morning dew.
あさなぎ 朝凪 a morning calm (on the sea).
あさね 朝寝 ¶朝寝する get up late; lie in bed (till) late in the morning;《英口語》have a lie-in.
あさねぼう 朝寝坊 a late riser.
あさはか 浅はか ¶浅はかな〈無思慮な〉thoughtless; shallow;《文》imprudent; short-sighted;〈愚かな〉silly;《文》unwise / 浅はかな考え a shallow idea; a superficial way of thinking. 文例 ⇩
あさはん 朝飯 ⇨ ちょうしょく.
あさばん 朝晩 morning and evening; day and night. 文例 ⇩
あさひ 朝日 the morning [rising] sun ¶朝日に匂う山桜花 wild cherry blossoms glowing in the morning sun. 文例 ⇩
あさましい 浅ましい〈恥ずべき〉shameful; disgraceful;〈卑しい〉contemptible;《文》base;《文》mean;〈惨めな〉miserable; wretched ¶浅ましい行為 a mean act;《文》shameful [despicable] conduct / 浅ましい世の中 a wretched world / 我が身を浅ましく思う be ashamed of *oneself* ((for what *one* has done)). 文例 ⇩
あざみ〖植〗a thistle.
あざむく 欺く deceive ⇨ だます. 文例 ⇩

あさめし 朝飯 ⇨ ちょうしょく ¶朝飯前の仕事〈比喩的〉an easy job [task]; a cinch;《英俗》a doddle. 文例 ⇩
あさもや 朝靄 a morning mist.
あざやか 鮮やか ¶鮮やかな clear《lines》; vivid《impressions》; bright《colors》;〈手際のよい, 見事な〉splendid《skill》; brilliant《technique》; fine《performance》/ 鮮やかな黄色 a vivid yellow / 鮮やかな勝利 a brilliant victory / 鮮やかな飛行ぶり skillful piloting / 鮮やかさ brightness; vividness / 鮮やかに clearly; brightly;〈見事に〉splendidly; skillfully. 文例 ⇩
あさやけ 朝焼け a (red) glow in the morning sky. 文例 ⇩
あさゆ 朝湯 (take) a morning bath.
あさゆう 朝夕 ⇨ あさばん.
あざらし〖動〗a [an earless] seal.
あさり〖貝〗an *asari* clam ★これに近い貝にcockleがある.
あさる 漁る look [search] for; hunt (for);〈動物が食べ物を〉scavenge ¶えさをあさり歩く prowl about for food; wander about in search of food / 残飯をあさる野良猫 a stray cat scavenging for kitchen waste / 古本をあさる hunt for secondhand books; poke around second-hand bookstores.
あざわらう 嘲笑う laugh at; sneer at; ridicule;《文》deride.
あし[1] 足, 脚 a foot (*pl.* feet) (足); a leg (脚); a paw (犬猫などの);〈たこなどの〉a tentacle; an arm;〈グラスの〉the stem;〈歩調〉step; pace ¶太い脚 thick [heavy] legs; plump legs (女の) / 足が遅い be slow on *one's* feet; be a slow walker [runner] / 足が達者である have strong legs; be a good [strong] walker / 足が立つようになる find *one's* feet [legs] / 足が地に着いている keep *one's* feet on the ground; be realistic / 予算から足が出る exceed the budget / 脚が長い have long legs; be long-legged / 足が早いを be quick on *one's* feet; be a fast walker [runner] / 脚が短い have short legs; be short-legged / 足が弱い have weak legs; be weak in the legs; be a poor walker / 足の裏 the sole (of *one's* foot); the bottom of

---

朝のこんな時間に人の家へ行くのですか. Are you really going out to visit [see] someone at this time of the morning? / 2人はそれから朝まで語り明かした. They talked for the rest of the night.
あさい 彼の英文学の知識は浅い. He has only a superficial knowledge of English literature. / 私はあの人とは交際が浅い. I only know him slightly. |《文》I am only slightly acquainted with him. / 会社は創立以来日がまだ浅い. It is not (very) long since the firm was established. / 春はまだ浅い. It is still [《文》as yet] early spring. / Spring has just set in. / 2人の間には浅からぬ関係がある. The two of them are on very familiar terms [are very close].
あさおき 朝起きは三文の得. The early bird catches the worm.〖諺〗
あさはか 死のうと思ったのは浅はかでした. It was silly of me to think of killing myself.
あさばん 朝晩はめっきり涼しくなった. It is quite cool these days in the mornings and evenings.
あさひ 僕の部屋には朝日がさし込む. My room catches [gets] the morning sun [sunlight].
あさましい 何という浅ましいことをしたのだろう. What a shameful thing to have done!
あざむく 明々と照明された室内は昼を欺く明るさであった. The room was illuminated so brilliantly that it looked as if it was in full daylight.
あさめし そんなことは朝飯前さ. I could do it before breakfast. | That's nothing. | Nothing could be easier. |《口語》It's as easy as pie.
あざやか その日の出来事は今も鮮やかに覚えている. I still vividly remember [《文》have a vivid recollection of] what happened on that day.
あさやけ 朝焼けの日には雨が降ると言われている. A red sky [glow]

one's foot / 足の甲 one's instep / 3本足のテーブル a three-legged table / 脚の太いズボン wide-legged trousers / 足の向くままに歩く walk at random; go wherever one's fancy takes one / 足の指å toe / 足を洗う wash one's feet; ⟨やめる⟩ wash one's hands of ⟨an affair⟩; quit ⟨the shady business⟩ / ⟨交通の⟩足を奪われる be deprived of (means of) transport / 足を組む cross one's legs / 足をすくう trip sb up ⟨組んでいた⟩足を解く unwind one's legs / 足を留めą stop; stay / ⟨流れなどに⟩足をとられる be swept [carried] off one's feet / 足を伸ばす stretch (out) one's legs / ⟨行程を⟩ go a little way further (to) / extend one's journey (as far as Kobe) / 何遍も足を運ぶ visit sb several times; 《文》 frequent ⟨a place⟩ / 足を早める quicken one's pace / ⟨疲れた⟩足を引きずって歩く drag one's weary feet; trudge ⟨along⟩ / ⟨競争仲間の⟩足を引っぱる do something to keep ⟨one's rival⟩ from succeeding; try to obstruct [《文》 frustrate] sb; try to stand in sb's way / 足を向ける 《文》 direct [turn, bend] one's steps (toward a place) / 足を緩める slacken one's pace / 足にまめができる get blisters on one's feet. 文例⇩

あし² 葦 《植》 a reed ¶あしの生い茂ったreedy [reed-grown] ⟨marshes⟩. 文例⇩

あじ¹ 味 (a) taste; (a) flavor; 《文》 (a) savor ¶…の味がする[する] 《文》 savor) of…; have a flavor of… / 味が変わる(悪くなる)turn sour [stale] / 良い味がする, 味がいい taste good [nice, sweet] / 妙な味がする have a strange taste / 味のある tasteful; ⟨含蓄のある⟩《文》 pregnant; suggestive / 味のない tasteless; insipid; ⟨くだらない⟩ dry; dull / 味のよい nice; tasty; delicious; 《文》 savory / 《文》 palatable / 物の味のわからない人 a person without a (discriminating) palate / 味の悪い bad-tasting; nasty; 《文》 unsavory; unpalatable / 味をしめる[覚える] get [acquire] a taste (for) / 味を付ける season / 味を付ける taste (to) / 味をみる taste; try [have] a taste of; sample; ⟨試食[飲]する⟩ try / 食べられるかどうかを味で見分ける tell by taste whether sth is edible or not / 味なことを言う

say something clever [witty] / 味なことをやる act smartly; do something impressive. 文例⇩

あじ² 《魚》 a horse mackerel.

アジ [⟨agitation⟩] ¶アジ演説 a propaganda [an inflammatory] speech / アジビラ a propaganda [an inflammatory] handbill [poster].

アジア Asia ¶アジアの Asiatic; Asian / アジア人 an Asiatic; an Asian / アジア(競技)大会 the Asian Games / アジア大陸 the Asian Continent.

あしあと 足跡 a footprint; a footmark ¶足跡を残す[つける] leave one's footprints / 足跡をたどって[つけて]行く follow (up) sb's footsteps; follow ⟨an elephant's⟩ tracks.

あしおと 足音 a footstep; a step ¶足音を立てる[立てない] walk noisily [silently] / 足音を立てて with noisy footsteps / 足音を立てずに with silent steps; ⟨walk⟩ without making a sound / 足音をあまり立てない人 a quiet [soft] walker / 足音をしのばせて with stealthy steps; ⟨move⟩ on cat's feet. 文例⇩

あしか 《動》 a sea lion; an eared seal.

あしがかり 足掛かり a footing; a foothold ¶⟨登山者などが⟩足掛かりを探す look for a foothold ⟨on a bare rock⟩; try to get a purchase with one's feet ⟨on a rock face⟩. 文例⇩

あしかけ 足掛 文例⇩

あしかけあがり 足掛け上り 《体操》 legging-up.

あじかげん 味加減を見る taste sth to see how it is seasoned.

あしかせ 足枷 fetters; shackles ¶足枷をはめられている be in fetters.

あしからず 悪しからず 文例⇩

あしきり 足切り ⟨入試の⟩ ¶足切りを行なう eliminate candidates who have failed to score a certain number of points (in the first test).

あしくび 足首 an ankle.

あしげ¹ 足蹴 ¶足蹴にする kick; give sb a kick.

あしげ² 葦毛 ¶葦毛の馬 a gray horse / 連銭葦毛の dapple-gray ⟨horses⟩.

あじけない 味気ない dull; flat; dreary ¶味気ない世の中 a dreary world; 《文》 wearisome life / 世の中が味気なくなる get tired of living. 文例⇩

あしこし 足腰 ¶足腰が立つうちは as long as

---

at sunrise is said to be a sign of rain.

あし¹ 彼は足がふらついていた。 He was unsteady on his feet. / パジャマの一方の脚に両脚を入れてしまった。I put both legs into one leg of my pajamas. / ミサゴが魚を足でつかんだ。 The osprey seized a fish in its talons [claws]. / とても疲れてそれ以上一歩も足が出なかった。 I was so tired that I couldn't walk another step. / 君の足なら5分で行ける。At your pace you can get there in five minutes. / その足で入院中の友人の見舞に行った。 He went directly to see his friend in (the) hospital, without coming home first. / 質に入れた時計から足がついた。The watch he had pawned put the police on the scent. / それで足がついて御用となった。 That supplied a clue which led to his arrest. / 学友の足もしだいに遠くなった。 His schoolmates began to keep away from him. / この記事を書くには随分足を使った。 It took a lot of legwork to write this article.

あし² 人は考える葦である。Man is a thinking reed.

あじ¹ それは何の味もしなかった。 It had no taste at all. / お味はいかがですか。| What do you think of it? | 狐は、一旦鶏の味を覚えると又

やって来る。 If foxes once taste a chicken, they will come back again. / この魚はまずまずの味だ。 This fish tastes pretty good. | This fish doesn't taste at all bad. / 風邪を引いて食べ物の味がわからない。 I've got a cold and I can't taste what I'm eating [and I've lost my sense of taste]. / この酒は強すぎてフランス料理のデリケートな味を殺している。 This liquor is too strong; it kills the delicate flavor of French cuisine. / 君のような人が貧乏の味を知っているはずはないよ。How could you know what it is like to be poor? / 競馬で味を占めるとなかなかやめられないもの

あしごしらえ　17　あじわう

one can move about / 足腰の立たない病人 a bedridden invalid.
あしごしらえ 足拵え ¶足ごしらえを厳重にする put on sturdy footwear (in preparation for a long hard climb).
あじさい 《植》a hydrangea.
あじさし 《鳥》a tern.
あしざま 悪し様 ¶悪し様に言う abuse *sb*; speak insultingly 《to, about》; 《文》speak ill of *sb*; paint *sb* black ⇨ **あっこう, わるくち**.
あししげく 足繁く ¶足繁く通う visit [go to] 《a place》frequently [very often]; pay frequent visits to 《a house》; 《文》frequent 《a bar》.
あした 明日 tomorrow ⇨ **あす**. 文例⇩
あしだい 足代 travel(ing) expenses; carfare, a fare.
あしつき 足つき the way *one* walks. 文例⇩
あじつけ 味付け seasoning; flavoring ¶味付け海苔 seasoned laver.
あしでまとい 足手纏い 〈係累〉《文》an encumbrance;〈邪魔物〉a nuisance; a hindrance;《口語》a drag ¶足手まといになる〈物が〉be a nuisance 《to *one*》;《文》《物・人に》妨げられる〉 be hindered 《by》;《文》be encumbered 《with》. 文例⇩
あしどめ 足留め ¶足留めする keep *sb* indoors;〈滞在させる〉persuade [《文》induce] *sb* to stay / 足留めを食う be stranded [marooned] 《in *one's* hotel because of a snowstorm》; be obliged [forced] to stay on 《at a place》.
あしどり 足取り 〈歩き方〉the way *one* walks; *one's* tread;《文》*one's* gait; 〈物события などの〉a movement ¶ゆっくりした足取りの slow-paced 《camels》/ 重い[軽い]足取りで with heavy [light] steps / 足どりを探る trace the movements 《of》/ 足どりを早める quicken [increase] *one's* step [gait].
あしなみ 足並み a pace; a step ¶足並みをそろえる 〈早さを〉keep pace 《with》;〈左右の足を〉fall [get] into step 《with》/ 足並みを乱す break [walk out of] step.
あしならし 足慣らし ¶足慣らしをする walk for practice.
あしば 足場 〈建築用の〉scaffolding; a scaffold; 〈足を掛ける所〉(a) footing (★複数にはしない); a foothold ¶足場を掛ける set up scaffolding / 足場を得る get [《文》gain,《文》secure] a foothold / 一歩一歩足場を確かめて岩壁をよじ登る climb a rocky cliff testing the footing for each step.
あしばや 足早な light-footed;《文》swift-footed / 足早な人 a quick walker; a light-footed person / 足早に at a quick [brisk] pace.
あしぶみ 足踏み ¶足踏みする step; stamp;〈行進を止めて〉mark time;〈進まない〉make no progress [headway]; be at a standstill.
あしもと 足下[元] ¶足下に at *one's* feet / 足下が危ない[ふらつく] be unsteady on *one's* feet [legs]; walk with unsteady [uncertain] steps; walk unsteadily [uncertainly] / 足下の明るいうちに〈日の暮れぬうちに〉before dark [nightfall];〈手後れにならないように〉before it is too late / 足下にも寄り付けない be nothing [nowhere near] as good as;《文》be far inferior 《to》; be no match 《for》/ 足下に付け込む, 足下を見る take unfair advantage of 《*sb's* helpless condition》/ 足下から鳥が立つようにabruptly;《文》precipitately. 文例⇩
あしゅ 亜種《生物》a subspecies 《単複同形》¶亜種の subspecific.
あしゅら 阿修羅《仏教》Asura ¶あしゅらのように with berserk(er) fury [rage];《go》berserk;《口語》like fury.
あしらい treatment; (a) reception (接待) ¶客あしらいがよい be hospitable;〈店が〉give good service.
あしらう 〈待遇する〉treat;《文》receive;〈操る〉handle; deal with;〈食品などを〉dress. 文例⇩
アジる stir up [instigate] *sb* 《to do》.
あしわ 足輪〈鳥の標識用の〉a leg band;《英》a ring.
あじわい 味わい ⇨ **あじ**¹ ¶味わいの深い言葉《文》a word [phrase] with a profound meaning;《文》a word [phrase] pregnant with meaning; an impressive remark.
あじわう 味わう taste; get a taste of;〈鑑賞する〉appreciate;〈享受する〉enjoy;〈経験する〉experience; go through ¶初めて味わう have *one's* first taste 《of hospital life》/ 味わうべき言葉 a significant remark. 文例⇩

だ. Once you have tasted the thrill of gambling on horse races, you can't easily get over it.
あしおと だれかがそっと近付いて来る足音がした. I heard the soft footsteps of someone coming toward me. / あれがお父さんの足音だ. Those are Father's footsteps.
あしがかり うちの会社はまだその地方にはほとんど足掛かりができていない. Our firm has scarcely even a toehold [foothold] in that province.
あしかけ 東京へ来てから足掛け 3 年になる. This is my third year in Tokyo.
あしからず どうぞあしからず. I hope you will not take it amiss. / 父の急病のため欠席いたしました. あしからずご了承下さい. Please excuse my absence; my father was suddenly taken ill.
あじけない 味気ない世の中になりましたなあ. All the spice has gone out of life, hasn't it?
あした あしたはあしたの風が吹く. Let tomorrow take care of itself. / 今日はともかく, あしたからはちょっと忙しくなる. After today I'm going to be pretty busy.
あしつき 足つきですぐ彼だとわかった. I recognized him at once by his walk.
あしでまとい こんな物を持っていては足手まといだ. If I take them, they will (only) get in my way.
あしもと 足もとに気を付けて下さい. Please be careful where you step. | Mind [Watch] your step! | Look where you're going!
あしらう 私たちは訪問したどの会社でも冷たくあしらわれた. We were given a cold reception at [《口語》We got the brush-off from] every company that we visited.
あじわう これは, はじめに 1 口味わったとこでは, とてもおだやかな味のワインですね. At first taste, this wine is very smooth.

あしわざ 足業〖柔道〗foot techniques.
あす 明日 tomorrow ¶明日の朝 tomorrow morning. 文例⇩
あずかり 預かり ¶〈勝負が〉預かりになる be called off as a draw; end in a tie [draw]; be drawn / 〈問題を〉預かりにしておく leave 《a matter》undecided; hold 《a subject》over (for further discussion) / 預かり物 something left in one's care [《文》charge]; something one is looking after 《for sb》/ 預かり証 a (temporary) receipt; 〈手荷物の〉a (claim) check.
あずかる¹ 与る 〈参加する〉take part [a hand] (in); 《文》participate 《in》; 〈分け前などに〉share [have a share] 《in》; 〈いただく〉《文》receive 《an invitation》¶相談にあずかる be consulted / …にあずかって力がある contribute to…; make for…; help toward 《an end, doing》; go far [a long way] toward…. 文例⇩
あずかる² 預かる 〈保管する〉keep; look after sth 《for sb》; 《文》receive sth in trust; take charge of sth; 《文》take sth in charge; 《文》be entrusted 《with》; 〈監督する〉be in charge 《of》; take care of 《a house》.
あずき 小豆 an adzuki bean ¶小豆色の reddish-brown / 小豆アイス adzuki-bean sherbet.
あずける 預ける leave sth in sb's care [charge]; 《文》entrust sb with sth [sth to sb]; deposit sth with sb ¶金を銀行に預ける put [deposit] money in a bank / 金を人に預ける entrust sb with one's money / 子供を預ける leave a child in sb's care / 荷物を預ける 《米》check one's baggage [《英》leave one's luggage (in a left-luggage office)] / …の所に預けてある be in sb's keeping [safekeeping] / 預け主 a depositor. 文例⇩
アスタチン〖化〗astatine.
あすなろ〖植〗a hiba arborvitae.
アスパラガス (an) asparagus (単複同形).
アスピリン (an) aspirin ¶アスピリンを2錠飲む take two aspirins.
アスファルト asphalt ¶アスファルトを敷く pave 《a road》with asphalt; asphalt 《the road surface》/ アスファルト道路 an asphalt(-paved) [《米》a blacktop] road; a tarmac road.

あずまや 東屋 an arbor; a bower; a summer-house.
あせ 汗 sweat; perspiration ¶汗がだらだら流れている〈顔などが〉be running [streaming] with sweat / 汗が噴き出す〈人が主語〉break out in sweat / 汗をかく[が出る] sweat; perspire / びっしょり汗をかく, 汗だくになる be wet [dripping] with perspiration; be drenched in sweat / 《口語》be all of a sweat / 〈運動をして〉大いに汗をかく sweat a great deal / 額の汗を拭う wipe (the) perspiration from one's brow / 汗にまみれた sweat-soaked 《laborers》/ 汗ばむ be 《文》become) moist with sweat; be slightly sweaty / 汗臭い smell [reek] of sweat / 汗水流して働く sweat blood; 《英俗》sweat [work] one's guts out / 汗みどろになっている be covered with sweat. 文例⇩
用法 Horses sweat; men perspire; ladies only flush. という言葉があるが, 一般に上品な人(特に女性)は sweat (動詞·名詞とも)を避けて perspire, perspiration を使う傾向がある. ただし, 逆に, そんなことは無意味だから, perspire, perspiration を絶対には使わないという人もある. 名詞用法の sweat は動詞用法に比べると, 上品な人の間でも多く使われる. 特に無冠詞あるいは定冠詞つきの場合がそうである. 不定冠詞つきの a sweat は in a sweat という句で使われるが, その場合はスポーツ選手や馬以外について言うのは, すこし下品とされる. 形容詞をつけて, たとえば, in a cold sweat (冷や汗をかいている)のように使うのは普通の用法である. 本項の文例は, 大部分が sweat の用法を示したものである. 上記の説明を文例で確かめられたい.
あぜ 畦 a ridge between rice fields ¶畦道 a path between rice fields.
アセチレン acetylene ¶アセチレンランプ an acetylene torch.
アセテート acetate.
あせも 汗疹 (have) prickly heat; (a) heat rash.
あせる¹ 焦る 〈急ぐ〉be in a hurry [《口語》rush]; be hasty; 〈もどかしがる〉be impatient; fret; 〈熱望する〉be eager 《for victory, to make up the loss》¶焦らない be in no hurry; keep cool. 文例⇩
あせる² 褪せる fade ¶色のあせた faded. 文例⇩

あす 彼の命は明日の日も知れない. His life is hanging by a thread. / 明日という日もある. Tomorrow is another day.
あずかる¹ 当社の今日の発展にはこれらの人々の努力があずかって力がある. What this company is today owes a great deal to the exertions of these people. / それは私のあずかり知る所ではない. I have nothing to do with the matter. / お招きにあずかってありがとうございます. Thank you very much for your invitation. / おほめにあずかって恐縮です. I feel most flattered by your compliment.
あずかる² この金を預かっておいてくれ. Look after [Keep] this money for me. / 彼は君から預かっ

ていた金を使い込んでしまったという話だ. I've heard that he has spent all the money you left in his keeping. / 艦長は数千人の生命を預かっている. The captain has the lives of several thousand people entrusted to him. / 私は5年生を預かっている. I am in charge of the fifth grade.
あずける 僕は F 銀行に100万円預けてある. I have (a deposit of) one million yen in the F Bank. / 本は2, 3日私に預けておきなさい. Leave the book with me for a few days. / 彼は息子を浅井先生のもとに預けた. He placed his son in the care of Mr. Asai.
あせ 脇の下に汗をかいた. I was sweating under my arms [in my armpits]. / 汗が顔をだらだら流

れていた. Sweat was pouring down his face. / His face was running with sweat. / 汗ぐっしょりだった. He was soaking with sweat. / 汗がワイシャツを通した. The perspiration wetted my shirt. / 額に玉の汗をかいていた. Drops of sweat stood on his forehead. | I saw the sweat beading on his forehead. / うんと汗をかけばその風邪は直る. A good sweat will cure your cold. / 我々は額に汗して食べている. We are getting our living by the sweat of our brows. / 彼は汗かきだ. He sweats easily. / 彼には大分汗をかかされたよ. He put me in a pretty sweat. / 壁が汗をかいていた. The wall was sweating [wet with condensation].

あぜん 啞然 ¶啞然とする be stunned《by》; be dum(b)founded; be flabbergasted; be struck dumb with astonishment / 啞然として in (utter) amazement;《文》in speechless wonder;《文》in open-mouthed surprise.

あそこ あそこに (over) there;《文》yonder; in that place / あそこまで as far as there; that far / あそこの木立ち the trees over there. 文例⇩

あそばせる 遊ばせる ⟨働かせないで⟩ have [leave] *sb* idle; let (the expensive equipment) sit idle ¶子供を遊ばせる ⟨面倒を見る⟩ look after [take care of] a child; ⟨あやす⟩ amuse a child / ⟨使わずにおく⟩ leave [have] *one*'s money lying idle. 文例⇩

あそび 遊び ⟨遊戯⟩ playing;《文》play; ⟨競技⟩ a game; a sport; ⟨気晴らし⟩ a pastime; (a) recreation; ⟨慰み⟩ (an) amusement; ⟨行楽⟩ holiday-making; ⟨機械の⟩ play ¶(機械の装置が)遊びが多すぎる have too much [《文》excess] play / 遊びに加わる join [enter into] the play / 遊びに出る go out to play / 遊びに行く go to see (a friend); visit (a place) for pleasure; ⟨遊覧に行く⟩ go on [make] an excursion《to》; go on a trip《to》; go on holiday / トランプの game of cards / 遊び相手⟨友達⟩ a playmate / 遊び相手がない have no one to play with / 遊びがてら partly for diversion [pleasure] / ⟨レジャーの⟩ leisure clothes; ⟨上着⟩ a sports coat / 遊び癖がつく get out of the way [habit] of working / 遊び事を pastime; ⟨勝負⟩ a game / 遊び盛りの子供 a child at a playful age / (学校の)遊び時間 a recess / 遊び好きの pleasure-[amusement-]loving / 遊び道具 a toy; a plaything / 遊び人 ⟨やくざ⟩ a gambler; ⟨道楽者⟩ a sporting man; a playboy (★「女遊びをする人」とは言わない) / 遊び半分に partly for fun;《文》half in sport / 遊び場 ⟨学校の⟩ a playground; ⟨大人の⟩ a place of amusement; an entertainment [amusement] district (地区). 文例⇩

あそぶ 遊ぶ ⟨遊戯をする⟩ play (★大人については言わない); make a game of《doing》; ⟨楽しむ, 気晴らしする⟩ enjoy [amuse] *oneself*; divert *oneself*; ⟨行楽で⟩ make a (pleasure) trip《to》; go on an excursion《to》; ⟨訪れる⟩ visit; ⟨遊び興じる⟩ make merry; ⟨ぶらぶらする⟩ be idle; idle (*one*'s time) away; do nothing ¶遊んでいる ⟨子供が⟩ be playing [《文》at play]; ⟨職がない⟩ be out of work; ⟨機械などが⟩ be not in use; lie [sit] idle / トランプをして遊ぶ play cards / 遊んでいる人 an idle man; an idler / ⟨失業者⟩ an unemployed person; the unemployed (総称) / 遊び歩く⟨回る⟩ spend *one*'s time in pleasure [on the town] / 遊んで暮らす live in idleness / ⟨安楽に⟩ live a life of ease / 一日中遊び暮らす spend the whole day playing [in amusements] / 遊び戯れる frolic. 文例⇩

あだ 仇 ¶あだを討つ[討つ] ⇨かたき(敵を討つ) / あだをする do *sb* harm [wrong];《文》do *sb* a disservice / (…が)身のあだとなる《文》be the cause of *one*'s ruin; ⟨文⟩ prove [be] *one*'s ruin / 恩をあだで返す《文》return evil for good. 文例⇩

アダージョ《音楽》(イタリア語) adagio.

あたい 価, 値 ⟨値段⟩ a price; ⟨価値⟩ value; worth ¶値する be worth (seeing);《文》be worthy (of mention); deserve (praise); ⟨文⟩ be deserving (of special attention);《文》merit《recommendation》/ 一読に値する be worth reading / 5万円の価がある be worth 50,000 yen. 文例⇩

あたいりく 亜大陸 a subcontinent ¶インド亜大陸 the Indian Subcontinent.

あたえる 与える give; let *sb* have *sth*; ⟨贈与する⟩ present *sth* to *sb*; present *sb* with *sth*; make *sb* a present of *sth*; ⟨授与する⟩ award;《文》confer (a title on *sb*); grant; ⟨給する⟩ supply; provide; allow (手当などを); ⟨割当てる⟩ allot; assign; ⟨課する⟩ set ¶賞を与える award *sb* a prize / 仕事を与える provide work for *sb*; provide *sb* with work / 問題を与える set (a pupil) a problem / それぞれに分け前を与える allot a share to each / 与えられた三角形 a given triangle. 文例⇩

あだおろそか 徒おろそか ¶あだおろそかに

あせる¹ 焦るな. Don't rush it. | Take your time about it. | Take it easy. | そんなに焦るには及ばない. There is no need to be in such a hurry. | 焦ると損をする. Haste makes waste. [諺]

あせる² アカデミー賞受賞の喜びに比べれば, ほかのことはすべて色あせたものに感じられた. Everything paled into insignificance by comparison with the joy of receiving the Academy Award.

あそこ ほら, あそこに! ⟨遠方⟩ Over there! | ⟨下方⟩ Down there! | ⟨上方⟩ Up there! | ⟨内⟩ In there! | ⟨外⟩ Out there!

あそばせる お前を遊ばしておくわけにはいかない. I cannot afford to have you idle.

あそび 用事がてら別府へ遊びに行った. I went to Beppu partly on business and partly for pleasure. / また遊びに来たまえ. Come and see me again. / 商売はまるで遊びです. We are doing practically no business. / ブルックリン橋の中央の継ぎ目には30センチもの遊びを持たせてある. The center joint of the Brooklyn Bridge allows for as much as one foot of play.

あそぶ 働いてばかりいて遊ばないと体に毒だ. It does you no good to do nothing but work. / 遊んではいられない. I can't afford to be idle. / 彼は失業してこの1年遊んでいる. He has had no work since he lost his job a year ago.

あだ 親切でしたことがかえってあだとなってしまった. What I had done out of kindness proved, unexpectedly, to have been a disservice to him. / 美貌があだとなった. Her beauty was her ruin.

あたい 彼の勇敢な行為は大いに賞賛に値する. His brave conduct deserves [entitles him to] high praise. / この方法によれば金星までの距離のかなり正確な値が得られる. By this method you can get [This method gives] a good value for the distance to Venus. / 次の方程式を解いてxの値を求めなさい. Solve the equation for x.

あたえる 彼は持っていた金を惜しみなく貧しい人々に与えた. He gave his money generously to the poor. / 1等賞は太郎に与えられた. (The) first prize went to Taro. / その手術は患者に少しも

[あ]

する make light of; do not do justice《to *sb* [*sth*]》. [文例⇩]

あたかも 恰も ⇨まるで.

あたたかい 暖[温]かい warm ¶暖かい色 a warm color / 暖かい冬 a mild winter / 温かい歓迎 a warm [hearty,《文》cordial] welcome / 温かい心 a warm [kindly] heart / 心の温かい kindhearted; warmhearted / 暖かく warmly / 暖かになる get warm; warm (up); grow warmer / 暖かにしている keep *oneself* warm. [文例⇩]

あたたかみ 暖[温]かみ warmth ¶心に温かみがある have a warm [kind] heart; be warm-hearted; be kindhearted / 心に温かみがない have a cold heart; be coldhearted. [文例⇩]

あたたまる 暖[温]まる get warm; warm [heat] up; be warmed; warm *oneself*《by [at] the fire》 ¶心温まる heartwarming《hospitality》/ 体の温まる飲物 a warming drink. [文例⇩]

あたためる 暖[温]める warm (up); heat (up) ¶温め直す rewarm; reheat; 〈飲食物を〉warm up [《米》over] / あらかじめ温めておく pre-heat / 心の中に温めておく mull《an idea》over; keep《an idea》in *one's* mind until《it》is fully developed;《文》incubate《a plan》.

アタッシェケース an attaché case.

あだっぽい 《文》coquettish;《文》voluptuous; inviting.

あだな あだ名 a nickname《for》 ¶…というあだ名がつく get [come by] the nickname of.../「赤シャツ」とあだ名される be nicknamed "Red Shirt" / あだ名をつける give *sb* a nickname / (人の)あだ名を呼ぶ call *sb* by *his* nickname.

アダプター an adapter.

あたふたと ¶あたふたと in a hurry [flurry]; helter-skelter.

あたま 頭 〈頭部〉the head; 〈頭脳〉a head; a brain (★複数形 brains で使われることが多い) ¶頭がいい be clever;《口語》be bright; have brains;《口語》have a good head on *one's* shoulders;《口語》be brainy / 頭が痛い have a headache / 頭が痛くなる get a headache《from too much reading》/ 頭がいる need [require] brains / 頭が変だ be crazy; be off *one's* head; be out of *one's* mind / 頭が変になる go off *one's* head / 頭が悪い be stupid;《米口語》be dumb;《口語》be thick; be dull; have no brains / 頭の奥に in the back of *one's* mind / 頭の回転の早い人 a quick-witted person; a quick thinker / 頭の回転の早さ quick-wittedness;《文》mental agility / 頭のてっぺんから足のつま先まで from head to foot; from top to toe / 頭を上げる raise *one's* head / 頭を抑える keep *sb* under control [under *one's* thumb]; hold [keep] *sb* down / 両手で頭を抱える bury [hold] *one's* head in *one's* hands / 頭をかく scratch *one's* head (★ scratch *one's* head は頭がかゆくてかくほかに, 困惑·不満·不可解などを表わす動作) / 頭を刈ってもらう have [get] *one's* hair cut; have [get] a haircut / 頭を下げる bow [lower] *one's* head / 丁寧に頭を下げて with a respectful [low] bow / 頭をたたき割る brain *sb* / 頭を垂れる hang (down) *one's* head / 頭を使う[働かす] use *one's* head [brains] / 頭を使う仕事 brainwork; mental work / 頭を使い過ぎる overtax *one's* brain / 頭を悩ます〈考えて〉rack [cudgel] *one's* brains《to *do*, over a question》; 〈心配して〉be worried《about, over》/ 頭をはねる take a cut [percentage]《of the profits》/ 頭に入れる put《an idea》into *one's* mind / 頭に浮かぶ come [spring] to mind; come into [enter] *one's* head; occur to *one* / 頭に置く take *sth* into consideration [account]; 〈忘れずにいる〉bear *sth* in mind / 頭にくる《口語》get mad;《俗》lose *one's* cool; 〈物事が〉offend *one*; irritate *one*; drive *one* crazy; 〈酒が〉go to *one's* head / 頭からはね付ける[否定する] give a flat refusal [denial]. [文例⇩]

[用法]「頭」を, a head ではなく, the head と記述してあるのは, 体の部分で head と称されるところのみを指し, それ以外の部分から区分していることが the によって示されるからである. 以上の理由で, この辞

苦痛を与えない. The operation does not cause the patient any pain.

あだおろそか ご恩のほど, あだおろそかにはいたしません. Thank you very much, sir. I will never forget your kindness.

あたたかい 何か温かい飲み物を下さい. Please give me something hot to drink. / この電気ストーブはとても暖かい. This electric heater gives a good heat. / 陽気が暖かになった. The weather has got warmer [has warmed up]. / 気持ちの大きい温かい人だった. He was a warm person with a big heart. / あの人たちについては, もっと温かい見方をしてあげるべきだと思います. I think you ought to take a more charitable view of those people.

あたたかみ 人間的温かみのある人だった. There was a lot of human warmth in him. / 不幸にして家庭の暖かみを知らない. Unfortunately he does not know what it is to have a happy home.

あたたまる 部屋はよく暖まっていた. The room was well heated. / 気体は加熱されると, 1度温まるごとにその七氏0度に於ける体積の約273分の1膨張する. When a gas is heated, each degree of warming causes it to expand by about $^1/_{273}$ of its volume at 0°C. / 故トレンチ氏に触れられたあなたのお言葉を, 心温まる思いで伺いました. Your mention of the late Mr. Trench warmed my heart.

あたま 頭が重い. I feel heavy in the head. / 頭隠して尻隠さずだ. That's behaving like an ostrich [like ostriches]. / 君たちはみんな頭隠して尻隠さずだ. You're a lot of ostriches, burying your heads in the sand and thinking you haven't been noticed. ★ダチョウの習性に関する俗信から. / サギが魚を捕えて頭から飲み込んだ. The heron caught a fish and swallowed it head first. / 毛虫が頭を下にしてぶら下がっていた. A hairy caterpillar was hanging, head downward. / (教室で先生に)指されないように頭を下げていた. I kept my head down so as not to be picked out. / 知的能力とは, たくさんのアイデアを頭に入れてその間の関係を理解する力のことだ, と言った人がある. Someone has said that intellectual ability consists in the power of holding [keeping] a large number of ideas in one's mind and seeing the relationships between them. / あの人の前では頭

あたまうち 頭打ち ¶(相場などが)頭打ちになる hit [reach] the [*its*] ceiling [peak]; peak. 文例⇩

あたまかず 頭数 ¶頭数が多い[少ない] there are a large [small] number (of); 《文》be large [small] in number / 頭数を数える count the number of people (present); count heads / 頭数をそろえる[増す, 減らす] make up [increase, reduce] the number.

あたまかぶ 頭株 a leader; a leading figure.

あたまきん 頭金 a down payment; a deposit ¶頭金を払う pay (50,000 yen) down (on a TV set).

あたまごし 頭越し 文例⇩

あたまごなし 頭ごなし ¶頭ごなしにしかる scold *sb* 《文》reprimand *sb*,《口語》tell *sb* off] without hearing *his* side of the story;《文》 condemn *sb* unheard.

あたまでっかち 頭でっかち ¶頭でっかちの top-heavy.

あたまわり 頭割り ¶頭割りで per head;《文》 per capita / 頭割りで費用を出す pay an equal share of [《英》go shares in] the expenses.

アダム Adam.

あたら regrettably ¶あたら命を失う lose *one*'s precious life. 文例⇩

あたらしい 新しい new; fresh; novel;〈最近の〉recent; latest; modern / 記憶に新しい be fresh in *one*'s memory / 新しい魚 fresh fish / 新しい考え a new idea / 新しいニュース hot news / 新しく newly;《文》anew; afresh / 新しくする renew;《文》renovate / 新しく建てた[造った] newly-built[-made] / 新しく来た人 a newcomer / 新しく来た先生 a new teacher / 茶を新しく入れかえる make fresh tea; make a fresh pot of tea. 文例⇩

あたらしがりや 新しがり屋 a novelty hunter.

あたらしがる 新しがる be fond of [hunt after] novelties.

あたらずさわらず 当たらず障らず ⇨あたりさわり ¶あたらずさわらずの返事をする give a bland [harmless] answer; make a reply that will cause no trouble [friction] anywhere.

あたり¹ 辺り 〈近所〉the neighborhood; the vicinity;〈方向〉the direction;〈…のころ〉about;…or thereabouts ¶辺りを見回す look around [about] / ここ[そこ]ら辺り around here [there]; in this [that] neighborhood; in these [those] parts / 次の日曜辺り about next Sunday / 一昨年辺り the year before last or thereabouts ¶辺り構わず with no thought for the people around *one*. 文例⇩

あたり² 当たり 〈的中〉a hit; a success;〈…に付き〉per ¶1人当たり per head [capita] / 1日当たり500円 500 yen a [per] day / (釣りで)当たりがある have a strike [bite] / 人当たりがいい[悪い]〈野球〉hit well [badly];〈人が〉be friendly [unfriendly] / 当たりをとる make a hit / 当たりくじ a winning ticket [slip]; a lucky [winning] number / 当たりそこないのファウル《野球》a glancing foul. 文例⇩

あたりきょうげん 当たり狂言 a hit; a successful play.

あたりげい 当たり芸 a successful performance.

あたりさわり 当たり障り ¶当たり障りのない事を言う make harmless [bland] remarks / 当たり障りのないようにする take care not to offend anybody.

あたりちらす 当たり散らす take out [《文》vent] *one*'s spite on everybody; snap at [take it out on, be cross with] everybody. 文例⇩

あたりどころ 当たり所 文例⇩

あたりどし 当たり年 a fruitful year; a good [lucky] year. 文例⇩

あたりはずれ 当たり外れ ¶当たり外れのある[ない]仕事 a risky [sure-fire] job. 文例⇩

あたりまえ 当たり前 ¶当たり前の 〈普通の〉usual; common; ordinary;〈当然の〉natural; proper;〈もっともな〉reasonable / 当たり前

が上がらない。I cannot hold up my head before him. / あの人の頭張りには頭が下がる。I take off my hat to him [I really respect him] for his perseverance. / あんな無礼なことを言われると頭に来る。It gets to me when he says that sort of insulting thing to me.

あたまうち 僕の給料は頭打ちになっている。My salary has reached the ceiling for my grade [rank].

あたまごし おれの頭越しに課長に話を持っていったんで、頭にきたんだ。I was angry because he went over my head to the section chief.

あたら あたら若い人を死なしてしまった。It's a pity [It's too bad] that he should have died so young. / あたら好機を逸した。

We missed a golden opportunity.

あたらしい 新しい話でもありますか。Any news? / この辞書は内容がすっかり新しくなった。This dictionary has been brought thoroughly up to date.

あたらしがりや 彼は新しがり屋だ。He is very fond of novelties. | He seizes at anything new.

あたり¹ 辺りにだれもいなかった。No one happened to be around [by]. / その女の人は若かった。20代の末から30代の初め辺りの年頃だった。She was young—somewhere in the late twenties or early thirties.

あたり² この機械を買ったのは当たりだった。This machine was a good [wise] choice. / (魚釣りで)当たりがあった。I had [There was] a bite. / (野球で)いい当たり! Good hit!

あたりちらす 彼女は夫に腹を立てて子供に当たり散らしていた。She was angry with [mad at] her husband and was taking it out [taking out her feelings] on her children. / あの人は何かにいら立っているらしく、何だかんだと私に当たり散らすんです。Something seems to be worrying him; he's forever on at me about one thing or another.

あたりどころ 投石を受けた警官1人が当たり所が悪くて死亡した。One of the policemen happened to be hit on a vital spot by a thrown rock, and died.

あたりどし 今年はカボチャの当たり年だった。We've had a bumper crop of pumpkins this year.

あたりはずれ この類の道具には当たり外れがあって、長いこと使い込んでみないと良し悪しはわから

の事 a matter of course / 当たり前の事と思う take it for granted 《that...》 / 当たり前なら under ordinary circumstances. 文例⇩

あたりや 当たり屋 《運のいい人》 a lucky person; 〈野球で〉 a batter in luck; 〈わざと自動車にぶつかる人〉 a person who deliberately gets knocked down by an automobile for the purpose of extortion; an automobile accident faker.

あたりやく 当たり役 (play) a successful part.

あたる 当たる 〈ぶつかる〉 bump [knock] 《into》; hit 《against》 (on, against); 〈触れる〉 touch; 〈さらされる〉 be exposed to 《rain》; 〈日・光が〉 shine on; 〈暖まる〉 warm *oneself* (at the fire); bask [bathe] 《in the sun》; 〈相当する〉 correspond (to); be equivalent (to); be worth 《a million yen》; 〈時日が〉 fall (on); 〈当てはまる〉 apply (to); 《文》 be applicable (to); 〈的中する〉 hit; be hit (by); strike; 〈予想などが〉 come true; 〈成功する〉 succeed; be [《文》 prove] a success; make a hit; 〈担当する〉 undertake; take *sth* in hand; take charge (of); 〈探る〉 sound (out); feel; 〈向かう, 対抗する〉 face; set *oneself* (up) against; deal with; 〈中毒する〉 disagree 《with *one*》 (食物が主語); be [get] poisoned 《by what *one* has eaten》 / 弾丸に当たる be hit by a bullet / 弾丸が真ん中に当たる hit 《the target》 right in the center / 〈推測が〉うまく当たる guess right; hit the mark / 当たらない 〈失敗する〉 fail; 《文》 be unsuccessful; 〈推測が〉 guess wrong; 〈弾丸が〉 miss 《the mark》 / 「重厚な」に当たる英語の English for '*jūkō-na*'; 〈食べた〉魚にあたる be made ill [sick] by eating spoiled fish / 暑さにあたる be affected by the (summer) heat / 水にあたる be poisoned [made ill] by bad water / つらく当たる treat *sb* unkindly [harshly]; be hard on *sb* / 当たってみる sound

sb (out) 《about [on] *sth*》; take *one*'s chance 《with *sb*》 / 辞書に当たってみる look up 《a word》 in a dictionary; consult a dictionary 《for the meaning [usage] of a word》 / 東[左]手に当たって to the east [left] / 日比谷の方角に当たって in the direction of Hibiya / この時に当たって on this occasion; 《文》 at this juncture / 本を選ぶに当たって in choosing [in the choice of] books. 文例⇩

あたん 亜炭 lignite; brown coal.

アチーブメントテスト 《take》 an achievement test.

あちこち here and there; 〈行ったり来たり〉 to and fro; up and down; 〈所々に〉 in places ¶あちこちの学校 several (different) schools / あちこちから集まる come from all over the place [《文》 far and wide, all quarters] / あちこちを見る look this way and that / あちこち旅をして回る travel from place to place; travel around [《英》 about] (the country).

あちら 〈あれ〉 that; 〈他方〉 the other; 〈先方〉 the other party ¶あちらに[で] 〈あそこ〉 there; 〈向こうの方〉 over there; 《文》 yonder / あちら側 (on) the other side / あちらこちら ⇨ あちこち. 文例⇩

あっ 〈驚き〉 Oh!; Dear me!; (Good) heavens!; 〈痛み, 熱さ〉 Ouch!; Wow! ¶あっと叫ぶ cry out; give a cry / あっと言う間に (less than) no time; in an instant; in the twinkling of an eye; before you can say Jack Robinson / あっと言わせる take *sb* aback; astonish; startle (the world); leave *sb* speechless / あっと言わせるような astounding; spectacular / あっと驚く be taken aback; be startled.

あつあつ 熱々 文例⇩

あつい¹ 厚い 〈分厚い〉 thick 《books》; heavy 《walls》; 〈手厚い〉 kind; 《文》 cordial; warm

---

ない. This kind of tool is like a lottery; you can't tell whether it is good or bad until you have used it for a long time.

あたりまえ 当たり前さ. Of course. | That goes without saying. | 彼が怒るのは当たり前だ. He may well be angry. | It is natural that he should be angry. / 彼が失敗したのは当たり前だ. It is no surprise that he has failed. / 彼女がよく眠れなかったのは当たり前だ. It's no wonder that she couldn't sleep well. | She could not sleep well, and no wonder. | 当たり前の事をしただけです. I did nothing more than what I ought to have done. / 当たり前なら彼は もう課長ぐらいにはなっているはずだ. He ought at least to be a section chief by now.

あたる 雨が窓に当たっていた. The rain was beating against the window. / 波が岩に当たって砕けていた. The waves were breaking on the rocks. / 石が頭

に当たった. A stone hit him on the head. / 第一撃は肩に当たった. The first blow caught him on the shoulder. / 気温の季節的変化は太陽光線が地球に当たる角度によって生じる. Seasonal changes in temperature are caused by the angle at which the sun's rays strike the earth. / この部屋はほとんど日が当たらない. This room gets very little sun [sunshine]. / この靴は指に当たる. These shoes pinch me in the toes. / 天皇誕生日は日曜日に当たる. The Emperor's Birthday falls on Sunday. / それに当たる英語はない. There is no English (equivalent) for it. / 彼を前衛画家と呼ぶのは当たらない. It is not accurate to call him an avant-garde painter. | The term 'avant-garde painter' doesn't fit him. / あの人はあなたの何に当たりますか. What relation is he to you? / そんなことをしたら失礼に当たる. That would be

impolite. / 今日の天気予報は当たった. Today's weather forecast proved right. / 最近の天気予報は大体8割は当たる. Weather forecasts are about 80 per cent accurate these days. / 当たらずといえども遠からずだ. You have guessed nearly right. | You're not far off [from] the truth. / 今年はすいかが当たった. Watermelons have turned out well this year. | We've had a bumper crop of watermelons this year. / 昨晩の音楽会は当たった. The concert last night was a success. / 会話の時間に僕が当たった. I was asked to speak in the conversation hour. / あちこち当たってみたが彼の居所はつかめなかった. I asked [made inquiries] at a number of places but could not find his whereabouts. / 両党は提携して自民党に当たった. The two parties joined hands against the Liberal Democratic Party. / 何かそこで食べた物に彼があたっ

¶厚く 〈厚さを〉thick; thickly;〈懇に〉warmly;《文》cordially; kindly / 厚くする thicken; make thicker / 厚く切る cut (meat) into thick slices / 厚く礼を述べる thank sb heartily [cordially] / 厚くもてなす《文》receive sb cordially; give sb a friendly [warm,《文》cordial] reception.

あつい[2] 熱[暑]い hot; warm; sultry (蒸し暑い); heated (熱した) ¶うんと熱いコーヒー piping hot coffee / 熱くする heat (up); warm (up) / 熱くなる get [《文》become] hot; heat (up) / 暑くなる get [《文》become] warm. 文例⇩

あつえん 圧延 rolling ¶圧延工場 a rolling mill.

あっか[1] 悪化 〈状態の〉a change for the worse;《文》(a) deterioration;〈風俗などの〉《文》degeneration; corruption ¶悪化する get [《文》become] worse; go from bad to worse;《文》deteriorate;〈病状が〉take a turn for the worse;〈事態が〉grow more serious / 悪化させる make sth worse; aggravate. 文例⇩

あっか[2] 悪貨 文例⇩

あつかい 扱い 〈待遇の〉treatment; service;〈取扱い〉dealing; handling ¶ひどい扱いを受ける be ill-treated;《口語》get a raw deal / 道具の扱いがうまい be clever [handy] with one's tools; use one's tools skillfully.

あつかう 扱う 〈遇する〉treat;〈取り扱う〉deal with; handle; manage;〈売買する〉deal in (toys);〈運用する〉work; use ¶扱いやすい[にくい] be easy [hard] to deal with; be handy [unwieldy,《文》refractory] / 公平に扱う treat sb fairly; give sb a fair deal / 〈新聞が〉大きく扱う splash (a story); play up (the news);《口語》give (a matter) the full treatment [a big write-up]. 文例⇩

あつかましい 厚かましい《口語》cheeky;《米口語》nervy; shameless;《文》brazen; impudent;〈押しの強い〉pushing ¶厚かましく shamelessly; impudently / 厚かましくも…する have the cheek [nerve, impudence] to do; be shameless [impudent] enough to do. 文例⇩

あつがみ 厚紙 cardboard; pasteboard.

あつがり 暑がり a person who is sensitive to [can't stand] the heat. 文例⇩

あつがる 暑がる complain of the (summer) heat; feel the heat.

あつかん 熱燗 hot sake ¶熱燗で一杯やる have some [a drink of] hot sake.

あっかん[1] 圧巻 the best part (of a book); the highlight (of the evening);〈傑作〉a masterpiece.

あっかん[2] 悪漢 a villain; a rascal; a scoundrel.

あつぎ 厚着 ¶厚着する wear a lot of clothes / 厚着をしすぎる wear too many clothes.

あつくるしい 暑苦しい sultry; unpleasantly hot; too warm for comfort; hot and close; sweltering; stuffy (部屋などが). 文例⇩

あっけ ¶あっけない (be) not long enough; (be) too little [short, soon, quick] / あっけない負け方をする be beaten too easily;《文》suffer a disappointing defeat / あっけなく all too soon [easily] / あっけに取られる be taken aback; be amazed; be dum(b)founded / あっけに取られて in open-mouthed astonishment; in amazement. 文例⇩

あつげしょう 厚化粧 (a) heavy [thick] make-up ¶厚化粧をしている wear heavy [too much] make-up; be heavily made up.

あっけらかん ¶あっけらかんとしている look as though one has nothing at all to do with (what is going on);《文》be [remain] quite indifferent (to sth).

あっこう 悪口 abuse;《文》vilification ¶悪口を浴びせる shower abuse on sb / 悪口雑言(ぞうごん)する curse and swear; call sb (all sorts of)

た. Something he ate there disagreed with him. / あたりはしないよ.〈食べた物について〉It won't do you any harm. / 当たって砕けろ. Take your chance. | Nothing venture nothing win.《諺》

あちら あちらへ着いたらすぐお手紙を下さい. Please write to me as soon as you arrive there.

あっ あっ！傘を車の中に忘れてきた. Damn! I have left my umbrella in the train. / あっ, 蛇だ. Look, there's a snake! / あっと言う間に花も散ってしまった. The cherry blossoms have gone all too soon.

あつあつ 2人は熱々だ. They are madly [passionately, desperately] in love with each other.

あつい[2] 僕は暑いのは平気だ. I don't mind the heat. / インドは恐ろしく暑い所だ. It is awfully hot in India. / 京都の夏は随分暑い. Summers are very hot in Kyoto. / 暑いですなあ. Isn't it hot?

あっか[1] 情勢は急速に悪化していた. The situation was fast deteriorating.

あっか[2] 悪貨は良貨を駆逐する. Bad money drives out good.

あつかう 扱いやすいように新機種は小型化された. For ease of handling, the new model has been made smaller. / 氏の演説は新聞紙上に大きく扱われた. His speech got a big write-up in the newspapers. / この本にはイギリスの政治, 経済, 歴史, 文化などの面が充分広く扱われている. The political, economic, historical and cultural aspects of Britain are well covered in this book. / 事柄が複雑過ぎるのでここでは扱えない. The matter is too complicated to go into here. / 手前共ではその手の品は扱っておりません. We don't deal in that line of goods.

あつかましい 何という厚かましいやつだ. What a nerve! | What cheek! | The nerve of him! / 厚かましいお願いですがこれを私の家へ届けて下さいませんか. I'm afraid I'm asking too much of you, but do you think you could take this to my home?

あつがり 君は暑がりだね. You do feel the heat, don't you!

あっかん[1] 部屋の中央に置かれた巨像は正に圧巻である. The effect of the massive statue placed in the center of the room is really overwhelming.

あつくるしい 昨夜は暑苦しくてよく眠れなかった. Last night I slept badly [didn't sleep well] because of the heat.

あっけ 休暇はあっけなく過ぎた. The vacation passed all too quickly. / 彼はあっけに取られてそこに座りこんでいた. He sat there speechless with amazement. / みんなあっけに取られて私の顔を見た. Everybody looked at me with blank disbelief.

names; use abusive language.

あつさ¹ 厚さ thickness ¶厚さが5センチある be five centimeters thick [in thickness]; have a thickness of five centimeters. 文例↓

あつさ² 暑さ heat; warmth ¶暑さに負ける suffer from [be affected by] the heat / 暑さをしのぐ stand the heat / 木陰に暑さを避ける shelter from the heat under a tree / 暑さしのぎに so as to forget the heat. 文例↓

あっさく 圧搾 compression ¶圧搾する press; compress / 圧搾器 a compressor / 圧搾空気 compressed air / 圧搾ポンプ a compressor pump.

あっさつ 圧殺 ¶国民の言論の自由を圧殺する suppress [snuff out] the people's freedom of speech; gag the people.

あっさり(と) 〈単純に〉simply; 〈簡単に〉briefly; 〈訳なく〉easily; 〈淡白に〉frankly; 〈潔く〉with (a) good grace ¶あっさりした simple; brief; light (軽い); plain (平淡な); frank (淡白な) / あっさりした色 a plain color / あっさりした人 a straightforward [frank] person; an open-hearted person / あっさりした食べ物 light food / あっさり片付ける dispose of《a matter》lightly; dismiss《a matter》out of hand.

あっし 圧死 ¶圧死する be crushed [squeezed] to death.

あっしゅく 圧縮 ¶圧縮する compress; condense.

あっしょう 圧勝 ¶圧勝する win an overwhelming [a crushing, a sweeping] victory《over》; overwhelm.

アッシリア Assyria ¶アッシリアの Assyrian / アッシリア人 an Assyrian.

あっする 圧する press (down); 〈圧迫する〉oppress; 〈威圧する〉overpower; overwhelm. 文例↓

あっせい 圧制 oppression (圧迫); tyranny (虐政) ¶圧制に苦しむ《文》groan under tyranny / 圧制を加える oppress; treat《the populace》highhandedly; 〈虐げる〉tyrannize / 圧制的 oppressive; tyrannical / 圧制者 an oppressor; a tyrant.

あっせん 斡旋 〈世話〉《文》good [kind] offices; services; 〈取り成し〉mediation ¶斡旋する use one's good offices / be [《文》render] a service; go between《two parties》/ 職を斡旋する help sb (to) find a job / 斡旋しようと申し出る offer one's good offices《to settle a dispute》/ 秋葉氏の斡旋により through the good offices of Mr. Akiba / 斡旋を頼む ask for sb's mediation / 斡旋者 a mediator; a go-between.

あっち ⇒ あちら.

あつで 厚手 ¶厚手の thick《paper》.

あっと ⇒ あっ.

あっとう 圧倒 ¶圧倒する overwhelm; overpower / 圧倒的に《文》overwhelmingly; 《文》overpoweringly / 圧倒的勝利をおさめる win an overwhelming [a sweeping] victory《over》/ 圧倒的多数で当選する be elected by an overwhelming majority.

アットホーム ¶アットホームな雰囲気 a home-like [homey] atmosphere.

アッパーカット 〈deal sb〉an uppercut.

あっぱく 圧迫 pressure; oppression ¶圧迫する press; 〈弾圧する〉oppress; suppress; (米) pressure /...に圧迫を加える put [《文》exert] pressure on...; 《文》bring pressure to bear on... / 圧迫を受ける be pressed; be pressured; 《文》be subjected to pressure / 圧迫を受けて under the pressure (of) / 圧迫感 an oppressive feeling; a sense of being oppressed. 文例↓

あっぱれ Well done! ¶あっぱれな splendid; 《文》admirable. 文例↓

アップ 〈上げること〉raising; lifting; 〈髪型〉an upsweep; an upswept hairdo; 〈クローズアップ〉⇒ クローズアップ ¶給料が5％アップになる get a 5% raise in (one's) salary / 髪をアップにしている wear one's hair up [upswept] / アップの写真をとる take a close-up (picture) (of).

あっぷあっぷ ¶あっぷあっぷする a gasp for breath; be about to drown / (会社などが)あっぷあっぷの状態だ be barely keeping itself afloat; be on the verge of bankruptcy.

アップリケ (an) appliqué.

アップルパイ (an) apple pie [《英》tart].

あつぼったい 厚ぼったい thick; heavy; bulky

あつさ¹ 厚さはどれ程か. How thick is it? / What is the thickness? / どれも厚さは同じである. They are all the same [《文》of uniform] thickness. / グリーンランドの氷河は所によって厚さ1.5キロメートル以上に達する. The Greenland glacier reaches a thickness of more than 1.5 kilometers in some places.

あつさ² この暑さでは歩けない. I can't walk about in this heat. / 今日の暑さはひどいです. How hot it is today! | Today's heat is terrible, isn't it? / 彼らは40度という暑さの中で働かねばならなかった. They had to work in the 40-degree heat.

あっする 威風堂々あたりを圧するものがあった. His stately appearance overawed everyone present.

あっせん どうぞよろしくご斡旋お願いします. Please do me a favor and use your influence for me.

あっち あっちへ行け. Go away! | Clear off [out]! | Get [Go] along with you!

あっとう この部門では西ドイツの製品が本品を圧倒している. In this sector, articles made in West Germany are driving Japanese goods out of the market.

あっぱく 当局は彼らを絶えず圧迫している. The authorities are constantly putting [《文》exerting] pressure on them.

あっぱれ あっぱれなお手並だ. Your performance does you credit.

アップリケ そのエプロンには花のアップリケがついていた. The apron had some flowers appliquéd on it.

あつまり 雨降りで集まりが悪かった. The rain made the attendance poor.

あつまる 集まれ! 「号令」Fall [Close] in! / パレードを見ようと人が集まった. People gathered to see the parade. / どこへ集まろうか. Where shall we meet? / 皆集まったか. Has everybody come? | Is everybody here? / このようにして水滴が集まって雲になるのです. In this way, water-

あつまり 集まり ‹集会› a gathering; a meeting; 《文》an assembly; 《口語》a get-together (親しい仲間の); a party; ‹出席者› an attendance; ‹群れ› a crowd ¶町内の集まり a gathering of neighbors. 文例↓

あつまる 集まる gather; come [get] together; ‹会する› meet; 《文》assemble; ‹群れる› crowd; swarm; ‹集中する› concentrate ((on)); center, converge ((on)) (一点に) ¶集まった金 the money collected; the contributions. 文例↓

あつみ 厚味 ⇨ あつさ¹. 文例↓

あつめる 集める get [bring, put] together; gather; ‹呼び集める› call together; ‹収集する› collect; make a collection of; ‹募集する› raise (a fund); recruit (factory hands); ‹集中さす› concentrate ((on)) ¶材料を集める gather materials (for) / 切手を集める collect [make a collection of] stamps / 寄付金を集める collect [《文》solicit] contributions / 世間の注目を集める attract public attention.

あつらえ 誂え ‹注文› an order; ‹品物› the article ordered; the order ¶あつらえの服 a suit made to order; a tailor-made [custom-made, tailored] suit / あつらえ向きの ideal; well-suited / あつらえ向きの品[人] the right thing [person] (for); just the thing [person] (for). 文例↓

あつらえる 誂える give an order ((to sb for sth)); place an order ((with sb for sth)); order ((an article at a store [from a maker])) (★ from は取り寄せる場合).

あつりょく 圧力 pressure ¶圧力をかける ‹物に› press; give [《文》apply] pressure ((to)); ‹人に› 《米》pressure sb ((to do [into doing])); 《文》bring pressure (to bear) on sb ((to do)); put pressure on sb ((to do)) / 圧力をかけられる be [come] under pressure ((to do)); be pressured ((to do [into doing])) / 圧力を緩める relax [reduce] the pressure ((on)) / 蒸気の圧力を上げる get up a head of steam / 圧力計 a pressure gauge; a manometer / 圧力団体 a pressure group / 圧力なべ a pressure cooker / 圧力なべで料理する pressure-cook ((beans)).

あつれき 軋轢 friction; 《文》discord; 《文》strife; 《文》(a) conflict; (a) collision; a clash ¶あつれきがある be in conflict / あつれきを来たす[生じる] produce [lead to] friction / あつれきを避ける avoid friction.

あて 当て ‹目当て› 《文》an object; an aim; 《文》an end; ‹期待› hope(s); expectation(s) ¶当てがはずれる ‹人が主語› be disappointed (in one's hopes); 《文》be frustrated; ‹対象が主語› prove a disappointment / 当てのない aimless / 当てもなく aimlessly at random / …を当てにする depend [rely, count] on; bank on; 《文》put [place] reliance on; put (one's) trust in; ‹期待する› expect; hope for / …を当てにして 《文》in expectation [anticipation] of …; on the promise of… / 当てになる reliable; trustworthy; ‹確実な› sure / 当てにならない unreliable; untrustworthy; treacherous ((footholds)); ‹不確かな› uncertain. 文例↓

-あて …宛 ¶沢田氏あての手紙 a letter addressed to Mr. Sawada / 研究社あての荷物 goods consigned to Kenkyusha / 本店あてに手紙を書く write(to) the head office / コナント氏あてに郵便為替を組む draw a postal money order for [in favor of] Mr. Conant / ビールを1人あて2本注文する order two bottles of beer for each person [per head].

あてうま 当て馬 a stallion brought near a mare to see whether the mare is in heat or to stimulate it into estrus; ‹競馬の› a horse raced as a rival to the favorite; ‹選挙の› a candidate run to put the favorite at a disadvantage.

あてがいぶち 宛てがい扶持 an allowance given at the employer's discretion.

あてがう 宛てがう ‹給与する› allow; supply; provide (for); ‹割り当てる› allocate ((to)); allot ((to)); 《文》assign ((to)); ‹付ける› apply ((to, on)); put [《文》over B] ¶望遠鏡に目をあてがう put one's eye to a telescope / 仕事をあてがう assign a task to sb / 子供に玩具をあてがう give a child a toy to play with. 文例↓

---

drops collect together to form a cloud. / 世間の同情が彼に集まった。Public sympathy focused on him. | He attracted a great deal of public sympathy. / 皆の目が彼に集まった。All eyes were turned on him.

あつみ 思春期になると男子は胸の厚みが増し肩幅が広くなる。At puberty, a boy's chest deepens and his shoulders widen.

あつめる 彼は美術書を集め始めた。He began to build up a library of books on art. / あの人はパイプをたくさん集めている。He has a large collection of pipes. / 僕ら3人の金を集めても 5,000 円しかなかった。We three had only 5,000 yen between us.

あつらえ その日はあつらえ向きの天気でした。We had ideal weather (on) that day.

あつれき 党員間に絶えずあつれきがある。There is constant friction among the members of the party. / その問題に関して社内に多大な[さまざまな]あつれきが生じた。A good deal of discord has [Various discords have] arisen in the company over the question.

あて 彼はこれという当てもなしに上京した。He went to Tokyo with no definite object in view. / 君は金を借りる当てがあるのか。Do you have anyone to whom you can turn for a loan? / 君が来ないので当てがはずれた。I was disappointed that you didn't come. / いつも今分の天気は当てにならない。The weather is changeable [unreliable] at this time of (the) year. / 4月には昇給するだろうとあてにしているんです。I'm figuring on (getting) a pay raise in April. / あの人の約束は少しも当てになりません。His promises cannot be trusted [relied on] at all. / あの人をあまり当てにしてはいけません。You mustn't expect too much from [of, out of] him. / (一般的に)人を当てにしてはいけません。You mustn't take people for granted.

あてがう 私はこの部屋をあてがわれた。This room has been assigned to me. / せんがうまく合うかどうかびんにあてがってみなさ

あてこすり 当て擦り an indirect attack [criticism]; covert sarcasm; (an) innuendo (pl. -es); (an) insinuation.

あてこする 当て擦る attack [criticize] *sb* indirectly; make an insinuating remark《about》; insinuate. 文例↓

あてこむ 当て込む expect; hope for; count [reckon, (米) figure] on ¶ …を当て込んで《文》in expectation [anticipation] of [that…]; in the hope that…. 文例↓

あてさき 宛て先 an address.

あてじ 当て字〈音だけで当てた字〉a Chinese character used as a phonetic symbol rather than for its meaning; 〈勝手な代用文字〉an arbitrarily used substitute character.

あてずいりょう, あてずっぽう 当て推量, 当てずっぽう a (random) guess; 《文》a guess; guesswork ¶ 当てずっぽうの haphazard / random / 当てずっぽうで《make a decision》by guesswork / 当て推量をする guess; make a (random) guess; 《文》hazard a conjecture / 当てずっぽうを言ってみる try a shot in the dark / 当てずっぽうでうまく言い当てる make a lucky shot [guess] (at the answer). 文例↓

あてつける 当て付ける ⇨ あてこする.

あてっこ 当てっこ a guessing competition ¶ 当てっこをする try and see who guesses right.

あてど ¶ あてどもなく《wander》aimlessly.

あてな 宛名 an address ¶ あて名の人 an addressee / あて名が違う be wrongly addressed / 手紙にあて名を書く address a letter (to) / あて名印刷機 an addressing machine.

あてにげ 当て逃げ a hit-and-run accident causing property damage.

アテネ Athens ¶ アテネの Athenian / アテネ人 an Athenian.

アデノイド 【解】 adenoids ¶ アデノイド症の子供 an adenoidal child.

あてはまる 当て嵌まる〈適用される〉apply 《to》; fit《the case》; hold true [good]《for》; be true《of》;〈該当する〉come under《this classification》; be fit《for》.

あてはめる 当て嵌める〈適用する〉apply《to》; fit;〈適応させる〉adapt. 文例↓

あてみ 当て身 ¶ 当て身を食わせる stun *sb* by a strike at a vital point.

あてもの 当て物〈なぞ〉a riddle;〈当てっこ〉guessing;〈当てがう物〉a covering; a pad.

あでやか 艶やか ¶ あでやかな charming; fascinating; attractive.

あてられる 当てられる〈悪い影響を受ける〉be affected by [suffer from]《the summer heat》;〈悩まされる〉be embarrassed《by》; be annoyed《by》.

あてる¹ 当[充]てる〈あてがう〉put;《文》place;《文》apply;〈ぶつける〉hit;《文》strike;〈命中させる〉hit;〈言い当てる〉guess《the answer》; make a guess (at);〈成功する〉succeed (in); make a (lucky) hit;〈割り当てる〉allot (to); allocate (to); assign (to);〈充当する〉appropriate (to, for) ¶ 日に当てる expose *sth* to the sun / 雨に当てないようにする protect *sth* from (the) rain / 額に手を当てる put *one's* hand to [《文》lay *one's* hand on] *one's* forehead / 受話器を耳に当てる hold the receiver to *one's* ear / ハンカチを口に当てる with *one's* handkerchief to [against] *one's* mouth; with *one's* mouth against a handkerchief / うまく当てる〈的を〉guess right /〈推測で〉guess right / 当て損う〈的を〉miss the mark;〈当て事を〉guess wrong / うまく選び当てる make a good [《文》happy] choice《of》/ その日を休養に充てる set the day aside for rest / (先生が)生徒に訳を当てる ask (a student) to translate (a passage) / (クラスで先生に)当てられる be picked (on) (to answer a question). 文例↓

あてる² 宛てる〈手紙などを〉address ¶ 木村氏にあてた手紙 a letter addressed to Mr. Kimura.

あてレコ dubbing ⇨ ふきかえ.

い). Put this cork to the mouth of the bottle and see whether it fits or not.

あてこする あれは実は僕を当てこすっているのだ. His remarks are actually directed at me in (in a roundabout way). | That remark was really a dig at me.

あてこむ 彼は祭りを当て込んで見世物を興行した. He put on a show backed [in the hope] that it would attract the festival crowd.

あてずっぽう 当て推量だがこれには鎌田氏が一枚からんでいるんじゃないかと思う. It's a long shot, but I think Mr. Kamata must have something to do with this.

あてはまる この規則はどの場合にも当てはまる. This rule applies to every case. / 一見したところではこれは実社会には全然当てはまらない無用の数学的概念と思われるかもしれない. At first glance this might seem a useless mathematical concept without any application to the real world. / これはすべての日本の役人に当てはまる. This goes for [is true of] every Japanese government official. / この法則の当てはまらない場合もある. There are exceptions to this rule.

あてはめる この規則をもっと広い範囲に当てはめてみてはどうだ. What do you say to applying this rule a wider application?

あてられる あの2人の仲のよさには当てられた. They were so demonstratively affectionate that it was embarrassing.

あてる¹ 彼は思わず叫び声を立てそうになって, あわてて口に手を当ててふさいだ. He felt a cry about to break from his throat and clapped a hand over his mouth. / これは息子の部屋に充ててある. This room is (set aside) for my son. / 僕は晩の9時から12時までの3時間を勉強時間に充てている. I allot three hours a day, from 9 p.m. to midnight, to my studies. / その収益は貧しい人々の救済に充てるのです. The proceeds will go to the relief of the poor. / 箱の中に何が入っているか当ててごらん. 3回はずれたらだめだぞ. I'll give you three guesses what's in the box. / うまく当てられた. You've guessed right!

あと¹ 愛犬が彼の後からついて来た. His pet dog followed at his heels. / 僕はそっと彼の後をつけた. I followed him noiselessly. / 僕は彼のすぐ後からその部屋に入った. I immediately followed him into the room. / 3歩後へ!『号令』Three steps backward! /

あと¹ 後 〈後方〉 the back; the rear; 〈将来〉 the future; 〈結果〉 the end; 《文》 the conclusion; the consequences; 〈残余〉 the rest; the others; 《文》 the remainder; 〈後任・後継〉 a successor ¶ 後の〈うしろの〉 back; rear; 〈次の〉 the next; the following; 〈後者の〉《文》 the latter; 〈以後の〉 later; 《文》 subsequent; 〈結果的〉《文》 consequent / 一番後の the (very) back (row); rearmost; 《文》 hindmost; 《文》 hindermost / 後に〔で〕 after; behind; back; backward(s); 〈以後〉 since; after; afterward(s); later; 《文》 subsequently; 〈後刻, 後ほど〉 later (on) / 数日あとに〈その時から〉after a few days; a few days later / 〈今から〉後数日で in a few days; a few days from now / 後に残る stay [remain] behind / 後に残される be left behind / 後に残った家族 the bereaved family / 後に下がる[退く] draw back; step back / 後になる drop [fall] behind 《the others》 / 一番後に来る be the last to arrive / 〈人の〉後について行く follow (on behind) sb / 〈人の〉後について回る tag round after sb / 後にする[回す] postpone; put off / 故郷を後にする leave one's home (behind one) / 後に座る〈後任になる〉succeed sb 《in his position, as manager》 / …のすぐ後に〈続いて〉right on the heels of… / 後は天に任せる leave the rest to Heaven / 後をも見ずに逃げる run away without [《文》 with never] a backward look / 〈人の〉後を受けて picking up where sb left off / 後から後から one after another; in rapid succession / 後々のためを図る provide for the future. 文例⇩

あと² 跡 〈印跡〉 a mark; a print; an impression; 〈汚点〉 a stain; 〈人・車・動物などの通った跡〉a track; 〈遺跡〉 a site; remains; ruins ¶〈汚れた〉指の跡 a fingermark / 歯の跡 (a) toothmark; teethmarks / 靴の跡 a shoe print; a footprint / かまれた跡 a bite; a mark made by biting / 蚊に刺されたあと a mosquito bite / 車の通った跡 the track of a car / 跡がつく leave a mark 《on》 / 〈家系の〉跡が絶える become extinct / 跡をとる succeed 《one's father》 as the head of the family / 跡を追う follow up sb; run after sb; trail 《the suspect》 / 跡を残す [残さない] leave one's traces [no trace] behind one / 跡をくらます cover (up) one's tracks [traces]; 《文》 conceal one's whereabouts / 跡を絶つ put an end to sth; wipe sth out (of existence); exterminate / 跡が付けられる be followed [shadowed, tailed] (by). 文例⇩

あとあし 後足 〈脚〉 a hind [back, rear] leg; a hind limb; 〈足〉 a hind [back, rear] foot; a hind paw; 〈海亀などの〉 a hind flipper ¶ 後足の爪〔趾〕a hind claw [toe] / 後足で立つ stand (up) on its hind legs; 〈馬が〉 rear (up) / 後足で砂をかけるようなことをする do something spiteful as one leaves 《one's job》. 文例⇩

あとあじ 後味 an aftertaste ¶ 後味がいい have [leave] a pleasant aftertaste / 後味が悪い have [leave] a bad [nasty] aftertaste; leave a bad taste in one's mouth (特に比喩的な表現で). 文例⇩

あとおし 後押し 〈後援〉 support; backing; 〈後援者〉 a supporter; a backer; 〈そそのかす人〉《文》 an instigator 《of a crime》; 〈車などの〉 a pusher ¶ 後押しする〈押す〉 push 《a cart》 / 〈後援する〉 support; back sb (up); stand behind sb; 〈そそのかす〉《文》 instigate; egg sb on (to do).

あとがき 後書き a postscript 《to a book》.

あとかた 跡形 traces; marks; 《文》 vestiges ¶ 跡形もなく without leaving any trace; 《vanish》 without trace / 跡形もなく壊される be completely destroyed / 《文》 be razed to the ground.

あとかたづけ 後片付け ¶ 後片付けする put 《things》 in order 《after a party》; clear away 《things after the job is finished》 / 食事の後片付けをする clear the table; 〈皿洗いをする〉 wash [do] the dishes; 《英》 wash up.

あとがま 後釜 a successor 《to》 ¶ 後がまに座

後から参ります. I will come after you. / 子象が母象の後にくっついて行くのが見られた. I saw a baby elephant tagging along behind its mother. / 彼はマフィンのあとにケーキを食べた. He followed up the muffin with a piece of cake. / そんなことは後でやればよい. That can be left till later. / That can wait. / 話の後が聞きたい. Tell me the sequel to that story. / こうなっては後へは引けない. I can't back down [《米》 off] now. / 後は引き受けた. I'll take over now. / You can leave it [the rest] to me (now). / 後はどうなろうと知らない. I don't care about the consequences. / そんなことをすると後がこわいぞ. You'll have to pay dearly for it. / There'll be the devil to pay. / 父が死んで彼は孤児に後に残

された. His father's death left him an orphan. / 今となっては後の祭りだ. It's too late now. / 《文》You came a day after [too late for] the fair. / あんなにこわい思いに会ったことは後にも先にもない. I have never been so frightened before or since. / 西田村までは車で行き, あとは歩いた. I went by car as far as Nishida Village and walked the rest of way. / ボーナスから10万円を家族旅行に使って, 後は全部貯金した. I spent 100,000 yen out of the bonus on a family trip and put all the rest in the bank. / この酒は後を引く. This sake is so good that you cannot help wanting more. / 後は野となれ山となれ. After us [me] the deluge!《諺》
あと² 少しも進歩の跡がない. It shows no evidence of progress. /

そのベッドにはまだ彼の寝ていた跡が残っていた. The bed still bore the imprint [held the impression] of his body. / 悪書の出版が跡を絶たない. There is no end to the publication of undesirable books. / その城の跡は今は立派な公園になっている. There is a fine park now where the castle once stood.
あとあし その犬は後足で立ち上がると高さが1メートル半以上ある. The dog stands more than 1.5 meters on its hind legs.
あとあじ そのちょっとした事件は治まったものの, 後味は悪かった. The petty affair died down, but it left a bad taste in my mouth.
あとかた 今では城の跡形もない. Nothing remains [There is nothing left] of the castle now.

あとくされ／あなうめ　28

あとくされ 後腐れ ¶後腐れのないようにする leave no seeds of future trouble.

あとくち 後口 〈後味〉 ⇒あとあじ ¶〈あとから来たもの〉a later arrival ¶後口に回す leave *sth* to be dealt with later on. 文例↓

あどけない innocent ;《文》cherubic ; childlike ; 〈うぶな〉《文》ingenuous ; naive ¶あどけない事を言う talk like a child ; say childish things／あどけなさ innocence ;《文》naiveté.

あとさき 後先 front and rear ; 〈始めと終わり〉beginning and end ; 〈順序〉an order ; 〈結果〉the consequences ; 〈文の〉the context ¶後先をよく考える《文》be prudent ; think of [(文) reflect on] the consequences／後先を考えない《文》be imprudent ; do not think of the consequences／後先を考えて物を言う think carefully before *one* speaks ; weigh *one's* words／後先に before and behind [after] ; front and rear／後先にする reverse 《the order》;《文》invert 《the position》／話が後先になったが I should have told you this first, but…／後先見ずの thoughtless ; rash ; reckless／後先見ずに recklessly ; blindly ;《文》improvidently ; with no thought for [regard to] the consequences.

あとざん 後産 the afterbirth.

あとしまつ 後始末 ¶後始末をする settle ; set 《matters》right ; wind up 《an affair》;《文》deal with the aftermath／倒産した会社の後始末をする wind up the affairs of a bankrupt company. 文例↓

あとずさり 後退り ¶後ずさりする step [draw, move] back.

あとぜめ 後攻め【野球】taking to the field first. 文例↓

あとち 跡地 the site 《of a demolished building》. 文例↓

あとちえ 後知恵 being wise after the event ; hindsight.

あとつぎ 跡継ぎ an heir (男) ; an heiress (女) ; a successor (to).

あとづける 跡付ける trace 《the footsteps of Alexander the Great》; confirm 《the history of the Heike's downfall》《by newly-collected evidence》.　　　　　　　　「son and heir.

あととり 跡取り ⇒あとつぎ ¶跡取り息子 *one's*

あとばらい 後払い deferred payment ¶後払いで買う buy *sth* on deferred terms.

アドバルーン an advertising balloon.

あとまわし 後回し ¶後回しにする leave *sth* until later ; leave *sth* over ; let 《a matter》wait ; delay 《doing》till later ; put *sth* off ; postpone ; defer／…より後回しにする take a back seat to 《another problem》. 文例↓

あとめ 跡目 ¶跡目を継ぐ succeed *sb* 《as the head master of the Utazawa school》; succeed to 《the family name》.

あともどり 後戻り 〈後退〉going back ; 〈退歩〉《文》retrogression ¶後戻りする 〈退く〉go [move, step] back ; back ; 〈引き返す〉turn back ; backtrack ; retrace *one's* steps ; 〈退歩する〉《文》retrogress.

アトラクション an attraction ; a side show.

アトリエ a studio (*pl.* -s) ; an atelier.

アドリブ an ad-lib ¶アドリブの ad-lib 《remarks》／アドリブをやる ad-lib ; improvise.

アドリアかい アドリア海 the Adriatic (Sea).

アドレス an address ¶営業所の[自宅の]アドレス *one's* business [home] address.

アドレナリン【生化】adrenalin.

あな 穴．孔 a hole ; an opening ; a slit (細長い) ; an eyelet (ひも穴) ; 〈獣類の〉a burrow ; 〈隙間〉a gap ; 〈欠損〉a deficit ; 〈欠点〉a fault ;《文》a defect ; 〈競馬の〉(pick) a dark horse ¶ぽっかりあいた穴 a gaping hole (木の中に虫が掘った)トンネル状の穴 a gallery／穴をあける[うがつ] make a hole (in) ; bore [drill] a hole 《with an awl》;〈損を〉cause a loss／木に穴をあける昆虫 a tree-boring insect／穴をふさぐ stop [close, cover] (up) a hole ; fill [stop] up a gap 《with rags》／穴を掘る dig a hole [pit] (in the ground) ; 〈動物が〉burrow ; dig a den／穴を掘ってその中に身を隠す dig in／穴のあくほど顔を見る stare [look hard] at *sb* ;《文》scrutinize *sb's* face／(電算機用)孔あけカード a punched [punch] card／(書類などの)穴あけ器 a punch. 文例↓

アナ(ー)キスト an anarchist.

あなうめ 穴埋め ¶穴埋めをする〈空白を〉fill

あとくち 初版の予約はもう締め切りで, 後口の申込みは来年3月から受付けるそうだ．I hear that the subscription list for the first edition has been closed, and that later subscriptions are to be accepted from next March.

あとしまつ 親父の借金の後始末が大変だった．I had a hard time paying off the debts that had been left by my father.

あとぜめ 延長戦になれば後攻めが有利だ．If you have to play extra innings, you're better off batting second [at the bottom].

あとち 米軍が立ち退いた後, その基地の跡地は公園になる．After the American troops have left, the site of the base will be converted into a park.

あとまわし それは後回しでよい．That can wait.／You can let it wait.

アドリブ 彼はせりふを忘れたのでアドリブで切り抜けた．He forgot his lines and ad-libbed.／そのジョークはアドリブだった．The joke was ad lib.

あな 硫酸が1滴こぼれて白衣に穴があいた．A drop of sulfuric acid ate a hole in my lab coat.／送水管に穴があいた．The water pipe sprang a leak.／地面に大きな穴をあける隕石もある．Some meteorites gouge out huge craters.／その計画は穴だらけだ．The plan is full of holes.／穴があれば入りたい気持ちだった．I wished the ground would open up and swallow me.／I wished I could sink through the floor.

あなうめ (試験に)穴埋め問題が出た．There were some questions with blanks to fill in.／There were some fill-in-the-blanks-type questions.

アナウンス 間もなく名古屋ですというアナウンスがあった．The

アナウンサー　　あばずれ

a blank [gap] ; 〈欠損などの〉make up 《a loss》; make up for 《the damage》; cover 《a deficit》; 《文》supply 《a deficiency》.
アナウンサー an announcer. ¶女性アナウンサー a woman announcer 《*pl.* women announcers》.
アナウンス an announcement. ¶アナウンスする announce.
あながち 強ち 〈必ずしも〉(not) necessarily ; (not) always ; 〈完全には〉(not) altogether ; (not) entirely ; 《文》(not) wholly. 文例⇩
あなぐま 穴熊 a badger.
あなぐら 穴蔵 a cellar.
アナクロニズム (an) anachronism ¶アナクロニズムの anachronistic.
用法 「アナクロニズム」は (an) anachronism で表わせるのだが、日本語では (an) anachronism で表わせるのだが、日本語では「時代遅れ」の意味であるのに対して、英語の anachronism はその時代にはあり得ないような、後の時代のものを持ち込む場合も含まれている。たとえば、Shakespeare switched on the electric light. と言えば anachronism の例になる。
あなご 〖魚〗a conger (eel).
あなた 貴方 you ; 〈夫婦・恋人などの呼びかけ〉(my) dear ; (my) darling ¶あなたの your 《friend》 ; 《a friend》 of yours / あなた方2人とも both of you / あなた様 sir ; madam / あなたまかせで depending entirely on others.
あなどり 侮り contempt ; scorn ; 《文》disdain ¶侮りを受ける be despised ; 《文》be held in contempt.
あなどる 侮る despise ; 《文》disdain ; 《文》hold *sb* in contempt ; make light of ¶侮り難い敵 a formidable enemy ; 《文》no mean adversary. 文例⇩
あなば 穴場 a good place not many people know about ¶はぜ釣りの穴場 a little-known place where good goby fishing can be found. 文例⇩
あなぼこ 穴ぼこ ⇨ あな ¶穴ぼこだらけの道 a potholed road.
あに[1] 兄 an elder [《米》older] brother ; a big brother ¶一番上[下]の兄 the youngest [eldest elder] brother / 兄の方のトム Tom, elder of the brothers / 兄弟子 a senior pupil / 兄嫁 *one*'s sister-in-law ; *one*'s elder brother's wife.
用法 英語では特に必要のない限り、兄弟姉妹のことを言うとき elder, younger はつけず、単に *one*'s brother ; *one*'s sister ですませる。英米では年齢の上下と関係なく兄弟姉妹同士は John, Mary のように呼び捨てにするのが普通。
あに[2] ¶あに図らんや 《文》contrary to *one*'s expectations ; to *one*'s surprise.
アニメ(ーション) animation ⇨ どうが.
アニリン 〖化〗aniline.
あね 姉 an elder [《米》older] sister ; a big sister ⇨ あに[1] 用法 ¶一番上の姉 the eldest [《米》oldest] sister / 姉様人形 a (simple) paper doll in bridal wear / 姉婿(❓) *one*'s brother-in-law ; *one*'s elder sister's husband / 姉娘 the elder daughter. 文例⇩
あねったい 亜熱帯 the subtropical [semitropical] zones ; the subtropics ; the semitropics ¶亜熱帯植物 a subtropical plant.
アネモネ 〖植〗an anemone ; a windflower.
あの that ; those ; the ¶あの時 then ; (at) that time / あの人 he ; she ; that person ; that [the] man [woman] / あの人たち they ; those people [men, women] / あの頃は in those days / あのように like that ; (in) that way / あのような男 a man like him [that] ; 《文》such a man as he.
あのう well ; let me see ; er-r-r-r.
あのてこのて あの手この手 ¶あの手この手で this way and that ; by various means ; by this means and that / あの手この手を使う [《文》resort to] all kinds of tricks ; use a variety of means.
あのね look here! ; 《米》say! ; 《英》I say! ; listen!
あのよ あの世 the other [next] world ; 《文》the afterlife ¶あの世で in the other [next] world ; 《文》in the beyond / あの世へ行く die ; go to Heaven ; 〈婉曲に〉leave this world ; pass to the other shore. 文例⇩
アノラック an anorak ; a parka.
アパート 〈部屋〉《米》an apartment ; 《英》a flat ; 〈建物〉《米》an apartment [a rooming] house ; 《英》a block of flats ⇨ マンション ¶アパート暮らしをする 《米》live in an apartment ; 《英》live in a flat / 高層アパート 《米》a multi-story apartment building [《英》block of flats].
あばく 暴く 〈暴露する〉expose 《a secret plan》 ; unmask 《a deception》 ; uncover 《a plot》 ; 《文》lay bare 《an evil design》 ; bring 《a secret》 to light ; 〈墓を〉open 《a grave》. 文例⇩
あばずれ ¶あばずれ女 a (real) bitch ; a shameless hussy. 文例⇩

P.A. announced [informed us] that we would soon arrive at Nagoya. ★ P.A. は public-address system の略.
あながち あながちそうとは限らない. It is not necessarily so. / 君の言うこともあながち無理ではない. What you say is not altogether unreasonable. / その事故はあながち彼だけの責任ではない. He is not wholly to blame for the accident.
あなどる 彼の法律の知識は侮り難い. His knowledge of the law is not to be made light of.

あなば T 温泉は観光客が素通りするところで、秋の行楽の穴場と言えましょう. The hot-spring resort at T is likely to be bypassed by sightseers, so it would be a good bet as a place (for you) to spend your autumn holidays.
あね 彼の奥さんは姉さん女房だ. His wife is older than him. ⇨よめ
あのう どういうわけで遅刻したのですか？—あのう、おなかが痛かったものですから. Why are you late?—Please, sir, I had a stomachache. / あのう、佐久間さん. I

say, Mr. Sakuma.
あのよ あの世まで持って行けるわけじゃなし、金を貯めたってつまらない. There's not much point in saving up money ; you can't take it with you when you go).
あばく あのうそつき、いつか正体をあばいてやる. Some day I'll catch him out, the cheat! | I'm determined to show up that liar some day.
あばずれ あの女はあばずれだ. She has no sense of shame. | She is a woman with no reputation to lose.

あばた a pockmark; a pit ¶あばた面 a pockmarked face. 文例⇩

あばら 肋 the ribs; the rib cage [case] ¶あばら骨 a rib. 文例⇩

アパラチアさんみゃく アパラチア山脈 the Appalachian Mountains; the Appalachians.

あばらや あばら屋 ⟨荒れはてた⟩ a dilapidated [tumbledown] house; a hovel; ⟨粗末な⟩ a miserable shack. 文例⇩

あばれうま 暴れ馬 an unruly [unmanageable] horse; ⟨逃げ出した⟩ a runaway horse.

あばれがわ 暴れ川 a river which often breaks [overflows] its banks.

あばれる 暴れる behave [act] violently [wildly]; rage; storm; ⟨もがく⟩ struggle ¶暴れ出す start acting violently; go on a [the] rampage; go berserk; get unruly; get riotous ⟨多数の人が⟩; ⟨おりなどを破って⟩ break loose ¶暴れ込む break [force *one's* way] into ⟨a house⟩ / 暴れ回る rush [run] about wildly; rage about. 文例⇩

あばれんぼう 暴れん坊 a hooligan; a rowdy; ⟪口語⟫ a roughneck; ⟪英⟫ a rough.

アバンギャルド the avant-garde; the vanguard.

アピール (an) appeal ¶アピールする appeal (to); make an appeal ⟨to the referee⟩. 文例⇩

あひさん 亜砒酸 ⟪化⟫ arsenious acid; ⟨無水亜砒酸, 俗に亜砒酸と呼ばれている猛毒⟩ arsenic trioxide; arsenious oxide; white arsenic ★英語では通俗にこの猛毒のことを単に arsenic と呼ぶ. たとえば He poisoned his wife with arsenic. のように言う.

あびせたおし 浴びせ倒し⟪相撲⟫ pushing down ⟨*one's* opponent⟩ by leaning on ⟨him⟩.

あびせる 浴びせる ⟨水などを⟩ pour [throw] ⟨water⟩ on [over]; ⟨悪口などを⟩ heap ⟨abuse⟩ on ¶⟨野球で⟩ヒット 10 本を浴びせる shower ten hits ⟨on the opposing team⟩ / 質問を浴びせる shower questions on *sb*; bombard *sb* with questions.

あひる ⟪鳥⟫ a ⟨domestic⟩ duck ¶みにくいあひるの子 an ugly duckling. 文例⇩

あびる 浴びる ⟨水を⟩ pour [dash] ⟨water⟩ over *oneself*; bathe ⟨in cold water⟩; ⟨光を⟩ bask ⟨in the sun⟩; be bathed ⟨in the moonlight⟩; be flooded ⟨with light⟩; ⟨受ける⟩ suffer ⟨an attack⟩; expose *oneself* ⟨to criticism⟩; be exposed ⟨to⟩; subjected ⟨to public censure⟩ ¶川で水を浴びる have a bathe [dip] in the river / ひとふろ浴びる have [take] a bath / ほこりを浴びる be covered with dust / 砲火を浴びる come under gunfire / 放射線を浴び過ぎて死亡する die from overexposure to radiation / 浴びるように酒を飲む drink like a fish.

あぶ ⟪昆⟫ a horsefly; a gadfly ¶あぶはち取らずになる fall between two stools.

アフガニスタン Afghanistan ¶アフガニスタンの Afghan / アフガニスタン人 an Afghan / アフガニスタン民主共和国 the Democratic Republic of Afghanistan.

あぶく 泡⇨あわ¹ ¶あぶく銭 easy money; unearned [easily gained] money.

アブサン ⟪酒⟫ absinthe.

アブストラクトアート abstract art.

アフターケア ⟪医⟫ aftercare.

アフターサービス after-sales service; ⟨automobile repair⟩ service; servicing ⟨on goods sold to customers⟩ ¶アフターサービスをする service ⟨a motorcar⟩; do [carry out] a service ⟨on⟩. 文例⇩

あぶない 危ない ⟨危険な⟩ dangerous; risky; ⟪文⟫ perilous; ⟨生命などが⟩ critical; ⟨be⟩ in danger ⟪文⟫ peril; ⟨疑わしい⟩ doubtful; questionable ¶危ない事をする run a risk; take a chance / 危ない目に会う be exposed to danger / 危ない所を助かる have a narrow escape / 危ない所を助けられる be rescued from danger / 危ない橋を渡る make a risky attempt; tread on dangerous ground; skate on thin ice / 危なく nearly; almost; ⟨be⟩ on the point of ⟨doing⟩ / 危ながる be afraid ⟨of⟩; feel uneasy ⟨about⟩; ⟪文⟫ fear. 文例⇩

あぶなげ 危な気 ¶危な気のない ⟨安全な⟩ safe; secure; ⟨しっかりした⟩ steady; sound; sure-footed ⟨判断など⟩; ⟨頼りになる⟩ reliable; trustworthy.

あぶなっかしい 危なっかしい ¶危なっかしい企て a risky [chancy] attempt / 危なっかしいはしご a shaky ladder / 危なっかしい足取りで歩く walk unsteadily / 危なっかしいフランス語を話す speak French haltingly. 文例⇩

あぶみ 鐙 a stirrup.

あばた 月面をあばたにしたのは隕石である. It was meteorites that pockmarked the moon [pocked the moon's surface]. / あばたもえくぼ. Love blinds a man to all imperfections. | Love is blind. ⟪諺⟫

あばら (やせて) あばら骨が見えていた. The ribs stood out on his chest. | You could count his ribs.

あばらや あばら屋にようこそお出で下さいました. Welcome to my humble dwelling!

あばれる そのカジキは釣り上げられるまで長い間猛烈に暴れた. The marlin put up a long, hard fight before it was landed.

アピール このコマーシャルは若い女性にアピールしようとしたものだ. This commercial is meant to appeal to young women. / この種の音楽は僕の心にアピールしなくなってしまった. Music of this sort has lost its appeal for me.

あひる あひるが鳴いている. A duck is quacking.

アフターサービス 小さい店の方がアフターサービスがいい. Small shops offer better after-sales service. / あの店はアフターサービスがよくないと評判だ. That store has a reputation for poor [unsatisfactory] servicing.

あぶない 危ない! | Look out! | Watch out! / 危ないよ. (Be) careful! / 危ないからやめろ. Stop. It's dangerous. / 橋が壊れていて危ない. The bridge is dangerously out of repair. / 戸を開け放しておいては危ない. It is not safe to leave the door open. / あの病人の容体は危ない. The patient is in a critical condition. / 成功するかどうかが危ないものだ. His success is doubtful. / 危ない空模様だ. The weather looks threatening. | It looks like rain. / そんなことをしては危ないよ. It is dangerous to do that sort of thing. / 危なかった. It was close. | It was a close thing [shave]. / 危なく車にひかれると

あぶら

あぶら¹ 油 oil ¶ (海面などに)浮いた油 an oil slick / 油が切れる run short of oil / 充分油がさしてあって楽に回る車 a well-oiled, smoothly running wheel / 油が付く get [be] oily [oil-stained] / 油の染み an oil stain / 油を流したような海 a glassy sea / 油をさす (引く, 塗る) oil (a machine); 髪に油をつける grease one's hair / 油を売る sell oil; ⟨怠ける⟩ idle one's time away; ⟨話⟩ loaf (about); dawdle / 油をしぼる press oil ((from)); ⟨叱る⟩ tell sb off; take sb to task; give sb a talking-to; ⟨文⟩ reprimand, scold / 火に油を注ぐ add fuel to the flames; throw [heap] fuel on the fire / 油で揚げる fry in oil / 油っ気のない oil-free; ⟨unoiled ⟨hair⟩ / 油だらけの, 油染みた oily; oil-stained; covered in [stained with] oil. 文例◊

あぶら² 脂 fat; tallow (蠟(ろう)状の); lard (豚の) ¶ 脂が乗る put on fat; ⟨仕事に⟩ warm up ((to one's work)) / (魚などが)脂が乗っている be fatty / 脂を塗る grease / 脂ぎった四十男 an oily-faced fleshy man in his forties / 脂染みた greasy; stained with grease / 脂っこい食物 rich food. 文例◊

あぶらあせ 脂汗 greasy sweat.

あぶらえ 油絵 an oil painting; ⟨画法⟩ oil painting ¶ 油絵の静物 a still life (painted) in oils / 油絵を描く paint in oils / 油絵画家 a painter in oils.

あぶらえのぐ 油絵の具 oils; oil paints [colors].

あぶらかす 油粕 oilcake.

あぶらがみ 油紙 oiled paper.

あぶらぐすり 油薬 (an) ointment.

あぶらげ 油揚げ a deep-fried *tofu* cutlet.

あぶらさし 油差し an oilcan.

あぶらしょう 脂性 ¶ 脂性の greasy ⟨skin⟩.

あぶらぜみ 油蟬 a large brown cicada.

あぶらな 油菜 rape.

あぶらみ 脂身 fatty meat.

あぶらむし 油虫 ⟨ごきぶり⟩ a cockroach; a black beetle; ⟨ありまき⟩ a plant louse.

アフリカ Africa ¶ アフリカ人 an African / アフリカ(人)の African / アフリカ大陸 the African Continent.

あぶる 炙る ⟨焼く⟩ broil (肉・魚などを); toast (パンなどを) ¶ 干したわかさぎを軽くあぶる toast dried smelts lightly / 火鉢で手をあぶる warm one's hands over a *hibachi* / ぬれた靴下を火にあぶって乾かす dry one's wet socks over [at] a fire.

アフレコ 〖映画・テレビ〗 postrecording; postscoring; dubbing.

あふれる 溢れる overflow; brim over ((with)); flood ¶ あふれそうに一杯になっている be full to the brim. 文例◊

あぶれる ⟨仕事に⟩ cannot [fail to] get a job [find work] ¶ 仕事にあぶれている be out of work [a job].

あべこべ ¶ あべこべの ⟨文⟩ contrary ⟨opinions⟩; opposite ⟨directions⟩ / あべこべに ⟨do⟩ the wrong way round; back to front; ⟨文⟩ inversely; ⟨順序を⟩ in reverse order; ⟨表裏を⟩ inside [the wrong side] out; ⟨上下を⟩ upside down; ⟨かえって⟩ instead; on the contrary / あべこべにする物を reverse; turn *sth* the other way; turn *sth* upside down (上下を); turn *sth* inside out (表裏を); ⟨物のやり方を⟩ get *sth* the wrong way round [back to front]; put [get] the cart before the horse (本末を顚倒する). 文例◊

アベック [<⟨フランス語⟩ *avec*=with] a (courting) couple; a couple on a date; a young man with his girlfriend; a girl with her boyfriend ¶ アベックで ⟨2人が⟩ together; ⟨go for a walk⟩ with one's boyfriend [girlfriend]; ⟨米⟩ with one's date; ⟨幾組も⟩ in couples; in pairs. 文例◊

アベマリア an Ave (Maria); (a) Hail Mary.

アペリティフ an aperitif.

あへん 阿片 opium ¶ アヘンを吸う smoke [eat] opium / アヘン常用者 an opium smoker [eater] / アヘン戦争 〖史〗 the Opium War / アヘン中毒 opium poisoning.

あほう 阿呆 a fool ⇨ばか.

あほうどり an albatross; ⟨口語⟩ a gooney bird.

アボカド 〖植〗 an avocado ⟨*pl.* -(e)s⟩; ⟨実⟩ an avocado (pear); an alligator pear.

アポロ 〖ギリシャ・ローマ神話〗 Apollo ¶ アポロ的 Apollonic; Apollonian / アポロ計画 Project Apollo.

あま¹ 尼 a nun; a priestess ¶ 尼になる become a nun; enter a convent / ⟨文⟩ take the veil / 尼寺 a convent; ⟨文⟩ a nunnery.

あま² 亜麻 flax ¶ 亜麻(製)の flax(en).

あま³ 海女 a woman diver ((for abalones)).

ころだった. I was nearly run over by a car. / 危なく溺れ死ぬところだった. I came near being drowned. / 危なくその列車に乗り遅れるところだった. I almost missed the train.

あぶなっかしい 彼は危なっかしい手つきで漬物を刻んでいた. He was awkwardly chopping the pickles. / 赤ん坊がはじめて危なっかしい足取りで歩いた. The baby took its first perilous steps.

あぶら¹ モーターの油が切れた. The oil in this motor has dried up. / The motor needs oiling. / 彼は途中で油を売っているに相違ない. He must be loitering on the way.

あぶら² 彼は脂の乗り切った年頃だ. He's in the prime of life. / 野村博士は45歳, 学者としては脂の乗り切った年齢である. Dr. Nomura is now 45, the best age for a scholar.

あふれる 豪雨のため川があふれた. The heavy rain caused the river to overflow (its banks). / 温泉は浴槽にあふれていた. The bath was running over with hot-spring water. / ホールは堂にあふれていた. The hall was filled [full] to overflowing. / 彼は喜びにあふれていた. He was brimming over with joy. / 彼女の目に涙があふれていた. Her eyes were filled [swimming] with tears.

あべこべ 君の手袋はあべこべだよ. You have your gloves on the wrong hands. / それでは私が聞いている話とまるであべこべだ. That's quite contrary to what I've heard. / 彼はお礼を言われるつもりでいたのに, あべこべにしかられた. He expected to be thanked, and got scolded instead.

アベック 公園にはアベックがたくさんいた. There were a lot of young couples in the park.

あまあし 雨脚 文例⇩

あまい 甘い 〈味が〉(be, taste) sweet ; sweet-flavored ; 〈甘やかす〉soft ; 《文》indulgent ; fond ; 〈お人好しの〉gullible ; simple-minded ; 〈鍛えが〉(be) not well tempered ¶甘い物《米》candy ;《英》sweets / 甘い物が好きである have a sweet tooth / 甘い母親 a fond [an indulgent] mother / 甘い考え《文》excessive optimism ; overoptimism ; too optimistic thinking / 甘い言葉にだまされる fall for sb's honeyed words / 子供に甘い を such [[《文》overindulgent, too permissive]] with one's children / 甘くする sweeten / 子供を甘く育てる bring up a child (too) indulgently ; spoil a child / 女に甘い have a soft spot for women / 甘く見る〈口語〉think sb (is) a soft touch [an easy mark] ;《文》hold sb cheap ; think sb easy to deal with. 文例⇩

あまえる 甘える behave like a spoilt child ; 〈犬などが〉fawn on 〈its master〉/ 人の親切に甘える be too dependent on sb's kindness / 甘えた調子で物を言う speak in a wheedling voice. 文例⇩

あまえんぼう 甘えん坊 a wheedling child.
あまがえる 雨蛙 〈動〉a tree frog [toad].
あまがさ 雨傘 an umbrella.
あまがっぱ 雨合羽 ⇒ かっぱ¹.
あまから 甘辛 ¶甘辛の salted and sweetened.
あまかわ 甘皮 〈植〉the endocarp ; 〈つめの〉the cuticle.
あまぐ 雨具 rainwear ; 〈レーンコート〉a raincoat ; 〈傘〉an umbrella. 文例⇩
あまくだり 天下り ¶天下りの recommended from high quarters ; appointed by orders from above / 天下り人事 the appointment [《口語》parachuting] of a former government official to a high position in 《a private company》.
あまくち 甘口 ¶甘口の酒 (a) sweetish sake / 甘口のみそ miso with a mildly salty taste.
あまぐつ 雨靴 rain boots [shoes].
あまぐも 雨雲 a rain cloud.
あまぐり 甘栗 sweet roasted chestnuts.
あまごい 雨乞い ¶雨乞いをする pray for rain ; offer prayers for rain / 雨乞いの儀式 rain-making rituals.

あまざけ 甘酒 amazake ; a sweet drink made from fermented rice.
あまざらし 雨曝し ¶雨ざらしの weather-beaten / 雨ざらしにする expose sth to the rain [weather] ; leave sth in the rain.
あまじお 甘塩 ¶甘塩のさけ lightly-salted salmon.
あます 余す leave (over) ; spare ; save (節約する) ¶小遣いを余す save something from one's pocket money / 金を余さず使う spend all one's money / 余す所なく《文》exhaustively ; thoroughly. 文例⇩
あまずっぱい 甘酸っぱい sour-sweet ★sweet-and-sour と言うのは中華料理の酢豚 (sweet-and-sour pork) の味.
アマゾンがわ アマゾン川 the Amazon ¶アマゾン川〈流域〉の Amazonian.
あまた 数多 ⇒ たくさん, たすう.
あまだい 甘鯛 〈魚〉a tilefish.
あまだれ 雨垂れ raindrops ¶雨だれの音 the pattering of raindrops / 雨だれ式でタイプライターを打つ type by the hunt-and-peck method ; 〈一本指で〉type with one finger.
あまちゃ 甘茶 hydrangea tea.
アマチュア an amateur ¶アマチュア無線家 a radio amateur ; a (radio) ham.
あまつさえ besides ;《文》moreover ; in addition.
あまったるい 甘ったるい too sweet ; sugary ¶甘ったるい言葉 honeyed words ;《口語》sweet talk / 甘ったるい芝居 a sentimental play.
あまったれ 甘ったれ ⇒ あまえんぼう.
あまったれる 甘ったれる ⇒ あまえる.
あまど 雨戸 〈引き戸〉a sliding door ; 〈シャッター〉a shutter ¶雨戸を開ける[閉める] slide shutters [doors] open [shut].
あまどい 雨樋 〈横樋〉a gutter ; 〈堅樋〉《米》a downspout ;《英》a downpipe.
あまとう 甘党 a person who prefers cakes and candies to alcoholic drinks. 文例⇩
あまなっとう 甘納豆 sweetened adzuki beans.
あまに 亜麻仁 linseed ¶亜麻仁油 linseed oil.
あまねく 普く 〈一般に〉《文》universally ; 〈広

あまあし 夏の夕立は雨脚が早い. A summer shower comes on fast. / 雨脚が激しくなった. The rain became heavier. / 雨脚が衰えて小降りになった. The rain slackened to a drizzle.
あまい コーヒーは甘くしたのが好きだ. I like my coffee sweet. / この漬物は塩が甘い. There isn't enough salt [Not enough salt has been used] in these pickles. | These pickles have not been salted enough. / 武田先生は点が甘い. Mr. Takeda is generous in his marking. / そんなことで彼が妥協すると思ったら考えが甘い. You're a real optimist if you expect him to compromise on such terms.
あまえる うちの子は甘えてしようがありません. My child has got quite spoilt. / お言葉に甘えて明日お うかがいいたします. Thank you very much for your kind invitation. I'll come and see you tomorrow.
あまぐ 山の天候は変わりやすいから雨具は用意して行くべきだ. Since the weather in the mountains is changeable, you should carry something to protect you from the rain. / 今日は雨具を持って来なかった. I haven't brought any rain things with me.
あます 余すところたった 100 円だ. We have only one hundred yen left. / 総選挙まで余すところわずか 2 日となった. Only two days remain before the general election.

あまとう 僕は甘党だ. 〈甘い物を好む〉I have a sweet tooth. | 〈酒を飲まない〉I don't drink.
あまみず 街路には雨水が流れていた. The streets were running with rain.
あまもり ひどく雨漏りがする. The roof leaks badly. | There is a bad leak in the roof.
あまやかす 子供を甘やかすとだめになる. Spare the rod and spoil the child. [諺]
あまやどり 近くの喫茶店に雨宿りに駆け込んだ. I ran into a nearby coffee shop to shelter from [get out of] the rain. / 降り出したので木の下で雨宿りした. It started to rain, so we took cover under a tree.

の) offal; bony parts ¶あらを捜す pick holes 《in》; find fault 《with》; find flaws 《in》.

あら² Oh!; Why!; Good gracious!; Dear me!

あらあらしい 荒々しい rough; harsh; violent ¶荒々しい気性 《文》 a violent [an unruly] temperament / 荒々しい言葉 harsh [violent] words [language] / 荒々しく roughly; harshly; violently.

あらい¹ 洗い 〈せんたく〉 washing ¶洗いがきく stand washing; be washable / 鯉の洗い slices of carp washed in cold water.

あらい² 粗い wild; rough; harsh; violent; 《文》 rude; heavy 《波が》 strong 《風が》 ¶気性の荒い人 a rough-natured [quick-tempered] person / 言葉遣いが荒い be rough in one's speech / 荒く roughly; harshly; violently. 文例⇩

あらい³ 粗い coarse; rough ¶目の粗い網 a large-mesh(ed) net; a net with large meshes / 粗い縞 large stripes / 地の粗い織物 coarse cloth; (a) fabric with a loose weave / きめの粗い肌 a rough skin.

あらいおけ 洗い桶 〈大型の〉 a washtub; 〈台所のしの〉 《米》 a dishpan; 《英》 a washing-up bowl.

あらいおとす 洗い落とす wash off [out] 《a stain》 ¶《頭を洗ったあとで》シャンプーを洗い落とす rinse off the shampoo.

あらいがみ 洗い髪 文例⇩

あらいぐま 洗い熊 《動》 a raccoon; a racoon; 《口語》 a coon.

あらいざらい 洗い浚い ¶洗いざらい持って行く take everything away; leave nothing behind / 洗いざらいぶちまける confess everything; tell the whole story (down to the last detail) / いい所も悪い所も洗いざらい書く draw sb warts and all; paint sb with all his faults. 文例⇩

あらいざらし 洗い晒し ¶洗い晒しのジーパン (a pair of) blue jeans faded from repeated washing.

あらいさる 洗い去る wash away.

あらいそ 荒磯 〈岩の多い〉 a rocky coast; 〈波の荒い〉 a wave-beaten shore.

あらいだす 洗い出す wash out 《dirt》.

あらいたてる 洗い立てる rake up 《sb's past》; ferret out 《sb's secret》; 〈細かく調べる〉 examine sth closely.

あらいながす 洗い流す wash away; flush (out).

あらいもの 洗い物 〈食後の〉 dishes to be washed; 《英》 washing up; 〈洗濯物〉 the wash; washing; laundry ¶《食後の》洗い物をする do the dishes [《英》 washing-up]; 《英》 wash up.

あらう 洗う wash; 《文》 cleanse ¶手や顔を洗う wash one's face and hands; have a wash; 《米》 wash up / 目を洗う bathe one's eyes (in warm water) / 髪を洗う wash [shampoo] one's hair / 《波が》デッキを洗う sweep the deck / 素性を洗う inquire into sb's past / 洗い立ての newly [freshly] washed. 文例⇩

あらうみ 荒海 a rough [stormy] sea.

あらかじめ 予め beforehand; in advance; ahead of time ¶あらかじめ通知する give previous notice / あらかじめ注意する give warning / あらかじめ用意する have sth ready beforehand; make preparations in advance / あらかじめ選んでおいた材料 the preselected material. 文例⇩

あらかせぎ 荒稼ぎ ¶荒稼ぎをする make money hand over fist; 《俗》 make a pile [bundle]; make quick money; 《口語》 rake it in; 《口語》 clean up; 〈泥棒が〉 make [have] a good haul.

あらかた 〈大部分〉 for the most part; mostly; 〈ほとんど〉 almost; 〈概略〉 on the whole. 文例⇩

あらかべ 荒壁 a rough-coated wall.

アラカルト à la carte.

あらぎょう 荒行 rigorous ascetic exercises.

あらくれ 荒くれ ¶荒くれ男 a rough [rowdy] fellow / 荒くれ仕事 a rough job.

あらけずり 粗[荒]削り ¶あら削りの rough-planed[-hewn] / 〈洗練されていない〉 unrefined. 文例⇩

あらげる 荒げる ⇨ あららげる.

あらさがし あら捜し faultfinding; 《口語》 nitpicking ¶あら捜しをする find fault 《with》 ⇨ あら¹ (あらを捜す).

あらし 嵐 a storm; a windstorm; 《文》 a tempest; 〈豪雨〉 a rainstorm ¶ひどいあらし a

---

meeting the union's demands.

あら² あら, まあ. Dear me! / や, そんなばかなわよ. Why, it can't be! / あら!何でしょう, 地震かしら. There! What's that? An earthquake? / あらあら, あそこをご覧. Look, look! over there! / あら!そうですか. Really? | Oh! Is that so?

あらい¹ 波が荒い. The sea is rough [running high]. / あの家は平和な家庭で, 荒い言葉一聞かれない. Not a single angry voice is ever heard in that happy home.

あらいがみ 彼女は洗い髪姿でいた. She had just washed her hair and it was still unarranged.

あらいざらい お互いに洗いざらい ぶちまけて話し合いたいと思う. I want to have it out with you.

あらう この色は洗ってもきれいい. This color is fast when washed. / そのしみは洗っても取れなかった. The stain would [did] not wash out. / 波が岸を洗っていた. The sea was washing [lapping] (against) the shore.

あらかじめ ハンターたちはその獲物がどこへ向かっているのかをあらかじめ知っていて, 手頃な場所で待ち伏せていた. The hunters, with advance knowledge of where the herd was headed, lay in ambush at a convenient spot.

あらかた この時期には村の男たちはあらかた都会へ出かせぎに行ってしまう. Most of the menfolk leave the village to work in the cities at this time of (the) year. / 仕事はあらかたけりがついた. The work is nearly finished.

あらけずり この文はあら削りだ. This writing lacks polish.

あらし 嵐になりそうだ. The weather looks stormy. / 嵐が起こった. A storm came on. / 嵐が吹きすさんでいる. The storm is raging. / 嵐はやんだ. The storm has blown over [calmed down]. / The storm is over. / 嵐で庭がひどく荒れてしまった. The garden has been badly ravaged by the storm. / この新説の発表は論戦の嵐を巻き起こした. The an-

あらしまわる violent [heavy] storm / あらしの夜 a stormy night / あらしの前の静けさ the calm [lull] before a storm / あらしのような拍手 thunderous applause; a storm of applause / あらしに会う be caught in [overtaken by] a storm. 文例⇩
あらしまわる 荒らし回る storm through ((the land)); ravage ((the whole town)).
あらす 荒らす 〈荒廃させる〉lay waste; ruin; devastate; 〈害する〉harm; do (severe) damage [harm] ((to)); 《文》wreak havoc ((on)); damage; 〈襲う〉raid; make a raid ((on)); 〈略奪を働く〉loot; 《文》sack; 《文》pillage; 《文》despoil; 〈押し入る〉break into ((a bank)); 〈皮膚を〉roughen ¶〈洪水・あらしなどが〉作物を荒らす damage [do damage to, work havoc with] the crops. 文例⇩
アラスカ Alaska (略: Alas.) ¶アラスカの Alaskan.
あらすじ 粗筋 an outline [a plot summary] ((of a story)) ¶〈連載小説の〉前回までの粗筋 the story so far / 話の粗筋を述べる give an outline of the story. 文例⇩
あらせいとう 〘植〙a stock.
あらそい 争い 〈競争〉(a) competition; (a) rivalry; a contest; 〈論争〉a dispute; an argument; a controversy; 〈けんか〉a quarrel; a fight; 〈不和〉《文》(a) discord; (a) conflict; 《文》strife ¶争いの種をまく sow the seeds of discord.
あらそう 争う 〈競争する〉compete [《文》vie] ((with sb for sth)); 《文》contend ((with [against] sb for sth)); 〈論争する〉argue [《文》dispute] ((with sb about [over] sth)); have a dispute [an argument] ((with sb about [over] sth)); 《文》engage in a controversy; 〈けんかする〉quarrel ((with sb about [over] sth)); fight ((with [against] sb for sth)); 〈仲たがいする〉be in conflict [《文》discord] ((with)) ¶法廷で争う go to law ((with, against)); 《文》contest (the issue) at law / 勝ち[功名]を争う《文》contend for victory [honors] / 議席を争う contest a seat (in the House) / …をする try to be the first to do; try to get ahead of other people ((in doing)) / 争われぬ事実《文》an undeniable [indisputable] fact / 争われぬ証拠《文》incontrovertible [incontestable] evidence [proof].

あらた 新た ⇒あたらしい ¶新たに afresh; newly; 《文》anew; 〈再び〉(over) again / 記憶を新たにする refresh one's memory / 決意を新たにする make a fresh determination / 再び新たに始める start all over again; start afresh; 《文》begin anew.
あらたか ⇒れいげん².
あらだつ 荒立つ 〈事が〉《文》be aggravated; be made worse; 〈怒る〉be excited.
あらだてる 荒立てる make ((a matter)) worse; 《文》aggravate ¶事を荒立てないようにする handle things carefully; go out of one's way not to stir up trouble; let sleeping dogs lie; 《文》seek an amicable settlement ((of)).
あらたまる 改まる 〈新しくなる〉be renewed; 〈変わる〉change; be changed; be altered; 〈改正される〉be revised; 〈改善される〉be improved; 〈矯正(きょうせい)される〉be reformed; be corrected; 〈病状が〉take a turn for the worse; take a serious turn; 〈儀式ばる〉stand on ceremony; become formal ¶改まった席で on a formal occasion / 改まった言葉使いをする use formal language. 文例⇩
あらためて 改めて 〈更に〉(over) again; 〈別の時に〉another time; on another occasion; 〈新たに〉afresh; 《文》anew. 文例⇩
あらためる 改める 〈変える〉change; alter; 〈一新する〉renew; 〈矯正する〉innovate; 〈矯正する〉correct; reform; 〈修正する〉revise; correct; 〈改善する〉improve; 〈調べる〉examine; inspect ¶方針を改める change one's plan [policy, course of action] / 誤りを改める《文》correct an error / 規則を改める revise the regulations / 行ないを改める mend one's ways; turn over a new leaf / 金額を改める check [《文》verify] the amount. 文例⇩
あらっぽい 荒っぽい ⇒あらい² ¶荒っぽい事をする use violence; 《口語》play (it) rough; 〈荒っぽく取り扱う〉handle sth roughly.
あらて 新手 a new worker [employee]; 〈兵〉a fresh force; reinforcements; 〈新方法〉a new way [method] ((of doing)).
あらと 粗砥 a rough grindstone.

nouncement of this new theory loosed [blew up] a storm of comment and dispute.
あらす 部屋の中はひどく荒らされていた. The room was found to have been completely ransacked. / その古墳は荒らされて副葬品は何もなくなっている. The ancient tomb has been completely plundered [pillaged] of its grave goods.
あらすじ 話の粗筋はできた. 細かいことはこれからだ. I've worked out the bare bones of the story; now I'm going to fill in the details.
あらそい 2人の間にはいつも争いが絶えない. They are constantly battling [at odds] with each other. / 金の分配のことで彼らの間に争いが起こった. A dispute arose among them about the distribution of the money.
あらそう これは一刻を争う問題だ. The problem does not admit of [does not brook] a moment's delay. / 今は一分一秒を争う時だ. We haven't a moment to lose. / 事実は争われない. We cannot deny the fact. | There is no gainsaying the fact. | 年は争われない. Age will tell. | There is no contending against age.
あらたまる 年が改まった. The new year has come round. / 改まってお願いしたいことがあります. I have one thing that I must ask you particularly to do for me.
あらためて いずれ改めてお話ししましょう. Let's talk about it some other time. / ここで改めて説くまでもない. It needs no repetition [reiteration] here. / 何も改めて申し上げることはありません. I have nothing particular to say.
あらためる この悪習は改めねばならない. This evil practice must be abolished.
あらっぽい 荒っぽいまねはするなよ. Cut out the rough stuff! / こんなことでは らちが あかない. 一つ荒っぽい手を使ってみるか. We're getting nowhere this way. Now let's try throwing our

[あ]

あらなみ 荒波 raging waves; rough waters; a heavy sea ¶(船が)荒波にもまれる be tossed about by angry waves / 世間の荒波にもまれる《文》suffer the hardships of life; be buffeted about in the world.

あらなわ 荒縄 a straw rope.

あらぬ ¶あらぬ疑いをかけられる be wrongly [《文》falsely] suspected《of theft》/ あらぬ方を見る look off into space [the air]; 〈顔を背ける〉look away / あらぬ事を口走る talk wildly; say crazy things. [文例⇩]

あらぬり 粗塗り (a) rough coating; a first coat ¶粗塗りをする give《the wall》a first coat《of plaster》.

アラバマ Alabama (略: Ala.) ¶アラバマ州の人 an Alabamian; an Alabaman ★土地の人は Alabamian の方を好んで用いる.

アラビア Arabia ¶アラビア(人)の Arabian; Arabic / アラビア馬 an Arab / アラビア海 the Arabian Sea / アラビア語(の) Arabic / アラビアゴム gum arabic / アラビア人 an Arabian; an Arab / アラビア数字 Arabic numerals [figures] / アラビア半島 the Arabian Peninsula / アラビア文字 Arabic script / アラビア夜話〘書名〙*The Arabian Nights*; *The Thousand and One Nights*; *The Arabian Nights' Entertainments.*

アラブ an Arab ¶アラブ化する Arabize; Arabicize / アラブ首長国連邦 the United Arab Emirates / アラブ諸国 the Arab States.

アラフラかい アラフラ海 the Arafura Sea.

アラベスク〘美術·音楽·バレー〙an arabesque.

あらまき 新巻き ¶新巻きの鮭 a lightly salted salmon.

あらまし 〈概略〉an outline; the gist; 〈ざっと〉roughly; about; 〈ほとんど〉almost; nearly ¶計画のあらましを述べる give an outline of the plan. [文例⇩]

アラモード à la mode ¶アップルパイ アラモード《米》(an) apple pie à la mode.

あらもの 荒物 household utensils such as buckets, brooms, dustpans, etc. ¶荒物屋〈人〉a dealer in household goods; 〈店〉a household goods store.

あらゆる all; every (possible) ¶あらゆる種類の人 all sorts of people / あらゆる手段を尽くす try every possible means / あらゆる点で《文》in all respects; 《文》in every respect / 問題をあらゆる角度から検討する study a problem from all angles.

あららげる 荒らげる ¶声を荒らげる raise *one's* voice《in anger》/ 声を荒らげて in an angry voice.

あらりょうじ 荒療治 〈治療〉a drastic treatment; 〈思い切った手段〉a drastic remedy; drastic measures ¶事態収拾のため荒療治を行なう take drastic measures to save the situation.

あられ 霰 hail; a hailstone; 〈菓子〉very small rice biscuits [crackers]. [文例⇩]

あられもない unladylike; 《文》unbecoming《to a woman》; 《文》indecorous; 《文》immodest ¶あられもない姿で眠っている be sleeping in an untidy manner.

あらわ ¶あらわな open; unconcealed / あらわに〈公然と〉openly; publicly; 〈明白に〉plainly; clearly; 〈露骨に〉bluntly / 肌もあらわに not properly [decently] covered; dressed scantily; 〈裸で〉naked / あらわにする《文》lay bare; 《文》reveal; expose; show.

あらわす[1] 表[現]わす 〈示す〉show; 《文》manifest; display; indicate; 〈証明する〉prove; 〈暴露する〉《文》disclose; 《文》reveal; betray; expose; 〈表現する〉express; 《文》give expression to; 〈代表する〉represent; stand for; 〈象徴する〉symbolize ¶名を現わす become famous; make *one's* name / 手腕を現わす show *one's* ability / 怒りを表わす betray *one's* anger / 考えを言葉に表わす put *one's* thoughts into [express *one's* thoughts in] words. [文例⇩]

---

weight about (a bit).

あらぬ 彼はあらぬ方を見ていた. He was looking in the wrong direction.

あらまし 会議の結果はあらまし次のとおりである. The results of the conference may be summarized as follows.

あられ あられが降っている. It is hailing. / あられがパラパラと屋根に音を立てていた. Hailstones were clattering on the roof.

あらわす[1] これは彼の正直さを表わしている. This shows [is evidence of] his honesty. / それをどう言って表わしてよいかわかりません. I don't know how to put it into words. / この記号は何を表わすのか. What does this sign stand for? | What is this a sign for?

あらわす[2] 彼は社会学に関する数冊の書物を著わした. He has written [He is the author of] several books on sociology.

あらわれ それは彼の妻に対する愛情の現われだった. It was an expression of his love for his wife. / それは彼の 10 年間の努力の現われだった. It was the fruit of ten years' effort on his part.

あらわれる 月が雲間から現われた. The moon came out from behind the clouds. / 乱世には英雄が現われる. Turbulent ages produce heroes. / 現代生活のさまざまなストレスが身体の病気となって現われる. The various stresses of modern life find their expression in physical illness. / 驚きの色が彼の表情に表われた. A look of surprise came over his face. / 酒を飲むと本性が現われる. Liquor [Alcohol] reveals one's true self. | 《ラテン語》*In vino veritas.*

あり 会場は蟻のはい出るすきもないような警戒ぶりだった. The security in [around] the hall was very tight. | The hall was very closely guarded. / 蟻の穴から土手も崩れる. A small leak will sink a great ship. 〘諺〙| For want of a nail, the rider was lost. (★ 'For want of a nail, the shoe is lost; for want of a shoe, the horse is lost; for want of a horse, the rider is lost.' というのがつづまってできた).

ありありと 彼はその光景をありありと目に見えるように語った. He gave us a graphic account of the scene. / 苦悩の色がありありと表情に現われていた. His mental anguish was plainly visible in his expression. | His face plainly registered (his) distress.

ありあわせ 夕食はあり合わせですませましょう. Let's make dinner from [with] whatever we have in the house. / あり合わせの物しかないけれど, 僕のところで晩飯を食べないか. Won't you come

あらわす² 著わす write [publish] 《a book》. 文例⇩

あらわれ 現われ an expression ; a sign ; 《文》a manifestation. 文例⇩

あらわれる 現[表]われる 〈姿を現わす〉appear ; make one's appearance ; present [show] one-self ; turn up ; emerge ; 〈見えてくる〉come in sight [into view] ; 〈表に現われる〉show *itself* ; 〈文〉be revealed ; 〈文〉be exposed ; 〈発見される〉be found (out) ; 〈文〉be discovered ¶世に現われる become known [famous] ; 〈名を上げる〉make one's name ; 〈文〉attain distinction / 世に現われずに死ぬ live and die in obscurity.

あらんかぎり 有らん限り ¶あらん限りの声を張り上げて at the top of one's voice / あらん限りの手段を 〈文〉resort to every possible means / あらん限りの力を出す put out [《文》forth] all one's strength / あらん限りの能力を尽して to the best of one's ability ; as best one can.

あり 蟻 an ant ¶ありの巣 an ant(s') nest / あり塚 an anthill ; an ant mound. 文例⇩

アリア《音楽》an aria.

ありあまる 有り余る 〈物が主語〉be more than enough ; 《文》be superabundant ; 《文》be in excess ; 〈人が主語〉have more than enough ; have too many [much] ; 〈たくさんの〉over-flowing ¶金がありあまるほどある have more money than one can spend ; have enough money and to spare ; have money to burn.

ありありと distinctly ; clearly ; vividly ¶…がありありと目に浮かぶ remember *sth* vividly ; 《文》have a vivid recollection of…. 文例⇩

ありあわせ 有り合わせ ¶有り合わせの available ; ready [to, on] hand / 有り合わせのさかなで一杯やる have a drink with whatever food is available to go with it. 文例⇩

ありうる 有り得る be possible ¶あり得る事

a possibility. 文例⇩

ありか 在り処 〈ある所〉the place (where) *sth* is (kept) ; 〈居所〉one's whereabouts (★ 単数複数両様に扱われる) ; 〈隠れ場所〉one's hiding place ¶ありかを突き止める find (out) where *sth* [*sb*] is ; locate ; track down.

ありかた 在り方 ¶政党のあり方 what a political party should be ; a political party as it ought to be.

ありがたい 有り難い kind ; welcome ; 《文》gracious ¶有り難い贈り物 a welcome [《文》much appreciated] gift / 有り難い説教 《文》an edifying sermon / 有り難くない客 an unwelcome guest / 有り難いことに fortunately ; luckily / 有り難く思う be thankful [grateful] 《to *sb* for *sth*》; be obliged 《to *sb*》; appreciate 《*sb*'s kindness》/ 有り難く頂戴する accept *sth* with thanks. 文例⇩

ありがたがる 有り難がる 〈感謝する〉be thankful 《for》; feel grateful 《to *sb* for *sth*》; show one's gratitude 《to *sb* for *sth*》; appreciate ; 《文》be appreciative of *sth* ; 〈尊ぶ〉value ; prize ; make much of ; set great store by 《人(に)似り難がられない仕事 a thankless job [《文》task].

ありがたなみだ 有り難涙 ¶有り難涙をこぼす 《文》shed tears of gratitude.

ありがたみ 有り難味 value ; 《文》virtue ¶有り難みを知る realize the value 《of *sth*》. 文例⇩

ありがためいわく 有り難迷惑 misplaced kindness ; an unwelcome favor. 文例⇩

ありがち 有り勝ち ¶有り勝ちの 《文》frequent ; common ; not uncommon / 有り勝ちである be apt [prone] to happen / 職人に有り勝ちの癖 a habit often found in a workman. 文例⇩

ありがとう ¶ありがとうと手を振る wave one's thanks 《to *sb* for *sth*》/ (手伝いなどをして)両親にありがとうと言われる earn one's parents' thanks. 文例⇩

ありがね 有り金 the money in [on] hand ;

---

and have supper with us, if you don't mind taking potluck?

ありうる 5月の末に霜が降りるとはまずないが,しかしあり得ることだ. Frost is possible, though not probable, at the end of May./ それは大いに[全く]あり得ることだ. It is quite[entirely] possible./ それはまずあり得ないことだ. That is highly improbable.| That is most unlikely (to happen).| That is a virtual impossibility.

ありか 行先をくらました殺人容疑者はいまだにありかが知れない. The whereabouts of the fleeing murder suspect is [are] still unknown.

ありがたい そう言って下さるのは有り難い. It is very kind of you to say so. | そうして頂ければ有り難い仕合わせです. I would be very grateful if you would do so./ 有り難い, 雨がやんだぞ. Thank God! It's stopped raining. / 君が

この役を引き受けてくれるか. それは有り難い. You man you're going to take on the job? That's very kind of you. Thank you. / お手紙有り難く拝読いたしました. Thank you very much for your kind letter. | 漢方薬の有り難いところはここだ. Herein lies the virtue of a herbal medicine. / 親というものは有り難いものだ. We really owe a great deal to our parents. / 電卓というものは有り難いものだ. What a blessed device [happy invention] the pocket calculator is! / 木村さんのご親切を有り難いと思わないのか. Don't you appreciate [feel any gratitude for] Mr. Kimura's kindness? / Don't you think you ought to be grateful to Mr. Kimura for his kindness?

ありがたみ はじめて親の有り難みがわかった. I realized for the first time how much I owe (to)

my parents. / 私は友人の有り難みを知っている. I know what a good thing it is to have friends. / 病気になって初めて健康の有り難みがわかる. You don't appreciate the value [importance] of good health until you lose it.

ありがためいわく それは有り難迷惑だよ. Thank you for nothing!/ 彼も有り難迷惑なことをしてくれたものだ. I must say he did me a disservice, though I know he meant well.

ありがち 学生には有り勝ちのことだが,彼もあればあるだけ使ってしまう. As is often the case with students, he never saves anything out of the money he gets.

ありがとう ありがとう. Thank you. | 〈軽い言い方〉Thanks. / どうもありがとう. Thank you very much.|〈くだけた言い方〉Thanks a lot [million]. / 結構な品をお送り下さいましてありがとうござい

ありきたり 在り来たり ¶ありきたりの〈在来の〉conventional; customary;〈ありふれた〉common; usual;《口語》just another;〈普通の〉ordinary.

ありくい [動] an anteater.

ありさま 有様〈状態〉a state; a condition;〈事情〉circumstances;〈光景〉a spectacle; a scene ¶今の有様では as things are [stand] (now); the way things are (at the moment); in the present state of things ; in [under] the present circumstances / …の有様を述べる give an account of…. 文例⇩

ありじごく [昆] an ant-lion larva.

ありしひ 在りし日 the old days;《文》bygone [former, past] days ¶ありし日の事ども 思い出の past / ありし日の有倉教授 the late Professor Arikura while he was still alive / ありしひをしのぶ think of bygone days [the past].

ありそう 有りそう ¶ありそうな probable; likely / ありそうもない improbable; unlikely / ありそうな話 a likely [《文》plausible] story. 文例⇩

アリゾナ Arizona (略: Ariz.) ¶アリゾナ州の人 an Arizonan; an Arizonian.

ありだか 有り高〈金〉the amount in [on] hand;〈品〉goods in stock; goods in [on] hand.

ありつく find; get; come by ¶ご馳走にありつく be treated《to a dinner》/ 仕事にありつく find employment [a job];《口語》land a job.

ありったけ all that *one* has [there is] ¶ありったけの all; as many《containers》as *one* has; as much《money》as *one* has / ありったけの声で叫ぶ shout at the top of *one's* voice / ありったけの力を出す put out [《文》exert,《文》put forth] all *one's* strength.

ありてい 有り体 ¶ありていに言えば to tell the (plain) truth; frankly speaking; not to put too fine a point on it ; the blunt fact is that… / ありていに白状する confess (to) everything ; make a clean breast of *sth*.

ありとあらゆる 有りとあらゆる ⇨ あらゆる.

ありのまま 有りのまま ¶ありのままの〈そのままの〉as it is [stands];〈飾らない〉plain;〈誇張のない〉《文》unexaggerated;〈むき出しの〉bare;《文》undisguised / ありのままに〈そのままに〉as it is;〈飾らずに〉plainly;〈率直に〉frankly; candidly;〈隠さず〉openly;《文》without concealment;〈誇張なく〉without exaggeration / ありのままの事実 a bare [plain] fact; the unvarnished [plain] truth / ありのままを言う tell [speak] the truth; give an honest account (of). 文例⇩

アリバイ an alibi ¶アリバイがある have an alibi / アリバイをでっち上げる fake an alibi / アリバイを立証する prove *sb's* alibi / アリバイを突き崩す break *sb's* alibi. 文例⇩

ありふれた common (or garden); run-of-the-mill; commonplace; familiar;《文》trite ¶ありふれた事 a commonplace event; an everyday affair / ありふれた話 a well-known story;《文》a twice-told tale.

ありまき [昆] an aphid; an ant cow; a plant louse.

ありもしない nonexistent;《文》spurious; unreal ¶ありもしないことを言い立てられる have a false story told about *one*; have a groundless rumor put around about *one*.

ありゅう 亜流 an (inferior) imitator.

ありゅうさん 亜硫酸 [化] sulfurous acid ¶亜硫酸ガス sulfurous acid gas.

アリューシャンれっとう アリューシャン列島 the Aleutian Islands; the Aleutians.

ありんさん 亜燐酸 [化] phosphorous acid.

ある¹ 或 one; a; some; a certain (★ a certain は知っているがはっきり名を出したりしたくないときに用いる) ¶ある人 a certain

---

ました. Thank you very much for the nice present you sent me. / (店頭で顧客に)毎度ありがとうございます. Thank you, sir [madam]. ★ この場合, 日本語での「ありがとうございます」と「ありがとうございました」の違いを英語に移しかえることはできない.

ありがね 有り金を全部はたいてその家を手に入れた. He spent all the money he had to his name and obtained the house.

ありきたり ありきたりの料理の本とは違います. This isn't just another cookbook.

ありさま 難民は実に惨めな有様だ. The refugees are in a wretched condition. / 事故の現場はさんたんたる有様で, どこから後片付けに手をつけてよいかわからなかった. The scene of the accident was in such a mess that they did not know where to begin clearing up.

ありそう 大いにありそうなことだ. That's quite probable [very likely]. / そんなことはまず絶対にありそうもないように見える. The odds seem to be overwhelmingly against such an eventuality.

ありのまま ありのままを言いたまえ. State the facts as they are. / 彼は出来事をありのままに話した. He gave us a straightforward account of what happened.

アリバイ 彼らには皆完全なアリバイがあった. They all had watertight alibis. / 彼のアリバイが崩れた. His alibi broke down.

ある² その家には広い庭がある. The house has a large garden (to it). / この家にはガスがある. Gas is laid on in this house. / その本は今しがた確かに机の上にあった. I am sure I saw the book on the desk a minute ago. / この「人間探知機」は人の汗に含まれるあるかないかの少量のアンモニアに反応する. This 'man detector' reacts to the vanishingly small quantities of ammonia in human perspiration. / 寺は丘の上にある. The temple stands on a hill. / 公園は市の中央にある. The park lies in the center of the town. / 家の後ろに小川がある. A stream runs behind my house. / その語はたいがいの辞書にある. The word is given [found, listed] in almost all dictionaries. / 化学繊維というものは 40 年以上の昔からあった. Synthetic fibers have been in existence for more than forty years. / この種の装置には色々の型[名]のものがある. Devices of this sort come in various types [go by various names]. / 決定権は理事会にある. The power of decision resides in the board of directors. / それは長さ 3 メートル, 重さ 30 キロある. It measures three meters in length and weighs thirty kilograms. / その地所は 30 平方メートルある. The lot covers thirty square meters. /

ある person; someone (誰か) / ある時 once / (おとぎ話で)昔々ある時のこと once upon a time / ある日 one day / ある所で at a certain place / ある意味では in a sense / ある程度(まで) to a certain extent; to some degree.

ある² 有[在]る 〈…である〉 be; 〈存在する〉 there is [are]; 《文》 exist; 《文》 be found; 〈所在する〉 《文》 be situated; 《文》 stand (山・建物など); 《文》 lie (都市・国などが); run (道・川が); 〈所有〉 have; 《文》 possess; own; keep; 〈設備の〉 《文》 be equipped (with); 〈付属する〉 have sth attached (to); 〈起こる〉 happen; 《文》 occur; 《文》 take place; 〈催される〉 be held; 〈…に存する〉 《文》 lie in; 《文》 consist in ¶音楽の才能がある have a gift for music / ふろ場がある 〈建物が主語〉 have [be provided with] a bathroom / ほとんど無しかの建物 or no (money); little, if any, (money); 《文》 few, if any, (books); 《文》 few or no (books) / 惨事のあった所 the scene of a disaster / …さえあれば with; if one has [had]; if there is [was, were] / どんなことがあろうと whatever happens [may happen]; come what may / あるだけ ⇒ ありたけ. [文例る]

あるいは 或いは 〈または〉 or; either...or; 〈おそらくは〉 perhaps; probably; maybe; 〈ひょっとして〉 possibly ¶これかあるいはそれ (either) this or that / あるいはまた or again. [文例る]

あるがまま ⇒ ありのまま ¶物事をあるがままに受け取る take things as they are [come].

アルカリ 《化》 (an) alkali ((pl. -(e)s) ¶アルカリ性[度] alkalinity / アルカリ性の alkaline / アルカリ性にする alkalize; alkalify / アルカリ性土壌 alkaline soil / アルカリ性反応 an alkaline reaction.

アルカロイド 《化》 an alkaloid.

アルキメデス Archimedes ¶アルキメデスの原理 Archimedes' principle.

あるく 歩く walk; step ¶歩いて学校へ行く walk to school; go to school on foot / 歩いて帰る walk home; go home on foot / 歩けるようになる 〈幼児が〉 start walking [to walk]; 《文》 become able to walk; 〈病人などが〉 find [get back on] one's feet; start [be able] to walk again / 歩かせる walk (a child) / バッターをフォアボールで歩かせる walk a batter on balls / 歩き方 the way one walks; one's walk [step] / 歩き回る walk [go] about; pace around [about]; wander; gad about (遊び歩く). [文例]

アルコール alcohol ¶アルコール(性)の alcoholic / 飲用[薬用]アルコール potable [medicinal] alcohol / アルコール飲料 a [an alcoholic] drink / アルコール中毒 alcoholism / アルコール中毒患者 an alcoholic / アルコール中毒にかかっている be addicted to alcohol; be an alcoholic / アルコールランプ a spirit lamp / アルコール漬けの標本 a specimen (preserved) in alcohol [spirits] / (呼気による)アルコール量測定器 《米》 a drunkometer; 《英》《商標名》 a Breathalyzer.

アルゴン 《化》 argon.

アルジェリア Algeria ¶アルジェリア(人)の Algerian / アルジェリア人 an Algerian / アルジェリア民主人民共和国 the Democratic and Popular Republic of Algeria.

アルゼンチン Argentina ¶アルゼンチンの Argentine; Argentinean / アルゼンチン共和国 the Argentine Republic / アルゼンチン人 an Argentine; an Argentinean.

アルト 《音楽》 alto ¶アルト歌手 an alto ((pl. -s)).

アルバイト [<《ドイツ語》 Arbeit=work] a (side) job; (side) work; a part-time job; 《口語》 moonlighting (学生以外の) ¶アルバイトをする work (part-time); 〈自分の職業以外に〉 take on another [an extra] job; 《口語》 moonlight /

その本はどこの本屋にもある。You can get the book [The book is to be had] at any bookstore. / 本会の会員には種々の特典がある。The members of this society enjoy various privileges. / これだけの金があれば当座は間に合う。This sum will be enough for immediate expenses. / そこへ行ったことがあるか。Have you ever visited the place? / Have you ever been there? / 昨夜火事があった。A fire broke out last night. / 私の不在中に色々の事があった。All sorts of things happened while I was away [in my absence]. / その会はいつあるか。When is the meeting to be held? / 学校は4時まである。We have school until four o'clock. / 明日英語の試験がある。We have an examination in English tomorrow. / そんなことがあるものか。How can that be? / That's impossible! / 人もあろうに君がそう言うとは！To think that you, of all people, should say so! / 友人はかくありたいものだ。That's what a true friend ought to be like. / どうかそうありたいものだ。I hope so. / 夢であれかしと思う。I wish it were all a dream. / 幸福は満足にある。Happiness consists in contentment.

あるいは ウィルソン教授にあるいは会えるかもしれないと思って研究室へ行ってみた。I went to Prof. Wilson's office on the chance of finding [that I might find] him there. / あるいはそうかもしれない。It may well be so. / That is not impossible.

あるく 駅からずっと歩きましたか。Have you walked all the way from the station? / 駅までは歩いて10分です。It is ten minutes' [a ten-minute] walk to the station. / It takes ten minutes to get to the station on foot. / バスの停留場は家から歩いて5分とかからない。The bus stop is within five minutes' walk of my house. / うちの赤ちゃんが今日はじめて歩きました。Our baby took its first steps today. / その湖は歩いて簡単に行けるところにある。The lake is within easy walking distance. / 体を休めた方がいい。明日はたくさん歩かなければならないから。You'd better get some rest; you've a lot of walking to do tomorrow. / じきにまた起きて歩けるようになるよ。You will soon be up and about again. / 医者は2週間以内に歩けるようにしてあげると言った。The doctor said he would have me on my feet in a fortnight. / はえはどうして天井を歩けるのかしら。I wonder how flies manage to walk on the ceiling. / あの人は小児麻痺でうまく歩けなくなったので。He had an attack of polio, which has made walking difficult for him. / その時点でピケット博

アルパカ / **あれる**

アルバイトをして学校を出る work *one's* way through school / アルバイトで得た金で北海道旅行に行く go on a trip to Hokkaido with the money *one* has earned / アルバイト学生 a working student. 文例↓

アルパカ 【動】an alpaca; 〈織物〉alpaca.

アルバニア Albania ¶アルバニアの Albanian / アルバニア人 an Albanian / アルバニア人民社会主義共和国 the People's Socialist Republic of Albania.

アルバム an album; a photograph [photo] album ¶アルバムに写真を貼る fix [stick] a picture in an album.

アルピニスト an alpinist.

アルファ alpha ¶プラスアルファ 《10,000 yen》 plus something; 《(the agreed amount) and a little extra [more]》 / アルファ付きで勝つ win 《(a game)》 with (part of) the last inning left / アルファ粒子[線] 【物】an alpha particle [ray]. 文例↓

アルファベット the alphabet ¶アルファベット順に並べる arrange alphabetically [in alphabetical order].

アルプス the Alps ¶アルプスの Alpine / 日本アルプス the Japan Alps.

アルペン アルペン競技【スキー】the Alpine events / アルペンホルン an alphorn; an alpenhorn.

アルマイト anodized aluminum ★アルマイトは和製英語.英語の alumite は明礬(みょうばん)石.

あるまじき 《文》unworthy 《of a gentleman》; 《文》unbecoming 《to a student》. 文例↓

アルマジロ 【動】an armadillo (pl. -s).

アルミ(ニウム) 《米》aluminum, 《英》aluminium ¶アルミサッシュ an aluminum sash [window frame] / アルミホイル tin [aluminum] foil.

アルメニア Armenia ¶アルメニアの Armenian / アルメニア人 an Armenian.

あれ[1] 荒れ 〈あらし〉a storm; 〈荒天〉stormy [rough, heavy] weather; 〈皮膚の〉roughness; chapping ¶皮膚の荒れを防ぐ keep the skin from chapping [becoming chapped]. 文例↓

あれ[2] that; it; 〈複数で〉they; those ¶あれこれ this or [and] that; one thing or another / あれやこれやと考えた末 after thinking this way and that 《over a matter》; after a great deal of thought / あれから, あれ以来 since then; from that time / あれでも even so; for all that; despite everything / あれほど (much); 《文》to that extent [degree] / あれほどの such 《a great scholar》 as that; 《a rich man》 like that. 文例↓

あれ[3] ¶〈あれっ〉Look!; Listen!; 〈驚き〉Oh no!; (Good) Heavens! / あれっ! と叫ぶ give a cry of amazement / あれあれと言う間にwhile *one* is looking on in blank amazement.

あれい 亜鈴 (a pair of) dumbbells.

あれくるう 荒れ狂う 〈風・波などが〉rage; rampage; 〈人が〉go berserk ¶荒れ狂う海 angry [raging] waves [waters].

アレグレット 【音楽】allegretto.

アレグロ 【音楽】allegro.

あれしょう 荒れ性 ¶荒れ性の人 a person whose skin is susceptible to chapping. 文例↓

あれち 荒れ地 wasteland; barren land.

あれの 荒れ野 a wilderness; wild land.

あれはてる 荒れ果てる 〈建物などが〉fall into [go to] ruin; 《文》fall into disrepair; 〈土地が〉run [go] wild ¶荒れ果てた 〈建物などが〉dilapidated; ruined; run-down; tumbledown; 〈土地が〉waste / 荒れ果てている 〈建物などが〉 be in a dilapidated state [ruinous condition]; 《文》be in utter disrepair; 〈土地が〉lie waste. 文例↓

あれほうだい 荒れ放題 ¶荒れ放題になっている〈建物が〉《文》be left to utter dilapidation; 〈土地が〉be left to run [go] wild ⇒あれはてる.

あれもよう 荒れ模様 文例↓

あれる 荒れる 〈海・天候が〉get [《文》become] rough [stormy]; 〈土地が〉go [run] wild; 〈建物が〉fall into [go to] ruin; get [《文》become] dilapidated; 〈皮膚が〉become rough; get chapped (ひびが切れる); 〈人が〉behave violently ¶荒れた家 a dilapidated house; 《文》a house in decay / 荒れた庭 a neglected [a badly-kept, 《文》an ill-kept] garden / 荒れた土地 wasteland. 文例↓

アルバイト 士は従来の研究法を捨て,新しい道を歩きだしたのです. At that point, Dr. Pickett discarded his old line of research and struck out in a new direction.

アルバイト 彼はアルバイトに忙しくて勉強ができない. He is too busy with his job to attend to his schoolwork.

アルファ 年末手当は 2 か月分プラスアルファだ. The year-end allowance will be the equivalent of something over two months' wages.

あるまじき 学生にあるまじき行為だ. Students ought not do that sort of thing. | It is improper for a student to behave in such a way.

あれ[1] このクリームはお肌の荒れによく効きます. This cream is good for chapped skin.

あれ[2] あれくらいのことなら僕だってできると思うよ. I think I can do that much. / あれっぱかりのことで腹を立てることないだろう. Why do you get angry over a trivial matter like that? / 彼はあれこれと彼女を慰めようとつとめた. He tried this way and that to comfort her. / あれやこれやで忙しい. I am very busy with all sorts of things to do. / あれやこれやとやってみた. I tried one thing and another [this, that and the other]. / あれやこれやで新聞も読めなかった. What with visitors' calls and children crying, I couldn't even read the newspaper. / あれ以来[あれっきり]彼に会わない. I never saw him after that. | That was the last I saw of him. / 私はあれからずっと丈夫です. I have been in good health ever since. / 僕は英語はあれほど上手には話せない. I can't speak English as well as he can. / あれほど注意してやったのにあの男はまたやり損なった. For all my warnings he bungled again. / あれほど努力したのに失敗したとは気の毒なことだ. It's a pity that he has failed in spite of trying so hard. / あれほどのばかとは思わなかった. I hadn't thought that he was as foolish as that /《口語》he was that

アレルギー (an) allergy ¶アレルギーを起こす食品 allergenic food / アレルギーになる develop an allergy 《to》/ アレルギー性の allergic 《to sth》/ アレルギー性疾患 an allergic disease; an allergy / アレルギー反応 (an) allergic reaction.

あろう ¶…であろう will; probably; may; I think (that); surely (きっと); I hope (よい事を予想して); I fear (気づかって); it seems [appears] (らしい); どんな事があろうと whatever may happen; come what may / それが本当であろうなかろうと whether (it is [《文》be]) true or not.

アロハ(シャツ) an aloha shirt.

あわ¹ 泡 a bubble; foam; froth ¶ビールの泡 froth [bubbles] on beer; the head on beer / 泡だらけの, 泡の多い foamy / frothy / 泡が立つ ⇨ あわだつ / 口から泡を吹く froth [foam] at the mouth / 泡を食う get flustered; lose one's head; lose one's presence of mind / 泡を食って逃げる be taken by surprise and take to one's heels. 文例⇩

あわ² 粟 《植》millet ¶(肌が)粟立つ ⇨ とりはだ / 粟粒 a grain of millet.

あわい 淡い 〈味の〉light; 〈色の〉light; pale; 〈光などの〉faint; pale; 〈はかない〉《文》fleeting; 《文》passing ¶色が淡いbe light in color / 淡い哀愁を帯びた詩《文》a poem with a touch of [tinged with] melancholy / 淡い望み a faint hope. 文例⇩

あわさる 合わさる 〈結合する〉join; combine; be put together / 〈閉じる〉close; 《文》become closed.

あわせ 袷 a lined *kimono*.

あわせかがみ 合わせ鏡 ¶合わせ鏡をする look at *oneself* in two mirrors held against each other.

あわせめ 合わせ目 a joint; a seam (縫い目など).

あわせる¹ 合わ[併]せる 〈集める〉put [bring] together; 〈加える〉add 《to》; 〈足す[sum up]〉; 〈併合する〉merge; 〈結合する〉join (together); 《文》unite; combine 《A with B》; 〈混合する〉mix; 〈配合する〉match 《colors》; 〈適合させる〉fit [《文》adjust]《A to B》; bring 《A》into line (with B) / 2枚の板を2枚合わせる put two boards together / 手を合わせて祈る join one's hands in prayer / 双眼鏡を自分の目に合わせる adjust the binoculars (correctly) to suit one [one's eyes] / ダイヤルの目盛りを5に合わせる set the dial at 5 / ラジオを合わせる tune in the radio 《to the BBC》/ (録画の)音声を画面に合わせる synchronize the sound with the picture / 合わせて 〈合計して〉in all; all told; 〈いっしょに〉altogether; 〈つけ加えて〉in addition / 音楽に合わせて手をたたく clap one's hands in time to the music / ピアノに合わせて歌う sing along to the [sb's] piano(-playing) / 靴を足に合わせて作る make shoes to measure. 文例⇩

あわせる² 会わせる let 《A》see 《B》; get 《A》to meet [see] 《B》; make 《A》meet 《B》¶2人を会わせる arrange a meeting between the two.

あわただしい 慌ただしい busy; hurried; 〈あわてた〉flustered ¶慌ただしい一日を送る pass a busy day / 慌ただしい旅行 a hurried trip; a whirlwind tour / 慌ただしい一生 a short [brief, 《文》fleeting] life / 慌ただしく hurriedly; hastily; in a hurry [flurry] / 慌ただしさ hustle and bustle; hurry and flurry. 文例⇩

あわだち 泡立ち 文例⇩

あわだつ 泡立つ bubble; foam; froth; 〈せっけんが〉lather. 文例⇩

あわだてき 泡立て器 an eggbeater; a [an egg] whisk.

あわだてる 泡立てる beat up a froth; 〈卵・クリームなどを〉whip (up); 〈せっけん水を〉froth up (the soapy water).

あわてもの 慌て者 a hasty person.

あわてる 慌てる 〈まごつく〉be confused; be flustered; be flurried; 《口語》get rattled; lose one's head [presence of mind]; panic; 〈急ぐ〉be in a hurry [rush] ¶少しも慌てない keep quite cool; keep one's head [《米口語》cool, 《文》composure]; be [stay] quite unruffled / 慌てて, 慌てふためいて in a fluster / 慌てて逃げる run away in a fluster [in confusion];

---

foolish]. / あれでなかなかユーモアのある人なのだ. He is a humorist in his own way. / あれでも小説家だ. He is a novelist of a sort [after a fashion].

あれしょう 彼女は荒れ性だ. Her skin chaps easily.

あれはてる 庭は荒れ果てている. The garden is utterly neglected [overgrown].

あれもよう 荒れ模様だ. It looks as if we're going to have a storm. | There are signs of a storm coming on. / これから荒れ模様になるぞ. We're heading for stormy [wild] weather.

あれる 海が荒れている. The sea is rough. / 毎年今restaurants天気が荒れる. We have stormy weather at this time every year. / 水仕事をすると手が荒れる. Washing and doing the dishes will chap your hands.

アレルギー 日本人の核アレルギーを直さなければいけないなどという人もある. There are some who assert that it is necessary to cure Japanese of their allergy to nuclear energy.

あわ¹ 泡が出来る[消える]. A bubble forms [breaks, bursts]. / このビールは泡がよく立つ. This beer has a good head.

あわい 月が淡く光っていた. The moon was shining wanly.

あわせる¹ 高見山は僕たち4人を合わせたより重い. Takamiyama is heavier than the four of us put together. / みんなのお金を合わせてもたった5千円だった. We had only 5,000 yen between [among] us. / 君に合わせる顔がない. I'm ashamed to look you in the face. / 世間様に合わせる顔がない. How can I hold my head up in public?

あわせる² 父は私をその人に会わせなかった. My father would not allow me to see the man.

あわただしい その年もあわただしく暮れた. The year passed all too quickly.

あわだち この石鹸は泡立ちがいい[悪い]. This soap lathers well [does not lather well].

あわだつ 岩に当たる波が泡立っていた. Waves were foaming

あわばこ 泡箱《物》a bubble chamber.
あわび《貝》an abalone.
あわや ¶あわやと思う間もなく in (less than) no time; in an instant; in the twinkling of an eye ¶《文例》(spring).
あわゆき 淡雪 light snow; a light snowfall (in spring).
あわよくば if there is a chance; if things go well; ¶if fortune [luck] favors one.
あわれ 哀れ〈悲哀〉sorrow; pathos; 〈惨めさ〉misery ¶哀れな pitiful; 《文》pitiable; miserable; 《文》wretched; poor; sad; pathetic / 哀れっぽい 《文》plaintive《music》; 《文》mournful《songs》/ 聞くも哀れな物語 a touching [pathetic] story / 哀れを誘う [を催す] have [take] pity《on》; feel pity《for》; 《文》be moved to pity《by the sight of...》. 文例↓
あわれみ 哀れみ pity; 《文》compassion; mercy ¶哀れみ深い《文》compassionate; 《文》merciful; sympathetic / 哀れみをかける pity; take pity on sb; 《文》treat sb with compassion / 哀れみを乞う appeal for sb's pity; beg sb for mercy.
あわれむ 哀れむ pity; take [have] pity《on》; 《文》feel pity《for》; 《文》have compassion《on》; sympathize《with》¶哀れむべき ⇒あわれ（哀れな）.
あん¹ 案〈考え〉an idea; 〈計画〉a plan; a scheme; 〈提案〉a proposal; 〈草案〉a draft; 〈議案〉a bill ¶案を立てる[作る] work out [《文》devise] a plan / 案を出す present [submit] a plan; make a suggestion / 案にたがわず as one expected; 《文》as was expected; 《口語》sure enough / 案に相違して 《文》contrary to what one expected [one's expectations]; against all expectation(s).
あん² 庵 a hermitage; 〈僧庵〉a monastery; 〈庵室〉a hermit's cell.
あん³ 餡 sweet bean paste ¶あんパン a bun filled with bean paste.
あんあんり 暗々裡 ¶暗々裡に〈黙って〉tacitly; 〈秘かに〉secretly.
あんい 安易 ¶安易な easy; easygoing / 安易な考え方 an easygoing way of thinking / 安易に妥協する make an easy compromise / 安易にものを考える take things easy.
あんいつ 安逸《文》idle ease; 《文》indolence ¶安逸な idle; 《文》indolent / 安逸をむさぼる, 安逸な生活を送る live in idleness; lead an idle life.
あんえい 暗影 a shadow; (a) gloom ¶暗影を投じる《文》cast a shadow [pall]《over》.
あんか 安価 cheapness; a low [moderate] price ¶安価な cheap; low-priced; 《文》low [moderate] in price; inexpensive / 安価な娯楽 cheap recreation / 安価に cheaply; 《文》at a low [moderate] price; 《buy sth》cheap. 文例↓
アンカー〈リレーの〉the anchor (man) (on a team) ¶アンカーをつとめる anchor《a relay team》. 文例↓
あんがい 案外 ¶案外な unexpected; surprising / 案外に unexpectedly; 《文》contrary to one's expectations [to what one (had) expected]; surprisingly / 案外に思う be surprised (at the result) / 案外難しい be more difficult than one (had) expected. 文例↓
あんかけ 餡掛け food dressed with a thick starchy sauce.
あんかっしょく 暗褐色 dark brown; 《文》dun ¶暗褐色の dark-brown; dun-colored.
アンカラ Ankara.
アンカレ(ッ)ジ Anchorage.
あんかん 安閑 ¶安閑として idly; in idleness; 《文》indolently / 安閑として暮らす pass one's time in idleness; idle one's time away. 文例↓
あんき¹ 安危 ¶国家の安危の分かれる時 a national crisis / 国の安危にかかわる問題 a matter affecting the security of the nation; an issue on which the fate of the nation depends. 文例↓
あんき² 暗記 ¶暗記する learn [get] sth by heart; 《文》commit sth to memory / 暗記している know [have got] sth by heart / 機械的暗記 rote memorization; learning by rote / 暗記物 memory subjects / 暗記力《one's powers of》memory; 《文》retentive power / 暗記力が強い[弱い] have a good [bad, poor] memory.
あんぎゃ 行脚 ¶行脚する travel on foot; go on a walking tour [a pilgrimage] / 行脚の僧 an itinerant priest.
あんきょ 暗渠 a culvert.
アングラ ¶アングラ映画[劇場] an underground film [theater].
あんぐり ¶あんぐり口を開けて with one's mouth wide open / 《文》agape / 驚いて口あん

---

beat a hasty retreat / 慌てて戸外へ飛び出す rush out of doors in alarm / 慌てずに calmly; 《文》composedly; without panic(king).

against the rocks.
あわてる あわてるな。Don't panic. | Don't get excited. | Take it easy. / 私はあわてて電車を乗り違えた。In my hurry I took the wrong train. / 彼らは試験間際になって急にあわて出した。They got flustered just before the examination.
あわや あわや彼はおぼれようとするところであった。He was very nearly [near being] drowned.
あわれ あの子にもその子の両親を失った。The poor boy lost both his parents. / 少女の小さな棺の前にそなえられた人形がひとしお哀れをさそった。The doll placed before the small coffin of the girl added a pathetic note.
あわれむ 彼はさもさような顔をして,「彼らの無知は哀れむべきものだ」と言った。He said superciliously, 'Their ignorance is to be pitied'.
あん¹ 案に相違した。My expectations were disappointed. | 《結果が》The results were disappointing.
あんか この種の薬品は最近では比較的安価に製造されるようになった。It has become possible of late to make drugs of this sort at relatively low cost.
アンカー《競泳で》アンカーの山田君が飛び込んだ。Yamada, the anchor man, dived in for the last lap.
あんがい 案外な成績だった。The result was a surprise. / そいつは案外難しいぞ。It'll be more difficult than you think. / 兄の病気は案外重い。My brother is more seriously ill than I imagined. / 損失は案外わずかだった。The loss was far less than we feared.

アングロサクソン ぐりである be agape with wonder ; be left in open-mouthed amazement.
アングロサクソン ¶アングロサクソン民族 the Anglo-Saxon race ; the Anglo-Saxons.
アンケート [<《フランス語》enquête=inquiry] ¶a questionnaire ¶アンケートをとる send out [obtain information by means of] questionnaires / アンケート調査 a questionnaire survey / アンケート用紙に記入する fill out a questionnaire.
あんけん 案件 a matter ; an item ¶重要案件 an important item (on the agenda).
あんこ 餡子 ⇨ あん³ ¶あんこ玉 a bean-paste ball.
あんこう 《魚》an anglerfish ; an angler ¶あんこう鍋 anglerfish meat served hot with vegetables in a pot.
あんごう 暗号 a cipher ; a code ¶暗号で書く write in code [cipher] / 暗号化する code ; encode / 電信暗号 a telegraphic code ; a cable code / 暗号(文)を解く〈暗号帳で〉decipher ; 〈敵の通信などを〉crack [break] a code / 暗号文を普通文に直す decode a message / 暗号帳 a code book / 暗号電報を打つ send a code(d) telegram ; wire sb in code.
アンコール an encore ¶アンコールする call for [demand] an encore / アンコールを受ける receive [get] an encore / アンコールに答えて「小犬のワルツ」を弾く play 'Valse du petit chien' as an encore / アンコール曲 an encore. 文例⇩
あんこく 暗黒 darkness ; blackness ¶暗黒の (pitch-)dark ; black ; gloomy / 社会[人生]の暗黒面 the dark [seamy] side of society [life] / 暗黒街 the underworld ; gangland / 暗黒時代 a dark age ; a black period / 《西洋史》the Dark Ages.
アンゴラ Angola ¶アンゴラ人民共和国 the People's Republic of Angola.
あんさつ 暗殺 (an) assassination ¶暗殺する assassinate / 暗殺を企てる plan to assassinate sb ; make an attempt on sb's life / 暗殺者 an assassin. [livery.
あんさん¹ 安産 ¶安産する have an easy delivery.
あんざん² 暗算 mental arithmetic [calculation] ¶暗算をする do a sum [sums] in one's head ; make a mental count 《of》.
あんざんがん 安山岩 andesite.

アンサンブル an ensemble.
あんじ 暗示 a hint ; a suggestion ¶暗示する hint ; suggest ; give [drop] a hint / 暗示的な, 暗示に富んだ thought-provoking / 暗示にかかりやすい be suggestible ; 《文》be susceptible [amenable] to suggestion. 文例⇩
あんしつ 暗室 a (photo) darkroom.
あんじゅう 安住 ¶現在の地位に安住している be content with one's present position / 安住の地を求める seek a place where one can live in peace / 宗教に安住の地を得る find (one's) peace in religion.
あんしゅつ 案出 ¶案出する《文》devise ; invent ; think [work] out ; 《文》contrive / 案出者 an inventor ; 《文》an originator.
あんしょう¹ 暗唱 recitation ¶暗唱する recite ; repeat from memory.
あんしょう² 暗礁 a sunken [submerged] rock ; a reef ¶暗礁に乗り上げる〈船が〉strike [run on] a rock ; be stranded on a reef ; 〈計画・交渉などが〉reach [come to] (a) deadlock ; be deadlocked. 文例⇩
あんしょうばんごう 暗証番号 one's (personal) code number.
あんじる 案じる be anxious 《about, for》; be concerned 《about, over》; worry 《about, over》; be afraid 《of》; 《文》fear. 文例⇩
あんしん 安心 〈心配のないこと〉peace of mind ; freedom from care ; 〈ほっとすること〉relief ¶安心し切っている be quite free from care [anxiety, fear] / 安心する feel easy 《about》; 《文》feel at ease ; 《文》feel relieved ; stop worrying 《about sth》; 〈大丈夫と思う〉feel reassured ; 《文》be [rest] assured ; be confident 《of, that...》/ 安心して at (one's) ease ; 《文》without anxiety ; 〈die〉in peace ; feeling relieved / 大いに安心したことには to my great relief / 安心させる put sb at his ease ; ease sb's mind ; 《文》relieve sb of his anxiety / 安心できる人 a reliable [trustworthy] person / 安心できない人 an unreliable [untrustworthy] person / 安心感 a sense of security / 安心立命を得る《文》attain spiritual peace. 文例⇩
あんず 《植》an apricot.
あんせい 安静 rest ; 《文》repose ¶安静を要する〈病気が主語〉require rest in bed / 安静にしている[を保つ] lie quietly ; keep quiet / 安静療法 a rest cure. 文例⇩

あんかん 安閑としてはいられない. This is no time for idling.
あんき¹ 身の安危などを顧みてはいられなかった. I couldn't worry about my own safety.
アンコール 彼は3回アンコールされた. He was called back to the stage three times. / アンコール！アンコール！ Encore! Encore!
あんじ この事件から暗示を得て小説を書いた. This event gave him the idea [suggested the plot] for his novel.
あんしょう² そんなわけで, 彼らの結婚生活は暗礁に乗り上げてしまった. That is how their marriage went onto the rocks.
あんじる 案じるより産むがやすし. Fear is often worse than the danger itself.
あんしん 彼が無事に到着したので安心した. His safe arrival set my mind at ease. / その知らせで大いに安心した. I was greatly relieved at the news. / 病人はもう安心だ. The patient is out of danger. / あまり安心はできないよ. Don't be too sure of it. / 仕事が進めばもう安心だ. Now that we've got (on) this far with the work,

we can take things easy. / 大丈夫合格するから安心したまえ. I can assure you that you will pass the exam. / あの人なら安心して仕事を任せられるよ. You may trust him to do the work for you. / 一同無事ですからご安心下さい. I am glad to tell you that we are all safe.
あんせい 医師は絶対安静を命じた. The doctor prescribed complete rest for him. / 彼女は結核の治療中で, 昼食後1時間の安静時間をとらなければならなかった. She was under treatment for tu-

あんせん 暗線 《物》《スペクトルの》 a dark line.
あんぜん 安全 safety; security ¶安全な safe; 《文》secure; free from danger / 安全に safely; in safety / 身の安全を図る look to one's own safety / 安全感 a sense of security / 《電気の》安全器 a cutout; a circuit breaker / 安全規則 safety regulations; 《交通の》road safety rules / 安全係数 a factor of safety; a safety factor / 安全策をとる take precautions; play it safe / 安全施設 safety facilities / 安全週間 Safety Week / 安全性 safety / 安全地帯 a safety zone; 《道路の》an island; a traffic [《米》safety] island; 《英》a refuge / 安全ベルト a safety belt / 座席の a seat belt / 安全帽 a crash helmet / 安全率 a safety factor (of 99.99%). 文例⇩

あんぜんうんてん 安全運転 safe [careful] driving ¶安全運転をする drive safely [carefully].
あんぜんかみそり 安全剃刀 a safety razor ¶安全剃刀の刃 a (safety-)razor blade.
あんぜんきじゅん 安全基準 safety standards.
あんぜんけん 安全圏 ¶《競争で》安全圏に入る get [secure] a safe lead.
あんぜんそうち 安全装置 a safety device [system]; 《銃の》a safety catch; 《口語》a safety ¶《銃に》安全装置をかける put (a gun) on safety; put the safety catch on / 《銃の》安全装置をはずす push off the safety (catch).
あんぜんだいいち 安全第一 ¶安全第一でやる act on the principle [basis] of safety-first. 文例⇩
あんぜんピン 安全ピン a safety pin ¶安全ピンで留める fasten 《a crape to one's sleeve》with a safety pin / 安全ピンをはずす unfasten a safety pin.
あんぜんべん 安全弁 a safety valve. 文例⇩
あんぜんほしょう 安全保障 security ¶集団安全保障 collective security / 安全保障条約 a security treaty [pact] にちゃい.
あんそく 安息 rest; 《文》repose ¶安息日 the Sabbath (Day).
あんだ 安打 a hit ⇒ヒット.
アンダーシャツ 《米》an undershirt; 《英》a vest.
アンダースロー 《野球》an underhand [underarm] throw [delivery]; underhand [underarm] pitching ¶アンダースローで投げる throw (the ball) underhand [underarm].
アンダーライン an underline ¶アンダーラインする underline 《a word》; underscore 《a phrase》.
あんたい 安泰 peace; security ¶国家の安泰 the peace and security of the nation.
あんたん 暗澹 ¶暗澹たる dark; gloomy. 文例⇩
アンダンテ 《音楽》andante.
あんち 安置 ¶安置する install; 《文》enshrine; 《棺を》lay in state. 文例⇩
アンチグア(・バーブーダ) Antigua and Barbuda ¶アンチグア人 an Antiguan.
アンチテーゼ 《<《ドイツ語》Antithese》an antithesis 《pl. -theses》.
アンチノック ¶アンチノック剤 antiknock; an antiknock agent [compound].
アンチモン, アンチモニー 《化》antimony.
あんちゃく 安着 safe arrival ¶安着する《人が》arrive safe (and sound); arrive safely [in safety]; 《品物が》arrive in good condition.
あんちゅうもさく 暗中模索 ¶暗中模索する grope in the dark; be at sea; be at a loss 《as to what to do》.
あんちょく 安直 ⇒あんか.
あんちょこ ⇒とら(とらの巻).
アンツーカー 《フランス語》en tout cas 《tracks》.
あんてい 安定 stability; steadiness ¶職業の安定 job security / 物価の安定 stabilization of prices / 安定する become stable; be stabilized / 安定している be stable / 安定を保つ[失う] maintain [lose] its [one's] stability; keep [lose] its [one's] equilibrium [balance] / 安定を欠く be unstable; 《文》lack stability / 生活の安定を得る secure one's livelihood; find a sure means of making one's living / 安定感のある[ない] stable [unstable]; secure [insecure] / 経済の安定成長期 a period of stable economic growth / 安定勢力 a stabilizing force.
あんていばん 安定板 《飛行機の》a stabilizer ¶垂直安定板 a (vertical) fin; a vertical stabilizer / 水平安定板 a horizontal stabilizer.
アンデス ¶アンデス山脈 the Andes / アンデス地方の Andean.
アンテナ an aerial; an antenna 《pl. -s》(★複

berculosis and had to take an hour's rest after lunch.
あんぜん ここにいれば安全です. This place is safe from any danger. | We are out of danger here.
あんぜんきじゅん 放射能が原子力委員会の定めた安全基準を上回った. The radioactivity rose above the safety levels established by the Atomic Energy Commission.
あんぜんけん 《選挙で》安全圏に入っている. Mr. Ito is safe to win the seat. |《米俗》Mr. Ito is home free. |《英口語》Mr. Ito is home and dry.
あんぜんだいいち 安全第一.《標語》Safety first.
あんぜんピン ポケットに先のはずれた安全ピンが入っていた. 安全どころじゃない. There was an open safety pin in my pocket. That's not what I call [not my idea of] safety!
あんぜんべん この種の競技は人間の闘争本能に対する安全弁になっていると言える. It can be said that competitive sport of this sort is a safety valve for man's fighting instinct.
あんたん 前途は暗澹たるものだ. The future looks gloomy.
あんち 像は台の上に安置してある. The statue rests on a pedestal. / 氏の遺骸は本願寺に安置されている. His body lies in state in the Honganji Temple.
アンテナ 家々の屋根にテレビの高いアンテナが立っている. Television aerials [TV antennas] are sticking up high on the roofs of the houses.
あんとう 党員の間に暗闘が絶えない. There is a constant secret feud among the members of the party.
あんな 彼女があんなひどいことを言うとは思わなかった. I never expected her to say such spiteful things. / あんなに働かなくてもいいのに. He doesn't have to work as hard as that [《口語》work that hard]. / どうしてあんな事をしなければならなかったのだろう. Why did he have to do what he

あんてん 暗転 《劇》a dark change.

あんど 安堵 relief;《文》reassurance ⇒あんしん ¶安堵の胸をなで下ろす feel greatly relieved.

あんとう 暗闘 a secret feud;《文》veiled enmity. 文例○

アンドラ 《自治国》Andorra ¶アンドラの An-

アンドロゲン 《生化》an androgen. ┌dorran.

アンドロメダ 《ギリシャ神話》Andromeda ¶アンドロメダ座 〈星座〉Andromeda / アンドロメダ星雲 the Andromeda Galaxy.

あんな such; that; that sort [kind] of; like that ¶あんな本 that sort [kind] of book (★口語では that sort of a book と冠詞をつけて言うこともある) / あんな男 a man like him / あんな美しい絵 such a beautiful picture;《文》so fine a picture / あんなに so; like that; (in) that way. 文例○

あんない 案内 〈導き〉guidance;〈招待〉(an) invitation;〈報せ〉《文》an advice; a notice ¶案内する guide sb; act as sb's guide;《文》conduct; lead; 先に立って案内する lead the way (to) / 道を案内する show sb the way / 案内して見せる conduct [show] sb over [round] (the school) / give sb a tour ((of the factory) / 部屋の中へ[席へ]案内する show [usher] sb into the room [to his seat] / ご案内のとおり as you know / 〜の案内で under sb's guidance / 案内係 a clerk at the information desk; 〈座席への〉an usher; an usherette (女性) / 案内書 a guide book ((to the National Museum)) / a guide ((to Atami)) / 案内業者 (tourist) guide / 案内所 an information bureau [center]; an inquiry office / 案内状 a letter [note] of invitation; an invitation / 案内図 〈所在地などの〉an information map; a guide map; 〈観光用の〉a sightseeing map / 〈駅の中などの〉案内板 a direction board. 文例○

あんに 暗に indirectly;《文》implicitly;《文》tacitly ¶暗に知らせる suggest; hint; drop a hint / 暗に指す《文》allude to; hint at. 文例○

あんのじょう 案の定 as one expected; as expected;《文》as was expected;《口語》sure enough. 文例○

あんのん 安穏 ¶安穏な peaceful; quiet;《文》tranquil / 安穏に peacefully; quietly;《文》tranquilly.

あんば 鞍馬 〈器具〉a pommel horse;《米》a side horse;〈種目〉the pommel [side] horse.

あんばい ¶こんなあんばいに in this way [《口》manner]; like this / このあんばいで行くと if things go on like this [at this rate] / いいあんばいに fortunately; luckily. 文例○

アンパイヤ an umpire ¶アンパイヤをする act as umpire ((for a game)); umpire ((a game)).

アンバランス 《文》imbalance ¶アンバランスの unbalanced.

あんぴ 安否 safety ¶安否を尋ねる inquire [ask] after 《sb, sb's health》/ 安否を気遣う worry [be concerned] about sb's safety. 文例○

あんぶ 鞍部 〈山の〉a saddle; a col.

あんぷ 暗譜 ¶暗譜で弾く play ((a sonata)) from memory [without music].

アンプ 《電》an amplifier. 文例○ ┌pule.

アンプル 〈注射液などの〉an ampoule; an am-

あんぶん 案分 ¶案分する《文》divide (distribute) proportionally ((among)); 案分比例 proportional distribution.

アンペア 《電》an ampere; an amp ¶アンペア計 an ammeter / アンペア数 amperage.

あんぽ 安保 ⇒にちべい（日米安全保障条約）¶安保闘争 the campaign against the Japan-U.S. Security Treaty.

あんぽう 罨法《医》fomentation ¶罨法をする foment; apply a poultice [compress] (to).

あんま 按摩 〈人〉a masseur (男); a masseuse (女);〈術〉massage ¶あんまをする massage sb; give sb a massage / あんまをしてもらう have [get] a massage; have oneself massaged / あんまをとる call in a masseur.

あんまく 暗幕 a black curtain. 文例○

あんまり ⇒あまり(に).

あんみつ 餡蜜 mitsumame topped with sweet bean paste.

---

did? / 僕はあんな偉い人を見たことがない。I never saw a greater man than him in my life. ⇒より² 用法

あんない 町中を案内してあげた。I showed him all round the town. / 彼は私を立派なホテルに案内した。He took me to a fine hotel. / 途中までご案内しましょう。I'll go part of the way with you. / お席までご案内いたしましょう。May I show you to your seat? / 中へ[出口まで]ご案内して下さい。Show the gentleman in [out], please.

あんに 彼は暗に金を要求したのだ。He made an indirect demand for money.

あんのじょう 案の定彼はそこにいた。Sure enough, he was there. / 急行は案の定混みこんで席はなかった。As I had feared, the express train was very crowded and I couldn't get a seat. / 私の決意を家族に告げると、案の定皆びっくりした。I announced my decision to my family and they were predictably alarmed.

あんばい すべていいあんばいに運んだ。Everything went all right. / いいあんばいにけがをしなかった。I am glad I didn't get hurt. / 万事適当にあんばいしてくれたまえ。Please arrange everything as you think fit.

あんぴ 彼はたびたび両親に手紙を書いて安否を尋ねる。He often writes to his parents asking how they are getting on. / 紀州沖で遭難した人たちの安否は未だに不明です。The fate [What has become] of the people shipwrecked off Kishu is still unknown.

アンプ そこではアンプでボリュームを一杯に上げたロックバンドの演奏が行なわれていた。A rock band was playing there, with amplifiers full on.

あんまく お客様に映画を見せるために窓に暗幕を張った。We blacked out the windows to show a movie to our guests.

あんまり そりゃあんまりだ。That's too much. | That's going too far. / そんなことをするとは君もあんまりだ。It is too heartless [unkind] of you to do such a thing.

あんみん 安眠 a quiet [good, sound] sleep ¶安眠する sleep quietly [well, soundly]; have a good [quiet] sleep; have a good night [night's sleep] / 安眠ができない cannot get a good [quiet] night's sleep; have [pass] a bad night / 安眠を妨害する disturb sb's sleep. 文例⇩

あんもく 暗黙 ¶暗黙のうちに《文》tacitly / 暗黙の了解《文》a tacit understanding. 文例⇩

アンモナイト〖古生物〗an ammonite.

アンモニア〖化〗ammonia ¶アンモニア水 ammonia water; aqueous ammonia.

あんや 暗夜 a dark night ¶暗夜に乗じて under (the) cover of night [darkness].

あんやく 暗躍 ¶暗躍する《文》engage in secret maneuvers; be active behind the scenes.

あんよ《小児語》a tootsie ¶あんよする toddle.

あんらく 安楽 ease; comfort ¶安楽な comfortable; easy / 安楽に暮らす live in (ease and) comfort; live in easy circumstances; live comfortably / 安楽椅子 an easy chair; an armchair / 安楽死 euthanasia; mercy killing.

あんるい 暗涙 ¶暗涙にむせぶ《文》shed silent tears.

い

い¹ 井 ⇨ いど¹. 文例⇩

い² 亥〈十二支の〉(the Year of) the Boar.

い³ 医 文例⇩

い⁴ 胃 the stomach ¶胃が丈夫である[弱い] have a strong [weak] stomach; have a good [weak] digestion / 胃が悪い have stomach trouble / 胃が痛む have a stomachache; have a pain in one's stomach / 胃の gastric / 胃の内容物を調べる examine the contents of 《an animal's》 stomach.

い⁵ 異 ¶異を唱える[立てる] make [raise] an objection (to) / 異うにたりない be not surprising.

い⁶ 〈心〉a mind; 〈意志〉《文》(a) will; (an) intention; 〈意味〉a sense; (a) meaning; 〈注意〉attention ¶意のままにする do as one pleases [likes]; have sth one's own way / 意に介する《文》heed;《文》give heed (to); mind; worry (oneself) (about, over) / 意に介しない do not mind [care about];《文》be indifferent to / 意に反する be against one's will / 意に満たない be unsatisfactory / …に意を用いる be careful about [of]…; pay attention to…; take sth into account [《文》consideration] / 意を安んじる feel at ease / 意を強くするに足りる be reassuring; be encouraging / 意を迎える curry favor with sb;《文》ingratiate oneself with sb. 文例⇩

い⁷ 藺〖植〗a rush.

イ〖音楽〗〈音名〉A ¶イ長[短]調 (in) A major [minor].

-い …位 a place; a rank; a position ¶第4位の the fourth-ranking《Dodgers》/ 2位になる take [win,《文》gain] second place; be placed second / 〈競技で〉finish [come] second; come in second (place); finish (a race) in second place / 3位に落ちる drop to third place / 第1位である be [stand, rank] first; head [top] the list (of) / 第5位である be fifth [in fifth position]. 文例⇩

あんみん 薬を飲んだら安眠ができた。The medicine gave me a good sleep. / そのステレオを止めてくれ。安眠妨害だ。Turn off the stereo. I can't sleep for it.

あんもく 2人の間には暗黙の了解が成立していたのだ。There was an unspoken agreement [a tacit understanding] between the two of them.

あんよ (幼児に)あんよは上手! What a clever boy [girl]!

い¹ 井の中のかわず大海を知らず。The frog in the well knows nothing of the great ocean.

い³ 医は仁術。Medicine is a benevolent art.

い⁶ 僕は人が何と言おうと意に介しない。I don't care what people may say about me.

-い オリンピックのメダルは3位までの入賞者にだけ与えられる。Medals are awarded only for the first three places in the Olympics. / 彼は4分15秒フラットで第2位であった。He came in second in 4:15 flat. / 第3位はT大学が獲得した。Third place went to T University. / 彼はずっと遅れて4位だった。He was [came (in)] a bad [poor] fourth.

いあわせる だれも居合わせなかった。No one happened to be about [nearby].

いい 彼の提案には大いにいい所がある。There's a good deal of merit in [a lot to be said for] his proposal. / (ある事柄について)そこがいい所なんだ。That's the beauty [charm] of it. / 彼のどこがいいんだい。What do you see in him? / あの男のいい所は気取りのないことだ。What I like about him is that he doesn't put on airs. / あの男にはどこもいい所がない。I see nothing good in him. / いい事を聞かしてくれた。Many thanks for your valuable information. / いい事ばかりはない。We must take the evil with the good. / Life is not all fun. / Life is not all beer and skittles. / 〖諺〗僕は行かないでいい事をした。I am glad I wasn't there. / 今にいい事もあるさ。Bad times will not last forever. / It is a long lane that has no turning. 〖諺〗 / Let us hope for the best. / 彼は僕の知らないのをいい事にしてだました。He took advantage of my ignorance and cheated [deceived] me. / 彼はいい時に死んだ。He was lucky to die when he did. / いい時に来てくれた。You've come at just the right moment. / いい物をあげよう。Here's something nice for you. / 彼女はいい声だ。She has a sweet voice. / 寒い冬の夜に熱い風呂に入るのは気持ちがいい。It feels good to have a hot bath [A hot bath feels good] on a cold winter night. / 今日は少し気分がいい。I feel better today. / 朝の散歩は身体のためにいい。A walk in the morning will do you good. /〈それでいい〉〈よろしい〉All right. /〈充分だ〉That's enough. /〈間に合う〉That will

いあい 居合 the art of drawing *one's* sword, cutting down *one's* opponent and sheathing the sword, all in one motion [stroke].

いあつ 威圧 ¶威圧する overpower; overawe; browbeat / 威圧的な overbearing; highhanded.

イアトニー 胃アトニー《医》gastric atony.

いあわせる 居合わせる happen [《文》chance] to be (present) ¶居合わせた1人 one of those present. 文例員

いあん 慰安 〈慰め〉(a) consolation; (a) comfort;《文》(a) solace;〈気晴らし〉(a) recreation;〈娯楽〉an amusement ¶慰安する console;《文》solace; comfort / 慰安を求める seek solace 《in religion》/ 慰安会 an entertainment.

いい good; nice; fine; 〈優れた〉excellent; 〈快い〉《文》pleasing; pleasant; 〈美しい〉beautiful; pretty; 〈香り・味・色などが〉sweet; 《文》agreeable; 〈貴重な〉precious; valuable; 〈適切な〉proper; right; suitable ¶読みいい be easy to read / いい天気 fine [lovely, beautiful] weather ★ lovely は天気について以外は女性専用語 / いい男《美男子》a handsome man / 〈好漢〉a nice fellow /《米口語》a regular guy / いい女 a beautiful [pretty, good-looking] woman; an attractive woman;《口語》a (good-)looker / いい物 ⇨いいかた / いい事 a good thing / いい気持ちで〈人が主語〉feel good; be comfortable; 〈物が主語〉《new clothes》feel nice (pleasant, good) / いいことずくめ ⇨**-ず くめ** / いい日を選ぶ choose a lucky day / 〈病気が〉いい方に向かう get better; take a turn for the better;《文》take a favorable turn / いい時に、いい所へ at the right [《文》a favorable] moment / …だといい I wish; I hope / …してもいい〈自分が〉do not mind doing;〈他人が〉can [may] do ★ くだけた会話では may より can を使うのが普通 / …しなくてもいい do not have to *do*; need not *do*; do not need to

do / 人がいい be good-natured / …と言ってもいいくらいだ be no better than《a plagiarism》; be as good as《finished》; be virtually《extinct》/ ずっといい much [far] better / …の方がいい prefer《A to B》; like《A》better《than B》/ …する方がいい had better [best] *do* / …しない方がいい had better not *do*. 文例員

いいあい 言い合い a quarrel; a dispute; a squabble (些細な事についての) ¶言い合いをする quarrel《with sb, about [over] sth》; have a quarrel [words]《with》;《文》dispute《with sb about sth》; cross swords《with sb》; squabble《with sb about sth》.

いいあてる 言い当てる guess right; make a good guess; hit the mark.

いいあやまり 言い誤り ⇨いえこない、いちがい.

いいあらそい 言い争い ⇨いあい.

いいあらためる 言い改める correct *oneself*; express《the idea》in a different way; put《it》in another way.

いいあらわす 言い表わす express; put《an idea》into [in] words; give expression to《*one's* thoughts》; describe ¶言葉では言い表わせない be indescribable;《文》be inexpressible; be beyond words / 言葉では言い表わせないほど美しい be indescribably beautiful; be beautiful beyond words [《文》expression]. 文例員

いいあわせる 言い合わせる arrange [make arrangements] in advance [beforehand];《文》prearrange ¶言い合わせたように《文》as if by common consent;《文》as if prearranged;

イーイーカメラ an electric-eye camera.

いいえ 〈答が否定の時〉no; 〈答が肯定の時〉yes. 文例員

いいおく 言い置く ⇨いのこす.

いいおくる 言い送る 〈書面で〉write (to); send a letter《to》; 〈伝言する〉send sb word

---

do / もう着いてもいい頃だ. It is about time they arrived. / バッキンガム宮殿へ行くにはこの道でいいですか. Is this the right way to Buckingham Palace? / そのくらいのことはわかってもいい年頃だ. He's old enough to know that much. / 私がいいように取り計らいましょう. I will see that everything goes well. / そのことは彼に黙っていた方がいいと思った. I thought it best [better] not to tell him anything about it. / 君のいいようにしなさい. Do as you please [like]. / どうしていいかわからない. I don't know what to do. / I am at a loss (as to) what to do. / どうしたらいいですか. What should I [we] do? / What would be best? / 1千万円あればいいなあ. If only [I wish] I had ten million yen. / 明日まで天気がもてばいいが. I do hope it'll keep fine till tomorrow. / 早く試験が終わればいいのに. I'll be glad to get the exam over. / 君はアメリカへ行くといい. I advise you to go to America. / 太郎に手伝わせたらいいでしょう. Why don't you [Why not] get Taro to help you? ★ Why don't you… には「なぜ…しないのか」となじるような気持ちも含まれない / 僕は日本にいる方がずっといいと思う. I think I had much better stay in Japan. ★ 相手に向かって You had better… と言うのは命令的に聞こえるので注意を要する. Why don't you stay…?, I advise you to…, Wouldn't it be better if you stayed…? などの言い方をする方がいい. / もうしばらく待ってもいいだろう. It won't hurt to wait a little longer. / 君はいつ行ってもいい. You can [may] leave at any time. / 明日は来なくてもいい. You don't have to [needn't] come tomorrow. / There is no need for you to come tomorrow. / 1つ取ってもいいですか. May I take one? / 窓を開けてもいいですか.—いいですよ. Do you mind if I open [Would you mind my opening] the window? —No, not at all. / やってみてもいい. I don't mind having a try [口語] giving it a go]. / 〈酒を〉一杯いかがです.—いいですね. Will you have a glass?—I don't mind if I do [Well, I wouldn't say no]. / いいか、これは秘密だぞ. Mind you, this is a secret. / いいかい、忘れちゃだめだよ. Don't forget that. It's important. / (かくれんぼで)もういいかい.—まあだだよ. (Are you) ready?—No, not yet.

いいあらわす その光景は「悲惨」の2字よりほかに言い表わす言葉がない. 'Horrible' is the only word to describe the scene. / その時は言葉では言い表わせないほど悩んだ. I went through indescribable mental anguish at that time.

いいえ お住まいは東京ですか.—いいえ、違います. Do you live in Tokyo?—No, I don't. / 豚肉は嫌

いいおとす 言い落とす ⇒いいもらす.
いいおよぶ 言い及ぶ refer [《文》 allude] to; make a reference to; mention; 《文》 make mention of.
いいおわる 言い終わる finish speaking.
いいかえす 言い返す talk [answer] back; retort. 文例↓
いいかえる 言い換える say [《文》 express] *sth* in different words; put 《it》 in another way; 《文》 rephrase [reword] 《the statement》 ¶言い換えれば (to put it) in other words; to put it differently; that is (to say); 《文》 namely. 文例↓
いいかお いい顔
いいがかり 言い掛かり a trumped-up [false] charge [accusation] ¶言い掛かりをつける accuse *sb* falsely; make a false charge (against); 〈けんかをふっかける〉pick a quarrel 《with》 ⇒いんねん (因縁をつける).
いいかける 言い掛ける be (just) going to speak; have *sth* on the tip of *one's* tongue ¶言い掛けてやめる check *oneself* before the words are out of *one's* mouth; stop in the middle of a sentence. 文例↓
いいかげん いい加減 〈いい加減な〈無責任な〉irresponsible;〈本気でない〉halfhearted;〈でたらめな〉random;〈あいまいな〉vague;〈根拠のない〉groundless ¶いい加減な返事 a vague answer / いい加減な事を言う talk irresponsibly; say irresponsible things / いい加減な処置をとる take halfway measures / ちょうどいい加減の大きさ (just) the right size / いい加減に〈でたらめに〉at random;〈不徹底に〉halfway;〈身を入れずに〉halfheartedly / 仕事をいい加減にやる scamp *one's* work. 文例↓
いいかた 言い方 a manner [way] of speaking [saying *sth*]; how to put 《it》; an expression; (a) (different) wording (★ 複数にはしない) ¶更に別の言い方をすれば to put it still another way ⇒いいかえる. 文例↓
いいかねる 言い兼ねる find 《it》 hard to say; dare not say; hesitate to say. 文例↓
いいかわす 言い交わす 文例↓
いいき 好いき ¶いい気な〈呑気な〉easygoing; happy-go-lucky;〈得意な〉conceited;〈ひとりよがりの〉《文》 self-complacent / いい気になる be puffed up (by); be elated 《with success》; be self-complacent. 文例↓
いいきかせる 言い聞かせる 〈命じる〉 tell *sb* to do;《文》 instruct *sb* to do;《文》 bid *sb* do;〈説得する〉persuade;〈忠告する〉advise;〈戒める〉warn;《文》 admonish. 文例↓
いいきみ いい気味
いいきる 言い切る 〈断言する〉 say [《文》 state] positively [definitely]《that...》; declare 《that...》;《文》 assert 《that...》;〈言い終わる〉 finish saying 《it》; finish *one's* sentence. 文例↓
いいぐさ 言い草 words; remarks; what *sb* says ¶彼の言い草ではないが as he would say. 文例↓
いいくるめる 言いくるめる quibble; explain away ¶さぎをからすと言いくるめる (try to) persuade *sb* that black is white.
いいこ いい子 a good child [boy, girl] ¶自分ばかりいい子になる earn praise [credit] due to somebody else [other people]; escape the blame (for *one's* actions) at somebody else's [other people's] expense.
いいこめる 言い込める talk [argue] *sb* down; argue *sb* into silence; defeat *sb* in argument.
いいさす 言いさす

イージーオーダー ¶イージーオーダーの服 a semi-order-made [semi-custom-made, semi-

---

いですか.—いいえ 好きです. Don't you like pork?—Yes, I do. / もう一杯いかがですか.—いいえ, もう充分いただきました. Won't you have some more?—No, thank you. I have had enough already.

いいおくる デービス氏にその由を言い送りましょう. I will write (to) Mr. Davis to that effect.

いいかえす 彼は私に激しくくってかかって, 悪いのは君の方で自分ではないと言い返して来た. He came back at me with a violent protest, saying that it was my fault, not his.

いいかえる 言い換えれば, 現代企業は多数の人から集めた金で, 自分たちの活動をまかなっている. Put another way, modern enterprises finance their activities with the money collected from a great number of people.

いいかお そうたびたびお金を借りに行っては, いい顔はされなくなるよ. You'll wear out your welcome if you go and borrow money from him too often. / ああした連中にはそうそういい顔ばかりしてはいられない. I cannot always make myself pleasant to the likes of him. / 値引きを承知はしたものの, いい顔はしなかった. He did agree to reduce the price, but he wasn't very pleased about it. / 彼はこの辺ではいい顔だ. He has (got) a lot of influence here. / 《赤ん坊に》いい顔をしてごらん. Make a funny face, dear.

いいかける 今何を言いかけたのですか. What were you going to say?

いいかげん もういい加減によせ. Oh, (why don't you) lay off! / That's enough. / 冗談もいい加減にしろ. Enough of your jokes! / 僕は物事をいい加減にするのは嫌いだ. I hate to do things by halves. / あの男にはいい加減愛想がつきた. I am quite disgusted with him.

いいかた 彼は目上に対する物の言い方を知らない. He does not know the proper way to speak to his superiors. / ほかに言い方がありますか. Is there any other way of saying it?

いいかねる 何とも言い兼ねる. I don't know what to say. / I'm at a loss for words. / 僕はその断わりを言い兼ねた. I could not bring myself to refuse it.

いいかわす 2人は固く言い交した仲だ. They have exchanged vows of eternal love. | They are firmly pledged to each other.

いいき あれで自分の務めは果たしたつもりなんだから, いい気なもんだ. He thinks he has already done his share of the work. How easygoing can you get?

いいきかせる 今後は気を付けるように言い聞かせます. I will tell him to be more careful in (the) future. / 僕がいくら言い聞かせても彼はだめだ. I have given him any amount of advice, but it never does any good.

いいきみ いい気味だ. It serves him right! / 《口語》 Serve(s) him right!

いいきる この失敗はあながち彼1人のせいだとは言い切れない. It is impossible to say definitely

いいしぶる 言い渋る hesitate [be reluctant] to say.

いいしれぬ 言い知れぬ unspeakable ;《文》inexpressible ; indescribable. 文例↓

いいすぎる 言い過ぎる say too much ; go too far (in saying) ;〈過大に〉exaggerate ;〈非難する〉criticize too severely ¶…といっても言い過ぎではない It is not too much to say that… ; It is no exaggeration to say that…. 文例↓

いいすてる 言い捨てる say sth as one leaves (the room) [goes away, goes out] ; make a parting shot [remark]. 文例↓

イースト yeast ¶イースト菌 yeast.

いいそこなう 言い損なう ¶言い損ないをする ⇒ いいそこなう

いいそこなう 言い損なう make a mistake in one's use [choice] of words ;〈失言する〉make a slip of the tongue ;〈言いそびれる〉⇒ いいそびれる

いいそびれる 言いそびれる fail to mention sth ; fail to tell sb sth ; miss one's [a] chance to tell sb sth ; forget to say sth.

いいだくだく 唯々諾々 ¶唯々諾々として〈言われるままに〉at sb's beck and call ;〈おとなしく〉obediently ;《文》submissively ; tamely.

いいだしっぺ 言い出しっぺ 文例↓

いいたす 言い足す add ;《文》say sth in addition ; make an additional remark.

いいだす 言い出す〈言い始める〉begin to speak ; start talking ; break the ice (言いにくいことを) ;〈口に出す〉come out with (a foolish remark) ; blurt sth out ;〈提議する〉propose ; suggest. 文例↓

いいたてる 言い立てる《文》assert ;《文》make an assertion ; declare ¶欠点を言い立てる point out the faults (of the machine) (one by one).

いいちがい 言い違い《文》a misstatement ; a slip (of the tongue) ¶言い違いをする make a slip of the tongue.

いいつかる 言い付かる ¶(…するように)言い付かっている have been told [ordered] 《to do》; have orders 《to do》.

いいつくす 言い尽くす tell everything [the whole story] ; say everything there is to say [to be said] ;《文》exhaust (a subject) ; leave nothing unsaid ¶言い尽くせない《文》inexpressible ; indescribable. 文例↓

いいつくろう 言い繕う gloss over (one's faults) ; make an excuse (for one's mistake) ; explain away (one's strange behavior).

いいつけ 言い付け〈命令〉an order ; a command ;〈指図〉directions ; instructions ¶言いつけどおりにする do as one is told ;《文》bid ; follow sb's [the] instructions / 親の言いつけに従う[背く] obey [disobey] one's parents.

いいつける 言い付ける〈命じる〉tell [order] sb 《to do》;《文》bid sb 《do》;〈告げ口する〉tell (sb's parent) ; tell (on sb).

いいつたえ 言い伝え a tradition ; a legend ¶昔からの言い伝え an ancient [old] tradition / 曽祖父の代からの言い伝えによると according to a tradition from my great-grandfather's time / …という言い伝えがある Tradition [Legend] has it that…

いいつたえる 言い伝える〈伝説を〉hand sth down by word of mouth ;〈伝言する〉send word 《that…》;〈うわさを〉spread (a rumor). 文例↓

いいとし いい年 文例↓

---

that he is the only one to blame for the failure.

いいぐさ 何という言い草だ。How dare you speak to me like that?

いいこ ジョニーは今日はいい子にしていました。Johnny has been good today. / いい子だ、泣くな。Don't cry, there's a good boy. / 坊やはいい子だ ねんねしな。Sleep, baby, sleep.

いいしれぬ あの男のために私は言い知れぬ苦しみを味わいました。I can't tell you what agonies [how much] I suffered on his account.

いいすぎる それは少々言い過ぎだろう。I think that's putting it a little too strongly. / You're going a bit too far, aren't you? / 僕の言い過ぎでした。お許し下さい。I overstepped the mark in saying that sort of thing to you. Please excuse me.

いいすてる そう言い捨てて彼は部屋から飛び出して行った。Flinging this [remark] over his shoulder, he stormed out of the room.

いいだしっぺ 言い出しっぺだから君からやりたまえ。You said it first [You brought it up], so you do it first.

いいだす 彼はいったん言い出したらなかなかきかない。Once he has declared his intention [said what he intends to do], there's no budging him. / 君が思い切ってそれを言い出してくれたので助かった。It was a great help to us that you had the courage to say that [come out with it].

いいつくす それは一言で言い尽くせる。It can be summed up in one word. / その探検隊の苦労はとうてい言い尽くせるものではない。The hardships the expedition went through cannot be described in words. / お礼は言葉では言い尽くせません。I cannot thank you enough for your kindness. / その景色の美しさは言葉では言い尽くせない。The view is beautiful beyond description.

いいつける 5時にヒギンズ氏を駅まで出迎えるよう言いつけられました。I was told to meet Mr. Higgins at the station at five. / ご用がありましたらいつでもお言いつけ下さい。Whenever you want me, I am at your service. / 君のお父さんに言いつけるぞ。I'll tell your daddy (on you). / そんなことをすると言いつけるぞ。If you do that, I'll tell.

いいつたえる 言い伝えでは地球が球形であることをピタゴラスがはじめて唱えたことになっている。Tradition credits Pythagoras with being the first to suggest the idea that the earth is spherical in shape.

いいつたえる その話は今なおお美談として言い伝えられている。The story is still told to this day with undiminished admiration. / そのことは次から次へとこっそり言い伝えられた。It was whispered from mouth to mouth.

いいとし あの人もいい年になった。He's no longer young. / 大田さんは55といういい年をしながらプラモデルに凝っている。Mr. Ota, even at the age of 55, is still taken up with building plastic models. / いい年をしてみっとも

いいなおす 言い直す correct *oneself*; put [《文》express] (the idea) differently; rephrase (the question);《文》restate (*one's* proposal).

いいなか 好い仲 ¶いい仲である be in love ((with));《文》be on intimate terms ((with)). 文例⇩

いいながら 言いながら ¶こう言いながら《文》so saying; with this [these words] 言いながら though; although; even though.

いいなずけ *one's* fiancé (男); *one's* fiancée (女);《文》*one's* husband-[wife-]to-be ¶…いいなずけになっている be engaged [《文》betrothed] to….

いいならわし 言い習わし 〈言い伝え〉⇒いいつたえ; 〈よく使われる表現〉a common saying; 〈決まった語法〉an idiom; a set phrase. 文例⇩

いいなり 言いなり ¶(次第)になる do as *one* is told (to) ((by sb));《文》do *sb's* bidding; be at *sb's* beck and call;《口語》be under *sb's* thumb;《口語》eat out of *sb's* hand.

いいにくい 言いにくい ¶言いにくい事 a delicate matter [subject] / 言いにくそうに hesitantly. 文例⇩

いいぬけ 言い抜け《文》an evasion; an evasive answer; 〈口実〉an excuse. 文例⇩

いいぬける 言い抜ける make [give] an evasive answer; talk *oneself* out of ((the difficulty)); explain away ((the incriminating signature)).

いいね 値 (at) the asking price [(at) the price asked [named]; the seller's price.

いいのがれ 言い逃れ ⇒いいぬけ.

いいのこす 言い残す ¶leave word [a message] ((with sb)); 〈遺言で〉state in *one's* will ((that…)); 〈言い落とす〉forget to say [mention].

いいはなつ 言い放つ 〈はっきり〉《文》declare;《文》assert;《文》state positively; say sth once and for all; 〈思い切って〉《文》venture to say ((that…)). 文例⇩

いいはる 言い張る insist ((on, that…));《文》maintain (steadfastly) ((that…)); keep saying ((that…)).

イーピーレコード an EP (extended-play) record.

いいひらき 言い開き (an) explanation ⇒べんかい ¶言い開きする explain *oneself*; (try to) justify *oneself* [*one's* stand]. 文例⇩

いいふくめる 言い含める tell sb beforehand [in advance] ((what he is to do)); give sb careful instructions; instruct sb carefully [《文》minutely] ((about, concerning)).

いいふらす 言い触らす spread ((a story)) ((around)); set ((a rumor)) afloat; circulate ((a rumor)). 文例⇩

いいふるす 言い古す ¶言い古された言葉 a worn-out [《文》hackneyed] phrase / 言い古されたしゃれ a stale joke.

いいぶん 言い分 *one's* say; what *one* has to say; a claim;《have》a case; 〈異議〉an objection; 〈不平〉a complaint ¶自分の言い分を通す get *one's* way; carry *one's* point / 両方の言い分を聞く hear both sides (of the story) / 言い分を述べる state *one's* case. 文例⇩

いいまかす 言い負かす talk sb down ⇒いいこめる. 文例⇩

いいまぎらす 言い紛らす quibble;《文》equivocate;《文》prevaricate.

いいまわし 言い回し a turn of phrase; the way *one* says sth;《文》a mode of expression; (a) wording (★複数にする) ¶うまい言い回し a clever [an apt] expression; a well-turned phrase. 文例⇩

いいもらす 言い漏らす forget to say [mention]; leave sth unsaid.

いいよう 言い様 ⇒いいかた ¶言い様のない indescribable;《文》inexpressible; unspeakable.

いいよどむ 言い淀む hesitate to say; hem and haw.

いいよる 言い寄る《文》woo; court; make《文》amorous) advances to ¶(いやだという女に)しつこく言い寄る force *one's* attentions on ((a woman)).

いいわけ 言い訳 〈わび〉an apology; an excuse;《口語》an alibi; 〈口実〉a pretext;《文》a plea; 〈弁明〉an explanation; 〈弁護〉a defense ¶苦しい言い訳 a poor [lame] excuse / 言い訳する make an excuse [apology]; apolo-

---

ない. You ought to know better at your age. | Be [Act] your age!

いいなか あの2人はいい仲だ. They are in love with each other. | They are lovers [sweethearts].

いいならわし そう言うのが言いわしになっている. That is the usual way of saying it.

いいにくい 彼には言いにくいことだったようだ. He seems to have found it hard [awkward] to say. / あの人にそうは言いにくいよ. I hesitate to say that to him.

いいぬけ あの男は言い抜けがうまい. He can talk his way out of anything.

いいのこす 彼は何も言い残して行かなかった. He left no message.

いいはなつ 「あんたが私のことをどう思おうと知ったこっちゃない」と彼は警官に向かって言い放った. 'I don't give a damn what you think about me,' he spat out at the policeman.

いいひらき あんなことをして言い開きができるだろうか. How can he justify behavior like that?

いいふらす 彼はKさんは泥棒だとさかんに言い触らしていた. He was telling everybody that Mr. K was a thief. / 彼は病気のように言い触らされていた. It was put about that he was ill.

いいぶん それについては少々言い分がある. I have a word or two to say about it. / 言い分を聞かずに人を責めるのはよくない. You should not condemn a person unheard. / 双方共に言い分がある. There are two sides to the argument. | There are arguments on both sides. / 僕の言い分も聞いてくれ. Let me state my case. / もっともな言い分だ. There's a lot (of truth) in what he says. | His point is well taken.

いいまかす 女房には言い負かされておく方が家庭の平和にはいい. It is advisable, for the sake of peace in the home, to leave one's wife with the last word.

いいまぎらす 彼は話題を変えて巧みに言い紛らしてしまった. He changed the subject and skillfully evaded the point.

いいまわし 着想はよいが言い回し

いいわすれる

gize (for a mistake); explain [justify] *oneself*; 《口語》put out an alibi (for being late) / 病気だ[知らなかった]と言い訳する 《文》plead illness [ignorance] / 言い訳がましい (say *sth*) defensively / 言い訳の手紙 a letter of apology / 言い訳の立たない 《文》inexcusable; 《文》unjustifiable / 言い訳に by way of excuse; in explanation (of).

いいわすれる 言い忘れる forget to say [mention].

いいわたし 言い渡し 〈宣告〉a sentence; a judgment; 《文》a pronouncement; 〈命令〉an order; a command; 〈告知〉an announcement. 文例⓪

いいわたす 言い渡す 〈宣告する〉sentence 《a prisoner to death》; 〈命じる〉order; 〈告げる〉tell; give *sb* to understand (that...) ¶ 判決を言い渡す give judgment [a decision]; pronounce [pass] sentence (on) / 無罪を言い渡す acquit *sb* of the charge.

いいん[1] 医院 《米》a doctor's [physician's] office; 《英》a (doctor's) surgery / 〈医師が2人以上の〉a clinic ¶ 藤田医院 Dr. Fujita's office ★ 日本では看板にも「藤田医院」と書くが、英語では'N.C. Feedler, M.D.'というように医師の名前と学位を書く.

いいん[2] 委員 a member of a committee; 《米》a committeeman; 〈代表〉a delegate ¶ 委員の1人である be on [be a member of] a committee / 委員会 a committee; a commission / 委員会を招集する call a meeting of the committee; call a committee into session / 委員会を開く hold a committee meeting / 委員会を設ける form [set up] a committee / 7人委員会 a seven-member committee; a committee of seven / 委員長 a chairman; a chairperson / 副委員長 the vice-chairman [cochairman, assistant chairman] of a committee / 委員長を勤める chair a committee. 文例⓪

いう 言う say; 〈話す〉talk about; 〈伝える〉tell; 〈述べる〉《文》state; 《文》remark 《on *sth*, that...》; 〈言明する〉declare; 《文》assert; 〈呼ぶ〉call ¶ 礼を言う 《文》express *one's* gratitude; thank *sb* / 金の事を言う talk [speak] about money / よく[悪く]言う speak well [badly, 《文》ill] of *sb*; say good [bad] things about *sb* / 言うべきでないことを言う say something inappropriate [that would be better left unsaid]; 《口語》speak out of line / 言うことがなくなる run out of things to say; run out of words / 言いたい事で物が言えなくなる lose *one's* speech / ...せよと言う 〈命令する〉tell [order] *sb* to do; 〈忠告する〉advise *sb* to do; 〈説得する〉persuade *sb* to do / ...するなと言う 〈命令する〉tell *sb* not to do; forbid *sb* to do; 〈忠告する〉advise *sb* not to do; 〈説得する〉talk *sb* out of doing; 《文》dissuade *sb* from doing / 人の言うことを聞く listen to what *sb* says; take *sb's* advice (助言を); 〈聞き入れる〉obey [be obedient to] *sb*; do what one is told to (do) / いうことを聞かない disobedient (students); naughty 《children》; 《文》fractious 《horses》; unruly (hair) / ...と言われている It is said that...; They [People] say...; I hear; I am told that... / 言う事とする事が違う say one thing but do another; talk in one way but act in another / 言うにいわれぬ unspeakable; indescribable; indefinable / 言うに足りぬ insignificant; 《文》trifling / 言うまでもなく of course; 《文》needless to say / ...は言うまでもない It goes without saying that...; It need scarcely [hardly] be said that... / ...は言うまでもなく not to mention [speak of]...; to say nothing of...; let alone... / ...と言ってもよい We can safely say that...; 《文》It may safely be said that...; It is not too much to say that... / 私に言わせれば in my opinion; if you ask me / 彼自身の言うところによると by his own account / 言わず語らずの内に 《文》tacitly / 《文》by tacit understanding / ...と言わぬばかりに 《文》as if [as much as] to say that...; as if [though] (he were...) / ...とはいえ though (it is...); even if (it were...); granting [admitting] that... / 言いたい事 what *one* wants [has] to say / 言いたい事を言う speak *one's* mind; say [have] *one's* say / 木村という人 a man called [《文》named] Kimura; a Mr. Kimura / ...と言って ⇨ -といって. 文例⓪

がまずい。The idea is good, but it is not very aptly expressed. / 言い回しは君に委せる。Phrase it any way you like.

いいよう 言い様が悪いと怒られるぞ。Watch your language or you'll catch it! / You'll be in trouble if you're not careful about your language. / 何とかに言い様もあったろうに。You could have said it (in) some other way. / 物に言い様だ。There is more than one way of putting it. / 言い様のない苦しみでした。I can't tell you the agonies I suffered.

いいわけ その言い訳は通らない。We cannot accept such an excuse. / それは言い訳にはならない。That is no excuse. / どんな事情があってもその言い訳にはならない。There are no circumstances that could justify it. / 彼は言い訳がましい事は一切言わなかった。He did not say a word in defense of himself.

いいわたし 10月5日に彼に判決の言い渡しをする。Judgment will be passed [handed down] on him on October 5.

いいん[2] 委員会は今その問題を審議している。The committee is in session on that question. / アンドルーズ氏を委員長として委員会が新設された。A committee has been set up under the chairmanship of Mr. Andrews.

いう この子はまだ物が言えない。This child can't talk yet. / 何と言われました。Pardon me? / 君の言うとおりだ。What you say is true. / You are quite right. / だから言わないことじゃない。I told you so! / Didn't I tell you? / 彼は言ってみれば、無冠の帝王ですよ。He is an uncrowned monarch, in a manner of speaking. / 彼は英語は言うまでもなくドイツ語も知っている。He knows German, to say nothing of English. / だれかがそう言っているだけで人を非難するのはよろしくない。One shouldn't criticize someone merely on someone else's say-so. / その他は言うに足りない。The rest are not worth mentioning. / 言うに言われぬほどきれい

いえ 家 〈家屋〉 a house ; 〈家庭〉 *one's* (family) home ; 〈一家〉 a family ; 〈世帯〉 a household ¶住む家がない have no house to live in / 家の domestic《affairs》; household《economy》; family《matters》/ 家の外で out of [outside] the house ; out-of-doors ; outdoors / 家の中で in [inside] the house; indoors / 家のない人たち homeless people / 家を持つ make *one*'s home《at》; settle down / 家を明ける 〈旅行などで〉 stay away (from home); 〈立ち退く〉《文》vacate a house / 家を出る 〈出勤などで〉 leave the house; 〈子供が独立して〉 leave home; 〈家出する〉 ⇨いえで / (戦争などで)家を棄てて逃げる run away from [《文》flee *one's*] home / 家にいない be out ; be away from home ; be not at home / 家に帰る go [come] home / 家にいる be [stay] (at) home ; stay [keep] indoors / 同じ家に住む live in the same house《as *sb*》; live under the same roof《as *sb*》/ 金持ちの[貧しい]家に生まれる be born rich [poor] ; be born into a rich [poor] family / 家ごとに at [in] every house ; at every door. [文例⇩]

いえか 家蚊 a house mosquito.

いえがら 家柄 〈家の格〉 the (social) standing [status] of a family ; 〈家系〉《文》lineage ; 《文》birth ¶家柄がよい come from a good family; 《文》be of good birth / 家柄のよい人 a person from a good family ; 《文》a well-born person.

いえき 胃液 gastric [stomach] juices [liquids] ¶胃液の分泌 gastric secretions.

いえじ 家路 ¶家路を急ぐ hurry home ; 《文》hurry along on *one's* homeward journey / 家路につく start [set out] for home.

イエス yes ¶イエスかノーかの決定 a yes-no decision / イエスかノーかと尋ねる ask for a decision one way or the other ; ask for an answer yes or no.

イエスキリスト Jesus Christ.

イエズスかい イエズス会 the Society of Jesus ¶イエズス会士 a Jesuit.

イエスマン a yes-man.

いえだに 家だに a rat mite.

いえつき 家付 ¶家付きの娘 an heiress ; the daughter of the house.

いえで 家出 ¶家出する run away from home; leave home / 家出している be missing from home / 家出少女[少年] a runaway girl [boy] ; a girl [boy] who has run away from home / 家出人 a runaway.

いえばえ 家蠅 a housefly.

イエメン Yemen ¶イエメンの Yemeni / イエメン・アラブ共和国 〈北イエメン〉 the Yemen Arab Republic / イエメン人 a Yemeni / イエメン民主人民共和国 〈南イエメン〉 the People's Democratic Republic of Yemen.

いえもと 家元 the head of a school《of *Noh* players》; the school head ; 〈宗家〉 the head [representative] family of a school《of Japanese dancing》.

いえやしき 家屋敷 a house and land; an estate; *one's* property ; 〈農家の〉《米》a homestead.

いえる 癒える ⇨なおる.

いえん 胃炎 gastritis.

イオ 〈木星の衛星〉 Io.

いおう 硫黄 sulfur; sulphur ¶硫黄の sulfurous; sulfureous ; sulfuric / 硫黄泉 a sulfureous spring.

イオニア Ionia ¶イオニア柱式 the Ionic order.

イオニウム 〖化〗 ionium.

だ. It is too beautiful for words. / 彼は驚いて物が言えなかった. He was speechless with astonishment. / (落ち着きを取り戻して)ようやく物が言えるようになった. I found my voice at last. / 何がつらいといって貧乏ほどつらいものはない. There is nothing as hard to bear as poverty. / 私の言う事がわかりますか. Do you understand me? / 何を言おうとしているんだい. What are you driving [getting] at? / それはだれにも言わないでくれ. Don't tell anyone [say anything to anyone] about it. | Keep it under your hat. / あの人は今日は来られないと言ってよこした. 〈手紙または伝言で〉 He wrote to say [has sent me word] that he cannot come today. / 私がそう言っていたとあの人に伝えて下さい. Tell him that from me. / 言いたい事があるなら遠慮なく言わせろ. If he has anything to say, let him speak out. / 言うだけのことを言ってやろうと心に決めていた. I was determined to have my say. / さっさと正直に言ってしまえよ. Come on! Out with it! / 行くと言ってきかなかった. He insisted on going. / 私はだれの言う事も聞かない. I don't take orders from anybody. | I'm my own boss. / その時以来, 左手が言うことをきかなくなった. I have lost the use of my left hand since then. / 金銭上の事は言いにくい. It is embarrassing to speak about money (matters). / 病人はもう危険はないと医者が言った. The doctor pronounced the patient out of danger. / このことは自動車についても言える. This also holds good for automobiles. | This is true of cars, too. / こんなことを僕が言うとおかしいかね. Does this sound funny coming from me? / 彼女は頭が痛いと言って何も食べようとしなかった. She refused to eat, pleading a headache. / 思うことがうまく言えなかった. I could not express myself satisfactorily. / 春だというのに, まだだいぶ寒い. Though it is spring, [It is spring now, but] it is still pretty cold. / ベニスはよくアドリア海の女王と言われる. Venice is often called [referred to as] the Queen of the Adriatic. / 忙しいですか.—忙しいと言えば忙しいし, 忙しくないと言えば忙しくないですね. Are you busy?—In one way you could say I'm busy, then in another way (you could say) I'm not. / 英語では梅を何と言いますか. What is the English for '*ume*'? / 英語では 'a handsome woman' と言いますか. Do you ever speak of 'a handsome woman' in English? / (言い方に困って)何と言いましょうか. How should I put it? / あの人は君が言うほどの悪人ではないよ. He is not such a bad sort as you make him out to be. | He is not as bad as you paint him. / 彼の書いたのは何という本ですか. What is the title of his book? / 僕には原氏というよい友人がある. I have a good friend in Mr. Hara. / 小説と言えば君は漱石の「坊っちゃん」を読んだかね. Talking [Speaking] of novels, have you ever read *Botchan* by Soseki? / この町には公園というほどの物はない. There are no parks to speak of [worth mentioning] in this town. / 色合いといい柄といい申し分なしだ. It is perfect both in color and pattern. / だがこのことは, 言うは易く行なうは難しであった.

いおり 庵 a hermitage ¶いおりを結んでいる live in a hermitage ((in, at)); 〈隠遁する〉《文》 seclude *oneself* ((in, at)).

イオン 《化》an ion ¶陰イオン an anion; a negative ion / 陽イオン a cation; a positive ion / イオン化する ionize / イオン交換樹脂 an ion exchange resin.

いか¹ 以下 ¶以下の 〈数量が〉...or [and] below [less]; 《文》not exceeding; 〈下記の〉following; 《文》undermentioned / 5歳以下の小児 children of five and under; children less than six years old / 千円以下で for 1,000 yen or less; for not more than 1,000 yen / 校長以下用務員に至るまで from the principal down to the janitors / 中流以下の below the middle class / 以下同様 and so forth [on]. 文例⇩
用因 children under five years of age も children less than five years old も「5歳未満」の意味になる.「10キロメートル以下の距離」を a distance of under ten kilometers と言っても日常的にはさしつかえないが, 正確には a distance of ten kilometers or less と言う.

いか² 医科 the medical department ¶医科の学生 a medical student / 医科大学 a medical college.

いか³ 《動》a cuttlefish ((*pl.* -(es)); a squid ((*pl.* -(s)) ¶いかの甲 a cuttlebone.

いが 毬 a bur(r); a (chestnut) case.

いがい¹ 以外 ～ほか ¶...以外に 〈...を除いて〉except (for); 《文》excepting; 《文》with the exception of; 《文》excluding; but; 〈...の外にも〉besides; 《文》in addition to. 文例⇩
用因 1) except の次に来る人称代名詞は目的格になるが, but は前置詞とも接続詞とも考えられて, たとえば no one but him とも no one but he とも使われる, ただし後者は《文》である. また, この意味の but は no, all, nobody, anywhere, everything などの語のあと, または who, where, what など疑問詞のあとで使う.
2)「...があるという点を除いては」という意味の時は必ず except for とする: Your composition is quite all right except for two or three spelling mistakes.

いがい² 遺骸 《文》the (mortal) remains ((of *sb*)); the (dead) body ((of *sb*)).

いがい³ 意外 ¶意外な unexpected; 《文》unlooked-for; unforeseen; 〈偶然の〉accidental / 意外な結末で終わる物語 a story with a surprise ending / 意外な所で会う meet *sb* where *one* least expected to / 意外に(も) unexpectedly; against all [《文》contrary to (all)] expectation(s); to *one's* surprise / 意外かもしれないが contrary to what you might think / 意外に早く earlier than expected [《文》than was expected] / 意外に思う 〈驚く〉be surprised ((at)); 〈落胆する〉be disappointed ((at)). 文例⇩

いかいよう 胃潰瘍 a stomach [gastric] ulcer. 文例⇩

いかが 如何 ⇨ どう⁴. 文例⇩

いかがわしい 〈怪しげな〉《文》questionable; 《文》dubious; suspicious; 〈みだらな〉indecent; obscene; immoral ¶いかがわしい商売 a shady business / いかがわしい人物 a questionable character / いかがわしい場所 a disreputable place.

いかく 威嚇 《文》(a) menace; a threat; 《文》intimidation ¶威嚇する threaten; 《文》menace; intimidate; browbeat / 威嚇的に 《文》menacingly; threateningly / (動物の)威嚇の姿勢をとる assume a threat posture / 威嚇射撃

But this was easier [sooner] said than done. / 言わぬが花. The less said about it the better.

いえ このあたりも今一面に家が立ってしまった. This neighborhood is completely built up now. / おれが日に15時間も働いているからこそ, この家が持っているのだぞ. I work fifteen hours a day, mind you, to keep a roof over your heads. / 私の夢は自分の家を持つことです. My dream is to have a house of my own [my own house]. / 家の物を売る権利はお前にはない. You have no right to sell things out of the house.

いか¹ 気温はセ氏10度以下である. The temperature is below 10℃. / それは1万円以下では出来ない. It will cost at least 1万円. / この規定に違反する者は3か月以下の禁錮刑に処せられる. Any person who violates these regulations is liable to imprisonment of up to three months. / 以下は彼の話である. The following is his story. | Here [This] is his story. / 当時の情況を以下に記す. The situation at that time is described in the pages that follow. / 以下

次号. To be continued. / 以下略. The rest is omitted. / 50ページ以下参照. See p. 50 ff. ★ ff. は and the following pages と読む.

いがい¹ この庭園は月曜日以外は一般に開放されている. The garden is open to the public (on) every day except Monday. / ケアリー先生は大学で授業のある日以外はたいてい自宅で勉強しておられます. Professor Cary is generally studying at home except when he has classes at college. / ジョンは最後の1問以外は全部の問に答えた. John answered all the questions except (for) [with the exception of] the last. / あの方については, ある商社の社長さんだということ以外何も知りません. I know nothing about him except (for the fact) that he is the president of some business firm. / キャシー以外は皆うれしそうだった. Everyone looked happy except (for) Cathy. | Everyone but Cathy looked happy. / 地球上の水のうち3パーセント以外はすべて海にある. All but 3 per cent of the water on Earth is in the oceans. / ジョイス以外のだれがそんなことを言うだろう

か. Who but Joyce would say such a thing? / ここには私以外にはだれもいません. There's no one here but [other than] me. ★ other than に続く人称代名詞は目的格が普通. ⇨より! 用因 / これ以外に何か面白い小説をお持ちですか. Do you have any other interesting novels? / 彼は給料以外に相当な収入がある. He has a considerable income besides [in addition to] his salary.

いがい³ 兄の病気は意外に重かった. My brother was more seriously ill than I had imagined. / これは意外だ. I did not expect this. | This is a surprise. / 君にここで会うとは全く意外だ. I didn't expect to [that I would] meet you here. / その小説は意外な結末で終わった. The novel had a surprise dénouement [a twist at the end]. / 意外にも私の言ったことが人々に誤解された. To my surprise, they misunderstood me [what I said].

いかいよう 彼は胃潰瘍にかかっていた. He had a stomach ulcer.

いかが ご機嫌いかがですか. How are you getting along? | 〈あいさつ〉How are you? / 今日はご気

をする fire warning shots. [文例⇩]
いがく 医学 medical science; medicine ¶医学的に medically / 医学の進んだ国 a medically advanced country / 医学上の medical / 医学界 the medical world; medical circles / 医学生 a medical student / 医学士〈人〉a bachelor of medicine;〈学位〉Bachelor of Medicine (略: M.B., B.M.) / 医学者 a medical scientist / 医学博士〈人〉a doctor of medicine;〈学位〉Doctor of Medicine (略: M.D., D.M.) / 医学部 the medical department / 医学部進学課程 the premedical course.
いかくちょう 胃拡張 gastric dilation; dilation of the stomach.
いがぐりあたま いがぐり頭 a close-cropped head.
いかさま〈欺瞞(ぎまん)〉trickery; (a) fraud;《文》(an) imposture;〈にせもの〉a counterfeit;《口語》a fake;〈勝負での〉foul play ¶いかさまの《文》false; sham;《文》spurious;《俗》phon(e)y / いかさま師 a cheat; a swindler.
いかさよう 異化作用〘生物·生理〙catabolism.
いかす[1] 生かす〈生き返らす〉revive; bring *sb* back [《文》restore *sb*] to life;〈活用する〉make the most of《*one's* opportunities》; make the best use of《the fund》 ¶生かしておく keep《a fish》alive; let *sb* live;〈殺さない〉spare《*sb, sb's* life》;〈生気を与える〉give life to《the picture》/ (校正などで) 一度消した言葉を生かす restore a deleted word / 金を生かして使う spend *one's* money wisely [for useful purposes]; make good [the best] use of *one's* money. [文例⇩]
いかす[2]《口語》be cool;《米》be neat;《俗》be groovy;《俗》be way-out;〈外見が〉look great [《英》a treat]. [文例⇩]
いかすい 胃下垂 gastroptosis; downward displacement of the stomach.
いかだ 筏 a raft ¶いかだに乗って行く go《down a river》by [on a] raft; raft《down a river》/ いかだを組む make a raft《of logs》/ いかだ乗り a raftsman / 丸太をいかだに組んで川下へ送る raft logs down the river / いかだで運ぶ carry *sth* on a raft; raft *sth*《to》.
いがた 鋳型 a mold ¶鋳型に注ぎこむ cast [pour]《metal》into a mold / 鋳型を外す strip a mold《from a casting》.
いかつい 厳つい stern《looks》; square《shoulders》 ¶いかつい顔をしている have a stern face; be hard-[stern-]faced.
いかに 如何に〈どういう風に〉how?;《文》in what way?;〈どれほど〉how?; how much?;〈どれほど…でも〉however; whatever ⇨どんな(どんなに) ¶いかにして…すべきか how to *do*.
いかにも 如何にも〈実に〉indeed; really;〈確かに〉certainly; surely; to be sure;〈はなはだ〉very; extremely ¶いかにもうれしそうに《文》with evident joy. [文例⇩]
いかほど 如何程 ⇨いくら, どの[2] (どのくらい).
いがみあい 啀み合い〈けんか〉a quarrel; wrangling;〈反目〉a feud.
いがみあう 啀み合う〈けんかする〉quarrel [wrangle]《with》;〈反目し合っている〉be at daggers drawn《with》;《文》feud [be at feud]《with》.
いかめしい 厳しい〈厳粛な〉solemn; stern;《文》grave;〈威厳のある〉dignified;《文》majestic;〈堂々たる〉《文》stately; magnificent;〈こわそうな〉forbidding ¶いかめしい顔つき a stern look [face] / いかめしい建物 an imposing [a stately] building / いかめしく《文》gravely; sternly;《文》with dignity;《文》with a dignified air. [文例⇩]
いカメラ 胃カメラ a gastrocamera.
いかもの〈にせ物〉a fake; a bogus [《文》spurious] article;〈異常な食べ物〉freak food ¶いか物食い an eater of unusual [bizarre] food; a gastronomic adventurer.
いからせる 怒らせる ¶肩を怒らせる square *one's* shoulders / 肩を怒らせて歩く swagger (along) / 目を怒らせる give *sb* an angry look; glare《at》.
いがらっぽい irritating; acrid.
いかり[1] 怒り anger; (a) rage;《文》wrath; indignation ¶怒りが解ける *one's* anger cools;〈人が主語〉relent《toward》/ 怒りを抑える restrain [hold in,《文》contain] *one's* anger / 怒りを抑えられなくなる give way to (*one's*) anger [rage] / 怒りを静める calm [《文》quell,《文》appease] *sb's* anger / 怒りを爆発させる explode into angry words;《俗》blow *one's* top / 怒りをぶちまける《口語》take it out《on》;《文》vent [wreak] *one's* anger《on》/ 怒りを招く[に触れる] arouse *sb's* anger; offend *sb*;《文》

分はいかがですか.〈病人に〉How do you feel today? / 近頃はいかがですか.《口語》How's everything? | 《口語》How's things? (★ How's は How is の縮約形であるから, この文は明らかに非文法的であるが, 一般によく使われる) / ご商売はいかがです. How's business? / (客に)お茶を一杯いかがです. Won't you have a cup of tea? / この夏には北海道旅行はいかがですか. What do you say to [How about] (taking) a trip to Hokkaido this summer? / 箱根旅行はいかがでしたか. How did you enjoy your trip to Hakone? | 《口語》How was Hakone? / これはいかが致しましょう. What shall I do with this? / 上着をお脱ぎになったらいかがです. Won't you [Why don't you] take your coat off?
いかく 殺すぞと言って威嚇すれば彼らは何でもするだろう. If threatened with death, they will do anything.
いかす[1] この事業の成功を見るまで父を生かしておきたかった. I wish my father could have lived to see the success of this enterprise. / モデルを生かすも殺すもカメラマンの腕次第だ. It depends entirely on the cameraman's skill whether the model is used to advantage or not.
いかす[2] その新しいドレス, いかすじゃないか. You really look great in your new dress!
いかにも いかにもありそうな事だ. That is more than probable. / いかにも彼の言いそうな事だ. It is just like him to say so.
いかめしい 彼はいつもいかめしい顔つきをしている. He always looks as grave as a judge. / 入口にはいかめしい顔をした守衛が立っていた. A guard stood at the door with a stern, set face.

incur *sb*'s wrath / 怒りに燃える burn with anger.

いかり² 錨 an anchor ¶ **いかりを下ろす** drop anchor; lower an anchor; anchor 《at》 / いかりをかけている ride [lie, be] at anchor / いかりを上げる weigh [raise the] anchor; pull up [haul in] an anchor / いかり索 an anchor cable.

いかる 怒る ⇨ **おこる**¹ ¶ **肩が怒っている** have square shoulders.

いかれる 〈やられる〉 be beaten 《by》; 〈(部品などが)故障する〉 break down; 〈ほろりとする〉 be touched 《by》; get sentimental 《over》; 〈ほれこむ〉 be (dead) gone 《on a girl》 ¶ **いかれている** 〈頭がおかしい〉 be touched in the head; 〈故障している〉 be out of order; 《米俗》 be shot [snafu]; 《英俗》 be buggered.

いかん¹ 移管 (a) transfer of jurisdiction [authority] ¶ **移管する** place 《a matter》 under the authority [control] of another department; transfer.

いかん² 偉観 a fine [grand] sight.

いかん³ 遺憾 ¶ **遺憾な** 〈嘆かわしい〉 regrettable; 《文》 deplorable; 《文》 lamentable; 〈不満足な〉 unsatisfactory / **遺憾のない** 〈完全な〉 perfect; (most) satisfactory; 〈充分な〉 thorough / **遺憾なく** 〈完全に〉 perfectly; 《文》 to perfection; (most) satisfactorily; 〈充分に〉 fully / **遺憾なく才能を発揮する** 《文》 give full play to *one*'s abilities / **遺憾ながら** I regret [am sorry] to say that…; 《文》 to my regret / **遺憾とする** [に思う] regret; be sorry 《that》; 《文》 feel bad 《about》 / **(…は)誠に遺憾(千万)である** It is a great pity 《that…》; 《文》 It is really regrettable 《that…》; 《文》 It is greatly to be regretted 《that…》. 文例⇩

いかん⁴ 如何 what?; how? ¶ **…のいかんを問わず** 《文》 regardless [irrespective] of 《whether…》. 文例⇩

いがん 胃癌 (a) cancer of the stomach; gastric cancer.

いがんたいしょく 依願退職 ¶ **依願退職する** resign *one*'s post [duties] (voluntarily).

いき¹ 生き 〈鮮度〉 freshness; 〈校正用語〉 stet (略: st.) ¶ **生きのいい魚** a fresh fish / **生きの悪い魚** a fish that is no longer fresh.

いき² 行き ¶ **行きは船で帰りは電車にする** go by boat and come back by train / **…行きの** 《a train》 (bound) for 《Tokyo》; 〈荷物〉 《the baggage》 (booked) for 《Aomori》 / **神戸行きの切符** a ticket to Kobe. 文例⇩

いき³ 息 〈呼気〉 a [*one*'s] breath; 〈呼吸〉 breathing ¶ **まだ息がある** be still breathing; be still alive / **…の息がかかっている** have the backing of 《the Prime Minister》 / **息が切れる** get out of breath; lose *one*'s breath [wind] / **息が臭い** have bad [foul] breath / **息が苦しい** have difficulty (in) breathing; breathe with difficulty / **息が長く続く**[続かない] be long-[short-]winded; *one*'s wind is strong [weak] / **息が詰まる** be choked; be stifled / **息のあるうちに** while *one* is alive / **息の続く限り** to *one*'s last gasp; as long as *one* has any breath [wind] left in *one* / **息の根を止める** kill; 《文》 take [put an end to] *sb*'s life / **息を切らして** out of breath, panting; breathless(ly) / **息を殺して[詰めて]** hold *one*'s breath / **息を殺して** with bated breath; in breathless excitement [suspense] / **息をする** breathe 《through *one*'s nostrils》 / **息を吸う** breathe in; draw in *one*'s breath; take in breath; 《文》 inhale / **息を(入れる)** draw a (deep) breath / **〈休む〉** 《口語》 take [have] a breather; take a pause [short rest] / **息をつく暇もない** do not have time to breathe / **息を飲むような** breathtaking; thrilling / **息を吐き出す** breathe out; give out breath; 《文》 exhale / **息をはずませる** gasp; pant (for breath) / **息を引きとる[が絶える]** 《文》 breathe *one*'s last (breath) [dying breath]; 《文》 expire; die / **息を吹き返す** come to (life); come [be brought] round / **息もつかずに** without taking breath; 〈一息に〉 at a stretch / **息もつかずに飲み干す** drain 《a glass》 at a draft [《口語》 in one go]. 文例⇩

いき⁴ 域 〈地域〉 a region; 〈範囲〉 limits; 〈段階〉 a stage; 〈水準〉 a level ¶ **…の域に達する** reach the stage of…; 《文》 attain the level of… / **…の域を出ない** be no better than 《an amateur singer》.

いき⁵ 意気 〈元気〉 spirit(s); 《文》 heart; 〈士気〉 morale ¶ **意気盛んな** high-spirited / **意気揚揚としている**(軒昂(けんこう)) be in high spirits; be elated 《at the victory》; be flushed 《with (*one*'s) success》 / **意気消沈する** lose heart [courage]; be dispirited / **意気投合する** 《文》 find a kindred [congenial] spirit in *sb*; 《口語》 hit it off

---

いかん³ こういう事故が頻発するのは遺憾な事だ。 It is a matter for regret that such accidents should happen so frequently. / このホテルは設備の点は遺憾ないだ。 The appointments in this hotel leave nothing to be desired. / 遺憾ながら参会できません。 I am sorry, but I am unable to attend the meeting.

いかん⁴ 奈々子の運命やいかん。 What will be the fate of Nanako? / それはいかんの先方の態度やいかんによって決すべき事である。 We should make our decision on the basis of [according to] their attitude. | The decision we make should depend on their attitude. / それはいかんともなしがたい。 It can't be helped. | There is no help for it.

いき² この電車はどこ行きですか。 Where is this train for? | Where does this train go to?

いき³ 彼女は息が切れて言葉をとぎらせた。 She stopped talking, quite out of breath. | She stopped for lack of breath. / 我々は一刻も早くと息もつがずに駆けつけた。 We hurried on without stopping to recover our breath. / この部屋は息が詰まりそうだ。 This room is stifling. / 吐く息が白く見えた。 Their breath showed as little white puffs in the air. | I could see (the plumes of) their breath. / 辞書の編集は息の長い仕事だ。 Compiling a dictionary requires a long-sustained effort. / 2人はぴったり息が合っていた。 They were [made] a perfect pair. / 彼の作品はクリスティーの模倣の域を出ない。 His works are no better than [little more than] imitations of Christie.

(well) together [with each other]. 文例↓

いき⁶ 遺棄 《文》abandonment ; 《文》desertion ¶ 遺棄する abandon ; desert ; leave 《a dead body》unattended.

いき⁷ 粋 いきな stylish ; smart(-looking) ; 《文》chic ; fashionable / 帽子をいきに傾けてかぶっている be wearing one's hat at a rakish angle.

いぎ¹ 威儀 ¶ 威儀を正して 《文》in a dignified [solemn] manner ; 《文》in state.

いぎ² 異議 (a) an objection ; a protest ; 〈不賛成〉《文》dissent / 異議がある[ない] have an [no] objection 《to》/ 異議なく without objection ;〈異議を唱える者なく〉nem. con.(★ ラテン語 nemine contradicente の略)/ 満場異議なく unanimously / 異議を唱える[さしはさむ] object 《to》; raise an objection 《to》; protest 《about, against》; make a protest 《against》;《文》express dissent 《from》/ 異議を申し立てる lodge a protest [an objection] 《against》/〈法廷での〉異議申し立て a formal objection ; an exception. 文例↓

いぎ³ 意義 (a) meaning ; (a) sense ; 《文》significance ⇨ いみ ¶ この意義深い日に 《文》on this memorable day. 文例↓

いきあう 行き会う meet sb (by chance) ; come across [upon] sb ; 〈すれ違う〉pass sb.

いきあたりばったり 行き当たりばったり ¶ 行き当たりばったりの random ; haphazard ; hit-or-miss ; unplanned ;〈のんきな〉happy-go-lucky / 行き当たりばったりにやる play it [sth] by ear ; do in a haphazard way [at random]. 文例↓

いきいき 生き生き ¶ 生き生きした 〈新鮮な〉fresh ;〈活気のある〉lively ;《文》animated ;〈活発な〉active ;〈真に迫った〉lifelike ; vivid / 生き生きした表現 a vivid expression ;《文》a graphic description / 生き生きと full of life ; vividly / 生き生きとさせる refresh ;《文》enliven.

いきうつし 生き写し ¶ 生き写しである be the (very) image 《of》; be the living [《口語》spitting] image 《of》; be an exact copy 《of》. 文例↓

いきうま 生き馬 ¶ 生き馬の目を抜くような sharp ; shrewd / 生き馬の目を抜くようなことをする go in for [use] sharp practice. 文例↓

いきうめ 生き埋め ¶ 生き埋めになる be buried alive.

いきえ 生き餌 〈飼料〉a living thing given as food (to a kept animal) ; live feed ;〈釣りの〉live bait.

いきおい 勢い 1.〈力〉power ; force ;〈気力〉energy ; vigor ; spirit ; life ; drive ;〈勢力〉(an) influence ; authority ;〈はずみ〉(an) impetus ; momentum ;〈傾向〉a tendency ; a trend ¶ 勢いがつく be enlivened ;《文》gain vigor [force] ; be encouraged / 勢いのいい, 勢いのある〈力のある〉powerful ;〈元気な〉spirited ; vigorous; full of life ;〈活発な〉lively ; animated / 勢いのない lifeless ;《文》spiritless ; dull ;《文》enervated / 勢いよく《文》with great force ; vigorously ; with vigor [spirit, strength] ; in high spirits / 勢いをつける《文》enliven ; encourage ; cheer [brace] sb up / 勢いをそがれる be discouraged ; be dispirited / 勢いを増す gather strength [momentum] / 勢いに乗ずる take advantage of the circumstances ; follow up one's advantage 《over sb》/ この勢いで進めば if things go on at this rate / 時の勢いで by force of circumstances / 酒の勢いで under the influence of liquor. **2.**〈必然的に〉《文》necessarily ;《文》of necessity ; inevitably ;〈自然と〉naturally ; as a natural result [consequence].

いきがい 生きがい ¶ 生きがいがある[ない] have something [nothing] to live for / 生きがいのある生活をする live a useful life ; lead a worthwhile life ; live to some purpose / 生き

いき⁵ その意気だ. That's the spirit. / 人生意気に感ず. Heart is won by heart. / 私は全く意気消沈してしまった. My heart quite failed me. / 2人はすっかり意気投合して, はしご酒に及んだ. We decided that we liked each other a lot [that we were kindred spirits] and went barhopping.

いぎ²〈議長のことば〉異議ありませんか. ―異議なしと認めます. Has anyone any objection? ―I see no objection. / 異議あり. Objection! / 異議なし. No objection! / 僕は異議はない. I have no objection (to it). / I have nothing to say against it. /〈裁判長のことば〉異議の申し立てを認めます[却下いたします]. Objection sustained [overruled].

いぎ³ ゼロの発見は数学史上大きな意義のある出来事であった. The discovery of zero was an event of great significance in the history of mathematics. / この20年ほどの間に生態学は新しい意義を帯びるものとなった. In the past twenty years or so ecology has taken on a new significance.

いきあたりばったり あの男は何をするにも行き当たりばったりだ. He leaves everything to chance.

いきうつし 君は30年前のお父さんに生き写しだ. You look exactly as your father did thirty years ago. / 彼女はクララに生き写しだった. She was Clara to the life.

いきうま 東京は生き馬の目を抜くような所から気をつけなさい. You must keep your wits about you [be wide-awake] in Tokyo, or you will be taken in by some sharp practice or other.

いきおい この町の人口は大変な勢いで増えている. The population of this town is increasing at a great rate. / その運動は勢いを失って自然消滅してしまった. The movement died, having run out of momentum. / 彼は酒の勢いで部長に食ってかかった. Grown bold on sake, he turned on the chief of his department. / それは自然の勢いである[勢いのしからしむるところだ]. That is the natural course of events. | It is only natural that it should be so. / 彼らは勢いこんでその仕事に取りかかった. They set about the work with great élan [determination].

いきがい 野生動物の研究が彼の生きがいとなっている. The study of wild animals is his (whole) life.

いきかえる 雨で草木が生き返った. The rain has revived the plants.

いきがかり 今までの行き掛かりは忘れることにしましょう. Let's forget all that has happened between us. | Let's let bygones be bygones. / その場の行き掛かりでやむを得ず承諾したのです. The

いきかえり 行き帰り ¶学校の行き帰りに on the [one's] way to and from school ⇒おうふく.

いきかえる 生き返る revive; return [come, 《文》be restored] to life; come around ¶生き返ったような気持ちがする feel quite refreshed; 〈安心して〉breathe freely (again). 文例⇩

いきがかり 行き掛かり ¶行き掛かりで[上] under the [by force of] circumstances.

いきがけ 行き掛け ¶行きがけに on one's way 《to》; in going 《to》; in passing. 文例⇩

いきかた¹ 行き方 a way of life [living]; a lifestyle; how to live (as a scholar).

いきかた² 行き方 〈やり方〉one's way [《文》manner] of doing things; one's method; 〈方針〉《文》a course; a line (of conduct) ¶独自の行き方をする take one's own line [course]. 文例⇩

いきき 行き来 〈通行〉comings and goings; traffic ⇒おうらい; 〈交際〉《文》association ¶行き来する come and go; 〈交際する〉associate 《with》; be on visiting terms 《with》/ 行き来しない do not associate 《with》; 〈絶交する〉part company 《with》. 文例⇩

いきぎれ 息切れ ¶息切れする get [《文》become] short of breath; be winded / 息切れしている be out of breath; be breathless /《口語》be puffed / すぐに息切れしやすい be short-winded. 文例⇩

いきぐるしい 息苦しい 〈場所が〉be stuffy; be stifling; be suffocating; be close; 〈呼吸が苦しい〉have difficulty (in) breathing; breathe with difficulty.

いきごみ 意気込み enthusiasm; eagerness;《文》ardor. 文例⇩

いきごむ 意気込む be enthusiastic 《about》; be intent [《文》bent] on 《doing》; have a great interest 《in》; be eager [determined] 《to do》 ¶大いに意気込んで with great enthusiasm.

いきさき 行き先 〈目的地〉one's destination; the end of one's journey; 〈行った[行く]場所〉the place where one has gone [is going]; 〈所在〉one's whereabouts. 文例⇩

いきさつ 〈事の起きた順序〉the sequence of events; 〈事情〉the circumstances; 〈詳細〉particulars; details. 文例⇩

いきじびき 生き字引 a walking dictionary [encyclopedia].

いきすぎ 行き過ぎ ¶行き過ぎをやる ⇒いきすぎる / 行き過ぎにならないように気をつける take care not to go too far. 文例⇩

いきすぎる 行き過ぎる 〈通り過ぎる〉go [walk] past [beyond]; 〈度を越す〉go too far; overreach [overleap] oneself. 文例⇩

いきせききる 息せき切る ¶息せき切ってbreathlessly; panting; gasping; puffing and blowing; out of breath.

いきだおれ 行き倒れ a person dying [lying dead] on the street ¶行き倒れになる fall ill [dead] on the street.

いきち 生き血 blood of a living person [animal].

いきちがい 行き違い 〈手紙などの〉crossing; 〈誤解〉a misunderstanding; 〈不和〉(a) disagreement ¶行き違いになる 〈人が〉miss each other (on the way); 〈手紙などが〉cross; 〈失敗する〉go wrong; fail.

いきづかい 息遣い breathing ¶息づかいが荒い breathe hard [heavily]; pant / 息づかいが苦しい have difficulty (in) breathing / 息づかいが普通に戻る get one's breath (back [back again]). 文例⇩

いきつく 行き着く arrive at [in]; reach; get to. 文例⇩

いきつけ 行きつけ ¶行きつけの床屋 one's favorite barber; the barbershop that one pa-

---

circumstances compelled me to give my consent.
いきがけ 行きがけの駄賃こいつももらってやれ. I'll have this one, too, before I go.
いきかた¹ 私は主婦としての私の生き方を変えるべきではないかと思いました. I wondered if I ought to change my way of living [my life pattern] as a housewife.
いきかた² それは私の行き方ではない. That's not my way (of doing things). / これは首相としては新しい行き方だ. This is a new line [departure] for the Prime Minister.
いきき 通りは人の行き来がなかった. The street was deserted. / あの男とは行き来しない方がよい. I would advise you to avoid his company.
いきぎれ 長い間働きづめで息切れの態(てい)である. We've been working quite a long time and could do with a breather now.
いきごみ 初めの意気込みはどこへやら. They have lost most of their initial enthusiasm.
いきごむ 彼は今度ひとも優勝すると意気込んでいた. He was (dead) set on winning the championship.
いきさき 行き先を知らせておいて下さい. Please keep me informed about your whereabouts.
いきさつ どういういきさつなのか私にはわからない. I don't know how it came about.
いきすぎ それは行き過ぎだ. That's going too far.
いきすぎる 居眠りをして駅を2つ行き過ぎてしまった. I was carried two stops beyond my destination while I was napping. / 彼の動きから察するに彼は自分でもこの件では行き過ぎたことを認めていたようだった. His move suggested that he thought he had gone too far [overstepped the mark] in this case. / それはたしかにいい考えだが, 行き過ぎてはいけない. That's certainly a good idea, but it mustn't be pushed too far.
いきちがい 手紙が途中で行き違いになったに相違ない. Our letters must have crossed in the mail. / 2人の間に何か行き違いがあったらしい. There seems to have been some misunderstanding between them.
いきづかい ペギーの息づかいが普通に戻った. Peggy's breathing was normal again.
いきつく そんなことをいつまでもやっていると, 行き着く所は刑務所だぞ. If you go on doing things like that, you'll land up in prison one day. / とうとう行き着く所へ行き着いてしまった. I knew all along that we'd come to this pass, and here we are.

いきづまり 行き詰まり (a) deadlock; a stalemate; 《文》 an impasse ¶行き詰まりを打開する find a way out of the deadlock [impasse]; break the deadlock [stalemate]. 文例⇩

いきづまる¹ 行き詰まる come [be at] a dead end; reach [be in] a deadlock [a stalemate, 《文》 an impasse]; be stalemated; be deadlocked; be at the end of one's tether. 文例⇩

いきづまる² 息詰まる ¶息詰まるような 《文》 oppressive 《silence》; thrilling 《scenes》; breathtaking 《skill》.

いきどおり 憤り ⇨いかり¹, ふんがい.

いきどころ 行き所 ¶行き所がない have nowhere to go; be turned adrift (in the world).

いきとどく 行き届く 〈注意深い〉 be careful; 《文》 be attentive to details; 〈思いやりがある〉 be tactful; be considerate; 〈完全である〉 be complete; be perfect. 文例⇩

いきどまり 行き止まり the dead end (of a road); 〈袋小路〉 a blind alley; a dead-end street; a cul-de-sac ¶行き止まりになる come to a dead end; end.

いきながらえる 生き長らえる live on; 〈長生きする〉 have a long life; (not) live long; 〈生き残る〉 survive ¶90歳まで生き長らえる live to the ripe old age of ninety; live to ninety (years of age).

いきなり 《文》 abruptly; suddenly; all of a sudden; out of the blue; 〈準備なしで〉 without preparation; 〈予告なしに〉 (hit sb) without warning; without notice.

いきぬき 息抜き (take, have) a rest; 《口語》 a breather; (a) breathing space. 文例⇩

いきぬく 生き抜く survive (a war); live through (an era); 〈天寿を全うする〉 live out one's life. 文例⇩

いきのこり 生き残り a survivor 《of a war》.

いきのこる 生き残る survive 《a disaster》; outlive 《others》.

いきのびる 生き延びる 〈生き残る〉 survive 《a war》; outlive 《others》; 〈命拾いして〉 live on borrowed time; 〈長生きする〉 live to an old age [for many years].

いきはじ 生き恥 ¶生き恥をさらす live in disgrace; 《文》 live ignominiously.

いきぼとけ 生き仏 a living Buddha; a saintly person.

いきまく 息巻く rage 《at, against》; storm. 文例⇩

いきむ 息む 〈便所で〉 strain (at stool); 〈分娩時に〉 bear [push] down.

いきもの 生き物 a living thing; a (living) creature; 〈動物〉 an animal; 〈総称〉 life ¶色々な生き物 various forms of life. 文例⇩

いきょう¹ 異教 heathenism; paganism ¶異教の heathen; pagan / 異教徒 a heathen; a pagan.

いきょう² 異郷 《文》 a strange land; a foreign country.

いぎょう 偉業 a great undertaking [achievement].

いきょく¹ 医局 a medical office ¶医局員 (a member of) the medical staff / 医局長 a senior assistant on the medical staff (of the surgical department).

いきょく² 委曲 ⇨いさい¹ ¶委曲を尽くす give all the details (of); go into particulars; give a full account (of).

イギリス England; Britain ⇨えいこく ¶イギリス英語 British English; 〈イギリス英語独特の語句やイディオム〉 a Briticism / イギリス海峡 the (English) Channel / イギリス連合王国 the United Kingdom (of Great Britain and Northern Ireland) (略: U.K.).

いきりたつ いきり立つ get angry; lose one's temper; 《文》 become indignant; 《文》 be enraged; be in a rage; 《口語》 be up in arms (over, about).

いきる 生きる live; exist ¶90歳まで生きる live to be ninety (years old); live to the age

---

いきづまり この交渉を行き詰まりのままにさせておくわけにはゆかない. We cannot afford to leave the negotiations deadlocked.

いきづまる¹ そういうことではやがて行き詰まるにきまっている. You're on a hiding to nothing. / 資金不足で事業はすっかり行き詰まってしまった. Our enterprise has got completely bogged down for want of funds.

いきとどく 庭の手入れが行き届いている. The garden is tended with great care. / それは皆私が行き届かないからです. It is all due to my lack of care [attention]. | It is all my fault.

いきぬき 仕事の息抜きに昨日は音楽会に行って来た. I went to a concert yesterday to take my mind off [to get away from] my work.

いきのこり 彼はビクトリア時代の生き残りだ. He is a holdover from [relic of] the Victorian age.

いきまく 彼は私と法廷で争うと息巻いた. He declared threateningly that he would bring an action against me.

いきもの 言葉は生き物だ. The words we use have lives of their own.

いきる 彼は今生きるか死ぬかの瀬戸際だ. He is hanging between life and death. / 僕だって80まで生きないものでもあるまい. I don't see why I shouldn't see eighty. / その化石を見た時, この動物は生きていた時にはどんな姿をしていたのかなと思った. When I saw the fossil, I wondered how the animal had looked in life [when it was alive]. / やっと飛騨の山中に落ち延びることができた. He managed to escape to the mountains in Hida alive [with his life]. / この肖像はまるで生きているようだ. This portrait is really lifelike. / 彼の小説の中の人物は生きている. The characters in his novels ring true. / 彼との契約はまだ生きている. The contract with him still holds. / その法律は今でも生きている. That law is still in effect.

いきわたる みんなに行き渡るだけのワインがありますか. Is there enough wine to go around?

いく すぐ行くよ. 〈相手の方へ〉 I'm coming in a minute. | I'll be right over. | I won't be long. / 〈他の場所へ〉 I'll go at once. / 本郷へはどの道を行ったらよいでしょうか. Which street should I take (to go) to Hongo? / この通りを行くと上野に出ます. This street leads [goes] to Ueno. / 私もあなたと同じ方へ行きます. I'm

いきわかれ

of ninety / 生きるか死ぬかの問題 a matter of life and death / 生きている be living; be alive / 米を食って生きている live [《文》subsist] on rice / 生きているうちに while one lives [is alive]; during one's life / 生きて帰る come back [return] alive / 生きた魚 a live fish / 生きた手本 a living model [example] / 生きた心地がしない be beside *oneself* with fear;《文》be in mortal fear. 文例⑥

いきわかれ 生き別れ (a) separation (《from sb》) ¶生き別れになる part (from sb) in life.

いきわたる 行き渡る 〈広がる〉spread [《文》extend] all over (a place); reach every part of (the country); 〈普及する〉《文》prevail; 〈分配される物が皆に〉go around [round]. 文例⑥

いく 行く go; come; 〈訪ねる〉call (on sb, at sb's house); visit;《文》pay sb a visit; 〈出席する〉attend (a meeting); 〈…に向かって去る〉leave for (Kyoto); 〈道が〉…へ通じる lead to (the station); go to (Nagoya) ¶東京へ行く列車 a train (bound) for Tokyo / 横浜からホンコンへ行く船 a ship bound from Yokohama to Hong Kong / 学校[教会]へ行く go to school [church] / 泳ぎ[スキー, 釣り]に行く go swimming [skiing, fishing] / 歩いて行く walk (to); go on foot / 電車[バス, 飛行機, 船]で行く go by train [bus, plane, boat] ★ go (to a place) on [in] a train [a bus, etc.] という言い方もある. その場合の前置詞は《米》では on,《英》では in / 〈事に当たって〉行くところまで行く go to the very limit; 〈口語〉go all the way / 〈★「肉体関係を持つ」という意味で使う場合には, 続けて with sb という形でも使う〉 / 行ったり来たりする come and go; shuttle (between the two capitals) ⇒うまく / 〈物事がうまく行く〉⇒うまく. 文例⑥

囲団「行く」に当たる英語は一般的には go だが, 話相手の所へ行く場合には, 相手を中心にした言い方をして come を用いる. たとえば,「明日遊びに行っていいですか」は Can I come and see you tomorrow?

となる. ともすると, Can I go … tomorrow? というような誤りをし勝ちだから注意を要する. 以上のことは take と bring の区別にも当てはまる. take は「持って行く」, bring は「持って来る」だが,「明日, 君のところへ持って行くよ」は I'll bring it to you tomorrow. であって, …take…ではない.

いく- 幾… 〜なん- ¶幾通りもの all sorts [kinds] of; various / 幾重にも〈折重ね〉several times over; 〈頼む時〉《文》humbly; 《文》earnestly; 幾久しく for ever; 《文》eternally. 文例⑥

イグアナ《動》an iguana.

いぐい 居食い ¶居食いする live in idleness.

いくえい 育英 ⇒きょういく ¶育英事業 educational work / 育英資金 a scholarship / 日本育英会 the Japan Scholarship Foundation.

いぐさ 藺草《植》a rush.

いくじ¹ 育児 child-rearing[-raising]; child [baby, infant] care ¶育児書 a book on child-rearing / 育児法 a method of child-rearing.

いくじ² 意気地 ¶意気地のない spineless; backboneless; timid; cowardly; weak-kneed / 意気地がない have no backbone [《口語》guts]; 《俗》be chicken;《文》lack spirit [nerve] / 意気地なし a coward; a timid [《文》poor-spirited] creature.

いくしゅ 育種 (selective) breeding 《of animals [plants]》.

いくせい 育成 ¶育成する〈育てる〉bring up; rear; raise; 《文》nurture, 〈助成する〉《文》foster; encourage; 《文》promote.

いくた 幾多 ¶幾多の many; 《文》numerous; a (great) number of.

いくつ 幾つ〈幾個〉how many?; 〈幾歳〉how old? ¶幾つかの some; several / 幾つもの many; a great many; any number of; a (large) number of; many a (thing) / 〜たくさん / 幾つでも any number of; ever so many / 幾つでもあなたが欲しいだけ as many as you want [like]. 文例⑥

いくど 幾度 how often?; how many times? いく- 今日は幾日ですか. What day of the month is it (today)? / 京都に幾日ご滞在でしたか. How long [many days] did you stay in Kyoto? / 幾日も好天気が続いた. We have had a long spell of fine weather. / 幾重にもおわびを申します. A thousand pardons! | Please accept my sincerest apologies. / 幾久しくとお祝い申し上げます. I wish you both everlasting happiness and prosperity. | I wish you a very happy married life.

いくしゅ 鳩は帰巣能力の高いものを選んで育種されてきた. Pigeons have been selectively bred for their homing ability.

いくつ もう幾つ欲しいのですか. How many more do you want? / 12掛ける5は幾つですか. What [How much] is twelve times five? / 東京には大学が幾つもある. There are any number of

---

going your way. / 頂上までどのくらいかかりましょうか. —1時間半で行けますよ. How long will it take (me) to get to the top?— You can get there [make it] in one and a half hours. / ここから歩いてほんの5分で行かれます. It's only five minutes' walk [a five-minute walk] from here. / バスで行けば10分です. It's ten minutes by bus. | It's a ten-minute ride on a bus. | インドへ行ったことがありますか. Have you ever been to India? / どこへ行って来ました. Where have you been? / 彼はアメリカへ行った. He has gone to America. / 行ってまいります. Good-bye. / 行ってらっしゃい. Good-bye; have a nice day. | 〈遊びに出かける人に〉(I hope you) have a good time. | 〈旅行に行く人に〉I hope you have a nice [pleasant] trip. / むしゃくしゃしながら教室

へ行った. I carried my outraged feelings into the class. | このまま行くと, 我々は地球を人が住めないようにしてしまうかもしれない. The way we are going, we may well make the earth uninhabitable for man. / ここでコーヒーを飲んで行こう. Let's have a (cup of) coffee here. / そうは行かないよ〈君の思うようにはさせない〉You're not getting away with that! | 〈結果がそうはならない〉It won't work out that way. | 結果は思いどおりに行かなかった. The results fell short of our expectations. / 彼を名差して非難するところまでは行かなかった. They stopped short of mentioning him by name in their criticism. / 節約もそこまで行くとけちに近い. Thrift, when carried to that extent, borders on stinginess. / さあ, 行くぞ. 〈行動を起こすとき〉Here goes [we go]!

[い]

⇨なんど¹. [文例⇩]

いくどうおん 異口同音 ¶異口同音に《文》with one voice ;《文》with one accord ; unanimously. [文例⇩]

いくび 猪首 ¶猪首の bullnecked.

いくぶん 幾分 〈幾らか〉some ; something ; 〈一部分〉a part;《文》a portion ¶収入の幾分かを貯蓄する save something from *one's* income / 幾分か 〈部分的に〉《文》partially ; partly ; 〈やや, 多少〉rather ; to some extent ;《文》to a certain degree ;《文》somewhat. [文例⇩]

いくら 幾ら 〈量, 額〉how much?; what《is the price》?; 〈数〉how many? ¶1ポンド[ダース]幾らで売る sell by the pound [dozen] / 1日幾らで払われる be paid by the day / (金を)幾ら出しても, 幾らもらっても at any price / 幾ら…しても 〈譲歩〉however…*one does* [《文》may *do*] ; 〈…にもかかわらず〉for [with] all《our efforts》;《文》despite ;《文》in spite of / 幾ら働いても however hard *one* works [may work] / 幾ら金があっても however rich *one* is [may be] / 幾ら長く[遅く]ても at the longest [latest] / 幾らでも as much [many] as *one* likes ; any amount [number] of ; 〈金額〉any sum ; any price / 幾らか〈多少〉some ; 〈やや〉《文》somewhat ; a little ; 〈幾分〉to some extent;《文》in some measure; 〈一部分〉in part. [文例⇩]

イクラ [<《ロシヤ語》*ikra*] salmon roe.

いけ 池 a pond ¶不忍の池 Shinobazu Pond.

いけい 畏敬 《文》reverence ;《文》awe (and respect) ¶畏敬する《文》revere;《文》hold *sb* in awe ; stand in awe of *sb* / 畏敬の念を起こさせる awe-inspiring《portraits》/ 畏敬の念に打たれる《文》be struck with awe.

いけいれん 胃痙攣 convulsions of the stomach ; (stomach) cramps ¶胃けいれんを起こす get stomach cramps.

いけがき 生け垣 a hedge ¶生け垣で囲う hedge (in)《a garden》/ 生け垣を作る plant a hedge.

いけす 生け簀 a fish preserve ; a live-box ; a well (漁船の).

いけすかない いけ好かない disgusting ; nasty;《米口語》creepy《people》.

いけづくり 生け作り a freshly-killed fish served whole with its meat cut in slices.

いけどり 生け捕り ¶生け捕りにする ⇨いけどる.

いけどる 生け捕る catch [capture]《a tiger》alive.

いけない 〈してはならない〉must not *do* ; 〈すべきでない〉should not *do* ; ought not to *do* ; 〈…しなくてはならない〉must *do* ; 〈すべきである〉should *do* ; ought to *do* ; 〈禁止されている〉be forbidden ;《文》be prohibited ; 〈だめである〉be no good ; be wrong ; 〈役に立たない〉be useless ;《文》be of no use ; won't do ¶…するといけないから so that…will [may] not ; so as not to *do* ; for fear (that)… ;《文》lest…should. [文例⇩]

[用法] must と have to は「…しなければならない」「…することがどうしても必要だ」の意であるが, should はするかしないかは, それをする人の判断に任せるという感じであって, むしろ「…した方がいい」に近い. 明日の朝一番列車で出かける予定の息子に向かって, 明日は早いから「早く寝た方がいいですよ」「早く寝ないとだめですよ」と母親が言うとすれば You should go to bed early tonight. でよい. これを表現をきつくして「早く寝なくてはいけません」と言うことがありうるように, 英語でも You must… と言うことはある. しかし, 「明日の朝は早く起きなくてはいけません」は You must [have to] get up early tomorrow morning. であって, これを You should… と言うのは適切ではない. なぜならば, 早く起きなければ一番列車に間に合わないわけで, そうするかしないかを判断する余地は息子にはないからである.

いけにえ 生け贄 ⇨ぎせい¹ ¶いけにえにする

---

universities in Tokyo. / このアクセサリーのうちの幾つかをあなたに上げましょう. You may have some of these accessories. / お幾つですか. How old are you? / 彼の方が僕より幾つか年上だ. He is some years older than me [I am]. ⇨より² [用法]. / あの人は40幾つかだ. He's forty-odd years old. | He's forty-something.

いくど この絵は幾度見ても飽きない. I never tire of gazing at this picture. / 彼には幾度となく警告をしたが効き目がなかった. I warned him any number of times, but to no effect.

いくどうおん 彼らは異口同音に「そうだ!」と叫んだ. They all cried 'Yes' with one voice [in chorus].

いくぶん 今日は幾分気持ちがいい. I feel a little better today. / これで幾分か荷が軽くなったようだ. This seems to have lightened the burden somewhat.

いくら 値段は幾らですか. How much is it? | What is the price? / 幾らぐらいかかりましょうか. How much will it cost? / 幾らで買ったのか. What did you pay [give] for it? | How much did you get it for? / 全部で幾らになりますか. What does it come [amount] to? / その本なら幾ら出しても欲しい. I will pay any price to obtain that book. / 幾ら金を出しても幸福は買えない. No amount of money can buy happiness. / 彼らは幾ら働いても生活が困難だ. They find it hard to make a living [make ends meet], however hard they work. / 幾ら勇敢な人でもそれはできない. Even the bravest man could not do that. / 幾ら何でもあんまり無礼だ. There's no excuse for that sort of rudeness. / 幾らなんでもその金は受け取れません. I can't bring myself to accept the money. / 金は欲しいだけ幾らでもやる. I will give you as much money as you want. / 時間は幾らでもある. I have all the time in the world. / ブルックス先生の講義は幾らかわかった程度です. I understood only a part of Professor Brooks's lecture. / もう幾らも残っていない. There aren't many [There isn't much] left now. / 上京してから幾らもたたない. It is not long since I came up to Tokyo. / 駅までは幾らもない. The station isn't far.

いけない 5時までに帰って来なければいけないよ. You must be back by five. / この部屋ではタバコを吸ってはいけないことになっています. You are not supposed to smoke in this room. / 時計を直さなくてはいけない. The clock needs repairing. / 雨が降るといけないから傘を持って行きなさい. Take your umbrella (just) in case it rains [it should rain]. / いけない, いけないと思いながら,

いけばな 生け花〈生けること〉 ikebana; (the Japanese art of) flower arrangement; 〈生けた花〉arranged flowers ¶生け花を習う take lessons in flower arrangement.

いける¹ 生ける living; alive ¶生けるがごとき lifelike / 生けるごとく as if (it) was [were] alive; 《文》as if alive / 生きとし生けるもの all living things; 《文》all God's creatures (great and small) / 生けるしかばね a living corpse.

いける² 活ける arrange (flowers in a vase).

いける³ 埋ける〈物を〉bury sth《in the ground》; 〈火を〉cover (charcoal) with ash.

いける⁴〈酒が飲める〉can drink; can take one's drink; be a drinker; 〈よい〉nice; good; not bad (at all); not so [half] bad.

いけん¹ 意見〈考え〉an opinion; an idea; a view;〈提案〉a suggestion;〈忠告〉(a piece of) advice;〈いさめ〉《文》a reproof;《文》a reprimand;《口語》a piece of one's mind;《文》(a) remonstrance;《文》(an) admonition ¶意見する〈忠告する〉give advice (to);〈いさめる〉《口語》tell sb off;《文》reprove;《文》reprimand;《文》admonish 《sb for his carelessness》;《文》remonstrate 《against sb's behavior, with sb about his conduct》/ 意見の衝突 a conflict [clash] of opinion / 意見が合う《文》be of the same opinion; agree 《with sb about a matter》/ 意見が合わない disagree 《with sb》; differ 《with sb about [on, over] a question》/ 意見を述べる give [state, express,《文》voice] one's opinion / 意見を聞く[尋ねる] ask sb's opinion [views] / 意見を交換する exchange views [opinions] 《with sb on a subject》/ 意見を受け入れる accept sb's opinion;〈忠告を〉accept [take] sb's advice. 文例⬇

いけん² 違憲 (a) violation of the constitution ¶違憲性 unconstitutionality / 違憲立法 unconstitutional legislation.

いげん 威厳《文》dignity ¶威厳のある dignified;《文》majestic / 威厳のある人《文》a man of dignified appearance / 威厳のない undignified / 威厳を保つ maintain [keep] one's dignity. 文例

いご¹ 以後〈今後〉after this; from now on; in future;《文》hereafter;〈将来は〉in the future ¶…以後は[の] since…; after ★現在完了のあとには since を使うのが正しい: This is the greatest national event we have had since the Olympics. (オリンピック以後最大の国家的行事だ) / それ以後 since then; after that (time); from that time onward / 4月8日以後 on and after April 8 / (それから)以後の出来事 later [《文》subsequent] events. 文例⬇

いご² 囲碁 (the game of) go.

いこい 憩い ⇒きゅうけい¹, きゅうそく¹ ¶憩いの場 a place of recreation and relaxation 《for the citizens》.

いこう¹ 以降 ⇒いご¹.

いこう² 衣桁 a clothes [dress] rack; a clotheshorse.

いこう³ 威光 authority; power; influence ¶親の威光で through the influence of one's parents [father, mother].

いこう⁴ 移行 ¶移行する shift 《to》; move 《to》;《文》proceed 《to》.

いこう⁵ 移項《数》(a) transposition ¶移項する transpose (a term).

いこう⁶ 意向 one's [an] intention; one's idea [mind] ¶…する意向である intend to do; be inclined to do; have a mind to do / 意向を探る sound sb (out) 《about [on] sth》. 文例⬇

いこう⁷ 遺稿 one's posthumous manuscripts; the writings left by the deceased ¶K氏の遺稿を整理する edit the unpublished writings left by the late Mr. K.

つい, 彼の言いなりになってしまった. I let him persuade me against my better judgment. / お兄さんがご病気ですか, そりゃいけませんね. Your brother is ill? That's too bad. / 君がいけないんだ. It's your fault. | You are to blame. / このペンはいけないな. This pen won't do. Give me another. / ばねがいけないのです. Something is wrong [the matter] with the spring. / 僕はもういけない.〈万事休したか〉I can't go any further [do any more]. | That's me finished! / 何ていけない子だろう. What a naughty child you are!

いける⁴ 僕はあまりいける口じゃない. I'm not much of a drinker.

いけん¹ それについては別段意見がない. I have no opinion of my own about that. / そのことには僕は意見を述べるわけにいかない. I am not in a position to comment on that matter. / それは絶対に不可能だというのが僕の意見だ. I am of the opinion that it is absolutely impossible. / その点では君と同意見だ. I agree [I'm in agreement] with you on that point. /《口語》I can go along with you on that. / その問題では皆の意見がまちまちである. Opinion is divided on that question. / その問題については我々の意見が一致しない点が多い. There is considerable disagreement among us on the subject. / 政府部内には鋭い意見の対立がある. There are sharp differences (of opinion) within the Cabinet. / 教授会ではA案よりもB案の方とするという意見の方が強かった. The weight of opinion among the faculty was on the side of Proposal B rather than Proposal A.

いげん 氏の態度にはどことなく威厳がある. There is something dignified in his bearing. / そんな事をすると君の威厳にかかわる. That would be beneath your dignity.

いご¹ 以後こんなことをしてはいけません. You must not do a thing like this again. / 来週の火曜以後は家におります. I'll be at home on and after next Tuesday. / 44歳以後, ムンクはずっと精神に異常を来たしていたと言ってよい. From 44 years of age, Munch was almost continuously psychotic.

いこう³ 戦前の日本では父親の威光は大したものだった. In prewar Japan a father used to have great authority over his family. / その威光は遠く領外にも及んだ. His power was felt far outside the boundaries of his domain.

いこう⁶ この計画に関するあなたのご意向はいかがですか. What do you think of this plan? / 彼には辞任の意向はありません. He has no intention of resigning

いこう / いさめる

いこう[8] 憩う rest; take a rest ⇨ きゅうけい[1], きゅうそく[1].

イコール 文例↓

いこく 異国 a foreign country;《文》a strange land ¶異国風の exotic / 異国情緒 an exotic mood / 異国趣味 exoticism.

いごこち 居心地 ¶居心地がよい〈場所が主語〉be comfortable (to live in); be snug; be cozy;〈人が主語〉feel at home / 居心地が悪い〈場所が主語〉be uncomfortable;〈人が主語〉be uncomfortable; be ill at ease.

いこじ 意固地 ¶いこじな obstinate; stubborn; cross-grained. 文例↓

いこつ 遺骨 sb's remains; sb's (funeral) ashes ¶遺骨を拾う pay off one's old scores.

いこん 遺恨 a grudge; spite;《文》enmity ¶遺恨がある have [《文》bear] a grudge《against sb》/ 遺恨を晴らす pay off one's old scores; get one's revenge [《文》revenge oneself]《on one's father's murderer》; be revenged《on sb for sth》.

イコン【美術】an icon.

いごん 遺言【法】a will ⇨ ゆいごん ¶遺言者〈男〉a testator;〈女〉a testatrix / 遺言執行者 a testamentary executor.

いざ now; well; come (now) ¶いざとなれば《文》if compelled;《文》when occasion demands;《文》in case of need / いざ鎌倉という時には in an emergency;《口語》in a pinch; when it comes to the point [《口語》crunch];《口語》when the chips are down; when it comes to a showdown / いざという時の用意をしておく provide against emergencies《文》a time of necessity, a rainy day》; prepare for the worst / 人はいざ知らず私は as for me; for my part;《文》I, for one,《am of the opinion that...》. 文例↓

いさい[1] 委細 details;《文》particulars;〈事情〉the whole circumstances [story] ¶委細を話す tell everything about《a matter》; go [enter] into details [particulars]; give all the details《of》. 文例↓

いさい[2] 異彩 ¶異彩を放つ be conspicuous;《文》cut a conspicuous figure; stand out prominently (among others). 文例↓

いさかい ⇨ けんか[2].

いざかや 居酒屋 a bar;《米》a saloon;《英》a pub;《英》a public house.

いさき【魚】a grunt.

いさぎよい 潔い〈男らしい〉manly;〈未練がましくない〉sportsmanlike ¶潔く〈雄々しく〉manfully;〈未練なく〉with (a) good grace;《give in》gracefully; in a sporting spirit / 潔く負ける be a good loser; accept defeat cheerfully [with (a) good grace].

いさぎよし 潔し ¶潔しとしない be too proud to do;《文》disdain to do [doing]; be ashamed to do.

いさく 遺作 one's posthumous work(s).

いざこざ (a) trouble; a quarrel; difficulties ⇨ ごたごた.

いささか 些か a little; a bit; slightly; somewhat ¶いささかの a little; slight; insignificant / いささかも...ない not... in the least; not...at all. 文例↓

いさましい 勇ましい brave;《文》courageous;《文》valiant;〈男らしい〉manly;〈勇壮な〉stirring; dashing ¶勇ましい行ない《文》a heroic act / 勇ましいラッパの音 a stirring flourish of trumpets / 勇ましく bravely;《文》courageously;《文》valiantly.

いさみあし 勇み足【相撲】(losing a match by) stepping out of the ring unintentionally;〈比喩的に〉overreach oneself; overleap. 文例↓

いさみはだ 勇み肌 ¶勇み肌の《文》chivalrous;《文》gallant; dashing; spirited;《文》(a man) of dash and spirit.

いさむ 勇む be encouraged (by); brace oneself up;〈意気が揚がる〉be in high spirits;〈馬などが〉prance ¶勇んで in [full of] high spirits;《口語》full of beans. 文例↓

いさめ 諌め (a piece of) advice;《文》(a) remonstrance;《文》(an) admonition;《文》counsel.

いさめる 諌める advise《sb not to do》;《文》remonstrate《against sb's behavior, with sb

---

his post.

イコール 2プラス5イコール7. Two and five make [is] seven. | Two plus five equals seven. | 7−3=4 Three from seven is [leaves] four. | Seven minus three equals [is, leaves] four. | 6×5=30 Six times five is thirty. | 6 multiplied by 5 equals 30. | 15÷3=5 Three into fifteen goes five times. | 15 divided by 3 equals [is] 5.

いこじ とめると彼はますますいこじになってけります. If you try to talk him out of doing it, he will only stick to it all the more obstinately.

いざ 私はフランス語はひどい片言ですけれども、いざとなればなんとかなります. My knowledge of French is very limited, but I will be able to get by [take care of myself] when I have to [when it is necessary]. | My French is pretty dreadful, but at a pinch I expect I'll manage. / そのくらいの金は何とか出せると思っていたが、いざ細かい計算をしてみると、だめだった. At first he thought he could afford that much, but when it came to the actual counting of pennies he found he couldn't. / いざとなると、あの男は意気地なしだ. When it comes to the crunch [In a crisis], he has no backbone. / ほかの人はいざ知らず、彼に限って疑う余地はない. However it may be with other people, he is quite above suspicion.

いさい[1] 委細面談. Further details at interview. | Particulars to be arranged personally. / お手紙の件委細承知いたしました. The contents of your letter have been carefully noted.

いさい[2] 彼は独特のひげで異彩を放っていた. We couldn't miss his characteristic beard.

いささか 私はそれを聞いていささか驚いた. The news was a bit of a surprise to me. / 彼はいささかも恥じる様子はなかった. He did not seem to be the least bit ashamed. / この言葉はいささかの真理を含んでいる. This statement contains a grain of truth.

いさみあし はじめがうまく行ったのに調子付いて、勇み足をやってしまった.〈仕事などで〉I was carried away by my initial success and overstepped the mark.

いさむ その報告に一行は勇み立っ

いざり **躄** a cripple.

いざる **躄る** carry oneself on one's knees [haunches].

いさん¹ **胃酸** stomach acids ¶胃酸過多の hyperacid / 胃酸過多症 hyperacidity.

いさん² **遺産** property left [by]; a legacy; a bequest; an inheritance ¶遺産を残す leave [《文》bequeath] a fortune [an estate] / 遺産を継ぐ inherit [come into] (one's father's) property; succeed to an [sb's] estate / 遺産相続 inheritance / 遺産相続人 an heir (to property); an inheritor; a legatee (遺言状による). 文例⇩

いし¹ **石** (a) stone; a pebble (小石);《米口語》a rock;《宝石》a precious stone; a jewel ¶石の多い, 石だらけの stony; full of stones; pebbly (beaches) / 石にかじりついても at any cost; by any means; by sheer perseverance / 石うす a stone mortar [mill] / 石垣 a stone wall / 石切場 a (stone [rock]) quarry; a stone pit / 石ころ a pebble; a stone;《米口語》a rock / 石段 (a flight of) stone steps / 石造りの built of stone; stone((-built))(houses) / 石燈籠 a stone lantern / 石屋 〈石商〉a dealer in stone; 〈石工〉a stonemason; a stonecutter. 文例⇩

いし² **医師** ⇨いしゃ¶ 医師の資格のある人 a person licensed to practice medicine / 医師会 a medical association / 医師国家試験 the National Examination for Medical Practitioners / 医師法 the Medical Act.

いし³ **意志** (a) will;《文》volition ¶意志が強い be strong-willed; have a lot of will power; have a strong [an iron] will / 意志が弱い[薄弱である] have a weak will; be weak-willed / 意志薄弱な人 a weak-willed person; a person with no [not much] will power / 意志の力 will power; strength of will / 意志に反して against one's will / 自分の意志で of one's own accord [free will]; voluntarily / 意志決定 decision-making / 意志決定者 a decision-maker.

いし⁴ **意思** an intention; a wish; a purpose ¶意思が疎通する communicate with (one's children); understand each other / 意思を貫徹する carry out one's intention;《口語》have [get] one's own way / 意思能力《文》mental capacity / 意思表示をする《文》indicate one's intention;《文》express one's will.

いし⁵ **遺志** (one's father's) dying [last] wish (★この英語は「臨終に際しての最後の願い」というより広い意味で使える);《文》the desire [wish] of the deceased ¶亡父の遺志を果たす《文》carry out the intention of one's (deceased) father.

いじ¹ **意地** 〈根性〉will power; backbone; 〈誇り〉pride; 〈体面〉《文》honor ¶意地がある have a strong will; have guts [backbone] / 意地(が)きたない be mean; be greedy; be grasping;《文》be avaricious / 意地がない have no guts [backbone]; be spineless / 意地の悪い unkind; spiteful;《口語》mean;《文》malicious; ill-natured; bad-tempered / 意地の悪いことをする be unkind [《口語》nasty,《口語》mean] (to sb) / 意地を通す have one's own way / 意地を張る do not give in; be obstinate; be stubborn / 意地になって〈頑固に〉obstinately; stubbornly; 〈ひねくれて〉《文》perversely / 意地比べ a test [battle, clash] of wills (between)) / 意地悪 〈性質〉《文》maliciousness; spite; spitefulness;〈状態〉《文》ill will; 〈人〉a spiteful [a malicious,《文》an ill-natured] person / 意地悪く spitefully;《文》ill-naturedly; perversely; 〈運悪く〉unfortunately; unluckily. 文例⇩

いじ² **維持** maintenance; preservation; support; upkeep ¶維持する maintain; preserve; support; keep (up); sustain / クラブを維持する keep a club going / 維持費 (the cost of) maintenance; maintenance costs; upkeep. 文例⇩

いじ³ **遺児** a child left after its father's [mother's] death; 〈孤児〉an orphan ¶K氏の遺児 the children of the late Mr. K.

いしあたま **石頭** 文例⇩

いさん² 彼女は祖父から多額の遺産をもらった. She received a large inheritance from her grandfather.

いし¹ 道に石が敷いてある. The road is paved [flagged] with stone. / 石段を上がると赤い鳥居があります. A flight of stone steps leads you to a red torii. / 石に矢の立つためしもある. Nothing is impossible to a determined mind. | Where there's a will, there's a way. [諺] / 石の上にも三年. Perseverance will win in the end.

いじ³ そうしたのは私の意志ではなかった. I was compelled to do [　] inst my will. | I didn't do it because I wanted to. / 彼は意志の強い人だ. He is a strong-willed man [a man with a will of iron]. / あの男には自分の意志というものがない. He has no will of his own.

いし⁴ 両者は意思の疎通を欠いている. They do not understand each other. | There is a lack of understanding [a communication gap] between them. / 世代間に意思が疎通しなくなった. Communication between the generations has broken down. / そういう意思は毛頭ありません. I have no such intention at all.

いし⁵ 故人の意思により供花の儀はご辞退申し上げます. 《掲示》No flowers by request.

いじ¹ 男の意地としてやり通さなければならない. My sense of honor obliges me to carry [see] it through. / 彼はつまらない意地を張って意見を改めようとしなかった. He persisted in his opinion out of foolish pride. / 彼は止めるとかえって意地になる. Trying to dissuade him only makes him more obstinate.

いじ² 維持費が高くつく. The cost of maintenance comes high. / 維持費が払い切れない. I cannot pay the upkeep.

いしあたま あいつは石頭だ. 〈ぶつかって〉His skull is as hard as granite. 〈頑固だ〉He is as obstinate as a mule. / 彼は石頭だ. He is pig-headed. | 〈純〜〉He is really thickheaded [thickskulled].

いしき 意識 consciousness; awareness; *one's* senses ¶意識する《文》be conscious of; feel; be aware of / 意識のある[ない] conscious [unconscious]; aware [unaware] 《of》/ 意識の流れ the stream of consciousness / 意識を失う lose consciousness; lose *one's* senses; faint;《口語》pass out / 意識を回復する recover [regain] consciousness 《*one's* senses》; come to 《*oneself* [*one's* senses]》; come around [round] / 意識を深める deepen *one's* awareness 《of》/ 意識下の subconscious / 意識的に consciously; deliberately; intentionally; on purpose. 文例⊕

いしけり 石蹴り hopscotch ¶石けりをする play (at) hopscotch.

いじける 〈畏縮する〉cower; grow timid;〈ひねくれる〉《文》become perverse;〈草木が〉be stunted ¶いじけた心 a warped [《文》perverse] mind [personality].

いしだい 石鯛 a (false) parrot fish.

いしだたみ 石畳 (a) stone pavement [flooring]; flagstones ¶石畳の道 a stone-paved road / 石畳になっている be paved [floored] with stone [flagstones]; be flagged.

いしつ 異質 ¶異質の different in kind;《文》of a different nature;《文》heterogeneous;〈外来の〉foreign《to》extraneous《to》.

いしづき 石突き the ferrule 《of an umbrella》.

いしつぶつ 遺失物 a lost article; lost property ¶遺失物取扱所《米》the lost and found (office);《英》a lost property office.

いしばし 石橋 a stone bridge ¶石橋をたたいて渡る《文》make assurance double sure; act with the utmost caution.

いじめる 苛める ill-treat; treat *sb* harshly; be hard on *sb*; be cruel to (a dog); tease; annoy; bully 〈弱い者を〉. 文例⊕

いしもち 〔魚〕a croaker; a drum.

いしゃ¹ 医者 a doctor; a medical practitioner (開業医); a physician (内科医); a surgeon (外科医) ★ 単に a doctor と言っては博士の意味とまぎらわしい時は区別をつけるために、a medical doctor という ¶医者を開業している practice medicine / 医者を迎える(呼ぶ) call (in) a doctor; send for a doctor (呼びにやる) / 次から次と医者を変える go from one doctor to another / 医者に見てもらう see [《文》consult] a doctor / 医者にかかっている be under the care of a doctor; be under medical treatment;《英口語》be under the doctor 《for hepatitis》.

いしゃ² 慰謝 (a) consolation;《文》(a) solace ¶慰謝する console;《文》solace / 慰謝を求める[見出す] seek [find] solace 《in religion》/ 慰謝料 compensation; damages; consolation money.

いじゃく 胃弱 dyspepsia; indigestion ¶胃弱の人 a dyspeptic / 胃弱である be dyspeptic; suffer from indigestion; have a weak stomach.

いしゅ 異種 a different kind [species]; a different variety.

いしゅう 異臭 a nasty [a foul,《文》an offensive] smell;《口語》a stink;《文》a stench ¶異臭を放つ give out a foul smell [stench]; stink.

いじゅう 移住 migration (人種・動物などの); emigration (外国への); immigration (外国よりの);〈転居〉a move; (a) removal ¶移住する a migrate; settle 《in》; emigrate 《to》(外国へ); immigrate 《into》(外国から);〈転居する〉move / 移住者[民] an emigrant; an immigrant; a settler / 移住地〈行き先〉the place where *one* is going to live;〈移住した所〉the place in which *one* has settled. 文例⊕

いしゅがえし 意趣返し ¶意趣返しをする get [have] *one's* revenge 《on *sb*》;《文》revenge *oneself* [be revenged]《on *sb* for *sth*》; retaliate 《against *sb*》; get even 《with *sb*》; have [get] *one's* own back 《on *sb*》. 文例⊕

いしゅく¹ 委縮 ¶委縮する 〈物が〉wither; shrink; shrivel;〈器官が〉become atrophied; atrophy.

いしゅく² 畏縮 ¶畏縮する shrink [flinch]《from》;《文》quail《before, at》; cower《before》;《文》be daunted《by》; be dispirited.

いじゅつ 医術 (the art of) medicine.

いしょ 遺書 〈書き置き〉a note left behind (by a deceased person); a farewell note; a suicide note (自殺者の);《文》a testamentary letter (特定の人に宛てた);〈遺言書〉a will; *one's* last will and testament.

いしょう¹ 衣装 clothes; dress;〈時代・地方などに固有の〉(a) costume ¶現代衣装のハムレット a modern-dress version of *Hamlet*; *Hamlet* in modern dress / 衣装をつける dress *oneself* 《in》; put on the costume 《of Benkei》/ 時代劇の衣装をつけた俳優 an actor wearing

---

いしき その問題が再び彼の意識の前面に押し出されてきた。The problem once again rose to the surface of his consciousness [came to the front of his mind]. / 病院に担ぎ込まれた時、彼は意識不明だった。He was unconscious [senseless] when he was carried into the hospital. / 彼は死ぬ 3 時間前まで意識があった。He was conscious [retained his consciousness] until three hours before his death. / 多くの人は自分

people are hardly aware of the danger they are in.
いじめる そんなにいじめないでくれ。Don't be so mean to me [hard on me].
いしゃ¹ 目が悪くて医者にかかった。I had eye trouble and saw the doctor. / 医者の不養生。Physician, heal thyself!【諺】
いじゅう ダム工事のため、村民は何代も住みなれた村から移住させられた。To make way for the construction of a new dam, they

tions.
いしゅがえし これは彼が意趣返しにした事だ。He has done this in revenge [by way of retaliation].
いしょう¹ 彼女はマリー・アントワネットの衣装をつけていた。She was costumed as Marie Antoinette.
いじょう¹ 以上. 〈終わり〉Concluded. [《通信》Over. / これ以上言う事はない。I have nothing more to say. / 20 歳以上の方でないと応募できません。Candidates

historical costume / 芝居の衣装 a theatrical [stage] costume / 嫁入り衣装 a bride's outfit / 衣装好みの fond of clothes / 衣装持ちである have a lot of clothes ; 《文》 have a large wardrobe / (芝居の)衣装方 a costumer / 衣装屋 a costumier. [文例⇩]

いしょう[2] 意匠 a design ¶意匠を作る draw [make] a design / 意匠を凝らした elaborately designed [《文》 wrought] / 意匠権 design right / 意匠登録 registration of a design.

いじょう[1] 以上 ¶以上の〈数量が〉 more than; over ; above ; 〈程度が〉 beyond ; past ; further 《than》; 〈上記の〉《文》 the above(-mentioned); the 《book》 mentioned above ; 《文》 foregoing ; 《文》 aforesaid ; 《文》 the said / …する以上は 〈…だから〉 since… ; now that… ; seeing that… ; 〈…する限りは〉 so long as… ; 〈…したからは〉 once… ; 〈いやしくも(…するからは)〉 if…at all / 6歳以上の子供 children of six years and up [upward] ; children from six years up; children, six years and over; children over six years old / 500円以上千円まで from 500 to 1,000 yen / 収入以上の暮らしをする live beyond [above] *one's* income / 想像以上である be more than *one* can imagine. [文例⇩]

[用法] たとえば，複数の定義をするのに，「2つもしくはそれ以上」というのを英語では more than one と簡単に言える．もっと大きな数について，たとえば100以上と言うとき日本語では多く100を含むが，英語で more than [over, above, upward of] 100 と言えば100は含まないので，正確を期するならば not less than 100 ; 100 or more ; 100 and over と言う必要がある．しかし，日常的には more than, over で充分間に合う．

いじょう[2] 委譲 transfer; 《文》 devolution ¶(権限などが)委譲される be transferred [passed] 《to *sb*》; 《文》 devolve 《on *sb*》.

いじょう[3] 異状 〈故障〉 something wrong ; 《nothing is》 the matter ; an accident ; 〈変化〉 (a) change ; 〈狂い〉 disorder ; 〈身体の〉《文》 (an) indisposition ; (a) disorder ¶異状がある something is wrong 《with》; 〈脈拍などが〉 be abnormal ; 〈機械などが〉 be out of order ; 〈人が〉《文》 be indisposed / 精神に異状がある be mentally disturbed ; be (mentally) deranged / 異状がない be all right; be normal; be in good order / 異状のある abnormal ; 〈故障のある〉 wrong ; faulty ; 《文》 defective ; 〈狂っている〉 《文》 disordered ; deranged (精神などの) ; 〈病に冒された〉 affected ; 《文》 diseased. [文例⇩]

いじょう[4] 異常 ¶異常な〈普通でない〉 unusual ; extraordinary ; 《文》 singular ; abnormal ; 〈著しい〉 remarkable ; 〈非凡な〉 uncommon / 異常気象 abnormal weather / 異常接近〘航空〙 a near miss.

いしょく[1] 衣食 food and clothing ; 〈生計〉 a living ; a livelihood ¶衣食住 food, clothing and shelter. [文例⇩]

いしょく[2] 委嘱 ¶委嘱する ask [《文》 request] *sb* 《to *do*》; commission 《a painter to paint a mural》 / …の委嘱によって at the request of… / 委嘱作品 a commissioned work. [文例⇩]

いしょく[3] 移植 transplanting; transplantation; 〘医〙 a transplant ; grafting ¶移植する transplant ; graft 《skin》 / 腎臓移植を受ける receive a kidney transplant / (皮膚·臓器の)被移植者 the (graft) recipient ; the host.

いしょく[4] 異色 ¶異色の out of the ordinary ; uncommon; unconventional; unusual; unique; 《文》 singular.

いじらしい 〈愛らしい〉 lovable ; sweet ; 〈無邪気な〉 innocent ; 〈哀れな〉 pitiful ; touching ; pathetic.

いじる 弄る 〈指で〉 finger ; fumble ; 〈もてあそぶ〉 play [toy] with 《*one's* food》; 《口語》 mess [fool] (about) with 《the equipment》; tamper [tinker] with 《a tool》; monkey [fiddle] (about [around]) with 《a machine》; 〈触れる〉 touch ; handle. [文例⇩]

いしわた 石綿 asbestos.

いしん[1] 威信 prestige ; 《文》 dignity ¶威信を傷つける injure the prestige 《of》; let *sb* down / 威信を失墜する lose *one's* dignity / 威信を保つ maintain *one's* prestige [dignity] / 威信にかかわる affect *one's* prestige [dignity]. [文例⇩]

いしん[2] 維新 ⇨ めいじ[2] (明治維新).

いじん 偉人 a great man.

いじんしゅ 異人種 an alien [a different] race.

いしんでんしん 以心伝心 《文》 tacit understanding ; telepathy ¶以心伝心で《文》 tacitly ; by telepathy ; telepathically. [文例⇩]

いす 椅子 a chair ; 〈長[寝]椅子〉 a sofa ; a lounge ; a couch ; 〈地位〉 a post ; a position ¶(食堂の)子供用高椅子 a high chair / 椅子の腕[背, 脚, 座部] the arm [back, legs, seat] of a chair / 大臣の椅子 the portfolio 《of education》 / 教授の椅子を占めている hold a chair

---

以上出していた. The jet plane was flying at more than [doing better than] 500 mph. / 以上が氏の論説の大要である. The above is the gist of his article. / 生きている以上は働かねばならない. So long as we live, we have to work. / 何事もいったん決心した以上はあくまでもやり通す人だ. Once he makes up his mind to do something, he never stops until he achieves it.

いじょう[3] エンジンに異状がある. Something is wrong [the matter] with the engine. | The engine is out of order. / 部屋の中は何の異状もなかった. Everything was in good [perfect] order in the room. | I didn't notice any sign of disturbance in the room. / 悲しみのあまり精神に異状を来たしたらしい. Grief has apparently deranged his mind.

いしょく[1] 衣食足って礼節を知る. Fine manners need a full stomach.

いしょく[2] 彼はN響から交響曲の作曲を委嘱された. He received a commission from the NHK Symphony Orchestra to compose a symphony.

いじる 単に行政機構をいじるだけでは実効は上がらないであろう. Nothing practical would be gained by merely fiddling about with the machinery of government.

いしん[1] 我が国の威信を保ち得るかどうかという場合である. Our national prestige is at stake.

いしんでんしん お互いの心は以心伝心で何となくわかっていた. We were in some kind of telepathic communication (with each other).

いすか 《鳥》a crossbill ¶いすかの嘴(はし)と食い違う be at cross-purposes.
いずこ ⇒どこ ¶いずこも同じ be the same.
イズベスチヤ Izvestia.
いずまい 居住まい ¶居住まいを正す sit up straight; straighten *oneself*.
いずみ 泉 a spring; a fountain ¶知識の泉 《文》a font [fount] of knowledge.
イスラエル (the State of) Israel ¶イスラエル人〈現代の〉an Israeli (*pl*. -lis, (集合的) -li); 〈古代イスラエル王国の〉an Israelite / イスラエル(人)の〈現代の〉Israeli; 〈古代の〉Israelite.
イスラム ¶イスラム教 Islam / イスラム教徒 a Muslim; ((*pl*. -s)) / イスラム世界 the Islamic world; 《throughout》Islam.
いずれ 何れ 〈どちら〉which ⇒どちら, どれ; 〈どのみち〉anyway; anyhow; at any rate; 〈いずれまた〉some other time; another time; 〈やがて〉in (course of) time; sooner or later (早晩); 〈結局〉after all ¶真偽いずれにもせよ whether it is true or not; いずれの場合においても in all cases; in either case (2つの場合) / いずれかのうち one of these days; before (too) long. 文例↓
いすわる 居座る 〈居続ける〉stay on (at); 〈留任する〉stay [《文》remain] in the same position [in office]; 〈権力の座に〉stay [《文》remain] in power.
いせい¹ 威勢 〈元気〉spirit; dash; 〈勢力〉power; influence; authority ¶威勢のいい (high-) spirited; dashing; lively; snappy; energetic; vigorous; full-blooded / 威勢のない《文》spiritless; listless; lifeless / 威勢をつける encourage; cheer up / 威勢よく in high spirits; vigorously; 《口語》full of go. 文例↓
いせい² 異性 the other [opposite] sex ¶初めて異性を知る have *one*'s first sexual experience / 異性に目ざめる be sexually initiated; 《文》undergo *one*'s sexual initiation / 異性関係 relations [relationships] with the opposite sex / 異性体《化》an isomer.
-いせい ...以西 ¶箱根以西に[の, は] (to the) west of Hakone; (at) Hakone and westward.
いせいしゃ 為政者 an administrator; a statesman.
いせえび 伊勢蝦 a (spiny) lobster.
いせき¹ 移籍 ¶(プロスポーツの選手が)移籍される be transferred (to the Tigers).
いせき² 遺跡 remains; ruins ¶先史時代の遺跡 a prehistoric site. 文例↓
いせつ 異説 a different view [theory]; 《文》conflicting views [theories] ¶異説を立てる 《文》dissent from (the orthodox theory).
いせん 緯線《地理》a parallel (of latitude); a latitude line.
いぜん¹ 以前 〈今から見て〉ago; 〈その時から見て〉before; since; 〈かつて〉once; on an earlier occasion; 〈昔〉《文》formerly; 《文》in former times ⇒もと ¶ ...以前は...だった [した] used to be... [*to do*] / 以前の《文》former; previous; past; one-time / 以前のとおり as before / ずっと以前に long ago; a long time ago / 以前よりも (work harder) than before [*one* used to]. 文例↓
いぜん² 依然 〈依然として〉still; as...as ever; as ((it) was) before; as (it) used to be / 依然として変わらない be [《文》remain] unchanged. 文例↓
いせんじょう 胃洗浄 ¶胃洗浄を行なう administer a stomach pump (to *sb*); carry out a gastric lavage.
いそ 磯 a beach (浜); (a) shore (岸); the seashore ¶磯伝いに along the beach / 磯魚 an inshore fish / 磯釣り fishing from the rocks on the shore; (go) surf fishing / 磯料理 a seafood meal [dish].

いす 彼は社長の椅子をねらっているのだ。He's got his eye on the job of president of the company.
いずこ インフレはいずこも同じ, パリでも人々の悩みの種だ。People are suffering from inflation in Paris, just as everywhere else.
いずれ いずれそんな事になるだろうと思った。I expected as much. | That's what I expected. / いずれそのうちにご返事いたします。I will send you an answer one of these days.
いせい 全く威勢のいい男だ。He's a really energetic fellow. |《口語》He's a real live wire. / 口先は威勢がいいが気の小さい男なのだ。He certainly uses aggressive language but in reality he's something of a coward.
いせき この付近には歴史上の遺跡が多い。This neighborhood abounds in historic sites. / 城は荒廃してわずかに遺跡だけが残っている。Nothing is left of the castle but ruins.
いぜん¹ 僕らはずっと以前からの知り合いです。We have known each other for a long time. / 以前何度も行ったことがあるのでその辺の地理はよく知っていた。I was familiar with the neighborhood, as I had been there several times before. / この彫刻は紀元 500 年以前のものと考えられている。This sculpture is dated A.D. 500. / 彼は以前とはまるで変わった人間になった。He has become quite a different man. / 以前と比べて今は暮らしがずっと楽になった。We are much better off than we used to be.
いぜん² この契約は依然有効であるThis contract holds good even now.
いそいそ(と) チャイムが鳴ると, 彼女はいそいそと立ち上がって玄関にジムを迎えた。At the sound of the chimes, she sprang to her feet [stood up with alacrity] and went to the door to greet Jim.
いそうろう 居候三杯目にはそっと出し。The nonpaying lodger puts out his bowl very diffidently for a second refill of rice.
いそがしい 年末は商店は忙しい。The shops are busy toward the year-end. / 今日は一日中忙しかった。I've had a busy [full] day today. | I've been busy [on the go] since morning. / 私はいろいろ忙しいので散歩する暇もありません。I have so many things to attend to that I have no time even to take a walk. / お忙し

いそいそ(と) delightedly ; joyfully ; 〈進んで〉《文》with a will ; willingly ; 《文》with alacrity. 文例⇩

いそう¹ 位相 【電・物】a phase ¶位相が合っている[いない] be in [out of] phase (with) / 位相幾何学 topology / 位相差 a phase difference / 位相差顕微鏡 a phase(-contrast [-difference]) microscope.

いそう² 移送 ¶移送する transport ; 《文》convey ; carry ; transfer.

いそうがい 意想外 ⇨ **よそう**¹ (予想外).

いそうろう 居候 a lodger (with a family) who pays nothing for his board and lodging ; 〈賤んで〉a sponger ; 《米口語》a freeloader ; 《英口語》a scrounger ¶居候をする live rent-free ; live off [sponge on] sb ; 《米口語》freeload (on sb) / 居候生活《米口語》freeloading. 文例⇩

いそがしい 忙しい be busy ; be occupied ; be engaged (仕事中) ¶忙しい仕事 pressing work ; urgent business / 仕事に忙しい be busy [at] one's work / 試験の準備に忙しい be busy preparing for the examination ★ busy のあとは直ちに doing をつける. be fully occupied. be busily engaged と言えば be busily engaged in doing を続ける / 忙しく, 忙しそうに busily ; in a hurried manner / 忙しく暮らす lead a busy life / 忙しく立ち働く busy oneself (in (doing)).

いそぎ 急ぎ《文》haste ; hurry ¶急ぎの hurried ; hasty ; 〈さし迫った〉pressing ; urgent / 急ぎの注文 an urgent order / 急ぎ足で with hurried [hasty] steps ; at a quick pace / 急ぎ足になる quicken one's pace.

いそぎんちゃく 【動】a sea anemone.

いそぐ 急ぐ hurry (up) ; 《文》hasten ; 《口語》step on it ★ make haste は文例に挙げたような場合にしか使わない. step on it は「アクセルを踏む」の意味の転用で go faster の意 ¶できるだけ急ぐ hurry as much as one can ; 《文》make as much haste as possible / 仕事を急ぐ hurry [speed] up one's work / 道を急ぐ hurry on one's way ; hurry along / 成功を急ぐ be in a hurry [too eager] for success / 急いだあまり in one's hurry ; in a hurry (in) ; 《文》in haste ; 〈あわてて〉hastily ; hurriedly ; 〈猶予なく〉without delay / 急いでいる be in a hurry ; 〈口語〉be in a rush ; 《文》be in haste / 急いで立ち去る hurry off [away] / 急いで出かける hurry out / 急いで帰る hurry back ; 〈家に〉hurry [《文》hasten] home / 急がせる hurry up [on] ; 《文》hasten ; speed. 文例⇩

いぞく 遺族 a bereaved family ; 《文》the family of the deceased ¶戦死者の遺族 the war bereaved / 遺族年金 a survivor's pension.

いそしむ 勤しむ ⇨ **はげむ** ¶仕事にいそしむ《文》work diligently [assiduously] / 読書にいそしむ devote oneself to [bury one's head in] one's books.

イソップものがたり イソップ物語 Aesop's Fables.

いそん 依存 ¶依存する depend (on) ; 《文》be dependent (on) ; rely (on) / ...に依存するところが大きい depend [rely] heavily on... / 依存度 dependence (on) ; reliance (on). 文例⇩

いぞん 異存 ⇨ **いぎ**² ¶異存がある have an objection (to) / 異存がない have nothing to say (against) ; have no objection (to). 文例⇩

いた 板 a board ; a plank (厚板) ; 〈金属板〉a plate ; a sheet (薄い) ; a slab (平板状の石・金属など) ¶板を張る, 板張りにする board (over) ; lay boards (on) / 板張りの boarded ; board-lined (walls) / 板で囲う, 板囲いする board up [in] ; enclose with boarding / 板についている be at home (in) / 板石 a stone slab ; a flagstone (敷石用) / 板戸 a wooden door / 板塀 a board fence.

いたい¹ 遺体《文》the remains ; the (dead) body ¶遺体を安置する lay out the remains / 遺体を収容する recover the remains / 遺体で見つかる be found dead / 遺体安置所 a mortuary. 文例⇩

いたい² 痛い 〈痛む〉hurt ; be painful ; be sore ; be tender ; smart (ぴりぴり痛む) ; 〈つらい〉be trying ; be hard to bear ¶頭[腹]が痛い have a headache [stomachache] ; have [feel] a pain in one's head [stomach] / 目[のど]が痛い have sore eyes [a sore throat] / 触ると痛い 〈患部が

ところをおじゃま致しました. Excuse me for having taken up your precious time. / お忙しいところをおいでいただきまして有り難うございました. Thank you very much for coming, right in the middle of your day.

いそぐ 急げ! Hurry up! | Be quick! / 彼はひどく急いでいた. He was in a great hurry [big rush]. / なぜそんなに急ぐのか. Why are you in such a hurry? | What's the [your] rush? / 別に何も急ぐことなんかいらない. I'm in no hurry. | I'm not in any rush. / どんなに急いでいる時でも, 彼は結核して病床の私を見舞ってくれた. However much of a hurry he was in, he always found time to visit me in my sickbed. / 物事は急いではだめだ.

It's no good rushing things. / 急ぐことはない. There's no hurry. / 別に急ぐ仕事ではなかった. There was no urgency about the job. / 急いで持っておいで. Bring it here quick. / (物語などの途中で)ところで, 話の先を少々急ぎましょう. But let's hurry [rush] things a little. / 急がばまわれ. More haste, less speed. 【諺】 | Make haste slowly. 【諺】 | The farthest [longest] way about is the nearest way home. 【諺】

いそん 米国の国防は主としてミサイルに依存している. For its defense, the U.S. places its main reliance [depends chiefly] on missiles. / 大気中の空気に全く依存せずにエンジンが開発されて, 初めて潜水艦の建造が可能になったのだった. It was the de-

velopment of an engine which could operate in total independence from atmospheric air that made possible the construction of the submarine.

いぞん ご異存がなければそのようにさせていただきます. I'll do it that way, if you don't mind. / 少しも異存はない. I have not the slightest objection (to it).

いた 彼の先生ぶりも板についてきた. Now he looks quite at home before the blackboard. / 背広姿が板についていない. A business suit looks [sits] well on him. / まだ背広姿が板についていない. He doesn't look comfortable [at home] in a business suit yet.

いたい¹ 遺体の引き取り手がない. No one has claimed the body.

主語〉 be sore to the touch / 痛い敗北をこうむる suffer a stinging defeat / 痛い目にあう suffer; have a bitter experience / 痛い目にあわせる teach sb a lesson; give sb a good thrashing; make sb suffer [smart] [for it] / 〈人の〉痛い所〈弱点〉 one's weak point; 〈触れられたくないところ〉 one's sore [sensitive] spot [point] / 痛い所を突く strike sb at his most vulnerable point / 痛くもかゆくもない 〈事が主語〉 do not affect one at all; 〈自分が主語〉《口語》don't give a damn;《口語》couldn't care less / 痛くもない腹を探られる be unjustly suspected;《文》incur groundless suspicion / 痛さ a pain.
文例D
用法 「痛い所を突く」を touch sb on the raw とすると「突いた」ことよりも、むしろそれに対する相手の反応、たとえば怒りの、激しさが予想される表現となる。

いだい 偉大 ¶偉大な great; grand / 偉大な業績 a great achievement.

いたいいたいびょう 痛い痛い病 *itai-itai* [ouch-ouch] disease, so called because of its extremely painful effects, caused by cadmium poisoning from industrial wastes in Toyama Prefecture.

いたいけ innocent; helpless ¶いたいけな少女《文》a girl of tender age.

いたいたしい 痛々しい pitiful; pathetic ¶見るも痛々しいほどやせている be painfully thin.

いたがね 板金 a metal plate; sheet metal.

いたガラス 板ガラス plate glass (厚手の); sheet glass (薄手の).

いたがる 痛がる complain of a pain ¶痛がって泣く cry with pain [in one's pain]. 文例D

いたく 委託《文》trust;《文》charge;《文》commission; 〈販売の〉consignment ¶委託する《文》entrust sth with sth [sth to sb]; put [《文》place] sth in sb's charge; commission sb to do; 〈商品を〉consign (goods for sale to a firm) / 委託加工 processing on commission / 委託金 money in trust; a trust fund / 委託研究 contract research / 委託販売 consignment sale / 委託販売する sell (goods) on commission / 委託品 consigned goods; a consignment.

いだく 抱く 〈腕に〉hold [take] (a child) in one's arms;《文》embrace; 〈心に〉entertain;《文》cherish;《文》harbor;《文》nurse; hold ¶不安の念をいだく feel uneasy / 大望をいだく have an ambition.

いたけだかに 居丈高に domineeringly; high-handedly; overbearingly;《口語》in a high and mighty manner ¶居丈高になる take [《文》adopt,《文》assume] an overbearing attitude.

いたご 板子 a plank ¶板子一枚下は地獄である have only a plank between *one* and perdition; be only four inches from death.

いたしかた 致し方 ⇒しかた.

いたしかゆし 痛し痒し ¶痛しかゆしである be in a dilemma (a fix, an awkward position); be faced with a difficult choice (between two alternatives).

いたじき 板敷き a board floor.

いたす 致す 〈する〉do; 〈もたらす、招く〉《文》bring about; lead to.

いたすだれ 板簾 a Venetian blind ¶板すだれを下ろす let down (the slats of) a Venetian blind.

いたずら¹ 悪戯 〈悪さ〉(a piece of) mischief; an escapade; 〈悪ふざけ〉a prank; a practical joke; a trick ¶悪質ないたずら malicious mischief / いたずら半分に half for [in] fun / いたずら(を)する do mischief; be mischievous; play a trick [joke, prank] (on); 〈もてあそぶ〉play with (fire); 〈女性に〉molest / いたずらをしている[始める] be in [get into] mischief / いたずらをさせないでおく keep (a boy) out of mischief / いたずらっ子 a mischievous boy; a child full of mischief / いたずら盛りの男の子 a boy at his most mischievous age ¶いたずら書き ⇒らくがき / いたずらっぽい目つきをして with impish eyes; with mischief in one's eyes. 文例D

いたずら² 徒ら ¶いたずらに 〈無益に〉pointlessly; in vain; to no purpose; uselessly; 〈当てもなく〉aimlessly; 〈安閑と〉idly / いたずらに日を暮らす live in idleness; idle one's time away / いたずらに金を使う spend money uselessly; waste [throw away] one's money / いたずらに騒ぎ立てる make a great fuss [《文》make much ado] about nothing.

いただき 頂 the top; the summit; the peak; 〈頭・帽子の〉the crown ¶山の頂に at the top of a mountain.

いただく 頂く 〈かぶっている〉wear (a crown); be crowned (with); be capped (with); 〈頂戴

いたい² おお痛い。Ouch! It [That] hurts! / どこが痛いのですか。Where does it hurt? / Where's the pain? / 痛くはなかったですか。I hope I didn't hurt you. / 少しも痛くない。It doesn't hurt at all. / やむを得ず200万円支払ったが、これは痛かった。I had to pay two million yen, though it broke my heart to (do it). / 痛い所をついたね。You've got me there! / You've found my weak point, haven't you! / そこが彼の痛い所なんだ。That's a sore point with him. / He's very sensitive [口語 touchy] about it [that]. / 彼が失敗したところで、僕は痛くもかゆくもない。I couldn't care less [It doesn't matter to me at all] whether he has failed or not.

いたがる 先生、患者がひどく痛がっています。Doctor, the patient is in terrible pain!

いたずら¹ 彼らは何かいたずらをたくらんでいる。They are up to something [some mischief or other].

いただく その山は頂上に雪を頂いている。The summit of the mountain is covered with snow. / The mountain is crowned with snow. / その協会は宮様を会長に頂いている。The society has a Prince as its president. / この本を頂いてもいいですか。Can I have this book? / 全部で3,500円頂きます。That will be [The price is] 3,500 yen altogether. / ドアを閉めていただけませんか。May I trouble you to shut the door? / 充分頂きました。Thank you. I have had enough. ★食事を始めるときの「いただきます」の英語では言わない / この小説はセンチメンタル過ぎて、私にはいただけませんな。

いたたまれない

する〉 have ; get ;《文》receive ; accept ; take ; be paid ;〈...してもらう〉get *sb* to *do* ; have *sb do* ;〈飲食する〉have ; eat ; drink ; take ¶ありがたく頂く accept *sth* gratefully [with thanks] / 雪を頂く山 a snow-capped[-crowned] mountain / ...していただきたい I would like [I want] you to *do* /〈遠慮しながら〉I wish you would *do*. 文例◯

いたたまれない 居たたまれない be unable to stay (on) ¶居たたまれなくする make it (too) hot (for *sb*). 文例◯

いたち【動】a weasel ¶えぞいたち a Siberian ermine / 本土いたち a Japanese mink.

いたちごっこ《be in》a vicious circle ¶物価と賃金のいたちごっこ a wage-price spiral.

いたチョコ 板チョコ a bar of chocolate.

いたって 至って very (much) ;《文》exceedingly ; extremely.

いたで 痛手 a severe [serious] wound ;〈大打撃〉a heavy [hard] blow ¶痛手を負う be seriously [badly] wounded ;〈傷を〉sustain a serious wound ;〈打撃を受ける〉get a severe blow ; be hard hit 《by》/ 痛手を負わせる《on》; inflict a wound《on》/ 痛手を与える give *sb* a heavy blow.

いだてん 韋駄天 ¶韋駄天走りに走る run like (a streak of) lightning.

いたのま 板の間〈床〉a wooden floor ;〈部屋〉a room with a wooden floor.

いたばさみ 板挟み ¶板挟みになる be caught [placed] in a dilemma 《between》; be torn between conflicting demands.

いたぶき 板葺 ¶板ぶきの shingle-roofed 《houses》/ 屋根を板ぶきにする cover the roof with shingles / 板ぶき屋根 a shingle roof.

いたまえ 板前 a cook ; a chef.

いたましい 痛ましい〈哀れな〉sad ; pitiful ;《文》pitiable ; touching ; pathetic ;〈惨めな〉miserable ; wretched ¶見るも[聞くも]痛ましい《文》heart-rending ;《文》harrowing.

いたみ 痛[傷]み a pain ; an ache ; a sore ; a smart (ひりひりする痛み) ; a sting [stinging pain] (刺すような痛み) ;〈心痛〉pain ;《文》a grief ;〈損傷〉damage ; a bruise (果物などの) ¶激しい痛み a severe [a sharp,《文》an acute] pain / 痛みを感じる[感じない] feel a [no] pain ⇨いたむ² / 痛みを軽くする ease 《文》allay the pain ; make the pain easier / 痛み止め a painkiller ;【医】an anodyne. 文例◯

いたみいる 痛み入る〈恐縮する〉be [feel]

71

いたる

greatly [extremely] obliged 《to *sb*》;〈すまないと思う〉be very sorry 《for》;〈恥じ入る〉feel ashamed 《of》. 文例◯

いたむ¹ 悼む mourn ;《文》grieve 《for》;《文》lament ;〈惜しむ〉regret ¶友の死を悼む mourn [lament] (over) the death of *one's* friend / 悼むべき《文》lamentable.

いたむ² 痛[傷]む have [《文》suffer from] a pain ;〈局部が〉ache ; hurt ; be sore ; be tender ; smart (ひりひりする) ;〈損傷をうける〉be hurt ; be damaged ;〈腐敗する〉go bad ; spoil ; be spoiled ;〈英口語〉go off ; go sour (牛乳が) ¶歯[頭]がひどく痛む have a bad toothache [headache] / *one's* tooth [head] aches terribly / 腹が痛む feel a pain in *one's* stomach ; have a stomachache / 傷んだ[傷みかかった]肉 tainted [stale] meat / 傷みやすい品〈壊れもの〉a fragile article ;〈なまもの〉perishable goods ; perishables. 文例◯

いため 板目〈板の木目〉the grain [veins] of a board ;〈柾(まさ)目に対して〉a cross grain.

いためつける 痛め付ける deal *sb* a severe blow ; treat *sb* harshly ; take *sb* to task.

いためる¹ 炒める fry ; frizzle (かりかりになるまで) ¶いため物 fried food.

いためる² 痛める, 傷める〈傷つける〉hurt ; injure ;〈そこなう〉spoil ; damage ;《文》impair ;〈悩ます, 苦します〉pain ; worry ;《文》afflict ¶心を痛める be troubled [《文》pained]《by》; be worried《about》; trouble [worry] *oneself* 《about》.

いたらない 至らない〈行き届かない〉imperfect ; unsatisfactory ;〈経験不足な〉inexperienced ;〈不注意な〉careless ; not attentive enough ¶至らない所 *one's* faults ; *one's* shortcomings.

いたり 至り the height 《of folly》¶若気の至りで carried away by *one's* youthful enthusiasm [《文》ardor]. 文例◯

イタリア Italy ¶イタリアの Italian /〈地図で見た〉イタリアのかかとの部分 the heel of Italy / イタリア共和国 the Republic of Italy / イタリア語 Italian / イタリア人 an Italian.

イタリック〈活字〉italic type ;《printed in》italics ¶イタリック(体)にする italicize ; put in italics. 文例◯

いたる 至る〈来る〉come ;〈到着する〉arrive 《at, in》; reach ; get《to》;〈及ぶ〉come《to》; 《to》; extend《to》;〈(...するように)なる〉begin

---

This novel is too sentimental for my liking [to suit me].
いたたまれない 恥ずかしくて居たたまれなかった. I was too ashamed to stay on [stay there any longer].
いたって 私は至って字が下手です. My writing is very poor.
いたましい それは見るも痛ましい光景だった. It was a harrowing sight.
いたみ 痛みが取れた. The pain has gone. | It doesn't hurt any more [longer]. | 彼女は突然胃に

激しい痛みを覚えた. She suddenly felt a severe pain in her stomach. | A terrible pain took her suddenly in the stomach. | 品物の傷みは思ったよりひどかった. The goods were far more badly damaged than had been expected.
いたみいる 大変お手数をかけて痛み入ります. I am very sorry to have given you so much trouble.
いたむ² どの歯が痛みますか. Which tooth is it that hurts [that is giving you the pain]? /

霜で葉が傷んだ. The frost has nipped the leaves. | 私の家は古くなって方々傷んでいる. My house is an old one and there are quite a few places that need repair. / 牛乳は傷みやすい. Milk spoils [goes sour] easily.
いたり 大成功の由, 慶賀の至りに存じます. I should like to congratulate you most sincerely on your achievement.
イタリック〈引用文に注記して〉イタリックは本稿筆者のもの. (Present) author's italics. | My italics.

to *do*; 〈結果が…に〉なる〉end [〈文〉result] (in); 〈口語〉end up *doing*; lead (to) / …と信ずるに至る come to believe that... / 発狂に至らしめる drive *sb* mad / …に至るまで to...; up [down] to...; until...; till... / 今に至るまで until now; to this day; up to the present (time) / 社長から守衛に至るまで from the president down to the doorkeepers / ここに至って at this point / 至る所 everywhere; wherever *one* goes; all over the place; 〈文〉 throughout (the country) / 世界の至る所から from all parts [every corner] of the world. 文例❶

いたれりつくせり 至れり尽くせり ¶至れり尽くせりである be perfect; be thorough; leave nothing to be desired. 文例❶

いたわり 労り 〈思いやり〉consideration; 〈同情〉sympathy; 〈親切〉(a) kindness (shown to an old woman).

いたわる 労る 〈思いやりを示す〉be considerate (to); 〈慰める〉console; 〈大事にする〉take (good) care of; be kind (to); treat *sb* kindly.

いたん 異端 (a) heresy; heterodoxy ¶異端者 a heretic.

いち¹ 一 one; 〈数〉(greater [smaller] than) unity ¶第1 the first / (トランプの)ハートの1 the ace of hearts / 一から十まで in everything; 〈文〉in every particular; 〈文〉all without exception / 一も二もなく〈すぐに〉readily; without a second thought; 〈文句なしに〉without asking questions; without question; 〈きっぱり〉pointblank; flatly / 一も二もなく断わる refuse flatly; give *sb* a flat refusal / 一か八かやってみる take *one's* chance (on (doing) *sth*); take a risk; chance it / 一を聞いて十を知る 〈口語〉be quick on the uptake; have a very perceptive mind / 一対一の会談 a man-to-man talk / 一対一の対応 a one-to-one correspondence. 文例❶

いち² 市 a market; a fair ¶市の立つ日 a market day / 市へ出す take (*one's* produce) to market.

いち³ 位置 〈場所〉a place; a position; a location; 〈地位〉a position; 〈身分〉*one's* status; standing; 〈立場〉a place; a stand ¶位置がよい[悪い] be in a good [bad] position; 〈文〉be well [badly, ill] situated [located] / 位置を変える change [shift] (*one's*) position / (船などで)星を観測して自分の位置を知る get [get a fix by the stars / 位置につく take *one's* position [place]; go into [take up] position / 位置エネルギー 〈物〉potential energy / 位置付け placement (of different occupational categories).

いちあん 一案 an idea; a plan. 文例❶

いちい¹ 一位 the first place [rank]; 〈文〉the foremost place [position] ¶一位を占める rank [stand] first; be at the top (of *one's* class); head [top] the list (of); 〈文〉hold the foremost place (among).

いちい² 〈植〉a (Japanese) yew (tree).

いちいち 一々 〈一つ一つ〉one by one; 〈文〉severally; 〈ことごとく〉every one (of them); 〈文〉without omission; 〈詳しく〉in detail; fully. 文例❶

いちいん 一員 a member (of).

いちいんせい 一院制 the single-chamber [unicameral] system.

いちえん 一円 ¶関東一円で throughout [all over] the Kanto region.

いちおう 一応 〈仮に〉tentatively; 〈さし当たり〉for the present; for the time being; at least; 〈まず〉in the first place; first; 〈一度〉once ¶今一応 once more; again / なお一応相談の上で after further consultation / 一応目を通す run (*one's* eyes) through.

いちがいに 一概に 〈十把一からげに〉sweepingly; wholesale; 〈無差別に〉〈文〉indiscriminately; 〈無条件に〉〈文〉without reservation; unconditionally. 文例❶

いちがつ 一月 January (略: Jan.).

いたる 道は箱根をへて三島に至る。The road leads to Mishima via Hakone. / 本線はまだ開通の運びに至らない。This line is not yet open to traffic. / やがて彼をよく知るに至った。I soon got to know him better. / それがもとで彼は一大발足をなすに至った。That led him to make a great discovery. / 経営方針の誤りから1億円の欠損を見るに至った。The adoption of an unwise business policy resulted in a deficit of ¥100 million. / 事ここに至っては策のほどこしようがない。Now that things have come to this pass, there is nothing that can be done to remedy the situation. / あの会社はほとんど全国至るところに支店がある。That company has branches in almost every part of the country. / 微細な点に至るまで注意が払われていた。Attention was paid to the minutest details.

いたれりつくせり 彼らは安藤氏から至れり尽くせりのもてなしを受けた。They received every imaginable [every sort of] service from Mr. Ando. | They were waited on hand and foot by Mr. Ando.

いち¹ 体育の先生は、「一二、一二」と掛け声をかけた。The physical education teacher called out, 'One-two, one-two.' / 知者には一を聞いて十を知る。A word to the wise is enough. 【諺】/ 一を聞いて十を知るという君ではないか。One word should be enough to a man of your intelligence. / あの人の命令に一から十まで服従する訳にはいかない。I cannot obey him in everything. / 彼は一も二もなく同意した。He was only too glad to consent. / 一か八かやってみよう。I'll give it a try, sink or swim.

いち² この通りに毎朝市が立つ。Every morning a fair is held on this street. / 今日は市の立つ日だ。This is the day for the fair.

いち³ 位置について。〈作業場などで〉Places! / 位置について、用意、ドン。〈競走の号令〉On your marks, get set, go! 〈正式〉Ready, steady, go! (子供の運動会の)/ 警察署は町の中央に位置している。The police station is [located, situated] in the center of the town.

いちあん それは確かに一案だ。That's certainly a possibility [a good idea]. / それも一案として考慮に値する。That is worth considering as an alternative.

いちいち する前に一々私に断わるには及ばない。You don't have to tell me everything that you are going to do.

いちがん 一丸 ¶一丸となって united ; in a body. 文例⇩

いちがんレフ 一眼レフ a single-lens reflex camera.

いちく 移築 ¶移築する dismantle 《a historic building》 and reconstruct 《it》 at a different place. 文例⇩

いちぐう 一隅 ¶一隅を a nook.

いちげい 一芸 ¶一芸に秀でる be a master of an art ; 《文》 be proficient 《in sth》. 文例⇩

いちげき 一撃 ¶一撃を加える a blow ; a hit ¶一撃の下に at [with] one [a single] blow / 一撃を加える give [deal] sb a blow. 文例⇩

いちげん 一元 ¶一元的 unified / 一元化する unify / 一元論《哲》 monism.

いちげん² 一言 ⇒いちごん ¶一言居士《文》 a ready critic ; a person who has something to say on anything and everything.

いちご¹ 一期 ¶50歳を一期として 《die》 at the age of fifty.

いちご² 一語 a (single) word ¶一語一語 《translate sth》 word by word ; 《read it out》 one word at a time.

いちご³ 苺 《実》 a strawberry ; 《植物》 a strawberry (plant) ¶いちご畑 a strawberry field / いちごクリーム strawberries and cream.

いちころ 一ころ ¶一ころでやっつけてしまう trounce ; beat sb hands down ; 《口語》 walk (all) over sb ; 《英口語》 knock spots off sb ; 《俗》 clobber sb.

いちごん 一言 a (single) word ; one word ⇒ひとこと ¶一言する speak [say] a word 《about》 / 一言もない have no word to say in excuse [to offer in apology] / 一言のもとにはねつける reject 《sb's request》 pointblank [flatly] / 一言半句もゆるがせに weigh one's words carefully ; be very careful in one's choice of words. 文例⇩

いちざ 一座 《人々》 the party ; all those present ; 《文》 the (whole) company ; 〈劇団〉 a company (of players) ; a troupe.

いちじ¹ 一字 one letter ¶一字一句そのとおりに literally ; 《文》 verbatim.

いちじ² 一次 ¶一次の first ; primary / 第1次吉田内閣 the first Yoshida Cabinet / 一次方程式 a linear [first-degree, simple] equation / 一次産業［産品］ primary industries [products] / 一次試験 a first-stage examination / 一次冷却水 primary [first-stage] coolant.

いちじ³ 一事 one thing ¶一事不再理《法》 the principle of not debating the same matter twice during the same session ; a prohibition against double jeopardy. 文例⇩

いちじ⁴ 一時 〈時刻〉 one o'clock ; 〈かつて〉 (at) one time ; once ; 〈しばらく〉 for the time [while] ; 〈当分〉 for the present ; for the time being ¶一時的(的) temporary ; 《文》 impermanent ; 《文》 momentary ; 《文》 passing / 一時預かり所〈劇場・レストランなどの〉 a cloakroom ; 〈駅・空港などの〉《米》 a checkroom ;《英》 a left luggage office / 一時預かり証 a claim check / 一時預けにする leave 《one's baggage》 at a 《station》 checkroom / 一時帰休制 a layoff system / 一時金 a lump-sum payment / 一時しのぎ a makeshift ;《文》 a temporary expedient ; a stopgap (measure) / 一時逃れの言い訳を言う make an excuse to gain [buy] time / 一時払い payment in a lump sum. 文例⇩

いちじく 〈木〉 a fig tree ; 〈実〉 a fig.

いちじつ 一日

いちじゅん 一巡 ¶一巡する make a tour of 《the whole building》 ; make a [the] circuit of 《the lakeshore》 / 始めに戻るを be back 《come back to》 where one started / 打者一巡する go once through 《their》 batting order.

いちじょ 一助 ¶一助となる be helpful 《to sb, in doing》 ; be of some help 《toward》. 文例⇩

いちじょう 一条 ¶一条の光線 a streak of light / 一条の煙 a wisp of smoke.

いちじるしい 著しい remarkable ;《文》 marked ; conspicuous ; striking ;《文》 salient ;《文》 pronounced ;《文》 notable ¶著しい対照 a strik-

---

いちおう 一応彼の意見を聞いてみなければならない。 We cannot go without at least asking his opinion. / 念のため一応書類を調べてみて下さい。 Please run through the papers to make sure. / 一応もっともな言い分だが、それで皆の賛成が得られると思うか。 That sounds reasonable, to be sure, but do you think everybody will agree to it?

いちがいに 一概にそうとばかりは言えない。 One cannot make that kind of sweeping generalization. / そう一概にけなすものではない。 You should not run them down so indiscriminately.

いちがん これは SF と推理小説と歴史を打って一丸としたような作品だ。 This work is science fiction, mystery, and history all in one [rolled into one].

いちく これは飛騨の民家を移築したものです。 This is an old house brought over from the Hida district and reassembled here.

いちげい 何事も一芸に秀でるのは容易なことではない。 It is no easy matter to be a master of any art [make oneself master of any art].

いちげき あごに一撃かと食らわせてやった。 I dealt [landed] him one on the jaw.

いちご 一期一会。〈茶道の教え〉 Treasure every meeting, for it will never recur.

いちころ この手でいけば彼は一ころだ。 With this trick you're sure to get him. / 彼は彼女の魅力に一ころだった。 He fell for her in a big way.

いちごん 一言ごあいさつ申し上げます。 Ladies and gentlemen, may I say a few words to you by way of greeting. / 会議の席上で彼は一言も発言しなかった。 He did not utter a word [kept absolute silence] throughout the conference. / 一言半句も他人にもらすな。 Do not breathe a word [syllable] of it to anyone. / ここで当時のローマの法律について一言しておく必要があると思う。 I think the topic [subject] of Roman law at that time calls for some comment here.

いちじ³ 一事が万事だ。 You can judge all the rest by this single instance.

いちじ⁴ 一時は盛んなものだった。 He was prosperous in his day. / 彼は昔better days. He has seen better days.

いちじつ その事にかけてはあちらは君より一日の長がある。 He is a little more experienced than you in that line.

いちじょ 本書が英語研究者の一助となるならば幸いである。 I would feel amply rewarded for my ef-

ing [sharp] contrast / 著しく remarkably ; 《文》 markedly ; strikingly.

いちじん 一陣 ¶一陣の風 a gust of wind.

いちず 一途 ¶一途な人 a single-minded person / 一途に 〈心をこめて〉 with all *one's* heart ; wholeheartedly ; 〈盲目的に〉 blindly ; 〈単純に〉 simply / 一途に思いこむ be obsessed with the idea 《that...》.

いちぜん 一膳 〈一杯〉 a bowl 《of rice》 ; 〈一対〉 a pair 《of chopsticks》.

いちぞく 一族 *one's* (whole) family ; the 《Minamoto》 clan ; 〈親族〉 relatives ; 《文》 kinsmen ¶一族郎党を引き連れて with *one's* family and followers.

いちぞん 一存 ¶一存で at *one's* own discretion ; on *one's* own responsibility. [文例⇩]

いちだ 一打 〖野球〗 a [one] hit ¶一打同点のチャンス a chance to even the score with one hit. [文例⇩]

いちだい 一代 〈一世代〉 one [a] generation ; 〈一生〉 *one's* lifetime ¶一代で築き上げた財産 a fortune of *one's* own making / 一代の英雄 the greatest hero of the age / 一代記 a biography ; a life / 一代雑種 an F_1 hybrid. [文例⇩]

いちだいじ 一大事 a serious [《文》 grave] matter ; 《文》 a matter of great [some] consequence ; an emergency ⇨ たいへん[2]. [文例⇩]

いちだん[1] 一団 a group ; a party ; a body ; 〈劇団〉 a troupe ¶一団となる form a group ; band [bunch] together ; bunch up (together) / 一団となって in a body [group] ; 《文》 en masse. [文例⇩]

いちだん[2] 一段 〈階段の〉 a step ; 〈はしごの〉 a rung ; a round ; 〈階級の〉 a degree ; a grade ; 〈章句の〉 a paragraph ⇨ だん[2] ¶一段上がる[下がる] rise [fall] a degree / 一段と進歩する 《文》 make further progress ; take a step forward / 一段と声を張り上げる raise *one's* voice a pitch higher. [文例⇩]

いちだんらく 一段落 ¶一段落する reach a stage where *one* can take a rest 《from *one's* work》 ; be settled for the time being ; complete the first stage 《of the work》 ; 《口語》 break the back of 《a job》.

いちど 一度 〈1回〉 once ; one time ; 〈ある時に〉 once ; on one occasion ¶一度に 〈一回に〉 at a time ; at a stretch (続けて) ; 〈一挙に〉 all at once ; at a stroke ; 〈いっしょに〉 all together ; 〈同時に〉 at the same time / 一度に1つ[2つ]ずつ 《deal with》 one [two] at a time / 一度で 〈一回の試みで〉 at one try ; on the [*one's*] first try ; at a [one] go / 1年に1度 once a year / 今一度 once more ; (once) again / 一度きり 〈1回だけ〉 only once ; 〈今回限り〉 (just) for once ; 〈これを限りに〉 once (and) for all / 一度ならず more than once ; again and again ; repeatedly / 一度も 〈...しない〉 never ; not once. [文例⇩]

いちどう[1] 一同 all ; the whole 《staff》 ¶我々一同 all of us / 家族一同 all *one's* family / 職員生徒一同 the teachers and pupils ; the whole school / 一同を代表して on behalf of everybody. [文例⇩]

いちどう[2] 一堂 ¶一堂に会する gather [meet together] in a hall [room].

いちどき 一時 ⇨ いちど, いちじ[4].

いちどく 一読 ¶一読する read 《a book》 through ; look 《a report》 over ; run *one's* eyes over 《a paper》. [文例⇩]

いちなん 一難 [文例⇩]

いちに 一二 one or two ¶1, 2年 a year or two ; one or two years / 1, 2度 once or twice. [文例⇩]

いちにち 一日 a [one] day ; 〈終日〉 all day (long) ; the whole day ; from morning till [to] night ¶1日か2日で in a day or two / 1日分の仕事 a day's work / 1日3回 three times a day / 1日置きに every other day ; on alternate days / 一日増しによくなる get better every day [day by day] / 一日延ばしに延ばす put *sth* off from day to day / 一日千秋の思いで待つ wait impatiently 《for *sb's* arrival》 ;

---

forts if this book proved helpful to students of English.

いちぞん こういう重大なことは君の一存で決めてはいけない. You ought not to decide such a serious matter by yourself.

いちだ 一打逆転のチャンスだ. With one hit we can turn the tables (on them). / この一打に勝敗がかかっている. Whether they win or lose depends on the next swing of the bat.

いちだい 彼は一代で巨額の財産を作った. He amassed an enormous fortune in the course of his lifetime. / それは氏一代の失策だった. That was the greatest mistake of his whole career.

いちだいじ これは一大事だ. This is serious. / 国家の一大事だ. The fate of the country is at stake.

いちだん[1] シャラーが先頭になり他の5人の走者が一団となってそれを追っている. Schaller has taken the lead, with the other five bunched behind him.

いちだん[2] あのドレスだと彼女は一段と魅力的に見える. That dress adds to her beauty. | She looks even more charming [attractive] in that dress.

いちど 一度見ればたくさんだ. One look is enough. / 一度このルールを呑み込んでしまえばあとはむずかしいことはない. Once you understand this rule, you will have no further difficulty. / 一度に2つの事をするな. Do not attempt to do two things at a time.

いちどう[1] 一同承諾した. They all gave their consent. / ご成功を家族一同と共にお祝い申し上げます. My family joins with me in congratulating you on your success.

いちどく この一節は一読しただけでは理解できないでしょう. I doubt if you'll be able to understand this paragraph on first reading. / この本は一読の価値がある. This book is (well) worth reading.

いちなん 一難去ってまた一難. Out of the frying pan into the fire. 〖諺〗

いちに 彼はこの町で一二を争う金持ちだ. He is one of the richest men, if not the richest man, in this town.

いちにち 一日一善. 〖標語〗 One good deed a day. / 春の一日家族連れで軽いハイキングに出かけた. One day in spring [One spring day] I went on a gentle hike with my family. / 朝は桜の花が一日中で一番美しく見える. The cherry blossoms appear to best advantage in [during] the morning. / 一日として彼が実験室に出かけな

いちにん 一任 ¶一任する leave *sth* entirely to *sb* [*sb's* discretion];《文》entrust *sb* with *sth*; give *sb* a free hand to *do*. 文例⇩

いちにんしょう 一人称《文法》(in) the first person ¶一人称単数[複数] the first person singular [plural] / 一人称小説 [<《ドイツ語》*Ich-Roman*] a first-person novel.

いちにんまえ 一人前〈1人分〉a portion for one person;〈食事の〉one helping (of soup) ¶1人前千円 1,000 yen per person [portion] / 一人前の〈1人分の〉for one person;〈成人した〉grown-up; adult;〈独立の〉independent; self-supporting;〈資格充分な〉full-fledged [《英》fully-fledged]《sailors》/ 一人前の賃金をとる receive pay at the full rate / 一人前になる〈成年に達する〉come of age;《文》attain manhood [womanhood]; become a man [woman];〈独立する〉become independent; stand on *one's* own (two) feet. 文例⇩

いちねん¹ 一年 one [a] year ¶1年に1度 once a year; annually / 1年に1度の annual; yearly / 一年中 all the year round [through]; throughout [all through] the year; all year (long); at all times of the year; the year (whole) round [through] / 1年生 a first-year student /《米》a first-grade pupil (小学校の);《米》a freshman (大学・高校等の);《英》a fresher (大学の);〈初心者〉a beginner / 小学一年生になる《米》enter [start] the first grade;《英》start school / 一年生議員〈代議士〉a newly elected Dietman / 一年生植物 an annual plant; an annual.

いちねん² 一念〈熱心〉enthusiasm;《文》zeal;〈決意〉determination;〈願い〉《文》an ardent wish ¶一念こめて…する *do* with *one's* whole heart; make a concentrated effort to *do*.

いちば 市場〈常設の〉a shopping center [precinct];〈定期的に開かれる〉a market; a marketplace ¶魚[青物]市場 a fish [vegetable] market.

いちはつ《植》an iris; a fleur-de-lis (*pl.* fleurs-).

いちはやく 逸早く quickly; promptly; without (a moment's) delay. 文例⇩

いちばん 一番〈第1位〉No. 1; the first (place);〈勝負〉a game; a round; a bout ¶一番の first (diagram); (figure) (number) one; the best (player) / クラスで1番の生徒 the best student in the class / 1番になる get [take] first place; come (in) [finish] first / ためしに一番やってみる have a go [try] (at (*doing* *sth*)) / 一番大きい the largest (piece) / 一番先の the front (desk); the first;《文》the foremost / 一番後の the rear; the last; (the seat) furthest [nearest the] back;《文》the hindmost / 一番手 the first (person) (to *do*) / 一番鶏 the first crow of the cock / 一番乗り the first (person) to arrive / 1番バッター《野球》the lead-off man / 1番星 the first star of evening / 1番列車 the first train. 文例⇩

いちひめ 一姫 文例⇩

いちびょう 一病 文例⇩

いちぶ¹ 一分 ¶一分のすきもない watertight《reasoning》/ 一分のすきもない服装をしている be impeccably dressed.

いちぶ² 一部〈一部分〉a part; a portion; a section;〈印刷物の〉a copy ¶一部の過激派《apart from》a small group [section] of extremists / 一部の人たち some people / …の一部をなす form (a) part of… / 一部修正する make a partial amendment《of the regulations》.

いちぶいちりん 一分一厘 ¶一分一厘も違わない be quite the same; be exactly alike; be identical;《英口語》there is not a hap'orth of difference《between》.

いちぶしじゅう 一部始終 all the details; everything《about》¶一部始終を語る《文》give full particulars《of》; give a complete [full] account《of》; tell the whole story. 文例⇩

いちべつ¹ 一別 ¶一別以来 since I saw you last; since we last met;《文》since last

い日はなかった. Not a day passed that he did not go [without his going] to the laboratory.

いちにん 私は学校の経営を一任されている. I have been put in sole charge of the affairs of the school. | The management of the affairs of the school has been entrusted to me.

いちにんまえ あの男を一人前の人間にしてやろう. I will make a man (out) of him.

いちねん 1年は365日だ. There are 365 days in a year. | A year has 365 days. / 1年の計は元旦にあり. New Year's Day is the day for planning [making plans for] the coming year. | Decisions made on New Year's Day are the key to a successful year.

いちはやく 彼はそれを聞いていち早く駆けつけた. Directly he heard of it he rushed to the place. / 彼はいち早くそれを利用した. He was quick to take advantage of it.

いちばん 彼はクラスで1番だ. He is top of the class. / 彼は数学では(クラスで)1番だった. He was top in mathematics. | He was best in the class in mathematics. / 彼は試験に1番で及第した. He passed the examination first on the list. | He came first in the examination. / 私の買った宝くじは当たりくじと1番違いだった. The number on the lottery card I had bought turned out to be the very next one to the winning number. / 私はこれが一番好きだ. I like this best. / 黙っているのが一番だ. You had best keep silent. / 碁を一番やろうか. Shall we have a game of *go*? / 1957年のスプートニクの打ち上げでソ連は宇宙開発競争の一番乗りを果たした. The Soviet Union was first off the mark [scored a first] in the space race with the launching of Sputnik in 1957.

いちひめ 俗に一姫二太郎と言う. It is commonly said that it is good to have a daughter first and then a son.

いちびょう 一病息災. People with a slight ailment will be more careful and live longer than those who are never ill.

いちぶ² これは彼の収集のほんの一部に過ぎない. This is only (a) part of his collection. / 彼は一部の人には評判が悪い. He is spoken badly of in some quarters.

いちぶしじゅう 彼は一部始終を知っている. He knows all [everything] (there is to know) about it.

いちべつ² 一瞥 ¶一瞥する glance 《at, on》; cast a glance 《at》; shoot a look 《at》 / 一瞥して at a glance. 文例↓

いちぼう 一望 ¶一望千里の海原 an unlimited [a boundless] expanse of ocean / 一望の中に収める command a (sweeping) view of; have a bird's-eye view of. 文例↓

いちまい 一枚 a sheet [piece] (of paper); a copy (of a photograph) ¶皿1枚 a [one] plate / 役者が一枚上である be a cut above *sb*; be one up on *sb* / 一枚加わる get in on the [*sb's*] act; weigh in (議論やけんかに) / (劇団の)一枚看板 a box-office draw. 文例↓

いちまつ 一抹 a touch 《of melancholy》; a tinge 《of sadness》 ¶一抹の不安を感じる feel slightly uneasy; feel some [a certain] anxiety 《about》.

いちまつもよう 市松模様 checks; a check [《米》checkered, 《英》chequered] pattern ¶市松模様の checked; 《米》checkered 《英》chequered.

いちみ 一味 〈徒党〉(fellow) conspirators; 〈一団〉a gang 《of robbers》. 文例↓

いちみゃく 一脈 ¶一脈相通じるものがある have something in common 《with》.

いちめい¹ 一名 〈1人〉one person; 〈別名〉another [a second] name; an alias ¶一名...という名も知られる...; also called... 文例↓

いちめい² 一命 ⇒いのち.

いちめん 一面 a surface; a side; 〈全面〉the whole surface; 〈様相〉《文》an aspect; 〈文〉a phase; 〈新聞の〉the front [first] page ¶顔一面に all over *one's* face / 一面の火となる be completely enveloped in flames / 一面においては... on the other hand... / (新聞が)第一面で報道する report *sth* on the front page; make a front-page report of *sth*. 文例↓

いちもうさく 一毛作 single-cropping 《of rice》. 文例↓

いちもうだじん 一網打尽 ¶一網打尽に捕える make a wholesale [summary] arrest 《of》; round up 《a gang of criminals》.

いちもく 一目 〈基盤の〉a point ¶一目置く 《文》acknowledge *sb's* superiority 《to *oneself*》; 《文》yield the palm 《to》 / 一目瞭然である be quite obvious; be as plain as day [as a pikestaff, as the nose on your face].

いちもくさん 一目散 ¶一目散に at full speed; as fast as *one's* legs can carry *one* / 一目散に逃げる run (away) for *one's* [dear] life; take to *one's* heels; show *sb* a clean pair of heels.

いちもつ 一物 《俗》*one's* prick ¶胸に一物ある have an ulterior motive; have an axe to grind; have some plot [《文》further design] in *one's* mind.

いちもん¹ 一文 a penny; a farthing ¶一文惜しみの penny-pinching / 一文なしになる become penniless; 《俗》go (flat [《英》stony]) broke; 《俗》be cleaned out.

いちもん² 一門 〈一族〉a family; a clan; 〈家族〉*one's* kinsfolk; 〈宗派〉the whole sect ¶平門 the Taira clan; the Tairas.

いちもんいっとう 一問一答 (a series of) questions and answers. 文例↓

いちもんじ 一文字 ¶一文字に in a straight line / 口を一文字に結ぶ set *one's* lips / 口を一文字に結んで with *one's* lips closed tight [firmly set].

いちや 一夜 ¶一夜にして in one [a single] night / 一夜を明かす〈寝て〉pass a night 《at, in》; 〈寝ずに〉sit [stay] up all night / 一夜漬け〈漬け物〉pickles salted overnight; 〈勉強〉cramming (for an examination).

いちやく 一躍 ¶一躍して a [one] bound; at a jump [a leap] / 一躍世界第2位になる jump to [vault into] second place (as an exporter of cars).

いちゃつく flirt 《with》; 《口語》make up 《to》; 〈2人が主語〉bill and coo.

いちゃもん ¶いちゃもんをつける pick a fight [quarrel] with *sb*; needle 《*sb* about *sth*》; niggle 《at *sb*》; find fault 《with *sb* [*sb's* actions]》; pick holes 《in what *sb* has done》.

いちゅう 意中 *one's* mind; 《文》heart, intention] ¶意中の人 the person *one* is thinking

---

いちべつ² 彼は僕には一瞥もくれないで去った。He went away without taking any notice of me.

いちぼう 頂上からは周囲の景色を一望の中に収めることができる。From the summit we can get a full view [The summit commands a panoramic view] of the scenery in the surrounding country.

いちまい これはとてもいい機械だと思っていたが、こんど出た新型はその又一枚上を行くものだ。I have regarded this as a very good machine, but the new model that has recently come out has gone one better. / 行政整理は内閣の一枚看板だ。Administrative personnel reduction is the only policy the present Government has to its name. / 彼はその謀略に一枚嚙んでいた。He had a hand [was involved] in the plot.

いちみ 彼はその一味に加わっていた。He was one [a member] of the group. | He was a party to the plot.

いちめい 料金はご1名様300円です。The charge is 300 yen each [per head].

いちめん その話には聞くも涙の一面がある。The story has a sad side to it. / 彼の行為は非難すべきだが、一面また同情すべき所もある。Of course he should be blamed for what he did, but, on the other hand, he also deserves our sympathy. / 空は一面黒雲におおわれている。The sky is completely covered with dark clouds. / 池には氷が一面に張っている。The pond is frozen over. / この事件は全米の新聞の第一面のニュースになった。The affair hit [made] the front pages of newspapers throughout the U.S.

いちもうさく この土地では一毛作しかできない。The land yields only one crop a year.

いちもく あの人には一目も二目も置いている。I admit that he is in every way my superior. | I can't hold a candle to him.

いちもん¹ 一文惜しみの百失い。Penny wise and pound foolish. 〈諺〉| To lose [spoil] the ship for a hap'orth of tar.

いちもんいっとう 記者会見で次のような一問一答が行なわれた。問..., 答... The following questions and answers were exchanged [The following exchanges took

of ; 〈恋人〉《文》the man [girl] closest to *one's* heart / 意中を明かす open [《文》bare] *one's* heart《to》; 《文》disclose *one's* intention《to》; 《文》unbosom *oneself*《to》.

いちょ 遺著 a posthumous work.

いちよう 一様 ¶一様の 〈均一の〉 uniform ; equal ; even ; 〈同一の〉 the same ; identical / 一様の服装をしている be all dressed alike / 一様に《文》uniformly; equally; evenly ; alike; in the same way. [文例⇩]

いちょう[1] 医長 the head physician [doctor].

いちょう[2] 胃腸 the stomach and intestines ¶胃腸が悪い[丈夫だ] have poor [good] digestion / 胃腸病 a gastrointestinal disorder / 胃腸薬 a medicine for the digestive organs [for the digestion] ; a digestive.

いちょう[3] 〔植〕a ginkgo《*pl.* -es》; a maidenhair tree.

いちよく 一翼 ¶一翼を担う play a [*its, one's*] part《in the industrialization of the region》; contribute《to the progress of medical science》; have a share《in this country's foreign trade》.

いちらん 一覧 ¶一覧する take [have] a look at ; look [read] through ; run (*one's* eyes) through / 一覧払い為替手形 a bill payable at [on] sight ; a sight [demand] bill [draft] / 一覧後30日払い payable at thirty days after sight / 一覧表 a table ; a list. [文例⇩]

いちらんせいそうせいじ 一卵性双生児 identical twins.

いちり 一理 [文例⇩]

いちりいちがい 一利一害 [文例⇩]

いちりつ 一律 ¶一律に 〈均等に〉《文》uniformly ; evenly ; 〈無差別に〉 impartially / 一律7％の昇給 an across-the-board wage increase of 7 per cent. [文例⇩]

いちりづか 一里塚 a milestone ; a milepost.

いちりゅう 一流 ¶一流の 〈第一級の〉 first-class ; first-rate ; 《文》of the first class [rank, order] ; top-ranking ; (one of) the best ; foremost ; 〈…特有の〉《文》peculiar《to》; characteristic《of》/ 一流会社 (one of) the top-ranking companies / 一流校 (one of) the best(-known) schools. [文例⇩]

いちりょうじつ 一両日《for》a day or two ¶一両日中に in a day or two.

いちりん 一輪 〈花〉 a (single) flower ¶(花が) 1輪2輪と咲き始める come out one by one / 一輪ざし a single-flower vase.

いちる 一縷 ¶一縷の望み《there is》a ray of hope.

いちるい 一塁 first base ¶一塁に出る get [go] to first base ; make [reach] first base / 一塁手 the first baseman / 一塁手をやる play first base / 一塁線 the first base line.

いちれい[1] 一礼 ¶一礼する make a bow.

いちれい[2] 一例 an example ; 《文》an instance ¶一例を挙げれば for example [instance] ; to take [《文》cite, give] an [a single] example / 多くのうちの一例を挙げれば to take one example of many. [文例⇩]

いちれつ 一列 a line ; a row ; a rank (横の) ; a file (縦の) ¶一列に並ぶ form [stand in] a line [row, 《英》queue (バスなどを待って)] / 一列縦隊で進む march (in) single file.

いちれん 一連 ¶一連の a series of《questions》; a chain of《events》/ 一連番号 consecutive numbers / 一連番号をつける number《the cards》consecutively.

いちれんたくしょう 一蓮託生 ¶一蓮託生である《文》share *sb's* fate ; 《口語》be in the same boat.

いちろ 一路 ¶一路サンフランシスコに向かう head [go] straight for San Francisco.

いちわ 一羽 ¶一羽の雀 a sparrow.

いつ when? ; (at) what time? ; how soon? ⇨ いつか[2], いつでも, いつにない, いつのまにか, いつまで, いつも ¶いつごろ about what time? / いつから since when? ; how long? ; from what time? / いつぞや 〈先日〉 the other day ; some time ago ; 〈かつて〉 once / いつなんどき at any moment [time]. [文例⇩]

いつう 胃痛 a pain in the stomach ; (a) stomachache.

いつか[1] 五日 five days ¶5月5日 May 5 (★

---

place] at the news conference : —Q...., A....

いちやく 氏はその小説を書いて一躍文壇に名を成した. He leaped to literary fame by writing that novel. / 種痘の発見でジェンナーはイギリスの田舎の無名の一開業医から, 一躍, 国際的に有名になった. The discovery of vaccination catapulted Jenner from the obscurity of a rural British practice into international fame.

いちよう これらすべてを一様に律する訳にはいかない. We can't apply the same rule to all of them.

いちらん ご一覧に供します. I submit this for your inspection. / ご一覧の上お返し下さい. Please return it to me after looking through it.

いちり 彼の言うことも一理ある. There is some truth in what he says.

いちりいちがい 新政策には一利一害がある. The new policy has both advantages and disadvantages [merits and demerits].

いちりつ それは一律には扱えない. They cannot be treated in the same way. / 本俸の2か月分プラス一律2万円がボーナスとして支給された. Twice the amount of the basic monthly salary with an uniform addition of 20,000 yen was given as a bonus.

いちりゅう 彼は現代一流の物理学者だ. He is one of the most eminent physicists of the day. / これは彼一流の文体である. This is his characteristic style.

いちれい[2] これはほんの一例に過ぎない. This is only one instance among many. | This is simply a case in point.

いつ 奈良はいつ行ってもいいところだ. We find Nara pleasant [We enjoy Nara] whenever we visit it. / 彼はいつ行っても留守だった. Every time I called, he was out. / いつ頃からここに来ているのですか. How long have you been staying here? / それからいつしか10年が経った. Ten years had passed before we were aware of it. / いつ出発しようか.—いつでもいい. When shall we start? —Any time will do. / それはいつ出来上がりますか. When will it be ready [finished]? / いつとはなしに眠ってしまった. Without realizing it I fell asleep. / いつなりとお出で下さい. Come any

いつか (May (the) fifth と読む); the fifth of May.

いつか[2] 〈未来の〉 some time; sometime; at some future time; (at) some time or other; some day; someday; one day; 〈過去の〉 some time; sometime; (at) some time or other; once; one day; the other day (先日); 〈時が来れば〉 in due course; in time; 〈いつのまにか〉 ⇒ いつのまに ¶ またいつか some other time [day] / 来週のいつか some [sometime] next week / いつかそのうち one of these days; soon; before long; in the near future / いつかしら (at) some time or other; 〈早晩〉 sooner or later; 〈結局〉 in the long run. 文例⇩

いっか 一家 a family; a household; 〈家族〉 one's family ¶ 一家の主人 the master of a house; the head of a family / 一家の収入 the family income / 一家を成す 〈構える〉 make a home of one's own; 〈芸術家などが〉 make a name; establish one's fame 〈as a novelist〉; develop a style of one's own / 浜田一家 the (whole) Hamada family; (all) the Hamadas / 一家言 an (independent) opinion of one's own / 一家心中 a suicide of an entire family. 文例⇩

いっかい 一介 ¶ 一介の a mere 〈student〉; only 〈a salesman〉. 文例⇩

いっかい[2] 一回 〈1度〉 once; one time ⇒ いちど; 〈勝負の〉 a round; a game; a bout 〈拳闘などの〉; the first inning (野球の) ¶ 1週に1回 once a week / 1回で〈1度に〉 at a time / 〈1回の試みで〉 in one try 〈口語〉 go, attempt; 〈pass the test〉 at one's first attempt [go]; 〈succeed in sth〉 on one's first try / 1回戦 〈の第一試合〉 the first game; 〈トーナメントの〉 the first round / (薬の)1回分 a dose.

いっかい[3] 一階 〈米〉 the first floor; 〈英〉 the ground floor; 〈公共建築物などの〉 the street floor; the main floor (デパートなどの) ★〈英〉では the first floor は「二階」. ⇨ かい[6] 用法

いっかく[1] 一角 a corner; 〈動〉 a narwhal ¶ 天の一角を見つめる gaze fixedly at the sky.

いっかく[2] 一廓 a block.

いっかくじゅう 一角獣 a unicorn.

いっかくせんきん 一攫千金 ¶ 一攫千金をたくらむ人 a person who plans to make quick money; a get-rich-quick schemer / 一攫千金を夢見る dream of making a fortune at a stroke.

いっかせい 一過性 ¶ 一過性の temporary; 〈文〉 transitory.

いっかつ[1] 一括 ¶ 一括する 〈引っくるめる〉 lump together; 〈概括する〉 sum up; summarize / 一括して in a lump; 〈文〉 collectively / 一括契約 a blanket contract / 一括提案 a package proposal / 一括払い a lump-sum payment; (a) payment in a lump sum. 文例⇩

いっかつ[2] 一喝 ¶ 一喝する thunder (out); roar.

いっかな ⇒ いかに(どうしても).

いっかん 一巻 a volume; a book ¶ 第1巻 the first volume; Volume One; Vol. I. 文例⇩

いっかん[2] 一貫 ¶ 一貫した consistent / 一貫して consistently; from first to last / 一貫している be consistent / 一貫作業 one continuous operation / 一貫生産の integrated 〈steelworks〉. 文例⇩

いっかん[3] 一環 ¶ 一環をなす be [〈文〉 form] a link in the chain (of events); form a part of (the campaign).

いっき[1] 一気 ¶ 一気〈呵成(いつ)〉に at a [one] stretch (stroke); 〈at a breath〉 / 一気に飲み干す drink 〈one's sake〉 down [up] in a single draft [gulp] / 一気に丘を駆け登る run up a hill at a dash; run right up to the top of a hill / 一気に3時間しゃべりまくる rattle on nonstop for three hours. 文例⇩

いっき[2] 一揆 a riot; an uprising ¶ 一揆を起こす rise in a riot.

いっき[3] 一騎 a (single) horseman ¶ 一騎打ち (a) single combat; a man-to-man fight [combat] / 一騎当千のつわもの a mighty warrior.

いっき[4] 逸機 missing a chance [an opportunity].

いっきいちゆう 一喜一憂 ¶ 一喜一憂する be

---

time you like. / いつなんどき彼が来るかもしれない. He may come at any moment. | He is expected (at) any minute.

いつか[1] 国によっては既に官公でも週5日制を実施している. In some countries, government offices too have instituted the five-day week.

いつか[2] いつかまたお目にかかりたいものですね. I hope we'll meet again some day. / いつか日曜日に会おうじゃないか. Let's meet some Sunday. / 君は去年のいつか私の所に来たことがあるね. I remember you came to see me sometime last year. / 同じ質問を受けた覚えがある. I remember I was once asked the same question. / いつか後悔しますよ. You will regret it sooner or later. | The time will come when you'll be sorry.

いっか 彼は一家をあげてブラジルに移住した. He emigrated to Brazil with all his family. / 彼は英語学者として一家をなしている. He has an established reputation as a scholar of English.

いっかい[1] 私は一介の教師にすぎない. I am a mere schoolteacher.| I'm only a schoolteacher.

いっかつ[1] 3つの法案が一括上程された. Three bills were brought up together for discussion.

いっかん[1] そんなことになったら私の生涯は一巻の終わりだ. It is as much as my career is worth if I should let it happen. / この事件で彼の一生は一巻の終わりとなってしまった. This incident closed the book on [〈英〉 put paid to] his career.

いっかん[2] 彼は終始一貫労働者の味方であった. He remained a staunch friend of the workers throughout his long career. / 彼の行為には一貫性がない. His conduct lacks consistency.

いっき[1] この詩は一気呵成に書いたものである. This poem was composed at one sitting.

いっきいちゆう そんなつまらことに一喜一憂するのは愚かだ. It's silly to let yourself be affected by such trivial matters.

いっきゅう 氏は今日の分子生物学者の中で第一級の人物である. He is in the first rank of molecular biologists at the present time.

いっきょう それも一興だろう. It'll be fun to do that.

いつく 彼は家に居着かない. He doesn't stay at home much.

いっけん これで一件落着. It is all

glad and sad by turns; 《文》cannot put *one's* mind at ease / 一喜一憂しながら restlessly; in suspense. 文例⇩

いっきゅう 一級 ¶ 第一級の first-class; first-rate ⇨ **いちりゅう** / 一級酒 first-class *sake* / 一級品 first-class goods / 一級品のカーペット a first-quality carpet. 文例⇩

いっきょ 一挙 ¶ 一挙に at a [one, a single] stroke; at one effort; at one (fell) swoop; all at once / 敵を一挙に粉砕する beat [crush] the enemy at a blow / 一挙一動、一挙手一投足 《文》*one's* every action; everything *one* does / 一挙一動に注意する〈自分の〉be careful about [《文》prudent in] every little thing *one* does; 〈人の〉watch every movement 《of》 / 一挙両得をねらう aim to kill two birds with one stone; try to make *sth* serve two ends.

いっきょう 一興 文例⇩

いつく 居着く settle (down); come to stay; stay permanently [a long time]. 文例⇩

いつくしみ 慈しみ love; affection ¶ 慈しみ深い affectionate; loving; 《文》tender; 《文》merciful.

いつくしむ 慈しむ love; be affectionate 《to》; 〈大事にする〉treat tenderly [kindly]; 〈哀れむ〉pity; take pity on ¶ 慈しんで世話をする take loving care of 《the orphans》.

いっけい 一計 ¶ 一計を案じる think [work] out a plan.

いっけん¹ 一件 an affair; a matter; a case ¶ 一件書類 all the papers [documents] relating to a case; a dossier 《on a criminal case》. 文例⇩

いっけん² 一見 ¶ 一見する have [take] a look 《at》; glance 《at》 / 一見(して) at a glance; at (a) first glance; at first sight; on first sight [viewing]; 〈見た所は〉apparently; seemingly / 一見の価値がある be worth seeing [《口語》taking a look at]. 文例⇩

いっけん³ 一軒 ¶ 一軒の家 a house / 一軒ごとに回って歩く call at every house; go from door to door; make a house-to-house visit / 一軒家 a solitary [an isolated] house.

いっこ¹ 一己 ¶ 私一己の考えで on my own responsibility [judgment]; at my (own) discretion.

いっこ² 一戸 ⇨ **いっか** ¶ 一戸建ての家 a detached house.

いっこ³ 一個 one; a piece ¶ 一個 10 円 ten yen each [apiece] / 1 個いくらで売る sell *sth* at so much each [apiece] ★ sell watermelons by the piece と言うと、切った西瓜を 1 切れいくらで売るという意味になる.

いっこ⁴ 一顧 ¶ 一顧の価値もない be quite worthless;《文》be beneath (*one's*) notice / 一顧も与えない《文》give no heed 《to》; take no notice [account] 《of》.

いっこう¹ 一行 a party; a company; 〈俳優などの〉a troupe ¶ 安田氏一行 Mr. Yasuda and his party / 一行の人々 the members of the party / 一行に加わる join the party. 文例⇩

いっこう² 一考 ¶ 一考する《文》give thought to *sth*; give *sth* some thought; think *sth* over; think about *sth*; consider *sth*. 文例⇩

いっこう³ 一向 ¶ 〈少しも〉(not) at all;《文》(not) in the least;《not》a bit; 〈全く〉quite;《unaware》. 文例⇩

いっこく¹ 一国 ¶ 一国一城の主(あるじ) a feudal lord. 文例⇩

いっこく² 一刻 ¶ a minute; a moment; an instant ¶ 刻一刻と every moment / 一刻も早く without a moment's delay; at once; as soon as possible / 一刻も早く…する lose no time in doing. 文例⇩

いっこく³ 一刻 ¶ 一刻な〈頑固な〉bigoted; stubborn; obstinate; 〈わがままな〉《文》willful.

いっさい 一切 〈全部〉all; the whole; 〈一切の事物〉everything; 〈否定〉(not) anything; nothing; 〈全く〉《文》wholly; entirely ¶ 一切の all; whole; entire; every / 一切の関係を断つ cut off all relations 《with》 / 一切…しない never *do*; do not *do* at all / 一切合切 the whole lot 《of》. 文例⇩

いつざい 逸材 an outstanding student [scholar, etc.]; a talented person;《文》a person of (ex-

---

settled. | The case is closed.
いっけん² それは地図を一見すれば明瞭にわかる. A glance at the map shows that clearly. / 一見正直そうだが、そうでないのだ. He is not as honest as he looks [as he appears to be]. / この仕事は一見見える程にはやさしくない. This job is not as easy as it looks at first. / 一見そう見えるだけのことである. That is only a surface impression.
いっけん³ スターンさんの家は 1 軒置いて隣です. Mr. Sterne lives two doors away from us [lives next door but one to us].
いっこう¹ 一行は 3 名であった. The party consisted of three people. | There were three of us. / ザイルが不意に切れて、一行 7 名のうち、4 名が遭難死した. Their rope gave way all of a sudden

and four of the seven men were killed in the tragedy.
いっこう² これは一考を要する問題だ. This is a matter that demands [calls for] our careful consideration. / ぜひご一考を煩わしたい. Please give some consideration to the matter.
いっこう³ 私はいっこうに存じません. I know nothing at all [absolutely nothing] about it. / 彼が何と言おうといっこうに構わない. I don't care a bit [I couldn't care less] what he says. / その薬を飲んだがいっこうに良くならない. I am no better for taking the medicine.
いっこく¹ 部長ともなると、一国一城の主で安易な妥協はしない. The chief of a department, with his pride in his position and the interests of his men to protect,

does not make easy compromises.
いっこく² 一刻を争う. Not a moment is to be lost. | There is no time to lose. / この病人は一刻も早く入院させなければいけない. It is most urgent that this patient be hospitalized. / スペースシャトルの打上げ時刻は刻一刻と近づいていた. T-time for the launch of the space shuttle was rapidly approaching. / 一刻千金である. Every moment is precious.
いっこく³ そんな一刻な事を言うな. Don't be so obstinate [《英口語》bloody-minded].
いっさい 本件には私は一切関係がありません. I have nothing whatever to do with this affair. / 宿泊費その他一切でいかほどになりますか. How much will it cost, including the hotel charges and

ceptional) talent ¶クラーク氏門下の逸材の1人 one of Mr. Clark's most talented pupils.
いっさく- 一昨… ¶一昨日 the day before yesterday / 一昨年[夜] the year [night] before last / 一昨昨日 three days ago.
いっさつ[1] 一冊 a copy《of the Bible》(1部)；《be complete in》one volume (1巻) ¶一冊物 a one-volume edition《of Shakespeare's works》. [文例⇩]
いっさつ[2] 一札 ¶一札入れる〈約定書を〉give a written promise《to, that...》；〈借用証を〉write an IOU. 「もくさん.
いっさん 一散 ¶一散に at full speed ⇨いち
いっさんか 一酸化〘化〙 ¶一酸化物 (a) monoxide / 一酸化炭素 carbon monoxide / 一酸化炭素中毒で死ぬ die of carbon monoxide poisoning.
いっし[1] 一矢 ¶一矢を報いる get a blow in; 〈議論で〉make [give] a telling reply [response].
いっし[2] 一糸 ¶一糸乱れず in precise order；《give cheers》in perfect coordination / 身に一糸もまとわずに stark-naked; with not a stitch [nothing] on.
いっし[3] 一指 ¶一指も触れさせない do not allow *sb* to lay (even) a finger on *sth*；《文》keep *sth* inviolate.
いっしき 一式 a (complete) set《of》 ¶家具一式 a (full) set [a suite] of furniture / 茶器一式 a tea set [service].
いっしゃせんり 一瀉千里 ¶一瀉千里に《文》with great rapidity; in a hurry; at full stretch / 一瀉千里に仕事をかたづける rush through *one's* work [a job].
いっしゅ 一種 a kind; a sort; a species《単複同形》; a variety ¶一種の a kind [sort] of / (あまり感心できない)一種の茶 tea of a kind [sort]; tea of sorts / 第1種郵便物 first-class mail matter. [文例⇩]
いっしゅう[1] 一周 ¶一周する go [walk, travel] round; make a round《of》; make a [one, the] circuit《of》/ 世界を一周する travel round the world; make a round-the-world trip / 一周してもとのところに戻る come full circle《to》/ 一周忌 the first anniversary of *sb's* death / 1周年記念祭 the first anniversary《of》. [文例⇩]
いっしゅう[2] 一蹴 ¶一蹴する〈しりぞける〉refuse《a request》flatly; reject; turn down《a proposal》;〈勝つ〉beat *sb* easily.
いっしゅう(かん) 一週(間)《for》a week ⇨しゅう[4].
いっしゅん(かん) 一瞬(間)《in》an instant [a moment] ⇨しゅんかん. [文例⇩]
いっしょ 一緒 ¶一緒に〈共に〉together;〈…と共に〉with...; along with...; together with...;《文》in the company of...; 〈並んで〉alongside...; 〈同時に〉at the same time; (all) at once; simultaneously; 〈ひとまとめに〉all together;《文》en masse; in the lump / 一緒にする put together; 〈まぜる〉mix up; 〈混同する〉confuse [《文》confound]《A with B》/ 一緒になる join (up with)《a party》; meet; 〈結婚する〉get married [《口語》get spliced]《to *sb*》;《文》become man and wife / 一緒に住む live together; live in the same house as *sb* / 一緒に歌う sing in chorus / …と一緒に行く go with *sb*;《文》accompany *sb*; keep *sb* company / 手紙と一緒に送る send *sth* (together) with a letter / 一緒になって…する join *sb* in *doing*. [文例⇩]
いっしょう[1] 一生 *one's* (whole) life; a lifetime ¶せみの一生 the cicada's life cycle / 一生の間 throughout (*one's*) life; all *one's* life; as long as *one* lives / 一生の仕事 *one's* lifework [life's work] / 一生の望み《文》*one's* lifelong desire / 一生のお願いですから for goodness' [pity's] sake / 一生の別れ a parting for life / 一生を終える end *one's* days [life] / 一生を送る[過ごす] live out *one's* life《in Tokyo》/ 一生を捧げる devote [dedicate] *one's* life《to the study of cancer》/ 一生に1度のチャンス the chance

---

everything? / 火事で一切合切焼いてしまった. I've had my possessions burned in the fire, lock, stock, and barrel.
いっさつ[1] この問題を全面的に論じようとすればそれだけで1冊の本になる. A full discussion of this subject would require a volume to itself.
いっしゅ 稲は草の1種である. The rice plant is a kind of grass. / 彼は一種の天才である. He is a genius in a sense. / その物語には一種カフカ風な所がある. There is something Kafkaesque in the story. / 彼の文章には一種独特の魅力がある. His style is marked by a charm all his own.
いっしゅう[1] 飛行機は市の上空を1周した. The plane circled over the city. / (長距離レースで)トムは最後の1周でジョンに抜かれた. Tom was overtaken by John on the final lap. / 地球は1年かかって太陽を1周する. The earth goes [revolves] round the sun once in a year. | It takes the Earth a year to go once around the sun.
いっしゅん(かん) それは一瞬の出来事であった. It all happened in a moment [flash]. / 列車が通過するほんの一瞬前に何とか車を踏切りから出した. They managed to move the car from the level crossing a split second before the train came through. / 彼は突っ込んで来た車の前から跳び退いて, 正に一瞬の差で助かった. He jumped out of the way of the oncoming car and managed to save himself by the skin of his teeth [with only seconds to spare].
いっしょ 僕らは学校が一緒でした. We were at school together. / (教師が生徒に)さあ, 一緒に. Now, all together. / キューバは北海道と九州を一緒にしたほどの大きさである. Cuba is as large as Hokkaido and Kyushu put together. / だれか私と一緒に行ってもらいましょう. I will get someone to go with me. / ではご一緒しましょうと言って彼も立ち上がった. He also stood up with an offer to accompany us. / 皆一緒になって歌った. We all joined in the song. / 私も子供たちと一緒になって遊んだ. I joined in the children's game.
いっしょう[1] これだけの本は一生かかっても読み切れないだろう. There are more books here than one can read in one's lifetime. / この屈辱は一生忘れないだろう. I will not forget this humiliation for the rest of my life. / この仕事は一生続くだろう. This work will take my lifetime. / こんな事は一生のうちに二度とあるまい. A thing like this will never hap-

いっしょう of a lifetime; a once-in-a-lifetime chance / 一生独身で通す be single /《文》remain unmarried] all one's life; live and die a bachelor (男が). 文例↓

いっしょう² 一笑 ¶一笑に付する laugh 《a matter》off [away]; shrug 《a matter》off.

いっしょう³ 一将 文例↓

いっしょうけんめい 一生懸命 ¶全力をあげて) with all one's might;《文》with might and main; do as well as one can;〈専心に〉with one's whole heart;〈死に物狂いに〉for one's [dear] life; desperately ¶一生懸命にやる try as hard as one can; do one's best [《文》utmost] /…に一生懸命になっている be determined to do; be intent on doing / 一生懸命に走る run as fast as one's legs can carry one; run for all one is worth / 一生懸命に働く〈勉強する〉 work hard; work as hard as one can.

いっしょく¹ 一色 one color ¶赤一色に塗りつぶす paint sth all (in) red.

いっしょく² 一食 a [one] meal. 文例↓

いっしょくそくはつ 一触即発 ¶一触即発の状態 a touch-and-go [an extremely delicate] situation. 文例↓

いっしん¹ 一心 ¶一心(不乱)に wholeheartedly; with one's whole heart; heart and soul; intently /…に一心になる be intent 《文》bent] on sth; devote oneself to sth; be absorbed in sth / 一心に祈る pray with one's whole heart;《文》offer a fervent prayer 《for sth, that…》/ 一心不乱に勉強する concentrate on one's work / 一心に耳を傾ける listen intently (to); be all ears; hang on sb's words /…したい一心から out of sheer desire to do. 文例↓

いっしん² 一身 ¶一身上の相談をする consult sb about one's personal affairs / 一身上の都合で退職する resign for personal reasons.

いっしん³ 一新 ¶一新する renew;《文》renovate; revolutionize (根本的に); change sth completely. 文例↓

いっしん⁴ 一審 the first trial ¶第一審裁判所 a court of first instance.

いっしんいったい 一進一退 ¶一進一退の now advancing and now retreating; fluctuating.

いっしんきょう 一神教 monotheism. 文例↓

いっすい 一睡 ¶一睡もしない do not sleep a wink; have a sleepless night.

いっする 逸する〈失う〉lose;〈逃がす〉miss; let sth slip [go];〈それる〉stray [《文》deviate] 《from a course》¶逸してはならない機会 an opportunity not to be missed; a golden opportunity.

いっすん 一寸 ¶一寸先も見えない cannot see one's hand in front of one's face《because of the fog》; cannot see an inch ahead 《of one》/ 一寸先も見えない吹雪 a blinding snowstorm.

いっすんぼうし 一寸法師 Tom Thumb (英国童話の); Jack Sprat (マザーグース童謡集の).

いっせい¹ 一世〈1代目の移民〉an issei (pl. -(s));〈その時代〉the time; the age [day] ¶ヘンリー1世 Henry I.

いっせい² 一斉 ¶一斉に〈一緒に〉all together; in unison;〈同時に〉all at once; simultaneously;〈異口同音に〉in chorus;《文》with one voice; unanimously ¶一斉検挙 a wholesale [blanket] arrest;《口語》a roundup / 一斉射撃 a volley (of fire); a fusillade / 一斉射撃をする fire a volley [fusillade]; deliver a volley of fire (against). 文例↓

いっせいちだい 一世一代 ¶一世一代の once in a lifetime / 一世一代の大仕事 the greatest work of one's lifetime. 文例↓

いっせき 一石 ¶一石を投じる create a stir 《in》/ 一石二鳥 (a case of) killing two birds with one stone.

いっせつ¹ 一節〈文章の〉a paragraph; a passage;〈詩の〉a stanza;〈歌の〉a verse.

いっせつ² 一説 ¶一説によれば according to

---

pen again in my lifetime.

いっしょう³ この仕事のようなのを「一将功成って万骨枯る」と言うのだ。The saying, 'A general climbs to fame on the bodies of thousands of nameless soldiers,' fits this sort of job very aptly.

いっしょく¹ 町は大統領歓迎の一色に塗りつぶされた。The whole town was enveloped in an atmosphere of welcome for the President. | The whole town was enthusiastically involved in preparations to greet [for the visit of] the President.

いっしょく² 1日1食はお米をやめてパンにしています。I eat bread instead of rice for at least one meal every day. / 動物園のゴリラは一食にどのくらい食べると思いますか。How much food do you think a zoo gorilla eats at a single meal?

いっしょくそくはつ 両国間の関係は一触即発の危機にある。Relations between the two countries are strained to breaking point. / パレスチナ人問題は他のいずれの国際問題よりも大きな一触即発の危険をはらんでいる。The Palestinian problem is potentially more immediately explosive than any other international question. / カリブ海全域が一触即発の危険をはらんでいた。The whole Caribbean region was a tinderbox.

いっしん¹ 夫婦は一心同体である。Husband and wife are one flesh.

いっしん³ 気分を一新するために1週間田舎へ行って来たい。I need a week in the country to restore my spirits [to put me back in top form].

いっしんいったい 氏の病状は一進一退。Sometimes he gets a little better but then he has a relapse [gets worse again]. | He's better one minute [day] and worse the next. / 戦いは一進一退であった。The struggle seesawed to and fro.

いっすい 昨夜はほとんど一睡もしなかった。I hardly got a wink of sleep last night.

いっすん 一寸先はやみの世の中だ。Nobody knows what may happen tomorrow. / 一寸の虫にも五分の魂。Even a worm will turn. [諺]

いっせい² 市内でスピード違反の一斉取締まりが行なわれている。A citywide crackdown on speeding offenses is now going on.

いっせいちだい それは恐らく彼の一世一代の名演説であったろう。It was perhaps the finest speech he ever made in his lifetime. / それは彼女にとって一世一代の(晴れの)日であった。It was the happiest [greatest] day of her life. / For her, it was a day to

いっせん / いっちょうら

いっせん¹ 一戦 〈戦い〉a battle; an engagement; 〈勝負〉a game; a contest; a bout ¶この一戦 this battle we are going to fight; this single battle (to decide the issue) / 一戦を交える fight [《文》engage in] a battle 《with》; have a fight 《with》; have a game 《of go with》/ 最後の一戦を試みる put up a last-ditch fight 《against》.

いっせん² 一線 ¶明確な一線を画する draw a clear [sharp, firm] line [distinction]《between》.

いっそ 文例↓

いっそう¹ 一層 more; still [even] more; all the more / 一層努力する make even greater efforts; work harder (than ever). 文例↓

いっそう² 一掃 ¶一掃する sweep away; clear (away [off]); wipe [stamp] out;《口語》get rid of;《文》eradicate / 夏物一掃大売出し a clearance sale of summer goods.

いっそく 一足 a pair (of shoes).

いっそくとび 一足飛び ¶一足飛びに at [with] a [one] bound; in one stride; in a single leap.

いったい¹ 一体 〈一体全体〉(how, what, why) on earth [《口語》the hell, in the world] / 一体に generally; generally speaking; on the whole / 一体になる《文》become one with...; be united 《文》integrated with...; identify (oneself) with... / 一体となって in a body; as one / 一体化 unification; integration / 一体感 (a feeling of) identification 《with》; a sense of unity. 文例↓

いったい² 一帯 a stretch (of open country); a tract (of land) / この辺一帯 the whole neighborhood [district] / 北海道一帯に all over Hokkaido.

いったい³ 一隊 a party (of mountaineers); a company (of soldiers); a (police) squad.

いつだつ 逸脱 《文》(a) deviation;《文》(a) departure ¶逸脱する stray [《文》depart,《文》deviate]《from》/ 権限を逸脱する overstep one's authority (規範を)逸脱した行動 deviant behavior.

いったん¹ 一端 〈片端〉one end; 〈一部〉a part ¶感想の一端を述べる tell something of what one thinks 《about sth》.

いったん² 一旦 once ¶一旦承諾した以上は Once you have agreed [《文》consented], ... 文例↓

いっち 一致 agreement; 〈合致〉《文》accord; consistency; 〈符合〉《文》coincidence; 〈同意〉《文》consent; 〈協同〉union; unity; cooperation ¶一致する agree 《with》; 《文》be consistent 《with》; 〈符合する〉coincide 《with》; tally 《with》; be in keeping 《with》/ 全員の意見が一致する reach 《a》consensus 《on a matter》/ 全員の一致した意見では The consensus (of opinion) is that... / 一致しない disagree 《with》; differ 《from》/ 一致した行動をとる act in unison [《文》concert] / 一致を欠く lack unity / 一致協力する cooperate 《with》;《文》unite (our) efforts; join forces 《with》; work together / 一致団結 union; solidarity; total cooperation / 一致点 a point of agreement [identity].

いっちゃく 一着 the first (person [runner, etc.]) to arrive [come in]; the first (arrival); 〈着物の〉a suit (of clothes); a pair (of trousers) ¶1着になる finish [come in] first; be the first to come in.

いっちゅうや 一昼夜 a whole day and night ¶一昼夜ぶっ通しで働く work all day and night; work around [round] the clock / 一昼夜交代勤務 a 24-hour shift.

いっちょういっせき 一朝一夕 ¶一朝一夕に in a (single) day; in a short time; in a short [brief] space of time.

いっちょういったん 一長一短 文例↓

いっちょうら 一帳羅 〈持っている唯一の服〉the only proper (suit of) clothes one has; 〈晴

---

remember.

いっそ そんな高い家賃を出すのならいっそ家を建てる。I would rather [sooner] build myself a house than pay such a high rent. / あの男はいっそのこと細君と別れた方がいい。He might as well get divorced from his wife. / そんなことをするくらいならいっそのこと死んでしまいます。I'd die before I'd do something like that.

いっそう¹ 彼は手術したために一層悪くなった。He got even worse because of the operation. / 正直なだけに一層同情される。We sympathize with him all the more because he is honest.

いったい¹ 彼は一体英語を知っているのか。Does he know any English at all? / 一体事の原因はどうなのです。What is the real cause of the affair? / 僕の机で一体何をしているんだ。Just what are you doing at my desk? / 一体何のつもりでそんな事をするのですか。What on earth do you mean, doing such a thing? / 観客との一体感が役者たちの演技を一層充実したものとしているようであった。The actors' sense of unity with the audience seemed to add even greater depth to their performance.

いったん¹ これで彼の性格の一端が知れよう。This should enable you to get a glimpse of his character.

いったん² 一旦した約束は破るわけにいかない。A promise once made cannot be broken.

いっち 専門家の間ではこれは比較的新しい隆起だということで一般に意見が一致している。There is general agreement [a general consensus] among experts that it is quite a recent upheaval. / この点について我々は必ずしも一致していない。We are not entirely in agreement on this point. / 彼らの話が一致しない。Their stories do not tally. | Their stories do not square with one another [do not square]. / デューラーが当時のドイツ最大の画家であることはすべての人の一致した意見である。Dürer is by common consent Germany's greatest artist of that time. / 両委員会の調査結果は実質的に一致している。The findings of the two committees are in substantial agreement. / 実験の結果は理論的計算で前以て得られていた値とよく[みごとに]一致した。The result of the experiment gave good agreement [was in beautiful agreement] with the value that had been obtained by theoretical calculation. / 彼らは利害の一致によって結びついてい

いっちょくせん 一直線 ¶一直線にin a straight line; as the crow flies / 一直線に進む go straight on; make straight 《for》; make a bee-line 《for》.

いつつ 五つ ⇨ご¹ ¶五つ子 quintuplets;《米口語》quints;《英口語》quins.

いっつい 一対 a pair 《of》; a couple 《of》 ¶1対のナイフとフォーク a knife and fork.

いっつう 一通 a copy 《of a document》 ¶1通の手紙 a letter.

いつづける 居続ける stay on 《at one's friend's house》;《文》remain in residence 《in the same neighborhood》.

いって 一手 〈将棋などの〉a move ¶一手に引き受ける undertake 《a task》single-handed / 一手販売店 a [the] sole agency / 一手販売人 the sole agent [distributor] 《of the article for Japan》.

いってい 一定 ¶一定の fixed;《文》specific; definite; regular; settled;〈標準の〉standard;〈ある程度の〉a certain (amount of) /〈一定の書式〉a set [《文》prescribed] form / 一定の収入 a regular [fixed] income / 一定の職業 a regular occupation; a steady job / 一定の場所 a fixed place / 一定する fix; set; define;《文》unify (統一する); standardize (標準化する) / 一定していない irregular; unsettled / 一定不変の《文》invariable; fixed (and unchangeable); permanent. 文例⇩

いってき 一滴 a drop 《of water》 ¶1滴ずつ drop by drop. 文例⇩

いってつ 一徹 ¶一徹な obstinate; stubborn; headstrong / 老いの一徹で with the obstinacy [stubbornness] of an old man 《of his age》.

いつでも 〈いつなんどきでも〉(at) any time;〈常に〉always; all the time; at all times; ever ¶…する時はいつでも every time one does / いつでも…しない never do. 文例⇩

イッテルビウム 《化》ytterbium.

いってん¹ 一点 a point; a speck; a dot;〈1個〉one; an article ¶1点入れる score a point; score a run (野球で) / 質問に対して一点一点答える answer the question point by point. 文例⇩

いってん² 一天 文例⇩

いってん³ 一転 ¶一転する〈1回転する〉turn round;〈変わる〉undergo a complete [sudden] change.

いってんばり 一点張り ¶努力一点張りで through [《口》by dint of] sheer effort / 一点張りで押し通す persist in doing; stick to 《a single policy》. 文例⇩

いっと 一途 ¶上昇の一途をたどる keep [go] on increasing; rise [go up] steadily.

いっとう¹ 一投 文例⇩

いっとう² 一党 ¶一党独裁 one-party rule / 一党一派に偏しない nonpartisan; nonparty.

いっとう³ 一等 〈等級〉the first class [rank, grade];〈第1位〉the first place;〈最も〉most ¶1等で旅行する travel first class;《船の》travel in a first-class cabin / 1等星 a star of the first magnitude / 1等賞を獲得する win (the) first prize.

いっとう⁴ 一頭 ¶馬一頭 one [a] horse / 1頭立ての馬車 a one-horse carriage / 一頭地を抜く surpass; excel; tower 《over》;《文》cut a conspicuous figure 《among》;《文》stand unrivaled 《among》; stand [be] head and shoulders 《above》.

いっとうりょうだん 一刀両断 ¶一刀両断にする cut sb in two with a single stroke of one's sword;〈比喩的に〉do without beating about the bush; come straight to the point and do.

イットリウム 《化》yttrium.

いつにない unusual ¶いつになく unusually;《文》as is unusual [rarely the case] with 《sb, sth》.

いつのまにか いつの間にか before one knows [is aware]; without one's knowledge; unnoticed. 文例⇩

る. They are united by a community of interest. / 我々が全員一致協力すれば計画は成功するだろう. If we all hang together, our plan will succeed.

いっちょういっせき これは一朝一夕に解決される問題ではない. This is not a problem that can be solved [settled] overnight [in a short time]. / 大事は一朝一夕に成るものではない. Rome was not built in a day. 〔諺〕

いっちょういったん これらの計画はどれも一長一短がある. Each of these plans has its merits and demerits.

いって 〈将棋で〉1手で2つの駒は取れない. You cannot take two pieces in one move.

いってい うちの人は帰宅の時間が一定していない. My husband is irregular in [as regards] the time he comes home. / 価格は一定していません. 作りによって多少の違いがあります. The price is not uniform; there are small differences according to the type. / クラブの会合は毎月一定の日に開かれます. The club meets on a fixed day each month.

いってき その時彼女は一滴の涙も流さなかった. She did not shed a single tear at the time.

いつでも いつでも出発できるようになっている. We are ready to start at a moment's notice. / 上京するといつでも叔父の家に泊まる. Whenever I go up to Tokyo, I stay with my uncle. / 彼はいつでもその冷静かつ公平な態度を失わない. He never loses his cool, impartial attitude.

いってん¹ 一天にわかにかき曇った. The sky suddenly became overcast.

いってん² 太陽の光がマッチの先の一点に集まるようにレンズを当てなさい. Hold the lens so that the sunlight comes to a point on the tip of the match. / 空に一点の雲もない. There is not a speck of cloud in the (whole) sky. / 心に一点のやましい所もない. I have a clear conscience.

いってんばり 彼は知らぬ存ぜぬの一点張りで押し通した. He persisted to the last in denying his knowledge of the matter.

いっとう¹ 観衆は一投一打にどっと歓声を上げた. The spectators burst into uproarious cheers at every throw of the ball and every swing of the bat.

いつにない 彼はいつになく元気がなかった. He was in low spirits, which was quite unusual for him.

いつのまにか 冬休みもいつの間にか過ぎてしまった. The winter vacation has passed all too soon.

いっぱ 一派 a school; a party; a faction; a sect 《宗派》 ¶田中一派 the Tanaka faction; Tanaka and his followers.

いっぱい¹ 一杯 〈分量〉a cup; a glass ¶コーヒー1杯 a cup of coffee / 水1杯 a glass of water / 1杯の飯 a bowl of rice / さじに1杯 a spoonful 《of》/ 一杯にする fill (up) 《a glass with water》/ 一杯になる be filled up; be full 《of》/ 1杯やる have a drink / 座りこんでゆっくり一杯やる sit over one's sake [drink] / 水をコップに一杯つぐ fill a glass with water / 今年一杯までは by the end of this year / 一杯食わす cheat; take sb in; play a trick 《on sb》/ 一杯機嫌の (slightly) drunk; tipsy; 《口語》tight; 一杯機嫌で 《口語》(somewhat) under the influence; under the influence of liquor; 《文》in one's cups.

いっぱい² 一敗 ¶一敗地にまみれる suffer a (crushing) defeat 《at the hands of...》/ 9勝1敗 nine wins and one defeat.

いっぱく 一泊 ¶一泊する pass [spend] a night 《at, in》; stay overnight 《at, in》; put up 《at a hotel》for the night / 1泊旅行をする make an overnight trip to Hakone.

いっぱし ¶いっぱしの competent enough; pretty good / いっぱし役に立つ be fairly useful; be serviceable enough.

いっぱつ 一発 a (single) shot ¶1発の銃声 the sound [report] of a gun / 1発撃つ fire a shot / 1発で打ち止める kill 《a bird》with a single shot [one's first shot] / 一発必中 を期する aim carefully so as to hit the target with one's first shot / (運動の選手などが)一発をねらう chance it. 文例 ⇩

いっぱん¹ 一半 ¶一半の責任がある be partially responsible [to blame] 《for》.

いっぱん² 一般 ¶一般の general; universal; 〈通例の〉common; ordinary; usual / 一般の学生 students in general; ordinary students; the average student / 一般の人々、一般大衆 the general public; people [the public] at large; the man in the street / 一般に generally (speaking); universally; 《通例》commonly; usually; 〈概して〉as a (general) rule; on the whole /(庭園などが)一般に開放されている be open to the (general) public / 世間一般に知れ渡る become public knowledge; become known to a wide public / 一般用[向き]の for popular [general] use / 一般向きに書かれた天文学の本 a book on astronomy (written) for the lay reader; a popular book on astronomy / 一般化する generalize; popularize / 一般会計 the general account / 一般教育 general education / 一般消費税 a general excise tax / 一般職 regular government service / 一般人 an ordinary person; ordinary people; the (general) public; the man in the street. 文例 ⇩

いっぴき 一匹 ¶一匹の犬 one [a] dog / 一匹狼 a lone wolf.

いっぴつ 一筆 ¶一筆書き送る write a few lines 《to》; drop [send] a line 《to》.

いっぴょう 一票 ¶一票を投じる cast a vote [ballot]. 文例 ⇩

いっぴん¹ 一品 ¶料理を一品追加注文する order another [an additional] dish / 一品料理 an à la carte dish.

いっぴん² 逸品 a fine [superb] article ¶全収集中の逸品 the gem of the whole collection.

いっぷ 一夫 ¶一夫一婦制 monogamy / 一夫一婦の monogamous / 一夫多妻制 polygamy / 一夫多妻の polygamous.

いっぷう 一風 ¶一風変わった odd; queer (★男性について He is queer. と言うと「あの人はホモだ」の意味になる); eccentric; strange; out of the ordinary; unconventional. 文例 ⇩

いっぷく 一服 〈薬の〉a dose; 〈タバコの〉a

いっぱい¹ ウイスキーをもう1杯いかがです。Won't you have a little [some] more whisky? | Won't you have another [some more]? ★このように、another のあとの glass of whisky は言わないのが自然。「ウイスキー1杯」は a whisky と言えるから、この場合、言いたければ another whisky と言ってもいい。/ 一杯やりながらその問題を話し合った。We discussed the matter over a drink. / コップは一杯であふれそうだ。The glass is full to the brim [to overflowing]. / もうおなかが一杯です。I can't eat another thing. / 彼女は目に涙を一杯ためていた。Her eyes were filled [brimming] with tears. / それを終えるには年内一杯かかる。It will take all this year to complete it. / 彼女の生命は今年一杯もたないだろう。She probably won't live [see] the year out. / スタンドは観衆で一杯だった。The stands were packed with spectators. / この本には誤植が一杯ある。There are a lot [a great number] of misprints in this book. / その結果を見たときは一杯食わされたと思った。I felt cheated when I saw the result. / 私は彼女にまんまと一杯食わされたのだった。I had been simply taken in by her.

いっぱつ あごに1発パンチを食らった。I got a punch on the jaw.

いっぱん² 女性は一般に子供は好きだ。Women generally love children. / 一般に女子の方が男子よりも語学に上達する。Generally speaking, girls make better linguists than boys. / このデザインは一般向きでない。This design will not go down well with the general public. / これらの作品は、これまであまり一般の人の目にはつかなかったが、決して捨てたものではない。These works, though they have not been much in the public eye, are by no means worthless. / 一般論に終始して各論に至らなかった。We only discussed generalities, without going into specifics.

いっぴつ ご帰国のご予定を一筆お知らせ下さい。Please write and let me know when you are coming back.

いっぴょう この会議では我々は平等に一票を行使する権利があります。We all have an equal right to vote in this assembly. / 選挙区によって一票の持つ重みに差がありすぎる。The differences in the weight of one vote between different constituencies are too great.

いっぷう 彼は一風変わった芸術家だ。He is an artist with something eccentric about him [with a difference].

いっぷく² その光景はさながら一幅の絵巻物である。The scene looks just like a picture scroll.

いっぺん 病勢が一変した。His disease has suddenly taken a new turn. / 形勢は一変して味方に有

smoke; a puff ¶一服する〈タバコを〉 have a smoke;〈休む〉 have [take] a (little) rest; take [have] a breather / 一服盛る poison *sb*.

いっぷく² 一幅 a scroll. [文例⇩]

いつぶす 鋳潰す melt down《old coins》.

いっぺん¹ 一片 a piece; a fragment; a scrap ¶一片の良心もない男 a man without even a trace [《文》modicum] of conscience.

いっぺん² 一辺 ¶一辺の長さが 10 センチの正方形 a square ten centimeters on a side; a square, 10 cm each side.

いっぺん³ 一変 ¶一変する change completely; undergo a complete change; be transformed / 態度を一変する change *one's* attitude altogether [entirely]. [文例⇩]

いっぺん⁴ 一遍 ⇨いちど.

いっぺん⁵ 一編 a piece《of poetry》.

いっぺんとう 一辺倒 whole-hearted devotion to one side ¶ソ連一辺倒である be an out-and-out supporter of Soviet Russia; be totally committed to Russia [the Soviet cause].

いっぽ 一歩 a step ¶改善の第一歩 the first step toward improvement / 1 歩 1 歩 step by step / 1 歩ごとに at every step / 1 歩進む[退く] take a step forward [backward] / 一歩も譲らない do not yield an inch / …より一歩先んじている be one jump ahead of *sb*; go *sb* one better. [文例⇩]

いっぽう¹ 一方〈片方〉 one side; one hand; 〈他の側〉 the other side [hand]; 〈(当事者の)片方〉《文》a party; 〈他の一方〉《文》the other party; 〈話かわって〉 on the other hand (★日本語の「一方では」は, 英語ではこう言うべきことが多い. 機械的に on one hand としないこと); in the meantime; meanwhile ¶一方の話ばかり聞く hear [listen to] only one side of the story / 一方に片寄る lean to one side / 一方に偏している be one-sided / 一方では…他方では… on the one hand… on the other (hand)… / 一方的な one-sided; unilateral《action》; lopsided《contests》/ 一方的勝利を収める win a runaway [an easy] victory / 一方からだけしか透視できない窓 a one-way window / 一方通行 one-way traffic / 一方通行路の入口 the entrance to [of] a one-way street. [文例⇩]

いっぽう² 一報 ¶一報する《文》inform《*sb* of *sth*》; let《*sb*》know. [文例⇩]

いっぽん 一本 〈1 個〉 one; a piece; 〈1 瓶〉 a bottle ¶チョーク 1 本 a piece of chalk / 鉛筆 1 本 a pencil / 一本とる gain a point《over》; score a point《against》/ 一本とられる be beaten; lose a point [round]《in an argument》/ 一本足で立つ stand on one leg / (野球で)一本足の打撃姿勢をとる take the flamingo [one-legged] stance / 一本気な single-minded / 一本立ちになる become independent; stand on *one's* own (two) feet / 一本調子の monotonous; 〈物のやり方が〉 unimaginative / 一本釣り pole-and-line fishing / 一本松 a solitary pine tree / 一本道 a straight [direct] road; a road without a fork all along. [文例⇩]

いつまで how long?; till when? ¶いつまでに《文》by when?; when《will it be ready》by? (★会話ではこの言い方が普通); by what time [day]?; how soon? / いつまでも〈永久に〉 forever [《英》for ever]; for good; eternally; 〈好きなだけ〉 as long as *one* likes; 〈無期限に〉 indefinitely / いつまで経っても for a long, long time; 《口語》《not》 in a month of Sundays. [文例⇩]

いつも always; 《口語》forever; 〈平常〉 usually; as a rule; 〈習慣的に〉《文》habitually; 〈必ず〉《文》invariably; 〈…するたびに〉 whenever…; every time… ¶いつも…しない never *do* / いつも(ながら)の usual; 《文》habitual; 《文》customary / いつものように as usual; in *one's*

利となった. The tide turned in our favor. / 相対性理論は宇宙観を一変させた. The theory of relativity brought about a revolutionary change in man's view of the universe.

いっぽ 疲れて足が一歩も先へ出なかった. I was so tired that I was unable to take another step. / 我々はさらに一歩を進めて代替エネルギーの実用化を計らなければならない. We must go a step further and try to put alternative energy sources into practical use. / 一歩誤れば一大事となる. A single mistake [false step] would have grave consequences. / 市当局は問題の解決に向かって大きく一歩前進した. The city authorities have taken a big step toward the solution of the problem. / ここまで来れば線文字 B の完全解読まではほんの一歩だった. From this it was only a step to the complete decipherment of the linear B script. / これは氏のこれまでの作品から一歩も出ていない. This is little better than any of his previous works. / 自殺の一歩手前で救われた. He was on the point [verge] of killing himself, when a helping hand was extended to him.

いっぽう¹ 一方は平面で他方は円錐状になっている. It is plane on one side and conical on the other. / 物価は上がる一方だ. Prices keep on [never stop] rising. / 病人は悪くなる一方です. The patient is getting worse and worse. / 一方通行. 〖掲示〗One Way (Only).

いっぽう² ご一報あり次第係員を参上させます. Our representative will be sent to you on receipt of your notice. / 事件の第一報が入ったのは昨日の午後 11 時だった. It was at 11 o'clock last night that the first report of the incident came in.

いっぽん こいつは一本やられた. That's one to you [him]! / 一本突っ込まれて返答に窮した. I was at a loss how to reply to this telling thrust. / 彼は一本立ちで充分やって行ける. He can get on very well by himself. / ここから村までは一本道です. This road leads [goes] direct to the village. / 父は正直一本やりで通して来ました. My father has never deviated from the path of honesty all his life.

いつまで いつまで東京にご滞在ですか. How long are you going to stay in Tokyo? / なるほど今我々は繁栄を享受しているが, 問題はこれがいつまで続くかということだ. It is true that we are enjoying prosperity, but the question is 'how long will it last?' / この理想の達成にはいつまでかかるかわからない. This ideal will take an eternity to be realized. / いつまで待っても返事が来なかった. I waited and waited, but got [received] no answer. | However long I waited, no reply came.

usual way / いつもと違って unusually ; 《文》 contrary to *one's* [the] normal custom [habit] / いつもより早く earlier than usual. [文例⇩]

いつわ 逸話 an anecdote. [文例⇩]

いつわり 偽り 〈うそ〉 a lie ; 《文》 a falsehood ; 〈作り事〉 《文》 a fabrication ; 〈虚偽〉 《文》 a deceit ¶偽りを言う ⇨ **いつわる** / 偽りであることを示す prove 《it》 to be false ; give the lie to *sb* [*sth*] / 偽りの false ; untrue ; fictitious / 偽りのない honest ; true ; sincere.

いつわる 偽る 〈うそを言う〉 lie ; tell a lie ; 〈よそおう〉 《文》 feign 《ignorance》; pretend 《that..., to be...》; 〈あざむく〉 deceive ¶事実を偽る lie about [《文》 misrepresent] the facts / 名を偽る assume a false name / 病気と偽る 《文》 feign illness ; pretend to be ill / 偽って by [on, under] false pretenses / ...と偽って under [on] the pretext 《of, that...》.

イデオロギー [<《ドイツ語》 *Ideologie*] (an) ideology ¶イデオロギー的 ideological / イデオロギー論争 an ideological dispute.

いてざ 射手座 〔天〕 Sagittarius ; the Archer ⇨ ざ 文例.

いてつく 凍てつく freeze ¶いてついた道 a frozen [an icy] road / いてつくような風 a freezing cold wind.

いてん 移転 a change of residence ; a move 《to》; (a) removal ; 〈権利などの譲渡〉 (a) transfer ¶移転する move ; 《英》 move house / 新居[田舎]に移転する move into a new house [into the country] / 移転先 *one's* new address / 移転通知 a notice of (*one's*) change of address. [文例⇩]

いでん 遺伝 heredity ; (genetic) inheritance ; (hereditary) transmission ¶遺伝の法則 the laws of heredity / 遺伝する be inherited ; run in the family [blood] / 遺伝的欠陥 a genetic defect [fault, flaw] / 放射能による遺伝的障害 genetic damage caused by radioactivity / 遺伝因子 a genetic factor / 遺伝学 genetics / 遺伝形質 a genetic trait [character, endowment] / 遺伝子 a gene / 遺伝子工学 genetic engineering / 遺伝病 a hereditary disease [disorder] ; an inherited [a genetic] disease. [文例⇩]

いと[1] 糸 (a) thread (縫い糸) ; yarn (紡ぎ糸) ; a string (たこ糸, 楽器の弦) ; a line (釣糸) ¶糸を紡ぐ spin yarn ; spin thread 《out of cotton》/ 針に糸を通す thread a needle / (釣りをする人が)糸をたれる cast [drop] *one's* line / (手術後に)糸を抜く take out [remove] the stitches / (陰で)糸を引く pull strings [wires] / 糸で吊す hang *sth* 《from the ceiling》 with thread / 糸くず waste thread ; cotton [silk] waste. [文例⇩]

いと[2] 意図 an intention ; an aim ¶...の意図を持って with the intention of *doing* ; 〔法〕 with intent to *do* / 意図する intend to *do* ; aim 《at *sth* [to *do*]》 / 彼の意図したとおりに just as he intended [designed] ; 《文》《to shape things》 to his own design / 意図的に on purpose ; intentionally ; deliberately ; 《文》 by design.

いど[1] 井戸 a well ¶深く掘った井戸 a deep-drilled well / 井戸の水をくむ draw water from a well / 井戸を掘る sink [dig] a well / 井戸端会議 housewives' gossip ; 《join》 a group of gossiping women / 井戸水 well water / 井戸屋 a well-digger.

いど[2] 緯度 latitude ¶高[低]緯度地方 high [low] latitudes / 緯度線 a parallel. [文例⇩]

いとう 厭う 〈嫌う〉 dislike ; hate ; detest ; loathe ; 〈いやになる〉 be disgusted with ; get tired [《文》 weary, sick] of ¶労をいとう spare *oneself* / 骨折りをいとわない 《文》 spare no pains ; do not mind taking the trouble 《to *do*》 / ...するのをいとわない do not mind *doing* ; be ready [willing] to *do*.

-いとう ...以東 ¶東京以東の[に, は] (to the) east of Tokyo ; (at) Tokyo and eastward.

いどう[1] 異同 a difference ; 《文》 (a) dissimilarity.

いどう[2] 異動 a change ¶異動を行なう make changes 《in the staff》 / 大異動 a wholesale change 《of the membership》; a 《Cabinet》 reshuffle.

いどう[3] 移動 a movement ; a transfer ; 〈民族や動物の群れの〉 (a) migration ¶移動する move ; transfer ; shift 《*one's* position》 / ゲルマン民族の大移動 〔西洋史〕 the Germanic [Gothic] migration / 移動撮影 〔映画・テレビ〕 a moving [travel] shot / 移動申告[証明] a report [certificate] of *one's* change of residence / 移動性高気圧 a migratory anticyclone / 移動大使 a roving ambassador. [文例⇩]

いときりば 糸切歯 an eyetooth 《*pl.* -teeth》; a canine tooth.

いとぐち 糸口 〈始まり〉 a beginning ; a start ;

いつも 私はいつも7時に起きて8時に朝食をとることにしている. I make it a rule to get up at seven and have breakfast at eight. | I make a practice of getting up at seven and having breakfast at eight. / 彼は来る時はいつも何か手みやげを持ってくる. He never calls on me without bringing something as a present. / いつもこの単語の使い方に自信が持てない. I'm never certain about the use of this word. / 彼女は今日はいつもと違う. She is not herself today. / その講義中, ディクソン博士はいつもの元気旺盛な姿に見えた. During the lecture, Dr. Dixon looked [appeared] his usual vigorous self. / いつもと変わったことはない. Nothing unusual has happened. / いつもならば今頃はみな退社している時刻だ. If this were an ordinary day, everyone would have gone home by this time.

いつわ あの人には面白い逸話がある. An amusing anecdote [story] is told about him.

いてん 左記に移転いたしました. We have moved to the following address.

いでん 彼の場合は母方の遺伝が出たのです. He takes after his mother's side of the family.

いと[1] (釣りで)大きな魚がかかって, 糸を全部繰り出したがけっきょく糸を切られてしまった. A big fish took out the whole length of my line and then broke it (on [for] me).

いど[2] 米国のその地方は北海道と同緯度だ. That part of the United States is in the same latitude as Hokkaido.

いどう[3] ヒラメは生まれた時には頭の両側に目があるが, 成長するにつれて片方の目が反対側に移動する. The flounder starts life

いとこ a (first) cousin ★ cousin は正式には日本語の「いとこ」を指すが、英語の日常語では、もっと意味の範囲が広く、「またいとこ」(second cousin)、「またまたいとこ」(third cousin) などから、いとこの配偶者なども含む ¶いとこの子 a first cousin once removed / いとこ同士の結婚 (a) marriage between cousins; (a) (cross-)cousin marriage.

いどころ 居所 《住所》 one's address; 《行方》 where one is; one's whereabouts. 文例⇩

いとしい 《文》beloved; dear ¶いとしく思う《文》think tenderly of; one's heart goes out to 《a child》.

いとしご いとし子《文》 one's beloved child.

いとすぎ 糸杉 a cypress (tree).

いとぞこ 糸底 the rim at the bottom 《of a porcelain cup》.

いととんぼ 糸とんぼ 〖昆〗 a damselfly.

いとなみ 営み 〈仕事〉 (a) business; an occupation; 〈活動〉 an activity; 《文》 a pursuit; an act.

いとなむ 営む 〈挙行する〉 perform 《a religious service》; hold 《a ceremony》; 〈経営する〉 run 《a hotel》; carry on 《an enterprise》; conduct 《business》; keep 《a store》; 〈従事する〉《文》engage in 《trade》;《文》follow 《an occupation》.

いとのこ 糸のこ a fret saw ¶糸のこの刃 a fret-saw blade.

いとま 暇 time; 〈閑暇〉 leisure (time); time to spare 〜ひま ¶いとまを告げる、いとまごいをする take one's leave; take leave 《of sb》; say good-bye (to); 《文》 bid farewell (to) / いとまごいに行く make a farewell call 《on sb》; pay a farewell call 《to sb》. 文例⇩

いとまき 糸巻き a (thread) spool; a bobbin; a reel ¶糸巻きに糸を巻く reel thread; wind thread on a spool [bobbin].

いとみみず 〖動〗 a tubifex (pl. -es)).

いどむ 挑む challenge sb 《to a fight》; defy sb 《to do》; give sb [throw down] a challenge 《to a duel》 ¶けんかをいどむ pick a quarrel 《with》.

いとめ 糸目 ¶金に糸目をつけずに regardless of expense. 文例⇩

いとめる 射止める 〈獲物を〉 shoot 《a tiger》 dead; bring down 《a bird》; 〈異性を〉《文》win (the heart of) 《a girl》;《口語》hook;《文》gain 《a lady's》 hand.

いとやなぎ 糸柳 a weeping willow.

いとわしい 厭わしい disagreeable; disgusting; detestable; distasteful; abominable; loathsome.

いな 否 no;《文》nay ¶否と答える say no;《文》answer in the negative / 否とは言わせない refuse to take no for an answer / 財産があると否かにかかわらず whether one is wealthy or not [《文》no]. 文例⇩

-いない …以内 ¶…以内の[に] within; less [not more] than;《米口語》inside of / 5千円以内の金額 a sum less than [《文》not exceeding] 5,000 yen / 5分以内に[で] within [in less than] five minutes / 5分以内に は「5分で」「5分たったら」の意. 文例⇩

いないいないばあ ¶いないいないばあをする play peekaboo [英]peepbo].

いなおる 居直る 〈強気に出る〉《口語》come out fighting; take [《文》assume] the offensive; take [《文》assume] an aggressive attitude [stance]; take a 'so what!' attitude; 〈脅迫的態度をとる〉 take [《文》assume] a threatening attitude ¶居直り強盗 a thief who threatens violence when detected. 文例⇩

いなか 田舎 the country; the countryside; 〈地方〉 a rural district; the provinces;《故郷》one's home; one's hometown; one's home village ¶田舎の rural;《文》rustic; provincial (★ provincial は人について言うと「田舎くさい」という意味になる) / 田舎の景色 rural scenery / 田舎から出たての 《young men》 fresh from the country / 田舎へ行く go into [down to] the country / 田舎へ帰る〈帰省する〉 go home; go back to the country / 田舎へ引っこむ retire into the country / 田舎くさい[じみた] countrified / 田舎言葉 a provincial [country] dialect / 田舎言葉丸出しで話す speak [talk] broad / 田舎住まい rural [country] life; living in the country / 田舎育ちの reared [brought up] in the country; country-bred / 田舎なまりで話す speak with a provincial accent / 田舎風の rustic / 田舎風に 《do》 country fashion / 田舎回りをする 〈劇団などが〉 make a country [provincial] tour; get the

---

with an eye on either side of its head, but, as it grows, one eye migrates to the other side.

いとぐち これが彼の出世の糸口となった. This paved the way for his future success. / 彼の発言がその後の交渉の糸口となった. His remark broke the ice for further negotiations.

いどころ 彼は居所を言わなかった. He didn't give me his address. / 彼の行方はいまだにわからない. His whereabouts is [are] still unknown.

いとま あまりにも突然の事故だったので前後をかえりみるいとまがなかった. The accident happened too suddenly for me to have time to think what I should do. / もうこれでおいとまします. I must say good-bye now. / I think I should be going now.

いとめ 彼は「金に糸目はつけない」という態度を取った. He took the attitude that money was no object.

いな この問に対する答は断じて否である. The answer to this question is an emphatic 'no'. / 孔子は中国、否、世界の偉人である. Confucius is one of the greatest teachers that China, nay, the world has ever produced.

-いない これらのホテルはみな駅から車で10分以内の所にある. These hotels are all (situated) within ten minutes' drive of the station. / 論文の長さは3千語以内とする. The paper should not exceed 3,000 words in length.

いなおる 私のこの作品はいわゆる専門家からだいぶ批判を受けましたが、この頃は、ではこれで何ることができますかと居直っています. This work of mine has been severely criticized by the so-called experts, but I laugh in their faces these days, asking

いながらにして in [from] one's home; from one's seat; without stirring. 文例⇩

いなご 〖昆〗a locust.

いなさく 稲作 〈稲の栽培〉rice farming [cultivation]; 〈出来高〉a rice crop ¶稲作地帯 a rice-producing district.

いなす parry (a question); dodge (an attack) skillfully; handle (one's opponent) cleverly.

いなずま 稲妻 (a flash of) lightning ¶稲妻のように as quick as lightning; with lightning speed / 稲妻形に zigzag; in a zigzag line. 文例⇩

いなせな dashing; stylish; dapper; rakish.

いななき 嘶き a neigh; a whinny; a bray (ろばの).

いななく 嘶く neigh; whinny; bray (ろばが) ¶一声高くいななく give a loud neigh.

いなびかり 稲光 (a flash of) lightning. 文例⇩

いなほ 稲穂 an ear of a rice plant.

いなむ 否む 〈否定する〉deny; 〈断わる〉decline; refuse. 文例⇩

-いなや …否や …するや否や 〈早速〉as soon as; 《文》no sooner...than; 《文》hardly [scarcely] ...when; the moment [instant]...; 〈…かどうか〉whether...or not 《文》no). 文例⇩

いならぶ 居並ぶ sit in a row ¶居並ぶ面々all those present; the whole company.

いなり 稲荷 the god Inari (originally a god of harvests, later worshipped as the guardian deity of an area) ¶稲荷ずし flavored boiled rice wrapped in fried bean curd.

-いなん …以南 ¶仙台以南の[に, は] (to the) south of Sendai; (at) Sendai and southward.

イニシアチブ an initiative ¶イニシアチブを取る take the initiative (in doing).

イニシアル one's initials ¶イニシアルの署名をする initial (a document). ¶bring [ship] in.

いにゅう 移入 ¶移入する import; introduce;

いにん 委任 《文》trust; 《文》charge; 《文》commission ¶委任する 《文》entrust [charge] sb with (a matter); leave [《文》entrust] (a matter) to sb / 権限の委任 delegation of authority / 委任状 a letter [power] of attorney.

イニング 〖野球〗an inning.

いぬ 犬 a dog; 〈回し者〉a spy; 〈十二支の戌〉(the Year of) the Dog ¶犬の canine / 犬をひいて運動させる take a dog for a walk; walk a dog / 雌犬 a bitch; a she-dog / 子犬, 犬ころ a puppy; a pup / 犬かきで泳ぐ swim with a dog paddle; dog-paddle / 犬小屋 a doghouse; a kennel / 犬ぞり a dog sled [sledge] / 犬猫病院 a pets' hospital / 犬張り子 a papier-mâché dog / 犬屋〈店〉a kennel; 〈人〉a kennelman.

いぬくぎ 犬釘 a spike.

いぬじに 犬死に ¶犬死にする 《文》die to no purpose; die uselessly [《文》in vain].

いね 稲 a rice plant ¶稲の栽培[取り入れ] rice cultivation [harvesting] / 稲を刈る cut [mow] rice (plants); reap [harvest] rice / 稲刈り harvesting rice / 稲科植物 (true) grasses.

いねむり 居眠り a doze; a nap ¶居眠りする doze; take a nap / 居眠りを始める doze off (to sleep); fall [go off] into a doze; nod [drop] off / 居眠り運転をする doze (off) [fall asleep] at the wheel [while driving].

いのいちばん いの一番 ¶いの一番に first of all; 《口語》first thing. 文例⇩

いのこる 居残る stay [《文》remain] behind; 〈残業する〉work overtime ⇒ざんぎょう.

いのしし 猪 a wild boar.

イノシンさん イノシン酸 〖化〗inosinic acid / イノシン酸ソーダ sodium inosinate.

いのち 命 life ¶命が危ない one's life is in danger; [《文》be in peril of one's life / 命のある[ない] living [lifeless] / 命のある限りは as [so] long as one lives / 命の糧(?) 《文》the staff of life / 命の洗濯 recreation; 《文》refreshment of spirit / 命を惜しむ 《文》take sb's life; kill / 命を惜しむ 《文》hold one's life dear / 命をかける, 命がけでやる risk [stake] one's life; do at the risk of one's life / 《文》命を危くする, 命に関わる endanger one's life / 命を助ける save sb's life; 〈ゆるす〉spare sb's life / 命をつなぐ support oneself; manage to keep body

---

them if they could match it.

いなか 私は田舎で暮らす方が好きだ. I prefer country life. / ここは都会に近い割にひどく田舎くさい. This place is very countrified considering that it is so close to town.

いながらにして いながらにして富士が眺められる. We can enjoy a view of Mt. Fuji from our own room.

いなずま 稲妻が空[雲間]を走った. Lightning streaked across the sky [between the clouds].

いなびかり 稲光がした. There was a flash of lightning. | Lightning flashed. / 北の空でときどきぴかぴかっと稲光がした. I saw occasional flashes of lightning in the northern sky.

いなむ 私は否みかねた. I hesitated [I could not find it in my heart] to refuse. / この事実を否むことはできない. There is no denying this fact. | The fact is undeniable.

-いなや 彼は僕の姿を見るや否や出て行った. He had no sooner caught sight of me than he went out. / コリンズ氏の発言が終わるや否や, ドブソン氏が「議長!」と言いながら立ち上がった. The moment Mr. Collins finished speaking, Mr. Dobson stood up, calling, 'Mr. Chairman!'

いにん 私の不在中は事務上の事はいっさい伊藤さんに委任してあります. All business is in Mr. Ito's charge during my absence.

いぬ 犬畜生にも劣ったやつだ. He is worse than a beast. / 犬も歩けば棒にあたる. The dog that trots about finds a bone. 〖諺〗

いのいちばん 彼がいの一番にやって来た. He was the first to come./ 明日の朝いの一番にそれをやりましょう. I'll do it first thing tomorrow morning.

いのち 心配で命が縮まる思いだった. Worry was killing me. / 君の吸うタバコの一本一本が君の命を縮めているのだ. Every cigarette you smoke is a nail in your coffin. / 僕は命が惜しい. Life is

and soul together / 命を取りとめる escape death; ⟨病人が⟩ pull through / 命よりも大切だ⟨文⟩be dearer [more precious] (to one) than life itself / 命からがら逃れる barely escape with one's life / 命ごいする plead for one's life / 命知らず a daredevil / 命知らずの reckless; daredevil; careless about one's personal safety / 命綱 a lifeline / 命取りの fatal; ⟨文⟩ mortal / 命取りになる be [prove] fatal (to one) / あやうく命拾いする have a narrow [hairbreadth] escape; miss ⟨being killed⟩ by a hairsbreadth. 文例⇩

いのり 祈り (a) prayer; ⟨食事前後の⟩ (a) grace.

いのる 祈る ⟨祈禱する⟩ pray ⟨to⟩; say [offer] a prayer; say grace ⟨before or after a meal⟩; ⟨望む⟩ wish. 文例⇩

いはい 位牌 a mortuary tablet.

いはつ 遺髪 the hair of the deceased.

いばら 茨 ⟨植⟩ a thorn; a bramble; a brier; a briar ¶いばらの道をたどる tread a thorny path. 文例⇩

いばる 威張る ⟨高ぶる⟩ be proud; ⟨文⟩ be haughty; ⟨口語⟩ be stuck up; ⟨もったいぶる⟩ stand on one's dignity; give oneself airs; put on airs; ⟨豪語する⟩ talk big; brag; ⟨誇る⟩ be proud ⟨of, that...⟩; pride oneself ⟨on⟩ ¶威張った arrogant; ⟨文⟩ haughty; overbearing / 威張って歩く swagger; strut ⟨about, along⟩; 威張り散らす be domineering; lord it over ⟨one's subordinates⟩; ⟨口語⟩ throw one's weight around. 文例⇩

いはん 違反 ⟨規則の⟩ (a) violation; ⟨文⟩ (an) infringement; ⟨文⟩ a transgression; an offense; ⟨約束の⟩ (a) breach; ⟨命令の⟩ disobedience ¶違反する act [be] against ⟨a law⟩; break ⟨one's promise, a contract⟩; disobey ⟨the orders⟩; ⟨文⟩ violate ⟨a regulation⟩; offend against ⟨the rules⟩ / 違反者 an offender ⟨against the law⟩; ⟨文⟩ a violator ⟨of the rules⟩. 文例⇩

いびき 鼾 a snore ¶いびきをかく snore / 大いびきをかく snore loudly [terribly]. 文例⇩

イヒチオール ⟨薬⟩ ichthammol; ⟨商標名⟩ Ichthyol.

いびつ 歪 ¶いびつの distorted; crooked / いびつになる get [⟨文⟩ become] warped [distorted]; warp.

いひょう 意表 ¶意表に出る take [catch] sb by surprise; do something unexpected.

いびょう 胃病 (a) stomach trouble; a disorder of the stomach.

いびる ⇒ いじめる.

いひん 遺品 an article left by the deceased.

いふ¹ 畏怖 awe; dread ¶畏怖の念を起こす stand in awe ⟨of⟩ / 畏怖の念を起こさせる put sb in awe ⟨of⟩ / 畏怖の念に打たれた awe-struck; ⟨文⟩ awe-stricken.

いふ² 異父 ¶異父兄弟 half brothers / 異父姉妹 half sisters.

用法 英語では「異父」と「異母」を普通は区別しない. 区別する必要のあるときは one's brother [sister] by a different father [mother] と言う. また, here is half brothers [sisters] と区別して「実の兄弟[姉妹]」と言いたいときは full brothers [sisters] と言う.

イブ Eve.

いふう 威風 ¶威風堂々たる ⟨文⟩ majestic; imposing; ⟨文⟩ stately / 威風堂々と ⟨文⟩ majestically; in state; in a dignified [stately] way [⟨文⟩ manner]. 文例⇩

いぶかしい 訝しい ⇒ あやしい ¶いぶかしそうに dubiously; suspiciously; questioningly.

いぶかる 訝る ⇒ あやしむ.

いぶき 息吹き ¶春の息吹き a touch [feeling] of spring in the air / 青春の息吹き an expression [⟨文⟩ emanation] of youthful energy. 文例⇩

いふく 衣服 clothes; dress; ⟨総称⟩ clothing.

いぶくろ 胃袋 the stomach.

いぶし 燻し ⟨燻蒸(くんじょう)⟩ fumigation; ⟨酸化⟩ oxidization ¶いぶしをかける fumigate; oxidize / いぶし銀 oxidized silver. 文例⇩

いぶす 燻す smoke; fumigate; ⟨酸化する⟩ oxidize.

いぶつ¹ 異物 a foreign body; an alien substance.

いぶつ² 遺物 a relic; remains; ⟨文⟩ vestiges ¶過去の遺物 a relic of the past / 封建時代の遺物 a hangover [⟨米⟩ holdover] from the feudal times.

イブニングドレス an evening dress [gown].

いぶる 燻る smoke; smolder; be smoky (部屋などが). 文例⇩

いぶんし 異分子 ⟨文⟩ a foreign [an alien] ele-

---

dear to me. / あの人は僕にとっては命の恩人だ. I owe him my life. / それは僕の命にもかかわる問題だ. It is a matter of life and death for me. | It is as much as my life is worth. / 彼は好奇心のために危うく命を失うところだった. His curiosity nearly cost him his life. / シーザーは判断を誤ったために命を落とした. Caesar paid for his miscalculation with his life. / それは彼の命取りになるだろう. It will be the end of him. / 言われたとおりにしろ, さもなくと命がないぞ. Do as I tell you, or you're a dead man. / 命あっての物種. While there's life, there's hope. ⟨諺⟩ / 命長ければ恥多し.

The longer you live, the more shame you suffer.

いのる ご成功を祈る. I wish you success.

いばら その後の彼の一生はいばらの道であった. His life thereafter was full of trials and tribulations.

いばる 別に威張れた話じゃない. It's nothing to be proud of.

いはん それは規則違反だ. That's against the rules. / 彼は交通違反で罰せられた. He was punished for a traffic offense.

いひょう 彼はしばしば人の意表に出るような事をする. He often does things that surprise people.

いふう 威風あたりを払って, ダリウス王は玉座についていた. Ra-

diating power, King Darius sat on the throne.

いぶき 柔らかい日差しに皇居のお堀の水もぬるみ, 春の息吹きが感じられる. The soft sunshine has taken the icy chill off the waters of the Imperial Palace moat, and makes us feel [and there is a feeling in the air] that spring is not far away.

いぶし 彼の演技にはいぶし銀のような味がある. His performance impresses us with a skill that is quiet and restrained rather than obvious.

いぶる たきぎがいぶって燃えない. The wood only smolders and will not burn.

ment ; an outsider《人》.

いへき 胃壁 the walls of the stomach ; the stomach walls [lining].

イベリアはんとう イベリア半島 the Iberian Peninsula ; Iberia.

いへん 異変 〈事故〉an accident ; 〈変事〉an emergency ; a disaster ; a calamity.

いぼ[1] 疣 《have》a wart ; a verruca (*pl.* -cas, -cae) ¶ いぼいぼの warty / いぼじ blind piles.

いぼ[2] 異母 ¶ 異母兄弟 half brothers / 異母姉妹 half sisters ⇨ いふ[2].

いほう 違法 〈違法の〉illegal ; unlawful / 違法行為 an illegal act ; a violation of the law ; 〈官吏の〉【法】(a) malfeasance. 文例⇩

いほうじん 異邦人 a foreigner ; a stranger ; an alien.

-いほく …以北 ¶ 京都以北の[に, は] (to the) north of Kyoto ; (at) Kyoto and northward.

いま[1] 今 〈現在〉the present ; the present time [day] ; this time [moment] ; now ¶ 今は now ; at present ; at the present time ; at the moment ; nowadays ; these days (★ in these days of nuclear power generation のように of …を伴うとき以外は in はつけない. in those days (あのころ)は in を伴う)／たった今 just now ; a moment ago / 今すぐ at once ; immediately ; in a moment / 今の〈現在の〉present ;《文》existing ;〈今日の〉of the present day ; present-day ; of today ; current《English》/ 今の有様では as the matter stands ; as things are / 今のうちに before it is too late / 今のところ for the present ; for the moment ; for the time being ; at present / 今しばらく a little longer / 今一度 once more [again] / 今頃, 今時分 ⇨ いまごろ / 今一人(の人) another person ; the other person (2人の中の) / 今でも, 今なお even now ; still ; as yet ; 〈否定の形で〉(not) yet / 今となっては now that things have come to this pass / 今で言う… what is now called… / 今では (by) now ; nowadays / 今から10年前に ten years ago / 今から50年たてば (in) fifty years from now ; in fifty years' time / 今から考えてみると, 今にして思えば when I think of 《it》now ; looking back (to [on] 《it》) now ; 《文》in retrospect / 今さら ⇨ いまさら / 今頃 ⇨ いまごろ / 今に ⇨ いまに / 今にも ⇨ いまにも / 今まで ⇨ いままで / 今もって ⇨ いまだに. 文例⇩

いま[2] 居間 a living room ; 《英》a sitting room ¶ 居間兼寝室《英》a bed-sitter [bed-sitting-room, bed-sit].

いましい 忌ま忌ましい vexing ;《文》vexatious ; annoying ; provoking ; galling ; cursed ; confounded ¶ いましい雨 annoying rain / いましましそうに in vexation (at) ; as if 《he》is annoyed ; disgustedly / いましましがる be vexed [annoyed] 《by, at》;《文》be chagrined 《at》.

いまがわやき 今川焼 a Japanese muffin containing bean jam, served hot.

いまごろ 今頃 (about) this time ; at this time of day [night, (the) year] ¶ 明日の今頃 about this time tomorrow ; tomorrow this time / 今頃はもう now ; by now ; by this time. 文例⇩

いまさら 今更 〈今になって〉now ; after such a long time [《文》so long a time] ; 〈事ここに至っては〉now that things have come to this pass ¶ 今更らしく as if 《it》were [was] something new / 今更言うまでもないが… It is hardly necessary to say [mention], but…

いましめ 戒め 〈訓戒〉《文》(an) admonition ; 《文》(a) remonstrance ;〈教訓〉a lesson ;〈警告〉(a) warning ; 〈禁戒〉a caution ¶ …の戒めを守る follow *sb*'s instructions / …を戒めとする take warning from… 文例⇩

いましめる 戒める 〈諭す〉《文》admonish 《*sb* against doing wrong》;《文》remonstrate 《with *sb* on the dangers of overwork》; 〈警告する〉warn 《*sb* of danger》; caution 《*sb* against a

---

いほう 彼らのしていることは商業道徳に反するかもしれないが, 違法ではない. What they are doing may be contrary to commercial ethics, but it is not against the law [they are still (acting) within the law].

いま[1] 今は秋です. It is autumn now. / それには今が絶好の時だ. Now is the best time for doing it. / 時計は今ちょうど8時を打っている. The clock is just striking eight. / 彼らは今のイラクに住んでいた. They were living in what is now Iraq. / 今から10日ほど前のことだった. It was about ten days ago. / 今から行って電車に間に合うかしら. I wonder if I can make the train if I start now. / Do I have time to catch the train? / 今からでも遅くはない. Even now, it's not too late. / 今から思えばあの時すでに彼は死を決していたのだろう. Looking back now, I can see that he had already decided to kill himself at that time. / おじは今(し)方着いたばかりです. My uncle has just arrived [came just now]. / 今行きます. I will come in a minute. / I'm coming. / 電車が今出るところだった. The train was about to start [on the point of leaving]. / 今一つの方を下さい. Let me have the other one. / 彼の説明には今一つすっきりしないところがある. There is something about his explanation that I find difficult to swallow [that sticks in my throat]. / 彼の来るのを今や遅しと[今か今かと]待った. I waited impatiently [eagerly] for him to come.

いまごろ 毎年今頃は非常に雨が多い. Every year about this time we have a great deal of rain. / 今頃はもう奈良に着いているに違いない. He must have arrived in Nara by now.

いまさら 今更仕方がない. It can't be helped now. / Nothing can be done about it now. / 今更のように常識の必要を感じた. I felt all the more keenly the need for common sense.

いましめ これは私にとって良い戒めとなった. It was a valuable lesson to me.

いまだ いまだかつて150歳まで生きた人はない. No man has ever lived to the age of 150.

いまだに いまだに返事がない. I still haven't had an answer. / そこはいまだに空地になっている. The lot is still vacant even now.

いまどき 今時珍しい人だ. He's a man of a type rarely to be met with nowadays.

いまに 今に見ろ. You'll have to pay for this. / 今にわかるよ. Wait and see. / Time will tell [show]. / 今に報いがある[ひどい目に会う]よ. He'll get his comeuppance one of these days.

いまにも 船は今にも沈みそうだっ

いまだ 未だ ⇨まだ ¶いまだかつてない偉い人 the greatest man that ever lived. 文例⇩

いまだし 未だし ¶いまだしの感がある leave something to be desired; be not yet quite satisfactory.

いまだに 未だに still; even now. 文例⇩

いまどき 今時 〈今の時代に〉nowadays; these days; at the present age; 〈こんな時刻に〉at this time of night [day]; at this hour of the night [morning, day, evening] ¶今時の〈youngsters〉nowadays [《of》today]; present-day 《students》. 文例⇩

いまに 今に 〈将来〉in《the》future; 〈間もなく〉soon; before long; 〈そのうち〉one of these days; 〈やがて〉by and by; in 《course of》time; 〈いつか〉some day; someday ⇨いつか². 文例⇩

いまにも 今にも every moment; (at) any moment ¶今にも…しそうである be going [about] to do; be on the point [brink, verge] of doing; be ready to do. 文例⇩

いままで 今迄 (up) until now; till now; up to the present ¶今までは, 今までのところ so far / 今までにない事件 an unprecedented incident. 文例⇩

いまわ ¶いまわの時 one's dying hour; one's last hour / いまわの際に on one's deathbed; in one's death hour / いまわの際まで until one's last moment. 文例⇩

いまわしい 忌まわしい disgusting; detestable; loathsome; abominable;《文》odious;《文》repugnant ¶忌まわしい事件 a scandal.

いみ 意味 (a) meaning; (a) sense;《文》significance;《趣旨》(a) point;《文》the effect;《文》the purport;《文》the import ¶意味する mean;《文》signify; imply (暗に) / 真の意味で in the true sense (of the word) / ある意味では in a sense / …という意味の手紙 a letter to the effect that… / 意味のない meaningless; senseless; pointless; empty 《words》/ 意味を取る make sense out of 《a signal》; interpret 《a passage》/ 意味を取り違える get the meaning wrong; mistake the meaning; misinterpret; misunderstand / 意味をなさない do not make sense / 意味ありげな significant; meaning / 意味ありげに in a meaning manner / 意味深長な expressive《glances》; suggestive《words》;〈意味深い〉meaningful; full of [《文》pregnant with] meaning;《文》of profound significance / 意味合い a shade of meaning / 意味内容 the semantic content (of a term); 意味論《言語》semantics.

いみきらう 忌み嫌う ⇨いむ.

いみことば 忌み言葉 a word considered to be unlucky; a taboo word.

いみじくも 〈見事に〉《文》exquisitely; admirably; 〈適切に〉aptly. 文例⇩

いみづける 意味付ける give sense (to); make sense of sth; make (it) significant; put sth in context. 文例⇩

いみょう 異名 another name; 〈あだ名〉a nickname ¶…と異名をとる also go by the name of…; be nicknamed [《文》dubbed]….

いみん 移民 〈移住〉emigration (外国への); immigration (外国からの); 〈移住者〉an immigrant (外国からの); an emigrant (外国への); a settler (未開地への) ⇨いじゅう.

いむ 忌む 〈忌み嫌う〉hate;《文》abhor; loathe; detest; 〈避ける〉shun; avoid; 〈禁止する〉taboo; 〈断つ〉《文》abstain (from) ¶忌むべき abominable; detestable; loathsome.

いむしつ 医務室 a medical office.

イメージ an image ¶イメージアップする improve the image 《of》/ イメージチェンジを計る try to change one's (public) image. 文例⇩

た. The boat was on the point [verge] of sinking. / 今にも降りそうだ. It looks like rain.

いままで 今まで何をしていたんだい. What have you been doing all this time [while]? / あんな美人は今まで見たことがない. I have never seen such a beautiful woman in my life. | She is the most beautiful woman I ever saw.

いまわ いまわの際に彼はこう言った. These were his dying words.

いまわしい 聞くも忌まわしい事だ. It is odious even to hear of it.

いみ それはどういう意味ですか. What do you mean by that? | How do you mean? / ここを君はどういう意味に取るか. How do you interpret this passage? / この言葉にそんな意味はない. This word does not have any such meaning. / これは単に意味のない数字の羅列にすぎない. This is merely a meaningless row of numbers. / この電報の意味は全くわからない. I can't make head or tail of this telegram. | I can't make out what this telegram says. / 彼は生きることに意味が見出せないと言った. He said he saw no purpose in living. / 別に深い意味でそう言ったわけではない. I did not mean anything serious when I said that. / その会合は政治的意味を含んだものではない. The meeting has no political implications. / そんなことをしても意味[大して意味]がない. There is no sense [not much point] in doing that. / そのような方策を取っても経済的にも意味がないだろう. Such measures would not make economic sense. / こうした規定は全く意味がなくなった. All meaning has gone out of these regulations. / そのような実験は人類の破滅を意味するかもしれない. Such experiments might spell the end of the human race. / 彼女は意味ありげに彼の顔をちらりと見た. She shot a meaning glance at him. / 'Skinny' というと 'slim' というのとは意味内容が違う. The word 'skinny' has different connotations from the word 'slim'.

いみじくも 「忘れな草」とはいみじくも名付けたものである. The flower is aptly called 'forget-me-not'. | The name 'forget-me-not' is an inspired one.

いみづける こうした研究によって, 彼は一見無意味に思われた野性の猿の行動を意味付けることができた. By these studies he was able to make sense out of [bring sense into] what had appeared to be the aimless behavior of monkeys in the wild state.

イメージ 有名人について世間の人はきまったイメージを抱いている. People have a set picture in

いも 芋 〈じゃがいも〉 a potato 《pl. -es》; 〈さつまいも〉 a sweet potato; 〈里いも〉 a taro 《pl. -s》 ¶いも畑 a sweet-potato field [patch] / いもづる sweet-potato vines / いもづる式に one after another. 文例⇩

いもうと 妹 a (younger) sister ⇨ あに 囲碁 ¶一番末の妹 one's youngest sister / 妹娘 one's younger daughter.

いもちびょう いもち病 【植物病理】rice blast.

いもの 鋳物 a casting; an article of cast metal ¶鋳物工場 a foundry / 鋳物師 a founder.

いもむし 芋虫 a green caterpillar.

いもり 【動】 a newt.

いや¹ 〈否定〉 no ⇨ いいえ; 〈肯定〉 yes; 〈ちゅうちょう〉 Well, ... ¶いやでも応でも ⇨ いやおうなし. 文例⇩

いや² 嫌 ¶嫌な〈不快な〉 disagreeable; 《口語》 nasty; unpleasant; disgusting; 《文》 odious; offensive; 〈好ましくない〉 《文》 undesirable; unwelcome; 〈忌まわしい〉 hateful; loathsome / 嫌な天気 bad [nasty, foul] weather / 嫌なにおい a bad [a nasty, an offensive] smell / 嫌な顔をする frown; scowl; look offended [《口》displeased] / 嫌なやつ an unpleasant [a disgusting, an odious] fellow / 嫌になる become disgusted 《with》; 〈飽きる〉 get [《文》 become] sick [tired, 《文》 weary] of; 《口語》 get [《文》 become] fed up 《with》 / 世の中が嫌になる lose interest in life; become sick [《文》 weary] of life. 文例⇩

いやいや 嫌々 against one's will; unwillingly; reluctantly; grudgingly ¶いやいや承諾をagree 《to sth》 against one's will; give one's unwilling consent.

いやおうなし 否応なし ¶いやおうなしに whether one likes it or not; willy-nilly / いやおうなしに...させる force [compel] sb to do; make sb do by force.

いやがうえにも 弥が上にも all the more; more 《for》; 《文》 harass; do spiteful [nasty] things

いやがらせ 嫌がらせ harassment; pinpricks 〈些細な〉 ¶嫌がらせの電話 pestering telephone calls / 嫌がらせをする make trouble 《for》; 《文》 harass; do spiteful [nasty] things 《to sb》; annoy / 嫌がらせを言う ⇨ いやみ. 文例⇩

いやがる 嫌がる dislike; hate; be unwilling [reluctant] to do; fight shy of sth. 文例⇩

いやく¹ 医薬 (a) medicine; a medicinal drug ¶医薬分業 separation of dispensing from medical practice.

いやく² 違約 (a) breach of contract; a breach of promise (特に婚約の) ¶違約する break a promise [a contract]; break [go back on] one's word / 違約金 (pay) damages for (one's) breach of contract; a penalty.

いやく³ 意訳 (a) free translation ¶意訳する translate freely; make a free translation.

いやけ 嫌気 ¶嫌気がさす 《口語》 get sick (of); tire [get tired] (of); become disgusted 《with》. 文例⇩

いやしい 卑[賤]しい 《文》 humble; low; 〈文〉 menial; 《文》 lowly; 〈卑劣な〉 《文》 base; 《文》 mean; 〈野卑な〉 vulgar; coarse ¶金銭に卑しい be mercenary / 卑しい心 a base mind; a mean spirit / 卑しい言葉づかい a vulgar expression / 賎しい仕事 a low-prestige job; menial work / 卑しからぬ respectable; decent. 文例⇩

いやしくも at all; in the least; ever ¶いやしくも...以上は since...; now that...; 〈一旦〉 once... / いやしくもそれをする以上は if you do it at all. 文例⇩

いやしむ 卑しむ despise; look down on sb; 《文》 hold sb in contempt ¶卑しむべき contemptible; despicable; 《文》 base; 《文》 mean.

いやす 癒す heal (a wound, sb of his disease); cure (a disease); quench (one's thirst); remove (the pain); work off (one's frustration).

いやに awfully; terribly ¶いやに頭が痛い have a bad [nasty] headache. 文例⇩

いやはや 〈驚き・嘆息など〉 Oh!; Oh dear!; Dear me!

イヤホ(ー)ン an earphone ¶イヤホ(ー)ンをつける[している] put on [wear] an earphone / イヤホ(ー)ンでラジオを聞く listen to the radio

---

their minds about how famous people look. / そんなことをすれば、必ず我が社のイメージダウンになる。That is bound to hurt our company's image [reputation].

いも プールはいもを洗うような混雑だった。The crowd was splashing and jostling each other in the swimming pool.

いや¹ いや、それは違う。No, you are wrong. / No, it isn't. / 君が悪いんじゃないんだ。―いや、そうなんだ。It isn't your fault.―Yes, it is.

いや² 嫌な知らせを聞いて飯がまずくなった。The bad news spoilt my dinner. / あの男の顔を見るのも嫌だ。I hate the very sight of him. / 自分ながら嫌になった。I am disgusted with myself. / だいぶ嫌な目に会った。I had a pretty rotten time. / それを思い出すと嫌になる。It makes me sick to think of it. / 会社の嫌なことがあっても、決してそれを家まで持って帰るなどということはしない。I never take my problems home with me from the office. / 問題は嫌というほどある。We have more than enough of problems. / 日照りが続いたと思ったら、こんどは嫌というほど雨が降った。After a long spell of dry weather, it rained with a vengeance [《米俗》like all get-out].

いやがらせ 我々の仲間はまだ少ないので、彼らに対して嫌がらせ程度のことしかできない。There are still too few of us to have much more than nuisance value against them.

いやがる 彼は完全主義なので人に嫌がられるのだ。His perfectionism puts people off.

いやく³ 彼の訳はあまりに意訳に過ぎる。His translation is too free.

いやけ そろそろこの仕事に嫌気がさしてきた。I'm growing [getting] tired of this job.

いやしい どんなに身分の賎しい者にもそれなりの権利はある。A cat may look at a king. 《諺》

いやしくも いやしくも良心のある人なら、できる事ではない。A man who has a particle of conscience could not do that.

いやに いやに寒いね。It's awfully cold, isn't it? / その男はいやに落ち着き払っていた。The man remained provokingly cool.

いやみ 彼の文章は嫌味だ。His style is mannered (and artificial).

いやみ 嫌味 〈不快〉《文》disagreeableness；《文》offensiveness；〈皮肉〉sarcasm；〈きざ〉《文》affectation；〈悪趣味〉bad taste ¶嫌味のある offensive；disagreeable；〈皮肉な〉sarcastic／嫌味のない agreeable；pleasant；〈気取りのない〉《文》unaffected；〈あか抜けした〉refined／嫌味を言う say disagreeable things；make sarcastic [cutting] remarks (on)；say something to hurt sb's feelings. 文例①

いやらしい 〈不快〉unpleasant；disagreeable；disgusting；repulsive；〈みだらな〉indecent；《文》lewd；dirty；dirty-minded；smutty (jokes)；《文》lascivious ¶いやらしい目つきで見る leer (at)／いやらしい流し目をする cast lascivious glances (at)／女性にいやらしい事を言う say improper things to a girl；make improper suggestion to a woman／女性にいやらしいことをする molest a woman；take liberties with a girl. 文例①

イヤリング an earring ¶耳たぶの下に垂れるイヤリング a drop earring／イヤリングをつけている wear earrings.

いゆう 畏友 one's respected friend.

いよいよ 愈々〈ますます〉more and more；still more；all the more；increasingly ⇒ます ます；〈遂に〉at last；at length；〈結局〉after all；〈本当に〉really；positively ¶いよいよ繁栄する become more and more prosperous／いよいよという時に〈最後に〉at the last moment；〈やっと間に合って〉at the eleventh hour；〈きわどいところで〉just in time；in the nick of time／いよいよとなれば if it comes to that；when the time comes；〈窮すれば〉if things come to the worst／いよいよという時まで延ばす postpone (a matter) to the last moment [minute]. 文例①

いよう¹ 威容 an imposing [a dignified, a majestic] appearance ¶ソ連軍の威容を示す分列行進 a march-past displaying the great power of the Soviet armed forces.

いよう² 異様 ¶異様な strange；queer；odd；grotesque；bizarre／異様に見える look queer [strange].

いよく 意欲 (a) will；(a) desire；《文》volition ¶…しようという意欲が盛んである have a strong will [desire] to do；be eager to do／…しようという意欲を起こさせる give sb an incentive to do／意欲を減退させるもの《文》a disincentive (to do)／意欲的な《文》highly [strongly] motivated；enthusiastic；enterprising. 文例①

いらい 依頼〈願い〉a request；〈委託〉a commission；〈信用〉trust；〈頼ること〉《文》reliance ¶依頼する request；make sb a request；ask (sb to do)；〈…に頼る〉rely on／弁護士に依頼する leave (a matter) to a lawyer／依頼に応じる agree to [grant, comply with] sb's request／依頼に応じて on request／ご依頼により at your request／依頼状 a letter of request；a written request／(弁護士などの)依頼人 a client. 文例①

-いらい …以来 since…¶それ以来 since then；from that time on [onward]；ever since. 文例①

いらいら いらいらする become irritated；get [《文》become] nervous [fretful]；fret (about, at, for, over)；〈あせる〉grow impatient／いらいらしている be irritable；be irritated；be nervous；be impatient；be on edge；《口語》be edgy／いらいらしながら nervously；impatiently；agitatedly／いらいらさせる irritate；make sb irritated；get [jar] on sb's nerves. 文例①

イラク Iraq ¶イラク共和国 the Republic of Iraq／イラク人 an Iraqi.

いらくさ 刺草 《植》a nettle.

イラスト an illustration.

イラストレーター an illustrator.

いらだつ 苛立つ〈じれる〉be irritated；be nettled；fret；〈もどかしがる〉grow impatient；lose (one's) patience ¶いら立って in a fret；impatiently／神経をいら立たせる get [jar] on sb's nerves ⇒ いらいら.

いらっしゃい 〈お出でなさい〉Come in；《口語》Come on in；〈こちらへどうぞ〉This way, please；〈ようこそ〉Welcome!；〈店員が客に〉Can [May] I help you, sir [madam]?；What can I do for you, sir [madam]? 文例①

いやらしい まあ！いやらしいわね。Oh, you are horrible!

いよいよ 風はいよいよ激しくなった。The wind blew harder and harder.｜この正月から毎日日記をつけるつもりでいたが、いよいよ始めてみると容易ではなかった。I had intended to keep a diary every day from New Year's Day on, but when I actually started it, I found it very hard to keep it up.｜いよいよ夏らしくなった。Summer has begun in real earnest.｜いよいよ運が向いてきたぞ。My luck seems to have turned at last.｜Things look as if they are starting to go my way.

いよう¹ 巨大なアスワン・ハイ・ダムは堂々たる威容を誇っている。The huge Aswan High Dam overwhelms us with its imposing bulk.

いよう² 私は一種異様な恐怖感に襲われた。I was struck with an indescribable sensation of horror.｜A strange fear came over me.｜異様に聞こえるかもしれないがしかし事実だ。It may sound strange, but it is true.

いよく 大学に入ってから始めた外国語をマスターするのは非常に困難だが、意欲さえあれば決して不可能ではない。It is very hard to master a foreign language that you begin to learn after entering college, but it is by no means impossible provided that the will is there.

いらい 放送局から劇の脚本を書くことを依頼された。The broadcasting company commissioned me to write a play.｜彼は依頼心が強すぎる。He relies on other people too much.

-いらい この家に来て以来ずっとこの家に住んでいる。I have lived in this house ever since I came to this city.｜こちらに住むようになって以来、多くの人と知り合いになりました。I have made friends with a lot of people since I have lived here.

いらいら 彼は気がいらいらしていた。He was [His nerves were] on edge.｜彼女の来るのが遅いので彼はいらいらしていた。He was impatient at her delay.｜彼はいらいらがこうじて頭が変になりかかっていた。His nerves were driving him crazy.

いらっしゃい さあ、いらっしゃい、いらっしゃい。〈呼び込みの声〉

いらっしゃる 〈来る〉 come; call; 〈行く〉 go; 〈居る〉 be; 〈…である〉 be. 文例⬇

イラン Iran ¶イランの Iranian / イラン回教共和国 the Islamic Republic of Iran / イラン人 an Iranian.

いり 入り 〈入る事〉 entering; 〈入場者〉 an attendance; an audience; 〈始まり〉 the beginning ¶日の入りまでには by sunset / 彼岸の入り the beginning [first day] of the equinoctial week / 入りが多い[少ない] 〈会などが〉 there is a good [poor] attendance (at the meeting); 〈劇場などが〉 draw [have] a large [poor] audience; there is a good [poor] house. 文例⬇

-いり …入り ¶5万円入りの財布 a wallet containing 50,000 yen / さし絵入りの小説 a story with illustrations / (タバコの)20個入りの箱 a 20-pack carton / (ビールなどの)1ダースのりのケース a 12-bottle crate / 2リットル入りのびん a 2-liter bottle.

いりあい 入り会い ¶入会権 right of common; commonage / 入会地 common land; a common.

いりうみ 入り海 〈湾〉 a bay; 〈入り江〉 an (ocean) inlet.

いりえ 入り江 an inlet; an arm of the sea.

いりおもてやまねこ 西表山猫 an Iriomote wildcat.

いりぐち 入り口 an entrance (to); a way in; 〈戸口〉 a door [doorway] (to); 〈門〉 a gate [gateway] (to); 〈港〉 the mouth of [entrance to] a harbor / 高速道路の入り口 the entrance ramp; 〔(英)〕 the slip road to an expressway / 入り口で at the entrance [door]. 文例⬇

いりくむ 入り組む get [be, 〔文〕 become] complicated; be tangled ¶入り組んだ complicated; 〔文〕 intricate; tangled; involved.

イリジウム 〔化〕 iridium.

いりたまご 炒り玉子 scrambled eggs.

イリノイ Illinois (略: Ill.) ¶イリノイ州の人 an Illinoisan.

いりひ 入り日 the setting sun.

いりびたり 入り浸り ¶入り浸りである be a constant visitor [guest] (at); spend all one's time (at).

いりまじる 入り交じる mix 《with》; be mixed (together [up]); be mingled 〔文〕 intermingled《with》. 文例⬇

いりみだれる 入り乱れる be jumbled (together) ¶入り乱れて in confusion; in disorder / 入り乱れて戦う engage in a melee.

いりむこ 入り婿 ¶入り婿になる marry into one's wife's family.

いりゅう¹ 遺留 ¶遺留品 things left behind / 遺留分 the portion (of the property) to which one is legally entitled.

いりゅう² 慰留 ¶慰留する persuade sb not to resign; persuade sb to stay in office; 〔文〕 dissuade sb from resigning.

いりよう 入り用 ⇒ひつよう.

いりょう¹ 衣料 clothing; garments; clothes ¶衣料費 clothing expenses / 衣料品店 a clothing store.

いりょう² 医療 medical treatment [care] ⇒ちりょう² ¶医療器械 medical appliances [instruments] / 医療技術の発達 an advance in medical technology / 医療給付 a medical benefit / 医療施設 medical facilities / 医療班 a medical team / 医療費 medical expenses; a doctor's bill / 医療品 medical supplies.

いりょく 威力 〈力, 勢〉 power; 〔文〕 might; 〈権力〉 authority; 〈勢力〉 influence ¶威力のある powerful; mighty; formidable / 威力をふるう 〔文〕 exercise [wield] one's power [authority] (over); 〔口語〕 throw one's weight around / 威力業務妨害 forcible obstruction of business; obstructing business by force.

いる¹ 炒る parch; roast ¶豆をいる roast [parch] beans / 茶をいる roast [toast] tea.

いる² 居る 〈存在する〉 be; there is [are]; exist; 〈居住する〉 live; occupy (a room); 〈滞在する〉 stay; 〈棲息する〉 live; inhabit (a place); be found; 〈現に…している〉 be doing; be at (play); be in 《motion》 ¶仕事をしている be

---

Walk up! Walk up! / いらっしゃる 鈴木さんはこの頃めったにいらっしゃいません。Mr. Suzuki rarely comes to see me these days. / よくいらっしゃいました。Welcome! / I'm glad you've come. / あなたもいらっしゃるのですか。Are you going, too? / アーノルドさんはいらっしゃいますか。Is Mr. Arnold in [at home]?

いり 梅雨の入りはいつですか。When does the rainy season set in? / 会場はもうすでにかなりの入りだった。The hall was already well filled. / その映画は大そう入りがいらない。The picture seems to be quite successful [doing very nicely] at the box office. / 初日はわずか7分の入りだった。On the opening day only seven tenths of the seating capacity was filled.

-いり このびんは2リットル入りです。This bottle holds two liters.

いりぐち この入り口からは入れません。No entrance by this door.

いりまじる 彼は母親に対して, 愛情, 憎悪, 甘え, 憤りなどの入り交じった気持ちを抱いている。His feelings toward his mother are ambivalent—love, hate, dependence and resentment all at the same time.

いる² 日本にはおおかみがいますか。Is the wolf found in Japan? / この部屋はむし暑くてとてもいられない。This room is so hot and sticky that I can't possibly stay here. / (帰らないで)もう少しいたまえ。Stay a little longer. / 市内に千人余りの外国人がいる。There are over 1,000 foreigners living [〔文〕 residing] in the city. / 私はおじの家にいます。I live with my uncle. / あの家には恐ろしい犬がいる。They keep a fierce dog. / あたりにだれもいなかった。No one happened to be [about, around]. / 大学教授も大勢いた。A number of university professors were also present. / あの人は私のいない所で悪口を言っているらしい。It appears that he talks [says unpleasant things] about me behind my back. / 君がいないのでみんな寂しがっていた。We all missed you very much. / あなたがいないと家が寂しい。The house is lonely without you. / ずっとパリにいたのかね。—いたりいなかったりだよ。Have you been in Paris all this time?—Off and on. / 彼女が無事かどうか早く知りたくていても立ってもいられない。I am dying [I can't wait] to know whether she is safe or not. / 子供たちは庭で遊んでいる。The children are playing out

いる working; be at work / 商売をしている be engaged in business / 怠けている stay [《文》remain] idle / ...のいる所[此]で in the presence of... / いないな be not in [here, there, etc.] 《文》be absent; be away 《from home》/ ...せずにはいられない cannot help [keep from] doing, 《文》cannot (help) but do.

いる³ 要る 〈人が主語〉 need; must have; 《文》be [stand] in need of; 《文》require; want (欲する) (★「要る」には need,「要らない」には do not want が適切な場合が多い); 〈物が主語〉be necessary; be needed; be required. 文例⇩

いる⁴ 射る shoot ¶矢を射る shoot an arrow / 的を射る hit a target.

いる⁵ 鋳る cast (a bell); mint 《coins》. 文例⇩

いるい 衣類 clothing; clothes; garments. 文例⇩

いるか 《動》a dolphin (マイルカなど, 鼻先のとがったもの); a porpoise (スナメリなど, くちばしのしないもの).

いるす 居留守 ¶居留守を使う pretend not to be in [at home]; pretend to be out. 文例⇩

いれあげる 入れ揚げる try to win 《a woman's》 affection by lavishing money on 《her》.

いれい¹ 異例 an exceptional [《文》a singular] case; an exception ¶異例の exceptional; 《文》unprecedented (先例のない).

いれい² 慰霊 ¶慰霊祭 a memorial service (for the war dead) / 慰霊塔 a war memorial; a cenotaph (built in memory of war victims).

いれかえ 入れ替[換]え 〈取り換え〉 replacement; 〈交替〉 shifting; 〈列車の〉 switching; shunting.

いれかえる 入れ替[換]える 〈取り換える〉 change; replace 《an old thing with a new one》; substitute (the right word for the wrong one); 〈新しくする〉 renew; 〈入れ直す〉 put sth in afresh; 〈列車を〉 switch; shunt ¶〈劇場で〉観客を入れ替える shift the audience / 心[魂]を入れ替える reform (oneself); 《口語》mend one's ways. 文例⇩

いれかわり 入れ代[替]わり ¶入れ代わりに in place of; as a substitute for / 入れ代わり立ち代わり one after another; by turns.

いれかわる 入れ代[替]わる change places 《with sb》; take sb's place; replace [relieve] sb.

イレギュラー イレギュラーな irregular.

いれぐい 入れ食い 〈釣り〉 文例⇩

いれずみ 入れ墨 a tattoo ⇒ほりもの ¶入れ墨をする tattoo.

いれぢえ 入れ知恵 ¶入れ知恵する suggest an idea (to); give sb a hint; put an idea into sb's head; prime (a witness).

いれちがい 入れ違い ¶入れ違いになる pass sb as one enters (a building); pass each other (at the entrance).

いれちがえる 入れ違える put sth in the wrong place; 《文》misplace.

いれば 入れ歯 an artificial [a false] tooth ¶入れ歯をする have a false tooth put in / 入れ歯をしている wear false teeth / 入れ歯をはめる [はずす] put in [take out] one's false teeth / 総入れ歯 (full) dentures / 数本つないだ入れ歯 a partial denture. 文例⇩

いれもの 入れ物 《文》 a receptacle; a container; 《文》a vessel; something to put (it) in. 文例⇩

いれる 入れる 〈中に〉 put in [into]; let sb [into (the room)]; 〈加える〉 add (to); 〈はめこむ〉 set (in); 《文》insert; 〈詰める〉 stuff; 〈収容する〉 《文》accommodate; hold; take in 《a patient》 ¶綿を入れる stuff [wad] (clothes) with cotton wool / 生徒を入れる admit students / (親が)子供を学校へ入れる send a child to school / コーヒーを入れる make [brew] coffee / スイッチを入れる switch (an electric stove) on / 人の説を入れる accept sb's view / 要求を入れる agree [《文》accede] to sb's demand / 利息を入れて[入れずに] 10万円 100,000 yen inclusive [exclusive] of interest.

いろ 色 a color; 〈色合い〉《文》a hue; a tint;

---

in the garden. / 笑わずにはいられなかった. I could not help laughing [help but laugh].

いる³ 僕は50万円要る. I must have 500,000 yen. / その仕事にはかなり人手が要る. The work will require [take] quite a number of hands. / もうこの本は要らなくなった. I don't want this book any more. / 私の暮らしには車は要らない. The way I live, I can do without a car. / 要らない世話をやくな. Mind your own business! / 君は要らない事をしたよ. You didn't need to do that. | That was quite [totally] unnecessary!

いる⁵ この像は青銅で鋳たものだ. This statue is cast in bronze.

いるい この地区の人々は食糧も乏しく, 住居も劣悪で, 充分な被服もない. The people of this area are ill fed, ill sheltered and ill clothed.

いるす 彼に会って来たって? 僕は居留守を使ったんだ. You've been to see him? Well, he was not at home to me.

いれかえ 当館は入れ替え制です 〈映画館の掲示〉 Ticket valid for one program only. / 入れ替えなし.〈同上〉Ticket valid throughout day of issue. | 〈英〉Continuous programme.

いれかえる お茶を入れ替えましょうか. Shall I make some fresh tea?

イレギュラー ボールがイレギュラーした.〈野球〉The ball took a bad bounce.

いれぐい 入れ食いだった. The fish took the bait as fast as I could get the hook into the water. | I had a bite with every cast of my line.

いれずみ その水夫は腕にいかりの入れ墨をしていた. The sailor had an anchor tattooed on his arm.

いれちがい 田中と入れ違いに山田が来た. Yamada came in just after Tanaka had left. / 手紙が入れ違いになった. My letter crossed (with his). | Our letters crossed.

いれば 私の歯は入れ歯ではありません. These are my own teeth.

いれもの それを持って行くのに何か入れ物が欲しい. I want something to carry it in.

いれる この箱には何が入れてあるのですか. What do you keep in this box? / 紅茶にミルクをお入れになりますか. Do you take milk in your tea? / この講堂は2千人入れられる. This hall seats [will hold] 2,000 people. / 彼は快く私の請いを入れた. He willingly complied with my request. / 彼の教えは少しも世にいれられなかった. The public would not listen

いろあい a tinge; 濃淡 a shade; 〈肌の〉a complexion; 〈様子〉a look; 《文》an air ¶色が濃い[淡]い be deep [light] in color / 〈肌の〉色が白[黒]い be fair [dark]; have a fair [dark] complexion / ありとあらゆる色の《pencils》of every color of the rainbow / 〈肌の〉色の白い fair(-complexioned) / 日焼けして色が黒くなる get 《文》 become] tanned; get sunburnt / 色が変わる change color; 〈あせる〉be discolored; fade / 色を失う lose color; turn pale 《with fear》/ ...の色を帯びる be tinged with 《red》/ 色を付ける〈着色する〉color; give color to; paint; tint; 〈譲歩する〉give in a little; make some concession; add something extra 《to sb's regular pay》/ 憤然として色をなす turn red with anger / 疲労の色を見せる look tired. 文例⇩

いろあい 色合い a shade; 《文》a hue; a tint; a tinge; the tone (of a color) 〈色調〉. 文例⇩

いろいろ 色々 ¶いろいろ(に) in many [various] ways; variously / いろいろな various; all sorts of; of different [all] kinds [sorts]; various kinds of; a variety of; 〈雑多な〉miscellaneous / いろいろな動物 various [different kinds of] animals / いろいろと手を尽くす do everything one can think of; try every (possible) means. 文例⇩

いろう¹ 遺漏 《文》(an) omission; 〈見落とし〉(an) oversight ¶遺漏なく without omission; 〈徹底的に〉thoroughly; 〈文〉exhaustively / 遺漏なく調べる《文》make an exhaustive investigation 《of》. 文例⇩

いろう² 慰労 ¶店員慰労の会を催す give a party by way of rewarding one's employees for their services / 慰労休暇 a special holiday given in recognition of one's services / 慰労金 (get) a bonus; a reward for one's services.

いろえんぴつ 色鉛筆 a colored pencil.

いろおとこ 色男 〈美男子〉a handsome man; 〈女にもてる男〉a lady-killer. 文例⇩

いろか 色香 ¶女の色香に迷う fall a victim to the charms of a woman; be infatuated with a woman.

いろがみ 色紙 colored paper.

いろきちがい 色気違い a sex maniac.

いろけ 色気 〈関心〉interest in the opposite sex; 〈魅力〉sex appeal; glamor ¶色気がつく begin to think of the opposite sex [of girls, of boys]; reach adolescence / 色気のある 《文》sexually attractive; sexy / 色気のない女 a woman with no sex appeal; a sexless woman / 色気のない返した短篇小説 a curt [brusque] answer / お色気を利かした短篇小説 a spicy short story / ...に色気たっぷりである have a good mind to do; be very interested 《in》.

いろごと 色事 a love affair; 《文》an affair of the heart; 〈文〉an intrigue ¶色事師 a rake; a lady-killer; 《文》a Don Juan.

いろじかけ 色仕掛け ¶色仕掛けで by using one's sexual charm (for an ulterior purpose). 文例⇩

いろしゅうさ 色収差 〖光〗chromatic aberration.

いろじろ 色白 ¶色白の fair(-complexioned).

いろずり 色刷り color printing ¶色刷りの鳥類図鑑 a book of birds illustrated in color [with color illustrations] / 色刷りにする print (a picture) in color.

いろづく 色付く 《文》acquire [take on] a color; 〈紅葉する〉turn red [yellow]; break into color; color.

いろっぽい 色っぽい erotic; seductive; sexy; 《文》amorous; 〈文〉coquettish.

いろつや 色艶 (a) color; 〈肌の〉a complexion; 〈光沢〉luster ¶肌の色つやがいい have a healthy [good] complexion / 色つやが悪い have an unhealthy complexion; look pale.

いろどり 彩り 〈着色〉coloring; 〈配色〉a color scheme.

いろとりどり 色とりどり ¶色とりどりの〈複数のものが〉of various colors; 〈1つのものが〉multicolored; 《文》varicolored; 〈種類が〉various kinds of 《clothes》.

いろどる 彩る color; paint; 〈染める〉dye. 文例⇩

いろなおし 色直し 〈結婚式の〉the bride's changing of dresses (at the wedding dinner).

いろは the iroha; the Japanese syllabary; 〈初歩〉the ABC; 《文》the rudiments ¶〈物事を〉いろはから始める begin from the beginning / 囲碁をいろはから習う learn the rudiments of the game of go as an absolute beginner.

いろめ 色目 ¶色目を使う cast a flirtatious

---

to [heed] his teachings. / スト中の労働者は要求がいれられたのでみな就業した. The strikers, their demands having been met, all returned to work. / 私の家族は私自身を入れて7人です. My family has seven members, counting [including] myself.

いろ それは何色ですか. What color is it? / 何色の糸が欲しいのですか. What color thread do you want? / それは色が桜草に似ている. It resembles a primrose in color. / これを緑色に染めてもらいたい. I want it dyed green. / タコはその居る場所によって体の色を変える. The octopus changes color according to its surroundings. / 犬は色の som が識別できない. Dogs cannot see colors [see in color, perceive colors]. | Dogs do not possess color vision. / 彼はその知らせに色を失った. All the color left his face when he heard the news.

いろあい デザインも色合いも申し分がない. It's perfect in both design and coloring.

いろいろ 行ってみるといろいろの人がいますよ. You will find all sorts of people there. / 菊には種類もいろいろある. There are a number of varieties of chrysanthemum. / こんなにいろいろな事を覚えたって何になるものか. What is the good of learning all these things? / いろいろやることがある. I've got lots of things to do. / 彼はいろいろやってみたあげく, その発明に成功した. He succeeded in the invention after many trials and errors. / 理由はそれこそいろいろある. There are many, many reasons for it. / いろいろ質問された. They plied me with questions. / 日本ではいろいろの事が変わった. Things have changed in Japan. / 世間はいろいろだ. It takes all sorts (of people) to make a world. / いろいろありがとう. Thanks for everything.

[《文》coquettish] glance《at》;《口語》make eyes《at》; eye *sb*; ogle《at》.

いろめがね 色眼鏡《a pair of》colored glasses; 〈サングラス〉sunglasses ¶色眼鏡で物を見る look on *sth* from a biased viewpoint [《文》with a jaundiced eye].

いろめく 色めく 〈活気づく〉become lively [animated]; liven up; 〈興奮する〉get excited; grow agitated.

いろもの 色物 〈着色品〉a colored article; 〈生地〉colored fabrics.

いろよい 色良い ¶色よい返事 a favorable answer.

いろり 囲炉裏 a hearth; a fireplace ¶囲炉裏を囲んで座る sit round the fire / 囲炉裏端で by the fireside. [文例⇩]

いろわけ 色分け 〈分類〉(a) classification; (a) division; 〈複雑な配線や図版などの色彩による区別〉color-coding ¶色分けをする classify; sort; divide; color-code / 色分け地図 a colored map.

いろん 異論 〈反対〉an objection; a protest ¶異論を唱える object《to》; raise an objection《to, against》; take exception《to》. [文例⇩]

いわ 岩 (a) rock; a crag (ごつごつした) ¶岩の多い rocky; craggy / 岩のごろごろした斜面 a rock-strewn slope / 自然のままの岩に彫った仏像 an image of Buddha carved in the surface of a living rock.

いわい 祝い congratulation(s); 〈祝い事〉a celebration; festivities; 〈祝祭〉a festival ¶…の祝いに in celebration of…; to congratulate… / 祝い酒 a celebratory drink / 祝い状 a letter of congratulation; a congratulatory letter / 祝い箸 special festive chopsticks. [文例⇩]

いわう 祝う congratulate《*sb* on *his* success》; offer *one's* congratulations《to *sb* on *his* recovery》; 〈事柄を〉celebrate [commemorate]《an event》; hold a celebration; observe《a festival》¶勝利を祝う celebrate [《文》rejoice over] a victory / …を祝って in celebration of…; to congratulate….

いわかん 違和感《文》a sense of incompatibility; a feeling that *one* does not belong《in a place》. [文例⇩]

いわく 曰く 〈言う〉say; 〈理由〉a reason; a cause; 〈来歴〉a history ¶いわくがあって for certain reasons / いわくありげな《文》meaning(ful);《文》disingenuous / いわくつきのダイヤモンド a diamond with a history attached to it. [文例⇩]

いわし 鰯 a sardine ¶いわしの缶詰め《米》canned [《英》tinned] sardines. [文例⇩]

いわしぐも 鰯雲 a cirrocumulus《*pl.* -li》.

いわずかたらず 言わず語らず ¶言わず語らずのうちに《文》tacitly;《文》by tacit understanding;《文》implicitly; by implication.

いわずもがな 言わずもがな 〈言うべきでない〉ought not to say; 〈言うまでもない〉⇨ いう (…は言うまでもない). [文例⇩]

いわだな 岩棚 a rock ledge [shelf, platform].

いわな 岩魚 a char(r).

いわば[1] 岩場〖登山〗a craggy place.

いわば[2] 言わば《文》so to speak;《文》as it were;《文》in a manner of speaking; 〈ある意味では〉in a sense ¶いわば…のようなものである may (possibly) be compared [《文》likened] to….

いわゆる 所謂 the so-called…; what is called…; what you [they] call…. [文例⇩]

いわれ 〈理由〉a reason; a cause; 〈由緒〉a history; an origin ¶いわれのない《文》baseless《rumors》; unfounded《allegations》; 〈無理な〉unreasonable; unjustified / いわれなく without any reason [cause]. [文例⇩]

いわんや 言わんや much [still] more [less (否定)]; not to mention [speak of]; to say nothing of; let alone. [文例⇩]

いん[1] 印 〈印章〉a seal; 〈スタンプ〉a stamp ¶印を押す put [《文》affix] *one's* seal《to》.

いん[2] 因 ⇨ げんいん[1].

いん[3] 陰 the negative ¶陰に陽に《文》implicitly and explicitly; publicly and privately; in every possible way. [文例⇩]

いん[4] 韻 a rhyme ¶韻を踏む rhyme《with》.

いんいんめつめつ 陰々滅々 ¶陰々滅々とした gloomy and depressing.

いんうつ 陰鬱 ¶陰鬱な gloomy; depressing; dreary; cheerless; dismal / 陰鬱な空 an overcast [《文》a leaden] sky / 陰鬱な雲 heavy [sullen] clouds / 陰鬱な天候 gloomy [miserable] weather / 陰鬱な顔をしている look gloomy

---

いろう[1] 万事遺漏のないようにしなさい. See that nothing goes amiss.

いろおとこ (ふざけて)いよう, 色男! Aren't we handsome today!

いろじかけ 彼女は色仕掛けで彼から情報を得ようとした. By turning on her charm, she tried to get information out of him.

いろどる 西の空が夕日に美しく彩られていた. The western sky was beautifully colored by the setting sun.

いろり いろりの上に大きななべがかかっていた. A large pot hung over the hearth.

いろん 僕には別に異論はない. I have no objection to it. | I take no particular exception to it.

いわい お祝いに一杯やりましょう. Let's celebrate (the occasion) with a drink. / ご卒業をお祝い申し上げます. I offer you my congratulations on your graduation.

いわかん 違和感を感じた. I felt out of place.

いわく いわく言い難し. It is a hard question. | That is hard to explain.

いわし いわしの頭も信心から. Anything can be deified.

いわずもがな 言わずもがなのことを言ってしまった. I oughtn't to have said that. | I'd have been better leaving that unsaid.

いわゆる いわゆる人間学というものが単なる学問より大切だ. The 'science of humanity' is more important than mere book learning.

いわれ 僕がそれをしなければならないといういわれはない. There is no reason why I must do it. | There's no law that says I've got to do it.

いわんや 彼は代数も幾何も知らぬ, 言わんや三角法をやだ. He knows neither algebra nor geometry, let alone trigonometry.

いん[3] 寺の鐘が陰にこもってごーんと鳴った. There boomed the

[い]

[depressed, glum] / 陰鬱に gloomily ; drearily ; dismally.
いんえい 陰影 a shadow ; shade ; 〈画の〉 shade(s) ¶陰影をつける shade 《a picture》; put in the shadings.
いんおうご 印欧語 an Indo-European language.
いんか 引火 ¶引火する《文》ignite ; catch [take] fire / 極めて引火しやすい be highly inflammable / 引火点 the flash(ing) point.
インカ ¶インカ人 an Inca 《*pl.* -(s)》 / インカ帝国 the Inca Empire.
いんが[1] 因果 cause and effect ; 〈運命〉 fate ; 〈不運〉 misfortune ¶因果な unfortunate ; unlucky / 因果なことに as ill luck would have it ; to make matters worse / 因果とあきらめる resign *oneself* to *one's* fate [《文》lot] / 因果を含める《文》tell *sb* to reconcile *himself* to *his* lot ; persuade *sb* to accept *his* fate / 因果応報《文》retribution ; 《文》retributive justice / 因果関係 the relation of cause and effect ; a causal relationship 《between》; causality / 因果律 the law [principle] of causality [causation]. [文例⇩]
いんが[2] 陰画〘写真〙a negative (picture).
いんがい 院外 ¶院外の outside the Diet / 院外団 members 《of the Liberal Democratic Party》 who have no seat in the Diet.
いんかく 陰核〘解〙the clitoris.
いんがし 印画紙〘写真〙printing paper.
いんかしょくぶつ 隠花植物 a cryptogam ; a flowerless plant.
いんかん 印鑑 〈印章〉 *one's* seal ; 〈押した形〉 a seal impression ¶印鑑を届ける have *one's* seal impression registered / 印鑑証明 a certificate of *one's* seal impression.
いんき 陰気 ¶陰気な gloomy ; dismal ; 《文》melancholy ; 《文》cheerless / 陰気な顔をしている wear a gloomy [long] face ; look melancholy [《口語》blue] / 陰気臭い部屋 a gloomy(-looking) room. [文例⇩]
インキ ⇨インク.
いんぎ 院議 〈議決〉 a decision of the House ; 〈討議〉 a debate in the House ¶院議に付する send 《a bill》 to the floor.
いんきょ 隠居 〈引退〉 retirement (from active life) ; 〈人〉 a person retired from active life ¶隠居する retire (from active life).
いんきょく 陰極〘電〙the negative pole ; the cathode ¶陰極管 a cathode(-ray) tube / 陰極線 cathode rays.
いんきん 陰金〘医〙ringworm (in the groin) ; tinea cruris.
いんぎん 慇懃 ¶いんぎんな〈丁重な〉 polite ; courteous ; civil / いんぎんに politely ; courteously / いんぎん無礼である be polite 《to *sb*》 on the surface but actually contemptuous 《of *him*》; be unctuous but insulting ; be (offensively) obsequious.
インク ink ¶インクのしみ an ink stain / インクの香も新しい新聞 a newspaper fresh from the press / 赤インクで書く write in red ink / ペンとインクで書く write with (a) pen and ink / インク消し an ink eraser / インクびん a bottle of ink ; an ink bottle.
イングランド England.
いんけい 陰茎 the penis 《*pl.* penises, penes》.
いんけん 陰険 ¶陰険な sly ; wily ; 《文》guileful ; 《文》insidious ; treacherous ; underhand / 陰険な手段を用いる use subtle tricks ; play a deep game. [文例⇩]
いんげんまめ 隠元豆 a kidney bean ; 《英》a haricot (bean).
いんこ〘鳥〙a parakeet ; a macaw (こんごういんこ) ; a cockatoo (ぼたんいんこ).
いんご 隠語 secret language ; 《thieves'》 cant.
いんこう 咽喉 the throat.
いんごう 因業 ¶因業な〈無情な〉 hardhearted ; heartless ; merciless ; pitiless / 因業な大家(おおや) a harsh [grasping] landlord.
インコース〘陸上競技〙an inner [the inside] lane 《of a track》 ¶インコースの球を投げる〘野球〙pitch a ball close to the batter.
いんさつ 印刷 printing ; presswork ¶印刷する print ; put into print / 印刷したばかりの fresh [damp] from the press / 印刷になっている be in print / 印刷に付する print *sth* ; have *sth* printed / 印刷に付される be printed ; go to press ; find 《its》 way into print / 印刷中である be in (the) press / 印刷に出す send 《a manuscript》 to the press / 印刷インク printing [printer's] ink / 印刷機 a (printing) press ; a printing machine / 印刷技術 a printing technique / 印刷業 the printing industry / 印刷所 a printing office [house, shop] / (書物などの1度の)印刷部数 a pressrun ; a run / 印刷物 printed matter ; 《英》printed papers / 印刷屋 [工] a printer / 印刷用紙 printing paper. [文例⇩]
いんさん 陰惨 ¶陰惨な gruesome ; horrible ; grim.
いんし[1] 因子 a factor.
いんし[2] 印紙 a stamp ¶100円の印紙 a 100-yen stamp / 印紙をはる put a stamp 《on》; 《文》affix a stamp 《to》 / 印紙税 stamp duty.
いんじ 印字 ¶印字する print ; type (out) / (コンピューターなどの)印字機 a printer.
インジウム〘化〙indium.
いんしつ 陰湿 ¶陰湿な〈性格などが〉 spiteful ; malicious ; 〈手段などが〉 underhand ; 《文》insidious ; 〈場所が〉 damp.
いんしゅ 飲酒 drinking ¶飲酒運転 drunken driving ; driving 《a car》 while intoxicated [un-

---

dismal sound of a temple bell.
いんが[1] 僕は何の因果でこう苦しむのだろう. What have I done to deserve to suffer like this? / 因果な性分だ. One cannot help one's nature. / 親の因果が子に報いる. The sins of the fathers are visited upon the children.
いんき そんな陰気な話はもうやめましょう. Let's stop talking about such gloomy subjects. / 子供が死んで家中が陰気になった. The death of the child cast a shadow over the whole family.
いんけん 陰険なやつだ. He's a sly old fox.
いんさつ 印刷が鮮明だ. It is clearly printed. / 自分の名が印刷になっているのを見たときはうれしかった. I was pleased to see my name in print. / 印刷物在中. 〈封筒の上書〉. Printed matter. | 《英》Printed papers.
いんしょう[2] ロンドンの印象はい

いんしゅう 因習 (a) convention ¶因習的な conventional / 因習を打破する do away with conventionalities / 因習にとらわれている《文》be a slave to convention; be bound by convention.

インシュリン 【薬】insulin ¶インシュリンショック insulin shock.

いんしょう¹ 印章 a seal; a stamp.

いんしょう² 印象 an impression ¶あざやかな[ぼんやりした]印象 a vivid [vague] impression / …という印象を与える give [《文》convey] the impression that…; strike one as ((unnatural)) / いい印象を与える give a good impression ((to sb)); make a good impression ((on sb, on sb's mind)); impress sb favorably / 印象を残す leave an impression ((on sb's mind)); leave sb with an impression ((of)) [the impression ((that…))] / 第一印象 one's [the] first impressions ((of)) / 印象的な impressive; striking / 印象主義【芸術】impressionism / 印象派 the impressionist school; the impressionists / 後期印象派 the postimpressionists / 印象批評 impressionistic criticism. 文例⇩

いんしょく 飲食 ¶飲食する eat and drink / 飲食物 food and drink / 飲食店 an eating house [place]; a restaurant. 文例⇩

いんしん 陰唇 【解】the labia (★ labium の複数形); the lips of the vulva ¶大[小]陰唇 the labia majora [minora].

いんすう 因数 【数】a factor ¶因数に分解する factorize [factor] ((an expression)); resolve [break up] ((a quantity)) into factors / 因数分解 factorization.

いんずう 員数 the (total) number ¶員数をそろえる fill up the number; make up the numbers ((of)).

インスタント ¶インスタントコーヒー instant coffee / インスタント食品 convenience [precooked, fast] food(s) / インスタントラーメン precooked Chinese noodles.

インスピレーション (an) inspiration ¶インスピレーションを受ける receive [get] an idea [one's inspiration] ((from)); be inspired ((by)). 文例⇩

いんせい 陰性 ¶陰性の〈気質が〉gloomy; 〈反応が〉negative; 〈病気が〉dormant.

いんぜい 印税 royalties ((on a book)).

いんせき¹ 引責 ¶引責辞職する take the responsibility on oneself and resign.

いんせき² 姻戚 ¶姻戚関係にある be related by marriage ((to)).

いんせき³ 隕石 a meteorite.

いんぜん 隠然 ¶隠然たる〈隠れた〉《文》latent; 〈事実上の〉《文》virtual / 隠然たる勢力 (a) latent power.

いんそつ 引率 ¶引率する lead; be in charge of ((a party)) /…を引率して leading a party of…; at the head of… / 引率者 a leader. 文例⇩

インターカレッジ ¶インターカレッジの intercollegiate.

インターセプト 【蹴球】an interception ¶インターセプトする intercept ((a forward pass)).

インターチェンジ an interchange ¶クローバー型インターチェンジ a cloverleaf (interchange).

インターナショナル 〈国際労働者同盟〉the International (Working Men's Association); 〈歌〉the Internationale.

インターハイ an inter-high school ((athletic)) competition.

インターバル an interval ¶インターバル練習 training [practicing] with regular intervals of rest.

インターフェア 【競技】interference ¶インターフェアする interfere (in the play of the opposing team, with a member of the opposing team).

インターホン 〈装置〉an intercom; an intercommunication system; 〈送受器〉an intercommunication phone.

インターン an intern(e) ¶インターンとして勤務する serve one's internship ((at a hospital)); intern.

いんたい 引退 ¶引退する retire (from active life) / 引退している live in retirement.

インダス ¶インダス川 the Indus River / インダス文明 the Indus (valley) civilization.

インタビュー an interview ¶インタビューする interview sb; have an interview ((with)) / インタビューする[される]人 an interviewer [interviewee]. 文例⇩

インチ an inch ((略: in.)) ¶5フィート8インチ five feet eight inches; 5 ft. 8 in.; 5′8″. 文例⇩

いんちき 〈だますこと〉cheating; 〈にせもの〉a fake ¶いんちきな fake; bogus; 《俗》phon(e)y / いんちきをやる cheat; fake.

いんちょう 院長 the director ((of a hospital)); the president ((of an academy)).

インディアナ Indiana ((略: Ind.)) ¶インディアナ州の人 an Indianan.

インディアペーパー India paper.

インディアン an Indian; an American Indian; a Red Indian.

インディオ an Indian → インディアン.

いんてつ 隕鉄 meteoric iron.

インテリア 〈内部〉the interior ¶インテリアデザイナー an interior designer / インテリアデザイン interior design.

インテリ(ゲンチャ) 〈総称〉intellectuals; 《文》

かがでしたか. What was your impression of London? / あのときの印象は忘れられない. I'll never forget the impression I received at that time.

いんしょく 夏は飲食物に気をつけなさい. Be careful about what you eat and drink in summer.

インスピレーション その時インスピレーションがわいた. Just then I had an inspiration [《米》a brainstorm《英》a brainwave].

いんそつ 先生は生徒たちを引率して遠足に行った. The teacher went on a short trip with his pupils.

インタビュー その時には盛んに写真にとられたりインタビューされたりした. At that time I was always being photographed and interviewed.

インチ 彼は身長が6フィート1インチある. He is six feet one inch tall. | He is[stands] six-foot-one.

the intelligentsia; 〈1人〉an intellectual; an educated person ¶インテリ向きの雑誌 a highbrow magazine / インテリ女性 an intellectual [educated] woman.

いんでんき 陰電気 negative electricity.

いんでんし 陰電子 an electron.

インド India ¶インドの Indian / インド共和国 the Republic of India / インド語 〈公用語〉Hindi / 東[西]インド諸島 the East [West] Indies / インド人 an Indian / インド洋 the Indian Ocean.

いんとう 咽頭 《解》the pharynx (*pl.* -rynges, -ynxes) ¶咽頭炎 pharyngitis.

いんどう 引導 ¶引導を渡す say a requiem 《for a departed soul》; 〈覚悟させる〉tell sb to prepare for the worst; 〈終わらせる〉put an end to; 《文》give sb the coup de grace.

いんとく 隠匿 ¶隠匿する《文》conceal; hide; 〈かくまう〉shelter.

インドシナ インドシナ半島 Indochina; the Indochinese Peninsula.

イントネーション (an) intonation ¶イントネーション曲線 an intonation contour.

インドネシア Indonesia ¶インドネシアの Indonesian / インドネシア共和国 the Republic of Indonesia / インドネシア語 Indonesian / インドネシア人 an Indonesian.

イントロダクション an introduction; 〈ポピュラー曲の〉《口語》an intro (*pl.* -s).

いんとん 隠遁 ¶隠遁する retire from the world; live in retirement; 〈世を捨てる〉renounce the world; 〈文〉be a recluse; a hermit.

いんない 院内 ¶院内の[で] inside the House [Diet] / 院内総務《米》the floor leader; 《英》a (party) whip.

いんにく 印肉 an inkpad; a stamp pad.

いんにん 隠忍 ¶隠忍自重する be patient; endure; put up with. 文例⇩

いんねん 因縁 〈宿命〉fate; (a) destiny; 〈由来〉the origin; the history; 〈ゆかり〉《文》affinity; connection ¶因縁とあきらめる resign *oneself* to one's fate / 浅からぬ因縁がある be deeply related 《to》; be closely connected 《with》/ 因縁をつける pick a fight [quarrel] 《with sb》; invent a pretext for a quarrel 《with sb》.

いんのう 陰嚢 the scrotum (*pl.* -tums, -ta).

いんび 隠微 ¶隠微な obscure; 《文》latent; hidden; cryptic; 〈微妙な〉subtle.

いんぶ 陰部 the genital area; 〈婉曲に〉the private parts; the privates ¶外陰部 the external genitals.

インファイト 《ボクシング》infighting.

インプット 《コンピューター》input 《to》.

インフルエンザ influenza;《口語》(the) flu ¶インフルエンザにかかる get [catch,《文》contract] influenza / インフルエンザにかかっている have [be suffering from] influenza; have flu; be sick with the flu. 文例⇩

インフレ(ーション) inflation ¶インフレの昂進率 the rate of inflation; an inflation rate / インフレを来たす[抑える] cause [check] inflation / 悪性インフレ vicious [virulent] inflation / インフレ傾向[政策] an inflationary tendency [policy] / インフレ対策 counter-inflation measures.

いんぶん 韻文 〈散文に対して〉verse;《詩》a poem; poetry (総称) ¶韻文で書く write 《a play》in verse.

いんぺい 隠蔽 ¶隠蔽する《文》conceal; hide; cover (up).

いんぼう 陰謀 a plot;《文》an [a secret] intrigue; (a) conspiracy (共謀) ¶陰謀を企てる[たくらむ] plot; lay a plot;《文》intrigue 《against》; conspire 《against》/ 陰謀家 a schemer; a conspirator.

いんめつ 隠滅 ¶隠滅する destroy 《evidence》.

いんもう 陰毛 pubic hair.

いんゆ 隠喩 a metaphor.

いんよう¹ 引用 quotation ¶引用する quote 《from a book》; cite 《an instance》¶シェイクスピアの作品の一節を引用する quote (a passage from) Shakespeare / 引用する価値のある quotable / 引用句[文] a quotation;《口語》a quote / 引用符 quotation marks;《口語》quotes / 引用符でくくる put in quotation marks [quotes]; enclose in inverted commas. 用語 ' ' を single quotation marks, " " を double quotation marks という. また引用文を読み上げるときは, はじめに quote, 終わりに unquote と言って, 引用文の開始と終結を明らかにする. 簡単で丁寧な場合には単に quotes とだけ言えばよい.

いんよう² 陰陽 the (interacting) principles of Yin and Yang; the positive and negative [male and female] principles.

いんよう³ 飲用 ¶飲用する drink / 飲用の for drinking / 飲用に適する be fit [good] to drink; be drinkable / 飲用に適さない be unfit to drink.

いんりつ 韻律 〈詩の〉(a) meter; 〈リズム〉(a) rhythm.

いんりょう 飲料 a drink;《文》a beverage ¶飲料水 drinking water; water to drink. 文例⇩

いんりょく 引力 〈天体の〉gravitation; (the force [pull] of) gravity; (a) gravitational force [power, pull]; 〈物体間の〉(gravitational) attraction; (an) attractive force ¶引力の法則 the law of gravitation / 引力を及ぼす exert a

---

いんにん 彼は隠忍自重して機の熟するのを待った. He waited patiently for the time to be ripe [for the opportunity to mature].
インフルエンザ インフルエンザが大いにはやっている. There's a lot of flu about.
いんよう¹ 次にロングフェローの詩が数行引用されている. Next we find a few lines quoted from Longfellow. / 私の言葉は前後を無視して引用された. I was quoted out of context.
いんりょう 飲料水.《掲示》Drinking water.
うえ¹ 宇宙では上も下もないから身体の向きは問題にならない. In space there is no up or down, so

one's bodily position is immaterial. / あの建物の右上を飛行機が飛んでいる. There's an airplane flying above and to the right of that building. / 彼はワイシャツの袖をひじの上までまくり上げていた. His shirt sleeves were rolled up above [past] his elbows. / 彼は私の一枚上を行っ

gravitational pull [influence] 《on *sth*》/ 引力に逆らって against [in defiance of] (the force of) gravity / 太陽[地球]の引力 solar [terrestrial] gravitation / 引力圏 the 《moon's》 sphere of gravitation; the gravitational field 《of the earth》.

いんれき 陰暦 the lunar calendar ⇨ きゅうれき.

う

う¹ 卯 〈十二支の〉 (the Year of) the Hare.
う² 《鳥》 a cormorant ¶うの目たかの目で (search) with sharp [keen] eyes.
ウイークエンド a weekend ⇨ しゅうまつ¹.
ウイークデー a weekday.
ウイーン [<《ドイツ語》*Wien*] Vienna ¶ウィーンの Viennese.
ういういしい 初々しい fresh; unsophisticated.
ういきょう 茴香 《植》 a fennel. ¶ ⇨ うぶ.
ウイグル ¶ウイグル語 Uighur / ウイグル人 a Uighur; the Uighur people (総称).
ういざん 初産 one's first childbirth.
ウイスキー whisky ¶ウイスキーをストレートで飲む drink whisky straight [neat].
ウイスコンシン Wisconsin (略: Wis., Wisc.) ¶ウイスコンシン州の人 a Wisconsinite.
ウイット wit ¶ウイットのある witty.
ういまご 初孫 one's first grandchild.
ウイルス a virus ¶風邪のウイルス the common cold virus / ウイルス病 a virus [viral] disease / ウイルス学 virology.
ウインカー 〈車の〉 direction indicators; blinkers; winkers. 「give *sb* a wink.
ウインク a wink ¶ウインクする wink 《at》
ウインタースポーツ winter sports.
ウインチ a winch; a hoist ¶ウインチで持ち上げる[下ろす] winch *sth* up [down].
ウインドー ⇨ ショーウインドー.
ウインドブレーカー 《商標名》 《米》 a Windbreaker / 《英》 a windcheater.
ウインナ ⇨ ウイーン ¶ウインナコーヒー coffee served with a large quantity of fresh cream / ウインナソーセージ a wienerwurst;《米》 a wiener;《米口語》 a weenie.
ウーマンリブ women's liberation [lib];《運動》 the women's liberation [lib] movement ¶ウーマンリブの活動家 an activist in the women's liberation movement;《口語》 a women's libber. 「suit.
ウール wool ¶ウールの服 a woolen [wool]
ウーロンちゃ ウーロン茶 oolong. 「well.
ううん 〈いいえ〉 no;〈ためらいを表わして〉 うーん ¶うーんとうなる groan; give a groan うーんと言って倒れる fall with a groan.

うえ¹ 上 〈上部〉 the upper part;〈表面〉 the surface;〈頂上〉 the top;〈山の〉 the summit 〈上部・上方の〉 up; upward; upper;〈高い〉 higher 《than》;〈…以上の〉 more than; above; over; beyond;〈すぐれた〉 better 《than》;《文》 superior 《to》;〈年上の〉 older 《than》 / 一番上の the topmost; the uppermost / ページの右上のすみ the top right-hand corner of the page / 上の地位 a higher position / 10歳より上の子供たち children of ten years and upward / …の上に[を] 〈表面に接して〉 on;《文》 upon;〈表面から離れて〉 over; above;〈上方に〉 up / 机の上の[上にある]本 the book on [on top of] the desk ★ 本の中や下にある本との区別をはっきり付けたいときに, on the desk でなく, on top of the desk と言う / 入口の上の看板 a signboard over the entrance / 上を下への大騒ぎである be in complete [utter] confusion; be like an upturned anthill / 頭の上を飛ぶ fly overhead [over *one's* head] / 人の上に立つ lead others / 上の方に[へ] upward / 上に述べたように as we have said [as was mentioned] above / 上から下まで from top to bottom / 上から3行目 the third line from the top / 上からの命令 an order from above / 上から下へ[下から上へ] 順番に in descending [ascending] order / …の[した]上に besides…;《文》 in addition to…; on top of…; as well as …／…した[である]上は since…; now that…; seeing that… / 試験の上で on [after] examination / 十分に考慮した上で《文》 after due consideration / 酒の上で under the influence of drink [liquor] / 山の上で at the top of a mountain. 文例⬇

うえ² 飢え hunger; starvation ¶飢えをしのぐ stave [keep] off 《*one's*》 hunger.
ウェーター a waiter.
ウエーティングサークル 《野球》 the on-deck circle; the next batter's box.
ウエーデルン 《スキー》 wedeling ¶ウエーデルンをする wedel.
ウエート weight ¶ウエートを置く〈重視す

た. He went one better than me. ⇨ より¹ 囲例 / 上を見ればきりがない. Don't compare yourself with those above you. | Don't aspire too high. | 英文を書く力は彼の方が君より上だ. He is better than you at writing English. | 上には上がある. There is no limit to excellence. | Greatness is com- parative. / 彼は私より3つ年が上です. He is three years older than me [I am]. ⇨ より² 囲例 /《文》 He is my senior by three years. / 上の方の妹が子供みたいに訳がわからなかったので, 僕は腹を立ててしまった. I got angry, because my older sister was acting like a child. / もうこの上申し上げるこ

とはありません. I have nothing more to say. | I have nothing to add to what I have already said. / 彼は実業家である上に音楽家でもあった. Besides being a businessman, he was a musician. | He was a businessman, and a musician as well. / 道に迷った上に雨にまで降られた. We lost our

ウエートレス / うかされる

る〉 give [《文》attach] (greater) importance (to); 〈強調する〉《文》lay emphasis (on); emphasize.
ウエートレス a waitress.
ウエーブ 〈髪の〉a wave ⇒パーマ(ネント). 文例⬇
ウェールズ Wales ¶ウェールズの Welsh / ウェールズ語 Welsh / ウェールズ人〈男〉a Welshman;〈女〉a Welshwoman;〈全体〉the Welsh.
うえかえ 植え替え transplanting; transplantation.
うえかえる 植え替える transplant.
うえき 植木〈庭木〉a garden plant [tree];〈鉢植えの〉a pot [potted] plant ¶植木ばさみ〈a pair of〉garden shears / 植木鉢 a flowerpot / 植木屋 a gardener (庭師); a nurseryman (苗木屋).
うえこみ 植え込み a planting; (a) shrubbery (低木);¶植え込みのある庭 a garden planted with trees.
うえした 上下 ⇒じょうげ ¶上下になる〈逆さになる〉be upside down; be topsy-turvy.
うえじに 飢え死に ¶飢え死にする die of [from] hunger; starve to death.
ウエスタン〈西部劇〉a Western;〈音楽〉country(-and-western) music.
ウエスト the waist ¶ウエストがほっそりしている have a slim waist / ウエストライン the waistline. 文例⬇
ウエストバージニア West Virginia (略: W. Va.) ¶ウエストバージニア州の人 a West Virginian.
うえつける 植え付ける plant; bed out;〈心に〉《文》implant. 文例⬇
ウエット ウエットな sentimental.
ウエディング ¶ウエディングケーキ[ドレス] a wedding cake [dress].
ウエハース a wafer.
ウェリントン Wellington
うえる¹ 植える plant ¶庭にばらを植える plant a garden with roses.
うえる² 飢える be [go] hungry; be starving;〈欲しがる〉be hungry (for); long [《文》thirst] (for); hanker (after, for) ¶飢えた hungry; starved; famished / 愛情に飢えている be starved of [hungry for] affection / 愛情に飢えている子供 a love-starved child / 知識に飢えている be thirsty for knowledge. 文例⬇

ウエルターきゅう ウエルター級 the welterweight class ¶ウエルター級の選手 a welterweight.
うお 魚 ⇒さかな¹ ¶魚市場 a fish market / 魚座〈天〉Pisces; the Fishes ⇒さ 文例.
うおうさおう 右往左往 ¶右往左往する go this way and that; run about in confusion.
ウオーターシュート a water chute.
ウオーミングアップ warming up; a warm-up ¶ウオーミングアップをする warm up.
ウオツカ vodka.
うおのめ 魚の目 a corn.
うか 羽化《昆》emergence ¶羽化する emerge / 羽化したばかりの蝶 a newly-emerged butterfly.
うかい¹ 迂回 ¶迂回する make a detour; detour; take [go (to a place)] by a roundabout route [course]; bypass (skirt around) (a town) / 5キロ迂回する make a detour of five kilometers / 工事現場を迂回して行く make a detour to avoid a construction site.
うかい² 鵜飼い〈事〉fishing with cormorants; cormorant fishing;〈人〉a cormorant fisherman.
うがい 嗽 ¶うがいする rinse (out) (one's mouth); gargle / うがい薬 a gargle; (a) mouthwash.
うかうか ⇒うっかり ¶うかうかしている be careless; be not paying attention;《文》be inattentive; be off one's guard. 文例⬇
うかがい 伺い〈訪問〉a call; a visit;〈質問〉an inquiry; a question ¶伺いを立てる ask for sb's instructions.
うかがう¹ 伺う〈訪れる〉call on sb; call at (sb's house); visit; pay sb a visit;〈問う〉ask 《sb about sth》; inquire 《whether..., 《文》of sb about sth》;〈聞く〉hear; be told. 文例⬇
うかがう² 窺う〈機会を〉watch [wait] for (a chance);〈探知する〉spy on;〈推測する〉《文》infer; gather; guess;〈のぞく〉peep into [through] ¶機会をうかがっている be on the watch [lookout] for an opportunity; be biding one's time / 形勢をうかがう wait and see how things go [how the wind blows]. 文例⬇
うかされる 浮かされる be carried away 《by》;

---

way, and, what was worse still, we were caught in a shower.
ウエーブ 彼女の髪には自然にウエーブがついている。Her hair has a natural wave [is naturally wavy].
ウエスト 彼女のウエストは70センチだ。She is [measures] 70 centimeters around the waist. / 彼女は若い頃に比べてウエストがだいぶ太くなった。Her waistline is much bigger than it was when she was young.
うえつける こうした考えが彼らの心にしっかりと植え付けられている。These ideas are firmly implanted [rooted] in their minds.
うえる² 妻子を飢えさすわけにはいかない。I can't let my family go hungry. / 人々は飢えてやせ細っている。The people are thin with hunger.
うかうか うかうかするな。Look sharp! / 今はうかうかしている時じゃない。This is no time for hanging about.
うかがう¹ 今夜お伺いいたしましょう。I'll be over tonight. / もう一つお伺いしたい事がございます。I have one more question to ask you. / 彼よりその事をあなたからお伺いしたように申しております。He says that he heard it from you. / 父がご出発の日時をお伺いするようにと申しております。My father would like to know when you are leaving.
うかがう² 彼がこの提案を受諾する意志がないことは、あんなことを言ったことからもうかがえる。It can be gathered from what he said that he has no intention of accepting this proposal. / 彼らが間違っているということはこの事からはっきりとうかがえる。This indicates [shows] unquestionably that they are in the wrong.
うかされる 彼は競馬熱に浮かされている。Horse-racing fever has taken hold of him. | He has caught the racing fever.
うかつ うかつな事をした。It was very careless [stupid] of me to do

うかす 浮かす ⇒うかべる.

うかつ 迂闊 ¶うかつな〈無思慮〉thoughtless;〈不注意〉careless;《文》inadvertent;〈愚か〉stupid / うかつに〈無思慮〉thoughtlessly;〈不注意〉carelessly; inadvertently;〈愚か〉stupidly. 文例⇩

うがつ 穿つ〈掘る〉dig; bore; excavate; drill ¶うがったことを言う make apt [penetrating] remarks / うがった推測をする make a shrewd guess. 文例⇩

うかぬかお 浮かぬ顔 a gloomy [glum, troubled] look ¶浮かぬ顔をする look gloomy [blue, troubled]; pull a long face.

うかびあがる 浮かび上がる〈水面に出る〉surface; come [rise] to the surface; break the surface;〈一旦沈んだものが〉be afloat (again);〈表面化する〉come to the front;〈下の地位から〉rise [emerge] from obscurity.

うかぶ 浮かぶ float (on the water, in the air);〈浮上する〉⇒ うかびあがる, うきあがる ¶心に浮かぶ come [spring] to mind; occur to one / ちらりと心に浮かぶ flash across one's mind / 浮かんでいる be afloat; be floating / 浮かぶ瀬がない have no chance to get on in the world.

うかべる 浮かべる float; set (a boat) afloat; sail (a toy boat) ¶悲しみの色を浮かべる look sad / 両眼に涙を浮かべて with tears in one's eyes / 口許に微笑を浮かべて with a smile on one's lips.

うかる 受かる pass (an examination).

うかれる 浮かれる〈ご機嫌である〉be very happy; be in high spirits; be in good [top, fine] form; be quite delighted;《口語》be tickled pink;〈騒ぐ〉make merry; have a frolic; be on the spree ¶酔って浮かれる be happily [cheerfully] drunk; be merry / 浮かれ歩く go out on a spree [binge]; go out [be] on the town.

うがん 右岸 (on) the right bank (of).

ウガンダ Uganda ¶ウガンダの Ugandan / ウガンダ共和国 the Republic of Uganda / ウガンダ人 a Ugandan.

うき¹ 雨期[季] the rainy [wet] season; the rains (熱帯の); the monsoon (season) (インドの). 文例⇩

うき² 浮き〈釣の〉a float;〈浮標〉a buoy ¶浮きをつける tie [fix] a float (to).

うきあがる 浮き上がる surface; rise [come] to the surface (of); break the surface. 文例⇩

うきあし 浮き足 ¶浮き足立つ〈逃げ腰になる〉be ready to run away; show every sign of taking to one's heels;〈自信を失う〉lose confidence;〈あわてる〉be disconcerted.

うきうき 浮き浮き ¶浮き浮きと buoyantly; cheerfully; with a light heart. 文例⇩

うきくさ 浮き草 duckweed; a floating weed (一般に).

うきぐも 浮き雲 a floating [drifting] cloud.

うきしずみ 浮き沈み ⇒ ふちん, えいせいすい. 文例⇩

うきす 浮き巣 a floating nest.

うきたつ 浮き立つ be buoyant; be cheered up ¶心を浮き立たせる cheer up; enliven;《文》exhilarate. 文例⇩

うきでる 浮き出る ⇒ うきあがる, うかびあがる.

うきな 浮き名 ¶浮き名を流す[立てられる] one's love affairs are [become] the talk of the town; get a reputation as a philanderer.

うきぶくろ 浮き袋〈水泳用の〉a (rubber) swimming ring;〈救命用の〉a life buoy [ring];〈魚の〉an air bladder ¶浮き袋をして泳ぐ swim with the help of a rubber ring.

うきぼり 浮き彫り a (carved [sculptured]) relief; (a) relief sculpture [carving] ¶浮き彫りにする carve in relief;〈浮き立たせる〉bring [throw] sth into 《sharp》 relief / 浮き彫りになる stand out in 《bold》 relief / 浅[高]浮き彫りの像 a sculpture in low [high] relief / 中浮き彫りの像 a sculpture in bas-relief.

うきみ¹ 浮き身 floating (motionless) on one's back.

うきみ² 憂き身 ¶憂き身をやつす devote oneself 《to》; give oneself over 《to》; be absorbed 《in》.

うきめ 憂き目 ¶憂き目を見る have a hard time; go through hardships; suffer misery 《from》.

---

that. | I should have known better. / 彼にうかつな事を言うな. Be careful [Watch your words] when you talk to him.

うかつ それはいささかうがち過ぎた観察だ. You are reading a bit too much into the situation.

うかぶ 綿のような雲が空に浮かんでいた. Fleecy clouds floated in [were sailing across] the sky. / 霧の中から船の姿が大きく浮かんで見えた. A ship loomed large through the fog. / ジョージという名の男が捜査線上に浮かんで来た. A man named George loomed up as a suspect as the investigation progressed. / 会社からあんな不当な扱いをされたのでは彼も浮かばれまい. He must be finding it hard to get over his resentment at having received such unfair treatment from the company. / これで母の霊も浮かばれるでしょう. This will set my mother's soul at rest. / 君がそんなに亡くなったお父さんも浮かばれない. You will make your father turn in his grave. / これで彼はもう一生浮かばれまい. This has ruined his career, I'm sure.

うき¹ 雨期になった. The rainy season has [The rains have] set in.

うきあがる 青空に富士山がくっきり浮き上がって見える. Mt. Fuji stands out in bold relief against the blue sky. / 我が国の今日の政治は大衆からすっかり浮き上がっている. Politics in our country today is far from being based upon the real needs of the general public. / 彼らはあまりに急進的で大衆から浮き上がっている. They are so radical that they are not attuned to the needs of the people.

うきうき 退院の時は私の心は浮き浮きしていた. My heart was singing as I left the hospital.

うきしずみ 彼は浮き沈みが激しい. With him it's up one minute and down the next.

うきたつ その吉報に彼らは浮き立った. They were buoyed up by the good news.

うきよ 浮き世 the world; life; 〈はかないものとしての〉this transient [fleeting] world ¶浮き世がいやになる get [grow, 《文》become] sick [tired] of life / 浮き世の 《文》worldly; 《文》earthly / 浮き世の煩わしさ 〈苦労〉worldly cares; 〈騒がしさ〉《文》the turmoil of this mortal life / 浮き世の習い [常] the way of the world / 浮き世のはかなさ 《文》the transience [transitoriness] of human life / 浮き世を捨てる renounce the world. 文例↓

うきよえ 浮世絵 an *ukiyoe*; a picture [color print] of everyday life in the Edo period.

うきわ 浮き輪 ⇒うきぶくろ.

うく 浮く 〈浮かぶ〉float; 〈浮き上がる〉surface; come [rise] to the surface; 〈余る〉be left over; 〈節約になる〉be saved ¶油の浮いたシチュー a stew swimming with grease / 歯の浮くような音を立てる make a noise that sets *one*'s teeth on edge. 文例↓

うぐい 〈魚〉a dace (*pl*. ~(s)).

うぐいす 〈鳥〉a bush warbler ¶うぐいすの谷渡り the flight of a bush warbler from valley to valley; 〈鳴き声〉the song of a bush warbler in flight. 文例↓

ウクライナ the Ukraine ¶ウクライナの Ukrainian / ウクライナ人 a Ukrainian.

ウクレレ 〈楽器〉a ukulele.

うけ[1] 受け 〈気受け〉popularity; 《文》favor; reception; 〈囲碁・将棋〉defense; a defensive move ¶受けが良い[悪い] be popular [unpopular] (with); go down well [badly] (with); 《文》be in favor [disfavor] (with); 〈文〉be in good [bad] repute (with) / 受けに回る go on the defensive. 文例↓

うけ[2] 有卦 ¶有卦に入る enjoy a run of good luck.

うけあい 受[請]け合い ⇒ほしょう[2]. 文例↓

うけあう 受[請]け合う 〈引き受ける〉undertake; take on 《a task》; 〈保証する〉《文》assure; guarantee; answer [vouch] for; give *one*'s word for.

うけい 右傾 ¶右傾する lean to the right.

うけいれ 受け入れ 《文》receiving; 《文》acceptance ¶(留学生・難民などの)受け入れ国 a host [receiving] country / 受け入れ態勢を整える[が整っていない] make (full) preparations [be not (yet) ready] to receive [for receiving].

うけいれる 受け入れる accept; get; receive; 〈同意する〉《文》assent to; 《文》comply with; 〈聞き入れる〉grant [《口語》go along with] 《*sb*'s request》; listen to ¶一般に受け入れられる be generally accepted; 《文》find [win, gain, meet with] general acceptance / 受け入れやすい[難い] 〈事が主語〉be acceptable [unacceptable] to *one*; go down well [hard] with *one*. 文例↓

うけうり 受け売り ¶受け売りする tell *sb* *sth* at second hand; echo 《*sb*'s words》/ 受け売りの知識 secondhand knowledge [information]. 文例↓

うけおい 請負 a contract (for work) ¶請負で under [by] contract / 請負に出す give out a contract (for the work); put (the work) out to contract / 請負人[師] a contractor / 請負仕事 a contract job.

うけおう 請け負う a contract (for the work, to *do*); get [《文》receive] a contract 《for *sth* from *sb*》; 〈引き受ける〉undertake; take on ¶請け負わせる give *sb* a contract (for); let a contract (to *sb*); farm (the work) out (to *sb*). 文例↓

うけこたえ 受け答え ¶受け答えする answer; give an answer 《to》 ⇒こたえ, へんじ[1].

うけざら 受け皿 a saucer. 文例↓

うけだす 受け出す 〈質物を〉redeem; take *sth* out of pawn.

うけだち 受け太刀 ¶受け太刀になる be [be put] on the defensive.

うけたまわる 承る 〈聞く〉hear; listen to; be told; 〈知る, 理解する〉know; understand; 〈命令を〉《文》receive 《a command》; 〈注文などを〉take 《an order》.

うけつぐ 受け継ぐ inherit 《*sth* from *sb*》; succeed to 《*one*'s father's business》; be the heir [《文》be heir] to 《an estate》; take over 《a task》. 文例↓

うけつけ 受付 〈受理〉《文》acceptance; 《文》

うきよ これが浮き世の常だ. Such is the way of the world. / とかく浮き世はままならぬ. If wishes were horses, beggars would ride. 【諺】

うく この木切れの方がそっちのよりよく浮く[浮かない]. This piece of wood floats higher [lower] than that. / それで千円浮く. That means a saving of 1,000 yen. | You can save 1,000 yen that way.

うぐいす その廊下はうぐいす張りになっていた. The hallway floor planking was specially sprung to emit creaking noises when trodden on.

うけ[1] その本は批評家の受けが良かった. The book was well received by the critics. | The book found favor with the critics.

うけあい 彼の成功は受け合いだ. I am [It is] absolutely certain that he will succeed. / 彼が明日ここへ来ることは受け合いだ. I bet [Depend on it,] he'll come here tomorrow.

うけあう よし, 私が受け合った. All right, I will answer for it. / 彼の人物は私が受け合う. I will answer for his character. / 品質の上等なことは受け合います. We guarantee the high quality of our goods.

うけいれ 老人はそういう新しい考えを受け入れない. Old people are not receptive toward such new ideas. / そういう提案ならソ連も受け入れるだろう. That sort of proposal will be acceptable even to the Soviet Union. / 当時はまだそのような思想を受け入れる世の中ではなかった. The times were not yet ready for such ideas.

うけうり 彼の考えは先生の考えの受け売りに過ぎない. His opinion is a mere echo of his teacher's.

うけおう 彼はその家の建築を5千万円で請け負った. He has contracted to build the house for 50 million yen.

うけざら 野党が自民党から政権を奪うことは不可能だ. 第一, 受け皿が出来ていない. There is no possibility that the opposition will seize the reins of government from the Liberal Democratic Party. In the first place, they are not ready to take them over yet.

うけつける 受け付ける 《文》receive; accept (a proposal); take up (an appeal) 《受け付けない〈拒絶する〉》refuse; reject; turn down; 〈耳を貸さない〉turn a deaf ear (to); 〈平気である〉be immune [《文》impervious] (to). 文例⇩

うけとめる 受け止める catch (a ball); stop the blow (from one's enemy's sword); 〈提案などを〉react (to); take.

うけとり(しょう) 受取(証) a receipt 《for》¶受取を書く make out a receipt (for) /受取を出す give sb a receipt (for) /受取手形【商】a bill receivable /受取人 a recipient; a remittee (送金の); a payee (手形の); a beneficiary (保険金などの); a consignee (貨物の); an addressee (郵便物の).

うけとる 受け取る 〈受ける〉get; 《文》receive; accept; 《文》come [be] to hand (物が主語); 〈解する〉take; interpret; understand; 〈信じる〉believe ¶…を受け取り次第《文》on receipt of (the goods). 文例⇩

うけながす 受け流す parry; fend off; turn aside ¶質問の鋒先をやんわりと受け流す take the edge off sb's questions with skilful [flexible] answers.

うけみ 受け身 passiveness; 《文》passivity; 【文法】the passive (voice); 【柔道】a break-fall ¶受け身の defensive; passive /受け身になる go onto [be on] the defensive; lose the initiative.

うけもち 受け持ち ¶受け持ちの教師 the teacher in charge of the (first-year) class; 〈生徒の立場からみて〉one's (homeroom) teacher /受け持ちの生徒 the pupils in one's care [charge] /受け持ち区域 a district assigned [allotted] to one; 〈警官などの〉one's beat; 〈セールスマンなどの〉one's territory. 文例⇩

うけもつ 受け持つ take [be in] charge of; have sth in [under] one's charge ¶受け持たせる allot; allocate; 《文》assign; put sb in charge of sth.

うける 受ける 〈得る,与えられる〉《文》receive; be given; have; take; get; 《文》obtain; 〈受け止める〉catch (a ball); make a defensive move (囲碁・将棋で); 〈支える〉prop [shore] up; 〈被る〉《文》suffer (an injury); 《文》sustain (damage); 《文》incur (a loss); 〈承諾する〉accept (a proposal); 〈人気を得る〉be popular (among, with); go down well (with); 《文》be well received; take (well) (with); (口語) catch on (with) ¶試験を受ける take [sit for] an examination /手術を受ける have [《文》undergo] an operation (for appendicitis) ★undergo に比べて、過去形の underwent はなお一段と文語的なので、なるべく使うのを避けた方がよい /訪問を受ける have a visit (from) /受けて立つ accept sb's challenge (and do); 《文》take [pick] up the gauntlet. 文例⇩

うけわたし 受け渡し (a) delivery; 〈譲渡〉(a) transfer.

うけわたす 受け渡す deliver; hand over; transfer.

うげん 右舷【海】the starboard ★船上で船首に向かって右側をいう ¶右舷(の方向)に (sight a steamer) to starboard.

うご 雨後 ¶雨後のたけのこのように出る crop up like mushrooms after a rain; mushroom; increase rapidly (in number).

うごうのしゅう 烏合の衆 a (mere) rabble; a disorderly crowd; a [an undisciplined] mob (騒々しい).

うごかす 動かす move; stir; 〈移動さす〉《文》remove; shift; 〈変更する〉change; alter; 〈運転する〉《文》start [set] (a machine) in motion; put (a motor) into action; operate; work; 〈心を〉move; touch; affect ¶動かされやすい be easily affected [moved, influenced] /お世辞に心を動かされない be above [immune to] flattery /誘惑に心を動かされない《文》be proof against temptation /動かし得ない事実 an undeniable [indisputable] fact /動かし難い決意《文》(an) unshakable resolution /動かし難い証拠《文》(an) incontrovertible [incontestable] proof. 文例⇩

うけだす その当時私たちは5月になるとオーバーを質に入れ、10月になると受け出したものでした。 In those days we used to pawn our overcoats in May and take them out in October.

うけたまわる その計画の詳細を承りたいと思います。Please let me know [tell me about] the details of the plan. / 何の役に立つのか、ひとつ承りたいものです。What's the use of it, I'd like to know?

うけつぐ 彼の演じた弁慶の型は今でも受け継がれている。His portrayal of Benkei still lives on in the performances of the actors of today.

うけつけ 受付.【掲示】Information.

うけつける 願書は2月5日から受け付けます。Applications will be accepted on and after the 5th of February. / フランス科学アカデミーが永久運動装置の設計図を一切受け付けないことにしたのは遠く1775年のことである。It was as long ago as in 1775 that the French Academy of Sciences closed its doors to all perpetual-motion designs. / 私の胃はそうした食物は受け付けなかった。My stomach revolted at such food.

うけとめる あなたはその報道をどのように受け止められましたか。What was your reaction to the news?

うけとる そうとしか受け取れません。There is no other interpretation [reading] to be placed on it. | It can't be taken in any other way. / 君は僕の言ったことを間違って受け取ったのだ。You got me wrong.

うけもち このクラスはどなたの受け持ちですか。Who teaches this class? | Who is in charge of this class?

うける 彼は至るところで盛んな歓迎を受けた。He received [met with] a hearty welcome everywhere. / そのショーは上演早々から若者に受けた。The show was an instant hit with young people.

うごかす 彼らを動かしていた動機は全く金銭的なものだった。The motives actuating [driving] them were purely mercenary. / 何物も彼の決心を動かすことはできな

うごき 動き (a) movement; (a) motion; 〈変化〉a change; 〈動向〉a drift; a trend ¶人の心の表面に現われない動き the inner workings of the human mind / 動きがとれない 〈混雑して〉cannot move [stir] (an inch); be tied up (in traffic); be bogged down (in the mud, on a question); 〈窮地に陥る〉be in a predicament [fix] / 借金で動きがとれないまで be deep in debt; 《口語》be up to one's ears [eyes] in debt. 用例⇩

うごきまわる 動き回る move [get] about.
うごく 動く move; stir; shift; 〈機械などが〉work; go; run; 〈揺れる〉shake; swing; sway; 〈変わる〉change; vary; 〈心が〉be moved; be touched; be affected; 〈左右される〉be influenced; be swayed; 〈動揺する〉waver; 《文》vacillate ¶動いている be moving; 《文》be in motion / 電気で動く機械 a machine run by electricity / 電池で動く時計 a battery-operated clock; a clock powered by a battery / 動かないでいる remain still [《文》stationary]; be at standstill; 《文》be at rest; stay put / 動かなくなる stop moving [going, running]; come to a standstill / 〈故障で〉break down; go out of action / 〈動物などが〉凍りついたようにじっとして動かなくなる freeze / 折れた腕が動かないように添え木を当てる set a broken arm in splints to hold it in position / 腹が一杯で動けなくなるまで食う eat *oneself* to a standstill / 動かぬ証拠《文》(an) incontestable proof; hard [《文》immutable] evidence. 用例⇩
うごめく wriggle; squirm ¶得意の鼻をうごめかす look triumphant; be elated 《with success》.
うこん 《植》(a) turmeric.
うさ 憂さ gloom; 《文》melancholy; sadness; 《文》sorrow ¶憂さを晴らす divert *one*'s mind from *one*'s cares; drive away [《文》dispel] *one*'s gloom / 酒に憂さを紛らす[忘れる] drown *one*'s sorrows (in drink) / 憂さ晴らしに for amusement; as a [by way of] diversion; to distract *one* from *one*'s grief.
うさぎ 兎 a rabbit; a hare (野うさぎ) ¶うさぎの肉 〈eat〉rabbit / (イソップ物語の)うさぎと亀 the Hare and the Tortoise / うさぎ小屋 a rabbit hutch / うさぎ小屋のような家の集まったごちゃごちゃした町 a warren of narrow streets / うさぎ跳び jumping along in a squatting position.
うさんくさい うさん臭い suspicious; questionable; 《口語》shady ¶うさん臭そうに見る look suspiciously at *sb*.
うし 牛 〈総称〉cattle; 〈雌〉a cow; 〈雄〉a bull; 〈去勢牛〉a bullock; 《米》a steer (食肉用); an ox (*pl.* oxen) (荷車用); 〈子牛〉a calf (*pl.* calves); 〈十二支の丑〉(the Year of) the Ox ¶食肉用の牛 beef cattle / 牛の歩みのごとく at a snail's pace / 牛の皮 cowhide / 牛を飼う keep cows; raise cattle / 牛に引かれて善光寺参り be led to do good by some accidental event / 牛小屋 a cow shed.
うじ 氏 〈血統〉(a) lineage; birth; family; 〈家名〉a family name ¶氏と育ち nature and nurture. 用例⇩
うじ 蛆 a maggot; a grub ¶うじがわいている〈物・場所が主語〉be infested with maggots.
うじがみ 氏神 a guardian [tutelary] deity [god] (of a place).
うしかもしか 《動》a gnu (*pl.* -(s)); a wildebeest (*pl.* -(s)).
うじこ 氏子 people under the protection of the community deity.
うしなう 失う lose; miss; 《文》be deprived of ¶父を失う lose [《文》be bereaved of] *one*'s father / 信用を失う lose *one*'s credit (with *sb*); lose the confidence (of *sb*); 《文》fall into discredit 《with *sb*》/ (人類進化上の)失われた環(ゎ) the missing link. 用例⇩
うしみつどき 丑三つ時 ¶草木も眠る丑三つ時に in the dead of night; in the small hours of the morning; in the wee (small) hours.
うじゃうじゃ ⇨ようよ.
うしろ 後ろ the back; the rear ¶後ろ back; rear; hind (feet) / 後ろの席[ドア] a back [rear] seat [door] / (劇場などの)後ろの方の席 a seat toward the back / 後ろに[で, の] behind; at the back [in the rear] (of); 《米口語》(in) back of; after / 後ろに倒れる fall down backward / 後ろに回る get behind 《a tree》/ (オートバイなどの)後ろに乗る ride pillion /

かった. Nothing could shake his resolution [make him change his mind].
うごき 彼の演技には無駄な動きは全くなかった. There was absolutely no wasted motion in his performance. / 車が泥にはまって動きがとれなくなった. The car got stuck [bogged down] in the mud. / 当時両国は領土問題をめぐって動きのとれない状況だった. At that time the two countries were in a stalemate over their territorial claims. / 世論の動きを見なければならない. You must watch the movement of public opinion.
うごく なおよく研究してみると, この気体は猛烈に熱く, そして激しく動いていることがわかった. This gas, on closer study, proved to be ferociously hot and in violent movement. / そこを動くな. Stay (right) where you are! / エレベーターは動いていない. The elevator is not working [is out of operation]. / 彼の社長就任は動かないところだ. It is quite certain that he will become the president.

うじ 氏より育ち. Birth is much, but breeding is more. 〈諺〉
うしなう 私はトムという友人を失った. I lost a friend in Tom. / 彼はその仕事に人命を失った. The work cost him his life. / 彼女は自動車事故で息子を失った. She had her son killed in a car accident. / 彼もまた一個の英雄たるを失わない. He might well be called a hero.
うしろ 写真をとりますからそこに並んで下さい. 小さい人が前に, 大きい人は後ろに. Now let me take a picture. Please line up there, short ones in front, tall ones at the back. / 後ろから見ると大きな田舎家のような家だ. From the back it looks like a large country house.
うしろがみ 後ろ髪を引かれる思いで生徒たちと別れた. I tore myself from my pupils with an aching heart.

うしろがみ 後ろ髪 ¶後ろ髪を引かれる思いがする feel as if one had one's heart behind; find it hard to tear [wrench] oneself away from ⟨sb, a place⟩.

うしろぐらい 後ろ暗い ⟨うさん臭い⟩《文》questionable; shady; suspicious; ⟨内密の⟩ underhand;《文》clandestine ¶何か後ろ暗いことをしている be involved in something shady. 文例↓

うしろすがた 後ろ姿 ⟨後ろから見た姿⟩ the back view ⟨of sb⟩; ⟨遠ざかりゆく姿⟩ the retreating figure ⟨of sb⟩ ¶後ろ姿を見送る gaze after sb.

うしろだて 後ろ盾 ⟨後援⟩ backing; support; ⟨後援者⟩ a supporter; a backer; a patron ¶後ろ盾になる back sb up; support / 後ろ盾にもつ have sb behind one [at one's back]. 文例↓

うしろで 後ろ手 ¶後ろ手に縛る bind [tie] sb's hands [arms] behind him [his back].

うしろまえ 後ろ前 ¶セーターを後ろ前に着る put one's sweater on back to front [backward].

うしろむき 後ろ向き ¶後ろ向きになる turn backward; turn one's back to sb / 後ろ向きの物の考え方 a backward-looking way of thinking. 文例↓

うしろめたい 後ろめたい ⇨ うしろぐらい.

うしろゆび 後ろ指 ¶後ろ指を差される《文》have the finger of derision pointed at one; be talked about contemptuously [with scorn];《文》be an object of ⟨public⟩ contempt.

うす 臼 a mortar. ¶臼でつく pound ⟨rice⟩ in a mortar.

うす- 薄... ¶薄ばかの half-witted / 薄緑 light green / 薄紫 pale purple.

うず 渦 ⇨ うずまき ¶渦の中に引き込まれる be drawn into a whirlpool / 渦を巻く whirl; eddy; swirl ⟨流れが⟩; curl ⟨煙が⟩ / 興奮の渦に巻いて in a whirl [swirl] / 興奮の渦を巻き起こす raise a storm of excitement. 文例↓

うすあかり 薄明かり dim [faint] light; ⟨たそがれ⟩ twilight; ⟨夜明けの⟩ morning twilight. 文例↓

うすい 薄い ⟨厚さが⟩ thin; ⟨色が⟩ light; pale; faint; ⟨稀薄な⟩ weak;《文》tenuous; ⟨少ない⟩ little; small ¶薄いコーヒー weak coffee / 薄いスープ thin soup / 薄くする ⇨ うすめる / 薄く切る ⇨ うすぎり / 薄くなる get《文》become thin [thinner]; thin. 文例↓

うすうす 薄々 ⟨少し⟩ a little; slightly; ⟨かすかに⟩ dimly ¶薄々覚えている dimly remember;《文》have a dim recollection ⟨of⟩ / 薄々感づく become vaguely aware ⟨of⟩; get a scent ⟨of⟩; have an inkling ⟨of⟩.

うずうず ¶うずうずする be impatient ⟨to do⟩;《文》be burning with a desire ⟨to do⟩;《口語》be itching [raring] ⟨to do⟩;《口語》have an itch ⟨to do⟩.

うすがみ 薄紙 thin paper ¶薄紙をはぐように very gradually; little by little; by slow degrees.

うすかわ 薄皮 a thin skin; a thin coating [membrane]; a film ¶みかんを剝いて薄皮を全部取り除く peel a tangerine and remove all the inner membranes.

うすぎ 薄着 ¶薄着する be thinly [lightly] dressed.

うすぎたない 薄汚ない dirty; grubby.

うすきみ 薄気味 ¶薄気味の悪い weird; uncanny; eerie.

うすぎり 薄切り a (thin) slice ⟨of⟩ ¶薄切りにする cut into (thin) slices; cut《meat》thin; slice (thinly).

うずく 疼く ache; smart; tingle; throb with pain; ⟨比喩的に⟩ fester; rankle. 文例↓

うずくまる 蹲る crouch; squat down.

うすぐも 薄雲 thin [fleecy, gauzy] clouds; a wisp of cloud.

うすぐもり 薄曇り slightly cloudy weather. 文例↓

うすぐらい 薄暗い dim; gloomy ¶薄暗い所で ⟨たそがれなどの⟩ in the dusk [twilight] ⟨of the evening⟩; ⟨灯火の⟩ in dim [poor] light; / まだ薄暗いうちに出かける start [leave ⟨a place⟩] before dawn / 薄暗い部屋 a dimly-lit [《文》an ill-lit] room. 文例↓

うしろぐらい 後ろ暗い事は何もしていない. I have a clear conscience.

うしろすがた 逃げて行く彼の後ろ姿がちらりと見えた. I caught a glimpse of his back as he ran away./後ろ姿はお父さんそっくりだ. From the back [In back view] he looks quite like his father.

うしろだて 彼は知事という後ろ盾を得た. He found a supporter in the governor.

うしろむき 道標が後ろ向きになっていた. The guidepost stood facing away from the path. / 彼は政治家として前向きより後ろ向きの人物だった. As a politician he looked backward rather than forward.

うず 煙が渦を巻いて上がっている. The smoke is curling up.

うすあかり その薄明かりで踏み跡を見付けるのは大変だった. It was really hard to find the trail in that faint light.

うすい 彼の髪も薄くなってきた. His hair is thinning [is going thin]. / 彼の頭のてっぺんの髪が薄い. His hair is thin on top. / チンパンジーは生まれた時は色が薄く, 年をとるにつれて濃くなる. Chimpanzees are born with light-colored coats, which darken with age. / お茶は薄くして下さい. I like my tea weak. / 利益は薄いが, 数でこなしてゆく. The profit is small, but we make up for it by high turnover. / この問題は僕には興味が薄い. The subject is of little interest to me. / ベースアップは上に薄く下に厚くすべきだ. The percentage of the wage increase should be smaller for the higher-ranking staff and larger for the lower.

うずく 歯がひどくうずく. My tooth aches horribly [《口語》like anything, 《俗》like hell]. / 屈辱の思い出が今なお彼の胸中にうずいている. The memory of the insult still rankles with him.

うすぐもり 今日は薄曇りだ. It is a bit cloudy today.

うすぐらい 日がかげって空は既に

うすくらがり 薄暗がり ¶薄暗がりで in the semidarkness [half dark]; 〈たそがれの〉in the dusk [twilight] 〈(of the evening)〉; 〈灯火の〉in the poor [dim] light.

うすげしょう 薄化粧 ¶薄化粧する put on light make-up / 薄化粧した富士山 Mt. Fuji lightly covered with snow. 文例⇩

うすごおり 薄氷 thin ice. 文例⇩

うすずみ 薄墨 ¶薄墨色の gray;《文》leaden 〈skies〉.

うすたかく 堆く high; in a heap [pile] ¶うずたかく積む pile [heap] up high; pile 〈goods〉mountain-high / うずたかく積まれた本 heaps [piles] of books.

うすっぺら 薄っぺら ¶薄っぺらな〈薄い〉thin; flimsy;《文》tenuous;〈浅薄な〉shallow; superficial;〈軽薄な〉frivolous / 薄っぺらな教養 a thin veneer of education / 薄っぺらな議論 a flimsy [tenuous] argument.

うすで 薄手 ¶薄手の thin; thinly-made; light 〈paper〉.

うすばかげろう 【昆】 an ant lion.

うすび 薄日 soft sunbeams.

うずまき 渦巻〈小さい〉an eddy; a swirl;〈大きい〉a whirlpool; a vortex 《pl. -texes, -tices》;〈模様〉a whorl.

うすまく 渦巻く eddy; whirl; swirl (流れが).

うずまる 埋まる ⇒うまる. 文例⇩

うすめ¹ 薄目 ¶薄目をあける open one's eyes slightly / 薄目をあけて with one's eyes slightly open; (look) through half-closed eyes;《文》(look) from under lowered lids.

うすめ² 薄め ¶薄めの〈茶などが〉rather thin; 〈色が〉rather light [pale] ⇒ うすい, うすめ.

うすめる 薄める make sth thin [thinner]; thin 〈paint〉;《文》attenuate; rarefy; dilute; water sth down (水で).

うずめる 埋める ⇒ うめる ¶ハンカチに顔を埋めて泣く cry [《文》weep] into one's handkerchief. 文例⇩

うすもの 薄物〈薄織〉a transparent fabric; 〈silk〉gauze;〈薄い着物〉light clothes [clothing];《文》a light garment.

うずもや 薄靄 (a) thin [gauzy] mist.

うずもれる 埋もれる be buried 〈under〉; be covered 〈with〉 ¶雪にうずもれる be snowed in [up, under]; be covered with snow; be buried in snow / 世にうずもれる live in obscurity.

うすよごれる 薄汚れる get a little dirty; come to appear slightly soiled (all over) ¶薄汚れたシーツ a dirty [grubby] bed sheet.

うずら 【鳥】 a quail ¶うずらの卵 a quail's egg.

うすらぐ 薄らぐ〈光が〉get [grow,《文》become] dim [faint];〈痛みなどが〉lessen;《文》abate;〈興味などが〉decline; flag;〈情熱などが〉cool (down) ⇒ うすれる. 文例⇩

うすらさむい 薄ら寒い chilly; slightly cold; coldish.

うずらまめ うずら豆 mottled kidney beans.

ウスリー the Ussuri River.

うすれる 薄れる〈色が〉fade; get [《文》become] fainter [less distinct] ⇒ うすらぐ.

うすわらい 薄笑い〈give〉a faint [thin] smile.

うせつ 右折 ¶右折する turn right; turn to the right. 文例⇩

うせる 失せる〈消失する〉disappear; vanish; be gone;〈紛失する〉be lost; be missing.

うそ¹ 嘘〈人をだますための〉a lie; a fib (たわいのない);〈本当でないこと〉《文》a falsehood; an untruth;〈作り事〉《文》a fabrication ★ 相手に向かって「うそでしょう」と言うのを、英語で You must be a liar. とか That is [must be] a lie. とか言えば相手の人格をひどく傷つけることになる。You don't mean it, do you? と言うのがいい。¶うその false; untrue / うそのような話 an incredible story / うそをつく lie 〈about〉; tell a lie [falsehood]〈about〉/ うそを教える give sb false [wrong] information 〈about〉/ うそ八百を並べる tell a pack of lies 〈about〉. 文例⇩

うそ² 【鳥】 a bullfinch.

わずかに薄暗くなっていた。The sun was obscured, and there was already a touch of darkness in the sky.

うすげしょう 彼女はブルーのドレスを着、薄化粧をして姿を見せた。She appeared in a blue dress and with just a (light) touch of make-up.

うすごおり 池に薄氷が張った。The pond was thinly coated with ice. / 池に薄氷が張った。A thin coat of ice formed on the pond.

うずたかく 机上には書類がうずたかく積んであった。The desk was piled high with papers.

うすび 雲間から薄日がもれていた。A little sunlight was coming through the clouds.

うずまる 今日の新聞の第1面は米大統領来日の記事でうずまっている。Today's paper devotes its entire front page to the news of the U.S. President's visit to this country.

うずめる 彼女は母のひざに顔をうずめた。She buried her head in her mother's lap.

うすらぐ 寒さも薄らいだ。It isn't as cold as it was. | It has become less cold. / その薬のおかげで痛みが薄らいだ。The medicine eased [《文》alleviated] the pain. / 時とともに悲しみも薄らぐ。Time blunts the edge of sorrow.

うせつ 右折禁止。《掲示》No right turn.

うそ¹ それは全然うそだ。It's all a complete lie. | There is no truth (whatsoever) in it. / 彼の話にうそが混じっていることは間違いない。Part of his story cannot possibly be true. / うそだと思うかもしれないが、私は彼女より 10 も若いんだぜ。Believe it or not, I am ten years younger than her. ⇒ より² 用法 / うそつけ！ Don't be silly! | Don't talk rubbish [nonsense]! / 彼はうそがばれても平気なものだった。He didn't turn a hair when he was caught out in a lie. / そのうそをつくろうために、彼はその上塗りにまたうそをつかなければならなかった。In order to cover up his lie, he had to lie still further. / うそじゃないよ、彼は彼女と会う約束をつい忘れていたんだ。You can take it from me that he just forgot his appointment with her. / その金が欲しくないと言えばうそになりますが、今の私には金よりも時間の方が貴重なのです。I would be a liar if I said I don't want the money, but time is more precious to me than money at the moment. / 2 時間近くも雨は激しく降っていたが、突然うそのように晴れ上がった。It had been rain-

うぞうむぞう　有象無象　the rabble; the ragtag and bobtail.

うそつき　嘘つき　a liar　¶うそつきだと言う　call sb a liar; accuse sb of telling a lie;《文》give the lie to sb. 文例⇩

うそはっけんき　嘘発見器　a lie detector　¶うそ発見器で調べられる　be given a [the] lie-detector test.

うそぶく〈そらとぼける〉pretend not to know;《文》pretend [feign] ignorance;〈豪語する〉talk big; brag.

うた　歌〈詩〉a poem; poetry (総称);〈短歌〉a tanka;〈歌謡〉a song;〈歌うこと〉singing　¶歌を歌う　sing (a song);〈鼻歌で〉hum a tune;〈小声で〉croon (a song) / 歌を歌いながら仕事をする　sing at one's work / 歌を歌って赤ん坊を寝かせつける　sing a baby to sleep / 歌を詠む　write [compose] a tanka [poem] / (平安時代の)歌合せ　a poetry contest / 歌心がある　have a poetic turn of mind / 新年歌会始め　the New Year's Poetry Party (held at the Imperial Court). 文例⇩

うたい　謡　⇒ようきょく².

うたいて　歌い手　a singer; a vocalist.

うたいもんく　歌い文句　a slogan; a catchword; a catch phrase.

うたう¹　歌う　sing;〈吟じる〉recite; chant;〈鳥が〉sing; warble　¶歌い出す　begin to sing; start singing; break into song.

うたう²　謳う〈賞揚する〉《文》extol;《文》sing the praises of;〈述べる〉《文》state; express　¶うたわれる　be famous [《文》famed] (for);《文》be reputed (to be...);〈悪名を〉be notorious (for);《悪名を》/ 天才とうたわれる　be reputed to be [have the reputation of being] a genius.

うたがい　疑い〈疑念〉(a) doubt;〈疑問〉a question;〈嫌疑〉(a) suspicion;〈不信〉(a) distrust; (a) mistrust　¶疑いもない　undoubted; unquestionable;《文》indubitable; undeniable / 疑いの目で見る　view [look on, regard] sth [sb] with suspicion / 疑い(も)なく　without [beyond] (a) doubt; undoubtedly; doubtless; no doubt; without [beyond (all)] question / 一点の疑いもなく　without any doubt; beyond all [the] shadow of a doubt / 疑いを抱く〈疑念〉have [feel,《文》entertain] doubts (about); be doubtful (of, about); be skeptical (of, about);〈嫌疑〉have a suspicion (that...); suspect ((sb of murder)); be suspicious (of);〈不信〉do not trust; have a distrust [mistrust] (of);《文》be distrustful [mistrustful]《of》/ 疑いを受ける[招く] be suspected (of murder); fall [come] under suspicion (of theft);《文》incur sb's suspicion / 疑いを起こさせる〈疑念〉raise a doubt (in sb's mind); make sb doubt;〈嫌疑〉arouse [《文》excite] suspicion (in sb's mind); rouse [arouse] sb's suspicion / 疑いをかける　cast [throw] one's doubt (on); fix one's suspicions (on) / 疑いを晴らす　clear oneself of the charge (of theft);〈事が主語〉dispel one's doubts / ...の疑いで　on suspicion of (being a spy); on a charge of (murder) / 疑い深い　suspicious; skeptical; incredulous (looks); distrustful. 文例⇩

うたがう　疑う〈疑念〉doubt; be doubtful (of); have doubts (about);〈嫌疑〉suspect (sb of murder); be suspicious (of);〈不信〉distrust;《文》be distrustful [mistrustful] (of); be skeptical (about, of)　¶疑わない　have no doubt (of, as to); do not doubt ((but) that...);《文》make no doubt (of, that ...) / 少しも疑わずに　without the least [a slight] suspicion (of). 文例⇩

用法　同じ「疑う」でも doubt と suspect では意味も使い方も違う。I doubt whether [《口語》if, that] it is true.｜I doubt its truth. は、「(本当だと言われているが)本当かどうか怪しいものだと思う」の意味であるが、I suspect that it is true.｜I suspect it to be true. は「(うそだと言われているが)本当なのではないかなと思う」という意味になる。

うたがわしい　疑わしい〈疑念のある〉doubtful; questionable; dubious;〈不確実な〉uncertain;〈信頼できぬ〉unreliable;〈怪しい〉suspicious　¶疑わしそうに　doubtfully; incredulously; suspiciously; with suspicion / 疑わ

---

ing hard for nearly two hours, but it stopped suddenly as if by magic [it stopped so suddenly and so completely that you could hardly believe it]. / うそも方便. Circumstances may justify a lie. / その手で行かなくてはうそだ. You really ought to take that step. | That's the only way to do it.

うそつき　うそつきは泥棒の始まり. Show me a liar, and I will show you a thief. 【諺】| He that will lie will steal. 【諺】

うた　彼女は歌がうまい. She is a good singer. | 歌は世につれ, 世は歌につれ. Songs and the times change together.

うたう¹　彼は音痴で, 満足に歌が歌えない. He is tone-deaf and cannot carry a tune. | 少年たちは声高らかに歌いながら行進して行っ

た. The boys marched along in full song. | 彼らは歌っては飲み, 飲んではジョークを飛ばした. Between their songs they drank, and between drinks they cracked jokes.

うたう²　この事は決議の中でうたっておく必要がある. Mention must be made of this in the resolution.

うたがい　すっかり疑いが晴れた. All my doubts have vanished [been dissipated]. | 彼の誠実さについては疑いをいれる余地もない. There is no room (left) for doubt as to his honesty. | His honesty is above suspicion. | 立証があまりにも明確で疑いをさしはさむ余地は全くなかった. It was too clearly proved to admit of any doubt. | 近日中に両社が合同することは疑いない. There is no doubt that the two firms will

merge in the near future. / この山にウラン鉱があることはもはや疑いない. The existence of uranium ore in this mountain is no longer in doubt. | 彼は強盗の1人として疑いをかけられている. He is under suspicion as one of the robbers. | 彼に疑いがかかった. Suspicion fell on him. | He fell under suspicion.

うたがう　僕は自分の目を疑った. I couldn't believe my (own) eyes. | この本は通常彼の作とされているが, この原稿の発見によって彼が作者であったかどうか疑われるようになった. The book is usually ascribed to him, but the discovery of this manuscript has thrown doubt on its authorship. | 疑う余地がないとして受け入れられた. It was accepted as being beyond doubt.

うたぐち 歌口 the mouthpiece [embouchure] ((of a flute)).

うたごえ 歌声 a singing voice.

うたたね 転た寝 a doze;((口語))a snooze ¶うたた寝する doze (off); nod off; drop off (to sleep);((口語))snooze;((口語))take a snooze.

うだつ ¶うだつが上がらない cannot get on [rise] in the world.

うだる 茹だる be boiled ¶暑さにうだる feel oppressed by the heat; swelter / うだるような暑さ the sweltering heat ((of the tropical night)) / うだるように暑い日 a sweltering hot day.

うたん 右端 the right end ¶((写真・図版などで))右端の((the person)) on the extreme right; ((the figure)) at the far right.

うち 内 ⟨内部⟩ the inside;((文))the interior; ⟨家⟩ a house; ⟨自宅⟩ one's home [house] ¶うちの者 one's people [family];((米口語))one's folks / おうちの方 your family;((米口語))your folks / うちへ帰る go home, come [get] home / うちを出る leave home [the house] / 内に[で]((文))within; inside;⟨屋内に⟩indoors;⟨…の[している]間に⟩while; during;⟨経過すれば⟩in; in the course of;⟨自宅に⟩at home;⟨…の中で⟩between; among; amid(st); in / 内にいる⟨屋内に⟩stay indoors;⟨自宅に⟩be [stay] (at) home; be in / 内にいない⟨屋内に⟩stay outdoors;⟨自宅に⟩be away from home ; be out / 若いうちに while (one is) young / 貧苦のうちに育つ be raised in a poor home /((文))be bred in poverty / 拍手かっさいのうちに amidst the applause ((of the audience)) / 雨が降らないうちに before it rains / 暗くならぬ[夜の明けぬ]内に before dark [daybreak] / 内から⟨内部から⟩((be locked)) on the inside [((from within));⟨中から⟩((select)) out of [from among] ((many candidates)). 文例↓

うちあい¹ 打ち合い ⟨ボクシング⟩ an exchange (of punches [blows]);⟨球技⟩ a rally.

うちあい² 撃ち合い an exchange of shots; a gun battle.

うちあう 撃ち合う exchange shots ((with)).

うちあげ 打ち上げ ⟨花火の⟩ sending [shooting] up;⟨ロケットの⟩ (a) launching; a launch; ⟨興行の⟩ the close [end] ((of a run of performances)) ¶(ロケットの打ち上げ 10 秒後[前]に ten seconds after [before] launch; at T plus [minus] ten (★Tは T-time (打ち上げ時間)の略) / ロケットの打ち上げ台[場] a launching pad [site] / 打ち上げ花火 a rocket; a skyrocket. 文例↓

うちあけばなし 打ち明け話 a confidential talk;(exchange) confidences.

うちあける 打ち明ける take sb into one's confidence ;((文))disclose [reveal, confide] ((a secret to sb)); confide in sb ;((文))make a confidant [confidante (女)] of sb ¶心を打ち明ける speak one's mind (to); open [((文))unburden] one's heart (to);((文))unburden oneself ((of one's secrets));((文))unbosom oneself (to) / 何もかも打ち明けて言える tell [confess] everything (to) / 打ち明けて言えば to be frank [candid] with you ; frankly speaking. 文例↓

うちあげる 打ち上げる shoot [send] up; ⟨ロケットを⟩ launch;⟨波が物を⟩ throw [((文))cast] sth on the shore; wash sth ashore;⟨興行を⟩ finish; close ¶人工衛星を打ち上げる launch an artificial satellite; put an artificial satellite into the sky / フライを打ち上げる ⟨野球⟩ fly [hit a fly] ((into left field)) ★この意味の fly は fly, flied, flied と変化する。 文例↓

うちあわせ 打ち合わせ a previous arrangement ¶打ち合わせをする make arrangements beforehand ((with sb for a matter)); arrange ((a matter with sb, that...)) / 打ち合わせ会⟨予備会談⟩((hold)) a preliminary assembly [meeting];⟨相談会⟩((have)) a consultation. 文例↓

うちあわせる 打ち合わせる ⟨物を⟩ beat [strike, clap] ((sticks)) together;⟨下相談をする⟩ ⇒うちあわせ (打ち合わせをする) ¶前々から打ち合わせたとおり as arranged [prearranged]; according to previous arrangements.

うちいり 討ち入り ¶討ち入りする break (into); make a raid (on).

うちいわい 内祝い a family celebration;⟨贈り物⟩ a present given on the occasion of a family celebration.

うちうち 内々 ⇒うちわ¹.

うちうみ 内海 an inland sea.

うちおとす 打[撃]ち落とす shoot (bring) down ((an enemy plane));((口語))down ((a flying bird)).

うちおろす 打ち下ろす bring (a stick) down ((on sb's head)). 文例↓

うちかえす 打ち返す hit [((文))strike] back;

うたがわしい 彼が本当にそんなことをしたかどうかはなはだ疑わしい。It is very doubtful [It is open to serious question] whether he really did such a thing. / 彼の挙動には少しも疑わしい所がない。His behavior is above [beyond] suspicion.

うち 君のうちはどこですか。Where do you live? / 彼はうちにばかり閉じこもっている。He is a regular stay-at-home. / うちから歩いてたった 5 分の所です。It is only five minutes' walk from home. / 1 キロも行かないうちにわか雨に会った。I had not gone a kilometer before I was caught in a shower. / 彼は 10 日のうち 7 日は釣りに出かけていた。He was out fishing on seven days out of ten. / 現代のアメリカの作家の中ではスタインベックが一番好きです。I like Steinbeck best of all the modern American writers. / この本は彼の代表作のうちに入る。This book counts among his major works.

うちあげ その宇宙船は打ち上げ準備中であった。The spacecraft was being readied for launch. / (ロケットの)打ち上げ時には地球と火星との距離は約 2 億キロであった。The Earth and Mars were about 200 million kilometers apart at launch. / 打ち上げ前 5 秒, 14 秒, 13, 12, 11, 10, 9 … 点火! T minus 15, 14, 13, 12, 11, 10, 9 … Ignition!

うちあける あの人は何でも私に打

うちかかる 打ち掛かる strike (out) at sb;〈飛び掛かる〉pounce on sb.

うちかけ¹ 打ち掛け ¶打ち掛けにする〈囲碁〉leave a game of go unfinished for the day.

うちかけ² 袿 a long overgarment (worn by a bride).

うちがけ 内掛け〔相撲〕¶相手を内掛けで倒す throw down one's opponent by putting one's leg between his legs and leaning on him.

うちかつ 打ち勝つ beat [《文》conquer]《the enemy》; overcome 〔get over, surmount〕《obstacles》;〔ボクシング〕outbox《one's opponent》;〔野球〕outhit《the opposing team》⇨ かつ.

うちがわ 内側 the inside; the inner part ¶内側の inside; inner;《文》interior / トラックの内側のコース the inside lanes; the lanes on the inside of a track / 内側に on the inside; inside;《文》within;《文》inward / 〈ドアなどが〉内側に開く open inward(s) / 内側からかぎをかける lock (a door) on the inside [《文》from within]. 文例⇩

うちき 内気《文》a retiring [reserved] disposition; shyness ¶内気な bashful; shy; retiring; reserved.

うちき² 打ち気〔野球〕¶打ち気充分である be determined to hit the ball / バッターに打ち気なしと見る decide that the batter is not going to [has no mind to] hit.

うちきず 打ち傷 a bruise ⇨ だぼくしょう.

うちきり 打ち切り ¶打ち切りになる come to an end [《文》a close]. 文例⇩

うちきる 打ち切る leave [break, call] off (the talks); bring (a matter) to an end [a close]; discontinue; close;《口語》drop; axe (a project); wind up (a discussion). 文例⇩

うちきん 内金 (a) down payment; (a) part [partial] payment ¶内金として5千円払う pay 5,000 yen down; give 5,000 yen as part payment.

うちくび 打ち首 ¶打ち首にする behead;《文》decapitate; cut sb's head off.

うちけし 打ち消し《文》(a) denial;《文》(a) negation ¶打ち消しの negative《expressions》.

うちけす 打ち消す deny;《文》give a denial to (the rumor);《文》negate; contradict.

うちゲバ 内ゲバ violence within a (student) sect;《文》internal strife.

うちげんかん 内玄関 a side door.

うちこむ 打ち込む 〈くぎなどを〉drive [knock] 《a nail》in [into];〈太刀を〉strike;〈テニス・卓球などを〉smash;〈弾丸を〉shoot [fire] (into);〈熱中する〉apply [《文》devote] oneself 《to》; be absorbed [《文》engrossed] (in); be keen (on);〔野球〕ピッチャーを打ち込む collect hits off a pitcher. 文例⇩

うちころす 打〔撃〕ち殺す〈殴り殺す〉beat [club] sb to death;〈射殺する〉shoot sb dead.

うちじに 討ち死に ¶討ち死にする die [killed,《文》fall] in battle [《文》on the field of battle]; die fighting.

うちじゅう 家中〈家族〉the whole family; all (the members of) the family;〈家の中〉(search) all over the house.

うちたおす 打ち倒す〈殴り倒す〉knock [《文》strike] sb down;《口語》floor sb (with one's fist [a blow]);〈政府などを〉overthrow.

うちだし 打ち出し〈興行の〉the close;〈細工〉embossing; embossed work.

うちだす 打〔撃〕ち出す〈発砲する〉open fire (on);〈タイプライターで〉type [tap] out;〈模様を〉emboss;〈閉演する〉end; close;〈政策などを〉work [hammer] out;〈発表する〉announce; lay out;《文》set forth. 文例⇩

うちつける 打ち付ける knock; hit; beat;《文》strike ⇨ ぶつける;〈くぎなどを〉drive (a nail into a wall);〈くいに板を打ち付ける〉nail a board to a post. 文例⇩

うちつづく 打ち続く long;《文》long-continued ¶打ち続く不幸 a series of misfortunes.

うちづら 内面 ¶内面が悪い be surly [bad-tempered] at home.

うちでし 内弟子 a pupil living [boarding] in the home of his master; an apprentice ¶内弟子を取る take apprentices / 内弟子になる serve one's apprenticeship with [under] sb; be apprenticed to sb.

うちでのこづち 打ち出の小槌 a mallet of luck; a horn of plenty; a cornucopia.

うちとける 打ち解ける be frank [open, candid] (with sb) ¶打ち解けて話す have a friendly chat [heart-to-heart talk] (with); talk freely (to) / 打ち解けた調子で in a chatty [familiar] tone / 打ち解けない be uncommunicative; be reserved;《口語》be standoffish. 文例⇩

うちどめ 打ち止め ¶打ち止めにする〈興行などを〉bring (the show) to a close [an end] /

ち明けて話す. He keeps nothing secret from me.

うちあげる 岩田投手の第2球を香川が打ち上げ, ライト大山これを取ってワンアウト. Kagawa lofted Iwata's second pitch to right fielder Oyama for the first out.

うちあわせる 鈴木さんが婚礼のことで打ち合わせに来た. Mr. Suzuki came to arrange about the wedding.

うちおろす〈座禅をしている〉彼の肩に警策が打ち下ろされた. The stick descended on his shoulder.

うちかえす 波が岸辺に打ち返してきた. Waves were rolling onto the beach.

うちがわ その箱は外側は緑で内側は黄色です. The box is green outside and yellow inside.

うちきり この件はその日の晩は打ち切りになった. The subject was closed [dropped] for the evening.

うちきる〈親からの〉送金が打ち切られた. My allowance was cut off.

うちこむ 神経がひどく疲れていて仕事に打ち込めないのです. My nerves are so worn out that I cannot put my heart into my work.

うちだす テレタイプがクーデターのニュースを打ち出していた. A teletype was clicking out the news of the coup d'état.

うちつける 荒波にもまれて舟は岩に打ち付けられた. The boat was battered against a rock by the heavy surf.

うちとける 彼はだれとでも打ち解

パチンコの機械を打ち止めにする play out a pachinko machine.

うちとる 討ち取る 〈殺す〉kill;〈文〉slay;〈負かす〉beat; defeat ¶バッターを3球3振に討ち取る strike out a batter on three straight pitches.

うちぬき 打抜き ¶打抜き型 a die / 打ち抜き機 a punch; a punching machine.

うちぬく 打[撃]ち抜く 〈貫通する〉pierce; penetrate;〈穴をあける〉punch (a hole); perforate;〈型で〉stamp out (a coin);〈弾丸で〉shoot through (a target).

うちのめす 打ちのめす 〈口語〉beat sb to a pulp;〈口語〉beat sb up;〈口語〉finish sb. 文例⇩

うちのり 内法 the internal [inside] measurement(s) (of) ¶内法が10センチある be 10 centimeters across [wide] on the inside.

うちひも 打ち紐 a braid.

うちべんけい 内弁慶 a lion at home and a mouse abroad. [the castle walls.

うちぼり 内堀 an inner moat; a moat within

うちまく 内幕 〈内情〉inside information (on);〈口語〉the lowdown (on) ¶内幕を語る give sb inside information [the lowdown] / 内幕を知っている have inside knowledge (of); have got the lowdown (on) / 芸術家の世界の内幕に通じている be in the know about the artistic world / 内幕話 an inside story [account, report] (of); a behind-the-scenes story. 文例⇩

うちまくる 撃[打]ちまくる 〈銃砲を〉fire [blaze] away (at the enemy); fire (guns) by volleys (一斉射撃で);〈野球〉hit the ball (pitcher) all over the park; loose off a barrage of hits;〈ボクシング〉loose off a barrage of blows (to one's opponent's face).

うちまた 内股 the inside of the thigh ¶内股に歩く walk pigeon-toed; walk with one's toes turned in [inward].

うちみ 打ち身 a bruise.

うちみず 打ち水 ¶打ち水する sprinkle 《the lane》 with water; water 《the garden》.

うちやぶる 打ち破る ⇨やぶる, まかす.

うちゅう¹ 宇宙 the universe; the cosmos;〈大気圏外の〉(outer) space / 宇宙の《the origin》of the universe; universal;〈文〉cosmic;〈空間の〉spatial / 宇宙に打ち上げる launch [put, send]《a man》into space / 大宇宙 the macrocosm [microcosm] / 宇宙医学 space medicine / 宇宙開発競争 a space race / 宇宙開発計画 a space development project [program] / 宇宙科学 space science / 宇宙科学者 a space scientist / 宇宙カプセル a space capsule / 宇宙空間 space / 宇宙航法 space navigation; astronautics / 宇宙時代 the space age; the age of space / 宇宙銃 a space gun / 宇宙食 space food / 宇宙人〈他の星から地球を訪れる想像の生物〉a visitor from (outer) space; an alien / 宇宙塵【天】cosmic dust;〈通俗に〉space [interstellar] dust / 宇宙ステーション a space station / 宇宙生物学 exobiology / 宇宙船 a spaceship; a spacecraft (単複同形) / 宇宙線【物】cosmic rays / 宇宙大爆発生成論 the big-bang theory / 宇宙探査 space [celestial] exploration / 宇宙探査機 a space probe / 宇宙飛行 (a) space flight / 宇宙飛行士 an astronaut; a spaceman [spacewoman]; a cosmonaut (ソ連の) / 宇宙服 a space suit / 宇宙兵器 a space weapon / 宇宙歩行[遊泳]をする take a space walk; walk in space / 宇宙無限膨脹説 the steady-state theory / 宇宙旅行 (go on) space [interplanetary] travel; a journey into space; a voyage across space.

うちゅう² 雨中 ¶雨中に in the rain / 雨中にもかかわらず in spite of the rain; though it is raining.

うちょうてん 有頂天 ¶有頂天になる go into raptures [ecstasies] (over); be beside oneself with joy; walk [tread] on air; be in (the) seventh heaven.

うちよせる 打ち寄せる 〈波が〉dash against; wash 《the shore》; break on 《the rocks》; surge in 《from the Pacific》 ¶浜辺に打ち寄せられた色々なもの debris washed in from the sea. 文例⇩

うちわ¹ 内輪 ¶内輪の 〈内々の〉private;〈控え目の〉moderate / 内輪のこと a family [private] affair / 内輪の恥をさらけ出す wash one's dirty linen in public / 内輪で among ourselves [themselves]; in private; privately / 内輪に見積もる make a low [moderate, conservative] estimate (of) / 内輪に見積もって at a conservative [moderate] estimate / ごく内輪に言って to say the least (of it) / 内輪に暮らす live within one's means [in a modest way] / 内輪げんか[もめ]をする have a family quarrel; quarrel among themselves [ourselves]. 文例⇩

うちわ² 団扇 a (paper) fan ¶うちわを使う fan oneself.

うちわけ 内訳 a breakdown 《of the total expenditure》 ¶内訳を示す itemize; give sb a breakdown 《of a figure》 / 内訳明細書 an itemized statement. 文例⇩

けて話をする。He talks quite freely with everybody. / 彼はなかなか他の人と打ち解けようとしなかった。He wouldn't come out of his shell.

うちどめ この相撲一番にて本日の打ち止め。This is the last match for today.

うちのめす 全く打ちのめされたような気持ちだった。I felt completely shattered.

うちまく 彼は政界の内幕を知っていた。He knew what was going on behind the scenes [what the score was] in the political world.

うちよせる 浜にはうねりが打ち寄せていた。Waves were rolling in across the beach. / 波がひたひたといそに打ち寄せている。Waves are lapping the beach.

うちわ¹ あなたは内輪の人だからこの事をお知らせしておきます。I'll let you in on this, since you're one of the family. / 結婚式はごく内輪の者だけでやりました。We invited only the closest members of our family to our wedding. / 彼の財産は内輪に見積もって約2億円はある。A conservative estimate of the value of his property is about 200 million yen.

うちわけ 支出の内訳は30項目以上になる。The expenditure breaks down [is broken down] into more than 30 items.

うつ 打[撃, 討]つ〈たたく〉hit; beat; knock;〈(文)strike〉; give [deal] sb a blow; slap〈平手で〉;〈心を〉touch; move; impress;〈時を〉strike;〈発射する〉fire; shoot; take a shot(at);〈興行する〉give [present, perform] (a play); run [stage] (a show);〈攻撃する〉attack;〈(文)assault〉;〈破る〉defeat; destroy;〈征服する〉〈(文)conquer〉,〈(文)subjugate〉/頭を打つ hit sb on the head / 2 時を打つ strike two / 5 発撃つ fire [let go] five shots / 右腕を撃たれる be shot in the right arm / そばを打つ make buckwheat vermicelli / 庭に水を打つ sprinkle the garden with water; water the garden /感に打たれる be moved [impressed, touched] (by); be struck with wonder [admiration]. 文例⇩

うつうつ 鬱々 ¶うつうつと gloomily; cheerlessly / うつうつとして楽しまない be depressed; be in low spirits; mope. 文例⇩

うっかり 〈気づかずに〉carelessly; thoughtlessly; inadvertently;〈ぼんやりして〉absent-mindedly;〈気を許して〉in an unguarded moment;〈我知らず〉in spite of *oneself*;〈軽率に〉rashly ¶うっかりしゃべる inadvertently talk about *sth*; blurt out《a secret》; let《the truth》slip out. 文例⇩

うつくしい 美しい beautiful; lovely; fine; pretty(可愛い);〈容貌が〉handsome; good-looking;〈(文)comely〉;〈魅力的な〉charming;〈印象的な〉picturesque;〈気高い〉noble;〈清い〉pure ★ handsome は通例男性について「端麗な」の意で用い、女性には beautiful, pretty を用いる。a handsome woman と言うと、体つきが立派で生気と気品のある女性の意味 /形の美しい shapely; well-formed / 心が美しい be sweet-natured (主に女性が); have a heart of gold / 美しい声で in a sweet voice / 美しい所 a beautiful place /〈(文)a place of great beauty〉/美しく〈(文)beautifully〉; charmingly / 美しくする beautify / 美しさ beauty.

うっけつ 鬱血 congestion (of blood) ¶鬱血する be congested (with blood).

うつし 写し a copy; a (facsimile) transcript (謄写物);〈副本〉a duplicate;〈複製〉a reproduction; a facsimile ¶写しをとる make a copy [duplicate] (of); copy.

うつす[1] 写[映]す〈謄写する〉copy; take [make] a copy [facsimile] (of); transcribe;〈模写する〉imitate; copy; reproduce; trace;〈描写する〉describe;〈(文)depict〉; picture;〈写真を〉photograph; take a photograph [picture] of;〈影を〉reflect; project; cast ¶映画をスクリーンに映す project [throw] a picture onto the screen / 湖に影を映す be reflected [mirrored] in the lake / 写真を写してもらう have *one's* photograph taken. 文例⇩

うつす[2] 移す move [remove] (to, into); transfer (to); shift (to);〈付託する〉refer 《a matter to the committee》; remit 《a case to the higher court》;〈容器に〉pour [empty] (into);〈病気を〉infect 《sb with a disease》; give 《sb one's cold》; pass 《a disease on to sb》¶注意を移す turn [divert, distract] *one's* attention《from A to B》/計画を実行に移す put [carry] a plan into effect 《(文)execution》/本店から支店へ移される be transferred from the head office to a branch.

うっすら 薄ら〈薄く〉thinly; lightly; slightly; faintly ¶うっすらと目をあけて with *one's* eyes slightly open / うっすらと雪化粧した富士山 Mt. Fuji lightly powdered with snow. 文例⇩

うっせき 鬱積 ¶鬱積した pent-up (feelings); bottled-up (bitterness).

うっそう 鬱蒼 ¶うっそうたる thick; dense;〈(文)luxuriant〉/うっそうと thickly; densely;〈(文)luxuriantly〉/うっそうと葉の生い茂ったニレの木 a densely leafed elm / うっそうとした森林 a dense forest.

うったえ 訴え〈訴訟〉a lawsuit; a suit; an action;〈告訴〉a charge; an accusation;〈訴願〉a petition; an appeal; a complaint ¶損害賠償の訴え a suit for damages; a《3,000,000 yen》damage suit / …の訴えで at the suit of…; on complaint of….

うったえる 訴える ¶〈訴訟を起こす〉sue 《sb for sth》; take sb to court 《for sth》; bring [file] an action [《(文)a suit》] 《against sb》; go to law 《against sb》;〈口語〉have the law 《on sb》;〈苦情を言う〉complain (about, of);〈正義などに〉appeal to ¶裁判所に訴える file a suit with the court 《against sb for sth》; bring an action in the court 《against sb for sth》; take *one's* case to the court of law / 警察に訴える lay a complaint before the police; lodge [file] a complaint with the police / 頭痛を訴える complain of a headache / 暴力に訴える 《(文)resort to [have recourse to] violence; use force》/世論に訴える appeal to public opinion. 文例⇩

うっちゃり 打っちゃり《相撲》the trick of leaning back and carrying *one's* opponent round

---

うつ 雨が窓を激しく打っていた。The rain was beating [drumming] hard against the window. / いま打ったのは何時ですか。What hour did it [the clock] strike? / もっと何かほかに打つ手がありそうなものだ。There ought to be some other measures we [they] can take. / 彼について一心に打たれるのは、彼の仕事に対するひたむきな情熱である。What impresses me most about him is his single-minded devotion to his work.

うつうつ その日一日私は家でうつうつとしていた。I moped in the house all day.

うっかり うっかり手紙に切手を張るのを忘れた。I carelessly forgot to put a stamp on the letter.

うつす[1] 私は新しいカードを取ってその一文を写し取った。I took a new card and copied out the whole sentence. / 彼は鏡に自分の姿を映して見た。He looked at himself in the mirror. / テレビは世相をそのまま映しているという人もある。Some people say that television is holding up a mirror to life.

うっすら 彼女の額にうっすらと汗がにじんだ。A light film of perspiration formed on her forehead.

うったえる 彼は詐欺で訴えられた。He was accused of fraud. / この種の絵は民衆の日常生活を生

うっちゃる 打っちゃる 〈捨てる〉throw [cast] away;〈あきらめる〉give up; abandon;〈放任する〉neglect; lay aside; leave [let] alone; let sb [sth] be ¶物事をうっちゃらかしにしておく let things slide.

うつつ 現つ ¶うつつを抜かす be infatuated 《with, by》; give *oneself* up 《to gambling》; be besotted 《by a girl》;《口語》be dead gone 《on a woman》/ 夢にもうつつにも waking or sleeping; awake or asleep.

うってかかる 打って掛かる hit (strike) out at *sb*;《口語》lash out at *sb*;《口語》take a swipe at *sb*.

うってかわる 打って変わる change completely;《文》undergo a complete change ¶打って変わった人間となる become a different [new] man / 打って変わった態度に出る take [《文》adopt] a completely changed [an entirely different] attitude.

うってつけ 打って付け ¶打って付けの the very [the most suitable] (thing, person for *sth*). 文例◎

うってでる 打って出る 〈軍勢が〉sally out; make a sally [sortie]; 〈選挙などに〉《米》run 《for》;《英》stand 《for》; declare *one's* candidacy 《for》;〈乗り出す〉make *one's* debut ¶政治家として打って出る launch into politics;《文》enter on a political career. 文例◎

うっとうしい 〈陰気な〉gloomy; depressing; miserable;〈どんよりした〉dull; oppressive ¶うっとうしい天気 miserable [depressing, oppressive] weather.

うっとり ¶うっとりする be fascinated [《文》enraptured, entranced] 《by, with》; be in raptures 《over》/ うっとりと 《文》absorbedly; spellbound; in raptures; in rapt admiration; in a trance. 文例◎

うつびょう 鬱病 (a) (psychotic) depression ¶うつ病にかかっている suffer from [be afflicted with] depression; be depressed / うつ病患者 a depressive.

うつぶせ 俯せ ¶うつぶせに倒れる fall on *one's* face; fall prone 《to the floor》/ うつぶせになる lie on *one's* face; lie prone.

うっぷん 鬱憤 pent-up feelings [《文》sentiments]; resentment; a grudge ¶うっぷんを晴らす settle old scores 《with》;《口語》get *one's* own back 《on》;《口語》revenge *oneself* 《on sb for sth》;《文》wreak *one's* wrath 《on》; work off *one's* grudge 《on》/ うっぷんをもらす let out [《文》give vent to] *one's* pent-up feelings 《against》;《文》vent *one's* spleen.

うつぼ【魚】a moray (eel).

うつぼつ ¶うつぼつたる pent-up; irresistible / うつぼつたる野心 a burning [《文》vaulting] ambition / うつぼつたる冒険心を抱いている be burning with enterprise.

うつむく 俯く 〈顔を伏せる〉hang (down) [bow, droop, bend] *one's* head;〈伏し目になる〉look down;《文》cast down *one's* eyes.

うつむけ 俯け ¶うつむけに on *one's* face; face downward; in a prone position.

うつり 映り 〈映像〉a reflection;〈配合〉harmony ¶映りがよい match [go well 《with》]; harmonize 《with》.

うつりが 移り香 a lingering scent.

うつりかわり 移り変わり (a) change;《文》(a) transition ¶季節の移り変わり the turn of the seasons / 世の中の移り変わり the changing times.

うつりかわる 移り変わる change;《文》undergo changes ¶移り変わる景色を車窓から眺める gaze at the changing [passing] scenery through the train window.

うつりぎ 移り気 ¶移り気な fickle; unreliable;《文》capricious;《文》inconstant;《文》volatile.

うつる¹ 映[写]る 〈投影する〉be reflected [mirrored] 《in》;〈配合がいい〉go well 《with》;〈似合う〉suit;《文》become;〈調和する〉harmonize 《with》;〈写真が〉be taken; come out (well) ¶鏡に映る be reflected in a well. / この部屋にはこの家具は映りが悪い. The furniture doesn't go well with this room.

うつる² 庭の松の木の影が障子に映った. The shadow of the pine tree in the garden fell on the *shoji*. / この部屋の2つの鏡に自分の姿が幾つも幾つもどこまでも続いて映っているのに気が付いた. He noticed that his own reflection was being repeated endlessly in the two mirrors of the room. / この写真に写っている女の子は僕の妹です. The girl in this picture is my sister.

うつる³ 私は今の家を移ろうと思っている. I am thinking of moving out of my house. / 堀河天皇の治世は11世紀が12世紀に移る時期であった. The reign of the Emperor Horikawa covers the period when the 11th century

---

き生きと描いているので非常に訴えるところがある. Paintings of this kind have considerable appeal, as they vividly depict the everyday life of ordinary people. / この音楽は私の心に少しも訴えてこない. This music has no appeal for me. | This music does not appeal to me at all.

うっちゃる 私をうっちゃっといて下さい. Leave [Let] me alone. / うっちゃっておけ. 別に迷惑はかからない. Let him be; he's doing no harm. / あんな人たちが何と言おうとうっちゃっておきなさい. Don't mind whatever they say about you. / あんな所に傘がうっちゃってある. Somebody's gone and left an umbrella there.

うってつけ 彼はそこの仕事にはうってつけの人だ. He is just the man [He is the right person] for the job. / 彼にはうってつけの仕事だ. This is just the job for him. | This is the sort of job he is best fitted to undertake. / これこそうってつけの品だ. This is just what we want. | This will fill the bill perfectly.

うってでる 彼は青森から代議士に打って出る意向を明らかにした. He has announced his intention to run for the Diet from Aomori.

うっとり 彼女はその音楽にうっとりと耳を傾けていた. She was listening ecstatically to the music. | She was miles away, listening to the music.

うつり この地区はテレビの映りがよくない. TV reception isn't good [is unsatisfactory] in this area. / この2つの色は映りがよい. These two colors go together well. / この部屋にはこの家具は映りが悪い. The furniture doesn't go well with this room.

うつる¹ 庭の松の木の影が障子に映った. The shadow of the pine tree in the garden fell on the *shoji*. / この部屋の2つの鏡に自分の姿が幾つも幾つもどこまでも続いて映っているのに気が付いた. He noticed that his own reflection was being repeated endlessly in the two mirrors of the room. / この写真に写っている女の子は僕の妹です. The girl in this picture is my sister.

うつる³ 私は今の家を移ろうと思っている. I am thinking of moving out of my house. / 堀河天皇の治世は11世紀が12世紀に移る時期であった. The reign of the Emperor Horikawa covers the period when the 11th century

うつる² 移る〈移転する〉move《to a place, into a house》;〈職場・学校などを〉transfer《to another department》;〈変わる〉change; shift;〈転じる〉pass《into, to》; turn《to》;〈感染する〉catch《a disease from sb》; be infected《with diphtheria》;〈火事が〉spread《to》¶(病気が)次々にうつる pass [be passed] from person to person / うつる病気 an infectious [《口語》a catching, a contagious] disease. 文例↓

うつろ 空ろ〈うつろな〈からっぽの〉hollow; empty;〈ぼんやりした〉vacant; blank / うつろな顔つき《wear》a vacant [blank] look / うつろな気分になる feel hollow. 文例↓

うつわ 器〈容器〉a container; a vessel; a receptacle;〈器量〉caliber;《文》capacity ¶(人物の)器が大きい[小さい] be a man of high [poor] caliber. 文例↓

うで 腕〈上腕〉an arm;〈腕前〉ability(★しばしば複数形で使われる);〈技〉《文》capacity ¶腕のある〈腕利きの〉skilled; talented; competent; able; capable / 腕のない incapable; incompetent / 腕を折る have one's arm broken / break one's arm / 腕を組む〈自分の〉fold one's arms;〈人と〉put one's arm through sb's; link arms with sb / 腕を組んで《walk》with one's arms folded; with folded arms;〈人と〉linking arms;《walk》arm in arm《with》/ 腕をつかむ grab [seize] sb by the arm / 交互に腕を伸ばしてよじ登る climb arm over arm《up a cliff》/ 腕をふるう use [display] one's skill《in》/ 腕に十分に play to one's abilities [talent]《in》/ 腕をみがく improve one's skill; 腕に覚えがある be confident of one's ability [skill] / 包みを腕にかかえる hold a parcel under [in the crook of] one's arm / 腕にすがって歩く walk on sb's arm (for support) / 腕によりをかける put all one's skill《into sth》/ 腕次第で according to one's ability. 文例↓

うでぎ 腕木〈軒などを支える〉a bracket;〈信号の〉an arm;〈電柱などの〉a crosspiece.

うできき 腕利き ⇨うで(腕のある).
うでぐみ 腕組み ⇨うで(腕を組む).
うでくらべ 腕比べ ¶腕比べをする try one's skill [ability, strength]《against sb》; meet sb at a trial of skill《in》; compete《with [against] sb at (doing) sth》.
うでずく 腕ずく ¶腕ずくの strong-arm《methods》/ 腕ずくで by force /《文》by main force; by brute strength.
うでずもう 腕相撲 Indian wrestling; arm-wrestling ¶腕相撲をする Indian-[arm-]wrestle《with》.
うでたてふせ 腕立て伏せ《米》a pushup;《英》a press-up ¶毎朝腕立て伏せを30回やる do 30 pushups every morning.
うでだめし 腕試し ¶腕試しをする try one's skill [hand]《at》.
うでっぷし 腕っ節 muscular power; brawn ¶腕っ節の強い男 a man of great physical strength; a brawny fellow.
うでどけい 腕時計 a watch; a wristwatch ¶腕時計のバンド a watch strap.
うでまえ 腕前 ⇨うで.
うでまくり 腕捲り ¶腕まくりする roll [pull, turn] up one's sleeves; bare one's arms / 腕まくりして with one's sleeves rolled up.
うでる 茹でる ⇨ゆでる.
うでわ 腕輪 a bracelet; a bangle.
うてん rainy [wet] weather; a rainy [wet] day ¶雨天の場合は in case of rain; if it rains / 雨天のため owing to [on account of] the rain / 雨天続き a long spell of rainy weather / 雨天体操場 a gymnasium (pl. -siums, -sia); a gym. 文例↓
うど《植》an udo (plant) ¶うどの大木 a big useless fellow.
うとい 疎い〈疎遠である〉《文》be estranged [alienated]《from》;〈不案内である〉do not know much《about》;《口語》be not well up《in》;《文》know little《of》;《文》be ignorant《of》;《文》be unacquainted《with》¶世事に疎い do not know much about the world. 文例↓

passed into [gave way to] the 12th. / それから話は財政問題に移った. Then they moved onto [passed on to] the financial problems. / では次の章に移りましょう. Well, let's go on to the next chapter. / 彼の情熱が課員の全員にうつった. His enthusiasm infected all the members of the section. / 隣の家に火が移った. The fire spread to the house next door. / その茶は彼女のクリームのにおいが移っていて飲めなかった. The smell of her skin cream had got into the tea and spoiled it.

うつろ 彼の笑い声がうつろに響いた. His laughter rang hollow. / その男は何の返事もせずうつろな目付きであらぬ方をじっと見ていた. The man made no answer, but just stared vacantly into space.

うつわ 彼は首相の器ではない. He does not have quite the stature [have it in him] to be Prime Minister. / 私はその器ではありません. I am not up to it [not equal to the task].

うで 彼は腕が短いのでテニスの選手にはなれないと思っていた. He thought he wouldn't make a tennis player because he was short in the arm. / 腕が鳴るよ. I'm burning to try my hand at it. / I'm [My fingers are] itching to do it. / 彼はチェスが好きで, 腕を上げるために毎日2時間はチェスの本を読んでいる. He's very fond of chess and, hoping to improve his game, spends at least two hours every day poring over books on chess. / あの大工の腕は確かだ. That carpenter surely knows his job. / 腕によりをかけてやってみましょう. I'll try and do it to the best of my ability. / 彼はいわゆる腕一本でたたき上げた人です. He is what is called a self-made man.

うでくらべ よし, それでは腕比べをしよう. Well then, let's try and see which of us can do it better.

うでだめし あの男の腕試しにこの仕事をやらせてみよう. Let's give that fellow a tryout on this job.

うてん 雨天順延. To be postponed in case of rain.

うど あいつはうどの大木さ. He is like a great tree that is good for nothing but shade.

うとい 田舎で長い間独り暮らしをしていたので, 彼は世間に疎くなっていた. He was out of things, having lived alone for so many years in the country.

うとうと ❶うとうとする〈うたた寝を始める〉doze off; drop off (to sleep); fall into a doze〈眠気を催す〉feel drowsy [sleepy].

うどん noodles ❶うどん粉(wheat) flour / うどん粉病 mildew (on roses) / うどん屋〈店〉a noodle shop /〈人〉a noodle vendor [maker].

うとんじる 疎んじる neglect;《文》slight; treat *sb* coldly;《文》give *sb* the cold shoulder; keep *sb* at arm's length.

うながす 促す〈催促する〉urge; press;〈刺激する〉《文》stimulate; spur; goad;〈促進する〉prompt; quicken ❶進歩を促す quicken [accelerate] the progress《of》/ 返事を促す press *sb* for an answer.

うなぎ 鰻 an eel ❶うなぎを食べる eat eel / うなぎどんぶり a bowl of eel and rice / うなぎ屋 an eel restaurant / うなぎの寝床のような家 a long, narrow house / うなぎのぼりになる rise [《文》advance] rapidly; spiral up; rocket (up);《口語》skyrocket.

うなされる have a nightmare [bad dream] ❶うなされて大声を上げる cry out in *one's* sleep.

うなじ 項 the nape (of the neck).

うなずく nod (*one's* head)《to, at》;〈同意する〉agree《to》❶うなずいて承認する[同意を示す] nod *one's* agreement [《文》assent]《to》/ そのとおりですとうなずく《文》give an affirmative nod. 文例⇩

うなだれる droop [hang down] *one's* head ❶深くうなだれる bow *one's* head low.

ウナでん ウナ電〈send〉an urgent telegram.

うなり 唸り〈うめきの〉a groan; a moan;〈ほえ声〉a roar; a growl; a howl;〈独楽(ﾃﾞ)などの〉humming;〈はちなどの〉a buzz; buzzing; a drone; droning;〈機械などの〉buzzing; a roar (騒がしい);〈弾丸などの〉whizzing ❶うなりを立てる〈風が〉howl;〈蜂などが〉hum;〈弾丸などが〉whiz(z);〈はちなどが〉buzz; drone /〈弾丸などが〉うなりを立てて飛ぶ zip through the air. 文例⇩

うなる 唸る〈うめく〉groan; moan;〈猛獣が〉roar; howl; growl;〈犬が〉snarl ❶うなるほど金を持っている have a mint of money;《口語》be rolling [wallowing] in money [in it].

うに〈動〉a sea urchin; an urchin;〈食品〉《seasoned》sea urchin eggs [roe].

うぬぼれ 自惚れ (self-)conceit;《文》vanity ❶うぬぼれた (self-)conceited; vain;《口語》big-headed;《米口語》swelled-headed;《英口語》swollen-headed / うぬぼれが強い be full of *oneself* [*one's* own importance].

うぬぼれる 自惚れる be vain; be conceited; have a high opinion of *oneself*;《文》be puffed up with conceit [vanity];《口語》be a bighead;《米口語》have a swelled head;《英口語》have a swollen head.

うね 畝 a ridge;〈織物・編み物の〉a rib.

うねうね ❶うねうねした winding; meandering; zigzag;《文》sinuous;《文》tortuous ❶うねうねと流れる meander [wind (*its* way)] 《across the plain》. 文例⇩

うねり〈波動〉(a) wave motion;〈起伏〉《文》undulation;〈屈曲〉winding;〈波の〉heaving sea; a swell; a roller (大うねり). 文例⇩

うねる〈土地が〉undulate;〈道・川などが〉wind; meander;〈波が〉swell.

うのみ 鵜呑み ❶うのみにする swallow [bolt] *sth* whole [without chewing *it*].

うは 右派 the right wing; the right-wingers; the right-wing faction《of》❶右派の right-wing; rightist.

うば 乳母 a (wet) nurse.

うばいあい 奪い合い a scramble《for》.

うばいあう 奪い合う a scramble《for》; fight《over》❶予算を奪い合う fight《文》contend, struggle for a larger share of the budget.

うばいかえす 奪い返す take [win] back; recapture.

うばいさる 奪い去る take away; carry off.

うばいとる 奪い取る take《by force》; snatch [《文》wrest] *sth*《away》from *sb*; rob [《文》deprive] *sb* of *sth*;〈略奪する〉plunder; pillage; loot ❶王位を奪う usurp the throne / 生命を奪う take *sb's* life / 心を奪われる be fascinated [《文》enraptured, carried away]《by》; lose *one's*

うなずく 2人はさかんにうなずき合いながら話していた。They were talking to each other with a great deal of nodding. / 彼の説明にはうなずけないところがある。His explanation is not entirely convincing.

うなり トラックがうなりを立てて街道を走っている。Trucks are roaring along the highway.

うなる その絵を見たときには思わずうなってしまった。I could not suppress a grunt of admiration when I saw the picture. / ジェフに買えないものなんてないよ。何しろ金はうなるほどあるんだから。Jeff can afford anything; he's simply rolling in it.

うぬぼれる 彼は自分では秀才だとうぬぼれている。He flatters himself that he's got a lot of brains. / 彼女は町内で指折りの美人だとうぬぼれている。She fancies herself as one of the most beautiful women in the neighborhood.

うねうね 美術館の外には多勢の人がうねうねと列を作っていた。A long queue of people snaked along the outside of the art gallery.

うねり 海はうねりが高い。There is a strong swell.

うのみ 彼らはその話をうのみにした。They swallowed the story hook, line and sinker. / They took the whole story on trust [on faith].

うばう その室内のけんらんたる装飾は我々の目を奪った。The gorgeous decorations of the room dazzled our eyes.

うま ナポレオン軍は6月24日徒歩および馬でワルシャワを発した。Napoleon's army left Warsaw by foot and horse on June 24. / 彼は大分馬に乗ったのでがにまたになっていた。He was bowlegged from so much horseback riding. / あの男とはうまが合わない。I don't get on well [hit it off] with him. / 彼はどこの馬の骨だかわからない男だ。Nobody knows where he comes from [who he is]. / 彼にいくら説いてもまるで馬の耳に念仏だ。Our advice was like water off a duck's back to him. / Giving him advice was like preaching to the deaf.

うまい うまい!Splendid!] That's fine! / この桃のうまそうなこと。

うばぐるま 乳母車 《米》a baby carriage [buggy]; 《英》a perambulator; 《英口語》a pram ¶乳母車を押して行く wheel a baby carriage.

うぶ ¶うぶな〈無邪気な〉innocent; naive; 《文》artless; simple; unsophisticated;〈経験の浅い〉inexperienced; green / うぶな娘 an innocent [《文》ingenuous] girl.

うぶぎ 産着 clothes for a newborn baby.

うぶげ 産毛 downy [fine soft] hair《on one's cheek》; down.

うぶごえ 産声 the first cry of a newborn baby; the birth cry (of the space age) ¶産声を上げる give [《文》utter] one's first cry /〈生まれる〉be born; see the light (of day).

うぶゆ 産湯 ¶産湯をつかわせる give《a newborn baby》its first bath.

うま 馬 a horse;〈小型の〉a pony;〈十二支の午〉(the Year of) the Horse / 馬の《文》equine / 馬の手入れをする[口を取る] groom [hold] a horse / 馬を飼う[調教する] keep [train] a horse / 馬を止める pull up [rein in] one's horse / 馬を慣らす break in a horse / 馬にくらを置く[蹄鉄を打つ] saddle [shoe] a horse / 馬に乗る ride a horse; get on [mount] a horse / 馬に乗って (go) on horseback / 馬に馬具をつける[水をやる] harness [water] a horse / 馬から落ちる fall off [be thrown from] one's horse / 馬から降りる get off [《文》dismount from] a horse / 馬市 a horse fair / 馬方 a (packhorse) driver / 馬小屋 a stable ⇒うまや. 文例⇩

うまい 甘い[旨い]〈美味な〉sweet; nice;《be taste》good; delicious (非常に);《文》palatable;〈上首尾の〉successful;〈幸運な〉lucky;〈上手な〉skillful; clever;《be》good (at);《be》at home (in, on);〈適切な〉well-chosen; apt;《文》felicitous;《文》happy;〈すばらしい〉splendid; excellent; fine;〈金になる〉profitable;《文》lucrative ¶うまい考え a good [《文》happy, capital] idea / うまい物 dainty food; a delicacy; a goody;《米》a tidbit;《英》a titbit / うまい事を言う say nice [clever] things / 字がうまい one's writing is good;《文》write a good hand / 英語がうまい be good at English; speak English well;《文》have a good command of English / うまい汁を吸う《口語》make a good thing out of (a public project);《口語》milk (profits from) sth / うまい仕事 a profitable [《俗》juicy] job / うまそうな appetizing; tempting / うまそうに食べる eat sth as if one was enjoying it [《口語》with apparent relish]. 文例⇩

うまく 旨く〈美味に〉deliciously;〈巧みに〉well; skillfully; cleverly;《文》aptly;〈首尾よく〉successfully;〈運よく〉luckily ¶うまく行く go well [all right];《口語》come off (well); work out (nicely); succeed;《口語》do [turn] the trick / うまく行けば if things go well; with luck / うまく行かない go wrong [《文》amiss] / うまくやる make a good [fine] job (of sth);《口語》make a go (of); manage sth successfully [satisfactorily]; be successful (in). 文例⇩

うまごやし 《植》(a) clover.

うまさ 旨さ deliciousness;《文》palatability.

うまづら 馬面《a man with》a long, equine face;《口語》a horseface ¶馬づらの《口語》horse-faced.

うまとび 馬跳び leapfrog ¶馬跳びをする play leapfrog; leapfrog.

うまのり 馬乗り ¶馬乗りになる sit astride sb.

うまみ 旨味 taste; flavor;〈妙味〉(a) charm; the beauty (of) ¶うま味のある〈誘惑的な〉《文》alluring; tempting;〈もうかる〉profitable;《文》lucrative.

うまや 馬屋, 厩 a stable ¶馬屋に入れる put (a horse) in a stable; stable (a horse).

うまる 埋まる be buried (under);〈一杯になる〉be filled (up) (with).

うまれ 生まれ〈出生〉birth;〈家柄〉《文》lineage; a family;〈出生地〉one's birthplace ¶生まれの卑しい lowborn / 生まれのよい well-born / ドイツ生まれのフランス人 a German-born Frenchman / 生まれ故郷 one's birthplace; one's hometown. 文例⇩

How nice these peaches look! / 彼の家へ行くといつもうまいものを出す。He always feeds his guests well. |《文》He keeps a good table. / そいつは話がうますぎる。That's too good to be true. / おごる者久しからずとはうまいことを言ったものだ。It is well said that pride goes before a fall. / うまいことを言うわね。It's nice to hear that.

うまく こうするとずっとうまく食べられます。This will improve its flavor a great deal. | This will make it a lot more palatable. / 試験はうまく行った。I did well in the examination. / 何もかもうまく行った。Everything went well with us. | Everything turned out [went off] all right. / 物事うまく行っていないと感じた。I sensed that things were not going as they should. / 家の庭でトマトを栽培しようとしたんだが、あまりうまく行かなかった。I tried to raise tomatoes in my garden, but without without much success. / それをやってみたが、うまく行くこともあり、さほどでないこともあった。It has been attempted with varying degrees of success. / この辺からようやく事がうまく行き始めた。From about now, things began to go better. |《文》Here at last success began to attend us. / 彼は今度の仕事はなかなかうまくやっている。He is making out well in his new job. / そのやり方ではあまりうまく行かないだろう。You won't get very far, doing it that way. / とかく物事はうまく行かぬものだ。Things go by contraries in this world. / うまくやったねえ! What a lucky fellow you are! / 彼は校長とうまく行っていない。He is not getting along with the principal.

うまる その谷が堆積物で埋まったのは更新世初期のことと考えられている。It is surmised that the valley was choked with sediments in the Lower Pleistocene.

うまれ お生まれはどちらですか。Where do you come from? | Where are you from? / 彼は英国人だ。He is an Englishman by birth [origin]. | He is originally from England. / 彼はカリフォルニア生まれのカリフォルニア育ちだ。He was born and bred

うまれあわせる 生まれ合わせる happen to be born ((in the year of...)).

うまれかわり 生まれ変わり 《再生》《文》rebirth;《文》regeneration; ⟨化身⟩ a reincarnation ((of)).

うまれかわる 生まれ変わる be born again; be reborn; ⟨別人のようになる⟩ become a new man. 文例↓

うまれそこない 生まれ損い a good-for-nothing. 文例↓

うまれつき 生まれつき ⟨天性⟩ one's nature; ⟨生まれながらに⟩ by nature; naturally; ⟨生まれた時から⟩ from birth ¶生まれつきの能力 an inborn [a native] ability / 生まれつききちょうめんな性質 be methodical [a methodical person] by nature ★ by nature という句は形容詞又は名詞に添えて使うもので, I don't like medicine by nature. のように動詞に添えて使うことはできない。こういう場合は下の文例のように言う。

うまれつく 生まれつく be born ((a musician)). 文例↓

うまれながら 生まれながら ¶生まれながら(に) by nature; naturally / 生まれながらの 《文》innate; inborn; born; natural;《文》native;《文》inherent.

うまれる 生まれる be born; come into being [existence, the world];《文》see the light; ⟨生じる⟩ result ((from)); be a result [a product, an outgrowth] ((of)) ¶金持ち[貧乏]に生まれる be born rich [poor]; have [《文》be born of] rich [poor] parents / 生まれてはじめて for the first time in one's life / 生まれたばかりの子供 a newborn baby / 生まれたばかりの子馬 a newly-born foal; a foal (still) wet from its mother / 自分の生まれ育った町 the town where one was born and bred. 文例↓

うみ¹ 海の親 one's true [real] parent; ⟨創始者⟩ the founder; the originator; the inventor / 生みの苦しみ ((experience)) the pains [《文》pangs] of childbirth; ⟨比喩的⟩ the throes of creation. 文例↓

うみ² 海 the sea; an ocean (大洋); ⟨すずりの⟩ the well ¶火の海 ⇒ひのうみ / 海の男 a sailor; a seafaring man / 海の家 a seaside clubhouse ((owned by a company)) / 海の魚 a saltwater fish / 海のない国 a landlocked country / 海のものとも山のものともしかない be [hang] in the balance; be (quite) in the air;《文》be in a nebulous condition; be (still) an unknown quantity / 海に出す take [put] a ship to sea / 海に落ちる fall into the sea; ⟨船から⟩ fall overboard / 海に囲まれた国 a country surrounded by (the) sea / 海へ行く go to the seaside / 海千山千のしたたか者 an old fox. 文例↓

うみ³ 膿 pus; purulent matter ¶押して膿を出す squeeze [press] the pus out of ((a boil)). 文例↓

うみおとす 生[産]み落とす ⇒うむ³.

うみかぜ 海風 a sea breeze [wind].

うみがめ 海亀 a sea turtle.

うみだす 生み出す ⇒うむ³ ¶新しい理論を生み出す hatch (out) [《文》formulate] a new theory. 文例↓

うみづり 海釣り sea fishing.

うみどり 海鳥 a seabird; a seafowl.

うみなり 海鳴り the rumbling of the sea.

うみねこ 海猫 [鳥] a black-tailed gull.

うみびらき 海開き the opening of the sea-bathing season ((at)). 文例↓

うみべ 海辺 the seashore; the seaside; the beach (浜); the coast ¶海辺の町 a seaside town.

うみへび 海蛇 a sea snake.

うむ¹ 有無 ⟨存在⟩ existence; presence; ⟨諾否⟩ yes or no ¶有無を言わせず《文》peremptorily; forcibly; willy-nilly / 有無相通じる supply each other's wants; fill each other's needs.

うむ² 倦む ⇒あきる ¶うまずたゆまず tirelessly; untiringly;《文》with untiring [dogged] perseverance.

うむ³ 産[生]む bear; give birth to;《文》be delivered of ((a baby)); ⟨動物が⟩ breed; ⟨産卵する⟩ lay ((eggs)); spawn (魚が); ⟨...を生じる⟩

---

in California. | He is a Californian born and bred. / あなたは何年生まれですか. When were you born? / 彼は生まれ故郷の秋田へ帰った. He has returned to his native Akita.

うまれあわせる いい時代に生まれ合わせたものだ. How lucky I am to have been born in these times!

うまれかわる この次生まれ変わってくるとしたら, 男になりたいですか女になりたいですか. If you could be born again [have your time over again], would you like to be a man or a woman? / 彼は全く生まれ変わったようになった. He is quite another man now.

うまれそこない この里生まれ損いめ. You useless bastard!

うまれつき 私は生まれつき薬嫌いで, めったに薬を飲まない. I have an innate dislike for medicine and seldom take any.

うまれつく あの人はああのように生まれついているのだ. He's born that way. | That's the way he's made.

うまれながら 彼は生まれながらの詩人である. He is a born poet. | He was born a poet. | Nature cut him out for a poet.

うまれる 鈴木さんのところに男の子が生まれた. The Suzukis had a baby boy. / 月曜日には子供が生まれる予定だった. The baby was due to arrive on Monday. / 彼らには子供が2人あって, もう1人生まれようとしていた. They had two children and another was on the way. / 生まれたとき目方が3キロあった. The baby weighed three kilograms at birth. / 1878年に生まれ, 1968年に亡くなったアプトン・シンクレアは問題小説『ジャングル』の作者として知られている. Upton Sinclair, whose dates are 1878 to 1968, is known for his problem novel, *The Jungle*. / ヒラメは生まれたときには普通の魚と同じように体を縦にして泳いでおり, 目も両側についている. The flounder starts life swimming upright in the ordinary way, with an eye on either side of its head. / 象の子は生まれてから数分すると立つことができる. An elephant calf can stand on its legs within a few minutes of birth. / 彼女は生まれたまんまの姿でそこに立っていた. She stood there in her birthday suit. / また英語雑誌が生まれた. Another English magazine has ap-

うむ　119　うら

produce; bring forth; give rise to; 《文》yield ¶利子を生むbear [yield] interest (at 5 per cent) / 産み立ての卵 a new-laid [fresh] egg. 文例⇩

うむ⁴　膿む pus forms [gathers] ((in the wound); 〈傷が主語〉fester ⇨かのう¹.

ウムラウト【言語】(an) umlaut ¶ウムラウト符号 an umlaut sign.

うめ　梅〈木〉an ume tree; 〈実〉an ume; a Japanese apricot; 〈花〉an ume blossom ★梅は従来plumとされているが、これは正しくない。¶梅酒 spirits flavored with ume; ume liquor / 梅干し a pickled ume / 梅見に行く go to see [view] ume blossoms.

うめあわせ　埋め合わせ amends; (a) compensation ¶埋め合わせに to make up [make amends] for; by way of compensation ¶埋め合わせをする make up [make amends] ((to sb, for sth); cover [make good] ((the loss). 文例⇩

うめき(ごえ)　呻き(声) a groan; a moan; moaning ¶うめき声をあげる ⇨うめく.

うめく　呻く groan; moan; give a groan [moan] ¶苦痛にうめく groan with pain.

うめくさ　埋め草 a (space) filler; a fill-in. 文例⇩

うめたて　埋め立て (land) reclamation ¶埋め立て工事 reclamation work / 埋め立て地 reclaimed land [ground].

うめたてる　埋め立てる reclaim (land from the sea); fill up (a pond with earth); fill in (a moat).

うめる　埋める 〈土の中などに〉bury ((in, under)); 〈すき間などを〉fill up [in]; plug (up); stop ((a gap)); 〈埋め合わせる〉make up [make amends] ((for)); cover [make good] ((the loss) ¶土の中に浅く[深く]埋める bury sth lightly [deeply] in the ground.

うもう　羽毛 feathers; plumes; plumage (集合的); 〈綿毛〉down ¶羽毛のある feathered.

うもれぎ　埋もれ木 bogwood ¶埋もれ木細工 bogwood work.

うもれる　埋もれる ⇨うずもれる.

うやうやしい　恭しい respectful; reverent; 《文》deferential ¶恭しく respectfully; reverently; 《文》deferentially / 恭しくおじぎをする make a respectful bow ((to)); 《文》make a profound obeisance ((to).

うやまう　敬う respect; 《文》esteem; honor; 《文》revere; 《文》venerate; 《文》hold sb in esteem [reverence]; look up to; pay respect to ¶神を敬う worship [《文》revere] God / 敬うべき《文》worthy of respect; 《文》venerable.

うやむや ¶うやむやな返事をする give a vague reply; do not commit oneself / 事をうやむやにしておく leave a matter unsettled [《文》undecided] (and do nothing definite about it). 文例⇩

うようよ in swarms ¶うようよしている〈場所が主語〉swarm [be crowded] ((with)); crawl [be alive] ((with)).

うよきょくせつ　紆余曲折〈錯雑〉complications; 〈波乱〉《文》vicissitudes (of life) ¶紆余曲折を経て after many twists and turns.

うよく　右翼〈思想上の〉the right wing; right-wingers; rightists; 〖野球〗right field ¶右翼手 a right fielder / 右翼団体 a right-wing organization / 右翼思想の持ち主である be right-wing in one's opinions / 右翼への3塁打 a triple into right field.

うら　裏 the back; the reverse [wrong] side; the underside (下側); the inside (内側); 〈背後〉the back; the rear; 〈衣服の〉the lining ¶硬貨の裏 the back [reverse, tail] of a coin / 第3回の裏〖野球〗the second [last] half of the third inning / 彼の言葉の裏の意味 the hidden meaning [the implication] of his words / 裏をかく outwit [outfox] sb; frustrate [foil] 《sb's scheme, sb in his plan》 / 裏をつける line (a coat with fur) / 心の裏を見すかす read sb's thoughts; see through what sb has in his mind / 上着の裏にバッジをつけている wear a badge on the inside of one's coat / 裏で[に] at the back ((of)); 《米口語》in back ((of)); in the rear; behind / 裏へ回る go to the rear (of the house); go round to the back (door). 文例⇩

---

peared. / こんなすばらしい部屋に泊まったのは生まれてはじめてだわ. This is the most splendid room I've ever stayed in.

うみ¹　生みの親より育ての親. One's foster parents are dearer than one's real mother and father.

うみ²　海が荒れそうだ. There is going to be a heavy [rough] sea. / 結果はまだ海のものとも山のものともわかりかねます. It is as yet too early to predict the result.

うみ³　傷が膿を持った. Pus formed [gathered] in the wound. / 膿がじくじく出ている. Pus is oozing out. / 腕の傷から膿が出ていた. He had a running sore on his arm. / この際、政界にたまっているすべての膿を出してしまうべきだ. At this juncture all the cor-ruption that has been poisoning the political life of the nation should be brought out into the open.

うみだす　これは安川氏の頭から生み出されたものだ. This is Mr. Yasukawa's brainchild.

うみなり　海鳴りがしている. The sea is rumbling.

うみびらき　湘南海岸は明日海開きだ. The Shonan beach will be opened to bathers tomorrow.

うむ³　彼女は昨日子供を生んだ. She had a baby yesterday. / 彼女は子供を5人生んだ. She is the mother of five children. / 彼は日本が生んだ最大の歴史家である. He is the greatest historian that Japan has ever produced. / 金は金を生む. Money begets money. / このニュースは色々な憶測を生んだ. The news has given rise to all sorts of speculation.

うめあわせ　このような動物を飼育して子孫のために残すのはよいことには違いないが、世界の森から彼らが姿を消してしまったことに対しては、あまり埋め合わせにはならない. It is certainly a good thing to keep these animals alive in captivity for posterity, but that is small compensation for their disappearance from the forests of the world.

うめくさ　何か埋め草が欲しい. I want something to fill up the space.

うやむや　この問題はうやむやになってしまった. The question remained pending for a long time and was forgotten at last.

うら　鏡は裏に水銀が塗ってある.

うらうち 裏打ち lining; backing ¶裏打ちする line (a coat with silk); back (a map with strong paper).

うらおもて 裏表 both sides ⇒ひょうり ¶裏表のある人 a double-dealer; ⟨偽善者⟩ a hypocrite / 裏表のある行動をとる play a double game / 政界の裏表を知っている know the inside of the political world; know the political world inside out. 文例↓

うらかいどう 裏街道 a byroad; a byway ¶人生の裏街道を歩いてきた人 a person who has seen the dark [seamy] side of life.

うらがえし 裏返し ¶裏返しにする turn (a card) over; turn (a sock) inside out; ⟨上下を⟩ turn (a table) upside down / 答案用紙を裏返しに置く place one's test paper face down [downward] (on the desk) / 靴下を裏返しにはく put one's socks on inside [wrong side] out. 文例↓

うらがき 裏書き (an) endorsement; ⟨確証⟩ (a) confirmation ⇒うらづけ ¶裏書きする endorse; ⟨確証する⟩ confirm (a fact); corroborate; support / 手形に裏書きをする endorse a bill / 裏書き人 an endorser. 文例↓

うらかた 裏方 ⟨芝居の⟩ a property man; ⟨口語⟩ a propman.

うらがね 裏金 money used in secret; a secret fund. 文例↓

うらがわ 裏側 ⇒うら ¶月の裏側 the other [hidden, far, dark] side of the moon.

うらきど 裏木戸 a back door.

うらぎり 裏切り (a) betrayal; treachery ¶裏切り行為 an act of treachery; a breach of faith; ⟨口語⟩ a sell-out / 裏切り者 a betrayer; a traitor; ⟨密告者⟩ an informer; ⟨口語⟩ a stool pigeon.

うらぎる 裏切る ⟨文⟩ betray; ⟨文⟩ turn traitor to sb; ⟨口語⟩ double-cross (one's friends); play a double game with sb; ⟨口語⟩ sell out on sb; break faith with sb; be unfaithful to (one's husband) ¶期待を裏切る ⟨主格・相手が主語⟩ disappoint [fall short of, be contrary to] one's expectation(s). 文例↓

うらぐち 裏口 the back [rear] door [entrance]; the kitchen door (台所口) ¶裏口取引き back-door dealings / 裏口から出る go out by [through, at] the back door / 裏口入学をする get into [⟨文⟩ obtain admission to] (a college) by the back door.

うらごえ 裏声 a falsetto (pl. -s) ¶裏声で歌う sing (in) falsetto.

うらごし 裏漉し a strainer ¶裏ごしする strain (the potatoes).

うらさく 裏作 a secondary crop.

うらじ 裏地 a lining; a cloth [fabric] backing.

うらしま 浦島 ¶浦島太郎のような人 a Rip Van Winkle.

うらづけ 裏付け ⟨支持⟩ backing; support; ⟨確認⟩ ⟨文⟩ endorsement; confirmation; ⟨証明⟩ proof; ⟨文⟩ corroboration; ⟨文⟩ substantiation; ⟨保証⟩ (a) guarantee; (a) security; ⟨米⟩ ⟨a⟩ collateral (見返り) ¶⟨議論などが⟩充分な裏付けがある ⟨文⟩ be well [soundly] substantiated; be well supported ⟨⟨by the evidence⟩⟩ / 事実の裏付けのない議論 an argument not based [founded] on fact; an argument unsupported [⟨文⟩ unsubstantiated] by the facts. 文例↓

うらづける 裏付ける back (up); support; give [⟨文⟩ lend] support to; bear out; endorse; ⟨文⟩ substantiate; ⟨文⟩ lend substance to ¶言葉を行為で裏付ける back up one's words with deeds.

うらて 裏手 ¶裏手の[に] at the back ⟨⟨of⟩⟩; ⟨⟨米口語⟩⟩ (in) back of; in the rear ⟨⟨of⟩⟩; behind.

うらどおり 裏通り a back street [alley, lane].

うらない 占い fortunetelling; divination ¶占い者 a fortuneteller / ⟨水脈や鉱脈を探る⟩ 占い棒 a dowsing [divining] rod.

うらなう 占う tell sb's fortune; divine (the future); forecast (from tea leaves) ¶占ってもらう have one's fortune told ⟨⟨by⟩⟩; consult a fortuneteller ⟨⟨about sth⟩⟩.

うらなり 末成[生]り a fruit grown near the top end of the vine; ⟨顔の青白い人⟩ a man with a pale face.

ウラニウム ⇒ウラン

うらにわ 裏庭 a back [rear] garden; ⟨米⟩ a backyard; ⟨米⟩ a yard.

うらばなし 裏話 an inside story.

Mirrors have a backing of quicksilver. / 裏を見よ。Please turn over. (略: P.T.O.) / 鍵は缶の裏についています。⟨伯語の表記⟩ Key on bottom. / 裏がある。There are wheels within wheels.

うらおもて この布は裏表の見分けがつかない。I cannot tell which is the right side of this material.

うらがえし コックさんがポークチョップを投げ上げると、裏返しになってフライパンに戻って来た。The cook threw the pork chops up in the air, and they landed in the pan the other way up.

うらがき この事実は彼の無能を裏書きするものである。This fact proves his incompetence.

うらかた これだけの規模の国際会議になると、裏方さんたちの苦労は大変なものである。An international conference of this scale requires a great deal of effort on the part of the people working behind the scenes. / この計画の実現については、彼は終始裏方的な存在に過ぎなかった。His role in the implementation of the project was an inconspicuous one, which never brought him into the limelight.

うらがね 同社は佐藤氏に5千万円の裏金を払った。The company paid Mr. Sato 50 million yen under the table. / 何億円もの裏金が動いたということだ。It is reported that hundreds of millions of yen in dirty money has changed hands.

うらぎる 結果は僕らの期待を裏切った。The results failed to come up to our expectations. / 何か裏切られたような気がした。I felt cheated. / 彼は僕らの信頼を裏切らなかった。He showed [proved] himself worthy of our trust.

うらづけ 貴君の論拠となる事実の裏付けがないと思います。I want to know what facts you have to support [corroborate] your argument.

うらはら 彼は言うこととすることが裏腹だ。He says one thing and does another. | He does not live up to his words.

うらはら 裏腹 ¶《裏腹な》opposite; reverse / …とは裏腹に《文》contrary to….

うらばんぐみ 裏番組 a program on a different channel (broadcast to compete with a popular program).

うらびょうし 裏表紙 a back cover.

うらぶれる get shabby; go downhill; go to seed ¶うらぶれた生活をしている《文》live in poverty; be down and out; be down at heel.

うらぼん 盂蘭盆 ⇨ぼん².

うらまち 裏町 a back street.

うらまど 裏窓 a back [rear] window.

うらみ¹ 恨み bitterness; ill feeling; a grudge; resentment; 〈憎悪〉hatred; 〈悪意〉malice; 〈敵意〉《文》enmity; hostility ¶恨みをいだく have [harbor, feel] a grudge 《against》; bear malice / 恨みを買う《文》incur sb's enmity [hatred] / 恨みを晴らす have [《口語》get] one's revenge 《on sb》; revenge oneself 《on sb》; settle [pay off] old scores 《with sb》; square accounts 《with sb》/ 恨み(言)を言う complain 《to sb about sth》/ 恨み重なる敵 one's mortal [deadly, sworn] enemy / 恨みつらみの数々を並べ立てる list all [《文》enumerate] one's complaints 《against》; complain about [of] one thing after the other. 文例↓

うらみ² 憾み regret; a matter for regret ⇨いかん³. 文例↓

うらむ 恨む have [bear] a grudge against sb; feel bitter about sb; 《文》think ill of sb; feel resentment at sth ★現代英語では bear sb ill will とは言わないが、bear sb no ill will の方はごく普通に使われる。 文例↓

うらめ 裏目 ¶裏目に出る produce a result opposite to what one has intended; 《one's plans》backfire. 文例↓

うらめしい 恨めしい〈非難をこめた〉reproachful; 〈残念そうな〉rueful; regretful ¶恨めしそうに reproachfully; with a rueful look. 文例↓

うらもん 裏門 a back [rear] gate.

うらやま 裏山 a hill at the back [in the rear] 《of one's house》.

うらやましい 羨ましい〈うらやむべき〉enviable; 〈うらやましがる〉envy; be envious of ⇨うらやむ ¶うらやましがらせる make sb envious 《of sth》;《文》excite envy 《in sb》; become the envy of sb / うらやましそうな目つき an envious look / うらやましそうに enviously; 《look》with envy. 文例↓

うらやむ 羨む envy; be envious of ¶成功をうらやむ envy sb's success; envy sb for his success; envy sb his success; feel envy at sb's success / うらやむに足りない unenviable. 文例↓

うららか 麗らか ¶うららかな bright (and clear); beautiful; fine; glorious.

ウラル ¶ウラル山脈 the Ural Mountains; the Urals / ウラルアルタイ語族 the Ural-Altaic languages.

ウラン《化》uranium ¶濃縮ウラン enriched uranium / 超ウラン元素 a transuranic element / ウラン鉱 uranium ore.

うり¹ 瓜 a gourd ¶瓜二つである be like two peas in a pod;《口語》be the spitting image 《of one's father》; be exactly alike; be the picture 《of one's mother》; be one's double. 文例↓

うり² 売り sale; selling ¶売りに出す put sth on sale; place sth on the market; offer [put up] sth for sale / 売りに出されている be on sale; be up for sale; be in [on] the market.

うりあげ(きんだか) 売り上げ [金[高]] sales; proceeds; turnover; takings ¶売り上げ伝票 a sales slip. 文例↓

うりあるく 売り歩く peddle; hawk;《文》cry 《one's wares》.

うりいそぐ 売り急ぐ be eager to sell; sell in haste.

うりおしむ 売り惜しむ hold back 《goods》 from the market; hold off selling 《goods》; be unwilling to sell sth (in expectation of better prices). 文例↓

うりかい 売り買い ⇨ばいばい.

うりかけ(だい)きん 売り掛け(代)金 money due from accounts.

うりきれ 売り切れ a sellout ¶売り切れになる be sold out; be [go] out of stock. 文例↓

うりこ 売り子 a salesman; a salesgirl; a sales-

うらみ¹ さあ、これで恨みっこなしだ。Now we are quits. / これで恨みっこなしということにしよう。Let's call it quits.

うらみ² この措置はいささか手遅れのうらみがある。I am afraid this measure has been taken [left] a little too late.

うらむ 僕は人に恨まれるようなことは何もしていない。I have done nothing to incur anyone's enmity. / だれも恨むかけにはいかない。I have only myself to blame [thank] for it.

うらめ その計画が裏目に出て、彼は大損をした。The plan backfired (on him), and he lost a great deal of money. / することなすこと裏目に出た。Everything he did went against him.

うらめしい 彼が一言もとりなしてくれないのがうらめしかった。I thought it was awfully unkind of him not to put in a single good word for me. / 「うらめしや」と言って幽霊が現れた。The ghost appeared, saying, 'I have not forgotten the wrong you did me.'

うらやましい まあおうやましいこと。How I envy you! / 彼の新しい車は近所みんなにうらやましがられている。His new car is the envy of all his friends.

うらやむ 2人は人もうらやむ仲であった。Their happy marriage was the envy of all their neighbors.

うり¹ 瓜のつるになすびはならぬ。You cannot make a silk purse out of a sow's ear. 〔諺〕

うりあげ(きんだか) 売り上げが大分ふえて[減って]いる。Sales have picked up [fallen off] considerably. / わが社の売り上げ高は最近急激に年総額100億円まで伸びた。The sales figures of our firm recently soared to an annual total of ten billion yen.

うりおしむ 生産者は値上がりを予想して売り惜しんでいる。Producers are holding off selling in anticipation of a rise in price.

うりきれ 売り切れ。〔掲示〕Sold out. / (鉄道で)本日の座席指定券は売り切れました。All the reserved seats for today have been sold.

うりことば 売り言葉 ¶売り言葉に買い言葉 《give [pay] sb》 tit for tat. 文例↓

うりこみ 売り込み promoting the sales 《of a product》 ¶強引な[やんわりとした]売り込み a hard [soft] sell / 売り込みの腕 《aggressive》 salesmanship. 文例↓

うりこむ 売り込む sell; find a market [an outlet] 《for》; 《口語》push 《one's wares》; 〈評判になる〉become well known; make a name ¶新人歌手を売り込んでスターにする build up a new singer to stardom / 多年売り込んだ店 a store which has customers of long standing. 文例↓

うりざねがお 瓜実顔 an oval face.

うりさばく 売り捌く sell; dispose of.

うりだし 売り出し 〈安売り〉a bargain sale / 〈特売〉a special sale; 〈蔵払い〉a clearance sale / 歳末大売り出し a year-end sale / 売り出しの作家 an up-and-coming writer.

うりだす 売り出す 〈品物を〉offer *sth* for sale; put *sth* on sale; place *sth* on the market; market 《a machine》; 〈名前を〉become popular; 〈名が〉rise in fame. 文例↓

うりつくす 売り尽くす sell out; 《文》exhaust one's stock 《of》.

うりつける 売り付ける sell *sth* to *sb*; 〈無理に〉push 《one's wares》; 〈粗品品などを〉《口語》palm *sth* off on [onto] *sb*; foist (off) *sth* on *sb*; fob *sb* off with *sth*.

うりて 売り手 a seller ¶売り手市場 a sellers' market.

うりとばす 売り飛ばす sell (off [away]); dispose of.

うりね 売り値 a selling price.

うりば 売り場 the place where *sth* is sold; a counter; 〈デパートなどで催し物会場などと対照して〉a sales floor; 〈店の一隅の,通常廉価品の〉a (slipper) floor / 《米》a store; 《英》a shop ¶売り場監督[主任] a floor [section] manager; 《米》a floorwalker; 《英》a shopwalker.

うりはらう 売り払う sell [trade] off; dispose of.

うりひろめる 売り広める enlarge [extend] the market 《for》; 〈広告する〉advertise.

うりもの 売り物 an article for [on] sale ¶売り物になる be salable; be marketable; be fit for sale / 美貌(ぼう)を売り物にする capitalize on *one*'s beauty 《good looks》. 文例↓

うりや 売り家 a house for sale.

うりょう 雨量 (a) rainfall; 【気象】precipitation ¶東京の年間平均雨量 the average annual rainfall in Tokyo / 雨量の多い[少ない]地域 a region of high [low] rainfall / 雨量計 a rain gauge.

うりわたす 売り渡す sell *sth* (over) to *sb*; 〈譲渡する〉transfer *sth* to *sb*.

うりん 雨林 a rain forest ¶熱帯雨林 a tropical rain forest.

うる[1] 売る 〈販売する〉sell; deal in 《silk goods》; 〈処分する〉dispose of; 〈裏切る〉betray ¶高[安]く売る sell *sth* dear [cheap]; sell *sth* at a high [low] price / 1つ100円で売る sell at 100 yen each 《apiece》 ★ sell at 100 yen a piece と言うと,「ひと切れ100円で売る」の意味になる / 2千円で売る sell for 2,000 yen / 1ダース幾らで売る sell by the dozen / 名を売る win *oneself* a reputation; make a name for *oneself*; become popular [widely known] / 国を売る sell [betray, 《文》turn traitor to] *one's* country.

うる[2] 得る ⇨える ¶大いに得るところがある gain a great deal; 〈学ぶ〉learn a great deal 《from》 / 少しも得るところがない gain nothing 《from, by》 / …し得る 〈可能〉can *do*; be able to *do*; be capable of *doing*; 〈許可〉may *do* ⇨できる. 文例↓

うるう 閏 ¶閏年 a leap [an intercalary] year / 閏秒 a leap second.

うるおい 潤い 〈湿気〉moisture; damp; wetness; 〈利潤〉gain(s); (a) profit ¶潤いのある声 《文》a mellifluous voice / 潤いのある眼 liquid eyes / 潤いのない dry / 潤いのない生活をする 《文》lead a prosaic life. 文例↓

うるおう 潤う be moistened; get [《文》become] wet [moist]; 〈利益を受ける〉profit 《文》gain benefit 《by》.

うるおす 潤す 〈湿らす〉wet; moisten; 〈利する〉profit; benefit.

ウルグアイ Uruguay ¶ウルグアイの Uruguayan / ウルグアイ人 an Uruguayan / ウルグ

うりことば 売り言葉に買い言葉でやり合っているうちに殴り合いになった. The exchange of harsh words developed into an exchange of blows.

うりこみ 販売競争の過熱化を抑えるために関係各社間に販売協定が結ばれた. In order to cool down the sales war a sales agreement has been made between the firms concerned. / 同社は学校関係への売り込みを策している. They are aiming for the educational market.

うりこむ あの店は長年かかって売り込んで来た. They have built up a good business over the years.

うりだす これは来年の3月までには売り出されることでしょう. This will go on sale by next March. / 彼はこの作で売り出した. This book won [earned] him a name as a writer.

うりもの 売り物.『掲示』For sale. / あの車は売り物と書いてある. That car has a for-sale sign on it. / あの料理屋はこれを売り物にしている. That restaurant's specialty is lobster.

うりょう 昨日の雨量は30ミリだった. We had thirty millimeters of rain yesterday. / この地域は雨量が多い. The rainfall in this area is heavy. / この地方では年によって雨量が大きく異なる. In this district there is a great variation from year to year in the amount of rain. / 当時はこの地域の雨量は現在よりも多かったようである. It appears that this region received more rainfall in those days than it does today.

うる[2] 私はこの本を読んで大いに得る所があった. I have learned a great deal from this book. / これ以上交渉を続けても何ら得るところはあるまい. You will gain nothing from further negotia-

うるさい

アイ東方共和国 the Oriental Republic of Uruguay.

うるさい 〈厄介な〉 annoying; bothering; troublesome; worrisome; 〈騒々しい〉 noisy; 《文》 clamorous; boisterous; 〈しつこい〉 persistent; 《文》importunate;〈あら捜し好きの〉faultfinding; 《文》 captious; 〈好みが難しい〉 (be) particular (about); (be) hard to please; 《口語》 fussy; 《文》 fastidious ¶ うるさく persistently; annoyingly; 《文》 importunately / うるさく質問する plague [pester] sb with questions / うるさそうに as if one is irritated; with an annoyed look; with a bored air. 文例⇩

うるさがた 煩さ型 《口語》a nit-picker;《口語》an old woman (男について言う);《文》 a fastidious [captious] person; a faultfinder.

うるし 漆 lacquer; japan ¶漆の木 a Japanese lacquer [varnish, sumac] tree / 漆にかぶれる[負ける] react to lacquer by coming out in a rash / 漆を塗る lacquer; japan / 漆塗りの lacquered; japanned / 漆職人 a lacquer worker / 漆細工 lacquerware.

うるち 粳 〈米〉 nonglutinous rice.

ウルトラC a supremely difficult maneuver (in gymnastics).

うるむ 潤む be wet [moist,《文》dimmed] (with tears). 文例⇩

うるわしい 麗しい beautiful; lovely; charming; graceful; elegant.

うれい 憂[愁]い 〈憂愁〉《文》grief; sorrow; 《文》distress;〈苦悩〉trouble;《文》affliction; 〈心配〉anxiety; fear; apprehension(s);〈危険〉 danger ¶ …の愁いがある[ない] there is some [no] fear of...; be in danger of [safe from]... / 愁いに沈む be overwhelmed with sorrow;《文》 be disconsolate (at, over); be in deep grief (over) / 愁い顔 (wear, have) a sad [troubled] look.

うれうべき 憂うべき 〈嘆かわしい〉《文》grievous; deplorable; 《文》 lamentable; 〈警戒すべき〉 alarming. 文例⇩

うれえる 憂[愁]える 〈心配する〉 fear; be anxious (about); be apprehensive (about, of, for); worry (about, over);〈嘆く〉《文》grieve (for, over);《文》be distressed (at).

うれくち 売れ口 〈販路〉an outlet (for); a market (for); 〈売れ行き〉sale(s); demand;

〈職〉《obtain》employment ¶売れ口がある be marketable; be salable; be in demand / 売れ口がない be unmarketable; be unsalable; be not in much demand / 売れ口を捜す[見付ける] seek [find] a market [an outlet] (for an article).

うれしい 嬉しい joyful; delightful;《文》glad (tidings); happy 《events》;〈うれしく思う〉 be glad; be delighted; be pleased; be happy ¶うれしい知らせ happy news 《of success》 / うれしそう[うれしげ]に joyfully; delightedly / うれしくて for joy; with delight / うれしい事に(は) to one's delight [joy] / うれしさ joy; delight; gladness / うれしさの余り in one's joy [delight]. 文例⇩

うれしがらせ 嬉しがらせ ¶うれしがらせを言う flatter; say nice things (to); tickle sb's vanity;《口語》jolly sb (along).

うれしがる 嬉しがる be glad; be pleased; be delighted; be happy;《文》rejoice (over) ¶うれしがらせる make sb happy; please; delight;《文》gladden. 文例⇩

うれしなき 嬉し泣き ¶うれし泣きに泣く cry [weep] for joy; cry with joy.

うれしなみだ 嬉し涙 ¶うれし涙を流す shed tears of joy [happy tears] / うれし涙にむせぶ be choked with tears of joy.

ウレタン 《化》urethane ¶ウレタンフォーム urethane foam.

うれっこ 売れっ子 a popular person; a person who is much sought after.

うれのこり 売れ残り unsold goods; dead stock;〈婚期を逸した娘〉an old maid.

うれのこる 売れ残る 〈品物が〉 be [go,《文》 remain] unsold;〈女が〉be left on the shelf; 《文》remain unmarried.

うれゆき 売れ行き sale(s); demand ⇒ うれる ¶売れ行きがいい[悪い] sell [do not sell] well; be a good [poor] seller; be [not in much] demand; there is a good [poor] demand (for). 文例⇩

うれる 売れる sell; be in demand;〈市場性がある〉be marketable; be salable;〈名が〉become popular; become well known ¶よく売れる be [do] well; have [《文》enjoy] a good [large] sale; there is a good demand 《for》/ どんどん売れる sell like hot cakes / 高く売れ

---

tions with them.

うるおい この新しい趣味が彼の生活に潤いを与えた. His new hobby lent a little interest to his otherwise drab life. / この絵は彼の研究室に潤いを与える唯一のものだった. The painting was the only thing to relieve the severe atmosphere of his laboratory.

うるさい 世間の口はうるさい. People will talk. / なんてうるさいはえだろう. What a nuisance this fly is! / うるさいぞ! Shut up! | Hold your tongue! / うるさいな. ほっといてくれ. Don't bother me. Just leave me alone!|

Get out of my hair!

うるむ 彼女は目を潤ませていた. Her eyes were filled with tears. / その哀れな少女の悲しい物語にすべての人が目を潤ませた. The sorrowful story of the poor girl brought a tear to everybody's eyes.

うれうべき 憂うべき事態に立ち至った. It is deplorable [a matter for great regret] that things should have come to this pass.

うれしい お目にかかれてとてもうれしいです. I am very glad to see you. / 今日はとてもうれしそうですね. You look very happy to-

day. / その知らせを聞いて彼はうれしくて口もきけなかった. He was speechless with joy at the news. / うれしさはほどほどしかった. I nearly wept for joy.

うれしがる (新しく買った物を手にして喜んでいる夫に)あなたって, 本当にうれしがり屋さんね. You're just like a child with a new toy!

うれゆき 彼の小説は相変わらず売れ行きがよい. His novels continue to sell well [enjoy a large sale]. / このためにこの本の売れ行きが悪くなるようなことはあるまい. This will not hurt the sales

うろうろ ¶うろうろする ⇨ うろつく, うろたえる.

うろおぼえ うろ覚え 《have》 a vague memory 《of》; 《have, retain》 an uncertain [a dim, a faint, a hazy] recollection 《of》.

うろこ 鱗 a scale ¶うろこのある, うろこ状の scaled; scaly ¶うろこを落とす scale 《a fish》; remove the scales from 《a fish》うろこ雲 ⇨ けんせきうん.

うろたえる lose one's head [one's presence of mind]; be upset; be flurried; be flustered; be thrown into confusion ¶うろたえて逃げる run away helter-skelter; hurry off in confusion / うろたえない keep calm; stay [《文》remain] unruffled; keep one's head [one's presence of mind].

うろつく loiter; hang about [around] 《a house》; prowl 《about, around》; be on the prowl.

うろん ¶うろんな suspicious(-looking); questionable / うろんに思う suspect.

うわあご 上顎 the upper jaw; 〈口蓋〉the roof of the [one's] mouth; the palate.

うわがき 上書き 〈箱などの〉an inscription; a superscription; 〈宛名〉an address ¶封筒に上書きを書く address [direct] a letter 《to sb》.

うわき 浮気 ¶浮気な 〈移り気な〉flighty; fickle; 〈淫奔な〉《文》wanton; 〈不貞な〉《文》inconstant; unfaithful / 浮気をする have an affair 《with》; be unfaithful [《文》false] to one's husband [wife]; 《米口語》play around / 浮気者〈男〉a philanderer;〈女〉a flirt.

うわぎ 上着 a coat; a jacket;〈総称〉outerwear (下着に対して) ¶背広の上着 a suit jacket / 上着を着て with one's coat [jacket] on; in one's coat / 上着を脱いで with one's jacket off; in one's shirt sleeves.

うわぐすり 釉薬 glaze ¶釉薬をかける glaze 《pottery》; enamel 《a brooch》.

うわぐつ 上靴 ⇨ うわばき.

うわごと 譫言 ¶うわごとを言う talk in (a) delirium / うわごとを言い出す fall into (a) delirium.

うわさ 噂 (a) rumor; (a) report; (a) gossip; hearsay ¶嫌なうわさ an ugly rumor / うわさする talk [gossip]《about》/ うわさを聞く hear a rumor《that...》/ うわさを立てる spread [start] a rumor; set a rumor afloat / うわさを立てられる, うわさに上る be talked [gossiped] about; become the talk of the town (町中の) / ...といううわさだ, うわさによれば...だ rumor has it that...; there is a rumor [story] going around that...; word has spread [got around] that...; it is said [rumored, reported] that...; they say [I hear, I am told] that.... 文例8

うわすべり 上滑り ¶上滑りの superficial; shallow.   「of home-brew).

うわずみ 上澄み the top clear part 《of a bottle

うわずる 上擦る 〈声が〉sound hollow; ring false / 上擦った声で in a shrill, excited voice.

うわぜい 上背 ⇨ せい⁶, たけ¹.

うわついた flippant; frivolous.

うわ(っ)かわ 上側 the upper side; the surface.

うわ(っ)ちょうし 上っ調子 ¶上っ調子の flippant; frivolous.

うわ(っ)つら 上(っ)面 ⇨ うわべ ¶上っ面をなでる (merely) scratch [skim] the surface 《of an affair》.

うわっぱり 上っ張り a smock;《英》an overall.

うわづみ 上積み ¶上積みする load [pile]《A》on top of 《B》;〈上乗せする〉⇨ うわのせ.

うわて 上手〈優れた人〉a better hand 《at sth》; one's superior (in sth) ¶上手に出る get the upper hand of sb; outdo / ...より上手である be better 《at sth》than sb;《文》be superior (to);《文》surpass;《文》excel / 一枚上手である 《口語》be a cut above sb / 上手を持つ〈囲碁・将棋で〉play as a superior player; have a handicap (of four stones) (in a game of go) / 上手投げ〈相撲〉throwing one's opponent using one's outside arm;【野球】an overhand throw (delivery).

うわぬり 上塗り ¶上塗りする give the final [last] coat 《of paint》;〈釉薬(?)をかける〉glaze / 恥の上塗りをする add to one's shame.

うわのせ 上乗せ ¶上乗せする add (2,000 yen) to 《the amount previously offered》; top 《their

---

of the book.

うれる これなら黙っていても2万円には売れる. You'll have no problem in selling this for 20,000 yen. / それは安いのでよく売れた. It had a good sale because of its low price. / この種の書物は我が国では類書がないから間違いなく売れるでしょう. A book of this kind would have no rivals and would have an assured sale in this country. / 今度の本は少なくとも20万部は売れるだろう. The sales of the new book will reach at least 200,000 copies.

うわさ 彼が近く辞任するだろうといううわさが立っている. There is a rumor afloat [Word has got out] that he will soon resign. / そのうわさはたちまち広まった.

The rumor spread fast. / うわさの広まるのは早いものだ. News travels fast. / バートン氏が蒸発したというのが近所中のうわさ話になっている. The mysterious disappearance of Mr. Burton is the talk of the neighborhood. / それ以来彼女のうわさは絶えた. She has not been heard of since. / 学校中そのうわさで持ち切っていた. It was the sole topic of conversation at the school. | I set all the school buzzing. / うわさをすれば影がさす. Talk of the devil, and he is sure to appear. 【諺】★この諺、日常会話では前半までしか言わないのが普通.

うわべ 彼は物事の上辺だけしか見ない. He looks only at the surface of things. / 物事は上辺だけ

ではわからない. Appearances are deceptive. / この仕事は上辺は実にたやすいように見える. On the face of it, the job looks easy enough. / 両者は確かによく似ているが, 似ているのは上辺だけだ. The two look very similar, but the veneer of similarity is very thin. / 彼は上辺は平静を装って私の部屋から出て行った. He went out of my room with an outward appearance of calm. / ゴードンのステラに対する愛情は上辺だけのもので, 心の底では彼女を憎んでいたのだ. Gordon's affection for Stella was only a front; in his heart of hearts he hated her. / 彼は正直そうだが, 実は悪賢い男なのだ. His cunning is hidden behind a facade of

うわのそら 上の空 ¶上の空で inattentively; absent-mindedly; vacantly / 上の空で聞く listen to sb with only half one's mind; pay almost no attention to 《sb's talk》.

うわのり 上乗り riding 《a truck》 on the top of the load; 〈人〉a person riding 《a truck》 on the top of the load.

うわば 上歯 an upper tooth.

うわばき 上履き (a pair of) (indoor) slippers.

うわばり 上張り ¶上張りする face (a wall with tiles); coat 《with》; veneer (a table with mahogany).

うわべ 上辺 〈外面〉《文》the exterior; 〈表面〉the surface; 〈外部〉the outside; 〈外観〉outward appearance [show] ¶上辺は outwardly; seemingly; to all appearances; on the surface / 上辺の outward; apparent; superficial (皮相の) / 上辺を飾る put a (surface) gloss on sth; 《体裁をつくろう》keep up appearances / 上辺だけの友人らしさ surface friendliness / 上辺だけで判断する judge sb [sth] only by appearances.

うわまえ 上前 ¶上前をはねる take a percentage [《口語》a cut]《from》;《俗》take a rake-off.

うわまわる 上回る be more [better] than;《文》exceed; top;〈技量など〉《文》surpass;《文》excel.

うわむき 上向き ¶上向きになる〈上を向く〉look [turn] upward;〈相場などが〉rise; show an upward tendency;〈事業などが〉be improving; be on the upswing; look up. 文例⇩

うわめ 上目 ¶上目を使う glance up [upward] 《at》.

うわやく 上役 a senior official; one's superior;《口語》(the) high-[higher-]ups.

うん¹ 運 (a) destiny; (a) fate;〈巡り合わせ〉fortune; luck; chance ¶運がいい[悪い] be lucky [unlucky]; be in [out of] luck / 運が向いている be down on one's luck / 運のいい lucky; fortunate / 運の悪い unlucky; unfortunate / 運よく fortunately; luckily; by good luck [fortune]; as (good) luck would have it / 運よく…する have the good fortune to do; be lucky enough to do / 運悪く unfortunately; unluckily; by ill fortune; as (ill) luck would have it / 運を試す try one's luck; take a chance / 運を天に任せる leave (a matter) to chance; trust to luck [chance]. 文例⇩

うん² yes; all right; well;〈ふうん〉h'm ¶うんと言う say yes; agree;《文》reply affirmatively;《文》consent [give one's consent]《to》/ うんとうなずく nod (one's) agreement [《文》assent]《to》/ うんうん言って…する sweat (over, at) / うんうんうなりながら (with a great deal of) grunting and groaning / うんともすんとも言わない say nothing at all;《文》make no response whatever; keep silent 《about》;《俗》clam up. 文例⇩

うんえい 運営 management; operation; administration;《文》conduct ¶運営する manage; operate; run / 運営費 operational [operating] expenses / (会議体の)運営委員会 a steering committee. 文例⇩

うんか 《昆》a leafhopper.

うんが 運河 a canal; a shipping [navigation] canal ¶運河を開く construct [build, dig, cut] a canal 《through, across》/ 運河通行税 canal dues.

うんかい 雲海 a sea of clouds.

うんきゅう 運休 suspension [stoppage] of (the) (bus) service. 文例⇩

うんこう¹ 運行 revolution 《of a planet》; movement 《of a heavenly body》 ¶運行する revolve [go, move, orbit, travel] 《round [around] the sun》/ その地区一帯を運行しているバス the buses that cover the area.

うんこう² 運航 service ¶運航する run; ply 《between》/ 別府高松間を運航している船 a ship that plies between Beppu and Takamatsu.

うんこう³ 雲高 the height of the cloud ceiling; the ceiling.

うんざり ¶うんざりする be [feel] disgusted 《with, at》; be sick and tired 《of》;《口語》be fed up [fed to the teeth] 《with》;《物が主語》bore [《文》weary] one to death;《口語》bore the pants off one. 文例⇩

---

honesty.

うわまわる 総額は1千万円をはるかに上回っている。The sum total is well over ten million yen. / 輸出が輸入を2千万ドル上回った。Exports exceeded imports by 20 million dollars. / 彼は自己最高記録を1.5秒上回る記録で優勝した。He won the championship, bettering his personal best (time) by 1.5 seconds.

うわむき 物価は上向きだ。Prices are going up [are on the rise].

うん¹ 私に運が向いてきた。Luck has turned in my favor. / 気にするな，そのうちに運が向くよ。Never mind; your luck'll turn one day. / 彼には運がない。Luck is running against him. / 今夜は運がいい[悪い]。I am in [out of] luck tonight. / それ以上は運が続かなかった。My luck didn't hold out. / 彼の運の尽きだった。His number was up then. | That sealed his fate. / チェスは運に左右されることのないゲームだ。Chess is a game that has no element of chance. / 自動車にはねられたが，運よく骨1本折らなかった。He was knocked down by a car, but fortunately he had no bones broken. / そいつはひどく運が悪かったなあ。That's very rough [tough] luck on you. / あの人は子供運が悪かった。He had no luck with children. / His children were a real trial to him. / 何事にも運不運がある。Luck plays a part in everything.

うん² 彼はただうんとかううんとか言うだけだった。He answered with nothing more than the barest of negatives and affirmatives. / 彼女は色々な事をくどくどと話したが，どれもうんうんと聞いてやれば済む話だった。She talked tediously on about various subjects which required no more than a grunt or two out of me. / 今朝はあの男うんともすんとも言わなかった。I haven't heard a peep out of him this morning.

うんえい このクラブはうまく運営されている。This club is well run.

うんきゅう 20本以上の列車が運休になった。More than 20 trains were canceled.

うんざり 彼の退屈な長談義にはほとほとうんざりした。His tedious

うんさん 運算 ⇨ えんざん, けいさん¹.

うんさんむしょう 雲散霧消 ¶雲散霧消する disperse like mist; go up in smoke; vanish like smoke [into thin air].

うんじょうびと 雲上人 《文》dwellers among the clouds; courtiers.

うんすい 雲水 an itinerant monk [priest].

うんせい 運勢 fortune; luck; *one's* star ¶運勢がいい[悪い] be born under a lucky [an unlucky] star / 運勢を見る tell [read] *sb's* fortune / 運勢を見てもらう have *one's* fortune told (by); consult a fortuneteller. 文例↓

うんそう 運送 transport; transportation; 《文》conveyance; carriage; forwarding; shipment ⇨ ゆそう² ¶運送する transport; 《文》convey; carry; forward; ship / 運送業 the express [forwarding] business; the transport industry / 運送料 ⇨ うんちん / 運送屋〔店〕 a forwarding [shipping] agency; 〈人〉a forwarding [shipping] agent; a carrier; 《米》an expressman.

うんだめし 運試し a trial of luck ¶運試しをする try *one's* luck [fortune]; 《口語》chance it. 文例↓

うんちく 蘊蓄 *one's* stock of knowledge; 《文》erudition ¶うんちくのある人《文》a man of profound knowledge; 《文》an erudite person / うんちくを傾ける apply *one's* whole stock [store] of knowledge 《to the task》. 文例↓

うんちん 運賃 〈旅客の〉a fare; 〈貨物の〉a shipping [forwarding, carrying] charge; freight (on); carriage (on) ¶運賃先[前払いで]《send goods》carriage forward [prepaid] / 運賃表〈旅客の〉a fare table; 〈貨物の〉a freight list. 文例↓

うんでい 雲泥 ¶雲泥の差がある be as different as chalk and cheese; there is a world of difference [all the difference in the world] (between).

うんてん 運転 working; operation; running; (in) service; driving(車の) ⇨ うんよう ¶運転する work; operate; drive (an automobile); set 《a machine》going [in motion]; run / 自動車を運転する drive a car; take [be at] the wheel / 代わって(自動車の)運転を引受ける take over the wheel / 自動車運転の教習を受ける take driving lessons; take a driving course / 運転が開始される〈機械が〉be started; be placed in operation; 〈鉄道などが〉be put in service / 10 分間の運転間隔を保つ run (trains) at ten-minute intervals / 運転技術 driving skill; *one's* skill as a driver / 運転休止中の機械 a machine out of operation [service] / (自動車の)運転教習所の教師 a driving instructor / 運転系統 a (bus) route / 運転資金 working capital / 運転手〈電車などの〉《米》a motorman; 《英》a driver; 〈自動車の〉《米》a driver; a chauffeur (お抱えの); 〈タクシーの〉a taxi [cab] driver; 〈口語〉a cabby; 〈機械の〉an operator / 運転台〈電車などの〉《米》motorman's cab; 《英》the driver's cab; 〈トラックなどの〉the driver's cab [seat] / (自動車の)運転免許をとる get [《文》obtain] *one's* driving license / (自動車の)運転免許試験を受ける take a driving test.

うんと 〈たくさん〉a great deal; a lot; very much; 《文》abundantly ⇨ たくさん 囲因; 〈力いっぱい〉with all *one's* might; 〈したたか〉severely; soundly; hard; 〈遙かに〉far (better); (better) by far; 《口語》way (better) ¶うんと殴る give *sb* a good thrashing [beating] / うんとしかってやる give *sb* a good talking-to / 金がうんとある have lots [《口語》heaps, 《口語》loads] of money.

うんどう 運動 〈物理的な〉motion; movement; 〈体育上の〉exercise(s); athletics; sports; games; 〈社会的な〉a movement; a drive; a campaign; canvassing (勧誘・遊説などの); lobbying(議員に対する) ¶運動する〈物体が〉move; 〈体育上の〉exercise; take (plenty of) exercise; 〈奔走する〉make a movement [drive] (for); carry on [carry out, 《文》conduct] a campaign (for); 〈勧誘の〉canvass (for); 〈選挙の〉electioneer / 〈議員に対して〉lobby / 運動の法則 the laws of motion / 運動のために散歩をする take a walk for (the sake of) exercise; 《戯言》take a constitutional (運動不足の中年紳士が) / 運動中の物体 a body in motion / 大いに運動をする take a lot [a great deal] of exercise / 軽い[適度の]運動をする take light [moderate] exercise / 激しい運動をする exercise hard / 犬に運動をさせる exercise [walk] *one's* dog; take *one's* dog for a walk [run]; give a run [walk] to *one's* dog / 運動を起こす start [launch] a campaign [drive, movement] (for, against).

¶運動員〈選挙の〉a canvasser; a campaigner; an election agent / 運動エネルギー【物】kinetic energy / 運動家 an activist (in a political movement); a crusader (for women's rights) / 運動記者 a sports columnist [report-

---

talk bored me stiff [bored the life out of me, 《口語》bored the pants off me].

うんせい 今年は僕の運勢はいい[悪い]. I am told that this year will be lucky [unlucky] for me.

うんだめし うまく行くかどうかわからないが, 運試しにやってみよう. I don't know if we can pull it off, but let's chance it.

うんちく これは彼がうんちくを傾けた作だ. He has poured his whole stock of knowledge into this book.

うんちん 運賃無料.『掲示』Carriage [Freight] free. / この小荷物の運賃は幾らになりますか. How much would you charge for shipping this parcel? / What does the carriage on this parcel come to?

うんてん このバスの運転間隔は 10 分です. The buses on this route run every ten minutes. / そのエレベーターは運転休止になっていた. The elevator was out of action [was not working].

うんちん 運賃無料.『掲示』Carriage [Freight] free. / この小荷物の運賃は幾らになりますか. How much would you charge for shipping this parcel? / What does the carriage on this parcel come to?

うんどう 運動をすると食が進む. Exercise gives you a good appetite. / 水泳は全身の筋肉を使うのでいい運動である. Swimming is a good form of exercise, because it uses every muscle in [of] the body. / その改革に対する反対運動を開始した. They mounted a campaign [started agitating] against the reform.

うんどうかい 学校の運動会は来週だ. The school sports are next

うんどうかい 運動会 a sports meeting；《英》《school》sports／《陸上競技会》an athletic meeting〔《米》meet〕 ¶運動会の行なわれる日 a sports〔《米》field〕day／運動会を催す hold a sports meeting. 文例↓

うんどうぶ 運動部 〈学校の〉an athletic club；〈新聞社の〉the sports department. ¶《新聞社の》運動部長 the sports editor.

うんどうぶそく 運動不足 lack〔shortage〕of exercise. ¶運動不足のために through lack of exercise；《文》through insufficient exercise／運動不足である be short of exercise. 文例↓

うんぬん 云々 and so on〔forth〕; etc. ¶うんぬんする comment 《on》; criticize.

うんのう 蘊奥 ¶蘊奥をきわめる《文》delve into the mysteries 《of》; master the secrets 《of》; make *oneself* an authority 《on》.

うんぱん 運搬 ⇨ うんそう ¶運搬する carry；《文》convey; transport.

うんぴつ 運筆 the use of *one's* brush 〔pen〕.

うんめい 運命《文》(a) destiny；《文》(a) fate；《文》(a) lot；《文》doom (悪い) ¶運命づけられている《文》be destined 《to *do*, for the teaching profession》; be doomed 《to failure》／不幸な運命《文》ill-fated《love》／運命のいたずら a quirk 〔an irony〕of fate／運命の日《文》the fateful 〔fatal〕day／運命の女神 Fortune；《ギリシャ・ローマ神話》the (three) Fates／運命を開拓する carve out *one's* own future; mold 〔fashion〕*one's* own destiny／運命を決する《文》determine the destiny 《of》／運命を左右する affect the fate 《of》; sway 〔influence〕the destiny 《of》／運命を共にする throw 〔《文》cast〕in *one's* lot with *sb*／運命とあきらめる resign *oneself* 〔submit〕to 《*one's*》fate／運命線〔手相〕the line of Fate 〔Destiny, Saturn〕／運命論者 a fatalist. 文例↓

うんも 雲母【鉱】mica.

うんゆ 運輸《文》conveyance; (public) transport; transportation; traffic ⇨ ゆそう² ★a public conveyance と言うと，バス・タクシーなど 1 台の交通機関の意味になる ¶運輸会社 a transit company／運輸省〔大臣〕the Ministry 〔Minister〕of Transport.

うんよう 運用 ¶運用する〈用いる〉use; make use of；〈適用する〉apply 《to》；〈実施する〉put into practice 〔effect〕；〈投資する〉invest 《in》／施設をうまく運用して行く keep the facilities in good working order／英語の運用能力を高める improve *one's* working knowledge of English.

え

え¹ 柄 〈道具の〉a handle；〈機械の〉a grip; a hilt〈刀の〉; a shaft〈やりの〉／傘の柄 the handle of an umbrella／ほうきの柄 a broomstick; a broom handle／長い柄のついたスプーン a long-handled spoon／柄を付ける fit〔put〕a handle《to》.

え² 絵，画 a picture; a drawing（彩色してない），a painting（彩色），a sketch（略画），an illustration（さし絵）¶私の母の絵〈母を描いた絵〉a picture of my mother；〈母が持っている絵〉a picture of my mother's；〈上記のどちらの意味にも用いて〉my mother's picture／ピカソの絵 a picture by Picasso／絵のような picturesque；《文》graphic《description》／絵のように美しい be as pretty as a picture／絵を描く draw a picture; make a drawing／〈彩色の〉paint a picture; paint *sth*／馬の絵を描く draw (a picture of) a horse／絵を描くのがうまい be good at drawing 〔painting〕／絵にかいた餅 (be nothing but) pie in the sky. 文例↓

え³ 餌 〈えさ〉(a) bait；〈food〉food ¶カナリヤの餌 canary seed／餌をやる feed 《hens》. 文例↓

---

week.／昨日僕たちの学校で運動会があった。Yesterday was our school 〔school's〕field day.｜《英》We had the sports (day) at our school yesterday.／運動会の 100 メートル競走で優勝した。I won the hundred-meter dash in the sports.

うんどうぶそく 君は運動不足だよ。You don't get enough exercise.

うんめい その計画は始めから失敗する運命だったのだ。The plan was foredoomed to failure.／彼らの運命は前もって定まっていた。Their destiny was foreordained.／彼らの運命は決まった。Their fate was sealed.／船長は船と運命をともにした。The captain went down with his ship.

え² これは何の絵ですか。What is this a picture of?／〈一見してわからない絵について〉What is this (picture) meant to be?／この絵はだれの作ですか。Who painted this picture?｜Who is this picture (painted) by?／この絵はまるで絵になっていない。This picture is no good.｜What sort of a picture is this!／まるで絵から抜け出たようだ。She looks as if she had stepped out of a picture.／〈テレビの〉画がよく見えない。I can't get a good picture.｜The picture is no good.

え³ この鳥の餌は何ですか。What does this bird feed on?

-え …重 -fold ¶2重の[に] double; 《文》two-fold.

エアカーテン an air curtain.
エアコン an air-conditioner.
エアターミナル an air terminal.
エアバス an airbus.
エアポケット an air pocket.
えい¹ 嬰《音楽》¶嬰ロ長[短]調 (in) B sharp [major [minor]].
えい²《魚》a ray.
えい³ ¶えいと叫んで with a cry [yell] / えいとばかりに〈思い切って〉decisively.
えいい 鋭意《文》diligently;《文》earnestly;《文》assiduously.
えいえい 営々 ¶営々と《文》assiduously; strenuously; busily / 営々として働く work hard.
えいえいじてん 英英辞典 an English dictionary; a dictionary of English explained in English.
えいえん 永遠 eternity;《文》perpetuity;《文》permanence; immortality (不滅) ¶永遠の《文》eternal;《文》perpetual; permanent; everlasting;《不滅の》《文》immortal / 永遠の平和 a lasting [permanent] peace / 永遠に forever; for good;《文》eternally;《文》perpetually / 永遠性《文》permanency;《文》timelessness.
えいが¹ 映画 a picture; a film;《米》a motion [moving] picture;《米》a movie ¶（アマチュアが）自分で撮った映画 a home movie / 映画の cinematic / 映画の台本 a film [movie] script; a scenario (《pl. -s》) / 映画を見に行く《米》go to a movie [the movies];《英》go to the pictures [cinema] / 映画を見ている watch a film [movie] /〈映画館にいる〉be at the movies [pictures, cinema]; sit in a movie / 映画音楽 film music / 映画化する make a movie (version) of; make (a novel) into a movie [film] / 映画界 the motion-picture [movie] world;《英》the film world; movie circles;《米》the movies;《英》the cinema / 映画界に入る enter the movie world; go into the movies / 映画会社 a movie company / 映画館 a movie [motion-picture] theater [house];《英》a cinema / 映画監督 a movie director / 映画祭 a film festival / 映画撮影所 a movie [film] studio / 映画撮影用カメラ a motion-picture camera; a cinecamera / 映画産業 the movie [motion-picture, film] industry / 映画俳優 a movie [film, screen] actor [actress] / 映画ファン a movie [cinema] fan. 文例 ↓
えいが² 栄華〈繁栄〉prosperity;〈豪華〉《文》splendor;《文》pomp ¶栄華を極める be at the height of [《文》zenith] of one's prosperity; live in splendor.
えいかいわ 英会話 English conversation; conversation in English ¶英会話がうまい speak English well; be good at speaking English / 英会話の練習をする practice speaking English / 英会話学校 a school of spoken [conversational] English; a school of English conversation; an English conversation school.
えいかく 鋭角 an acute angle ¶…と鋭角をなす make an acute angle with…; be at an acute angle to… / 鋭角三角形 an acute-angled triangle.
えいかん 栄冠 the crown;《文》the laurels;《文》the palm ¶勝利の栄冠を戴く《文》be crowned with [win the laurels of] victory. 文例 ↓
えいき 鋭気〈気勢〉spirit;〈元気〉vigor; energy ¶鋭気を養う restore [build up] one's energy.
えいきゅう 永久 ⇒えいえん 永久不変の everlasting / 半永久的 semipermanent ((equipment)) / 永久運動 perpetual motion / 永久歯 [磁石] a permanent tooth [magnet].
えいきょう 影響 (an) influence; (an) effect; an impact ((on));〈波及的〉repercussions; consequences ¶よい[悪い]影響 a good [bad] influence;《文》a favorable [harmful] influence; a good [bad] effect / …に影響する[を及ぼす] influence…; affect…; have [《文》exert] an influence on…; have [produce] an effect on…; act [tell] on… / …の影響を受ける be affected [influenced] by… / …の影響で under the influence of…; owing to…;《文》in consequence of… / 影響力がある be influential ((with sb)), 《one's words》 tell ((with sb)). 文例 ↓
えいぎょう 営業〈業務〉business;〈商態〉trade; 〈販売〉sales;〈運営〉operation(s) ¶営業する do [carry on] business / 営業している be in business; be open for business / 営業案内 a pamphlet describing one's business (operations) / 営業時間 business (office) hours / 営業所 a place of business; a business office / 営業上の秘密 a trade secret / 営業スタッフ the sales staff ((of Kenkyusha)) / 営業税 a business tax / 営業成績 business [trading] results [performance] / 営業停止になる be ordered to suspend business; be (temporarily) closed down / 営業費 business [operating, running] expenses / 営業部 the sales department / 営業妨害 obstructing sb's business; interference with sb's business / 営業方針《(a company's)》business policy / 会社の営業方針を決める set company policies. 文例 ↓
えいご 英語 English; the English language; 〈単語〉an English word ¶英語がうまい[まずい] be good [no good, poor] at English; have a good [poor] command of English / 英語の English / 英語の手紙 a letter (written) in

---

えいが¹ ハムレットは映画でなら見たことがある. I have only seen *Hamlet* as a movie.
えいかん 彼女はミスユニバースの栄冠をかち得た. She was crowned Miss Universe.
えいきょう 彼はフランスの音楽に強い影響を与えて来た. He has had [《文》exerted] a strong influence on French music. / 東京地方には今夜台風の影響があるでしょう. Tokyo will feel the effect of the typhoon this evening. / 出版界は不況の影響をもろに受けた. The publishing business was hard hit by the depression.
えいきょう この種の容器は既に営業用に使用されている. Containers of this kind are already in commercial use. / あの店は日曜には営業しない. That store is closed on Sundays. / 改築中は隣で営業いたします. We shall be carrying on business next door during rebuilding. / あの店の営業時間は10時から5時までだ. That store is open from 10 a.m. to 5 p.m. / わが社の後半期の営業成績は良好であった. Our company has done very good business during the last half year. / そこへ駐車しないでくれ. 営業妨害だ. Don't park your car there. It's

えいこう　English / 英語の先生 a teacher of English ; an English teacher (★ English にアクセントを置いて an Énglish teacher と言う。an English téacher と言うと「イギリス人の先生」の意味になる) / 英語を話す speak English / 英語を話す[用いる]国民 an English-speaking people / 英語で話す[書く] speak [write] in English / 英語学 English linguistics / 英語教育 the teaching of English / 英語劇 a theatrical performance given in English / 英語圏 the English-speaking world. 文例⇩

えいこう¹　曳航　¶曳航する tow《a ship》; take [have]《a ship》in tow.

えいこう²　栄光　glory ; honor　¶栄光に輝く be covered in glory ;《文》be crowned with glory.

えいごう　永劫　⇨ えいえん　¶永劫回帰《哲》Eternal Recurrence / 永劫不変の《文》eternal ; everlasting ;《文》immutable.

えいこうだん　曳光弾　a tracer (bullet).

えいこく　英国　England ; Great Britain (★ 英本島、すなわち England, Wales, Scotland) ; the United Kingdom (of Great Britain and Northern Ireland)(略 : U.K.)　¶英国の English ; British / 英国特有の語(句) a Briticism / 英国国旗 the Union Jack / 英国人 an Englishman ; an Englishwoman (女性) ;《米》a Britisher ;《総称》the English / 英国製の made in England ; English-made.

えいこせいすい　栄枯盛衰　prosperity and decline ; rise and fall ; ups and downs [《文》vicissitudes] of life. 文例⇩

えいさい　英才　《才能》talent ; genius ; 〈人〉a gifted [talented] person ;《文》a man of talent　¶英才教育 special education for the gifted.

えいさくぶん　英作文　《学課》English composition ;《書いたもの》an English composition [essay] ; an essay in English /《和文英訳》Japanese-English translation　¶英作文の練習をする do exercises in English composition ; practice writing English.　「lish poetry.

えいし　英詩　an English poem ;《総称》English-

えいし²　衛視　《国会の》a Diet guard.

えいじしんぶん　英字新聞　an English-language (news)paper ; a newspaper in English.

えいしゃ¹　映写　projection　¶映写する project [throw, show]《a picture》on a screen ; screen《a film》/ 映写機 a projector / 映写技師 a projectionist / 映写の running time《for a film》/ 映写室 a projection room / 映写幕 a (projection) screen. 文例⇩

えいしゃ²　泳者　a (competitive) swimmer　¶《リレーの》第1[2]泳者 the first [second] swimmer《of the Japanese relay team》).

えいじゅう　永住　permanent residence　¶永住する live [《文》reside] permanently《in》/ 永住している live permanently《in Japan》;《文》be in permanent residence《at》/ 永住の地 one's permanent home / 永住権 the right of permanent residence / 永住者 a permanent resident.

えいしょう　詠唱　《音楽》an aria.

えいしょく　栄職　〈地位〉a high [《文》an honorable] position ;〈職業〉《文》an honorable profession.

えいじる　映じる　〈反映する〉be reflected《in》; be mirrored《in, on》;〈印象を与える〉impress　¶外国人の目に映じた日本 Japan as seen by foreigners. 文例⇩

えいせい¹　衛生　hygiene ; sanitation ;〈健康〉health　¶衛生的な《文》sanitary ; hygienic / 衛生によい good for [《文》beneficial to] the health ; healthy ; wholesome / 衛生に害のある insanitary ; unwholesome ; unhealthy ; bad for [《文》injurious to] the health / 衛生に注意する look after [be careful about] one's health / 衛生学 hygiene / 衛生材料 medical supplies / 衛生施設 sanitary facilities / 衛生思想の発達していない国 a country whose people have a poor idea of sanitation / 衛生状態 sanitary conditions / 衛生状態を保つ maintain hygiene《in a building》/ 衛生兵 a medical orderly. 文例⇩

えいせい²　衛星　a satellite　¶衛星国 a satellite (country [state]) / 衛星中継 tv by [via] satellite relay / 衛星通信 satellite communications / 衛星都市 a satellite city [town].

えいせいちゅうりつ　永世中立　《maintain》permanent neutrality　¶永世中立国 a permanently neutral country [state].

えいぜん　営繕　building and repairs　¶営繕課 the building and repairs section.

えいそ　英ソ　Britain and the Soviet Union　¶英ソの Anglo-[British-]Soviet《relations》.

えいぞう　映像　〈テレビなどの〉a picture ; an image ;〈水・鏡などの〉a reflection (in the mirror)　¶テレビの映像《transmit》television pictures / レーダーに映る映像 a blip on the radar screen. 文例⇩

えいぞく　永続　¶永続する last for a long time (★ これに対して、last long は否定文・疑問文で使うのが普通) ; continue ;《文》endure / 永続的 lasting ; permanent / 永続性《文》perpetuity ; permanence ; permanency.

えいたつ　栄達　distinction ; 《文》advancement (in life) ⇨ しゅっせ　¶栄達を求める seek distinction ; hanker after (worldly) fame.

---

in our way. / 営業中.《掲示》Open. / 平常どおり営業しております.《掲示》Business as usual.

えいご 「コンセント」は英語で何と言うか. What is the English for 'konsento'? /《句・文について》これを英語で何と言う. How do you put it in English? / あの人は英語を上手に話す. He speaks English well [fluently]. / あの人は英語がよくできる. He is good at [《文》proficient in] English. | He has a good knowledge of English. / この国では英語を使わない. English is not spoken in this country. / 自分の英語力をウィリアムズさんを相手にして試してみた. I tried (out) my English on Mr. Williams.

えいこせいすい 栄枯盛衰は世の習い. Life has its ups and downs.

えいしゃ¹ この映画の映写時間は2時間である. This film runs for two hours.

えいじる 東京は外国からの訪問者の目にはどう映じるだろう. What impression will Tokyo make on foreign visitors?

えいせい¹ この地域は衛生状態が悪い. The sanitation in this area is poor.

えいぞう できるだけシャープな映像が得られるようにカメラのレン

えいたん 詠嘆 ¶詠嘆する admire; express [give voice to] one's admiration (for).

えいだん¹ 英断 decision;《文》resolution;〈処置〉a decisive [《文》resolute] step ¶英断を下す make a decision; take a decisive step.

えいだん² 営団 a corporation.

えいち 英知 wisdom; intelligence (聡明);《文》sagacity (明敏).

えいてん 栄転 transference on promotion ¶栄転する be promoted [transferred] to a higher post.

エイト《ボートレース》an (Oxford) eight.

えいどく 英独 Britain and Germany ¶英独の Anglo-German.

えいびん 鋭敏 ¶鋭敏な sharp; keen; acute; sensitive;〈知力の〉quick-witted; shrewd / 鋭敏な感覚 keen [quick] senses / 鋭敏な頭脳の持主 a sharp-witted person; a person [possessor] of keen intellect. 文例⇩

えいふつ 英仏 Britain and France ¶英仏の Anglo-French.

えいぶん 英文《read》English;〈1つの文〉an English sentence ¶英文を書く write English / 英文で書く write sth in English / 英文科 the department of English language and literature / 英文解釈 construing an English text; understanding English / 英文和訳 translation from English into Japanese; (an) English-Japanese translation / 英文タイプ typing (in English) / 普通には in English をつけて言うことはない．特に必要があって，たとえば「和文タイプ」と区別しなければならない場合のような時の表現である．「英文タイピスト」も単に a typist である．必要があれば an operator of an English-language typewriter のような表現もできる． 文例⇩

えいぶんがく 英文学 English literature ¶英文学者 a scholar of English literature.

えいぶんぽう 英文法 English grammar ¶英文法の本 an English grammar. 文例⇩

えいへい 衛兵 a (military) guard; a sentry;《文》a sentinel ¶バッキンガム宮殿の衛兵交代を見物に行く go to see the Changing of the Guard at Buckingham Palace.

えいべい 英米 England and America; Britain and the United States ¶英米の English [British] and American; Anglo-American / 英米人 Englishmen and Americans / 英米法 Anglo-American law.

えいほう¹ 泳法 a style of swimming.

えいほう² 英法 (the) English law.

えいほう³ 鋭鋒 the brunt (of an attack [argument]) ¶鋭鋒をくじく blunt [take off] the edge (of); disarm (one's critics).

えいみん 永眠 eternal sleep [rest]; death ¶永眠する die; pass away [on]; go to one's final rest / 永眠の地 one's final resting place ★ 日本語の「永眠」と同様，die と death を除いてはここにある表現はすべて婉曲な言い方．

えいやく 英訳 an English translation [version] ¶英訳する translate [put,《文》render, turn] into English.

えいやっ えいやっと投げる throw (one's opponent) with a yell [with all one's might].

えいゆう 英雄 a hero (pl. -es) ¶英雄的行為《文》a heroic deed; an act of heroism / 英雄崇拝 hero worship. 文例⇩

えいよ 栄誉〈名誉〉honor; glory;《口語》kudos;〈名声〉fame;《文》renown ¶栄誉ある honorable; glorious / 栄誉をになう have the honor (of doing) / 栄誉礼を受ける receive the salute of a guard of honor.

えいよう 栄養 nutrition; nourishment ¶栄養のよい well-fed[-nourished] / 栄養になる，栄養分に富む nutritious; nourishing / 栄養的にバランスのとれた食事 a nutritionally balanced diet / 栄養価《a》 nutritive [nutritional] value;（be low in）food value / 栄養学 dietetics; nutritional science / 栄養士 a dietician; a dietitian / 栄養失調 malnutrition / 栄養素 a nutrient / 栄養分 a nutritious [nourishing] substance; a nutriment / 栄養不良 undernourishment / 栄養不良の undernourished; ill-fed.

えいり¹ 絵入り ¶絵入りの illustrated; pictorial.

えいり² 営利 profit-making; moneymaking;《文》gain ¶営利にきゅうきゅうとしている be engrossed in moneymaking;《文》be intent on gain;《俗》be on the make / 営利を目的とする[しない] profit-making [nonprofit] (《organizations》) / 営利を念頭に置かずに without any thought of gain [profit] / 営利会社[事業] a commercial company [enterprise] / 営利主義 commercialism.

えいり³ 鋭利 ¶鋭利な sharp; keen / 鋭利な刃物 a sharp-edged tool.

えいりょう 英領 (a) British territory;〈直轄植民地〉a Crown Colony ¶旧英領 an ex-British [a former British] territory / 英領バージン諸島 the British Virgin Islands.

えいりん 映倫 the Commission for the Administration of the Motion Picture Code of Ethics.

えいりんしょ 営林署 a local forestry office.

えいれんぽう 英連邦 the (British) Commonwealth (of Nations).

えいわじてん 英和辞典 an English-Japanese dictionary.

えいん 会陰《解》the perineum (pl. -nea).

ズを調節しなさい．Adjust the camera lens so that you get the sharpest possible image.

えいだん¹ この件については一大英断を下す必要がある．This matter calls for decisive [drastic] measures.

えいてん ご栄転おめでとうございます．Let me congratulate you on your promotion.

えいびん 犬は嗅覚が鋭敏だ．Dogs have an acute sense of smell. | Dogs have a keen nose.

えいぶん 彼は英文が上手だ．He writes English well. | His written English is (very) good.

えいぶんぽう これは今までに読んだ中で一番いい英文法の本だ．This is the best English grammar (book) I've ever read.

えいゆう 英雄色を好む．All great men are also great lovers [womanizers].

ええ ええ，ようございますとも．Yes, with pleasure. | Certainly.

えがく 作者は女王を残忍な女として描いている．The author por-

ええ〈承諾, 肯定〉yes ; oh, yes! ;〈疑問〉eh? ; what? ; (I beg your) pardon? ;〈ためらい〉well; let me see ; er…. 文例▶

エーカー an acre.

エーゲかい エーゲ海 the Aegean Sea ¶エーゲ海諸島 the Aegean Islands.

エース an ace ;〈最もすぐれた選手〉a leading player ;〈野球〉the top [first-line, outstanding] pitcher《on a team》¶〈トランプの〉ダイヤのエース the ace of diamonds.

エーテル《化》ether.

エーデルワイス《植》an edelweiss.

ええと let me see ; well ; er….

エービーシー the alphabet ;〈初歩〉the ABC《of chemistry》¶エービーシー順に《arrange》in alphabetical order ; alphabetically.

エープリルフール〈万愚節〉April [All] Fools' Day ;〈かつがれた人〉an April fool.

エール a (school, college) yell ¶エールを交換する exchange yells.

えがお 笑顔 a smiling [beaming] face ¶無理に笑顔を作る force a smile / 笑顔になる smile / 笑顔で迎える greet sb with a smile.

えかき 絵かき a painter ; an artist.

えがく 描く draw ; paint〈彩色して〉;〈絵にかく〉make a picture [painting] of ;〈円などを〉describe ;〈三角形などを〉construct ;〈略図を〉sketch ;〈グラフに〉plot (out)《sth on squared paper》;〈描写する〉《文》depict ; describe ¶心に描く picture sth to oneself ; form a mental picture《of》; envision. 文例▶

えがたい 得難い be hard [difficult] to get [obtain] ; cannot be easily obtained [found] ; be beyond one's reach ¶得難い品 a rare thing ; a rarity / またと得難い好機 a golden opportunity ; a rare chance / an opportunity that may never come again [that should not be missed].

えがらっぽい acrid ; pungent. 文例▶

えき[1] 易 fortunetelling ; divination ¶易を見てもらう have one's fortune told / 易占 divination lore.

えき[2] 益〈利益〉benefit ; good ;〈収益〉《文》gain ; profit ;〈便益〉advantage ;〈効用〉use ; service ¶益する[益になる] be of use [service]《to》;〈益を与える〉benefit ; profit ; do sb good / なんの益(する所)もない do sb no good ;《文》be of no benefit / 益のある《文》beneficial ; useful ;《文》advantageous / 益のない useless ;《文》fruitless ; of no use. 文例▶

えき[3] 液〈液体〉(a) liquid ;〈流動体〉(a) fluid ;〈液汁〉juice (特に果物の) ;〈分泌液〉a secretion ;〈溶液〉a solution.

えき[4] 駅 a (train) station ; a railroad [railway] station ;《米》a depot ¶駅員 a station employee ;《総称》the station staff / 駅売りの(newspapers) sold at a railroad station / 駅留めの(a parcel) to be called for / 駅ビル a building built over [near] a railroad station (housing a shopping complex) / 駅前広場 a station square [plaza]. 文例▶

えきか 液化 liquefaction ¶液化する〈物を〉liquefy ;〈物が〉be liquefied ; liquefy ; become liquid / 液化ガス liquefied [liquid] gas / 液化石油ガス liquefied petroleum gas (略: LPG) / 液化天然ガス liquefied natural gas (略: LNG).

えきがく 疫学 epidemiology.

エキサイト ¶エキサイトする get [be] excited.

エキシビションゲーム an exhibition game [match] ¶エキシビションゲームをやる play an exhibition (game).

えきしゃ[1] 易者 a fortuneteller.

えきしゃ[2] 駅舎 a station (building [house]).

えきじょう 液状 ¶液状の liquefied ; liquid〈soap〉; fluid〈substances〉;〈sulfur〉in liquid form / 液状になる go into [change to, be converted to] a liquid state ⇒えきか.

エキス an extract [essence]《of beef》.

エキストラ an extra ;《文》a supernumerary ;《口語》a super ¶エキストラをやる appear [play] as an extra《in a movie》.

エキスパート an expert《in, at》.

エキスパンダー an [a chest] expander. 文例▶

エキゾチック ¶エキゾチックな exotic.

えきたい 液体 (a) liquid ; (a) fluid ¶液体空気[燃料] liquid air [fuel].

えきちゅう 益虫 a useful [《文》beneficial] insect.

えきちょう[1] 益鳥 a useful bird.

えきちょう[2] 駅長 a stationmaster《at Tokyo》¶駅長室 the stationmaster's office.

えきでんきょうそう 駅伝競走 a long-distance relay road race.

えきばしゃ 駅馬車 a stagecoach ; a stage.

えきびょう 疫病 an epidemic ;《文》a pestilence ; a plague.

えきべん 駅弁 a box lunch sold at a railroad station ¶駅弁大学 a minor local college ;《口語》a Mickey Mouse university [college].

えきり 疫痢 children's dysentery.

エクアドル (the Republic of) Ecuador ¶エクアドルの Ecuadorian / エクアドル人 an Ecuadorian.

えくぼ a dimple ¶えくぼのある顔 a dimpled face. 文例▶

えぐる 抉る scoop out ; gouge out ;〈摘発する〉expose ¶えぐって穴をあける bore a hole (through) ; hollow out《a log》/ 丸木をえぐってカヌーを作る hollow a canoe out of a log.

エクレア〈菓子〉an éclair ; a chocolate éclair.

えげつない〈あくどい〉mean ; grasping ; greedy ;〈下品な〉vulgar ;〈いやな〉nasty ; disgusting.

エゴ ego ; self.

---

trays the queen as a cruel woman. / この小説は18世紀の庶民の生活をよく描いている。This novel gives a good picture of the life of the common people in the eighteenth century.

えがたい 得難い人物です。He is a type of man rarely to be met with.

えき そんな事をして何の益になるのか。What is the use [good] of doing a thing like that?

えき 渋谷までは1駅です。You only have to ride the train one stop to Shibuya.

エキスパンダー このエキスパンダーのばねを5本全部付けたままではとても広げられない。I cannot for the life of me stretch this expander with all five strands on.

えくぼ 彼女はにっこりするとえくぼができる。Her face dimples when she smiles.

エゴイスト a selfish [self-centered] person; an egoist; 《文》an egocentric person. 文例⇩
エゴイズム selfishness; egoism.
えこう 回向 ¶回向する hold a memorial service (for);《文》say prayers for the repose of sb's soul.
えごころ 絵心 ¶絵心がある〈描く力が〉have an aptitude for painting;〈見る目が〉have an eye for the picturesque.
えこじ ⇨いこじ.
エコノミークラス the economy class ¶エコノミークラスの航空券 an economy-class air ticket / エコノミークラスで行く go economy(-class).
エコノミックアニマル a nation dedicated to economic success (to the exclusion of all other objectives).
えこひいき 依怙贔屓 favoritism;《文》partiality ¶えこひいきの unfair;《文》partial / えこひいきの ない fair; impartial / えこひいきする show favoritism [partiality] (toward); be partial ((to)); treat sb with undue favor.
えさ 餌 food;〈釣りの〉(fish) bait;〈誘惑物〉a lure; a bait ¶釣針に餌をつける bait a hook ((with a worm))/〈動物が〉餌を採る feed (itself) / 餌をやる feed ((an animal))/(動物に) 餌をやる時間 feeding time / 餌をやり過ぎる overfeed ((one's pets))/ 雀の餌にパン屑をやる feed crumbs to sparrows / 野鳥のために餌台 を設ける put up a bird table [feeder] / 餌場 〈野生動物の〉a feeding ground [area] /〈餌付けの〉a feeding station /〈家畜の〉a feeding area [station]. 文例⇩
えじき 餌食〈肉食動物の〉a prey;〈犠牲〉a victim ¶…の餌食となる become the prey of…; become the victim of…/ 鮫の餌食になる become food for sharks / 餌食にする prey on.
エジプト Egypt ¶エジプトの an Egyptian / エジプトアラブ共和国 the Arab Republic of Egypt / エジプト人 an Egyptian.
えしゃく 会釈 a bow ¶《文》(a) salute ⇨あいさつ ¶会釈する bow ((to));《文》(a) salute; make a bow; salute / 軽く会釈する bow slightly; greet ((sb)) with a nod; nod ((one's head)) ((to sb))/ 会釈を交わす exchange bows.
エスエフ 〈ジャンル〉science fiction (略: SF); 《口語》sci-fi ¶エスエフ映画 a science fiction picture [film] / エスエフ作家 a science-fiction writer / エスエフ小説 a science-fiction novel [story].
エスオーエス (send out) an SOS.
エスカルゴ《フランス語》an escargot; an edible 「snail.
エスカレーター an escalator ¶上[下]へ行くエスカレーター an up [a down] escalator.
エスカレート ¶エスカレートする escalate. 文例⇩
エスキモー an Eskimo (pl. -mos, -mo) ¶エスキモー語 Eskimo.
エステル《化》an ester.

エスプリ esprit.
エスペラント Esperanto ¶エスペラント使用者 an Esperantist.
えせ- false; would-be; sham; mock ¶えせ紳士 a would-be gentleman.
えそ 壊疽《医》gangrene ¶壊疽の[にかかった] gangrenous.
えぞまつ《植》a Yeddo [Japanese] spruce.
えそらごと 絵空事〈非現実的なこと〉《文》a castle in the air [in Spain] ;〈つくりごと〉《文》a fiction;《文》(a) fabrication.
えだ 枝 a branch;〈大枝〉《文》a bough;《文》a limb;〈細枝〉a twig ¶枝を下ろす[切る] lop off [down] branches; prune a tree /(木が)枝を広げる spread its branches (out) / 枝振りのいい松 a pine tree with gracefully-shaped branches. 文例⇩
えたい 得体 ¶得体の知れない strange(-looking); mysterious / 得体の知れない人〈何を考えているのかわからない〉《文》an enigmatic person;〈見知らぬ人〉a stranger / 得体の知れない病気 an unaccountable [unaccounted-for] disease.
えだげ 枝毛 a split hair ¶枝毛をトリートメントする treat the split ends of one's hair.
えだは 枝葉 ⇨しよう⁶.
えだまめ 枝豆 (young) soybeans in the pod.
えたり 得たり ⇨しめた ¶得たり賢し[得たりや応]と…する lose no time (in) doing; seize the opportunity to do; pounce on ((sb's slip of the tongue)) and do.
えだわかれ 枝分かれ ramification ¶枝分かれする branch off ((from)); ramify.
エタン《化》ethane.
エチオピア Ethiopia ¶エチオピアの Ethiopian / エチオピア人 an Ethiopian.
エチケット etiquette; (good) manners ¶…するのがエチケットだ It is good manners [《文》proper etiquette] to do; Etiquette requires that… /…はエチケットに反する It is not good etiquette to do; It is a breach of etiquette to do / エチケットを知っている[守る] know [observe] the rules of etiquette.
エチュード《音楽》an étude; a study.
エチル《化》ethyl ¶エチルアルコール ethanol; ethyl alcohol.
エチレン《化》ethylene ¶エチレングリコール ethylene glycol.
えつ 悦 ¶悦に入る be pleased ((about));《文》rejoice ((at, over)); glow with self-satisfaction; gloat ((over)); smile to oneself.
えっ eh!; what!; well!; oh!
えっきょう 越境《文》(a) border transgression ¶越境する cross the frontier ((into));《文》transgress the border ((of a neighboring state))/ 越境入学する gain admission into a school in a school district other than one's own.
エックスせん エックス線 X-rays ¶X線にかける X-ray; give sb an X-ray; make an X-ray

---

エゴイスト あいつはエゴイストだ。He is selfish.
えさ かえると虫を餌にしている。Frogs feed on insects. / シジュウカラは1日に体重の30パーセントの餌を必要とする。It needs 30 per cent of its own body weight in food daily. / 冬の間は野鳥のために餌を出しておいてやります。We put out food for the birds during the winter.
エスカレート そのちょっとした衝

えづけ **餌付け** ¶餌付けをする make 《monkeys》 take to feeding.

えっけん **越権** ¶越権行為をする exceed [overstep] one's authority;《文》exceed the prerogatives of one's office. 文例⇩

エッジ 《スキー・スケート》an edge ¶エッジを利かす edge; use the edges 《of one's skis》.

エッセンス (an) essence.

エッチ ¶エッチな〈人が〉dirty-minded;《文》salacious;〈話・本などが〉《口語》dirty〈jokes〉; smutty〈talk〉; lewd;《文》salacious; indecent. 文例⇩

えのき 榎 a nettle tree; a hackberry.

えっちらおっちら 《文》laboriously; with a great deal of effort ¶えっちらおっちら歩いて行く trudge (along).

エッチング an etching.

えっとう **越冬** ¶越冬する pass the winter; winter (at) / 南極越冬隊 the wintering party in the Antarctic.

えつねん **越年** ¶越年する see the old year out / 越年性植物 a biennial (plant).

エッフェルとう エッフェル塔 the Eiffel Tower.

えつらん **閲覧** ¶閲覧する read; peruse / 公衆の閲覧に供する provide《books》for public reading / 閲覧室 a reading room / 閲覧者 a reader / 閲覧票 a call slip.

えて **得手** one's forte ⇒とくい¹ ¶得手に帆を上げる get the wind in one's sails; be in one's element;《文》be on song.

エディプスコンプレックス 《心理》an Oedipus complex.

えてかって **得手勝手** ¶得手勝手な selfish;《文》egoistic;《文》egotistical / 得手勝手な人 a selfish person / 得手勝手なことをする have one's own way; do just what one wants [as one likes]; be selfish (about sth); act selfishly;《文》follow one's own wishes (regardless of others).

えてして ⇒とかく ¶えてして…し勝ちだ be apt [liable, prone] to do; be given to doing.

エデン Eden ¶エデンの園 the Garden of Eden.

えど **江戸** Edo ¶江戸っ子 a native of Edo [Tokyo] / 江戸時代 the Tokugawa [Edo] period.

えとく **会得** ¶会得する〈理解する〉understand; grasp (the meaning of);〈習得する〉learn《how to do》; master《the art of...》.

エトロフ Iturup Island.

エナメル enamel ¶エナメル靴〈男性用〉patent-leather shoes;〈女性用〉enameled shoes.

エヌジー 《映画》N.G. ★ no good の略 ¶エヌジーを出す spoil [ruin] a sequence.

エネルギー 《物》energy ¶エネルギーを与える energize / 省エネルギー energy-saving; energy-conserving / エネルギー保存の法則 the law of the conservation of energy / エネルギー革命 an energy revolution; a revolutionary change in the forms of energy used / エネルギー危機 an energy crisis / エネルギー源 an energy source; a source of energy / エネルギー資源 energy resources / エネルギー事情 the energy situation / エネルギー需要 the demand for energy; energy needs / エネルギー政策[問題] an energy policy [problem].

エネルギッシュ [<《ドイツ語》energisch] ¶エネルギッシュな energetic;《a man》with a lot [great deal] of energy.

えのぐ **絵の具** colors; paints ¶絵の具を塗る paint; color / 絵の具皿 a dish for mixing paints / 絵の具箱 a paint box.

えはがき **絵葉書** a picture postcard 《of Tokyo Tower》; a postcard [post card]《with a view of Hakone》 ★ 正式には picture postcard だが, 日常語では picture を省いて言う ¶絵葉書になりそうな風景 picture-postcard scenery.

えび 《動》a lobster (いせえび); a prawn (車えび); a shrimp (小えび) ¶えびのように腰の曲がった老人 an old man bent almost double with age / えびでたいを釣る use [throw] a sprat to catch a mackerel /〈飛び込み競技の〉えび形 the jackknife (dive) ★ 複数形は jackknives ではなくて jackknifes / えびフライ fried prawns.

エピソード an episode; an anecdote (逸話).

えびちゃ **えび茶** ¶えび茶(色)の maroon; reddish brown.

えびら 箙 a quiver《of arrows》.

エフエム FM [fm] ¶frequency modulation の略 ¶FM 放送 FM broadcasting; an FM broadcast (一回の) / FM 放送局[ラジオ] an FM station [radio].

えぶくろ **餌袋**〈鳥の〉a crop; a gizzard (砂嚢).

えふだ **絵札**〈トランプの〉a picture card;《米》a face card;《英》a court card.

えふで **絵筆** a paintbrush.

エフビーアイ 〈米国連邦捜査局〉FBI [F.B.I.] ★ Federal Bureau of Investigation の略.

エプロン an apron; a kitchen apron ¶エプロンをしている wear [be in] an apron / 白いエプロンをした岡村夫人 white-aproned Mrs. Okamura / エプロンで手を拭く wipe one's hands on one's apron.

エペ 《フェンシング》an épée; an epee.

えへへ 〈笑い声〉he, he!

エベレスト Mt. Everest.

えへん ahem! ¶えへんとせき払いする hem; clear one's throat.

エホバ Jehovah.

えほん **絵本** a picture book.

突がエスカレートして本格的な市街戦になった. The minor clash escalated to serious street fighting.

えだ 枝がたいそう広がっている. The branches spread far and wide.

えっけん それは君, 越権だよ. You've no right to do that.

エッチ あの人エッチだ. He's got a dirty mind, hasn't he?

えつねん 2千万円もあれば越年できるでしょう. Twenty million yen would tide us over into the

えま 絵馬 a votive picture [tablet] of a horse.
えまき(もの) 絵巻(物) a picture scroll. 文例⇩
えみ 笑み a smile ¶笑みを浮かべて with a smile; smiling(ly).
エミュー 《鳥》an emu. ┌erald.
エメラルド (an) emerald ¶エメラルド色 em-┘
えもいわれぬ えも言われぬ 《文》indescribable; 《文》indefinable.
えもの 獲物 〈狩猟の〉 game; 《文》quarry; a bag; spoils 〈of a chase〉; 〈肉食動物の〉 a prey (animal); a quarry; a kill (殺した); 〈漁の〉 a catch; a haul; 〈略奪品〉 booty ¶獲物が多い[少ない] have plenty of [do not have much] game; have a good [poor] bag [catch] / 獲物の多い場所 a place rich in game / 獲物を捕える take game / 獲物を仕止める make a kill. 文例⇩
えもんかけ 衣紋掛け a (coat) hanger.
えら 鰓 the gills 《of a fish》 ¶(俗に人について) えらが張っている be square-jawed / えらで呼吸する動物 a gill-breathing animal / えらぶた a gill cover.
エラー 〈野球などの〉 an error ¶投球のエラー a throwing error / エラーをやる make an error / ショートのエラーで3塁セーフになる be safe on third base on an error by the shortstop.
えらい 偉い 〈偉大な〉 great; 〈すぐれた〉《文》superior; 《文》eminent; important; 〈大した, ひどい〉 serious; awful; terrible; 〈激しい〉 violent; severe; hard ¶偉い人 a great man / 偉い損 a serious [heavy] loss / えらい仕事 hard work / えらい目に会う have a hard time / 偉くなる become important [a great man]; 《文》achieve [come to] greatness; succeed (in the world). 文例⇩
えらそう 偉そう ¶偉そうな self-important; important-[proud-]looking / 偉そうに self-importantly; with an air of importance; proudly / 偉そうなことを言う talk big / 偉そうに見える look self-important.
えらぶ 選ぶ choose 《between two things, something from [out of] other things》; opt 《for sth, to do》; 《文》elect 《to do》; 〈選抜する〉《文》select 〈選出する〉 elect; 〈より分ける〉 sort; assort ¶日を選ぶ select [choose] a day / AよりBを選ぶ prefer B to A; choose B over A / 生きて恥を受けるよりはむしろ死

を選ぶ prefer death to dishonor; would rather die than live in disgrace / 委員長に選ばれる be elected (the) chairman of the committee. 文例⇩
えり 襟 〈首, 襟元〉 the neck; 〈洋服の〉 a collar ¶あわてて着行たためにコートの襟が立っている one's coat collar is turned up / 襟の開いたシャツ an open-neck(ed) shirt; a shirt open at the neck / 襟をつかむ seize [take] sb by the collar [lapels] / オーバーの襟を立てる turn up the collar of one's overcoat / 襟を正して聞く listen with respectful attention / 襟がよごれのついたワイシャツ a shirt with a dirty collar.
えりあし 襟足 the nape of 《a woman's》 neck.
エリート 〈個人〉 a member of an [the] elite; 〈総称〉 the elite 《of society》; an elite group ¶パワーエリート the power elite 《inside the government》 / エリート意識が強い have a strong sense of being one [a member] of the elite / エリートコースを歩む be on course for membership of the elite; be destined for high [higher] things / エリート主義 elitism / エリート主義の教育制度 an elitist education system.
えりくび 襟首 the nape [back] of the neck ¶襟首をつかまえる seize sb by the scruff of the neck.
えりぐり 襟ぐり the neckline ¶襟ぐりの深いドレス a low-cut dress.
えりごのみ 選り好み ⇨よりごのみ.
えりしょう 襟章 a collar badge.
えりぬき 選り抜き ⇨よりぬき.
えりまき 襟巻 a muffler; a comforter.
えりもと 襟元 ¶襟元が寒い feel cold around one's neck.
える 得る get; have; 《文》obtain; 《文》acquire; 《文》secure; 《文》procure; 〈見つける〉find; 〈努力を払って〉earn; 〈勝利などを〉win; 《文》gain; 〈受ける〉《文》receive; 〈...し得る〉can do; be able to do ¶賛成を得る receive [meet, secure] sb's approval / 協力を得る obtain cooperation 《from sb》 / 信用を得る gain [win] sb's confidence / 地位を得る get [《文》attain] a position / 知識を得る acquire knowledge / ...せざるを得ない must do; have to do; cannot help doing; cannot (help) but do; be forced [obliged, compelled] to do. 文例⇩
エルエル a language laboratory [lab].

---

new year.
えまき(もの) 伝統を誇るその祭の日には大勢の見物人の前で古式による行列の王朝絵巻が繰り広げられる. On the day of the age-old festival the scene of an ancient procession unrolls before a large crowd of spectators like a scroll from the Heian era.
えもいわれぬ えも言われぬ景色だ. The scenery is beautiful beyond description. | The view beggars (all) description.
えもの 獲物はうさぎが1匹だけだった. I got [shot] nothing but a hare. / (平地よりも)山の方が獲物が多いですよ. You'll find better hunting in the mountains.
えらい 偉いぞ! Well done! / 偉い事をやったのだなあ. Now you've done it [something]. / あの男は今に偉くなるよ. He will make a name for himself some day. / 彼は自分を偉いと思っている. He thinks highly [has a high opinion] of himself. / えらい降りだね! What a downpour! | Doesn't it rain! / 表はえらい人出だ. There are great crowds [large numbers] of people out in the street. / (どうも)えらい事になったねえ! We're really in the soup [We're in a real fix] now, aren't we?
えらぶ 彼が選んだのはローストビーフと野菜サラダだった. His choices were roast beef and vegetable salad. / これらの手段のどれを選ぶのもあなたの自由です. You have a free choice between these alternatives. / 彼に言われたとおりにする以外に選ぶ道はありませんでした. I had no choice but to do as he had told me.
える その肖像を見る人は皆襟を正

エルグ 〖物〗 an erg.
エルサルバドル (the Republic of) El Salvador ¶エルサルバドルの Salvadoran; Salvadorian.
エルサレム Jerusalem.
エルピーレコード an LP (*pl.* LP's, LPs); an LP record; a long-playing record.
エルビウム 〖化〗 erbium.
エレキギター an electric guitar.
エレクトロニクス electronics ¶エレクトロニクス産業 the electronics industry.
エレベーター 《米》 an elevator;《英》a lift ¶(運転者のついていない)自分で動かすエレベーター a self-service elevator / エレベーターに乗る take an elevator《to the fifth floor》/ go up [down] in an elevator / エレベーターの所在階数表示器 an elevator indicator / エレベーターを運転する run [operate] an elevator / エレベーターを呼ぶボタン the down [up] elevator button / エレベーターつきの[のない]アパート an elevator [a walk-up] apartment house / 貨物[業務用]エレベーター a freight [service] elevator / エレベーターガール an elevator operator. 文例⇩

エロ ¶エロな erotic;〈わいせつな〉obscene; dirty; off-color.
えん¹ 円〈円形〉a circle;〈貨幣の〉a yen (記号: ¥) ¶円を描く draw [describe] a circle / 円運動 (in) a circular movement / 千円紙幣 a thousand-yen note / 円相場 the exchange rate of the yen; the yen rate (in New York).
えん² 宴 ⇒えんかい². 文例⇩
えん³ 縁 〈関係〉《文》a relation; (a) relationship; (a) connection;〈きずな〉ties;《文》bonds;〈結婚〉marriage;《文》the marriage knot;〈宿縁〉《文》karma; fate ¶…と縁が近い[遠い] be closely [distantly] related to… / 縁を結ぶ form a connection (with);〈結婚する〉marry;《文》contract a marriage (with) / 縁を切る cut [《文》sever] one's connection(s) (with); break with (the past); disown (one's son) / 不思議な縁で by a curious turn of fate / …とは縁もゆかりもない be a complete stranger to…; have nothing to do with… / …と縁続きである be related to… / 縁遠い娘 a girl who has [has had] very little prospect [chance] of marriage. 文例⇩
えんいん 遠因 a remote [distant] cause.
えんえい 遠泳 a long(-distance) swim.

えんえき 演繹 〖論〗deduction ¶演繹する deduce / 演繹的 deductive;〈a priori〉/ 演繹的に deductively; a priori / 演繹法 the deductive method [process].
えんえん¹ 炎々 ¶炎々と燃え上がる blaze up / 炎々と aflame; in flames; in a blaze; (all) ablaze.
えんえん² 延々 ¶延々4時間に及んだ試合 a game that went on for [lasted, took] as long as four hours.
えんか¹ 塩化 〖化〗chloridation ¶塩化する chloridate / 塩化物 a chloride / 塩化ビニール vinyl chloride.
えんか² 演歌 a popular song with a melody of traditional Japanese type.
えんかい¹ 沿海 ¶沿海の coastal; inshore / 沿海漁業 inshore fishery.
えんかい² 宴会 a dinner (party); a banquet; a feast ¶宴会を催す give a dinner (party); hold [give] a banquet / 宴会場 a banquet(ing) hall. 文例⇩
えんがい 塩害 salt damage ¶塩害を受ける〈農作物が〉be damaged by (the infiltration of) seawater;〈電気の磁子などが〉be damaged by the briny air.
えんかく¹ 沿革 the history (of);〈発達〉the (origin and) development (of).
えんかく² 遠隔 ⇒えんぽう ¶遠隔の地 an out-of-the-way [《文》a distant] place / 遠隔操作 《under》 remote control / 遠隔操作する operate 《a machine》 by remote control / 遠隔地貿易 long-distance trade.
えんかつ 円滑 smoothness;〈融和〉《文》harmony ¶円滑な smooth;《文》harmonious / 円滑に smoothly;《文》harmoniously;〈故障なく〉without a hitch / 円滑にする《文》facilitate; smooth. 文例⇩
えんがわ 縁側 a veranda(h) ¶縁側に出る go out onto the verandah.
えんかん 鉛管 a lead pipe ¶鉛管工事 plumbing.
えんがん 沿岸 (on, along) the coast; (on, along) the shore ¶沿岸漁業 coastal [inshore] fishery / 沿岸警備隊 the coast guard / 沿岸航路 a coastal [coastwise] route / アメリカの大西洋沿岸地方 the Atlantic seaboard of the United States. 文例⇩
えんき¹ 延期 (a) postponement ¶延期する

す. It is a really awe-inspiring portrait.
える このような新しい考えをどこで彼は得たのだろうか. Where did he come by an original idea like this? / それは彼が経験によって得た教訓だ. That is a lesson he learned from experience.
エレベーター そのエレベーターを止めてください. Hold that elevator, please! / エレベーターが途中で止まった. The elevator stopped between floors.
えん 宴たけなわであった. The feast was at its height. | The party was in full swing.
えん³ 彼とは縁を切ることにした. I made up my mind not to have anything more to do with him. | I decided to have done with him. / 僕は金に縁がない. Money and I are strangers. / 縁があったらまたお目にかかりましょう. I hope our paths will cross again. / これをご縁にまたどうぞお出かけください. I hope to see more of you. / およそ現実とは縁違いの提案だった. It was an entirely unrealistic proposal. / 縁は異なもの味なもの. Strange and inscrutable is the way two people are brought together into wedlock.
えんかい² 昨夜は宴会に出ていた. I was at a party last night. / 大小宴会承ります.《広告》Large and small parties catered for.
えんかつ 2人の仲は円滑に行かない. They don't get on well together. | Things are not going very smoothly between them. / 万事円滑に運んだ. Everything went smoothly.
えんがん その町は日本海の沿岸にある. The town lies on (the coast of) the Sea of Japan.

えんき postpone ; put off ; defer 《payment》; adjourn 《a meeting》/ 期限を延期する extend [《文》prolong] the term / 延期になる be put off ; be postponed 《until》; be deferred 《until》. 文例⇩

えんき² 塩基 《化》a base.

えんぎ¹ 演技 performance ; acting ¶演技を抑える underact ; underplay 《a part》/ (必要以上に)大げさな演技をする overact ; overplay 《a part》/ りっぱな演技を見せる perform *one's* part well ; give an excellent performance / (監督の)演技をつける direct the action 《of an actor》/ 演技者 a performer / 演技派の女優 an actress who relies on her acting skills (rather than on her good looks).

えんぎ² 縁起 〈前兆〉an omen ; 〈由来〉the history ; the origin ¶縁起のいい lucky ; 《文》auspicious / 縁起の悪い unlucky ; 《文》ill-omened ; ominous ; 《文》inauspicious / 縁起をかつぐ be superstitious / 縁起直しに for better luck / 縁起物 a mascot ; a bringer of good luck. 文例⇩

えんきょく 婉曲 ¶婉曲な roundabout ; indirect ; euphemistic / 婉曲な言い回し a euphemism 《for》/ 婉曲に言う tell *sth* in a roundabout way.

えんきょり 遠距離 a long [great] distance ¶遠距離から射撃する shoot 《at the enemy》at long range.

えんきん 遠近 ¶遠近を問わず regardless [irrespective] of distance / 遠近画法 perspective drawing / (絵に)遠近感を与える give [supply] perspective 《to a painting》/ (絵は)遠近法に適っている[いない] be in [out of] perspective.

えんぐみ 縁組 〈婚姻〉a marriage (alliance) ; a match ; 〈養子の〉adoption ¶縁組する 《文》contract a marriage 《with》; marry (into a family).

えんぐん 援軍 ¶援軍を送る send reinforcements 《to》.

えんけい¹ 円形 a round shape ; a circle ¶円形の circular ; round / 円形に in a circle / 円形劇場 an amphitheater ; a theater in the round.

えんけい² 遠景 a distant view 《of》; (in) the background (絵などの).

えんげい¹ 園芸 gardening ; horticulture ; floriculture (花の栽培) ¶園芸を上手のある be a good gardener ; 《米》have a green thumb ; 《英》have green fingers / 園芸家 a horticulturist ; a horticultural expert / 園芸植物 a garden plant / 園芸用具 gardening tools.

えんげい² 演芸 (variety) entertainment ; 〈演技〉a performance ¶演芸場 an entertainment hall ; 〈寄席〉a variety [music] hall.

エンゲージリング an engagement ring.

えんげき 演劇 〈芸術の一部門〉theater (arts) ; dramatic arts ; 〈上演〉a theatrical performance ; 〈作品〉a drama ¶(大学で)演劇を専攻する major in theater [drama] / 演劇をやる present a play ; perform a play on the stage / 演劇界 the theatrical world ; theatrical circles / 演劇人 a man of the theater / 演劇博物館 a theater museum / 演劇批評家 a drama critic.

エンゲルけいすう エンゲル係数 《経》Engel's coefficient.

えんこ¹ 縁故 〈関係〉《文》relation ; connection ; 〈人〉a relative ; a relation ¶縁故をたどって through *one's* friends [relatives] / 縁故採用 hiring *sb* through personal connections.

えんこ² ¶えんこする 〈すわる〉sit down ; 〈自動車などが〉break down 《on the road》; be stranded.

えんご 援護 backing ; protection ; support ¶援護する back (up) ; protect ; support ; give support to / 援護射撃のもとに under covering fire 《from artillery》.

えんこん 怨恨 ⇒うらみ¹.

えんざい 冤罪 a false charge [accusation] ¶えん罪をこうむる be falsely charged 《with burglary》; be falsely accused 《of murder》. 文例⇩

えんさん 塩酸 《化》hydrochloric acid.

えんさん 演算 an operation ¶演算を行なう carry out an operation.

えんし 遠視 ¶遠視(眼)である 《米》be far-sighted ; 《英》be long-sighted / 遠視用の眼鏡 (a pair of) glasses for the far-sighted.

えんじ¹ 園児 〈幼稚園の〉a kindergarten pupil [child].

えんじ² 臙脂 〈色〉dark red.

えんじつてん 遠日点 《天》the aphelion 《pl. -lia》.

エンジニア an engineer.

えんじゃ 縁者 ⇒しんるい² ; 縁者びいき nepotism / 縁者びいきの 《文》nepotistic.

えんしゅう¹ 円周 circumference ¶円周率 the ratio of the circumference of a circle to its diameter ; pi (記号 : π).

えんしゅう² 演習 〈練習〉(a) practice ; an exercise ; (a) drill ; a seminar (大学での) ; 〈軍隊の〉(drill) maneuvers ; exercises ¶富士演習場 the Fuji maneuvering ground.

えんじゅく 円熟 ¶円熟する mellow 《with age》; mature ; ripen / 円熟した 《文》mature ; ripe ; fully-developed / 円熟の域に達する 《文》attain maturity / 円熟味を増す get 《文》become] mellower 《with age》. 文例⇩

えんしゅつ 演出 direction ¶演出する direct ;

えんき¹ 天候の回復するまでスペースシャトルの打上げは延期すると発表された。A hold was announced on the launching of the space shuttle until the weather cleared.

えんぎ² 縁起でもないことを言うな。Don't say things like that. It might bring bad luck.

えんざい それはえん罪だ。I am innocent of the charge. / 彼らはえん罪に泣いている。They are victims of a false accusation.

えんじゅく 年月を経て彼は円熟した人物になった。The years have [Time has] mellowed him.

えんしゅつ 大統領の記者会見はきめ細かに演出されたものだった。The president's press conference was a carefully stage-managed affair.

えんじる 氏は世界の指導者としての役割を最後まで演じた人であった。He played out his part as a

えんじょ 　137　　**えんたくかいぎ**

stage / 演出家[者] a director;《米》a producer / 演出効果 stage effects / 演出ヘルムート・ライナー directed by Helmuth Reiner.

えんじょ 援助 help;《文》aid; assistance; support ¶援助する[を与える]《文》assist; give assistance (to); support; help, aid; back (up)（後援する）/ 援助の手をさしのべる stretch out [lend] a helping hand (to);《文》extend assistance (to) / 援助を求める ask [appeal to] sb for assistance [help] / 海外援助計画 a foreign aid plan [program] / 経済[財政, 食糧]援助 economic [financial, food] aid / 被援助国 an aid-receiving nation; an aid-recipient country.

えんしょう¹ 炎症 (an) inflammation ¶炎症を起こす cause inflammation;〈患部が主語〉become [be] inflamed.

えんしょう² 延焼 ¶延焼する〈火が〉spread ((to));〈建物が〉catch fire / 延焼を防ぐ check the spread of the fire / 延焼を免れる escape the fire [spreading flames].

えんしょう³ 艶笑 ¶艶笑談 a comic story with an erotic content / 艶笑文学 humorous erotic literature.

えんじょう 炎上 ¶炎上する go up in flames /（飛行機が）墜落炎上する crash into flames.

えんじる 演じる perform (a play); play [act] (a part); commit (a blunder) ¶スカーレット・オハラを演じる play (the part of) Scarlett O'Hara. 文例◊

えんしん 遠心 ¶遠心的 centrifugal / 遠心分離機 a centrifuge / 遠心力 centrifugal force.

えんじん¹ 円陣 ¶円陣を作る form a circle; stand [sit] in a circle.

えんじん² 猿人 an ape man; (a) pithecanthropus (*pl.* -pi).

エンジン³ an engine ¶エンジンをかける start [turn on] an engine / エンジンを止める[切る] stop [switch off] an engine / エンジンをかけたままにしておく leave the engine running. 文例◊

えんすい 円錐 a cone ¶円錐形の conic(al) / 円錐曲線 a conic section.

えんずい 延髄《解》the medulla oblongata (*pl.* medulla oblongatas, medullae oblongatae); the medulla (*pl.* -las, -lae).

えんすいこ 塩水湖 a salt(-water) lake.

エンスト an engine stall [failure]. 文例◊

えんせい¹ 遠征 an expedition;〈運動選手の〉a visit; a tour ¶遠征する make [go on] an expedition;〈侵入する〉invade;〈運動選手が〉go on a tour (to [of] the U.S.A.); tour (Britain); visit /（相手の土地へ行ってする）遠征試合 an away match / 遠征隊 an expedition; an expeditionary team /〈運動選手の〉a visiting team.

えんせい² 厭世《文》being weary of life [the world]; pessimism ¶厭世的な pessimistic / 厭世自殺をする despair of life and kill *oneself*; kill *oneself* in despair.

えんぜつ 演説 a speech; an address; an oration (荘重な);〈演説をすること〉public speaking ¶演説する make [deliver] a speech [an address]; speak (before an audience); orate / 演説の原稿作成者 a speech writer / 演説家 a (public) speaker; an orator / 演説会は oratorical [a speech] meeting / 演説会場 a hall where a speech meeting is held / 演説口調で《文》in an oratorical [a declamatory] tone. 文例◊

エンゼルフィッシュ an angelfish (*pl.* -es).

えんせん 沿線 ¶沿線の along [on] the railroad line.

えんそ 塩素《化》chlorine ¶塩素で殺菌する chlorinate ((the water)) /（水道の）塩素注入所 a chlorination station.

えんそう 演奏 a (musical) performance; a rendering; a rendition;〈1人の演奏家の，または特定の作曲家の作品の〉a recital;〈演奏法〉execution ¶演奏する perform; give a performance [recital]; play (a sonata) / ピアノを演奏する play the piano / あまり演奏されないオネゲルの交響曲 little-played symphonies of Honegger / 演奏家 a performing musician / 演奏会を催す give a concert [recital] / 演奏会形式のカルメン a concert version of 'Carmen' / 演奏旅行 a concert [playing] tour / 演奏者 a performer; a player.

えんそく 遠足 an [a day] excursion; (a school) trip; a hike; an outing; a picnic ¶遠足に行く go on an excursion [a picnic, an outing]; take [go on] a trip / 遠足に連れて行く take ((children)) on an excursion. 文例◊

えんたい 延滞〈遅滞〉(a) delay;〈滞納〉arrears ¶延滞する be delayed; be in arrears / 延滞金 (money in) arrears / 延滞利子 overdue interest.

えんだい¹ 演題 the subject of an address [a speech, a lecture] ¶「言語と精神」という演題で話す speak on (the subject of) 'Language and Mind'.

えんだい² 縁台 a bench ¶縁台将棋 a game of *shogi* played on a bench in the street.

えんだい³ 遠大 ¶遠大な far-reaching;《文》lofty; ambitious / 遠大な計画 a grand [far-reaching] program / 遠大な志[抱負] a great ambition; lofty aspirations.

えんだか 円高〈相場〉a high yen rate;〈円価の上昇〉a rise in the exchange rate of the yen ⇨えんやす ¶円高差益 a profit accruing from a rise in the yen rate. 文例◊

えんたくかいぎ 円卓会議 a round-table con-

---

leader of the financial world.

エンジン エンジンがかかった[かからなかった]. The engine caught [wouldn't catch]. |《英》The engine fired [wouldn't fire]. / 何となく仕事にエンジンがかからない. I don't know why, but [For some reason or other] I can't get (myself) started [going] on the work. / 僕はエンジンのかかるのが遅いんだ. I'm a slow starter.

エンスト エンストを起こした. The engine stalled [stopped].

えんぜつ あれほど下手くそな演説は聞いたことがない. That was the worst(-delivered) speech I have ever heard.

えんそく 学校の遠足で相模湖へ行った. We went to Lake Sagami on a school excursion.

えんだか このところしばらく円高が続いている. The yen has been strong for some time now. / 急激な円高をもたらしていた日本の貿

えんだん¹ 演壇 a platform; a rostrum 《pl. -trums, -tra》 ¶演壇に立つ stand on the platform; take the rostrum.

えんだん² 縁談 a proposal to introduce prospective marriage partners; an offer of marriage; a marriage proposal ¶縁談がある have an offer of marriage / 縁談をまとめる arrange a marriage. 文例⇩

えんちてん 遠地点 《天》apogee ⇨ きんちてん ¶遠地点に達する reach apogee.

えんちゃく 延着 delayed [《文》belated] arrival; 〈送った品の〉 delay in delivery ¶延着する arrive late; be delayed (in arrival). 文例⇩

えんちゅう 円柱 a column; a pillar ¶円柱のあるギリシア神殿 a columned Greek temple / 円柱形[状]の columnar.

えんちょう¹ 延長 〈延ばすこと〉extension; prolongation; 〈長さ〉length ¶延長する prolong (a meeting); lengthen (a line); extend (a railroad line); draw out * prolong は主に時間を延ばす意. lengthen は物の長さを延ばす意. extend はどちらの場合にも使える / 3メートル延長する make sth three meters longer; extend sth by three meters / (野球の)延長戦 an extra-inning game [contest] / (野球の)延長戦をやる play extra innings. 文例⇩

えんちょう² 園長 the principal 《of a kindergarten》; the curator 《of a zoo》.

えんてん 炎天 hot [broiling] weather ¶炎天にさらされて歩く walk in [under] a burning [scorching] sun.

えんでん 塩田 a saltpan ¶塩田法 salt drying.

えんとう¹ 円筒 a cylinder ¶円筒形の cylindrical / (古代オリエントの)円筒印章 a cylinder seal.

えんとう² 遠投 《野球》《make》a long throw.

えんどう¹ 沿道 〈道筋〉the route; 〈道路〉the road ¶沿道の[に] along the route [road]; by the roadside. 文例⇩

えんどう² 豌豆 a pea.

えんどく 鉛毒 《suffer from》lead poisoning.

えんとつ 煙突 a chimney; 〈機関・汽船の〉a funnel; 〈暖炉の〉a stovepipe ¶煙突の笠 a chimney cowl / 2本煙突の船 a two-funneled ship;《口語》a two-stacker.

エントリー an entry ¶エントリーをすませる enter oneself (for a contest).

えんにち 縁日 the day for [of] the fair; a festival day ¶縁日の露店 a fair stall / 縁日の商人 a stall keeper (at a fair).

えんのした 縁の下 the space under the floor ¶縁の下の力持ちを演じる do a thankless task [job]; labor in the background.

えんばく 燕麦 《植》oats.

えんばん 円盤 a disk; a disc; 〈円盤投の〉a discus ¶空飛ぶ円盤 〈そら〉/ 円盤投げ the discus (throw) / 円盤投げの選手 a discus thrower / 円盤投げの世界記録保持者 the world-record holder in the discus.

えんぴつ 鉛筆 a pencil ¶HBの鉛筆 an HB pencil / 消しゴム付きの鉛筆 a pencil with an eraser tip / 先が丸くなった鉛筆 a blunt pencil / 芯の堅い[柔かい]鉛筆 a hard-[soft-]lead pencil / 鉛筆の書き込み penciled notes / 鉛筆の先 the point of one's pencil; a pencil point / 鉛筆の芯 the lead of a pencil / 鉛筆をなめる wet a pencil on the tip of one's tongue / 鉛筆で書く write in [with a] pencil / 赤[青]鉛筆 a red [blue] pencil / 鉛筆入れ a pencil case / 鉛筆画 a pencil drawing / 鉛筆削り a pencil sharpener.

えんびふく 燕尾服 a swallow-tailed coat;《口語》《wear, be in》tails;《口語》a swallowtail; a tailcoat.

えんぶきょく 円舞曲 a waltz.

えんぶん 塩分 salt content 《of seawater》¶塩分を含んだ saline; salty / 塩分を除く remove salt (from); desalinate; desalinize; desalt.

えんぼう¹ 遠望 a distant view 《of Mt. Fuji》¶遠望する 〈遠方から見る〉get [have] a distant view of 《Mt. Asama》; view [look at] sth from a distance; 〈遠くを見る〉gaze into the distance.

えんぼう² 遠謀 a far-sighted plan ¶遠謀深慮の far-sighted; foresighted ⇨ しんりょ.

易尻の黒字を減らすべきだとアメリカ及び EC 諸国が要求しはじめた. The U.S. and the EEC nations have begun to demand that Japan (should) reduce[eliminate] her trade surplus, which has resulted in a steep appreciation of the yen.

えんだん² 縁談で友人の家を訪ねた. I visited my friend's home to tell him of a prospective marriage partner for him. / 縁談をまとめたいと思って山田文子さんに会いました. I met Miss Fumiko Yamada with a view to arranging her marriage.

えんちゃく 列車は2時間延着した. The train arrived two hours late. | The train was two hours behind time [schedule].

えんちょう 地下鉄の延長工事で車は通れなかった. Traffic was disrupted by work on a subway extension. / EF が EB と等しくなるように線分 AE を F まで延長せよ. Extend AE to F so that EF equals EB. / 試合は延長戦になった. The game went into extra innings.

えんどう¹ パレード見物の群衆で沿道は大変な混雑だった. The route of the parade was thickly lined with crowds of spectators.

えんぼう¹ そこからはアルプスの峰々を遠望することができる. From there you can get a distant view of the peaks of the Alps.

えんぼう そんな遠方まで会いには行けない. I can't go all that way to see him.

えんまく 本心を見透かされないように彼はあれこれとさかんに煙幕を張った. He tried one thing after another by way of a smoke screen so as not to have his real intentions seen through [not to give himself away].

えんまん 2人の夫婦仲は非常に円満だ. They get on very well together. / ストライキは円満に解決した. The strike was settled amicably.

えんらい² 遠雷がとどろいていた. Thunder was rolling in the distance.

えんりょ 彼は私に対してどこか遠慮している. There is something reserved in his manner toward me. / ジュリアンと僕との間には何の遠慮もない. Julian and I don't need to hold anything back [hide anything] from each other. | There is no reserve be-

えんぽう 遠方 〈遠距離〉a great [long] distance; a long way; 〈遠い所〉a distant place;《文》a far country ¶遠方の distant; faraway /《文》far; remote / 遠方に far away [off]; a long way off; in the distance / はるか遠方に in the far-off distance / 遠方から来る come a long way 《from》;《文》come from afar / 遠方から見ると be seen from a distance.

えんま 閻魔《サンスクリット語》*Yama*; the King of Hell ¶えんま帳 a teacher's mark [grade] book / えんま帳につける put 《a grade》 down in *one's* (mark) book.

えんまく 煙幕 a smoke screen ¶煙幕を張る lay (down) a smoke screen.

えんまん 円満 ¶円満な《文》harmonious; peaceful / 円満な家庭 a happy home / 円満な人格《文》a well-integrated [an integrated] personality / 円満な紳士 an amiable gentleman / 円満退職する resign of *one's* own free will; resign with *one's* reputation [good name] intact / 円満に《文》harmoniously; smoothly; peacefully. 文例⇩

えんむすび 縁結び marriage ¶縁結びの神 a god of [who presides over] marriage.

えんめい 延命 ¶内閣の延命を図る try to prolong the life of the cabinet.

えんやす 円安〈相場〉a low yen rate;〈円価の下落〉a fall in (the exchange rate of) the yen ⇨えんだか ¶円安を招来する bring about a depreciation of the yen (in the international money markets).

えんゆうかい 園遊会 ¶園遊会を催す give [hold] a garden party.

えんよう¹ 援用 ¶援用する〈条文などを〉invoke《a clause》;〈引用する〉quote《an article》; cite《a precedent》.

えんよう² 遠洋 the open sea (far from land) ¶遠洋漁業 pelagic [deep-sea] fishery / 遠洋航海 ocean navigation / 遠洋航海に出る[出ている] set out [be] on a long cruise.

えんらい¹ 遠来 ¶遠来の客《文》a visitor from afar.

えんらい² 遠雷 distant thunder ¶遠雷のとどろき the distant boom [roll] of thunder / 遠雷のような音 a booming sound; a boom. 文例⇩

えんりょ 遠慮 〈控える〉reserve; diffidence ¶遠慮する 〈差し控える〉 be reserved; hold back;〈固苦しくする〉stand on ceremony;〈ためらう〉hesitate;〈人の気持ちに〉respect [spare] *sb's* feelings /〈席をはずす〉go away; stay out 《of the room》;《口語》make *oneself* scarce / 批評を遠慮する《文》refrain from criticizing / 遠慮のない unreserved;《文》unconstrained; free;〈率直な〉frank; candid; outspoken / 遠慮のない話だが to be frank with you / 遠慮なく without reserve; frankly;〈気楽に〉at (*one's*) ease;〈腹蔵なく〉freely / 遠慮なく言う speak straightforwardly; do not mince matters / 遠慮会釈なく ruthlessly; mercilessly / 遠慮深い modest; shy / 遠慮勝ちに modestly. 文例⇩

えんるい 塩類 salts ¶塩類泉 a saline spring; a mineral salt spring.

えんろ 遠路 a long way [distance]. 文例⇩

お

お 尾 a tail; a brush (きつねなどの太い尾); a train (くじゃくなどの) ¶尾が長い[短い] have a long [short] tail / 尾の長い[短い] long-[short-]tailed 《monkeys》/ 尾を振る wag *its* tail (犬が); swish *its* tail (牛などが) /(事柄が)尾を引く leave (*its*) traces; have a lasting effect; be not over and done with. 文例⇩

オアシス an oasis 《*pl.* oases》 ¶砂漠のオアシス an oasis in the desert ★この句は比喩的にも使う。 文例⇩

tween Julian and me. / ここでは何のご遠慮もいりません。You can feel at home in our house. / 遠慮していたら, なんにもいい事ないですよ。Modesty will get you nowhere. / まだおなかはすいていたが, 2つめのパイは悪いと思って遠慮した。Although I was still hungry, I refused a second piece of pie out of politeness. / どうぞ遠慮なくお上がり下さい。Please help yourself (to the cookies). / さあさあ, 遠慮なんかしないで, 1つ取りなさい。Come on, come on! Do take one! / ご用の向きがございましたらいつでもどうぞ遠慮なくお申し付け下さいまし。I am always at your service. / ちょっと聞きたい事があるんだが。—遠慮なく聞けよ。May I ask you something?—Ask away! / わからない事があったら, 遠慮なく聞いて下さい。Ask me whenever you are in doubt. / 私はその人に遠慮して言いたい事も言わなかった。Out of deference to him I did not say as much as I should have liked to. / だんだんと村の人々は私に遠慮なく物を言うようになってきた。Little by little, the villagers opened up to me. / 我々は彼の政策を遠慮なく批判した。We criticized his policy without pulling any punches. / 彼は長老たちに遠慮してすこし離れた所にかしこまって座っていた。He sat stiffly a respectful distance away from the elders. / 彼は遠慮勝ちな人だ。He has rather a retiring nature. / おタバコはご遠慮下さい。Please [Kindly] refrain from smoking. / ちょっとこの席を遠慮してくれないか。Could you leave us alone for a few minutes?

えんろ 出発の際は空港まで遠路わざわざお見送り下さいましてまことにありがとう存じます。Many thanks for (your kindness in) coming all the way to the airport to see me off when I left.

お ボス猿は尾をぴんと上げていばって歩いていた。The leader of the troop of monkeys was walking proudly with his tail held stiffly backward. / 前の日のいさかいがまだ尾を引いていた。The bickering of the day before was still having its aftereffects on them.

オアシス この公園はこのあたりのサラリーマンたちのオアシスとなっている。This park is an oasis for

おあずけ お預け ¶お預けを食う be kept waiting ((for)) / お預けになる 〈延期される〉 be postponed ; be put off.

おい¹ 老い ⇨ろうねん ¶老いも若きも (both) young and old (alike) / 老いの悲しみ the sorrow of old age.

おい² 甥 a nephew ((of [to] sb)).

おい³ hullo ; hey ; ((米)) say ; ((英)) I say ; look here ; listen. 文例⇩

おいあげる 追い上げる 〈上方に〉chase ((a bear)) up ((into a tree)) ; 〈競走で〉move up ((behind sb)) ; 〈迫る〉threaten to catch up with sb [((英)) catch sb up].

おいうち 追い打ち ¶追い打ちをかける 〈敗走する敵に〉attack [fire at] the routed enemy ; 〈ひるんでいる相手に〉give an additional blow ((to the already daunted opponent)).

おいえげい 御家芸 one's (traditional) specialty ; ((文)) one's forte (得手).

おいえそうどう 御家騒動 a family quarrel [trouble] ; ((文)) family strife.

おいおい¹ 追々 〈少しずつ〉gradually ; by degrees ; little by little ; 〈やがて〉by and by ; in (course of) time.

おいおい² ¶おいおい泣く cry bitterly ; cry one's heart out.

おいおとす 追い落とす gain in power and unseat ((the president of the party)).

おいかえす 追い返す drive ((sb)) back ; ((文)) repel ; ((文)) repulse ; order sb back (命令して) ; 〈訪問者などを〉send sb away ; show sb the door (戸を指さして出て行けと). 文例⇩

おいかける 追い掛ける run after sb ; ((文)) pursue ; chase.

おいかぜ 追い風 a following [favorable] wind ; a tailwind ¶追い風を受けて帆走する sail [run] before the wind. 文例⇩

おいこし 追い越し ¶追い越し禁止区域 a no-passing [((英)) no-overtaking] zone / 追い越し車線 a passing lane ; ((英)) an overtaking lane. 文例⇩

おいこす 追い越す pass ; get ahead of sb ; leave sb behind ; outrun ; ((文)) outstrip ; overtake ; 〈しのぐ〉outdo ; ((文)) surpass ¶はるかに追い越す get far ahead of sb ; outdistance. 文例⇩

おいこみ 追い込み the last spurt ; the last [final] lap ; ((印刷)) a run-on ¶最後の追い込みをかける put out [on, ((文)) forth] a last spurt / 最後の追い込みに入る [入っている] go into [be on] the last stage (of the work).

おいこむ¹ 老い込む grow old ; ((文)) age ; grow weak from age ; get ((文)) become) decrepit. 文例⇩

おいこむ² 追い込む drive [chase] ((into)) ; ((印刷)) run on ¶窮地に追い込む drive [force, put] sb into a corner ; corner sb.

おいさき¹ 生い先 (a child's) future ; the years lying ahead ((of the boy)).

おいさき² 老い先 ¶老い先短い老人 an old man who does not have many years to live.

おいしい ⇨うまい 文例⇩

おいしげる 生い茂る 〈草木が主語〉grow thick(-ly) [((文)) luxuriantly] ; 〈場所が主語〉be thickly covered with ((trees)) ; be overgrown [((文)) rank] with ((weeds)) ¶木のおい茂った丘 a thickly-[heavily-]wooded hill.

おいすがる 追い縋る run up to sb from behind ; try not to be left behind. 文例⇩

おいせまる 追い迫る gain on sb ; run sb close [((文)) hard] ; be hot on the heels of sb.

おいそれと 〈すぐに〉at a moment's notice ; readily ; 〈考えなく〉thoughtlessly ; 〈無造作に〉casually ; in an offhand way ; 〈簡単に〉easily.

おいだす 追い出す turn [drive, force (力ずくで)] sb out ; ((口語)) throw [kick] sb out ; 〈地位から〉((文)) oust (sb from a position) ; 〈解雇する〉fire ; ((文)) dismiss ; ((文)) discharge ; ((口語)) sack ; ((口語)) give sb the sack ; 〈借家人を〉eject [evict (法に訴えて)] ((a tenant)) from ((the house)).

おいたち 生い立ち 〈成長〉⇨せいちょう² ; 〈経歴〉one's background ; one's personal history ; 〈幼少時代〉one's childhood ¶子供の生い立ちを見守る watch how a child grows up ; watch over a growing child.

おいたてる 追い立てる 〈追いやる〉send [drive] sb away ; hustle ; ((口語)) shoo sb away [out] ; 〈急がせる〉hurry sb (up) ; 〈借家人を〉eject [evict (法に訴えて)] ((a tenant)) from ((the house)) ¶馬を追い立てる urge a horse forward [on].

おいちらす 追い散らす drive away ; disperse ((a crowd)) ; 〈潰(かい)させる〉((文)) rout ; ((文)) put ((the enemy)) to flight [rout].

おいつく 追い付く catch up with sb ; ((英)) catch sb up ; overtake ; gain on sb (段々と) ★

---

the office workers around here.

おあずけ お預け. 〈犬に向かって言うことば〉Trust! / Wait (for it)! / 彼はまるでうまそうな肉を前にしてお預けを食った犬みたいだった. He was [looked] like a dog which has been put on trust for an appetizing piece of meat.

おい³ おいおい, そんな夢のような話じゃないよ. Come on now ; be realistic!

おいかえす 彼女が家を飛び出して里に戻ると, 母親からさっさと帰りなさいと追い返された. No sooner had she run home to mother than she was sent packing off back to her husband.

おいかぜ 風は追い風だ. The wind is favorable.

おいこし 追い越し禁止. 〖標示〗 No passing. / ((英)) No overtaking.

おいこす (会社で)彼は何人もの後輩に追い越されてしまった. He has been outstripped by quite a few men younger than him. ⇨より² 用法 / He has seen a good many younger men promoted ahead of him.

おいこみ ラルフはパトリックの猛烈な追い込みを退けて優勝した. Ralph won the championship against a strong challenge from Patrick.

おいこむ¹ 今から老い込んじゃいけないよ. It's too early to think of yourself as an old man.

おいしい コーヒーをおいしくいただきました. I enjoyed the coffee (very much). / 朝ご飯をおいしく食べられるように僕は毎朝散歩します. I go out for a walk every morning, to work up a good appetite for my breakfast.

おいすがる 追いすがる報道陣を振り切って彼は車に乗り込んだ.

おいつめる 追い詰める get close behind sb; 〈追跡して〉run (a criminal) down; 〈窮地に〉corner; drive [force, put] sb into a (tight) corner; 《文》drive [bring] sb to bay.

おいて 於いて at; in; on; 〈関して〉in; as for; 《文》as to; 《文》in point of; … on the part of... ¶本郷において at Hongo / 東京において in Tokyo / 学問において(は) in point of learning / 文明の程度においては as to the level of the civilization.

おいで お出で ¶お出でになる ⇨くる¹, いく, いる² / お出でお出でをする beckon (to) sb.

おいてきぼり 置いてきぼり ¶置いてきぼりにする[を食う] leave sb [be left] behind.

おいぬき 追い抜き ¶(自転車競走の)団体追い抜き競技 a team pursuit event [race].

おいぬく 追い抜く ⇨ぬく.

おいはぎ 追い剥ぎ a highwayman.

おいはらう 追い払う drive [turn, send] (the onlookers) away; disperse (a mob); 《文》repel (the enemy); fight off (the enemy); get rid of; 〈悪魔などを〉exorcise (evil spirits from a place); 〈地位から〉expel 《文》oust (sb from a position).

おいぼれ 老いぼれ a feeble-minded old man; a senile old fool; 《文》a dotard.

おいぼれる 老いぼれる go senile; get 《文》become] decrepit ⇨もうろく.

おいまわす 追い回す run after sb; chase sb about; 〈つきまとう〉follow sb around; hang about sb; pester (a girl); 〈激しく使う〉order sb about.

おいめ 負い目 《文》indebtedness ¶負い目を感じる 《文》feel beholden (to sb); feel that one has a debt to pay (to sb).

おいもとめる 追い求める pursue (an ideal); 《文》seek after (worldly pleasures).

おいやる 追い遣る send [drive] sb away; 〈命令して〉order sb off ¶死に追いやる drive sb to [to commit] suicide.

おいらく 老いらく ¶老いらくの恋 love in old age.

おいる 老いる grow old; age ¶老いてますます盛んである be going strong [《文》be hale and hearty] despite one's age.

オイル oil ¶オイルショック the oil shock / オイルダラー《経》the petrodollar; petrodollars / オイルフェンス an oil fence / オイル焼き slices of meat fried in oil.

おいろなおし お色直し ⇨いろなおし.

おう¹ 王 a king; a ruler; 《文》a sovereign; 《文》a monarch; a magnate (ことに産業界の) ⇨おうさま, こくおう ¶百獣の王 the king of beasts / 自動車王 an automobile magnate [king].

おう² 翁 an old [《文》aged] man ¶尾崎翁 old Mr. Ozaki.

おう³ 追う 〈追いかける〉go [run] after; chase; 《文》pursue; 〈後について行く〉follow; trail; track; 〈追い払う〉drive sb away; 〈追い出す〉turn [drive, 《口語》kick] sb out ¶牛を追う drive cattle / 名声を追う go after [《文》pursue] fame / 流行を追う follow the fashion / 激しく追う go [run] in hot pursuit of sb; follow sb closely ¶…の跡を追っている be on the track [trail] of (a bear, a criminal) / 仕事に追われる be swamped [pressed] with work / 時間に追われる be pressed for time; time presses/順序を追って in order / 《文》in due order / 年を追って year after year; from year to year; each year / 日を追って day by day; daily / 追いつ追われつの接戦 a seesaw game [match].

おう⁴ 負う 〈背負う〉carry [have] sth on one's back; 《文》bear (a heavy burden); 〈お陰をこうむる〉owe sb for sth; 《文》be indebted to sb for sth; 〈費用などを負担する〉bear (the costs); foot (the bill); 〈任務や義務などを〉shoulder; take on; 《文》assume; 《文》be charged with ¶重傷を負う be [get] severely [seriously] wounded [injured]; get a bad wound (on one's arm); 《文》receive a serious injury (to one's leg) / …の義務を負う be obliged to do; 《文》be under (an) obligation to do / …に負う所が多い be greatly indebted [owe a great deal] to sb for sth.

おうい 王位 the throne; the crown; 《文》kingship ¶王位を奪う[継承する] usurp [succeed to, inherit] the throne / 王位を捨てる abdicate (from) the throne / 王位を譲る resign one's throne to (one's son); pass the throne on to (one's younger brother) / 王位にある be on the throne / 王位につく take [《文》accede to,

---

Shaking off the reporters who followed him about, he got in the car.

おいそれと おいそれと引受けられるような仕事じゃない. I'll have to have a think before I take on the job. / そんな大金を貸してくれと言ったって, おいそれと貸せるもんじゃない. I can't lend you such a big sum of money just for the asking.

おいつく この分野で日本はアメリカに追い付き追い越せと長年努力してきた. Japan has been making efforts for quite a number of years to catch up with and surpass the United States in this field. / 今さら悔んでも追い付かない. It's too late for regrets. | It's no use [good] crying over spilt milk.

おいで どうぞこちらへお出で下さい. Come [Step] this way, please./ようこそお出で下さいました. I am very glad that you have come. / 土曜日にお出で下さいませんか. ご一緒に食事でもと思いますのですが. Will you come over on Saturday and have dinner with us? / ワイルドさんはおいでですか. Is Mr. Wilde in [at home]?

おう³ この1敗でソ連チームは今度は一転して追う立場になった. The tables have been turned by this defeat and now the Russian team is in the position of having to come from behind. / 私はこの仕事に追われていて読書する暇もない. I'm under such pressure from this work that I have no time for reading.

おう⁴ 今日あるのは彼の父に負う所が極めて多い. He owes a lot [is deeply indebted] to his

おういつ 横溢 ¶横溢する be full of ; be filled with ; be overflowing with / 元気横溢している be full of vigor [health (and life)], 《口語》 pep, 《口語》 beans.

おうえん 応援 〈援助〉《文》 aid ; 《文》 assistance ; help ; reinforcement (増援) ; 〈支持〉 support ; backing ; 〈声援〉 cheering ; 《米口語》 rooting ¶応援する《文》 aid ; 《文》 assist ; help ; give help [《文》 aid] (to) ; reinforce ; support ; back (up) ; cheer ; 《米口語》 root (for) ; 盛んに応援する cheer (one's team) vigorously / 応援を頼む ask sb for help [support, 《文》 aid] / 応援演説 (make) a campaign [vote-getting] speech (for a candidate) / 応援団 a cheering party ; 《米口語》 rooters / 応援団長 a cheerleader.

おうおう 往々 〈時折〉 sometimes ; occasionally ; now and then ; from time to time ; 〈たびたび〉 often ; 《文》 frequently ; more often than not ¶学生に往々見られることであるが as is often the case with students. 文例⇩

おうか 謳歌 ¶謳歌する sing [chant] the praises of ; 《文》 glorify ; 《文》 extol(l) ; 《文》 eulogize / 青春を謳歌する openly enjoy the joys of youth.

おうが 横臥 ¶横臥する lie (down).

おうかくまく 横隔膜 【解】 the diaphragm ; the midriff.

おうかっしょく 黄褐色 yellowish brown.

おうかん 王冠 a (royal) crown ; 〈瓶の〉 a crown cap ¶王冠をいただく〈かぶる〉 wear a crown ; 〈王位につく〉 be crowned king [queen].

おうぎ 扇 a (folding) fan ¶扇を使う use a fan ; fan oneself / 扇形の fan-shaped / 扇形に広がる fan (out).

おうきゅう 応急 ¶応急の 〈急場の〉 emergency 《supplies》 ; 〈一時的〉 temporary ; 〈間に合わせの〉 stopgap ; makeshift / 応急策をとる take emergency measures ; 《文》 employ a temporary expedient / 応急処置 (make) temporary repairs / 応急手当 (give) first aid (to).

おうけ 王家 a royal family [house] ¶ (古代エジプトの)王家の谷 the Valley of the Kings [Tombs].

おうけん 王権 royal authority [power(s)] ; 《文》 the royal prerogative ; 《文》 regal power ; 《文》 a sovereign right [privilege] ¶王権神授説 《西洋史》 (the doctrine of) the divine right of kings.

おうこう[1] 王侯 the king and feudal lords ¶王侯貴族のような生活をする live like a lord [prince].

おうこう[2] 横行 ¶横行する be rampant ; overrun (the town) ; 〈場所が主語〉 be infested with (robbers).

おうこく 王国 a kingdom ; a monarchy.

おうごん 黄金 gold ; 〈財〉 money ¶黄金の gold ; golden / 黄金時代 the golden age ; 〈全盛期〉《文》(in) one's palmy days / 黄金分割 the golden section [mean].

おうざ 王座 the throne ¶王座を占める win the (intercollegiate) championship ; hold the premier position [first place] ; be at the top (of).

おうさま 王様 a king ; 《文》 a monarch ; 〈敬語〉 His Majesty (the King) ; Your Majesty.

おうし 雄(牡)牛 a bull ; 〈去勢した〉 an ox (pl. oxen) ¶牡牛座 【天】 Taurus ; the Bull ⇒文例.

おうじ[1] 王子 a Royal prince ; a prince of the blood (royal).

おうじ[2] 皇子 an Imperial prince ¶天皇の第二皇子 the second son of the emperor.

おうしつ 王室 Royal family [household].

おうじゃ 王者 a king ; 《文》 a monarch ; 〈優勝者〉 the champion ¶陸の王者慶応 Keio, kings of the athletic(s) field / 王者の貫録充分だ be a worthy champion ; 《文》 have dignity and power well worthy of the championship.

おうしゅ 応手 〈囲碁・将棋などでの〉 a response ¶応手として…と指す respond (to one's opponent's move) with….

おうしゅう[1] 応酬 《文》 a response, a reply ; an answer ; 〈文〉 a riposte (当意即妙な) ; 〈反駁〈はん〉〉 a retort ¶野次の応酬 an exchange of heckling / 応酬する《文》 respond ; reply ; make a (sharp) retort.

おうしゅう[2] 押収 seizure ; confiscation ¶押収する seize ; confiscate.

おうしゅう[3] 欧州 Europe ⇒ヨーロッパ ¶欧州共同体 the European Community (略: EC) / 欧州経済共同体 the European Economic Community (略: EEC) ; 〈通称〉 the Common Market.

おうじゅほうしょう 黄綬褒章 a Yellow Ribbon Medal.

おうじょ[1] 王女 a Royal princess ; a princess of the blood (royal).

おうじょ[2] 皇女 an Imperial princess ¶天皇の第二皇女 the second daughter of the emperor.

おうしょう 王将 〈将棋〉 a king.

おうじょう 往生 ¶往生する〈死ぬ〉die ;《文》breathe one's last ;《口語》give up the ghost ;《俗》kick the bucket ; 〈屈服する〉give in (to) ;《文》yield ; 〈閉口する〉be at one's wits' end ; be in a fix ; be nonplus(s)ed / 大往生を遂げる die a calm [peaceful] death / 往生際が悪い accept defeat with (a) bad grace ; be a bad loser. 文例⇩　　　　「race(s).

おうしょくじんしゅ 黄色人種 the yellow

おうじる 応じる 〈答える〉 answer ; reply [《文》

おうしん おうふく

respond 《to》; 〈承諾する〉accept; agree [《文》consent] 《to》; 《文》comply 《with》; 〈かなう〉meet ¶質問に応じる answer a question / 提案に応じる accept [agree to, consent to] a proposal / 要求に応じる comply with a request / 時代の要求に応じる 《文》meet the demand[s] of the times / 招待[注文]に応じる accept an invitation [order] / 懸賞募集に応じる enter a prize contest / 収入[能力]に応じて according to *one's* income [ability] / 必要に応じて as occasion demands; as the need arises / 呼ぶ声に応じて in answer to the call / 多数の要望に応じて in response to [《文》in compliance with] numerous requests.

おうしん[1] 往信 a message sent out to get a reply; 〈往復葉書の〉the original message of a reply-paid postcard.

おうしん[2] 往診 a house call [visit] ¶夜間の往診 a night call [visit] / 往診する make a house call [visit] 《on *sb*》; go and see 《a patient》 at 《his》 home / 往診中である be out [away] on *one's* rounds [*one's* round of sick calls] / 往診料 the doctor's fee for a visit. 文例

おうせい 旺盛 ¶元気旺盛である be full of vigor [health (and life), 《口語》beans]; be brimming over with vitality / 食欲旺盛である have a good [an excellent] appetite.

おうせいふっこ 王政復古 the Restoration of Imperial Rule; 〈英国王チャールズ二世の〉the Restoration.

おうせつ 応接 a reception ¶応接する 《文》receive 《a visitor》; see / 応接室[間] a drawing room. 文例

おうせん[1] 応戦 ¶応戦する fight back; 〈砲撃で〉return the 《enemy's》 fire; 〈挑戦に応じる〉accept [take up] the challenge.

おうせん[2] 横線 ¶横線を引く cross 《a check》 / 横線小切手 a crossed check.

おうぞく 王族 a royal family; 《a member of》 royalty.

おうだ 殴打 beating; 《法》battery ¶殴打する hit; beat; 《文》strike; give [deal] *sb* a blow 《on the head》(一撃する); drub; give *sb* a drubbing (袋叩きにする).

おうたい[1] 応対 ¶応対する receive 《callers》; wait on 《customers》; 〈相手にする〉deal with *sb* / 応対がじょうず[へた]である be good [awkward] at dealing with people. 文例

おうたい[2] 黄体 《生理》a corpus luteum (*pl.* corpora lutea) ¶黄体ホルモン progesterone; corpus luteum hormone.

おうたい[3] 横隊 a rank; a line ¶2列横隊に整列する form [be drawn up in] a double line / 4列横隊になる form (up) four deep.

おうだん 黄疸 《医》jaundice ¶黄疸にかかった人 a person who has [who is suffering from] jaundice.

おうだん[2] 横断 crossing ¶横断する cross; go [walk, travel, sail, run, fly] across; 《文》traverse / 横断歩道 a pedestrian crossing; 《米》a crosswalk; 《英》a zebra crossing / 押しボタン式横断歩道 a push-button (pedestrian) crossing; 《英》a pelican crossing (★ *pedestrian light controlled crossing* の最後の *con* を *can* に変えて作られた語) / 道路に張られた横断幕 a banner strung across [slung over] a street / 横断面 a cross section.

おうちゃく 横着 ¶横着な 〈怠惰な〉lazy; 〈ずうずうしい〉cheeky; 《文》brazen / 横着をきめこむ shirk [neglect] *one's* duties.

おうちょう 王朝 a dynasty ¶(映画などの)王朝物 a Heian period piece ⇒ えまき 文例.

おうて 王手 〖将棋〗王手 check ¶王手する check [give check to] 《(the opponent's) king》 / 王手されて逃げる get out of check / 逆王手 return check / 両(明き)王手 double (discovered) check / 王手飛車取りをかける fork 《(the opponent's) king and rook》《with *one's* bishop》. 文例

おうてっこう 黄鉄鉱 〖鉱〗iron pyrites; 〈通俗に〉fool's gold.

おうてん 横転 ¶横転する turn over and lie on *its* side; 〈ごろごろと〉roll sideways; 〈飛行機が〉do [make] a roll.

おうと 嘔吐 vomiting ¶嘔吐する vomit; 《口語》throw up; 《口語》throw [bring] up 《*one's* food》 / 嘔吐を催す ⇒ はきけ (吐き気を催す).

おうどいろ 黄土色 ocher ¶黄土色の ocher.

おうとう 応答 ⇒ こたえ, こたえる[1], へんじ[1].

おうどうこう 黄銅鉱 〖鉱〗copper pyrites.

おうとつ 凹凸 ¶凹凸のある uneven ⇒ でこぼこ.

おうねん 往年 ¶往年の 《文》former; one-time. 文例

おうひ 王妃 a queen; an empress.

おうふう 欧風 ¶欧風の 《a house》 in (the) European style.

おうふく 往復 ¶往復する go 《to Kobe》 and return [come back]; go to and from 《a place》; get there and back; make a round trip 《to, between》; 〈通う〉run 《between》; 《文》ply 《between》(船が) / 日に2往復する make two round trips a day 《between A and B》 / 往復とも歩く walk 《to a place》 and back; walk both ways / 学校(会社)へ往復の途中 on *one's* way to and from school [work, the office] / (機械の部分の)往復運動 a to-and-fro [back-and-forth] motion; a reciprocating motion / 往復はがき a reply-paid postcard; 《米》a double postal card / 往復切符《米》a round-trip ticket; 《英》a return ticket / 往復便 a shuttle service. 文例

---

car.

おうせつ 問い合わせの手紙が殺到して応接にいとまがなかった。So many letters of inquiry poured in that we had our hands full answering them.

おうたい[1] ロドニーは今客の応対で忙しい。Rodney is busy receiving visitors. / その店員は客の応対が悪いといって売場主任にしかられた。The salesclerk was reprimanded by the floorwalker because of his lack of courtesy to customers.

おうて 王手! Check! / 王手がかかっている。The king is in check.

おうねん 彼は往年の名投手である。He was once a famous pitcher.

おうふく 横浜まで往復幾らですか。How much is it to Yokohama and back? / (切符は) 片道300円,

おうぶん¹ 欧文 writing in a Western language ¶欧文電報 a telegram in a Western language.

おうぶん² 応分 ¶応分の〈適当した〉appropriate;〈文〉due; reasonable;〈資力・能力に応じた〉《文》〈assistance〉according to one's means [ability] / 応分の寄付をする contribute 《to a fund》what [as much as] one can afford / 応分の処遇を与える give [《文》render] sb his due.

おうへい 横柄 arrogance; haughtiness; insolence ¶横柄な arrogant; haughty; insolent; supercilious; overbearing / 横柄に構える assume an attitude of arrogant superiority《toward》. 文例⇩

おうべい 欧米 Europe and America; the West ¶欧米の European and American; Western / 欧米諸国 Western countries / 欧米人 Europeans and Americans; Westerners.

おうぼ 応募〈寄付などの〉subscription;〈入学などの〉application ¶応募する apply《for》; subscribe《for, to》/ 自分から進んで応募する volunteer《for》/ 応募者 an applicant; a subscriber.

おうほう 応報 ⇨おう¹(因果応報), むくい.

おうぼう 横暴 ¶横暴な oppressive; tyrannical; despotic;〈高圧的な〉overbearing; highhanded;〈不当な〉unreasonable / 横暴を極める tyrannize《over》; behave very high-handedly.

おうむ a parrot; a cockatoo ¶おうむ返しに言う repeat [echo] sb's words (mechanically [like a parrot]); parrot sb's words.

おうむがい 貝 a nautilus (pl. -luses, -li); a chambered [pearly] nautilus.

おうめん 凹面 a concave surface ¶凹面の concave / 凹面をなしている be concavely curved / 凹面鏡 a concave mirror.

おうよう 応用 (practical) application ¶応用する apply《science to industry》; put (knowledge) to practical use; put (theories) into practice / 応用できる can be applied《to》;《文》be applicable《to》/ 応用の範囲が広い《文》have wide applicability;《文》be widely applicable; have a wide range of application;《文》be of wide application / 応用できない cannot be applied《to》;《文》be inapplicable《to》/ 応用化学[物理学] applied chemistry [physics] / 応用問題 a question to test (the students') ability to use (their) knowledge in practice;〈練習問題〉exercises. 文例⇩

おうらい 往来〈交通〉traffic;〈道路〉a road; a street ¶往来する come and go / 人の往来 (there are a lot of) comings and goings / 人の往来が絶える〈道路が主語〉be deserted / 往来の激しい道 a busy [crowded] street.

おうりょう 横領〈公金などの〉《文》(a) misappropriation;《文》embezzlement ¶横領する《文》usurp;《文》misappropriate (public money); embezzle (money from the company where one is working);〈蜻蛉に〉《文》appropriate (government money) / 横領罪で逮捕される be arrested on a charge of embezzlement.

おうりょく 応力〈機・物〉stress.

おうりょくしょく 黄緑色 yellowish green; olive (color).

おうりん 黄燐〈化〉yellow [white] phosphorus.

おうレンズ 凹レンズ a concave lens.

おえらがた お偉方 important people;〈口語〉VIPs;《文》dignitaries;《文》personages;《文》exalted personalities;〈俗〉bigwigs.

おえる 終える end; finish; complete; get [be] through (with);〈遂行する〉《文》accomplish;〈卒業する〉graduate (from);〈文〉¶大学の課程を終える complete [pass through] a [one's] university course / 1日の仕事を終えて after a day's work. 文例⇩

おお O; oh;〈うむ〉well;〈応答〉yes; all right. 文例⇩

おおあくび 大欠伸 ¶大あくびをする give [let out] a big [huge] yawn.

おおあじ 大味 ¶大味である have not much flavor; be flat (to the taste).

おおあせ 大汗 ⇨あせ 用法 ¶大汗をかく sweat [perspire] heavily [《文》copiously];〈骨を折る〉(have to) make a great effort. 文例⇩

おおあたり 大当たり ¶大当たりする[をとる]〈大成功をおさめる〉be a great [big] success; be a big [smash] hit; pull off a great coup;

往復なら550円です。It costs 300 yen single and 550 yen round trip [〈英〉return]. / ヨークまで2等往復1枚下さい。〈米〉One second-class round-trip ticket to York, please. | 〈英〉A second-class return to York, please. / 往復20キロある。It's twenty kilometers there and back. / 彼は始終東京と大阪の間を往復している。He is constantly going back and forth between Tokyo and Osaka.

おうへい 彼は部下に横柄である。He lords it over his men.

おうよう 彼のこの発明は、今日、産業界の各方面で広く応用されている。This invention of his is finding wide application today in various fields of manufacturing industry. / エジソンは実地に応用できないと思われるアイデアは軽蔑した。Edison scorned ideas for which he could see no practical application.

おえる クリスタル博士は南米の旅行を終えてこのほど帰国した。Dr. Crystal has recently returned home from his tour of South America.

おお お痛い。Ouch, it hurts! / おお、そうか。Really, is that so?

おおあせ 彼を同意させるのに大汗をかいた。I had a real job coaxing him into accepting our conditions.

おおあたり このところ田中君は大当たりだ。Tanaka is really in luck these days. / その劇は大当たりだった。The play was a great (box-office) success. / 今年は彼の商売は大当たりだった。This has been a bonanza year for his business.

おおあめ 大雨が降った。It rained heavily. | There was a downpour.

おおあれ ちゃんとした事を言うのか。何かちゃんとしたわけがあるのかい。-もちろん大ありさ。Why do you say things like that? Is there any good reason for it? — Sure. There are any number of (reasons). [You bet there are!]

おおあれ 海は大荒れになった。The sea got very rough. / 今日の土俵は大荒れだった。The formbook was thrown out of the window at today's sumo. | Today's sumo tournament saw a number of

おおあな 大穴 〈大きな穴〉a big [large] hole; 〈大きな欠損〉(suffer,《文》incur) a great loss;《文》(cause) a heavy deficit ¶大穴を当てて have a big win《on the race》/《競馬で》大穴をねらう bet on a dark horse.

おおあめ 大雨 a heavy rain; a downpour / 大雨洪水注意報 a heavy rain and flood warning. [文例⇩]

おおあり 大有り [文例⇩]

おおあれ 大荒れ〈大あらし〉a heavy storm. [文例⇩]

おおい¹ 覆い a cover (for a sofa); a covering ¶覆いのある covered / 覆いのない uncovered; bare / 覆いをする cover / 覆いを取る take the cover off 《sth》; uncover;《文》bare.

おおい² 多い have [there are] a lot of (rooms); lots of [《文》many] (people do);《文》be great in number; be numerous (in, with); be rich (in);〈頻度〉be frequent ¶多くの〈数〉a lot of (houses), a large [good, great] number of (people); many (mistakes); numerous (vehicles);〈量〉a lot of (butter); a great deal [amount] of (money); plenty of (food) ★「多くの」の意味で多く(数), much (量)を肯定平叙文で使うのは《文》. 会話では a lot of と言うのが自然 ⇨たくさん [用法] / 多くは mostly; for the most part; generally / 主にもに mainly; chiefly; largely / 多くとも at most; at the outside / 数[量]が多くなる increase in number [quantity].

[用法]「…が多い[は少ない]」を英語で言うには, 日本語とはかなり文構成を異にする.「そう考える人が多い[は少ない]」は A lot of [Not many] people think so. |《文》Many [Few] people think so. が一番普通. これを People who think so are many [few]. とは言わない. 英語にはまた, 個が集まった結果を示す名詞, 例えば a number (数), a class (クラス), a population (人口), an audience (聴衆), a circulation (新聞などの発行部数) などが数多くあり, これらの語について「多い」「少ない」を言うには, 数ではなく大きな(size)について言うことになるので, large [great], small が使われる.「日本は人口が多い」は Japan has a large population. であり,「出席者の数は意外に多かった[少なかった]」は The number of people present was surprisingly large [small]. である. 日本語の「多い」は, 頻度を言うことも少なくない. その場合は, 英語では frequent(ly) や often が使われる.「日本は地震が多い」Earthquakes are frequent in Japan. /「この語は長さについて使われることが多い」This word often [frequently] refers to length. 以上の他にも,「日本は山が多い」Japan is a mountainous country. などの言い方もあって,「多い」の英訳は, その都度判断を要する. 日本語の「多く」は, 単に「数が多い」の意味だけではなく,「全体の中で比率が大きい」の意味で使われることもよくある. その場合は a lot of や many は必ずしも適当ではなく, most を使うほうがよい.「多くの日本人が今では集団住宅に住んでいる」Many [A lot of] Japanese are living in apartments nowadays. /「今でも多くの日本人は木造家屋に住んでいる」Most (of the) Japanese are still living in wooden houses.

おーい hullo!; hello!;〈船員が他の船を呼ぶ声〉ahoy!

おおいかくす 覆い隠す hide sth from sight with a cover; hide [《文》conceal] sth under a cover.

おおいそぎ 大急ぎ ¶大急ぎの urgent; pressing / 大急ぎの注文 a rush order / 大急ぎの用事で on urgent business / 大急ぎで hurriedly; in a great hurry;《口語》in a (big) rush;《文》in great haste; at great speed;《口語》double-quick / 大急ぎで仕事をする rush one's work. [文例⇩]

おおいちばん 大一番 ¶優勝の行方(ゆくえ)を大きく左右する大一番 a big match [bout] which will greatly affect the final destination of the championship.

おおいに 大いに very much; very; greatly; considerably; highly;《文》exceedingly;《文》to a considerable degree; to a great [large] extent;《文》in (a) great [large] measure ★We were much surprised. のように much を肯定平叙文で単独に使うのは《文》⇨たくさん [用法] ¶大いに喜ぶ be very delighted; be highly pleased / 大いに違う be widely different (from) / 大いに必要としている badly need sth;《文》be in great need (of). [文例⇩]

おおいばり 大威張り ¶大いばりできる have nothing to be ashamed of;《文》be well worthy of 《one's status》; more than deserve 《the pro-

---

upsets.

おおい² 新幹線の神戸以西はトンネルがひじょうに多い. There are a very large number of tunnels [Tunnels are frequent] west of Kobe on the Shinkansen. / 同じ間違いがなんと多いんだろう. It's astonishing how often the same mistake has been made! | How often he's [they've] made the same mistake(s)! / この車は5人乗りだから1人多すぎる. This car is meant for five people, so there is one too many of us [so we are one too many]. / この学校では女子の方が男子よりずっと多い. In this school boys are far [greatly] outnumbered by girls. / 多ければ多いほどよい. The more the better. / 田口さんは僕より収入が多い. Mr. Taguchi earns more than me [than I do]. ⇨より² / 田口さんの収入は私のより多い. Mr. Taguchi's income is bigger [larger] than mine. / 父は家族が多かったから大変だった. Father had to work hard since he had a large family to support. / こういう蛙は日本には多い. These frogs abound in Japan. | Japan abounds in these frogs. / この地方からは多くの鉱物が出る. An abundance of mineral products come from this district. / この夏は雨が多かった. We have had a lot of rain this summer. / 西暦2000年になると世界の人口は今よりずっと多くなっている. By the year 2000 the world's population will have become a lot larger than it is now. / 人体は水分を多く含んでいる. The human body contains a large amount of water. / レモンにはビタミンCが多い. Lemons are rich in vitamin C. / 彼は遅刻が多い. He often [frequently] comes late. / 子連れの未亡人には苦労が多い. Life is hard [tough] for a widowed mother.

おおいそぎ 大急ぎでこれを斎藤さんの所へ届けて下さい. Please take this to Mr. Saito as quickly as you can. / 彼は電車に遅れないように大急ぎで出かけた. He hurried out so as to be in time for the train. / 大急ぎで警官が現場に駆け付けたが間に合わなかった. The police rushed to the scene but it was too late.

おおいに それはこの事件と大いに

おおいり 大入り a large attendance ⇒ おおあたり、まんいん ¶大入り袋 a full-house bonus. 文例⇩

おおう 覆う cover; overlay;〈覆い隠す〉hide;《文》conceal; cover up;〈包む〉wrap;《文》envelop;《文》mantle;《文》veil;〈さえぎる〉screen; keep (the sun) off ¶両手で顔をおおう cover one's face with one's hands; bury [hide] one's face in one's hands (頭を垂れて) / 両手で耳を覆う cover one's ears with one's hands; put [《文》place] one's hands over one's ears / 山頂を覆う雲 clouds hanging over the top of the mountain / 一面雲に覆われる be clouded over; be overcast; be filled [《文》overspread] with clouds / 一面雪に覆われる be blanketed [covered all over] with snow.

おおうつし 大写し【映画】a close-up (picture) ¶大写しにする bring sb [sth] into close-up; make a close-up (picture) (of) / 大写しをとる take a close-up (of). 文例⇩

おおうなばら 大海原 a vast expanse of sea.

おおうりだし 大売出し ⇒うりだし.

オーエス〈綱引きの掛け声〉Heave! Heave!

オーエル an office girl ¶ある銀行に勤めているオーエル a girl [woman] working in a bank.

おおおく 大奥 the shogun's harem [seraglio].

おおおじ 大伯[叔]父 a greatuncle; a granduncle.

おおおとこ 大男 a big man; a giant (of a man). 文例⇩

おおおにばす【植】a royal water lily; a water platter.

おおおば 大伯[叔]母 a greataunt; a grandaunt.

おおおんな 大女 a big woman; a woman of large build; a giantess (巨人).

おおがかり 大掛かり ¶大掛かりな large-scale (projects) / 大掛かりに on a large [grand] scale.

おおかぜ 大風 a storm; a typhoon.

おおかた 大方〈多分〉probably; perhaps; maybe;〈ほとんど〉almost; nearly; more or less;〈大部分〉for the most part; mostly. 文例⇩

おおがた 大型 ¶大型の big; large;《文》of large size; large-sized; king-size(d) / 超大型の extra-large; supersize(d) / プロ野球界の大型新人 a rookie of great promise in the pro baseball world / 大型トラック a heavy-duty truck.

おおかみ 狼 a wolf (pl. wolves). 文例⇩

おおがら 大柄 ¶大柄の〈体格が〉large;《文》of large build /〈模様が〉large-patterned.

おおかれすくなかれ 多かれ少なかれ in [to a] greater or less(er) degree; to a greater or less(er) extent.

おおきい, おおきな 大きい, 大きな big; large; great; grand;〈強大な〉《文》mighty;〈巨大な〉huge; gigantic; enormous; colossal; vast;〈広大な〉《文》extensive;《文》spacious;〈声の〉loud ¶大きい間違い a big [great, serious,《文》gross] mistake / 大きな過ち a grave error / 子牛と同じくらい大きい犬 a dog about as large as [about the size of] a calf / 大きいものから小さいものへと順に並べる arrange (books) in decreasing order of size [in order of decreasing size] / 望みが大きい have a great ambition; have high hopes / 大きい声で in a loud voice / 大きな顔をする look (as if one is) important / 大きなことを言う brag; boast;《口語》talk big / 大きな字で書く write large [in large letters] / 大きく〈大規模に〉in a big [large] way; on a large [grand] scale / 大きくする make sth larger;《文》enlarge; magnify; extend (拡張する) / 災害を大きくする make the disaster worse; add to [《文》aggravate,《文》compound] the disaster / 大きくなる get bigger; grow larger;《文》increase in size;〈成長する〉grow (up); get [grow,《文》become] taller;〈養育される〉be brought up;〈増大する〉expand;〈重大化する〉get [《文》become] serious;《文》assume serious proportions / 大きくなりすぎた都市 an overgrown city / 気が大きくなる take courage;《文》become emboldened / 大きくなって上着が着られなくなる outgrow one's coat / 大きく言う exaggerate / 大きく言う venture [《文》make bold] to say…; state boldly (that …); make a bold statement [declaration] / 大きく商売をする carry on a large business; do [carry on one's] business in a big way / 家計に大きく響く seriously affect one's household finances / 目を大きく見開いて with one's eyes wide open / 大きめの largish. 文例⇩

おおきさ 大きさ (a) size;《文》magnitude;〈寸法〉dimensions;〈かさ〉bulk;〈容積〉volume;〈音量〉volume; loudness;《文》amplitude ¶いろいろな大きさの石 stones of various sizes / 猫くらいの大きさの動物 a cat-sized animal / 大きさの違う靴 different-sized shoes / 大きさは幅5メートル長さ6メートルである

関係がある. That has a great [good] deal to do with this affair. / 大いに感激した. I was (greatly) impressed. / 今夜は大いに飲もうじゃないか. Let's make a night of it [《俗》go on the booze] tonight.

おおいばり これだけの成功をおさめたのだから大いばりじゃないか. Having achieved this much success, you have every right to be pleased with [proud of] yourself. / このバラなら大いばりで展示会に出品できる. This rose can be entered with perfect confidence for the exhibition.

おおいり 大入り満員.【掲示】House Full. / この芝居は大入りだった. The play drew big crowds [a large audience, a full house]. / こんな大入りは見たことがない. I never saw the house so full. / 今度の芝居は大入り請け合いだよ. I bet the new play will be a great draw.

おおう 壁はつたに覆われている. The wall is covered [overgrown] with ivy. / それは覆うべからざ

る事実だ. That is an undeniable fact. | There is no disguising the fact.

おおうつし 大写しにすると花弁の色模様がはっきりわかる. A close-up clearly shows the color pattern of the petal.

おおおとこ 大男総身に知恵が回りかね. More brawn, less brain.

おおかた 大方そんな事だろうと思った. I thought as much. / 家は大方でき上がった. The house is nearly finished.

おおかみ 男はみんな狼よ. Beware

オーキシン 〖植・化〗(an) auxin.

おおく 多く ⇨ おおい².

おおぐい 大食い 〈事〉〖文〗gluttony;〈人〉a big [heavy] eater; a glutton ¶大食いの gluttonous.

おおぐち 大口 ¶大口の注文 a big order / 大口の取引 a large transaction;《口語》a big deal / 大口をきかす with one's mouth wide open / 大口をたたく brag; boast;《口語》talk big.

おおぐまざ 大熊座〖天〗Ursa Major; the Plow;《米》the Big Dipper;《英》the Great Bear.

おおくら 大蔵 ¶大蔵大臣 the Minister of Finance; the Finance Minister;《英》the Chancellor of the Exchequer / 大蔵省 the Ministry of Finance;《英》the Exchequer.

オーケー《承諾の言葉》《口語》O.K.; all right;《承諾》《口語》an O.K.(pl. O.K.'s); an okay;(an) approval ¶オーケーする《口語》O.K. [okay](a plan); approve (a proposal) ★ O.K. の過去形は O.K.'d, 現在分詞形は O.K.'ing となるが, okayed, okaying を使うほうがよい / オーケーをもらう get an O.K.(on a proposal); get〖文〗sb's approval.

おおげさ 大袈裟 ¶大げさな exaggerated; overdone (身振り動作など);〈言葉が〉big (talk);〖文〗high-flown (speech);〖文〗hyperbolic / 大げさに exaggeratedly;〈大仕掛けに〉on a large scale / 大げさに言う exaggerate; overstate;《口語》pile it on;《口語》lay it on thick [with a trowel] / 大げさに述べる describe (an event) in exaggerated terms; give an overdrawn description (of).

オーケストラ an orchestra ¶50人編成のオーケストラ a 50-piece[-member] orchestra / オーケストラの伴奏で to an orchestral accompaniment.

おおごえ 大声 ¶大声で in [with] a loud voice; loudly / 大声で叫ぶ give a loud cry / 大声を出す raise one's voice; speak loudly; shout / 大声で指図する shout instructions.

おおごしょ 大御所 a leading [an outstanding] figure ¶文壇の大御所〖文〗the doyen of《Japanese》men of letters.

おおごと 大事 a serious [〖文〗grave] matter; an alarming incident ¶大事になる get [〖文〗become] serious; assume serious proportions. 〖文例⇩〗

おおざけ 大酒 ¶大酒を飲む drink heavily [hard];《俗》booze / 大酒飲み a heavy [hard] drinker;《俗》a boozer.

おおさじ 大さじ a tablespoon ¶大さじ1杯の砂糖 a tablespoonful [one tablespoon] of sugar ⇨ さじ¹.

おおざっぱ 大雑把 ¶大ざっぱな rough; broad; sketchy (descriptions) / 大ざっぱに in a rough-and-ready manner [way, fashion] / 大ざっぱに言って broadly [roughly] speaking; in a broad way / 大ざっぱに言って正しい be broadly true / 大ざっぱに見て at a rough estimate [guess] / 大ざっぱに見積もる estimate roughly; make a rough estimate (of).

おおさわぎ 大騒ぎ〈喧騒〉an uproar;〈混雑〉〖文〗a turmoil;〈騒動〉〖文〗a tumult; a great disturbance [commotion,《口語》fuss] ⇨ さわぎ ¶大騒ぎをする be in an uproar [a turmoil]; make a tumult; make [put up] a (great) fuss (about, over); make much ado (about).

おおしい 雄々しい〈男らしい〉manly;〈勇敢な〉brave;〖文〗heroic;《口語》gallant ¶雄々しく like a man; bravely;〖文〗heroically;〖文〗gallantly.

オージー a former (female) student 《of》;《米》an alumna (pl. -nae);《英》an old girl.

おおしお 大潮 the spring tide(s).

おおじかけ 大仕掛け ¶大仕掛けの large-scale / 大仕掛けに[で]on a large [grand] scale.

おおしごと 大仕事 a big job;〖文〗a great task. 〖文例⇩〗

おおじだい 大時代 ¶大時代な very old-fashioned; antiquated. 〖文例⇩〗

おおすじ 大筋 an outline ⇨ あらすじ, たいりゃく.

オーストラリア Australia ¶オーストラリアの Australian / オーストラリア人 an Australian.

オーストリア Austria ¶オーストリアの Austrian / オーストリア人 an Austrian / オーストリアハンガリー帝国〖史〗the Austro-Hungarian Empire.

おおずもう 大相撲〈興行〉a grand *sumo* tournament;〈熱戦〉a prolonged [long-drawn-out] bout with both wrestlers exerting their full strength.

おおせ 仰せ ¶仰せに従って〖文〗in obedience to your [his, her] wishes [instructions];〖文〗at your [his, her] instance. 〖文例⇩〗

---

of men. They're all wolves.|Men are only after one thing.

おおきい A は B よりどれほど大きいか. How much larger is A than B? / ボビーは歳の割りには大きい. Bobby is big for his age. / 大きくなったねえ.《子供に向かって》How you've grown! /《小さい子供に》You're a big boy [girl] now, aren't you! / 大きくなったら何になりたい. What do you want to be when you grow up? / もう少し大きい声でおっしゃって下さい. Please speak a little louder. | Please speak up. / 事件が大きくなりそうだ. The affair threatens to become serious. / それは大きい痛手だ. It's a terrible blow.

おおきさ すべての物は温度の変化によって大きさが変わる. Everything changes (in) size with a change in temperature. / この模型は50分の1の大きさに作られている. This model is made to a scale of 1/50. is one-fiftieth と読む /(手ぶりをしながら) このくらいの大きさの箱だったよ. It was a box about this big.

おおごと これは大事だ. This is serious!

おおしごと そいつは大仕事だ. That's quite an undertaking [a job]. / これから先が大仕事だ. We've got a lot to do yet.

おおじだい 何とまあ大時代な話だろう. What an anachronism!

おおせ 仰せのとおりです. You are quite right, sir [madam]. / 仰せに従いましょう. I'll do as you tell me. | I shall obey your orders.

おおぜい 大勢 ¶大勢の a great [large] number of; many ⇒たくさん 囲法 /大勢の家族 a large family / 大勢で in (great) numbers; in crowds. 文例⇩

おおぜき 大関 a *sumo* wrestler of the second highest rank.

-おおせる manage (to do); succeed (in doing); finish (doing) ¶逃げおおせる manage to get away; 《文》 make good *one's* escape.

おおそうじ 大掃除 (a) (spring) house cleaning; a spring-clean; spring-cleaning ¶大掃除をする do a general (house) cleaning; clean house.

オーソドックス ¶オーソドックスな orthodox.

おおぞら 大空 the sky [skies]; 《文》 the vault of heaven;《文》 the canopy of the heavens; 《文》 the firmament.

オーダーメード ¶オーダーメードの made-to-order; custom-made; custom-built; 〈服が〉(custom-)tailored; tailor-made.

おおだい 大台 文例⇩

おおだすかり 大助かり 文例⇩

おおだてもの 大立者 a leading [prominent] figure; a leader; a magnate;《俗》a bigwig ¶財界の大立者 a financial magnate; a mogul of the business world / 政界の大立者 a conspicuous figure in the political world; one of the political leaders (of the nation).

おおちがい 大違い 〈相違〉a great difference; 〈誤り〉a great mistake ¶大違いだ be very different (from); be a far cry (from); there is a great difference (a world of difference) (between). 文例⇩

おおづかみ 大掴み ⇒おおざっぱ.

おおっぴら 大っぴら ¶おおっぴらに openly; in public ⇒こうぜん¹(公然と).

おおつぶ 大粒 a large drop (of rain) ¶大粒の汗 a large bead of sweat / 大粒の涙 a large tear.

おおづめ 大詰め 《文》the denouement; 〈劇などの〉the final [last] scene [act]; 〈終わり〉the end ¶大詰めになる[近づく] come [draw] to an end [a close].

おおて 大手 major companies [firms]; big enterprises ¶私鉄大手5社 the five biggest private railway companies.

おおで 大手 ¶大手を振って in triumph; 〈罰せられずに〉《文》with impunity / 大手を広げて立ちはだかる stand in *sb's* way with *one's* arms spread out [wide].

オーディオ ¶オーディオの audio / オーディオファン an audiophile; an audio fan [enthusiast,《俗》freak].

オーディション an audition ¶オーディションを受ける have an audition; audition 《for a part》.

おおでき 大出来 a great [big] success. 文例⇩

おおどうぐ 大道具 (stage) setting; a (set) scene ¶大道具係 a sceneshifter; 〈大道具を作る人〉 a stage carpenter.

おおどおり 大通り a main [principal] street; 《英》a high street.

オートクチュール [<《フランス語》*haute couture*] a dress (ordered) from a high-class dress shop [a couturier].

オートバイ a motorcycle;《英口語》a motorbike ★ motorbike は《米》では小型のものを言う.

オードブル an hors d'oeuvre (*pl.* -(s)).

オートボルタ (the Republic of) the Upper Volta;《フランス語》*la Haute-Volta* ¶オートボルタの Voltaic.

オートミール oatmeal;〈煮た〉porridge.

オートメーション automation ¶オートメーションで (operate the equipment) by automation / 完全に [高度に] オートメーション化された工場 a fully [highly] automated factory.

オートレース 〈オートバイの〉a motorcycle race; 〈自動車の〉a motor [an auto] race ¶オートレースの選手 〈オートバイの〉 a motorcycle rider; 〈自動車の〉 a racing driver.

オーナー an owner (of a professional baseball team) ¶オーナードライバー a (private) motorist;《英》an owner-driver.

おおなた 大鉈 a large hatchet ¶大なたを振るう make a drastic cut (in the budget); slash [prune] (the personnel) severely.

オーバー¹〈外套〉an overcoat.

オーバー²〈表現などが〉オーバーな exaggerated;《文》overdrawn ¶〈予算額などを〉オーバーする go over [beyond] (the budgeted amount);《文》exceed (the limit); be more than (one million yen).

オーバースロー 〈野球〉an overhand throw [delivery, pitch].

オーバーハング〈登山〉an [a rock] overhang.

オーバーホール an overhaul ¶オーバーホールする overhaul (an engine).

おおばこ 〈植〉a plantain.

おおはば 大幅 ¶大幅な下落 a big fall (in prices) / 大幅な賃上げ a big [《文》substantial] raise in pay / 大幅な削減 a sharp cut;《文》a drastic retrenchment. 文例⇩

おおばん¹ 大判 ¶大判の large-sized.

おおばん² 大盤 〈囲碁・将棋の解説用〉a demonstration board.

おおぜい 彼は大勢の前で恥をかかされた. He was insulted in public.

-おおせる この仕事は彼にはやりおおせまい. He will not be equal to this job. | He is unlikely to be up to it.

おおだい 彼の年収は初めて1千万円の大台を越えた. His income for the year exceeded the ten million yen mark for the first time in his life. / 同紙は発行部数を300万の大台に乗せた. The circulation of the paper has hit the three million mark.

おおだすかり そうしてくれれば大助かりだ. That would be a great help to me. / 君が手伝ってくれるので大助かりだ. Your assistance takes a lot of the weight off my shoulders.

おおちがい 見ると聞くでは大違いだった. What I actually saw was something quite different from what I had heard. / そうなれば大違いだ. That makes all the difference in the world.

おおでき 大出来,大出来. Well done! | Good for you!

おおはば 彼は100メートルの自由型で自分の持つ51秒3の世界記録を大幅に上回る49秒44のタイムを出した. He was timed at

おおばんぶるまい 大盤振る舞い ¶大盤振る舞いをする give a big feast; hold [throw] a sumptuous party; wine and dine ((the visitors)) in a big way.

オービー a former student; 《米》an alumnus ((pl. -ni)); 《英》an old boy.

おおびけ 大引け《株式》the close ¶大引けの相場 the closing prices [quotations] / 大引けに at the close (of the market). 文例⇩

おおひろま 大広間 a (great) hall.

おおぶね 大船 a big boat. 文例⇩

おおぶり 大振り ¶大振りする overswing.

おおぶろしき 大風呂敷《事》bragging; boasting; 《人》a braggart ¶大風呂敷をひろげた talk big; brag; 《米口語》blow one's (own) horn; 《英口語》blow one's own trumpet.

オーブン an oven.

オープン an open. ¶オープンする ⇒ かいぎょう², かいてん² / オープンゲーム an open game / オープン戦 an exhibition game / オープンカー an open car / オープンサンド(イッチ) an open sandwich / オープンシャツ an open shirt / オープンショップ《労》an open shop.

おおべや 大部屋 a large room; 〈劇場などの〉a greenroom; an actors' common room ¶大部屋俳優 a utility actor [actress].

オーボエ an oboe. ¶オーボエ奏者 an oboist.

おおまか 大まか 〈概略の〉rough; broad; 〈おうような〉generous; free [《文》liberal] ((with one's money)); openhanded / 大まかに言えば broadly [roughly] speaking; in general terms / 大まかに見積もる make a rough estimate ((of)).

おおまじめ 大真面目 ¶大まじめな[で] in all seriousness; 《文》in real [deadly] earnest; 《文》very much in earnest.

おおまた 大股 ¶大股に歩く take [walk with] long steps [strides]; stride (out).

おおまわり 大回り ⇒ まわりみち ¶大回りをする make a big [long] detour ((by way of Kanazawa to reach Kyoto)).

オーマン Oman ¶オーマンの Omani / オーマン国 the Sultanate of Oman / オーマン人 an Omani.

おおみず 大水 ⇒ こうずい.

おおみそか 大晦日 (on) New Year's Eve.

オーム 《電》an ohm ¶オームの法則 Ohm's law / オーム計 an ohmmeter.

おおむかし 大昔 ancient times [days]; 《文》great antiquity ¶大昔の習慣《文》a custom of remote antiquity / 大昔は a long, long time ago; (many) ages ago; 《文》in the remote past / 大昔から《文》from [since] time immemorial; 《文》since very remote times; 《文》since antiquity.

おおむぎ 大麦《植物》barley; 《穀粒》a barleycorn.

おおむこう 大向こう the gallery ¶たいしゅう¹ ¶大向こうの人気をねらう play to the gallery.

おおむね 概ね ⇒ たいがい², だいたい¹.

おおむらさき 〈日本の国蝶〉a giant purple butterfly.

おおめ 大目 ¶大目に見る 〈許容する〉tolerate; let sb off (lightly); 《口語》give sb a break; condone; 〈見のがす〉overlook; pass over; let (it) pass [go]; 〈見て見ぬふりをする〉wink [《文》connive] at.

おおもじ 大文字 a capital letter; 《印刷》an uppercase letter ¶大文字で書く write ((a word)) with [in] capital letters; capitalize ((a letter)). 文例⇩

おおもて 大持て ¶大持てである be very popular ((with, among)); 《文》be greatly sought after. 文例⇩

おおもと 大本《本源》the original source ((of)); the real root ((of)); 《根本》the foundation; the basis ((pl. bases)).

おおもの 大物 someone who matters; an important figure; 《俗》a bigwig; 《俗》a big shot; 〈猟や釣りの〉big game ¶大物政治家 a big-name politician / 大物釣り big-game fishing.

おおもり 大盛り a large helping [serving] ((of noodles)).

おおや 大家 the owner [proprietor] of a rented house; a landlord; a landlady ((女)).

おおやけ 公 ¶公の public; 〈公式の〉official; 〈正式の〉formal / 公に publicly; in public; openly; officially; formally / 公にする publish; make ((the news)) public [《文》widely known]; announce ((a decision)) officially; 〈明るみに出す〉bring sth to light / 公になる be published; be made public / 〈明るみに出る〉《文》come to light. 文例⇩

おおやすうり 大安売り a special bargain sale ¶大安売りする sell sth at a greatly reduced price; sell sth dirt cheap.

おおゆき 大雪 a heavy snow [snowfall]. 文例⇩

おおよう 大様 ¶大様な big-hearted; generous; 《文》magnanimous; indulgent; forgiving / 金使いが大様である be generous [《文》liberal] with one's money / 大様に構える take a tolerant [《文》benevolent] attitude ((toward)); 《文》act magnanimously [with (a show of) magnanimity].

おおよそ 大凡 ⇒ およそ, だいたい¹.

おおよろこび 大喜び ¶大喜びで with great

49.44 in the 100 meters freestyle, well inside his own world record of 51.3.

おおびけ 大引けの相場はどんなぐあいでしたか. Tell me how the market closed.

おおぶね 私がお引受けした以上大船に乗った気持ちでいて下さい. Now that I've taken on the job, you can rest easy and leave it all to me [you can put your full trust in me and forget all about it].

おおもじ ドイツ語では名詞は最初の文字を大文字で書く. In German, nouns are spelled with a capital initial.

おおもて そのバーで彼は大もてだった. He was a big hit with the girls at that bar.

おおもの 業界では大物なのだ. He is very important in this [our] trade. / この子は(将来)大物になるぞ. This boy will make a name for himself when he grows up. / 今度の内閣は大物ぞろいだ. The new Cabinet is an array of big [famous] names. / 栃の花は大物食いだ. Tochinohana is no respecter of the official rankings.

おおやけ 彼の著述は生前には公にされなかった. His works did not see the light until after his death.

おおゆき 昨日大雪が降った. It

オーライ all right; O.K.

おおらか ¶おおらかな《文》benevolent; big-hearted;《文》magnanimous.

オール an oar ¶オール受け a rowlock;《米》an oarlock.

オールスター ¶オールスターキャスト『映画』an all-star cast / オールスターゲーム『野球』an all-star game.

オールスパイス allspice.

オールドミス an old maid; a spinster ★ old miss は和製英語.

オールバック《with one's》hair combed straight back from one's forehead.

オーレオマイシン『薬』chlortetracycline;『商標名』Aureomycin.

オーロラ an aurora (pl. -ras, -rae)〈南極の〉an aurora australis; southern lights;〈北極の〉an aurora borealis; northern lights.

おおわざ 大業 ¶〈相撲・柔道などで〉大業を掛ける make a daring attack 《on one's opponent》.

おおわらい 大笑い a loud [an uproarious] laugh; a hearty [good] laugh; a burst [roar] of laughter ¶大笑いをする have a hearty laugh 《at, over》; roar with laughter.

おおわらわ 大童 ¶試験の準備に大わらわである be very busy preparing for an examination / 大わらわになって働く work like a horse;《文》exert oneself to the utmost; make a great [furious] effort.

おか¹ 丘 a hill;〈小さい〉a hillock; a hummock.

おか² 陸 land; the shore ¶〈船が〉陸に着く make land.

おかあさん お母さん a [one's] mother;〈呼びかけの語〉Mother (ややあらたまった言い方);〈小児語〉Mam(m)a;〈米口語〉Mom;〈米口語〉Momma;〈英口語〉Mum;〈英口語〉Mummy (主に女性・子供が使う).

おかえし お返し a return gift ¶お返しに《give sth》in return《for a present received》. 文例☟

おかえり お帰り 文例☟

おかかえ お抱え ¶お抱えの運転手 a chauffeur in one's employ / お抱えの弁護士 a lawyer on a retainer; a retained lawyer / お抱え新聞 a kept newspaper《of the Liberal Democratic Party》.

おかくず おが屑 sawdust.

おかげ お陰 ¶お陰をこうむる〈恩恵をうけている〉owe《sth to sb》; be in sb's debt《for》;《文》be indebted《to sb for sth》;〈利益を得る〉profit [《文》benefit]《by sth》/ …のお陰で thanks to …;〈原因・理由で〉owing to …; because of …; due to …;〈世話で〉through sb's good offices ★ thanks to は本来、よい事について言う表現だが、最近は悪いことについて言う方がむしろ多くなっている. 文例☟

おかしい〈面白い〉amusing; funny;〈おどけた〉comic(al);《文》droll;〈ばかばかしい〉ridiculous; ludicrous; laughable;〈奇妙な〉strange; queer; odd;〈怪しい〉suspicious ¶頭がおかしい be queer in the head; be crazy / おかしい事には《文》strange to say; oddly [curiously] enough / おかしさをこらえる resist an impulse to laugh; suppress one's laughter; keep a straight face. 文例☟

おかしがる〈面白がる〉be amused《by, at》;《口語》be tickled《at, by》;〈不思議がる〉wonder《at》.

おかしらつき 尾頭付き a fish served whole 《complete with head and tail》.

おかす¹ 犯[侵]す〈罪を〉commit;《文》perpetrate;〈規則などを〉break; offend《against》;《文》violate;〈侵害する〉trespass on;《文》infringe (on);〈婦女を〉rape;《文》violate;〈侵入する〉invade; raid; make a raid on ¶罪を犯す〈法律上の〉commit [perpetrate] a crime; be guilty of《murder》;〈道徳上の〉commit a sin; sin《against》/ 権利を侵す infringe on sb's rights / 版権を侵す infringe a copyright / 侵すべからざる《文》inviolable《rights》/ 犯し難い《文》dignified《old gentlemen》.

おかす² 冒す〈危険を冒す run a risk; risk [《文》brave] (a) danger / 生命の危険を冒して at the risk of one's life / 風雨を冒して in spite of the wind and rain / 病に冒される be affected [attacked] by a disease. 文例☟

おかず a (side) dish. 文例☟

おかっぱあたま おかっぱ頭 ¶おかっぱ頭の少女 a girl with bobbed hair.

おかどちがい お門違い ¶お門違いをする go

---

snowed heavily [hard] yesterday. / 近年珍しい大雪だ. It is the heaviest snowfall we have had in [for] years. ★ in は《米》, for は《英》.

おかえし お返しに何を上げたらいいだろうか. What shall we give in return for his present? / 20円のお返しになります. Here is your 20 yen change.

おかえり お帰りなさい.〈あらたまった場合〉Welcome home! |〈勤やめ学校から帰った者に〉Hullo, dear.

おかげ この仕事がうまくいったのは全くのお陰です. We owe our success in this work entirely to you. / お陰様でみんな元気です. We're all fine, thank you. / お陰様で水害を免れました. Fortunately we were not affected by the flood. / 本県の農業事情が改善されたのは田宮氏のお陰である. It is (entirely) thanks to Mr. Tamiya that the state of agriculture in this prefecture has improved. | Mr. Tamiya was instrumental in improving agricultural conditions in this prefecture. / この事故のお陰で私たちが乗った列車は3時間も遅れてしまった. The accident was responsible for our train being three hours late. | Thanks to the accident, our train ran three hours behind schedule. / あの男のお陰で不愉快な思いをした. I had a thin time thanks to that fellow.

おかしい 何がおかしい. What's (so) funny? / おかしくてたまらなかった. It was so funny that I could not help laughing. / おかしな人. You are a strange man! / 彼がそんなに怒っているとはおかしい. It is strange that he should be so angry. / おかしなことに彼はその事については何も言わない. The odd thing is that he says nothing about it. / 日本で言うビアガーデンというもののおかしなところは, それが庭でも何でもないことです. The

おかぶ お株　¶お株を奪われる be beaten at *one's* own game；〈文〉be outdone 《by *sb*》in *one's* own forte.

おかぼ 陸稲　rice [a rice plant] grown in a dry field.

おかまい お構い　¶お構いなしに regardless of《expense》；〈文〉without regard to《time and place》；ignoring [disregarding]《the wishes of other people》. 文例⇩

おかみ 〈宿屋の〉the landlady；〈料亭の〉the hostess；the proprietress (経営者).

おがみたおす 拝み倒す　win *sb* over by pleading with *him*《文》by *one's* entreaties.

おがむ 拝む　〈礼拝する〉worship；bow (to)；〈祈願する〉pray (to)；〈拝見する〉see；look at　¶手を合わせて拝む join *one's* hands in prayer.

おかめ 〈お多福〉a woman with a round face, plump cheeks, and a flat nose；〈醜い女〉a plain [an ugly,〈米〉a homely] woman.

おかめはちもく 岡目八目　文例⇩

おから tofu [bean-curd] refuse；the edible meal-like residue left after the production of *tofu* [bean curd].

オカリナ an ocarina.

おがわ 小川　a (small) stream；a brook；a brooklet；a rivulet.

おかわり お代わり　another [a second] helping；a refill；〈飲み物の〉another cup (of coffee)　¶お代わりをくださいと言う ask for another helping / お代わりをくださいと言って茶碗を出す hold out *one's* bowl for a refill.

おかん 悪寒　¶悪寒がする feel [tremble with] a chill；have a shivering fit.

おかんむり お冠　¶お冠である be cross [《文》displeased]《with *sb*, about *sth*》；be in a bad temper [mood] / ひどくお冠である be as cross as two sticks [as a bear with a sore head] / お冠を曲げられる be offended《by》；take offense《at》；take *sth* amiss.

おき¹ 沖　¶沖に[で] in the offing；offshore；out at sea / 3キロ沖で three kilometers offshore [off the shore] / 銚子沖で off (the coast of) Choshi / 沖へこぎ出す pull out to sea / 沖釣り offshore fishing.

おき² 燠　embers；live charcoal [coals].

-おき …置き　¶1日置きに every other [second] day / 4時間置きに every four hours；at intervals of four hours；at four-hour intervals / 1行置きに on every other line；on alternate lines / 2メートル置きにくいを立て plant stakes two meters apart [at intervals of two meters]. 文例⇩

おきあがりこぼし 起き上がり小法師　a daruma doll made so as to right itself when knocked over.

おきあがる 起き上がる　get up；〈文〉rise；〈床(とこ)の上に〉sit up in 《one's》bed；〈転んで〉pick *oneself* up　¶やっと起き上がる scramble to *one's* feet.

おきあみ 【動】a krill (単複同形).

おきかえる 置き換える　〈取り換える〉replace 《A with B》；〈場所を移す〉move [shift]《*sth* from…to…》；change the position (of)；〈並べ換える〉rearrange.

おきがさ 置き傘　a spare umbrella kept at *one's* place of work.

おきご 置き碁　a game of *go* played with a handicap.

おきざり 置き去り　¶置き去りにする leave *sb* behind (one)；desert *sb*《島などに》置き去りにされる be marooned (on an island). 文例⇩

オキシダント 【化】an oxidant.

オキシフル (hydrogen) peroxide.

おきだす 起き出す　get out of bed；《文》leave *one's* bed.

おきちがえる 置き違える　put *sth* in the wrong place；misplace.

おきっぱなし 置きっ放し　¶置きっぱなしにする leave *sth* where *it* is (and do nothing about *it*) / 鍵を机の上に置きっぱなしにして外出する go out leaving *one's* keys (lying) on *one's* desk.

おきて 掟　〈規定〉a rule；〈法律〉a law；〈規則〉a regulation.

おきてがみ 置き手紙　¶置き手紙をする leave a letter [note]《for *sb*》.

おきどけい 置き時計　a clock (to stand on a table, etc.).

おきどころ 置き所　⇨おきば(しょ)　¶身の置き所

---

funny thing about the Japanese 'beer gardens' is that they are not gardens at all. / おかしいなあ、もうとっくに来る時分だのに。Why is he so long (in) coming, I wonder? / 私の口から言うのもおかしいですが、うちの息子はとてもいい子ですよ。My son is a very good boy, though I say it myself.

おかす² 彼は肺を冒している。His lungs are affected. | He has lung trouble.

おかず 今晩のおかずは? What's [What are we having] for dinner tonight?

おかどちがい 僕を責めるのはお門違いだ。You are laying the blame at the wrong door. | You're barking up the wrong tree if you think I'rロ to blame. / 100万円貸せだって、お門違いだよ。Will I lend you one million yen? You are talking to the wrong man!

おかまい どうぞお構いなく。Please don't put yourself to any trouble for my sake. / せっかくお出で下さいましたのに何のお構いも致しませんで。Thank you for coming. I hope you've enjoyed your visit. / あの男は人の迷惑などいっこうお構いなしだ。He never thinks about the trouble he is causing (to) other people. / 僕はそんなことはお構いなしだ。I don't give a damn for things like that. | That's none of my business.

おかめはちもく 岡目八目。Onlookers can read the game (far) better than the players themselves.

-おき 電車は5分置きに走っています。The trains run every five minutes [at five-minute intervals].

おきざり 君がもう5分遅かったら、私たちは君を置き去りにして出発するところだった。If you had been five minutes later, we would have left without you.

おきだす 僕が家を出たときはまだ

おぎない に苦しむ do not know where to put *oneself*.

おぎない 補い 〈補充〉 a supplement;《文》 a complement;〈補償〉《文》 reparation; (a) compensation.

おぎなう 補う 〈欠乏を〉 make up (for);〈欠員を〉 fill up 《a vacancy》;〈埋め合わせる〉 compensate for; make good;〈補足する〉 supplement (*one's* income by doing a side job) ¶ 欠損を補う make good [make up] the loss; make up [《文》 supply] the deficit. 文例⇩

おきなおる 起き直る sit up (in bed).

おきなかし 沖仲仕 a stevedore;《米》 a longshoreman;《英》 a docker.

おきにいり お気に入り ¶ お気に入りの favorite; pet; darling. 文例⇩

おきぬけ 起き抜け ¶ 起き抜けに as soon as *one* gets up; (the) first thing in the morning.

おきば(しょ) 置き場(所) a place (for);〈小屋〉 a shed ¶〈物がふえすぎて〉 置き場がなくなる run out of storage space /〈駅前などの〉 自転車置き場 a parking place for bicycles. 文例⇩

おきまり お決まり ¶ お決まりの usual;《文》 customary; *one's* inevitable (red hat);《文》 the same old (excuse, menu);《口語》 conventional;《文》 stereotyped; stock;〈十八番の〉 *one's* favorite (parlor trick). 'ent.

おきみやげ 置き土産 a parting [good-by] present.

おきもの 置き物 an ornament (for) ¶ 床の間の置き物を an ornament for [in] the *tokonoma*;〈比喩的に〉 a (mere) figurehead. 文例⇩

おぎゃあ ¶ おぎゃあと泣く cry;《文》 mewl (弱々しく) / おぎゃあと生まれる be born [arrive in the world] with a cry / おぎゃあと生まれた時からずっと ever since *one's* first cry as an infant.

おきる 起きる 〈起床する〉 get up; get out of bed;《文》 rise;〈目を覚ます〉 wake up;《文》 awake;〈転んで〉 pick *oneself* up;〈事件が〉 happen; take place;《文》 occur; break out;〈火が〉 be kindled; be made ¶ 目ざまし時計で起きる be woken [awakened] by the alarm clock / 病気がよくなって起きられるようになる get well enough to leave *one's* bed [to get on *one's* feet] / 寝ないで起きている〈眠らずにいる〉 lie awake;〈起きている〉 sit [stay] up. 文例⇩

おきわすれる 置き忘れる leave *sth* (behind); put *sth* in 《a place》 and forget where (*it* is); mislay. 文例⇩

おく¹ 奥 the inner part; the inside;《文》 the interior; the heart; the depths (森などの) ¶ 奥の部屋 a back [rear] room; an inner [inside] room / 奥へ通す show *sb* into a room / 森の奥深くに deep in the forest / 森の奥深く分け入る go deep into a forest. 文例⇩

おく² 億 one [a] hundred million ¶ 10億(米) a billion;《英》 a thousand million / 数億年 several hundred millions of years.

用法 数詞の用法に英米間にこのような相違があるのは不便なので a billion は近頃イギリスでも 10億の意味で(特に科学記事, 経済記事で)段々使われるようになり, たとえば In this book, a billion is taken to equal a thousand million. というような断わり書きのある本さえもこのごろは見受けられるようになっている. この傾向は今後一層強まり, 米国式の用法が一般化することが予想される. a trillion (1兆) の用法についても同じことが言える.

おく³ 置く put (down);《文》 place; lay (横に); set (すえる);〈残しておく〉 leave;〈放任する〉 let; leave;〈設ける〉 establish; set up;〈貯蔵する〉 hold; keep;〈配置する〉 post 《a sentry》; station 《a garrison》;〈別にする〉 set apart;〈かえる〉《文》 engage; keep ¶ 事務所を置く have (*its*, *one's*) office (in the building) / トロントに工場を置く site [《文》 locate] a plant in Toronto / 下宿人を置く take in boarders; have lodgers in *one's* house /〈数学で〉 x=3 と置く put x=3 / 置いて来る[行く] leave *sth* behind (*one*); leave *sth* for [with] *sb* / そのままにしておく leave *sth* as *it* is; let *sth* alone [be] / 1日置いて次の日 the day after next / …をおいて except (for)…; apart from…; but…. 文例⇩

おくがい 屋外 ¶ 屋外の outdoor; open-air; outside / 屋外での in the open (air); outdoors; out of doors / 屋外に置かれるように作られた彫刻 a sculpture intended for an outdoor setting / 屋外スポーツ outdoor sports.

おくぎ 奥義 (be initiated into) the secrets [mysteries] (of).

おくざしき 奥座敷 ⇒ おく¹ (奥の部屋). 文例⇩

おくさま 奥様 〈呼びかけ〉 madam; Mrs. 《Robinson》;〈召し使いなどの言葉〉 ma'am.

だれも起き出していなかった. No one was stirring when I left home.

おぎなう 彼の勤勉さはその才能の不足を補って余りあるものだった. His capacity for hard work more than made up for his lack of talent.

おきにいり 彼は先生のお気に入りだ. He's the teacher's favorite [pet].

おきば(しょ) もっと大きいステレオが欲しいことは欲しいんだけれど, 僕の部屋は狭くて置き場所がない. I would certainly like a bigger stereo system, but there is no place to put it in my small room.

おきもの 社長といっても彼は床の間の置き物同然なんだ. He is president only in name.

おきる 父はさりげない調子で, 明日は早く起きてもらいたいと言った. My father told me casually that he wanted me up early the next day. / 起きて待っているこ とはないさ. 帰りは遅くなると思うから. Don't wait up (for me). I'll probably be late back. / こんなに遅くまで起きて何をしているのですか. What are you doing up so late? / もう1週間もすれば起きて歩けるようになるでしょう. She will be up and about in a week. / 起きている間は, たいていこの仕事をしています. I spend most of my waking hours on [doing] this work.

おきわすれる 会社の机の上にライターを置き忘れて来た. I left my lighter on my office desk.

おく¹ 庭の奥に木造の小屋があった. There was a wooden shed at the bottom of the garden. / 心の奥には彼女と離婚したいという気持ちがあった. In the back of his mind was the thought of divorcing her.

おく³ その機械を買う金はあるが, 置く場所がない. We have enough money to buy the machine with,

おくじょう 屋上 the housetop; the roof ¶屋上庭園 a roof garden. 文例↓

おくする 臆する fear; flinch [《文》shrink] 《from》(★主に否定文で使う); feel [be] afraid [shy] 《of》;《文》quail《at》/ 臆せずに without flinching;《文》dauntlessly;《文》undaunted.

おくせつ 臆説《文》an opinion [a theory] based on conjecture. 文例↓

おくそく 憶測 a guess;《文》a conjecture;《文》a surmise;《文》a supposition; speculation ¶憶測する guess;《文》surmise;《文》conjecture; make a guess [conjecture]; speculate 《about, on》/ あえて憶測を試みる hazard a guess / 多分に憶測の域を出ない be little better than guesswork [a guess];《文》be largely conjectural. 文例↓

おくそこ 奥底 ¶奥底の知れない人物《文》a person of very profound character; an inscrutable person;《口語》a deep one / 心の奥底では at the bottom of one's heart; in one's heart of hearts; in [at] the back of one's mind.

オクターブ《音楽》an octave ¶1オクターブ上げる[下げる] raise [drop]《the tune》an octave.

オクタンか オクタン価 an octane number [value, rating] ¶オクタン価の高い high-octane《gasoline》;《gasoline》with a high octane rating.

おくち 奥地 the interior; the back regions ¶奥地の upcountry《farms》/ 奥地へ《go》upcountry;《head》for [toward, into] the interior / 奥地で《live》upcountry / アマゾン流域の奥地で in the innermost depths of the Amazonian region.

おくづけ 奥付 〈書物の〉a colophon; an [a publisher's] imprint.

おくて¹ 奥手 ¶奥手の〈性的に〉slow in sexual development / 奥手である be slow to mature

おくて² 晩稲 late rice.   [[in maturing].

おくない 屋内 ¶屋内の indoor / 屋内に置く観賞用植物 a house plant / 屋内で indoors;《文》within doors / 屋内運動場 a gymnasium《pl. -siums, -sia》;《口語》a gym / 屋内スポーツ indoor sports.

おくに お国 ⇒くに ¶お国言葉[なまり] a dialect;《文》a provincialism; a local accent / お国自慢をする boast about one's country [birthplace]. 文例↓

おくのいん 奥の院 the inner shrine; the (inner) sanctuary; the innermost sanctum; the holy of holies.

おくのて 奥の手 ¶《まだ出さない》奥の手がある have a card up one's sleeve / 奥の手を出す play one's trump (card).

おくば 奥歯 a back tooth; a molar ¶奥歯に物のはさまったような言い方をする talk as if one were hiding [《文》concealing] something; be not quite frank《with sb》.

おくび 噯気;《医》eructation ¶おくびを出す[漏らす] belch / おくびにも出さない do not breathe a word《of》; keep mum《about》;《口語》keep it under one's hat.

おくびょう 臆病 cowardice; timidity ¶臆病な cowardly; timid;《口語》chicken;《文》chicken-hearted[-livered]; lily-livered;《文》faint-hearted / 臆病風に吹かれる lose one's nerve;《口語》be in a funk;《俗》go [turn] chicken / 臆病者 a coward; a craven;《俗》a chicken.

おくぶかい 奥深い deep;〈深遠な〉《文》profound;《文》abstruse;《文》recondite.

おくまった 奥まった secluded;《文》sequestered;《文》inmost.

おくまんちょうじゃ 億万長者 a billionaire; a multimillionaire.

おくみ 衽 a gusset; a gore.

おくめん 臆面 ¶臆面もなく impudently; brazenly; shamelessly;《文》unashamedly;《文》audaciously / 臆面もなく…する have the cheek [face, nerve, impudence] to do.

おくゆかしい 奥床しい〈慎み深い〉reserved; restrained; modest;〈洗練された〉refined;〈上品な〉《文》graceful;〈優雅な〉elegant;〈紳士的な〉《文》gentlemanlike.

おくゆき 奥行き depth ¶奥行きのある deep. 文例↓

おくら 御蔵 ¶御蔵にする do not make sth public;《文》keep sth from seeing the light; shelve《sth》;《米》table《a bill》.

オクラ《植》(an) okra;《米》(a) gumbo《pl. -s》.

おくらせる 遅[後]らせる delay; put off;《文》retard ¶時計を1時間遅らせる put [set, turn] a clock back one hour.

---

but no space to house it. ⇒おきば(しょ) / 《商店で》この商品なら置いておいて損はしないと思う。 I believe these goods will earn their keep. / このお茶は薄すぎるから少し出るまで置いておきなさい。 This tea is too weak; let it stand for a while. / 言わずにおく方がよかろう。 It is better left unsaid. / お前を遊ばせておくことはできません。 I cannot afford to have you idle. / 彼をおいてはそれをなし得る者はない。 Apart from him, there's no one who can do it. | No one but him [《文》he] can do it.

おくざしき 熱海は東京の奥座敷といった所で，東京の商社が接待の宴会に利用することが多い。 Atami is an annex, as it were, to Tokyo, and Tokyo business firms often give parties there to entertain their customers.

おくじょう 屋上屋を架するようなものだ。 That's like putting a fifth wheel on a coach.

おくせつ 言語の起源に関しては幾つかの憶説がある。 Several theories have been postulated about the origin of speech.

おくそく 彼が閣内にとどまるか否かについてさまざまな憶測が行なわれた。 There was considerable conjecture [Speculation was rife] as to whether he would stay in the cabinet or not. / 現段階ではどのようにでも憶測できる。 At this stage, one guess is as good as another.

おくに お国はどちらですか。 Where [What country] do you come from? / お国では皆さまお変わりもありませんか。 Is everybody at home well? / 皆が盛んにお国自慢をやった。 They vied with each other in singing the praises of their home countries.

おくび (このことは)おくびにも出すなよ。 Mum's the word! | Keep it under your hat.

おくゆき 家は間口7間奥行き12

オクラホマ Oklahoma (略: Okla.) ¶オクラホマ州の人 an Oklahoman.

おくりおおかみ 送り狼 a man who pretends to escort a woman home and molests her.

おくりかえす 送り返す send back; return.

おくりがな 送り仮名 *kana* added after a Chinese character to show its Japanese inflection.

おくりこむ 送り込む send 《troops》 into 《a battlefield》; 〈付き添って〉see [《文》escort] *sb* to 《a place》¶金星に探測機を送り込む send a probe to Venus.

おくりさき 送り先 the destination; the address; a consignee (荷受け人).

おくりじょう 送り状 an invoice ¶送り状を作る make out an invoice; invoice 《a shipment of goods》.

おくりだし 送り出し 【相撲】 pushing (*one's* opponent) out of the ring from behind.

おくりだす 送り出す 〈物を〉send out; forward; 〈見送る〉show [see, bow (丁重に)] *sb* out; see *sb* to the door ¶子供を学校へ送り出す send a child off to school.

おくりとどける 送り届ける ⇒ **おくる**[1].

おくりにん 送り人 a sender; a consignor (荷の); a remitter (金の).

おくりむかえ 送り迎え ¶社長を車で送り迎えする take the president to the office and back home by car / 幼稚園へ行く子供の送り迎えをする take a child to and from the kindergarten.

おくりもの 贈り物 a gift ¶贈り物をする give [send] *sb sth* as a present [gift]; make *sb* a present of *sth*; present *sth* to *sb* [*sb* with *sth*] / 贈り物にかけるリボン a gift-wrapping ribbon.

おくる[1] 送る send; 〈品物を〉forward; dispatch (船や貨車で); 〈派遣する〉dispatch; 〈見送る〉see [send] off; 〈送金する〉remit; 〈送り届ける〉see [take, 《文》escort] *sb* to 《a place》に; 〈及〉pass; speed, 《口語》put in ¶玄関まで送る see [《文》accompany] *sb* to the door / (人を)家まで送る see *sb* home; 〈歩いて〉walk *sb* home; 〈車で〉drive *sb* [give *sb* a ride] home; take *sb* home in *one's* car / 悲惨な生活を送る lead [live] a wretched life / 旧年を送り新年を迎える see the old year out and the new year in. 文例⇩

おくる[2] 贈る 〈贈呈する〉give [send] *sb sth* as a present [gift]; make *sb* a present of *sth*; present *sth* to *sb* [*sb* with *sth*]; 〈授与する〉confer [《文》bestow] 《a doctor's degree》 on *sb*; grant 《a pension to *sb*》; award 《a prize to *sb*》.

おくれ 遅[後]れ a (time) lag; (a) delay ¶後れを取る 〈負ける〉be beaten; 《文》be defeated; 〈及ばない〉get [fall, lag] behind 《*sb*, in *sth*》; be outstripped [outdistanced] 《by》/ だれにも後れを取らない be second to none; give 《yield》first place to no one / 後れを取らないようにする keep up 《with》; keep [stay] abreast 《of》/ 遅れを取り戻す catch up 《with *sb*, on [with] *one's* work》.

おくれげ 後れ毛 loose [stray] hair [《文》locks].

おくればせ 後れ馳せ ¶後ればせの《文》belated / 後ればせに 《文》belatedly / 後ればせながら though a little (too) late; 《文》though belated.

おくれる 遅[後]れる be late 《for》; be behind time [schedule]; be delayed; 〈期限に〉be overdue / 〈流行・時勢に〉get [fall, lag] behind 《the times》; 〈学問・仕事など〉be behind 《in》; 〈知能・学力が〉be backward; 〈人後に落ちる〉be outstripped [outdistanced] 《by》; 《文》yield to *sb*; 〈時計が〉lose; go [be] slow ¶電車に遅れる miss [be late for] a train / 学校に遅れる be late for school / (時計が)1 日に 10 分遅れる lose ten minutes a day / 時勢に遅れないようにする keep abreast of [up with] the times / 文化の遅れた部族 a culturally retarded tribe.

おけ 桶 〈洗濯用などの〉a tub; 〈手おけ〉a pail; a (wooden) bucket ¶おけ 1 杯の水 a pail [pailful] of water / おけ屋 a cooper.

おこえがかり お声掛かり ¶…のお声がかりで《文》at the instance of…; on the recommendation of….

おこがましい 〈なまいきな〉impudent; cheeky; 《文》presumptuous; 〈片腹痛い〉laughable; ridiculous ¶おこがましくも…する take the liberty of *do*ing; have the cheek [be impudent enough] to *do*.

おこげ お焦げ burnt [scorched] rice.

おこさまランチ お子様ランチ a lunch for children.

おこす 起こ[興]す 〈倒れたものを〉raise; set up; pick 《a child》up; 〈目をさまさす〉wake (up); 《文》awake; 《文》awaken; arouse; 〈設立する〉set up; establish; start; found; 〈開始する〉open; begin; start; launch; 〈企てる〉

間だ. The house has a frontage of 7 *ken* and a depth of 12 *ken*. / 彼の学問は間口は広いが奥行きがない. His knowledge is wide but shallow.

おくる[1] 様々な番組が NHK から世界各地に向けて送られている. A large variety of programs are [is] being sent [beamed] out from the NHK to all parts of the world.

おくれ 今朝の新幹線は軒並み最高 2 時間の遅れが出たということだ. Delays of up to two hours were reported on all *Shinkansen* trains this morning. / 今月は仕事の遅れを取り戻すために頑張らなくてはならない. This month I must work hard to catch up on my work.

おくれる 電車は 20 分遅れた. The train was twenty minutes behind time [schedule]. / 彼は僕より遅れて来た. He came later than me. ⇒ **より**[1] 囲囲 / 僕は仕事がひどく遅れている. I am behind with [in] my work. / 1 か月間病気で休んだから, 遅れた所を取り返すために勉強しなければならなかった. I stayed away from school for a month because of illness, so I had to work hard to make up for (the) lost time. / 僕の時計は 5 分遅れている. My watch is five minutes slow.

おこす 明日朝 7 時に起こして下さい. Please call me at seven tomorrow morning. / 子供たちを夜遅くまで起こしておかない方がいい. You ought not to keep the children up late at night.

おこなわれる この規則は今でも行

promote ; organize ; 〈ひき起こす〉《文》give rise to ; lead to ; cause ; trigger off ; 〈発生させる〉produce ; 《文》generate; 〈土などを〉plow; break ; 《文》till 《the ground》 ¶ 転んだ人を起こす set *sb* on *his* legs ; 〈助け起こす〉help *sb* up [to *his* feet] / 貧困から身を起こす rise from poverty / 摩擦によって熱を起こす produce heat by friction / 興味を起こす begin to take an interest 《in》 / 好奇心を起こさせる arouse [《文》excite] *sb's* curiosity / 脳貧血を起こす have an attack of cerebral anemia. [文例⇩]

おこぜ 〘魚〙 a scorpion fish ; a stingfish ; a stonefish.

おごそか 厳か ¶ 厳かな solemn ; stern ; 《文》grave ; 《文》austere ; 《文》majestic ; 《文》awe-inspiring / 厳かに solemnly ; 《文》with solemnity ; 《文》gravely.

おこたる 怠る 〈閑却する〉neglect ; 《文》be negligent [neglectful] 《of》; fail to attend 《to》; 〈なまける〉be idle ; be lazy ¶ 義務を怠る neglect *one's* duties / 手紙の返事を怠る 〈1回〉fail to answer a letter; leave a letter unanswered ; 〈常習的に〉be bad at [《文》be remiss in] answering letters / 怠りがちである be apt to neglect 《*one's* duties》 / 怠りなく 〈勤勉に〉《文》diligently ; 〈忠実に〉faithfully.

おこない 行ない 〈行為〉an act; an action; 《文》a deed ; 〈品行〉behavior ; 《文》conduct ¶ 行ないのいい well-behaved ; 《文》well-conducted / 行ないの悪い人 a badly-behaved person; 《文》a person of bad behavior [conduct] ; 《口語》a bad character / 行ないを改める reform ; 《口語》mend *one's* ways ; 《口語》turn over a new leaf ; 《文》reform *one's* conduct.

おこなう 行なう 〈する〉do ; 〈実行する〉《文》practice ; put *sth* into practice ; carry out ; 〈果たす〉perform ; 〈挙行する〉hold ; give ¶ 試験を行なう give an examination / 式を行なう perform [hold] a ceremony / 考えたことを実際に行なう put an idea into practice.

おこなわれる 行なわれる 〈実行される〉be done ; be put into practice ; be carried out ; 〈実施される〉come into [be put in] force ; take effect ; 《文》become effective ; 〈挙行される〉take place ; be held ; come off. [文例⇩]

おこのみ お好み ⇨ **このみ**[2] ¶ お好み食堂 a variety restaurant ; a specialty-restaurant arcade (食堂街).

おこのみやき お好み焼き a thin, flat cake of unsweetened batter fried with various ingredients.

おこぼれ お零れ ¶ おこぼれにあずかる get [have] (only) a tiny share of 《the profits》.

おこらせる 怒らせる make *sb* angry [《口語》mad] ; offend [《文》give offense to] *sb* ; 《文》anger ; provoke ; get *sb's* hackles up ; make *sb's* hackles rise.

おこり 起こり 〈起原〉the origin ; the source ; the beginning ; 〈原因〉the cause. [文例⇩]

おごり 奢り 〈ぜいたく〉luxury; extravagance; 〈馳走〉a treat ¶ おごりにふける live extravagantly ; go in for [《文》indulge in] luxury [luxurious living] ; 《口語》live the life of Riley. [文例⇩]

おこりだす 怒り出す fly [get] into a rage [passion] ; flare up ⇨ **おこる**[1].

おこりっぽい 怒りっぽい quick to take offense ; quick-[short-, hot-]tempered ; 《口語》touchy ; 《文》irascible.

おこる[1] 怒る 〈腹を立てる〉get angry 《with *sb*, at [about] *sth*》; be offended 《at》; take offense; lose *one's* temper ; 《口語》get mad 《with *sb*, at *sb* [*sth*]》; 《口語》blow *one's* top ; 〈叱る〉⇨ **しかる** ¶ 真赤になって[火のように]怒る be red [flushed] with anger / 怒って angrily ; 《文》in anger ; 《口語》in a huff ; 〈ひどく〉in a (fit of) rage / 怒っている be angry ; be in a bad temper ; 《口語》be mad. [文例⇩]

おこる[2] 起こ[興]る 〈事件などが〉happen; take place ; turn up (思いがけぬ事が) ; 《文》occur ; 〈戦争・火事などが〉break out ; 〈生じる〉《文》come into existence [being] ; spring up ; 〈栄える〉rise 《to greatness》; 《文》prosper ; 〈起因する〉result 《from》; 《文》arise [stem] 《from》; 《文》originate 《in》; 〈病気が〉have an attack [a fit] of 《asthma》 ¶ どんな事が起こっても no matter what happens ; whatever happens [may happen]. [文例⇩]

おごる[1] 奢る 〈ぜいたくする〉live in luxury ; be extravagant ; 〈ごちそうする〉give *sb sth* as a treat ; treat *sb* to *sth* ; stand [buy] *sb* 《a dinner》; 《口語》set *sb* up to 《a beer》 ¶ 口がおごっている be very finicky [particular, fussy, fastidious] about *one's* food / ビフテキをおごる 〈自分で〉treat *oneself* to [《口語》splurge on] a steak ; 〈人に〉treat *sb* to a steak. [文例⇩]

おごる[2] 驕る be arrogant ; 《文》be haughty ; 《口語》be a bighead ; 《口語》have a big head ;

なわれている. This rule is still in force. / この地方ではいろいろの古い習慣が今も行なわれている. A number of ancient customs still exist [are still maintained] in this part of the country. / 激しい戦闘が行なわれている. Bitter fighting is going on.

おこり 事の起こりはこうだ. This is how it started.

おごり もう1杯やりたまえ. これは僕のおごりだ. Have another drink. This one is on me.

おこる[1] そんなつまらないことで怒るなよ. Don't let such a trifling thing put you out. / 昨夜のことで彼女はまだ怒っているかしら. I wonder if she is still sore at me about what happened last night.

おこる[2] 次の週にどんな事が起こるかだれにもわからなかった. No one knew what was in store the following week. / その戦争はどうして起こったのですか. What caused [was the cause of] the war? / 最近の汚職事件は起こるべくして起きたものだ. The recent scandal occurred, just as it was bound to. / さらにまた不穏な事件が起ころうとしていた. Another disturbing incident was in the making. / 君の胃の病気は飲み過ぎから起こるのだ. Your stomach trouble comes from drinking too much.

おごる[1] これは僕がおごるよ. This is on me. / 僕に昼飯をおごらせてくれたまえ. Let me buy your lunch for you. / 僕がおごるからもう1杯やれよ. Have another drink on me.

《米口語》have a swelled head; 《英口語》have a swollen head ¶勝って驕らない be modest about *one's* victory. 文例⇩

おさえ 押[抑]え 〈重し〉a weight; 〈圧力〉(a) pressure; 〈防止〉(a) check; 〈にらみ〉control ¶抑えがきかなくなる lose control of; 〈対象が主語〉get out of control [hand].

おさえこみ 押え込み 《柔道》immobilization (on the mat); a mat hold.

おさえこむ 押え込む hold [pin] down 《*one's* opponent》 (on the mat).

おさえつける 押え付ける 〈押しふせる〉press [hold, pin] down; 〈抑圧する〉put down; suppress; check; bring *sb* under control; 《口語》get [have] *sb* under *one's* thumb; 《口語》clamp down on 《the rioters》.

おさえる 押[抑]える 〈押えつける〉press [hold] down; 〈制止する〉stop; check; hold *sb* in check; 《文》curb; restrain 《keep》 《*sb* from doing》; 〈調子を〉lower; tone down; 〈捕える〉catch; arrest; 〈差し押える〉⇒さしおさえる ¶怒りを抑える hold back [keep down, suppress, repress] *one's* anger; control *one's* temper / 自分(の気持ち)を抑える restrain [check, contain] *oneself*; hold [rein] *oneself* in; take a grip on *oneself* / 費用を10万円以下に抑える keep the expenses below [from exceeding] 100,000 yen / 物価の上昇を5%以下に抑える prevent prices from rising more than five per cent / ヒット3本に抑える limit [hold] 《the opposing team》 to three hits / 抑え難い uncontrollable; 《文》irrepressible; 《文》irresistible. 文例⇩

おさおさ ¶警戒おさおさ怠りない keep a sharp lookout 《for an attack from the enemy》; guard 《the President's person》 closely 《文》jealously / 用意おさおさ怠りない be fully prepared 《for》; make every 《possible》 preparation 《for》.

おさがり お下がり 〈衣服〉clothes handed down 《from *one's* sister》; 《口語》a hand-me-down 《from》; 《英口語》a reach-me-down 《from》.

おさき お先 文例⇩

おさきぼう お先棒 ¶お先棒をかつぐ《文》act as *sb's* instrument 〔willing tool〕.

おさげ お下げ ¶髪をお下げにしている wear *one's* hair in plaits [《米》braids] / お下げ髪の少女 a girl with a plait [two plaits] (of hair) hanging down her back. 文例⇩

おさと お里 〈実家〉*one's* parents' home; 〈素性〉*one's* origin(s) ¶お里が知れる 〈人が主語〉give *oneself* away; betray *oneself* [*one's* character] 《by *one's* behavior》; 〈事柄が主語〉give *one* away.

おさない 幼い 〈幼少の〉very young; 《文》infant; 〈子供らしい〉《文》childlike; 〈幼稚な〉childish; infantile ¶幼い考え a childish idea / 幼い時に when 《one was》 very young [a child]; as a child; in *one's* childhood [《文》infancy]; very early in life / 幼い時から from [(ever) since] *one's* childhood; from childhood.

おさながお 幼顔 what *one* looked like as a child. 文例⇩ 「[heart].

おさなごころ 幼心 a childish [child's] mind

おさなともだち 幼友達 ⇒ おさななじみ.

おさななじみ 幼なじみ a friend [playmate] of *one's* childhood; a childhood friend.

おさなり お座なり お座なりの careless; 《文》perfunctory; slapdash / お座なりに in a perfunctory [slapdash] manner / お座なりを言う say anything that comes into *one's* mind [just to suit the occasion]; make irresponsible remarks. 文例⇩

おさまり 収[納]まり ¶収まりが着く 〈落着する〉be settled; be fixed up; 《文》come to a settlement; 〈終わる〉come to an end / 収まりをつける 〈解決する〉settle; fix up; 《文》bring *sth* to a settlement; 〈終止符を打つ〉put an end [《文》a period] to *sth*; round off 《an argument》.

おさまりかえる 納まり返る 〈満足している〉be quite content 《with *one's* position》; 〈平気でいる〉remain [be] unruffled ¶納まり返って with a self-satisfied air; 《文》complacently.

おさまる 治[収, 納, 修]まる 〈世の中が〉be at peace; 〈静まる〉subside; calm [die] down; 《米》quiet down; 《英》quieten down; 〈火事などが〉be got under (control); 〈鎮圧される〉be put down; be suppressed; 〈落着する〉come to an end [《文》a settlement]; be settled ¶社長に納まる take *one's* position [take up *one's* post] as president / 〈物が〉納まるべきところに納まる fall into place / 〈食物が〉胃に納まる stay in the stomach / 安楽椅子に納まる be settled [《文》ensconced] in an armchair / 納まらない 〈不満である〉be [feel] dissatisfied [discontented] 《with》. 文例⇩

おさめ 納め ¶納めの the last 《fair》; the closing 《session》.

おさめる 治[収, 納, 修]める 〈統治する〉rule

おごる² 驕る者[平家]は久しからず. Pride goes before a fall. 諺
おさえる はしごをしっかり押えていてくれ. Steady the ladder firmly. / 会社は労組に完全に抑えられている. The firm is under the thumb of the labor union.
おさき どうぞお先へ. You go first, please. | After you. / お先に失礼. Excuse me for going first. / お先真っ暗だ. 〈見通しが立たない〉I cannot tell with any certainty how things will turn out. | 〈見通しは絶望的だ〉There is absolutely no hope for the future. | The future looks black.
おさげ 彼女は髪をお下げにしていた. Her hair hung in two plaits.
おさながお 彼はどこか幼顔が残っている. He still retains some traces of his childhood features.
おさなごころ 幼心にも非常に悲しかった. Child as I was [Even as a child], I felt very sad.
おさなり あの男の言うことはお座なりで当てにならない. He cannot be trusted, for he does not take responsibility for what he has said.
おさまる その仕事に必要な材料はあまり多くはなくて, 大きめの段ボール箱1つに収まった. The material we needed for the work was not much; it all went into one largish cardboard box. / 風が収まった. The wind has dropped. / あらしは収まった. The storm has spent itself [lost its force]. / この薬を飲めば痛みはじきに治まります. If you take this medicine, your pain will soon go. / この騒ぎもそのうちに

おさらい　157　おしえる

[《文》reign] over; govern; 〈鎮定する〉put down; suppress; 〈管理する〉manage; 〈奉納する〉offer; 〈納付する〉pay; 〈納品する〉deliver; supply; 〈しまう〉put away [in]; keep; store; 〈受ける〉accept; 〈解決する〉settle; finish; 〈得る〉get (hold of); 《文》obtain; 《文》gain; 《文》reap 《the fruits of *one's* efforts》; 〈学業を〉follow 《文》pursue ¶ 家を治める manage a household / もめ事を治める make [patch] up a quarrel / 利益を治める make [《文》realize] a profit / 勝利を治める win [《文》gain] a victory 《over》/ 元の所に納める put *sth* back in *its* place / 月謝を納める pay *one's* school fees / 学業を修める follow *one's* course of study; pursue *one's* studies.

おさらい 〈復習〉a review; 《英》revision; 〈稽古〉a rehearsal ¶ (稽古事の)おさらい会 a show [concert] given by the pupils 《of》/ おさらいをする review [《英》revise] *one's* lessons; have a run-through 《of》; rehearse (a play); 《文例》

おさん お産 〔〕→**さん**.　｜have a rehearsal.

おし¹ 押し 〈押すこと〉a push; 〈ずうずうしさ〉push; 《文》audacity; 〈おもし〉a weight ¶ 押しする give *sb* a push / ひと押しに土俵から押し出す put 《*one's* opponent》out of the ring at one push / 押しの強い pushing; aggressive; 《口語》pushy; 《文》audacious / 押しが利く have 《some》 influence 《with》; be influential 《among》/ 押しをする put a weight on; press / 押し相撲 a pushing specialist 《among *sumo* wrestlers》. 《文例》

おし²唖 a mute; a dumb person.
おじ 伯(叔)父 an uncle.
おしあいへしあい 押し合いへし合い ¶ 押し合いへし合いする hustle and jostle; push and shove. 《文例》

おしあう 押し合う push [jostle] one another.
おしあける 押し開ける push 《a door》 open; 〈むりに〉force 《a locked door》open.
おしあげる 押し上げる push [《文》thrust] up ¶ 物価を押し上げる push [force] up the prices.
おしあてる 押し当てる press [push]《A against [on] B》¶ 目にハンカチを押し当てる hold a handkerchief to *one's* eyes / ドアに耳を押し当てる press *one's* ear against the door.

おしい 惜しい 〈残念な〉regrettable; 〈残念である〉《文》It is to be regretted 《that...》; It is a pity [《文》a matter for regret]《that...》; It is too bad 《that...》; 〈大切な〉precious; valu-

able; 《文》(a book that is) dear to one (★ この意味の dear は名詞の前にはつけない); 〈もったいない〉too good 《for》¶ 惜しそうに unwillingly; grudgingly; reluctantly. 《文例》

おじいさん 〈祖父〉 a grandfather; a grandpa; a granddad (★ grandpa and granddad は口語・小児語); 〈老人〉an old man.

おしいただく 押し戴く hold *sth* up reverently before *one*.

おしいる 押し入る break into; force *one's* way into; 〈夜盗が〉burgle; 《米》burglarize.

おしいれ 押し入れ 《米》a closet; 《英》a store cupboard.

おしうり 押し売り 〈事〉high-pressure selling; aggressive peddling (of goods); 〈人〉a high-pressure salesman; a peddler who uses aggressive methods to achieve a sale ¶ 押し売りする peddle 《*one's* goods》 in an aggressive and persistent way; force [press] *sb* to buy *sth* / 押し売り的商法 aggressive [high-pressure] salesmanship; the hard sell. 《文例》

おしえ 教え 〈教訓〉《文》teachings; 《文》a precept; a lesson; 〈教義〉a doctrine ¶ 孔子の教え the teachings of Confucius / 教えを受ける take lessons (in piano); be taught 《by》; study 《under *sb*》; learn 《French from *sb*》/ 教えを守る 《文》abide by *sb's* precepts / 教えに従う follow *sb's* teachings / 教え方 a method of teaching; how to teach 《foreign languages》/ 教え子 *one's* (former) pupil.

おしえこむ 教え込む train 《*sb* how to do》; plant (an idea) in 《*sb's* mind》; 《文》implant [instill] (an idea into [in *sb*]); 《文》inculcate (an idea in *sb*, *sb* with an idea) ¶ ...であると教えこまれる be taught to believe that....

おしえる 教える teach; give lessons (in); 《文》instruct; 〈知らせる〉tell 《*sb* (that...), *sb* about *sth*》; 《文》inform 《*sb* of *sth*, *sb* (that...)》; 〈示す〉show; point out (指し示す); 〈説く〉preach; 〈説明する〉explain; 〈教育する〉educate; 〈指導する〉guide; coach ¶ フランス語を教える give *sb* lessons in French; teach *sb* French / ピアノを教える give *sb* lessons in piano [piano lessons] / (教室で)ハムレットを教える read Hamlet with *one's* students / 道を教える tell [show] *sb* the way (to a place); 《文》direct *sb* to (a place) ★ tell は言葉で, show は地図を書いて又は案内して, 教える, の意味. direct はどの場合も含む. 《文例》

治まるだろう. The fuss will blow over in time. / 事態が治まるまで待とう. Let's wait until things cool down [off].
おし 商売は押しの一手. Push is everything in business.
おしあいへしあい 人々は押し合いへし合いしながらその電車に乗り込んだ. The people got into the train with a lot of pushing and shoving.
おしい 国家のために惜しい人を失った. His death is a great loss to the country. / 捨てるには惜し

い. It's too good to be thrown away. / 惜しいことに彼は若くして死んでしまった. It's too bad that he died young. / この古ズボンなら泥でよごれても惜しくない. I don't mind getting this old pair of pants soiled with mud. / ピントを合わせていたら惜しい所で逃げられて郭公の写真を撮り損なった. I couldn't take a picture of the cuckoo, as it flew away just when I had got it in focus. / 女優になれるものならばどんな犠牲を払っても惜しくありませんわ. I

would give anything in the world to be an actress. / 試験が済むまでは1時間でも惜しい. I grudge even an hour until the examination is over. / 命が惜しかったらそこを動くな. Stay where you are, if you want to stay alive.
おしうり 押し売りお断わり.〈貼札〉No Peddlers or Salesmen. |《米》No Solicitors. |《英》No Hawkers.
おしえる 何をしたらいいのか教えて下さい. Tell me what to do. / これにはずいぶん教えられたよ. I've

おしかえす ― おしのける

おしかえす 押し返す push [force] back.
おしかけにょうぼう 押し掛け女房 [文例↓]
おしかける 押し掛ける 〈訪問する〉call on sb without notice [without a previous appointment]; 〈会合などに〉go ((to a party)) uninvited; invite oneself ((to a party)); (《口語》) crash [gate-crash] ((a party)); 〈大勢で〉throng ((to a place)). [文例↓]
おじぎ お辞儀 ¶お辞儀する bow ((to)); make a bow [(《文》) an obeisance] ((to)) / 腰をかがめて丁寧にお辞儀をする make a polite bow [bow politely] from the waist / お辞儀し合う exchange bows ((with)). [文例↓]
おしきせ お仕着せ clothes provided ((for workers)) by the employer; (a) livery (貴族の召使いなどが着るそろいの).
おじぎそう 【植】a mimosa; a sensitive plant.
おしきる 押し切る 〈ずうずうしく〉brazen it out; face ((the matter)) out ¶反対を押し切る overcome [steamroller] the opposition ((of)) / 反対を押し切って for all [in spite of] sb's opposition.
おしくも 惜しくも to one's regret [(《文》) chagrin]; regrettably ⇒ おしい ¶惜しくも敗れる ⇒ せきはい.
おしげ 惜しげ ¶惜しげもなく generously; freely; (《文》) liberally; unsparingly; (《文》) without stint / 惜しげもなく金を使う lavish money on ((luxuries)); (《口語》) spend money like water [as if there's no tomorrow, as if it's going out of fashion].
おじけ 怖じ気 ¶怖じ気がつく 〈怖がる〉get frightened [scared]; lose courage [one's nerve]; (《口語》) go [get] into a (blue) funk ⇒ おじける.
おじける 怖じける be afraid ((of)); be frightened ((at, of)); be scared ((of)); (《文》) fear; (《文》) quail (with fear) ((at)); 〈しりごみする〉shrink [recoil] ((from)).
おしこみごうとう 押し込み強盗 a housebreaker.
おしこむ 押し込む 〈詰める〉push [shove, squeeze, stuff, jam] sth into ((a container)) ¶口に食物を押し込む stuff [cram] food into one's mouth.
おしこめる 押し込める 〈閉じ込める〉shut sb up; (《文》) confine; 〈押し込む〉⇒ おしこむ ¶(大勢の人が)狭い部屋に押し込められる be crowded into a small room.
おしころす 圧し殺す crush sb to death ¶声を圧し殺して in a (hoarse) subdued voice.
おじさん 小父さん (《小児語》) a man; 〈呼びかけ〉Mister!; Sir! ¶よそのおじさん a (strange)

gentleman.
おしすすめる 押[推]し進める push on [ahead] ((with a plan)); go [move] ahead with ((a project)) ⇒ すいしん³.
おしたおす 押し倒す push sb down.
おしだし 押し出し ¶押し出しののっぱな男 a fine-looking man; (《文》) a man of fine appearance [dignified presence] / (野球で)押し出しの1点をあげる force in a run with a bases-loaded walk / 押し出し絵の具 tube paint. [文例↓]
おしだす 押し出す push [force, (《文》) thrust, press, squeeze] out ¶土俵の外に押し出す push ((one's opponent)) out of the ring / 歯みがきをチューブから押し出す squeeze toothpaste out of [from] the tube.
おしたてる 押し立てる 〈掲げる〉hoist; put up; display; 〈支持する〉back (up); support ¶赤旗を押し立てて (march) with red flags held up high.
おしだまる 押し黙る ⇒ だまりこくる.
おしつける 押し付ける 〈圧する〉press [push] ((A)) against ((B)); 〈上から〉press sth down; 〈強制する〉force; compel; 〈品物などを〉press [foist, force] sth on sb ¶壁に押しつける press [hold] sb against the wall / 仕事を押しつける force [off-load] work on(to) sb / 責任を押しつける shift [off-load] the responsibility ((onto sb [sb's shoulders])); (《口語》) pass the buck ((to)) / 自分の考えを人に押しつける force [foist] one's opinions [ideas] on sb. [文例↓]
おしっこ ¶おしっこをする wee-wee (小児語); (《口語》) piddle; (《文》) pee; (《俗》) piss / おしっこを漏らす wet one's pants.
おしつぶす 押し潰す crush; smash; squash; steamroller ((sb's opposition)). [文例↓]
おしつまる 押し詰まる [文例↓]
おしとおす 押し通す 〈遂行する〉push [force, carry] ((one's plan)) through; 〈主張する〉persist ((in doing)) to the end / 〈頑張り通す〉hold out [(《口語》) hang on] to the bitter end; (《文》) endure to the last ¶信念を押し通す stick to one's belief(s) to the last [end] / ずうずうしく押し通す brazen it out; face ((the matter)) out.
おしどり 【鳥】a mandarin duck ¶おしどり夫婦 a couple of lovebirds.
おしながす 押し流す wash [carry] away. [文例↓]
おしのける 押し退ける push [shove] sb [sth] aside [away, out of the way]; (《文》) thrust sb [sth] aside; nudge sb aside; 〈ひじで〉elbow sb aside [out of the way]; 〈取って代わる〉take

---

learned a lot from this. | This was a real lesson to me. / この機械の操作を教えて下さい. Show me how to operate this machine.
おしかけにょうぼう 彼女は押し掛け女房だ. She browbeat [bullied] him [her husband] into marrying her. | She was the one who was enthusiastic about the marriage [who was keen to get married].
おしかける あの時はトイレットペーパーを買いに主婦たちがスーパーに押し掛けたものでした. I remember how housewives mobbed [made a run on] the supermarkets to buy toilet paper.
おじぎ (子供に) お辞儀はどうしたの. Where are your manners?
おしだし フォスター氏は押し出しが堂々としていた. Mr. Foster was a fine [an imposing] figure of a man.
おしつける うちの嫁は子供を私に押しつけて芝居見物に行きました. My daughter-in-law wished her children on me and went to the theater. / 彼女は嫌な家事を夫に押しつけた. She landed the unpleasant household chores on her husband. / 書き言葉の規則を話し言葉に押しつけてはいけない. The rules of the written language must not be forced onto

おしのび お忍び ¶お忍びで…に行く visit 《a place》 incognito; pay an incognito visit to….

おしば 押し葉 a pressed plant [leaf].

おしはかる 推し量る ⇨ すいそく.

おしばな 押し花 a pressed flower.

おしべ 雄蕊 《植》a stamen.

おしボタン 押しボタン a push button ¶押しボタン戦争 push-button warfare.

おしぼり お絞り a small damp towel (served to a guest at table).

おしまい ⇨ しまい². 文例⇩

おしまくる 押し捲くる push and push; keep pushing to the end (最後まで).

おしみない 惜しみない generous; 《文》unstinted (praise); 《文》unstinting (aid) ¶惜しみなく 〈おしげ(惜しげもなく), おしむ(惜しまずに).

おしむ 惜しむ 〈出し惜しむ〉 be not generous [free] 《with》; 《文》be ungenerous 《with》; grudge; begrudge; be sparing 《with [《文》of]》; be mean [stingy] 《with》; 〈残念に思う〉regret; be [feel] sorry 《for》; 《文》lament; 〈嫌がる〉be unwilling; be reluctant ¶命よりも名を惜しむ value [prize] honor above life / 別れを惜しむ be unwilling [《文》loath] to part from sb; be reluctant to leave sb / …するために努力を惜しまない spare no effort to do ★ spare は do not spare; spare no 《expense》の形で常に否定形で使う / 金を惜しまない lavish money on 《luxuries》; 《口語》splash (out) (on) / 賞賛を惜しまない be liberal [lavish] with one's praise; give unstinted praise 《to》/ 惜しまずに generously; lavishly; 《文》unsparingly; ungrudgingly; 《文》without stint / 費用を惜しまず regardless of expense / 惜しむべき regrettable; deplorable; 《文》lamentable / 惜しむらくは It is a pity that…; 《文》It is to be regretted that…. 文例⇩

おしめ ⇨ しまい².

おしめり お湿り ⇨ あめ¹. 文例⇩

おしもどす 押し戻す push [press, force] back; 〈突き返す〉reject.

おしもんどう 押し問答 ¶押し問答する bandy words 《with》; argue 《with sb about sth》.

おじや rice gruel seasoned with miso or soy sauce.

おしゃか ¶おしゃかになる prove [turn out, end up] a failure; be found to be no good.

おしゃぶり a teething ring; 《米》a pacifier; 《英》a dummy; 《英》a comforter ★ teething ring は固いもの(ほとんどプラスチック製), dummy と comforter はゴムかプラスチック製の乳首のようなもの, pacifier は両方を言う.

おしゃぶる 押し破る break 《the door》open; break [force one's way] through (the gate).

おしゃべり 〈事〉chattering; a talk; idle talk; (a) chat; chitchat; gossip (うわさ話); 〈人〉《口語》a chatterbox; 《口語》a nonstop talker; a gossip; 《口語》a blabbermouth (秘密を守れない) ¶おしゃべりな talkative; chatty; gossipy / おしゃべりする chatter; chat; have a chat; gossip; blab (秘密を漏らす).

おしゃま 《文》precocity ¶おしゃまな女の子 a precocious girl; 《英口語》a (little) madam.

おしやる 押し遣る push [《文》thrust] sb [sth] away [aside].

おしゃれ 〈事〉dressing up; 《文》personal adornment; making up (化粧); 〈人〉a person who spends (too) much time and money on his clothing and personal appearance; 〈男〉a dandy ¶おしゃれをする dress (oneself) up; look [make oneself] smart; 〈女性が〉《口語》doll oneself [be dolled] up.

おじゃん ¶おじゃんになる fall through; come to nothing; be ruined.

おしょう 和尚 a Buddhist priest (in charge of a temple).

おじょうさん お嬢さん a young lady; 〈人の娘をさして〉your [his] daughter; 〈当人に呼びかけて〉young lady; miss (商人や使用人などが) ¶川上さんのお嬢さん Mr. Kawakami's daughter / かわいいお嬢さん a sweet [《米口語》cute] little girl / お嬢さん育ちの人 a naive [an unsophisticated] woman; a woman who knows nothing about the world.

おしょうばん お相伴 ¶お相伴する share [take part, 《文》participate] 《in》; 《文》partake 《of a meal》 ★ partake は非常に文語的だが, 日常会話でもおどけて使うことがある).

おしょく 汚職 corruption; 《米》graft; 〈贈収賄〉bribery ¶汚職を生む breed graft and corruption / 汚職事件 a corruption case [scandal]; a graft [《口語》payoff] scandal / 汚職を行なった政治家 a corrupt politician.

おしよせる 押し寄せる close [swarm] in 《on sb》; crowd (to a place); rush for (the door); 〈波が〉surge [beat, rush] (on) ¶サインを求めて押し寄せる mob [crowd around, press around] (a famous singer) for 《his》autograph.

おしろい (face) powder ¶おしろいをつける put powder on (one's face); powder (one's

---

speech. / 押しつけがましいお願いで恐れ入りますが, 明日は私の代わりに会に出ていただけませんでしょうか. I don't mean to force you, but I'd be very much obliged if you would attend the meeting in my place tomorrow.

おしつぶす 私は人込みで押しつぶされそうだった. I was almost squashed flat [squeezed out of shape] in the crowd.

おしつまる いよいよ今年も押し詰まってあと experienced数日になりました. The year is drawing to its close, with only a few days left.

おしとおす 最後まで知らぬ存ぜぬの一点張りで押し通した. He persisted in denying all knowledge of it to the last. / 独身で押し通した. He remained single all his life.

おしながす 橋は洪水で押し流されてしまった. The bridge was swept away by the flood.

おしまい (こうなっては)もうあの男もおしまいだ. The game is up for him. | That cooked his goose (for him). | He's done for.

おしむ 寸暇を惜しんで勉強した. He gave every spare moment to his studies.

おしめり けっこうなお湿りですな. This rain is most welcome, isn't

face) / おしろいっ気のない女 a woman wearing no make-up at all / おしろい刷毛 a powder puff. 文例⇩

おしろいばな 【植】a four-o'clock.

オシログラフ 【電】an oscillograph.

オシロスコープ 【電】an oscilloscope.

おしわける 押し分ける push ((them)) apart ¶人を押し分けて行く[進む] push [force, elbow] one's way through a crowd; shove through a crowd.

おす[1] 雄 a male ((animal)); a he ¶雄の male; he-((whales)); billy ((goats)); dog ((foxes)); bull ((whales, elephants)); buck ((rabbits)); cock ((sparrows)) ★これらの形容詞は全部名詞としても使える。例: That elephant is a bull. / 雄猫 a tomcat; a tom (cat). 文例⇩

おす[2] 押す ⟨押す⟩ push; shove; give *sth* a push [shove]; ⟨圧する⟩ press ¶下に押す push [press] down; 《文》depress ((a lever)) / 呼び鈴を押す press the bell button / (相撲で)押し負ける be outpushed ((by)) / 人に押されながら電車に乗り込む be jostled aboard a train / バスの中でぎゅうぎゅう押される be squeezed [squashed] in a bus / 押すな押すなの混雑である be crowded [jammed] with people / 病を押して in spite of *one's* illness / 押しも押されもしない acknowledged ((masters)); ((a scholar)) with an [((文)) of] established reputation. 文例⇩

おす[3] 推す ⟨推断する⟩ 《文》infer [deduce] ((from)); gather; conclude; judge ((by, from)); ⟨憶測する⟩ guess; 《文》surmise; ⟨推薦する⟩ recommend ¶種々の事情から推して everything [all things] taken together ((it seems that ...)) / …に推されて on the recommendation of.... 文例⇩

おすい 汚水 dirty [filthy, foul] water; polluted water; ⟨下水⟩ sewage; slops (流しの) ⇨げすい / (台所・洗面所などの)汚水管 a soil [waste] pipe / 汚水処理 sewage treatment [disposal].

おずおず(と) timidly; nervously; 《文》faintheartedly.

おすそわけ お裾分け ¶お裾分けする give *sb* part [a share, 《文》a portion] ((of something *one* has received as a gift)); share *sth* with *sb*.

オスマントルコ 〈オスマントルコ族 the Ottoman Turks / オスマントルコ帝国 【史】the Ottoman Empire.

オスミウム 【化】osmium.

おすみつき お墨付き ⟨書類⟩ a paper bearing the signature ((of the *shogun*)); ⟨保証⟩ a guarantee ((of *sb*)); ⟨約束⟩ a promise.

オスロ Oslo.

オセアニア Oceania. ¶オセアニアの Oceanian.

おせおせ 押せ押せ ¶押せ押せムードで riding ((along)) on the crest of the wave; *do* caught up in the mood ((without stopping to think)).

おせじ お世辞 an empty [insincere] compliment; flattery; 《口語》blarney ¶お世辞に[as a] compliment / お世辞を言う pay compliments ((to)); say nice things ((to)); flatter; 《口語》lay it on ((with *sb*)) / お世辞のない所を(申しますと) frankly speaking; to be frank ((with you)) / お世辞たっぷりの《文》adulatory; unctuous. 文例⇩

おせちりょうり お節料理 festive food for the New Year.

おせっかい ¶おせっかいな interfering; meddlesome; 《文》officious; 《口語》nosey [nosy] / おせっかいな人 an interfering [a meddlesome, an officious] person; a busybody; 《英》a nosy parker / おせっかいな店員 an overkind salesclerk / おせっかいをやく interfere ((in)); meddle ((in [with] *sb's* affairs)); 《口語》poke *one's* nose ((into *sb's* business)). 文例⇩

おせん 汚染 contamination ((of water supplies)); (air) pollution ¶工場廃液による河川の汚染 industrial pollution of a river / 汚染する be contaminated; be polluted; be tainted / 汚染された polluted ((air)); contaminated ((water)); tainted ((food)) / 汚染する contaminate; pollute; taint / ひどく汚染されている be heavily polluted / 放射能に汚染された空気 air contaminated by radioactivity / 汚染を取り除く decontaminate / 汚染物質 a pollutant; a

---

it?
おしろい 彼女はおしろいをつけすぎている。She has too much powder [make-up] on.
おす[1] この猫は雄ですか雌ですか。Is this cat a he or a she?
おす[2] 押さないで下さい。Please don't push (against me). / 日本チームはソ連チームに終始押され気味だった。The Japanese team was under pressure from the Soviets all through the game.
おす[3] 服装から推して、その女性は土地の人ではなさそうに思われた。Judging from her dress, I didn't think she could be a native of the locality.
おせおせ 先月神田君が病気で3週間ほど休んだので仕事が遅れで押せ押せになり、期限に追われて大忙だ。As Kanda was off sick for about three weeks last month, the progress of the work has been delayed, and now that the deadline is drawing near the pressure is really on us.
おせじ「すてきね」と彼女は言ったが、それはほんのお世辞だった。'It's nice,' she said, just to please him. / そんなお世辞を言ってもだめですよ。Flattery will get you nowhere. | You can't get round me with flattery, you know. / このスープはうまい。お世辞でなく。This soup is good. Really good. | お世辞にも美人とは言いかねる女だった。She couldn't be called good-looking, (not) by any standards.
おせっかい 余計なお世話だ。It's none of your business. | Mind your own business!

おそい あの男、遅いなあ。What a long wait we're having for him. / 今から行ってはもう遅い。It is too late to start now. / 彼は1日遅くやって来た。He came a day too late. / 会社から遅く戻ることがよくある。He is often late (coming) home from the office. / 彼女は夜遅くまで寝ない。She doesn't go to bed till late (at night). / 彼女は夜遅くまで勉強する。She works (until) late at night. / こんなに遅くどこへ行くんだ。Where are you going at this time of night? / (会合などに遅刻して)どうも遅くなりました。Excuse me for being late.
おそう 恐ろしい災難が一家を襲った。A dreadful disaster befell the family.
おそで 今日は遅出だ。I don't have

おそい 遅い ⟨時刻が⟩ late; ⟨動作が⟩ slow; 《文》tardy ¶進歩が遅い make slow progress / *its* progress is slow / 来るのが遅い be slow in coming / 頭の回転が遅い be slow-witted / be dull / 今や遅しと待つ wait impatiently ⟨for⟩ / 夜遅く late at night / 夜遅くまで (until) late at night; late [till late,《文》far] into the night / 遅くなる ⟨時刻が⟩ get [grow] late; ⟨人や物事などが⟩ be late for ⟨school⟩; be behind time [schedule] / 遅く(とも) at (the) latest / おそかれ早かれ sooner or later. 文例⇩

おそう 襲う ⟨襲撃する⟩ attack; make an attack on;《文》assail; assault; storm;⟨餌食を⟩ fall [pounce] on;⟨敵地などに侵入する⟩ raid; make a raid into; invade;⟨病気・災害などが⟩ strike; hit;《文》visit ¶恐怖に襲われる be seized with fear; have [get] a fright / 暴風雨に襲われる⟨場所が主語⟩ be hit [visited] by a storm;⟨人が主語⟩ be caught in [overtaken by] a storm / 突然激痛に襲われる have a sudden attack of severe pain. 文例⇩

おぞけ ¶おぞけを振るう be horrified ⟨at the thought⟩.

おそざき 遅咲き ¶遅咲きの late ⟨flowers⟩; late-flowering ⟨cherries⟩.

おそじも 遅霜 a late frost ¶⟨作物などが⟩遅霜の被害を受ける be damaged by a late frost.

おそで 遅出 (*one's* turn for) late attendance (at the office). 文例⇩

おそなえ お供え an offering;⟨もち⟩ a rice-cake offering.

おそばん 遅番 (on) the second [late] shift ⇨ はやばん

おそまき 遅蒔き ¶遅まきの (too) late; belated ⟨efforts⟩ / 遅まきながら though a little too late; (somewhat) belatedly. 文例⇩

おぞましい hideous; hateful; horrifying; nauseating;⟨口語⟩creepy.

おそらく 恐らく probably; maybe; perhaps; as likely as not; (very [most]) likely ★副詞としての likely は単独で使われることは少なく, very や most を伴うのが普通⟩;⟨十中八九⟩ in all likelihood [probability];⟨心配して⟩ I'm afraid; I fear;⟨疑いを持って⟩ I suspect. 文例⇩

おそるおそる 恐る恐る ⟨こわごわ⟩《文》fearfully; timidly; nervously;⟨用心して⟩ cautiously; gingerly (特に物に手を触れるとき).

おそるべき 恐るべき ⇨ おそろしい

おそれ 恐れ ⟨恐怖⟩ (a) fear; terror;⟨文⟩dread; horror;⟨懸念⟩《文》apprehension(s); anxiety;⟨畏怖⟩《文》awe;⟨危険⟩ (a) danger; (a) risk ¶…の恐れがある be in danger of…; it is feared ⟨that…⟩; there is the possibility (danger) ⟨of…, that…⟩ / 恐れを知らない fearless;《文》dauntless;《文》intrepid / 恐れをなす dread; be frightened [scared] ⟨at⟩; be intimidated ⟨by⟩;《文》stand in awe [fear] ⟨of⟩. 文例⇩

おそれいる 恐れ入る ⟨恐縮する⟩ be sorry ⟨for⟩; be abashed; feel small;⟨感謝する⟩ be much obliged ⟨to⟩; thank ⟨*sb* for *sth*⟩;⟨閉口する⟩ be [feel] embarrassed;《文》be confounded;⟨驚く⟩ be astonished; be surprised ¶恐れ入りますが Excuse [Pardon] me, but… / 恐れ入りますが…して下さいませんか I am sorry to trouble you, but would you mind *doing*? 文例⇩

おそれおののく 恐れ戦く tremble with fear;《文》shudder with awe ¶恐れおののいて in fear and trembling;《文》in abject fear.

おそれる 恐れる be afraid ⟨of⟩;《文》be fearful ⟨of⟩; dread;《文》fear;⟨ぎょっとする⟩ be frightened [scared] ⟨at⟩ ¶恐れている be afraid [in fear] ⟨of⟩;《文》stand [be] in awe ⟨of⟩ / …を恐れて for fear ⟨of, that…⟩;《文》fearful ⟨of, that…⟩ / 恐れない be not afraid ⟨of⟩;《文》be unafraid ⟨of⟩;《文》be fearless ⟨of⟩; have no fear ⟨of⟩; defy ⟨death⟩ ★ be fearless of *sth* は《文》だが, 「何ものも恐れない」の意味で He is fearless. のように言うのは《文》ではない. 文例⇩

おそろい お揃い ¶おそろいで together;⟨大勢で⟩ in a body ⇨ そろう²(そろって) / おそろい

---

to go to the office early today.

おそまき ロージャーは遅まきながらアーネストに追いつこうと最近頑張り始めた. Roger got off to a slow start, but he has recently been trying really hard to catch up with Ernest.

おそらく 恐らく明日は帰って来るでしょう. He will very [most] likely come back tomorrow. / 恐らくこれはこの種のものでは最上のものだろう. This is the best of the kind, I dare say. / 恐らく彼は承知しないでしょう. I'm afraid he won't agree.

おそれ 暴風雨になる恐れがある. It is likely that we shall have stormy weather. | There are signs of an approaching storm. / 余病を併発する恐れはない. There is no fear of complications setting in. / 彼のけんまくに恐れをなしてだれも寄り付かなかった. Everyone was so frightened by his angry look that they did not dare to go near him. / 彼女の凄腕にはだれでも恐れをなしている. Everybody is in awe of her shrewdness.

おそれいる これはどうも恐れ入ります. I am sorry to have given you so much trouble. / これはご親切に, 恐れ入ります. I am very much obliged to you. | Thank you. It's very kind of you. / 君の言い訳のうまいのには恐れ入る. You are a past master at making excuses, I must say. | I can only admire your clever excuses. / あれで英文学の大家だとは恐れ入った. Just think of his calling himself an authority on English literature! / 僕がその金を払うだろうと思っているんだから恐れ入るよ. Now, if you please, he expects me to pay for it. | And—would you believe it?—he expects me to foot the bill. / いや, 恐れ入りました. 仰せのとおりです. Well, I'm staggered [I stand corrected]. It's just as you say. / 彼の長話には恐れ入ったよ. I was bored stiff by his long tedious talk.

おそれる 君に何も恐れることはない. You have nothing to be afraid of. / 病気になるのを恐れ過ぎるのはよくない. It's foolish to worry too much about falling ill. / アホウドリは人間を恐れない. Albatrosses are not shy of human beings.

の服 suits made of [cut from] the same cloth / おそろいの服を着た2人の少女 two girls in matching [identical] ⟪blue⟫ dresses. [文例⇩]

おそろしい 恐ろしい 〈こわい〉 frightening; terrifying; bloodcurdling (血も凍るような); 〈ひどい〉 fearful; dreadful; frightful; terrible; ⟪口語⟫ awful; 〈兇悪な〉 fierce; ferocious; 〈恐るべき〉 formidable; ⟪文⟫ awesome; ⟪文⟫ redoubtable; 〈途方もない〉 tremendous; stupendous; enormous; ⟪口語⟫ terrific ¶恐ろしい目つきをする look menacingly ⟪at *sb*⟫ / 恐ろしい人出 a tremendous crowd; an enormous turnout (of people) / 恐ろしいスピードで at a terrific speed / おそろしく 〈ひどく〉 fearfully; dreadfully; frightfully; terribly; ⟪口語⟫ awfully; 〈非常に〉 very; extremely; ⟪文⟫ exceedingly / おそろしく暑い very [awfully] hot / 恐ろしく金がかかる be terribly [fearfully] expensive. [文例⇩]

おそろしがる 恐ろしがる ⇨ **おそれる**.

おそろしさ 恐ろしさ fear; terror; horror ¶恐ろしさに for [from, out of] fear / 恐ろしさのあまり気を失う faint in terror / 恐ろしさのあまり口もきけなくなる be struck dumb with fright. [文例⇩]

おそわる 教わる be taught ⟪history by Mr. A⟫; learn ⟪English from Mr. B⟫; study ⟪chemistry under Prof. C⟫; take lessons ⟪in piano from Miss D⟫. [文例⇩]

オゾン 〖化〗 ozone ¶海岸で胸一杯にオゾンを吸う breathe in lungfuls of ozone at the seaside.

おたく お宅 your house; your home; 〈あなた〉 you ¶お宅のお子さん your child [children]. [文例⇩]

おたずねもの お尋ね者 a person wanted by the police; ⟪文⟫ a fugitive from justice; ⟪口語⟫ a man on the run.

おたちだい お立ち台 〈皇居の〉 the Balcony of Appearances.

おだて 煽て flattery; ⟪口語⟫ soft soap; ⟪英口語⟫ flannel ¶おだてに乗る be taken in by [⟪文⟫ fall a prey to] flattery / おだてに乗りやすい be easily flattered; be (very) susceptible to flattery / おだてに乗らない be above flattery; ⟪口語⟫ cannot be soft-soaped [⟪英⟫ flannelled]; be proof against flattery. [文例⇩]

おだてる 煽てる ⟪口語⟫ soft-soap *sb*; ⟪英口語⟫ flannel *sb*; 〈そそのかす〉 incite ⟪*sb* to an act, to *do*⟫; egg *sb* on ⟪to *do*⟫; wheedle [cajole] ⟪*sb* into *doing*⟫; 〈追従を言う〉 flatter ¶おだてられて ⟪文⟫ at *sb's* instigation.

おたふく お多福 〈醜い女〉 a plain [⟪米⟫ homely] woman.

おたふくかぜ お多福風邪 mumps ⟪単数扱い⟫ ¶お多福風邪にかかる get mumps.

おだぶつ お陀仏 ¶お陀仏になる die; ⟪口語⟫ pop off; ⟪俗⟫ kick the bucket; ⟪俗⟫ be a goner.

おだまき 〖植〗 a columbine.

おたまじゃくし お玉杓子 〖動〗 a tadpole; 〈音符〉 a musical note.

おためごかし お為ごかし an act of ostensible kindness done in *one's* own interest ¶おためごかしに ⟪文⟫ ostensibly for *sb's* good; as if *one* meant well toward *sb*.

おだやか 穏やか ¶穏やかな calm; quiet; peaceful; mild; gentle; ⟪文⟫ tranquil; 〈穏当な〉 moderate; 〈相当の〉 reasonable; 〈円満な〉 friendly; ⟪文⟫ amicable / 穏やかな海 a calm [quiet] sea / 穏やかな気候 a mild [⟪文⟫ genial] climate / 穏やかな解決 an amicable settlement / (食物が)穏やかな味である be mild [bland] in taste / 穏やかならぬ serious; threatening; alarming; ⟪文⟫ disquieting / 穏やかに quietly; calmly; peacefully; gently; 〈穏当に〉 moderately; 〈円満に〉 ⟪文⟫ amicably / 穏やかになる calm [quiet] down; become calm; abate; 〈風波が〉 be lulled / 穏やかに流れる川 a gently flowing river; a river with a gentle current. [文例⇩]

オタワ Ottawa.

おだわらひょうじょう 小田原評定 an inconclusive conference; a long [⟪文⟫ protracted] debate which achieves nothing.

おち 落ち 〈遺漏〉 a slip; ⟪文⟫ an omission; 〈要点〉 the punch line ⟪of a joke⟫; 〈終結〉 the end ¶落ちなく ⟪文⟫without omission; fully; in full / 結局…が落ちだ end (up) [⟪文⟫ result] in ⟪failure⟫; lead to ⟪friction⟫.

おちあう 落ち合う 〈集合する〉 meet; come together; 〈偶然に出あう〉 come across [⟪文⟫ upon] *sb*. [文例⇩]

おちいる 陥る fall [get] into; be led into ¶危険に陥る get into danger / 全くの混乱状態に陥る ⟪文⟫ fall into utter confusion / 誘惑に陥る give in [⟪文⟫ yield, ⟪文⟫ succumb]

おそろい おそろいでどちらへ. Where are you two [all] going? / 日曜日には必ず奥さんとおそろいで外出する. He goes out with his wife every Sunday.

おそろしい この間のような恐ろしい思いをしたことはなかった. I have never had such a frightening experience as I had the other day. / 恐ろしかったの何のって, 私は人が首を斬り落とされるところを見てしまったのだ. Horror of horrors! I saw with my own eyes a man's head being cut off. / おそろしく寒い晩だった. It was an awfully cold night. / 熱心は恐ろしいもので彼は1年あまりでフランス語をものにした. Enthusiasm can make a man achieve wonders; he mastered French in a year or so.

おそろしさ あまりの恐ろしさに彼は歯の根も合わなかった. He was so terror-stricken that his teeth chattered. / がんの恐ろしさをはじめて知った. I realized for the first time how dreadful cancer is.

おそわる ドイツ語はだれに教わったのですか. Who taught you German? / 私の電話番号をどこで教わったのですか. 電話帳には出ていないはずですが. Where did you get my phone number? I'm sure it's not in the book. / だれに教わらなくてもタイプライターくらいは打てるようになりますよ. You can teach yourself typewriting, you know.

おたく ブラウンさんのお宅はこちらですか. Is this Mr. Brown's residence? / 結構なお宅ですな. You have a nice home here. / (スミス夫人に向かって) 今, ご主人はお宅ですか. Is Mr. Smith at home? / お宅では皆様いかがでい

おちおち ¶おちおち眠れない do not [cannot] sleep well [peacefully]; do not have a good [quiet] night; sleep badly [restlessly]; pass a bad [wakeful] night / おちおちしていられない cannot just do [be doing] nothing; 《文》cannot remain idle.

おちぐち 落ち口 〈滝の〉 the sill [lip] (of a waterfall); 〈下水などの〉 an outfall.

おちくぼむ 落ち窪む sink (in); cave in ¶落ちくぼんだ deep-set (eyes); hollow [sunken] (cheeks).

おちこぼれ 落ちこぼれ a student who cannot keep up with the class (in mathematics); 〈中途退学する〉 a (school) dropout.

おちこむ 落ち込む fall in; 〈屋根・地盤などが〉 cave in; sink; 〈気持ちが〉 get depressed; 《口語》feel down [blue].

おちつき 落ち着き presence of mind; 《文》composure; 《文》self-possession ¶落ち着きのある calm; 《文》placid; self-possessed; 《文》composed; 《文》serene / 落ち着きのない restless; nervous; fidgety; flurried (あわてた) ¶落ち着きを失う lose one's head [presence of mind]; get [《文》become] restless; be flustered [《文》become] restless; be flustered / 落ち着きを失わない ⇒ **おちつきはらう** / 落ち着きを取り戻す regain one's presence of mind; 《文》recover one's composure. 文例⇩

おちつきはらう 落ち着き払う stay quite unruffled; be as cool as a cucumber; 《文》remain perfectly composed ¶落ち着き払って coolly; quite calmly; cool, calm, and collected; 《文》equably; 《文》with perfect composure.

おちつく 落ち着く settle (down); 〈定住する〉 make one's home; come to stay 〈here〉 (《口》先に); 〈新しい家や部屋などに〉 settle [get settled] in; 〈心の平静を失わない〉 keep one's head [presence of mind]; keep calm; 《俗》keep [do not lose] one's cool; 〈心の平静を取り戻す〉《口語》pull oneself together; 《文》recover [regain] one's composure; 〈静まる〉 go [《文》become] calm [quiet]; calm [quiet] down; subside; 《文》abate ¶落ち着いた calm; self-possessed; 《文》quiet; 《文》contained; 《文》collected / 落ち着いた柄 a quiet pattern / 落ち着いた気分で in a calm [collected] frame of mind / 落ち着いて calmly; 《文》collectedly; 《文》composedly; 《文》with composure / 落ち着いて…する settle down to (one's studies); 落ち着かない feel nervous [uneasy]; be ill at ease; be fidgety (そわそわしている). 文例⇩

おちつける 落ち着ける quiet [《英》quieten] sb (down); calm sb (down); soothe (one's nerves) ¶気を落ち着ける calm [《文》compose] oneself; collect one's senses / 腰を落ち着けて…にかかる settle down to (one's work).

おちど 落ち度 〈失策〉 a mistake; a slip; 《口語》a slip-up; 《文》a fault; 《文》an error; 〈罪〉blame ¶落ち度がある be to blame; be at fault / 落ち度のない blameless / 自分の落ち度を認める accept [take] the blame for one's actions [for what one has done wrong]; own up (to having done) / 人の落ち度にする lay [put] the blame (for sth) on sb. 文例⇩

おちのびる 落ち延びる run away; escape (to); 《文》flee; make good [《文》effect] one's escape (to).

おちば 落ち葉 〈rake up〉 fallen [dead] leaves.

おちぶれる 落ちぶれる fall [sink] low; go down in the world; 《文》fall into reduced circumstances; 《口語》go to the dogs ¶落ちぶれている have fallen (very) low; 《口語》be down and out; 《口語》be down on one's luck; 《文》be in reduced circumstances / 落ちぶれた一家 a family now fallen on evil days / 落ちぶれた人 《口語》a down-and-out; 《口語》a man (who is) down on his luck. 文例⇩

おちぼ 落ち穂 gleanings; fallen ears (of barley) ¶落ち穂を拾う glean / (ミレーの)「落ち穂拾い」'The Gleaners'.

おちめ 落ち目 ¶落ち目の政治家 a politician who is down on his luck; a politician on the downgrade / 落ち目になる go [be] down on one's luck; 〈人気などが〉 go into a [be on the] decline; be on the wane; be out of luck. 文例⇩

おちゃ お茶 ⇒ちゃ ¶お茶の時間 〈午後の〉(at) teatime; 〈コーヒーなどを飲む休憩時間〉a coffee [tea] break / お茶の先生 a tea master, a tea-ceremony teacher / お茶を濁す 〈いいかげんにやっておく〉do sth in a halfhearted [makeshift] way; 〈態度を明らかにしない〉give an evasive reply; reply evasively; 《口語》fudge one's answer [the issue]; 《口語》pussy-

---

らっしゃいますか. How is your family? | How are your people?

おだて あの男にはおだてがきかない. It's no use trying to soft-soap [《英》flannel] him. | Flattery will get you nowhere with him. | He is impervious to flattery.

おだやか 君が彼の前でそんなことをするのは穏やかでないと思う. I think it improper for you to act that way in his presence.

おちあう そこで落ち合おうという約束は果たされなかった. The rendezvous was not kept. / その村は千曲川と犀川の落ち合う所にある. The village is situated at the junction of the rivers Chikuma and Sai [where the rivers Chikuma and Sai meet].

おちつく この絵はこの部屋では落ち着きが悪い. The painting is out of keeping with this room.

おちつく 当分ここに落ち着くつもりです. We'll make our home here for some time to come. / まあ落ち着きたまえ. Cool [Calm] down. | 〈怒るな〉《口語》Keep your hair on. / この部屋は気が落ち着かない. I don't feel at home in this room. / 彼もあの会社の重役になって, これで落ち着くところへ落ち着いたわけだ. He has found his proper level as one of the directors of that firm. / 結局現状維持に落ち着くことになるでしょう. I think we will, after all is said and done, settle for the maintenance of the status quo.

おちど 私の方に落ち度はない. There is no fault on my part.

おちぶれる まだそこまでは落ちぶれない. I haven't sunk as low as that yet.

おちめ 彼も落ち目になった. His fortunes have begun to decline. |

おちゃっぴい 〈おしゃべり〉《口語》a chatterbox；〈ませた娘〉a precocious girl.

おちょぼぐち おちょぼ口 a button of a mouth ¶おちょぼ口をする purse [pucker] up *one's* lips.

おちる 落ちる 〈落下する〉fall；drop；come [go] down；〈橋など〉give way；〈壁など〉crumble；〈屋根など〉fall [cave] in；〈日が〉set；sink；〈城などが〉fall；〈漏れる〉be omitted；be left out；be missing；〈取れる〉come off [out]；〈劣る〉be not as good as；《文》be inferior (to)；〈落第する〉fail ⇨らくだい；〈手に入る〉fall into (*one's* hand)；〈柔道で〉fall unconscious；pass out ¶椅子から落ちる fall off a chair／木から落ちる fall [drop] from a tree／〈人が〉fall out of a tree／はしご段から落ちる fall down the stairs；fall downstairs／〈雨が〉ぽつぽつ落ちる fall in drops／〈成績が〉5 番に落ちる go down to fifth place／客足が落ちる 〈店が主語〉lose (*its*) customers [《文》custom]. 文例⇩

おつ 乙 〈第 2〉 the second；B；〈成績の〉B；good；〈後者〉《文》the latter ¶乙な stylish；smart；chic；〈結構な〉nice；fine／乙な事を言う make witty [clever] remarks／乙に澄ます put on airs；act affectedly；《文》strike an affected pose／乙に澄ましてプルーディに primly；〈偉ぶって〉in a superior way；with a superior air [an air of superiority].

おっかなびっくり ¶おっかなびっくりで timidly；in great fear ⇨びくびく.

おつき お付き ¶お付きの者 an attendant；a person in attendance ⟨on a prince⟩.

おっくう ¶おっくうな〈事が〉bothersome；troublesome；tiresome／おっくうがる think it too much trouble to *do*；《俗》think *sth* is a (real) drag；find it a great bother to *do*；be too lazy to *do*.

オックスフォード Oxford ¶オックスフォード大学 Oxford University；〈正式名〉the University of Oxford／オックスフォード大学の出身者 an Oxford man [woman]；《文》an Oxonian (★今では Oxonian はやや気取った言い方とされている).

おつげ お告げ an oracle；a revelation；a divine message ¶神様のお告げで《know *sth*》through divine revelation.

おっしゃる ⇨いう. 文例⇩

おっちょこちょい a careless [hasty] person；《口語》a scatterbrain；《口語》a birdbrain.

おっつかっつ おっつかっつの much [about, nearly] the same；nearly equal. 文例⇩

おっつけ 追っ付け soon；by and by；before long.

おって¹ 追っ手 pursuers；a pursuing party；《米》a posse ¶追っ手をかける send a party of pursuers after *sb*.

おって² 追って later (on)；afterward(s).

おってがき 追って書き a postscript (略：P.S.).

おっと¹ 夫 a husband ¶夫のある女 a married woman.

おっと² oh. 文例⇩

おっとせい 《動》a fur seal.

おっとり ¶おっとりした〈上品な〉《文》urbane；《文》well-bred；gentlemanly（男が）；ladylike（女が）；《口語》smooth；〈おだやかな〉《文》mild-mannered；unassuming；《文》unpretentious；《文》undemonstrative.

おてあげ お手上げ ⇨《手を挙げる》¶お手上げだ be finished；《口語》be done for；《口語》have had it；《英口語》have had *one's* chips.

おでこ 〈額〉the forehead；the brow；〈突き出た額〉a prominent [bulging] forehead ¶おでこの〈a boy〉with a prominent forehead.

おてだま お手玉 a beanbag ¶お手玉をする toss [play with] beanbags.

おてつき お手付き ¶（カルタ遊びで）お手付きをする touch a wrong card.

おてのもの お手の物 《文》*one's* forte；*one's* specialty ¶…はお手の物である〈人が主語〉be quite at home in 《English》；《文》be well versed in 《chess》；be in *one's* element 《doing, when...》；〈事が主語〉be *one's* line.

おてもり お手盛り ¶お手盛りの計画 a plan made to suit *oneself*. 文例⇩

おてやわらか お手柔らか ¶お手柔らかに

Luck has begun to go against him.／彼の人気もとうに落ち目になっている. His popularity has been on the wane for a long time.

おちゃ あんなやつを負かすのはお茶の子さいさい〈だ〉. I can beat him hands down.／それくらいはお茶の子さいさい〈だ〉.《俗》That's a cinch.／《英俗》That's a piece of cake.

おちる 彼は 20 メートルのところから地上に落ちた. He fell twenty meters to the ground.／軒から雨垂れがぽたぽた落ちている. Rainwater is dripping from the eaves, tap, tap, tap.／冬になるといたいの木の葉が落ちる. In winter most trees are stripped of their leaves.／そこに落ちているのは何ですか. What's that lying there?／昨夜のひどい風で木の実がみな落ちた. That big wind last night shook all the fruit off the tree.／橋は落ちていた. The bridge was down.／桟敷が落ちてけが人が数名出た. The gallery gave way and several people were injured.／アテネはスパルタの手に落ちた. Athens fell to Sparta.／このしみはどうしても落ちない. This stain won't come out.／これは見本より落ちる. This does not come up to the sample.／近頃私は語学の力が落ちてきている. My language ability is regressing these days.

おっしゃる ふん，おっしゃいましたね. You don't mince (your) words, do you!｜Well, that's a fine remark, I must say.／私で役に立つ事がありましたらおっしゃって下さい. If there is anything I can do for you, please let me know.／そうおっしゃるのでしたら（そういたしましょう）. As you wish.

おっつかっつ その 2 つではおっつかっつといったところだろう. I

おてん 汚点 a blot; a stain; a taint; a blemish; a flaw ¶汚点をつける put a blot (on) / 汚点を残す leave a stain (on) / 名声にぬぐうべからざる汚点を残す〈事柄が主語〉《文》leave an indelible stain on *one's* name [reputation].

おでん vegetables, fish dumplings and various other articles of food stewed in a thin soy soup, and served hot.

おてんきや お天気屋 a temperamental [moody] person;《文》a man of moods.

おてんば a tomboy;《文》a hoyden ¶おてんばな tomboyish;《文》hoydenish.

おと 音 a sound;〈騒音〉a noise; a din ¶波の音 the roar of the waves; the booming of the sea / 音を出す make [《文》produce] a sound / 音を立てる make (a) noise / 音を立てて noisily / 音を立てないで noiselessly; softly. 文例↓

おとうさん お父さん a [*one's*] father;〈呼びかけの語〉Father (ややあらたまった言い方);《口語》Dad;《口語》Daddy (主に女性・子供が使う);《米口語》Pop;《米口語》Poppa ★ 男性では成人すると Daddy と言うのをてれくさくなって Dad と言うようになる人が多いが,女性では Daddy という呼び方を一生使う人は珍しくない.

おとうと 弟 a (younger) brother; *one's* little [《米口語》kid] brother ⇨あに[1] 用法 ¶末の弟 *one's* youngest brother. 文例↓

おとおし お通し a relish; an hors d'oeuvre (《pl.》-(s)).

おどおど ¶おどおどする be nervous; be frightened;《文》be in fear;《口語》have the jitters / おどおどして timidly; nervously;《文》timorously.

おどかし 脅かし a threat;《文》a menace; intimidation.

おどかす 脅かす threaten;《文》menace; intimidate; browbeat;〈びっくりさせる〉frighten; scare;《口語》throw a scare into *sb* / 殺すぞと脅かす threaten to kill *sb*; threaten *sb* with death. 文例↓

おとぎ お伽 ¶おとぎの国 (a) fairyland / おとぎ話 a fairy tale [story]; a nursery tale / おとぎ話の世界 a fairy-tale world; (a) never-never land.

おどけ《文》a pleasantry; an attempt at humor ⇨どけ ¶おどけ者 a joker; a wag.

おどける joke; be funny; play the fool ¶おどけた funny; humorous;《文》droll; facetious / おどけて as a joke; jokingly; in fun;《文》in sport; humorously.

おとこ 男 a man (*pl.* men);《口語》menfolk (複数);〈男性〉the male sex;〈やつ〉a fellow;《米口語》a guy;《英口語》a chap;〈情夫〉*one's* lover ¶面白い男 an amusing fellow / 男だけの世界 the male-only world (the *sumo* stables) / 男だけのパーティー a stag party / 男がすたる (should) be ashamed (of *oneself*); cannot live with *oneself* / 男の / 男らしい; masculine; male / 男の中の男《文》a man among men / 男のような mannish《women》/ 男の先生 a man teacher (*pl.* men teachers) / 男の文学 man's literature; literature for men / 男の子〈少年〉a boy;〈赤ん坊〉a baby boy; a boy baby / 男を下げる lose face; disgrace *oneself*; cannot [can no longer] hold *one's* head up (in public) /《文》fall in (the) public estimation [esteem] / 男を上げる do something *one* can be proud of; perform [pass] with flying colors /《文》rise in (the) public estimation [esteem] / 男にほれられるような男 a man's man / 男にする make a man of *sb* / 一人前の男になる become a man; come of age;《文》attain manhood / 男らしい manly; masculine / 男らしくない 男らしからぬ unmanly; effeminate / 男らしくする be a man; behave [act] like a man / 男親 a father / 男気のある chivalrous / 男嫌い〈人〉a man-hater / 男心 a man's feelings / 男坂 the steeper of the two uphill paths (leading to a shrine) / 男盛りに in the prime of manhood / 男所帯 a womanless household; a bachelor's home / 男伊達(㊥) a 'knight of the town' who is ready to defend the lower classes against bullying *samurai* / 男たらし《文》a femme fatale (*pl.* femmes fatales);《文》a siren; a flirt / 男友達 a boyfriend; a man friend (*pl.* men friends) / 男ぶりのいい handsome; good-looking / 男まさりの spirited [strong-minded]《women》/ 男持ちの gentlemen's《watches》; men's《umbrellas》/ 男物 men's things;〈衣類〉men's wear /（女性が）男物のセーターを着ている be

---

don't think there's much to choose between the two. | It is very difficult to say which of the two is better. / 私は当時 40 歳, 大田さんもおっつかっつの年頃だったと思う. I was forty then, and Mr. Ota, I think, was not far from it.

おっと[2] おっとどっこい, その手は食わんよ. Oh, I know that little game of yours. / おっと待った. Wait a bit. | Just a moment!

お手あげだ お手上げだ. I don't know what to do. | Nothing can be done about it. / その事件については教員一同お手上げの態だった. The faculty threw up its hands in despair over that incident.

おてもり 議員のお手盛り増俸案が昨夜可決された. Last night the assemblymen passed the bill to raise their own pay.

おてやわらか お手柔らかに願います. Don't be too hard on me, please. |〈競技で〉I hope you won't give me too hard a game.

おと 何か音がしましたか. Did you hear anything? / その音が何だかわかりますか. Can you identify this sound? / 大きな音がして木が倒れた. The tree came down with a loud crash. / 波が岸辺を洗う音が遠くに聞こえた. The lapping of the water against the shore could be heard in the distance. / 彼が多年の努力によって築き上げた事業が, 今, 音を立てて崩れ始めたのだった. The business which he had built up with years of effort was now disintegrating like a great edifice collapsing to the ground.

おとうと 清水さんも私も木内先生の門下で, 私の方が弟弟子です. We are both pupils of Master Kiuchi. I started to study under him later than Mr. Shimizu did.

おどかす 800万円かかるって, おど

wearing a man's sweater / 男役 〈宝塚などの〉 a male role [part] / 男やもめ a widower. 文例下

おとさた 音沙汰 news; a letter; 《文》 tidings.

おどし 脅し ⇒おどかし ¶ただの脅し an idle threat / 〈動物の〉脅しの姿勢をとる assume a threat posture / 脅し文句 threatening words; 《口語》tough talk.

おとしあな 落とし穴 a pitfall (trap); a pit (trap) ¶野獣を捕えるための落とし穴 a game pit / 落とし穴の仕掛けてある問題 a catch question (in an examination) / 落とし穴に落ちる[かかる] fall [walk] into a pit [trap] ★ pit はほとんどの場合文字どおりの意味にしか解されないが、trap の方は文脈によって比喩的な意味にもなる. 文例下

おとしいれる 落とし入れる, 陥れる trap; 《文》ensnare; 《文》entrap; 〈城などに〉《文》take; 《文》carry; 《文》reduce ¶人を謀略で落とし入れて…させる trick sb [entrap sb by a trick] into doing / 落とし入れられる be trapped; 《文》be ensnared; 《文》be entrapped; be caught in a snare (set by sb).

おとしだね 落し胤 a bastard (child); an illegitimate child.

おとしだま お年玉 money given as a gift at the New Year; a New Year's present [gift] ¶お年玉つき年賀はがき a New Year's lottery postcard.

おとしたまご 落とし卵 poached eggs.

おとしぬし 落とし主 the owner of a lost [found] article. 文例下

おとしぶた 落とし蓋 《料理》¶落とし蓋をする place a small lid directly on the food (to be boiled in a pot).

おとしもの 落とし物 a lost article; lost property.

おとす 落とす 〈高所から〉drop; let sth fall; throw sth down 〈失う〉lose; 〈取り去る〉take away [off]; 《文》remove; 〈控除する〉deduct; 〈脱漏する〉leave out; 《文》omit; 〈名声・品質などを〉lower; 《文》degrade; 《文》debase; 〈失墜する〉take 《something》away; [《文》detract] from 《one's reputation》; 〈競売で〉knock sth down 《to sb》(競売人が); make a successful bid (for sth) (せり手が) ¶財布[命]を落とす lose one's wallet [life] / いくさに《大いに》世間の評判を落とす〈人が主語〉fall a little [a great deal] in (the) public estimation / ボールを落とす miss [fail to catch] the ball / 試合を落とす lose a game / あごひげを落とす shave off one's beard / 〈得意で〉角を落とす《米口語》spot 《one's opponent》a kaku / 《英》give sb a kaku / 声を落として in a subdued voice. 文例下

おどす 脅す ⇒おどかす ¶脅して承知させる terrify sb into agreeing [《文》compliance]; browbeat sb into accepting 《the proposal》/ 脅して追い払う scare [threaten] sb off / 脅したりすかしたりして with threats and coaxings; using the carrot and the stick.

おとずれ 訪れ ⇒ほうもん² ¶春の訪れ the coming of spring. 文例下

おとずれる 訪れる ⇒ほうもん² (訪問する).

おととい 一昨日 (the) day before yesterday ¶おとといの朝 the morning before last.

おととし 一昨年 the year before last ¶おととしの夏 (in) the summer before last.

おとな 大人 a man (pl. men); a woman (pl. women); an adult; 《小児語》a grownup ¶大人の adult; grown-up / 大人の遊び a game for adults / 大人になる grow up (to be a man [woman]) / become a man [woman] / 大人びている look like a grownup; be precocious (ませている) / 大人げない《文》(be) unworthy of a grown man [woman]; 〈子供じみた〉childish; 《文》puerile. 文例下

おとなしい gentle; mild; meek; good-tempered; 〈従順な〉obedient; 《文》docile; 〈物静かな〉quiet; 〈行儀のよい〉well-behaved; 〈なれた〉tame; 〈色調などの〉quiet; sober ¶おとなしく gently; meekly; obediently; 〈静かに〉quietly / おとなしくする behave (well [properly]); behave oneself; act as one should (do); 〈子供が〉be a good child [boy, girl]; be good / おとなしくしている keep quiet; be on

---

かすなよ. It will cost eight million yen, you say? No kidding!

おとこ 赤ちゃんは男ですか女ですか. Is the baby a boy or a girl? / 〈赤ん坊を見せながら〉どうだ立派な男の子だろう. Isn't he a fine big man? / さすが男だ, よく言った. Spoken like a man! / 男らしくないやつだな. He's not much of a man, is he? / 男らしくしろ. Be a man! / 伊藤君の方がお前よりよっぽど男らしいぞ. Ito is much more of a man than you are. / 彼は男泣きに泣いた. He wept in spite of himself. / いよう, 相変わらずの男ぶりだね, チャーリー. I see you haven't lost your looks, Charlie. / 彼女はずっと男嫌いで通して来た. She always declared that she would have nothing to do with men. / 男やもめにうじがわく. A widower cannot look after himself properly [keep the house clean and tidy].

おとさた それっきり彼から音さたがない. I have heard nothing from him since.

おとしあな この種の広告に不用意に飛びつくと落とし穴にかかることがある. This sort of advertisement can hold pitfalls for the unwary. / この問題は一見やさしい. ところが, ここに落とし穴があるのだ. This question looks easy at first glance. Here, however, is the catch.

おとしぬし その金の落とし主はまだ現われない. As yet no one has appeared to claim the money.

おとす あれっ, クレジットカードがない. どこかで落としてしまったのかもしれない. Oh, my credit card is missing! I may have dropped it somewhere. / 彼は名簿を読み上げるときに私の名を落とした. He skipped [missed] my name in calling the roll.

おとずれ 春の訪れも近い. Spring will soon be here. | Spring is just around the corner.

おとな その展覧会の入場料は大人1人500円です. The admission to the exhibition is 500 yen per adult. / 大人になるまではそういう所へ行ってはいけません. You shouldn't go to such a place until you are grown up [an adult]. / ジョンは大人にならないうちに死んだ. John did not live to [see] adulthood [manhood]. / その裁判事件で彼は大人になった. The lawsuit made a man (out) of him. / あの娘はもう子供じゃな

おとなしのかまえ 音無しの構え ¶音無しの構えでいる take [do] nothing and wait for an opportunity;《口語》lie low.
おとめ 乙女 《文》a maiden; a (young) girl; a virgin〈処女〉 ¶乙女座《天》Virgo; the Virgin
おとも お供 ⇒とも².
おとり 囮〈鳥〉a decoy (bird);〈誘い〉a lure; a bait ¶おとりに使う use (a bird) for calling [for a caller, as a decoy];〈人を〉use [《文》employ] sb as a decoy;《口語》put sb〈in a criminal organization〉as a plant / おとり捜査 an undercover operation [investigation];《米口語》a sting.
おどり 踊り a dance; dancing ¶踊りがうまい be a good dancer; dance well / 踊りの師匠 a dancing master [mistress] / 踊り子 a dancer;〈ショーの〉a showgirl; a chorus girl / 踊り場 a dance floor;〈階段の〉a landing.
おどりあがる 躍り上がる spring [jump] up; leap [jump] to one's feet ¶躍り上がって喜ぶ jump for joy; dance with joy.
おどりかかる 躍りかかる spring [jump] on sb.
おどりこむ 躍り込む〈飛び込む〉jump [leap] into;〈乱入する〉rush [burst] into.
おどりでる 躍り出る jump (to the top place in a contest).
おとる 劣る 《文》be inferior (to); be worse (than); compare unfavorably ((with)) ¶だれにも劣らない be second to none ((in batting)); be as (skillful) as the next man. 文例⊕
おどる 踊[躍]る〈踊りを踊る〉dance;〈跳ねる〉jump; leap; spring ¶喜びに胸を躍らせて with one's heart leaping (up) for joy / 急流に躍る鮭 a salmon leaping a rapid / 踊り出す begin to dance; go [break] into a dance. 文例⊕
おとろえ 衰え weakening; (a) decline ¶健康の衰えを感じる feel that one's health is getting worse [deteriorating];《文》sense a decline in one's health.

おとろえる 衰える〈衰弱する〉get [《文》become] weak; lose vigor; waste away; flag;《文》be enfeebled;〈なえしおれる〉wither; fade;〈衰退する〉decline; decay;《文》wane;〈火や風などの勢いが〉subside; slack off;《文》wane;〈勇気などが〉sink ¶人気[健康]が衰える one's popularity [health] declines;《文》decline in popularity [health] / 衰えかけている be declining; be failing;《口語》be going downhill / 勢いが衰えず《文》with unabated vigor. 文例⊕
おどろかす 驚かす surprise; astonish; startle; amaze;〈ぎょっとさせる〉shock; give sb a start;〈怖がらせる〉frighten; terrify; scare;〈騒がす〉create a sensation [stir]. 文例⊕
おどろき 驚き surprise; astonishment;〈驚嘆〉amazement; wonder;〈恐怖〉fright; horror; terror ¶驚きの目を見張る stare in wonder (at). 文例⊕
おどろく 驚く〈びっくりする〉be surprised [astonished, amazed] ((at, to see)); be taken aback;〈ぎょっとする〉be shocked; get a start [turn];〈怖がる〉be frightened; be alarmed; take alarm ((at));〈驚嘆する〉wonder ((at));《文》marvel ((at)) ¶驚くべき surprising; startling; astonishing; amazing; wonderful; marvelous / 驚くに当たらない事実 an unsurprising fact / 驚くに足りない It is no [little,《文》small] wonder that... / 驚いたことには to one's surprise [astonishment, dismay] / 驚いて物が言えない be struck dumb; be speechless with surprise / 驚いて叫ぶ cry out in surprise [astonishment] / 驚きあわてる be frightened out of one's wits ((by, at)). 文例⊕
おないどし 同い年 ¶同い年である be the same age as...;〈双方が主語〉《文》be of an age / 同い年の人 a person of the same age(-group) as one / 彼と同い年くらいの少年たち boys about his age.
おなか お腹 the stomach;《口語》one's inside(s);《小児語》one's tummy ⇒はら² ¶おなかの子 the child one [sb] is expecting. 文例⊕
おなが 尾長《鳥》an azure-winged magpie.

い. 大人だ. She's no longer a child. She's a grown woman. / 小さな子供に向かって悪態をつくなんて, それがいい大人のすることですか. Are you calling a little boy names? That's a fine manly way to behave! [Why don't you act your age?]
おとなしい おとなしくしないとどこへも連れて行かないよ. If you don't behave (yourself), I won't take you anywhere. / いずれおとなしくなるよ. He'll tame down in time. / 錦蛇はおとなしい動物でいいペットになる. Indian pythons are unaggressive creatures and make good pets.
おとる バレーダンサーは技術が確かでなければならないが, それに劣らず大切なことは, 音楽に対して敏感なことである. Ballet danc-

ers must have accurate technique, but it is no less important that they (should) be sensitive to music. / 今日も昨日に劣らず寒い. Today is just as cold as yesterday was. / 畜生にも劣ったやつだ. He is worse than an animal.
おどる 彼は笛に合わせて踊った. He danced to the flute. / 要するに, 君は彼に踊らされていたんだ. The fact is that you've been made to dance to his tune.
おとろえる 彼の健康は既に衰えかけていた. His health was already declining [failing]. / 彼の人気は非常に衰えている. His popularity is very much on the wane [《俗》is on the skids]. / 彼は近頃めっきり衰えた. He has lost a great deal of his vigor lately. / 彼女の仕事に対する意欲と能力は老年に

なっても衰えなかった. Her willingness and ability to work did not drop off even in her old age.
おどろかす そのニュースには全くもって驚かされたよ. The news has quite bowled me over.
おどろき これを聞いたときの両親の驚きはどんなだったろう. How [You can imagine how] surprised his parents were when they heard! / あの人がまだ40歳とは驚きだ. It comes as a surprise to learn that he is only forty.
おどろく その知らせには全く[ちょっぴり]驚いた. The news gave me quite a turn [gave me a bit of a turn]. / 彼の腕前には驚き入った. I was filled with admiration for his skill.
おなか 彼女は大分お腹が大きい. She is very obviously in the fam-

おながどり 尾長鶏 a long-tailed rooster.
おながれ お流れ ¶お流れになる be given up; be dropped; be called off;《文》prove abortive.
おなじ 同じ〈同一〉the same; one and the same; self-same; identical;〈等しい〉equivalent (to);〈同様の〉similar (to);《文》like;《俗》kindred;〈共通の〉common ¶ほとんど同じである be much [almost] the same (as); there is not much to choose between《them》/ 同じ高さである be [《文》be of] the same height; be as high as... /死んだも同じである be as good as dead / 泥棒と同じだ be no [little] better than a thief / 同じことを何度も言う say the same thing again and again; repeat *oneself* / 同じ条件で on equal terms / 同じに[く] in the same way [manner];《文》likewise; similarly;《文》alike; equally; as well. 文例⇩
用法 the same...as は「同種」, the same...that は「同一」を意味するという説があるが, 実際はそのような区別は行なわれていない. 意味の区別は文脈によって決まる. たとえば He wears the same necktie as [that] he wore yesterday はどちらも「同一」の意味である. ただし, 現代英語では一般に that よりも as が好まれる. また, あとに動詞が続かないときは, 当然ながら, as しか使えない.

おに 鬼 an ogre; a demon;〈鬼ごっこの〉it ¶仕事の鬼 a demon for work;《文》an indefatigable worker / 鬼のような《文》fiendish; cruel;《文》inhuman;《文》demoniacal / 鬼のような人間 a devil (of a man);《文》a human fiend / 鬼の首を取ったように triumphantly [《文》*one's*heart]; 《文》steel *oneself* [*one's* heart] against pity. 文例⇩
おにがわら 鬼瓦 a ridge-end tile.
おにごっこ 鬼ごっこ ¶鬼ごっこをする play tag《with》.
おにび 鬼火 a will-o'-the-wisp; a jack-o'-lantern.
おにひとで〖動〗a crown-of-thorns starfish.
おにゆり〖植〗a tiger lily.
おね 尾根 a ridge; a spur (横に張り出した).
おねじ 雄ねじ a male screw.
おの 斧 an ax(e); a hatchet (手おの) ¶斧を加える take an axe to《a tree, the budget》.
おのおの 各々 各々 ⇨ 文例⇩
おのずから 自ずから〈自然と〉naturally; as a matter of course;〈ひとりでに〉《文》of *itself*; of *its* own accord ¶おのずから明らかな ob-

vious;《文》self-evident;《文》axiomatic. 文例⇩
おののく 戦く shudder ⇨ ふるえる.
おのぼりさん お上りさん a visitor (to Tokyo) from the country;《米口語》a (country) hick.
おのれ 己 ⇨ じぶん¹.
おは 尾羽 ¶尾羽打ち枯らしている〈貧乏している〉《文》be in reduced circumstances;《口語》be down and out;〈身なりが〉be shabbily dressed; be down at heel.
おば 伯叔母 an aunt ¶おばちゃん《小児語》an auntie.
おばあさん〈祖母〉a grandmother; a grandma;《小児語》a granny;〈老婦人〉an old woman [lady] ¶おばあさん子 a child spoiled by his [her] grandmother.
オパール opal.
オハイオ Ohio ¶オハイオ州の人 an Ohioan.
おばけ お化け ⇨ ばけもの.
おはこ〈えて〉*one's* favorite (party [parlor]) trick; *one's* specialty;《文》*one's* forte ¶おはこを出す perform [《口語》trot out] *one's* regular party trick.
おばさん 小母さん a (middle-aged) lady ¶よそのおばさん a (strange) lady.
おはじき〈玉〉a tiddlywink; a counter;〈遊び〉《play》(a Japanese game resembling) tiddlywinks.
おはち お鉢 a container [tub] for boiled rice;〈順番〉*one's* turn. 文例⇩
おばな 雄花 a male flower [blossom].
おはなばたけ お花畑〈高山の〉a field of alpine flowers.
おばね 尾羽〈鳥の〉tail feathers.
おはよう お早う Good morning! ¶お早うと言う wish [《文》bid] *sb* good morning; say good morning (to).
おはらいばこ お払い箱 ¶お払い箱になる《文》be dismissed; be [get] fired;《口語》be sacked;《口語》get the sack.
おび 帯 an obi; a belt; a sash (女帯); a girdle (腰帯) ¶帯を締める[解く, 結ぶ] put on [undo, tie] an obi / 帯に短したすきに長しである be good for neither one thing nor the other.
おびあげ 帯揚げ a bustle for an obi.
おびえる 脅[怯]える be frightened (of, at); be scared (of);《口語》get the wind up.
おびきいれる 誘き入れる lure [decoy, entice] *sb* into《a place》.

---

ily way. | She looks as if her baby is due pretty soon. |〈少しユーモラスに〉She is very pregnant.
おなじ 僕は君と同じ辞書を持っている. I have the same dictionary as yours. / 今日行っても明日行っても同じだ. It makes no difference whether you go today or tomorrow. / これは僕にとっては死刑の宣告だ. This is as good as a death sentence to me. / 生を愛し死を恐れることは人も動物も同じだ. Love of life and fear of death are common to man and beasts. / 趣味が同じところから彼らは親しくなった. They became friends as a result of the interests they had in common. / 僕だって同じ人間だよ. I am no less a man than you are.
おに 鬼に金棒だ. That would really clinch it for us [give us the edge]. | That would give us a decisive advantage. / 鬼の目にも涙. Even the hardest heart will sometimes be moved to pity. / 鬼の居ぬ間に洗濯. When the cat's away, the mice will play. /〈諺〉

「鬼も十八, 番茶も出花」というが, あの子もこのごろきれいになった. She looks quite pretty these days. 'Sweet sixteen,' you know. /〈鬼ごっこで〉君が鬼だよ. You're it.
おのおの 人には各々長所と短所とがある. Each person has his merits and demerits.
おのずから 事実はおのずから明らかである. The facts speak for themselves.
おはち 僕にお鉢が回って来た. My turn has come (round).

おびきだす 誘き出す lure [decoy, entice] sb out of (a place).

おびきよせる 誘き寄せる lure [entice] sb to come toward one.

おひたし お浸し ¶ほうれんそうのおひたし boiled spinach ((eaten with soy sauce)).

おびただしい 夥しい 〈多数の〉a great many; a great number of;《文》innumerable; countless; 〈莫大な〉vast; immense; enormous ¶おびただしい人出 an enormous turnout of people / おびただしく in great numbers; abundantly;《文》profusely;《文》copiously / おびただしく出血する bleed copiously.

おひつじ 雄[牡]羊 ⇨ ひつじ ¶牡羊座《天》Aries; the Ram ⇨ さ 文例.

おびどめ 帯留〔帯締め〕a sash band; 〈飾り〉an ornament worn over an obi.

おひとよし お人好し a softhearted [good-natured] person; 〈だまされやすい人〉a credulous person; an easy mark;《口語》a soft touch ((金を借りやすい)). 文例

おびふう 帯封 a wrapper ¶帯封をする put a (mailing) wrapper around (a newspaper).

おびやかす 脅かす 〈脅迫する〉threaten;《文》menace; 〈恐れさせる〉frighten; scare; intimidate. 文例

おひゃくど お百度 ¶お百度を踏む walk back and forth a hundred times before a shrine offering a prayer each time; 〈比喩的に〉make repeated calls on sb (to ask a favor).

おひょう 〘魚〙a (Pacific) halibut ((pl. -(s)).

おひらき お開き ¶お開きにする break up;《文》adjourn; close (a party).

おびる 帯びる wear [《文》bear] ((a sword)); carry; 〈委任される〉《文》be entrusted [charged] ((with)); 〈含む〉have; 〈持つようになる〉take on ((a new meaning)); 〈…の気味がある〉have a trace ((of)); be tinged ((with)); 〈憂いを帯びている〉wear a sorrowful look; look sad / 赤味を帯びた reddish; tinged with red / 重要な使命を帯びて on an important mission.

おひれ 尾鰭 ¶尾ひれをつける 〈誇張する〉exaggerate;《口語》stretch ((the facts)); 〈潤色する〉《文》embellish [add embellishments to] ((one's account)); embroider ((a story)); dress up ((one's adventure)); add made-up details ((to a story)).

オフィス an office ¶オフィス街 a street lined with office buildings; a business district ((地区)).

おぶう 負ぶう carry ((a child)) on one's back; have ((a baby)) strapped to one's back.

おふくろ お袋 one's mother ¶お袋の味 the taste of home cooking.

オブザーバー an observer.

おぶさる 負ぶさる be carried on sb's back; 〈頼る〉rely [depend] ((on)).

オフセット 〔印刷〕offset (printing) ¶オフセット(印刷)にする offset / オフセット印刷機 an offset press.

おふだ 御札 a charm ((お守り)); an amulet ((護符)); a talisman ((まじない札)).

おぶつ 汚物 filth; dirt; muck.

オブラート 〔＜《ドイツ語》Oblate〕a wafer ((for wrapping a dose of powdered medicine)) ¶不快な事実をオブラートに包む sugar-coat an unpleasant fact.

おふる お古 a used article; 〈衣類〉(his brother's) hand-me-downs;《英》(her sister's) reach-me-downs.

おべっか flattery;《口語》soft soap;《英口語》flannel ¶おべっかを言う[使う] flatter; curry favor with sb; fawn on sb;《口語》soft-soap sb;《口語》butter sb up;《英口語》flannel sb / おべっか使い a flatterer;《文》a sycophant; a toady.

オペック 〔石油輸出国機構〕OPEC ★ the Organization of Petroleum Exporting Countries の略.

オペラ an opera ⇨ かげき² ¶グランドオペラ a grand opera / オペラ歌手 an opera singer / オペラグラス opera glasses.

オペレッタ an operetta.

おべんちゃら ⇨ おべっか.

おぼえ 覚え 〈記憶〉memory; 〈回想〉《文》recollection;《文》remembrance; 〈感じ〉a sense; 〈経験〉(an) experience; 〈気受け〉(a) favor ¶覚えがよい[悪い] 〈理解〉be quick [slow] at learning ((things)); be a quick [slow] learner / 〈記憶〉have a good [poor] memory / 覚えがある remember; recall / 〈悪事について〉身に覚えのないことだと言う insist on [《文》assert] one's innocence; say that one is [《文》declare oneself (to be)] innocent of ((a crime)) / 覚えがめでたい《口語》be in sb's good books;《文》be in sb's favor / 覚えがめでたくない be out of favor with sb;《口語》be in sb's bad books. 文例

おぼえがき 覚え書き 〈備忘録〉a memorandum

おひとよし 私はそれほどのお人好しではありませんよ. I'm afraid you greatly overrate my good nature. / そんな話でだまされるなんて,君もずいぶんお人好しだ. It's pretty naive of you to be taken in by such a story.

おびやかす 同国に戦乱の続く限り極東の平和は脅かされるであろう. So long as the war goes on in that country, it will be a menace to the peace of the Far East. / 我々のチームは彼らを大いに脅かすことであろう. Our team will pose them a real threat.

おぼえ あの人に会った覚えがある. I remember meeting him. / 僕も同じような目にあった覚えがある. I've had a similar experience. / こんなに寒い3月は今まで覚えがない. I have never known such a cold March as this. / 中国のこの地方では,これまでに白人を見た覚えのある人は1人もない. In this part of China no white man has been seen in living memory.

おぼえる その本を子供の時に読んだことを覚えている. I remember reading [having read, that I read] the book when I was a child. / 彼は人の名前をよく覚える[覚えない]たちだ. He has a good memory for names [is no good at remembering names]. / 学校で習った幾何でどなたも覚えていることと思いますが, どんな三角形でもその3つの角の合計はいつも180度です. As everybody will remember from school geometry, the sum of the three angles of any triangle is always 180 degrees. / 食事がとてもうまかった

おぼえる　　　　　　　　　　　　　　　　　　　　　170　　　　　　　　　　　　　　　　　おめずおくせず

《pl. -dums, -da》; a memo 《pl. -s》; 〈外交文書〉 a note; a memorandum ¶覚え書きを送る [手交する] send [deliver] a note 《to》/ (各国の代表が署名した)共同覚え書き a collective note.

おぼえる 覚える 〈記憶する〉 remember; 《文》 commit (a fact) to memory; memorize; 〈暗記する〉 learn by heart; 〈習得する〉 learn; 《文》 acquire (a new technique); master (完全に); 〈感じる〉 feel (a pain) ¶覚えている〈人が主語〉 remember, recall; have [bear, keep] sth in mind; 〈事が主語〉 live in one's memory; はっきりと[ぼんやり]覚えている remember clearly [vaguely]; 《文》 have a vivid [dim] recollection (of). (前ページから)

オホーツクかい オホーツク海 the Sea of Okhotsk.

おぼしい 思しい ¶その子の父とおぼしい人物 a man who is apparently [who appears to be] the boy's father.

おぼしめし 思し召し 〈お考え〉 your opinion; 〈御意〉 your wishes [《文》 will, 《文》 pleasure] ¶おぼしめしがある be interested in sb; 《口語》 fancy (a girl).

オポチュニスト an opportunist.

おぼつかない 〈疑わしい〉 uncertain; doubtful; dubious; 〈見込みのない〉 unlikely; almost hopeless ¶おぼつかない足どりで with unsteady steps [《文》 gait] / おぼつかない英語で in faltering [shaky] English. 文例⇩

おぼれる 溺れる 〈水に〉 drown; be drowned; 〈耽溺(たんでき)する〉 indulge 《in》; be addicted 《to》; 《口語》 be hooked 《on a girl, on gambling》 ¶女におぼれる be infatuated with a woman / 子供の愛におぼれる dote on one's children. 文例⇩

おぼろ 朧 ¶おぼろげに vaguely; faintly; dimly; indistinctly / おぼろげに記憶している remember dimly; have a hazy recollection of / おぼろ月夜 a night with a hazy moon.

おまいり お参り ⇒ さんけい².

おまえ お前〈君〉 you; 〈妻に〉 dear; darling; 〈子供に〉 my child [boy] ¶ my son, my daughter はこの意味ではほとんど使われない。

おまけ 〈追加〉 an addition; 〈景品〉 something thrown in ¶おまけに in addition 《to》; on top of sth; into the bargain; 《文》 moreover; besides; 〈その上困ったことに〉 to make matters worse / …をおまけに付ける throw in sth (for good measure). 文例⇩

おまつり お祭り ⇒ まつり。

おまもり お守り an amulet; a (good-luck) charm; a talisman ⇒ まもり ¶災難よけのお守り a charm against [to ward off] evils.

おまわり お巡り 《口語》 a cop ⇒ けいかん² ¶お巡りさん an [a police] officer.

おみき お神酒 (a) libation; *sake* offered to a god.

おみくじ お神籤 a written oracle ¶おみくじを引く consult an oracle.

おみずとり お水取り the water-drawing ceremony; the rite of drawing sacred water.

おむつ a diaper; 《英》 a nappy; (a baby's) napkin ¶汚れたおむつ a wet [soiled] napkin / おむつをする put a diaper on (a baby); diaper (a baby) / 赤ん坊のおむつを取りかえる change the baby's diaper; change the baby / おむつカバー a diaper cover / おむつかぶれ diaper [nappy] rash / 貸しおむつ業 (be engaged in) diaper service.

オムレツ an omelet; an omelette.

おめ お目 ¶お目にかかる〈会う〉 see; meet; 《敬語》 have the honor [pleasure] of seeing sb / お目にかける show; 《文》 submit sth to [for] sb's inspection. 文例⇩

おめい 汚名 《文》 a stigma (pl. -mas, -mata); 《文》 a stain upon one's honor; 《文》 dishonor; disgrace ¶汚名をこうむる〈人が主語〉 suffer [《文》 incur] disgrace (for); 《文》 be maligned; 〈事が主語〉 bring disgrace on (one's own head) / 汚名をそそぐ[すすぐ] clear one's name; remove the disgrace that has (been) attached to one's name.

おめおめ(と) 〈恥じもせず〉 unashamedly; shamelessly; 〈屈辱的に〉《文》 ignominiously; 〈おとなしく〉 tamely; 《take abuse》 lying down. 文例⇩

おめかし ⇒ おしゃれ。

おめしれっしゃ お召し列車 the Imperial train.

おめずおくせず 怯めず臆せず fearlessly; 《文》

ので、この店の名は一つ覚えておこうと思った. I found the meal so good that I made a mental note of the name of the restaurant. / そんな言い方をどこで覚えたんですか. Where did you pick up such an expression? / 覚えていろ！（このままではすまないぞ） You'll pay for this! | You won't get away with this! | You (just) wait!

おぼしめし 幾らですか。—おぼしめしで結構です。 How much?—Whatever (price) you care to pay.

おぼつかない あの人の全快はおぼつかない。 There is little hope for his recovery. / 彼の成功はおぼつかないと私は思う。 I don't think he is likely to succeed.

おぼれる 彼はおぼれそうになった少女を助けた. He saved a little girl from drowning. / おぼれるものは藁(わら)をもつかむ. A drowning man will clutch [catch] at a straw. 《諺》

おまけ 彼はおまけに身体を悪くした. What was worse, he damaged his health. / 彼は僕のことを日本一のばか者だと言った. For good measure, he added that I was the damnedest fool in the world.

おめ 伊藤ですが佐藤さんにお目にかかりたいとおっしゃって下さい。 Will you please tell Mr. Sato that Ito would like to see him?

おめおめ(と) おめおめこのような辱しめを受けるような彼らではあるまい. They will not take this humiliation lying down.

おめでた (出産の時)谷さんのお宅では近々おめでたがあるそうだ。 I hear that Mrs. Tani is expecting a happy event shortly.

おめでとう クリスマスおめでとう。—おめでとう。 Merry Christmas to you.—The same to you [And to you].

おもい¹ 彼女はひとりあれこれと思いにふけっていた. She was deep in her own thoughts. / 彼は思いにふけりながらその部屋を後にした. He left the room thinking deeply [deep in thought]. / 私が思いにふけっていると突然ドロシーに声をかけられた. Dorothy broke in on my reverie. / 思いは3

おめだま　お目玉　¶お目玉をちょうだいする〈口語〉be told off ((by)); be scolded ((by)); 〈口語〉get a (good) telling-off [talking-to] ((from)); 〈口語〉catch it (hot); 〈米口語〉be bawled out; 〈英口語〉have a strip torn off ((one)).

おめでた　a matter for congratulation; 〈文〉an auspicious event; 〈出産〉a happy event. 文例◊

おめでとう　Congratulations!; 〈誕生日に〉Happy birthday (to you)!; Many happy returns of the day! ¶おめでとうを言う give [offer] one's congratulations ((to)) / おめでとうと背中を叩かれる get a congratulatory pat on the back ((from a friend)). 文例◊

おめみえ　お目見え　〈俳優の〉(an actor's) first public appearance; a debut.

おもい¹　思い　〈考え〉(a) thought; 〈心〉mind; heart; 〈感情〉feelings; an emotion; sentiment; 〈愛情〉love; affection; 〈願望〉a desire; a wish; (a) hope; 〈期待〉expectation(s); 〈想像〉imagination; 〈経験〉an experience ¶思いがかなう have one's wish (come true); 〈文〉attain one's desire / 思いのままに as one likes [〈文〉pleases]; 〈文〉at will / 思いをはせる think about (home) / 思いを凝らす concentrate one's mind ((on)) / 思いを寄せる fall in love ((with)); take a fancy ((to)) / つらい思いをする have a bitter experience / 〈口語〉have a hard [thin] time (of it) / 思いにふける be lost [buried] in thought; 〈口語〉be miles away. 文例◊

おもい²　重い　〈目方が〉heavy; 〈重大な〉serious, important; 〈文〉weighty; 〈文〉grave; 〈罰などが〉severe; 〈気分が〉depressed ¶頭が重い one's head feels heavy; feel heavy in the head / 病気が重い be seriously [critically] ill / 重い罪 a serious [grave] crime / 重い罰 a severe punishment / 重い負担 a heavy burden / 重い地位 an important position / 重い足を引きずって歩く walk heavily [wearily], plod [trudge] ((along)) / 重くする〈目方を〉make sth heavier; add to its weight / 〈悪化さ せる〉make ((the situation)) worse; 〈文〉aggravate / 重くなる〈目方が〉get [〈文〉become, grow] heavy [heavier]; 〈文〉increase in weight; 〈病気が〉get [〈文〉become] worse [serious]; take a turn for the worse / 重く用いる give sb a position of trust / 重そうな heavy-looking ((packages)). 文例◊

おもいあがる　思い上がる　get conceited; have a high [good] opinion of oneself; 〈口語〉get stuck-up ((about)); 〈口語〉get too big for one's boots [breeches]; 〈文〉be puffed up ((with)); 〈米口語〉get a swelled head; 〈英口語〉get a swollen head ¶思い上がった conceited; 〈口語〉big-headed; 〈米〉swelled-headed; 〈英〉swollen-headed; 〈口語〉stuck-up. 文例◊

おもいあたる　思い当たる　〈事が主語〉occur to ((one, one's mind)); strike one; 〈人が主語〉call [bring] sth to mind; recall; remember; think of; 〈悟る〉realize. 文例◊

おもいあまる　思い余る　〈どうしてよいかわからない〉be at a loss [all at sea] ((as to what to do)); be unable to make up one's mind; 〈我慢できなくなる〉cannot stand sth any longer.

おもいあわせる　思い合わせる　¶かれこれ思い合わせる consider [weigh up] ((all the issues)); take ((various things)) into consideration [account].

おもいいれ　思い入れ　¶〈役者が〉思い入れする strike a (meditative) pose / 思い入れたっぷりに with a lot of posing for effect.

おもいえがく　思い描く　⇒そうぞう²(想像する).

おもいおこす　思い起こす　⇒おもいだす.

おもいおもい(に)　思い思い(に)　each in his own way; 〈文〉each according to his own fancy [taste].

おもいかえす　思い返す　〈もう一度考える〉think sth over (again); think back ((on sth)); reconsider; 〈考え直す〉think better of sth; change one's mind ((about)). 文例◊

おもいがけない　思いがけない　unexpected; unforeseen; 〈文〉unlooked-for; 〈偶然の〉accidental ¶思いがけない出合 a chance meeting / 思いがけない訪問客 an unexpected

---

年前ダンスパーティではじめて彼女に会った日に帰って行った。His thoughts went back three years to the day when he first saw her at a dance. / 僕がそんなことをするなんて思いも及ばないことだ。I cannot see myself doing a thing like that. / やっと思いがかなった。At last my wish has come true. / この一事をもってしても、この国の現状に対して彼らがいかに大きな不満を抱いているか、ただし思い半ばに過ぎるであろう。You can easily imagine from this incident alone how deep their dissatisfaction is with the present conditions in this country. / 彼はずいぶん母親思いだ。He is a very affectionate son to his mother. | He is very good to his mother.

おもい²　私はその会合の席から重い心を抱いて帰って来た。I came away from the meeting with a heavy heart. / その知らせを聞いて僕は気が重かった。The news weighed heavily on my mind.

おもいあがる　成功に思い上がって、ひどくうぬぼれ者になってしまった。Success went to his head, and he became very conceited.

おもいあたる　そう言われれば思い当たることもある。この間彼の様子がすこし変だと思った。That reminds me—some days ago, I thought he was behaving a little strangely. / 何か私に言い忘れたことがありますか。いや、今のと ころ、思い当たりません。Is there anything you forgot to tell me? —No, not that I can think of.

おもいおもい(に)　彼らは思い思いに帰途についた。Each of them started out on his way home. / 彼らは思い思いの職業を選んだ。They each chose an occupation to their own liking. / 幕が下りると、彼らは席を離れて思い思いに劇場内の食堂へ行った。When the curtain fell, they left their seats and went to the theater's restaurants as the fancy took them.

おもいかえす　彼は前の日にした仕事のことを思い返していた。He was casting his mind back over the work that he had done the

おもいきり／おもいつめる

visitor / 思いがけない出来事 an unforeseen [unlooked-for] event / 思いがけなく unexpectedly; contrary to what one expected [《に》 to one's expectations]; by chance [accident]. 文例⇩

おもいきり 思い切り ⟨あきらめ⟩《文》resignation; ⟨決心⟩《文》decisiveness; ⟨思う存分⟩ to one's heart's content; ⟨力一杯⟩ with all one's might; to the best of one's ability ¶思い切りがいい be decisive; be quick to make decisions; 《文》be prompt in decision / 思い切りが悪い be indecisive; 《口語》shilly-shally; 《文》lack decision / 思い切りよく decisively; 《文》with decision; with (a) good grace. 文例⇩

おもいきる 思い切る ⟨あきらめる⟩《文》resign oneself (to one's fate); ⟨断念する⟩ give up; abandon; ⟨決心する⟩ decide; make up one's mind (to do) / 大学進学を思い切る give up the idea of going on to college / 思い切って…する dare [《文》venture] to do; 《文》make so bold as to do; take the plunge and do / 思い切らせる ⟨説得して⟩ persuade sb not to do; put sb off doing; 《文》dissuade sb from doing / 思い切った bold [《文》resolute] step / 思い切った処置 drastic measures. 文例⇩

おもいこむ 思い込む ⟨…のつもりでいる⟩ be under the impression that…; imagine that…; 《口語》get it into one's head that…; be convinced that…; be possessed with the idea that…; ⟨固く信じて⟩; ⟨心を注ぐ⟩ set one's heart on (a matter); be bent (on doing) ¶無論…のことと思い込む take it for granted that….

おもいしる 思い知る ⟨悟る⟩ see; realize; come home to one (事が主語); ⟨懲りる⟩ know sth to one's cost; ⟨文⟩ remember; learn a lesson (from) (★ learn one's lesson の方が learn a lesson よりもずっと多く使われるが, その場合, あとに何も続けて言わないのが普通. learn a lesson の場合でも, あとの from 以下を言わないこともある).

おもいすごす 思い過ごす worry too much 《about》; ⟨取り越し苦労⟩ meet trouble halfway.

おもいだしわらい 思い出し笑い ¶思い出し笑いをする recall sth and smile over it; smile over sth that happened in the past; 《文》smile reminiscently.

おもいだす 思い出す recall; call [bring] sth to mind; recollect; remember; 《文》think of; hit on ¶思い出させる remind sb of sth; put sb in mind of sth / ときどき思い出したように勉強する work by fits and starts [in snatches]. 文例⇩

おもいたつ 思い立つ ⟨思い付く⟩ think of doing; 《口語》take it into one's head to do (あとのことをよく考えずに); ⟨決心する⟩ decide to do; make up one's mind to do; 《文》resolve to do. 文例⇩

おもいちがい 思い違い (a) misunderstanding; 《文》(a) misapprehension ¶思い違いをする misunderstand; take (it) wrong; 《口語》get (hold of) the wrong end of the stick. 文例⇩

おもいつき 思い付き a plan; an idea; a suggestion ¶いい思い付き a good [《文》happy] idea. 文例⇩

おもいつく 思い付く think of sth; hit on (a plan); take [get] it into one's head (to do, that…) ¶偶然に思い付く stumble on (an idea) / 突然思い付く it strikes one (to do, that…).

おもいつめる 思い詰める be obsessed 《with》; ⟨よくよく考える⟩ brood over (a matter); ⟨身を焦がす⟩ be consumed with (grief, a desire to do); torment oneself with the thought (of); ⟨悲しむ⟩ take sth to heart.

---

day before.

おもいがけない 昨日思いがけなく小学校時代の友人が訪ねて来た. To my surprise, I had a visit yesterday from a friend of mine who went to primary school with me. / ここであなたにお会いしようとは全く思いがけませんでした. You are the last person I expected to meet here. | Fancy meeting you here! / 彼の鋭い言葉は私にとって思いがけないものであった. His sharp remarks took me unawares [by surprise].

おもいきり 彼はそのドアを思い切り強くけとばした. He kicked at the door with a vengeance. / 思い切り食べた. I ate my fill.

おもいきる あの人は思い切ったことをやる. He does daring things. / 彼はずいぶん思い切ったことを言う男だ. He is really an outspoken fellow.

おもいこむ あの男はいったんこうと思い込んだらいつでもああなんだ. He's always like that once he gets an idea into his head. / いったんこうと思い込んだら最後彼は決して心を動かさない. Nothing can make him change his mind once he has reached a decision.

おもいしる これで思い知るだろう. This will teach him a lesson. / あとで思い知らせてやる. You'll pay for this!

おもいすごす それは君の思い過ごしだよ. You're imagining things. | It's all in your mind.

おもいだす その事は今でもときどき思い出す. The affair still comes to my mind now and then. / 彼女は 2 人が子供だった頃のハリーを思い出した. She remembered Harry from when they were children (together). / 私には思い出せません. I can't remember it. | It has escaped [slipped] my memory. / You put me in mind [remind me] of my brother. / のですっかり様子が変わっていたので彼だということがなかなか思い出せなかった. The change in him was so great that I could hardly recognize him. / 顔は知っているのだが, 何時どこで会った人だか思い出せない. I know his face, but I can't place him. / 以前に何かの雑誌で見た店の名を彼は一生懸命思い出そうとした. He racked his brains for the name of a store that he had once seen in some magazine. / それで思い出したけれど田原さんに電話をかけなければいかないんだ. That reminds me that I must make a phone call to Mr. Tawara. / この場面はミルトンの失楽園よりもダンテの地獄界を思い出させる. The scene is more suggestive of Dante's *Inferno* than Milton's *Paradise Lost*.

おもいたつ 急に思い立ってやってみたくなった. I suddenly took it into my head to try it. / 彼女は自分から言ってそうしようと言い出したのです. It was on her own initiative that she offered to

おもいで 思い出 《文》recollections; memories ¶幼い頃の遠い思い出 a distant childhood memory / 思い出にふける 《文》indulge in reminiscences / 思い出の《記念すべき》《文》memorable; 〈思い出の多い〉(a place) associated with [full of memories of] 《one's happy childhood》/ 思い出の記 one's memoirs [reminiscences] / 昔の思い出話をする talk [reminisce] about the good old days. 文例⇩

おもいどおり 思い通り 思いどおりに as one likes [《文》pleases]; 《文》at one's pleasure; to one's satisfaction / 思いどおりにする have one's own way (in a matter); do just as one wants to. 文例⇩

おもいとどまる 思い止まる abandon [give up] (the idea of marrying her); 〈思い止まらせる〉refrain from doing ¶思い止まらせる persuade sb not to do; 《文》dissuade sb from doing; talk sb out of doing.

おもいなおす 思い直す ⇨ おもいかえす, かんがえなおす ¶思い直して on second thoughts [《米》thought].

おもいなし 思いなし 文例⇩

おもいなやむ 思い悩む 〈悩む〉be worried [troubled] (about) ⇨ なやむ; 〈当惑する〉be at a loss 《what to do》; be at one's wits' end.

おもいのこす 思い残す ¶思い残すことは何もない have nothing to regret [to look back on with regret]. 文例⇩

おもいのほか 思いの外 unexpectedly; 《文》beyond (all) expectation(s); more...than one expected [imagined, thought, feared]. 文例⇩

おもいめぐらす 思い巡らす turn 《a matter》over in one's mind; think sth over; think of (this and that); 《文》ponder (on [over]) sth; 《文》ruminate over [on, about] sth.

おもいもよらない 思いも寄らない 〈予期しない〉⇨ おもいがけない; 〈問題外である〉be out of the question; 〈想像できない〉be inconceivable; be unthinkable; be unimaginable. 文例⇩

おもいやり 思いやり 〈同情〉sympathy; compassion; 〈察し〉thoughtfulness; consideration ¶思いやりのある thoughtful; sympathetic 《toward》; considerate 《toward》 《of people's feelings》; kind 《to》/ 他人の気持ちに対して思いやりがある be thoughtful; 《文》be considerate of the feelings of others / 思いやりのない inconsiderate; thoughtless; unkind; uncharitable; unsympathetic / 思いやりを示す show consideration (for). 文例⇩

おもいやる 思いやる sympathize with; feel for; be considerate toward; show consideration for; 〈立場に〉enter into sb's feelings ¶思いやられる 〈心配である〉feel anxious (about); be concerned (about); 〈想像がつく〉may [can] be (easily) imagined; 《文》be imaginable. 文例⇩

おもいわずらう 思い煩う worry (about, over); be worried [concerned] (about); feel anxious (about).

おもう 思う 〈考える〉think (of, about, over); consider; 〈信じる〉believe; 〈判断する〉judge; 〈感じる〉feel; 〈みなす〉regard sth [sb] (as); look upon sth [sb] (as); put [set] sth [sb] down (as); 〈予期する〉expect; 〈想像する〉imagine; suppose; fancy; figure; 《口語》guess; 《口語》reckon; 〈誤認する〉take [mistake] (A for B); 〈積もりである〉intend [mean] to do; be going to do; think of doing; plan to do [on doing]; have a mind to do; 〈願う〉want; wish; 〈欲する〉desire; 〈希望する〉hope; 〈懸念する〉fear; be afraid (that...); 〈いぶかる〉wonder (if, whether...); 〈怪しむ〉suspect; doubt ⇨ うたがう 囲読; 〈気にかける〉mind; care (★ care は否定文・疑問文のみで使う)

---

do it. / 思い立ったが吉日. Strike while the iron is hot. 〔諺〕| Never put off till tomorrow what you can do today. 〔諺〕| Procrastination is the thief of time. 〔諺〕

おもいちがい 君は思い違いをしている. You are mistaken. | You are (laboring) under a false impression. | You've got it wrong. / これは思い違いで買ってしまったのだ. I bought this under a misapprehension.

おもいつき 単なるこの場の思い付きではだめだ. よく練った案がほしいんだ. A mere impromptu idea won't do. I want a properly-thought-out plan.

おもいつく うまいことを思い付いた. A bright idea occurred to me [flashed into my mind]. | I hit on a good idea. / 一体どうしてそんなことを思い付いたのだ. What on earth put that into your head? / (それ以上何も思い付かなかった. I had entirely run out of ideas. / 後から思い付いて車寄せを付け足したのです. The porch was added (to the building) as an afterthought.

おもいで この旅行はいつまでも楽しい思い出となるでしょう. This trip will stay with us as a happy memory. / 私たちにとって, 夢のような子供の世界はもう思い出の中にかすんでしまったのです. For us, that magic world of childhood has already faded into memory. / 祖父は思い出の品々を部屋に飾って若かりし日をしのんでいるのです. Setting out his personal memorabilia in his room, my grandfather relives his earlier years.

おもいどおり 君の思いどおりにはなるまい. Things are unlikely to turn out as you want.

おもいなし 思いなしか今日は浮かぬ顔をしていた. It may be my imagination, but he looked seedy today.

おもいのこす これで思い残すことは何もない. Now I can die without any regrets.

おもいのほか 成績は思いのほか悪かった. The results did not come up to my expectations. | The results fell short of my expectations.

おもいもよらない 彼女と結婚するなんて思いも寄らなかった. I cannot see myself marrying her. / そんなことは思いも寄らなかった. I never dreamed of it. / 君がそんなことを言おうとは思いも寄らなかった. That is the last thing I expected to hear from you.

おもいやり こんなに寒い部屋にこういつまでも待たせるなんて, 彼女も実に思いやりのない女だ. It is very thoughtless of her to keep us waiting so long in a cold room like this.

おもいやる 私は彼の心中を思いやって黙っていた. I kept silent out of regard for his feelings. / 今からそんなことでは行く末が思いやられる. The way you are going on, I feel uneasy about how you

おもうぞんぶん 〈記憶する〉remember;〈回想する〉《文》recollect;〈好きである〉love;fall in love (with);take a fancy (to)(軽い意味で) ¶よく思う think well of / 悪く思う think badly [《文》ill] of;take (it) amiss / どこかへ旅行に行きたいと思う feel like going on a trip somewhere / 思ったほど難しくない be not as hard as one expected [feared] / …を思って at the thought [idea] of… / …しようと思って with the intention of doing / 思うように[とおりに]as one wishes;to one's satisfaction;satisfactorily.　文例⬇

おもうぞんぶん 思う存分 to one's heart's content;to one's complete satisfaction;《文》to the full;《文》heartily;as much as one likes [wishes, desires] ¶思う存分食べる[飲む]eat [drink] one's fill / 思う存分人生を楽しむ enjoy life to the full.

おもうつぼ 思う壺 ¶思う壺にはまる〈事が〉turn out just as one wished;〈人の術中に陥る〉play into sb's hands.　文例⬇

おもおもしい 重々しい solemn;dignified;《文》grave ¶重々しい口調で in a grave tone;weighing one's words / 重々しく《文》gravely;solemnly;〈もったいぶって〉with a self-important air;《speak》pompously.

おもかげ 面影 〈顔つき〉《文》a visage;a face;looks;〈幻影〉an image;〈痕跡〉a vestige;a trace ¶昔の面影がない be no longer what (it) used to be;be a mere shadow of one's former self / 古武士の面影がある remind sb of a samurai of ancient times.　文例⬇

おもかじ 面舵 《海》¶面舵をとる put the helm (to) starboard;starboard the helm.　文例⬇

おもき 重き ¶重きをなす be a leading figure (in);have influence (with);carry weight (with);〈尊敬される〉be thought highly of;《文》be (highly) esteemed;《文》be held in high esteem / 重きを置く〈重点を置く〉lay [put] stress [emphasis] on;emphasize;〈重視する〉attach importance to;set 《great》store by;give 《due》weight to / 重きを加える gain [grow] in importance.

おもくるしい 重苦しい heavy;gloomy;oppressive ¶胸が重苦しい have a heavy feeling [feel heavy] in one's [the] chest / 重苦しい雰囲気 an oppressive atmosphere / 重苦しい空模様 a gloomy [sullen] sky.

おもさ 重さ weight ¶重さを計る weigh sth / 重さが100キログラムある weigh 100 kilograms;be 100 kilograms in weight.

おもし 重し a weight ¶石を重しにのせる place [put] a stone as a weight on sth;put sth under a stone / 重しで押さえる weight sth down.

おもしろい 面白い 〈興味のある〉interesting;〈楽しませる〉(it is) fun (doing, to do)(★ fun は名詞);〈おかしい〉amusing;〈こっけいな〉funny;〈愉快な〉delightful;pleasant;〈奇妙な〉curious;queer;odd;〈満足な〉satisfactory;《文》favorable;〈有望な〉promising;hopeful;encouraging ¶面白い思い付き an interesting idea / 面白いように売れる〈物が主語〉sell like fun [hot cakes] / 面白く〈おかしく〉amusingly;〈興味をもって〉with interest;〈楽しく〉delightfully;with pleasure [enjoyment] / 面白く過ごす have a good [pleasant, enjoyable, delightful] time / 面白くない〈面白みのない〉uninteresting;dull;boring;flat;〈味のない〉《文》prosaic;〈不愉快な〉unpleasant;〈思わしくない〉unsatisfactory;《文》unfavorable;discouraging;〈望ましくない〉undesirable;unsavory 《reputation》 / …に対して面白くない感情を抱く have [hold] a grudge against sb;harbor ill feeling against sb;《口語》have it in for sb / 面白くなくなる〈事が主語〉get [become] uninteresting [dull];lose its relish [《文》savor] 《for one》;〈人が主語〉lose interest (in) / 面白そうに looking [as if one is] interested;《文》

---

will end up.
おもう 君はあの人をどう思いますか. What do you think of him? / 英語では充分思うことが言えない. I cannot express everything I want to say in English. / 僕はそうは思わない. I don't think so. | I don't see it like that. / こんどは成功したいものだと思います. I hope I will succeed this time. / 思っただけでも身震いがする. I shudder at the mere thought of it. / 私は彼が間違っていると思います. I believe [am of the opinion] that he is in the wrong. / 君がここにいるとは思わなかった. I had no idea that you were here. / 僕が自分でここへやって来るのだと思っていました. I was under the impression that she was coming here in person. / この件については君は万事承知のことと思う. I take it that you know everything about this matter. / 私は彼をドイツ人だと思った. I took him for [had him down as] a German. / 僕は自動車を買おうかと思っている. I am thinking of buying a car. / 東京へ出てみようと思った. He took it into his head to go up to Tokyo. / 彼を解雇しようなどとは思っていない. I have no intention of dismissing him. / 思うようにばかりは行かないものだ. You can't always have things your own way. / あんなやつは死んでしまえばいいと思った. I wished him dead and gone.

おもうつぼ (結果は)彼の思う壺になった. He got what he wanted. | Things went his way.

おもかげ 彼は父親の面影にそっくりだ. He is the very image [picture] of his father. / 今の彼にはかつての美青年の面影がある. He retains nothing of the handsome youth that he was. / あの町へ行っても繁栄を誇った昔の面影はもう全く見られない. If you visit the town, you will find that it no longer has [retains] any vestige of its former glory.

おもかじ 面舵.《号令》Starboard (helm)! | 《米》Right! / 面舵一杯. Hard starboard!

おもさ それはどのくらいの重さですか. How much does it weigh? | What weight is it? / その薬は同じ重さの金に匹敵する価値があると言われていた. The medicine was said to be worth its weight in gold. / 彼はその地位の責任の重さに耐えかねているかのように見えた. He looked as if he was weighed down by the responsibility of his position.

おもしろい 彼は実に面白い男だ. He is a very interesting man. | He is great fun. | He is full of fun. / そんなことは僕には少しも面白くない. That sort of thing

おもしろおかしい　面白おかしい ⇨ こっけい、おもしろい ¶面白おかしく話す tell a story in a very amusing way. 文例⇩

おもしろがる　面白がる be amused ((at, with, by)); enjoy; 《文》 take delight ((in)); 《文》 delight ((in)); 《文》 find pleasure ((in)) ¶子猫をじゃらして面白がる amuse *oneself* by playing with a kitten / しゃれを聞いて面白がる be amused at a joke / 面白がらせる amuse; 《文》 delight; entertain.

おもしろさ　面白さ ⇨ おもしろみ.

おもしろはんぶん　面白半分 ¶面白半分に for fun; in fun; in joke [《文》jest];《口語》for a lark.

おもしろみ　面白味 interest; fun ¶冗談の面白味 (see) the point of a joke / 面白味のある [ない] ⇨ おもしろい (面白い、面白くない) / 面白味を添える add interest [spice] 《to the story》.

おもたせ　お持たせ ⇨ おくりもの. 文例⇩
用法 英米には手土産を持って行く習慣はないし、たとえ何か持って来た場合でもその場で開けるか、日本式の弁解はしない。むしろ、The cake looked so nice that I thought we'd have it right away. というような事を言う。逆に、その人のプレゼント以外のものを用意していて、それを出そうと思っている場合に、弁解する必要を感じて、Oh, what delicious-looking strawberries! We'll have them for tea tomorrow. I have an apple pie in the oven for dinner tonight. のような事を言う。下の文例は日本語の直訳を示したもの。

おもだった　主立った main; 《文》 principal; leading; 《文》 chief; important; prominent.

おもちゃ　a toy ¶《比喩的に》a plaything ¶おもちゃの自動車 a toy car / おもちゃのお金 play money / おもちゃにする play [toy, trifle] with; make a toy [plaything] of / おもちゃ箱 a toy box [chest] / おもちゃ屋 《店》《米》a toy store; 《英》a toyshop; 《人》a toy dealer.

おもて　表 《表面》the surface; the face; the right side (衣類などの); the obverse [head] (貨幣の); 《顔》the face ⇨ かお; 《外面》the outside; 《文》the exterior; 《外見》the outward appearance; 《前面》the front; 《通り》the street ¶表の戸 the front [street] door / 表を出して [上にして] (the) right side up [up]; (lay a card) face up / 表に[で] out of doors; outdoors; outside (the house); 《文》without; 《米》on the street; 《英》in the street / 7回の表で 《野球》at the top [in the first half] of the seventh inning.

おもてかんばん　表看板 《うわべのみせかけ》《文》a mask; a pretext; 《名目上の長》a figurehead ⇨ かんばん.

おもてぐち　表口 the front entrance ¶表口から入る enter at [by] the front door.

おもてげい　表芸 ¶表芸は落語だ be a storyteller by profession.

おもてげんかん　表玄関 (the) entrance hall ¶東京の表玄関 the main gateway to Tokyo.

おもてざた　表沙汰 ¶表ざたにする 《公表する》 make *sth* public; 《文》 bring 《a matter》 to light; 《裁判ざたにする》 go to law 《against *sb* about *sth*》; 《文》 bring a suit 《against *sb* for *sth*》 / 表ざたにしないで解決する settle 《a matter》out of court / 表ざたになる be made public; 《文》 come to light; be brought before the court.

おもてだつ　表立つ become [be made] public; come out in the open ¶表立たないようにする keep *sth* out of the public eye; keep *sth* under wraps / 《自分が》表立たないようにしている take a back seat; be self-effacing. 文例⇩

おもてどおり　表通り 《家の前の通り》the street in front of *one's* house; 《大通り》a main street.

おもてむき　表向き ¶表向きは 《表面上は》《文》ostensibly; 《公式に》officially; for the record; 《公表する事として》for the public; 《口語》for public consumption / 表向きの理由 the surface reason 《for》. 文例⇩

---

has no interest for me [does not interest me] at all. / 旅行は面白かったかい。Did you enjoy the trip? / 今夜はとても面白かった。I had a lot of fun this evening. | I enjoyed the evening very much. / 今日の新聞に何か面白いことがありますか。Is there anything interesting in today's paper? / ただ面白いから人形作りをやっているんです。I make dolls just for the fun of it. / この本は非常に面白く読んだ。I read this book with great interest. | I very much enjoyed (reading) this book. / これは単に面白い話としてお聞かせします。I'm going to tell you this merely as a matter of interest. / こんな音楽会は行っても面白くないよ。There's no fun [interest] in going to a concert of this sort. / そのショーは面白くなかった。The show was not much fun. / たくさん釣れれば魚釣りは面白いものだ。Angling is fun when you have a good catch. / 狩猟なんてどこが面白いのか僕にはわからない。I don't see the fun of [what fun there is in] hunting.

おもしろおかしい　人生は面白おかしい事ばかりではない。Life is not all beer and skittles.

おもしろみ　僕には碁の面白味がまだ本当にはわからない。I don't as yet see the real appeal of the game of go. / クリケットの面白味はどういうところにあるのですか。What are the interesting points of cricket? | What (is it that) makes cricket interesting?

おもたせ　お持たせで失礼でございますが。Please excuse me for serving you with what you brought us.

おもちゃ　人間の眼は実によくできていて、それに比べれば、どんなに精巧なカメラでも子供のおもちゃのように思われる。The human eye is so well made that it makes the most sophisticated camera seem a child's toy by comparison.

おもて　表は暗い。It is dark outside. / まだ充分よくなっていないから表へ出てはいけません。You are not well enough to go out yet. / 表で人だかりがしている。There is a crowd on the street. / うちの子はほかの子供たちと表で遊んでいる。My son was out playing with some other children.

おもてだつ　その件については自民党内にまだ表立った動きはない。There is no obvious activitiy in the Liberal Democratic Party yet concerning the matter. | There are as yet no visible signs of the Liberal Democrats doing anything about it.

おもてむき　表向きはそういう話になっています。That is what has been officially announced. | That

おもてもん 表門 the front gate.

おもな 主な main;《文》chief;《文》principal; leading; major; important ¶主な産物 principal [staple] products / 主な会員 leading members.

おもなが 面長 ¶面長な long-faced;《a man》with a long face.

おもに[1] 重荷 a heavy load [《文》burden];〈厄介物〉《文》an encumbrance ¶心の重荷 a load on one's mind / 重荷を下ろす《文》be relieved of a burden;〈心の〉have a load off one's mind; feel relieved; take a load off one's mind (事が主語) / 重荷を背負う《文》shoulder a burden; carry a heavy load on one's shoulders.

おもに[2] 主に 〈主として〉mainly;《文》principally;《文》chiefly;〈大体において〉in the main;〈たいがい〉mostly; for the most part; generally.

おもはゆい 面映ゆい be [feel] embarrassed. 文例⇩

おもみ 重み 〈重量〉weight;〈重要性〉importance; weight;〈貫録〉《文》dignity; weight ¶重みのある 《an idea》of weight; dignified (貫録のある) / …に重みを加える give added weight to《the opinion》/ 重みが増す grow in importance; gather weight.

おもむき 趣 〈雅趣〉《文》grace; elegance; (a) charm;〈趣意〉⇒しゅい[1], しゅし[2] ¶講演の大体の趣 the gist [《文》tenor,《文》general purport] of a speech / 趣のある《文》tasteful; elegant; attractive / 趣のない tasteless; insipid; flat; dull; uninteresting / 趣を異にする be different (from). 文例⇩

おもむく 赴く 〈行く〉go;《文》proceed;《文》betake oneself 《to》;〈なる〉become; get; grow ¶救援に赴く go to sb's rescue / 欲望の赴くままに行動する《文》give free rein to one's desires.

おもむろに 徐ろに 〈ゆっくりと〉slowly; in a leisurely manner;〈慎重に〉deliberately;〈少しずつ〉by (slow) degrees; gradually;〈静かに〉gently;〈辛抱づよく〉patiently.

おももち 面持ち ⇒かおつき.

おもや 母屋 the main building.

おもやつれ 面やつれ ¶面やつれする grow thin in the face / 面やつれのした haggard(-looking).

おもゆ 重湯 rice water; thin rice gruel.

おもり 重り 〈はかりの〉a weight;〈釣り糸の〉a (fishing) sinker;〈測鉛〉a plumb; a sounding lead ¶網につける重り a (net-)sinker / 釣り糸に重りをつける weight a line. 文例⇩

おもわく 思惑 〈考え〉thought;〈意図〉an intention;〈目的〉a purpose;《文》an end in view;〈投機〉speculation;〈口語〉spec ¶思惑が外れる〈事が主語〉《文》come [fall] short of one's expectation(s);〈人が主語〉《文》be disappointed in one's expectation(s); miscalculate / 思惑どおりになる turn out just as one wished / 他人の思惑を気にして《act》out of concern for others' opinions / 思惑買い speculative buying / 思惑買いをする buy sth on speculation [spec]. 文例⇩

おもわしい 思わしい satisfactory; suitable;《文》desirable;〈気に入った〉to one's liking [taste] ¶思わしくない unsatisfactory; unsuitable; disappointing. 文例⇩

おもわず 思わず《文》involuntarily; in spite of oneself. 文例⇩

おもわせぶり 思わせ振り ¶思わせぶりな half-concealed; tantalizing;〈性的に〉suggestive.

おもわせる 思わせる make [have] sb think [believe]《that…》;〈印象を与える〉give sb the impression 《that…》; strike [impress] 《sb as…》;〈思い起こさす〉remind 《sb of sth》; bring [call] sth to mind;《文》be reminiscent of;《文》be evocative [suggestive] of ¶変だなと思わせる strike one as strange.

おもわぬ 思わぬ unexpected; unlooked-for.

おもわれる 思われる 〈と見える〉seem (to be); appear (to be); look《expensive, as if it is expensive》;〈と聞こえる〉sound;〈印象を与える〉strike [impress]《one as》;〈みなされる〉be regarded《as》;〈愛される〉be loved;《文》be yearned for ¶人によく[悪く]思われる be well [badly,《文》ill] thought of by others / 私には…と思われる It seems [appears] to me that…. 文例⇩

おもんじる 重んじる 〈重視する〉value; think

---

is the official version. / 彼は表向きは異議を唱えなかった。He raised no objection openly [in public].

おもに[1] これで心の重荷がおりた。That is a load off my mind. | This is one weight lifted from my mind. / その借金がその人の重荷になっていた。The debt lay like a heavy weight on his mind.

おもはゆい 彼のほめ言葉が面映ゆかった。His words of praise embarrassed me. / 只今は司会者の方から身に余るお言葉をいただきまして、まことに面映ゆく存じております。Mr. Chairman has said rather too many nice things about me; I wish he had spared my blushes.

おもみ その家は雪の重みのために倒壊した。The house collapsed under the weight of snow. / 彼の言うことは重みがある。What he says carries weight.

おもむき 冬枯れの景色にもまた趣がある。A desolate winter scene has a charm of its own. / 古い水車がその庭に趣を添えていた。An old water wheel graced the garden.

おもり 起き上がり小法師は底に重りがつけてあるので、傾けると必ず起き上がる。The 'daruma' doll, being weighted on the bottom, always returns to an upright position when tipped over.

おもわく 彼には何か思惑があるらしい。He apparently has some ulterior motive.

おもわしい 思わしい品がみつからない。I cannot find one that will do. / 結果があまり思わしくありません。I am not quite satisfied with the result. / 彼の健康は思わしくない。He is not in the best of health. / 仕事の進み具合が思わしくない。The work isn't progressing as well as it might. | The work is not making as much progress as it should.

おもわず 思わず吹き出してしまった。I burst out laughing in spite of myself. / 思わず「まさか!」と言ってしまった。I heard myself

[make] a great deal [《文》much] of ; give [attach] importance to ; give weight to ; set (great) store by ; 〈文〉respect ; honor ; 《文》esteem ; 〈文〉hold *sb* in high respect [regard] ¶何よりも健康を重んじる value health above everything else / 軽んじない make light of ; slight ; have no regard for.

おもんぱかる 慮る consider ; be thoughtful [concerned] (about) ;〈気づかう〉fear ; be apprehensive (about) ;《文》have apprehensions 《about》¶将来をおもんぱかる take thought for the future.

おや¹ 親 a parent (★ただし、単数ではあまり使われない) ;〈父〉a father ;〈母〉a mother ;〈両親〉*one's* parents ;〈トランプの〉the dealer ;〈ばくちの〉the banker ¶親の《文》parental ; *one's* parents' (house) ;《文》paternal (父の) ;《文》maternal (母の) / 親の愛 parental love [affection] / 親のない子 a child with no parents ; an orphan ; a parentless child / 貧しい親を持った子供 a child of poor parents / 親を養う[失う] support [lose] *one's* parents / 親を大切にする be kind to *one's* parents / 親を粗末にする be unkind to *one's* parents / 親をとも思わない defy [《文》slight] *one's* parents / 親に従う obey [be obedient to] *one's* parents / 親にそっくりの子 a child who is very like [who is a perfect copy of] his father [mother] ; a chip off the old block (★父親に似た男の子の意味で男性が用いる表現) / 親になる become a father [mother] ;《文》enter parenthood. 文例⇩

おや² Oh! ; Why! ; Good heavens! ; Oh dear! ;《米》Gee (whizz)! ;〈主として女性が用いる〉Dear me! 文例⇩

おやおもい 親思い ¶親思いである be considerate [devoted] to *one's* parents [mother, father].

おやがいしゃ 親会社 a parent company [corporation].

おやがかり 親掛かり ¶親掛かりの身である be dependent on *one's* parents.

おやかた 親方 a master ; a chief ; a boss ;〈相撲部屋の〉a stable master ¶左官の親方 a master plasterer / 親方日の丸《an attitude》of dependence on the government. 文例⇩

おやがわり 親代わり ¶親代わりに in place of *sb's* parents ;《文》(act) as surrogate parent ;《ラテン語》(act, be) *in loco parentis*.

おやこ 親子 parent and child ¶親子の縁 the ties between parent and child [parents and children] / 親子関係 a parent-child relationship. 文例⇩

おやこうこう 親孝行 ⇒こうこう².

おやごころ 親心《文》parental love [affection] ¶親心から out of *one's* love for [out of kindness to] *one's* child. 文例⇩

おやこどんぶり 親子丼 a bowl of rice with chicken, egg, and vegetables.

おやじ 親父 *one's* father ;《俗》the old man ;〈老人〉an old man ;〈身分〉*one's* boss ;〈主人や部課長など〉《口語》the old man ;《口語》the boss.

おやしお 親潮 the *Oyashio* [Okhotsk] current.

おやしらず 親知らず〈知恵歯〉a wisdom tooth ¶親知らずが生える cut (one of) *one's* wisdom teeth.

おやすみ お休み 文例⇩

おやだま 親玉 a boss.

おやつ お八つ (afternoon) tea ; a snack ; between-meals refreshments ¶おやつの時間 (at) teatime / おやつを食べる have tea. 文例⇩

おやどけい 親時計 a master [control] clock.

おやどり 親鳥 a parent bird.

おやばか 親馬鹿 (the ludicrous behavior of) a fond parent (doting parents). 文例⇩

おやふこう 親不孝 ⇒ふこう¹.

おやぶね 親船 a mother ship ⇒おおぶね.

おやぶん 親分 a boss ; a chief ; a leader ¶親分肌の《文》magnanimous ; big-hearted / 親分風を吹かせる be bossy.

おやま an actor who plays female roles.

おやみ 小止み ¶小止みなく without a break ; without (a) letup ;《文》ceaselessly. 文例⇩

おやもと 親元[許] *one's* [*one's* parents'] home ;《文》*one's* parental roof ¶親元を離れる leave *one's* home [parental roof] / 親元へ引き渡す hand *sb* over to *his* parents.

おやゆずり 親譲り ¶親譲りの inherited from *one's* parents ; hereditary / 親譲りの財産 in-

---

saying, 'Well, I never!' / 思わずそう言ってしまったのです。The words just escaped my lips.

おもわぬ 彼は相手を侮っていて、思わぬ不覚を取った。He had underrated his opponent's strength, and suffered an unexpected defeat.

おもわれる 雨が降りそうに思われる。It looks like rain. / 一般に芸術家は気分屋だと思われている。Artists are generally supposed to be temperamental.

おや¹ 色々な精神的・肉体的特徴が親から子へと伝わる。Various mental and physical traits are passed on from parent to child. / 親を見れば子がわかる。Know the breed and know the dog. / この親にしてこの子あり。Like father, like son. | Like mother, like daughter. / 親はなくとも子は育つ。Nature is a good mother. / 親の因果が子に報いる。The sins of the fathers are visited upon the children. / 親の心子知らず。A child does not know how deeply concerned his parents are about him. / 親の光は七光。It's a great help to have a famous parent.

おや² おや、だれかな。Oh, who could that be? / おやもう11時だ。Why! It's eleven o'clock already!

おやかた あの連中は親方日の丸だ。They can always fall back on the government.

おやこ 彼女は親子程も年の違う男と結婚した。She married a man (who was) old enough to be her father.

おやごころ それが親心というものだろう。That is what parental love means [is all about].

おやすみ お休みなさい。Good night.

おやつ では、おやつにしましょう。Let's stop for a coffee [cup of tea].

おやばか これが親ばかというものでしょう。This is the way fond parents behave, I suppose.

おやみ 雨が小やみなく降り続い

おやゆび 親指 〈手の〉 a thumb; 〈足の〉 a big toe.

およぎ 泳ぎ swimming ⇨ すいえい ¶泳ぎに行く go swimming 《in a river》; go 《to a river》 for a swim [《英》bathe] / 泳ぎがうまい[へただ] be a good [poor] swimmer. 文例⇩

およぐ 泳ぐ swim; have a swim [《英》bathe]; ¶よろめく totter / からだが泳ぐ lose one's balance / 岸に泳ぎ着く swim to the shore / 泳ぎ回る swim about / 泳ぎ渡る swim across 《a river》 / 犯人を泳がせておく leave the culprit at large. 文例⇩

およそ 凡そ 〈約〉about; nearly; roughly; approximately; 〈大まかに言って〉generally [broadly] speaking; 〈大抵〉generally; as a rule / 〈全く〉quite; entirely; altogether; 《not》 at all ¶およその 《rough》 《estimates》; approximate 《numbers》. 文例⇩

およばれ お呼ばれ ⇨ しょうたい³.

および 及び and; as well as ¶A 及び B (both) A and B; B as well as A.

およびごし 及び腰 ⇨ およびこし 文例⇩

およぶ 及ぶ 〈達する〉 reach; amount 《to》; come [run] (up) 《to》; 〈わたる〉《文》 extend 《to, over》; range 《over》; 〈言及する〉 refer 《to》 ¶及ばない 〈達しない〉 do not amount 《to》; fall short 《of》; 〈匹敵しない〉《文》 be inferior 《to》; fall behind; be no match 《for》 / 全く想像も及ばない be beyond all imagination / 及びもつかない 〈事が主語〉 be beyond one's power [ability]; 〈人が主語〉 be not equal to 《the job》; be no match 《for》 / …するに及ばない need not do / 及ぶものがない have no equal [rival]; 《文》 be [stand] unrivaled; be second to none. 文例⇩

およぼす 及ぼす ¶影響[感化]を及ぼす influence; 《文》 exert [exercise] one's [an] influence on; have an effect on; affect / 害を及ぼす harm; damage; 《文》 do [cause] harm to.

オラトリオ 《音楽》 an oratorio 《pl. -s》.

オランウータン 《動》 an orang-utan; an orangoutang.

オランダ Holland; 〈公式名〉 the Netherlands ¶オランダ(人)の Dutch / オランダ語 Dutch / オランダ人 a Dutchman; a Dutchwoman 《女》; a Hollander; a Netherlander; 〈総称〉the Dutch.

おり¹ 折り 〈折箱〉 a small wooden box (for packing food).

おり² 折り 〈場合〉 an occasion; 〈機会〉 an opportunity; a chance ¶…した折り when…/ その折り, 折りから, 折りしも at that time; just then; 《文》 on that occasion / 折りがあれば 《文》 when (the) opportunity arises [presents itself] / 折りも折り(とて) just at the moment / いつか折りを見て at a convenient time / 折りさえあれば…する take every opportunity to do / 折りに触れて at times; occasionally; now and then / 折りよく[あしく] fortunately [unfortunately]; as luck would have it (★ この句は文脈によって, 「運よく」の意味にも「不運にも」の意味にもなる) / 折り折り ⇨ おりおり. 文例⇩

おり³ 澱 〈飲み物の〉 dregs; lees; grounds; 〈一般に〉(a) sediment (★ 複数形にはしない).

おり⁴ 織り fabric; (a) texture; (a) weave ¶精巧な織りの finely-woven (cloth); 《文》《cloth》 of exquisite weave / 目の荒い[細かい] 織りの loosely-[close-]woven (cloth); coarse [fine-textured] (fabric); (cloth) with a [《文》 (a)] coarse [close] texture.

おり⁵ 檻 a cage 《猛獣の》; a pen 《家畜の》; 〈牢獄〉a prison; a jail; a cell 《独房》 ¶輸送用の檻 a transport [carrying] cage / 檻の中の, 檻に入れられた caged 《animals》 / 檻の中で生れた《animals》 born behind bars; 《chimpanzees》 born in captivity.

-おり …折り ¶2つ折りにする fold in two [down]; double 《a newspaper》 over [down].

おりあい 折り合い ¶折り合いがよい get on well 《with》; be on good terms 《with》 / 折り合いがつく come to terms 《文》 an accommodation 《with》; reach an understanding [agreement] 《with》 / 折り合いをつける settle (the matter); 《文》 effect a (peaceful) settlement of (a dispute); 〈妥協する〉 compromise 《with》.

た. It rained without (a) letup.

おやゆずり 彼の語学の才能は親譲りだ. He inherited his language ability from his parents [father, mother]. | His aptitude for languages comes [is an inheritance] from his father.

およぎ もう一泳ぎしよう. Let's have another swim.

およぐ 向こうの小島まで泳いで行こう. Let's swim out to that small island over there. | あなたはどんな泳ぎ方ができますか. What kind of swimming strokes can you do?

およそ その町の人口はおよそ3万人です. The population of the town is about thirty thousand. | The town has a population of some thirty thousand [of thirty thousand or so]. | およそその見当です. You're about right. | That's about the size of it. | そんなことをしたっておよそ意味がない. It is quite meaningless to do a thing like that. | It makes no sense at all to do such a thing. / およそばかげた話だ. That's utter nonsense. | It is the height of absurdity. | 君は大方ここだろうとおよその見当で来た. I came on the chance that I might find you here.

およびごし 彼は及び腰でその本を取ろうとした. He half rose from his chair and leaned [bent] forward to reach for the book. / そんな及び腰ではこの問題の解決できない. Such an irresolute attitude will not do if you are to settle this matter. | You need to be more decisive to resolve this problem.

およぶ 伝えられる所によれば損害は数百万ドルに及んだという. The damage reportedly amounted to [ran into the] millions of dollars. / 負傷者は200名に及んだという. It is said that as many as two hundred people were injured. / 会期は3週間に及ぶ予定. The session will extend over a period of three weeks. / 及ぶ限りのことはしたのですが, だめでした. I tried everything in my power, but to no purpose. / その仕事をやりかけてみて, 私の力には及ばないと悟った. I tried to do the job and found in no time that it was beyond me. | As soon as I

おりあう 折り合う 〈話がまとまる〉 come to terms [an understanding] 《with》; reach an agreement 《with》; 〈妥協する〉 compromise 《with》; meet *sb* halfway; 〈譲歩する〉 make concessions 《to》; 〈仲よくする〉 get on [along] 《with》; 《口語》 hit it off (well) 《with》. [文例⇩]

おりいって 折り入って ¶折り入って頼む beg *sb* to *do*; plead with [《文》 entreat] *sb* to *do*. [文例⇩]

オリーブ 〘植〙 an olive ¶オリーブ畑 an olive grove / オリーブ油 olive oil.

おりえり 折り襟 〈襟〉 a lapel; 〈カラー〉 a turned-down collar.

オリエンテーション 《文》 (an) orientation ¶新入生に対するオリエンテーション orientation [an orientation session] for incoming freshmen.

オリエンテーリング orienteering.

オリエント the Orient ¶オリエントの Oriental / オリエント学者 an Orientalist.

おりおり 折々 sometimes; at times; occasionally.

オリオンざ オリオン座 〘天〙 Orion.

おりかえし 折り返し 〈襟の〉 a lapel; 〈ズボンの〉 《米》 a cuff 《on a trouser leg》; 《英》 a turn-up; 〈本のカバーの〉 a flap; 〈水泳の〉 a turn; 〈歌の〉 a refrain; 《文》 a burden ¶折り返し返事を出す answer by return (《米》 of mail [《英》 of post]) / 折り返し運転 (a) shuttle service / (マラソンの)折り返し点 《at》 the turn / 折り返し列車 a shuttle train. [文例⇩]

おりかえす 折り返す turn up [down]; fold back; 〈引き返す〉 turn back; 〈(競泳で)ターンをする〉 turn; make a 《good》 turn.

おりかさなる 折り重なる lie on top of one another [each other]; 《文》 lie one above another [the other] ¶折り重なって倒れる fall down on top of one another [each other]; fall down in a heap.

おりかさねる 折り重ねる fold 《the sheets of paper》 and pile 《them》 up.

おりがみ 折り紙 〈技術〉 *origami*; the art of folding paper into various figures; 〈紙〉 (colored) paper for folding ¶折り紙で鶴を折る fold a piece of paper into the figure of a crane / 折り紙つきの certified as genuine; guaranteed; 〈悪名高い〉 notorious.

おりこむ[1] 折り込む turn [tuck] in ¶ビラを新聞に折り込む insert leaflets in the newspapers / (本の)折り込みページ a foldout (page).

おりこむ[2] 織り込む weave 《into》; work 《into the fabric》; 〈考慮に入れる〉 take *sth* into account [consideration]; make allowance(s) for ¶話の中に織り込む weave 《a fact》 into a story / 勘定に織り込む reckon *sth* in *one's* calculations; count *sth* in / 新しく提案されたアイデアを計画に織り込む 《文》 incorporate the newly suggested ideas into the plan. [文例⇩]

おりたたみ 折り畳み ¶折り畳み椅子 a folding [collapsible] chair; 〈キャンプ用の〉 a camp chair / 折り畳み傘 a folding [telescopic] umbrella.

おりたたむ 折り畳む fold (up) ¶折り畳むことのできる座席 a folding seat; a bucket seat (飛行機やバスなどの) / 折り畳んでしまい込めるベッド a foldaway bed. [文例⇩]

おりづめ 折り詰め food packed in a small wooden box; 〈弁当〉 a box lunch.

おりづる 折り鶴 a folded-paper [an *origami*] crane.

おりまげる 折り曲げる bend; turn 《*one's* skirt》 up; turn 《*one's* lapels》 down ¶本のページを折り曲げる fold [turn] down the corner of a page; dog-ear a book.

おりめ[1] 折り目 a fold; a crease 《in *one's* trousers》 ¶折り目をつける crease / きちんと折り目のついた well-creased 《trousers》 / 折り目正しい 〈きちんとした〉 well-mannered; 〈丁重な〉 polite; 《文》 courteous; 〈固苦しい〉 formal / 客に折り目正しくあいさつする receive a guest with a formal [polite] greeting.

おりめ[2] 織り目 texture ¶織り目の荒い[細かい] coarse-[close-]woven; with a [《文》 of (a)] coarse [close] texture.

おりもの[1] 下り物 a (vaginal) discharge; 〈月経〉 the menses.

---

launched out on the business, I knew I was out of my depth. / その国の工業の生産性は欧米諸国にはるかに及ばない. The productivity of that country falls far [a long way] short of that of Western countries. / こと数学にかけては, あの人にはとても及びもつきません. When it comes to mathematics, I can't [am not fit to] hold a candle to him. / 人間の嗅覚は犬にはとうてい及ばない. Man's sense of smell is nowhere near as acute [nothing like as good] as that of the dog. / 同じような機械は色々あるが, 正確さの点でどれもこの機種には遠く及ばない. There are large numbers of similar appliances but not one comes within miles of this model in respect of accuracy. / 彼女の記録は世界記録に 0 秒 3 及ばなかった. Her time was three tenths of a second off the world record. / 談たまたまこの事に及んだ. He happened to touch on this subject. / 急ぐには及ばない. There is no hurry. | You needn't hurry. / 辞退なさるには及びません. There is no reason for you to decline the offer. / ご心配なさるには及びません. There's no call for you to worry. / 及ばずながらご尽力いたしましょう. I will do what little I can to help you.

おり[2] 京都へ行った折り宮田氏を訪ねました. I called on Mr. Miyata when I made a visit to Kyoto./ またとない折りだ. This is the best chance you'll ever get. | You'll never have such an opportunity again.

おりあう 値段の点で折り合わなかった. We couldn't agree on the price. / アメリカはどういう条件なら折り合うつもりだろうか. What terms is the U.S. willing to settle for?

おりいって 折り入ってお願いしたいことがあるのですが. I have a special favor to ask (of) you.

おりかえし 列車は東京・静岡間を折り返し運転をしている. Trains are operating a shuttle service between Tokyo and Shizuoka.

おりこむ[2] そのような可能性は織り込み済みだった. Such possibilities had been allowed for.

おりたたむ この椅子は折り畳むと

おりもの² 織物 cloth(s); (textile) fabrics; textiles; woven stuff ¶織物業〈製造〉be engaged in] textile manufacture; 〈販売〉be in the textile 〔《米》dry goods, 《英》drapery〕 business / 織物工業 the textile industry.

おりる 降[下]りる get [go, come, step] down; 《文》descend; 〈乗り物から〉get off [out]; leave 《the bus》; 《文》alight 《from》 ¶山を下りる go down a hill; descend a mountain / 急いで階段を下りる hurry down the stairs / 階下に降りる go [come] downstairs / 電車から降りる get [step] off a train; alight from a train / タクシーから降りる get out of a taxi / ゲームを降りる quit [drop out of] the game. 文例⇩

オリンピック the Olympic Games; the Olympics; 《文》the (15th) Olympiad ★ The Olympic Games と the Olympics は構文上単数にも複数にも扱われる ¶日本代表としてオリンピックに出場する represent Japan in the Olympic Games / オリンピックで金メダルを獲得する win a gold medal at the Olympics / 近代〔冬季〕オリンピック the modern [Winter] Olympics / オリンピック記録 an Olympic record / オリンピック選手 an Olympic sportsman / オリンピック組織委員会 the Olympic Organizing Committee (略: O.O.C.) / 国際オリンピック委員会 the International Olympic Committee (略: IOC) / 日本オリンピック委員会 the Japanese Olympic Committee (略: J.O.C.) / オリンピック村 an Olympic village.

おる¹ 折る break (off); snap (ぽきりと); 《医》fracture (骨を); 〈畳む〉fold; 〈曲げる〉bend; turn down 《a collar》 ¶右腕を折る break *one's* right arm; have [get] *one's* right arm broken / 2つに折る fold 《a sheet》 in two; double 《a blanket》 / ページのすみを折る fold [turn] down the corner of a page; dog-ear 《a book》 / 手紙を折る fold (up) a letter / 花を折る pick 〔《文》pluck〕 a flower / ひざを折る fall (down) [go down] on *one's* knees.

おる² 織る weave ¶糸を織って布にする weave thread into cloth / アルパカの毛で織った布 a fabric woven from the wool of the alpaca.

オルガン an organ ¶オルガンを弾く play the organ / オルガン奏者 an organist.

オルグ an organizer.

オルゴール 〈<《オランダ語》orgel〉《米》a music box; 《英》a musical box.

オルドビスき オルドビス紀 《地質》the Ordovician period.

おれ 俺 ¶俺はお前の間柄である be on a first-name basis.

おれいまいり お礼参り ¶お礼参りをする pay a visit of thanks to a shrine [temple]; 〈やくざなどが〉call on *sb* to settle old scores with *him*.

おれきれき お歴々 notables; 《口語》big names; 《俗》bigwigs ⇒おえらがた.

オレゴン Oregon (略: Oreg.) ¶オレゴン州の人 an Oregonian.

おれる 折れる break; be broken; give way; snap (ぽきっと); 《医》fracture (骨が); 〈畳まる〉be folded; be doubled (2つに); 〈譲歩する〉give in (to); 《文》yield (to); 〈妥協する〉compromise (with) ¶3つに折れる be folded [broken] in three / (曲がり角で)右に折れる turn to the right / 折れて出る meet *sb* halfway; make concessions. 文例⇩

オレンジ an orange.

おろおろ ¶おろおろする be flustered; do not know what to do; 《口語》dither; 《口語》be all of a dither; be uneasy; be nervous / おろおろ声で in a faltering [trembling, quavering] voice.

おろか¹ 愚か ¶愚かな ⇨ばか. 文例⇩

おろか² ¶…(は)おろか 〈言うまでもなく〉not to speak of; not to mention; to say nothing of; let alone. 文例⇩

おろし 卸 wholesale trade [business] ¶卸で売る[買う] sell [buy] *sth* wholesale / 卸値で at the wholesale price / 卸売り市場 a wholesale market / 卸売り物価指数 a wholesale price index / 卸商 a wholesale merchant [dealer] / 卸売業者 a wholesaler.

-おろし …下ろし a wind blowing down 《Mt. Akagi》.

おろしがね 下ろし金 a grater.

おろす 降[下]ろす, 卸す take [bring, put] down; lower; 〈荷を〉unload; discharge (船荷を); 〈カーテン・幕などを〉pull down; drop; 〈車から〉set 《a passenger》 down; let 《a passenger》 off; drop; 〈新品を〉wear [put on, use] *sth* for the first time; 〈卸売りする〉sell *sth* wholesale; 〈堕胎する〉have an abortion (performed) ¶はしごを下ろす let down a ladder / 旗を下ろす lower [haul down] a flag / ボートを下ろす lower a boat; 〈水の上に〉launch a boat; get a boat on the water / なべ

ぺしゃんこになる. This chair folds flat.

おりる ご乗車は降りる方が済むまでお待ち下さい. Please let passengers off the train first. / 鳥が地面に降りている. A bird is on the ground.

おる 彼は新聞を2つに折って手に持ち、その記事を繰り返し読んだ. He folded the paper in two [in half], held it before him, and read the news over and over again.

おれる その板は乗ったら折れた. The plank gave way beneath my feet. / 双方が折れて出たので話は円満に解決した. The matter was amicably settled because they made mutual concessions.

おろか¹ 私は愚かにもその男を信用してしまった. I was foolish enough to trust him.

おろか² 彼はウイスキーはおろかビールも飲まない. He does not drink beer, let alone [never mind] whisky. / 彼はフランス語はおろか英語も話せない. He can't speak English, to say nothing of [let alone] French.

おろす (運転手に向かって)そこの角のところで降ろして下さい. Please drop me at the corner over there.

おろそか ご親切は決してあだおろそかにはいたしません. I will never forget the kindness you have shown me.

おわせる 彼は自分の責任を僕に負わせた. He shuffled off his responsibility onto me.

を下ろす take a pot off [from over] the fire ; take [《文》 remove] a pot from the stove [heat] / 新しいシャツを下ろす wear a new shirt (for the first time) / 木の枝を下ろす trim [prune, lop] off the branches of a tree / 銀行 預金から 10 万円下ろす withdraw ¥100,000 from *one's* bank account / 大根を下ろす grate a radish / 手を貸して降ろしてあげる help *sb* off ((a car)); help [《文》 hand] ((an old woman)) down from [out of] ((the bus)) / 配役[役職]から 降ろされる 《文》 be deprived [relieved] of *one's* role [position]. 文例⇩

おろそか ¶おろそかな 《文》 negligent ; 《文》 neglectful ; careless ; 《文》 remiss / おろそか にする 〈なおざりにする〉 neglect ; 《文》 be negligent [neglectful] of ; 〈注意を払わない〉 pay no attention to ; 〈軽んじる〉 make light of ;《文》 slight / おろそかにしない 〈よく注意 する〉 pay careful attention to ; 〈重視する〉 think [make] a great deal [a lot, 《文》 much] of / (受けた恩を)あだやおろそかに思わ ない be grateful [thankful] ((to *sb* for *sth*)). 文例⇩

おわせる 負わせる 〈背負わせる〉 put *sth* on *sb's* back ; make *sb* carry *sth* ; 〈負担させる〉 《文》 charge [《口語》 saddle] (*sb* with a duty) ; 〈責任を負わせる〉 lay (the responsibility on *sb*) ; 〈傷を〉《文》 in- flict (injuries on *sb*) ; give (injuries) ¶ 大任 を負わせる entrust [《文》 charge] *sb* with an important task / 責めを負わせる lay [put] the blame on *sb* for *sth* ; lay *sth* at *sb's* door ; 罪 を負わせる lay the guilt on *sb* / 費用を負わ せる bear the expenses [foot the bill(s)]. 文例⇩

おわり 終わり an end ;《文》 a close ; a finish ; 〈結末〉 a conclusion ;《文》 an expiration ; 〈期限の〉 expiry ¶ 終わりの last ; final ; 《文》 conclud- ing ;《文》 terminal / 終わりから 2 番目の next to the last ; last but one / 終わりまで till the end ;《文》 to the last / 終わりまで聞く hear *sb* out / 芝居を終わりまで見る sit out [through] a play / 終わりに finally ; at the end [conclusion] (of) / 終わりに近づく draw to a close / 終わりごろに toward the end [close] ((of)) / 終わりにする bring *sth* to an end [a close]; finish ; wind *sth* up / 終わりを告げる ⇒ **おわる** / 終わり値 〈証券市場などでの〉 the closing price. 文例⇩

おわる 終わる 〈終了する〉 end ;《文》 close ; come [be brought] to an end [《文》 a close] ; be over ;《文》 terminate ; 〈完了する〉 be fin- ished ; be completed ; 〈完了させる〉 finish ; complete ; get through with ; bring *sth* to an end ; 〈完結させる〉 conclude ; 〈期限が〉 run out ; expire ; 〈結局…になる〉 end [《文》 re- sult] in ¶ 仕事を終わる finish [get through with] *one's* work / 失敗に終わる end (up) in [as a] failure / 本を読み終わる have read through [finish reading, be through with] a book / 学 校が終わってから after school (is over) / 検 死が終わるまで until after the inquest / こ の週の終わらぬうちに before the week is out. 文例⇩

おん¹ 音 a sound ¶ 漢字を音で読む read a Chinese character phonetically.

おん² 恩 〈恩恵〉 a favor ;《文》 a benefit ; an obligation ; 〈感謝の念〉 a debt of gratitude ; 〈親切〉 kind- ness ¶ 恩がある, 恩になっている be in *sb's* debt ;《文》 be indebted to *sb* ; be under an obligation to *sb* ; owe *sb* a debt of gratitude ; 《口語》 owe *sb* / 恩に着せる make a favor of *sth* ; emphasize the favor one has done to *sb* ; dwell [harp] on how grateful *sb* should be to *one* / 恩を知る be grateful ((to *sb*, for *sb's* kindness)) / 恩を返す ⇒ **おんがえし** / 恩を仇(た゜) で返す 《文》 return evil for good ; repay kind- ness with ingratitude / 恩を施す do *sb* a favor ; do a favor for *sb* / 恩着せがましい patroniz- ing / 恩知らず 〈事〉 ingratitude ; 〈人〉 an un- grateful person / 恩知らずの ungrateful. 文例⇩

おんあんぽう 温罨法 a hot [warm] compress [poultice] ⇒ **あんぽう**.

おんいき 音域 a pitch extent ; 〈音楽〉 a regis- ter ¶ 高[低]音域 the upper [lower] register (of this instrument).

おんいん 音韻 a vocal sound ¶ 音韻組織 the sound system ((of a language)) / 音韻変化 (a) phonetic change / 音韻論 phonology.

おんかい 音階 a (musical) scale ¶ 音階を弾く [歌う] play [sing] scales / 五音音階 a penta- tonic scale / 七音音階 a seven-note scale / 長 [短]音階 the major [minor] scale / 音階練習を する practice scales ((on the piano)).

おんがえし 恩返し ¶ 恩返しをする repay an obligation ; repay *sb* for *his* kindness ;《文》 requite *sb's* favor / 恩返しに…する do in re- turn for *sb's* kindness ; do out of gratitude to *sb*. 文例⇩

おわり 終わりに臨んで, 皆さま方 のこのご事業に私共は進んで協力 する意志のあることを重ねて申し 上げたいと存じます。In conclu- sion [In concluding my speech], I wish to assure you again that we are willing to cooperate with you in this enterprise of yours. | 彼は演説の終わりにこう言った。 He ended his speech with these words. / 彼は私に終わりまで言う な、と言った。'O.K. Don't worry,' he said, cutting me off in midsentence.
おわる 彼の努力の試みは結局無駄に終 わった。Everything he did came to nothing. | His efforts were all in vain. / そこで物語は突然に終 わっている。At that point the story comes to an abrupt end. / 同窓会は校歌の大合唱で終わった。 The alumni meeting was round- ed off by everyone singing the school song together.
おん² ご恩は決して忘れません。I will never forget your kindness [what you have done for me]. | 彼はだれの恩も受けていないと 思っている。He thinks he is un- der obligation to no man. | He doesn't feel beholden to any- body. / もしそうしてくれたなら いつまでも恩に着るよ。If you would do that for me, I'd be eternally grateful.
おんいき 鳥は人間と大体同じ音域 の音が聞きとれる。Birds can hear within roughly the same range as man.
おんがえし 何か恩返しをしなけれ ばならない。I must do something

おんがく 音楽 music ¶音楽的な musical;《文》melodious / 音楽が分からない do not understand music; cannot appreciate music; be not musical / 音楽の先生 a music teacher; a teacher of music / 音楽映画 a musical (film) / 音楽家 a musician / 音楽会 a concert;〈独奏・独唱〉a recital / 音楽学 musicology / 音楽学校 a school [an academy] of music; a conservatory / (映画などの)音楽監督 a music [musical] director / 音楽教育 musical education; music training / 音楽好き a music lover; a lover of music / 音楽好きの music-loving / 音楽性 musicianship / 音楽隊 a band / 音楽堂 a concert hall / 音楽評論家 a music critic / 音楽理論 musical [music] theory.

おんかん 音感 ¶音感がいい have a good ear for music / 絶対音感《have》absolute [perfect] pitch / 音感教育 acoustic [auditory] training.

おんぎ 恩義 ⇒おんけい.

おんきゅう 恩給 a (public employees') pension ¶恩給がつく become entitled to a pension / 恩給をもらう get [《文》receive, be granted] a pension; be pensioned (by the state) / 恩給で暮らす live on a pension / 恩給生活者 a pensioner / 恩給制度 a pension system.

おんきょう 音響 a sound; a noise (騒音) ¶大音響と共に爆発する explode with a loud noise [《口語》bang,《文》report] / 音響効果 a sound [an acoustic] effect;《improve》the acoustics 《of a hall》(劇場などの)音響効果がいい have good acoustics / 音響測深機 an echo sounder. [文例⇩]

オングストローム 〖物〗an angstrom (unit).

おんけい 恩恵 a favor;《文》a benefit ¶恩恵を施す do sb a favor; do a favor for sb / 恩恵を受ける benefit (from, by);《文》receive benefit 《from》/ 恩恵をこうむっている be in sb's debt;《文》be indebted 《to》. [文例⇩]

おんけつどうぶつ 温血動物 a warm-blooded animal.

おんけん 穏健 ¶穏健な moderate;《文》temperate; sensible / 穏健派 (the) moderates.

おんこう 温厚 ¶温厚な gentle; mild(-mannered).

おんさ 音叉 〖物〗a tuning fork.

オンザロック (whisky) on the rocks.

おんし 恩師 one's (former) teacher.

おんししょう 恩賜賞 the Imperial Award 《of the Japan Academy of Arts》.

おんしつ¹ 音質 tone quality.

おんしつ² 温室 a greenhouse; a hothouse; a glasshouse; a forcing house (促成栽培用の) ¶温室で咲かせる force 《a plant》to bloom in a hothouse / 温室効果〖気象〗the greenhouse effect / 温室栽培の grown under glass; hothouse (fruit). [文例⇩]

おんしゃ 恩赦 a (free) pardon ⇒たいしゃ¹, とくしゃ ¶恩赦に浴する《文》be granted (an) amnesty; be pardoned /《文》receive a pardon.

おんしょう 温床 a hotbed; a (cold) frame; a forcing bed (促成栽培用の) ¶犯罪の温床 a hotbed of crime.

おんじょう 温情 a warm heart; (a) kindly feeling ¶温情ある kindly; warm-hearted / 温情主義 paternalism.

おんしょく 音色 (a) tone color; (a) timbre ⇒ねいろ.

おんしん 音信 correspondence;《文》a communication;〈手紙〉a letter. [文例⇩]

おんじん 恩人《文》a benefactor ¶命の恩人 a person to whom one owes one's life. [文例⇩]

オンス an ounce (略: oz.).

おんすい 温水 warm water ¶温水プール a heated (swimming) pool.

おんせい 音声 (a) voice; a speech [phonetic] sound ¶音声学 phonetics / 音声学者 a phonetician / 音声多重放送 a television broadcast using two audio frequencies; a sound multiplex television broadcast.

おんせつ 音節 a syllable ¶音節に切る divide 《a word》into syllables; syllabify; syllabicate / 単[2, 3, 多]音節の[からなる] monosyllabic [dissyllabic, trisyllabic, polysyllabic] (words) / (日本の仮名のような)音節文字 a syllabic (character [symbol]); a syllabary (五十音図).

おんせん 温泉 (a) hot [thermal] spring ¶温泉に行く visit [go to] a hot-spring resort / 伊香保温泉 the spa of Ikaho / 温泉場 a hot-spring resort; a spa;《文》a watering place / 温泉町 a hot-spring town / 温泉宿 a hot-spring hotel. [文例⇩]

おんそ 音素 〖言語〗a phoneme ¶音素論 phonemics.

おんそく 音速 the speed [velocity] of sound ¶音速の壁を破る break the sound [sonic] barrier / 音速の2倍で飛ぶ fly at twice the speed of sound; fly at Mach 2 / 音速を越える[に達する] exceed [reach] sonic speed / 音速に近い near-sonic (speeds) / 音速以下の subsonic.

おんぞん 温存 ¶温存する keep;《文》preserve;《文》retain; set aside [apart] (for later use).

おんたい 温帯 the temperate zones ¶温帯植

---

in return for his kindness.

おんきょう 彼はオペラ座は大きいものほど音響効果が悪い. The bigger an opera house is, the worse are its acoustic properties. / このホールは音響効果がとてもよい [悪い]. The acoustics of this hall are very good [bad].

おんけい 彼には非常な恩恵をこうむっています. I owe him a great debt of gratitude. / 私の両親は高等教育の恩恵を受けなかった. My parents didn't have the benefit of higher education. / この発明は人類にとって一大恩恵になるだろう. This invention will prove a great boon to mankind. / 現代化学が錬金術になにがしかの恩恵をこうむっていないとは言えない. Modern chemistry is not without some obligation to alchemy.

おんしつ² 彼は温室育ちだ. He has been brought up on a bed of roses. |《英》He has spent his life wrapped in cotton wool.

おんしん あれ以来まるきり音信不通です. I have heard nothing from him since.

おんじん あなたは私の命の恩人です. I owe you my life.

おんせん 温泉を掘り当てた. A hot spring was tapped.

おんてい 彼女の歌は音程がしっかりしている. She sings with a sure ear for pitch. / 彼女は高いC

物 a temperate (zone) plant / 温帯地方 the temperate regions [latitudes] / 温帯低気圧 an extratropical cyclone.

おんだん 温暖 ¶ 温暖な warm ; mild ; temperate ; 《文》 genial / 温暖な土地に住む live in a temperate climate / 温暖前線 a warm front.

おんち 音痴 ¶ 音痴である be tone-deaf ; 〈通俗に〉 have no ear for music / 方向音痴である have no sense of direction.

おんちゅう 御中 Messrs. (★ Messieurs の略) ¶ 後藤商会御中 Messrs. Goto & Co. / 明治大学御中 (To) Meiji University.

おんちょう[1] 音調 〈調子〉 a tune ; 〈音色〉 a tone ; 〈音質〉 (a) timbre ; 〈ふし〉 (a) melody ; 〈リズム〉 (a) rhythm ; 〈言葉の〉 (an) intonation ¶ 音調のよい pleasant (to the ear) ; 《文》 melodious ; 《文》 euphonious 《phrases》.

おんちょう[2] 恩寵 〘キリスト教〙 grace 《of God》 ; 《divine》 favor ¶ 神の恩寵により by the grace of God / 神の恩寵を受ける receive [enjoy] divine favor / 神の恩寵を失う lose God's favor ; fall out of God's favor.

おんてい 音程 〘音楽〙 an [a musical] interval ¶ 音程が合って[狂って]いる be in [out of] tune ; be on [out of] pitch. [文例⇩]

おんてん 恩典 a special favor ; a privilege (特典) ¶ 恩典に浴する 《文》 receive [be granted] a special favor.

おんど[1] 音頭 ¶ 音頭を取る lead 《a chorus, a cheer》 ; 〈比喩的に〉 take the lead ; call the tune / 音頭取り 〈歌の〉 a chorus leader ; 〈主唱者〉 a leader. [文例⇩]

おんど[2] 温度 (a) temperature ¶ マイナス30度という温度 a temperature of −30° / (物体の)温度が上がる rise [increase] in temperature / (物体の)温度が下がる fall [drop] in temperature / 温度の変化 (a) temperature change [variation] / 温度を計る[調整する] take [adjust] the temperature 《of》 / 一定の[高い, 低い]温度で at a fixed [high, low] temperature / 一年の平均温度 the annual mean temperature / 温度計 a thermometer / 温度調節 temperature control / 温度調節装置 a temperature control (system) ; 〈サーモスタット〉 a thermostat. [文例⇩]

[用法] 英米では科学的な話以外の日常の用語としては, 気温·体温などの温度はセ氏 (centigrade) でなくカ氏 (Fahrenheit) が使われる. たとえば「温度は室内で80度だ」The temperature is 80 degrees indoors. のように.

おんとう 穏当 ¶ 穏当な 《文》 proper ; 《文》 just ; right ; reasonable ; 《文》 appropriate ; 《文》 fitting / 穏当な処置 appropriate measures / 穏当な要求 a reasonable claim.

おんどく 音読 ¶ 音読する read aloud.

おんどり 雄鳥 a cock (bird) ; 〈鶏の〉 《米》 a rooster ; 《英》 a cock.

おんな 女 a woman 《*pl.* women》 ; a female ; 〈総称〉 woman ; womankind ; 《文》 the gentle [fair, weaker] sex (★ 一般的に言って 《文》 ではあるが, 皮肉な意味で, またはおどけてならば日常会話でも使う) ; 〈情婦〉 a [*one's*] mistress ; 〈愛人〉 *one's* woman ¶ 女の woman ; female ; feminine ★ a woman doctor, a woman worker などの複数形は women doctors, women workers となる. a lady doctor ならば lady doctors と後の名詞だけを複数形にする / 女の子 〈娘〉 a daughter ; 〈若い女〉 a girl ; 〈子供〉 a (little) girl ; 〈赤ん坊〉 a baby girl / 女のような 《文》 womanish ; effeminate / 女を知らない 〈童貞である〉 be a virgin ; have never had anything to do with women [girls] (★「性的経験がない」という意味と,「女性とつきあったことがない」という意味のどちらにも使える) / (成長して)一人前の女になる grow into a woman ; reach [《文》 attain] womanhood / 女ばかりの会合 《口語》 a hen party / 女らしい 《文》 womanly ; ladylike ; feminine / 女親 a mother / 女形 ⇨ おやま / 女客 a woman [lady] visitor [guest, customer] / 女嫌い 〈事〉 《文》 misogyny ; 〈人〉 a woman-hater ; 《文》 a misogynist / 女坂 the gentler of the two uphill paths 《leading to a shrine》 / 女盛りである[を過ぎている] be in [past] the prime of womanhood / 女事務員 an office girl ; a female clerk / 女主人 〈主婦〉 the mistress (of the house) ; 〈店の〉 the proprietress ; 〈宿屋の〉 the landlady / 女達 women ; 《口語》 womenfolk / 女だてらに woman as she is [was] ; unlike a woman / 女たらし a lady-killer ; 《文》 a Don Juan ; 《文》 a philanderer / 女友達 a girlfriend ; a woman [lady] friend / 女文字の手紙 a letter in a woman's writing [《文》 written in a female hand] / 女持ち[女物]の ladies' 《watches》 ; women's 《sweaters》 ; 《umbrellas》 for ladies' use. [文例⇩]

おんなごころ 女心 a woman's mind [heart] ¶ 女心の機微 the delicate workings of a woman's mind / 女心を解しない男 a man who does not understand the female mind. [文例⇩]

おんなで 女手 [文例⇩]

おんねん 怨念 a deep-seated [《文》 consuming]

音程が下がる[低い D で音程が上がる]. She goes flat on her high C [goes sharp on her low D].

おんど[1] 大田さんが音頭を取ってこの企画をスタートさせたのです. Mr. Ota took the lead in getting this program started. | This program was launched at the instigation of Mr. Ota.

おんど[2] 温度が30度に上がった. The temperature rose [went up, climbed (up)] to 30 degrees. / 温度が5度に下がった. The temperature fell [went down, dropped] to 5 degrees.

おんな 一般に女の方が男より長生きする. Generally speaking, women live longer than men. / どうだい, いい女じゃないか. Well, don't you think she's beautiful? | 《口語》 Look! A real looker [A sight for sore eyes], isn't she? / 彼女には女らしいところがない. There is little of the woman in her. / 女三人寄ればかしましい. Where there are women and geese, there wants no noise. 〘諺〙 / 女やもめに花が咲く. Young widows attract men.

おんなごころ 女心と秋の空. A woman's mind and winter wind change oft. 〘諺〙

おんなで 彼女は女手一つで2人の子供を大学にまでやった. Woman as she was, she worked hard and earned enough money to send

おんのじ

grudge ¶怨念を抱く bear sb a grudge ; have [bear, 《文》harbor] a grudge (against).

おんのじ 御の字 文例⇩

おんぱ 音波 a sound wave.

おんばひがさ 乳母日傘 ¶乳母日傘で育てられる be brought up by overprotective parents ; be raised like a hothouse plant.

おんぴょうもじ 音標文字 a phonetic sign 《symbol, alphabet》.

おんびん¹ 音便 a euphonic change 《in the pronunciation of a Japanese word》. ¶音便で for the sake of euphony ; euphonically.

おんびん² 穏便 ¶穏便に〈円満に〉《文》amicably ; peaceably ;〈内々に〉out of court ; between the parties concerned /穏便に済ます settle 《a matter》 out of court ; reach an amicable settlement 《with》.

おんぶ 負んぶ ⇒おぶう, おぶさる.

おんぷ 音符《音楽》a (musical) note ⇒がくふ ¶全音符《米》a whole note ;《英》a semibreve /二分音符《米》a half note ;《英》a minim /四分音符《米》a quarter note ;《英》a crotchet /八分音符《米》an eighth note ;《英》a quaver /十六分音符《米》a sixteenth note ;《英》a semiquaver /三十二分音符《米》a thirty-second note ;《英》a demisemiquaver /六十四分音符《米》a sixty-fourth note ;《英》a hemidemisemiquaver.

おんぷう 温風 ¶(機械装置で)温風を送る send a warm current of air《to》.

おんぼろ ¶おんぼろの shabby《suits》; worn-out《clothes》; dilapidated《huts》;〈ぼろぼろの〉ragged ; tattered /おんぼろ自動車 a battered old car ;《口語》a jalopy ;《俗》a heap.

おんめい 音名《音楽》a pitch name.

おんやく 音訳 transliteration ¶音訳する transliterate《Sanskrit words with Roman letters》.

オンライン《コンピューター》¶オンラインの[で] on-line /オンラインシステムのある銀行 a bank with on-line equipment《銀行や交通機関で用いる》オンライン実時間処理方式 an on-line real time system.

おんりょう¹ 音量 the volume《of the radio music》¶音量を上げる[下げる] turn the volume up [down] ; turn the volume high [low] /音量を最大にしてステレオをかける play a stereo at top [full] volume ;《口語》play a stereo 《at》 full blast /音量測定器 a sound-level meter. 文例⇩

おんりょう² 怨霊 a vengeful [an unquiet] ghost.

おんわ 温和 ¶温和な〈人柄など〉gentle ; quiet ; mild-tempered ;《文》benign ;〈気候など〉mild ;《文》clement /温和な気候 a mild [genial] climate /温和な人柄の《man》with a gentle nature.

か

か¹ 可〈成績などが〉fairly good ; passable(★一般に C で表わす)¶可もなく不可もない be neither good nor bad ; be indifferent /可とする approve (of). 文例⇩

か² 科〈学科〉a department ;〈専攻課程〉a course ;〈動植物の〉a family /英語科 the department of English ; the English department /猫科 the cat family.

か³ 蚊 a mosquito(pl. -(e)s)¶蚊が多い〈場所が主語〉swarm with mosquitoes /蚊のような足 spindly [very thin] legs /蚊の鳴くような声で in a very faint [thin] voice /蚊をたたく swat [slap] a mosquito /蚊に食われる be bitten [stung] by a mosquito /蚊に食われたあと a mosquito bite /蚊に刺されたほどにも思わない couldn't care less《about》; do not care a bit [《文》whit]《about》. 文例⇩

か⁴ 課〈学業での〉a lesson ;〈事務機構の〉a section ¶第5課 Lesson 5 ; the fifth lesson /課員 the staff of a section /課長 the chief [head] of a section ; a section chief.

-か あるいは...か, あるいは if... ; (either...) or... ; whether...or... ¶これかあれか this or that /...するかしないかに《文》scarcely [hardly] (had he spoken) when. 文例⇩

が¹ 我 ¶我の強い人 a self-assertive[-willed] person /我を折る give in [《文》yield]《to sb's opinion》/我を張る be self-willed ; stick to one's opinion.

が² 蛾 a moth.

---

her two children to college. /家には女手がない. Our family has no women to do the household chores [to take care of the housekeeping].

おんのじ そうなりゃ御の字だ. I can't ask for more than that. / I could wish for nothing better than that.

おんりょう¹ そのつまみは音量調節用です. That knob is the volume control.

か¹ 2者のうちいずれを選ぶも可. You may choose either of the two. /彼は行くとして可ならざるはなしだ. He is equal to anything. /可とする者は10名, 否は3名だった. There were ten ayes against three noes. /可とするものの多数. The ayes have it.

か³ 今夜は蚊がひどい. The mosquitoes are terrible tonight. /あたりには蚊がぶんぶん言っていた. Mosquitoes were buzzing [humming] all around. /耳元へぷーんと飛んで来た蚊をたたいた. I hit [slapped] out at a mosquito which came droning toward my ear.

-か あれはだれか. Who is he? /寝不足のためか頭が重い. I feel heavy in the head, probably because I'm short of sleep. /おや! 杉山君じゃないか. Oh, it's you, Sugiyama! /散歩しようじゃないか. What do you say to [How about] taking a walk? /風呂が沸いたかどうか聞いて下さい. Please ask whether the bath is ready. /雨が降るかどうかわからない. I can't tell whether it is going to rain or not. /君が帰るか帰らな

-が¹ 《主語を示す》 ¶形が似ている have a similar shape to *sth*; 《文》resemble *sth* in shape / 足が速い[遅い] be quick-[slow-]footed ; 《文》be quick [slow] of foot / 耳が遠い be hard of hearing ★ be slow of foot, be sharp of eye などの of が《文》であるが, be hard of hearing は成句として熟しているので《文》ではない / テニスが上手だ be good at tennis; be a good tennis player. 文例⇩

-が² 《しかし》but; (and) yet; however; though; although; while; nevertheless;〈そして〉and. 文例⇩
用法 「小山という者ですがご主人いらっしゃいますか」 My name is Koyama. Is your husband in? /「昨日あのレストランに行ってみましたが, 大変おいしかったですよ」 I went to that restaurant yesterday; the food was very good. のように,「が」に「しかし」という対立・対照の意味のない場合には, 接続詞なしで, ピリオド又はセミコロンで区切る方が適切な場合が多い.

かあ 〈からすの鳴き声〉 cawing; a caw ¶かあかあ鳴く caw.

カー a car ⇨ じどうしゃ ¶カーステレオ car stereo equipment; a car stereo (system) / カーフェリー《米》an automobile ferry ;《英》a car ferry ★ car ferry は《米》では鉄道車両運搬用の船 / カーラジオ a car [an auto] radio.

があがあ 〈あひるが〉quack ,〈かえるが〉croak.

カーキいろ カーキ色 khaki.

カースト (a) caste ¶カースト制度 the caste system.

ガーゼ gauze.

かあつ 加圧 ¶加圧する apply pressure 《to》; pressurize / 加圧して熱する heat 《a solution》under pressure.

カーディガン a cardigan.

カーテン a curtain ¶窓のカーテン a curtain (at a window); a window curtain / カーテンを開ける open the curtains; pull [draw] the curtains back [aside]; pull [draw] the curtains apart / カーテンを閉める close [draw] the curtains; pull [draw] the curtains to; pull [draw] the curtains together / カーテンで仕切る draw the curtain off 《a part of the room》/ カーテンリング[レール, ロッド] a curtain ring [rail, rod].
用法 「明かりをつける前にカーテンを閉めなさい」 Draw the curtains before you put the light on. というように, draw the curtains は主として「カーテンを閉める」意であるが,「その朝はお手伝いさんが8時半にやって来て, カーテンを開けました」 The maid came in at 8:30 that morning and drew the curtains. というように, 場合によっては「カーテンを開ける」意にもなり得るため, 紛らわしさを避けるためには,「カーテンを開ける[閉める]」には, open [close] the curtains を使う方がいい.

カード 〈紙〉a card; a slip (of paper) ;〈スポーツの〉組合せ〉a card ¶好カード an [a box-office] attraction ;《米》a drawing card / カード索引 〈事〉card-indexing ;〈物〉a card index / カード(式)目録 a card catalog / カードケース a card case [cabinet].

ガード¹ 〈鉄橋〉a girder bridge; a railroad bridge (over a road) ¶ガードの下をくぐる pass under a railroad bridge.

ガード² 《ボクシング》one's guard ¶ガードが固い have a strong guard.

ガードマン a (security) guard; a watchman ¶ガードマンの詰め所 a guardroom.

カートリッジ a cartridge ¶カートリッジを入れ替える put a new cartridge 《in》.

ガードル a girdle.

ガードレール a guardrail; a crash barrier.

カートン a carton 《of cigarettes》.

ガーナ Ghana ¶ガーナ共和国 the Republic of Ghana / ガーナ人 a Ghanaian; a Ghanian / ガーナ(人)の Ghanaian; Ghanian.

カーニバル a carnival.

カーネーション 《植》 carnation.

カーバイド 《化》 (calcium) carbide.

カービンじゅう カービン銃 a carbine ¶自動カービン銃 a machine carbine.

カーブ 〈曲線〉a curve; a curved line ;〈道路の〉a bend; a curve ,《野球》a curve (ball) ¶カーブする 〈線が〉curve ; 《文》describe a curve ;〈道が〉bend (to the right) ;〈自動車などが〉turn; make a turn / ゆるい[鋭く曲がる]カーブを投げる pitch a slow [sharply-breaking] curve / 急カーブ a sharp bend [turn]; a hairpin bend (U字形の). 文例⇩

カーペット a carpet ⇨ じゅうたん.

ガーベラ《植》a Transvaal daisy; a gerbera.

カーボベルデ ⇨ カボベルデ.

カーボン carbon ¶~たんそ ¶カーボン紙 carbon paper; a carbon (1枚の) / カーボン紙で写しをとる make a carbon (copy) 《of》.

カーラー a curler.

カール a curl; a ringlet ¶髪をカールする curl *one*'s hair / 髪をカールしている have *one*'s hair curled [waved] / カールが取れる lose (its) curl / カール用のピン[クリップ] a curler / カ

いかに彼が来た. He came immediately after you had left. | No sooner had you left than he came.
-が¹ キリンはくびが長い. The giraffe has a long neck. | 君が好きだ. I love you. | 月が出た. The moon rose.
-が² 傷は深いが致命傷ではない. The wound, though deep, is not fatal. | あの男は貧乏はしているが正直だ. He is poor but honest. | 太郎は勉強家だが次郎は怠け者だ. While Taro works hard, Jiro is idle. | 君はただ彼を嫌っているだけだが僕は憎んでいるのだ. I hate him, whereas you merely dislike him. | 私は昨日そこに行ったたいへん面白かった. I went there yesterday and had a very good time. | あの人は子供が5人ありますがみんな男の子です. He has five children, all boys. | 金があったら払うのだが. If I had the money, I would pay you.
カーテン 部屋に入って窓のカーテンを閉めた. She went into the room and closed [drew] the curtains.
カーブ カーブしているところを高速で走るのは危険である. It is not safe to go round a bend at high speed. | そのトラックは交差点の所で左に急カーブを切ろうとした. The truck tried to turn sharp left at the intersection.

ガール

ールペーパー curl papers (★ 通常複数形で用いられる). 文例⇩

ガール a girl ¶ガールスカウト 《総称》《米》the Girl Scouts;《英》the Girl Guides;〈一人〉《米》a girl scout;《英》a girl guide / ガールフレンド〈女友達〉a girl friend;〈恋人〉a girlfriend ★ 男性が my girlfriend と言うと「恋人」で, 単なる「女友達」は friend. 女性にとっての「女友達」は one's (girl) friend.

かい¹ 下位 a low(er) rank; a junior [《文》subordinate] position ¶下位の junior; low(er)-ranking;《文》subordinate / 下位に立つ rank lower than sb; be below [inferior to] sb in rank; be junior [《文》subordinate] to sb;《文》occupy [hold] a subordinate position to sb / 下位打者〈野球〉a batter at the bottom end of the order.

かい² 回〈度数〉a time;〈競技の〉a round; a game;〈野球〉an inning ¶1回 ⇨ いっかい² / 2回 ⇨ にかい¹ / (トーナメントの)第3回戦 the third round / (ボクシングなどの)10回戦 a bout [fight] of ten rounds; a ten-rounder / 7回の表[裏]〈野球〉(in) the first [second] half of the seventh inning;〈口語〉(in) the top [bottom] of the seventh / 何回も any number of times; time [again] and again. 文例⇩

かい³ 会〈会合〉a meeting;《文》a gathering; a party;〈団体〉a society; a club; an association ¶会を催す hold a meeting; hold [give] a party / 会を組織する organize [form] a society [an association]. 文例⇩

かい⁴ 貝 a shellfish (pl. -(e)s) ¶貝を掘る dig (for) shellfish [clams] / 貝細工 shellwork ⇨ かい⁵

かい⁵ 怪 a mystery; a wonder. しいがら.

かい⁶ 階 a floor;《米》a story;《英》a ground floor; the first story [《英》storey] / 2階《米》the second floor;《英》the first floor; the second story [《英》storey] / 最上階の部屋 a room on the top floor / 10階建てのビル《米》a ten-storied[-story] building;《英》a ten-storeyed[-storey] building. 文例⇩

用法 story [《英》storey] は建物を外から見た時の語で, floor は建物の内部にある各階の床. floor を使って「1階」「2階」「3階」と言う時,《米》では the first floor, the second floor, the third floor となるが,《英》では the ground floor, the first floor, the second floor となって,《米》と《英》では1つずつ数がずれるが, story [《英》storey] を用いる時は the first story [《英》storey], the second story [《英》storey], the third story [《英》storey] というように,《米》《英》でも数え方に違いはない.

かい⁷ 解〈説明〉(an) explanation;〈注解〉notes;〈解法〉a solution 《of, to》; a key 《to》.

かい⁸ 櫂 an oar; a paddle ¶かいをこぐ pull

カール カールが取れてしまった. My hair has lost its curl.

かい² 毎月1回会合を開いている. We hold a meeting [We meet] once a month.

かい³ 会は1時に散会した. The meeting broke up at one o'clock.

かい⁶ 事務所は何階にありますか. What floor is the office on? /

186

かいいれる

an oar / かいでこぐ row 《a boat》; paddle 《a canoe》.

かい⁹〈効果〉(an) effect; (a) result;〈価値〉worth;〈益〉use; benefit;《文》avail ¶かいがある be worth doing; it is worth (one's) while to do;〈報いられる〉be rewarded / かいがない be of no use [《文》avail]; be useless;《文》be in vain / かいのある worthwhile; rewarding / かいのない fruitless;《文》unavailing; unrewarding / 努力のかいもなく in spite of [for all] one's efforts.

-かい …界 a world; circles ¶各界の名士 notables from all spheres of society; various celebrities / 実業界 business circles / 動物[植物, 鉱物]界 the animal [vegetable, mineral] kingdom / 文学界 the literary world.

がい 害 harm; injury; damage; evil effects ¶飲酒の害 the bad [harmful] effects of drinking / 健康に害がある be bad for [《文》injurious to] (the) health / 害のある harmful;《文》injurious;《文》noxious / 害のない harmless; innocuous / 害を受ける be damaged 《by》; suffer damage 《from》/ 害になる do harm 《to》; be harmful [《文》injurious] 《to》.

-がい …外〈…の外側に〉outside;〈…を外れて〉out of ¶市外に outside the city; out of town / 専門外である be out of one's line.

かいあく 改悪 a change for the worse ¶憲法の改悪 an undesirable amendment to the constitution / 改悪する change sth for the worse; make sth worse.

がいあく 害悪 ⇨ がい.

かいあげ 買い上げ buying;《文》purchase ¶政府の米の買い上げ価格 the government's purchasing price for rice.

かいあげる 買い上げる buy;《文》purchase.

かいあさる 買い漁る hunt for sth; go round shopping for sth.

がいあつ 外圧〈外からの〉external [outside] pressure;〈外国の〉foreign pressure.

かいあつめる 買い集める spend money (in) collecting (old things).

ガイアナ Guyana ¶ガイアナ人 a Guyanese〈単複同形〉; a Guyanan / ガイアナ(人)の Guyanese; Guyanan.

かいいき 海域 a sea [an ocean] area.

かいいぬ 飼い犬 a house dog ¶飼い犬に手をかまれる have one's hand bitten by one's own [pet] dog;〈比喩的に〉be betrayed by one's trusted follower. 文例⇩

かいいれ 買い入れ buying;《文》(a) purchase ¶買い入れ価格 the purchase [purchasing] price.

かいいれる 買い入れる buy;《文》purchase;

このビルは何階建てですか. How many floors does this building have? / 2階と3階は止まりません.〈エレベーターガールの言葉〉We don't stop at floors two and three.

かい⁹ 勉強したかいがあって彼は試験に合格した. His hard work was rewarded with success in the examination. / 骨折ったかいがあった. I have not labored in vain. / そんな事をしてもかいがあるまい. I don't think it would be worth our while to do such a thing. / こんな本を読んだとて何のかいがあろう. What is the use [good] of reading a book like this?

〈仕入れる〉lay in.

かいいん¹ 会員 a member;〈全体〉a membership ¶会員が多い[少ない] have a large number of [do not have many] members; have a large [small] membership / 会員の資格を失う lose one's membership / 会員になる become a member; join 《a society》/ 正(準, 通常, 特別, 名誉, 終身)会員 a regular [an associate, an ordinary, a special, an honorary, a life] member / 会員制 a membership system / 会員制の 《a club》for members only / 会員名簿[章, 証] a membership list [badge, card]. 文例↓

かいいん² 改印 ¶改印する change one's (registered) seal.

かいいん³ 海員 a seaman; a sailor ¶海員になる become a seaman; go to sea / 海員組合 a seamen's union.

かいいん⁴ 開院 〈国会の〉the opening of a Diet session;〈病院の〉the opening of a hospital ¶(国会の)開院式 the opening ceremony of a Diet session.

かいうける 買い受ける buy;《文》purchase;《文》acquire sth by purchase.

かいうん¹ 海運 marine transportation [transport]; shipping ¶海運業 the shipping business [trade, industry] / 海運業者 a shipping agent [agency (店)]; shipping interests (総称).

かいうん² 開運 improvement of one's fortune ¶開運のお守り a good-luck charm / 開運を祈る pray for better fortune.

かいえん 開演 ¶開演する the performance begins; raise the curtain. 文例↓

がいえん¹ 外延 【論】extension; denotation.

がいえん² 外苑 the outer gardens ¶明治神宮外苑 the Outer Gardens of the Meiji Shrine.

かいおうせい 海王星 【天】Neptune.

かいおき 買い置き ¶買い置きの品 things laid [bought] in for future use; things kept in reserve; a reserve (of food) / 買い置きをする lay sth in for future use; keep sth in reserve. 文例↓

かいか¹ 開化 civilization;《文》enlightenment ¶開化した civilized;《文》enlightened.

かいか² 開花 flowering;《文》efflorescence ¶開花する come into flower [bloom]; flower; bloom; blossom; come out / 開花している be in flower [bloom] / 開花期 the flowering season. 文例↓

かいか³ 開架 〈事〉open [free] access to stacks [(book)shelves];〈書架〉open stacks [(book-)shelves] / 開架式図書館 an open-access library / 開架式図書室 an open-stack[-shelf] room.

かいか⁴ 階下 階下の一室 a downstair(s) room; a room downstairs / 階下に[で] downstairs / 階下へ行く go downstairs.

かいが 絵画 ⇒え² ¶絵画的な pictorial; picturesque (美しい) / 絵画館 a picture [an art] gallery.

がいか¹ 外貨 foreign currency ¶外貨の獲得 acquisition of foreign money / 日本の手持ち[保有]外貨 Japan's foreign-currency holdings [foreign-exchange reserves] / 外貨予算 a foreign exchange budget.

がいか² 凱歌 a triumphal song ¶凱歌を上げる win a triumph [victory] 《over the enemy》; triumph 《over the enemy》.

ガイガーけいすう ガイガー計数 【物】a Geiger count / ガイガー計数管 a Geiger counter.

かいかい 開会 ¶開会する open the meeting; begin 《its》 session; open; sit / 開会中である be open; be in session; be sitting / 開会の辞を述べる give [deliver] an opening address / 開会を宣言する declare 《the meeting》 open; call 《the meeting》 to order / 開会式 an opening ceremony. 文例↓

かいがい 海外 overseas [foreign] countries ¶海外の overseas; foreign / 海外に abroad; overseas;《文》over [beyond] the seas / 海外に旅行する go on a trip abroad; travel abroad / 海外から帰る return from abroad [overseas] / 海外経済[軍事]援助 overseas economic [military] aid / 海外市場 an overseas [a foreign] market / 海外事情 (knowledge of) foreign affairs / 海外版 an overseas edition / 海外貿易 ⇒がいこく(外国貿易) / 海外放送 overseas broadcasting; an overseas broadcast (1回の) / 海外旅行 overseas [foreign] travel; an overseas trip. 文例↓

がいかい¹ 外界 the outside world;《文》one's external environment ⇒がいぶ.

がいかい² 外海 the open sea.

かいがいしい brisk; spirited; plucky;《口語》spunky ¶かいがいしいって立ちである be fitted out for hard work / かいがいしく働く work briskly [actively].

かいかく 改革 (a) reform;《文》reformation; reorganization ¶改革する reform; reorganize; carry out a reform / 改革者 a reformer. 文例↓

がいかく 外角 【幾何】an exterior [external] angle;【野球】the outside ¶外角球 an outside ball.

がいかくだんたい 外郭団体 a fringe organization;〈官庁の〉an extra-departmental body [organization].

かいかた 買い方 〈人〉a buyer;【相場】a bull;〈方法〉how to buy [get a bargain].

かいいぬ 飼い犬に手をかまれるとはこのことだ。This is a case of a dog biting the hand that feeds it.

かいいん¹ 本会は1千名の会員を有する。This society has a membership of a thousand [has one thousand members]. / このゴルフ場は会員制になっています。This golf course is not open to non-members.

かいえん 午後5時開演。The curtain rises [is raised] at 5 p.m.

かいおき コーヒーの買い置きがなくなった。There isn't any coffee in the house.

かいか² 東京では桜の開花期は4月上旬です。In Tokyo the cherry blossoms come out in early April.

かいかい 議会は明日から開会される。The Diet opens [begins its session] tomorrow.

かいがい 彼は海外視察旅行から帰ったばかりのところだ。He has just returned from a tour of inspection abroad.

かいかく 彼らは直ちに教育制度の

かいかつ 快活 ¶快活な cheerful; jolly; light-hearted;〈きびきびした〉lively / 快活に cheerfully; with a light heart.

がいかつ 概括 a summary; (a) generalization ¶概括する summarize; sum up; generalize / 概括して言えば to sum up; in short; generally speaking.

かいかぶる 買い被る overestimate; overrate; think too highly of; give too much credit to; make too much of; have too high an opinion of. 文例◎

かいがら 貝殻 a shell ¶貝殻を拾う collect [gather] shells / 貝殻細工 shellwork / 貝殻追放《史》ostracism.

かいかん¹ 会館 a hall; an assembly hall ¶東京キリスト教青年会館 the Tokyo YMCA Hall.

かいかん² 快感 a pleasant feeling;《文》an agreeable sensation ¶快感を覚える feel good;《文》feel pleasure.

かいかん³ 開館 ¶開館する open / 開館している be open.

かいがん 海岸 the seashore; the seaside; the coast〈沿岸〉;〈浜辺〉the beach ¶海岸の町 a seaside town / 海岸に[で] on the shore; by the sea; at the seaside / 海岸に打ち上げられる be washed ashore / 海岸伝いに along the shore[coast] / 海岸線 the coastline; the shoreline;〈鉄道〉a coastal railroad / 海岸通り a road along the seashore; a promenade〈遊歩道〉.

がいかん¹ 外観 the outside [external] appearance;《文》the exterior;《文》externals; the look ¶建物の外観 the exterior [external appearance] of a building / 外観で人を判断する judge people by appearances [externals].

がいかん² 概観〈見渡すこと〉a general view [survey];〈輪郭〉an outline ¶概観する survey; take a general [bird's-eye] view of.

かいき¹ 回忌 an anniversary of *sb's* death ¶3[7]回忌 the second [sixth] anniversary of *sb's* death.

かいき² 回帰 ¶回帰する recur; revolve;〈帰る〉return; go back / 回帰熱 recurrent fever / 北[南]回帰線 ⇨ きた, みなみ.

かいき³ 会期 a term; a period ¶(国会などの)会期を延長する extend [prolong] the session. 文例◎

かいき⁴ 怪奇 (a) mystery; (a) wonder ¶怪奇な mysterious; strange; grotesque; bizarre / 怪奇小説 a mystery story; a ghost story; a thriller.

かいき⁵ 買い気《相場》(a) bullish feeling [sentiment].

かいぎ¹ 会議 a conference; a meeting; a council; a convention〈大会〉;〈会期中の〉a sitting; a session ¶会議を開く hold a conference [council, meeting]; sit in conference / 会議を招集する call [convene, convoke] a conference / 会議室[場] a conference room [hall]. 文例◎

かいぎ² 懐疑 doubt; skepticism ¶懐疑的 skeptical; incredulous (about) / 懐疑派 the skeptics / 懐疑論[主義]《哲》skepticism.

がいき 外気 the (open) air; (the) fresh air; the air outside ¶外気に当たる get some (fresh) air; get out in the (fresh [open]) air / 外気に当てる expose *sth* to the air; air *sth*.

かいきいわい 快気祝い ¶快気祝いをする give *sb* a present to thank *him* for *his* kindness while *one* was ill.

かいきしょく 皆既食 a total eclipse ((of the sun).

かいきゃく 開脚 ¶(跳馬の)開脚飛び《体操》the astride (straddle, vertical stride) vault / 開脚登高《スキー》herringboning.

かいぎゃく 諧謔《文》a jest; a joke; (a) pleasantry; humor ¶かいぎゃくを解する[解しない] have a [no] sense of humor / かいぎゃくをろうする crack jokes / かいぎゃく家 a humorist / かいぎゃく味のある humorous; jocular; witty.

かいきゅう¹ 階級 a class; (a) rank; a grade ¶階級が違う belong to different classes / 階級が上である〈軍人などが〉be senior to *sb* in rank / あらゆる階級の人 people of all classes / 階級の差別を撤廃[打破]する abolish [break down] class distinctions / 階級社会 a class society / 階級なき社会 a classless society / 階級意識 class consciousness / 階級意識が強い be very [strongly] class-conscious /〈軍人の〉階級章 a badge of rank / 階級制度 the class system / (行政官の)階級組織 the hierarchy ((of the Civil Service) /《文》class strife.

かいきゅう² 懐旧 nostalgia; yearning for the old days;《文》retrospection ¶懐旧談 reminiscences / 懐旧談をする talk about the past [*one's* past experiences]; reminisce. 文例◎

かいきょ 快挙 a heroic deed [feat].

かいきょう¹ 回教 Islam ⇨ イスラム(イスラム教) ¶回教寺院 a mosque / 回教徒 a Muslim.

かいきょう² 海峡 a strait (★ しばしば複数形で使われる); a channel ¶イギリス海峡 the English Channel / ドーバー海峡 the Strait(s) of Dover.

改革に乗り出した。They immediately set out to reform the education system.

かいかぶる 彼は私の力を買いかぶっていた。He had too high an opinion [had an exaggerated idea] of my abilities. / He gave me credit for more ability than I really had.

かいき³ 博覧会の会期はまだあと1か月あります。The exhibition will be open for another month. /

国会の会期は9月半ばまでである。The Diet will stay in session until mid-September.

かいぎ¹ やっと彼らを会議のテーブルに就かせることができた。At last I succeeded in getting them to the conference table. / いままでの問題について会議中です。They are now sitting in conference on [are now discussing] that question.

かいきゅう² その光景を見て懐旧

の情に堪えなかった。The sight brought memories of the past surging back to me. / 2人の旧友は懐旧談に楽しくひと時を過ごした。The two old friends had a very pleasant time listening to each other's reminiscences of [listening to each other reminiscing about] their youth.

かいきょう² 彼は肉屋を開業した。He set up as a butcher. / その店は明日から開業する。The store

かいきょう³ 懐郷 ¶懐郷の情に駆られる get [《文》become] homesick [nostalgic] 《for》.

かいぎょう¹ 改行 ¶改行する start a new paragraph [line] ★書き取りなどの際に「(ここで)改行せよ」というときは単に (New) paragraph. と言えばよい.

かいぎょう² 開業 ¶開業する start (a) business; establish *oneself* [set up] in business; set up as (a bookseller), open a store; 《医者・弁護士が》 start [go into] practice / 《医者・弁護士が》開業している be in practice / 開業医 a medical practitioner; a practicing doctor. 文例⇩

がいきょう 概況 the general situation [condition].

かいきょく 開局 ¶開局する 〈局を〉 open [set up, establish] a (new) post office [T.V. station, radio station] / 〈局が〉 start service. 文例⇩

かいきる 買い切る ¶ホテルの部屋を買い切る reserve [《英》book] all the rooms at a hotel / 切符を買い切る buy up all the tickets 《for the matinee》.

かいきん¹ 皆勤 perfect attendance 《for three years》 ¶皆勤する do not miss a single day; 《文》do not absent *oneself* for a single day / 皆勤者 a person who has not missed a day 《at work》.

かいきん² 解禁 removal of a ban [an embargo]; 〈猟などの〉 the opening of the shooting [fishing] season ¶解禁する remove [lift] the ban [embargo] 《on》 ★embargo は意味が通商などの禁止に限定されている. 文例⇩

がいきん 外勤 working away from [outside] the office / 《be on》 outside duty.

かいきんシャツ 開襟シャツ an open-necked shirt.

かいぐい 買い食い ¶買い食いする spend *one's* pocket money on candy [sweets].

かいくぐる 掻い潜る dodge *one's* way through 《the crowd》.

かいぐん 海軍 the navy (★単複両様の扱い) ¶海軍の naval / 海軍軍人 a navy man; naval personnel (集合的) ⇒すいへい² / 海軍工廠 a naval arsenal / 海軍士官 a naval officer / 海軍省[大臣] the Department [Minister] of the Navy.

かいけい¹ 会計 accounts; finance; 〈勘定書き〉 a bill; 〈支払い〉 payment ¶会計をする settle the account; pay the [*one's*] bill / 会計の accounts [accounting] section / 会計係 an accountant; an accounting clerk; 〈出納係〉 a cashier / 会計学 accounting / 会計監査人 an auditor / (団体の)会計幹事 a treasurer / 会計検査をする audit (a firm's) accounts / 会計検査院 the Board of Audit / 会計検査官 an auditor / 公認会計士 《米》 a certified public accountant (略: C.P.A., CPA) / 《英》 a chartered accountant (略: C.A.) / 会計主任 a chief accountant / 会計年度 a fiscal [《英》financial] year / 1983 会計年度 the 1983 fiscal year; fiscal 1983 / 会計簿 an account book / 会計報告 a treasurer's report; a financial report.

かいけい² 塊茎 《植》 a tuber ¶塊茎植物 a tuberous plant.

がいけい 外形 an external [outward] form.

がいけい 外径 an external [outside] diameter.

かいけつ 解決 (a) solution; (a) settlement ¶解決する solve; settle; 〈解決される〉 be settled; be solved; 《文》 come to a settlement / 交渉によって解決する negotiate a settlement 《with》 / 解決法を見出す find [work out] a solution 《to a problem》; find a way out of (a way of overcoming) 《the difficulty》. 文例⇩

かいけつびょう 壊血病 scurvy.

かいけん 会見 an interview; a meeting ¶会見する see; meet; interview; have a talk [an interview] 《with》 / 会見を申し込む ask for an interview 《with》 / 会見記 get an account of [a report on] an [*one's*] interview 《with》.

かいげん¹ 改元 ¶改元する change the name of an era.

かいげん² 戒厳 ¶戒厳司令官 the chief martial law administrator / 戒厳令 martial law / 戒厳令をしく proclaim martial law; place [put] (a city) under martial law / 戒厳令を解く lift [repeal, withdraw] martial law. 文例⇩

がいけん 外見 ⇨がいかん¹; うわべ.

かいこ¹ 蚕 a silkworm ¶蚕を飼う rear [raise] silkworms.

かいこ² 回顧 ⇨かいそう³ ¶横山大観回顧展 the Retrospective Exhibition of Taikan Yokoyama. 文例⇩

かいこ³ 解雇 《文》 dismissal; 《口語》 firing; 《口語》 sacking; 《口語》(give *sb*, get) the sack; 《文》discharge ¶解雇する 《文》 dismiss; 《口語》 fire; 《口語》 sack; 《文》 discharge / 解雇手当 a dismissal allowance; severance pay; 《英》 a redundancy payment / 1 か月前に解雇予告をする give *sb* one month's notice.

かいこ⁴ 懐古 ⇨かいこ². 文例⇩

かいこう¹ 回航 ¶回航する bring [take] a ship (to).

---

opens for business tomorrow.

かいきょく その日の水道使用量は都水道局始まって以来の記録であった. The quantity of water consumed on that day was the largest since the establishment [in the history] of the Metropolitan Government Waterworks Bureau.

かいきん² その事件は昨日記事解禁となった. The press ban on the case was removed yesterday. / さけ漁は来週解禁となる. The salmon season opens next week. | The open season on salmon starts next week.

かいけつ 事態は円満に解決した. The matter has been settled amicably [has been brought to an amicable settlement]. / それは僕が自分で解決すべき事です. That's something I must work out for myself. / 解決法を目下考慮中です. I am considering how to settle the matter.

かいげん² 同市は現在戒厳令下にある. The city is now under martial law. | Martial law has been proclaimed in the city.

かいこ² 回顧すればもう 20 年の昔となった. It was twenty years ago as I look back on it.

かいこ⁴ 年を取ると懐古趣味が強くなるものだ. The older we get, the more fondly we think of the past.

かいこう² 海港 a seaport.
かいこう³ 海溝 a [an ocean] deep [trench] ¶日本海溝 the Japan Deep / ミンダナオ海溝 the Mindanao Trench.
かいこう⁴ 開口 ¶開口一番…と言う[をする] one's first words are 《an appeal for money》; the first thing one says is 《that one intends to resign》; open one's speech with 《an attack on the Government》/ 開口部 an opening; 《文》 an orifice.
かいこう⁵ 開校 ¶開校する open [establish, found] a school / 開校記念日 the anniversary of the founding of the school.
かいこう⁶ 開港 ¶開港する open a port (to foreign trade) / 開港場《史》an open [a treaty] port.
かいこう⁷ 開講 ¶開講する begin a series of lectures 《on Western philosophy》; open a course 《in English》.
かいごう 会合 a meeting; a gathering; 《文》 an assembly; 《口語》a get-together 《親しい者同士の私的な》 ¶会合する meet; gather; assemble; 《口語》get together / 会合の場所 a meeting place; a rendezvous
がいこう¹ 外交 diplomacy ¶日本の対米外交 Japan's policy toward the United States / 外交的手腕 diplomatic talent [skill] / 外交員 a (traveling) salesman; 《英》a commercial traveller; a canvasser / 外交家〈交際上手〉a diplomatic person; a diplomatist / 外交官 a diplomat ¶外交官になる enter the diplomatic service / 外交官の特権 diplomatic immunity / 外交官試験 the Diplomatic Service Examination / 外交関係を断つ break off diplomatic relations 《with》/ 外交交渉 diplomatic negotiations; negotiations through diplomatic channels / 外交使節団 a diplomatic mission 《to France》/ 外交辞令を使う use diplomatic language; be (just) being diplomatic / 外交政策 (a) foreign policy / 外交団 the diplomatic corps / 外交文書 a diplomatic document / 外交ルートを通じて through diplomatic channels. 文例④
がいこう² 外項《数》an outer term.
がいこうせい 外向性《心理》extroversion ¶外向性の extrovert; extroverted 《★「陽気な」という程度の意味であるが, 一般的にも使われる》/ 外向性の人 an extrovert.
かいこく¹ 戒告 ¶戒告を与える give sb a warning; warn [caution] sb against sth.
かいこく² 海国 a maritime [sea] power.

かいこく³ 開国 the opening 《of Japan》《to the world》 ¶開国する open the country (to the world).
がいこく 外国 a foreign country [《文》land] ¶外国の foreign; overseas / 外国に[で]abroad; overseas / 外国へ行く go abroad / 外国へ向かう船 a ship outbound 《from Kobe》/ 外国から帰る return from abroad from a foreign country] / 外国語 a foreign language / 外国航路 an overseas route / 外国航路の船 a ship on a foreign run [an overseas route]; an ocean liner / 外国人 a foreigner; people from [in] other countries; 《法》an alien / 外国人嫌い 《文》 xenophobia; 〈人〉《文》a xenophobe / 外国製の foreign(-made) 〈cars〉; 〈goods〉 made abroad; 《文》〈articles〉of foreign make / 外国貿易 foreign [overseas] trade. 文例④
がいこつ 骸骨 a skeleton ¶がい骨のようにやせ衰える be reduced to a skeleton [to skin and bones].
かいこむ¹ 買い込む buy; 《文》purchase; lay in 《coal for the winter》.
かいこむ² 掻い込む ¶小脇にかい込む hold 《carry, take》sth under one's arm.
かいごろし 飼い殺し ¶飼い殺しにする just keep sb on the payroll.
かいこん¹ 悔恨 remorse 《for》; regret 《at》; 《文》 repentance 《for》; 《文》contrition 《for》.
かいこん² 開墾 reclamation ¶開墾する reclaim 《waste land》; bring 《waste land》 under cultivation / 開墾地 land brought under cultivation; reclaimed land.
かいさい¹ 快哉 ¶快哉を叫ぶ yell with delight; shout for joy.
かいさい² 皆済 ¶皆済する pay 《a debt》 in full; pay 《all one's debts》 off.
かいさい³ 開催 ¶開催する hold 《a meeting》; open 《an exhibition》 ¶開催中である be open; 〈会議などが〉be in session; 開催地 the place where a meeting [conference, etc.] is held; the site 《of an exposition》.
かいざい 介在 ¶介在する lie [stand] between.
がいさい 外債 a foreign loan ¶外債を募る[起こす] raise [float] a foreign loan.
かいさく¹ 改作 (an) adaptation 《from》 ¶改作する adapt 《King Lear for the Japanese stage》/ 改作者 an adapter. 文例④
かいさく² 開削 ¶開削する 〈掘る〉cut; excavate; 〈運河などを建設する〉build; 《文》 construct / 開削工事 excavation works.
かいさつ 改札 the examination of tickets ¶改

がいこう¹ 彼は保険の外交をやっている。He is selling insurance. | He is an insurance salesman. | 私の兄は外交官です。My brother is a diplomat [is in the diplomatic service].
がいこく その時僕は初めて外国の土を踏んだんです。That was the first time that I had set foot on foreign soil. | 外国語で思う事を表現するのはまことに難しい事 is very hard to express oneself in a language that is not one's own. / 彼は外国語が得意だ。He is good at languages.
かいさく¹ これは近松を改作したものだ。This is an adaptation from one of Chikamatsu's works.
かいさん¹ 国会は解散された。The Diet has been dissolved. | 集会は10時に解散した。The meeting rose [broke up] at ten o'clock.
がいさん この国の人口は概算5千万に達する。The population of the country is roughly estimated at 50,000,000. | At a rough estimate, the country has a population of 50,000,000.
かいし 試合開始は午後2時。Play begins [commences] at 2 p.m. | 本線は15日より運転を開始する。The line will be opened to traffic on the 15th.
かいして 生徒たちは概してよく勉強している。On the whole [For the most part] our students work

かいさん　札する　examine [punch] tickets at the barrier / 改札係　a ticket examiner [《英》collector] (in a railroad station) / 改札口　a ticket barrier　★日本では駅などの表示に wicket とあるが、「改札口」の英訳としては、これは適切でない。

かいさん¹　海産　¶海産食品　seafood / 海産物　marine products / 海産物商　a dealer in marine products.

かいさん²　開山　the founder of a temple.

かいさん³　解散　〈会合の〉breakup；〈議会の〉dissolution　¶解散する〈会合者が〉break up；disperse；〈国会を〉dissolve；〈国会が〉be dissolved / (国会の)解散権　the right to dissolve (the Diet).

かいざん　改竄　¶改ざんする　alter《the text》dishonestly；falsify《a receipt》；《俗》cook (the books)；juggle《figures》；《米》raise (a check).

がいさん　概算　a rough estimate　¶概算する　estimate roughly；make a rough estimate《of》/ 概算で　at a rough estimate；roughly. 文例⇩

かいし　開始　beginning；start；《文》commencement；opening　¶開始する　begin；start；《文》commence；open / 攻撃を開始する　open [mount] an attack (on, against) / 交渉を開始する　enter into negotiations《with》/ 作業を開始する　begin [start] work. 文例⇩

がいし¹　外資　foreign capital　¶外資系会社　a foreign-owned[-affiliated] corporation；a foreign firm / 外資導入　the introduction of foreign capital.

がいし²　碍子　an insulator.

がいじ　外耳　《解》the external ear　¶外耳炎　《医》otitis externa.

かいじけん　怪事件　a mystery；a mysterious event；a strange case [affair].

がいして　概して　generally (speaking)；in general；as a (general) rule；on the whole. 文例⇩

かいしめ　買い占め　cornering　¶買い占めをやる，買い占める　buy up (all the goods)；corner [make a corner in]《wheat》.

かいしゃ　会社　a company (略：Co.)；a (business) firm；《主に米》a corporation　¶会社を組織する　form [organize] a company / 会社に行く[出る]　go to work；〈事務系の人が〉go to the office (★ go to the [one's] company という言い方は不自然) / 会社に勤める　work for [be an employee of] a company [corporation] / 会社へ入る　join a company；enter (the service of) a corporation / 会社員　an employee [a clerk] of a company；an office [a white-collar] worker / 会社組織になる　be incorporated as a company / 会社法　《米》corporation law；《英》company law. 文例⇩

用법　「お仕事は」という質問に対する答としての「会社員です」に相当する英語はない。英米ではもう少し具体的に I work for a trading [securities] company. という形で答えるのが普通。

がいしゃ　外車　a foreign(-made) car；an imported car.

かいしゃく　解釈　(an) interpretation；(a) reading；〈説明〉(an) explanation　¶解釈する　interpret；explain / 善意[悪意]に解釈する　take 《sb's words》in good [bad] part；《文》interpret 《sb's action》favorably [unfavorably] / 間違って解釈する　take [interpret] sth wrongly；misinterpret；《文》put a wrong construction on sth；《口語》get the wrong end of the stick. 文例⇩

かいしゅう¹　回収　(a) withdrawal；(a) collection　¶回収する　collect《waste materials》；withdraw sth from circulation [sale]；〈通貨を〉call in (old 100-yen notes) / 貸付金[売り掛け金]を回収する　collect debts [bills] / (宇宙船の)回収予定地　a recovery area.

かいしゅう²　会衆　people gathered together；a congregation (特に教会の)；an attendance (会衆の数).

かいしゅう³　改宗　(a) conversion　¶改宗する　be converted to《Catholicism》；《米》convert to《Islam》/ 改宗させる　convert sb (to Christianity)；《文》proselytize sb / 改宗者　a convert (to Buddhism). 文例⇩

かいしゅう⁴　改修　repair(s)；improvement　¶改修する　repair《a building》；improve《a road》/ 改修工事　repair work.

かいじゅう¹　怪獣　a monster；a monstrous animal　¶怪獣映画　a monster film.

かいじゅう²　海獣　a sea [marine] animal.

かいじゅう³　懐柔　¶懐柔する〈抱き込む〉win sb over (to one's side)；〈なだめる〉appease；placate；conciliate / 懐柔策〈抱き込み策〉a measure to win sb over to one's side；〈宥和策〉《文》a conciliatory measure；an appeasement policy.

がいじゅう　害獣　a harmful [《文》noxious] animal；a pest；vermin (総称). 文例⇩

がいじゅうないごう　外柔内剛　¶外柔内剛の人　a man who is gentle in appearance but tough in spirit.

がいしゅつ　外出　¶外出する　go out / 外出しない　stay indoors [at home] / 外出の支度をする　get ready to go out / 外着　street clothes / 夜間外出禁止令　a curfew. 文例⇩

---

hard. / 小さな女の子は概して人形が好きだ。Little girls in general are fond of dolls. | Most little girls are fond of dolls. | 今年の作物の出来は概して良好である。This year's crops are on the whole excellent. / 彼の論旨は概して正しい。His argument is more or less correct.

かいしゃ　去年から彼はあの会社に勤めているのです。He began to work for that company last year.

かいしゃく　この文章はそう解釈するより他に解釈の仕様がない。The passage admits of no other interpretation [reading]. / 彼は英語の解釈力が足りない。His ability at reading English is poor.

かいしゅう²　会衆は多数[少数]であった。There was a large [small] attendance at the meeting.

かいしゅう³　彼の熱烈な説教は多くの人を改宗させた。His fiery sermon made [won] many converts to his faith.

がいじゅう　うさぎはどんなにかわいく見えても、農民には害獣に過ぎない。Rabbits may look cute, but to the farmers they are no more than vermin.

がいしゅつ　あいにくただいま外出しております。I'm sorry, he is out at the moment. / 昨日は雨で外出ができなかった。Rain kept me indoors yesterday. / 私は1人

かいしゅん 改悛 《文》repentance;《文》penitence; remorse ¶改悛する feel penitent;《文》repent; feel remorse.

かいしょ¹ 会所 〈囲碁などの〉a《go players'》club.

かいしょ² 楷書 the square [printed] style (of Chinese characters). 文例⇩

かいじょ 解除 〈解放〉release;〈解禁〉lifting ¶禁令を解除する lift [remove] a ban 《on》/ 警報を解除する call off an alert;〈空襲の〉sound the all-clear / 責任を解除する release sb from [relieve sb of] his responsibilities / 統制を解除する remove the control(s) (on); decontrol 《prices》.

かいしょう¹ 改称 ¶改称する change the name [title] 《to》; rename.

かいしょう² 快勝 ¶快勝する win a sweeping [an overwhelming] victory 《over》; have an easy win 《in a game》; win easily.

かいしょう³ 解消 《文》(a) dissolution; (a) cancellation ¶解消する dissolve; cancel; annul / 契約を解消する cancel [annul] a contract / 婚約を解消する break [call off] the [one's] engagement / 発展的解消を遂げる be dissolved in order that a better organization may be formed.

かいしょう⁴ かい性 ¶かい性のある able; resourceful / かい性のある亭主 a good provider / かい性のない shiftless; good-for-nothing. 文例⇩

かいじょう¹ 会場 the place 《for the meeting, where the party is to be held》; a venue;《開催地》the grounds; a site 《敷地》 ¶会場整理係 a marshal; a steward. 文例⇩

かいじょう² 回状 a circular (letter).

かいじょう³ 海上 ¶海上に[で] on the sea; at sea; during the voyage 《航海中》/ 海上生活 life at sea; a sailor's [《文》seafaring] life / 海上保安庁 the Maritime Safety Agency / 海上補給路 a maritime supply route / 海上保険 marine insurance / 海上保険会社 a marine insurance company / 海上輸送 transport by sea; marine transport. 文例⇩

かいじょう⁴ 開場 ¶開場する open; open the doors / 開場中である be open. 文例⇩

かいじょう⁵ 階上 ¶階上の一室 an upstair(s) room / 階上に[で] upstairs / 階上へ行く go upstairs.

かいじょう⁶ 階乗 《数》¶nの階乗 n!; n factorial; the factorial of n.

かいじょう⁷ 塊状 ¶塊状岩 a massive rock / 塊状溶岩 block lava.

がいしょう¹ 外相 ⇒がいむ（外務大臣）¶外相会議 a foreign ministers' conference / 外相級会談 talks at the foreign-minister level.

がいしょう² 外商 going round for orders ¶外商部 the large-[institutional-]customer department; the department (in a department store) dealing with large institutional customers.

がいしょう³ 外傷 an external wound [injury]; 〈特に身体に傷害を与える肉体の〉 a trauma (pl. -s, -mata).

がいしょう⁴ 街娼 a streetwalker.

かいしょうほう 海商法 maritime law.

かいしょく¹ 会食 ¶会食する have [take] a meal together;《文》dine together;《文》dine 《with》.

かいしょく² 海食 coastal erosion.

かいしょく³ 解職 ⇒かいにん，めんしょく.

がいしょく 外食 ¶外食する eat out.

かいしん¹ 会心 ¶会心の作 a work after one's (own) heart; a satisfactory work / 会心の笑みを浮かべる give [smile] a smile of satisfaction; smile complacently.

かいしん² 回診 ¶回診する go the rounds (of one's patients); do one's rounds.

かいしん³ 改心 ¶改心する 〈非を認める〉be penitent;〈行ないを改める〉mend one's ways; reform; turn over a new leaf / 改心した人 a reformed man. 文例⇩

かいしん⁴ 改新 《文》(a) renovation;《文》(a) reformation ¶大化の改新 the Taika Reform.

かいじん¹ 灰燼 ¶灰燼に帰する be reduced to ashes; be burnt [razed] to the ground.

かいじん² 海神 the god of the sea;《ギリシャ神話》Poseidon;《ローマ神話》Neptune.

がいしん 外心 《幾何》a circumcenter.

がいじん 外人 〈白人〉a Westerner; a European ⇒がいこく（外国人）¶外人部隊 a foreign legion.

かいじん(ぶつ) 怪人(物) a mystery man.

かいず 海図 a (nautical) chart ¶海図に載っていない島 an uncharted island.

かいすい 海水 seawater; brine ¶海水着 a bathing suit; a swimsuit /《英》a swimming costume / 海水プール a seawater swimming pool / 海水帽 a bathing cap.

かいすいよく 海水浴 sea bathing ¶海水浴をする bathe in the sea; have [take] a dip [《英》bathe] in the sea / 鎌倉で海水浴をする bathe

---

で外出を許される年頃になっていた. I was old enough to be allowed out by myself. / それに取りかかっている時は，電話がかかっても一切外出しないことにした. While I was involved in that, I was ' out ' to all telephone calls. / 全市に夜間外出禁止令が布かれた. A curfew was imposed on the city.

かいしょ² 楷書でお書き下さい. Please use block letters.

かいしょう⁴ たかが月に20万円ぐらい稼ぐのにふうふう言ってるなんて，あなたは本当にかい性なしだわ. You aren't much of a man if you can't pick up [make] a miserable two hundred thousand yen a month without all this whining. / あんたにかい性があればこんなみじめな暮らしを送らないですむのにねえ. We wouldn't have to lead such a wretched [miserable] life if you were half a man.

かいじょう¹ 会場はどちらですか.

Where is the meeting (going) to be held? / 会場は帝国ホテルにしました. We have chosen the Imperial Hotel as the place for the meeting. / ここが博覧会の会場になる所です. This is the site for the exhibition. / 会場整理のため入場料100円頂きます. A nominal charge of 100 yen will be made for admission.

かいじょう³ 海上つつがなく神戸に入港した. We arrived in Kobe after an uneventful voyage.

on the beach at Kamakura / 海水浴に行く go sea-bathing; go swimming (in the sea) /《1口》go for a swim [《英》a bathe] in the sea / 逗子(ず)へ海水浴に行く go swimming [bathing] at Zushi / 海水浴場 a bathing [swimming] beach; a bathing resort / 海水浴客 a sea bather. 用例⇩

かいすう 回数 the number of times ¶回数を重ねる repeat 《so many times》/ 回数券 a book [sheet] of tickets / 20回の回数券 a book of 20 coupons.

がいすう 概数 ¶概数で in round numbers [figures]; approximately.

かいする¹ 介する〈理解する〉mind; worry 《about》/ 少しも意に介しない do not care a bit 《what sb does》/《口語》could not care less 《about》/《口語》do not give [care] a damn 《what sb says about oneself》/ 友人A氏を介して through 《the good offices of》my friend Mr. A / 通訳を介して話す speak through [《文》with the aid of] an interpreter.

かいする² 解する〈理解する〉understand; see; make out;《文》comprehend;〈解釈する〉interpret; take sth 《as…》; take 《it that…》.

がいする 害する harm; hurt; injure; damage. 用例⇩

かいせい¹ 改正〈修正〉(a) revision; (an) amendment;〈変更〉(an) alteration; (a) change;〈改良〉(an) improvement ¶改正する〈修正する〉revise; amend 《the Constitution》;〈変更する〉alter; change;〈改善する〉improve / 刑法の一部を改正する make a partial amendment of the Criminal Code / 改正定価 the revised price. 用例⇩

かいせい² 改姓 ¶改姓する change one's family name.

かいせい³ 快晴 fine [fair] weather.

かいせいどうぶつ 海生動物 a marine [sea] animal.

かいせき 解析《数》analysis ¶解析する analyze / 解析幾何学 analytic(al) geometry.

かいせつ¹ 回折《物》diffraction ¶回折する diffract; be diffracted; undergo diffraction / 回折格子[スペクトル] a diffraction grating [spectrum].

かいせつ² 開設 ¶開設する establish; set up; open / 電話を開設する have a telephone installed 《in one's house》.

かいせつ³ 解説 (an) explanation; (an) interpretation; a commentary 《on》¶解説する explain; interpret; comment on 《the news》.

かいせつ⁴ 外接《幾何》¶外接する circumscribe 《a polygon》/ 外接円 a circle circumscribing 《a polygon》.

がいせつ 概説 general remarks; an outline ¶概説する give an outline 《of》.

カイゼルひげ カイゼル髭 a handlebar mustache.

かいせん¹ 会戦 a battle; an encounter; an engagement.

かいせん² 回線 a circuit ¶電話回線 a telephone circuit.

かいせん³ 改選 reelection ¶改選する reelect 《the members》/ 半数改選 election of half the members 《of the House of Councilors》.

かいせん⁴ 海戦 a naval [sea] battle ¶日本海海戦 the Battle of Tsushima [the Sea of Japan].

かいせん⁵ 疥癬《医》scabies; the itch.

かいせん⁶ 開戦 the opening of hostilities ¶開戦する open war [hostilities]《against》; make war 《on, against》.

かいぜん 改善 (an) improvement;《文》(a) betterment; a change for the better ⇨かいりょう ¶労働条件の改善 the improvement of working conditions / 改善する improve; make sth better; better. 用例⇩

がいせん¹ 外線《電》an outside wire [cable];〈電話の〉an outside line ¶外線工事 outside wiring. 用例⇩

がいせん² 凱旋 a triumphal return ¶凱旋する return in triumph [with glory]; make a triumphant return 《to》/ 凱旋門 a triumphal arch / 凱旋将軍 a general returning from a victorious campaign / 凱旋将軍のような歓迎を受ける receive [return to] a hero's welcome.

がいぜんせい 蓋然性 probability ¶蓋然性が高い be highly [very] probable.

かいせんどんや 回船問屋〈店〉a shipping agency;〈人〉a shipping agent.

かいそ¹ 改組 reorganization ¶改組する reorganize.

かいそ² 開祖 the founder 《of a sect [school]》.

かいそう¹ 回送 ¶回送する〈転送する〉forward; send on; redirect 《a letter》;〈車を空車のまま他へ運ぶ〉drive 《a bus》without passengers 《to the shed》/ 回送車 an out-of-service car [train];《米》a deadhead;〈故障車〉a car being returned for repairs.

かいそう² 会葬 ¶会葬する attend [be at] a funeral / 会葬者 people attending a funeral.

かいじょう⁴ 午後4時開場. Doors open at 4 p.m. / 開場前からたくさんの人が行列を作っていた. Lots of people were lining up in front of the theater before the doors opened.

かいしょく¹ 今晩は友人と会食の約束がある. I have a dinner engagement [an engagement to dine] with a friend this evening.

かいしん³ 彼は今ではすっかり改心している. He is truly penitent [is another man] now.

かいすいよく 私は夏はたいてい海水浴に行く. I usually go to the seaside in summer.

かいすう 彼の欠席の回数はどれほどですか. How often [many times] was he absent? / この線は列車運転の回数が以前より多くなった. We have more trains (running) on this line now than before.

かいする 過労は健康を害する. Overwork will injure your health. / 彼は人の感情を害することを何とも思わない. He thinks nothing of hurting other people's feelings.

かいせい¹ 今月5日から時間表が改正される. The revised timetable will go into effect on [from] the 5th of this month.

かいぜん 少しも改善の跡が見えない. It shows no sign of improvement. / 大いに改善の余地がある. There is plenty of scope [room] for improvement.

がいせん¹ 9を回すと外線につなが

かいそう[3] 回想 recollection; reminiscence ¶回想する look back on [over] ⟪the past⟫; think back to ⟪an event in the past⟫; recollect; recall *sth* to *one's* mind / (映画の)回想場面 a flashback / 回想録 ⟪write *one's*⟫ reminiscences; ⟪publish *one's*⟫ memoirs. [文例⇩]

かいそう[4] 回漕 ⇨かいうん[1] ¶回漕する transport ⟪goods⟫ by sea; ship.

かいそう[5] 快走 ¶快走する run [sail] fast [at an exhilarating speed]; scud ⟪across the waves⟫.

かいそう[6] 改装 redecoration; remodeling; a refit (特に船の) ¶改装する redecorate; refurbish; remodel; ⟪米口語⟫ do over; refit; convert / 店を改装する redecorate [refurbish, refit] a store / 喫茶店を改装してレストランにする remodel [convert] a tearoom into a restaurant. [文例⇩]

かいそう[7] 海藻 seaweed(s); marine plants.

かいそう[8] 階層 a class; a social stratum ¶あらゆる階層の人々 people of every class [on every social level]; ⟪文⟫ people from every walk [all walks] of life / 階層社会 a stratified society.

かいそう[9] 潰走 ¶潰走させる put ⟪the enemy⟫ to flight; rout; send ⟪the enemy⟫ flying.

かいぞう[1] 改造 (an) alteration; remodeling; reorganization ¶内閣の改造 a reshuffle in [of] the Cabinet; a Cabinet reshuffle / 改造する alter; remodel; revamp; reorganize; reshuffle ⟪the Cabinet⟫ / 倉庫を工場に改造する convert a warehouse into a factory.

かいぞう[2] 解像 〘写真〙 ¶解像度[力] resolution; resolving power / 高解像度写真 a high-resolution photograph.

がいそう 外装 〈包装〉 wrapping(s); 〈建物などの〉 (a) facing (material); the exterior (finish) ⟪of a building⟫; (a) cladding.

がいそうほう 外挿法 〘統計〙 extrapolation.

かいぞえ 介添え 〈助手〉 a helper; an assistant; 〈決闘の〉 a second; 〈花嫁の〉 a bridesmaid; 〈花婿の〉 a best man ¶介添えする help; assist; act as second.

かいそく[1] 会則 the regulations [rules] of a society.

かいそく[2] 快速 ¶快速の high-speed; fast / 快速(力) a high [great] speed / 1時間200キロの快速(力)で走る run at the high speed of 200 kilometers an hour / 快速船 a fast sailing ship / 快速艇 a speedboat / 快速電車 a rapid(-service) train. [文例⇩]

かいぞく 海賊 a pirate ¶海賊を働く commit piracy / 海賊行為 (an act of) piracy / 海賊船 a pirate ship / 海賊版 a pirate edition.

かいそん 海損 〘保険〙 sea damage; an average ¶共同[単独]海損 a general [particular] average.

かいだ 快打 〘野球〙 a clean hit.

かいたい 解体 〈分解〉 taking ⟪a machine⟫ apart [to pieces]; dismantling; 〈解消〉 (a) dissolution ¶解体する take [pull] ⟪a machine⟫ apart [to pieces]; dismantle ⟪a factory⟫; scrap [break up] ⟪a ship⟫; pull down ⟪a building⟫ / 財閥を解体する dissolve [break up] a *zaibatsu*.

かいだい[1] 改題 ¶改題する change the title ⟪of a book⟫ / …と改題して under the new title of….

かいだい[2] 解題 a bibliography ⟪of⟫; a bibliographical introduction ⟪to⟫.

かいたく 開拓 〈土地の〉 reclamation; 〈森林地の〉 deforestation; ⟪英⟫ disafforestation; 〈新分野の〉 pathfinding ¶開拓する reclaim ⟪wasteland⟫; open up ⟪Hokkaido⟫; put ⟪virgin land⟫ to the plow; clear ⟪land of forests⟫; blaze a trail ⟪in⟫ / 新市場を開拓する find [open up] a new market ⟪for⟫ / 運命を開拓する improve *one's* lot (by *one's* own efforts); carve out a career for *oneself* / 開拓者 〈入植者〉 a settler; a pioneer; 〈新分野の〉 a pioneer; a pathfinder; a trail-blazer / 開拓者的努力 a trail-blazing effort / 開拓地 reclaimed land.

かいだく 快諾 ¶快諾する[を与える] agree [⟪文⟫ consent] readily [willingly]. [文例⇩]

かいだし 買い出し 〈仕入れ〉 buying (wholesale); 〈日用品などの〉 shopping ¶買い出しする buy ⟪goods⟫ (wholesale); lay in ⟪provisions⟫ / 買い出しに出かける go ⟪to the market⟫ to buy [lay in] ⟪provisions⟫; go shopping ⟪in town⟫.

かいだす 掻い出す bail [ladle] out ¶船の水をかい出す bail water out of a boat; bail a boat out.

かいたたく 買い叩く ⟪口語⟫ beat ⟪the seller, the price of an article⟫ (right) down; drive a hard bargain with *sb* and get ⟪an article⟫ dirt cheap.

かいたて 買いたて ¶買いたての ⟪clothes⟫ that *one* has just bought; newly-bought ⟪furniture⟫.

かいだめ 買い溜め ¶買いだめする hoard (up); stock up ⟪on⟫.

かいだん[1] 会談 a talk; a conference ¶会談する talk together; have a talk ⟪with⟫; confer ⟪with⟫.

かいだん[2] 怪談 a ghost story; a tale of the supernatural.

かいだん[3] 階段 〈階と階との間の〉 (a flight of) stairs; 〈入口などの〉 steps ¶階段を昇る[降

ります. Dial 9, and you'll get an outside line.

かいそう[3] その当時を回想すれば夢のようだ. When I look back upon those days, it all seems like a dream. | The memories of those days come back to me as if they were the scenes of a dream.

かいそう[6] 船は改装のため目下ドック入りしている. The ship is now in dock for a refit.

かいそく[2] 東京高尾間には快速電車が走っている. A rapid-car service operates [is available] between Tokyo and Takao.

かいだく 彼は私の申し出を快諾した. He readily agreed to my request.

かいだん[3] 彼は階段を2段ずつ飛ぶように駆け上がった. He flew up the steps, two at a time.

がいたん まことに慨嘆に堪えない. It really is most regrettable [is a matter for great regret]. / 道徳の低下は実に慨嘆すべきものがある. The decline in public morals is simply deplorable.

かいちゅう[4] 懐中物ご用心. Beware of pickpockets.

かいちゅうでんとう 懐中電灯をつ

りる】 go up [down] the stairs / 階段の上で at the top [head] of the stairs / 階段の下で at the bottom [foot] of the stairs / 階段教室 a (lecture) theater. 文例⇩

がいたん 慨嘆 ¶慨嘆する《文》deplore; 《文》lament (over); regret / 慨嘆すべき deplorable; 《文》lamentable. 文例⇩

かいだんじ 快男児 a (jolly) good fellow.

がいち 外地 ⇨がいこく ¶外地勤務 overseas service.

かいちく 改築 rebuilding; remodeling; reconstruction ¶改築する rebuild; remodel / 改築中である be being rebuilt; be under reconstruction.

かいちゅう¹ 回虫 a roundworm; an ascarid ¶回虫がわく get roundworms / 回虫病 ascariasis.

かいちゅう² 改鋳 ¶改鋳する〈貨幣を〉remint (gold coins); recoin; 〈鐘を〉recast.

かいちゅう³ 海中 ¶海中に in [into, under, 《文》beneath] the sea / (船から)海中に落ちる fall overboard / 海中に沈む sink under [《文》beneath] the waves; go down (船が).

かいちゅう⁴ 懐中 ¶懐中鏡 a pocket mirror / 懐中時計 a watch / 懐中無一物である have no money with one. 文例⇩

がいちゅう¹ 外注 ¶(自社製品の)機械の部品を外注に出す place an order with an outside supplier for parts of a machine (produced in one's plant).

がいちゅう² 害虫 a harmful [an injurious, 《文》a noxious] insect; an insect that does harm to《the rice crop》; vermin (総称) ¶害虫の防除 pest control / 害虫を駆除する exterminate [get rid of] noxious insects.

かいちゅうでんとう 懐中電灯 an electric [a pocket] torch; a flashlight ¶懐中電灯をつける[消す] turn a torch on [off] / 懐中電灯で照らす put the light from a flashlight on 《an object》. 文例⇩

かいちょう¹ 会長 the president (of a society); the chairman (of the board of directors). 文例⇩

かいちょう² 回腸 【解】the ileum (pl. ilea).

かいちょう³ 快調 ¶(スポーツの選手などが)快調である be in top [the best] condition; be in good form [shape] ⇨ コンディション 田园 / 快調に進む make good [steady] headway; go along in top [high] gear; progress smoothly.

かいちょう⁴ 海鳥 a sea bird; a seafowl.

かいちょう⁵ 開帳 ¶賭場を開帳する run a gambling house / 秘仏を開帳する unveil a treasured Buddhist image.

かいちょう⁶ 諧調 melody; harmony ¶諧調の美 euphony.

がいちょう 害鳥 a harmful [an injurious] bird; a bird that does harm 《to the rice crop》; vermin (総称).

かいつう 開通 ¶開通する〈新線が〉be opened to traffic; 〈不通線が〉be reopened (for service) / 開通式 the formal opening 《of a railroad》. 文例⇩

かいづか 貝塚 a shell mound [heap, midden]; a kitchen midden.

かいつけ 買い付け buying; 《文》(a) purchase ⇨ かいいれ, かう² ¶買いつけの肉屋 one's butcher; one's favorite meat store. 文例⇩

かいつぶり 【鳥】a grebe.

かいつまむ 掻い摘まむ sum up; summarize ¶かいつまんで話す tell briefly; give the outline (of); outline; sketch / かいつまんで言えば in short [brief]; to sum up.

かいて 買手 a buyer; 《文》a purchaser ¶すぐ買手が付く find a ready sale [market]; find a buyer at once / 買手市場 a buyers' market. 文例⇩

かいてい¹ 改定 (a) revision ¶改定する revise 《the tariff》.

かいてい² 改訂 (a) revision ¶改訂する revise / 改訂版 a revised edition.

かいてい³ 海底 the bottom [bed] of the sea; the ocean floor [bed] ¶海底に沈む sink [go down] to the bottom of the sea / 海底火山 a submarine volcano / 海底電信 submarine telegraph / 海底電信で by cable / 海底電線を敷設する lay a submarine [an underwater] cable / 海底トンネル an undersea [a submarine] tunnel / 海底油田 a submarine oil field.

かいてい⁴ 開廷 ¶開廷する open [hold] the court / 開廷中である the court is sitting / 開廷日 a court day.

かいてき 快適 ¶快適な comfortable; pleasant; agreeable.

がいてき 外敵 a foreign enemy [invader] ¶外敵の攻撃を受ける suffer an attack from a foreign country; be attacked by a foreign enemy.

かいてん¹ 回転 (a) revolution; (a) rotation ¶回転する turn (go, move, spin) round; revolve; rotate; gyrate / 1回転する make one revolution [rotation, full turn]; turn full circle / 〈頭の回転が速い[遅い] be quick [slow] on the uptake / 毎分100回転のスピードで at 100 revolutions [revs] per minute (略: 100 r.p.m.) / 大回転《スキー》the giant slalom / 回

けて, 足元を照らしてくれた. She shone her torch on the floor in front of us.

かいちょう¹ 本協会の会長は沢田博士です. The society is under the presidency of Dr. Sawada.

かいつう 不通区間は5時間後に開通した. The damaged section was reopened to traffic [The train service in the damaged section was restored] five hours later. / 千歳橋の開通式は昨日行なわれた. The Chitose Bridge was opened with due ceremony yesterday.

かいつけ 値上りを見越して大量に小豆の買い付けをした. We made large purchases of adzuki in anticipation of a rise in its price.

かいて その作品には幾人もの買手がついたのに彼はそれを売らな

かった. He refused to sell the work, though he received several offers for it. / あの家はまだ買手がつかない. They still haven't found a buyer for that house. | That house is still unsold.

かいてい² その辞書に大改訂を施す必要があることを彼も認めた. He too admitted that the dictionary needed a drastic revision.

かいてん 転椅子 a revolving [swivel] chair / 回転運動 (set up) a rotary [rotatory] motion [movement]; revolution; rotation / 回転競技《スキー》the slalom / 回転資金 a revolving fund / 回転軸 the axis of rotation [gyration]; a pivot / (エンジンの)回転数を上げる rev up (an engine) / 回転盤 a turntable; a rotary table; a rotating [turning] disk / 回転ドア a revolving door / 回転木馬 ⇨ メリーゴーラウンド / 回転翼 〈ヘリコプターの〉a rotor (blade); 〈送風機の〉a wafter / 回転率〈資金などの〉the (rate of) turnover (of capital [merchandise]). 文例⇩

かいてん² 開店 ¶開店する open the store; the shop opens.

がいでん 外電 a foreign telegram; a dispatch 《from London》.

ガイド a guide ¶ガイドブック a guidebook; a guide.

かいとう¹ 回答 a reply; an answer ⇨ へんじ¹ ¶回答者 an answerer; 〈クイズ番組の〉a panelist; 〈アンケートの〉a respondent. 文例⇩

かいとう² 快刀 ¶快刀乱麻を断つ act decisively to solve a complicated problem; cut the Gordian knot.

かいとう³ 怪盗 a phantom thief.

かいとう⁴ 解凍 thawing(-out) ¶解凍する thaw [defrost] (frozen meat).

かいとう⁵ 解答 a solution (of [to] a problem); an answer (to a question) ¶解答する solve (a problem); answer (a question) / 正しい解答をする give the right [correct] answer;《文》answer correctly / 間違った解答をする give a wrong answer;《文》answer incorrectly / 試験問題解答 a key [(a set of) answers] to examination questions.

かいどう 街道 a highway; a main road;《英》a highroad ¶甲州街道 the Koshu Highway / 青梅街道 the Ome Road.

がいとう¹ 外套 an overcoat ¶厚い外套を着ている wear a heavy overcoat.

がいとう² 街灯 a streetlamp; a streetlight; 〈柱〉a lamppost.

がいとう³ 街頭 ¶街頭で《米》on the street;《英》in the street / 街頭演説 a speech made on a street corner; soapbox oratory / 街頭募金 collecting [《文》soliciting] contributions on the street / 街頭(録音)のインタビュー a 'man in the street' interview; a curbside interview.

がいとう⁴ 該当 ¶該当する〈条項などに当てはまる〉come [fall] under《Article 9》; 〈条項などが適用し得る〉《文》be applicable (to). 文例⇩

かいどく¹ 買い得 ¶お買い得品 a bargain; a good buy.

かいどく² 解読《文》decipherment; decoding ¶解読する break [crack]《the enemy's code》; decipher; decode / 暗号電報を解読する decipher a (coded) telegram.

用法 暗号を「解読する」には (a)「暗号の秘密を解く」と (b)「暗号文を普通文に直す」の意があるが, break は (a) の意味のみ, decipher, decode はどちらの意味にも使えるが, (b) の意味のことが多い.

がいどく 害毒《文》evil; harm;《文》an evil [a baneful] influence ¶社会に害毒を流す exert a baneful influence on society; corrupt society.

かいどり 飼い鳥 〈籠に入れて飼う小鳥〉a cage [captive] bird; 〈家禽〉a domestic fowl.

かいとる 買い取る buy;《文》obtain sth by purchase;《文》purchase ⇨ かう².

かいならす 飼い馴らす tame; domesticate.

かいなん 海難 a disaster at sea; a shipwreck ¶海難にあう〈船が主語〉meet with a disaster at sea; be wrecked; 〈人が主語〉be shipwrecked / 海難救助 sea rescue / 〈航空機の参加した〉air-sea rescue (略: A.S.R.) / 海難信号を発する radio an SOS; flash a distress signal / 高等[地方]海難審判庁 the Higher [Local] Marine Accidents Inquiry Agency.

かいにゅう 介入 intervention; interference ¶介入する intervene [interfere] (in a dispute); meddle (in a matter); step in. 文例⇩

かいにん 解任 ¶解任する relieve sb of his post; remove sb from his position.

かいぬし¹ 買い主 the buyer; the purchaser.

かいぬし² 飼い主 the owner; the keeper ¶飼い主のない犬 a stray [homeless] dog.

かいね 買い値 the purchase price.

かいねこ 飼い猫 a house cat.

がいねん 概念《文》a concept;《文》a conception; a general idea ¶概念化する《文》conceptualize / 概念的思考《文》conceptual thinking.

かいば 飼い葉 fodder; forage ¶馬に飼い葉をやる feed a horse; give a horse fodder / 飼い葉おけ a manger.

がいはく 外泊 ¶外泊する stay out overnight; sleep away from home.

がいはく² 該博 ¶該博な《文》extensive;《文》profound / 該博な知識 a wide knowledge (of); 《文》profound learning;《文》erudition. 文例⇩

かいばしら 貝柱 the adductor muscle (of shellfish, used as food).

かいはつ 開発 development; exploitation ¶開発する develop (land); exploit《natural resources》/ 新しいシステムを開発する develop

---

かいてん¹ 地球は約365日で太陽の周囲を1回転する. The earth makes one revolution round the sun in about 365 days.
かいてん² 開店は10時です. The store opens at 10. / まるで開店休業の状態だ. We [They] are open for business, but are doing virtually none at all.
かいとう¹ その問い合わせの手紙に対して彼らからは何の回答もなかった. They received no reply from him to their letter of inquiry. | Their letter of inquiry went unanswered by him.
がいとう⁴ それは刑法第57条に該当する. It comes under Article 57 of the Criminal Code.
かいどく¹ それはお買い得ですよ. It's a real bargain. | It's a really good buy.
かいにゅう 彼らは警察の介入に抗議してデモを行なった. They held a demonstration to protest against the police intervention.
がいはく² 氏の該博な知識には一同敬服しています. We all admire his erudition.
かいひ¹ 会費は年額4,000円です. Membership fees are 4,000 yen a year. / 会費5,000円は当日ご持参下さい. You are requested to bring 5,000 yen as expenses for

a new system / 開発援助 《increase》 development assistance / 開発中の 《開発段階にある》 機械 a machine which is under development [in the development stage] / 土地開発業者 a land developer / 開発銀行 a development bank / 宇宙開発計画 a space development program / 北海道開発庁 the Hokkaido Development Board.

かいばつ 海抜 ¶海抜1,000メートルである be 1,000 meters above sea level.

かいはん[1] 改版 《改訂》 (a) revision; 〈改訂本〉 a revised [new] edition ¶改版する revise 《the current edition》; issue a revised [new] edition.

かいはん[2] 解版 《印刷》 distribution of type ¶解版する distribute the type.

かいひ[1] 会費 membership fees [dues] ★「会費」は membership fees と複数形で使うことが多いが, 時には a membership fee と単数形をとることもある. dues は単数形はとらない ¶クラブの会費 club dues; 《英》 one's club subscription. 文例⇩

かいひ[2] 回避 《文》 avoidance; evasion ¶回避する avoid; evade / 責任を回避する evade [dodge] the responsibility 《for》 / 他国の紛争に巻き込まれることを回避する avoid [steer clear of] involvement in conflicts between other powers.

がいひ 外皮 《解・動》 an integument; a skin.

かいびゃく 開闢 ¶開闢以来 since the beginning [creation] of the world; since the beginning of time; since the dawn of history / 開闢以来の出来事 an unprecedented event.

かいひょう 開票 ¶開票する open the ballot boxes; count the votes / 開票所 [立会人] a ballot-counting office (witness). 文例⇩

がいひょう 概評 a general comment 《on》.

かいひょうき 解氷期 the thawing season.

かいひん 海浜 ⇨ うみべ, はま ¶海浜ホテル a seaside hotel.

がいぶ 外部 〈外側〉 the outside; 《文》 the exterior; 〈外界〉 the outside world ¶建物の外部 the exterior of a building / 外部の 《文》 external; outer; 《文》 exterior / 外部の人 an outsider / 外部から見ると when seen from the outside. 文例⇩

かいふう[1] 海風 a sea breeze.

かいふう[2] 開封 ¶開封する open 《a letter》 / 開封で送る send 《a letter》 unsealed.

かいふく 回復 〈健康の〉 recovery 《from illness》; recuperation 《after an illness》; 〈復旧〉 restoration ¶回復する 〈健康を〉 get well again; get better (★ get better はただ「快方に向かう」という意味に限らず,「完全に回復する」という意味でもよく使われる); recover 《from 《one's》 illness》; get over 《a disease》; 《文》 be restored to health; 《文》 regain [recover] one's health; 〈取り返す〉 get sth back; restore 《order》; redeem 《one's credit》; retrieve 《one's honor》 / 元気を回復する recover one's spirits [strength] / 回復期にある be in the convalescent stage; be convalescing; be getting better / 回復期にある患者 a convalescent (patient) / 回復力 〈病気からの〉 recuperative power. 文例⇩

かいふくしゅじゅつ 開腹手術 an abdominal operation.

かいぶつ 怪物 〈化け物〉 a monster; a goblin; 〈なぞの人〉 a mysterious figure; a dark horse ¶海の [に棲む] 怪物 a sea monster.

かいぶん 灰分 ash; the ash content 《of》.

がいぶん 外聞 ¶外聞の悪い disreputable; shameful; scandalous / 外聞をはばかる家庭の秘密 a skeleton in the cupboard. 文例⇩

かいぶんしょ 怪文書 an anonymous muckraking document.

かいへい[1] 皆兵 ¶国民皆兵制度 a universal conscription system.

かいへい[2] 海兵 a marine ¶海兵隊 a marine corps; 《米》 the Marines; 《英》 the (Royal) Marines.

かいへい[3] 開平 《数》 ¶開平する extract the square root 《of》.

かいへい[4] 開閉 ¶開閉する open and shut 《a window》 / 《電気の》 回路を開閉する make and break a circuit / 開閉器 a switch / 開閉器箱 a switch box. 文例⇩

かいへん 改変 (a) change; (an) alteration; (a) modification; 《文》 (a) renovation ¶改変する change; alter; modify; renovate.

かいべん 快便 regular motions [bowel movements]. 文例⇩

かいほう[1] 介抱 nursing; care ¶介抱する nurse; tend; look after; care for / 介抱泥を働く rob [《米口語》 roll] a drunk (while pretending to help him). 文例⇩

かいほう[2] 会報 a bulletin; the transactions [proceedings] of a society.

かいほう[3] 快方 ¶快方に向かう 〈人が主語〉 get better (★ get better には「完全に健康を回復する」の意味もある); 《文》 improve in health; 〈病気が主語〉 take a turn for the better; take a favorable [better] turn.

かいほう[4] 快報 good news ⇨ きっぽう.

かいほう[5] 開放 ¶開放する open; 〈開けたま

---

the evening.
かいひょう 私も開票に立ち会いました. I was among the witnesses when the votes were counted [when the ballot boxes were opened].
がいぶ 秘密が外部に漏れた. The secret leaked out.
かいふく 疲労回復にはよく眠るのが一番だ. The best way to recover from [get over] one's fatigue is

to sleep well. / 船は天候の回復を待っている. The boat is waiting for the weather to improve.
がいぶん 君, 外聞が悪いぜ, そんな所にしょっちゅう出入りしていると. You will damage [lose] your reputation if you frequent places like that. / そうなっては恥も外聞もなかった. I no longer cared what other people would think of me.

かいへい ドアは自動開閉式になっている. The door opens and shuts automatically.
かいべん 快食快食快眠は健康のしるし. A good appetite, sound sleep, and regular motions are the three signs of good health.
かいほう[1] あなたが介抱して下さらなかったら私は死ぬところでした. Had it not been for your care, I should have died.

かいほう まにしておく〉 leave 《the door》 open; 〈一般に〉 open 《a private garden》 to the public / 開放性結核 open tuberculosis / 《性質の》開放的な frank; open; straightforward; uninhibited. 文例⇩

かいほう⁶ 解放 release; 《文》liberation; 《文》emancipation ¶解放する release; free; 《文》liberate; set 《a prisoner》 free [at liberty]; let sb go [loose]; 《文》emancipate / 人民解放軍 the people's liberation army / 解放戦争 a war of liberation; a liberation war / 解放地区 a liberated district [area].

かいほう 解剖 〈医学上の〉 dissection; 〈死因調査の〉 a postmortem (examination); an autopsy ¶解剖する dissect; hold an autopsy [postmortem (examination)] 《on》/ 解剖に付する 《a body》 dissected; submit 《a corpse》 to dissection / 解剖学 anatomy / 解剖学的特徴 an anatomical feature / 解剖室 a dissecting [dissection] room / 解剖図 an anatomical chart [drawing] / 解剖台 a dissecting table / 解剖用具 dissecting tools. 文例⇩

がいほう 外報 foreign news; a foreign telegram ¶《新聞社の》外報部 the foreign news department.

かいほうせき 海泡石 【鉱】meerschaum; sepiolite.

かいぼり 搔掘り ¶かい掘りする drain the water out of 《a pond》; drain 《a well》 dry.

かいぼん 海盆 【地理】an ocean basin.

がいまい 外米 imported rice.

かいまき 搔い巻き a futon with sleeves.

かいまく 開幕 ⇨かいえん ¶開幕戦 an opening game; an (a season) opener.

かいまみる 垣間見る catch [have] a glimpse 《of》. 文例⇩

かいみょう 戒名 a posthumous Buddhist name.

かいむ 皆無 文例⇩

がいむ 外務 ¶外務省[大臣] the Department [Minister] of Foreign Affairs; the Foreign Office [Minister].

かいめい¹ 改名 ¶改名する change one's name 《to》; be renamed 《Masao》; 《文》 assume the new name 《of》.

かいめい² 解明 《文》elucidation; 《文》explication ¶解明する make 《a mystery》 clear; 《文》elucidate 《the meaning》; 《文》explicate 《a theory》; throw [shed] light on sth.

かいめつ 壊滅 〈破壊〉 destruction; 〈全滅〉annihilation ¶壊滅する be destroyed; be ruined; be wiped out; be annihilated / 壊滅的な打撃 a deadly [fatal] blow; a deathblow. 文例⇩

かいめん¹ 界面 【物】the interface 《between two liquids》 ¶界面化学 surface chemistry / 界面張力 【物】interfacial tension.

かいめん² 海面 the surface of the sea ¶海面温度 a sea-surface temperature / 海面気圧 the pressure of the atmosphere at sea level; sea-level (atmospheric) pressure.

かいめん³ 海綿 a (natural) sponge ¶海綿で吸い取る sponge up [off] 《spilled ink》/ 海綿状の spongy / 海綿動物 a sponge.

がいめん 外面 the outside; 《文》the exterior; the (exterior) surface ⇨ うわべ, ひょうめん.

かいもく 皆目 ⇨まったく.

かいもどす 買い戻す buy sth back; 《文》repurchase.

かいもとめる 買い求める ⇨かう².

かいもの 買物 〈買うこと〉a purchase; 〈米〉marketing; 《文》(a) purchase; 〈買い得品〉⇨かいどく¹ ¶買物をする do one's shopping 〈米〉marketing); 色々と [少しばかり]買物をする make various [some] purchases 《in a store》; do a lot of [some] shopping / 安い[高い]買物をする 《人が主語》 buy [get] sth at [for] less [more] than the market price; 〈品物が主語〉 be cheap [dear, expensive] 《at 1,000 yen》; be a good [bad] bargain [buy] 《at that price》/ 買物に行く go shopping 《in Shinjuku》/ 買物袋 a shopping [〈英〉carrier] bag.

かいもん 開門 ¶開門する open the gate.

がいや 外野 【野球】the outfield ¶外野手 an outfielder / 外野席 the outfield bleachers.

かいやく 解約 ¶解約する cancel a contract; annul an agreement / 定期預金を解約する cancel a time deposit / 保険を解約する cancel an insurance contract; surrender an insurance policy.

かいゆう¹ 回遊 ¶回遊する 〈人が〉 make a circular tour 《of Scotland》; tour (around) 《the Hokuriku region》; 〈英〉make a round trip to 《the Lake District》; 〈魚が〉 wander [move] about 《the open seas》; range 《the ocean》; make 《seasonal》 migrations / 回遊魚 a wandering [migratory] fish / 回遊(乗車)券 an excursion [a circular] ticket.

がいゆう 外遊 ⇨ようこう¹.

かいよう¹ 海洋 the sea(s); the ocean ¶海洋学 oceanography / 海洋気象台 a marine meteorological observatory / 海洋小説 a sea story / 海洋少年団 the Sea Scouts / 海洋性気候 an oceanic climate / 海洋生物学 marine biology / 海洋物理学 physical oceanography.

かいほう⁵ 開ական無用.【掲示】Please shut the door. | 〈防火扉などの〉This door must be kept closed at all times. / アメリカの社会が開放的であるに反して日本の社会は閉鎖的である。 Japanese society is closed, while that of America is open.

かいほう 死体を解剖した結果絞殺と判明した。 The postmortem showed that she had been strangled (to death).

かいまみる その言葉を聞いて彼女の執念のすさまじさをかいま見る思いがした。 Her words gave me a glimpse of her tremendous tenacity of purpose.

かいむ 取引は皆無だ。 There has been no trading at all. | Business has been nonexistent. / 彼は法律の知識が皆無だ。 He has not the slightest knowledge of the law.

かいめつ それは彼らの計画にとって壊滅的な打撃となった。 It proved to be the deathblow to their plans.

かいもの きょうはたくさん買物がある。 I have a lot of shopping to do. / 家内はスーパーまで買物に出かけました。 My wife has gone out to do some shopping in the supermarket.

かいよう² 潰瘍 an ulcer ¶潰瘍性の ulcerative 《diseases》.

がいよう¹ 外洋 ⇨ がいかい² ¶外洋漁業 deep-sea fishing [fishery].

がいよう² 概要 ⇨ がいりゃく.

がいようやく 外用薬 a medicine for external use [application].

かいらい¹ 界雷 《気象》a frontal thunderstorm.

かいらい² 傀儡 a puppet ¶かいらい政府 a puppet government.

がいらい 外来 ¶外来の (coming) from abroad; foreign; imported / 外来患者 an outpatient / 外来語 a loan [borrowed] word (from Dutch); a word of foreign origin / 外来思想 foreign ideas / 外来植物 an exotic plant.

かいらく 快楽 (a) pleasure ¶人生の快楽 the pleasures of life / 快楽を追う 《文》seek [pursue] pleasure / 快楽にふける 《文》give *oneself* up to pleasure / 快楽主義 hedonism; epicureanism / 快楽主義者 a hedonist; an epicurean.

かいらん¹ 回覧 ¶回覧する pass (a circular notice) on (to *sb*); send (a circular) round (to all the members); read (a magazine) in turn / 回覧雑誌 a magazine for circulating 《among》/ 回覧板 a notice for circulation.

かいらん² 壊乱 ¶風俗を壊乱する corrupt public morals.

かいり 乖離 ⇨ ゆうり³.

カイリ 海里 a nautical [sea] mile.

かいりき 怪力 fantastic (physical) strength; superhuman strength.

かいりつ 戒律 religious precepts; commandments.

がいりゃく 概略 〈概要〉an outline; a summary; a résumé (論文などの); 〈ほとんど〉almost, practically; 〈大ざっぱに言って〉roughly; in (rough) outline ¶概略を示す give an outline [the gist, a general idea] (of); make a summary (of); summarize / 概略を言えば roughly speaking. 文例⇩

かいりゅう¹ 海流 an ocean [a sea] current ¶日本海流 the Japan Current.

かいりゅう² 開立 《数》 ¶開立する extract the cube root 《of》.

かいりょう 改良 (an) improvement; (a) reform; 《文》betterment ¶改良する improve 《land》; improve on *sth*; reform 《a method》; make *sth* better / 改良品[種] an improved product [breed]. 文例⇩

がいりょく 外力 external [outside] force.

がいりん 外輪 ¶外輪山 the outer rim of a crater / 外輪船 a side-[paddle-]wheel steamer [boat]; a side-wheeler; a paddle-wheeler.

かいるい 貝類 shellfish ¶貝類学 conchology.

かいろ¹ 回路 《電》a [an electric] circuit ¶回路を開く open [break, cut off] a circuit / 回路を閉じる 《通じる》close [make] a circuit.

かいろ² 海路 a sea route ¶海路別府へ行く go to Beppu by sea; take a sea passage 《from Kobe》to Beppu.

かいろ³ 懐炉 a portable body warmer ¶かいろ灰 solid fuel for a body warmer.

カイロ Cairo.

がいろ 街路 a street; an avenue ¶街路樹 trees lining a street / 街路樹のある通り a tree-lined street.

かいろう 回廊 a corridor; a gallery.

がいろん 概論 an outline (of); an introduction (to).

かいわ 会話 (a) conversation ¶会話する talk [speak] 《to, with》; have a conversation [talk] 《with》/ 会話体で書いた本 a book written in a colloquial [conversational] style.

かいわい 界隈 the neighborhood; 《文》the vicinity ¶この界隈で[に] in this neighborhood [vicinity]; around here.

かいん 下院 〈一般に〉the Lower House [Chamber]; 〈米国の〉the House of Representatives; 〈英国の〉the House of Commons.

かう¹ 支う prop [shore] *sth* up; support *sth* with a prop [shore].

かう² 買う 〈買い求める〉buy; 《文》purchase; get; take; 〈認める〉appreciate; have a good [high] opinion of *sb*; 〈招く〉《文》incur; provoke ¶高く買う buy *sth* for [at] a high price; pay a lot (of money) for *sth* / 安く買う buy [get] *sth* cheap [for a low price]; do not pay [give] much for *sth* / 2千円で買う buy [get] *sth* for two thousand yen; pay [give] two thousand yen for *sth* / けんかを買う accept [take up] *sb's* challenge / 人の不興を買う get on the wrong side of *sb*; 《文》incur *sb's* displeasure / 怒りを買う offend *sb*; provoke *sb* [*sb's* anger] / 5千円で買おうと言う offer *sb* 5,000 yen for *sth* / 金で買える money can buy *sth*, 〈物が主語〉can be bought with money; can be got for money; 《文》be purchasable. 文例⇩

かう³ 飼う 〈飼育する〉raise 《sheep》; rear 《silkworms》; 〈飼っておく〉keep 《a dog》/ 〈食べさせる〉feed 《cattle on hay》.

カウボーイ a cowboy; 《米口語》a cowpuncher.

かうん 家運 the fortunes of a family ¶家運

がいりゃく 予定は概略次のとおり。The plan may be summarized as follows. / 彼の失脚の経緯は概略このようなものであった。Such, in (rough) outline, is the story of his downfall.

かいりょう この制度には改良の余地が[大いにある]。There is no [ample] room for further improvement in this system. / この方法なら確かに前の方法の改良になっている。This method is certainly an improvement on the previous one.

かう² 君にも1つ買って上げようか。Shall I get one for you too? / その馬は幾らで買ったの？ What [How much] did you pay for your horse? / 幸福は金では買えない。Money cannot buy happiness. / 100万円では大した車は買えない。You cannot get a very good car for a million yen. / A million yen will not buy a very good automobile. / 彼の恨みを買うようなことをした覚えはない。I certainly haven't done anything to incur his enmity. / 彼の誠実さは買ってやらなければならない。We must give him due credit for his good faith. / 君はあの男をずいぶん高く買っているんだね。You've got quite an

ガウン a gown.
カウンセラー a counselor.
カウンター¹ 〈店の〉a (service) counter.
カウンター² 〖ボクシング〗(get [《文》receive]) a counterblow.
カウント a count; counting ¶カウントする count / 7千カウントの放射能 7,000 counts of radioactivity / フルカウント〖野球〗a full count (of 3 and 2) / カウントアウトになる be counted out. 文例⇩

かえ 替え 〈代わり〉a substitute; a replacement; 〈交換〉(a) change ¶替えがきかない cannot be replaced; be irreplaceable.
かえうた 替え歌 a variation (of a song).
かえぎ 替え着 a change of clothes.
かえす¹ 返す 〈返却する〉return; give [hand] *sth* back; 〈金を〉pay back; repay; 〈元の位置へ〉put back; replace; 〈裏返すか〉turn *sth* over; 〈返送する〉send *sth* back ¶恩をあだで返す 《文》return evil for good. 文例⇩
かえす² 孵す 〈卵をひなにする〉hatch (out) 《an egg》; 〈卵を抱く〉sit on 《eggs》.
かえすがえす(も) 返す返す(も) 〈実に〉really; indeed; 〈はなはだ〉extremely; exceedingly. 文例⇩
かえズボン 替えズボン slacks; trousers; 〈予備の〉an extra pair of trousers (for a suit).
かえだま 替え玉 a stand-in; 《口語》a ringer (特に競技で) ¶試験に替え玉を使う get *sb* to take an examination for *one*; use a stand-in in an examination.
かえち 替地 a piece of land substituted 《for》; a substitute lot 《for》.
かえって 〈反対に〉instead of *doing*; (so) far from *doing*; 〈なおさら〉(all) the more [better, worse] 《for, because》. 文例⇩
かえで 〖植〗a maple (tree).

かえば 替刃 a (new) razor blade.
かえり 帰り 《文》(a) return; coming [going] home [back] ¶帰りが遅いを late home [back]; be late in coming back / 帰りを急ぐ hurry back [home] / 帰りがけに as *one* leaves; 《文》on taking *one's* leave / 帰り〔道〕に on *one's* way home [back] / 学校からの帰り道に on *one's* way home from school / 帰り支度をす る get ready [《文》prepare] to go home [back]. 文例⇩
かえりうち 返り討ち ¶返り討ちにあう 〈敵討ちで〉be killed by *sb* on whom *one* has been seeking revenge; be killed by *one's* intended victim; 〈比喩的に〉challenge *sb* to a fight [game] and get defeated.
かえりざき 返り咲き 〈花の〉blooming [blossoming] a second time; 〈復活〉a comeback ★木に咲く花の場合には blossoming を用い る ¶返り咲きする 〈花が〉bloom [blossom] again (out of season); 〈復活する〉come back 《to power》; make [stage] a comeback (to public life).
かえりつく 帰り着く arrive [get] home; return 《to》.
かえりみる 顧〔省〕みる 〈振り向く〉look back; 〈反省する〉think about *sb*; 《文》reflect on 《*one's* past conduct》; 〈回想する〉look back on [to] *sth* (in the past); 〈顧慮する〉take notice of; look to; think of ¶省みてやましい 所がない have a clear [an easy] conscience / 顧みて他をいう (give an evasive answer and try to) change the subject / 顧みない 〈顧慮しない〉disregard; ignore; pay no attention to; take no notice of / 一身を顧みない sacrifice *one's* life; act with total disregard for *one's* own interests. 文例⇩
かえる¹ 蛙 〖動〗a frog ¶かえる泳ぎ ⇒ひらおよぎ. 文例⇩
かえる² 変える 〈変更する〉change; alter; 〈改

---

opinion of him!
カウント (ボクシングの選手が) カ ウント9でようやく立ち上がった. He took a count of nine before getting up.
かえす 先日お貸しした本はいつ 返していただけますか. When will you give me back [return (me)] the book I lent you the other day? / 読んだら本を元の場 所に返しておいて下さい. Put the book back in its place [back where it was] when you are through with it.
かえすがえす(も) 君が目的が果 せなかったことは返す返すも残念 です. I'm extremely sorry [It is a thousand pities] that you couldn't achieve your objective.
かえって 休養するどころかかえっ ていつもより仕事に励んだ. Instead of taking a rest, he worked much harder than usual. / 吹雪 はやむどころか, かえって激しく なった. The snowstorm, far from

abating, increased in fury. / 忠告 をしたらかえって不興を買ってし まった. I gave him some good advice, but only incurred his displeasure. / 少量の酒ならかえって 薬ですよ. A little drink does you more good than harm. / 転地して かえって悪くなった. The change of air did him more harm than good. / If anything, he got worse for the change of air. / 知らなかっ たと言えば言う程度はかえって私 の言葉を疑った. The more I asserted my ignorance of the matter, the less he believed me.
かえり きょうはたいへん帰りが遅 い. He is unusually late coming home today. / 帰りは車で送って あげるよ. I'll see you home in my car. / (見せ物小屋などで)お 帰りはこちら. This way out! / 僕は散歩の帰り道で児玉さんに出 会った. On my way home from a stroll, I met Mr. Kodama.
かえりみる 顧みれば早や30年の

昔となった. Thirty years have passed since it took place. / 彼は 自分の仕事が忙しくて他を顧みる 暇がない. He is too busy with his work to attend to anything else.
かえる¹ かえるが鳴き出した. Frogs started croaking (to croak). / か えるのつらにしょんべんだ. It's like water off a duck's back. / か えるの子はかえる. Like father, like son. (諺)
かえる² どこまでも目的を変える な. Keep [Stick] to your purpose. / いったん下した命令だか ら変えるわけにはいかない. I've given the order, and it must stand. / 雨がひどいので日を変え て訪ねることにした. It rained so hard that we decided to visit him some other time.
かえる³ 何かほかの品とお換えに なってはいかがです. Would you take something else instead? / 僕 と立場を換えたら君はどうする.

かえる》 reform 《a system》; amend 《a regulation》 / 職を変える change *one's* occupation [job] / 道を変えて行く take a different [another] route. 文例⇩

かえる³ 代[換,替]える 〈転換する〉 change [turn, convert] 《A into B》; 〈交換する〉 exchange 《A for B》; 〈替りを立てる〉 substitute 《A for B》; put 《A》 in place of 《B》; replace 《A with B》 / 金に換える convert *one's* clothes》 into money / …に代えて in place of…; as a substitute for….

かえる⁴ 返[帰]る come [go] back [home]; get [be] back; return; 〈辞去する〉 leave; take *one's* leave; 〈元に復する〉 return [to] / われに返る come to *oneself*; come round [to]; recover *one's* senses / 帰らぬ過去 the irrevocable past / 帰らぬ旅に出る 《文》 depart from this world; 《文》 go on *one's* last journey. 文例⇩

かえる⁵ 孵る hatch (out); be hatched ¶卵からかえる hatch from [out of] the egg / 卵からかえったばかりのひよこ a newly-[freshly-] hatched chick; a chick fresh out of the shell [which has just hatched]. 文例⇩

かえん 火炎 a flame; a blaze ¶火炎に包まれる be envelped [wrapped] in flames / 火炎びん a petrol bomb; a Molotov cocktail / 火炎放射器 a flame thrower.

かお 〈顔面〉 a face; 〈目鼻立ち〉 *one's* looks; 《文》 *one's* features; 《文》 *one's* countenance; 〈表情〉 a look; 〈面目〉 *one's* honor ¶丸い[細い, 長い]顔 a round [narrow, long] face / 涼しい顔 すずしい 〈なに食わぬ顔〉 なにくわぬお / 顔が売れている be popular 《with, among》; 〈勢力がある〉 have a lot of influence 《in the city government, with the directors》 / 顔がきく have a lot of influence 《with, over, in》; have contacts 《in》; be very influential 《in》 / 顔が広い know a lot [large number] of people; be widely known; 《文》 have a wide acquaintance; have a large circle of acquaintances / 《人の》顔を見る look *sb* in the face / 顔を見合わせる look at each other; exchange glances / 顔を合わせる 〈会う〉 see; meet; 〈試合で〉 be matched [pitted] against *sb*; 〈役者が〉 appear in the same play / 顔を向き合わせて座る sit face to face with *sb* / 顔を真赤にする go [《文》become] red in the face; 〈恥じて〉 blush / 難しい顔をする look serious [grave] / 苦い顔をする look sour; scowl / 大きな顔をする look proud [haughty] / 《口語》 look as if *one* owned the place / 恐い顔をした女 a woman with a fierce look on her face / 顔を覚えている remember [recognize] *sb* / 顔を知っている know *sb* by sight / 顔を出す[見せる] 〈物陰などから〉 show *one's* face; 〈人中へ〉 appear 《in public》; turn [show] up; make [put in an appearance; 〈出席する〉 attend 《a meeting》; 〈訪問する〉 ⇨ かおだし (顔出しする) / 顔を立てる show deference 《to》; save *sb's* face [honor] / 顔をつぶす embarrass *sb*; make *sb* look foolish; 《文》 put *sb* out of countenance / 顔をつぶされる lose face; 顔にかかわる 〈事が主語〉 be beneath *one's* dignity; would reflect badly on *one*. 文例⇩

かおあわせ 〈集まること〉 meeting (together); 〈紹介〉 (an) introduction; 〈俳優の〉 appearance in the same play ¶顔合わせをする meet (together); be introduced to one another. 文例⇩

かおいろ 顔色 a [*one's*] complexion ¶顔色が白い[黒い] have a fair [dark] complexion / 顔色がいい[悪い] look [do not look] well / 顔色のいい[悪い]人 a person with a healthy [bad] complexion / 顔色を変える change color; 〈青くなる〉 go [turn] pale / 人の顔色をうかがう try to gauge [judge] *sb's* feelings [state of mind] 《from *his* expression》 / 人の顔色を読む read *sb's* expression [face]. 文例⇩

かおかたち 顔形 features; looks ⇨ ようぼう².

What would you do in my place?/ この千円札を100円硬貨10個に替えて下さい。 Please change [break] this 1,000-yen note into ten 100-yen coins. / 健康は何物にも換え難い。 Nothing can take the place of health. / Nothing is more precious than health. / いくら費用がかかっても彼の命には換えられない。 His life must be saved at any cost.

かえる⁴ お帰りなさい。〈旅行から帰ったとき〉 Welcome home! / 〈勤めから帰ったとき〉 Hullo, dear [darling]. / すぐ帰って来ます。 I won't be long. / 私は6時までに帰らなければならない。 I must be home by six o'clock. / それは彼が東京へ帰って2日後のことであった。 It happened two days after he got back to Tokyo. / 君ならもう帰ってもいい。 You can leave [be off] now. / 子供の頃に帰りたい。 I wish I were a boy again! / 悔やんでも返らぬことだ。 It's no use crying over split milk. / What is done cannot be undone. / その遺失物は持ち主に返った。 The lost article was restored to its owner.

かえる⁵ 卵がかえった。 The eggs have hatched (out). / ひなが2羽かえった。 Two chickens have hatched (out).

かお 私の顔を覚えているかね。 Do you recognize [remember] me? / 彼は僕の顔を穴のあくほど見た。 He looked hard at me. / 皆知らない顔ばかりだ。 They are all strangers to me. / 彼は顔で笑って, 心で泣いていた。 He was smiling, though he was sad at heart. / あいつは顔を見るのも嫌だ。 I can't bear the sight of him. / ちょっと顔を貸してくれませんか。 I'd like to have a few words with you. / Could I have your ear for a moment? / そうしなければ僕の顔が立たない。 It is a point of honor that I should do it. / ちゃんと顔にそう書いてある。 It's written all over your face. / それを聞いて顔から火が出るような気持ちだった。 I was deeply ashamed to hear it. / 怒りが顔に出た。 His face betrayed his anger [that he was angry]. / 何もかも心得ていると言うような顔をしていた。 He looked as if he knew all about it. / 彼は顔に似合わず穏やかな人物だ。 He has a gentle nature, though his looks belie it. / あの会社なら木に顔がきくと彼は言っている。 He says he has a great deal of influence in the corporation.

かおあわせ 2人はその試合が初顔合わせであった。 That was the first time they had been pitted against each other.

かおいろ それを見たとたんに彼の顔色が変わった。 The color left his

かおく 家屋 a house; a building ¶家屋税 a house tax.

かおじゃしん 顔写真 a photograph [picture] of sb's face;〈犯人の〉《米俗》a mug shot.

かおだし 顔出し ¶顔出しする show one's face; make [put in] an appearance;〈訪問する〉visit sb; call on sb; call at sb's (house); drop [look] in on sb (ひょっこり);〈出席する〉attend (a meeting);〈ご機嫌伺いをする〉pay one's respects to [a courtesy call on] sb. 文例↓

かおだち 顔立ち ¶one's (facial) features;〈顔〉a face ⇨ かお ¶顔立ちがいい be pretty; be handsome; have nice [pretty] features; be good-looking; have a handsome face ★ pretty は女性に限って、handsome はほとんど男性に限って用いられる.

かおつき 顔付き a [one's] face; a (sad) look (on one's face); looks;《文》features (目鼻立ち) ¶いかめしい顔付き a stern look / 心配そうな顔付きをする look worried. 文例↓

かおつなぎ 顔繋ぎ ¶顔つなぎする (call on sb) to maintain [keep up] one's contact(s).

かおなじみ 顔馴染み a familiar face; a friend ¶顔なじみである be on familiar terms with sb; be sb's (old) friend. 文例↓

かおぶれ 顔触れ a lineup;《文》the personnel ¶新内閣の顔ぶれ (a list of) the members of the new Cabinet.

かおまけ 顔負け ¶顔負けする be put to shame; feel embarrassed (at). 文例↓

かおみしり 顔見知り ⇨ しりあい ¶お互いに顔見知りである know each other by sight; have met before [previously];《文》be acquainted (with each other).

かおみせ 顔見世 one's debut; one's first appearance on the stage ¶顔見世興行 a show with an all-star cast.

かおむけ 顔向け

かおやく 顔役 a man of influence; a boss.

かおり 香[薫]り (a) smell; (a) scent;《文》an aroma ¶ばらの香り the scent [smell] of roses / コーヒーの香り the aroma of coffee / よい香りがする smell sweet [nice] / 香りのよい sweet-scented[-smelling];《文》fragrant; aromatic.

かおる 香[薫]る smell sweet;《文》be fragrant. 文例↓

がか¹ 画架 an easel.
がか² 画家 a painter; an artist.
がか³ 雅歌《聖書》The Song of Solomon [Songs].

かかあでんか 嚊天下

かかい 歌会 a gathering of tanka poets; a tanka party.

かがい 課外 ¶課外活動 extracurricular [after-school] activities / 課外授業 an extracurricular lesson (in Spanish).

かかい¹ 瓦解 a fall; a downfall; (a) collapse ¶瓦解する fall down; collapse; be ruined.

かかい² 画会〈絵を描く会〉a gathering of painters;〈絵の展覧会〉an art exhibition.

かがいしゃ 加害者 a wrongdoer;《文》an assailant (暴行などの); a murderer (殺人事件の).

かかえ 抱え ⇨ おかかえ ¶ひと抱えの薪 an armful [armload] of firewood / 幾抱えもある大木 a big tree measuring several spans of a man's arms around. 文例↓

かかえこむ 抱え込む ⇨ かかえる.

かかえる 抱える〈だいて持つ〉hold [carry] sth in one's arms [under one's arm];〈雇用する〉(人を) engage; have (320 men) on one's staff; keep ¶赤ん坊を抱える carry [hold] a baby in one's arms / 頭を抱えて with one's head between one's hands / 大勢の子供を抱えている have a large number of children to feed [to provide for] / …に抱えられている〈雇われている〉be employed by sb; be in sb's employ / 抱え主 the employer; the master. 文例↓

カカオ cacao ¶カカオの実 cacao beans.

かかく 価格 (a) price; (a) value ⇨ ねだん ¶価格協定 a price-maintenance agreement; an agreement to maintain the price of a commodity / 価格差 a price differential [difference] / 価格差補給金 subsidies to offset price differentials / 価格調整[統制] price adjustment [control] / 価格表 a price list / 価格表記郵便 mail matter with value declared / 価格表記郵便で出す send sth by insured mail.

かがく¹ 下顎 the lower [under] jaw ¶下顎骨 the (lower) jawbone.

かがく² 化学 chemistry ¶化学的 chemical / 化学的に chemically / 化学工業 the chemical industry / 化学合成 chemosynthesis / 化学構造 the chemical structure《of a medicine》/

---

face the instant he saw it.

かおだし ちょっと山本さんのところへ顔出ししてこよう. I will just make a call at Mr. Yamamoto's.

かおつき 彼の顔付きを見て、合格しなかったことを知った. I knew by the look on his face [could read in his face] that the result of the exam was disappointing.

かおなじみ あそこには君の顔なじみがたくさんいるよ. You will find plenty of familiar faces there.

かおまけ 玄人顔負けの見事な歌いっぷりだった. He sang so well that even a professional singer would have been put to shame

to hear him.

かおむけ 二度と世間に顔向けができない. I don't know when I will be able to show my face in public again.

かおる 庭にはばらの花が香っている. The garden is fragrant with the smell of roses.

かかあでんか あの家はかかあ天下だ. The wife wears the trousers [is the boss] in that house. / 彼の所はかかあ天下だ. He is a henpecked husband.

かかえ この木の回りは3抱えはあるだろう. It would take three men with outstretched arms to

encircle that tree.

かかえる 彼女は3人の子供を抱えて細々と暮らしている. She is making a bare living with three children to feed.

かがく² 水の化学式は H₂O である. The chemical formula for water is H₂O.

かかす 塩は一日も欠かすことができない. We cannot do without salt even for a single day.

かかと 靴下のかかとに穴が空いていた. There was a hole in the heel of my sock.

かがみ¹ 海面は鏡のようだった. The sea was as smooth as glass

かがく

化学製品 chemicals ; chemical products / 化学式[記号] a chemical formula [symbol] / 化学実験[実験室] a chemical experiment [laboratory] / 化学者 a chemist / 化学繊維 (a) synthetic [chemical] fiber / 化学調味料 a synthetic seasoning (agent) / 化学反応[作用] (a) chemical reaction [action] / 化学肥料 (a) chemical fertilizer / 化学兵器 a chemical weapon / 化学変化 a chemical change / 化学方程式 a chemical equation / 化学療法 chemotherapy / 化学物質 chemical substances ; chemicals / 化学薬品 pharmaceuticals ; pharmaceutical products. 文例↓

かがく³ 科学 science ¶科学的に scientifically / 科学映画 a science film / 科学界 scientific circles ; the world of science / 科学思想 scientific thought / 科学技術庁 the Science and Technology Agency / 科学者 a scientist ; a man of science / 科学戦 scientific warfare / 科学知識 scientific knowledge / 科学博物館 a science museum.

ががく 雅楽 *gagaku* ; (ancient) court music (and dance).

かかげる 掲げる 〈掲揚する〉hoist [put up] (a flag) ; hang out (a sign) ; 〈掲載する〉publish ; print ; carry.

かかし (set up) a scarecrow.

かかす 欠かす miss ; fail to attend ¶欠かさず regularly ; without fail / 一度も欠かさず会に出席する attend the meeting regularly [without fail] / 散歩を一日も欠かさない take a walk every day (without fail). 文例↓

かかと 踵 the heel ¶かかとの高い[低い]靴 high-[low-]heeled shoes ; shoes with high [low] heels. 文例↓

かがみ¹ 鏡 a mirror ; a looking glass ; 〈たるの〉a barrel head ¶鏡のような (sea) like a mirror ; glassy (sea) / 鏡のように滑らかな as smooth as glass / 鏡の間 a hall of mirrors / 鏡に映る be reflected in a mirror / 自分の姿を鏡で見る look at [see] *oneself* in a mirror / 鏡を見る[のぞく] look in a mirror / (たるの)鏡を抜く take out the barrel head ; open a barrel (cask). 文例↓

かがみ² 鑑 ⇒ もはん, てほん.

かがみいた 鏡板 a panel.

かがみもち 鏡餅 a round rice-cake (offered to a deity).

かがむ 屈む stoop ; bend forward ; crouch (うずくまる) ¶かがんで歩く walk with a stoop / かがんで花を摘む stoop [bend] (down) to pick up a flower / 腰のかがんだ老人 a man bent (down) with age. 文例↓

かがめる 屈める bend ; bow ¶身をかがめる bend (*oneself*) forward ; stoop ; crouch (うずくまるように) / 机の上に体をかがめる bend over *one's* desk. 文例↓

かがやかしい 輝かしい bright ; brilliant ¶輝かしい成功 a brilliant success / 輝かしい未来 a bright future.

かがやかす 輝かす make *sth* shine [bright] ; brighten (up) ¶目を輝かして with a gleam (of interest [hope]) in *one's* eye.

かがやき 輝き brilliance ; brightness ; glitter.

かがやく 輝く shine ; glitter ; sparkle ; 〈顔などが〉brighten (up) ; light up ¶朝日に輝く glitter in the morning sun / 輝き渡る shine all around. 文例↓

かかり 係り, 掛かり 〈担当者〉a person in charge ; 〈費用〉expenses ; charges ¶係の人, 係員 a clerk [an official] in charge / 係長 a subsection chief. 文例↓

かがり 縢り sewing (up) ; 〈つくろい〉darning ; a darn (ひとかがり) ; [製本] sewing ¶かがり糸 darning-thread ; binding thread / かがり針 a darning needle.

-がかり …掛かり ¶2日がかりで…する it takes *one* two days to *do* ; spend two days *doing* / 10人がかりの仕事 a job requiring 10 men ; a job which takes [requires] 10 men to do. 文例↓

かかりあい 係り合い ⇒ かんけい².

かかりあう 係り合う ⇒ かかわりあう.

かかりきり 掛かり切り ¶かかりきりになる[である] spend all *one's* time (on) ; give *one's* whole time 《to》; 〈文〉devote all *one's* energies 《to》. 文例↓

かかりつけ 掛かり付け ¶かかりつけの医者 *one's* (family) doctor.

かがりび 篝火 a bonfire ; a watch fire ; 〈漁の〉a fishing fire ¶かがり火をたく make a bonfire [watch fire].

かかる¹ 掛[懸, 架]かる 〈垂れ下がる〉hang 《on, from》; be suspended 《on, from》; 〈陥る〉fall into (a trap) ; be caught ; 〈着手する〉begin ; start ; set about 《work, *doing*》; 〈従事している〉〈文〉be engaged 《in》; be occupied 《with》;

かかる

[was like a mirror].
かがむ 彼はやれやれというようにかがんでそれを拾い上げた. He bent wearily and picked it up.
かがめる 身をかがめてその小型車に乗り込んだ. He crouched [bent himself down] to get into the small car.
かがやく 太陽がきらきら輝いている. The sun is shining brightly. / 空には星がきらきら輝いている. The stars are twinkling (up) in the sky. / 彼女の指には大粒のダイヤがきらきら輝いていた. A big diamond was sparkling on her finger. / 彼の顔は喜び[希望]に輝いた. His face brightened (up) [lighted up] with joy [hope].
かかり それは係の者によく注意しておきましょう. I will point it out to the people concerned [those who are in charge of the matter]. / これは僕の係ではありません[係が違います]. This is not my department. / 町に住むと掛かりが掛かる. It is expensive [costs a great deal] to live in town.
-がかり 3日がかりでその仕事を終えた. It took me three days [It cost me three days' labor] to finish the job. | I spent three days doing the job. / 本書は彼の5年がかりの労作である. This book is the product of five years' labor on his part. / It took him five years to write this book. / 4人がかりでその石を運んだ. It took [required] four men to carry the rock. | The four men carried the rock between them.
かかりきり この1週間その仕事に掛かり切りです. For the past week the job has taken all my time and

かかる 〈要する〉 need; require; take; cost; 〈…次第である〉 depend [hinge] (on); rest (with); 〈水などが〉はね掛かる splash (on) / 〈絵などが〉壁に掛かっている be hung [hanging] on the wall / 網に掛かる be caught [entangled] in a net / (魚が)針に掛かる be hooked; take the hook / 敵の計略に掛かる fall into the enemy's trap; play into the enemy's hands / お茶の用意に掛かる set about making tea / 医者に掛かる consult [see] a doctor; be under the care of a doctor / 費用が幾ら掛かっても at any cost; regardless of expense.

かかる[2] 罹る 〈病気に〉 fall [be taken] ill; catch (measles); get (cancer); suffer from (arthritis); (文) contract (mumps) ¶喘息にかかっている have [be suffering from] asthma / 病気にかかって死ぬ die of a disease. 文例↓

かかる[3] 〈このような〉such; like this ¶かかる人 such a man; a person like this.

-かかる 〈まさに…しようとする〉 be going to *do*; be about to *do*; be on the point of *do*ing. 文例↓

かがる 縢る sew (up); darn (繕う) ¶ほころびをかがる sew up an open seam.

-がかる ¶赤味がかった紫 reddish purple; purple inclining to red / 左翼がかっている lean [be inclined] toward the Left; be somewhat pink.

かかわらず 〈…であるのに〉though; although; in spite of; despite; (文) notwithstanding; no matter [how, what, who, etc.]; for [with] all; 〈…に関係なく〉regardless of; whether... or... ¶それにもかかわらず nevertheless; none the less; however / 雨天にもかかわらず in spite of [notwithstanding] the rain; though it is raining / 国籍のいかんにかかわらず (文) irrespective of (their) nationality. 文例↓

かかわり 係わり relation; connection ¶かかわりがある[ない] have something [nothing] to do with *sth* [*sb*]. 文例↓

かかわりあい 係わり合い ⇒ **かんけい**[2]. 文例↓

かかわりあう 係わり合う 〈巻き込まれる〉get [be] involved [entangled] (in); get mixed up (in); 〈関係する〉have something to do (with); have dealings (with). 文例↓

かかわる 係わる 〈…に関係する〉be concerned (in); have to do (with); have a hand (in); 〈関与する〉take part (in); 〈巻き込まれる〉get mixed up (in); be involved (in); 〈…に干渉する〉meddle [interfere] (in); 〈…に影響する〉affect; concern; 〈危ぶする〉endanger; (文) imperil ¶名誉にかかわる〈事が主語〉affect *one*'s honor [reputation]. 文例↓

かかん[1] 花冠 〔植〕the corolla (of a flower).

かかん[2] 果敢 ¶果敢な bold; daring.

かき[1] 下記 ¶下記の the following; (文) the undermentioned; (the men) mentioned below / 下記のとおり as follows.

かき[2] 火気 fire. 文例↓

かき[3] 火器 firearms ¶重火器 heavy firearms.

かき[4] 花器 〈花瓶〉a (flower) vase; 〈水盤〉a flower bowl.

かき[5] 牡蠣 an oyster ¶かき船 an oyster boat / かきフライ fried oysters / かき養殖 oyster farming [culture] / かき養殖業者 an oyster farmer / かき養殖場[床(ど)] an oyster farm [bed]. 文例↓

かき[6] 柿 〈実〉a (Japanese) persimmon; a *kaki*; 〈木〉a (Japanese) persimmon tree; a *kaki* tree ¶柿渋 the bitter [astringent] juice of the persimmon; persimmon tannin.

かき[7] 垣 〈囲い〉a fence; 〈生垣〉a hedge; 〈さく〉a railing ¶垣を巡らす put a fence around [round] (a tree); enclose [encircle] (a house) with a fence; 〈中へ入らせないようにするために〉fence off (a pond).

かき[8] 夏季[期] summer; summertime; the summer season ⇒ **なつ** ¶夏期用の for summer use / 夏期休暇 the summer vacation [holi-

---

energy.
かける[1] 上着がくぎに掛かっている. The coat is hanging on a peg. / 新月が低く西の空に懸かっていた. The new moon hung low in the western sky. / この河には橋が3つ架かっている. There are three bridges across this river. | Three bridges span this river. / すべては次の出方に掛かっている. Everything depends [hinges] on what they do next. / わが社の将来は掛かって君たちの双肩にあるのだ. The future of our firm rests on your shoulders. / 負担は全部私に掛かる. I have to bear all the expenses. / 私に疑いが掛かった. Suspicion fell on me. / さあ仕事に掛かろう. Come on, let's get to work. / 大工はいま屋根に掛かっている. The carpenters are at work on the roof now. / 彼は長年掛かって集めた本をあの火事で焼いてしまった. He had all his books, which had taken him years to collect, burned in the fire. / 彼が全快するまでにはまだ2,3週間は掛かるだろう. It will be two or three weeks before he gets well. / この本をかくのに私は3年掛かった. It took me three years to write this book. / この小包を航空便で送るとすると幾ら掛かりますか. How much does it cost to send this parcel by airmail? / 駅へ行くのに何分掛かりますか. How long [How much time] does it take to get to the station? / 大勢掛かってやっと犯人を取り押えた. The culprit was caught at last by the combined efforts of several men. / あの人に掛かったら駄目だ. You are no match for him. / 今や楽隊は何に掛かっていますか. What is on at the Yurakuza? / さあ, 掛かって来い. Come on! / これは田中氏自身の発明にかかる装置である. This apparatus is of Mr. Tanaka's own devising.

かかる[2] 一度その病気にかかるともう二度とかからないですみます. Those who have had the disease are permanently immune to it thereafter. / この旅行中に彼はひどい熱病にかかった. He was taken ill with a serious fever during this trip. / 彼女は流感にかかって寝込んでしまった. She came down with flu. / 君はいつからその病気にかかっているのですか. How long has it been troubling you?

-かかる 僕がちょうどそれをしかかっていたら, 彼から電話が掛かって来たのです. I was just going to do it when I got a call from him. / 太陽が出かかっています. The sun is about [beginning] to rise. / 船が沈みかかっている. The ship is sinking.

かかわらず 彼は大いに勉強したに

days] / 夏期講習会 a summer school.

かぎ[1] 鉤 a hook ¶かぎで引っかける hook《a fish》/ かぎの手になった right-angled / かぎ形の hook-shaped ; L-shaped / かぎ十字 a hooked cross ; a swastika.

かぎ[2] 鍵 a key ; 〈クロスワードパズルなどの〉 a clue (★ この場合には key は使えない) ¶1束のかぎ a bunch of keys《on a ring》/ かぎで錠を開ける unlock《a door》; open a lock with a key / かぎをかける lock《a suitcase》; turn a key on / かぎをかけておく keep *sth* under lock and key / スーツケースにかぎをかけないでおく leave a suitcase unlocked / かぎを錠前にはめる put the key in the lock / かぎを錠前に差したままにしておく leave the key in the lock / 問題解決の鍵を握っている hold the key to the solution of the question / かぎ穴 a keyhole. [文例⇩]

がき 餓鬼 〈餓鬼道の亡者(もうじゃ)〉 a hungry ghost ; 〈子供〉 a brat ; a little devil ¶餓鬼大将 the boss of the kids《of the neighborhood》; a bully (弱い者いじめの).

かきあげ 掻き揚げ a mixture of ingredients fried in batter.

かきあげる[1] 書[描]き上げる finish writing [drawing, painting].

かきあげる[2] 掻き上げる 〈くしで〉 comb up《*one's* hair》.

かきあつめる 掻き集める rake [scrape] up [together] ¶落葉をかき集める rake up fallen leaves / 金をかき集める scrape together a sum of money.

かぎあてる 嗅ぎ当てる smell [sniff] out.

かきあらためる 書き改める rewrite.

かきあらわす 書き表わす describe ; put *sth* in writing. [文例⇩]

かきあわせる 掻き合わせる adjust ¶着物の襟をかき合わせる adjust the neckband of *one's kimono* / 上着の襟をかき合わせる clutch *one's* lapels across *one's* chest [bosom].

かきいれ 書入れ 〈記入〉 an entry ; 〈注〉 (marginal) notes ¶書入れ時 the best [busiest, rush] season [hours]《for》. [文例⇩]

かきいれる 書き入れる write《*sb's* name》 in《on a voting slip》; fill in《an application》; enter (up)《an item in an account book》; make an entry of *sth*《in a register》 ¶本に注を書き入れる write notes in a book / (書類や問題の)空所に必要事項を書き入れる fill in the blanks ; 《米》 fill out [《英》 fill in]《a form》.

かきうつす 書き写す copy ; transcribe.

かきおき 書置き 〈書き手紙〉 a note [letter] left behind ; 〈遺書〉 a (written) will ; 《文》 a testamentary letter ¶書置きをする 〈置き手紙〉 leave a note [letter, message] behind ; 〈遺書〉 leave a will.

かきおくる 書き送る write [send] a letter《to》; write (to) *sb* ¶…と書き送る write to say that… ; send a letter saying that….

かきおとす 書き落とす omit *sth* (in writing) by mistake ; forget to write.

かきおろし 書き下ろし ¶書き下ろしの小説 a newly written novel.

かきおろす 書き下ろす ¶小説[脚本]を書き下ろす write a new novel [play]. [文例⇩]

かきかえ 書き換え 〈書き直し〉 rewriting ; 〈更新〉 (a) renewal ; 〈名義の〉 (a) transfer ¶(株式の)名義書き換えを停止する close the transfer ledger.

かきかえる 書き換える 〈書き直す〉 rewrite ; 〈証文を〉 renew《a bond》; 〈名義を〉 transfer ¶不動産を妻の名義に書き換える transfer *one's* estate to *one's* wife.

かきかた 書き方 〈書き様〉 how to write ; a way [style, 《文》 manner] of writing ; 〈書式〉 a form ; 〈習字〉 penmanship ; calligraphy. [文例⇩]

かききず 掻き傷 a scratch.

かきくどく 掻き口説く 〈こぼす〉 complain《about》; grumble《about, over》; 〈訴える〉 plead《for mercy》; beg《for help》.

もかかわらず試験に落第した. Although he had worked very hard, he failed the examination. / 病気にもかかわらず会議に出席した. He attended the meeting in spite of [despite] his illness. / 結果のいかんにかかわらず今すぐに着手しなければならないと思う. I think we should set about it at once, no matter what the consequences. / あれほどのベテランにもかかわらず, 彼はどうしてよいのかわからなかった. With [For] all his experience, he had no idea what to do with it. / 晴雨にかかわらずまいります. Rain or shine, I will come.

かかわり その事件とは何のかかわりもありません. I had nothing to do with that incident.

かかわりあい 当方には全く係わり合いのない事だ. We have nothing to do with the matter. | That is no concern (whatsoever) of ours.

かかわりあう そんな事に係わり合いたくない. I don't want to get involved [mixed up] in that business.

かかわる 今の場合はそんな事にかかわってはいられない. This is no time to be concerning ourselves with such things. / この件にはかかわらないほうがいい. You had better keep out of [stay away from] this affair. / その病気は命にかかわるようなことはない. The disease will not prove fatal.

かき[2] 火気厳禁. 〖掲示〗 Caution : Flammable.

かき[5] 'r' のつかない月のかきは食べられない. You should only eat oysters when there is an 'r' in the month.

かぎ[2] 訪ねて行ったらかぎがかかっていて留守だった. I found him out, with the door locked. / かぎをゆっくり回すと, ドアがぐーっと開いた. He gave the key a slow turn and the door swung open. / 入口のかぎ穴から部屋の中をのぞこうとした. He tried to look [peep] into the room through the keyhole.

かきあらわす その美観は筆では書き表わせない. The beauty of the sight is beyond description.

かきいれ その本にはページごとにたくさん書入れがしてあった. The book had a large number of notes written in on every page. / その日の彼の日記にはなにも書入れがなかった. There was no entry in his diary for that day. / 秋は農家の書入れ時だ. Autumn is the busiest season for farmers.

かきおろす これは明治座4月興行のために特に書き下ろしたものだ. This play was specially written for the April show at the Meijiza.

かきかた この届けは書き方が間違っている. This report is not

かきくもる 掻き曇る be overcast ; be clouded over.

かきくわえる 書き加える add 《further comments, that…》; put additional words [phrases] 《in one's report》; insert [《文》interpolate] 《a few words in one's essay》; 〈追って書きを〉write a postscript 《to a letter》.

かきけす 掻き消す scratch out ; 〈音を〉drown ¶かき消すように姿が見えなくなる vanish (into thin air). 文例⇩

かきことば 書き言葉 written language ; literary Japanese [English, etc.] ⇒ぶんご.

かきこみ 書き込み ⇒かきいれ.

かきこむ 書き込む ⇒かきいれる.

かぎざき 鉤裂き a tear ; a rent ; a rip (大きい) ¶くぎに引っかけてかぎ裂きをこしらえる tear 《one's coat》on a nail.

かきさし 書きさし ¶書きさしの原稿 an unfinished [a half-finished] manuscript.

かきしるす 書き記す write [put] sth down ; take a note of sth ; enter sth 《in a diary》; put sth on record ; record.

かきそえる 書き添える add 《that…》; 〈追って書きを〉write a postscript to 《a letter》. 文例⇩

かきそこない 書き損ない a mistake in writing ; a slip of the pen.

かきそこなう 書き損なう make a mistake in writing ; write 《a word》incorrectly [wrong] ; spoil [make a mess of] 《three sheets of paper》.

かきぞめ 書き初め (do) a special piece of calligraphy for the New Year.

かきそんじ 書き損じ ⇒かきそこない.

かきだし 書き出し the opening sentence [paragraph, passage] ; the beginning. 文例⇩

かきたす 書き足す ⇒かきそえる.

かきだす 掻き出す rake (the ashes from the fireplace).

かぎだす 嗅ぎ出す smell [sniff] sth out.

かきたてる¹ 書き立てる 〈盛んに書く〉splash 《a story on the front page》; write sth up (big) 《in a newspaper》(通常良い意味で) ; 〈個条書きにする〉《文》enumerate ; 《文》itemize ; make a list of 《sb's misdeeds》. 文例⇩

かきたてる² 掻き立てる 〈ストーブの火などを〉stir [poke] 《the fire》; give 《the fire》a poke ; 〈そそる〉stir ; arouse ¶オーバーの襟をかき立てる turn up the collar of one's overcoat / 興味をかき立てる arouse [whip up] interest 《in》. 文例⇩

かきたま 搔き玉 egg soup.

かきちらし 書き散らし scribblings ; scrawlings ; a scrawl.

かきちらす 書き散らす scribble ; scrawl. 文例⇩

かきつけ 書付 〈覚え書〉a note ; 〈文書〉a document ; a paper ; 〈勘定書〉a bill.

かきつける 書き付ける write [take, note, 《文》set, put, jot] sth down ; make notes [a note] of sth.

かぎつける 嗅ぎ付ける scent ; smell ; sense ; get wind of ; 〈見つける〉detect.

かぎっこ 鍵っ子 a door-key [latchkey] child.

かぎって 限って ⇒かぎる.

かきつばた 【植】an iris (pl. irises) (★ irides は「眼の虹彩」の意の時の iris の複数形) ; a flag.

かきとめ(ゆうびん) 書留(郵便) 《米》registered letter ; 《米》registered mail ; 《英》registered post ¶書留で出す send 《a letter》by registered mail [《英》post] ; register 《a parcel》/ 書留にして有る have [get] 《a parcel》registered ; register 《a letter》/ 書留速達 a registered letter by express / 書留料 the registration fee ; the charge for registration.

かきとめる 書き留める write [note, take, put, jot] sth down ; put sth on record ; record ; make notes [a note] of sth.

かきとり 書き取り (a) dictation ¶英語の書き取りをやらせる give 《the class》an English dictation. 文例⇩

かきとる 書き取る write [take, note] sth down ¶書き取らせる dictate 《a passage to the class》; have 《a stenographer》take sth down.

かきなおし 書直し rewriting ; a rewrite ; 〈清書〉a fair copy.

かきなおす 書き直す rewrite ; 《米》write sth over (again) ; 《英》write sth again ; 〈清書する〉make a fair copy (of) ; write 《an essay》out fair. 文例⇩

かきながす 書き流す write sth rapidly ; dash sth off.

かきなぐる 書きなぐる scribble sth out ; dash sth off.

かきならす¹ 掻き均す rake sth (smooth) ; smooth [level] 《the ashes》.

かきならす² 掻き鳴らす strum [thrum] (on) 《a guitar》; twang away 《at a guitar》(盛んに).

かきにくい 書きにくい 〈字や絵が〉be difficult written in the proper form.

かきくもる 一天にわかにかき曇った. The sky suddenly became overcast. | The sky was suddenly filled with (dense) clouds.

かきけす その姿はかき消すように消えた. The figure suddenly vanished./ 彼の声はかき消されて聞こえなかった. The din drowned his voice.

かきそえる 一両日中に上京すると書き添えてあった. He added that he was coming up to town in a day or two. / 私が昨日帰ったことを書き添えておいて下さらない. Will you please put a postscript [a p.s.] to your letter saying that I got home yesterday.

かきだし この小説の書き出しはうまい. This novel opens with a fine piece of writing.

かきたてる¹ 新聞はその事件を盛んに書き立てた. The newspapers gave a lot of space to the affair. | The newspapers splashed their stories about the case.

かきたてる² 彼はストーブの火をかき立てて燃え上がらせた. He poked up a blaze in the stove. / この話はその少年の想像力をひどくかき立てた. This story really stirred the boy's imagination.

かきちらす これは気の向き次第に書き散らしたものです. These are only stray notes written at random.

かきとり 今日はフランス語の書き取りがある. We have a French dictation today.

かきなおす これは最初の原稿をすっかり書き直したものです. This is a complete rewrite of his first draft.

かきにくい 今はその事は書きにくい. I don't think it proper [ad-

かきぬく　書き抜く　take out [extract, 《文》excerpt] (a passage) from (a book).
かきね　垣根　a fence; a hedge (生け垣) ⇨ かき[7] ¶垣根をめぐらした fenced-off (gardens) / 垣根越しに 《look》 over a fence.
かきのこす　書き残す　〈書き置きする〉 leave a note [message, letter] (behind); 〈書かないまに残す〉 leave (the last two pages of one's manuscript) unfinished.
かぎばな　鉤鼻　a hooked [《文》 an aquiline] nose　¶かぎ鼻の hook-nosed.
かぎばり　鉤針　a hook.
かきはん　書き判　a written seal; a signature.
かきまぜる　掻き混ぜる　stir; mix (A) up (with B).
かきまちがい　書き間違い　a mistake in writing; a slip of the pen; (a) misspelling (綴りの).
かきまちがえる　書き間違える　write (a character) incorrectly; make a mistake in writing (sb's name); make a slip of the pen; misspell (a word) (綴りを) / あて名を書き違える address (a letter) wrongly.
かきまわす　掻き回す　〈かくはんする〉 stir (up); churn (milk) / 〈捜して〉 ransack (a room); rummage (in) / さじでかき回す stir (one's coffee) with a spoon / 引き出しの中をかき回す rummage in the drawer / 会社をかき回す throw the company into confusion. 文例⇩
かきみだす　掻き乱す　disturb; confuse ¶秩序をかき乱す disturb the peace and order (of).
かきむしる　掻き毟る　tear; rip; 《文》 rend ¶はらわたをかきむしるような heartrending / はらわたをかきむしられる思いがする one's heart is wrung 《with grief, at the news》. 文例⇩
かきもの　書き物　〈事〉 writing; 〈書類〉 a paper; a document; 〈1人の人の全著作〉 writings ¶書物にする put sth down in writing [in black and white]; 《文》 commit sth to writing / 書き物にしておく keep a written record (of); 《文》 have sth down in black and white / 書き物をする write; do 《some》 writing / 書き物用の机 a writing desk.
かきもらす　書き漏らす　⇨ かきおとす.
かぎゃく　可逆　¶可逆反応 (a) reversible reaction. / 可逆性 reversibility.
かきゃくせん　貨客船　a cargo-passenger boat [ship, steamer].
かきゅう¹　下級　a lower [low] class [grade] ¶下級の lower(-grade); 《officials》 in the lower echelons / 下級官庁 a subordinate office / 下級吏員 a minor official; 《総称》 lower-level[-echelon] (government) officials / 下級裁判所 a lower [an inferior] court / 下級生 a lower-grade boy [girl].
かきゅう²　火急　¶火急の urgent; pressing; imminent / 火急の場合には in an emergency; in case of emergency / 火急の用事があって on urgent business.
かきょう¹　佳境　the most interesting part 《of a story》; the climax (of a story). 文例⇩
かきょう²　華僑　an overseas Chinese.
かぎょう¹　家業　〈代々の職業〉 one's father's occupation [trade]; 〈自分の職業〉 one's occupation [trade, profession] ¶家業を継ぐ succeed one's father in the family occupation [trade].
かぎょう²　課業　a task; a lesson; schoolwork.
かきょく　歌曲　a song (in the classical style) ¶ドイツの歌曲 a German song; 《ドイツ語》 a lied (pl. lieder).
かきよせる　掻き寄せる　⇨ かきあつめる.
かぎり　限り　a limit; limits; 《文》 bounds ¶限りがある there is a limit (to our patience) / 数[紙面]に限りがある the number [space] is limited; be limited [restricted] in number [space] / 限りがない there is no limit 《to human progress》; 《文》 know no limits [bounds] / 限りのない unlimited; 《文》 boundless; infinite / 放蕩(½)の限りを尽くす 《文》 run the whole gamut of dissipation / 限りなく without limit; limitlessly; endlessly; infinitely; 〈非常に〉 extremely / …する限り (for) as long as one does [continues to do] / …しない限り unless [until] one does / できる限り as far [much] as possible; as much as one can; to the best of one's ability / 声を限りに at the top of one's voice / 命のあらん限り as long as one lives / 事情の許す限り as [so] far as circumstances permit / 私の知っている限りでは as [so] far as I know; to the best of my knowledge.
かぎる　限る　〈制限する〉 set a limit 《to》; limit sth 《to》; restrict sth 《to》; 〈最上である〉 be the best (for); be the only way 《to do》　¶日を限る〈日取りを決める〉 fix [set] a date / 〈日

visable] to write about it now. | This is not the place [proper occasion] for me to write about it.
かきまわす　彼は風呂の湯を手でかき回していた。He was churning the bath water with his hand.
かきむしる　それを聞いて胸をかきむしられる思いがした。The news wrung my heart.
かきょう¹　話はいよいよ佳境に入った。Now we come to [we've reached] the most interesting part of the story.
かぎょう¹　家業は次男が継いだ。His second son succeeded him in the business.
かぎり　我々の能力には限りがある。Our abilities are limited. | There is a limit to our abilities [to what we can do]. | 欲には限りがない。There is no limit to our desires. | Avarice knows no bounds [limits]. / 授業料は本月25日限り納付の事。Tuition fees must be paid not later than the 25th of this month. / できる限りいたします。I will do everything in my power [all I can]. / 彼はそのとき何か言いましたか。―私の知っている限りでは, 何も言いませんでした。Did he say anything then?—Not that I know of. / 健全な批判力を持っている限り読む本の種類はたいして問題にならない。As [So] long as you have sound judgment, it matters comparatively little what kinds of books you read. / 私に関する限りそれは本当ではありません。As far as I am concerned, it is not true. / 本券は1枚1人に限り有効。This ticket admits one person only. / 見渡す限り月見草が咲いていた。There were evening primroses as far as the eye could see

かきわける 掻き分ける push [shove, 《文》thrust]《the thick undergrowth》 aside ¶群衆をかき分けて進む elbow [push, plow] one's way through the crowd.

かぎわける 嗅ぎ分ける tell [《文》distinguish]《A》from《B》by smell.

かきわり 書き割 stage setting ; a set scene.

かきん 家禽 a domestic fowl ; poultry (総称).

かく¹ 角〈角度〉an angle ;〈四角〉a square ;〈将棋の〉a bishop ¶角ばった square ; angular / 角に切る cut sth square / 五寸角の柱 a pillar five inches square. 文例◎

かく² 画〈字の〉a stroke ¶4画の字 a character of four strokes.

かく³ 核〈細胞, 原子などの〉a nucleus《pl. nuclei》;〈核心〉a kernel ; a core ¶核の傘 the《American》nuclear umbrella / 核アレルギー nuclear allergy / 核エネルギー nuclear energy / 核家族 a nuclear family / 核クラブ《join》the nuclear club / 核攻撃を加える make a nuclear attack《on》/ 核時代 the nuclear age / 核閃光 a nuclear《fission》flash / 核戦力 nuclear capability / 核装備する nuclearize《a submarine》/ 核装備しうる nuclear-capable《aircraft》/ 核燃料 nuclear fuel / 核爆弾[弾頭] a nuclear bomb [warhead] / 核廃棄物 nuclear waste(s) / 核反応 (a) nuclear reaction / 核物理学 nuclear physics / 核兵器 a nuclear weapon ;〈総称〉nuclear arms [weaponry] / 核(兵器)拡散防止条約 the nuclear nonproliferation treaty [pact] / 核(兵器)保有国 a nuclear power [state] / 核粒子 a nucleon ; a nuclear particle. ★核実験, 核戦争, 核爆発, 核武装, 核分裂, 核融合は別見出し.

かく⁴ 格〈格式〉standing ; status ; a rank ; a class ;〈資格〉capacity ;〈決まり〉a rule ;《文法》a case ¶格が上がる[下がる] rise [fall] in rank / 格が違う be in [belong to] a different class《from》; be on different levels. 文例◎

かく⁵ 欠く〈不足して〉be short of ; need ; lack ;《文》want ;《文》be wanting [lacking]《in》; be short《of》; be missing (物が主語) ;〈怠る〉neglect ; fail《in》;〈砕く〉chip《the rim of a bowl》; crack《ice》¶義理を欠く neglect [fail to perform] one's social duty / 欠くべからざる indispensable《to》; essential《to》;《文》requisite《to》/ 欠くべからざる necessities ; necessaries ;《口語》a must. 文例◎

かく⁶ 書く write《a letter, a story》; compose《a poem》;《文》pen《an article》;〈書き記す〉write [put] down ;〈記述する〉describe ;〈描く〉draw ; paint (彩色して) ¶インクで書く write in ink / 鉛筆で書く write with a pencil [in pencil] / 雑誌に書く write for a magazine / 随筆を書く write an essay / 地図を書く draw a map / 領収書を書く write [make] out a receipt / 手紙に…と書いてある the letter says [it says in the letter] that…. 文例◎

かく⁷ 掻く〈体などを〉scratch《one's back》;〈落葉などを〉rake《up》《the dead leaves》;〈耳を〉pick《one's ear》;〈水を〉paddle ;〈雪などを〉shovel [remove]《the snow from the road》. 文例◎

かく⁸ 各 each ; every ⇒かくじ.

かく⁹ 斯く ¶かく(して)thus ; so / かくのごとき《incidents》like this ; such《matters》/ かくのごとく《文》thus ; like this ; in this way /《этот manner》/ かくなる上は since it has come to this ; now that things have come to this pass.

かく- 隔… every other [second] ¶隔週[日] every other [second] week [day].

かぐ¹ 家具 (household) furniture ¶家具一点 a piece [an article] of furniture / 家具一式 a set of furniture / 家具を入れる put furniture in《a room》; furnish《a room》/ 家具付きの部屋 a furnished room / 家具屋〈人〉a dealer in [maker of] furniture /〈店〉a furniture store.

かぐ² 嗅ぐ smell ; scent ; sniff (at)《a rose》. 文例◎

がく¹ 学〈学問〉learning ;〈知識〉knowledge ¶学のある人 a knowledgeable [《文》learned] person / 学と名の付くもの '-ics' and '-ologies'.

がく² 萼《植》a calyx《pl. -es, calyces》¶がく片 a sepal.

がく³ 額〈掛け額〉a tablet ;〈画〉a framed picture ;〈額縁〉a frame ¶油絵の額 a framed oil painting / 額を掛ける hang a (framed) picture《on the wall》/ 額にする, 額縁に入れる frame《a picture》; set《a picture》in a frame / 額縁 a (picture) frame.

がく⁴ 額〈分量〉a sum《of money》; an amount《of expenditure [output]》¶莫大な額に達する

[reach].
かぎる これに限る. This is just the thing for me. / 海水浴なら葉山に限る. Hayama is the best place for sea bathing. / 君は黙っているに限るよ. You had better [best] keep silent. / 彼らの活動は狭い範囲に限られている. Their activities are restricted within narrow limits. / 演説は5分間に限られている. Speeches are limited to five minutes. / 品物は高くさえあれば良いとは限らない. An article is not always good just because it is dear (expensive). / 警察官だからといってみな勇敢だとは限らない. Not all policemen are brave. / 本当でないとも限らない. It may possibly be true. / 何事に限らず全力を注げ. Whatever you do, do your best. / あの人に限ってそんなことはしない. He is the last man to do such a thing. / 私はその日に限って帰りが遅かった. I came home late on that particular day.
かく 90度の角を直角という. An angle of 90° (ninety degrees) is called a right angle.

かく⁴ そのホテルはほかとは格が違う. That hotel is in a different class from the rest.

かく⁵ 彼は常識を欠いている. He lacks [is short of] common sense.

かく⁶ 何か書く紙を持っていますか. Do you have some paper to write on? / このペンは書きよい. This pen writes well [smoothly]. / 彼は自分の名も書けない. He can't even spell his own name. / 英語の書ける人が欲しい. I want a man who writes good

かくあげ 格上げ ¶格上げする raise [《文》elevate] (a section) to the status of (a department); promote sb to a higher rank; upgrade.

かくい¹ 各位 Sirs ¶会員各位へ to the members.

かくい² 隔意 ⇨ えんりょ, ふくそう.

がくい 学位 a [an academic] degree ¶医学博士[文学修士]の学位 the degree of Doctor of Medicine [Master of Arts] / 学位を授ける grant [award] sb a degree; confer a degree on sb / 学位を取る get [take, 《文》obtain, 《文》receive] a degree 《from Harvard University, in engineering at Cambridge》 / 学位を取るために勉強する study [work] for a degree (in economics) / 学位を持っている have [《文》hold] a degree / 学位論文 a thesis for a degree.
文例 ⇩

かくいつ 画一 uniformity ¶画一に uniformly / 画一にする make sth uniform; standardize / 画一的教育 uniform education / 画一化 standardization.

かくいん 客員 a guest (member) ¶客員教授 a visiting [guest] professor.

かくう 架空 ¶架空の〈虚構の〉fictitious; fictional; 〈空想上の〉imaginary / 架空の人物 a fictitious character 《in a novel》; an imaginary personage 《in a play》/ 架空の物語 a fictional account of a journey to Mars).

かくえき 各駅 ¶各駅に停車する stop at every station (on the way) / 各駅停車の列車 a local [《英》stopping] train.

がくえん 学園 an educational institution; a school ¶学園祭 a campus [school] festival / 学園紛争 a campus dispute; 《文》campus strife.

かくかい 各界 every sphere [field] of life; various circles.

かくかい 各階 ¶各階の on [of] every floor / 各階止まりのエレベーター an elevator that stops at every floor.

かくかい 角界 the *sumo* world.

かくがい 閣外 ¶閣外の[に] outside the Cabinet.

がくがい 学外 ¶学外の outside the university [campus].

かくかく so and so ¶かくかくの such and such.

がくがく ¶ひざががくがくする one's knees

shake (under one); 歯ががくがくする a tooth comes [becomes] loose.

かくがり 角刈り a square cut [haircut] ¶角刈りにする have one's hair cut square.

かくぎ 閣議 a Cabinet meeting ¶閣議にかける put (a matter) to the Cabinet [a Cabinet meeting]; 《文》submit (a matter) to [lay (a matter) before] a Cabinet meeting / 定例[臨時]閣議 a regular [special] Cabinet meeting.

がくぎょう 学業 one's studies; one's schoolwork ¶学業に励む work hard (at one's lessons) / 学業成績 a school record; 《文》scholastic performance.

がくげい 学芸 arts and sciences; 〈学問芸術の素養〉《文》literary and artistic attainments ¶学芸大学 a university of arts and sciences; a teachers' college / 〈新聞社の〉学芸部 the arts, science and entertainment department.

がくげき 楽劇 a musical drama.

かくげつ 隔月 ¶隔月に every other [second] month; in alternate months / 隔月発行の雑誌 a bimonthly magazine.

かくげん¹ 格言 a proverb; a maxim; a saying ¶格言にいわく A [The] proverb says that... / 格言にもあるとおり as the saying goes [has it]. 文例 ⇩

かくげん² 確言 ¶確言する say [state] positively [definitely]; 《文》assert; 《文》affirm; (cannot) say for certain.

かくご 覚悟 〈決心〉(a) resolution; 〈あきらめ〉resignation; 〈用意〉readiness; 《文》preparedness ¶覚悟する make up one's mind 《to sth, to do》; be ready [prepared] 《for》 / 覚悟している〈心を決めている〉be determined 《to do》; 《文》be resolved 《to do, that...》; 〈心構えができている〉be ready [prepared] 《for》; 〈観念している〉be resigned 《to one's fate》 / 覚悟の自殺 a premeditated suicide.

かくごおり 角氷 〈冷蔵庫で作る〉an ice cube.

かくさ 格差 a gap; a differential ¶所得[給与]の格差をなくする abolish pay [earnings] differentials.

かくざい 角材 《米》rectangular lumber;《英》rectangular timber.

がくさい 学債 (issue) a school bond.

がくさいてき 学際的 interdisciplinary 《collaboration》.

かくさく 画策 ¶画策する〈計画する〉plan; 《文》project; scheme; lay a plan [scheme];

English. / 彼は今新しい小説を書いている。He is working [at work] on a new novel. / この本を書いた緒方氏は元新聞記者である。Mr. Ogata, the author of this book, used to be a newspaperman. / 手紙にはこう書いてある。The letter goes like this. | This is what it says in the letter. / あれは何と書いてあるのですか。What does that say? / 彼はちょっと絵も描く。

かく⁷ 犬が前足で土をかいている。A dog is pawing the ground. / 鶏は土をかいて虫をあさる。Hens scratch the ground for worms.

かぐ² ちょっとそれをかいでみた。I took a sniff at it. / 犬がその郵便ポストをくんくんかいでいた。A dog was sniffing (at) the mailbox.

がくい アイゼンハウアー大統領はデリー大学で名誉法学博士の学位を贈られた。President Eisenhower was awarded an honorary law degree at Delhi University. / 彼の Ph.D. の学位はロンドン大学で取ったものです。He got his Ph.D. from London University.

かくげん¹ 格言にもあるとおり、「時は金なり」だ。Time is money, as the proverb goes.

かくご 何事があろうとも私は覚悟を決めている。Whatever may happen, I am prepared for it. / そのためには職を賭する覚悟である。I'm ready to risk my career for it. / いよいよこれからが試練だと覚悟を決めた。I steeled myself for the ordeal. / この仕事にかかるにはよほどの覚悟が必要である。The undertaking will require

かくさげ 格下げ ¶格下げする lower the status 《of》; reduce sb to a lower position [rank]; downgrade; demote.

かくざとう 角砂糖 cube [lump] sugar ¶角砂糖1個 a lump (of sugar); a (sugar) cube.

かくさん[1] 拡散〖物〗diffusion; 〈核兵器などの〉proliferation ¶気体の拡散 the diffusion of gases / 拡散する diffuse; proliferate / 核兵器の拡散を防ぐ check the spread [proliferation] of nuclear weapons; prevent nuclear proliferation ⇒ かく[3]（核兵器）拡散防止条約).

かくさん[2] 核酸〖生化〗nucleic acid ¶デオキシリボ核酸 deoxyribonucleic acid (略: DNA)（★略称で言うのが普通）/ リボ核酸 ribonucleic acid (略: RNA)（★略称で言うのが普通）.

かくし 隠し a pocket ⇒ポケット.

かくじ 各自 each (one); everyone ¶各自の each; respective; individual; 《文》several; one's own / 各自に each; respectively; individually; 《文》severally. [文例⇩]

がくし[1] 学士 a university graduate [man]; a bachelor ¶ 〈人〉a bachelor of arts; 〈学位〉Bachelor of Arts (略: B.A.) / (日本)学士院 the Japan Academy / 学士会員 a member of the Academy; an academician / 学士号 a bachelor's degree / 学士入学を認める allow a graduate of a different department to enter one's department as an undergraduate.

がくし[2] 学資 ⇒がくひ.

かくしあじ 隠し味 ¶隠し味に醤油を少し入れる put a small amount of soy sauce in sth as a hidden flavor.

かくしカメラ 隠しカメラ a hidden [concealed] camera; a candid camera.

かくしき 格式〈位〉status; social standing; 〈法式〉formality; formalities; a rule ¶格式ばる〈形式ばる〉stick to formalities; stand on ceremony; be strictly formal / 〈偉そうにする〉stand on one's dignity.

がくしき 学識 scholarship; 《文》learning ¶学識がある《文》be a learned [an erudite] scholar / 学識経験者 people of experience or academic standing.

かくしげい 隠し芸 a parlor trick; one's party piece. [文例⇩]

かくしごと 隠し事 a secret ¶隠し事でもあるかのように as though [as if] one had [has] something to hide. [文例⇩]

かくしだて 隠し立て ¶隠し立てする keep sth (secret) from sb; hide [《文》conceal] sth from sb / 隠し立てをしない be frank; be candid / お互いに隠し立てをしない have no secrets from each other; keep nothing (secret) from each other. [文例⇩]

かくしつ[1] 角質 of horny; keratinous.

かくしつ[2] 確執《文》discord; a feud ¶確執がある be at odds 《with sb [each other]》; there is a feud (a lot of ill feeling) [between them].

かくじつ[1] 隔日 ¶隔日に every other [second] day; on alternate days.

かくじつ[2] 確実 ¶確実な〈確かな〉certain; sure; 〈信頼すべき〉reliable; trustworthy; 〈安全な〉sound; safe / 確実な会社 a reliable firm / 確実な証拠 positive proof / 確実な商売 [投資] a sound business [investment] / 確実な情報 reliable information / 確実な方法 a sure [safe] method / …を確実と思う be confident [sure] of 《sb's success》; be sure [certain] that 《sb will succeed》 ⇒ かくしん[2] / 確実に〈確かに〉certainly; surely; for certain; 〈しっかりと〉securely / 確実にする make sure 《(that...)》; ensure. [文例⇩]

かくじっけん 核実験 nuclear (weapons) testing; 〈1回の〉a nuclear (weapons [arms]) test ¶核実験の禁止 a ban on nuclear tests; a nuclear test ban / 核実験の自発的停止 a (self-imposed) nuclear test moratorium (一定期間の) / 核実験を行なう carry out a nuclear test / 核実験を再開する resume nuclear testing / 空中[大気圏内]核実験 a nuclear test in the air [atmosphere] / 地下核実験 underground nuclear testing / 核実験禁止協定 a nuclear test ban agreement / 核実験場 a nuclear testing ground.

かくしどり 隠し撮り taking a photograph [picture] with [by means of] a hidden camera.

かくしマイク 隠しマイク a hidden [concealed] microphone; 《口語》a bug.

がくしゃ 学者 a scholar; 《文》a learned man; 《文》a savant (大学者) ¶学者らしい scholarly / 学者ぶった pedantic. [文例⇩]

かくしゅ 各種 ¶各種の various; 《wines》of every kind; all sorts [kinds, descriptions] of / 各種学校 a school in the 'miscellaneous' category.

かくしゅう 隔週 ¶隔週に every other [second] week; 《英》fortnightly / 隔週発行の雑誌 a biweekly [fortnightly] (magazine).

かくじゅう 拡充 (an) expansion ¶拡充する expand.

---

real resolution on your part. / そのときはしょせん命はないものと覚悟を決めていた. I had given up all hope of life then.

かくし 各自の部署に就け. Go to your posts. / 各自弁当持参のこと. Everyone to bring his own lunch.

かくしげい 僕はお座敷でやるような隠し芸は知らないんです. I don't have any party pieces. / いた芸だね. 君にそんな隠し芸があるとは知らなかったよ. Well, that's quite a trick! I didn't know you had such a hidden talent.

かくしごと 彼は僕に何か隠し事をしているに違いない. I'm sure he is keeping something (secret) from me. | He must be holding out on me.

かくしだて 君には少しも隠し立てなんかしない. I keep nothing from you.

かくじつ[2] この話には確実な根拠があるのだ. I have the news on good authority. / 彼の当選は確実だ. It is certain [a certainty] that he will win the election. / これで彼が外務大臣に任命されることは確実となった. This has ensured his appointment as Foreign Minister. | His appointment as Foreign Minister a certainty. / この報告はまだ確実とは言えない. This report remains to be confirmed.

がくしゃ 彼は学者肌のところがあ

がくしゅう　学習　〈習い覚えること〉learning；〈勉強〉work；study　¶学習する〈習い覚える〉learn；〈勉強する〉work；study / 日本語を学習している外国人 a foreigner who is learning Japanese；a foreign student of the Japanese language / 学習曲線〖心理〗a learning curve / 学習辞典 a learner's [learners'] dictionary / 学習帳 a workbook / 学習指導要領 the (official) course [curriculum] guidelines / 学習塾 a small private institute where primary and/or secondary school pupils are given supplementary lessons after school hours；a (private) cramming school；a crammer / 学習能力 learning ability / 学習理論 a learning theory.

がくじゅつ　学術　science；〈学識〉《文》learning；scholarship　¶学術的 academic；scientific / 日本学術会議 the Science Council of Japan / 学術雑誌 a learned [scientific] journal / 学術団体 an academic society；a learned body [society].

かくしょ　各所　¶各所の[に] in every [each] place；in various places. 文例⇩

かくしょう　確証　conclusive [solid] evidence；(a) positive [convincing] proof　¶確証する prove definitely；give positive proof 《of sth, that…》/ 確証のない報道 an unconfirmed report / 確証を握る secure positive evidence 《to show that…》. 文例⇩

がくしょう　楽章　〖音楽〗a movement　¶第一楽章 the first movement 《of the *Pastoral Symphony*》.

かくしん[1]　革新　(a) reform；(an) innovation　¶革新する reform；make a reform 《in》；《文》innovate / 革新政党 a reformist [progressive] (political) party / 革新派 the reformists；a reformist group.

かくしん[2]　核心　the core；the kernel；〈要点〉the point；the nub　¶事の核心 the (very) core of a subject / 問題の核心に触れる get to the heart [core] of the matter [problem] / 《俗》get down to the nitty-gritty.

かくしん[3]　確信　(a) conviction；a firm belief；confidence (自信)　¶確信する believe firmly；be sure [certain, convinced, confident] 《that …, of sth》/ 確信犯 a prisoner of conscience. 文例⇩

用法　sure と certain が区別なく用いられることもあるが, 区別する場合は, sure の方は主観的判断もしくは直観に基づいて, certain は客観的事実や証拠に基づいて,「確信」のもてることを表わす. 又 convinced は証拠や他人の言葉に基づいての「確信」を示すこともあるが, 多くの場合, 他人がどんなことを言おうと, どんな証拠をあげようと, 自分の「確信」の揺るぎのないことを表わしている. confident は「自信」の深さを強調している語.

かくじん　各人　each (person)；every one 《of you》.

かくす　隠す　hide；《文》conceal；〈覆い隠す〉cover；〈遮り隠す〉screen；〈秘密にする〉keep [《文》conceal] sth from sb；keep sth secret [back] from sb；〈かくまう〉shelter；give refuge to sb；〈見えなくする〉put sth out of sight；keep sth from sight　¶姿を隠す disappear；go out of sight；hide (*oneself*) 《behind the screen》/ 事実を隠す suppress [cover up] a fact / 年を隠す hide [conceal] one's age；make a secret of one's age / 見えないところに隠す hide [conceal] sth from view / 隠さない make no secret of sth / 隠さずに without concealing 《one's feelings》；frankly；candidly / 何を隠そう to tell the truth. 文例⇩

かくすい　角錐　〖数〗a pyramid.

かくする　画する　〈線を(を)引く〉draw；〈区画する〉mark the limits 《of》；mark sth off　¶一線を画する make a clear distinction 《between》；draw a line of demarcation 《between》/ 新時代を画する mark a new epoch；be epoch-making.

かくせい[1]　覚醒　(an) awakening　¶覚醒する〈目が覚める〉wake (up)；awake；〈迷いから覚める〉lose one's illusions；come to one's senses；〈比喩的に〉《文》awake 《to sth》/ (人を)覚醒させる awaken sb to sth；〈迷いから〉rid [《文》conceal] sb 《of his mistaken idea》/ 覚醒剤 a stimulant.

かくせい[2]　隔世　¶隔世遺伝 atavism；(a) reversion；(a) throwback. 文例⇩

がくせい[1]　学生　a student　¶学生運動 a student movement / 学生街 the students' quarter / 学生会館 a student union building / 学生活動家 a student activist / 学生参加 student participation / 学生時代 one's school [student] days / 学生証 a student's identification card；《口語》an ID (card) / 学生生活 student [college] life / 学生大会 a students' convention [general meeting] / 学生服 a school uniform / 学生部長 a dean of students. 文例⇩

がくせい[2]　学制　an educational system　¶学制改革 (a) reform of the educational system.

かくせいき　拡声器　(loud)speaker；〈携帯用の〉《米》a bullhorn；《英》a loudhailer；a megaphone (電気の)；〈場内・機内などの放送装置〉a public address system；a PA [P.A., p.a.]

る[少しもない]. He has something [nothing] of the scholar about him.

かくしょ　市内各所に出水があった. There were floods in various parts of the city. / Several parts of the city were flooded.

かくしょう　彼の仕業だという確証でもあるのかね. Do you have any positive proof that he did it?

かくしん[3]　知は力なりと僕は確信している. I firmly believe [It is my firm belief] that knowledge is power. / 僕は君の成功を確信している. I am sure [certain] that you will succeed [be successful]. / 僕は彼は潔白だと確信している. I am convinced that he is innocent [convinced of his innocence]. / そのときの彼の言葉に, 僕はその手紙を書いたのは彼なのだという確信を深めた. What he said then confirmed me in my opinion that he was the writer of the letter.

かくじん　各人各様のやり方でやった. Each of them tried his own way of doing it.

かくす　君には何一つ隠していることなんかない. I am not hiding [keeping] anything from you.

かくせい[2]　当時を思うと隔世の感がある. When I think of those days, I feel I am living in a completely different age.

がくせい[1]　本学の学生数は3千名で

がくせき(ぼ) 学籍(簿) a school [college] register ¶学籍簿から削る strike sb's name off the school register.

かくぜつ 隔絶 ¶隔絶する be completely separated [isolated] (from); 《文》 be far removed 《from》.

がくせつ 学説 a theory; a doctrine ¶新学説を立てる set up [《文》 formulate] a new theory.

かくぜん 画然 ¶画然たる distinct; clear.

がくぜん 愕然 ¶愕然とする be amazed; be shocked; be [《文》 stand] aghast (at).

かくせんそう 核戦争 (a) nuclear war ¶核戦争の脅威 a nuclear threat / 人類を核戦争による絶滅から防ぐ save mankind from nuclear extinction [annihilation].

がくそく 学則 school regulations.

かくだい 拡大 magnification; enlargement ¶拡大する 〈大きくする〉 magnify; enlarge; 〈広がる〉 spread; expand / 生産を拡大する increase [boost] the production (of) / 拡大委員会 a meeting of a committee with enlarged membership / 拡大解釈する stretch the meaning of 《the law》; 《口語》 bend 《the rules》 / 拡大再生産 reproduction on an enlarged scale; enlarged reproduction.

がくたい 楽隊 a band; 〈吹奏楽の〉 a brass band.

かくだいきょう 拡大鏡 a magnifying glass ¶拡大鏡で見る observe [look at] *sth* under a magnifying glass.

かくたる 確たる ⇨ たしか (確かな).

かくたん 喀痰 《医》 expectoration ¶喀痰検査 the examination of *sb's* sputum.

かくだん 格段 ⇨ かくべつ. [文例⇩]

がくだん[1] 楽団 an orchestra; a band ¶楽団員 a member of an orchestra.

がくだん[2] 楽壇 the musical world; musical circles.

かくち 各地 every [each] place; 〈諸地方〉 various places [districts] ¶世界各地から from every corner [all parts] of the world.

かくちゅう 角柱 《数》 a prism; 〈四角な柱〉 a square pillar.

かくちょう[1] 拡張 extension; expansion; enlargement ¶拡張する extend; expand; enlarge; increase / 街路を拡張する widen a street / 業務を拡張する extend [expand] *one's* business / 〈領土などの〉拡張政策 expansionism; an expansionist policy.

かくちょう[2] 格調 〈文章などの〉 a tone; a style ¶格調の高い演説 《文》 a high-toned speech / 格調の高い文章 《文》 a literary composition written in a lofty [an exalted] style.

がくちょう 学長 a president; 《英》 a vice-chancellor ⇨ そうちょう[2] ★.

かくづけ 格付け grading; rating ¶格付けする grade; rate / 格付け検査 a grading test.

かくてい 決定; 《文》 settlement ¶確定する 〈決まる〉 become definite [certain]; be decided (on); be settled; be fixed (on); 〈決める〉 decide on; settle; fix (on) / 確定した fixed; decided; definite / 確定的に definitely; conclusively / 確定案 a final draft / 〈所得税の〉確定申告 (file) a [one's] final (income tax) return (for the year). [文例⇩]

カクテル a cocktail ¶カクテルグラス a cocktail glass / カクテルドレス a cocktail dress / カクテルパーティー a cocktail party.

かくど 角度 an angle ¶45度の角度で[に] at an angle of 45° / 角度を計る measure the angle (of) / あらゆる角度から検討する study 《a problem》 from all angles. [文例⇩]

がくと 学徒 a student; a scholar ¶学徒援護会 the Students' Assistance Association.

かくとう[1] 格闘 a (hand-to-hand) fight; a melee ¶〈数人の〉格闘する a fight (hand to hand) 《with》; grapple 《with》 / 格闘技 (a) combative sport.

かくとう[2] 確答 ¶確答する answer [《文》 reply] definitely; give a definite answer [reply]. [文例⇩]

がくどう 学童 a schoolchild; 〈男〉 a schoolboy; 〈女〉 a schoolgirl.

かくとく 獲得 《文》 acquisition ¶獲得する 《文》 acquire; 《文》 obtain; 《文》 secure; gain; get.

かくない 閣内 ¶閣内の[で] within the Cabinet; inside the Cabinet / 閣内不統一を招く [引き起こす] invite [cause] disunity within the Cabinet.

がくない 学内 ¶学内の[に] in the university; within the campus, 《米》 on (the) campus / 学内運動競技大会 intramural sports.

かくにん 確認 confirmation ¶確認する confirm; 《文》 ascertain / 真偽を確認する 《文》 ascertain the truth 《of a report》 / 報道を確認する confirm a report / 〈ホテルなどの〉予約を確認する confirm *one's* reservation(s) / 再確認する ⇨ さいかくにん / 確認書 a note of confirmation. [文例⇩]

かくねん 隔年 ¶隔年に every other [second] year; in alternate years.

がくねん 学年 a school [an academic] year; 〈学級〉 a class; 《米》 a grade ¶学年試験 an annual examination. [文例⇩]

ある. This college has a student body of 3,000 [an enrollment of 3,000 (students)].

かくだい 戦火が拡大しないように全力を尽くさねばならない. We must do all we can to prevent the war from spreading.

かくだん 両者の間には格段の違いがある. There is a marked [great] difference between them.

かくてい 方針はまだ確定していない. The course to be taken has not yet been decided upon. | The policy isn't [hasn't been] fixed definitely yet. / 最高裁は上告を却下し, 彼の死刑判決は原審どおり確定した. The Supreme Court rejected his appeal, confirming the death sentence previously passed on him. / 彼の辞任は確実である. It's certain that he will resign.

かくど この問題をそれとは別の角度から眺めてみると, 又違った様相を呈するであろう. The matter will look different if you look at it from another [a different] angle.

かくとう[2] 大臣は確答を避けた. The minister avoided committing himself in his answer.

かくにん その報道はまだ確認されていない. The report has not been confirmed yet.

かくのう 格納 ¶格納する house / (航空機の)格納庫 a hangar.

かくは 各派 〈政党〉 each party ; 〈派閥〉 each faction ; 〈流派〉 each school ; 〈宗派〉 each sect [denomination] ¶各派交渉会 〈政党間の〉 an interparty liaison meeting ; 〈党内の〉 an intraparty liaison meeting.

がくは 学派 a school ¶マンチェスター学派 the Manchester school.

かくばくはつ 核爆発 a nuclear explosion [blast] ¶核爆発を行なう set off a nuclear explosion [blast] / 核爆発装置 a nuclear device.

がくばつ 学閥 an academic [a school] clique ¶(会社内などで)学閥を作る form an exclusive group of graduates of a [the same] university.

かくばる 角張る ⇨しかく[1](四角張る) ¶角張った顔 a squarish face.

かくはん 攪拌 ¶かくはんする stir 《cream》; churn 《milk》; beat 《eggs》.

がくひ 学費 school expenses ¶学費を出す pay *sb's* [provide *sb* with *his*] school expenses; pay for *sb's* education. [文例⇩]

かくびん 角瓶 a square bottle.

かくぶ 各部 each [every] part [section, department].

がくふ 楽譜 music ; a (musical) score ¶1枚の楽譜 a sheet of music / 楽譜が読める (be able to) read music.

がくぶ 学部 a faculty ; 《米》 a department (★《米》では faculty を「教員全体」の意でも使うので「学部」を a department と呼ぶ場合が多い) ¶学部長 a dean.

がくふう 学風 〈伝統〉 academic traditions; 〈研究法〉 a method of study ; 〈学校の気風〉 the character [atmosphere] of a college [school].

かくぶそう 核武装 nuclear armament(s) ¶核武装する arm *itself* with nuclear weapons ; 《口語》 go nuclear / 核武装の撤廃 nuclear disarmament / 核武装をしている国 a nuclear power / 核武装を禁止する denuclearize 《a country》 / 非核武装化 denuclearization / 核武装禁止[非核武装]地域 a nuclear-free [denuclearized] zone / 核武装競争 a nuclear arms race.

かくぶんれつ 核分裂 〖物〗 nuclear fission ; 〖生物〗 nuclear division [fission] ¶核分裂生成物 a fission product / 核分裂物質 fissionable materials.

かくへき 隔壁 a partition (wall) ; 〈船・鉱山の〉 a bulkhead.

かくべつ 格別 ¶格別の particular ; special ; exceptional (破格の) ; 〈目に立つ〉 marked ; noticeable / 格別に particularly ; in particular ; (e)specially ; exceptionally. [文例⇩]

かくほ 確保 ¶確保する make sure of 《*one's* position》; 《文》 secure 《a seat》; ensure [《米》 insure] 《safety》.

かくほう 確報 a definite [reliable] report.

かくぼう 角帽 a (square) college cap ; 〈房飾りのついた〉 a mortarboard.

がくぼう 学帽 a school cap.

かくほうめん 各方面 ¶社会の各方面の人々 all classes of people ; 《文》 people in all walks of life / 各方面に in every direction [《文》 quarter] ; in all directions [《文》 quarters].

かくまう 匿う shelter ; give shelter [《文》 refuge] to *sb* ; take *sb* under *one's* wing.

かくまく 角膜 〖解〗 the cornea ¶角膜炎 keratitis / 角膜移植 transplantation of the cornea ; a corneal transplant.

がくむ 学務 school [educational] affairs ¶学務課 the educational affairs section.

かくめい 革命 a revolution ¶革命が起きる a revolution breaks out / 革命の[的] revolutionary / 革命を起こす[実行する] start [carry out] a revolution / 革命家 a revolutionary / 革命軍[政府] a revolutionary army [government]. [文例⇩]

がくめい 学名 a scientific name ; 〈動物の〉 a zoological name ; 〈植物の〉 a botanical name ¶学名の付け方 nomenclature.

がくめん 額面 face [par] value ¶額面価格で at par (value) / 額面以上[以下]で above [below] par (value) / 額面どおりに受け取る take 《a report》 at (its) face value / 額面割れの株 shares below par (value).

がくもん 学問 〈勉学〉 learning 《law》 ; study 《of Chinese classics》 ; 〈学業〉 studies ; 〈科学〉 science (総称) ; 〈学術の1分野〉 a science ; an academic discipline ; 〈学識〉 《文》 learning ; scholarship ; 〈知識〉 knowledge ¶学問のある人 《文》 a learned person ; 《文》 a man of learning / 学問のない人 an uneducated [《文》 unlettered] person ; a man with little [not much] learning / 学問のための学問 learning for its own sake / 学問の自由 academic freedom / 学問をする learn ; study / 学問をさせる give *sb* an education / 学問を鼻にかける be proud of *one's* learning [scholarship] / 学問上 scientifically. [文例⇩]

がくや 楽屋 a dressing room (出演の準備のための) ; a greenroom (休憩のための) ¶楽屋で in the dressing room ; backstage ; behind the

---

かくねん 日本では学年は4月1日に始まり翌年の3月31日に終わる. In Japan the school year begins on April 1st and ends on March 31st of the following year.

がくひ 学費を出してあげようと言ってくれた. He offered to pay for [to finance] my education.

かくべつ 格別変わったこともない. There's nothing new in particular. | There have been no changes worth special mention. / この数か月間は格別のこともなく過ぎた. The last few months have been rather uneventful. / 格別用事もございません. I have nothing (in) particular to do. / この暑さは格別です. This heat is exceptional. / 格別寒いとも思いません. I don't feel so very cold. / 暑い日の生ビールの味はまた格別だ. Draft beer tastes especially good [There is nothing like draft beer] on a hot day.

かくめい マイクロエレクトロニクスは産業界に革命をもたらそうとしている. Microelectronics is on the point of revolutionizing the industrial world.

がくもん 彼はなかなか学問ができる. He is a good scholar. / これらの現象は学問的にはあまり興味がない. These phenomena are of

かくやく 楽屋落ち an in [inside] story／楽屋口 a stage door／楽屋話をする tell an inside story.

かくやく 確約 a firm [definite] promise ¶確約する promise positively; give *sb* one's word (to do); commit *oneself* (to do).

かくやす 格安 ¶格安な cheap; inexpensive; low in price; 格安に cheap; at a low price／格安品 low-priced goods／〈買い得品〉a bargain.

がくゆう 学友 a schoolmate; a schoolfellow; a fellow student ¶学友会〈在学生の〉a students' association／〈卒業生の〉《米》an alumni [alumnae] association;《英》an old boys' [girls'] association.

かくゆうごう 核融合 nuclear fusion ¶核融合爆弾 a (nuclear) fusion bomb.

かくよう 各様 ⇨かくじん 各人.

がくようひん 学用品 school supplies [things].

かぐら 神楽 *kagura*; sacred (*Shinto*) music and dance.

かくらん 攪乱 disturbance ¶攪乱する disturb; throw 《the enemy》 into confusion [disorder].

かくり 隔離 isolation ¶隔離する isolate; separate; set *sb* apart 《from》;〈海外からの旅行者で伝染病の疑いのある人などを〉put [keep] *sb* in quarantine／隔離患者 a patient kept in isolation; an isolated patient／隔離病院[病棟] an isolation hospital [ward].

がくり 学理 (a) theory; a scientific principle ¶学理を実地に応用する put (a) theory into practice.

かくりつ¹ 確立《文》establishment ¶確立する establish. 文例⊕

かくりつ² 確率《数》a probability ¶確率の法則 the laws of probability. 文例⊕

かくりょう 閣僚 a member of the Cabinet; a Cabinet minister ¶閣僚の1人である hold a portfolio [a seat in the Cabinet]／閣僚級会談 a conference at ministerial level; a minister-level conference [talk].

がくりょく 学力 academic [scholastic] ability 《文》attainment ¶学力がある[ない] be a good [poor] scholar／大卒以上の学力がある have a higher level of academic ability than the average university graduate／学力検査 an achievement test. 文例⊕

かくれ 隠れ ¶隠れもない〈明白な〉obvious;《文》patent;〈名高い〉well-known; notorious〈悪名で〉／隠れもない事実 an obvious [a patent] fact／隠れキリシタン《日本史》a crypto-Christian; an underground Christian／隠れ場[家] a hiding place;《文》a place of concealment [shelter];《口語》a hide-out;《口語》a hideaway／隠れみの a cloak of invisibility;〈比喩的に〉a cloak (for); a cover (for). 文例⊕

がくれい 学齢 school age ¶学齢に達する[達しない] reach [be under] school age／学齢に達した[達しない]子供 a child of [under] school age; a school-aged (preschool) child.

がくれき 学歴 *one's* educational background; *one's* academic background [career] ¶学歴のない人 a person who has had no regular schooling [no formal education]／学歴を問わずに regardless [irrespective] of educational background／学歴社会 a society which sets a greater value on the academic career of an individual than on his real ability.

かくれる 隠れる hide (*oneself*);《文》conceal *oneself*;〈避難する〉take《文》seek refuge;〈見えなくなる〉disappear; be lost to [from] sight; go out of sight; become invisible ¶ベッドの下に[ドアの後ろに]隠れる hide (*oneself*) under the bed [behind the door]／隠れた岩 a hidden rock; a sunken rock（海中に）／ひそかに in secret; secretly;〈かこつけて〉under the cloak (of); under cover (of)／慈善の美名に隠れて under the cloak of charity／隠れている lie concealed; be [lie, stay,《文》remain] in hiding. 文例⊕

かくれんぼう 隠れん坊《play》hide-and-seek.

かくろん 各論 an itemized discussion ¶各論に入る go into the detail(s) [particulars] (of a subject) ⇨ そうろん.

かぐわしい 香しい fragrant; sweet-smelling[-scented].

がくわり 学割〈運賃などの割引き〉a student(s') discount;〈その運賃など〉a student fare [rate];〈証明書〉a certificate of qualification for a student(s') discount.

がくんと with a jerk; suddenly（急に）¶（車などが）がくんと止まる jerk to a stop; stop with a jerk; come to a lurching halt（★荷物を高く積んだ車などが，急停止した時，車体や

---

little academic interest.／学問に王道なし．There is no royal road to learning. 諺⊕

かくりつ¹ その著書によって哲学者としての彼の名声は確立した．The book established his fame [reputation] as a philosopher.

かくりつ² そのような事の起こる確率は 1/4 である．The event has a probability of 0.25.／The probability is one in four that such a thing will happen.

がくりょく この試験を受けるにはまだ学力が足りない．His academic ability is not yet equal to the examination.／近年大学生の学力低下がはなはだしいと言われている．It is said that there has been a marked decline in the levels of academic attainment of university students.

かくれ 彼らの隠れ家を突き止めるのに1週間かかった．It took us a week to locate [discover] their hideaway [hiding place].／公共性を隠れみのにして利権追求を図っている．They are pursuing profits under the cloak [cover] of the public interest.

かくれる 月が雲に隠れた．The moon went [disappeared, hid itself] behind the clouds.／彼は追っ手に追われて洞穴の中へ隠れた．Driven by his pursuers, he took refuge in a cave.

かけ² それはちょっとしたかけだけれど，やってみる値打ちはある．It's a bit of a gamble, but it's worth trying.

-かけ それはまだ書きかけだ．I haven't finished writing it yet.／I've just only started (writing) it.

かげ² レンブラントは陰を有効に使うことができた画家だ．Rembrandt was a painter who could use shade to good effect.／白帆が島の陰になった．The white sail has gone [disappeared] be-

かけ¹ 掛け 《掛け売り》credit;《掛け金》an account; a bill;《掛けそば》buckwheat noodles in soup ¶掛けで売る[買う] sell [buy] sth on credit [《英口語》tick] ⇒ かけうり.

かけ² 賭 betting; gambling; a gamble ¶かけをする make a bet (on); gamble 《at cards, on horse races》 ⇒ かける / かけに応じる take [accept] a bet [wager] / かけで勝つ[負ける] win [lose] a bet [wager] / かけ金 a bet;《文》a wager / かけマージャンをやる play mahjong for money [stakes]. 文例Ø

-かけ …掛け ¶吸いかけの紙巻きたばこ a half-smoked cigarette / 食いかけの菓子 a half-eaten cake / やりかけの仕事 unfinished work / 帽子掛け a coat hook; a peg; a hat rack [stand]〈スタンド状の〉. 文例Ø

かげ¹ 鹿毛〈色〉fawn;a fawn color;〈馬〉a fawn-colored horse.

かげ² 陰 (the) shade /〈陰の声〉〈ラジオ・テレビの〉the mystery voice / 人の陰になる〈背後に隠れる〉be hidden [《文》concealed] behind sb;〈光をさえぎる〉be [stand] in sb's light / 木の陰に[で](sit) in the shadow of a tree;〈下〉(take) shelter) under a tree;〈後〉《hide》behind a tree / 陰になり日向になりして both openly and secretly / 陰で behind sb's [sb's] back; in secret; behind the scenes. 文例Ø

かげ³ 影〈投影〉a shadow;〈月・灯火などの光〉light;〈映像〉a reflection; an image;〈形跡〉a trace ¶影が薄い look as if one were shadowed by death / 影が薄くなる one's presence hardly makes itself felt [is hardly noticed]; fade away;《文》undergo an eclipse; be pushed into the background; be thrown into the shade / 影の形に添うように《文》as the shadow follows the form / …の影を映す《文》mirror the image of …; reflect … / 影を落とす《文》cast [throw] a [one's, its] shadow (on, over) / 影を潜める hide;《文》conceal oneself; disappear; vanish / 影も形も見えない there is no sign (of him); not a trace (of him) is to be seen; be nowhere to be seen. 文例Ø

がけ 崖 a precipice; a cliff; a bluff ¶がけの縁に立つ stand on the edge [lip] of a precipice [cliff] / がけから落ちる fall over a precipice / がけ崩れ a landslip; a landslide.

-がけ ¶命がけで at the risk of one's life / 帰りがけに on one's way home / 定価の8がけで at 80 per cent of the price / 4人がけの椅子 a bench for four (persons) /〈座席に〉3人がけで座る sit three in [to] a seat.

かけあい 掛け合い〈交渉〉negotiations;〈話・歌などの〉a dialogue; a duet ¶掛け合い漫才 a comic dialogue.

かけあう 掛け合う negotiate 《with sb on [about, over] sth》 ¶値段を掛け合う bargain [haggle] 《with sb》about the price.

かけあがる 駆け上がる run [rush] up ¶2階へ[階段を]駆け上がる run [rush] upstairs [up the stairs].

かけあし 駆け足 a run;〈馬の〉a canter; a gallop ★馬の駆け足のうち gallop が最も速い走り方で, canter はそれに続く. はしる ¶駆け足で at a run;〈兵隊が〉(march) at the double;〈馬が〉at a gallop [canter] / 駆け足になる break into a run;〈馬が〉break into a gallop [canter]. 文例Ø

かけあわせる 掛け合わせる〈倍する〉multiply 《3 by 2》;〈交配する〉cross 《a tiger with [and] a lion》.

かけい¹ 火刑 ⇒ ひあぶり.

かけい² 家系 one's (family) line;《文》(a) lineage; (a) pedigree ⇒ いえがら, けい¹ ¶3代前まで家系をたどる trace sb's family line through three generations.

かけい³ 家計〈経済〉household economy; family finances;〈生計〉living; livelihood ⇒ せいけい¹ ¶家計が豊か[困難]である be well [badly] off;《文》be in easy [straitened] circumstances / 家計費 household expenses /〈予算〉a family budget / 家計簿 an [a household] account book / 家計簿をつける keep (household) accounts.

かけうり 掛け売り selling on credit [《英口語》tick] ⇒ かけ¹.

かげえ 影絵 a shadow picture.

かけおち 駆け落ち (an) elopement ¶駆け落ちする elope (run away) 《with one's lover》.

かけおりる 駆け下りる run down;〈坂を〉run downhill ¶階下に[階段を]駆け下りる run downstairs [down the stairs].

かけがえ 掛け替え a substitute ¶掛け替えがない cannot be replaced; be irreplaceable / 掛け替えのない命《文》one's precious life / 掛け替えのない子 one's dearest child. 文例Ø

hind the island. / 少し左へ寄ってくれないか, 陰になるから. Please move a little to the left; you are in my light. / この事件の陰にこれか黒幕がいるに違いない. There must be someone behind this affair. / 陰ながら君の成功を祈ります. I am praying for your success. / 陰ながら案じておりました. I was anxious about you, though I didn't tell you in so many words.

かげ³ 松の木の影が障子に映った. The shadow of a pine tree fell on the shoji. / そう言えばこの間会った時どことなく影が薄いような気がした. Now I come to think of it, when I last met him I fancied he hadn't long to live. / 新しいスーパーができて, 今まであったスーパーは影が薄れてしまった. The new supermarket has put the old one in(to) the shade. / この事件は両国間の友好関係に暗い影を投ずるであろう. The event will cast a (dark) shadow on the friendly relations between the two countries. / 犯人の影も見えなかった. We could not find even a trace of the culprit.

かけあし 駆け足進め! [号令] At the double. March! / 駆け足で出て行った. He started off at a run. / 春はもう足許までやって来る. Spring is just around the corner.

かけあわせる 雄のライオンと雌のとらとを掛け合わせて出来たものがライガーである. The cross between [The offspring of] a male lion and a female tiger is a liger.

かけうり 掛け売りお断わり. [掲示] No credit given. | Cash only.

かけがえ 掛け替えのない品だから

かけかえる　掛け替える　replace ¶軸を掛け替える change a hanging scroll for a new one; hang a new scroll / 橋を掛け替える rebuild a bridge.

かけがね　掛け金　a latch ¶掛け金をかける[外す] latch [unlatch] 《the door》.

かげき¹　過激　¶過激な〈極端な〉extreme; radical; 〈乱暴な〉violent / 過激な思想 radical [extreme] ideas / 過激に走る go to extremes; be too radical [violent]; go too far / 過激派 (the) radicals; (the) extremists / ロシア革命の〉the Bolsheviks / 過激分子 a radical element (★しばしば複数形で使われる).

かげき²　歌劇　(an) opera ⇒オペラ ¶軽歌劇 an operetta; a light opera / 喜歌劇 ⇒きがげき / 歌劇団 an opera company [troupe] / 〈宝塚などの〉a girls' operetta troupe [company] / 歌劇場 an opera house; 〈宝塚などの〉an operetta house.

かけきん　掛け金　〈割賦金〉an installment; 〈保険の〉a premium ¶月千円の掛け金をする pay monthly installments [premiums] of 1,000 yen.

かげぐち　陰口　backbiting ¶陰口をきく[たたく] talk about sb behind his back; say unkind [spiteful, 《口語》nasty] things about sb behind his back; backbite sb.

かけくらべ　駆け比べ ⇒かけっこ.

かけごえ　掛け声　a shout 《to mark time, of encouragement》; a call; a yell ¶掛け声を掛ける〈呼び掛けて〉shout 《to》; call out 《to》; 〈拍子をとって〉shout time; 〈励まして〉shout encouragement; 〈ほめて〉shout applause. 文例⇩

かけごと　賭け事　gambling ⇒かけ², ばくち. 文例⇩

かけこみ　駆け込み ¶駆け込み乗車 rushing to get on a train [bus].

かけこむ　駆け込む　run [rush] into [in]; 〈逃げ込む〉seek refuge [shelter] 《in a Buddhist temple》.

かけざん　掛け算　(a) multiplication ¶掛け算をする multiply; do multiplication.

かけじく　掛軸 ⇒かけもの.

かけす　《鳥》a jay.

かけず　掛図　a wall chart; a wall map (地図).

かげぜん　陰膳　¶陰膳を据える set a meal for an absent person (to pray for his safe return).

かけだし　駆け出し　a fledgling; a cub ¶駆け出しの医者 a newly-fledged doctor / 駆け出しの音楽家[劇作家] a fledgling musician [dramatist] / 駆け出しの記者 a cub reporter. 文例⇩

かけだす　駆け出す　〈外へ〉run [rush] out; 〈走り始める〉start running; break into a run; bolt 《馬などが驚いて出る》.

かけつ　可決　¶可決する pass [approve] 《a bill》; carry 《a motion》 / 可決される be passed; be carried. 文例⇩

かけつけ　駆け付け　¶かけつけ3杯飲む 《口語》drink three cups of sake on the trot.

かけつける　駆け付ける　run [rush] (to).

かけっこ　駆けっこ　a (foot)race ¶駆けっこをする have [run] a race 《with》; race 《with》.

がけっぷち　崖っ縁　the edge [lip] of a precipice [cliff] ⇒がけ.

かけて　〈…にわたって〉(extending) over…; 〈(…から)…におよんで〉(from…) to [till]…; 〈…に誓って〉by 《God》; on 《文》upon》《my honor》¶秋から冬にかけて from (late) autumn to [till] (early) winter / 週末にかけて over the weekend / …にかけては〈の点では〉《文》in point of…; in the matter of…; when it comes to…. 文例⇩

かけどけい　掛け時計　a wall clock.

かけとり　掛け取り ⇒しゅうきん.

かけぬける　駆け抜ける　〈後から〉run past sb from behind; 〈走り抜ける〉run through 《a gate》.

かけね　掛け値　an inflated [a fancy] price; 〈誇張〉(an) exaggeration ¶掛け値のない net; honest / 掛け値のない所を言う state things [the facts] as they are; 《口語》call a spade a spade; give one's honest opinion 《about》 / 掛け値を言う ask an inflated price (to leave scope for haggling [for reducing the price later]); 〈誇張する〉exaggerate. 文例⇩

注意しなさい。Handle it with care; it can't be replaced if it's broken. / 彼はうちの会社にとって掛け替えのない人だ。He is absolutely invaluable [an irreplaceable asset] to the company.

かけごえ その新計画は結局掛け声だけに終わった。There had been considerable fanfare about the adoption of the new plan, but in the end it came to nothing [fizzled out].

かけごと 僕はかけ事は嫌いだ。I'm not a betting man.

かけだし その事件があったのは私がまだ記者として駆け出し時代のことだった。It was in my days as a cub reporter that the incident occurred.

かけつ 議案は投票の結果200票対70票で可決された。The bill was passed by a vote of 200 to 70.

かけつける 私は犯行現場に駆け付けた。I hurried [rushed] to the scene of the crime.

かけて 男子の面目にかけてやってみせる。On my honor I assure you I will do it. / 学問にかけては彼は僕より上だ。In learning he is superior to me. / テニスにかけては彼はだれにも負けない。When it comes to tennis, he is second to none [there's no one to beat him].

かけね 掛け値は一切致しません。All our prices are the lowest possible. ¶掲示》All prices net. / 掛け値のないところで幾らですか。What is the lowest price you can possibly offer me? いたところ、彼は余り学問は出来ない。To be candid, [It's no exaggeration to say that] he is not a very good [not much of a] scholar.

かけはなれる 君の提案は現実とはかけ離れた理想論に過ぎない。What you propose is little more than idealism, bearing no relation to the realities of life. / 私は自分の趣味とは全くかけ離れた仕事をしている。I am engaged in a job quite foreign to my taste.

かけひき こういう問題を扱う時は多少は駆け引きを使わなければならない。When we are dealing with a problem like [such as] this, we have to use a little diplomacy. / その辺の駆け引きは難しい。That is where tact is needed.

かげひなた 人に対して陰ひなたがあってはいけない。Don't be one thing in front of a person and another behind his back. / あのボー

かけのぼる 駆け上る run up;〈坂を〉run uphill ¶二階へ[階段を]駆け上る run upstairs [up the stairs].

かけはし 掛け橋 〈仮設〉a temporary bridge;〈比喩的に〉a bridge 《between the two generations, connecting two countries》⇨はし³.

かけはなれる 懸け離れる 〈距離が〉be far [wide] apart ; be a long way from ;〈文〉be distant 《from》;〈性状などが〉be (widely) different 《from》;〈文〉be (far) removed 《from》. 文例☟

かけひ 筧 a [an open] water pipe ; a conduit.

かけひき 駆け引き 〈値段の〉bargaining ;〈戦略〉tactics ; strategy ;〈策略〉tricks ;〈外交術〉diplomacy ¶駆け引きをする bargain [haggle] 《with sb about the price》; use diplomacy / 駆け引きのある cunning / 駆け引きのない honest ; straightforward ; straight-dealing. 文例☟

かげひなた 陰日向 陰ひなたのある two-faced ; double-dealing ;《口語》two-timing / 陰ひなたなく faithfully. 文例☟

かけぶとん 掛け布団 a quilt.

かげべんけい 陰弁慶 ⇨うちべんけい.

かげぼうし 影法師 a shadow ; a silhouette.

かげぼし 陰干し ¶陰干しにする dry *sth* out of direct sunlight ; air [dry] *sth* in the shade ; shade-dry *sth*.

かけまわる 駆け回る 〈走り回る〉run [move] about [around] ;〈忙しく暮らす〉be busy 《doing》; busy *oneself*《(in) doing》; bustle about ; be on the move. 文例☟

かけもち 掛け持ち ¶掛け持ちする do two or more jobs at the same time ; have part-time jobs in two or more places / 3校掛け持ちで教える teach at three different schools.

かけもの 掛物〈掛軸〉a *kakemono*; a hanging picture [scroll] ¶掛物の軸 a roller (for a *kakemono*).

かけよる 駆け寄る run up to sb.

かけら 欠けら a (broken) piece ;《文》a fragment ¶ガラスのかけら a piece of broken glass / 割れた皿のかけら a fragment of a broken dish / かけらもない there is not a trace [an ounce, a flicker] 《of...》.

かげり 陰〔翳〕り a cloud 《on sb's happiness》⇨くもり. 文例☟

かける¹ 欠ける 〈壊れる〉break ; be broken ; chip ; be chipped ;〈不足する〉lack ; be short of [《文》wanting in]《common sense》;〈月が〉wane ¶縁の欠けた湯呑み a chipped cup / 注意が欠けている be not as careful as one should be ; be careless. 文例☟

かける² 書ける can [be able to] write ¶〈筆が〉よく書ける write well.

かける³ 掛〔架〕ける 〈つるす〉hang ;《文》suspend ; hook 《かぎに》;〈架設する〉lay ;《文》construct ; build ; install ;〈腰掛ける〉sit 《on [in] a chair》; sit down ;〈散布する〉sprinkle 《on, over》;〈注ぐ〉pour 《on》;〈心配などを〉give《sb trouble》;〈ひもなどを〉tie (up)《sticks with a rope》; put (a cord) round *sth* ;〈掛け算する〉multiply 《4 by 2》;〈かぶせる〉put [throw] *sth* on [over]; spread [lay] *sth* on [over]; cover *sth* with 《a cloth》¶看板を掛ける hang [put] up a [one's] signboard / 帽子をくぎに掛ける hang [put] one's hat on a peg / 壁[屋根]にはしごを掛ける put [lean] a ladder up against a wall / 〈屋根の〉the edge of the roof] / 窓にカーテンを掛ける hang curtains in a window / 肩に手を掛ける put [lay] one's hand on sb's shoulder / ラジオをかける turn [switch] the radio on / やかんを火にかける put a kettle on (the fire) / ソースをかける put [pour] sauce on 《the oysters》/ 会議に掛ける submit 《a matter》to a conference / 多額の費用を掛ける spend [lay out] a large amount of money 《on》/ (椅子に)掛けたままでいる stay [《文》remain, keep] seated. 文例☟

かける⁴ 駆ける ⇨はしる.

かける⁵ 賭ける bet 《on a horse》; bet [stake, put]《¥100,000 on a horse》;《文》wager ;〈危険を冒す〉risk ¶命をかけて at the risk of one's life / 金をかけて[かけずに]トランプをする play cards for money [for love].

-かける〈...し始める〉begin to *do* [*doing*];

イは陰ひなたがある. That waiter works hard only when his manager is watching.
かけまわる 一日方々駆け回った. I have spent the whole day visiting one place after another. / 子供たちは家の中を駆け回った. The children ran about the house.
かげり 日本の経済にかげりが見えてきた. There are some signs [indications] of Japan's economy declining [going downhill].
かける¹ あの男に欠けているのは勇気だ. What he lacks [needs] is courage. / 要するに君の失敗は熱意が欠けていたためなのだ. When you came down to it, your failure was due to your lack of enthusiasm. / このシリーズ物は1冊欠けている. One volume is missing from this series. / 月は欠け始め た. The moon is on the wane.
かける² 大学を卒業しても手紙一本満足に書けない者がいる. There are some university graduates who cannot write a decent letter.
かける³ 寒いから布団をよく掛けて寝なさい. It is very cold, so you must cover yourself up well. / どうぞお掛け下さい. Won't you have a seat [chair], please? |《会議などで》Please take your seats. / 彼はどうぞお掛け下さいという身振りをした. He motioned me to a chair. / 彼の病気は医者に掛けてもだめだ. His disease is past medical help [aid, treatment]. / 大変ご面倒をお掛けしてすみません. I am sorry to give you [put you to] so much trouble. / 彼は家具に大分金を掛けた. He laid out a great deal of money on his furniture. / 幾ら時間を掛けてやってもいい. You may take as much time as you like. / 5掛けるの3は15. Five times three is fifteen. | Five (multiplied) by three make(s) fifteen. | Three fives are fifteen. ★ Five times three is fifteen. は数式では5×3=15となる. 掛け算の読み方は×を常に times と言い, 前が1や0であっても time とは言わない. /3に幾つを掛けると24になるか. What must you multiply 3 by to get 24?
かける⁵ あの男はきっとあそこにいる. 1万円かける. 10,000 yen that you find him there. / さいころのひと振りに身を滅ぼす. There are some fools who gamble a large fortune on a single throw of the

かける start to *do* [*doing*]；⟨…しようとする⟩ be about [going] to *do*；be on the point of *doing* ¶読みかける begin [start] reading／わかりかける begin to understand／破産しかける be on the edge [verge, brink] of bankruptcy. 文例⇩

かげる 陰る ⟨暗くなる⟩ darken; get dark；⟨日・月が⟩ be clouded; be obscured. 文例⇩

かげろう¹ 陽炎 heat haze. 文例⇩

かげろう² 〖昆〗 a mayfly ¶かげろうのような ⟪文⟫ ephemeral；⟪文⟫ short-lived.

かげん¹ 下弦 ¶下弦の月 a waning [an old] moon.

かげん² 加減 ⟨調節⟩ adjustment; fixing (up)；⟨程度⟩ a degree; an extent；⟨料理の味付け⟩ seasoning；⟨足し算と引き算⟩ addition and subtraction ¶加減する ⟨調節する⟩ adjust; fix；⟨適度にする⟩ ⟪文⟫ moderate; keep *sth* within bounds；⟪文⟫ be temperate (in)／少し加減が悪い do not feel very well; feel slightly ill ⟪文⟫ indisposed／風呂の加減を見る see how hot the bath is／うつむき加減で bending slightly forward／加減乗除 addition, subtraction, multiplication and division; the four rules of arithmetic. 文例⇩

かこ 過去 the past；⟪文⟫ bygone days；⟨前歴⟩ one's past (life) ¶過去の past；⟪文⟫ bygone／過去の人 (口語) a has-been；(口語) (one of) yesterday's men／過去のある人 a person with [who has] a past／遠い過去において in the distant past／過去に生きる live in the past／過去3年間 for [during] the past [last] three years／過去完了(時制) 〖文法〗 the past perfect (tense)／(動詞の)過去形 〖文法〗 the past [preterite] tense (form) (of a verb)／過去時制 〖文法〗 the past tense; the preterite (tense)／過去分詞 〖文法〗 a past participle. 文例⇩

かご¹ 加護 divine protection ¶神の加護を求める call upon [pray to] God for help [protection].

かご² 籠, 籃 ⟨鳥かご⟩ a cage; a coop (伏せかご)；⟨編みかご⟩ a basket; a hamper ¶1籠の果物 a basket(ful) of fruit／かごの鳥 a bird in a cage; a caged bird／かごを編む make a basket／かご細工 basketwork／かご抜け詐欺を働く swindle *sb* and escape by another door.

かご³ 駕籠 a *kago*; a palanquin ¶かごで行 く go ⟪to Kyoto⟫ by palanquin／かごかき a palanquin bearer.

かこい 囲い an enclosure; a paling; a fence; a pen (家畜を入れる) ¶囲いの内に[で] within [inside] the enclosure；in the compound／囲いをする enclose; fence round [around]; rail [rope] off.

かこう¹ 下降 ⟪文⟫ a descent; a fall; a drop；⟨景気などの⟩ a decline; a downturn ¶下降する go [come] down; drop; fall；⟪文⟫ descend／下降線をたどる[描く] describe a downward curve；⟨衰える⟩ be on the decline [wane]／⟨減少する⟩ be on the decrease.

かこう² 火口 a crater ¶火口丘 a volcanic cone／火口原[壁] a crater basin [wall]／火口湖 a crater lake. 文例⇩

かこう³ 加工 processing ¶加工する process／加工業 the processing industries／加工業者 a processor／加工工場 a processing plant／加工賃[費] processing charges [costs]／加工品 processed goods.

かこう⁴ 花梗 〖植〗 a flower stalk; a peduncle.

かこう⁵ 河口 the mouth of a river; an estuary. 文例⇩

かこう⁶ 河港 a river port.

かこう⁷ 囲う ⟨囲む⟩ ⇒かこむ；⟨貯蔵する⟩ store; keep ⟪apples⟫ in storage；⟨めかけを⟩ keep ⟪a mistress⟫.

かごう 化合 (chemical) combination ¶化合する (chemically) combine ⟪with⟫; be brought into (chemical) combination ⟪with⟫／化合物 a (chemical) compound. 文例⇩

かごう 雅号 a pen name；⟪フランス語⟫ a *nom de plume* ⟪pl. *noms de plume*⟫.

かこうがん 花崗岩 granite.

かこく 苛酷 ¶苛酷な severe; hard; harsh；⟪文⟫ rigorous; cruel／苛酷な取り扱いをする be hard ⟪on⟫; be harsh ⟪to, with⟫; deal cruelly [severely] ⟪with⟫.

かこちょう 過去帳 a family register of deaths.

かこつ 託つ ⟨こぼす⟩ complain ⟪about, ⟪文⟫ of⟫; grumble ⟪about⟫；⟨嘆く⟩ ⟪文⟫ lament (over) *sth* ¶身の不運をかこつ lament (over) one's misfortunes.

かこつける 託ける make *sth* the pretext [excuse] ⟪for⟫; use *sth* as a pretext ¶…にかこつけて pretending ⟪that…⟫; on [under] the

---

dice.

-かける 彼は何か言いかけてやめた. He started to say something, but checked himself.／駅に着いた時電車は発車しかけていた. The train was starting [about to move], when I got to the station.／どうやら英語がわかりかけてきたらしいね. It seems that you are beginning to understand English.

かげる 陽が陰った. The sun has gone behind the clouds.／月が陰った. The moon was veiled by the clouds.

かげろう¹ かげろうが立っている. The air is shimmering with the heat.／前方の道路にかげろうが立っていた. Heat waves were shimmering above the road ahead.

かげん² お風呂の加減はいかがですか. How is the bath?／今日はお加減はいかがですか. How do you feel today?／陽気の加減か頭痛がする. I've a headache; it's probably because of the weather.／このスープは味加減がいい. The seasoning in this soup is just right.／彼の世間を知らなさ加減には驚く. How little he knows of the world!

かこ それも今は過去の事になってしまった. It is a thing of the past now.／過去は問わないことにしよう. Let bygones be bygones.／*make* の過去形は *made* である. The past tense [preterite (form)] of *make* is *made*.

かこう² 墜落した飛行機の残骸は三原山の火口の縁で発見された. The wreckage of the plane was sighted on the lip [rim] of the crater of Mt. Mihara.

かこう⁵ 新潟は信濃川の河口にある. Niigata stands at the mouth of the Shinano (River).

かごう 水素は酸素と化合して水と

かこみ　囲み　a siege ¶囲みを解く raise the siege《of a town》/ 囲みを破る break through the besieging army / (新聞の)囲み記事 a boxed article [report].

かこむ　囲む　〈取り巻く〉enclose; surround; encircle; 〈軍隊が〉besiege; lay siege to 《a town》 ¶テーブルを囲む sit around a table / 三方山に囲まれている be surrounded by hills on three sides / 陸地に囲まれた港 a landlocked harbor. 文例⇩

かこん　禍根　《文》the root of the evil; the source(s) of trouble ¶禍根を除く eliminate the root of the evil; remove the source(s) of (the) trouble. 文例⇩

かごん　過言　¶…といっても過言でない It is not too much to say that…; It is no exaggeration to say that…; It can [may] safely be said that….

かさ¹　笠　〈頭にかぶる〉a woven hat (of rushes or bamboo); 〈電灯の〉a (lamp)shade; 〈きのこ類の〉a cap ¶煙突のかさ a (chimney) cowl. 文例⇩

かさ²　毬　〈松の実などの〉a (pine) cone.

かさ³　傘　〈雨傘〉an umbrella; 〈日傘〉a parasol; a sunshade ¶きちんと巻いた傘 a neatly furled umbrella / おちょこになった傘 an umbrella blown inside out 《by the wind》/ 傘の柄 the handle of an umbrella / 傘の骨 an umbrella rib / 傘をさす put up an umbrella / 傘を広げる open an umbrella / 傘をすぼめる shut [close] an umbrella / 傘を持って行く take [carry] 《an》umbrella with one / 傘立て an umbrella stand / 傘屋〈店〉an umbrella shop; 〈人〉an umbrella seller. 文例⇩

かさ⁴　嵩　〈容積〉bulk; volume; 〈量〉quantity ¶かさのある bulky; unwieldy / かさにかかって arrogantly; highhandedly; overbearingly.

かさ⁵　暈　a halo (pl. -(e)s); a ring.

かさあな　風穴　a windhole; an air hole ¶風穴をあける 〈銃などで〉《口語》fill sb [drill sb through] with lead; 〈口語で〉run sb through.

「ちき／火災保険 ⇨ かさいほけん.

かさい　火災　⇨ かじ ¶火災報知器 ⇨ かさいほう

かさい　家財　household effects [goods] / 家財(道具)をまとめて引っ越す move 《to the country》with all one's belongings

[household goods] / (火事の際)家財(道具)を持ち出す save one's household effects.

かさいほうちき　火災報知器　a fire alarm (box) ¶火災報知器で知らせる sound a fire alarm / 火災報知器をいたずらする sound a false alarm.

かさいほけん　火災保険　fire insurance ¶火災保険をかける insure one's house [have one's house insured] against fire / 火災保険会社(証券) a fire insurance company [policy]. 文例⇩

かさかさ　¶かさかさ鳴る rustle; make a rustling sound / (皮膚などが)かさかさしている 〈脂気がない〉be dry; 〈荒れている〉be rough to the touch [feel].

がさがさ　rustlingly; with a rustle [rustling sound] ¶がさがさする rustle. 文例⇩

かざかみ　風上　¶風上の windward; upwind / 風上に toward the wind; windward; upwind / 風上に向かう face the wind [to windward] / 人の風上にも置けないやつ a person who is not fit for one's company; a person who is not fit to be called a [《文》is not worthy of the name of] 《scholar》. 文例⇩

かさく¹　佳作　a good [fine] piece (of work); 〈選外になった〉a work of which honorable mention is made;《表示》Honorable mention.

かさく²　家作　《米》a house for rent;《英》a house to let.

かさく³　寡作　¶寡作である《文》be far from prolific; produce one's works at rare intervals.

かざぐるま　風車　〈おもちゃの〉《米》a pinwheel;《英》a windmill; 〈米をついたり水を汲んだりする〉⇨ ふうしゃ. 文例⇩

かざごえ　風邪声　a voice that is hoarse [husky] from a cold.

かささぎ　〖鳥〗a magpie.

かざしも　風下　¶風下の downwind; leeward / 風下に down the wind; downwind; leeward (of) / 風下にある lie (to) leeward 《of》; be downwind (of, from).

かざす　翳す　hold sth up over one's head ¶高くかざす hold sth up high;《文》hold sth aloft / 火に手をかざす warm one's hands at [over] the fire / 目の上に手をかざす shade one's eyes with one's hand / 明かりにかざして見る hold

---

なる。Hydrogen combines with oxygen to form water.

かこつける　彼は父親の病気にかこつけて2日ばかり休ましてくれと言った。He wanted to take a couple of days off on the pretext of his father's illness.

かこむ　山にすっかり囲まれているので，この港には風一つ吹いてない。This harbor is so closed in by the hills that not a breath of air comes in.

かこん　こういう事が続出するのを放置しておくと，将来に大きな禍根を残すことになろう。If we do nothing to prevent things like this from happening over and over again, there will be a tremendous bill to pay some time in the future.

かさ¹　彼は親の威光をかさに着て威張っている。He fancies himself [thinks he's important] merely because his father is famous.

かさ³　彼らは皆傘をさしていた。They all had their umbrellas up. / 3人で1つの傘に入って行った。We went on our way, three to an umbrella.

かさ⁵　月にかさがかかっている。The moon has a ring [halo] around it.

かさいほけん　その家には2千万円

の火災保険がついている。The house is insured against fire for 20,000,000 yen.

がさがさ　くまかやぶからがさがさ出て来た。A bear came crashing out of the thicket.

かざかみ　ここは風上だから火事は大丈夫だろう。I hope we are safe, as this house stands to windward of the fire. / 教師の風上にも置けぬやつだ。He is an absolute disgrace to the teaching profession.

かざぐるま　彼女の手に持っていた風車がそよ風にくるくると回っていた。The pinwheel in her hand was whirling [revolving] in the

がさつ ¶がさつな rough; unpolished; 《文》unmannerly.

かさなる 重なる be piled up; lie on top of one another; overlap each other ¶不幸が重なる have one misfortune after another; have a series of misfortunes / 用事が重なる be swamped [snowed under] with work [business] / 重なり合って倒れる fall on top of one another. 文例⇩

かさねがさね 重ね重ね repeatedly; frequently; over and over (again); over [again and] again ¶重ね重ねの repeated; a series of / 重ね重ねの不幸 a series of misfortunes / 重ね重ね面倒をかける frequently put [be forever putting] *sb* to trouble.

かさねぎ 重ね着 ¶シャツを3枚重ね着する wear three undershirts one over another.

かさねる 重ねる 〈積む〉pile [heap] up; put 《books》on top of each other [of one another]; 《文》place 〈articles〉one upon another; 〈繰り返す〉repeat ¶重ねて 〈積み重ねて〉in piles [layers]; one on top of the other (2つ); on top of one another (3つ以上); 〈繰り返して〉repeatedly / 新聞紙を2枚重ねて包む wrap *sth* in two thicknesses [in two sheets] of newspaper / 日を重ねる spend many days [day after day]. 文例⇩

かさばる 嵩張る be bulky ¶嵩張った bulky; unwieldy.

かさぶた 瘡蓋 a (dried) scab.

かざみ(どり) 風見(鶏) a weather [wind] vane; a weathercock (雄鶏の飾りのある).

かさむ 嵩む 〈増す〉pile up; 《文》increase (in amount [volume]); 〈金額が〉run [go, mount] up (to a large sum); 〈文〉借金がかさむ *one's* debts increase [mount up]; 〈人が主語〉get deeper (and deeper) in debt.

かざむき 風向き 〈風の吹く方向〉the direction of the wind; the wind direction; 〈形勢〉the situation; 〈機嫌〉《文》*one's* humor ¶風向きがいい[悪い] 〈形勢〉the situation is in [not in] *one's* favor; 《文》the situation is favorable [unfavorable] to *one*; 〈機嫌〉be in a good [bad] temper [mood]; 《文》be in good [ill] humor / 風向きを知る 〈風の方向〉know which way the wind blows; 〈形勢〉see which way the wind blows [the cat jumps].

かざよけ 風除け a windbreak. 文例⇩

かざり 飾り 〈装飾〉an ornament; a decoration; 〈衣装の〉(lace) trimmings ¶新年のお飾り New Year's decorations; 〈鏡餅〉⇨ かがみもち / 飾りの ornamental; decorative / レースの飾りのついた服 a dress trimmed with lace / 飾りのない simple; plain; 《文》unadorned / 飾りに for decorative purposes / 飾りだな a display shelf (for trophies); a whatnot / 飾りボタン an ornamental button; a fancy button (変わり型の). 文例⇩

かざりけ 飾り気 《文》affectation ¶飾り気のない unaffected; 〈率直な〉plain; frank; straightforward; candid. 文例⇩

かざりたてる 飾り立てる decorate *sth* ornately [gaudily]; deck out; dress up (服装を) ⇨ かざる ¶宝石で身を飾り立てる deck *oneself* out with jewels; 《文》adorn *oneself* with jewels.

かざりつけ 飾り付け decorations; arrangements ¶店の飾り付け shop decorations; window dressing / クリスマスツリーに飾り付けをする decorate a Christmas tree.

かざりつける 飾り付ける decorate 《a room》; arrange 〈flowers〉; dress (a shopwindow).

かざりまど 飾り窓 ⇨ ショーウインドー

かざりもの 飾り物 〈装飾品〉an ornament; a decoration; 〈名目だけの存在〉a figurehead. 文例⇩

かざる 飾る decorate; 《文》ornament; 《文》adorn; dress (陳列窓を); embellish (潤色する); 〈陳列する〉put *sth* on show; exhibit; display; 〈気取る〉give *oneself* [put on] airs ¶言葉を飾る use fine language; 《文》use fair words / 部屋を絵で飾る decorate a room with pictures / 宝石で身を飾る adorn *oneself* with jewels. 文例⇩

用法 adorn は特に人について用いられることが多いが, decorate や ornament は人には用いることができない.

かさん 加算 addition ¶加算する 〈加える〉add; 〈算入する〉include / 加算税 an additional tax.

かざん 火山 a volcano (*pl.* -(e)s) ¶火山の volcanic / 火山学 volcanology / 火山活動 volcanic activity / 火山国 a volcanic country / 火山岩 volcanic rock / 火山測候所 a volcanological observatory / 火山弾 【地質】a volcanic bomb / 火山灰 volcanic ash / 火山脈[帯] a

---

breeze.

かさなる 今年は子供の日と日曜日とが重なっている。Children's Day falls on Sunday this year.

かさねる 重ねて質問します。Let me ask another question. / この事は重ねて申すまでもありません。I don't think I need to repeat it.

かざむき 風向きが北に変わったのでわが家は類焼を免れた。The wind having shifted [veered around] to the north, my house was saved from the fire. / どうも風向きが悪くなってきたぞ。Things are turning [starting to go] against me.

かざよけ これらの樹は家の風よけになる。These trees protect [shelter] the house from the wind.

かざり それは飾り井戸なんですよ。That is a false well, put there for decorative purposes.

かざりけ 彼は少しも飾り気がない。He is quite unaffected [without affectation]. / He is quite a plain, modest man.

かざりもの 彼は飾り物の社長さ。He is the president of the firm in name only; he has practically no authority. / He is merely a figurehead president.

かざる 一束の花が食卓に飾ってあった。The table was ornamented with a bunch of flowers. / ウィンドーに色々の品が飾ってある。Various goods are on show [display] in the window. / 彼のようなうわべを飾る人は嫌いだ。I don't like showy [ostentatious] people like him.

かさん 利子を加算すれば100万円以上になる。It comes [amounts] to more than a million yen if you include the interest.

かし 河岸を変えて飲み直そうじゃないか。Let's go to a different bar

かさんか 過酸化 ¶過酸化水素 hydrogen peroxide / 過酸化物 (a) peroxide.
かさんめいし 可算名詞《文法》a countable noun ¶不可算名詞 an uncountable noun.
かし¹ 下肢 the lower limbs; the legs.
かし² 仮死 suspended animation; apparent death ¶仮死状態にある be in a (temporary) state of apparent death.
かし³ 河岸 a riverside; a river bank; ⟨魚市場⟩ a fish market ¶向こう河岸 (on) the opposite [other] side of the river / 河岸を変える try [go to] another place [somewhere else]. 文例⇩
かし⁴ 菓子 confectionery (総称); ⟨生菓子⟩ (a) cake; ⟨パイ類⟩ pastry; ⟨糖菓⟩ ⟨米⟩ candy;《英》sweets ¶菓子折り a box of cakes / 菓子器 a cake box (★形が丸くても box と言う) / 菓子皿 a tea plate / 菓子パン a sweetened bun / 菓子屋⟨店⟩ a confectionery;《米》a candy store;《英》a sweet shop; ⟨人⟩ a confectioner.
かし⁵ 貸し ⟨貸付金⟩ a loan; ⟨売り掛け金⟩ a bill; ⟨賃貸⟩ hire; rent ¶貸し衣装 ⇨ かしいしょう / 貸し金庫 a safe-deposit box (for rent) / 貸し自転車 a bicycle for rent; a rental bicycle / 貸し席 a room for [on] hire / 貸しボート a boat for [on] hire / 貸し別荘[店舗] a villa [store] for rent. 文例⇩
かし⁶ 歌詞 the words of a song; the (song) lyrics.
かし⁷ 樫《植》an oak (tree) ¶かしの実 an acorn.
カし⁸ カ氏 ¶カ氏72度 72 degrees Fahrenheit; 72°F / カ氏寒暖計 a Fahrenheit thermometer.
かじ¹ 火事 a fire ¶大火事 a big [large] fire;《文》a conflagration / 火事が起こる a fire breaks out [《文》occurs,《文》takes place] / 火事を起こす cause [start] a fire / 火事に遭う suffer from a fire / 火事で焼ける be burned in a fire; be destroyed by fire / 火事見舞いに行く call on sb to express one's sympathy after a fire / 火事場 the scene of a fire / 火事場泥棒 a looter; a thief at a fire / 火事場泥棒を働く loot [steal sth] at a fire / ⟨比喩的に⟩ fish in troubled waters. 文例⇩
かじ² 加持 ⟨まじない⟩ an incantation; ⟨信仰治療⟩ faith healing; a faith cure ¶加持祈禱を行なう perform incantations; practice faith healing.
かじ³ 家事 housework (★狭義には,家の中の掃除・整理の意で,炊事を含まない); housekeeping; domestic duties [chores] ¶家事の手伝いをする help ⟨one's mother⟩ with the housework / 家事の見習をする learn housekeeping under sb / 家事をする do housework [household tasks]; keep house / 家事を取り締まる be in charge of the affairs of the household.
かじ⁴ 舵 ⟨舵板⟩ a rudder; ⟨舵柄⟩ a tiller; ⟨舵輪⟩ a (steering) wheel ¶かじを取る steer《a boat》; be at the tiller; ⟨操る⟩ manage; control; ⟨国を⟩ be at the helm (of state) / かじを誤る steer a ship in the wrong direction; take a wrong course / かじ取り ⟨事⟩ steering; ⟨人⟩ a helmsman; a steersman; ⟨ボートの⟩ a cox; a coxswain. 文例⇩
がし 餓死 death from hunger; starvation ¶餓死する die of hunger; starve [be starved] to death.
かしいしょう 貸衣装 costumes for rent [hire] ¶貸し衣装のタキシードを着て現われる appear in a hired dinner jacket / 貸衣装屋 a dress hire firm; ⟨芝居・仮装用の⟩ a costumer; a costumier.
かじか 鰍 ⟨魚⟩ a miller's-thumb; a sculpin.
かじか(がえる) 河鹿(蛙) a kajika frog.
かしかた 貸方《簿記》the credit [creditor] (略: cr.); the credit [creditor] side ¶貸方に記入する enter《an item》on the credit side; enter [place, put] 《a sum》to sb's credit; credit 《a sum》to sb / 貸方残高 a credit [creditor] balance / 貸方票[勘定,記入] a credit note [account, entry].
かじかむ go numb [be numbed] with cold. 文例⇩
かしかり 貸し借り borrowing and [or] lending ⇨ たいしゃく. 文例⇩
かしかん 下士官 ⟨陸軍⟩ a noncommissioned officer; ⟨海軍⟩ a petty officer.
かじき ⟨魚⟩ a spearfish (まかじき); a swordfish (めかじき); a sailfish (ばしょうかじき).
かしきり 貸切り ⟨予約した⟩ reserved;《英》booked / 貸切りバス[飛行機] a chartered bus [plane]. 文例⇩
かしきん 貸金 a loan ¶貸金を回収する collect [call in] loans.

---

and start drinking again, shall we?
かし⁴ これは食べる菓子じゃなくて見る菓子だ. This is a cake for looking at, not for eating.
かし⁵ 彼に10万円ほど貸しがある. He is in my debt to the tune of 100,000 yen. | He owes me 100,000 yen. / 彼には貸しがあるからいやは言わないだろう. He's in my debt, so he's unlikely to refuse.
かじ¹ 火事はどこだ. Where is the fire? / 君の家が火事だ. Your house is on fire. / ゆうべ近所に火事があった. There was a fire near my house [in our neighborhood] last night. / 私は火事に遭ったことはない. I have never had [experienced] a fire. / その火事は風呂屋が火元だった. The fire started in a public bathhouse. / その火事で150戸焼失した. One hundred and fifty houses were destroyed in the fire. / 火事で蔵書を全部焼いてしまった. I had all my books burned in the fire.
かじ⁴ かじが利かない. The ship doesn't answer to the helm. / 彼のような有力者がかじ取りになったのだから, もう大丈夫だ. Now that we've got a strong man like him at the helm, things are sure to go well.
かじかむ 指がかじかんでペンが持てない. My fingers are so numbed [stiff] with cold that I can't hold my pen.
かしかり これで君とはもう貸し借りなしだ. Now we are all square. | (口語) Now we be quits.
かしきり この車両は貸切りだ. This carriage [car] is reserved.

かしぐ 傾ぐ ⇨ かたむく.
かしげる 傾げる ⇨ かたむける ¶首を少しかしげる[かしげて] put [with] one's head a little to one side.
かしこい 賢い wise; clever;《口語》bright; intelligent;《文》sagacious,《米》smart ¶賢く wisely; cleverly;〈如才なく〉tactfully / 賢く立ち回る act smartly / 賢そうな intelligent-looking.
かしこうせん 可視光線 visible rays (of light).
かしこし 貸越し〈当座預金の〉an overdraft ¶貸越しになっている〈当座預金が〉be overdrawn.
かしこまる 畏まる〈正座する〉sit straight [upright, respectfully].
かしずく wait on sb;《文》attend on sb.
かしだおれ 貸倒れ a bad [an irrecoverable] debt ¶貸倒れになる become irrecoverable / 貸倒れ準備金 a bad debt reserve.
かしだし 貸出し lending; a loan; an advance ¶貸出しをする make a loan (to);〈貸出し〉lend [loan] out / 図書館の貸出しを利用する use the lending [loan] service of a library / (図書館の本などが)貸出しになっている be out on loan.
かしだす 貸し出す ⇨ かしだし (貸出しをする).
かしちん 貸賃〈土地・家屋・テレビなどの〉rent;〈乗物などを〉hire; a hire charge.
かしつ[1] 加湿 humidification ¶加湿器 a humidifier.
かしつ[2] 過失〈失策〉a fault;〈誤り〉a mistake;《文》an error; a blunder;〈不慮の事〉an accident;〈怠慢〉negligence ¶過失を犯す blunder;《文》commit an error; make a mistake [a blunder] / 過失傷害罪 accidental [unintentional] infliction of injury / 過失致死罪 (a) homicide by misadventure.
かじつ 果実 (a) fruit;《法》fruit(s).
がしつ 画室 ⇨ アトリエ.
かしつけ 貸付 lending ¶貸付金 a loan; an advance / 貸付信託 a loan trust.
かしつける 貸し付ける ⇨ かす[2].
かして[ぬし] 貸し手[主] the lender;〈金貸の〉the creditor;〈不動産の〉the lessor; the landlord; the landlady (女) (★ ただし法律的な話などでは男女ともに landlord と言う).
かじぼう 梶棒 shafts ¶梶棒1本をさす時はもちろん a shaft.
かしほん 貸本 a book to loan out;《米》a book for rent;《英》a book for hire ¶貸本屋《米》a rental library;《英》a commercial lending library.
かしま 貸間《米》a room for rent;《英》a room to let. 文例⇩
かしましい 姦しい noisy;《文》clamorous.

カシミヤ cashmere ¶カシミヤのコート a cashmere coat.
かしや 貸家《米》a house for rent;《英》a house to let ¶貸家を捜す hunt [look] for a house for rent / 貸家に住む live in a rented house / 貸家札 a 'for rent' [《英》'to let'] notice.
かしゃ 貨車《米》a freight car;《英》a goods wagon [van] ¶貨車1両分 a carload (of freight);《英》a wagonload (of goods).
かじや 鍛冶屋〈人〉a blacksmith; a smith;〈仕事場〉a smithy; a blacksmith's shop.
かしゃく[1] 仮借 ¶仮借なく without mercy; ruthlessly;〈手をゆるめずに〉mercilessly; relentlessly; unsparingly.
かしゃく[2] 呵責 ¶良心のかしゃくに悩む one's conscience pricks one;《文》feel the pricks of conscience; be tormented by a guilty conscience.
かしゅ[1] 火酒 spirits;《文》ardent spirits.
かしゅ[2] 歌手 a singer; a vocalist.
かじゅ 果樹 a fruit tree ¶果樹園 an orchard; a fruit farm / 果樹栽培 fruit growing [cultivation] / 果樹栽培業者[果樹園経営者] a fruit grower [farmer].
かしゅう 歌集 a collection of tanka [poems]; an anthology (選歌集); a song book (唱歌集).
かじゅう[1] 加重 weighting;《法》aggravation ¶加重する weight; aggravate / 加重平均《統計》a weighted average [mean].
かじゅう[2] 果汁 fruit juice;〈果汁入り飲料水〉a fruit drink.
かじゅう[3] 荷重《機》load ¶荷重試験 a load test.
がしゅう 画集 a book of paintings [drawings] ¶レンブラント画集《書名》Collected Paintings of Rembrandt.
かしょ 箇所〈場所〉a place; a spot;〈地点〉a point;〈部分〉a part; a portion; a passage (文章の) ¶同じ箇所に in the same place;〈注解などに記して〉loc. cit. (★ ラテン語 loco citato の略).
かじょ 花序《植》inflorescence.
かしょう[1] 仮称 a tentative [provisional] name ¶…と仮称する call [name] sth … tentatively [provisionally, for the time being].
かしょう[2] 河床 the riverbed.
かしょう[3] 過小[少] ¶過小評価する underestimate; underrate; belittle.
かしょう[4] 歌唱《事》singing;〈歌〉a song ¶歌唱力 one's skill as a singer / 歌唱力がある be a talented singer.
かじょう[1] 下情 ¶下情に通じている《文》be well acquainted with the life of the (common)

かしこまる かしこまりました. Certainly, sir. | Very good, sir. / そんなにかしこまるには及ばない. Don't stand on ceremony so much.
かしつ[2] それは過失でなく, 故意にしたことである. It was not done by accident, but by design. / 出火の原因は過失か放火か. Was the fire accidental or deliberate?
かしま 貸間あり.《掲示》《米》Rooms for rent. |《英》Rooms to let.
かしや 貸家.《掲示》《米》For rent. |《英》To let.
かしょ 彼は数箇所に傷を受けた. He was wounded [injured] in several places. | He received several wounds.

かしら 頭右[左, 中]!《号令》Eyes right [left, front]!
-かしら 本当かしら. I wonder if it's true. / 彼はどうなったのかしら. I wonder what's become of him.
かしらもじ 文章のはじめの語は頭文字で書きなさい. Begin the first word in a sentence with a capital

かじょう people [the living conditions of the masses].
かじょう² 過剰 《文》(an) excess; a surplus; 《文》overabundance ¶過剰の too much; excessive;〈余計な〉superfluous; excess / 過剰人員 superfluous personnel;《文》supernumeraries / 人口過剰 surplus population / 過剰投資 overinvestment /（薬剤の）過剰投与《医》overdosage / 過剰投与する overdose.
かじょう³ 渦状 ⇨ うずまき ¶渦状星雲 a spiral nebula / 渦状紋〈指紋の〉a whorl.
かじょう⁴ 箇条〈項目〉an article; a clause; an item;〈規約〉a provision ¶8箇条の要求 an eight-point demand / 10箇条より成る consist of ten articles / 箇条書きにする itemize.
がしょう¹ 画商 a picture [an art] dealer ¶画商の店 an art shop; a (commercial art) gallery.
がしょう² 賀正 ⇨ きんがしんねん.
がじょう 牙城 a stronghold (of conservatism);《文》a bastion (of reaction) ¶敵の牙城に迫る threaten the enemy's citadel [fort].
かしら 頭〈頭部〉the head;〈首脳〉the head; a leader; a chief; a boss (親分) ¶人の頭に立つ become [be looked up to as] a leader; lead others. 文例⇩
-かしら I wonder (if [whether, how, when, where, who, what]...). 文例⇩
かしらもじ 頭文字〈初めの1字〉the first letter (of a word);〈名前の〉one's initials;〈大文字〉a capital letter ¶頭文字を組み合わせて作った略語 an acronym（ 例えば the United Nations Educational, Scientific, and Cultural Organization の略語 UNESCO のようなもの）/ 頭文字で書く write in capitals [capital letters] / 頭文字で書き起こす capitalize《a word》/ 頭文字で（略式の）署名をする initial《a paper》.
かじりつく 齧り付く〈食い付く〉fasten one's teeth in; bite (at);〈すがり付く〉hold on to; cling to ¶仕事にかじり付く stick at one's job [work].
かじる 齧る bite (at); gnaw (at); nibble (at); crunch (rice crackers)（ばりばり音を立てて）¶りんごをかじる munch an apple /（ねずみなどが）壁をかじって穴をあける gnaw a hole through [in] a wall / …を少しかじっている〈知っている〉have a smattering of《Latin》; know a (little) bit of《French》/ かじり取る bite [nibble] off. 文例⇩
かしわ 柏《植》an oak (tree) ¶柏もち《菓子》a rice cake wrapped in an oak leaf;〈寝かた〉sleeping rolled up in a single quilt.
かしわで 柏手 ¶柏手を打つ clap one's hands《in worship at a Shinto shrine》.
かしん¹ 家臣 a vassal; a retainer.

かしん² 過信 ¶過信する put [《文》place] too much confidence (in); be overconfident (in) / 自己の能力を過信する have too much confidence in oneself; overestimate one's own abilities.
かじん¹ 佳人 a beautiful woman. 文例⇩
かじん² 家人 one's family; one's people. 文例⇩
かじん³ 歌人 a poet.
かす¹ 滓, 渣〈おり〉dregs; lees; grounds (特にコーヒーの);〈浮きかす〉scum;〈くず〉refuse ¶くず ¶かす汁 soup with a sake lees base / かす漬け vegetables [fish] pickled in sake lees.
かす² 貸す〈金品を〉lend;《米》loan;〈用立てる〉《文》accommodate sb (with money);〈掛け売りする〉give sb credit;〈家・土地を賃貸する〉《米》rent;《英》let;〈家・土地以外の物を賃貸する〉《米》rent out;《英》hire out;〈電話などを〉let sb use ¶知恵を貸す give advice [《文》counsel (to) / 手を貸す give [lend] sb a helping hand / 時を貸す give [allow] sb [sth] time / 部屋を貸す rent [《英》let] a room to sb / 耳を貸す《文》lend one's ear《to》;《文》give ear《to》; listen《to》. 文例⇩
用法 lend は持ち運びのできるものを「貸す」時に用い, 電話など持ち運びのできないものを「貸す」時には let sb use《one's telephone》とする. 家・土地などを「貸す」時は《米》では rent, 《英》では let が普通で稀に《米》も rent を用い, 家・土地以外の物の賃貸には《米》では rent out, 《英》では hire out を使う.
かず 数 a number ¶数が多い the number of《students》is large; there are [is] a large number of《people》;《文》be large in number / 数が少ない the number of《students》is small; there are not many《people》;《文》be small [few] in number / 数がふえる the number of《jobless people》grows [increases];《文》grow [increase] in number / 数がわからなくなる lose count《of》/ 数を間違える count wrong(-ly); miscount the number《of children》/ 数をそろえる make up the number(s)《of》; get [《文》secure] the number《of people [items]》required / 数に限りがある there are (only) limited numbers [a limited number] of《tickets》;《文》be limited in number / 数に物を言わせて by sheer weight [force] of numbers / 数に入れる count sb [sth] (in); include sb [sth] in the number / 数に入れない do not include sb [sth]; count sb [sth] out / 物の数に入らない be insignificant; count for nothing; do not count / 数でこなす《商業上》make profits through [by means of] quantity sales [high turnover] / 物の数とも思わない make [think] nothing of; take no account of / 数多く《文》(appear) in large numbers / 数限りない in-

letter.
かじる ねずみがりんごをかじっていた. I found a rat gnawing at an apple. / 彼は何でも少しずつかじっている. He knows something [a bit] about everything. / 彼は高校でドイツ語を少しかじっていた. He learned a little German in [《英》at] high school.

かじん¹ 佳人薄命. Beauty and long life seldom go hand in hand.
かじん² 家人の留守中に泥棒が入った. The house was broken into while the people were out.
かす² 彼に10万円貸してくれと頼まれた. He asked me for a loan of [to lend him] 100,000 yen. / 彼は青山にある家を人に貸して, 自

分は大磯に引っ越した. He rented out his house in Aoyama and moved to Oiso. / この部屋なら月5万円で貸せる. This room rents for 50,000 yen a month. / ちょっとそれを貸してごらん. Let me have it. | Let me see. / 電話を貸していただけますか. May I use the telephone?

ガス (a) gas; 〈濃霧〉 (a) (dense [thick]) fog ¶〈海や山で〉ガスが発生する a fog rises / ガスのメーター a gas meter / ガスをつける [消す] turn the gas on [off] / ガス状の gaseous / ガス壊疽(えそ)〖医〗gas gangrene / ガス壊疽菌 a gas bacillus / ガス会社 a gas company / ガス管 (本管) a gas main (本管) / ガスこんろ a gas heater / ガス室 〈第2次世界大戦でナチスドイツが処刑用に造った〉a gas chamber / ガスストーブ a gas stove [heater] / ガス代 gas charges [rates]; one's gas bill (請求書) / ガス台 a gas ring [burner] / ガスタービン a gas turbine / ガスタンク a gas tank; (英) a gasholder / ガス中毒 gas-poisoning / ガス灯 a gaslight; a gaslamp / ガス爆発 a gas explosion / ガスマスク a gas mask / ガス漏れ a gas leak; an escape of gas / ガス屋 a gasman; 〈検針員〉a gas-meter reader; 〈集金人〉a gas-bill collector; 〈取付け係〉a gas fitter / ガス湯わかし器 a gas water heater; (英) a geyser / ガスライター a gas lighter / ガスレンジ a gas cooker [range]. 文例⇩

かすい 河水 river water ¶河水の増減 the rise and fall of water in a river.

かすいぶんかい 加水分解〖化〗hydrolysis ¶加水分解する hydrolyze; be hydrolyzed.

かすか 微か ¶かすかな 〈はっきりしない〉faint; dim; (文) indistinct; 〈少しの〉slight / かすかな希望 a faint [slight] hope / かすかに 〈ぼんやり〉faintly; dimly; (文) indistinctly; 〈少し〉slightly. 文例⇩

かすがい 鎹 a clamp; a cramp (iron). 文例⇩

かすかす ¶すれてる ¶かすかすのりんご a juiceless [dry] apple.

カスタード custard ¶カスタードプリン a [an egg, a baked] custard; a crème caramel (キャラメルソース付きの).

カスタネット (a pair of) castanets.

カステラ [く《ポルトガル語》pão de Castella] sponge cake.

かずのこ 数の子 herring roe.

カスピかい カスピ海 the Caspian Sea.

かすみ 霞 (a) haze; (a) mist ¶かすみのかかった hazy; misty / かすみを食って生きる live on air / かすみ網 a (Japanese) mist net. 文例⇩

かすむ 霞む grow hazy [dim]; be misted; be blurred. 文例⇩

かすめる 掠める 〈奪う〉rob; plunder; 〈体に触れて過ぎる〉graze; 〈すれすれに飛ぶ〉skim ¶〈弾丸が〉肩先をかすめる go [whiz] past one's shoulder / 人目をかすめて stealthily; (文) by stealth; (口語) on the sly. 文例⇩

かすり 絣 a splashed pattern ¶かすりの着物 a kimono with splashed patterns.

かすりきず 掠り傷 a scratch ¶かすり傷を受ける get a scratch (on the hand). 文例⇩

かする¹ 科する impose ((a fine on sb)); inflict ((a penalty on sb)).

かする² 掠る graze.

かする³ 課する ¶〈税を〉lay [levy] ((a tax on sth)); 〈仕事を〉set [(文) assign] sb (a task); impose ((a task on sb)) ¶宿題を課する set [(文) assign] (one's pupils) homework.

かすれる 掠れる ¶〈声が〉get [(文) become] hoarse [husky]; 〈ペンが〉be scratchy; 〈文字などが〉be (faint and) patchy.

かせ¹ 枷 shackles; fetters (足かせ); handcuffs (手かせ) ¶かせをかける shackle; 〈足かせ〉fetter; 〈手かせ〉handcuff; put handcuffs on sb.

かせ² 桛 a reel.

かぜ¹ 風 a wind; a breeze (微風); a draft (外から吹込む風); a current of air ★wind は主として自然現象の風に限られる。扇風機の風は wind ではなく, a current of air. a current of air は自然の風,人工の風を問わない. draft は一般に「すき間風」と訳されるが,もっと意味が広く,室内や車内に窓などから吹き込んで来

かず 生徒の数は600に近い. The number of students is close on six hundred. / これは数ある中の一例に過ぎない. This is only one instance among many. / 犠牲者は何千という数にのぼった. Victims numbered in the thousands.

ガス 私の家にはガスが引いてある. We have gas laid on in the house. / ガスがついている. The gas is on. / ガスは消えている. The gas is off. / 1か月にどれ程ガスを使いますか. 〈分量〉How much gas do you use [burn] a month? / 〈料金〉What is your monthly gas bill? / How much a month do you pay for gas? / ガス臭いのに気がついて台所へ行って見ると,ゴム管の割れ目から漏れていた. I smelled gas and went to the kitchen to find it escaping from a crack in the pipe. / 貸家: ガス,水道完備. 〈掲示〉House for Rent: with all main services.

かすか 寺の鐘の音かすかに聞こえる. The sound of the temple bell can be faintly heard. / You can just hear the faint sound of the temple bell. / 筑波山が遠くにかすかに見える. Mt. Tsukuba is dimly visible in the distance. / その事はかすかに覚えています. I have a faint recollection [dim memory] of it.

かすがい 子はかすがい. Children are said [supposed] to bring [hold] their parents together.

かすみ 山々にかすみがかかっていた. A haze [mist] lay [hung] over the hills.

かすむ 涙で目がかすんだ. My eyes misted with tears. / Tears blurred [dimmed] my eyes. / 年を取ると目がかすむ. One's sight grows dim with age.

かすめる 1羽の鳥が水面をかすめて飛び去った. A bird skimmed over the water.

かすりきず 彼はかすり傷一つ受けなかった. He escaped without a scratch (on him).

かぜ¹ 風が吹いていた. The wind was blowing. / 風が出た. The wind rose [sprang up]. / また風が出てきた. The wind is getting up again. / 風が強まった. It began to blow harder. / The wind grew stronger. / 風がやんだ. The wind fell [dropped, died down]. / 風がちょっと静まった. There was a

かぜ る風も draft である ¶ 一陣の風 a blast [gust] of wind / かすかな風 a breath of air; a light gentle wind [breeze] / 激しい風 a violent [high] wind; a stiff breeze / 身を切るような風 a cutting [biting, nipping] wind / 風の強い[ない]日 a windy [windless] day / 風の神 the god of the wind / どうした風の吹き回しか by a curious turn of events; for some reason or other / 風の便りに聞くと I heard say that…; It has come to my ears that… / 風を通す[入れる] let 《O》 admit) fresh air (into); ventilate; air (clothes, a room) / 風をくらって逃げる beat a hasty retreat; take to *one's* heels / 風を物ともせず in the teeth of the wind / 風に向かって《walk》in [against] the wind / 風になびく草 the grass waving in the wind / 風に翻る flutter in the wind / 風に運ばれて来る come [《文》be borne] in on the wind; be blown in / どこ吹く風と澄ました顔をしている look [pretend to be] quite unconcerned. 文例⇩

かぜ² 風邪 (a) cold; 《医》the common cold ¶ 風邪を引く catch (a) cold; take (a) cold / ひどい風邪を引く catch a bad cold / 風邪を引いている have a cold / 風邪を引いて寝ている be in bed [be down, be laid up] with a cold / 風邪を引きかけている be getting [coming down with] a cold / 風邪を引き直す catch a fresh cold / 風邪気味だ have a slight [a touch of] cold / 風邪薬 (a) cold medicine [cure].

かぜあたり 風当たり ¶ 風当たりが強い 〈風が主語〉 blow hard 《against the house》; 〈場所が主語〉 be wind-swept; be windy; 〈人や事が主語〉 be under attack [pressure]; be criticized; 《文》be subject to criticism. 文例⇩

かせい¹ 火星 《天》Mars ¶ 火星の Martian / 火星人 a Martian. 文例⇩

かせい² 火勢 the force of the fire [flames].

かせい³ 加勢 〈助力〉backing up; support; help; 〈援助〉assistance; aid; 〈援兵〉reinforcements ¶ 加勢する back *sb* up; support; help; 《文》assist; 《文》aid; 〈肩を持つ〉take sides with; side with.

かせい⁴ 仮性 ¶ 仮性近視 false myopia [near-sightedness].

かせい⁵ 苛性 《化》¶ 苛性カリ[ソーダ] caustic potash [soda].

かせい⁶ 家政 〈家庭を治めること〉housekeeping; 〈家庭の経済〉domestic economy ¶ 家政が上手[下手]である be a good [bad] housekeeper [housewife, 《米》homemaker] / 家政を処理する keep house; manage *one's* household / 家政科[学部] a course in [the department of] domestic science / 家政学 domestic science; home economics / 家政婦 a (paid) housekeeper / 《英》a daily help.

かぜい 課税 〈事〉taxation; 〈税〉a tax ¶ 課税する tax; impose [levy] a tax [duties] 《on *sb* [*sth*]》 / 個人の所得に課税する tax the income of an individual / 重く課税する tax 《luxury goods》heavily; impose a heavy tax 《on》 / 課税の対象となる be subject to taxation; be taxable; be an object of taxation / 課税価額 the taxable amount; the assessed value (額) / 課税所得 taxable income / 課税品 a taxable article; 〈税関での〉a dutiable article / 課税率 a tax rate.

かせいがん 火成岩 《地質》igneous rock.

カゼイン 《化》casein.

かせき 化石 a fossil; fossil remains 《of early man》 ¶ 生きた化石 a living fossil / 動物[植物]の化石 a fossil animal [plant] / 化石になる fossilize / 化石学 fossilology / 化石学者 a fossilologist / 化石層 a fossiliferous stratum / 化石燃料 fossil fuels.

かせぎ 稼ぎ 〈働き〉labor; work; 〈稼ぎ高〉 (*one's*) earnings; 〈人の〉income ¶ 稼ぎに出る go to work; hire *oneself* out / 時間稼ぎに to gain time / 稼ぎ口 work; a job / 稼ぎ手 〈一家の〉the breadwinner; the provider; 〈よく働く人〉a hard worker. 文例⇩

かせぐ 稼ぐ 〈精出して働く〉work hard; 〈働いて金を得る〉earn 《a sum of money》; 〈働いて暮らしを立てる〉work for *one's* living; earn *one's* living ¶ 1日に5千円稼ぐ make [earn] 5,000 yen a day / よく稼ぐ work hard; be a hard worker / 時間を稼ぐ play for time; gain time 《to plan *one's* tactics》. 文例⇩

---

lull in the wind. / 風は少しも[そよとの風も]ない。There is not a breath of air. / 大変な風だ。It is blowing a gale. / There is a strong wind. / 風はどの方向から吹いていますか。Which direction [quarter] does the wind blow from? / 風は西から吹いている。The wind is blowing from the west. / 風が南に変わった。The wind has shifted to the south. / 窓に風が当たる。The wind is blowing against the window. / その窓は閉めないで。少し風を入れた方がいいから。Don't close that window. Let a little air circulate. / 帽子を風に飛ばされた。I had my hat blown off (by the wind). / ろうそくの火が風に揺らめいた。The candlelight flickered in the wind. / 風でともし火が消えた。The wind blew out the light. / 子供は風の子。Children are open-air creatures. / Children are happy to be outdoors in all weathers [whatever the weather]. / 人生は、風の吹き回し次第で、どうなるか分からないものだ。We live haphazard lives subject to the varying winds of fortune.

かぜ 風邪がなかなか抜けない。I can't get rid of my cold. / 君の風邪がうつった。You've given me your cold. / I've caught your cold. / 僕のは普通の風邪で、流感じゃない。Mine is the common cold, not flu.

かぜあたり 地位が上がると世間の風当たりも強くなるものだ。People judge you more severely [are harder on you] the higher [further up] you get on the social ladder.

かせい² 火勢が強い。The flames are raging furiously. / 火勢が衰えた。The fire has gone down.

かせい⁶ 1週間程家政婦に来てもらおう。I'll have a woman in to keep house for me for a week or so.

かせぎ 彼はいい稼ぎになる仕事を見つけた。He found a job that carried good pay. / あの家ではたった一人の稼ぎ手に死なれた。That family has lost their only support.

かせぐ 稼ぐに追いつく貧乏なし。

かせつ¹ 仮設 ¶仮設住宅 a temporary dwelling; temporary housing (総称).

かせつ² 仮説 a hypothesis 《pl. -potheses》 ¶仮説の hypothetical /…という仮説に基づいて on the hypothesis that… / 仮説を立てる set up a hypothesis; hypothesize.

かせつ³ 架設 construction; building ¶架設する《文》construct (a railroad); build (a bridge); lay (a cable); install (a telephone).

カセット a (tape) cassette; 〈録音した〉a cassette recording ¶カセットテープ a cassette tape / カセットテープレコーダー a cassette (tape) recorder.

かぜとおし 風通し ventilation ¶風通しがいい[悪い] be well [poorly] ventilated; be airy [close, stuffy].

かせん¹ 下線 an underline ¶下線を引く underline [underscore] 《a word》/ 下線を引いた部分 an underlined [underscored] part.

かせん² 化繊 ⇨ かがく² (化学繊維).

かせん³ 河川 rivers ¶河川の改修 river improvement / 河川系 a river system / 河川工事 river conservation work / 河川敷(ｼｷ) a (dry) riverbed.

かせん⁴ 架線 〈事〉overhead [aerial] wiring; 〈線〉an overhead (power) line ¶架線工事 wiring work / 架線工夫《米》a lineman;《英》a linesman.

かせん⁵ 寡占《経》oligopoly ¶買手寡占《経》oligopsony / 寡占経済 oligopolistic economy / 寡占市場 an oligopolistic market.

かぜん 果然 sure enough; as one thought [expected]; as was expected.

がぜん 俄然 suddenly; all of a sudden.

かそ 過疎〈人口の〉depopulation ¶人口の過疎に悩む suffer from depopulation / 過疎地域 a depopulated area.

かそう¹ 下層 a lower [an underlying] layer [stratum] ¶下層雲(ｳﾝ) lower clouds / 下層階級 the lower classes / 下層社会 the lower strata of society; (the language of) the gutter / 下層土 subsoil.

かそう² 火葬 (a) cremation ¶火葬にする cremate; burn (a dead body) to ashes / 火葬場 a crematory;《英》a crematorium 《pl. -s, -toria》.

かそう³ 仮装 (a) disguise; (a) fancy dress ¶仮装する disguise oneself 《as》; be disguised 《as》/ 仮装行列 a fancy-dress parade / 仮装舞踏会 a costume [fancy-dress, masked] ball;《文》a masquerade.

かそう⁴ 仮想 imagination; (a) supposition ¶仮想する imagine; assume; suppose / 仮想の imaginary / 仮想敵国 a hypothetical [potential] enemy.

かそう⁵ 家相 the 'physiognomy' of a house (regarded as lucky or unlucky); the divination of the auspices of a house from its position, etc.

がぞう 画像 〈テレビの〉a picture;〈肖像〉a portrait;《文》one's likeness.

かぞえうた 数え歌 a counting(-out) rhyme.

かぞえかた 数え方 the counting system; a way [《文》manner] of counting ¶日本流の数え方で according to the Japanese way of counting (ages); by Japanese count. 文例⑥

かぞえどし 数え年 ¶数え年で7つを be in one's seventh (calendar) year ★英語で「数え年」をわかりやすく説明するには the same way that you count the ages of horses in the West と言うのも一法である。子馬が生まれたら a yearling, 正月を過ぎたら a two-year-old と言う.

かぞえる 数える count; reckon; calculate;《文》number ¶10 数える count ten / 100 から逆に数える count back from a hundred to one / 素早く数える make a quick count (of the cars) / (金などを)数えて出す count out (10 five-dollar bills) / 明日から数えて 50 年前に fifty years ago tomorrow /…の中に数えられるを be counted [《文》numbered] among… / 世界の大発明家の中に数えられる rank [be reckoned] among the world's greatest inventors / 数え立てる[上げる] count [reckon] up;《文》enumerate / 数え違えになう miscount; count (the pages) wrong(ly) / 数え直す count again / 数え切れない countless; innumerable;《文》numberless;《be》too numerous to count / 数え切れなくなる〈人が主語〉lose count of;〈物が主語〉become [get to be] too numerous to be counted. 文例⑥

かそく 加速 ¶加速する accelerate; increase speed; speed up / 加速器 an 《electron》 accelerator / 加速度《物》acceleration / 加速度的に at an increasing tempo; with increasing speed.

かぞく¹ 家族 a family;《口語》one's people [《米》folks] ¶家族が多い〈少ない〉 have a large [small] family / 家族の一員 one [a member] of the family /…の家族の一員となる enter the family of 《Mr. Jones》/ 家族を養う support one's family / 家族として扱う treat sb as [as if he were] a member of one's family / 8人家族 a family of eight / 家族意識 a sense of family / 家族会議 a family council / 家族計画〈産児制限による〉family planning; planned parent-

---

A hard worker will never know [is a stranger to] poverty.

かぞえかた 戦前の日本では年齢の数え方はヨーロッパとは違っていた。In prewar Japan we counted our age in a different way from Europeans.

かぞえる 幾つまで数えられるかね。How high can you count (to)? / そんな人は数えるほどしかいない。Men like that can be counted on the fingers of one hand.

かぞく¹ うちは家族数が多い。My family is very large. / うちの家族はみんな口ベたた。My family are all poor talkers. / 私は大勢の家族を養わねばならない。I have a large family to support. / 家族の者がテレビを見ている時に、自分だけ学校の宿題をやらなくてはならないのはつらいことだ。It is hard to have to do one's homework when the rest of the family are [is] watching television. / 家族計画が普及して家族数の減少が急速に進むであろう。The spread of family planning will speed up the decline in family size.

かた¹ この方がスミスさんです。This (gentleman) is Mr. Smith. / あなたがこの手紙に書いてある方ですか。Are you the gentleman mentioned in this letter?

かぞく / かだい

かぞく¹ 家族 /家族構成 family structure / 家族連れの旅行 a family trip / 家族制度 the family system / 家族向きのレストラン a family restaurant. 文例⑨

用法 family に呼応する動詞は, family を一つの集合体として意識するか, それを構成している家族を個別的に意識しているかによって, 単数形にも複数形にもなる. 従って, How is your family? とも How are your family? とも言える.

かぞく² 華族 〈男〉a nobleman ; a peer ; 〈女〉a noblewoman ; a peeress ; 〈総称〉the nobility ; the peerage.

かそせい 可塑性 ¶可塑性素材 plastic materials ; plastics.

ガソリン 《米》gasoline ; 《英》petrol ; 《米口語》gas ¶ガソリンを食う車《口語》a gas-guzzler / ガソリンエンジン a gasoline [《英》petrol] engine / ガソリンスタンド a filling [service] station ; 《米》a gas station ; 《英》a petrol station / ガソリンスタンドの店員 a filling-station attendant.

かた¹ 方 〈…気付け〉care of (略：c/o) ¶この方 this ; 《文》this gentleman [lady] / 伊東様方山田様 Mr. Yamada, care of [c/o] Mr. Ito. 文例⑨

かた² 片 ¶片をつける 〈仕事などの〉finish ; get through with ; 〈問題の〉settle 《a question》; 〈借金の〉pay ; clear off.

かた³ 形, 型 〈形式〉(a) form ; 〈形状〉(a) shape ; 〈仕立て方〉(a) cut ; (a) make ; 〈大きさ〉(a) size ; 〈模様〉a pattern ; a design ; 〈様式〉a style ; (a) type ; 〈ひな型〉a model ; 〈鋳型〉a mold ; 〈担保〉(a) security ¶柔道の型 judo forms / 形が崩れる get out of shape ; lose shape / 形が崩れない keep [retain] its shape / 1979年型のキャデラック a 1979(-model) Cadillac ; a Cadillac of the 1979 model / 型のごとく[通り] 《文》in due form ; formally / 型を取る model 《a tooth in wax》/ 型を破る flout the conventions ; break with tradition / 貸金の形に取る take 《a watch》as security for the loan / 型にはめる standardize / 型にはまった stereotyped ; conventional / 型にはまらない unconventional ; 《口語》offbeat ; 〈自由な〉free. 文例⑨

かた⁴ 肩 the shoulder ¶山の肩 a mountain shoulder / 肩がいい《野球》(an outfielder) with a powerful throw / 肩が凝る[張る] one's shoulders are stiff ; have stiff shoulders ; 〈比喩的に〉feel uncomfortable [ill at ease] / 肩の凝る読み物 solid [serious] reading / 肩の凝らない読み物 light reading / 肩の力をぬく relax ; 《口語》take it easy / 肩の張ったsquare-shouldered / 肩を怒らす square one's shoulders / 肩を貸す lend sb one's shoulder ; give sb a shoulder / 肩をすくめる shrug one's shoulders / 肩を叩く tap [pat] sb on the shoulder / 肩を持つ, …に肩を入れる side 《with》; take sides 《with》; support ; back up / …と肩を並べる rank with… ; can compare with… ; equal 《sb in sth》/ 肩にする[かつぐ] shoulder ; carry [《文》bear] sth on one's shoulder / …を肩にして《a gun》on one's shoulder / 肩で息をする breathe hard ; pant / 肩で風を切って歩く strut [swagger] along. 文例⑨

かた⁵ 潟 〈外海と分離してできた湖〉a lagoon ; 〈浦〉an inlet.

かた⁶ 過多 《文》(an) excess ; 《文》(a) superabundance ; too much ¶供給過多 an excess of supply ; oversupply.

-かた …方 ¶歩き方 a [one's] way [《文》manner] of walking ; the way one walks ; 《文》a [one's] gait / 話し方 one's way of speaking ; the way one speaks / 将棋の指し方 how to play shogi. 文例⑨

がた ¶がたが来る get [《文》become] (old and) rickety ; become weak in the joints / がたの来た車 an old and decrepit car ; 《口語》an old crock ; a rattletrap / 《英》an old banger.

かたあげ 肩揚げ (make) a tuck at the shoulder.

かたあし 片足[脚] one foot [leg] ¶片足の人 a one-legged person / 片足で立つ stand on one leg.

かたあて 肩当て a shoulder pad.

カタール (the State of) Qatar.

かたい 堅[固, 硬]い 〈石など〉hard ; solid ; 〈肉など〉tough ; 〈きつい〉tight ; 〈硬直した〉stiff ; 〈堅固な〉strong ; firm ; 〈厳正な〉strict ; rigid ; 〈信頼し得る〉reliable ; trustworthy ; 〈堅実な〉safe ; steady ; honest ; 〈確実な〉sure ; certain ; 〈品行の〉《文》honorable ; 《文》upright ; 〈貞操の〉chaste ⇒ かたく² ¶頭が固い〈頑固〉be obstinate ; be stubborn ; 〈旧弊〉be too conservative ; 〈鈍い〉be thickheaded ; be thick-skulled / 口が堅い ⇒ くち / 堅い人〈正直な〉an honest [a straight] person ; 〈堅実な〉a steady [trustworthy] person / 固い結び目 a tight knot / 固い握手をかわす shake hands with a firm grip / 固い決心《文》a firm resolution [resolve] / 固い誓い[約束] a solemn oath [promise] / 堅い読み物 serious [solid] reading. 文例⑨

かだい¹ 過大 ¶過大な《文》excessive ; too much ; 〈法外な〉unreasonable / 過大に評価する overestimate ; overrate.

かた² あの事件はまだ片がつかない. That affair is not settled yet.
かた³ 彼は自分の家屋敷を形にして金を借りた. He borrowed money on the security of his real estate.
かた⁴ これで肩の荷がおりたよ. That's [It has taken] a load off my mind. / 私はひどく転んで肩を外した. I had a bad fall and dislocated my shoulder. / 東京もこの点ではヨーロッパのどんな大都市とも肩を並べることができる. In this respect Tokyo can compare with any large city in Europe. / 景色では日本と肩を並べる国は少ない. There are few countries that can rival Japan in scenic beauty. / その野牛は肩までの高さが1メートル半近くあった. The buffalo was [stood] about 1.5 meters tall at the shoulders.
-かた あの男の笑い方が気にくわない. I don't like the way he smiles.
かたい この肉は堅い. This meat is tough. / この家の地盤は固い. This house stands on firm ground. / もうけは少なくても堅い商売だ. The business is sound, though it doesn't make a lot of money. / 彼の文章は堅い. His style is too stiff. / 彼の当選は堅い. He is sure to win the elec-

かだい² 課題 〈題目〉a subject ; a theme ; 〈問題〉a problem ; 〈任務〉a task ; an assignment ; 〈宿題〉homework ; 〈練習問題〉exercises ¶解決すべき課題 a problem to be solved [((文))awaiting solution] / 課題を与える set sb a task ; give sb an assignment ((of 10 arithmetic problems)).

-がたい …難い 〈困難である〉it is hard (difficult) to do ; 〈到底できない〉it is impossible to do ¶避けがたい unavoidable ; inevitable / 忍びがたきを忍ぶ bear the unbearable. 文例⇩

がだい 画題 〈題材〉the subject of [for] a painting ; 〈表題〉the title of a painting.

かたいじ 片意地 〈強情〉stubbornness ; obstinacy ; pigheadedness ; 〈偏屈〉perversity ; ((口語))mulishness ; ((英口語))bloody-mindedness ¶片意地な stubborn ; obstinate ; pigheaded ; headstrong ; perverse ; ((口語))mulish ; ((英口語))bloody-minded / 片意地になる get [grow, ((文))become] obstinate.

かたいっぽう 片一方 ⇨ かたほう.

かたいなか 片田舎 a remote country place ; an out-of-the-way place.

かたいれ 肩入れ ⇨ かた⁴ (肩を入れる).

かたうで 片腕 〈片方の腕〉one arm ; 〈信頼する者〉one's right-hand man ; one's right hand ¶片腕の人 a one-armed person. 文例⇩

かたえくぼ 片笑窪 a dimple on one cheek.

かたおち がた落ち a slump ; ((口語))take a nose dive ; ((口語))nose-dive ; fall [drop, decline] (away) badly [seriously]. 文例⇩

かたおもい 片思い unrequited [((文))unreciprocated, unreturned, one-sided] love. 文例⇩

かたおや 片親 one parent ¶片親のない子供 a child with only one parent living.

かたがき 肩書 a title ; 〈学位〉a degree ¶肩書のある with a title [handle] to one's name / 肩書のない untitled ; without any title. 文例⇩

かたかけ 肩掛け a shawl ; a wrap ; a stole (婦人用の毛皮または羽毛の,長いもの) ¶肩掛けをかける put a shawl on / 肩掛けをかけている wear a shawl.

かたかた 〈かたかたいう音〉a clatter ; clattering / かたかた鳴る clatter.

かたがた¹ 方々 〈人々〉all (ladies and) gentlemen ; all people [persons].

かたがた² 〈…をかねて〉partly…and partly… ; 〈同時に〉at the same time ¶商用かたがた東京見物に来る come to Tokyo partly on business and partly for sightseeing. 文例⇩

がたがた with a rattling [clattering] noise ¶がたがたする rattle ; clatter ; 〈揺れる〉shake ; be shaky ; jolt (車などが) / がたがた震える tremble (with fear) ; shiver ((with cold)) / がたがたの rickety ; shaky. 文例⇩

かたかな 片仮名 katakana ; the square form of kana ; 〈個々の〉a katakana character ⇨ かな.

かたがみ 型紙 a (paper) pattern (for a dress) ; a dress pattern ((for a child's suit)).

かたがわ 片側 one side ¶道の片側を歩く keep to one side of the road. 文例⇩

かたがわり 肩代わり 〈肩代わりする〉shoulder (sb's debts) ; take over (the business).

かたき 敵 an enemy ; ((文))a foe ¶敵をとる [討つ] revenge oneself on sb (for a wrong) ; get [take, have] one's revenge on sb ; ((口語))get even with sb ; ((口語))get one's own back on sb / 親の敵を討つ avenge [take revenge for] one's father's death / 江戸の敵を長崎で討つ get one's revenge [((口語))one's own back] on sb in a roundabout way / 敵討ち revenge ; vengeance / 敵役 (an actor playing) the villain's part [role] ; ((口語))a heavy. 文例⇩

かたぎ¹ 堅気 ¶堅気の honest ; respectable ; decent ¶堅気で暮らす live honestly ; earn [make] an honest living / 堅気になる leave [quit] one's life of sin [crime] ; go straight. 文例⇩

かたぎ² 気質 character ; (a) temperament ¶学生かたぎ the way students think [feel, behave] / 学者[芸術家]かたぎの人 a man of a scholarly type [an artistic temperament].

かたく¹ 家宅 ¶家宅侵入罪 (the charge of) housebreaking / 家宅捜索 a house [((文))domiciliary] search ; ((口語))a raid / 家宅捜索する search sb's house (for sth) / 家宅捜索を受ける ((文))be subjected to a search ; have one's house searched.

かたく² 堅[固,硬]く 〈物体が〉hard ; 〈しっかりと〉tight(ly) ; fast ; firmly ; 〈強固に〉strongly ; 〈きっぱり〉decisively ; positively ; 〈厳重に〉strictly ; rigidly ¶卵を固くゆでる boil an egg hard / 堅[硬]くなる get [((文))become] hard ; harden ; get [go, grow, ((文))become] stiff ; go solid (糊などが) ; 〈人前などで〉get nervous ; freeze (up) (on the platform) ; get stage fright (役者などが) / 身を固くする go rigid / 固く握る grasp sth firmly ; take a firm grip of [on]

---

tion. | It is (almost) certain that he will win the election.

-がたい 情欲は制し難い. Passions are hard to control. / このような行為は許し難い. Such conduct is hardly excusable.

かたうで 彼がいなくなって片腕がもがれたような気がする. I miss him keenly ; he was like a right arm to me.

がたおち 先月は売上げががた落ちだった. Sales declined [slumped] sharply last month. / あんな本を出したので彼の評判はがた落ちになった. His new book ruined his reputation.

かたおもい 結局彼の片思いに終わった. His love was not returned after all.

かたがき 日本ではまだまだ肩書が物を言う. The handle to one's name still counts for a great deal in Japan.

かたがた² 近所へ用足しかたがた彼を訪ねた. I called on him as I had business in that neighborhood.

かたかた 風で窓ががたがたした. The windows rattled in the wind. / ひざがたがた震えた. My knees knocked together.

かたがわ 片側通行. 〚掲示〛One side closed to traffic. | (英)Single line traffic.

かたき 2人は敵同士だ. They are enemies. / いつかは敵をとってやる. I'll get even with him someday.

かたぎ¹ 彼女はバーのマダムだが, どこか堅気の女のようなところが

かたくな　頑な ⇨ がんこ.
かたくり　《植》a dogtooth violet　¶かたくり粉 dogtooth violet starch;〈今日普通に市販されているじゃがいもを原料にした〉potato starch.
かたくるしい　堅苦しい〈人が〉formal; stiff(-mannered); strait-laced;《口語》stuffy;〈規則などが〉strict; rigid; hard and fast;〈雰囲気が〉uncomfortable; formal; strained　¶堅苦しい規則 hard and fast rules / 堅苦しいこと[あいさつ]は抜きにする do without《文》dispense with] (the) formalities; do not stand on ceremony. 文例⇩
かたぐるま　肩車　¶肩車に乗る ride on sb's shoulders; ride pickaback [piggyback] on sb / 肩車に乗せる have [hold] (a child) on one's shoulders; ride [carry] (a child) pickaback.
かたこう　形鋼 a steel section; a steel beam (大型の).
かたごし　肩越し　¶肩越しに人を見る look at sb over one's shoulder.
かたこと　片言 a smattering《of English》¶片言を言う[でしゃべる] talk like a baby; use baby talk; speak broken Japanese [English] in a faltering manner / 片言まじりの英語で語る talk (about sth) in broken English.
がたごと　¶がたごと走る rattle [clatter] along.
かたさ　堅[固]さ〈石などの〉hardness;《文》solidity;〈肉などの〉toughness;〈革などの〉stiffness;〈きつさ〉tightness;〈身持ちの〉steadiness;《文》chastity.
かたさき　肩先　¶肩先を切られる get [《文》receive] a cut in the shoulder.
かたじけない　忝い ⇨ ありがたい.
かたず　固唾　¶かたずをのむ hold one's breath; with bated breath; with breathless [intense] interest;《await sth》expectantly.
かたすかし　肩透かし　¶肩透かしを食わせる dodge; sidestep;《口語》fool《the police》.
かたすみ　片隅　¶片隅に in a corner.
かたずみ　堅炭 hard charcoal.
かたたたき　肩叩き　¶肩叩きをする put pressure on sb to resign [to leave his job]; give sb the hint (that he ought to leave).
かたち　形〈形状〉(a) form; (a) shape;〈姿〉(an) appearance; a figure　¶形が崩れる[崩れない]

lose [hold] its shape / 形が変る change shape [form] / 形の同じような《hilly》hills) with a similar shape [form];《文》《bowls》similar in shape [form] / 軍艦の形をした小島 an islet shaped like [in the shape of] a warship / …の形をとる take [assume] the form [shape] of … / 本の形で《be published》in book form;《come out》as a book. 文例⇩
かたちづくる　形作る form; shape ⇨ けいせい.
かたちばかり　形ばかり　¶形ばかりのお礼 a slight token of (one's) gratitude / 形ばかりのお祝いをする celebrate《one's birthday》just for form's sake.
かたちんば　片ちんば ⇨ びっこ　¶片ちんばの靴 an odd pair of shoes.
かたづく　片付く〈整う〉be put in order; be put [set] to rights; be in (good) order; be tidy;〈処理される〉be settled; be disposed of; be cleared off;〈完了する〉be finished; end; come [《文》be brought] to an end;〈縁づく〉be married off; get married (to a rich man); marry《a doctor, into a good family》. 文例⇩
がたつく ⇨ がたがた (がたがたする).
かたづける　片付ける〈整とんする〉put [set] (one's affairs) in order; tidy sth up;〈取り去る〉clear [take] sth away; remove; get sth out of the way (邪魔物を);〈しまう〉put sth away (いつも置いてある所へ); put sth back (元の所へ);〈解決する〉settle (a dispute); solve (a problem);〈処分する〉dispose of; get rid of;〈完結する〉finish; put an end to sth; bring sth to an end; get sth over (with) (面倒な事を);〈嫁にやる〉marry off (all one's daughters); marry (one's daughter) to (a rich man);〈殺す〉do away with sb; kill;《俗語》bump sb off;《米俗》rub sb out　¶食器を片付ける clear away the table things; clear the table. 文例⇩
かたっぱし　片っ端　¶片っ端から one after another;《文》one and all;《口語》《eat》the whole lot;《take》whatever one can lay (one's) hands on.
かたつむり　a snail　¶かたつむりの殻 a snail shell / かたつむりの通った跡 a snail track / かたつむりのようにのろのろと《go along, walk》at a snail's pace.
かたて　片手 one hand　¶片手をポケットに突っ込む stick [《文》thrust] one's hand into one's pocket / 片手にかばんを, 片手にかさを持つ hold a briefcase in one hand and an

---

ある. Though she runs a bar, she has a streak of the lady in her.
かたく²　扉は堅く閉じてあった. The door was shut tight. / 彼は口を固く閉ざして語らなかった. He shut his mouth tight, and refused to tell [say a word]. / 校則は堅く守らねばならない. The school regulations must be strictly observed. / 彼は校長の前へ呼ばれて堅くなった. He felt nervous [ill at ease] when he was summoned in front of the principal. / 彼の

口付けを受けた時彼女は身を固くした. She went rigid when he kissed her.
かたくるしい　固苦しい事は大嫌いだ. I can't stand formalities.
かたち　それはどんな形をしているの. What shape is it? / 形は魚に似ている. It's shaped like a fish. | It has a shape like a fish. / それは色々の形で現われる. It appears in various [a variety of] forms.
かたちんば　この靴は片ちんばだ. These shoes are not [do not

make] a pair.
かたづく　部屋はきちんと片づいていた. I found the room in good order.
かたづける　この仕事は今年中に片付けなければならない. I must finish this work by the end of the year. / どうぞその本箱へ片付けておいて下さい. Please put it away in the bookcase there. / その椅子が邪魔だから片付けろ. Get that chair out of the way. / この問題から片付けよう.

かたておち　片手落ち　¶片手落ちの inconsistent；〈不公平な〉one-sided；unfair；biased；《文》partial. 文例⇩

かたてま　片手間　¶片手間に〈手のすいたときに〉in one's spare [leisure] time；《文》in one's leisure hours；〈副業として〉as a side job [line]；《口語》on the side／仕事の片手間に in the intervals of one's work；when one has a spare moment (from one's work). 文例⇩

かたとき　片時　a (single) moment；an instant ¶片時も忘れない do not forget sth even for a moment. 文例⇩

かたどる　象る　model [pattern]《a paperweight》on [after]《a tortoise》；imitate ¶琵琶湖にかたどって池を造る make a pond in the shape of Lake Biwa.

かたな　刀　a sword；〈日本刀〉a katana　¶刀を抜く draw [unsheathe] a [one's] sword／刀を(さやに)納める sheathe [put up] a [one's] sword／刀を構えて向かい合う face each other with drawn swords／刀を差している [《文》bear] a sword (at one's side)／刀折れ矢尽きるまで as long as one has one's weapons／刀かじ a swordsmith／刀傷 a sword cut [wound].

かたながれ　片流れ　¶屋根の傾斜 sloping one way only　¶片流れ屋根 a pent [shed] roof；a lean-to《pl. -tos》.

かたなし　形無し　⇨だいなし. 文例⇩

かたならし　肩慣らし　warming up；a warm-up ¶肩慣らしをする warm up；limber up.

かたねり　固練り　¶事　giving sth the consistency of thick paste by kneading [churning]／〈物〉(a) thick paste.

かたば　片刃　of a single-edged.

かたはい　片肺　one lung　¶片肺で飛行を続ける continue the flight with only one engine working.

かたはし　片端　an edge；one end　¶片端に寄る step aside／片端から ⇨かたっぱし.

かたはだ　片肌　¶片肌脱ぐ〈肩を〉bare one shoulder；〈助力する〉give [《文》render] assistance ((to))；lend sb a helping hand；use one's influence ((for)).

かたはば　肩幅　the breadth of one's shoulders；《洋裁》the width across the shoulders ¶肩幅が広い[狭い] be broad [narrow] across the shoulders；〈人体〉have broad [narrow] shoulders；be broad-[narrow-]shouldered.

かたばみ　《植》a wood sorrel；an oxalis.

かたはらいたい　片腹痛い　〈事が主語〉be ridiculous；be absurd；be laughable.

カタパルト　a catapult　¶カタパルトで発射する catapult (a plane).

かたひざ　片膝　¶片ひざを立てる raise one knee／片ひざをつく kneel down on one knee.

かたひじ　肩肘　¶肩肘張る[怒(いか)らす] try to look big [tough]；swagger.

がたぴし　¶がたぴしする rattle／がたぴしと戸を開ける open a door with a lot of noise；rattle a door open.

かたぶつ　堅物　a (too) serious [a strait-laced] person.

かたぶとり　固太り　¶固太りの女 a solidly-built woman. 文例⇩

かたほう　片方　〈片側〉one side；〈片方の物 the other one；〈対の〉one of a pair；the pair [fellow]《to this glove》；〈組の〉one [the other] party.

かたぼう　片棒　¶片棒を担ぐ take part ((in))；be a partner ((in))；have a hand ((in)).

かたぼうえき　片貿易　one-way [unbalanced, unilateral] trade.

かたまり　塊　a lump；a mass；a clod（土の）；〈集団〉a clump；a cluster；a group；a crowd ¶粘土の塊 a lump of clay／うその塊 a pack of lies／ここにひと塊あそこにひと塊 in groups；in clusters. 文例⇩

かたまる　固まる　〈固くなる〉harden；get [go, 《文》become] hard [firm, solid]；set（液状の物が）；〈凝結する〉congeal；〈塊になる〉turn into [《文》become] a solid [hard] mass；lump；cake；〈集まる〉gather (together)；huddle together；bunch (up) together；〈自分を限定する〉get into a rut；get into a fixed way (of life) ¶4,5人ずつ固まって in groups [knots] of four or five. 文例⇩

かたみ[1]　形見　a keepsake；a memento《pl. -(e)s》¶形見に持っている keep sth as a memento ((of))／形見分けをする distribute mementos ((of the deceased)) among ((the relatives)). 文例⇩

かたみ　肩身　¶肩身が狭い feel ashamed [inferior]. 文例⇩

Let's solve [dispose of] this problem first.／これはつまらない問題だといって片付けるわけにはいかない. This problem can hardly be dismissed as unimportant.

かたておち　決して片手落ちではしない. Of course I won't discriminate against either of them.／彼だけ助けるなんて片手落ちだ. It's unfair of you only to help him.

かたてま　これは片手間でできるような仕事ではない. This isn't a job which can be done in your spare time.

かたとき　片時も君のことを忘れることはない. You are always present in my thoughts [mind].

かたなし　この不景気で(うちの)商売は形無しさ. The depression has ruined our business.／彼女にかかっては あの男も形無しだ. She twists him round her little finger.／He's like putty in her hands.

かたはらいたい　彼が人に倹約を説くなんて片腹痛いよ. I am amused by the idea of his preaching thrift to others.

かたぶとり　彼女は中肉中背で固太りだった. She was a woman of medium height and build, with a certain solidity to her.

かたほう　荷が片方に少し寄り過ぎている. The load is a little too much to one side.／彼は片方の耳が聞こえない. He is deaf in one ear.／片方の靴はどこにあるのか. Where is the pair [fellow] to this shoe?／片方の言う事だけでは判断できない. I can't judge fairly by hearing only one side of the story.

かたまり　あの男は欲の塊だ. He is avarice personified.

かたまる　のりが固まった. The paste has gone hard [solid].／石膏は早く固まる. Plaster of Paris sets quickly.／これで会社の基礎

かたみち 片道 one way ¶片道乗車券《米》a one-way ticket;《英》a single (ticket) / 片道料金《米》a one-way fare;《英》a single fare.

かたむき 傾き 〈傾斜〉《文》inclination; slope; slant; 〈傾向〉a tendency ((to, toward)); a trend; a leaning; 〈性向〉an inclination;《文》a bent ¶…の[…する]傾きがある be apt to *do*; be liable to *do*; have a tendency to *do*; be given to doing. 文例↓

かたむく 傾く 〈傾斜する〉lean ((to, toward)); slope; incline ((to, toward)); 〈船などが横に〉list; careen; 〈衰える〉decline; wane; 〈日・月が〉decline; go down; sink ¶左に傾く lean to the left; 〈船が〉lean to port. 文例↓

かたむける 傾ける 〈かしげる〉tilt; incline; 〈器具などを〉tip; slant; 〈心を〉devote *oneself* to *sth*; concentrate (*one's* attention) on *sth* ¶耳を傾ける listen to ((*sb*, what *sb* says)) / 杯を傾ける have a drink [cup of *sake*].

かため¹ 片目 one eye ¶〈相撲で〉片目が明く score *one's* first win (after successive defeats) / 片目が見えない be blind in [《文》of] one eye / 片目の人 a one-eyed person.

かため² 固め 〈防備〉defense; 〈警固〉guard; 〈誓い〉a pledge ¶固めの杯を交わす exchange cups of *sake* as a pledge of friendship [partnership]; 〈夫婦が〉《文》exchange nuptial cups.

かため³ 固め ¶固めにゆでる boil ((eggs)) rather hard [on the hard side].

かためる 固める 〈固くする〉make *sth* hard [harder]; harden; 〈強化する〉strengthen; 〈堅固にする〉solidify; consolidate (*one's power*); 〈締める〉tighten; 〈凝結させる〉congeal; coagulate; 〈集める〉collect; mass ((together)); 〈防御する〉defend; fortify; 〈警固する〉guard ((a gate)) ¶基礎を固める strengthen the basis [(of)] / 結束を固める strengthen the unity ((of the party)) / 決心を固める make a firm decision ((to *do*)) / 身を固める (get married and) settle down / よろいに身を固める be dressed [clad] in armor.

かためん 片面 one side ¶片面レコード a single-faced[-sided] record [disc].

かたやき 堅焼き ¶堅焼きの hard-baked; hard / 堅焼きせんべい a hard rice cracker.

かたやぶり 型破り a departure from old custom [the usual way of *doing*]; 《文》unconventionality ¶型破りの unconventional; unusual.

かたよる 偏る, 片寄る 〈傾く〉lean ((to, toward)); incline ((toward)); 〈偏する〉be biased; be one-sided; be prejudiced ((against, in favor of)); 《文》be partial ((to)) ★「片寄った」という意味の partial は《文》で, 日常語としてはほとんど使われないが,「片寄らない」の意の impartial は日常語として盛んに使われる ¶片寄らない impartial; unprejudiced; fair. 文例↓

かたらい 語らい 〈談話〉a talk; a chat; 〈約束〉a promise; a vow.

かたりあう 語り合う talk [chat] ((with *sb*)); have a talk [chat] ((with *sb*)). 文例↓

かたりあかす 語り明かす talk the night away; talk all (through the) night.

かたりぐさ 語り草 a topic (of conversation); the talk of the town [neighborhood]; a legend (in the village). 文例↓

かたりくち 語り口 the way *one* tells ((a story)); *one's* way of reciting (a *joruri*).

かたりつがれる 語り継がれる be passed [handed] down [on] from generation to generation; be passed down the ages from mouth to mouth.

かたりて 語り手 a narrator; a storyteller; a reciter (義太夫などの).

かたりと with a clatter; clatteringly.

かたりべ 語り部 《日本史》a clan [family] of (professional) narrators [reciters] of legends and folktales in the service of the Imperial Court in early Japan; a Court remembrancer; 〈広く〉a storyteller.

かたる¹ 語る talk; chat; tell; 《文》relate; 《文》narrate; 〈節をつけて〉recite; chant ⇒はなす² ¶経験を語る tell of *one's* experiences / 昔を語る talk about the old days ((about bygone days)) / 語るに落ちる inadvertently reveal ((*one's* secret, that…)); let slip [let it out] ((that…)) / 語るに足りない be beneath *one's* notice; be not worth mentioning. 文例↓

かたる² 騙る swindle; deceive; cheat ¶金をかたり取る swindle money out of *sb*; swindle *sb* out of *his* money / 名前をかたって under [assuming] a false name.

カタル 《医》catarrh ¶カタル性の catarrhal (pneumonia).

カタルシス (a) catharsis ((*pl.* -tharses)).

も固まった. This means that the corporation is on a firm [secure] footing [foundation] now.

かたみ¹ これが父のただ一つの形見です. This is the only thing I have to remember my father by.

かたみ² あんな親戚があるかと思うと肩身が狭い. I am ashamed of having a fellow like that among my relatives. / これで君のお父さんも肩身が広くなるだろう. You've given your father something to make him proud of you at last.

かたみち 長野まで片道1枚下さい.《米》A one-way ticket to Nagano, please. |《英》A single to Nagano, please.

かたむき 今の青年はとかく労働を嫌う傾きがある. The young men of today are apt [have a tendency] to dislike physical labor.

かたむく 塔は少し東に傾いている. The tower leans somewhat toward the east. / 彼はその意見に傾いている. He leans toward that opinion. / 日が西に傾いている. The sun is sinking in the west. / 彼の運勢も傾いてきた. His fortune is waning [on the wane].

かたよる 食事が片寄らないようにしなければいけません. You must have a balanced diet.

かたりあう 今夜は大いに語り合おうではないか. Let's have a good long talk tonight, shall we?

かたりぐさ 彼の英雄的な行為は今でも町の人々の語り草になっている. The people of the town still talk about his heroic deeds. / これは後世の語り草となろう. This story will be handed down to posterity.

かたる¹ 野村さんは, 彼自身の語るところによれば, 英語を話すのはいつも苦が手であった. Mr. Nomura, by his own account, was never good at speaking Eng-

カタログ a catalog(ue) (of books) ¶カタログに載せる put [《文》place] (an item) on [in] a catalog; list (an article) in a catalog / 商品の価格を記載したカタログ a priced catalog / カタログ記載値段 the list price.

かたわ 片輪 a cripple; a deformed person ★日本語同様英語の方も差別語.

かたわら 傍ら <そば> the side ⇒そば¹ / <…する一方で> besides; while / 傍らから <a filing cabinet> at *one*'s side [elbow] / …の傍らから by the side of…; beside…; by…; near [close, hard] by / 道の傍らに by the wayside [roadside] / 傍らに寄る step aside [to one side]. 文例↓

かたわれ 片割れ <砕片> a fragment; a broken piece; <仲間の1人> one of the (same) party [group] ¶敵の片割れ one of the enemy.

かたん 加担 <援助> assistance; support; <参加> participation; <共謀> conspiracy ¶加担する <援助する> assist; 《文》aid; support; <味方する> take sides with *sb*; side with *sb*; <関与する> take part 《文》participate] in *sth*; be involved in *sth*; have a hand [part] in *sth* [doing]; be a party to *sth* / 加担者 an accomplice; a conspirator. 文例↓

かだん¹ 果断 (prompt) decision; 《文》resolution ¶果断な decisive; 《文》resolute; drastic; bold / 果断な処置を採る take resolute steps [drastic measures].

かだん² 花壇 a flower bed.

かだん³ 華壇 the world of floral artists.

かだん⁴ 歌壇 the world of *tanka* poets.

がだん 画壇 the art world; art circles.

カタンいと カタン糸 (a reel of) cotton thread; machine [sewing] cotton.

がたんと with a bang [bump] ¶(車両などが)がたんと動き出す jerk [get jerkily] into motion / がたんと止まる jerk to a stop / がたんと落ちる ⇒がたおち.

かち¹ 価値 value; worth; merit ⇒ねうち ¶使用価値 value in use / 価値観 (*one*'s) values / 価値基準 a standard of value / 価値体系 a value system; a set of values / 価値判断 (a) value judgment; 《文》evaluation (評価) / 価値論 〖哲〗 axiology. 文例↓

かち² 勝ち a victory; a win (競技での) ⇒しょ

うり, かつ³ ¶勝ちを譲る give *sb* the game. 文例↓

-がち <とかく…する> be apt [prone, liable] to *do*; be given to *doing*; <容易に…する> easily *do*. 文例↓

かちあう かち合う <衝突する> clash [collide] with; <祝日などが日曜日などと> coincide (with); fall on (a Sunday). 文例↓

かちいくさ 勝ち戦 a victory; 《文》a victorious battle [war] ⇒しょうり.

かちうま 勝ち馬 a winning horse; a winner.

かちえる 勝ち得る ⇒かくとく.

かちかち ¶かちかち鳴る <時計が> ticktack; ticktock; <固い物が> click; clack; clatter / 凍って[乾いて]かちかちになる be frozen [dried] hard / (緊張して)身体がかちかちになる go 《文》become] rigid (with [from] nervous tension); be petrified.

かちき 勝ち気 《文》an unyielding spirit ¶勝ち気な女 a woman of spirit; a strong-minded[-spirited] woman.

かちく 家畜 a domestic animal; a farm animal (農家の); livestock (総称) ¶家畜の改良 improvement of livestock / 半ば家畜化した動物 a semi-domesticated animal / 家畜学 animal husbandry / 家畜病院 a veterinary hospital; <犬猫の> a pets' hospital.

かちこす 勝ち越す have more wins than losses; have already won more than half *one*'s matches; <相手に対して> lead [have beaten] *sb* by 《three》matches.

かちすすむ 勝ち進む win (*one*'s way) through (to the semifinals).

かちっぱなし, かちとおす 勝ちっ放す, 勝ち通す win 《three》straight [consecutive] victories [games, matches]; have a 《long》winning streak.

かちどき 勝ち鬨 ¶勝ちどきをあげる raise [give] a shout of victory (triumphant shout).

かちとる 勝ち取る ⇒かくとく.

かちなのり 勝名乗り ¶(力士が)勝名乗りを受ける be declared winner.

かちにげ 勝ち逃げ ¶勝ち逃げする clear off [run away] with *one*'s winnings; get out (of the game) while *one* is ahead [winning].

かちぬきせん 勝ち抜き戦 a tournament; 《英》a

---

lish.
かたわら 彼は学校へも出るし, 傍ら家でも教えている. Besides teaching at school, he gives private lessons at home. | He gives private lessons at home, while also teaching at school.

かたん この争いには僕はどちらにも加担したくない. I'll be neutral in this dispute. | I refuse to take sides in this dispute.

かち¹ 彼の行為は大いに褒めてやる価値がある. His conduct deserves the highest praise. / 彼らの作品は当時日本では一般に価値を認められていなかった. Their work was generally unappreciat-

ed in Japan in those days. / 四分音符は八分音符2個の価値を持っている. A quarter note has the value of two eighth notes.

かち² この勝負は君の勝ちだ. The game is yours. / 試合は 3対2で早稲田の勝ちになった. Waseda won the game [The game ended in a Waseda victory] by three runs [goals, points] to two. / この勝ちに乗じて彼らはさらに敵の司令部目差して進撃した. They followed up their victory by advancing on the enemy's headquarters.

-がち 若い者は極端に走りがちだ. Young people are apt to go to extremes. / とかく空腹になるとかん

しゃくを起こしがちになる. One is more prone to lose *one*'s temper when *one* is hungry. / この病気は子供にありがちだ. Children are liable [susceptible] to this disease. / 6月中は雨がちでした. We had a lot of rain in June. | It rained a great deal in June. / 宅は留守がちでございます. My husband is away from home most of the time.

かちあう 試験とかちあってその会に出られなかった. The meeting clashed with my examinations, so I could not attend it.

かちかち 夜回りの鳴らす拍子木がかちかち鳴った. Click-clack went

かちのこる 勝ち残る 〈予選に〉survive an elimination match ; 〈勝ち進む〉win (one's way) through (to the finals) ¶勝ち残った選手 a survivor.

かちほこる 勝ち誇る be triumphant ; 《文》exult in [at] one's victory ; be elated with success ¶勝ち誇って triumphantly ; in triumph.

かちぼし 勝ち星 a win / 勝ち星をあげる have a win / 勝ち星を数える count one's wins [how many wins one has achieved] ; count the number of victories to one's credit.

かちまけ 勝ち負け ⇨ しょうはい¹, しょうぶ¹.

かちめ 勝ち目 ¶勝ち目がある stand [have] a good [fair] chance of winning 〈the battle [game]〉; the chances [odds] are in one's favor / 勝ち目がない stand [have] no chance of winning 〈the battle [game]〉; the chances [odds] are against one / 勝ち目のない戦い a hopeless war ; a lost cause ; 〈試合〉a losing game. 文例↓

かちゃかちゃ ¶かちゃかちゃ鳴る clang.

がちゃがちゃ ¶がちゃがちゃさせる[音を立てる] clatter ; clank ; rattle. 文例↓

がちゃんと ¶がちゃんと音を立てる clang ; clank ; crash / がちゃんと音をたてて with a crash / 皿が割れるがちゃんという音 the crash of a breaking dish [plate] / がちゃんと電話を切る slam the receiver down ; ring off. 文例↓

かちゅう¹ 火中 ¶火中の栗を拾う risk one's neck [life] / 火中に投じる throw sth into the fire ; 《文》commit sth to the flames ; 〈身を〉plunge (oneself) into the flames. 文例↓

かちゅう² 渦中 ¶渦中に巻き込まれる 《文》be drawn into the vortex (of war) ; be involved [entangled, embroiled] in (a quarrel). 文例↓

かちょう¹ 家長 the head of a family ; a patriarch ; a matriarch 〈女〉¶家長制度 the patriarchal system.

かちょう² 課長 ⇨ か¹.

がちょう 〈鳥〉a goose 《pl. geese》¶がちょうの雄 a gander ; a male goose / がちょうのひな a gosling ; a young goose. 文例↓

かちょうおん 可聴音 an audible sound.

かちょうきん 課徴金 a surcharge.

かちりと with a click ¶かちりと音を立てる click. 文例↓

かちんと with a clink [clack] ¶かちんと鳴る clink ; click. 文例↓

かつ¹ 活 ¶活を入れる 〈柔道で〉apply the (judo) technique of resuscitation ; resuscitate ; 〈元気づける〉cheer sb up ; encourage sb ; put some backbone in sb ; 〈口語〉give sb a pep talk ; 《口語》buck sb up / 死中に活を求める try to find a way out of the terrible difficulty.

かつ² 渇 ⇨ かわき¹.

かつ³ 勝[克]つ win ; win [gain] a victory (over) ; be [come off] victorious [a winner] ; 〈征服する〉conquer ; 〈負かす〉defeat ; beat ; get the better of ; 〈克服する〉overcome ; 《文》surmount ; 〈勝る〉《文》surpass ; be superior to ; 〈優勢である〉《文》prevail ; predominate ¶戦いに勝つ win a battle ; win [gain] the day / 敵に勝つ defeat [win a victory over] the enemy / 競技[競走]に勝つ win a game [race] / 議論に勝つ win [get the better of sb] in an argument / 訴訟に勝つ win a case [lawsuit] / 困難に勝つ overcome [《文》surmount, get over] a difficulty / 己れに克つ conquer [control] oneself ; get control of oneself / 勝ったり負けたりしながら with varying turns of fortune / 勝っておごらず負けて悪びれない win with modesty and accept defeat gracefully. 文例↓

かつ⁴ 且 besides ; moreover ; also ; and (★多くの場合強勢を伴って) ; at the same time ; both...and... ; ...as well as... ¶必要かつ充分な条件〈数・論〉necessary and sufficient conditions / 面白くかつ有益である be both 《文》at once) interesting and instructive ; be instructive as well as interesting. 文例↓

カツ ⇨ カツレツ.

かつあい 割愛 ¶割愛する 〈省略する〉leave out ; 《文》omit ; 〈譲る〉spare sb sth ; spare sth for sb ; 〈他の職場に転じることを認める〉release sb ; allow [《文》permit] sb to resign (in order to take up another job). 文例↓

かつお 鰹 〈魚〉a [an oceanic] bonito 《pl. -(s)》¶かつお節 (a piece of) dried bonito ; 〈削った物〉dried bonito shavings.

かっか¹ 閣下 〈二人称〉Your Excellency 《pl. Your Excellencies》; 〈三人称〉His Excellency

---

the clappers of the night watchman.

かちめ 勝ち目は7分3分だ。The odds are seven to three that we will win the game. / 勝ち目がない[ある]. The odds are against me [are in my favor].

がちゃがちゃ 皿をがちゃがちゃさせるな。Don't make such a clattering noise with the plates.

がちゃんと 石ががちゃんと窓ガラスを破って飛び込んだ。A stone came crashing through the window.

がちょう がちょうがああがあ鳴いた。The geese cackled.

かちりと ドアがかちりと締まった。The door clicked shut.

かちんと その言葉がかちんときた。The remark really got my goat [made me mad].

かつ³ 早稲田は9対5のスコアで慶応に勝った。Waseda defeated [beat] Keio by 9 runs to 5. / Waseda beat Keio 9-5. / 病気には勝てない。No one can win against disease. / 議論には悪に勝つ。I am no match for him in argument. / 結局善は悪に勝つ。Virtue will triumph over vice in the end. / この絵は赤味が勝っている。Red dominates in this picture. / 勝てば官軍。Nothing succeeds like success. 諺 / Losers are always in the wrong. 諺 / 勝って兜の緒を締めよ。Don't relax your guard after you've won the battle [fight].

かつ⁴ 彼は知識もありかつ経験も豊かだ。He has experience as well as knowledge. / He has both knowledge and experience. / かつ笑い、かつ語りつつ、最後の夕べを楽しく過ごした。Now laughing and now talking, we enjoyed our last evening together.

かつあい 萩にも立ち寄りたかったが、列車の都合で割愛して帰った。I wished to visit Hagi on the way home too, but the train service obliged me to deny myself the

かっか ⇒ **かっと** ¶ かっかする〈怒りで〉burn (with anger); fume; flush crimson (with indignation);《口語》get mad (with [at] sb for sth).

がっか¹ 学科〈科目〉a subject of study (on a school curriculum);〈課程〉a course of study; a school course ¶ 学科試験 examinations in academic subjects.

がっか² 学課 a lesson; schoolwork ¶ 学課を復習する《米》review [《英》revise] one's lessons / 学課を予習する prepare one's lessons.

かっかい 各界《文》every walk of life ¶ 各界の代表者 representatives of every sector of society.

がっかい¹ 学会 a learned [scientific] society ¶ 学会に出る attend a meeting《of the Japan Cancer Society》/ 日本英文学会 the English Literary Society of Japan.

がっかい² 学界 academic circles; the academic world ¶ 学界に認められる gain academic recognition (as...). 文例↓

かっかく 赫々 ¶ かっかくたる brilliant;《文》glorious.

かっかざん 活火山 an active [a live] volcano.

かつかつ¹〈ひづめの音〉clip, clop; clippety-clop.

かつかつ²〈辛うじて〉(only) just; barely ¶ かつかつの生活をする make a bare living; live on the edge of subsistence. 文例↓

がつがつ voraciously; hungrily ¶ がつがつ食う eat voraciously [ravenously, like a pig]; devour; gobble [wolf] down /〈金銭などに〉がつがつしている be greedy for《money, fame》.

かっかと ⇒ **かっか²** ¶ かっかと燃える burn hot [brightly] / 火をかっとおこしておく keep the fire well alight / ほおがかっかとほてる one's cheeks burn [blush]《with shame》;〈事が主語〉make one blush; bring a blush to one's cheeks.

がっかり ¶ がっかりする〈失望する〉be disappointed (about [at] sth, with [in] sb);〈落胆する〉lose heart; be heartbroken; be disheartened;《文》be cast down ¶ がっかりさせる〈失望させる〉disappoint;〈落胆させる〉make sb lose heart; discourage. 文例↓

かっき 活気 vigor; spirit; energy; animation ¶ 活気が付く get [《文》become] lively [animated, active] / 活気のある lively; full of life; pleasure. / 紙面の都合で挿し絵は割愛しました. Space did not permit us to insert the illustrations.

がっかい² 氏は学界のために大いに功労があった. He has done a great deal for [rendered great services to] the cause of learning [science].

かつかつ² 彼は駅に駆けつけて列車にかつかつ間に合った. He rushed to the station and got there just in time for the train. / 会員はかつかつ100人ぐらいにはなるでしょう. The membership will barely reach 100.

がっかり なぜそんなにがっかりしているのか. Why are you so depressed? / 計画が失敗したと聞いて私はがっかりした. I lost heart [My heart sank] when I heard of the failure of our plan. / 彼女が留守だったのでがっかりした. To my disappointment, I found that she was not at home. / あの男にはがっかりしたよ. I am disappointed in [with] him. He is a disappointment to me.

かっき 将来の志望について語った時彼の話の何と活気に満ちていたことか. How full of life [animated; spirited; active / 活気のない spiritless; lifeless; dull;《文》inert / 活気を添える, 活気付ける put (new) life into sth [sb]; give life to; enliven;《文》animate; stimulate; inspire / 活気に乏しい be lacking spirit [life].

がっき¹ 学期 a (school) term;《米》a session; a semester (二学期制の) ¶ 第一学期 the first term / 学期中 during (the) term; in term / 学期末に at the end of (the) term.

がっき² 楽器 a musical instrument; an instrument.

かつぎあげる 担ぎ上げる carry sth up; lift sth up on one's shoulder.

かつぎこむ 担ぎ込む carry《a wounded person》into《a hospital》.

かつぎだす 担ぎ出す carry sth out of《a house》;〈比喩的に〉have sb《as candidate》.

かっきてき 画期的 epoch-making.

かつぎまわる 担ぎ回る carry sth about.

かつぎや 担ぎ屋〈行商人〉a peddler;〈迷信家〉a superstitious person.

がっきゅう¹ 学究 ⇒ **がくしゃ**.

がっきゅう² 学級 a class ¶ 学級委員 a class officer / 学級文庫 a classroom library / 学級閉鎖 temporary closing of classes.

かっきょ 割拠 ¶ 割拠する each holds his own sphere of influence ⇒ **ぐんゆうかっきょ**.

かっきょう 活況 activity; briskness; prosperity. 文例↓

がっきょく 楽曲 a (musical) composition; a piece of music.

かっきり just; exactly; precisely;〈時間が〉sharp; punctually ¶ 1万円かっきり just 10,000 yen; neither more nor less than 10,000 yen / 2時かっきりに promptly at 2 o'clock; at 2 o'clock precisely; on the dot of 2; at 2 sharp [on the dot, prompt]. 文例↓
用法 on the dot (of 2) と at (2) on the dot の使い方を厳しく区別するとすれば, He came on the dot of 2. というように on the dot (of 2) は過去の出来事の叙述に用いることが多く, at (2) on the dot は Please arrive at 2 on the dot. というように将来のことについての命令・打ち合わせに使われることが多い.

かつぐ 担ぐ〈肩に〉carry;《口語》bear sth on one's shoulder;〈だます〉take sb in; play a trick on sb;〈ふざけて〉play a joke on sb;《口語》pull sb's leg;〈迷信深い〉be superstitious ¶ 重い荷を担いで with a heavy burtion] he was when he talked about his hopes for the future!

かっきょう 市場は活況を呈している. The market is active [brisk].

かっきり 幕が5時かっきりに開く. The curtain rises at 5 sharp [on the dot].

かつぐ 彼らに担がれて, そんな時期に学部長に就任する気持ちになったのです. It was because I was prevailed upon by them that I decided to assume the office of dean at that juncture.

がっくり それを聞いて父はがっくりきた. Father's spirits sagged

がっく den on *one*'s shoulder / 銃を担いでいる have a gun on *one*'s shoulder / …を会長に担ぐ have *sb* as the president 《of the society》. 文例⇩

がっく¹ 区 a school district ¶学区制 the school district system.

がっく² 楽句 a (musical) phrase.

かっくう 滑空 gliding; a glide ¶滑空する glide.

がっくり ⇨ らくたん, がっかり ¶がっくりとうなだれる drop *one*'s head (on *one*'s chest); hang *one*'s head down. 文例⇩

かっけ 脚気 beriberi ¶脚気が起こる get beriberi / 脚気心 heart failure from beriberi.

かつげき 活劇 《場面》a fighting scene;《映画》an action film /《けんか》a scuffle ¶活劇を演じる《映画で》play [act out,《文》enact] a fighting scene;《取っ組み合いをする》fight (with); scuffle (with).

かっけつ 喀血 [医] hemoptysis ¶喀血する spit [expectorate, cough up] blood.

かっこ¹ 各戸 ¶各戸に at every door; from door to door.

かっこ² 各個 ¶各個に each; individually; respectively /各個撃破する defeat 《*one*'s opponents》 one by one.

かっこ³ 括弧 《丸形》a parenthesis (*pl*. -theses); a round bracket /《角形》a (square) bracket;《山形》(〈 〉) an angle bracket /《大括弧》a brace;《二重》a double parenthesis ★いずれも通常は複数形で用いられる ¶括弧に入れる put 《a word》 in parentheses [brackets] / 括弧つきの民主主義 democracy in quotes [inverted commas].

かっこ⁴ 確固 ¶確固たる firm; determined;《文》resolute / 確固として firmly;《文》determinedly;《文》resolutely. 文例⇩

かっこ⁵ ⇨ かっこう¹ ¶かっこいい 《俗》cool;《俗》groovy.

かっこう¹ 格好 〈形〉(a) shape; (a) form;〈見掛け〉appearance(s) /〈値段などの〉moderate; reasonable;〈適当な〉suitable; fit /格好がよくなる improve in appearance; look better /格好が崩れる look worse; get out of shape / 格好の(いい) attractive; nice-looking; nicely-[pleasantly-]shaped [formed]; shapely (legs); stylish (clothes); well-cut (suits) / 格好の悪い ugly; unattractive;〈形の〉《文》ill-formed;《文》unseemly;〈姿の〉clumsy;〈仕立の〉ill-cut / 格好をつける try to look good [clever, smart] / 格好よく見える look nice 《《文》well》;《文》cut a fine [good] figure / 格好よく作る make *sth* so that *it* looks attractive [nice] / 30 格好の人 a person about thirty years old.

かっこう² 郭公 [鳥] a cuckoo.

かっこう³ 滑降 《スキー》a descent ¶滑降競技 a downhill race.

がっこう 学校 a school ⇨ だいがく ¶学校が引けてから after school (hours); after school is over /学校をやめる leave [drop out of] school / 学校を卒業する leave [finish] school; complete the school course /《米》graduate from school / 学校のある日に on school days / on days when *one* has school / 学校にいた時, 学校時代に when *one* was in [at] school (★ in は《米》, at は《英》); in *one*'s school days / 学校に入る enter a school / 学校に通う[行く] go to school; attend school /学校で《場所》at school; in school (校舎内で);《米》in school;《英》at school / 子供を学校へ上げる[出す] send [put] *one*'s child [boy, girl] to school / 学校かばん〈肩にかけたりする〉a school satchel / 学校教育 school education; schooling / 学校差 (a) disparity in academic standards》 among schools / 学校債 (issue) a school bond / 学校新聞 a school paper / 学校生活 school life / 学校文法 school grammar / 学校友達 a schoolfellow; a schoolmate; a friend from *one*'s school days / 学校放送〈テレビ・ラジオの〉a school(s) broadcast [program]; the school hour(s). 文例⇩

かっこく 各国〈それぞれの国〉every [each] country [nation];〈諸国〉various [all] countries [states]. 文例⇩

がっこつ 顎骨 [解] the jawbone; the maxilla 《*pl*. -lae》.

かっこむ 搔っ込む ¶朝飯をかっ込む bolt (down) [rush] *one*'s breakfast; have [make] a hasty breakfast.

かっさい 喝采 cheers ⇨ はくしゅ (拍手かっさい) ¶かっさいする cheer; give *sb* a cheer / 立ち上がってかっさいする give *sb* a standing ovation / かっさいを博する draw a cheer 《from》; win applause; receive an ovation 《from》/ かっさいに答える acknowledge the cheers 《of the audience》. 文例⇩

[Father was very downcast] at the news.

かっこ⁴ アメリカのイギリスに対する支持は確固たるものである。The United States is firm [steady] in its support of the United Kingdom.

かっこう² 掛け軸が掛かっていないと床の間は格好がつかないものだ。It takes a hanging scroll to make a *tokonoma* [ceremonial alcove] look its best [look as it should]. / こんな格好では人前に出られない。I am not fit to be seen. / 素手で帰るわけにはいかない, 何とか格好をつけてもらおう。I cannot leave empty-handed. You must give me something to save my face.

がっこう 君は学校は どこですか。What school do you go to [attend]? / 明日から学校は夏休みになる。School breaks up tomorrow for the summer vacation. / 明日は学校がない[学校は休みだ]。We have no school tomorrow. / 僕は毎朝7時に出て学校へ行きます。I leave home for school at seven every morning. / 弟は東京の学校へ行っています。My brother is at school in Tokyo. / 学校へ傘を忘れてきた。I've left my umbrella at school. / あの人は学校教育を少しも受けなかった。He never had any schooling. | He never went to school. / 君の学校生活についてもう少し話して下さい。Please tell me a little more about your life at school.

かっこく 各国それぞれの風俗習慣がある。Each country has its own manners and customs.

かっさい 壇上に彼を見せると盛んなかっさいがわき起こった。He was heartily cheered when

かつさい 滑剤 a lubricant.
がっさく 合作 ¶合作する〈共同する〉collaborate 《with sb on sth》; cooperate 《with sb in sth》; 〈著述を〉write (a book) jointly 《with sb》; coauthor (a book).
がっさん 合算 ¶合算する add up [together].
かつじ 活字 (a piece of) printing [movable] type; type ¶5号活字 No. 5 type / 活字の大きさ (a) type size / 細かい活字(のもの)を読む read fine print / 活字を組む set up type; compose type / 活字を拾う pick out type(s) / 新しい活字を作らせる have (a) new type cut [made] / 活字にする put (an article) into print; print [put] (a manuscript) in type / 活字に組む set up 《manuscripts》(for printing) / 大きい[小さい]活字で印刷する print in large [small] type / 大きい活字の国語辞典 a Japanese dictionary in large print / 活字体で書く print (one's name); use [write in] block letters. 文例参
かっしゃ 滑車 a pulley ¶滑車台 a pulley block.
ガッシュ 〈絵の具及びそれを用いる画法〉gouache; 〈絵〉a gouache ¶ガッシュで描く paint in gouache.
がっしゅうこく 合衆国 the United States (of America) (略: the U.S.(A.)) ⇨アメリカ.
がっしゅく 合宿 ¶合宿する lodge [board] together; 〈練習所に〉stay together in a camp 《for training》/ 合宿所 a training camp.
かつじょう 割譲 (a) cession ¶割譲する cede (a part of its territory to another country).
がっしょう¹ 合唱 (a) chorus ¶合唱する sing together [in chorus] / 男[女, 混]声合唱 a male [female, mixed] chorus / 男声合唱曲 a chorus for men's [male] voices / 合唱隊[団] a chorus; a choir (教会の) / ウィーン少年合唱団 the Vienna Boys' Choir.
がっしょう² 合掌 ¶合掌する join one's hands in prayer.
かっしょく 褐色 brown ¶褐色の brown.
がっしり ¶体格ががっしりしている be sturdy; be strongly [powerfully, solidly] built / 肩幅の広い体のがっしりした男 a broad-shouldered, heavy-set man.
かっすい 渇水 (a) drought; (a) shortage of water; a water shortage ¶渇水期 a period of water shortage; the dry season (乾季).
がっする 合する join (together) (into one); combine 《with》; unite 《with》.

かっせい 活性 ¶活性化《化》activation / 活性化する revitalize (the economy); 《化》activate / 活性炭 activated carbon [charcoal].
かっせき 滑石 talc; talcum ¶滑石粉 talcum powder; talc.
かっせん¹ 合戦 a battle ¶川中島の合戦 the Battle of Kawanakajima.
かっせん² 割線 《数》a secant.
かっそう 滑走 〈飛行機の〉《start》the roll; 〈氷や雪の上の〉sliding ¶滑走する〈飛行機が〉roll; 〈氷や雪の上を〉slide / 滑走路 a runway.
がっそう 合奏 ¶合奏する play in concert / 二[三, 四]部合奏 a duet [trio (pl. -s), quartet].
カッター a cutter ¶カッターシャツ a long-sleeved sport shirt.
がったい 合体 ¶合体する unite [be united] 《with》; combine [be combined] 《into one》; coalesce 《with》; be incorporated (into a larger town).
かったん 褐炭 brown coal; lignite.
がったんごっとん 〈汽車の音〉clickety-clack.
かつだんそう 活断層《地質》active faulting ¶活断層地帯 a zone [region] of active faulting.
がっち 合致 ⇨いっち.
かっちゅう 甲冑 armor.
がっちり ¶がっちりした〈体格が〉⇨がっしり; 〈抜け目のない〉shrewd; hard-headed; canny; 《口語》smart; 〈締まり屋の〉stingy; tightfisted; close-fisted / がっちりとスクラムを組む form a tight scrum [scrummage]; 〈団結する〉band closely together 《to do》.
ガッツ guts ¶こんじょう¹ ¶ガッツポーズをする hold up one's fists in triumph.
かつて once; (at) one time; before; 《文》formerly ¶もと (もとは ★) ¶かつての former; one-time; ex- (premier). 文例参
かって¹ 勝手〈台所〉a kitchen ¶勝手口 the kitchen [back, service] door / 勝手道具 kitchen utensils [things]; kitchenware / 勝手仕事をする do kitchen work / 勝手元 ⇨かってむき.
かって² 勝手〈自分の都合〉one's own convenience; 〈気まま〉one's own way; selfishness; willfulness ¶勝手な〈利己的な〉selfish; self-seeking; 〈人の言うことを聞こうとしない〉self-willed; 《文》arbitrary; wayward / 勝手なまねをする have one's own way; do what [as] one likes [wishes, pleases] / 勝手に〈気ままに〉as one pleases [likes, wishes, chooses]; selfishly; willfully; by choice [preference]; 〈自由意志で〉freely; of one's (own) free will;

---

he appeared on the platform.
かつじ これは何号活字ですか. What size is this type? / 自分の書いたものが活字になったのはうれしいものだ. It is a real thrill to see oneself [one's writing] in print. / その印刷機も古く活字もかすれていた. The presswork was performed on an old press from worn type.
かつて かつてそこには稲荷のほこらがあった. There used to be an Inari shrine there. / あの家はか

つて伊藤氏の所有だった. At one time that house belonged to Mr. Ito. / That house once belonged to Mr. Ito. / あんな偉い人はいまだかつて見たことがない. He is the greatest man I have ever seen.
かって² ここは勝手知ったる我が家のようなものだ. I know my way around [about] this place as well as if it were my own house. / 彼はその仕事を勝手にやらせてくれた. He gave me a free hand to do the job. / 世間の人にはな

んとでも勝手に言わせておくがいい. Let people say what they like. / どうぞご遠慮なく. Suit yourself. / Please yourself. / You are welcome to it [to do so]. / それが嫌なら, あとは勝手にしなさい. Take it or leave it. / You can like it or lump it. / If you don't like it, you can go jump in the lake. / 自分の物をどうしようと僕の勝手だ. I can do what I like with my own property. / 行くも, 留まるも, お前の勝手だ. You are

かってっこう

of one's own accord; 〈独断で〉at one's (own) discretion; 〈無断で〉arbitrarily; 〈無断で〉without leave [permission] / 人の物を勝手に使う make free use of sb's things; 《文》appropriate sb's things for one's own use / 勝手が違う 〈人が主語〉be out of one's element; 〈物が主語〉be not in one's line / 勝手を知っている 〈物事のを〉know the ropes; know how to do; 〈場所などの〉be familiar with (a place); know one's way about [around] ((in) the town) / 仕事の勝手を飲み込める 《口語》get the hang of one's work [job] / 自分の勝手をはかる 《文》consult one's own convenience; be self-seeking / 勝手ながら…する take [allow oneself] the liberty of doing / 勝手気ままにさせておく let sb have his own way; leave sb to do what he likes. 「tite. 文例⤵

かってっこう 褐鉄鉱 limonite; brown hema-

かってでる 買って出る volunteer (to do); take it upon oneself (to do); volunteer [offer] one's services (as mediator); constitute oneself (trouble-shooter). 文例⤵

かってむき 勝手向き one's (financial) circumstances ¶勝手向きがいい be well off; 《文》be in easy [prosperous] circumstances; 《口語》be on easy street / 勝手向きが苦しい be badly off; 《文》be in poor [difficult] circumstances.

がってん 合点 ➾がてん. 文例⤵

かっと ¶かっとなる lose one's temper; fly into a passion [sudden rage]; suddenly take offense; be overcome by anger; 《口語》boil; 《俗》blow one's top [《米》stack] / かっとなって in a (fit of) temper; in a rage / 両眼をかっと見開く open one's eyes wide. 文例⤵

カット 〈小さな挿絵〉a woodcut; 〈映画などの〉切取り cutting; a cut; 〈庭球・卓球〉a cut ¶カットする〈削除する〉cut; cross out; bluepencil; 〈球を〉cut (the ball).

ガット[1] 〈腸線〉gut; catgut.

ガット[2] 〈関税と貿易に関する一般協定〉GATT (★ the General Agreement on Tariffs and Trade の略).

かっとう 葛藤 trouble; 《文》discord; (a) conflict ¶心[感情]のかっとう (undergo) mental [emotional] conflict / かっとうを生じる〈事が主語〉cause trouble; 《文》breed discord.

かつどう 活動 activity; action ¶学生たちの学内での活動 student activities on [within] the campus / 活動する be active; play [take] an active part (in) / 活動させる bring sth into play; 《文》call sth into action / 活動中である be in action; 〈火山が〉be in activity / 活動の舞台 the stage for [sphere of, field of] one's activities [activity, action] / 活動を開始する go into action; come into play; 〈軍隊などが〉begin operations / 活動家 an (anti-war) activist / 活動力 energy; vitality. 文例⤵

カットグラス cut glass.

かっとばす かっ飛ばす slam [clout, smack out] (a homer).

カットバック〈映画〉a cutback ¶カットバックする cut back (to).

かっぱ[1] 合羽 [<〈ポルトガル語〉capa] a raincoat; a waterproof (coat); 〈主に英〉a mackintosh; a raincape (袖なしの).

かっぱ[2] 河童 a kappa; a water [river] sprite; 〈人〉a (good) swimmer ¶陸(お)に上がったかっぱ a fish out of water. 文例⤵

かっぱつ 活発 ¶活発な lively; brisk; sprightly; active; full of life / 活発な議論を戦わせる have an animated [a lively] discussion ((about sth, with sb)) / 活発に actively; briskly; lively / 活発にする make (a chemical reaction) active; activate (a chemical reaction) / 動作が活発である be brisk (in one's movements).

かっぱらう 掻っ払う《俗》swipe; filch;《口語》pinch;《口語》lift; snatch (a woman's handbag); shoplift.

かっぱん 活版〈印刷〉type-printing;〈活字〉type ¶活版で印刷する print with type / 活版屋〈人〉a printer;〈店〉a printing shop.

がっぴょう 合評 a joint review ¶合評会 a meeting for jointly reviewing ((the month's magazine articles)).

カップ a cup; a trophy (優勝杯) ¶カップケーキ a cupcake.

かっぷく 格幅 build; physique ¶格幅がいい be stout; be stoutly built.

カップル a couple.

がっぺい 合併 (a) combination; (a) consolidation; (an) amalgamation; (a) merger ¶合併する combine; consolidate; amalgamate; merge / 町村合併 the consolidation of smaller municipalities (to form a larger one) / 合併号 a combined number ((for January and February)) / 合併集合《数》a union; a join / 合併授業 teaching a combined class / 合併症 a complication. 文例⤵

用法 会社・企業の「合併」という時、最も普通に用い

---

free to [It's up to you whether you] go or stay. / 甚だ勝手ですがお先に失礼させていただきます。Please excuse me for leaving before you.

かってでる そんな役を買って出る者がいるもんか。I'm sure no one will volunteer to play that role.

がってん がってんだ。All right. / O.K.

かっと あの人はすぐかっとなるたちだ。He is very quick-tempered. | He loses his temper easily.

かつどう 阿蘇山は今なお活動していて、いつ噴火するかもしれぬ。Mt. Aso is still active and may erupt at any time. / 水泳は体全身の筋肉を活動させる。Swimming brings nearly all the muscles of the body into play.

かっぱ[2] かっぱの川流れ。Even the best swimmer sometimes gets drowned. | Homer sometimes nods.〖諺〗

かっぱつ 彼女は女の子にしては少し活発過ぎる。She is a bit too active for a girl.

がっぺい 田中先生の倫理の講義はA, B, C 3クラス合併で行なわれます。Mr. Tanaka's lecture on ethics is given to the three classes A, B, and C combined. / A, B両社は合併してC社となった。A and B Companies (were) merged [amalgamated] to form C Company. / B社はA社に(吸収)合併された。B Company was merged into A Company. / 大丈夫合併

かっぽ 闊歩 ¶闊歩する stride; strut; swagger (about).

かつぼう 渇望 《文》a strong [an eager] desire (for); a craving (for); a longing (for); thirst (for) ¶渇望する《文》have a strong desire (for); 《文》desire *sth* eagerly; be eager for; long [thirst] for; 《文》crave for.

かっぽう 割烹 ⇒りょうり ¶割烹着 a cook's apron / 割烹旅館 a hotel priding itself on its restaurant [cuisine].

がっぽん 合本 copies 《of a magazine》bound together in one volume.

かつやく 活躍 activity; action ¶活躍する be active (in); take [play] an active part (in); 《文》participate actively (in). 文例↓

かつやくきん 括約筋 《解》a sphincter (muscle) ¶肛門括約筋 the anal sphincter.

かつよう 活用 practical use; application; 《文法》inflection (語尾の); declension (名詞の); conjugation (動詞の) ¶活用する put [turn] 《knowledge》to practical use; apply 《scientific discoveries to industrial production》; 《文》utilize 《one's experience》; make good use of 《one's abilities in a job》; 《文法》inflect; decline; conjugate / フルに活用する make full use of *sth*.

かつようじゅ 闊葉樹 ⇒こうようじゅ.

かつら 桂《植》a katsura (tree).

かつら 鬘 a wig; false hair ¶かつらを着けている wear a wig / かつら師 a wig maker. 文例↓

かつりょく 活力 energy; vitality; 《文》vital power [force]; 《口語》(plenty of) go.

かつれい 割礼 circumcision ¶割礼を施す circumcise *sb*.

カツレツ a fried cutlet ¶ポーク[チキン]カツレツ a fried pork [chicken] cutlet.

かつろ 活路 ¶活路を開く[見いだす] find a way out 《of the difficulty》; cut *one's* way 《through the enemy》.

かて 糧 food; bread ¶心の糧《文》spiritual nourishment / その日その日の糧を得る earn *one's* daily bread.

かてい¹ 仮定 an assumption; (a) supposition ¶仮定する assume; suppose; presume / …と仮定して assuming [supposing] that…; on the assumption [supposition] that…/ …と仮定しても (even) granted [granting] that… / 仮定法《文法》the subjunctive mood. 文例↓

かてい² 家庭 a home; a family; a household ¶家庭の平和[不和] domestic peace [trouble, 《文》discord] / 家庭の事情 for family reasons / 家庭を持つ make [start] a home; get married and settle down / 家庭的 homely 《atmosphere》; domestic 《type》; family-oriented 《men》/ 家庭科 domestic science / 家庭環境 one's family [home] background [environment] / 家庭教育 home training [education] / 家庭教師 ⇒かていきょうし / 家庭経済 household [domestic] economy / 家庭裁判所 a domestic (relations) court / 家庭常備薬 a household medicine / 家庭人 a family man / 家庭生活 home [family, domestic] life / 家庭争議 a family dispute; family [domestic] trouble / 家庭風の home-style 《meals》/ 家庭訪問 (a round of) calls at the homes of *one's* pupils / 家庭問題 home problems / 家庭用 for home [household, domestic] use / 家庭用品 household utensils [articles] / 家庭欄《新聞の》the household topics [the homemaking] page / 家庭料理 home cooking. 文例↓

かてい³ 過程 a process; a course; a stage ¶…の過程をたどる go through the process [stage] of… / 生産[製造]過程 a production [manufacturing] process.

かてい⁴ 課程《学科》a course;《全教科》a curriculum (*pl.* -s, -la) ¶高等学校の課程を修了する finish [complete, go through] the whole course of a high school. 文例↓

かていきょうし 家庭教師 a private teacher; a (private) tutor ¶家庭教師について勉強する study under a tutor / 家庭教師を雇う take on [《文》engage] a tutor / 家庭教師をする teach 《a boy》at 《his》home; tutor.

カテーテル catheter.

カテゴリー《論》a category ⇒はんちゅう.

かててくわえて かてて加えて 〈その上〉moreover; besides; in addition; on top of 《that》; 〈一層困ったことに〉to make matters worse. 文例↓

ガテマラ ⇒グアテマラ.

-がてら 文例↓

かでん¹ 家伝 ¶家伝の hereditary; 《techniques》handed on within the family / 家伝薬

症さえ起こらなければ病気はじきに治りますよ。I assure you that your disease will soon be cured if no complications arise [set in].

かつやく きょうの試合では彼が一番活躍した。He made the biggest impact [was the outstanding player] in today's game. / 彼は将来産業界で活躍したいと希望している。He hopes to play an active part in the industrial world.

かつら² かつらなんかしていないよ。This is my own hair (that I'm wearing)!

かてい¹ AB が CD に等しいと仮定してみよう。Let's assume [suppose] that AB is equal to CD. / それが事実だと仮定しても君の考えは間違っている。Even granted [granting] that it is true, you are still in the wrong.

かてい² 彼女は社交的というよりむしろ家庭的だ。She is domestic rather than sociable. / 彼は家庭的には全く恵まれなかった。His home life was anything but blissful.

かてい 右の者は本校所定の課程を修了したことを証明する。This is to certify that the above-mentioned has completed the prescribed course of this school.

かててくわえて かてて加えて雨まで降り出してきた。To make matters worse, it began to rain.

-がてら 今度の金曜日に京都に商用がてら遊びに行ってきます。I'm going to Kyoto next Friday partly on business and partly for

a medicine prepared from a family recipe.
かでん² 荷電 electric charge ¶荷電粒子 a [an electrically] charged particle.
がてん 合点 ⇒なっとく ¶合点が行かない様子で looking unconvinced; looking as if (he) is still in doubt; dubiously; doubtfully / 合点の行かない puzzling; strange;《an explanation》that does not make sense [hold water]. 文例⇩
がでんいんすい 我田引水 drawing water to one's own mill; turning sth to one's own advantage. 文例⇩
かと 過渡 ¶過渡的な transitional / 過渡期 ⇒かとき.
かど¹ 角〈曲り角〉a corner; an angle;〈人柄の〉the rough edges (of one's character); abrasiveness ¶〈性格の〉角が取れる〈事を主語〉smooth (down) the rough edges of one's character / 角のある〈人柄について〉abrasive《personality》; difficult《people》/ 角の取れた affable; sociable / 角の欠けた chipped / 角を取る round off the (sharp) corners / 角を曲がる turn [go round] a corner / 角に[で] on [at] the corner / 角地 a corner plot [(米) lot] / 角店[屋敷] a store [house] on [at] the corner; a corner store [house]. 文例⇩
かど² 門 the gate; the door ¶門ごとに at every door; from door to door.
かど³ 廉〈罪科〉a charge;〈疑い〉(a) suspicion;〈理由〉grounds;〈点〉a point ¶...した廉で on a charge of 《murder》; on the ground that....
かど⁴ 過度 ¶過度の too much;《文》excessive;《文》immoderate / 過度の労働[勉強] overwork /《文》excessive work; too much work / 過度に too much;《文》excessively /《文》to excess;《文》immoderately / 過度に眼を使う overtax one's eyes.
かとう¹ 下等 ¶下等な low; inferior;〈卑劣な〉mean;〈粗野な〉coarse;〈下品な〉vulgar / 下等な人間 a mean-spirited fellow;《文》a person of low character / 下等動物[植物] lower animals [plants].
かとう² 過当 ¶過当な《文》excessive;〈法外な〉exorbitant;〈不当な〉undue; undeserved / 過当競争 excessive competition.
かとう³ 果糖〖化〗fructose; fruit sugar.
かどう¹ 可動 ¶可動の movable; mobile / 可動軌条 a slide [movable] rail / 可動橋 a movable bridge.
かどう² 華道 the art of flower arrangement.
かどう³ 歌道 (the art of) tanka poetry.

かどう⁴ 稼働《文》operation; work ¶稼働中である〈人・機械が〉be working;〈人が〉be at work;〈機械が〉《文》be in operation / 稼働人口 the manpower / 稼働日数 the number of days worked.
かとうせいじ 寡頭政治 oligarchy.
かとき 過渡期 a transition(al) period; a period [an age] of transition.
かとく 家督 ¶家督を相続する succeed to a house; succeed《one's father》as the head of the family; inherit the family property [estate] / 家督を譲る transfer the headship of the family (to).
かどぐち 門口 ¶門口に at the door [gate]. 文例⇩
かどづけ 門付け a strolling singer [musician] ¶門付けする sing [play music] from door to door (for money).
かどで 門出《文》departure; setting off [out] ¶門出する set out [off] (on a trip); leave home;〈世に出る〉start in life;〈事業などに乗り出す〉launch into《a business career》/ 門出を祝う wish [bid] sb Godspeed; wish sb a good trip.
かどばる 角張る〈角が突き出ている〉be angular; have sharp corners;〈四角張る〉≒しかく¹.
かどばん 角番 a game (of shogi) in which the title is at stake; a game (of go) on the outcome of which the handicap for the games thereafter depends;〈比喩的に〉(be in) a make-or-break situation.
かどまつ 門松 the New Year's decorative pine trees [branches] ¶門松を立てる put [set] up decorative pine trees at the gate (for the New Year); decorate the gate with pine branches (for the New Year).
カドミウム〖化〗cadmium.
カドリール a [the] quadrille ¶カドリールを踊る dance the quadrille.
かとりせんこう 蚊取り線香 a mosquito (repellent) coil.
カトリック ¶カトリック教 Catholicism / カトリック教会 the (Roman) Catholic Church / カトリック教徒 a (Roman) Catholic.
ガドリニウム〖化〗gadolinium.
カトレア〖植〗a cattleya.
かどわかす ⇒ゆうかい¹《誘拐する》.
かとんぼ 蚊とんぼ a crane fly; a daddy longlegs (単複同形).
かな 仮名 (a) kana; the Japanese syllabary ¶仮

---

pleasure. / 私は昨日上野公園の花見がてら大石君を訪問した。I visited Oishi yesterday while I was out viewing the cherry blossoms in the Ueno Park.
がてん 彼の言う事はどうも合点が行かない。I can't buy what he says. / What he says doesn't convince me. / なぜそうなるのか合点が行かない。I can't see how that can be so. / もっと合点が行くように説明してくれ。Explain it to me some other way, so that I get your point.
がでんいんすい 我田引水のようですが、わが国において英語教育は今後ますますその重要性を増すことと思います。Though I say it myself, I think the teaching of English will become more important in this country.
かど¹ 最初の角を左にお曲がりなさい。Take the first turning on the left. | Turn to the left at the first corner. / ポストはこの通りの角にある。The mailbox is on the corner of this street. / そう言っては角が立つ。That would arouse bitterness [cause needless offense]. | That would sound unnecessarily harsh. / 人中へ出るようになれば彼も角が取れてくるだろう。Mixing with other people will smooth down his rough edges [make him better company]. | Association with others will make him more affable [his company more congenial].
かどぐち 彼を門口まで送って出た.

かなあみ 金網 wire netting; wire gauze (目の細かい).

かない 家内 〈妻〉 one's wife; 〈家族〉 a family; one's people [《米》folks] ¶家内の domestic; family; household / 家内で[一同] the whole family; all the members of one's family / 家内安全を祈る pray for the well-being of one's family / 家内工業 home manufacturing; a home [household, domestic] industry.

かなう 叶う[適, 敵]う 〈できる〉 can do; be equal to 《doing, the task》; be [lie] in one's power (事が主語); 〈願いなどが〉《文》be fulfilled; 《文》be realized; be heard; 〈適合する〉 suit 《one's taste》; answer [serve] 《the purpose》; meet 《one's wishes》; 〈一致する〉 agree 《with》; 《文》 accord 《with》; be consistent 《with》; 〈匹敵する〉 match; be a match 《for》; be equal 《to》; can compare 《with》 ¶願いがかなう one's wish is realized [fulfilled] / 〈神仏への祈りが〉 one's prayer is answered [heard] / わびがかなう one's apologies are accepted [by] / 道理にかなう accord [be consistent] with reason / 法にかなう 《文》 conform to the law / 心にかなった after one's fancy [one's (own) heart] / かなう事なら if possible; if it is in my power / かなわない 〈できない〉 be unable to do; be not equal to 《doing, the task》; be beyond one's power (事が主語); 〈対抗できない〉 be no match for...; can't match [stand comparison with].... 文例↓

かなえ 鼎 a tripod kettle ¶かなえの軽重を問われる one's ability is doubted [called in question].

かなえる 叶える grant 《sb's request [petition]》 ⇒ かなう.

かなきりごえ 金切り声 ¶金切り声を出す let out a scream [shrill cry]; scream; shriek / 金切り声で in a shrill voice.

かなきん 金巾 [《ポルトガル語》 canequim] 《米》 unbleached muslin; 《英》 calico.

かなぐ 金具 metal fittings; 〈金属製の部分〉 metallic [metal] parts ¶金具を打つ[つける] nail [fix] metal fittings 《on》.

かなくぎ 金釘 an iron nail ¶金くぎ流で書く have bad [clumsy, crabbed] writing; 《文》 write a bad [clumsy, crabbed] hand.

かなくさい 金臭い 〈味が〉 have a metallic taste; taste metallic; 〈においが〉 smell metallic.

かなぐし 金串 a metal skewer [spit].

かなくそ 金屎 slag; dross.

かなぐりすてる かなぐり捨てる fling [《文》cast] off; throw away.

かなけ 金気 〈鉄分〉 iron contained 《in water》; 〈味〉 a metallic taste.

かなしい 悲しい sad; unhappy; 《文》 sorrowful; 《文》 mournful; 〈哀れな〉 touching; pathetic; plaintive (声・音調などが); 〈嘆かわしい〉《文》 lamentable ¶悲しい顔付きをする look sad [unhappy, 《文》 sorrowful]; have a sad look on one's face / 悲しい思いがする, 悲しくなる feel sad [《文》 sorrowful] / 悲しいかな 《文》 alas! / 嬉しいときも悲しいときも in joy and in sorrow / 悲しい事に Sad to say, ...; Unfortunately, ...; It is a pity that... / 悲しそうに, 悲しげに sadly; with a sad look; sorrowfully; mournfully; 〈say〉 plaintively. 文例↓

かなしさ 悲しさ sadness; sorrow; 《文》 grief ¶悲しさの余り in [《文》 the excess of] one's grief [sorrow]. 文例↓

かなしばり 金縛り ¶金縛りになっている be bound hand and foot (by the contract); be tied [chained] down (by the regulations of the company).

かなしみ 悲しみ sorrow; sadness; unhappiness; 《文》 grief; distress; 〈悲嘆〉《文》 lamentation; mourning ¶悲しみに沈んでいる be sunk in grief. 文例↓

かなしむ 悲しむ feel sad [unhappy]; feel sorrow 《for》; be grieved 《at》; 〈気の毒に思う〉 feel sorry 《for》; regret; 〈嘆く〉《文》 lament; deplore ¶人の不幸を悲しむ feel sorry for sb's misfortune / 悲しんで 《文》 in sorrow; sorrowfully / 悲しむべき 〈悲しい〉 ⇒ かなしい; 〈遺憾な〉 regrettable. 文例↓

かなた 彼方 ⇒ あちら ¶はるかかなたに far in the distance; far off [away] / 海のかなたに beyond [across] the sea.

カナダ Canada ¶カナダの Canadian / カナダ

I saw him out as far as the gate.
かな この仮名遣いは間違っている. This use of kana is wrong [mistaken].
かなう 私の身にかなう事なら何でもいたします. I will do anything in my power for you. / 祈願がかなって彼女の息子は無事に戦地から帰った. Her prayers were answered and her son came home safely from the front. / それは願ったりかなったりです. That's just what I have been wishing for. / 理想にかなった人は少ない. Very few people measure up to our ideal. / 僕もテニスは得意だが君にはかなわない. I'm good at tennis, too, but I'm no match for you [but you are more than a match for me]. / 棒高飛びでは彼にかなう者は一人もいない. He has no equal when it comes to pole vaulting. | As a pole jumper he is unrivaled [second to none]. / こんなに大勢が相手ではとてもかなわない. There is no way we can win [no contending] against such heavy odds. / こう暑くてはかなわない. I can't stand this heat. | This heat is unbearable [more than I can put up with].
かなしい 悲しいかなわが友今やなし. Alas! my friend is no more! / それを思うと悲しくなる. It grieves me [It makes me unhappy] to think of it. / The thought of it makes me unhappy [sad]. / あまり悲しくて涙も出なかった. I was too overwhelmed with grief even to weep. / 彼女は悲しげにじっと私を見た. She gazed at me with a sad look.
かなしさ 彼女の胸は悲しさで一杯であった. Her heart was filled with grief.
かなしみ 時がたてば彼女の悲しみも和らぐことだろう. I hope time will take the edge off her sorrow.

かなだらい 人 a Canadian / フランス系カナダ人 a French Canadian.
かなだらい 金盥 a metal basin; 〈洗面器〉a metal washbowl [washbasin].
かなづち 金槌 a hammer ¶金づちでくぎを打つ drive a nail with a hammer; hammer a nail (in the board). 文例⇩
カナッペ a canapé.
かなつぼまなこ 金壺眼 deep-set staring eyes.
かなつんぼ 金聾 ¶金つんぼの stone-deaf; as かなてこ 鉄梃 a crowbar. | deaf as a post.
かなでる 奏でる play (the koto).
かなとこ 金床 an anvil.
かなぶん(ぶん)〔昆〕a (Japanese) drone beetle.
かなめ 要 〈扇の〉the pivot; 〈要点〉a main [vital, pivotal] point; the point ¶かなめ石 a keystone.
かなもの 金物 〈器物〉iron [metal] goods; hardware; ironware; 〈金具〉metal fittings ¶金物屋〈店〉a hardware store; 〈英〉an ironmonger's (shop); 〈人〉a hardware merchant; 〈英〉an ironmonger.
かならず 必ず 〈きっと〉certainly; surely; without fail; 〈是非とも〉by all means; 〈常に〉always; invariably; 〈必然的に〉〈文〉necessarily; inevitably ¶必ず…するbe sure to do; never fail to do; do without fail / 必ず…することに決めている make a point of doing; make it a rule to do / 必ずしも…でない be not always [necessarily]…. 文例⇩
かなり considerably (higher); rather 〈expensive〉; 〈口語〉a good bit (taller); 〈口語〉good and (short); 〈口語〉pretty (good) ★「かなり」は fairly と訳す傾向があるが, fairly は意味が弱く適訳ではない ¶かなりの considerable (expense); quite a (task); a lot of (people); quite a bit of (time) / かなりの大金 a sizable [considerable] sum of money / かなりの収入 a decent [respectable] income / かなり長い間 (for) quite a long time (a while); for a considerable time / かなり大きな家 rather a [a rather] large house; a pretty big house; a good-sized house. 文例⇩
カナリヤ〔鳥〕a canary.
がなる shout [bark] (at) ¶(拡声機などが)がなり立てる blare (out).
かに 蟹 〔動〕a crab ¶かにのはさみ ⇨ はさみ / かににはさまれる be nipped [bitten] by a crab /

かに缶〈米〉canned crab; 〈英〉tinned crab; a can [tin] of crab meat / かに工船 a crab-canning boat / かに座〔天〕Cancer; the Crab ⇨ざ 文例 / かに族 backpackers / かに漁 crab fishing; crabbing. 文例⇩
かにく 果肉 flesh; pulp (柔らかい).
がにまた 蟹股 ¶がにまたの bowlegged; bandy-legged / がにまたで歩く walk bowlegged [bandy-legged].
かにゅう 加入 joining; entry; 〈文〉admission; 〈電話の〉having a telephone installed ¶加入する join (an association); become a member of 〈a club〉; 〈電話に〉have a telephone installed; be [have oneself] put on the telephone / 国連に加入させる seat (a newly independent country) in the United Nations / 加入者 a member; 〈電話の〉a (telephone) subscriber.
カヌー 〈舟〉a canoe; 〈事〉canoeing; 〈競技〉a canoeing event ¶カヌーをこぐ paddle a canoe / カヌーで川を下る canoe down a river / カヌー競漕 a canoe race.
かね[1] 金 〈金銭〉money; 〈財産〉〈文〉wealth; 〈文〉riches; 〈金額〉a sum; 〈金属〉(a) metal ¶たくさん[わずか]の金 a large [small] sum of money / 金がある have plenty of money; be rich; be well off / 金がない have no money; be poor; be badly off / 金が有り余っている have more money than one can spend; 〈口語〉be rolling in money; have so much money (that) one doesn't know what to do with it / 金が掛かる cost [take] (one) a lot of money; be expensive / 金の問題 a matter of money / 金の入る道 a source of income [revenue] / 金が入る〈人が主語〉come into (a lot of) money / 金を掛ける spend money (on clothes) / 金をこしらえる raise money [funds] (for) / 金を寝かす let money lie idle / 金に困っている 〈口語〉be pressed for [short of] money; 〈口語〉be hard up (for money); have (got) money problems / 〈文〉be in financial difficulties / …を金にする make money out of sth; turn sth into money / 金になる be profitable; be paying; there is money (in sth) / 金にならない仕事 unprofitable work; a job that does not pay / 自分の金で at one's own expense / 金で済むことなら if money can settle (it) / 金で買う buy sth with money / 金で地位につく buy oneself

---

かなしむ 彼はその試みが失敗に終わったと聞いて悲しんだ. It made him sad to hear [He learned to his sorrow] that the attempt ended in a failure. / 彼女は息子の死を悲しんで泣いた. She wept over her son's death. / 今はいたずらに悲しんでいる時ではない. This is no time (for us) to be giving way to our grief.
かなづち 彼は金づちだ. He cannot swim a stroke. | He can't swim any more than a pig can fly.
かならず 食事の前に必ず手を洗いなさい. Be sure to wash your hands before meals. / 彼は必ず失敗する. He is bound [certain, sure] to fail. / 彼は朝飯前に必ず1時間散歩をする. He makes it a rule to have an hour's walk before breakfast. / 彼らは会えば必ずけんかをする. They never meet without quarreling. / 勝敗は必ずしも数の多少にはよらない. Success in battle does not always depend on numbers. / 人は金があるからといって必ずしも幸福であるとは限らない. Because a man is rich it does not necessarily

follow that he is happy.
かなり 今朝はかなり雪が降った. Quite a bit of snow fell this morning. / 彼はかなり自由に英語を話す. He speaks English very [rather] well. / 日本の知識人で自分たちの文化は外国人には容易に理解され得ないと誤解している者がかなり多い. Quite a number of Japanese intellectuals are under the false impression that their culture can hardly be appreciated by foreigners.
かに かには甲羅に似せて穴を掘る. The crab digs a hole that fits

かね² 鐘, 鉦 a bell;＜どら＞a gong ¶放課の鐘 the closing bell / 鐘が鳴る a bell rings [sounds]; ＜教会の＞ the bells ring [chime] / 鐘の音＜寺の＞ the sound [peal] of a temple bell; ＜教会の＞ the chimes of the church bells / (教会の)鐘の ひも 《pull》 the bell rope / 鐘を鳴らす ring [sound] / 鐘を強く strike [toll] a bell / 鉦や太鼓で探す make every effort to find sb [sth]; look [search] for sb [sth] for all one is worth / 鐘突き a bell ringer / 鐘突き堂 a bell house. 文例⇩

かねあい 兼ね合い ¶千番に一番のかね合い an extremely difficult [delicate] affair / …との かね合いで keeping [with] 《the budget》 in mind; in view of 《the financial situation》. 文例⇩

かねいれ 金入れ ＜銭箱＞ a cashbox; a till; ＜財 布＞ a purse; a pocketbook; a wallet (札入れ).

かねかし 金貸 a moneylender; a usurer (高利貸し) ¶金貸しをする run a moneylending business.

かねがね ⇨ かねて. 文例⇩

かねぐり 金繰り ¶金繰りがつかない can't (manage to) raise the funds 《for》. 文例⇩

かねじゃく 曲尺 ＜大工の＞ a metal measure; a carpenter's square; ＜鯨尺に対して＞ the regular shaku (= 30.303 cm).

かねずく 金ずく ¶金ずくで＜金の力で＞ by using money as one's weapon [bait]; by power of money; ＜金を出して＞ for money. 文例⇩

かねそなえる 兼ね備える ¶AとB(と)を兼ね 備える have both A and B; have B as well as A [A as well as B] ⇨ –ばかり 囲語.

かねつ¹ 加熱 ¶加熱する heat / 加熱殺菌する sterilize (milk) by heating.

かねつ² 過熱 ¶過熱する overheat; superheat (液体を蒸発させないで沸騰点以上に熱する). 文例⇩

かねづかい 金遣い ¶金遣いが荒い spend money lavishly [wastefully]; be too free [generous] with one's money; 《口語》 throw [fling] one's money about [around]; 《口語》 spend money like water; 《俗》 spend money like it's going out of fashion / 金遣いの荒い人 an extravagant person; a spendthrift; a big [lavish] spender.

かねづまり 金詰まり (a) shortage of money [funds]; financial pressure; ＜金融市場の＞ tight money ¶金詰まりである be short of fund; be pressed [pinched] for money. 文例⇩

かねづる 金蔓 ¶金づるをつかむ find a supplier of funds (a financial supporter).

かねて ＜前もって＞ before; 《文》 previously; beforehand; ＜既に＞ already; ＜しばらく前から＞ for some time (past) ¶かねて計画していた 旅行 the trip one has been planning to make for some time (past); 《文》 one's intended [contemplated] trip / かねての望み 《文》 one's long-cherished desire / かねての計画どおり according to the prearranged plan [program]. 文例⇩

–かねない …兼ねない ⇨ かねる.

かねばなれ 金離れ ¶金離れがいい be generous [liberal, free] with one's money; be open-handed / 金離れが悪い be stingy; be tight-fisted; be close-fisted. 文例⇩

かねまわり 金回り ¶金回りがいい have plenty of money; be well off; be in funds / 金回 りが悪い be short of money; 《口語》 be hard up (for money); be badly off.

かねめ 金目 ¶金目の物 a valuable article. 「valuables.

かねもうけ 金儲け making money; moneymaking ¶金もうけがうまい be clever [good] at making money.

かねもち 金持ち a rich [wealthy] person; 《文》 a person of wealth [means] ¶金持ちの rich; wealthy; 《文》 affluent; 《文》 opulent / 金持ち の家に生まれる be born rich [into money] / 金持ちになる get [grow,《文》 become] rich; make a fortune [《口語》pile] / 大金持ちになる get very rich; 《文》 accumulate [amass, achieve] great wealth; become a millionaire / 大変な金持 ちである be fabulously rich; 《文》 have a

---

[suits] its shell.
かね¹ 僕は外套が欲しいけれども買う金がない。 I want an overcoat, but I have no money to buy one (with). / そんなぜいたくな車を買うだけの金の余裕がない。 I cannot afford (the money for) such an expensive car. / この家には大分金が掛かりました。 It took a lot of money to build this house. / 金の持ち合わせがない。 I have no cash on [with] me. / 金の生る木 はない。 Money does not grow on trees. / 金の切れ目が縁の切れ目。 When poverty comes in at the door, love flies out at the window. 《諺》 / この計画は金を食うぞ。 I'm afraid this project will simply eat money. / この仕事は少しも金にならない。 There's no money in this job. / 彼は金で動くような人じゃない。 He can't be bought. / この世に金で動かぬ人 はいない、と彼はうそぶいた。 He said cynically that every man has his price. / 幾ら金を出しても幸福は買えない。 No amount of money can buy happiness. / 彼は子供の教育には金を惜しまない。 He doesn't begrudge what he has to pay for his childrens' education. / 君のためなら喜んで金を出そう。 Since it's you who's asking for money, I'll gladly let you have it. / 金がいるんならいつでも用立てましょう。 If it's money you need, you only have to ask. / 彼らは金は出すが口は出さない。 They open their checkbooks without opening their mouths too much. | They are generous with their money, but sparing with their advice. / 金は天下の 回りもの。 Money moves from pocket to pocket. | If money can be lost, it can also be regained.

かね² ほら、鐘が鳴っている。 Listen! There goes the bell! / 教会 の鐘が10時を告げた。 The church bells struck [rang] ten.
かねあい 千番に一番の兼ね合いだ。 It's a one-in-a-thousand chance.
かねがね 彼女が美人だということはかねがね耳にしていた。 I have often heard about her beauty. / パリへ行ってみたいとかねがね思っていた。 It has been my long-cherished desire to visit Paris.
かねぐり 金繰りはだれがつけるのか。 Who is going to raise the funds for it?
かねずく 金ずくで彼女に「うん」と言わせたのさ。 It was money that induced her to welcome his advances [to agree to his suggestions]. | ＜結婚の申し込みの場合＞ It was his money that made her accept him [say 'yes'] (when he proposed).

かねる 《具備する》combine [unite] 《A with B》; 〈役立つ〉serve both as 《A and B》; 〈兼職する〉hold 《a post》 in addition to one's regular one; hold 《two posts》 at once 《文》 simultaneously, 《文》 concurrently ¶書斎と客間とを兼ねた室 a room serving both as a study and a drawing room / 首相と外相を兼ね る hold the portfolio for Foreign Affairs concurrently with the premiership / 用事と遊びを兼ねて partly on business and partly for pleasure; on business combined with pleasure. 文例↓

-かねる 〈ためらう〉hesitate to do; be unwilling [reluctant] to do; 〈できない〉cannot do; cannot [《文》 can ill] afford to do; be not in a position to do; be unable to do ¶…しかねない be quite capable of doing; do not scruple to do / どんな悪事もしかねない be not capable of any crime / あの人なら…しかねない I wouldn't put it past him [her] to do / 申し上げかねますが…. Excuse me, but…. 文例↓

かねん 可燃 ¶可燃性 combustibility; flammability / 可燃性試験 a flammability test / 可燃性の combustible; flammable / 可燃物 combustibles; (in)flammable materials.

かの 彼の ⇨あの ¶かの地 that place [country]; there.

かのう¹ 化膿 《医》 suppuration; the formation [discharge] of pus ¶化膿する suppurate; 〈傷が〉fester; 〈できものが〉come to a head / 化膿した festering 《sores》; 《医》 purulent 《lesions》 / 化膿菌 suppurative [pyogenic] microorganisms.

かのう² 可能 ¶可能性 possibility; 〈潜在的な〉potential; 《文》 potentialities / 可能な、可能性のある possible / 大いに売り上げを伸ばす可能性のある 《an invention》 with a big sales potential / 可能性のない not possible; impossible / 可能性を開発する develop one's potential [potentialities] / 可能にする make sth possible; enable sb 《to do》 / 可能性事 a possibility. 文例↓

かのこ 鹿の子 ¶鹿の子絞り dappled cloth / 鹿の子まだらの dappled; white-spotted.

かのじょ 彼女 she; 〈恋人〉one's girlfriend; 《口語》 one's girl ¶彼女は[が] she / 彼女の[に、 を] her / 彼女のもの hers.

かば 樺 ¶かば色 reddish yellow / かばの木 a birch tree.

かば² 河馬 《動》 a hippopotamus 《pl. -muses, -mi》; 《口語》 a hippo 《pl. -s》 ¶こびとかば a pygmy hippopotamus.

カバー 〈おおい〉a cover; 〈本の〉a jacket; a dust cover [jacket, wrapper]; 《スポーツ》 covering ¶カバーする 《スポーツ》 cover 《second base》; 〈償う〉meet 《sb's expenses》; make up 《a loss》 / カバーをかける cover 《a chair》; put the cover on 《the machine》 / タイプのカバーを取る take the cover off a typewriter (★ take off the cover of a typewriter とはあまり言わない) / カバーガール a cover girl / カバーチャージ a cover charge.

かばう 庇う 〈守る〉protect [shield] sb 《from harm》; take sb under one's wing; 〈とりなす〉plead for sb; stick up for sb; take sb's part; cover up for sb 《過失などを隠蔽して》. 文例↓

がばがば ¶《靴などが》がばがばだ be too large 《for one》.

がはく 画伯 ⇨がか² ¶横山大観画伯 the master artist Taikan Yokoyama.

かばしら 蚊柱 a column of swarming mosquitoes.

がばと ¶がばと跳ね起きる spring [jump, start] to one's feet; spring up 《from one's bed》.

かばやき 蒲焼 a (split and) broiled eel [loach]; a spitchcock ¶蒲焼にする (split and) broil 《an eel》.

かばり 蚊鉤 a [an artificial] fly ¶蚊ばりで釣る fly-fish; fish [angle] with a fly.

かはん¹ 河畔 the banks of a river; the riverside ¶河畔のホテル a riverside hotel. 文例↓

かねる² 日本の経済は少々過熱気味である。Japan's economy is overheating somewhat.

かねづまり 金詰まりで今しばらくはその計画もこれ以上は進められない。Money is so tight [We are so short of funds] we won't be able to go ahead with the project for some time.

かねて かねて聞いていたよりはどすぐ [よほど] すぐれていた。It was far better than I had heard. / おうわさはかねてから田中さんからお聞きしておりました。I've often heard [I've heard a lot] about you from Mr. Tanaka.

かねばなれ 人は金をたくさん持っているときより持っていないときの方が金離れのいいことがある。People are sometimes more generous when they don't have much money than when they have plenty.

かねもうけ その仕事は大して金もうけにならない。There isn't much money (to be made) in that business.

かねもち 金持ち苦労多し。Care follows wealth. | Much coin, much care. 《諺》 / 金持ちけんかせず。A rich man never quarrels.

かねる 彼は1人で校長、教頭、用務員をみな兼ねている。He is principal, teacher, and janitor, all in one. / この書斎は応接間も兼ねている。This study serves as a drawing room, too. / 監査役は取締役を兼ねることはできない。An auditor may not at the same time be a director.

-かねる 遺憾ながらご依頼に応じかねます。I regret to say that I am not in a position to comply with your request. / 忙しかったので彼の招待には応じかねた。I was so busy that I was unable to accept his invitation. / それだけはいたしかねます。I will do anything but that. / あの男ならそんな事もしかねない。I wouldn't put it past him. / 目的を遂げるためにはどんな事でもしかねない男だ。He will stop at nothing [He would go to any lengths] to achieve his objective [ends].

かのう² 成功の可能性はまずない。Their chances of success are very slim [virtually nil]. | They have only a slim chance of making good. / 彼のような男は善にも悪にも大きな可能性を生来備えている。A man like him has a great potential for either good or evil.

かばう 彼は手を挙げて身をかばった。He raised his arm to protect [shield] himself from the blow. / だれも私をかばってくれない。No one takes my part.

かはん¹ ロンドンはテムズ河畔に

かはん² 過半 ⇨ かはんすう.
かばん 鞄 a bag; a satchel (学生用で肩にかけたりする); 〈書類などを入れる〉 a briefcase; an attaché case (平たくて固い); 〈旅行用の〉 a (travel) bag; a suitcase (四角い) ¶ かばんに詰める put 《things》 in [into] a bag; pack a bag / かばん持ち 《口語》 a sidekick; a flunky (軽蔑的).
がばん 画板 a drawing [drafting] board.
かはんしん 下半身 the lower half of the body.
かはんすう 過半数 the greater part [number] 《of》; the majority; more than half 《the members》 ¶ 過半数を得る get [win, 《文》 obtain] a [an absolute] majority / 国会で過半数を占める hold a majority in the Diet. [文例⇩]
かひ 可否 〈是非〉 right or wrong; 〈当否〉 《文》 propriety; 《文》 advisability; 〈賛否〉 ayes and noes; pros and cons; for and against ¶ 可否の投票 votes for and against 《a bill》 / 可否の論 the pros and cons 《of a question》 / …の可否を論じる discuss [argue about] the propriety [advisability] of… / 投票で可否を決する decide 《a matter》 by vote; put 《a matter》 to the [a] vote; take a vote 《on a matter》. [文例⇩]
かび¹ 黴 (a) mold ¶ 青かび green mold / 白かび 〈食品などにつく〉 mold; 〈本·カメラ·植物の葉などにつく〉 mildew / かびが生える, かびる go [get, 《文》 become] moldy / かびが生えた, かびた moldy; mildewed / かびだらけである[になる] be covered with mold [mildew] / かびを取り除く get the mold [mildew] off *sth*; 《文》 remove the mold [mildew] 《from》 / かび臭い musty; fusty; 〈古臭い〉 stale / かび菌 a mold (fungus).
かび² 華美 〈華やかさ〉 splendor; magnificence; 〈けばけばしさ〉 pomp; gaudiness ¶ 華美な splendid; pompous; showy; gaudy / 華美な服装をする be gaily [flashily, gaudily] dressed.
かひつ 加筆 ¶ 加筆する touch up; retouch; 〈原稿などに〉 revise; correct.
がびょう 画鋲 《米》 a thumbtack; 《英》 a drawing pin ¶ 画鋲でとめる 《米》 tack [《英》 pin] 《a poster to the wall》.
かびる 黴びる ⇨ かび¹.
かびん¹ 花瓶 a (flower) vase ¶ 花瓶にさす put 《dahlias》 in a vase.
かびん² 過敏 ¶ 過敏な too sensitive 《to, about》; 《文》 hypersensitive 《to, about》; nervous (神経が); allergic 《to》 (アレルギー症) / 過敏症 hypersensitivity 《to》; allergy 《to》.
かふ¹ 火夫 ⇨ かま¹ (かまたき).
かふ² 下付 ¶ 下付する grant 《a license》; issue 《a passport》.
かふ³ 寡婦 ⇨ みぼうじん, やもめ.
かぶ¹ 株 〈切り株〉 a stump; 〈根〉 roots; 〈(会社の資本の一部としての)株式〉 stock [shares] 《in a company》; 〈株券〉 《米》 a stock (certificate); 《英》 a share (certificate); 〈しにせののれん〉 goodwill ¶ (比喩的に)株が上がる *one's* stock rises [goes up]; 〈事が主語〉 《文》 raise *one* in the public esteem / 株を買う[売る] 《米》 buy [sell] stocks; 《英》 buy [sell] shares / 株を10,000株買う buy 10,000 shares 《of a company》 / (植物の)株を分けてふやす multiply 《a plant》 by division [dividing *its* roots] / 株に手を出す dabble in stocks; play the (stock) market / 株でもうける[損する] make [lose] money on the stock market / 株屋 a stockbroker. [文例⇩]
かぶ² 蕪 〖植〗 a turnip.
かぶ³ 下部 the lower part ¶ 下部構造 the understructure; a substructure / 下部組織 a lower branch 《of an organization》; an infrastructure.
がふ 画布 《a piece of》 canvas.
かふう 家風 a family custom [tradition]; the ways of a family ¶ 家風に合わない be out of keeping with the ways of the [*one's*] family.
がふう 画風 *one's* style of painting; *one's* brushwork.
カフェイン 〖化〗 caffein(e) ¶ カフェイン抜きの caffeinless [caffein-free] 《coffee》.
かぶか 株価 the price of a stock; a stock price ¶ 株価指数 the price index of stocks.
がぶがぶ ¶ がぶがぶ飲む drink a great deal of 《water》; drink 《beer》 in great drafts; guzzle 《beer》.
かぶき 歌舞伎 the *kabuki* ¶ 歌舞伎役者 a *kabuki* actor.
かぶきもん 冠木門 a roofed gate.
かふく 禍福 fortune and [or] misfortune; good and [or] bad [《文》 ill] luck. [文例⇩]
かふくぶ 下腹部 the abdomen; 〈陰部〉 ⇨ いんぶ.
かぶけん 株券 《米》 a stock (certificate); 《英》 a share (certificate).
かぶさる 被さる hang over; cover. [文例⇩]
かぶしき 株式 stock; shares ⇨ かぶ¹, かぶけん ¶ 株式を発行する issue shares / 株式を募集する offer shares for subscription / 株式会社 a joint-stock company; 《米》 a stock company [corporation] ★ 社名に書く場合は, 《米》 …, Inc.; 《英》 …Co., Ltd. と略記する / 株式市況[相場] stock quotations [prices] / 株式市場 the

---

ある. London is situated on the Thames.
かはんすう 合格者の過半数は大学出身者であった. The majority of the successful candidates were university graduates.
かひ この問題に対して可否の論が色々とあった. There were a lot of opinions, pro and con, on this question. / 投票の結果は可否相半ばした. The votes were equally divided.
かぶ¹ B社の株は現在700円になっている. B Company shares stand at 700 (yen). / 僕はあの会社の株を持っている. I have some shares in that company. | I have some of that company's stock. / 彼はP社の株を買い占めているというこうわさだ. Rumor has it that he is buying up the shares of P Company. / 学生間では彼の株が急に上った. His stock [reputation] with the students has soared [risen sharply].
かふく 禍福はあざなえるなわのごとし. Good and ill luck are next-door neighbors [are closely interwoven].
かぶさる 彼が休んだので, 仕事がこっちにかぶさって来て, 今日は一日中忙しかった. He has been away, so we have been that much busier all day.
かぶる 女性は屋内でも帽子をかぶったままでいていい. It is all

カフス cuffs ¶カフスボタン cuff links; ⟨縫い付けの⟩ sleeve [cuff] buttons.

かぶせる 被せる cover *sth* ⟨with earth⟩; plate *sth* ⟨with gold⟩; put ⟨a quilt⟩ on [over] *sb* ¶歯に金をかぶせる put a gold crown on a tooth; crown a tooth with gold / 罪をかぶせる ⇨つみ¹(罪を着せる).

カプセル ⟨薬・人工衛星の⟩ a capsule.

かふそく 過不足 ¶過不足のない neither too much nor too little; just enough / 肉付きが過不足がない be neither too fat nor too thin.

かぶと 兜 a (war) helmet ¶かぶとを脱ぐ take *one's* helmet off; ⟨比喩的に⟩ admit defeat; ⟨文⟩ give *sb* best.

かぶとがに 【動】 a horseshoe crab.

かぶとむし 甲虫 a beetle.

かぶぬし 株主 a stockholder; a shareholder ¶株主総会 a general meeting (of a company [corporation]); a stockholders' [shareholders'] meeting.

かぶばんしゅうごう 可付番集合 【数】 an enumerable set.

かぶら 蕪 【植】 a turnip.

カプリチオ 【音楽】 a caprice; a capriccio (*pl.* -s, -ci).

かぶりつき 嚙り付き ⟨劇場の⟩ the front row of the orchestra seats; front-row seats on the main floor.

かぶりつく 嚙り付く fasten *one's* teeth ⟨on⟩; bite ⟨into⟩.

がぶりと ¶がぶりとかみつく sink *its* [*one's*] teeth into ⟨*sb's* arm⟩.

かぶりもの 被り物 headgear.

かぶる 被る ⟨帽子を⟩ put ⟨*one's* hat⟩ on; ⟨布団などを⟩ pull ⟨the quilt⟩ over *one's* head; ⟨写真⟩ be fogged ¶帽子をかぶってみる try a hat on / 帽子をかぶっている have a hat on; wear [be wearing] a hat / 帽子をかぶっていないは bareheaded; be hatless / 帽子をかぶらないで外出する go out without *one's* [without a, with no] hat on / 帽子をかぶりなおす adjust *one's* hat / セーターを頭からかぶって pull [⟨文⟩ draw] a sweater over *one's* head / ほこりをかぶる be covered with dust / 水をかぶる ⟨体に⟩ pour water over oneself; ⟨畑などに⟩ be under [covered with] water; ⟨文⟩ be submerged / 罪をかぶる ⇨つみ¹(罪を着る). 文例⇩

がぶる ⟨船などが⟩ pitch ¶がぶって寄る 【相撲】 force *one's* opponent out with repeated shoves.

かぶれる ⟨漆などに⟩ react ⟨to lacquer⟩ by coming out in a rash; be poisoned ⟨by a sumac(h)⟩; ⟨米口語⟩ get poison ivy; get [⟨文⟩ contract] a rash ⟨from a medicine⟩; ⟨…に感化される⟩ be influenced ⟨by *sb*⟩; ⟨口語⟩ go overboard for ⟨the British way of life⟩ ¶アメリカ[英国]かぶれの人 an Americanized [Anglicized] person.

かふん 花粉 pollen ¶花粉症 【医】 pollinosis.

かぶん¹ 過分 ⟨過度の⟩ ⟨文⟩ excessive; ⟨不相応な⟩ undeserved; ⟨文⟩ unmerited; ⟨文⟩ undue. 文例⇩

かぶん² 寡聞 文例⇩

かぶんすう 仮分数 an improper fraction.

かべ 壁 a wall; ⟨障壁⟩ a (blank) wall; a barrier ¶壁のない wall-less; open-sided / 壁を塗る plaster a wall; ⟨塗料で⟩ paint a wall ⟨green⟩ / 壁を破る ⟨比喩的に⟩ break the ⟨two-hour⟩ barrier; make a breakthrough / 壁に絵を掛ける hang a picture on the wall / ⟨困難などの⟩壁に突き当たる run into [come up against] a stone [brick] wall / 壁で仕切る ⟨ふさぐ, 囲む⟩ wall *sth* off [up, in] / 壁一重隔てて with a wall between ⟨us⟩ / 壁板 a wall panel [board]; ⟨総称⟩ wall paneling / 壁新聞 a wall newspaper / 壁土 plaster; wall mud. 文例⇩

かへい 貨幣 ⟨通貨⟩ money; currency; ⟨硬貨⟩ a coin ¶貨幣価値 the value of money / 貨幣経済 (a) money economy / 貨幣制度 the monetary system / 貨幣単位 a monetary [currency] unit.

かべかけ 壁掛け a tapestry; a wall-hanging.

かべがみ 壁紙 wallpaper ¶部屋に緑色の壁紙を張る (wall)paper a room in green; cover the walls of a room with green wallpaper.

かべん 花弁 a petal ⇨ はなびら.

かほう¹ 下方 ¶下方に below; down (below); downward.

かほう² 加法 【数】 addition ⇨ たしざん.

かほう³ 果報 ⟨good⟩ fortune ¶果報者 a lucky [fortunate] person [fellow]. 文例⇩

かほう⁴ 家宝 an heirloom; a family treasure.

がほう 画報 an illustrated magazine; a pictorial (magazine).

かほうわ 過飽和 【化】 supersaturation ¶過飽和溶液 a supersaturated solution.

がぼがぼ ¶がぼがぼいう[音を立てる] squelch.

かほご 過保護 overprotection; overprotectiveness ¶過保護児童 a pampered child; an overprotected child. 文例⇩

---

right for women to keep their hats on indoors. / あの帽子はもう少し左にかぶるといい。Your hat should [needs to] go a little more to the left. / 船は波をかぶり始めた。The boat began to ship water.

かぶん¹ こんなに過分なお礼を頂戴して恐縮です。I am afraid I hardly deserve this sort of remuneration.

かぶん² その事はまだ寡聞にして存じません。I've heard nothing about it yet.

かべ この壁にびょうで物をとめることはお断わり。〈掲示〉 No thumbtacks to be used on this wall. / 彼が初めて400メートル競走で45秒の壁を破った。He was the first man to crack the 45 second barrier for 400 meters. / 技術上の壁を突き破らなければ我々の目的は達成できない。We need a technological breakthrough if we are to achieve our purpose. / 交渉は厚い壁に突き当たってしまった。The negotiations have come up against a brick wall. / 壁に耳あり。Walls have ears. 〈諺〉

かほう³ 果報は寝て待て。Everything comes to those who wait. 〈諺〉

かほご 彼らは独り息子に対して少々過保護のようだね。They seem to be a bit too protective toward their only son. / 彼は母親の過保護から逃げるために寮に入ろうと決心した。He made up his mind

かぼそい か細い ⟨細い⟩ slender; slim; ⟨弱い⟩ delicate; fragile; ⟨かすかな⟩ faint; feeble ¶か細い声 (in) a feeble voice.

かぼちゃ a pumpkin.

カボベルデ (the Republic of) Cape Verde ¶カボベルデ人 a Cape Verdian.

ガボン Gabon ¶ガボン共和国 the Gabonese Republic / ガボン人 a Gabonese.

かほんか 禾本科 ¶禾本科植物 (true) grasses.

かま¹ 釜, 窯 ⟨炊事用の⟩ a pot; ⟨湯沸かし⟩ a kettle; a ca(u)ldron (両側に取っ手のついた大型の); ⟨汽缶⟩ a boiler; ⟨かまど⟩ a furnace; an oven; ⟨陶器やれんがを焼く⟩ a kiln ¶飯をたくかま a rice-cooker; a pot [cooker] for boiling rice / 茶の湯のかま a teakettle / 一つかまの飯を食う⟪文⟫ break bread with sb; live under the same roof as sb (1人が主語) / live under the same (a single) roof (その全員が主語) / かまたき a stoker; a fireman; a boilerman / 窯元 a potter / かまゆで boiling in a caldron.

かま² 鎌 a sickle; a reaping hook; a scythe (大きな) ¶かまで稲を刈る reap rice with a sickle / かまをかける trap [trick] sb (into telling the truth); put a leading question to sb.

がま¹ 蒲 ⟪植⟫ a cattail; a reed mace. 文例⇩

がま² ⟪動⟫ a toad ¶がまの脂(ｱﾌﾞﾗ) toad's grease.

かまう 構う ⟨意に介する⟩ mind, care about; be concerned about; trouble [concern] oneself about; pay attention to; take notice of; ⟪文⟫ give [pay] heed to; ⟨からかう⟩ tease; ⟨干渉する⟩ meddle in [with]; interfere in [with]; ⟨相手にする⟩ have something to do with; ⟨待遇する⟩ entertain; ⟪文⟫ be attentive to; ⟨世話する⟩ care for; look after ¶費用を構わず regardless of expense; without regard to cost. 文例⇩

かまえ 構え ⟨身構え⟩ a posture; a pose; ⟨構造⟩ structure; construction; ⟨様式⟩ a style; ⟨外観⟩ an appearance. 文例⇩

かまえる 構える ⟨身構える⟩ get set (to do); ⟪文⟫ assume a posture (of defense); ⟨用意する⟩ get [make] ready (to do); be [⟪文⟫ stand] ready [prepared] (for); ⟨一家を⟩ run (a house); set up (house) ¶尊大に構える put on airs; put on [⟪文⟫ assume] an air of superiority [hauteur] / のんきに構える take things easy / 批評家然と構える pose as a critic / 銃を構えて with a [one's] rifle at the ready.

かまきり ⟪動⟫ a (praying) mantis.

がまぐち がま口 a purse; a pocketbook; ⟨小銭入れ⟩ a change [coin] purse.

かまくび 鎌首 ¶⟨蛇が⟩鎌首をもたげる raise its head.

かまくら a festival observed in the middle of January in northern Japan, featuring snow huts in which children play house.

かまける be busy ⟨doing, with sth⟩; be occupied ⟨in doing, with sth⟩; be taken up ⟪with doing [sth]⟫.

-がましい look like...; sound like... ¶指図がましいことを申し上げるようですが It's not for me to dictate to you [to tell you what to do], but... / 未練がましく with (a) bad grace. 文例⇩

かます¹ ⟨わら・むしろの袋⟩ a straw bag.

かます² ⟪魚⟫ a barracuda (pl. -(s)).

かまち 框 ⟪建⟫ a frame; ⟨戸の⟩ a doorcase; a doorframe ¶窓のかまち a window frame.

かまど 竈 a kitchen range; a cooking stove.

かまとと ⟪事⟫⟪文⟫ feigned [pretended] innocence; ⟨人⟩ a girl who plays the (sweet) innocent [who pretends innocence].

かまぼこ 蒲鉾 boiled fish paste ¶かまぼこ形の semicylindrical / かまぼこ兵舎 (米) a Quonset hut; (英) a Nissen hut.

がまん 我慢 ⟨忍耐⟩ endurance; patience; ⟨頑張り⟩ perseverance; ⟨寛容⟩ tolerance; ⟨自制⟩ self-control; self-restraint ¶我慢する ⟨忍耐する⟩ be patient ⟪with sb⟫; endure; bear; stand; put up with; ⟨自制する⟩ control [restrain] oneself; ⟨寛容する⟩ tolerate / 腹が立つのを我慢する suppress [⟪文⟫ contain] one's anger / 泣きたいのを我慢する hold [keep] back one's tears; ⟪文⟫ forbear from crying [to cry] / 我慢できない can't stand (it) (any more [longer]); ⟨物・相手が⟩ be unbearable; be intolerable; be insufferable / 我慢強い patient; persevering / 我慢会 an endurance contest.

かみ¹ 上 ⟨上部⟩ the top; the upper part; ⟨上流⟩ the upper stream ¶上は校長から下は用務員に至るまで from the principal down to the janitor / 上半期 the first half of the year; the first half year / 上の句 ⟨歌の⟩ the first half (of a tanka poem).

かみ² 神 ⟨一神教の⟩ God; ⟨多神教の⟩ a god; a goddess (女神); ⟪文⟫ a deity ¶縁結び[商売

---

to be a boarder in order to escape his mother's overprotection [overprotectiveness].

かま² 随分かまをかけた質問だね. That's a very leading question. / いくらかまをかけられても僕はしゃべらなかった. I refused to be drawn.

かまう 人が僕の事を何と言おうと構わない. I don't care [mind] what people say about me. / 君が何をしようと構わない. I don't give [care] a damn what you do. / ここでタバコを吸っても構いませんか. Do you mind my smoking [if I smoke] here? / 今出かけてもいいし, もう少し後でも構いません. It doesn't matter whether we start now or a little later. / 幾日ご滞在なさっても構いません. You may stay with us (for) as long as you like. / 失敗したって構うものか. Who cares if we fail? / 彼は服装を構わない. He is careless about his appearance. / あんなやつに構ってなんかいられない. I won't have anything to do with such a fellow. | I've no time to waste on a man like him. / 彼は私の事を少しも構ってくれなかった. He paid no attention to me. / 私には構わないでくれ. Leave me alone. | Let me alone [be].

かまえ 彼の家は構えが立派だ. His house has an imposing appearance.

かまける 子供にかまけて本を読むひまもないのよ. I'm so busy looking after my children (that) I've no time for reading. / 仕事にかまけてごぶさたしておりまし

の神 the god of marriage [commerce] / 神の divine; heavenly / 神のなせる業(ﾜｻﾞ) God's work(s) [handiwork] / 神の国 the kingdom of God [Heaven] /《書名》*The City of God* / 神を信じる believe in God / 神に祈る pray to God 《for *sth*, that…》/ 神にまつろう worship *sb* [*sth*] as a god; deify / 神に導かれる be guided by God; be divinely guided / 神かけて誓う swear by God.

かみ[3] 紙 paper ¶紙1枚 a sheet [piece] of paper / 紙のように薄く切る slice *sth* paper thin / 紙を張る paper 《a box》/ 紙に書く write *sth* [put *sth* down] on paper / 紙に包む wrap *sth* [do *sth* up] in paper / 紙一重の差 a very fine line [slight difference]《between》/ 紙入れ〈札入れ〉a wallet;〈婦人持ちの〉《米》a pocketbook / 紙押え棒《タイプライター・印刷機などの》a bail bar / 紙切れ a piece [scrap, strip, slip] of paper / 紙細工 paperwork / 紙製品 paper products / 紙タオル a paper towel / 紙包み a paper parcel [package] / 紙つぶて a paper pellet / 紙テープ (a) paper tape; a paper streamer (見送り用などの) / 紙挟み a folder [file] / 紙挟み《厚紙を2つに折った》a folder / 紙袋 a paper bag [《米》sack] / 紙巻タバコ a cigarette / 紙屋〈店〉a paper store;〈人〉a dealer in paper. 文例図

かみ[4] 髪 hair (of the head) ¶髪が薄くなる one's hair is thinning / 髪の毛 a hair / 髪の毛がまっすぐな straight-haired / 髪を分ける[くしけずる] part [comb] one's hair / 髪をなで付ける comb one's hair / 髪をブラシで梳かす brush (down) one's hair / 髪を刈ってもらう have [get] one's hair cut [trimmed]; have a haircut / 髪をゆう dress [fix, do up] one's hair / 髪を長く伸ばして[短くして]いる wear one's hair long [cut short]. 文例図

かみ[5] 加味 ¶加味する tinge [season] *sth*《with》/ 法に人情を加味する《文》temper justice with mercy.

かみあう 嚙み合う bite each other;〈歯車が〉mesh《with, into》; engage《with》;《歯科》occlude (上下の歯が) /〈歯車が〉嚙み合っている[いない] be in [out of] gear [mesh] /〈議論などで人が〉be (arguing) on the same wavelength [on different wavelengths] / かみ合わせる clench 《one's teeth》; engage 《cogwheels》;〈けんかさせる〉set《dogs》fighting (each other). 文例図

かみあぶら 髪油 hair oil; brilliantine.

かみがかり 神憑り ¶神がかりの possessed by the supernatural;《狂信的》fanatical / だんだんと神がかり状態になる work *oneself* into a trancelike state.

かみかくし 神隠し ¶神隠しに遭う be spirited away [off].

かみかざり 髪飾り a hair ornament.

かみかぜ 神風 a divine wind ¶神風特攻隊 a *kamikaze* [suicide] corps / 神風運転手 a *kamikaze* (daredevil, reckless) (taxi) driver.

かみがた[1] 上方 Kyoto and (its) neighborhood [vicinity]; the Kyoto-Osaka area [district].

かみがた[2], **かみかたち** 髪型, 髪形 a hair style;〈女性の〉a coiffure;《口語》a hairdo (*pl*. -s) /〈男子の〉a haircut ¶魅力的な髪型をしている have a nice [an attractive] hairdo; one's hair looks very nice.

がみがみ ¶がみがみ言う snap [snarl] 《at》;《俗》give it to *sb* (hot [stiff]);〈主に女性が〉nag《at》/ がみがみ言いとばす《口語》give *sb* a good telling-off [a piece of one's mind];《口語》give *sb* hell;《文》scold *sb* vehemently / がみがみ女[女房] a nagging woman [wife].

かみきりむし かみきり虫 a long-horned beetle; a longicorn.

かみきる 嚙み切る bite [gnaw] off; cut *sth* off with one's teeth / 舌をかみ切る bite through one's tongue / 縄をかみ切る bite [gnaw] a rope through [in two].

かみくず 紙屑 waste paper ¶紙くずかご《米》a wastebasket;《英》a wastepaper basket / 紙くず同然だ be no better than waste paper; be not worth the paper it's written on (契約・条約などが).

かみくだく 嚙み砕く crunch; crush *sth* with one's teeth;〈やさしくする〉simplify ¶かみ砕いて説明する explain *sth* in plain language.

かみこなす 嚙みこなす chew; masticate;〈理解する〉digest.

かみころす 嚙み殺す bite《an animal》to death ¶あくびをかみ殺す stifle [suppress] a yawn.

かみざ 上座 the top [highest] seat; an upper seat; the seat [place] of honor ¶上座を占める take the seat of honor; sit at the top [head]《of the table》; take the top seat; sit above *sb*.

かみさびた 神さびた awe-inspiring; holy; sacred.

かみさま 神様 ⇒ かみ[2] ¶校正の神様 an ace proofreader; the king of the proofreaders 《in

---

た. I've been too busy with my work to pay you a visit.
-がましい こんな事を言うと干渉がましいのですが、他人になってそんな事をしない方がよいと思います. I know this sounds like interference [as if I'm interfering], but I would like to persuade you not to get involved.
がまん この条件で当分我慢してくれたまえ. Please put up with these terms for the time being. / 痛くて我慢しきれなくなった. He could no longer stand the pain. / これは到底我慢できない. This is too much for me [more than I can bear]. / 君にはもう我慢ができない. I have lost patience with you. | I've had enough of you. | I can't put up with you any longer.
かみ[1] この川の1キロほど上に橋がある. There is a bridge about one kilometer up this river.
かみ[2] その時実際にどんな事が起こったか、神ならぬ身の知るよしもない. No one will ever know what actually happened at that moment.
かみ[3] 天才と狂人の差は紙一重だ. Genius is but one remove from madness.
かみ[4] もう少し髪の手入れをしたまえ. You should take a bit more care of your hair. / 髪も洗って下さいね.〈美容院で〉I'd like a shampoo too, please.
かみあう 2人の議論がどうもかみ合わないようだ. They seem to

かみしばい 紙芝居 a picture-story show ¶紙芝居のおじさん a picture-story showman.

かみしめる 噛み締める chew 《one's food》 well;〈心で〉think about sth;《文》meditate on; digest ¶先生の言葉をよくかみしめて聞く take what one's teacher says to heart.

かみしも 裃 a kamishimo; a ceremonial dress worn by the samurai ¶かみしもを着る〈儀式張る〉/ かみしもを脱いで〈儀式張らずに〉without ceremony;〈寛いで〉at 《one's》 ease.

かみすき 紙漉き 〈事〉papermaking;〈人〉a papermaker ¶紙すき場 a paper mill.

かみそり 剃刀 a razor ¶かみそりの刃 a razor's edge ¶〈替刃〉a razor blade / かみそりのように鋭い《be》as sharp as a razor; razor-sharp / かみそりのように鋭い男 a very shrewd man; an acute fellow / かみそり負けする get razor rash / かみそり砥(と) 〈石の〉a (razor) hone;〈革の〉a (razor) strop.

かみだな 神棚 a household Shinto altar.

かみつ 過密 overcrowding; overpopulation (人口の) ¶過密ダイヤ an overcrowded railroad schedule / 過密都市 an overcrowded [overpopulated] city.

かみつく 噛み付く bite [snap] at ¶足にかみ付く bite sb in the leg / 〈犬などが〉がぶりとかみ付く sink its teeth into 《sb's leg》/ かみ付くように言う〈人に〉snap [snarl] at sb;〈ひどく叱る〉jump on sb [down sb's throat];《口語》bite sb's head off;〈言葉を〉snap [spit] (it) out.

かみて 上手〈かみ,うえ〉¶舞台上手 the left stage; the right stage as seen from the audience.

かみなり 雷 thunder; a thunderbolt (雷電) ★ thunder は「雷鳴」のみを意味し,「稲光」 lightning とは別. a thunderbolt は音と光の双方を指す ¶雷が落ちる 《場所などが主語》be struck by lightning ⇒らくらい/雷の音 a peal [roar, roll] of thunder / 雷を落とす〈どなる〉thunder at sb / 雷にうたれる be struck by lightning / 雷親父 a bad-tempered [《文》an irascible] old man; a thunderer. 文例↓

かみびょうし 紙表紙 a paper cover ¶紙表紙の本 a paperback (book); a book (bound) in paper covers.

かみふぶき 紙吹雪 confetti; ticker tape ¶紙吹雪をまく throw confetti [ticker tape] 《over a procession》.

かみやすり 紙鑢 sandpaper; emery paper ¶粗い[細かい]紙やすり coarse [fine] sandpaper / 紙やすりで磨く polish sth with sandpaper; sand [sandpaper] sth (down).

かみゆい 髪結い〈事〉hairdressing;〈人〉a (ladies') hairdresser ¶女髪結い a female hairdresser; a coiffeuse.

かみよ 神代 the age of the gods; the mythological age ¶神代の昔から since the age of the gods; from [since] time immemorial.

かみわける 噛み分ける understand ¶世の中の酸いも甘いもかみ分けた人 a man who has tasted the sweets and bitters of life; a man of the world.

かみわざ 神業〈神技〉a superhuman feat;〈奇跡〉a miracle. 文例↓

かみん 仮眠 ¶仮眠する take [have] a nap.

かむ¹ 擤む ¶鼻をかむ blow one's nose.

かむ² 噛む〈かみつく〉bite;〈そしゃくする〉chew;《文》masticate ¶食物をよくかむ chew one's food well / 〈波が〉岩をかむ dash against a rock / 犬にかまれる be bitten by a dog / かんで含めるように教える teach sb sth carefully (in easily understandable terms); take great pains to give sb a clear idea of sth. 文例↓

ガム 《a stick of》 (chewing) gum ⇒チューインガム.

がむしゃら ¶がむしゃらな reckless; daredevil / がむしゃらに勉強する work frantically [《口語》like mad].

カムチャツカ Kamchatka; the Kamchatka Peninsula.

カムバック a comeback ¶カムバックする make a [one's] comeback; come back 《to power》.

カムフラージュ (a) camouflage;〈比喩的に〉a smokescreen ¶カムフラージュする camouflage 《a military vehicle》; disguise 《one's real intentions》.

かめ¹ 亀 a tortoise; a turtle (海がめ) ¶かめの甲 the shell of a tortoise; tortoiseshell (べっこう細工の材料としての). 文例↓

かめ² 瓶 an earthenware pot; a jar (広口の); a jug (取っ手と注ぎ口の付いた).

かめい¹ 加盟 joining; entry (into) ¶加盟する join (the Federation); become a member (of the League) / 国連に加盟させる seat 《a newly independent country》in the United Nations / 加盟国〈国際団体の〉a member nation (of the United Nations);〈条約の〉a signatory (power) 《to a treaty》/ 加盟者 a member / 加盟団体 a member [an affiliated] organization.

かめい² 仮名〈仮につけた名〉a fictitious name;〈偽名〉an assumed [a false] name; a pseudonym ¶…という仮名を使って under the name [pseudonym] of….

かめい³ 家名 ¶家名をあげる raise the repu-

---

be talking at cross purposes.
かみなり あの雷はどこに落ちましたか. Where did the lightning strike? / 雷が来そうな曇り空だった. It was heavy and thundery. / 雷が鳴った. It thundered. | Thunder rolled [rumbled, cracked]. / 雷が今にも落ちそうな激しい音でごろごろと鳴った. Thunder rolled with menacing crashes.
かみわざ あれは全く神業だった. I didn't think such a feat was humanly possible.
かむ² 彼はまるでかんで吐き出すようにそう言って部屋を出て行った. Spitting out this remark, he went out of the room.
かめ¹ 亀の甲より年の功. Sense comes with age. | Years bring wisdom. | The older the wiser. [諺]
がめん (テレビで)途中画面が切れましたことをお詫び申し上げます. We apologize for the temporary loss of vision [your picture]. |〈テロップなどによる表示〉Temporary fault on vision.
かも いいかもがやって来た. やつに一つ試してみよう. Here's an

カメオ　a cameo 《pl. -s》.
がめつい　greedy; tightfisted;《口語》tight.
カメラ　a camera ¶カメラを向ける point [aim, level] one's camera at sb [sth] / カメラに収める photograph; take a photograph [picture]《of》/ 水中カメラ an underwater camera / カメラ気違い a photography enthusiast;《俗》a camera [photography] freak / カメラマン a cameraman / カメラ屋 a camera store [shop].
カメルーン　Cameroon; Cameroun ¶カメルーンの Cameroonian / カメルーン人 a Cameroonian / カメルーン連合共和国 the United Republic of Cameroon.
カメレオン《動》a chameleon.
かめん　仮面 ⇨めん¹ ¶仮面をかぶる wear a mask / …の仮面をかぶって under the mask [cloak] of… / 仮面を脱ぐ pull [throw] off the [one's] mask / 仮面をはぐ unmask (a villain); expose (an imposter) / 仮面舞踏会 a mask(ed) ball; a masquerade.
がめん　画面 a picture;《映画・テレビ》the picture; the screen ¶(テレビの)画面が暗い the picture is not bright enough /(映画・テレビで)画面に入っていく enter [get into] the picture; come on / 画面から消える go [get] out of the picture (off the screen).
かも　鴨《鳥》a (wild) duck; a drake (雄);〈だまされやすい人〉《口語》an easy mark [victim];《口語》a sucker ¶かも猟に行く go duck-shooting [-netting]. 文例⇩
かもい　鴨居《建》a lintel.
かもく¹　科[課]目〈学課〉a subject;〈課程〉a course (of study); a curriculum (pl. -la, -lums)〈全体〉;〈項目〉an item ¶入試科目 the subjects of the entrance examination《for a university》.
かもく²　寡黙《文》taciturnity; reticence ¶寡黙な《文》taciturn; reticent;《文》uncommunicative / 寡黙な人 a taciturn [reticent] person; a man of few words.
かもじ　false hair; a switch.
かもしか《動》〈日本産の〉a (Japanese) serow;〈アフリカ・アジア産の〉an antelope.
かもしだす　醸し出す produce ⇨かもす ¶家庭的な雰囲気をかもし出す produce [create] a homey atmosphere.
-かもしれない　may [might] (be, do); perhaps; maybe; possibly; I am afraid / …した[だった]かもしれない may have done [been]. 文例⇩
用法　「…かもしれない」を may の代わりに might を使って言うのは、そうなる見込みが非常に乏しいと感じられる場合. The sky is cloudy, and it may rain before evening.(空がくもっているから、晩までに雨になるかもしれない) / Though the sun is shining now, it might rain before evening.(今は日が照っているが、これでも晩までに雨になるかもしれない).
かもす　醸す〈醸造する〉brew;〈引き起こす〉cause;《文》bring about;《文》give rise to ¶物議をかもす ⇨ぶつぎ.
かもつ　貨物 freight;《英》goods;〈船荷〉(a) cargo (pl. -(e)s) ¶貨物駅《米》a freight depot;《英》a goods station / 貨物係 a freight clerk /(飛行機の)貨物室 a hold / 貨物自動車《米》a (motor) truck;《英》a (motor) lorry / 貨物船 a cargo ship [boat, steamer]; a freighter / 貨物取扱所 a freight [《英》goods] office / 貨物引替証 a consignment sheet / 貨物輸送機 a cargo plane; a freighter / 貨物列車 a freight train;《英》a goods train.
かものはし《動》a duckbill.
かもめ　鷗《鳥》a seagull; a (common) gull.
かもん　家紋 a family crest.
かや¹　茅《植》plants used for thatching; thatch (plants) ¶かやぶき屋根 a thatched roof.
かや²　榧《植》a kaya (tree); a Japanese nutmeg (tree).
かや³　蚊帳 a mosquito net ¶蚊帳をつる[はず]す put up [take down] a mosquito net / 蚊帳をつって寝る sleep under a mosquito net.
がやがや　noisily;《文》clamorously ¶がやがやする〈騒ぐ〉make a noise / がやがやいう人の声 the confused murmuring of voices. 文例⇩
かやく　火薬 gunpowder; powder ¶黒色火薬 black powder / 火薬庫 a (powder) magazine; an explosives warehouse / 火薬製造工場 an explosives plant [factory]; a powder(-manufacturing) plant [factory].
カヤック〈舟〉a kayak;〈競技〉kayaking ¶女子カヤックシングルス[ダブルス] women's 〈500-meter〉kayak singles [doubles].
かやり(び)　蚊遣り(火) a smoky fire used against [to keep off] mosquitoes;〈主に の〉a smudge ¶蚊やり火をたく make a smudge (to keep mosquitoes off); smoke mosquitoes away.
かゆ　粥 (rice) gruel ¶かゆをすする eat gruel / かゆを煮る boil rice into《thick, thin》gruel. 文例⇩
かゆい　痒い itchy; itching;〈かゆく感じる〉feel [be] itchy; itch ¶かゆい所をかく scratch an itch [itchy place] / かゆい所をかいてやる scratch sb where he itches / かゆい所へ手が届く be very helpful; be very attentive [considerate];〈物・行為が主語〉be all that one could ask (for) / かゆみを complain of itching. 文例⇩

---

easy mark [a sucker] coming. Let's try it on him.
-かもしれない　明日は雪かもしれない. It may snow [We may have snow] tomorrow. | I'm afraid we'll have snow tomorrow. / 彼女は家にいないかもしれない. She may not be at home. / 君の言うとおりかもしれない. Maybe [Perhaps] you are right. / 本当もしれないよ. Who knows but it may be so? / 私の言い付けたことを忘れたのかもしれない. He may have forgotten my orders. / さもなかったら命を落としたかもしれない. Otherwise he might well have lost his life.
がやがや　がやがやしていて彼の話が少しも聞き取れなかった. I could not catch a word of his speech owing to the noise.
かゆ　若い時は貧乏でかゆをすすって暮らした. When he was young, he was so poor that he virtually had to live on gruel.
かゆい　背中がかゆい. My back itches. | I've got an itch in my

かゆみ 痒み an itch; an itching sensation ¶ かゆい ¶ かゆみ止め(の薬) a medicine to stop [control] itching;〖医〗an antipruritic.

かよい 通い〈船の〉〖文〗plying; a run;〈通勤〉living out;〈通帳〉a passbook ¶ 通いのお手伝いさん a live-out [daily] maid / アメリカ通いの船 a steamer on the American line [run]. 文例⇩

かよう¹ 歌謡 a song.

かよう² 通う〈往復する〉go to and from 《a place》;〈船などが〉ply 《between, from...to ...》;〈電車などが〉run;〈通勤・通学する〉go to 《school, work》; attend 《school, church》, commute 《to work, between Kamakura and Tokyo, from Kamakura to Tokyo》(近郊から);〈しばしば行く〉go to 《a place》often; visit 《a place》frequently;〖文〗frequent 《a place》;〈血などが〉circulate ¶ 歩いて学校に通う walk to (and from) school / (郊外から)電車で通う commute by train / 瀬戸内海を通う汽船 a steamboat plying on the Inland Sea / 新宿・中野間を通うバス a bus which runs between Shinjuku and Nakano / 通い慣れた道 a familiar road / 心が通う〖文〗《one's appeal》evokes a sympathetic response from sb;〖文〗《one's appeal》strikes a sympathetic chord in sb / (2人の)心が através し合っている〖口語〗be on the same wavelength (as each other);〖文〗be sympathetic 《congenial》spirits. 文例⇩

かよう³ 斯様 ¶かような〉こんな.

かようきょく 歌謡曲 a popular song ¶ 歌謡曲歌手 a popular singer.

がようし 画用紙 (a sheet of) drawing paper; cartridge paper (厚手の).

かようせい 可溶性〈他の液体の中に溶け得る性質〉solubility;〈金属などが熱で融ける性質〉fusibility ¶ 可溶性の soluble; fusible.

かようび 火曜日 Tuesday (略: Tu., Tues.) ⇒にちようび(の) 用法.

がよく 我欲 self-interest;〖文〗selfish desire;〖文〗egoism.

からい か弱い weak; delicate;〖文〗frail; tender; helpless.

から¹ 空 ¶空の empty / 空にする empty 《a bag of its contents》; make 《a box》empty / 空になる be emptied;〖文〗become empty / 空である be empty; have nothing in [inside] it,〖文〗contain nothing. 文例⇩

から² 殻〈穀物の〉a husk;《米》a hull;〈貝類・果実の〉a shell;〈ナッツの〉(a nut)shell;〈抜け殻〉castoff skin; a slough ¶ 卵の殻 an eggshell / 自分の殻の中に閉じこもる withdraw into one's shell [oneself] / 殻を持った動物 a shelled animal / 自分の殻を破る break out of one's shell.

から³〈全く〉⇒ からきし. 文例⇩

から⁴〈人〉from;〈場所〉from; out of;〈時〉from; at; in; on (and after)《某日から》; since (以来);〈数〉from;〈原料・材料〉from; out of 《★製品になったとき材料の質がかなり変化している時には from を, 変化していない時には of または out of を用いる》;〈動機〉from; out of;〈原因・理由〉as; since; because; owing to;〈判断の基準〉from; by ¶ 友人から手紙を受け取る get [have,〖文〗receive] a letter from a friend / イギリスから帰る come back from England / 東京から大阪まで from Tokyo to Osaka / 15ページ[第3章]から始める begin at page 15 [with the third chapter] / 馬から落ちる be thrown from [off] one's horse / 階段から落ちる fall down the stairs / がけから落ちる fall over a precipice / 窓から外を見る[中をのぞき込む] look out of [look in at] the window / 裏口から出入する go in and out by [at] the back door / 子供のときから知っている know sb from childhood [from when he was a child] / 1時から手があく be free after one o'clock / 朝から晩まで from morning till night / 10歳から15歳までの子供 children (ranging) from ten to fifteen years old / 責任感から out of [from] a sense of duty / 好奇心から out of curiosity. 文例⇩

---

back.

かよい 昔は住み込みのお手伝いさんがいたのですが、今の人は通いです。We used to have a maid who lived in, but our present one lives out.

かよう² 彼はどの学校に通っていますか。What school is he attending? / 毎朝バスで会社へ通っています。I go to work by bus every morning.

から¹ 財布をあらためて見たら中は空だった。I examined the purse, and found it empty.

から³ 彼はから意気地がない。He has no guts at all.

から⁴ だれから買ったの？ Who did you buy this from? / だれから聞きましたか。Who told you? / 君の事は野田さんから聞きました。I heard about you from [through] Mr. Noda. / 君から始めたまえ。You go first. / 君からこんなひどい待遇を受けようとは思わなかった。I did not expect such hard treatment at your hands. / 犬がテーブルの下からのこのこ出てきた。A dog crept out from under the table. / 月が窓から差し込んだ。The moon shone (in) through the window. / 風は東から吹いている。The wind is coming [blowing] from the east. / 太陽は東から出る。The sun rises in the east. / その火事は風呂屋から出た。The fire started in a bathhouse. / 私は15メートルのところから鳥を撃った。I shot the bird from a distance of fifteen meters. / ここから富士山がよく見えます。We can get a fine view of Mt. Fuji from here. / この写真は長浜から見た琵琶湖の風景だ。This photo is Lake Biwa as seen from Nagahama. / 彼は少年時代から利口だった。He was clever from childhood. / 新学期は4月から始まる。The new school term begins in April. / 試験は午前9時から始まります。The examination begins at 9 in the morning. / 午後から手がすきます。I'll be free in the afternoon. / 英語を始めてから4年になる。It is four years since I began studying English. / 願書は3月10日から受け付ける。Applications will be accepted on and after March 10. / 運賃は9月1日から値上げになります。The fares will be raised on September 1st. / 水曜日から金曜日まで京都に3泊したいのでホテルを予約して下さい。Please reserve us a room at a hotel in Kyoto for three nights from Wednesday through Friday. / 酒は米からつくる。Sake is made from rice. / 刃物は鋼鉄からつくる。Edge tools are made of [out of] steel. / 煙か

がら¹ 柄 〈模様〉 a pattern; a design; 〈体格〉 build; 〈品位〉 dignity ¶柄が大きい be burly; be big; 《文》be of large build / 柄の悪い男 a lout; a vulgar fellow / 柄にもない be out of character; be unlike [not like] one / 時局柄 in view of the current situation / 場所柄も考えずに without any [taking no] thought of where one is [of the occasion]. 文例↓

がら² 〈スープの材料などにする〉 chicken bones.

カラー¹ 〈色〉 (a) color ¶カラー写真 a color photo(graph) [picture] / カラースライド a color slide [transparency] / カラーテレビ color television; 〈受像機〉 a color TV (set) / カラーフィルム a color film.

カラー² 〈襟〉 a (shirt) collar ¶ソフトカラー a soft collar / カラーボタン a collar button; 〈取り外しのできる〉 a collar stud.

がらあき がら空き ⇨ がらがら²(がらがらに空いている).

からい 辛い 〈カレーなどが〉 hot; 〈塩辛い〉 salty; salt ⇨ しお(塩辛い, 塩辛く煮る) ¶点が辛い be severe in marking [giving marks]. 文例↓

からいばり 空威張り bluster; (a) bluff; an empty boast ¶空威張りする bluster; bluff.

からうり 空売り 〔取引〕 selling short; a short sale.

カラオケ 《spend the evening (in)》 singing to a taped accompaniment.

からかい ⇨ からかう ¶からかい半分に (half) in fun; banteringly.

からかう make fun of sb; poke fun at sb; play a joke on sb; 《口語》pull sb's leg; banter; tease; 《口語》kid ¶猫をからかう tease a cat. 文例↓

からかさ a bamboo-and-paper umbrella ⇨ かさ³.

からかみ 唐紙 a (paper-covered) sliding door; a sliding screen.

からから¹ ¶からからに乾いた dry as a bone; bone-dry; parched; dried-up (干上がった).

からから² ¶からからと笑う laugh loudly; burst into (a roar of) laughter / からからと鳴る clatter.

がらがら¹ 〈おもちゃの〉 a rattle ¶がらがら音がする make a rattling sound; rattle; clatter /(荷車が)道をがらがら通る rattle along the road. 文例↓

がらがら² 〈すいているさま〉¶がらがらに空いている there are very few 《passengers aboard the ship, spectators in the theater》; be nearly empty of 《passengers, spectators》; 〈劇場などが〉 be very thinly attended. 文例↓

がらがらへび がらがら蛇 〔動〕 a rattlesnake.

からきし quite; utterly; (not) at all ¶からきし知らない know nothing (at all) about sth; 《文》be utterly ignorant of sth / からきしだめだ[役に立たない] be of no use at all; be quite useless. 文例↓

からくさもよう 唐草模様 an arabesque (pattern [design]).

からくじ 空鬮 ¶空くじを引く draw a blank ticket (in the lottery). 文例↓

がらくた useless [worn-out] articles; junk; rubbish.

からくち 辛口 ¶辛口の dry 《wine》.

からくも 辛くも barely; narrowly ¶辛くも逃れる barely escape; have a narrow escape.

からくり 〈仕掛け〉 mechanism; 〈計略〉 a trick; 《口語》a dodge.

からげ 絡げ a bundle; a sheaf ¶ひとからげにする tie 《goods》 into one bundle; bundle 《articles》 (all) up together.

からげる 絡げる 〈しばる〉 tie up; bind; 〈まくりあげる〉 tuck up ¶しりをからげる tuck up one's skirt.

からげんき 空元気 《make》a show of courage; 〈酒の上の〉《show》Dutch courage.

からころ clip-clop ¶からころと with a clatter / からころと歩く clop 《along the street》.

からさお 殻竿 a flail ¶からさおを打つ thresh

らは何も生まれない. Nothing can be made out of nothing. / こんな事故の起こったのは君の怠慢からだ. The disaster happened because [as a result] of your negligence. / 今年は気候が良くないからりんごは不作だろう. Owing to the bad weather this year, the apple crop will be poor. / 地面がぬれているからきっと雨が降ったんだわ. It must have rained, since the ground is wet. / それだから聞きたいのだ. That is why I want to know. / 東大出だからといって有能だとは限らない. A man is not necessarily competent simply because he graduated from Tokyo University. / 彼がいなくなったからにはもう怖いものはない. Now that he is gone, I have no one to fear. / 彼の地位からくる威厳がある. His very appearance is dignified. / 式が始まるから10分前からあった. There was more than ten minutes before the ceremony began. / それは1つ3万円からする. They are worth no less than 30,000 yen apiece. / 値段は5本で5千円から2万円まである. They vary [range] in price from 5,000 to 20,000 yen. / 彼の家は駅から歩いて5分以内のところにある. His house is within five minutes' [a five-minute] walk of the station. / むこうから車が来たよ. There's a car coming (the other way).

がら¹ これが今流行の柄です. This is the pattern that is in fashion at the moment. / 彼がそんなことをするなんて柄にもないことだ. It was quite unlike him to do such a thing. | It was quite out of character for him to do something like that. / 僕は職業柄旅行することが多い. My job means that I often have to travel. | My business involves a lot of traveling.

からい このカレーは僕には辛過ぎる. This curry is too hot for me.

からかう からかわないで下さい. Don't tease [《米》kid] me, please. / ちょっと君をからかっただけですよ. It was only a joke. | We were only having a little fun with you.

がらがら¹ 材木がからがらと音を立てて崩れた. The stack of lumber collapsed noisily.

がらがら² 連絡船はがらがらだった. The ferryboat had very few passengers on board. | There were very few passengers aboard the ferry. / その劇場はがらがらに空いていた. The theater was very thinly [poorly] attended.

からきし 商売はからきし暇だ. Business is very slow.

からくじ 空くじはありません.

からさわぎ 空騒ぎ ¶空騒ぎをする make a (great) fuss [make much ado] about nothing.

からし 芥子 mustard ¶からし漬け (aubergines) pickled in mustard / からし菜 a leaf [an Indian] mustard.

からす¹ 烏 a crow; a raven (大がらす) ¶からすが鳴く a crow caws; a raven croaks / からすの行水をする have a quick dip (in the bath); take a hurried bath. 文例◊

からす² 枯らす〈草木を〉let (the grass) wither; blight;〈材木を〉season ¶よく枯らした材木 well-seasoned timber.

からす³ 涸らす〈池などを〉dry up;〈井戸などを〉empty;〈文〉exhaust;〈財源などを〉drain.

からす⁴ 嗄らす ¶しゃべって[どなって]声をからす talk [shout] oneself hoarse / 声をからして in a hoarse voice; hoarsely.

ガラス glass ¶ガラスの破片 a piece of broken glass; a glass splinter (とがった) / 網入りガラス wired glass / 安全ガラス safety glass / ガラスの陳列ケース a glass [glazed] showcase / ガラス張りの glazed〈cases〉; glassed-in (display shelves);〈比喩的に〉(open and) aboveboard / ガラス器 glassware / ガラス切り a glass cutter / ガラス工場 a glass factory; a glassworks / ガラス細工 glasswork / (ガラスを細長い管で吹いて作る) ガラス職人 a glass blower / ガラス玉 a glass bead / ガラス戸 a glass [glazed] door / ガラス戸のはまった本箱 a glass-fronted bookcase / ガラス瓶 a glass bottle / ガラス粉 glass dust; powdered glass / ガラス屋〈人〉a glazier;〈店〉a glass store [shop]. 文例◊

からすうり【植】a snake gourd [cucumber].

からすぐち 烏口 a drawing [ruling] pen.

からすみ dried mullet roe.

からすむぎ 烏麦〈穀物〉oats;〈植物〉an oat (plant).

からせき 空咳 (have) a dry cough; a hacking cough (続けて出る).

からせじ 空世辞 ¶空世辞を言う pay empty compliments (to); tickle [appeal] to sb's vanity by complimenting [saying nice things to] him.

からだ 体〈肉体〉the body;〈体格〉physique; build;〈体質〉constitution;〈健康〉health ¶からだ中 from head to foot; all over (全面に) / からだがよくなる get well [better];《文》improve in health / 体の bodily; physical / からだの具合がいい be quite well;《文》be in good health / からだの具合が悪い be ill; be sick ⇒びょうき ★;《口語》be in a bad way;《文》be in bad [poor] health / からだの弱い人《文》a person with a weak constitution; a person who is in delicate health / からだのがっちりした strongly [sturdily] built 〈men〉;《文》(a man) of strong [solid] build; sturdy / からだをこわす lose one's health; make oneself ill (無理をして);〈事が主語〉damage [injure, ruin] one's health / からだを大事にする take (good) care of oneself; be careful about one's health / からだをつくる build up one's physique / からだを休める take [have] a rest; rest (oneself) / からだを張って...する do at the risk of (losing) one's life;《口語》lay one's life on the line to do / からだにいい[悪い]be good [bad] for one (the health, one's health); be wholesome [unwholesome];《文》be beneficial [injurious] to (one's) health / からだつき one's figure. 文例◊

からたち【植】a trifoliate orange.

からちゃ 空茶 ¶空茶を出す serve tea by itself [without cakes].

からっかぜ 空っ風 a dry wind.

からっきし ⇒からきし.

からっと ⇒からりと ¶からっと揚げる fry (prawns) crisp.

カラット a carat; a karat ★ karat は carat の異体ではあるが,《米》では宝石には carat を, 金の場合には karat を用いて,区別する ¶5カラットのダイヤモンド a 5-carat diamond; a diamond of five carats.

からっぽ ⇒から¹.

からつゆ 空梅雨 a dry [rainless] rainy season.

からて¹ 空[唐]手 karate;〈with〉karate blows ¶空手チョップを見舞う give sb a karate chop.

からて² 空手 for empty-handed;〈獲物なしで〉with an empty bag (狩猟); without a catch (釣り);〈資金なしで〉without funds.

からてがた 空手形〈issue〉a fictitious [bad] bill;〈約束〉an empty promise [pledge].

からとう 辛党 a drinker.

からに 空荷 ¶空荷で帰る return unloaded;〈船が〉return in ballast; return light.

からねんぶつ 空念仏 ¶空念仏に終わる end in [prove to be] nothing but empty talk. 文例◊

Every ticket wins a prize.

からす¹ それでも風呂に入ったつもりか。からすの行水じゃないか。Do you call that a bath? More like a cat and a promise! / 彼女の髪はからすのぬれ羽色だ。Her hair is jet-black.

ガラス 学校の財政運営はガラス張りであるべきだ。The administration of financial affairs in educational institutions should be completely open and aboveboard.

からだ この洋服は僕のからだに合わない。This coat does not fit me. / そんなに無理をするとからだをこわすよ。You'll make yourself ill if you push yourself so hard. / こう忙しくてはからだが持たない。I'm afraid I'll break down under the pressure of work. / 粗悪な食事と過労で,彼はからだを悪くしてしまった。His health had been undermined by bad food and overwork. / (競泳で) 彼は僕をからだ一つ抜いていた。He was a full length ahead of me. / それには彼がちょうどおあつらえ向きのからだつきだと思った。I thought he was [had] just the build for it.

からねんぶつ 首相の行政改革も空念仏に終りそうだ。I'm afraid the Premier's promise to carry out the administrative reforms will prove to be nothing but idle [empty] talk.

からまる つたが木の幹に絡まっている。Ivy was twined around the tree trunk. / 糸が絡まった。The thread has got tangled. / 針金が私の足に絡まった。My foot caught [got entangled] in some wire.

からみあう 2人は指と指を絡み合わせながら,歩いて帰った。They walked home with their fingers

カラビナ 〖登山〗 a carabiner; a snap ring.
からぶき 乾拭き ¶からぶきする rub (the table) with a dry cloth; dust (the furniture).
からふと 樺太 Sakhalin.
からぶり 空振り ¶空振りする〈野球で〉swing [strike] at the ball and miss;〈ボクシングで〉swish the air.
からぼり 空堀 a dry moat.
からまつ 唐松 〖植〗a (Japanese) larch (tree).
からまる 絡まる 〈巻きつく〉twine around; entwine; wind *itself* round;〈もつれる〉get caught in《the wire》; get entangled [entangle *itself*] in《the net》. 文例⇩
からまわり 空回り ¶空回りする〈車・エンジンが高速で〉race;〈機械が低速で〉idle; run idle;〈議論が〉(the argument) goes round and round and gets nowhere.
からみ 辛味 a sharp (pungent, hot) taste; bite;〈塩味〉a salty taste.
-がらみ …搦み ¶四十がらみの男 a man about forty years of age; a fortyish man.
からみあう 絡み合う be intertwined; be locked together;〈もつれる〉get entangled 《in》; be in a tangle. 文例⇩
からみつく 絡み付く 〈巻きつく〉twine [coil] *itself* around;〈まといつく〉cling [hang on] to *sb* [*sth*]. 文例⇩
からむ 絡む〈絡まる〉⇨ からまる;〈けんかを吹きかける〉pick a quarrel《with》¶人情に絡まれて out of pity [sympathy] 《for》;〈文〉unable to harden *one's* heart enough. 文例⇩
からめて 搦め手 the back gate; the postern ¶からめ手から攻める attack (a castle) in the rear;〈比喩的に〉approach [go about] *sth* in a roundabout way.
からりと ¶からりと晴れた空 a clear [cloudless] sky. 文例⇩
がらりと ¶〈全く〉entirely; completely;〈突然〉suddenly; all of a sudden ¶がらりと戸を開ける fling a (sliding) door open (without warning).
がらんがらん ¶がらんがらんと鳴る clang / がらんがらんと鳴る鐘の音 the clanging of a (school) bell.
がらんと ¶がらんとした empty; bare; deserted / がらんとしている look empty [bare]. 文例⇩
がらんどう ¶がらんどうの hollow; empty.

かり[1] 仮 ¶仮の〈臨時の〉temporary; provisional;〈急造の〉improvised / 仮の世〈文〉[this] transient world / 仮に〈一時的に〉temporarily; provisionally; for the time being;〈試験的に〉tentatively; by way of experiment;〈見習いに〉on trial / 仮に…とすれば suppose…; supposing《that it is…》; if… / 仮に…としても (even) if…;〈even〉granted [granting] that… / 仮にも〈しぼらくでも〉(not) even for a time [an instant];〈いやしくも〉at all / 仮営所 a temporary office (place of business) / 仮親 foster parents / 仮建築 a temporary building / 仮採用 appointment on trial [probation]; a provisional appointment / 仮執行 provisional execution / 仮条約〖協定〗a provisional treaty [agreement] / 仮処分《make》provisional disposition;〈裁判所の〉差止命令=a provisional [temporary] injunction / 仮政府 a provisional government / 仮登記 provisional registration / 仮入学を許される be provisionally admitted (to a school); be admitted《to a school》on probation / 仮払い金 a temporary payment / 仮免状〖許〗a temporary [provisional] license / 仮領収証 a temporary [an interim] receipt. 文例⇩

かり[2] 狩り hunting; a hunt ⇨ りょう[2] ¶とら [きつね] 狩り tiger [fox] hunting / 紅葉狩り ⇨ もみじ.

かり[3] 借り a debt; a loan; a bill (買物代金の) ¶借りがある be in debt to *sb* (for 100,000 yen); owe *sb* (50,000 yen) / 借りを返す pay [repay] *one's* debts; pay *one's* bill;〈比喩的に〉get even [square] with *sb*; get *one's* own back on *sb* / 借りをつくる run [fall] into debt.

かり[4] 雁 〖鳥〗⇨ がん[1].

カリ 〖化〗 potassium ¶カリ肥料 (a) potash fertilizer.

かりあげる 刈り上げる 〈髪を〉cut [trim]《*sb's* hair》short ¶髪を短く刈り上げてもらう have *one's* hair cut short.

かりあつめる 駆り集める gather together; round up; muster; mobilize.

かりいしょう 借衣装 hired clothes; clothes for hire.

かりいれ 刈り入れ a harvest; harvesting; reaping ¶刈り入れする harvest; reap; gather in / 刈り入れ時 the harvest; harvest time. 文例⇩

---

entwined.
からみつく スカートが足に絡み付いて歩きにくかった。 My skirt clung to my legs, making it difficult to walk.
からむ 彼は酒癖が悪くて限度を越すと人に絡んでくる。 He can't hold his liquor, and turns unpleasant [nasty] after he passes his limit.
からりと 空がからりと晴れた。 It [The weather] has cleared up.
がらりと 彼はその時以来がらりと人が変わった。 He has completely changed since then.
がらんと 家の中はがらんとしてだれもいなかった。 The house was deserted.

かり[1] この世は仮の宿に過ぎない。 This world is but a place of passage. / それは仮につけた名です。 That is the name that it has been given provisionally. / 仮にそうしておこう。 Let's leave it like that for the present. / 仮に君の言うことが事実としても、弁解にはならない。 Even granting that what you say is true, that is no excuse. / あの人が仮にもそんなことをしようとは思われない。 I can't bring myself to believe that he, of all people, would ever do such a thing.
かり[3] あの店には大分借りがあるんだ。 I've run up a large bill at that bar. / いつかこの借りを返してやるからな。 I'll get even with [get my own back on] you for this some day.
かりあつめる 仲間を駆り集めて彼を応援しよう。 Let's round up [mobilize] our friends to help him.
かりいれ 刈り入れ時でとても忙しい。 We are very busy as it is harvest time.

かりいれきん 借入金 a loan (of money) 《from a bank》.

かりいれる 借り入れる ⇨ かりる.

かりうける 借り受ける ⇨ かりる.

カリウム 【化】 potassium ⇨ カリ.

ガリウム 【化】 gallium.

カリエス 【医】 caries ¶脊椎(梵)カリエス ⇨ せきつい.

かりかた 借方 【簿記】 the debit [debtor] (略: dr.); the debit [debtor] side ¶借方に記入する debit 《a sum of money》 against sb 《sb's account》; enter 《an item》 on the debit side [to sb's debit] / 借方勘定 a debtor account / 借方残高 a debit balance.

かりかぶ 刈り株 stubble ¶刈り株だらけの stubble-covered 《fields》.

かりかり ¶かりかりした 〈食べ物などが〉 be crisp / かりかりになる get [go, 《文》become] crisp; crisp (up) / かりかりかむ[食べる] crunch (on) 《hard crackers》.

がりがり noisily ¶がりがり音を立てる grate 《on the stones》; make [produce] a rasping noise [sound]; 《ペンが》make [produce] a scratching sound / がりがりひっかく scratch 《a mosquito bite》 / がりがりかむ crunch (on) 《a bone》; munch.

がりがりもうじゃ 我利我利亡者 a greedy [grasping] person.

かりぎ 借り着 borrowed clothes.

カリキュラム a curriculum 《pl. -la, -s》.

かりきる 借り切る charter 《a bus》; reserve [book] all 《the rooms on the second floor》.

かりこし 借越し a debit balance; 《当座預金の》an overdraft; overdrawing.

かりこみ 狩り込み a roundup 《of tramps by the police》 ¶一斉狩り込みをやる make a large-scale roundup of 《drug traffickers》.

かりこむ 刈り込む 〈頭髪を〉 cut; crop 〈短く〉; 〈草木を〉 prune; trim; pollard 〈枝を全部〉; 〈芝生を〉 mow.

かりしゃくほう, かりしゅっしょ 仮釈放, 仮出所 (release on) parole; conditional release ¶仮釈放する, 仮出所させる release 《a prisoner》 on parole; parole 《a prisoner》 / 仮出所中の人 a person on parole; a parolee.

カリスマ charisma ¶カリスマ的 charismatic.

かりずまい 仮住まい a temporary residence ¶仮住まいする live [《文》reside] temporarily 《at》.

かりそめ ¶かりそめの 〈一時の〉 temporary; 《文》 transient; 〈ささいな〉 trivial; trifling; slight / かりそめの恋 a passing fancy; 《文》 transient affection / かりそめの病 a slight illness / かりそめにする make light of; 《文》 slight; neglect / かりそめにも 〈つかの間を〉 for a moment; 〈いつでも〉 even in the slightest degree; 〈決して…しない〉 (not) on any account; on no account; 《not》 ever do.

かりたおす 借り倒す ⇨ ふみたおす.

かりだす¹ 借り出す borrow; have the loan of 《a book》; 〈図書館の本などを〉 take [check] out ¶《図書館の本などが》借り出すことができる be available for loan / 学校図書館から借り出した本 a book out on loan from the school library.

かりだす² 狩[駆]り出す 〈獲物を〉 hunt out [up]; 〈犯人を〉 round up; comb out ¶きつねを穴から狩り出す draw a fox from its lair / 投票に駆り出す get 《the voters》 out to the poll.

かりたてる¹ 狩り立てる hunt up [out]; run [chase] 《a fox》.

かりたてる² 駆り立てる 〈動物を〉 drive《cattle along the road》; 〈むりやり…させる〉 drive sb to do; urge [spur] sb on to do ¶国民を戦争に駆り立てる urge the nation [drive the people] to war.

かりちょういん 仮調印 initialing ¶仮調印する initial 《a treaty》.

かりちん 借り賃 〈不動産・物品の〉 (a) rent; 〈物品・乗り物の〉 hire; a hire charge.

かりて 借り手 a borrower; 〈土地・家屋の〉 a tenant ¶すぐに借り手がつく soon [easily] find a tenant / 借り手がつかない be [stay, 《文》 remain] untenanted [unrented].

かりとじ 仮綴じ (a) temporary binding; 〈紙装〉 paper binding ⇨ かみびょうし ¶仮とじにする bind 《the papers》 temporarily [in a temporary cover] / 仮と じ本 a temporarily bound book.

かりとり 刈取 ⇨ かりとる ¶刈取機 a reaping [harvesting] machine; a reaper (and binder); a harvester.

かりとる 刈り取る 〈刈る〉 mow; cut down; 〈取り入れる〉 reap; gather in; harvest.

かりぬい 仮縫い basting; tacking; 〈サイズ合わせ〉 (a) fitting ¶仮縫いする baste; tack; have a (first) fitting.

かりば 狩場 ⇨ りょう《猟場》.

かりばし 仮橋 a temporary bridge.

カリパス (a pair of) cal(l)ipers.

がりばん がり版 a mimeograph ¶がり版で刷る mimeograph 《an article》; make [run off] copies 《of a manifesto》 on a mimeograph.

カリフォルニア California (略: Calif., Cal.) ¶カリフォルニアの Californian / カリフォルニア州の人 a Californian.

カリブかい カリブ海 the Caribbean (Sea).

かりそめ かりそめにもそんな心を起こしてはならない。Not for a moment must you think of doing anything like that. / かりそめにもそんな事を言ってはならない。On no account must you say such a thing.

かりぬい 仮縫いはいつ出来ますか。When will it be ready for a first fitting? / 洋服屋が間もなく仮縫いにやってくる。The tailor will soon be here to give me a fitting.

かりもの この外套は借り物だ。This overcoat is not mine.

がりゅう 僕のタイプは我流だ。The way I type is self-taught. / 我流でいいからやりたまえ。Go ahead and do it in your own way.

かりる 借りた物は返さねばならない。One must pay one's debts. / この傘をお借りできますか。May [Could] I borrow this umbrella? / ちょっとお電話をお借りできますか。May I use your telephone for a moment, please? / あなたのお力を借りることができれば幸せで

カリフラワー a cauliflower.
がりべん がり勉 《米口語》grinding;《英口語》swotting ¶がり勉屋《米口語》a grind;《英口語》a swot.
かりほうたい 仮包帯 a temporary bandage [dressing] ¶仮包帯を施す dress 《sb's wound》temporarily / 仮包帯する a dressing [an aid] station.
カリホルニウム 《化》californium.
かりもの 借り物 something that is borrowed [is not one's own] ¶借り物の意見 a borrowed opinion. 文例⇩
かりゅう¹ 下流 the lower reaches [course] 《of a stream》¶ここから3キロ下流に three kilometers downstream [down the river] from here.
かりゅう² 顆粒 a granule ¶顆粒状の granular; granulated 《sugar》.
がりゅう 我流 ¶我流でやる do in one's own way. 文例⇩
かりゅうかい 花柳界 the gay quarters; the world of the geisha.
かりゅうど 狩人 ⇨りょう² 《猟師》.
かりょう¹ 科料 a fine ¶500円の科料に処せられる be fined 500 yen.
かりょう² 加療 ¶加療中である be under medical treatment.
がりょう 雅量 《文》magnanimity; generosity ¶雅量のある generous;《文》magnanimous; broad-minded; tolerant.
かりょく 火力 《火の力》heating [thermal] power;《銃火器の力》firepower ¶火力において勝る《文》surpass 《the enemy》in firepower; outgun《the enemy》/ 火力発電 thermal power generation / 火力発電所 a thermal power station [plant].
かりる 借りる borrow sth《from sb》; have [get,《文》obtain, take] the loan of sth;《賃借りする》hire《a boat》; rent《a house, land》; lease《land》;《電話などを》use《sb's telephone》 ⇨ かす² 囲み ¶力を借りる ask for《sb's》help / 知恵を借りに行く go to sb for advice /...の言葉を借りて言えば in sb's phrase; to borrow [use] sb's words /家を1軒借りる rent [take the lease of] a house / 劇場を1晩借りる hire a theater for one evening. 文例⇩
かりん 花梨《植》a Chinese quince (tree).
かりんさん 過燐酸《化》¶過燐酸塩 (a) superphosphate / 過燐酸石灰 superphosphate of lime / 過燐酸肥料 (a) superphosphate fertilizer; superphosphate(s).
かりんとう fried dough cookies.
かる¹ 刈る《頭髪などを》cut; trim; crop《短かく》;《羊毛を》shear《a sheep》; clip off《the wool》;《稲などを》reap;《草を》mow;《樹木を》trim; prune ¶髪を短く刈る cut sb's hair short [close]; crop sb's hair / 髪を刈ってもらう have one's hair cut [trimmed]; have [get] a haircut. 文例⇩
かる² 駆る drive《a car》; urge《a horse》on《with a whip》; spur on《a horse》¶車[馬]を駆って...へ行く drive [ride] to《a place》/ 恐怖の念に駆られる《文》be stricken [seized] with fear / 功名心に駆られる be driven《文》motivated,《文》prompted》by ambition / 好奇心に駆られて out of curiosity. 文例⇩
-がる《...と感じる》feel;《...したいと思う》want;《文》desire;《ふりをする》pretend ¶面白[寂し]がる feel amused [lonely] / 寒がる《寒いとこぼす》complain of the cold /《寒さに感じやすい》be sensitive to the cold / 行きたがる want [be anxious] to go / 強がる pretend to be tough; bluff.
かるい 軽い light;《ちょっとした》slight; not serious, trifling;《楽な》easy ¶目方が軽い weigh light; be light (in weight) / 口が軽い《文》be indiscreet; be too talkative /《口語》be a blabbermouth / 軽い病気 a slight illness [《文》indisposition] / 軽い食事 a light meal / 軽いしゃれ a little joke / 軽い過失 a minor error [fault] / 軽い読物 light reading / 軽い気持ちで《do》casually [without much thought];《do》without [not] taking it too seriously. 文例⇩
かるいし 軽石《a piece of》pumice (stone) ¶軽石でこする rub《one's heel》with pumice; pumice《one's heel》.
カルカッタ Calcutta.
かるがるしい 軽々しい《軽率な》thoughtless; careless; hasty; rash;《文》imprudent;《浮薄な》light; frivolous; flippant ¶軽々しい事をしない《文》be discreet;《文》be prudent / 軽々しく lightly;《文》indiscreetly; hastily; rashly; without much thought;《文》without due reflection / 軽々しく人の言うことを信じる believe what one hears too easily; be credulous. 文例⇩
かるがると 軽々と lightly; easily; without《any》effort; effortlessly ¶大きな石を軽々と持ち上げる lift up a huge stone easily [as if it were as light as a feather].
カルキ [く《オランダ語》kalk] bleaching powder ¶カルキ臭い《tap water》smelling of chlorine.
かるく 軽く lightly; softly《そっと》; easily《容易に》¶軽くする lighten《a load》; relieve [lessen]《pain》/ 船荷を軽くする lighten a ship of her cargo / 軽く考える take sth lightly; make light of sth / 軽く背をたたく tap sb on the back / 茶碗に軽く2杯の飯 two tightly-filled bowlfuls of rice / 軽く2勝する win two games easily [hands down]. 文例⇩

す. I should appreciate your help. / この家は借りているのです. This house is not mine. It is rented. / この家は田中さんから月10万で借りています. I've rented this house from Mr. Tanaka for 100,000 yen a month.
かる¹ 20分で刈ってもらえますか. Can you give me a haircut in twenty minutes?
かる² 彼は車を駆って現場に急行した. He hurried [rushed] to the scene in his car.
-がる めんどうがってやらないだけだ. He just thinks that it is too troublesome.
かるい 今度の風邪は軽い. The colds that are about at the moment are not serious.
かるがるしい He always weighs his words carefully.
かるく 心も軽く家を出て行った. He left home with a light heart. / これでいくらか肩の荷が軽くなった. This has taken some of the weight off my mind.

かるくち 軽口 a pleasant joke; a pleasantry ¶軽口をたたく crack a joke.

カルシウム 《化》calcium.

カルタ [<《ポルトガル語》*carta*] *karuta*; traditional Japanese playing cards ⇒ **トランプ** ¶カルタ1組 a pack [《米》deck] of *karuta* / カルタを取る play *karuta*; have [play] a game of *karuta* / カルタ会 a *karuta* party.

カルタゴ Carthage.

カルチャーショック (a case of) culture shock.

カルテ [<《ドイツ語》*Karte*] (a patient's) (clinical) records; a (clinical) record card [sheet].

カルテット 《音楽》a quartet(te).

カルデラ 《地質》a caldera; a crater ¶カルデラ湖 a crater lake.

カルテル [<《ドイツ語》*Kartell*] 《経済》a cartel ¶カルテルを作る form a cartel; cartelize / カルテルを解く dissolve [break up] a cartel ¶ (of steel companies) / 不況カルテル a (business) recession cartel / …とカルテル協定を結ぶ make [《文》conclude] a cartel agreement with….

かるはずみ 軽はずみ ⇒はずみ

カルメやき カルメ焼き [<《ポルトガル語》*caramelo*] foam candy.

かるやき 軽焼き a wafer.

かるわざ 軽業 acrobatics; acrobatic feats; an acrobatic performance ¶軽業をする perform [do] acrobatics / 軽業的に acrobatically / 軽業師 an acrobat.

かれ 彼 ¶彼は[が] he / 彼の, 彼のもの his / 彼に[を] him.

がれ scree ¶がれ場 a scree-covered slope; a scree; a talus.

かれい¹ 家令 a (house) steward.

かれい² 鰈 《魚》a (right-eyed) flounder; a flat-fish.

かれい³ 華麗 ¶華麗な splendid; magnificent; gorgeous / 華麗さ splendor; magnificence; gorgeousness.

カレー curry ¶カレー粉 curry powder / カレーライス curry and rice / カレー料理 curried food; a curry.

ガレージ a garage.

かれえだ 枯枝 a dead [withered] branch [twig].

かれき 枯木 a dead [withered] tree. 文例⇩

がれき 瓦礫 rubble; debris ¶がれきの山 a heap of rubble.

かれくさ 枯草 dead [withered] grass.

かれこれ 〈あれやこれや〉this and that; one thing and [or] another; 〈およそ〉about; around; nearly; almost ¶かれこれ言う talk [say things] (about); 〈批評する〉criticize; comment (on); 〈苦情を言う〉grumble (about); complain (about, of); 〈異議を唱える〉object (to) / かれこれ言わずに without question [《文》demur]; with (a) good grace / かれこれするうちに (in the) meantime; meanwhile. 文例⇩

かれつ 苛烈 ¶苛烈な severe; relentless.

かれの 枯野 a desolate field.

かれは 枯葉 a dead [withered] leaf.

かれら 彼等 ¶彼らは[が] they / 彼らの their / 彼らのもの theirs / 彼らに[を] them.

かれる¹ 枯れる 〈草木が〉wither; die; be dead; 《文》be blasted; 〈材木が〉be seasoned; 〈老熟する〉mature (with age) ¶枯れた withered; dead; 〈材木・人などが〉seasoned. 文例⇩

かれる² 涸れる 〈水が〉dry up; run [go] dry (井戸や流れの); 〈尽きる〉run out; 〈人が〉be exhausted ¶かれることのない泉 a perennial spring. 文例⇩

かれる³ 嗄れる 〈声が〉get [go, grow] hoarse [husky]. 文例⇩

かれん 可憐 ¶可憐な 〈哀れな〉pitiful; pitiable; 〈愛らしい〉pretty; lovely; sweet;《米》cute.

カレンダー a calendar ¶カレンダーを1枚はぎ取る tear a sheet off the calendar / カレンダーをめくる turn over a calendar / 卓上[壁掛け]カレンダー a desk [wall] calendar.

かろう¹ 家老 a chief retainer (of a feudal lord); a minister (of a *daimyo*).

かろう² 過労 overwork ¶過労になるまで働く work too hard; overwork (oneself) / 過労を感じる feel overworked. 文例⇩

がろう 画廊 a picture [an art] gallery.

かろうじて 辛うじて barely; narrowly; with difficulty; just manage (to *do*) ¶かろうじて逃れる have a narrow [hairbreadth] escape; escape narrowly [by the skin of one's teeth] / かろうじて試験に及第する pass an examination with difficulty;《口語》(just) scrape through an exam / かろうじて生計を立てる make [earn] a bare living;《口語》scrape a living. 文例⇩

かれき 枯木も山のにぎわい。The more the merrier. / 枯木も山のにぎわいだというので僕も連れて来られたのさ。I've been brought here simply to pad out the numbers [to swell the crowd].

かれこれ その案にはだれもかれこれ言わなかった。No one raised any objection to the plan. / かれこれ6時です。It's about [around] six o'clock. | It's getting on for six.

かれる¹ この木は枯れている。This tree is dead [withered]. / この植木は水不足で枯れかかっている。This plant is dying from lack of water. / 霜にあってもこの植木は枯れない。Frost won't kill [blight] these plants. / 彼の芸は年と共に枯れてきた。The years have matured his art.

かれる² 井戸の水がかれてしまった。The well has run dry [has dried up].

かれる³ 風邪を引いて声がかれてしまった。My voice is hoarse from a cold.

かろう² 彼は過労のため病気になった。He fell ill from overwork.

かろうじて 彼はかろうじて目的を達した。He barely achieved [managed to achieve] his object. / 私はかろうじて助かった。I was saved by the skin of my teeth.

かわ¹ 川の水が増した。The river has risen [swollen]. / 川があふれた。The river has overflowed its banks. / 淀川は大阪市中を流れ、大阪湾に注ぐ。The Yodo flows through Osaka and empties into Osaka Bay. / この川は十和田湖から流れ出ている。This river comes from Lake Towada. | This river rises [has its source] in Lake Towada.

かわ² 彼は人間の皮をかぶったけだものだ。He's no better [more] than an animal.

カロチン 〖化〗 carotene; carotin.

かろやか 軽やか ¶軽やかな light; airy / 軽やかに lightly; airily / 足取りも軽やかに 《walk》 with light steps.

カロリー 〖物〗 a calorie ¶カロリーが多い, カロリー価が高い have a high calorific value; be high in calories / カロリーが少ない, カロリー価が低い have a low calorific value / 1日3,000カロリーの食事をとる take a 3,000 caloric diet [eat 3,000 calories of food] per day / 低[高]カロリーの食事 《be on》 a low-[high-]calorie diet / カロリー含有量 caloric [calorie] content / カロリー摂取量 (a) calorie intake.

かろん 歌論 an essay on *waka* poems; an essay in Japanese poetics.

ガロン a gallon.

かろんじる 軽んじる 〈軽くみる〉 make [think] light of; 《文》 slight; neglect; do not attach much importance to; 《文》 attach little importance to; 〈さげすむ〉 despise; look down on ¶人命を軽んじる make light of [attach little importance to] human life.

かわ[1] 川, 河 a river; 〈流れ〉 a stream; 〈小川〉 a brook; a rivulet ¶川の水 river water / 川のほとりにあるホテル a hotel on a river; a riverside hotel / 川に沿って, 川伝いに along a river / 川をさかのぼる[下る] go up [down] a river / 川を渡る cross a river; wade across a stream (かちわたる) / 隅田川 the Sumida (River); the (River) Sumida. 文例↓

かわ[2] 皮, 革 〈表皮〉 the 《one's》 skin; 〈獣皮〉 a hide; 〈なめし革〉 leather; 〈樹皮〉 bark; 〈果皮〉 (a) rind; peel; 〈皮膜, 薄皮〉 film ⇨けがわ ¶りんごの皮 the rind of an apple; apple peel / みかんの皮 orange peel / トマト［バナナ］の皮 tomato [banana] skin / パンの皮 the crust of bread / ふとんの皮 《文》 ふとん / 皮のような 《an appearance》 like leather; 《文》 leatherlike; leathery / 皮のついたままのじゃがいも a potato in its skin; a potato in its jacket / 皮をはぐ［むく］ skin 《a chicken》; peel 《an orange》; pare 《an apple》 / 木の皮をはぐ take the bark off 《a tree》; bark 《a tree》 / 皮ごと食べる eat 《a tomato》 skin and all [with the skin on] / 革工場 a tannery / 革細工 leatherwork / 革細工人 a leatherworker / 皮製品 leather goods [products] / 皮製の leather 《bags》 / 皮むきナイフ a paring knife / 革屋 〈店〉 a leather store; 〈人〉 a leather dealer; 〈なめし工〉 a tanner. 文例↓

がわ a side; 〈時計のふた〉 a 《silver》 case ¶…の側につく take sides with…; side with …; be on the side of… / 左側 the left(-hand) side / 北側 on the north side / 使用者側の怠慢により owing to neglect of duty on the part of the management. 文例↓

かわあそび 川遊び 〈子供たちの〉 an outing to the riverside; picnicking at the riverside; 〈泳ぎ〉 swimming [bathing] in a river; 〈船での〉 boating [rowing] in a river.

かわいい 可愛い 〈愛らしい〉 sweet; 《米口語》 cute; pretty; 〈愛している〉 dear; darling; 〈小さい〉 tiny ¶かわいい女の子 a cute [lovely, charming] little girl; 〈若い女性〉 an attractive young girl / かわいい人形 a cute doll / かわいい声 in a sweet voice / かわいい顔をしている be pretty; be cute; be lovely. 文例↓

かわいがる 可愛がる love; pet; make a pet of 《a boy》; be affectionate to *sb*; treat *sb* with love [affection]; 〈抱いたりして〉 caress; fondle. 文例↓

かわいげ the charm of an innocent child. 文例↓

かわいさ 可愛さ 文例↓

かわいそう 可哀そう ¶かわいそうな 〈哀れむべき〉 poor; pitiable; pitiful; 〈惨めな〉 miserable; wretched; 〈感動させる〉 pathetic; touching; 〈無慈悲な〉 cruel; pitiless / かわいそうな話 a sad [pathetic] story / かわいそうなことをする［目にあわせる］ be cruel to *sb*; treat *sb* cruelly; do something cruel to *sb* / …をかわいそうに思う pity *sb*; feel sorry [《文》 pity] for *sb*. 文例↓

かわいらしい 可愛らしい ⇨ かわいい ¶かわいらしい子供 a lovely [《米》 cute] little child / かわいらしい時計 a tiny watch.

かわうお 川魚 a river [stream, freshwater] fish.

かわうそ 〖動〗 an [a river] otter.

かわえび 川蝦 a river [freshwater] shrimp.

かわおび 革帯 a leather belt.

かわかす 乾かす dry ¶火で乾かす dry *sth* over [at] the fire / 天日で乾かす dry *sth* in the sun / 衣類を外につるして乾かす hang clothes

---

がわ 学校は川のこちら[向こう]側にある. The school is on this [the other] side of the river. / 彼は私の右側に座った. He sat on my right (side). / 彼の家の南側はガラス工場である. His house is bounded on the south by a glass factory. / 我々の側には異論はない. There is no objection on our part. / 日本は第一次世界大戦では連合[国側]について参戦した. Japan entered the First World war on the side of the Allied Powers.

かわいい 子供というものはかわいいものだ. Nothing is sweeter than a child. / あの女の子を見て. なんてかわいいんでしょう. Look at that little girl! Isn't she cute! [What a darling she is!] / 僕のところの犬は毎朝駅まで迎えに来る. かわいいものだね. My dog follows me to the station every morning. Cute [Charming], isn't it? / かわいい子には旅をさせよ. A pampered child learns little; the best education is to be forced out into the world.

かわいがる 梅津夫人は彼女をわが子のようにかわいがった. Mrs. Umezu loved her as if she were [was] her own daughter. / 彼は先生にかわいがられている. He is his teacher's pet. | He is a favorite with his teacher. / 彼はその犬を非常にかわいがっている. The dog is his great pet.

かわいげ あの子はかわいげがない. There is nothing of the charming child about that boy.

かわいさ 子にいさ余って憎さ百倍. The greatest hate springs from the greatest love. 〖諺〗

かわいそう かわいそうに! Poor thing [man, girl, boy] ! / かわいそうにあの子をごらん. Look at that poor boy. / かわいそうに思って彼を逃してやった. I set him free out of pity.

かわかぜ 川風 a river breeze [wind].
かわかみ 川上 the upper reaches [course] of a river ¶川上へ up the river [stream]; upriver; upstream.
かわき¹ 渇き thirst ¶のどの渇きを覚える feel thirsty / のどの渇きをいやす quench [《文》relieve, 《文》slake] one's thirst.
かわき² 乾き ¶乾きが早い dry easily [fast].
かわぎし 川岸 ⇨ かわばた.
かわきり 皮切り 〈始め〉 the beginning; the start ¶皮切りに…する start [begin] by doing; start the ball rolling by doing. 文例⇩
かわぎり 川霧 a river fog [mist].
かわく¹ 渇く be [feel] thirsty ¶のどが渇く be thirsty; one's throat is dry; be dry.
かわく² 乾く dry; get [《口》become] dry; be parched ¶乾いた dry; parched / 乾いたタオル a dry towel / 乾いたくちびる parched lips. 文例⇩
かわぐつ 革靴 leather shoes.
かわさんよう 皮算用 ¶取らぬたぬきの皮算用をする count one's chickens before they are hatched.
かわしも 川下 the lower reaches [course] of a river ¶川下へ down the river [stream]; downstream.
かわす¹ 交わす exchange ¶あいさつを交わす exchange greetings 《with》/ 言葉を交わす talk 《with》; exchange a few words 《with》;《文》enter into conversation 《with》/ 情を交わす《文》have an intimate [a sexual] relationship 《with》.
かわす² 躱す dodge; avoid; sidestep ¶体をかわして…をそらす dodge [sidestep] ¶a blow].
かわず 蛙 ⇨ かえる¹.
かわせ 為替 exchange ¶外国[内国]為替 foreign [domestic] exchange / ドル[円]為替 dollar [yen] exchange ⇨ でんしん(電信為替), ゆうびん(為替受取人 the payee / 為替管理 exchange control / 為替銀行 an exchange bank / 為替差益[差損] an exchange profit [loss] / 為替尻(じり) an exchange balance; a balance of exchange / 為替手形 a bill of exchange / 為替振出人 the sender / 為替レート ⇨ かわせそうば
かわせそうば 為替相場 a rate of exchange; an exchange rate ¶1ドル220円の為替相場で at the (exchange) rate of 220 yen to the U.S. dollar.
かわせみ 〔鳥〕 a kingfisher.
かわぞこ 川底 the bottom of a river; the riverbed; the stream bed.
かわった 変わった 〈違った〉 different; another; 〈色々な〉 various; 《口》 diverse; 〈特別の〉 particular; 〈異常な〉 unusual; uncommon; 《things》 out of the ordinary; 〈奇妙な〉 odd; strange; queer; 《文》 curious ¶変わったことが好きである be fond of novelty; care for anything new / 色々変わった品 a variety of articles / 変わった人 ⇨ かわりもの. 文例⇩
かわづり 川釣り river fishing.
かわと 革砥 a (razor) strop ¶革砥でとぐ sharpen (a razor) on a strop; strop (a razor).
かわどこ 川床 the riverbed; the stream bed.
かわとじ 革綴じ 〈総革〉 leather binding; 〈背革〉 quarter binding in leather ¶革とじの本 〈総革〉 a leather-bound book; a book bound in leather; 〈背革〉 a book quarter-bound in leather.
かわなみ 川波 ripples on a river.
かわはぎ 〔魚〕 a filefish.
かわばた 川端 a riverside; a riverbank ¶川端に by (on) a river; on the bank(s) of a river / 川端柳 a riverside willow (tree).
かわはば 川幅 the width of a river. 文例⇩
かわばり 革張り ¶革張りの leather-covered 《chairs》.
かわひも 革紐 a (leather) strap; a thong; 〈犬をつなぐ〉 a leash.
かわびょうし 革表紙 a leather cover; 〈皮とじ〉 leather binding ¶革表紙の本 a leather-bound book; a book bound in leather.
かわびらき 川開き a river carnival [festival] 《at Ryogoku》.
かわぶくろ 革袋 a leather bag; 〈酒を入れる〉 a wineskin.
かわぶね 川船 a riverboat; a rivercraft 《単複同形》.

かわかみ ここから3キロほど川上に村が1つある. There is a village about three kilometers up the river from here.
かわきり この試合が今シーズンの皮切りです. This game is the season opener. / 熊本を皮切りに九州一円を講演して回った. He went on a lecture tour of Kyushu starting in [with] Kumamoto.
かわく² 着物が乾いた. The clothes have dried.
かわった 彼はいつもと少しも変わった様子がなかった. There was nothing unusual about him. | He looked his usual self. / 彼女はこれまでと全く変わった歌い方をした. She sang in a different way from how she had ever sung before. / 何か変わった事でもないかい. What's the news? | Is there any news? / 別段変わった事もない. Nothing in particular.|Nothing to speak of. / 変わった事がなければよいが. I hope nothing has happened. | I hope there hasn't been an accident. / 何か変わった事があったらすぐに必ず電話をくれ. If anything happens, be sure to call [《英》ring] me at once.
かわはば 川幅は約10メートルだ. The river is about ten meters across [wide].
かわり¹ この部屋は事務室の代わりになる. This room will serve for the office. / これはつえの代わりになる. This will do for a walking stick. / 私の代わりに息子をやります. I will send my son instead of me. / My son will go in my place [《文》stead]. / 彼が病気になったので, 僕がその代わりをしなければならなかった. He fell ill, so I had to substitute for him. / 君の代わりにだれか雇わなくてはならないことになるだろう. We'll be obliged to hire someone in your place. / 英語を教わる代わりに彼女に日本語を教えている. I taught her Japanese in exchange for English. / 値段は少し高いが, その代わり持ちがいい. This wears better, though it's a bit expensive. / 彼は敵も多い代わりに味方も多い. He has as many friends as enemies. / 教えるのは骨が折れる代わりに楽しみがある. The pleasure of teaching makes up for the toil.

かわべ[べり] 川辺[縁] ⇨ かわばた.
かわむこう 川向こう ¶川向こうの[に] on the opposite [other] side of the river; across the river.
かわも 川面 the surface of a river.
かわやなぎ 川柳 《植》a purple willow (tree).
かわら¹ 瓦 a tile ¶かわらで屋根をふく roof 《a house》with tiles; tile the roof / 屋根がわらを葺く家 a roofing tile / 棟がわら a ridge tile / かわらぶきの家 a tile-roofed house / かわら屋〈かわらを売る店〉a tile store;〈売る人〉a tile dealer;〈かわらを焼く人〉a tile maker; a tiler;〈ふく人〉a tiler / かわら屋根 a tiled roof.
かわら² 川[河]原 a dry riverbed.
かわらけ unglazed earthenware.
かわり¹ 代[替]わり 〈代用品〉a substitute;〈代人〉a proxy; a deputy;〈交替者〉a relief;〈代償〉compensation ¶二の替わり a second program / 代わりがきかない cannot be replaced; be irreplaceable / 代わりの〈代用の〉substitute;〈別の〉alternative; another;〈新しい〉fresh / 人の代わりをする take sb's place; act in sb's place; substitute for sb / …の代わりに in place of…; instead of…; on behalf of…; for…; as (a) substitute for…;〈文〉in its [sb's] stead;〈代償〉in return for…;〈埋合わせ〉to make up for…;〈交換〉in exchange for… / …の代わりになる serve as [for]…; answer [serve] the purpose of…; do duty for … / 人の代わりに行く go instead of sb;《文》go in sb's stead / 替わり狂言 the program for the next month. 文例⇩
かわり² 変わり 〈変化〉a change;〈相違〉a difference;〈異状〉something wrong;〈変事〉an accident ¶変わりがない〈変化なし〉be [《文》remain] unchanged;〈異常なし〉nothing is the matter 《with》; be all right;〈健康に〉be (perfectly) well / 変わりなく〈変化なく〉without a change;〈相変わらず〉constantly;〈一様に〉《文》uniformly;〈永久に〉for ever;〈事なく〉uneventfully; peacefully;〈元気に〉well / 変わりなく 変わりなく暮らす get along well [fine, all right]. 文例⇩
かわりあう 代わり合う relieve each other; take turns 《to do》⇨ こうたい¹. 文例⇩
かわりだね 変わり種 something [somebody] out of the ordinary; a novelty; an exception; an exceptional case; a variant〈変種・変形〉⇨ かわりもの.
かわりばえ 代わり映え 文例⇩
かわりはてる 変わり果てる be completely changed; 《文》undergo a complete change ¶変わり果てた姿になる〈死ぬ〉become dead and cold.
かわりばんこ 代わり番こ ⇨ こうたい¹ (交替に).
かわりみ 変わり身 ¶変わり身が早い be quick to adapt (to new [changing] circumstances);《口語》be (very) quick on one's feet.
かわりめ 変わり目 a change; a turning point ¶陽気の変わり目 the turn of the seasons / 学期の変わり目 the end [beginning] of a school term / 世紀の変わり目 the turn of the [a] century. 文例⇩
かわりもの 変わり者 an odd [a queer] fellow; an eccentric (person).
かわりもよう 変わり模様 a fancy pattern.
かわる¹ 代わる take sb's place; replace sb;〈交代する〉relieve sb ¶…に代わって for…; in sb's place; in (the) place of…; instead of …; on [《米》in] behalf of…; …になり代わって in the name of…;〈…の後任に〉in succession to… / 代わる代わる ⇨ こうたい¹ (交替に). 文例⇩
かわる² 変わる〈変化する〉change;《文》undergo a change; be altered;〈変動する〉vary;〈修正される〉be amended; be revised;〈…に変形する〉change [turn]《into》; be turned [transformed]《into》;〈違う〉be different《from》;《文》differ《from》 ¶変わらない be [remain] unchanged; be the same (as before);《文》be constant (in one's opinion) / 気が変わる change one's mind / 話が変わる change the (pass on) to another) subject / 話変わって / ははなし 変わりやすい changeable; variable; unsettled;〈心の〉fickle;《文》inconstant;《文》capricious;〈気分の〉moody;《文》volatile ⇨ かわった. 文例⇩
かん¹ 缶《米》a can;《英》a tin (can); a canis-

かわり² 時間制に変わりはない. There is no change in the timetable. / だれも国を思う心に変りはない. Love of our homeland is common to us all. / この2つ少しも変わりはない. There is not a bit of difference between them. / They are exactly the same. / お変わりはありませんか. How are you? / How are you getting along?
かわりあう 2人は代わり合って父の看護をした. They nursed their sick father between them. / They took turns to nurse their father.
かわりばえ 何も代わり映えがしない. It's none the better for the change. / The change has brought (about) no improvement.
かわりめ 時候の変わり目になると右ひじの関節が痛む. At the turn of the seasons the pain comes back to my right elbow. / 僕は出し物の変わり目ごとに歌舞伎座に芝居を見に行く. I go to the Kabukiza theater every time there is a change of program.
かわる¹ ちょっと僕と代わってくれないか. Just take my place, will you? / 機械は完全には人力に代わり得ない. Machinery cannot completely take the place of human labor. / 母に代わって私がご案内いたします. I'll show you around in my mother's place [《文》stead]. / 父に代わって厚く御礼申し上げます. I would like to thank you heartily on behalf of my father.
かわる² 風が南に変わった. The wind has shifted [veered] to the south. / もうじき潮が変わる. The tide will soon turn. / 彼の気分は毎日変わる. His mood varies from day to day. / 10月1日から規則が変わる. The new regulations will come into force on and after October 1st. / 君はこの前会ったときと大して変わっていない. You haven't changed much since I saw you last. / 彼は今では全く人が変わってしまった. He is quite another [a different] man now. / 毛虫はちょうやがに変わる. Caterpillars turn into butterflies or moths. / これは先ほどのとは変わっている. This is different from the one I saw a little while ago. / 今は昔と事情が変わっている. Things are not

かん / かんい

かん² 巻 a volume;〈映画の〉a reel ¶第1巻 the first volume; vol. 1 /〈映画の〉reel 1 /〈映画の〉5巻物 a five-reel picture [film]; a five-reeler / 全20巻の漱石の作品集 a set of Soseki's works in 20 volumes / 何巻もある英語辞典 a many-[multi-]volume English dictionary.

かん³ 勘 (an) intuition;《口語》a hunch ¶勘がいい[悪い] be quick [slow] to understand;《口語》be quick [slow] on the uptake;《口語》be quick [slow] to catch on / 外国語に対する勘がいい have a good linguistic sense / 勘を働かす use one's intuition;《口語》play a [one's] hunch / 勘で分かる know sth by intuition; feel sth in one's bones. 文例◎

かん⁴ 貫 a kan (=3.75 kg).

かん⁵ 棺 a coffin;《米》a casket. 文例◎

かん⁶ 寒 midwinter; the cold season; the coldest season [days] of the year (大寒). 文例◎

かん⁷〈間隙〉an interval;〈期間〉a period;〈…の間〉for; during; in;〈…の中間〉between (二者の); among (三者以上の) ⇒あいだ 囲み ¶10年間 for ten years / 過去20年間に during [in] the past twenty years /〈劇場などでの〉5分間の休憩 five minutes' [a five-minute] intermission / 間髪をいれず《…するやいなや》just as; no sooner...than /《瞬間に》(as) quick as lightning (a flash, thought); in (less than) no time. 文例◎

かん⁸ 感 (a) feeling; (a) sensation; emotion;〈感服〉admiration;〈印象〉an impression ¶感極まる be filled (overcome) with emotion; be deeply moved [touched] (by) / 感極まって涙を流す be moved to tears / 感極まった声で in a voice charged with emotion.

かん⁹ 管 a pipe; a tube; a duct (導管).

かん¹⁰ 歓 ¶歓を尽くす enjoy oneself to the full;《口語》have a most enjoyable time.

かん¹¹ 燗 ¶かんをする heat [warm]《sake》/ かんをして飲む drink《sake》warm [hot].

かん¹² 癇 ¶かんの強い〈怒りっぽい〉irritable; testy; peevish (子供が);〈神経質な〉nervous / かんの強い子供 a peevish child / かんの強い馬 a high-spirited horse / かんにさわる〈事が主語〉irritate; offend; provoke;《口語》get on one's nerves;《文》cut one to the quick.

かん¹³ 観〈外観〉an appearance; a look;〈光景〉a spectacle; a sight;〈見方〉a view; an outlook ¶…の観がある appear《to be...》; look like...; seem《to be..., that...》/ 中国観 one's view of China. 文例◎

かん¹⁴ 簡 ¶簡にして要を得ている be brief and to the point.

かん¹⁵ 環 a ring; a link (鎖の); a handle (たんすなどの).

かん¹⁶ 漢〈中国の王朝〉Han ¶前漢 the Former [Western] Han / 後漢 the Later [Eastern] Han / 漢民族 (the) Han Chinese; the Chinese.

がん¹ 雁〖鳥〗a wild goose. 文例◎

がん²癌〖医〗(a) cancer ¶のどにがんができる get cancer of the throat; get a cancer in the throat / がんの組織 cancer tissue / がんで死ぬ die of cancer / 市政のがん a cancer [a curse] in the municipal administration / 舌がん cancer of the tongue / 肺がん lung cancer / がん患者 a cancer patient / がん細胞 a cancer cell / がん年齢 the cancer-prone age. 文例◎ 囲み よくある「がん」については lung cancer, stomach cancer のように言い, 比較的珍しい「がん」については cancer of the bladder [liver] のように言うのが普通. 医学的に改まって言う時には cancer of the stomach の形で言う傾向がある.

がん³ 願〈祈願〉a prayer;〈願望〉a wish;〈誓〉a vow ¶願をかける offer a prayer with a vow《to a deity, at a shrine》; make a vow《to a deity》. 文例◎

ガン ⇒ピストル ¶ガンさばきがうまい handle one's gun skillfully [well] / ガンマニア〈人〉a gun maniac.

かんい¹ 官位 office and rank; (an) official rank.

かんい² 簡易 simple; simplified; easy; plain / 簡易にする simplify / 簡易裁判所 a summary court / 簡易宿泊所 a cheap lodging house;《米》a cheap rooming house;《米》

---

what they used to be. / その時から彼の僕に対する態度が変わった. From then on his attitude to me changed [was different]. | From that time his attitude toward me underwent a change. | 今では都会も田舎も生活にたいに変わらない. Nowadays there is little difference between town and country in the way people live. / 今頃の天気は変わりやすい. The weather is quite unsettled [changeable] at this time of (the) year. / 彼は気が変わりやすい. He is a man of moods.

かん³ どうしてわかったんですか. 一勘だよ, 太郎君. How did you know?—It was a hunch [I felt it in my bones], Taro.

かん⁵ 棺をおおうて事定まる. Call no man great before he is dead. | A man's true worth is known only when he is laid to rest.

かん⁶ 寒が明けた. The coldest part of the year is over. / 来週から寒に入る. The coldest season sets in next week.

かん⁷ 展覧会は10日から5日間開かれる. The exhibition will be held for five days beginning on the 10th.

かん⁸ 彼は感極まって声も出なかった. His heart was too full for words. | He choked up and was unable to speak. / 彼は感に堪えない様子であった. He seemed to have been struck by a feeling of deep admiration.

かん¹³ 君はこの前会ったときとは全く別人の観がある. You look [appear] quite different from the last time I saw you. / 全市が一大公園の観がある. The whole city strikes us as one big park.

がん¹ がんの群がかぎになり, さおになりして鳴きながら北に渡って行った. A flock of wild geese honked their way north, flying now in single file and now in a V (shape).

がん² 舌にがんができた. He's got cancer of the tongue.

がん³ 願がかなってうれしい. I'm delighted that my prayers were heard [answered]. / 息子の病気が治るようにと浅草の観音様に一生茶断ちの願をかけた. She took a vow to the Kannon at Asakusa that she would abstain from drinking tea for life if her prayers for the recovery of her son were answered.

かんい¹ 私が学問が好きになったのは祖父の感化です. My grandfather inspired me with a love of learning. | My love of learning is

かんいっぱつ 間一髪 ¶間一髪のところで逃れる escape by the skin of one's teeth; have a hairbreadth [very narrow] escape.

かんいん 姦淫 (commit) adultery ⇒かんつう¹.

かんえつ 観閲 ¶観閲する review the troops [fleet (船を)] / 観閲式 a review of the troops [fleet].

かんえん 肝炎 【医】hepatitis.

がんえん 岩塩 rock salt ¶岩塩を掘る mine salt.

かんおけ 棺桶 a coffin; 《米》a casket ¶片足を棺桶に突っ込んでいる have one foot in the grave.

かんか¹ 感化 influence ¶感化する influence; 《文》exert influence on; inspire / 感化される [を受ける] be influenced [by] / よい[悪い]感化を与える have [《文》exert] a good [a bad, 《文》an evil] influence 《on》 / …の感化を受けて under the influence of…. 文例 ↓

かんか² 管下 ¶管下にある be under the jurisdiction [control] 《of》.

がんか¹ 眼下 ¶眼下に[の] under [below] one's eyes / 全市を眼下に見下ろす overlook the whole city; command a view of the city below. 文例 ↓

がんか² 眼科 〈学問〉ophthalmology;〈病院の〉the department of ophthalmology ¶眼科医 an ophthalmologist; an oculist; an eye doctor [specialist] (通俗に).

がんか³ 眼窩 【解】the eye socket; the orbit (of the eye).

かんかい 官界 the official world; official circles; officialdom ¶官界にある[入る] be in [go into,《文》enter] government [public,《英》the civil] service.

かんがい¹ 干害 drought damage ¶干害を受ける suffer from (a) drought.

かんがい² 感慨 strong feelings;《文》deep emotion ¶感慨にふける be overcome by deep emotion / 感慨深げに with deep emotion; feelingly / 感慨無量である be deeply moved;《文》one [one's heart] is filled with deep emotion. 文例 ↓

かんがい³ 管外 ¶管外の outside the jurisdiction [control] 《of》.

かんがい⁴ 灌漑 irrigation ¶かんがいする irrigate; water / かんがいの便がある be well irrigated [watered]; have good irrigation facilities / かんがい工事 irrigation works / かんがい用水 irrigation water / かんがい用堀割[水路] an irrigation ditch [canal].

がんかい 眼界 〈視野〉the range [field] of vision;〈見晴らし〉《文》a prospect ⇒しや.
文例 ↓

かんがえ 考え 〈思考〉thinking; (a) thought;〈着想〉an idea; a notion;〈熟考〉consideration; deliberation; reflection;〈沈思〉meditation;〈判断〉judgment;〈思慮〉discretion;《文》prudence; sense;〈意見〉an opinion; a view;〈信念〉a belief;〈意図〉an intention;《文》a design;〈趣向〉a plan;〈期待〉expectation(s); hope;〈願望〉(a) wish;《文》(a) desire;〈想像〉imagination ¶うまい考え a clever [bright,《文》happy] idea / 考えの足りない] thoughtless; unwise; ill-advised;《文》imprudent / 考えが進んでいる have advanced ideas / 考えがつく〈まとまる〉get a definite idea;〈決心する〉make up one's mind 《to do》 / 考えが変わる change one's mind / 考えを述べる express one's opinion; speak one's mind / 考えを起こす think of 《doing》; take it into one's head 《to do》 / 考えに沈む be lost in thought / 私の考えでは in my opinion [view]; to my mind; to my way of thinking / …という考えで with a view to doing; for the purpose of doing; with the idea of doing / 後先の考えなく recklessly; thoughtlessly / 別にどうという考えもなく without any definite idea; aimlessly.

かんがえかた 考え方 one's way of thinking;〈見方〉one's point of view;〈解き方〉a solution 《of [to] a problem》; how to solve 《a question》 ¶考え方のしっかりした人々 level-headed [sensible] people. 文例 ↓

がんか¹ 丘の上から港内を眼下に見下ろすことができる。The hill commands a bird's-eye view of the harbor.

かんがい² 彼は無量の感慨をこめてその追悼の辞を書いた。He wrote the memorial address from the fullness of his heart. / 往時を回想すれば感慨無量である。When I look back on [over] the past, a thousand emotions crowd in on me.

がんかい 森を出ると急に眼界が開けた。A wide prospect opened [revealed itself] as I came out of the forest.

かんがえ 彼は時代よりも一歩進んだ考えを持っていた。His ideas were ahead of the times. / 私の考えはそうでない。I think otherwise [《口語》different]. / そんな考えでいられては困る。It won't do for you to have ideas like that. / あなたのお考えはいかがです。What is your opinion? / 私の考えをお聞かせ下さい。Let me have your thoughts on it. / 彼にはまた彼の考えがあろう。He may have an opinion of his own. / それはいい考えだ。That's a good idea. / 今のところ渡米の考えは全くありません。I have no intention of going to America at present. / 父は私を医者にする考えでいる。My father intends me to be a doctor. / 彼はなかなかよい考え方をしている。He has pretty sound judgment. / 私一人の考えで決めるわけにはいきません。I can't decide it (either way) at my own discretion. / 考えのない事をしたものだ。How rash of him to have done such a thing! / それを考えに入れていなかった。I reckoned without that. | I didn't take that into consideration [account]. / お前がどうしても嫌だと言うなら私にも考えがある。You absolutely refuse (to do it), do you? We'll see about that! / 考えなしにそんな発言をしたのでまことに申し訳ありません。I'm very sorry that I used those words without thinking (first).

かんがえかた 君の考え方は正しい。You are right (to think so). / 今の若い人は我々とは考え方が違う。Young men of today have a different way of thinking from ours.

かんがえごと

かんがえごと 考え事 something to think about; 〈心にかかる事〉(a) concern; worries ¶考え事がある have something to worry about; be worried about something; have something (that weighs) on *one*'s mind / 考え事をする think about something / 考え事にふける be sunk [lost] in thought. 文例⇩

かんがえこむ 考え込む be sunk [lost, absorbed] in thought; brood over *sth*; 〈途方に暮れる〉be at a loss [what to do]. 文例⇩

かんがえだす 考え出す 〈思いつく〉think out 《a plan》; think of 《an idea》; think up 《an excuse》; devise 《a plan》〈考え始める〉begin to think. 文例⇩

かんがえちがい 考え違い 〈誤解〉(a) misunderstanding; a mistake; 〈間違った考え〉a mistaken [《文》an erroneous] idea ¶考え違いをする misunderstand; mistake / 私の考え違いでなければ〈記憶が〉if I remember rightly; 〈考え方が〉if I am not mistaken. 文例⇩

かんがえつく 考え付く 〈考え出す〉hit [strike] on 《a plan》; think of; think out; devise; 〈思い出す〉recall; remember; call *sth* to mind. 文例⇩

かんがえなおす 考え直す reconsider; rethink; think *sth* over (again); think better of *sth* ¶考え直して on second thoughts [《米》thought]. 文例⇩

かんがえぬく 考え抜く think 《a matter》out [through]; rack *one*'s brains 《over a question, for a plan》.

かんがえぶかい 考え深い thoughtful; 《文》prudent; 《文》discreet.

かんがえもの 考え物 〈一考を要する問題〉a problem; a question; 〈なぞ〉a puzzle; a riddle; 〈難問〉a tricky [difficult] problem; 《口語》a hard [tough] nut to crack. 文例⇩

かんがえよう 考え様 〈考え方〉*one*'s way of thinking; 〈見解〉*one*'s point of view. 文例⇩

かんがえる 考える 〈思考する〉think 《of, about, that...》,《文》on); 〈信じる〉believe; 〈意図する〉intend (to *do*); think of 《*doing*》have *sth* in mind; 〈予期する〉expect; hope; 〈懸念する〉fear; 〈判断する〉judge; conclude; 〈想像する〉imagine; suppose; 〈...と見なす〉consider (*sb* (to be) a fool, that *sb* is a fool); regard 《*sth* as stupid》; take 《*sb* for a madman》; look on 《*sb* as a friend》; 〈...ではないかと疑う〉suspect; 〈...ではあるまいと疑う〉doubt; 〈考慮する〉consider; think 《a matter》over; turn 《a matter》over (in *one*'s mind); 〈考えに入れる〉take *sth* into consideration [account]; 〈熟慮する〉think [ponder] over *sth*; 《文》reflect on *sth* ¶考えてみると when you come to think of it; when you look at it / 先の事を考える think about [of] the future / よく考える think hard [carefully] about *sth*; give a great deal of thought to *sth* / まじめに考える think seriously about *sth*; 《文》give serious thought [consideration] to *sth* / じっくり考えるstop to think 《about *sth*, about *doing*》; give *sth* plenty of thought / ...と考えられている it is thought that... / 考えられる conceivable / 考えられぬ unthinkable; inconceivable. 文例⇩

かんかく¹ 間隔 a space; an interval ¶間隔を置く[明ける] leave a space 《between》/ 間隔を詰める narrow the distance [space] 《between》; 〈競走で追いつく〉catch up with *sb* / 2メートルの間隔を置いて at intervals of two meters; two meters apart 《from each other》/ 一定の間隔を置いて at regular intervals / 15分間隔で at 15-minute intervals; at intervals of 15 minutes.

かんかく² 感覚 a sense; (a) sensation; (a) feeling ¶感覚が鋭い have a keen sense 《of dis-

---

かんがえごと 彼は考え事をしていて食事をするのも忘れてしまった。He was so absorbed in thought that he even forgot to take his meal [forgot to eat].

かんがえこむ 何をそんなに考え込んでいるんだ。What has made you so thoughtful? / 彼はまたも机に向かってその問題を考え込んだ。He sat down again at his desk brooding over the matter.

かんがえだす そんな事を考え出したら切りがない。If you start thinking of things like that, you will get nowhere.

かんがえちがい 木戸君もその場に い合わせたと思ったのは私の考え違いだった。I was mistaken in thinking [I was under the mistaken impression] that Kido was there too. / あの人の世話になろうなどと思ったら考え違いだ。You can't expect any help from him.

かんがえつく うまいことを考え付いた。I hit on a good idea. | A bright idea occurred to me.

かんがえなおす それが実情だとすると少々考え直さなければいけない。If that's the way things are, I may have to do a little reconsidering. / 考え直してみて止めることにした。On second thoughts, I gave it up.

かんがえもの それが得策か否かは考え物だ。It is doubtful whether it is a wise plan or not. / そいつは考え物だ。That is a difficult one [question]. | I would advise against it.

かんがえよう 物は考えようだ。Everything depends on your way of thinking. / それは考えようでどうにでもとれる。It may be taken any way, depending (on) how you think of it.

かんがえる まあ考えてもごらん。Just [Only] think about it. 何を考えているのか。What are you thinking about? / 彼女はいつも考えるより先に言葉が口から出てしまうのだった。She never thought before she spoke. / 君が考えて良いと思ったようにしたまえ。You may do as you think [see] fit. / 彼の申し出をどう考えていいのかわからなかった。I didn't know what to make of his offer. / よく考えればこの問題の答えはわかったはずだ。You could have answered this question if you'd thought about it. / ちょっと考えさえすれば、それがいんちきだという事ぐらいわかるろう。A moment's thought [consideration] should be enough for you to see that it is phoney. / 彼は一人で何か一生懸命考えていた。He was thinking away to himself. / 彼が何を考えているのかさっぱりわからない。I have no idea what's going on inside his head [what's in his mind]. / あんな男のことなんか考えないようにしなさい。Keep your mind off him. | Keep him off your mind. / 考えてみると、それができるのは彼だけだということがわかった。When I came to think of it, he was the

かんがく　have a (keen) feeling 《for color》／感覚が古い one is [one's ideas are] behind the times／感覚を失う go [be numb [dead]; lose all feeling [sensation] 《in one's toes》; be numbed 《with cold》／美的感覚 a sense of beauty; an (a)esthetic sense／感覚的の sensuous 《quality of music》; sensual 《pleasures》／感覚器官 a sense organ／感覚中枢 the sensory [sense] center; the sensorium 《pl. -s, -ria》. 文例⇩

かんがく　漢学 the study of the Chinese classics; Sinology; Chinese studies ¶漢学者 a scholar of the Chinese classics; a Sinologist.

かんかつ　管轄 jurisdiction; control ¶管轄する have [《文》exercise] jurisdiction 《over》; control／…の管轄下にある fall under the jurisdiction of…; be under the control of…;《文》belong in the competence of…;《法廷の》…の管轄内[外]である be within [outside] the jurisdiction of…;〈問題が〉be within [beyond] the competence of…／管轄官庁 the competent [proper] authorities／管轄権 jurisdiction. 文例⇩

かんがっき　管楽器 a wind instrument ⇒きんかんがっき, もっかんがっき.

かんがみる　鑑みる ¶…にかんがみて in view of…; in consideration of…; in the light of…. 文例⇩

カンガルー〈動〉a kangaroo《pl. -(s)》.

かんかん¹〈音〉¶〈鐘が〉かんかん鳴る clang.

かんかん²〈日が照りつけたり，炭火がおこっているさま〉¶かんかんおこった炭火 glowing [red-hot] charcoal／かんかんになって怒る fly into a rage [passion];《口語》blow one's top. 文例⇩

カンカン〈踊り〉the cancan ¶カンカンを踊る do the cancan.

かんがん　宦官 a eunuch.

がんがん ding-dong; clang-clang ¶がんがん鳴る[鳴らす] ring ding-dong; sound loudly [noisily]; clang. 文例⇩

かんかんぼう　かんかん帽 a boater; a straw hat.

かんき¹　乾期[季] the dry season.

かんき²　換気 ventilation ¶換気する ventilate／換気がいい[悪い] be well [badly] ventilated／部屋の換気をする ventilate [air] a room／換気扇 a ventilating fan; an extractor fan《特に家庭用の》／換気装置 a ventilator; a ventilation system. 文例⇩

かんき³　寒気 the cold ⇒さむさ. 文例⇩

かんき⁴　喚起 ¶喚起する《文》awaken; rouse; arouse; excite／注意を喚起する call sb's attention 《to》／世論を喚起する rouse [stir up] public opinion 《against a policy》.

かんき⁵　歓喜 (great) joy; delight ¶歓喜する be very glad 《to hear that…》;《文》rejoice 《at [over] good news》／歓喜して〈dance〉for joy; in great delight.

がんき　雁木〈雪国の〉a covered alley.

かんきだん　寒気団〔気象〕a cold air mass.

かんきつるい　柑橘類 citrus fruits.

かんきゃく¹　閑却 ¶閑却する neglect;《文》be neglectful of; ignore; disregard.

かんきゃく²　観客〈野球場などの〉a spectator;〈劇場の〉(a) member of the audience; an audience《観客全体》;〈入場者〉a visitor ¶観客が多い there is a large audience 《in the hall》;〈出し物などが〉draw a large audience [a good house]／観客が少ない there is a small audience 《in the theater》;〈出し物などが主語〉have a small [meager] audience; have a thin house／観客席 the seats (for the audience [spectators, public]). 文例⇩

かんきゅう¹　乾球 ¶乾球温度計 a dry-bulb thermometer.

かんきゅう²　感泣 ¶感泣する《文》be moved

---

only person who could do it.／考えただけでもたまらない。I can't bear to think of it.｜The very thought of it upsets [worries, frightens] me.／僕の地位は君が考えるほど好ましいものではない。My position is not as enviable as you suppose.｜こんな事になろうとは少しも考えなかった。I never thought that it would come to such a pass.／よく考えて口をきくものだ。Think [Consider] carefully before you speak.｜You must weigh your words.／その年になったらもう少ししたことを考えそうなものだ。You should know better at your age.／その事を考えれば考える程まずます不安になるので，もうその事は考えないことにした。The more I think about it, the more uneasy I feel, so I've decided not to give it any more thought.／考えておきましょう。I'll see [think] about it.｜I'll think it over.／まだ若いということも考えてやらなければいけない。You must make allowance(s) for his youth.／よく考えてみると，彼の言葉をうのみにした僕たちの方が少々軽率だった。On reflection, I found that it had been rather hasty of us to take him completely at his word.

かんかく² 1時間も外に立っていたので足の感覚がなくなってしまった。I have lost all feeling in my feet [My feet are numb] after standing outside for a whole hour.／大脳が体から感覚情報を受け取る。The cerebrum receives sensory messages from the body.

かんかつ　その問題は我々の管轄外の事である。The matter doesn't come within our jurisdiction.｜《法廷の審議事項について》The case is beyond our competence.

かんがみる　彼の失敗にかんがみて，我々は新たな方法を案出しなければなるまい。In view of his failure, we should work out a new approach.

かんかん²　日がかんかん照っていた。The sun was blazing down [shining for all it was worth].／彼は武夫のことをかんかんに怒っていた。He was very angry with [in a great rage at] Takeo.

がんがん　頭ががんがんする。I've got a splitting headache.｜耳ががんがん鳴っている。I've a ringing in my ears.｜My ears are ringing.

かんき²　換気のために窓を開けなさい。Open the windows and let some fresh air in [and air the room].

かんき³　寒気が甚だしい[厳しい]。It is extremely [bitterly] cold.

かんきゃく²　観客は皆若い人ばかりだった。The audience was made up entirely of young people.｜The audience were all young.　★《観客》の一人一人を念頭に置いて言うとき，audience に呼応する動詞は複数形になることがある／この芝居は初日以来日ましに観客が増えてきている。Ever since its opening night

to tears ⟪by, with⟫; ⟪文⟫ shed tears of gratitude ⟪for⟫.
かんきゅう³ 緩急 ¶緩急よろしきを得る be tactful ⟪in dealing with...⟫.
がんきゅう 眼球 the eyeball.
かんきょう¹ 感興 interest; fun ¶感興がわく get [⟪文⟫ become] interested ⟪in⟫ / 感興のおもむくままに as *one's* fancy dictates [takes *one*] / 感興をそそる 〈事が主語〉 arouse [excite] *one's* interest ⟪in⟫; attract [capture] *one's* fancy / 感興をそぐ 〈事が主語〉 spoil the fun; kill *one's* interest. [文例⇩]
かんきょう² 環境 (an) environment; surroundings; a milieu ⟪*pl.* -s, -x⟫ ¶(近所の)環境がいい[悪い] be in a good [an undesirable] neighborhood / 環境医学[衛生学] environmental medicine [hygiene] / 環境汚染 the pollution of the environment / 環境基準 the environmental standard ⟪for sulfurous acid gas⟫ / 環境庁 ⟪the Director General of⟫ the Environment Agency / 環境破壊[保護] the destruction [protection] of the environment / 環境保護論者 an environmentalist / 環境問題 an environmental problem.
かんきょう³ 艦橋 the bridge ⟪of a warship⟫.
かんぎょう 勧業 ¶日本勧業銀行 the Hypothec Bank of Japan / 勧業債券 a hypothec debenture.
がんきょう 頑強 ¶頑強な stubborn; dogged; persistent; die-hard ⟪rightists⟫ / 頑強に stubbornly; doggedly; persistently / 頑強に抵抗する resist stubbornly [vigorously]; put up (a) stubborn resistance.
かんきり 缶切り ⟪米⟫ a can opener; ⟪英⟫ a tin opener.
かんきん¹ 桿菌 ⇨ バチルス.
かんきん² 換金 ¶換金する convert [turn] ⟪goods⟫ into money; ⟪文⟫ realize ⟪*one's* securities⟫; 〈現金に換える〉 cash ⟪a check⟫; have [get] ⟪a check⟫ cashed.
かんきん³ 監禁 imprisonment; confinement ¶監禁する imprison; ⟪文⟫ confine; place *sb* in [under] confinement; put [keep] *sb* under lock and key / 自宅に監禁する place *sb* under house arrest / 不法監禁 illegal detention.
がんきん 元金 the principal.
かんく 管区 a district under ⟪its⟫ jurisdiction; 〈警察の〉 ⟪米⟫ a ⟪police⟫ precinct ¶管区気象台 a district meteorological observatory.
がんぐ 玩具 ⇨ おもちゃ.
がんくつ 岩窟 a (rock) cave; a cavern; a grotto ⟪*pl.* -(e)s⟫ ¶岩窟王 〔書名〕 *The Count of Monte Cristo*.
がんくび 雁首 〈きせるの〉 the bowl ⟪of a pipe⟫; 〈首・頸〉 the head ¶がん首をそろえる (do no more than) sit silently ⟪at a meeting⟫.
かんぐる 勘繰る guess *sb's* true intentions [hidden motives]; suspect ⟪that...⟫.
かんけい¹ 奸計 ⇨ かんさく ¶奸計をめぐらす make crafty plans.
かんけい² 関係 〈関連〉 (a) relationship; (a) connection; (a) relation; 〈情交〉 ⟪文⟫ (sexual) relations; 〈影響〉 influence ¶精神と物質との関係 the relation between mind and matter / 関係する[がある] 〈つながりがある〉 be related ⟪to⟫; relate ⟪to⟫; be connected ⟪with⟫; have something to do ⟪with⟫; 〈情交〉 have (sexual) relations ⟪with⟫; have an affair ⟪with⟫; 〈関与する〉 ⟪文⟫ participate ⟪in⟫; take part ⟪in⟫; have a hand ⟪in⟫; be involved ⟪in⟫; 〈影響する〉 have influence ⟪on⟫; affect / 陰謀に関係する participate [have a hand] in a scheme; be (a) party to a plot / 関係がない have no relation ⟪to⟫; have nothing to do ⟪with⟫; be unrelated ⟪to⟫ / ストレスに関係のある病気 stress-related diseases / 関係を樹立する establish ⟪trade⟫ relations [connections] ⟪with⟫ / 関係を断つ sever [break off] *one's* [the] connections [relations] ⟪with⟫; 〈手を洗う〉 wash *one's* hands of ⟪*sb, sth*⟫ / ...と[に]関係なく irrespective of...; regardless of...; ⟪文⟫ independently of... / 関係詞 〖文法〗 a relative / 関係者 〈関与者〉 the persons [parties] concerned; a participant (参加者); 〈利害の〉 an interested party / 関係書類 the relevant documents; (all) the documents related ⟪to the matter⟫ / 関係代名詞[形容詞, 副詞] 〖文法〗 a relative pronoun [adjective, adverb] / 関係当局 the authorities concerned; the competent authorities / 関係法規 the related laws and regulations. [文例⇩]
かんげい 歓迎 a welcome; a reception ¶歓迎する welcome; give a welcome to *sb*; ⟪口語⟫ give *sb* the glad hand / 心から歓迎する give *sb* a warm [hearty] welcome [reception] / 熱烈に歓迎される ⟪文⟫ be enthusiastically received [welcomed]; get [⟪文⟫ receive] an enthusiastic [a rousing, a rapturous] welcome [reception] / 歓迎される[されない]客 a welcome [an un-

---

this play has been drawing bigger and bigger audiences. / そのような劇はこの劇場へ来る観客層には受けない. A play of that sort would not appeal to the type of audience that come to this theater.
かんきょう¹ この小説は私になんの感興もそそらない. This novel has no interest for [does not appeal to] me.
かんけい² 物価の高下は主として需要と供給の関係によって定まる. The prices of commodities are largely determined by the relation between supply and demand. / 個人対家族の関係は家族対社会の関係に似ている. The individual is to the family what the family is to the community. / 彼女は自分に関係があることだけしか注意しなかった. She noticed nothing but what related to [concerned] herself. / 両者の間には密接な関係がある. There is an intimate relationship [a close connection] between them. | The two are closely connected. / あなたはあの方とどういうご関係ですか. 〈親戚関係〉 How are you related to him? | 〈交際上〉 What is your relationship [connection] with him? / 僕はあの男とは一切関係がない. I have nothing to do [am not involved] with him. / 2人は前から関係があったらしい. It seems that they have had (sexual) relations [have been intimate] (with each other) for a long time. / もうあの女とは何の関係もない. It's all over as far as she is concerned. | I'm through with

かんげいこ 寒稽古 midwinter exercises [training] (in judo).

かんげき¹ 間隙 〈すきま〉 a gap; 《文》 an aperture; 〈仲たがい〉 a break; 《文》 a breach of friendship; 〈文〉 (an) estrangement ¶間隙を縫って歩く thread *one's* way through 《the crowds》 / 間隙を生じる 〈事が主語〉 cause an estrangement 《between them》.

かんげき² 感激 strong [《文》 deep] emotion ¶感激する 《文》 be deeply moved [touched] 《by》; be very [《文》 deeply] impressed 《by, at, with》 / 感激の場面 a dramatic [moving, touching, soul-stirring] scene / 感激の涙を流す 《文》 be moved to tears.

かんげき³ 観劇 playgoing; theatergoing ¶観劇に出かける go to the theater; go to see a play / 観劇会 a theater party.

かんげざい 緩下剤 《医》 a laxative.

かんけつ¹ 完結 《文》 completion; (a) conclusion ¶完結する 〈終える〉 complete; 《文》 conclude; finish; end; bring *sth* to an end [to completion]; 〈終わる〉 be completed; 《文》 be concluded; be finished; come to an end [a conclusion]. 文例⇩

かんけつ² 間欠 ¶間欠的に intermittently; by fits and starts; off and on / 間欠泉 a geyser / 間欠熱 intermittent fever.

かんけつ³ 簡潔 ¶簡潔な brief; concise; terse / 簡潔に説明する explain *sth* briefly [《文》 in brief].

かんけん 官憲 〈当局〉 the (government) authorities; government officials; 〈警察〉 the police (authorities).

かんげん¹ 甘言 《文》 honeyed words; 《米口語》 sweet talk; (words of) flattery ¶甘言を弄する 《文》 use fair [sweet] words; 《口語》 soft-soap *sb*; 《米口語》 sweet-talk *sb* / 甘言に乗る be taken in by *sb's* honeyed words.

かんげん² 換言 ¶換言すれば in other words; that is (to say); 《文》 namely.

かんげん³ 還元 〈もとに戻すこと〉 restoration; 《化・論》 reduction; 〈分解〉 resolution; 〈酸化物の〉 deoxidization ¶還元する restore *sth* 《to *its* original state》; reduce *sth* 《to *its* components》; resolve *sth* 《into *its* elements》; 《化》 deoxidize; reduce / 利益を社会に還元する return 《the company's》 profits to society / 還元できない irreducible / 還元炎[剤] a reducing flame [agent].

かんげん⁴ 諫言 《文》 remonstrance; 《文》 expostulation; 《文》 admonition ¶諫言する 《文》 remonstrate [expostulate] with *sb* 《on [about] *his* folly》; 《文》 admonish *sb* 《against being impatient, not to do things like that》.

かんけん 頑健 ¶頑健な very strong; robust; sturdy.

かんげんがく 管弦楽 orchestral music ¶管弦楽団 an orchestra / 管弦楽法 orchestration.

かんこ 歓呼 ¶歓呼する cheer; shout for joy / 歓呼の中に amid hearty cheers / 歓呼の声をあげる give a shout of joy.

かんご¹ 看護 nursing; the care (of the sick); nursing care ⇒ かんびょう ¶看護人 a (sick) nurse; 〈男の〉 a male nurse / 看護婦 ⇒ かんごふ / 看護の科学 the science of nursing / 看護学生 a student nurse / 看護学校 a nurses' school [college]. 文例⇩

かんご² 漢語 a Chinese word [expression] ¶漢語を使う use Chinese words [expressions].

かんこ 頑固 ¶頑固な 〈強情な〉 obstinate; stubborn; mulish; die-hard 《conservatives》; 〈偏屈な〉 bigoted; 〈病気が〉 persistent; 〈習慣などが〉 《文》 inveterate / 頑固なせき[風邪] a persistent cough [cold]. 文例⇩

かんこう¹ 刊行 publication ¶刊行する publish; issue; bring out / 刊行物 a publication / 定期刊行物 a periodical.

かんこう² 甘汞 《化》 calomel.

かんこう³ 敢行 ¶敢行する dare [venture] 《to do》.

かんこう⁴ 感光 《写真》 exposure (to light) ¶感光させる expose 《the film》 (to light) / 感光剤 a photosensitizer / 感光紙 sensitized [photosensitive, light-sensitive] paper / 感光色素 light-sensitive [photosensitive] pigments / 感光度[性] photosensitivity.

かんこう⁵ 慣行 ⇒ ならわし, しゅうかん³.

かんこう⁶ 観光 sightseeing ¶観光する go sightseeing; see the sights (of a town); 《口語》 do (the town, Paris) / 観光の季節 a tourist season / 観光の名所 tourist attractions / 京都へ観光に行く go to Kyoto to see the sights / 観光案内所 a tourist information center; 《表示》 Tourist Information / 観光客 a sightseer;

---

her now. / 君の病気はこの天候に関係があるのだろう。I think your illness has something to do with this weather. / この質問は本件に関係がない。The question has no bearing on [is irrelevant to] this matter. / それは君の関係した事ではない。It is no concern of yours. | It is none of your business. / 気候の関係でこの植物は日本ではよく育たない。Because of the climate, this plant does not grow well in Japan.

かんげい 駅は彼を歓迎する人々で一杯だった。The station was filled with people who had come to welcome him. / 彼らはいつも我々を歓迎してくれた。They always gave us a hearty welcome. | They never failed to make us welcome. / この品は一般から大歓迎を受けている。This product is meeting with great public favor. / 投稿歓迎。Contributions (from readers) are cordially invited. / 歓迎ニューヨーク・ヤンキーズ。Welcome the New York Yankees.

かんけつ¹ もう1冊で完結です。〈全集などが〉 One more volume will complete the set. | 〈双書が〉 One more book will complete the series. / 次号完結。To be concluded (in our next issue).

かんСЯ 彼は頑健だ。He enjoys robust health.

かんご¹ あの病人には手厚い看護が必要です。That patient needs careful nursing [good nursing care].

がんこ そんな頑固な事を言うな。Don't be so obstinate.

がんこう a tourist / 観光業者 a travel [tourist] agent / 観光コース a tourist route / 観光局 a (national) tourist bureau / 観光産業 tourism; the tourist industry / 観光団 a tourist [sightseeing] party [group] / 観光地[ホテル] a tourist resort [hotel] / 観光都市 a tourist city [town] / 観光バス[船] a sightseeing bus [boat] / 観光旅行 a (sightseeing) tour.

がんこう 眼光 ¶眼光が鋭い be sharp-eyed; have keen [《文》penetrating] eyesight / 眼光紙背に徹する (be able to) read between the lines.

かんこうちょう 官公庁 government and municipal offices; public agencies ¶官公庁労働者組合 the Government and Public Workers Union (略: GPWU).

かんこうへん(しょう) 肝硬変(症)《医》cirrhosis (of the liver).

かんこうれい 箝口令 ¶箝口令をしく hush up 《a scandal》; order sb to keep silent 《about》; order sb not to mention sth.

かんこく¹ 勧告 (a piece of) advice; 《文》counsel; (a) recommendation ¶勧告する advise; 《文》counsel; recommend; give sb advice [《文》counsel]; 〈…するように促す〉urge [call on] sb 《to do》/ …の勧告を受けて[に従って] on sb's advice / 勧告書 a written advice. 文例

かんこく² 韓国 the Republic of Korea (略: ROK); Korea / 韓国の (South) Korean / 韓国人 a (South) Korean.

かんごく 監獄 ⇨けいむしょ.

かんこどり 閑古鳥 ⇨かっこう¹. 文例

かんごふ 看護婦 a (sick) nurse ¶准看護婦 a practical nurse / 正看護婦 a trained [graduate, registered] nurse / 《英》a staff nurse / 派出看護婦 a visiting [hired] nurse / 病院看護婦 a hospital nurse / 看護婦長 a chief [head, supervising] nurse; 《英》a sister / 看護婦会 a nurses' agency.

かんこんそうさい 冠婚葬祭《on》ceremonial occasions.

かんさ 監査 〈検査〉inspection; 〈会計の〉an audit; auditing ¶監査する inspect; 〈経理を〉audit 《the company accounts》/ 監査証明 an audit certificate / 監査役〈会社の〉an auditor.

かんさいき 艦載機 a carrier-based[-borne] (air)plane [aircraft]; carrier-based[-borne] aircraft (総称).

かんさい(ちほう) 関西(地方) the Kansai region.

かんざいにん 管財人 a [an official] receiver.

かんさく 奸策 a shrewd [dirty] trick; a sinister scheme [《文》design]; 《文》a sly artifice ¶奸策をろうする《文》use wiles; play a dirty trick 《on sb》.

がんさく 贋作 a counterfeit ⇨にせ.

かんざけ 燗酒 warmed [heated] sake ⇨かん¹¹.

かんざし 簪《wear》an ornamental hairpin.

カンザス Kansas (略: Kans., Kan.) ¶カンザス州の人 a Kansan.

かんさつ¹ 監察 inspection ¶監察官 an inspector.

かんさつ² 観察 observation ¶観察する observe; watch; look at / 私の観察する所では according to my observation; as I see [look at] it / よく観察すれば…であることが分かる close [careful] observation shows [reveals] that … / 観察を誤る make an incorrect observation / 観察眼がある have an observant eye 《for》/ 観察記録を書く write one's observations 《on wild birds》/ 観察力 one's powers of observation. 文例

かんさつ³ 鑑札 a license ¶犬の鑑札 a dog license / 鑑札を受ける take (out) a license 《to keep a dog》/ 鑑札を下付する grant a license / 無鑑札の unlicensed 《bars》,《doing business》without a license / 鑑札料 a license fee.

かんざまし 燗冷まし sake that has cooled down after being warmed [heated].

かんさん¹ 閑散〈ひっそりしているさま〉quietness; 〈不活発〉dullness; inactivity ¶閑散とした〈ひっそりした〉quiet; 〈不活発な〉dull; inactive; slack.

かんさん² 換算 conversion; change ¶換算する convert 《into》; change 《into》/ トン数に換算して in terms of tonnage / 換算表 a conversion table / 換算率 a conversion ratio; an exchange rate (外国為替の). 文例

かんし¹ 冠詞《文法》an article ¶定[不定]冠詞 a definite [an indefinite] article / 定[不定]冠詞をつける give 《a noun》a definite [an indefinite] article. 文例

かんし² 漢詩 a Chinese poem; 〈総称〉Chinese poetry.

かんし³ 鉗子《外科》a forceps《単複同形》.

かんし⁴ 監視 watching; observation; 〈監督〉supervision; 〈特に刑法上の〉《文》surveillance ¶監視する watch; keep (a) watch on; keep an eye on; observe; 〈…がないかと見張る〉watch (out) for 《traffic offenses》/ 行動を監視する watch [keep (a) watch on] sb's move-

---

かんこく¹ 彼は辞職の勧告を受けた. He was advised [called on] to resign.

かんこどり その温泉場は閑古鳥が鳴く寂しさだった. The hot-spring resort was quite deserted. / 証券市場は閑古鳥が鳴いている有様だ. Virtually no business is being done in the stock market.

かんさつ² 私の観察は正しかった. My observation has proved correct. / 彼の観察眼は鋭い. He has a sharp, observant eye. / 彼はその植物の観察記録を取っていた. He kept a record of his observations on that plant.

かんさん² 円に換算するとおよそ3万円になる. The sum will come to about 30,000 yen in Japanese currency. / 僕の車の現在までの走行距離は1万キロ, マイルに換算して6,250マイルである. The distance my car has covered up to now is 10,000 kilometers, or 6,250 miles.

かんし¹ この名詞は不定冠詞を取らない. This noun does not take an indefinite article.

かんし¹ ミサイルの実験はレーダーおよび無線による監視網によって比較的容易に探知できる. Missile tests can be detected with relative ease by a radar and radio surveillance system.

かんじ² (会合などで)今夜の幹事はだれ. Who are the organizers of the party this evening? | Who is in charge of this party?

かんじ³ (何となく)何か恐ろしい事

かんし⁵ 環視 ⇨ しゅうじん²(衆人環視の中で).

かんじ¹ 漢字 (a) *kanji* ; a Chinese character [ideograph] (used in Japanese writing) ¶漢字で書く write in *kanji* / 漢字制限 restriction on the use of *kanji*.

かんじ² 幹事 a manager ; a secretary ; an organizer (会合などの) ¶幹事長 a secretary-general ; a chief secretary (社債発行などの)幹事(証券)会社 a managing underwriter. 文例⇩

かんじ³ 感じ ⟨感覚⟩ feeling ; a sense, ⟨手触り⟩ the touch ; the feel ; ⟨印象⟩ an impression ; ⟨心持ち⟩ a feeling ; ⟨効果⟩ an effect ¶感じが鈍い be thick-skinned / 感じがない have lost all (the) feeling (in *one's* hands) ; cannot feel (the pain) ; feel dead ; 《文》be insensible (to) ; be numb ¶《文》benumbed (with cold) / 感じのいい人 a pleasant [an agreeable, a nice] person / 感じの悪い人 an unpleasant [a disagreeable, 《口語》a nasty] person / 明るい感じの絵 a cheerful picture / 感じを与える impress *sb* as ((being) a kind man) ; strike *sb* as (silly). 文例⇩

かんじいる 感じ入る be deeply impressed [struck] (by, with) ⇨ かんしん²(感心する).

がんじがらめ ¶がんじがらめにする bind *sb* firmly (hand and foot) / 規則でがんじがらめになっている be hedged about [around] with rules and regulations ; be bound hand and foot by strict and complex laws.

かんしき 鑑識 ⟨めきき⟩ judgment ; ⟨犯罪の⟩ (criminal) identification ¶美術品の鑑識にすぐれている be a good judge of [have an eye for] objects of art ; be a connoisseur of works of art / (警視庁などの)鑑識課 the (Criminal) Identification Section / 鑑識眼 (have) a critical [《文》discerning] eye (for).

かんじき snowshoes.

がんしき 眼識 a critical [《文》discerning] eye ; 《文》discernment ¶眼識がある have an eye (for works of art) ; be a connoisseur (of old furniture).

ガンジス(がわ) ガンジス(川) the Ganges ; the Ganga.

がんじつ 元日 (on) New Year's Day.

かんしつけい 乾湿計 a psychrometer ; a wet and dry bulb hygrometer [thermometer].

かんしつぞう 乾漆像 a dry-lacquered image (of the Buddha).

かんして 関して ¶…に関して on… ; about … ; as to… ; concerning… ; regarding… ; in [with] regard to…. 文例⇩

かんじとる 感じ取る perceive ; scent ⟨danger⟩ ; take in. 文例⇩

かんしゃ¹ 官舎 an official residence.

かんしゃ² 感謝 thanks ; gratitude ¶感謝する ⟨有り難く思う⟩ be thankful [grateful] (to *sb* for *his* services) ; appreciate ⟨*your* kindness⟩ ; ⟨礼を言う⟩ thank *sb* (for *his* help) ; give *one's* thanks (for) ; 《文》express ⟨*one's*⟩ gratitude (for) ; 《文》express [show] *one's* appreciation (of *sb's* services) / 感謝のしるしに as a token [《文》in token] of *one's* gratitude / 感謝の涙を流す《文》shed tears of gratitude / 感謝決議(pass) a vote of thanks / 感謝祭《米国の》Thanksgiving (Day) / 感謝状 a letter of thanks [appreciation]. 文例⇩

かんじゃ 患者 a patient ; a case ⟨of cholera⟩ ; a sufferer ⟨from rheumatism⟩ ; a subject (of an operation) ¶患者名簿 a sick list ; ⟨入院患者の⟩ a list of (in)patients. 文例⇩

かんしゃく 癇癪 a temper ; a fit of anger [bad temper] ; a tantrum (幼児の) ; a passion ¶かんしゃく持ち hot-[quick-, short-]tempered ; irritable ; 《文》irascible / かんしゃくを起こす lose *one's* temper ; fly into a passion [tantrum] / かんしゃくを押える control [keep] *one's* temper / かんしゃく玉 a (fire)cracker / かんしゃく玉が破裂する burst into a fit of rage ; explode with anger ; 《口語》blow *one's* top. 文例⇩

かんしゅ¹ 看守 《米》a (prison) guard ; 《米》a jailer ; 《英》a prison officer ; 《英》a (prison) warder ¶婦人看守《米》a female guard ; 《英》a (prison) wardress.

かんしゅ² 看取 看取する《文》perceive ; notice ; detect ; find ; see.

かんしゅ³ 緩手 ⟨碁・将棋の⟩ an ineffective [a wasted] move.

かんしゅ⁴ 艦首 the bow(s) (of a warship) ★ bows と複数形になることが多い.

かんじゅ 甘受 甘受する be resigned to ⟨*one's* fate⟩ ; submit (tamely) to ⟨*sb's* demand⟩ ; take ⟨an insult⟩ lying down.

かんしゅう¹ 慣習 ⇨ しゅうかん³ ¶慣習法 (the) customary law ; (the) common law (英米の).

かんしゅう² 監修 (editorial) supervision ¶監

が起こりそうそうな感じがする. I have a feeling (in my bones) that something terrible is going to happen. / あの人に会ってどんな感じがしましたか. How did he strike you? / とてもいい感じの人です. He impressed me favorably [as being a decent man]. / 僕の感じでは、彼は参加する意志はないようだ. It is my impression that he has no mind to join us. / 触った感じでわかった. I could tell by the feel.

かんして 私はその事に関しては何も知らない. I know nothing about it. / この件に関して何かご意見がおありでしょうか. What do you have to say in [with] regard to this matter?

かんじとる 彼女は振り向かなくても自分の後ろで何が起きているかは感じ取っていた. She took in what was going on behind her without turning her head.

かんしゃ² 感謝の言葉もありません. I don't know how to express my thanks. / I can never thank you enough. / ご好意を深く感謝いたします. I thank you from the bottom of my heart for your kindness. / I am deeply grateful to you for your kindness.

かんじゃ 横浜市内にコレラ患者が3名発生した. Three cases of cholera occurred in Yokohama. / あのお医者さんは患者が多い. The doctor has a large practice.

かんしゃく 彼はかんしゃくを起こして私を殴ったことがある. He

かんしゅう

修する supervise 《the compilation of a dictionary》/ 武藤博士監修のもとに編集される be compiled under the (general) supervision of Dr. Muto / 監修者 a general [supervising] editor; an editor-in-chief.

かんしゅう[3] 観衆 spectators; onlookers; 《劇場の》(a member of) the audience ⇒ かんきゃく[2].

かんじゅく 完熟 full ripeness [maturity] ¶完熟する come to [《文》 attain] full maturity; ripen into full maturity / 完熟した fully ripe [ripened].

かんじゅせい 感受性 sensitiveness; 《文》 sensibility ¶感受性が強い 《情操面で》 have [be a person of] real [great] sensibility; 《他人の批判などに》 feel very sensitive (to criticism); 《影響を受けやすい》 be very impressionable / 感受性の鈍い thick-skinned; stolid.

かんしょ[1] 甘蔗 《植》a sugar cane ¶甘蔗糖 cane sugar.

かんしょ[2] 甘藷 《植》a sweet potato.

かんしょ[3] 寒暑 heat and cold; 《温度》 temperature.

がんしょ 願書 an [a written] application ¶願書を出す file [present, send in] an application (for an export license).

かんしょう[1] 干渉 interference; (an) intervention; meddling ¶干渉する interfere (in sb's affairs); intervene (in); meddle (in, with) / だれの干渉も受けない be one's own master / 干渉計 《光》an interferometer / 干渉縞(ﾂ) interference fringes / 干渉好きの interfering 《neighbors》; 《people》 in the habit of interfering in other people's affairs; meddlesome. 文例も

かんしょう[2] 完勝 a complete victory ¶完勝する win [score] a complete victory 《over》.

かんしょう[3] 感傷 sentiment; sentimentality ¶感傷的 sentimental / いやに感傷的な too sentimental; mawkish / 感傷的になる get [《文》 become] sentimental; sentimentalize 《about [over] one's childhood》 / 感傷家 a sentimentalist / 感傷主義 sentimentalism. 文例も

かんしょう[4] 管掌 ¶管掌する take [be in] charge of 《a matter》; have 《a matter》 in

268

かんじょう

charge; manage / 政府管掌健康保険 Government-managed health insurance.

かんしょう[5] 緩衝 ¶緩衝器 a shock absorber; 《鉄道車両の》a buffer (★複数形で使用されることが多い) / 緩衝国 a buffer (state) 《against》 / 緩衝地帯 a buffer [neutral] zone; 《create》a buffer 《against》.

かんしょう[6] 癇性 ¶癇性な《神経質な》nervous; 《ひどくきれい好きな》particular [fussy] about cleanliness; 《怒りっぽい》hot-tempered.

かんしょう[7] 環礁 an atoll ¶エニウェトク環礁 the Eniwetok atolls.

かんしょう[8] 観照 《文》contemplation.

かんしょう[9] 観賞 観賞する admire; enjoy ¶観賞魚 an aquarium fish / 観賞植物 a decorative [house] plant.

かんしょう[10] 鑑賞 《文》appreciation ¶鑑賞する read 《poetry》; listen to 《music》; see [watch] 《a play》; 《良さがわかる》(can) appreciate 《Shostakovich》/ 鑑賞的に appreciatively; with appreciation / 鑑賞力がある have a keen [real] appreciation 《of art》; have an eye 《for beauty》; have an ear 《for music》/ 名画鑑賞会 a special show of well-known films.

かんじょう[1] 冠状 ¶《心臓の》冠状動脈[静脈] the coronary arteries [veins] / 冠状動脈血栓症 (a) coronary thrombosis / 冠状動脈 a coronary.

かんじょう[2] 勘定 《計算》counting; reckoning; calculation; 《会計》accounts; 《支払い》payment; settlement; 《勘定書き》a bill; 《米》a check ¶勘定する 《計算する》count; reckon; calculate; 《払う》pay [settle] a bill [an account] / 金を勘定する count money / 勘定が下手[上手]である be bad [good] at figures [calculating] / 勘定をためる run up bills 《in a store》/ たまった勘定をとり立てる collect long-standing bills [accounts] 《from》/ 勘定に入る[入らない] count [do not count] / 勘定に入れる take sth into account [consideration] / 勘定に入れない leave sth out of one's calculations; reckon without sth; take no account [thought] of sth / …の勘定に付ける put [《the expenses》(down)] to sb's account / 勘定書きを持って来させる ask [call] for one's bill / 勘定取り a bill collector / 勘定日 a settle-

---

once struck me in a fit of rage [passion]. / かんしゃくを押えるのが大変だった。It cost me a tremendous effort to keep my temper.

かんしょ[3] その国は寒暑の差がはだしい。The country is marked by a wide range of temperature between the hottest and coldest periods of the year.

かんしょう[1] 子供にはあまり干渉しない方がよい。Children ought to be left alone [to themselves] sometimes.

かんしょう[3] 外交交渉には感傷などの入り込む余地は全くない。There's no room for sentiment in diplomatic negotiations.

かんじょう[2] 勘定すると月3万円の割になる。It works out at 30,000 yen a month. / お勘定はいくら。What is the bill? | 《口語》What's the damage? | How much do I owe you? / 勘定はめいめい別にして下さい。Separate bills 《米》 checks], please. / 勘定は全部で幾らになるかね。How much will they be altogether? | How much does the whole account come to? / お勘定をして下さい。My bill [《米》 check], please. / 《貸金の》勘定をそういつまでも待つわけにはまいりません。I can't afford to let accounts run on. / このワインは僕の勘定につけておいて下さい。Please charge this wine to

my account [bill]. | Put this wine on my check, please. / 彼は勘定ずくでそうしただけの事だ。He did it on his calculation as to what effects it would have on his interests.

かんじょう[4] 彼女はそれまで彼に対してこのような感情を抱いたことは一度なかった。She had never felt like this [felt this way] toward him before. / 彼の話を聞いてこれまで眠っていた彼女の宗教的感情が目覚めた。His speech roused [stirred up] her latent religious feelings [emotions].

かんじょう[5] 彼に会った時の感触ですが, 彼は私たちの提案を違わず受諾するだろうと思います。

かんじょう ment day. 文例⇩
かんじょう³ 感状 a citation.
かんじょう⁴ 感情 feeling(s); emotion (理性に対する); sentiment (感傷, 情操); passion (激情) ¶感情が高まる[激する] one's feelings run high; get excited [worked up] / 感情を押える control one's feelings; 《文》repress [suppress] one's emotions; contain oneself [《文》one's passions] / …の感情を無視する do not consider [have no regard for] sb's feelings / 感情を害する《他人の》hurt [wound] sb's feelings; offend sb;《自分が》be offended (by); take offense 《at》/ 感情に走る be carried away by [give way to] one's feelings / 一時の感情に駆られて on the impulse of the moment; impulsively / 強い国民感情に支配される be swayed [influenced] by strong public sentiment [feeling] 《against the U.S.》/ 対日感情 sentiment toward Japan / 感情的 sentimental; emotional / 感情的に物を考える think with one's heart (rather than one's head) / 感情的になりやすい be excitable; be apt to get excited / 感情移入《心理・美学》empathy / 感情家 an emotional person; a person who is easily swayed by his feelings [《文》stirred by emotion] / 感情線《手相の》the line of Heart / 感情論 an emotionally-charged[-loaded] argument. 文例⇩
かんじょう⁵ 管状 ¶管状の tubular (in form).
かんじょう⁶ 環状 ring-shaped; circular / 環状7号線 Loop 7 / 環状線《電車の》a belt [loop] line / 環状道路 a loop [ring] road;《米》a belt highway.
がんしょう¹ 岩漿 《地質》magma.
がんしょう² 岩礁 sunken rocks; a (shore) reef.
がんじょう 頑丈 頑丈な strong; sturdy; burly; strongly-built[-made];《どっしりした》massive / 頑丈な体付きの若者 a powerfully-built young man.
かんじょうきん 桿状菌 ⇨ バチルス.
かんしょく¹ 官職 ⇨ こうしょく¹.
かんしょく² 間食 eating between meals ¶間食をする eat [have a snack] between meals.
かんしょく³ 閑職《文》a sinecure; an unimportant post; an easy [《口語》a cushy] job.
かんしょく⁴ 寒色 a cold color.
かんしょく⁵ 感触《手触り》the touch; the feel;

《感じ》a feeling ⇨ てざわり, かんじ³. 文例⇩
がんしょく 顔色 ⇨ かおいろ ¶顔色なからしめる put sb to shame; put [cast, throw] sb in [into] the shade.
かんじる 感じる 《知覚する》feel; be aware [conscious] (of);《感動する》be impressed (by, with); be moved [touched] (by) ¶痛みを感じる feel a pain (in one's chest) / 空腹を感じる feel hungry / 困難を感じる find [have] difficulty (in doing); find it difficult to do / 不便を感じる《文》experience [suffer] inconvenience / 人の恩に感じる appreciate [be moved by] sb's kindness / 感じない《文》be insensitive (to pain); be dead (to all sense of shame);《感動しない》be unmoved [unaffected] (by) / 感じやすい《敏感な》tender-hearted; sensitive; impressionable; easily moved (by);《激しやすい》excitable / 感じやすい娘心 a girl's tender heart. 文例⇩
かんしん¹ 寒心 ¶寒心すべき alarming; deplorable; regrettable / …は寒心にたえない《文》It is a matter for regret that…; It is deplorable [regrettable] that….
かんしん² 感心 ¶感心な admirable;《文》praiseworthy;《文》laudable / 感心する admire; feel admiration (for); be struck with admiration; be very [deeply] impressed (with, by) / 感心させる《文》evoke admiration from sb; impress sb favorably / 感心して聞く listen to (sb's speech) admiringly [《文》with admiration] / あまり感心しない《人が主語》be not very happy [satisfied, pleased] (with);《口語》do not think much of sth;《事が主語》be not very satisfactory. 文例⇩
かんしん³ 関心 concern; (an) interest ¶…の関心の的となる occupy the interest [attention] of… / 関心を持つ be interested (in); take (an) interest (in) / 関心を持たない have no interest (in); be indifferent (to) ⇨ むかんしん 関心事 a (matter) of concern. 文例⇩
かんしん⁴ 歓心 ¶歓心を買う curry favor with sb; make up to sb;《文》(try to) win sb's favor.
かんじん 肝心 ¶肝心な《主要な》main; essential (to);《重大な》important; crucial; vital / 肝心(かなめ)な事点 the main [vital, crucial] thing [point]; the most important thing

---

When I talked with him, I got the feeling that he will accept our offer before long.
かんじる 何かがさっとするように私の右肩に触れるのを感じました。I felt something brush against my right shoulder. / この時ほど自分の無知を強く感じたことはない。Never had I realized my ignorance more keenly than I did then. / 彼女はだれかに尾行されていることを感じていた。She was aware that someone was following her. / 彼はいくら親切に言ってやっても感じるような男じゃない。All our kind words will be lost on him. / 感じる所あって彼 の申し出を断わることにしました。Something has happened and I have decided to refuse his offer.
かんしん² 感心, 感心! Well done! Good for you! / 私が留守のあいだ, 花に水をやってくれたとは, 感心だ。It was sensible of you to water the flowers while I was away. / あなたの勉強ぶりには私もほとほと感心しました。I am deeply impressed by your hard work. / あまり腹のすいたとき強い酒を飲むのは感心しできません。It is not very good idea to drink strong liquor on an empty stomach. / 僕はマトンはあまり感心しない。I don't care much for [think much of] mutton. / あの人の感心な点は決して人の悪口を言わないことだ。It must be mentioned to his credit [What I like about him is] that he never speaks badly about other people.
かんしん³ 私はそういう事には全然関心を持ちません。I have no interest in that sort of thing. / その実験には彼らも深い関心を示しました。They showed deep interest in that experiment, too. / 彼らはコンピューターの可能性に対する関心を強めている。They are taking an increasing interest in the possibilities of the computer.

かんじんもと　勧進元 a promoter.
かんすい¹　冠水 ¶冠水する be covered with water; be submerged; be flooded.
かんすい²　完遂 《文》successful execution;《文》completion ¶完遂する《文》bring sth to a successful conclusion; complete; carry sth through / 目的を完遂する《文》attain one's object;《文》accomplish one's purpose.
がんすい　含水 ¶含水炭素 ⇒たんかすいぶつ / 含水量 the water content《of a substance》.
かんすう　関数【数】a function ¶関数方程式 a functional equation / 関数論 the theory of functions.
かんする　関する 〈関係する〉be connected with; be concerned with; be related to; bear on; 〈影響する〉affect《sb's honor》¶宗教に関する書物 a book on religion / 宗教(which is) concerned with religion / 環境衛生に関する法律 laws regarding [concerning] environmental sanitation / 私に関する限り as [so] far as I am concerned / われ関せずという態度を取る《文》assume an attitude of indifference《to, toward》. 文例◊
かんせい¹　完成 《文》completion;《文》accomplishment ¶完成する〈終える〉finish; complete;《文》accomplish; round out;《文》bring sth to completion 〈終わる〉be finished; be completed;《文》be accomplished / 完成に近い be nearly finished [complete];《文》be approaching [nearing] completion / 完成品 a finished product; finished goods. 文例◊
かんせい²　官製 ¶官製はがき an official [a government] postcard /《米》a postal card ⇒しせい(私製はがき ★).
かんせい³　乾性 ¶乾性油 drying oil / 乾性肋膜炎 dry pleurisy.
かんせい⁴　感性 sensitivity;《文》sensibility.
かんせい⁵　管制; controlling ¶管制官 a [an air-traffic] controller /（空港の）管制塔 a control tower.
かんせい⁶　慣性【物】inertia ¶慣性の法則 the law of inertia.
かんせい⁷　歓声 a shout of joy; a cheer ¶歓声をあげる shout for joy; give [let out] a cheer. 文例◊
かんせい⁸　閑静 ¶閑静な quiet; peaceful;《文》tranquil / 閑静な所 a quiet [secluded] place [spot]. 文例◊
かんぜい　関税 customs; customs duties; a (customs) duty; a tariff　★ customs duties と複数形を取ることが多い ¶関税をかける impose [levy]《customs》duties《on imported goods》/ 横浜関税局 the Yokohama Customs Bureau / 関税障壁を設ける[除く] erect [remove] a tariff wall [customs barrier] / 関税同盟 a customs union / 関税率 a tariff rate.
がんせいひろう　眼精疲労 eyestrain; fatigue of the eyes.
かんせき　漢籍 a book in classical Chinese; a Chinese book.
がんせき　岩石 (a) rock; stones and rocks ¶岩石の多い rocky / 岩石学 petrology / 岩石層 a rock layer [stratum].
かんせつ¹　間接 ¶間接の[的] indirect / 間接(的)に indirectly; at second hand /（X線の）間接撮影 miniature radiography / 間接照明 indirect [concealed] lighting / 間接税 an indirect tax / 間接選挙 indirect election / 間接貿易 indirect trade / 間接目的語【文法】an indirect object【文法】/《米》indirect discourse /《英》indirect speech. 文例◊
かんせつ²　関節【解】a joint ¶関節の articular [ligaments] / 関節をくじく dislocate a joint / 関節炎 arthritis / 関節痛 arthralgia. 文例◊
がんぜない　頑是ない innocent; helpless;《文》artless.
かんせん¹　汗腺【解】a sweat [perspiratory] gland.
かんせん²　感染 infection; contagion（接触による）¶感染する be infected《with cholera》; contract《a disease》by infection; catch《a disease from sb》/ 感染性の infectious; contagious / 感染経路 an infection route.
かんせん³　幹線 a trunk [main] line ¶新幹線 ⇒しんかんせん / 幹線道路 a main [principal, trunk] road; an arterial road.
かんせん⁴　観戦 ¶観戦する〈軍隊の作戦を〉observe《military operations》; 〈ゲームを〉watch《a baseball game》/ 観戦記 a witness's account《of a game》.
かんぜん¹　完全 ¶完全な perfect; complete / 完全に perfectly; to perfection; 〈すっかり〉quite; entirely; wholly; fully; completely / 完全にする perfect; make sth perfect;《文》bring sth to perfection / 完全無欠な perfect and faultless; absolutely perfect / 完全雇用 full employment / 完全主義者 a perfectionist / 完全燃焼 perfect combustion / 完全犯罪[試合] a perfect crime [game]. 文例◊
かんぜん²　敢然 ¶敢然と bravely; fearlessly;《文》dauntlessly;《文》undaunted; manfully / 敢然と…する do bravely; be brave enough to

かんじん そこが肝心なところだ。That's the point. / 彼は大事業を計画しているが肝心の金がない。He is planning to start a big enterprise, but does not have the necessary funds to start it with. / 肝心な時にあいつはいなくなる。Just when we really need him, he's nowhere to be found.
かんする 私に関する限りきょうでも明日でも出発できます。As far as I'm concerned, I can leave either today or tomorrow. / 彼のおかしな行動に関するうわさは僕も耳にしている。I've heard the rumor concerning his strange behavior, too.
かんせい¹ 死ぬまでにはこの事業を完成したいものだ。I hope to see the work accomplished before I die.
かんせい⁷ 彼の姿が見え始めると、群衆から大歓声が上がった。The crowd cheered wildly [Great shouts of joy arose from the crowd] when he came in sight.
かんせい⁸ 近所は閑静で郊外のようですよ。Our neighborhood is so quiet that you feel as if you were way out of town.
かんせつ¹ その話は間接に聞いたのです。I had the news at second hand. / 私はその事件には間接に

がんぜん 眼前 ⇨め¹(目の前で) ¶(景色などが)眼前に展開する open out before one [one's eyes].
かんぜんちょうあく 勧善懲悪 poetic justice ¶勧善懲悪小説 a didactic [moralistic] novel.
かんそ 簡素 ¶簡素な simple; plain (and simple) / 簡素化する simplify.
がんそ 元祖 〈創始者〉the originator; the founder; 〈発明者〉the inventor.
かんそう¹ 完走 ¶完走する〈競走で〉run the whole distance; stay the course (in a marathon); (manage to) complete [finish] the course [race].
かんそう² 乾燥 drying ¶乾燥する〈乾かす〉dry (up); season (木材などを); desiccate (脱水する) /〈乾く〉be [((文)) become] parched [dry]; dry (up) / 乾燥した dry; dried; parched; 〈土地が〉arid / 乾燥器[機] a drier; a drying machine / 乾燥剤 a desiccant / 乾燥室 a drying room / (不毛の)乾燥地帯 an arid region / 異常乾燥注意報 a dry-weather warning / 乾燥野菜 dehydrated vegetables / 乾燥バナナ a dried banana.
かんそう³ 感想 one's thoughts; one's impression(s); ((文)) one's sentiments ¶感想をのべる state [give] one's impressions (of); give one's thoughts (on); express one's sentiment(s) (on); remark (on) / 感想文 a (written) description of one's impressions. 文例⇩
かんそう⁴ 歓送 ¶歓送する give sb a hearty send-off / 歓送会 a send-off [farewell] party (in honor of Mr. Kanda).
かんぞう¹ 甘草 〔植〕licorice; ((英)) liquorice ¶甘草エキス licorice extract.
かんぞう² 肝臓 〔解〕the liver ¶肝臓の hepatic.
がんぞう 贋造 ((文)) counterfeiting; forgery ¶贋造する ((文)) counterfeit; forge / 贋造紙幣 a forged [counterfeit] (bank) note.
かんそうきょく 間奏曲 an interlude; an intermezzo (pl. -s, -mezzi).
かんそうじゅつ 観相術 (the art of) physiognomy.
かんそく 観測 (an) observation; a survey ¶観測する observe; survey; 〈初めて〉sight (a new star) / 私の観測では in my opinion; to my mind; as I see [look at] it / 観測気球 an observation balloon; 〈気象用の〉a sounding balloon; 〈比喩的〉a trial balloon; ((フランス語)) a ballon d'essai (pl. ballons d'essai) / 観測記録 a record of one's observations (of, on) / 観測者 an observer / 観測所 an observatory;

〈臨時の〉an observing station / 観測資料 observational data / 観測地点 an observation point [site] / 観測網 an observation network. 文例⇩
かんそん 寒村 a lonely [an impoverished, a deserted] village.
カンタータ 〔音楽〕a cantata.
かんたい¹ 寒帯 the Frigid Zones ¶南[北]寒帯 the South [North] Frigid Zone / 寒帯動物 a polar [an arctic] animal.
かんたい² 歓待 a warm [cordial] reception; a (hearty) welcome; hospitality ¶歓待する give sb a cordial reception [hearty welcome]; entertain [((文)) receive] sb warmly; welcome. 文例⇩
かんたい³ 艦隊 a squadron (小); a fleet (大) ¶艦隊勤務をする do one's sea time.
かんだい 寛大 broad-mindedness; generosity; ((文)) magnanimity; ((文)) liberality; ((口語)) bigheartedness; ((文)) tolerance ¶寛大な generous; ((文)) magnanimous; liberal; forgiving; 〈容認する〉tolerant / 寛大に generously; ((文)) magnanimously; 〈寛容に〉tolerantly / 寛大に扱う deal leniently with sb; ((文)) show clemency to sb.
がんたい 眼帯 a patch (over one's eye).
かんたいへいよう 環太平洋 ¶環太平洋地震帯 the circum-Pacific earthquake belt / 環太平洋諸国 the Pacific basin countries.
かんだかい 甲高い high-pitched ((tones)); shrill [reedy] ((voices)); sharp ((cries)).
かんたく 干拓 land reclamation by drainage ¶干拓する reclaim land (from the Bay of Kojima) / 干拓工事 reclamation works / 干拓地 reclaimed land.
かんたん¹ 肝胆 ¶肝胆相照らす間柄である be inseparable [bosom, great] friends like David and Jonathan / 肝胆相照らして語り合う have a heart-to-heart talk (with).
かんたん² 感嘆 admiration ((for, of)); wonder ¶感嘆する admire; marvel (at); wonder (at); be struck [filled] with wonder [admiration] / 感嘆すべき admirable; wonderful; marvelous / 感嘆符 〔文法〕an exclamation mark [point] / 感嘆文 〔文法〕an exclamatory sentence; an exclamation. 文例⇩
かんたん³ 簡単 〈複雑でないこと〉simplicity; 〈短いこと〉brevity ¶簡単な〈複雑でない〉simple; ((主に英)) straightforward; 〈短い〉brief; short; 〈手軽な〉light; 〈容易な〉easy / 簡単に simply; briefly; ((文)) in brief / 簡単にする simplify; make [cut] sth short / 簡単に言え

関係がある. I am indirectly concerned in the affair.
かんせつ 右腕の関節が外れた. I had my right arm put out of joint. | I dislocated my right arm.
かんぺき¹ 何事によらず完全は望まれない. Perfection cannot be expected in anything. / 建築はまだ完全には出来上がっていない. The building is not quite finished yet.

かんそう³ 滞米中のご感想はいかがですか. How did America strike you? | What were your impressions of America? / その件については別に感想はありません. I've no particular comments to make on that subject.
かんそく その地位には田中氏が任命されるだろうというのが一般の観測である. It is generally believed that Mr. Tanaka will be

appointed to the post.
かんたい² 彼女は到るところで歓待された. She was warmly received wherever she went. / 彼は清水夫妻の歓待を受けた. He enjoyed the hospitality of Mr. and Mrs. Shimizu.
かんたん² その像を見てただただ感嘆した. I was filled with wonder [admiration] at the sight of the statue. | I gazed at the statue in

かんだん¹ 間断 ¶間断なく incessantly;《文》ceaselessly;《文》unceasingly; continuously; without a break.

かんだん² 閑談 an idle talk; a chat;《口語》a confab ¶閑談する have a chat (confab)《with》; chat《with》. 「talk [chat]《with》.

かんだん³ 歓談 ¶歓談する have a pleasant がんたん 元旦 New Year's Day.

かんだんけい 寒暖計 a thermometer. 文例⇩

かんち¹ 好知 cunning; craft; wiles ⇒ たける¹ (好知にたけている).

かんち² 寒地 a cold region [district] ⇒かんれい¹(寒冷地) ¶寒地植物 a psychrophyte.

かんち³ 感知 ¶感知する《文》perceive; be [《文》become] aware of sth; sense [scent《danger》] / 感知器 [装置] a (smoke, heat) sensor.

かんち⁴ 関知 ¶関知する be concerned (in); have something to do with sb [sth] / 関知しない have no concern《in》; have nothing to do with sb [sth]. 文例⇩

かんちがい 勘違い a mistake; (a) misunderstanding; a mistaken idea ¶勘違いをする guess wrong; misunderstand; mistake [take]《A》for《B》;《口語》get (hold of) the wrong end of the stick.

がんちく 含蓄 implication; significance; overtones ¶含蓄のある significant;《文》meaningful;《文》pregnant with meaning / 含蓄のある言葉 a phrase pregnant with (hidden) meaning; an expression full of overtones.

かんちゅう 寒中 ¶寒中に during the coldest season; in the depth(s) of winter / 寒中水泳 midwinter swimming.

がんちゅう 眼中 ¶眼中にない [置かない] take no account [notice] of; think nothing of; disregard. 文例⇩

かんちょう¹ 干潮 ⇒ひきしお.

かんちょう² 官庁 a government office [agency] ¶官庁街 the district where (most of) the government offices are located / 官庁用語 official terminology [jargon]; officialese.

かんちょう³ 管長 the superintendent priest; the chief abbot.

かんちょう⁴ 館長 a director; a superintendent ¶図書館長 a (chief) librarian / 博物館長 the director of a museum.

かんちょう⁵ 艦長 〈大型艦の〉the captain《of a battleship》;〈小型艦の〉the commander《of a torpedo boat》¶艦長室 the captain's cabin.

かんちょう⁶ 灌腸 an enema ¶灌腸する give [《文》administer] an enema《to》/ 灌腸器 [液] an enema.

かんつう¹ 姦通 adultery ¶姦通する commit adultery《with》.

かんつう² 貫通 ¶貫通する go [《文》pass] (right) through; pierce; penetrate. 文例⇩

カンツォーネ《音楽》a canzone 《pl. -s, -ni》.

かんづく 感付く sense [scent, smell]《danger》; have [get] an inkling of (the intrigue); be [《文》become] aware of (sb's plan).

かんづめ 缶詰《米》canned food [goods];《英》tinned food [goods] ¶さけの缶詰 canned salmon / 缶詰を開ける open a can / 缶詰にする pack《meat》in a can [《英》tin] /《米》can《英》tin; 〈比喩的に〉confine sb in a room / 缶詰業者 a canner / 缶詰工業 the canning industry / 缶詰工場 a canning plant [factory]; a cannery.

かんてい¹ 官邸 an official residence.

かんてい² 艦艇 war vessels; warships.

かんてい³ 鑑定 judgment; an expert opinion 〈専門家の〉;〈訴訟の〉legal advice;〈評価〉appraisal; estimation ¶鑑定する judge; give an (expert) opinion 《on》;〈価格を〉estimate / 筆跡を鑑定する give an expert opinion on sb's handwriting / 鑑定してもらう have sth appraised 《by》; have an expert look at sth / 鑑定者 [人] a judge;〈美術品の〉a connoisseur;〈法廷の〉an expert witness / 鑑定書 a written statement of an expert opinion 《on a work of art, sb's handwriting》.

がんてい 眼底 the eyeground;《解》the fundus (of the eye) ¶眼底検査(法)《医》funduscopy / 眼底出血 (a) hemorrhage in the eyeground.

かんてつ 貫徹《文》accomplishment;《文》realization ¶貫徹する carry through [out]; put sth into effect;《文》accomplish; achieve;《文》realize;《文》attain / 初志を貫徹する realize [carry out] one's original intention.

カンテラ a (hand) lantern.

かんてん¹ 寒天〈食品〉agar(-agar) ¶寒天培養基 an agar culture medium.

かんてん² 寒天〈空模〉(in) freezing [cold] weather; a bleak wintry sky.

かんてん³ 観点 a point of view; a viewpoint; a standpoint; an angle ⇒けんち ¶観点が違う have a different point of view; view [look at] sth differently [from a different angle] / この観点から考えると from this point of view;

---

admiration [wonder].
かんたん² この電報はあまり簡単すぎて意味がわからない。This telegram is too brief to be clear. / 食事は簡単に済ませう。Let's have a light meal. / 象は1頭だけで重さ2トンの木材を引っぱるぐらいは簡単にやってのける。A single elephant will make light work of pulling a two-ton log.
かんだんけい 寒暖計は今何度に上がっていますか。How high has the thermometer risen now? / 寒暖計は室内で七氏25度を示している。The thermometer reads [stands at, registers] 25°C in the shade. / ここでは真夏でも寒暖計が30度に上がることはめったにない。The thermometer seldom goes over 30 degrees here even at the height of summer.
かんち⁴ それは僕の関知するところではない。It is no concern of mine. | It's none of my business.

がんちゅう 彼には僕の存在などてんで眼中になかった。He completely ignored me [discounted my presence]. / あんなやつは僕の眼中にない。He is beneath my notice.
かんつう² 彼は胸部に貫通銃創を受けた。He was shot through the chest.
かんでん ぬれた手で触ると感電するよ。You'll get a [an electric] shock if you touch it with your

かんでん 感電 ¶感電する get a [an electric] shock / 感電死する be (accidentally) electrocuted; be killed by an [die of] electric shock.
かんでんち 乾電池 a dry cell [battery].
カント ¶カント哲学 Kantian philosophy.
かんど 感度 sensitivity ¶感度がいい be sensitive (to). 文例⇩
がんと ¶がんと一発くらわす give sb a hard [severe] blow (on the jaw);《口語》punch [belt] sb (in the nose).
かんとう¹ 完投《野球》¶完投する pitch the whole game [the full nine innings]; go the (whole) distance.
かんとう² 巻頭 the beginning [opening page] of a book ¶巻頭言 a foreword; a preface; a prefatory note / 巻頭論文 the opening article (of a magazine). 文例⇩
かんとう³ 敢闘 ¶敢闘する fight bravely [《文》gallantly,《文》courageously]; put up a manly fight《against》/ 敢闘賞 a fighting-spirit award / 敢闘精神が旺盛(ｾｲ)である have plenty of fight in one.
かんとう⁴ 関東 ¶関東地方 the Kanto region / 関東大震災 the Great (Kanto) Earthquake of 1923.
かんどう¹ 勘当 ¶勘当する disown; disinherit; cut (one's son) off ([《文》] with a shilling).
かんどう² 間道 〈抜け道〉a secret path;〈わき道〉a byroad;〈近道〉a short cut.
かんどう³ 感動 → かんげき² ¶感動する be impressed (by, with); be touched (by) / 感動させる《文》move (sb to tears); touch sb's heart / 感動的な moving; touching. 文例⇩
かんとうし 間投詞《文法》an interjection.
かんとく¹ 感得 ¶感得する〈悟る〉realize;《文》perceive; be [《文》become] aware [conscious] of;〈感づく〉sense.
かんとく² 監督〈事〉supervision; control;《文》superintendence; direction;〈人〉a supervisor; a superintendent; a supervisor;〈試験の〉《米》a proctor;《英》an invigilator;〈職工・工夫の〉a foreman;〈スポーツの〉a manager;〈映画の〉a director ¶監督する superintend; supervise; control; oversee; direct; look after; be in charge [take charge] of /…の監督の下に under the supervision [direction, control] of… / 黒沢氏監督の映画 a film directed by Mr. Kurosawa / 試験の監督をする《米》proctor /《英》invigilate an examination /（映画の）助監督 an assistant director / 監督官庁 the competent authorities.
かんどころ 勘所〈楽器の〉a position (on the fingerboard);〈急所〉a vital point ¶勘所を押える grasp [do not miss] the point.
がんとして 頑として stubbornly; firmly;《文》obdurately ¶頑として動かない stand as firm as a rock; do not budge an inch / 頑として応じない refuse (sb's offer) firmly;《文》be obdurate in one's refusal ((to do)) / 頑として聞き入れない will not listen (to); turn a deaf ear ((to)). 文例⇩
カントリークラブ a country club.
かんな 鉋 a plane ¶かんなをかける plane (a board) / きれいにかんなをかける plane (a board) smooth / かんなで削る plane away [off, down] / かんなくず《⁺》(wood) shavings.
カンナ《植》a canna.
かんない¹ 管内 ¶管内に[で] within [throughout] the jurisdiction [district] (of).
かんない² 艦内 ¶艦内を調べる search the warship for sth [sb].
かんなん 艱難 hardships;《文》privations; difficulties;《文》trials;《文》tribulations ¶艱難にあう go through hardships;《口語》have a rough time / 艱難に耐える endure hardships; 艱難辛苦 trials and tribulations; hardships. 文例⇩
かんにん 堪忍〈我慢〉patience;《文》forbearance;〈勘弁〉forgiveness; pardon ¶堪忍する〈我慢する〉be patient (with sb); put up with sth;〈許す〉pardon; forgive; overlook ★ pardon も forgive も「人」及び「罪」などを目的語に取り得るが, overlook の目的語には「人」はなり得ない / 堪忍できない〈我慢〉have no patience with sb [sth]; cannot put up with sth; be unbearable（対象が主語）; be more than one can stand（事が主語）;〈勘弁〉cannot forgive [overlook]; be unpardonable（事が主語）/ 堪忍袋の緒が切れる can no longer put up with sth; lose (all) patience with sb;〈事が主語〉be the last straw;《文》exhaust one's patience. 文例⇩
カンニング ¶カンニングする cheat in [on] an exam;《口語》crib / カンニングペーパー a crib.
かんぬき 閂 a bolt; a bar ¶かんぬきをかける bar [bolt] ((the gate)) / かんぬきをはずす unbar [unbolt] ((the gate)).
かんぬし 神主 a Shinto priest.
かんねん 観念〈考え〉an idea; a notion;《文》

---

wet hands [when your hands are wet].
かんど 感度はいかがですか. どうぞ,《トランシーバーなど》How do you read me? Over.
かんとう² 今月号の巻頭に彼の論文が出ている. The current issue of the magazine opens with his essay.
かんどう³ 彼らの厚い友情には深く[ひどく]感動した. The strength of their friendship moved me profoundly [a great deal].
かんとく² 監督をいっそう厳重にせよ. Stricter supervision should be exercised.
がんとして 彼の失敗は我々の忠告を頑として聞き入れなかった結果だった. His failure was the inevitable result of his obstinacy in ignoring our advice.
かんなん 彼女は艱難辛苦して子供を育て上げた. She managed to bring up her children under great difficulties. | 艱難なんじを玉にす. Adversity is the best school.《諺》
かんにん ならぬ勘忍するが勘忍. True patience lies in bearing the unbearable. / あの男には, もう勘忍袋の緒が切れた. I've lost all [I'm out of] patience with him. | I've reached the limit of my patience with him. | He has exhausted my patience.
カンニング 彼はフランス語の試験

がんねん　元年 the first year of (Showa).

かんのう¹ 完納 ⟨税金などの⟩ full payment ¶完納する pay (the fine) in full; pay the whole amount of (the tax).

かんのう² 官能 the senses ¶官能の喜び sensual pleasure / 官能的 sensual / 官能主義 sensualism.

かんのう³ 間脳 【解】 the diencephalon; the interbrain.

かんのう⁴ 感応 ⟨生理上の⟩ sympathy; response; ⟨神仏の⟩ response; ⟨電気の⟩ induction ⇨ ゆうどう ¶感応する ⟨共感する⟩ sympathize (with); ⟨…にこたえる⟩ respond (to); ⟨神仏が⟩ hear (our prayer).

かんのん 観音 *Kannon*; *Kwannon*; the Goddess of Mercy ¶観音開きの戸 (a cupboard with) hinged double doors / 観音開きの窓 a casement (window).

かんぱ¹ 看破 ¶看破する see through (a fraud); penetrate (*sb's* disguise); read (*sb's* thought). 文例⇩

かんぱ² 寒波 a cold wave. 文例⇩

カンパ a campaign; a drive ¶資金カンパ fund-raising campaign [drive]; a campaign for raising funds (for).

かんぱい¹ 完敗 a complete [comprehensive, crushing] defeat ¶完敗する be comprehensively beaten; suffer a complete defeat; 《口語》be beaten hollow.

かんぱい² 乾杯 a toast ¶乾杯する drink a toast (in honor of *sb*); drink (*sb's* health); toast [drink to] (*sb*, *sb's* health) / 乾杯の音頭(おんど)をとる propose a toast (to). 文例⇩

かんぱく 関白 a *kampaku*; a senior regent; the chief adviser to the Emperor ¶亭主関白 ⇨ ていしゅ 文例.

かんばしい¹ 芳しい ⟨香りの⟩ sweet(-smelling); 《文》fragrant; ⟨評判など⟩ good; 《文》favorable ¶芳しくない ⟨評判など⟩ poor; bad; 《文》unfavorable; ⟨よくなない⟩ bad; ⟨恥ずべき⟩ shameful; scandalous. 文例⇩

かんばしった 甲走った sharp; shrill.

カンバス 【画布】 (a) canvas.

かんばつ 干ばつ a drought; a long spell [period] of dry weather ¶干ばつの被害 drought damage / 干ばつ地域 a drought-stricken area.

がんばり 頑張り endurance; 《文》tenacity ¶頑張りが利く persevere (in, with); 《文》be tenacious; be tough / 頑張りが利かない give in [up] easily / 頑張り屋 a person who perseveres (with *his* task); a sticker; 《米口語》a bitter-ender.

がんばる 頑張る ⟨根気よくやる⟩ persevere (in, with); ⟨主張する⟩ persist (in); insist (on); ⟨固守する⟩ stick (to, at); ⟨踏ん張る⟩ hold out; hang [hold] on; stand firm; hold [stand] *one's* ground; ⟨競技などで⟩ put up a good fight ¶最後まで頑張る stand [fight] it out; struggle to the bitter end; keep it up; 《主に英》keep *one's* end up. 文例⇩

かんばん¹ 看板 ⟨a signboard; a sign; ⟨事務所・医院などの⟩ a doorplate ¶質屋[床屋]の看板 a pawnbroker's [barber's] sign / 看板を出す hang up [out] a sign; 《米》hang out [up] *one's* shingle (医者・弁護士などが) / 看板を塗り変える repaint a signboard; ⟨比喩的に⟩ change *one's* colors / 看板に偽りなしである ⟨物が⟩ be true to *its* name; can be taken at face value / ⟨人が⟩ sail under *one's* true [own] colors / (酒場などが) 看板にする close (for the day) / 看板倒れである be not as good as *it* looks [is reputed to be] / 看板屋 a sign maker [painter] / 看板役者 the (only) box-office star (of a theatrical troupe).

かんぱん¹ 甲板 a deck ¶甲板に出る go [come] on deck / 上[下]甲板 the upper [lower] deck. 文例⇩

かんぱん² 乾板 【写真】 a dry (photographic) plate; a plate.

カンパン 乾パン hardtack; 《米》ship biscuit; 《英》ship's biscuit.

がんばん 岩盤 bedrock; a rock bed; solid rock.

かんび¹ 甘美 ¶甘美な sweet.

かんび² 完備 ¶完備している be well supplied with (books on Japanese art); be fully equipped (with a public-address system); be complete (with furniture). 文例⇩

かんぴ 官費 ¶官費で at government expense.

ガンビア (the Republic of) The Gambia ¶ガンビアの Gambian / ガンビア人 a Gambian.

かんびょう 看病 ¶看病する nurse; 《文》tend; attend (on); look after ¶寝ずに看病する sit up with [attend] (a sick person) all through the night / 看病疲れ fatigue as a result of nursing [tending] a sick person for a long (period

---

でカンニングをしてつかまった。He was caught cheating [cribbing] in his French exam.

かんねん 君は幸福ということについて誤った観念を持っている。You have the wrong idea about [a mistaken notion of] happiness. / 彼は時間の観念がない。He has no sense of time.

かんぱ¹ 一目で彼が偽善者だということを看破した。I saw at a glance that he was a hypocrite.

かんぱ²寒波が関東地方を襲った。A cold wave hit the Kanto region.

かんぱい² 乾杯! Your health! | Good health! | Prosit! | 《英》Cheers! / 新郎新婦のために乾杯いたしましょう。Let's toast the bride and bridegroom! / 平井教授の健康を祝して乾杯いたしましょう。Let's drink to the health of Prof. Hirai | Allow me to propose the health of Prof. Hirai!

かんばしい 彼の学校の成績はあま り芳しくない。He is not doing very well at school.

がんばる 頑張れ! ⟨へばるな⟩ Hold out! | Bear up! | ⟨弱音を吐くな⟩ Never say die! | ⟨その調子⟩ Keep it up! | Keep going! | Keep at it! / 救助隊が来るまで頑張るんだ。We must hold out [hang on] till help comes.

かんばん 看板は何時ですか。What time do you [does the bar] close? / 彼女はあのタバコ屋の看板娘だ。

かんぴょう 干瓢 dried gourd shavings.
かんびょう 眼病 an eye disease; eye trouble.
かんびょうき 間氷期〖地質〗an interglacial period [epoch]; an interglacial.
かんぶ 患部 the affected [diseased] part; the seat of a disease.
かんぶ² 幹部 an executive; a leader; a leading [principal] member; the (managing) staff (総称); 〈軍隊などの〉a cadreman; (a member of) a cadre ¶最高幹部 the top executives / 中堅幹部 a middle-grade executive; a cadre (集合的) / (ソ連最高会議の)常任幹部会 the presidium / 幹部会議 an executive council; a staff conference [meeting] / 幹部候補生 a (military [naval]) cadet / 〈企業の〉an executive trainee; a trainee executive.
かんぷ¹ 完膚 ¶完膚なきまで〈徹底的に〉thoroughly;〈跡形もなく〉beyond recognition;〈痛烈に〉scathingly; unsparingly.
かんぷ² 還付 ¶還付する return; refund (a tax).
かんぷう¹ 完封 (口語) a whitewash; (米) a shutout ¶完封する〈相手の動きなどを〉suppress [paralyze] (the enemy's movement);〈スポーツ〉(口語) whitewash; (《米口語》) blank; (《米》) shut out (the opposing team).
かんぷう² 寒風 a cold [chilly] wind ¶身を切るような寒風 a cutting [biting, piercing] wind. 文例↓
かんぷく 感服 admiration ⇒ かんしん² ¶感服すべき admirable;《文》praiseworthy.
かんぶつ 乾物 dry foods [provisions]; groceries ¶乾物屋〈人〉a grocer;〈店〉(米) a grocery (store);((英)) a grocer's (shop).
かんぶまさつ 乾布摩擦 (have) a rubdown with a dry towel.
カンフル camphor ¶カンフル注射をする give [《文》administer] a camphor injection (to).
かんぶん 漢文〈書いたもの〉Chinese writing;〈文学〉Chinese classics [classical literature] ¶漢文で書いてある本 a book written in classical Chinese.
かんぺいしき 観兵式 (hold) a parade [military review].
かんぺき¹ 完璧 ¶完璧な perfect; flawless; impeccable / 完璧の域に達する reach (the stage of) perfection / 完璧を期する aim at [for] perfection.
かんぺき² 癇癖 ¶癇癖の強い short-[quick-]tempered; irritable;《文》irascible.
がんぺき¹ 岸壁 a quay (wall); a wharf (pl. wharves, wharfs); a pier ¶岸壁に横付けにな

る come [be brought] alongside the quay.
がんぺき² 岩壁 (the face of) a rock cliff; a rock wall [face].
かんべつ 鑑別 ¶鑑別する distinguish《A from B, between A and B》; tell《A from B》¶ひよこの雌雄を鑑別する sex chickens / 練馬少年鑑別所 the Nerima Juvenile Classification Office.
かんべん¹ 勘弁 ¶勘弁する pardon; forgive; excuse《sb's error, sb for his error》; overlook《sb's error》⇒ かんにん ★;〈我慢する〉bear; put up with; tolerate (寛容する) / 勘弁できない unpardonable; inexcusable; intolerable. 文例↓
かんべん² 簡便 ¶簡便な〈簡単な〉simple;〈便利な〉handy; convenient.
かんぼう 官房 the secretariat ¶大臣官房 the Minister's Secretariat / 官房長 the director of the Minister's Secretariat; a chief secretary.
かんぼう² 感冒 ⇒ かぜ².
かんぽう¹ 官報 a [an official] gazette.
かんぽう² 漢方 traditional Chinese medicine ¶漢方医 a doctor of Chinese medicine / 漢方薬 a herbal medicine.
がんぼう 願望 ⇒ ねがい(こと), のぞみ.
かんぽうしゃげき 艦砲射撃 bombardment by [from] a warship.
かんぼく 灌木 a shrub; a bush ¶灌木の茂み a shrubbery.
カンボジア Cambodia;〈正式の国名〉Democratic Kampuchea ¶カンボジアの Cambodian / カンボジア人 a Cambodian.
かんぼつ 陥没 (a) subsidence; a cave-in; (a) collapse ¶陥没する cave [fall] in; subside; sink; collapse / 道路の陥没箇所 a cave-in in the road.
かんぽん 完本 a complete (and unabridged) edition; an unexpurgated edition (無削除の) ¶5巻物の完本 a complete set of five volumes.
がんぽん 元本 the capital; the principal.
ガンマせん ガンマ線〖物〗gamma rays; γ-rays.
かんまつ 巻末 (at) the end of a book [volume].
かんまん¹ 干満 the ebb and flow (of the tide) ¶干満の差 the range of the tide; a tidal range. 文例↓
かんまん² 緩慢 ¶緩慢な slow(-moving); sluggish; dull; inactive / 動作が緩慢である be slow-moving; be slow in one's movements. 文例↓
がんみ 玩味 ¶玩味する〈風味を〉taste; relish; savor;〈真価を〉appreciate / 熟読玩味する ⇒ じゅくどく.

She is the draw at that cigar store.
かんぱん¹ 波が甲板を洗った。Waves washed [swept] the deck.
かんぷう² この家は広告にはガス・水道完備と書いてあったはずだが。Your ad says that this house is complete with gas and water services, doesn't it?
かんびょう 手厚い看病のかいもなく彼女は昨夜亡くなった。She died last night, all the care taken of her proving of no avail.
かんぷう² 寒風肌を刺すばかりであった。The wind was piercingly cold.
かんべん¹ 今度だけ勘弁して下さい。Please forgive me, just this once. / 勘弁してよ。Give me a break! | Have a heart! / もう勘弁できない。I cannot stand this any longer. | This is more than

I can bear. | That's the limit. / それだけはご勘弁を願います。I will do anything but that.
かんまん¹ 潮には1日2度の干満がある。The tide rises and falls twice a day. / 有明海は潮の干満の差が甚だしい[3メートル余もある]。The tidal range is very great [more than three meters] in the Sea of Ariake.
かんまん² 金融が緩慢だ。The

かんみりょう 甘味料 a sweetener.
かんむり 冠 a crown; a coronet 《小型の》.
かんめ 貫目 〈目方〉 ⇨ めかた; 〈貫〉 ⇨ かん⁴.
かんめい¹ 感銘 (an) impression ¶感銘する be (strongly) impressed (with, by); be moved [touched] (by) /〈事が主語〉 be (strongly) impressed on *one*'s mind; make a deep impression on *one* [*one*'s mind]. 文例⇩
かんめい² 簡明 ¶簡明な concise; terse; brief and to the point. 文例⇩
がんめい(ころう) 頑迷(固陋) ¶頑迷(固陋)な bigoted; wrong-headed; stupid and obstinate [stubborn].
がんめん 顔面 the face ¶顔面けいれん a facial tic / 顔面神経 facial nerves / 顔面神経痛 facial neuralgia / 顔面まひ facial paralysis.
かんもう 冠毛 〈鳥の〉 a crest;〈たんぽぽ・あざみなどの種子〉 a pappus ((*pl*. pappi)).
がんもく 眼目 〈要点〉 the (main) point; the gist; 〈主眼〉 the primary [main] object.
がんもどき a fried bean curd cake with vegetables and other ingredients in it.
かんもん¹ 喚問 a summons ((*pl*. -ses)) ¶喚問する summon *sb* (for examination).
かんもん² 関門 a barrier ((to success in life)); a gateway ((to the Far East)) ¶入学試験の関門をパスする get through the entrance examination ((and enter Sophia University)).
かんやく¹ 完訳 a complete translation.
かんやく² 簡約 ¶簡約する condense; abridge; simplify / 簡約した simplified; concise / 研究社簡約英和辞典《書名》 *Kenkyusha's Concise English-Japanese Dictionary*.
がんやく 丸薬 a pill.
かんゆ 肝油 cod-liver oil.
かんゆう 勧誘 〈誘い〉 (an) invitation; 〈説得〉 persuasion; 《文》 (an) inducement; 〈運動〉 canvassing ¶勧誘する 〈誘う〉 invite *sb* ((to *do*)); 〈勧める〉 persuade *sb* ((to *do*, into *doing*)); induce *sb* ((to *do*)); 《文》 solicit *sb* ((for donation)); canvass ((for subscriptions)) / 勧誘員〈選挙などの〉 a canvasser;〈注文取り〉 a (door-to-door) salesman; a canvasser.
がんゆう 含有 ⇨ ふくむ² ¶銀の含有量 the silver content ((of a sample of ore)).
かんよ 関与 《文》 participation ¶関与する 《文》 participate (in); take part (in); have [take] a hand (in); be concerned (in).
かんよう¹ 肝要 ¶肝要な 〈重要な〉 important; 《文》 of (vital) importance; vital; 〈不可欠の〉 essential; 《文》 indispensable; necessary.
かんよう² 涵養 ¶涵養する cultivate ((a love of nature)); develop ((a taste for fine arts)); build up ((character)).

かんよう³ 寛容 tolerance; toleration; open-mindedness ¶寛容な tolerant; open-minded; permissive; lenient.
かんよう⁴ 慣用 common use; usage ¶慣用の common; usual; in common [everyday] use;〈語句の〉 idiomatic / 慣用音 the traditional [popularly accepted] pronunciation ((of a *kanji*)) / 慣用語句 an idiom; an idiomatic expression. 文例⇩
かんようしょくぶつ 観葉植物 a foliage plant.
がんらい 元来 〈本来〉 originally; primarily; 〈本質的に〉 essentially; in *itself*;〈本当は〉 really; properly speaking;〈生まれつき〉 by nature;〈初めから〉 from the first [start, beginning].
かんらく¹ 陥落 fall; surrender;〈降格〉 demotion ¶陥落する 〈陣地などが〉 fall; surrender;〈格下げになる〉 be reduced to a lower rank; be demoted (to).
かんらく² 歓楽 pleasure; mirth ¶歓楽を追う pursue [《文》 seek] pleasure / 歓楽街 an entertainment district;〈赤線地帯〉 a red-light district.
かんらん 観覧 viewing; inspection ¶観覧する see; view; inspect / 観覧が自由である be open to visitors [for public inspection] / 観覧券 an admission ticket / 観覧者 a spectator; a visitor / 観覧車 〈遊園地の〉 a Ferris wheel / 観覧席 a seat; the stands / 観覧料 an admission fee; admission. 文例⇩
かんらんせき 橄欖石 olivine;〈透明濃緑色の宝石〉 peridot.
かんり¹ 官吏 ⇨ こうむいん.
かんり² 管理 〈支配, 取締まり〉 administration; management; control; supervision;《文》 superintendence;〈保管〉 charge; care ¶管理する administer ((the foreign affairs of a country)); manage ((the business affairs of a company)); control ((foreign exchange)); superintend ((a public institution)); take [have] charge of ((*sb*'s property)); take care of ((a building)) / 政府の管理下にある be under government control / 管理局 an administrative bureau / 管理者 an administrator; a manager; a superintendent; an executor (遺産などの); the management (集合的) / 管理職 (a person holding) an administrative [a managerial] position; the management (集合的) / 中間管理職 a middle manager; the middle management (集合的) / (アパートなどの)管理人 a caretaker; a concierge; 《米》 a janitor.
がんり 元利 (the) principal and interest.
がんりき 眼力 insight; power(s) of observation. 文例⇩

---

money market is sluggish.
かんめい¹ 彼の演説は聴衆に非常な感銘を与えた. His speech had a great impression on the audience. / The audience was greatly impressed by his speech.
かんめい² 文は簡明を尊ぶ. Brevity is the soul of writing.
かんよう⁴ この表現は現代英語の慣用法では正しいとされている. This expression is sanctioned by current English usage.
がんらい この本は元来子供に読ませるためのものだ. This book is intended essentially for young people [as juvenile reading]. / これらの物質は元来有毒なものではない. These substances are not poisonous in themselves. / 彼は元来正直な男だ. He is honest by nature. / 人間は元来社会的動物である. Man is born a social animal.
かんらん 観覧料300円.【掲示】Admission: 300 yen.
がんりき 彼が実際にやっていることはその説く所とは大違いだ, と

かんりゃく 簡略 ¶簡略な〈簡単な〉simple; brief;〈略式の〉informal / 簡略にする simplify 《the procedure》.

かんりゅう¹ 貫流 ¶貫流する flow [run] through 《a vast plain》.

かんりゅう² 乾留 dry distillation;〈石炭の〉carbonization.

かんりゅう³ 寒流 a cold current.

かんりゅう⁴ 還流 a return current; a back flow [current];『金融』(a) reflux ¶還流する return 《to normal circulation》; flow back.

かんりょう¹ 完了 《文》completion; finishing ¶完了する〈終える〉complete; finish;〈終わる〉be completed; be finished; be over / 現在 [過去] 完了 (時制) 『文法』the present [past] perfect (tense). 文例↓

かんりょう² 官僚 a government official; a bureaucrat;〈総称〉(the) bureaucracy; officialdom ¶官僚的, 官僚主義の bureaucratic / 官僚政治 bureaucratic government / 官僚主義 bureaucracy.

がんりょう 顔料〈絵の具〉paints; colors;〈塗料〉pigments.

かんるい 感涙 ¶感涙にむせぶ《文》be moved to tears.

かんれい¹ 寒冷 ¶寒冷な cold; chilly / 寒冷前線『気象』a cold front / 寒冷地 a cold (northern) district / 寒冷地手当 a cold-district allowance.

かんれい² 慣例 (a) custom; a usual practice; a precedent (先例) ¶慣例の customary; usual / 慣例を破る break (with) the custom / 悪い慣例を残す make a bad precedent / 慣例に従 う follow [《文》observe, 《文》conform to] the established procedures;《口語》go [do things] by the book / 慣例に従って according to one's custom; as is the custom with one. 文例↓

かんれき 還暦《celebrate》one's 60th birthday.

かんれん 関連 ⇒かんけい² ¶…に関連して in connection with…; in relation to…; with reference to… / 関連産業 related industries [businesses] / 関連事項《文》related [relevant] matters /《文》matters relevant to the subject / 関連質問〈議会での〉an interpellation on related matters /《文》related matters / 関連性 relevance; relevancy / 関連性がある be relevant 《to》; have relevance 《to, for》/ 関連性がない be irrelevant 《to》; have no relevance 《to, for》. 文例↓

かんろく 貫録 presence; dignity ¶貫録がある be [look] dignified; have 《a lot of 〔considerable〕》presence / 貫録がない lack [《文》be wanting in] dignity.

かんわ 緩和 easing; relief;《文》mitigation;《文》alleviation ¶国際間の緊張の緩和 the easing of strained relations [political tensions] between nations; détente / 緩和する ease; relieve;《文》mitigate;《文》alleviate / 制限を緩和する relax [ease] restrictions 《on trade》/ 要求を緩和する moderate one's demand 《for higher wages》. 文例↓

かんわきゅうだい 閑話休題 (but) to return to our subject, …; (well,) to resume the thread of my talk, ….

かんわじてん 漢和辞典 a dictionary [lexicon] of kanji [classical Chinese] explained in Japanese.

き

き¹ 木〈樹木〉a tree; a shrub (低木);〈木材〉wood;《米》lumber;《英》timber ¶木の wooden; (made) of wood / 木の茂った山 a (densely) wooded hill / 木を見て森を見ず cannot see the wood for the trees / 木に竹を接(つ)いだような〈つじつまの合わない〉incongruous;〈不適当な〉out of place / 木によって魚を求める attempt [try to do] the impossible; fish for the moon / 木で鼻をくくったような返事をする give sb a curt [《文》brusque] reply.

き² 生 ¶生の〈純粋の〉pure; undiluted; unmixed;〈なまの〉raw / ウイスキーを生で飲む drink whisky straight《英》neat.

き³ 気〈精神, 心〉spirit; (a) mind;〈気分〉one's feelings; a mood;〈気質〉(a) nature;《文》a disposition;〈意志〉will;〈意向〉an intention; a mind;〈注意〉attention;〈空気〉air; atmosphere ¶なんの気なしに unintentionally; casually; without meaning anything (by it) / 気は心で as a small token 《of one's gratitude [friendship]》/ 気は確かである be sane; be in possession of one's senses; be in one's right mind.

¶気が合う〈2人以上が主語〉get along well [hit it off] (together);《文》be kindred spirits;〈相手と〉get on [along well 《with》]; hit it off 《with》/ 気がある〈関心が〉be interested 《in》; take an interest 《in》;〈意向が〉be [feel] inclined (to do);〈異性に〉be interested 《in》; be keen 《on》;《口語》fancy sb / 気が大きい be generous; be large-[big-]hearted / 気が重い〈事が主語〉lie heavy on

---

いうことぐらい大した眼力がなくともわかる. It doesn't take particularly keen insight [acute observation] to see that there is a vast gulf between what he says and what he actually does.

かんりょう 仕事は今月一杯に完了する. The work will be finished [completed] by the end of this month. / 仕事は完了したかね. Have you done all your work?

かんれい 彼らは何事も慣例通りにしかやらない. They always go [do things] by the book.

かんれん 君の質問は我々の当面の問題とは何の関連性もない. Your question has no relevance to the matter we are talking about now.

かんわ これらの徴候から判断してこの交通難もいずれは緩和されることであろう. From these indications I think that eventually these traffic problems will ease.

one's mind ; 《口語》 have got *one* down ; 〈人が主語〉 be [feel] depressed [down] / 気が変わる change *one's* mind / 気が変わりやすい be always [forever] changing *one's* mind ;《文》be fickle ;《文》be irresolute / 気が利く be sensible ;《口語》be smart ; be tactful (人扱いが)〈思いやりがある〉be considerate ; be thoughtful / 気が気でない[もめる]feel uneasy (anxious)《about》; worry [feel worried]《about》; 〈事が主語〉have [keep] *one* in (a state of) suspense (はらはらさせる) / 気がくじける lose heart ; be disheartened ; be discouraged / 気が進む ⇨ 気が向く / 気が済む be satisfied《with》/ 気がする feel ; think ; fancy ;《口語》reckon ; 〈予感する〉have a feeling ;《口語》hunch《that...》/ 気が立つ be [get] excited《at, over》; get worked up《about》/ 気が立っている be nervous [worked-up, on edge]《about》/ 気が小さい be timid ;《文》be faint-hearted / 気が違う〈ふれる,変になる〉⇨ きちがい,くるう / 気が散る〈事が主語〉distract *one* [*one's* attention] / 気がつく〈気づく〉⇨ きづく / 正気づく come to (*oneself*) ; come round ; recover [regain] consciousness [*one's* senses] / 気が転倒する be upset ; be flurried ; lose *one's* presence of mind / 〈驚いて〉be frightened out of *one's* wits / 気が遠くなる ⇨ 気を失う / 気が遠くなるような金額 an astounding [《口語》a mind-boggling] sum of money / 気がとがめる《文》*one's* conscience pricks *one* ; suffer from a guilty conscience ; feel uneasy / 気がない〈関心が〉have no interest (in) ; do not care《for》/ 〈意向が〉have no mind to *do* ; have no intention of *doing* / 気が長い be patient ; have a lot of patience / 気が抜ける〈気落ちする〉⇨ 〈ビールなどが〉go flat ; 〈茶・コーヒーなどが〉lose *its* flavor ; 〈物事が〉go [get, 《文》become] stale [insipid] / 気が早い〈速断する〉be hasty ; be rash / 〈短気である〉be short-[quick-]tempered / 気が引ける feel ashamed ; feel small《in *sb's* presence》; feel inferior《before *sb*》; be ill at ease ; be [get,《文》become] self-conscious / 気がふさぐ〈人が主語〉be [feel] depressed / 〈事が主語〉depress *one* / 気が短い be short-[quick-]tempered ; have a quick [short] temper / 気が向く feel inclined to *do* ; feel like *doing* / 気が向くと when (*one* is) in the (right) mood《to *do*, for *sth*》; when the fancy [mood, urge] takes *one* / 気が向かない[進まない] be unwilling [reluctant] to *do* ; be in no mood《to *do*, for *sth*》/ 気が楽になる be [feel] relieved ; have a load (taken) 〈*sth* is a load〉off *one's* mind / 気が若い be young in [at] heart.

¶気の合った《文》congenial《friends》;《文》kindred《spirits》/ 気の荒い hot-tempered ; quarrelsome / 気の多い《a man》with a lot [a large number] of interests ⇨ 気の変わりやすい / 気の多い人 a man of many interests ⇨ 気の変わりやすい / 気の置けない相手 a person *one* can feel [*one* feels] at (*one's*) ease with / 気の置けない友達《文》an intimate [a bosom] friend / 気の変わりやすい《文》capricious ; whimsical ; fickle / 気の利いた〈利口な〉clever ; smart ;《文》tasteful / 気の利いた贈り物 a well-chosen gift / 気の利いた事を言う say nice things / 気の利かない〈頭の鈍い〉dull(-witted) / 〈趣のない〉tasteless / 〈不体裁な〉clumsy ; awkward / 気のつく〈注意深い〉observant ; 〈親切な〉kind ; considerate / 気の強い〈丈夫な〉brave ;《文》stout-hearted ; 〈大胆な〉bold ; daring / 気のない indifferent ; half-hearted / 気の練れた人 a person with an even [《文》a genial] temper ; an even-tempered [《文》equable] person / 気の向いた事をする follow *one's* own whim [《文》inclination,《文》bent] / 気の向くままに as *one's* [the] fancy takes *one* ;《文》as *one's* whim dictates / 気のもめる〈はらはらさせる〉suspenseful ;〈心配な〉uneasy / 気のよい good-natured / 気の弱い timid ;《文》timorous ; faint-hearted.

¶気を入れてやる buckle down to《*one's* job》; get down to business and *do* ; do in

き[3] その雨はいつまで降る気なんだろう. I wonder when it will (decide to) stop raining. / 承知したと言いたい気も大分あった[ないではなかった.] I had a good mind [half a mind] to accept the offer. / その時はやってみる気もあった. I was ready [willing] to undertake it at that time. / 彼を怒らせる気はすこしもなかった. I had no thought [intention] of offending him. / 窓を締めてください, あの音楽が聞こえて気が散りますから. Shut the window, please. That music distracts me [my attention]. / その知らせを聞いて彼はすっかり気が転倒してしまった. The news quite upset him. | He was very (much) upset by the news. / 忙しい間は気が張っていたせいかどうやら病気にならなかった. Maybe it was because my nerves were at full stretch, but I managed to keep well while I was busy on that job. / こんな身なりで外へ〔人中に〕出るのは気が引ける. I am ashamed to go out [I don't think I am fit to be seen,] dressed like this. / こんな所でぼんやり待っているのも気が利かない話だ. There is no sense in waiting here doing nothing. / 彼は気が向くと何時間でも続けて机に向かっている. When the urge takes him, he is at his desk for hours on end. / 彼は気が大き過ぎる. He is generous to a fault. / そんな事をする彼の気が知れない. I can't understand why he should do such a thing. / 彼は何でも自分でしなければ気が済まない. He is not satisfied unless he does everything by himself. / 借金を返して気が済んだ. Paying off the debt eased my conscience. / 休日はほかの日より日が短い気がする. A holiday always seems to pass more quickly than a weekday [an ordinary day]. / どこかであの人に会ったような気がする. I fancy I have met him somewhere. / 気がついて見ると, 救急車でどこかへ運ばれて行くところだった. The first thing I knew was that I was being carried somewhere in an ambulance. / 家へ帰るまで, 時計をなくしたことに気がつかなかった. I did not miss my watch till I got home. / それに気がつかなかった. I didn't notice [never noticed] it. | It had escaped my notice. / それはいいところへ気がついた. That's a good idea. / 気がとがめてとてもそんな事はできません. I can't,

earnest ;《文》be attentive 《to one's duties》/ 気を失う faint ;《文》swoon ; lose consciousness ; black out ; pass out / なぐられて気を失う be beaten [knocked] senseless [unconscious] / 気を取り直して落ち着ける calm oneself ;《口語》pull oneself together ;《文》regain one's composure / 気を落とす lose heart ; be discouraged ; be disheartened / 気を変える change one's mind / 気を利かして…する be sensible enough to do ; have the sense to do / 気を配る pay attention 《to》; be watchful for /《文》with one accord ; with [in] one mind / 気を確かに持つ keep one's senses ; brace oneself (元気を出す) / 気を使う worry [bother] 《about》; take 《sb's feelings》 into consideration / 気をつける take care 《of》; be careful 《about》; keep an eye 《on》; ⟨用心する⟩ watch [look] out ; be on one's guard / 気をつけて carefully ; cautiously / 気をつけをする[している] stand to [at] attention / 気を取られる have one's attention caught 《by》; be distracted [preoccupied] 《by》; ⟨熱中する⟩ be absorbed 《in》; be intent 《on》/ 気を取り直す take (new [fresh]) heart ; pull oneself together ; regain control of oneself /《文》collect oneself / 気をのまれる be overawed 《by》/ 気を吐く make a good showing ; be very successful 《in》/ 気を晴らす cheer oneself up ⇒ きばらし / 気を引く catch [attract] sb's attention ; arouse sb's interest /気を引いてみる sound sb (out) (on [about] sth) ; try to arouse sb's interest (in a subject) / 気を引き立てる cheer sb up ; encourage / 気を回す ⟨疑う⟩ suspect ; be suspicious / ⟨しっとする⟩ be jealous 《of》/ ちょっと気を持たせる give sb just a little [a glimmer of,《文》some slight] hope / 気をもむ worry (oneself) 《about》; be anxious 《about》/ 気をもませる ⟨事が主語⟩ worry one ; keep one in suspense (はらはらさせる) / 気を許す be off one's guard / 気をゆるめる relax one's attention / 気をよくする be pleased 《by》; get [take]

(great) satisfaction 《from》/ 気を悪くする offend [give offense to] sb ;《文》displease sb ; hurt sb's feelings / ⟨不快に思う⟩ be offended [take offense] 《at》;《文》be displeased 《by》.

¶ 気に入る ⟨人が主語⟩ like ; be pleased 《with》; take a fancy 《to》; ⟨物が主語⟩ please one ; catch [take] one's fancy ;《口語》be in one's good books / 気に入った家 a house that suits one [《文》is to one's taste] / 気に入られる be loved 《by》; 《口語》gain sb's favor ;《文》find [win] favor with sb / 気に入らない ⟨人が主語⟩ do not like ; be not fond of ; be dissatisfied [displeased] 《with》; ⟨物が主語⟩ do not please one ; be not to one's taste [liking] / 気に入り ⇒ おきにいり / 気にかかる ⇒ 気にかける ⇒ 気にする / 気にくわない ⟨物事が主語⟩《文》be disagreeable 《to》; be unsatisfactory (不満足) ; ⟨人が主語⟩ be not pleased 《with》; be dissatisfied [《文》displeased] 《with》/ 気に障る ⟨事が主語⟩ offend one ;《文》displease one ; hurt one's feelings / 気にする worry [bother] 《about》; be nervous 《about》; ⟨苦にする⟩ take sth to heart / ⟨心にかける⟩ have sth at heart / 気にしない do not mind (★ mind は否定文・疑問文に用いられるのが普通) ;《文》care nothing 《for》;《文》be indifferent 《to》/ 気にとめる pay attention 《to》; take notice 《of》/ 気にとめない pay no attention 《to》; take no notice 《of》; do not mind ; pay [《文》give] no heed 《to》/ 気になる ⟨物事が主語⟩ be [weigh] on one's mind ; worry one ; ⟨人が主語⟩ feel uneasy 《about》; be anxious 《about》/ …する気になる take it into one's head to do ; bring oneself to do / …する気にならない do not feel like doing ; be in no mood to do ; cannot bring oneself to do ; cannot find it in one's heart to do / 気に病む worry [be anxious] 《about》.

き⁴ 忌 ⟨喪⟩ (a period of) mourning ; ⟨年忌⟩ an

---

in all conscience, do such a thing. / 彼は気の荒い人だ. He has [is a man with] a violent temper. / 何事も気の持ちよう一つだ. Everything depends on how you look at it. / 気の利いたデザインだ. It is an attractive design. / 全く気が置けない人だ. I feel completely at (my) ease [at home] in his presence. / それは君の気のせいだ. It's your imagination. / いつも伊豆へ行くから, 今度は一つ気を変えて信州へ行こうじゃないか. We always seem to go to Izu. How about going to Shinshu this time, for a change? / 彼女は気を利かしてその男に主人は今日は留守ですと言った. She had the sense to tell him that her husband was away that day. / 気をつけっ!《号令》

Attention! / 病気にならないように気をつけなさい. Take care not to make yourself ill. / 以後は気をつけます. I will be more careful in future. / 階段を降りるとき足元に気をつけなさい. Watch your step when you go down the stairs. / では気をつけて行っていらっしゃい. ⟨旅立つ人などに⟩ Good luck! | ⟨フランス語⟩ Bon voyage! / あの男にはまだ気を許せない. I don't trust him completely yet. / I can't yet put my complete confidence in him. / そのケーキはお気に入りましたか. How do you like the cake? / 私はどちらも余り気に入らないよ. I don't think much of either of them. / I don't like either of them very much. / 物事は自分の気に入るようにばかりいくものではない. Things don't

always go as one would wish. / そんな事はわざわざ気に留める程の事ではない. I don't think it is worthy of serious notice [attention]. / 試験の結果が気にかかる. I am worried about my examination results. / 何がそんなに気にくわないのだ. What are you so annoyed [upset] about? | What am I supposed to have done? / 父の健康がひどく気になった. I was very worried about my father's health. | My father's poor health lay heavy on my mind. | どうして自殺する気になったのだろう. What induced him to kill himself? | I wonder what drove him to suicide. / そんな事をする気にはとてもなれない. I couldn't bring myself [find it in my heart] to do such a thing. | I can't imagine [see] myself doing

き

anniversary of sb's death ¶祖父の三回[周]忌 the second anniversary of one's grandfather's death.

き[5] 季 a season ⇨ きせつ.

き[6] 奇 ¶奇を好む be deliberately unconventional; 〈文〉be averse to following the beaten path; be eccentric / 奇をてらう make a display of one's eccentricity [〈文〉unconventionality].

き[7] 紀 【地質】a period ¶石炭紀 the Carboniferous period.

き[8] 記 〈記述〉an account; a description; 〈歴史〉a history; a chronicle; annals (年代記); 〈記録〉a record.

き[9] 黄 yellow.

き[10] 基 【化】a group; a radical.

き[11] 期 〈時代〉a period; an age; 〈期日〉a date; a time; 〈期間〉a period; a term; 〈会期〉a session; 〈病気の〉a stage ¶2期勤める serve two terms (as President). 文例⇩

き[12] 機 〈機会〉an opportunity; a chance; an occasion; 〈時〉a time; 〈飛行機〉〈米〉an airplane; 〈英〉an aeroplane; a plane ¶機を失う[逸する] miss [lose] an [one's] opportunity; miss [lose] a [one's] chance; let a chance slip (away) [go] / 機を見るに敏である be quick to seize an opportunity / 機に乗じる take advantage [〈文〉avail oneself] of an [the] opportunity. 文例⇩

ぎ 義 ⇨ せいぎ.

ギア ⇨ ギヤ.

きあい 気合い a yell; a shout ¶気合いをかける cheer; shout [yell] at sb / 気合いもろとも打ち込む bring down one's sword with a yell / 気合い負けする be overawed by sb.

ぎあく 偽悪 ¶偽悪家〈文〉a person whose malevolence is no more than a pose; a person whose bark is worse than his bite.

きあけ 忌明け the end [expiration] of the period of mourning.

きあつ 気圧 atmospheric [air] pressure ¶気圧の谷 a trough of low (atmospheric) pressure; a low pressure trough / 50気圧に相当する圧力 a pressure of 50 atmospheres / 気圧計 a barometer / 気圧配置 the distribution of atmospheric pressure. 文例⇩

ギアナ Guiana ⇨ ガイアナ ¶ギアナの Guianese.

きあわせる 来合わせる happen to come [pass by]; come by chance. 文例⇩

きあん 起案 ¶起案する draft [draw up] a plan (for); prepare [make out] a draft plan (for).

ぎあん 議案 a bill; a measure ¶議案を国会に提出する introduce a bill in the House; submit a bill to the Diet.

きい[1] 貴意 your wishes [〈文〉will, request].

きい[2] 奇異 ¶奇異な strange; queer; singular; odd.

きー ⇨ きーきー. 文例⇩

キー a key ¶タイプライターのキーをたたく tap [pound 強く] the keys of a typewriter / 電信のキーをたたく operate telegraph keys / キーステーション a key station / キーパンチャー a keypuncher / キーポイント a key point / キーホールダー 〈キー鎖状の〉a key holder; 〈リングの〉a key ring.

きいきい, きーきー ¶きいきいいう creak; squeak; screech / きいきいいう音 a creaking [squeaking] sound [noise] / きーきー声 a squeaky [screechy] voice / きーきー声で話す squeak; screech.

ぎいぎい ¶ぎいぎいいう音〈きしむ音〉a creak; 〈すれる音〉a grating [rasping] sound [noise] / ぎいぎいいう音する creak; grate; rasp.

きいたふう 利いた風 ¶利いた風な事を言う talk knowingly [in a smart-alecky way].

きいちご 木苺【植】a raspberry.

きいっぽん 生一本 ¶生一本の〈酒が〉pure; undiluted / 生一本な〈性格が〉straightforward; honest.

きいと 生糸 raw silk.

きいろ 黄色 yellow ¶黄色い yellow / 黄色い声 a shrill voice / 黄色がかった yellowish.

きいん 起因 ¶起因する be caused by; be due to; 〈文〉originate in; spring [〈文〉result, arise] from.

ぎいん[1] 議院 ⇨ ぎかい, こっかい[1] ¶議院運営委員会 the House Steering Committee.

ぎいん[2] 議員 a member of an assembly; an assemblyman; 〈国会の〉a member of the Diet; a Dietman; a Dietwoman (婦人); 〈米〉a Congressman; 〈英〉a member of Parliament; an M.P. ¶議員会館 the Diet Members' Office Building / 議員提出法案 a (private) member's bill / 議員立法 legislation at the instance of House members.

---

such a thing.

き[11] その議案は今期の国会に提出されるだろう。The bill will be submitted to the present session of the Diet.

き[12] 機が熟するまで待つべきだ。We should wait until the time is ripe. / 機を見てそれを実行しましょう。I will carry it out at the first (available) opportunity. | I will put it into effect as soon as an opportunity presents itself.

ぎ 義を見てせざるは勇なきなり。To see what is right and not to do it is to lack courage.

きあつ 昨日の気圧は980ミリバールだった。The barometer registered [stood at] 980 mb [millibars] yesterday. / 今年は北陸地方は気圧の関係で雨が多い。This year the Hokuriku region has a lot of rain due to the prevailing pattern of atmospheric pressure.

きあわせる 彼はちょうどいいところへ来合わせた。He happened to come [make his appearance] at just the right moment.

きい 遺憾ながら貴意に添いかねます。We regret to inform you that we cannot comply with your request.

きー 自動車がきーといって止まった。A car screeched to a halt.

きいん この病気は多く過労と睡眠不足に起因する。This disease is, in most cases, caused by overwork and lack of sleep.

きえる 風でろうそくが消えた。The candle was blown out by the wind. / 山の雪は消えてしまった。The snow disappeared from the mountains. / まだ雪は消えない。There is still snow on the ground. / 字が消えて読めない。

キウイフルーツ a kiwi (fruit [berry]).

きうけ 気受け ¶気受けがいい[悪い] be popular [unpopular] 《with》;《文》be in [out of] favor 《with》.

きうん 機運〔傾向〕a tendency; a trend;〈機会〉an opportunity; a chance.

きえ 帰依 ¶帰依する become a (devout) believer 《in Buddhism》;《文》embrace 《Christianity》.

きえい¹ 気鋭 ¶気鋭の spirited; energetic ⇒ しんしん²(新進気鋭の).

きえい² 機影 the sight of an airplane ¶機影を現わす〈飛行機が主語〉come into view; come in sight; appear /機影を没する〈飛行機が主語〉go out of sight; disappear.

きえいる 消え入る ¶消え入るような声で言う speak in a faint [《文》scarcely audible] voice / 消え入るばかりに泣く cry bitterly; cry *one's* heart out.

きえる 消える disappear;〈火が〉go out;〈電灯が〉go off [out];〈雪などが〉melt (away);〈音が遠ざかって〉die away;〈摩滅する〉wear away;《文》be effaced ¶消えたタバコ a dead [burnt-out] cigarette / 消え失せる vanish; disappear; fade away [out] / 消え残る雪 lingering snow.

きえん¹ 気炎〈意気〉high spirits;〈議論〉a heated argument ¶気炎を上げる[《文》argue heatedly 《for, against》;〈大言する〉talk big.

きえん² 奇縁 a strange turn of fate; a (curious) coincidence.

きえん³ 機縁 ⇒ きっかけ.

ぎえんきん 義援金 a contribution; a donation ⇒ きふ¹.

きえんさん 希塩酸 dilute hydrochloric acid.

きおいたつ 気負い立つ be eager 《to *do*》;《文》be on *one's* mettle 《for success, to *do*》.

きおう¹ 既往 ⇒ かこ ¶既往症 a disease which *one* had in the past.

きおう² 気負う ⇒ きおいたつ ¶気負い過ぎる be too eager 《to *do*, for success》.

きおく 記憶 (a) memory;《文》remembrance;《文》(a) recollection(想起) ¶記憶する〈覚えている〉remember; be [《文》live] in *one's* memory〈事が主語〉;〈忘れないようにする〉keep [bear] *sth* in mind;〈覚える〉learn [get] *sth* by heart;《文》commit *sth* to memory; memorize / 記憶すべき《文》memorable《events》/ 記憶(力)がいい[悪い] have a good [bad, poor] memory / 私の記憶に誤りがなければ if I remember rightly [correctly]; if my memory serves me right(ly) [doesn't deceive me] / 記憶に新たである be fresh in *one's* memory / 記憶を失う lose *one's* memory / 記憶術 (the art of) mnemonics / 記憶喪失症〔医〕amnesia / 記憶装置《コンピューター》a memory [storage] (unit) / 記憶違い a lapse of memory / 記憶中枢 a memory center / 記憶容量《コンピューター》memory [storage] capacity. 文例①

きおくれ 気後れ nervousness;《文》diffidence ¶気後れがする lose *one's* nerve; be [feel] daunted 《by》;《文》become [be] diffident. 文例①

きおち 気落ち ⇒ らくたん, がっかり.

きおん 気温 (an) air [atmospheric] temperature ¶気温の変化 a change of [in the] temperature. 文例①

ぎおん 擬音 a sound effect (★ 複数形で用いられることが多い) ¶擬音係 a sound-effects man.

きか¹ 気化 vaporization; evaporation; gasification ¶気化する vaporize; evaporate; gasify / 気化熱〔物〕the heat of vaporization.

きか² 帰化 naturalization ¶帰化する be naturalized 《in Japan, as a Japanese citizen》/ 帰化植物 a naturalized plant / 帰化人 a naturalized Japanese [Englishman]; a Japanese [an Englishman] by naturalization / 帰化人である be Japanese [English] by naturalization.

きか³ 幾何 ⇒ きかがく ¶幾何級数 ⇒ とうひきゅうすう.

きが 飢餓 hunger; starvation ¶飢餓にひんする, 飢餓線上にある be starving; face [be threatened with] starvation; be on [live at] the verge of starvation / 飢餓賃金 starvation wages. 文例①

ぎが 戯画 a caricature ¶戯画に描く, 戯画化する caricature.

きかい¹ 棋界 the go [shogi] world.

きかい² 機会 an opportunity; a chance; an occasion ¶機会あるごとに at every opportunity; whenever the opportunity arises [presents itself] / 機会のあり次第に at the first opportunity / 機会を待つ[ねらう] wait [watch

---

The characters are defaced and unreadable. / それを見て彼女の顔から微笑が消えた. The smile left her face when she saw it. / はっと思うとその姿はかき消すように消えてしまった. In a twinkling the figure vanished completely. / その事が頭[心]から消えない. It is indelibly impressed on my mind. / I cannot put it out of my mind.

きおく 彼の彼のこの作品によってもっともよく記憶されるだろう. He will be remembered best for this work. / もはやこの町にはそのことを記憶している人はいない. It is no longer remembered by anyone now living in this town. / このコンピューターは 256 K の記憶容量がある. This computer has 256 K of memory. ★ K=1024 bytes / 年を取ると記憶力が鈍る. Age dims our memory. / Our memory deteriorates with age.

きおくれ 賃上げを要求するつもりだったのに, 社長の前に立ったら気後れしてしまった. I was going to ask for a raise, but I lost my nerve when I stood in front of the boss.

きおん 気温がセ氏15度に上がった[下がった]. The temperature rose [went down] to 15°C. / まだ早春だというのに日中の気温が25度にもなることがあった. Though it was still early spring, daytime temperatures reached 25°C.

きが これらの外国からの援助がなければ, 彼らは飢餓に近い状態に陥るであろう. Without this aid from abroad [foreign countries] they would be reduced to near starvation.

for] a [*one's*] chance 《to *do*》 / 機会を捕える seize [catch] an opportunity 《of *doing*, to *do*》 / 機会を逸する miss [lose, overlook] an [*one's*] opportunity ; let a [*one's*] chance slip / 機会を利用する[に乗じる] take advantage [《文》 avail *oneself*] of an opportunity / またの機会に (at) some other time ; some time later / 機会均等主義 the principle of equal opportunity. [文例⇩]

きかい[3] 機械, 器械 a machine ; machinery (総称) ; 〈仕掛け〉 a mechanism ; works (時計などの) ; 〈医療などの〉 an instrument ; an appliance ; (an) apparatus (★ apparatus は複数形を取ることはまれ) ¶ パチンコの機械 a pinball machine / 米をつく機械 a machine for hulling rice / 機械のような machinelike / 機械を動かす start a machine ; set a machine in motion ; operate [run] a machine / 機械で動くおもちゃ a mechanical toy / 機械で読み取り可能な 〖コンピューター〗 machine-readable 《input texts》 / 機械的に mechanically / 機械油 machine oil / 機械編み[縫い]の machine-knitted[-sewn] / 機械化 mechanization / 機械化する mechanize / 機械化部隊 a mechanized unit / 機械技師 a mechanical engineer ; a mechanician / 機械技術 machine [mechanical] technology / 機械工 a mechanic / 機械工学 mechanical engineering / 機械工業 the machine industry / 機械工場 a machine shop [factory] / 機械時代 the machine age / 機械製の machine-made ; made by machinery / 器械体操 apparatus gymnastics / 機械文明 (a) machine civilization / 機械力 mechanical power / 機械論的宇宙観 〖哲〗 a mechanistic view of the universe.

きかい[4] 奇怪 ¶ 奇怪な strange ; mysterious ; uncanny ; weird ; monstrous / 奇怪な風説 a wild rumor.

きがい[1] 危害 an injury ; harm ¶ 危害を加える harm [hurt, injure] *sb* ; do *sb* harm ; 《文》 inflict an injury on *sb* / 危害をこうむる be harmed [injured] 《by》 ; 《文》 receive [sustain] an injury 《from》 / 危害を免れる escape unhurt [with a whole skin].

きがい[2] 気概 spirit ; 《文》 mettle ; 《口語》 guts ; backbone ; pride ¶ 気概がない have no spirit [backbone] / 気概のある (high-)spirited ; 《文》 mettlesome ; plucky ; proud ; 《俗》 gutsy / 気概のある男 《文》 a man of mettle [pluck] ; a man with plenty of guts [courage] (in him) / 気概を示す show *one's* mettle [pluck].

ぎかい 議会 an assembly ; 〈国会〉 a national assembly ; the Diet (日本の) ; Congress (米国の) ; Parliament (英国の) ⇨ こっかい[1] ¶ 議会主義 parliamentarism / 議会政治 parliamentary government / 議会制度 the parliamentary system / 議会制民主主義 parliamentary democracy.

きがえ 着替え a change of clothes ; spare clothes ¶ 着替えの下着 a change of underclothes ; spare underwear / 着替えをする change (*one's* clothes) / 着替え室 a changing room.

きかえる 着替える change (*one's* clothes) ¶ セーターを脱いでブレザーに着替える change from *one's* [a] sweater into a blazer. [文例⇩]

きかがく 幾何学 geometry ¶ 幾何学的[の] geometric(al) / 幾何学的に geometrically / 幾何学式庭園 a formal garden / 幾何学模様 a geometric pattern.

きがかり 気掛かり (an) anxiety ; a worry ; concern ¶ 気掛かりになる, 気掛かりである 〈人が主語〉 feel anxious [uneasy] 《about》 ; worry [be concerned] 《about》 ; 〈事が主語〉 worry *one* ; be [《文》 weigh] on *one's* mind. [文例⇩]

きかかる 来かかる (happen to) come along [pass by].

きかく[1] 企画 a plan ; planning ⇨ けいかく ¶ 企画課[室] the planning section [office] / 企画性 the ability to make plans.

きかく[2] 規格 a standard ¶ 規格を統一する standardize / 規格化 standardization / 規格外の nonstandardized ; 〈規格に達しない〉 substandard ; below (the) standard / 規格判 a standard size / 規格品 standardized goods [articles].

きがく 器楽 instrumental music.

ぎがく 伎楽 *gigaku* ; an ancient masked drama.

きがけ 来がけ ¶ 来がけに on *one's* way here ; when *one* comes [is coming].

きかげき 喜歌劇 〈グランドオペラに対して〉 (a) comic opera ; 〈オペレッタ〉 an operetta.

きかざる 着飾る dress (*oneself*) up ; be gaily [gaudily] dressed ; be in *one's* (Sunday) best.

きガスるい 希ガス類 〖化〗 rare gases.

きかせる[1] 利かせる ¶ 凄みを利かせる ⇨ すごむ / 塩を利かせる season 《food》 with salt ; put salt in 《food》. [文例⇩]

きかせる[2] 聞かせる tell ; let *sb* hear [know] 《about, of》 ¶「故郷の空」を歌って聞かせる sing 'Comin' through the Rye' for *sb* / ピ

きかい[2] 機会は二度と来ない. An opportunity once lost is lost for ever. / 今こそ世界におけるわが国の地位を改善すべき絶好の機会だ. This is a golden opportunity for Japan to improve her position in the world. / この旅行ではきっとフランスの農村の生活を見る機会があることと思います. I'm sure the trip will give us the opportunity of seeing some of France's rural life. / この機会を利用してロンドン滞在中我々一行に示されたご好意の数々に対しまして皆様に謝意を表したいと存じます. Let me take this opportunity of thanking you for the kindnesses you showed us all during our stay in London.

きかえる 入浴をすませ, 着物を着替えてから, 彼女は出て行った. Having bathed and changed, she went out.

きがかり そう聞くとちょっと気がかりだ. The news is a bit worrying.

きかせる[1] もっと塩を利かせて下さい. Put in more salt, please.

きかせる[2] 何か面白い話を聞かせてください. Tell us an interesting story, please. / これは子供に聞かせる話ではない. This story should not be told to [is not fit for the ears of] children. / 彼に聞かせるつもりではなかったのだ. It was not meant for his

アノを弾いて聞かせる play the piano for sb / 本を読んで聞かせる read sb a book ; read a book to sb / 聞かせどころ〈最高潮〉the climax 《of a story》; the most moving part 《of a song》; 〈芸の見せ場〉the part 《of a musical composition》where one can display one's skill [《文》virtuosity]. 文例⇩

きがた 木型 a wooden model [pattern] ¶帽子の木型 a (hat) block / 靴の木型〈靴を作るための〉a (shoemaker's) last ; 〈型がくずれないようにするための〉a shoe tree [stretcher].

きがね 気兼ね ¶気がねする feel hesitant [uneasy, uncomfortable, 《文》diffident, ill at ease] 《in sb's presence, about doing》; have scruples 《about [in] doing》; 《文》have regard 《for sb's feelings》; 《文》show constraint 《toward sb, in sb's presence》(態度に表わして) / …に気がねして out of regard [consideration] for 《sb's feelings》; 《文》in [out of] deference to 《public opinion》/ 気がねしないで feel at 《one's》ease 《in sb's presence》; be self-assured ; act naturally ; do not worry 《about》; 《文》have no regard [consideration] 《for sb's feelings》(人の気持を考えない); have no scruples 《about doing》(手段を選ばない). 文例⇩

きがまえ 気構え readiness ; 《文》preparedness ¶気構えができていない be not ready [prepared] 《for sth, to do》.

きがる 気軽 ¶気軽に light-heartedly ; cheerfully ; 《文》with a light heart ; 《文》readily. 文例⇩

きかん¹ 気管 〖解〗the trachea (pl. -s, -cheae); the windpipe ¶気管の tracheal / 気管切開 tracheotomy.

きかん² 季刊 ¶季刊の quarterly ; published [issued] quarterly / 季刊誌 a quarterly ; a quarterly journal [magazine].

きかん³ 汽缶 (a steam) boiler ⇨ ボイラー ¶汽缶室 a boiler room ; 〈船の〉a stokehold ; a fireroom.

きかん⁴ 奇観 ¶奇観を呈する present a wonderful sight [《文》a singular spectacle].

きかん⁵ 既刊 ¶既刊の already [previously] published [issued].

きかん⁶ 帰還 a return (home); repatriation (外国から本国への) ¶帰還する return ; return [come] home ; be repatriated / 帰還者 a returnee ; a repatriate / 帰還兵 a returned [repatriated] soldier. 文例⇩

きかん⁷ 基幹 ¶基幹産業 basic [key] industries.

きかん⁸ 期間 a term ; a period (of time) ⇨ きげん³. 文例⇩

きかん⁹ 旗艦 a flagship.

きかん¹⁰ 器官 〖生物〗an organ ¶生命の維持に重要な器官 a vital organ / 器官疾患 an organic disease.

きかん¹¹ 機関 〈エンジン〉an engine ; 〈手段〉a means (単複同形); 〈団体・組織などの〉an organ ; 〈施設〉facilities ; 〈組織〉a system ¶党の機関 the apparatus [organs] of the party / 審議機関 a deliberative body [organ] / 機関庫 an engine shed / 機関室 an engine room / 機関車 a locomotive ;《口語》a loco (pl. -s);《英》an engine / 機関長 the chief engineer.

きがん 祈願 (a) prayer ¶祈願する pray 《for the safety of one's son》/ 祈願をこめる《文》offer (up) a fervent prayer 《for the return of one's health》/ 祈願文 〖文法〗an optative sentence.

きかん 技官 a technical official [officer].

ぎがん 義眼 a false [an artificial, a glass] eye.

きがんかいせき 奇岩怪石 fantastically-shaped rocks.

きかんき 利かん気 ¶利かん気の《文》spirited ;《文》unyielding ; stiff-necked.

きかんし¹ 気管支 〖解〗the bronchi (sing. bronchus); the bronchial tubes ¶気管支の bronchial / 気管支炎 bronchitis / 気管支カタル bronchial catarrh / 気管支鏡 a bronchoscope.

きかんし² 機関士 〈鉄道の〉《米》an [a locomotive] engineer ;《英》an engine driver ; 〈商船の〉an engineer ¶一等機関士 a first engineer.

きかんし³ 機関紙[誌] an organ ¶政党[組合]の機関紙[誌] a party [union] organ.

きかんじゅう[ほう] 機関銃[砲] a machine gun ¶機関銃で掃射する rake 《the enemy position》with machine-gun fire ; machine-gun / 機関銃のように質問を浴びせる fire off questions in rapid succession / 重[軽]機関銃 a heavy [light] machine gun / 機関銃手 a machine-gunner. 文例⇩

きかんぼう 利かん坊 a naughty [《文》an unruly] child.

きき¹ 危機 a crisis (pl. crises); a critical moment ¶政治的[財政上の]危機 a political [financial] crisis / 危機をはらむ be very critical ;《文》be fraught with danger / 危機を乗り切る〈人が主語〉get over a crisis ; 〈金な

---

ears. / あの喫茶店ではいい音楽を聞かせるそうだ。They say we can listen to good music in that tearoom. / 彼ののどはなかなか聞かせるね。He has a very good voice, doesn't he?

きがね 彼はなんだか気がねしているみたいネ。He doesn't really seem at his ease with us [them]. / 気がねしないでいつまでもいたまえ。Make yourself at home and stay with us as long as you please.

きがる あのお医者さんは夜中でも気軽に来てくれます。That doctor never shows any reluctance in coming out even in the middle of the night. / いつでもお気軽にお立ち寄り下さい。You are always welcome at my house.

きかん⁶ 帰還者は家族の者に涙で迎えられた。The returnees were welcomed by their families in tears.

きかん⁸ この勤務の期間はどのくらいの予定ですか。How long is this appointment for? / For how long am I to hold this post? / その建築工事は完成までには彼らの予想よりずっと長い期間がかかった。The building work took much longer to complete than they had expected.

きかんじゅう 機関銃がタタタタと鳴った。'Rat-tat-tat' went a machine gun.

どが主語〉tide *one* over a crisis / 危機を緩和する ease a crisis / 危機に陥る[陥っている] fall into [be in] crisis / 危機にひんする be in a critical situation / 危機に直面する face a crisis / 危機に臨んで at a crisis; in an emergency / 危機一髪である be in imminent danger; be touch-and-go; hang by a thread [hair] / 危機一髪というときに at the critical moment; in the nick of time / 危機一髪で助かる escape《death》by a hairsbreadth [by the skin of *one's* teeth]; have a narrow [hairbreadth] escape. [文例⇩]

き

きき[2] 鬼気 ¶鬼気迫る ghastly; bloodcurdling; unearthly.

きき[3] 喜々, 嬉々 ¶喜々として merrily;《文》joyfully; cheerfully; happily.

ぎぎ 疑義 a doubt ¶疑義を抱く have [《文》entertain] doubts《about, as to》/ 疑義を正す check doubtful points; 〈人に〉ask *sb* a question《about, as to》; ask *sb* for an explanation [《文》for elucidation]《of a matter》.

ききあきる 聞き飽きる be [get, grow] tired [《口語》sick] of hearing. [文例⇩]

ききあわせる 聞き合わせる ⇨ **といあわせる**.

ききいる 聞き入る listen attentively to《what *sb* says》 ¶ラジオに聞き入る listen attentively to the radio;《口語》be [have *one's* ear] glued to the radio.

ききいれる 聞き入れる 〈要求·願いを〉agree to [《文》grant,《文》comply with]《*sb's* request》; accept《*sb's* resignation》; 〈忠告を〉take [follow]《*sb's* advice》 ¶聞き入れない reject [refuse to accept]《*sb's* suggestion》; turn a deaf ear to《*sb's* advice》. [文例⇩]

ききうで 利き腕 the arm *one* feels more comfortable using [*one* uses more skillfully] (than the other); *one's* dominant arm [hand]; 〈右腕〉the right arm.

ききおとす 聞き落とす ⇨ **ききもらす**.

ききおぼえ 聞き覚え ¶聞き覚えのある[ない]声 a familiar [strange] voice. [文例⇩]

ききおぼえる 聞き覚える learn《a language》by ear; pick up《English》.

ききおよぶ 聞き及ぶ hear [learn, know] about [of] ¶お聞き及びのとおり as you must have heard; as you know.

ききかえす 聞き返す ask *sb* back; throw a question back《at *sb*》.

ききかじり 聞き齧り a smattering《of》. [文例⇩]

ききかじる 聞き齧る get a smattering《of》; get a superficial knowledge《of》.

ききかた 聞き方 [文例⇩]

ききぐるしい 聞き苦しい《an accent》which is disagreeable [unpleasant, offensive] to listen to [《文》to the ear]. [文例⇩]

ききこみ 聞き込み (a piece of) information;《文》information [intelligence] obtained by inquiry ¶聞き込み(捜査)を続ける go on trying to get [obtain] more information《about, on, as to》;《口語》keep [carry, go] on with the legwork.

ききこむ 聞き込む 〈人が主語〉get [《文》obtain] information (by inquiring); find out《about》; hear《of, about》; get wind of (偶然に); 〈事が主語〉《文》reach [come to] *one's* ear(s);《文》come to *one's* knowledge. [文例⇩]

ききざけ 利き酒 *sake* [wine] tasting ¶利き酒をする test the quality of *sake* by tasting; taste wine / 利き酒をする人 a *sake* [wine] taster.

ききじょうず 聞き上手 a good listener.

ききしる 聞き知る learn《about, of, that...》; know《about,《文》of》.

ききずて 聞き捨て ¶聞き捨てにする overlook; ignore; pass over《*sb's* rude remarks》/ 聞き捨てにならない unpardonable;《文》inexcusable.

ききそこない 聞き損ない ⇨ **ききちがい**.

ききそこなう 聞き損なう ⇨ **ききもらす**.

ききたがる 聞きたがる be inquisitive [curious]《about》; be curious [anxious] to hear [know].

ききだす 聞き出す 〈聞いて知る〉obtain《information》by questioning; (make inquiries and) find out《the truth》; worm《a secret》out of *sb*; 〈聞き始める〉begin to listen to. [文例⇩]

ききただす 聞きただす 〈確かめる〉make sure

きき[1] 危機は去った. The crisis is over [has passed]. / 内閣は今や重大な危機に直面している. The Cabinet is now facing a serious crisis. / 国際的危機感は緩和された. There has been an easing of the atmosphere of international crisis.

ききあきる もうそんな話は聞き飽きた. I've heard enough of that.

ききいれる いくら懇願してもがんとして聞き入れてくれなかった. He wouldn't listen [turned a deaf ear] to our entreaties. | He was immune to our pleas.

ききおぼえ 彼は聞き覚えでいろいろの歌を知っている. He knows a lot of songs which he has picked up by hearing others sing.

ききかじり 彼は聞きかじりでいろいろの事を知っている. He has picked up bits of disconnected knowledge here and there.

ききかた それは君の聞き方が悪いんだ. The way you put the question was not clear enough. | That's because you put the question badly.

ききぐるしい 彼のあの発言は聞き苦しかったよ. It made me feel uncomfortable to hear him say it. | Hearing him say that made me feel uncomfortable.

ききこむ 彼について何か聞き込んだ事でもあるかね. Have you heard anything about him?

ききだす 彼女からは何も聞き出せなかった. I couldn't extract any information from her. / 我々はその問題について彼の意見を聞き出そうとした. We tried to find out his opinion [sounded him out] on that question.

ききちがい 余りにも思いがけない知らせなので, 私の聞き違いではないかと思った. The news was such a surprise that I could hardly believe my ears.

ききつける その物音を聞きつけて人々が駆けつけた. At the noise people rushed to the scene. / 彼の帰郷を聞きつけて, 昔の教え子たちが大勢やって来た. Many of his old pupils came to see him when they heard that he had come home. / 彼のなまりはそれ

ききちがい

of 《the expected arrival time》; 《文》ascertain 《the truth》; 〈問う〉inquire (about) 《*sb's* reason for *doing*》.

ききちがい 聞き違い ¶聞き違いをする hear *sb* [*sth*] wrong; mishear; 〈誤解する〉misunderstand 《what *sb* says》.

ききつける 聞きつける 〈物音を〉hear; catch 《the sound》; 〈聞き込む〉(happen to) learn [hear] 《about, of》; get wind of 《偶然に》; 〈聞き慣れた〉⇨ ききなれる. 文例↓

ききづたえ 聞き伝え hearsay ¶聞き伝えで知る know by hearsay; hear tell 《that..., of *sth*》.

ききづらい 聞き辛い 〈聞き取りにくい〉⇨ ききにくい;〈聞くにたえない〉⇨ ききぐるしい.

ききて 聞き手 a hearer; a listener;〈聴衆〉an audience.

ききとがめる 聞き答める find fault with 《what *sb* says》; (happen to) hear *sb* mention *sth* and blame *him* [take *him* to task] for it.

ききどころ 聞き所 〈話などの〉the point; the most important part;〈音楽の〉the finest [most beautiful] passage(s).

ききとどける 聞き届ける grant [《文》comply with]《*sb's* request》; accept《*sb's* resignation》. 文例↓

ききとり 聞き取り understanding spoken English [French, etc.]; aural [listening] comprehension (語学教育での) ¶聞き取りの試験 an aural comprehension test／聞き取りの練習 listening practice; an aural comprehension drill／聞き取り用の[に書かれた]文章 a passage 《of English》for listening practice. 文例↓

ききとる 聞き取る catch《*sb's* words》; follow *sb* ¶聞き取れない〈聞こえない〉can't be heard;《文》be inaudible;〈人が主語〉can't hear. 文例↓

ききなおす 聞き直す inquire [ask] again.

ききながす 聞き流す take no notice (of); pay no attention (to);《文》give no heed (to).

ききなれる 聞き慣れる get used [accustomed] to hearing ¶聞き慣れた[慣れない]声 a familiar [strange] voice; a voice that is familiar [unfamiliar] to *one* [《文》*one's* ear].

ききにくい 聞きにくい 〈聞き取りにくい〉be

ききょう

difficult [hard] to hear; be indistinct;〈尋ねにくい〉be an awkward question to ask;〈聞き苦しい〉⇨ ききぐるしい.

ききふるした 聞き古した well-worn; hackneyed; stale; trite.

ききほれる 聞き惚れる《文》listen to《a song》with rapt attention;《文》be enraptured [charmed]《by a melody》; be lost [absorbed] in 《the music》.

ききみみ 聞き耳 ¶聞き耳を立てる prick up *one's* ears; listen for《a sound》.文例↓

ききめ 効[利]き目 an effect;〈薬などの〉《文》efficacy ¶効き目のある effective; telling;〈薬など〉《a medicine》that works;《文》efficacious／すばらしい効き目がある be extremely effective;〈薬などが〉be most efficacious;《口語》work wonders／効き目がない do *sb* no good; have no effect (on). 文例↓

ききもの 聞き物 something worth hearing;〈呼び物〉a feature (program) ¶今日のラジオの聞き物 today's radio choice.

ききもらす 聞き漏らす fail to hear [catch]《a word》; miss《a word》.

ききやく 聞き役 ⇨ ききて. 文例↓

ききゃく 棄却 ¶棄却する dismiss《a case》;《口語》throw《a suit》out of court.

ききゅう[1] 危急 an emergency; a crisis (*pl.* crises)⇨ きき[1] ¶危急の critical／危急の場合に in case of [in an] emergency; in time of danger [need]／危急を救う save *sb* from imminent danger／危急存亡のとき an [a time of] emergency; a critical moment [《文》hour]. 文例↓

ききゅう[2] 気球 a balloon ¶気球を揚げる fly [send up] a balloon／気球に乗って昇る go up [《文》ascend] in a balloon. 文例↓

ききゅう[3] 帰休 ⇨ いちじ (一時帰休制).

ききょ 起居 *one's* daily life ¶起居をともに live (together) with [under the same roof as] *sb*.

ききょう[1] 気胸 〈医〉pneumothorax ¶人工[自然]気胸《spontaneous》pneumothorax／気胸療法 a pneumothorax treatment.

ききょう[2] 奇矯 ¶奇矯な eccentric; erratic／奇矯な振る舞いをする behave in an eccentric fashion.

を聞きつけている人にだってとてもおかしい時があるんだ。His accent sometimes sounds very funny even to people who are used to (hearing) it.

ききとどける 彼らは何回も請願したが，ついに聞き届けられなかった。Their frequent petitions all went unheeded.

ききとり 英語の聞き取りの練習のために FEN の放送を聞いています。I listen to FEN broadcasts in order to improve my comprehension of [to get used to hearing] spoken English.

ききとる 君の言う事がよく聞き取れなかった。I didn't really catch what you said. ｜ I could hardly

follow you. ／騒音で彼の言葉がよく聞き取れなかった。The noise was so loud that his words were almost inaudible.

ききにくい 本人に直接聞けと言うの。それは聞きにくいよ。You say I should ask him about it directly? I don't think I dare [could].

ききみみ ルーシーはトランプで独り占いをしながら того会話に聞き耳を立てているらしかった。Lucy seemed to be keeping an ear turned toward our conversation while she was playing solitaire.

ききめ 薬はすぐ効き目があった。The medicine worked almost at once. ｜ The medicine quickly

took effect.

ききやく 聴衆は彼の話を一言半句も聞き漏らすまいと一心に傾聴した。The audience listened intently [attentively] so that they would not miss a single word of what he said.

ききやく 今度は僕が聞き役に回って，奥さんのことで彼がぐちるのを聞いた。Then it was my turn to listen to him grumble about his wife.

ききゅう[1] 国家危急存亡のときであった。We were facing a national crisis.

ききゅう[2] 気球がふくらんだ。The balloon filled out. ／彼らは気球に乗って英仏海峡を横断しようと

ききょう³ 帰京 ¶帰京する come [go] back to Tokyo; return to [be back in] Tokyo.

ききょう⁴ 桔梗 〘植〙a balloonflower; a (Chinese) bellflower.

ききょう⁵ 帰郷 homecoming ¶帰郷する go [come] home; return (to *one's*) home.

きぎょう 企業 an [a business] enterprise; an undertaking ¶日本の海外企業 Japan's overseas enterprises / 大企業 a large(-scale) [major] enterprise; a large corporation [company]; a big firm [business] / 民間[国営]企業 a private [government, state] enterprise / 企業イメージ a corporate image / 企業化する produce (goods) on a commercial basis / 企業家 an entrepreneur / 企業心に富んだ人 〘文〙a man of enterprise / 企業整備 industrial readjustment.

ぎきょう 義俠 〘文〙chivalry ¶義俠的な 〘文〙chivalrous / 義俠心 a chivalrous spirit.

ぎきょうだい 義兄弟 〈義理の兄弟〉a brother-in-law (*pl.* brothers-); 〈盟友〉a sworn brother.

ぎきょく 戯曲 (a) drama; a play ⇨げき².

きぎれ 木切れ a piece [chip, splinter] of wood.

ききわけ 聞き分け ¶聞き分けのよい reasonable 《men》; obedient [docile] 《children》/ 聞き分けのない unreasonable 《women》; naughty 《boys》.

ききわける 聞き分ける 〈道理を〉listen to reason; be reasonable; 〈納得する〉understand; 〈区別する〉tell 《the difference》by hearing. 文例⇩

ききん¹ 飢饉 a famine; a crop failure (凶作); 〈不足〉(a) shortage; 〘文〙a dearth ¶水ききん a water shortage.

ききん² 基金 〈資金〉a fund (for); 〈基本財産〉an endowment; 〈財団〉a foundation ¶基金を設ける establish a fund; set up a foundation / 基金を贈る donate a fund to 《a college》; endow 《a hospital》.

ききんぞく 貴金属 noble [precious] metals ★空気中で酸化せず, 化学変化をほとんど受けない金属, という意味では noble metals. これらの金属が産出量も少なく, 高価であるという意味では precious metals.

きく¹ 〘植〙a chrysanthemum ¶菊の御紋章 the Imperial chrysanthemum crest; the crest of an open chrysanthemum with sixteen complete rays / 菊科植物 a composite (plant); the *Compositae* (総称) / 菊人形 a chrysanthemum figure.

きく² 利[効]く 〈効き目がある〉be effective; have an effect 《on》; take effect 《on》; be good 《for》; tell [act, work] 《on》; 〘文〙be efficacious (★薬について使う); 〈機械などが〉work; 〈くぎが〉hold; 〈将棋のこまが〉command 《a square》; 〈わさびなどが〉be pungent; bite ¶鼻が利く have a keen nose / 修理が利かない be beyond repair / 左手が利かなくなる lose the use of one's left arm. 文例⇩

きく³ 聞[聴]く 〈傾聴する〉listen; listen to 《*sb*, what *sb* says》; 〈聞こえる〉hear (人が主語); 〈聞き知る〉learn 《about, of, that...》; 〈問う〉ask; inquire; 〈照会する〉make inquiries 《about》; 〈忠告などを〉follow; take; 〈願い・要求などを〉grant; 〘文〙comply with; 〈訴えを〉hear ¶ラジオを聞く listen to the radio / 親の言うことを聞く obey *one's* parents / 人の言う事を聞かない do not take advice from others; 〘文〙give no heed to others' counsel / よく聞く名前 a familiar name / 聞くところによれば from what I hear; I hear [I'm told] 《that...》/ ... といって聞かない insist 《on, that...》; persist 《in》.

きぐ¹ 危惧 fear; misgivings; 〘文〙apprehensions ¶危惧の念を抱く feel [〘文〙entertain] misgivings 《about》; be apprehensive 《about, of》.

きぐ² 器[機]具 a tool; an implement; an instrument; an appliance.

きくいも 菊芋 〘植〙an [a Jerusalem] artichoke.

きぐう¹ 奇遇 an unexpected [a chance] meeting.

きぐう² 寄寓 ¶寄寓する live [stay] 《with *sb*》.

きくぎ 木釘 a wooden peg.

ぎくしゃく ¶ぎくしゃくしている do not

した. They tried to cross the English Channel by balloon.

ききょう⁵ 私は毎年1度は帰郷することにしています. I make it a rule to return [come home] to my village [town] once every year.

ききわける イギリス人の英語とアメリカ人の英語を聞き分けられますか. Can you tell English spoken by an Englishman from that spoken by an American?

きく² あの人にはおどしは利かない. He is not a man to be intimidated. / その薬は私に少しも効かなかった. The medicine had no effect on me. / 年を取ると目が利かなくなる. One's eyesight begins to fail with age. / 脳の片側に損傷を受けると体の反対側が利かなくなるのが普通である. Damage to one side of the brain usually leads to loss of function on the opposite side of the body. / ブレーキが利かなかったからだ. It's because the brakes wouldn't [refused to] work. / 費用は10万円では利かないだろう. It will cost more than 100,000 yen.

きく³ 〔僕の言うことを〕君は聞いていなかったね. You weren't listening, were you? / おうわさは田中さんからよくお聞きしております. I've heard a lot about you from Mr. Tanaka. / 彼は物陰で聞いているところでそう言った. He said it in my hearing. / それだけ聞けばたくさんだ. That's enough from you. / 君の成功を聞けば御両親はさぞお喜びになるでしょう. Your parents must be very happy to hear of your success [at the news of your success]. / あの方はたいへん誠実な人だったと聞いております. I'm told [that] [I was given to understand that] he was a man of integrity. / 彼が英語を話すのを聞いていると英国人と思えるくらいです. To hear him speak English, you'd think he was [you would take him for] an Englishman. / 私は自宅で金子氏の放送講演を聞いていた. I was listening to Mr. Kaneko's radio lecture at my own house. / 理由が聞きたい. I want to know the reason. / ちょっと警察で聞いてみよう. I will just inquire at the police station. / 何も聞かないで, さっさとやって

move [work] smoothly ; be jerky [not smooth] 《in its movement》.
きくず 木屑〈木片〉a chip [small piece] of wood ; 〈かんなくず〉(wood) shavings.
きぐすり 生薬 a herbal medicine.
きくずれ 着崩れ ¶着崩れする lose 《its》 shape (through long wear) ; become the worse for wear / 着崩れしたドレス a worn-out dress.
きぐち 木口〈用材の質〉the quality of timber used ; 〈切り口〉⇒こぐち².
きぐつ 木靴 sabots ; clogs ; wooden shoes.
ぎくっと ⇒ぎくりと.
きぐみ¹ 木組み〈組み方〉wood joinery ; 〈組んだもの〉a wooden frame(work) ; timbering.
きぐみ² 気組み〈心構え〉こころがまえ ; 〈意気込み〉⇒いきごみ.
きぐらい 気位 ¶気位が高い be proud. 文例⇩
きくらげ 〈植〉a jew's-ear.
ぎくりと ¶ぎくりとする start 《at》; be startled (by, at) / ぎくりとさせる make sb start ; give sb a start ; strike terror into sb's heart(強い恐怖心を与える). 文例⇩
きぐろう 気苦労 worry ; care ¶気苦労が絶えない always have something to worry about ; one's life is full of cares [worries]. 文例⇩
きけい¹ 奇形〈文〉(a) malformation ; (a) deformity ¶奇形児 a deformed [malformed] child.
きけい² 奇計 a cunning plan ; a clever scheme.
ぎけい 義兄 a brother-in-law《pl. brothers-》.
ぎげい 技芸 arts and crafts.
きげき 喜劇 a comedy ; (a) farce(笑劇) ¶喜劇的 comic(al) ; farcical / 喜劇映画 a comic film [picture] / 喜劇作者 a writer of comedies ; a comic writer / 喜劇俳優[役者] a comedian ; 〈男〉a comic [comedy] actor ; 〈女〉a comic [comedy] actress. 文例⇩
きけつ¹ 既決 ¶既決の decided ; settled / 既決囚 a convict ; a convicted prisoner / 既決書類入れ an out-tray.
きけつ² 帰結〈結末〉a conclusion ; an end ; 〈結果〉a result ; a consequence ; 〈条件文の〉『文法』an apodosis 《pl. -oses》¶当然の帰結として as a natural result [consequence] / …は当然の帰結である It naturally follows that… ; The logical conclusion is that…
ぎけつ 議決 a decision ; a resolution ¶議決する decide (on) ; vote (for, against, that…) / 議決機関 a legislative organ / 議決権 the right to vote. 文例⇩
きけん¹ 危険 (a) danger ; 〈文〉(a) peril ; (a) risk ; 〈文〉a hazard ¶危険な dangerous ; 〈文〉perilous ; risky ; 〈文〉hazardous ; unsafe ; adventurous (冒険的な) / (動物などの)危険を知らせる声 a danger call / 危険を免れる[脱する] escape from [get out of] danger / 危険を冒す brave danger ; run a risk / 一か八かの危険を冒す take a chance [risk] / 危険に陥る get into danger [a dangerous situation] / 危険に落とし入れる〈事が主語〉endanger ; 〈文〉jeopardize ; 〈文〉put one in jeopardy / 危険に際して in case [time] of danger / 身を危険にさらす expose oneself to danger ; 〈口語〉risk one's skin / 危険にひんしている be in danger / 危険視する regard sb [sth] as dangerous / 危険作業 dangerous work ; a hazardous job / 危険思想 dangerous ideas [thoughts] / 危険状態 a dangerous [critical] condition / 危険信号 a danger signal / 危険人物 a dangerous man [character] ; a security risk (国の安全上の) / 危険性 danger ; dangerousness / 危険地帯[区域] a danger area [zone, spot] / 危険物〈法〉a dangerous object [thing] ; 〈運送の際の表示〉explosives and combustibles / 危険分子 dangerous elements. 文例⇩
きけん² 棄権〈投票の〉abstention (from voting) ; 〈権利の〉〈文〉abandonment [renunciation] of one's right ; 〈競技の〉〈文〉default ; absence ¶棄権する〈投票を〉abstain from voting ; stay away from the poll ; 〈権利を〉abandon [give up, 〈文〉renounce] one's right ; 〈競技で〉withdraw [scratch] (from a contest) ; be absent / 棄権者 an abstainer ; a nonvoter / 棄権率 an abstention rate. 文例⇩
きげん¹ 紀元 an era ; an epoch ¶西暦紀元前50年に in 50 B.C. (★ B.C. は before Christ の略) ⇒せいれき.

れ. Don't ask questions ; just do it ! / 彼は帰ると言って聞かなかった. He insisted on going home. / 聞くと見るとでは大変な違いだ. What a difference (there is) between what I heard and what I see now ! / 聞くは一時の恥,〈聞かぬは末代の恥〉. Better ask than go astray.
きぐう これは奇遇ですね. Fancy meeting you here [again])!
きくずれ この服はいつまで着ても着崩れはしません. This suit will keep [won't lose] its shape however long you wear it.
きぐらい 彼女は気位が高いからそんなことはしません. She is too proud [too much of a lady] to do something like that.
ぎくりと 彼は居眠りしていたに違いない, 私の声を聞いてぎくりとしたから. He must have been dozing, for he started at the sound of [when he heard] my voice.
きぐろう 田舎暮らしは気苦労がない. Country life is free from care. | You have no worries when you live in the country.
きげき 実人生でもこういった喜劇がしばしば演じられることがある. Comic scenes like this are often enacted in real life.
ぎけつ 会員は会長不信任を議決した. The members passed a vote of no confidence in the president.
きけん¹ この家は木造だから火事のときは危険だ. This house would be dangerous in time of fire, as it is built of wood. / れを生で食べるのは危険だ. It is dangerous to eat them raw. / この森では道に迷う危険はない. There is no risk of losing your way in the woods. / この種の仕事にはある程度の危険はつきものである. Running some risks is unavoidable in this kind of work. / この事業には少しも危険がない. There is no risk in this enterprise. / 彼は危険が身に迫るのを知らなかった. He was not aware of the approaching danger. / 患者はまだ危険な状態にある. The patient is not yet out of danger.
きけん² 投票の結果は原案に賛成するもの24, 反対6, 棄権1であった. There were 24 votes for the bill, 6 against, and 1 absten-

きげん² 起源[原] the origin; the beginning ¶起源する originate (in); take *its* rise (in); have *its* origin [roots] (in); be traceable (to) / 起源を尋ねる trace *sth* to *its* origin [source]. 文例↓

きげん³ 期限 〈期間〉《文》a term; a period; 〈期間の切れる時点〉a time limit; a deadline ¶期限が来る[になる]〈支払いの〉become [fall] due; 〈満期になる〉mature / 期限が切れた[満了した]とき when the term expires [runs out]; on [at] the expiration [expiry] (of the lease); at [on] maturity / 期限を定める[切る] set [fix] a time limit [a deadline] (for); 《文》set [fix] a term (to) / 一定の期限内に within a definite period of time / 期限つきの with a 《one-year》 time limit [deadline]. 文例↓

きげん⁴ 機嫌 (a) humor; a mood ¶機嫌がいい be in a good humor [mood]; be cheerful / 機嫌が悪い be in a bad [《文》an ill] humor [mood]; 《口語》be cross; 《文》be displeased; 《文》be out of humor / 機嫌よく cheerfully; in a good humor / 機嫌をとる humor; please; 〈へつらう〉flatter; 〈気に入ろうとする〉curry favor with *sb*; 《文》ingratiate *oneself* with *sb* / 機嫌をそこねる offend; 《文》displease; hurt *sb's* feelings; put *sb* in(to) a bad mood [《文》out of humor] / 機嫌を直す get into a better mood [temper]; come around; regain [recover] *one's* temper (かんかんに怒っていた人が) ⇒ごきげん.

きご 季語 a season word [phrase].

きこう¹ 気孔 a pore; 〈植物の〉a stoma 《*pl.* -mata, -s》; 〈昆虫の〉a stigma 《*pl.* -s, -mata》.

きこう² 気候 climate; 〈天候〉weather; 〈季節〉a season ¶不順な気候 unseasonable weather / 大陸[海洋, 島嶼(ﾄｳ)]性気候 a continental [an oceanic, an insular] climate / 気候の変化 a climatic change / 気候の変わり目に at the change of the seasons. 文例↓

きこう³ 奇行 eccentric behavior [《文》conduct]; 《文》an eccentricity ¶奇行に富む be full of eccentricities [amusing anecdotes].

きこう⁴ 紀行 an account of a trip [journey]; a record of [book about] *one's* travels ¶紀行作家 a travel writer.

きこう⁵ 起工 ¶起工する begin [start] the construction 《of a bridge》; 〈船を〉lay the keel 《of》; 〈建築を〉lay the cornerstone 《of》; 〈土木工事を〉break ground 《for》 / 起工式〈建築の〉[the keel 《船の》]; the ground-breaking ceremony (土木工事の). 文例↓

きこう⁶ 帰港 ¶帰港する return to port.

きこう⁷ 寄港 ¶寄港する call [touch, stop] 《at》; make a call 《at》 / 寄港地 a port of call.

きこう⁸ 寄稿 (a) contribution ¶寄稿する contribute 《to a newspaper》; write 《for a magazine》 / 寄稿家[者] a contributor.

きこう⁹ 機構 〈仕組み〉a mechanism; machinery (運営の); 〈制度〉a system; 〈構造〉structure; 〈組織体〉an organization ¶国際連合の複雑な機構 the complex mechanism [machinery] of the United Nations / 行政の機構 the machinery of government / 経済の機構 the economic structure [《口語》setup] / 機構を改める reorganize [revamp] the system.

きごう¹ 記号 a mark; a sign; a symbol ¶記号論 semiotics; semiology / 記号論理学 symbolic [mathematical] logic.

きごう² 揮毫 〈書〉writing; 〈画〉painting; drawing ¶揮毫する 〈書を〉write; 〈画を〉draw; paint.

ぎこう¹ 技工 a craftsman ¶(歯科の)技工士 a dental technician.

ぎこう² 技巧 (technical) skill; technique ¶技巧を凝らす give full play to *one's* technique [skill]; 《文》exercise *one's* utmost skill / 大変な技巧家 an artist [a painter, etc.] of great skill; a great technician (特に絵画・音楽の). 文例↓

きこうし 貴公子 a young nobleman; 《文》a scion of the nobility ¶貴公子然たる princely [noble-looking] 《young men》.

きこえ 聞こえ 〈外聞〉reputation; fame; 《文》renown; 〈音声〉sonority ¶聞こえがいい sound nice [decent, respectable]. 文例↓

きこえよがし 聞こえよがし

きこえる 聞こえる 〈人が主語〉(can) hear; catch 《the sound》; 〈音が主語〉《文》be audible; be heard; reach *one's* ear(s); 〈響く〉sound; 〈知られる〉be well known ¶皮肉に聞こえる sound ironical / 本当らしく[うそのように]聞こえる ring true [false] / 聞こえない 《文》be inaudible; cannot be heard / 聞こえる[聞こえない]ところで in [out of] *one's* hearing / 呼べば聞こえるところに within call

---

tion. | The vote was 24 to 6 with 1 abstention.

きげん² その起源は不明である. Its origin is unknown. | It is of unknown [uncertain] origin. / この珍しい風習の起源は徳川時代にさかのぼる. The origin of this curious custom can be traced [This strange custom dates] back to the Tokugawa period.

きげん³ この契約の期限は1年である. The contract holds [is] good for one year. / この仕事には別に期限はない. There is no time limit for completing this job. / 期限前にこの仕事を仕上げておこうじゃないか. Let's get the job done before the deadline.

きこう² 当地の気候は温和で健康によい. The climate here is mild and healthy. / そこは気候の変化が激しい. The place is subject to extreme [violent] climatic changes.

きこう⁵ 一昨年起工した大橋はこのほど竣工した. The construction of the Ohashi bridge, which was begun [started] the year before last, has just been completed.

ぎこう² 文章家がどんなに技巧を凝らしてもその神秘な美しさを表現することはできない. No amount of technique on the writer's part could express its mysterious beauty.

きこえ そう言った方が聞こえがいい. It would sound better.

きこえよがし 彼女は聞こえよがしに僕の悪口を言った. She deliberately spoke badly of me in my hearing.

きこえる ひばりの声が聞こえた. I heard a lark singing. / 足音が聞こえなくなった. The footsteps

きこく [earshot]. 文例⇩

きこく 帰国 帰国する return [come back] to one's country; go [come, get] home / 帰国の途につく leave for home / 帰国子女の教育問題 the educational problems of children who have returned from abroad.

ぎごく 疑獄 a bribery case; a corruption scandal;《米》a graft case.

きごこち 着心地 着心地がいい[悪い] be comfortable [uncomfortable] to wear. 文例⇩

きごころ 気心 気心が知れない be a stranger (to one); be unreliable / 気心の知れた familiar; old and tried; reliable. 文例⇩

ぎごちない awkward; clumsy; stiff;《文》constrained ¶ぎごちない態度で awkwardly; stiffly; in a constrained manner / ぎごちない文章 an awkward [a stilted] style.

きこつ 気骨 ⇨ きがい².

きこなし 着こなし 着こなしがうまい[まずい] dress well [badly]; wear one's clothes well [badly]. 文例⇩

きこのいきおい 騎虎の勢い ¶騎虎の勢いで having no choice but to carry on; being unable to change one's line of action.

ぎこぶん 擬古文 a pseudoclassical style.

きこむ 着込む 《たくさん着る》put on warm clothes; dress (oneself) warmly; wrap up well [warmly];〈着る〉⇨ きる².

きこり 樵 a woodcutter.

きこん 既婚 ¶既婚の married / 既婚者 a married person.

きざ 気障 ¶きざな〈気どった〉affected;〈おつに澄ました〉prim; mincing〈歩き方や口のきき方など〉;〈うぬぼれた〉conceited;〈人を見くだす〉snobbish;〈学者ぶった〉pedantic;〈けばけばしい〉flashy; showy.

きさい¹ 奇[鬼]才 ¶きさい remarkable talent; unusual ability;〈人物〉a [《文》a singular] genius; an outstandingly talented person.

きさい² 記載 mention;〔簿記〕entry ¶記載する mention; record;〈新聞雑誌が〉carry; print;〈帳簿に〉enter / 記載事項 items mentioned / 記載漏れ an omission.

きさい³ 起債 flotation of a loan ¶起債する float [raise] a loan; issue bonds.

きざい 機[器]材《機械・器具の材料》materials for the manufacture of machinery [implements];《機械・器具と材料》machinery [implements] and materials.

きさき 后 an empress; a queen.

ぎざぎざ notches;〈貨幣のふちの〉ridges((cut on the edge of a coin)); milling ¶ぎざぎざのある notched; corrugated; milled.

きさく 気さく ¶気さくな〈率直な〉frank; candid; openhearted;〈愛想のよい〉cheerful and friendly; sociable; (a person who is) easy to get on with;《米口語》folksy.

ぎさく 偽作 a forgery; a fake;〈文学作品〉《文》an apocryphal work;《文》a work of spurious authorship.

きざし 兆し〈徴候〉a symptom; a sign; an indication;〈前兆〉an omen. 文例⇩

きざす 兆す show signs [symptoms] (of); give indications (of).

きざみ 刻み〈刻み目〉a notch; a nick;〈タバコ〉cut [shredded] tobacco ¶刻み(目)をつける notch; nick /(電話料金などが)秒刻みで計算される be calculated by the second.

きざむ 刻む〈切り刻む〉cut sth (fine); chop sth (up);〈肉などを〉mince; hash;〈彫刻する〉carve; engrave; chisel; inscribe(碑文などを). 文例⇩

きさん 起算 ¶起算する reckon (count,《文》compute) from (a date) / 起算日 the base [initial] date for reckoning (a period of time); the date from which a period of time is reckoned.

ぎさん 蟻酸 《化》formic acid.

きし¹ 岸〈川の〉the bank;〈海・湖の〉the shore;〈海の〉the coast;〈池などの〉the border ¶岸を離れて off (the) shore / 岸に[へ] ashore; on shore. 文例⇩
用法 川の「岸」は bank. shore は海や湖のような大きな水の広がりの「岸」をさすが, ミシシッピー川のような大河の広さを強調したい時に(特に詩や小説で)その「岸」を shore ということがある. coast は海岸線としての「岸」.

きし² 棋士 a (professional) go [shogi] player.

きし³ 旗幟 ⇨ はた, のぼり² ¶きしを鮮明にする make one's attitude clear; state《文》define,《文》clarify one's position (on a matter).

きし⁴ 騎士〈中世ヨーロッパの〉a knight ¶騎士道《文》chivalry / 騎士道にかなった《文》chivalrous.

きじ¹ 生地, 木地〈織物〉texture; stuff;〈布〉(plain) cloth;〈木目〉the grain;〈塗物の〉the

---

died away. / 水の上だと声は遠くまで聞こえるものだ. Voices carry a long way [a great distance] over water. / 電話口でお声が聞こえません. I cannot hear you (properly). / ラジオをかけたら, ダンス音楽が聞こえて来た. I turned on the radio, and dance music came on. / 君の発音はフランス語らしく聞こえないね. Your pronunciation doesn't sound much like French. / 彼の話は本当らしく聞こえた. His story rang true [had the ring of truth].

きごこち 今度の服の着心地はいかが. How does your new coat feel?

きごころ お互いに気心のよくわかった仲だ. We are close friends, well used to each other's ways. / いつまでつきあっても気心のわからない男だ. I still don't understand him, for all my long acquaintance with him.

きこなし 彼女は着こなしが上手だ. She knows how to wear her clothes. | She dresses well [stylishly].

きざし インフレの兆しが見えている. There are indications that prices will go up. | There is every indication of a rise in prices.

きざむ 時計が時を刻んでいた. A clock was ticking (away). / この事は私の心に深く刻みこまれた. This was deeply engraved on my mind [my memory].

きし¹ 波が岸を打っていた. The waves were beating [dashing] against the shore. / 琵琶湖の岸に沿って松林が長く並んでいた. There were long rows of pine trees flanking the shore of Lake Biwa.

unlacquered wood ; the base for (applying) the lacquer ; 〈陶磁器の〉 biscuit ; bisque ; earthenware [porcelain] ready for glazing ¶洋服の生地 〈男物〉 suit material ; suiting ; 〈女物〉 dress material / ワイシャツの生地 shirting / 生地のままの plain ; unvarnished (ニスを塗ってない) ; unglazed (うわぐすりを塗ってない) / 生地の見本 a material sample / 生地屋 〈店〉 《米》 a dry-goods store ; 《英》 a draper's (shop) ; 〈人〉 《米》 a dry-goods merchant ; 《英》 a draper.

きじ² 記事 〈新聞の〉 a news story [item] ; a report ; a piece [an article] 《on the freedom of the press》 ; 〈叙述〉 (a) description ; an account ¶記事を載せる print [give] an account 《of》 ; carry a story [news item] / 記事を書く write [do] an article [a report] 《on》 / 記事をとる get [take hold of] [obtain] news ; get copy (種を) / 記事を差し止める place a ban on the publication of the news 《of》 / 記事差し止め a press ban ; 《英》 an embargo 《on an article [a topic]》. 文例⇩

きじ³ 雉 〈鳥〉 a pheasant.

ぎし¹ 技師 an engineer ¶土木[機械, 鉱山]技師 a civil [mechanical, mining] engineer.

ぎし² 義士 〈忠臣〉 《文》 a loyal retainer ; 〈正義の人〉 a righteous [an upright] person.

ぎし³ 義姉 a sister-in-law (pl. sisters-).

ぎし⁴ 義肢 an artificial [a false] limb.

ぎし⁵ 義歯 ⇒いれば.

ぎじ 議事 (parliamentary) proceedings ¶議事の進行をはかる expedite (the) proceedings / 議事に入る[を閉じる] open [close] a sitting ; start [close] proceedings / 議事堂 an assembly hall ; 〈国会の〉 the Diet Building ; 《米》 the Capitol ; 《英》 the Houses of Parliament / 議事日程 the order of the day ; an agenda / 議事録 the minutes (of the proceedings) ; 〈国会の〉 the (official) record of the proceedings of the Diet ; the Diet Record. 文例⇩

ぎじ- 疑似... false ; suspected ; para- ¶疑似コレラ paracholera ; a suspected case of cholera.

きしかいせい 起死回生 ¶起死回生の霊薬 a wonderful medicine capable of reviving the dead ; a miracle [wonder] drug / 起死回生のホームランを放つ hit a homer to pull the game out of the fire.

ぎしき 儀式 〈式典〉 a ceremony ; 《文》 a function ; 〈宗教上の〉 《文》 a rite ; a service ; (a) ritual ¶儀式を行なう hold [perform] a ceremony / 儀式ばる be ceremonious ; stand on ceremony. 文例⇩

ぎしぎし ¶ぎしぎしいう [音がする] creak ; squeak ; make a creaking sound.

きしつ 気質 ⇒しょう¹.

きじつ 期日 a (fixed) date ; 《文》 an appointed day ; 〈期限〉 a due date ; a time limit ⇒げん³ ¶出発の期日を決める fix [decide on] the date of one's departure.

きじばと 雉鳩 〈鳥〉 a rufous turtledove.

ぎじ(ばり) 擬餌(鉤) 〈虫に似せた〉 a [an artificial] fly ; 〈水中で使う〉 a lure ; a spinner (回し転する).

きしむ 軋む creak ; squeak.

きしゃ¹ 汽車 a (railroad) train ; 〈電車・ディーゼル車に対して〉 a steam train ⇒れっしゃ ¶博多行の汽車 a train for Hakata ; the Hakata train / 汽車の旅 a train journey ; a railroad trip / 汽車の窓から見た景色 a scene (viewed) from a train window / 汽車ぽっぽ a choo-choo (train) ; 《英》 a puff-puff.

きしゃ² 記者 a journalist ; a newspaperman ; a reporter (探訪記者) ; a correspondent (通信員) ; 〈編集者〉 an editor ; 〈執筆者〉 a writer ¶朝日新聞の記者 a reporter for [on] the Asahi / 新米記者 a cub reporter / 婦人記者 a newspaperwoman ; a woman reporter (pl. women reporters) / 記者会見 a press [news] conference / 記者会見をする give [hold, call] a press conference ; meet the press / 記者クラブ a press club / 記者席 a press box (議場・競技場などの) ; a press gallery (議会の) / 記者団 a press corps. 文例⇩

きしゃく 希釈 《化》 dilution ; attenuation ¶希釈する dilute ; attenuate / 希釈液 a weak [diluted] solution.

きしゅ¹ 気腫 《医》 emphysema ¶肺気腫 pulmonary emphysema.

きしゅ² 旗手 a standard-bearer ; a flag-bearer (オリンピックなどでの) ¶ダダイズムの旗手 the standard-bearer of Dadaism [the Dadaist movement].

きしゅ³ 機首 the nose of an airplane ¶機首を下げる [上げる] nose down [up] ; lower [pull up] the nose / 機首を北に向ける turn north(ward) ; head for the north.

きしゅ⁴ 機種 〈飛行機の〉 kinds [types] of airplanes.

きしゅ⁵ 騎手 a rider ; a horseman ; a jockey (競馬の).

きじゅ 喜寿 ¶喜寿の祝いをする celebrate one's [sb's] 77th birthday.

ぎしゅ 義手 an artificial [a false] arm [hand].

きしゅう¹ 奇習 a strange custom.

きじ² けさの「朝日」にその火事の記事が出ている. This morning's Asahi carries an account of the fire. | The fire is reported in this morning's Asahi. / 新聞の記事を全面的に信じることはできない. You can't believe everything you read in the (news)papers. / これは確かに面白い記事になる. This will make an interesting news item, I'm sure. / これだけの事件がたった3行の記事にしかならないのはおかしいと思った. I thought it strange that this incident only got three lines in the newspaper. / この記事は本日正午まで差し止めになっていた. This article had been suppressed until today's noon.

ぎじ 議事進行! Order! Order!

ぎしき これは儀式の場合に使う衣装です. These costumes are used on formal [ceremonial] occasions.

きしゃ² 辞任の意思はないと記者団に語った. He told the press that he had no intention of resigning.

ぎじゅつ 外国語で話すことも一つの技術である. Speaking a foreign language is an art, too. / それにはほどの技術を要する. It requires a great deal of technical skill. / それは技術的に不可能

きしゅう[2] 奇襲 a surprise [《口語》 sneak] attack 《on Pearl Harbor》 ¶奇襲する make a surprise attack [raid] 《on》; take 《the enemy》 by surprise.

きじゅう 機銃 a machine gun ⇨きかんじゅう[ほう] ¶機銃掃射する machine-gun; strafe (飛行機で).

きじゅうき 起重機 a crane; a derrick (船の) ¶起重機でつり上げる lift [hoist] *sth* with [by means of] a crane.

きしゅく 寄宿 ¶寄宿する lodge [board] 《at *sb's* house, with *sb*》 ¶寄宿生 a boarding student; a boarder / 寄宿舎 《米》 a dormitory; 《口語》 a dorm; a hostel.

きじゅつ[1] 奇術 conjuring tricks; magic ⇨てじな ¶奇術を行なう do conjuring [magic] tricks / 奇術師 a conjurer; a magician.

きじゅつ[2] 記述 (a) description; an account ¶記述する describe; give an account 《of》 / 記述的 descriptive / 記述文法 descriptive grammar.

ぎじゅつ 技術 an art; (a) skill; (a) technique; 〈科学·工業の〉 technology; technics (学問としての) (★ technics は単数扱い); 〈学科〉 manual training ¶高度の技術 high [advanced, sophisticated] technology / 技術の進歩 technological [technical] advance [improvement(s)] / 技術の導入 introduction [importation] of foreign techniques / 技術家[者] a technical expert; a technician; a technologist; 〈技師〉 an engineer / 技術革新 (a) technological innovation / 技術教育 technical education / 技術協力 technical [technological] cooperation / 技術提携 (an agreement for) technical cooperation; 《口語》 a technical tie-up / 技術料 a technical fee. [文例⇩]

きじゅん[1] 帰順 ¶帰順する submit 《to》; 《文》 return to *one's* former allegiance / 帰順を誓う 《文》 swear [pledge] allegiance 《to the ruler》.

きじゅん[2] 基準 a standard; 《文》 a criterion 《*pl.* -teria》; a yardstick ¶基準の standard / 基準価格 a standard price / (物価統計などの)基準期間[時] the base period / 基準賃金 standard wages / 基準点 〘測量〙 a point of reference; a reference point. [文例⇩]

きしょう[1] 気性 《文》 a disposition; nature; temperament ⇨きだて ¶気性の激しい人 a man of violent moods; a person who is subject to violent changes of mood. [文例⇩]

きしょう[2] 気象 weather (conditions); 《文》 atmospheric phenomena ⇨てんき[1] ¶気象の変化 a change in the weather [in weather condition] / 気象衛星 a weather satellite / 気象学 meteorology / 気象観測[情報, データ] weather [meteorological] observation [information, data] / 気象観測船 a weather ship / 気象写真 a weather picture 《from a satellite》 / 中央気象台 the Central Meteorological Observatory / 気象台員 a weatherman / 気象庁 the Meteorological Agency / 気象通報 a weather report. [文例⇩]

きしょう[3] 希少 ¶希少価値 《have》 scarcity [rarity] value / 希少物資 scarce goods [materials].

きしょう[4] 起床 ¶起床する get out of bed; get up; 《文》 rise (from *one's* bed).

きしょう[5] 記章 a medal; a badge (会員章など) ¶従軍記章 a war [service] medal.

きじょう[1] 机上 ¶机上の空論 an armchair theory [plan]; a mere [an empty] theory; an impractical proposition.

きじょう[2] 機上 ¶機上の人となる board [get on (board)] an airplane; enplane / 機上から眺める look down from an airplane; get [have, take] a bird's-eye view 《of a city》 from an aircraft.

きじょう[3] 気丈 ¶気丈な 《文》 courageous; 《文》 stouthearted.

ぎしょう 偽証 false evidence [《文》 testimony] ¶偽証する give false evidence; 《文》 bear false witness 《against》; 〈偽証罪を犯す〉 commit perjury; perjure *oneself* / 偽証罪 perjury.

ぎじょう 議場 an assembly hall; the chamber; 《on》 the floor (of the House). [文例⇩]

きしょうさん 希硝酸 dilute nitric acid.

ぎじょうへい 儀仗兵 a guard of honor.

きしょく[1] 気色 ¶気色が悪い 〈人が主語〉 feel sick [disgusted] 《at the sight》; 〈物が主語〉 be disgusting; be unpleasant; 《文》 be displeasing / 気色の悪い 〈不快な〉 disgusting; 《文》 odious; 〈不吉な〉 ominous; 〈気味の悪い〉 creepy; eerie; gruesome.

きしょく[2] 寄食 ¶寄食する sponge on *sb*; be *sb's* hanger-on; be a parasite on *sb* ⇨いそうろう. [文例⇩]

きしょく[3] 喜色 a pleased [《文》 joyful] look.

きしる 軋る 〈きーきー〉 creak; squeak; 〈がりがり〉 grate; rasp.

きしん[1] 帰心 ¶帰心矢のごとし be very anxious [eager] to go [get] home; 《文》 have an irresistible longing for (*one's*) home.

きしん[2] 寄進 ⇨きふ[1].

きじん 奇人 an eccentric (person); an odd [a strange] fellow.

だ. It is technically impossible. / 交渉は若干の技術的な問題で行き詰まっている. The negotiations have reached a deadlock on a few technicalities [technical points]. / 技術者の不足はますます甚だしくなりつつある. The dearth of technicians is growing more and more serious.

きじゅん[2] これを基準にして我々の環境の変化を測定することができる. This is a standard against [a yardstick by] which we can measure the changes in our environment. / どのような基準から見てもそれは異常である. It is abnormal by any standard(s).

きしょう[1] どんな気性の人ですか. What sort of (a) man is he? / 私の気性として物事を半端にしておけない. It is not in my nature to leave anything half done.

きしょう[2] 10月上旬にしては異常な気象で, 我々が旭川に着いた時は吹雪だった. The weather was abnormal for early October; we arrived at Asahikawa in driving snow.

ぎじょう 議場は混乱に陥った. The floor was thrown into disorder.

きしょく[3] 喜色満面にあふれていた. He was all smiles. | He was beaming.

ぎしん 疑心 ⇨ぎねん. 文例⇩
ぎじん 擬人 ¶擬人化する personify / 擬人法 personification.
きす¹ 《魚》a sillaginoid (fish).
きす² 期す ⇨きする².
キス a kiss (on the cheek) ¶キスする kiss 《sb on the mouth》; give sb a kiss / キスを返す kiss sb back /「お休みなさい」のキスをする kiss (a child) good night / 投げキスをする blow [throw] sb a kiss.
きず 傷, 瑕 〈からだの〉an injury; a wound; a cut (切り傷); a scratch (かき傷); a scar (傷跡); 〈品物の〉a chip; a flaw; a scratch (傷跡); 〈欠点〉a fault; 《文》a defect; 〈弱点〉a weakness ⇨けが 用因 ¶軽い[重い]傷 a slight [serious] injury / 傷ひとつない flawless; perfect / 傷をつける 〈からだに〉⇨きずつける; 〈品物などに〉damage; ruin; spoil / 傷を負わずに 《escape》 unhurt; 《get away》 with a whole skin.
きずあと 傷跡 a scar ¶戦争の傷跡 the scars of the war / みけんに傷跡がある have a scar on one's forehead; one's forehead is scarred [《文》 bears a scar]. 文例⇩
きずいしょう 黄水晶 《鉱》citrine.
きずいせん 黄水仙 《植》a jonquil.
きすう¹ 奇数 an odd [uneven] number ¶奇数回 an odd number of times / 奇数日 odd days.
きすう² 基数 〈序数に対する〉a cardinal number; 〈1から9までの数〉a fundamental number.
きすうほう 記数法 (a system of) numerical notation.
ぎすぎす ¶ぎすぎすした 〈やせた〉skinny; scrawny; 〈感じが〉stiff; 《文》unaffable.
きずく 築く ¶build; construct; 《文》erect; raise ¶築き上げる build [work] up (a good business); establish (one's reputation).
きずぐすり 傷薬 an ointment.
きずぐち 傷口 a wound ¶傷口の開いた傷 an open [a gaping] wound / 傷口を縫う stitch [sew up] a wound. 文例⇩
きずつく 傷つく be [get] injured [wounded]; 〈心が〉be hurt ⇨きずつける 用因.
きずつける 傷つける injure; wound; 《文》inflict a wound (on); 〈心を〉hurt ¶名声を傷つける harm [hurt, 《文》injure] sb's reputation [good name].
きずな 絆 《文》bonds; ties ¶友情のきずな the bonds [ties] of friendship.

きずもの 傷物 damaged goods; a damaged [《文》flawed, defective] article / a reject (普通の販路では売れない品物); ¶傷物にする damage; spoil; 〈娘を〉《文》ruin (a girl).
きする¹ 帰する 〈…帰着する〉come to; end [《文》result] in; lead to; 〈…のせいにする〉put (one's failure) down to; 《文》attribute [ascribe] (one's failure) to (one's poor health) ¶失敗に帰する prove a [end in] failure / …の手に帰する fall into sb's hands / 帰するところ after all; when all is said (and done); in the end; in the final analysis. 文例⇩
きする² 期する 〈期待する〉expect; 〈確信する〉be sure [confident] 《about, of, that…》; 〈決心する〉decide; 《文》determine; resolve; 〈覚悟している〉be prepared for 《the worst》; be ready to do ¶期せずして unexpectedly; accidentally; by chance / 期せずして…する happen [chance] to do. 文例⇩
きせい¹ 気勢 spirits; enthusiasm 《文》ardor (意気込み) ¶気勢があがる 〈人が主語〉be in good [high] spirits; be in great [great, fine] form; 〈事が主語〉encourage; cheer / 気勢をそぐ 〈事が主語〉dispirit; discourage; dampen one's enthusiasm [ardor]. 文例⇩
きせい² 奇声 ¶奇声を発する give [《文》utter] a strange sound; squeal.
きせい³ 帰省 ¶帰省する go [come, return] home / 休暇で帰省している be home on holiday.
きせい⁴ 既成 ¶既成の existing; 《文》accomplished / 既成の事実 a fait accompli (pl. faits accomplis); an accomplished [established] fact / 既成政党 the existing [established] political parties.
きせい⁵ 既製 ¶既製品 ready-made goods [articles] / 既製服 ready-to-wear [ready-made] clothes; a ready-to-wear suit [dress].
きせい⁶ 寄生 parasitism ¶寄生する live on [with] (its host); be parasitic [a parasite] on (a tree) / 寄生虫 〔動物, 植物〕a parasite; a parasitic worm [animal, plant] / 寄生虫学 parasitology / 寄生虫駆除剤 a paraciticide.
きせい⁷ 規制 control; 《文》regulation ¶規制する control; 《文》regulate / 法的規制を加える impose legal controls (on) / 自己規制 voluntary control [restrictions] 《on her car exports to the U.S.》.
ぎせい¹ 犠牲 a sacrifice; 〈被害者〉a victim, 〈身代わり〉a scapegoat ¶犠牲となる be sacrificed; be a victim 《of》; 《文》fall (a) vic-

---

ぎしん 疑心暗鬼を生ず. Suspicion begets ugly fears.
きず 傷はひどく痛んだ. The wound hurt badly [like hell]. / そんな事をしたらあの人にきずがつきます. That would reflect on his good name. / このつや出しを塗っておけばきずがつきません. This polish will protect it from scratches.
きずあと 戦争の傷跡がまだ残っている. The country has not yet recovered from the effects of the war. | The country still bears the scars of the war.
きずぐち 傷口がふさがった. The wound has closed.
きする¹ 彼の主張も帰する所は同じだ. What he says comes to the same thing.
きする² 2人は再会を期して別れた. They parted, promising to meet again. / 2人の考えは期せずして一致した. They happened to have the same view of it. | Their views coincided with each other.
きせい¹ その知らせを聞いて大いに気勢があがった. The news cheered us greatly.
ぎせい¹ 彼女は我が子のために自分の幸福を犠牲にした. She sacrificed her happiness for her son. / どんな犠牲を払ってもやり遂げるつもりです. I am determined to see it through to the bitter end. | I will [am going to] get

ぎせい tim《to》/ 犠牲を払う make sacrifices《for》/ 多大の犠牲を払う pay dearly [a heavy price] 《for》/ 犠牲にする sacrifice [《文》make a sacrifice of]《oneself, one's happiness》/ …を犠牲にして the sacrifice [cost] of … / 犠牲的精神 be full of》the spirit of self-sacrifice / 犠牲者 a victim;〈事故などの〉a casualty / 犠牲バント[フライ]【野球】a sacrifice bunt [fly] ⇨ぎだ.[文例↓]

ぎせい² 擬制【法】a (legal) fiction ¶擬制資本 fictitious [watered] capital.

ぎせいご 擬声語 an onomatopoeic word; an onomatopoeia.

きせかえにんぎょう 着せ替え人形 a dress-up doll.

きせき¹ 奇跡 a miracle; a wonder ¶奇跡を行なう work [perform] miracles; work [do] wonders / 奇跡的に miraculously / 奇跡的に死を免れる escape death by a miracle.[文例↓]

きせき² 軌跡【数】a locus (pl. loci);〈比喩的〉tracks ¶軌跡を求める derive a locus /〈軌跡をたどる follow the tracks《of…, left by…》.

ぎせき 議席 a seat (in the House) ¶議席を獲得する[有する] win [have] a seat (in the House) / 議席につく take one's seat.[文例↓]

きせつ 季節 a season ¶桜の季節 the cherry-blossom season / 季節の移り変わり the turn(-ing) of the seasons / 季節の花 flowers of the season / 季節の変化 the change of the seasons / 季節を問わず in all seasons, in and out of season / 季節的に seasonally; according to the season / 気候の季節的変化 seasonal changes of climate / 季節向きの suitable for the season;《文》seasonable / 季節はずれの out of season;《文》unseasonable / 季節遅れの behind the season / 季節風 a seasonal wind; a monsoon (インド洋・南アジアの) / (ホテルなどの)季節料金 a seasonal rate / 季節労働者 a seasonal laborer [worker].[文例↓]

きせつ 既設 ¶既設の established; existing / 既設線 lines in operation.

きぜつ 気絶 ¶気絶する lose consciousness [one's senses]; faint / なぐって気絶させる knock sb unconscious [out, senseless].

キセノン【化】xenon.

きせる 着せる〈着物を〉dress;《文》clothe;〈覆う〉cover;〈めっきする〉plate; coat;〈罪を〉lay (the blame on sb); fasten (a crime on sb); charge《sb with an offense》¶上着を着せて見てやる try a coat on sb / 着せてやる help sb into《his coat》, help sb (on) with《his coat》.

キセル [＜《カンボジア語》khsier (管の意)] a (tobacco) pipe ¶キセルをする steal a train ride (to Nikko) by paying only for the first and last sections of the ride; go (to Atami) by train without paying for the middle part of the journey.

きぜわしい 気忙しい restless, fidgety ⇨せっかち.[文例↓]

きせん¹ 汽船 a steamship; a steamer; a liner (定期船) ¶汽船で行く go (to Honolulu) by steamer; take a steamer (to) / 汽船勝山丸 the S.S. Katsuyama Maru (★ S.S. は steam-ship の略で, [éses] と発音する) / 汽船会社 a steamship company.

きせん² 棋戦〈トーナメント方式の〉a go [shogi] tournament /〈一局〉a game of go [shogi].

きせん³ 貴賤 high and low.

きせん⁴ 機先 ¶機先を制する forestall《one's rival, sb's attempt》; get a start on [the start of] sb.

きぜん 毅然 ¶毅然たる《文》dauntless;《文》resolute; firm / 毅然として《文》dauntlessly;《文》resolutely; firmly;《文》with fortitude.

ぎぜん 偽善 hypocrisy ¶偽善を行なう behave hypocritically,《文》practice hypocrisy; be a [《文》play the] hypocrite / 偽善的 hypocritical / 偽善者 a hypocrite.

きそ¹ 起訴 prosecution; indictment ¶起訴する prosecute [indict] sb (for a crime); charge sb《with a crime》/ 起訴状 a bill of indictment; an [a written] indictment / 起訴猶予にする suspend [shelve] an indictment; leave a charge on the file.

きそ² 基礎 the foundation; the basis (pl. bases); the base ¶基礎的 fundamental, basic / 基礎を…に置く, 基礎は…にある be based [founded] on…; rest on… / 基礎を作る[築く] lay the foundation(s)《of》; lay the groundwork《for》/ 基礎を固める consolidate the foundation(s)《of》; put《the project》on a firm basis / 基礎にある lie at the base [foundation]《of》/ 基礎医学 the basic medical sciences / 基礎学科 primary subjects (of study) / 基礎科学 (a) basic science / 基礎工作 spade-work; groundwork / 基礎控除 basic deduction (from taxable income) / 基礎体温【生理】the basal body temperature (略: BBT) / 基礎知識 an elementary [a basic, a fundamental] knowledge《of》; a grounding《in》.[文例↓]

きそう¹ 奇想 a fantastic idea;[文例↓]《文》a conceit

---

my way at any cost. |《文》I intend to achieve my objective, come what may.

きせき¹ 奇跡でもなければ病人はとても助かるまい. Nothing short of a miracle will save the patient.

ぎせき 今度の総選挙で民社党は議席を20から30に増やした. The Democratic Socialist Party increased their representation in the House from 20 to 30 at the last general election.

きせつ¹ この季節はいつも風が強い. It generally blows hard at this time of (the) year. / 季節に少し早過ぎる大雪に見舞われた. We had a heavy snowfall a bit earlier than normal. | Heavy snow fell unseasonably early (that year). / 日本人は父祖伝来の鋭い季節感を失いつつある. The Japanese are losing the keen sense of the seasons which they inherited from their fathers.

きぜわしい 締切日が迫って来たので気ぜわしい思いをしています. I feel pressed for time as the deadline is drawing near.

きせん³ 職業に貴賤なし. All occupations [All honest trades] are equally honorable.

きそ² 今や本校の基礎も固まった. Our school is now firmly established. / 英語の基礎が十分できている. He has a good grounding in English.

きそう¹ 奇想曲 a capriccio 《pl. -s》. 文例⇩

きそう² 起草 ¶起草する draft; draw up / 起草委員会 a drafting committee / 起草者 a drafter.

きそう³ 競う compete [《文》contend, 《文》vie] 《with sb for sth》 ¶競って買い求める compete with others in buying sth.

きぞう¹ 寄贈 presentation; 《文》donation ¶寄贈する present 《sb with sth, sth to sb》; donate [make a donation of] 《a sum of money to the school》/ 寄贈品 a gift; a present / 寄贈本 a presentation copy.

ぎそう¹ 偽[擬]装 (a) camouflage ¶偽装する camouflage; 擬装爆弾 a booby trap (bomb) / 偽装網 a camouflage net.

ぎそう² 艤装 rigging ¶艤装する rig 《a ship》; fit 《a ship》 out (for sea).

ぎぞう 偽造 forgery; counterfeiting; 《文》fabrication ¶偽造する forge; counterfeit; 《文》fabricate / 偽造品 a forged [《文》spurious] article; a forgery / a counterfeit; a fake.

きそうかん 気送管 a pneumatic [dispatch] tube.

きそうほんのう 帰巣本能 the homing instinct.

きそく¹ 気息 ¶気息奄(えん)々としている gasp for breath; breathe feebly / 死にかかっている be more dead than alive; be on one's [its] last legs / 気息音 《音声》an aspirate.

きそく² 規則 a rule; a regulation ★rulesあるいは regulations と，複数形で使うことが多い ¶規則を定める make [lay down, 《文》establish] rules [regulations] / 規則を守る observe [obey] the rules; 《文》conform to the regulations / 規則に違反する，規則を破る go against [break, disobey, 《文》violate] the rules / 極めて規則的に very regularly; 《文》with great regularity / 規則正しい生活をする lead a well-regulated life; have very regular habits / 規則違反 a breach of the rules / 規則動詞 《文法》a regular verb. 文例⇩

きぞく 帰属 《復帰》reversion; return; 〈所管〉jurisdiction; 〈所属〉belonging ¶帰属する 〈復帰する〉revert 《to》; be restored 《to》; 〈所管に入る〉come under the jurisdiction 《of》; 〈所属〉belong 《to》 / 帰属意識 (a feeling of) identification 《with》; a sense of belonging / R 島の帰属問題 the question of the title to R Island.

きぞく 貴族 〈1 人〉a noble; a nobleman; a noblewoman 《女》; a peer; a peeress 《女》; 〈総称〉the nobility; the aristocracy; the peerage ¶貴族の noble; aristocratic / 貴族に列せられる be raised to the peerage [nobility] / 貴族的な aristocratic.

ぎそく 義足 an artificial leg; a wooden [《口語》peg] leg.

きそん¹ 既存 ¶既存の existing 《facilities》.

きそん² 棄損[毀]損 damage; injury ¶棄損する damage; injure; 《文》impair ⇒めいよ (名誉棄損する，名誉棄損).

きた 北 (the) north ¶北の north; northern / 北に 〈離れて北方に〉to the north 《of》; 〈境を接して〉on the north 《of》; 〈北部に〉in the north 《of》/ 東京の北にある lie (to the) north of Tokyo / 北に向かって進む go (toward the) north / 北へ (to the) north; northward / 北向きの家 a house facing north / 北回帰線 the tropic of Cancer.

ぎだ 犠打 《野球》a sacrifice hit [bunt]; a sacrifice. 文例⇩

ギター a guitar ¶ギターを弾く play the guitar / ギター奏者 a guitarist.

きたい¹ 気体 a gaseous body; (a) gas ¶気体の gaseous / 気体の分子 a gas molecule / 気体になる become [turn into] a gas.

きたい² 期待 expectation(s); anticipation; hope(s) ¶期待する hope for; expect; 〈予期する〉bargain for (通常否定文で); 〈心待ちに〉hope for; look forward to 《sth, doing》; 〈当てにする〉count on / ...を期待して in anticipation [expectation] of...; in the hope (that..., of doing) / 期待をかける put one's hopes in [on]; 《文》place [lay] one's hopes (on) / (事が)期待を裏切る，期待はずれになる 《文》run counter to one's expectation(s); fall short of one's expectations / disappoint one; let one down / 期待に添う come [measure] up to 《one's》 expectation(s). 文例⇩

きたい³ 機体 〈エンジン以外の全体〉the airframe; 〈胴体〉the body; the fuselage.

ぎたい 擬態 《生物》(biological) mimicry; mimesis ¶擬態語 《言語》a mimetic word.

ぎだい 議題 a subject [topic] for discussion ¶議題となる come [be brought] up for discussion [debate]; be placed on the agenda; be mooted.

きたえる 鍛える 〈刀剣を〉forge; temper; 〈鍛練する〉drill; train ¶身体を鍛える harden oneself [one's body] / 腕を鍛える improve one's skill; train oneself (in an art). 文例⇩

きそう¹ 奇想天外だ. It is a most unexpected [original] idea.

きそく² この学校は規則がやかましい. The rules in this school are very strict [are strictly enforced]. / 何事も規則ずくめに行くものではない. Not everything goes by rule.

きた アメリカ合衆国は北はカナダに接している. On the north, the United States of America borders on Canada.

ぎだ 彼の犠打で 2 者進塁した. His sacrifice moved both runners along.

きたい² 彼の期待ははずれた. His hopes were disappointed. / あまり彼に期待してはいけない. You must not expect too much of [from] him. / 結果は期待したほどではなかった. The result fell short of my expectations [was not as good as I had expected]. / 彼は大いに我々の期待に答えてくれた. He did just what we hoped. | He did exactly what was expected of him. / こんなにうまく行くものとは期待していなかった. We did not bargain for such a big success.

きたえる 皮膚を鍛えると，極度の寒さにも耐えることができる. Our skin can be so hardened that it can stand extreme cold.

きたきり 僕は着た切り雀だ. I've nothing to wear except the clothes I have on [I am standing up in].

きたく¹ もう間もなく帰宅すると

きたかぜ 北風 a north [northerly] wind; a wind from the north.
きたきり 着た切り
きたく¹ 帰宅 ¶帰宅する〈帰って行く〉go home;〈帰って来る〉come [return] home;〈帰りつく〉get home. 文例⊘
きたく² 寄託《文》(a) deposition;《法》bailment ⇒いたく ¶寄託する deposit *sth* with 《a bank》;《文》entrust *sb* with *sth*;《文》commit *sth* to *sb's* care.
きたぐに 北国 the northern provinces.
きたけ 丈丈 the length of one's dress.
きたす 来たす cause; bring about; lead to; give rise to; end [《文》result] in.
きたたいせいよう 北大西洋 the North Atlantic (Ocean) ¶北大西洋条約 the North Atlantic Treaty / 北大西洋条約機構 the North Atlantic Treaty Organization (略: NATO) ★ NATO は [néitou] と発音する。 「new.
きたて 来たて ¶来たての newly-arrived;
きだて 気立て《文》(a) disposition;(a) nature;(a)temperament ¶気立てのいい[悪い]good-[ill-]natured / 気立てのやさしい tender-hearted; softhearted;《a person》with a gentle disposition. 文例⊘
きたない 汚い〈不潔な〉dirty; grubby; soiled;〈卑劣な〉mean(-spirited);《文》ignoble;〈卑怯な〉foul; unfair;〈けちな〉tightfisted; stingy ¶汚い勝ち方をする win by foul play / 汚いことをする use underhand methods;《口語》play dirty /《口語》do the dirty on *sb* / 汚い手を使う use [play,《口語》pull] a mean [dirty] trick / 汚い(手を使う)やつ a mean(-minded) fellow;《口語》a (real) bastard;《英口語》a nasty piece of work. 文例⊘
きたる 来たる ¶〈次の〉next; coming; forthcoming ¶来たる20日に on the 20th (of this month) / 来たるべき総選挙 the forthcoming general election.
きたん 忌憚 ¶忌憚のない frank; outspoken; candid;《文》unreserved / 忌憚なく《文》without reserve; frankly / 忌憚なく言えば to be frank (with you); frankly speaking. 文例⊘
きだん 気団《気象》an air mass ¶寒[暖]気団 a cold [warm] air mass.
きち¹ 吉 good luck [fortune]. 文例⊘
きち² 危地 a dangerous [《口語》perilous] position; a critical situation ¶危地に陥る[を脱する] get into [out of] danger.
きち³ 既知 ¶既知の (already-)known / 既知数 a known quantity.

きち⁴ 基地 a base ¶永久[海軍, 軍事, 駐留, 燃料補給]基地 a permanent [naval, military, garrison, fueling] base.
きち⁵ 機知 wit ¶機知のひらめき a flash of wit / 機知に富む be full of wit; be witty.
きちがい 気違い〈狂気〉madness; insanity;〈狂人〉a madman; a madwoman (女); a lunatic;〈熱狂〉a mania [craze, fad] (for);〈熱狂者〉a maniac;《俗》a nut (case);《俗》a loony ¶気違いになる go [《口語》become] mad [insane]; lose *one's* head / 気違いのようになって frantically; frenziedly;《口語》like mad / 気違いじみた mad; crazy; frantic; wild / カー気違い a car maniac [《口語》nut,《俗》freak] / カメラ[写真]気違い a camera [photography] bug / 気違いざた (an act of) madness [insanity]. 文例⊘
きちきち ¶きちきちに詰まっている be closely packed 《with》; be jam-packed 《with people》/ 時間きちきちに just in time 《for the train》; on the dot;《at 3 o'clock》sharp.
きちく 鬼畜 a brute of a man ¶鬼畜のような fiendish; brutal.
きちにち 吉日 a lucky [《文》an auspicious,《文》a propitious] day.
きちゃく 帰着 ¶帰着する〈帰ってくる〉return; come back;〈けっきょく...になる〉arrive at 《a conclusion》; result [end] in; resolve *itself* into [to]; add up to; boil down to / 議論の帰着点 the logical conclusion of an argument. 文例⊘
きちゅう 忌中《表示》In Mourning.
きちょう¹ 記帳〈記入〉register; (an) entry;〈署名〉a signature ¶記帳する〈帳簿に〉register; enter up 《an item in the account book》; make an entry 《of *sth*》;〈署名する〉sign [enter] *one's* name 《in the visitors' register》/ 記帳係 an entry clerk; a bookkeeper.
きちょう² 機長 a pilot; the captain 《of the crew》.
きちょう³ 基調 the keynote; the underlying tone ¶経済の基調 the basic economic conditions (of Japan) / ...の基調をなす form the keynote of... / 基調演説 a keynote address [speech] / 基調演説をする人 a keynote speaker. 文例⊘
きちょう⁴ 貴重 ¶貴重な precious; valuable / 貴重品 an article of value;《総称》valuables.
ぎちょう 議長 the president; the chairman; the chairperson; the chairwoman (女); the Speaker (衆議院の); the President (参議院の)

思います。I expect he will be home before long.
きだて 彼女は気立てはよいが, 気がきかない。She has a good heart, but not [is naturally sweet tempered, but hasn't] much sense.
きたない その手は汚いぞ。That's a dirty trick! | That's playing dirty! / カンニングするなんて汚いやつだ。It was despicable of him to cheat in the exam.
きたん 賛成かどうか忌憚なく言っ

てくれたまえ。Tell me frankly whether you are for or against it.
きち¹ 万事上々吉だ。Everything is going very well.
きちがい 気違いでもなければそんな事はすまい。No one in his right mind would do such a thing. / そんな事をしたら気違いに刃物を持たせるようなものだ。It's like giving a loaded revolver to a lunatic. / 彼の行為は気違いじみている。His conduct

borders on insanity. / この吹雪の中を山に登るなんてまったく気違いさただ。It is sheer madness to try to climb the mountain in such a snowstorm.
きちゃく それはけっきょく金の問題に帰着する。In the end it is [resolves itself into] a question of money.
きちょう³ これが両国間の関係の基調となった。This set the tone for the relations between the

きちょうめん

¶議長になる take [be in] the chair; preside over 《a meeting》; chair 《a meeting》/ 野田氏を議長として with Mr. Noda in the chair. 文例⇩

きちょうめん 几帳面 ¶きちょうめんな 《文》 punctilious; 《文》 scrupulous; conscientious.

きちれい 吉例 ¶吉例により according to (annual) custom.

きちんと 〈正確に〉 accurately; exactly; 〈整頓して〉 neatly; tidily; 〈かっきり〉 punctually; sharp; 〈滞りなく〉 regularly; 〈きちょうめんに〉《文》 scrupulously; 《文》 punctiliously ¶(洋服などが体に)きちんと合う fit one perfectly [snugly, like a glove] / きちんと3時に just [exactly, punctually] at three (o'clock); 《口語》 on the dot of three; at three sharp [《口語》 on the dot]; きちんとする put [set] (things) right; put [set] (a room) in order; tidy (up) 《one's room》; straighten out 《one's personal affairs》; きちんとした in good order; orderly; neat; tidy ¶きちんと座る 〈背筋をのばして〉 sit straight; 〈(机などに)正面に〉 sit square (to one's desk); きちんと支払う be regular [punctual] in paying 《one's rent》; きちんと片づいた部屋 a tidy room. 文例⇩

きちんやど 木賃宿 a cheap lodging house; 《米俗》 a flophouse; 《英俗》 a dosshouse.

きつい 〈きびしい〉 severe; intense; hard; 〈窮屈な〉 tight; close; 〈勇気のある〉 brave; 《文》 courageous; 《文》 stouthearted; 〈勝気な〉 strong-minded; 〈力のある〉 strong ¶きつい顔をする look stern; frown at sb / きつい仕事 hard [heavy] work; a tough [demanding] job / 目つきのきつい男 a sharp-[hard-]eyed man. 文例⇩

きつえん 喫煙 smoking ¶喫煙する smoke; have a smoke / 喫煙室 a smoking room / 喫煙者 a smoker. 文例⇩

きつおん 吃音 ⇨ どもり.

きづかい 気遣い ⇨ しんぱい. 文例⇩

きづかう 気遣う ⇨ しんぱい(心配する) ¶…を気遣って for fear of (making mistakes); in fear of (attack by the press) / 気遣わしげに anxiously; with anxious looks. 文例⇩

きっかけ 〈機会〉 a chance; an opportunity; 〈手はじめ〉 a start; a beginning; 〈芝居の〉 a cue ¶…をきっかけに taking advantage of…; with (this) as a start / きっかけをつかむ seize an opportunity (to do, of doing). 文例⇩

きっかり exactly; precisely; just; sharp ¶5時きっかりに exactly at five o'clock; at five sharp; 《口語》 on the dot of five / きっかり1万円 exactly [just] 10,000 yen.

きづかれ 気疲れ 《文》 mental fatigue; worry ¶気疲れする 《文》 be mentally fatigued; suffer from nervous strain.

きっきょう 吉凶 good or bad [《文》 ill] luck; fortune ¶吉凶を占う tell sb's fortune; 《文》 read good omens or bad (from natural phenomena). 文例⇩

キック a kick ¶キックする kick 《the ball》/ キックオフ 《フットボール》 a kickoff / キックボクシング kick boxing.

きづく 気付く notice; 《文》 take notice (of sth); become aware (of sth, that…); 《文》 perceive; realize (that…); find (out); 〈感づく〉 sense; suspect ¶人に気づかれずに without being noticed by anyone; (come in) unnoticed; without attracting anyone's attention. 文例⇩

ぎっくりごし ぎっくり腰 (have) a strained back.

きつけ 着付け ¶着付けをしてやる dress 《a girl》 ¶手伝って help sb get dressed; 着付け室 〈洋服売場の〉 a fitting room [booth].

-きづけ …気付 care of (略: c/o)… ¶研究社気付 青木様 Mr. Aoki, c/o Kenkyusha. 文例⇩

きつけ(ぐすり) 気付け(薬) a stimulant; a tonic; 《文》 a restorative.

きっさき 切っ先 the point [tip] (of a sword).

きっさてん 喫茶店 a tearoom; a coffee shop; a café.

ぎっしり close(ly); tight(ly); fully ¶ぎっしり詰まっている be closely packed (with); be cram-full [crammed full] (of notes); 〈劇場などに人で〉 be crowded to capacity / ぎっしり詰まったスケジュール a full [crammed] sched-ule.

キッス ⇨ キス.

きっすい¹ 生粋 ¶生粋のtrueborn; dyed-in-the-wool; pure; genuine / 生粋のアメリカ人 a natural-born American citizen; a one-hundred-percent American. 文例⇩

---

two countries.

ぎちょう 議長! 〈呼び掛け〉 Mr. Chairman!

きちんと 出掛ける前に机の上をきちんと片づけておきなさい。 Put your desk in order [Tidy your desk properly] before you go out, will you?

きつい これまで彼女にきついことを言ったことはない。 I have never spoken a harsh word to her. | この靴はきつ過ぎる。 These shoes are too tight. | These shoes pinch. / その仕事は彼には少々きつ過ぎないか。 Isn't the work [job] a bit too hard [tough] for him?

きつえん この病気には喫煙の習慣のある人の方がはるかにかかりやすいのです。 Habitual smokers are far more likely to contract this disease.

きづかい この企てが失敗する気遣いはありません。 There is no danger [You needn't worry] that this scheme will fail [go wrong].

きづかう 彼の病気は気遣うほどのものではありません。 His illness is nothing serious [to worry about]. / 彼が回復するかどうか気遣わしい。 I am afraid he may not recover. / 母親のことが気遣われてならなかった。 The thought of his mother lay heavy on his heart.

きっかけ 話し出すのによいきっかけだった。 It was a good chance to broach [bring up] the matter.

きっきょう 昔の人は獣骨を焼いて吉凶を占った。 Ancient people baked bones of animals to divine whether fortune would be good or bad.

きづく 間もなく自分の間違いに気づいた。 It wasn't long before I realized that I had been wrong. / だってベッドの下をみることに気づかなかったんですもの。 It was because it didn't [It just didn't] occur to me to look under the bed. / 当店のサービスでお気づき

きっすい² 喫[吃]水 《米》draft;《英》draught ¶喫水の深い[浅い]船 a deep-[light-, shallow-]draft ship / 喫水 17 フィートの船 a ship of 17 feet draft; a ship which draws 17 feet / 喫水線 a waterline / 満載喫水線 the load (water-)line. 文例⇩

きっする 喫する〈飲む・食う〉⇨のむ，くう²;〈受ける・被る〉suffer ¶惨敗を喫する suffer [《文》sustain] a crushing defeat.

きづた 木蔦 《植》(an) ivy.

きづち 木槌 a wooden hammer; a mallet.

ぎっちょ ⇨ひだり(左利きの人).

きっちょう 吉兆 a good [lucky] omen;《文》happy augury.

きっちり exactly; perfectly;〈堅く〉tight(ly); closely;〈時間が〉punctually; sharp; just ¶きっちり1時間 exactly (just) an hour /〈服などが〉きっちり合う fit one like a glove [to a T] / きっちりふたをする cover sth tight(-ly); keep sth tightly covered. 文例⇩

きつつき《鳥》a woodpecker.

きって 切手 a (postage) stamp ¶60円の切手 a sixty-yen stamp / 切手を張る stamp (a letter); put a stamp on (an envelope) / 切手を張り宛名を書いた封筒 a stamped and addressed envelope / 切手アルバム a stamp album / 切手収集 stamp-collecting; philately / 切手収集家 a stamp collector; a philatelist. 文例⇩

-きっての ¶社内きっての敏腕家 the ablest man in the whole office / 日本の財界きっての大立者 the most influential of all Japanese financiers.

きっと¹〈間違いなく〉surely; certainly; undoubtedly; without fail; must《be, have done》. 文例⇩

きっと²〈けわしい顔つきになって〉sharply; sternly ¶きっとなる straighten oneself; straighten one's face; look stern / きっとなってにらみつける cast a sharp [hard] glance (at).

キッド kid ¶キッドの靴 kid shoes.

きつね 狐《動》a fox; a vixen (雌) ¶きつねの毛皮 (a) fox fur / きつねの襟巻 a fox-fur muffler / きつねの嫁入り a shower when the sun is shining / きつねにばかされる [つかれる] be bewitched [possessed] by a fox / きつ ねにつままれたように with a look of utter amazement; with a flabbergasted look / きつね色にこんがりと焼く do sth to a beautiful brown; brown sth lightly《over a fire》/ きつねつき a person possessed by a fox [an evil spirit] / きつね火 a will-o'-the-wisp; a jack-o'-lantern.

きつねざる《動》a lemur.

きっぱり〈はっきり〉clearly; distinctly;〈断固として〉positively; decidedly ¶きっぱりした返事 a definite reply / きっぱり断わる refuse flatly [outright, once (and) for all]; give a flat refusal;《文》decline positively. 文例⇩

きっぷ¹ 切符 a ticket; a coupon (ticket)《切り取り式の》¶切符を買う buy [get] a ticket《for Osaka, to a theater》/ 切符を買う人の行列 a ticket line《英》queue] / 切符を切るpunch [clip] a ticket / 切符売場 a ticket office [《米》cage];《英》a booking office; a box office (劇場の).

きっぷ² 気風 ⇨きふう¹, きまえ ¶気風のいい男 a generous [an openhearted, a big-hearted] man;《口語》a great [《米》regular] guy.

きっぽう 吉報 good news;《文》joyful [glad] tidings. 文例⇩

きづまり 気詰まり ¶気詰まりである feel ill at ease.

きつもん 詰問 close questioning; a searching inquiry; cross-examination ¶詰問する examine [question] sb closely; demand (an explanation》 from [《文》of] sb; cross-examine sb.

きづよい 気強い reassuring; encouraging ⇨こころよい.

きてい¹ 既定 ¶既定の established; fixed / 既定方針どおりに according to the prearranged plan [program].

きてい² 規定〈規則〉regulations; rules ⇨きく²;〈条項〉provisions ¶規定する《文》prescribe; provide《《文》stipulate》(that...) / 規定の《文》prescribed; regular;〈制定の〉regulation (fare) / 規定に従って according to [《文》in conformity with] the rules / (体操競技の)規定種目 compulsory exercises / (病人などの)規定食 a (prescribed) diet / (飛び込み競技の)規定飛び込み compulsory [required] dives. 文例⇩

の点は何なりとお聞かせ下さい。『掲示』 Any comments regarding our service will be welcomed.

-きづけ 武蔵大学気付で手紙をくれたえい。Write (to) me care of Musashi University.

ぎっしり スタンドは観客でぎっしりだった。The stands were crowded.[The stands were solidly filled] with spectators. /本箱には本がぎっしり詰まっていた。The bookcase was packed with books.

きっすい¹ 彼は生粋の東京人です。He is a true Tokyoite. | He was born and bred in Tokyo.

きっすい² この船は喫水が深い[浅 い]. This boat has a deep [shallow] draft. | This boat draws a lot of [does not draw much] water.

きっちり あの時計はきっちり合っています。That clock is exactly right.

きって 60円切手を3枚下さい。(Give me) three 60-yen stamps, please. / この手紙はいくらの切手をはればいいですか。What is the postage on this letter? / あの手紙は切手が不足だったかもしれない。I'm afraid I have understamped the letter.

きっと¹ きっとそうだよ。Are you sure? / あの男はきっとあのパチンコ屋にいるよ。I'll bet he's [I'm sure you will find him] in that pachinko parlor. / きっと電池がきれてるんだろう。The battery must be dead.

きっぱり 君はきっぱり決めなさっちゃいけない。You must make up your mind once (and) for all.

きっぷ¹ 切符のない方は入場できません。『掲示』 Admission by ticket only.

きっぽう 君に吉報をもってきたよ。I have some (very) good news for you.

きてい² 生徒は全部寄宿舎へ入る

きてい[3] 基底 a base; a foundation ⇨きばん, きほん.

ぎてい 義弟 a brother-in-law 《*pl.* brothers-》.

ぎていしょ 議定書 a protocol.

きてき 汽笛 a (steam) whistle; 《英》 a hooter; a siren ¶工場の汽笛 a factory whistle; 《英》 a hooter / 汽笛を鳴らす sound [blow, give] a whistle; whistle. [文例⇩]

きてん[1] 機[気]転 quick-wittedness ¶機転がきく[きかない] be quick-[dull-]witted; have the sense (enough) [lack the sense] to *do* / とっさの機転で using *one's* brains quickly.

きてん[2] 起[基]点 〈鉄道の〉 the railhead; 〈距離測量の〉 the starting [base] point ¶日本橋を基点として距離を測る measure the distance with Nihonbashi as (the) starting point. [文例⇩]

ぎてん 疑点 a doubtful point; a doubt; 〈問題点〉 a moot point [question].

きでんりょく 起電力 electromotive force (略: E.M.F., e.m.f.).

きと[1] 企図 ⇨くわだて.

きと[2] 帰途 ¶帰途に on *one's* way home [back]; 〈旅行の〉 on *one's* return trip / 帰途につく leave [start] for home; start on *one's* way home.

きど 木戸 〈小門〉 a wicket (gate); 〈入口〉 a gate; a door ¶木戸御免である have a free pass 《to a theater》; be on the free list 《of a theater》 / 木戸銭 ⇨にゅうじょう[2] (入場料).

きどあいらく 喜怒哀楽 ¶喜怒哀楽を顔に表わさない do not betray *one's* feelings [emotions].

きとう[1] 気筒 〘機〙 a (steam) cylinder ¶6気筒エンジン a 6-cylinder(ed) engine.

きとう[2] 祈禱 a prayer; grace (食前の) ⇨いのり ¶祈禱する pray 《for》; say *one's* prayers; 〈食前に〉 say grace / 祈禱会 a prayer meeting / 祈禱師 a shaman; an exorcist (悪魔ばらいの) / 祈禱書 a prayer book; 〈英国教会または同系統教会の〉 The Book of Common Prayer.

きとう[3] 亀頭 〘解〙 the glans (of the penis).

きどう[1] 軌道 〈天体·人工衛星の〉 an orbit; an orbiting [orbital] path; 〈線路〉 a (railroad) track ⇨せんろ ¶地球を回る人工衛星の軌道 the orbit of a [an artificial] satellite around the earth / 地球の周囲を軌道を描いて回転している衛星 a satellite orbiting (around) the earth; an earth-orbiting satellite / (逆推進ロケットで) 軌道を離脱する leave [go out of] (*its*) orbit / 軌道に乗る 〈人工衛星などが〉 go into [《文》 achieve] orbit; 〈仕事などが〉 be [get] started along the right lines; get going / 軌道に乗っている 〈人工衛星などが〉 be in orbit; 〈仕事などが〉 be well under way; be a going concern / 軌道に乗せる 〈人工衛星などを〉 put [《文》 place] 《a satellite》 in [into] orbit; orbit 《a satellite》; 〈仕事などを〉 set 《a business corporation》 on 《its》 way / 人工衛星を打ち上げて軌道に乗せる launch [lift] a satellite into orbit / 楕円[真円]軌道 an elliptical [a circular] orbit / 同期[惑星間]軌道 a synchronous [an interplanetary] orbit / 軌道速度 orbital speed [velocity] / (宇宙船の) 軌道飛行 an orbital flight. [文例⇩]

きどう[2] 機動 ¶機動性 mobility; maneuverability / (警察)機動隊 the riot police; 〈その一隊〉 a riot squad 《of Kyoto Prefectural Police》 / 機動隊員 a riot policeman / 機動部隊 a mechanized unit; 〈特殊任務を持った〉 a task force / 機動力 mobile power.

きどうこう 輝銅鉱 chalcocite.

きどうらく 着道楽 love of finery [fine clothes].

きとく[1] 危篤 ¶危篤である be dangerously [critically] ill; be in a critical condition; 〈入院患者が〉 be on the danger [critical] list / 危篤に陥る 〈人が主語〉 fall into a critical condition; 〈病気が主語〉 take a critical turn. [文例⇩]

きとく[2] 奇特 ¶奇特な 〈感心な〉 《文》 praiseworthy; 《文》 commendable; 《文》 laudable; 〈公共心のある〉 public-spirited / 奇特な寄進者 a pious benefactor.

きとくけん 既得権 〈権利〉 vested rights; 〈権益〉 vested interests.

きどり 気取り affectation; posturing ¶気取りが少しもない be not at all [not in the least] affected; be quite without [free from] affectation / 夫婦気取りでいる[暮らす] behave as [live together like] man and wife / 気取り屋 an affected person; 〈しゃれ者〉 a dandy.

きどる 気取る 〈重々しい様子をする〉 give *oneself* [put on] airs; 〈…ぶる〉 pose as 《a lady》; 《文》 affect 《the hero》; pretend to be 《a scholar》 ¶気取った affected / 気取らない unaffected; free from affectation; unassuming / 気取って歩く walk in a prim, affected way [manner]; walk with mincing steps [in a

---

規定になっている. The rule is that all students should live in the dormitory. / 第10条及び11条の規定は次の場合にはこれを適用しない. The provisions of Articles 10 and 11 shall not apply in the following cases.

きてき 汽笛が鳴っている. The whistle is blowing. | There goes the whistle. / 汽笛一声新橋駅を出た. The train pulled out of Shinbashi Station with a whistle.

きてん[2] 本線は郡山を起点として新津に至る. This line starts at Koriyama and ends [terminates] at Niitsu.

きどう[1] 地球は約365日と1/4で軌道を一周する. The earth completes its orbit in about 365 1/4 days. / ソ連の宇宙飛行士チトフはボストーク2号に乗って地球を回る軌道を17周した. The Russian cosmonaut Titov made seventeen orbits [made a seventeen-orbit flight] around the earth in Vostok II. / ロケットは軌道に乗せるために必要な秒速7,600メートルに加速された. The rocket was accelerated to its orbital velocity of 7,600 meters per second. / 日本の民主主義も軌道に乗ってきた. Democracy has come to stay in Japan. / うちの会社もようやく軌道に乗ってきた. We can now safely say that our firm is a going concern.

きとく[1] 母危篤の電報を受け取り, 急いで帰郷した. I received a

きどるい 希土類 《化》 ¶希土類元素 a rare-earth element [metal].

きない 機内 ¶機内で in [inside] an airplane / 機内食 a meal served on a plane; an in-flight meal.

きなが 気長 ¶気長な slowgoing; leisurely; patient / 気長に patiently; with patience; 《文》without haste / 気長にやる do *sth* slowly [in a leisurely fashion]; take *one's* time (in *doing*, over *sth*); go [take it] easy.

きながし 着流し ¶着流しで in *kimono* with no *hakama* on; in *one's* everyday clothes.

きなくさい きな臭い〈人が主語〉smell smoke; smell something smoldering [burning]. 文例⬇

きなこ 黄な粉 soybean flour.

きなん 危難 (a) danger; 《文》(a) peril; 〈遭難〉distress ⇒きけん[1].

ギニア Guinea ¶ギニアの Guinean / ギニア人 a Guinean / ギニア人民革命共和国 the People's Revolutionary Republic of Guinea / ギニアビサウ共和国 the Republic of Guinea-Bissau / 赤道ギニア共和国 the Republic of Equatorial Guinea.

キニーネ quinine.

きにゅう 記入 (an) entry ¶記入する enter (*one's* name in the list); make an entry (of an item in a ledger); fill in (the form) / 記入漏れ an omission. 文例⬇

きにん 帰任 ¶帰任する return [go back, come back] to *one's* post.

きぬ 絹 silk ¶絹の silk (stockings); made of silk /絹のような silky (texture); 《文》silken (hair) /絹の道《史》the Silk Road [Route] / 絹を裂くような声 a piercing cry; a scream; a shriek /絹糸〈縫い糸〉silk thread;〈織物用〉silk yarn /絹織物 silk goods; silk(s) /絹地 silk cloth [stuff, fabrics]; silk /絹商人 a silk merchant /絹張りの洋傘 a silk umbrella / 絹物を着ている be dressed in silk.

きぬけ 気抜け ⇒ほうしん², き³(気が抜ける) ¶気抜けしたように〈茫然と〉absent-mindedly;〈しょんぼりと〉dejectedly.

きぬずれ 衣擦れ ¶衣擦れの音 the rustle [rustling, swishing] of *one's* dress [skirts] / 衣擦れの音をさせて歩く rustle (along).

きね 杵 a pestle; a pounder ¶杵でつく pound (rice) with a pestle; crush (grains) with a pounder.

きねづか 杵柄 ¶昔とったきねづかで using

**[《文》] utilizing *one's* experience from the past.

きねん 記念 commemoration ¶記念する commemorate /記念の commemorative; memorial /記念に in memory [《文》commemoration] (of); to commemorate;〈形見に〉as a token [keepsake] /記念館 a memorial hall / 記念切手 a commemorative stamp /記念号 a commemoration number; a special number issued in memory of (the late Prof. Kozu) / 記念祭 a commemoration; an anniversary / 記念写真 a souvenir [commemorative] picture [photograph] /記念樹 a memorial tree /記念出版 a commemorative publication /記念碑 a monument; a cenotaph (死者のための) / 記念碑的な monumental /記念日 a memorial [commemoration] day; an anniversary /記念品 a souvenir; a memento (*pl.* -(e)s); a keepsake (形見) /記念論文集 essays (contributed) in celebration of (the 10th anniversary of…); a festschrift. 文例⬇

きねん 疑念 doubt; (a) suspicion; misgivings (不安) ⇒うたがう田園.

きのう¹ 昨日 yesterday ¶先週の昨日 a week ago yesterday /〈主に英〉yesterday week / 昨日の朝[午後] yesterday morning [afternoon] / 昨日の晩 yesterday [last] evening; last night ⇒よる¹ ★ ¶昨日の新聞 yesterday's paper. 文例⬇

きのう² 帰納 《論》induction ¶帰納する make an induction (from the facts) /帰納的に inductively /帰納的推理 inductive reasoning / 帰納法 induction; the inductive method.

きのう³ 機能 a function;《文》a faculty ¶機能する function; work /機能を発揮する fulfill *one's* [*its*] function /機能的 functional / 機能的疾患 a functional disease /機能訓練 functional training /機能検査 a functional test /機能主義 functionalism /機能障害 a functional disorder /機能低下[不全] (a) malfunction.

きのう 技能 (technical) skill;〈能力〉ability ¶技能がすぐれている be highly skilled (in) / 技能のある skilled; able /技能をみがく improve *one's* skill /技能オリンピック the International Vocational Training Competition /技能賞《相撲》the technique award.

きのこ 茸 a mushroom; a toadstool (有毒な) ¶きのこ取りに行く go out to gather [hunt] mushrooms (in the woods); go mushrooming

---

telegram informing me of my mother's critical condition, and hurried home. /父危篤すぐ帰れ.〈電文〉Father critical return immediately.

きどる そんなに気取るなよ. Don't give yourself such airs. /彼は鼻もちならぬ気取ったやつだ. I can't stand his affected manners.

きない 機長が機内放送を通じて乗客に飛行位置を告げた. The captain told the passengers over the aircraft's P.A. system where they were flying.

きなくさい きな臭いぞ. There's a smell of something smoldering. / きな臭くなってきた. There are signs of the approach of war. | The threat [danger] of war is growing.

きにゅう 記入済み.〈表示〉"Entered."

きねん 記念に写真を撮ろうじゃないか. Let's have our photograph taken to commemorate this occasion. / わが校は昨日創立60周年記念祭を行なった. Our school celebrated the 60th anniversary of its foundation yesterday.

きのう¹ 僕がこの学校へ入ってからもう3年になる. まだほんの昨日のように思っているのだ. It is already three years since I entered this school, but it seems like only yesterday. /それは昨日今日の事ではない. That isn't something that happened yesterday. |《文》That is by no means a matter of recent occurrence. /

《in the woods》/ (原爆の)きのこ雲 a mushroom cloud. 文例⇩

きのどく 気の毒 ¶気の毒な unfortunate 《people》; 《口語》poor (Mr. Smith); 《文》pitiable 《wretches》 ¶気の毒がる[に思う] feel [be] sorry (for *sb*); pity ★人を「気の毒」に思う気持を表わすには, 英語では名詞 (people, Mr. Smith) の前に poor をつけた形で表わすのが最も普通. 例:「お気の毒にスミスさんは…」(Poor Mr. Smith...) ⇒ どうじょう 用法. 文例⇩

きのぼり 木登り ¶木登りをする climb (up) a tree / 木登り魚 a climbing perch; a walking fish. 文例⇩

きのみ 木の実 ⇒ このみ¹

きのみきのままで 着のみ着のままで with only the clothes *one* happens to be wearing; without anything but what [the clothes] *one* stands up in. 文例⇩

きのめ 木の芽 〈木の新芽〉a (leaf) bud; 〈さんしょうの芽〉a leaf bud of Japanese pepper ¶木の芽時 the budding season / 木の芽楽(がく) bean curd baked and spread with *miso* and pepper leaf buds.

きのり 気乗り ¶気乗りする take an interest [be interested] 《in *sth*》; feel inclined to *do*; feel like *doing*; be willing to *do*; 〈熱中する〉get 《文》become] enthusiastic 《over, about, for》; warm up 《to *one's* work》/ 気乗りがしない do not take interest 《in》; 《文》take little interest 《in》; have no inclination to *do*; be reluctant to *do*; be in no mood to *do*.

きば¹ 牙 a tusk 《象・いのししなどの》; a fang 《犬・おおかみなどの》 ¶きばをむく snarl 《at》/ きばにかける, きばをたてる fang; strike *its* tusks [fangs] 《into》.

きば² 木場 a lumberyard.

きば³ 騎馬 ¶騎馬巡査 a mounted policeman / 騎馬戦 《play》a mock cavalry battle / 騎馬民族 an equestrian [a nomadic] people.

きはく¹ 気迫 ¶気迫がある[ない] be full of [have no, 《文》be lacking in] spirit.

きはく² 希薄 ¶希薄な 〈薄い〉thin; weak; 〈水などで薄めた〉dilute(d); 〈気体が〉rarefied; 〈くまれな〉rare; 〈希少の〉thin; sparse / 高山の希薄な空気 the rarefied air of the high mountains / 人口の希薄な地域 a sparsely [thinly] populated [《文》peopled] area / 希薄にする thin 《a liquid》; rarefy 《a gas》; dilute 《a solution》; attenuate 《a liquid》. 文例⇩

きばく 起爆 ¶起爆装置 a triggering device 《for a nuclear blast》; a detonator / 起爆剤 the initial explosive; a detonator / 起爆剤となる〈事が主語〉trigger 《a revolution》.

きばこ 木箱 a wooden box [chest].

きはつ 揮発 ¶揮発する[させる] volatilize / 揮発しやすい, 揮発性の volatile / 揮発油 volatile oil(s); benzine (ベンジン); naphtha (ナフサ).

きばつ 奇抜 ¶奇抜な original; unconventional; novel. 文例⇩

きばむ 黄ばむ grow yellowish; be tinged with yellow ¶黄ばんだ yellowish; sallow(顔色など).

きばらし 気晴らし (a) pastime; (a) diversion; (a) recreation ¶気晴らしをする divert *oneself*; take *one's* mind off *one's* troubles [worries, work]; amuse *oneself*.

きばる 気張る 〈努力する〉exert [strain] *oneself*; make an effort 《to *do*》; 〈はずむ・おごる〉treat *oneself* to *sth*; 《口語》splurge on 《an expensive meal》; 《英口語》lash out on 《a new dress》; give 《a generous tip》/ 大いに気張ってスポーツカーを買う splurge on [《文》allow *oneself* an extravagance and buy] a sports car. 文例⇩

きはん 規範 〈手本〉a model; an example; 〈判断などの規準〉a standard; 《文》a criterion 《*pl.* -ria》; 《文》a norm ¶規範的 normative / 規範文法 normative [prescriptive] grammar.

きばん 基盤 a base; a basis 《*pl.* bases》; a foundation ¶しっかりした基盤の上に置く put 《the finances of a college》on a firm basis / …を基盤とする be based [founded] on… 文例⇩

きはんせん 機帆船 a motor-powered sailing vessel; a motor sailing vessel; a motor sailer.

きひ 忌避 〈徴兵などの〉evasion; 〈法律上の〉a challenge ¶忌避する 〈避ける〉evade; avoid; shun; 〈裁判官などを〉challenge 《the judge》.

きび¹ 黍 〔植〕millet ¶きび団子 a millet dumpling

昨日の敵は今日の友. Yesterday's enemy is today's ally.

きのこ 私はきのこの栽培をやっています. I'm a mushroom grower.

きのどく それはお気の毒ですね. I'm sorry to hear that. / まあお気の毒な. What a pity! / That's too bad! |〈相手に対して〉Poor you! / You poor thing! / お気の毒ですがご依頼に応じかねます. I'm sorry I can't oblige you. |《文》I regret to say that I cannot comply with your request. / 気の毒に思って5千円貸してやった. I took pity on him and lent him ¥5,000.

きのぼり これらの動物は皆木登りが上手である. These animals are all good tree climbers.

きのみきのままで 私どもは着のみ着のままで焼け出されました. We escaped from the scene of the fire, dressed just as we were, unable to save anything from the flames.

きはく² 高山では平地より空気が希薄だ. The air is thinner [more rarefied] on the mountains than on the plains.

きばつ 何か奇抜な趣向で人をあっと言わしてやりたいものだ. What I want is some original idea to set people back on their heels.

きばらし 東京に行けば気晴らしにはこと欠かない. You'll find plenty in Tokyo to divert you [take your mind off your troubles].

きばる もう5万円気張れば最新型のが買えるのに. If you paid 50,000 yen more, you could get the latest model.

きばん これが彼らの生活の基盤になっている. This forms the basis of their livelihood. / 両国の首脳は, 懸案解決のための共通の基盤を求めるために, なお一層の努力

きび² 機微 secrets; inner workings ¶人情の機微に通じている have a keen insight into human nature.

きびき 忌引 absence from work [school] due to mourning ¶学校を忌引する absent oneself from school on account of a death in one's family.

きびきび ¶きびきびした〈動作の〉energetic; brisk; lively;《口語》zippy;〈言動の〉crisp; pithy; vigorous ¶きびきびしたしゃべり方 a crisp manner of speaking / きびきびした文章 a crisp style. 文例⇩

きびしい 厳(酷)しい severe;〈厳格な〉strict; rigid;〈苛酷な〉harsh; hard;〈容赦ない〉unsparing; relentless;〈激烈な〉intense ¶きびしい師匠 a hard master / きびしい先生 a stern teacher / きびしい暑さ intense heat / きびしい寒さ severe cold / きびしく severely;〈厳格に〉strictly; rigidly;〈細かに〉closely / きびしく促成する press sb hard for sth / きびしく罰する punish sb severely / きびしさ severity; intensity; sternness. 文例⇩

きびす 踵 the heel ¶きびすを返す[めぐらす] turn back; retrace one's steps / きびすを接して《follow》(hot [hard]) on the heels of…;《occur》one after another in quick succession.

きびたき 【鳥】 a narcissus flycatcher.

きひつ 偽筆〈書〉forged handwriting;〈画〉a forged picture ¶偽筆の forged; counterfeit.

きびゅうほう 帰謬法【論】《ラテン語》 reductio ad absurdum ¶帰謬法で証明する prove sth by reductio ad absurdum.

きびょう 奇病 a strange disease [case].

きひん¹ 気品《文》dignity;《文》grace; elegance; refinement ¶気品のある dignified;《文》graceful; elegant; refined. 文例⇩

きひん² 貴賓 a distinguished [《文》an honored] guest; a guest of honor ¶貴賓席 seats reserved for distinguished guests;〈皇族のための〉a royal box.

きびん 機敏 ¶機敏な〈心の働きが〉smart; shrewd;〈動作が〉quick; prompt ¶機敏な商人 a shrewd man of business / 動作が機敏である be quick [agile] in one's movements.

きふ¹ 寄付 (a) contribution; (a) donation ¶寄付する contribute 《1,000 yen to the community chest》; subscribe 《a large amount of money to a fund》; donate 《10 million yen to a school》; make a donation [gift] 《of 100 dollars to a hospital》/ 寄付を募る raise subscriptions; collect contributions / 寄付金 a contribution; a donation; a gift of money / 寄付者 a donor; a contributor; a subscriber. 文例⇩

きふ² 棋譜 the record of a game of go [shogi].

きぶ 基部 the base; the foundation; the basal part 《of a column》.

きふ 義父 a father-in-law 《pl. fathers-》.

きふう¹ 気風〈個人の〉character;《文》(a) disposition; (a) temperament;〈社会の〉《文》(an) ethos;《精神》spirit;〈特性〉《文》traits; characteristics.

きふう² 棋風 one's way [style] of playing go [shogi].

きふく 起伏 ups and downs;《文》undulations ¶起伏する rise and fall; roll;《文》undulate / ゆるやかに起伏する山々 gently undulating hills / 起伏のある平野 an undulating [a rolling] plain / 起伏の多い生涯 a life full of ups and downs. 文例⇩

きぶくれ 着膨れ ¶着ぶくれする be thickly dressed [《文》clad]; bundle oneself up (in heavy warm clothing) / 着ぶくれラッシュ the rush-hour congestion made worse by people's thick winter clothes.

きふじん 貴婦人 a (titled) lady; a noblewoman ¶貴婦人らしい ladylike 《manners》.

ギプス [<《ドイツ語》*Gips*=gypsum] a (plaster) cast ¶ギプスをはめる〈自分が〉be in plaster [a plaster cast]; wear [have 《one's leg》 in] a (plaster) cast;〈人に〉put 《sb's leg》 in plaster [a plaster cast] / ギプスをはめた子供 a child in plaster [a cast].

きぶつ 器物〈容器〉a vessel;〈器具〉a utensil;〈家具〉furniture.

キブツ 〈イスラエルの集団農場〉 a kibbutz 《pl. -butzim》.

きふほう 記譜法【音楽】musical notation.

きふるし 着古し old [used, worn-out, cast-off] clothes. 文例⇩

キプロス Cyprus ¶キプロスの Cypriot(e) / キプロス共和国 the Republic of Cyprus / キプロス人 a Cypriot(e).

きぶん 気分〈気持ち〉(a) feeling;《文》(a)

をすることを約束した. The prime ministers of the two countries pledged further efforts to search for common ground that could lead to a solution of the long-pending issues between them.

きびきび あの人の言うことはきびきびしている.〈話し方が〉He has a crisp way of speaking. ｜ 〈話の内容が〉What he says is always terse and to the point.

きびしい 彼は生徒にはとてもきびしいそうだ. I hear he is very strict with his pupils. / その学校では生徒に対する監督がきびしい. That school exerts rigorous discipline over its students. / 君はきびし過ぎる. You are too hard on [too demanding with] him. / 規則が最近きびしくなった. The regulations have been tightened up [have been made more rigorous] recently. ｜ このような北国での生活環境はきびしいものだ. Living conditions are harsh in these northern districts.

きひん¹ 彼女にはどことなく気品がある. There is something refined about her. /《口語》She's got real class. / この絵は気品に乏しい. The painting is lacking in grace.

きふ¹ 彼はその施設へ100万円寄付した. He made a donation of one million yen to that institution. / 社殿の修理の費用にご寄付を願います. Please give something toward the fund for repairing the shrine.

きふく 海運業は起伏の波の大きい事業である. The merchant marine is a highly cyclical [a boom and slump] industry.

きふるし これはおやじの着古しをもらったのだ. This is an old suit of my father's. ｜ This is a hand-me-down [《英》reach-me-down] from my father.

ぎふん sentiment ; a mood ; 《雰囲気》 an atmosphere ¶気分がいい feel good [well, all right]；《前よりも》feel better / 気分が悪い［すぐれない］do not feel well [good]; feel ill [bad, 《口語》poorly, 《文》unwell]; 《口語》feel rotten (ひどく); feel sick (★主に吐き気がする時にいう) / お祭り気分で in a festive mood / その時の気分次第で according to the mood of [to how one feels at] the moment / 気分を出す create an atmosphere 《suitable to the occasion》/ 気分を転換する divert *oneself* / 気分転換をして for recreation; for a change / 気分屋 a moody [temperamental] person; a man [《文》creature] of moods. 文例⇩

ぎふん 義憤 《文》righteous indignation ¶義憤を感じる *one's* blood boils with righteous indignation (at, over, about); 〈事が主語〉 offend *one's* sense of justice.

きへい 騎兵 a cavalryman; a trooper; cavalry (総称).

きへき 奇癖 a strange [an eccentric] habit.

きべん 奇［詭］弁 《文》sophistry; 《文》(a) sophism ¶奇弁をろうする use [employ] sophistry [sophisms]; chop logic 《with *sb*》/ 奇弁家 a sophist.

きぼ 規模 (a) scale ¶大［小］規模な large-[small-]scale 《undertakings》;《business》on a large [small] scale;《文》《a project》of large [small] dimensions / 大［小］規模に on a large [small] scale; in a large [small] way / 規模を拡大［縮小］する enlarge [reduce] the scale 《of》/ 世界的規模で on a world [global] scale. 文例⇩

ぎぼ 義母 a mother-in-law (*pl.* mothers-).

きほう¹ 気泡 ⇨ あわ¹.

きほう² 気胞 〈魚の〉an air [a swimming] bladder; a (fish) sound; 〈植物の〉an air vesicle.

きほう³ 既報 ¶既報のとおり《文》as previously [already] reported [announced].

きぼう 希望〈望み〉(a) hope;〈願望〉(a) wish;《文》(a) desire;〈抱負〉《文》(an) aspiration; (an) ambition;〈期待〉expectation(s);〈要求〉(a) request; a demand ¶希望する hope (to do, that...); hope for *sth*; wish (to do, to do); 《文》desire (*sth*, to do);《文》aspire to [after] *sth*;〈期待する〉expect / 希望どおりに〈自分の〉as *one* wishes [wished];〈相手の〉《文》as requested;〈相手の〉《文》at *sb's* request / 希望のない hopeless / ...の希望を抱いて in [with] the hope of doing [that...] / 希望を達する *one's* wish is granted;《文》realize [gratify] *one's* wishes;《文》attain *one's* desires / 希望を述べる express the hope (that...);《文》lay *one's* wish before *sb* / 希望を掛ける lay [hang, fasten] *one's* hope(s) on *sb* [*sth*] / 希望を捨てる despair 《of *sth* [doing]》; give up 《all》hope / 希望に満ちて［燃えて］いる be hopeful; be full of hope / 希望に応じる［添う］《文》do [go along with] what *sb* wants;《文》meet *sb's* wishes / 希望に生きる live in hope(s) / 希望に反して against [contrary to] *one's* wishes / メーカーの希望価格 a maker's recommended price (略: MRP) / 希望者 a person who wants [《文》desires, wishes] to do;〈志願者〉an applicant; a candidate / 入会希望者 an applicant [a candidate] for membership / 希望条件《文》the terms desired / 希望的観測 wishful thinking. 文例⇩

囲みhope は少なくとも主観的には 実現可能と思える事柄を，期待をこめて願望している時に用いられるのに対して，wish の方は事柄の可能性とは無関係に，または実現不可能と思える事でも，そうあって欲しいと思う時に用いられる．desire は wish より強い欲求を表わす．なお hope の後に that-clause が続く場合は wish の場合と異なって直説法が用いられる．

ぎほう 技法 (a) technique ¶技法上の問題 technical problems.

きぼうほう 喜望峰 the Cape of Good Hope.

ぎぼし 擬宝珠〈手すりや欄干の飾〉an ornamental cap 《on a bridge post》; an onion-shaped ornament 《on the railings》;〈ゆり科の多年生植物〉a hosta.

きぼね 気骨 ¶気骨が折れる be a great strain on *one's* mind; be tiresome; be irksome.

きぼり 木彫り wood carving; a wood carving (作品);〈木版などの〉wood engraving; a wood

---

きぶん 今日はご気分はいかがですか．How do you feel today? / 今日は何となく気分がすぐれない．I don't feel good [well] today. / 彼女はひどく疲れていて，ダンスをしようという気分ではなかった．She was so tired that she was in no mood for dancing. / 戸外へ一歩出てみるとまたちょっと気分が違う．A step out of town and you will find yourself in a different atmosphere. / 今夜は気分を変えて外で食事をするのはどうかね．How [What] about eating out this evening for a change?

きぼ その事業はよほど規模が大きいに違いない．The business is certainly run on a very extensive scale. / それ程の規模の戦争はそれまでの歴史上かつてなかった．A war of such magnitude had never been seen in our history.

きぼう 彼の希望は化学者になることだ．He hopes to become a chemist. / どうやって患者に回復の希望を与えようかと思い悩んだ．He was quite at a loss as to how to give his patient some hope of recovery. / それは希望どおりに行かなかった．It did not turn out as I wished. / 僕の希望はめちゃくちゃになった．My hopes were shattered [dashed, ruined]. / 本人の希望で外国旅行をさせた．I sent him abroad at his own request. / 希望の曙光さえ見えなかった．There was not even a gleam of hope. / この実験の成功はいかなる癌も一〇〇パーセント治る日が来るという希望を抱かせてくれる．The success of this experiment holds out hope that the day will come when anykind of cancer will be completely curable. / 彼女の目は希望に輝いていた．Her eyes gleamed with hope. / Hope gleamed in her eyes.

きほん もう一度基本から始めよう．Let's get back to the basics [fundamentals] (of archery).

きまぐれ 彼は全くの気まぐれでそうしたのだ．He did so out of pure caprice. / 一時の気まぐれから彼は船員になった．He went to sea on a mere whim [on the spur of the moment].

きまずい 2人の仲が少し気まずくなっている．They are not getting along as well as they used

きほん 基本 〈基礎〉a foundation ; a basis 《pl. bases》;〈基礎的な事柄〉《文》fundamentals ; basics ;〈基準〉a standard ¶英語を基本から始める study English from the basics / 基本的 fundamental ; basic / 基本的人権 fundamental [basic] human rights / 基本的に fundamentally ; basically / 基本給 base [basic] wages [pay] ; a base [basic] salary / (学校などの)基本金[財産] an endowment / 基本条件 a basal condition.

ぎまい 義妹 a sister-in-law 《pl. sisters-》.

きまえ 気前 ¶気前のいい generous ;《文》liberal ; openhanded / 気前よく generously ; liberally / 気前よく金を使う be free [generous] with *one's* money ; lavish *one's* money 《on》/ 気前を見せる act generously ; show *one's* generosity 《with *one's* money》.

きまぐれ 気紛れ a whim ;《文》a caprice ;《文》a whimsy ; 〈浮いた気持ちの〉¶気まぐれな fickle ;《文》capricious ; whimsical / 気まぐれな天気 changeable [variable] weather / 気まぐれな人間 a moody person ; a man of moods ; a capricious [whimsical] person / …の気まぐれで at *sb*'s whim(s). 文例⇩

きまじめ 生真面目 ¶生まじめな very serious [《文》earnest] ; (be) serious (almost) to a fault.

きまずい 気まずい ¶気まずい思いをする feel embarrassed [awkward]. 文例⇩

きまつ 期末 the end of a term ; a term end ¶期末に at the end of the term ; at the term end / 期末試験 a term-end examination.

きまま 気儘 ¶気ままな《文》wayward ;《文》willful ; self-willed / 気ままに暮らす live an easy [a carefree] life / 僕の気ままでのんきなカウボーイの生活 the free and easy life of a footloose cowboy / 気ままをする have *one's* own way ; act as *one* pleases.

きまり 決まり 〈決定〉a settlement ;〈取り決め〉an arrangement ; an agreement ;〈秩序〉order ;〈規定〉rules ; regulations ;〈習慣〉a habit ; a custom ⇨ おきまり ¶決まりの ⇨きまる (決まった), おきまり (お決まりの) / 決まりのない disorderly ; irregular / 決まりが悪い feel awkward ; be [feel] embarrassed ; be ashamed ;《文》be abashed / 決まりがつく〈決着がつく〉be settled ; be brought to an end ;〈話がつく〉come to an agreement [to terms] ;〈整う〉be put in order / 決まりをつける〈決着をつける〉settle ;《文》conclude ;《文》bring (a matter) to a conclusion [an end] ;《口語》sort (a matter) out ;《口語》sort things out /〈話をつける〉arrange / 決まり悪そうに bashfully ; in [with] some embarrassment / 決まりきった〈定まった〉fixed ;〈当たり前の〉too common ;〈明らかな〉plain ; self-evident / 決まり手〈相撲の〉a winning trick / 決まり文句 a cliché ; a hackneyed expression. 文例⇩

きまる 決まる 〈決定する〉be decided ; be settled ; be fixed ;〈話がつく〉be arranged ; be agreed on ¶ …によって決まる depend on… ;《文》be determined by… / …に決まっている〈必ず…だ〉be certain [sure, bound] to *do* ;〈運命である〉be doomed (to failure, to fail) ;《文》be destined to *do* ;〈当然である〉it is natural (for *one* to *do*, that *one* should *do*) / 決まった regular ; fixed ; definite / 決まって always ;《文》invariably ; regularly / 決まって…する always *do* ; make it a rule to *do* ; be in the habit of *doing*. 文例⇩

ぎまん 欺瞞《文》(a) deception ; (a) fraud ¶欺瞞する deceive ⇨ だます / 欺瞞的 deceptive ; fraudulent.

きみ¹ 気味 〈心持ち〉(a) feeling ; (a) sensation ;〈…の気味〉a touch 《of》; a dash ; a shade ; a tinge ; a suspicion ⇨ いいきみ ¶気味の悪い weird ; uncanny ; eerie ; creepy / 疲れ気味である be rather [a little] tired / 風邪気味である have a touch of cold ; have [be suffering from] a slight cold. 文例⇩

きみ² 黄身 the yolk [yellow] (of an egg) ; (an) egg yolk ¶黄身の2つある卵 a double-yolked egg.

きみ³ 君 you ;〈呼びかけ〉Hey, you! ; Hey

---

to. | A certain coolness has come over their relationship.

きまま 子供は気ままにさせておくべきではないと思います。I don't believe in giving children their own way. | I don't think we should allow children to have their own way.

きまり 引っ越したばかりで家の中がまだ決まりがつかない。I have only just moved in and haven't had time to put things in order. / 朝食前に散歩するのが彼の決まりだ。He makes it a rule to go out [He is in the habit of going out] for a stroll before breakfast. / それがこういう場合の決まり文句だ。That is the usual phrase [conventional expression] used on such occasions.

きまる それは前もってちゃんと決まっていたのだ。It was all arranged beforehand. / 会議は木曜日の晩に決まった。The meeting has been fixed for Thursday evening. / 条件はまだ決まらない。The terms have not yet been agreed on. / 彼は成功するに決まっている。He is sure [certain, bound] to succeed. | It is certain that he will succeed. / 生あるものはやがては亡びるものと決まっている。It is in the course of nature that living things should die sooner or later. / 僕の朝食はいつも牛乳1本にパン3切れと決まっている。My breakfast always consists of one bottle of milk and three slices of bread. / 金があるから幸福だとは決まっていない。A rich man is not always [necessarily] happy. / 奇妙な事に僕が外出しようとするといつも決まって雨が降り出す。Strangely [Oddly] enough, it never fails to start raining whenever I try to go out. / 彼女にはもう決まった人がいる。She already has someone she's going to get married to. | 彼女の身なりはみごとに決まっていた。Her dress was in perfect taste.

きみ¹ このごろは地震が頻繁で気味が悪い。The large [The increase in the] number of earthquakes lately is rather disturbing [unsettling]. / 彼女は少々太り気味だ。She is on the heavy side. | She is rather [somewhat] overweight.

きみがよ 君が代 *Kimigayo*; the Japanese national anthem.

きみじか 気短 ¶気短な〈短気な〉short-[quick-]tempered;〈性急な〉impatient; hasty; rash.

きみつ¹ 気密 ¶気密の airtight / 気密室 an airtight chamber;〈飛行機の〉a pressure [pressurized] cabin;〈潜水艦の〉a pressure hull.

きみつ² 機密〈状態〉secrecy;〈事柄〉secret information; a secret ¶軍事[外交]上の機密 a military [diplomatic] secret / 機密の secret; confidential; classified (国家などの) / 機密を漏らす let [leak] out a secret / 機密費 secret (service) funds / 機密文書[書類] confidential [classified] documents [papers]. 文例⇩

きみどり 黄緑 yellowish green.

きみゃく 気脈 ¶気脈を通じる conspire (with); have a secret [《文》tacit] understanding (with);《文》be in collusion (with);《文》establish [be in] secret communication (with). 文例⇩

きみょう 奇妙 ¶奇妙な strange; queer; odd ⇒みょう, ふしぎ / 奇妙なことに strangely [oddly] enough;《文》strange to say. 文例⇩

ぎむ 義務 (a) duty; an obligation ¶…する義務がある ought to *do*; be bound (in duty) to *do*; have [be under] an obligation to *do*;《文》be obligated to *do*; it is up to *one* to *do* / 義務の観念, 義務感 a sense of duty / 義務を負わせる put [place] *sb* under an obligation (to *do*) / 義務を怠る neglect *one's* duties / 義務を尽くす[果たす] do *one's* duty;《文》fulfill *one's* obligations;《文》discharge *one's* duties / 社会に対する義務を果たす do *one's* duty by society / 義務的の《文》obligatory; compulsory / 義務教育 compulsory education. 文例⇩

きむずかしい 気難しい be hard to please; be particular [《文》fastidious, choosy, fussy] (about) ¶気むずかしい老婦人 a difficult old lady.

きむすめ 生娘〈処女〉a virgin;〈うぶな娘〉an innocent [unsophisticated] girl.

キムチ〈朝鮮料理〉*kimchi*; Korean pickles.

きめ¹ 木目 grain ¶きめの荒い coarse《skin》; rough-[coarse-]grained / きめの細かい fine(-grained); close-grained; smooth [delicate]《skin》. 文例⇩

きめ² 決め ⇒きまり ¶月[時間]決めで by the month [hour] / 決め玉《野球》(a pitcher's) best pitch.

きめい 記名 ¶記名する sign *one's* name / 記名捺印する sign and seal《a document》/ 記名投票 an open ballot.

ぎめい 偽名 a false [an assumed] name; an alias (特に犯罪者の) ¶…という偽名で under the false name of….

きめこむ 決め込む〈勝手に思い込む〉assume (that…); jump to the conclusion (that…); take it for granted (that…); presume (*sb* [*sth*] to be…, that…);〈ふりをする〉assume (an innocent air);《文》affect; pretend (to be…, that…); pose (as)〈知らぬ顔の半兵衛を決め込む pretend [《文》feign] ignorance.

きめつける take *sb* to task (for *sth*);《口語》give *sb* a piece of *one's* mind.

きめて 決め手 a conclusive factor; a decisive fact;《口語》a clincher;《証拠》conclusive [decisive, clinching] evidence;《将棋などの》a clinching move. 文例⇩

きめる 決める〈決定する〉decide (to *do*, that…, on *sb* [*sth*], between A and B);《文》determine; fix (the date for *sth*, on *sb* [*sth*]);《口語》make it (A (rather than B));〈結着をつける〉settle;〈協定をする〉arrange; agree (to *do*, on *sth*);〈日時を〉set;《文》appoint;〈選ぶ〉choose;〈決心する〉make up *one's* mind (to *do*); set *one's* heart on *sth* [*doing*];《文》resolve to *do*;《文》be resolved (to *do*, on *doing*) ¶…することに決めている make a point of *doing*; make it a rule to *do*. 文例⇩

きめん 鬼面 ¶鬼面人を驚かす〈事が主語〉startle《people》by *its* strange appearance; be startling in *its* outward appearance (but not in *its* intrinsic nature).

きも 肝, 胆〈肝臓〉the liver;〈度胸〉courage; spirit; pluck;《口語》guts ¶肝の太い bold; daring; plucky / 肝がすわっている be brave;

きみ³ あ, 君か. Oh, it's you, (Tanaka)!

きみつ² それは機密事項になっている. That is classified information.

きみゃく 2人はひそかに気脈を通じていた. There was a secret understanding between them.

きみょう この薬は奇妙に頭痛に効く. This medicine is remarkably effective for headaches.

ぎむ そうしなければならない法律上の義務はない. I have [am under] no legal obligation to do so. / 私の公の行為を当局者以外に説明するのはないと思う. I don't feel called upon to explain my official actions except to the proper authorities.

きめ¹ 彼女の肌はきめがなめらかだ. Her skin is very smooth [has a velvety texture]. / きめの細かい対策を講じたい. We ought to consider measures to cover every eventuality [possible contingency].

きめて それが決め手になって彼は勝負をあきらめた. It proved the final clincher that persuaded him to give up (the struggle).

きめる それは君の決めることだ. It's up to you to decide. / You must decide. / まだなんとも決めずにおいた方がよい. You had better leave it undecided [in the air]. / 彼のネクタイの選択を最終的に決めるのはいつも奥さんだった. His wife always had the final say in the choice of his ties. / 彼は医者になるつもりで, 絶対そう決めている. He wants to be a doctor. He's absolutely set on it. / 彼は日曜には働かないことに決めている. He makes it a rule not to work on Sundays. / その家を借りることに決めて来た. I have arranged to rent the house. / 水曜日に決めよう. Let's make it Wednesday. / パーティーには和服を着て行くことに決めた. She decided to [that she would] go

きもいり have a lot of pluck [guts] / 胆を冷やす be frightened; 胆をつぶす be amazed; be astounded; be frightened out of one's wits / 胆をつぶすような amazing; astounding; 《口語》 mind-boggling 《事が主語》 be deeply impressed 《with, by》; 《事が主語》 be brought home to one; be engraved in [《文》 deeply impressed on] one's mind / 《うなぎの》肝吸い eel liver soup / 肝試し a test of sb's courage. 文例⇩

きもいり 肝煎り 〈世話〉 《文》 good [kind] offices; 〈主催〉 sponsorship; 《文》 auspices ¶…の肝煎りで 〈世話〉 through the good [kind] offices of 《Mr. Kudo》; 〈主催〉 under the sponsorship [auspices] of…; sponsored by….

きもち 気持ち 〈感じ〉 a feeling; a sensation; 〈気分〉 a mood ¶気持ちがいい 《事が主語》 be comfortable; be pleasant; be agreeable; 〈人・事が主語〉 feel good / 気持ちが悪い 〈事が主語〉 be unpleasant; be disagreeable; 〈人が主語〉 feel ill [unwell, funny] (気分がすぐれない); feel sick (吐き気がする) / 気持ちを引き締める brace oneself (up) 《to do, for a task》; 《文》 gird up one's loins 《to do》/ 気持ちを悪くする 《事が主語》 be [feel] hurt 《at sb's words, by sb》; 《人の》 hurt 《sb, sb's feelings》; put sb in a bad mood / 泣きたいような気持ちになる feel like crying / 気持ちよく 〈愉快に〉 pleasantly; cheerfully; 〈渋らずに〉 willingly; with (a) good grace; 〈やかましい事を言わずに〉 without quibbling [making any difficulties]. 文例⇩

きもったま 肝っ玉 ⇨きも ¶肝っ玉の太い 〈大胆な〉 daring; bold; plucky; 《文》 audacious; 〈太っ腹の〉 large-minded / 肝っ玉の小さい 〈臆病な〉 timid; cowardly; 《文》 white-livered; 〈狭量な〉 narrow-minded.

きもの 着物 〈和服〉 a kimono; 〈衣服〉 clothes; 《文》 clothing; dress ¶夏の軽い着物 light clothes for summer wear / 着物の寸法を計る measure sb for his clothes / 着物を着る put on one's clothes; get into one's clothes; dress oneself / 急いで着物を着る rush into one's clothes; throw one's clothes on / りっぱな [みすぼらしい] 着物を着ている be well [poorly] dressed / 着物を脱ぐ take one's clothes off; get undressed; undress (oneself).

きもん¹ 鬼門 〈北東の方角〉 the 'demon's gate'; the quarter lying to the northeast of one's position, superstitiously believed to be unlucky; 〈苦手〉 にがて.

きもん² 旗門 《スキー》 a (slalom) gate.

ぎもん 疑問 〈疑心〉 (a) doubt; 〈問題〉 a problem; a question ¶疑問の doubtful; questionable; 《文法》 interrogative / 疑問がある there is some doubt 《as to, about, whether…》; be open to question / 疑問の余地がない be beyond question; there is no doubt [question] 《about, that…》 / 疑問を抱く have (one's) doubts 《about》; doubt 《sb's honesty, whether…》 / 疑問を提出する pose [put up] a question / 疑問代名詞 an interrogative pronoun / 疑問符 a question [an interrogation] mark / 疑問文 an interrogative sentence. 文例⇩

ギヤ (a) gear ¶ギヤを入れる put (the car) in gear / ギヤをセカンド [バック] に入れる put 《the car》 in second [reverse] (gear); get into second [reverse] (gear) / ギヤを入れかえる change 《米》 shift] gear(s) / ギヤをサード [トップ] に切りかえる change (up) into third [top] (gear) / ギヤレバー a gear lever; 《米》 a gearshift. 文例⇩

きゃあきゃあ ⇨きゃっ ¶きゃあきゃあ笑う scream with laughter 《at》; squeal with mirth [delight] 《at》; laugh merrily 《at》.

ぎゃあぎゃあ ¶ぎゃあぎゃあ泣[鳴]く scream; squeal; squall (幼児や鳥などが); squawk (鳥が); caterwaul (猫などが) / ぎゃあぎゃあ反対する cry out against sth.

きやく 規約 〈協約〉 an agreement; 〈規定〉 rules.

きゃく 客 〈訪問客〉 a caller; a visitor; 〈招いた客〉 a guest; 〈宿屋などの〉 a guest; 〈下宿人〉 a lodger; 〈弁護士などの〉 a client; 《文》 clientele (総称); 〈商店・レストランなどの〉 a customer; a patron (常客) (総称); 〈乗客〉 a passenger ¶用談に来た客 a business visitor / 客がある have a caller [visitor]; have company / 客に会う see [receive] a caller [visitor] / 客足が遠い attract very few customers; do not do much business / 客足がつく attract

---

きも この事を肝に銘じておきなさい. You must always keep this fact in mind. | Let this lesson be engraved on your mind.

きもち 早朝だったので空気も気持ちがよく涼しかった. Since it was early in the morning the air was refreshingly [pleasantly] cool. | 少々気持ちがよくない. I don't feel very well. | I feel a little unwell [a bit funny]. | I don't quite feel myself. | それを見ただけで気持ちが悪くなった. The mere sight of it made me feel sick. / お嬢さんをお嫁にやるのはどんなお気持ちですか. How does it feel to be the father of a bride?/ 顔を洗うといい気持ちになりますよ. A wash will freshen you up. | 私の所にいるときは彼は気持ちよく働いていました. He was a willing worker while he was working for me.

きもったま 座って話をしているうちにだんだん肝っ玉がすわってきた. As I sat talking with him I began to gather courage.

きもの 私は着物なんか構いません. I don't care how I dress.

ぎもん 疑問があったらなんでも尋ねなさい. Ask me whenever (you are) in doubt. / その点は疑問はない. There is no doubt about that. / 疑問が氷解した. My doubts have been dispelled. / その記事を読んだうえ, 私には幾つかの疑問が残った. When I read the article, I was left with several questions. / 彼が成功するかどうかは疑問だ. There is some doubt as to [It is doubtful] whether he will succeed. / 彼がその理論に疑問を投げかけた最初の人であった. He was the first to question [cast doubt on] the theory.

ギヤ 事故の時, ギヤはどこに入れていましたか. —セカンドです. What gear were you in at the

ぎゃくじょう 逆上 ¶逆上する the blood rushes to *one's* head; be beside *oneself* 《with rage》.

ぎゃくしょうばい 客商売 the entertainment [hotel, restaurant] business.

ぎゃくしょく 脚色 dramatization ¶脚色する dramatize 《a story》; adapt 《a novel》 for the stage [screen]; make a stage [screen] version of 《a story》/ 脚色者 a dramatizer; an adapter.

ぎゃくすいしんロケット 逆推進ロケット a retrorocket ¶逆推進ロケットに点火する retrofire.

ぎゃくすう 逆数 【数】 a reciprocal (number). 文例⇩

ぎゃくずき 客好き 〈事〉 hospitality; 〈人〉 a hospitable person ¶客好きである be fond of company; like entertaining guests; be hospitable.

ぎゃくすじ 客筋 ⇨きゃくだね.

ぎゃくせいせっけん 逆性石鹸 invert soap.

ぎゃくせき 客席 〈劇場などの〉 a seat 《in a theater》; 〈タクシーの〉 a passenger seat.

ぎゃくせつ 逆説 a paradox ¶逆説的 paradoxical.

ぎゃくせん 客船 a passenger boat [ship]; 〈大洋航路の定期船〉 a (passenger) liner.

ぎゃくせんでん 逆宣伝 counterpropaganda ⇨せんでん.

ぎゃくせんび 脚線美 ¶脚線美の女 a woman with shapely legs.

ぎゃくたい 客体 【哲】 the object.

ぎゃくたい 虐待 ill-treatment; cruelty ¶虐待する treat *sb* cruelly; ill-treat; 《文》 maltreat; be cruel 《to animals》.

きゃくだね 客種 ¶客種が良い[悪い] have a good [low] class of customers; have customers from the upper [lower] classes (of society).

ぎゃくたんち 逆探知 ¶逆探知する trace (the call).

きゃくちゅう 脚注 a footnote ¶脚注を施す put [give] footnotes (to); footnote 《an essay》.

ぎゃくちょう 逆調 an unfavorable [《文》 adverse] condition ¶貿易の逆調 an unfavorable balance of trade.

ぎゃくて 逆手 【柔道】 a reverse armlock ⇨さかて[1] ¶逆手を取ってやり込める go onto the offensive by saying 《that…》; counter *sb*'s attack by charging 《that…》; counterattack and argue *sb* down.

ぎゃくてん 逆転 (a) reversal; 《口語》 a turnabout; 【気象】 (an) inversion ¶気温の逆転 a temperature [thermal] inversion / 逆転する be reversed; 【気象】 be inverted / 逆転勝ちす

ぎゃく

[draw] customers / 客扱い hospitality; entertainment; 〈宿泊などの〉 service / 〈店などの〉客あしらいがよい[悪い] the service (in that store) is good [bad]; [they] give good [poor] service.

ぎゃく 逆 the opposite; 《文》 the converse; 《文》 the inverse; the reverse ¶逆の contrary 《winds》; reverse 《order》; opposite 《directions》/ 逆に 《文》 conversely; 《文》 inversely; the other way around [about] / 逆にする reverse 《the order》; 〈上下を〉 turn *sth* upside down; 〈表裏を〉 turn *sth* inside out / 逆に並べる put [《文》 place] (the numbers) in reverse order / 逆に向く turn around; face in the opposite direction; face the other way. 文例⇩

ギャグ a gag ¶ギャグを飛ばす toss off a gag; crack jokes.

きゃくいん[1] 客員 ⇨かくいん. 「ん[4].

きゃくいん[2] 脚韻 【詩学】 an end rhyme ⇨い

きゃくえん 客演 ¶客演する make *one's* guest appearance 《in a show》; appear [perform, play] as guest (on the stage).

ぎゃくかいてん 逆回転 spinning the opposite way; 【テニス・卓球】 backspin; 【スケート】 a counter.

ぎゃくこうか 逆効果 ¶逆効果になる have the opposite effect [result] to what was intended; defeat *its* own end [purpose].

ぎゃくこう(せん) 逆光(線) backlight ¶逆光で写真を撮る take a picture into [against] the sun.

ぎゃくコース 逆コース 〈反対方向の道〉 the reverse course; 〈反動〉 (a) reaction ¶逆コースを行く take the reverse course; go in the opposite direction; 〈時代に逆行する〉 go against the times; swim [row] against the stream / 逆コースの傾向がある 《文》 show a reactionary tendency.

ぎゃくさつ 虐殺 (a) slaughter; (a) massacre ¶虐殺する slaughter; butcher; massacre.

ぎゃくさん 逆算 ¶逆算する count backward 《to》; calculate back 《to》.

きゃくしつ 客室 〈旅館の〉 a guest room; 〈旅客機の〉 a (passenger) cabin; 〈船の〉 ⇨せんしつ ¶(旅客機の)客室乗務員 a cabin crew.

きゃくしゃ 客車 a passenger car [coach, 《英》 carriage]; 《米》 a day coach (寝台車と区別して); 〈列車〉 a passenger train.

ぎゃくしゅう 逆襲 a counterattack; a counteroffensive ¶逆襲する counterattack; make [launch] a counterattack (on, against); 〈やり返す〉 counter; 〈言い返す〉 retort 《that…》.

文例⇩

---

time of the accident?—(I was in) second.

きゃく 金子さんの家は今お客様が来ているらしい. Mr. Kaneko seems to have a visitor [guest]. / 今夜田舎からお客様が来ることになっている. I'm expecting a visitor from my hometown this evening. / 社長はただ今お客様でございます. The President has somebody with him at the moment. / 〈相手に食事代などを払わせまいとして〉今日はあなたはお客様ですよ. You're my guest today. | It's [The meal is, The drinks are] on me today. / お客様は神様です. The customer is king [is always right]. / あの店は客が多い. That store has [attracts] a lot of customers. |

That restaurant is well patronized.

ぎゃく 逆もまた真である. The reverse is also true. / 不眠症から偏頭痛になることもあるし, その逆の場合もある. Sometimes insomnia causes migraine, and sometimes it is the other way around [about].

ぎゃくしゅう 我々の賃上げ要求に

きゃくど 客土 earth brought from some other place (to improve the soil).

きゃくどめ 客止め ¶客止めの盛況である bring in [play to] a capacity audience / 客止めにする stop selling tickets ; close the box office.

きゃくひき 客引き 〈事〉touting ; 〈人〉a tout ; a barker (見世物の) ¶客引きをする tout (for customers) ; 《文》solicit custom.

ぎゃくひれい 逆比例 ⇒はんぴれい.

きゃくほん 脚本 〈芝居の〉a playbook ; a (play) script ; 〈映画の〉a scenario 《pl. -s》; a (film) script ¶脚本作者 a scriptwriter ; 〈芝居の〉a playwright ; 〈映画の〉a scenario writer.

きゃくま 客間 a drawing room.

ぎゃくもどり 逆戻り (a) reversion ; a relapse (病気などの) ¶逆戻りする go back (to one's earlier state) ; 〈引き返す〉go [turn] back ; retrace one's steps ; 〈退歩する〉《文》relapse 《into one's old habits》. 文例⇩

ぎゃくゆしゅつ 逆輸出 reexport ⇒ゆしゅつ.

ぎゃくゆにゅう 逆輸入 reimport ⇒ゆにゅう.

ぎゃくよう 逆用 ¶逆用する turn 《the enemy's propaganda》to one's own advantage.

きゃくよせ 客寄せ an attraction ¶客寄せに to attract customers ; as an attraction.

ぎゃくりゅう 逆流 (a) backflow ; (a) return flow ; a back ¶《文》an adverse current ¶逆流する flow backward [upstream].

きゃくりょく 脚力 the strength of one's legs ; one's walking ability.

ギャザースカート a gathered [shirred] skirt.

きゃしゃ 華奢 ¶きゃしゃな《文》《a person》of slight build ; slightly-[lightly-]built ; delicate ; slim ; slender ; fragile.

きやすい 気安い ⇒こころやすい ¶気安い人 a person with whom one need not stand on ceremony ; 《文》one's intimate friend ⇒したしい ★

キャスチングボート ¶キャスチングボートを握っている hold the decisive vote ; have [hold] the balance of power ★英語の casting vote は可否同数の際の議長の決定票.

キャスト 〈配役〉the cast (of characters).

きやすめ 気休め ¶気休めに for conscience' sake ; to ease one's mind ; 《文》to allay one's anxiety / 気休めに薬を与える give [《文》administer] a placebo to 《a patient》just to satisfy him [for its psychological effect].

きゃたつ 脚立 a stepladder.

キャタピラ a caterpillar (tread).

きゃっ ¶きゃっと叫ぶ shriek ; scream ; give [《文》utter] a shriek [scream] / きゃっきゃっと笑う scream with laughter / (猿が)きゃっきゃっと鳴く chatter.

ぎゃっ ¶ぎゃっと叫ぶ yell ; squawk (鳥が). ⇒きゃあきゃあ

きゃっか 却下 (a) rejection ; (a) dismissal ¶却下する reject 《a petition》; dismiss 《an appeal》; turn down 《sb's request》; 〈裁判長が〉overrule 《an objection from the defense》.

きゃっかん 客観 《哲》the object ¶客観的に objectively / 客観化する objectify / 客観性 objectivity / 客観情勢 objective circumstances / 客観テスト an objective test.

ぎゃっきょう 逆境 ¶逆境にある《文》be in adversity ; 《文》be in [under] adverse circumstances. 文例⇩

きゃっこう 脚光 footlights ¶脚光を浴びる be in [move into, be thrown into] the limelight ; be spotlighted ; be highlighted.

ぎゃっこう 逆行 ¶逆行する go [move] backward ;《文》retrogress ;《文》retrograde ;〈反する〉run counter 《to》/ 時代に逆行する go against the times ; swim [row] against the stream.

キャッシュ cash ¶キャッシュカード a cash card.

キャッチフレーズ a catch phrase.

キャッチボール catch ¶キャッチボールをする play catch.

キャッチャー 《野球》a catcher 《on a high-school team》¶キャッチャーをつとめる catch [be (a) catcher] 《for the Yankees》.

キャッチャーボート 《捕鯨》a catcher.

キャップ 〈帽子〉a cap ;〈万年筆などの〉a cap ; a point protector ¶(炭坑夫の)キャップランプ a cap lamp.

ギャップ a gap ¶世代間の[時間的]ギャップ a generation [time] gap / ギャップを埋める fill [stop, close] a gap.

キャディー 《ゴルフ》a caddie ; a caddy ¶キャディーをやる caddie 《for a golfer》/ キャディー料 a caddie [caddying] fee.

ギャバジン gabardine.

キャバレー a cabaret.

きゃはん 脚絆 ⇒ゲートル.

キャビア caviar(e).

キャビネ 〈判〉the cabinet size ;〈写真〉a cabinet photograph.

対して彼らは一時帰休という脅しで応戦してきた. They countered our demand for higher wages by threatening to lay us off.

ぎゃくすう 5の逆数は 1/5 である. The reciprocal of 5 is $1/5$.

ぎゃくてん 形勢が逆転して我々に有利となった. The situation changed [The tide turned] to our advantage. / 一打逆転のチャンスだ. One hit would turn the tables in our favor. / 必勝と思われたゲームがそのエラーで残念ながら逆転負けになってしまった. The error turned what seemed like certain victory into a disappointing defeat.

ぎゃくもどり まるで中世に逆戻りしたような感じだ. It's as if we were back in the Middle Ages.

きやすめ 来年もう一度やってみることができると思えば少しは気休めになります. It gives me some consolation to think that I can try again next year.

ぎゃっきょう 彼は小さい時から逆境と戦ってきた. From early

キャプテン a captain ⇒ しゅしょう¹.
キャブレター a carburetor.
ぎゃふん ¶ぎゃふんと言わせる argue sb into silence; talk sb down;《口語》squelch / ぎゃふんと言う be beaten hollow; be brought to one's knees;《口語》throw in the towel [sponge].
キャベツ a cabbage;《a head of》cabbage.
きゃら 伽羅〈香〉eaglewood; agalloch; aloeswood;〈木〉an eaglewood [agalloch, aloeswood] tree.
ギャラ a guarantee; a (guaranteed) fee《to an entertainer》.
キャラコ calico.
キャラバン〈隊商〉a caravan ¶キャラバンシューズ light mountain-climbing shoes.
キャラメル a caramel ¶キャラメルをなめる chew a caramel.
キャリア〈職業上の経歴〉a career;〈経験〉experience ¶法律家としてのキャリア one's career in law [as a lawyer] / キャリア15年の教師 a teacher with fifteen years' experience / キャリアウーマン a career woman [girl].
きゃんきゃん ¶きゃんきゃん鳴く[ほえる]〈犬などが〉yelp; yap.
ギャング a gangster ¶ギャングの一団 a gang of robbers.
キャンセル (a) cancellation ⇒とりけし ¶キャンセルする cancel《one's subscription》⇒とりけす / キャンセル待ちを be on the waiting list.
キャンデー (a piece of) candy;《英》a sweet;〈総称〉(sell) candies;《英》sweets ¶棒の先につけたキャンデー a lollipop.
キャンパス (a) campus ¶キャンパスで on (the) campus.
キャンピングカー a camper;《英》a motorized caravan.
キャンプ a camp; camping ¶キャンプする camp (out) /キャンプに行く go (out) camping / キャンプ場 a campsite; a campground / キャンプ生活 camping(-out) / キャンプファイア (around) a campfire / キャンプ用具 camping equipment.
ギャンブル gambling ⇒ばくち.
キャンペーン a campaign ⇒うんどう.
キャンベラ Canberra.
きゆう 杞憂 imaginary [needless] fears;《文》groundless apprehensions.
きゅう 九 ⇒く¹ ¶9倍 nine times.
きゅう² 旧 ¶旧の; 《文》former / 旧の元日 New Year's Day according to the lunar calendar / 旧に復する be restored to its former state.
きゅう³ 灸 moxa cautery; moxibustion ¶きゅうを据える burn moxa on《the skin》; cauterize《the skin》with moxa; give sb moxa treatment /〈比喩的に〉punish [《文》chastise] sb for sth; scold sb for [about] sth.
きゅう⁴ 急〈危急〉(an) emergency; a crisis (pl. crises); (a) danger;〈緊急〉urgency ¶急な〈緊急の〉urgent; pressing;〈突然の〉sudden;〈険しい〉steep;〈急角度の〉sharp;〈流れの早い〉《文》swift; rapid / 急を要する be urgent; be pressing; need immediate attention / 急を告げる〈警報を出す〉give [raise] the alarm;〈猶予できない〉be urgent;《文》admit of no delay / 急を救う help sb out of danger / 急に〈直ちに〉quickly; immediately; at [on] short notice;〈急いで〉hastily;《文》in haste;〈突然に〉suddenly; all of a sudden;〈予告なしに〉without warning / 急に止まる stop short / 急に金がいる be in urgent need of money. 文例⇩

きゅう⁵ 級〈階級〉a class; a grade;〈学年〉a class;《米》a grade;《英》a form ¶2級上[下]である〈学年が〉be two grades senior [junior]《to sb》;〈等級が〉be two classes higher [lower]《than sb》/ アリゾナ級の戦艦 a battleship of the Arizona class / 大臣級の人物 a person of ministerial caliber / エジソン級の発明家 an inventor of the order of Edison / メガトン級の核爆発 a nuclear explosion in the megaton range / 大使級会談 a conference at the ambassadorial level; an ambassador-level talk.

きゅう⁶ 球〈球体〉a sphere; a globe;〈まり〉a ball;〈電球など〉a bulb. 文例⇩

キュー〈玉突きの〉a cue;〈合図〉a cue ¶キューを出す give sb a cue; cue sb.

ぎゆう 義勇 ¶義勇軍 a volunteer army / 義勇兵 a volunteer.

ぎゅう¹ 牛 ⇒ぎゅうにく, うし ¶牛缶 canned beef;《英》tinned beef / 牛丼 a bowl of rice topped with beef / 牛鍋〈すき焼〉sukiyaki;〈なべ〉a sukiyaki pan / 牛皮 cowhide.

ぎゅう²〈音〉a creak; a squeak ¶ぎゅうぎゅう鳴る creak; squeak / ぎゅうぎゅう詰め込む squeeze《things》into《a narrow place》; pack《things》like sardines / ぎゅうぎゅう詰めの電車 a jam-packed car / ぎゅうぎゅう言う目にあわせる make sb cry (for) mercy; bring sb to his knees.

きゅうあい 求愛 courting;《文》courtship ¶求愛する court;《文》woo /〈鳥の〉求愛ダンス a courtship [mating] dance.

きゅうあく 旧悪《文》one's past misdeed(s); one's old crime(s) ¶旧悪を暴く expose sb's past misdeeds; rake up sb's secret past. 文例⇩

きゅういん 吸引〈吸いこむこと〉absorption; suction;〈引きつけること〉attraction

---

childhood he had to struggle against adverse circumstances.
きゅう⁵ その丘は東側よりも西側の方が坂が急だ. The hill rises more steeply from the west than from the east. / 母校の急を救え. Come to the rescue of your alma mater in her [at her time of] crisis. / 急な用事ができた. Some urgent business has turned up.
きゅう⁶ ピッチャー, 振りかぶって, 第5球. Winding up, the pitcher throws the fifth pitch.
きゅうあく 彼の旧悪が露顕した. His past crime came to light.
きゅうか² 彼は休暇をとって山へ行った. He went off to the mountains on vacation. / 休暇は楽しく過ごしました. I've had a nice vacation [《英》holiday].
きゅうかい 国会は1月10日まで休会に入ることに決した. The Diet decided to adjourn (its session) until the 10th of Janu-

きゅうえん ¶吸引する〈吸い込む〉absorb; suck (in);《文》imbibe /〈引きつける〉attract; draw / 吸引力〈吸う力〉sucking force;〈引力〉attraction.

きゅうえん[1] 休演 ¶休演する〈出し物を〉suspend the performance ((of a play));〈役者が〉do not [fail to] appear (on the stage); do not perform [give a performance] (that night).

きゅうえん[2] 救援 relief; (a) rescue ¶救援する relieve; rescue / …の救援に赴く go to the rescue of… / 救援を求める ask for help; call on sb for help / 救援隊 a relief [rescue] party / 救援投手 a relief pitcher;《俗》a fireman / 救援物資 relief goods.

きゅうか[1] 旧家 an old family.

きゅうか[2] 休暇 a holiday, a vacation;〈賜暇〉(a) leave ★夏休みや冬休みなどの休暇を言う時,《米》では the summer [Christmas] vacation といい,《英》では高校までは the summer [Christmas] holidays, 大学になると the summer [Christmas] vacation というのが普通 ¶休暇をとる take [get] leave (of absence) /《米》take a vacation;《英》take a holiday / 3日間の休暇をとる take [have] three days off; take a three days' vacation [《英》holiday] / 休暇を過ごす spend one's vacation [《英》holidays] ((in Switzerland)) / 休暇をとって旅行している be away on vacation [《英》on holiday] / 休暇で帰国[帰省]している be home on leave [on furlough] (特に軍人や海外勤務の公務員など). 文例

きゅうか[3] 毬果《植》a cone.

きゅうかい 休会 (an) adjournment; a recess ¶休会になる be adjourned; adjourn; recess; go into recess / 休会明けの国会 the first session of the Diet after the recess.

きゅうかく 嗅覚 the sense of smell ¶嗅覚が鋭い have a keen nose; have a good [《文》an acute] sense of smell.

きゅうがく 休学 (a year's [term's]) leave of absence ((from school)) ¶休学する take time off school; take (a year) off school; take (a year's) leave of absence / 1年間の休学届を出す apply for a year's leave of absence.

きゅうかくど 急角度 ¶急角度に (turn) at an acute [a sharp] angle; (bend) sharply [in a sharp curve].

きゅうかざん 休火山 a dormant [an inactive, a quiescent] volcano.

きゅうがた 旧型 an old model [type].

きゅうかん[1] 旧館 the old [older] building.

きゅうかん[2] 休刊 ¶休刊する suspend (discontinue) publication. 文例

きゅうかん[3] 休館 ¶休館する close ((the museum)) / 休館になる close; be closed.

きゅうかん[4] 急患 an emergency case ¶急患で往診に出ている be away on an emergency call.

きゅうかんち 休閑地 a fallow field; fallow land; land lying fallow.

きゅうかんちょう 九官鳥 a hill myna(h).

きゅうき 吸気〈事〉inhalation of air;〈空気〉air breathed in. ¶(ジェットエンジンの)吸気口 an intake (duct).

きゅうぎ 球技 a ball game.

きゅうきゅう[1] 救急 first aid ¶救急用の first-aid ((medicines)) / 救急車 an ambulance (car) / 救急箱 a first-aid kit [box] / 救急病院 an emergency hospital.

きゅうきゅう[2] 汲々 ¶きゅうきゅうとしている《文》be intent ((on making money)); be eager ((to please one's employer)).

きゅうきゅう[3] ¶きゅうきゅう鳴る creak; squeak.

きゅうきょ[1] 旧居 one's old house;《文》one's former residence.

きゅうきょ[2] 急遽 in a hurry,《文》in haste ⇒ いそぐ (いそいで).

きゅうきょう[1] 旧教 ⇒ カトリック.

きゅうきょう[2] 窮境 ⇒ きゅうち[2].

きゅうぎょう 休業〈店の〉closing down;《文》suspension of business;《文》closure;〈工場などの〉a shutdown /〈休暇〉a holiday ¶休業する〈人が〉take a holiday; take a day off; 〈店が〉be closed (to business); 《文》suspend business [operations]. 文例

きゅうきょく 嬉遊曲《音楽》a divertimento (pl. -tos, -ti).

きゅうきょく 究[窮]極 ¶究極の《文》ultimate; final; last / 究極のところ after all; when all is said and done /《文》ultimately; in the last [final] analysis. 文例

きゅうきん 給金 ⇒ きゅうりょう[2] ¶(力士が)給金を直す have [score] more wins than losses (and get a raise in one's pay).

きゅうくつ 窮屈 ¶窮屈な〈狭い〉narrow;〈固い〉tight;〈固苦しい〉stiff; formal;〈気づまり〉《文》constrained; ill at ease / 窮屈な規則 rigid regulations / 狭くて窮屈である〈場所が主語〉be too cramped for comfort;〈人が主語〉feel cramped in a confined space. 文例

きゅうけい[1] 休憩 (a) rest; a (rest) break; (a) recess;〈旅館での〉a short stay;〈幕間〉an intermission;《英》an interval ¶正午[10分間]の休憩 a noon [ten-minute] recess / 休憩する take a rest [recess, break] / 仕事を止めて休憩する rest [take a rest] from (one's) work / (長距離バスの)休憩のための停車 a rest stop / 休憩時間 a recess;《英》an intermission;《英》an interval / 休憩室 a resting room; a lounge (ホテルなどの) / 休憩所

---

ary. / 国会は休会中です。The Diet is in recess now.

きゅうかん[2] 本紙は明日休刊いたします。There will be no issue of this paper tomorrow.

きゅうぎょう 本日休業。《掲示》Closed today. / 当分の間休業いたします。《掲示》Closed until further notice.

きゅうきょく 究極の責任は学長にある。Ultimate responsibility lies with the president.

きゅうくつ このズボンは腰のところが少々窮屈だ。The trousers feel [are] a bit tight around the waist. / そんな窮屈なことは抜きにしましょう。Let's not bother with such formalities. / 知らない家へ行くと窮屈なものだ。One feels ill at ease in a stranger's house. / 私には日本の社会が少々窮屈に感じられた。I found Japanese society a bit too confining [restricting].

きゅうけい¹ a resting place;〈劇場などの〉a lobby. 文例⇩

きゅうけい² 求刑 ¶求刑する demand [propose]《five years' imprisonment》for《the accused》.

きゅうけい³ 球形 a spherical [globular] shape ¶球形の spherical; globular; globe-shaped.

きゅうけい⁴ 球茎《植》a corm.

きゅうげき¹ 旧劇 ⇨かぶき.

きゅうげき² 急激 ¶急激な sudden; abrupt; drastic (徹底的な); radical (急進的な) / 急激に suddenly; abruptly; drastically (徹底的に).

きゅうけつ 給血 ⇨けんけつ.

きゅうけつき 吸血鬼 a vampire; a bloodsucker (比喩的に).

きゅうご 救護《文》relief; aid ¶救護する《文》relieve;《文》aid / 救護所 a first-aid station / 救護班 a relief party [squad] / 救護班のテント a medical tent.

きゅうこう¹ 旧交 ¶旧交を温める renew one's (old) friendship《with》.

きゅうこう² 旧稿 ¶旧稿を書き改める rewrite one's old manuscript.

きゅうこう³ 休校 ¶休校する close《the school for the time being》/ 休校になる be closed.

きゅうこう⁴ 休耕 ¶休耕にする leave《a field》fallow [idle] / 休耕中である lie fallow [idle] / 休耕期間 a fallow period / 休耕田 a fallow field; a field lying fallow.

きゅうこう⁵ 休講 ¶休講する cancel one's lecture(s) [class(es)]; do not attend school; cannot meet one's class. 文例⇩

きゅうこう⁶ 急行〈列車〉an express (train) ¶7 時 30 分の急行 the 7:30 [seven-thirty] express / 急行する rush [hurry,《文》hasten]《to》/ 急行で行く take an express《to a place》by express / 急行券 an express ticket / 急行停車駅 an express station / 急行バス[エレベータ] an express bus [elevator] / 急行料金 an express charge / 普通[特別]急行列車 an ordinary [a limited] express (train).

きゅうこうか 急降下《航空》a (steep) dive; a nose dive (故意でない) ¶急降下する nose-dive; zoom down / 急降下に移る plunge into a dive / 急降下爆撃 dive bombing / 急降下爆撃する dive-bomb / 急降下爆撃機 a dive bomber.

きゅうこく 急告 an urgent notice. 文例⇩

きゅうごしらえ 急拵え ⇨きゅうぞう¹.

きゅうこん¹ 求婚 a proposal [an offer] of marriage;《文》courtship ¶求婚する ask sb to marry one; propose (marriage)《to a girl》;《文》ask for《a lady's》hand; court;《文》woo / 求婚広告 an advertisement for a spouse.

きゅうこん² 球根 a bulb ¶球根植物 a bulbous plant /《俗に》a bulb.

きゅうこんりょこう 旧婚旅行 a second honeymoon.

きゅうさい¹ 休載 ¶休載する do not carry [publish] / 休載になる be not published; do not appear《in a newspaper》.

きゅうさい² 救済《文》relief; help;《文》aid;〈魂の〉salvation ¶救済する help; give relief [aid]《to》;《文》relieve; save / 難民を救済する give relief [extend a helping hand] to the refugees / 救済策[法] relief measures; a remedy / 救済事業 relief work / 救済資金 relief funds.

きゅうさく 旧作 one's old [earlier] work.

きゅうし¹ 九死 ¶九死に一生を得る have a narrow [hairbreadth] escape from death; escape death by a hairsbreadth [by the skin of one's teeth].

きゅうし² 旧師 one's former teacher.

きゅうし³ 休止 ¶休止 (a) pause;《文》(a) suspension;《文》a halt; (a) rest ¶休止する〈止まる〉stop; pause;《文》halt; come to a standstill [halt];〈止める〉stop; suspend;《文》discontinue;〈休息する〉rest / 大[小]休止する《軍》take a long [short] rest / 休止符《音楽》a rest; a pause.

きゅうし⁴ 臼歯 a molar (tooth);《口語》a grinder ¶小臼歯 a premolar (tooth) / 第 1 [2] 大臼歯 a first [second] molar.

きゅうし⁵ 急死 (a) sudden [《文》(an) untimely] death ¶急死する die suddenly;《文》meet with an untimely death.

きゅうし⁶ 急使 an express messenger; a courier.

きゅうじ 給仕〈事務室の〉an office boy;〈食事の〉a waiter; a waitress (女);〈ホテルの〉a page (boy);《米》a bellboy;《米口語》a bellhop;〈船の〉a cabin boy; a steward;〈列車の〉a boy;《米》a porter ¶給仕する wait on sb at the [に me] table; serve《at a dinner party》/ 給仕なしで食事する wait on oneself at table. 文例⇩

きゅうしき 旧式 ¶旧式の of the [an] old type [style]; old-fashioned; out-of-date; outdated.

きゅうしつ 吸湿 moisture absorption ¶吸湿性が強い be highly hygroscopic / 吸湿剤 a desiccant; a moisture absorbent.

きゅうじつ 休日 a holiday; a day off ⇨やすみ ¶休日に仕事に出る go to work on a holiday / 休日で遊びに出ている人 a holidaymaker; a holidayer / 休日気分で in (a) holiday mood.

きゅうしゃ¹ 厩舎 ⇨うまや.

きゅうしゃ² 鳩舎 a dovecot(e); a pigeon house.

きゅうしゃ³ 牛舎 a cowshed.

きゅうしゅう¹ 吸収《文》absorption;〈同化〉《文》assimilation ¶吸収する absorb; suck in;《文》imbibe;〈同化する〉assimilate / 知識を吸収する absorb [soak up] information《about, on》/ 吸収力[性]のある absorbent;《文》absorptive / 吸収スペクトル an absorption

---

きゅうけい—10 分間.〈映画館などの表示〉Intermission—10 minutes.

きゅうこう³ 山下教授本日休講.《掲示》Professor Yamashita's lectures [classes] for today are canceled.

きゅうこく 急告—本日第 2 時限終了後全員校庭に集合のこと.《掲示》Urgent—All students are to assemble in the schoolyard after the second period.

きゅうじ ご婦人方から先に給仕したまえ.Serve the ladies first. / わが家では食事の時はいつも長女

spectrum.
きゅうしゅう² 急襲 a surprise [sudden] attack; a raid ¶急襲する make a surprise [sudden] attack (on); raid; storm.
きゅうじゅう 九十 ninety ¶90番目の ninetieth / 90代の人 a nonagenarian.
きゅうしゅつ 救出 ⇨ きゅうじょ, すくう ¶救出作戦 a rescue operation.
きゅうじゅつ 弓術 archery ¶弓術家 an archer.
きゅうしょ 急所 〈生命にかかわる所〉 a vital spot [part]; 《文》 the vitals (総称) / 〈要点〉 a vital [key] point; 〈痛い所〉 a sore [tender] spot; 《文》 the quick; 〈弱点〉 a weak [vulnerable] spot ¶急所を突く hit sb on a fatal spot / 急所を蹴る kick sb in the crotch [groin] / 〈弾丸などが〉急所をはずれる miss the vital organs / 急所を突いた[はずれた]質問 a question that is to the point [beside the mark] / 急所を握っている have a hold over sb.
きゅうじょ 救助 (a) rescue; relief; 《文》 aid ¶救助する rescue; save; relieve; 《文》 aid / 人命を救助する save a life / 救助を求める ask [call] for help [aid] / 〈大声で〉 cry for help / 救助におもむく go to sb's rescue / 救助作業 rescue work / 〈遭難船の〉救助信号 an SOS (call) / a distress call [signal] / 救助船 a lifeboat; a rescue boat [ship] / 〈高層建築物などの火災時に用いる〉救助袋 an escape chute.
きゅうしょう 旧称 the old name; the former title.
きゅうじょう¹ 休場 〈劇場などの〉 closure 《of a theater》; 〈人の〉 absence 《from the ring [stage]》 ¶休場する 〈劇場などが〉 be closed (for a month); 〈力士が〉 stay away from [do not appear in] the ring; 〈役者が〉 do not appear on [《文》 absent oneself from] the stage.
きゅうじょう² 宮城 ⇨ こうきょ.
きゅうじょう³ 球場 ⇨ やきゅう(野球場) ¶後楽園球場 the Korakuen Stadium.
きゅうじょう⁴ 球状 ⇨ きゅうけい³.
きゅうじょう⁵ 窮状 distress; a wretched condition; 《文》 a sad [sorry] plight.
きゅうしょうしょう 急上昇 a sudden rise 《in prices》; 【航空】 a steep climb; a zoom; zooming ¶急上昇する rise suddenly [sharply]; shoot up; 【航空】 climb steeply; zoom.
きゅうしょく¹ 休職 temporary retirement ¶休職になる be suspended from one's job [duties].
きゅうしょく² 求職 job hunting ¶求職する look for [《文》 seek] employment; look [hunt] for a job / 求職者 a job hunter [seeker] / 求職人口 the number of persons seeking employment / 求職欄 [広告] a situations-wanted column [advertisement].
きゅうしょく³ 給食 ¶給食する provide [supply] 《the workers》 with meals; provide lunch 《for schoolchildren》 / 学校給食 (provision of) school meals [lunch].
ぎゅうじる 牛耳る control 《an organization》 (completely); have 《an organization》 under one's thumb; 《口語》 lead sb by the nose.
きゅうしん¹ 休診 ¶休診する accept no patients; close the office [《英》 surgery] 《for the day》.
きゅうしん² 求心 ¶求心的 centripetal / 求心力 centripetal force.
きゅうしん³ 急進 ¶急進的 radical; extreme / 急進思想 radical ideas / 急進主義 radicalism / 急進派 the radicals.
きゅうしん⁴ 球審 【野球】 a ball [plate] umpire; an umpire-in-chief.
きゅうじん¹ 九仞 ¶九仞の功を一簣(³)に欠く fail to reap the fruits of one's long exertion by grudging a little effort [making a careless error] at the last stage.
きゅうじん² 求人 a job offer; 《文》 an offer of a situation ¶求人側の要求[条件] hiring requirements [terms] / 求人広告 a situations-vacant advertisement; 《口語》 a help-wanted ad. 文例⓭
きゅうす 急須 a teapot.
きゅうすい 給水 water supply [service] ¶給水する supply 《a town》 with water / 給水管 a water pipe; a service pipe (引き込み管); a feed pipe (ボイラーの) / 給水本管 a water [service] main / 給水制限 restriction(s) on water supply / 給水車[船] a water wagon [boat]; a water tender / 給水栓 a hydrant / 給水弁 [ポンプ, タンク] a feed valve [pump, tank].
きゅうすいかん 吸水管 a suction pipe; a siphon.
きゅうすう 級数 【数】 a series ⇨ とうさきゅうすう, とうひきゅうすう.
きゅうする¹ 給する supply [provide, 《文》 furnish] 《sb with sth》; allow 《sb money for sth》.
きゅうする² 窮する 〈貧乏する〉 grow [get, 《文》 become] poor; 《文》 be reduced to poverty; 〈金に〉 be short of money; be hard up / 〈当惑する〉 be at a loss; be at one's wits' end; 〈くっぱ詰まる〉 be driven to the wall; be in a fix ¶返答に窮する be at a loss for an answer; do not know what answer to make. 文例⓭
きゅうせい¹ 旧姓 one's previous [《文》 former] name; 〈女性の結婚前の姓〉 one's maiden name ¶伊藤淑子, 旧姓矢野 Mrs. Yoshiko Ito, née Yano / 千葉正雄, 旧姓須田 Masao Chiba, formerly Suda.
きゅうせい² 急性 ¶急性の acute 《pneumonia》.
きゅうせいぐん 救世軍 the Salvation Army ¶救世軍の軍人 a Salvationist.
きゅうせいしゅ 救世主 the Saviour; the Redeemer; the Messiah.

が給仕してくれますよ. In my family my eldest daughter always serves at table.
きゅうしん¹ 本日休診. 〖掲示〗 Closed today. | 《英》 No surgery today.
きゅうじん² 求人. 〖掲示〗 Help wanted. | 本学の学生には求人の申し込みが多い. There are lots of job offers for the undergraduates of this university.
きゅうする² 私は彼の処置に窮した. I did not know [I was in a quandary as to] what to do with him. | 窮すれば通ず. There is

きゅうせい(ど) 旧制(度) the old [former] system ¶旧制高校 a higher school under the old system of education.

きゅうせかい 旧世界 the Old World.

きゅうせき 旧跡 a historic spot; a place of historic interest;〈遺跡〉ruins ⇨めいしょ(名所旧跡).

きゅうせきほう 求積法 〖数〗stereometry (体積の); planimetry (面積の).

きゅうせつ 急設 ¶急設する install《a telephone》hurriedly; lay《a cable》speedily.

きゅうせっき 旧石器 a paleolith ¶旧石器時代 the Paleolithic era; the Old Stone Age / 旧石器時代人 Paleolithic man (総称).

きゅうせん 休戦 《文》(a) suspension [cessation] of hostilities; a cease-fire; a truce; an armistice (平和交渉のための) ¶休戦する stop fighting (temporarily);《文》suspend [call off] hostilities; make a truce《with》;《文》conclude an armistice《with》/ 休戦協定 a cease-fire agreement; an armistice; a truce.

きゅうせんぽう 急先鋒 ¶…の急先鋒である be an active leader of 《the revolt》; be in the van [forefront] of《the movement》.

きゅうそ 窮鼠 文例⇩

きゅうそう 急送 ¶急送する send [《米》ship] sth by express; dispatch《a message》;《米》express《the goods》(運送会社便で).

きゅうぞう¹ 急造 ¶急造する build hurriedly;《文》construct in haste / 急造の hurriedly [hastily] built [constructed]; improvised / 住宅急造計画 a crash housing program (for urban residents).

きゅうぞう² 急増 a sudden [rapid, sharp] increase ¶急増する increase suddenly [rapidly].

きゅうそく¹ 休息 (a) rest;《文》repose ¶休息する rest; take a rest;《文》repose.

きゅうそく² 球速 the speed of a pitched ball;《a pitcher's》pace ¶球速を変える〈投手が主語〉change《one's》pace.

きゅうそく³ 急速 ¶急速な fast; rapid; quick; swift; prompt / 問題の急速な解決を望む hope for a prompt solution of the problem / 急速に進歩する make rapid progress.

きゅうたい¹ 旧態 the old [《文》former] state of things ¶旧態をとどめない《文》leave no trace of its former state; be changed beyond recognition / 旧態依然としている be [《文》remain] unchanged (as it was).

きゅうたい² 球体 a sphere; a spherical body; a globe.

きゅうだい 及第 ¶及第する pass《an examination》; make the grade; pass muster (基準に達する)/ 及第者 a successful examinee [candidate] / 及第点をとる get [obtain, receive] a pass [passing] mark [《米》grade]. 文例⇩

きゅうだん¹ 糾弾 (a) denunciation;《文》censure;〖法〗(an) impeachment ¶糾弾する denounce ; 《文》censure ;〖法〗impeach.

きゅうだん² 球団 (a corporation owning) a professional baseball team.

きゅうち¹ 旧知 an old friend [acquaintance].

きゅうち² 窮地 a predicament; an awkward position ¶窮地に陥る《口語》get into a scrape [fix, hole]; be forced into a (tight) corner;《文》find oneself in serious [desperate] straits / 窮地を脱する get out of difficulty [trouble]. 文例⇩

きゅうちゃく 吸着 adsorption ¶吸着する adsorb / 吸着剤 an adsorbent.

きゅうちゅう 宮中 the (Imperial) Court ¶宮中で at Court.

きゅうちょう¹ 級長 the president of a class; a class president.

きゅうちょう² 窮鳥 a bird in distress. 文例⇩

きゅうつい 急追 hot pursuit ¶急追する be in hot pursuit of sb; press hard on sb;《文》pursue《the enemy》hotly [closely].

きゅうっと ⇨きゅっと ¶きゅうっと一杯やる take [have] a long drink of《one's sake》; take [have] a long draft of《beer》.

きゅうてい¹ 休廷 ¶休廷する the court does not sit; 〈人が主語〉hold no court; adjourn the court (until). 文例⇩

きゅうてい² 宮廷 the Court ¶宮廷画家 a court painter (to Henry VIII)/ 宮廷生活 court life / 宮廷文学 court literature.

きゅうていしゃ 急停車 ¶急停車する〈車が主語〉stop suddenly [short]; come [be brought] to a sudden stop;〈運転者が主語〉bring (a car, a train) to a sudden stop;《口語》stamp [slam] on the brakes; put on [《文》apply] the emergency brake.

きゅうてき 仇敵《文》a [one's] mortal [sworn] enemy ⇨かたき.

きゅうてん 急転 ¶急転する change suddenly; take a sudden turn / 急転直下 suddenly; all at once;《口語》all of a sudden. 文例⇩

きゅうでん 宮殿 a palace.

きゅうとう 急騰 a sudden [sharp] rise (in prices); a jump ¶急騰する rise suddenly [sharply]; shoot up; jump (to 600 yen).

きゅうどう¹ 弓道 ⇨きゅうじゅつ.

きゅうどう² 旧道 the old road.

ぎゅうとう 牛刀 ¶にわとりを割(さ)くに牛刀をもってする kill a fly with a hand grenade.

きゅうどうしゃ 求道者《文》a seeker after truth.

きゅうなん 救難 (a) rescue ¶救難作業 rescue work.

---

always some way out of difficulty if you really look [one really looks] for one.

きゅうそ 窮鼠猫をかむ. Even a worm will turn. | A stag at bay is a dangerous foe.

きゅうだい 彼は文部大臣としてはまずまず[辛うじて]及第だろう. I think he just about gets a pass(ing) mark as Education Minister.

きゅうち² そのために彼は窮地に立つことになった. That put him in a very awkward position [《口語》in rather a hole).

きゅうちょう² 窮鳥懐に入れば猟師も殺さず. Even the huntsman refrains from killing a poor bird which has flown into his bosom for refuge.

きゅうてい 今日は休廷だ. The court will not sit today.

きゅうてん 事件は急転直下解決した. The matter has suddenly

ぎゅうにく 牛肉 beef.
きゅうにゅう 吸入 《文》inhalation ¶吸入する《文》inhale; breathe in; suck (in) / 吸入器 an inhaler; an inhalator / 〈患者に〉吸入(器)をかける have 《a patient》inhale (vaporized) medicine by means of an inhaler.
ぎゅうにゅう 牛乳 (cow's) milk ¶牛乳で育てる feed [raise] 《a baby》on cow's milk; bring up 《a baby》on the bottle / 子供に牛乳を飲ませる give a baby a bottle / 牛乳びん a milk bottle / 牛乳屋〈店〉a dairy; 〈販売者〉a milk dealer; 〈配達人〉a milkman.
きゅうねん 旧年 the old [past] year; last year.
きゅうは 旧派 the old school.
きゅうば 急場 an emergency; a crisis 《pl. crises》¶急場に間にあわせる fill [meet] the immediate needs (the needs of the moment); 《文》devise a makeshift / 急場をしのぐのに役立つ〈物が主語〉tide one over a crisis; pull one through a difficulty / 急場を助ける help sb out of a crisis; help sb in distress. 文例⇩
キューバ Cuba ¶キューバのCuban / キューバ共和国 the Republic of Cuba / キューバ人 a Cuban.
ぎゅうば 牛馬 horses and cows ¶牛馬のようにこき使う work sb hard; sweat 《one's workers》.
きゅうはく¹ 急迫 ¶〈事態が〉急迫する grow [《文》become] tense [critical, acute].
きゅうはく² 窮迫 ⇨きゅうぼう ¶財政が窮迫している be in financial difficulties.
きゅうはん 旧版 an old [earlier] edition.
きゅうばん 吸盤 a sucker.
ぎゅうひ 求肥 〈菓子〉Turkish delight.
キューピー 〈商標名〉a Kewpie doll.
キュービズム 《美術》cubism ⇨ りったい (立体派).
きゅうひせい 給費生 a scholarship student; a student on a scholarship.
キューピッド Cupid.
きゅうびょう 急病 a sudden (attack of) illness ¶急病にかかる be suddenly taken ill / 家族に急病人がでる have a sudden illness in one's [the] family.
きゅうふ 給付 〈支給〉⇨しきゅう²; 〈保険などの〉(a) benefit.
きゅうぶん 旧聞 old [stale] news.
きゅうへい 旧弊 ¶旧弊な人 an old fog(e)y.
きゅうへん 急変 〈突然の変化〉a sudden change [turn]; 〈変事〉an emergency; an accident ¶急変する change suddenly; 《文》undergo a sudden change; 〈病状が〉take a sudden turn for the worse.
きゅうほう¹ 臼砲 a mortar.
きゅうほう² 急報 an urgent message; 〈警報〉an alarm ¶急報する report promptly; send an urgent message (to); 〈を知らせる〉give [raise] the alarm. 文例⇩
きゅうぼう 窮乏 poverty; 《文》want; 《文》destitution; 《文》privation; 《文》indigence ¶窮乏している be poor; be badly off; 《文》be in needy [straitened] circumstances; 《口語》be on one's uppers / 窮乏に陥る become poor; 《文》be reduced to poverty.
きゅうほせんじゅつ 牛歩戦術 〈議場などでの〉delaying, stonewalling tactics.
きゅうみん 休眠 《生物》dormancy; quiescence.
きゅうむ 急務 urgent [pressing] business; a pressing [crying] need.
きゅうめい¹ 究明 ¶究明する study; investigate; inquire ((into)) / … の原因を究明する clear up [look deep into] the causes of….
きゅうめい² 救命 ¶救命具 a life jacket [《米》vest] (胴衣); a life belt (ベルト形の); 《米》a life preserver(胴衣・ブイなども含めて、広く浮くもの); 〈総称〉survival equipment / 救命胴衣 a life jacket [《米》vest] / 救命ボート〈いかだ〉a life raft; 〈短艇〉a lifeboat.
きゅうめん 球面 a spherical surface ¶球面幾何学[三角法] spherical geometry [trigonometry]; spherics.
きゅうやくせいしょ 旧約聖書 the Old Testament.
きゅうゆ 給油 〈機械への〉oiling; lubrication; 〈燃料の補給〉refueling ¶給油する〈人が主語〉oil [lubricate] 《wheels》; refuel 《an airplane》; 〈飛行機が主語〉refuel / 給油機 a tanker plane / 給油所 an oil depot; 〈ガソリンスタンド〉a filling [《米》gas, 《英》petrol] station ⇨ ガソリン / 給油タンク an oil-feeding tank. 文例⇩
きゅうゆう¹ 旧友 an old friend.
きゅうゆう² 級友 a classmate.
きゅうよ¹ 給与 〈手当て〉an allowance ⇨ きゅうりょう² / 給与所得 (an) earned [(a) wage] income / 給与水準 a pay [wage] level / 給与体系 a pay [wage] structure [system].
きゅうよ² 窮余 ¶窮余の一策として as a (means of) last resort; 《文》as a desperate shift.
きゅうよう¹ 休養 (a) rest; 《文》recuperation (病後の) ¶きゅうそく¹ ¶休養施設 vacation [rest and recreation] facilities; recuperation facilities (病後の). 文例⇩
きゅうよう² 急用 ¶急用で on urgent [pressing] business. 文例⇩
きゅうらい 旧来 ¶旧来の customary; long-established; customary ¶旧来の陋習を破る do away with the conventionalities of the past.
きゅうらく 及落 success or failure (in an ex-

---

been settled.
きゅうば 500万円あればこの急場がしのげる. Five million yen will tide me over [see me through] this crisis.
きゅうほう² 急報により警官が2人現場に駆けつけた. At the report two policemen rushed to the scene.
きゅうゆ 保有外貨の流出を抑えることはわが国目下の急務である. It is an urgent necessity for our country to check the drain on its foreign exchange reserves.
きゅうゆ 給油のため約1時間アンカレッジに立ち寄った. We [The aircraft] made a refueling stop of about an hour at Anchorage.
きゅうよう¹ 1週間自宅でゆっくり休養したまえ. Take a week's rest at home, (John).
きゅうよう² なにか急用があったら電話で知らせて下さい. Please let me know by telephone if

きゅうらく　314　ぎょう

amination); the result of an examination; examination results. 文例⇩

きゅうらく² 急落 a sudden drop [fall];《文》a sharp [steep] decline; a slump ¶急落する drop suddenly [sharply]; slump (to 600 yen).

きゅうり 《植》a cucumber; a gherkin (ピクルス用の小さい) ¶きゅうりもみ sliced cucumbers seasoned with vinegar.

きゅうりゅう 急流 a fast-flowing [《文》rapid, 《文》swift] stream; a fast [《文》swift] current; 〈激流〉rapids.

きゅうりょう¹ 丘陵 a hill; a hillock ★ hillock の方が hill よりも小さい ¶丘陵地帯 hill [hilly] country.

きゅうりょう² 給料 pay; a salary; wages;《文》remuneration ★ salary は普通月給で, サラリーマンなどに銀行振込みで支払われることが多い. wages は筋肉労働者などに現金で支給される週給をさし, pay はその両方の意を含む. pay に対する《文》の remuneration ¶高い[安い]給料 a high [low, small] salary; high [small] pay / 給料がいい〈会社などが主語〉pay well; pay good wages;〈人が主語〉be well paid / 給料が上がる〈人が主語〉get a salary increase [《口語》rise] / 給料をもらう get [《文》receive] one's salary (from) / have one's wages paid / 月20万円の給料をもらう draw [get] a monthly salary of 200,000 yen (from a firm) / 給料日 a payday / 給料袋 a pay envelope;《英》a pay packet. 文例⇩

きゅうれき 旧暦 the old [lunar] calendar. 文例⇩

きゅっと ¶きゅっと締める tighten (a rope) / 胸がきゅっとなる feel a tug at one's heartstrings; get a lump in one's throat. 文例⇩

ぎゅっと tightly; firmly ¶ぎゅっと縛る bind [tie] sth fast (with a rope) / ぎゅっと手を握る squeeze sb's hand.

キュラソー curaçao.

キュリー《放射能の単位》a curie (略: Ci) ¶キロキュリー a kilocurie / マイクロキュリー a microcurie / ミリキュリー a millicurie.

キュリウム《化》curium.

きよ 寄与 ⇨ こうけん⁴. 文例⇩

きよ¹ 居 ¶居を定める[構える] settle (in, at);

《文》take up residence [one's abode] (in, at).

きよ² 虚 ¶虚に乗じる, 虚をつく catch sb off (his) guard;《文》take advantage of sb's unpreparedness.

きよい 清い clean; clear; pure;《文》chaste (行状が潔白な); platonic (love).

きょう¹ 紀要 a bulletin; transactions; proceedings ¶語学研究所紀要 the Bulletin of the Institute of Language Teaching.

きょう² 起用 ¶起用する〈任命する〉appoint sb《to a position of responsibility》;〈昇任させる〉promote sb (to a higher rank).

きょう³ 器用 ¶器用な skillful; clever;《文》dexterous / 器用に skillfully; cleverly;《文》dexterously / 手先が器用である be clever with one's hands [fingers] / 手先の器用さ skill with the hands;《文》manual dexterity. 文例⇩

きょう¹ 今日 today;《文》this day ¶今日という今日 this very day / 10年前の今日 ten years ago today; this day ten years ago / 今日の午後 this afternoon / 今日の朝刊新聞 today's *Asahi* /（こともあろうに）今日に限って today of all days / 今日までは [until] today;《文》up to [up until] this day / 今日中に in the course of today; before the day is out; by the end of the day. 文例⇩

きょう² 凶 bad [《文》ill] luck;《文》ill fortune. 文例⇩

きょう³ 経 a sutra; the Buddhist scriptures ¶お経を読む recite [chant, read] a sutra / お経料 a priest's fee.

きょう⁴ 卿 Lord; Sir ¶藤原頼通卿 Lord Yorimichi Fujiwara; Yorimichi, Lord Fujiwara.

きょう⁵ 興 ¶興が乗る get [《口語》become] interested (in); warm up (to one's work) / 興を添える〈事が主語〉add to the fun (of); heighten one's interest (in) / 興をさます[ぐ] spoil the fun (of); kill one's interest (in); dampen [cool down] one's enthusiasm (for). 文例⇩

-きょう …強 a little over [more than]《fifty》; something over《2 pounds》¶5メートル強 a little [bit] longer than five meters; just over 5 meters.

ぎょう¹ 行〈文章の〉a line ¶行を改める begin a new line [paragraph] / 行間をあける

---

there is any urgent business for me.

きゅうらく¹ それで及落が決まるだろう. Your success will depend on it. / まだ及落がわからない. I don't yet know whether I've passed or failed.

きゅうりょう² 彼の給料は幾らくらいか. What is his salary? / How much [What] salary does he get [draw]? / 同社が従業員に支払う給料は総額1千万円に達する. The monthly payroll of the firm amounts to 10 million yen. / 彼は2年間病気で長期欠勤したが, その間会社は彼に給料を半額支給していた. He could not attend the office for two years because of illness, but the firm kept him on half pay.

きゅうれき この地方では今でも旧暦を用いている. In these parts they still use [go by] the old calendar.

きゅっと 突然ブレーキのきーっと鳴る音を聞けば, だれでも胸をきゅっと締めつけられるような気持ちがする. The sudden sound of brakes squealing will tighten anyone's stomach.

きよ これが世界の人口問題の解決に寄与する所は多大であろうと思う. I believe this will go a long way toward solving the world's population problem.

きょう³ 日本人の方がイギリス人よりも手先は器用だ. The Japanese are better [cleverer] with their hands than the English. |《文》The Japanese have greater manual dexterity than the English. / 器用貧乏. Versatility never pays.

きょう¹ 今日は何日ですか. What day of the month is it [today]? | What is the date? / 今日は11月3日です. Today [This] is the third of November. / 今日は金曜日だ. It is Friday today. | Today is Friday. / 今日から新学年が始まった. A new school year began

leave space between (the) lines ; 《印刷》space out / 行数 the number of lines ; linage (原稿などの).

ぎょう² 行 〈修行〉religious austerities; 〈勤行〉a service ¶行をする practice asceticism [religious austerities].

きょうあく 凶[兇]悪 ¶凶悪な atrocious; fiendish ; brutal; 《文》heinous ¶凶悪犯〈罪〉a vicious [《文》heinous] crime ; 〈人〉a vicious criminal.

きょうあつ 強圧 pressure ¶強圧を加える put pressure [《文》bring pressure to bear] on *sb*; 《文》coerce [《米》(high-)pressure] *sb* 《into *doing*》/ 強圧手段 highhanded [《文》coercive] measures ; a strong-arm method.

きょうあん 教案 a (draft) teaching program.

きょうい¹ 胸囲 *one's* chest measurement ; 《文》the girth of the chest ¶胸囲を計る take *sb's* chest measurement ; measure *sb's* chest. 文例⇩

きょうい² 脅威《文》a menace ; a threat ¶脅威となる[を与える] threaten [《文》menace] 《a country with war》; be a menace 《to》; be [pose] a threat 《to》/ …の脅威にさらされる be exposed to the menace of 《atomic war》. 文例⇩

きょうい³ 強意 ⇨ きょうちょう³ ¶強意語《文法》an intensive (word) ; an intensifier.

きょうい⁴ 驚異《文》(a) wonder ; a miracle ; a marvel ¶驚異的な wonderful; surprising; amazing ; astounding ; marvelous ; miraculous ¶驚異の目を見張る stare in wonder 《at》. 文例⇩

きょういく 教育 education ; 〈訓練〉training ; 〈教養〉culture ¶教育する educate ; train / 教育の[的] educational / 教育のある educated; cultured / 教育のない uneducated ; illiterate (文盲の) / 教育の機会均等 equal educational opportunity / 教育を受ける get [《文》receive] *one's* education 《at a college》; be educated 《at a school》/ 最高の教育を受けた人 a man of the highest education / 教育委員 a member of a board of education / 教育委員会 a board of education ; a school board / 教育映画 an educational film / 教育家[者] an educator ; an educationist ; an educationalist / 教育界 the educational world ; educational circles / 教育学 pedagogy ; pedagogics / 教育学部 the de-partment of education / 教育課程 ⇨ カリキュラム / 教育玩具 an educational toy / 教育機関 an educational institution [establishment] / 教育基本法 the Fundamentals of Education Act / 教育行政 education administration / 教育施設 educational facilities / 教育実習 teaching practice ; student teaching / 教育実習生 a student [trainee] teacher / 教育心理学 educational psychology / 教育制度 an education(al) [a school] system / 教育大学 a university of education / 教育庁〈東京都の〉the Office of Education / 教育長 the superintendent of education [schools] 《in Tokyo》/ (ラジオ・テレビの)教育番組 an educational program / 教育費 educational [school] expenses / 教育ママ a mother who is obsessed with her children's education ; a mother who persistently pushes her children to study [work]; an education-minded mother. 文例⇩

きょういん 教員 a teacher ; 〈初・中等学校の〉a schoolteacher; a schoolmaster (男); a schoolmistress (女); 〈全体〉the (teaching) staff ¶英語の教員 a teacher of English ; an English teacher / 体育の教員 a physical education [P. E.] teacher / 教員免許状 a teacher's license / 教員室 a staff [teachers'] room / 教員養成計画 a teacher-training program. 文例⇩

きょうえい 競泳 a swimming race [match, competition] ; 〈種目〉a swimming [《米口語》swim] event ¶競泳選手 a (competitive) swimmer.

きょうえん¹ 共演 ¶共演する play [appear, feature] together 《in a film》; 〈スターが〉co-star / ポール・ニューマンとロバート・レッドフォード共演の映画 a film co-starring [jointly featuring] Paul Newman and Robert Redford / 共演者〈スター〉a co-star.

きょうえん² 競演 a contest ; a competitive performance ¶競演する compete 《with》; play opposite 《another actor》.

きょうえん³ 供[饗]宴 a banquet ; a feast ; a dinner.
きょうおう 供応〈もてなし〉an entertainment ; a treat ; 〈宴会〉a dinner ; a feast ; a banquet ¶供応する treat *sb* to a dinner 《by way of bribing *him*》; 《文》entertain *sb* at dinner.

きょうか¹ 狂歌 a comic *tanka*.

---

today.
きょう² おみくじは凶と出た. The fortunetelling slip read 'unlucky'.
きょう³ その事件で，パーティーの興がすっかりさめてしまった. The incident took all the fun out of the party.
ぎょう その句は1ページの6行目にある. You will find the phrase in the sixth line [on line 6] of the first page.
きょうい¹ 彼は胸囲が90センチある. He measures [is] 90 centimeters around the chest.
きょうい² それは我が国の安全にとって重大な脅威となるであろう. It constitutes a grave menace to the safety of our nation, I fear. | I am afraid it will seriously threaten the security of this country. / 当時オーストリアはフランスの攻撃の脅威にさらされていた. Austria was under constant threat of attack from France at that time.
きょうい⁴ 彼があの岩を持ち上げるのを見た時は本当に驚異だった. It was a real eye-opener to me when I saw him lift that rock. | I was filled with wonder at the sight of him lifting that rock. / 最近10年間の日本の目覚ましい工業の発展に彼らはひとしく驚異の眼を見張った. They were all amazed at the wonderful progress of Japanese industry in the last ten years.
きょういく 彼は息子に立派な教育を受けさせたいと思った. He wanted to give his son a good education. / 多少は教育も受けました. I have had some education. / 日本は教育程度が高い. The Japanese have a high standard of education.
きょういん 彼は小学校の教員です. He is a primary school teach-

きょうか² 強化 ¶強化する strengthen 《the nation's defense》; reinforce 《a bank》;《文》intensify 《propaganda》; step up 《an advertising drive》; build [《米俗》beef] up 《the country's military strength》;《文》consolidate 《one's position》;〈食品を〉fortify [enrich] 《food with vitamins [minerals]》/ 強化合宿 camp training / 強化合宿に入る[入っている] live together [be] in a training camp / 強化ガラス tempered glass / ビタミン強化食品 vitamin-enriched[-fortified] food / 強化プラスチック reinforced plastics.

きょうか³ 教化 ¶教化する educate; civilize;《文》enlighten.

きょうか⁴ 教科 〈科目〉a subject;〈課程〉a course of study; a curriculum 《pl. -s, -la》⇨ カリキュラム.

きょうかい¹ 協会 a society; an association ¶日本ラスキン協会 the John Ruskin Society of Japan.

きょうかい² 教会 a church ¶教会の鐘 church bells / 教会へ行く go to church / 教会で結婚する be married in church / 教会員 a member of a church; a church member / 教会音楽 church music / 教会堂 a church / 教会暦 the ecclesiastical calendar.

きょうかい³ 境界 a boundary; a border ★boundary が, 2つの地方の厳密な意味での「区分線」をさすのに対して, border は漠然とその「区分線のあたり」を意味することが多い ¶境界を定める fix the boundary (line) (between) / 境界争い a boundary dispute / 境界線 a boundary (line) (between) ; a dividing line (between);《文》a line of demarcation (between). 文例8

きょうがい 境涯 〈境遇〉circumstances;〈身分〉《文》one's station in life.

ぎょうかい 業界 the industry; the trade ¶タクシー業界の人 people in the taxi trade / 業界新聞 a trade paper. 文例8

ぎょうかいがん 凝灰岩 〖地質〗(a) tuff.

きょうかいし 教誨師 〈刑務所の〉a (prison) chaplain.

きょうかく¹ 夾角 〖幾何〗an included angle.

きょうかく² 侠客 a 'knight of the town'; a professional gambler (in the Edo period).

きょうかく³ 胸郭 the chest; the thorax 《pl. -es, thoraces》¶胸郭が広い[狭い] have a broad [narrow] chest.

きょうがく 共学 coeducation ⇨ だんじょ.

きょうがく² 驚愕 ⇨ おどろき, おどろく.

ぎょうかく 仰角 an angle of elevation.

きょうかしょ 教科書 a textbook;《米》a schoolbook ¶歴史の教科書 a history text(book) / 教科書版 a text(book) edition.

きょうかたびら 経帷子 a (burial) shroud ;《文》a winding sheet.

きょうかつ 恐喝 ⇨ おどかし, おどかす.

きょうかん¹ 凶[兇]漢 〈悪人〉a villain; a ruffian;《米》a hoodlum;〈殺人者〉a murderer; a killer;〈暗殺者〉an assassin.

きょうかん² 共感 sympathy; (a) response ¶共感を感じる feel sympathy (for, toward); sympathize 《with》/ 共感を得る win [get, gain,《文》secure] sb's sympathy / 共感を呼ぶ arouse [《文》excite, gain] sb's sympathy.

きょうかん³ 教官 a teacher; an instructor ¶自動車学校の教官 a driving instructor.

きょうき¹ 凶[兇]器 an offensive [a dangerous, a deadly, a lethal] weapon ¶走る凶器 a weapon on wheels / 凶器準備集合罪で逮捕される be arrested on the charge of assembling with offensive weapons.

きょうき² 共起 〖言語〗cooccurrence.

きょうき³ 狂気 ⇨ きちがい.

きょうき⁴ 狂喜 ¶狂喜する be wild [beside oneself] with joy 《at the news》; go [fall] into raptures (at, over).

きょうき⁵ 侠気 《文》a chivalrous spirit ¶侠気のある 《文》chivalrous.

きょうき⁶ 狭軌 〖鉄道〗a narrow gauge ¶狭軌鉄道 [線路] a narrow-gauge railroad [track, line].

きょうぎ¹ 協議 《文》conference; consultation ¶協議する talk 《with sb over sth》; consult [confer] 《with》/ 協議会 a conference; a council / 協議事項 a subject of discussion ; a matter for consultation ; an item on the agenda / 協議離婚 (a) divorce by agreement [(mutual) consent]. 文例8

きょうぎ² 狭義 a narrow sense ¶狭義の教育 education in the narrow sense (of the word).

きょうぎ³ 経木 a paper-thin sheet of wood ¶経木の折り a box of paper-thin wood (for packing food).

きょうぎ⁴ 教義 a doctrine; (a) dogma;《文》a tenet ¶教義学上の doctrinal; dogmatic / (キリスト教の)教義問答 〈事〉《文》catechism ; 〈本〉a catechism.

きょうぎ⁵ 競技 a game; a (competitive) sport ; 〈試合〉a match ; a contest ; a competition ; 〈種目〉an event ¶競技をする have [play] a game [match] / 競技に加わる take part in a contest / 競技会 〈運動の〉an athletic meeting [《米》meet]; a contest ; a competition ; 〈技術などの〉a contest ; 競技施設 athletic facilities / 競技者 a contestant ; a player / 競技場 a sports ground

---

er. | He teaches in a primary school.

きょうかい³ リオグランデ川がアメリカ合衆国とメキシコの境界になっている。The Rio Grande forms the boundary between the U.S. and Mexico.

ぎょうかい その新発明は業界の話題になっている。The new invention is the talk of the trade.

きょうぎ¹ 両国政府がこの問題で直ちに協議に入ることに同意した。They agreed that the two Governments would immediately begin consultations regarding the matter.

ぎょうぎ 彼は行儀が悪い[を知らない]。He has no manners. / そんな行儀がありますか。Where are your manners! / 今日のパーティーではお行儀よくしましたか。Did you behave (yourself) at the party today? / 人が話をしているのにあくびをするなんてずいぶん行儀が悪いね。How ill-mannered you are to yawn when I am talking to you! / 君の行儀はまったくなってない。Your manners are absolutely deplorable.

きょうきゅう この類の品の供給は

[field, park]; a (sports) stadium.
ぎょうぎ 行儀 manners; behavior ¶行儀のいい well-mannered[-behaved] / 行儀の悪い badly-behaved; ill-mannered; ⦅文⦆ unmannerly / 行儀をよくする behave *oneself*; behave well [properly] / 行儀よくすわる sit properly / 行儀を習う learn manners [how to behave]; cultivate good manners / 行儀作法 (good) manners; ⦅文⦆ (matters of) etiquette. [文例⇩]
きょうきゃく 橋脚 a (bridge) pier.
きょうきゅう 供給 supply; service (電気·ガス·水道の) ¶供給する supply [provide, ⦅文⦆ furnish] *sb* with *sth* / 油の供給を受ける be supplied with oil ⦅by⦆; get [⦅文⦆ derive] *its* supply of oil ⦅from⦆ / (水道などの)供給区域 a service area / 供給源 a source of supply / 供給者 a supplier; a provider / 供給不足[過多] a short [an excessive] supply; an undersupply [oversupply] / 供給路 a supply route; a channel of supply. [文例⇩]
ぎょうぎょうしい 仰々しい 〈言葉などが〉 exaggerated; ⦅文⦆ bombastic; 〈見かけが〉 pompous; ⦅文⦆ grandiose; ⦅文⦆ ostentatious ¶仰仰しい肩書き a high-[grand-]sounding title / 仰々しく ⦅文⦆ ostentatiously; exaggeratedly / 仰々しく言う exaggerate; overstate ⦅*one's* case⦆. [文例⇩]
きょうきん[1] 胸筋 〔解〕 a pectoral (muscle).
きょうきん[2] 胸襟 ¶胸襟を開く confide in *sb*; take *sb* into *one's* confidence; ⦅文⦆ bare *one's* heart [soul] to *sb*; ⦅文⦆ unbosom *oneself* to *sb* / 胸襟を開いて語る talk with *sb* without reserve; have a heart-to-heart talk with *sb*.
きょうく 教区 〈キリスト教の〉 a parish ¶教区の教会 a parish church / 教区民 a parishioner; 〈総称〉 the parish.
きょうぐ 教具 teaching tools.
きょうぐう 境遇 〈身の上〉 circumstances; ⦅文⦆ *one's* lot; 〈環境〉 environment; surroundings ⇨みのうえ, かんきょう[2]. [文例⇩]
きょうくん 教訓 〈教え〉 the teachings ⦅of Confucius⦆; ⦅文⦆ a precept; 〈訓話〉 a lesson; a moral (寓(ぐう)意的の); 〈教える事〉 instruction ¶教訓を得る learn a lesson ⦅from⦆ / 教訓を引き出す draw a moral ⦅from a story⦆ / 教訓になる 〈事柄が主語〉 teach *one* a lesson; be a [an object] lesson to *one*; teach *one* ⦅to be more careful⦆ / 教訓的な instructive; ⦅文⦆ edifying. [文例⇩]
きょうげき[1] 京劇 classical Chinese opera [drama].
きょうげき[2] 挟撃 a pincer attack ⇨はさみうち ¶挟撃作戦 a pincer movement.
きょうけつ 供血 ⇨けんけつ.
ぎょうけつ[1] 凝血 〈事〉 coagulation of blood; blood clotting; 〈血〉 coagulated [clotted] blood; a clot of blood; ⦅文⦆ gore ¶凝血する blood clots [coagulates, congeals]; 〈事が主語〉 coagulate [clot, congeal] blood.
ぎょうけつ[2] 凝結 〈液体の〉 coagulation; congealment; congelation; setting (セメントの); 〈気体の〉 condensation ¶凝結する 〈液体が〉 coagulate; congeal; set (セメントが); 〈気体が〉 condense.
きょうけん[1] 狂犬 a mad dog; a rabid dog (狂犬病にかかった) ¶狂犬病 rabies; hydrophobia / 狂犬病の予防注射をする give ⦅a dog⦆ an antirabies serum injection.
きょうけん[2] 強肩 ¶強肩の外野手 an outfielder with a powerful throw.
きょうけん[3] 強権 state power ¶強権を発動する ⦅文⦆ invoke the power of (the) law; ⦅文⦆ institute vigorous action ⦅against⦆.
きょうけん[4] 強健 ¶強健な strong; healthy; ⦅文⦆ robust / 強健な人 a healthy person; ⦅文⦆ a person of robust health.
きょうげん 狂言 〈能狂言〉 a *Noh* farce; 〈芝居〉 a play; 〈作りごと〉 a fake; a trick ¶狂言自殺 a sham suicide / 狂言回し a subsidiary character (in a *kabuki* play) essential for the development of the plot.
きょうこ 強固 ¶強固な firm; secure; solid; strong / 意志の強固な人 a strong-willed person / 強固にする strengthen ⦅the defense⦆; make ⦅*one's* footing⦆ secure; consolidate ⦅*one's* position⦆.
ぎょうこ 凝固 solidification; coagulation; curdling (牛乳などの); setting (セメントなどの); 〔物〕 congelation ¶凝固する solidify; coagulate; congeal; clot; 〈牛乳などが〉 curdle; 〈セメントなどが〉 set / (牛乳などの)凝固剤 a coagulating agent; a coagulant.
きょうこう[1] 凶[兇]行 〈暴行〉 (an act of) violence; 〈殺害〉 (a) murder ¶凶行に及ぶ 〈乱暴する〉 do violence to *sb*; 〈殺害する〉 commit murder; murder *sb*.
きょうこう[2] 恐慌 a ⦅financial⦆ panic; (a) panic fear; a scare; (an) alarm ¶恐慌を引き起こす cause [bring on] a panic / 恐慌を来たす 〈人が主語〉 get into a panic ⦅about⦆; panic (★ panicked, panicking と変化する); be seized with panic [fear]; be panic-stricken; be alarmed; be scared.
きょうこう[3] 胸腔 〔解〕 the thorax ⦅*pl.* -es, thoraces⦆; the thoracic cavity.
きょうこう[4] 強行 ¶強行する force; enforce /

いつも充分あった[不足していた]. Things of this kind were always in plentiful supply [in short supply]. / インドネシアは日本の主な液化天然ガスの供給地である. Indonesia is the country from which Japan obtains the major part of its supplies [is Japan's main supplier] of liquefied natural gas.

ぎょうぎょうしい あの人の言う事は仰々しい. He has an exaggerated way of saying things.

きょうぐう 人間は境遇に左右される. Man is a creature of circumstances. / 今の境遇ではとてもそんなことはできない. In my present circumstances I cannot possibly afford to do it. | My present circumstances will not allow me to do so.

きょうくん これを教訓に, 今後はもっと慎重にしたまえ. Let it be a lesson to you. I hope you will be more careful in future. / 彼には無謀運転はやめろというい教訓になるだろう. Maybe that will teach him [that will be an object lesson to him] not to drive so recklessly.

強行突破する force [《口語》 bulldoze] *one's* way through 《the enemy's line》. [文例⇩]

きょうこう[5] 教皇 ⇨ほうおう[1].

きょうこう[6] 強硬 ¶強硬な strong; firm; 《文》 resolute / 強硬な決議文 a strongly-worded resolution / 強硬な手段を取る take strong [drastic] measures / 強硬な態度を取る take a firm attitude 《toward》; stand firm 《against》 / 強硬に反対する oppose *sth* stubbornly; offer [raise, set up] strong opposition 《to》 / 強硬派 the hard-liners; the hawks / 強硬路線を取る take a hard [hawkish] line.

きょうごう[1] 強豪 a veteran (player).

きょうごう[2] 競合 rivalry; competition ⇨せりあう ¶競合脱線 (a) derailment caused by a combination of factors.

ぎょうこう 僥倖 luck; a piece [stroke] of good luck; a windfall ¶僥倖にも by (good) luck; luckily; as (good) luck would have it. [文例⇩]

きょうこうぐん 強行軍 a forced march; 〈比喩的に〉 an exhausting trip 《around Europe》.

きょうこく[1] 峡谷 a gorge; a ravine; a glen (特にスコットランドやアイルランドでの); a canyon (大峡谷).

きょうこく[2] 強国 a (great) power ¶世界の強国 the powers of the world; the world powers.

きょうこつ 胸骨 〖解〗 the breastbone; the sternum 《*pl.* -s, -na》.

きょうさ 教唆 incitement; 《文》 instigation; 〖法〗 abetment ¶教唆する incite [《文》 instigate] *sb* 《to *do*》; 〖法〗 abet *sb* 《in a crime》.

ぎょうざ 餃子 ⇨ギョーザ.

きょうさい[1] 共催 ¶…の共催で 《文》 under the joint auspices of…; cosponsored by 《A and B》.

きょうさい[2] 恐妻 《文》 (servile) submission to *one's* wife ¶恐妻家 a henpecked [submissive] husband.

きょうざい 教材 teaching materials.

きょうさいかい[くみあい] 共済会[組合] a mutual aid association; a (mutual) benefit society; 《英》 a friendly society.

きょうさく[1] 凶作 a bad [poor] crop [harvest]; a crop [harvest] failure. [文例⇩]

きょうさく[2] 狭窄 〖医〗 stricture; stenosis.

きょうさく[3] 競作 ¶競作する compete [《文》 vie] 《with each other》 in composing [drawing, writing].

きょうざつぶつ 夾雑物 impurities.

きょうざまし 興冷まし ⇨きょうざめ.

きょうざめ 興醒め ¶興ざめなことをする spoil the fun [pleasure]; 《口語》 put a damper 《on the party》; 《口語》 throw a wet blanket 《over, on》 / 興ざめなことを言ったりする人 a killjoy; 《口語》 a spoilsport; 《口語》 a wet blanket. [文例⇩]

きょうさん[1] 共産 ¶共産化する 〈他の人を〉 communize; 〈自分が〉 go [turn] communist / 共産圏諸国 countries in the Communist bloc; Communist bloc countries / 共産主義 communism / 共産主義の communist(ic) / 共産主義者 a communist / 共産主義社会 a communist society / 共産制 《primitive》 communism / 共産党 the Communist Party / 共産党員 a communist / 共産党同調者[シンパ] a Communist sympathizer; a fellow traveler / 共産党宣言 the Communist Manifesto.

きょうさん[2] 協賛 〈賛成〉 approval; 〈支持〉 support; 〈後援〉 cosponsorship; 〈協力〉 cooperation ¶協賛する 〈賛成する〉 approve 《a plan》; 〈支持する〉 support 《a campaign》; 〈後援する〉 cosponsor 《a contest》; 〈協力する〉 cooperate 《with》.

きょうさん[3] 強酸 a strong acid.

ぎょうさん 仰山 ⇨たくさん, ぎょうぎょうしい.

きょうし 教師 〈学校の〉 a teacher; 〈(精神的)指導者〉 a teacher; 《文》 a mentor; 《文》 a preceptor; 〈師匠〉 a master ⇨きょういん, せんせい[2] ¶教師稼業 schoolteaching / 教師用指導書 a teacher's manual. [文例⇩]

きょうじ 教示 teaching; 《文》 instruction ¶教示する teach 《*sb* how to *do*》; 《文》 instruct 《*sb* in *sth*》.

ぎょうし 凝視 ¶凝視する stare 《at》; gaze 《at》; fix [fasten] *one's* eyes 《on》.

ぎょうじ[1] 行司 a *sumo* referee ¶行司溜(だま)り a seat (near the ring) for a waiting referee.

ぎょうじ[2] 行事 an event; 《文》 a function ¶学校の行事予定 a schedule for the activities of the school year.

きょうしきょく 狂詩曲 〖音楽〗 a rhapsody.

きょうしつ 教室 a schoolroom; a classroom ¶121番教室 Room 121 / 教室管理 classroom control. [文例⇩]

きょうしゃ 強者 a strong man; 〈総称〉 《文》 the strong; 《文》 the powerful.

きょうじや 経師屋 a paper hanger.

ぎょうしゃ 業者 a trader; a tradesman; 〈総称〉 the trade ¶関係業者 the traders concerned.

ぎょうじゃ 行者 《文》 an ascetic.

きょうじゃく 強弱 〈強さ〉 strength; power; 〈音の〉 loudness; 〈音声の〉 (a) stress; (an) accent.

きょうしゅ 興趣 ⇨きょうみ, おもむき.

きょうじゅ[1] 享受 《文》 enjoyment ¶享受する

きょうこう[4] 政府は同法案を国会で強行可決した. The government rammed [railroaded] the bill through the Diet.

ぎょうこう 僕が合格したのは僥倖です. It was by mere [pure] chance that I passed the examination. / 僥倖をたのむな. Don't rely on chance.

きょうさく[1] 今年は米は凶作だ. This year's rice crop has been a failure.

きょうざめ 興ざめなことを言うなよ. Don't be a spoilsport.

きょうし 教師になろうと決心した動機は? What has made you decide to be a teacher [to go into teaching]? / ある予備校で教師にならないかと言われた. I was offered a teaching post at a certain prep school. / 1960年以来僕は日本の大学で教師をしている. Since 1960 I have been on the faculty of a Japanese university.

きょうしつ 外国語は教室だけでは学べない. Foreign languages cannot be learned in class alone.

きょうじゅ[2] あの方はなんの教授だか知っていますか. Do you know what he is a professor of? /

きょうじゅ 《文》enjoy; have / 健康を享受する be in [《文》 enjoy, have] good health.

きょうじゅ 教授《事》teaching;《文》instruction;〈人〉a professor ⇨ きょうし ¶教授する teach sb (Japanese history);《文》instruct sb (in cooking); give lessons (in French) / 大沢教授 Professor [Prof.] Osawa / プリンストン大学の英文学の教授 a professor of English literature at [in] Princeton University / 教授会〈会議〉a faculty meeting [council];〈団体〉《米》the faculty; the professorate; the professoriate / 教授陣 the professors;《米》the faculty; the teaching staff (of a university) / 教授法 a teaching method; how to teach (English). 文例⇩

ぎょうしゅ 業種 a type of industry; a category of business [trade] ¶業種別に区分する classify by industry.

きょうしゅう 郷愁 homesickness;《文》nostalgia ¶郷愁を感じる be homesick; feel nostalgic [nostalgia] (for). 文例⇩

きょうしゅう² 強襲 an assault; a violent attack ¶強襲する assault; storm / 三塁強襲のヒットを放つ《野球》《口語》slug a hit too hot for the third baseman to handle.

ぎょうしゅう 凝集《文》cohesion; condensation ¶凝集する cohere; condense / 凝集力 (a) cohesive force; cohesion.

きょうしゅうじょ 教習所 a training school (for) / 自動車教習所 a driving school.

きょうしゅく 恐縮 ¶恐縮する〈好意・骨折りに感謝する〉feel obliged [《文》indebted] (to sb for his trouble); be grateful (to sb for his kindness);〈すまなく思う〉be sorry to trouble [for troubling, for having troubled] sb;〈恥じ入る〉feel small; be [feel] ashamed [embarrassed]. 文例⇩

ぎょうしゅく 凝縮 condensation ¶凝縮する condense.

きょうしゅつ 供出 delivery《of rice to the government》¶米を供出する deliver rice《to the government》/ 供出を割り当てる allot [allocate] a fixed quantity (of rice) to be delivered.

きょうじゅつ 供述《法》testimony; (a) statement ¶供述する testify《that..., for [against] sb》; state / 供述書 a written statement.

きょうしょ 教書〈大統領〉a message;〈法王の〉a (papal) bull /《米国大統領の》年頭教書 ⇨ ねんとう¹.

ぎょうしょ 行書 gyosho; the semicursive style of writing Chinese characters.

きょうしょう¹ 協商《外交》an entente ¶協商を結ぶ conclude an entente《with》/ 協商国 a party to the entente; the entente (集合的).

きょうしょう² 狭小 ¶狭小な narrow; small; limited.

きょうじょう 教条 ⇨ きょうぎ⁴ ¶教条主義 dogmatism; doctrinarianism / 教条主義者 a dogmatist; a doctrinarian; a doctrinaire.

ぎょうしょう 行商 peddling; hawking ¶行商する peddle; hawk / 行商人 a peddler; a pedlar; a hawker.

ぎょうじょう 行状 ⇨ ひんこう.

きょうしょく 教職 the teaching profession ¶教職につく[ある]《文》enter [follow] the teaching profession; become [be] a teacher / 教職員 the staff of a school; school personnel / 教職員組合 a school staff union / 教職課程 a teacher-training [a teaching, an education] course / 教職志望者 an applicant for a teaching post; a person who wants to become a teacher [to enter the teaching profession].

きょうじる 興じる amuse oneself (by doing); have fun ¶笑い興じる laugh gaily [merrily,《文》in merriment].

きょうしん 共振《物》(a) resonance; (a) sympathetic vibration (音叉(おんさ)の).

きょうしん² 狂信 fanaticism ¶狂信的 fanatical;〈人〉fanatic / 狂信者 a fanatic; a fanatical believer (in).

きょうしん³ 強震 a severe [violent] earthquake; a severe (earthquake) shock ¶強震計 a strong-motion seismograph. 文例⇩

きょうじん¹ 狂人 ⇨ きちがい.

きょうじん² 強靱 ¶強靱な strong; tough; stiff.

きょうしんざい 強心剤 a cardiotonic drug; a heart stimulant.

きょうしんしょう 狭心症《医》angina (pectoris).

ぎょうずい 行水 ¶行水を使う have [take] a quick bath in a washtub (in summer).

きょうすいびょう 恐水病 ⇨ きょうけん¹ (狂犬病).

きょうする 供する ¶閲覧に供する submit《document》for sb's inspection / 茶菓を供する serve tea and cake.

きょうせい¹ 共生《生物》symbiosis ¶共生する live together [symbiotically] / 共生関係 a symbiotic relationship.

きょうせい² 教生 a student [trainee] teacher.

きょうせい³ 強制《文》compulsion;《文》coercion ¶強制する compel; force;《文》coerce / 強制して...させる compel [force] sb to do;《文》coerce sb into doing / 強制されて under

---

彼は以前法政大学でドイツ語の教授をしていたことがある。He was once a professor of German at Hosei University. / その頃私はスタンフォード大学の教授だった。At that time I was on the faculty of Stanford University [at Stanford]. / 今一番重要なのは**教授陣**を強化することだ。What is most important to us now is to strengthen the teaching staff of our university.

きょうしゅう¹ 彼はパリ時代を思い返して郷愁を感じた。He looked back with nostalgia on the days when he lived in Paris. | He felt nostalgic when he remembered his life in Paris.

きょうしゅく これは恐縮です。It is very kind [good] of you. | I am very much obliged to you. / 恐縮ですがこれを写して下さい。I am sorry to trouble you, but could you [do you think you could] copy this for me? / 自らの誤りを指摘されて大いに恐縮した。I felt deeply ashamed when he pointed out my mistake.

きょうしん³ 昨夜当地に強震があった。We had a very strong

きょうせい compulsion / 強制的 compulsory; forced;《文》coercive / 強制的に forcibly; by force [compulsion] / 強制執行《法》compulsory execution; attachment (差し押え) / 強制執行令状 a writ of compulsory execution;《差し押えの》a writ of attachment / 強制収容する put *sb* into custody; confine《foreign nationals》in a camp / 強制収容所 a concentration camp / 強制送還 deportation / 強制保険 compulsory insurance / 強制力 compelling power [force] /《法的な》legal force / 強制労働 forced labor / 強制わいせつ行為《法》(an) indecent assault. 文例⇩

きょうせい⁴ 強勢 emphasis; (a) stress; an accent ¶ 強勢のある音節 an accented [stressed] syllable / 強勢を置く put [lay, place] emphasis [stress]《on》; emphasize; accent《a word on the first syllable》.

きょうせい⁵ 矯正 ¶ 矯正する reform; correct; cure; set [put] *sth* right / 悪癖を矯正する cure [break] *sb* of a bad habit / 矯正法《文》a remedy; a cure / 矯正視力 corrected eyesight.

ぎょうせい 行政 administration ¶ 行政の手腕 administrative ability / 行政上 administratively / 行政改革を行なう carry out an administrative reform; reform the administration / 行政学 public administration / 行政官 an executive officer; an administrative official / 行政管理庁 the Administrative Management Agency / 行政機関 an administrative organ [body] / 行政協定 an administrative agreement / 行政権 administrative power [authority] / 行政指導 administrative guidance / 行政整理 administrative readjustment / 行政訴訟 administrative litigation / 行政法 administrative law. 文例⇩

ぎょうせき 業績《scholarly》achievements;《sales》results ¶ 立派な業績を上げる get [《文》achieve] good《business》results; produce brilliant《scientific》achievements.

きょうせん 胸腺《解》the thymus (gland).

きょうそ 教祖 the founder of a religion [religious sect].

きょうそう¹ 競争 (a) competition; a contest; rivalry ¶ 競争する compete《with *sb* for *sth*, with [against] *sb* in *sth*》; rival《*sb* in *sth*》; contest《an election》/ 激しい競争 (a) keen [severe, cutthroat] competition; a tight race / 競争相手 a competitor; a rival / 競争価格 a competitive price / 競争圏内にある have a chance in the competition; be in the running / 競争圏外に落ちる have no chance in the competition; be out of the running / 競争試験 a competitive examination / 競争場裡《文》an arena of competition / 競争心 a spirit of rivalry;《文》emulation / 競争率 the ratio of successful (applicants) to total applicants. 文例⇩

きょうそう² 競走 a race ¶ 競走する run [have] a race《with》; race (against) *sb* / 競走に出る run [compete] in a race; enter [take part in, go in for] a race / 競走に出す enter《a car》in a race; race《a horse》/ 競走に勝つ[負ける] win [lose] a race / 100メートル競走 a 100-meter race [dash] / 競走用自動車[自転車] a racing car [bicycle]; a racer. 文例⇩

きょうそう³ 強壮 ¶ 強壮な strong;《文》robust; sturdy / 強壮剤 a tonic.

きょうぞう 胸像 a bust ¶ ルイ十四世の胸像 a portrait bust of Louis XIV.

ぎょうそう 形相 a《fierce》look.

きょうそうきょく¹ 狂想曲 ⇨ カプリチオ.

きょうそうきょく² 協奏曲 a《violin》concerto《*pl*. -s》.

きょうそく 脇息 an armrest ¶ 脇息に凭(もた)る lean on an armrest.

きょうそくぼん 教則本《音楽》a primer; a manual.

きょうそん 共存 coexistence ¶ 共存する coexist; exist together; live and let live / 共存共栄主義 the principle of mutual coexistence [live-and-let-live].

きょうだ 強打 ¶ 強打する hit *sb* hard; deal *sb* a heavy blow;《口語》wallop;《口語》belt;《米口語》slug / 胸を強打される get [《文》receive] a hard blow on the chest / 強打者《野球》a hard [powerful] hitter;《米口語》a slugger.

きょうたい 狂態《文》shameful [disgraceful] conduct ¶ 狂態を演じる behave scandalously.

きょうだい¹ 兄弟, 姉妹 a brother (男); a sister (女);《社会・人類》a sibling ⇨ 用語 ¶ 兄弟[姉妹]の〈男の〉brotherly;《文》fraternal;〈女の〉sisterly / 曾我兄弟 the brothers Soga; the Soga brothers / 兄弟[姉妹]愛 fraternal [sisterly] love / 兄弟[姉妹]げんか a quarrel between brothers [sisters] / 兄弟分 a sworn brother;《米口語》a buddy;《英口語》a mate. 文例⇩

用語 日本語では5人兄弟の1人に「ご兄弟は何人ですか」と聞く時, 自分を含めて数えて「5人です」という答が返るのが普通であるが, 英語では How many brothers and sisters do you have? という問いには, 尋ねられた方は, 自分を含めずに Four,

---

earthquake here last night.

きょうせい³ 強制されて契約書に署名したのです。I signed the contract under compulsion. / 彼に強制的にそうさせた。I forced him to do it.

ぎょうせい 現在の市長は行政の手腕に欠けている。The present mayor is an incompetent administrator [has no administrative ability].

きょうそう¹ 選挙の競争は激しかった。The election was sharply contested. / 学問ではあの人と競争できない。I am no match for him [I cannot rival him] as a scholar. / この値段ではアメリカに輸出しても競争にならない。At these prices we can't expect our exports to be competitive in the American market. / これらの国は労働力が安いので, 日本にとって容易ならぬ競争相手になりつつある。These countries with their cheap labor are offering serious competition to Japan. / Japan is having [meeting] serious competition from these countries where labor is cheap. / 輸出価格の上昇は世界市場における競争力を弱める。Higher export prices will weaken our competitive position in world markets.

きょうだい² 鏡台 a dressing table.
きょうだい³ 強大 ¶ 強大な powerful; strong; 《文》mighty.
きょうたく¹ 供託 ¶ 供託する deposit 《money in a bank, with sb》/ 供託金 a deposit; deposit money.
きょうたく² 教卓 a teacher's desk.
きょうたん 驚嘆 admiration;《文》wonder ¶ 驚嘆する admire;《文》wonder [marvel]《at》; be struck with admiration [wonder] / 驚嘆すべき《文》admirable; wonderful; marvelous. 文例⇩
きょうだん¹ 教団 an [a religious] order.
きょうだん² 教壇 the platform ¶ 教壇に立つ stand on the platform;〈教える〉be a teacher;《米》teach school / 教壇生活 a teacher's life.
きょうち 境地 〈あきらめの境地に達する《文》come to accept one's fate with resignation / 新しい境地を開く break new [fresh] ground 《in a field of investigation》; open up a new field 《in literature》.
きょうちくとう《植》an oleander.
きょうちゅう 胸中 ¶ 胸中の[に]in one's mind [heart] / 胸中を察する feel for sb; appreciate sb's feelings; sympathize with sb.
ぎょうちゅう 蟯虫 a pinworm; a threadworm.
きょうちょ 共著〈事〉collaboration; joint authorship;〈書物〉a joint work ¶ ...と共著で〈write a book〉in collaboration with...;《written》under joint authorship with... / 共著者 a collaborator; a coauthor; a joint author.
きょうちょう¹ 凶兆 a bad [《口》an evil] omen.
きょうちょう² 協調 cooperation; harmony (調和); conciliation (妥協) ¶ 協調する cooperate;《文》act in concert [union]《with》;《文》act harmoniously《with》/ 協調的 cooperative;《文》harmonious《with》/《文》conciliatory.
きょうちょう³ 強調 emphasis; stress ¶ 強調する emphasize; stress; lay [《文》place, put] emphasis [stress]《on》/ underscore; point up.
きょうつい 胸椎《解》the thoracic vertebrae.
きょうつう 共通 ¶ 共通の common / 全体に共通の性質《文》a characteristic common to all / ...と共通に in common with... / 共通一次試験 the common first-stage (university entrance) examination. 文例⇩
きょうてい¹ 協定 an agreement; a convention; a pact; arrangements ¶ 協定する agree on《the terms》; make arrangements《with》/ 協定が成立する〈当事者が主語〉reach [arrive at, come to] an agreement《with》/ 協定を結ぶ[廃棄する]《文》conclude [abrogate] an agreement《with》/ 協定価格 an agreed price / 協定書 (a copy of) a written agreement. 文例⇩
きょうてい² 教程〈課程〉a course of study; a curriculum 《pl. -la, -s》;〈教本〉a textbook; a manual.
きょうてい³ 競艇 a speedboat [motorboat] race.
きょうてき 強敵 a powerful [formidable] enemy [rival]. 文例⇩
きょうてん 経典 教典 ⇨ きょう³, せいしょ².
ぎょうてん 仰天 ⇨ びっくり.
きょうてんどうち 驚天動地 ¶ 驚天動地の earthshaking; astounding.
きょうと 教徒 a believer 《in》; a follower 《of》.
きょうど¹ 匈奴《史》the Hsiung-Nu; the Huns.
きょうど² 郷土 one's native province; one's (old) home; one's birthplace ¶ 郷土愛 love for [of] one's home province / 郷土玩具 a folk toy / 郷土芸能 a performing art peculiar to a locality / 郷土史 (a) local history / 郷土色 local color / 郷土人形 a local doll / 郷土料理 local [country] dishes.
きょうど³ 強度 strength; intensity (光などの) ¶ 強度の strong (glasses); powerful (lenses); intense (light) / 強度の近眼である be very nearsighted [shortsighted] / (材料の)強度試験 a strength test (on a sample of steel).
きょうとう 共闘 a joint struggle ¶ 共闘する struggle jointly《for, against》; form [present] a united front《against》/ 共闘委員会 a joint struggle committee 《for, against》.
きょうとう² 教頭 a head teacher.
きょうどう 共[協]同 cooperation; collaboration; partnership ¶ 共同する cooperate《with》; work together; team up《with》; join forces [hands]《with》;《文》act in concert [union]《with》/ 共同して in cooperation [conjunction,《文》concert]《with》; jointly / 共同の common; joint; united; public (公共の) / 共同の精神 a spirit of cooperation; a cooperative spirit / 共同の敵 a common enemy 《of Japan and China》/ 協同一致して in unanimous cooperation / 共同海損《保険》general average (略: G.A., g.a.) / 共同管理 joint control;《国際法》condominium / 協同組合 a cooperative society; a (producers') cooperative;《口語》a co-op / 協同組合店 a cooperative store;《口語》a co-op / 共同経営 joint management / 共同決議〈衆参両院の〉a joint resolution / 共同研究 joint [group] research(es);

きょうそう² あの山の頂上まで競走しよう. I'll race you [Let's have a race] to the top of that hill.
きょうだい¹ 彼は5人兄弟の上から2番目だった. He was the second oldest [eldest] of five brothers. | 兄弟は他人の始まり. When it comes down to it, brothers are little better than strangers. | In the final analysis, blood is no thicker than water.
きょうたん 彼はその難問を解いて人びとを驚嘆させた. He solved the difficult problem to the wonder and admiration of all.
きょうつう 彼らは共通の利害で結ばれている. They are bound together by common interests. | What binds them together is their community of interest. / 両者の間にはどこか共通点がある. The two have something in common with each other).
きょうてい¹ 日米間に協定が成立した. An agreement was reached between America and Japan. / 各新聞社が協定して広告料を値上げした. All the newspapers raised their advertisement rates by agreement.
きょうてき 日本チームは準決勝で強敵アメリカチームと対戦する.

a joint study / 共同作業 group work / 共同作戦 concerted operations / 共同事業 a joint enterprise [undertaking] / 共同社会 a community / 共同生活 community life; communal life [living]; living together / 共同正犯 an accomplice ⇨ きょうはん / 共同声明 《issue》a joint statement / 共同責任 ＜委員会・内閣などの＞ corporate [collective] responsibility / 共同戦線を張る form [present] a united [common, joint] front 《against》; join forces 《with》; 《文》make common cause 《with》/ 共同体 a community / 共同電話 (a telephone on) a party line / 共同便所 a public lavatory [convenience]; (a) public) comfort station / 共同謀議《法》(a) conspiracy / 共同募金 the community chest / 共同募金運動 a community-chest (fund) drive / 共同墓地 a (public) cemetery. 文例⑩

きょうとうほ 橋頭堡 a bridgehead; a beachhead (海浜の) ¶橋頭堡を築く establish a bridgehead [beachhead].

きょうねん 享年 one's age at death. 文例⑩

きょうばい 競売 (an) auction; (a) sale by [《米》at] auction ¶競売する[にかける] put up (an article) to auction [for sale]; auction (an article) (off); sell (an article) by [《米》at] auction / 競売場 an auction room / 競売人 an auctioneer.

きょうはく 脅迫 a threat;《文》(a) menace; intimidation (相手の弱味につけこんでゆすりなどすること);【法】duress ¶脅迫する threaten;《文》menace;＜相手の弱味につけこんで＞ intimidate; blackmail (金をゆする目的で) /殺すと言って脅迫する threaten sb with death; threaten to kill sb / 脅迫して…させる intimidate [blackmail] sb into doing / 脅迫されて…する do under duress / 脅迫的な threatening; menacing / 脅迫状 a threatening letter / 脅迫電話 (receive) a threatening telephone call. 文例⑩

きょうはくかんねん 強迫観念 an obsession; a persistent idea ¶強迫観念に悩む suffer from an obsession / …という強迫観念にとりつかれる be obsessed by [with] the idea [thought] that....

きょうはん 共犯＜事＞《文》complicity (in a crime); ＜人＞ an accomplice (of [with] sb in a crime) ¶事前[事後]共犯＜人＞【法】an accessory before [after] the fact. 文例⑩

きょうふ¹ 恐怖 (a) fear; terror; (a) fright;《文》(a) dread; (a) panic (恐慌) ¶恐怖に襲われる be terrified;《文》be seized with fear; be terror-[panic-]stricken / 恐怖を感じる be afraid of; fear; dread; be frightened [terrified]《at》/ 恐怖映画 a horror film / 恐怖心を抱かせる strike terror into sb's heart;《文》inspire dread [terror] in sb; scare; frighten / 恐怖症 a phobia《about water》; (a) morbid fear 《of women》/ 赤面恐怖症 erythrophobia / 対人恐怖症 anthropophobia / 閉所恐怖症 claustrophobia / 恐怖政治 terrorism; a reign of terror / 恐怖政治をしく rule《one's country》by fear.

きょうふ² 教父 ＜初期キリスト教の神学者＞ a Church Father; ＜洗礼時の名付け親＞ a godfather.

きょうぶ 胸部 the chest; the breast; ＜昆虫などの＞ the thorax (pl. -es, thoraces); the thoracic region ⇨ むね² ★ ¶胸部疾患 a chest disease.

きょうふう 強風 a strong [high] wind; a gale ¶(木などが)強風で吹き倒される be blown down in [by] a gale / 強風注意報 a gale warning.

きょうへん 共編 coeditorship ¶A氏とB氏の共編による辞典 a dictionary (jointly) edited by Mr. A and Mr. B / 共編者 a coeditor; a joint editor.

きょうべん¹ 強弁 ¶強弁する＜無理な理屈を言う＞《文》reason against reason; ＜言い張る＞ insist obstinately《on doing, that…》.

きょうべん² 教鞭 ¶教鞭をとる be a teacher《at》; teach at a school;《米》teach school.

きょうほ 競歩 competitive walking; a walking race; a (20-kilometer) walk ¶競歩選手 a walker.

きょうぼう¹ 共謀 (a) conspiracy;《文》collusion ¶共謀する plot together; conspire 《with》;《文》collude《with》/ …と共謀して in conspiracy [collusion] with… / 共謀者 a conspirator; an accomplice.

きょうぼう² 凶[兇]暴 ¶凶暴な brutal; ferocious; savage.

きょうぼう³ 狂暴 ¶狂暴な violent; frenzied.

きょうほん 狂奔 ¶狂奔する make desperate [frantic] efforts《to do》; be absorbed in《doing》/ 金策に狂奔している be busy raising money.

きょうみ 興味 (an) interest ¶興味のある interesting;《文》《a subject》of some interest / 興味のない uninteresting;《文》of no interest; dull ¶興味を覚える[持つ] be [feel] interested《in》; take an interest《in》/ 興味を起こさせる ＜事が主語＞ rouse [arouse,《文》awaken,《文》excite] one's interest《in》/ 興味を引く＜事

In the semifinals the Japanese team faces tough opposition from the American team.
きょうどう 費用は共同で負担することに皆同意した。We agreed that we would bear the expenses jointly. / 彼らは4人共同で車を買った。They bought a car between the four of them.
きょうねん 原氏は昨日池袋の自宅で死去された。享年75歳。Mr. Hara died at his home in Ikebukuro yesterday, aged 75.
きょうばい 競売はいつ行なわれますか? When will the auction take place? / それは競売で買ったのです。I bought it at an auction.
きょうはく 彼は裁判ざたにするぞと言って私を脅迫した。He threatened me with a lawsuit. | He threatened to take me to court. / 彼は私を脅迫して10万円取っていった。He blackmailed me out of 100,000 yen. / 脅迫されていた約束だから、守る必要はないはずだ。I don't think we need keep the promise, since it was made under duress.
きょうはん 彼が共犯者だと聞いて皆びっくりした。We were all surprised to hear that he was an accomplice [he had had a hand

きょうむ 教務 〈学校の〉 academic affairs [administration]; 〈宗門の〉 educational affairs ¶教務課 the instruction section.

ぎょうむ 業務 business; work ¶業務の拡張 expansion of business / 業務に励む apply oneself to one's work / 業務管理 business control [management] / 業務用の for business use [purposes]. 文例⇩

きょうめい 共鳴 〈事〉resonance; 〈音〉a sympathetic sound; a resonance; 〈共感〉sympathy ¶共鳴する 〈物体が〉be resonant 《with》; resonate; 〈人が〉sympathize [feel] 《with》; be in sympathy 《with》/ 共鳴を引き起こす cause [produce, set up] resonance(s); 〈人の心に〉strike a sympathetic chord 《in sb》; arouse [call forth] a response 《in sb's heart》/ 共鳴者 a resonator; a sympathizer; 〈特に共産主義の〉 a fellow traveler / (楽器の)共鳴板 a sound(ing) board; a resonator. 文例⇩

きょうもん 経文 the text of a sutra; 〈経典〉a sutra; Buddhist scriptures.

きょうやく¹ 共訳 ¶共訳する translate《a book from the French into Japanese》jointly [in collaboration]《with》/ ...共訳 translated《from the Russian into English》by...and....

きょうやく² 協約 ⇒ きょうてい¹ ¶団体協約 a collective agreement.

きょうゆ 教諭 a teacher.

きょうゆう 共有 joint [common] ownership ¶共有する own jointly; hold [have] sth in common / 共有者 a joint owner; a co-owner / 共有地 common [communal] land; a 《village》 common / 共有物〔財産〕common property.

きょうよ 供与 ¶供与する ⇒ あたえる / 借款を供与する give [grant] sb a loan 《of 10 billion yen》;《文》extend credit to sb.

きょうよう¹ 共用 ¶共用する share 《the bathroom》with sb / 共用の for common use; common.

きょうよう² 強要 ¶強要する force [compel,《文》coerce] sb《to do》.

きょうよう³ 教養 culture; education ¶教養のある educated;《文》cultured;《文》(a person) of culture / 教養のない (a person) without any [with no] culture; uncultured; uneducated / 教養を身につける improve oneself;《文》acquire some culture / 教養を高める raise one's cultural level / 教養を豊かにする enrich [broaden] one's education [mind]《by traveling abroad》/ 教養課程 a general education course / 教養(学)部 the college of liberal arts [general education]; the liberal arts school / 教養小説《ドイツ語》a Bildungsroman; an educational novel / 教養番組〈ラジオ・テレビの〉 an educational [a cultural] program. 文例⇩

きょうらく 享楽 ¶享楽する enjoy《the pleasures of the senses》/ 享楽的 pleasure-loving[-seeking]; given up to pleasure / 享楽主義 hedonism / 享楽主義者 a hedonist / 享楽生活を送る live a life of pleasure.

きょうらん 狂乱 frenzy; madness ¶半狂乱 ⇒ はんきょうらん.

きょうり¹ 郷里 the place where one was born and brought up; one's (old) home; one's native village [town]; one's birthplace ¶郷里の新聞 a newspaper from (back) home / 郷里の父 one's father back (at) home / 郷里の母に手紙を出す write home to (one's) mother / 郷里へ帰る go [come] home. 文例⇩

きょうり² 教理 a doctrine;《文》a tenet; a dogma.

きょうりきこ 強力粉 strong flour.

きょうりゅう 恐竜〔古生物〕a dinosaur ¶恐竜時代 the age of the dinosaurs.

きょうりょう¹ 狭量 ¶狭量な narrow-minded; intolerant;《文》illiberal.

きょうりょう² 橋梁 a bridge ⇒ はし³ ¶橋梁工学 bridge engineering.

きょうりょく¹ 協力 cooperation ¶協力する cooperate《with》; work together;《文》unite one's efforts《with》; join forces [hands]《with》;《文》make common cause《with》;《口語》play ball《with》/ ...と協力して in cooperation [《文》concert, partnership] with... / 協力者 a cooperator; a collaborator. 文例⇩

きょうりょく² 強力 ¶強力な strong; powerful;《文》potent;《文》mighty / 強力接着剤 a high-strength adhesive / 強力ビタミン剤 a high-potency [concentrated] vitamin preparation.

きょうれき 教歴 one's teaching experience; one's career [experience] as a teacher.

きょうれつ 強烈 ¶強烈な《文》intense; strong; severe / 強烈な一撃 a powerful [crushing] blow; a vicious punch / 強烈な色彩 hot [loud] colors.

ぎょうれつ 行列 〈列〉a procession;〈行進〉(a) procession; (a) parade; (a) march;〔数〕a

---

in the crime.
きょうみ そんな絵は私には興味がない。That sort of picture does not interest [appeal to] me. | I've no interest in paintings like that [of that sort].
ぎょうむ その電車の運転手は業務上過失致死傷の疑いで逮捕された。The motorman of the train was arrested on a charge of professional negligence resulting in injury and [or] death.
きょうめい ブルーノ・ワルターは現代音楽の傾向に共鳴しなかった。Bruno Walter was out of sympathy with modern trends in music.
きょうよう³ 彼はかなり教養がありそうだ。He seems to be a man of some culture.
きょうり¹ ご郷里はどちらですか。May I ask where you come [are] from? | 彼の郷里は鹿児島です。His home is in Kagoshima. | He comes [hails] from Kagoshima.
きょうりょく¹ 多くの人びとの協力によって工事は完成した。The construction was completed thanks to the united efforts of a great number of people. | A large number of people cooperated in getting [to get] the construction work done.

matrix《pl. matrices, matrixes》 ¶(買物などの)行列を作る form a line [《英》 queue]; line up;《英》queue (up) / 行列を作って歩く march in procession; parade / 行列式〘数〙 a determinant.

きょうれん 教練 (a) military drill.

きょうわ 共和 ¶共和国 a republic / 共和制(度) republicanism / 共和政治 republican government / 共和政体 a republican system [form] of government / (米国の)共和党 the Republican Party;《口語》the Grand Old Party (略: the G.O.P.) / 共和党員[主義者] a Republican.

きょうわおん 協和音〘音楽〙(a) consonance; (a) concord.

きょえい(しん) 虚栄(心) vanity ¶虚栄心の強い vain / 女性の虚栄心をくすぐる毛皮製品 furs that flatter women's vanity.

ぎょえん 御苑 an Imperial garden ¶新宿御苑 the Shinjuku (Imperial) Gardens.

ギョーザ 餃子 spiced minced pork wrapped in a small pancake and steamed or fried.

きょか 許可 permission;《文》leave;〈承認〉approval; sanction;〈免許〉(a) license;〈入学・入場の〉admission ¶許可する permit; give *sb* leave《to *do*》;〈承認する〉approve (of);《文》sanction;〈免許する〉license;〈入場・入学を〉admit *sb*《to [into] a place》/ 許可を得て by permission《of the authorities》;《do business》under license / 許可を得ずに without permission [leave] / 許可証 a license; a permit. [文例⇩]

ぎょかい(るい) 魚介(類) fish and shellfish; seafood.

きょがく 巨額〈金額〉an enormous [a colossal] sum (of money);〈量〉a huge amount; a vast quantity.

ぎょかく 漁獲〈事〉fishery;〈取れ高〉a《big》haul; a《good》catch ¶さけの漁獲割当量《Japan's》salmon catch quota.

きょかん 巨漢 a giant (of a man); a big man [fellow].

ぎょがんレンズ 魚眼レンズ a fisheye lens.

きょぎ 虚偽《文》(a) falsehood ¶虚偽の《文》false; untrue / 虚偽の陳述《文》a false representation;《文》(a) misrepresentation / 虚偽の申し立をする make a false statement《of *sth*, that...》;《文》misrepresent《*one's* age》.

ぎょき 漁期 a fishing [an open] season.

ぎょきょう 漁況 ¶漁況放送 a fishery [fishing] report (on the radio).

ぎょぎょう 漁業 fishery; the fishing industry ¶漁業会社 a fishery company / 漁業権 fishing rights / 日ソ漁業協定 the Soviet-Japanese Fisheries Agreement / 漁業協同組合 a fishermen's cooperative (association); a fishing [fishery] cooperative / 200 カイリ漁業専管水域《Canada's》200-mile fishing zone; (the area within)《Japan's》200-mile fishing limits.

きょきょじつじつ 虚々実々 ¶虚々実々の戦い a match between equally shrewd people;《it is》diamond cut diamond. [文例⇩]

きょきん 拠金 a contribution ¶拠金する contribute money《to a fund》.

きょく[1] 曲〈音楽〉music;〈1 曲〉a piece of music;〈節(ふし)〉a tune; a melody;《文》an air.

きょく[2] 局〈官庁の〉a bureau; a department;〈電話の〉a telephone exchange;《米》the central;〈郵便局〉a post office;〈放送局〉a broadcasting [radio, T.V.] station;〈囲碁などの勝負〉a game ¶局に当たる take charge of《an affair》; deal with the situation.

きょく[3] 極〈地球・磁気の〉a pole;〈窮まる所〉the climax; the extreme;《文》the extremity;《文》the culmination;〈絶頂〉the height;《文》the zenith;〈どん底〉the bottom;《文》the nadir ¶極の polar / 極の方に poleward / 貧窮の極に達する《文》be reduced to extreme poverty / 疲労の極に達する be utterly exhausted.

ぎょく 漁区 a fishing ground [area].

ぎょぐ 漁具 a fishing implement; fishing gear [tackle].

きょくいん 局員〈官庁の〉an official; the staff of a bureau (全体);〈郵便局などの〉a《post-office》clerk; the staff《of a post office》(全体).

きょくう 極右 the extreme right ¶極右分子 extreme right-wing elements; ultranationalists; ultraconservatives.

きょくがい 局外 ¶局外の outside;《文》external / 局外に立つ stand outside;《文》keep aloof《from》/ 局外者 an outsider; a third party.

きょくげい 曲芸 acrobatics; an acrobatic feat; a stunt; a trick (動物の) ★acrobatics は単複両様に扱われる ¶曲芸をやる do stunts《on horseback》/ 曲芸師 an acrobat; a tumbler / 曲芸飛行 stunt flying; aerobatics; aerial acrobatics. [文例⇩]

きょくげん[1] 局限 ¶局限する《文》localize; limit *sth*《to》;《文》set limits to *sth*.

きょくげん[2] 極言 ¶極言する go so far as to say《that...》; go to the length(s) of saying《that...》/ 極言すれば to put it strongly [at its most extreme].

きょくげん[3] 極限〈限界〉a limit;《文》bounds;〈極端〉《文》an extremity ¶極限に達する

きょか 先生の許可を得てからそうしなさい. Ask permission from your teacher to do that. | Ask your teacher for [your teacher's] permission to do it. / ここで写真を撮るにはその筋の許可を得なければならない. You must apply to the authorities for permission to take photographs here.

きょきょじつじつ 正に虚々実々というところだった. It was (a case of) diamond cut diamond.

きょくげい 曲芸を覚えるのには長年の訓練が必要だ. It takes years of training to learn acrobatics. | Acrobatics require(s) long training.

きょくげん[3] 極限状況のもとでいかなる行動を取るかは自分たちでもわからない. We cannot know how we will act when pushed to the limit.

ぎょくせき このクラスの学生は玉石混交だ. The students of this class are of very uneven ability.

きょくせつ 幾多の曲折を経て交渉がようやく妥結した. After many twists and turns the negotiations achieved a settlement.

きょくたん 彼らがロックアウトと

きょくさ **極左** the extreme left ¶極左分子 extreme left-wing elements; extremists of [on] the left.

ぎょくざ **玉座** the throne.

ぎょくさい **玉砕** ¶玉砕する《文》die a hero's death;《文》die the death of a hero / 玉砕を期する《文》seek an honorable death rather than an ignoble surrender;《文》choose death over dishonor / 玉砕攻撃 a suicidal attack; a banzai charge.

きょくしゃほう **曲射砲** a howitzer.

きょくしょ **局所** ⇒きょくぶ.

きょくしょう **極小** the minimum《pl. -ma, -s》¶極小の minimum / 極小にする minimize ⇒きょくだい.

ぎょくせき **玉石** ¶玉石混淆である be a mixture [jumble] of good and bad; be a jumble of wheat and tares [chaff and grain]. 文例◊

きょくせつ **曲折** 〈曲りくねり〉bending; winding; twists and turns;〈変化〉《文》vicissitudes; ups and downs;〈錯綜〉complications ¶曲折する bend; curve; wind; zigzag; meander 〈道・川など〉.

きょくせん **曲線** a curved line; a curve ¶曲線を描く describe a curve; curve / 曲線座標《数》curvilinear coordinates / 曲線美の女 a woman with a beautiful [a voluptuous, an attractive] figure;《口語》a curvaceous woman.

きょくそう **極相**《生態》a climax ¶極相に達する reach its climax.

きょくだい **極大** the maximum《pl. -ma, -s》¶極大の maximum / 極大にする maximize / 極大と極小《数》the maximum and minimum / 極大極小問題 a maximum-minimum problem.

きょくたん **極端** extreme; radical;《文》excessive / 極端な extremely; too far /《文》to excess / 極端に走る go to extremes [《口語》excess]; go too far / 極端から極端へ走る go from one extreme to another / 極端論者 an extremist. 文例◊

きょくち¹ **局地** a local area; a locality ¶局地的 local / 局地化[解決]する《文》localize《a war》. 文例◊

きょくち² **極地** the polar regions ¶極地植物 an arctic plant / 極地探検 a polar expedition.

きょくち³ **極致** perfection;《文》the culmination /《文》the ideal of beauty / 完成の極致《文》the acme of perfection. 文例◊

きょくちょう **局長** 〈官庁の〉the chief of a bureau;〈電話局などの〉the head of a telephone office [broadcasting station]; a postmaster 局長室 局長. 便/取締.

きょくていおん **極低温** a very [an extremely] low temperature ¶極低温物理学 very low temperature physics.

きょくてん **極点** ⇒きょく³.

きょくど **極度** ¶極度の《文》utmost; extreme; maximum / 極度の神経衰弱にかかる have a nervous breakdown of the severest [worst] kind / 極度に extremely;《文》to the highest degree;《文》to the utmost.

きょくとう **極東** the Far East ¶極東の Far Eastern.

きょくどめ **局留め** ¶局留めで手紙を出す send a letter poste restante [《米》to general delivery].

きょくのり **曲乗り** 〈自転車の〉trick [stunt] cycling; a bicycle trick;〈曲馬の〉circus [stunt] riding;〈飛行機の〉stunt flying; aerobatics ¶曲乗りをする do stunt riding [cycling, flying].

きょくばだん **曲芸団** a circus ⇒サーカス.

きょくばん¹ **局番** an exchange number.

きょくばん² **極板** a pole plate.

きょくび **極微** ¶極微の infinitesimal; microscopic.

きょくぶ **局部** 〈一部〉a (limited) part;〈局地〉a local area;〈患部〉the affected part [region];〈陰部〉the private parts;《口語》the privates ¶局部的 local / 局部的に locally / 局部麻酔 local an(a)esthesia. 文例◊

きょくめい **局名** 〈放送局の〉the name of a (broadcasting) station;〈無電の〉a call sign; call letters ¶局名のアナウンス《ラジオ・テレビ》station identification; a station break.

きょくめん¹ **曲面** a curved surface.

きょくめん² **局面** 〈碁や将棋の〉the position; the state of the game;〈情勢〉the situation;〈段階〉a phase ¶局面が一変する《文》the situation assumes [takes on] a new aspect / 局面を打開する break the deadlock; bring a deadlock to an end. 文例◊

きょくもく **曲目** a program; the selection《for a concert》. 文例◊

きょくよう **極洋** the polar seas ¶極洋漁業 polar-sea fishery [fishing].

きょくりつ **曲率**《数》(a) curvature ¶曲率が大きい[小さい] have a large [small] (amount of) curvature.

きょくりょう **極量** 〈薬の〉a maximum dose ¶極量以上に睡眠薬をのむ take an overdose of sleeping tablets.

きょくりょく **極力**《文》to the utmost; to the

いう極端なことまでしようとは思わなかった。Little did I think that they would take [resort to] the extreme step of a lockout. / 両極端は一致する。Extremes meet.〔諺〕

きょくち¹ 昨日の雨はほんの局地的なものだった。Yesterday's rainfall was limited to a very small area.

きょくち³ 心中は愛の極致であると彼は論じた。He argued that double suicide is the sublime culmination of love.

きょくぶ 直接患者の指に局部麻酔をかけてその手術を行なった。The operation was performed under a local anesthetic, injected directly into the patient's finger.

きょくめん² その事件で局面が一変した。The incident completely changed the situation. |《口語》After that had happened, it was a whole new ball game. / 我々は局面の展開を注目している。We are watching the development of the situation. | We are keeping an eye on developments [on how things develop].

きょくもく 皆さま次の曲目は『荒

ぎょくろ 玉露 high-quality green tea.

きょくろん 極論 ⇨ きょくげん².

ぎょぐん 魚群 a school [shoal] of fish ¶魚群探知機 a fish-finder.

きょこう¹ 挙行 ¶挙行する hold [give] 《a reception》; perform 《a ceremony》/ 挙行される be held; take place; come off. 文例⇩

きょこう² 虚構 an [a complete] invention; 《文》a fabrication; 《文》(a) fiction ¶虚構の made-up; invented; fictitious; false. 文例⇩

ぎょこう 漁港 a fishing port.

きょこくいっち 挙国一致 national unity ¶挙国一致内閣 a government of national unity. 文例⇩

きょしき 挙式 ¶挙式する hold a ceremony; 〈結婚を〉celebrate [《文》solemnize] the wedding 《of...and...》.

きょしてき 巨視的《物・数・経》macroscopic; 〈見方が〉comprehensive; 《文》all-inclusive ¶巨視的に見る take a broad view《of》; see sth in broad perspective / 巨視的経済学 macroeconomics / 巨視的理論《経》a macroscopic theory.

ぎょしゃ 御者 a driver; a cabman; a coachman ¶御者台 the driver's seat; the coach box.

きょじゃく 虚弱 ¶虚弱な the weak; delicate; feeble; 《文》infirm / 身体が虚弱である《文》have a weak constitution; be in delicate health.

きょしゅ 挙手〈敬礼〉a military salute; 〈採決の〉a show of hands ¶挙手する raise one's hand; show one's hand 〈採決で〉/ 挙手の礼をする〈片手を高く挙げて〉raise one's hand in salute; 〈軍隊式に〉salute; give [make] a (military) salute / 挙手によって採決する vote《on a question》by a show of hands. 文例⇩

きょしゅう 去就 ¶去就を明らかにする make one's attitude [position]《on a topic》clear; make it clear where one stands; 《文》define [clarify] one's attitude《to》; commit oneself《on》/ 去就を決する decide on one's course of action / 去就に迷う do not know which course to take; be in two minds《about, as to, whether》.

きょじゅう《文》residence;《文》dwelling;《文》abode ¶居住する live《at, in》;《文》dwell《at, in》;《文》reside《at, in》;《文》be domiciled《at, in》; inhabit《a place》/ 居住者 a resident; a (town-)dweller; an inhabitant / 居住人口 the resident population《of an area》/ 車などが〉居住性が良い be comfortable (to ride in) / 居住地 one's place of residence.

きょしょう 巨匠 a (great) master ¶画壇の巨匠 a great painter.

ぎょしょう 漁礁 a rocky place under the water where fish tend to gather ¶人工漁礁 a man-made gathering-place for fish.

ぎょじょう 漁場 a fishing ground [spot]; a fishery.

きょしょく 虚飾《文》ostentation; (an) affectation; (a) display; (a) show ¶虚飾的な showy;《文》ostentatious; flashy / 虚飾のない《文》unaffected; plain.

きょしん 虚心 ¶虚心(坦懐)に〈率直に〉frankly;《文》without reserve; 〈偏見なく〉without [free from] prejudice; open-mindedly.

きょじん 巨人 a giant;《文》a titan ¶財界の巨人 a leading figure in financial circles; a financial magnate / 巨人症《医》gigantism; giantism.

きょすう 虚数 an imaginary number ¶虚数単位 the imaginary unit ($\sqrt{-1}$, 記号: i).

ぎょする 御する〈馬や馬車を〉drive《a horse, a carriage》; 〈操る〉manage; handle; 〈制御する〉control ¶意のままに御する control sb at will; have sb at one's beck and call; twist sb around [round] one's (little) finger / 御しやすい easy to manage [deal with]; manageable;《文》tractable / 御し難い hard to manage [deal with]; unmanageable;《文》unruly;《文》intractable.

きょせい¹ 去勢 castration; emasculation ¶去勢する castrate; emasculate; geld (人間以外の動物を); 〈精神的に〉《文》effeminate; tame / 去勢牛 a bullock; a castrated bull / 去勢馬 a gelding; a castrated horse.

きょせい² 虚勢 a false show of power [influence, courage]; a bluff ¶虚勢を張る make a false show of power [courage]; put on a bold [brave] front; bluff; make a bluff.

きょせき【考古】a megalith ¶巨石文化 (a) megalithic culture.

きょぜつ 拒絶 (a) refusal; (a) rejection; (a) denial ¶拒絶する refuse; deny; turn down /《法》引受け[支払い]拒絶証書 a protest for nonacceptance [nonpayment] / 拒絶反応 rejection;《have》an allergy《to studying》. 文例⇩

ぎょせん 漁船 a fishing boat.

きょぞう 虚像《光》a virtual image; 〈一般に〉a false image.

ぎょそん 漁村 a fishing village.

きょたい 巨体 a big body; one's [its] bulk.

きょだい 巨大 ¶巨大な huge; enormous; gi-

「城の月」でございます. Ladies and gentlemen, our next number is 'The Moon over the Ruined Castle.'

きょこう¹ 式典は予定どおり挙行された. The ceremony went off [ahead] as planned.

きょこう² 彼の話は全くの虚構だ. His account is complete fiction [is totally fictitious].

きょこくいっち 国民は挙国一致して国難に立ち向かった. The (whole) nation rose to the national crisis as one man.

きょしゅ 原案に賛成の方は挙手を願います. Those in favor of the proposal, raise their hands. | I call for a show of hands on this motion.

きょぜつ 拒絶反応が始まった. Rejection set in.

ぎょっと その物音を聞いて彼はぎょっとした. He jumped at the noise. | The noise startled him. | The noise gave him a start [quite a turn].

きょどう 彼は挙動不審で警官に調

ぎょたく

gantic; colossal; monstrous / 巨大科学 big science / 巨大細胞[分子] a giant cell [molecule] / 巨大都市 a megalopolis.
ぎょたく 魚拓 (make) an ink rubbing of a fish.
きょだつ 虚脱 『医』(physical) collapse; prostration;〈無気力〉lethargy;〈無関心〉apathy ¶虚脱状態にある〈無気力である〉be in a state of lethargy;〈無関心である〉be sunk in apathy;〈ぼう然としている〉be utterly absent-minded; be in a state of absolute bewilderment.
きょっかい 曲解 (a) distortion;《文》a strained interpretation ¶曲解する distort [《文》pervert]《the meaning of a passage》; twist《sb's words》.
きょっかん 極冠『天・地学』a polar cap.
きょっけい 極刑〈最も重い刑罰〉the maximum penalty;〈死刑〉⇨しけい[1].
きょっこう 極光 ⇨オーロラ.
ぎょっと ¶ぎょっとする[なる] jump; be startled; be frightened; start; have one's heart in one's mouth [throat]. 文例⇩
きょてん 拠点〈基地〉a base;〈陣地〉a position; a strong point.
きょとう 巨頭 a leader; a prominent figure ¶財界の巨頭 a financial magnate; a leading financier [businessman] / 巨頭会談[会議] a summit [top-level] talk [conference].
きょどう 挙動〈振舞〉behavior;《文》conduct;《文》demeanor;〈行動〉actions; doings ¶〈体操などで〉一挙動で in a single movement / 挙動不審である act [behave] suspiciously. 文例⇩
ぎょどう 魚道〈魚群が常に通る道筋〉a regular course for fish;〈ダムなどに設けた〉a fishway; きょとっきょとっ ⇨きょろきょろ. ┃a fish ladder.
きょとんと ¶きょとんとして with a stupid [vacant] look; with a look of amazement; vacantly / きょとんとした顔をする look stupefied [vacant].
ぎょにく 魚肉 fish (meat).
きょねん 去年 last year ¶去年の5月に last May; in May (of) last year; a year ago last May.
用法 6月過ぎに, 単に last May と言うと今年の5月を指すこともあるので, それを避ける場合には in May (of) last year 又は a year ago last May と言う.
きょひ[1] 巨費 ¶巨費を投じる invest [sink] a huge sum of money (in) / 巨費を投じて at a great cost ★「10億円の巨費を投じて」というように, 具体的な大きな金額が添えられる時は, at a cost of one billion yen といって, great をつけないのが英語としては自然.
きょひ[2] 拒否 (a) denial; (a) rejection; (a) re-

327

ぎょろう

fusal; (a) veto (pl. -es) ¶拒否する deny; reject; refuse; turn down; veto / 拒否権を行使する exercise one's veto power / 拒否権を用いて葬り去る veto《a proposal》; block《a proposal》with a veto. 文例⇩
ぎょふ 漁夫 a fisherman ¶漁夫の利を占める《文》fish in troubled waters.
ぎょふん 魚粉 fish meal.
ぎょほう 漁法 a fishing method; how to catch fish; how to fish for《salmon》.
きよほうへん 毀誉褒貶 praise and [or] blame 《文》censure); (various) criticisms.
きょまん 巨万 millions ¶巨万の富を築く pile up [《文》amass] vast [immense] wealth; become a millionaire (multimillionaire).
ぎょみん 漁民 fishermen; fisherfolk.
きょむ 虚無 nothingness;〈虚無的な〉nihilistic / 虚無主義 nihilism / 虚無主義者 a nihilist.
きょめい 虚名 an empty name; a false [《文》spurious] reputation.
きよめる 清める purify;《文》cleanse; make sth pure;〈厄払いをする〉exorcize.
ぎょもう 漁網 a fishing net.
ぎょゆ 魚油 fish oil.
きょよう 許容 ¶許容する allow;《文》permit / 放射能の許容限度 the maximum permissible dose of radiation.
きょらい 去来 ¶去来する come and go;《文》recur (in one's mind).
ぎょらい 魚雷 a torpedo (pl. -es) ¶魚雷を発射する fire [launch] a torpedo (at) / 魚雷艇 [発射管] a torpedo boat [tube].
きよらか 清らか ⇨きよい.
きょり 距離 (a) distance;〈間隔〉an interval ¶距離がある be distant; be (ten miles) away / (競争相手との)距離が開く〈勝つ〉get a good [long] lead (on);〈負ける〉lag behind《one's opponent》/ 少し[3キロメートル]の距離を置いて at a short distance [at a distance of three kilometers] / (競走で)距離を詰める catch up on《one's opponent》/ 距離感 a sense [feeling] of distance / 距離競技〈スキー〉a distance race / 距離計(測定器) a range finder. 文例⇩
きょりゅう 居留 ¶居留する live [《文》reside] (in) / 居留地 a settlement; a concession / 居留民《Japanese》residents (in, at).
ぎょりゅう 魚竜『古生物』an ichthyosaur.
ぎょるい 魚類 fishes ¶魚類学 ichthyology.
きょれい 虚礼《文》dead forms; empty [hollow] formalities ¶虚礼を廃止する abolish [do away with] empty formalities.
ぎょろう 魚労[撈] ⇨ぎょぎょう ¶魚労長 a chief fisherman / 魚労民族 a fishing [piscatory] people.

べられた. The police called on him to account for his strange behavior.
きょひ[2] この決議もソ連の拒否権発動によってだめになるだろう. The resolution will be killed by the Russian veto.
きょり 東京から横浜までの距離はどのくらいありますか. How far is it from Tokyo to Yokohama? | What is the distance between Tokyo and Yokohama? / 交通機関が発達するほど, 世界の距離は短縮される. The world grows smaller as the means of transportation improve. | Advances in transportation shrink distances. / あの人のような腕前になるにはまだまだ距離がある. I have a long way to go before I even approach his skill. / 我々の考えには大きな距離がある. We are very different [poles apart] in our opinions. / 彼からある程度の距離を保っていた方がいいよ. You had better keep some distance from him.

きょろきょろ ¶きょろきょろする look around (restlessly); stare about / あたりをきょろきょろ捜す look around for *sth*.

ぎょろぎょろ ¶ぎょろぎょろ見回す look around [about] (*one*) staringly [with *one's* eyes rolling].

きらい¹ 機雷 an underwater [a submarine] mine; a mine / 機雷に触れる hit [strike] a mine / 機雷を敷設する lay [place] mines / 係留機雷 a moored mine / 浮遊機雷 a floating [surface] mine / 機雷原 a minefield / 機雷敷設艦 a minelayer.

きらい² 嫌い 〈嫌悪〉 a dislike 《of, for》; (a) distaste 《for》; 〈憎悪〉 (a) hatred 《for》; 《文》 (an) aversion 《to, for》; 〈気味・傾向〉 a suspicion; a tendency ¶嫌いな物 what *one* does not like / 嫌いである dislike; hate; detest; 《文》 abhor ¶きらう 《用法》/ 嫌いになる come to dislike *sth*; no longer like *sth* [*sb*]; do not like *sth* [*sb*] any longer [more]; come to have a dislike 《of, for》; take a dislike 《to》; 《文》 develop an aversion 《to, for》/ …の嫌いがある 〈…という欠点がある〉 be open to the charge of…; 〈少々…である〉 be slightly [somewhat] …; smack of…; there is a suspicion that…. 文例

きらう 嫌う do not like; dislike; hate; detest; 《文》 abhor ¶嫌われる be disliked [hated] by *sb*; 《口語》 be in [get into] *sb's* bad [black] books; 《文》 be in [get into] *sb's* bad graces. 文例

《用法》dislike と比べて、hate も detest も abhor もずっと意味が強いが、《口語》では hate は dislike とほとんど同じ意味で用いられることがある。

きらきら brilliantly; glitteringly ¶きらきらする glitter; sparkle; twinkle 〈星など〉 / シャンデリアの明かりを受けてきらきら輝いているダイヤモンド a diamond sparkling [glittering] in the light of the chandelier. 文例

ぎらぎら glaringly; dazzlingly; garishly ¶ぎらぎらする glare; dazzle / ぎらぎらする光 glaring [dazzling] light.

きらく 気楽 ¶気楽な 〈のんきな〉 easygoing; happy-go-lucky / 〈安楽な〉 comfortable; easy; carefree / 気楽に暮らす live in comfort [ease]. 文例

きらす 切らす 〈人が主語〉 run out of 《gas》; 〈品物が主語〉 be out of stock. 文例

きらびやか ¶きらびやかな gorgeous; gaudy; gay.

きらぼし きら星 ¶きら星のように居並ぶ外国の使臣たち 《文》 a galaxy [an impressive array] of foreign ambassadors.

きらめく ⇒きらきら (きらきらする) ¶空にきらめく星 stars twinkling in the sky.

きり¹ 切り limits; 《文》 bounds; an end ¶切りのない endless; 《文》 boundless; 《文》 limitless / 切りのいい 〈悪い〉ところ a good [an inconvenient] place to leave off / 切りをつける put a stop [an end] 《to》; settle. 文例

きり² 桐 a paulownia ¶きり箱 a box (made) of paulownia wood.

きり³ 錐 a gimlet (T字型の取っ手のあるもみぎり); an awl (靴屋などが使う突きぎり); an auger (らせん形の木工ぎり); a drill (金属・石などをうがつ); an ice pick (氷割り用の) ¶きりで穴をあける bore a hole in *sth* with a gimlet.

きり⁴ 霧 (a) fog; (a) mist (薄い) / 〈しぶき〉 spray ¶海[地上]の霧 (a) sea [ground] fog / 深い[濃い]霧 (a) dense [thick] fog / 霧がかかっている[立ちこめた, 流れる]谷間 《文》 a mist-hung[-filled, -swept] gorge / 霧のかかった朝 a misty morning / 霧の深い日 a foggy day / 霧を吹く 《flowers》; spray water 《on, over》/ 霧に深く包まれている be wrapped [enveloped] in a dense fog; lie deep in fog / 霧吹き a spray(er); an atomizer. 文例

-きり ⇒-だけ.

ぎり 義理 (a) (social) duty; (an) obligation ¶義理の父 *one's* father-in-law / 義理のおじ *one's* uncle by marriage / 義理を欠く 《文》 fail in [to perform] *one's* social duties [obligations] /…に対して義理を立てる do *one's* duty by *sb* / 義理と人情の板ばさみになる be torn between love and duty; do not know whether *one* should choose love or duty / 義理で from a sense of duty / 義理堅い have a keen [strong] sense of duty [obligation] / 《文》 have a meticulous regard for social duties / 義理知らずである have no sense of duty; be ungrateful. 文例

きらい 猫は嫌いだが, 犬は嫌いじゃない。I don't like cats but I do like dogs. / 彼は羊の肉が嫌いで決して口にしない。He [hates] mutton and never eats it. / なぜ急に彼が嫌いになったの。Why did you take such a sudden dislike to him?

きらう ほかの人があんなに嫌っていた仕事をなぜ彼が引き受けたんだろう。What made him take a job which nobody else would have anything to do with [would touch (, with a barge pole)]? / Why did he undertake the task when everyone else fought shy of it? / 彼はクラスで一番の嫌われ者だ。He is the most hated [disliked] boy in our class.

きらきら 湖は月光できらきらしていた。The lake glistened [sparkled] in the moonlight.

きらく (訪問客などに対して)気楽にしたまえ。Make yourself at home [comfortable]. / (余りあせらないで)気楽にやるんだね。Take it easy (, Tony)! / What's the rush [hurry]? | There's no rush!

きらす まだ少し小銭を切らしまして。I'm sorry I have no small change.

きり¹ ここは切りがいい[悪い]。This is a good [an awkward] place to leave off. / 切りのいい所でやめなさい。Stop when it is convenient [when you get to a convenient place]. / 甘やかせば切りがない。There has to be a limit to our indulgence toward him. / 人の欲には切りがない。Avarice knows no bounds. / 上を見れば切りがない。You'll never be satisfied if you compare yourself with those above you.

きり⁴ 細かい霧が立ち始めた。A fine mist began to form. / 霧が薄れた。The fog [mist] thinned. / 霧が晴れた。The fog [mist] cleared [lifted, cleared away]. / 空港は一面に厚く霧に包まれていた。The airport was shrouded in

きりあう 切[斬]り合う fight with swords; cross swords 《with》.

きりあげ 切り上げ ⇨ きりあげる ¶平価の切り上げ (a) revaluation 《of the Japanese yen》.

きりあげる 切り上げる 〈終わりにする〉 bring *sth* to an end; stop; close; finish; wind up; 〈端数を〉round 《a number》up [raise 《a number》]《to the nearest whole number》; 〈平価を〉revalue 《the yen》. 文例⇩

きりうり 切り売り ¶切り売りする sell《things》by the piece [slice] / 学問の切り売りをする peddle [hawk] *one's* knowledge; dispense measured doses of knowledge 《to》.

きりおとす 切り落とす cut [chop] off 《the end of a stick》; cut 《a branch》away 《from the tree》.

きりおろす 切り下ろす ¶刀を切りおろす cut down 《on *sb's* head》with *one's* sword.

きりかえ 切り換え 〈変更〉a change; 〈転換〉a changeover; a switchover; 〈電気の〉switching; 〈更新〉(a) renewal 《of the license》.

きりかえす 切り返す counterattack 《on, against》; make a counterattack 《against, on》; counter 《*sb's* demand for higher wages by threatening to dismiss *him*》.

きりかえる 切り換える 〈変える〉change; 〈転換する〉change [switch] over 《to》; 〈新たにする〉renew / 〈電気を〉switch / 頭を切り換える change *one's* way of thinking / ラジオ[テレビ]を他の局に切り換える change the channel; switch over 《to the NHK》 / 話題を切り換える change the subject; switch the conversation 《to another subject》. 文例⇩

きりかかる 切[斬]り掛かる attack [jump on] *sb* with *one's* sword; attempt to strike *sb* with *one's* sword; slash at *sb*.

きりかぶ 切り株 〈樹木の〉a (tree) stump; 〈稲などの〉(a piece of, a clump of) stubble.

きりきざむ 切り刻む cut [chop] 《a cabbage》up into pieces; hash 《beef》.

きりきず 切り傷 a cut; a gash 《大きな》; 【医】an incised wound ¶ひたいの切り傷の跡 a (knife)scar on *one's* forehead.

きりきり ¶きりきり回る spin fast / 頭がきりきり痛む have a splitting [piercing] headache / こめかみがきりきり痛む feel [have] a piercing [drilling] pain in *one's* temple / 忙しくてきりきり舞いする be frightfully busy 《with *one's* work》.

ぎりぎり[1] ¶ぎりぎりの最低値段 the lowest (possible) price; the (rock-)bottom price / ぎりぎりの時間に at the last moment; just [barely] in time 《for the last train》; at the eleventh hour. 文例⇩

ぎりぎり[2] ¶ぎりぎり歯を鳴らす grind *one's* teeth.

きりぎりす 【昆】a (long-horned) grasshopper; a katydid.

きりくず 切り屑 chips; ends ¶材木の切りくず chips of wood; wood chips.

きりくずす 切り崩す cut through 《a mountain》; level 《down》《a hill》(平らにする); break 《a strike》; split 《the opposition party》; undermine 《the solidarity of the opposition》.

きりくち 切り口 〈木口〉a cut end; 〈断面〉a section; 〈傷などの〉an opening; a slit (細長い).

きりこうじょう 切り口上 ¶切り口上で述べる speak in a clipped and formal manner.

きりさげ 切り下げ ¶〈平価の〉(a) devaluation 《of the yen》.

きりさげる 切り下げる reduce; lower; cut down; 〈平価を〉devalue 《the U.S. dollar》.

きりさめ 霧雨 a (fine) misty rain; a drizzle; a drizzly rain. 文例⇩

キリシタン [〈ポルトガル語〉*Cristão*] 〈教え〉Christianity in feudal Japan; 〈信者〉a Christian in feudal Japan ¶隠れキリシタン ⇨ かくれ / キリシタン文学 early Christian literature in Japan.

ギリシャ Greece ¶ギリシャの Greek / ギリシャ共和国 the Hellenic Republic / ギリシャ語 Greek / ギリシャ人 a Greek / ギリシャ正教 the Greek [Eastern] Orthodox Church.

きりすてる 斬り捨て ¶斬り捨て御免 the right to cut *sb* down [to slay *sb* with impunity].

きりすてる 切り捨てる 〈切る〉cut down; 〈殺す〉《文》put *sb* to the sword; 〈文》slay; 〈省略する〉omit ¶端数を切り捨てる omit [ignore, discard] fractions; round 《a number》down [reduce 《a number》] 《to the nearest whole number》/ 小数 2 位以下を切り捨てる omit the figures below the second decimal place.

キリスト (Jesus) Christ ¶キリスト教 Chris-

---

dense fog. / 空港は霧にとざされため, 空の便が再開するまで 2 時間も待たされた。The airport was fogbound, so we had to wait two hours for flights to restart.

-きり この辺にいるアメリカ人はあの人 1 人きりです。He is the only American living in this neighborhood. / これきりですか。Is this all? / これっきり言わないが, こんなばかなまねはやめなさい。I warn you, once and for all, that this foolishness must stop. / あれっきり彼女には会っていない。It was the last time I saw her. / I haven't seen her since. / それっきり何の消息もない。I have heard nothing more from him.

ぎり 彼には義理があったので, そうしたんです。I am duty-bound to him, so I did it. / 義理にもそうしなければならない。I am duty-bound to do so. / この金は義理にも受け取れない。I can't, in all conscience, accept this money. / 義理も人情も知らぬやつだ。He is a man lost to all sense of duty and humanity. / あの人は義理堅いんで弱るよ。He is a bit overconscientious in performing his social duties.

きりあげる もう 1 本飲んで切り上げよう。Let's have one last [final] bottle. / 今日の仕事はこんで切り上げよう。Let's call it a day. / こんな場所は早く切り上げよう。Let's get out of here soon.

きりかえる 簡単に頭を切り換えるような男じゃない。He's not the kind of man to change his way of thinking easily.

ぎりぎり[1] 最低ぎりぎりで幾らですか。What is the very lowest price you will take? / 締め切りぎりぎりにやっと間に合った。I barely managed to make the deadline.

きりさめ 霧雨が降っている。It is

きりたおす 切り倒す fell 《a tree》; cut [《文》hew] 《a tree》down.

きりだし 切り出し 《小刀》a short straight-bladed knife (with the cutting edge set at an angle).

きりだす 切り出す 〈話などを〉begin to talk 《about》; broach 《a subject》; 〈木を〉cut down 《trees》and haul 《them》out; 〈石を〉quarry 《marble from Carrara》.

きりたつ 切り立つ ¶切り立った崖(姜) a sheer [perpendicular] cliff; a bluff.

きり[1] 起立 〈号令〉Stand up! ¶起立する stand up; rise (to *one's* feet) / 起立投票にかける take a rising vote 《on a question》.

きり[2] 規律 《文》order; discipline; 〈規則〉rules; regulations ¶規律を守る observe [keep] discipline; observe [conform to] the rule(s) / 規律正しい orderly; well-disciplined / 規律正しく 《文》in good order; in an orderly manner. 文例 4

きりつける 切り付ける 〈切りかかる〉cut [slash] at *sb* (with a knife).

きりっと きりっとした〈服装などの〉smart; spruce; neat (and trim); 〈輪郭の〉clear-cut / 服装がきりっとしている be smartly [sprucely] dressed.

きりづま(やね) 切妻(屋根) 《建》a gable roof.

きりつめる 切り詰める 〈短くする〉shorten; cut *sth* short; 〈節減する〉cut down; 《文》curtail; 《文》retrench; reduce ¶暮らしを切り詰める curtail [cut down, cut back (on)] *one's* living expenses; reduce *one's* family budget / 切り詰めた暮らしをする 《文》live frugally; 《文》lead a frugal life.

きりどおし 切り通し a (road) cutting; a (road) cut; an excavation.

きりとりせん 切り取り線 the line along which to cut 《a section》off; 〈点線〉a dotted line; 〈ミシン目〉a perforated line; 〈表示〉Cut here.

きりとる 切り取る cut off [out, away]; 《文》excise; tear off (破って); ¶新聞記事を切り取る clip [cut out] an article from a newspaper; make a newspaper clipping [《英》cutting].

きりぬき 切り抜き 《米》a clipping; 《英》a cutting ¶新聞の切り抜き a newspaper clipping [《英》cutting] / 切り抜きを貼る scrapbook.

きりぬく 切り抜く cut [clip] (out) 《from》.

きりぬける 切り抜ける cut [fight] *one's* way through 《the besieging enemy》; find *one's* way out of 《the difficulty》; get over 《a difficulty》; come [struggle] through 《a crisis》. 文例 4

きりは 切り羽 《鉱山》a coal [working] face; a face ¶〈鉱夫などが〉切り羽で働く work at the face.

きりばこ 霧箱 《物》a cloud chamber.

キリバス Kiribati ¶キリバス共和国 the Republic of Kiribati.

きりばな 切り花 cut flowers.

きりはなす 切り離[放]す cut off [apart]; separate; 《文》detach; 《文》sever; uncouple (連結したものを); undock (宇宙船を) ¶…から切り離して apart [separately] from…; independently of…/ 切り離せない 《文》be inseparable 《from》. 文例 4

きりはらう 切り払う clear 《the land of trees》; cut 《the dead wood》away 《from the trees》; 〈枝を〉prune 《twigs from the tree》.

きりばり 切り張り ¶切り張りする patch 《a paper screen》; put a patch on 《a hole in a *shoji*》.

きりひらく 切り開く〈切開する〉cut *sth* open; 〈開拓する〉clear 《waste land》¶自分の運命を切り開く create [carve out] *one's* own future; hew [carve] out a career for *oneself* / 道を切り開いて進む cut [《文》hew] *one's* way [a path] 《through the jungle》.

きりふだ 切り札 〈トランプの〉a trump (card); 〈最後の手段〉*one's* last resort ¶切り札で切る play a trump 《on an ace》; trump 《*one's* opponent's card》/ 切り札を出す play a trump 《on a king》/〈奥の手を出す〉play *one's* trump card [*one's* ace]. 文例 4

きりぼし 切り干し〈大根〉dried (fine) strips of radish; 〈さつま芋〉dried slices of sweet potato.

きりまわす 切り回す manage 《household affairs》; run 《a store》; control 《a company》.

きりみ 切り身 a slice [cut] 《of salmon》.

きりむすぶ 切り結ぶ cross swords 《with》.

きりめ 切り目 ¶切り目をつける make a notch 《in》; notch; 《料理》score 《the meat》.

きりもみ 錐揉み 《航空》a (tail)spin ¶きりもみ状態で墜落する fall in a spin / きりもみ

---

drizzling. | A drizzly rain is falling.

きりつ[2] 学校の規律が乱れている。School discipline is not as it should be. / 軍隊は規律が厳重だ。Discipline is strictly enforced in the army. | Military discipline is very strict.

きりぬける 今までにも苦しい時代がたびたびありましたが、どうやら切り抜けてきました。We have often had hard times, but we've always managed to come [pull] through. / 5,000 万円あればこの急場を切り抜けることができるのですが。I'm sure 50 million yen will tide us over our present crisis.

きりはなす これはその問題とは切り離して論議すべきである。This question must be discussed separately from that one. / 世界の現状では政治と経済を切り離して考えることはできない。In the present state of affairs of the world, politics cannot be separated [dissociated] from economics.

きりふだ ハートが切り札です。Hearts are trumps. / 彼女は最後まで切り札を手放さなかった。She held the trump card [The trump card remained] in her hand to the very end.

きりょう 彼女は歌もうまいし器量もいい。She is a good singer and has (good) looks as well.

きりょう 技量は充分あるのだが、まだ経験が足りない。He is capable enough, but lacks experi-

きりもり 切り盛り management ¶切り盛りする ⇨ **きりまわす** / 家事の切り盛りの上手な婦人 a good housewife [housekeeper].

きりゅう¹ 気流 an air [atmospheric] current ; a current [stream] of air ; an air stream ; ⟨an⟩ airflow (航空機などの表面を流れる) ¶気流に乗る[乗って上昇する] ride [soar on] an air current.

きりゅう² 寄留 《文》temporary residence ¶寄留する live [《文》reside] temporarily (at a place, with sb) / 寄留地 a place of temporary residence / 寄留届 a report of one's temporary residence.

きりゅうさん 希硫酸 dilute sulfuric acid.

きりょう 器量 ⟨容貌(ぼう)⟩ looks ; 《文》features ; ⟨才能⟩ ability ; talent ; 《文》caliber ¶器量のいい good-looking ; ⟨女が⟩ beautiful ; ⟨主に男が⟩ handsome ; personable / 器量のよくない plain ; ugly ; 《米》homely / 器量人《文》a man of ability [high caliber].

ぎりょう 技量 ability; skill; competence ¶技量のある《文》able ; capable ; skilled / 技量を充分に発揮する give full play to one's abilities / 技量を磨く improve one's skill. 文例』

きりょく 気力 ⟨元気⟩ energy ; spirit ; vigor ; ⟨活力⟩ vitality ; ⟨勇気⟩ 《文》mettle ; pluck ; ⟨意志力⟩ will power ¶気力がある be energetic ; be full of vigor / 気力がない be spiritless ; do not have the energy to do / 気力が衰える one's energy [will power] fails one ; lose one's vigor [spirit] ; 《文》become enervated / 気力だけで《successed》by sheer force of will.

きりわける 切り分ける cut and divide ; ⟨肉料理を⟩ carve ⟨roast beef⟩.

きりん ⟨動⟩a giraffe ; ⟨中国の伝説上の動物⟩a legendary Chinese animal with a single horn, a deer-like body, horse-like hoofs, and an ox-like tail ; ⟨足の早い馬⟩a fast horse ¶きりん児 a (child) prodigy ; a wonder child.

きる¹ 切る cut ; carve ⟨roast beef⟩ ; hash (細かに刻む); saw (のこぎりで); clip [shear] (はさみで); slice (薄く); ⟨切り倒す⟩ fell ⟨trees⟩ ; cut down ; ⟨切符を⟩ punch ⟨tickets⟩ ; 《英》clip ; ⟨電気などを⟩ turn [switch] ⟨the light⟩ off ; ⟨電話を⟩ hang up ; 《英》ring off ; ⟨途中で止める⟩ pause ; stop ; break off ; ⟨トランプを⟩ shuffle ; riffle (2群に分けて両方から); cut (1回だけ) ¶ナイフ[ガラスの破片]で指を切る cut one's finger with a knife [on a piece of broken glass] / 10秒を切る run ⟨a hundred yards⟩ in under [in less than] 10 seconds ; break 10 seconds ⟨for the hundred meters⟩ / 身を切るような風 a cutting [piercing] wind / 切っても切れない関係にある be closely [《文》intimately] bound up ⟨with⟩. 文例』

きる² 着る ⟨着用する⟩ put on ; slip into ⟨a dressing gown⟩ (っとっと); ⟨着ている⟩ wear ; have on ; be dressed [《文》clad] (in white) ; ⟨罪を⟩ be charged with ⟨a crime⟩ ; take the blame [responsibility] for ⟨a crime⟩ (進んで) ¶りっぱな服を着ている be finely dressed / 着物を着たままで寝る sleep in one's clothes ; sleep with one's clothes on / ためしに着てみる try ⟨a coat⟩ on. 文例』

キルティング 《洋裁》quilting.

ギルド 《史》a guild ¶ギルドの会員 a guild member ; a guildsman / 職業ギルド a trade [craft] guild / ギルド商人 a guild merchant.

きれ 切れ ⟨布⟩ cloth ; material ; ⟨小片⟩ a piece ; a bit ; a fragment (断片); a slice (薄片); a scrap (切れ端) ¶木綿の切れ ⟨a piece of⟩ cotton cloth / ケーキ1切れ a piece [slice] of cake / パンの薄い1切れ a slice of bread / 切れのいい技(わざ) a cleanly [smartly] executed play [fall, trick].

きれあじ 切れ味 sharpness ⟨of a blade⟩ ¶切れ味がいい be sharp; cut well / 切れ味のいい文章を書く write in an incisive style / ナイフの切れ味を試す try a knife to see how well it cuts [will cut]. 文例』

きれい 奇麗 ¶きれいな ⟨美しい⟩ beautiful ; pretty ; fine ; ⟨容貌の⟩ handsome ; good-looking ; 《文》comely ; ⟨清潔な⟩ clean ; ⟨澄んだ⟩ clear ; pure ; ⟨整った⟩ tidy ; neat / きれいに beautifully ; finely ; ⟨清潔に⟩ clean ; ⟨きちんと⟩ neatly ; tidily / ⟨まったく⟩ all ; entirely ; completely / きれいにする ⟨美しくする⟩ make sth beautiful ; 《文》beautify ; ⟨飾る⟩ decorate ; 《文》adorn ; ⟨清潔にする⟩ clean ; make sth clean ; 《文》cleanse ; ⟨片づける⟩ put sth in order ; make sth tidy ; tidy up / きれいに書く write neatly / ⟨清書する⟩ make a fair copy ⟨of⟩ / きれいに忘れる forget all about sth ;《口語》clean forget sth / 借金をきれいに返す clear [pay off] one's debts / きれいごとで済ませる avoid complications ; whitewash ⟨an affair⟩ / きれい好きな cleanly ; tidy ; house-proud (主婦が). 文例』

---

ence. / 彼らは技量は伯仲である。They are equal to each other in skill.

きる¹ 彼はおので右脚をひどく切った。He gave himself a nasty cut on the right leg with a hatchet. / 電話を切らないで待っていて下さい。Hold [《口語》Hang] on, please ! | Hold the line, please !

きる² この暑さでは上着を着ていられない。I can't keep my coat on in this heat. / 彼女は彼の着ていたグレーのスーツをちらりと見た。She glanced at the gray suit he was wearing [he had on]. / 出席したくないわ、だって着て行く物がないんですもの。I don't want to attend the party, as I've nothing to go in [to wear (to it)].

きれあじ このかみそりは切れ味が悪い。This razor has lost its edge.

きれい こんなにきれいな花を見たことがない。I have never seen such a beautiful flower. / きれいなナプキンを下さい。Give me a clean napkin, please. / 正々堂々と戦ってきれいに負けるさ。Play fair and be a good loser. / 出掛ける前に部屋をきれいに片付けなさい。Tidy [Straighten] up your room before you go out. / 犬は皿をきれいになめた。The dog licked the plate clean. / 本ではきれいごとに書いてあるが、実情はけしからん話だった。This book glosses it over, but in reality it was a real scan-

ぎれい 儀礼 courtesy; 《文》etiquette ¶儀礼的に訪問する pay a courtesy call 《on》[a courtesy visit 《to》].

きれぎれ 切れ切れ ¶切れ切れの broken; disconnected; 《文》fragmentary / 切れ切れに in (broken) pieces; 《口語》in bits; 《文》in fragments. 文例⇩

きれこみ 切れ込み a cut; a notch.

きれじ[1] 切れ地 (a piece of) cloth.

きれじ[2] 切れ痔 bleeding piles.

きれつ 亀裂 a crack 《in the earth》; a crevice; a cleft; a fissure ¶亀裂を生じる crack; fissure / 亀裂を深める deepen the split 《in a group, between A and B》.

-きれない …切れない ¶いくら褒めても褒め切れない cannot praise sb [sth] too much; cannot speak too highly 《of》 / 食べ切れない be more than one can eat. 文例⇩

きれなが 切れ長 ¶切れ長の目 slit [almond] eyes.

きれはし 切れ端 a broken piece; a scrap; a chip; a fragment.

きれま 切れ間 ⇒きれめ ¶雲の切れ間 a gap [break, 《文》rift] in the clouds.

きれめ 切れ目〈切れた所〉《文》a rift; a gap; a break; 〈話などの〉a pause; an interval; 〈詩や音楽の〉a caesura; 〈尽きるところ〉an end.

きれもの 切れ者《文》an able man; a shrewd man (of business).

きれる 切れる〈鋭利である〉be sharp; cut well; 〈すれて〉wear; be worn out; 〈切断される〉break; come apart; snap 《糸などが》; 〈破壊する〉collapse; give way;《電話が》be cut off; be disconnected; 〈尽きる〉run out; 《文》be exhausted; be out of stock 《商品が》; 〈不足する〉run [be] short 《of》; 〈期限が〉expire; fall due; 〈才気がある〉be shrewd;《口語》be sharp; be very able; be bright; have a sharp mind ¶手の切れるような 1万円札 a crisp 10,000-yen note / 油の切れた機械 a machine which has run out of oil [that needs oiling]. 文例⇩

きろ[1] 岐路〈分かれ道〉a forked road; 〈十字路〉a crossroads ¶人生の岐路に立つ stand [be] at the crossroads of [a turning-point in] one's life.

きろ[2] 帰路 ⇒きと[2].

キロ- ¶キログラム a kilogram (略: kg); a kilo (pl. -s) / キロサイクル a kilocycle (略: kc) / キロトン a kiloton (略: kt) / キロバイト a kilobyte (略: K) / キロビット a kilobit (略: K) / キロメートル a kilometer (略: km) / キロリットル a kiloliter (略: kl) / キロワット a kilowatt (略: kW) / キロワット時 a kilowatt-hour (略: kWh). 文例⇩

きろく 記録 a record;〈文書〉a document;〈古(公)文書〉archives;〈年代記〉a chronicle;〈議事録〉minutes ⇒しんきろく, せかい（世界記録）¶記録する《文》record; write sth down; put sth on record;《文》chronicle / 記録を作る set [establish] a record [new mark]《in》/ 記録を破る break [smash, beat, better] the (Olympic) record (heat); record-breaking (output) / 記録的な, 記録破りの record (heat); record-breaking (output) / 記録的短時間で in record time / 自己最高記録 one's personal best [record]; one's best performance / 優勝記録 the winning record;〈競走などの〉the winning time / 記録映画 a documentary film [movie]; a documentary / 記録係 a scorer; a scorekeeper;〈映画などの〉a continuity man [girl];〈計時係〉a timekeeper /《文》a recording device; a recorder / 記録保持者 a record holder (in [for] the high jump). 文例⇩

ギロチン a guillotine ¶ギロチンにかける guillotine.

ぎろん 議論〈立論〉(an) argument;〈討議〉(a) discussion;〈討論〉(a) debate;〈論争〉(a) dispute; (a) controversy ¶筋の通った議論 a consistent argument / 激しい議論 a heated debate /, 議論する argue 《that…, against [for, about, over] sth, with sb》; discuss 《sth with sb》; debate 《(on [about]) sth with sb》; dispute 《about sth》/ 徹底的に議論して解決する argue sth out [thoroughly] 《with sb》; have it out 《with sb》; thrash [thresh] out 《a problem》/ 議論のために議論する argue for argument's sake / 議論の相手になる meet sb in argument / 議論のある問題 a matter of argument [debate, controversy]; a moot point [question] / 議論の余地のない《文》inarguable;《文》indisputable / 議論をとことんまで押し進める pursue an argument to its logical conclusion / 議論に勝つ [負ける] win [lose] an argument; have [get] the best [worst] of an argument / 議論好きな argumentative;《文》

---

dal. / 彼はきれい好きだ。 He is very tidy. | He has neat habits.

きれぎれ 隣の部屋の話し声が切れ切れに聞こえてきた。 Snatches of conversation could be heard from the next room.

-きれない この部屋に 100人は入り切れない。 This room is too small to contain a hundred men. / 使い切れないほど金がある。 He has more money than he can spend.

きれる ナイフが切れなくなった。 My knife has lost its edge. / この糸が切れた。 The string of the kite has broken [snapped]. / 雲が切れてきた。 The clouds are breaking. / 話が途中で切れた。 We were cut off in the middle of our conversation. / あと 2 日で契約の期限が切れます。 The contract expires [runs out] in two days. / それでは元値が切れます。 That would be below cost.

キロ- 東京大阪間のキロ数はどのくらいになりますか。 What is the distance between Tokyo and Osaka in kilometers?

きろく 彼の記録は 4分 28秒 4だった。 His record was [He was timed at] 4:28.4. / そのためには注意深く観察し忠実に記録を取ることが必要だ。 It calls for careful observation and faithful record-keeping. / 彼は 400メートルを 46秒 5の記録で優勝した。 He won the 400 meters [the 400-meter race] with a time of 46.5 seconds.

ぎろん 議論百出してついに決定を見るに至らなかった。 There were so many disputes that we could not come to a decision. / 2 人の子供が竹が木か草かで議論していた。 The two boys were discuss-

きわ 際 〈端〉 an edge; a brink; a verge; 〈そば〉 a side.

ぎわく 疑惑 (a) doubt; (a) suspicion ⇒ **ぎねん**, **うたがい**.

きわだつ 際立つ be conspicuous; be prominent; stand out ¶際立った conspicuous; prominent; striking; 《文》 salient.

きわどい 〈危険な〉 dangerous; risky; tricky; 《文》 hazardous; 〈間一髪の〉 close; hairbreadth; 〈微妙な〉 delicate; 〈みだらな〉 verging on indecency; suggestive ¶きわどい芸当をやる make a risky attempt; 〈法や道徳にすれすれの〉 sail near [close to] the wind / きわどい勝負 a close game [contest] / きわどい時に[所で] in the nick of time; at a critical moment / きわどい判定 a dubious [debatable] decision. 文例◐

きわまりない 窮[極]まりない be infinite; be endless ¶危険極まりない be extremely dangerous.

きわまる 窮[極]まる 〈終わる〉 end; come to an end; 〈極度に達する〉 reach [be carried to] an extreme ¶不都合極まる be quite [absolutely] outrageous / 極まるところを知らない there is no end to ⟨his avarice⟩; 《文》 know no bounds. 文例◐

きわみ 極み ¶遺憾の極みである be most regrettable.

きわめて 極めて very; extremely; 《文》 exceedingly; in the extreme ¶極めて寛大である be very [exceedingly] generous; be generous in the extreme.

きわめる 究[窮, 極]める 〈研鑽する〉 study [investigate] sth thoroughly; master; 〈果てまで行く〉 go to the end (of); go to extremes ¶頂上を極める reach [《文》 attain] the summit ⟨of a mountain⟩ / 真相を究める get at the truth [to the bottom] ⟨of an affair⟩ / 暴虐を極める 《文》 be tyrannical in the extreme / 残忍を極める be most cruel / 口を極めて賞する speak of sb in the highest terms; be very loud in one's praises of sb. 文例◐

きわもの 際物 ¶際物の ⟨a novel⟩ on the (short-lived) topic of the day; 《文》 ephemeral ⟨publications⟩.

きん¹ 斤 a kin (=600 g).

きん² 金 gold; ¶金の gold; made of gold; 《文》 golden / 金のような golden / 金の卵を産むがちょう ⟨kill⟩ the goose that lays the golden eggs; the golden goose / 金を含む auriferous / 同じ目方の金に等しい値打ちがある be worth its weight in gold / 金色の gold(en-colored) / 金細工 goldwork / 金細工師 a goldsmith / 金時計 a gold watch / 金ペン a gold pen [nib].

きん³ 菌 a germ; 《医》 a bacterium ⟪pl. bacteria⟫; a bacillus ⟪pl. bacilli⟫.

きん⁴ 筋 ⇒ **きんにく** ¶後頭筋 a posterior head muscle / 筋ジストロフィー muscular dystrophy.

きん⁵ 禁 《文》 (a) prohibition; a ban ⟪on smoking⟫ ¶禁を犯す break [《文》 violate] the ban [prohibition].

ぎん 銀 silver ¶銀の silver; made of silver / 銀色の silver; silvery / 銀鉱石 silver ore / 銀細工 silverwork / 銀細工師 a silversmith / 銀時計 a silver watch. 文例◐

きんあつ 禁圧 suppression; 《文》 (a) prohibition; a ban ⟪on sth⟫ ¶禁圧する suppress; prohibit; ban.

きんいつ 均一 uniformity ¶均一の uniform / 千円均一で ⟨sell⟩ at a flat rate [uniform price] of 1,000 yen / 均一値段 a uniform [flat] price. 文例◐

きんいん¹ 近因 an immediate [a proximate] cause.

きんいん² 金印 a gold seal.

きんえい 近影 sb's recent [latest] photograph [picture].

きんえん¹ 近縁 ¶…と近縁関係にある, …の近縁種である be closely related to…; be a near relation [close relative] of….

きんえん² 筋炎 《医》 myositis.

きんえん³ 禁煙 ¶禁煙する stop [give up, 《米口語》 quit, 《文》 abstain from] smoking / 禁煙の掲示[サイン] a no-smoking sign. 文例◐

きんか¹ 近火 a fire in one's neighborhood.

きんか² 金貨 a gold coin [piece].

ぎんか 銀貨 a silver coin [piece].

ぎんが 銀河 the Milky Way; the Galaxy ¶銀河系 the galactic system / 銀河系外星雲 an external galaxy.

きんかい¹ 近海 《文》 the adjoining [near] seas;

---

ing whether bamboo is a tree or a (type of) grass. / それが本当に有毒かどうかは議論のあるところだ. Whether it is really toxic is a matter of controversy [a moot point]. | There is controversy as to whether it is really toxic. / 暴力じゃなくて議論でこい. Use arguments, not violence.

きわどい きわどいところで終電に間にあった. I was just in time for the last train. / 彼はきわどいところで助かった. He escaped narrowly. | He had a narrow escape.

きわまる 物窮まれば変ず. When matters develop beyond a certain point [reach extremes], changes are bound to occur. / 無礼極まるやつだ. What a rude fellow he is!

きわめる 広くすべての事を知ると共に, 一事を究めよ. Know something about everything and everything about something.

ぎん 朝起きて見たら一面の銀世界だった. I awoke to find the whole place covered with 《文》 mantled in] snow.

きんいつ 市電の運賃は 140 円均一です. A flat fare of 140 yen [uniform 140-yen fare] is charged on the streetcars here.

きんえん 禁煙. 『掲示』 No smoking. / 教室内では禁煙です. Smoking is prohibited [is not allowed] in the classrooms. / 「禁煙」のサインがついているうちはおタバコはご遠慮下さい. Please refrain from smoking while the 'No Smoking' signs are on.

きんか 昨Е近火のところ, 早速お見舞い頂きまして, ありがたくお礼申し上げます. Thank you very much for your kind inquiry after

home [the neighboring] waters ¶銚子の近海で in the sea near Choshi; off Choshi / 近海漁業 inshore fishery [fishing] / 近海もの[魚] an inshore fish.

きんかい[2] 金塊 a lump [nugget] of gold (未鋳造の); a gold ingot (鋳塊); a gold bar (棒状の); gold bullion (総称).

き

ぎんかい 銀塊 a silver ingot (鋳塊); a silver bar (棒状の); silver bullion (総称).

ぎんかいしょく 銀灰色 silver gray ¶銀灰色の silver-gray.

きんかぎょくじょう 金科玉条 a golden rule ¶金科玉条とする stick fast 《to》; recognize no other authority 《than》; 《文》 adhere strictly 《to》.

きんがく[1] 金額 a sum [an amount] (of money). [文例⇩]

きんがく[2] 菌学 mycology.

きんかくし 金隠し the front screen (of a lavatory pan).

きんがしんねん 謹賀新年 (I wish you) a Happy New Year.

ぎんがみ 銀紙 silver paper; aluminum [tin] foil.

きんかん[1] 近刊 ¶近刊の〈新刊の〉 recently published 《books》; 《magazines》 just out; 〈近日出版の〉 forthcoming; 《米》 upcoming; in preparation / 近刊予告 an announcement of books in preparation [of forthcoming books].

きんかん[2] 金柑 〘植〙 a kumquat; a cumquat; a Chinese orange.

きんかん[3] 金冠 〈歯の〉 a (gold) crown ¶金冠をかぶせる crown 《a tooth》 with gold.

きんがん 近眼 shortsightedness; nearsightedness; myopia ¶近眼の shortsighted; nearsighted; myopic / 近眼の人 a shortsighted [nearsighted] person / 近眼鏡 spectacles for shortsightedness.

きんかんがっき 金管楽器 a brass instrument ¶(管弦楽の)金管楽器部 the brass(es).

きんかんしょく 金環食 an annular eclipse (of the sun).

きんかんばん 金看板 〈看板〉 a signboard with gilt lettering; 〈特筆するもの〉 a feature; 〈人〉 a star; an ace.

きんき 禁忌 (a) taboo; tabooing ¶配合禁忌の薬品 incompatible drugs.

ぎんき 銀器 silverware; 〈食器〉 (table) silver (集合的).

きんきじゃくやく 欣喜雀躍 dancing [jumping] for joy.

ぎんぎつね 銀狐 〘動〙 a silver fox.

きんきゅう 緊急 ¶緊急の urgent; pressing 《business matters》; 《a》 crying 《need》 / 緊急の際[時]には in an emergency / 緊急会議《hold》 an urgent [emergency] conference / (議会での)緊急質問 an emergency interpellation / 緊急措置[対策] 《take》 emergency measures; 《devise》 urgent countermeasures / 緊急逮捕 (an) arrest without (a) warrant / 緊急逮捕される be arrested on the spot / 緊急動議 《put》 an emergency resolution [urgent motion] / (領空侵犯機発見の際の)緊急発進 scrambling; a scramble / 緊急避難 emergency evacuation.

きんぎょ 金魚 a goldfish ¶金魚鉢 a goldfish basin; 〈ガラスの〉 a goldfish bowl / 金魚藻 hornwort / 金魚屋 a goldfish seller [vendor].

きんきょう 近況 〈状況〉 the present [recent] situation; 〈安否〉 how *one* is getting along. [文例⇩]

きんきょり 近距離 a short distance ¶近距離の所にある be a short distance away 《from here》 / 近距離で 《see *sth*》 at close quarters; 《fire》 at short [close] range / 近距離列車 a local train.

きんぎん 金銀 〈金と銀〉 gold and silver; 〈金銭〉 money.

きんく 禁句 a taboo word [phrase].

キングサイズ ¶キングサイズの king-size(d) 《cigarettes》.

きんけい[1] 近景 a short-[close-]range view 《of》.

きんけい[2] 錦鶏 〘鳥〙 a golden pheasant.

きんけつびょう 金欠病 lack of money; poverty ¶金欠病にかかっている be short of money [funds]; 《口語》 be broke; 《俗》 be strapped for cash.

きんけん[1] 近県 neighboring prefectures.

きんけん[2] 金権 the power of money; financial influence ¶金権政治 plutocracy.

きんげん[1] 金言 an adage; a maxim.

きんげん[2] 謹厳 ¶謹厳な stern; serious; 《文》 grave; solemn / 謹厳な人 《文》 a grave person; a man of strict morals.

きんけんちょちく 勤倹貯蓄 thrift and saving.

きんこ[1] 金庫 a safe; a strongbox; 〈銀行などの金庫室〉 a vault ¶金庫破り 〈行為〉 safebreaking; safecracking; 〈人〉 a safebreaker; a safecracker. [文例⇩]

きんこ[2] 禁固 imprisonment; confinement ¶禁固5ヵ月の刑に処せられる be sentenced to five months' imprisonment.

きんこう[1] 近郊 《in》 the suburbs 《of》; 《on》 the outskirts 《of》 ¶京都及びその近郊 Kyoto and (its) environs / 近郊の neighboring.

きんこう[2] 均衡 balance; equilibrium ¶均衡を保つ[失う, 破る] keep [lose, upset] the balance / 均衡を保っている be balanced; be in balance [equilibrium] / 均衡予算 a balanced budget. [文例⇩]

きんこう[3] 金工 〈工芸〉 metalworking; 〈人〉 a metalworker; a metalsmith; a craftsman in metal.

きんこう[4] 金鉱 〈鉱石〉 gold ore; 〈鉱山〉 a gold mine ¶金鉱を発見する discover gold (deposits).

---

us when a fire broke out in our neighborhood yesterday.

きんがく[1] 金額にして3万円ぐらいのものです. It is valued at about 30,000 yen.

きんきょう ご近況お知らせ下さい. Please let me know how you are getting along.

きんこ[1] その金庫はダイヤル式で, 数字の組合わせを知らないので開けられなかった. The safe had a combination lock, which I couldn't open as I didn't know the combination.

きんこう[2] 両超大国間のこの微妙な力の均衡が保たれている限りは安全だ. We are safe as [so] long as this fine balance of power

きんごう 近郷 the neighboring districts; the surrounding countryside.

ぎんこう 銀行 a bank ¶銀行に預金する deposit money in a bank / 銀行に預金が100万円ある have a bank account of 1,000,000 yen; have ¥1,000,000 (deposited) in the [a] bank / 銀行と取り引きを始める[止める] open an [close *one's*] account with a bank / 銀行員 a bank clerk / 銀行家 a banker / 銀行業 banking; the banking business / 銀行業務 banking services / 銀行強盗を働く rob [《俗》stick up] a bank.

きんこつ 筋骨 ¶筋骨たくましい muscular; well-muscled; brawny; powerfully-built.

きんこんいちばん 緊褌一番 ¶緊褌一番…する brace *oneself* 《for a task》; 《文》 gird up *one's* loins to *do*.

きんこんしき 金婚式 a golden wedding ¶金婚式を祝う celebrate 《our, their》 golden wedding.

ぎんこんしき 銀婚式 a silver wedding.

きんざい 近在 ⇨ きんごう.

きんさく¹ 近作 *one's* latest work [product].

きんさく² 金策 ¶金策する raise money; get a loan (of money) 《from》.

きんざん 金山 a gold mine.

ぎんざん 銀山 a silver mine.

きんし¹ 近視 ⇨ きんがん ¶近視眼的な政策 a shortsighted [myopic] policy.

きんし² 金糸 gold thread; spun gold.

きんし³ 菌糸 【植】 a hypha 《*pl.* -phae》 ¶菌糸体 a mycelium 《*pl.* -lia》.

きんし⁴ 禁止 《文》 (a) prohibition 《against, on》; a ban 《on》; an embargo 《*pl.* -es》; (a) taboo 《against, on》 ¶禁止する forbid 《*sth*, *sb* to *do*》; prohibit 《*sth*, *sb* from *doing*》; ban; 《文》 interdict; put an embargo on *sth* ⇨ きんじる 回国 禁止を解く withdraw the prohibition against *sth*; lift [remove] the ban [embargo] on *sth*. 文例⇩

きんじ 近似 ¶近似計算 approximation / 近似値 an approximate value [quantity]; an approximation.

ぎんし 銀糸 silver thread; spun silver.

きんじさん 禁治産 ⇨ きんちさん.

きんしつ 均質 homogeneity ¶均質の homogeneous / 均質化する homogenize.

きんじつ 近日 soon; shortly; one of these days.

きんじつてん 近日点 【天】 the perihelion 《*pl.* -helia》.

きんじて 禁じ手 ⇨ はんそく.

きんじとう 金字塔 〈ピラミッド〉 a pyramid; 〈偉大な業績〉《文》 a monumental achievement; 《文》 a monument 《of learning》; a landmark 《in Japanese criticism》 ¶出版界の金字塔 a monumental publication.

きんしゃ 金紗 silk crepe.

きんしゅ¹ 金主 a financial backer [supporter] ¶金主になる finance 《an enterprise》; give *sb* financial support.

きんしゅ² 筋腫 【医】 (a) myoma 《*pl.* -s, -mata》.

きんしゅ³ 禁酒 《文》 (total) abstinence from drink; temperance (★正確には「節酒」の意であるが、実際には「禁酒」の意で使われる) ¶禁酒する stop [give up, 《米口語》 quit, 《文》 abstain from] drinking; 《俗》 go on the (water) wagon; swear off drinking (誓いをたてて) / 禁酒の誓いをたてる[破る] take [break] the pledge / 禁酒を破る start drinking again; 《俗》 come off the (water) wagon / 禁酒運動 a temperance movement / 禁酒家 an [a total] abstainer; a teetotaler (絶対的の) / 《アメリカの》 禁酒郡 a dry county / 禁酒主義 teetotalism; prohibitionism / 禁酒法 《米国史》 the prohibition law; Prohibition.

きんじゅう 禽獣 birds and beasts; (dumb) animals ⇨ けだもの.

きんしゅく 緊縮 (strict) economy; 《文》 austerity; 《削減》 curtailment; 《文》 retrenchment ¶緊縮する economize, 〈削減する〉 《文》 curtail; cut down; 《文》 retrench / 緊縮生活 《lead》 an austere life; 《文》 《practice》 austerity / 緊縮政策 a policy of austerity [retrenchment]; a belt-tightening policy.

きんじゅんび 金準備 the gold reserve.

きんしょ 禁書 a forbidden [banned] book ¶禁書目録 a list of forbidden books; 〈カトリックの〉 the Index (of Prohibited Books).

きんじょ 近所 the neighborhood; the vicinity ¶近所の neighboring; nearby / 近所の人 a neighbor / 近所の子供たち the neighborhood children / 近所の寺 a nearby temple; a temple in *one's* neighborhood / 近所に in the neighborhood 《of》; nearby; about [near, 《米》 around, 《英》 round] here [there] / 近所迷惑 a nuisance [an annoyance] to the neighbors / 近所づきあいする associate 《with *sb*》 as neighbors; be on neighborly terms. 文例⇩

きんしょう 僅少 ⇨ わずか.

ぎんしょう 吟唱[誦] recitation; chanting ⇨ きんじる.

きんじょうてっぺき 金城鉄壁 《文》 an impregnable fortress.

きんじる 禁じる 〈禁止する〉 forbid 《*sth*, *sb* to *do*》; 《文》 prohibit 《*sth*, *sb* from *doing*》; ban; 《文》 interdict; 〈押える〉 suppress; check ¶失笑を禁じ得ない cannot help laughing / 喜びの念を禁じ得ない cannot contain *oneself* for joy. 回国「禁じる」の意で最も一般的な英語は forbid. prohibit は法律や規則などによって「禁じる」の意であり、ban もほぼそれに近いが、宗教や道徳などの観点から言われることもある。 interdict は教会が教

---

between the two superpowers is maintained.

きんし この薬品の販売は法律によって禁止されています。 The sale of this drug is prohibited by law. / いかなる国の核実験も禁止するよう国連に訴えた。 We appealed to the United Nations to ban nuclear tests in any country.

きんじょ ご近所まで参りましたのでちょっとお寄りしました。 I have just dropped in, as I happened to be passing (this way).

きんじる 僕は酒を禁じられている。 I have been forbidden to drink (alcohol). / 未成年者の喫煙は法律で禁じられている。 The law

ぎんじる 権によって「禁じる」の意が強い.

ぎんじる 吟じる sing; chant; recite.

きんしん¹ 近親 a close relative; a near relation ¶近親結婚 (a) consanguineous marriage; (a) marriage between close relatives / 近親相姦 incest / 近親相姦的[の] incestuous. 文例◇

きんしん² 謹慎 《悔悟》《文》repentance; 《文》penitence (for *one's* sins); 〈行ないを慎むこと〉good behavior; 〈監禁〉house arrest; 《法》domiciliary confinement ¶謹慎する〈悔悟する〉《文》repent ((of) *one's* sins); 《文》be penitent; 〈行ないを慎む〉behave (*oneself*); be on *one's* best behavior / 謹慎を命じられる be put on *one's* best behavior; be confined to *one's* house.

きんせい¹ 近世 ⇨ きんだい.

きんせい² 均整 symmetry ¶均整のとれた symmetric(al); well-balanced; well-proportioned.

きんせい³ 金星 Venus.

きんせい⁴ 禁制 ⇨ きんし¹ ¶禁制の forbidden; 《文》prohibited; taboo(ed) / 禁制品 prohibited [banned] goods; 〈貿易上の〉contraband (goods).

きんせき 金石 ¶金石学 epigraphy / 金石文 an epigraph; an inscription engraved on stone or other durable material.

きんせつ 近接 ¶近接する《文》approach; 《文》draw near; come [go] close (to) / 近接している be [stand] close 《文》adjacent (to); 《文》be contiguous 《to, with》; be near / 近接の neighboring 《文》adjacent / 近接未来《文法》immediate [near] future.

きんせん¹ 金銭 money; cash ⇨ かね¹ ¶金銭（上）の問題 a money 《pecuniary》matter; a question [matter] of money / 金銭登録器 a cash register. 文例◇

きんせん² 琴線 ¶心の琴線に触れる〈事柄が主語〉touch [pull at, tug at] *one's* heartstrings.

きんせんか 《植》a pot marigold.

きんそく 禁足 ¶禁足を命じる order *sb* to stay in one place [at home] (for five days).

きんぞく¹ 金属 (a) metal ¶金属（製）の (made of) metal; metallic / 金属性の音 a metallic sound / 金属加工 metalworking / 金属元素 a metallic element / 金属工業 the metalworking industry / 金属製品 metal goods; hardware / 金属組織学 metallography / 金属探知器 a metal detector.

きんぞく² 勤続 continuous [long] service ¶30年勤続する serve (in a firm) for thirty years / 勤続手当 a long-service allowance / 勤続年数 the length of (*one's*) service. 文例◇

きんそん 近村 neighboring [nearby] villages.

きんだい 近代 the modern period; recent [modern] times ¶近代の modern / 近代的 modern; modernistic / 前近代的な premodern / 近代化 modernization / 近代化する modernize / 近代音楽《建築》modern music [architecture] / 近代史 modern history / 近代思想 modern ideas / 近代主義 modernism / 近代人 modern people / 近代戦 modern warfare / 東京国立近代美術館 the Tokyo National Museum of Modern Arts.

きんだか 金高 ⇨ きんがく.

きんだん 禁断 ¶禁断の木の実《文》(the) forbidden fruit / 禁断症状 withdrawal symptoms.

きんちさん 禁治産《法》incompetency ¶禁治産の宣告を受ける be declared incompetent / 禁治産者 an incompetent / 準禁治産者 a quasi-incompetent.

きんちてん 近地点《天》the perigee (point). 文例◇

きんちゃく 近着 ¶近着の洋書 Western books which have just arrived.

きんちょ 近著 *one's* latest work.

きんちょう¹ 禁鳥 a protected bird.

きんちょう² 緊張 strain; tension ¶緊張する get [《文》become] tense; be strained; 《口語》be on edge / 緊張した strained; tense / 緊張した空気 a tense atmosphere / 緊張を緩和する relieve [ease] the tension (of) / 国際間の緊張緩和 the easing [relief] of international tensions; détente / 緊張を欠く lack seriousness. 文例◇

きんちょう³ 謹聴 ¶謹聴する listen to *sb* attentively [《文》with attention].

きんてい¹ 欽定 ¶欽定憲法 the (Japanese) Imperial Constitution / 欽定訳聖書 the Authorized [the King James] Version (of the Bible).

きんてい² 謹呈 ⇨ そうてい.

きんでい 金泥 gold paint ¶金泥の屏風（びょう）a gold-painted folding screen.

ぎんでい 銀泥 silver paint ¶銀泥の silver-painted.

きんてき 金的 ¶金的を射止める〈弓矢で〉hit the bull's eye; 〈大成功する〉succeed brilliantly. 文例◇

きんでんず 筋電図《医》an electromyogram (略: EMG).

きんとう¹ 近東 the Near East ¶近東諸国 the countries of the Near East.

きんとう² 均等 equality; 《文》uniformity ¶均等に equally; 《文》uniformly; evenly / 均等にする equalize; make *sth* equal; 《口語》even

---

prohibits minors from smoking.

きんしん¹ あの方は野田さんの近親です。He is closely related to Mr. Noda.

きんせん¹ 彼とは金銭上の関係は全くない。I have never had any financial dealings with him.

きんぞく² 彼は永年勤続者として社長から表彰された。He was officially commended by the president for his long service with the company.

きんちてん その人工衛星は、地球からの距離が近地点で65マイル、遠地点で200マイルの長円軌道を描いている。The artificial satellite is in an elliptical orbit 65 miles above the earth at perigee and 200 miles at apogee.

きんちょう² 対ソ関係はきわめて緊張していた。Relations with Russia were very strained. / 彼は緊張した顔つきで考え込んだ。His face grew tight with thought. / 冷戦の緊張が高まった [high up]. / その町へ入ったら緊張感がみなぎっていた。A tense atmosphere could be felt everywhere in the town. / 彼は

ぎんなん a ginkgo nut.

きんにく 筋肉 ¶[手[腕]の]筋肉 a hand [an arm] muscle / 筋肉の muscular / 筋肉のよく発達した well-muscled; muscular; 《文》 sinewy; brawny / 筋肉注射 an intramuscular injection / 筋肉痛 muscle pain(s); myalgia / 筋肉疲労 muscular fatigue / 筋肉労働 manual labor / 筋肉労働者 a manual worker. 文例 ⇩

きんねん 近年 《文》of late years; in recent years. 文例 ⇩

きんのう 勤王 loyalty to the Emperor ¶勤王家 a supporter of the Imperial cause.

きんば 金歯 a gold tooth ¶金歯を入れてもらう have a gold tooth put in; have a tooth capped with gold.

きんぱい 金杯 a gold cup [goblet].

ぎんぱい 銀杯 a silver cup [goblet].

きんばえ 金蠅 〔昆〕a green-bottle (fly).

きんぱく¹ 金箔 (a piece of) gold leaf (薄い); gold foil (厚手の).

きんぱく² 緊迫 tension; strain ¶緊迫する become tense [《文》acute]; grow strained / 緊迫した情勢[空気] a tense situation [atmosphere].

ぎんぱく 銀箔 (a piece of) silver leaf (薄い); silver foil (厚手の).

きんぱつ 金髪 blonde (女の) [blond (男の)] hair; golden [fair] hair ¶金髪の golden-[fair-]haired; blond (men); blonde (women).

ぎんぱつ 銀髪 silver(y) [gray] hair ⇒しらが.

ぎんばん 銀盤 a skating rink ¶銀盤の女王 《文》the queen of the ice. ‾‾ing.

きんぴか 金ぴか ¶金ぴかの gilded; glitter-

きんびょうぶ 金屛風 a gilt folding screen; a folding screen covered [decorated] with gold leaf.

きんぴん 金品 money and [or] other articles.

きんぶち 金縁 〈眼鏡の〉gold rims; 〈額縁〉a gilt frame ¶金縁眼鏡をかけている wear [be in] gold-rimmed spectacles.

ぎんぶち 銀縁 〈眼鏡の〉silver rims ¶銀縁眼鏡 silver-rimmed spectacles.

ぎんぶら 銀ぶら a stroll on the Ginza (street).

きんぷん 金粉 gold dust.

ぎんぷん 銀粉 silver dust.

きんべん 勤勉 hard work; 《文》diligence; 《文》industry ¶勤勉な hardworking; 《文》diligent; 《文》industrious / 勤勉に働く work hard [《文》diligently] / 勤勉家 a hard worker.

きんぺん 近辺 ⇒ふきん².

きんぽうげ 〔植〕a buttercup.

きんぼし 金星 〔相撲〕a win made against a grand champion; a glorious victory.

きんボタン 金ボタン a brass button ¶金ボタンの学生 a student in a brass-buttoned uniform.

きんほんい(せい) 金本位(制) the gold standard.

ぎんほんい(せい) 銀本位(制) the silver standard.

きんまきえ 金蒔絵 gold lacquer ¶金蒔絵の箱 a gold-lacquered box [casket].

ぎんみ 吟味 〈調べ〉(a) close examination [investigation]; 〈試し〉a test; 〈精選〉careful selection ¶吟味する 〈調べる〉examine closely; 《文》investigate minutely; 〈試す〉put sth to the test; test; 〈精選する〉select sth with care [carefully] / よく吟味した品 a choice article. 文例 ⇩

きんみつ 緊密 ¶緊密な close; 《文》intimate / 緊密な連絡を保つ keep in close contact 《with》/ 緊密に提携して in close cooperation 《with》.

きんみゃく 金脈 (shady) sources of funds ⇒きんしゅ¹.

きんむ 勤務 《文》service; 《文》duty ¶勤務する work; 《文》do duty / 1日24時間勤務する work 24 hours a day; work a 24-hour day / 勤務中である be on duty [at work] / 勤務先 one's place of work [《文》employment] / 勤務時間 office [business, working] hours / 勤務成績 one's service record / 勤務地手当 a service-area allowance / 勤務年限 the length of one's service / 勤務評定 (a teacher's) efficiency rating / 勤務評定書 an efficiency rating report.

きんむく 金無垢 ¶金むくの of pure [solid] gold.

きんめっき 金めっき gilding; gold-plating ¶金めっきする gild; plate sth with gold / 金めっきの gilt; gilded; gold-plated.

ぎんめっき 銀めっき silvering; silver-plating ¶銀めっきする plate sth with silver; silver.

きんモール 金モール gold lace [braid] 《for a military officer's uniform》.

きんもくせい 〔植〕a fragrant olive.

きんもじ 金文字 gold [gilt] letters; gilt lettering (on a sailor's cap).

きんもつ 禁物 (a) taboo; a prohibited [forbidden] thing; something to be carefully avoided; 〈有害物〉a harmful [《文》an injurious] thing; a poison.

きんゆ 禁輸 an embargo on the export [import] 《of》.

全力を傾けて両国間の[ソ連との]緊張緩和を計ろうとした。He put all his efforts into trying to arrange a détente [a relaxation of the tension] between the two countries [with Russia]. / ソ連の首相は世界の緊張緩和のために頂上会談を提案した。The Soviet Premier suggested a summit meeting for the alleviation of world tensions.

きんちょう³ 謹聴謹聴. Hear! Hear!

きんてき やつも金的を射止めたもんだ。大金持ちの娘と結婚したなんて. To the envy of all of us, he married a rich heiress.

きんにく 水泳はほとんど全身の筋肉を働かせる. Swimming brings nearly all the muscles of the body into active play.

きんねん 今日は近年にない寒さでした. This is the coldest weather we have had in recent years [for years].

きんみ 材料は充分吟味してあります. They are manufactured from the choicest materials.

きんもつ 油っこい物はその患者には禁物だ. Fatty food is bad for

きんゆう

きんゆう 金融 finance ; circulation of money ; financing (融資) ¶金融を引き締める tighten credit [the money market] / 金融緩和政策 an easy-money policy / 金融引き締め政策 a tight-money policy / 金融界 the financial world ; financial circles / 金融機関 a financial [banking] institution / 金融業 financial [money-lending] business / 金融業者 a financier ; a moneylender ; a money broker / 金融恐慌 a financial panic / 金融公庫 a finance corporation / 金融市場 the money market / 金融資本 financial capital / 金融資本家 a financial capitalist / 金融政策 (a) financial policy. 文例⇩

ぎんゆうしじん 吟遊詩人 ⟨西洋史⟩ a wandering minstrel ; ⟨南仏の⟩ a troubadour ; ⟨北仏の⟩ a trouvère ; ⟨ドイツの⟩ a minnesinger.

きんよう 緊要 ¶緊要な important ; ⟨文⟩ of vital importance ; essential ⟨to⟩ ; ⟨文⟩ indispensable ⟨to⟩.

きんよう(び) 金曜(日) Friday (略 : Fri.) ⇨ ちよう(び) 囲碁 ¶13日の金曜日 Friday the thirteenth.

きんよく 禁欲 ⟨文⟩ asceticism ; ⟨文⟩ continence (特に性欲の) ¶禁欲する ⟨文⟩ control [repress] one's bodily desires ; practice asceticism ; ⟨性欲を⟩ practice continence / 禁欲主義 asceticism / 禁欲主義者 an ascetic.

きんらい 近来 ⇨ ちかごろ, さいきん². 文例⇩

きんらん 金襴 gold brocade ¶金襴どんす gold-brocaded satin damask.

きんり 金利 ⟨利子⟩ interest (on money) ; ⟨利率⟩ a rate of interest ¶金利を引き上げる [下げる] raise [lower] the interest rate [the rate of interest] / 金利生活者 《フランス語》 a rentier. 文例⇩

きんりょう¹ 禁猟 prohibition of hunting ¶禁猟期 a closed season ; 《英》 a close season / 禁猟区 a (game) preserve ; a (bird, wildlife) sanctuary.

きんりょう² 禁漁 prohibition of fishing ¶禁漁期 a closed season (for trout) ; 《英》 a close season / 禁漁区 an area closed to fishing ; a no-fishing area [zone] / ⟨海の⟩ a marine preserve.

きんりょく¹ 金力 the power of money [wealth]. 文例⇩

きんりょく² 筋力 muscular strength [power].

きんるい 菌類 fungi (*sing.* fungus).

きんれい 禁令 ⟨文⟩ a prohibitory [an interdictory] decree ; ⟨文⟩ a prohibition ⟨against⟩ ; a ban ⟨on⟩.

きんろう 勤労 work ; labor ; service ¶勤労意欲 the will to work / 勤労階級 [大衆] the working classes [masses] / 勤労感謝の日 Labor Thanksgiving Day / 勤労者 a worker ; a working person ; a laborer ; working people (総称) / 勤労所得 (an) earned income / 勤労所得税 the earned income tax / 勤労奉仕 labor service.

く

く¹ 九 nine ¶第9 the ninth.

く² 区 ⟨市の⟩ a ward ; ⟨区域⟩ a district ; a section ¶新宿区 Shinjuku Ward / 区議会 a ward assembly / 区立図書館 a ward library. 文例⇩

く³ 句 a phrase ; an expression ; ⟨詩の⟩ a line (1 行) ; a verse (1 節) ; ⟨俳句⟩ a haiku.

く⁴ 苦 ⟨苦痛⟩ (a) pain ; suffering(s) ; ⟨文⟩ an affliction ; ⟨心配⟩ anxiety ; worries ; (a) trouble ; cares ; ⟨困苦⟩ hardship(s) ; ⟨文⟩ privation ¶苦になる weigh on one's mind ; make one anxious ; ⟨文⟩ cause one anxiety / 苦にする take *sth* to heart ; worry [be worried] ⟨about⟩ ; be anxious ⟨about⟩ / 苦にしない take (it) easy ; do not mind (it) ; think little [nothing] of *sth* / 苦もなく easily ; ⟨文⟩ with ease ; without trouble [difficulty]. 文例⇩

ぐ¹ 具 ⟨手段⟩ ⟨文⟩ a means ; a tool ; ⟨汁・五目飯などの種⟩ ingredients ¶…を政争の具とす

る make political capital of….

ぐ² 愚 ⟨文⟩ folly ; stupidity ; silliness ¶愚の骨頂 the height of stupidity [folly] ; sheer folly / 愚にもつかない absurd ; ridiculous / 愚にもつかない事を言う talk nonsense [rubbish, rot].

ぐあい 具合 ⟨状態⟩ a condition ; a state ; ⟨方法⟩ a manner ; a way ¶天気具合 weather conditions / いい具合に ⟨幸いに⟩ luckily ; happily / 具合がいい [悪い] ⟨調子が～⟩ be in good [be out of] order ; nothing [something] is wrong ⟨with⟩ ; ⟨都合が～⟩ be convenient [inconvenient] ; suit [do not suit] one / 体の具合がいい feel well. 文例⇩

グアテマラ (the Republic of) Guatemala ¶グアテマラの Guatemalan / グアテマラ人 a Guatemalan.

グアム Guam (Island).

くい¹ 杭 a stake ; a post ; a pile ; piling (集合

---

the patient. / 彼の前で競馬の話は禁物だ。You must never talk [must avoid talking] about horse racing in his presence.

きんゆう 金融がひっぱくしている [緩慢である]。Money is tight [easy].

きんらい この本は彼の近来の傑作

だ。This is one of the best books he has written in recent years. / 近来の大雨だ。We haven't had such a heavy rain for some time [these last few months].

きんり 金利が高い [安い]。Money is dear [cheap].

きんりょく¹ 彼は金力で左右され

る人間ではない。He is the last man to be influenced by money.

く² このバスは1区90円(で)a section. The bus fare here is 90 yen (for) a section.

く⁴ その事は苦にしないでもよい。Don't trouble yourself about the matter. / 苦は楽の種。No cross,

くい ¶杙を打つ drive in a pile [stake] / 杭を立てる put up a post / 杭穴 a posthole ; a stake hole / 杭打ち piling ; pile driving / 杭打ち機 a pile driver.

くい² 悔い ⇒こうかい⁴ ¶悔いを残す leave something to be regretted [that *one* will regret] later.

くいあげ 食い上げ ⇒めし 文例.

くいあらす 食い荒らす eat (several dishes) by halves ; eat messily ; spoil *sth* by eating *it* ; eat *sth* ravenously.

くいあらためる 悔い改める 《文》repent 《of *one's* sinful life》; 《文》be penitent ; reform ; turn over a new leaf ; mend *one's* ways.

くいあわせ 食い合わせ ¶食い合わせが悪い have a harmful effect when eaten together.

くいいじ 食い意地 ¶食い意地が張っている be greedy ; 《文》be gluttonous.

くいいる 食い入る ⇒くいこむ ¶食い入るように見つめる stare into 《*sb's* face》.

クイーン a queen ¶ダイヤのクイーン《トランプ》the queen of diamonds.

くいかけ 食い掛け ¶食いかけの 〈a fish〉 left half-eaten ; half-eaten [picked-over] 《dishes》.

くいき 区域 an area ; a district ; a zone ¶…の区域内で within the limits of... ; inside the boundary of....

くいきる 食い切る bite off ; cut *sth* off with *one's* teeth. 文例↓

ぐいぐい strongly ; vigorously ; 《文》unremittingly ; 《文》unsparingly ; on and on ¶ぐいぐい進む push forward [on (and on)] / ぐいぐい押す push [press] hard / ぐいぐい飲む drink hard ; drink in large drafts.

くいけ 食い気 ⇒しょくよく.

くいこみ 食い込み 〈損失〉《文》a deficit ; a loss ; 〈蚕食〉inroads 《on, into》.

くいこむ 食い込む 〈むしばむ〉eat 《*one's* way》 into ; gnaw into ; 〈侵入する〉《文》encroach 《on》; 〈めり込む〉dig into 《the bark》; 〈損失を起こす〉cause a deficit ¶時間(蓄え)に食い込む make inroads into [on] *one's* time [savings] / 肉に食い込む足のつめ an ingrowing toenail.

くいさがる 食い下がる hang [hold] on 《to *one's* opponent》; persist 《in an attack》; refuse to back down ; stand *one's* ground ; 〈質問で〉harass 《a minister》with persistent questions.

くいしばる 食いしばる set [clench] 《*one's* teeth》.

くいしんぼう 食いしん坊 a glutton ; 《口語》a greedy pig ; 《文》a gourmand ¶食いしん坊な greedy ; gluttonous.

クイズ a quiz ; a quiz game ¶クイズ番組《ラジオ・テレビ》a quiz program [show] / クイズ番組の回答者 a competitor 《on a quiz show》/ クイズ番組の司会者 a quizmaster / クイズゲーム a quiz game 《competition》.

くいすぎる 食い過ぎる eat too much ; overeat 《*oneself*》; eat more [have more to eat] than is good 《for *one*》.

くいだおれ 食い倒れ ¶食い倒れになる ruin *oneself* (financially) by *one's* extravagance in food ; eat *oneself* out of house and home.

くいだめ 食い溜め ¶食いだめする stuff *oneself* with food so that *one* can go without eating for some time.

くいたりない 食い足りない 〈充分に食べてない〉have not had enough to eat ; have not eaten enough ; want to eat more ; 〈不満足である (対象が主語)〉be unsatisfactory ; leave something to be desired.

くいちがい 食い違い a conflict ; 〈矛盾〉《文》a discrepancy ; inconsistency ; 《文》discordance ; 〈衝突〉a collision ; 〈相違〉(a) difference 《in views》.

くいちがう 食い違う 〈合わない〉run counter 《to》; 《文》be in discord 《with》; 〈衝突する〉collide [clash] 《with》; 〈うまく行かない〉go wrong 《with *one*》; go against *one* ¶意見が食い違う 《the parties'》 opinions differ ; differ 《in》/ 〈お互いの〉話が食い違う be (talking) at cross-purposes.

くいちぎる 食い千切る bite off.

くいちらす 食い散らす eat untidily [messily] ; leave *one's* food in a mess.

くいつく 食い付く bite (at) ¶食いついて離れない stick fast [like a leech] 《to》.

くいつくす 食い尽くす eat all 《*one's* provisions》; eat everything 《*one* has in the house》; 《文》consume ; run through 《《文》exhaust》 《*one's* stocks of rice》.

ぐい(っ)と with a jerk ¶ぐいと引く[押す] pull [push] with a (sudden) jerk ; give *sth* a good [smart] pull [push] / ぐいっと飲む drink 《*one's* whisky》at a gulp ; take a pull at 《*one's* sake》; 《俗》have a snort 《of Scotch》.

くいつなぐ 食いつなぐ ⇒くのばす.

くいつぶす 食いつぶす eat oneself [*sb*] out of house and home ¶財産を食いつぶす run through *one's* fortune / 資本を食いつぶす live on *one's* capital.

くいつめる 食い詰める be not able to make a living any longer ; 《文》be reduced to poverty ; 《口語》be down and out ; be (down) on *one's* uppers ; 《俗》go broke (無一文になる).

くいどうらく 食い道楽 〈事〉the enjoyment of good food 《《文》the pleasures of the table》; 《文》epicurism ; 《文》gastronomy ; 〈人〉a gourmet ; 《文》an epicure ; 《文》a gastronome.

くいとめる 食い止める check ; hold [keep

---

no crown. 【諺】| No pains, no gains. 【諺】

ぐあい 様子はどんな具合ですか。How are things going? | 万事具合よく行っている。Everything is going well [all right]. | 仕事がどんな具合かこれから見に行くところです。I'm going to see how their work is coming along. | この家は具合よく出来ている。This house is conveniently planned. | この機械は具合が悪い。This machine is not working properly. | Something is wrong with this machine. / 引出しの具合が悪い。The drawers do not run [move] smoothly. | こういう具合にやるんだ。Do it this way [like this]. / 肉はちょうどいい具合に焼けている。The meat is done to a turn.

くいきる これはとても食い切れな

くいな 《鳥》 a waterrail.
くいにげ 食い逃げ ¶食い逃げする run away without paying one's bill; bilk 《an eating house》.
くいのこし 食い残し leftover food; leftovers [leavings] 《at the table, from the dinner》.
くいのこす 食い残す leave 《a dish》 half-eaten [unfinished].
くいのばす 食い延ばす eke out 《one's food [savings]》; save one's provisions; economize in the use of 《materials》.
くいはぐれる 食いはぐれる 〈食事時に〉 miss one's meal [dinner]; 〈失職する〉 lose one's job; 《文》 lose one's means of livelihood. 文例④
くいぶち 食い扶持 しょくひ.
くいほうだい 食い放題 ⇒たべほうだい.
くいもの 食い物 〈食べ物〉 food; 《文》 provisions; 《俗》 grub ¶食い物にする prey on sb; live on [off] sb / …を食い物にする at the expense of….
くいる 悔いる しゅくい⁴.

くう¹ 空 〈空中〉 the air; 〈虚空〉 space; 《文》 the void; 〈空虚〉 emptiness ¶空の空なるもの《文》 vanity of vanities / 空をつかむ claw [grasp at, clutch at] the air / 空を打つ beat the air; hit empty air / 空を切る cut the air / 空に消える vanish 《disappear》 into thin air [the air] / 空対空ミサイル an air-to-air missile.
くう² 食う 〈食べる〉 eat; have; 《文》 take; 〈常食する〉 live on 《rice》; 〈生活する〉 live 《on, by》; earn [make] one's living; 〈虫などが〉 bite; gnaw; 〈(魚が)えさを〉 bite; 〈芝居などで共演者を〉 steal 《the show》 from sb; upstage sb ¶食える 〈食べて安全〉 be eatable [fit to eat]; 〈結構うまい〉 be eatable; 〈食用になる〉 be edible / 食うか食われるかの戦い a life-and-death struggle; a struggle with no quarter given or taken / 食うために働く work for one's bread / ようやく食っている scratch a living; eke out a precarious living; barely manage to keep body and soul together / 食うに困る find it hard to make a living; be badly off / 食うや食わずの生活である live on the bare subsistence level; be on the edge [verge] of starvation / 食うに困らない have enough to live on; be comfortably off / なに食わぬ顔を
する wear [put on] an innocent look; 《文》 feign [pretend] ignorance; assume a nonchalant air; try to look as if nothing had happened / 食ってかかる turn on sb; defy sb; challenge sb / 人を食ったことを言う talk big; tell a tall story [tale]. 文例④
くうい 空位 a vacancy; a vacant post ¶空位になっている be vacant / 王位の空位期間 an interregnum (pl. -s, -na).
ぐうい 寓意 a moral; a hidden meaning ¶寓意物語 a parable; a fable.
くういき 空域 《five miles of》 airspace.
クウェート (the State of) Kuwait ¶クウェートの Kuwaiti / クウェート人 a Kuwaiti.
くうかん 空間 space; 〈余地〉 room ¶空間的 spatial / 空間と時間上の 《哲・物》 spatiotemporal 《order》 / 空間感覚 have a sense of space.
くうかんち 空閑地 vacant land ⇒ あきち.
くうき 空気 air; 〈雰囲気〉 an atmosphere ¶空気の流通のいい[悪い] well-[poorly-]ventilated; airy [stuffy] / 空気の通らない airtight; airproof / 空気を入れる let 《fresh》 air in; 《文》 admit air / 〈タイヤに〉 pump up 《a tire》 / 空気を入れ替える air 《a room》 / 空気を抜く let the air out of 《a tire》; 《文》 deflate / 空気を抜いた evacuated 《glass bulbs》 / 空気中の酸素 atmospheric oxygen / 空気穴 an air vent [hole] / 空気入れ an [a tire] inflator; a bicycle pump 《自転車用》 / 空気銃 an air gun / 空気浄化機 an air purifier / 空気調節 air conditioning / 空気調節する air-condition / 空気を抜いた装置 an air conditioner; air-conditioning equipment / 空気伝染 infection by air; aerial [airborne] infection / 空気まくら an air [a pneumatic] cushion / 空気力学 aerodynamics / 空気冷却器 an air cooler. 文例④
くうきょ 空虚 ¶空虚な empty; 《文》 vacant; hollow.
ぐうぐう 〈いびきの音〉 z-z-z ¶ぐうぐう寝ている be fast [sound] asleep / ぐうぐういびきをかく snore loudly / 〈空腹で〉腹がぐうぐう鳴る one's stomach growls [rumbles] 《with hunger, for breakfast》.
くうぐん 空軍 an air force; the air service ¶空軍の行動 air action / 空軍基地 an air (force) base / 空軍力 《文》 airpower [might].
くうこう 空港 an airport ¶羽田空港 Haneda Airport / 空港ビル the terminal building.
ぐうじ 宮司 the chief priest of a Shinto shrine.
くうしゃ 空車 an empty car [taxi]. 文例④

い. This is more than I can eat.
くいとめる 風が強くて彼らは火の手を食い止めることができなかった. On account of the violent wind they were unable to check the spread of the flames.
くいはぐれる あれだけ英語ができれば食いはぐれることはない. His knowledge of English will always provide him with an income. | With a knowledge of English like his he will never be short of a job.

くう² 彼らは野菜を盛んに食う. They are great eaters of vegetables. | こうなったら食うか食われるかだ. This is a kill-or-be-killed situation. / 心配するな, あの男にとって君を取って食いはしない. Don't worry. He won't eat [bite] you. / あの男は何をして食っているのか. What does he do for a living? / この事業は金を食う. This job eats money. | This

is a very costly enterprise. / この車はずいぶんガソリンを食う. This car is very heavy on gas. | This car simply drinks gasoline. / 〈魚釣りで〉今日はよく食う. The fish are biting well today. / 〈魚釣りで〉今日はさっぱり食わない. I haven't had a bite today. / 彼は食う物も食わずに息子を教育した. He denied himself all the comforts of life to give his son an education. / その手は食わな

くしゅう 空襲 an air raid; an air [《文》aerial] attack ¶空襲する make an air raid (on); air-raid; attack (a town) from the air / 空襲警報 an air-raid alarm [warning]; 〈警戒警報〉(a yellow alert) に対して〉 a red alert / 空襲警報のサイレン an air-raid siren.

くしゅうごう 空集合 《数》an [the] empty set; a [the] null set.

くしょ 空所 (a) space; a blank (space). 文例区

ぐうすう 偶数 an even number ¶偶数の even(-numbered). 文例区

グーズベリー 《木》a gooseberry bush; 〈実〉a gooseberry.

ぐうする 遇する 〈扱う〉treat; deal with; 〈接待する〉entertain; receive.

くうせき 空席 a vacant [an unoccupied] seat; 〈地位〉a vacant post; a vacancy; an opening; 〈余地〉room.

くうぜん 空前 ¶空前の unprecedented; 《文》unexampled; unheard-of; 《文》unparalleled; record-breaking; 《文》epoch-making; epochal / 空前絶後の the first and probably the last... / 空前絶後の名画 the greatest film of all time. 文例区

ぐうぜん 偶然 (a) chance; accident; 《文》fortuity; 〈同時発生〉(a) coincidence ¶偶然の accidental; chance; casual; 《文》adventitious / 偶然の一致 a coincidence / 偶然の要素 a chance factor / 偶然に出来事 an accident / 偶然に by chance [accident]; accidentally; unexpectedly; casually / 偶然出会う happen to meet; meet by chance; come [run] across; 《口語》bump into. 文例区

くうそ 空疎 ¶空疎な empty; 《文》poor in content [substance]; 《文》unsubstantial.

くうそう 空想 a [an idle] fancy; a daydream; (a) fantasy; a vision; imagination ¶空想する fancy; daydream; imagine / 空想をたくましくする give full play to one's fancy; let one's imagination run away with one / 空想にふける fall into the [lost in] thought [《口語》(a) reverie]; be given to daydreaming (癖として) / 空想的 fanciful; imaginary; Utopian / 空想家 a daydreamer; a visionary. 文例区

ぐうぞう 偶像 an idol; an icon ¶偶像崇拝 idolatry; idol worship / 偶像破壊 iconoclasm / 偶像破壊者 an iconoclast.

ぐうたら an idler; a loafer; a good-for-nothing; 《米口語》a bum; 《英口語》a layabout ¶ぐうたらな lazy; idle; good-for-nothing.

くうち 空地 vacant ground; a vacant lot.

くうちゅう 空中 the air ¶空中の aerial; in the air / 空中に in the air; in midair / 空中滑走する glide (in the air); volplane; plane / 空中給油 refueling in the air; air-to-air refueling / 空中査察 (an) aerial inspection / 空中衝突 a midair collision / 空中戦 an airfight; an aerial combat [dogfight] / 空中浮遊微生物 aeroplankton / 空中ブランコ a trapeze / 空中分解する disintegrate in midair; come apart while flying / 空中放電 atmospheric discharge / 空中楼閣 (build) castles [a castle] in the air.

ぐうっと ¶ぐうっと飲む take a long gulp [drink] (of beer, from the bottle).

くうていたい 空挺隊 airborne troops; paratroops.

クーデター a coup d'état (pl. coups d'état, coup d'états); a coup ¶クーデターを行なう carry out a coup d'état; pull (off) a coup.

くうてん 空転 《機》¶空転する race; run idle / 議論が空転する argue in a circle; the argument goes round and round and gets nowhere.

くうでん 空電 《通信》atmospherics; static; strays ¶空電除去装置 a static eliminator.

くうどう 空洞 a cave; 〈くぼみ〉a cavity; a hollow; 《医》a vomica (pl. -cae) ¶空洞化する become hollow; lose [《文》become devoid of] substance / 空洞化した議会 parliamentary democracy in name only [reduced to mere form].

ぐうのね ぐうの音 ¶ぐうの音も出ないようにする 〈黙らせる〉silence sb; 《口語》sit on sb; 《口語》squelch sb; 〈やっつける〉《口語》beat sb hollow; 《文》sort sb out.

くうはく 空白 〈印刷物などの〉a blank; (a) blank space; 〈比喩的に〉a (political) vacuum ¶力の空白 a power vacuum.

くうばく[1] 空爆 (aerial) bombing; 〈空襲〉an air raid ⇨ くうしゅう.

くうばく[2] 空漠 ¶空漠たる 〈広い〉vast; 《文》boundless; 〈ぼうっとした〉vague; hazy.

ぐうはつ 偶発 ¶偶発する happen; 《文》occur [come about] by chance / 偶発的(な) accidental; 《文》contingent; 《文》episodic / 偶発事件 an accident; 《文》a contingency / 偶発戦争 accidental warfare / (the danger of) war through accident.

くうひ 空費 ¶空費する waste; idle [fritter] (one's time) away. 文例区

くうふく 空腹 ¶空腹である[を感じる] be

くうぶん 空文 a dead letter; a (mere) scrap of paper. 文例↓

クーペ a coupé; a coupe.

くうぼ 空母 ⇒ こうくう³ (航空母艦).

くうほう¹ 空包 (fire) a blank (cartridge).

くうほう² 空砲 (fire) a blank charge [shot].

クーポン a coupon; a voucher (食券・宿泊券) ¶クーポン券 a coupon ticket; a voucher.

くうゆ 空輸 air transportation; air [《文》aerial] transport; transport by air; an airlift; air delivery ¶空輸する transport by air [by plane]; airlift (a corps); fly (goods to a remote town) / 空輸作戦 airlift (operations) / 空輸部隊 an airborne unit [corps].

クーラー 〈水などを冷やすもの〉 a 《water》cooler; 〈冷房機〉 an air conditioner.

くうらん 空欄 a blank column; a blank (space) ¶空欄に書き込む fill in the blanks.

くうりくうろん 空理空論 《文》 vain speculation; empty [impractical] theories.

くうれいしき 空冷式 ¶空冷式の air-cooled 《engines》.

くうろ 空路 an air route [lane]; an airway ¶空路名古屋から東京に帰る fly back to Tokyo from Nagoya. 文例↓

くうろん 空論 an empty theory ¶机上の空論 ⇒ きじょう¹.

クーロン 《電》 a coulomb (略: C).

ぐうわ 寓話 a fable; an allegory.

クエーカー a Quaker; a member of the Society of Friends.

クエーサー 《天》 a quasar.

クエート ⇒ クウェート.

くえき 苦役 〈労働〉 hard work; 《文》 toil; drudgery; 〈どれい生活〉 slavery; 〈懲役〉 ⇒ ちょうえき.

くえない 食えない ⇒ くう²; 〈悪賢い〉 shrewd; 《口語》 smart (and wide-awake); cunning; crafty.

くえんさん 枸櫞酸 《化》 citric acid.

クオーターバック 【フットボール】 a quarterback ¶クオーターバックを勤める quarterback 《for a team》.

くかい¹ 区会 a ward assembly ¶区会議員 a member of the [a] ward assembly.

くかい² 句会 a haiku gathering.

くかく 区画 〈区分け〉 division; 《文》 demarcation; 〈1区画〉 a section; a division; a compartment; a block (市街の); 〈土地の〉 a lot [plot] (of land); 〈界限〉 the boundary; the limits ¶区画する divide; partition; demarcate; mark off 《one lot from another》 / 区画整理 replanning of streets; readjustment of town lots.

くがく 苦学 ¶苦学する work one's way through school [college]; 《文》 study under adversity / 苦学生 a working [self-supporting] student.

くがつ 九月 September (略: Sept.).

くかん 区間 a section ¶《国鉄の》電車区間 a train section.

くき 茎 a stalk; a stem.

くぎ 釘 a nail; 〈枕木用の〉 a spike ¶くぎの頭 a nailhead / くぎを打つ nail; drive (in) a nail / くぎを抜く pull [draw] out a nail; unnail / 一本くぎをさす 《念を押す》 remind sb of sth; 〈警告する〉 give sb a warning / くぎ抜き 《ペンチ型の》 (a pair of) pincers (nippers); 《かなこ型の》 a nail puller [extractor] / くぎ抜き付きの金づち a claw hammer. 文例↓

くぎづけ 釘付け ¶くぎづけにする nail up [down]; fasten with nails; 〈値段を〉 peg (the price at ¥800) / その場にくぎづけになる stand riveted to [transfixed on] the spot / 走者を塁にくぎづけにする hold a runner on base. 文例↓

くきょう 苦境 《文》 distress; 《文》 adverse circumstances; a painful position; 《文》 a predicament; 《口語》 a fix; a dilemma ¶苦境を救う help sb out of his difficulties / 苦境にある[立つ] be in a fix; be in trouble [distress, difficulties] / 苦境に陥る get into trouble [《口語》 hot water].

くぎょう 苦行 penance; asceticism; mortification of the flesh ¶苦行する do penance; practice asceticism [mortification]; mortify one's flesh [body].

くぎり 区切り 〈句読〉 punctuation; 〈間(ま)〉 a pause; a break; 〈終わり〉 an end; a spot ¶仕事に区切りをつける break off [call a halt to] one's work; 《口語》 call it a day; 《口語》 knock off.

くぎる 区切る 〈文章を〉 punctuate; mark off 《by a comma》; 〈仕切る〉 divide (off); partition (off) ¶区切って読む read (a text) with pauses between phrases.

くぎん 苦吟 ¶苦吟する rack one's brains (for a good line of verse).

くく¹ 九々 ¶九々(の表) the multiplication table; 《口語》 (learn) one's tables.

くく² 区々 〈文〉 various; 《文》 diverse; conflicting (reports). 文例↓

くぐりど 潜り戸 a side door [gate]; a wicket (gate).

くくる 括る tie [do] up; bind; fasten; bundle; cord (up) (a box) (ひもで); strap (皮ひもで) ⇒ しめくくる.

くぐる 潜る go [《文》 pass] through [under

だ. It is an intolerable [a frightful] waste of time.
くうふく 空腹にまずいものなし. Hunger is the best sauce. 《諺》
くうぶん その条約は空文化している. The treaty is now a dead letter [a mere scrap of paper].
くうろ 氏は成田を出発, 空路ハワイに向かった. He flew from Narita toward Hawaii.
くぎ くぎがよく利かない. The nail isn't holding (fast).
くぎづけ 驚きのあまりその場にくぎづけになった. Surprise nailed him to the spot. / 彼らの眼はテレビにくぎづけになっていた. Their eyes were glued to the television.

くげ 公卿, 公家 a court noble.

くけい 矩形 a rectangle ¶矩形の rectangular.

くける 絎ける blindstitch.

くげん 苦言 candid advice ; a bitter pill (for sb to swallow) / 苦言を呈する give sb candid advice ;《文》exhort sb (to do);《文》remonstrate with sb (about sth). 文例◊

ぐねん 具現 ⇨ たいげん², じつげん.

くこ 【植】a Chinese matrimony vine.

くさ 草 grass ; a herb (有用な) ; a weed (雑草) ¶1本の草 a blade of grass / 草の生えた grass-grown ; grassy ; weedy (雑草の) / 草の根 a grass root / 草の根を分けて捜す leave no stone unturned / 草の根デモクラシー grass-roots democracy / 草の実 grass seed / 草を刈る cut [mow] grass / 草を取る, 草むしりをする weed (a garden) /《家畜が》草を食う feed on grass ; graze / 草ぼうぼうの overrun [overgrown,《文》rank] with grass [weeds].

くさい 臭い offensive (smells) ; stinking (drains) ; bad (smells) ; foul (breath) ;《口語》smelly ;《文》evil-smelling ;《文》malodorous ;〈…臭い〉smell of (sake) (★ smell は動詞) ;〈怪しい〉suspicious (-looking) ;《口語》fishy ¶臭いにおいがする smell nasty ; give out a bad smell /《文》smell offensive ; stink (ひどく) ;〈臭い物にふたをする〉hush up (a scandal) ; sweep (a troublesome problem) under the rug. 文例◊

くさいきれ 草いきれ the stifling smell of grass (in the summer heat).

くさいろ 草色 (light) green ; yellowish green ; grass green.

くさかり 草刈り mowing ¶草刈りする cut the grass (with a sickle) ; mow (the grass) / 草刈りがま a sickle ; a scythe (長柄の).

くさき 草木 plants ; vegetation ¶草木も眠るうしみつ時に ⇨うしみつどき.

くさくさ くさくさする feel wretched (depressed) ; be out of sorts.

くさけいば 草競馬 a local horse race.

くさす 腐す run sb down ; criticize ; speak badly about sb ;《文》speak ill [disparagingly, slightingly] of sb ;《文》disparage.

くさち 草地 grassland.

くさとり 草取り weeding ¶草取りをする weed (a field).

くさば 草葉 ¶草葉の陰で《文》under the sod ; in the grave.

くさばな 草花 a flowering plant ; a flower.

くさはら 草原 a grassy plain ; a meadow ; a green field.

くさび 楔 a wedge ; a chock (輪やたるの) ¶くさびを打つ drive in a wedge / 敵陣にくさびを打ち込む drive a wedge between the enemy lines ; split the enemy lines apart / くさび形文字 cuneiform script (writing).

くさぶえ 草笛 a reed pipe.

くさぶかい 草深い grass-grown ; grassy ;〈草の〉weed-grown ; weedy ¶草深い田舎 an out-of-the-way village ; the remote countryside ;《口語》(live out in) the sticks.

くさぶき 草ぶき ¶草ぶき屋根 a thatched roof ; a (roof of) thatch / 草ぶきの家 a thatched house [cottage].

くさみ 臭味 a bad [an unpleasant, a nasty] smell ;《文》an offensive odor ;〈気取り〉(be free from) affectation ¶臭みがある smell (unpleasant) ; have a strong smell ;《文》be ill-smelling ;〈気取っている〉be affected ;〈きざだ〉have a dash [touch] of (pedantry) ; smack [《文》savor] of (self-conceit).

くさむら 叢 the grass ; a thicket.

くさもち 草餅 a rice-flour dumpling mixed with mugwort.

くさやきゅう 草野球 sandlot baseball.

くさらす 腐らす allow (meat) to spoil [rot,《文》putrefy] ; corrode (腐食させる) ¶気を腐らす《文》become weary (of) ;《文》be sick at heart ; be depressed ; be disheartened ; lose heart.

くさり 鎖 a chain ¶鎖をはずす undo the chain ; unchain / 鎖でつなぐ chain (a dog) up ; put (a prisoner) in chains / 鎖でつないだ犬 a dog on a chain. 文例◊

ぐさりと ¶短刀でぐさりと刺す stab sb with a dagger ;《文》plunge a dagger (into).

くさる 腐る〈腐敗する〉go bad [rotten] ; rot ; spoil ;《文》decompose ;《文》decay ;〈卵が〉addle ; be addled ;〈牛乳などが〉go [turn] sour ;〈肉などが〉《文》putrefy ;〈魚などが〉go stale ;〈気が〉⇨くさらす《気を腐らす》¶腐った rotten ; bad ; stale ; addled / 腐っていない材木 sound timber / 腐りやすい spoil [go bad] easily [quickly] ; soon go bad ¶腐らない be perishable / 腐らない keep good / 金を腐るほど持っている《口語》be rolling in money [《俗》it] ; have money to burn.

くされえん 腐れ縁〈断ち難い関係〉《文》an inseverable [a fated] relationship ;《口語》a friendship that one is stuck with [can't get out of] ;〈不幸な関係〉an unfortunate relationship [entanglement (特に異性との)] ¶腐れ縁とあきらめる give up hope of breaking off [《文》severing] one's relations (with sb).

くさわけ 草分け〈先駆者〉a pioneer ; a pathfinder ; a trailblazer ;〈初期の開拓者〉an early settler ;〈考案者〉the originator.

くし¹ 串 a spit (大きい) ; a skewer ¶くしにさす spit ; skewer / 魚をくしにさして焼く broil [grill] a fish on a skewer.

くく² この点については意見が区々に分かれている。Opinion is divided [Opinions differ] on this point.

くぐる 犬が垣根をくぐって入って来た。A dog crept in through the hedge.

くげん 貴君に一言苦言を呈したい。I'd like to give you my frank opinion for your own good.

くさい ガス臭いぞ。I smell gas. /（悪事などをかぎつけて）臭いぞ。I smell a rat.

くさり 犬は鎖でつないである。The dog is on a chain [is chained up].

くさる この魚は明日の朝までには腐ってしまう。This fish will not

くし²　駆使　¶駆使する use freely / 多くの資料を駆使する make free [the most] use of abundant data / 英語を自由に駆使できる have a good command of English.

くし³　櫛　¶くしの歯の teeth of a comb / くしの歯を引くように起こる crop up [happen, 《文》occur] in rapid succession / くしを入れる comb 《one's hair》/ くしを入れてない uncombed; disheveled /《文》unkempt / くしをさす wear a comb (in one's hair).

くじ　籤　〈引く物〉a lottery ticket /《文》a lot;〈くじ引き〉a raffle (福引き) / くじを引く draw lots / くじに当たる win (a prize) in a lottery [raffle]; draw [have, get] a winning ticket [number] (in a lottery [raffle]) / くじにはずれる draw [have, get] a losing ticket [number] / くじで決める draw lots [straws] to decide (who does, whether...); decide by drawing lots [《文》by lot] / くじ運が強い〈弱い〉be lucky [unlucky] in lotteries; often win something [never win anything, never have any luck] in raffles. 文例⇩

囲み　a lot はくじびきで各人が引く「くじ」を意味し, 具体的には a ticket, a number, a straw などである. lot は一定の慣用句の中でしか使われないと言ってもよく, 単数形では (decide) by lot と言うらしい. これも decide by drawing lots と言うことの方が多い. 複数の lots も draw lots 以外にはあまり使われない. 事がらとしての「くじびき」には, lottery と raffle があるが, あたると金がもらえる宝くじ的なものが lottery, 品物がもらえる福引き的なものが raffle である.「くじにはずれる」は draw a blank という語をぴったりのように思われるが, この成句は現代英語では専ら比喩的に「成果をあげない」の意味で使われていて,「空くじを引く」の意味には使われない.

くじく　挫く　〈手足をねんざする〉sprain; wrench;〈脱臼する〉dislocate;〈計画などを〉《文》frustrate [disappoint]《sb's plans [hopes]》; baffle [frustrate] sb;〈勢い・勇気を〉dispirit (★受動態で使うのが普通); unnerve. 文例⇩

くしげずる　梳る　comb.

くじける　挫ける　〈気が〉be discouraged; be disheartened; be dispirited; lose heart [courage].

くしざし　串刺し　¶串刺しにする skewer 《a piece of meat》; spit 《chicken》/ 串刺しになった魚 a fish on a skewer.

くじゃく　〖鳥〗a peacock; a peahen (雌).

くしゃくしゃ　¶くしゃくしゃにする crumple (up) (paper); rumple up [tousle] 《one's hair》;《米口語》muss (up) 《one's hair》/ くしゃくしゃにして丸める crumple 《a piece of paper》into a ball.

ぐしゃぐしゃ　¶ぐしゃぐしゃの〈ぬれた〉drenched;〈水けを含んだ〉sloppy; sopping (wet);〈どろどろの〉pulpy; muddy / ぐしゃぐしゃに壊れる be crushed out of shape.

ぐしゃっと　¶ぐしゃっとつぶれる be crushed to a pulp.

くしゃみ　sneezing; a sneeze　¶くしゃみをする, くしゃみが出る sneeze; have a sneezing fit (発作ざまに). 文例⇩

くじゅう¹　苦汁　¶苦汁をなめる have [《文》suffer] a bitter experience;《口語》have a hard time (of it).

くじゅう²　苦渋　¶苦渋に満ちた表情 (wear) a deeply-troubled look.

くじょ　駆除　extermination; destruction; stamping out　¶駆除する exterminate; stamp out; get rid of; rid [clear] 《a house of vermin》.

くしょう　苦笑　¶苦笑する smile wryly [a wry smile]; give a forced laugh.

くじょう　苦情　〈不平〉a complaint; a grievance;〈反対〉objection(s)　¶苦情を言う make a complaint 《about sth, against sb》; complain 《to sb of sth》/ 苦情 make [raise] objections 《to》/ 苦情処理 (a) grievance procedure;《文》a procedure for the redress of grievances.

ぐしょう　具象　⇨ **ぐたい**　〈具体的(な)〉concrete; figurative / 具象画 a representational painting / 具象化する exteriorize; reify.

くじら　鯨　a whale　¶ごんどうくじら a pilot [black] whale; a blackfish / ざとうくじら a humpback whale / しろながすくじら a blue whale; a sulphur-bottom (whale) / せみくじら a right whale; a Greenland [bowhead] whale / ながすくじら a finback; a fin whale / はくじら a toothed whale / ひげくじら a baleen [whalebone] whale / まっこうくじら a sperm whale; a cachalot / くじら尺 a cloth measure.

くしん　苦心　pains; hard work　¶苦心する〈骨を折る〉take pains (over); work hard /《文》make strenuous efforts 《to do》/〈頭を悩ます〉rack one's brains / 苦心して by hard work; painstakingly; with great pains; with considerable effort / 苦心の作《文》the [a] fruit of much labor [great efforts] / 苦心談 an account of the pains one has taken 《to do》. 文例⇩

ぐしん　具申　¶具申する report (on a matter) / 意見を具申する offer one's opinion 《to one's superiors》.

---

keep overnight. / 彼は根性が腐っている. He is corrupt at heart. / 腐っても鯛. An old eagle is better than a young crow.

くじ くじで行く人を決めよう. Let us draw lots to decide who goes. / (競技の)組み合わせはくじで決められた. The pairings were drawn by ballot. / くじが当たった. The lot fell on me.

くじく 手首をくじいた. I have sprained my wrist.

くじける 彼は1度や2度の失敗でくじけるような人間ではない. He is not the sort of man to be discouraged by a failure or two.

くしゃみ 昨日(君のうわさをしていたのだが)くしゃみが出なかったか. Were your ears burning yesterday?

くしん この著作には大分苦心の跡が見える. The author seems to have taken great pains over this work.

ぐずぐず ぐずぐずしてはいられない. We have no time to lose. / ぐずぐずしていると列車に遅れるぞ. Hurry up, or you'll miss the train. / 何をぐずぐずしているのだ. Why on earth have you been so long? | What's taken you so long [all this time]? / ぐずぐずするな. Look sharp! | Be quick! | Make it snappy!

くすぐったい およし, くすぐったい. Stop! It tickles! / 足[耳]の

くず¹ 屑 rubbish; waste; trash; rags (ぼろ); junk (古道具など); scraps (かけら); crumbs (パンの) ¶金属のくず scrap [junk] metal / 人間のくず the scum of the earth; the dregs of humanity; a good-for-nothing / くず糸 waste thread / くず入れ〈駅や公園の〉a trash basket [box]; 《英》a litter bin / くずかご《米》a wastebasket; 《英》a wastepaper basket / くず鉄 scrap iron; scrap / くず拾い a ragpicker; a ragman / くず屋 a ragman; 《米》a junkman; 《英》a rag-and-bone man.

くず² 植 an arrowroot ¶くず餅 a pudding-like arrowroot cake / くず湯 arrowroot gruel (★現在一般に使用されているのは、原料がじゃがいもであるから、potato starch gruel と言うべきだろう).

ぐず〈のろま〉《米》a slowpoke; 《英》a slow-coach; 《文》a laggard; 〈意志の弱い人〉a weak-willed person; 〈優柔不断な人〉《文》an irresolute person; 〈ぐずぐず言う人〉a wishy-washy person; 《英口語》a wet ¶ぐずである be slow; 《文》be a laggard; have no spirit.

くすくす ¶くすくす笑う giggle; titter; 《米》snicker; 《英》snigger.

ぐずぐず〈のろく〉slowly; lazily; idly; 〈ためらって〉hesitatingly ¶ぐずぐずする〈のろい〉be slow; dawdle over 《one's breakfast》; 《文》be tardy; 〈わざと〉stall; 《口語》drag one's feet; 〈立ち去らない〉hang around; loiter; 《文》linger; 〈ためらう〉hesitate; 〈態度が不決断〉《口語》dilly-dally; shilly-shally / ぐずぐずせずに without hesitation [delay]; straight off / ぐずぐず言う grumble 《at, that...》; mutter 《about, that...》; complain 《about, that...》. 文例⇩

くすぐったい《one's ears》tickle ★「くすぐったい」を tickling で形容詞として表わすことはしない ¶くすぐったくなる be ticklish; be sensitive to tickling. 文例⇩

くすぐり〈くすぐること〉tickling; titillation; 〈冗談〉a joke; a gag.

くすぐる tickle ¶わきの下をくすぐる tickle sb under the arms [in the armpits].

くずす 崩す〈破壊する〉destroy; demolish; pull down; level (down) (平らにする) ¶山を崩して道を開く cut a road through a hill / ひざを崩す sit at ease; make oneself at home / 1万円札を崩す change [break] a 10,000-yen note (into small money) / 字を崩して書く write a character in the running style. 文例⇩

くすだま くす玉 a decorative paper ball 《for festive occasions》.

ぐずつく 文例⇩

くすねる steal; pilfer; filch; 《口語》pinch; 《口語》lift; 《口語》snitch; 《英口語》nick ⇒ぬす

くすのき 〈植〉a camphor tree.

くすぶる 燻る smoke; smolder ¶日米の間でくすぶっている問題 The situation that is smoldering between Japan and the U.S. / 家にくすぶっている stay indoors [at home]; do not enjoy the outdoor life / 平社員でくすぶっている《文》remain [live the humdrum life of] a mere clerk.

くすり 薬 (a) medicine; a drug; a pill (丸薬); an ointment (軟膏); 〈陶器の〉glaze; 〈ためになるもの〉benefit; 〈利益〉good ¶薬を飲む take medicine / 薬になる be good 《for》; do one good / 薬瓶 a medicine bottle / 薬屋〈店〉a pharmacy; 《米》a drugstore; 《英》a chemist's (shop); 〈人〉a pharmacist; 《米》a druggist; 《英》a chemist / 薬湯 a medicated [medicinal] bath.

くすりゆび 薬指 the third finger; the ring finger (主に左の).

ぐずる〈むずかる〉fret (赤ん坊が); be peevish; 《英》grizzle.

-くずれ ¶ボクサーくずれ《口語》an ex-boxer who has gone to the dogs; a degenerate ex-boxer / 作家くずれの大学教師 a failed writer turned university teacher.

くずれる 崩れる collapse; give way; break; fall to pieces [《口語》bits]; come [fall] apart; be destroyed; 〈落ち込む〉cave [fall] in; sink down; 〈形が〉get out of shape; 〈天気が〉change for the worse; break (晴天つづきの後); 〈相場が〉break; slump ¶さわると崩れる crumble to the touch / 崩れ落ちる tumble down / 崩れかかった crumbling 《walls》. 文例⇩

くすんだ dark; 《文》somber; 《文》dull-hued; dim (light).

くせ 癖 a (personal) habit; a [one's] way; a peculiarity; 〈悪癖〉a vice; a weakness ¶癖がつく get [fall] into a habit / 喫煙の癖がつく fall into the habit of smoking; take to smoking / ...する癖がある have [be in] the habit of doing / 癖をつける form a habit / 癖を直す 〈人の〉cure sb of his habit; get sb out of his habit; 〈自分の〉break [get out of, overcome, get over] one's habit 《of》; get rid [break oneself] of a habit / ...の癖に when; though; in spite of 《being...》 / つい癖で...する do...from [out of, by force of] habit. 文例⇩

すぐったい. My feet [ears] tickle. / あんな事を言われて何だかくすぐったかった.〈ほめられて〉I felt I hardly deserved his praise.

くずす 20ドル札をくずしていただけませんか. Could you give me change for a 20-dollar bill?

ぐずつく 天気はここ2,3日ぐずつくでしょう. The weather will remain unsettled for the next few days.

くすり この薬を飲めば病気が直る. This medicine will cure you [your illness]. / 何の薬ですか. What is this good for? / この失敗は彼にはいい薬になるよ. This failure will teach him a lesson [will be a lesson to him]. / 少し厳しすぎたかな. Have I been too harsh on him? / あの男は人情味などというものは薬にしたくもない. He hasn't an ounce of human kindness in him.

くずれる 地震で土手が崩れた. The earthquake destroyed the embankment. / 屋根が雪の重みで崩れ落ちそうになっていた. The roof was in danger of giving way under the weight of the snow.

くせ それが彼の癖なのだ. It's a habit of his to do that. | That's

くせげ 癖毛 (naturally) wavy [curly] hair; frizzy [kinky] hair (細かく縮れた).

くせもの 曲者《悪漢》a rascal; a rogue;《老獪(ゔ)な人》an old fox;《盗賊》a burglar; a thief; a robber;〈怪しいやつ〉a suspicious(-looking) fellow.

くせん 苦戦 a hard fight; a desperate battle;〈競技などの〉a close contest; a losing game (負けになる) ¶苦戦する fight against heavy odds; have a tough game; be in trouble.

くせんてい 駆潜艇 a (submarine) chaser.

くそ ⇨ふん².

くそどきょう 糞度胸 ¶くそ度胸のある foolhardy; daredevil.

くそべんきょう 糞勉強 ¶くそ勉強する grind (away)《at examination subjects》; cram《for an exam》;《米》bone up《on a subject, for an exam》;《英》swot《at a subject, for an exam》.

くそまじめ 糞真面目 ¶くそまじめだ be too serious; be serious to a fault.

くそみそ 糞味噌 ¶くそみそに言う run sb [sth] down; call sb every name [everything] under the sun.

くだ 管 a pipe; a tube;《plastic》tubing ¶酔って管を巻く babble [blather] drunkenly.

ぐたい 具体 具体的 concrete; physical; definite / 具体的に言えば to put it concretely / 具体案 a definite plan / 具体化する〈事が〉take (concrete) shape; shape up; materialize;〈事を〉give shape (to);《文》put (a plan) into effect / 具体策《文》a concrete measure. 文例⇩

くだく 砕く break sth (into pieces); smash; crush; shatter;〈すって〉grind sth into powder;〈ついて〉pound; pulverize (粉に) ¶心を砕く rack one's brains; think and think《about》.

くたくた ¶くたくたに疲れる be worn out; be (utterly) exhausted; be dead tired;《口語》be dog-tired;《米俗》be pooped (out);《英俗》be knackered / くたくたに煮る reduce (cabbage) to (a) pulp by boiling. 文例⇩

くだくだしい tedious; lengthy ¶くだくだしく tediously; at (great) length.

くだける 砕ける break; be broken; be smashed; be crushed ¶当たって砕ける take a risk [chance] / 砕けた〈壊れた〉broken; smashed;〈平易な〉easy; plain;〈愛想よい〉affable;〈親しみやすい〉familiar (language); friendly / 砕けた説明 a straightforward explanation / 砕けた態度で in a free and easy manner; with a friendly attitude. 文例⇩

ください 下さい ¶…を下さい I would like (a box of matches), please; May I have (a glass of water), please / …して下さい Will [Would] you please do ¶ 人にものを頼むときの「…して下さい」という丁寧な気持ちは please によって表わされる。

くださる 下さる〈与える〉give;《文》confer [bestow] sth (on me); 〈…して下さる〉《文》be kind [good] enough to do;《文》have the kindness to do. 文例⇩

くだす 下す〈下ろす〉let down; lower;〈命令を〉give; issue;〈判決を〉deliver (a judgment); pass (sentence);〈負かす〉defeat; beat; down ¶腹を下す have diarrhea; have loose bowels.

くたばる〈死ぬ〉《俗》kick the bucket;《俗》cash in (one's checks [chips]);《俗》croak;《英俗》snuff it.

くたびれる get [《文》become] tired;《文》be fatigued ⇨つかれる¹ ¶くたびれた靴 tired [well-worn] shoes; shoes rather the worse for wear. 文例⇩

くだもの 果物 a fruit; fruit (総称) ★複数の fruits は違った種類の果物を言うときにしか使わないし、その場合でも various kinds of fruit とか different sorts of fruit のように言うのが普通 ¶果物屋《店》a fruit store [shop];《人》a fruiterer.

くだらない 下らない〈取るに足りない〉worthless; rubbishy; trashy;《文》trifling; insignificant;〈ばかげた〉absurd; silly; senseless;〈無益な〉idle; useless ¶下らない物 rubbish; mere trash; garbage / 下らない事を言う talk rubbish [nonsense].

くだり¹ 下り a descent; going down ¶天竜下り shooting the Tenryu Rapids / ライン下り a Rhine cruise; a boat trip down the Rhine / 下り列車[線, ホーム] a down train [line, platform]. 文例⇩

くだり² 条 a passage; a line.

くだりざか 下り坂〈道の〉a downward slope; a downhill road;〈下火〉《文》a decline;《文》an ebb ¶下り坂になる〈道が〉slope [go] down; go [run] downhill;〈衰える〉《文》decline;《文》wane; be on the wane [decline]; be in decline;〈天気が〉break. 文例⇩

くだる 下る〈降りる〉go [come, get] down;《文》descend;〈下降する〉fall; drop;〈命令な

どが〉be given; be issued;〈以下である〉be less than; be below [under];〈劣る〉be not as good《as》;《文》be inferior《to》;〈降参する〉surrender《to》;《文》yield《to》 ¶川を下る go down a river / 山を下る go [get, climb] down a mountain / 腹が下っている have loose bowels / 3千を下らない be not less than 3,000. [文例⇩]

くだん 件 ¶くだんの〈問題の〉《文》《the case》 in question;〈前述の〉《文》the said《man》; the above-mentioned.

[用法] 英語では「すでに話題にのぼった…」の意は，多くの場合単に the … で表わすことも可能である．

くち 口 the [*one's*] mouth; the [*one's*] lips (唇);〈言葉〉words; speech;《文》tongue;〈味覚〉*one's* taste;《文》*one's* palate;〈器物の〉a mouth; a mouthpiece; a spout (湯沸かしなどの); a nozzle (ホースの); a tap (たるの);〈開口部〉an opening;〈通行口〉a door; a gate (門); an entrance (入口); an exit (出口);〈就職口〉a job; a position; an opening; a vacancy;〈割前〉a share;〈種類〉a sort.

¶口がうまい be glib-[smooth-]tongued;《文》be fair-spoken / 口が重い be a man [woman] of few words;《文》be slow of speech;《文》be incommunicative [taciturn] / 口がかかる be offered a position / 口が堅い be close-mouthed; be tight-lipped;《文》be discreet / 口が軽い have a loose tongue; be talkative;《口語》be a blabbermouth / 口がきけなくなる find *oneself* unable to speak《for terror》; lose *one's* tongue; be tongue-tied (★ tongue-tied は lose *one's* tongue ほどではなく，「どもって」という程度) / (再び) 口がきけるようになる find *one's* tongue / 口が臭い have bad breath / 口が肥えている[おごっている] be hard to please where (*one's*) food is concerned; be particular [fussy] about *one's* food;《文》have a discriminating palate;《文》be (something of) a gourmet / 口がすべる blurt *sth* out; let *sth* fall [drop]; say *sth* thoughtlessly / つい口がすべって…と言う be careless enough to say…; let it slip that… / 口が達者である be glib(-tongued); have a glib tongue; be a glib talker / 開いた口がふさがらない be dum(b)founded; be speechless《with surprise》; be struck dumb / 口が悪い be sarcastic; have a sharp [nasty] tongue.

¶口の oral.

¶口を開ける open *one's* mouth;〈栓を〉uncork《a bottle》/ 口を大きく開ける open *one's* mouth wide / 口をきく speak [talk]《to》;〈仲裁する〉mediate《between》;〈世話する〉use *one's* influence《for》;〈取りなす〉put in a (good) word《for, on *sb's* behalf》;〈仲人をする〉act as go-between《for [between] A and B, in the matter of》/ 大きな口をきく boast; brag;《口語》talk big; be boastful / 口を切る be the first to speak; break the silence; break the ice《(by) saying…》(初対面の人々がみな遠慮している場合など) / 口をきわめてほめる《文》be loud in *sb's* praise [in *one's* praises of *sb*]; speak of [praise] *sb* in the highest possible terms; praise *sb* to the skies / (仕事の)口を捜す look for a job;《文》seek employment / 口をすぼめる purse (up) *one's* lips / (びんなどに)口をする cork《a bottle》/ 口をそろえて〈一斉に〉in chorus;《文》with one [a single] voice;〈一致して〉unanimously / 口を出す put a word in;〈干渉する〉butt in; interrupt; intrude / 口をつける taste / 口を慎む be careful of *one's* language; be careful what *one* says; control *one's* tongue / 口をとがらす pout / 口をとがらして言う say *sth* with a pout / 口を固く閉ざす shut *one's* mouth tight(ly); clamp *one's* lips together / 口を閉ざして語らない shut *one's* mouth and stay silent; keep silent / 口を閉じる shut *one's* mouth;〈黙る〉stop [《文》cease] talking;《口語》shut up / 口をぬぐってすましている《文》feign innocence [ignorance] / 口をはさむ put a word in;《cannot》get a word in (edgeways) / 口を割る confess《to》; let out《*one's* idea》.

¶口に合う suit *one*;《文》be to *one's* taste / 口にする〈言葉を口に出す〉speak [talk] of; mention; refer to; let《the name of *sb*》fall;〈食べる〉eat; take;〈味わう〉taste / 口にすべからざる《a topic》that should [must] not be mentioned; unmentionable.

¶口で《reported》by word of mouth;《文》《express》orally / 口では言い表わせないほど more than *one* can say;《文》more than tongue can tell; beyond description; indescribably.

¶(人の)口から聞く hear《it》from *sb* [《文》*sb's* lips] / 口から口へと伝わる pass from mouth to mouth. [文例⇩]

ぐち 愚痴 a [an idle] complaint; a grumble;《口語》a moan ¶ぐちっぽい whining;《文》querulous《men》/ ぐちっぽい人 a complainer; a grumbler;《口語》a moaner / ぐちをこ

くだける あの人は砕けた英語で流暢(りゅうちょう)に話す. He speaks fluent, colloquial English.

ください (食卓で)塩を取って下さいませんか. Would you please pass me the salt? | May I trouble you for the salt? / 窓を閉めて下さいませんでしょうか. Would you mind closing the window?

くださる このお金は私に下さるのですか. Is this money for me? / 私の願いを聞いて下さればまことにありがたい. I hope you will be kind enough to grant my request.

くたばる くたばってしまえ. Drop dead! | Go to hell [the devil]!

くたびれる それを見上げていて首がくたびれた. I got a stiff neck from looking up at it.

くだり[1] 次の下りは何時ですか. What time is the next down train? / そこで道は下りになる. The road slopes down [goes downhill] from there.

くだりざか 彼の人気は既に下り坂だ. His popularity is already in decline. / 今晩あたりから天気は下り坂になるでしょう. This fine weather will not last [hold (up)] till tomorrow.

くだる 前進命令が下った. We were ordered to advance.

くち とたんに彼はぴったり口を閉ざしてしまった. He shut up at once like a clam. / 口から先に生まれて来たようなやつだ. He must have been born talking. / 彼女は自分の口からそう言ったの

くちあけ 口開け the opening (of business); 〈たるなどの〉broaching.

くちあたり 口当たり ¶口当たりがいい[悪い] taste nice [nasty]; taste pleasant [unpleasant]; 《文》be pleasant [unpleasant] to the taste; 《文》be palatable [unpalatable] / 口当たりのいい人 a smooth talker; a soft-soaper.

くちうつし 口移し〈食物の〉mouth-to-mouth feeding ¶口移し(に)する feed from mouth to mouth; transfer (food) from *one's* mouth to *sb's* / 〈人工呼吸の〉口移し法 the mouth-to-mouth method (of resuscitation); 《口語》《give *sb*》the kiss of life.

くちうら 口裏 ¶口裏を合わせる make sure 《their》stories agree; arrange not to contradict each other; arrange beforehand to tell the same story [say the same thing] (to the police).

くちえ 口絵 a frontispiece.

くちかず 口数 ¶口数が多い be talkative; 《文》be loquacious; talk [be given to talking] too much / 口数の少ない silent; 《文》incommunicative; 《文》taciturn; 《文》reticent; 《文》(a man) of few words. 文例↓

くちがね 口金 a cap; a clasp (かばんの); a base (電球などの); 《機》a mouthpiece.

くちがる 口軽 a loose-tongued person.

くちき 朽ち木〈立ち木〉a decayed tree; 〈木材〉decayed wood.

くちきき 口利き〈調停〉mediation; 〈結婚などの〉matchmaking; acting as go-between ¶人に口ききを頼む〈調停を〉ask *sb* to mediate [act as peacemaker]; 〈尽力を〉《文》ask *sb* to use *his* good offices (on *one's* behalf) ⇒くち(口をきく).

くちぎたない 口汚ない foul-mouthed; abusive ¶口汚なくののしる call *sb* names; 《文》abuse *sb*. 文例↓

くちく 駆逐 ¶駆逐する《文》expel; drive away [out]; 《口語》get rid of.

くちくかん 駆逐艦 a destroyer.

くちぐせ 口癖 ¶口癖のように言う always say; keep saying; be never tired of saying. 文例↓

くちぐち 口々 ¶口々に〈各自〉individually; separately; 《文》severally; 〈異口同音に〉unanimously.

くちぐるま 口車 ¶口車に乗る be taken in by *sb's* glib talk [《口語》slick talk, 《文》honeyed words].

くちげんか 口喧嘩 (have) a quarrel [words] 《with *sb*》⇒ けんか². 文例↓

くちごたえ 口答え back talk; a retort ¶口答えをする talk back (to *sb*); answer (*sb*) back; retort; 《口語》give *sb* back talk. 文例↓

くちコミ 口コミ ¶口コミで by word of mouth; by mouth-to-mouth advertising; 《learn about *sth*》on [through] the grapevine.

くちごもる 口籠もる〈つかえる〉falter; be stuck for a word; hesitate (in speaking); hem (and haw); 〈もぐもぐ言う〉mumble ¶口ごもりながら言い訳をする mumble (out) an excuse.

くちさがない 口さがない gossipy; fond of gossip; 〈口の悪い〉《文》slanderous; abusive ¶口さがない連中 gossipmongers; scandalmongers.

くちさき 口先 ¶口先のうまい smooth-tongued; oily; 《文》fair-spoken / 口先だけの insincere; 《文》specious / 口先ばかり大胆である be full of brave talk [words]; be all bark and no bite / 口先だけは完全軍縮に賛意を表する pay [lend] lip service to the principle of complete disarmament.

くちさびしい 口寂しい feel the need for something to chew [to put in *one's* mouth].

くちずさむ 口ずさむ hum (a tune); sing [croon] to *oneself*.

くちぞえ 口添え recommendation; 《文》good offices ¶口添えする recommend; put in a (good) word for [on behalf of] *sb*.

くちだし 口出し ⇒ くち(口を出す). 文例↓

くちつき 口付き〈口の形〉the shape of *one's* mouth; 〈口ぶり〉⇒ くちぶり / 口付きの巻きタバコ a cigarette with a (cardboard) mouthpiece; 〈フィルター付き〉a filter-tip [《英》a tipped] cigarette.

だ. I heard it from her own lips. / その怪物は口が耳まで裂けていた. The mouth of the monster extended from ear to ear. / そのときは口がきけなくなってしまった. Words failed me at that time. / なんだって私にそんな口のきき方をするのか. How dare you talk to me like that! / 赤ん坊がやっと口をききはじめた. The child has only just started to speak. / 彼の方が専ら話し手で, こちらは口をはさむこともろくにできなかった. He monopolized the conversation and I couldn't [could hardly] get a word in edgeways. / 口は災いのもと. Confine your tongue, lest it confine you. 《諺》| Don't let your mouth get you in trouble! / 口は災いのもとだよ. Just look back at the mess you're in and you'll find that your tongue started it. / そう言う口の下からまたうそをついた. Almost in the same breath, he told another lie. / 山上の垂訓を語った口の下から, 彼は軍備拡張を唱えた. He preached about the Sermon on the Mount, and in the next breath he called for expansion of armaments. / はっきり口に出して認めたわけではない. He did not admit it in so many words. / 口にするにはあまりばかげていた. It was too idiotic for words. / 彼はうまいことを言うが口だけ. He's full of fine talk, but it is all talk and no action [it's nothing but hot air]. / 口も八丁手も八丁. He is not only eloquent but also very efficient. / おしろいの面が彼女に向かって口をぱくぱくやった. The big lion mask mouthed at her. / 1日4千円でメッセンジャーボーイの口がある. There is an opening for a messenger boy at 4,000 yen a day. / 僕はいい口が見つかった. I have found a good job. / この口は品切れになりました. This lot is now out of stock.

ぐち 彼は絶えず不景気だとぐちをこぼしている. He is constantly complaining about the poor state of business. / それはぐちというものだ. That's crying over spilt milk.

くちづけ 口付け ⇨ キス.
くちつたえ 口伝え 〈口授〉 oral instruction; 〈伝承〉 oral transmission; (a) tradition ¶口伝えに by word of mouth ⇨ くちコミ; 〈昔から〉 by (oral) tradition / 口伝えの orally-transmitted (sagas).
くちどめ 口止め ¶口止めする forbid sb to say anything (to anybody) about sth; impose silence on sb; muzzle sb / 口止め料 hush money. 文例⇩
くちとり 口取り ⇨ つまみ.
くちなおし 口直し ¶口直しをする take away the aftertaste / 口直しに to take the nasty taste out of one's mouth.
くちなし 〖植〗 a Cape jasmine; a gardenia.
くちば 朽ち葉 a dead [decayed] leaf ¶朽ち葉色〖フランス語〗 feuille morte; foliage brown.
くちばし 嘴 a beak; a bill ¶先がかぎのように曲がったくちばし a hooked beak / くちばしをいれる meddle [interfere] in; put (poke, 〖文〗 thrust) one's nose into / まだくちばしの黄色い若者 an inexperienced [〖文〗 a callow] young man / 〖口語〗 a greenhorn. 文例⇩
くちばしる 口走る say 〈something senseless〉; 〈うっかり口に出して言う〉 let 〈a secret〉 slip [out]; blurt out.
くちはてる 朽ち果てる rot [rust] away; 〈人が〉 die in obscurity.
くちはばったい 口幅ったい ¶口幅ったいことを言う talk big; 〖俗〗 shoot off one's mouth.
くちび 口火 〈導火線〉 a fuse (火縄銃などの); a train (爆薬の); 〈火を移すために燃やしておく〉 a pilot light [flame] ¶口火を切る 〈開始する〉 begin; touch off; trigger off / …の口火になる spark sth (off). 文例⇩
くちひげ 口髭 〖wear〗 a mustache.
くちひも 口紐 〈袋の〉 a drawstring.
くちびる 唇 a lip ¶薄い [厚い] 唇 thin [full] lips / 上 [下] 唇 the upper [lower] lip.
くちぶえ 口笛 a whistle ¶口笛を吹く whistle; give a whistle.
くちぶり 口振り 〈言い方〉 the way one talks; one's way of talking; 〈ほのめかし〉 a hint ¶君の口ぶりでは (by) the way you talk. 文例⇩

くちべた 口下手 a poor talker.
くちべに 口紅 (a) lipstick ¶口紅のついた lipstick-stained 《cigarette stubs》 / 口紅をつける put lipstick on (one's lips); put on lipstick / 口紅をつけている wear lipstick. 文例⇩
くちまね 口真似 mimicry ¶口まねする mimic sb [the way sb talks]; imitate sb's way of speaking / 口まねがうまい be a good mimic ⇨ こわいろ.
くちもと 口元 the mouth ¶口もとに微笑を浮かべて with a smile playing about one's lips [mouth].
くちやかましい 口喧しい nagging 《wives》; sharp-tongued; faultfinding; critical; 〖文〗 censorious; 〈細かい〉 particular ¶口やかましく言う nag (at); find fault (with).
くちやくそく 口約束 ¶口約束をする give one's word (to); make a verbal promise [agreement]; promise by word of mouth.
ぐちゃぐちゃ 〈ぐちゃぐちゃの pulpy; too soft; 〈水っぽい〉 sopping (wet); sloppy.
くちゅう 苦衷 〈苦悩〉 〖文〗 mental suffering; 〖文〗 the anguish of an unresolvable dilemma; 〈苦しい立場〉 a difficult situation, a predicament; a painful position ¶苦衷を察する sympathize with sb in his predicament.
ちゅうざい 駆虫剤 an insecticide; (an) insect powder (粉末) ⇨ さっちゅうざい; 〈虫下し〉 a vermifuge; an anthelmint(h)ic.
くちょう¹ 口調 a tone ¶口調が悪い do not sound pleasant; be unpleasant to the ear; 〖文〗 lack euphony / 口調のよい well-sounding; rhythmical; 〖文〗 euphonious / 演説口調で 〖文〗 in an oratorical tone. 文例⇩
くちょう² 区長 the headman [chief] of a ward.
ぐちょく 愚直 simple (and honest); honest to a fault.
くちる 朽ちる decay; rot ¶朽ちた rotten; decayed / 朽ちかけた crumbling; moldering.
くちわ 口輪 a muzzle ¶口輪をする muzzle 《a dog》; put a muzzle on 《a dog》.
くつ 靴 shoes (短靴); boots (深靴) ¶靴1足 a pair of shoes / 靴を脱ぐ take one's shoes off / 靴をはく put one's shoes on / 靴をみがく polish shoes; 〖米〗 shine shoes. 文例⇩

くちかず 彼女は口数の少ない人だった. She was one of those people who never say much.
くちきたない 彼女は口汚ないでいやだ. She is so foul-mouthed that I can't stand her.
くちぐせ 父は「金が欲しい, 金が欲しい」と口癖のように言っていた. Father never opened his mouth without saying, 'I wish I had more money.' / 「全くだ」というのが彼の口癖だ. He has a way of saying, 'Quite so.' | 'Quite so' is a pet phrase of his.
くちげんか 口げんかで済んだ. They quarreled violently but didn't come to blows.
くちごたえ 彼は子供には口答えを許さなかった. He would not

take any back talk from his children. | He never let his children answer (him) back.
くちだし 余計な口出しをするな. Mind your own business.
くちどめ 口止め料に 5 万円払った. I bought his silence for 50,000 yen.
くちばし この話にはくちばしを入れるなと言ったではないか. I thought I told you to keep out of this!
くちはばったい 口幅ったいことを言うようですが, 仕事の腕では東京中の仲間のだれにもひけをとりません. I may seem to be talking big, but in my professional skill I give best to no-one in the whole city of Tokyo.

くちび それが第一次世界大戦の口火となった. This touched [triggered] off the First World War. | This led to World War I.
くちぶえ 彼は口をすぼめて口笛を吹き出した. He pursed his lips in a whistle.
くちぶり 彼は何でも知っていそうな口ぶりだ. He talks as if he knew everything.
くちべに 彼女はいつも歯に少し口紅がついていた. There was always a little lipstick on her teeth. / 学校では口紅をつけることは許されない. The school does not let girl pupils wear lipstick.
くちょう¹ この方が口調がいい. This sounds better.
くつ この靴は窮屈だ. These shoes

くつう 苦痛 (a) pain；《文》a pang (劇痛)〈〉いたみ ¶精神的苦痛《文》mental anguish / 苦痛のあまり呻き声を立てる give a moan of pain；moan in one's pain / 苦痛を与える cause sb pain；《文》inflict pain (on)；hurt sb / 苦痛を感じる feel (a) pain；suffer pain / 苦痛に堪える bear [《文》endure] the pain. 文例⇩

くつおと 靴音 ¶靴音が聞こえる hear sb's footsteps；hear sb walking (in his shoes).

くつがえす 覆す upset；overturn，turn over；capsize (船を)；〈打倒する〉overthrow ¶定説を覆す explode [overthrow, disprove] the established theory / 判決を覆す reverse a sentence.

くつがえる 覆る overturn；be upset；be overturned；〈船が〉capsize.

くつがた 靴型 a shoe [boot] tree.

クッキー 《米》a cookie；《英》a biscuit.

くっきょう 屈強 ¶屈強な strong；sturdy；robust；wiry (筋肉質の).

くっきょく 屈曲 bending；winding；〈海岸線などの〉an indentation；irregularities ¶屈曲する be crooked；bend；wind / 屈曲した crooked；winding；zigzag(ging) / 屈曲部 an elbow；an elbow-shaped bend.

くっきり distinctly；clearly；boldly；《文》in bold [strong] relief；《文》with crystal clarity；〈著しく〉conspicuously；remarkably. 文例⇩

くっきん 屈筋《解》a flexor (muscle).

ぐつぐつ ¶ぐつぐつ煮る boil (the beans) gently；simmer.

くっさく 掘削 ¶掘削する dig out [through]；excavate / 掘削機 an excavator；a [an earth] scraper / 掘削装置 drilling rigs.

くっし 屈指 ¶屈指の leading；《文》foremost；prominent；《文》preeminent / 屈指の良港 one of the best seaports 《along the coast》. 文例⇩

くつした 靴下 socks (短い)；stockings (長い) ¶靴下 1 足 a pair of socks [stockings] / 〈靴を脱いで〉靴下だけになって in one's stockings；in one's stockinged feet / 靴下止め《米》garters；《英》suspenders.

くつじゅう 屈従《文》(servile) submission；《文》subservience ¶屈従する submit [《文》yield, 《文》succumb] (to)；bend the knee [(to)] / 屈従的な《文》submissive；《文》subservient.

くつじょく 屈辱 (a) humiliation；(a) disgrace；(a) shame；(an) indignity；an insult；〈敗北〉a defeat ¶屈辱的な humiliating；shameful / 屈辱をこうむる be disgraced；be humiliated；be insulted / 屈辱を忍ぶ put up with [swallow] an insult.

クッション a cushion ¶クッションのいい椅子 a soft, comfortable chair / クッションをつける cushion 《a seat》.

くっしん 屈伸 ¶屈伸する bend and stretch；〈関節などが〉flex / ひざの屈伸運動をする do knee bends. 文例⇩

くつずみ 靴墨 shoe polish.

ぐっすり ¶ぐっすり寝る sleep soundly / ぐっすり眠っている be fast [sound, heavily] asleep.

くっする 屈する〈曲げる〉bend；〈負ける〉《文》yield (to)；give in (to)；《文》bow (to)；《口語》cave in；〈たじろぐ〉《文》be daunted (by)；shrink (from) ¶身を屈して…する stoop to do / 逆境に屈しない bear up well under difficult [《文》adverse] circumstances / 屈せずに undauntedly.

くつずれ 靴擦れ (get) a shoe sore.

くっせつ 屈折《光学》refraction ¶屈折する be refracted；undergo a refraction bend / 彼の例の屈折した論理 that convoluted logic of his / 屈折語《言語》an inflectional [inflective] language / 屈折度の異なる光線 differently refrangible rays / 屈折率 a refractive index；an index of refraction.

くっそう 屈葬 (a) crouched [flexed] burial.

くつぞこ 靴底 the sole (of a shoe).

くったく 屈託〈心配〉worry；care；〈退屈〉boredom；《文》ennui ¶屈託する〈心配する〉be worried (about)；〈退屈する〉get [《文》become] bored [《文》weary] / 屈託がない have no cares [worries]；be free from care [worry]；be carefree.

ぐったり ¶ぐったり疲れる be tired out；be dead tired；be exhausted / ぐったりと椅子に座る sit limply in a chair；slump down onto [into] a chair / ぐったりしている be slumped 《over one's desk》.

くっつく stick (cling, 《文》adhere) (to).

くっつける〈合わせる〉join；put together；〈接合する〉attach；〈粘着する〉stick；paste (のりで)；glue (にかわで)；〈取りつける〉fix.

くってかかる 食って掛かる turn [round] on sb；go at sb；fly [lash out] at sb.

ぐっと〈一息に〉at a gulp；〈大いに〉《文》much；a great deal；〈強く〉tightly；firmly ¶ぐっと飲む《口語》gulp 《one's beer》 down；〈一息に〉drink sth at a gulp / 〈長く〉take a long drink 《from a bottle》 / ぐっと引っぱる give a strong [good] pull 《at the rope》 / 胸にぐっとくる come home to one；touch one. 文例⇩

くつぬぐい 靴拭い a doormat；〈鉄の〉a shoe [mud] scraper.

グッピー《魚》a guppy.

くつひも 靴紐 a shoelace；《米》a shoestring；a bootlace (編み上げの) ¶靴ひもを結ぶ fasten [tie] one's shoelaces；lace (up) one's

---

pinch me [are too tight]. / (靴磨きが)だんな、靴をみがきませんか。Give your shoes a shine, sir?
くつう 苦痛を感じなくなった。The pain has gone [has left me]. / 父の厄介になっているのは苦痛だ。It is distressing for me to be dependent on my father.

くっきり 雪の積もった峰がその輪郭を青空にくっきりと浮かべている。The snowcapped peaks stand clearly outlined [stand out in bold relief] against the blue sky.
くっし 日本は世界屈指の工業国だ。Japan is one of the greatest industrial countries in the world.

くっしん しゃくとりむしは屈伸して進む。The measuring worm progresses by alternately looping and straightening its body.
くってかかる 彼は怒って僕に食ってかかった。He turned on me in a fury.
ぐっと それでぐっとよくなった。

くっぷく 屈服 《文》 submission; (a) surrender ¶屈服する《文》 yield (to); surrender 《to》; give in (to); submit (to).

くつブラシ 靴ブラシ a shoe [boot] brush.

くつべら 靴箆 a shoehorn; <長いもの> a long shoehorn.

くつみがき 靴磨き <事> shoe polishing;<人> a bootblack;《英》a shoeblack ¶靴磨きの少年《米》a shoeshine boy / 靴磨き用の布 a shoe rag.

くつや 靴屋 <店>《米》a shoe store;《英》a shoe shop;<人> a shoemaker.

くつろぐ 寛ぐ relax; make oneself at home [comfortable]; take oneself at ease; unbend ¶くつろいで at one's ease; in a relaxed mood,《文》without reserve.

くつわ 轡 a bit ¶くつわを並べて (ride) abreast;(run) side by side.

ぐでんぐでん ¶ぐでんぐでんに酔っぱらっている be dead [blind, rolling] drunk;《口語》be plastered [canned];《口語》be drunk [《英俗》pissed] out of one's mind;《英俗》be as pissed as a newt.

くどい <長ったらしい> long-winded; tedious; lengthy;<しつこい> insistent;《味が》importunate;<味が> heavy ¶くどく<冗長に> tediously;<繰り返して> repeatedly;<しつこく> insistently;《文》importunately; inquisitively (根掘り葉掘り). 文例⬇

くとう¹ 句読《法》punctuation; pointing ¶句読を切る punctuate / 句読点 punctuation marks.

くとう² 苦闘 a bitter [an uphill] struggle; a hard fight ¶苦闘する fight [struggle] hard [desperately].

くどう 駆動 ¶四輪駆動の自動車 a four-wheel-drive vehicle / 前輪駆動の自動車 a front-wheel-drive car / 駆動軸 a drive shaft / 駆動力 driving power.

くどく¹ 功徳 <恵み>《文》benevolence;<善行>《文》a pious [charitable] deed; good works;《文》(a) merit;《文》virtue ¶功徳を施す do an act of charity / 功徳を積む accumulate good deeds; earn (a great deal of) merit (for one's generosity). 文例⬇

くどく² 口説く <せがむ> badger sb 《for, to do》; pester;《文》importune;《文》solicit 《sb's help》;<勧める> urge sb (to do);<異性を>《口語》make a play《米》(pitch) (for a girl);《英口語》chat (a girl) up; court (a woman) ¶口説き落とす persuade sb 《to do, into doing》; induce sb to do; win sb over; bring [talk] sb round;<異性を> win sb's affections;《口語》get off with 《a girl》;《俗》score with 《a girl》;《口語》《do not》 get anywhere with 《a girl》.

くどくど ¶くどくど言う dwell 《on a subject》; harp on 《a matter》;《口語》go on 《and on》《about a matter》; labor 《the point》.

ぐどん 愚鈍 ¶愚鈍な stupid; dull; thick-headed.

くないちょう 宮内庁 the Imperial Household Agency ¶宮内庁長官 the Director of the Imperial Household Agency.

くなん 苦難 suffering(s); hardship(s);《文》distress.

くに 国 <国土> a country; a land;<国家> a state; a nation;<国籍> one's nationality;<故国> one's (home) country;<故郷> one's (old) home; the part of the country (that) one comes from; one's home province; one's birthplace ¶武蔵の国 Musashi province; the province of Musashi / 国の両親 one's parents at home / 国を思う心 one's love for one's country / 国へ帰る[を出る] go [leave] home / 国へ手紙を書く write home / 国柄 national character [characteristics]. 文例⬇

くにく 苦肉 ¶苦肉の策 the last resort; a desperate measure taken under the pressure of necessity.

くにもと 国許 one's home.

ぐにゃぐにゃ ¶ぐにゃぐにゃの soft; spineless;《flabby (muscles)》; limp;《文》flaccid.

くねくね ⇒くねる(くねった) ¶くねくねと (run) (in a) zigzag;《twist》like a snake.

くねる be crooked;<曲がりくねる> twist and turn; zigzag; wind; meander ¶くねった crooked; full of twists and bends;《文》tortuous;《文》sinuous / 体をくねらせて踊る do a sinuous dance.

くのう 苦悩 suffering(s); distress; (an) affliction; anguish; agony; trouble ¶苦悩する be anguished; be in agony / 苦悩に満ちた《文》anguished 《conscience》.

くはい 苦杯 ¶苦杯をなめる《文》drink a bitter cup;《文》drink the cup of humiliation;<負ける> suffer a defeat.

くばる 配る distribute; hand [pass] out; deal (out) 《cards》; serve (out) 《food》;<配達する> deliver.

くび 首 <<くび> a neck;<頭> a head ¶首のない死体 a headless corpse / 首をすくめる shrug one's shoulders; duck one's head (銃弾をよけるなど) / 窓から首を出す lean out of the window; stick [poke] one's head out of a window / 首を突っ込む poke one's head inside 《a room》;<かかわり合いを持つ> take part (in); have a hand (in); have one's finger in the pie / 首を縦に振る nod (one's head);<同

くつひも 靴ひもがゆるんだ。The shoelace came loose.

くどい 彼の文はくどい。His style is rather wordy. / くどいようですが明日は7時に必ず来て下さい。Excuse me for repeating myself, but I will expect you at 7 o'clock.

くどく¹ 功徳を積むことによって救いが得られると一般に信じられた。It was generally believed that salvation could be earned by good works.

くなん この時は彼らにとってまさに苦難の時であった。These were indeed hard times for them.

くに 農は国のもとである。Agriculture is the foundation of the nation. / この費用は国の負担です。This is a charge on the national treasury. | The government bears the whole expense of this.

ぐび 具意する nod *one's* agreement ((to)); agree ((to)); 《文》give (*one's*) assent ((to)) / 首を横に振る shake *one's* head; 〈拒絶する〉refuse; 〈扇風機が〉oscillate / 首をかしげる put *one's* head on one side; look doubtful [quizzical] / 首をひねる rack *one's* brains; think hard / 首を伸ばす crane *one's* neck ((to get a better view)) / 首を長くして待つ wait impatiently; wait for [look forward to] *sth* with impatience / 首を切る cut off *sb's* head; behead *sb*; 〈解雇する〉sack; give *sb* the sack; 《米》fire; 《文》dismiss / 人の首にかじりつく throw both arms round *sb's* neck / 首になる get the sack; be sacked; 《米》be fired; 《文》be dismissed. 文例⬇

ぐび 具備 ¶具備する〈備わっている〉《文》be furnished ((with)); 〈持っている〉《文》possess; have; 《文》be possessed of.

くびかざり 首飾り a necklace; a neck ornament; a necklet; a choker (幾重にも巻きつけた真珠のネックレスなど).

くびがり 首狩り headhunting ¶首狩り族 headhunters.

くびき 軛 a yoke ¶くびきにつながれた2頭の牛 a pair of yoked oxen.

くびきり 首切り 〈断頭(%)〉《文》decapitation; beheading; 〈解雇する〉the sack; 《文》dismissal ⇒くび(首を切る) ¶首切り反対を叫ぶ protest against the dismissal of workers.

くびくくり 首縊り ⇒くびつり.

くびじっけん 首実検 identification ((of a suspect)) ¶首実検をする identify ((a suspect)) / 首実検に立ち合う attend an identification parade (面通しで).

ぐびじんそう 虞美人草 ⇒ひなげし.

くびすじ 首筋 the back [nape] of the neck ¶首筋をつかまえる take [《文》seize] ((a cat)) by the scruff of the neck ★ scruff はつかまえる対象としての「首筋」のときに使う。

くびったけ 首っ丈 ¶首ったけである be madly [deeply] in love ((with)); be head over heels in love ((with)).

くびっぴき 首っ引き ¶辞書と首っ引きで (do *one's* homework)) constantly looking words up in a dictionary; looking up every other [virtually every] word in a dictionary; with a dictionary in one hand.

くびつり 首吊り hanging *oneself*; 〈人〉a person who has hanged himself.

くびねっこ 首根っこ ⇒くび ¶首根っこをおさえる grab [《文》seize] *sb* by the neck; 〈比喩的に〉《口語》have [get] *sb* by the short hairs; have *sb* under *one's* thumb.

くびれる 《文》be constricted; be pinched in ¶くびれたウエスト a pinched-in waist / ひょうたんのくびれた所 the narrow part of a gourd.

くびわ 首輪 a necklace; a choker; 〈犬の〉a collar.

くぶ 九分 〈十分の九〉nine tenths; nine parts; 〈百分の九〉nine per cent; 9% ¶九分どおり almost; nearly all / 九分九厘 almost certainly; in all probability. 文例⬇

くふう 工夫 a device; 〈計略〉a contrivance; 〈計画〉a plan; 〈手段〉《文》a means (単複同形) ¶工夫する《文》devise ((a plan)); 《文》contrive ((a means)); invent; plan; think out; use *one's* brains / 工夫をこらした計画案 a fully worked-out plan / 新工夫の《文》newly-devised. 文例⬇

くぶん 区分 〈分割〉(a) division; 〈分類〉(a) classification; sorting ¶区分する divide ((into)); partition (off); 〈分類する〉classify; sort (out).

くべつ 区別 〈差異〉(a) distinction; (a) difference; 〈差別〉discrimination; 〈分類〉(a) classification; (a) division ¶区別する tell [know] (one from the other); tell (them) apart; distinguish ((between A and B, A from B)) / 男女の区別なく without (any) [making no] distinction of sex; 《文》irrespective [regardless] of sex.

くべる put [throw] (logs) on [in] the fire.

くぼち 窪地 a sunken place; a depression; a basin.

くぼみ 窪み a hollow (place); a depression ¶目のくぼみ the hollows around the eyes.

くぼむ 窪む become hollow [depressed]; 〈陥没する〉cave in; sink ¶くぼんだ hollow; sunken / 目のくぼんだ人 a person with sunken [deep-set] eyes.

くま¹ 隈 〈隅, 奥〉a corner; a nook; a recess; 〈陰〉a dark [shady] area [place]; 〈ぼかし〉shading. 文例⬇

くま² 熊 《動》a bear ¶くまの皮 (a) bearskin / くまの胆(%) bear's gall bladder (dried and used as a medicine) / くま祭り a bear-sacrifice festival; the ritual killing of a bear.

くまで 熊手 a rake; 〈竹製の〉a bamboo rake ¶熊手でかく rake.

くまどる 隈取る 〈濃淡をつける〉shade off; 〈役者が顔を〉make up (*one's* face).

くまなく 隈無く all over; 《文》throughout; everywhere; in every nook and cranny [corner] ¶くまなく捜す search everywhere; hunt [search] high and low; leave no corner unsearched; leave no stone unturned; comb (a district for suspects). 文例⬇

くまんばち 《昆》⇒すずめばち.

くみ 組 〈級〉a class; 〈仲間〉a company; a party; a team (競技の); a crew (こぎ手の); a gang (悪者の); 〈労働者の〉a gang; a crew; a team 〈1そろい〉a set ((of wine glasses)); 〈1対〉a pair; 《印刷》composition; typesetting ¶準決勝の第1組 heat No. 1 of the semifinals / トランプ1組 a pack 《米》deck)) of cards / 茶器1組 a tea set [service] / 1組の椅子 a set

---

くび 彼はいろいろな事に首を突っ込みすぎる。He has too many irons in the fire. | He has his fingers in so many pies. / 彼は借金で首が回らない。He's up to his neck [head over heels] in debt.

くぶ もう九分どおり出来た。It is practically [90 per cent] ready.

くふう 何かうまい工夫はありませんか。Have you got any good ideas?

くま¹ 彼女の目の下にはくまができていた。There were dark rings [circles] under [beneath] her eyes.

くまなく 月はくまなくあたりを照

ぐみ 【植】a goumi ; a *gumi* ; an oleaster.

くみあい 組合 an association ; a guild (同業の) ; a union (労働者などの) ¶**労働組合**〈ろうどうくみあい〉 労働組合 a unionist ; a union member / 組合活動 union activities / 組合規約 union charter [constitution] / 組合専従員 a full-time union officer ; a paid union official / 組合費 union dues / 組合労働者〈総称〉organized [union] labor.

くみあう 組み合う 〈取っ組み合う〉grapple [come to grips] (with) ; 〈協同する〉band [club] together ; cooperate (with).

くみあげる[1] 汲み上げる draw (up) (water from a well) ; pump up (ポンプで).

くみあげる[2] 組み上げる finish setting up (the frame) ; 【印刷】make up a page).

くみあわせ 組み合わせ (a) combination ; (an) assortment ; 〈競技の〉matching ¶**組み合わせ錠** a combination lock.

くみあわせる 組み合わせる combine ; assort ; join [unite, group] together ; 〈競技で〉match [pit] (A against B) ; bracket (A and B) together / 指を組み合わせる lace [lock] one's fingers together [up].

くみいれる 組み入れる ⇒ くみこむ, へんにゅう.

くみうち 組み打ち a grapple ¶**組みうちする** grapple [close, struggle] (with).

くみかえ 組み替え rearrangement (of classes) ; 【印刷】recomposition ;【生物】recombination (遺伝子間の) ¶**組み替える** ⇒ くみかえる.

くみかえる 組み替える rearrange (classes) ; 【印刷】recompose ; reset ;【生物】recombine (linked genes).

くみかわす 酌み交わす drink with sb.

くみきょく 組曲 【音楽】a suite.

くみこむ 組み込む put in ; program (instructions into the computer) ; 《文》integrate (into) ; 《文》internalize.

くみする 組みする 〈味方する〉take sb's side ; be on the side of ; side with ; support ; align oneself with (the workers) ;《文》subscribe to (sb's opinion) ; 〈関係がある〉take part (in) ;《文》participate (in) ¶**組みしやすい[がたい]** be easy [hard] to deal with.

くみだす 汲み出す bail [scoop, ladle] out (water) ; pump out (ポンプで).

くみたて 組み立て construction ; structure ; 〈構成〉《文》constitution ; 〈機械の〉assembling ;《文》erection ¶**組み立て工** an assembler ; an assemblyman / 組み立て工場 an assembly shop [plant] / 組み立て材料一式 a do-it-yourself kit / 組み立て式の本箱 a sectional [knockdown] bookcase.

くみたてる 組み立てる put [fit, piece] together ; assemble ;《文》construct ;《文》erect. 文例⇩

くみちょう 組長 a head ; a leader ; 〈職工の〉a foreman.

くみつく 組み付く grapple (with) ; seize hold of ; tackle.

くみとり 汲み取り dipping up ¶**(便所の)くみ取り口** an opening for collecting night soil / 汲み取り車 a night-soil [《俗》honey] cart [wagon] / くみ取り人 a night-soil man.

くみとる 汲み取る 〈水などを〉draw [dip] up ; drain ; ladle (ひしゃくで) ; 〈事情を〉take (the circumstances) into consideration ; make allowance(s) for ¶**屎尿**〈しにょう〉**をくみ取る** collect [dip up] night soil / 心をくみ取る feel with sb ; understand sb's feelings ; sympathize with sb's feelings.

くみはん 組み版【印刷】typesetting ; composition ; a form ; 〈英〉a forme ¶**組み版にする** set (up) type ; put (a manuscript) in type.

くみひも 組み紐 a braid ; a braided [plaited] cord.

くみふせる 組み伏せる hold [get, pin] sb down ; pin [wrestle] sb to the ground [floor].

くみほす 汲み干す drain (a well) (out).

くみわけ 組み分け dividing (pupils) into groups [classes] ; (a) grouping.

くみん 区民 the inhabitants of a ward.

ぐみん 愚民 ignorant [《文》uninformed] people ;《文》the unlettered masses ¶**愚民政策** 《文》an obscurantist policy.

くむ[1] 汲む dip [scoop] up ; draw ; ladle (ひしゃくで) ; pump (ポンプで) ; 〈斟酌〈しんしゃく〉する〉⇒ **くみとる** ¶**井戸の水をくむ** draw water from a well / くみ立ての水 water fresh from the well / くめども尽きぬ泉 an inexhaustible spring.

くむ[2] 組む 〈組み立てる〉assemble ; put [fit, piece] together ; 〈活字を〉set (up) in (7-point) type ; put (an article) in type ; 〈協同する〉unite [join forces] (with) ; team up (with) ; 〈2人ずつ〉pair (off [up]) (with) ; 〈取り組む〉be matched (against) ; meet (対戦する) ; 〈編む〉braid (a cord) ; 〈交差する〉cross (one's legs) ¶**腕を組む** 〈自分の〉fold one's arms ; 〈人と〉link one's arm in sb's / 腕を組んで歩く walk arm in arm (with) / 手を後ろで組む clasp one's hands behind one's back / …と組んで together with sb ; in partnership with sb ; 〈共謀して〉in conspiracy [league] with sb. 文例⇩

くめん 工面 工面する manage (to do) ; make shift (to do) ; raise (money).

くも[1] 雲 a cloud ; 〈総称〉the clouds ¶**雲の峰** a gigantic column of clouds ; a bank of clouds / 雲のない cloudless ; unclouded / 雲の多い cloudy (days) / 雲のかかった月 the clouded moon / 雲をつかむような vague ; hazy ; elusive / 雲におおわれる be covered with clouds ; be clouded over / 雲におおわれた

らしていた. Everything was bathed in bright moonlight.
くみたてる 元どおり組み立てる自信がなければ, 分解してはだめだ. Don't take it apart unless you are sure you can put it together again.
くむ 彼は腕を組んで考えにふけっていた. He was sitting [standing] with folded arms, lost in thought. / こんどは君と組もうか. Shall I [make a team] with you this time? / 彼は組んだ両手に頭をのせて椅子にそり返った. He clasped his hands behind

くも 【動】a spider ¶くもの糸 a spider's thread / くもの巣 a spider('s) web; a cobweb / くもの子を散らすように逃げる run away《(文)flee, (文)disperse》(helter-skelter) in all directions; scatter like birds. 文例⇩

くもがくれ 雲隠れ ¶雲隠れする disappear; go [be] missing; hide *oneself*.

くもがたじょうぎ 雲形定規 a curved rule; a French curve.

くもすけ 雲助 (a ruffian of) a palanquin bearer.

くもつ 供物 (文) a votive offering; an offering 《to the spirits of *one's* ancestors》.

くalso 雲間 ¶雲間から現われる appear from behind the clouds; break [get] through the clouds; ⟨飛行機が⟩ break cloud / 雲間に隠れる disappear [go] behind the clouds; be hidden by the clouds.

くもまく 蜘蛛膜 【解】 the arachnoid (membrane); the arachnoidea ¶くも膜下出血 subarachnoid hemorrhage.

くもゆき 雲行き (the look of) the sky; ⟨形勢⟩ the situation; things; the turn of affairs [things, events]; the development of events ¶雲行きを見る see how the wind blows; watch the turn of events. 文例⇩

くもらせる 曇らせる cloud; ⟨不透明にする⟩ make *sth* dim [opaque]; dim; blur; ⟨色を⟩ dull. 文例⇩

くもり 曇り ⟨空の⟩ cloudy [gray] weather; a cloudy sky; ⟨陰影⟩ a shadow; a blur (鏡などの) / 曇りのち晴れ ⟨予報⟩ cloudy, fine [fair] later / 曇りのない clear / 曇りのない目で見る see *sth* with unclouded eyes / 曇りがちの mainly [predominantly] cloudy 《weather》/ 曇りガラス frosted glass.

くもる 曇る become cloudy [overcast]; cloud (over); ⟨もうろうとなる⟩ become dim; be clouded; ⟨レンズやガラスが水蒸気で⟩ get fogged [misted]; ⟨顔が⟩ cloud; ⟨声が⟩ falter; be choked with sobs.

くもん 苦悶 agony; (文) anguish ¶苦悶する be in agony [anguish]; writhe (in agony) / 苦悶の表情 an agonized look.

ぐもん 愚問 a silly [stupid, foolish] question.

くやくしょ 区役所 a ward office.

くやしい、くやしがる 悔しい、悔しがる feel bitter 《about, at》; regret; feel [be] vexed [(文) chagrined] 《at》★ 日本語には「悔しい」は話者自身、「悔しがる」は話者以外の人物が主語のときに使われるという区別があるが、英語にはこれに相当する区別はない / 悔し紛れに out of spite [vexation]; (文) to give vent to *one's* chagrin / 悔しさに、悔しさのあまり in *one's* frustration [vexation] / 悔し涙 tears of vexation; regretful tears. 文例⇩

くやみ 悔やみ ⟨弔慰⟩ (文) condolence(s); ⟨後悔⟩ (文) repentance; (a) regret ¶悔やみを述べる express [offer] *one's* condolences 《to *sb* on a sad event》; express *one's* sympathy 《for the bereaved family》/ 悔やみ状 a letter of condolence [sympathy] 《on the death of…》. 文例⇩

くやむ 悔やむ ⟨後悔する⟩ (文) repent (of); regret; be sorry (for); ⟨悲しむ⟩ (文) lament; (文) mourn (for, over); ⟨弔う⟩ sympathize [commiserate, (文) condole] with *sb* 《on *his* bereavement》. 文例⇩

くゆらす 燻らす smoke 《a cigar》; pull (away) 《at *one's* cigar》.

くよう 供養 a memorial service ¶供養する hold a memorial service (for); hold [say] a mass (for).

くよくよ くよくよする worry 《about, over》; fret 《about》; brood 《over》. 文例⇩

くら¹ 鞍 a saddle ¶鞍を置く[降ろす] saddle [unsaddle] 《a horse》; put a saddle on 《a saddle off》《a horse》/ 鞍にまたがる take [get into] the saddle; get onto [(文) mount] *one's* horse / 鞍敷き a saddlecloth; a pad.

くら² 蔵、倉 a warehouse; a storehouse ¶倉

くも¹ 山陰から大きな雲がわき上がってきた。A huge cloud rose [raised its head] from behind the mountain. / 雲が出て来た。Clouds are gathering. / 空が曇ってきた。The sky is getting overcast. / 雲が晴れた。The clouds lifted [cleared]. / 空には一点の雲もない。There is not a speck of cloud in the sky. / 雲が低く垂れている。The clouds are hanging low. / 雲足が大そう早い。The clouds are moving fast.

くも² 見るとくもが巣をかけていた。I saw a spider spinning its web. / 電線がくもの巣のようだ。Telegraph wires are stretched like cobwebs.

くもゆき 雲行きが怪しい[険悪だ]。The clouds have an ugly look. | his head and leaned back in his chair.

くもらせる 彼は顔を曇らせた。He frowned. | His face took on a troubled look.

くもる 一天にわかにかき曇った。The sky was suddenly overcast. / 湯気で窓ガラスが曇っている。The windowpanes are all steamed up. | The windows are misted over from the steam. / 息で眼鏡が曇った。My breath fogged my glasses. / 彼女の目は涙で曇った。Her eyes were blinded with tears. | Tears blurred her eyes.

くやしい ああ悔しい。How maddening [disappointing]! / 試験に落ちたのは本当に悔しかった。It was a bitter disappointment to fail the exam. / 1列車おくれに立ったと聞いて悔しかった。I heard, to my vexation, that he | 形勢が〉The situation is getting serious.

had left on the train just before mine. / 悔しかったらこのとおりにやってみろ。I dare you to do exactly the same thing.

くやみ 真心からお悔やみ申し上げます。Please accept my sincere condolences.

くやむ 悔やんでも始まらない。It is no use crying over spilt milk.

くよくよ くよくよするな。Don't worry! | Take it easy! | Cheer up! / 成績が悪かったからといってあんまりくよくよしなさんな。Don't let your bad grades bother [worry] you too much!

くらい¹ 小数点の上は、下から順に一、十、百、千…の位です。The first figure to the left of the decimal point represents the number of units, the second, the number of tens, the third of hundreds,

くらい

に入れる store; put ((one's furniture)) in storage [store]; warehouse / 蔵払い〈売り出し〉a clearance sale.

くらい¹ 位〈階級〉(a) grade; (a) rank; 〈王位〉the throne; the crown; 〈品位〉《文》dignity; 《数》the position ((of a figure)); a numerical position; the ((fourth)) place ((of decimals)) (小数点以下の) ¶ 位する rank; be ranked; 〈位置する〉be ((in, at)); 《文》be situated [located] ((in, at)); stand / 首位[第2位]に位する rank first [second]; head [stand second on the list ((of))] / 位が高い[低い] be high [low] in rank / 位の高い人《文》a person of high rank / 大佐の位まで昇進する rise [advance] to the rank of colonel. 文例

くらい² 暗い〈場所が〉dark; gloomy; 〈灯火が〉dim; 〈知らない〉《文》be ignorant ((of)); be unfamiliar ((with)); be a stranger ((to)); 《口語》be in the dark ((about)) ¶ 暗いうちに[から] before daylight [daybreak] / 暗い気持ちになる feel gloomy / 暗くする darken; make dim; dim [lower] ((the light)) / 暗くなる get [((の))become] dark [dim]; be overcast ((空が曇って)) / 暗くなってから[ならないうちに] after [before] dark. 文例

-くらい〈ほとんど〉almost; ...or thereabouts; 〈比較〉almost as...as; so...as; 〈程度〉so...that; so...as to do /〈いっその事〉rather; sooner...than; 〈少なくとも〉at least ¶ これくらい this [so] much / どのくらい how much [many, long, far] / 死んだと言ってもいいくらいだ be as good as [be all but] dead.

-ぐらい ⇨ -くらい.

グライダー((maneuver)) a glider; a sailplane

くらいどり 位取り ¶ 位取りを間違える mistake the position of a figure; get the number of zeros [the position of the decimal point] wrong.

くらいまけ 位負け ¶ 位負けする〈自分の地位に〉cannot live up to one's position [rank]; 〈相手の地位能力に威圧される〉be overawed ((by)).

クライマックス((reach)) a [the] climax ¶ クライマックスへと盛り上げる build ((a drama)) (up) to a climax.

くらう 食らう ⇨ くう².

グラウンド a ground; a playground (学校の); a (playing [sports]) field ¶ 野球のグラウンド a baseball ground; a ballpark / グラウンドマナー ground manners.

くらがえ 鞍替え ¶ くら替えする change one's quarters [job]; change sides; switch over from ((one job)) to ((another)); 別派にくら替えする desert one's faction to join another.

くらがり 暗がり〈暗い所〉a dark place; the dark;〈暗やみ〉¶ 暗がりで in a dimly-lit place; ((read)) in a poor light; 〈暗やみで〉in the dark.

くらく 苦楽 ¶ 苦楽を共にする《文》share one's lot ((with sb)).

クラクション〔商標〕a Klaxon; a horn ¶ クラクションを鳴らす sound one's Klaxon [horn]; honk.

くらくら ¶ くらくらする feel dizzy [giddy]. 文例

ぐらぐら ¶ ぐらぐらする totter; be shaky; be unsteady; 〈決心が〉waver;《文》vacillate; 〈机などが〉be wobbly / ぐらぐらする椅子 a rickety chair.

くらげ a jellyfish; a medusa (pl. -sae, -s) ¶ くらげのかさ the umbrella [bell] of a jellyfish.

くらさ darkness; gloom. 文例

くらし 暮らし〈生計〉a living; a [one's] livelihood;〈暮らし向き〉one's circumstances ¶ 暮らしを立てる ⇨ くらす / 一家の暮らしを立てる support [maintain] one's family / 月15万円で暮らしを立てる live on 150,000 yen a month / よい暮らしをする make a good living / 暮らしに困る cannot [can hardly] manage (to live) on one's income;《文》be in needy [straitened] circumstances; be hardly able to make (both) ends meet / 暮らし向きがいい[悪い] be well [badly] off / 人々の暮らし方 the way people live. 文例

グラジオラス〔植〕a gladiolus (pl. -li, -luses).

---

the fourth of thousands, etc.

くらい² 電灯が暗い。The lamp is dim [not very bright]. / 朝の4時はまだ暗い。It is not light enough [still dark] at four in the morning. / 暗いところで本を読むのは眼に悪いよ。It is bad [isn't good] for your eyes to read in poor light. / このごろは暗くなるのが早い。Darkness falls earlier now. / 暗くてもう字が読めない。It is too dark [There isn't enough light] to read any more. / 空が暗くなってきた。The sky is getting overcast. / 僕はこの辺の地理に暗い。I am new to this part of the town.

-くらい どのくらいかかったか。〈費用が〉How much did it cost? / 〈時間が〉How long did it take? / ここから箱根までどのくらいありますか。How far is it from here to Hakone? / 車で1時間くらい。It's an hour's ride, more or less. | (It's) about an hour by car. / もう半マイルもいくらいだ。It is scarcely half a mile further. / この地方の産物と言ってはまずこれくらいのものだ。These are about all the products of the locality there are. / 日本人であれくらい英文を書く人は少ない。Few Japanese can write English as well as that. / お茶の一杯ぐらいは出してもいいのに。They might at least offer us a cup of tea. / 実にいい景色で君に見せたいくらいだった。It really was a fine view. You should have seen it. / そんなことをするくらいならいっそ死んだ方がましだ。I would sooner [rather] die than do that. / その場でぶんなぐってやりたいくらいだった。I could have hit [I almost felt like hitting] him on the spot. / 安くて？ 僕には高すぎるくらいだ。Cheap, you say? It's almost too expensive for me!

くらくら 頭がくらくらした。My head reeled [swam]. | My head went round.

ぐらぐら あの人はいつもぐらぐらしている。He has no definite ideas. | He never knows his own mind. / 突然ぐらぐらときた。The earth suddenly shook. | I suddenly felt the house shake. / やがて湯がぐらぐら煮たってきた。The water eventually came to a rolling boil.

くらさ 彼は少しも暗さがなかった。He didn't seem to have a care in the world. | He looked a completely happy man.

くらし 田舎の方がずっと暮らしが

くらしきりょう 倉敷料 storage (charges); godown rent.

クラシック a classic;〈総称〉classics ¶クラシックな classic(al) / クラシック音楽 classical music.

くらす 暮らす〈生活する〉live; make a [one's] living; earn [get, make] a livelihood;〈過す〉get on [along]; spend *one's* time, a day) ¶安楽に暮らす live comfortably [in comfort] / むつまじく暮らす get on [along] very well together; be very happy together / 忙しい日を暮らす live [lead] a busy life / ぶらぶら日を暮らす idle [dawdle] *one's* time away; loaf. 文例❺

クラス a class ¶英語のクラス an English class / 1万トンクラスの船舶 vessels of the 10,000-ton class / クラス委員 a class officer [representative] / クラス会 a class meeting;〈卒業生の〉a class reunion / クラス討論 a class discussion.

グラス〈ガラス〉a glass;〈コップ〉a glass;〈眼鏡〉glasses ¶グラスを合わせる touch glasses / グラスファイバー glass fiber; fiber glass.

グラタン《フランス語》gratin ¶マカロニグラタン macaroni *au gratin* / グラタン皿 a baking dish.

クラッカー〈菓子〉a (soda) cracker;〈爆音を発するおもちゃ〉《pull》a cracker (bonbon).

ぐらつく〈よろめく〉totter; reel;〈揺れる〉shake;〈不安定》be unsteady; be shaky; be rickety;〈動揺する〉《文》vacillate; waver. 文例❺

クラッチ〈機〉a clutch ¶クラッチを入れる release [let in] the clutch / クラッチを切る disengage [push down] the clutch; declutch.

くらに 倉荷 warehouse goods ¶倉荷証券 a warrant;《米》a warehouse receipt;《英》a warehouse certificate.

グラニューとう グラニュー糖 granulated sugar.

グラビア〈版〉(photo)gravure.

クラブ〈団体〉a club; a clubhouse (建物);〈トランプ〉《the ace of》clubs;〈ゴルフ棒〉a club ¶クラブ員 a member of a club); a clubber / クラブ活動 club [extracurricular] activities.

グラフ a graph; a graphic chart; a diagram ¶グラフにする make a graph (of) / 棒[線]グラフ a bar [line] chart / グラフ用紙 graph [section, plotting] paper.

グラフィック ¶グラフィックアート the graphic arts / グラフィックデザイナー a graphic artist [designer].

クラフト ¶クラフト紙 kraft (paper).

-くらべ 比べ〈力比べ a contest of (physical) strength / 知恵比べ ⇒ちえ / たけ比べ comparing heights with each other.

くらべもの 比べ物 ¶…とは比べ物にならない cannot compare [be compared] (with); be no match (for). 文例❺

くらべる 比べる compare (A and B, A with [to] B); make a comparison (between A and B); contrast (A with B) (対照する) ¶力を比べる measure *one's* strength (with) / …と比べれば in [by] comparison with…; (as) compared with…. 文例❺

グラマーガール a glamour girl.

くらます 暗ます〈隠す〉hide;《文》conceal;〈目を〉blind; dazzle;〈欺く〉deceive ¶姿[あと, ゆくえ]をくらます disappear; cover *one's* tracks; conceal [hide] *oneself*; go into hiding.

くらむ 暗む get [grow, be] dizzy [giddy];〈くらがくらされる〉be dazzled; be blinded ¶目の暗むような高所 a giddy height / 金に目が暗む be blinded by the lure of money / 目も暗むばかりの閃光 a blinding flash.

グラム a gram (略: g).

くらやみ 暗闇 ¶暗やみで in the dark; in darkness.

クラリネット a clarinet ¶クラリネット奏者 a clarinet(t)ist; a clarinet player.

くらわす 食らわす ¶1発食らわす give *sb* a punch [blow]; hit *sb* with *one's* fist;《口語》let *sb* have it [one]; punch *sb*.

クランク a crank ¶クランクを回す crank (an engine); turn a crank / クランクインする《映画》start filming / クランクシャフト a crankshaft.

グランプリ《フランス語》the *grand prix*;《win》the grand prize.

くり¹ 栗〈実〉a chestnut;〈木〉a chestnut tree ¶くり拾いに行く go chestnut-gathering / くり色の chestnut; nut-brown; maroon.

くり² 刳り a hollow; a scoop ¶襟の刳りの深さ the depth of *one's* neckline.

くり³ 庫裏 the priests' living quarters.

くりあげる 繰り上げる advance; move up;〈運算で数を上位に〉carry (1) ¶期日を繰り上げる advance [move up] the date (from …to…).

くりあわせる 繰り合わせる〈時間を〉make time;〈都合を〉arrange matters; manage to do.

クリーニング〈洗濯〉laundry;〈ドライクリーニング〉(dry) cleaning ¶クリーニングに出す take (*one's* suit) to the cleaner's; send (*one's* shirts) to the laundry / クリーニング屋〈店〉a laundry; a (dry-)cleaner's;〈人〉a cleaner; a laundryman / クリーニング代 a laundry [(dry-)cleaning] charge.

楽だ. Living is much easier in the country. / 以前より暮らしが楽になっている人が多い. Many people are better off than they used to be.

くらす こればっちの金では暮らせない. I cannot live on such a small sum of money. / いかがお暮らしですか. How are you getting along? / 休暇中はどこで暮らしましたか. Where did you spend your vacation? / 彼は余生を田舎に引っ込んで暮らした. He lived the remainder of his life in rural retirement.

ぐらつく 机がぐらついて書きにくい. The table is so wobbly that I can hardly write. / 彼の決心は ぐらつかなかった. He remained firm in his resolution.

くらべもの 地球は, 大きさでは, 木星とてんで比べものにならない. The earth does not begin to compare with Jupiter for size.

くらべる 2人を比べると一方はまるで子供だ. He is a mere boy beside [by the side of] the other.

クリーム 〈食品〉cream;〈化粧品〉《face, hand》cream ¶クリームをつける cream 《one's face》; apply cream to 《one's hands》/ クリーム状の creamy; creamlike / 生クリーム fresh cream / クリーム色 cream (color) / クリーム色の cream-colored; cream 《curtains》/ クリーム色に塗る paint 《a door》cream / クリームパンな bun with a cream filling.

くりいれる 繰り入れる transfer 《a sum of money from...to...》; put in ¶翌年度の予算に繰り入れる carry 《a sum》over to the next year's budget.

グリーン 〈色〉green;〘ゴルフ〙the (putting) green.

クリーンアップトリオ 〘野球〙numbers 3, 4 and 5 in the batting line-up; a trio of sluggers ★ cleanup trio は英語ではなく, 4番打者を the cleanup man [batter, hitter] というが, 3番, 5番を含めた言い方はない.

グリーンランド Greenland.

くりかえし 繰り返し 〈反復〉repetition; a repeat;〘文〙reiteration;〈歌の〉a refrain ¶繰り返しの多い repetitive;〘文〙repetitious.

くりかえす 繰り返す repeat;〘文〙reiterate; do over again ¶同じことを繰り返す repeat the same thing / 繰り返して repeatedly / 3度繰り返して読む read three times over / 繰り返し繰り返し again (time) and again; over and over (again).

くりからもんもん ¶くりからもんもんが彫ってある be tattooed [have tattoo pictures] all over 《one's body》.

くりくり ¶くりくりした目 big, round eyes / 目をくりくりさせる goggle one's eyes / くりくり坊主になる 〈頭を剃って〉have one's head shaved [clean-shaven];〈髪を刈って〉have a close crop haircut.

ぐりぐり a hard lump 《under the skin》.

くりげ 栗毛 ¶栗毛の馬 a chestnut [bay] (horse); a sorrel.

クリケット (play) cricket.

グリコーゲン 〘化〙glycogen.

くりこし 繰り越し a transfer;〈次期への〉a carry-over ¶前葉[前期]より繰り越し〘簿記〙brought forward (略: BF)/ 次葉[次期]への繰り越し〘簿記〙carried forward (略: CF)/ 繰り越し金〈前期からの〉the balance [amount of money] brought forward 《from the previous account》;〈次期への〉the balance [amount of money] carried forward 《to the next account》.

くりこす 繰り越す transfer 《to, from》;〈次へ〉carry forward [over] 《to》;〈前より〉bring forward [over] 《from》.

くりごと 繰り言 ¶繰り言を言う tell the same story over (and over) again;〈不平を言う〉grumble 《about, of》; complain 《about, of》/ 返らぬ繰り言を言う〘文〙indulge in vain [useless] regrets.

くりこむ 繰り込む 〈繰り入れる〉⇒くりいれる;〈乗り込む〉march [parade, stream] in [into].

くりさげる 繰り下げる 〈ずらす〉carry [take, move] down;〈繰り延べる〉⇒くりのべる.

クリスタル crystal ¶クリスタルガラス crystal glass.

クリスチャン a Christian.

クリスマス Christmas; Xmas ¶ Christmas Day (当日)¶クリスマスを祝う keep [observe] Christmas / クリスマスプレゼント a Christmas present [gift]/ クリスマスイブ (on) Christmas Eve / クリスマスカード[ケーキ, ツリー] a Christmas card [cake, tree]. 用例⇩

グリセード 〘登山〙a glissade ¶グリセードする glissade.

グリセリン 〘化〙glycerol; glycerin(e).

くりだす 繰り出す ¶ロープを繰り出す pay [let] out the rope / 新手を繰り出す send out fresh troops; reinforce 《the guards》/ 威勢よく繰り出す〘文〙sally forth / 繰り出し梯子 an extension [aerial] ladder.

クリップ 〈紙ばさみ〉a (paper) clip;〈髪の〉a curling pin; a curler. 用例⇩

くりど 繰り戸 a sliding door.

クリニック 〈診療所〉a clinic.

グリニッジ グリニッジ標準時 Greenwich Mean Time (略: GMT); Greenwich Time.

くりぬく 刳り抜く hollow [scoop, gouge] out ¶目玉をくり抜く gouge sb's eyes out.

くりのべる 繰り延べる postpone; put off 《a meeting》; defer 《payment》.

くりひろげる 繰り広げる unroll; unfold; spread [open] (out); develop ¶ (競技で)大観衆の前で熱戦を繰り広げる play an exciting game in front of [watched by] a huge crowd of spectators.

クリプトン 〘化〙krypton.

クリミア the Crimea ¶クリミア半島[戦争] the Crimean Peninsula [War].

くりょ 苦慮 ¶苦慮する〈苦心する〉rack [cudgel] one's brains;〈心労する〉be anxious [worried] 《about》; worry 《oneself》《about, over》.

グリル a grill (room).

クリンチ 〘ボクシング〙a clinch; clinching ¶クリンチする clinch / クリンチしている《boxers》in a clinch.

グリンピース peas.

くる¹ 来る come;〈顔を出す〉turn [show] up;〈着く〉reach; arrive 《at, in》; come in (列車が); arrive;〘文〙come to hand (手紙などが);〈近づく〉〘文〙approach; get [come,〘文〙draw]

どっちが長く水の中にいられるか比べっこをしよう. Let's see which of us can remain under water longer. / 彼は足に比べて胴が長すぎる. His body is too long for his legs. / 飛んでいる鳥はその流線形の故に, 飛行機と比べたくなるが, 実は大きな違いがある. The flying bird, with its streamlined shape, invites comparison with the airplane, but there are major differences.

くりあわせる 万障お繰り合わせの上ご出席下さい. Your attendance is earnestly requested. / 彼から面会を求めきたが, 時間の繰り合わせがつかない. He wants to see me, but I can't find the time for it.

クリスマス クリスマスおめでとう. Merry Christmas! | A merry Christmas to you! | グリーンさんはクリスマスプレゼントに本をくれました. Mrs. Green gave me a book for Christmas.

クリップ 彼女は髪にクリップをつけたまま台所仕事をしていた.

くる near; 〈訪れる〉visit; call (on *one*, at *one's* house); come to see *one*; 〈季節が〉come (round); set in; 〈…になる〉《文》become; grow; get; come to *do*; 〈起因する〉come of [from]; be due to; be caused by 「取りに[連れに]来る come [call] for / 取って来る go and get; fetch; collect / ラテン語から来た言葉 a word derived from Latin; a word with a [(《文》of] Latin origin / 面白くなってくる get [《文》become] interesting. 文例↓

くる² 刳る 〈穴などを〉bore (a hole); hollow out; scoop [gouge] out.

くる³ 繰る 〈巻く〉reel; wind; 〈紡ぐ〉spin; 〈ページを〉turn over (pages); 〈雨戸を繰る slide the storm doors into place / 綿を繰る gin (out) cotton.

ぐる an accomplice ⇨ **きょうぼう**¹ ¶《口語》be in cahoots 《with》; plot together 《with》;《文》conspire 《with》;《文》act [be] in league [collusion] 《with》/ …とぐるになって《口語》in cahoots with...;《文》in league [conspiracy, collusion] with....

くるい 狂い 〈狂気〉madness; 〈手順の〉disorder; confusion; 〈故障〉something wrong 《with one's watch》;《文》a malfunction / 〈ゆがみ〉(a) warp 「狂いが来る〈ゆがむ〉be warped; 〈機械などが〉go wrong; get out of order;《文》malfunction / 少しの狂いもなく正確に with faultless precision / 狂い死にする be raving / 狂い咲きの花 a flower blooming out of season. 文例↓

くるう 狂う 〈気が〉go mad; lose *one's* reason; go [《文》become] insane;《口語》lose [go out of] *one's* mind;《口語》go crazy;《俗》go off *one's* head;《機械が》get out of order; go wrong;〈計画が〉be upset; go wrong;〈調子が〉go [get] out of tune;〈ゆがむ〉warp;〈的がはずれる〉go wild; miss the mark 「気が狂っている be mad; be insane; be (mentally) deranged;《口語》be crazy;《俗》be cracked [《英》crackers];〈楽器の〉調子が狂っている be out of tune / 狂わせる〈気を〉drive *sb* mad;《口語》unhinge *sb's* mind;〈手はず・計画などを〉upset; frustrate; throw (the plan) into disorder. 文例↓

クルー 『ボート』a crew.

グループ a group; a circle ¶ グループを作る form a group; group (together) / グループに分ける divide into 《four》 groups; group (into) / 小グループ a subgroup.

くるくる ¶ くるくる回る turn [go] round and round; twirl; spin.

ぐるぐる round and round; in circles ¶ ぐるぐる回る[回す] turn round and round; spin round; circle; wheel / ぐるぐる巻く wind [twine] (a cord) round *sth*.

くるしい 苦しい 〈苦痛な〉painful; 〈つらい〉trying; 《文》distressing; 〈困難な〉hard; difficult; 《口語》tough; 〈当惑させる〉embarrassing; awkward; 〈困窮した〉needy; 《文》distressed [straitened] (circumstances); 〈無理な〉far-fetched; 《文》strained; 《文》forced ¶ 息が苦しい have difficulty in [with *one's*] breathing; breathe with difficulty / 苦しい言い訳 a lame [forced, poor] excuse / 苦しい立場にある be in a difficult [an awkward] position / 苦しい目にあう have a hard [trying] time (of it) / 苦しがる complain of a pain in *one's* chest); be in great pain. 文例↓

くるしさ 苦しさ ⇨ **くるしみ**.

くるしまぎれ 苦し紛れ ¶ 苦しまぎれに in *one's* pain [agony]; driven by pain [《文》distress]; in desperation (やけになって).

くるしみ 苦しみ 〈苦痛〉(a) pain; (a) sting (刺されたような); 〈難儀〉suffering(s); trouble(s); 《文》distress; 〈苦悩〉agony; 《文》anguish.

くるしむ 苦しむ suffer 《from》; feel [be in] pain; 《文》be afflicted 《with》; be tormented 《by》; 〈もだえる〉groan; suffer agony; writhe (in agony); 〈困る〉be troubled 《with》; be in trouble; 《文》be distressed 《by》; 〈悩む〉be worried 《by》; worry (*oneself*) 《about, over》; 〈骨折る〉try hard; take pains ¶ 圧制に苦しむ groan under oppression.

くるしめる 苦しめる torment; torture; 〈悩ます〉《文》distress; worry; 〈病気などが〉hurt *sb*; give *sb* pain; 〈いじめる〉bully; treat *sb* harshly; 〈迫害する〉persecute ¶ 貧乏に苦しめられる be distressed by poverty.

グルタミン 『化』glutamine ¶ グルタミン酸ソーダ monosodium [sodium] glutamate.

グルテン 『化』gluten ¶ グルテン状の glutenous.

くるびょう 佝僂病 rickets; rachitis ¶ 佝僂病にかかっている人 a person suffering from rickets; a rachitic (person).

くるぶし 踝 the ankle.

くるま 車 〈車輪〉a wheel; 〈ピアノなど, 重い家具につける〉a castor; 〈乗り物〉a vehicle; 《文》a conveyance; 〈自動車〉a car; a mo-

---

She was doing kitchen work with curlers in her hair [with her hair (up) in curlers].

くる¹ 春が来た. Spring has come [is here]. / さあ, 来たまえ. Come along! / さあ来い. Come on! / そう来なくっちゃ. Now you're talking! | That's the way to talk! | もうじきに正月が来る. The New Year is just around the corner. / バスが来ました. Here comes our bus. | The bus is coming. / 何の用でここへ来たか. What has brought you here? | What are you here for? / あらしが来そうだ. We are going to have a storm. / 友人を迎えに空港へ行って来ました. I have been to the airport to meet a friend. / 彼の病気は食い過ぎから来るのだ. His illness is a result of overeating. / 雨が降って来た. It's starting to rain. / 大分冷えて来た. It's getting quite cold.

くるい 私の目に狂いはない. There is nothing wrong with my judgment. What has brought you here? / あらしが来そうだ. We are going to have a storm. / 友人を迎えに空港へ行って来ました. I have been to the airport to meet a friend. / 彼の病気は食い過ぎから来るのだ. His illness is a result of overeating. / 雨が降って来た. It's starting to rain. / 大分冷えて来た. It's getting quite cold.

くるい 私の目に狂いはない. There is nothing wrong with my judgment.

くるう 悲しさのあまり彼女は気が狂った. Grief has turned her brain. / 気が狂いそうだ. I'm going off my head. / この時計は 1 年に5秒以上は狂わない. This watch does not vary more than five seconds per year. / 予算が狂った. The estimate was wrong [too low].

くるしい いまその時が私のもっとも苦しい時代だった. That was the worst time of my life. / 1日10

torcar ; an automobile ; 〈荷車〉a cart ¶列車の先頭[最後部]の車 the front [back] car of a train / 車で行く go by car / 車を引く pull [draw] a cart / 車を締め出した地域 a vehicle-free area / 車賃[代] a fare. [文例⇩]

くるまいす 車椅子 〈病人用の〉a wheelchair ; an invalid chair.

くるまえび 車えび a prawn.

くるまざ 車座 ¶車座になる sit in a circle [ring] 《around》.

くるまよせ 車寄せ a porch ; a carriage entrance ; 《文》a porte-cochere.

くるまる be wrapped up 《in a blanket》; wrap [tuck] *oneself* up 《in》.

くるみ 〈木〉a walnut (tree) ; 〈実〉a walnut ¶くるみ割り (a pair of) nutcrackers / 組曲「くるみ割り人形」the *Nutcracker Suite*.

-ぐるみ including... ; ...and all ¶家族ぐるみ with all (the members of) *one's* family / 着物ぐるみ clothes and all. [文例⇩]

くるむ wrap 《in》; tuck up 《in》.

くるめる 〈一括する〉lump [put] 《everything》 together ; 〈含める〉include ¶全部くるめて (all) in all ; all taken together ; all told ; in total.

くるり ¶くるりと回る[向きを変える] turn round [around] ; pivot (quickly).

ぐるり ⇨まわり ¶ぐるりに[を] round ; around / ぐるりを取り巻く surround completely / ぐるりと後を振り向く turn right round.

くれ 暮れ 〈日暮れ〉nightfall ; dusk ; 〈年末〉the year-end ; the end of the year ¶暮れのボーナス a year-end bonus / 秋の暮れのある夕べ one evening late in autumn / 暮れ方に at sunset [dusk, nightfall] ; toward evening. [文例⇩]

クレーター a 《lunar》 crater.

グレートブリテン Great Britain ¶グレートブリテンおよび北部アイルランド連合王国 the United Kingdom of Great Britain and Northern Ireland (略 : U.K.).

クレープ crepe ; crape ; 《フランス語》*crêpe* ¶クレープペーパー crepe paper.

グレープフルーツ a grapefruit 《*pl.* -(s)》.

クレーム a claim (for damages) ¶クレームをつける make [put in] a claim for damages [compensation] ; 〈苦情·異議を出す〉make a complaint ; raise [《文》lodge] an objection 《to》 ★英語の claim には「苦情」「異議」の意味はない / クレームに応じる meet a claim for damages.

クレーン a crane ⇨きじゅうき.

クレオソート creosote.

くれぐれも 呉れ呉れも 〈切に〉《文》earnestly ; 〈繰り返し〉repeatedly ; over and over (again) ; again [time] and again. [文例⇩]

グレコローマン 〖レスリング〗the Greco-Roman style.

クレジット a credit ¶クレジットカード a credit card.

グレシャム ¶グレシャムの法則〖経〗Gresham's law.

クレゾール ¶クレゾール石鹼液 saponated cresol solution / クレゾール水 cresol water.

ぐれつ 愚劣 ¶愚劣な stupid ; foolish ; senseless / 愚劣な話 silly talk ; nonsense ; rubbish.

くれない 紅 deep red ; crimson.

グレナダ (the State of) Grenada.

クレバス 〈氷河·雪原の〉a crevasse.

クレムリン the Kremlin.

クレヨン (a) crayon ¶クレヨンでかく draw 《a sketch》 with crayons [in crayon(s)] / クレヨン画 a crayon drawing ; a drawing in crayon(s).

くれる[1] 呉れる 〈与える〉give ; let *one* have ; 〈...してくれる〉*do* for *one* ¶...をくれと言う ask for *sth* / ...してくれと言う ask *sb* to *do*. [文例⇩]

くれる[2] 暮れる 〈日が〉get [grow] dark ; 〈年が〉end ; come to an end ; close ; run [be] out ¶日が暮れてから[暮れぬうちに] after [before] dark / 涙に暮れる be in (floods of) tears ; weep *one's* eyes out. [文例⇩]

ぐれる go astray ; 《文》stray from the right path ; 《文》fall into evil ways ¶ぐれた若者 a delinquent youngster.

クレンザー a cleanser.

ぐれんたい 愚連隊 (a gang of) hooligans ; 《米口語》hoodlums ; 《英俗》(young) yobbos.

くろ 黒 ¶黒(の) black ; 〈有罪の〉guilty ⇨くろい / (囲碁で)黒を持つ play black 《in a game of *go*》 / 黒っぽい dark ; blackish / 墨黒々と書く write in deep [jet] black.

くろい 黒い black ; 〈浅黒い〉dark ; 《文》dusky ¶(人が)色が黒い have a dark complexion / 黒くする blacken / 黒くなる get [go, 《文》become] black ; blacken / 日に焼けて黒くなる be [get] sunburnt [(sun)tanned] / 黒く染める[塗る] dye [paint] *sth* black.

くろう 苦労 〈難儀〉trouble(s) ; hardship(s) ;

時間の仕事は苦しくてたまらない. I cannot stand the strain of working ten hours a day. / 苦しい時の神頼み. Once on shore, we pray no more. 〖諺〗| The danger past and God forgotten. 〖諺〗

くるま 9時きっかりにホテルまで車を差し向けましょう. I'll send a car to the hotel at nine sharp. / この通りは車はあまり通らない. There is very little traffic along this street. / 道路を横断する時は車に注意するんですよ. Watch for the passing traffic when you cross the street.

-ぐるみ この花は鉢ぐるみ800円です. This flower is 800 yen including [with] the pot.

くれ 暮れのうちは忙しくてお訪ねできません. I'm afraid I won't have time to pay you a visit before the New Year.

くれぐれも くれぐれもご両親によろしく. Please give my best regards to your parents. / くれぐれもお体をお大事に. Please take good care of yourself.

くれる[1] これは私にくれるの? Is this (a gift) for me? / ちょっとこれ持っていてくれないか. Just hold this for me, will you? / だれが費用を出してくれるのか. Who pays [foots the bill for] your expenses?

くれる[2] 途中で日が暮れた. Night fell while we were on our way. | The sun went down before we got there. / 6時ごろに日が暮れ

ぐろう suffering(s);〈骨折り〉《文》toil; labor;《文》pains;〈心配〉care(s); anxiety; worries ¶浮き世の苦労 the troubles [cares] of life / 苦労する have a hard time (of it); suffer [《文》undergo, go through] hardships;〈手数がかかる〉have trouble;〈骨折る〉work hard;《文》toil; take pains;〈心配する〉be worried [anxious] (about) / 苦労して得た hard-earned (experience) / 苦労の多い full of cares [troubles] / 苦労のない free from care; carefree; untroubled / 苦労の種 a cause of trouble; 苦労の種をかける put a thorn in one's flesh [side] / 苦労をかける put sb to (a lot of) trouble; give sb trouble; worry sb;《文》cause sb anxiety / 苦労人 a man of the world / 苦労性な (tend to) worry too much; take things too seriously; be a (natural) worrier. 文例①

ぐろう 愚弄 ridicule; fool; make a fool of; make fun of; mock (at); jeer (at); jibe (at); taunt.

くろうと 玄人 an expert (on sth, in doing);〈専門家〉a professional; a specialist (in);〈商売女〉a woman of the entertainment trades ¶玄人気質(かたぎ) professionalism. 文例①

クローカス《植》a crocus (pl. -es, -ci).

クロース cloth; book[binder's] cloth ¶クロース装 cloth binding / クロース装のclothbound; bound in cloth.

クローズアップ《映画》a close-up; a close shot; a close-up view (of the moon) ★ close-upの発音は [klóusʌp] ¶クローズアップする take a close-up (of) / クローズアップで (show sth) in close-up / 大きくクローズアップされる be highlighted; be in the limelight; be in the news [the public eye]; come to the fore.

クローズドショップ《労》a closed shop.

クローバー a clover ¶四つ葉のクローバー a four-leaf[-leaved] clover / クローバーインターチェンジ a cloverleaf (interchange).

グローバル ¶グローバルな global《views》.

くろおび 黒帯 a black belt. 文例①

グローブ〈野球の〉a glove ★ 発音は [glʌv] ¶グローブコンパートメント〈自動車の〉a glove compartment.

クロール《水泳》the crawl (stroke) ¶クロールで泳ぐ crawl (across a pool); swim the crawl.

クローン《生物》a clone ¶クローンを造る produce clones (of); clone (a mammal).

くろかみ 黒髪 black hair.

くろこ 黒子《歌舞伎》a kabuki stagehand dressed in black who assists the actors in various ways during the performance.

くろこげ 黒焦げ ¶黒焦げになる be charred; be burned (black).

くろざとう 黒砂糖 raw [unrefined] sugar; Barbados [muscovado] sugar.

くろじ 黒字 ⇒りえき ¶黒字である be in (the) black / 黒字になる go into the black.

くろしお 黒潮 the Kuroshio current; the Japan current.

くろしょうぞく 黒装束 ¶黒装束で dressed in black.

くろしろ 黒白 ⇒しろくろ.

クロスカントリー(レース) a cross-country race;(a) cross-country.

くろずむ 黒ずむ get [go,《文》become] black [blackish]; blacken;〈色調が〉get [《文》become] dark; darken ¶黒ずんだ dark; darkish; blackish / 目の縁が黒ずんでいる have dark circles [rings] around one's eyes.

クロスワードパズル(do) a crossword puzzle ¶クロスワードパズルの鍵 crossword-puzzle clues ★ この場合 key は使えない.

くろだい 黒鯛 a black porgy.

グロッキー(become) groggy.

グロテスク ¶グロテスクな grotesque; bizarre.

くろぬり 黒塗り ¶黒塗りの《漆で》blacklacquered;《ペンキで》black-painted.

くろパン 黒パン brown bread; rye bread.

くろビール 黒ビール black beer; porter; stout.

くろびかり 黒光り black luster ¶黒光りする shine black.

くろぼし 黒星〈しるし〉a black spot [dot];〈射的の〉the bull's-eye;〈負け星〉a defeat [black] mark;〈負け〉a defeat;〈失敗〉a failure ¶黒星を取る《文》suffer a defeat; be beaten;《口》be defeated.

くろまく 黒幕〈黒い幕〉a black curtain;〈背後で糸を引く人〉a wirepuller ¶黒幕になる pull the wires [strings] (from behind); be [work] behind the scenes; mastermind (a revolt).

クロマニョンじん クロマニョン人《人類》(a) Cro-Magnon man.

くろまめ 黒豆 a black soybean.

くろみ 黒味 ¶黒味がかった blackish; dark(-ish).

クロム《化》chromium; chrome ¶クロムめっきの chrome-[chromium-]plated / クロムイエロー chrome yellow.

ます. It gets dark about six. / 日が暮れかかっている. Night is coming on. / 日が暮れかかっていた. It was nearly dark. | The light was failing.

くろう この家を建てるのに私がどんなに苦労したか、お前らにはわからぬだろう. You don't know what I had to go through to build this house. / タクシーをとるのに苦労したよ. I had trouble getting a taxi. / わたしゃ, ほんとに苦労が絶えないよ. My worries are unending [endless]. / 彼は苦労が絶えない. He is never free from care. / 名簿に全部眼を通すのはひと苦労だ. It is quite a job to go through the list. / ご苦労さまでした. Many thanks for your trouble.

くろうと あなたの料理は玄人だ. Your cooking is virtually of professional standard. / これでは玄人はだしだ. This would put even a professional to shame. / 彼は玄人なみにギターがひける. He plays the guitar to a professional standard.

くろおび スパイサー氏は黒帯だ. Mr. Spicer is [has] a black belt in judo.

くろやま お屋の店の前は黒山の人だかりだった. A large crowd of people gathered in front of the vegetable store. | The street in front of the vegetable store

くろめ 黒目 the iris (and pupil) of the eye.
くろめがね 黒眼鏡 dark glasses.
くろやき 黒焼き ¶黒焼きの charred《newts》.
くろやま 黒山 [文例⇩]
クロレラ〘植〙a chlorella (alga).
クロロホルム chloroform ¶クロロホルムをかける chloroform《a cat》.
クロロマイセチン〘薬〙Chloromycetin ★これは商品名. 正式の薬名は chloramphenicol.
くろわく 黒枠 black borders [edges]; ‹死亡通知などの› mourning borders ¶黒枠の black-edged[-framed] / 黒枠の広告 an obituary (notice) / 黒枠のはがき a mourning card.
クロワッサン《フランス語》a *croissant*.
くろんぼ(う) 黒ん坊 ⇨**こくじん** ¶くろんぼコンテスト a suntan contest.
くわ[1] 桑 a mulberry (tree) ¶桑の実 a mulberry / 桑を摘む pick mulberry leaves / 桑畑 a mulberry field [plantation].
くわ[2] 鍬 a hoe ¶くわを入れる break ground; plow; hoe; cultivate《land》;《文》put《land》to the plow / くわ入れ式 a ground-breaking ceremony.
くわい〘植〙an arrowhead.
くわえる[1] 加える add《one number to another》; ‹合計する› sum [add] up; ‹含める› include; ‹危害などを› give《damage》;《文》inflict ¶速力を加える gather speed; speed up;《文》gain velocity / 危害を加える inflict an injury《on》. [文例⇩]
くわえる[2] 銜える take [hold, have] *sth* in *one's* mouth [between *one's* teeth] ¶くわえタバコで with a cigarette in the corner of *one's* mouth; cigarette in mouth / 指をくわえて見ている look on enviously《at》. [文例⇩]
くわがた(むし)〘昆〙a stag beetle.
くわけ 区分け ⇨**くぶん**.
くわしい 詳しい ‹詳細な› full; detailed; minute; ‹その上の› further; ‹正確な› exact; accurate ¶詳しい事 details; particulars; ‹その上の詳細› further information [particulars] / …に詳しい know《a subject》thoroughly [well]; have a detailed knowledge of…; be knowledgeable about…;《文》be well versed in…; be at home in [on]…; be well informed about [of]…; be well acquainted with… / 詳しく ‹詳細に› minutely; in detail; ‹充分に› fully; in full; ‹正確に› exactly; accurately. [文例⇩]
くわす 食わす ⇨**くわせる**.
くわずぎらい 食わず嫌い ¶食わず嫌いである dislike [reject]《*sushi*》without even having tried it; have a prejudice [be prejudiced]《against》.
くわせもの 食わせ物 ‹物› a fake; a sham;《文》a counterfeit; a phon(e)y; ‹人› an imposter; a cheat; a hypocrite (偽善者).
くわせる 食わせる ‹食物を› feed《an animal on oats》; feed《oats》to《an animal》; ‹扶養する› support; feed; keep; provide for; ‹食らわす› give *sb*《a box on the ear》¶一杯食わせる ⇨**いっぱい**[1]. [文例⇩]
くわだて 企て ‹計画› a plan; a project;《文》a design; ‹試み› an attempt; ‹事業› an undertaking; an enterprise; ‹陰謀› a plot;《文》an intrigue.
くわだてる 企てる ‹計画する› plan; scheme;《文》project; ‹意図する› intend; have *sth* in mind;《文》purpose《(making [to make]) an attempt》; ‹試みる› attempt; try; ‹着手する› undertake. [文例⇩]
グワッシュ ⇨**ガッシュ**.
くわり 区割り demarcation; marking of boundaries ⇨**くぶん**.
くわわる 加わる join (in); take part [《文》participate] in; have a hand in《a game》; ‹増加する› grow [gain,《文》increase]《in》¶一行に加わる join [be with] the party. [文例⇩]
くん[1] 訓 the native Japanese reading [rendering] of a Chinese character ¶訓で読む read [pronounce]《a Chinese character》with《its》Japanese reading.
くん[2] 勲 ¶勲1等 the First Order of Merit.
-くん …君 ‹敬称› Mr.《Araki》; Master《Taro》(少年に) ★例えば, 加藤文雄という人を「加藤君」と呼ぶときは (Mr.) Kato でよいが, 「文雄君」は Fumio と呼び捨てにして, Mr. は付けない. 親しい間柄では個人名を呼び捨てにするのが英語の習慣である.
ぐん[1] 軍 an army; a force; troops.
ぐん[2] 郡 a county ¶郡部 rural districts (not included within town or city boundaries).
ぐん[3] 群 ⇨**むれ** ¶群をなす crowd; flock; swarm / 群をなして in a group [groups]; in swarms; in herds; in flocks; in schools (魚が) / 群を抜く《文》rise [be] above the common herd;《文》be of towering stature; distinguish *oneself*; be outstanding; come out on top《of》/ 群を抜いてそびえる木 a tree towering above its neighbors / 群論〘数〙group theory; the theory of groups.
ぐんい 軍医 an army [a naval] surgeon.
くんいく 訓育 education; discipline; character building.

---

was black [solid] with people.
くわえる[1] 5に6を加えよ. Add 6 to 5. / 2に3を加えると5だ. Two and three make five. / 私を加えて一行10人. The party numbered ten, including myself.
くわえる[2] 大きな黒犬が何か白いものをくわえて走って行った. I saw a big black dog running off with something white in its mouth.
くわしい (広告文などで)詳しいことは直接お尋ね下さい. Apply in person for further particulars. / 詳しいことは手紙で申し上げます. I will give you full information by letter. / そのような事柄については, この辞書の方が詳しい. This dictionary gives more information on that sort of thing.
くわせる 馬に湿ったまぐさを食わせるな. Never feed wet hay to the horse. / あの店ではうまいビフテキを食わせる. That restaurant serves good steaks.
くわだてる 彼の企てたことは何でも成功する. He succeeds in everything he undertakes [turns his hand to].
くわわる 雨に風さえ加わった. In addition to the rain, the wind began to blow. / 暑さが日増しに加わってきた. It is getting hotter and hotter every day. / 列車は下り坂でスピードが加わった. The train gained speed as it went down the slope.

ぐんか 軍歌 a military [martial, marching] song.

くんかい 訓戒《文》admonition;《文》exhortation; a lecture; warning ¶訓戒する《文》admonish [exhort]《sb to do》; caution; warn.

ぐんがくたい 軍楽隊 a military band ¶海軍軍楽隊 a naval band / 軍楽隊長 a band master.

ぐんかん 軍艦 a warship; a man-of-war《pl. men-》¶軍艦旗 a naval ensign.

ぐんき¹ 軍紀[規] military [naval] discipline ¶軍紀を守る[乱す] maintain [offend against] military [naval] discipline.

ぐんき² 軍旗 the (regimental) colors; a battle flag; a standard; an ensign.

ぐんきものがたり 軍記物語 a war tale; a military romance.

ぐんきょ 群居 live gregariously [together, in flocks] / 群居本能 the herd instinct ⇒ぐんせい².

くんくん sniff, sniff! ¶くんくん嗅ぐ sniff (at); give a sniff (at) / くんくん泣く《小犬が》whine.

ぐんぐん〈着々〉steadily; at a great rate; increasingly; by leaps and bounds;〈見る見る〉rapidly ¶ぐんぐん上達する make steady [rapid] progress /〈競走で相手を〉ぐんぐん引き離す quickly outdistance《the other runners》/ ぐんぐん伸びる grow taller and taller《背が》; expand steadily《事業が》.

くんこう 勲功《文》distinguished [meritorious] service(s);《文》merits; exploits (of war) ¶勲功をたてる render distinguished services《to the state》; distinguish *oneself*《in》.

ぐんこう 軍港 a naval port.

ぐんこくしゅぎ 軍国主義 militarism ¶軍国主義の militaristic / 軍国主義者 a militarist.

くんし 君子《文》a man of virtue [noble character]; a (true) gentleman ¶君子ぶる《文》assume a virtuous air. 文例あり

くんじ¹ 訓示 instruction(s); briefing(行動開始前の) ¶訓示する instruct; give instructions.

くんじ² 訓辞《文》an admonitory speech; (an address of) instructions ¶卒業式における校長の訓辞 the principal's address on commencement day.

ぐんじ 軍事 military affairs ¶軍事上の military; strategic / 軍事援助 military aid / 軍事教練 military training (drill) / 軍事行動 military operations [action]; hostile operations / 軍事顧問 a military adviser / 軍事裁判 military trial [court, tribunal] / 軍事施設 military establishments [installations] / 軍事政権 a military regime [junta] / 軍事同盟 a military alliance / 軍事評論家 a military commentator / 軍事力 military [armed] strength; armaments. 文例あり

ぐんしきん 軍資金《軍費》war funds;〈運動費〉campaign funds.

くんしゅ 君主 a monarch; a sovereign ¶君主政体 monarchy.

ぐんじゅ 軍需 ¶軍需工場 a munitions [an arms] factory [works, plant]; a war plant / 軍需産業 the munitions industry; war industries / 軍需品 munitions; war supplies.

ぐんしゅう¹ 群衆 a crowd (of people);《文》the multitude;《文》a throng;〈大衆〉《文》the masses ¶群衆に紛れて逃げる slip away in the crowd.

ぐんしゅう² 群集 a large group of people; a mob;《生態》a [an ecological] community ¶群集心理 mob [mass, crowd] psychology ¶群集心理 the group [crowd] mind / 群集本能 the herd instinct.

ぐんしゅく 軍縮 disarmament; arms reduction ¶完全軍縮 total [complete] disarmament / 軍縮会議 a disarmament conference / 軍縮会談 disarmament talks.

くんしょう 勲章 a decoration; an order; a medal ¶勲章を着けている wear a decoration / 勲章を授ける confer [award] a decoration [an order]《on *sb*》; decorate *sb*《with an order》. 文例あり

ぐんしょう 群小 ¶群小の minor;《文》lesser;《文》petty; insignificant / 群小作家 minor [lesser-known] writers.

ぐんじょういろ 群青色 ultramarine.

ぐんじん 軍人 a serviceman;〈陸軍〉a soldier;〈海軍〉a sailor;〈空軍〉an airman;〈将校〉a military [naval] officer;〈全体〉members of the armed forces ¶陸海軍軍人 soldiers and sailors / 職業軍人 a professional soldier; a career officer(将校).

くんずほぐれつ ¶くんずほぐれつの乱闘になる wrestle [tussle, grapple] wildly《with》; scuffle fiercely together.

くんせい 燻製 ¶燻製の smoked《salmon》.

ぐんせい¹ 軍政 (under) military administration [government] ¶軍政を敷く establish a military administration; impose military rule《on》/ 軍政府 a military government.

ぐんせい² 群生 群生する〈動物が〉live in flocks [herds];〈植物が〉grow gregariously [in crowds] / 群生の gregarious / 群生動物 gregarious [social] animals.

ぐんぜい 軍勢〈兵数〉the number of soldiers;〈軍〉an army; troops ¶3万の軍勢 an army 30,000 strong / 敵の軍勢 the enemy forces.

ぐんそう 軍装〈平時の〉(in) military uniform;〈戦闘時〉battle dress [kit] ¶完全軍装で in full kit [gear].

ぐんぞう 群像〈彫刻〉a sculptured group ¶ラオコーン群像 the Laocoön group.

くんし 君子は豹変す。A wise man changes his mind, a fool never.《諺》/ 君子危うきに近寄らず。A wise man never courts danger. | Discretion is the better part of valor.《諺》

ぐんじ この島は軍事的に見てきわめて重要である。This island is of great strategic importance. | This island is very important in military terms.

くんしょう 宇宙飛行士の胸には, 首相の手で勲章が飾られた。The premier pinned a medal on the breast of the cosmonaut.

ぐんゆうかっきょ 日本の政界は群雄割拠だ。The political world of Japan is an arena of rival bosses, each with his own sphere of influence.

け¹ スープの中に毛が1本入って

ぐんぞく 軍属 a civilian employee of the army [navy]; a civilian war worker.

ぐんたい 軍隊 〈軍〉 armed forces; an army; troops ¶軍隊に入る enter [enlist in] the army / 8千人の軍隊 an army 8,000 strong; an 8,000-man army / 軍隊蟻(がり) 〈昆〉 an army [a driver, a legionary] ant / 軍隊行進曲 a military march / 軍隊生活 (an) army [(a) military] life / 軍隊生活をする serve in the army.

-ぐんだり ¶能登くんだりまで行く go as far as [all the way down to] Noto.

ぐんと ¶ぐんとよくなる improve markedly; become far [much] better.

くんとう 薫陶 〈訓練〉 discipline; training; 〈教育〉 education ¶薫陶する discipline; drill; train; 〈教育する〉 educate; breed up / …の薫陶を受ける 〈文〉 be under sb's tutelage.

ぐんとう¹ 軍刀 a military sword; a saber.

ぐんとう² 群島 a group of islands; an archipelago (pl. -(e)s) ¶マライ群島 the Malay Archipelago / マーシャル群島 the Marshal Islands.

ぐんばい 軍配 a military leader's fan; a sumo referee's fan (行司の) ¶…に軍配を上げる give a decision in favor of sb; declare sb the winner.

ぐんばつ 軍閥 a military clique.

ぐんび 軍備 armaments; military preparedness ¶軍備の増強 military [arms] buildup / 軍備を縮小[拡張]する reduce [increase] armaments / 軍備拡張[縮小] expansion [reduction] of armaments / 軍備競争 an arms [armaments] race / 軍備制限 arms control / 軍備撤廃 disarmament; demilitarization.

ぐんぶ 軍部 the military authorities; the military.

くんぷう 薫風 《文》 a balmy breeze.

ぐんぷく 軍服 a military [naval] uniform ¶軍服を着ている be in (military) uniform / 軍服姿の将校 an officer in uniform; a uniformed officer.

ぐんぽうかいぎ 軍法会議 a court-martial (pl. courts-martial, court-martials) ¶軍法会議を召集する call a court-martial / 軍法会議にかける try (a soldier) by court-martial; court-martial (a soldier).

ぐんむ 軍務 military service [duty] ¶軍務に服する serve in the army [navy]; perform military duties.

ぐんもん 軍門 ¶軍門にくだる surrender ((to)); 《文》 capitulate; be defeated ((by)).

ぐんゆうかっきょ 群雄割拠 rivalry of warlords ¶群雄割拠の時代 the age of rival chiefs [warlords]. 文例⑨

ぐんよう 軍用 ¶軍用の military; for military use [purposes]; war (戦争用の) / 軍用機 a military plane; a warplane; combat aircraft (総称) / 軍用犬 an army [military] dog / 軍用道路 a military road / 軍用列車 a troop train.

ぐんらく 群落 〈生態〉 a colony.

くんりん 君臨 ¶君臨する 《文》 reign ((over)); rule ((over)) / 映画界に君臨する dominate [lord it over] the film world.

くんれい 訓令 ¶訓令する[を発する] instruct; give [issue] instructions [orders] / …の訓令に基づいて on the instructions of….

くんれん 訓練 training; (a) drill; practice; (training) exercises; discipline ¶訓練する train; drill; discipline / よく訓練されている be highly disciplined; be well trained / 訓練を受ける be trained ((in)); train ((for)); 《文》 undergo training [discipline] / 猛訓練 hard [intensive] training / 訓練生 a trainee.

くんわ 訓話 《文》 a moral discourse; 《文》 an admonitory lecture.

け

け¹ 毛 (a) hair; down (うぶ毛); 〈羽毛〉 a feather; down (綿毛); 〈獣毛〉 fur; 〈羊毛〉 wool ⇨ かみ⁴(髪の毛) ¶毛が生える hair grows ((on one's legs)) / 毛が抜ける hair falls [comes] out; 〈人が主語〉 lose one's hair / 毛のシャツ a woolen undershirt / 毛がない hairless; bald / 毛ほども (not) a particle ((of)). 文例⑨

け² 気 〈気配〉 a sign; an indication; 〈気味〉 a touch; 〈痕跡〉(にき) a trace. 文例⑨

け³ 卦 a divination sign ⇨ うらない, はっけ.

-け …家 ¶徳川家 the Tokugawa House [family]; the Tokugawas.

げ 下 〈下等〉 the low class [grade]; 〈下巻〉 the last [second, third] volume ¶下の下 the worst [poorest] of all; 〈人について〉 the lowest of the low; the dregs of humanity; 《米俗》 the pits (of the world). 文例⑨

けあい 蹴合い ⇨ とうけい³ ¶鶏に蹴合いをさせる hold a cockfight.

けあがり 蹴上がり 〈器械体操〉 a kip ¶蹴上がりをする perform a kip; kip.

けあげる 蹴上げる kick up.

けあな 毛穴 pores (in the skin).

けあみ 毛編み ¶毛編みの knitted in wool; woolen / 毛編みのセーター a knitted (woolen) sweater; a (woolen) jersey sweater.

いた. I found a hair in my soup. / 彼には君らに対する同情心などは毛ほどもない. He doesn't have a particle [grain] of sympathy for you. / 毛を吹いて疵を求めない方がいいよ. (You know what they say.) People who live in glass houses shouldn't throw stones.

け² そんな気もない. There is not the slightest suspicion of it.

げ そんな事をするような人間は下の下だよ. A person who would do something like that is the lowest of the low [the dregs of humanity] / そういう手段は下の下だ. That is the worst possible measure that could be taken.

けい¹ 兄 ⇒ あに ¶吉田兄 Mr. Yoshida. [文例⇩]

けい² 刑 a punishment; a penalty; a sentence (宣告) ¶刑の適用 the application of a punishment / 刑の執行を猶予する suspend (the execution of) a sentence / 刑を宣告する pronounce [pass] a sentence on *sb* / 刑を減じる reduce [commute] a sentence ((to six months)) / 懲役5年の刑に処する sentence (a prisoner) to five years at [((英))with] hard labor / 刑に服する serve [submit to] a sentence. [文例⇩]

けい³ 系 〈系統〉a system; 〈血統〉a family line; 《文》lineage; 〖数〗a corollary ¶河川系 a river system / ドイツ系のアメリカ人 an American of German descent [extraction]; a German-American / 保守系の候補者 a conservative candidate.

けい⁴ 計 〈計画〉a plan; a scheme; 〈計略〉a plot; 〈合計〉the total; 〈計器〉a meter; a gauge ¶計3万円になる be 30,000 yen in total [in all, all told]; total 30,000 yen.

けい⁵ 罫 a (ruled) line ¶罫のある紙 ruled [lined] paper / 罫のない紙 plain [unruled] paper / 罫を引く rule lines ((on a sheet of paper)).

げい 芸 〈技芸〉an art; 〈たしなみ〉《文》an accomplishment; 〈演技〉a performance; 〈曲芸〉a trick ¶芸が細かい pay careful attention to detail(s) [to the details ((of))] / 犬に芸を教える teach a dog tricks. [文例⇩]

ゲイ ¶ゲイバー a gay bar / ゲイボーイ a (young) homosexual [《口語》gay].

けいあい 敬愛 ¶敬愛する love and respect; 《文》hold *sb* in high esteem [regard].

けいい¹ 経緯 〈いきさつ〉details; particulars; circumstances; 〈経度と緯度〉longitude and latitude ¶経緯儀〖測量〗a theodolite.

けいい² 敬意 respect; 《文》regard; 〈敬愛〉homage ¶敬意を表する defer ((to)); pay *one's* respects ((to)); do [pay, offer] homage ((to)) / …に敬意を表して as a mark of respect for…;

out of respect for…; in [out of] deference to…; in honor of….

げいいき 芸域 ¶芸域が広い be very versatile. [文例⇩]

けいえい 経営 〈管理〉management; administration; 〈運営〉operation ¶経営する manage (a firm); run (a company); 《文》conduct (business); carry on (an enterprise); keep (a store); operate (a mine) / ホテルを経営する keep [run] a hotel / 経営の才 administrative [executive] ability; a talent for managing (a bank) / 経営学 business administration [studies] / (労使の)経営協議会 a joint management council / 経営コンサルタント a management consultant / (労働者の)経営参加 worker participation (in management); industrial democracy [codetermination] / 経営者 a manager; an executive; 〈店主〉a proprietor / 経営者と労働者〈集合的に〉(conflicts between) labor and management / 経営費 operating [running] costs [expenses]. [文例⇩]

けいえん 敬遠 ¶敬遠する keep *sb* [hold *sb* off] at a (respectful) distance; give *sb* a wide berth; shy away from *sth*; 〖野球〗walk [pass] (a batter) intentionally.

けいえんげき 軽演劇 light comedy.

けいおんがく 軽音楽 light music.

けいか 経過 〈事の〉progress; 《文》course; development; 〈時日の〉passing; 《文》passage; 《文》a lapse; 〈期限の〉《文》expiration ¶事件の経過 the development of an affair / 経過する〈事が〉progress; develop; 〈時日が〉pass; go by; 《文》elapse; 〈期限が〉expire / 10年の歳月が経過して after (a lapse of) ten years / (病人が)経過良好である be making satisfactory progress; be doing well [fine]. [文例⇩]

けいが 慶賀 ¶慶賀する congratulate *sb* ((on *his* success)); offer *one's* congratulations ((to *sb* on *his* success)) / …は慶賀すべきことである It is a matter for congratulation that…. [文例⇩]

けい¹ 兄たりがたく弟たりがたし,というところだ. There's little [not much] to choose between them. | They are (about) equal [on a par].

けい² この罪で有罪と決まれば最高懲役10年の刑を受けることになる. Conviction under this charge carries a maximum penalty of 10 years in prison.

げい 芸は身を助く. Accomplishments are a lifelong benefit to their possessor.

けいい² 彼の意見に敬意を表さなくてはいけないか. このことについては彼は我々のだれよりも経験豊かなのだから. We must defer to his opinion, for he has more experience in this matter than any of us. / 石井先生の所へちょっと敬意を表しに行かないか. What do you say to visiting Mr. Ishii just to pay our re-

spects?

げいいき 彼は芸域が広くて, 悲劇ばかりでなく喜劇の役でも立派にこなす. He is a very versatile actor: he can play a comic part [role] just as capably as (he does) a tragic one.

けいえい 彼の経営よろしきをえて事業は大いに発展した. Under his capable [excellent] management the business has grown more and more prosperous. / その会社は経営難に陥っている. The firm is in financial difficulties [is finding it difficult to keep going]. / 彼はその学校の経営面の一切を担当している. He runs all the business end of the school.

けいか (病人の夫を持った奥さんに向かって)ご病人の経過はいかがですか. How is your husband doing? / 有り難う, 経過は良好でございます. もう大丈夫ですわ.

He is coming along fine, thank you. He is out of danger now. / 交渉の経過が報告された. The progress of the negotiations was reported to them. / 期限が経過しましたのでこの切符は無効です. This ticket is no good; it has expired.

けいが 首尾よく合格なさいました由, 慶賀の至りに存じます. Allow me to offer you my hearty congratulations on your success in the examination. / 暑さきびしき折から皆さまご壮健の由, 慶賀の至りに存じます. I am very glad to hear that all your family are in good health in spite of the intense (summer) heat. ★英米には, こういう暑中見舞い的なあいさつをする習慣はない.

けいかい¹ 夕刻から暴風になる恐れがありますから沿岸一帯は警戒を要します. Stormy weather is

けいかい¹ 警戒 〈用心〉 caution ; (a) precaution ; 〈見張り〉 watch ; (a) lookout ; 〈警護〉 guard ; 〈警告〉 (a) warning ; a caution ¶ 警戒する〈用心する〉 be cautious about ((sth, doing)) ; take precautions (against) ; 〈見張る〉 look out ((for pickpockets)) ; watch ((for a thief)) ; be on the watch ((for)) ; guard ((against)) ; be on one's guard ((against)) / 警戒を厳重にする keep a strict [close] watch ((on)) / 警戒をゆるめる lower one's guard ((against)) ; 〈文〉 relax one's vigilance ((against)) / 警戒警報 a preliminary alert / 警戒色 【動】〈事〉 warning [sematic] coloration ; 〈特定の色〉 a warning [sematic] color ((動物の発する)) 警戒声[音] (give) an alarm cry [note] / 警戒水位 the danger level ((of a river)) / (警察が)警戒線[網]を張る form [throw] a police cordon ((around an area)) / 警戒線を突破する break [slip (こっそりと)] through a police cordon / 警戒態勢につく be (put) on the alert ((for)) ; be alerted ((in case…)). 文例⇩

けいかい² 軽快 ¶軽快な light ; nimble ; airy / 軽快な足取りで with a light (and springy) step ; light-footedly / 軽快な調べ a lilting tune. 文例⇩

けいがい 形骸 a ruin ; a wreck ¶形骸化した民主主義 democracy that has become a dead letter ; democracy stripped of all its contents ; a mere shell of democracy. 文例⇩

けいかく 計画 a plan ; a project ; a scheme ; a program ¶計画する plan / 計画どおりに according to plan ; as planned [scheduled] / 計画的な intentional ; deliberate ; calculated ; 《文》premeditated (犯罪が) / 計画的に deliberately ; on purpose ; intentionally ; 《文》by design / 計画中である〈事業が〉be in the planning stage ; be on foot ; 〈人が〉be planning ((an operation)) ; 《文》have sth in contemplation / 計画を立てる lay [form, work out] a plan [scheme] ; make [plan] a program / 計画を実行する carry out [《文》execute] one's plan / 5 ヵ年計画 a five-year plan [program] / 計画経済 (a) planned economy / 計画変更 a change of plan. 文例⇩

けいかん¹ 景観 ⇨けしき, ながめ²

けいかん² 警官 a policeman ; a police officer ; 《英》a (police) constable ; 〈総称〉the police (★ the police は複数扱い) ¶警官隊 a police force [squad]. 文例⇩

けいがん 慧眼 a keen [sharp] eye ; 《文》(keen) insight ; (good) judgment ; 《文》acumen. ¶慧眼な keen-[sharp-]eyed ; quick-sighted ; 《文》perceptive ; 《文》discerning. 文例⇩

けいかんしじん 桂冠詩人 a poet laureate.

けいき¹ 刑期 a term of imprisonment ; a prison term ¶刑期をつとめる serve one's term of imprisonment ; 《口語》do time (in Urawa Prison) / 刑期をつとめ上げる serve one's full term in prison ; serve out one's sentence.

けいき² 計器 a meter ; a gauge ; an instrument ¶航海[工業]用計器 a nautical [an industrial] instrument / 計器着陸 (an) instrument [(a) blind] landing / 計器板 an instrument board ; a dashboard (自動車・航空機などの) / 計器飛行 an instrument [a blind] flight ; instrument [blind] flying.

けいき³ 契機 【哲】a moment ; 〈機会〉an opportunity ; a chance ¶これを契機として with this as a turning point [a trigger] ; taking [《文》availing oneself of] this opportunity.

けいき⁴ 景気 〈世間の〉(the) times ; things ; 〈商況〉business ; the market ; 〈状況〉activity ; prosperity ¶景気がいい 〈商況〉(the) times are good ; business [the market] is brisk ; 〈威勢〉be lively [perky, jaunty] ; be in high spirits / 景気のいい音楽 lively music / 景気のいいことを言う talk big / 景気づく get [grow, 《文》become] active ; liven up ; be enlivened / 景気をつける liven up ; enliven ; brighten / 景気よく騒ぐ go on the [have a] spree / 景気よく金を使う lavish one's money ((on)) ; spend money lavishly ((on)) / 景気後退 a recession ; a

---

expected toward evening, so precautions should be taken along the coast. / あの男は警戒した方がいいよ。You should watch [keep an eye on] him. | You must be on your guard against him. / 病人は今一番警戒を要するときだ。The patient is in the most critical stage. / 財界筋は新政策に対して警戒的である。Financial circles are wary of the new policy. / 我我は昨日から24時間警戒態勢に入っている。We have been on 24-hour alert since yesterday.

けいかい² 彼は動作が軽快だ。He is nimble [quick] in his movements.

けいがい 今ではその寺は形骸すら留めていない。Nothing remains of the temple now. / わが国の仏教は今や形骸ばかりになってしまったと彼は嘆いている。He bemoans the fact that Buddhism has been reduced to a shell in this country. / 彼は、この法律はすでに形骸化しているので廃止すべきである、と主張した。He argued that the law had become a dead letter and should be repealed.

けいかく その計画はうまく行った。The plan worked (well). / そこに鉄道を敷設する計画がある。There is a plan afoot [A plan is on foot] to construct a railroad there. / その事件で計画がすっかり狂ってしまった。The accident has upset [frustrated] all our plans. / 夏休みの計画を何か立てましたか。Have you made any plans for the summer vacation? / 父と京都へ行く計画です。I am planning to go [on going] to Kyoto with my father. | 万事計画どおりに行った。Everything went according to plan. | Everything worked out exactly as scheduled. / その暴動は周到に計画されたものらしい。The riot seems to have been carried out according to a well-laid plan. / その事業はまだ計画中の段階です。The project is still in the planning stage. / 生産が計画目標に1割不足であった。Production was ten per cent short of the planned target. / 彼のやることには計画性がない。There is neither plan nor system in anything he does.

けいかん²50人の警官が事故の現場に派遣された。Fifty policemen were dispatched to the scene of the accident.

けいがん 彼のような慧眼の人にかかっては隠しだてしてもむだだ。It's no use trying to conceal anything from him ; he has such keen perception. | Nothing can

けいきゅう　軽気球　a balloon ⇒ ききゅう².

けいきへい　軽騎兵　⟨1人⟩ a light cavalryman; a hussar; ⟨隊⟩ light cavalry.

けいきょ　軽挙　a rash [reckless] act ¶軽挙妄動(ﾎﾞｳﾄﾞｳ)を慎む⟪文⟫ behave [proceed] prudently / 軽挙妄動を戒める warn *sb* against rashness.

けいきんぞく　軽金属　light metals.

けいく　警句　a witty [clever] remark; a witticism; an epigram; ⟪口語⟫ a crack ¶警句を吐く make a witty remark ⟪about⟫; ⟪口語⟫ make a crack ⟪about⟫ / 警句集 a collection of epigrams.

けいぐ　敬具　Yours truly [faithfully]; Sincerely yours.

けいけい　炯々　¶眼光けいけいたる having piercing [penetrating] eyes; with a piercing look ⟪文⟫⟪語⟫.

けいけい²　軽々　¶軽々に ⇒かるがるしい (かるがるしく).

げいげき　迎撃　迎撃する lie in wait [ambush] ⟪for⟫; ambush; waylay; intercept ⟪raiding bombers⟫ / 迎撃機 an interceptor / 迎撃用ミサイル an interceptor missile.

けいけん¹　経験　(an) experience ¶経験する experience; go through; ⟪文⟫ undergo / 直接の経験 direct [firsthand, personal] experience / 苦い経験 (a) bitter experience / 英語教授の経験がある have taught English; ⟨経験を積んでいる⟩ have (some) experience [in [of]) teaching English / 英語教授の経験がない have no experience of teaching English; have never taught English / 経験のある ⟨a person⟩ who has *done*; ⟨a person⟩ who has experienced [has (had) experience of] *doing* / 経験のない ⟨a person⟩ with no experience of *doing*; ⟨a person⟩ who has never *done* / 経験の豊かな[浅い] experienced [inexperienced] / 経験を積む gain ⟪文⟫ acquire (new) experience / add to [increase, build up, ⟪文⟫ enrich] *one*'s experience / 経験を生かす make good use of *one*'s experience / 経験に富む turn *one*'s experience to good account / 経験に富む experienced ⟪in⟫; ⟪文⟫ have considerable [rich, wide] experience ⟪of teaching, in politics⟫ / 経験に乏しい be inexperienced ⟪in⟫ (★ be inexperienced の後に in... が続くと⟪文⟫); do not have much experience ⟪of, in⟫; ⟪文⟫ lack experience ⟪of, in⟫ / 私の経験では in my experience / 経験で知る know *sth* from (*one*'s) experience; learn *sth* by experience / 経験的に empirically / 経験的知識 empirical knowledge / 経験者 a person with [who has] experience ⟪of living overseas⟫; a person who had *done*; ⟨経験を積んだ⟩ a person with (long) experience ⟪in⟫; ⟨熟練労働者⟩ an experienced worker / 経験談をする tell a story [give an account] of *one*'s experiences; ⟪文⟫ relate *one*'s experiences / 経験哲学 empirical philosophy / 経験論[主義]【哲】 empiricism.
文例図

けいけん²　敬虔　¶敬虔な pious; devout / 敬虔な祈りを捧げる pray devoutly ⟪before the altar⟫.

けいげん　軽減　(a) reduction; ⟪文⟫ (a) decrease; ⟪文⟫ mitigation ¶軽減する lighten; reduce; relieve; ⟪文⟫ decrease; ⟪文⟫ alleviate; mitigate ⟪an offense⟫ ⟪罪を⟫; commute ⟪a sentence⟫ ⟪刑を⟫. 文例図

けいこ　稽古 ⟨練習⟩ practice; training; exercise; a rehearsal ⟪演技の⟫; ⟨学習⟩ study; learning; ⟨授業⟩ a lesson ⟪in⟫ ¶稽古する ⟨練習する⟩ practice; train; do exercises; rehearse ⟪演技を⟫; ⟨学ぶ⟩ study; learn; take lessons ⟪in⟫ / ピアノを稽古する ⟨授業を受ける⟩ take piano lessons; ⟪文⟫ lessons in (the) piano; ⟨自分で⟩ do (*one*'s) piano practice; practice on the piano / …について声楽の稽古をする take voice [vocal] lessons from *sb* / 稽古をつける give *sb* lessons ⟪in⟫; train; teach; coach *sb* ⟪in fencing⟫ / よく稽古をつんだ演技 a well-rehearsed performance / 稽古着 a suit for ⟪*judo*⟫ practice / 稽古場 a place where lessons are given; a drill [rehearsal] hall / 稽古日 a [the] day for *one*'s ⟪*samisen*⟫ lesson; a day when one has a ⟪dancing⟫ class.
文例図

けいご¹　敬語　an honorific (expression [word]); a term of respect ¶敬語を使って話す use respect language [polite expressions].

けいご²　警護　ごえい.

けいこう¹　経口【薬】¶経口投与 ⟪doses for⟫ oral administration / 経口避妊薬 an oral con-

---

get past his eagle eye.

けいき⁴　景気はいかがですか。⟨商売が⟩ How's business? / ⟨一般に⟩ How's everything? / ⟪口語⟫ How's things? / そんなに景気が悪いのかね。Are things so very bad? / 景気がよくなってきた。Business is looking [picking] up.

けいけん¹　こんな寒さはこれまでに経験したことがない。This is the coldest weather I've ever experienced. / 私が経験した範囲ではこれが最良の方法である。In my experience this is the best method. / 私は子供をなくしたつらい経験がある。I know what it is to lose a child. / 私はこういう仕事には経験がない。I've no experience of [I'm new to] this kind of work. / 何事も経験だと思ってその仕事を引き受けることにした。I decided to take the job on just for the experience of it. / その失敗がいい経験になった。The failure was a good lesson to me. / 僕の経験からするとそれはほとんど不可能だね。It is next to impossible, as I know from (my own) experience. / 彼は自分の経験談を話してくれた。He told us of his experiences. / まさに「経験者は語る」というものだ。These facts are known only to those who have had firsthand experience.

けいげん　そうなれば我々の負担も大いに軽減されることだろう。It will greatly lighten [⟪文⟫ alleviate] our burden.

けいこ　僕は3年間柔道を稽古した。I got training in *judo* for three years. / 僕はそのアメリカ

けいこう² 傾向 〈傾き〉a tendency 《to, toward》; a trend ; 〈心などの〉an inclination ; 《文》a disposition ¶傾向がある tend [have a tendency] to *do* ; have an inclination to *do* ; be apt to *do* / 保守的傾向がある tend [lean] toward conservatism ; be rather conservative 《in *one*'s views》/ 傾向を示す develop [show] a tendency to *do* / 傾向的《文》tendentious / 傾向文学 committed 《left-wing》literature. 文例⇩

けいこう³ 携行 ¶携行する carry [take] *sth* with *one* ⇨ たずさえる.

けいこう⁴ 蛍光 fluorescence ¶蛍光を発する fluoresce ; be fluorescent ; generate fluorescence / 蛍光灯 a fluorescent light [lamp] / 蛍光塗料[染料] (a) fluorescent paint [dye] / 蛍光板 a fluorescent screen.

げいごう 迎合 ¶迎合する cater to *sb*'s wishes [feelings]; alter [adjust] *one*'s opinions and behavior to please *sb* / 迎合主義者 a timeserver ; an opportunist.

けいこうぎょう 軽工業 light industries.

けいこく¹ 渓谷 a (steep-walled) valley ; a ravine ; a gorge ; a canyon ⇨ たに 図.

けいこく² 警告 (a) warning ; a caution ; 《文》(an) admonition ¶警告する warn 《*sb* of [against] *sth*, (not) to *do*, that…》; caution 《*sb* against [for] *sth*, that…》; give *sb* a warning 《of *sth*, that…》;《文》admonish 《*sb* for [against] *sth*》/ 厳重な警告を発する issue [send out] a stern warning 《to》. 〔*pl.* -iae, -ias〕

けいこつ¹ 脛骨 〖解〗the shinbone ; the tibia

けいこつ² 頚骨 〖解〗the bones of [in] the neck; the cervical [neck] vertebrae.

げいごと 芸事 accomplishments.

けいさい 掲載 ¶掲載する publish ; print ; carry 《the news》/ 新聞に掲載される appear [be reported] in a newspaper / その論文の掲載誌 the magazine which carries the article. 文例⇩

けいざい 経済 〈国などの〉an economy ; 〈倹約〉economy ; 〈財政〉finance ¶時間の経済 economy of time / 経済的な economical / 経済上の economic ; financial / 経済上[的に] economically ; financially ; 〈節約して〉with economy / 経済家 a man with a strong [keen] sense of economy ; a thrifty [《文》frugal] person ;〈主婦〉a good [careful] housekeeper / 経済界 the economic world ; financial [economic] circles / 経済外交 economic diplomacy / 経済学 (the science of) economics / 経済学者 an economist / 経済学博士〈人〉a doctor of economics ;〈学位〉Doctor of Economics / 経済学部 the economics department / 経済閣僚 Cabinet ministers in charge of economic affairs ; economic ministers / 経済閣僚懇談会 an economic ministers' conference / 経済活動 economic activities / 経済観念 a sense of economy / 経済企画庁 the Economic Planning Agency / 経済危機 an economic [a financial] crisis / 経済機構[制度] an economic structure [system] / 経済記者 a financial reporter ; a reporter of financial news /〈国連の〉経済協力開発機構 the Organization for Economic Cooperation and Development (略: OECD) / 経済原論 the principles of economics / 経済史 (an) economic history / 経済事情[状態] economic conditions ; the economic [financial] situation 《of Japan》/〈個人の〉经済 (the state of) *one*'s finances / 経済生活 economic life / 経済政策 (an) economic policy / 経済成長率 the rate of 《Japan's》economic growth / 経済戦 an economic war /〈車の〉経済速度 an [the most] economical speed / 経済大学 a college of economics / 経済大国 a big [great] economic power / 経済地理 economic geography / 経済封鎖 an economic blockade /〈新聞の〉経済面[欄] the financial page [section, columns] / 経済問題 an economic problem / 経済力 economic power [strength]. 文例⇩

けいさつ 警察 the police ;〈警察署〉a police station ¶警察の保護を受ける get [receive] police protection / 警察へ届ける[訴える] report [complain] to the police / 警察へ突き出す[引き渡す] deliver *sb* [hand *sb* over] to the police / 警察学校 a police school / 警察官 a police officer ; a policeman / 警察犬[国家] a police dog [state] / 警察権 (exercise, abuse) the police authority [power] / 警察署長 a police chief ;《米》a (town, city) marshal ;《英》a chief constable / 警察制度 a police system / 警察庁 the National Police Agency / 警察手帳 a policeman's notebook / 警察力 police force. 文例⇩

けいさん¹ 計算 calculation ; computation ; reckoning ; counting ¶計算する calculate ; com-

---

婦人を稽古台にして会話の練習をした. I practiced my English conversation on the American lady. / 彼女はノーマン氏についてピアノの稽古をした. She took piano lessons from [studied the piano under] Mr. Norman.

けいこう² 近頃の学生には保守的傾向が強くなった. Nowadays there is a growing conservative tendency among the students.

けいさい それは昨日の読売新聞に掲載された. It appeared [came out] in yesterday's *Yomiuri*. / この論文は数回にわたって朝日新聞に掲載された. This article was serialized [printed in serial form] in the *Asahi*.

けいざい そんな事は経済が許さない. I am not rich enough to afford it. / ごく経済にやっても月20万円はかかります. We can't live on less than 200,000 yen a month, whatever economies we practice. / ガスは電気より経済です. Gas is more economical than electricity. / 彼女は経済観念が発達している. She has a highly developed sense of economy. / これは両国の経済(制度)の違いから来ていると思う. I believe this is a result of the different economic systems of the two countries.

けいさつ 警察の者ですが…. I'm from the police. / とうとう警察の手が回った. At last the law caught up with him. / やつは警察ににらまれている. The police are keeping an eye on him. / そのすりは警察に引っ張って行かれた. The pickpocket was taken

けいさん pute; reckon; count; 〈合計する〉add up / 計算が早い[遅い] be quick [slow] at figures [accounts] / 計算を間違える miscalculate; miscount; get *one's* sums wrong; make a mistake in (*one's*) calculation(s) / 計算に入れる take *sth* into account [consideration (比喩的にのみ)] / 計算に入れない do not take *sth* into account; reckon without *sth*; leave *sth* out of *one's* reckoning / 計算係 an accountant / 計算機 a computer; a calculator; a calculating [an adding] machine → コンピューター / 計算尺 a slide rule / 計算書 a statement (of accounts). 文例◎

けいさん² 珪酸, ケイ酸 【化】 silicic acid ¶ケイ酸塩 (a) silicate.

けいさんぷ 経産婦 a multipara (*pl*. -rae); a primipara (*pl*. -s, -rae) (1回の).

けいし¹ 軽視 ¶軽視する make light of; think [make] little of; 《文》 slight; neglect; 《文》 belittle; 《文》 minimize. 文例◎

けいし² 罫紙 ruled [lined] paper.

けいし³ 警視 a police superintendent ¶警視総監 the Superintendent-General [Chief Commissioner] of the Metropolitan Police / 警視庁 the Metropolitan Police Board.

けいじ¹ 刑事 a (police) detective ¶刑事上の criminal; penal / 刑事裁判所 a criminal court / 刑事事件 a criminal case; a penal offense / 刑事事件専門の弁護士 a criminal lawyer / 《米》 (attorney) / 刑事訴訟 a criminal action [suit] / 刑事訴訟法 the Criminal Procedure Act.

けいじ² 計時 time; clock ¶ (競技・競泳の)計時係員) a timer; a timekeeper / (競泳の)電気計時機 an automatic (touch) timer [timing machine].

けいじ³ 掲示 a notice ¶掲示する[を出す] post (up) [put up, tack up] a notice 《on the wall》 / 掲示板 《米》 a bulletin board / 《英》 a notice board. 文例◎

けいじ⁴ 啓示 (a) revelation ¶啓示する reveal / 啓示宗教 a revealed religion.

けいじ⁵ 慶事 a happy [《文》 an auspicious] event; 《文》 a matter for congratulation.

けいじ⁶ 繋辞 【論】 a copula.

けいじか 形而下 ¶形而下の physical; 《文》 concrete.

けいしき 形式 (a) form; (a) formality ¶形式的な superficial; formal; 《文》 perfunctory /

形式的に, 形式上 formally; for form's sake; as a matter of form; 《文》 perfunctorily / 正当な形式を踏む go through [《文》 observe] the proper [《文》 due] formalities / 形式にこだわる[とらわれる] 〈手続き・文書などで〉 insist on [stick to, be fussy about, 《口語》 be sticky about] the proper forms [procedure(s), formalities]; 〈儀礼上〉 be too formal; stand on ceremony / 形式張らないで without formality [ceremony] / 形式主義者 a formalist / 形式主語[目的語] 【文法】 a formal subject [object] / 形式論[主義] formalism / 形式論理 formal logic. 文例◎

けいじじょう 形而上 ¶形而上の metaphysical / 形而上学 metaphysics / 形而上学者 a metaphysician.

けいしゃ¹ 珪砂 silica sand.

けいしゃ² 傾斜 an inclination; a slant; a slope (勾配(ぶ)); 〈船の〉 a list; 〈地層の〉 a dip ¶傾斜する incline; lean; slant; tilt; 〈道路が〉 slope; 〈船などが〉 list; careen (ひどく); 〈地層が〉 dip / ゆるやかに傾斜している incline gently; 〈土地が〉 slope gradually; shelve (down, up) / 傾斜した inclined; slanting; sloping / 傾斜角 an angle of inclination / 傾斜生産方式 the priority production system / 傾斜度 a gradient; 《米》 a grade / 傾斜面 an inclined plane; an incline. 文例◎

けいしゃ³ 鶏舎 a hen [chicken] house.

けいしゅ 警手 〈踏切の〉 a gateman [an attendant] (at a railroad crossing); 《英》 a (level-)crossing keeper.

げいじゅつ 芸術 (an) art; 〈美術〉 fine arts ¶芸術のための, 芸術至上主義 art for art's sake / 芸術的 artistic / 芸術院 the Japan Art Academy / 芸術院賞 an Art Academy prize [award] / 芸術映画 an art film / 芸術家 an artist / 芸術活動 art activities / 芸術写真 an artistic photograph / 芸術大学 an art college / 芸術哲学 the philosophy of art / 芸術品 an object [a work] of art. 文例◎

けいしょう¹ 形象 a shape; a figure; 【美学】 an image.

けいしょう² 敬称 an honorific [a courtesy] title; 〈呼びかけ方〉 a form of address ¶敬称を省略して呼ぶ call *sb's* name without (using) *his* title.

[marched off] to the police station. / 彼は警察官の制服を着ていた. I found him in police uniform.

けいさん² 運賃は距離で計算する. Fares are reckoned by distance. / 計算が合わなかった. The accounts did not tally. / 第3問は計算問題であった. The third question required a numerical calculation.

けいし¹ 彼は小さい事でも決して軽視しなかった. He never made light of small [little] things.

けいじ³ 学校は明日は休みだとい

う掲示が出ている. There is a notice up announcing that there is no school tomorrow.

けいしき あまりに形式にとらわれるとかえって精神を没却することになる. Excessive adherence to form can render a work lifeless. / それはどういう形式で発表にしますか. In what form will it be published?

けいしゃ² 船は浸水いよいよ甚だしく40度から80度にまで傾斜した. More and more water poured into the ship, and her list increased from 40 to 80 degrees. /

ロケットは赤道に対して31度の傾斜で発射された. The rocket was launched with an inclination to the equator of 31 degrees.

げいじゅつ 芸術は長く人生は短い. Art is long, life is short. 【諺】/ 彼には芸術家肌の所がある. There is something of the artist in him. | He has an artistic temperament.

けいしょう³ そこは景勝の地として知られている. The place is known [famous] for its beautiful scenery.

けいしょう⁷ これは現代消費社会

けいしょう³ 景勝 ❶景勝の地 a scenic spot; 《文》a place of scenic beauty. 文例⇩

けいしょう⁴ 軽症 a slight illness; a mild case (of measles) ❶軽症のうつ病にかかっている have a touch [slight attack] of depression.

けいしょう⁵ 軽傷 a slight injury [wound] ❶軽傷を負う be slightly injured [wounded] ((in the head)) / 軽傷者 a slightly injured [wounded] person;《集合的に》 the slightly injured [wounded].

けいしょう⁶ 継承 succession; inheritance ❶継承する succeed to ((the throne)); inherit ((the estate)); take over ((the assets)) / 継承者 a successor ((to)); an heir ((to)).

けいしょう⁷ 警鐘 an alarm bell ❶警鐘を打ち鳴らす ring [sound] an alarm (bell); 〈比喩的に〉sound [give, raise] the alarm. 文例⇩

けいしょう⁸ 軽少 ❶軽少の little; slight;《文》trifling. 文例⇩

けいじょう¹ 刑場 a place of execution; a scaffold (処刑台) ❶刑場の露と消える be executed; die on the scaffold.

けいじょう² 計上 ❶計上する〈合計する〉add up;〈当てる〉appropriate ((a sum of money for sth)) / 体育館の建設費として2億円を計上する appropriate ¥200 million for the building of the gymnasium.

けいじょう³ 計上 ❶計上する かたち.

けいじょう⁴ 経常 ❶経常の ordinary; current; working / 経常費 (the) operating [working, running] expenses; ordinary expenditure / 経常予算 the ordinary [working] budget.

けいじょう⁵ 警乗 ❶警乗する police [mount guard on] ((a train)).

けいじょうみゃく 頸静脈《解》the jugular 「(vein).

けいしょく 軽食 a light meal; a snack ❶軽食堂 a snack bar;《米》a luncheonette;《米》a lunchroom.

けいしん¹ 敬神 respect [reverence] for God;《文》piety ❶敬神の念 a pious feeling; piety; fear of God / 敬神の念の厚い《文》pious;《文》devoutly religious;《文》God-fearing.

けいしん² 軽信 credulity; credulousness;《文》over-ready credence ❶軽信する be too ready to believe ((that...)); be gullible [credulous] enough to believe ((that...));《文》give (too) ready credence ((to)).

けいしん³ 軽震 a weak earthquake.

けいず 系図 a genealogical table [chart]; a family tree;〈系譜〉a genealogy; lineage ❶系図が正しい come from a good family;《文》be a person of good birth;《文》come from a family of pedigree / 系図を調べる trace *sb's* genealogy [descent] back ((to the founder of *his* family)).

けいすう¹ 計数 ⇨けいさん¹ ❶計数に明るい be good at figures.

けいすう² 係数《数・物》a coefficient ❶吸収係数 the absorption coefficient; the coefficient of absorption / 摩擦係数《機》the coefficient of friction.

けいせい¹ 形成 formation ❶形成する form; shape; mold; make; compose;《文》constitute / 形成期《文》the formative period ((of a nation)) /《文》the formative years ((of an individual))/ 形成外科 plastic surgery. 文例⇩

けいせい² 形勢〈状勢〉the situation; the state of affairs [things];〈見込み〉the prospects ❶形勢を観望する watch the situation [the development of affairs]; see how the land lies; see how [which way] the wind blows;〈日和見する〉sit on the fence;《口語》(wait and) see which way the cat jumps / 目下の形勢では as things are; as matters stand. 文例⇩

けいせき 形跡〈痕跡(こんせき)〉traces; marks;〈証拠〉signs; evidence ❶形跡を留めない leave no trace behind / 形跡をくらます cover up *one's* traces. 文例⇩

けいせつ 螢雪 文例⇩

けいせん¹ 係船《事》mooring;《船》a boat [ship] moored ((to a buoy, at a pier)); a laid-up [an idle] ship (休航船) ❶係船する moor a boat [ship] ((at, to)) / 係船料 a mooring fee.

けいせん² 経線《地理》a line of (terrestrial, geographical) longitude; a meridian.

けいせん³ 罫線 a ruled line ⇨けい⁵.

ケイソ ケイ素《化》silicon.

けいそう¹ 係争〈争い〉(a) dispute;《文》contention;〈裁判〉a lawsuit ❶係争中である be in dispute; be at issue;〈法廷で〉be pending in court;《法》be sub judice / 係争中の問題 a question at issue; a pending problem / 係争点 a point at issue; a disputed point.

けいそう² 珪藻《植》a diatom ❶珪藻土 diatomaceous earth; kieselguhr.

けいそう³ 軽装 light clothes [clothing,《文》dress] ❶軽装する be lightly dressed [《文》clad]. 文例⇩

への一大警鐘である. This should be a grave warning to the consumer society of today.

けいしょう⁸ ほんの軽少ですがお礼のしるしです. Please accept this as a token of my gratitude.

けいせい¹ それらの家々が一小集落を形成している. Those houses form [make up] a small community. / 彼の性格を形成したのは彼が少年時代を送ったこの環境であった. His character has been molded [shaped] by the environment in which he passed his boyhood.

けいせい² 形勢はどうかね. What is the situation? | Which way is the wind blowing? |〈勝負の〉What are the chances? / 形勢がいい[悪い]. The prospects are bright [gloomy]. | Things look hopeful [dismal]. / 形勢は一変して味方の不利 [有利] となった. The tide turned against us [in our favor]. / 形勢はますます不利だ. Things are going from bad to worse.

けいせき 泥棒は裏口から入った形跡がある. There are signs that the thief [traces of the thief's having] entered the house by the back door.

けいせつ 皆様が螢雪の功成って今日めでたく卒業の日を迎えられましたことを心からお喜び申し上げます. Let me offer you my hearty congratulations on the successful completion of your studies, achieved after long years of steady application.

けいそう³ できるだけ軽装で出かけようじゃないか. Let's go out

けいそく 計測 ¶計測する measure.

けいぞく 継続 (a) continuation;《文》continuance;〈更新〉(a) renewal ¶継続する〈続く〉continue; last;〈続ける〉continue; go on with《one's work》;〈更新する〉renew /〈新聞・雑誌の〉購読を継続する renew one's subscription 《for》/ 継続的 continuous; uninterrupted / 継続的に continuously; without interruption / 継続期間 (a period of) duration / 10ヵ年継続事業 an undertaking extending over ten years; a ten-year program / 法案を継続審議にする carry a bill over to [until] the next session. 文例⇩

けいそつ 軽率〈軽はずみ〉rashness; hastiness;〈不注意〉thoughtlessness; carelessness;《文》imprudence ¶軽率な〈軽はずみな〉rash; hasty;〈不注意な〉careless; thoughtless;《文》imprudent / 軽率なことをする act [behave] hastily [rashly]; do something rash; take a rash step;《文》commit a rash act / 軽率に信じる believe too readily《that…》;《文》be credulous enough to believe《that…》.

けいだ 軽打 ¶〖野球〗a light hit.

けいたい¹ 形態 (a) form; (a) shape ⇨ かたち ¶形態学〖生物〗morphology / 形態素〖言語〗a morpheme.

けいたい² 携帯 ¶携帯する carry; bring [take] sth with one; have sth with [on, about] one / 携帯用の, 携帯に便利な portable《radios》/ hand《cameras》; pocket《dictionaries》/ 携帯燃料 canned [〖英〗tinned] fuel / 携帯品 one's belongings;《文》one's personal effects; hand baggage [luggage] / 携帯品預かり所 a cloakroom; [〖米〗a checkroom. 文例⇩

けいだい 境内 the precincts; the grounds. 文例⇩

げいだん 芸談 an artist's talk on his art.

けいだんれん 経団連〈経済団体連合会〉the Federation of Economic Organizations.

けいちゅう 傾注 ¶全力を傾注する devote oneself entirely《to》; concentrate one's efforts [energies]《on》.

けいちょう¹ 軽重〈relative〉importance ¶軽重を計る weigh the importance [《文》gravity] of sth.

けいちょう² 傾聴 ¶傾聴する listen (attentively) to《sb's talk》; be all ears [attention] / 傾聴に値する be worth listening to.

けいちょうふはく 軽佻浮薄 ¶軽佻浮薄な flippant; frivolous.

けいつい 頸椎〖解〗the cervical [neck] verte-「brae.

けいてき 警笛 an alarm whistle; a (warning) horn;〈自動車の〉a (car) horn ¶警笛を鳴らす whistle a warning; sound the alarm;〈自動車が〉sound [blow, toot] its [one's] horn; honk.

けいでんき 継電器 a relay.

けいと 毛糸 woolen yarn; worsted (yarn); wool ¶毛糸の靴下 woolen [worsted] socks / 毛糸の玉 a ball of (knitting) yarn / 毛糸で靴下を編む knit wool into socks; knit socks out of wool.

けいど¹ 軽度 ¶軽度の slight / 軽度に slightly;《文》to a slight degree.

けいど² 経度 longitude (略: long.).

けいとう¹ 系統〈組織〉a system;〈血統〉《文》lineage; descent;〈党派〉a party; a clique ¶系統を立てる《文》systematize; make sth systematic / 系統を引く be descended《from》;〈気質などが主語〉be inherited《from》; run in the family / 系統的 systematic; methodical / 系統的に systematically; methodically / バスの運転系統 bus (service) routes / 神経[消化器]系統 the nervous [digestive] system / 系統樹〖生物〗a genealogical [family] tree / 系統発生〖生物〗phylogeny; phylogenesis.

けいとう² 傾倒 ¶傾倒する devote oneself《to》;《文》be wholly devoted《to》;〈人に〉admire; adore;《文》have a great esteem (for) / 全力を傾倒する concentrate all one's energies《on》. 文例⇩

けいとう³ 鶏頭〖植〗a cockscomb.

げいとう 芸当 a performance; a feat (難しい); a stunt (離れわざ) ¶危ない芸当をする〈曲芸を演じる〉perform a risky feat [stunt];〈危ない事をする〉make a risky attempt; skate on thin ice.

げいどう 芸道 an art ¶芸道に励む《文》devote oneself to the refinement of one's art.

けいどうみゃく 頸動脈〖解〗the carotid (artery).

げいなし 芸なし a person with no accomplishments at all.

げいにん 芸人 an artiste; an [a professional] entertainer.

げいのう 芸能 public entertainment; the performing arts ¶芸能界 show business [《口語》biz]; the entertainment world / 芸能界の人々 people in show business / 芸能人 ⇨げいにん. 文例⇩

けいば 競馬 (horse) racing;〈1回の〉a horse race ¶競馬を見に行く go to the races / 競馬

---

as lightly-equipped as possible.

けいぞく 今の仕事を継続してやってみます。I will go on with my present work. / この企画の継続に大賛成です。We are all for the continuance of the project. / この薬は継続的に使用しないと効果が現われない。This drug doesn't take effect if it is not used continuously.

けいそつ 彼女の聞いている所でその話をするなんて彼も軽率だった。It was imprudent [thoughtless] of him to mention it in her hearing. / 何事も軽率にしてはいけない。Use prudence in whatever you do.

けいたい² この辞書は携帯に便利である。This dictionary is handy to carry. / 賊は凶器を携帯していなかった。The robber had [carried] no weapon with him.

けいだい 豪徳寺の境内はとても静かだった。It was very peaceful [quiet] within the precincts of Gotokuji Temple.

けいとう² 現象学を系統的に研究しようと思う。I intend to make a systematic study of phenomenology.

けいとう² 彼は漱石に傾倒している。He is an ardent admirer [a devoted reader] of Soseki.

けいはいびょう

にかける bet (money) on a horse ; bet on [《米》play the horses] / 競馬でもうける[損をする] make [lose] money on the horses [the turf] / 競馬で身上をつぶす race one's fortune away / 競馬界 a racehorse ; 競馬界 the racing world ; racing circles ; the turf ; 競馬狂 a turf fan ; a racing man / 競馬場 a racecourse ; a race track / 競馬新聞 a racing form ; 《英》a racing (news)paper.

けいはいびょう 珪肺病 《医》silicosis ¶珪肺病患者 a silicosis sufferer [victim].

けいはく 軽薄 《浮薄》frivolity ; flippancy ; 〈移り気〉fickleness ¶軽薄な《浮薄な》frivolous ; flippant ; 〈移り気〉の fickle.

けいはつ 啓発 《文》enlightenment ; education ¶啓発する 《文》enlighten ; 《文》illuminate ; educate / 知能を啓発する improve [cultivate] one's mind ; 《文》develop one's intellectual [mental] faculties. 文例◎

けいばつ 刑罰 a punishment ; a penalty ¶刑罰を加える punish ; inflict a punishment [penalty] on sb.

けいはんざい 軽犯罪 a minor offense ¶軽犯罪法 the Minor Offenses Act.

けいはんちほう 京阪地方 the Keihan district ; the Kyoto-Osaka area.

けいひ¹ 桂皮 cassia (bark).

けいひ² 経費 《費用》expense(s) ; cost(s) ; 〈支出〉expenditure(s) ; (an) outlay ¶経費がとてもかかる[かさむ] cost a lot of money ; be very expensive / 経費の都合で for financial reasons / 経費を節減する reduce [cut down (on)] costs [expenses] ; 《文》curtail [retrench] expenditures / 経費削減計画 a cost-reduction program [plan].

けいび¹ 警備 guard ; defense ¶警備する guard 《a building against [from] robbers》; keep [stand] guard 《at the entrance, over a house》; defend ; police / 警備が厳重である be strictly guarded ; be heavily policed / 警備に立っている be on guard (duty) [at the gate] / 警備員 a guard / 警備隊 a garrison ; guards / 警備保障会社 a security company [agency] ; (private) security service.

けいび² 軽微 ¶軽微な slight ; trifling ; negligible.

けいひん¹ 景品 a (free) gift ; 《米》a giveaway ¶景品を出す offer gifts [《米》giveaways] / 景品付き売り出し a sale with free gifts [giveaways] / 景品券 a gift coupon.

けいひん² 京浜 ¶京浜工業地帯 the Keihin manufacturing district / 京浜地方 the Keihin district ; the Tokyo-Yokohama area.

371

けいみょう

げひんかん 迎賓館 a guest house.

けいふ¹ 系譜 a genealogy ; a pedigree ; 《文》lineage 〈血統〉¶日本浪漫主義の系譜をたどる trace the descent of Japanese Romanticism back (to).

けいふ² 継父 a stepfather.

けいぶ¹ 頸部 《解》the neck ; the cervix (pl. -vixes, -vices) ¶頸部の cervical.

けいぶ² 警部 a police inspector ¶警部補 an assistant (police) inspector.

げいふう 芸風 〈特徴〉the style [characteristics] 《of one's performance [acting]》; 〈伝統〉the artistic tradition 《of the Kanze School》.

けいふく 敬服 ¶敬服する admire ; have a high opinion of sb [sth] ; think highly of sb [sth] ; 《文》hold sb [sth] in high esteem ; 《文》esteem sb [sth] highly / 敬服すべき admirable ; 《文》worthy of admiration [esteem]. 文例◎

けいふぼ 継父母 (one's) stepparents.

けいふん 鶏糞 fowl droppings.

けいべつ 軽蔑 contempt ; scorn ; disdain ¶軽蔑する despise ; feel contempt [scorn] for sb ; 《文》slight ; 《文》disdain ; look down on sb ; 《文》hold sb in contempt ; 《口語》look down one's nose at sb ; 《文》scorn / 軽蔑すべき contemptible ; despicable / 軽蔑的な contemptuous ; scornful ; 《文》disdainful. 文例◎

けいべん 軽便 ¶軽便な convenient ; handy / 軽便鉄道 a light railway.

けいぼ¹ 敬慕 ¶敬慕する love and respect ; adore ; admire.

けいぼ² 継母 a stepmother.

けいほう¹ 刑法 the criminal law ; 〈刑法典〉the criminal [penal] code ¶刑法上の罪 a criminal [penal] offense / 刑法学者 a scholar of [an expert in] the criminal law / 刑法改正運動 a movement [campaign] for penal reform.

けいほう² 警報 a warning (signal) ; an alarm (signal) ¶警報を出す give [raise, sound] the alarm (for a fire) ; issue a (flood, storm) warning / 警報を解除する cancel a (tsunami) warning ; 〈空襲〉give [sound] the all clear / 警報器 an alarm.

けいぼう 警棒 《米》a (policeman's) nightstick ; 《米》a billy (club) ; 《英》a (policeman's) truncheon.

けいぼうだん 警防団 volunteer guards ; 《米》a vigilance committee ; 《米》a vigilante corps.

けいま 桂馬 《将棋》a (chess) knight ; 《囲碁》a knight jump.

けいみょう 軽妙 ¶軽妙な light (and easy) ; witty ; clever ; smart / 軽妙なしゃれ a witty joke / 軽妙に lightly ; wittily. 文例◎

げいのう 彼が芸能界で成功したのはあの奇妙な形をした大きな鼻のおかげだった. It was that big, odd-shaped nose that made him a success in show business [in the field of entertainment].

けいはつ 僕が氏の著書を読んで大いに啓発されるところがあった. His book enlightened me on a lot of points. / I've learned a lot from his book.

けいひ² この企画を成功させるためなら経費は惜しまないつもりだ. I will spare no expense to make this project a success. / この仕事は経費倒れになりやしないかと心配している. I'm afraid that the cost of this project will prove prohibitive [will be its undoing].

けいふく 彼の博学には敬服する. I admire (him for) his erudition.

けいべつ 彼はそれを見てさも軽蔑したように笑った. When he saw it, he gave a scornful laugh. / '政治屋' という言葉は軽蔑的な意味で使われる. 'Politician' is used in a derogatory sense.

けいみょう なかなか軽妙な筆致だ. It is written in a light and

けいむしょ 刑務所 a prison; a jail;《英》a gaol ¶刑務所に収容する[送る] put *sb* in prison; send *sb* to prison; imprison / 刑務所に入っている be in prison;《口語》be behind bars / 刑務所長 the governor [《米》warden] of a prison. 文例⇩

げいめい 芸名 a stage [screen] name.

けいもう 啓蒙《文》enlightenment ¶啓蒙する《文》enlighten; educate / 啓蒙的《文》enlightening; illuminating;〈初歩の〉elementary / 啓蒙運動 a campaign for enlightenment /〈十八世紀ヨーロッパの〉the Enlightenment / 啓蒙時代[期] the (Age of) Enlightenment / 啓蒙哲学[文学] the philosophy [literature] of the Enlightenment.

けいやく 契約 a contract; an agreement; a promise ¶契約する[を結ぶ] contract (to *do*, with *sb* for *sth* [*doing*]); make [《文》enter into] a contract 《with》; make an agreement 《with》/ 契約を守る[履行する] fulfill [carry out] a contract [promise] / 契約を破る[解除する] break [dissolve] a contract / 3 年間の契約で work (for a firm) on [under] a three-year contract / 裏契約 a secret agreement (made in connection with a formal contract) / 仮契約 a provisional contract / 契約違反《a》breach of contract / 契約者 a party to a contract / 契約書 a (written) contract. 文例⇩

けいゆ 経由 ¶...を経由して, ...を経由する; by way of... ¶シベリア経由でモスクワに行く go to Moscow via [by way of] Siberia.

けいゆ 軽油 gas oil; light oil.

げいゆ 鯨油 whale oil.

けいよう[1] 形容 ;〈叙述〉description ;〈事物の特徴などを言い表わす語〉an epithet ;〈比喩〉a figure of speech; a figurative expression ¶形容する〈叙述する〉describe;〈比喩的に言う〉《文》express *sth* figuratively /〈事物が〉形容するに言葉がない be beyond [《文》beggar] description; be too 《beautiful》for words / 形容語[辞] an epithet / 形容詞 an adjective / 形容詞句[節] an adjective phrase [clause].

けいよう[2] 掲揚 ¶掲揚する hoist; put up; fly / 国旗を掲揚する hoist [put up] a national flag.

けいよう[3] 京葉 ¶京葉工業地帯 the manufacturing district between Tokyo and Chiba; the Tokyo-Chiba industrial zone [belt].

けいらん 鶏卵 an [a hen's] egg.

けいり 経理 accounting ¶経理部[課] the account department [section].

けいりゃく 計略 a plan; a scheme; a trick; a plot;《文》a design;《文》a stratagem ¶計略をめぐらす make [work out] a plan; devise a scheme [stratagem] / 計略にかかる fall into *sb's* trap; step into a snare set by *sb*. 文例⇩

けいりゅう[1] 係留 ¶係留する moor 《at》/〈船が〉係留してある be moored 《at the pier, to a buoy》; be riding at 《its [her]》moorings / 係留気球 a captive balloon / 係留場 moorings / 係留ブイ[柱] a mooring buoy [post].

けいりゅう[2] 渓流 a mountain torrent [stream].

けいりょう[1] 計量 measuring; weighing (重さの) ¶計量する measure; weigh / 計量器 a meter; a gauge; a weighing machine (重量の) / 計量経済学 econometrics / 計量経済学者 an econometrician / 計量コップ a measuring cup [glass].

けいりょう[2] 軽量 ¶軽量の light (cargo); lightweight (*sumo* wrestlers) / 軽量級の選手《スポーツ》a lightweight.

けいりん 競輪 a bicycle [cycle] race ¶競輪にかける bet on cycle races / 競輪場 a cycling stadium; a cycle-race track / 競輪選手 a professional cyclist; a cycle racer.

けいるい 係累《文》encumbrances; dependents (扶養家族) ¶係累が多い have [be encumbered with] a large family / 係累のない unencumbered;〈独身の〉unmarried.

けいれい 敬礼 a salute ¶敬礼をする salute (an officer); give [make] a salute 《to》/ 敬礼を受ける take the salute 《of one's men》; receive a salute 《from》.

けいれき 経歴 *one's* (past) career [record]; *one's* personal history;《文》*one's* (personal) antecedents ¶《選挙の》経歴放送[公報] a broadcast [bulletin] of the candidates' careers. 文例⇩

けいれつ 系列 a series; a system ¶企業の系列化 the grouping of enterprises / 三井系列の会社 a business firm of [belonging to, affiliated with] the Mitsui group; an affiliate of the Mitsui group.

けいれん 痙攣 a convulsion; a spasm; a twitch; cramp (脚などの筋肉の); a tic (顔面の) ¶けいれんする, けいれんを起こす〈全身が〉go into convulsions; have a convulsive fit [seizure];〈手などが〉move spasmodically; twitch (ぴくぴくする); get cramp (in *one's* leg); be seized with cramp / けいれん性の convulsive; spasmodic / けいれん的にふるえる quiver convulsively [spasmodically] / けいれん性まひ spastic paralysis.

けいろ[1] 毛色 the color of *one's* [*its*] hair; hair

---

easy style. | The writer has a happy, light touch.

けいむしょ そんなことをしていると最後には刑務所行きだぞ。You'll land up in prison if you go on that way.

けいやく 契約(の期限)が切れた。The contract has expired [terminated]. / 当社は市当局と新庁舎建築の契約を結びました。We have made a contract with the city government to build [for building] a new city hall. / その事については契約書には何も言っていない。Nothing is said about it in the contract.

けいりゃく 計略は図に当たった。The scheme succeeded. | The plan worked well. / 計略がはずれた。The scheme [plan] failed.

けいれき あの人は一体どういう経歴の人でしょう。I'd like to know (something) about his past career. / 彼は多彩な経歴の持ち主だ。He has had a very varied [checkered] career. / 彼は経歴がいいからどこにでも口があるだろう。His past record is so good that he'll be able to find a job anywhere.

けいろ[2] その発達の経路はちょっと複雑だ。The stages it has gone through in its development are

けいろ color;〈動物の〉the color of the fur; the coat color ¶毛色の変わった queer; odd; strange; curious; out of the ordinary / 毛色の変わった人 a person who is out of the common run; an odd [a strange] fellow; an oddity.

けいろ² 経路〈筋道〉a course; a route; a channel;〈段階〉a stage;〈過程〉a process ¶同じ経路をたどる follow the same course / バスの運転経路 a bus (service) route / 情報経路 a channel of information. 文例↓

けいろう 敬老 respect for the old [aged] ¶敬老の日 Respect-for-the-Aged Day; Old People's Day / 敬老の念から in [out of] deference to sb's age.

けう 稀有 ¶稀有の rare; unusual; uncommon;〈前例のない〉unprecedented; unheard-of.

けうら 毛裏 ¶毛裏の外套 a fur-lined overcoat.

げえ ¶(吐こうとして)げえという retch;《米》keck.

ケーキ (a) cake ¶ケーキ1切れ a piece [slice] of cake / 誕生日のお祝いのケーキ a birthday cake / ケーキにナイフを入れる cut the《wedding》cake. 文例↓

ゲージ a gauge.

ケース a case ¶ケースワーカー a caseworker. 文例↓

ゲート a gate;〈競馬の〉《米》a (starting) gate;《英》starting stalls ⇒もん¹, ていり (出入口). 文例↓

ゲートル〈巻きゲートル〉puttees;〈昔ヨーロッパ人が着用した皮製のゲートル〉gaiters ¶ゲートルを巻く put on [do up] one's puttees.

ケープ a cape.

ケーブルカー〈車両〉a cable car; a funicular railway coach;〈鉄道〉a cable [funicular] railway ⇒ロープウエイ ¶ケーブルカーで頂上まで行く reach the (mountain) top by cable car [by funicular].

ゲーム a game ¶ゲームの理論 game(s) theory / 2ゲーム半のゲーム差がある be 2 and a half games ahead of [behind]《the Tigers》. 文例↓

けおされる 気圧される be overawed; feel small (in sb's presence).

けおとす 蹴落とす ¶階下へけ落とす kick downstairs / 同僚をけ落として出世する win promotion at the expense of one's colleagues.

けおり 毛織り ¶毛織りの woolen / 毛織物 woolen goods [cloth, fabrics, textiles]; wool / 毛織物業 the woolen textile industry / 毛織物製造業者 a woolen manufacturer / 毛織物商 a woolen merchant.

けが 怪我〈負傷〉an injury; a wound; a cut (切り傷);《文》a hurt ¶大けが a serious injury [wound] / ちょっとだけが a slight injury / けがの功名 a lucky [chance] hit; a fluke / けがをする get [be] hurt; be injured; be wounded; get a cut / けがをさせる injure; hurt;《文》inflict an injury [a wound] on sb / けがを免れる escape (without) injury; get off unhurt / けが人 an injured [a wounded] person;〈総称〉the injured; the wounded. 文例↓
囲み「けがをする」と言っても、軽いけがの場合には get hurt; hurt oneself, 交通事故などによる「けが」には be injured, 戦争などの場合の「けが」には be wounded が使われる.

げか 外科 (the science of) surgery;〈病院の〉the surgical department ¶外科医 a surgeon / 外科手術 《undergo》a surgical operation; (need) surgery.

げかい 下界〈地上〉the earth;〈この世〉this world ¶下界を見おろす look down on the earth.

けがす 汚す〈名誉などを〉disgrace; bring disgrace on;《文》dishonor;《冒とくする》《文》defile;《文》profane (a temple) ¶家名を汚す bring disgrace on [be a disgrace to] one's family.

けがらわしい 汚らわしい〈忌まわしい〉disgusting; loathsome; repulsive; detestable;〈わいせつな〉dirty. 文例↓

けがれ 汚れ〈不浄〉《文》uncleanness;《文》impurity;《文》defilement;《文》pollution 〈汚点, 汚辱〉a stain; a blot;〈罪〉(a) sin ¶汚れのない《文》undefiled; spotless; clean; pure;《文》unsullied / 汚れを知らぬ少女 an innocent girl. 文例↓

けがれる 汚れる《文》be defiled;《文》be polluted;《文》become unclean ¶汚れた《文》unclean;《文》polluted / 汚れた金 ill-gotten gains; dirty [tainted] money / 汚れた一生 a sinful life.

けがわ 毛皮 (a) fur ¶毛皮の外套[襟巻] a fur coat [comforter] / 毛皮商 a furrier.

げき¹ 劇 a play; (a) drama ¶ラシーヌの劇 a play by Racine; a Racine play / 劇にする, 劇化する dramatize; adapt [turn] (a novel) into a play; make a dramatic version of《a story》/ 劇的な dramatic / 劇的に dramatically / 劇映画 a film with a dramatic story; a story film / 劇画 a comic strip with a dramatic story / 劇作家 a dramatist; a playwright / 劇作法 dramatics; dramaturgy / 劇詩 dramatic poetry / 〈1篇〉a dramatic poem / 劇団 a theatrical

---

ケーキ 太るからケーキは食べ過ぎないように. Don't eat too much cake, or you'll put on weight.

ケース この種の問題はケースバイケースで処理したいと思う. We'll deal with questions of this kind separately, on a case-by-case basis [depending on the circumstances].

ゲート 日本航空402便ロンドン行きのお客様は15番ゲートまでお進み下さい. Will passengers on Japan Air Lines flight 402 for London please make their way to gate fifteen. / 各系ゲートイン完了.《競馬で》They're all in.

ゲーム ゲームセット.《テニス》Game and set. | 〈一般に〉That's it! | The game's over [up]!

けが おけがをなさいましたか. Are you hurt? | Have you hurt yourself? / 乗客にけがはなかった. The passengers were unhurt. / あれはけがの勝ちさ. He won the game by a fluke.

けがらわしい 見るも汚らわしかった. It was odious to look at. | It was a really disgusting sight.

けがれ そんな物を取るのは手の汚れだ. I will not soil my hands with such things.

げき

company [troupe] / 劇団 the stage ; the theatrical world / 劇中劇 a play within a play / 劇評 dramatic criticism / 劇作家 a drama critic / 劇文学 dramatic literature.

げき² 檄 〈訴え〉 an [a written] appeal ; 〈回状〉 a circular ; 〈宣言書〉 a manifesto ((*pl.* -(e)s)) ¶檄を飛ばす issue a manifesto ((declaring that...)) ; send out circulars ((appealing to the workers for financial aid)).

げきえつ 激越 ¶激越な violent ; fiery ; 《文》 vehement / 激越な口調で in a fierce tone of voice ; 《文》 vehemently.

げきか 激化 ¶激化する get [《文》 become] (more) violent [serious] ; 《文》 intensify ; 《文》 be aggravated.

げきげん 激減 a sharp [marked] drop [fall, 《文》 decrease] ¶激減する a drop [《文》 decrease, fall off] sharply.

げきしょう 激賞 high praise ¶激賞する praise *sb* highly [to the skies] ; 《文》 be very loud [warm] in *one's* praise of *sth*.

げきじょう¹ 劇場 a theater ; a playhouse ¶劇場街 a theater district [quarter].

げきじょう² 激情 strong feeling(s) ; passion ¶激情に駆られて in a fit of passion.

げきしょく 激職 ⇨ 激務.

げきしん 激震 a severe [violent] shock [earthquake] ; [地震] a very disastrous earthquake. [文例⇩]

げきする 激する 〈興奮する〉 get [be] excited ; 〈怒る〉 be enraged ; fly into a passion (急に) ; 〈流れなどが〉 dash (against) ; 〈言葉などが〉 get [grow, 《文》 become] violent ¶岩に激する水 water dashing against the rocks / 激しやすい excitable ; inflammable ; hot-tempered.

げきせん 激戦 〈戦闘〉 a fierce battle ; desperate fighting ; 〈競争〉 a hot contest ¶激戦する fight hard [desperately] (with, against) ; fight a fierce [hard] battle (with) / (選挙の)激戦区 a closely contested constituency / 激戦地 the scene of a hard-fought battle. [文例⇩]

げきぞう 激増 a sudden [marked] rise [increase] ¶激増する increase suddenly [《文》 markedly] ; 〈水量が〉 rise [swell] rapidly.

げきたい 撃退 ¶撃退する drive [beat] ((the enemy)) back ; 《文》 repel ; 《文》 repulse.

げきちん 撃沈 ¶撃沈する (attack and) sink ((a ship)) ; send ((a ship)) to the bottom.

げきつい 撃墜 ¶撃墜する shoot [bring] down ((a plane)) ; 《口語》 down ((a plane)).

げきつう 激痛 (feel) an acute [a sharp] pain ((in the chest)).

げきど 激怒 violent anger ; rage ; fury ¶激怒する be enraged ; fly into a passion.

げきどう 激動 ¶激動する a shake violently ; 〈社会などが〉 be thrown into turmoil [《文》 a ferment] / 激動の年 a year of violent (political) change ; 《文》 a tumultuous year ; 《文》 a year of ferment.

げきとつ 激突 a crash ; a clash ¶激突する collide violently ((with)) ; crash ((into)) ; clash ((against)). [文例⇩]

げきは 撃破 ¶撃破する defeat ; crush ; smash.

げきはつ 激発 a sudden fit (of passion) ; an outburst (of temper).

げきぶん 檄文 ⇨ 檄².

げきへん 激変 a sudden [violent] change ; 《文》 a sea change ¶激変する change suddenly [violently] ; undergo a sea change.

げきむ 激[劇]務 〈職務〉 a busy post ; 〈仕事〉 hard work ; 《文》 an arduous task ¶激務についている be engaged in taxing work ; hold a busy post / 激務に倒れる break down under [《文》 succumb to] the strain of hard work.

げきやく 劇薬 〈強い薬〉 a powerful medicine ; 〈毒薬〉 (a) poison.

けぎらい 毛嫌い ¶毛嫌いする be prejudiced [biased] ((against)) ; have a prejudice ((against)) ; 《文》 have an antipathy ((to)).

げきりゅう 激流 a rapid [swift] current ; a violently rushing stream ; a torrent ¶激流に押し流される be swept away by a swift current.

げきれい 激励 (an) encouragement ¶激励する encourage *sb* ((to do)) ; cheer *sb* (on) / 激励の言葉 words of encouragement / 激励演説 a speech of encouragement ; 《口語》 a pep talk.

げきれつ 激烈 ⇨ はげしい.

げきろう 激浪 raging [angry] waves ; high [heavy] seas ¶激浪にさらわれる[のまれる] be swept away by the angry waves.

げきろん 激論 〈議論〉 a hot argument ; a heated discussion ; 〈口論〉 heated words ¶激論する argue hotly ((with *sb* about *sth*)) ; 《文》 discuss *sth* vehemently ((with *sb*)) ; have a heated discussion ((with *sb* about *sth*)).

げくう 外宮 the Outer Shrine of Ise.

けくず 毛くず flocks ; bits of down.

けけん 怪訝 ¶けげんな dubious ; suspicious / けげんそうに dubiously ; suspiciously.

げこ 下戸 [文例⇩]

げこくじょう 下克[剋]上 ¶下克上の時代 the period characterized by inferiors [those below] overthrowing their superiors [those above].

げきしん 昨夜東京に激震があった. A severe earthquake (shock) was felt in Tokyo last night.

げきせん なおも激戦が続いた. The war raged on. / ここは第2次世界大戦中の激戦地だった. A fierce battle was fought here during World War II.

げきぞう 需要が激増した. The demand (for it) showed a sharp [marked] increase. / 事故の件数が激増した. The number of accidents has increased sharply. | Accidents have increased enormously in number.

げきとつ 自由民主党と社会党の国会での激突は避けられないだろう. A clash between the Liberal Democrats and the Socialists in the Diet seems unavoidable.

げきろん 原子力発電所の安全性について激論がたたかわされた. They were engaged in a heated controversy as to the safety of nuclear power plants.

げこ 僕は下戸だ. I don't drink.

けし 彼にはけし粒ほどの良心もない. He doesn't have an ounce of conscience in him.

けしいん 手紙には6月1日付けのボストンの消印が押してあった. The letter was postmarked Boston June 1.

けさ¹ 今朝 the morning ¶今朝から since morning / 今朝早く early this morning.

けさ² 袈裟 a (Buddhist priest's) stole ¶袈裟がけに斬る cut *sb* down slantwise from the shoulder.

げざ 下座 〈寄席(蕊)などの〉 the musicians' box on the left side of the stage in a *yose*.

げざい 下剤 a purgative (medicine) ; a cathartic ; a laxative (緩下剤) ¶下剤をかける 〈自分で〉 use a purgative ; 〈他人に〉 administer a cathartic to *sb*.

げさく 戯作 〈江戸時代の〉 popular [lowbrow] literature [fiction] ¶戯作者 a popular novelist [writer].

げざん 下山 ¶下山する 〈山をおりる〉 go down [climb down, 《文》 descend] a mountain ; 〈寺を去る〉 leave a temple.

けし 〈植〉 a poppy ¶けし粒 a poppy seed / けし粒ほどの as small as a pinhead. 文例⇩

げし 夏至 the summer solstice.

けしいん 消印 a postmark ; a cancellation stamp [mark] ¶消印を押す postmark 《a letter》; cancel 《a stamp》 with a postmark ; 《英》 frank 《a letter》 / 消印器 a canceler. 文例⇩

けしかける 〈犬などを〉 set 《a dog》 on *sb* ; 〈扇動する〉 incite [《文》 instigate] *sb* 《to do》; egg [spur] *sb* on 《to do》.

けしからん 〈無礼な〉 rude ; impertinent ; insolent ; insulting ; shameful ; 〈許し難い〉 unpardonable ; inexcusable ; 〈無法な〉 outrageous ; 〈恥ずべき〉 disgraceful ¶怪しからん振る舞いをする behave rudely [outrageously] ; 〈他人に〉 take liberties with 《a woman》.

けしき 景色 scenery ; a landscape ; 〈眺め〉 a view ; a scene ¶田舎の景色 rural scenery / 美しい景色 beautiful scenery ; a picturesque [charming, lovely] view / 夜の景色 a night scene / 景色のいい場所 a beauty spot; a place with beautiful scenery ; a place commanding a fine view. 文例⇩

けしきばむ 気色ばむ get angry [《口語》 mad] ; 《文》 become indignant ; bristle with anger.

げじげじ 〈動〉 a house centipede ¶げじげじのように嫌われる be hated like a scorpion [viper] / げじげじ眉毛 thick [bushy] eyebrows.

けしゴム 消しゴム an eraser ; an india [India] rubber ; 《英》 a rubber ¶消しゴムで消す rub out (a pencil mark) with an eraser.

けしずみ 消し炭 used charcoal ; (charcoal) cinders.

けしとぶ 消し飛ぶ 〈飛び去る〉 fly off [away] ; 〈投げ飛ばされる〉 be hurled [scattered] away.

けしとめる 消し止める put 《a fire》 out ; 《文》 extinguish ; get 《a fire》 under (control).

けじめ ⇨ くべつ ¶けじめをつける make a distinction (between A and B) ; distinguish 《A from B, between A and B》 / 公私のけじめをつける draw a (sharp) line between *one's* public and private life. 文例⇩

げしゃ 下車 ¶下車する get off 《the train》 ; get out of 《the car》; leave 《the train》; 《文》 alight from 《the train》.

げしゅく 下宿 〈事〉 lodging ; 〈場所〉 *one's* lodging(s) ; 《主に英口語》 digs ¶下宿する lodge [be a lodger] 《at *sb's* house, with *sb*》; 《米》 room 《at *sb's* house, with *sb*》; 〈まかないつきで〉 board [be a boarder] 《with *sb*, at *sb's* house》 / 下宿を変える change *one's* lodgings / 下宿人 〈間借りだけの〉 a lodger ; 《米》 a roomer ; 〈まかないつきの〉 a boarder ; a paying guest (★下宿屋が, 単に商売としてやっているのではないと思わせるための婉曲的表現) / 下宿屋 a boarding house ; a lodging [《米》 rooming] house / 下宿をする run [keep] a boarding [lodging] house ; take in paying guests / 下宿料 the charge for (board and) lodging ; the rent (for a room). 文例⇩

げしゅにん 下手人 the murderer ; 《文》 the perpetrator of the murder. 文例⇩

げじゅん 下旬 the last ten days (of a month) ¶7月下旬に toward the end of July ; late in July.

けしょう 化粧 (a) make-up ¶化粧する make (*oneself*) up ; put on (*one's*) make-up ; 《口語》 do *one's* face ; 《口語》 put *one's* face on (おどけて言う時) / 化粧している 〈化粧中である〉 be putting on *one's* make-up ; 《口語》 be doing *one's* face ; 〈化粧した顔をしている〉 wear make-up / 化粧を全く[ほとんど]していない wear no [hardly any] make-up / 化粧を直す fix *one's* make-up / 化粧を落とす take off [take out] *one's* make-up / 化粧下 a make-up base ; foundation cream / 化粧水 toilet water [lotion] / 化粧せっけん toilet soap / 化粧台 a dressing table / 化粧道具 a toilet set / 化粧道具入れ a vanity case [bag] ; a dressing case / (贈答品を入れる)化粧箱 a fancy [presentation] box / 化粧箱入りの gift-boxed 《ties》 / 化粧品 〈総称〉 cosmetics ; toiletries (★石けん・歯ブラシなども含む) ; 〈その1つ〉 a cosmetic / 化粧品店(会社) a cosmetic store [firm] / 化粧部屋[室] a dressing room ; a powder room (便所と一緒の) / 化粧回し a *sumo* wrestler's ornamental apron / 化粧れんが a dressed

---

けしき 窓から見た景色はすばらしい。 The view from the window is magnificent. / この沿線には景色のいい所が多い。 There is a lot of beautiful [fine] scenery along this railroad line. / そこは景色の美しさで知られている。 The place is noted for its scenic beauty. / 景色の点ではそのあたりの田舎がおもしろみがない。 Scenically, the countryside is not interesting. | The countryside has nothing interesting to offer in the way of scenery.

けじめ あの子は勉強する時と遊ぶ時のけじめがない。 He doesn't know when to work and when to play.

げしゅく 僕は学校の近所に下宿した。 I have taken a room near the school. / 君の所の下宿料は幾らですか。 What [How much] do you pay [do they charge you] for board and lodging? / 僕の下宿料は1か月5万円です。 Board and lodging cost me 50,000 yen a month.

げしゅにん 下手人はだれだと思うか。 Who do you think committed the murder?

けじらみ 毛じらみ 〘昆〙a crab [pubic] louse; a crab.

けしん 化身 《文》(the) incarnation; 《文》(the) embodiment ¶悪魔の化身 the incarnation [embodiment] of evil; the devil incarnate.

けす 消す put 《the fire》 out; switch off 《the light》; turn off 《the gas》; 《文》 extinguish; 〈筆跡を〉erase; rub out 《pencil marks》(消しゴムで); wipe out (黒板拭きなどで); 〈線などを引いて〉cross 《strike》 (a word) out; 〈酸性・塩などを中和する〉counteract; neutralize; 〈殺す〉kill; murder; 《口語》liquidate; 《俗》rub out ¶火を消す put the fire out; extinguish the fire; 〈火事を〉get a fire under (control) / 吹いて[踏んで, たたいて]消す blow [trample, beat] out 《the flames》 / 毛布を掛けて火を消す smother the fire with a blanket / いやなにおいを消す get rid of [destroy, remove] a bad smell / カレンダーの日付に印をつけて消して行く mark off the dates on the calendar / 黒板のチョークの字を消す erase the chalk marks on [wipe the chalk marks off] the blackboard; clean [《米》erase] the blackboard / 文字をなすって消す blot a letter. 文例⇨

げす 下種 a vulgar fellow; a boor ¶げす張っている be vulgar; be boorish. 文例⇨

げすい 下水 〈排水溝〉a sewer; a drain; 〈設備〉a sewerage system; sewerage; drainage; 〈汚水〉sewage ¶下水管 a sewer pipe; a drainpipe / 下水工事 drainage [sewerage] works / 下水処理場 a sewage (treatment) plant.

ゲスト a guest ¶ゲストとして出演する make a guest appearance (in a show).

けずね 毛脛 hairy shins [legs].

けずり 削り ¶鉛筆の削りくず pencil shavings / 削り節 shavings of dried bonito.

けずる 削る 〈刃物で〉shave 《wood》, plane 《a board》 (かんなで); sharpen (a pencil) (とがらす); 〈削除する〉cross out; strike out [off]; erase; delete; 〈削減する〉reduce; cut (pare, whittle) down; 《文》curtail ¶リストから名前を削る strike sb's name off the list / 予算を削る reduce [cut down] the budget.

げせわ 下世話 ¶下世話に言う as they say in the vernacular. 文例⇨

げせん 下船 ¶下船する leave the ship; 〈上陸する〉go [come] ashore.

げそく 下足 footwear; shoes (removed before entering a Japanese restaurant, etc.) ¶下足札 a check [tally] for one's shoes / 下足番 a (checkroom) attendant in charge of (customers') footwear.

けた 桁 〈梁〉a beam; a crossbeam; a girder (橋などの); 〈そろばんの〉a reed; 〈単位〉a figure; 〈位どり〉a place ¶けたが違う be widely different [poles apart] (from); be in a different class (from); stand no comparison (with); be no match (for) / 4けたの数 a four-digit[-figure] number; a number with four figures [digits] / 1けた下[上]げる move a figure one place to the right [left] / けたはずれの天才 a man of extraordinary genius / けたはずれの安値 a fantastically [ridiculously] low price. 文例⇨

げた 下駄 (a pair of) geta; (wooden) clogs ¶下駄をはいて歩く go in geta / 下駄を預ける leave a matter in sb's hands; leave an affair [《文》the transaction of a matter] to sb [sb's discretion] / 下駄箱 a shoe [footwear] cupboard / 下駄屋 a geta store.

けたおす 蹴倒す kick sb down.

けだかい 気高い 《文》noble; 《文》high-minded; dignified; refined; 《文》lofty ¶気高さ refinement; 《文》nobility.

けたたく ¶けたたく笑う cackle.

けたたましい 〈騒々しい〉noisy; loud; wild; 〈鋭い〉piercing; shrill ¶けたたましいサイレンの音 the loud screech of a siren / けたたましく noisily; loudly; wildly.

げだつ 解脱 〘仏教〙emancipation [deliverance] from worldly attachments; salvation from the bondage of this world.

けだもの 獣 a beast; 《文》a brute ¶獣のような人 a beast of a man; a brute.

けだるい listless; lazy; 《文》languorous; 《文》languid ¶ぽかぽかしたけだるい春の日 a warm, lazy spring day / けだるさ listlessness / 《文》languor; 《文》lassitude.

げだん 下段 〈寝台車の〉the lower berth ¶刀を下段に構える hold one's sword low.

けち¹ 〈しみったれ〉stinginess; 《英》meanness; 《文》niggardliness; tightfistedness; 〈人〉a stingy [《米》cheap, 《英》mean] fellow; a miser; 《米俗》a tightwad ¶けちな, けち臭い

けしょう 一心不乱に働いているときの女性には化粧では得られない美しさがある。In a woman who is engaged heart and soul in her work we find a beauty that cannot be attained by the use of cosmetics. / 化粧品売場の女の子に聞いてみるのはどうだろう。Why don't you [we] ask the girls at the cosmetic(s) counter about it?

けす なぜ音を消してテレビを見ているの? Why are you watching TV with the sound off?

げす げすの後知恵。Fools are wise after the event.

げせわ 下世話に言うわれ鍋にとじ蓋だ。Every Jack has his Jill, as the common [popular] saying goes.

けた 2人とも金持ちだがけたが違う。They are both rich, but there's no comparison between them. / 君の答は1けた間違ってやしないかね。You've got one figure too few [many] in your answer, haven't you? / I'm afraid your answer is one figure [digit] too short [long].

けたたましい 庭からけたたましい叫び声が聞こえて来た。A shrill cry was heard in the garden. / 戸を開けるとベルがけたたましく鳴り響いた。When the door was opened, the bell rang noisily.

けつあつ 血圧が最低80最高130から最低120最高180に跳ね上がった。My blood pressure shot up from 130/80 to 180/120. ★ 130/80 は 130 over 80 と読む。

けついん 欠員が生じた。A vacancy occurred. | A position became vacant.

けつえき 運動すると血液の循環がよくなる。Exercise improves the

〈しみったれな〉 stingy; niggardly; miserly; close-fisted; tightfisted /〈みみっちい〉cheap;《英》mean;〈見すぼらしい〉poor; shabby / けちな考え a narrow-minded idea / けちな贈り物 a poor gift / けちけち金をつかう be tight [stingy,《英》mean] with one's money; spend [use] (one's) money carefully [sparingly,《文》frugally] / けちけちせずに金を使う be free [generous, liberal] with one's money; spend [use] (one's) money freely [liberally,《文》without restraint] / けちけちして金をためる save money by pinching and scraping [by penny-pinching,《文》by living frugally].

けち[2] 〈不吉〉 bad [《文》ill] luck ¶けちがつく《米口語》there is a jinx 《on》;〈事が主語〉bring bad luck 《to》;《口語》jinx / けちをつける〈水をさす〉throw [pour] cold water 《on, over》;〈難くせをつける〉find fault 《with》; criticize;《文》cavil 《at》;《口語》crab 《about》;〈けなす〉belittle; disparage.

ケチャップ ketchup;《米》catsup.

けちらす 蹴散らす 〈散らかす〉scatter sth by kicking it;〈敗走させる〉rout 《the enemy》; put 《the enemy》to rout.

けちんぼう けちん坊 a miser; a stingy [《米》cheap] fellow;《米俗》a tightwad.

けつ[1] 決〈決定〉(a) decision;〈採決〉a vote ¶決を採る put sth to the vote; take a vote on sth.

けつ[2]《米俗》the butt;《米卑》the ass;《英俗》the bum;《英卑》the arse ⇒ しり[1].

けつあつ 血圧 blood pressure ¶血圧が高い [低い] have《a》high [low] blood pressure / 血圧を計ってもらう have [get] one's blood pressure measured / 血圧計 a sphygmomanometer / 血圧降下剤 a hypotensive drug; a depressor / 血圧測定 sphygmomanometry. 文例 ⇩

けつい 決意 ⇒けっしん ¶決意を新たにする make a fresh resolve 《to do》.

けついん 欠員 a vacancy; a vacant position [post]; an opening ¶欠員を補充する fill a vacancy. 文例 ⇩

けつえき 血液 blood ¶O型の血液 O-group[-type] blood / 血液の循環 the circulation of the blood;《通俗に》(improve) one's [the] circulation / 血液型 a blood group [type] / 血液型をきめる type sb's blood / 同じ血液型を用いる〈輸血・手術などで〉match (a patient's) blood group / 血液銀行 a blood bank / 血液検査 a blood test. 文例 ⇩

けつえん 血縁 ⇒けつぞく.

けっか 欠課 ¶欠課する〈病気などで〉be absent from (do not come to) a class;〈さぼる〉《口語》cut a class.

けっか 結果 a result; a consequence; an effect;〈成果〉《文》fruit(s); a product;〈終末〉the end ¶最終の結果 a final [an end] result / その結果 consequently; in consequence; as a result / …の結果 as a [the] result of… / 結果が…となる result [end] in… / 結果論〈一般に〉being wise after the event;《論》a posteriori reasoning.

けっかい 決壊 ¶決壊する collapse; give way; be broken. 文例 ⇩

けっかく 結核 tuberculosis;《口語》T.B.（★T.B. は tuberculosis の略ではあるが, tuberculosis は医学の専門用語で, 日常語としては T.B. というのが普通. 結核にかかる get T.B.; contract tuberculosis / 結核性の tubercular; tuberculous / 結核患者 a tuberculosis patient; a case of tuberculosis / 結核菌 a tubercle bacillus / 結核療養所 a sanatorium [sanitarium] for tuberculosis; a T.B. sanatorium (hospital).

げつがく 月額 a monthly sum [amount].

けっかふざ 結跏趺坐 (assume, sit in) the lotus position.

けっかん[1] 欠陥 a defect; a fault; a flaw; a shortcoming ¶欠陥のある defective; faulty / 欠陥のない faultless; flawless; perfect / 欠陥を指摘する point out defects 《in a machine》; indicate flaws 《in an argument》/ 欠陥車 a defective car; a car with a (structural) defect. 文例 ⇩

けっかん[2] 血管 a blood vessel.

けつがん 頁岩 shale.

げっかん 月刊 ¶月刊の monthly / 月刊雑誌 a monthly (magazine). 文例 ⇩

けっき 血気 ¶血気盛んである be hot-blooded;《文》be full of youthful vigor; be in one's prime / 血気にはやる《文》be driven [carried away] by youthful ardor / 血気にはやって…する do impetuously.

けっき 決起 ¶決起する rouse oneself to action / 決起大会 a rally.

けつぎ 決議 a resolution; a decision ¶決議

---

circulation (of the blood). / あなたの血液型は何ですか. What is your blood group [type]? / 私の血液型は AB 型です. My blood group [type] is AB.

けつ[2] 試験の結果は今日発表になります. The results of the examination will be published today. / その結果はどうなるのやら私にはわかりません. I have no idea how it will turn out [what the result will be]. / これは多年苦心の結果この発明を完成したのだ. This invention is the fruit of many years of hard work [effort]. / 結果的には, 1 週間もたたぬうちに彼は首になってしまった. As things turned out, he was fired before the week was out. / それは結果論だよ. You're just being [It's easy to be] wise after the event. / 結果論だがその政策の失敗の原因はこの国の経済成長力の見通しの甘さにあった. Although this was not obvious until after the event, [With the advantage of hindsight it was clear that] the policy failed because of [an] the overoptimistic estimates of this country's potential for economic growth. / そういう結果になることは初めからわかりきっていた. It was a foregone conclusion.

けっかい 数か所で堤防が決壊した. The banks collapsed [were broken] in several places.

けっかん スペインのカルロス二世は心身共に欠陥があった. Charles II of Spain was defective in both mind and body.

げっかん その雑誌は月刊だ. The magazine comes out once a month. / The magazine is issued [published] monthly.

けっきゅう resolve 《that..., on [against] *doing*》; pass [adopt, carry] a resolution 《that..., on *do*, for [against] *doing*》; decide 《that..., on *doing*》; vote 《that..., to *do*》/ 可決議する〈決議の文句〉Be it [It is] resolved that... /決議案を提出する[決議文を手渡す] move [hand over] a resolution / 決議機関 a decision-making body [organ] / 決議事項 resolutions.

けっきゅう¹ 血球 a blood corpuscle [cell] ⇒ せっけっきゅう、はっけっきゅう ¶血球計算〈do, carry out〉a blood count.

けっきゅう² 結球《植》a head; a heart ¶よく結球したキャベツ a cabbage with a good head [a solid heart].

げっきゅう 月給 a (monthly) salary ¶月給を取る draw [get] a (large, small) salary 《from a firm》/ 20万円の月給で〈work〉at [for] a salary of 200,000 yen a month / 月給取り a salaried worker [man]; a white-collar worker / 月給日 a payday / 月給袋 a pay envelope [《英》packet]. 文例⇩

けっきょ 穴居 ¶穴居する live [《文》dwell] in a cave / 穴居時代 the cave period [age] / 穴居人 a cave man [dweller]; a troglodyte / 穴居生活 cave dwelling; a troglodytic life; troglodytism.

けっきょく 結局 when [after] all is said and done; finally; 《文》in the final analysis, 《文》ultimately; after all; in the end; in the long run. 文例⇩

囲碁「結局」の意味の after all は、He did come back after all. (結局帰って来た)のように文末で使う。after all を文頭に使うと、たとえば After all, he did come back. は「とにかく帰って来ることは帰って来たんだから、まあいいじゃないか」という意味になる。

けっきん 欠勤 absence 《from》; 《文》nonattendance 《at》¶欠勤する be absent 《oneself》《from work》; do not go [come] (to the office) / 欠勤者 an absentee; those absent / 欠勤届 a report [notice] of absence / 欠勤届を出す report *one's* absence (to). 文例⇩

けづくろい 毛繕い ¶〈動物が〉毛づくろいする groom *itself*.

げっけい 月経 menstruation; the menses; a (menstrual) period; 《通俗に》a [*one's*] period ¶月経中の女 a menstruating woman; a woman who is having her [a] period; 〈婉曲に〉a woman who is indisposed [unwell] / 月経帯 a sanitary napkin / 月経痛 menstrual pain / 《米》cramps]; period pains / 月経不順 menstrual irregularity; irregular menstruation / 月経閉止期 ⇒ こうねんき. 文例⇩

げっけいかん 月桂冠 a laurel wreath ¶月桂冠を得る《文》win *one's* laurels; 《文》carry off the palm.

げっけいじゅ 月桂樹《植》a laurel (tree); a bay tree ¶(乾燥した)月桂樹の葉《料理》a bay leaf.

けっこう¹ 欠航〈船舶の〉the cancellation of a sailing; 〈飛行機の〉the cancellation of a flight. 文例⇩

けっこう² 血行 the circulation (of the blood); ¶血行をよくする improve the circulation (of the blood) / 血行障害 (an) interruption in the circulation (of the blood).

けっこう³ 決行 ¶決行する carry out (a plan); make (a night assault); 《文》put (*one's* vow) into effect.

けっこう⁴ 結構 pretty [fairly] well; tolerably; well enough ¶結構な〈よい〉nice; good; fine; excellent; 〈すばらしい〉splendid; wonderful; 〈美味な〉delicious; sweet / 結構な品 a fine article; 〈贈り物〉a handsome [nice] present [gift] / 結構な天気 fine [nice, delightful] weather / 結構な御身分である be in an enviable [a very good] position; 《口語》be sitting pretty / それはいかにも結構だが... That's [It's] all very well, but... (★ 不満足・不同意を表わすときの決まり文句) / 結構飲める be fairly good to drink / 結構悪くない be not so [too] bad.

けっこう¹ 欠号 a missing number 《of a periodical》.

けっこう² 結合《文》(a) union; (a) combination; 《化》bonding ¶結合する《文》unite; combine 《with》; join 《with, together》; link (together [up]); 《化》bond 《with, together》/

けつぎ その決議案は国連総会で賛成多数で可決された. The resolution was carried by a majority when put [submitted] to the U.N. General Assembly.
げっきゅう うちの社員は全員月給で、日給は一人もおりません. Our workers are all paid by the month; none (of them) by the day.
けっきょく 結局どうなりましたか. How did it end [turn out]? / 結局彼は応じなかった. In the end he didn't consent. / この材料を使う方が結局は安くつくよ. It will be cheaper in the long run to use this material.
けっきん 頭痛のため今日は欠勤します. I have a headache and cannot come to work [the office] today. / 彼は病身でとかく欠勤がちだ. He has poor health, so he is irregular in his attendance at the office [so his attendance record is poor].
げっけい 普通女性は月経がないとわかった時初めて妊娠に気付くのである. A woman doesn't usually realize [isn't usually aware] that she is pregnant until she misses a menstrual period.
けっこう³ 連絡船[青森行 32便]は猛吹雪のため欠航になった. The sailing of the ferry [Flight 32 for Aomori] was canceled owing to the snowstorm.
けっこう⁴ それは結構. That's good [nice, fine]! / それで結構. That'll do. / おれの言うとおりにすると言うなら結構. If you do what I tell you, well and good. / どうしても自分の好きなようにしたいと言うなら、それも結構だ. If you insist on having it your own way, well and good. ★ この well and good は日本語の「それも結構」と同じく、皮肉をこめて、「それならこちらにも考えがある」の意となる. / 結構なものをいただきまして誠に有り難う存じます. Thank you so much for your nice present. / 現在の地位で結構です. I am quite content with [in] my present position. / その新政策は結構ずくめというわけにはいかなかった. The new policy was not

分子の結合 the bonding of molecules.
げっこう¹ 月光 moonlight ¶月光の曲《曲名》the *Moonlight Sonata* / 月光を浴びた moonlit 《gardens》; moonlight 《scenes》/ 月光を浴びて in the moonlight.
げっこう² 激高 ¶激高する get [be] excited; 《文》be incensed; be enraged; 《文》become indignant; 激高して with [in] great excitement; in a fit of passion.
けっこん¹ 血痕 a bloodstain ¶血痕のついた bloodstained.
けっこん² 結婚 (a) marriage; 《文》matrimony; 《文》a (marital) union ¶結婚する marry; get married / …と結婚する marry sb; get married to sb / 結婚ほやほやの just-married (young couples) / 結婚させる marry (one's daughter to a rich man); give (one's daughter) away (in marriage) (to); 《文》make (them) man and wife / 結婚の相手 《文》a marriage [marital] partner; 《文》one's spouse / 結婚の誓い(make) (one's) marriage [《文》nuptial] vows / 結婚の申し込み a proposal [an offer] of marriage 《to》/ 結婚を申し込む propose (marriage) to 《a girl》; make an offer of marriage (to) / 結婚を承諾する accept (sb's) (marriage) proposal / 結婚を解消する dissolve one's marriage《to, with》; divorce (one's spouse) / 幸福な結婚をする make a happy marriage《with, to》/ 結婚祝いの品 a wedding present [gift] / 結婚記念日 a wedding anniversary / 結婚行進曲 a wedding march /〈メンデルスゾーンの〉the *Wedding March* / 結婚式 a wedding [《ぢ》marriage] (ceremony) / 結婚式を挙げる hold [《文》celebrate] a wedding / 結婚生活 married life / 結婚制度 a marriage system / 結婚相談 marriage [marital] counseling / 結婚相談所 a matrimonial agency / 結婚適齢期 (a) marriageable age / 結婚届 けを出す have one's marriage registered / (蜂などの)結婚飛行 a nuptial flight / 結婚披露(ろ)宴 a wedding reception [breakfast, dinner] ★ breakfast と言っても「朝食」の意味ではない / 結婚費用 wedding expenses / 結婚指輪 a wedding ring. 文例①
けっさい¹ 決済 ⇨ けっさん, しはらい.

けっさい² 決裁 approval; decision; 《文》sanction ¶決裁する approve; 《文》sanction; decide 《on》/ 決裁を仰ぐ submit 《a matter》for sb's approval.
けっさく 傑作 a masterpiece; one's best work; 《フランス語》a chef d'oeuvre (pl. chefs d'oeuvre); 〈大失策〉a serious [gross] mistake; a blunder ¶傑作をやらかす make a complete fool [ass] of oneself; 《米俗》pull a boner. 文例①
けっさつ 結紮《外科》ligation ¶結紮する tie (up) (a blood vessel); ligate.
けっさん 決算 settlement of accounts ¶決算する settle [balance] the accounts; close the books / 決算日 a settling day / 決算報告 a statement of accounts.
げっさん 月産 monthly production; (a) monthly output ¶月産…である produce [yield, manufacture] 《1,000 tons of fertilizer》monthly [a month, per month].
けっし 決死 ¶決死の覚悟でいる be ready [prepared] to die / 決死の覚悟で進む advance in the face of death / 決死隊 a suicide corps.
けつじ 欠字 an omitted word; an omission; 《印刷》a blank (type).
げつじ 月次 ¶月次報告 a monthly report.
けっしきそ 血色素《生化》hemoglobin.
けつじつ 結実 fruition; fructification; 〈比喩的に〉《文》fruition ¶結実する bear fruit; fruit; 〈比喩的に〉bear fruit; produce (good) results.
けっして 決して ¶決して…し[で]ない definitely not…; by no means…; not…in the least; not…at all; …on no account; never… (★ never には時間の観念が含まれていて, 単なる否定の強調ではない). 文例①
けっしゃ 結社 an association; a society; a fraternity ¶結社の自由 freedom of association / 結社を作る form [organize] an association.
げっしゃ 月謝 monthly tuition; a (monthly) tuition fee.
けっしゅう 結集 ¶結集する concentrate《in a place》; rally 《around the flag》. 文例①

---

an unmixed blessing. / もっとビールをいかが. —いやもう結構. Will you have some more beer? —No, thank you. / 有り難う, みんな達者です. —それは結構です. We are all very well, thank you. —I'm glad to hear that. / それには5千円もあれば結構です. Five thousand yen will be enough for the purpose. / イギリスの夏も結構です. The summer *is* quite hot in England. / 結構なご身分ですね. How [That must be] very nice for you! | Aren't we sitting pretty then! / 日光を見ないうちは結構と言うな. Don't use the word 'marvelous' until you've seen Nikko. | Until you've seen Nikko, you haven't seen anything.

★ 英語の諺に, See Naples and die. というのがあるので See Nikko and die. と言っても通じる.
けっこん 彼は2度の結婚で 6人の子持ちになっていた. He had six children by two successive marriages. / 彼女はいい結婚をしていた. She married well. / 今日はこの神社で8組も結婚式があった. There were no less than eight marriages [weddings] in this shrine today.
けっさく 彼の昨日のスピーチは傑作だったね. His speech yesterday was a masterpiece [was quite incredible]. ★ masterpiece といっても日本語の「傑作」と同じように, 文字どおりの意味のほかに,「こっけいなものだった」とい

う皮肉の意がこめられている場合もある. quite incredible の方はほとんどの場合「(信じられないほど)ひどいものだった」の意.
けっして 彼女を説得して彼との結婚を思いとどまらせるのは決して容易なことではない. It is by no means easy to persuade her not to marry [《文》dissuade her from marrying] him. / 彼は決して悪くない. He is in no way to blame. / あの人は決してそんな事をする人じゃない. He is the last person to do such a thing. / 決してあなたを忘れません. I'll never forget you.
けっしゅう 彼らは総力を結集して難局に当たった. All of them joined forces in an all-out effort to surmount the crisis.

げっしゅう 月収 a monthly income. 文例⇩

けっしゅつ 傑出 ¶傑出する be outstanding ((at, in)); 《文》 excel ((at, in)); 《文》 be preeminent / 傑出した prominent; distinguished; marked; outstanding; 《文》 preeminent. 文例⇩

けっしょ 血書 ¶血書する write ((a petition)) in one's own blood.

けつじょ 欠如 a shortage ; (a) lack ; 《文》 (a) want ; 《文》 (a) deficiency ⇨ かく⁵, かける¹.

けっしょう¹ 血漿 blood plasma ; serum.

けっしょう² 決勝 ¶決勝戦 the final round [match, game]; the final(s); a play-off (同点又は引き分けの時の) / 決勝戦に進出する go into the finals; reach [《口語》make] the finals / 決勝戦出場者 a finalist / 決勝線 the finishing line / 決勝点に達する get to [reach] the finishing line ; break the (finishing) tape.

けっしょう³ 結晶 《作用》 crystallization ; 〈結晶体〉 a crystal; 〈成果〉 fruit(s) ¶結晶する crystallize ((into)) / 愛の結晶 《文》 the fruit of ((their, our)) union / 結晶学 crystallography / 結晶形 (a) crystal form. 文例⇩

けつじょう 欠場 ¶欠場する 〈競技会などに〉 do not take part [《文》participate] ((in)); do not play [compete, etc.] ((in)); do not enter ((for an event)).

けっしょうばん 血小板 〖解〗a (blood) platelet ; a thrombocyte.

けっしょく¹ 欠食 ¶欠食児童 undernourished [poorly-fed] children.

けっしょく² 血色 (a) complexion ; color ¶血色がいい one's color is good ; look well ; have a good [healthy, 《文》ruddy] complexion / 血色が悪い one's color is pale ; look pale [unwell]; have a pale [sallow] complexion. 文例⇩

げっしょく 月食 an eclipse of the moon ; a lunar eclipse. 文例⇩

げっしるい 齧歯類 〖動〗rodents.

けっしん 決心 determination ; 《文》 resolution ¶決心する make up one's mind ((to do)); decide ((to do, on doing, that...)); 《文》 determine ((to do, on doing, that...)) / 固く決心している be firmly determined [《文》resolved] ((to do)); be dead [quite] set on ((doing)) / 決心がつかないでいる be hesitating ((about doing, what to do)); be in two minds ((about sth, whether to do or not)); be undecided ((about)) / 決心が鈍る one's resolve [《文》resolution] weakens / 決心を固める resolve firmly ((to do)); make a firm resolution ; stiffen one's resolve / 決心を翻す give up one's resolution ; change one's mind. 文例⇩

けっしん² 結審 the conclusion of a hearing. 文例⇩

けっする 決する 〈決める〉 decide ((to do, on doing, that...)); 《文》 resolve ((to do, on doing, that...)); 《文》 determine ((to do, on doing, that...)); 〈決まる〉 come to a decision ; be decided ((on)); 〈判定する〉 judge ¶決しかねる be unable to make up one's mind ((to do)); hesitate ((about doing)).

けっせい¹ 血清 (a) serum (pl. -s, sera) ¶血清学 serology / 血清肝炎 serum hepatitis / 血清注射 (a) serum injection / 血清療法 serum treatment [therapy]; serotherapy.

けっせい² 結成 ¶結成する form ; organize / 結成大会 an inaugural meeting [rally].

けつぜい 血税 a tax paid by the sweat of one's brow.

げっせかい 月世界 the lunar world; the moon.

けっせき¹ 欠席 absence ; 《文》 nonattendance ; 《文》 nonappearance ; 〖法〗default ¶欠席する be absent ((from)); 《文》 absent oneself ((from)); fail to attend ; do not appear ; 〖法〗default / 欠席がちである have a poor attendance record / 欠席判決 judgment by default [in one's absence] / 欠席裁判を受ける be tried in one's absence [《ラテン語》 in absentia] / 欠席者 an absentee ; 〈裁判の〉 a defaulter / 欠席届 a report [notice] of nonattendance [absence] / 欠席率 (the rate of) absenteeism. 文例⇩

けっせき² 結石 〖医〗a (renal) calculus (pl. -li); a stone (in the bladder).

けっせん¹ 血栓 〖医〗a blood clot ; a thrombus (pl. -bi) ¶血栓症 ((cerebral, coronary)) thrombosis.

けっせん² 血戦 a bloody battle ; a desperate fight.

けっせん³ 決戦 a decisive battle ; 〈競技の〉 a [the] decider ; the deciding match [game, set, race] ; 〈引き分けの後の〉 a play-off ; a run-off

---

げっしゅう この仕事は月収20万円になります。I get 200,000 yen a [per] month by doing this work. | This job brings (me) in 200,000 yen a month.

けっしゅつ 漢学者として彼は傑出していた。He was quite outstanding [had no peer] as a scholar of classical Chinese.

けっしょう³ この作は彼の多年の努力の結晶である。This work is the fruit of many years' labor on his part.

けっしょく² じきに彼は血色もよくなり体重も増えた。His color soon improved, and he started to put on weight.

げっしょく あしたの晩は月食があります。There is to be a lunar eclipse tomorrow night. / 今月食だ。The moon is in eclipse.

けっしん¹ 最後まで戦う決心だ。I am determined to fight to the last. / どんなに説いても彼は決心を翻さなかった。Despite all my arguments, he stuck to his decision. / そのため彼の決心がぐらついた。That shook his resolution.

けっしん² 結審になった。The hearing was concluded [wound up].

けっせき¹ ゆうべから頭が痛くて今日は欠席してしまった。I have been suffering from a headache since last night, and I couldn't attend (school) today. / やむを得ない事情のため本日の会には欠席いたします。I regret to say that I am prevented by unavoidable circumstances from attending [being prevented at] today's meeting. / 来週は欠席させていただきます。I won't be able to come next week. / 彼は欠席裁判で死刑の判決を受けた。He was sentenced to death in absentia.

けっそく 目的達成のため我々はますます同じ結束を固くしなければならない。We must strengthen our unity [stick together with even greater resolution] in order to

けつぜん　決然　¶決然たる decisive; determined; firm;《文》resolute ∥ 決然と(して) decisively; in a decisive manner; firmly;《文》resolutely.

けっせんとうひょう　決選投票　¶決選投票を行なう hold a second [final, decisive] ballot (for an office);《口語》hold a run-off (between the two most successful candidates)).

けっそう　血相　⇒かおいろ　¶血相を変える change color ∥ 血相を変えて〈怒って〉with a menacing look;〈真っ青になって〉with a pale face.

けっそく　結束　《文》union; unity　¶結束する band [stick] together; unite; be united ∥ 結束して in a body; unitedly ∥ 結束して事に当る unite in doing; make a united effort to do. 文例⇩

けつぞく　血族 a blood relative [relation]　¶血族関係 blood relationship; ties of blood; consanguinity ∥ 血族結婚 (a) consanguineous marriage ∥ 代々血族結婚をしている家族 an inbred family.

げっそり　¶げっそりする〈気を落とす〉be disheartened; be disappointed ∥〈やせる〉lose a lot of weight; grow very thin.

けっそん　欠損〈不足額〉a deficit;〈損失〉a loss　¶欠損を生じる[きたす] suffer [result in] a loss ∥ 欠損を補う cover [make up (for)] a loss. 文例⇩

けったい　結滞《医》a pause [an intermission] in the pulse. 文例⇩

けったいな　⇒おかしい.

けったく　結託 (a) conspiracy;《文》collusion ¶結託する conspire (with);《文》collude ((with))∥ ...と結託して in conspiracy [collusion] with....

けったん　血痰《bring up》bloody phlegm.

けつだん　決断 (a) decision; (a) determination; (a) resolution ¶決断する decide ((to do, on doing, that...));《文》resolve ((to do, that...));《文》determine ((to do, that...)) ∥ 決断が早い be prompt in one's [make quick] decisions ∥ 決断力のある人 a decisive person;《文》a man of decision ∥ 決断力に乏しい lack decision;《文》be irresolute. 文例⇩

けつだんしき　結団式 an inaugural meeting [rally] (to celebrate the formation [organization] of a party [delegation]).

けっちゃく　決着〈終結〉a conclusion; an end;〈解決〉(a) decision; (a) settlement　¶決着がつく end; come to an end; be settled ∥ 決着がつかない be still [《文》remain] unsettled; be pending ∥ 決着をつける settle; bring sth to an end [a conclusion]. 文例⇩

けっちょう　結腸《解》the colon.

けっちん　血沈〈反応〉blood sedimentation [precipitation];〈速度〉a blood sedimentation [precipitation] rate ¶血沈を計る measure the precipitation of sb's blood.

けってい　決定 (a) decision; (a) settlement;《文》(a) determination; (a) conclusion ¶決定する〈きめる〉decide ((to do, on doing, that...)); settle ((that..., on sth)); fix ((on sth));《文》determine ((to do, that...));〈きまる〉be decided (on); be settled [《文》determined]; come to [reach] a decision ∥ 日取りを決定する fix [set] the date (for) ∥ 決定的 definite; final; decisive ∥ 決定的瞬間 a crucial moment ∥ 決定権 the say;〈権利〉the right to decide;〈力〉the power of decision ∥ 決定打〈野球の〉a winning hit;〈議論などの〉a remark that decides an argument;《口語》a clincher ∥ 決定版 a definitive edition ∥ 決定論《哲》determinism. 文例⇩

けってん　欠点〈きず〉a fault; a defect; a blemish;〈弱点〉a flaw;〈落第点〉a failure [fail] mark ¶欠点のある faulty; defective ∥ 欠点のない faultless; flawless; perfect ∥ 欠点がない be free from faults; be perfect ∥ 欠点を捜す find fault with sb [sth]. 文例⇩

けっとう¹　血統 a family line; (a) pedigree;《文》blood; (a) lineage ¶血統がよい〈動物が〉have a good pedigree;《文》be of good stock [of a good line] ∥〈人が〉come from a good family; be of good stock [family] ∥ 血統のよい[血統書つきの]犬 a pedigree dog ∥

けっそん このために 1 千万円の欠損となった。This caused a deficit of 10 million yen. / 欠損続きで皆がっかりだ。A series of losses [One loss after another] has discouraged us all.

けったい 脈に結滞があった。His pulse was beating intermittently. / His heart was skipping beats.

けつだん だれにも瞬間的に決断を下さねばならぬときがあるものだ。There are times when one has to make a snap decision. / 決断力に欠ける人は責任ある地位にはつけない。A man who lacks decision cannot hold a position of responsibility.

けっちゃく 戦いは決着がつかなかった。The battle was [proved] inconclusive.

けってい 遠足はこの次の土曜日と決定した。The date of our excursion was fixed for next Saturday. / 彼の後任はすでに決定した。His successor has already been chosen. / 決定権は君にある。The decision is in your hands. / It rests [lies] with you to decide. / この問題では彼には決定権はなかった。He had no say in this matter. / 彼の言葉が決定打となった。His remark clinched [decided] our argument. / これこそ近代歌劇場の決定版だ。This is the last word in modern opera houses.

けってん それがあの人の欠点だ。〈性格の〉That is a blemish in his character. |〈弱点〉That is his weak point. | 欠点のない人はない。No one is free from faults. |《文》There is no man but has some faults. | 地震の多いのが日本の欠点だ。The frequency of earthquakes is one serious drawback of Japan. / 早口だけが欠点で、いい先生だ。The only thing we have against him is that he speaks too fast, but he is a good

けっとう フランス人の血統である be of French extraction [descent]. 文例⇩

けっとう² 血糖 sugar in the blood; blood sugar ¶血糖値を下げる lower the level of sugar in the blood; lower sb's blood-sugar level.

けっとう³ 決闘 a duel; a shoot-out (ガンマン同士の) ¶決闘する duel [fight a duel]《with sb, over sth》/ 決闘を申し込む challenge sb to a duel / 決闘の申し込みに応じる accept sb's challenge to a duel / 決闘者 a duelist / 決闘用ピストル a dueling pistol.

けっとう⁴ 結党 the founding [formation] of a party ¶結党する found [form, organize] a party / 結党の精神 the principles on which a political party is formed [organized] / 結党式 the ceremony of inauguration《of a new political party》.

ゲットー a ghetto (pl. -s).

けつにょう 血尿〈尿〉bloody urine;〈症状〉hematuria.

けっぱい 欠配《配給品の》nondelivery of rations;〈給料の〉nonpayment of wages. 文例⇩

けっぱく 潔白 ¶潔白な〈罪のない〉innocent;《文》guiltless;〈清廉な〉《文》upright ⇒せいれんけっぱく / 身の潔白を証拠だてる prove [establish] one's innocence;《文》vindicate oneself《from a charge of theft》. 文例⇩

けっぱつ 結髪 hairdressing ⇒かみ⁴《髪を結う》.

けつばん 欠番 a missing number.

けっぱん 血判 ¶血判する seal 《a written pledge》with one's blood.

けっぴょう 結氷 ice formation; freezing ¶結氷する ice forms; freeze [be frozen] over / 結氷を防ぐ prevent ice formation; deice.

げっぷ¹ 月賦 payment in [by] monthly installments; monthly payments ¶月賦で買う[売る] buy [sell]《a TV set》on the installment plan [《英》on hire purchase] / 月賦で2千円ずつ払う pay《for an article》in monthly installments of 2,000 yen《over a period of 18 months》/ 月賦販売 installment selling;〈方法〉《米》the installment plan;《英》hire purchase. 文例⇩

げっぷ² belching; a belch;《口語》a burp ¶げっぷが出る《人が主語》belch;《口語》burp /《赤ん坊に》げっぷをさせる burp《a baby》.

けつぶつ 傑物 a great man;《文》a giant among men;《文》a man of great caliber.

けっぺき 潔癖《excessive》fastidiousness; a love of [an obsession with] cleanliness ¶潔癖家 a stickler for cleanliness; a person who is fastidious about cleanness; a person who has very strict ideas of cleanliness [《文》probity].

けつべつ 訣別 ⇒ わかれ, わかれる.

けっぺん 血便 bloody feces.

けつぼう 欠乏 (a) shortage; (a) scarcity; (a) lack;《文》(a) want ¶欠乏する be [run] short of sth; lack; be lacking in sth;《文》want;《文》be wanting in sth;《文》be deficient in sth /《ビタミンなどの》欠乏症 a《vitamin-》deficiency disease. 文例⇩

げっぽう 月報 a monthly report [bulletin]. 文例⇩

けつぼん 欠本 a missing volume.

けつまく 結膜《解》the conjunctiva (pl. -s, -vae) ¶結膜炎 conjunctivitis / 流行性結膜炎 epidemic [contagious] conjunctivitis; pinkeye.

けつまつ 結末〈終わり〉an end;《文》a close; a conclusion;〈落着〉settlement;〈結果〉a result;《文》an issue; an outcome;〈物語などの〉《文》the denouement; the catastrophe (悲劇的な) ¶結末がつく come to an end [a conclusion]; be settled / 結末をつける bring sth to an end [a conclusion, a close]; put an end to sth; settle.

げつまつ 月末 the end of the month ¶月末に[近くなって] at [toward] the end of the month.

けづめ 蹴爪《鶏などの》a spur.

げつめん 月面 the surface of the moon ¶月面車 a lunar rover; a moon buggy [car] / 月面図 a selenographic chart / 月面歩行 a moon [lunar] walk.

けつゆうびょう 血友病 hemophilia ¶血友病患者 a hemophiliac.

げつよう(び) 月曜(日) Monday (略: Mon.) ⇒ にちようび.

けつらく 欠落〈欠如〉(a) lack;《文》(a) want;〈脱漏〉(an) omission ⇒ かく⁵, かける¹, ぬける.

けつれい 欠礼 ¶欠礼する fail [《文》omit] to pay one's compliments [to offer one's greetings].

げつれい¹ 月例 ¶月例の monthly / 月例委員

---

teacher.

けっとう¹ その血統は今は絶えてない。The (family) line has died out [become extinct].

けっぱい これで1週間欠配だ。We have had no rations for a week.

けっぱく 彼は自分は潔白であると言い張った。He insisted that he was innocent [that his hands were clean].

げっぷ¹ 彼は2年月賦でピアノを買った。He bought a piano on the installment plan to be paid for over a period of two years.

けつぼう 彼らは資金が欠乏しているようだ。They seem to be short of funds.

けっぽん この全集は1冊欠本になっている。One volume is missing from this set.

げつまつ 月末までにはこの仕事を終わります。I'll finish this work by the end of this month [before the month is out].

けつれつ 交渉は決裂した。The negotiations broke down.

けつろん この事故の責任は彼らにある、と結論せざるを得ない。It is hard to escape [We are driven to] the conclusion that they are to blame for the accident. / この ことからその船はフロリダ沖で沈没したに違いない、という結論に達したのだ。From this we concluded [drew the conclusion] that the ship must have sunk off Florida. / 彼らは両案の長所短所を論じたが、結論に達しなかった。They had an inconclusive debate about the relative merits (and demerits) of the two proposals.

げてもの 陶器が好きだと言っても、彼には下手物趣味だ。It's true that he's fond of porcelain, but actually what he likes are inexpensive, folksy things rarely noticed by ordinary people.

げつれい 月齢 the age of the moon.

けつれつ 決裂 a breakdown ; (文) (a) rupture ¶決裂する break down ; be broken off ; (文) come to [end in] (a) rupture.

けつろ 血路 ¶血路を求める[開く] find a way out 《of the difficulties》; cut [fight] one's way 《through the enemy line》.

けつろん 結論 a conclusion ; a concluding remark (講演などの) ¶結論する, 結論に達する, 結論を下す conclude 《that...》; reach [arrive at, come to] the conclusion 《that...》; form [draw] the conclusion 《that...》/ 結論を急ぐ[早まる] jump to conclusions ; form a hasty conclusion / 結論として in conclusion ; to conclude. 文例⇩

げてもの 下手物 〈工芸品〉a piece of folkcraft ; 〈変ったもの〉a strange [an odd] thing. 文例⇩

げどく 解毒 〖医〗detoxification ; detoxication ¶解毒する counteract [neutralize] poison ; detoxify ; detoxicate / 解毒剤 an antidote ; a detoxicant.

けとばす 蹴飛ばす 〈足で〉send sb flying with a kick ; kick ; 〈断わる〉reject ; refuse ; turn down.

けどる 気取る ⇨ きづく, かんづく.

けなげ 健気 ¶けなげな 〈雄々しい〉heroic ; brave ; くりっぱな〉admirable ; (文) laudable.

けなす run sb down ; abuse ; disparage ; (文) speak slightingly [ill] of sb.

けなみ 毛並み 〈毛の生えぐあい〉the lie of 《a dog's》hair ; 〈血筋〉lineage ¶毛並みが 〈動物が〉have a good [fine] coat of fur [hair] ; 〈出身が〉come of a good family ; be a person of high birth.

げなん 下男 a (male) servant ; a manservant 《pl. menservants》.

ケニア Kenya ¶ケニアのa Kenyan / ケニア共和国 the Republic of Kenya / ケニア人 a Kenyan.

けぬき 毛抜き (a pair of) tweezers ¶毛抜きでとげを抜く pluck [pull] a thorn out 《of one's finger》with tweezers.

げねつ 解熱 ¶解熱する lower [reduce] sb's temperature ; alleviate fever / 解熱剤 an antifebrile (drug) ; an antipyretic ; a febrifuge.

けねん 懸念 fear ; anxiety ⇨ しんぱい. 文例⇩

けば (a) nap ; fluff ¶けば立てる raise a nap (on) ; fluff (up) / けば立った《cloth》with a nap ; nappy ; fluffy.

けはい 気配 an indication ; a sign. 文例⇩

けはえぐすり 毛生え薬 a hair restorer.

けばけばしい showy ; gaudy ; loud ¶けばけばしい色のシャツ a loud [violent-colored] shirt / けばけばしく装う dress oneself showily ; be gaudily [flashily] dressed.

げばひょう 下馬評 common gossip ; (a) rumor ¶下馬評では according to rumor ; rumor has it that.... 文例⇩

けばり 毛鉤 a [an artificial] fly.

ゲバ(ルト) 〖〈ドイツ語〉Gewalt〗 violence ; force ⇨ ぼうりょく / ゲバ棒 a stave (carried by an activist student).

げびた 下卑た ⇨ げひん (下品な).

けびょう 仮病 (a) pretended [(口語) faked, (文) feigned] illness ¶仮病を使う pretend to be ill ; (文) feign illness.

げひん 下品 ¶下品な vulgar ; (文) low ; (文) mean ; 〈卑わいな〉dirty. 文例⇩

けぶかい 毛深い hairy 《legs》; shaggy 《dogs》.

ケベック Quebec.

けぼり 毛彫り hairlines (on an engraving).

けまり 蹴鞠 〈遊び〉*kemari* ; a type of football played by courtiers in ancient Japan ; 〈まり〉a football.

けむ 煙 ⇨ けむり ¶けむに巻かれる 〈あっけにとられる〉be bewildered ; be mystified.

けむい 煙い smoky. 文例⇩

けむくじゃら 毛むくじゃら ⇨ けぶかい.

けむし 毛虫 a hairy caterpillar ; a woolly bear (caterpillar) ¶毛虫のように嫌う hate sb like poison.

けむたい 煙たい 〈煙い〉⇨ けむい ; 〈気がねな〉文例⇩

けむり 煙 smoke ¶一条の煙 a wisp of smoke / もうもうたる煙 clouds [volumes] of smoke / 煙が立ちこめる〈場所が主語〉be filled with smoke / 煙と消える〈希望などが〉go up in smoke ; 〈跡形なく消える〉vanish [melt] into thin air / 煙を出す give out [pour out, (文) emit] smoke / 煙に包まれる be enveloped [(文) wreathed] in smoke / 煙に巻かれる be overcome by smoke / 煙に巻かれて死ぬ be suffocated [choked] to death by smoke / 煙

けねん 私は彼が試験に落ちしないかと懸念している。I am worried that he will fail the examination. / その点については一切ご懸念は無用です。You may set your mind at rest on that point. / 彼はまた戦争になるのではないかという憂色を表明した。He expressed anxiety that war would break out again.

けはい その家には人のいる気配が全くなかった。There was no sign of life in the house. / 彼には自殺なんかしそうな気配は少しもなかった。There was nothing in his look or manner to show that he would commit suicide. / あらしになりそうな気配があった。There were indications of a coming storm [that a storm was coming]. / 人の来る気配がした。I sensed someone approaching.

げばひょう 下馬評では彼が副総裁に選ばれるだろうということだ。The talk is [There are rumors] that he will be elected vice-president.

けびょう 彼の病気は仮病だ。His illness was a fake [was nothing more than play-acting].

げひん あんな口のきき方をするなんて, 下品な女だねえ。It's very vulgar of her to speak like that. / 見る物すべてに値段を言うなんて下品なことだ。It's bad taste to put a price on everything.

けむい 煙いなあ。What a lot of smoke ! / 煙くて涙が出た。The smoke made my eyes water.

けむたい 煙たい男だ。I always feel ill at ease in his presence. / 僕をそんなに煙たがらなくてもいいだろう。Don't fight shy of me like that. / 若い同僚たちはたいがい彼を煙たがっていた。His younger colleagues were rather afraid of him.

けむる 煙る ⟨くすぶる⟩ smoke; smolder; ⟨かすむ⟩ be hazy; appear dim 《in the distance》. 文例⇩

けもの 獣 a beast; an animal ¶けもの道 an animal [a game] trail.

けやき 〘植〙 a keyaki; a Japanese tree of the genus Zelkova.

けやぶる 蹴破る kick 《a door》in [open]; break 《a door》open by kicking it.

けら 〘昆〙 a mole cricket.

ゲラ 〘印刷〙 a galley ¶ゲラ刷り a galley proof; a proof (sheet).

けらい 家来 a retainer; a vassal; a follower; one's men (総称).

げらく 下落 a fall; a decline ¶石炭価格の下落 a fall [decline] in the price of coal / 下落する fall (off); decline; go [come] down.

けらけら ¶けらけら笑う cackle. 文例⇩

げらげら ¶げらげら笑う guffaw; give a horse-laugh; cackle.

ケラチン 〘化〙 keratin.

けり ¶けりがつく be settled; be brought to an end / けりをつける settle; finish; bring sth to an end. 文例⇩

げり 下痢 〘医〙 diarrhea ¶下痢している have loose bowels; suffer from [have] diarrhea / 下痢止めa medicine for diarrhea.

ゲリラ ¶ゲリラ戦 guerilla warfare [fighting] / ゲリラ戦術 guerilla tactics / ゲリラ部隊 a guerilla band / ゲリラ兵 a guerilla.

ける 蹴る ⟨足で⟩ kick; give sth [sb] a kick; ⟨拒絶する⟩ reject; refuse; turn down ¶波をけって進む plow (through) the waves / 馬にけられる be kicked by a horse; get a kick from a horse. 文例⇩

ゲル 〘化・物〙 (a) gel.

ケルト ¶ケルト語 Celtic / ケルト人 a Celt / ケルト人[語]の Celtic.

ゲルマニウム 〘化〙 germanium.

ゲルマン ¶ゲルマン人 a German; a Teuton / ゲルマン民族 the Germanic peoples [races].

ケルン 〘登山〙 a cairn.

げれつ 下劣 ¶下劣な ⟨文⟩ base; ⟨文⟩ mean; low. 文例⇩

けれど(も) but; however; though; although; (and) yet ¶粗末だけれども住み心地のいい部屋 a humble but comfortable room; ⟨文⟩ a comfortable, though humble, room. 文例⇩

けれん ⟨俗受けをねらった演技⟩ playing to the gallery; ⟨はったり⟩ showing off; ⟨ごまかし⟩ a trick.

ゲレンデ [<⟪ドイツ語⟫ Gelände] a ski slope ★複数形で使われることが多い.

ケロイド a keloid (scar) ¶ケロイド(状)の keloidal / 背中がケロイドになっている have keloid scars on one's back.

けろりと ⟨すっかり⟩ entirely; ⟨平気で⟩ nonchalantly; as if nothing had happened. 文例⇩

けわしい 険しい ⟨傾斜が急な⟩ steep; ⟨文⟩ precipitous; ⟨厳しい⟩ severe; grim ¶険しい山道 a steep [rugged, treacherous] mountain path / 険しい顔をする look sternly 《at》; scowl 《at》.

けん¹ 件 a matter; an affair; a case (訴訟などの); a subject (問題) ¶盗難件数 the number of cases of theft. 文例⇩

けん² 妍 beauty ¶妍を競う ⟨文⟩ vie 《with one another》in beauty.

けん³ 券 a ticket; a coupon ⇒きっぷ¹.

けん⁴ 県 a prefecture ¶県の prefectural / 県花 a prefectural flower / 県下の[で] in [throughout] the prefecture / 県外の[で] outside the prefecture / 三重県人会 an association of people from Mie Prefecture / 県税 a prefectural tax. 文例⇩

けん⁵ 剣 a sword ⇒かたな.

けん⁶ 兼 ¶総理大臣兼外務大臣 Prime Minister and (concurrently) Minister of Foreign Affairs / 書斎兼応接間 a study-cum-drawing room, a room used both as a study and for receiving visitors; a study in which one also sees one's guests.

けん⁷ 険 ¶険のある stern (looks); strong (features); stinging 《words》.

けん⁸ 圏 a sphere; a range; a bloc ¶…の圏内[外] within [out of] the sphere [range] of… / (当選・入賞などの)圏内[外]にある be in [out of] the running ⇒とうせん.

けん⁹ 間 a ken (=1.82 m) ¶間数 the length [breadth] 《of a room》in ken.

けん¹⁰ 腱 〘解〙 a tendon.

けん¹¹ 鍵 ⟨ピアノなどの⟩ a key ¶黒[白]鍵 a

けむり 煙突から煙が出ている. Smoke is rising from the chimney. | The chimney is giving out smoke. / 屋根から煙がもうもうと立ち上っていた. Dense smoke was pouring up from the roof. / 彼はタバコの煙をぷっと彼女の顔に吹きかけた. He blew cigarette smoke into her face. / 100万円が煙になった. A million yen went up in smoke.

けむる 東山は雨に煙っていた. The Higashiyama Hills could be seen only dimly in the rain.

げらく 砂糖の値段は2割方下落した. The price of sugar has fallen [declined] by 20 per cent. / 物価は下落の傾向にある. Prices are coming down [tending to fall].

けり 何とかうまく話のけりをつけてもらいたい. I want you to settle the matter somehow.

ける 彼は席をけって退席した. He stormed indignantly out of the room.

げれつ 彼は品性が下劣だ. He has a mean character.

けれど(も) 最善を尽くしたのだけれどもうまくは行かなかった. I did my utmost, but it didn't come off [turn out well]. / それはたしかに困難な時期ではあったけれども, 楽しい時もあったのだ. It was certainly a difficult time; however, there were amusing moments. / 彼は若いけれどもなかなか考えがある. Though he is young [Young as he is], he is no fool. / 彼は全力を尽くしたけれども失敗した. He failed, for all his efforts. / 今夜はお伺いします. 長居はできませんけれど. I will come tonight; I cannot stay long, though.

けれん けれん(味)の多い男だ. He is quite a showman.

けろりと 病気がけろりと直ってしまった. He has recovered (from

black [white] key.

-けん …軒 ¶この通りの2,3軒先に 《be》 a few doors up [down] this street / 僕の家から3軒目に 《live》 three doors from my house;《live》three doors away from me.

げん¹ 言 a word; a remark; a statement ¶言を左右にする do not commit *oneself*;《文》equivocate / 言を左右にして on one pretext or another.

げん² 弦 〈弓の〉 a bowstring; 《幾何》a chord.

げん³ 舷 the side of a ship; the gunwale; the gunnel.

げん⁴ 絃 a string; a chord.

げん⁵ 現 ¶現に〈現実に〉 actually; 〈自分の目で〉with *one's* own eyes; 〈例えば〉for instance / 現内閣 the present Cabinet.

げん⁶ 減 ¶5割減になる reduce [《文》decrease, be reduced] by 50 per cent.

げん⁷ 厳 ¶厳に strictly; rigidly / 厳に過ぎる be too strict [severe]. 文例⇩

げん⁸ 験〈ききめ〉⇒ きため;〈縁起〉⇒ えんぎ².

げん⁹ 元《中国史》Yüan ¶元朝 the Yüan dynasty.

けんあく 険悪 ¶険悪な〈天候などが〉 threatening; stormy; 〈事態が〉 serious;《文》grave / 険悪な空 a threatening sky. 文例⇩

げんあつ 減圧 reduction of pressure; decompression ¶減圧する reduce the pressure《of》; decompress.

けんあん 懸案 an outstanding [a pending] problem [question] ¶多年の懸案 a long-pending[-standing] question / 日米間の懸案 a problem pending between Japan and the United States. 文例⇩

げんあん 原案 〈議案〉the original bill; 〈計画〉the original plan; 〈草案〉a draft ¶原案を作成する make [prepare] a draft (plan)《of》/ 原案どおり可決する pass 《a bill》in 《its》original form [without amendment].

けんい 権威 〈権力〉 authority; power; 〈大家〉an authority 《on》¶親の権威 parental authority / 世界的権威 a world authority 《on》/ 権威のある authoritative;《文》(a scholar) of authority / 自分の言葉に権威を添えるための引用 quotations to lend [give] authority to *one's* statement / 権威主義 authoritarianism / 権威主義者 an authoritarian / 権威筋《according to》authoritative sources. 文例⇩

けんいざい 健胃剤 ⇒ しょうか²(消化剤).

けんいん¹ 牽引 traction ¶牽引する pull;《文》draw; haul / 牽引車 a tractor / 牽引力 (force of) traction; pulling power [force].

けんいん² 検印 ¶検印を押す put *one's* seal [stamp] (of approval)《on》;《文》affix a seal [stamp] (of approval)《to》. 文例⇩

げんいん¹ 原因 a cause;〈根源〉the origin; the source ¶…に原因する be caused by…; start [《文》arise] from…; be due to…; result from… / 原因を究明する try to find the cause 《of》/ 原因を *sth* to *its* origins / 原因結果 cause and effect. 文例⇩

げんいん² 減員 ¶減員する reduce the staff [personnel]《by 10 per cent》.

けんうん 絹[巻]雲《気象》a cirrus 《*pl*. -ri》; a cirrus cloud.

けんえい 県営 ¶県営の prefectural 《housing developments》.

げんえい 幻影 ⇒ まぼろし.

けんえき¹ 検疫 quarantine; medical inspection ¶検疫を受ける be quarantined; be put in quarantine / 検疫所[官, 期間] a quarantine station (officer, period).

けんえき² 権益 (rights and) interests ¶権益を守る protect *one's* interests《in a foreign country》.

げんえき¹ 原液 an undiluted solution 《of》.

げんえき² 現役 ¶現役の軍艦 a warship in commission; a warship on [in] active service / 現役の将校 an officer on [in] active service; an officer on the active list / 現役の選手 a player on the active list / 《受験生が》現役で合格する pass 《a college entrance examination》directly on graduation (from high school).

けんえつ 検閲 〈刊行物などの〉censorship;〈点検〉inspection ¶新聞の検閲 press censorship / 検閲する 〈刊行物などを〉censor;〈点検する〉inspect; examine / 検閲を受ける be censored; be submitted for [《文》subjected to] censorship / 検閲を通る pass censorship [the censor] / 検閲を受けていない uncensored《news》/ 検閲にひっかかりそうな censorable《language》/ 検閲済みの censored《news》/ 検閲係[官]〈刊行物の〉a censor;〈検査官〉an inspector.

けんえん 犬猿 ¶犬猿の仲である《A and B》are like cat and dog; be on bad terms《with》. 文例⇩

---

his illness) very quickly. / 彼はけろりとして帰って来た。 He returned home as if nothing had happened.

けん¹ あの件はどうなりましたか。What became of that matter?

けん⁴ 彼は千葉県人です。 He comes from [He's a native of] Chiba Prefecture.

けん⁷ それは厳として存在する事実だ。 It is an undeniable fact [a grim reality].

けんあく 事態が険悪になってきた。 The situation has become serious [has been getting uglier]. / 天候がはなはだ険悪だ。 The sky looks very threatening.

けんあん その問題はまだ懸案になっている。 The question is still unsettled. / これは未だに両国間の懸案になっている厄介な問題だ。 This is a very difficult problem outstanding between the two countries.

けんい 彼は部下に対して権威がない。 He has no authority over his subordinates. / この問題に関して権威のある書物が欲しい。 I want to get an authoritative book on this subject.

けんいん² この本には著者の検印がない。 This book does not have the author's seal [imprint].

げんいん¹ どういう原因で戦争が起こったのか。 What has caused [was the cause of] the war? / 病気の原因は食事にビタミンが不足しているためかもしれない。 The disease may be due to a diet poor in vitamins. / A dietary deficiency of vitamins may be responsible for the disease.

けんえん 2人は犬猿の仲だ。 They are at daggers drawn (with each other). / They always fight like

けんお 嫌悪 (a) hatred; (a) dislike; disgust; 《文》 an aversion / 《文》 repugnance ¶嫌悪する hate; dislike; detest; 《文》 abhor; loathe / 嫌悪すべき hateful; detestable; disgusting; loathsome; abominable / 嫌悪の念をいだく have a hatred (for); have [feel] an aversion (to). 文例⇩

けんおん 検温 ¶検温する take sb's temperature / 検温器 a (clinical) thermometer.

けんか 堅果 【植】a nut.

けんか ＜口論＞ a quarrel; a squabble (くだらない); 《口語》 a fight; ＜論争＞ a dispute; ＜暴力を含んだ＞ a fight; a brawl (荒々しい); a scuffle (つかみ合い) ¶けんかする＜quarrel [have a quarrel]《with sb over [about] sth》; have words《with》; ＜仲たがいする＞ fall out 《with sb over sth》; ＜暴力を用いる＞ fight; scuffle / けんかの種 the reason for [cause of] a quarrel; a bone of contention / けんかを仕掛ける[売る, 吹っかける] pick [《文》 seek] a quarrel [fight] with sb / けんかを買う accept a [sb's] challenge (to a quarrel); 《文》 pick [take] up the gauntlet / けんかになる ＜口語に＞ start quarreling; get into an argument [《文》 altercation]《with sb over sth》; turn into a quarrel (事が主語); ＜なぐり合いの＞ start fighting; get into a fight《with》; come to blows《with》; turn into a fight (事が主語) / けんか腰になる take a truculent [defiant] attitude / けんか好きな quarrelsome / けんか別れする part (from sb) in anger. 文例⇩

げんか 言下 ¶言下に答える answer [reply] promptly; make a prompt reply / 言下に否定する ＜直ちに＞ deny promptly; ＜きっぱりと＞ deny flatly.

げんか 原価 the cost (price) ¶原価で at cost / 原価以下で below cost / 原価計算 cost accounting / 原価計算係 a cost accountant [clerk].

げんが 原画 an original picture [painting].

けんかい 見解 an opinion; a view ¶見解が一致する have [《文》 hold] the same opinion 《as》; agree《with》; see eye to eye《with》; 《文》 be at one《with》 / 見解を異にする have a different opinion《from》; disagree《with》. 文例⇩

けんかい 県会 a prefectural assembly ¶県会議員 a member of a prefectural assembly.

けんがい 懸崖 an overhanging cliff; a precipice ¶懸崖作りの菊 a cascade chrysanthemum.

げんかい 限界 limits; a limit; 《文》 bounds ¶限界を置く[定める] set limits [a limit]《to》; limit / 限界効用逓減の法則《経済》the law of diminishing marginal utility / 限界生産力 marginal productivity. 文例⇩

げんがい 言外の implied; unexpressed ¶言外の意味をとる catch the implied meaning 《of》; read between the lines.

けんかく[1] 剣客 a swordsman; a fencer.

けんかく[2] 懸隔 ⇒へだたり.

けんがく 見学 ¶見学する visit [tour]《a factory》(for information); 《体育の授業などを＞ observe; look on / 見学に行く make a field trip to《a museum [shipyard]》 / 見学旅行をする make a study [investigative] tour of [around]《Europe》.

げんかく[1] 幻覚〈作用〉hallucination; ＜幻に見える物＞ a hallucination; a hallucinatory image ¶幻覚剤 a hallucinatory [hallucinogenic] drug; a hallucinogen.

げんかく[2] 厳格 ¶厳格な strict; stern; 《文》 rigorous; severe / 厳格な父親 a stern [strict] father / 厳格な区別《make》 a sharp distinction《between》 / 厳格に strictly; sternly; 《文》 rigorously; severely. 文例⇩

げんがく[1] 弦楽 string music ¶弦楽合奏団 a string orchestra [band] / 弦楽四重奏(団) a string quartet.

げんがく[2] 衒学《文》pedantry ¶衒学的 pedantic.

げんがく[3] 減額 (a) reduction; a cut; 《文》 (a) curtailment ¶減額する reduce; cut down (on); 《文》 curtail.

げんかしょうきゃく 減価償却 depreciation ¶減価償却準備積立金 a depreciation reserve.

けんかしょくぶつ 顕花植物 a phanerogam; a flowering plant.

げんがっき 弦楽器 a stringed instrument.

けんがみね 剣が峰 ¶剣が峰に立つ be in a desperate state; be in a tight corner; have one's back to [against] the wall / (相撲で)剣が

---

cat and dog. | They live a cat-and-dog life.

けんお 彼はその光景を嫌悪の目で見た。He viewed the scene with loathing [repugnance, distaste].

けんか[2] 僕が間に入って2人のけんかをとめてやった。I stepped in and settled [made up] the quarrel between them. / 売られたけんかなら買ってやる。I will do it if I am dared to. / 部屋に入って来た時はずいぶんとけんか腰だったぜ。You sure had a chip on your shoulder when you came into my room. / けんか両成敗。It takes two to make a quarrel. / ここはけんか両成敗だ。I think

you're both in the wrong. | I'd say it was six of one and half a dozen of the other (between you).

けんかい[1] それは見解の相違だ。It's a matter of opinion. / この時点でという見解が生じた。At this point there emerged a clear divergence of views. / この問題に関しては見解がまちまちである。Opinion is divided [There is a diversity of views] on this question.

げんかい 物には限界がある。There is a limit to everything. / 僕は自分の力の限界がわかった。I learned the limits of my ability. |

I recognized my own limitations.

げんかく[2] 彼は生徒に対してとても厳格だ。He is very severe [strict] with his pupils. / 彼は厳格な家庭に育った。He was brought up very strictly [in a strict family]. | He had a very strict upbringing.

げんかん 自動車はゆっくりと玄関に着いた。The automobile drew slowly up to the door. / 成田は日本の玄関である。Narita is the gateway to Japan. / 彼女に会おうとしたが玄関払いを食わされた。I tried to see her, but was not allowed in the house [but had the door slammed in my face].

けんがん 検眼 an eye examination; 〈視力検査〉an eyesight test; optometry (視力計を用いての); ophthalmoscopy (検眼鏡を用いての) ¶ 検眼する examine sb's eyes; 〈視力を検査する〉test sb's eyesight / 検眼鏡 an ophthalmoscope.

げんかん[1] 玄関 〈入口〉the (front) door; the (front) entrance; the porch; 〈玄関の間〉(entrance) hall [vestibule] ¶ 玄関から入る enter at the front door / 玄関払いをくわす turn 《a visitor》 away at the door; refuse to let [show] 《a visitor》 in / 玄関番 a doorkeeper. 文例⊕

げんかん[2] 厳寒 severe [intense] cold ¶ 厳寒の候に in the middle [depths] of winter; in the coldest season.

けんぎ[1] 建議 〈提議〉a proposal; a suggestion; 〈進言〉《文》a memorial (to the government); 《文》representations ¶ 建議する〈申し出る〉propose; suggest; 〈進言する〉present a memorial (to); make representations (to).

けんぎ[2] 嫌疑 suspicion ⇒ うたがい, ようぎ.

げんき[1] 元気 vigor; energy; vitality; 《口語》pep ¶ 元気な 高-spirited; vigorous; spry; cheerful / 元気な赤ちゃん a bouncing baby / 元気な老人 a spry [hale and hearty (健康な)] old man / 元気がつく, 元気づく cheer [《口語》buck] up; take heart, 〈病人が〉recover one's strength / 元気のない depressed; low-spirited; cheerless / 元気を出す cheer [《口語》buck] up; brace oneself up / 元気をつける cheer sb up; encourage; 《文》put sb on his mettle / 元気になる 〈明るくなる〉cheer up; become cheerful; 〈気持ちよくなる〉be refreshed; 〈勇気が出る〉take heart; 〈病人が〉get well [better]; pick up; recover one's [《文》enjoy good health] / 元気よく in high spirits; cheerfully / 元気一杯[あふれるばかり]である be full of vigor [《口語》pep, 《口語》beans]; 《口語》have plenty of bounce. 文例⊕

げんき[2] 原器 〈度量衡の〉the 《meter》 standard.

げんぎ 原義 the original meaning 《of a word》.

けんせい 嫌気性〈生物・生理〉¶ 嫌気性の anaerobic (bacteria).

けんきゃく 健脚 ¶ 健脚である be a good walker.

けんきゅう 研究 research(es); (a) study; research work [effort]; 〈調査〉(an) investigation; (an) inquiry ¶ 研究する study; make a study (of); do [conduct] research (on, in); make [carry out] research(es) (into); research (on, into); 〈調査する〉investigate; inquire 《into》 / 研究を発表する 〈出版物で〉publish the results of one's research work (in a bulletin); 〈口頭で〉read a [one's] paper (on) / 研究員[生] a research worker [student] / 研究家[者] a student [scholar] (of) / 研究科 a (post)graduate course / 研究会 a society for the study of 《English poetry》 / 研究課題 a research task / 研究活動 research activities / 研究室 a study (room); an office (教授個人の); 〈実験室〉a laboratory / 〈口語〉a lab / 研究所 a (research) laboratory; an [a research] institute / 研究助成金 a research grant / 研究資料 material [data] for one's research; research material / 研究団体 a research organization [body] / 研究図書館 a research library / 研究発表会 a meeting for reading research papers / 研究費 research funds [expenses] / 研究報告 a report of (one's) research; a research paper (報告書) / 研究方法 a method of study [research] / 研究領域 an area of study [investigation]; a research area / 研究旅行 a study trip / 研究論文 a research paper (on); a study (on); a dissertation (学位論文); a treatise (学術論文); a monograph (専攻論文). 文例⊕

囲語 study は, He spent the whole afternoon in study. / The plan is under study now. というように, 研究又は学習という行為そのものをさす時は無冠詞で用いられる。また対象を深く調べる, 又調査の結果を論文にまとめる程の気持ちをこめて「研究」という時は, He wanted to make a study of American history. というように, a study の形になる. また書きあげられた「研究論文」をさす時も a study で, He is writing a study on Shakespeare's plays. と言うが, 自分の研究課題または科目を広くさす場合は, He pursued his studies with more enthusiasm at Princeton. というように複数形となるのが普通である. research については, do research

---

げんき[1] 一杯やると元気が出るよ. A cup of sake will give you a lift [pep you up]. / 彼はいつもの元気がなかった. He wasn't his usual (sprightly) self. | He wasn't feeling himself. | He didn't look himself. / だんだん元気が出て, ベッドの上に起き上がれるぐらいになった. Gradually I picked up, and became well enough to sit up in bed. / 元気を出せ! Cheer up! | Keep your chin up! / お元気ですか. How are you? / とても元気です. 〈上の返事〉Fine, thank you. | Never better, thanks. / 彼は元気よく歩いて帰って行った. He walked home in high spirits. / もっと元気よく歌うんだ. Put more spirit into your singing!

けんきゅう 彼はトマス・ハーディ研究のためにイギリスに留学した. He went (over) to England to pursue his study of Thomas Hardy. / ハーバードでピュリタニズムの研究をしています. I'm doing some research [I'm working] on Puritanism at Harvard. / それは大いに[さらに]研究すべき問題である. The subject demands close [further] investigation. / 何か簡単な方法はないかと目下研究中です. My researches have been directed toward finding a simpler method. / さらによく研究した結果その星は太陽の10倍の大きさがあることがわかった. The star, on closer study, proved to be ten times as large as the sun. | Further research showed [Further study revealed] that the star was ten times the size of the sun. / 彼は何事につけても研究心が旺盛だ. He has an inquiring mind and is very curious about everything. / ヘンリー・アダムズに関する研究論文を日本アメリカ文学会で発表した. He read [gave] a paper on Henry Adams to the American Literature Society of Japan.

げんきゅう 言及 reference ¶言及する refer to; mention; make 《no》 mention of; touch on 〈短かく〉 ★ make mention of は否定文で使われるのが普通.

げんきゅう² 原級 《文法》the positive degree; 〈同じクラス〉 the same class ¶原級に留める keep 《a student》 in the same class for another year; make 《a student》 repeat 《the first-year course》.

けんぎゅう(せい) 牽牛(星) 《天》Altair.

けんきょ¹ 検挙 ¶検挙する arrest; 《口語》nab; round up 〈一斉に〉/ 一斉[大量]に検挙する make a wholesale [mass] arrest 《of》; round up 《narcotics traffickers》. 文例⇩

けんきょ² 謙虚 modesty; 《文》humility ¶謙虚な modest; humble.

けんぎょう 兼業 a side job; a sideline; business on the side ¶兼業する follow [《文》pursue] 《another trade》as a side job [on the side] / 兼業農家 〈農業を主とする〉 a farmer with a side job; 〈農業を従とする〉 a person who does farming on the side.

げんきょう¹ 元凶 the ringleader; 《文》the prime mover.

げんきょう² 現況 ⇒げんじょう².

げんぎょう 現業 site [shop-floor] operations; 〈三公社五現業などという時の〉 a government enterprise (engaged in manufacture or processing); a nonclerical government department ¶現業員 a nonclerical [blue-collar] worker.

けんきょうふかい 牽強付会 ¶牽強付会の《文》forced 《views》; far-fetched 《opinions》.

げんきょく 原曲 the original work [version].

けんきん 献金 giving [《文》contribution of, 《文》donation of] money; a contribution; a donation; 〈教会・集会などでの〉(take) a collection ¶献金する contribute [donate] money 《to》/ 献金を集める collect contributions (from) / 《make [take (up)] a collection [for the relief fund]》/ 献金箱 a contribution [collection] box; 〈教会の〉 an offertory box.

げんきん¹ 現金 cash; ready money; hard cash ¶小切手を現金にかえる cash a check; have [get] a check cashed / 現金で買う buy 《an article》 for cash / 現金で払う pay 《for an article》 in cash / 現金な人 a calculating person / 現金書留 registered mail for cash / 現金書留で送金する send (¥2,000) (in cash) by registered mail / 現金収入 《have》a cash income / 現金正価 a cash price / 現金取引 cash transactions / 現金輸送車 a car [van] used for transporting cash; a security vehicle.

げんきん² 厳禁 ¶厳禁する prohibit [forbid] sth strictly. 文例⇩

げんけい¹ 原形 the original form ¶原形に復す《文》be restored to its original form / 原形をとどめない[失う] have no trace [《文》vestige] of its original form; lose its original form / 原形質《生物》protoplasm / 原形不定詞《文法》a bare infinitive.

げんけい² 原型 a prototype (工学・発生学などの); an archetype (文学・美術などの).

げんけい³ 減刑 ¶減刑する a commute (a death sentence to life imprisonment); reduce 《a sentence of 20 days solitary confinement to 10 days》.

けんげき¹ 剣戟 ¶剣戟の響き the clash of swords [《文》arms].

けんげき² 剣劇 〈芝居〉a sword-fighting play; 〈映画〉an action film featuring sword fighting.

けんけつ 献血 donation of blood ¶献血する donate [give] blood 《to》/ 献血者 a (blood) donor.

けんげん¹ 権限 power(s); authority;《法》competence ¶権限を与える authorize sb (to do); give sb [《文》vest sb with] (the) authority (to do) / 広範な権限を持っている have wide powers [broad authority] (to do) / 権限を越える《法》exceed one's competence [authority, powers]; be outside [beyond] the competence (of the court). 文例⇩

けんげん² 顕現《文》(a) manifestation.

けんけんごうごう 喧々囂々 ¶けんけんごうごうたる noisy; uproarious;《文》clamorous / けんけんごうごうと noisily; uproariously;《文》clamorously.

けんご 堅固 ¶堅固な strong; solid; secure; firm;《文》steadfast / 堅固に strongly; firmly; securely / 堅固にする strengthen; make sth firm [solid]. 文例⇩

げんご¹ 言語 (a) language; speech ⇒ことば ★「言語」一般のことは language であるが, ある1国の「言語」という時は a [the] language となる ¶言語学 linguistics / 言語学者 a linguist / 言語教育 language education / 言語社会学 sociolinguistics / 言語習慣 speech [lin-

---

けんきょ¹ 彼は選挙違反で検挙された. He was arrested for violations of the election law.

げんきん¹ 現金でお買い上げの節は5分引きに致します. Prices are subject to 5 percent discount for cash. / 赤ん坊って現金なものだ. お乳をのませたらもう泣き止んだ. A baby is so simple and innocent; it stopped crying as soon as it was put to its mother's breast.

げんきん² 実験室内での喫煙は厳禁です. Smoking is strictly prohibited in the laboratory.

けんげん¹ どのような権限があってそんな命令をするのか. On what authority do you give such orders? / この問題の審議は当委員会の権限外のことだ. It is not within the competence of the committee to consider the matter.

けんけんごうごう 議論が沸騰して議場はけんけんごうごうとなった. The hall resounded with argument.

けんご 立派な仏教学者になりたいという彼の道心は堅固だから決して迷うことはあるまい. He is so firmly resolved to become a great Buddhist scholar that nothing will divert him from his purpose.

げんご¹ 言語を持つのは人間だけである. Man alone has the gift of speech. / その風景の美しさは

げんご [guistic] habits / 言語障害 a speech impediment [defect]; an impediment in one's speech / 言語心理学 psycholinguistics / 言語地理学 linguistic geography; geographical linguistics / 言語年代学 glottochronology / 言語能力 language [linguistic] ability [abilities, competence]. 文例⇩

げんご² 原語 the original word [language] ¶ホーマーを原語で読む read Homer in the original.

けんこう 健康 health; fitness ¶健康な healthy/ 健康が衰える one's health declines [fails] / 健康を損なう one's health breaks down; 〈事が主語〉injure [ruin, undermine] one's health; 〈人が主語〉fall [《文》become] ill / 健康を回復する get one's health back; recover [《文》regain] one's health; get fit again / 健康を増進する improve one's health / 健康を保つ keep fit; keep [《文》maintain (to)] one's health / 健康を祝して乾杯する drink (to) sb's health; toast sb [sb's health] / 健康にいい be good for one [the health] / 健康に悪い be bad for one [the health] / 《文》be injurious to [hurt] one's health / 健康に適している be healthy; be wholesome; suit one's health / 健康に注意する take (good) care of oneself [one's health] / 健康である be healthy; be well; be in good health; 《文》enjoy good health / 健康でない、健康がすぐれない be not well; be in bad [poor] health / 健康管理 health care 《for the aged》/ 健康状態 (the condition of) one's health / 健康色 a healthy complexion / 健康食 (be on) a healthy food diet / 健康食品店 a health food store / 健康診断 a medical [health] examination; a (physical) checkup / 健康相談 a health consultation / 健康体 a healthy body; 《be in》a healthy condition / 健康地 a healthy place / 健康美 healthy beauty / 健康法 how to keep fit / 健康保険 health insurance / 健康保険に入っている have (health) insurance; be on the health insurance list / 健康保険医[証] a health insurance doctor [card] / 健康優良児 a prize-winning child in a health contest. 文例⇩

けんごう 剣豪 a great swordsman; a master fencer.

げんこう¹ 言行 speech and action; words and deeds ¶言行録 a memoir. 文例⇩

げんこう² 原稿 a manuscript (略: MS, pl. MSS); a typescript (タイプで打った); copy (印刷に回すばかりになった); 〈投稿〉a contribution; 〈草案〉a draft ¶原稿を書く write [prepare] a manuscript / 原稿を募る invite [《文》solicit] contributions 《for [to] a magazine》/ 原稿用紙 manuscript paper; a writing pad (綴ってある) / 原稿料 a fee for an article [a manuscript, something one has written]; copy money / 原稿生活をする live by writing [《文》by one's pen] / (新聞社の)原稿整理係 a copyreader; a copy editor.

げんこう³ 現行 ¶現行の教科書 the textbooks now in use / 現行制度 the present system / 現行法規 the existing laws; the regulations now [at present] in force.

げんこう⁴ 元寇 〖日本史〗the Mongolian Invasions (of 1274 and 1281).

げんごう 元号 ⇒ねんごう.

けんこうこつ 肩胛骨 〘解〙the scapula 《pl. -lae, -las》; the shoulder blade.

げんこうはん 現行犯 a crime committed in the presence of a policeman ¶現行犯で逮捕する catch sb in the act of (committing a theft); catch (a thief) red-handed [《文》in flagrante delicto].

けんこく 建国 the founding of a country [state] ¶アメリカ建国の父たち《米国史》the Founding Fathers of America / 建国記念の日 National Foundation Day.

げんこく 原告 〘法〙a plaintiff; a complainant; an accuser.

げんこつ 拳骨 a fist ¶拳骨を固める clench one's fist / 拳骨でなぐる hit [《文》strike] sb with one's fist.

げんごろう 〘昆〙a diving beetle.

げんこん 現今 ¶現今は now; today; at present; nowadays / 現今の present(-day); current; of today.

けんこんいってき 乾坤一擲 ¶けんこんいってきの勝負をする stake everything one has 《on sth》; take a chance 《on sth》.

けんさ 検査 (an) inspection; (an) examination; a test; a checkup (医学的な); an overhaul (機械などを分解して調べる); an audit (会計の) ¶検査する inspect; examine; test; check; overhaul; audit / 視力を検査する test sb's eyesight / 検査を受ける have [《文》undergo] an examination; be examined; be inspected; have 《one's eyes》 tested / 検査官 an inspector; an examiner; 〈会計の〉an auditor / 検査技術 testing technique(s) / 検査役〘相撲〙an advisor to a sumo referee. 文例⇩

けんざい¹ 建材 building material(s).

けんざい² 健在 ¶健在である 〈健康である〉

全く言語に絶する. The beauty of the scenery beggars description. | The scenery is beautiful beyond description.

けんこう 近ію ごきげんいかがですか. How is your health lately? / 有り難う, 健康そのものです. I am in excellent health, thank you. / ご健康を祝しまして.〈乾杯の時の言葉〉Here's to you! | Your health! / 病気になってはじめて健康の有り難みがわかる.

You cannot appreciate the blessing of health until you lose it. / 彼女のほおは健康で赤く輝いていた. Her cheeks were rosy with health. / 健康上の理由で彼は学部長を辞任した. He resigned his post as dean for health reasons. / これが私の健康法です. This is what I do to keep fit.

げんこう¹ 彼の言行は一致しない. His deeds do not match his words. | He says one thing and

does another. / 彼は言行一致の人だ. He is a man of his word.

げんこう² 原稿のままでもかまわない, 君の論文を一日も早く読みたいものだ. I'd like to read your article as soon as possible; I don't mind [care] if it is still in manuscript. / 原稿料は 1 ページ幾らでお支払いいたします. You are paid for your manuscript at so much a page.

けんさ 鉄分が含まれていないかと

けんざい be well; be in good [excellent] health; 《口語》 be going strong; 《(選手などが)好調である》 be in good condition; be in form; 《口語》 be in good shape; 〈引退しない〉 be on the active list.

けんざい³ 顕在 ¶顕在化する 《文》 become actual [manifest]; 《文》 be actualized.

けんざい¹ 原罪 《キリスト教》 original sin.

けんざい² 現在 〈名詞〉 the present time; 〈副詞〉 at present; at the present time; 《米》 presently; currently; (here and) now ★presently は《英》でも at present の意味で使われるようになったが,そういう使い方はずさんだとして避ける人も ● 現在の present; existing; current / 現在まで up to now; until today; to date / 1980 年 10 月 1 日現在の東京の人口 the population of Tokyo as of October 1, 1980 / 現在(時制)《文法》the present (tense) / 現在高 the amount in [on] hand / 現在地 the place where *one* is now [at present] / 現在分詞《文法》a present participle. 文例 ⇩

げんさいききん 減債基金 a sinking fund.

けんざかい 県境 a prefectural boundary ¶群馬県と新潟県の県境 the Gunma-Niigata border; the boundary (line) between Gunma and Niigata prefectures.

けんさく¹ 検索 reference;《コンピューター》(information) retrieval ¶検索する refer to 《a dictionary》; look up 《a word》 in 《a dictionary》; search 《a thesaurus》 for 《the right word》 / 検索に便であるbe easy to refer to; be handy for reference. 文例 ⇩

けんさく² 献策 (a) suggestion; (a piece of) advice ¶献策する suggest 《that...》; submit a plan 《to》; advise 《the premier on his policy-making》.

げんさく 原作 the original (work) ¶原作者 the original (original) author [writer] 《of a novel》. 文例 ⇩

けんさつ¹ 検札 inspection [examination] of tickets ¶検札係 a ticket inspector.

けんさつ² 検察 ¶検察側の証人 a witness for the prosecution / 検察官 a public prosecutor ⇒けんじ¹ / 最高東京地方検察庁 the Supreme [Tokyo District] Public Prosecutors Office / 検察当局 the prosecution.

けんざん¹ 剣山 a kenzan; a pinholder.

けんざん² 検算 ¶検算する check [go over, verify] the accounts;《数》prove 《one's answer》.

げんさん 減産 〈自然的〉 a fall [《文》decrease] in output [production]; 〈人為的〉 a cut in [(a) reduction of] production [output].

げんさんち 原産地 the place [country] of origin; the (original) home. 文例 ⇩

けんし¹ 犬歯 a dogtooth; a canine (tooth).

けんし² 剣士 a swordsman; a fencer.

けんし³ 検死 an [a coroner's] inquest; a post-mortem (examination); an autopsy ★post-mortem も autopsy も死体を解剖して死因を調べることを意味し, inquest は post-mortem や autopsy の結果に基づいて行なわれる死因の審理で, 裁判の一種 ¶検死する hold an inquest over 《a corpse》; perform a post-mortem [an autopsy] on 《the body》 / 検死官 a coroner;《米》a medical examiner.

けんし⁴ 絹糸 ⇒きぬ(絹糸).

けんじ¹ 検事 a public prosecutor ¶検事正 a chief public prosecutor / 検事総長 the Public Prosecutor General;《米》the Attorney General.

けんじ² 堅持 ¶堅持する hold fast [《文》adhere] 《to》;《文》maintain firmly.

げんし¹ 幻視 a (visual) hallucination.

げんし² 原子 an atom ¶原子の atomic / 原子価 (a) valence; (a) valency / 原子核 an atomic nucleus ⇒かく³ / 原子雲 an atomic cloud / 原子構造 atomic structure / 原子爆弾 an atom(ic) bomb; an A-bomb / 原子番号 an atomic number / 原子病 radiation sickness / 原子物理学 atomic physics / 原子量 atomic weight / 原子力 ⇒げんしりょく / 原子炉 an atomic pile; a (nuclear) reactor / 原子論 the atomic theory;《古代ギリシア哲学の》atomism.

げんし³ 原始 ¶原始的 primitive; primeval / 原始キリスト教 primitive [early] Christianity / 原始時代 the primitive age / 原始人 (a) primitive man; a primitive / 原始林 a primeval forest.

げんし⁴ 原紙 〈謄写版の〉 a stencil; (a sheet of) stencil paper ¶原紙を切る cut a stencil.

げんし⁵ 減資 ¶減資する reduce the capital 《from...to...》.

けんしき 見識 〈意見〉 views; an opinion; 〈眼識〉《文》discernment; 〈気位〉pride; self-respect ¶見識がある[高い]〈自分の意見を持っている〉have an opinion of *one's* own; 〈眼識がある〉have an eye 《for paintings》;《文》be discerning; be a person of considerable insight; 〈自尊心がある〉have considerable self-respect; be proud / 見識ばる stand on *one's* dignity;《文》assume an air of (self-) importance. 文例 ⇩

げんしち 言質 ⇒げんち¹.

その砂を検査してみた. He tested the sand for iron. / 検査済. 《表示》Inspected. / O.K.

けんざい² ご両親はご健在ですか. Are your parents still alive?

げんざい² 多くの人は現在にのみ生きている. Many people live only in the present. / 米国の国民総生産は現在, 年額約9千300億ドルである. The U.S. gross national product is currently around $930 billion a year. / I drink は現在時制だ. 'I drink' is in the present tense. / 現在地を地図でさがして調べた. We studied the map to find out where we were.

けんさく¹ 利用者の検索の便を計って, この辞書にはサムインデックスがついている. This dictionary is thumb-indexed in order to make it easy for the user to look up words in it.

げんさく 彼はその小説の所々に手を加えてみたが, その改作は原作より幾分見劣りするものだった. He rewrote his story here and there, but the revised version proved a bit inferior to the original.

げんさんち タバコの原産地はアメリカ大陸である. The American continent is the original home

けんじつ 堅実 ¶堅実な steady; sound / 堅実な投資 a sound investment / 堅実に steadily.

げんじつ 現実 《文》(an) actuality; (a) reality ¶厳しい人生の現実 the stern [hard, harsh] realities of life / 現実の actual; real / 現実を直視する face (up to) reality / 現実から逃避する[遊離している] escape from [be out of touch with] reality / 現実的な realistic; down-to-earth / 現実主義 realism.

げんしゅ¹ 元首 the head of state; 《文》a sovereign.

げんしゅ² 原酒 unprocessed *sake*.

げんしゅ³ 厳守 ¶厳守する keep [《文》observe] strictly / 規則を厳守する observe the rules strictly [to the letter] / 時間を厳守する be very punctual.

けんしゅう 研修 (in-service) training; 〈新入社員などの〉an induction course ¶研修する study / 研修所 a [an in-service] training institute / 研修生 a trainee.

けんじゅう 拳銃 a pistol; a gun; 《米》a handgun; a revolver (連発式の) ⇨ピストル ¶拳銃の撃ち合い an exchange of gunfire / 《米》a gunfight / 拳銃を向ける point [aim, 《文》level] a gun (at); cover sb with a pistol / 拳銃を突きつけて[突きつけられて] at the point of a pistol; at gunpoint / 拳銃で撃つ fire a gun (at); shoot sb with a pistol.

げんじゅう 減収 a fall [《文》decrease] in income [yield, output]. 文例⇩

げんじゅう 厳重 ¶厳重な strict; severe; rigid / 厳重に strictly; severely; rigidly / 厳重に見張る keep (a) strict watch (on, over); guard 《the gate》strictly.

げんじゅうしょ 現住所 one's present address; where one is living at present.

げんじゅうみん 原住民 a native; an aborigine; an aboriginal.

けんしゅく 厳粛 ¶厳粛な serious; solemn; 《文》grave. 文例⇩

けんしゅつ 検出 ¶検出する detect [find] 《strontium 90》(by chemical analysis) / 検出器[装置] a detector.

けんじゅつ 剣術 ⇨けんどう².

げんしょ 原書 the original ¶シェイクスピアを原書で読む read Shakespeare in the original.

けんしょう 肩章 a shoulder strap; an epaulet(te) (主に軍服の).

けんしょう¹ 検証 〈実証〉《文》(a) verification; 〈検査〉(an) inspection; a test; probate (遺言の) ¶検証する verify; inspect; test; probate (遺言を) / 実地検証 ⇨じっち.

けんしょう² 腱鞘 【解】the sheath of a tendon; a tendon sheath ¶腱鞘炎 tenosynovitis.

けんしょう³ 憲章 a charter ¶大憲章《英国史》(the) Magna Charta [Carta]; the Great Charter.

けんしょう⁴ 懸賞 a prize; a reward ¶懸賞をつける offer a prize [reward] (for); 〈犯人などに〉set [put] a price (on the offender's head) / 懸賞に当たる win [carry off] a prize (in a contest) / 懸賞課題[問題] a subject [problem] for a prize contest / 懸賞金 prize money; a reward / 懸賞小説 a prize(-winning) novel / 懸賞当選者 a prize winner.

けんじょう¹ 献上 ¶献上する present 《sth to sb, sb with sth》; make sb a present of sth / 献上品 a gift; a present.

けんじょう² 謙譲 modesty; 《文》humility ¶謙譲な modest; humble / 謙譲の美徳 the virtue of modesty / 謙譲の美徳を発揮する behave modestly [with modesty].

げんしょう¹ 現象 a phenomenon (*pl.* -mena, -s) ¶現象学【哲】phenomenology. 文例⇩

げんしょう² 減少 (a) reduction; a fall; drop; 《文》(a) decrease; (文)(a) diminution ¶収入の減少 a decrease [reduction] in income / 減少する reduce; 《文》decrease; 《文》diminish; lessen; fall off; be reduced.

げんじょう¹ 原状 the original state; 《文》the former condition; 【法】《ラテン語》the *status quo ante* ¶原状に復する return [restore] sth to *its* original state;【法】reestablish [restore matters to] the *status quo ante*.

げんじょう² 現状 the status quo; the present [existing] condition [state of things] ¶現状のままにしておく leave sth as *it* is / 現状では in [under] the present [existing] circumstances; with the existing state of affairs; as matters now stand / 現状維持 maintenance of the status quo / 現状維持協定 a standstill [status quo] agreement. 文例⇩

げんじょう³ 現場 ⇨げんば.

げんしょく¹ 原色 a primary color ¶三原色 the three primary colors.

げんしょく² 現職 the present post [office] ¶現職の serving 《officials》;《文》incumbent;《a policeman》on the active list [in active service] / 現職にとどまる remain [stay] in (one's present) office; stay on the job.

げんしょく³ 減食 ¶減食する eat less;《文》reduce one's diet.

げんしりょく 原子力 nuclear [atomic] energy ¶原子力で動く atomic-powered; nuclear-powered / 原子力推進の nuclear-propelled /

---

of tobacco. | Tobacco is native [indigenous] to the American continent.

げんし ネプツニウムの原子番号は93である。The atomic number of neptunium is 93.

けんしき 時代に一歩先んじた見識を持たねばならない。We must keep a step ahead of the times in our outlook. / そんなこ

とをしては僕の見識にかかわる。It would be beneath my dignity to do such a thing.

げんしょう 本年の米作は約100万トンの減収となった。The rice crop this year shows a decrease of about a million tons.

げんしゅく 式は極めて厳粛に行なわれた。The ceremony was conducted with great [the utmost]

solemnity. / 社殿の前に立つと厳粛な気分に打たれた。We felt awed as we stood in front of the shrine.

げんしょう 当地でも同じような現象が認められた。A similar phenomenon was noted [observed] here.

げんじょう 世界の現状と未来について論じ合った。We discussed

けんじる (国連及び米国の)原子力委員会 the Atomic Energy Commission (略: AEC) / 原子力エンジン an atomic engine / 原子力協定 an atomic energy agreement / 原子力時代 the atomic age / 原子力船 a nuclear(-powered) ship [vessel] / 原子力潜水艦 a nuclear(-powered) submarine; an atomic(-powered) submarine / 原子力発電 nuclear [atomic] power generation / 原子力発電所 a nuclear [an atomic] power station [plant] / 原子力平和利用 peaceful uses of nuclear [atomic] energy / 原子力平和利用計画 an atoms-for-peace program / 原子力ロケット a nuclear-powered rocket.

けんじる 献じる ⇨ さしあげる, けんじょう¹(献上する).

げんじる 減じる ⟨引く⟩ subtract 《2 from 5》; deduct 《10% from *sb's* salary》/ ⟨減らす⟩ decrease; reduce; ⟨減る⟩ 《文》decrease; 《文》diminish; ⟨罪を⟩ commute 《*sb's* punishment from death to life imprisonment》.

けんしん¹ 検針 meter-reading ¶検針する check [read] a 《gas》 meter / 検針係 a 《gas-》meter reader.

けんしん² 検診 (a) medical examination ¶結核の集団検診 a group [mass] tuberculosis [T.B.] examination.

けんしん³ 献身 self-sacrifice; devotion ¶献身する devote [sacrifice, dedicate] *oneself* 《to》 / 献身的な self-sacrificing; devoted / 献身的に devotedly / 献身的に尽くす serve *sb* faithfully; devote *oneself* 《to》.

けんじん¹ 堅陣 a strong position; a stronghold ¶敵の堅陣を抜く capture [《文》carry] the enemy's strong position.

けんじん² 賢人 a wise man; a sage.

けんしん 原審 ⇨ かきゅう¹(下級裁判所), げんはんけつ.

げんじん 原人 a hominid; Early [Dawn] Man.

けんすい 懸垂 《体操》chinning exercises; a pull-up ¶懸垂をやる do chinning exercises 《on an iron bar》; chin *oneself* (up); do a pull-up.

げんすい¹ 元帥 〈陸軍〉《米》a general of the army; 《英》a (field) marshal; 〈海軍〉《米》a fleet admiral; 《英》an admiral of the fleet.

げんすい² 減水 ¶減水する ⟨川などが⟩ fall; subside; recede.

げんすい³ 減衰 〈物・化・電〉 attenuation ¶減衰する be attenuated / 減衰器 《電》an attenuator.

けんずいし 遣隋使 《日本史》a Japanese envoy to Sui Dynasty China.

げんすいばく 原水爆 atomic and hydrogen bombs; A- and H-bombs; nuclear and thermonuclear bombs ¶原水爆禁止世界会議[大会] a World Conference [Rally] Against Atomic and Hydrogen Bombs / 原水爆戦争 nuclear [atomic and hydrogen] warfare.

げんすうぶんれつ 減数分裂 《生物》meiosis; reduction division.

げんすん(だい) 原寸(大) actual [natural] size ¶原寸大の full-scale[-size(d)]; 《文》of full size / 原寸図 a full-scale drawing.

げんせ 現世 this world [life] ¶現世の[的] (this-)worldly; 《文》earthly; 《文》mundane; 《文》of this life / 現世では[における] in this world; in life; 《文》(on) this side of Paradise.

けんせい¹ 牽制 〈抑止〉a check; restraint; curbing; 《軍》containment; 〈陽動〉diversionary action; a feint operation; 《野球》a check; a pick-off throw ¶牽制する 〈抑える〉check; restrain; 《軍》contain; 〈陽動する〉make a feint / ランナーを牽制する 《野球》check a runner (by a tossing motion); peg a runner (on the base) / 牽制球 《野球》a pick-off throw / 牽制攻撃 a containing attack.

けんせい² 権勢 ⇨けんりょく ¶権勢欲 greed [《文》(a) lust] for power.

けんせい³ 憲政 constitutional government; constitutionalism ¶憲政の常道 the regular procedures of constitutional government.

げんせい¹ 原生 ¶原生動物 a protozoan 《*pl.* -s, -zoa》; a protozoon 《*pl.* -zoa》/ 原生林 a virgin [primeval] forest.

げんせい² 現世 ⇨げんせ.

げんせい³ 厳正 ¶厳正な ⟨きびしい⟩ strict; rigid; ⟨公正な⟩ (strictly) fair; impartial / 厳正に ⟨きびしく⟩ strictly; rigidly; ⟨公正に⟩ fairly; fair and square; impartially / 厳正中立 (observe, keep) strict neutrality.

げんぜい 減税 reduction of taxes; a tax reduction [cut] ¶減税する reduce [cut] taxes / 戻し減税 a tax rebate.

けんせき 譴責 《文》a reprimand; 《文》a rebuke; 《文》a reproof ¶譴責する 《文》rebuke; 《文》reprove / 譴責処分を受ける receive an official reprimand 《for》.

げんせき 原石 ¶ダイヤモンド[ルビー]の原石 (a) diamond [ruby] in the rough.

けんせきうん 絹(巻)積雲 a cirrocumulus 《*pl.* -li》; a cirrocumulus cloud.

けんせつ 建設 〈建物などの〉building; construction; 《文》erection; 〈設立〉establishment; 〈創設〉founding ¶建設する build; 《文》construct; erect; 〈設立する〉establish; 〈創設する〉found / 建設中である be being built / 建設中で[in course of] construction / 建設的 constructive / 建設会社 a construction company / 建設機械 a construction machine; construction machinery (集合的) / 建設業 the building [construction] industry / 建設業者 a builder; a building contractor / 建設現場 a construction site / 建設工事 construction work / 建設工事に当たる where the world is and where it is going.

げんすい² 川が減水し始めた. The level of the river has begun to fall [subside].

けんせつ 関係当局はようやく建設的な方向に一歩踏み出すことを決定した. The authorities concerned have at last decided to make a constructive move.

けんぜん 健全なる精神は健全なる身体に宿る. A sound mind in a sound body. 《諺》

けんそく そのデモで多数の検束者が出た. A large number of demonstrators were detained by the police.

けんぜん 労働者 a building [construction] worker / 建設者〈建物などの〉a builder ;〈創設者が〉a founder / 建設省[大臣] the Ministry [Minister] of Construction / 建設費 construction [building] costs.

けんぜん 健全 ¶健全な healthy; sound; wholesome / 健全な読み物 healthy [wholesome] reading / 健全な発達を遂げる make sound development / 健全財政 sound finance ; a healthy [balanced] budget (予算). 文例⇩

げんせん¹ 源泉 the source ; ¶知識の源泉《文》a fount of wisdom / 源泉課税《米》(a) withholding tax ;《英》pay-as-you-earn (略: PAYE) / 源泉徴収 deducting tax from income at source ; withholding / 源泉徴収票 a certificate of tax deducted (at source).

げんせん² 厳選 ¶厳選する select [screen] carefully; hand-pick / 厳選した choice《goods》; select《members》; carefully screened《students》; hand-picked《drivers》.

げんぜん 厳然 ¶厳然と〈いかめしく〉solemnly ; sternly ;《文》with dignity ;〈紛れもなく〉(as) clear as day / 厳然と構える adopt a stern manner ;《文》assume a grave air / 厳然たる事実 an undeniable fact.

げんそ 元素 an [a chemical] element ¶元素記号 the (chemical) symbol for an element.

けんそう 喧騒 ⇨ さわぎ, さわがしい.

けんぞう 建造 building ; construction ¶建造する build ;《文》construct / 建造中である be being built ;《文》be under [in course of] construction ;〈船が〉be on the stocks (at Uraga) / 建造物 a building ;《文》an edifice (堂々とした).

げんそう¹ 幻想 a fantasy; an illusion; a vision ;《文》a reverie ¶幻想的な fantastic / 幻想曲 a fantasia ; a fantasy.

げんそう² 現送 ¶現送する transport cash《to》.

げんそう³ 舷窓 a porthole.

げんぞう 現像《写真》developing ; development ¶現像する develop《a reel of film》/ 現像不足の underdeveloped《negatives》/ 現像液 developing fluid ; developer / 現像皿 a developing tray.

けんそううん 巻[絹]層雲《気象》a cirrostratus《pl. -ti》; a cirrostratus cloud.

けんそく 検束 ⇨ けんきょ, たいほ². 文例⇩

げんそく¹ 原則 a principle ; a fundamental rule ¶原則として in principle; as a (general) rule / 同じ原則により on the same principle. 文例⇩

げんそく² 舷側 the (ship's) side ¶舷側に《draw up》alongside the ship.

げんそく³ 減速 ¶減速する reduce speed [the speed《of a machine》]; slow down ; decelerate / 減速ギヤ a reduction gear.

げんぞく 還俗 ¶還俗する return to secular life ; renounce the cloth.

けんそん 謙遜 modesty ;《文》humility ¶謙遜な modest ; humble / 謙遜する be modest ; be humble《toward》/ 謙遜家 a modest person. 文例⇩

げんそん¹ 玄孫 a great-great-grandchild.

げんそん² 現存 ¶現存する exist ; be in existence / 現存の existing ; living. 文例⇩

けんたい¹ 倦怠 boredom ;《文》fatigue ; weariness ; tedium ;《文》languor ;《文》ennui ¶倦怠を感じる be [feel] tired [weary]《of》; be bored《by, with》;《文》become fatigued / (夫婦が)倦怠期になる get bored with each other [with *their* marriage] ;《文》become weary of married life.

けんたい² 献体 ¶献体する give [donate] *one's* body (after death)《to a hospital, for medical research》.

けんだい 見台 a bookrest.

げんたい 減退 a decline《in energy》; failing《of memory》; loss《of appetite》¶減退する decline ; subside ; fall off / 食欲が減退する lose *one's* appetite.

げんだい 現代 the present day; modern times; today ;《史》the contemporary period [age] ¶現代の contemporary; present-day; current; of our own time / 現代の日本 contemporary [present-day] Japan / 現代的 modern; modernistic / 現代英語 current [present-day] English / 現代作家 a contemporary writer / 現代史 contemporary history / 現代人 men of today / 現代性 modernity / 現代版 a modern version《of Italian Renaissance architecture》/ 現代文 contemporary writings / 現代文学 contemporary literature.

けんだくえき 懸濁液《物・化》a suspension《of starch and water》.

ケンタッキー Kentucky (略: Ken., Ky.) ¶ケンタッキー州の人 a Kentuckian.

けんだま 剣玉 a cup and ball ¶剣玉をやる play at cup and ball.

けんたん¹ 兼担 ⇨ けんにん¹.

けんたん² 健啖 a hearty appetite ¶健啖家 a big [hearty] eater. 文例⇩

げんたん 減反 ¶減反する reduce [cut down]《rice》acreage.

けんち 見地 a standpoint; a point of view ¶この見地から見れば from this point of view ; seen [viewed] in this light [from this angle]. 文例⇩

げんち 言質 ¶言質を与える give *one's* word《to do, that...》; commit *oneself*《to do》/ 言質を取る make [have] sb promise [《文》pledge, give *his* word]《to do, that...》/ 言質をとられないように話す avoid [speak without] committing *oneself* ; make a noncommittal state-

---

けんぞく¹ 金の貸し借りはしないというのが僕の原則だ．It's my principle [I make it a rule] neither to borrow nor to lend money.

けんそん 彼は謙遜しながら自分のしたことを話した．He spoke in a modest way of what he had done. / ご謙遜でしょう．You're too modest!

げんそん² これはその件に関する現存する最古の史料です．This is the oldest historical document extant on the subject.

けんたん² 君の健啖ぶりには驚くねえ！What an appetite you have!

けんち 教育的見地から見ればこの計画には欠点がある．From the educational point of view I find

ment. 文例⇩

げんち² 現地 ¶現地で[の] on the spot / 現地調査 an on-site inspection / 現地時間 local time / 現地人 a native / 現地調査 a field survey; (a piece of) field work [research]; an on-the-spot investigation / 現地報告 a field report; a report from the scene (of disaster).

けんちく 建築 〈事〉building; construction; 〈文〉erection / 〈物〉a building / 〈文〉a structure; architecture (総称) ¶建築する build; 〈文〉construct; 〈文〉erect; put [set] up / 建築上の architectural / (建物が)建築中である be being built; 〈文〉be under [in course of] construction / 建築家 an architect / 建築会社 a building [construction] company / 建築学 architecture / 建築技師 an architect / 建築技術 building techniques / 建築基準法 the Building Standards Act / 建築業 the building [construction] industry; (be in) the building trade / 建築業者 a builder; a building contractor / 建築現場 a building [construction] site / 建築工事 construction work / 建築材料 building materials / 建築史 (a) history of 《Japanese》architecture; (an) architectural history (of Japan) / 建築費 the cost of construction; building costs [expenses] / 大建築物 a large [big] building / 〈文〉an edifice / 建築法規 the building code / 建築様式 a style of building [architecture] / 建築用地 a building [housing] lot. 文例⇩

けんちじ 県知事 a prefectural governor ¶愛知県知事K氏 Mr. K, Governor of Aichi Prefecture.

げんちゅう¹ 原虫 ⇒ げんせい¹ (原生動物).

げんちゅう² 原注 notes found in the original (book, text) and not added to by the translator; original notes.

けんちょ 顕著 ¶顕著な conspicuous; remarkable; marked; striking; prominent; 〈文〉notable / 顕著な功績 〈文〉distinguished services 《to》/ 人口の顕著な増加 a marked increase in population.

げんちょ 原著 the original ¶原著者 the author; the writer.

けんちょう¹ 県庁 a prefectural office [government] ¶県庁の所在地 the seat of the prefectural government.

けんちょう² 県鳥 a prefectural bird.

けんちょう³ 堅調 〈取引〉a bullish tone.

げんちょう 幻聴 (an) auditory hallucination.

けんちょうぎ 検潮儀 a tide gage [register].

けんつく けんつくを食う be [get] scolded 《by》;〈口語〉catch it 《from》;〈口語〉get a rap on [over] the knuckles 《from》.

けんてい 検定 〈認可〉official approval [《文》sanction];〈検査〉(an) examination ¶検定する 〈認可する〉give official approval [sanction] 《to》; approve / 〈試験する〉examine / 検定試験 a (state) licensing examination / 文部省検定済みの中学校用教科書 a textbook approved by the Ministry of Education for use in junior high schools / 検定料 a fee for official examination. 文例⇩

げんてい 限定 limitation ¶限定する limit; restrict; set limits [a limit] to;〈意味などを〉〈文〉qualify / 限定詞〈文法〉a determiner / 限定出版 limited publication / 限定戦争 (a) limited war / 限定相続〈法〉qualified acceptance of heritage / 限定版 a limited edition (of 300 copies).

けんてん 圏点 ¶圏点をつける mark 《a word》with a small circle.

けんでん 喧伝 ¶喧伝される 《文》spread abroad; be widely known.

げんてん¹ 原典 the original (text) 《from which a translation or quotation is made》.

げんてん² 原点〈測量〉the datum [fiducial] point;〈座標軸の〉the origin (of the coordinate axes);〈出発点〉the starting point ¶原点にたちかえる go back to the starting point;〈口語〉start (again [〔米〕over]) from scratch.

げんてん³ 減点 ¶減点する subtract 《10 marks》 from *sb*'s marks; give *sb* a demerit [bad] mark / 減点法〈レスリングなどの試合の〉the bad-mark system.

けんでんき 検電器 an electroscope.

げんど 限度 a limit;〈文〉bounds ¶限度を設ける limit; set limits [bounds] 《to》/ 限度を超える go beyond [overstep] the limits [bounds] / 1万円を限度とする be limited to 10,000 yen / 500万円を限度として within the limit(s) of 5 million yen.

けんとう¹ 見当 〈ねらい〉aim;〈見積もり〉an estimate;〈推測〉a guess;《文》(a) conjecture;〈方向〉a direction; bearings ¶見当をつける〈ねらう〉take aim at; aim at;〈見積もる〉estimate;〈推測する〉guess / 40見当の人 a person (who is) about 40 years old [《文》of age]; a person of 40 or thereabouts / 見当違いをする miss *one*'s aim; guess wrong; make

---

some shortcomings in this plan.

げんち¹ 言質を与えてしまったので今さら引っ込みがつかない。I've committed myself to it and I can't draw back now.

けんちく この建物はルネサンス様式の建築である。The building is a specimen of Renaissance architecture. / 会社から低利の建築資金を借りることができた。I succeeded in obtaining a low-interest building loan from my company. / その土地は建築用地として売りに出ている。The land is being offered for building.

けんてい 本書は高等学校用として文部省の検定済みです。This book has been approved by the Ministry of Education for use in senior high schools.

げんど 物事にはすべて限度がある。There is a limit to everything. | Everything has its limits.

けんとう¹ まあそんなところでしょう。You are [That's] about right. / 費用の大体の見当はどんなもので

しょう。About how much do you reckon the expenses at? | What is your rough estimate of the cost? / 費用は200万円見当だ。The cost will be ¥2 million or thereabouts. / 少しも見当がつかない。It is impossible to make even a wild guess. | I haven't the faintest [remotest] idea. / 彼を殺害した犯人がだれなのかまるで見当がつかない。Who actually murdered him is anybody's guess. / 彼の財産はどれほどあるか見当

けんとう / 見当違いの方へ行く go in the wrong direction.

けんとう² 拳闘 boxing ⇨ ボクシング.

けんとう³ 軒燈 a lantern hanging from the eaves (of a Japanese house); a door lamp.

けんとう⁴ 健闘 a good fight;〈努力〉〈文〉strenuous efforts ¶健闘する fight bravely; fight [put up] a good fight;〈努力する〉make strenuous efforts.

けんとう⁵ 検討〈研究〉(an) examination; (an) investigation; study;〈討論〉(a) discussion ¶検討する〈研究する〉examine; investigate; inquire [go] into; study;〈討論する〉discuss; thrash out (a question). 文例⇩

けんどう¹ 県道 a prefectural road [highway].

けんどう² 剣道 (Japanese) fencing; swordsmanship ¶剣道の先生[道場] a fencing master [school] / 剣道の達人 a master fencer [swordsman].

げんとう¹ 幻灯 a slide;〈昔の〉a magic lantern ¶幻灯機 a slide projector.

げんとう² 舷灯 a sidelight.

げんどう¹ 言動 ¶言動が正しい〈文〉be upright in word and deed / 言動を慎む be careful about how one speaks and behaves [《文》in one's speech and behavior] / 感情を言動に現わす〈文〉betray one's emotions in speech and action.

げんどう² 原動 ¶原動機 a prime mover; a motor / 原動力〈動力〉motive power [force]; 〈推進力〉driving [moving] force.

けんとうし 遣唐使《日本史》a Japanese envoy to Tang Dynasty China.

ケントし ケント紙 Kent paper.

けんどじゅうらい[ちょうらい] 捲土重来 ¶捲土重来する《文》resume one's activities with redoubled energy [efforts]; try again even harder.

げんなま ⇨ げんきん¹.

げんなり ¶げんなりする《口語》be fed up (with); be bored (to death) (by, with).

けんにょう 検尿《医》examination of the urine; a urine test ¶検尿する examine sb's urine.

けんにん¹ 兼任 ¶兼任する《文》hold the additional [concurrent] post (of); also hold the post (of);《文》serve concurrently (as). 文例⇩

けんにん² 堅忍 ¶堅忍持久 dogged perseverance; untiring patience / 堅忍不抜《文》(indomitable) perseverance;《文》fortitude / 堅忍不抜の persevering;《文》indefatigable;《文》indomitable.

けんのう¹ 献納 ¶献納する offer; present; contribute.

けんのう² 権能〈権限〉⇨ けんげん¹;〈権利〉⇨ 「けんり」.

げんのしょうこ《植》a cranesbill.

けんのん 剣呑 ¶けんのんな〈危険な〉dangerous; risky;《文》hazardous;《文》perilous / 〈不安な〉unsafe; insecure; precarious / けんのんがる think (it) dangerous [risky]. 文例⇩

げんば 現場 the scene (of a murder) ¶現場の教師 a schoolteacher actively engaged in teaching (as opposed to educational administration) / 現場を押さえられる be caught red-handed ((while one is committing a crime); be caught in the act [of stealing] / 現場に到着[急行]する arrive at [rush to] the scene《of the murder》/ 現場で on the spot / 現場監督 a field overseer; a site foreman.

げんばい 減配 ¶減配する〈配当を〉reduce a dividend《from...to...》.

けんばいき 券売機 a ticket vending machine.

けんぱき 検波器 a (wave) detector.

げんばく 原爆 ⇨ げんし²(原子爆弾) ¶原爆記念館 the atom bomb museum / 原爆症 illnesses caused by atomic-bomb radiation.

げんばつ 厳罰 a severe [heavy] punishment; a harsh penalty ¶厳罰に処する punish sb severely;《文》inflict a severe punishment on sb.

けんばん 鍵盤 a keyboard ¶鍵盤楽器 a keyboard [keyed] instrument.

げんばん¹ 原板《写真》a negative (plate).

げんばん² 原盤 a master disc [record].

げんはんけつ 原判決 the decision [judgment] of the lower court ¶原判決を棄却する reverse [quash] the decision [judgment] of the lower court; overrule the original decision [judgment].

けんびきょう 顕微鏡 a microscope ¶高倍率の顕微鏡 a powerful [high-powered] microscope / 1千倍の顕微鏡 a microscope of 1,000 magnifications; a 1,000-power microscope / 顕微鏡で見る see [look at] sth under [through] a microscope / 顕微鏡で調べる examine sth with a microscope / 顕微鏡的 microscopic / 顕微鏡検査 a microscopic examination [test] / 顕微鏡写真 a photomicrograph;〈術〉photomicrography / 顕微鏡写真機 a photomicrographic camera; a photomicroscope.

けんぴつ 健筆 ¶健筆を揮う《文》wield a powerful [facile] pen / 健筆家 a prolific [productive] writer.

つかない. It is impossible to form any estimate of his probable assets. / 君が大方ここにいるだろうと見当をつけてやって来た. I came because I thought there was a good chance of finding you here. / 深い森に入り込んで方角の見当がつかなくなった. We lost our bearings in a dense forest. / 僕から金を借りようなんて見当違いだ. If you expect to borrow money from me, you are barking up the wrong tree [you've got another think coming]. / それは見当違いの推測だ. Your guess is wide of the mark. / こんなことに力こぶを入れるのは見当違いだ. You're misguided in laying emphasis on things of this sort.

けんとう⁵ 政府筋は対策を検討中である. Measures are now under review in government circles. / 鉄鋼価格の値上げを業界が熱心に検討している. An increase in the steel price is under active consideration in the industry.

けんにん¹ 外相は首相が兼任する. The Prime Minister concurrently holds the portfolio for Foreign Affairs.

けんのん そんなけんのんなことをするな. Don't take risks of that sort.

げんば 兇行の現場から血のついたタオルが発見された. A blood-stained towel was found at the

げんぴん 現品 the article in question; this article (on display) ⇨ げんぶつ.

けんぶ 剣舞 《perform》a sword dance.

けんぷ 絹布 silk; silk cloth.

げんぷう 厳封 ¶厳封する seal up [off]; seal tightly.

げんぶがん 玄武岩 basalt ¶玄武岩台地 a basaltic plateau.

げんぷく 元服 a ceremony to celebrate *sb's* coming of age.

けんぶつ 見物 sightseeing; a visit ¶見物する see; look at; see [《口語》do] the sights 《of Kyoto》; visit; 〈傍観する〉look on / 芝居を見物する see a play / 東京見物をする see [do] the sights of Tokyo / 見物席 a seat; the stands (総称) / 見物人 〈名所などの〉a sightseer; a visitor; 〈観客〉a spectator; the audience (総称); 〈傍観者〉an onlooker. 文例⇩

げんぶつ 現物 the actual thing [article]; 〈取引〉spot goods ¶現物を見ずに〈buy an article〉sight unseen; 《trade》without seeing the goods / 現物給与 (a) payment [an allowance] in kind / 現物取引 a spot transaction.

ケンブリッジ Cambridge ¶ケンブリッジの Cambridge《students》; Cantabrigian / ケンブリッジ出身者を a Cantabrigian (★今ではCantabrigian はやや気取った言い方となっている) / ケンブリッジ大学 Cambridge University.

けんぶん¹ 見聞〈知識〉information; knowledge;〈経験〉experience;〈観察〉observation ¶見聞する observe / 見聞が広い [狭い] be well-informed [badly informed]; have seen a great deal [very little] of life / 見聞を広める add to *one's*〈stock of〉information [knowledge]; see more of life [the world].

けんぶん² 検分 (an) inspection; (an) examination ¶検分する inspect; examine; look [see] over.

げんぶん 原文〈本文〉the text;〈原書の文〉the original (text) ¶原文のまま《ラテン語》sic / 原文で読む read《a novel》in the original / 原文に忠実に訳す make a faithful translation of the original. 文例⇩

用法 sic は誤りや疑問のある文を引用する時に,その誤りと思われる語又は句の次に,通常角括弧の中に入れて付記する。例: Henry Adam [sic], author of *The Education of Henry Adams*.

げんぶんいっち 言文一致 unification of the written and spoken language ¶言文一致体で書く write in colloquial Japanese.

けんぺい¹ 権柄 ¶権柄ずくで in an overbearing way [manner];《文》peremptorily;《文》imperiously.

けんぺい² 憲兵〈陸軍〉a military policeman (略: an MP); a soldier [an officer] of the military police; the military police (略: MP) (総称);〈海軍〉a shore patrol(man) (略: an SP); the shore patrol (略: SP) (総称) ¶憲兵司令官〈陸軍の〉a provost marshal.

けんぺいりつ 建蔽率 the building-to-land ratio.

けんべん 検便 (an) examination of the feces; a stool examination ¶検便する examine *sb's* stool [feces] / 検便用の便 a sample of feces.

げんぼ 原簿 the original register; the book in which the original entry was made [is found].

けんぽう¹ 拳法 boxing (as one of the Japanese martial arts).

けんぽう² 憲法 the constitution ¶憲法(上)の constitutional / 憲法を制定[改正]する establish [amend] the constitution / 日本国憲法 the Constitution of Japan / 憲法違反 a breach of the constitution / 憲法違反の unconstitutional / 憲法改正 revision [amendment] of the constitution /〈一つの〉an amendment to the constitution; a constitutional amendment / 憲法学者 a constitutional scholar [lawyer]; an expert in [a scholar of] constitutional law / 憲法記念日 Constitution Day / 憲法制定会議 a constitutional assembly [convention].

げんぽう¹ 減法〈数〉subtraction ⇨ ひきざん.

げんぽう² 減俸 a pay cut; a reduction in *one's* salary ¶減俸される have *one's* salary reduced (by 10 per cent, from…to…); have *one's* pay cut.

けんぼうじゅっすう 権謀術数 trickery;《文》wiles; Machiavelli(ani)sm ¶権謀術数を用いる resort to trickery [wiles].

けんぼうしょう 健忘症 forgetfulness ¶健忘症である be forgetful; have a poor [short, weak] memory.

けんぼく 原木 trees used as material《for pulpwood》.

けんぽん 献本〈事〉presentation of a copy《to》;〈本〉a presentation [complimentary] copy ¶献本する present a copy《of *one's* book》to *sb*; present *sb* with a copy《of *one's* book》.

けんぽん 原本 the original.

けんま 研磨 ¶研磨する polish; grind; whet / 研磨機 a grinder; a grinding machine; a polisher〈レンズなどの〉.

げんまい 玄米 unpolished [uncleaned, unmilled] rice ¶玄米パン a whole-rice bun.

けんまく 文例⇩

---

scene of the murder.

けんぶつ 京都は見物する所が多い. There are lots of sights to see [places worth seeing] in Kyoto. / この町の見物は全部済ませてしまった. I've done all the sights in the town. / その家の前に見物人の山が築かれた. Crowds of curious people gathered in front of the house. / その行列には大勢の見物人が集まった. The procession drew crowds of spectators.

げんぶん 原文は次のようになっている. The original text runs [reads] as follows [like this].

けんまく 彼は女のけんまくにたじろいだ. He was staggered by the vehemence with which the woman spoke.

けんめい² それは賢明な策ではない. That would not be wise [sensible]. / 論争中ずっと沈黙を守った方が賢明だったろう. He would have been better advised to maintain silence throughout the controversy.

げんめい¹ それは言明の限りでない. I am not in a position to make any comment on it. | No comment.

げんまん ¶げんまんをする hook *one's* little finger with *sb's* (as a token of a promise) ⇨ ゆびきり.
げんみつ 厳密 ¶厳密な strict; close;《文》rigorous;《文》rigid / 厳密な意味で in the strict sense of the word / 厳密に strictly; closely;《文》rigidly / 厳密に言えば strictly speaking / 厳密な科学的定義 a rigorously scientific definition / 厳密に調査する examine [investigate]《a matter》closely;《文》make a close examination of《a matter》.
けんみん 県民 an inhabitant [a citizen] of a prefecture ¶県民税 the prefectural (residents') tax.
けんむ 兼務 ⇨ けんにん[1].
けんめい[1] 件名 a subject; subject matter ¶件名索引[目録] a subject index [catalog(ue)].
けんめい[2] 賢明 ¶賢明な〈賢い〉wise; intelligent;《文》prudent;《文》sagacious;〈思慮深い〉discreet;《文》judicious;〈得策な〉advisable;《文》well-advised ¶賢明な処置を取る act wisely. 文例⇩
けんめい[3] 懸命 ⇨ いっしょうけんめい ¶懸命の努力をする make all-out efforts《to *do*》/ 懸命に戦う fight hard [desperately].
げんめい[1] 言明 ¶言明する declare; state / 言明を避ける make no comment《on》. 文例⇩
げんめい[2] 厳命 ¶厳命する give *sb* a strict order《that...》; strictly order *sb*《to *do*》.
げんめつ 幻滅《文》disillusion(ment);《文》disenchantment ¶幻滅の悲哀《文》the sorrow of disillusionment; a sad disillusionment / 幻滅を感じる be [get,《文》become] disillusioned [disenchanted]《with》. 文例⇩
げんめん[1] 原綿 raw cotton.
げんめん[2] 減免 reduction of and exemption from《taxes》.
げんもう 原毛 raw wool.
けんもほろろ ¶けんもほろろの curt; blunt;《文》brusque ¶けんもほろろのあいさつをする〈返事をする〉answer [reply] curtly [《文》brusquely];〈拒絶する〉refuse [turn down]《*sb's* request》flatly; give *sb* a flat [point-blank] refusal; rebuff *sb*.
げんもん 舷門 a gangway.
けんもんじょ 検問所 a checkpoint.
げんや 原野〈平野〉an uncultivated field; a plain;〈荒野〉wasteland; a wilderness (★《米》では wilderness は「荒野」「砂漠地帯」のみならず,「森林地帯」をも含めて, すべて太古のままの自然の姿をとどめている未開拓地を意味する).
けんやく 倹約《文》economy; economizing;《文》thrift;《文》frugality ¶倹約な economical; thrifty;《文》frugal / 倹約する save《oil》; use《energy》carefully; economize《on oil》; be frugal《with *one's* money》/ 費用を倹約する save expenses / 倹約して金をためる save money by economizing《on》/ 倹約して暮らす live without waste [wasting anything]; lead a frugal life / ガソリンを倹約して使う economize on gasoline / 倹約家 a thrifty [frugal] person. 文例⇩
げんゆ 原油 crude oil [petroleum].
けんよう 兼用 ⇨ けん[6] ¶兼用する use *sth* both as...and... / 兼用になる serve [can be used] both as...and.... 文例⇩
けんようすい 懸壅垂 ⇨ こうがい[2] (口蓋垂).
けんらん 絢爛 ¶けんらんたる gorgeous; brilliant; dazzling; gaudy. 文例⇩
けんり 権利 a right; a claim (請求権); a title (所有権を主張し得る資格); a privilege (特権); authority (権能) ¶権利と義務 rights and duties; claims and obligations / 権利がある have a [the] right《to *sth*, to *do*》; be entitled《to *sth*, to *do*》/ 権利を行使[乱用]する《文》exercise [abuse] *one's* rights / 権利を主張する insist on [《文》assert] *one's* rights; lay [assert *one's*] claim《to》/ 権利を侵害する infringe on *sb's* rights / 権利つき[落ち]の〘取引〙cum [ex] rights / 権利金 a premium;〈借家などの〉key money / 権利書 a title deed; a certificate of title. 文例⇩
げんり 原理 a principle ¶経済学の原理 the principles of economics.
けんりつ 県立 ¶県立高等学校 a prefectural high school.
げんりゅう 源流 ⇨ みなもと.
けんりゅうけい 検流計〘電〙a galvanometer.
けんりょう 見料 a《fortuneteller's》fee.
げんりょう[1] 原料 raw materials.
げんりょう[2] 減量 ¶減量する〈量を減らす〉reduce the quantity《of》;〈体重を減らす〉reduce *one's* weight;《口語》reduce / (選手などが)減量に苦しむ have a hard time reducing (*one's* weight).
けんりょく 権力 power; authority ¶権力のある powerful; influential / 権力のない powerless; uninfluential / 権力の座を追われる[から落ちる] be driven [fall] from power / 権力を握る seize power / 権力を振るう exercise [《文》wield] *one's* authority [power]《over》/ 権力に飢えている be hungry for power / 権力意志〘哲〙the will to power / 権力者 a man of power [influence]; those in power / 権力闘争 a struggle for power. 文例⇩

げんめつ 政治に幻滅を感じている青年が多い. There are a lot of young people who are disillusioned with politics.
けんやく 倹約すれば月10万円はかからない. I can get along on less than ¥100,000 a month if I am careful (about my expenses). / 倹約すればそのアパートを借りても暮らして行けると思った. I thought that with economy I could afford the apartment. / こんな寒いときは灯油をそう倹約しなくてもいい. You needn't be frugal [sparing] with kerosene in such cold weather.
けんよう この書斎は客間兼用です. I also use this study for receiving guests.
けんらん けんらん豪華な祭典だった. The festival was rich in pageantry.
けんり 債権者は貸し金の返済を要求する権利がある. A creditor has the right to demand payment of the debts which others owe him. / 彼にはそんなことをする権利はない. He has no right [business] to do that.
けんりょく 彼らの不和は権力争い

けんるい 堅塁 a stronghold ⇨ けんじん¹.
けんろう 堅牢 strong; solid; stout; durable (長持ちする).
げんろう 元老 《政界の》 an elder statesman; 〈古株〉 a senior member; an elder; a grand old man.
げんろん¹ 言論 speech ¶言論の自由 freedom of speech [opinion]; 〈出版の〉 freedom of the press / 言論界 the press / 言論機関 organs of expression [public opinion]; mass media / 言論戦 a war of words; 《文》 a verbal battle; 〈白熱の討議〉 a heated discussion.
げんろん² 原論 the principles (of economics).
げんわく 幻惑 ¶幻惑する dazzle; fascinate.

こ

こ¹ 子 a child 《pl. children》; 《文》 an offspring 《複数同形》; 《口語》 a kid; 〈男の子〉 a boy; a son; 〈女の子〉 a girl; a daughter; 〈動物の〉 the young; a cub; 〈魚の集合的〉 roe ¶子としての義務 one's duty as a son [daughter]; 《文》 (one's) filial duty / 子連れのおおかみ a wolf with its young ⇨ こども. 文例⇩
こ² 戸 ¶50戸の村 a village of fifty houses.
こ³ 弧 an arc ¶弧を描く draw [describe] an arc; 〈弧をなす〉 form an arch.
こ⁴ 個 a piece ★ piece は単位としての「個」ではなく,物の「部分」を意味する.したがって「すいか3個」は three watermelons. three pieces of watermelon は「すいか3切れ」である ¶せっけん5個 five pieces [cakes] of soap / なし3個 three pears. 文例⇩
こ⁵ 粉 ⇨ こな ¶(干し柿などが)粉を吹く have a bloom ((on it)) / 身を粉にして働く keep one's nose to the grindstone; work one's fingers to the bone; work hard.
こ⁶ 湖 ⇨ みずうみ ¶琵琶湖 Lake Biwa.
こ-¹ 小... small; 〈ほとんど〉 nearly ¶小一時間 nearly [almost] an [one] hour.
こ-² 故... ¶故スミス氏 the late Mr. Smith.
ご¹ 五 five ¶第5の fifth / 5倍の《文》 fivefold 《as large》;《文》 fivefold;《文》 quintuple / 5分の1 one-fifth.
ご² 碁 (the game of) go ¶碁を打つ play [have a game of] go / 碁石 a go stone / 碁盤 a go board. 文例⇩
ご³ 語 a word; a term (用語); a language (国語).
-ご ...後 ¶それから2年後 after two years; two years later [after] / 50年後の世界 the world 50 years from now [《文》 hence] / 今から3週間後に three weeks from now; in three weeks.
コアセルベート 《物・化》 a coacervate.
コアラ 《動》 a koala (bear).

こい¹ 恋 love ¶恋する love sb; be in love with sb / 恋を知る know what it is to be in love / 恋に破れる be disappointed in love;《文》 fail to win sb's heart / 恋仲である [になる] be [fall] in love (with each other). 文例⇩
こい² 鯉 a carp 《pl. -(s)》 ¶鯉の滝上り a carp swimming up a waterfall / こいのぼり a carp streamer.
こい³ 故意 ¶故意の deliberate;《文》 intentional;《文》 willful; studied / 故意に《文》 intentionally; deliberately; purposely; on purpose; 〈知りつつ〉 knowingly / 故意か偶然か《文》 whether by design or by accident. 文例⇩
こい⁴ 請い a request;《文》 an entreaty ¶請いをいれる grant [《文》 comply with] sb's request / ...の請いにより at [《文》 in compliance with] the request of sb.
こい⁵ 濃い 〈色の〉 dark; deep 《green》;〈液の〉 thick (soup); strong (coffee);〈化粧の〉 heavy 《make-up》;〈関係の〉 close ¶濃いお茶 strong tea / 濃いまゆ thick eyebrows / 濃くする〈色を〉 deepen; 〈液体を〉 thicken; 〈飲み物を〉 make (the coffee) strong / 茶を濃くいれる make tea strong.
ごい 語彙 a vocabulary ¶語彙を豊かにする enrich [increase, build up] one's vocabulary. 文例⇩
こいがたき 恋敵 a rival in love.
こいぐち 鯉口 the mouth of a sword sheath ¶鯉口を切る loosen one's sword (slightly in its sheath) for immediate use.
こいごころ 恋心 one's love (for sb); 〈恋を知る〉 《文》 the awakening of love.
ごいさぎ 五位鷺 a night heron.
こいし 小石 a small stone [《米》 rock]; a pebble; 〈集合的〉 gravel (砂利) ¶小石の多い pebbly (roads); shingly (beaches).
こいじ 恋路 ¶恋路の邪魔をする《文》 thwart

がもとであった. The disagreement between them was caused by their struggle for power.
こ¹ いい子だ,いい子だ. There's [That's] a good boy [girl]! / 子を持って知る親の恩. Only after becoming a parent yourself do you realize how much you owe [how indebted you are] to your own parents. / 子はかすがい. Children are a bond between their parents.
こ⁴ 桃は1個売りします. We [They] sell peaches at so much each [apiece].
ご² 街路が碁盤の目のように走っている. The streets of the city cross each other at right angles. | The city is built in a grid [gridiron] pattern.
-ご 朝食後すぐに出かけた. We got away right after breakfast. / 約束の期日はわずか3日後に迫っていた. The appointed date was now only three days away.
こい¹ 恋に上下の隔てなし. Love makes men equal. | Love is a leveler. / あなたは恋をしたことがありますか. Have you ever been in love? / 恋は思案のほか. Love and reason do not go together. | One cannot love and be wise. 《諺》

こいしい 恋路の邪魔をされる《文》be crossed in love.
こいしい 恋しい dear; dearest; sweet; darling;《文》beloved ¶ …が恋しい miss…; long for;《文》sigh [pine] for….
こいしがる 恋しがる miss *sb* [*sth*]; long for 《*one's* lover》;《文》sigh [pine] for *sth*;《文》yearn after 《*one's* old home》.
こいしたう 恋い慕う ⇨ こいしがる.
こいつ this man [fellow, chap,《米》guy]. 文例⇩
こいにょうぼう 恋女房 a wife *one* married for love.
こいぬ 小犬〈小さい犬〉a little dog;〈犬の子〉a puppy; a pup.
こいびと 恋人〈男〉*one's* boyfriend; *one's* boy;〈女〉*one's* girlfriend; *one's* girl.
こいぶみ 恋文 a love letter [note];《フランス語》a billet-doux (pl. billets-).
コイル 〈電〉a coil.
コイン 〈貨幣〉a coin ¶ コインランドリー《米》a laundromat;《英》a launderette / コインロッカー a coin(-operated) locker.
こう¹ 公 ⇨ こうしゃく¹.
こう² 甲〈かめ・えび・かにの〉a shell;【動】a carapace;〈足の〉the instep;〈手の〉the back;〈甲乙の〉(grade) A. 文例⇩
こう³ 功〈功績〉《文》merits;《文》services; distinguished service; credit;《文》a meritorious deed;〈成功〉(an) achievement;《文》success ¶ 1年の功 the merit of age [accumulated experience] ⇨ かめ¹ / 功を争う claim credit (for an invention) / 功を急ぐ be too eager for success / 功を立てる《文》render meritorious [distinguished] service; distinguish *oneself* / 功成り名とげる《文》accomplish *one's* object and make *oneself* a name; win name and fame. 文例⇩
こう⁴ 劫《囲碁》ko; an alternate-capture situation.
こう⁵ 効〈効力〉《文》efficacy;《文》virtue; benefit; good;〈成果〉an effect; a result;《文》fruits ⇨ こうか² / 効を奏する take effect; be [《文》prove] effective; be successful; work (well);《口語》do the trick.
こう⁶ 幸 ¶ 幸か不幸か《文》for good or for evil; luckily or unluckily; fortunately or unfortunately.
こう⁷ 香 (an) incense ¶ 香をたく burn incense.
こう⁸ 候〈時候〉a season; weather ¶ 春暖の候 (in) the mild spring weather.
こう⁹ 港 ⇨ みなと ¶ 新潟港 the port of Niigata; Niigata Port; Niigata Harbor.
こう¹⁰ 項〈条項〉a clause; a paragraph;〈予算表などの〉an item;【数】a term ¶ 方程式の1項 a member of an equation / 2 [3, 多]項式 a binomial [trinomial, polynomial] expression / 第1条第2項に該当する come under Clause 2, Article 1 [Subsection 2, Section 1].
こう¹¹ 稿 a draft; a manuscript ¶ 稿を起こす begin writing / 稿をあらためて《discuss the subject further》in another article.
こう¹² 綱【生物】a class ⇨ もん¹.
こう¹³ 鋼 steel ⇨ こうてつ².
こう¹⁴ 請う ask; request; beg;《文》entreat;《文》solicit (for) ¶ 援助を請う ask for *sb's* help [assistance]; appeal to *sb* for help [《文》aid]; call for help / 許しを請う beg *sb's* pardon; ask to be forgiven / 物を請う ask [beg] *sb* for *sth* / 請われるままに at *sb's* request; as requested. 文例⇩
こう¹⁵ 斯う〈このように〉so; like this; (in) this way;《文》thus ¶ こう言って《文》so saying; with this / こうなった以上は now that things have come to this (pass). 文例⇩
ごう¹ 号〈番号〉a number; an issue《雑誌などの》;〈名称〉a title;〈雅号〉a pen name ¶ 第1号 number one; No. 1 /「文芸春秋」の1月号 the January number [issue] of the *Bungei-Shunju*; the *Bungei-Shunju* for January.
ごう² 合〈量目〉a go (=0.18l);〈面積〉a go (=0.33m²) ¶ 5合目 the fifth (uphill) station 《of Mt. Fuji》.
ごう³ 郷 ⇨ 文例⇩
ごう⁴ 業《仏教》karma ¶ 業が深い be sinful / 業を煮やす be vexed (at); get [《文》become] irritated (at, by); be impatient 《with [of]》; lose *one's* temper.
ごう⁵ 壕 a trench; a dugout;〈防空壕〉a shelter.
こうあつ¹ 高圧〈電気の〉high tension [voltage];〈蒸気などの〉high pressure;〈圧制〉highhandedness; oppression ¶ 高圧的に highhandedly / 高圧ガス high-pressure gas / 高圧手段 highhanded measures / 高圧線 a high-tension wire [line];《米》a high-voltage cable; a power cable / 高圧電流 a high-tension current.
こうあつ² 降圧 ¶ 降圧変圧器 a step-down transformer / 降圧剤【医】a hypotensive drug; a depressor.
こうあん¹ 公安 public peace (and order); public safety [security] ¶ 公安委員 [委員会] a public safety commissioner [commission] / 公安官《鉄道の》a public security officer / 公安

こい 故意にやったわけでないのだから許してくれたまえ。Please forgive me; I meant no harm.
ごい 彼は語彙が豊富だ。He has an extensive [a large] vocabulary. / もう少し使用語彙を多彩にしなさい。Try to use a more varied vocabulary.
こいしい ああ、あなたが恋しい！ How I miss you! / I miss you very much.
こいつ こいつめ！ You devil [rascal]! / Damn you !
こう² 彼は手の甲が毛むくじゃらだった。The backs of his hands were hairy. / He had hairy hands.
こう³ 小倉氏の功によるところ大である。Much of the credit belongs [should go] to Mr. Ogura.
こう¹⁴ こうまでばかとは思わなかった。I didn't think he was so [《口語》this] stupid. / こうしてはいられない。I cannot go on like this. / There is no time to lose. / 僕のやり方はこうだ。This is how I go about it. / こうして片田舎に住んでいるとめったに客はない。Living as I do in an out-of-the-way place, I rarely have visitors.
ごう³ 郷に入っては郷に従え.

こうあん 条令 a public safety [security] regulation.
こうあん² 考案 a plan; a device; an idea ¶ 考案する plan; design; devise; contrive / 考案者 a designer.
こうい¹ 行為 〈行動〉 an act; an action; 《文》 a deed; *one's* doings; 〈行状〉 behavior; 《文》 conduct ¶ 行為にあらわす carry out; 《文》 execute; 《文》 translate 《an idea》 into action / 行為者 《文》 a doer; 《文》 a performer 《of a deed》 / 行為能力 (legal) capacity.
こうい² 好意 goodwill; good wishes; kindness; 《文》 favor ¶ 好意ある kind; friendly; well-disposed/好意の忠告 well-meant advice / 好意的に out of goodwill [kindness]; in a friendly way / 好意を持つ be well disposed [《文》 favorably disposed] 《toward》; be friendly [warm] 《to》; wish *sb* well; have a liking 《for》 / 好意を無にする do not [《文》 fail to] return [respond to] *sb's* kindness. 文例⇩
こうい³ 攻囲 (a) siege ¶ 攻囲する besiege; lay siege to / 攻囲軍 a besieging army.
こうい⁴ 皇位 the (Imperial) Throne ¶ 皇位を継ぐ succeed to the throne / 皇位につく[上る] come to [《文》 accede to, 《文》 ascend] the throne.
こうい⁵ 厚意 kindness; 《文》 favor ¶ …の厚意により through the courtesy [kindness, good offices] of….
こうい⁶ 校医 a school physician [doctor].
こうい⁷ 高位 a high rank ¶ 高位に上る rise to [reach, 《文》 attain] a high rank / 高位高官の人 people [men] in high places; 《文》 people [persons] of (high) rank and office; dignitaries ⇒ こうかん.⁷
ごうい 合意 (mutual) agreement; 《文》 mutual [common] consent ¶ 国民の[一般的]合意 a national [general] consensus / 合意の上で by mutual [common] consent / 合意に達する come to [arrive at, make, reach] an agreement 《with》. 文例⇩
こうゆう this; of this kind [sort]; like this ¶ こういうこと this sort of thing; a thing like this; a thing [an affair] of this sort; such a thing (as this).
こういき 広域 a wide [large] area ¶ 広域捜査 a search 《for a suspected criminal》 conducted over a very wide area; a search across a number of police districts.
こういしつ 更衣室 a dressing [locker] room; a changing-room.
こういしょう 後遺症 an aftereffect 《of an injury》; 〔医〕 a sequela 《*pl.* -lae》.
こういつ 後逸 ¶ 後逸する 〔野球〕 let (the ball) pass; miss [fail to catch] (a grounder).
こういっつい 好一対 ¶ 好一対を成す make a good pair [match].
こういってん 紅一点 《文》 the only member of the fair sex 《among》; the only woman in the group [《文》 company].
こういん¹ 工員 a (factory) worker [hand]; 《文》 an operative.
こういん² 光陰 文例⇩
こういん³ 拘引 (an) arrest; custody 《拘留》 ¶ 拘引する arrest; take *sb* to 《a police station》.
ごういん 強引 ¶ 強引な overbearing; 《文》 coercive 《measures》; highhanded; 《文》 (over-)assertive; 〔口語〕 pushy / 強引に 〈力ずくで〉 by force; 《文》 by main force; forcibly; 〈高圧的に〉 overbearingly; highhandedly; 〈理も非もなく〉 without rhyme or reason / 強引に事を進める push (the matter) ahead / (国会で) 法案を強引に通過させる ram a bill through the House.
こうう 降雨 a rainfall; (a) rain ¶ 降雨量 (the amount of) rainfall; a rainfall 《of 50 millimeters》 / 降雨林 《文》 うりん. 文例⇩
ごうう 豪雨 a heavy rain [rainfall]; a downpour. 文例⇩
こううん 幸運 (a stroke of) good fortune; (good) luck ¶ 幸運な fortunate; lucky / 幸運にも fortunately; luckily; by (good) luck; 《文》 by a happy chance / 幸運にも…する be lucky enough to *do*; 《文》 have the (good) fortune to *do* / 幸運児 a lucky fellow. 文例⇩
こううんき 耕運機 (drive, run) a cultivator.
こうえい¹ 公営 ¶ 公営の public; municipal / 公営にする place [bring] 《an undertaking》 under public [municipal] management / 公営ギャンブル municipally operated gambling / 公営住宅 public housing.
こうえい² 光栄 (an) honor; 《文》 glory; a privilege (特典) ¶ 光栄ある glorious; 《文》 honorable; 《文》 honored / …するの光栄に浴する have the honor of *do*ing; have the pleasure [honor] to *do*.
こうえい³ 後衛 〔軍〕 the rear (guard); 〔テニス〕 the back player; 〔フットボール〕 a back; a full-back ¶ 後衛の rearguard 《action》 / 後衛をつとめる fight a rearguard action.
こうえき¹ 公益 the public good [benefit, interest(s)] ¶ 公益を図る work for [《文》 pro-

---

When in Rome, do as the Romans do. 〔諺〕
こうい² そのご好意だけで結構です。I will take the will for the deed. / It's the thought that counts. / せっかくの好意が悪意にとられた。My good intentions were taken amiss. / 彼は新聞で好意的に書かれている。He is painted in a good light by the press. / 掲載写真は村山文夫氏のご好意による。The photographs are reproduced by courtesy of Mr. Fumio Murayama.
ごうい その問題については日本の財界では一般的な合意はまだ全く得られていない。There is no general consensus among financiers in Japan about it.
こういう こういうふうにしなさい。Do it like this [(in) this way]. / それはこういうわけさ。I'll tell you what.
こういん² 光陰矢のごとし。Time flies (like an arrow).
こうう 当地の昨日の降雨量は30ミリであった。Thirty millimeters of rain fell here yesterday. | The precipitation here yesterday registered 30 millimeters.
ごうう 非常な豪雨であった。It rained heavily [in torrents]. | The rain fell in sheets.
こううん 幸運を祈る。Good luck (to you)! | I wish you (the best of) luck.

mote] the public good / 公益事業 public utility works / 公益質屋 a public [municipal] pawnshop / 公益法人 a public-service corporation. [文例⇩]

こうえき[2] 交易 trade ⇨ ぼうえき.

こうえつ 校閲 reading (and correcting) ⟪*sb's* manuscript⟫ ¶校閲する read (and correct); look over ⟪a manuscript⟫ / 校閲係 〈新聞社の〉 a proofreader.

こうえん[1] 公園 a park; a public garden ¶日比谷公園 Hibiya Park.

こうえん[2] 公演 a public performance ¶公演する perform publicly [before an audience]; present [give, stage] ⟪a play⟫; put ⟪a play⟫ on; put ⟪a play⟫ on the stage.

こうえん[3] 好演 good acting; an excellent performance ⟪of a play⟫.

こうえん[4] 後援 support; backing; ⟪文⟫ patronage; assistance; help; ⟪文⟫ aid ¶後援する support; give support [backing] to; back up; help; aid / 後援続かず… for lack of further reinforcements / …の後援のもとに with the support [help] of…; supported [⟪文⟫ aided] by…; 〈主催〉 ⟪文⟫ under the auspices of…; sponsored by… / 後援会 〈芸能人などの〉 *one's* fan club / K氏の後援会を作る organize a society in support of Mr. K / 後援者 a supporter; a backer; a patron / 後援団体 a supporters' organization.

こうえん[5] 講演 a lecture; ⟪文⟫ an address; a talk ¶講演する give [deliver] a lecture ⟪on⟫; give a talk ⟪on⟫; lecture ⟪on Shakespeare⟫ / 講演会 a lecture meeting / 講演者 a lecturer; a speaker / 講演料 a lecturer's fee / 講演旅行 a lecture tour.

こうえん[6] 高遠 ¶高遠な ⟪文⟫ lofty; ⟪文⟫ noble; high(-flown) ⟪thinking⟫; ⟪文⟫ exalted; high-minded.

こうお 好悪 *one's* likes and dislikes; ⟪文⟫ partiality.

こうおつ 甲乙 〈差異〉 (a) difference; 〈差別〉 discrimination ¶甲乙のない equal / 甲乙をつける grade; discriminate ⟪between⟫ / 甲乙をつけないで equally; all alike. [文例⇩]

こうおん[1] 恒温 (a) constant temperature ¶恒温恒湿の ⟪a room⟫ with [held at] constant temperature and humidity.

こうおん[2] 高音 〘音楽〙 a high tone; a high-pitched sound; a note in the high key ¶高音部 the treble / 高音部記号 a treble [G] clef / 高音部符表 the treble staff.

こうおん[3] 高温 (a) high temperature ¶高温多湿の気候 a climate of high temperature and high humidity.

ごうおん 轟音 a roaring sound; a deafening roar.

こうか[1] 工科 the engineering department ¶工科大学 a technical [an engineering] college; an institute of technology.

こうか[2] 効果 (an) effect; effectiveness; 〈薬などの〉 efficacy; 〈結果〉 a result ¶効果がある have an effect ⟪on⟫; be effective; do *sb* good; 〈薬などが〉 ⟪文⟫ be efficacious; take effect / 効果がない have [produce] no effect ⟪on⟫; be ineffective; be ineffectual; be fruitless; get nowhere; be no use; ⟪文⟫ be of no avail; 〈薬などが〉 ⟪文⟫ be inefficacious / 効果を収める get [⟪文⟫ obtain] good results; 〈事柄が〉 produce satisfactory results / 効果てきめんである bring an immediate result ⟪on⟫; 〈薬が〉 take instant effect ⟪on⟫; work wonders. [文例⇩]

こうか[3] 校歌 a school [college] song.

こうか[4] 高価 a high price ¶高価な high-priced; expensive; costly.

こうか[5] 高架 ¶高架の elevated; overhead; high-level / 高架線[鉄道] ⟪米⟫ an elevated railroad; ⟪米口語⟫ an L [el]; ⟪英⟫ an overhead railway / 高架線を走る列車 ⟪米⟫ an elevated train; ⟪英⟫ an overhead railway train / 高架道 a high-level road; 〈他の道路・鉄道の上を越える〉 an overpass; ⟪英⟫ a flyover.

こうか[6] 降下 (a) descent; a fall; a drop; (a) landing (着陸) ¶降下する descend; land (着陸する).

こうか[7] 硬化 ¶硬化する stiffen; harden; go solid (糊などが) / 態度を硬化させる stiffen *one's* attitude / 硬化ゴム ebonite; vulcanite / 硬化症 〘医〙 sclerosis ⟪of the arteries⟫.

こうか[8] 硬貨 a coin; metallic currency; a ⟪ten-yen⟫ piece; 〘経済〙 hard currency.

こうが[1] 高雅 ¶高雅な refined; elegant.

こうが[2] 黄河 〈中国〉 the Hwang Ho; the Yellow River.

ごうか 豪華 ¶豪華な splendid; gorgeous; luxurious; ⟪口語⟫ classy ⟪hotels⟫; ⟪口語⟫ posh ⟪dinner parties⟫ / 豪華船 a luxury liner / 豪華版 a deluxe edition. [文例⇩]

こうかい[1] 公海 the high seas; 〘国際法〙 the open sea; international waters ¶公海上で核実験を行なう conduct nuclear tests over international waters.

こうかい[2] 公開 ¶株式の公開 public offering

こうえい[2] 光栄です. I feel [am] honored. / お目にかかれて, とても光栄です. I'm very honored [It is a great honor] to meet you. / 私どものささやかな会にご光来いただけましたら, この上ない光栄でございます. The honor would be entirely mine, if you would attend my little party. / この会に列することをえましたのは私の大いに光栄とするところであります. I esteem it a great honor [I feel highly honored] to be present at this meeting. | It is a great privilege for me to attend this meeting.

こうえき[1] 公益優先. The public interest must come first [must take priority].

こうおつ 両者はほとんど甲乙がつけがたい. There is little to choose between the two. | It is hard to say which of the two is better.

こうか[2] その効果が表われるには, 時間がかかります. It will be some time before its effects make themselves felt. / それは公衆の福祉を増進する上に非常に効果がある. It will go a long way toward promoting public welfare. / そんなことをしてもあの男には効果はあるまい. That will cut no ice with him.

ごうか 今夜のごちそうは豪華版だった. We had a big [grand] dinner this evening.

こうかい of stocks; a public sale of shares / 公開の (gardens) open to the public; open (meetings); public (exhibitions) / 公開の席で in public / 公開する open to the public; ⟨新しい発明品などを⟩ unveil; ⟨映画などを⟩ release; ⟨陳列する⟩ exhibit; put *sth* on view (to the public) / 一般に公開されている be open [on view] to the public / (大学の)公開講座 an extension [((英)) extramural] lecture [course] / 公開市場 an open market / 公開状 an open letter / 公開討論会 an open forum / 公開練習 『ボクシング』 a public workout / 公開録音 a public recording.

こうかい[3] 降灰 ⟨火山の爆発などに伴う⟩ a fall of ash; falling ash (灰).

こうかい[4] 後悔 ((文)) repentance; (a) regret; remorse / 後悔する ((文)) repent (of); regret; be sorry (for) / …したことを後悔する be sorry for [regret] doing [having *done*]; regret [be sorry] that *one did*. 【文例⇩】

こうかい[5] 航海 navigation; (a) (sea) voyage; (a) sailing; ⟨巡航⟩ a cruise ¶ 航海する ⟨船・人が⟩ sail; make a voyage (to); ((文)) voyage; ⟨人が⟩ take (a) passage (on board) the Queen Elizabeth / 航海中である ⟨人が⟩ be on a voyage; ⟨船・人が⟩ be (out) at sea / 航海士 a mate; a navigation officer / 一等航海士 a chief mate; a first mate [officer] / 二[三]等航海士 a second [third] mate [officer] / 大航海時代 ((史)) the Age of Great Voyages / 航海術 (the art of) navigation / 航海灯 navigation [running] lights / 航海日誌 (keep) a (ship's) log; a logbook. 【文例⇩】

こうかい[6] 紅海 the Red Sea.

こうかい[7] 黄海 the Yellow Sea.

ごうかい[1] 口外 ¶ 口外する let (a secret) out; betray; reveal; tell; ((文)) disclose / 口外しない keep (a secret); keep (a matter) to *oneself*; keep (it) a secret; keep mum about (a matter). 【文例⇩】

ごうかい[2] 口蓋 ((解)) the palate; the roof [vault] of the mouth / 口蓋の palatal / 軟[硬]口蓋 the soft [hard] palate / 口蓋垂 the uvula ((*pl*. -las, -lae)).

ごうかい[3] 公害 (environmental) pollution (環境汚染); (a) public nuisance (軽犯罪的) ★ 日本語の「公害」は英語の public nuisance の直訳ではあるが, この英語は今では法律用語としてしか使われず,「公害」のような日常語ではない. (environmental) pollution は正確には「騒音」「地盤沈下」などを含まないで「公害」ほど意味は広くないが, 通俗には日本語の「公害」とほぼ同じ意味で使われている. ¶ noise pollution (騒音公害)はこの英語の語彙の欠如をおぎなうための造語であるが, 言葉使いに厳格な人は好まない ¶ 公害の被害者 a pollution victim / 公害をひき起こす cause harm to the public / 公害を除去する remove (air and water) pollutants / 二次公害 secondary pollution / 無公害の pollution-free ((cars)); non-polluting ((technology)) / 低公害車 a low-pollution car / 公害対策 anti-pollution measures / 公害反対運動 an anti-pollution movement / 公害反対運動の活動家 an anti-pollution activist / 公害防止法 anti-pollution laws / 公害病 a pollution disease / 公害問題 a pollution problem.

こうがい[1] 坑外 ¶ 坑外の[に, で] above ground; on the surface / 坑外作業 surface work / 坑外夫 a surface worker.

こうがい[2] 郊外 (in) the suburbs (of); (on) the outskirts (of) ¶ 東京の郊外に住む live in the suburbs [a suburb] of Tokyo / 郊外居住者 a suburban resident; a suburbanite / 郊外生活 life in the suburbs; suburban life / 郊外電車 a suburban train. 【文例⇩】

こうがい[3] 校外 ¶ 校外の[に, で] outside (the) school; out of school.

こうがい[4] 梗概 an outline; a synopsis ((*pl*. -opses)); a summary ¶ 梗概を示す give an outline (of); outline; summarize.

こうがい[5] 港外 ¶ 港外の[に, で] outside the port [harbor] / 港外に停泊する lie at anchor off the harbor.

こうがい[6] 構外 ¶ 構外の[に, で] outside the premises [grounds, compound].

ごうかい 豪快 ¶ 豪快な dynamic; superb; beautiful; exciting; heroic.

ごうがい 号外 an extra [a special] (edition) ¶ 号外を発行する issue an extra.

こうかいどう 公会堂 a public [town] hall; a civic auditorium ((*pl*. -riums, -ria)).

こうかがく 光化学 ((物)) photochemistry ¶ 光化学スモッグ photochemical smog.

こうかく 口角 ¶ 口角泡を飛ばす have [((文)) engage in] a heated discussion.

こうがく[1] 工学 engineering; engineering science ¶ 応用[機械, 精密, 電気, 土木]工学 practical [mechanical, precision, electrical, civil] engineering / 工学部 the department of technology [engineering (science)] / 工学博士 ⟨人⟩ a docter of engineering; ⟨学位⟩ Doctor of Engineering (略: D.Eng.) / 工学修士 ⟨人⟩ a master of engineering; ⟨学位⟩ Master of Engineering (略: M.Eng.) / 工学士 ⟨人⟩ a bachelor of engineering; ⟨学位⟩ Bachelor of Engineering (略: B.Eng.).

こうがく[2] 光学 optics ¶ 光学ガラス optical glass / 光学兵器[器械] an optical weapon [instrument].

こうがく[3] 後学 ¶ 後学のため for *one's* information; for future use [benefit].

こうかい 彼は今まで怠けたのを後悔している. He is regretting his idleness [laziness]. | He is sorry that he has been idle. / あとになって後悔しないように, 若いうちにしっかり勉強しておきなさい. Do as much learning as possible while you are young, so that you will have no regrets later on. / 後悔先に立たず. One is always sorry after the event. | It is no use crying over spilt milk. 【諺】

こうかい 航海中は穏やかであった. We had a calm voyage [passage]. | The sea crossing was calm.

こうかい[1] 一言たりとも口外してはならん. Don't say anything to anybody about it. | Don't breathe a word of it to anyone.

こうがく⁴ 高額 a large amount [sum] 《of money》 ¶高額所得者 a large income earner; people in the higher brackets.

ごうかく 合格 success in an examination; passing an exam ¶合格する〈試験に〉pass 《an exam》; get through 《a test》;〈物が〉come up to the standard [mark]; stand the test;〈採用される〉be accepted ¶合格した successful candidate [applicant] / 合格点 a passing mark;〈人の〉the qualifying marks [score] / 合格率 the ratio of successful applicants; the (examination) pass rate.

こうかくか 好角家 a sumo fan [enthusiast].

こうがくしん 向学心 love of learning;《文》a desire to learn [for learning] ¶向学心に燃える《文》be an ardent lover of learning; have a strong interest in learning; be keen on learning.

こうがくねん 高学年 the higher [upper] classes [grades, forms].

こうかくるい 甲殻類《動》Crustacea ¶甲殻類の動物 a crustacean.

こうかくレンズ 広角レンズ a wide-angle lens ¶超広角レンズ a super-wide-angle lens.

こうかつ 狡猾 ¶こうかつな cunning; sly (as a fox); tricky; artful; crafty; wily / こうかつな手段 sharp practice; a shrewd trick / こうかつに立ち回る act craftily.

こうかん¹ 公刊 publication ⇒ かんこう¹, しゅっぱん¹. 文例⇩

こうかん² 公館 Government establishments ¶在外公館 〜 さいかん.

こうかん³ 好感 a good feeling; goodwill;〈好印象〉a good [《文》favorable] impression ¶好感を与える impress sb favorably; make a favorable impression (on sb) / 好感を抱くbe favorably [kindly, well] disposed toward sb; have [《文》entertain] a friendly feeling toward sb.

こうかん⁴ 好漢 a good [nice] fellow;《米口語》a regular guy.

こうかん⁵ 交換 (an) exchange; (an) interchange; give-and-take;〈物々交換〉barter;《口語》a swap;〈置き換え〉substitution; replacement;《数》commutation;〈手形の〉clearing ¶交換する exchange 《A for B》; make an exchange; give 《A for B》; give and take; barter [trade] 《A for B》;《口語》swap 《stamps》; substitute 《A for B》; clear 《bills》 / 中古の車を売って新車と交換する trade a used car in for a new one / …と交換に in exchange [return] for… /（電話の）自動 [手動] 交換 automatic [manual] switching / 交換学生 [教授] an exchange student [professor] / 交換価値 an exchange [exchangeable] value; exchangeability / 交換手 a telephone [switchboard] operator / 交換条件 a bargaining point /（電話の）交換台 a switchboard /（手形の）交換高 exchanges / 交換法則《数》the commutative law / 交換用部品 replacement (units and) parts / 交換レンズ《写真》an interchangeable lens. 文例⇩

こうかん⁶ 交歓 ¶交歓する exchange courtesies (greetings, good wishes) 《with》; fraternize 《with》 ⇒ しんぜん².

こうかん⁷ 高官 a high (government) official;《文》a (high) dignitary.

こうかん⁸ 鋼管 a steel pipe [tube]; steel tubing (総称).

こうがん¹ 紅顔 ¶紅顔の《文》rosy-cheeked; youthful / 紅顔の美少年《文》a fair [handsome] youth;《文》an Adonis.

こうがん² 厚顔 impudence; shamelessness ¶厚顔無恥の impudent; unabashed; shameless; thick-skinned.

こうがん³ 睾丸《解》the testicles; the testes (sing. testis) ¶こうがんの testicular / 副こうがん the epididymis (pl. -mides) / こうがん炎 orchitis; testitis.

ごうかん 強姦 (a) rape ¶強姦する rape;《文》commit rape 《upon》;《文》violate / 強姦罪 rape; criminal assault / 強姦犯人 a rapist.

こうがんざい 抗癌剤 an anticancer drug.

こうかんしんけい 交感神経 a sympathetic nerve ¶交感［対交感］神経系 the sympathetic [parasympathetic] nervous system.

こうかんど 高感度 supersensitivity ¶高感度フィルム a fast [supersensitive] film.

こうかんばん 後甲板 the quarterdeck; the afterdeck.

こうき¹ 公器 a public institution; a public organ (新聞など).

こうき² 広軌 a broad gauge ¶広軌鉄道 a broad-gauge railroad.

こうき³ 好機 a good [golden] opportunity; a good [《文》favorable] chance ¶好機を捕らえる take [seize] an opportunity;《文》avail oneself of an [a perfect] opportunity / 好機を逸する miss [lose] an opportunity [a chance]; let a chance go [slip]. 文例⇩

こうき⁴ 光輝 ¶光輝ある brilliant; shining;《文》glorious.

こうき⁵ 後記 a postscript (略：P.S., p.s.) ¶編集後記 the editor's postscript.

こうき⁶ 後期 the latter term; the latter [second] half year;《米》the second semester ¶ (3学期制の学校の) 後期 印象派 the post-impressionists / 後期ギリシャ語 late Greek.

こうき⁷ 香気 (a) fragrance;《文》an aroma; a sweet smell ¶香気のある《文》fragrant;《文》aromatic; sweet-smelling / 香気を発す smell sweet;《文》emit [send forth] fra-

---

Don't let it go any further. | Mum's the word!

こうがい 郊外の膨張によって都市生活そのものが変わりつつある。City life itself is being altered by the growth of the suburbs.

こうかん¹ 彼からの情報はすでに公刊されているものばかりである。All the information he gave me was [He told me nothing that wasn't] already in public print.

こうかん⁵ このビルには交換台がある。There is a (telephone) switchboard serving this building. / 私はスミス氏と日本語と英語の交換教授をした。I taught Mr. Smith Japanese in return [exchange] for lessons in English.

こうき³ このような好機は二度と来ないだろう。A chance like this

grance [a sweet smell].
こうき[8] 校旗 a school banner [flag].
こうき[9] 綱紀 〈国政の規律〉 official [government] discipline; 〈秩序〉 public order; law and order ¶綱紀の乱れ the deterioration of (official) discipline / 綱紀を正す《文》improve the moral fiber 《of》; tighten discipline 《among》/ 綱紀粛正 the enforcement of official discipline.
こうき[10] 高貴 ¶高貴な high; noble / 高貴な方《文》a person of high rank [of (noble) birth]; 《文》a high personage / 高貴の生まれである be born into a noble family; 《文》be high-born.
こうぎ[1] 広義 ¶広義に解釈する take 《it》 in the broad [wide] sense (of the word).
こうぎ[2] 抗議 a protest; an objection (反対); an exception (異議); a complaint (苦情) ¶抗議する protest [make a protest] 《to *sb* against *sth*》; 《米》protest 《the war in Vietnam》; offer [raise] an objection 《to》; object 《to》; take exception 《to》; complain ★「…に反対して抗議する」は protest against 《the war》 が英米共に通じる一般的な形だが, 《米》では protest 《the war》 の形も使われる / 強硬に抗議する make a strong [stiff] protest; give a strong-worded warning / 抗議を申し込む lodge [file, 《文》enter] a protest 《with *sb* against *sth*》/ 抗議集会 a protest meeting [rally] / 抗議デモ 《stage》 a protest demonstration [parade]; 《join in》 a march of protest 《against the war》/ 抗議文を手交する hand a protest note 《to *sb*》. [文例⇩]
こうぎ[3] 講義 a lecture 《on》 ¶講義する lecture 《on》; give a lecture 《on》; give a course 《in French》 (連続的の) / 講義の準備をする prepare *one's* lecture / 講義に出席する attend a lecture / 講義録 a correspondence course; a transcript of lectures. [文例⇩]
ごうき 剛毅 《文》fortitude ¶剛毅な《文》stouthearted; hardy; sturdy.
ごうぎ 合議 consultation ¶合議する confer 《with》; consult together 《about》/ 合議の上で《文》after consultation; 《文》by mutual consent / 合議制 a council system.
こうきあつ 高気圧 high (atmospheric) pressure ⇨ きあつ.
こうきしん 好奇心 curiosity ¶激しい好奇心 burning curiosity / 好奇心の強い curious; full of curiosity; inquisitive / 好奇心から[に駆られて] out of curiosity / 好奇心をひく[そそる] arouse [《文》excite] *one's* curiosity.
こうきゅう[1] 好球 〖野球〗a good pitch ¶好球を見のがす miss a good pitch.
こうきゅう[2] 考究 〈調査〉(an) investigation; (an) inquiry; 〈研究〉research(es); (a) study; 〈考慮〉consideration ¶考究する investigate; inquire into; study; make researches 《on, into》; consider; think over. [文例⇩]
こうきゅう[3] 恒久 ¶恒久の lasting; everlasting; permanent; eternal; perpetual / 恒久化する《文》perpetuate / 恒久平和 (a) permanent peace.
こうきゅう[4] 高級 ¶高級の high-class[-grade]; higher; advanced; quality 《papers》; 《口語》posh 《hotels》; 《口語》classy 《restaurants》; expensive 《restaurants》/ 高級官吏 higher [high-ranking] officials; government officials in the higher echelons / 高級車 a deluxe car; a luxury automobile / 高級住宅地 an exclusive residential district / 高級船員 an officer (of a ship); 〈集合的に〉the quarterdeck / 高級品《文》an article of quality; (high) quality goods [articles]. [文例⇩]
こうきゅう[5] 高給 a high [big] salary; high pay ¶高給を取る draw a high salary 《from a firm》; be highly paid.
こうきゅう[6] 硬球 〖テニス·卓球·野球〗a regulation ball.
ごうきゅう 剛球 〖野球〗a fast [speed] pitch; a smoke ball ¶剛球投手 a strong-armed pitcher; a smoke-ball hurler.
こうきゅうび 公休日 a (public) holiday.
こうきょ 皇居 the Imperial Palace ¶皇居前広場 the Palace Plaza.
こうきょう[1] 公共 ¶公共の public; common / 公共の福祉 public welfare / 公共の利益を図る《文》promote the public good; work for the public benefit [in the interests of the public] / 公共企業体 a public corporation / 公共財産 public property / 公共事業 a public undertaking [enterprise]; a public utility; public works; (public) utilities / 公共施設 public [community] facilities / 公共心 public spirit; a sense of public duty [morality] / 公共心のある public-spirited / 公共心に訴える appeal to the (citizens') sense of public morality / 公共団体 a public body [organization] / 公共投資 (a) public investment / 公共輸送機関 public transportation [《英》transport] / 公共料金 fees for public services; public utility charges [rates] (電気·水道料金など).
こうきょう[2] 好況 ⇨こうけいき ¶好況と不況の循環 the cycle of boom and bust / 好況産業 a boom(ing) industry / 好況時代 prosperous days [times]; boom times.
こうきょう[3] 交響 ¶交響的(な) symphonic 《jazz》/ 交響曲[楽] a symphony / 交響楽団 a symphony orchestra / 交響詩 a symphonic poem.
こうぎょう[1] 工業 (an) industry; manufacturing industry ¶工業の industrial; technical; manufacturing / 工業用の for industrial use [purposes]; industrial 《diamonds》/ 工業化す

---

will never come [offer itself] again. / 好機逸すべからず. Seize the opportunity while you can.
こうぎ[2] なぜ日本人が牛肉の値段を下げろと激しく抗議しないのか, 私にはわからない. I cannot understand why the Japanese do not protest loudly [vociferously] against high beef prices.
こうぎ[3] 岡野教授は来学期から「ハムレット」を講義する. Professor Okano will read 'Hamlet' with us next term.
こうきゅう[2] その計画はまだ考究中だ. The scheme is still under investigation.
こうきゅう[4] 壁紙を変えるだけで, この部屋は高級な感じが出ます

こうぎょう **工業化する** industrialize 《a country》; produce 《goods》 on a commercial basis / 工業界 industrial circles; the industrial world / 工業化学 industrial chemistry / 日本工業規格 the Japanese Industrial Standard (略: JIS) / 工業技術 industrial technology / 工業高等学校 a technical high school / 工業高等専門学校 a technical junior college / 工業国 an industrial nation [country] / 工業生産高 《Russia's》 industrial output / 工業製品[生産] industrial goods [production] / 工業大学 a technical college; a college [an institute] of technology / 《英》 a polytechnic / 工業地帯 an industrial area [zone] / 工業デザイナー an industrial designer / 工業都市 an industrial [a manufacturing, a factory] town [city] / 工業用地 an industrial site.

こうぎょう² 鉱業 mining; the mining industry ¶鉱業会社 a mining company / 鉱業家 a mine owner [operator].

こうぎょう³ 興行 〈1回の〉 a performance; a show; 〈事業〉 show business ¶興行する perform; give a performance; produce 《a play》; show [run] 《a play》/ 興行化する adapt 《a story》 for the stage; 〈映画化〉 film 《a story》/ 一月興行 the January program; the bill for January / 長[短]期興行 a long [short] run / 興行界 the entertainment world / 興行価値 box-office value / 興行権 performance [production] rights / 〈芝居の〉 stage [dramatic] rights / 興行師 an impresario 《pl. -s》; a show proprietor [manager]; a showman / 興行主 a promotor / 興行収益 box-office profits / 興行税 an entertainment tax / 興行成績 a box-office record / 興行物 a show; a (public) performance; an exhibition. 文例⇩

こうぎょうしょ 口供書 《法》 an affidavit.

こうぎょく 紅玉 〈宝石〉 a ruby; 〈りんご〉 a Jonathan (apple).

こうきん¹ 公金 public money [funds] ¶公金を横領する embezzle public money / 公金費消 embezzlement [misappropriation] of public money.

こうきん² 拘禁 detention; confinement; custody; imprisonment ¶拘禁する detain; confine; keep [hold] sb in custody; hold sb under arrest; imprison.

ごうきん 合金 an alloy ¶合金にする alloy 《metals, silver with copper》; make an alloy of 《copper and tin》/ 超合金 a superalloy.

こうきんせい 抗菌性 antibacterial.

こうく 鉱区 a mining area; a mine lot.

こうぐ 工具 a tool; an implement ¶工具1式 a set [kit] of tools.

こうくう¹ 口腔 ⇒こうこう¹ ¶口腔外科 oral surgery.

こうくう² 高空 ¶高空で high (up) in the air; 《文》 at a high altitude.

こうくう³ 航空 aviation; flying ¶航空医学 aviation [aeronautical] medicine / 航空宇宙局 ⇒ナサ / 航空宇宙産業 the aerospace industry / 航空会社 an airline company / 航空学[術] aeronautics / 航空機 a flying machine; an airplane; 《英》 an aeroplane; an aircraft 〈単複同形〉/ 航空基地 an air base / 航空券 a plane [an air(line)] ticket / 航空工学 aeronautical engineering / 航空士 an aerial navigator / 航空自衛隊 the Air Self-Defense Force / 航空施設 air navigation facilities / 航空写真 an aerial photograph / 航空写真術 aerial photography; aerophotography / 航空書簡 an aerogram; an air letter / 航空測量 aerial surveying; an aerial survey 〈1回の〉/ 航空隊 a flying [an aviation] corps / 航空灯 a navigation light / 航空灯台 an aerial lighthouse / 航空標識 a radio [an aerial] beacon / 航空(郵)便 air mail / 航空便で手紙を出す send a letter 《to Hawaii》 by air mail; airmail a letter / 航空母艦 an aircraft carrier; a carrier / 航空輸送 ⇒くうゆ / 航空力学 flight dynamics / 航空料金 an air fare / 航空路 an air [aerial] route [line]; an airway; 《航空》 an air lane.

こうぐう 厚遇 a warm 《《文》 cordial》 reception; kind treatment; hospitality ⇒ゆうぐう.

こうぐうけいさつ 皇宮警察 the Imperial Guards.

こうくつ 後屈 《医》 retroflexion 《of the uterus》.

こうくん 校訓 《文》 school precepts; a motto for school discipline.

こうぐん 行軍 a march; marching ¶行軍する march / 行軍中である be on the march.

こうげ 高下 〈身分の〉 rank; 〈品質の〉 quality; 〈相場の〉 fluctuations ¶身分の高下を問わず 《文》 irrespective of rank.

こうけい¹ 口径 ¶口径20インチの大砲 a gun of twenty-inch caliber; a 20-inch gun / 38口径のピストル a 38-caliber revolver; a 38.

こうけい² 光景 a spectacle; a sight; a scene ¶光景を呈する present a 《fine, pitiful》 spectacle.

こうけい³ 後継 ¶後継内閣 the incoming Cabinet / 後継者 a successor 《to》; 〈嗣子〉 an heir 《to》; an heiress 〈女〉. 文例⇩

こうげい 工芸 (artistic) handicraft(s); industrial art ¶工芸家 a craftsman / 工芸技術 craft skills; craftsmanship / 工芸美術 applied fine arts / 工芸品 a craft object; an art work; craft products.

ごうけい 合計 the (sum) total; the total amount [sum]; an aggregate 《of》 ¶合計する add [sum] up; total / 合計して in all; altogether; all told / 合計...になる total...; add [make] up to.... 文例⇩

上. A change of wallpaper is all that is required to give a feeling of quality to this room.
こうぎょう³ その芝居は20日間興行された. The play ran for twenty days [had a twenty-day run]. / その劇の上演に当たって劇場主はまず第一に興行成績を心配した. The proprietor of the theater looked first to the box office before mounting the play. / 興行成績は上乗だった. It was a great box-office success.
こうけい³ あの人の後継者はだれになるだろうか. Who will succeed him [to his post]?
ごうけい 支出は合計50万円になった. The expenditure totaled

こうけいき 好景気 (a wave of) prosperity; good times; a boom (にわか景気) ⇨ けいき⁴.

こうげき 攻撃 an attack 《on》; an assault; a raid; 〈非難〉a charge; 《文》(a) censure ¶攻撃する attack; assault; make an attack [assault]《on》; 《文》give battle 《to》; take the offensive 《against》; fall on (襲いかかる); go at (非難する); 《文》censure, criticize; denounce; speak [talk, write] against; 〈野球〉go [come] to bat ¶攻撃を開始する open [launch] an attack 《on, against》; mount an offensive / 攻撃を受ける be [come] under attack [fire] 《from one's opponents》/ 攻撃的な offensive, aggressive / 攻撃側〈野球〉the team at bat / 攻撃姿勢 an offensive posture / 攻撃用兵器 offensive weapons [arms] / 攻撃力 striking power [ability]; offensive power. 文例❹

こうけつ 高潔 ¶高潔な《文》noble(-minded);《文》high-minded[-principled] / 高潔な人《文》a person of noble character;《文》a high-minded man. 文例❹

ごうけつ 豪傑 a hero (pl. -es); a larger-than-life figure; an outstanding [extraordinary] man [character]; 〈風変りな人物〉a character ¶豪傑肌 larger than life / 豪傑笑い a broad [hearty] laugh; a guffaw.

こうけつあつ 高血圧 high blood pressure; hypertension ⇨ けつあつ.

こうけっか 好結果 a good [successful] result; (a) success ¶好結果を得る[生む] obtain [produce] satisfactory [good] results.

こうけん¹ 公権 civil rights; citizenship ¶公権を剥奪(ハクダツ)される be deprived of one's civil rights; be disfranchised / 公権剥奪[停止] deprivation [suspension] of civil rights; disfranchisement.

こうけん² 効験《文》efficacy; (an) effect ⇨ ききめ, こうのう² ¶効験あらたかな《文》wonderfully efficacious; 《文》of miraculous efficacy; wonder 《drugs》.

こうけん³ 後見〖法〗guardianship ¶後見をする act as guardian 《for》; look after 《children》/ 後見を受けている be (placed) under the guardianship 《of》; be in ward 《to》/ 後見人〖法〗a guardian; 〈演技者の〉a prompter / 被後見人 a ward.

こうけん⁴ 貢献 (a) contribution; services ¶貢献する contribute to 《…》; render services 《to》; go a long way [far] toward 《solving the problem》; do (a lot) for 《national welfare》; help 《sb (to) do》.

こうげん¹ 公言 ¶公言する declare 《that..., oneself to be》; quote《oneself》out (to be);《文》profess (to know, one's belief that...);《文》avow《oneself to be》/ …と公言してはばからない have no hesitation in stating [declaring] that....

こうげん² 光源 a light source; a source of light; 〖物〗an illuminant.

こうげん³ 抗原〖生理〗an antigen ¶抗原菌 an antigenic organism.

こうげん⁴ 広[高]言 tall [big] talk; a brag; a boast ¶高言を吐く talk tall [big]; brag 《about, of》; boast 《about, of, that...》.

こうげん⁵ 高原 a plateau (pl. -s, -eaux); a tableland; high plains ¶志賀高原 Shiga Heights / 高原地帯 a plateau area; plateau country / 高原療養所 an alpine sanatorium.

ごうけん¹ 合憲 ¶合憲性 constitutionality / 合憲的 constitutional.

ごうけん² 剛健 ¶剛健な strong and sturdy; virile; manly / 剛健な気風を養う《文》cultivate the spirit of fortitude and manliness.

こうげんびょう 膠原病 collagen disease.

こうこ¹ 公庫 the municipal [state] treasury; 〈金融公庫〉a finance corporation.

こうこ² 好個 ¶好個の excellent; fine; good; ideal / 好個の一例 a good [a fine, an appropriate] example;《文》a pertinent instance; a case in point.

こうご¹ 口語 spoken language; colloquial speech [language]; (a) colloquialism ¶口語の spoken; colloquial; conversational / 口語体で書く write in colloquial style.

こうご² 交互 ¶交互の〈相互の〉mutual;《文》reciprocal; 〈交替の〉alternate / 交互に mutually;《文》reciprocally; alternately; by turns.

ごうご 豪語 ¶豪語する boast; brag; talk big.

こうこう¹ 口腔〖解〗the mouth; the oral cavity ¶口腔衛生 oral [dental] hygiene.

こうこう² 孝行〖旧〗filial piety [duty] ¶孝行する[である] be dutiful to [thoughtful about] one's parents; be a good son [daughter]. 文例❹

こうこう³ 後攻〈野球〉⇨ あとぜめ.

こうこう⁴ 航行 navigation; sailing; a cruise (巡航) ¶こうかい³ ¶航行できる[できない]川 a navigable [an unnavigable] river. 文例❹

こうこう⁵ 高校 ⇨ こうとうがっこう ¶高校生 a (senior) high-school student;〈米〉a senior high student / 〈米〉a high schooler / 高校卒業生 a high school graduate. 文例❹

こうこう⁶ 煌々 ¶こうこうたる brilliant;

[amounted to, ran up to] 500,000 yen.

こうけいき 市場は好景気だ。The market is quite lively.

こうげき 首相は党内の実力者から猛烈に攻撃された。The Prime Minister came under heavy fire [a blistering attack] from influential members of his party. / 彼の品行は世間から攻撃されるだ

ろう。His conduct will lay him open to public censure. / 攻撃は最良の防御である。Attack is the best form of defense.

こうけつ だれもが氏の高潔な精神に敬意を払った。Everybody respected him for the nobility of his mind.

こうこう² 孝行をしたいときには親はなし。When one would be filial, one's parents are gone. | A son never thinks of his parents until it is too late.

こうこう⁴ この川は人吉まで航行ができる。This river is navigable as far as Hitoyoshi.

こうこう⁵ 彼は高校しか出ていない。He has had only a high-school education. / 彼女とは高校でいっしょだった。We went to

bright / こうこうと brilliantly; brightly.

こうこう⁷ 然々 so and so; such and such ¶こうこういう人 such and such a person / こうこうしろと言う tell *sb* to do so and so.

こうごう 皇后 an empress; a queen; 〈女帝と区別して〉 an empress [a queen] consort ¶皇后陛下 Her Majesty [H. M.] the Empress.

ごうごう ¶ごうごうたる roaring; rumbling; thundering / ごうごうたる音 a roaring [rumbling] sound; a roar; a rumble / ごうごうたる反対の声 an uproar [《文》a loud clamor] against 《the measure》; 《arouse》 stormy opposition 《to》 / ごうごうと鳴る roar; rumble. 文例⇩

こうごうしい 神々しい divine; 《文》 godly; holy; awe-inspiring.

こうごうせい 向光性 〖生物〗 ⇨ こうじつせい.

こうごうせい 光合成 〖植〗 photosynthesis.

こうこうど 高高度 ¶高高度の high-altitude 《aircraft》 / 高高度飛行 high-altitude flying.

こうこうや 好々爺 a good-natured [genial] old man.

こうこがく 考古学 archaeology ¶考古学的資料 archaeological evidence / 考古学者 an archaeologist.

こうこく¹ 公告 a public [an official] notice [announcement] ¶公告する notify [announce] publicly.

こうこく² 公国 a dukedom; a principality.

こうこく³ 広告 (an) advertisement; 《口語》 an ad; 〈宣伝〉 publicity; 〈ポスター〉 a poster; 〈ビラ〉 a bill ¶広告する advertise; announce; give publicity to / 三行広告 ⇨ さんぎょうこうこく / 広告業 the advertising business [industry] / 広告業者 an advertising agent; 広告塔 〈街路の〉 a poster column; 〈屋上などの〉 an advertising pillar / 広告主 an advertiser; 〈ラジオ・テレビの〉 a sponsor / 広告収入 advertising revenue / 広告放送 a commercial broadcast; 〈文句〉 a commercial (message) / 広告欄 an advertisement [ad] column / 広告料 advertisement rates. 文例⇩

こうこく⁴ 抗告 〖法〗 a protest; a complaint; an appeal ¶抗告する complain 《against a decision》; appeal 《from a decision》; file a protest 《against》.

こうこつ 恍惚 ¶こうこつとなる be in raptures [ecstasies] 《over》; be enchanted [《文》 enraptured, 《文》 entranced] 《by》; be carried away 《by》 / こうこつの 《文》 in an ecstasy; in raptures; enchanted / こうこつ状態になる go into trances [fits]; fall into a (deep) trance.

こうこつかん 硬骨漢 《文》 a man of unyielding spirit.

こうこつぶん[もじ] 甲骨文[文字] 〖考古〗 inscriptions on animal bones and tortoise carapaces.

こうさ¹ 考査 〈試験〉 a test; an examination ¶考査する examine.

こうさ² 交差 crossing; intersection; 〖遺伝〗 crossing-over ¶交差する cross 《intersect》 《each other》 / 交差線 a cross line / 交差点 a crossing; an intersection; a crossroads (四つ辻); a junction (線路の).

こうざ¹ 口座 an account ¶銀行に口座を開く open a bank account [an account with a bank] / 口座を閉じる close *one's* account.

こうざ² 高座 ¶高座に出る perform [play] on the stage; face an audience.

こうざ³ 講座 a course (of lectures); 〈大学の〉 a (professorial) chair ¶講座を設ける create [establish, found] a chair 《of》 / 国文学の講座を担当している hold [occupy] the chair of Japanese literature 《at Tokyo University》 / 音楽講座 lectures on music / ラジオ英語講座 a radio English course.

こうさい¹ 公債 a public loan [debt]; 〈証書〉 a public (loan) bond ¶1千億円の公債を募集する float [raise] a loan of 100 billion yen / 公債を発行する issue bonds.

こうさい² 光彩 《文》 luster; 《文》 brilliancy ¶光彩を放つ give off pretty colors; 《文》 shed luster; shine; 〈比喩的に〉 《文》 cut a brilliant figure; stand out 《among others》 / 光彩を失う lose *its* luster; 〈比喩的に〉 《文》 go into (temporary) eclipse.

こうさい³ 交際 company; friendship; 《文》 association; 《文》 society; 《文》 acquaintance ¶交際する keep company 《with》; go around [about] with *sb*; go about together ★いずれの表現も,「友人と」と「男女が」の両方に使える / 善い[悪い]人と交際する keep good [bad] company / 交際が広い know a lot of people; have a wide [large] circle of friends [acquaintances] / 交際を結ぶ form a friendship 《with》; get acquainted 《with》 / 交際を断つ break (off) [cut, 《文》 sever] relations [*one's* friendship] 《with》 / 交際好きの sociable; fond of company [society] / 交際家 a sociable person / 交際費 entertainment expenses; 〈企業の〉 an expense(s) account [allowance]. 文例⇩

こうさい⁴ 虹彩 〖解〗 the iris (*pl.* -es, irides) ¶虹彩炎 iritis.

こうざい¹ 功罪 《文》 merits and demerits [faults]. 文例⇩

こうざい² 鋼材 steel materials; structural steel (建築用); rolled steel (圧延鋼).

こうさく¹ 工作 〈製作〉 construction; engineer-

---

high school together. / I was at high school with her. / その本は高校2年のときに読んだ。I read the book in my second year of high school.

ごうごう 遠くにごうごうと列車の音がした。I heard the distant rumble of a train.

こうこく³ それは店の良い広告になる。That will make our shop better known to the public. この雑誌は広告が減って経営難に陥っている。The magazine is suffering from financial difficulties owing to a loss of advertising.

こうさい³ 石田さんとは親しく交際してきました。I have been very close to [on very close terms with] Mr. Ishida. / 彼はあまり人と交際しない。He generally keeps to himself. / あの人は多くのイギリス人と交際している。He has a lot of acquaintances among Englishmen.

こうざい¹ その政策は功罪相半ばする。The merits and demerits of the policy offset each other

こうさく ing work; 〈学科〉handicraft; 〈策動〉(political) maneuvering ¶工作する construct; make; 〈策動する〉maneuver; scheme; 《文》engineer (a plot) / 準備工作をする pave the way (for); prepare the ground (for) / 工作機械 a machine tool.

こうさく² 交錯 〈入り交じること〉mixture; blending; 〈錯綜(㌛)〉《文》complication ¶光と影の交錯 the interplay of light and shadow / 交錯する cross [mingle with] each other; be complicated.

こうさく³ 耕作 cultivation; farming; 《文》tillage ¶耕作する cultivate; farm; 《文》till (fields); plow (land) / 耕作に適した arable; tillable / 耕作地 arable land.

こうさく⁴ 鋼索 (a) wire rope ¶鋼索鉄道 a funicular (railway).

こうさつ¹ 考察 《文》consideration; (an) examination; (a) study; observations ¶考察する consider; examine; study; inquire into; weigh (the consequences).

こうさつ² 絞殺 strangulation ¶絞殺する strangle; murder sb by strangulation.

こうさん¹ 公算 probability; likelihood ¶…の公算が大きい there is a strong probability that…; there is every likelihood [indication] that…; (the) chances are that….

こうさん² 降参 surrender; 《文》submission ¶降参する give in (to); surrender (to); 《文》submit (to); 《文》yield (to); give up (the fight [struggle]) / 〈閉口する〉give up; be beaten; 《口語》be floored; 〈口語〉be stumped / 降参したと言う admit [《文》admit one's] defeat; 《米口語》cry uncle. 文例あ

こうざん¹ 高山 a high mountain ¶高山植物 an alpine plant; 〈相〉alpine flora / 高山病 mountain [altitude] sickness.

こうざん² 鉱山 a mine ¶鉱山技師 a mining engineer / 鉱山業 the mining industry; (engage in) mining / 鉱山業者 a mine operator; a mine-owner / 鉱山町 a mining town / 鉱山労働者 a mine worker; a miner.

こうさんきん 抗酸菌 an acid-fast bacterium (*pl.* -ria).

こうさんぶつ 鉱産物 a mineral product; minerals ¶鉱産物の豊富な mineral-rich (provinces); (areas) rich in mineral resources.

こうし¹ 小牛 a calf (*pl.* calves) ¶小牛の肉 veal / 小牛皮 calf (leather); calfskin (高級品).

こうし² 公私 ¶公私を区別する keep one's private and public life [affairs] separate; 《文》make a proper distinction between the public and private (domain) / 公私を混同する confuse [mix up] private and public [official] matters [affairs]; 《文》fail to distinguish [make a proper distinction] between the public and private (domain [spheres of life]) / 公私ともに both officially and privately.

こうし³ 公使 a minister ¶ウルグアイ駐在日本公使 the Japanese Minister to [in] Uruguay / 公使館 a legation / 公使館員 (a member of) the legation staff.

こうし⁴ 光子 《物》a photon.

こうし⁵ 行使 ¶行使する exercise (one's rights); use; make use of / 選挙権を行使する exercise one's right to vote / 武力を行使する 《文》resort [appeal] to arms; use force; take military action.

こうし⁶ 格子 〈戸の〉(a) lattice; 〈窓の〉latticework; 〈鉄の〉a grid; a grating / 格子縞(㌛) cross stripes / 格子戸 a lattice door [window].

こうし 講師 a lecturer (in sociology at Waseda University); 〈講演の〉a speaker; a lecturer; 〈シンポジウムの〉a panelist; the panel (講師団) ¶大学の英語の講師 a university lecturer in English / 時間講師 a part-time lecturer / 専任講師 a full-time lecturer; 《米》an instructor.

こうし 孔子 Confucius.

こうじ¹ 工事 construction; construction work; engineering work ¶工事中である be under [in course of] construction / 工事現場 a construction site / 工事事務所 a construction work office; a site office (工事現場の) / 工事費 the cost of construction; construction costs [expenses]. 文例あ

こうじ² 小路 an alley; a lane; a narrow street.

こうじ³ 公示 (a) public announcement; an official [a public] notice ¶公示する publish; make public; make sth known to the public.

こうじ⁴ 好餌 文例あ ¶好餌となる 《文》fall an easy prey [victim] (to); become an easy victim (of); 〈口語〉be an easy mark for (the confidence tricksters).

こうじ⁵ 後事 〈将来の〉future affairs; 〈死後の〉one's affairs after one's death ¶後事を託す ask sb to look after one's affairs when one is gone [while one is away].

こうじ⁷ 麹 *koji*; malted rice; malt (麦の).

ごうしがいしゃ 合資会社 a limited partnership ¶合資会社木村商会 Kimura & Co., Ltd.

こうしき¹ 公式 〈数学の〉a formula (*pl.* -s, -lae) ¶公式の formal; official / 公式に formally; officially / 公式的な考え方 a stereotyped way of thinking / 公式試合 a regular game [match] / 非公式試合 an exhibition game / 〈野球〉公式球 formalism / 公式訪問 a formal visit; 〈元首などの〉a state visit. 文例あ 「(ball).

こうしき² 硬式 ¶硬式球 regulation-ball (base-

[balance each other (out)].

こうさん² 降参だ! I give up. / I give in. / 彼は20分で降参した. He gave up [gave in (to his opponent)] after 20 minutes. ★give up は難問などに挑戦して「降参する」の意味にも使える.

こうじ¹ その工事の完成に約7年を要した. It took about seven years to complete the work. / 工事中.〈掲示〉Under construction [repair]. / 〈人がいるという意味で〉Men working [at work]. / この先工事中.〈掲示〉Construction ahead. / Road works.

こうじ⁴ 好事魔多し. Clouds always follow the sunshine. | There's many a slip 'twixt (the) cup and (the) lip. 〈諺〉

こうしき¹ それはまだ公式に発表されていない. It has not been

こうせい 高姿勢 《文》《assume》a high posture; a highhanded [an overbearing] attitude [manner].

こうしつ¹ 皇室 the Imperial Household [House, Family].

こうしつ² 硬質 ¶硬質の hard / 硬質ガラス [ゴム] hard glass [rubber].

こうしつ³ 膠質 ¶膠質の gluey; glutinous; gelatinous; 《物・化》colloid(al).

こうじつ 口実 an excuse; a pretext; a pretense ¶もっともらしい口実 a plausible excuse;《文》a specious pretense / へたな口実 a poor [flimsy, weak] excuse / 口実を作る[設ける] make [find] an excuse [a pretext] (for being late) / …を口実として on the pretext of…; with the excuse that…. 文例⇩

こうじつせい 向日性《植》(positive) heliotropism ¶向日性植物 a heliotropic plant.

こうしゃ¹ 公社 a public corporation ¶日本交通公社 the Japan Travel Bureau / 日本専売公社 the Japan Tobacco & Salt Public Corporation.

こうしゃ² 巧者 ¶巧者な clever; skillful;《文》dexterous;《文》adept / 相撲巧者の位登山 wily Masuiyama.

こうしゃ³ 後者《文》the latter ¶後者の《文》latter.

こうしゃ⁴ 降車 ⇒げしゃ ¶降車口 the exit; the way out / 降車ホーム an arrival platform.

こうしゃ⁵ 校舎 a schoolhouse; a school building.

ごうしゃ 豪奢 ¶豪奢な sumptuous; luxurious; extravagant; magnificent; grand.

こうしゃく¹ 公爵 a duke; a prince (日本・ドイツなどの) ¶公爵夫人 a duchess; a princess.

こうしゃく² 侯爵 a marquis ¶侯爵夫人 a marchioness.

こうしゃく³ 講釈 a lecture; 〈講談〉storytelling ¶講釈する give a lecture (on); explain / 講釈師 a (professional) storyteller.

こうしゃほう 高射砲 an antiaircraft gun.

こうしゅ 攻守 offense and defense; 〈野球〉batting and fielding ¶攻守同盟 an offensive and defensive alliance. 文例⇩

こうしゅう¹ 口臭 (have) bad [foul] breath;《医》halitosis ¶口臭がある have bad [foul] breath.

こうしゅう² 公衆 the general public; the public (at large);《文》the masses (一般大衆) ¶公衆の public;《文》communal / 公衆の前で in public / 公衆の利益になる be in [serve] the public interest(s) / 公衆衛生 public health [hygiene] / 公衆電話 a public telephone; a pay phone;〈室〉a (public) telephone booth; 〈英〉a telephone [call] box / 公衆道徳 public morality [morals] / 公衆便所 a public lavatory

⇒トイレ / 公衆浴場 a public bath; a bathhouse.

こうしゅう³ 講習 a (short) course; a class ¶講習を行なう〈受ける〉give [take] a course 《in [of] first aid》/ 講習会 a short course; a lecture class; a (summer, winter) school / 講習生 a student. 文例⇩

こうしゅうは 高周波《電》high frequency (略：H.F., HF).

こうしゅけい 絞首刑 (death [execution] by) hanging ¶絞首刑の判決 a hanging verdict; a death sentence / 絞首刑の宣告をうける be sentenced to death by hanging / 絞首刑に処せられる be put to death by hanging; be hanged.

こうしゅだい 絞首台 ¶絞首台に上がる《文》mount the gallows [scaffold].

こうじゅつ¹ 口述 dictation ¶口述の《文》oral;《文》verbal;《a message given》by word of mouth / 口述する《文》state orally; dictate 《a letter to one's typist》/ 口述試験 an oral examination; 《大学の》a viva voce (examination);〈英口語〉a viva / 《公聴会の》口述人 a witness 《before a Diet committee》/ 口述筆記 writing down at sb's dictation; dictation;〈書いたもの〉notes《of de Saussure's three courses》.

こうじゅつ² 後述 ¶後述する say [mention, describe, 《文》touch upon] later.

こうじゅほうしょう 紅綬褒章 a Red Ribbon Medal.

こうしょ 高所 a height;《文》an eminence;《文》an elevation;《文》an elevated spot ¶高所恐怖症《have》a fear of heights;《医》acrophobia.

こうじょ 控除 (a) deduction; subtraction ¶控除する deduct [subtract]《from》; take away; cut off / 控除できる deductible《expenses》/ 控除額 an amount deducted《from》; a deduction《from》; an abatement《of the tax》. 文例⇩

こうしょう¹ 口承 (an) oral tradition ⇒でんしょう.

こうしょう² 公称 ¶公称の《文》nominal; official.

こうしょう³ 公傷 an injury incurred [sustained] while on duty [at work].

こうしょう⁴ 交渉 negotiation(s); bargaining;〈関係〉《文》relation; connection ¶交渉する negotiate《with sb about sth》; confer [bargain]《with》/ …と交渉がない have no connection with…; have nothing to do with… / 交渉の場に就く sit at the negotiating table / 交渉を続ける carry on negotiations《with》/ 交渉を打ち切る break off negotiations《with》/ 交渉に入る[を開始する] start [《文》enter (into)] negotiations《with》/ 交渉による解決 a negotiated solution《of a dispute》. 文例⇩

---

officially announced yet. / それは公式どおりには行かない。That cannot be done out of a textbook.

彼は何かと口実をこしらえては義務を避けようとする。He always tries to shirk his duty on some pretext or other.

攻守所を変えた。The tables were turned.

私は軽井沢で催された3週間の夏期講習に出席した。I attended a three weeks' summer class held at Karuizawa.

印税は必要経費として30パーセント控除してよい。You can deduct 30 per cent from royalties as necessary expenses.

目下交渉中だ。Negotiations are under way. / これ以上先方と交渉を続けても無益だ。

こうしょう⁵ 考証 (a) historical investigation [inquiry, study] ¶考証する study (で《文》) ascertain) the historical evidence (for).
こうしょう⁶ 哄笑 loud laughter; a loud laugh; a roar of laughter; a guffaw ¶哄笑する laugh loudly; roar with laughter; guffaw. 文例日
こうしょう⁷ 校章 a school badge [pin].
こうしょう⁸ 鉱床 a [an ore] deposit.
こうしょう⁹ 高尚 ¶高尚な high; 《文》 lofty; 《文》 noble; 《文》 uplifted; 〈上品な〉 refined; elegant; 〈well-〉cultivated (taste).
こうじょう¹ 口上 〈伝言〉 word (of mouth); a message; 〈芝居の〉 a prologue ¶口上を述べる give [deliver] a (verbal) message / 口上で伝える 《文》 inform 《sb of sth》 by word of mouth / 口上書 a verbal note; 〔外交〕(フランス語) a note verbale (pl. notes verbales).
こうじょう² 工場 a factory; a works; a plant; a workshop ¶工場経営 factory [works] management / 工場主 a factory owner / 工場地帯 a factory [an industrial] district [area] / 工場長 a factory [works] manager / 工場排泄物 industrial [factory] waste; industrial effluent (液体の) / 工場閉鎖〔労働争議における〕a lockout; 〈不景気・倒産による〉《文》a (factory) closure; a shutdown; a closedown / 工場用地 an industrial site / 工場渡し〔商〕 ex works [factory, mill, plant]; free at factory / 工場渡し値段 the ex-works price; the factory [mill] price.
こうじょう³ 向上 improvement; progress; 《文》(self-)advancement / 体位の向上 (a) improvement in physique / 地位の向上 a rise in position / 向上する improve; better oneself; advance; rise; 《文》be elevated / 向上させる improve; raise; 《文》elevate / 生活の向上を図る try to improve one's living condition; try to get [gain] a better life (for oneself) / 向上心 a desire to improve oneself; ambition.
こうじょう⁴ 荒城 a ruined castle ¶荒城の月〔曲名〕The Moon over the Ruined Castle.
こうじょう⁵ 厚情 kindness; 《文》favor. 文例日
こうじょう⁶ 恒常 《文》constancy ¶恒常の constant; everlasting / 恒常性 constancy; 〔生理〕homeostasis.
ごうじょう 強情 《文》obstinacy; stubbornness ¶強情な obstinate; stubborn; headstrong; uncompromising; stiff-necked; bullheaded / 強情を張る be obstinate; be stubborn; insist (on doing) (…すると言い張って); persist (in doing) (やめると言ってもきかない). 文例日
こうじょうせん 甲状腺 〔解〕the thyroid gland [body] / 甲状腺炎 thyroiditis / 甲状腺ホルモン thyroid hormone; thyroxine(e).
こうじょうにん 公証人 a notary (public) 《pl. notaries (public)》.
こうしょく¹ 公職 《文》(a) public office; an official post [position] ¶公職を離れる leave office; leave public life / 公職にある[つく] hold [take up] (a) public office; be in [enter] government service / 公職にある人 an office-holder; a holder of (public) office / 公職に選ばれる be elected to public office / 公職選挙法〔法〕the Public Officers Election Act; the Representation of the People Act.
こうしょく² 好色 ¶好色の 《文》amorous; 《文》lewd; 《文》lustful; dirty-minded / 好色家 a lewd man; 《文》a sensualist; 《文》a satyr / 好色文学 erotic literature / 好色物〈西鶴などの〉fiction dealing with amorous adventures.
こうしょく³ 交織 a combined [mixed] weave ¶綿毛交織 a wool-cotton [half-wool] (fabric).
こうしょくじんしゅ 黄色人種 the yellow race(s).
こうじる¹ 高じる grow worse; 《文》be aggravated; 《文》grow in intensity ¶高じて…になる develop into….
こうじる² 講じる 〈講義する〉lecture (on); give a lecture (on); 〈案出する〉《文》devise [conceive] 《a plan》; think out [find] 《a solution》; 〈手段をとる〉take 《measures》; 《文》adopt; 《文》resort to.
こうしん¹ 交信 an exchange of messages; communication; correspondence ¶交信する exchange (radio) messages 《with》; 《文》be in communication 《with》; 《文》communicate 《with》; correspond 《with》; 《文》conduct [open] correspondence 《with》 / …と無電で交信中である be in radio communication with….
こうしん² 行進 a march; a parade ¶行進する march; 《文》proceed; parade / 行進曲 a march / 結婚[葬送]行進曲 a wedding [funeral] march.
こうしん³ 更新 《文》(a) renewal; 《文》(a) renovation ¶更新する renew 《one's driving license》; 《文》renovate / 記録を更新する break a record; make [establish] a new record; 〈自分の〉better [improve on] one's own record / 更新できる renewable.
こうしん⁴ 後進 〈後輩〉a junior; a younger man ¶後進のために道を開く (resign to) make room for one's juniors; give younger men a chance / 後進国 a backward nation

---

There is no point in going on talking with them any more.
こうしょう⁶ あの人の冗談に一座は哄笑した。His jokes set the company roaring with laughter. | His jokes had them rolling in the aisles.
こうしょう⁹ 学問は人格を高尚にする。Learning ennobles [elevates] the character.
こうじょう⁵ 色々ご厚情にあずかりありがたくお礼申し上げます。Thank you for all the kindness you have shown me.
ごうじょう あの男はどこまでも強情を張って誤りを通そうとした。He obstinately refused to admit his mistake.
こうしん⁴ 石田氏は後進のために勇退すべきだ。Mr Ishida should step down in favor of a younger man.
こうしん⁵ 明日の夕食会においてくだされば幸甚に存じます。I should be very happy if you would come to dinner tomorrow evening. / 至急ご手配下されば幸甚でございます。Your prompt attention would be appreciated.
こうじんばんじょう 風が少し強く吹けば黄塵万丈の街と化しうる。Whenever the wind blows a little hard, we find the streets

こうしん⁵ 高進 (a) rise; (an) acceleration;〈インフレなどの〉《文》aggravation; ¶高進する rise; accelerate;〈病勢が〉grow worse; take a turn for the worse.

こうじん¹ 公人 a public man [figure] ¶公人としての生活 one's public life.

こうじん² 幸甚 ¶幸甚である be very glad [happy];《文》deem (it) a favor;《文》be much obliged. 文例⇩

こうじん³ 後塵 ¶後塵を拝する play second fiddle (to);《文》be subordinate (to); take second billing (to).

こうしんじょ 興信所 an inquiry office [agency]; a (private) detective agency ¶商業興信所 a credit bureau; a commercial (inquiry) agency.

こうじんばんじょう 黄塵万丈《raise》a cloud of dust. 文例⇩

こうじんぶつ 好人物 a good-natured person.

こうしんりょう 香辛料 (cooking) spice(s) ¶香辛料を加える spice (food); season with spice.

こうず 構図 composition 《of a painting》;《文》compositional arrangement ¶構図がいい[悪い] be well [poorly] composed [designed, planned].

こうすい¹ 香水 a perfume; scent ¶香水をつける perfume; scent; put scent on 《one's handkerchief》/香水をつけている wear scent / 香水瓶 a bottle of perfume [scent] / 香水吹きa scent spray; an atomizer / 香水風呂 a perfumed bath. 文例⇩

こうすい² 硬水 hard water.

こうずい 洪水 a flood;《文》an inundation;《文》a deluge (大洪水);〈洪水の水〉floodwaters ¶書物の洪水 a flood [deluge, spate] of books / 車の洪水 a torrent of automobiles / 洪水に遭う suffer from flooding;〈家・田畑などが〉be flooded;《文》be inundated; be under water. 文例⇩

こうすいりょう 降水量《気象》(a) precipitation. 文例⇩

こうすう 恒数《物》a constant.

こうずか 好事家 a dilettante 《pl. -ti》;《文》an amateur 《of》;〈収集家〉a collector.

こうせい¹ 公正 justice; fairness;〈公平〉impartiality ¶公正な《文》just; fair;《文》righteous; fair-minded; impartial / 公正を期して in order to do (full) justice 《to》; in fairness 《to》/ 公正に振舞う act fairly 《toward sb》/ 公正取引委員会 the Fair Trade Commission.

こうせい² 更生 revival;《文》(a) rebirth;《文》regeneration;《文》rejuvenation;《文》rehabilitation ¶更生する be born again;〈新生活に〉start one's life all over;《文》be rehabilitated; remake one's life; turn over a new leaf. 文例⇩

こうせい³ 更正 correction; revision;《文》rectification.

こうせい⁴ 攻勢 ¶攻勢の offensive / 攻勢をとる take the offensive 《against》/ 攻勢に転じる change [switch] to the offensive / 平和[労働]攻勢 a peace [labor] offensive / 攻勢防御 active [offensive] defense.

こうせい⁵ 後世 after [coming] ages;〈人〉future generations;《文》posterity ¶後世に名を残す earn one's place in history. 文例⇩

こうせい⁶ 厚生 public [social] welfare ¶厚生事業[施設] welfare work [facilities] / 厚生省[大臣] the Ministry [Minister] of Welfare / 厚生年金 the Welfare Pension.

こうせい⁷ 恒星 a fixed star ¶恒星時 sidereal time.

こうせい⁸ 校正 proofreading ¶校正する read [correct] proofs; proofread 《an article》; do proofreading / 校正中に訂正する make corrections in [on] the proof(s) / 校正係 a proofreader / 校正刷り proofs; a proof (sheet) (1枚の) / 校正刷りで読む read 《his book》in proof / 校正段階で削る delete 《the words》at the proof stage.

こうせい⁹ 構成 making; (a) make-up; (a) construction; structure; composition; (an) organization;《文》formation; a setup ¶構成する《作る》make; compose;《文》construct;《文》structure; organize; form;〈出来ている〉《文》consist [be composed] of / 構成員《文》a constituent (member); a member 《of a community》/ 構成主義《美術》constructivism / 構成比《統計》a component [distribution] ratio / 構成分子 a constituent element; a component.

ごうせい¹ 合成《物》composition 《of forces》;《化》synthesis ¶合成する compose; compound; synthesize / 合成音 a synthetic sound / 合成語 a compound (word) / 合成ゴム synthetic rubber / 合成写真 a composite (photograph) 《of wartime scenes》/ 合成酒 synthetic sake / 合成樹脂 plastics; synthetic resins / 合成繊維 synthetic fiber(s) / 合成洗剤 a synthetic detergent / 合成物質 a synthetic substance. 文例⇩

---

turned into sandy deserts.

こうすい¹ 彼女がつけている香水を彼はぴたりとあてた。He accurately guessed the perfume she was wearing.

こうずい この雨が止まないと洪水になる。If it goes on raining, we are going to have a flood.

こうすいりょう ツンドラ地帯のほとんどは、年間降水量がわずか200ミリほどである。The tundra receives only about eight inches of precipitation a year. | The annual precipitation in the tundra is about eight inches.

こうせい² なんとかあの子を更生させてやりたいと思っています。I am hoping to give him a fresh start (in life).

こうせい⁵ アリストテレスの「詩学」は後世に広く影響を及ぼした。Aristotle's Poetics has had a wide influence down the ages. / オリンピックの起源や後世になってそれが復活した話は、私たちすべてスポーツを愛する者にはすこぶる興味深い。The story of the Olympic games, of their origin and latter-day revival, greatly interests all of us who love sport.

ごうせい¹ このトレーは合成樹脂です。This tray is plastic. / 現代

ごうせい² 豪勢 ¶豪勢な grand; great; luxurious; 《口語》plush.
こうせいしょうしょ 公正証書【法】a notarized [an authentic] deed ¶公正証書にする authenticate [notarize] 《a document》.
こうせいのう 高性能 ¶高性能の high efficient; high-powered 《gasoline》; high-performance 《aircraft》.
こうせいぶっしつ 抗生物質 an antibiotic.
こうせき¹ 功績 《文》a meritorious deed; 《文》distinguished service; an achievement; 《栄誉》credit ⇨こうろう ¶功績を立てる render distinguished service 《to the state》/ 自分の功績だと主張する claim (the) credit (for). [文例⇩]
こうせき² 洪積【地質】¶洪積世 the Pleistocene epoch / 洪積層 a diluvium 《pl. -s, -via》; a diluvial formation.
こうせき³ 航跡 a wake 《behind a sailing ship》; a furrow; a track;【航空】a flight path; 〈飛行機雲〉a vapor trail; a condensation trail; a contrail.
こうせき⁴ 鉱石 an ore; a mineral 《通俗に》; 〈受信機検波用の〉a crystal ¶鉱石受信機【ラジオ】a crystal set / 鉱石標本 mineralogical specimens / 鉱石粉砕機 an ore crusher.
こうせきうん 高積雲【気象】an altocumulus 《pl. -li》.
こうせつ¹ 公設 ¶公設の public; municipal 《市営の》/ 公設市場 a public [municipal] market.
こうせつ² 巧拙 skill; 《文》dexterity.
こうせつ³ 降雪 a snowfall. [文例⇩]
ごうせつ¹ 合接【論】conjunction.
ごうせつ² 豪雪 (a) heavy snow; a heavy snowfall.
こうせん¹ 口銭 〈手数料〉(a) commission; 〈歩合〉a percentage; 〈仲買の〉brokerage ¶口銭を取る take [get, receive] a commission 《on the sale of...》.
こうせん² 公選 public election; election by popular vote ¶公選する elect by popular vote.
こうせん³ 交戦 〈戦争〉a war; 《文》hostilities; 〈戦闘〉a battle; 《文》an engagement; combat; an action ¶交戦する fight 《against, with》; 《文》engage in a battle 《with》; 《文》join battle 《with》/ 交戦を回避する avoid action / 交戦中である be fighting 《against, with》; be at war 《with》/ 交戦権 《文》 《文》(renounce) the right of belligerency / 《文》belligerent rights / 交戦国 warring [belligerent] nations [powers]; 《文》the belligerents / 交戦状態 (be in) a state of war; 《文》belligerency / 交戦地帯 a war zone.
こうせん⁴ 光線 a ray [beam] 《of light》; light.
こうせん⁵ 抗戦 resistance ¶抗戦する resist; 《文》offer resistance 《to》.
こうせん⁶ 鉱泉 a mineral spring; 〈水〉mineral water.
こうぜん¹ 公然 ¶公然の open; public / 公然の秘密 an open secret / 公然と openly; in public.
こうぜん² 昂然 ¶昂然として triumphantly; proudly; with one's head up [high]; head high ¶昂然としている hold one's head high.
ごうぜん 傲然 ¶傲然と arrogantly; haughtily; proudly / 傲然と構える 《文》assume a haughty attitude [air].
こうせんてき 好戦的 ¶好戦的な warlike; 《文》bellicose.
こうそ¹ 公訴 public action; prosecution ¶公訴する prosecute.
こうそ² 控訴 an appeal 《to a higher court》¶控訴する appeal 《against a decision, from a lower to a higher court》/ 控訴状 a petition of appeal.
こうそ³ 酵素 an enzyme; a [an unorganized] ferment ¶酵素の enzymatic 《action》/ 酵素学 enzymology.
こうぞ【植】a kozo; a paper mulberry.
こうそう¹ 抗争 《文》(a) contention 《with each other, for power》; (a) conflict; 《文》strife; rivalry; (a) dispute; (a) struggle; 〈抵抗〉resistance ¶抗争する contend [strive] 《with, for, against》; struggle 《against》; 《文》dispute; resist.
こうそう² 後送 ¶後送する send back 《to the rear》/ (軍人が)傷病のため本国に後送される be invalided home; be sent home as an invalid.
こうそう³ 高僧 〈徳の高い〉《文》a priest of 《high》 virtue; 〈位の高い〉a high priest; 《文》a prelate.
こうそう⁴ 高層 ¶高層雲【気象】an altostratus 《pl. -ti》/ 高層気流 an upper air current / 高層建築 a high [high-rise, tall, multistory] building.
こうそう⁵ 構想 《文》(a) conception; an idea; a plot, a plan ¶構想が浮かぶ 《文》conceive an idea [a plan] / 構想を立てる 《文》formulate a plan [plot] / 構想を練る work over one's plan [plot, ideas] / 《文》elaborate a plan.
こうそう⁶ 宏壮 ¶宏壮な grand; imposing; magnificent.
こうぞう 構造 ¶structure; (a) construction; (a) make; 〈組織〉《文》constitution; organization ¶構造上の structural; organic / 構造上欠陥がある 《文》have a structural defect; 《文》be structurally defective / 構造改革 structural reform / 構造言語学 structural linguistics / 構造式【化】a structural 《constitutional, graphic》

は合成物質の時代だ。This is the age of synthetics.
こうせき¹ この偉業を達成したのは幾百人ものの科学者の功績である。The credit for this great accomplishment belongs [goes] to hundreds of scientists.

こうせつ³ この冬は降雪2メートルに及んだ。Snow fell two meters deep [to a depth of two meters] this winter. | There was [We had] two meters of snow this winter.
こうそく³ 強制された約束には拘束力がない。A promise made under duress is not binding. / 事情の変化を見た今日では, 我々は従来の方針には拘束されない。Under today's altered situation we are not bound by our past policies.

ごうそう 豪壮 ¶豪壮な magnificent; grand; imposing; important-looking.

こうそく¹ 光束 〖光〗luminous flux.

こうそく² 光速 the speed [velocity] of light; light speed.

こうそく³ 拘束 (a) restriction; (a) restraint; binding; control ¶拘束する restrict; restrain; bind; put sb under control; cramp / 拘束時間 〖労働〗portal-to-portal hours [time] / 拘束力 (binding) power [force]; authority. 文例⇩

こうそく⁴ 校則 school regulations.

こうぞく¹ 皇族 a member of the Imperial Family; an Imperial prince [princess]; ⟨全体⟩ royalty.

こうぞく² 後続 ¶後続の following; 《文》succeeding / 後続部隊 reinforcements.

こうぞく³ 航続 ¶航続距離 a (cruising [flying]) range [radius] (of 1600 km) / 航続時間 the duration of a cruise [flight]; endurance / 航続時間記録 an endurance record / 航続力 (a) cruising [flying] power [capacity]. 文例⇩

ごうぞく 豪族 (the head of) a powerful family [clan]; a baronial family.

こうそく(ど) 高速(度) a high speed; superspeed; rapid transit (交通) ¶高速度で at high speed / 高速撮影用映画カメラ a high-speed cinecamera / 高速中性子炉 a fast neutron reactor / 高速道路 《米》a freeway; an expressway; a speedway; a superhighway; 《英》a motorway; a turnpike (有料の) / 高速度映画 a slow-motion picture / 高速度鋼 high-speed steel.

こうた 小唄 a Japanese ballad accompanied on 「the samisen.

こうだ 好打 ¶(make) a good hit.

こうたい¹ 交代〔替〕《文》(an) alternation; (a) change; a shift (工具などの); a relay; a relief (番兵などの) ¶交代する 〈交代でする〉take turns; take one's turn (at, in doing); ⟨交代をする⟩ take sb's place; change places 《with one's partner》; relieve (each other) / ピッチャーを交代する change pitchers / 1時間交代にする take turns at one-hour shifts / 交代で[に] by turns; in turn; in relays; alternately; in rotation (with) / 昼夜交代で働く work in shifts day and night; work in relays round the clock / 8時間の3部交代で働く work in three shifts of eight hours [three eight-hour shifts] / 1日3交代制で on a three-shift(-a-day) basis.

こうたい² 抗体 〖生理〗an antibody ¶…に対する抗体を作り出す build up antibodies to sth.

こうたい³ 後退 (a) retreat; 《文》retrogression; 《文》regression ¶景気の後退 (a) recession / 後退する go [move, fall] back; back (away); recede; retreat; ⟨船が⟩ go astern / 車を後退させる drive a car in reverse (gear); back a car up / (自動車の)後退灯 reversing [《米》back-up] lights. 文例⇩

こうだい 広大 ¶広大な vast; 《文》extensive; immense; magnificent; grand / 広大無辺の 《文》boundless ⟨universe⟩; 《文》illimitable ⟨ocean⟩; 《文》immeasurable ⟨space⟩; infinite ⟨wisdom of God⟩.

こうたいごう(へいか) 皇太后(陛下) (Her Imperial Majesty) the Empress Dowager.

こうたいし 皇太子 the Crown Prince / 英国皇太子 the Prince of Wales / 皇太子妃 the Crown Princess.

こうだか 甲高 ¶甲高の ⟨靴が⟩ high-backed; ⟨足が⟩ high in the instep.

こうたく 光沢 《文》luster; (a) gloss ⇨つや ¶光沢のある glossy; 《文》lustrous; shiny.

ごうだつ 強奪 ¶強奪する rob sb of sth / 銀行から300万円を強奪する rob a bank of three million yen ★rob は「不法に奪う」ことで、暴力が伴わない「盗む」の意味にも使うことができる。

こうたん 降誕 ⟨キリストの⟩ the Nativity ¶キリスト降誕祭 Christmas.

こうだん¹ 公団 a public corporation ¶公団住宅 an apartment house built by the Housing Corporation.

こうだん² 後段 ⟨物語などの⟩ the latter part (of a tale) ¶後段に述べるごとく as described later; 《文》as referred to hereinafter; 《文》as is stated [touched upon] in a later chapter.

こうだん³ 降壇 ¶降壇する leave the platform [rostrum, pulpit].

こうだん⁴ 講談 a (battle) story; 《文》a historical narrative ¶講談師 a (professional) storyteller.

ごうたん 豪胆 ¶豪胆な 《文》stouthearted; daring; strong-nerved; 《文》dauntless; fearless.

こうだんし 好男子 ⟨美男子⟩ a handsome man; a good-[fine-]looking man; ⟨好漢⟩ a good [nice] fellow; 《米口語》a regular guy ¶非常な好男子 a really good-looking man.

こうだんしゃ 高段者 a high-dan[-rank]holder; a high-ranking (go, shogi) player.

こうち¹ 拘置 ¶拘置する detain; hold [keep] sb in custody / 拘置所 a prison; a detention center; a jail; 《英》a gaol.

こうち² 高地 highland(s); high country; an upland; heights; a hill; ⟨高原⟩ a tableland; a plateau (pl. -s, -eaux).

こうち³ 耕地 cultivated [plowed] land; a cultivated field [area]; plowland; land under cultivation; ⟨耕作に適した⟩ arable land ¶耕

こうぞく³ その飛行機は航続30時間に及んだ. The plane remained in the air for thirty hours. / コンコルドは航続距離4,000マイルで. Concorde has a 4,000-mile range [a range of 4,000 miles].

こうたい¹ だれか代代してくれる人はないか. Is there anyone who will take my place? / 交代の来るまで私はここを離れることができない. I can't leave my post till my relief comes. / 長距離旅行のあいだ, 私たちは交代で車の運転をした. We took turns at driving [at the wheel] on the long journey. / 24時間交代では. The shifts were twenty-four hours on, twenty-four hours off.

こうたい³ 1歩後退するには必ず2歩前進することにしよう. Let's make it a rule never to take one

こうち 地整理 the consolidation [adjustment] of arable land holdings / 耕地面積 cultivated acreage. 　　　　　　　　　　　　　[rate.

こうち⁴ 巧致 ¶巧致な《文》exquisite; elaborate.

こうちく 構築 ¶構築する build; construct;《文》erect / 構築物 a structure.

こうちし 後置詞【文法】a postposition.

こうちゃ 紅茶 (a cup of) tea ★日常生活では紅茶をいちいち black tea とは言わない / 紅茶を入れる make (a cup [pot] of) tea / 紅茶茶わん a teacup.

こうちゃく 膠着【言語】agglutination ¶膠着する stick (to);《文》adhere (to);【言語】agglutinate / 膠着語【言語】an agglutinative language / 膠着状態にある be deadlocked; be at a deadlock [stalemate] / 膠着状態に陥る become deadlocked; reach (a) deadlock.

こうちゅう 甲虫 a beetle.

こうちゅうじつど 高忠実度 high fidelity (略: hi-fi) ⇒ ハイファイ.

こうちょう¹ 好調 ¶好調の satisfactory;〈選手などが〉in good condition [shape]; in form ⇒ コンディション 用法.〖文例⏎〗

こうちょう² 紅潮 ¶紅潮する flush (up); blush; go red [pink].

こうちょう³ 校長〈中学・高校の〉a principal;〈小学校の〉a schoolmaster [schoolmistress (女)];〈主に英〉a headmaster [headmistress (女)]; the head ¶校長室 the principal's office / 校長代理 an acting [a deputy] principal. 〖文例⏎〗

こうちょう⁴ 高潮 (the) high tide;〈頂点〉the climax ¶高潮に達する reach a [the] climax.

こうちょうかい 公聴会 (hold) a public [an open] hearing.

こうちょうどうぶつ 腔腸動物【生物】a coelenterate.

こうちょく 硬直 ¶硬直する stiffen; get [《文》become] stiff [rigid] / 硬直した rigid; stiff.

こうちん 工賃 wages; pay; cost of (labor).

こうつう 交通〈往来〉traffic;〈運輸〉transportation;《英》transport ¶交通の便を図る improve transportation facilities / 交通の妨害になる obstruct [block] traffic / 交通を緩和する relieve [ease] (the) traffic congestion / 交通を整理する control [regulate] traffic / 交通を遮断する block (up) (a street) / 交通安全 road [traffic] safety / 交通安全運動 a road safety campaign / 交通安全週間 Traffic Safety Week / 交通違反《be fined ￥10,000 for》a traffic offense; violation of traffic regulations; (be arrested on) a traffic charge / 交通機関 a means of transportation; transport facilities; public transport / 交通規則 traffic rules [regulations]; the rule of the road / 交通公社 the Japan Travel Bureau (略: JTB) / 交通事故 a traffic [road] accident / 交通事故による死者 traffic deaths; (the number of) deaths on the roads / 交通渋滞 traffic congestion; a traffic jam [snarl] / 交通巡査 a traffic policeman;《英》a policeman on point [traffic] duty / 交通信号 a traffic signal [light] / 交通整理 traffic control / 交通整理の警官 a policeman directing traffic [on traffic duty] / 交通費 transportation expenses /《米》a carfare (乗車賃) / 交通問題 a traffic problem / 交通量 (the volume of) (wheeled) traffic / 交通量の多い道路 a road where the traffic is heavy; a busy [crowded] street.〖文例⏎〗

ごうつくばり 業突張り a pigheaded person; a mule; a diehard;〈けちん坊〉a skinflint; a miser.

こうつごう 好都合 ¶好都合な《文》favorable; convenient; fortunate / 好都合に well; all right /《文》favorably; successfully / 好都合である suit (one, one's convenience).〖文例⏎〗

こうてい¹ 工程 the progress [stage] of work;〈過程〉a (manufacturing) process.

こうてい² 公定 ¶公定の official; legal / 公定価格 an official price / 公定歩合 the official [bank] rate.

こうてい³ 公邸 an official residence.

こうてい⁴ 行程 (a) distance; a journey; a march.〖文例⏎〗

こうてい⁵ 肯定《文》affirmation ¶肯定する《文》affirm; answer "yes"《文》in the affirmative); agree;《文》acknowledge / 肯定的 affirmative / 肯定文【文法】an affirmative sentence.

こうてい⁶ 皇帝 an emperor ¶皇帝の imperial.

こうてい⁷ 高弟 the best [a leading] pupil [disciple].

こうてい⁸ 高低《文》undulations (起伏); unevenness (でこぼこ); rise and fall (上がり下がり); fluctuations (相場の); (a) pitch (modulation) (音の); height (高さ) ¶高低のある undulating (plains); uneven (land); fluctuating (markets) / 高低のない even; level.

こうてい⁹ 校訂 revision; recension ¶校訂する revise / 校訂者 a revisor / 校訂本 a revised edition [text]; a recension.

こうてい¹⁰ 校庭 a schoolyard; a school playground (小学校の);〈構内〉the school [college] grounds; the campus (大学の).

こうてい¹¹ 航程 the distance covered (by a step back without taking two (steps) forward.

こうちょう² 初めのうちは、すべて好調に運んだ. At first, everything went well.

こうちょう³ かねてから彼の夢は校長になることであった. His dream had been to get a headship.

こうつう そこは交通の便がいい [悪い]. The place is easy [hard] to get to. | Transport facilities there are very convenient [inconvenient]. / 交通が便利になったので郊外に住む人が多くなった. As the means of transportation have improved, a greater number of people now live in the suburbs. / 交通がほとんど途絶した. Traffic is at an almost complete standstill [is almost completely paralyzed]. / 交通量が少なかったので、時速70キロで走れた. As the traffic was light [As the road was not congested], we were able to do 70 (kilometers an hour) [70 km/h]. / ここでは交通機関はバスしかない. The bus is the only form of public transport here.

こうでい 拘泥 ⇨ こだわる.
ごうてい 豪邸 a (palatial) mansion.
こうてき¹ 公的 public; official ¶公的地位 a public position.
こうてき² 好適 ¶好適な ideal; good; best; suitable; …に好適である be suitable for…/スキーの好適地 an ideal place for skiing.
こうてきしゅ 好敵手 a good match [rival]; 《文》 a worthy opponent.
こうてつ¹ 更迭 a change; a switch; a reshuffle; a shakeup ¶更迭する change 《the members》; switch 《the commanders》; reshuffle 《the Cabinet》. 文例⇩
こうてつ² 鋼鉄 steel.
こうてん¹ 公転 revolution 《of the earth around the sun》¶公転する revolve 《around the sun》; move [go] around the sun / 公転周期 a period of revolution 《of fifty years》; an orbital period / 公転速度 an orbital speed. 文例⇩
こうてん² 交点 an intersection point; 《天》 a node.
こうてん³ 好転 ¶好転する change [take a turn] for the better; 《文》 take a favorable turn; improve; 《口語》 pick [look] up 《商況などが》. 文例⇩
こうてん⁴ 荒天 stormy [rough] weather.
こうてん⁵ 高点 a high mark [score] ¶最高点をとる win [get] the highest mark / 最高点で当選する be elected 《to the Diet》with the largest number of votes; head the list of successful candidates ⇨ さいこう⁶ (最高点).
こうでん¹ 公電 an official telegram.
こうでん² 香典 an obituary [a condolence] gift; incense money ¶香典返し a token of acknowledg(e)ment of an obituary present received.
こうでんかん 光電管 a phototube; a photocell; a photoelectric cell. ─tron.
こうでんし 光電子 《電子工学》a photoelec─
ごうてんじょう 格天井 a coffered ceiling.
こうてんてき 後天的 acquired 《immunity》; learned 《behavior patterns》.
こうど¹ 光度 luminous intensity; luminosity; (the degree of) brightness ¶星の光度 the magnitude [brightness] of a star / 光度0.2 a magnitude of 0.2 / 光度計 a photometer.
こうど² 高度 〈高さ〉 an altitude; (a) height ¶高度の〈高い〉 high; 〈強力な〉 strong; powerful; intense; high-degree; 〈進んだ〉 advanced; high-grade; high 《civilizations》 / 〈飛行機が〉高度を上げる[下げる] gain [lose] altitude / 高度に発達した highly-developed 《technology》 / 高度計 an altimeter / 高度差 (a) height difference; (a) difference in elevation / 経済の高度成長 high growth of the 《Japanese》 economy; (a) high level [rate] of economic growth / 高度成長期 a high-growth period. 文例⇩
こうど³ 硬度 hardness; solidity ¶硬度計 a durometer.
こうとう¹ 口頭 ¶口頭で orally; by word of mouth; 《文》《be examined》 viva voce / 口頭試問 an oral [a viva voce] examination; 《英口語》 a viva / 口頭弁論 oral pleadings [proceedings].
こうとう² 好投 《野球》 good [fine] pitching ¶好投する pitch well [expertly].
こうとう³ 高等 ¶高等の high; higher; advanced; 〈高級の〉 high-grade[-class] / 高等科 an advanced course / 高等教育 higher education / 高等教育機関 an institution of higher education [learning] / 高等裁判所 a high court / 高等数学 higher [advanced] mathematics / 高等生物 higher forms of life / 高等動物 a higher animal; animals of the higher orders.
こうとう⁴ 高踏 ¶高踏的 highbrow; high-toned 《journals》.
こうとう⁵ 高騰 a sudden [steep] rise (in prices); a jump (in prices) ¶高騰する rise (suddenly); soar; take a jump.
こうとう⁶ 喉頭 《解》 the larynx 《pl. -es, larynges》 ¶喉頭の laryngeal; laryngal / 喉頭炎 laryngitis / 喉頭音 《音声》 a guttural sound / 喉頭癌(ガン) 〔結核〕 laryngeal cancer [tuberculosis].
こうどう¹ 公道 a highway; a public road; a thoroughfare.
こうどう² 行動 behavior; action; an act; 《文》 conduct; a movement ¶行動する; act; behave; 《文》 conduct oneself / 行動の型 a behavioral pattern / 行動を共にする act [《口語》go along] with sb; act together; 《文》act in concert [line] 《with》 / 行動を起こす go [get, move] into action / 行動をとる take action 《against》 / 〈考えなどを〉行動に移す 《文》 translate 《an idea》 into action; carry out; 《文》 execute / …に対して直接軍事行動をとる take direct military action against… / 行動科学 behavioral science / 行動圏 《生態》 the [its] home range / 行動主義 《心理》 behaviorism / 行動人 a man of action / 行動特性 a behavioral characteristic / 行動半径 a radius of action [operation]; a cruising [an action] radius / 行動方針 the course of action. 文例⇩

こうつごう 万事好都合に行った。 Everything went well [all right, smoothly]. / それなら大いに〈おさら〉好都合です。 That will suit me fine [even better].
こうてい 東京から列車で半日の行程だ。 It is a half day's train journey from Tokyo. / 一行は1日の行程平均25キロメートルの速さで進んだ。 The party covered 25 kilometers a day on average.
こうてつ¹ 局長級の大変動があった。 There was a sweeping change of top-ranking officials.
こうてん¹ 地球は365日と4分の1で1公転する。 The earth goes around the sun in 365 and a quarter days.
こうてん³ 局面は好転してきた。 The tide is turning in our favor.
こうど² 機は羽田に着陸のため高度を下げ始めた。 The plane began to descend for the landing at Haneda. / これには高度の精密さが必要である。 This requires a high order of accuracy.
こうどう² 彼の行動は紳士的であった。 He behaved like a gentleman. / 反政府軍は再び行動を開始した。 The anti-government

こうどう³ 坑道 〖鉱山〗〈横の〉a (mining) gallery; a roadway; a drift (炭層に沿った);〈縦の〉a pit; a shaft.

こうどう⁴ 黄道 〖天文〗the ecliptic ¶黄道帯 the zodiac.

こうどう⁵ 講堂 a lecture hall [room]; an auditorium (*pl.* -s, -ria).

ごうどう 強盗〈人〉a robber;《米口語》a holdup man;《口語》a mugger (路上での);〈行為〉(armed) robbery; mugging ¶強盗に襲われる be robbed ★主語は人はずかりでなく、a bank, a train など建物・乗物がなりうる / 強盗を働く commit (a) robbery / 銀行[列車]強盗 a bank [train] robber. 文例⊕

ごうどう 合同 (a) combination; (a) union;〈企業・組織などの〉〖文〗amalgamation; merger;〖数〗congruence ¶合同する join; combine;〖文〗unite (into one body, with others) / 合同して jointly;〖法〗conjointly / 合同して事業を行なう join (hands)(with *sb*) in an enterprise; make a joint effort / 合同の joint; united; combined;〖数〗congruent《triangles》/ 合同事業 a joint undertaking.

こうとうがっこう 高等学校 a (senior) high school ⇒ こうこう³ ¶高等学校で in [《英》at] high school / 工業[商業,女子,農業,普通]高等学校 a technical [a commercial, a girls', an agricultural, an academic] high school.

こうとうぶ 後頭部 the back of the head;〖解〗the occipital region.

こうとうむけい 荒唐無稽 ¶荒唐無稽の nonsensical; absurd; foolish; preposterous; fantastic.

こうどく¹ 購読 ¶購読する subscribe《to》; take (a newspaper) ¶購読を続ける renew *one's* subscription《to, for》/ 購読者 a subscriber / 購読料 subscription (rates). 文例⊕

こうどく² 講読 reading; translation ¶大学でシェークスピアを講読する read Shakespeare (with *one's* class) at the university.

こうとくしん 公徳心 (have) a sense of public duty [morality].

こうどくそ 抗毒素 an antitoxin.

こうとりくみ 好取組 a well-matched contest [game]; a good [an interesting] match ¶本日の好取組 today's feature bouts.

こうない¹ 坑内 (in) the pit [shaft] ¶坑内出水 mine-flooding / 坑内水 mine water / 坑内労働者 an underground [a face] worker.

こうない² 校内 ¶校内に[で] in the school; in the school [college] grounds;《米》on (the) campus (大学の).

こうない³ 構内 (on) the premises;《in》the precincts [compound];《in》the grounds;《on》the campus (大学の) ¶駅構内 the (station) yard.

こうないえん 口内炎 〖医〗stomatitis; inflammation of the oral mucosa.

こうなん 後難 future trouble ¶後難を恐れる fear the consequences / 後難を恐れて for fear of aftereffects.

こうにゅう 購入 ¶購入する ⇒ かう².

こうにん¹ 公認 official recognition [approval]; authorization; certification ¶公認する recognize officially; authorize / 公認会計士《米》a certified public accountant (略: C.P.A., CPA);《英》a chartered accountant (略: C.A.) / 公認候補者 a recognized [authorized] candidate / 公認世界記録 an official world record / 公認プール a regulation-size pool. 文例⊕

こうにん² 後任 a successor《to a post》¶後任の校長 the incoming principal / 後任になる succeed *sb*; succeed to *sb's* post; take *sb's* place / …の後任として in succession to *sb*; to succeed *sb*; as the successor to *sb*. 文例⊕

こうねつ 高熱 (an) intense heat;〈体の〉a fever; a high temperature ¶高熱に冒される get [have, come down with] a fever [a (high) temperature].

こうねつひ 光熱費 heating and lighting expenses; expenses for light and fuel.

こうねんびょう 黄熱病 ⇒ おうねつびょう.

こうねん¹ 光年 〖天〗a light-year (略: lt-yr).

こうねん² 後年《将来》in years to come; in the future;〈その後〉later; afterward; in later years;〈晩年〉in *one's* later years.

こうねんき 更年期 the critical age [time of life];〈女性の〉the menopause;〈婉曲的に〉the change of life;《口語》the change ¶更年期障害 a menopausal disorder.

こうのう 効能 (an) effect;〖文〗efficacy;〖文〗virtue; good; use ¶効能が現われる take effect;〖文〗prove efficacious; work / 効能のある〖文〗efficacious; effective; good《for》; useful / 効能のない ineffective;《be》no good; useless / 効能書 a statement of virtues / 効能書ほどでもない be not as good as *it* is claimed to be. 文例⊕

こうのとり 〖鳥〗a stork.

こうのもの 香の物 pickles; pickled vegetables.

ごうのもの 剛の者〈強い人〉a strong man;〈勇者〉a brave man.

こうは¹ 光波 〖物〗light waves.

こうは² 硬派 a hard-liner; (one of) the hard-line party [elements];〈不良少年〉a young rough [tough] ¶硬派の記者 a reporter [news-

---

forces moved into action again.

ごうとう 今, 強盗にやられました. We have just had a robbery. / 最近銀行がいくつも強盗にやられた. A number of banks have been robbed recently.

ごうどう 1つの三角形の3辺の長さが他の三角形の3辺の長さとそれぞれ相等しい時は, この2つの三角形は合同である. Two triangles are congruent if the three sides of one are equal in length respectively to the three sides of the other.

こうどく¹ この新聞は購読者が多い. This paper has a large circulation. / お払い込みの購読料は8月号で切れます. なお引き続きご愛読下さいますよう, お願い申し上げます. Your subscription expires with the August number. We shall be very happy if you will kindly renew it.

こうにん¹ 氏は自由民主党から候補者として公認を得ている. He [His candidature] has the endorsement of the Liberal Demo-

こうば [paperman] dealing with serious topics.
こうば 工場 ⇨ こうじょう².
こうはい¹ 交配 mating;〈異種交配〉hybridization; crossing; crossbreeding ¶交配する mate (one breed with another); hybridize; cross; crossbreed / 交配種 a crossbred (dog [horse, etc.]); a hybrid.
こうはい² 光背 ⇨ ごこう.
こうはい³ 荒廃 waste; ruin;《文》devastation ¶荒廃する go to [fall into] ruin; be devastated; fall into (a state of) disrepair; be laid waste / 荒廃した ruined; devastated / 荒廃している lie in ruins; be laid waste /〈建物など手入れが足りずに〉be out of repair.
こうはい⁴ 後輩 one's junior; younger men.
[文例 ⇩]

こうばい¹ 公売 (a) public sale [auction] ¶公売に付する put sth up for public sale [for sale by public auction]; put sth up for [《米》at] auction; sell sth by [《米》at] auction.
こうばい² 勾配〈傾斜〉a slope; an incline;〈鉄道の〉a gradient;《米》a grade;〈屋根の〉a pitch ⇨ けいしゃ, さか¹ ¶急な[緩い]勾配 a steep [gentle] slope / 30 度の勾配で at [with] an incline [a gradient] of 30 degrees; inclined at an angle of 30°.
こうばい³ 紅梅 a Japanese apricot with red blossoms.
こうばい⁴ 購買《文》purchase; buying ¶購買する《文》purchase; buy;《文》procure / 購買組合 a cooperative (society);《口語》a co-op / 購買組合の売店 a cooperative (store);《口語》a co-op / 購買心をそそる《文》induce (a customer) to buy; arouse [excite] consumer(s') interest / 購買部〈学校などの〉a cooperative store;《口語》a co-op / 購買力 buying [purchasing] power.
こうばいすう 公倍数 a common multiple ¶最小公倍数 the least [lowest] common multiple (略: L.C.M., l.c.m.).
こうはいち 後背地《地理》the hinterland.
こうはく 紅白 red and white ¶紅白の幕 a red-and-white-striped curtain; a curtain in red and white stripes / 紅白試合 a contest between two groups / NHK 紅白歌合戦 the annual contest between male and female popular singers on New Year's Eve sponsored and broadcast by the NHK.
こうばく 広漠 ¶広漠たる vast; wide;《文》extensive / 広漠たる草原 an immense expanse of grassland.
こうばしい 香ばしい pleasant-[nice-]smelling;《文》fragrant; aromatic.
ごうはら 業腹 ¶業腹に思う be vexed ((at, with)); resent.

こうはん¹ 公判 a (public) trial [hearing] ¶公判を開く hold (a) court / 公判に付する bring (a case) to trial; try (a case) / 公判中である be on trial / 公判廷 the court (of trial).
こうはん² 甲板 ⇨ かんぱん¹ ¶甲板員 a deck hand.
こうはん³ 後半 the latter [second] half ¶後半期 the second half (of 1982) / 後半生 the latter half of one's life.
こうはん⁴ 広範 ¶広範な《文》extensive; broad; wide-ranging (studies); far-reaching (reforms);《文》far-flung (influence).
こうばん¹ 交番 a police box.
こうばん² 鋼板 a steel sheet (薄い); a steel plate (厚い).
ごうはん 合板 (a sheet of) plywood ¶プリント合板 printed plywood.
こうはんい 広範囲 ¶広範囲にわたる cover a wide range ((of)) / 広範囲にわたる知識《文》extensive knowledge.
こうひ¹ 工費 the cost of construction ¶総工費 6 千万円で at the total cost of ¥60,000,-000.
こうひ² 口碑 (oral) tradition; a legend; folklore ¶口碑に伝わる be handed down by tradition (orally, by word of mouth).
こうひ³ 公費 ¶公費で at (the) public [government] expense.
こうび¹ 交尾 copulation ¶交尾する copulate; mate; pair / 交尾中のとんぼ mating dragonflies / 交尾期 the mating [pairing] season [time, period].
こうび² 後尾 the rear; the tail; the stern (船尾) ¶後尾 rear; back;〈船尾の〉aft / 後尾灯 a taillight.
ごうひ 合否 success or failure;《文》acceptance or rejection;〈結果〉the result ¶合否を知らせる let sb know (by wire) whether he has passed the exam.
こうヒスタミンざい 抗ヒスタミン剤 an antihistamine.
こうひょう¹ 公表〈公布〉(an) official announcement;〈発表〉publication ¶公表する announce (officially); publish;《文》make sth public [known]; release / …と公表された It was officially announced [learned] that….
[文例 ⇩]
こうひょう² 好評 a favorable reception [opinion, notice, comment]; popularity;《文》public favor ¶好評の《文》of good repute; well-received; popular / 好評である be popular ((with));《文》be favorably spoken of;《文》enjoy popularity / 好評を博する win [gain] popularity / 好評を博す gain public favor.
[文例 ⇩]

---

cratic Party.
こうにん² 君の後任を捜すのはむずかしい. You are a hard man to replace.
こうのう その薬は私にはすこしも効能がなかった. The medicine had no effect on me. / この薬自体には何の効能もないが, 他の薬の吸収を助ける役をする. This medicine has no effect in itself, but it helps other medicines to be absorbed.
こうはい⁴ 彼は僕らよりずっと後輩だ. He is many years our junior.
こうひ¹ その橋は工費 5 億円を要した. The bridge was constructed at a cost of 500 million yen.
こうひょう¹ 疑惑を解くため事件の真相を直ちに公表すべきである. To clear suspicion, the facts of the case should be laid before the public at once.
こうひょう² この本は学生の間で

こうひょう³ 降雹 a hailstorm.

こうひょう⁴ 講評 (a) review; (a) criticism ¶講評する comment on; review; criticize.

こうびん 後便 ¶後便で in *one's* next letter; 《米》by the [*one's*] next mail; 《英》by the next post.

こうふ¹ 工夫 a laborer; a workman; a construction worker; 《英口語》a navvy.

こうふ² 公布 《文》promulgation; proclamation; (official) announcement ¶公布する 《文》promulgate; 《文》proclaim; make *sth* public; announce officially; issue.

こうふ³ 交付 ¶交付する deliver; grant; issue (a passport to [for] *sb*) /交付金 (give) a grant(-in-aid); a subsidy.

こうふ⁴ 坑夫 a (coal) miner.

こうふ⁵ 鉱夫 a mine worker.

こうぶ 後部 the rear; the hind (back) part; 〈船の〉the stern ¶後部の back; rear /後部に at [in] the rear /後部座席 the rear [back] seat.

こうふう 校風 the traditions of the school ¶校風に反する be against the best traditions of the school.

こうふく¹ 幸福 happiness; well-being; welfare; 〈幸運〉good luck [fortune] ¶幸福の追求《文》the pursuit of happiness /幸福な happy; 〈幸運な〉lucky; fortunate /幸福に暮らす lead [live] a happy life; live happily /幸福感 a feeling of happiness; a sense of well-being; 《心理》euphoria. 文例⤓

こうふく² 降伏 (a) surrender; 《文》capitulation ¶降伏する surrender (to); 《文》capitulate (to); 《文》yield (to); give in (to) /…という条件で降伏する capitulate (to the enemy) on [under] the condition that… /降伏を呼びかける call on *sb* to surrender /条件付[無条件]降伏 a conditional [an unconditional] surrender /降伏文書 an instrument of surrender. 文例⤓

こうぶつ¹ 好物 *one's* favorite dish [food].

こうぶつ² 鉱物 a mineral ¶鉱物の mineral /鉱物の標本箱 a mineralogical cabinet /鉱物界 the mineral kingdom /鉱物学 mineralogy /鉱物資源 mineral resources /鉱物質 mineral matter /鉱物綿 mineral [slag] wool.

こうふん¹ 口吻 *one's* way [manner] of speaking ⇨くちぶり.

こうふん² 興奮 excitement; agitation ¶興奮する be [get] excited; be worked up (over *sth*) /興奮しやすい excitable; (be) easily excited [agitated] /興奮して in excitement; excitedly /興奮させる excite; 《文》stimulate; get *sb* excited /《口語》worked up /興奮を静める calm *sb* down; 《文》allay *sb's* excitement /興奮剤 a stimulant; 《口語》a pep pill /《俗》an upper. 文例⤓

こうぶん 構文 a construction; the construction of a sentence; sentence structure.

こうぶんし 高分子 ¶高分子化学 (high) polymer chemistry /高分子化合物 a highly polymerized compound /高分子物質 a (high) polymer; a macromolecular substance.

こうぶんしょ 公文書 an official document [paper]; archives (保存された) ¶公文書偽造 forgery of an official document /国立公文書館 the National Archives.

こうぶんぼ 公分母 a common denominator ¶最小公分母 the lowest [least] common denominator (略：L.C.D., l.c.d.).

こうべ 頭 the head ¶頭を垂れて hang *one's* head /頭を垂れて with *one's* head down.

こうへい¹ 工兵 an engineer.

こうへい² 公平 impartiality; fairness; justice ¶公平な fair (and square); just; unbias(s)ed; impartial (opinions); evenhanded (treatment); 《文》equitable (treatment); unprejudiced (views) /公平に impartially; fairly; justly /公平を欠く be unfair (to); do *sb* an injustice (to) /公平無私な fair and disinterested. 文例⤓

こうへん 後編〈後半〉the latter part (of a book);〈続編〉a sequel (to).

こうべん 抗弁〈反対〉a protest;《法》a refutation;〈被告の〉a plea; (a) defense ¶抗弁する〈反論する〉protest; refute (the accusation);〈被告が〉make a plea; defend *oneself*.

ごうべん 合弁 ¶合弁の joint; under joint management /日中合弁事業 a Japanese-Chinese joint enterprise.

こうほ 候補〈立候補〉candidacy;《英》candidature ¶候補に立つ be a candidate for (the next Presidency);《米》run (as a candidate) (in the coming election, for President);《英》stand for (Parliament) /候補者 a candidate /(政党が) 候補者を立てる put up (50) candidates (in the coming general election) /候補者名簿 a list of (eligible) candidates;〈政党の〉《米》a slate; a ticket /候補地 a site proposed (for). 文例⤓

こうぼ¹ 公募〈募金などの〉a public appeal (for contributions);〈株式などの〉an offer for public subscription;〈求人の〉public advertisement (of a post) ¶公募する advertise for

---

非常に好評だ. This book is very popular with [among] the students.

こうひょう³ 昨日千葉県下に降雹があった. Yesterday it hailed [there was a hailstorm] in Chiba Prefecture.

こうふく¹ そのころの私は幸福の絶頂にあった. At that time my cup of happiness was full.

こうふく² それでは全面的降伏になる. That would mean a complete capitulation to the enemy. / 彼らは降伏のしるしに両手を上げて小屋から出て来た. They came out of the hut, their hands up in surrender.

こうぶつ² 私はかきが大の好物だ. I am very fond of [have a liking for] oysters. | Oysters are my special favorite. | I have a taste for oysters.

こうふん² 彼はそのことで今興奮している. He is in a state of excitement [is very wrought up] about it. / 強いコーヒーを飲んだので, 興奮して眠れなかった. My nerves were so stimulated by the strong coffee that I could not get to sleep.

こうへい² 黒田氏に対して公平を失することのないように言っておくが, 氏は事態を収拾するために

こうぼ 《candidates for a post》; raise 《a fund》 by subscription ; offer 《stocks》 for public subscription.

こうぼ² 酵母 yeast ; ferment ¶ 酵母菌 a yeast fungus.

こうほう¹ 公法 public law.

こうほう² 公報 an official report [dispatch, bulletin] ; an official gazette 《官報》.

こうほう³ 広報 《public》 information ; publicity ; public relations 《略：P.R.》 ¶ 広報課 a public relations department [section, office] / 広報活動 publicity [information] activities ; public relations / 広報官 a public relations 《affairs》 officer.

こうほう⁴ 後方 ¶ 後方に backward ; 《後ろに》 in [at] the rear ; at the back ; behind / 後方基地 a rear base / 後方勤務 service in the rear [at the base].

こうほう⁵ 航法 navigation ¶ 計器[星の観測による]航法 instrumental [celestial] navigation.

こうぼう¹ 工房 a studio 《pl. -s》;《フランス語》 an *atelier* ; a workshop.

こうぼう² 光芒 a shaft [beam] of light.

こうぼう³ 攻防 offense and defense ¶ 攻防戦 an offensive and defensive battle.

こうぼう⁴ 興亡 rise and fall ; ups and downs ; existence 《存亡》. [文例⇩]

こうぼう⁵ 弘法 [文例⇩]

こうぼう¹ 号砲 《fire》 a signal gun. [文例⇩]

ごうほう² 合法 ¶ 合法(性) legality ; lawfulness / 合法的 lawful ; legal / 合法的に lawfully ; legally / 合法化する legalize.

ごうほう³ 豪放 ¶ 豪放な manly and openhearted.

こうぼく¹ 公僕 a public servant ⇨ こうむいん.

こうぼく² 坑木 〈鉱山の〉 a pit prop.

こうぼく³ 香木 〈木〉 an aromatic tree ;〈材〉 fragrant wood.

こうぼく⁴ 高木 〈植〉 a tree.

こうま 小(子)馬 〈小さい馬〉 a pony ;〈子馬〉 a foal, a colt 《雄》; a filly 《雌》.

こうまい 高邁 ¶ 高邁な 《文》 high ; 《文》 lofty ; 《文》 noble / 高邁な理想 a lofty ideal / 高邁の精神の人 a high-minded person / 識見が高邁である have exalted ideas.

こうまん 高慢 〈自尊〉 pride ;〈尊大〉 haughtiness ; arrogance ;〈生意気〉 impertinence ; sauciness ¶ 高慢な proud ; haughty ; arrogant ; impertinent ; saucy / 高慢の鼻を折る humble *sb* ;《口語》 make *sb* eat dirt [humble pie] / 高慢ちきな顔をする look self-important [conceited] ;《口語》 look stuck-up ;《口語》 look snooty.

ごうまん 傲慢 haughtiness ; arrogance ;《文》 overweening pride ¶ 傲慢な arrogant ; haughty ; overbearing ;《口語》 stuck-up / 傲慢無礼な insolent.

こうみゃく 鉱脈 a vein (of ore) ; a lode ¶ 鉱脈を掘り当てる strike a vein 《of gold》.

こうみょう¹ 功名 a great exploit [achievement] ;《文》 a glorious deed ;〈名声〉 credit ; 《win, gain》 distinction 《fame》 ¶ 功名を争う compete [《文》vie] with each other 《to do》; claim credit 《for》/ 功名心 ambition ;《文》 aspiration.

こうみょう² 光明 light ;〈希望〉《a ray of》 hope ¶ 前途に光明がある have a bright [rosy] future (ahead of *one*) ; *one's* prospects are [future is] bright.

こうみょう³ 巧妙 ¶ 巧妙な skillful ; skilled ; clever ; ingenious / 巧妙に skillfully ;《文》 with skill [dexterity] ; cleverly ; ingeniously.

こうみん 公民 a citizen ¶ 公民館 a public hall ; a community center / 公民権 citizenship ; civil rights / 公民権運動 a civil rights movement.

こうむ¹ 公務 official [public] business [duties] ; government [official] affairs ¶ 公務による傷害[疾病] an injury [a disease] incurred in the line of duty / 公務で旅行する travel on official business / 公務多忙のため owing to the pressure of *one's* official duties / 公務執行妨害 interference with a government official in the exercise [performance] of his duties. [文例⇩]

こうむ² 校務 school affairs [business, duties].

こうむいん 公務員 〈1人〉 a public [civil] servant [official] ; a government employee ;〈全体〉 the public [civil] service ★ public も civil も《英》《米》にも通じるが,《米》では public が,《英》では civil が普通.

こうむてん 工務店 a building [civil engineering] firm ;〈人〉 a building contractor ; a builder.

こうむる 被る 《文》 suffer ;《文》 undergo ;《文》 sustain ;《文》 be subjected to ;《文》 receive ; have ; get ¶ 恩義をこうむる receive favors [kindness] ;《文》 enjoy *sb's* patronage / 損害をこうむる sustain [suffer, have] a loss ; be damaged.

こうめい 高名 ⇨ ゆうめい¹. [文例⇩]

ごうめいがいしゃ 合名会社 an unlimited [a general] partnership ¶ 合名会社佐藤商会 Sato & Co.

こうめい(せいだい) 公明(正大) fairness ; justice ; openness ; fair play ¶ 公明正大な fair

---

最善の努力を尽くされたのだ. In fairness [To do justice] to Mr. Kuroda, I must tell you that he has done everything he could do to save the situation.

こうほ 彼は会長の後継者として第一候補である. He is first in line to succeed the President of the Society. / その地位に対しては候補者が多数ある. There are a lot of candidates for the position.

こうぼう⁴ それは国の興亡を賭けた一戦だった. It was a battle on which the fate of the country hung.

こうぼう⁵ 弘法にも筆のあやまり. Homer sometimes nods. [諺] / 弘法筆を選ばず. A poor workman blames his tools. [諺]

ごうほう¹ 号砲一発,皆一斉にスタートした. At the report of the gun they all started off.

こうむ¹ 労働者たちは殴打暴行ならびに公務執行妨害の理由で逮捕された. The laborers were arrested on assault and battery charges and for obstructing the police in the performance of their duties.

こうめい ご高名は伊藤さんからかねがね承っておりました. I have heard a lot about you from Mr. Ito.

こうめいとう (and square); honest; open (and aboveboard); 《文》upright;《文》just;《文》honorable / 公明正大に fairly; honestly;《文》honorably;《文》justly / 公明正大にやる do things [deal with the matter] in a fair [an honorable, an honest] way; play fair; play the game / 公明選挙 a clean election. 文例⇩

こうめいとう 公明党 the Komeito; the Clean Government Party.

こうもう¹ 膏肓 ¶病膏肓に入る〈人が主語〉become a slave to [of] (a habit);〈事が主語〉take hold of sb;《文》become incorrigible.

こうもう² 孔孟 ¶孔孟の教 the teachings of Confucius and Mencius; Confucianism.

ごうもう 剛毛 a bristle.

こうもく 項目 a head; an item (and a subitem); a point;〈条項〉a clause; a provision ¶項目に分ける itemize / 5項目からなる要求 a five-point demand. 文例⇩

こうもり 《動》a bat.

こうもりがさ こうもり傘 an umbrella.

こうもん¹ 肛門 《解》the anus;《動》the vent;〈婉曲的に〉the back passage ¶肛門の anal 《diseases》/ 肛門科 proctology / 肛門鏡 a proctoscope.

こうもん² 校門 the gate of a school; a school gate.

ごうもん 拷問《physical, mental》torture;《口語》the third degree ¶拷問にかける torture;《文》put sb to torture;《口語》give sb the third degree; third-degree sb.

こうや¹ 荒野 a wilderness; a waste; wasteland.

こうや² 紺屋〈人〉a dyer;〈店〉a dyer's. 文例⇩

こうやく¹ 口約 ¶口約する give one's word;《文》make a verbal promise.

こうやく² 公約 a (public) commitment [promise,《文》pledge] ¶公約する commit [《文》pledge] oneself (publicly) (to do); make a public commitment / 党[選挙]の公約を実行する carry out [make good] a campaign [election] pledge [promise].

こうやく³ 膏薬〈はり膏薬〉a plaster;〈軟膏〉(an) ointment ¶膏薬をはる put a plaster on (a cut);《文》apply a plaster to (a wound) / 膏薬をはぐ take a plaster off;《文》remove a plaster.

こうやくすう 公約数 a common divisor [factor] ¶最大公約数 the greatest common divisor (略: G.C.D.); the highest common factor (略: H.C.F.).

こうやまき 高野まき《植》an umbrella pine, a parasol pine [fir].

こうゆ¹ 香油 perfumed [scented] hair oil.

こうゆ² 鉱油 mineral oil.

こうゆう¹ 交友 a friend; an acquaintance; a companion ¶交友関係を調べる find out [investigate] what company sb keeps; check up on sb's associates.

こうゆう² 校友 a schoolmate; a schoolfellow;〈同窓生〉a graduate;《米》an alumnus (pl. -ni);《米》an alumna (pl. -nae)(女);《英》an old boy [girl] ¶校友会〈団体〉an alumni [old boys] association; a graduates' association;〈会合〉an alumni [old boys'] meeting [reunion] / 校友会雑誌 an alumni magazine [bulletin, gazette].

ごうゆう 豪遊 ¶豪遊する go on an extravagant spree; spend money in a royal style;《俗》have a blowout.

こうゆうち 公有地 public(-owned) land.

こうよう¹ 公用 official [government] business; an official duty [mission];〈使用〉(for) public use ¶公用で on official business.

こうよう² 効用〈用途〉use; usefulness; good;《文》utility;〈効能〉an effect.

こうよう³ 紅[黄]葉〈葉〉red [yellow] leaves (of autumn);《文》tinted autumnal leaves;〈色〉autumnal tints [colors] (of yellow and gold) ¶紅葉する turn red [yellow]; be tinged with red [yellow]; put on 《their》autumn colors.

こうよう⁴ 高揚 (spiritual) uplift; a (psychological) lift ¶高揚する《文》exalt; enhance; uplift; whip up (war spirit).

こうようご 公用語 an official language (of an international conference).

こうようじゅ 広葉樹 a broad-leaved tree.

ごうよく 強欲 ⇨よくばり.

こうら 甲羅 a shell; a carapace ¶甲羅を干す bask [brown one's back] in the sun.

こうらく 行楽 an excursion; a picnic; an outing; a pleasure trip; holiday-making ¶行楽に行く go on an excursion [a pleasure trip]; have an outing / 行楽客 a tourist;《米》a vacationer;《米》a vacationist;《英》a holidaymaker;《英》a tripper / 行楽地 a tourist [vacation, holiday] resort.

こうり¹ 小売り retail(ing); retail sale ¶小売りをする retail; sell (at) retail / 小売り業 retail trade / 小売り商(人) a retail dealer; a retailer / 小売り店 a retail store [shop] / 小売り値段 a retail price. 文例⇩

こうり² 公理《数》an axiom.

こうり³ 功利《文》utility ¶功利的《文》utilitarian; down-to-earth; practical; unsentimental;《米俗》hard-nosed / 物事を功利的に考える take a utilitarian view of things; view things in a practical [down-to-earth] way / 功利主義 utilitarianism.

こうり⁴ 行李 a wicker suitcase.

こうり⁵ 高利 ¶高利で at high interest; at a high [《文》usurious] rate of interest; at an extortionate [exorbitant] rate of interest (不当に高く) / 高利貸し〈事〉moneylending;〈人〉a moneylender;《文》a usurer;《米口語》a loan shark.

こうめい(せいだい) 彼は常に公明正大だ. He is always fair and upright [open and aboveboard] in his dealings.

こうもく それはこの項目にはいる. It comes under this heading. | It belongs in [to] this category.

こうや² 紺屋の白ばかま. The tailor's wife is worst clad.【諺】|The shoemaker's wife goes barefoot.【諺】

こうようa 山々は燃えるように紅葉していた. The hills were ablaze [aflame] with autumn tints.

ごうり 合理 ¶合理(性)《文》rationality / 合理的 rational; reasonable / 合理化する rationalize; make sth more rational [reasonable] / 産業の合理化 rationalization of industry; industrial rationalization / 合理主義 rationalism; 〈無駄なことをしない〉 practical-mindedness, pragmatism / 合理主義者 a rationalist; a practical-minded person; a pragmatist.

ごうりき 強力 a (mountain) guide; a mountain carrier.

こうりつ¹ 公立 ¶公立の public; prefectural (府県立の); municipal (市立の).

こうりつ² 効率 efficiency ¶効率のいい[悪い] efficient [inefficient].

こうりつ³ 高率 a high rate ¶高率の関税 a high tariff.

こうりゃく 攻略 capture; 《文》conquest; 〈侵略〉(an) invasion ¶攻略する《文》carry (the enemy's position); capture (a city); take (a fortress); by storm, conquer (a country).

こうりゃん 高粱 kaoliang; (Chinese) sorghum.

こうりゅう¹ 交流 【電】an alternating current (略: AC); 〈交換〉interchange ¶文化の交流 cultural exchange [interchange] (between) / 人事の交流 an interchange of personnel (between) / 交流電動機 an AC [alternating current] motor / 交流発電機 an AC [alternating current] generator.

こうりゅう² 拘留 detention; custody ¶拘留する detain; take sb into custody; hold [keep] sb in custody; 《口語》lock sb up / 拘留中であるbe in detention; be (kept) in custody.

こうりゅう³ 興隆 rise; prosperity ¶興隆する rise; prosper; flourish.

ごうりゅう 合流 ¶合流する join; merge; meet; 〈川が〉flow [run] together; flow into each other; 〈加わる〉join (a party); link up (with); merge [be merged, 《文》unite] (with, into one group) / 合流点 the junction [confluence] (of two rivers); a meeting place (of two civilizations).

こうりょ 考慮 consideration; (careful) thought ¶考慮する《文》give consideration [thought] to; consider; think over; take account of; take sth into account [consideration] / 考慮中である〈人が主語〉be considering sth; have sth under consideration / 〈事が主語〉be under consideration / 考慮しない[に入れない] take no thought [account] of; leave sth out of consideration [account].

こうりょう¹ 香料 〈薬味〉spice(s); 〈芳香物〉(a) perfume; essence; 〈香典〉⇨ こうでん.

こうりょう² 校了 ¶〈校正の符号〉OK ¶校了にする OK (the proofs) / 校了刷り an OK'd proof; a press proof.

こうりょう³ 綱領 〈眼目〉a general plan; general principles; 〈摘要〉an outline; a summary ¶政党の綱領《米》a party platform; 《英》a party programme.

こうりょう⁴ 稿料 ⇨ げんこう²(原稿料).

こうりょう⁵ 荒涼 ¶荒涼たる《文》desolate (and forlorn); dreary; bleak; deserted; wild.

こうりょく 効力 (an) effect; 〈法律などの〉force; validity; 〈薬などの〉effect; 《文》efficacy ¶効力のある effective; 《文》efficacious; valid / 効力のない ineffective; null and void (法律契約などが) / 効力を生じる come into force [effect]; take effect / 効力を失う lose effect [its validity]; become invalid [null and void]. 文例⇩

ごうりょく 合力 【物】a resultant (force).

こうりん 降臨 〈キリストの〉Christ's coming; Advent ¶降臨節 Advent.

こうるさい 小うるさい fussy (about one's clothes); particular (about); hard to please; priggish (作法・言葉使いなどに); 〈こがみがまし言う〉nagging.

これい¹ 恒例 an established custom; a usual [time-honored] practice ¶恒例の customary; usual / 恒例により《文》as is customary (with us); as usual.

こうれい² 高齢 《文》an advanced age ¶高齢にもかかわらず in spite of (his) great age / 80の高齢で at the great age of eighty / 高齢者 an old [《文》aged] person; 《文》a person of advanced age; 〈集合的に〉old people; 《文》the aged.

ごうれい 号令 a (word of) command; an order ¶天下に号令する《文》hold sway over the country / 号令をかける give [shout] an order; give a (word of) command / 号令台 a drill platform.

こうれつ 後列 the rear (rank); the back row.

こうろ¹ 行路 a path; a course ¶人生行路《文》the (thorny) path of life; 《文》life's journey.

こうろ² 香炉 an incense burner.

こうろ³ 航路 a sea [sailing] route; a course; 〈定期便〉a line; a service ¶〈大洋上の〉常用航路 a sea-lane / 定期航路 a regular line [service] / 航路標識 a beacon; a channel mark.

こうろう 功労 (distinguished) service(s); 《文》merits; 〈文〉meritorious deeds ¶功労のある《文》meritorious / 功労を立てる distinguish oneself (in war); 《文》render distinguished service (to the state) / 功労により in recognition of sb's services / 功労者《文》a man [person] of merit.

こうろうきょう 公労協 〈公共企業体等労働組合協議会〉the Council of the Public Corporations and Government Workers Unions.

こうろん¹ 口論 a dispute; a quarrel; a wrangle; an argument; an exchange of words ¶口論する quarrel [argue, 《文》dispute] (with sb about sth); have an argument [a dispute] (with); have words (with); exchange words. 文例⇩

こうり¹ この品物は小売りで1個100円で売れる。These articles retail at [for] 100 yen apiece. / 小売りお断り。〈掲示〉Wholesale 《英》Trade (sales) only.

こうりょ まだ考慮してみる余地がある。It leaves some room for consideration. / その点については充分考慮した。We have given careful consideration to that point.

こうりょく その契約は3年間効力を有する。The contract holds good [is valid] for three years.

こうろん¹ 2人の間で激しい口論

こうろん² 公論 public opinion; the consensus (of opinion).
こうろんおつばく 甲論乙駁 ¶甲論乙駁する argue for and against 《a matter》.
こうわ 講和 peace; (a) reconciliation (和解) ¶講和する make [《文》conclude] peace 《with》/ 単独講和 a separate peace / 講和会議 a peace conference / 講和条件 conditions [terms] of peace / 講和条約 《conclude》 a peace treaty 《with》; a treaty of peace.
こうわ 講話 a lecture; a talk ¶講話をする deliver [give] a lecture 《on》; lecture 《on》.
こうわん 港湾 harbors ¶港湾施設 harbor [port] facilities / 港湾労働者 a dock worker; 〈荷役〉 a stevedore; 《米》 a longshoreman; 《英》 a docker.
こえ¹ 声 a voice; 〈叫び声〉 a cry; 〈鳥などの〉 notes; a song ¶声なき民の声 the voice of the silent majority; 《文》the opinion of the inarticulate masses / 虫の音 the singing of insects / 太い[細い]声 a deep [thin] voice / 声がいい have a sweet [fine] voice / 声の大きい[優しい] loud-soft-spoken; loud-soft-voiced / 声を出して読む read aloud / 声を忍んで泣く sob / 声を立てる let out [《文》utter] a shout [cry] / 声をかける call out 《to》; hail; 〈ひとこと〉 say something [a word] 《to》 / 声を限りに at the top of one's voice / 声をそろえて 《文》 with one voice; in chorus 《unison》 / 声をはずませて in a lively [an animated] voice / 声をひそめる lower one's voice / 声をひそめて in whispers; under one's breath / 小さい[低い]声で in a low voice; in whispers; in an undertone / 大きい[高い]声で in [with] a loud voice; loudly / 大きな声では言えないが between ourselves [you and me (and the gatepost)] / 声変わりする one's voice changes [breaks, cracks]. 文例⇩
こえ² 肥 ⇨ こやし ¶肥だめ[おけ] a night-soil [tank [bucket].
ごえい 護衛 a bodyguard; an escort; 〈集団〉 guard; escort ¶護衛する guard; escort / 駆逐艦に護衛された船団 a convoy with a destroyer escort / 護衛付きで under escort [guard] / 護衛艦 an escort ship [vessel]; a naval escort / 護衛兵 a guard. 文例⇩
ごえいか 御詠歌 a pilgrim's [Buddhist] hymn.
こえだ 小枝 a twig; 〈葉や花のついた〉 a sprig 《of holly》; 〈花枝〉 a spray 《of cherry blossom》.

こえる¹ 肥える 〈太る〉 get [grow] fat [stout]; put on [gain] flesh ⇨ ふとる; 〈土地が〉 grow fertile [rich] ¶肥える 〈身体の〉 fat; stout; 〈土地の〉 fertile / 目が肥えている have an eye 《for the beautiful》; 《文》 be quite a connoisseur 《of》 / 耳が肥えている have an ear 《for music》 / 口[舌]が肥えている be particular [《口語》choosy] about one's food; 《文》have a discerning palate; be something of a gourmet.
こえる² 越える pass; cross; go over [across, beyond]; 〈乗り越える〉《文》 surmount; get over; overcome; 〈超過する〉《文》 exceed; pass; be over; be above; be more than; 〈優越する〉《文》surpass; 《文》 excel ¶40歳を超えている be over forty; be more than forty years old; 《口語》be on the wrong side of forty / 川を越えて across a river. 文例⇩
こおう 呼応 ¶呼応する 《文》act in concert 《with》; respond 《to》 / …に呼応して in concert with…; in response to….
ゴーカート a go-cart; a kart.
コーカサス the Caucasus ¶コーカサス人 a Caucasian / コーカサス山脈 the Caucasus Mountains.
コークス 《《ドイツ語》Koks》 coke.
ゴーゴー the gogo (dance) ¶ゴーゴーを踊る dance [do] the gogo; gogo.
コース a course; a lane (トラック・プールの); a fairway (ゴルフの); 〈道筋〉 a route ¶第1コース Lane No. 1 / 《競泳の》コースを分ける 浮き lane buoys. 文例⇩
ゴースト 《テレビ》 a ghost; ghosting.
コーチ coaching; 〈人〉 a coach ¶コーチする coach (a team).
コーチゾン 《薬》 cortisone.
コーチャー a coach; 《野球》 a coacher (一塁と三塁の) ¶コーチャーボックス a coach's [coaching] box.
コーチン 《鶏》 a Cochin.
コート¹ 〈上着・外套〉 a coat.
コート² 〈球技の〉 a 《tennis, basketball》 court.
コード¹ 〈電気の〉 《米》 (a) cord; 《英》 (a) flex; a cable 〈太い〉.
コード² 〈電信の暗号〉 a code ¶コードブック a code book.
コートジボアール the Ivory Coast; Côte d'Ivoire ¶コートジボアール共和国 the Republic of Ivory Coast.
コードバン cordovan (leather).
こおどり 小躍り ¶小躍りして喜ぶ jump

が交された. Strong words were exchanged between them. / 口論からなぐり合いになった. They proceeded from words to blows. / 私たちは口論などしたことは一度もありません. We've never had a hard [cross] word between us.
こえ¹ うちのカナリヤはいい声で鳴きます. My canary sings sweetly. / 彼女は「助けて!」と叫ぼうとしたが声が出なかった. She tried to cry 'Help!' but her voice failed her [but had no voice]. / やっと声が出た. At last

I found my voice. / 声がかれてしまってまるで出ない. I am so hoarse that I can hardly speak above a whisper. / 彼は偉大な声楽家だったが, 今ではもう声が出ない. He was once a great singer, but his voice is gone now. / 彼女は自分が聞いた話を残らず声をひそめて彼に聞かせた. She repeated to him with bated breath all she had heard. / 彼は彼女に対して声を荒らげたことは一度もない. He has never raised his voice to her. / 少年の声は思春期

になると声変わりがして太くなる. A boy's voice changes [breaks, cracks] and becomes deeper at puberty. / 「彼って来いよ」と彼は私たちに声をかけた. He called to us to come in. / その制度に対しては改革の声が高い. There are loud calls for a reform of this system.
ごえい 首相が駅に着くまで警官が護衛した. The Premier went to the station under police escort.
こえる² その村は川[山]を越えたところにある. The village lies

[dance] for joy.

コーナー a corner ¶コーナーキック《サッカー》a corner (kick).

コーヒー coffee ¶ひいたコーヒー ground coffee / コーヒーの出しがら coffee grounds / コーヒーを入れる make coffee / コーヒー(を入れる)道具 coffee things / ブラックコーヒー black coffee / ミルク入りコーヒー coffee with milk ; 《英》white coffee ; 《フランス語》café au lait / コーヒー茶わん a coffee cup / コーヒー店 a coffee shop / コーヒーひき a coffee grinder [mill] / コーヒー豆 coffee beans / コーヒー沸かし a coffee-maker.

コーラ cola ; kola.

コーラス a chorus ⇒がっしょう¹.

こおらす 凍らす freeze.

コーラン the Koran.

こおり 氷 ice ¶氷が張りつめる be frozen over / 氷の張った frozen 《lakes》; ice-covered 《rivers》; ice-bound 《harbors》(氷に閉ざされた) / 氷のような[ように冷たい] icy ; ice-cold / 氷の刃(゙) a gleaming [shining] blade / 氷を入れたウイスキー whisky with ice [on the rocks] / 氷をかく shave (a block of) ice / 氷を砕く crush ice / 氷で冷やす cool *sth* with ice ; ice 《a bottle of beer》/ 氷小豆[いちご] a bowl of shaved ice with boiled adzuki beans [strawberry syrup] / 氷砂糖 rock [《英》sugar] candy ; crystallized sugar / 氷詰めにする pack 《fish》in ice / 氷まくら an ice pillow / 氷水 〈冷やした、または氷を浮かべた水〉iced [《米》ice] water ; 〈かき氷〉shaved ice with 《sugar, fruit》syrup / 氷屋 〈店〉an ice shop ; 〈人〉an ice dealer ; 《米》an iceman. 文例⇩

こおりつく 凍り付く freeze to [on] *sth* ; be frozen fast [hard] (to) ¶凍り付いた道 a frozen street. 文例⇩

こおる 凍る freeze ; be frozen over (一面に) ¶堅く凍る freeze (up) solid.

ゴール the goal ; 《バスケットボール》a basket ¶(球技で)ゴールを決める make [score, win] a goal ; 《バスケットボールで》make a basket ; sink a shot / ゴールインする reach [hit] the goal ; finish / ゴールキーパー a goalkeeper.

コールガール a call girl.

コールサイン 《通信》a call sign.

コールスロー 《料理》coleslaw.

コールタール coal tar ; tar ¶コールタールを塗る tar.

コールテン corduroy ; corded velveteen ¶コールテンのズボン corduroy pants ; (a pair of) corduroys.

ゴールデンアワー 《テレビ》(at, in) (the) prime time ; (the) peak viewing time [period].

ゴールデンウイーク the Golden Week (from April 29 through May 5, both of which are public holidays).

コールドクリーム cold cream.

コールドゲーム 《米》a called game. 文例⇩

コールドパーマ a cold wave ; 《英口語》a cold perm.

コールドミート cold meat.

ゴールドラッシュ a gold rush.

コールマネー 【金融】call money.

コールローン 【金融】a call loan ; a demand loan.

こおろぎ 〖昆〗a cricket. 文例⇩

コーンフレーク cornflakes.

こが 古雅 ¶古雅な classical ; 《文》antique and refined.

こがい¹ 子飼い ¶子飼いの 《an animal》reared from young ; hand-reared 《calves》/ 〈比喩的に〉《an apprentice [a pupil]》trained from boyhood ; 《a worker》trained within the firm.

こがい² 戸外 ¶戸外で in the open air ; out of doors ; outdoors / 戸外へ出る go outside [outdoors, out of doors] / 戸外運動 outdoor [open-air] exercise [sports].

ごかい¹ 五戒 【仏教】the five commandments (against murder, lust, theft, lying and intemperance).

ごかい² 誤解 (a) misunderstanding ; misinterpretation ¶誤解する misunderstand ; have a false idea (of) ; mistake ; 《口語》get (hold of) the wrong end of the stick ; 《悪くとる》take *sth* [*sb*] amiss ; 《口語》get *sb* [*sth*] wrong / 誤解される be misunderstood / 誤解されやすい 〈人が〉be liable to cause misunderstanding ; 〈人が〉be apt to be misunderstood ; 〈語句などが〉be misleading. 文例⇩

ごかい³ 〖動〗a lugworm.

こがいしゃ 子会社 a subsidiary (company).

コカイン 《化》cocain(e) ¶コカイン中毒 cocainism ; cocaine addiction [poisoning].

ごかく 互角 ¶互角の equal ; even ; evenly-[well-]matched / 互角の勝負 a close [well-matched] game / 互角に渡り合う prove *oneself* a good match [《文》a worthy opponent

---

across the river [beyond the hills]. / その問題を持ち出すと、必ず越えがたい壁にぶつかった。Whenever we brought up the problem, we came up against an insuperable wall. / 聴衆は千人を超えた。The audience exceeded [was over] a thousand.

コース 東京は台風のコースに入るかもしれない。Tokyo may lie in the course of the typhoon.

こおり 今夜は氷が張るだろう。It will freeze tonight. / スケートができるほど氷が固く張っている。The ice is strong enough to skate on. / 夏になると北極海の氷が割れて流れ出す。When summer comes the ice in the Arctic Ocean breaks up and begins to drift.

こおりつく 凍り付くような寒さだ。It is freezing (cold).

こおる 池も一面に凍った。The pond is frozen over. / 寒くて身体が凍りそうだった。I was chilled to the bone.

コールドゲーム 大雨のため、コールドゲームになった。The game was called because of heavy rain.

こおろぎ こおろぎが鳴いている。I hear a cricket chirping.

ごかい² どうかこの点誤解のないようにして頂きたい。Please let there be no misunderstanding about this. / 文意は明瞭で誤解の恐れはない。The meaning is clear and unmistakable. / この点について彼らの誤解を解かねばならない。I must remove their misunderstandings on this point. / 彼女のことを冷たい女だと思って

ごがく　語学 (study of languages) 語学が達者である be good at [《文》 proficient in] languages; be a good linguist / 語学の才能がある[ない] 《文》 have considerable [no] linguistic talent; have an [no] aptitude for (foreign) languages / 語学教育 language teaching [education] / 語学教師 a language teacher / 語学者 a linguist / 語学力 language ability.

ごかくけい　五角形 ⇨ ごかっけい.

こかげ　木陰 ¶木陰で in the shade of a tree; under a tree. 文例⇩

コカコーラ 《商標名》 Coca-Cola; Coke.

-ごかし ¶親切ごかしに under pretense of kindness / おためごかしに as if one meant well.

こがす　焦がす　burn; scorch; 〈きつね色に〉brown 《the meat》; singe (毛髪を); char (黒焦げにする).

こがた　小形型 ¶小型の small-sized; small; pocket (dictionaries); miniature; midget (〈く小型の) / 小型化 miniaturization / 小型化する miniaturize / 超小型化 microminiaturization / 小型乗用車 a small [compact] car; a minicar.

こがたな　小刀 a knife (pl. knives); 〈折り畳み式の〉a pocketknife; a penknife; a jackknife (大形の).

こかつ　枯渇 ⇨かれる², つきる. 文例⇩

ごがつ　五月　May ¶五月の節句 the Boys' Festival / 五月人形 dolls for the Boys' Festival.

ごかっけい　五角形 a pentagon.

こがね　小金 ¶小金をためる make a small fortune; lay by a sizable sum of money.

こがねむし　黄金虫 《昆》 a scarabaeid (beetle); a scarab; 〈日本の〉 a Japanese gold beetle [bug] ★アメリカの a gold beetle は, 日本の「こがねむし」とは別物.

こがら　小柄 ¶小柄の rather [《文》 somewhat] small; smallish; 《文》of small stature [build]. 文例⇩

こがらし　木枯らし a cold [wintry] wind; nipping [biting] winter wind.

こがれる　焦がれる　long (pine, 《文》yearn) for sth [sb]; be dying for sth [sb] ¶...に会いたいと思い焦がれる be dying to see sb; would give anything [a lot] to see sb.

ごかん¹　五感 the (five) senses.

ごかん²　語感 〈人の〉sensitivity to words; 〈語の与える感じ〉a nuance; (a) tinge; 《文》connotation ¶語感が鋭い be very sensitive to [have a keen sense of] language; be able to distinguish between delicate shades of meaning / 語感を養う develop a feeling for language.

ごかん　語幹 the stem (of a word).

ごがん³　護岸 shore [bank] protection; 〈川の〉 a river wall; 〈海岸の〉 a seawall; a sea bank ¶護岸工事 shore [bank] protection works / 護岸堤防 an embankment; a dyke [《米》dike].

こかんせつ　股関節 《解》 a hip joint; a coxa (pl. coxae) ¶股関節脱臼 dislocation of the hip joint.

こき¹　古希 ¶古希の祝いをする celebrate one's seventieth birthday.

こき²　呼気 expiration; breathing.

ごき¹　語気 a tone (of voice) ¶語気を荒らげて in an angry tone / 語気を荒らげる speak harshly; raise one's voice / 語気を強めて (speak) emphatically / 語気鋭く sharply.

ごき²　誤記 (make) an error in writing; a slip of the pen / 〈記入の〉 a misentry.

ごぎ　語義 the meaning of a word.

こきおろす　扱き下ろす　abuse [criticize, attack] sb severely; denounce; disparage; run sb down; 《米》score; lash; 《口語》lambast; 《口語》give sb a tongue-lashing [a roasting].

ごきげん　御機嫌 ⇨きげん⁴ ¶ご機嫌を伺う ask [inquire] after sb's health; pay one's respects to sb.

こきざみ　小刻み ¶小刻みに〈少しずつ〉bit by bit; little by little; piecemeal; a little at a time; 〈小またに〉《walk》with short, quick steps.

こきつかう　扱き使う　work [drive] sb hard; sweat (one's employees); have sb at one's beck and call (あごで使う).

こぎつける　漕ぎ着ける　〈船を〉row 《a boat》up to (a pier); 〈運びをつける〉get to [reach] 《a working stage》; manage (contrive) (to do). 文例⇩

こぎって　小切手 《米》 a check; 《英》 a cheque ¶1万円の小切手 a check for 10,000 yen / 小切手で払う pay by check / 小切手を振り出す [切る] issue [write out, make out] a check / 小切手を現金に換える cash a check / 横線[支払い保証]小切手 a crossed [certified] check / 小切手帳 a checkbook.

ごきぶり 《昆》 a cockroach ¶ごきぶりの出る台所 a cockroach-ridden kitchen.

こきみ　小気味 ¶小気味のいい smart; neat; refreshing / 小気味よく 〈痛快に〉smartly;

いるとしたら, 君の誤解だ. If you think she is cold-hearted, you are mistaken.

ごかく　君は吉田君となら互角だ. You are a match for Yoshida.

こかげ　日光を遮る木陰がなかった. There were no trees to shield us from the sun. / その木が涼しい木陰を与えてくれた. The tree gave [《文》afforded] us a cooling shade.

こがす　炎は天を焦がした. The flames almost scorched the sky.

こかつ　戦争は国の財産を枯渇させる. War is a great drain upon a country's resources.

こがら　彼はどちらかと言えば小柄の方だった. He was, if anything, below average height.

ごきげん　ご機嫌いかがですか. How are you (getting along)? / 《病人に》 How do you feel today? / ではご機嫌よう. Good-by! / Take it easy! Good luck! / Have a nice trip! / Bon voyage! / あの人はご機嫌の取りにくい人だ. He is hard to please. / 放っておきなよ, じきにご機嫌が直るから. Leave her alone, and she will soon come around [her good humor will soon return]. / 小林君はハワイで大変楽しい思いをして, すこぶるご機嫌で帰って来た. Kobayashi

こきゃく 顧客 ⇒とくい¹, きゃく.

こきゅう¹ 呼吸 〈息〉a breath; breathing;『生理』respiration; 〈こつ〉a knack; a trick; the (right) way (of doing); the secret (of, for) ¶呼吸する breathe / 呼吸を覚える get the knack [hang] (of); learn the trick (of); learn the ropes / 呼吸を合わせる keep time (with) / 呼吸運動 breathing exercises / 呼吸器 the respiratory organs / 呼吸困難 (have) difficulty in breathing; difficult breathing / 呼吸数 a breathing rate.

こきゅう² 胡弓 a Chinese fiddle.

こきょう 故郷 〈人の〉one's (old) home; one's hometown; one's birthplace ¶第二の故郷 one's second home; a home (away) from home / 故郷に帰る go [go back, return] home. 文例⇩

こぎれ 小切れ a small piece of cloth.

こぎれい 小奇麗 ¶小ぎれいな neat; trim; tidy.

こく¹ 石 〈単位〉a koku (=180 l).

こく² ¶こくがある 〈酒が〉have plenty of body; be full of body / こくのあるワイン full-bodied wine. 文例⇩

こく³ 扱く hackle (flax); thresh [thrash] (rice); strip (off) (leaves).

こく⁴ 酷 ¶酷な severe; hard; harsh; cruel; 酷なことをする treat sb harshly [cruelly]; be hard [rough] on sb.

こぐ¹ 扱ぐ pull up (a plant) by the roots.

こぐ² 漕ぐ row (a boat); work at the [one's] oars; pull the oar; 〈自転車を〉pedal (a bicycle); pump the pedals (of a bicycle) (強く); 〈ぶらんこを〉pump (a swing) ¶舟をこぐ row a boat; 〈居眠りする〉nod (while dozing) / こぐ手を休める rest on one's oar(s) / 沖へこぎ出す pull [put] out to sea / こぎ戻す row back / こぎ手 an oarsman; a rower.

ごく¹ 語句 words and phrases. 文例⇩

ごく² 極く 〈甚だ〉very; extremely; 《文》exceedingly; 〈最も〉most; 〈全く〉quite ¶ごく小さい very small; tiny / ごく内輪に見積もって at the lowest estimate.

ごくあく 極悪 ¶極悪(非道)の extremely wicked; atrocious; 《文》villainous; 《文》heinous; 《文》nefarious / 極悪人 an utter [a thoroughgoing, 《文》a consummate] villain; 《文》a scoundrel of the deepest [blackest] dye.

こくい 国威 national prestige [dignity] ¶国威を高める〈傷つける〉enhance [damage, 《文》impair] the national prestige (of Japan).

ごくい 極意 ¶極意をきわめる master the secret (of); 《文》be initiated into the mysteries (of an art).

ごくいん 極印 a stamp; a brand ¶殺人犯の極印を押される be branded (as) a murderer.

こくう 虚空 the (empty) air [sky]; empty space ¶虚空をつかむ grasp at the air [at thin air]; clutch at nothing / 虚空を見つめる stare into space [at nothing] / 虚空に消える vanish into thin air; disappear into nothingness.

こくうん 国運 《文》the destiny [fate] of a nation ¶国運の隆盛〈衰退〉the prosperity [decline] of the nation; the rise [fall] of the nation.

こくえい 国営 ¶国営の government-managed[-run]; state-operated / 国営にする put [place] (an enterprise) under government [state] management; nationalize / 国営化 nationalization / 国営事業 a government [state, national] enterprise.

こくえき 国益 national interest(s) ¶国益を計る promote the national interest / 国益となる serve the best interests of the nation. 文例⇩

こくえん 黒鉛 〖鉱・化〗graphite; plumbago; 〈通俗に〉black lead.

こくおう 国王 a king; 《文》a monarch; 《文》a sovereign ¶スウェーデン国王 the King of Sweden / 国王殺害 regicide.

こくがい 国外 ¶国外に[で] outside the country; abroad; overseas / 国外に追放する expel sb from the country; exile.

こくがく 国学 the study of Japanese classical literature ¶国学者 a Japanese classical scholar.

こくぎ 国技 a national sport [game].

こくげん 刻限 the fixed [appointed] time ¶刻限を過ぎた past [beyond] the time (for).

こくご 国語 〈1国の言語〉a language; 〈日本語〉the Japanese language; Japanese ¶2[3]か国語が話せる人 a bilingual [trilingual] person / 国語学 Japanese philology [linguistics] / 国語審議会 the Japanese Language Council / 国語問題 problems concerning [《文》pertaining to] the Japanese language. 文例⇩

ごくごく ¶ごくごく飲む drink (water) in big gulps [swallows]; take a long pull (at the bottle) / ごくごくいう音 a gurgle (in the

---

had a very good time in Hawaii and came back all smiles. / (酔っている人などに向かって)今夜はずいぶんご機嫌ですね。You are very pleased with yourself this evening, aren't you？

こぎつける やっとの事で先方と妥協にまで漕ぎ着けた。With great difficulty we have managed to reach an agreement with them.

こきょう 僕の故郷は浜松です。I come from Hamamatsu.

こく² この酒はとてもこくがある。This sake has plenty of body (to it).

こく⁴ そんな言い方をしては少し酷だよ。That's putting it a bit too strong. ¦ I wouldn't put it quite like that.

こぐ² 湖でボートをこぎたい。I want to have a row on the lake. ¦ I'd like to go boating at the lake. / 第2位のボートが一こぎごとに追いついて行く。The second boat is gaining at every stroke.

こくえき その政策がはじめて取られた当時は、それは明らかに国益に適うものであった。When the policy was introduced, it was clearly in the national interest.

こくご 彼は英語の外に数ヵ国語が話せる。He can speak several

こくさい throat of a man drinking water》.

こくさい¹ 国債《負債》a national debt [loan]; 〈証券〉a national [government] bond ¶国債を償還する redeem [sink] a national loan / 国債を発行する issue a national loan / 国債を募集する raise [float] a national loan.

こくさい² 国際 ¶国際的(な) international / 国際的に internationally / 国際化する internationalize / 国際会議 an international conference [congress] / 国際会議場 an international conference hall / 国際感覚を身につける acquire an international way of thinking; gain an understanding of other peoples' way of looking at things / 国際関係 international [diplomatic] relations / 国際管理 《place an island under》 international control / 国際競技 an international game [match, competition] / 国際協定 an international agreement; an accord / 国際協力 international cooperation / 国際空港 an international airport / 国際刑事警察機構 the International Criminal Police Organization (略: ICPO); Interpol / 国際結婚 a mixed marriage / 国際語 an international [a world, a universal] language / 国際公法《法》public international law / 国際試合 an international match / 国際児童年 the International Year of the Child (略: IYC) / 国際私法《法》private international law; the conflict of laws / 国際司法裁判所 the International Court of Justice (略: ICJ) / 国際社会 international society; the world community; the community 《文》 family) of nations / 国際情勢 the international situation / 国際色豊かな集まり a gathering with a markedly international character / 国際人 a cosmopolitan; a citizen of the world / 国際政治 international [world] politics / 国際線を飛行中の旅客機 an airliner on an international flight / 国際組織[団体] an international organization / 国際通貨基金 the International Monetary Fund (略: IMF) / 国際電話をかける make an international [overseas] (phone) call 《to New York》/ 国際都市 a cosmopolitan city / 国際紛争 an international dispute / 国際法 international law / 国際放送 international broadcasting; an international broadcast (1回の) / 国際見本市 an international trade fair / 国際問題 an international problem; a diplomatic issue / 国際労働機構 the International Labor Organization (略: ILO). 文例⇩

ごくさいしき 極彩色 ¶極彩色の richly colored; 《illustrations》in full color.

こくさいしゅうし 国際収支 international pay-

ments ¶国際収支の赤[黒]字 an unfavorable [a favorable] balance of international payments; a 《large [massive]》 balance of payments deficit [surplus] / 国際収支の不均衡を是正する correct the imbalance of international payments / 国際収支を改善する improve 《its》 balance of payments.

こくさいれんごう 国際連合 the United Nations (略: UN) ⇒こくれん.

こくさく 国策 (a) national [state] policy ¶国策の線に沿って in line with (the) national policy / 国策を遂行する carry out (a) national policy.

こくさん 国産 ¶国産の domestic; home-produced[-manufactured]; made in Japan / 国産品 a home [domestic] product; an article of Japanese make / 純国産品 an all-Japanese product.

こくし 酷使 ¶酷使する work [drive] sb hard; be a hard master; sweat 《one's workers》/ 身体を酷使する overwork; drive oneself relentlessly / 頭脳を酷使する overtax one's brains / 〈物心〉酷使に耐える stand (up to) [withstand] rough use. 文例⇩

こくじ¹ 告示 a notice; a bulletin; an announcement ¶告示する 《文》 notify; give notice 《of, that...》; announce / 大蔵省告示第2号 Notification No. 2 of the Ministry of Finance.

こくじ² 国事 affairs of state; national [state] affairs ¶国事に携わる take part in affairs of state.

こくじ³ 国璽 the Great Seal; the Seal of State.

こくじ⁴ 酷似 《文》 (a) close resemblance [similarity] 《between》 ¶酷似する be very [extremely] like sth; 《文》 resemble sth closely; bear a close resemblance 《to》.

こくしょ 酷暑 intense 《文》 torrid] heat (of summer) ¶酷暑の候 the hot season.

こくじょう 国情 the conditions of a country; the state of affairs in a country ¶中国[アメリカ]の国情 《know nothing about》Chinese [American] affairs; 《文》《be conversant with》things Chinese [American]. 文例⇩

ごくじょう 極上 ¶極上の the best; choicest; first-rate / 極上の牛肉 prime (cuts of) beef / 極上品《文》an article of the finest [highest] quality, the best of its kind. 「powder.

こくしょく 黒色 black ¶黒色火薬 black

こくじょく 国辱 a national disgrace; a disgrace to a [the, one's] country [nation]. 文例⇩

こくじん 黒人 a black; a black person; a Negro 《pl. -es》 ★ black という語がかつて持っ

languages besides English.

こくさい² 日本人はもっと国際性を持たなければいけないと彼は言った. He said that the Japanese ought to be more internationally minded. / これは国際問題に発展しそうだ. This is likely to develop into an international issue.

こくし 探検隊用の車両は頑丈で荒地での酷使に耐えるものでなければ

ばならなかった. The vehicles to serve the expedition had to be strongly built and be able to stand up to the rigors of use over rough terrain.

こくじょう それは日本の国情に合わない. It does not fit in with the actual situation in Japan.

こくじょく あの男のやったことは正に国辱ものだ. What he has

done is really a disgrace to our nation.

こくせい² 日本の人口は1980年10月1日の国勢調査によると117,057,000人であった. Japan's population was 117,057,000 according to the results of the national census taken on Oct. 1, 1980.

こくせき 彼の国籍はどこですか. What is his nationality? | What

こくすい 国粋 ¶国粋的 nationalistic / 国粋主義 nationalism ; ultranationalism. ていた軽蔑的なニュアンスはなくなり, 今では最も普通に用いられる. Negro は《米》では差別語なので使わない方が安全 ¶黒人の科学者 a black scientist / 黒人霊歌 a Negro spiritual.

こくせい[1] 国政 national administration; state politics; 《文》statecraft ¶国政を担当する《文》assume the reins of government;《文》take the helm of state / 国政を担当している《文》be at the helm of state / (国会の)国政調査権 the right to conduct investigations in relation to government.

こくせい[2] 国勢 the state of a country ¶国勢調査を行なう take a national census / 国勢調査員[票] a census taker [form]. 文例⇩

こくぜい 国税 a national tax ¶国税庁 the National Tax Administration Agency.

こくせき 国籍 nationality; citizenship ¶国籍を取得する acquire 《United States》nationality / 国籍を喪失する lose *one's* 《Japanese》nationality / 無国籍者 a stateless person / 国籍不明の 《an airplane》of unknown nationality. 文例⇩

こくせんべんごにん 国選弁護人 a court-appointed lawyer ¶国選弁護人をつける assign a defense counsel 《to a defendant》.

こくそ 告訴 a complaint; an accusation; legal proceedings; a legal action ¶告訴する accuse 《sb of a crime》; bring a suit [charge] 《against》; lodge a complaint 《against》; take legal steps 《against》; sue 《sb for damages》/ 告訴状 a letter [bill] of complaint.

こくそう[1] 国葬 a state [national] funeral ¶国葬にする give [《文》accord] *sb* a state funeral; hold a state funeral for *sb*.

こくそう[2] 穀倉 a granary ¶穀倉地帯 a granary.

こくぞうむし 《昆》a rice weevil.

こくたい 国体〈国家形態〉the structure of a state; the national polity 《of a country》;〈国民体育大会〉the National Athletic Meet.

こくたん〈植〉an ebony;〈材〉ebony.

こくち 告知 a notice;《文》a notification; an announcement ¶告知書 a notice.

こぐち[1] 小口〈端〉an end;〈品物の〉a small lot;〈小額〉a small amount ¶小口注文 a petty order.

こぐち[2] 木口 the cut end 《of a piece of wood》 ¶木口3寸の松材 a piece of pine wood 3 inches across.

こくちょう[1] 国鳥 a national bird. 文例⇩

こくちょう[2] 国蝶 a national butterfly. 文例⇩

こくちょう[3] 黒鳥 a black swan.

ごくちょうたんぱ 極超短波 a microwave.

ごくつぶし 穀潰し an idler; a good-for-nothing 《fellow》; a ne'er-do-well.

こくてい 国定 ¶国定の state; national / 国定公園 a semi-national [quasi-national] park.

こくてつ 国鉄 the Japanese National Railways (略: JNR) ¶国鉄総裁 the President of the National Railways Corporation.

こくてん 黒点 a dark [black] spot;〈太陽の〉a sunspot ¶太陽黒点の活動の最も盛んな時期 a period of maximum sunspot activity.

こくでん 国電〈電車〉a National Railways [JNR] local (electric) train;〈運行〉the National Railways local (electric) train service.

こくど 国土 a country;〈領土〉a territory; 《文》a realm;《文》a domain ¶国土開発 (national) land development / 国土計画 national land planning / 国土地理院 the Geographical Survey Institute. 文例⇩

こくどう 国道 a national road [highway] ¶国道8号線 Route 8.

こくない 国内 ¶国内の home; domestic; internal; inland / 国内に[で] in [within] the country / 国内事情 internal [domestic] affairs / 国内消費 home [domestic] consumption / 国内向け放送 the home service 《of the NHK》. 文例⇩

こくなん 国難 a national crisis.

こくはく 告白 (a) confession ¶愛の告白《文》a declaration of love / 告白する confess (to);《文》own (to);《口語》own up (to); admit; acknowledge / 罪を告白する confess (to) *one's* crime [sin]; confess that *one* has committed a crime;《文》confess *oneself* guilty. 文例⇩

こくはつ 告発 (a) prosecution; (an) accusation; (an) indictment; a (criminal) charge ¶告発する prosecute [《文》indict] 《sb for an offense》; accuse 《sb of a crime》; charge 《sb with a crime》/ 告発される be prosecuted [indicted] (for);《文》come under indictment.

こくばん 黒板 a blackboard;《米》a chalkboard ¶車付きの黒板 a rolling blackboard unit / 黒板に書いて示す demonstrate *sth* on [by using] the blackboard / 黒板〈に書いたものを〉をふく clean《米》erase) the blackboard / 黒板ふき《米》an [a blackboard] eraser;《英》a (black-)board rubber.

こくひ 国費 national expenditure [outlay] ¶国費を節減する cut governmental spending / 国費で at (the) government [national] expense.

こくび 小首 ¶小首をひねる[かしげる] bend [《文》incline] *one's* head slightly on [to] one side. 文例⇩

---

nationality is he? / 国籍はアメリカだが, 血統はドイツ人だ. He is American by nationality, but of German ancestry. / あの船の国籍は⽇本だ. That steamer sails under the Japanese flag.

こくちょう[1] 日本の国鳥は雉である. Japan's national bird is the pheasant.

こくちょう[2] 日本の国蝶はおおむらさきである. Japan's national butterfly is the giant purple (butterfly).

こくど 狭い国土にかかわらず, 日本人は東アジアで最高の生活水準に到達した. Despite their limited territory [land area], the Japanese have attained the highest living standards in East Asia.

こくない 国内線を飛行中の旅客機が乗っ取られた. A passenger plane was hijacked on an internal [a domestic] flight.

こくはく それは無知を告白するようなものだ. That amounts to a confession of your own ignorance.

こくび 本当かしらと問いたげに小首をかしげてこちらを見た. She bent her head a little to one

ごくひ 極秘 strict secrecy; ¶極秘の strictly confidential; 〈公文書・軍事事項など〉 top-secret; 《米》highly classified / 極秘のうちに with utmost secrecy / 極秘の事項 a close secret; 〈軍事上の〉a top secret / 極秘にする keep 《a matter》a close secret.

ごくび 極微 ⇨ きょくび.

こくびゃく 黒白〈色〉black and white; 〈正邪〉good and bad; right and wrong ¶黒白をつける make it clear whether *sth* is right or wrong; decide the issue / 黒白を争う argue 《(文)dispute》about which is right.

こくひょう 酷評 severe [sharp, scathing] criticism; 《文》strictures ¶酷評する criticize severely; pass harsh [incisive] criticism 《on》; 《文》pass strictures 《on》; 《文》castigate.

こくひん 国賓 a guest of the state; a national [state] guest.

こくふ 国富 national wealth [resources] ¶『国富論』《書名》*The Wealth of Nations*.

こくふく 克服 ¶克服する conquer; overcome; 《文》surmount; get over *sth*.

こくぶん 国文 the Japanese language / 国文学 Japanese literature / 国文(学)科 a Japanese literature course / 国文学史 the history of Japanese literature; 〈書物〉a history of Japanese literature / 国文法 Japanese grammar.

こくべつ 告別 《文》leave-taking; parting ¶告別する say good-by(e) 《to》; 《文》take 《one's》 leave 《of》; 《文》bid farewell 《to》 / 告別式 the final service (for the dead) 《before cremation or burial》; a funeral.

こくほう[1] 国法 the national law; the laws of the country; the law of the land.

こくほう[2] 国宝 a national treasure ¶国宝の指定を受ける be designated a national treasure / 国宝的人物 a national asset.

こくぼう 国防 national defense ⇨ ぼうえい / 国防会議 (a meeting of) the National Defense Council / 国防省 the department [ministry] of defense / 《米国の》国防総省 the Department of Defense; the Pentagon.

ごくぼそ 極細 ¶極細の万年筆 an extrafine-pointed (fountain) pen.

こぐまざ 小熊座〈星座〉Ursa Minor; 《米》the Little Dipper; 《英》the Little Bear.

こくみん 国民 a nation; a people; 〈人民〉the people; the nation; 〈1 人〉a 《British》national, a citizen 《of the United States》 ¶国民的の national / 国民の祝日 a national holiday / 世界の諸国民間の文化交流を促進する promote cultural exchanges between different peoples of the world / 国民皆兵制度を敷く introduce universal conscription / 国民感情 (a) national sentiment; national feeling / 国民休暇村 a 'village' for the people's recreation 《established within a national or semi-national park》 / 国民金融公庫 the People's Finance Corporation / 国民経済 the national economy / 国民健康保険《略》national health insurance / 国民宿舎 an inexpensive hotel operated by a local government; a people's hotel / 国民所得 the national income / 《最高裁判所判事の》国民審査 the popular review 《of the Supreme Court justices》 / 国民性 the national character [traits] 《of》; the characteristics of a nation / 国民生活 the life of the people; the people's living / 国民総生産 the gross national product 《略: GNP》 / 国民体育大会 the National Athletic Meet / 国民投票 a (national) referendum; a plebiscite / 国民投票を行なう hold a referendum 《on a matter》 / 国民投票で決定する decide 《a question》by referendum [plebiscite] / 国民年金 the National Pension.

こくむ 国務 (the) affairs of state; state affairs ¶国務大臣 a minister of state; 《無任所の》a minister without portfolio / 《米国の》国務省 the Department of State; the State Department / 《米国の》国務長官 the Secretary of State.

こくめい[1] 国名 the name of a country.

こくめい[2] 克明 ¶克明な 〈忠実な〉faithful; 〈良心的な〉conscientious; 〈細密な〉minute; detailed; 〈綿密な〉《文》scrupulous; 〈勤勉な〉《文》diligent / 克明に faithfully; conscientiously; minutely; in detail; 《文》scrupulously; 《文》diligently.

こくもつ 穀物 (food) grain; cereals; 《英》corn ¶穀物価格 grain [cereal] prices.

こくゆう 国有 state ownership ¶国有の state-[government-]owned / 国有にする nationalize / 国有化 nationalization / 国有財産 national [state] property / 国有鉄道 a government [national, state] railway ⇨ こくてつ / 国有地 nationally-owned land / 国有林 a state forest.

こくようせき 黒曜石 《鉱》obsidian.

ごくらく 極楽 (the Buddhist) paradise; 《文》the abode of the blessed; 《文》the home of the happy dead ¶極楽往生をする[遂げる] die a peaceful death / 極楽鳥 a bird of paradise.

ごくり ¶ごくりと飲む gulp 《one's beer》(down); take a big gulp 《of coffee》.

こくりつ 国立 ¶国立の national; state; government / 国立劇場 [公園, 大学, 博物館, 病院] a national theater [park, university, museum, hospital].

こくりょく 国力 national power [strength];

---

side and looked quizzically toward me as if questioning the truth of my remark [of what I had said].

こけ 庭石にこけがついてきた. The garden stones have become moss-grown.

こげくさい 何か焦げ臭いぞ. I can smell something burning.

こけつ 虎穴に入らずんば虎児を得ず. Nothing venture, nothing win [gain]. 《諺》

こげつく 彼は不用意に掛け売りをして焦げ付きを作ることが多かった. He was careless about selling his goods on credit and was often saddled with bad debts.

こげつく ご飯がかまの底に焦げづいていた. The rice got scorched and stuck to the bottom of the pot.

ごはん「ズボン」の語原はフランス語です. The word '*zubon*' is derived [comes] from French. / この言葉の語原は明らかでない.

こくるい 穀類 (food) grains ; cereals.

こくれん 国連 the United Nations (略:UN) ¶国連安全保障理事会 the United Nations Security Council (略:UNSC) / 国連軍 the United Nations [UN] forces / 国連経済社会理事会 the United Nations Economic and Social Council / 国連憲章 the United Nations [UN] Charter / 国連事務局[事務総長] the Secretariat [Secretary-General] of the United Nations / 国連総会 the United Nations General Assembly / 国連大学 the United Nations University / 国連分担金 《Japan's》 financial contribution to the United Nations / 国連貿易開発会議 the United Nations Conference on Trade and Development (略:UNCTAD) / 国連本部 the United Nations [UN] Headquarters.

こくろん 国論 public opinion [sentiment] ⇨ よろん ¶国論を統一する create [《文》achieve] a national consensus ; 《文》unify public opinion.

ごぐん 語群 《文法》a word group.

こぐんふんとう 孤軍奮闘 ¶孤軍奮闘する fight alone [unsupported] ; put up a solitary struggle.

こけ 苔 《植》(a) moss ; a moss plant ; 〈地衣〉lichen ; 〈舌の〉fur ¶こけ蒸した mossy ; moss-grown[-covered]. 文例⇩

ごけ¹ 後家 a widow ¶後家になる become a widow ; be widowed / 死ぬまで後家で通す remain a widow for the rest of *one's* life.

ごけ² 碁笥 a go-stone container.

こけい 固形 ¶固形の solid / 固形スープ a soup cube / 固形燃料 solid fuel / 固形物〈固体〉a solid body ; a solid ; 〈食物〉solid food.

ごけい 語形 《言語》a word form ; the form of a word ¶語形変化法 a paradigm / 語形変化[論] accidence.

こけおどし こけ威し 《文》an ostentatious display ; a (mere) show ; (a) bluff ¶こけおどしの showy ; high-sounding 〈文体·肩書など〉.

こけくさい 焦げ臭い 〈においが〉smell burnt ; have a burnt smell ; 〈食べて〉taste burnt ; have a burnt taste. 文例⇩

こけこっこー 〈cry〉cock-a-doodle-doo.

こけし *kokeshi* doll ; a wooden doll with a spherical head, a cylindrical body, and no limbs attached (originally a folkcraft product of the Tohoku region).

こげちゃいろ 焦げ茶色 dark brown (color).

こけつ 虎穴 文例⇩

こげつき 焦げ付き a bad debt ; 《文》an irrecoverable loan. 文例⇩

こげつく 焦げ付く 〈物が〉burn onto *sth* ; burn and stick to *sth* ; 〈貸しなどが〉become uncollectable [《文》irrecoverable] ¶焦げ付かないフライパン a nonstick frying pan. 文例⇩

こげめ 焦げ目 ¶焦げ目をつける grill 《a cut of fish meat》until the surface gets (slightly) burned.

こけらおとし こけら落とし the (formal) opening of a new theater.

こける 〈頬が〉sink ; 《文》be sunken ; be hollow ¶頬がこけている have hollow [sunken] cheeks.

こげる 焦げる scorch ; burn ; be scorched ; be burned ¶真黒に焦げる be scorched black ; be charred / 焦げた burnt 《wood》; scorched 《linen》; singed 《hair》.

こけん 沽券 ¶こけんにかかわる 〈事が主語〉be beneath *one's* dignity.

ごけん 護憲 ¶護憲運動 a movement for the defense of the Constitution ; a movement opposing revision of the Constitution.

ごげん 語原[源] the derivation [origin] of a word ; etymology ¶語原を調べる trace a word to its origin ; study the etymology 《of》/ 語原学 etymology / 通俗[民間]語原(説) folk etymology / 語原辞書 an etymological dictionary. 文例⇩

ここ¹ 個々 ¶個々の individual ; 《文》several / 個々に one by one ; each ; individually ; 《文》severally.

ここ² ¶ここに[で] here ; in [at] this place / ここへ here ; to this place / ここから from here ; from this place / ここまで here ; up to here [this point] ; so [《文》thus] far / ここかしこ here and there / ここかしこをさまよう wander from place to place / ここら辺に about [around] here ; in this neighborhood / ここ数日〈今まで〉(for) the last few days ; these few days ; 〈今後〉the next few days / ここ 4, 5 年間〈過去〉for the last [past] four or five years ; 〈未来〉for four or five years to come / ここしばらく for the time being ; for some time to come / ここぞという時に at the critical [psychological] moment / ここだけの話だが between you and me ; between you, me, and the gatepost ; between ourselves ; just in confidence (I'll tell you that...). 文例⇩

ごご 古語 an archaic word ; an archaism.

ごご 午後 ¶午後に in the afternoon / 今日[その日]の午後 this [that] afternoon / 明日[昨日]の午後 tomorrow [yesterday] afternoon / ある日の午後に one afternoon / 土曜の午後に on Saturday afternoon [afternoons (毎週)] / 午

The etymology of this word is doubtful. | The origin of this word is unknown.
ここ¹ 個々について言えばなかなか優秀な生徒がいます。Individually speaking, we have some excellent students.
ここ² あなたはここの係ですか。Are you in charge here? / ここが加納さんが事故に会った場所です。This is where Mr. Kano had [met] his accident. / ここに置くよ。I'll put it here. | 〈物や金を渡すとき〉Here it is [you are], then ! / 今日はここまでにしておきましょう。That will do for today. | Let us leave off here. / さあ、ここだと思った。I thought that the right moment had arrived. / 事すでにここに至っては騎虎の勢い止むを得ない。Now that things have come to this pass, there is no choice for us but to take the plunge. / これは

ココア cocoa.

ごごう 古豪 an old campaigner; a veteran.

ごこう 後光 a halo 《around the head of a saint》《pl. -(e)s》; an aureole ¶後光のさしているキリストの絵 a painting of Christ with his head surrounded by a halo.

こごえ 小声 ¶小声で in a small [low] voice; in a whisper; in an undertone; under *one's* breath / 小声になる lower *one's* voice. 文例◯

こごえる 凍える be numb [《文》benumbed] with cold; be chilled (to the bone) ¶凍え死ぬ be frozen to death; freeze to death; die of cold.

ここく 故国 *one's* homeland; *one's* home country.

こごし 小腰 ¶小腰をかがめる bow slightly; make a slight bow.

ここち 心地 〈感じ〉a feeling; 《文》a sensation; 〈気分〉a mood ¶心地よい comfortable; pleasant; 《文》agreeable / 夢見る心地である feel as if the whole thing were a dream. 文例◯

こごと¹ 小言 〈叱責〉(a) scolding; 《文》a rebuke; 〈お説教〉a lecture; 〈あら捜し〉fault-finding ¶小言を言う scold; 《文》rebuke; lecture; give [read] *sb* a lecture 《about *sth*》; find fault with / うんと小言を言ってやる give *sb* a good talking-to; give *sb* a piece of *one's* mind / 小言を言われる〔食う〕be scolded 《by》; 《口語》catch it 《from》. 文例◯

こごと² 戸毎 ¶戸ごとに at every door [house]; from door to door.

ここのか 九日 〈9日間〉nine days; 〈第9日〉the ninth day ¶5月9日 May 9; the ninth of May.

ここのつ 九つ ⇨く¹.

こごむ 屈む stoop; bend down [over].

ココやし 【植】〈実〉a coconut; 〈木〉a coconut palm; a coco 《pl. -s》.

こころ 心 (the) mind; 〈心情〉(the) heart; 〈精神〉(the) spirit; 〈考え〉a thought; 〈意志〉will; 〈注意〉care; attention; 〈気持ち〉a mood; 〈なぞの〉the answer ⇨き³ ¶心は至ってよい be a very good fellow at heart [bottom]; have a very good heart / 心が定まらない be in two minds 《about *sth*》 / 心の中で at [in] *one's* heart / 心の狭い narrow-minded; intolerant / 心の広い broad-minded; tolerant / 心の正しい right-minded / 心のままを率直に語る speak (straight) from the [*one's*] heart / 心を動かされる be moved [touched] 《by》 / 心を引く attract; appeal to / 心を悩ます worry 《about》; be anxious [worried] 《about》 / 心を決める make up *one's* mind 《to *do*, to *sth*》 / 心を入れかえる[改める] turn over a new leaf; reform / 心を尽くす do *one's* best / 心を捕える 〈事が主語〉capture the imagination 《of》; captivate *one* / …に心を向ける give [apply] *one's* mind to…; give [turn] *one's* attention to… / 心を合わせて 《文》with one accord; 《文》in concert 《with》 / 心をこめる give *one's* whole mind [heart] 《to》 / 心にかかる 〈事が主語〉trouble *one*; weigh on *one's* mind; 〈人が主語〉be anxious [worried] 《about》 / 心に留める[かける] bear *sth* in mind; be mindful 《of》; take 《a matter》 to heart / 心に抱く harbor; 《文》cherish; 《文》entertain / ふと心に浮かぶ 〈人が主語〉hit on; think of; 〈事が主語〉occur to *one*; cross [come across] *one's* mind; spring to mind / 心にかなう suit *one* [*one's* taste]; be to *one's* liking / 心にかなった 《a house》after *one's* own heart / 心からの, 心をこめた sincere; warm; hearty (welcome); 《文》cordial / 心から, 心をこめて 〈衷心から〉sincerely; from the bottom of *one's* heart; from the heart; 《文》cordially; 〈熱心に〉with a will / 心ひそかに secretly; inwardly / 心ゆくまで to *one's* heart's content; as much as *one* likes; to the full / 心ゆくまで話し合う talk with *sb* to *one's*

ここだけの話として聞いてもらいたい. This is just between you and me. | This shouldn't go any further.

ごご 午後はたいてい近くの池まで散歩に行けます. In the afternoon(s) [《米》Afternoons] I usually go for a walk to a pond near by. / ムーア氏が午後一杯車で町を案内してくれた. Mr. Moore drove me around the town all afternoon.

こごえ 彼等は用心して小声で話していた. They were talking in guarded whispers.

ここち 生きた心地がしなかった. I felt more dead than alive.

こごと¹ 夜そんなに遅く帰るとお母さんに小言を言われるよ. You will catch it from your mother if you come home so late at night.

こころ オフィスで働いていても, 心は山〔ゴルフ場〕に飛んでいた. He was working in his office, but his heart was in the mountains [on the golf course]. / 実に心の美しい人だ. He has a heart of gold. / 彼の演説は英国の大衆の心を捕えた. His speech captured the British popular imagination. / 彼の言うことなど心に留めるな. Don't mind [Don't take any notice of] what he says. / 私をお心におかけ下さいまして, ありがとうございます. Thank you very much for thinking of me. / 彼は父の跡を継ごうと心に決めている. He has his heart set on following in his father's footsteps. / あの場合は心にもない事を言わなければならなかったのだ. On that occasion I had to say something that I didn't really feel. / 心にもないことを言ってしまったと彼女は悔やんでいる. She is sorry for having said what she did not really mean. / その知らせを聞いて私はひどく心を痛めた. The news pained me a great deal. / ご成功を心からお祝い申し上げます. I should like to offer you my hearty congratulations on your success. / 氏の新著は日本の伝統芸能である狂言の生きた心に触れるものである. His new book goes right to the living heart of *kyogen*, one of the traditional performing arts of Japan.

こころあたり どこでそれをなくしたのか心当たりはありませんか. Do you have any idea where

こころあたり 心当たり ¶心当たりがある (happen to) know of / 少しも心当たりがない have no [do not have the slightest] idea ((of)) / 心当たりのへ問い合わせる inquire everywhere *one* can think of [at every likely place]. 文例⇩

こころある 心有る〈考え深い〉thoughtful；《文》thinking；〈用心のいい〉《文》prudent；《文》provident；far-sighted；〈思いやりのある〉considerate；thoughtful；humane.

こころいき 心意気 spirit；《文》disposition；a turn of mind ¶浪花っ子の心意気を示す show the spirit [enterprising mind] of the citizens of Osaka.

こころえ 心得〈知識〉knowledge；information；〈理解〉understanding；〈規則〉rules；regulations；〈注意〉directions ¶修学旅行中の心得 the rules to observe on [the dos and don'ts for] the school trip / 夏休みの心得 how to spend the summer vacation / 多少フランス語の心得がある have some knowledge of [a grounding in] French / 課長心得 an acting chief of a section / 心得違いをする do wrong；behave badly；misbehave (*oneself*)；《文》misconduct *oneself* / 心得顔をする a look wise [knowing] / 心得顔に with a knowing look；in a knowing manner；as if *one* knew everything [all about it].

こころえる 心得る〈知る〉know；understand；be aware ((of))；《文》be well informed ((concerning))；〈思う〉regard *sth* as...；consider *sth* (to be)...；take *sth* for.... 文例⇩

こころおきなく 心置きなく〈遠慮なく〉《文》without reserve；frankly；freely；〈心配なく〉without anxiety；free from care ¶心置きなく話す speak without reserve；open [pour out] *one's* heart ((to *sb*)). 文例⇩

こころおぼえ 心覚え〈記憶〉《文》remembrance；memory ⇨ おぼえ。¶心覚え、おぼえ〈覚え書き〉a reminder；notes ¶心覚えにする as a reminder；to help [as a help to] *one's* memory.

こころがけ 心掛け〈態度〉an [a mental] attitude；〈注意〉attention；care；〈努力〉(an) effort ¶心がけのいい sensible；《文》right-minded；〈注意深い〉careful；《文》prudent；〈経済上〉《文》provident / 心がけの悪い thoughtless；《文》wrong-headed；〈不注意な〉careless；《文》imprudent；〈経済上〉《文》improvident. 文例⇩

こころがける 心掛ける〈留意する〉bear [keep] *sth* in mind；be careful to *do*；take good care to *do*；〈つとめる〉try to *do*；〈志す〉endeavor to *do*；aim to *do* [at *doing*].

こころがまえ 心構え an [a mental] attitude；〈用意〉preparation ¶心構えができている be prepared [ready] ((for)) / 心構えをする prepare *oneself* ((for))；get ready ((for))；《文》hold *oneself* in readiness ((for)). 文例⇩

こころがわり 心変わり a change of mind [heart]；《文》inconstancy；〈裏切り〉treachery ¶心変わりする change *one's* mind；〈裏切る〉betray；turn traitor ((to)).

こころくばり 心配り alertness；watchfulness；keeping an eye out ((for *sth*)) ⇨ き³(気を配る).

こころぐるしい 心苦しい painful；regrettable ¶心苦しく思う〈人が主語〉be [feel] sorry ((for))；regret；〈事が主語〉be painful；《文》prick *one's* conscience. 文例⇩

こころざし 志〈大望〉(an) ambition；《文》(an) aspiration；〈希望〉a wish；a desire；(a) hope；〈決心〉《文》(a) resolution；〈意志〉《文》(a) will；〈意図〉(an) intention；a motive；《文》a design；〈目的〉《文》an object；an aim；a purpose；〈好意〉kindness；goodwill；〈贈り物〉a (small) present [gift] ¶志と違う〈人が主語〉《文》be frustrated in *one's* ambition；〈事が主語〉go wrong [《文》awry]；do not turn out as [the way] *one* hoped；《文》prove contrary to *one's* expectations / 志を立てる set up an aim in life；《文》resolve [aspire] ((to *do*)) / 志を遂げる《文》attain *one's* aim；《文》accomplish [achieve] *one's* object [purpose]. 文例⇩

---

you lost it? / 適任者のお心当たりがありますか。Do you have anyone in mind fit to fill the position?

こころえる 考古学者としてちゃんとした発掘をするには心得ておかなければならないことがたくさんある。It takes a lot of know-how for an archaeologist to carry out an excavation properly. / 心得たものだ。He knows his business. ¦ He knows what he is about [what he's doing, what's what]. / このわしを何と心得ているか。What do you take me for? / 自分を何と心得ているか。Who do you think you are? / 委細心得ました。I'll see that everything is all right.

こころおきなく どうぞお心置きなくいつまでもご滞在下さい。Please make yourself at home and stay with us as long as you please.

こころがけ その心がけはよいが実行しなければなんにもならない。That's very good as an idea, but it will get you nowhere unless it is translated into action. / 緊急事態になった時にあわてないためには、ふだんの心がけが大切です。It is important always to be prepared for the worst, if you are not to get flustered in an emergency. / (ふだんの)ふだんの心がけが悪いものだから、旅行先で雨にたたられてしまった。My trip has been spoiled by the rain；maybe this is a punishment for my sins.

こころがける これからはデーモン夫人には逆らわないよう、大いに心がけます。I will try hard [do my utmost] not to give offense to Mrs. Damon from now on.

こころがまえ 彼のその発見が偶然の発見だったことは事実であろう。しかし、それは、ふだんから心構えのできている人にだけ恵まれる偶然なのだ。It must be true that he made the discovery by accident. But the 'accident' was one of those that favor only the receptive mind.

こころぐるしい それを思うと心苦しい。It gives me pain [It pains me] to think of it. ¦ My conscience pricks me when I think of it.

こころざし 彼は志を遂げずしてなしく死んだ。He died before he could realize his ambition. / 彼は父の志を継いで政界に入った。

こころざす

こころざす 志す intend to *do*; aim 《at *sth*, to *do*》;《文》aspire to [after] 《fame》; set *one's* heart [mind] on 《learning》;〈決心する〉resolve to *do*; make up *one's* mind 《to do》¶外交官を志す aspire [aim] to be a (career) diplomat.

こころじょうぶ 心丈夫 ¶心丈夫である〈人が主語〉feel secure [safe, reassured];〈事が主語〉be reassuring.

こころづかい 心遣い consideration (for); thoughtfulness; care;《文》solicitude.

こころづくし 心尽くし〈親切〉kindness; attention;〈心遣い〉care;《文》solicitude; thoughtfulness; consideration;〈尽力〉efforts;《文》good offices.

こころづけ 心付け a tip; a gratuity ⇨チップ[1]. 文例⇩

こころづよい 心強い heartening; reassuring; encouraging ¶心強く思う feel reassured (by); feel secure [safe]; take heart 《at》.

こころない 心ない〈無思慮な〉thoughtless; unthinking;〈慎重を欠く〉indiscreet;《文》imprudent;〈無情な〉heartless; hard; cruel;〈思いやりのない〉unfeeling; inconsiderate. 文例⇩

こころならずも 心ならずも against *one's* will; unwillingly; reluctantly; in spite of *oneself*; against *one's* better judgment.

こころにくい 心憎い〈見事な〉excellent;《文》admirable; perfect;〈奥ゆかしい〉tasteful; graceful ¶心憎いばかりに irresistibly; remarkably well;《文》with flawless perfection.

こころね 心根〈気持ち〉*one's* (inmost) feelings; *one's* heart;〈性質〉*one's* nature;《文》*one's* disposition ¶心根の優しい人 a good-hearted person; a person with [who has] a heart of gold.

こころのこり 心残り ¶心残りがする regret; feel sorry (for); think that *sth* is [《文》feel *sth*] regrettable; feel [be] reluctant 《to leave》/ 心残りがない have nothing to regret; feel no regret(s). 文例⇩

こころばかり 心ばかり 文例⇩

こころぼそい 心細い helpless;《文》forlorn;〈見込みのない〉hopeless;〈寂しい〉lonely;〈人を落胆させるような〉discouraging; disheartening ¶心細いことを言う say discouraging things / 心細く思う feel helpless; feel lonely.

こころまかせ 心任せ ¶心まかせにする have *one's* own way; do as *one* pleases [likes] / 心まかせになる〈他人の〉be at *sb's* mercy;〈自分の〉have *sth* at *one's* disposal.

こころまち 心待ち ¶心待ちに待つ (eagerly) look forward to (a letter);《口語》can't wait for (New Year's). 文例⇩

こころみ 試み〈ためし〉a trial; a try;〈試験〉a test;〈実験〉an experiment;〈企て〉an attempt ¶試みに tentatively; by way of experiment / 試みに使ってみる try *sb* [*sth*] out;《口語》give *sth* [*sb*] a try; give *sth* [*sb*] a trial; employ *sb* on trial.

こころみる 試みる try; have [make] a trial (of); have [make] a try 《at》; try *one's* hand 《at》;〈試す〉test; put *sth* to the test;〈企てる〉attempt 《to do》; make an attempt 《at》.

こころもち 心持ち ⇨きもち;〈少し〉a little (larger); a bit (longer); a trifle (shorter); a shade (better).

こころもとない 心許ない〈不安な〉uneasy; uncertain;〈危なっかしい〉unsafe; precarious;〈頼りにならない〉unreliable; untrustworthy ¶心もとなく思う feel uneasy 《about》; have misgivings 《about》.

こころやすい 心安い familiar; friendly; close ¶心安い友人《文》a bosom friend; a friend (that) *one* can say anything [open *one's* heart] to / 心安くなる make friends 《with》; strike up a close friendship 《with》/ 心安くしている be on familiar terms 《with》; be friends 《with》.

こころやり 心遣り〈思いやり〉consideration;〈同情〉sympathy. 文例⇩

こころよい 快い pleasant; agreeable; comfortable;《文》delectable; refreshing 〈爽快な〉¶(風景などが)目に快い《文》be pleasing to the eye / 快く〈愉快に〉pleasantly; agreeably; comfortably; cheerfully;〈喜んで〉gladly; readily; willingly / 快く承諾する agree [《文》consent] willingly [readily];《文》give *one's* ready consent (to) / 快く思う be pleased 《with》; be glad 《at》/ 快く思わない be [feel] hurt [offended] 《at》;《文》be displeased

---

He followed his father into politics. | He entered politics treading in his father's footsteps.

こころざし だけで結構です。Thank you very much, Mr. —. I will take the will for the deed. / ご親切なお志ばかりに有り難う存じます。Many thanks for your kindness. / これはほんの志ですがお納めください。Please accept this as a small token of my gratitude.

こころづくし お心尽くしの品ことにありがとうございます。Thank you very much for your thoughtful present.

こころづけ お心付けは固くお断りいたします。〔掲示〕Tips are not accepted under any circumstances.

こころない 心ない事をしたものだ。What a thoughtless thing to have done!

こころのこり 一人娘を残して死んで行くのは、夏子にとってさだめし心残りだったことであろう。It must have troubled Natsuko to die and leave an only daughter behind.

こころばかり ほんの心ばかりの品ですがお礼のしるしでございます。どうぞお受け取り下さい。Please accept this as a small token of my gratitude.

こころぼそい 君がいないと心細い。I feel helpless without you. / 旅費が2万円では心細い。Twenty thousand yen for our traveling expenses is discouragingly small.

こころまち 君が来るのを心待ちに待っていたのだ。I thought you would never come.

こころもち 心持ち関西なまりがある。He speaks with just a suggestion [trace] of a Kansai accent.

こころやり せめてもの心やりだ。That is one [the only] consolation.

こころよい 小川のせせらぎが耳に快かった。The murmur of the brook was music to my ears.

こcon 関東大震災はその惨害のひ

ここん 古今 ¶古今の ancient and modern; 《文》《heroes》of all times [ages] / 古今を通じて《文》through [in] all ages / 古今にその比を見ない have no parallel [equal] in history / 古今東西の作家 writers of all ages and countries. 文例⇩

ごこん 語根 the root of a word.

こさ 濃さ depth (色の); thickness (液の); strength (茶・コーヒーの);《密度》density.

ごさ 誤差 an (accidental) error ¶許容し得る誤差の幅 a tolerance; an (acceptable) error range / 誤差1ミリ以下である be in error by less than one millimeter; be correct [accurate] (to) within less than a millimeter. 文例⇩

ござ a mat; matting (総称) ¶ござを敷く spread a mat (on the floor).

コサージ(ュ) a corsage.

ごさい 後妻 one's second wife.

こさいく 小細工 ¶小細工をやる play cheap tricks (on);《文》resort to petty tricks. 文例⇩

コサイン《数》a cosine (略: cos).

こざかしい 小賢しい〈生意気な〉impertinent; 〈ずるい〉cunning; crafty; tricky;〈抜け目のない〉shrewd.

こざかな 小魚 a small fish.

こさく 小作 (farm) tenancy; tenant farming ¶小作する farm (land) as a tenant / 小作人 a tenant farmer;《米》a sharecropper.

こさじ 小匙 a teaspoon ¶小さじ2杯の塩 two teaspoonfuls [teaspoons] of salt ⇨さじ¹ ★.

コサック a Cossack.

こざっぱり ¶こざっぱりした neat (and clean); tidy; trim / こざっぱりとした服装をしている be neatly dressed.

こさめ 小雨 (a) light rain [rainfall]; a drizzle. 文例⇩

こざら 小皿 a small plate.

こさん 古参 a senior; a veteran; an old-timer ¶古参の senior; veteran. 文例⇩

ごさん¹ 午餐《文》(a) luncheon; (a) lunch ¶午餐会を開く give a luncheon (party).

ごさん² 誤算〈計算違い〉(a) miscalculation;〈見込み違い〉(a) misjudgment《of》¶誤算する miscalculate; miscount; make a mistake [《文》an error] in calculation; misjudge.

こし¹ 腰 the waist; the hips ⇨しり¹ 囲注 ¶腰が痛い have (a) backache; one's back hurts [is sore, is stiff] / 腰が重い be slow in starting work; be slow to act / 重い物を担って腰が切れない be unable to stand [walk] erect with a heavy load on one's shoulder(s) / 腰の曲がった老人 an old man bent [stooped,《英》stooping] with age / 腰の弱い weak-kneed / 腰の強いうどん firm noodles / 腰の低い modest; unassuming; polite / 腰を下ろす[掛ける] sit down;《文》seat oneself; take a seat / 腰を下ろしている be sitting [be in [on] a chair];《文》be seated / 腰を曲げる bend down [over]; stoop; bow / 腰を伸ばす straighten oneself / 腰を抜かす be paralyzed with fright; be petrified (with terror) / 腰を据えて仕事にかかる settle (down) to work / 腰を据えて飲み始める start drinking seriously [in earnest] / 話の腰を折る interrupt sb (at an interesting part of his story) / (洪水の水などが)腰まで来る be waist-deep.

こし² 輿 a palanquin; a litter.

こじ¹ 古寺 an old (Buddhist) temple; a temple with a long history.

こじ² 固持する persist in (a belief); stick [hold fast,《文》adhere] to (a principle).

こじ³ 固辞 ¶固辞する refuse [《文》decline] (an offer) firmly.

こじ⁴ 孤児 an orphan ¶孤児になる be orphaned; be left an orphan.

こじ⁵ 故事〈いわれ〉a historical fact; an origin; a source;〈口碑〉(a) tradition ¶故事熟語辞典 a dictionary of fables and phrases / 故事来歴 the origin and history (of).

こじ⁶ 誇示 ¶誇示する display; parade; make a display [parade] of; show off.

-ごし …越し ¶3年越しの工事 construction work that has continued [lasted] for three years / 20年越しの友人関係 a friendship of 20 years' standing / 友情20年 old / 山越しに across [beyond] the mountain / 垣

どいこと古今未曾有であった. The earthquake in the Kanto region was the most destructive on record. / ジョットーは古今を通じて最大の画家の一人と考えられている. Giotto is considered one of the greatest painters of all time.

ごさ ±1%程度の誤差は免れないようである. Errors of plus or minus 1 per cent or so seem to be unavoidable. / 18世紀の科学者は地球の大きさを誤差4%ないし5%以内の程度まで知っていた. Scientists in the 18th century knew the earth's size within an error of 4 or 5 per cent. / すべての人口統計は±5%の誤差を見込まなければならないという専門家もいる. Some experts say that all demographic statistics are accurate only to plus or minus 5 per cent. / 2つの町の間の距離を誤差20センチの範囲で測定するなどと言っても無意味である. It is meaningless to try to measure the distance between two towns to the nearest 20 centimeters.

こさいく 小細工はやめろ. None of your cheap tricks!

こさめ 小雨が降っている. It is drizzling. / 雨が2, 3時間はげしく降ってから小雨に変わった. It rained hard for two or three hours, and then turned to a light drizzle.

こさん 中田さんは私よりずっと古参です. Mr. Nakada has served here a lot longer than I have. ⇨よ⑦² / 平井さんはうちの会社では古参の方です. Mr. Hirai is one of the veterans in [longest-serving members of] our company.

こし¹ 列車はずいぶん混んでいたが幸いに腰を掛けることができた. The train was very crowded, but luckily I was able to find a seat. / その物音に驚いて彼女は腰を浮かした. Alarmed at the

ごじ　　　　　　　　　　　　　　　434　　　　　　　　　　　　　こじゅうと

根越しに見る look over the fence. [文例⑥]
ごじ 誤字 a misused [miswritten] character; [印刷] an erratum (pl. -ta).
こしあける 扱じ開ける wrench [pry, prize] open; ⟨錠を⟩ pick ¶箱の蓋をこじ開ける prize a box open; pry the top off a box / こじ開けられる心配のない錠 an unpickable [a pickproof] lock.
こしいた 腰板 a wainscot.
こしいれ 輿入れ ¶輿入れをする marry ((into a family)).
こしお 小潮 a neap tide; (at) the neap.
こしおび 腰帯 ⟨ひも⟩ a girdle; ⟨おび⟩ a (waist) sash.
こじか 子鹿 a fawn.
こしかけ 腰掛け a chair (椅子); a bench; a stool (床几(しょうぎ)); ¶腰掛け仕事 a temporary job. [文例⑥]
こしかける 腰掛ける ⇨こし¹ (腰を掛ける). [文例⑥]
こしき¹ 轂 the hub [nave] (of a wheel).
こしき² 古式 ¶古式の笑い [美術] an archaic smile / 古式にのっとり with the traditional [ancient] ((Shinto)) rites.
こじき 乞食 ⟨人⟩ a beggar; (文) a mendicant; ⟨行為⟩ begging ¶乞食の女[子] a beggar woman [child] / 乞食をする beg for a living; beg one's meals [(文) bread] ((from door to door)) / 乞食根性 a mean [mercenary] spirit. [文例⑥]
ごしき 五色 ¶五色の five-colored; multicolored ⟨tapes⟩; (文) ⟨garments⟩ of many colors.
こしぎんちゃく 腰巾着 an obsequious follower; a sycophant.
こしくだけ 腰砕け ¶腰砕けになる weaken [become weak-kneed] ((at the crucial moment)); lose one's nerve.
こしけ [医] leukorrhea; (口語) (the) whites.
ごしごし ¶ごしごしする rub [scrub] hard.
こしだか 腰高 ¶腰高に寄り進む (相撲) advance in an unstable [an excessively erect] posture, pushing one's opponent / 腰高障子 a tall-skirted shoji.
こしたんたん 虎視眈々 ¶虎視たんたんとねらう (文) watch vigilantly for ((a chance)); look for ((a position)) eagerly; look enviously ((at)); (文) cast covetous eyes ((on sth)).
こしつ¹ 固執 ¶固執する cling [(文) adhere] ((to)); hold [stick] fast ((to)); persist ((in)); ⟨言い張る⟩ insist ((on)).
こしつ² 個室 a single room; a private room (私室).

ごじつ 後日 in (the) future (⇨ こんご★); later; some (other) day ¶後日のために ⟨参考に⟩ for future reference; ⟨戒め[証拠]に⟩ as a warning [proof] for the future / 後日談 a sequel to sth.
こしつき 腰付き the way one carries oneself; one's posture; (文) a [one's] carriage.
ゴシック Gothic ¶ゴシック活字 Gothic (type); ((printed in)) black letter / ゴシック建築[様式] Gothic architecture [style].
こじつけ distortion (of the meaning); a strained [distorted] interpretation ¶こじつけの far-fetched; forced; strained.
こじつける strain [force] ((the meaning of a word)).
ゴシップ gossip ¶ゴシップの種になる give rise to ((a lot of)) gossip; cause ((some)) gossip / (新聞雑誌の)ゴシップ欄 a gossip column.
ごじっぽひゃっぽ 五十歩百歩 [文例⑥]
こしなげ 腰投げ a hip throw; (レスリング) a cross-buttock.
こしにく 腰肉 loin (of beef).
こしぬけ 腰抜け a coward; a weak-kneed person ¶腰抜け侍 a cowardly [chicken-hearted] samurai. [文例⑥]
こしひも 腰紐 a girdle; a cord tied round the waist.
こしぼね 腰骨 the hipbone.
こじま 小島 a small island; an islet.
こしまき 腰巻 a waistcloth.
こしまわり 腰回り one's hip (女) [waist (男)] measurement ¶腰回りをはかる take sb's hip measurement; measure sb's hips. [文例⑥]
こしもと 腰元 a lady's maid; a lady in waiting ((to Her Grace)).
こしゃく 小癪 ¶小しゃくな pert; impudent; cheeky.
こしゆ 腰湯 (take) a hip [sitz] bath.
こしゅ¹ 戸主 the head of a family.
こしゅ² 固守 ¶固守する ⟨陣地などを⟩ defend ⟨one's position⟩ stubbornly; ⟨固持する⟩ hold [stick] fast ((to)).
ごしゅいんせん 御朱印船 [日本史] a trading ship [vessel] authorized by the shogunate.
こしゅう 固執 ⇨こしつ¹.
ごじゅう¹ 五十 fifty ¶第50 the fiftieth / 五十音 the Japanese syllabary / 五十三次(つぎ) the fifty-three stages (on the Tokaido).
ごじゅう² 五重 ¶五重の fivefold; (文) quintuple ¶五重の塔 a five-storied pagoda / 五重唱[奏] a quintet(te).
こじゅうと¹ 小姑 one's sister-in-law ((pl. sisters-)); one's husband's sister.

---

noise, she half rose to her feet.
-ごし 彼には3年越し会わない。I have not seen him these three years. / 父は8年越しの病人です。My father has been ill for eight long years.
こしかけ 今の会社はほんの腰掛けさ。I'm working for this firm only for a time. / なに、ほんの腰掛け仕事さ。I don't mean to stay in this job for the rest of my life.
こしかける この電車で腰掛けられたことがない。I've never got a seat on this line.
こじき 乞食を三日すればやめられない。Let a man once be a beggar and he will be a beggar all his life.
ごじっぽひゃっぽ いずれも五十歩

百歩だ。There is little [not much] to choose between them. ｜ It's six of one and half a dozen of the other.
こしぬけ やつらは腰抜けだ。(口語) They are chicken. / 腰抜けぶりを発揮してじきに降伏してしまった。They soon gave in like the cowards they are.
こしまわり 腰回りが前より少し太

こじゅうと² 小舅 one's brother-in-law (pl. brothers-); one's husband's brother.
ごしゅきょうぎ 五種競技 the pentathlon ¶五種競技の選手 a pentathlete / 近代五種競技 the modern pentathlon.
こじゅけい 〖鳥〗a Chinese [bamboo] partridge.
ごじゅん 語順〖文法〗word order.
こしょ 古書 〈昔の本〉an old book；〈古本〉a secondhand [《米》used] book ¶古書展覧会 an exhibition of rare [old, antiquarian] books.
ごしょ 御所 an Imperial palace ¶御所車 a court carriage.
ごじょ 互助 mutual aid [help] ¶互助会 a mutual-aid association [society].
こしょう 小姓 a page (to Nobunaga).
こしょう² 胡椒 pepper ¶こしょうを振りかける sprinkle pepper on《meat》/ 黒[白]こしょう black [white] pepper / こしょう入れ a pepper pot.
こしょう³ 故障〈機械などの〉a breakdown；a fault；trouble；《文》a malfunction；〈障害〉a hitch；an obstacle；a hindrance；〈事故〉an accident；〈異議〉an objection ¶エンジンの故障 engine trouble / 電気の故障 (a) power failure / 故障する go wrong；develop trouble；break down / 故障している be out of order / 故障なく without a hitch；without trouble [accident]；smoothly；all right；well / 故障を申し立てる protest (against); object (to); raise an objection (to); take exception (to) / 故障車 a broken-down [disabled] car. 文例⇩
こしょう⁴ 湖沼 lakes and marshes.
こじょう¹ 弧状 arc-shaped / 弧状列島 a crescent-shaped [an arcuate] archipelago.
こじょう² 湖上 ¶湖上の[に] on the lake.
ごしょう 後生 《文》(the) life hereafter；《文》the hereafter；《文》the life to come ¶後生だから For God's [goodness', mercy's] sake / 後生大事に持っている treasure；《文》cherish / 後生大事に勤める serve 《one's employer》very faithfully.
ごじょう 互譲 ⇒ゆずりあい.
こしょく 古色 ¶古色蒼然(そうぜん)たる antique-looking；patinaed；timeworn.
ごしょく 誤植 a misprint；a printer's [typographical] error.
こしらえ 拵え〈出来〉make；workmanship；〈服装〉a getup；dress；an outfit；〈顔の〉a make-up ¶こしらえが立派な beautifully-made 《brooches》；《文》《a cabinet》of exquisite workmanship / こしらえ事《文》a fabrication；《文》a fiction；a made-up [《口語》cock-and-bull] story / こしらえ物 an imitation；a counterfeit；a sham；a fake.
こしらえる 拵える 〈作る〉make；《文》manufacture；〈建てる〉build；《文》construct；〈作り事をする〉make up；《文》fabricate；invent；《口語》cook up《a story》¶服を新しくこしらえる have a new suit made / 顔をこしらえる make oneself up；《口語》do one's make-up；put one's make-up on /《金をこしらえる（もうける）》make money；《調達する》raise money《for》/ こしらえ直す remake；reconstruct；remodel；make over. 文例⇩
こじらす 〈悪化させる〉make 《a disease》worse；《文》aggravate；〈複雑にする〉complicate ¶風邪をこじらしたのがもとで死ぬ die from a neglected cold. 文例⇩
こじれる 〈病気が〉get complicated；grow [get] worse；〈物事が〉get complicated；get entangled. 文例⇩
こじわ 小皺 fine wrinkles [lines]；crow's-feet (目尻の) ¶小じわのある finely wrinkled《skin》.
こしん 湖心 the center of a lake.
こじん¹ 故人《文》the deceased；《文》the departed.
こじん² 個人 an individual；〈私人〉a private person [individual, citizen] ¶個人の[の]個人的[の]individual；personal；private / 個人的な問題 a private affair；a personal matter / 個人関係 personal [interpersonal] relations / 個人企業 [商店] a private [one-man] enterprise [concern] / 個人経営の《a firm》under private management / 個人差 differences among individuals；individual variation / 個人主義 individualism / 個人崇拝 the personality cult / (体操の)個人総合競技 individual combined exercises / 個人タクシー an owner-driver taxi / 個人プレー individual play；〈勝手な〉an egoistic play. 文例⇩
ごしん¹ 誤診 a wrong [《文》an erroneous] diagnosis ¶誤診する make a wrong diagnosis；diagnose wrongly.
ごしん² 誤審〖法〗(a) miscarriage of justice；(a) misjudgment；〖競技〗a wrong (refereeing) decision ¶誤審する misjudge；give a wrong [mistaken] decision.
ごしん³ 護身 ¶護身用の[に] for self-defense；for use in self-defense / 護身術 the art of self-defense.
ごしんたい 御神体 a shintai；an object of worship housed in a Shinto shrine and believed to contain the spirit of a deity.
こじんまり ⇒こぢんまり.
こす¹ 越[超]す cross；go [get] across [over, past]；

くなった. I measure a bit more round the waist than I used to.
こしょう 故障中.〖掲示〗Out of order. / エンジンに故障がある. Something is the matter with the engine. / 途中で車のエンジンが故障した. Our car developed engine trouble on the way. / 山道でバスが故障して動かなくなった. The bus broke down on the mountain road.
ごしょう 後生だから少し黙っていてくれないか. For goodness' [mercy's] sake, keep quiet for a while!
こしらえる いつまでにこしらえてもらえますか. How soon can you let me have it?
こじらす これ以上話をこじらすわけにはいかない. We cannot allow the matter to get any more complicated [involved].
こじれる 風邪がこじれて肺炎になった. His cold developed into pneumonia.
こじん² 私は彼と個人的には何の関係もない. I have no personal relations with him. / 私たちは個人的な付き合いでした. We knew each other on a personal basis. /

こす pass; 〈年月を〉pass; spend; 〈超過する〉《文》exceed; be over; be more than; 〈まさる〉《文》surpass; be better than / 〈移転する〉《文》move (house); remove ⇒ひっこす. 文例⬇

こす² 濾す filter; strain ¶こして取る[除く] filter out (the grounds).

こすい¹ 湖水 a lake ¶湖水に面した lakefront (hotels); (a restaurant) on the lakefront.

こすい² 鼓吹する 〈吹き込む〉put (an idea) into sb's mind; 《文》inspire sb with (an idea); 《文》inculcate (an idea) in sb; 〈唱道する〉《文》advocate (nationalism).

こすい³ 狡い ⇒ずるい.

こすう¹ 戸数 the number of houses [families] ¶戸数300ばかりの村 a village of about 300 houses. 文例⬇

こすう² 個数 the number (of articles).

ごすう 語数 the number of words.

こずえ 梢 the top of a tree; a treetop. 文例⬇

コスタリカ Costa Rica ¶コスタリカの Costa Rican / コスタリカ人 a Costa Rican.

コスト cost ⇒げんか², ひよう ¶コストインフレ cost-push inflation.

コスモス《植》a cosmos.

コスモポリタン a cosmopolitan; 《文》a citizen of the world.

こする 擦る rub; scrub; 〈こすり取る〉scour ((off)); scrape ((off, away)); 〈刷毛⦅はけ⦆で〉brush ¶目をこする rub one's eyes (in surprise) / 手をこすり合わせて暖める rub one's hands (together) for warmth / 〈動物などが〉身体をこすりつける rub (itself) against (sb's leg).

ごする 伍する rank ((with, among)).

こすれる 擦れる ⇒する.

ごぜ 瞽女 a blind female strolling musician.

こせい 個性 《文》individuality; one's personality ¶個性がない lack individuality / 個性を伸ばす develop one's personality / 個性を発揮する show [display] one's individuality / 個性的な (a man) with a great deal of personality; (a work) marked by one's strong individuality.

ごせい¹ 悟性 understanding.

ごせい² 語勢 a tone (of voice) ¶語勢を強める emphasize; lay stress on (a word).

こせいだい 古生代《地質》the Paleozoic (era).

こせいぶつ 古生物 animals and plants of past geological periods; life on earth in earlier times ¶古生物学 paleontology.

こせき¹ 戸籍 a family register ¶戸籍に入れる[から抜く] have (sb's name) entered in [deleted from] the family register / 戸籍係 an official in charge of family registration; a registrar / 戸籍謄[抄]本 a copy [an abstract] of one's family register / 戸籍筆頭人 the head of a family (on the family register).

こせき² 古跡 a historic spot; a place of historical interest; 〈廃墟〉historic remains; ruins.

こせこせ ¶こせこせする be fussy ((about)); be anxious [worry, make a fuss] ((about trifles)).

こせつ ⇒こせこせ.

こぜに 小銭 (small) change; small money ¶小銭入れ a change purse. 文例⬇

こぜりあい 小競り合い 〈戦闘の〉a skirmish; 〈ごたごた〉a petty quarrel.

こせん 古銭 an old [ancient] coin ¶古銭学 numismatics / 古銭学者 a numismatist.

ごせん¹ 五線《音楽》¶五線紙 music paper; a music sheet / 五線譜 (in) staff notation.

ごせん² 互選 mutual election ¶互選する elect by mutual vote. 文例⬇

ごぜん 午前 the morning; 《文》the forenoon ¶午前10時に at ten in the morning; 「over./ a.m. ¶ごご 用법. 文例⬇

こせんきょう 跨線橋 an overpass; 《英》a fly-

こせんじょう 古戦場 an ancient battlefield; an old battleground.

-こそ 文例⬇

こぞう 小僧 〈寺の〉a young Buddhist monk; a young bonze / 〈年期奉公人〉an apprentice (boy); 〈子供〉a boy; a kid; a brat ¶小僧に行く be apprenticed ((to a dry goods merchant).

ごそう 護送 ¶護送する 〈囚人などを〉send sb under escort [guard]; 〈輸送船などを〉convoy / 護送車《米》a patrol wagon /《英》a prison van /《口語》a Black Maria. 文例⬇

こそく 姑息 ¶こそくな《文》temporizing; makeshift / こそくな手段 a half [《文》tempo-

---

彼は英国人について英語の個人教授を受けています。He is taking private lessons in English from an Englishman.

こす¹ 入学志願者は1万人を越した。The number of applicants for admission exceeded [was over] ten thousand. | これに越したものはない。Nothing can be better (than this). | There's nothing like this. | これに越したことはない。That is the best thing (for you to do).

こすう¹ 同市の戸数は8千, 人口は4万ある。The city has 8,000 houses with 40,000 inhabitants.

こずえ 風は松の梢を吹き渡っていた。The wind was blowing in the tops of the pine trees.

こぜに これを小銭に換えてもらえますか。Can you change [break] this into small money?

ごせん² 議長は委員の互選による。The chairman is elected by the committee from among its members.

ごぜん 午前中は在宅の予定です。I'll be at home in the morning. / 仕上げるのに午前中一杯かかります。It will take all [the whole] morning to finish it.

-こそ これこそ僕が求めていたものだ。This is the very thing [just the thing] I wanted. | 僕こそおわびを申し上げなければなりません。It is I, not you, that must apologize. / 年こそ若いが彼はなかなか有能だ。Young as he is, he is a very able man. / 今度こそうまくあってうまく成功しなければ。If we are going to succeed, it's now or never. | We must succeed this time or never. / それでこそ真の教育者だ。That would be worthy of an educator in the true sense of the word.

ごそう 犯人は列車で東京まで護送されてきた。The culprit traveled to Tokyo by rail, under police escort.

ごぞく 英語とフランス語はインドヨーロッパ語族です。English and French are of the Indo-European family.

ごぞく a family of languages ; a linguistic family ¶インドヨーロッパ[ウラルアルタイ]語族 the Indo-European [Ural-Altaic] family (of languages).
ごくろう 御苦労 〔文例⇩〕
ごそげる scrape off ¶靴の泥をこそげ落とす scrape the mud off one's shoes.
こそこそ stealthily ; secretly ; on the sly ¶こそこそ立ち去る sneak away [off] ; creep [sidle] away / こそこそ話す talk in a whisper [in whispers].
ごそごそ ¶ごそごそする 〈音がする〉 rustle ; 〈音を立てる〉 make a noise ; 〈動き回る〉 crawl about (with a rustling sound).
こぞって 挙って 〈皆いっしょに〉 in a body ; 〈一致して〉〈文〉 with one accord ; unanimously ; to a man. 〔文例⇩〕
こそどろ こそ泥 a sneak thief ; a pilferer ¶こそ泥を働く pilfer ; filch ; 〈米口語〉 snitch ⇨ せっとう ★.
こそばゆい ticklish ⇨ くすぐったい.
ごぞんじ 御存じ ¶ご存じのとおり as you know ; as you are well aware. 〔文例⇩〕
こたい[1] 固体 a solid (body) ; solid matter ¶固体の solid / 固体燃料 solid fuel / 固体物理学 solid-state physics.
こたい[2] 個体 an individual ¶個体群〈生物〉 a population / 個体差 an individual difference / 個体識別をする recognize ((the monkeys)) individually / 個体発生〈生物〉 ontogeny ; ontogenesis.
こだい[1] 古代 ancient [old] times ; the remote past ; remote ages ¶古代の ancient ;《文》 of antiquity / 古代史 ancient history / 古代人 ancient people ;《文》 the ancients.
こだい[2] 誇大 ⇨ ちょう ¶誇大広告 an extravagant advertisement ;《口語》 a puff / 誇大妄想狂〈病〉 megalomania ; 〈人〉 a megalomaniac.
ごたい 五体 ¶五体満足である have no physical defect (whatever).
こたえ 答 〈返事〉 an answer ; a reply ; 〈応答〉《文》 a response ;《文》 a rejoinder ; 〈解答〉 an answer ; a solution ¶答を出す get [work out] an answer [a solution] ((to a question)). 〔文例⇩〕
こたえる[1] 答える answer ; reply ; give a reply [an answer] ; 〈反応する〉 respond ((to)) ; 〈解く〉 solve ¶質問に答える answer a question / ...に答える in answer [reply,《文》 response] to.... 〔文例⇩〕
こたえる[2] 堪える ⇨ たえる[1] ¶こたえられない 〈我慢できない〉〈物・事が主語〉 be irresistible ; 〈たまらなくよい〉《口語》 be terrific ; be really 《米口語》 mighty [nice, fine] good.
こたえる[3] 徹える 〈身にしみる〉 come [be brought] home ((to one)) ; 〈影響する〉 affect ; tell ((on)) ; 〈つらい〉 be trying ((to)) ; be hard [rough] ((on)).
こだかい 小高い slightly elevated ¶小高い丘 a small [low] hill ; a hillock / 小高い所 a slightly higher place [area] ;《文》 a small [low] elevation [eminence] ; a height.
こだから 子宝 ¶子宝に恵まれている《文》 be blessed with children.
ごたく 御託 ¶御託を並べる 〈もったいぶって くどくどと話す〉 talk pompously [tediously] ((about)) ; pontificate ((on)) ; 〈好きなことを言う〉 say what one likes ((about)).
ごたくせん 御託宣 〔文例⇩〕
ごたごた 〈紛争〉 (a) trouble ; difficulties ; 〈混乱〉 confusion ; disorder ; a mix-up ¶ごたごたしている be in confusion [disorder] / ごたごたを起こす cause [stir up] trouble. 〔文例⇩〕
こだし 小出し ¶小出しに a little at a time ; in small quantities [amounts] ; bit by bit / 小出しに使う use a small amount [quantity] ((of sth)) at a time ; use sth sparingly ; 〈金を〉 spend a small sum ((of money)) at a time ; spend ((money)) sparingly.
こだち 木立ち a clump of trees ; a grove.
こたつ 火燵 a kotatsu ; a Japanese foot warmer (with a quilt over it) ¶こたつに入る warm oneself in a kotatsu / 掘りごたつ a sunken kotatsu / こたつやぐら a wooden frame for a kotatsu (which supports the quilt).
コダック《商標名》 a Kodak (camera).
ごたつく ⇨ ごたごた.
こだね 子種 〈精子〉 sperm ; 〈子供〉 children ;《文》 issue. 〔文例⇩〕

ごくろう たびたびご足労をおかけして申し訳ありません。 I'm sorry to have given you the trouble of coming over so often.
こぞって 委員会のメンバーはこぞってその案に反対した。 All the members of the committee were against the plan. | The committee was solidly opposed to the plan. | The members of the committee were against the plan to a man.
ごぞんじ こういう問題について書かれた何かいい本をご存じありませんか。 Do you know of any good book on the subject?
こたえ 何度も戸をたたいたが答がなかった。 I knocked at the door again and again but there was no response. | I knocked and knocked but no one came to answer the door. / 次の答を求む。 Answer [Give answers to] the following questions. / それでは答にはなっていない。 That is not quite the answer.
こたえる[1] どう答えていいのかわからなかった。 I didn't know what to say in reply [what answer I ought to give]. | I was at a loss for an answer. / 呼べば答えるほどの所にある。 It is within call [hailing distance] of my house. / 本書はこのような読者の関心に充分答えるものである。 The interest of this kind of reader is well served by this book.
こたえる[3] 過労がこたえ出した。 Hard work began to tell on him. / 階段を上るのは弱い心臓にはこたえる。 Climbing stairs is a strain on [can tax] a weak heart.
ごたくせん 金は自分で作りというご託宣だった。 His injunction was that I raise the funds myself.
ごたごた 例の騒ぎ以来あの会社はごたごたばかり続いています。 There's been nothing but trouble in that corporation since the scandal.
こだね 彼の子種を宿したことを知った。 She realized that she was pregnant by him.

ごたぶん 御多分 ¶ご多分にもれず like the rest ; like other people. 文例⇩

こだま 木霊 an echo 《pl. -es》 ¶こだまする echo ; be echoed. 文例⇩

ごたまぜ a disorderly mixture ; a jumble ; 《米》a hodgepodge ; 《英》a hotchpotch ; a mishmash ¶ごたまぜになる[なっている] be jumbled together ; be mixed up ; 《口語》be (all) higgledy-piggledy.

こだわる be particular about 《trifles》; stick to 《formality》¶古い習慣にこだわる be unable [unwilling] to discard old customs ; be wedded to the old way of doing things [to the old ways].

こたん 枯淡 《文》 refined simplicity ¶枯淡な simple and refined.

コタンジェント 《数》 a cotangent (略: ctn).

こち 《魚》 a flathead.

こちこち ¶こちこち〈の物が〉dry and hard ; 〈頭が〉hidebound ; obstinate ; 〈緊張した〉tense ; stiff / こちこちの保守主義者 a confirmed conservative / こちこちになる become dry and hard ; 〈緊張して〉get [go, 《文》become] stiff [tense] ; 〈凍って〉be frozen stiff.

ごちそう 御馳走 〈もてなし〉 a treat ; 〈饗宴(きょう)の〉 a dinner ; a feast ; 〈うまい物〉 delicious food ; good things (to eat) ; a delicacy ¶ご馳走する give a feast [dinner] ; treat 《sb to sth》; 〈料理店へ行って〉take sb out to dinner 〈客のために〉ご馳走を作る prepare something special [a treat] 〈for dinner〉/ ご馳走になる be treated 《to sukiyaki》; 〈訪問先で〉stay for 《dinner》.

こちゃく 固着 ¶固着する 《文》adhere 《to》; stick (fast) 《to》; be firmly fixed 《to》.

ごちゃごちゃ ¶ごちゃごちゃの confused ; mixed-up ; in a mess / ごちゃごちゃにする mix [jumble, mess] up ; throw 《a room》into confusion [disorder].

こちょう 誇張 (an) exaggeration ; (an) overstatement ¶誇張する exaggerate ; overstate / 誇張して exaggeratingly ; 《文》with exaggeration ; 《文》bombastically / 誇張的 exaggerated ; 《文》bombastic ; high-flown.

ごちょう 語調 a tone (of voice) ¶語調を強める[和らげる] raise [soften] one's voice.

こちら 〈場所〉 this place ; here ; 〈こちら側〉 this side / 〈この方面〉 this way / 〈この物〉 this (one) ; 〈この方〉 this ; 《文》 this gentleman [lady] ; 〈当方〉 we ; I. 文例⇩

こぢんまり ¶こぢんまりした居心地のいい部屋 a cosy [snug] room ; a compact little apartment / こぢんまりと暮らす live in a small way.

こつ¹ 骨 〈ほね, 遺骨〉 ⇒ ほね, いこつ ¶骨揚げをする gather sb's ashes / 骨癌(がん) bone cancer / 骨細胞 a bone cell / 骨状の bonelike ; bony.

こつ² 骨 〈呼吸〉 a knack ; the trick ¶こつを覚える get the knack [hang] (of) ; learn the trick (of) / こつを知っている have (got) the knack [the trick] (of). 文例⇩

ごつい 〈ごつごつした〉 rugged ; 〈手ごわい〉 tough ; hard to deal with.

こっか¹ 国花 a national flower.

こっか² 国家 a state ; a country ; a nation ¶国家的[の] national ; state / 国家的行事 a national event ; (on) a state occasion / 国家管理 state [government] control / 国家経済 the national economy / 国家警察 the state police / 国家権力 state power ; the power(s) of the state / 国家公務員 a government official ; a national public servant / 国家公務員法 the Government Officials Act / 国家財政 national finance(s) ; the finances of the state / 国家試験 a state examination 《for the license to practice medicine》/ 国家主義 nationalism / 国家主義者 a nationalist / 国家社会主義 state [national] socialism / 国家統制主義 statism.

こっか³ 国歌 a national anthem.

こっか⁴ 骨化 ossification ¶骨化する ossify ; be ossified.

こっかい¹ 国会 a national assembly ; 〈日本の〉 the (National) Diet ; 〈米国の〉 Congress ; 〈英国の〉 Parliament ¶国会を解散する dissolve the Diet / 第10国会を召集する call [convene, summon] the 10th session of the Diet / 国会議員 a member of the (National) Diet ; a Diet member ; a Dietman (男) ; a Dietwoman(女) ; 〈米国の〉 a member of Congress ; a Congressman (男) ; a Congresswoman (女) ; 〈英国の〉 a Member of Parliament ; an M.P. / 国会議事堂 the Diet Building ; 〈米国の〉 the Capitol ; 〈英国の〉 the Houses of Parliament / 国会議事録 the Diet Record / 国会図書館 the National Diet Library ; 〈米国の〉 the Library of Congress / 国会法 the Diet Act.

こっかい² 骨灰 bone ash.

ごたぶん 競馬狂のご多分にもれず, 彼も全財産をつぶしてしまった。He lost all he had, like other [as is usual with] racing men. / 氏もまたご多分にもれない。He is no exception.

こだま 銃声が山々にこだました。The report of his gun echoed over [reverberated through] the hills.

ごちそう 何のご馳走もありませんが。We have nothing special to offer you. / ご馳走様(でした)。I have enjoyed my meal very much. Thank you. / 〈飲食店などで〉それでは今日はご馳走になっておくとしよう。I'll let you pay the bill this time, if you insist.

こちら こちらへどうぞ。This way, please. / 学校は川のこちらですか。Is the school on this side of the river? / こちらに高橋さんという方はおいでになりませんか。Excuse me, but does a Mr. Takahashi live with you? / 〈電話で〉こちら田中です。(This is) Mr. [Miss] Tanaka speaking. / 〈アナウンサーが〉こちらは大阪です。This is Osaka. / こちらをいただきます。I'll take this (one).

こつ² じきにこつがわかります。You'll soon learn the trick [get the hang] of it. / それをするにはこつがある。There is a knack to it [in doing it].

こづかい² 父は月に1万円ずつ小遣いをくれます。My father gives me an allowance of 10,000 yen a month.

こっき² 家ごとに国旗を掲げている。The national flag is hoisted

こっかい³ 黒海 the Black Sea.
こづかい¹ 小使 《米》a janitor;《英》a caretaker.
こづかい² 小遣 ¶小遣い spending money; pocket money (主に子供の);《米》an allowance (主に子供・学生の); pin money (女性の) ¶小遣い帳 a petty cash book. 文例⇩

こっかく 骨格 a skeleton; bone [skeletal] structure ¶骨格のたくましい人 a sturdily-built man.

こっかん 酷寒 severe [bitter, intense] cold.

ごっかん 極寒 severe [intense] cold ¶極寒の季節 the coldest season;(in) the depth(s) of winter.

こっき¹ 克己 〈自制(力)〉self-control; self-restraint;《文》self-denial (★self-control や self-restraint が外からの刺激や誘惑を抑制できる能力を意味するのに対して, self-denial は, 自分のやりたいこともあえてしない, という積極的な意味を持つ);〈忍耐(力)〉《文》stoicism ¶克己心のある self-denying;《文》stoic(al).

こっき² 国旗 a national flag ¶国旗を掲げる hoist [fly, put up] the national flag / 国旗掲揚式 a flag-hoisting ceremony. 文例⇩

こづきまわす こづき回す 〈あちこちへ〉push [shove] sb around [about];〈手荒に扱う〉handle sb roughly;〈いじめる〉tease.

こっきょう¹ 国教 a state religion ¶国教会 the state [established] church / 国教徒〈英国の〉a member of the Church of England / 非国教徒〈英国の〉a nonconformist.

こっきょう² 国境 the boundary; the border;《主に英》the frontier ★frontier は《米》では普通には「辺境」の意で, 「国境」の意味で用いられることはまれ ¶国境を越える cross the border 《into another country》/ 国境侵犯 (a) border violation / 国境線 a boundary line; a borderline / 国境地帯 the border; a border area [region]; the borderland ★これらはみな複数で使うことが多い / 国境紛争 [問題] a boundary [border] dispute [problem]. 文例⇩

こっきん 国禁 ¶国禁の書 a book banned [forbidden] by state laws.

コック¹ 〈料理人〉a cook ¶コック長 a chef; a chief cook.

コック² 〈栓〉a cock.

こづく 小突く push; poke; shove; nudge ¶ひじでこづく elbow / 脇腹をこづく poke [nudge] sb in the ribs.

こっく〈かんれい〉刻苦(勉励) ¶刻苦(勉励)する work hard [《文》diligently];《文》apply oneself closely to《one's studies》.

こっくり ¶こっくり(と)うなずく nod 《one's head》in agreement [《文》assent]; nod 《one's》agreement [《文》assent]《(to)》/ こっくりこっくり居眠りをする nod in a doze; nod off / こっくりさん《use》a planchette.

こづくり 小作り ¶小作りの〈人が〉small;《文》of small stature;〈物が〉small(-sized).

こっけい 滑稽 ¶こっけいな〈おどけて面白い〉funny; humorous; comic(al);〈ばかげた〉laughable; ludicrous; ridiculous; absurd. 文例⇩

こっこ 国庫 the (National) Treasury;《文》the coffers of the State ¶国庫で負担する defray (the expenses) out of the National Treasury / 国庫債券 a Treasury bond / 国庫収入 National Treasury receipts; national revenues / 国庫補助(金) a state [government] subsidy. 文例⇩

-ごっこ ¶カウボーイごっこをする play cowboys and Indians / お店[学校]ごっこをする play shop [school].

こっこう 国交 diplomatic relations ¶国交を断絶する《結ぶ》break [establish, enter into] diplomatic relations 《with》. 文例⇩

ごつごうしゅぎ 御都合主義 opportunism; timeserving (事大主義); expediency (便宜優先の) ¶ご都合主義者 an opportunist; a timeserver.

こっこく 刻々 every moment [hour]; hourly ¶刻々変化する change [vary] every hour [from one hour to another]. 文例⇩

こつこつ ¶こつこつ仕事をする work hard; plod [plug] away 《at a task》/ こつこつ勉強する work hard [steadily,《文》assiduously] / 机をこつこつとたたく rap on a desk / 戸をこつこつとたたく音 a rap [knock] at [on] the door. 文例⇩

ごつごつ ¶ごつごつした〈でこぼこの〉rugged;〈角(ど)張った〉angular;〈堅い〉stiff / ごつごつした指 horny fingers.

こっし 骨子 the main point(s); the substance; the gist.

こつずい 骨髄 the marrow (of a bone); the bone marrow ¶恨み骨髄に徹している bear [《文》harbor] a deep grudge against sb / 骨髄炎

over every door. / 入口に両国の国旗が交差されていた. The flags of the two countries were crossed at the entrance. / その船はフランスの国旗を掲げていた. The ship was sailing under the French flag.

こっきょう² 芸術に国境なし. Art has [knows] no national boundaries. / クエートは北はイラクと国境を接している. Kuwait is bordered on the north by Iraq. / Iraq borders Kuwait on the north.

こっけい 彼が演説したなんてこっけいだね. What a joke it is that he should have made a speech in public! / こっけい味を出すためにそうしたのさ. I did that for comic effect.

こっこ 義務教育費は全額国庫負担とすべきである. The National Treasury should cover all the costs of compulsory education.

こっこう 日米間の国交はますます親善の度を加えてきた. The friendship between Japan and the U.S. has grown more cordial than ever. / イランはイスラエルと国交を断絶した. Iran broke off diplomatic relations with Israel.

こっこく 危険が刻々迫りつつあった. The danger was coming nearer every moment.

こつこつ 相変わらずこつこつやってるね. You are hard at it as ever. / 戸をこつこつたたく音がした. There was a rap [knock] on the door. / こつこつと歩く足音がした. Footsteps clacked along the street.

こっせつ 骨折 (a) fracture (of a bone) ¶骨折する break [fracture] a bone; have a bone broken [fractured] ★fracture はやや専門的な医学用語の気分がある / 腕を骨折する break [fracture] one's arm / 骨折を直す mend broken bones / 単純[複雑]骨折 a simple [compound] fracture.

こつぜん 忽然 ¶こつぜんと suddenly; all of a sudden; all at once.

こっそう 骨相 〈からだの〉 the skeletal structure; 〈頭骨の〉 the structure [shape] of the skull ¶骨相学 phrenology.

こっそり secretly; in secret; on the quiet [sly]; stealthily; 《文》 by stealth ¶こっそり知らせる tell sb secretly 《about sth》; 《口語》 tip sb off 《that…, about sth》 / こっそり立ち去る slip off; creep away; 《文》 go away [leave] unobserved. 文例⇩

ごっそり 〈全部〉 all; entirely; completely; 〈ほとんどすべて〉 almost all; 〈たくさん〉 a large number 《of》; a great [good] deal 《of》.

ごったがえす ごった返す 〈混乱する〉 be in confusion [a turmoil]; 〈混み合う〉 be crowded [jammed] 《with people》. 文例⇩

ごったに ごった煮 《米》 a hodgepodge / 《英》 a hotchpotch.

こっち ⇨ こちら. 文例⇩

こづち 小槌 a small mallet; 〈議長などが持つ〉 a gavel ⇨ うちでのこづち.

ごっちゃ ⇨ ごちゃごちゃ.

こっちょう 骨頂 ¶愚の骨頂 ⇨ ぐ².

こつつぼ 骨壺 a cinerary [cremation] urn; an urn.

こづつみ 小包 a parcel; a (postal) package ¶小包郵便 parcel post (略: P.P., p.p.) / 小包郵便で送る send sth by parcel post.

こってり thick(ly); heavy; rich. ¶こってりした thick; heavy; rich.

こっとう(ひん) 骨董(品) an antique; a curio (pl. -s); 〈時代遅れの人や物〉 a museum piece (軽蔑的) ¶骨董あさり[いじり] antique [curio] hunting [collecting] / 骨董収集家 a collector of antiques [curios] / 骨董趣味 antiquarianism / 骨董屋〈店〉 an antique [a curio] store; 〈人〉 an antique [a curio] dealer.

こつにく 骨肉 ¶こつにくの争い a family quarrel; 《文》 family discord.

こっぱ 木端 a chip; a splinter ¶こっぱみじんに砕く break sth to pieces [fragments]; smash sth to atoms [matchwood] / こっぱ役人 a petty official.

こつばん 骨盤 【解】 the pelvis ((pl. -ves)).

こっぴどく こっ酷く 〈scold〉 harshly; 〈criticize〉 severely; 〈beat〉 soundly; 〈rebuke〉 scathingly.

こつぶ 小粒 a small [fine] grain; a granule ¶小粒の fine; small; granular.

コップ [<《ポルトガル語》kop] a glass; a tumbler (脚(き)も取っ手もないもの) ¶コップ1杯分 a glass(ful) (of water) / 水をコップ1杯 a glass of water / コップの中のあらし a storm in a teacup. 文例⇩

こっぷん 骨粉 bone meal [dust].

コッペパン a roll.

コッヘル [<《ドイツ語》Kocher] a camp stove.

こつまく 骨膜 【解】 the periosteum ((pl. -tea)) ¶骨膜に達する傷 a cut [wound] deep enough to reach the bone / 骨膜炎 periostitis.

こづめ 小爪 the half-moon (of a nail); 【解】 the lunula ((pl. -lae)).

こづらにくい 小面憎い 〈いやな〉 disgusting; 〈癪にさわる〉 maddening; provoking; 〈生意気な〉 saucy; cheeky.

こつんと with a bump [clunk] ¶こつんと頭をぶつける bump [bang] one's head (against the doorframe).

ごつんと ¶ごつんと打つ bang [thump] (one's head) / ごつんとぶつける bump (one's head against a wall); crack (one's head on a post).

こて¹ 鏝 〈裁縫用〉 an iron; 〈理髪用〉 curling tongs; 〈左官用〉 a trowel; 〈はんだごて〉 a soldering iron ⇒ アイロン ¶髪にこてをあてる curl one's hair with tongs; singe one's hair / こて板 〈左官・石工の〉 a mortarboard; a hawk.

こて² 小手 gauntlets; fencing gloves; 〈よろいの〉 an arm guard ¶小手をかざす shade one's eyes with one's hand.

こっそり 彼は足音を立てないでこっそり入って来た。 He came in with stealthy [noiseless] steps.

ごったがえす 店はクリスマスの買物客でごった返していた。 The store was crowded with Christmas shoppers.

こっち もうこっちのものだ。 Success [The game] is ours.

コップ 茶さじ1杯の砂糖をコップ半杯の水に溶かしなさい。 Dissolve a teaspoonful of sugar in half a glassful of water.

こてい ダムができて、僕たちの村は湖底に沈んでしまった。 The dam has been built, and the water of the artificial lake has completely submerged our village.

こてさき こうなっては小手先の器用さでは間に合わない。 Mere cleverness will be of no use [won't do] in this situation.

こてん¹ この小説はアメリカ文学の古典としての地位を確立している。 This novel is now one of the established classics of American literature.

こてん² 氏は永井画廊で個展を開く。 He will have [hold, give] an exhibition of his pictures at the Nagai Gallery.

こと¹ 事の起こりは野球の試合であった。 The trouble originated in a baseball game. / 私の事はご心配なさいませんように。 Don't trouble yourself about me [on my account]. / 事ここに至っては計画を断念するより他にいたし方がない。 Now that things have come to this pass, there is no help for it but to give up our plan. / さあ事だ。 This is serious, I tell you. | Here's a pretty go! / 何か事があるとあの人の所に相談に行ってた。 When we were in some trouble or other, we used to go to him for advice. / この規則が適用できないこともある。 There are cases where this rule does not apply. / この本を読んだことがあります。 Have you ever read this book? / いつ会っても彼が本を持っていないことはない。 I have never seen him without a book. / 急ぐことはない。 You needn't [There's no

ごて 後手 ¶(囲碁・将棋で)後手を引く lose the initiative / 後手になる be forestalled / 後手で打つ[指す] take [have] the second move in a 《go, chess》 game.

こてい¹ 固定 fixing; 《標本などの》fixation ¶固定する fix; be fixed / 固定観念 a fixed idea 《on》 / 固定給[収入] a fixed salary [income] / 固定資産 fixed assets [property]; 『会計』permanent assets / 固定資産税 a fixed property tax / 固定票 a solid [an assured, a safe] vote ; solid [assured] support (全体).

こてい² 湖底 the bottom of a lake. 文例⇩

コデイン 《化》codeine.

こてきたい 鼓笛隊 a fife and drum [drum and fife] corps [band].

こてこて heavily ; thickly ¶こてこてと化粧する wear heavy make-up ; powder one's face thickly ; be heavily painted / 髪に油をこてこてと塗る plaster one's hair (down) with hair oil.

ごてごて ⟨こてこて⟩ ⇨ こてこて ; ⟨くどくど⟩ ⇨ くどくど.

こてさき 小手先 ¶小手先でごまかす use cheap tricks. 文例⇩

こてしらべ 小手調べ a trial ; a tryout ; ⟨競技などの⟩ a workout ¶小手調べに for [as a] trial.

こでまり 『植』a spir(a)ea.

こてん¹ 古典 classics ; ⟨個称⟩ a classic ¶古典的 classic(al) / 古典学者 a classical scholar ; a classicist / 古典語 a classical language / (ギリシャ・ローマの) 古典古代 Classical Antiquity / 古典主義 classicism / 古典派 the classical school ; the classicists / 古典物理学 classical physics / 古典文学 classical literature. 文例⇩

こてん² 個展 a one-man exhibition [show].

ごてん 御殿 a palace. 文例⇩

こてんこてん ¶こてんこてんにやっつける defeat sb completely ; 《口語》beat sb hollow ; 《口語》make mincemeat of sb.

こと¹ 古都 an ancient city [capital].

こと² 事 ⟨事物⟩ a thing ; ⟨事柄⟩ a matter ; an affair ; ⟨問題⟩ a question ; ⟨事実⟩ a fact ; ⟨出来事⟩ an incident ; an event ; ⟨事故⟩ an accident ¶えのけん事 榎本健一 Ken'ichi Enomoto, alias Enoken ; Ken'ichi Enomoto, popularly known as [by the name of] Enoken / 事あれかしと願う wish that something would happen / 事もあろうに of all things / 事を好むを bent on making trouble / 事を分けて話す reason with sb / 事によると possibly ; perhaps ; probably ; maybe / …する事にしている make it a rule to do ; make a rule of doing / …との事である it is said that…; they say…; I hear… / …を事とする make it one's business to do ; devote oneself to sth. 文例⇩

こと³ 琴 a koto ¶琴を弾く play the koto / 琴柱(ことじ) a bridge.

こと⁴ 糊塗 ¶糊塗する gloss over 《one's mistakes》.

-ごと ⟨そっくり⟩ …and all ; ⟨…とともに⟩ (together) with ; ¶骨ごと食べる eat 《fish》 bones and all.

ことあたらしく 事新しく ⟨新たに⟩ afresh ; 《文》anew ; ⟨重ねて⟩ again ; ⟨特に⟩ specially ; ⟨今さら⟩ now. 文例⇩

ことう 孤島 a remote and lonely island ; a desert island 《無人島》.

こどう 鼓動 a beat ; beating ; throbbing ; pulsation ¶心臓の鼓動 the [a] beat [throb] of the heart ; (a) heartbeat / 鼓動する beat ; throb. 文例⇩

ごとう 語頭 the beginning of a word ¶語頭の initial (letters) ; 《the th-sound》 at the beginning of a word / 語頭音 『音声』an initial sound. 文例⇩

こどうぐ 小道具 ⟨舞台上の⟩ (stage) properties ; 《口語》props ; ⟨役者が手に持つ⟩ hand props ¶小道具方 a property [《口語》prop] man [master].

ことかく 事欠く be short of 《money》; lack ; 《文》want ; be in want [need] of sth ¶生活に事欠く be unable to make one's living ; 《文》be in needy circumstances / 事欠かない have plenty of sth ; have no need [lack, shortage] of sth ; be in no need of sth. 文例⇩

ことがら 事柄 ⇨ こと².

ことぎれる 事切れる 《文》breathe one's last ; die. 文例⇩

(need to)] hurry. | 《文》There is no need for haste. / 彼は重体だということだ. He is said to be [I was told that he is] seriously ill. / 私のことですか. Do you mean me? / 一難去ってまた一難とはこの事である. This is an instance of 'Out of the frying pan into the fire.' / 3分のことで その電車に乗りそこねた. I missed the train by only three minutes. / 行ったことは行ったが会えなかった. I did go, but I wasn't able to see him. / 田中のことだから3時きっかりにやって来るよ. If I know Tanaka, he'll come here [make his appearance] at three sharp. / 高い金を出しただけのことはある. It is worth the high price I paid for it. / 何度その手紙を読み返してみたことか. How often I read that letter! / その本はことによったら神田の古本屋にあるかもしれない. You may be able to get [may possibly find] the book at one of the secondhand bookstores in Kanda. / 事によると彼は家にいるかもしれない. I'm afraid you may not find him at home.

ことあたらしく いまさら事新しく言うまでもない. It is too well known to be mentioned here.

こどう 心臓の鼓動が一瞬止まった. His heart stopped beating for a moment.

ごとう 英語における語頭の /ð/ は指示詞及び接続詞に限って生じる. Initial /ð/ in English is restricted to [appears only in] demonstratives and conjunctions. ★例: the, this, that, they, there, thus, then, though, than.

ことかく おれが生きている間はお前に事欠かせない. You'll lack [want for] nothing as long as I live. / 私は暮らしには事欠かない. I've enough to get along with. / 資金には事欠かない. We have [There is] no shortage of funds for it. / 言うに事欠いておれをうそつき呼ばわりした. He had the gall to call me a liar.

ことぎれる 発見した時彼はすでに事切れていた. When we found him, his heart had ceased to

こどく　孤独 《文》solitude; loneliness ¶孤独な《文》solitary; lonely;《米》lonesome / 孤独癖 shut-in (personality) / (a person) with [who has, 《文》of] a solitary temperament.

ごとく　五徳 a trivet.

ごどく　誤読 ¶誤読する read [interpret] 《a passage》wrongly; misread; misinterpret.

ことごとく　悉く all; entirely;《文》wholly; without exception ¶全員ことごとく unanimously (一致して); in a body (総勢で); to a man (最後の一人まで).

ことごとに　事毎に〈万事に〉in everything;〈いつでも〉whenever;〈必ず〉always;《文》invariably. 文例↓

ことこまかに　事細かに《文》minutely; in detail ⇒しょうさい².

ことさら(に)　殊更(に)〈特に〉especially; specially; particularly;〈わざと〉on purpose; deliberately;《文》intentionally;《文》advisedly (よく考えて) ¶ことさらに大事を取る despite all the precautions one can (against); be especially [extremely] cautious (about doing). 文例↓

ことし　今年 this year;《文》the present [current] year ¶今年の夏 this summer. 文例↓

ことたりる　事足りる ¶answer [serve] the purpose;《will》do; be enough. 文例↓

ことづかる　言付かる〈伝言を〉be asked to send word to sb 《that...》;〈物を〉be asked to hand sb sth [sth to sb]. 文例↓

ことづけ　言付け ⇒でんごん.

ことなかれしゅぎ　事なかれ主義 a peace-at-any-price principle.

ことなく　事なく uneventfully; quietly; smoothly; without a hitch [mishap].

ことなる　異なる〈違う〉《文》differ (from); be different (from);〈似ていない〉be not like sth [sb];《文》be unlike sth [sb];《文》be dissimilar (to, from);〈多様である〉vary; diverge ¶異なった different;《文》dissimilar; various; varied. 文例↓

ことに　殊に〈とりわけ〉especially; in particular;〈格別に〉exceptionally;〈何よりも〉above all (things); most of all. 文例↓

-ごとに　…毎に〈毎〉every; each;〈…する度ごとに〉whenever; every time ¶2日目ごとに every other day / 3年ごとに every three years; every third year /（電報で）5字を増すごとに《pay forty yen》for every additional five characters / 一雨ごとに every time it rains; with every rainfall. 文例↓

ことにする　異にする ⇒ことなる.

ことのほか　殊の外〈非常に〉《文》exceedingly; extremely;〈例になく〉unusually; exceptionally. 文例↓

ことば　言葉〈言語〉speech; language;〈単語〉a word;〈句〉a phrase;〈表現〉an expression;〈用語〉a term;〈国語〉a language;《文》a tongue ¶言葉の verbal / 言葉の多い wordy; talkative / 言葉の少ない《文》taciturn;《a man》of few words / 言葉静かに in a calm tone; calmly / 言葉巧みに with sweet [《文》honeyed, cajoling] words / 言葉を荒らげる speak harshly [in an angry tone] / 言葉を返す answer [talk] back; retort / 言葉を飾らず do not mince matters [one's words] / 言葉をかける speak to sb;《文》address sb / 言葉を交わす talk with sb; have a word with sb / 言葉を濁す《文》equivocate;《文》prevaricate / 考えを言葉に表わす express one's thoughts; put one's thoughts into words; think aloud [out loud] / 言葉に尽くせない《文》be indescribable;《文》be inexpressible;《文》be beyond (all) description. 文例↓

ことばがき　詞書〈和歌の〉a foreword (to a waka explaining how it was composed);〈絵巻物の〉a legend (to a picture scroll explaining what it depicts).

ことばじり　言葉尻 ¶言葉尻をとらえる trip sb up with [catch sb in] his own words.

ことばづかい　言葉遣い wording; language; use [choice] of words ¶言葉遣いに気をつけ

beat.

ことごとく　彼は所持金をことごとく使ってしまった. He spent all the money he had with him. / 彼が手がけた仕事はことごとく失敗でした. Everything he put his hand to proved a failure.

ことごとに　彼は事ごとに成功した. He succeeded in everything he attempted. / その問題では彼は事ごとに僕に反対する. Whenever we discuss the matter, he invariably opposes me.

ことさら(に)　その問題に関しては, 政府はことさらに沈黙を守っていた. The government maintained a studied silence on the problem.

ことし　今年はきっと豊作だよ. I'm sure we'll have a good harvest [a bumper crop] this year. / 今年も余すところ幾らもない. There are only a few days to go to the end of the year.

ことたりる　差し当たっては100万円もあれば事足りるだろう. A million yen will do for the present.

ことづかる　手紙をことづかって参りました. Here's a letter he asked me to hand (to) you.

ことなる　その点では彼らは獣とあまり異ならない. They don't differ much from the beasts in that respect. / 習慣は国によって異なる. Each country has its own customs. | Customs differ from one country to another. | So many countries, so many customs.《諺》

ことに　僕はパリが好きだ, 殊に秋は. I love Paris, especially in autumn.

-ごとに　電車は10分ごとに出ます. The trains leave every ten minutes [at intervals of ten minutes]. / オリンピックは4年ごとに開催される. The Olympic Games are held every four years. / 彼女は来る人ごとに同じ質問をした. She asked the same question of everyone that came along.

ことのほか　それを聞かれて先生は殊のほか喜ばれた. He was very [extremely] pleased to hear that. / この冬は殊のほか寒い. It is unusually cold this winter. | This is the coldest winter in years.

ことば　お言葉に甘えてお願い申します. I will avail myself of your kind offer. | お言葉ですが, 私は賛成できません. I'm afraid you will think me impertinent to say so, but I cannot agree with you. | With all due respect, I'm afraid I must disagree with you. / それが父親に向かって言う言葉か. Is that the way to talk to your father? / お礼の言葉もござ

こども be careful in *one's* speech [choice of words]; watch *one's* language; weigh *one's* words / 言葉遣いの丁寧[乱暴]な人 a civil-[rough-]spoken person.

こども 子供 a child (*pl.* children); 〈男〉a boy; 〈女〉a girl; 〈赤ん坊〉a baby; 〈文〉an infant; 〈息子〉a son; 〈娘〉a daughter; 〈子孫〉offspring; 〈文〉issue ¶子供がある have a child / 子供がない have no children of *one's* own; be childless / 子供ができない女 a sterile [barren] woman / 子供のときに in *one's* childhood; when one was a child; as a child / 子供のときから from (*one's*) childhood / 子供の日 Children's Day / 子供の時間〖テレビ・ラジオ〗the children's hour / 子供の使い〈比喩的〉a fool's errand / 子供向きの《films (intended)》for children; juvenile《reading》/ 子供っぽい childish; 〈文〉puerile / 子供らしい childlike / 子供だまし mere child's play; a puerile trick; kid stuff / 子供服 children's clothing / 子供部屋 a nursery; a child's [children's] room. 文例□

こともなげに 事もなげに casually; lightly ¶事もなげに殺す kill *sb* in cold blood.

ことよせて 事寄せて《文》on [under] the pretext (of);《文》on the plea (of) ¶…にかこつける.

ことり 小鳥 a (small [little]) bird ★ small, little などの形容詞はつけないですよ! ことが多い ¶小鳥をかごに入れて飼う keep a bird in a cage / 小鳥屋〈店〉a bird shop; 〈人〉a bird dealer.

ことわざ 諺 a proverb; a (common) saying; 〈金言〉《文》a maxim ¶諺にもあるとおり as the proverb says [goes, has it]; as the saying goes. 文例□

ことわり 断わり〈辞退〉《文》declining; 〈拒絶〉(a) refusal; (a) rejection; 〈言いわけ〉an excuse; 《文》a plea; 〈予告〉a notice; 〈許可〉leave; permission ¶断わりもなく〈予告なく〉without (previous) notice; without warning; 〈許可なく〉without leave [permis-

sion] / 断わり状〈拒絶の〉a letter of refusal; 〈わびの〉a letter of apology [explanation].

ことわる 断わる〈拒絶する〉refuse; reject; turn down; 〈謝絶する〉《文》decline; excuse *oneself* (from); 〈予告する〉give *sb* notice; warn. 文例□

こな 粉〈穀類の〉flour; meal (ふるいにかけていない); 〈状態〉powder; dust ¶粉にする powder; pulverize; reduce *sth* to powder; grind *sth* into powder; 〈穀類をひいて〉grind [mill]《grain》into meal [flour] / 粉おしろい (face) powder / 粉薬 powdered medicine; (a)《stomach》powder / 粉々[粉みじん]に砕く break [crush, smash] *sth* to pieces [atoms, to smithereens] / 粉炭 charcoal dust / 粉せっけん soap powder / 粉茶 dust tea / 粉ミルク milk powder; powdered [dried] milk / 粉屋 a flour dealer; a miller (製粉業者) / 粉雪 powder(y) snow.

こなす〈処理する〉《can》cope [deal] with; manage; finish; 〈細かく砕く〉reduce *sth* to powder; grind *sth* into powder; 〈消化する〉digest ¶いろんな楽器をこなす can handle a variety of musical instruments / 数でこなす ⇨ かず / 役をこなす perform *one's* part creditably.

こなまいき 小生意気 ⇨ なまいき.

こなれ, こなれる ⇨ しょうか². ¶こなれた訳文 an idiomatic translation.

にくらしい 小憎らしい irritating; maddening; provoking;《口語》aggravating ⇨ にくらしい, しゃく(癪にさわる).

にもつ 小荷物〈主に米〉a package; 〈主に英〉a parcel.

コニャック cognac.

ごにん 誤認 ¶誤認する mistake 《A for B》;《文》misidentify《A as B》.

こにんずう 小人数 a small number of people; a few (people) ¶小人数のクラス a small class.

いません. I don't know how to express my thanks. / 初めてアメリカへ行ったときは言葉が通じなくて困りました. When I first went to the United States I had a hard time trying to make myself understood. / 君の感想を君自身の言葉で語るべきだ. You should describe what you thought about it in your own words. / あの人の言う事を言葉どおりにとってはいけない. You must not take him at his word. / その本に述べられている思想が非常に抽象的な言葉にむずかしい言葉で書かれていたので, ごくわずかの人しか理解できなかった. The book was so abstract in thought and difficult in language that only a few people could understand it. / 彼女はいまに近く子供ができるそうだ. She is going to have a baby before long. / 彼に, 子供は男の

子と女の子ではどちらがほしいか聞いてみた. I asked him whether he wanted a son or a daughter. / 僕はもう子供じゃない. I am no longer a child. / 彼を子供のときから知っている. I have known him from childhood. / 彼らは私を子供扱いにした. They treated me as if I was a child. / そんな子供だましの手には乗らないよ. You won't take me in by a childish [shallow] trick like that. / I'm too old a bird to be caught with chaff. / 子供心にも悲しくて涙が出た. Mere child as I was, it made me so sad that I cried.

ことわざ「郷に入っては郷に従え」という諺がある. The proverb says, ' When in Rome, do as the Romans do. '

ことわり 病気だからと彼は断わりの手紙をよこした. He sent us a

letter excusing himself on the ground of illness. / 掛け売り一切お断わり.〖掲示〗No credit given. | Sale on credit absolutely declined.

ことわる 忙しくて行かれないと断わって下さい. Tell him that I am too busy to go. / せっかくのお志ですがお断わりいたします. I am sorry I cannot accept your kind offer. / 自分の金を自分で使うのにだれに断わる必要があるのか. Do I have to ask anyone for permission to use my own money? / 彼は私に断わらずにしたのです. He did it without my permission.

こな このチョークは彼に踏まれて粉々になった. He stepped on the chalk and crushed it to powder. / 外は粉雪が降っていた. A fine snow was falling outside.

こなす この仕事は一日ではこなせ

こぬか 小糠 rice bran ¶小ぬか雨 (a) fine [drizzling, misty] rain; a drizzle.

コネ connections; (a) pull ¶コネがある have pull ((with [in] the firm)); (《口語》 have an in ((with sb)) / コネをつける set up (business) contacts ((in a company, with sb)). 文例⇩

コネチカット Connecticut (略: Conn.).

ごねどく ごね得. 文例⇩

こねる 捏ねる knead ((dough)); work ((mortar)); puddle (a wet mixture of earth).

ごねる make [raise] difficulties ((over)).

この this; these (複数); 〈現在の〉 present; 《文》current; 〈来たる〉 this; coming; 〈去る〉 last; past ¶君のこの時計 this watch of yours / このあたり このへん / このような ⇒こんな / この2, 3日 for the last [past] two or three days; these two or three days / この節 ⇒こんにち, このごろ / この程 ⇒このあいだ. 文例⇩

このあいだ この間 the other day; a few days ago; not long ago; recently; lately ¶この間の 《the accident》 《of》 the other day; recent; 《文》 late / この間の晩 the other evening [night] / ついこの間まで until quite recently. 文例⇩

このうえ この上 〈この外にも〉 besides;《文》moreover;《文》 in addition (to this); 〈いっそう〉 more;《文》 further ¶この上の 〈なおいっそうの〉《文》 further; more; 〈もっとよい〉 better;《文》 superior / この上は now; now (that) things have come to this [《文》 this pass] / この上ない the best [finest, greatest];《文》 superlative;《文》 matchless;《文》 peerless; first-rate / この上(も)なく most (of all); extremely / この上もなく幸福だ be as happy as (happy) can be. 文例⇩

このえ 近衛 ¶近衛師団 the Guards Division / 近衛兵 a guardsman; 〈総称〉 the (Imperial) Guards.

このかた¹ この方 〈以来〉 since ¶10年このかた for [in] the past [last] ten years; these ten years.

このかた² 〈この人〉《文》 this gentleman [lady].

このかん この間 meanwhile; in the meantime.

このくらい about this [so] much [many, large, long, wide, etc.];〈程度〉《文》to this degree [extent].

このごろ この頃 〈当今〉 now; nowadays; at present; these days (★ in these days of nuclear power generation [when people are traveling abroad in droves] などのように of... や when... の句・節をあとに伴うとき以外は these days の前に は付けない); 〈近頃〉 recently; lately; 《文》 of late;〈先頃から〉for some time past; these (last) few days ¶このごろの 〈当今の〉 〈young people〉 of today; present(-day); 〈近頃の〉 recent. 文例⇩

このさい この際 now;《文》at this juncture; on this occasion; under [in] these circumstances. 文例⇩

このさき この先 〈今後〉 from this time on;《文》 henceforth; in future; 〈将来〉 in the future ⇒こんご ★;《文》 hereafter;〈ここより先〉 beyond this (point). 文例⇩

コのじ コの字 ¶コの字型の U-shaped.

このしろ 〈魚〉 a gizzard shad.

このたび この度 this time ⇒こんど.

このつぎ この次 ¶この次の next / この次の土曜日に next Saturday; on Saturday next / この次に next; next time; another time (またの時). 文例⇩

このとおり この通り like this; in this way [《文》 manner]; as you see. 文例⇩

このとき この時 at this [that] time [moment]; then.

このは 木の葉 a leaf ((pl. leaves)); foliage (総称).

このば この場 here; this place ¶この場(here and) now / この場から from here.

このはずく 〈鳥〉 a scops owl; 〈アメリカ産の〉 a screech owl.

このぶん この分 ¶この分では 〈この調子では〉 at this rate; 〈今のありさまでは〉 as things are [stand]; (judging) from the present state

---

ないよ. You cannot do [finish] this job in a day.
コネ あの会社にはコネがある. I know a person who has some influence in that firm. / I've got an in to that company. / 彼はコネでその仕事をもらったのだ. He has got that job through his connections.

ごねどく ごね得だ. It sometimes pays to make trouble.

この 私はこの5年間一度も風邪を引いたことがありません. I haven't caught cold these five years. / この場合どうしたものでしょう. What do you think should be done in a case like this? / この父にしてこの子あり. Like father, like son.

このあいだ ついこの間の事でした. It happened just the other day. | It happened quite recently. / ド イツ語の勉強を始めたのはついこの間からなんです. I've only recently begun to learn German.

このうえ この上言うことはない. I have nothing more to say. / 父の喜びはこの上もなかった. Father's joy knew no bounds.

このかた¹ 生まれてこの方一度もそういうものにお目にかかったことはない. I've never seen anything like it in (all) my life.

このくらい このくらいの大きさ [高さ]だった. It was about this big [tall]. / このくらいで充分だろう. This much may be enough. / このくらい英文を上手に書ける人は少ない. Very few people can write English as well as this [write such fine English]. / 今日 So much [This will do] for today. / Let's leave off here today. / 2階 にはまだこのくらい本があるよ. I have as many more books [as many books again] as this upstairs.

このごろ このごろはとてもよく勉強している. He has been working very hard lately.

このさい この際だからしかたがない. There is no help for it under [in] these circumstances.

このさき この先お前はどうするつもりかね. What are your plans for the future? | What are you going to do from now on? / 郵便局ならすぐこの先です. The post office is only a little way from here.

このつぎ またこの次に行くとしよう. Let's go there some other time.

このとおり 私がやるとほれこのとおりうまくいく. See how well I

このへん この辺 この辺に near [about, around] here; in this neighborhood; in this part of the town [city, country] / どこかこの辺に somewhere near [around] here.

このほか この外《これに加えて》besides;《文》in addition (to this);《文》moreover;〈これを除いて〉except (for) this. 文例↓

このまえ この前 last time;《文》previously ¶この前の本;《文》previous [;《文》former / この前の日曜日に last Sunday; on Sunday last. 文例↓

このまぎれ 木の間隠れ ¶木の間隠れに見えるbe seen through the trees.

このましい 好ましい《文》desirable; nice; fine; agreeable ¶好ましくない《文》undesirable; disagreeable / 好ましからぬ人物 an undesirable (person);〈特に外交官として〉《ラテン語》(a) persona non grata ((pl. personae non gratae))(to, with).

このまま ¶このままにしておく〈現状のままにしておく〉leave sth as it is [stands];〈不問に付す〉pass over《sb's remarks》in silence; overlook《sb's bad behavior》. 文例↓

このみ[1] 木の実〈堅果〉nuts;〈漿果({しょう})〉berries;〈果物〉fruit(s).

このみ[2] 好み (a) liking; (a) taste; a fancy;〈希望〉a wish;〈注文・選択〉choice; preference ¶着物の好み one's taste for dress / 好みが難しい be fastidious [《口語》fussy] (in one's taste) / 〈物が〉好みにかなう suit [be to] one's taste; take one's fancy / お好みなら if you like [wish]. 文例↓

このむ 好む like; be fond of; have a liking [fancy, taste] for; (do not) care for;〈選択する〉prefer 《A to B》; choose 《A rather than B, A over B》 ¶好むと好まざるとにかかわらず whether one likes (it) or not; willy-nilly / 好んで〈望んで〉by [from] choice; by [for] preference;〈進んで〉of one's own accord; of one's (own) free will. 文例↓

このよ この世 this world [life]; the present life ¶この世の《文》worldly;《文》earthly;《文》mundane / この世の地獄 hell on earth;《文》a veritable hell / この世のものとも思われぬ unearthly / この世を去る die;《文》depart this life; pass away [on]《婉曲的に》/ この世で[に] in this world [life];《文》here below. 文例↓

このわた salted entrails of trepang.

こば 後場〔株式〕the afternoon session.

こばい 故買 ¶故買をする receive [deal in] stolen goods [property] / 故買者 a receiver (of stolen goods);《口語》a fence.

こばか 小馬鹿 ¶小ばかにする look down on sb; treat sb with contempt / 小ばかにしたように scornfully; contemptuously.

こはく 琥珀 amber ¶こはく色(の) amber / こはく織り taffeta.

こばこ 小箱 a small box; a casket (宝石などを入れる).

ごはさん 御破算 ¶ご破算にする〈そろばんで〉zero《one's abacus》;〈白紙に返す〉start afresh [《文》anew, all over again];《米》start over (again); start from scratch [with a clean slate]; make a fresh start ⇒ はくし[1].

こばしり 小走り ¶小走りに走る run with short steps; trot (along).

こはぜ a clasp ¶こはぜをかける[はずす] fasten [unfasten] the clasps《of one's tabi》.

こはだ〔魚〕a medium-sized gizzard shad.

こばな 小鼻 the wings of the nose. 文例↓

こばなし 小話 an anecdote.

こはば 小幅〈布〉single breadth;〈相場の変動などの〉a narrow range ¶小幅の値動き a small fluctuation in prices / 小幅物 cloth of single breadth.

こばむ 拒む〈拒絶する〉refuse; reject; turn down;《文》deny;〈反対する〉oppose; resist;〈防止する〉prevent《sb (from) doing》.

コバルト〔化〕cobalt ¶コバルト爆弾 a cobalt bomb / コバルトブルー cobalt blue.

こはるびより 小春日和 warm [《文》balmy] autumn weather; (an) Indian summer.

こはん 湖畔 ¶湖畔の lakeside (houses);《cab-

---

can do it. / これのとおり間違っているじゃないか. Don't you see your mistake?

このぶん この分では6月中には我々の仕事は片づくまい. At this rate, we won't be able to finish our job by the end of June. / この分なら明日は晴れるだろう. From the look of the sky, I think it will be fine tomorrow.

このほか この外にはありません. This is all I have.

このまえ この前会ったときは彼はとても元気でした. The last time I saw him, he was very well [in very good health]. / この前の家よりずっといい. This house is much better than the old one.

このまま このままここにいてもいいよ. You may stay here, if you like. / 〈着換えをしないで〉このままでは出かけられません. I cannot go out in these clothes [dressed like this].

このみ[2] 何か料理のお好みはありませんか. Is there any particular dish you like? / その他お好みにより調製いたします.〈メニューの添え書き〉Other dishes served to order. / 冷やお酒は僕のお好みではない. I'm not vey fond of drinking sake cold. / ジャズは僕の好みではない. Jazz isn't to my taste. / 彼は今自分の好みに一番合った仕事をしている. He's now doing the work most to his taste. / こしょうをお好みで〈加減〉加えて下さい. Add pepper to taste. / 〈服装に関して〉彼女の好みの色は黒です. She is (particularly) fond of black. / この2つの中ではどちらがお好みですか? Which of these two is your choice [preference]? / 我が社ではこのようにしてお客様のデザインの好みについての情報を得ております. In this way we get information about our customers' design preferences.

このむ 僕はバナナはあまり好まない. I don't care much for bananas. / 何を好んであんなことをしたのか. Why did you choose to do such a thing? / 特に甘いものを好む様子が見られた. They showed a marked liking [a strong preference] for sweet things.

このよ あれがこの世の見納めであった. That was the last I would see of him in life.

こばな 彼の小鼻がひくひく動いた. His nostrils twitched.

こばむ 来る者は拒まずだ. Any-

こばん ins) by [on] the lake / 湖畔に 《live》 by the lake; at the lakeside.

こばん 小判 a former Japanese oval gold coin; a *koban* ¶ 小判形の oval.

ごはん 御飯 〈炊いた米〉(boiled [cooked]) rice; 〈食事〉a meal ¶ ご飯を炊く boil [cook] rice / ご飯を食べる have [《文》take] *one's* meal / ご飯時に at mealtimes / ご飯蒸し a rice steamer. 文例▲

こばんざめ 〘魚〙 a remora; a sucking fish; a shark sucker.

こび 媚 〈へつらい〉(a piece of) flattery; 〈女性の〉《文》coquetry ¶ こびを売る flatter *sb* (to win *his* favor) / 〈女性が〉こびを呈する flirt 《with》; behave flirtatiously [《文》coquettishly] 《to》.

ごび 語尾 the ending [《文》termination] of a word ¶ 語尾がはっきりしない slur the ends of *one's* words [sentences] / 語尾の子音 a consonant in word-final position; a word-final consonant / 語尾変化 inflection; declension (名詞・形容詞の).

コピー a copy ⇒ うつし ¶〈広告などの〉コピーライター a copywriter.

こびき 木挽き a sawyer ¶ 木びき台 a sawhorse.

ゴビさばく ゴビ砂漠 the Gobi (Desert).

こひつじ 小羊 a lamb ¶ 神の子羊〈キリスト〉the Lamb of God.

こびと 小人 a midget; a pygmy; a dwarf (*pl.* -s, dwarves) (奇形の).

こびへつらう 媚び諂う ⇒ こびる, へつらう.

こびりつく stick [cling, 《文》adhere] 《to》 ¶ 泥のこびりついた靴 boots caked with mud; mud-caked boots. 文例▲

こびる 媚びる 〈へつらう〉flatter; curry favor with *sb*; 〈女性の〉flirt 《with》; 《文》play the coquette [《with》] ¶〈女の〉こびるような笑い a flirtatious [《文》coquettish] smile.

こびん 小鬢 sidelocks ⇒ びん³.

こぶ¹ 昆布 ⇒ こんぶ.

こぶ² 鼓舞 鼓舞する encourage; cheer; inspire 《*sb* to greater efforts》. 文例▲

こぶ³ 瘤 〈打撲による〉a bump; 〈はれ物〉a swelling; a lump; a wen (特に頭部の); 〈らくだの〉a hump; 〈木の〉a knot; a gnarl ¶ こぶだらけの木 a knotty [gnarled] tree. 文例▲

ごぶ 護符 ⇒ おまもり.

ごぶ 五分 〈半分〉half 《a sum》; fifty per cent; 〈100分の5〉five per cent ¶ 五分刈りにする have *one's* hair cut [cropped] short / 五分刈り頭 a short-cropped head; a crew-cut head / 五分五分の even; fifty-fifty / 五分五分の試合 an evenly-matched game / 五分五分になる〈仕返しなどの末〉get even 《with *sb*》; 《口語》be quits 《with》. 文例▲

こふう 古風 ¶ 古風な old-fashioned; antiquated; out-of-date; quaint.

ごふく(もの) 呉服(物) drapery;《米》dry goods ¶ 呉服商 a dealer in dry goods;《英》a draper / 呉服店《米》a dry goods store;《英》a draper's (shop).

ごぶさた 御無沙汰 (a) (long) silence;《文》neglect to write [call] ¶ ごぶさたする be silent;〈音信の〉fail [《文》neglect] to write;〈訪問の〉neglect to call / ごぶさたをわびる apologize for *one's* long silence [*one's* neglect to call on *sb*]. 文例▲

こぶし 小節 ¶ 小節の多い歌 a song full of grace notes.

こぶし² 古武士 an ancient warrior. 文例▲

こぶし 拳 a fist ¶ こぶしを固める clench *one's* fist / こぶし大の石 a fist-sized rock [stone].

こぶた 子豚 a young [baby] pig; a piglet.

こぶつ 古物 antiques;〈骨董〉(old) curios;〈使った物〉a secondhand [《米》used] article ¶ 古物商〈人〉a dealer in secondhand [《米》used] articles; a secondhand dealer;〈店〉a secondhand store.

こぶとり 小太り ¶ 小太りの女 a plump [buxom] woman.

こぶね 小舟 a small [light] boat;《文》a bark.

コブラ 〘動〙 a cobra.

コプラ 〈やし油の原料〉copra.

こぶり¹ 小振り ¶ 小ぶりの small-sized; smallish;《文》modest in size. 文例▲

こぶり² 小降り 文例▲

こふん 古墳 an ancient tomb (mound); a tumulus (*pl.* -es, -li).

こぶん¹ 子分 a follower;《文》an adherent; a henchman (暴力団などの);〈総称〉a following ¶ 子分が多い have a large following / 子分をふやす build up *one's* following.

こぶん² 古文 ancient [archaic] writings;〈古典〉classics.

ごふん 胡粉 Paris white.

ごぶん 誤文 an ungrammatical [《文》erroneous] sentence ¶ 誤文訂正 correcting (grammatical) mistakes in a sentence.

ごへい¹ 御幣 a wand with hemp and paper streamers (used in a *Shinto* ceremony) ¶ ご幣をかつぐ be superstitious.

---

body who comes will be welcome.

ごはん ご飯ですよ. Breakfast [Dinner, Supper] is ready!

こびりつく あの日の悲惨な光景が頭にこびりついて離れない. I cannot forget [erase from my memory] the cruel sight of that day. | The pitiable scenes of that day are (indelibly) engraved on my mind.

こぶ² 士気を鼓舞するのにはそれが一番だ. This is the best way to raise the morale of the men.

こぶ³ ひどく殴られて頭にこぶが出来た. I was beaten so hard that I got a lump on my head. / こぶが引っ込んだ. The bump has gone down. / 彼はこぶ付きの女と結婚した. He married a widow with a child (by her late husband).

ごぶ 当選するかどうか見込みは五分五分だね. I think it's an even chance that he will win the election.

ごぶさた 長い間ごぶさたいたしまして申し訳ありません. Please excuse me for my long silence.

こぶし² 彼には古武士の風格がある. He has something of the *samurai* about him.

こぶり¹ それよりはこの方が少し小ぶりだ. This is a bit smaller than that.

こぶり² 雪が小降りになってきた.

ごへい² 語弊 ¶語弊がある be misleading; be liable to be misunderstood / こういうと語弊があるかもしれないが... 《文》 I doubt the propriety of the word [expression], but....

こべつ¹ 戸別 ¶戸別に from house to house; from door to door / 戸別訪問をする visit from door to door; 〈選挙で〉 make a house-to-house canvass.

こべつ² 個別 ⇨ここ¹.

コペルニクス (Nicolaus) Copernicus ¶コペルニクスの地動説 the Copernican theory (of the universe) / コペルニクス的転回をする undergo a Copernican change.

ごへんけい 五辺形 a pentagon ¶五辺形の pentagonal.

コペンハーゲン Copenhagen.

ごほう¹ 語法 〈文法〉 grammar; 〈慣用法〉 usage; 〈表現法〉 an expression; 《文》 a mode [way] of expression; wording. 文例⇩

ごほう² 誤報 a false report; wrong information. 文例⇩

ごぼう 【植】 a burdock ¶ごぼう抜きにする pull sth out at a (single) stroke; 〈座り込み中の人を〉 pluck [lift] sb bodily out of (a group of sit-in demonstrators).

こぼうず 小坊主 a young bonze; a boy priest; a novice.

こぼく 古木 an old tree ¶松の古木 an old pine tree / 《文》 a pine tree that has seen many winters.

ごぼごぼ gurgling(ly) ¶ごぼごぼ音がする gurgle; burble.

こぼす 〈水などを〉 spill; drop; 《文》 shed 《tears》; 〈不平を言う〉 complain (about, of); grumble (at, over, about). 用法 spill の過去, 過去分詞形には spilled, spilt の 2 つがあるが, spilled は〈主に米〉, spilt は〈主に英〉.

こぼね 小骨 small [fine] bones ¶小骨の多い魚 a fish full of fine bones.

こぼれる 〈落ちる〉 fall; drop; spill ⇨こぼす 用法 〈あふれる〉 overflow; run over; 〈散らかる〉 be scattered; 〈〈刃などが〉欠ける〉 be chipped; be nicked.

ごほん ¶ごほんごほんとせきをする give [have] a hacking cough.

こぼんのう 子煩悩 a fond [good, loving] parent [father, mother] ¶子煩悩である love one's children dearly.

こま¹ 独楽 top ¶こまを回す spin a top.

こま² 駒 〈将棋の〉 a (chess)man; a piece; 〈楽器の〉 a bridge ¶〈将棋で〉駒を動かす make a move; move a piece / 駒を進める ⇨しんしゅつ¹ / 大[小駒] a major [minor] piece / 駒組 (a) formation.

こま³ 齣 〈フィルムの〉 a frame; 〈場面〉 a scene; 〈大学の授業の〉 a class.

ごま¹ 胡麻 【植】 a sesame; 〈実〉 sesame (seed) ¶ごまをする grind [crush] sesame (seeds); 〈へつらう〉 flatter; curry favor with; toady (to) / ごまあえ a dish dressed with sesame sauce / ごま油 sesame(-seed) oil / ごま塩 sesame and salt / ごま塩頭 (a man with) grizzled [pepper-and-salt] hair.

ごま² 護摩 【仏教】 ¶護摩を焚(ﾀ)く burn small pieces of wood on the altar to invoke divine help.

コマーシャル a commercial message [announcement]; a 《radio, TV》 commercial ¶コマーシャルの時間 a commercial break / コマーシャルソング a commercial song.

こまい 古米 old [long-stored] rice.

こまいぬ 狛犬 《a pair of》 (stone-carved) guardian dogs (placed at the gate or in front of a Shinto shrine).

こまかい 細かい 〈小さい〉 small; fine; 〈詳細な〉 detailed; 《文》 minute; full; 〈厳密に〉 strict; exact; close; particular; 〈金銭に〉 stingy; careful 《with one's money》; 《文》 thrifty ¶細かい印刷 small [close] print / 細かいお金 〈小銭〉 small change / 〈小額の金〉 a small sum of money / 細かい事 〈些事〉 《文》 a trifling matter; 《文》 a trifle; 〈詳細〉 《文》 a minute detail / 細かい注意 《文》 meticulous care; 〈指示〉 detailed instructions / 細かく, 細かに 〈細片に〉 to [in] pieces; 〈細部に〉 《文》 minutely; fully; in detail; 〈厳密に〉 closely; strictly / 細かく切る cut sth fine [into small pieces]; cut sth up / 細かく調べる examine sth closely / 細かく分ける subdivide sth (into smaller parts) / 千円札を細かくする change a 1,000-yen note (into 100-yen coins); break a 1,000-yen note. 文例⇩

ごまかし trickery; 《文》 (a) deception ¶ごまかしの false; 《文》 fraudulent.

ごまかす 〈だます〉 deceive; cheat; take sb in; 〈着服する〉 embezzle; pocket; 〈うまく逃げる〉 evade (a question); dodge (a tax) ¶勘定をごまかす cook up a bill / 年齢をごまかす lie about [《文》 misrepresent] one's age / 量目をごまかす give short measure [weight] / 笑ってごまかす laugh off 《sb's suspicions》. 文例⇩

The snow is letting [easing] up. | It isn't snowing so [is snowing less] hard. / 雨は小降りになって, 霧雨に変わった。 The rain eased to a fine misty drizzle.

ごほう¹ アメリカの語法ではその言い方は一般に認められている。 According to American usage, the expression is acceptable.

ごほう² それは誤報であった。 The report turned out to be [to have been] false. / その新聞にはときどき誤報が載る。 That paper often gives [carries] false reports.

こぼす 机にインキをこぼしてしまった。 I spilled some ink on the desk. / いまさらこぼしたってはじまらない。 It is no use crying over spilt milk. 【諺】

こぼれる テーブルをがたがたさせないで。 コーヒーがこぼれるから。 Don't shake the table, or the coffee will spill.

こまかい あの人は細かいところに気がつく。〈観察が〉 He is a shrewd observer. | 〈思いやりがある〉 He is very considerate of other people's feelings). / 彼は〈金銭の事に細かい。 He is very exacting in money matters.

ごまかす あの男に五千円ごまかされた。 I was cheated out of 5,000 yen by him. / そんなことを言ってもごまかされないぞ。 I'm not going to be put off [taken in] by anything like that.

こまぎれ 細切れ ¶肉のこまぎれ hashed [chopped] meat / こまぎれにしてもらう have (the meat) hashed [chopped].

こまく 鼓膜 〖解〗 the tympanum (*pl.* -na, -s); the tympanic membrane; the eardrum ¶鼓膜が破れる have *one*'s eardrum split [ruptured].

こまごま 細々 ¶こまごまと in (great) detail; in full; 〖文〗 minutely.

こましゃくれた 〈ませた〉 precocious; 〈生意気な〉 pert; saucy.

こまた 小股 ¶小股の切れ上がった女 a woman with a good figure / 小股に歩く walk with short, quick steps / 小股をすくう trip *sb* up / 小股取り〖レスリング・相撲〗 a trip.

こまづかい 小間使い a lady's maid.

こまどり 駒鳥 a Japanese robin.

こまねく 拱く ¶腕をこまねく fold *one*'s arms / 腕をこまねいて傍観する look on with folded arms; be an idle onlooker.

こまねずみ 〖動〗 a Japanese dancing [waltzing] mouse ¶こまねずみのように働く work like a beaver [bee].

こまむすび 小間結び 〖米〗 a square knot;〖主に英〗a reef knot; a flat knot.

こまめ 小まめ ¶こまめに働く work like a beaver [bee];〖口語〗beaver away (at *one*'s work);〖文〗work diligently.

ごまめ dried young anchovies ¶ごまめの歯ぎしり kicking against the pricks.

こまもの 小間物 fancy goods;〖米〗notions; 〖英〗haberdashery ¶小間物屋〈店〉 a fancy goods store [shop];〖米〗a notions store;〖英〗a haberdashery;〈人〉a fancy goods dealer; 〖英〗a haberdasher.

こまやか 濃やか ¶こまやかな warm [tender] (affection); close (friendship). 文例⇩

こまる 困る 〈難儀する〉 have difficulty (in doing); have trouble (doing); be in [get into] trouble; be in difficulties; have a hard time (of it); suffer (from); be hard put [〖文〗distressed] (by, with);〈貧窮する〉be badly off; 〈当惑する〉be embarrassed (by, with);〖口語〗be (put) on the spot; be perplexed (by); be put out (by);〈不便を感じる〉be inconvenienced ¶返答に困る do not know what answer to make; be at a loss for an answer / 食糧の欠乏で困る suffer from lack of food / 人に見られたら困る手紙 a compromising letter / 金に困っている be pressed [hard up] for money / The trouble is 《((that) ...)》;〈いっそう悪いことには〉to make matters worse / 困らせる 〈悩ます〉 trouble *sb* 《(with questions)》;〈当惑させる〉embarrass; put *sb* out;〖口語〗put *sb* on the spot;〈不便をかける〉inconvenience / 困り切る be nonplussed; 〖文〗be greatly perplexed; be in a bad [pretty] fix; be at *one*'s wits' end / 困り者 〈やくざ者〉a good-for-nothing (fellow);〈厄介者〉a nuisance; a black sheep.

こまわり 小回り ¶小回りがきく〈自動車が〉 have a small [tight] turning circle;〈比喩的に〉can adapt quickly to new circumstances; be very adaptable.

こみ 込み ¶〈付属品など〉すべて込みの値段 an all-in price / 込みで in the lump / 込み込み 15万円の月給 a monthly salary of 150,000 yen, inclusive of taxes; a gross salary of 150,000 yen.

ごみ 〈ちり〉 dust;〈くず〉 rubbish;〖米〗garbage;〖米〗trash; refuse;〖picnic〗 leavings ¶ごみの山 a rubbish heap / ごみ処理 waste [rubbish] disposal / ごみ捨て場〖米〗a garbage dump;〖英〗a rubbish tip; a dumping ground / ごみ取り車 a garbage cart [truck];〖英〗a dustcart / ごみ箱〖ため〗〖米〗a trash [a garbage, an ash] can;〖英〗a dustbin / ごみ屋〖米〗a garbage collector;〖英〗a dustman;〖英〗a dustbinman. 文例⇩

こみあう 込[混]み合う ⇨こむ.

こみあげる 込み上げる 〈吐きけを催す〉 retch; 〖文〗feel nausea;〈感情が〉〖文〗well up within *one*; be filled with (joy) (人が主語); fill *one*'s heart with (anger) (事が主語). 文例⇩

こみいる 込み入る be complicated; be entangled ¶込み入った〈複雑な〉 complicated; 〖文〗complex;〖文〗intricate;〈精巧な〉 elaborate. 文例⇩

ごみごみ ¶ごみごみしている be squalid; be messy / ごみごみした裏通り a squalid alley.

こみだし 小見出し a subtitle; a subheading.

こみち 小道 〈狭い道〉 a (narrow) path; a lane; 〈路地〉 an alley.

コミッショナー a commissioner.

こみみ 小耳 ¶小耳にはさむ〈人が主語〉happen to (over)hear《(that...)》;〈事が主語〉casually come to *one*'s knowledge.

こまやか 女性の方が男性より感情がこまやかだというのはうそだ. I don't think it's true that women have finer [more delicate] feelings than men.

こまる これは困りましたね. That's too bad. / この問題にはだれも困るだろう. This question would be difficult for anyone. / 君は肉以外のものは食べないんだから困る. The trouble with you is that you never eat anything but meat. / たださえ困っているところへ病人までできた. To make matters worse, one of them fell ill. / 彼がいなくては困るよ. We cannot do without him. / お宅の犬にほえられて困りました. Your dog gave me a bad time. / 雨が降ると困るから傘を持って行きなさい. Take an umbrella in case it rains. / 村の人は橋を流されて非常に困っている. The bridge was washed away, much to the inconvenience of the villagers. / 約束を守ってくれなくちゃ困る. You must keep your promise. / 困った事になった. Things have come to a pretty pass. | Now we are in a real fix〖口語〗in the soup. / そのうちに困った事になりますよ. You'll find yourself in trouble [in deep water] one of these days. / また一つ困った事がある. Here is another problem. / 困ったお天気ですね. Nasty weather, isn't it?

ごみ ごみ捨てるべからず. 〖掲示〗〈公園などで〉 No litter. |〈ごみ捨て場でない所に〉 No dumping (here).

コミューン a commune ¶パリコミューン《西洋史》the Commune (of Paris).

コミュニケ a communiqué ¶コミュニケを発表する[読み上げる] issue [read] a communiqué / 共同コミュニケ a joint communiqué.

コミュニケーション communication(s) ¶コミュニケーションの断絶 a breakdown in communication; a communication gap.

コミンテルン the Comintern ★ the Communist International の略.

コミンフォルム the Cominform ★ the Communist Information Bureau の略.

こむ 込む be crowded;《文》be congested;《文》be thronged 《with people》/ 込んだ電車 a crowded train / 手の込んだ elaborate 《workmanship》; intricate 《designs》. 文例◊

ゴム 〈樹液〉gum;〈弾性ゴム〉rubber;〈消しゴム〉《米》an eraser;《英》a rubber;〈歯に詰める〉gutta-percha ¶ゴムの木 a gum tree; a rubber plant [tree] / ゴムを引く coat *sth* with rubber; rubberize / ゴムを入れて伸縮自在にする elasticize 《a swimming suit》/ ゴム状の gummy; rubbery / ゴム用ゴムスタンプ a rubber stamp / ゴム園 a rubber plantation / ゴム靴 rubber shoes [boots] / ゴム底の rubber-soled 《shoes》/ ゴムのり gum (arabic); mucilage / ゴムひも (a piece of) elastic; an elastic (cord, string, tape) / ゴム製品 rubber goods / ゴム風船 a rubber balloon / ゴムボート a rubber boat [raft] / ゴムまり a rubber ball / ゴム輪 → わゴム.

こむぎ 小麦 wheat ¶小麦色の light-brown / 小麦色に日焼けした肌 a bronzed [beautifully (sun)tanned] skin / 小麦粉 (wheat) flour / 小麦畑 a wheat field.

こむすめ 小娘 a young girl; a slip of a girl.

こむそう 虚無僧 a mendicant Zen priest of the Fuke sect (, wearing a sedge hood and playing a *shakuhachi*).

こむらがえり ¶こむらがえりを起こす get [《文》be seized with] (a) cramp in the calf [leg] ★ a cramp は《主に米》, cramp は《主に英》.

こめ 米 rice ¶米をとぐ[炊く] wash [cook] rice / 米倉 a rice granary 〈warehouse, storehouse〉/ 米俵 a straw rice-bag / 米粒 a grain of rice / 米所 a rice-producing district / 米びつ a rice bin / 米屋〈店〉a rice store;〈人〉a rice dealer.

こめかみ《解》the temple.

こめつき 米搗き cleaning rice.

こめる 込める〈算入する〉count *sth* in; include;〈弾丸を〉load ¶銃に弾丸をこめる load [charge] a gun / 全身の力をこめて with all *one*'s strength / 心をこめて with all *one*'s heart; wholeheartedly. 文例◊

こめん 湖面 the surface of a lake.

ごめん 御免 ¶ごめんをこうむる《文》excuse *oneself* 《from doing》;《文》decline; beg off 《from *sth*》/ ごめんこうむって with your permission;《文》by your leave. 文例◊

ごめんたい 五面体 a pentahedron (*pl.* -s,-dra).

こも 薦 straw matting;〈1枚〉a straw [rush] mat ¶こもかぶり a *sake* cask wrapped in a rush mat / こも包みにする wrap *sth* in straw matting.

ごもく 五目 ¶五目並べ《play》gobang / 五目飯 Japanese pilaf; rice steamed in stock with vegetables (, fish and [or] chicken).

こもごも 〈かわるがわる〉by turns; alternately;〈あいついで〉one after another; in succession.

こもじ 小文字 a small letter;《印刷》lower case (略: l.c.); a lower-case letter.

こもち 子持ち〈妊婦〉a pregnant woman;〈親〉a parent ¶子持ちである〈妊娠している〉be pregnant; be expecting a child; be (big) with young 《獣が》; have spawn [roe]《魚が》;〈子供がいる〉have a family; be a mother [father] / 5人の子持ちである be the mother [father] of five children.

こもの 小物 〈こまごました品々や道具〉small articles;〈小人物〉a person of very little [no] importance; an unimportant [insignificant] fellow; small fry (集合的) ¶（自動車のダッシュボードにある）小物入れ a glove compartment. 文例◊

こもり 子守 a (dry) nurse; a nursemaid; a baby-sitter (留守居を頼まれる) ¶子守をする nurse [look after, take care of] a baby;〈留守居を頼まれて〉baby-sit / 子守歌 a lullaby; a cradle song / 子守歌を歌って子供を寝かす sing a child to sleep.

こもる 籠もる〈引きこもる〉shut *oneself* up 《in》; be confined 《to *one*'s room》;〈充満する（場所が主語）〉be full 《of》; be filled《with》¶（室内が）こもっている be stuffy; be close / 愛情のこもった言葉 affectionate words. 文例◊

こみあげる 熱いものがこみ上げてきた. Something hot welled up in my eyes.

こみいる 何かそこには込み入った事情があるに違いない. There must be some complicated circumstances behind it. / そうなると問題が込み入ってくるだろう. That will complicate the matter.

こみあう 込まないといけないから早く行こう. Let's go early to avoid the rush. | 〈自動車で〉Let's start early to avoid the traffic.

こめる その中には女中さんへのチップもこめてある. The tip for the chambermaid is included (in it). / 一心をこめてやれば何でも出来る. If you do it with your whole heart, you will succeed.

ごめん ごめん下さい. Hallo! | May I come in? / ごめんなさい.〈わびる時〉Sorry. | Pardon me. /〈座をはずす時〉ちょっとごめん下さい. Excuse me (for) a minute. / そんな事はごめんこうむりましょう. I would rather be excused from [not be involved in] that sort of thing. / お先へごめん下さい. Excuse me for going first [ahead]. / もう遅いからごめんこうむります. I must be going [With your permission I'll leave] now; it is so late.

こもの あの男は政治家としては小物だ. He is of no importance in political circles. | He is a small-time politician.

こもる タバコの煙が部屋に一杯にこもっている. The room is filled [heavy] with tobacco smoke. / 彼の一語一語には熱誠がこもって

こもれび 木洩れ日 sunlight filtering [sifting] down through the trees.

コモロ ¶コモロ諸島 the Comoro Islands; the Comoros / コモロ諸島の Comoro / コモロイスラム連邦共和国 the Federal Islamic Republic of the Comoros.

こもん 顧問 an adviser [advisor] (to); (米) a counselor ¶技術顧問 a technical advisor / 顧問団 an advisory group; (米) a brain(s) trust; 《口語》a think tank / 顧問弁護士 a legal adviser; a corporation lawyer (会社の); a family lawyer (家の).

こもんじょ 古文書 old (historical) documents; ancient [old] manuscripts ¶古文書学 paleography.

こや 小屋 a hut; a shed;〈掘っ建て小屋〉a shack;〈家畜の〉a pen;〈見世物の〉a booth; a《circus》tent;〈劇場の〉a theater ¶小屋を掛ける put up a shed;〈サーカスの〉hoist [put up] a big top.

こやぎ 小やぎ a kid; a young goat.

こやく 子役〈役者〉a child actor [actress];〈役割〉(play) a child's part.

ごやく 誤訳 (a) mistranslation;(a) wrong translation ¶誤訳する mistranslate; make a mistake [(an) error] in translation.

こやくにん 小役人 a petty official.

こやし 肥やし〈肥料〉manure; (a) fertilizer;〈下肥え〉night soil.

こやす 肥やす fertilize; enrich ¶私腹を肥やす⇒しふく² / 土地を肥やす make the soil fertile /〈肥料をやって〉fertilize the soil.

こやすがい 子安貝 a cowrie; a cowry.

こやま 小山 a (small) hill; a hillock.

こやみ 小止み a lull ¶小やみになる《文》abate; let up / 小やみなく incessantly; without letting up [(a) letup].

こゆう 固有〈特有の〉《文》peculiar (to); one's own;〈本来の〉《文》proper (to); 〈特性の〉《文》characteristic (of); typical《of》;〈生得の〉《文》inherent (in); native; inborn / 固有の性質 a characteristic; a peculiarity / 日本固有の動植物 plants and animals indigenous [native] to Japan / 固有名詞《文法》a proper noun. 文例⇩

こゆき 小雪 a light snowfall; a little snow.

こゆび 小指〈手の〉the little finger;《米口語》the pinkie;〈足の〉the little toe.

こよい 今宵 this evening; tonight.

こよう 雇用 employment; hire ¶雇用する employ; engage; hire; take (a worker) on / 雇用条件[契約] terms [a contract] of employment / 雇用主 an employer. 文例⇩

ごよう¹ 御用〈用事〉your business;〈注文〉your order ¶御用聞きに回る go the rounds of one's customers (taking orders); visit the customers on one's regular route / 御用納め the last business day of the year at the government offices / 政府の御用学者 a scholar kept [patronized] by the government / 御用組合 a company [kept] union / 御用商人[達(辛)] a purveyor (to the Imperial Household) / 御用邸 an Imperial villa / 御用始め the resumption [reopening] of office business after the New Year holidays. 文例⇩

ごよう² 誤用 (a) misuse;《文》(an) abuse;《文》(a) misapplication (適用の誤り) ¶誤用する misuse;《文》(a) misapply.

コヨーテ【動】a coyote.

こよみ 暦 a calendar;〈1冊の本になって、年中行事などが書かれているもの〉an almanac ¶暦の上では according to the calendar. 文例⇩

こより (a) paper string ¶こよりをよる twist 文例⇩ paper into a string.

コラージュ【美術】(a) collage.

コラール【音楽】a chorale.

こらい 古来 from old [ancient] times;《文》from time immemorial ¶古来の (age-)old; ancient; time-honored. 文例⇩

ごらいこう 御来光 the sunrise seen from the top of a high mountain.

こらえしょう 堪え性 ⇒にんたい (忍耐力).

こらえる 堪える〈我慢する〉bear; stand; put up with;《文》endure;〈忍耐する〉persevere; be patient;〈抑制する〉control; keep [hold] back ¶痛さをこらえる stand [《文》endure] the pain / 笑いをこらえる stifle [suppress] one's laughter / こらえ難い unbearable;《文》unendurable / こらえかねて unable to bear (it) any longer; running out of patience. 文例⇩

ごらく 娯楽 amusement(s); recreation(s); (a) pastime ¶娯楽雑誌 a magazine for amusement / 娯楽施設 amusement [recreational] facilities / 娯楽室 a recreation [games] room / 娯楽場 a place of amusement / (ラジオ・テレ

いた. His sincerity shone through in every word he spoke.

こゆう 神道は日本固有の宗教である. Shinto is the native religion of Japan.

こよう 女性の雇用の機会は非常に多くなっている. Employment opportunities for women have greatly expanded.

ごよう¹ 何かご用はありませんか. Can I do anything [What can I do] for you? | May [Can] I help you? / 太郎, お父さんが御用ですよ. Father wants you, Taro. / 何の御用ですか. What do you want with me? / 御用の方は裏口へお回り下さい. Visitors are requested to go to the back door. / ええ, お安い御用です. Certainly, with pleasure. / いつでも御用を勤めます. I'm always at your service. / 御用だ! You're under arrest.

こよみ 暦の上ではもう2週間前から春だ. Officially [According to the calendar], it has been spring for two weeks.

こら こら, 待て. Hey, you! Wait! / こら, そんなことはよせ. Look here! None of that.

こらい 人生七十古来まれなり. Man seldom lives to be seventy years old.

こらえる 彼は泣きたいのをじっとこらえた. He manfully held back his tears [《文》forbore to cry].

ごらん ちょっとこれをご覧. Just look at this. / それご覧. There! Didn't I tell you? / この町には別にご覧になるようなものはありません. There is nothing worth seeing in this town. / もう一度やってご覧. Try it again.

こりごり 借金はもうこりごりだ. I learned to my cost [I know by

こらしめ 懲らしめ (a) punishment; 《文》 chastisement; discipline ¶ 懲らしめのために as a lesson (to); for disciplinary purposes.

こらしめる, こらす[1] 懲らしめる, 懲らす〈罰する〉 punish; 《文》 discipline; teach sb a lesson; 《文》 chastise; 〈しかる〉 scold; 《口語》 give sb a (good) talking-to [telling-off].

こらす[2] 凝らす concentrate 《one's attention on sth》; devote 《oneself to sth》 ¶ 思いを凝らす 《文》 meditate [ponder] 《on》 / 工夫を凝らす work out 《文》 elaborate》 a plan; make an ingenious plan; 《文》 exercise one's ingenuity 《to do》 / ひとみを凝らす ⇒ひとみ.

ごらん 御覧 〈見よ〉 look!; 〈…してみよ〉 try (and do, doing); have a try [go] at 《doing》 ¶ ご覧のとおり as you see / ご覧に入れる show (it to you) / ご覧になる see; inspect.

こり[1] 梱 a bale; a package.

こり[2] 凝り stiffness (in the shoulders).

コリー a collie (dog).

ごりおし ごり押し ¶ ごり押しをやる 《口語》 railroad (a plan through a meeting); 《口語》 steamroller (the opposition).

こりかたまる 凝り固まる 〈凝結する〉 curdle; coagulate; 〈熱中する〉 be fanatical 《in one's beliefs》; be a bigot 《about religion》 / 熱中する》 be given up 《to》; be addicted 《to》; be absorbed 《in》.   「ing; smart.

こりこう 小利口 ¶ 小利口な clever; know-

こりごり 懲り懲り ⇒こりる ¶ こりごりだ have had enough (of); 《口語》 be sick (of); 《口語》 be fed up (to the back teeth) 《with》; 《俗》 have had a bellyful 《of》.

こりしょう 凝り性 ¶ 凝り性の 〈物事に熱中する〉 (a person) who tends to get immersed in [《口語》 go overboard for] anything he does 《undertakes》; 〈細かい〉 fastidious; finicky / 凝り性の映画監督 a very particular [finicky] film director.

こりつ 孤立 isolation ¶ 孤立する be isolated; stand alone; be friendless / 孤立した isolated; 《文》 solitary / 孤立語 【言語】〈同系統の言語のない言語〉 an isolated language; 〈中国語のような, 語形変化を持たない言語〉 an isolating language / 孤立主義 isolationism / 孤立政策 an isolationist policy.

ごりむちゅう 五里霧中 ¶ 五里霧中である be in a fog 《about》; be (all) at sea.

こりや 凝り屋 ⇒こりしょう.

こりゃ

ごりやく 御利益 divine help [grace].

こりょ 顧慮 consider; mind; pay attention to sth; take sth into consideration [account] / …を顧慮しないで without regard to …; regardless of…; without minding….

ごりょう 御陵 an Imperial mausoleum ¶ 多摩御陵 the Tama Mausoleum.

こりょうりや 小料理屋 a small restaurant; an eating house.

ゴリラ【動】a gorilla.

こりる 懲りる learn [grow wiser] by experience; find [know] sth to one's cost ¶ 失敗して懲りる learn a lesson from one's failure.

ごりん 五輪 ⇒オリンピック ¶ 五輪旗 the Olym-「pic flag.

コリントしき コリント式 【建】 the Corinthian order ¶ コリント式の柱 a Corinthian column.

こる 凝る 〈肩などが〉 get [grow, 《文》 become] stiff; 〈熱中する〉 be absorbed 《in》; be devoted [given up] 《to》; be crazy 《for》 ¶ 肩が凝る have a stiff shoulder; one's shoulder is [shoulders are] stiff; feel stiff in the shoulders / 競馬に凝っている have a passion for [《口語》 be hooked on] horse racing / 凝った elaborate 《designs》; 《文》 exquisite 《workmanship》.

コルク cork; 〈コルクの栓〉 a cork ¶ コルクの栓をする [抜く] cork [uncork] (a bottle) / コルクの栓をした瓶 a corked bottle / コルク抜き a corkscrew.

コルシカ (the island of) Corsica ¶ コルシカの Corsican / コルシカ人 a Corsican.

コルセット a corset.

コルネット【音楽】a cornet ¶ コルネット奏者 a cornet(t)ist.

ゴルフ golf ¶ ゴルフをする play golf; golf / ゴルフをする人, ゴルフ選手 a golfer / ゴルフに行く go golfing / ゴルフ場 golf links / ゴルフズボン plus fours / ゴルフ練習場 a golf practice range; a (golf) driving range.

コルホーズ《ロシア語》 a kolkhoz; a collective farm.

これ[1] this (pl. these) ¶ これで now; here; with this / これという理由もなく without

---

experience] what it is to be in debt. / イタリア料理はもうこりごりした. I don't think I'll have anything more to do with Italian food. / I've had a hideous experience with Italian food; it's been a lesson to me.
こりしょう あの人は本当に凝り性だ. He tends to get totally immersed [absorbed] in anything he undertakes. | 《口語》 Whatever he does, he always goes overboard [《俗》 goes the whole hog].
こりつ 孤立無援となってもなお彼は闘いを止めなかった. Deserted by all his friends, he fought on alone.
ごりむちゅう 仕事に就いて最初の1か月間は全く五里霧中だった. During my first month in my new job, I was completely at sea. / どうしたらいいのか五里霧中だよ. I don't have the foggiest idea [I'm quite at a loss as to] what to do.
こりゃ こりゃ大変だ. Oh, this is dreadful! / こりゃ驚いた. Really! This is a surprise (to me)!
ごりやく ご利益があった. My prayers were answered [heard].

こりょ 世間の取りざたなどは顧慮しない. I don't care at all what people say about me.
こりる 彼はこの一度の失敗に懲りて二度と相場に手を出さなかった. This single failure taught him what it is to dabble in speculation, and he never tried again after that. / どうぞ, これにお懲りにならずにおいで下さい. I hope I shall see more of you.
こる ダーウィンは興味を覚えるとあくまでそれに凝る性質であった. Charles Darwin's nature was to go heart and soul into any-

これ any particular reason / こればかりの so [such a] little [small, trifling] / これだけ, これぐらい〈数〉so many [few];〈量〉so much [little]; this much / これぐらいの高さの《a bookcase》about this tall / これっきり〈全部〉(this is) all;《(there is) no more /〈今度だけ〉(for) this once;〈2度と…しない〉never again / これほど雨が降っても for[(文) despite] all this rain / これから from now on ; after this ; hereafter ; in future / これからの《policy》from now on ; future 《events》/ これから 2 年すると in two years from now ;《文》two years hence ; in two more years / これこれの such and such / これまで〈今まで〉so far ;《文》thus far ; until now ; up to this day ; to date /〈ここまで〉《文》thus far ; up to this point / 生まれてからこれまでに (never) in *one's* life / これまでのように as before ; as ever / もうこれまでと思う give up all hope / これ見よがしに《文》ostentatiously ; for show ; to show off / これより先〈時〉before this ;《文》prior to this ;《文》previously ;〈話変わって〉meanwhile ;〈位置〉(up) ahead ; further on [ahead]; beyond this place. 文例⇩

これ²〈呼びかけ〉look here ; listen ; I say ;《米》say.

コレステロール【生化】cholesterol ¶ 低[高]コレステロール食品 low-[high-]cholesterol food.

コレラ cholera ¶ コレラ患者 a cholera patient ; a case of cholera / コレラ菌 a cholera germ [bacterium, bacillus]. 文例⇩

ころ¹ 頃〈時〉time ;〈およそ〉about ; around ;〈する頃〉when ; while ¶ その頃 in those days ; at the [that] time ; then / 若かりし頃 while [when] (*one* was) young / 10 時頃 (at) about [around] ten o'clock / 日暮れ頃 toward evening ; at nightfall.

ころ² a《log》roller.

ごろ 語呂 ¶ 語呂がいい sound pleasant [good, nice];《文》be pleasing to the ear ;《文》be euphonious /〈語呂が悪い〉sound unpleasant ; jar on *one's* ears [《文》on the ear] ;《文》lack euphony / 語呂合わせ a play on words ; a pun.

ゴロ【野球】a grounder ; a ground ball ¶ ゴロを打つ knock a grounder ; ground《to first》/ ゴロを打ってアウトになる ground out《to third》.

ころあい 頃合 ¶ 頃合の suitable《for》; (just) right《for》; fit《for》/ 頃合を計る calculate time ; time (*one's* actions) / 頃合を計って at the right moment ; in the nick of time.

コロイド【化】colloid ¶ コロイド状の colloidal / コロイド化学 colloid chemistry / コロイド溶液 a colloidal solution.

ころう 故[古]老〈老人〉an old man ;〈古くからの住人〉an old resident ¶ 村の故老 an old villager ; one of the oldest residents of the village.

ころがき ころ柿 a dried persimmon.

ころがす 転がす roll《a ball》; trundle《a barrel》;〈倒す〉throw *sb* down ; trip *sb* up (足をすくって).

ころがる 転がる〈回転する〉roll (over) ; trundle ;〈倒れる〉tumble [fall] down ;〈寝ころぶ〉lie down ; throw *oneself* down ¶ 転がり込む〈転がって入る〉roll into《a hole》;〈不意に現われる〉turn up (unexpectedly)《at *sb's* house》;〈口語〉land (*oneself*) on *sb* /〈思いがけなく手に入る(人が主語)〉come into《a big fortune》.

ごろく 語録 quotations《from》; the sayings《of Mao Zedong》;《文》analects《of》.

ころおちる 転げ落ちる fall [tumble] down [off].

ころげまわる 転げ回る roll [tumble] about ; toss about (in agony) ; writhe (about) (in agony) ; thrash about (のた打ち回る).

ころころ ¶ ころころ転がる roll over and

---

thing in which he was interested. / 凝っては思案にあたわず. Too much thinking will get you nowhere.

これ¹ これだけは本当だ. This much is true. / わが身を恥じるという気持ちなどこれっぽかりも持ち合わせていない男だ. He hasn't got an ounce of shame in him. | He is utterly lost to all [any] sense of shame. / これかと選択に迷った. I was at a loss which of them to select [which to choose from among them]. / これ以上の品はございません. This is the best of its kind. / これでおいとまします. I must say good-bye now. / これという絵は一つも持っておりません. I've no paintings worth mentioning to speak of]. / これでも私は幸福なのです. In my way [Such as I am], I'm a happy man. / これだけあれば当分これで間に合う. This will last me for some time. / 今日はこれまで. So much [That will be all] for today. / 僕の有り金はこれっきりだ. This is all the money I have (with me). / これほど悪いとは思わなかった. I didn't think [suspect] it was as bad as this. / これほど頼んでも聞いてもらえないのですか. Will nothing I say persuade you to agree? | Do you still mean to turn me down, however humbly I ask [however I plead with you]? / これほど言ってもまだ自分の間違いがわからないのか. Is this not enough to convince you that you are (in the) wrong? / これから駅へ行ってもその列車に間に合えしょうか. Won't I be too late for the train, if I go to the station now? / さあこれからが仕事の一番難しいところだ. Now, we come to the hardest part of the job. / これからだんだん寒くなる. The cold season is coming. | The weather is going to get colder. / 本当に暑いのはこれからだ. The hottest season has yet to come. / もうこれからはこういうことはいたしません. I will never do anything like this in future. / これこれの場合にはこれこれと言えと教えてくれた. He told me that on such and such an occasion I should say so and so. / 用事はこれこれしかじかとはっきり言いなさい. State your business clearly. | Say clearly what you have come here for. / 彼はこれまでよりよほどよく働いております. He is working much harder than before. / もうこれまでだ. It is all over for me [us]! / 彼はこれしきのことで驚くものか. He is the last man to be disconcerted by such a trifling matter. / これしきの事で決心を変えるつもりはない. It would

ごろごろ over / ころころと太った小犬 a chubby puppy.

ごろごろ ¶ごろごろする〈転がる〉roll /〈ぶらくらする〉idle *one's* time away; loaf around; lie about / ごろごろしている〈場所が主語〉be full of;《文》be strewn 《with》;〈物が主語〉be lying about (all over the place) /〈車が〉ごろごろ通る rumble along /〈雷などが〉ごろごろ鳴る rumble; roll /〈猫が〉のどをごろごろ鳴らす purr / ごろごろいう音 a rumbling sound; a rumble; a roll. 文例⇩

ころし 殺し killing; a murder (case) ¶殺し文句 a telling phrase [expression] / 殺し屋 a (professional) killer;《米俗》a hit man.

ころす 殺す〈生命を奪う〉kill;《文》take *sb's* life; murder;〈屠(ほふ)る〉slaughter; butcher;〈抑える〉suppress, stifle; smother;〈アウトにする〉put [throw, catch]《a runner》out ¶殺すと言っておどす threaten to kill [murder] *sb*;《文》threaten *sb* with death / 殺そうとする make an attempt on *sb's* life. 文例⇩

コロタイプ (a) collotype.

ごろつき〈乱暴漢〉a hoodlum;《米俗》a hood; a ruffian;〈ゆすり〉a blackmailer.

コロッケ a croquette.

コロナ a corona (*pl.* -s, -nae) ¶コロナ放電 (a) corona discharge.

ごろね ごろ寝 ¶ごろ寝する sleep [go to bed] with *one's* clothes on; lie dozing (in *one's* clothes).

ころばす 転ばす ⇨ ころがす.

ころぶ 転ぶ tumble [fall] (down); fall to the ground ¶石につまずいて転ぶ ⇨ つまずく. 文例⇩

ころも 衣〈着衣〉clothes;〈法衣〉a robe, a gown;〈天ぷら[フライ]の〉a batter [breadcrumb] coating /〈ケーキの〉frosting; icing ¶紫の衣をつけた高僧 a high priest in a purple robe / 衣をつける coat《fish》(in batter) / 衣をかける frost [ice]《a cake》/ 衣替(更)(ごろもがえ)え a sea-

sonal change of clothing; changing (*one's*) dress for the season.

コロラチューラ【音楽】coloratura ¶コロラチューラ歌手 a coloratura (soprano).

コロラド Colorado (略: Colo.) ¶コロラド州の人 a Coloradan.

ころりと〈他愛なく〉easily; with no [without (any)] effort;〈突然〉suddenly;〈すっかり〉clean; utterly ¶ころりと参る give up without struggle;《文》yield without (the least) resistance;〈女に〉fall head over heels in love 《with》.

ごろりと ¶ごろりと横になる throw *oneself* down; lie down.

コロン a colon.

コロンビア Colombia ¶コロンビアの Colombian / コロンビア人 a Colombian.

コロンビウム【化】columbium.

コロンブス Christopher Columbus ¶コロンブスの卵 the tradition that Columbus stood a raw egg on its end on the table; a thing that looks easy once it has been done / コロンブスの卵式に簡単に with the simplicity of Columbus' egg.

コロンボ Colombo.

こわい 怖い〈恐ろしい〉frightening;《口語》scary; fearful; dreadful; terrible;〈ぞっとするような〉bloodcurdling; hair-raising;〈恐れる〉こわがる ¶怖い顔をする look fierce [threatening]; scowl (glower)《at》/ 怖い目にあう be frightened《by》; get [have] a fright; have a terrible [dreadful] experience / 怖くなる be [get,《文》become] frightened;《文》be seized with fear. 文例⇩

こわい[2] 強い〈tough; hard; stiff ¶こわいご飯 hard boiled rice. 文例⇩

こわいろ 声色〈声の音色〉a (tone of) voice; a voice quality;〈物まね〉mimicking *sb's* voice; mimicry ¶声色を使う imitate [mimic, copy] *sb's* voice [way of talking] / 声色を使うのが

---

take more than this to make me change my mind. | これはこれは! Dear me! | Heavens! / これはこれはようこそ. Oh! How nice (it is) to see you! | Oh! How kind [nice] of you to come and see us!

これ[2] これ, 窓を閉めておくれ. I say, shut the window!

コレステロール そういうものを食べるとコレステロールが増える. That sort of food will raise the cholesterol level in your blood.

コレラ 世田谷区にコレラが発生した. A case of cholera has been reported from Setagaya Ward.

ころ[1] 元禄15年. It was in the 15th year of Genroku. | あの頃はもっと Things were much better in those days. | 〈感慨たっぷりに〉Those were the days! | 彼は9時前には起きない. He never gets up before [earlier than] nine o'clock. | また6時頃

お会いしましょう. I'll see you again (at) about six o'clock. / あの人を訪ねて大概会えるのはいつ頃でしょうか. What is the most likely time to find him at home?

ころがる こんな石ならその辺にいくらでも転がっている. There are rocks like this lying about anywhere around here. | There is nothing extraordinary about this rock. / 居候が転がり込んで来た.《口語》A freeloader has landed (himself) on me.

ごろごろ 重い荷馬車がごろごろ音を立てて橋を渡って行った. A heavy cart rumbled over the bridge. / 日曜日には家でごろごろしているだけだ. I spend my Sundays idly at home. | I just lie about the house on Sundays.

ころす 殺さば殺せ. Go on, then, kill me, if you dare.

ころぶ 彼は転んで片脚を折った. He broke his leg in a fall. / 転

んでもただは起きない男だ. He turns everything to good account. | 《俗》If he fell in a cesspit, he'd come up smelling of roses. / 転ばぬ先の杖. Prevention is better than cure.《諺》

こわい[1] 何も怖いものはない. There's nothing to be afraid of. / 私は雷が一番怖い. What I dread most is thunder. / 彼は怖いということを知らない. He doesn't know the meaning of (the word) 'fear.' | He does not know what fear is. / 怖い物見たさにのぞいて見た. Curiosity overcame fear, and he had a peep at it. / その崖の上から下をのぞいたら, 彼女は怖くなって口もきけなくなった. She was frightened speechless when she looked down from the top of the cliff.

こわい[2] ご飯が少しこわい. The rice is boiled rather hard.

こわがり(や) / こんきゅう

こわがり(や) 怖がり(屋) a timid person ; a coward.

こわがる 怖がる 《文》 fear ; be afraid 《of》; dread ; be in fear 《of》; be in a fright ¶怖がらせる frighten ; give *sb* a fright ; scare ; terrify ;〈おどす〉intimidate. 文例⇩

こわき 小脇 ¶小わきに抱える carry *sth* under *one*'s arm.

こわけ 小分け (a) subdivision ¶小分けする subdivide.

こわごわ timidly ;《文》with fear ; gingerly (特に, 物にさわる時).

こわざ ごわごわする be stiff《with starch》.

こわざ 小業 (one of) the minor techniques (of *judo*) ¶小業がきく be an expert in [a master of] the finer points [little tricks] 《of *sumo*》.

こわす 壊す 〈破壊する〉break ; destroy ; demolish ; smash ; damage ; ruin ; wreck ; pull [tear] (a house) down ;〈狂わす〉put (a machine) out of order ;〈計画などを〉spoil ; upset ;《文》frustrate ;《文》mar.

こわだんぱん 強談判 ¶強談判する make a strong-worded demand 《for payment》; make a strong protest 《to *sb* against *sth*》.

こわね 声音 a (tone of) voice.

こわばる get [《文》become] stiff ; stiffen (up) ¶こわばった stiff ; hard. 文例⇩

こわもて ¶こわもてがする be made much of [treated with deference] because people are frightened of *one* ;《文》achieve an apparent popularity through fear.

こわれ 壊れ 〈破損〉breakage ; wreckage ;〈破片〉a fragment ; a broken piece ¶壊れ物 a fragile article ; breakables. 文例⇩

こわれる 壊れる 〈砕ける〉break ; be broken ; come to pieces (ばらばらに) ;〈破損する〉be damaged ; be destroyed ;〈故障する〉get out of order ;〈計画などが〉fall through ; miscarry ;〈交渉などが〉be broken off ;《文》be ruptured ¶壊れた皿 a broken plate / 壊れやすい easily broken ; fragile ; frail. 文例⇩

こん¹ 根 〈数〉a root ;《化》a radical ;〈根気〉

こんき² ¶根のいる仕事 work which needs perseverance / 根を詰めて勉強する work [push *oneself*] rather too hard ; apply *oneself* a bit too closely to *one*'s studies / 根限り as long as *one*'s strength lasts ; with all *one*'s might / 根比べ an endurance contest ; a waiting game / 根比べをする have [《文》engage in] an endurance contest 《with》; see which [who] will hold out longer / 根気が続く have *one*'s patience exhausted [worn out] 《by》.

こん² 紺 dark [deep] blue ; navy blue ¶紺の deep-[navy-]blue.

こん- 今... this 《season》; the present 《term》.

こんい 懇意 ¶懇意な friendly ; familiar ; intimate (★ intimate は男女間の性的な関係を言う時に使われることが多いので注意) / 懇意になる get to know *sb* (well [better]) ;《文》become acquainted 《with》; make *sb*'s acquaintance / 懇意にしている be friends 《with》; be on friendly [intimate] terms 《with》. 文例⇩

こんいん 婚姻 ⇨けっこん ¶婚姻届 a notification of *one*'s marriage / 婚姻届を出す register *one*'s marriage.

こんかい 今回 ⇨こんど.

こんがい 婚外 ¶婚外交渉 extramarital sex [《文》(sexual) relations] 《with》.

こんがすり 紺絣 dark-blue cloth with white splash patterns.

こんがらかる 〈糸などが〉get [《文》become] entangled ;〈話などが〉get confused [mixed (up)] ;〈事件などが〉get [《文》become] complicated. 文例⇩

こんがり ¶こんがり(と)焼ける be done [cooked] to a beautiful brown ; be perfectly browned.

こんかん 根幹 〈基本〉the basis (*pl.* bases) ;〈中核〉the nucleus (*pl.* nuclei) ;〈基調〉the keynote.

こんがん 懇願 《文》(an) entreaty ¶懇願する《文》entreat ; implore ; plead (with *sb* to *do* [for *sth*]) ; beg. 文例⇩

こんき¹ 今期 this [the present] term [period] ¶今期国会 the present [current] session of the Diet.

こんき² 根気 《文》perseverance ; patience ⇨ **こん¹** ¶根気がいる need [《文》require] patience [perseverance] / 根気のよい persevering ; patient ; untiring / 根気よく patiently ;《文》with patience [perseverance] ; untiringly / 根気が尽きる run out of energy ; find *one*'s energy exhausted ; be unable to carry on any longer.

こんき³ 婚期 (the) marriageable age ¶婚期を逸する be past (the) marriageable age ; become an old maid / 婚期に達した娘 a girl of marriageable age.

こんきゅう 困窮 poverty ;《文》destitution ;《文》distress ¶困窮する get [《文》become] poor ; be reduced to poverty / 困窮している be poor ;《文》be destitute ; be badly off ;《文》

こわがる 間違いを怖がって話さないと、いつまでたっても英会話は上手になれない。You will never speak English well if you avoid speaking for fear of making mistakes. / 何も怖がる事はない。You have nothing to fear. / 彼は怖がって犬に近寄らなかった。He was afraid to come near the dog.

こわす これらの家を壊してその跡地にホテルを建てることになっている。These houses are coming [are to be pulled] down to make way for a hotel. / 深酒をすると胃を壊すよ。If you drink too much you'll get stomach trouble.

こわばる 彼女はむっつりと顔をこわばらせたままだった。Her face was set in a sulky look.

こわれ 壊れ物一取扱い注意. 《包装表記》Fragile — Handle with care. / 彼女をまるで壊れ物でも扱うように扱った。They handled her as if she were made of porcelain.

こわれる 壊れかかったような古い家だった。It was a tumbledown old house. | The house was very old and in a condition of near ruin. / このラジオは壊れている。This radio is out of order. / その縁談は壊れてしまった。The planned match has been broken off.

こんい 僕らはふとしたことから懇意になった。We got acquainted

こんきょ 根拠 a basis (*pl.* bases); ground(s); 《典拠》authority ¶根拠のある《文》well-grounded[-founded] / 根拠のない unfounded; groundless / 根拠地 a base (of operations). 文例⇩

ごんぎょう 勤行 a religious service.

こんく 困苦 hardship(s); 《文》privations; suffering(s) ¶困苦をなめる go through hardships; suffer privations / 困苦欠乏にたえる bear 《文》endure] hardships (and privations); live an austere life.

ゴング a gong.

コンクール [<《フランス語》*concours*] a (musical) contest; a competition ¶コンクールに参加する enter [《文》participate in] a contest.

コンクリート concrete ¶コンクリートの壁 a concrete wall / コンクリートで固める[を塗る] concrete (the road); cover (the path) with concrete / コンクリート打ち concreting / コンクリートミキサー a concrete [cement] mixer.

コングロマリット 《経営》a conglomerate.

ごんげ 権化《文》(an) incarnation ¶愛の権化 the incarnation of love; love incarnate.

こんけい 根茎《植》a rhizome.

こんけつ 混血 ¶混血の (a person) of mixed blood [race]; half-breed / 混血児 a child of mixed race / 日本人とイタリア人の混血児 a half-Japanese half-Italian child [boy, girl].

こんげつ 今月 this [《文》the current] month ¶今月15日に on the 15th of this month / 今月中に in the course of this month; before the month is out; by the end of the month.

こんげん 根源[元] ⇨ こんぽん ¶諸悪の根源 the root of all evil.

こんご 今後 after this;《文》hereafter; in (the) future ★ in future は「今までとは違って将来は」の意であるのに対して、in the future は単に「未来において」の意しか持たない ¶今後の future; coming ¶今後2年で (in) two years from now on;《文》two years hence / 今後ずっと from now on. 文例⇩

コンゴ the Congo ¶コンゴの Congolese / コンゴ人 a Congolese.

こんごう¹ 根号《数》a radical sign.

こんごう² 混合 mixing; mixture ¶混合する mix; mingle; blend / 混合酒 ⇨ カクテル / (テニスなどの)男女混合ダブルス mixed doubles / 混合肥料 (a) compound fertilizer / 混合物 a mixture; a mix; a blend.

こんごうしゃ 金剛砂 emery (powder).

こんごうづえ 金剛杖 a pilgrim's staff.

こんごうりき 金剛力 ¶金剛力の持ち主 a man who has unusual [《文》Herculean] strength.

コンコース a concourse.

ごんごどうだん 言語道断 ¶言語道断な outrageous; scandalous;《文》execable.

こんこんと¹ 昏々と ¶こんこんと眠る〈ぐっすり〉sleep fast [soundly]; sleep like a log [like a top]; 〈眠り続ける〉sleep on.

こんこんと² 滾々と ¶こんこんとわき出る gush [well] out [forth]; well up.

こんこんと³ 懇々と seriously;《文》earnestly; repeatedly(繰り返し)¶懇々と諭す《文》admonish *sb* repeatedly《against, for》; have a serious talk with *sb*.

コンサート a concert ¶コンサートを催す give a concert / コンサートマスター a concertmaster.

こんさいるい 根菜類 root vegetables; (edible) roots.

こんざつ 混雑〈雑踏〉a crush; crowdedness;《文》congestion;〈混乱〉confusion; disorder ¶混雑する be crowded;《文》be congested; be in confusion [disorder] / 交通の混雑を緩和する relieve [ease] traffic congestion; ease a traffic jam.

コンサルタント a (management) consultant.

こんじき 金色 ¶金色の golden(-colored).

こんじゃく 今昔 ¶今昔の感にたえない be struck by the effects of time [《文》by the changes wrought by time].

こんしゅう 今週 this week ¶今週中に in the course of the week; some time this week; before the end of this week.

こんじゅほうしょう 紺綬褒章 a Dark-blue Ribbon Medal.

こんじょう 根性〈性質〉(a) nature;〈気質〉《文》(a) temper;《文》(a) disposition;〈精神〉spirit;〈意志の力〉will power;《口語》guts;〈闘志〉fighting spirit;《口語》《頑張り》tenacity; doggedness ¶根性のある男 a man with (a lot of) guts / 根性(のあるところ)を見せる show spirit / 根性の腐った despicable;《文》base;《文》mean / 根性の曲がった perverse; cross-grained / 根性の悪い ill-natured / 根性を入れ換える reform. 文例⇩

---

with each other by pure chance. / 今後ご愛顧に願います。I'm very glad to know [to have met] you. / あの方とはご愛顧ですか。Do you know him well? | How well do you know him? / あの方とは特別にご愛顧に願っております。He is one of my best friends.

こんがらかる 頭がこんがらがって来。I'm getting confused.

こんかん 再三懇願したが許しを得られなかった。I pleaded with him again and again, but I could not get his permission.

こんきょ 彼がその招請を断わるだろうと信じるだけの充分な根拠がある。There are good grounds [We have a good reason] for believing that he will decline their invitation. / 根拠となるべき事実がない。We have no facts to go on. / 彼は何か根拠があってそう言ったに違いない。He must surely have some authority for what he said. / ここに書いてあることは歴史的事実を根拠としていない。What is written here has no basis in historical fact.

こんご 今後はもっと気をつけます。I will be more careful in future. / 今後は今後毎年15パーセントずつ増加するものと予想される。This amount is expected to increase by 15 per cent annually in the years ahead.

こんじょう¹ あの男には根性がな

こんじょう² 紺青 Prussian [deep] blue.
こんしょく 混色 mixed colors; (a) mixture of colors; a color blend.
こんしん¹ 混信 jamming (妨害などによる); interference; crosstalk.
こんしん² 渾身 ⇨ ぜんしん¹ ¶渾身の力をふりしぼって by using all *one*'s strength; with all *one*'s might;《文》with might and main.
こんしんかい 懇親会 a social gathering [meeting]; a social;《米》a sociable.
こんすい 昏睡 lethargic sleep;《医》(be in) (a) coma ¶昏睡状態に陥る become unconscious; fall [lapse] into a coma [comatose state]. 文例⬇
こんせい¹ 混成 ¶混成の mixed;《文》composite / 早稲田・慶応の混成チーム the Waseda-Keio combined team.
こんせい² 混声《音楽》mixed voices ¶混声四部合唱 a mixed chorus in four voices [voice parts].
こんせい³ 懇請《文》(an) entreaty;《文》an earnest request ¶懇請する《文》entreat; implore; ask; beg / …の懇請により at *sb*'s (earnest) request.
こんせき 痕跡 traces; marks;《文》vestiges ¶痕跡をとどめない leave no traces [marks] / 痕跡器官《生物》a vestigial [rudimentary] organ.
こんせつ 懇切 ¶懇切な〈親切な〉kind;《文》cordial; considerate;〈詳細な〉full;《文》minute; detailed / 懇切な説明 a minute [detailed] explanation / 懇切に kindly;《文》cordially;〈詳しく〉fully; in detail.
こんぜつ 根絶 extermination; eradication ¶根絶する root [stamp] out; exterminate; eradicate.
こんせん¹ 混戦 a confused [mixed] fight; a melee.
こんせん² 混線 ¶混線する get entangled [mixed up];〈電話で〉get [be] crossed. 文例⬇
こんぜん¹ 婚前 ¶婚前交渉 premarital sex;《文》premarital (sexual) relations [intercourse] (with).
こんぜん² 渾然 ¶こんぜんと《文》harmoniously;《文》in perfect harmony.
コンセンサス (build, reach) a consensus.
コンセント a (wall) socket; a [an electric] point;《米》a wall [service, convenience] outlet;《米》an outlet. 文例⬇
コンソメ consommé; clear soup.

こんだく 混濁 ¶混濁する get [《文》become] muddy [《文》turbid]; get muddled. 文例⬇
コンタクトレンズ a contact lens.
こんだて 献立 a menu;《文》a bill of fare.
こんたん 魂胆 an ulterior [underlying] motive; a secret [hidden] intention [《文》design] ¶何か魂胆があって for some hidden purpose. 文例⬇
こんだん 懇談 ¶懇談する have a familiar [friendly] talk (with); chat (with) / 懇談的に話す have an informal talk (with) / 懇談会 an informal gathering for discussion(s) (on, about).
コンチェルト《音楽》a (piano) concerto (*pl.* -s, -ti).
こんちゅう 昆虫 an insect ¶昆虫を採集する collect insects / 昆虫採集 insect collecting / 昆虫採集網に出掛ける go hunting for insects / 昆虫採集網 an insect net / 昆虫学 entomology / 昆虫学者 an entomologist / ファーブルの「昆虫記」*Entomological Souvenirs* by Jean Henri Fabre.
コンツェルン [<《ドイツ語》*Konzern*] a combine; a conglomerate.
コンテ¹〈クレヨンの一種〉conté (crayon).
コンテ²〈映画・放送の台本〉a continuity.
こんてい 根底 the basis (*pl.* bases); the foundation ⇨ こんぽん, どだい ¶…の根底をなす form the basis of…; be basic to… / 根底から《文》fundamentally;《文》radically; thoroughly;《口語》from the ground up / 根底からゆさぶる rock [shake]《the government》to《its》foundations.
コンディション〈身体の〉condition;〈競技成績のもとになる技術面の〉form ¶コンディションがいい [悪い] be in [out of] condition [form] /〈練習で〉コンディションを調えている [保っている] be [keep] in training / 絶好のコンディションである be in one's best condition; be in top form. 文例⬇
用法 He is in good condition, and he has been in training for the last month, but he has not been in form lately.〈身体の調子がいいし、この1か月はコンディションを落とさぬよう練習も積んできたが、最近は余り成績がよくない〉というように, be in condition は「身体の健康状態がいい」, be in training は「練習で〈いわゆる〉コンディションを整えている」, be in form は「健康・技術面での調子がよくて成績が上がっている」の意.
コンテスト a contest ¶美人コンテスト a beauty contest.

い. He has no guts.
こんすい 彼女はもう2日間も深い昏睡状態にある. She has been in a deep coma for two days.
こんせん 電話が混線している. The wires [lines] are crossed. / 話が混線してしまった. We found ourselves talking at cross-purposes.
コンセント ラジオを使いたいんだけれど, コンセントはどこにあるの. Where can I plug the radio in?
こんだく 意識が混濁した. His

consciousness faded [grew dim].
こんたん 突然辞任したりして, どういう魂胆なんだろう. What is his real reason for resigning so suddenly? / I wonder what underlies his sudden resignation.
こんてい 彼の学説はこの新説の出現で根底から覆された. His theory was completely exploded by the new theory. / The new theory knocked the bottom out of his theory.
コンディション〈成績が上がらなくて〉コンディションを落として

いる. He is not in form. / He's in poor form. / He can't find his (best) form. / 今夜一杯飲みに行かないか.一残念だけれど, 土曜のレースに備えてコンディションを整えているところだから. Would you like to go out for a drink tonight? —No, thank you. I'm in training for the race on Saturday.
こんど 今度は君の番だ. It's your turn (next). / また今度いらっしゃい. Come again some other time. / 今度からもっと気をつけ

コンテナ a container ¶ コンテナ化 containerization / コンテナ船 a container [cotainerized] ship [vessel].
コンデンサー 《電》a capacitor ; a condenser.
コンデンスミルク condensed milk.
コント [<《フランス語》*conte*] a (short) short story.
こんど 今度 〈このたび〉this time ; now ; 〈次の〉next time ; another time ; 〈近々〉shortly ; soon ; 〈このごろ〉lately ; recently ¶ 今度の〈現在の〉present ; new ; 〈次の〉next ; coming ; 〈先ごろの〉last ; recent / 今度の学長〈今度来た〉the new president ; 〈今度来る〉the incoming president / 今度の試験 the next [the coming [forthcoming] examination / 〈この間の〉the last [recent] examination / 今度の日曜日 next Sunday / 今度こそは this time ; now (for the first time) / 今度だけは for (this) once. 文例⇩
こんとう 昏倒 ¶昏倒する faint ; fall unconscious.
こんどう[1] 金銅 gilt bronze ¶金銅仏 a gilt bronze statue [image] of the Buddha.
こんどう[2] 混同 ¶混同する confuse [mix up, 《文》confound] 《A with B》; mistake 《A》for 《B》.
コンドーム a condom ; a sheath ; 《米》a prophylactic ; 《英口語》a French letter ; 《俗》a rubber.
ゴンドラ a gondola ¶ゴンドラの船頭 a gondolier.
コントラバス a contrabass ; a double bass ¶コントラバス奏者 a contrabassist.
コントラルト 《音楽》〈声〉contralto ; 〈歌手〉a contralto (*pl.* -s).
コンドル 《鳥》a condor.
コントロール control ¶コントロールがいい[悪い]球技〉have good [poor] control / コントロールタワー a control tower.
こんとん 混沌 chaos ¶混沌たる chaotic.
こんな こんな sort [type] of... ; this ; such ; 《文》such...as this ; of this kind [sort] ¶こんなにたくさん so many [much] / こんな具合に in this way [《文》manner] ; like this. 文例⇩
こんなん 困難 (a) difficulty ; trouble ; 〈労苦〉sufferings ; 《文》hardships / 困難な〈むずかしい〉difficult ; hard ; 〈めんどうな〉troublesome ; 〈つらい〉trying / 困難な状況 a difficult [tight] situation / 呼吸に困難を感じる have difficulty (in) breathing / 困難に打ち勝つ overcome [《文》surmount] difficulties / 困難である it is hard [difficult] for *one* to *do* ;〈人が主語〉find difficulty (in) *do*ing ; find it hard [difficult] to *do*. 文例⇩

こんにち 今日 today ; these days [times] ⇨こ のごろ ★ ¶生存競争の激しい今日 in these days when the struggle for survival is so fierce / 原子力時代の今日 in this age of atomic energy / 今日の学生 students of today ; today's students / 今日の日本 the Japan of today ; Japan today / 今日では nowadays ; now ; at present / 今日まで until today ; up to the present. 文例⇩
こんにゃく 《植》a konjak ; a konnyaku ; 〈食品〉paste made from konjak flour.
こんにゅう 混入 ¶混入する〈混ぜる〉mix 《A with B, A and B》; mingle ; 〈混じる〉get mixed (with).
こんねん 今年 ⇨ことし.
コンパ a party ; a social. 文例⇩
コンバイン a combine harvester ; a combine.
コンパクト a compact.
コンパス 〈両脚器〉(a pair of) compasses (片方の脚に鉛筆などを差し込む) ; dividers (両脚とも針になっている) ; 〈羅針盤〉a (mariner's) compass ¶コンパスが長い[短い] have long [short] legs ; be long-[short-]legged.
こんばん 今晩 this evening ; tonight. 文例⇩
コンビ (a) combination ¶...とコンビで in combination with... / 名コンビ a good [perfect, 《文》happy] combination.
コンビーフ corned beef.
コンビナート [<《ロシヤ語》*kombinat*] a [an industrial] complex ¶石油(化学)コンビナート a petrochemical complex.
コンピューター a [an electronic] computer ¶コンピューターにかける computerize ; put [feed] 《data》into a computer ; process 《information》by means of a computer / コンピューターで制御された機械 a machine under computer control ; a computer-controlled machine / アナログ[デジタル]コンピューター an analog [a digital] computer / コンピューター化 computerization / コンピューター技術 computer technology / コンピューター時代 the computer age / コンピューター制御装置 a computer-control system. 文例⇩

るんですよ. Be more careful in future. / 今度僕が行くとき連れて行ってやろう. I'll take you with me the next time I go.
こんな こんな事は二度と再びしません. I'll never do such a thing (as this) again. / こんなばかげたことないか. Nothing could be more absurd (than this). / 生まれてからこんな愉快なことはなかった. I've never enjoyed myself so much in my life. / こんな事になろうとは思わなかった. I didn't think things would come to this [《文》to such a pass].
こんなん こんなことをすれば君の立場が困難になる. That would put you in an awkward [a compromising, a difficult] position.
こんにち 今日は. 〈午前中〉Good morning! / 〈午後〉Good afternoon! / 〈気軽に〉Hello! / 彼の行方は今日に至るまで不明である. His whereabouts is [are] unknown to this day. / 文明の発達した今日にこんな事があってたまるものか. It is the last thing one would dream of in these civilized days. / 勤勉が氏をして今日あらしめたのだ. It is his hard work that has made him what he is today.
コンパ 今度の土曜日に新入部員の歓迎コンパを開こうじゃないか. Let's throw a party for the new members of our club next Saturday, shall we?
コンパス 彼はコンパスの長い足ですたすたと立ち去った. He strode away on his long legs.
こんばん 今晩は. Good evening.
コンピューター この部門のコン

こんぶ 昆布 *kombu*; tangle(weed); kelp ¶こんぶ漁 tangle(weed) harvesting [collecting].

コンプレックス〖精神分析〗a complex;〈劣等感〉an inferiority complex.

コンプレッサー〖機〗a compressor.

こんぶん 混文〖文法〗a compound-complex sentence.

コンペートー 金米糖 [<ポルトガル語> *confeito*] a type of small candy made by crystallizing sugar around a poppy-seed core.

こんぺき 紺碧 ¶紺碧の deep-blue.

コンベヤー a conveyor ¶コンベヤーベルト a conveyor belt.

コンボ a (jazz) combo (*pl.* -s).

こんぼう[1] 混紡 mixed spinning ¶混紡の mixed(-spun)《fabrics》/綿2割混紡のラシャ地 woolen fabric with 20 per cent of cotton.

こんぼう[2] 棍棒 a heavy stick; a club; a cudgel;〈警棒〉a truncheon ¶棍棒でなぐる hit [beat,《文》strike] *sb* with a heavy stick; club; cudgel(繰り返し).

こんぼう 梱包〈事〉packing;〈物〉a package ⇨にづくん.

こんぽん 根本〈基礎〉the foundation; the basis (*pl.* bases);〈根元〉the root; the origin; the source;〈本質〉the essence ¶根本的 basic; fundamental;《文》〈徹底的〉《文》radical; thorough / 根本的に basically;《文》fundamentally;〈徹底的に〉《文》radically; thoroughly / 根本原理 fundamental [basic] principles; fundamentals; ground rules / 根本問題 a fundamental [root] problem. 文例⇩

コンマ a comma ¶コンマで切る put [《文》insert, use] a comma《between》/ コンマ以下の人間 a person of no account; a nobody.

こんみょうにち 今明日 today and [or] tomorrow ¶今明日中に some time today or tomorrow.

こんめい 混迷 bewilderment;《文》stupefaction; bewildering confusion ¶混迷させる《文》stupefy; bewilder; confuse / 混迷に陥る be thrown into confusion.

こんもう 懇望《文》(an) entreaty;《文》an earnest request ¶懇望する plead《with *sb* to *do*》;《文》entreat; beg earnestly / ...の懇望によって at *sb's* earnest request. 文例⇩

こんもり ¶こんもりと thickly; luxuriantly / こんもり茂った森 thick woods.

こんや 今夜 this evening; tonight ¶去年の今夜 a year ago tonight. 文例⇩

こんやく 婚約 an engagement;《文》a betrothal ¶婚約する get [《文》become] engaged《to *sb*, to marry *sb*》/ 婚約を解消する break (off) *one's* engagement《with》/ 婚約期間 an engagement (period) / 婚約者 *one's* fiancé (男); *one's* fiancée (女);《文》*one's* betrothed / 婚約指輪 an engagement ring.

こんよう 混用 ¶混用する use《A》together [at the same time] with《B》; mix《A and B》.

こんよく 混浴 mixed bathing ¶混浴する《men and women》bathe together.

こんらん 混乱 confusion;〈口語〉a mix-up; disorder; chaos ¶混乱している be confused; be mixed up; be in confusion [disorder]; be chaotic / 火事場の混乱に乗じて in the confusion at the scene of the fire / 混乱状態 a state of confusion / 混乱状態に陥る be thrown into confusion [《文》disarray]. 文例⇩

こんりゅう 建立 ¶建立する build;《文》erect; set up; raise.

こんりんざい 金輪際 never; on no account. 文例⇩

こんれい 婚礼 ⇨けっこん[2](結婚式)¶(花嫁の)婚礼の衣装 a wedding [bridal] dress.

こんろ 焜炉 a portable cooking stove.

コンろんさんみゃく 崑崙山脈 the Kunlun mountains.

こんわかい 懇話会 a [an informal] gathering for discussion(s)《on, about》.

こんわく 困惑 ⇨とうわく.

さ

さ[1] 左 ¶左の〈次の〉the following / ...は左のとおり《文》be as follows; be given below / 左に掲ぐる事項《文》the particulars mentioned below.

さ[2] 差〈相違〉(a) difference;〈隔たり〉《文》(a) disparity;〈値開き〉a gap;〈値開き〉a margin;〈差し引き〉(a) balance;〈剰余〉the remainder;〈賃金の〉a (wage) differential;〈得票の差〉a majori-

---

ビューター化を一日も早く図るべきです。We must computerize this department as soon as possible. / パンチカードはコンピューターがじかに読み取ることができる媒体である。Punched cards are a machine-readable medium.

こんぽん 党分裂の根本原因は幹部の権力争いにあった。The root cause of the split in the party was [The split of the party had its origin in] the struggle for power among its leaders.

こんもう 木村氏の懇望もだし難く彼はついに承諾しました。He was unable to resist Mr. Kimura's entreaties, and finally consented.

こんや 今夜はこれで散会としよう。Let us break up for the night. / 今夜はこれで切り上げた方がよかろう。I think we'd better call it a night.

こんやく 婚約期間が長いのはよくない。I don't believe in long engagements.

こんらん 彼女は頭が混乱していて彼が何を言おうとしているのかはとんとわからなかった。In her confusion she could hardly make out what he was trying to say.

こんりんざい もうこんりんざいあの男には物を頼むまい。I will never, for the life of me, ask him to do anything for me again. / もうこんりんざいあいつには金を貸すものか。I'll be damned if I'll lend him money again.

さ[2] 一緒に行っていただいても、い

ty; a plurality (次位得票者との間の) ¶大きな差がある there is a great difference (between); 《文》differ greatly 《from》/ 差をつける (競技で引き離す) have [get] a lead 《of 20 meters on one's opponent》; 《差別する》 treat 《A and B》 differently; discriminate 《between》/ かなりの差をつけて by a considerable [solid] margin / 差を広げる〈競技で〉 increase [stretch] one's [the] lead / 差を求める〈数〉 find the remainder / わずかの差で by a narrow [slim] margin; by a small majority (選挙で) / 圧倒的な差で by an overwhelming margin / 甲乙の品質の差 the difference in quality between A and B / 年齢の差 (an) age difference;《文》(a) disparity in age. 文例⇩

さ[3] ¶さもないと ⇨ さもないと / さあらぬ体で as if nothing had happened.

ざ 座=せき[2] ¶座をはずす《文》excuse oneself (from the table); go [slip] out of the room / 権力の座についている人びと men in (positions of) power / 権力の座から引きずり下ろす unseat *sb*; dislodge *sb* [pull *sb* down] from the position of power. 文例⇩

さあ come on;〈さて〉well now;〈言いよどむ時〉well; let me see ¶さあさあ〈うながしの言葉〉come on, now.

サーカス a circus (show) ¶サーカスの小屋をかける pitch [put up] a circus / サーカスの団長[芸人] a circus master [performer] / サーカスを興行する put on [run] a circus / サーカス団 a circus troupe [company].

サーキット〈自動車レースの〉a (racing) circuit;〈電気回路〉a circuit.

サークル a circle ¶社会問題研究サークル a social problems study circle / サークルに入る join a club (★ join a circle とは言わない) / become a member of a 《poetry》circle (★ circle は単独に使わないで, その前に, 何のサークルであるかを示す語を付けて, a painting [photography, nature study] circle のように言うのが普通) / サークル活動 club [group] activities ★ circle activities とは言わない.

ざあざあ ¶ざあざあ水をかける pour water 《over, on》/ ざあざあ流れる flow with a rushing, gurgling sound / ざあざあ降りの雨 torrential [pouring] rain; a downpour. 文例⇩

サーチライト a searchlight ¶サーチライトを照らす[向ける] flash [turn, play] a searchlight (on).

サービス〈奉仕〉service;《球技》service ¶サ

ービスする provide *sth* extra [throw *sth* in] free of charge ★英語の service には「無料」「値引き」の意味はない / サービスエリア〈放送局・高速道路の〉a service area / サービス業 a service industry; a service job; サービスステーション a service station / 本日のサービス品 today's special / サービス部門 the service sector / サービス料 a service charge;〈レストランなどの〉a cover charge / サービス料込み service included. 文例⇩

サーブ〈テニスなどの〉a service; a serve ¶サーブがうまい[へただ] have a good [poor] serve / サーブを受ける receive the serve [service] / サーブをする serve (a ball).

サーフィン surfing ¶サーフィンをする人 a surfer / サーフィンに行く go surfing 《at Oiso》.

サーベル [<《オランダ語》*sabel*] a saber.

サーモスタット a thermostat.

サーロイン sirloin (steak).

さい[1] 才〈才能〉ability; a gift; (a) talent;《文》(an) aptitude; (a) genius ¶実務の才 business ability [《文》acumen] / 才のある able;《文》gifted; talented / 才のある人《文》a man of talent [ability] / 才を伸ばす develop one's talent / 才走った cocky; over-clever; smart-alecky / 才走った人《口語》a clever-dick; a smart aleck.

さい[2] 差異 = さ[2]. 文例⇩

さい[3] 菜 a side dish (eaten along with rice).

さい[4] 際 when;《文》on the occasion 《of》;《文》in case 《of》; if ¶出発の際に《文》at one's departure; when one sets out. 文例⇩

さい[5] 骰子 a dice (単複同形) ★ dice の単数形 die は今ではほとんど使われない古い形で, The die is cast. (さいは投げられた) という決まり文句にのみ残る ¶さいを振る throw dice (for a drink).

さい[6] 〈動〉a rhinoceros;《口語》a rhino《pl. -s》.

さい-[1] 再... re- ¶再発見する rediscover / 再保険 reinsurance.

さい-[2] 最... the most; the extreme ¶最下等(の) the worst / 最北部の the northernmost.

-さい ...歳 age; years ¶3歳の男児 a three-year-old boy; a boy of three [《文》of three years];《文》a boy three years old / 10歳の子供たち the ten-year-olds / 5歳のときに at the age of five;《文》at five years of age; at five years old / 16歳の時から from the age of sixteen / 7歳を過ぎるまで until after the age of

---

ただかなくても, どのみち大した差はありますまい. It will not make much difference whether you come with us or not. / 当地は寒暑の差が甚だしい所です. There are great extremes [changes] of temperature here. / 試合は1点差で我々の負けです. We lost the game by one point. / ゴールでは彼は相手に大きな差をつけていた. He had a long lead over his rival at the finish. / 次位の得票者に500票の

差をつけて当選した. He won (in) the election by a plurality of 500 votes.

ざ(星占いで)あなたは何座? What sign are you? / 僕は双子座です. I'm a Gemini.

さあ さあ来い. Come on! / さあ, そこだよ問題は. There, that's the question. / さあ, もう出かけようよ. Let's go. | Let's be off. / さあ, 東京に着いたぞ. Here we are in Tokyo.

ざあざあ ざあざあ雨が降って来

た. Rain came pouring down. | It began to rain in torrents [sheets].

サービス あの店はとてもサービスがいい[悪い]. The service in that store is very good [bad]. / これはサービスです. I will throw this in (free of charge). | This is on the house.

さい[4] 上京の際はお立ち寄り下さい. Please look me up when you come up to town [Tokyo]. / こういう際だからやむを得ない. It

seven [after age seven] / 6歳になるころには by the age of six; by the time *one* is six. [文例⇩]

ざい[1] 在 ¶在の者 a countryman; 《文》a rustic / 広島の在に住む live in a village near [on the outskirts of] Hiroshima.

ざい[2] 財 〈財産〉⇨ざいさん; 〔経済〕goods.

ざい- 在… ¶在英中 during *one's* stay in England; while (*one* is [was]) in England / 在米邦人 Japanese residents in America.

さいあい 最愛 ¶最愛の *one's* dearest [beloved] 《child》.

さいあく 最悪 the worst ¶最悪の場合には if [when] the worst comes to the worst; if [when] things come to the worst / 最悪の場合に備える prepare for the worst.

ざいあく 罪悪 〈法律上の〉a crime; 〈道徳·宗教上の〉(a) sin; a vice ¶罪悪感 a sense of sin [guilt]. [文例⇩]

ざいい 在位 ¶在位する be on the throne; reign / 長期間在位している国王 a long-reigning king / エリザベス一世の在位中に during [in] the reign of Queen Elizabeth I / 在位期間 the period of 《Queen Victoria's》 reign; when 《King George VI》 was on the throne.

ザイール (the Republic of) Zaire.

さいうよく 最右翼 〈もっとも可能性のある人·物〉the most likely one ¶優勝候補の最右翼 the probable [most likely] winner.

さいえん[1] 才媛 an intelligent [a talented] woman; 〈文才のある〉《文》a girl of literary talent; 〈学才のある〉《文》a girl with scholastic ability.

さいえん[2] 再演 ¶再演する stage [present] 《a play》 again; replay; 〈映画を〉show 《a movie》 again / 再演もの a repeat performance; a revival.

さいえん[3] 菜園 a vegetable [kitchen] garden; 〈大規模な〉《米》a truck farm; 《英》a market garden ¶家庭菜園を作る grow vegetables for *one's* family [for the house] / 菜園作り vegetable gardening.

さいか[1] 西下 ¶西下する go west from Tokyo; leave for the Kansai (region).

さいか[2] 裁可 《文》sanction; 《give *one's*》 approval.

ざいか[1] 在荷 (a) stock; goods in stock [store] ⇨さいこ ¶在荷過剰 excess stock; overstocking; a glut 《of eggs》 (on the market). [文例⇩]

ざいか[2] 財貨 money and property; 《文》wealth; 〈商品〉goods.

ざいか[3] 罪科 ⇨つみ[1], とが, ざいめい.

さいかい[1] 再会 meeting again; 《文》reunion ¶再会する meet again / 近い将来に再会を期して別れる part in the hope of meeting again before too long.

さいかい[2] 再開 ¶再開する reopen; 《文》resume.

さいかい[3] 際会 ¶際会する meet; face; be confronted by *sth.*

さいかい[4] 最下位 the lowest rank [position]; 〈順位の〉the tail end ¶最下位のチーム the tailender / 最下位である be the lowest in rank; 〈競技で〉be last; 《口語》be in the cellar (リーグ戦などで).

さいがい 災害 《文》a disaster; 《文》a calamity ¶災害をこうむる suffer from a disaster; be struck by disaster / 災害救助法 the Disaster Relief Act / 災害対策 measures to deal with natural calamities / 災害地 a disaster [an afflicted] area; a (disaster-)stricken [devastated] district / 災害手当 a casualty [an accident] allowance / 災害保険 accident insurance. [文例⇩]

ざいかい 財界 〈金融界〉the financial world; financial circles; 〈実業界〉the business world; (big-)business circles ¶財界人 〈金融家〉a financier; 〈実業家〉a businessman.

ざいがい 在外 ¶在外の overseas; 《文》resident [stationed] abroad / 在外研究員 a research student [worker] abroad / 在外公館 diplomatic establishments abroad; overseas agencies of the Ministry of Foreign Affairs / 在外資産 overseas [external] assets / 在外邦人 Japanese residents [nationals] abroad; overseas Japanese.

さいかいはつ 再開発 redevelopment ¶再開発する redevelop / (都市の)再開発区域 a redevelopment area.

さいかいもくよく 斎戒沐浴 ¶斎戒沐浴する 《文》perform *one's* ablutions; have a ceremonial wash; purify *oneself*.

さいかく 才覚 《have》 the wit(s) 《to *do*》 (★wit(s) は, 肯定平叙文では wits, 疑問文では wit(s), 否定文では wit となる); resources. [文例⇩]

ざいがく 在学 ¶在学する be in [at] school [college] / 在学中に while (*one* is [was]) at [in] school [college]; while (*one* is [was]) a student [an undergraduate] / 在学期間 《文》the period of attendance at school; *one's* school days / 在学証明書 a certificate of student status; 《口語》an [a student] ID card. [文例⇩]

さいかくにん 再確認 《文》reconfirmation ¶再確認する 《文》reconfirm; 《文》reaffirm.

さいかこう 再加工 reprocessing ¶再加工する reprocess; rework.

---

can't be helped under [in] the circumstances. | Things being how they are, we don't have any choice.

-さい 君は何歳になるの? How old are you? / 彼は30歳にはまだなるまい. I think he is still on this side of thirty. / 20歳以上の男子はみな収容所に送られてしまった. Men of twenty years and over were all sent to the concentration camp.

ざいあく トルストイは農民に対してある種の罪悪感を抱いていた. Tolstoy had some sort of guilt feeling toward the peasantry.

ざいか[1] 市場は在荷過剰である. The market is overstocked.

さいがい その地方に災害救助法が発動された. The Disaster Relief Act was invoked in that area.

さいかく その後はずっと自分の才覚一つで生活した. He lived ever after by his own wits.

ざいがく 本学在学生は約700名である. There are about 700 students (enrolled) at this college. | This school has an enrollment of about seven hundred.

さいき[1] 彼は才気かんぱつの人だ. He has a ready wit.

さいき[2] 彼は再起不能と宣告された. His case was pronounced (to

さいき¹ 才気 ¶才気のある《文》ingenious; smart; quick-witted /才気煥発(な)の《文》brilliant; 《文》resourceful; very intelligent. 文例⑪

さいき² 再起 a return to popularity [power, one's former position]; a comeback; 〈快復〉(a) recovery ¶再起する come back; make one's [stage a] comeback; 〈快復する〉recover; be [get] on one's feet again /再起不能である be past [beyond] hope of recovery; be disabled for life. 文例⑪

さいき- 再帰…. ¶再帰代名詞[動詞]《文法》a reflexive pronoun [verb].

さいぎ 猜疑 suspicion; jealousy (ねたみ) ¶さい疑の目で見る《文》look on sb with suspicion [with suspicious eyes] /さい疑心の強い suspicious 《of everything》; 〈ねたみ深い〉jealous 《of sb》.

さいきょ 再挙 ¶再挙を図る make another attempt; try to find another chance 《to do》.

さいきょういく 再教育 reeducation; retraining; 《文》reorientation; 〈現職者の〉in-service training ¶再教育する reeducate; retrain / 再教育コース a refresher course.

さいきん¹ 細菌 a bacillus (pl. -cilli); a bacterium (pl. -teria); a microbe; a germ ¶細菌の bacterial /細菌学 bacteriology /細菌学者 a bacteriologist /細菌検査 a bacteriological examination /細菌検査を行なう carry out a bacteriological examination 《on》/湘南海岸の細菌数 the bacteria count in the waters along Shonan beach /細菌戦 bacteriological [germ, microbe] warfare /細菌培養 germ culture; cultivation of bacteria /細菌兵器 a bacteriological weapon.

さいきん² 最近 ¶最近(に) recently; lately; 《文》of late ★ recently は, 過去時制又は現在完了時制の文で使う. lately は現在完了時制の文だけで, 主に疑問文, 否定文で用いる /最近5年間に in the last five years /最近の recent; the latest / 最近の流行 the latest fashion /つい最近まで until quite recently /「世界」の最近号 the latest number of the 'Sekai'. 文例⑪

さいきん³ 在勤 ¶在勤中《文》during one's service 《with the Japanese legation at Athens》/《文》while serving 《as Ambassador to Brazil》/ 海外在勤手当 a foreign service [an overseas] allowance.

さいく 細工 〈製作〉work; workmanship; craftsmanship; 〈作品を言う〉a piece of work; (a) handiwork; 〈術策〉《文》an artifice; 《文》a device; a trick ¶細工する work 《on bamboo, in silver》; 〈ごまかす〉use tricks; cook [make] up 《a story》; doctor / 色々な形に細工する work 〈glass〉into various shapes [forms] /細工が見事[粗末]である be superbly [poorly] made [worked] / 細工が上手な be of excellent [poor] workmanship / ろう細工 a waxwork. 文例⑪

さいくつ 採掘 mining; exploitation; working ¶採掘する mine 《gold, coal》; work [exploit] 《a mine》/ 採掘権 a mining concession; mining rights.

サイクリング cycling; bicycling ¶サイクリングに出かける go on a cycling tour; go cycling /サイクリング専用道路 a cycling road; a cycle track.

サイクル a cycle ¶4サイクル機関 a four-stroke engine.

サイクロトロン《原子物理》a cyclotron.

さいくん 細君 a wife (pl. wives).

さいぐんび 再軍備 rearmament ¶再軍備する rearm; 《文》remilitarize.

さいけいこく 最恵国 a most favored nation ¶最恵国待遇 most-favored-nation treatment / 最恵国待遇を与える give 《Japan》most-favored-nation status; treat 《Japan》as a most favored nation.

さいけいちょちく 財形貯蓄 'nest-egg' savings.

さいけいれい 最敬礼 ¶最敬礼をする make a deep [《文》profound] bow; bow from the waist.

さいけつ¹ 採血 drawing [collecting] blood ¶採血する gather [collect] blood 《from a donor》; 〈血液検査のために〉take blood samples; draw blood 《from a vein》.

さいけつ² 採決 voting; a vote 《on》; a division (議会などで) ¶採決する vote [take a vote] 《on》/採決を行なわずに without a vote [division] /採決に入る come to a vote /採決に付する put sth to a vote. 文例⑪

さいけつ³ 裁決 ⇒ さいだん ¶裁決書 a written verdict [decision].

さいげつ 歳月 time; years ¶歳月を経るに従って as days go by; with the passage of time; as time passes [goes by] / 《文》as the years pass [go by]. 文例⑪

さいけん¹ 再建 rebuilding; 《文》reconstruction; 《文》re-erection ¶再建する rebuild; reconstruct; 《文》re-erect; put [get] 〈the company〉back on 〈its〉feet /再建に乗り出す《文》embark on the reconstruction 《of》.

さいけん² 債券 a (loan) bond; a debenture ¶債券を発行[償還]する issue [redeem] bonds / 無記名債券 a bearer bond; a bond to bearer.

さいけん³ 債権 credit; a claim ¶債権がある

---

be) hopeless. / 彼が再起する見込は全くありません. There is no earthly chance of his making [staging] a comeback. / There is no possibility that he will make [stage] a comeback.

さいきん² 最近いつ彼にお会いでしたか. When did you see him last? / 最近では3か月前に行きました. The last time I went there was three months ago. / 最近ではそれは珍しくない. It isn't uncommon these days.

さいく この石は細工しやすい. This (kind of) stone is easy to work. / この帳簿はどうも細工されているように見える. It looks as though these accounts have been cooked up [as if someone has cooked these books]. / あの男は細工をやりすぎる. He is too much of a tactician.

さいけつ² 本問題に関して採決が行なわれた. A vote was taken on the question. / その決議案は採決の結果, 66対17で可決された. The vote on the resolution was 66 to 17 in 〈its〉 favor. / 決議の結果本案に対する賛成は30, 反対は50であった. The result of the voting was 30 for and 50 against the bill.

さいげつ この辞書を完成するのに

さいげん¹ 再現 《文》reappearance；《文》(a) reproduction ¶再現する〈現われる〉reappear；revive；〈現わす〉reproduce. 文例⓪

さいげん² 際限 limits；an end；《文》bounds ¶際限のない unlimited；《文》boundless；endless；《文》interminable / 際限なく endlessly；infinitely. 文例⓪

さいげん 財源 a source of revenue；a revenue source；(financial) resources；finances；means ¶新しい財源を求める look for a new source of revenue [income]. 文例⓪

さいけんとう 再検討 《文》(a) reexamination；《文》(a) reconsideration；《文》reappraisal；(a) review ¶再検討する reexamine；reconsider；《文》reappraise；review；restudy.

さいこ 最古 ¶最古の the oldest 《literature on the subject》.

さいご¹ 最後〈一番終わり〉the last；〈結末〉the end ¶最後の last；final；《文》ultimate / 最後の手段 the [one's] last resort [《文》resource] / 最後の勝利 the final [ultimate] victory / 最後の抵抗 (a) last-ditch resistance / 最後の点検 a last-minute checkup / 最後の努力 final [last-spurt] efforts / 最後の一人まで to the last man / 最後の晩餐《キリスト教》the Last Supper / 最後に〈一番後に〉last(ly)；〈終わりに〉finally；in conclusion / 最後には at (long) last；in the end；when all is said (and done)；in the long run / 最後まで to the end [last] / 人の話を最後まで聞く hear sb out；let sb finish his story / 芝居[余興,音楽会]を最後まで見る[聞く] sit a play [an entertainment, a concert] out / 最後通牒(ちょう)《文》(send, deliver) an ultimatum (pl. -tums, -ta) / 最後っぺ a parting shot. 文例⓪

さいご² 最期 one's last moment；one's death；《文》one's end ¶悲惨な最期を遂げる meet (with) a tragic end；die a sad [pitiful] death / 最期を見届ける watch sb die；(happen to) be present at sb's deathbed.

ざいこ 在庫 stock ¶在庫している〈物が主語〉be in stock [store]；be on hand；〈人が主語〉have (the goods) in stock [store] / 在庫調べ stocktaking / 在庫調べをする take stock [an inventory] of one's goods on hand；check the stock / 在庫帳 a stock book / 在庫品 goods in stock (on hand)；a stock (of toys)；在庫品がたくさんある[少ない] have a good [small] stock 《of glassware》 / 在庫品目録 a stock list；an inventory.

さいこう¹ 再考 《文》reconsideration；《文》rethinking ¶再考する reconsider；think (a problem) over again / 〈考え直す〉have second thoughts (about, on) / 再考の結果 on reflection；on second thoughts. 文例⓪

さいこう² 再校 《印刷》the second proof. 文例⓪

さいこう³ 再興 revival；《文》restoration ¶再興する revive；《文》restore (the country) (to greatness).

さいこう⁴ 採光 lighting ¶採光のよい[悪い]部屋 a well-[poorly-]lighted room.

さいこう⁵ 採鉱 mining ¶採鉱する mine / 採鉱機械 mining machinery.

さいこう⁶ 最高 ¶最高の the highest；maximum；《文》superlative；《文》supreme / 最高の地位にある人々 the top men (in the Soviet Union) / 最高価格 the highest price；the price ceiling (制限価格) / 最高学府 the highest seat of learning / 《文》the highest educational institution / 最高寒暖計 a maximum thermometer / 最高級品 top quality products / 最高記録 the best [highest] record；a new record；《口語》a new [an all-time] high / 最高検察庁 the Supreme Public Prosecutors Office / 最高限度を定める set an upper limit (to)；put a ceiling (on rents) (公的な) / 最高裁判所 the Supreme Court / 最高裁判所長官[判事] the Chief Justice [an associate justice] of the Supreme Court / 最高指導者の交代 a change at the top / 最高殊勲選手《野球》the most valuable player (略：MVP) / 最高首脳会議 a summit [top-level] conference / 最高司令官 the supreme commander；the commander in chief (略：C in C, C-in-C) / 最高点 the highest point；〈試験の〉the highest mark(s)；〈競技の〉the highest score；〈投票の〉the highest poll ⇨こうてん⁵. 文例⓪

ざいこう 在校 ⇨ざいがく.

ざいごう 罪業 ⇨つみ¹ ¶罪業を重ねる 《文》live a sinful life；《文》commit one sin after another.

ざいごうぐんじん 在郷軍人 an ex-soldier[-serviceman]；a reservist；《米》a veteran.

さいこうせい 再構成 《文》restructuring；《文》

10年の歳月を要した. It took ten years to complete the dictionary. / 歳月人を待たず. Time and tide wait for no man. 《諺》

さいげん¹ この劇は古代ギリシャ人が演じた形式をそのまま再現して上演されるものである. This play will be presented in exactly the same form as it was staged by the ancient Greeks.

さいげん² 際限もなく苦労が続いた. There was no end to our troubles. / いったん譲歩すると,

あとは際限がない. Once you give way, [Give way once and] there'll be no end to it.

ざいげん 給与改善の財源がない. We have no means of financing a raise in the wages.

さいけんとう 大統領は国防計画の再検討を命じた. The President ordered a review of the nation's defense plans.

さいご¹ 最後に彼がやって来た. He was the last to come. / こんど戦争が起こったら最後だろう.

Another war would [The next war will] be the end of us. / てっきり,これでおれも最後だと思った. I thought my time had come for sure. / これが結局主人の元気な姿を見る最後となりました. This was to be the last time I saw my husband alive. / 手紙の最後には私の成功を祈ると書いてあった. He closed his letter by wishing me success. / すきやきを作る時に野菜を入れるのは最後の最後にいたします. When you are cooking suki-

さいしょう ... ; 〈文才のある〉《文》a woman of a literary turn; 《文》a woman endowed with literary talent.

さいしょう 最小 ¶最小の the smallest; the least; (the) minimum; 《文》minimal / 最小限(度) the minimum / 最小限にする[押さえる, 減らす] keep [hold] ((the losses)) to a minimum; 《文》minimize; reduce ((the expenses)) to a [the] minimum / 最小公倍数 ⇨ こうばいすう. 文例⇩

さいじょう¹ 斎場 a funeral hall.

さいじょう² 最上 ¶最上の the best; the finest; the highest (quality); 《文》supreme; 《文》of the first order / 最上級 〈学級〉the highest [top] class; the highest grade;《文法》the superlative (degree).

ざいしょう 罪障 ⇨ つみ¹ ¶罪障を消滅する 《文》expiate one's sin(s) / 罪障消滅《文》expiation (of sin).

ざいじょう 罪状 ¶罪状の程度によって according to the degree of culpability / 罪状を認める[否認する] plead guilty [not guilty] to a criminal charge [to an offense] ⇨つみ¹.

さいじょうえい 再上映 a rerun ¶再上映する rerun ((a movie)); show ((a film)) again.

さいしょく¹ 才色 ¶才色兼備の婦人《文》a lady gifted with both wits [intelligence] and beauty; 《文》a beautiful and accomplished lady.

さいしょく² 菜食 a vegetable diet; a vegetarian meal ¶菜食する live on vegetables / 菜食主義[主義者] vegetarianism [a vegetarian].

ざいしょく 在職 ¶在職している hold office; be in office ⇨ さいにん¹, きんぞく¹. 文例⇩

さいしん¹ 再審 〈裁判〉a retrial; (a) review.

さいしん² 細心 ¶細心の《文》prudent; 《文》meticulous; careful;《文》scrupulous / 細心の注意をもって with the greatest (possible) care; 《文》scrupulously / 細心の注意を払う pay close attention ((to)).

さいしん³ 最新 ¶最新の the newest; the latest; up-to-date; hot (news) / 最新式の the latest [newest] style [model] of ((automobile)).

さいじん 才人《文》a man of talent [ability]; 〈才芸のある人〉《文》a man of accomplishments.

さいしんさ 再審査 (a) reexamination.

サイズ size ¶サイズが合う fit one; be one's size / サイズが合わない be not one's size / サイズが合うかどうか試めてみる try ((a jacket)) on for size / サイズを測る take the size ((of)) / サイズ表 the table of sizes. 文例⇩

ざいす 座椅子 a legless chair (used in a *tatami* room).

さいせい 再生 〈生き返ること〉⇨ そせい³;〈再び生まれること〉《文》(a) rebirth;《文》(a) second birth;《文》regeneration;〈廃品の〉recycling; reclamation;〈録音の〉(a) playback ¶再生する〈生き返る〉⇨ そせい³;〈廃品を〉recycle; reclaim;〈録音・録画を〉play back; reproduce; replay /〈録音・録画の〉再製装置 playback equipment / 再生能力《文》regenerative power(s) / 再生不能の《文》nonrenewable. 文例⇩

ざいせい¹ 在世 ¶在世中 in one's lifetime; 《文》in life; while one lives.

ざいせい² 財政 finance(s); financial affairs ¶財政が豊かである be well off; be in easy circumstances / 財政が困難であるか〈個人が〉be badly off; be hard up for money; be in a bad way financially; 〈国家などが〉be in financial difficulties / 財政を建て直す set [put] one's [one's] finances in order (by cutting down expenses) / 国家[家庭]の財政を握る hold the strings of the government [family] purse / 財政上の理由で on financial grounds; for financial reasons / 国家[地方]財政 national [local] finance / 財政的扶助 financial support [aid] / 財政扶助者 a financial supporter [backer] / 財政学 public finance; the science of finance / 財政顧問 a financial adviser / 財政状態 the financial condition ((of the nation)) / 財政政策 a financial [fiscal] policy / 財政整理 (re)adjustment of the finances / 財政通 a financial expert / 財政投融資計画 a national investment and loan program / 財政難におちいる get into financial trouble.

さいせいき 最盛期《文》the golden age; the peak period; the highest stage of development;〈出盛り〉the season; the best time (for) ¶最盛期である be at its peak; be at the height [《文》the zenith] of one's [its] prosperity; be in season.

さいせいさん 再生産 reproduction.

さいせき¹ 砕石 〈舗装用の〉macadam ¶砕石舗装の道路 a macadamized road.

さいせき² 採石 ¶採石する quarry / 採石場 a quarry; a stone pit / 採石夫 a quarryman; a quarrier.

ざいせき 在籍 ¶在籍する be on the (school) register [roll]. 文例⇩

さいせん¹ 再選 (seek) reelection ¶再選する reelect.

さいせん² 賽銭 a money offering ¶さい銭を

---

goya first, and then to Kyoto. / 彼がいかさま師だったということは僕は最初から知っていた。I knew all along that he was a fake.

さいしょう 建築費は最小(度) 2千万円は要るだろう。The construction will cost a minimum of ¥20,000,000.

ざいしょく 氏は本校に在職することと 20 年に及んだ。He has served [taught] in this school for twenty years.

サイズ 僕たちは服のサイズが同じだった。We wore [took] the same size. /（お帽子の）サイズはどのくらいでしょうか。What size do you take (in hats)? | What is your (hat) size?

さいせい トカゲの尻尾は切れても再生する。The lizard's tail regenerates (regrows) if cut off.

ざいせい² そんなぜいたくは私の財政が許さない。I cannot afford such luxuries.

ざいせき この大学には総数 6 千名の学生が在籍している。The college has a total enrollment of 6,000 students.

さいそく 彼にもう一度手紙をやってこの間の返事を催促しなくちゃ。I've got to write to him again, asking [and ask] for an answer to my previous letter.

さいこうちょう 最高潮 〈頂点〉 the climax; the peak; 《文》 the zenith ¶最高潮の場面 《文》 the climactic scene / 最高潮に達する reach the climax.

さいこうふ 再交付 a reissue; 《文》 a regrant ¶再交付する reissue; 《文》 regrant.

さいこうほう 最高峰 the highest peak ((of the Alps)) ¶画壇の最高峰 the greatest of all painters ((in Japan)).

さいこうりゅう 再拘留 《法》 (a) remand ¶再拘留する remand ((a suspect)) ((in custody)).

さいこうれつ 最後列 the (very) back [last] row; the rearmost row.

さいこよう 再雇用 《文》 reemployment ¶再雇用する 《文》 reemploy; rehire.

さいころ ⇨ さい⁵.

さいこん 再婚 《文》 remarriage; a second marriage ¶再婚する remarry; marry again.

さいさき 幸先 ¶幸先がいい[悪い] have [make] a good [bad] beginning [start]. 文例あり

さいさん 再三 ¶再三(再四) again and again; over and over (again); time and time again; repeatedly; more than once.

さいさん² 採算 ¶採算がとれる[とれない] be profitable [unprofitable]; be worth [not worth] one's while; pay [do not pay] ¶採算を無視して with no thought of profit / 採算価格 a break-even price.

ざいさん 財産 property; (material) possessions; a fortune (大財産); 《法》 an estate ¶100万ドルの財産がある be worth a million dollars / 財産をつくる make 《文》 amass] a fortune; build up one's savings (a nest egg) (貯蓄する) / 財産を継ぐ inherit [come into] sb's property / 財産を使い果たす spend all one's money [fortune] ((on)); run [go] through one's fortune / 財産を管理する administer [manage] sb's property / 財産家 《文》 a man of property [substance]; a rich [《文》 wealthy] person / 財産管理 property management; administration of property / 財産税 a wealth [property] tax / 財産相続 property inheritance / 財産分与 distribution of property / 財産目当てに結婚する marry for money; marry sb for his [her] fortune / 財産目録 an inventory (of property). 文例あり

さいし¹ 才子 a clever man; 《文》 a man of talent. 文例あり

さいし² 妻子 one's wife and children; one's family ¶妻子を養う[捨てる] support [desert] one's family.

さいし³ 祭司 a [an officiating] priest.

さいじ 細字 ¶細字で (be written) in small characters; (be) in fine writing; 〈活字〉 (print) in small type / 細字で書く write finely.

さいしき 彩色 ¶彩色を施す color / 彩色画 a colored picture; a picture in colors; a painting.

さいじき 歳時記 a glossary of seasonal terms for haiku composers, with illustrative verses.

さいけん 再試験 a reexamination; 《口語》 a make-up; a resit ¶再試験する reexamine; examine [test] again / 再試験を受ける take a reexamination; resit ((口語)) make up]) an examination (不合格科目の).

さいじつ 祭日 a national holiday; 《英》 a bank holiday; 〈宗教上の〉 a festival (day); a feast day.

ざいしつ¹ 在室 ¶在室している be in ((one's) room [office]).

ざいしつ² 材質 the quality of the material.

さいして 際して ⇨ さい⁴.

さいしゅ 採取 ¶採取する 〈選ぶ〉 pick; 〈取る〉 gather; fish for (pearls); extract / 採取経済 a collecting [gathering] economy.

さいしゅう¹ 採集 ¶採集する collect; gather / 採集家 a collector.

さいしゅう² 最終 ¶最終の the last (bus); the final ((examination)); the closing ((game)); 〈窮極の〉 《文》 ultimate ¶最終案 the final program [plan] / 最終結果 《文》 an end result / 最終製品 an end product / 最終兵器 an ultimate weapon / 最終列車 the last train.

ざいじゅう 在住 ¶在住する live ((in, at)); 《文》 reside ((in)) / 神戸に在住する外国人たち foreign residents of Kobe; 《文》 foreigners resident in Kobe.

さいしゅつ 歳出 annual expenditure.

さいしゅっぱつ 再出発 ¶再出発する make a fresh start; start afresh [over (again)).

さいしょ 最初 ¶最初の first; 《文》 initial; opening (games); 〈本来の〉 original; 〈一番早い〉 the earliest (visitor) / 最初は at first; 〈元来〉 originally / 最初から from the beginning [start, first] / 最初から始める begin at the beginning / 最初に in the first place; first; at the start [《文》 outset, beginning]. 文例あり

さいじょ 才女 an intelligent [a talented] wom-

---

yaki, greens should be added last of all. / 言い出したら最後あとへは引かない. Once he has come out with something he will never take it back.

さいこう¹ 再考の余地がない. There is no room for reconsideration.

さいこう² 要再校. Second proof required.

さいこう⁶ 今は最高の気分だ. I've never felt better. / きょうは最高の人出だった. A record number of people were out today. / この商売では最高で月収 30 万円でしょう. The monthly income in this trade will be [In this trade one could expect a monthly income of] ¥300,000 at best. | In this trade one can expect to earn a maximum of ¥300,000 a month. / こりゃあ最高だ. This is ideal [perfect]. | This leaves nothing to be desired. / 彼女はフランス語で最高点を取った. She got top marks in French.

さいさき そいつは幸先がいい. That's a good [promising] start.

ざいさん この屋敷を維持していくだけでも一財産かかるに違いない. It must cost a (small) fortune to keep up this mansion.

さいし¹ 才子多病. Whom the gods love die young. [諺]

さいしょ 最初に来たのはアーサーだった. Arthur was the first to come. / 最初名古屋へ行ってそれから京都へ行った. I went to Na-

あげる make a money offering《to a deity》/ さい銭箱 an offertory box [chest].

さいぜん[1] 最前 a (little) while ago ; just now ¶最前から for some time ; since a little while ago / 最前線《in》the front line ; the forefront / 最前列 the front row.

さいぜん[2] 最善 the best ¶最善を尽くす, 最善の努力を払う do *one's* best [《文》utmost] ; do everything in *one's* power.

さいそく[1] 細則 detailed rules ; subsidiary rules [regulations] ; bylaws.

さいそく[2] 催促 ¶催促する remind *sb*《of *sth*》; press [《文》urge] *sb*《to *do*》; 〈貸金を〉remind *sb*《of a debt》; dun *sb*《for the payment of a debt》/ 催促状 a reminder (letter). [文例⇩]

さいそしき 再組織 reorganization ; 《文》restructuring ¶再組織する reorganize ; 《文》restructure.

サイダー an aerated drink ; (a) soda pop ; 《英》(a) lemonade ★ cider はりんご酒 ¶サイダー瓶 a pop bottle.

さいたい 妻帯 ⇨けっこん[2] ¶妻帯者 a married man.

さいだい[1] 細大 ¶細大漏らさずに話す give a detailed [full] account of《the affair》; describe《an affair》in detail [《文》minutely, to the smallest detail] ; 《文》spare no detail.

さいだい[2] 最大 ¶最大の the greatest ; (the) maximum (最大限の) / 最大公約数 ⇨こうやくすう / 最大速力1時間200キロに達する reach [《文》attain] a maximum speed of 200 kilometers an hour / 最大多数の最大幸福 the greatest happiness of the greatest number. [文例⇩]

さいたく 採択 〈議案などの〉《文》adoption ; 〈選択〉《文》selection. ¶採択する《文》adopt ; select ; choose.

ざいたく 在宅 ¶在宅する be (at) home ; be in / 在宅日 *one's* at-home day. [文例⇩]

さいたん[1] 採炭 coal mining ¶採炭所 a colliery ; a coal mine / 採炭夫 a (coal-)face worker ; a collier / 採炭量 the output of coal.

さいたん[2] 最短 ¶最短の the shortest / 最短距離 the shortest distance / 最短コースを行く take the shortest route《to》.

さいだん[1] 祭壇《set up》an altar.

さいだん[2] 裁断 〈裁決〉(a) decision ; (a) judgment ; 〈洋服の〉cutting ¶裁断する judge ; decide《on》; 〈服を〉cut out《a dress》/ 裁断を仰ぐ[に任せる] leave [《文》submit]《a matter》to *sb's* judgment [for *sb's* decision] / 裁断を下す pass judgment《on》/ 裁断機 a cutter ; a cutting machine / 裁断師 a (tailor's) cutter ; a cloth-cutter.

ざいだん 財団 a foundation ¶財団の後援する foundation-sponsored《research》/ ロックフェラー財団 the Rockefeller Foundation / 財団法人 a foundation ; a foundational juridical person.

さいち 才知 wits ⇨さいかく★ ; intelligence ¶才知のある intelligent ; bright.

さいちゅう 最中 ¶最中(に) in the middle [midst] of ; 〈間に〉in the course of ; during ; while / 戦争の最中に in the midst of the war. [文例⇩]

ざいちゅう 在中 [文例⇩]

さいちょうさ 再調査 《文》(a) reinvestigation ; 《文》(a) reexamination ¶再調査する《文》reinvestigate ; 《文》reexamine.

さいてい[1] 最低 ¶最低の the lowest ; 《文》the lowermost ; 〈最小の〉(the) minimum ; 〈最悪の〉the worst / 最低に見積もる give the lowest possible estimate ; estimate《a repair job》at《¥200,000》at the minimum / 最低価格 the lowest [bottom] price ; the floor price (制限価格) / 最低寒暖計 a minimum thermometer / 最低記録 a record [new] low level ; 《口語》a new [an all-time] low / 最低生活 the minimum standard of living / 最低賃銀制 a minimum wage system / 最低必要条件 the minimum requirements. [文例⇩]

さいてい[2] 裁定 (a) decision ; an award ; 〈仲裁〉an arbitration ¶為替の裁定〔商〕arbitration of exchange / 裁定する《文》adjudge ; decide ; rule《on》; arbitrate ; award ; give an award《for, against》.

さいてき 最適 ¶最適の the most suitable ; the best suited ; 《文》the fittest / 最適条件《文》the optimum (conditions).

さいてん[1] 祭典 a festival ⇨さいれい.

さいてん[2] 採点 ¶採点する mark《test papers》; grade《students》; 《米》rate ; 〈競技の〉score / 100点満点で採点する mark《a paper》out of 100 / 採点が辛い[甘い] be severe [generous] in (*one's*) marking / 出席を採点に加味する consider a student's attendance record when awarding marks / 採点者 a marker / 採点表 a list of marks / 採点簿 a mark [grade] book.

さいでん 祭殿 a sanctuary ; a shrine.

さいど 再度 twice ; again ; for the second time ¶再度訪問する make a second visit《to》; 《文》revisit.

サイドカー 〈側車付きオートバイ〉a motorcycle combination ★ a sidecar は側車のみ.

さいどく 再読 ¶再読する read《a book》again ; 《文》reread. [文例⇩]

料理が遅いね. ちょっと催促してくれたまえ. Isn't the service slow! Hurry them up a little.

さいだい[2] 建築費は最大限3千万円だ. The building cost must not exceed ¥30 million.

ざいたく 彼は在宅しておりますがどなたにもご面会はできません. He's at home, but he won't see anybody. | He is in, but is not at home to anybody. / 日曜の午前中なら在宅しております. I stay at home on Sunday mornings.

さいちゅう 今は暑い最中だ. We are at the height of the hot season. / 食事の最中に停電になった. The lights went off [out] in the middle of the meal.

ざいちゅう 写真在中.〔表示〕'Photos (only).'

さいてい[1] あの会社の給料は月最低8万円です. The monthly salary in that firm is 80,000 yen at the lowest [is a minimum of ¥80,000]. / あんなことをするやつは最低の人間だよ. A man who does that sort of thing is the lowest of the low. |《米俗》A person who would behave like that is the pits (of the world).

さいどく その記事は再読する値打ちがある. The article is worth a second reading.

サイドスロー〖野球〗sidearm delivery [throwing].

さいとつにゅう 再突入 〈ロケットの大気圏への〉re-entry ¶大気圏に再突入する re-enter the atmosphere; make a 《successful》re-entry (into the atmosphere).

サイドブレーキ a hand brake.

さいなむ torment; torture;《文》harass.

さいなん 災難 〈不幸〉《文》a misfortune; a mishap;〈災禍〉《文》a calamity; a disaster;〈事故〉an accident ¶災難を免れる escape a disaster / 災難にあう meet with a misfortune. 文例⇩

さいにゅう 歳入 〈国家の〉revenue;〈個人の〉an annual income.

さいにん 再任《文》reappointment ¶再任する reappoint (sb to a post).

ざいにん¹ 在任 ¶在任中 while in office; during one's service 《as managing director with the Kobe Bank》.

ざいにん² 罪人 〈法律上の〉a criminal; an offender; a convict (既決の); a culprit (未決の);《文》a wrongdoer;〈道徳・宗教上の〉a sinner.

さいにんしき 再認識 ¶再認識する see sth in a new [fresh] light;《文》have a new [renew one's] understanding (of).

さいねん 再燃 ¶インフレの再燃《文》(a) recurrence of inflation / 再燃する rekindle; revive; be revived; come to the fore again / 再燃させる rekindle; revive 《old quarrels》;《文》reignite 《a border dispute》; reheat 《the international crisis》.

さいのう 才能 (a) talent; a gift; ability ¶音楽の才能がある have a gift [a talent, a knack] for music / 才能のある人 a talented [《文》an able, a gifted] person;《文》a man of talent / 才能を充分に発揮する give full play to one's talent / 才能を隠す《文》conceal one's ability; hide one's light [candle] under a bushel. 文例⇩

さいのかわら 賽の河原《仏教》the Children's Limbo;〈比喩的に〉《文》Sisyphean [《文》unavailing, futile] effort.

さいのめ 賽の目 〈さいころの点〉the spots [of] a dice; the pips /〈さいころ形の物〉small cubes; dice ¶さいの目に切る dice 《vegetables》; cut 《tofu》 into dice [small cubes].

さいはい 采配 ¶采配を振る(う) lead; direct;《文》command ¶take [be in] charge (of); take [be in] command (of);《口語》boss [run] the show. 文例⇩

さいばい 栽培 cultivation; culture; raising; growing; growth ¶栽培する cultivate; grow; raise / 栽培技術 cultivation techniques / 栽培漁業 aquaculture / 栽培者 a grower; a cultivator / 栽培植物 a domesticated [cultivated] plant. 文例⇩

さいばし 菜箸 large chopsticks for cooking and serving food.

さいはつ 再発 a relapse [recurrence, return] (of a disease) ¶再発する〈病気が主語〉recur; return; redevelop (腫瘍(しゅよう)が);〈人が主語〉have [suffer] a relapse [return] (of); have a second [another] attack of.

ざいばつ 財閥 a financial combine [group, clique];〈同族の〉a giant family concern; a zaibatsu;〈富裕階級〉the plutocracy ¶三井財閥 the Mitsui combine [zaibatsu] / 財閥解体 the dissolution of the zaibatsu.

さいはっこう 再発行 ¶再発行する reissue.

さいはて 最果て ¶最果ての the farthest; the remotest.

サイバネティックス cybernetics.

さいはん 再版 (a) reprint;〈第2刷〉a second impression;〈改版〉a second edition ¶再版する reprint / 再版になる run into a second impression.

さいばん 裁判 a trial; a hearing ¶裁判する judge; try;〈判決を下す〉decide on 《a case》; pass judgment on / 裁判の傍聴人 a spectator at a trial / 裁判を開く hold a court / 裁判を受ける be tried; face 《a trial》; come up for trial; be on trial / 裁判に勝つ[負ける] win [lose] a case [suit] ★ suit は民事訴訟, case は刑事訴訟であるが, 弁護士や裁判官から見れば, どちらも case となりうる / 裁判にかける bring sb to trial [justice]; try sb (in court) / 裁判官 a judge; a justice;〈一裁判所の裁判官全員〉the court; the bench / 裁判権 (have) jurisdiction 《over》 / 裁判ざた (court) proceedings;〈民事〉a lawsuit; an action;〈刑事〉a trial / 裁判ざたにする take 《sb, a matter》 to court; sue sb; bring an action 《against sb》; take [《文》institute] (legal) proceedings 《against sb》; go to law 《against sb》;《口語》have the law (on [onto] sb); prosecute sb 〈刑事事件で検察が〉/ 裁判ざたにしないで解決する settle 《a matter》 out of court [without going to law] / 裁判ざたになる come to [end up in] court; result in court action / 裁判事件 A court case / 裁判所〈建物〉a courthouse;〈法廷〉a (law) court; a court of justice / 裁判所長 the president of a court / 裁判長 the presiding [chief] judge;《米》the chief justice / 裁判手続き court procedure / 裁判費用 judicial costs. 文例⇩

さいはん(ばい) 再販(売) resale ¶再販価格 a resale price.

さいひ¹ 採否 ¶採否を決する〈議案などの〉vote on 《a bill》 / 採否を通知する《文》notify sb of the result (of his application).

さいひ² 歳費〈支出〉annual expenditure;〈国会議員の〉手当〉an annual allowance [salary].

さいなん 彼らにまたもや災難が振りかかった. Another calamity befell them. / あれ以来災難続きでした. I have had a series of misfortunes ever since.

さいのう 彼の才能は文学よりも機械いじりの方にあった. His gifts lay in a mechanical rather than a literary direction.

さいはい 彼は数百人の雇い人に采配を振るっている. He has hundreds of employees under his command. / だれかが陰で采配を振るっているに違いない. There must be someone pulling strings [wires] behind the scenes.

さいばい この辺ではタバコの栽培が盛んである. Tobacco is cultivated [grown] on a large scale in this part of the country.

さいばん 裁判は被告の勝訴に

さいひつ 才筆 《文》《wield》a brilliant pen ; ⟨才文才⟩ literary talent.

さいひょう 砕氷 ¶砕氷機 an ice crusher / 砕氷船 an icebreaker ; an iceboat.

さいひょうか 再評価 《文》reassessment ; 《文》revaluation ; 《文》(a) reevaluation ¶再評価する reassess ; 《文》reevaluate.

さいふ¹ 財布 《硬貨をいれる》a purse ; ⟨2つ折れになった札入れ⟩ a wallet ; a pocketbook ¶財布が軽い be short of money ; 《文》have a light purse ; ⟨口語⟩ be feeling the draft / 財布のひもを締める[緩める] tighten [loosen] one's purse strings / 財布をはたく spend one's last penny / 一家の財布を握っている hold the family purse strings ; manage the family's money affairs [the family finances] / (一家の)財布を握っている人 the purse holder.

さいふ² 採譜 ¶採譜する take (a folk melody) down in musical notation.

さいぶ 細部 details ; 《文》particulars ¶細部にわたって詳しく記述する describe sth in fine detail / 細部にわたって調べる go into detail(s) [particulars].

さいぶそう 再武装 rearmament ⇒ さいぐんび ¶再武装する rearm (itself) ; 《文》remilitarize (a country).

さいぶん(か) 細分(化) 《文》subdivision ; 《文》fragmentation ; 《文》ramification (分岐) ¶細分化する subdivide ; 《文》fractionize ; break into parts ; 《文》ramify.

さいべつ 細別 《文》subdivision ⇒ さいぶん(か) ¶細別する subdivide (into) ; 《文》itemize.

さいへん 細片 a slender [small] piece.

さいへんせい 再編成 reorganization ¶再編成する reorganize ; regroup.

さいほう 裁縫 sewing ; needlework ; ⟨仕立て⟩ tailoring ; dressmaking ¶裁縫が上手[へた]である be good [poor] at needlework ; be clever [awkward] with the needle / 裁縫をする do needlework ; sew / 裁縫台 a sewing table / 裁縫道具 sewing things / 裁縫ばさみ (a pair of) sewing scissors ; (sewing) shears (大形の).

さいぼう 細胞 〖生物〗 a cell ¶細胞の cellular / 細胞核 a (cell) nucleus (pl. -clei, -cleuses) / 細胞学 cytology / 細胞質 cytoplasm / 細胞組織 (the) cellular tissue / 細胞壁 the cell wall / 細胞分化 cell [cellular] differentiation / 細胞分裂 cell division / 細胞膜 cell membrane.

ざいほう 財宝 ⟨貴重品⟩ treasure(s) ; ⟨富⟩ 《文》riches ⇒ たから.

さいほうそう 再放送 a rebroadcast ; a repeat (performance) ; rebroadcasting ¶再放送する rebroadcast.

サイボーグ a cyborg ★ cybernetic organism からの合成語.

サイホン a siphon ¶サイホン作用 siphon effect ; siphonage / サイホン式コーヒー入れ a siphon coffee-maker.

さいまつ 歳末 the end of the year ; the year-end ¶歳末売出し[贈答品, 風景] a year-end sale [present, scene].

さいみつ 細密 《文》minute ; detailed ; fine ; close ; elaborate ⇒ せいみつ / 細密画 a miniature.

さいみん 催眠 ¶催眠剤 a sleeping drug [pill] ; a hypnotic [soporific] (agent) / 催眠術 hypnotism / 催眠術を施す hypnotize sb / 催眠術師 a hypnotist / 催眠療法 hypnotherapy / 催眠状態にある be in a hypnotic trance [state] ; be under hypnosis / 催眠状態からさます dehypnotize sb.

さいむ 債務 a debt ; an obligation ; liabilities ¶債務がある have debts (of 2 million yen) ; owe (sb 100,000 yen) ; stand [be] in sb's debt / 債務を果たす meet one's liabilities ; settle [pay] one's debts / 債務国 a debtor nation / 債務者 a debtor ; 〖法〗 an obligor / 債務不履行 default on [nonfulfillment of] an obligation.

ざいむ 財務 financial affairs ¶財務官 a financial commissioner / 財務局 the Financial Bureau / (米国の)財務省[長官] the Department [Secretary] of Treasury.

ざいめい 罪名 で on a charge of (fraud). 文例⇩

さいもく 細目 details ; 《文》particulars ; (specified) items ; specifications ¶細目にわたる go into details ; enter into particulars.

ざいもく 材木 wood (for building) ; ⟨挽(ひ)いた材木⟩ timber ; 《米》 lumber ¶材木を切り出す lumber ((in) a valley) / 材木にするために木を切る cut down trees for lumber / 材木置場 a lumberyard ; a timberyard / 材木商 a lumber [timber] dealer [merchant] / 材木流し lumber [timber] floating.

さいや 在野 ¶在野の (a party) out of office [power] ; non-Government (parties) ; (the parties) in opposition ; 在野党 ⇒ やとう¹.

さいやく 災厄 ⇒ さいなん.

さいゆしゅつ 再輸出 ¶再輸出する reexport.

さいゆにゅう 再輸入 ¶再輸入する reimport.

さいよう 採用 ⟨採択⟩ 《文》adoption ; ⟨任用⟩ 《文》appointment ; ⟨雇用⟩ 《文》employment ¶採用する adopt ((a plan)) ; accept ((a proposal)) ; introduce ((a system)) ; (start to) use ((a textbook)) ; employ ((a secretary)) ; 《文》engage / 採用試験 an examination for service / 採用通知 a notification of appointment / 不採用通知状 a rejection letter. 文例⇩

さいらい 再来 《文》a second coming [advent]. 文例⇩

ざいらい 在来 ¶在来の conventional ; old ; usual ; common ; ordinary / 在来種の native (strawberries) / 在来線 the old (Tokaido) line.

ざいりゅう 在留 ⇒ ざいじゅう ¶在留邦人 Japa-

た. The case was decided in favor of the defendant. / 事件は今裁判中です. The case is now on trial. / 裁判ざたは御免だ. We don't want to get involved with the courts. | I want to keep the courts [the law] out of this.

ざいめい 窃盗の罪名をきせられた. They charged him [He was charged] with theft.

さいよう タイピストとしてご採用下さい. I wish to offer my services as a typist. / ご投稿は遺憾ながら採用できません. The editor regrets that he is unable to make use of your contribution.

さいらい 彼はミルトンの再来だ. He is a second Milton. | He is

さいりょう¹ 最良 ¶最良の best; the ideal.
さいりょう² 裁量 discretion; decision ¶裁量に任せる leave sth to sb's discretion; give sb a free hand (in [concerning] sth) / 自分の裁量で at one's (own) discretion.
ざいりょう 材料 (a) material; stuff; 〈資料〉 data ⇒データ★ ¶材料を集める amass [collect] materials [data] (for) / 楽観[悲観]材料 an encouraging [a disheartening] factor / 材料試験 material(s) testing / 材料費 the cost of materials.
ざいりょく 財力 financial power; the power of money; money power; 〈財産〉 〈文〉 means; resources; 〈文〉 wealth ¶財力のある人 a man of means [wealth].
ザイル 〈<(ドイツ語) Seil〉 a rope ¶ザイルを岩にセットする belay a rope round [to] a rock.
さいるい 催涙 ¶催涙ガス tear gas / 催涙弾 a tear bomb [shell]; a tear gas grenade.
さいれい 祭礼 a festival; a fête; a festival rite ¶祭礼を行なう hold [celebrate] a festival (at the Hachiman Shrine).
サイレン a siren; a hooter (工場などの) ¶サイレンを鳴らす sound a siren; blow a hooter.
サイロ a silo (pl. -s).
さいろく 採録 ¶採録する select [extract] (a passage) and put (it) on record.
さいわい 幸い 〈幸福〉 happiness; 〈文〉 bliss; 〈文〉 felicity; 〈幸運〉 good luck [fortune] ¶幸いな lucky; 〈文〉 happy; 〈文〉 blessed; fortunate / 幸いに fortunately; luckily; by good luck [fortune]; 〈文〉 by a happy chance / 天候に幸いされる be favored by good weather. 文例⇩
サイン¹ 〈暗号〉 a sign; 〈合図〉 a signal; 〈署名〉 a signature; an autograph (有名人などの) ¶サインする sign (the hotel register); autograph (a book); sign one's name (on) / サインを送る signal; motion / サイン入りの写真 an autographed [a signed] photo / サイン帳 an autograph book [album] / サインペン a fiber-tipped pen / サインボール an autographed ball.
サイン² 〈数〉 a sine (略: sin).
ざいん 座員 a member of the company [troupe]; 〈総称〉 the company ¶座員一同に成り代わりまして representing [on behalf of] all the members of our troupe.
サウジアラビア Saudi Arabia ¶サウジアラビア王国 the Kingdom of Saudi Arabia / サウジアラビア人 a Saudi Arabian; a Saudi.
サウスカロライナ South Carolina (略: S.C.) ¶サウスカロライナ州の人 a South Carolinian.
サウスダコタ South Dakota (略: S.Dak., S.D.) ¶サウスダコタ州の人 a South Dakotan.
サウスポー 〖野球・ボクシング〗 a southpaw ⇒さとうしゃ.
サウナぶろ サウナ風呂 《have》 a sauna (bath).
サウンドトラック a soundtrack.
サウンドボックス a sound box.
さえ¹ 冴え ¶頭のさえ a sharp mind; 〈文〉 keen intelligence; a clear head / 腕のさえを見せる show [display] one's skill [dexterity] (in).
さえ² 〈すら〉 even ¶...さえすれば if only...; so long as... / 名前さえ書けない cannot even [so much as] write one's own name. 文例⇩
さえかえる 冴え返る be perfectly clear.
さえき 差益 marginal profits; a margin.
さえぎる 遮る interrupt sb; head sb off; obstruct 《the view》; bar (the way); cut off [out]; 〈文〉 intercept 《a stream》 ¶光を遮る block off the light / 人の言葉を遮る cut sb short [off]; interrupt sb / 道を遮る block [stand in] sb's way. 文例⇩
さえずり a song; a chirp; chirping; a twitter; twittering; 〈うぐいすなどの〉 a warble; warbling; 〈おしゃべり〉 chattering.
さえずる sing; chirp; chirrup; twitter; warble (うぐいすなどが); 〈しゃべる〉 chatter.
さえる 冴える 〈澄む〉 be clear; 〈熟練する〉 get skilled ¶さえた音色 a clear tone / 頭のさえた clear-headed; intelligent; 〈口語〉 be wakeful; be wide-awake / さえた色 a bright color / さえない色 a dull [somber] color / 気分がさえない feel depressed [down] / さえない顔をする pull [make] a long face; look miserable [blue] / 月のさえた夜 a bright moonlight night. 文例⇩
さお 竿 a pole; a rod ¶はかりのさお the (scale) beam; the arm of a balance / さおさすpole (punt) 《a boat》 / 小舟にさおさして川をさかのぼる punt up a stream / 時代の流れにさおさす 〈逆らわない〉 swim with the tide

---

Milton reincarnate.
サイレン 消防車がサイレンを鳴らしながら何台も走って行った. Fire engines scudded away with their sirens wailing. / 昼のサイレンが鳴った. The noon siren [hooter] blew. / サイレンが鳴り止んだ. The siren died.
さいわい 幸いにも私の試みは成功した. I was fortunate enough to succeed in my attempt. / 幸いなことにだれひとりけがはなかった. Mercifully no one was hurt. / 明日は幸い日曜日だからお伺いしましょう. It happens to be [Luckily it's] Sunday tomorrow, so I will come and see you. / お役にたてば幸いです. I shall be happy if I can be of any help (to you). / 心の清き者は幸なり. 〖聖書〗 Blessed are the pure in heart.
サイン¹ 飛行機から降りるやいなや, サイン攻めにあった. He was besieged by autograph hunters [seekers] the moment he stepped off the plane.
さえ² 孔子さえ欠点あるを免れなかった. Even Confucius was not free from faults. / 白味の魚でありさえすればどんなものでもよろしい. Any fish will do as [so] long as its meat is white. / ボタンを押しさえすればいい. You have only to press the button. / 君はただ一生懸命に勉強しさえすればいいのだ. All you have to do is (to) work hard. / 彼は暇さえあれば魚釣りだ. He goes fishing whenever he has time [a moment] to spare.
さえぎる 月が雲に遮られて見えなくなった. The moon was obscured [hidden] by the clouds. / 木立ちに遮られて向こうの景色がよく見えない. The view was obstructed [shut out] by a clump of trees. / 彼を遮って演説を思いとどまらせた. I headed him off

さおとめ 早乙女 〈田植えの娘〉 a rice-planting girl; 〈少女〉 a girl.

さか¹ 坂 a slope; an incline; a hill ¶坂の上に at the top [head] of a hill [slope] / 坂の下に at the bottom [foot] of a hill [slope] / 坂を上る[下る] go up [down] a slope; go uphill [downhill] / 七十の坂を越えている be on the wrong [other] side of seventy; be over seventy / 道が坂になっている〈上り〉 slope up [upward]; 〈下り〉 slope down [downward] / 上り坂 an uphill [upward] slope;《文》an ascent / 下り坂 a downhill [downward] slope;《文》a descent / 楽な坂 an easy slope / 緩やかな[急な]坂 a gentle [steep] slope / 坂道 a hill; a sloping road; a slope. 文例 ↓

さか² 茶菓 refreshments; tea and cakes ¶茶菓を出す serve light refreshments [tea and cakes].

さかあがり 逆上がり 《体操》forward upward circling (on the (horizontal) bar).

さかい 境 〈境界〉a border; a boundary; 〈国境〉the frontier ¶境を接する border (on); be bounded (by);《文》abut (on, against); share borders (with) / 境目 a boundary line; a borderline (between). 文例 ↓

さかえ 栄え 〈繁栄〉prosperity; 〈栄華〉glory ¶…に栄えあれ《文》May (Keio) flourish !

さかえる 栄える prosper; flourish; thrive; be prosperous. 文例 ↓

さかおとし 逆落とし 〈墜落〉a headlong fall; 〈攻撃〉a downhill rush.

さかき【植】a sakaki plant.

さがく 差額 the difference; the balance ¶差額を払う pay the balance / 貿易の差額 the balance of trade / 差額ベッド a bed incurring an extra charge.

さかぐら 酒蔵 a wine cellar [vault]; 〈酒造場〉a sake brewery.

さかご 逆子【医】《have》a breech delivery [birth]; (a) foot presentation.

さかさ(ま) 逆さ(ま) ¶逆さ(ま)の upside-down; inverted; reverse;《文》inverse / 逆さに upside down; the wrong way [side] up; 〈左右・前後逆に〉the wrong way round / 鉛筆を逆さに持つ hold a pencil by the wrong end / 逆さにする turn sth upside down [topsy-turvy];《文》invert; turn 《a bottle》bottom up / 逆さに置いた箱 an upended box / ABC を逆さに言う say the alphabet backward / 逆さまにぶら下がっている be hanging head down / 逆さ富士 an inverted image of Mt. Fuji (reflected in the water) / 逆さまつげ ingrowing eyelashes;【医】trichiasis. for. 文例 ↓

さがしもの 捜し物 something one is looking for.

さがしら 座頭 the leader of a troupe.

さがす 捜す look for; search for; have a look for;《文》seek; 〈捜索する〉hunt (up); trace; locate (所在を) ¶家の中を捜す search a house (for sth) / 引き出しの中を捜す search [rummage in] a drawer (for sth) / (辞書の) m のところを捜す search under m [the m's] / ポケットの中を手探りで捜す fumble [feel, fish] in one's pocket (for) / 職を捜す hunt [look] for a job / …を捜しに行く go in search [quest] of… / 捜し出す find [seek] out; discover, detect; locate / (人の)居所を捜し出す locate [find out] sb's whereabouts / 捜し回る look about (for); cast about [around] (for); scout around (for). 文例 ↓

さかずき 杯 a sake cup; a goblet (足付きの) ¶杯をさす[受ける] offer [accept] a cup / 杯を返す offer a cup in return / 杯をほす drain [empty] one's cup / 杯を合わす touch cups (with sb) / 杯に酒を注ぐ fill a cup.

さかぞり 逆剃り ¶逆ぞりをかける shave [use a razor] against the grain; shave upward.

さかだち 逆立ち 〈両手だけの〉a handstand; 〈頭もつけた〉a headstand ¶逆立ちする stand on one's hands [head]; do a handstand [headstand] / 逆立ちして歩く walk on one's hands. 文例 ↓

さかだつ 逆立つ stand on end; bristle up.

さかだてる 逆立てる bristle up (its hair); ruffle up (its feathers) ¶髪を逆立てて with one's hair erect [on end] / (犬などが)毛を逆立てて with raised hackles; with its hackles up.

さかだる 酒樽 a (sake) cask [barrel].

さかて¹ 逆手【体操】〈鉄棒の握り方〉the reverse [underhand] grip ¶短刀を逆手に持つ hold a dagger in a backhand grip.

さかて² 酒手 〈酒代〉drink [beer] money; 〈心付け〉a tip.

(from) making a speech.

さえる 月はさえ渡り海は静かであ る. The moon is bright and the sea calm.

さか¹ 家は坂を上り詰めた所にあ る. My house stands at the top of a hill. / 坂が緩くなった. The slope eased. / 一本の小道が緩やかな坂をなして彼の家の門まで続いていた. A lane rose gently [led in a slight gradient] to the gate of his house.

さかい この川が両県の境になっている. This river forms the boundary between the two prefectures. / そのさくが私の地所と彼の地所との境になっているので from his. / 浅間山は信州と上州との境にある. Mt. Asama stands on the boundary between Shinshu and Joshu.

さかえる あの店は栄えている. That store is doing good business. / 彼らはこしょうの取引で栄えた. They made their money from trade in pepper.

さがしもの 捜し物ですか. Are you looking for something?

さがす 町中くまなく行くえ不明になった犬を捜し回った. They combed the streets for the missing dog. / 家の中をくまなく捜したが見当たらなかった. I had a good search all over the house, but I could not find it. / その辺の店を捜してみよう. I think I'll shop around for it. / あの会社でタイピストを捜している. That firm is looking for a typist. / A typist is wanted [They need a typist] at that company.

さかだち 君が逆立ちしても, とても彼にはかなわないよ. You can try till you're blue in the face,

さかとびこみ 逆飛び込み〘水泳〙a headlong plunge [dive]; a header.

さかな[1] 魚 a fish《*pl.* -(es)》(★ two fishes のように, 具体的に数詞を伴う場合以外は, 複数形の fishes はあまり使われない);〈料理としての〉fish ¶魚3匹 three fishes / 数匹[たくさん]の魚 several [a lot of] fish / 魚の肉 fish meat / 魚の骨 a fish bone / 魚のたくさんいる川 a river teeming with fish / 魚屋〈人〉a fishmonger;〈店〉《米》a fish store;《英》a fish shop.

さかな[2] 肴 a side dish; a relish《taken with alcoholic drinks》.

[さ]

さかなで 逆なで ¶逆なでする rub《a cat》(up) the wrong way / (人の)神経を逆なでするようなことを言う say things that rub *sb* (up) the wrong way.

さかなみ 逆波 a head [chopping] sea.

ざがね 座金 a (metal) washer.

さかねじ 逆ねじ ¶逆ねじを食わせる retort《at [to] *sb*》; give a retort《to》; get back《at *sb*》; turn the tables《on *sb*》.

さかのぼる〈上流へ向かう〉go upstream; go up《a river》;〈過去に戻る〉go [trace] back《to the past》;〈遡及する〉《文》be retroactive [retrospective]《to》 ¶四月一日にさかのぼって《be effective》retroactive(ly) to April 1. [文例⇩]

さかば 酒場 a bar; a tavern;《米》a saloon;《英》a pub;《英》a public house ¶酒場の女 a bar girl.

さかまく 逆巻く roll; rage; boil ¶逆巻く怒とう《文》raging billows;《文》an angry [a turbulent] sea.

さかもり 酒盛り a drinking bout [party];《文》a carousal ¶酒盛りをする have a drinking party; have a drunken feast.

さかや 酒屋〈人〉a *sake* [wine] dealer [merchant];〈店〉a *sake* [wine] shop;《米》a package store;《英》an off-licence;〈醸造所〉a *sake* brewery.

さかゆめ 逆夢 [文例⇩]

さからう 逆らう〈反する〉go [act] against; oppose;〈従わない〉disobey;〈反抗する〉revolt [rebel]《against》; defy ¶時代に逆らう swim [go] against the tide [current] of the times / …に逆らって against; contrary to; in the face [teeth] of; in defiance of / 風に逆らって進む go in the teeth of the wind. [文例⇩]

さかり 盛り〈絶頂〉the height; the peak;《文》the zenith;〈人生の〉the prime of life;《in》*one's* prime;〈交尾欲〉heat (雌の); rut (雄の) ¶夏の盛り《in》high summer;《in》the height of summer / 盛りがついている be in rut [heat] / 盛りのついた牛 a cow in heat / 盛りを過ぎる be past *one's* [*its*] prime [best]; be on the decline [《文》wane] / 若い盛りに in the prime of (*one's*) youth / 盛りである〈花が〉be in full bloom [glory]; be at《their》best;〈果物が〉be in season;〈事が〉be in full swing. [文例⇩]

さかりば 盛り場 an amusement district;〈繁華街〉the busiest area (of town).

さがりめ 下がり目 downward-slanting eyes;〈衰勢〉a declining [falling] tendency [trend] ¶下がり目になっている〈物価などが〉show a downtrend [downward tendency];〈運などが〉be on the decline [《文》wane].

さがる 下がる〈垂れ下がる〉hang (down); dangle《from》;〈低下する〉go [come] down; drop; fall;〈衰える〉decline; sink;《文》wane;〈引き下がる〉leave; withdraw [《文》retire]《from》;〈後退する〉step back;〈退歩する〉fall off; deteriorate;〈位などが〉come down; be demoted《to》 ¶一歩下がる take a step backward / 腕が下がる *one's* skill falls off. [文例⇩]

さかん 盛ん ¶盛んな〈繁盛している〉prosperous; flourishing; thriving;〈上首尾の〉successful;〈活気ある〉busy; active; lively; vigorous;〈熱心な〉hearty; enthusiastic;〈激しい〉furious; hot;〈手広い〉《文》extensive; large;〈流行している〉popular / 盛んになる〈栄える〉prosper; flourish;〈活発になる〉become active; be in full flood;〈人気を得る〉become popular;〈勢いが増す〉gain force / 盛んに歓迎する welcome *sb* warmly; give *sb* a cordial reception. [文例⇩]

さがん[1] 左岸《on》the left bank《of》.

さがん[2] 砂岩〘地質〙sandstone.

さかん(や) 左官(屋) a plasterer ¶左官工事 plaster work; plastering.

さき[1] 先〈先端〉the point《of a pencil》; the tip《of a finger》; the end《of a stick》;〈目的地〉the [*one's*] destination;〈相手〉the other party; he; she; they;〈未来〉the future ¶これ

---

but you'll never get the better of him.

さかのぼる その当時にさかのぼって考えるとずいぶん愉快な事があった. When I look back on the time, I recall many exciting events. / 新給与は5月1日にさかのぼって支給される. The new pay scales are retroactive to May 1st. | The new salaries will be paid retrospectively from May 1. / この大学の設立ははるか12世紀にさかのぼります. The foundation of this university dates [goes] back to the twelfth century.

さかゆめ 夢は逆夢. Dreams go by contraries. / 夢には逆夢ということがある. Sometimes dreams mean the exact opposite of what happens in them.

さからう 彼は逆らわずに聞いていた. He listened without contradicting me.

さかり 海水浴は今が盛りだ. The sea-bathing season is now in full swing.

さがる 物価は常に上がる一方で, 下がることは決してない. Prices do nothing but rise [go up all the time]; they never come down. / 10年後には貨幣価値が今よりさらに下がっているのはほぼ間違いない. It is almost certain that the value of money will have gone even further down [will have declined even further] ten years from now. / 温度が急に下がった. There was a sharp drop in temperature. / 今度の試験で順位が5番下がった. I dropped [went down] five places in class after the recent examination.

さかん 彼の盛んな時代もあった. He has seen better days. / スキーが盛んだ. Skiing is all the rage [in great vogue]. / 適度の運動は血液の循環を盛んにする. Moder-

さき から先 from now on; in (the) future (⇒こんご★); 《文》hereafter / さおの先 the end of a pole / 先がとがっている be sharp [pointed] at the end / 先の〈元の〉《文》former; ex-; one-time;〈近頃の〉recent;《文》late / 水戸から3つ先の駅 the third station beyond Mito / 先のことを考える think of the future; think ahead [about one's future] / 先を争う try to be first;〈文〉rival sb for priority / …の先を行く be ahead of… / 先に〈以前に〉before; earlier (than); previous (to);《文》prior (to); 〈もと〉previously;〈文〉formerly;〈前もって〉beforehand; in advance / 何よりも先に first of all; before everything else / 100メートルほど先に about 100 meters along [ahead] / 先に立って歩く walk ahead of (others); lead the way / 先に述べたように《文》as mentioned earlier;《文》as previously stated / 外出先 the place where one has gone. 文例⇩

さき 左記 ¶左記の the following;《文》the (items) below / 左記のとおり《文》as follows. 文例⇩

さぎ¹ 詐欺 (a) fraud; a swindle; a trick; trickery ¶詐欺を働く swindle; practice [《口語》perpetrate] a swindle; commit a fraud 《on》/ 詐欺にかかる be swindled (by); fall a victim to a fraud / 詐欺で金を巻きあげる《文》defraud sb of his money; swindle money out of sb; cheat [swindle] sb out of (his) money / 詐欺師 a swindler; a confidence [《口語》con] man; a trickster; a sharper.

さぎ² 《鳥》〈白さぎ〉an [a white] egret; 〈青さぎ〉a (gray) heron;〈五位さぎ〉a night heron ¶さぎをからすと言いくるめる ⇒いいくるめる.

さきおととい three days ago [《口語》back]; two days before yesterday.

さきおととし three years ago [《口語》back]; two years before last.

さきがけ 先駆け〈先んじること〉the lead; the initiative /〈先駆者〉a pioneer /〈前ぶれ〉《文》a herald;《文》a harbinger; a forerunner ¶先駆けをする be the first (to do); take the lead [initiative] (in) / 流行の先駆けをする lead the fashion.

さきごろ 先ごろ ⇒せんじつ.

さきざき 先々〈未来〉the (distant) future;〈行く所々〉places one goes to ¶先々の事まで考える look far ahead [into the future]; think ahead about the future 《of》/ 行く先々でもてる be made much of wherever one goes.

サキソフォン ⇒サクソフォーン.

さきだつ 先立つ go ahead of; go [come] before; happen before;《文》precede ¶…に先立って before; earlier than;《文》previous [prior] to / 息子に先立たれる survive (outlive) one's son. 文例⇩

さきどり 先取り ¶先取りする〈あらかじめ受け取る〉take [receive] in advance;〈予想して行動する〉《文》anticipate (a new era).

さきばしる 先走る be forward (in, with);《口語》jump the gun; be too far ahead 《of》¶先走った男 a forward [presumptuous] man.

さきばらい 先払い〈到着払い〉payment [cash] on delivery;〈前払い〉payment in advance ¶先払いする pay in advance / 運賃先払いで carriage forward (先方); carriage paid (当方) / 料金先払いので C.O.D. (★ cash on delivery の略);《米》collect / 先払いで…を送る send sth cash on delivery;《米》send sth collect / 料金先払いで電話をかける《米》make a collect call;《米》call sb collect;《英》make a transfer-charge call;《英》phone sb reversing [and reverse] the charges / 郵便先払い postage payable on delivery. 文例⇩

さきぶと 先太 ¶先太に thickened toward the end; club-shaped.

さきぶれ 先触れ ⇒まえぶれ.

さきぼそ 先細 ¶先細の tapering / 先細の指 tapered fingers / 先細にする taper off [down, away].

さきぼそり 先細り ¶先細りになる go downhill; taper off / 先細りになって消滅する peter out; fizzle out.

さきほど 先程 ⇒さっき.

さきまわり 先回り ¶先回りする forestall sb; get [have] a start on sb;《文》anticipate sb in doing.

さきみだれる 咲き乱れる《文》bloom profusely [in profusion]. 文例⇩

さきもの 先物《相場》《buy》futures ¶先物買い purchase of futures /〈思惑買い〉speculation / 先物取引 dealings in futures.

さきやま 先山《鉱山》a coal-cutter.

さきゅう 砂丘 a (sand) dune; a sandhill.

さきゆき 先行き the future;《相場》future prospects.

ate exercise improves the circulation (of the blood). / 炉で火が盛んに燃えている。The fire is burning briskly in the fireplace. / 皆がまだ盛んに拍手しているのに、彼は壇を降りて来た。He came down from the platform while the applause was still at its height. / 昨夜のパーティーはなかなか盛んなものでした。The party last night was a great success.

さき¹ 尾の先が房になっている。The tail ends in a tuft. / 君はまだ先が長い。You have a long future ahead of you. / 荷物は先に送っておこう。I will send my baggage on ahead. / 費用の問題がなにより先だ。The question of expense is the first consideration. / 家は3軒先に住んでいる。He lives three doors away. / 箱根は小田原のどの先ですか。How far past Odawara is Hakone? / How far is Hakone beyond Odawara? / 彼らは何も先の当てがない。They've got nothing to look ahead to. / これから先は歩いて行きます。I will walk the rest of the way. / その先を話しな

さい。Go on with your story. / これは先の見込みがない。There is no future in this. | This has no future.

さき² 左記の品をお送り下さい。Please send us the undermentioned articles.

さきだつ 先立つものは金。Money is the first requisite.

さきばらい（電話で）料金先払いにして下さい。I'd like a collect call, please.

さきみだれる そこには花が咲き乱れている。The whole place is ablaze with flowering plants.

さぎょう 作業 work ¶作業をする work / 作業している be working [at work] / 作業仮説 a working hypothesis / 作業計画 a work project / 作業時間 working hours / 作業室 a workroom / 作業場 a workshop / 作業中(に) while at work / 作業班 a work [working] party ;〈軍隊の〉a fatigue party / 作業服 working clothes ;〈工具の〉overalls.

さぎょう 座興 ¶座興に to amuse [entertain] the company ; in [for] fun ; by way of a joke.

ざぎょう 座業 《文》 sedentary work ; a sedentary occupation [job].

さぎり 狭霧 a thin fog [mist, haze].

さきん 砂金 gold dust ; alluvial [placer] gold ¶砂金を採る〈なべで選り分けて〉pan gold ;〈砂を洗って〉wash for gold / 砂金採取 placer mining.

さきんじる 先んじる 〈先行する〉go ahead (of sb);《文》precede ; get a head start (on sb) ;〈先を越す〉forestall ;《文》anticipate ; get [have] a start (on sb) ; take the lead [initiative] (in doing) ¶…に先んじて in advance of ;《文》prior [previous] to ; before ; ahead of. 文例↓

さく¹ 作〈作品〉a work ;〈収穫〉a harvest ; a crop ; a yield ¶作がよい[悪い] have a good [bad] crop (of rice) ; have a rich [poor] harvest (of wheat) / セザンヌの作 a work by Cézanne ; a Cézanne / 一[二]番作 the first [second] crop.

さく² 柵 a fence ; a railing ; a paling ; a stockade ; fencing (集合的) ¶さくをめぐらす fence in [up] ; rail in ; palisade (a place) ; enclose (a place) with a palisade / さくを設ける set [put] up a fence (around) ; fence (around).

さく³ 策〈計画〉a plan ; a scheme ;〈政策〉a policy ;〈手段〉a step ;《文》a measure ;《文》a means (単複同形) ¶策が尽きる be at one's wits' end ; be at the end of one's resources / 策を施す take measures [steps] / 策を巡らす[講じる] work out [《文》devise] a scheme ; draw up a plan / 策をろうする《文》use artifice ; play tricks (on sb) / 策を誤る take a wrong step. 文例↓

さく⁴ 咲く bloom ; flower ; blossom ; come out [into flower] ; open ¶咲いている be in bloom [flower] ; be out ; be open / 咲き初める start flowering ; come into blossom / 咲きそろっている be in full bloom ; be at 《their》 best / 咲き誇る be in all 《their》 glory. 文例↓

さく⁵ 裂[割]く 〈裂く〉tear ; rend ; split ;〈切り裂く〉cut up ;《文》cleave ;〈引き離す〉cut off ;〈割き与える〉spare ;〈譲渡する〉cede (territory) ¶ずたずたに裂く tear 《a letter》 into shreds [to ribbons] ; tear 《a sheet of paper》up into fragments / 仲を裂く set 《A and B》 at odds ; alienate [estrange] 《A from B》 / 時間を割く spare time (for). 文例↓

さくい¹ 作為 ¶作為的〈人為的〉artificial ;〈故意の〉intentional ; deliberate / 作為動詞《文法》a factitive verb. 文例↓

さくい² 作意 〈創作などの趣向〉a central theme ;《フランス語》a motif ;〈作者の意図〉the intention of the author.

さくいん 索引 an index (pl. -dexes, -dices) ¶完全な[充分な]索引 fully-[well-]indexed 《atlases》/ 索引をつける index 《a book》; provide 《a book》 with an index / カード式[ABC 順]索引 a card [an alphabetical] index / 書物の索引 an index to a book / 索引カード an index card / 索引付きの[なしの]本 an indexed [unindexed, indexless] book / 他所参照用索引システム a cross-indexing system.

ザクースカ 《ロシア語》zakuski ★複数扱い. zakuska は zakuski の単数形だが, 英語では普通使われない.

さくおとこ 作男 a farmhand ; a farm worker [laborer].

さくがら 作柄 a harvest ; a crop ⇒さく¹ 作柄予想 crop [harvest] prospects ;〈予想収穫高〉the estimated crop (of rice).

さくがんき 削岩機 a rock drill.

さくぐ 索具 rigging ; tackle ¶索具を取り付ける rig 《a ship》.

さくげん 削減 ¶削減する cut (down) ; slice ;《文》curtail ;《文》retrench ; slash / 経費を削減する cut down (on) expenses / 予算の削減 budgetary cutbacks [cuts]. 文例↓

さくご 錯誤 a mistake ;《文》an error ¶錯誤に陥る make [commit] a mistake ;《文》fall into an error.

さくさく ¶さくさくする〈果物などが〉be crisp [crunchy] to eat ;〈汁気がない〉be not juicy [《文》succulent].

ざくざく ¶砂利の上をざくざく歩く crunch on gravel.

さくさん 酢酸 《化》 acetic acid ¶酢酸アミル pentyl [amyl] acetate ; banana oil / 酢酸塩 an acetate / 酢酸鉛 lead acetate.

さくし¹ 作詞 ¶作詞する〈流行歌などを〉write the words [lyrics] (for) / 《…氏》作詞 words [lyrics] by… / 作詞者 a lyric writer ; a songwriter.

さくし² 策士 a schemer ; a trickster ; a tactician ; a resourceful man. 文例↓

さくじつ 昨日 yesterday ⇒きのう¹.

さくしほう 作詩法 〈詩の作り方〉how to write

さきんじる 彼の思想ははるかに時代に先んじていた. His ideas were far ahead of his times. / 先んずれば人を制す. Take the lead, and you will win. | First come, first served.

さく³ 当を得た策ではない. That is [would be] unadvisable [unwise]. / こうなっては策の施しようがない. It is past remedying.

さく⁴ 花が咲いた. The flowers are out. / ぼたんがみごとに咲いている. The peonies are blooming beautifully [in magnificent bloom].

さく⁵ 私は胸を裂かれる思いをした. It was heartrending [enough to break my heart]. / 彼は忙しいところを時間を割いて出席してくれた. Busy as he was, he made time to attend the meeting.

さくい¹ この作品は作為の跡が露骨だ. This piece is too artificial.

さくげん 米国下院歳出委員会は海外援助に関する政府の要求額40億ドルのうち9億ドルを削減した. The House Appropriations Committee of the United States sliced $900 million out of the Administration's $4 billion foreign aid appropriation request.

ざくざく 大判小判がざくざく出てきた. Old gold coins came out in

さくしゃ 作者 the author; the authoress (女); the writer ¶作者不明の 《文》 of unknown authorship; anonymous. 文例↓

さくしゅ 搾取 exploitation ¶搾取する exploit; sweat sb; squeeze 《the poor》 / 搾取[被搾取]階級 the exploiting [exploited] class(es).

さくじょ 削除 ¶削除する 《文》 delete; eliminate; cancel; blot [cross, strike] out; blue-pencil / 名簿から削除する (sb's name) off the list / 無削除版 a complete and unexpurgated edition; an unabridged edition.

さくず 作図 ¶作図する draw a figure [chart, diagram]; 〖幾何〗 construct 《a triangle》; 〈数式をグラフに〉 plot / 作図問題 〖幾何〗 a construction problem.

さくせい 作成 ¶作成する make (out); draw up 《a document》; prepare 《a deed》; 〈契約・登記などを正式に〉 《文》 execute / 2通作成する make out 《a contract》 in duplicate.

さくせん 作戦 〈戦術〉 tactics; 〈戦略〉 strategy; 〈行動〉 (military, naval) operations ¶作戦上の strategic; operational / 作戦を練る elaborate [work out] a plan of operations / 作戦を誤る commit a strategic error / 直ちに作戦に使用できる be ready for operational use / 共同作戦 concerted operations; combined action / 作戦会議 a council of war / 作戦計画[基地] a plan [base] of operations. 文例↓

さくぜん 索然 ¶索然たる dry; dull; 《文》 devoid of interest.

さくそう 錯綜 ¶錯そうした complicated; intricate; knotty; entangled.

サクソフォーン a saxophone ¶サクソフォーン奏者 a saxophonist.

さくちゅうじんぶつ 作中人物 characters 《in a novel》.

さくつけ 作付け planting ¶作付け面積 the planted acreage; the area under cultivation.

さくてき 索敵 scouting; search operations ¶索敵行動 a reconnoitering [scouting] movement.

さくどう 策動 maneuvers; 《文》 machinations ¶策動する maneuver [intrigue] 《behind the scenes》; scheme [for power]; pull strings [wires] 《to get a post》 / 策動家 a schemer; an intriguer; a plotter 〈陰謀家〉.

さくにゅう 搾乳 milking ¶搾乳する milk 《a cow》 / 搾乳器 a milker; a milking machine / 搾乳場 a dairy.

さくねん 昨年 last year ⇒ きょねん.

さくばく 索漠 ¶索ばくたる dreary; bleak; desolate.

さくばん 昨晩 last night; yesterday evening ¶昨晩の火事 last night's fire.

さくひん 作品 a (piece of) work; a product; a production ¶芸術作品 a work of art / 文芸作品 a literary work.

さくふう 作風 a style ¶作風をまねる model one's style on sb's.

さくぶん 作文 〈作る事〉 composition; writing; 〈文章〉 an essay; a composition; 《米》 a theme ¶作文を書く write [make] an essay [a composition] 《on the theme…》; 《米》 write a theme. 文例↓

さくぼう 策謀 〈策略〉 《文》 (a) stratagem; a scheme; 〈陰謀〉 《文》 an intrigue; 《文》 machinations ¶策謀する scheme; plot / 策謀家 a schemer.

さくもつ 作物 crops; farm products; farm produce. 文例↓

さくや 昨夜 ⇒ さくばん.

さくら¹ 桜 〈木〉 a cherry tree; a *sakura*; 〈花〉 cherry blossoms [flowers]; 〈馬肉〉 horseflesh; horsemeat ¶桜色のpink; florid 〈complexion〉.

さくら² 《口語》 a shill; 〈大道商人の〉 a decoy; a fake buyer; 〈劇場の〉 a hired applauder; a claque 〈グループ〉; 〈競売の〉 a by-bidder ¶さくらになる act as a shill [decoy].

さくらそう 桜草 a primrose.

さくらん 錯乱 ¶精神が錯乱する go mad [distracted]; be mentally deranged; 《口語》 go [be] off one's head / 精神錯乱 dementia; 《a state of》 mental derangement; insanity. 文例↓

さくらんぼ a cherry ¶さくらんぼの種 a cherry stone.

さぐり 探り 〈探り針〉 a probe; a stylet ¶探りを入れる sound sb (out) 《on a subject》; tap 《sb's opinion》; 〈政治的に〉 put up a trial balloon [a *ballon d'essai*].

さぐりだす 探り出す smell [spy] out; worm [pry] 《a secret》 out 《of sb》 ¶人の意見を探り出す sound sb out 《on the idea》.

さくりゃく 策略 《文》 a stratagem; a trick; 《文》 a ruse; 《文》 an artifice; tactics; wiles ¶策略を巡らす devise a stratagem / 策略を用いる use artifice; play a (mean) trick 《on sb》 / 策略で[を用いて] 《escape》 by [with] a trick [stratagem] / 策略に富む be a shrewd tactician [schemer]. 文例↓

さぐる 探る 〈捜す〉 search for; fish for 〈information〉; 〈探りを入れる〉 spy on 《an enemy》; sound sb (out) 《on a subject》; 〈手で〉 feel [grope] for; 〈探査する〉 explore 《the ocean

---

plenty.

さくし² 策士策に溺れる. Too much scheming will be the schemer's downfall.

さくしゃ この詩の作者はだれですか. Who wrote [composed] this poem? / Who is this poem by?

さくせん 作戦が図に当たった. Our plan [ploy] worked remarkably well.

さくぶん 彼の財政計画も単なる作文に終わる運命にあった. His financial program was (fated) never to leave the drawing board.

さくもつ 作物ができなかった. The harvest failed. / この天気は作物によい[悪い]. This weather is good [bad] for the crops. / 今年は作物の出来が早い[遅い]. The crops are early [backward] this year.

さくらん これはきっとだれか精神の錯乱している人間のやった仕事だよ. This is the work, I am sure, of some poor creature with an unbalanced mind. / 彼は一時的に錯乱状態になって, 妻と息子を殺してしまった. He killed his wife and son in a fit of madness.

さくりゃく 彼らは勢力回復のためあらゆる策略を巡らしている. They are resorting to every stratagem to regain their influ-

さくれい 作例 an example 《of》; a model 《for》 ¶作例を示す give an example.

さくれつ 炸裂 (an) explosion; bursting ¶さく裂する explode; burst.

ざくろ 〖植〗 a pomegranate ¶ざくろの木 a pomegranate tree / ざくろ石 《鉱》 garnet.

さけ[1] 酒 liquor; drink; (an) alcoholic drink; 《俗》booze; 〈日本酒〉sake; 〈ぶどう酒〉wine ¶強い酒 hard liquor / 酒が強い can hold one's drink [liquor] / 酒が弱い cannot take one's drink [liquor] / 酒の勢いで under the influence of liquor / 酒の上のけんか a drunken brawl / 酒を飲む 〈日本酒〉drink sake / 〈飲酒〉drink (alcoholic beverages) / 酒を造る brew sake / 酒を断つ give up [《文》abstain from] drinking; 《口語》take [sign] the pledge; become a teetotaler [total abstainer]; 《口語》go [be] on the wagon / 酒びたりになる be steeped in liquor; be soaked in [sodden with] drink / 酒類 liquors; 《文》alcoholic beverages.
文例⇩

さけ[2] 鮭 〖魚〗 a salmon (単複同形) ¶燻《製》のさけ smoked salmon / さけ缶《米》canned [《英》tinned] salmon / さけます漁獲割当高 (Japan's) salmon catch quota (for 1981).

さげ- 下げ… ¶下げ札 a tag; a label / 下げ幕 a drop curtain.

さけい 左傾 ¶左傾する lean [incline] to the left; turn leftish [Red] / 左傾した left(-leaning); leftist; left-wing; radical; Red.

さけかす 酒粕 sake lees.

さけくさい 酒臭い smell [reek] of liquor ¶息が酒臭い have beery [alcoholic] breath; have liquor on one's breath.

さけくせ 酒癖 ¶酒癖がいい[悪い] be a good [bad] drunk.

さげすむ ⇨けいべつ.

さけのみ 酒飲み a (heavy) drinker; 《口語》a boozer; 《大酒飲み》a drunken sot; a tippler; a toper; a confirmed drunkard (飲んだくれ) ¶酒飲みになる take to drink / 酒飲み友だち a drinking companion.

さけび 叫び 〈大声〉a shout; a cry; an outcry; a yell; an exclamation; 〈悲鳴〉a shriek; a scream; 〈怒号〉a howl ¶改革の叫び a cry [clamor] for reform / …に対する反対の叫びが上がる an outcry is raised against 《the expansion of the airport》.

さけぶ 叫ぶ 〈大声を出す〉shout; cry (out); give 《a cry》 utter] a cry; yell; exclaim (感嘆して); 〈悲鳴をあげる〉shriek; scream; 〈不満・抗議で〉clamor ¶労働条件改善を叫ぶ cry for an improvement in working conditions / 賃金切下げ反対を叫ぶ cry [clamor] against the wage cut / 声をからして叫ぶ shout oneself hoarse / 産児制限を叫ぶ preach [《文》advocate] birth control.

さけめ 裂け目 a rent [rift, cleft] (in a cloud); a rip [tear, slit] (in a coat); a crack (fissure, chasm, crevice) (in the ground); a crevasse (in a glacier); a cleavage (in the rock).

さける[1] 裂ける split; tear; 《文》rend; burst (破裂する) ¶裂けやすい tear easily.

さける[2] 避ける 〈よける〉avoid; 《文》avert; ward off 《danger》; shun 《publicity》; 〈身をかわして〉dodge 《a blow》; 〈近寄らない〉keep [stay] away from 《danger》; stay clear of 《disputes》; 〈近づけない〉give a wide berth to sb; 〈責任などを〉shirk [sidestep] 《one's responsibilities》; 《文》evade 《an answer》; get around [round] 《difficulties》 ¶うまく避ける avoid sth neatly / 日を避ける shelter oneself [get shade] from the sun / 悪友を避ける avoid [keep away from] bad company / (見ぬ振りをして)わざと避ける cut sb (dead); 《口語》give sb the go-by / 明言を避ける take care not to commit oneself; steer clear of a definite commitment / 避け難い unavoidable; inevitable.

さげる[1] 下げる 〈つるす〉hang; 〈身につける〉wear 《a decoration》; bear 《a sword》; 〈下げさせる〉get [bring] down; lower; drop; let down; 〈位などを〉demote; reduce 《a soldier》 to a lower rank; 《米俗》bust 《a soldier to private》; 〈後退させる〉move sb back [backward]; 〈片づける〉clear; take away; 〈《預金を》引き出す〉draw [withdraw] 《money from a bank》; 〈交付する〉grant 《sb a license》 ¶頭を下げる lower one's head; bow / 値段を下げる lower [reduce, cut] the price / ぜんを下げる clear the table.
文例⇩

さげる[2] 提げる carry sth in one's hand; take sth with one.

さげん 左舷 port ¶左げん側に on the port side / 左げんに傾く list to port.

ざこ 雑魚 small fish [fry] ¶雑魚寝 ⇨ざこね.

ざこう 座高 one's sitting height.

さこく 鎖国 (national) isolation ¶鎖国する close the country; close the door (to foreigners) / 鎖国主義 an isolation policy; a policy of seclusion; a closed-door policy.

さこつ 鎖骨 〖解〗the collarbone; the clavicle.

さけ[1] 私は酒は飲みません。I do not drink. / 私は酒はだめです。I can't take hard liquor. / 酒を飲むのは結構です。酒に飲まれてはいけない。It's all right to drink, but don't let the drink take control. / 酒が回りはじめた。The sake began to take effect. / 酒が回るにつれて彼はぺらぺらしゃべり出した。The sake set his tongue wagging. / 酒は百薬の長。Sake is the best of all medicines.

さげる[1] 彼は頭を低く下げながら道路の反対側へ走った。Keeping his head down, he made a dash across the street.

ささいな 損失は些細なものだ。The loss is nothing to speak of.

ささげつつ ささげつつ！【号令】Present arms!

ささげる 亡き母にささぐ。〈著書の献辞〉To [Dedicated to] the memory of my late mother.

さざなみ 風が吹いて湖面にさざなみが立った。A puff of wind ruffled the surface of the lake.

ささる のどに魚の骨が刺さってしまった。I've got a fish bone stuck in my throat. | A fish bone has

ざこつ 座骨 〖解〗the hipbone; the innominate bone ¶座骨神経 the sciatic nerve / 座骨神経痛 sciatica; sciatic neuralgia.

ざこね 雑魚寝 ¶雑魚寝する all sleep together in a huddle.

ささ 笹 bamboo grass ¶笹の葉 a bamboo leaf / ささ舟 a bamboo-leaf boat / ささやぶ a bamboo bush.

ささい 些細 ¶些細な trifling; trivial; small; slight; insignificant / 些細な事 a trifle; a trifling [trivial] matter / 些細な事で怒る get angry at trifles / 些細な違い a slight difference / 些細な金 a petty sum (of money). 文例⇩

ささえ 支え a support; a prop; a stay.

ささえ 〖貝〗a turban [wreath] shell; a turbo 《pl. -s》¶ささえのつぼ焼きa turbo cooked in its own shell.

ささえる 支える〈持ちこたえる〉support; maintain; sustain; hold; keep; bear up;〈つっかいをする〉prop [bolster] up;〈食いとめる〉check〈the advance of the enemy〉¶柱で支える support (a wall) with a post / 一家を支える support [maintain] one's family / 城を支える hold a castle (against the enemy).

ささくれ a fine split;〈つめの根元の〉a hangnail; an agnail.

ささくれる split finely ¶神経がささくれる one's nerves get frayed.

ささげ 〖植〗a black-eyed pea; a cowpea.

ささげつつ 捧げ銃 ¶ささげつつをする present arms / ささげつつをして《stand》at the present arms. 文例⇩

ささげもの 捧げ物 an offering; a sacrifice (生けにえ) ¶ささげ物をする make an offering (to God); offer a sacrifice (to a deity).

ささげる 捧げる〈持ち上げる〉lift up; hold up;〈献上する〉give; offer; present;〈身心を〉devote;〈犠牲にする〉sacrifice ¶英語の勉強に一生をささげる devote one's life to the study of English / 国のために命をささげる give one's life for one's country / 祈りをささげる say [offer] a prayer / すべてを捧げる give everything [《口》one's all] to 《the cause of revolution》. 文例⇩

ささつ 査察 (an) inspection ¶査察する inspect; make an inspection (of) / 空中[現地]査察 an aerial [on-site] inspection.

さざなみ ripples; rippling waves; wavelets ¶さざなみが《立てる》ripple. 文例⇩

ささみ ささ身〈鶏の〉white [light] meat.

ささめき ⇨ ざわめき.

ささめゆき 細雪 a light [sparse] snowfall; fine-flaked snow.

ささやか ¶ささやかな tiny; small; little;《文》humble;《文》modest / ささやかな収入 a modest [small] income / ささやかに暮らす live in a small way.

ささやき a whisper; a murmur; murmuring ¶愛のささやき《murmur》sweet nothings;《文》soft whispers of love.

ささやく whisper; murmur; talk [say] in whispers; speak under one's breath [in an undertone] ¶耳にささやく whisper in sb's ear.

ささら a bamboo whisk.

ささる 刺さる stick; be stuck. 文例⇩

さざんか 〖植〗a sasanqua (camellia).

さし 差し ¶さしで〈2人で〉between two people;〈向かいあって〉face to face.

さじ¹ 匙 a spoon ¶1さじ a spoonful (of sugar) ★複数形は spoonfuls; spoonsful の2通りがあるが、後者は今は使われなくなっている / さじですくう spoon sth out [up] / さじを投げる give sth up as hopeless; throw in the towel [sponge]; despair of sth / さじ加減《調剤》a prescription; (a) dosage;《手加減》allowance; consideration / さじ加減をする make allowance(s)《for》; use one's discretion《in doing》/ さじ加減を誤る give a wrong prescription;《文》make an error《in doing》; miscalculate. 文例⇩

さじ² 瑣事 a trifle; a trivial matter; trivialities ¶瑣事にこだわる worry about trifles; be a stickler for [be particular about] trifles / 瑣事にこだわらない do not care about trifles.

ざし 座視 ¶座視する《文》remain an idle spectator; look on idly [doing nothing]. 文例⇩

さしあげる 差し上げる〈持ち上げる〉lift (up); raise;〈進呈する〉give;《文》present《sth to sb, sb with sth》; let sb have sth. 文例⇩

さしあたり 差し当たり〈当分〉for the moment [present]; for the time being;〈目下〉at present; at the [this] moment; just now. 文例⇩

さしいれ 差し入れ things sent in to a prisoner; a gift (from a patron) ¶郵便差入れ口 a letter drop / 差入れ屋 a prison caterer.

さしいれる 差し入れる〈挿入する〉insert; put sth into;〈刑務所で〉send sth in (to a prisoner).

さしえ 挿し絵 an illustration; a cut ¶挿し絵を入れる[かく] illustrate (a book) / 挿し絵入り[なし] illustrated [unillustrated] / 色刷りの挿し絵 a colored illustration / 挿し絵の説明 a caption / 挿し絵画家 an [a book] illustrator.

さしおく 差し置く〈放置する〉leave; leave sth as it is; leave [let] sth alone [be];〈無視する〉ignore; disregard; slight; go over sb's head (直属の上司などを) ¶何を差し置いても first of all; before everything (else). 文例⇩

---

stuck in my throat. / 靴にびょうが刺さったらしい。My shoe seems to have picked up a tack. / 靴の裏にびょうが刺さっていた。A thumbtack was embedded in the sole of the shoe.

さじ¹ 砂糖をもう2さじばかり入れて下さい。Please put two more spoonfuls of sugar in it.

ざし 君があの悪党の術中にみすみす陥るのを僕は座視するわけにはいかない。I can't stand by and see you play into the hands of that rascal. / 彼の窮境を座視するに忍びなかった。I couldn't leave him in the lurch.

さしあげる もっと肉を差し上げましょう。Let me help you to some more meat. / これはあなたに差し上げます。This is for you.

さしあたり 差し当たりこれで間に合う。This will do for the present. / It will serve our present purpose. / 差し当たりそれはいらない。I have no immediate need for it.

さしおく 僕らを差し置いて直接校

さしおさえ　差し押え attachment; (a) seizure; distraint; distress ¶差し押えを食う have ((one's property)) attached [placed under distraint] / 差し押えを解除する relieve ((sb's property)) from attachment / 差し押え令状 a warrant [writ] of attachment [seizure].

さしおさえる　差し押える distrain [attach, seize] ((sb's property for a debt)).

さしかえる　差し替え put (A) in the place of (B); replace (A with B) ¶花瓶の花を差し替える change the flowers in a vase ⇒ おきかえる, いれかえる.

さしかかる　差し掛かる come near (to); approach. 文例⇩

さしかけ¹　指し掛け ¶指し掛けにする <将棋を> leave a game of *shogi* unfinished for the day; adjourn ((the game)).

さしかけ²　差し掛け ¶差し掛け小屋 a penthouse; a lean-to shed ((against the house)) / 差し掛け屋根 a sloping [lean-to] roof.

さしかける　差し掛ける hold ((an umbrella)) over ((sb)); reach ((an umbrella)) over ((sb's head)).

さしがね　差し金 ¶…の差し金で <そそのかされて> ((文)) at ((sb's)) instigation / <入れ知恵で> on ((sb's)) suggestion. 文例⇩

さしき　挿し木 a cutting; <方法> (propagation by) cutting ¶挿し木をする make [plant] a cutting. 文例⇩

さじき　桟敷 ((劇場の)) a box (特等席); a gallery (天井さ敷) ¶正面さ敷 ((劇場の)) the dress circle.

ざしき　座敷 <部屋> a room floored with *tatami* mats; <客間> a reception room; a parlor ¶座敷に通す show [usher] ((sb)) into the parlor ((芸者に))お座敷がかかる be called; ((文)) have [be offered] an engagement.

さしきず　刺し傷 a stab wound; a stab; <針などの> a puncture ¶くぎの刺し傷 a nail wound.

さしこ　刺し子 a quilted coat; <縫い> quilting.

さしこみ　差し込み <挿入> ((文)) insertion; <電気の> a plug; <コンセント> an (electrical) outlet; a power point; a socket; <激痛> a spasm of pain; a griping pain; ((a fit of)) convulsions; a stitch (肋間(ろっかん)や脇腹の) ¶差し込みがくる feel [have] sharp pains ((in one's stomach)); be seized with a spasm.

さしこむ　差し込む <挿入する> ((文)) insert; put in [into]; thrust in; <プラグを> plug in; <痛む> have gripes; have a spasm of pain; <光が> shine [come, filter] in [into]. 文例⇩

さしころす　刺し殺す stab ((sb)) to death.

さしさわり　差し障り an obstacle; a hindrance; an impediment ¶差し障りがあるといけないから for fear of giving offense ((to)) / 差し障りのない <不快の念を与えない> innocuous; inoffensive; <どっちつかずの> innocuous; noncommittal.

さししめす　指し示す point to [at] ((sth)); point out ((an error)); indicate; show.

さしず　指図 directions; orders; instructions ¶指図する direct; order; give directions ((to)) / …の指図の下に under ((sb's)) directions / …から指図を受ける take orders from ((sb)) / 指図を仰ぐ ask ((sb)) for instructions / ああのこうのと指図がましくする order ((sb)) about; ((口語)) throw *one's* weight around; ((口語)) act bossily / 指図式手形 a bill payable to order; an order bill. 文例⇩

さしずめ ⇒ さしあたり. 文例⇩

さしせまる　差し迫る ((文)) be imminent; ((文)) be impending ¶差し迫った用事で on urgent business / 差し迫った危険 an imminent danger / 差し迫った問題 a pressing [an urgent] question / 時間に差し迫られる be pressed for time. 文例⇩

さしだす　差し出す <提出する> present ((an application)); submit ((a report)); hand [turn] in ((an article)); ((文)) tender ((one's resignation)); send ((one's card)); file ((a petition)); <送る> send; forward; <前へ出す> hold [stretch, reach] out; ((文)) extend ¶差出人 <手紙の> the sender / 差出人不明の手紙 an anonymous letter; a letter with no sender's name written on it.

さしちがえる¹　刺し違える stab each other ¶刺し違えて死ぬ die on each other's swords.

さしちがえる²　差し違える ((行司が)) make a wrong decision.

さしつかえ　差し支え <支障> a hindrance; an obstacle; <異議> (an) objection; <不便> an inconvenience; <困難> a difficulty; <先約> a previous engagement ¶差し支えない <構わない> may *do*; can *do*; be allowed to *do*; be justified in *doing*; <何とも思わない> do not mind *doing*; <不便を感じない> ((文)) experience no inconvenience; <困難でない> have no difficulty [trouble] ((in *doing*)); <先約がない> be free; be not engaged; <異議がない> have no objection ((to it)); <間に合う> ((文)) be sufficient; will do / …と言っても差し支えない

長と談判を始めた。He entered into direct negotiations with the headmaster over our heads.
さしかかる 峠にさしかかると自動車が故障を起こした。As we neared [approached] the pass, our car broke down.
さしがね きっとあいつの差し金だ。That fellow must have put him up to it [put the idea into his head].
さしき この木は挿し木ができますか。Can this tree be grown from a cutting?
さしこむ 月の光が窓から差し込んだ。The moonlight streamed in through the window. / 日光が部屋に差し込んだ。The sunlight found its way into the room.
さしず だれの指図でそんなことをしたか。Who told [ordered] you to do that? / 僕は人の指図なぞ受けるもんか。I will not be dictated to. / I won't take orders from anyone. / 「金5万円也」の小切手引換えに甲野太郎殿または指図人にお支払い下さい。Against this check pay Mr. Taro Kono, or order, fifty thousand yen only.
さしずめ さしずめ空飛ぶレストランと言ったところだ。It is, as it were, a flying restaurant.
さしせまる 約束の日が差し迫ってきた。The appointed day is close [near] at hand. / まあ、それが差し迫って必要という訳ではない。Well, I am in no immediate need of it.

さしつかえる　差し支える　〈支障がある〉be hindered from doing; 〈先約がある, 忙しい〉be engaged; 〈不便を感じる〉feel [suffer] ((some)) inconvenience; 〈困難である〉have difficulty (in doing); 〈なくて困る〉be short of (food); be hard up for (money). 文例↓

さして ⇒たいして¹. 文例↓

さしでがましい　差し出がましい　forward; ((口語)) pushy; impertinent; meddlesome; officious ¶差し出がましい事を言う make an impertinent [uncalled-for] remark / 差し出がましいことをする put oneself forward / 差し出がましいようですが I'm afraid this is none of my business, but….

さしでぐち　差し出口　¶差し出口をする butt [into]; stick [put] one's oar in; meddle with ((sb's business)).

さしでる　差し出る　⇒でしゃばる. 文例↓

さしとおす　刺し通す　pierce; ((文)) thrust ((a dagger)) home ¶刀で胸を刺し通す run a sword through sb's chest.

さしとめる　差し止める　〈禁止する〉prohibit; forbid; lay [place] a ban ((on)); 〈停止する〉suspend ¶新聞の発行を差し止める suspend the publication of a newspaper.

さしね　指し値　[商]the limits ¶指し値で買う [売る] buy [sell] at ((one's)) limit(s).

さしのべる　差し伸[延]べる　hold [stretch, reach] out ((one's hand)); ((文)) extend ((one's arm)) ¶…を取ろうとして手を差し伸べる reach out for sth / 援助の手を差し伸べる give sb a helping hand.

さしば　差し歯　[歯科]a post [dowel] crown.

さしはさむ　差し挟む　〈間に入れる〉((文)) insert; put sth between; 〈抱く〉have [((文)) harbor, ((文)) entertain] ((doubts)) ¶言葉を差し挟む put [get] a word in; interrupt [break into, cut into] ((other people's conversation)); get a word in edgewise ((普通否定語をともなって)) / 異議を差し挟む raise an objection ((to)); take exception ((to)).

さしひかえる　差し控える　〈控え目にする〉do not do too much; ((文)) do not do to excess; be moderate [((文)) temperate] ((in drinking)); ((文)) use moderation ((in eating)); ((文)) practice temperance ((in)); 〈…せずにおく〉withhold ((an announcement)); keep [((文)) refrain, ((文)) desist] from doing.

さしひき　差し引き　〈勘定の〉a balance; 〈控除〉(a) deduction; 〈潮の〉the ebb and flow ¶差し引き勘定をする balance ((an account)); strike a balance ((between the debits and credits)). 文例↓

さしひく　差し引く　take away [off]; deduct; subtract ¶給料から差し引く deduct ((a sum)) from sb's pay; take ((a sum)) off sb's salary.

さしまねく　差し招く　beckon (to) ((sb to come)).

さしまわす　差し回す　send ((a car)) (round) ¶宮内庁差し回しの自動車 a car sent round from the Imperial Household Agency.

さしみ　刺身　sashimi; sliced raw fish; slices of raw fish ¶まぐろの刺身 (a dish of) sliced raw tuna.

さしむかい　差し向かい　¶差し向かいに[で] face to face ((with)) / 差し向かいで話す have a face-to-face chat ((with)) / 差し向かいに座る take a seat opposite (to) sb.

さしむける　差し向ける　〈送る〉send sb (round); ((文)) dispatch.

さしもどす　差し戻す　send back; refer ((a case)) back ((to the original court)).

さしもの ⇒さがわ.

さしものし　指し物師　a joiner; a cabinetmaker.

さしゅ　詐取　¶詐取する obtain [get] ((money)) by fraud [on false pretenses]; swindle ((money from sb)); cheat ((sb out of sth)); ((文)) defraud ((sb of sth)).

さしょう¹　査証　a visa ¶旅券の査証を受ける get a visa on one's passport; get one's passport visaed / 入国[出国]査証 an entry [exit] visa / 査証係官 a visa officer.

さしょう²　詐称　¶詐称する assume sb's [a false] name; ((文)) represent oneself as…; give oneself out as…; misrepresent ((one's age)) / …と詐称して under the assumed [((文)) feigned] name of… / 学歴詐称 a false statement of one's academic career.

さじょう　砂上　¶砂上の楼閣 a house of cards; 〈実現性のない〉castles [build a castle] in the air.

ざしょう¹　座礁　¶座礁する run aground; run [be driven, be thrown] on a rock; go on the rocks; be stranded. 文例↓

ざしょう²　挫傷　⇒うちみ.

さしわたし　差し渡し　⇒ちょっけい².

さす¹　州　a sandbar; a sandbank.

さす²　刺す　〈突き刺す〉stick ((into, through)); pierce; stab; ((文)) thrust; 〈虫が〉sting; bite; 〈野球〉put ((a runner)) out; 〈縫う〉sew; stitch

---

さしつかえ　どちらでも差し支えありません. Either will do. / 酒もタバコも少しくらいでは差し支えないでしょう. A little alcohol or tobacco will do you no harm. / 休日はいくらあっても差し支えありません. You [One] can't have too many holidays. / こういう手段をとっても差し支えないと思う. I hope I am justified in taking this step.

さしつかえる　右手を包帯しているから書き物に差し支える. I have trouble in writing, as my right arm is bandaged. / よく眠らないと明日の仕事に差し支えます. If you don't get a proper night's rest you'll be unfit for tomorrow's work.

さして　今日の新聞にはさして面白い記事はない. There is nothing of special interest in today's paper.

さしでる　差し出たことはするな. Mind your own business. | This is none of your business.

さしひき　差し引き千円の得[損]だ. The balance is 1,000 yen to the good [bad]. / 差し引き勘定をすると私の方が得[損]になる. The balance of the account is in my favor [against me]. / 結局その政策の効果は差し引きプラスマイナスゼロということになるようだ. When we look at the balance sheet, the merits and demerits of this policy seem to even out.

ざしょう　船は台湾沖で座礁した. The ship went aground off Tai-

¶針で刺す prick ((one's finger)) with a needle / 布に針を刺す stick a needle into cloth / 小さな針に刺したちょうの標本 butterflies impaled on small pins / 本塁で刺す throw ((a runner)) out at home base / 蚊に刺される be bitten by a mosquito / はちに刺される be stung by a wasp. 文例⇩

さす³ 指 [差,刺]す 〈指示する〉 point to [at]; indicate; 〈指名[定]する〉 name; 《文》nominate; 《文》 designate; 〈挿入する〉《文》insert; put into [in]; 〈かざす〉 hold [put] up ((an umbrella)); 〈腰につける〉 wear ((a sword)); 〈杯を〉 offer ((a cup)); 〈注ぐ〉 pour ((into)); drop ((into)); 〈将棋を〉 play ((shogi)); 〈刺が〉 rise; flow; 〈日が〉 shine ((in, into, on)); 〈色が出る〉 be tinged with ((red)). 文例⇩

さすが さすがに大学者だけあって like the great scholar that he is; as might be expected of a great scholar, he... / さすがの英雄も hero as [though] he is.

さずかる 授かる 《文》 receive; 《文》 be gifted [endowed] with ((a talent)); be given [granted] ((a reward)); be awarded ((a prize)); 《文》 be blessed with ((a child)); 《文》 have ((a title)) conferred on one; 〈教わる〉 be taught ¶秘伝を授かる be initiated into the secrets ((of an art)) / 授かりもの a gift; a blessing; a godsend.

さずける 授ける grant ((a license to sb)); 《文》 confer ((a title on sb)); 《文》 invest ((sb with authority)); award ((a prize)); 〈教える〉teach; instruct ((sb in [on] sth)); 《文》 initiate ((sb into the secrets [mysteries] of an art)).

サスペンス suspense ¶サスペンスもの a thriller; a mystery story.

さすらい wandering ¶さすらいの身 a wanderer; an exile; a bird of passage / さすらいの生活 a wandering life.

さすらう wander; roam; 《口語》 knock about ((the world)).

さする 〈こする〉 rub; 〈なでる〉 pat; stroke; 〈あんまする〉 massage ¶顔をさする pass one's hand over one's face.

ざせき 座席 a seat ⇒ せき² ¶前[後]の座席 a front [back, rear] seat / 窓際[通路側]の座席 a window [an aisle] seat / 千人分の座席のある劇場 a 1,000-seat theater / 座席を取る get [hold, 《文》secure] a seat ((in a bus)) / 座席を替える change one's seat / 座席を予約する book [reserve] a seat ((in a theater)) / 座席を譲る offer [give up] one's seat ((to)) / 座席一覧図 the (theater) seat-plan / 座席指定券 a reserved-seat ticket / 座席調節用レバー a seat adjustment lever / 座席番号 the seat number. 文例⇩

させつ 左折 ¶左折する turn (to the) left.

ざせつ 挫折 a setback; a breakdown; (a) frustration; 〈気力の〉discouragement ¶ざせつする 〈計画など〉 miscarry; fail; break down; 〈気力が〉 be discouraged; be disheartened; lose heart / 挫折感 a sense of failure.

させる 〈強いて〉 make sb do; 《文》 cause sb to do; force [《文》compel] sb to do; 〈許し[放任]して〉 let sb do; 《文》 allow sb to do; 〈頼んで〉 have sb do; get sb to do. 文例⇩

させん 左遷 ¶左遷する relegate ((to)); 《文》 degrade ((to)); demote ((to)); 《米》 sidetrack.

ざぜん 座禅 Zen meditation (in a cross-legged position) ¶座禅を組む sit in Zen meditation [contemplation].

さぞ 〈どんなに〉 how; 〈きっと〉 surely; 《文》 indeed; no doubt; certainly. 文例⇩

さそい 誘い 〈招き〉 (an) invitation; 〈誘惑〉 (a) temptation; 〈誘引〉 (an) allurement; 《文》 (an) enticement ¶誘いをかける ⇨ さそう / 誘いをかけて聞き出す pump sb ((for information)) / 誘いに乗る be tempted ((to do)); fall a victim to sb's allurement. 「pump」

さそいみず 誘い水 ¶誘い水を差す prime ((a pump)).

さそう 誘う 〈招く〉 invite; ask; 〈誘いに寄る〉 call for sb; 〈促す〉《文》 induce; 《文》 call forth ((tears)); 〈誘惑する〉 tempt; entice; 《文》 allure; seduce ¶誘い出す lure [invite] out / 映画に誘う ask [invite] sb (to go) to the movies. 文例⇩

ざぞう 座像 a seated figure [statue].

さそくつうこう 左側通行 文例⇩

さそり a scorpion ¶さそり座 《天》 Scorpio; the Scorpion ⇨ さ 文例.

さた 〈指令〉 instructions; orders; 〈通知〉 a notice; news; 〈事柄〉 an affair ¶追ってきたさたを待つ wait for further instructions ((from)) / さたの限りである be absurd; be outwan.

さす² 後悔の念が胸を刺した. Remorse cut into my heart. / 虫に刺された跡がはれた. The place where I was stung [where the insect stung me] has swollen up.

さす³ 別にだれを指して言ったのでもない. I didn't mean anyone in particular. / 磁針は北を指す. The compass needle points to the north. / 彼女は日傘をさしている. She has a parasol up. / 早朝われわれは頂上を指して登った. We set out for the summit early in the morning.

さすが さすがは山田君だ. That's like Yamada. | That's Yamada all over. / さすがは久野君だけのことはある. That's only what you [one] would expect [have expected] of Kuno. / 覚悟はしながらも, 死刑と聞いて彼もすすがに顔色を変えた. Prepared as he was, he turned white the moment he heard himself sentenced to death. / さすがにプロだ. Now there's a real pro for you. / さすがに英国に3年いただけのことはある. He did not spend his three years in Britain for nothing.

ざせき この講堂には千人分の座席がある. This auditorium has seating accommodation for 1,000 people. | This hall has a seating capacity of 1,000. / ヨーロッパの歌劇場の多くは座席数2千以下である. Most opera houses in Europe have fewer than 2,000 seats.

ざせつ 彼の計画は挫折した. His plan miscarried [fell through]. | His plan didn't work out.

させる もう一度私にさせて下さい. Let me have another try. | Give me one more chance. / オーバーを直させました. I have had my overcoat mended. / 彼女が戻ったら, 電話させましょうか. Shall I have her call you back when she gets home? / 君にそんなことをさせようと思ったわけではない. I didn't mean you to do

さだか　⇨　あきらか

さだまる　定まる〈決まる〉be decided; be settled; be fixed;〈文〉be determined;〈天候が〉be settled; come to stay ¶定まった fixed; regular; definite／定まらぬ天候 changeable [unsettled,〈文〉fickle] weather. 文例⇩

さだめ　定め〈規定〉a law; a regulation; a rule;〈決定〉a decision;〈運命〉(a) destiny; (a) fate ¶定めなき〈確かでない〉uncertain〈変わりやすい〉changeable;〈文〉mutable;〈はかない〉〈文〉transient;〈文〉ephemeral;〈文〉evanescent／定めの時刻[場所]〈文〉the appointed hour [place]／特別の定めのないかぎり〈文〉unless otherwise provided [specified].

さだめし　定めし　probably; presumably; surely; no doubt. 文例⇩

さだめる　定める〈決める〉decide (on);〈文〉determine;〈文〉appoint (a place, an hour); fix (a date); lay down (a rule); provide; establish ¶方針を定める decide on one's policy／神によって定められた生涯《follow》a divinely ordained course of life.

さたん　左端　the left end ¶〈写真・図版などで〉左端の (the person) on the extreme left; (the figure) at the far left.

ざだん　座談　(a) conversation; a talk ¶座談が上手である be a good talker〈conversationalist〉／座談的に話す talk 《about sth》informally／座談会 a round-table talk 《on modern literature》; a discussion; a symposium《pl. -sia, -ums》.

さち　幸　⇨　さいわい　¶幸あれと祈る wish sb (good) luck; wish sb well; bless sb／幸薄き恋仲のふたり star-crossed lovers／海[山]の幸〈文〉the fruits of the sea [the countryside].

ざちょう　座長　the chairman;〈芝居の一座の〉the leader 《of a troupe》 ¶座長の席につく〈着いている〉take [be in] the chair／座長を勤める act as chairman; preside at [over] the meeting／座長に選ぶ elect sb chairman; put sb into the chair.

さつ　札　a bank note;《米》a bill; paper money ¶札で5万円 fifty thousand yen in notes／千円札 a 1,000-yen note／札入れ a wallet;《米》a pocketbook;《米》a billfold;《英》a notecase／札束 a roll [bundle] of notes／札びらを切る spend (one's) money recklessly [freely] (to show off).

-さつ　…冊　a volume (巻); a copy (部) ¶本2冊 two books; two copies (of the book)《同じ物》. 文例⇩

ざつ　雑　¶雑な〈粗雑な〉careless; slipshod; sloppy; slovenly／雑な文章 a slipshod style／雑な頭 a slovenly [〈文〉an undiscriminating] mind;〈人〉a person given to sloppy [careless] thinking; a careless [thoughtless] person／雑にできている poorly-made《shoes》;〈文〉《an article》of cheap [inferior] make.

さつい　殺意〈文〉murderous intent;《法》malice aforethought [prepense] ¶殺意を抱いて with murderous intent; with intent to kill sb.

さつえい　撮影　¶撮影する take a photograph [picture] of sb [sth]; photograph;〈映画を〉film [shoot]〈あ場面〉; make a film of 《a scene》／写真を撮影してもらう have [get] one's photograph taken／撮影機 a (movie) camera; a cinecamera／映画撮影所 a [film (movie)] studio (pl. -s)／《米》a lot／撮影済みのフィルム an exposed film. 文例⇩

さつきえき　雑役　odd jobs; chores ¶雑役夫 a general laborer; a handyman; an odd-job man;《米》a roustabout／雑役婦 a charwoman; a maid of all work.

ざつおん　雑音　noise;〈ラジオの〉radio noise;〈レコードの〉surface noise. 文例⇩

さっか　作家　a novelist; a writer; an author ¶女流作家 a woman novelist [writer]; an authoress.

ざっか　雑貨　miscellaneous goods; sundries; general goods [merchandise] ¶雑貨売り場《米》a notions counter／雑貨店 a general [《米》variety] store [shop].

サッカー　soccer;《英》(association) football ¶サッカーの選手 a soccer [football] player.

さつがい　殺害　¶殺害する kill; murder; put sb to death／殺害しようとする make an attempt on sb's life; try to kill sb／殺害者 a murderer (男); a murderess (女).

さっかく¹　錯角《数》alternate (interior) angles.
さっかく²　錯覚　an (optical) illusion; (a) hal-

---

anything of the sort.／どうか彼に成功させたいものだ. I do wish him success.／この物語を読んでいろいろ考えさせられた. The story gave me a lot to think about.｜The story gave me food for thought.

させん　彼の転任は左遷だ. His new appointment is a change for the worse.

さぜ　南極ではさぞかし寒いことであろう. How cold it must be in the Antarctic!／遠方からいらっしゃってさぞお疲れでございましょう. You must be tired after your long journey.

さそう　月に誘われて庭に出た. The moonlight tempted me out into the garden.

さそくつうこう　左側通行.【掲示】Keep to the left.

さた　正気のさたではない. He cannot be in his right mind.／旅行どころのさたではない. Traveling is out of the question.／先方から何のさたもない. I have heard nothing from him.

さだまる　人間のありようは食物によって定まる. A man is what he eats.／供給は需要によって定まる. Demand determines supply.

さだめし　ご旅行中はさだめし面白いことがあったでしょう. You must have had some interesting experiences during your trip.

-さつ　私は聖書を1冊買った. I bought a copy of the Bible.／その辞書は2冊になっています. The dictionary is in two volumes.

さつえい　この映画の撮影は8月初めに開始される予定です. Shooting on the film is scheduled to start in early August.／人気スターの小津さんは, 撮影の合間合間に台本を研究していた. Mr. Ozu, the popular star, studied his script between takes.／撮影禁止.【掲示】No photography.

ざつおん　裁判官は外の雑音に耳を貸してはいけない. The judge on

lucination ¶錯覚する have [be under] an illusion. [文例⇩]

ざつがく 雑学 《a man with》 a wide variety [a mass] of unorganized knowledge [information]; 《文》 encyclopedic knowledge. [文例⇩]

さっかしょう 擦過傷 an abrasion; a graze ¶擦過傷を負う 《文》 suffer [sustain] an abrasion; get a graze 《on the arm》.

サッカリン 〘化〙 saccharin.

ざっかん 雑感 *one's* impressions 《of》.

さつき 〘植〙 a dwarf azalea.

さっき 〈先刻〉 some time [a little while] ago ¶さっきから for quite a while; for some time / さっきまで until just a few minutes ago / さっきの話 what you mentioned a little while ago. [文例⇩]

ざつき 座付き ¶座付きの attached to a theater; belonging to a (theatrical) company / 座付き作者 a playwright writing specially for a company.

さっきだつ 殺気立つ grow excited; look menacing ¶殺気立った excited; bloodthirsty; menacing; ferocious / 殺気立った群衆 an excited crowd.

ざっきちょう 雑記帳 a notebook.

さっきゅう[1] 溯及 ⇨そきゅう.

さっきゅう[2] 早急 ¶早急に immediately; without delay; 《文》 without loss of time; at once; straight away; as quickly as possible.

ざっきょ 雑居 ¶雑居する live (close) together; 《文》 live cheek by jowl 《with》 / 雑居ビル a building housing a number of independent business concerns.

さっきょく 作曲 (musical) composition ¶作曲する compose; set 《a song》 to music; write music 《to a song》 / 作曲者[家] a composer. [文例⇩]

さっきん 殺菌 ¶殺菌する sterilize; disinfect; pasteurize (高温で) / 殺菌牛乳 sterilized [pasteurized] milk / 殺菌剤 a germicide; a disinfectant / 殺菌力 sterilizing power.

ざっきん 雑菌 unwanted bacteria (contaminating a culture [culture dish]).

サック 〈容器〉 a case 《for glasses》; 〈コンドーム〉 a condom; a (contraceptive) sheath ¶指サック 〈親指の〉 a thumbstall; 〈その他の指の〉 a fingerstall.

サックス 《口語》 a sax ⇨サクソフォーン.

ざっくばらん ¶ざっくばらんな frank; candid; outspoken; straightforward / ざっくばらんに frankly; candidly; outspokenly; straightforwardly / ざっくばらんに言えば frankly speaking; to be candid [frank] with you / ざっくばらんに意見を交換する have a frank and candid exchange of views 《with》.

さっくり ¶さっくりと混ぜる mix 《dough》 (lightly) taking care not to make 《it》 sticky.

ざっくり ¶ざっくりした布地 cloth with a very coarse weave / 肩口をざっくり切られている have a gash in the shoulder.

ざっけん 雑件 miscellaneous items [matters]; sundries.

ざっこく 雑穀 cereals ¶雑穀商 a dealer in cereals; a corn merchant [dealer].

さっこん 昨今 〈最近〉 recently; lately; 《文》 of late; 〈現在〉 nowadays; these days.

ざっこん 雑婚 〈異民族・異種族間の〉 (a) (racially) mixed marriage; (a) racial intermarriage; 〈乱婚〉 《文》 promiscuous sexual relations; promiscuity ¶雑婚する marry *sb* of (a) different race; 〈乱婚する〉 have promiscuous sexual relations 《with》.

さっさと promptly; quickly; fast; speedily; without wasting (*one's*) time; in a hurry ¶さっさと歩く walk quickly [briskly] / さっさと家へ帰る hurry home / さっさと出て行く clear out. [文例⇩]

さっし[1] 冊子 a booklet; a pamphlet (時事解説などの); a brochure (観光案内などの).

さっし[2] 察し 〈思いやり〉 consideration; sympathy; 〈推測〉 guess; 《文》 conjecture; 〈理解〉 understanding; 《文》 comprehension ¶察しがつく 〈推測できる〉 can guess [imagine]; 〈理解できる〉 can understand [make out] / 察しのいい 〈物わかりの早い〉 quick-witted; 《口語》 quick on the uptake; 《文》 perceptive; 〈思いやりのある〉 understanding; considerate / 察しの悪い 〈物わかりの鈍い〉 《文》 obtuse; 《口語》 slow on the uptake; slow-witted; thick-headed. [文例⇩]

サッシ a metal-framed glass sliding door [window]; 《英》 a patio door.

ざっし 雑誌 a magazine; a journal (専門的な); a periodical (定期刊行の) ¶雑誌の購読を申し込む send a subscription to a periodical / 雑誌をとる take [subscribe to] a magazine / 雑誌に寄稿する contribute (an article) to a magazine; write for a magazine / 月2回発行の雑誌 a fortnightly / 文芸雑誌 a literary magazine / 評論雑誌 a review / 医学雑誌 a medical journal / 雑誌記者 a magazine writer [reporter].

ざつじ 雑事 miscellaneous affairs ¶身辺雑事 *one's* personal [private] affairs.

ざっしゅ 雑種 a crossbreed; a cross 《between》; a hybrid ¶雑種の crossbred; hybrid; mongrel / 雑種強勢 〘生物〙 hybrid vigor; heterosis /

---

the bench should close his ears to the irresponsible criticisms of outsiders.

さっかく[2] 君が行くものと錯覚していたんだ. I was under the (mistaken) impression that you were going (to go).

ざつがく 彼は雑学の大家だ. He is a (virtual) storehouse of information.

さっき 君はさっきからどこへ行っていたの. Where have you been all this while? / さっきからずいぶん君を待っていたのだ. I have been waiting for you quite a while. / さっきの本をどこへ置いたか. Where did you put that book?

さっきょく その映画の音楽は佐藤氏の作曲だ. Mr. Sato wrote [did] the (musical) score for the film. / A氏作詞B氏作曲. Words by A, music by B.

さっさと さっさとやれよ! Get on with it! | Stop messing about! / さっさと言えよ. Come on, out with it! | Tell me right off.

さっし[2] お察しのとおり. You have guessed right. / あなたは察しのいい方だ. You are a good mind reader.

ざっしゅうにゅう / さっぱり

雑種犬 a mongrel (dog) / **雑種第一代**〖生物〗 the first filial generation (symb. F₁).

ざっしゅうにゅう 雑収入〈個人の〉(a) miscellaneous income;〈公共団体の〉miscellaneous revenues [receipts].

さっしょう 殺傷 ¶**殺傷する** kill and wound;《文》shed blood.

ざっしょく 雑食 ¶**雑食の**《動》omnivorous / **雑食動物** an omnivorous animal [feeder].

さっしん 刷新 (a) reform;《文》innovation;《文》renovation ¶**刷新する** reform;《文》innovate;《文》renovate / **人事の刷新を行なう** carry out a personnel reshuffle [shake-up].

さつじん 殺人 homicide; murder (殺意のある); manslaughter (殺意のない) ¶**2度殺人を犯す** commit two murders / **殺人的** deadly (heat); terrific (congestion); cutthroat (competition) / **殺人鬼** a bloodthirsty killer; a ghoul / **殺人狂** a homicidal maniac / **殺人罪を犯す** commit murder [homicide] / **殺人罪に問われる** be accused of murder / **殺人事件** a case of murder; a murder case / **殺人犯人** a homicide; a murderer (女); a murder suspect (容疑者) / **金品目当ての殺人犯** a murderer for gain / **殺人未遂** an attempted murder.

さっする 察する〈推測する〉guess;《文》conjecture;〈判断する〉judge;〈見てとる〉see; realize;《文》perceive; understand;〈想像する〉imagine; suppose;〈酌量する〉sympathize (with), feel (for);〈斟量する〉make allowance(s) for ¶**胸中を察する** enter into sb's feelings; read sb's thoughts [mind] / **察するところ** presumably; perhaps; I suppose (that...) / **うわさから察して** judging from rumors; from what I have heard (so far) / **彼の口振りから察して** from what he says...; I gather from his remarks that.... 文例↓

ざつぜんと 雑然と in disorder; in confusion; in a jumble; in a mess; in a confused way; at sixes and sevens; higgledy-piggledy. 文例↓

さっそう ¶**さっそうとした**《文》gallant; dashing; smart; jaunty / **さっそうたる馬上の英姿** a gallant figure on horseback / **さっそうと出かける** sail out (with a new hat on) / **さっそうと車で行く** drive off at a smart pace / **さっそうとしたスポーツカー** a racy sports car.

ざっそう 雑草 weeds / **雑草の生い茂った庭** a weed-infested[-grown] garden; a garden overgrown with weeds / **雑草を取る** weed (a garden). 文例↓

さっそく 早速 at once; immediately; right away; straight-away;《口語》straight off ¶**さっそく...する** lose no time in doing. 文例↓

さっそざい 殺鼠剤 (a) rat poison; ratsbane.

ざった 雑多 ¶**雑多な** unarranged; unorganized; unsorted / **雑多な人びと**《文》people of all sorts and conditions;〈群衆〉a mixed [miscellaneous] crowd of people.

ざつだい 雑題〈問題〉miscellaneous problems;〈題材〉miscellaneous subjects [themes].

ざつだん 雑談 idle [small] talk; light conversation; a chat ¶**雑談する** chat (with); have a chat (with);《口語》engage in chit-chat [small talk] (with).

さっち 察知 ¶**察知する** gather [《文》infer] (from); suspect;《文》perceive; sense; get wind [scent] of (a plot).

さっちゅうざい 殺虫剤 an insecticide; a vermicide; a pesticide ¶**殺虫剤噴霧器** an insecticide sprayer; an insect spray.

さっと〈急に〉suddenly;〈素早く〉quickly; in a quick gesture ¶**さっとあける** fling [throw] (a window) open / **さっと顔を赤らめる** blush all of a sudden / **さっと立ち上がる** stand up quickly; spring to one's feet. 文例↓

ざっと〈大略〉roughly; approximately; sketchily;〈概数で〉in round numbers;〈およそ〉about;〈簡単に〉briefly ¶**ざっと目を通す** go over (a paper); glance [run] over [through] (a letter);《口語》give sth the once-over (lightly) / **ざっと見積もる** make a rough estimate (of) / **ざっと話す** give a brief [bare] account (of); give sb a general idea (of). 文例↓

さっとう 殺到 ¶**殺到する** rush to (a place);《文》throng (a city); storm (a city); swoop down on (the enemy). 文例↓

ざっとう 雑踏〈人の群〉a crowd;〈文〉a throng; a jam;〈状態〉congestion ¶**雑踏する** be crowded [《文》thronged] (with people); be bustling / **雑踏する通り** a crowded [busy, bustling] street.

ざつねん 雑念 ¶**雑念を去る** put everything else [all other thoughts] out of one's mind;《文》banish [dismiss] worldly [all other] thoughts from one's mind.

ざつのう 雑嚢 a haversack; a duffel bag (円筒形で, 手提げ式).

ざっぱく 雑駁 ¶**雑ぱくな** loose (thinking); inconsistent (ideas);《文》incoherent;《文》desultory; patchy / **雑ぱくな知識** a scrappy [patchy] knowledge (of).

さつばつ 殺伐 ¶**殺伐な** (people) without (any) tenderness [human feelings];《文》inhumane (practices); barbarous (times).

さっぱり〈少しも〉(not) at all;(not) in the least;〈全然〉entirely; altogether; completely

---

さっする 彼の驚きは察するにあまりがある。You can imagine his surprise. / 彼女の顔つきから一切の事情を察することができた。I could read the whole story in her face.

ざつぜんと 本が雑然と彼の身のまわりに積んであった。Books were piled in a jumble around him.

ざっそう 庭一面に雑草が生えていた。The garden is overgrown [overrun] with weeds.

さっそく 私はさっそく仕事にとりかかった。I lost no time in getting to work. / 着いたらさっそくお手紙を出します。I'll write (to) you as soon as I arrive there.

さっと 風がさっと吹いた。There was a gust of wind.

ざっと 損害はざっと1億円の見込み。The (amount of) damage is roughly estimated at ¥100,000,-000. / 彼の年収はざっと5万ドルほどです。His year's income is about $50,000 in round figures [at a rough estimate]. / 彼にはざっと話してあります。I've told him of it in general outline.

さっとう 店には朝から客が殺到した。The store was crowded with

¶さっぱりする〈さわやかになる〉feel refreshed [(much) better]; 〈気が楽になる〉feel relieved / さっぱりした〈清潔な〉clean; tidy; neat; 〈淡泊な〉frank; openhearted / さっぱりした身なりをしている be neatly dressed. [文例⇩]

ざっぴ 雑費 sundry [miscellaneous] expenses; incidental expenses.

さっぷうけい 殺風景 ¶殺風景な〈もの寂しい〉dreary; bleak; 〈面白くない〉dull; drab; flat; 〈無趣味な〉tasteless; 《文》prosaic.

ざつぶん 雑文 《文》miscellanies (集めたもの); 〈随筆〉an essay ¶雑文家 a miscellanist.

さつまいも a sweet potato 《*pl.* -es》.

ざつむ 雑務 miscellaneous business [duties, tasks]; 〈日常の〉trivial everyday duties; routine duties ¶雑務に追われる *one's* time is occupied with routine business.

ざつよう 雑用 incidental tasks; odd jobs; 〈日常の〉《do》(household) chores ⇨ ざつむ. [文例⇩]

さつりく 殺戮 slaughter; butchery; (a) massacre; 《文》carnage ¶殺りくする slaughter; butcher; massacre / 大量殺りく mass murder; 《文》genocide / 殺りく戦 a war of (mass) slaughter.

ざつろく 雑録 miscellaneous records [notes, writings]; 《文》miscellanies; 《文》miscellanea.

さて well; now; and; 〈とかくするうち〉in the meantime; meanwhile ¶さては (well) then. [文例⇩]

さてい 査定 assessment ¶査定する assess 《*sb's* income at…》; make an assessment 《of》/ 査定価格 an assessed value [price].

サディスト a sadist.

サディズム sadism.

さておき 〈別として〉apart from; 《文》setting 《this question》 aside; 〈…は言うまでもなく〉to say nothing of; let alone ¶冗談はさておき joking aside [apart] / なにはさておき first of all; before everything [anything] else. [文例⇩]

さてつ[1] 砂鉄 iron sand.

さてつ[2] 蹉跌 a failure; a setback ¶さてつする fail; miscarry; fall through; hit a snag.

さと 里〈村落〉a village; 〈田舎〉the country; 〈故郷〉*one's* old home ¶里へ帰る〈嫁が〉go home to *one's* mother.

さとい 〈賢い〉intelligent; sharp-witted; 《口語》quick on the uptake; 〈鋭い〉sharp; keen; 《文》acute ¶利にさとい ⇨ り[2].

さといも 里芋 a taro 《*pl.* -s》.

さとう 砂糖 sugar ¶砂糖を入れる put sugar in 《*one's* coffee》; sugar; sweeten *sth* with sugar / 砂糖をかぶせる coat with sugar; ice; frost / (食卓用の)砂糖入れ a sugar bowl [《英》basin] / 砂糖きび (a) sugar cane / 砂糖漬けの preserved in sugar / 砂糖大根 a sugar beet / 砂糖煮にした candied 《fruits》/ 砂糖ばさみ 《a pair of》 sugar tongs / 砂糖水 sugared water. [文例⇩]

さどう[1] 作動 ¶作動する 《文》function; operate; work; run; go / 作動させる start; operate; 《文》put into operation / 作動し始める begin to work; start operating; 《文》go into operation / 作動中である 《文》be in operation.

さどう[2] 茶道 the tea ceremony.

さどう[3] 差動 〔物·機〕differential motion ¶差動(歯車)装置 a differential (gear).

さとおや 里親 a foster parent ¶一日里親になる act as 《a child's》 foster parent for the day / 里親制度 a foster-parent [foster-home] system.

さとがえり 里帰り a bride's (first) visit to her old [parents'] home ¶里帰りをする visit *one's* old home (for the first time) after *one's* marriage.

さとご 里子 ¶里子に出す put out 《*one's* baby》 to nurse 《with *sb*》; farm out 《a baby with *sb*》.

さとごころ 里心 ¶里心がつく get homesick; pine for *one's* home.

さとす 諭す 《文》admonish 《*sb* for *his* fault》; 《文》remonstrate 《with *sb* about *his* behavior》; warn 《*sb* not to *do*》; 〈理を説く〉reason 《with *sb* about *sth*》 ¶諭して…させる persuade *sb* to *do* / 諭して思いとどまらせる persuade *sb* not to *do*; 《文》dissuade *sb* from *doing* [an attempt]. [文例⇩]

さとり 悟り 〈理解〉understanding; 《文》comprehension; 〈悟道〉spiritual awakening [enlightenment]; 《the way to》 Buddhahood; 〈あきらめ〉《文》resignation ¶悟りがいい[悪い] be quick-[slow-]witted; 《口語》be quick [slow] on the uptake / 悟りを開く be spiritually awakened [enlightened]; attain higher perception [spiritual enlightenment]; 〈あきらめる〉take things philosophically [as they are]; resign *oneself* to the situation [《文》to *one's* lot] / 悟りに近付く be brought toward enlightenment. [文例⇩]

さとる 悟る〈理解する〉see; 《文》perceive; re-

---

customers from morning. / 注文が各方面から殺到した. We had a rush of orders from all quarters. | Orders poured in on us from all directions.

さっぱり 言いたい事を言ってしまったので胸がさっぱりした. Now that I have had my say, I feel much better (for it). / あの人たちが言うことは私にはさっぱりわからない. I cannot understand a word they say. | I can't make head or tail of what they're saying. / 僕は着る物でも食べ物でもさっぱりしたものが好きだ. In both food and clothing, I like things that are plain and simple.

ざつよう 何だかんだと雑用が多い. I have lots of things to do. | My time is taken up by one thing and another.

さて さてどうしよう. What shall I do now? / さてやってみるとなるとなかなかむずかしいものだ. When one comes to doing it, one finds it rather difficult.

さておき 彼らはぜいたく品はさておき日常の必需品にもことかいている. They lack the necessities of life, to say nothing of [let alone] luxuries. / 朝起きたらなにはさておきこれをしなさい. Do this (the) first thing in the morning.

さとう 紅茶には砂糖を入れましょうか. Do you take sugar in your tea?

さとす こちらがどんなに諭してきかせたところで, あの男には全くききめがない. No amount of reasoning has any effect on him.

さとり 彼はついに人生に対する悟

alize ; understand ; become aware [conscious] of ; 〈感づく〉 sense ; have an inkling of ; get wind of ; 〈…に覚める〉 awake to 《the danger》 ; 〈悟りを開く〉 さとり ¶ 過ちを悟る 《文》 be convinced of *one's* error / 事の重大性を悟る realize [become aware of] the seriousness [《文》 gravity] of the situation / …を悟らせる make *sb* realize *sth* ; open *sb's* eyes to *sth* / 悟られずに without being noticed ; without arousing suspicion. 文例⇩

サドル the saddle 《of a bicycle》.

さなえ 早苗 rice sprouts.

さながら ⇨ まるで. 文例⇩

さなぎ a chrysalis (*pl.* -lises, -salides) ; a pupa (*pl.* -pae, -pas) ¶ さなぎになる become a pupa ; pupate.

さなだ 真田 ¶ さなだ編み a plait ; a braid / さなだひも a braid.

さなだむし 真田虫 a tapeworm.

サナトリウム a sanatorium (*pl.* -ums, -ria) ; 《米》 a sanitarium (*pl.* -ums, -ria).

さのう 砂嚢 a sandbag ; 〈鳥の〉 a gizzard.

さは 左派 the left wing ; the left-wingers ; the leftists ¶ 左派の leftist ; left-wing.

さば 《魚》 a mackerel (単複同形) ¶ さばを読む cheat in counting ; lie about [《口語》 fudge, 《文》 misrepresent] 《*one's* age》.

さはい 差配 〈管理〉 charge ; 〈差配人〉 a landowner's [house owner's] agent ¶ 差配をしている act as *sb's* agent ; be in charge of 《a house》 on behalf of *sb*.

さばき 裁き (a) judgment ; (a) decision ¶ 裁きを受ける be judged ; be tried ; face trial.

さばく¹ 砂漠 a desert ¶ ゴビ砂漠 the Gobi (Desert).

さばく² 裁く 〈判決を下す〉 judge ; pass judgment 《on》 ; decide ; 〈審理する〉 try 《a case》 ; sit in judgment 《on》 ; 〈解決する〉 settle 《a question》.

さばく³ 捌く 〈売る〉 sell ; find a market 《for goods》 ; 〈処置する〉 dispose of 《a matter》 ; deal with ; 〈扱う〉 handle ; field 《questions》 ; 〈野球で球を〉 field ¶ ゴロ[フライ]をさばく field a grounder [fly ball] / さばき切れないほどの注文[仕事]がある be swamped with orders [work].

さばける 捌ける 〈売れる〉 sell ; be sold ; 〈世なれる〉 get used to the ways of the world ; know the world ¶ さばけた 〈世慣れた〉 worldly-wise ; 〈物わかりのいい〉 understanding ; 〈さっくばらんな〉 frank ; openhearted.

さばさば ⇨ さっぱり.

サハラさばく サハラ砂漠 the Sahara (Desert) ¶ サハラ砂漠の Saharan.

サハリン 〈樺太〉 Sakhalin.

サバンナ 《地理》 (a) savanna(h).

さび¹ 寂び 〈古色〉 an antique look ; 《文》 patina ; 〈閑寂〉 《文》 elegant [quiet] simplicity ¶ 寂びがつく get [《文》 acquire, take on] an antique look [a patina] / 寂びのある声 a deep, well-trained voice.

さび² 錆 rust ; 〈古色〉 さび¹ ¶ さびがつく ⇨ さびる / さびを落とす remove the rust 《from》 ; get the rust off ; derust / さび付いた rust-eaten 《machinery》 ; 《a knife》 fretted with rust / さび止め a rust preventive ; an antirust compound ; an anticorrosive / さび止めをする rust-proof. 文例⇩

さびしい 寂しい lonely ; lonesome ; 〈荒涼とした〉 desolate ; dreary ; 〈孤独な〉 《文》 solitary ; 〈人のいない〉 deserted ¶ 寂しさ (a feeling of) loneliness ; desolation / 寂しい顔 a cheerless countenance / 寂しい笑い a sad smile / 寂しく暮らす lead a lonely life / 寂しがり屋 a person who can't stand being alone ; a person who always needs company / 寂しがる feel lonely [《口語》 blue] / (★ lonely は形容詞であって, 副詞として使わない ; 〈いない人などを〉 miss *sb*. 文例⇩

ざひょう 座標 《数》 coordinates ¶ その点の座標 the coordinates of the point / 縦座標 an ordinate / 横座標 an abscissa (*pl.* -s, -cissae) / 座標系 《物》 a frame of reference / 座標軸 the axis of coordinates / 座標軸の回転[平行移動] rotation [translation] of axes.

さびる 錆びる get [go] rusty ; gather [form] rust ; rust ; be rusted / 〈しんからさびる be rusted through / さびた rusty ; rusted / さびない rustproof / 刀をさびないようにする keep a sword bright [free of rust].

さびれる 寂れる 〈町などが〉 become desolate [deserted] ; 〈店などが〉 become less prosperous ; lose popularity ; go downhill ¶ 寂れてゆく町 a declining town / 寂れた様子の deserted-looking / 寂れ果てた町 a deserted town ; a ghost town.

サファイア 《鉱》 sapphire ¶ サファイア針 a sapphire stylus [needle].

サファリ a safari ¶ サファリパーク a safari [wildlife] park.

ざぶざぶ 文例⇩

りが開けてきた. At last the great truth about life dawned upon him. / これで私は悟りを開いた. This has been an eye-opener to me. ǀ This has taught me a (vital) lesson.

さとる 彼は なかなか悟った 男だ. He is quite the philosopher. / 彼は悟られないように変装して行った. He went in disguise to avoid being detected.

さながら 富士山はさながら白扇を逆さにしたようだ. Mt. Fuji looks just like an inverted white fan.

さば きっと彼は5歳ばかりさばを読んでいるよ. 彼の言っている年齢の割にはとても老けて見えるもの. He looks much younger than he says he is ; I'm sure he is putting [adding] on five years or so.

さび² 驚いたことにそいつはすっかりさびついていましたよ. I found to my surprise that it was rusted solid (covered all over with rust). / 金具にはさびが深く食い込んでいた. Rust had eaten deeply into the metal parts.

さびしい 君がいなくなるととても寂しくなるよ. We will miss you badly. / 話相手がいなくて寂しい気がする. I feel lonely having no one to talk to.

さびれる 東京都内及びその周辺の桜の名所は だんだん 寂れてゆく. Many of the famous cherry-blossom resorts in and around Tokyo are losing popularity.

ざぶざぶ 彼の足のまわりで水がざぶざぶ音を立てた. The water

サブタイトル a subtitle ¶サブタイトルをつける subtitle (a book).
ざぶとん 座布団 a (floor) cushion.
サフラン 〖植〗 a saffron.
ざぶんと with a splash ¶ざぶんと水中に飛び込む plunge [plump] into water; jump into the water with a splash; make a splash dive.
さべつ 差別 discrimination ¶差別する[をつける] discriminate (in favor of A, against B) / 差別をもうけずに indiscriminately; without discrimination [《文》 distinction]; equally / 男女の差別 sex discrimination / 男女の差別なく irrespective of sex; men and women alike / 差別的 discriminatory; discriminating / 差別待遇 discriminatory treatment. 文例◎
さほう 作法 manners; 《文》 form; etiquette ¶食卓の作法 table manners / 作法を知っている be good-[well-]mannered / 作法を知らない have no manners; be ill-mannered; do not know the rules of [《文》 know nothing of] etiquette / 作法にかなう [はずれる] 《文》 conform to [offend against] the rules of etiquette / 作法に気をつける mind [be careful of] one's manners. 文例◎
サポーター 〈運動選手の〉 an athletic supporter; a jockstrap ¶膝[手首]のサポーター a knee [wrist] supporter.
サボタージュ 〖<《フランス語》 sabotage〗 a slowdown; a go-slow ★英語の sabotage は機械や建物に対する破壊行為 ¶サボタージュをする go slow; stage a slowdown; go on a go-slow.
サボテン 〖植〗 a cactus (pl. -tuses, -ti) ¶うちわサボテン a prickly pear.
さほど そんな (そんなに).
サボる 〈仕事を〉 loaf (on the job); 《米俗》 goof off; go slow; 〈学校を〉 play truant (from school); skip (school); cut (classes).
ざぼん 〖<《ポルトガル語》 zamboa〗 〖植〗 a shaddock; 《米》 a pomelo (pl. -s).
さま 様 〈様子・外観〉 looks; condition; shape ¶様になっている (be) in good shape; shapely / 様になっていない shapeless; unshaped; awkward; 《look》 less than perfect / 様変わりする be renewed; be converted; take on a different appearance. 文例◎

-さま …様 〈男子の〉 Mr. (Mister の略); Esq. (Esquire の略); Messrs. (フランス語 Messieurs の略, Mr. の複数); 〈女子の〉 Mrs. (Mistress の略); Miss (未婚の); Ms. (未・既婚を問わず). 文例◎
用法 Esq. は英国で私信に使う. 例えば John Smith 氏に個人的な用事で出す, 自宅宛の手紙には J. Smith, Esq. または John Smith, Esq. とするが, 仕事のことで勤め先の会社などにあてて出すときは Mr. J. Smith とする. Messrs. は Messrs. John Smith and Peter Brown のように使えると同時に, 日本語の「御中」に相当し, Messrs. Kenkyusha, Ltd. のように会社名などに付けることができる. Ms. (発音は [miz]) は, 女性だけが未婚と既婚を区別させられるのは不当だとする男女完全平等を主張する運動の産物であるが, 相手が結婚しているかどうかわからないときには便利なので, 次第に普及する傾向にある. ただし, 女性らしくないと, いやがる女性もいる.
ざま ⇨ ありさま. 文例◎
さまざま 様々な various; all sorts of; 《文》 diverse; 《文》 sundry; all manner of 《means》 ¶非常に様々な very diverse; a great variety of 《accessories》 / 様々な人 all sorts of people; 《文》 all sorts and conditions of men / 様々に in various [many] ways; 《文》 diversely.
さます¹ 冷ます 〈冷やす〉 cool; let sth cool [get cold]; 〈興などを〉 spoil; dampen ¶興を冷ます spoil sb's pleasure; put a wet blanket over 《the merry atmosphere》 / 熱を冷ます 〈事が主語〉 dampen one's enthusiasm [for sth]; put [《文》 cast] a damper on one's eagerness. 文例◎
さます² 覚ます 〈目を〉 《文》 awake; wake up; 〈人を〉 rouse [《文》 arouse] 《sb from sleep》; 〈迷いを〉 disillusion; disabuse 《sb of an idea》; 《文》 undeceive; 〈酔いを〉 sober sb up ¶目を覚ましている be (wide) awake; 〈寝床の中で〉 lie awake in bed. 文例◎
さまたげ 妨げ 〈事〉 obstruction; hindrance; 〈物〉 an obstacle; 《文》 an impediment ¶妨げもなく smoothly; without a hitch / 出世の妨げになる be an obstacle to one's success; stand [get] in one's way to success [in the way of one's career]; affect one's career / 勉強の妨げになる disturb sb's work; distract [disturb] sb when he is working [studying]. 文例◎
さまたげる 妨げる disturb 《sb's sleep》; prevent sb (from doing); hamper [hinder, 《文》

---

sloshed noisily round his legs.
さべつ 女性は差別されていたし, 今もされている. Women were and are discriminated against. / 君に差別をつけるわけではない. This is no discrimination against you. / 僕には君ら 2 人の間に差別をもうける気持ちはさらさらない. I have no intention of discriminating between you. / あの人は人に対して差別を設けない. He treats everyone alike.
さほう コーヒーを飲むときに音をたてるのは作法にかなっていない. It is bad manners to make a noise when you are drinking coffee.
さま 君が来ないと様にならないよ. The picture won't be complete if you don't come. / 彼がトレパンをはいてって様になるまい. Sweat pants won't look good [well] on him.
-さま そうなりゃ木村様々だ. If it does come off, I'll take my hat off to Kimura.
ざま なんたるざまだ. What do you think you're doing! / For shame! | Shame on you! / ざまを見ろ. Serves you right! | There you are!
さまざま 世はさまざま. It takes all sorts (of people) to make a world. / 人の心はさまざまだ. Many men, many minds.

さます¹ 熱ければ冷まして飲みなさい. If it's too hot, let it cool down before you drink it.
さます² 僕は夜中に幾度も目を覚ました. I had a wakeful night. / I slept fitfully. / 家へ連れ帰る前に彼の酔いを覚まそうとした. We tried to sober him up before taking him home.
さまたげ 遊びが仕事の妨げとなってはいけない. Don't let pleasure interfere with business. | Business before pleasure.
さまよう 彼の魂は今なおこの世にさ迷っている. His spirit still haunts this world.
さむい 寒くなりましたね. It's

さまつ impede| ((sb in his work); get [stand] in sb's way ¶成長を妨げる check [((文)) arrest] the growth (of).
さまつ 瑣末 ¶さ末な trifling; trivial.
さまよう さ迷う wander [roam] about ¶さよい歩く wander from place to place / 生死の境をさまよう ⇒ せい¹. 文例↓
サマリウム 《化》 samarium.
さみしい ⇒ さびしい.
さみだれ 五月雨 (an) early summer rain ¶さみだれに repeatedly; continually.
さむい 寒い cold; chilly ¶寒くなる get [grow] cold / 寒そうな chilly; wintry; bleak. 文例↓
さむがる 寒がる be sensitive to the cold; complain about [of] the cold ¶寒がり(屋) a person who is extremely sensitive to the cold; (口語) a cold-blooded person.
さむけ 寒気 a chill; a shivering fit; 〈悪寒〉《医》 ague ¶寒気がする have a cold fit; feel a chill; have the shivers; 〈物が主語〉 give one the shivers; give one the creeps (ぞっとして). 文例↓
さむさ 寒さ (the) cold; coldness ¶冬の寒さが始まると when the winter cold sets in / 寒さをしのぐ keep off [out] the cold / 寒さに弱い be very sensitive to [(文)) susceptible to the cold; be easily affected by cold weather / 寒さで震える shiver with [from] cold.
さむざむ 寒々 ¶寒々とした wintry; bleak. 文例↓
さむぞら 寒空 a wintry sky; cold weather.
さむらい 侍 a samurai; a warrior.
さめ 《魚》 a shark ¶さめ皮 sharkskin; shagreen (研磨用)/さめ肌 dry (scaly) skin.
さめざめ ¶さめざめと泣く 《文》 weep bitterly; cry one's heart [eyes] out; 《文》 give free vent to one's tears.
さめる¹ 冷める 〈冷たくなる〉 cool (down); get cold; 〈熱意などが〉 cool down; be damped. 文例↓
さめる² 覚める 〈目が〉 wake up; wake; 《文》 awake; come awake; be roused (物音などで); 〈悟る〉 come to one's senses; be disillusioned; be undeceived; 〈酔いが〉 sober up [down]; get [((文)) become] sober ¶夢から覚める come out of a dream / 目の覚めるような緑色 a

bright [vivid] green. 文例↓
さめる³ 褪める 〈色が主語〉 go [come] off; fade (away) / 〈物が主語〉 lose color; discolor; be discolored ¶さめない色 a fast [fadeless] color / さめやすい色 a fugitive [fading] color / 色のさめないようになっている fade-proof (fabrics). 文例↓
さも ¶さも満足そうに with evident satisfaction / さもおいしそうに as if (he) enjoys [likes] it greatly; with gusto; with keen relish. 文例↓
サモア Samoa ¶サモア島の Samoan / サモア人 a Samoan.
さもあらばあれ 《文》 be that as it may; at any rate.
さもしい selfish; self-seeking; 〈卑しい〉 self-interested; mean ¶さもしい根性 《文》 a mean mind; 《文》 one's baser self / さもしい心から 《文》 from base [sordid] motives / さもしいことをする stoop so low (as to do).
さもないと, さもなければ otherwise; if not; 《文》 or (else); or else. 文例↓
サモワール a samovar.
さもん 査問 ¶査問する examine; interrogate ((a suspect)); inquire into ((a matter)) / 査問委員会 an inquiry commission.
さや¹ 莢 a shell; a pod; a hull ¶さやをむく shell [pod] ((peas)) / 種子のさや a seed pod.
さや² 鞘 〈刀の〉 a sheath; a scabbard; 〈小刀の〉 a case; 〈差額〉 a margin; a difference; 〈相場〉 a spread; a markup (原価との) ¶刀のさやを払う draw [unsheathe] a sword; pull a sword out of its scabbard / 刀をさやに収める sheathe [put up] a sword / 元のさやに収まる 《文》 be reconciled ((with her former husband)).
さやいんげん French beans; 《英》 haricot (beans).
さやえんどう field [garden] peas.
ざやく 座薬 a suppository.
さゆ 白湯 (plain) hot [boiled] water.
さゆう 左右 right and left ¶左右する 〈支配する〉 control; 《文》 sway; 《文》 dominate; have [hold] the whip hand ((over sb)); 〈影響を与える〉 affect; influence; have [((文)) exert] an influence ((on)) / 左右を見る look right and left [both ways]; look around / 道路の左右に on either side [both sides] of the road / 左右に揺れる roll [sway] from side to side / 左右に分かれる part (to) right and left / 左右相称 《生

---

turned quite cold, hasn't it? / 私は寒いのは平気だ. I don't mind the cold. / 寒くないようにしていなさい. Keep yourself warm. / そんな薄着で寒くないですか. Aren't you cold in such thin clothes? / ふところが寒い. I'm short of cash.
さむけ 彼は少し寒気がすると言う. He says he is a bit [little] chilly.
さむざむ 彼はあてもなく寒々とした東京の町をさまよい歩いた. He wandered through Tokyo's cheerless winter streets with no particular object in mind.
さめる¹ スープが冷めないうちにどうぞ召上がってください. Do

go ahead with your soup before it gets cold. / 彼の野球熱もどうやらさめたらしい. He seems to have lost interest in baseball. / そのけんかでフィーの興が冷めてしまった. The quarrel threw a wet blanket over the atmosphere.
さめる² 僕は目が覚めやすい. I am a light sleeper. / 私は失敗して目が覚めた. My failure brought me to my senses. / 彼はまだその迷いから覚めていない. He hasn't come to his senses yet. / He has not awakened from the illusion yet.
さめる³ この色は洗ってもさめません. This color will stand washing.

さも さもありそうな事だ. That is very likely. / 彼としてはさもありなんというところだ. It was just like him to do that. / That was typical of him. / 彼女はさも不愉快そうにそっぽを向いた. She looked away as if she was disgusted.
さもないと もう出かける時間です. さもないと列車に間に合いませんよ. It's time to go now, or we'll miss the train. / 先に主任にことわっておきなさい. さもないとあとで面倒なことになるといけないから. Have a word with the manager first, or you may get into trouble later on. / 私はすぐ出

ざゆう 座右　座右の銘 a [one's] motto 《pl. -(e)s》/ 座右に置く have 《a dictionary》by one [one's side]; keep 《a book》at hand [one's elbow].

さよう¹ 作用 〈働き〉(an) action; working; 〈影響〉an effect; 〈機能〉《文》a function ¶作用する〈影響を与える〉act [《文》operate, work] 《on sth》; affect; 〈働く〉《文》function 《as》/ 作用し始める come into play / 作用反作用の法則 the law of (the equality of) action and reaction.

さよう² 〈しかり〉yes; 《文》quite so; 《文》indeed; 〈ええと〉well; let me see ¶さような ⇒そんな. 文例⇩

さよ(う)なら good-by(e); 《文》farewell; 《文》adieu; 《口語》so long; 《文》cheerio(h); bye-bye ¶さよならをする[言う] say good-by to sb / さよならと手を振る wave good-by to sb / さよならホーマー (belt in) a winning homer [a home run to snatch the game] in the bottom of the ninth (inning).

さよく 左翼 〈隊形〉the left wing [flank]; 〈政治上の〉the left (wing) (集合的); a leftist [left-winger] (個人); 〈野球〉the left field ¶左翼的〈leftist; left-wing / 左翼へフライを飛ばす fly to left / 新左翼 the New Left; 〈個人〉a New Leftist / 左翼団体[運動] a leftist organization [movement] / 左翼手〈野球〉a left fielder.

さより 〈魚〉a halfbeak.

さら 皿 a plate; a dish (★料理を盛ってあるのが a dish, その料理を直接分けて食器を使って食べるための皿が a plate である); 〈皿類の総称〉dishes; crockery; 〈はかりの〉a scalepan; a pan ¶皿に入れて出す serve sth in a dish [on a plate] / 皿に盛り分ける dish out 《potatoes》/ 皿で[から]食べる eat off [out of] a plate / 1皿 a plateful (of) / 〈同じ料理を〉2皿食べる have two helpings (of omelet) / 皿洗い〈行為〉dish-washing; 《英》washing-up; 〈人〉a dishwasher; 《英》a washer-up / 皿洗い機 a dishwasher / 食後の皿洗いをする wash the dishes (after a meal); 《英》wash up; 《英》do the washing-up / 皿ばかり a balance / 皿回しa dish-spinning trick.

さら ¶さらにある be (quite) common; (can) be found [met with] everywhere / さらにある出来事 a daily [an everyday] occurrence; a trivial matter. 文例⇩

さらいげつ 再来月 the month after next ¶来月か再来月(に) next month or the month after.

さらいしゅう 再来週 the week after next ¶再来週の土曜日 two weeks from Saturday.

さらいねん 再来年 the year after next.

さらう¹ 浚う clean (out) 《a well》; dredge 《a river》¶川をさらって死体を探す drag a river for a dead body.

さらう² 復習う go over; review; rehearse; run through ¶学課をさらう review one's lessons / ピアノをさらう practice on [at] the piano.

さらう³ 攫う 〈持ち去る〉carry sth off [away]; run [walk] away [off] with; 〈波が〉sweep [wash] away; 〈誘かいする〉kidnap; 《文》abduct ¶子供をさらう kidnap [carry off] a child / 〈たかなどが〉鶏をさらう make [fly] off with a chicken; pounce on a chicken and fly off with it / 勝ちをさらう walk [go] away with a victory / 金をさらって逃げる make off [run away] with sb's money. 文例⇩

さらがみ ざら紙 pulp paper; rough (printing) paper.

さらけだす さらけ出す let (a secret) out; 《文》disclose [divulge] 《a secret》; expose [betray] 《one's ignorance》; lay bare 《one's plans》¶手のうちをさらけ出す put [lay] one's cards on the table.

サラサ 〈《ポルトガル語》saraça〉printed cotton; print; chintz; calico ¶木綿[インド]サラサ cotton [India] print.

さらさら ¶〈木の葉が〉さらさら鳴る rustle /〈小川が〉さらさら流れる murmur; babble; burble. 文例⇩

ざらざら ¶ざらざらする feel rough; be sandy; be gritty (with sand) / ざらざらした手触り[感触] a rough [sandy] feel [texture].

さらし さらし首 sb's head (put) on public display / さらし粉 bleaching powder / さらし者になる 〈物笑いになる〉be kept on public display; be exposed to (public) ridicule; be pilloried (in the press); 〈罪人が〉be pilloried; sit in the stocks / さらし木綿 bleached cotton cloth. 文例⇩

さらす 〈漂白する〉bleach; 〈風雨・日光に〉expose ¶日にさらす expose sth to the sun / 危険に身をさらす put oneself in danger; expose oneself to danger / 風雨にさらされた ⇒ふうう.

サラセン ¶サラセン建築 Saracenic architec-

かけたが、さもないと彼に会えなかったろう. I went at once; otherwise I should have missed him.
さゆう 世界の歴史を左右するものは剣よりもむしろペンだ. The pen is mightier than the sword in shaping the history of the world. / 人間は環境に左右されやすい. Man is easily influenced by his surroundings.
さよう¹ なにか超自然的な力が作用しているかもしれない. Some supernatural power may be at work. / それは太陽光線の人体に及ぼす作用による. It is due to the action of the sun's rays upon the human body. / 作用あれば反作用あり. To every action, there is an equal and opposite reaction.
さよう² さようでございますとも. You are quite right, sir [madam].
ざら そんな事はざらだよ. It's by no means rare [uncommon]. / It happens a lot. / こんな犬はざらにいない. You will have to look a long way to find a dog like this. / こんな珍しい事はざらにはない. You won't get such a windfall every day.
さらう³ 彼は水泳中波にさらわれた. He was swept [carried] off by the waves while swimming.
さらさら 彼は即座に手紙をさらさらと書いた. He promptly wrote a letter with effortless ease. / 彼女が部屋を歩き回るとドレスがたえずさらさらと音を立てた. Her dress gave out a continual rustle as she walked about the room. / 木の葉がさらさらと風に鳴った. The leaves rustled in the wind.
さらし さらし者にはなりたくない.

さらそうじゅ／487／さわかい

ture / サラセン人 a Saracen / サラセン人の Saracen(ic).

さらそうじゅ 沙羅双樹 a sal (tree); a saul.

サラダ (a) salad ¶ハムサラダ a ham salad; ham and salad / 野菜サラダ a vegetable salad / サラダ菜 salad; lettuce / サラダ油 salad oil.

さらち さら地 《米》a vacant lot;《英》a vacant plot (of land).

さらに 更に〈再び〉(over) again; afresh;《文》anew;〈なお〉still more; further;《文》furthermore;《文》moreover;〈少しも〉(not) in the least;(not) at all ¶更に試みる try again; make another attempt. 文例⇩

さらば 〈さようなら〉《文》farewell;《文》adieu; good-by(e)《to Tokyo》.

サラブレッド 《馬》a thoroughbred (horse).

サラミソーセージ salami.

ざらめ ざら目〈砂糖〉granulated sugar (白色、こまかい粒子の); brown [demerara] sugar (赤ざらめ).

さらり ¶さらりと without hesitating; lightly; readily; smoothly / さらりと思い切る give *sth* up without regret /(手ざわりが)さらりとした silky; fine-grained.

サラリー a salary ¶月15万円のサラリーをもらっている draw [get,《文》receive] a salary of ¥150,000 a month (from *one's* firm) / サラリーマン a salaried [salary] worker; an office worker; a white-collar worker / サラリーマン階級 the salaried class ; the salariat(e). 文例⇩

サランラップ 《商標名》Saran Wrap; plastic cling film; saran wrappings.

サリー (インドの婦人の) a sari.

ざりがに a crayfish (*pl.* -(es));《米》a crawfish (*pl.* -(es)).

さりげない casual;《文》nonchalant ¶さりげなく in a casual manner; unconcernedly; nonchalantly / さりげない風をする look innocent;《文》feign indifference;《口語》play it cool. 文例⇩

サリチルさん サリチル酸《化》salicylic acid ¶サリチル酸ソーダ sodium salicylate.

さりとて nevertheless; for all that.

サリドマイド 《薬》thalidomide ¶サリドマイド(障害)児 a thalidomide baby.

さる¹ 猿 a monkey; an ape (類人猿);〈十二支の申〉(the Year of) the Monkey ¶猿のような apelike; monkeylike / 猿の腰掛け《植》a bracket [shelf] fungus / 猿知恵 superficial cleverness; shallow cunning / 猿まね an awkward [a poor] imitation / 猿回し[芝居] a monkey showman [show]. 文例⇩

さる² 去る〈離れる〉leave ; go away [off] ; quit ;〈捨てる〉desert ¶公職を去る retire [resign] from public life / 東京を北に去る 50 キロ 50 kilometers north of Tokyo / 今を去ること10年前 ten years ago / 去る 20 日 on the 20th of this month / 去る 3 月 last March ★ただし、たとえば 12 月に「去る 11 月」と言うとき last November では去年の 11 月の意味に誤解されるおそれがあって this (last) November と言うこともある。文例⇩

さる³ 然る〈ある〉a certain…. ⇨ある¹.

ざる (bamboo) sieve (basket) ¶ざる碁を打つ play a poor game of *go* (with) / ざる法 a law full of loopholes.

さるぐつわ 猿ぐつわ a gag ¶猿ぐつわをはめる gag *sb*; put a gag in *sb's* mouth.

さるすべり 《植》a crape myrtle; an Indian lilac;《囲碁》a monkey jump.

サルタン a sultan.

サルビア 《植》a salvia; a (scarlet) sage.

サルファ 《化》sulfa ¶サルファ剤 sulfa [sulfonamide] drugs.

サルベージ salvage; salvaging ¶サルベージ船 a salvage boat.

さるまた 猿股 (a pair of) underpants; briefs.

サルモネラきん サルモネラ菌 a salmonella (*pl.* -(s), -nellae) ¶サルモネラ菌による食中毒 salmonellosis.

さるもの さる者《文》a man of no common order. 文例⇩

-ざるをえない …ざるを得ない ¶…せざるを得ない〈余儀なく〉have to *do*; must *do*; have no choice but to *do*; be forced [compelled] to *do*;〈するまいとしても〉cannot help *doing*;《文》cannot but *do*;《文》cannot help but *do*. 文例⇩

されき 砂礫 grit; pebbles; gravel.

されこうべ a skull; a death's-head.

サロン¹ 〈談話室〉a saloon;〈社交的集まり〉a (literary) salon; a reception (held by a society hostess);(パリの現代美術展)the Salon ¶サロンマルキスト an armchair Marxist; a parlor pink.

サロン² 〈マライ人・ジャワ人の腰布〉a sarong.

さわ 沢〈沼地〉a swamp; a marsh;〈谷川〉a mountain stream.

さわかい 茶話会 a tea party.

I don't want to make a show [an exhibition] of myself.

さらす 雨にも日にもさらしてはいけない。You must keep it out of the rain and the sun.

さらに 更に悪いことには雨が降りだした。To make matters worse, rain began to fall.

サラリー 彼は月10万円のサラリーで雇われた。He was employed [taken on] at a salary of ¥100,000 a month.

さりげない 彼はさりげない調子でその問題に触れた。He referred to the matter as if it were nothing important [as if it were incidental].

さる¹ 猿が鳴いた。A monkey chattered [gibbered]./猿も木から落ちる。Homer sometimes nods. 【諺】

さる² 彼らの境遇は奴隷の状態をある事遠くなかった。Their condition was little short of slavery. / その結果、キューバもまた西欧の陣営を去ってしまった。As a result, Cuba, too, has become a defector from the Western camp./去る者日々にうとし。Out of sight, out of mind. 【諺】｜Seldom seen [Long absent], soon forgotten. 【諺】

さるもの 敵もさるものだ。This is no common enemy we have to deal with. | We have a tough [an ugly] customer to deal with.

-ざるをえない 緊急の用事だというので、すぐに行かざるをえなかった。I had to go straightaway because they said it was urgent. / つい本当のところを言わざるをえなかった。I could not help speaking the truth. / あとは運を天に

さわがしい 騒がしい 〈やかましい〉 noisy; boisterous;《文》clamorous; uproarious.〈物騒な〉《文》troubled;《文》turbulent.

さわがす 騒がす disturb;《文》agitate; alarm; cause anxiety (to); trouble ¶(事件が)世間を騒がす create [cause] a sensation / 町中を騒がす alarm [electrify] the whole town; set the whole town agog.

さわがれる 騒がれる be made much of; be lionized; be (much) sought after. 文例↓

さわぎ 騒ぎ 〈けんそう〉 a noise; an uproar;〈騒動〉(a) disturbance; trouble; a stir; a commotion;〈けんか〉 a quarrel; a fight; a brawl; a row;〈騒ぎ立てること〉 a fuss;〈興奮〉(an) excitement;〈大評判〉 a sensation ¶騒ぎを起こす make a disturbance;《口語》kick up [raise] a dust;〈ある事が〉 create [cause] a commotion [stir] / 騒ぎを大きくする add (fresh) fuel to the flames [fire] / コレラ[戦争]騒ぎ a cholera [war] scare.

さわぎたてる 騒ぎ立てる make a great fuss 《about》; shout [raise] an alarm; cry《murder》 ⇒さわぐ.

さわぐ 騒ぐ 〈騒々しくする〉 make a noise [racket];〈要求・反対して〉 clamor 《for, against》;〈騒動を起こす〉 kick up a row;〈興奮する〉 be excited;〈心配する〉 be alarmed;〈激する〉 be agitated;〈奔走する〉 rush [bustle] 《to do》; busy oneself 《about》;〈から騒ぎする〉 make a fuss《about》;〈遊興する〉 make merry; have a spree;《口語》make whoopee. 文例↓

ざわざわ ⇒ざわざわする ⇒ざわめく.

ざわつく ⇒ざわめく.

ざわめき a stir; (a) commotion; noises;〈人声〉 a hum [murmur] of voices.

ざわめく be noisy;《文》be astir;〈木の葉などが〉 rustle ¶ざわめかせる create a stir [commotion, flutter] (in, among). 文例↓

さわやか さわやかな fresh; refreshing; bracing;《文》invigorating;〈声の〉 clear;〈弁舌の〉 fluent;《文》eloquent ¶さわやかな朝 a crisp morning / 気分がさわやかになる feel refreshed.

さわら[1]〈植〉 a sawara cypress.

さわら[2]〈魚〉 a Spanish mackerel.

さわり 触り 〈触感〉 touch; feel;〈聞き所〉 the climax;〈最も moving passage (義太夫などの); the point (of a story).

さわり 障り 〈障害物〉 an obstacle;《文》a hindrance;〈害〉 harm;〈悪影響〉 a bad effect ¶障りがある be harmful (to); have a bad [《文》baneful] effect (on).

さわる[1] 触る touch; feel ¶指で触る finger; feel sth with one's fingers / 肩に触る touch sb on the shoulder / 触ると冷たい be cold to the touch [feel]. 文例↓

さわる[2] 障る 〈妨げる〉 hinder; interfere with; get in the way of;〈影響する〉 affect; tell (on);〈害になる〉 hurt; do one harm; be bad for (one's health) ¶人の気に障る hurt sb's feelings; offend [give offense to] sb.

さわんとうしゅ 左腕投手〈野球〉 a left-handed pitcher; a left-hander; a southpaw (pitcher).

さん[1] 三 three ¶第3 the third / 3度 three times;《文》thrice.

さん[2] 桟〈板の反りを防ぐための横木〉 a cross-piece;〈障子の〉 a frame;〈戸の〉 a bar ¶戸のさんを下ろす[外す] bar [unbar] the door.

さん[3] 〈出産〉(a) childbirth; (a) delivery ¶お産が軽い[重い] have an easy [a difficult] labor [delivery] / お産をする have [give birth to] a baby / お産で死ぬ die in childbirth. 文例↓

さん[4] 産〈産物〉 a product;〈財産〉 a fortune ⇒さいさん ¶産を成す make [《文》amass] a fortune;《口語》make a [one's] pile / 京都の産である come [《文》hail] from Kyoto / カリフォルニア産のオレンジ oranges grown [produced] in California / 外国[国内]産の小麦 foreign-grown [home-grown] wheat / 北海道産の熊 a bear from Hokkaido.

さん[5] 酸 an acid ¶酸類 acids.

さん[6] 算 ¶算を乱して《文》in great confusion;《文》in utter disorder.

さん[7] 賛 ¶絵に賛をする write a caption (legend) on a picture.

さん[8] 燦 ¶さんとして輝く shine brilliantly.

-さん[1] …山 Mt. [Mount] ¶富士山 Mt. Fuji.

-さん[2] 〈敬称〉 ⇒-さま.

さんい 賛意 ¶賛意を表する give [《文》express, show] one's approval (to sb, of a plan);《文》give one's assent (to). 文例↓

さんいつ 散逸 ¶散逸する get [be] scattered and lost.

さんいん 産院 a maternity hospital [home].

さんか 山窩 mountain gypsies in Japan.

さんか 参加 ¶参加する take part (in); join (a party);《文》participate (in); join in 《with

---

任せざるをえなかった. I had no choice but to leave the rest to chance.

さわがしい世の中が騒がしい. We are living in troubled times.

さわがれる おれも若いころは娘たちに少しは騒がれたものだよ. In my youth I excited some admiration among the girls. / この事件は新聞で大いに騒がれた. The case made a lot of noise in the papers.

さわぎ この騒ぎは何事だ. What's all this noise? / たちまち学校中は大騒ぎとなった. The whole school was instantly thrown into an uproar. / 騒ぎが収まるまではどうにもならなかった. We could do nothing until quiet [order] was restored. / 笑うどころの騒ぎではなかった. It was no laughing matter. / 騒いどころの騒ぎじゃないよ. 'Hot' isn't the word for it.

さわぐ 試験は20日からだから今から騒がなくてもいい. The examination begins on the 20th of this month, so you need not get worked up[nervous] yet. / コレラの発生で世間が騒ぎ出した. People got alarmed at the outbreak of cholera. / 内田夫人は少しも騒がなかった. Mrs. Uchida was quite unruffled.

ざわめく 町中はその知らせでざわめいていた. The whole town was buzzing with the news. / 氏が登壇すると聴衆がざわめいた. When he appeared on the platform, a stir ran through the audience. / 木の葉が微風にざわめいていた. The leaves were rustling in the breeze.

さんか them); enter 《a war》; sit in 《on a conference》/ 夏期講習に参加する be enrolled in a class at the summer school / 直接参加する take a direct part 《in》/ 参加を申し込む enter for 《a contest》/ 参加意識 a sense of participation / 参加国[チーム] a participating nation [team] / 参加者 a participant ; 〈競技の〉 an entrant. 文例◎

さんか⁴ 産科 〈学〉 obstetrics ; 〈病院の〉 the obstetrical department; the maternity division ¶産科医 an obstetrician / 産科病棟 a maternity ward.

さんか⁴ 惨禍 a disaster ; a calamity ; a catastrophe; 〈広域が火に包まれた〉《文》a holocaust ¶戦争の惨禍 the horrors of war ⇨ さんか².

さんか⁵ 傘下 ¶傘下の affiliated 《unions》; subsidiary 《companies》/ 総評傘下の労組 labor unions under the control [umbrella, influence] of the Sohyo [the General Council of Trade Unions of Japan].

さんか⁶ 酸化 《化》oxidation ; oxidization ¶酸化する〈他の物を〉oxidize; 〈その物が〉be oxidized / 酸化しやすい金属 an easily oxidizable metal / 酸化鉄 iron oxide / 酸化物 an oxide.

さんか⁷ 賛歌 《文》a paean ; a poem [song] in praise 《of》.

さんが 参賀 ¶参賀する go to the Imperial Palace and offer *one's* congratulations 《on the New Year》.

さんかい¹ 山海 ¶山海の珍味 《entertain *sb* with》all sorts of delicacies ; 《文》a sumptuous repast [feast].

さんかい 山塊 a mass of mountains ¶ヒマラヤ大山塊 the great Himalayan mountain massif.

さんかい¹ 散会 adjournment ¶散会する break up ; rise ; 《文》adjourn ; close. 文例◎

さんかい¹ 散開 《軍》deployment ¶散開する deploy; spread out / 散開している be dispersed 《in the field》; be in loose formation / 散開させる get 《the men》into open [extended] order.

さんかい¹ 三階 《米》the third floor [story] ; 《英》the second floor ⇨かい 回阶 ¶3階建ての家 a three-story[-storied] house ; a house with three stories. 文例◎

さんがい² 惨害 heavy [ruinous] damage ¶惨害を与える《文》wreak havoc on ; work havoc with 《the crops》/ 惨害をこうむる | suffer heavily from 《a storm》/ 水爆の惨害《文》an H-bomb holocaust / 戦争の惨害 the horrors

489 さんぎ

[ravages] of war.

さんがい 残がい the wreck ; the wreckage ¶飛行機の残がい the wreck [wreckage] of a plane; the remains of a wrecked plane.

さんかく¹ 三角 ¶三角 triangle ¶三角(形)の triangular ; three-cornered / 目を三角にする look angry ; give an angry look / 逆三角形 an inverted triangle / 三角関係 the eternal triangle; a love triangle / 三角関数 a trigonometric function / 三角巾(ん) a triangular bandage / 三角筋 《解》a deltoid (muscle)/平面[球面]三角《数》plane [spherical] trigonometry /三角定規 a set square ; a triangle / 三角州 a delta ⇨ デルタ / 三角錐 a trigonal [triangular] pyramid /三角測量 triangulation ; triangular surveying /三角点 ⇨ さんかくてん / 三角波 chopping waves / 三角比 a trigonometric ratio / 三角貿易 triangular trade / 三角翼 a delta wing.

さんかく² 参画 ¶参画する《文》participate in 《a project》; have a hand [in the planning of]; take part 《in a plot》; have a share 《in the execution of a plan》.

さんがく¹ 山岳 mountains ¶山岳会[部] a mountaineering [an alpine] club / 山岳地方 ⇨ さんち¹.

さんがく² 産額 the (amount of) production ; the output (of gold); the yield (of rice).

ざんがく 残額 ⇨ ざんだか ¶残額を支払う 〈残金を〉pay the remainder of the money due to *sb* ; 〈差額を〉pay the balance of *sb's* account.

さんかくてん 三角点 《測量》a triangulation point ¶三角点の標石 a stone triangulation marker.

さんがつ 三月 March (略: Mar.).

さんかっけい 三角形 a triangle ⇨ さんかく¹.

さんがにち 三が日 the first three days of the new year.

さんかん¹ 山間 ¶山間のへき地 a secluded [remote] place in [among] the mountains ; an out-of-the-way place in the mountains / 山間の湖 a mountain lake.

さんかん² 参観 ¶参観する visit ; inspect / 授業を参観する visit [inspect] a class 《at work》/ 工場を参観する pay a visit of inspection to a factory / 参観を許す[許さない] 〈場所が主語〉be open [closed] to visitors / 参観人 a visitor / 父母の参観日 a parents' visiting [open] day.

さんかんおう 三冠王 ¶三冠王になる 《野球》get [win] the triple crown.

さんぎ 算木 divining blocks.

さわり² この失敗は彼の名声に大きな障りとなった。His reputation will suffer greatly from this fiasco.

さわる¹ 触るんじゃありません! Don't touch! / 彼は自分の耳に触って見た。He felt at his ear. / それはそんなに冷たいかい。どれどれ、僕にも触らせてくれ。Is it that cold? Well, let me have a feel. / 触るべからず。[掲示] Hands off! / 触らぬ神に祟りなし。Let sleeping dogs lie.

さん¹ 彼女は近々お産をする。

She is going to have a baby. | 《口語》She is expecting.

さんい この理由から我々は彼の提案に賛意を表明した。For this reason we expressed our approval for his proposal.

さんか³ オリンピック大会には50カ国から5千人以上の選手が参加した。Fifty nations were represented by over 5,000 athletes in the Olympic Games. / われわれの日曜学校には400人の人が参加しております。Our Sunday school has an enrollment of 400. / 多くの大学生もこの新しい運動に参加した。Quite a few university students also joined in this new movement.

さんかい³ 何時に散会したか。When did the meeting break up? / 国会は午後7時に散会した。The House rose [adjourned] at seven in the evening.

さんかい¹ 私の部屋は3階です。My room is on the third floor 〔《英》second floor〕. / このエレベーター

ざんき 慚愧 ¶ざんきに堪えない be really ashamed of 《*oneself*, having done such a thing》.
さんぎいん 参議院 the House of Councilors ¶参議院議員[議長] the President [a member] of the House of Councilors.
さんきゃく 三脚 a tripod ¶三脚を立てる set *one's* tripod 《at a place, on a rock》/ 三脚椅子 a three-legged stool.
ざんぎゃく 残虐 (a) cruelty; 《文》(an) atrocity ¶残虐な cruel; heartless; brutal / 残虐なことをする do something cruel; commit an atrocity.
さんきゅう 産休 (on) maternity leave.
さんぎょう 産業 (an) industry ¶産業の industrial / 主要産業 the chief [key, major] industries / 第一次産業 (the) primary industries / 産業化する industrialize / 産業界 industrial circles; the industrial world / 産業開発 industrial development / 産業革命 the Industrial Revolution / 産業構造 industrial structure / 産業資本 industrial capital / 産業社会 industrial society / 産業スパイ a corporate [an industrial] spy / 産業地理 industrial geography / 産業転換 industrial conversion / 新産業都市 a new industrial city / 産業別組合 an industrial [《米》vertical] union.
[用法] industry は, 「産業」一般の意味では, Industry first developed in eighteenth-century England. (産業が最初に発達したのは 18 世紀の英国であった)のように不可算名詞。個々の産業の意味では, Shipbuilding is no longer a key industry. (造船業はもはや基幹産業ではない) / The industries of this country (わが国の諸産業)のように可算名詞扱い。各産業部門は the shipbuilding industry, the automobile industry のように the をつけて言う。
ざんきょう 残響 reverberation; 《反響》an echo 《*pl.* -es》.
ざんぎょう 残業 overtime [extra] work ¶残業する work overtime [extra hours] / 残業手当 overtime (pay); an allowance for overtime work.
さんぎょうこうこく 三行広告 a classified (three-line) advertisement [ad]; 《口語》a want ad ¶三行広告欄 the classified ad columns / 《口語》the want ads.
ざんぎりあたま ざん切り頭 a cropped head.
ざんきん 残金 ⇨さだか [文例⑨]
サングラス (a pair of) sunglasses ¶(wear) dark glasses.
さんけ 産気 ¶産気づく labor starts; 〈人が主語〉begin [go into] labor; begin to feel labor pains / 産気づいた女 a woman in labor.
ざんげ 懺悔 《悔悟》《文》penitence; 《文》repentance; 《告白》(a) confession ¶ざんげする 〈悔悟する〉《文》repent 《of *one's* sins》; 《告白する》confess 《*one's* sins to a priest》/ ざんげの生活 《文》a penitential [penitent's] life / ざんげ聴聞僧[室] a con-

fessor [confessional] / (ルソーの)懺悔録【書名】*Confessions*.
さんけい[1] 山系 a mountain system.
さんけい[2] 参詣 ¶さんけいする visit [pay a visit to] 《a temple》; make a pilgrimage 《to》/ さんけい人 a visitor 《to a shrine》; a pilgrim.
さんげき 惨劇 a tragedy; 《文》a tragic event; an atrocity ¶惨劇の現場 the scene of the tragedy.
さんけつ 酸欠 ⇨ さんそ (酸素欠乏).
ざんげつ 残月 the moon at dawn; the moon in the morning sky.
さんけん 散見 ¶散見する be found here and there; 〈人が主語〉come across *sth* occasionally [in places].
ざんげん 讒言 a false charge; (a) slander; 《文》(a) calumny ¶ざん言する give a slanderous account [report] 《of *one's* rival to *one's* master》; slander; make a false charge 《against》.
さんげんしょく 三原色 (the) three primary colors ¶三原色使用の trichromatic [trichromic] 《printing, photography》.
さんけんぶんりつ 三権分立 separation of (the three) powers (of administration, legislation, and judicature).
さんご[1] 産後 ¶産後の (convalescence) after childbirth; 【医】postpartum / 産後の肥立ちがいい[悪い] be doing well [badly] after childbirth.
さんご[2] 珊瑚 coral ¶さんごを採集する fish for coral / さんご海 the Coral Sea / さんご樹 a coral formation / さんご礁 a coral reef; an atoll 《環礁》/ さんご虫 a coral insect [polyp] / さんご島 a coral island.
さんこう 参考 reference; 《文》consultation ¶参考する refer to 《the notes》; consult 《a book》/ 参考のため for reference; for *one's* information / 参考になる provide [《文》furnish] *one* with useful information; give *one* food for thought; 〈助けになる〉be helpful 《to *one* in doing》/ (学習のための)参考書 a study-aid book / 参考書目 a bibliography / 参考資料 reference materials / 参考図書 a reference book [work] / 参考人 a witness / 参考品 a specimen for reference / 参考文献 references. [文例⑨]
さんごう 塹壕 a trench; a dugout ¶さんごうを作る[掘る] dig 《*oneself*》in; dig a trench; get entrenched.
さんごく 三国 ¶三国同盟 a triple alliance / 第三国 a third power / 三国一のおむこさん an ideal husband [son-in-law].
ざんこく 残酷 cruelty; brutality; atrocity ¶残酷な cruel; brutal; inhuman; merciless; harsh / 残酷に取り扱う treat *sb* cruelly [with brutality]; be cruel to *sb*.
さんさい 山菜 edible wild plants.

は 3 階で止まりますか。Does this elevator stop at the third floor?
ざんきん 残金は 2 千円だけです。2,000 yen is all (the money) there is left. | The balance is only 2,000 yen.
さんこう この本は英文学の研究におおいに参考になる。This book is a good guide to the study of English literature. / 私たちにはほとんど何の参考にもならない。It's hardly any help to us. | It offers us very little guidance. / ただ参考までに申し上げたにすぎ

ません。I said it only as [It was only] a suggestion. / それについては参考すべき文献がほとんどありません。There is very little literature to refer to about it.
さんさい[1] 湾内には大小の島々が散在している。The bay is studded

さんざい¹ 散在　¶散在する〈物が主語〉lie [be] scattered《all over the country》; be found here and there；〈場所が主語〉be dotted with 《sheep》.　文例⇩

さんざい² 散財　¶散財する spend money 《on》; squander [lavish] money 《on》; throw one's money away / 散財をかける put sb to great expense.

さんさく 散策 ⇨ さんぽ.

さんざし 山査子〈植〉a hawthorn.

ざんさつ 惨殺　¶惨殺する《文》cruelly murder; kill without mercy; butcher / 惨殺死体 a mangled body [corpse].

さんさろ 三差路 a three-forked road; a junction of three roads.

さんさん¹ 三々　¶三々五々 by twos and threes; in groups (of twos and threes) / 三々九度の杯をする exchange cups of sake at《their》wedding;《文》exchange nuptial cups.

さんさん² 燦々　¶さんさんたる bright; brilliant;《文》radiant / さんさんと陽の照る日 a bright sunny day / さんさんと降りそそぐ陽光 the brilliant rays of the sun.

さんざん 散々　¶散々な目に会う have a hard time of it / 散々〈に〉〈激しく〉severely; terribly;《容赦なく》mercilessly;《すっかり》thoroughly; utterly / 散々に負ける be beaten hollow; suffer a crushing defeat / 散々悩まされる be plagued [bored] to death《by》/ 散々ののしる《文》abuse [berate] sb roundly / 散々しかってやる《口語》tear into sb;《口語》tear a strip off sb / 散々 sb a good telling-off [scolding] / 散々人を待たす keep sb waiting a long time / 散々不平を並べる make all sorts of complaints; grumble one's fill / 散々迷惑をかける give sb [put sb to] a great deal [a lot] of trouble / 散々苦労したあげく after no end of trouble.　文例⇩

さんし 蚕糸 silk yarn [thread]　¶蚕糸試験場 a sericulture experimental station.

さんじ¹ 三次　¶第三次佐藤内閣 the third Sato Cabinet / 第三次産業《the》tertiary industries / 三次方程式 a cubic equation.

さんじ² 参事〈顧問〉a counselor; an adviser; a secretary　¶参事官 a councilor (of an embassy).

さんじ³ 惨事 a disaster; a tragedy; a disastrous accident; a tragic incident　¶惨事を引き起こす cause a terrible accident / 鉄道の惨事 a terrible railroad accident.

さんじ⁴ 賛辞 praise(s);《文》a eulogy;《文》a panegyric; a compliment　¶賛辞を呈する praise;《文》eulogize;《文》pay one's tribute (of praise)《to》; speak of sth in terms of high praise; pay compliments《to》/ 賛辞を惜しまない《文》give unstinted praise《to》.

ざんし¹ 残滓 leftovers; the residue; dregs 《液体の》¶封建主義の残滓 vestiges of feudalism.

ざんし² 惨死　¶惨死する meet with [come by] a tragic death;《文》be cruelly murdered.

ざんじ 暫時 for a (short) time; for some time;《for》a little while.

サンジカリズム syndicalism.

さんじげん 三次元 three dimensions　¶三次元の three-dimensional; three-D; 3-D.

さんしすいめい 山紫水明　¶山紫水明の地 a place famous for its natural [scenic] beauty; a scenic place.

さんじせいげん 産児制限 birth control　¶産児制限を行なう practice birth control.

さんしつ 産室 a delivery [lying-in] room (in a hospital).

さんしゃ 三者　¶三者会談 a tripartite meeting / 三者の ⇨ だいさん / 〈野球で投手が〉3者3振に打ちとる strike out three batters in order.

さんしゃく 参酌 ⇨ しんしゃく.

さんじゃく 三尺〈帯〉a kimono girdle; a waistband.

さんじゅう¹ 三十 thirty　¶第30 the thirtieth / 三十年戦争《世界史》the Thirty Years' War.

さんじゅう² 三重　¶三重の triple; treble;《文》threefold / 三重の塔 a three-storied pagoda / 三重苦 a triple handicap《of being blind, deaf, and dumb》;《文》triple distress / 三重結合〈化〉a triple bond / 三重唱〔奏〕《音楽》a trio (pl. -s).

さんじゅうごミリ 35ミリ〈フィルム〉a 35 millimeter [35-mm] film;〈カメラ〉a 35-mm camera. 〔Parallel.

さんじゅうはちどせん 三十八度線 the 38th

さんじゅうろっけい 三十六計　¶三十六計をきめこむ beat a retreat; take to one's heels; run away.　文例⇩

さんしゅつ¹ 産出　¶産出する produce; yield; 《文》bring forth / 産出額 the (amount of) production; the output (of gold).

さんしゅつ² 算出　¶算出する calculate; compute; work out.

さんじゅつ 算術 arithmetic　¶算術が得意だ [苦手だ] be good [poor] at sums; have a good [poor] head for figures / 算術的な do sums / 算術級数 ⇨ とうさきゅうすう / 算術計算 arithmetical computation;《perform》an arithmetical operation.

さんじょ 賛助 support;《文》patronage　¶賛助する support; back (up);《文》patronize / 賛助を求める [得る]《文》solicit [obtain] sb's support / 賛助会員 a supporting member / 賛助出演する appear as a guest (artist [star]).

ざんしょ 残暑 the lingering summer heat; the heat of late summer.　文例⇩

さんしょう¹ 三唱　¶万歳を三唱する give three cheers (for).

---

with islands, large and small.
さんざい 今日は一つ思い切り散財してやろうという気分だった. I was in an extravagant mood.
さんざん 大水で散々な目に会った. I had a terrible experience on account of the flood. / 試合は雨で散々だった. The match was quite spoilt by the rain.
さんじゅうろっけい 三十六計逃ぐるにしかず. The best thing to do now is to run away. | He that fights and runs away lives to fight another day. [諺] | Discretion is the better part of valor. [諺]
ざんしょ 今年は残暑がきびしい. The late summer heat is severe

さんしょう² 山椒 〖植〗《木》a Japanese pepper tree; a prickly ash; 《香辛料》Japanese pepper. 文例⇩

さんしょう³ 参照 ¶参照する compare ((with)); refer ((to)); consult; see / 参照((せよ))see; 《ラテン語》confer (略: cf.); 《ラテン語》vide (略: vid.) / (かっこ内で)その項参照 which see; 《ラテン語》quod vide (略: q.v.) ★これらのラテン語はほとんど決って略の形で使われる。

さんじょう¹ 山上 ¶山上の垂訓〖聖書〗the Sermon on the Mount.

さんじょう² 三乗〖数〗¶三乗する cube; raise ((a number)) to the third power [the power of 3] / 3乗根 the cube root / 3乗べき the third power ((of)). 文例⇩

さんじょう³ 参上 ¶参上する come to see ((you)); call ((on you, at your house)); visit.

さんじょう⁴ 惨状 a horrible [dreadful] scene [sight]; a miserable condition [state] ¶惨状を呈する ((文)) present a horrible spectacle [sight]; be in a wretched condition.

ざんしょう 残照 the afterglow.

さんしょううお 山椒魚 a salamander.

さんじょうき 三畳紀〖地質〗the Triassic period.

さんしょく¹ 三色 ¶三色の three-color; tricolor(ed) / 三色旗 a tricolor (flag) / 三色すみれ a pansy / 三色版 three-color printing.

さんしょく² 蚕食 ¶蚕食する encroach ((on)); make inroads ((on, into)).

さんじょくねつ 産褥熱〖医〗puerperal [childbed] fever.

さんじる 散じる scatter; disperse; 《金を》spend ((in, on)); squander ((on)) ¶酒にうつを散じる drown one's sorrows in drink.

さんしん 三振〖野球〗a strikeout ¶三振する be [get] struck out; strike out; ((口語)) fan / 三振させる ((a batter)) out; ((口語)) fan ((a batter)) / 14三振を奪う strike out 14.

ざんしん 斬新 ¶斬新な novel; original; ((文)) innovative ((products)).

さんすい¹ 山水《山と水》hills and waters; 《風景》a landscape; scenery ¶山水の美 natural [scenic] beauty / 山水画((法))(Chinese-style) landscape painting /((画))a (Chinese-style) landscape (painting) / 山水画家 a landscape painter.

さんすい² 散水 ¶散水する sprinkle ((the street)) with water; sprinkle water ((over the garden)) / 散水車 a water [motor, street] sprinkler; a sprinkler (truck).

さんすう 算数 ((算術)) arithmetic; ((計算)) calculation ⇒さんじゅつ.

さんすくみ 三すくみ ¶三すくみになる be in a three-cornered [tripartite] deadlock. 文例⇩

サンスクリット Sanskrit.

さんずのかわ 三途の川 the (River) Styx.

さんする¹ 産する produce; yield; turn out.

さんする² 算する ((文)) number; amount [come] to.

さんせい¹ 三世 a Sansei (sansei) ((pl. -(s)); a third-generation Japanese-American.

さんせい² 酸性 acidity ¶土壌の酸性 soil acidity / 酸性の acid ((soil)) / 酸性食品 acid foods / 酸性反応 (an) acid reaction.

さんせい³ 賛成 ¶賛成する approve of ((a plan)); give one's approval ((to)); agree ((to sb's proposal, with sb, with sb's opinion)); fall in with ((sb's views)); support ((a bill)); second ((a proposal)) / 賛成を得る gain [win] the approval ((of)); ((文)) meet (with) the approbation ((of)) / …に対して賛成反対の議論をする argue the pros and cons of… / 賛成演説 (make) a speech in support of ((a bill)) / 賛成者 a supporter / 賛成投票 vote for [in favor of] ((a bill)). 文例⇩

さんせいけん 参政権 suffrage; the franchise; the right to vote ¶参政権を与える give suffrage ((to women)); give [extend] the franchise ((to)) / 婦人参政権 woman suffrage.

さんせき 山積 ¶山積する lie in a heap [in piles]; accumulate; pile up. 文例⇩

ざんせつ 残雪 the remaining [unmelted] snow.

さんせん¹ 三選 ¶三選される be (re)elected ((Governor)) for the third (consecutive) term.

さんせん² 参戦 ¶参戦する enter [take part in, ((文)) participate in] the war; go to war / アメリカ側に参戦する enter the war on the American side / 参戦しない stay out of the war.

さんぜん 参禅 ¶参禅する practice Zen meditation (in a temple).

さんぜん² 燦然 ¶燦然たる brilliant; ((文)) radiant; ((文)) resplendent; dazzling / 燦然と輝く shine brilliantly [((文)) radiantly].

さんぜんさんご 産前産後 ¶産前産後の[に] before and after childbirth / 産前産後の休暇 (a) maternity leave.

さんそ 酸素 oxygen ¶酸素の欠乏に苦しむ suffer from oxygen starvation / 酸素吸入 oxygen inhalation / 酸素吸入器 an oxygen inhaler / 酸素吸入用マスク an oxygen mask / 酸素欠乏〖医〗hypoxia; anoxia / 酸素溶接 oxyacetylene

---

this year.

さんしょう² 山椒は小粒でもぴりりと辛い. Small he may be, but he is not a man to be trifled with.

さんしょう² 2の3乗は8. The cube of 2 is 8. / 2 cubed is 8.

さんじょう⁴ 被災地の住民の惨状は実にひどいものであった. The condition of the people in the stricken [disaster] area was quite appalling.

さんすくみ 三すくみの状態となった. The three parties came to a deadlock, each unable to establish its superiority over the other two.

さんせい³ 僕は君の意見に全く賛成です. I completely agree with your opinion. / 私は with you (100 per cent). / 僕の提案は全員の賛成を得た. My proposal received unanimous approval. / 賛成してくれて有り難い. I'm glad you saw it my way. / この計画に賛成してもらおうと思って彼を訪ねました. I called on him in the hope of interesting him in this plan. / 賛成の方は挙手を願います. Those in favor [The ayes] are requested to raise their hands. / 賛成は34, 反対は20. There were 34 ayes and 20 noes [34 for and 20 against the bill]. / 議案は賛成206 票反対178 票で通過した. The bill was passed with 206 in favor to 178 against. / 賛成者多数.〖議会〗The

さんそう 山荘 a mountain villa [retreat].
ざんぞう 残像 《心理》an afterimage;《光》persistence of vision.
さんぞく 山賊 a bandit;《文》a brigand / 山賊の巣くつ a bandits' den / 山賊の出没する場所 a bandit-ridden place; a place infested by bandits / 山賊行為 banditry;《文》brigandage.
さんそん 山村 a mountain village.
ざんそん 残存 ¶残存する survive; be still alive [in existence];《文》be extant; be left; remain / 残存者 a survivor / 残存種 a relict species.
ざんだか 残高 the balance; the remainder ¶銀行預金残高 the [one's] balance at the bank / 残高を全部引き出す draw the balance to nothing.
サンタクロース Santa Claus;《英》Father Christmas.
さんだつ 簒奪 usurpation ¶さん奪者 a usurper / さん奪する usurp (the throne).
サンダル (a pair of) sandals.
さんたん¹ 惨憺 ¶惨たんたる sad; wretched; miserable; horrible; tragic / 惨たんたる状態である《文》be in a very sorry plight / 惨たんたる敗北を喫する suffer a crushing defeat / 惨たんたる結果となる《事が主語》end in disaster (for one). 文例⇩
さんたん² 賛嘆 ¶賛嘆する admire;《文》extol; speak highly of; be filled with admiration (for). 文例⇩
さんだん¹ 三段 ¶三段構えの防御 a threefold defense / 三段式ロケット a three-stage rocket / 三段跳び《競技》the triple jump; the hop, step, and jump / 三段論法《論》a syllogism / 三段論法で論じる argue [reason] by syllogisms.
さんだん² 散弾 a shot ¶散弾銃 a shotgun.
さんだん³ 算段 ¶算段する manage; make shift / 金を算段する (manage to) raise some money.
さんち¹ 山地 mountain country (★「ある特徴を持った地域」の意味の country は不可算名詞); a mountainous region; a hilly district.
さんち² 産地 〈産物の〉a producing center [district]; 〈動植物の〉the home; the habitat ¶馬の産地 a horse-breeding center / タバコの産地 a tobacco-growing district / 産地直送のじゃがいも potatoes direct from the farm. 文例⇩
サンチャゴ Santiago.
さんちゅう 山中 ¶山中の[に, で] among [in] the mountains.
さんちょう 山頂 the summit [top] of a mountain; a mountaintop; a peak (とがった山の) ¶山頂に on the top [at the summit] of a mountain;《文》atop (Mt. Fuji). 文例⇩
さんてい 算定 ¶算定する〈計算する〉compute; calculate;〈見積もる〉estimate (the cost at ¥1,000,000);《文》appraise. 文例⇩
ざんてい 暫定 ¶暫定的の《文》provisional; temporary / 暫定的に《文》provisionally; temporarily; for the time being / 暫定案 a tentative [makeshift] plan / 暫定協定 a provisional agreement /《ラテン語》a *modus vivendi* (pl. *modi vivendi*) / 暫定措置 a temporary step; a stopgap measure / 暫定内閣 a caretaker cabinet / 暫定予算 a provisional budget.
サンデー a (chocolate) sundae.
さんど 三度 three times;《文》thrice ¶三度の食事 three (regular) meals (a day); daily meals / 三度に一度は (at least) once in three times / 三度三度(の食事に) at every meal / 3度目に for the third time.
サンドイッチ sandwiches ¶ハムサンドイッチ ham sandwiches / サンドイッチマン a sandwich man / サンドイッチマンがつけている広告板 sandwich boards.
さんとう 三等 the third class;〈第3位〉the third place ¶三等で旅行する travel [go] third-class /〈船で〉travel steerage / 三等重役 a third-rate business director / 三等親 a relation of the third degree.
さんどう¹ 参道 the approach [an entrance path] (to a *Shinto* shrine).
さんどう² 賛同 ¶賛同する approve of《a plan》; give *one's* approval to《a proposal》; support / 賛同を得る〈人が主語〉obtain *sb's* approval [《文》consent];〈事が主語〉meet with *sb's* approval / 賛同を得て with *sb's* approval [support] / 賛同を求める ask *sb's* approval《for a plan》.
ざんとう 残党《文》the remnants (of); survivors.
さんとうせいじ 三頭政治 a triumvirate.
さんとうぶん 三等分 ¶角の三等分《幾何》trisection of the angle / 三等分する cut [divide] into three equal parts; divide *sth* equally among three; trisect《an angle》.
サントメプリンシペ ¶サントメプリンシペ民主共和国 the Democratic Republic of São Tomé and Principe.
サントラ ⇨ サウンドトラック.
さんにゅう 算入 ¶算入する count [reckon] in; add in; include in.
さんにん 三人 ¶3人組 a trio (*pl.* -s) / 3人組

---

ayes have it.
さんせき 駅には滞貨が山積している。Piles of goods lie undelivered at the station. / 仕事が山積している。I have a lot of business to attend to.
さんたん¹ 焼け跡の光景は実に惨たんたるものであった。The ruins after the fire presented a really dreadful [horrible] sight. / 先日の台風でうちの庭の樹は実に惨んたるものだ。The recent typhoon has wrought terrible havoc with our garden plants.
さんたん² だれが彼の偉業に賛嘆を惜しむであろうか。Who can help admiring his great achievement?
さんち² 庄内は米の産地として名高い。Shonai is famous for the [its] production of rice.
さんちょう 山頂は一年中雪を頂いている。The mountain is crowned with snow all the year round.
さんてい その市場価格は現在日本では1トン当たり10万円と算定されている。Its market value in Japan at the present moment works out at ¥100,000 per ton.
さんど 彼は三度三度酒を飲む。He drinks *sake* with every (single) meal. / 碁が今や三度の飯より好きだ。The game of *go* is his

ざんにん の強盗 a gang of three robbers / 三人称単数《文法》 the third person singular.

ざんにん 残忍 ¶残忍な brutal; cold-blooded; cruel-hearted; cruel ⇒ さんぎゃく, さんこく.

さんねん 三年 three years ¶3年生 a third-year student;〈小学校の〉《米》a third-grade boy [girl];〈大学の〉《米》a junior.

ざんねん 残念 ¶残念な〈遺憾な〉unfortunate; regrettable; disappointing;〈口惜しい〉vexing;《文》mortifying / 残念ながら I'm afraid...; I am sorry [I regret] (to say) that... / 残念ながら…という結論に達した came to the reluctant conclusion that... /残念なことには unfortunately;《文》to one's (deep) regret; sad to say / 残念そうに regretfully / 残念がる, 残念に思う regret ((that...)); feel regret ((at)); be sorry /〈口惜しがる〉be vexed [mortified] ((at));《文》feel chagrin [be chagrined] ((at)) / 残念賞 a consolation prize. 文例⇩

さんば 産婆 a midwife (pl. -wives) ¶産婆術 midwifery / 産婆役を勤める《比喩的》serve as midwife to [assist in] ((the formation of an organization)).

サンバ〈ブラジルのダンス〉a samba ¶サンバを踊る dance the samba.

さんばい 三倍 three times ⇒ ばい 用法 ¶3倍する multiply (a number) by three; treble. 文例⇩

さんぱい 参拝 ¶参拝する visit ((a shrine)); enter ((a temple)) and pray before the altar / 参拝者 a visitor ((to a shrine)).

ざんぱい 惨敗 ¶惨敗する be beaten hollow;《文》be utterly [completely] defeated;《文》suffer a crushing [disastrous] defeat. 文例⇩

さんぱいきゅうはい 三拝九拝 ¶三拝九拝する bow repeatedly; kowtow.

サンパウロ São Paulo.

さんばがらす 三羽烏 a trio (pl. -s) ¶三羽烏らすの1人 one of the [a] trio.

さんばし 桟橋 a pier; a jetty;〈埠頭〉a wharf (pl. -s, wharves); a quay ¶桟橋に横づけになる come [go] alongside the pier / 桟橋まで見送る see sb off at the pier / 浮き桟橋 a landing stage; a floating pier [stage].

さんぱつ¹ 散発 ¶散発的《文》sporadic / 散発的発生 isolated [sporadic] outbreaks / 散発安打《野球》scattered hits / 散発的に《文》sporadically.

さんぱつ² 散髪 ¶散髪する have one's hair cut [trimmed]; have [get] a haircut / 散髪代 the price for [the charge for] a haircut. 文例⇩

さんばらがみ さんばら髪 loose and disheveled hair.

サンパン〈《中国語》舢板〉a sampan; a lighter.

ざんぱん 残飯 the leavings (of a meal); the leftovers ((from a dinner)); leftover rice [food].

さんはんきかん 三半規管《解》the three semicircular canals.

さんばんしょうぶ 三番勝負 a three-game[-round] match; a rubber (どちらかが2勝すれば終わりになる) ¶ブリッジの3番勝負をする have a rubber of bridge.

さんび 賛美 ¶賛美する admire; praise; glorify; sing sb's praises /口を極めて賛美する《文》extol sb to the skies / 全国民の賛美の的 an object of national admiration / 賛美歌 a hymn; a psalm / 賛美歌集 a hymnal; a hymnbook / 賛美者 an admirer.

さんぴ 賛否 approval and [or] disapproval; ayes and [or] noes ¶賛否を問う put (a question) to the vote / 賛否両論に耳を傾ける listen to the pros and cons ((of a matter)). 文例⇩

ザンビア (the Republic of) Zambia ¶ザンビアの Zambian / ザンビア人 a Zambian.

さんびゃく 三百 ¶三百代言《文》a pettifogger;《文》a pettifogging lawyer;《米口語》a shyster / 三百年祭 a tercentenary; a three-hundredth anniversary.

さんびょう 散票 scattered votes.

さんびょうし 三拍子《音楽》three-part time; (simple) triple time [measure] ¶三拍子そろった all-round;〈完全な〉consummate.

さんぴん 産品 ¶一[二, 三]次産品 primary [secondary, tertiary] products.

ざんぴん 残品 the remaining stock; unsold goods;〈たなざらし〉shopworn articles.

さんぶ 三部 ¶三部合唱[奏] a chorus [an ensemble] of three parts / 三部作 a trilogy

さんぷ¹ 産婦 a woman in childbed [in confinement] ¶産婦死亡率 (a) maternal mortality ★複数にはしない.

さんぷ² 散布 ¶散布する scatter; sprinkle; spray / 化学薬品の散布 chemical spraying / 散布器 a sprinkler; a sprayer.

ざんぶ 残部 the remainder;《文》the remnant; the rest; what is [are] left. 文例⇩

さんぷく 山腹 (on) a hillside [mountainside]; (on) the side of a mountain. 文例⇩

さんふじんか 産婦人科 obstetrics and gynecology ¶産婦人科の医者 an obstetrician and gynecologist.

さんぶつ 産物 a product; produce (★工業製品は products, 穀物, 牛乳, 羊毛など農場でできるものの総称が produce);〈成果〉a result;《文》the fruit(s) ((of long study)); an outcome.

ざんぶと ⇒ ざぶと. 文例⇩

---

ruling passion now. / 三度目の正直. Third time lucky.

さんにんよれば 三人寄れば文殊の知恵. Out of the counsel of three comes wisdom. | Two heads are better than one. 諺.

ざんねん 全く残念だ. It is a real disappointment. / あんなに若死にをして実に残念なことだ. What a pity [It's too bad, It's a shame]

that he (should have) died so young. / 試験に失敗して彼は非常に残念がった. He was deeply depressed at [really disappointed by] his failure in the examination. / まことに残念ながらお招きをお受けするわけにはゆきませんので. I'm so sorry I can't accept your kind invitation.

さんばい 炭素はヘリウムの3倍の

重さがある. Carbon is three times as heavy as helium. / 5の3倍は15です. Three times five is fifteen. | 5 multiplied by 3 is 15.

ざんぱい 前の選挙では私は対立候補に惨敗しました. In the last election I was swamped by the other candidate [my opponent].

さんぱつ² 彼は5か月前に散髪した

サンプラ 〘歯科〙 imitation platinum.
サンフランシスコ San Francisco.
サンプル a sample; a specimen;〈レストランの〉a model (★a sample は「実物見本」であって「模造品」の意味には使わない).
さんぶん¹ 三分 ¶三分する divide *sth* into three (parts) / 3分の1 one [a] third / 3分の2 two thirds. 文例⇩
さんぶん² 散文 prose ¶散文で書く write in prose / 散文的な《文》prosaic; matter-of-fact 《men》/ 散文家 a prose writer / 散文詩 a prose poem; prose poetry (総称).
さんぽ 散歩 a walk; a stroll ¶散歩する take a walk [stroll, turn]; stroll;《文》take the air / 散歩に行く go for a walk / 遠くへ散歩に出る take [go for] a long walk; go walking.
さんぽう¹ 三方〘神前の道具〙a small wooden stand (for placing an offering on).
さんぽう² 参謀〘軍の〙a staff officer; the staff (集合的);《相談役》an adviser; a counselor;《口語》a brain;《口語》the brains (集合的) ¶参謀会議を召集する call a council of war / 参謀総長 the Chief of the General Staff / 参謀本部 the General Staff Office.
さんぽう 三方 ¶三方山に囲まれている be surrounded by hills on three sides.
さんま〘魚〙a (Pacific) saury.
さんまい 三枚 ¶〈魚を〉三枚におろす fillet 《mackerels》; cut into fillets.
ざんまい 三昧 ¶ぜいたくざんまいに暮らす《文》live lapped in luxury / 読書ざんまいに過ごす be absorbed in reading; give all *one's* time to reading.
さんまいめ 三枚目〘劇・映画〙a comedian; an actor who plays comic roles.
サンマリノ the (Republic of) San Marino.
さんまん 散漫 ¶散漫な loose (thinking);《文》discursive《writings》;《文》desultory (reading);《文》diffuse《style》/ 頭の散漫な人 a loose-thinking person;〈心の集中力を欠いた人〉a scatterbrain.
さんみ 酸味 acidity; sourness ¶酸味がある have an acid taste; taste sour / 酸味のある sour; acid.
さんみいったい 三位一体〘宗教〙the Trinity; the Holy [Blessed] Trinity.
さんみゃく 山脈 a mountain range [chain] ¶飛騨山脈 the Hida mountains [mountain range].
ざんむ 残務 unsettled business;《文》affairs remaining unsettled [to be attended to] ¶残務を整理する wind up the affairs (of); settle [clear up] the remaining [《文》pending] business;〈会社清算の〉take on the work of liquidating《a company》.
さんめんきじ 三面記事 police [《米》city] news.
さんめんきょう 三面鏡 a three-sided [triple] mirror.
さんもん¹ 三文 ¶三文の値打ちもない be not worth a farthing [penny, fig, straw] / 三文小説 a cheap [pulp] novel /《米》a dime novel / 三文判 a ready-made seal / 三文文士 a hack (writer).
さんもん² 山門 the main gate of a Buddhist temple. 文例⇩
さんや 山野 fields and mountains; hills and valleys ¶山野を跋渉(ばっしょう)する roam the countryside;《文》range [roam over] hill and dale.
さんやく 三役〈相撲の〉the wrestlers of the three highest ranks (below 'yokozuna');〈政党などの〉the three key [top-ranking] officials (of).
さんやく² 散薬 powdered medicine; (a) powder.
さんゆこく 産油国 oil-producing countries [nations].
さんよ 参与〈役名〉a councilor ¶参与する take part [《文》participate] (in) / 経営に参与する have a voice in the management (of).
ざんよ 残余《文》the remainder (of); the rest; the balance; what is left (over) (from) ¶残余の remaining;《文》residual;《文》residuary.
さんようすうじ 算用数字 Arabic figures [numerals].
さんらん¹ 産卵 ¶産卵する lay eggs; spawn 《魚介類》》; blow (はえが) / 産卵のために海から川をさかのぼる魚 an anadromous fish / 産卵期 (at) egg-laying time; a laying period;〈魚の〉the spawning season [time] / 産卵場所 an egg-laying site.
さんらん² 散乱 ¶散乱する be [lie] scattered about;《文》disperse. 文例⇩
さんりゅう 三流 ¶三流の third-rate [-class].
ざんりゅう 残留 ¶残留する stay behind / 残留磁気 residual magnetism.
さんりん 山林 mountains and forests; a forest (on a mountain) ¶山林を造成する [伐採する] afforest [deforest] a mountain / 山林所得 an income from forestry.
さんりんしゃ 三輪車 a tricycle;《口語》a three-wheeler;《英口語》a trike.
さんるい 三塁〘野球〙third base ¶三塁手 a third-baseman / 三塁線 the third-base line / 三塁打 a three-base hit; a triple.
ざんるい 残塁〘野球〙¶残塁する be left on

きりだ. He hasn't had a haircut for five months. | His hair was last cut five months ago.
さんぴ その案には賛否両論がある. There are arguments both for and against the measure.
ざんぴん 残部少につきお早くご注文. Please order quickly, as stock is running out.
さんぷく ホテルは山腹にある. The hotel stands halfway up the hill.
さんぶつ その地の産物として取り立てて言うほどの物はない. The district produces nothing worth mentioning./これはローマン主義運動の一つの産物であった. This was an outgrowth of the Romantic Movement.
さんぶん¹ 学生たちで講堂は3分の1ほど埋まっていた. The hall was a third full of students./出席者の3分の2以上による多数決を要する. It requires a majority vote of two thirds or more of those attending [those present].
さんもん² 軍酒山門に入るを許さず. Leeks and liquor [Worldly distractions] are forbidden within the precincts of this temple.
さんらん² 空地には紙くずが散乱

サンルーム　а sunroom; a sun parlor.
さんれつ　参列　¶参列する attend; be present 〔at〕/ 葬式に参列する attend a funeral. 文例⇩

さんろく　山麓 《at》 the foot [base] of a mountain; the foothills (of Mount Fuji).
さんわおん　三和音 《音楽》a triad.

し

し¹ 士　¶廉潔(兢)の士 《文》a man of integrity [upright character].
し² 氏　〈氏族〉a family; a clan; 〈敬称〉Mr. (Kimura). ¶原, 森の両氏 Messrs. Hara and Mori / 平氏 the Taira family [clan]; the Tairas.
し³ 市　〈都市〉a city; a town; 〈行政区画〉a municipality ¶市の municipal; city / 仙台市 Sendai City; the city of Sendai / 市制をしく organize [be organized] as a municipality / 市当局 the municipal authorities.
し⁴ 史 ⇨れきし ¶現代[近代, 古代]史 contemporary [modern, ancient] history / 日本史 Japanese history; the history of Japan; 〈本〉a history of Japan.
し⁵ 四 four　¶四の五の言わずに ⇨ しのごの / 第4 the fourth.
し⁶ 死　(a) death; 《文》decease; 《文》demise ¶胃がんによる死 (one's) death from stomach cancer / 熱病による死 (one's) death of fever / 死の願望 a (romantic) death wish / 死の危険を冒す risk death / 死の恐怖[苦悶] the terror [agonies] of death / 死の商人 《文》a merchant of death / 死の灰 (radioactive) fallout / 死を覚悟する be prepared for death; be ready to die / 死を早める hasten sb's death / 死を免れる escape death / 死をもって償う 《文》atone for (one's crime) with death / …の死を悼む mourn (over) [regret] the death of… / 死に臨む[直面する] face death; look death in the face / 死に臨んで in one's last moments; on one's deathbed; when one is dying [about to die]. 文例⇩
し⁷ 師　a teacher; a master; 《文》one's mentor; 〈僧侶の尊称〉the Reverend [Rev(d).] (John Carpenter)　★この尊称はあとにクリスチャンネームを必要とする. また, the Reverend だけ独立で使うことはできない ¶師の恩を受ける have the favors [kindnesses] of one's teacher / 師と仰ぐ look up to sb as one's mentor / 師とする have sb for one's teacher.
し⁸ 詩　poetry (総称); a poem (1篇); verse (韻文) ¶詩を作る write [compose] a poem.
シ 《音楽》si; ti.
-し　and; besides; 《文》moreover; what with…, and (what with)….

じ¹ 字 〈文字〉a character; a letter (a, b, c など); an ideograph (表意文字); 〈手で書いた字〉(hand)writing; script; 〈文〉a hand; 〈印刷した字〉print　★ a letter は a word を構成する単位としての文字. 手書き・印刷の「字」を letter とは言わない. 「字を書く」「字を読む」も単に write, read であって, letters を添えない ¶細かい字 fine writing (手書き); small print (活字) / 字が上手[下手]である one's writing is good [poor]; 《文》write a good [poor] hand / 字が読めない cannot read / 字を書く write / 字を知らない be illiterate.
じ² 地　the ground (地面); land (土地); earth (土); soil (土壌); 〈囲碁〉(a) captured territory; 〈織り地の〉texture; weave; 〈文〉stuff ¶地がつんでいる have a close texture / 地の荒い[細かい] coarse [fine]; coarse-[finely-]textured; (cloth) with a coarse [fine] texture / 地の文 a descriptive [narrative] part [passage] / 探偵小説を地で行く act out a detective story / 白地に赤の模様 a red design on [against] a white background. 文例⇩
じ³ 次 《数》degree; 〈次の〉next; the following ¶第2次吉田内閣 the second Yoshida Cabinet.
じ⁴ 柱 〈琴の〉a bridge.
じ⁵ 時　〈時間〉an hour; 〈時刻〉o'clock; time ¶午前[午後] 4時に at four (o'clock) in the morning [afternoon]; at 4 a.m. [p.m.] / 1時半に at half past one / 8時半の汽車で行く go by the 8:30 [eight-thirty] train　★ 24時間制では零分は hundred と読む. 例えば, 9時 [0900] は (oh) nine hundred (hours), 14時 [1400] four-

---

していた. The vacant lot was littered with scraps of paper.
ざんるい　残塁なし. Nobody left on base.
さんれつ　参列者が多かった. A great many people were present. | There was a large attendance.
し⁶ 死は平等である. Death is a leveler. | All are equal in the grave. / 死は時を選ばない. Death keeps no calendar. / 死はやすく生は難し. It is easy to die for one's faith; it is hard to live up to it. / 彼は危うく死を免れた. He narrowly missed death. / 二死満塁. (野球) The bases are full with [and] two out.
し⁸ 秋に一葉の初めて枯れ落ちる姿も鋭い詩人の心には詩になるのである. To a keen-minded poet, the first fall of a single leaf in autumn spells a poem.
-し　雨は降るし, 泊まるところはないし, みじめな思いだった. It was raining so I had no room for the night, so I was really miserable. | What with the rain and having nowhere to stay, I had a dreadful time.
じ¹ その字はどう書くのですか. How do you write the character [spell the word]? / あいつの字はろくに読めないよ. His handwriting is almost illegible [unreadable]. / 眼鏡をかけないと小さい字が読めない. I can't read small print without (my) glasses. / 暗くて字が読めない. There isn't enough light to read (by). / 少なくともそこに字が書いてあるということはわかる. We can at least see that there is writing on

じ[7] 痔 hemorrhoids; piles ¶痔が悪い have [suffer from] hemorrhoids [piles].

じ 辞 ¶告別の辞 a farewell address / 辞を低くして humbly; politely.

しあい 試合 a match; a game; a competition; a bout (レスリングなど格闘技の); a tie (勝負き試合); a fight (ボクシングの) ¶野球の試合 a baseball game / 試合する play [have] a match [game] (with); play (with [against]) *sb* / 試合を申し込む challenge (a team) to a match; send *sb* a challenge to a game ((of tennis)) / 試合を承諾する accept a challenge to a game ((from)) / 試合に出る take part in a game / 第1試合 the first game; 〔野球〕〈ダブルヘッダーの〉 the opener.

じあい[1] 自愛 ¶自愛する take care of *oneself*. 文例⇩

じあい[2] 慈愛 affection; love ¶慈愛深い affectionate; loving; fond ((parents)); benevolent.

しあがる 仕上がる be finished; be completed; be ready.

しあげ 仕上げ finish; finishing;〈最後の〉the finishing touches [strokes] ¶仕上げをする give the finishing touches to [give the last finish (to)]; put a finish on ((the surface of stone, metal, etc.)) / 仕上げかんな a finishing [smoothing] plane / 仕上げ工 a finisher / 仕上げ塗り last coating; a finishing coat. 文例⇩

しあげる 仕上げる finish *sth* (off, up); complete; get through with ((one's work)); put *sth* into (*its*) final form /〈石や金属などの表面を〉dress. 文例⇩

しあさって two days after tomorrow; three days from now [《文》 hence].

ジアスターゼ〔生化〕diastase.

しあつけい 示圧計〔機〕a manometer; a pressure gauge.

しあつりょうほう 指圧療法 (practice, perform) finger-pressure therapy.

シアトー〈東南アジア条約機構〉SEATO ★ the Southeast Asia Treaty Organization の略. 発音は [sí:tou] ¶シアトー理事会 the SEATO Council.

シアトル Seattle.

じあまり 字余り ¶字余りの ((a *tanka*)) with an extra syllable [with extra syllables].

しあわせ 幸せ, 仕合わせ fortune; good fortune

[luck]; happiness; 《文》a blessing ¶幸せな lucky; fortunate; happy / 幸せに fortunately; happily / 幸せに生まれる be born under a lucky star / 幸せにも…する have the good fortune to *do* / 幸せ者 a lucky person [fellow]. 文例⇩

しあん[1] 私案 one's (private [personal]) plan; one's suggestion.

しあん[2] 思案 thought; 《文》consideration; meditation; 《文》reflection ¶思案する think (about); consider; 《文》meditate (on); ponder (over); 《文》reflect (on) / 思案に暮れる [ふける] be lost [sunk, buried] in thought; be absorbed in *one's* thoughts / 思案に余る, 思案投げ首のていである be at *one's* wits' end; be quite at a loss ((what to do)) / 思案顔で with a thoughtful look.

しあん[3] 試案 a draft (plan); a tentative plan.

シアン〔化〕cyanogen ¶シアン化物 a cyanide.

しい[1] 恣意 《文》arbitrariness; 《文》self-will ¶恣意的な arbitrary; self-willed; willful.

しい[2] 〔植〕a chinquapin ¶しいの実 a chinquapin; a sweet acorn.

じい[1] 示威 ¶示威的な threatening / 示威運動を行なう hold [stage] a demonstration.

じい[2] 次位 (the) second place ¶次位を占める rank second; hold second place.

じい[3] 自慰 masturbation.

じい[4] 侍医 a court physician; a physician (in ordinary) ((to the Emperor)).

じい[5] 辞意 ¶辞意が固い be determined [《文》firmly resolved] to resign / 辞意をもらす 《文》reveal [make known] *one's* intention to resign / 辞意を翻す reconsider *one's* resignation.

ジーエヌピー GNP ★ Gross National Product の略.

シーエム ⇨ コマーシャル.

しいか 詩歌 poetry (集合的); poems.

しいく 飼育 ¶飼育する keep; rear; raise; keep ((wild animals)) in captivity / 動物飼育係 an animal handler / 〈動物園の〉飼育係長 the head keeper / 飼育技術 handling and feeding techniques / 飼育者 a breeder; a raiser; a (bird) fancier / 飼育場 a (horse-)breeding farm.

じいしき 自意識 self-consciousness ¶自意識過剰の too [《文》excessively] self-conscious.

シーズン a season ¶野球[かき]のシーズン the baseball [oyster] season / シーズンの in season; in-season / シーズンオフ out of

---

it.
じ それは探偵小説を地で行ったようだった. It was just like a real-life detective story. / その話を一つ, 地で行こうじゃないか. Let's try and make that story come true.

しあい 試合は10回戦に及んだ. The game went into the tenth inning.

しあい[1] ご自愛ください Please look after [take good care of] yourself.

しあげ 仕上げは別の工場でやります. The finishing is done at another plant.

しあげる 1週間以内に仕上げてもらいたい. I want you to have it finished [ready] within a week.

しあわせ 君たちは平和なときに生まれて幸せだ. You are lucky to be living in peacetime. / 彼はいい息子を持って幸せだ. He is blessed with a good son. / 何が幸せになるかわからない. You never can tell what form [shape] good fortune will take [will come in]. / 君は行かないで幸せだった.

It was a good thing [It's a mercy] that you didn't go.

しあん 彼はどうしたらいいかといろいろ思案を凝らした. He racked his brains to see what he should do [what should be done]. / 名案はないものかと思案をめぐらしてみた. He cast about in his mind for a good plan. / ここが思案のしどころだ. This is the point we need to think about. | This is where we [I] have to stop and think. / ほかによい思案もない. I can't think of a better plan.

シーソー

season ; off-season / シーズン前の preseason. 文例⇩

シーソー a seesaw ; 《米口語》a teeter(-totter) ¶シーソーをして遊ぶ seesaw ; play on a seesaw / シーソーに乗る ride a seesaw / シーソーゲーム a seesaw game [match]. 文例⇩

しいたけ a shiitake mushroom.

しいたげる 虐げる oppress ; persecute ; tyrannize over ; treat cruelly ¶虐げられた人々 downtrodden people ; 《文》the oppressed.

シーツ a (bed) sheet.

しーっ hush! ; sh! ; shush! ; 〈犬などを追い払うとき〉shoo! ; scat! ¶しーっしーっと言って追い払う shoo (a cat) away.

シート 〈雨覆い〉a tarpaulin ; 〈切手の〉a sheet 《of postage stamps》; 〈座席〉a seat.

シード 〈競技〉to seed ¶シードする seed / シードされていない選手 an unseeded player / シード選手 a (top-, second-) seeded player [competition].

シートノック 〈野球〉fielding practice.

ジーパン 《wear》(blue) jeans ¶ジーパンをはいた《a young person》in (blue) jeans ; jeaned (teen-agers).

ジープ a jeep.

ジーメン an FBI agent ; 《米口語》a G-man.

じいや 爺や an old handyman.

シーラカンス 〈魚〉a coelacanth.

シール 〈封印紙〉a seal ; 〈シールスキン〉seal-skin.

しいる 強いる force ; 《文》compel ; 《文》coerce ; press ¶酒を強いる press sake on sb ; insist on sb having a drink / 服従を強いる compel sb to obey ; compel [force] sb's obedience / 自分の考えを人に強いる impose one's opinion on sb / 強いて by force, forcibly ⇨ むり(無理に) / 強いて…させる force [compel] sb to do / 強いられて by [on, under] pressure (from) ; 《文》under [on] compulsion. 文例⇩

しいれ 仕入れ stocking ; 《文》purchasing ; buying-in ; laying in stock ¶仕入れ係 a purchase clerk ; a buyer ; 〈大口〉a supplier ; a wholesaler 〈問屋〉/ 仕入れ高 quantity [value] of goods laid in / 仕入れ帳 a purchase book / 仕入れ値 [価格] the cost [buying] price / 仕入れ値[価格]で at cost / 仕入れ品 stock ; goods [stock] on hand.

しいれる 仕入れる lay [buy] in (a stock of) ; stock 《goods》¶仕入れてある keep [have] 《goods》in stock ; have a stock of. 文例⇩

じいろ 地色 a ground (color).

しいん¹ 子音 a consonant (sound) ¶無声[有声]子音 a voiceless [voiced] consonant.

しいん² 死因 the cause of (sb's) death ¶死因は…である 《the patient》died of 《heart failure》; sb's death was due to.... 文例⇩

しいん³ 試飲 試飲する sample 《wine》; try / 試飲会 a sampling party ; a wine-tasting. 文例⇩

シーン a scene.

じいん 寺院 a (Buddhist) temple ¶洞窟寺院 a cave temple / 寺院彫刻 temple sculpture 《of Southern India》.

ジーンズ ⇨ ジーパン.

じいんと ¶胸にじいんと来る be very touching ; touch one's heart.

じう 慈雨 a welcome [《文》beneficial] rain.

しうち 仕打ち 〈扱い〉treatment ; 〈行動〉an act ; an action ¶ひどい仕打ちをする do sb a bad turn ; treat sb badly ; 《文》maltreat. 文例⇩

しうんてん 試運転 a trial [test] run [trip] / 〈機械の〉test working ¶試運転用線路 a (full-scale) test line / 試運転を行なう make a trial [test] run 《of a car》.

シェア ¶日本で最大のシェアを占める have the largest market share 《of fountain pens》in Japan.

しえい¹ 市営 ¶市営の municipal / 市営住宅 a municipal dwelling house ; 《英》a council house / 市営バス a city bus.

しえい² 私営 ¶私営の privately-operated[-run] / 私営事業 a private enterprise.

じえい¹ 自営 ¶自営の independent ; self-supporting ; self-employed / 自営で 《do business》on one's own (account).

じえい² 自衛 self-defense ; self-protection ¶自衛上 in [by way of] self-defense / 自衛官 a uniformed member of the Self-Defense Forces / 自衛権 the right of [to] self-defense ; the right to defend oneself / 自衛行動をとる take action for self-defense [for one's own protection] / 自衛隊 the Self-Defense Forces / 陸上[海上, 航空]自衛隊 the Ground [Maritime, Air] Self-Defense Force.

シェーカー a (cocktail) shaker.

シェークスピア (William) Shakespeare ¶シェークスピアの Shakespearean.

シェークハンドグリップ 〈卓球〉the shake-hands grip.

シェーバー a shaver ; an electric razor [shaver].

シェービングクリーム shaving cream.

しえき 使役 《文》employment ¶使役する 《文》employ ; use / 使役動詞 《文法》a causative verb.

ジェスチャー ⇨ ゼスチャー.

ジェット ジェット(機)で行く go 《to London》by jet / ジェット機 a jet (air)plane ; 〈総称〉jets / ジェット機のキューンという音 the high whine of a jet plane / ジェット機の操縦士 a jet pilot / ジェット8基装の飛行機 an

---

シーズン シーズンオフには料金がずっと安くなる. The off-season rates are much lower.

シーソー 激しいシーソーゲームを演じた末に我がチームが勝利を収めた. Our team came out the victors after the lead had changed hands time and time again.

しいる 強いて帰ると言うならとめはしない. If you insist on going home, I won't stop you. / 甲乙しだが, 強いて言えばこの方が少し勝っている. There is little to choose between the two, but if pressed I would say that this is a shade better.

しいれる 英語の辞書はたくさん仕入れてあります. We have a large stock of English dictionaries.

しいん² 死因は何ですか. What was the cause of (his) death? | What did he die of?

しいん³ このぶどう酒はお気に召しますでしょうか. ちょっとご試飲下さい. Please taste [try] this wine to see if you like it.

しうち あの人からこんな仕打ちを

ジェットコースター eight-jet [eight-engined jet] plane / ジェットエンジン a jet engine ; a jet motor / ジェット気流 the jet stream / ジェット戦闘機[爆撃機] a jet fighter [bomber] / ジェット輸送機 a jet transport (plane) / ジェット旅客機 a jet airliner ; a jetliner.

ジェットコースター a roller coaster ;《英》a big dipper ;《英》a switchback (railway).

シェパード a German shepherd ;《英》Alsatian.

シエラレオネ Sierra Leone ¶ シエラレオネの Sierra Leonean / シエラレオネ共和国 the Republic of Sierra Leone / シエラレオネ人 a Sierra Leonean.

シェリーしゅ シェリー酒 sherry.

シェルパ a Sherpa (pl. -s)).

しえん¹ 支援 support ¶支援する support ; back sb (up) ;《文》aid / ...の支援を求める seek support from... / 精神的支援 moral support / 積極的支援 active [positive] support / 支援隊 a support party.

しえん² 私怨 (harbor) a personal grudge 《against》 ¶私怨を晴らす satisfy [work off] a personal spite [grudge] 《against》 / take one's grievance out on sb ;《文》avenge one's private grievance on sb.

しえん³ 紫煙 blue smoke (of tobacco) ¶紫煙をくゆらす have a leisurely smoke ; send up a curl of tobacco smoke.

しえん⁴ 試演 (give) a trial performance 《of a play》; a demonstration ; a preview.

しお¹ 塩 salt ¶塩が甘い do not have enough salt in (it) ;《文》be not sufficiently salted ; be not salty enough / 塩が辛すぎる be too heavily [well] salted ; be too salty / 塩の入っていない unsalted《butter》/ 塩を振りかける sprinkle salt on《fish》; sprinkle (fish) with salt / 塩をまく〈相撲で〉scatter salt ;〈不愉快な訪問者が帰ったあとへ〉throw out some salt / 塩入れ a saltcellar ;〈振り出し式の〉a salt shaker [sprinkler] / 塩加減の seasoning with salt / 塩辛い salty ;《文》salt / 塩辛く煮る cook with a lot of salt / 塩気 a salty taste ; saltiness / 塩胡椒(ｼﾞｮｳ)する season 《meat》 with pepper and salt / 塩魚 salt(ed) fish / 塩鮭 (a) salted salmon / 塩出しをする make (salted fish) less salty ; remove (some of) the salt from (the fish) (by soaking (it) in water) / 塩漬けにする salt (down) ; preserve [pickle] 《vegetables》 with [in] salt / 塩引きの salted ; salt-cured / 塩水 salt water ; brine / 塩焼きにする broil 《fish》 with salt. 文例⇩

しお² 潮〈海潮〉the tide ; a current (潮流) ¶潮の変わり目 the turning of the tide / 潮の差し引き the ebb and flow of the tide /〈鯨が〉潮を吹く blow [spout] (water) / 潮入りの川 a tidal river / 潮風 a sea [salt] breeze ; briny air / 潮だまり a tide [tidal] pool ; a rock pool. 文例⇩

しおから 塩辛 salted fish guts.

しおくり 仕送り ¶仕送りする supply [provide,《文》furnish] sb with sth ; send money to sb ; send sb an allowance / 月々8万円の仕送りで生活する[を受ける] live on [be given] a monthly allowance of 80,000 yen / 学資の仕送りをする provide [《文》furnish] sb with his school expenses / 仕送りを断つ stop sending money to sb ; cut off sb's allowance. [waves].

しおさい 潮騒 the sound [booming] of the sea

しおしお sorrowfully ; sadly ;《文》crestfallen ; in low spirits ;《文》with a heavy heart ; dejectedly. 文例⇩

しおどき 潮時〈好機〉an opportunity ; a chance ¶潮時を待つ wait for a favorable tide (to set sail) ; wait for an opportunity ; watch one's time / 潮時をはずす miss one's chance ; let a (good) chance slip / 潮時を見て...する take [seize] the opportunity to do. 文例⇩

しおひがり 潮干狩り shell gathering (at low tide [water]) ; digging for clams ¶潮干狩りに行く go seashell-[clam-]digging /《米》go clamming (at Enoshima). [crab.

しおまねき《動》a fiddler [beckoning, calling

しおらしい〈おとなしい〉gentle ; modest ;《文》meek ;〈かわいらしい〉sweet ;《文》tender ;〈哀れがる〉pathetic.

しおり〈書物の〉a bookmark ; a (book) marker ;〈案内〉a guide (to) ¶しおりを挟む put [slip] a bookmark between the pages [leaves] ; place a marker in a book.

しおりど 枝折り戸 a garden [wicket] gate made of branches and twigs.

しおれる 萎れる droop ; wilt ; wither ; fade ;〈心が〉be downhearted ; be depressed ;《文》be dejected ; be crestfallen ;《口語》be in the blues [dumps].

しおん¹ 歯音〈音声〉a dental (sound).

しおん²《植》an aster.

しか¹ 市価 the regular [normal] retail price ; the market price ¶市価千円の鉛筆削りを a pencil sharpener selling for 1,000 yen in the shops / 市価の2割引きで 20% off the market price [the regular price] / 市価の動き market movements [fluctuations].

しか² 歯科 dentistry ; dental surgery ¶歯科医 a dentist ; a dental surgeon / 歯科医院 a dentist's (office) ; a dental office [clinic] / 歯科大学 a dental college [university] / 歯科用器械 dentist's instruments / 歯科用治療設備 dental equipment.

受けようとは思わなかった. I didn't expect such treatment at his hands.
しお¹ この汁は塩辛い. There is too much salt in this soup. / 毎朝塩水を1杯飲みます. I have a glass of salt water every morning. / 塩加減はどうかと彼女はスープの味見をした. She tasted [had a taste of] the soup to see if there was enough salt in it.
しお² 潮が満ちている. The tide is high [right in]. / 潮が上げて[さして]いる. The tide is rising [coming in]. / 潮が引いている. The tide is going out [ebbing]. / 潮の変わり目に霧が音もなく川を上って来る. A fog steals up the river on the turn of the tide.
しおしおと それを聞いて彼はしおしおと部屋を出た. On hearing it he left the room, sad and dejected.
しおどき 物にはすべて潮時というものがある. There is a tide in the affairs of men. | There is a time for everything. / 引退するには今がちょうどいい潮時だ. I

しか³ 鹿 a deer《単複同形》;〈雄〉a stag;〈雌〉a doe;; a hind (赤鹿の);〈子〉a fawn《壁飾りの》しかの頭 a staghead / しかの皮 deerskin; buckskin / しかの角 an antler; a pair of antlers (1対) / しかの肉 venison.

-しか《...しか...ない only;《文》merely; no more than / 1つしかない万年筆 the only fountain pen one has. 文例④

しが 歯牙《...を歯牙にもかけない take no notice of...;《口語》do not give a damn [hang] for...; treat...with utter contempt [《文》disdain].

じか¹ 自家 one's own house [family] ¶自家居住者 a homeowner / 自家受精《生物》self-fertilization / 自家中毒 autotoxemia; autointoxication / 自家撞着(どうちゃく) self-contradiction / 自家製の homemade / 自家用車 a private car; an owner-driven car / 自家用の for private use; for home consumption; private; personal. 文例④

じか² 時価 the current price ¶時価で売る sell sth at the current market price. 文例④

じか³ 磁化《物》magnetization ¶磁化する magnetize.

じか⁴ 直 ¶じかに directly; at first hand ⇒ ちょくせつ / じかに着る (clothes) next [close] to one's skin / 直談判をする negotiate 《with sb》personally / (魚などを)直火で焼く broil [grill]《trout》over an open fire.

じが 自我 the [one's] self;《心理》(the) ego ¶自我の強い《文》egotistic;《文》egoistic; self-centered; self-willed / 自我の発展 self-development.

しかい¹ 市会 a municipal [city] assembly [council] ¶市会議員 a member of the municipal assembly;《米》a (city) councilman;《英》a city councillor / 市会議事堂 a city hall.

しかい² 司会 ¶司会する《文》preside at [over]《a meeting》; take the chair 《at a convention》; act as master [mistress] of ceremonies 《for》;《米口語》emcee《a show》/ 司会者《議長さ》 the chairman; the president;〈宴会の〉the toastmaster;〈テレビ放送などの〉the master [mistress] of ceremonies (略: m.c., MC, M.C.); a program host [hostess];《米口語》an emcee. 文例④

しかい³ 視界 the field [range] of vision; the visual field; view; visibility ¶視界を去る go out of view [sight] / 視界に入る come into view [sight].

しかい⁴ 死海 the Dead Sea ¶死海写本 the Dead Sea Scrolls.

しがい¹ 市外 ¶市外に out of town; outside (of) the town; in the suburbs; on the outskirts of a city / 市外局番《米・カナダ》an area code;《英》an STD code (★STD は Subscriber Trunk Dialling の略) / 市外電話 a long-distance [an out-of-town] call;《英》a trunk call.

しがい² 市街〈街路〉the streets;〈市〉a city; a town ¶市街戦 street fighting.

しがい³ 死骸 ⇒ したい¹.

じかい¹ 次回 next time ¶次回の the next (meeting).

じかい² 自戒 ¶自戒する caution oneself (against); take care (not to repeat the same error).

じがい 自害 ⇒じさつ.

じかい (さよう) 自壊(作用) disintegration.

しがいせん 紫外線《物》ultraviolet rays ¶紫外線療法 (an) ultraviolet treatment; ultraviolet light therapy.

しかえし 仕返し revenge; retaliation; tit for tat ¶仕返しする give [pay] tit for tat; revenge oneself 《on》; be revenged, get one's revenge 《on sb for sth》; retaliate 《on sb》; get even [square accounts]《with sb》; even the score ¶仕返しに in revenge [retaliation]《for》. 文例④

しかく¹ 四角 a quadrilateral; a four-sided figure;〈正方形〉a square ¶四角の four-sided / 四角張る be formal; be stiff; stand on ceremony / 四角張らずに《文》without ceremony; informally / 四角四面な prim; stuffy.

しかく² 死角 a dead angle; dead ground [space]. 文例④

しかく³ 刺客 an assassin; a killer ¶刺客の手に倒れる be assassinated;《文》fall (a) victim to an assassin.

しかく⁴ 視角《物》a visual angle; an angle of view [vision]; an optic angle.

しかく⁵ 視覚 (the sense of) sight; eyesight; visual sensation; vision; seeing ¶視覚型《心理》the visual type (記憶型の1つ) / 視覚芸術 visual arts. 文例④

しかく⁶ 資格〈要件〉qualification(s);〈権利〉a right; a claim;〈身分〉《文》capacity;〈能力〉

---

think that now is the time for me to step down from the stage.

-しか この商売を始めてまだ2年にしかならない. It's only [no more than] two years since I began this business. / それだけしか持っていない. That is all I have./そうとしか解釈できない. I cannot interpret it in any other way. / 若い時は一度しかない. You are only young once.

じか¹ この映画館には自家発電装置がある. This movie theater has a power plant of its own.

じか² その花瓶は時価100万円の 物だ. The vase is valued at a million yen today.

しかい² 会は中村氏の司会で開かれた. The meeting was opened with Mr. Nakamura in the chair.

しかい³ 視界をさえぎる物は何もなかった. There was nothing to interrupt the view.

しかえし この仕返しはきっとするぞ. I will pay you back [I will get my own back] for this.

しかく² そこは死角になっていて運転席から見えなかった. The spot was in the dead angle and couldn't be seen from the driver's seat.

しかく⁵ 漢字はアルファベットよりも視覚に訴える力が強い. Kanji have a stronger visual appeal than the alphabet.

しかく⁶ 荒木氏は代表委員の資格で答弁しました. Mr. Araki replied in his capacity as delegate. / 彼には成功するだけの資格がすべてそろっていた. He had every qualification for success. / 利益の分配にあずかる資格は僕にもある. I am entitled to a share in the profit. / 彼には当然この栄誉を担う資格がある. He can justly lay

しがく (文) competence ¶資格がある be qualified [competent] (for, to do); be eligible ((for membership)); have a right ((to do)) / 資格を与える give sb the qualification ((to do, as, for)); qualify sb ((to do, as, for)) / 資格を失う be disqualified ((from)) / 教員の資格をとる get [(文) obtain] a teacher's license; get [(文) obtain] a license for teaching ((in high school)) / …の資格で in the capacity of… / 個人の資格で in one's individual capacity / 資格(検定)試験 a qualifying examination / 資格審査 an examination of applicants' [candidates'] qualifications; a (preliminary) qualification exam; screening / 資格喪失 disqualification. 文例⊕

しがく¹ 史学 history; (the) study of history; historical science ¶史学科 a history course.

しがく² 私学 a private college [university].

じかく¹ 字画 the number of strokes ((in a Chinese character)).

じかく² 自覚 (文) self-knowledge; (文) (self-)awareness; (文) (self-)awakening ¶自覚する〈知る〉 (文) become conscious of; (文) become aware of 〈悟る〉 (文) realize; (文) awake to / 自覚症状 a subjective symptom. 文例⊕

じかく³ 耳殻 (解) the auricle; the pinna (pl. -s, -nae).

しがく(かん) 視学(官) a ((prefectural)) school inspector.

じがくじしゅう 自学自習 teaching oneself どくがく, じしゅう ¶自学自習を奨励する encourage ((the pupils)) to study by [for] themselves.

しかけ 仕掛け〈工夫〉 (文) a contrivance; a device; a mechanism; works; 〈からくり〉 a trick; a catch ¶仕掛けを考え出す make a device [contrivance] / 仕掛け花火 set fireworks; a set piece of fireworks (一個). 文例⊕

しかける 仕掛ける〈着手する〉 begin ((to do, doing)); start; set about;〈装置する〉 set (up); install ((an alarm system)); lay ((a mine));〈いどむ〉 challenge ((sb to a fight)); start ((a war on a country)) / …仕掛けている be going ((about)) to do; be on the point of doing / 仕掛けた仕事 the work in hand; work half-finished [left undone].

シカゴ Chicago.

しかざん 死火山 an extinct [a dead] volcano.

しかし but; however; still; (and) yet; (文) nevertheless. 文例⊕

しかじか 〈これこれ〉 so and so;〈等々〉 and so on [forth] ¶しかじかの such and such ((conditions)).

じがじさん 自画自賛 (文) self-praise ¶自画自賛する praise oneself; sing one's own praises; blow one's own trumpet; pat oneself on the back.

しかしながら ⇒しかし.

しかしゅう 詞華集 an anthology.

じかせん 耳下腺 (解) the parotid gland(s) ¶耳下腺炎 parotitis; mumps.

じがぞう 自画像 a self-portrait ¶自画像を描く paint [draw] one's own portrait.

しかた 仕方 a method; a way; (文) a means 〈用複同形〉 ⇒ -かた ¶仕方なしに〈いやいや〉 against one's will; reluctantly; unwillingly; 〈やむをえず〉 for lack of an alternative / 仕方なしに…する be obliged [forced, compelled] to do / …するより仕方がない there is nothing for it but to do; have no choice [option] but to do; 〈want very much [badly] to do; be dying to do. 文例⊕

じかた 地方〈はやし〉 an accompaniment ((to a dance)).

じかたび 地下足袋 rubber-soled socks with the big toe separate.

じがため 地固め ¶地固めする〈土地を〉 level the ground; prepare the ground ((for));〈行動の準備をする〉 lay the foundation ((for)); pave the way ((for)); prepare the ground ((for)).

しかつ 死活 life and [or] death;〈運命〉 fate ¶死活の闘争 (engage in) a life-and-death struggle / 死活問題 a matter of life or death; a life-and-death problem; a question of vital importance.

しがつ 四月 April (略: Apr.) ¶四月ばか〈人〉 an April fool;〈日〉 April [All] Fools' Day.

じかつ 自活 self-support ¶自活する support [(文) sustain] oneself; earn [make] one's (own) living / 自活の道 a means of supporting oneself; the way of making one's living.

しかつめらしい stiff and formal; (文) solemn; serious; priggish; (口語) starchy ¶しかつめらしい顔をする look as grave as a judge [an owl] / しかつめらしくお辞儀する make a formal bow.

---

claim to this distinction.

じかく² 自分の力の足りない事は自覚している。 I am conscious [well aware] of my lack of ability.

しかけ ひとりでに扉がしまるような仕掛けになっている。 The door is made [contrived] so as to close automatically.

しかし しかしおかしいね。It's strange, though. / しかし, いい天気だねえ。 Well, it's beautiful weather, isn't it? / しかし, 高見山はでっかいなあ。 Takamiyama really is a giant, isn't he?

しかた 彼はお辞儀の仕方も知らない。 He does not know how to make a proper bow. / 仕方がない。 It can't be helped. / There is no help for it. / 今さらそんな事を言ったってもう仕方がない。 It's no use [good] talking that way after the event. / この部屋は暑くて仕方がない。 It is unbearably hot in this room. / 出来た事は仕方がない。 What's done cannot be undone. / 仕方がないからこれを使っています。 I use this for want of a better one. / あんなばかじゃ仕方がない。 What can we do with a fool like that? / 若いんだから仕方がないよ。 You must make allowance(s) for his youth [inexperience]. / 千円ばかしじゃ仕方がない。 A thousand yen is nowhere near [nothing like] enough. / こんな事をしていても仕方がないよ。 I don't think this will get us anywhere. | We won't get anywhere like this. / 父親に言われて彼女は仕方なしに大学講師と結婚した。 She married a university lecturer under pressure from her father. / 外国語を物にするには一歩一歩覚

しかと 確と〈確かに〉certainly; for certain [sure];〈はっきりと〉clearly; distinctly;〈固く〉tightly; firmly.

しがない poor; wretched;《文》unnotable; humble.

じがね 地金 ground metal; the metal underneath;〈貨幣用金銀の〉bullion ¶地金を現わす betray *oneself*; reveal *one's* true character ⇒ほんしょう¹.

しかねる し兼ねる ⇒-かねる.

じがばち〖昆〗a (digger) wasp; a mud dauber.

しかばね 屍 ⇒しに¹.

しかばん 私家版 a privately printed book; a private (press) edition.

じかび 直火 ¶直火にかける heat *sth* on an open fire [flame].

しがみつく cling to; hold on; hold fast to; grip like a vice ¶首にしがみつく put [throw] *one's* arms around *sb's* neck.

しかめっつら しかめっ面 ¶しかめっ面をする frown [scowl] (at, on); knit *one's* brows; grimace (at); make grimaces [a wry face] / しかめっ面をして with a frown [grimace]; with knitted brows.

しかめる 顰める〖文例⇩〗

しかも 然も〈その上に〉moreover; besides; on top of (that); into the bargain; and...at that; and that; what is more; also; too;〈にもかかわらず〉and yet; for all that;《文》nevertheless. 〖文例⇩〗

じかやくろうちゅう 自家薬籠中 ¶自家薬籠中の物とする〈通暁する〉master; be at home (in); get complete control over *sth* /〈丸め込む〉get *sb* under *one's* thumb.

しからば 然らば if so;《文》if it be so; in that case; then.

しがらみ 柵 a weir ¶恋のしがらみ fetters [chains] of love.

しかり 然り ¶しかりと言う[答える] say [answer] yes;《文》answer in the affirmative;《文》affirm (*sb's* words).

しかる 叱る scold; tell *sb* off; give *sb* a telling-off;《文》chide;《文》reprove; give *sb* a scolding;《口語》give *sb* a piece of *one's* mind;《英口語》tear a strip off *sb* ¶叱りつける reprimand *sb* (for *sth*); dress *sb* down;《米口語》chew *sb* out / 叱られる be scolded;《口語》catch [get] it (from dad). 〖文例⇩〗

しかるに 然るに however; but;《文》nevertheless;《文》whereas; (while) on the other hand.

しかるべき 然る可き《文》due; proper;《文》fit; suitable; right;《文》appropriate;〈相当な〉respectable; decent;〈資格ある〉competent; qualified ¶しかるべき人物 a suitable [competent] person / しかるべき地位 a suitable position / しかるべく properly;〈適当に〉as *one* thinks best [fit]. 〖文例⇩〗

シガレット a cigarette ¶シガレットケース[ホールダー] a cigarette case [holder].

しかん¹ 士官 an officer ¶陸軍[海軍]士官 a military [naval] officer / 士官学校 a military academy.

しかん² 子癇〖医〗eclampsia.

しかん³ 史観 a view of history.

しかん⁴ 弛緩 slackness;《moral》laxness ¶弛緩する slacken / 弛緩した slack; slackened; lax.

しがん 志願〈申請〉an application;〈自ら進んですること〉volunteering ¶志願する apply (for); volunteer (for) / 志願者 an applicant; a candidate; a volunteer / 志願制度 the volunteer system / 志願兵 a volunteer.

じかん¹ 次官 a vice-minister; an undersecretary ¶文部次官 the Vice-Minister of Education.

じかん² 時間 an hour;〈時刻〉time ¶英語の時間 an English class [lesson] / 時間どおりに punctually; on time / 1時間ごとに at hourly intervals / 時間がたつ time passes [goes by, 《文》elapses] / 時間かせぎに play for time;《口語》stall / 時間を(厳重に)守る be punctual (to the minute) / 時間を取る take (a lot of) time / 時間を取らないdo not take much time / 時間に遅れるbe [come] late; be behind time / 時間に遅れずに in time / 時間に追われているbe pressed for time / ...の時間に間に合う be in time for (a train) / 時間外勤務[手当] overtime work [pay] / 時間外勤務をする work [do] overtime;《口語》put in extra hours / 時間稼ぎに to gain time / 時間感覚 time sense / 時間決めで (hire *sb*) by the

---

えていくより他に仕方がない。There is no other way of mastering a foreign language than to learn it step by step.

しかめる 苦痛に顔をしかめた。His face was distorted with pain.

しかも 10万円という手の切れるような1万円札で。He gave me 100,000 yen, and that in crisp 10,000-yen notes. / 英語で書いてある, しかも下手な英語で。It is written in English, and poor English at that. / 彼はそう言った, しかも驚いたことにそれを実行したのだった。He said he would, and what is more surprising, he did.

しかる 今みっちり叱ってやった所です。I have just given him a good telling-off [talking-to].

しかるべき 彼は私に感謝してしかるべきである。He ought to thank me for it. / しかるべく先方と話し合いなさい。Negotiate with them at your own discretion [as you think fit].

じかん² 時間がどんどんなくなっていった。The time ran out very fast. / もう学校へ行く時間だ。It is time to go to school now. / まだだいぶ時間がある。We still have plenty of time. / 数学の試験は時間が足りなかった。I was short of time during the exam in math. / それは時間との競走であった。It was a race against time. / 時間を持てあました。The time hung heavy [heavily] on my hands. / 時間がさっぱりわからなくなってしまった。I have lost all track of time. / 時間までに行けない。We won't be able to get there in time. / 大阪まで何時間かかりますか。How long does it take from here to Osaka? / 2時間目に数学がある。We have mathematics in the second period. / 列車は時間どおりに着いた。The train arrived on schedule [as scheduled, on time]. / 上野まで行くのにヘ

しき hour / 時間給〈時間〉 payment by the hour;〈出来高払いに対して〉hourly wages; time rates [wages] / 時間給水 restriction of water supply to certain hours / 時間芸術 arts based on tempo / 時間測定装置 a timing device / 時間帯 a time zone; a period of time / 時間つなぎ a (mere) time-filler / 時間表 ⇒ じこく²〈時刻表〉/ 時間割 a timetable; a schedule.

しき¹ 士気 fighting spirit; morale ¶士気を鼓舞する raise the morale《of the men》/ 士気阻喪する be [become] demoralized; one's morale is shaken; one's fighting spirit is weakened.

しき² 四季 the four seasons ¶四季の変化 the changes of the seasons / 四季を通じて all the year round; in [through] all seasons; throughout the year / 四季折々の眺め a view as it changes from season to season; the seasonal changes in the scenery / 四季咲きの perpetual《plants》/ 四季報 a quarterly (journal).

しき³ 式〈儀式〉a ceremony; rituals;〈文〉(文) rites;〈文〉a function; a celebration;《米》(inauguration) exercises;〈方法〉a method; a system;〈型, …風〉a style; a type;〈数理の〉an (algebraic) expression; a (chemical) formula (pl. -s, -lae) ¶式を挙げる[行なう] hold [have] a 〈wedding〉 ceremony; celebrate 《a wedding》/ 式で表わす formulate / ジョーンズ式発音符号 the Jones system of phonetic notation / ゴシック式建築 Gothic architecture / 式辞 (read, give) an address / 式場 the ceremonial hall [site] / 式服 ⇒ れいふく.【文例⇩】

しき⁴ 死期 the time [hour] of one's death;《文》one's last hour;《文》one's time [end] ¶死期を早める cause sb's early death; bring sb to an early grave;《文》hasten sb's death [end].【文例⇩】

しき⁵ 指揮 command;〈指図〉direction(s);〈監督〉《文》superintendence; supervision ¶指揮する command; lead; take command of《an army》;〈楽団を〉direct; conduct / …の指揮で《音楽》conducted by…;《文》under the baton of… / …の指揮下にある《文》be under the command [direction] of… / 指揮官 a commander / 指揮監督する direct and supervise / 指揮系統 a chain of command / 指揮者 a leader; a commander;〈音楽〉a conductor / 指揮台《音楽》a podium 《pl. -dia》; a (raised) platform / 指揮棒《音楽》a baton.

-しき -敷 ¶河川敷 a (dry) riverbed / なべ敷 a table mat.

しき《鳥》a snipe; a sandpiper.

じき¹ 自記 self-registering[-recording] ¶自記寒暖計 a self-registering thermometer.

じき² 次期 the next term [period] ¶次期国会 the next [coming] session of the Diet / 次期大統領 the President for the next term / 次期政権をねらう《文》aspire to take over the reins of government.

じき³ 時期〈時〉time; a period;〈季節〉a season; the time of (the) year ¶毎年この時期に at this time every year.【文例⇩】

じき⁴ 時機〈機会〉an opportunity; a chance; time;〈場合〉an occasion ¶時機を待つ《文》wait for a favorable opportunity; bide one's time; wait and see / 時機をうかがう watch for a chance [good opportunity] / 時機を捕らえる take [seize] an opportunity / 時機を逸する let an opportunity slip; lose [miss] one's chance.【文例⇩】

じき⁵ 磁気《物》magnetism ¶磁気を帯びた magnetic / 磁気あらし a magnetic storm / 磁気機雷 a magnetic mine / 磁気圏 the magnetosphere / 磁気測定 magnetometry / 磁気テープ (a) magnetic tape.

じき⁶ 磁器 porcelain; china(ware).

じき⁷ 直〈じきに〉〈すぐに〉in a moment; immediately;〈間もなく〉soon; in a short time; before long;〈近く〉close [near] by.【文例⇩】

じき 字義 ¶字義どおりの literal / 字義どおりに literally.

じき 児戯 ¶児戯に類する be (mere) child's play; be childish.

じき 時宜 ¶時宜にかなって[を得て]いる《文》be opportune; be timely.

しきい 敷居 the threshold (入口の); a doorsill (戸の); a window sill (窓の) ¶敷居をまたぐ cross [pass] the threshold.【文例⇩】

しきいき 識閾《心理》(below) the threshold of consciousness; the limen (pl. -s, limina) ¶識閾下の subliminal / 識閾上の supraliminal.

しきいし 敷石 a pavement;〈個々の〉a paving

なに時間がかかるはずがない。It can't take you that long to get to Ueno. / 彼らは時間の観念がない。They have no sense [idea] of time. / それは時間の問題に過ぎない。It is only a question [matter] of time.

しき³ それが田中式だ。That's Tanaka's way of doing things. | That's just like Tanaka. / 式場はどちらですか。Where is the ceremony (going) to be held?

しき⁴ 彼は死期が近付いている。He is on his deathbed. | His days are numbered.

じき³ この手の商売には今は時期がいい[悪い]。The times are right [not right] for this line of business. / この考えを実行に移すのはまだ時期が早い。It would be premature [It is still too early] to put this idea into practice.

じき⁴ あの本の出版は時機がよかった。The publication of that book was well-timed. / 時機を見て彼に忠告したまえ。Give him a warning when you have the opportunity. / 我々の飛躍すべき時機は到来した。The time has come when we should take bold steps. / 今はまだその時機ではない。The

じき⁷ もうじきに入梅になる。It will not be long before the rainy season sets in. / この子はじきに物を覚える。This boy is very quick to learn. / 試験はもうじきだ。The examination is nearly on us. / もうじき 12 時だ。It is almost [close on, getting on for] twelve o'clock. / 学校はここからじきだ。The school is only a short way from here. / もうじきだ。We are nearly there.

しきい この家の敷居は二度とまたぐな。Never show your face in this house again. | Never cross my threshold again. / ご無沙汰ばかりして敷居が高くなりました。Having neglected to visit you for so long, I feel awkard in coming

しきうつし 敷き写し (a) tracing ¶敷き写しする trace; make tracings (of).

しきがわ 敷き皮 a fur cushion; 《靴の》 an insole.

しきぎょう 私企業 a private firm [enterprise].

しききん 敷金 a deposit; caution money ¶敷金を入れる give [make, leave] a deposit; deposit caution money / 敷金3つ a deposit amounting [corresponding] to three months' rent.

しきけん 識見 ⇨ けんしき.

しきさい 色彩 a color; 《文》 a hue; a tint; coloring; 〈色合い〉 a tinge; 《文》 a tincture ¶政治的色彩のある politically-tinged 〈trade〉; (a decision) with political overtones [implications] / 政治的色彩のない (a club) with no political affiliations; 《文》 (a society) destitute of any political coloring / …の色彩を帯びた with a tinge of… / 色彩に乏しい colorless 〈くさえない〉 drab; dull / 色彩に富んだ (highly) colorful / 色彩感覚 color sensation / 〈審美的〉 (a color) sense.

しきし 色紙 a square piece of fancy paper (for writing a poem on).

じきじき 直々 直々の personal; direct / 直直に personally; in person.

しきしゃ 識者 well-informed people; 《文》 the wise [intelligent, informed]; 《文》 thinking people.

しきじゃく 色弱 《医》 (partial) colorblindness ¶色弱である be (partially) colorblind.

しきじょう 色情 sexual [《文》 carnal] passion [《文》 desire]; 《文》 lust ¶色情狂 《病》 erotomania; sex mania; 〈人〉 a sex maniac; an erotomaniac; a satyr (男); a nymphomaniac (女).

しきじりつ 識字率 a literacy rate.

しきそ 色素 coloring matter; 《生物》 (a) pigment ¶食用色素 food colors / 色素細胞 a pigment [pigmentary] cell; a chromatophore.

じきそ 直訴 直訴する make a direct appeal (to the Emperor); petition directly (to); go straight to the top.

しきたり 仕来たり a tradition; an institution; 《文》 a customary [conventional] practice ⇨ かんれい², ならわし.

ジギタリス 《植》 a foxglove; 《薬》 digitalis.

しきち 敷地 a (building) site; (a plot of) ground; (a building) lot ¶敷地を捜す[選ぶ] look for [choose, 《文》 select] a site (for).

しきちょう 色調 the tone of color; a color tone; color quality.

しきつめる 敷き詰める spread (gravel) all over 《the garden》; cover 《a road with gravel》; pave 《a path with flagstones》.

じきでし 直弟子 a direct disciple (of).

しきてん 式典 ⇨ しき³.

じきひつ 直筆 one's own handwriting; 《文》 an autograph writing (in facsimile) ⇨ じひつ.

しきふ 敷布 a (bed) sheet ¶敷布を敷く put [spread] a sheet (on the bed).

しきぶかん 式部官 a master of ceremonies.

しきぶとん 敷布団 a mattress.

しきべつ 識別 ¶識別(力) 《文》 discrimination; 《文》 discernment / 識別する distinguish [《文》 discriminate] (between A and B, A from B); tell (A from B); tell 《A and B》 apart; 《文》 discern; 〈…だと認める〉 identify; recognize / 識別できる distinguishable; recognizable / 識別しにくい indistinguishable; unrecognizable; hard to make out / 識別閾(⅟) 《心理・生理》 the threshold of difference.

しきま 色魔 a sex maniac.

しきもう 色盲 colorblindness ¶色盲の colorblind / 赤色盲の red-blind / 赤緑色盲 red-green colorblindness; Daltonism / 全色盲 total colorblindness.

しきもの 敷き物 a carpet; a rug; (a) floor covering; matting (畳類) ¶床に敷き物を敷く lay a carpet on the floor; cover the floor with a carpet; carpet the floor; spread a rug on the floor / 敷き物を敷いてない床 a bare [an uncarpeted] floor.

じぎゃく 自虐 《文》 self-persecution; 《文》 self-humiliation ¶自虐的な 《文》 self-tormenting.

しきゅう¹ 子宮 the womb; 《解》 the uterus (pl. -ri) ¶子宮の uterine / 子宮外妊娠 extra-uterine [ectopic] pregnancy / 子宮がん uterine cancer; cancer of the womb / 子宮筋腫 a myoma of the uterus / 子宮後屈 retroflexion [retroversion] of the uterus / 子宮内膜炎 endometritis.

しきゅう² 支給 ¶支給する provide [supply, 《文》 furnish] 《sb with sth》; allow; give; grant / 衣服を支給する provide [supply] sb with clothes / 月給15万円を支給する pay [give] sb a monthly salary of 150,000 yen / 旅費を支給する allow [pay] sb traveling expenses / 支給品 supplies.

しきゅう³ 四球 ⇨ フォアボール.

しきゅう⁴ 至急 ¶至急の urgent; pressing / 至急の場合 in urgent cases; in an emergency / 至急に urgently; at once; promptly; immediately; as quickly as possible; 《文》 without loss of time; 《文》 with dispatch; without delay; 《米》 in short order / 至急報 an urgent telegram (電報); an urgent call (電話) / 至急報[便]で打つ[送る] send 《a message, a package》 by express. 【文例】

しきゅう⁵ 死球 ⇨ デッドボール.

じきゅう¹ 自給 self-support; 《文》 self-sustenance ¶自給する support oneself; provide here.

しきゅう⁴ 何とぞ至急ご返事下さい. Kindly oblige me with an early answer. / 大至急でやってもらいたい. I want it finished as quickly as possible [with all possible speed]. / この傷は至急手当をしなければいけない. This wound needs prompt treatment. / 至急を要する手紙は必ず旅先へ回すこと. All letters requiring immediate attention must be forwarded to (the place) where I am staying.

しきゅうしき 知事の始球式で試合が開始された. The game was started [opened] by the governor tossing the first ball.

しぎょう 始業は午前9時, 終業は午後4時. School opens at 9 a.m. and closes at 4 p.m. | School

じきゅう for *oneself* / 自給自足 self-sufficing / 自給自足の self-sufficient 《文》-sufficing, -sustaining; self-contained / 自給率 (the degree of) self-sufficiency (in oil).

じきゅう² 持久 ¶持久戦 a long-drawn-out [《文》] protracted] struggle [war];《スポーツ》a game of endurance / 持久力 endurance, stamina; staying power;《文》tenacity; perseverance.

じきゅう³ 時給 payment by the hour ¶時給70円の昇給を要求する ask for a 70-yen-an-hour raise.

しきゅうしき 始球式 ¶始球式を行なう throw [pitch] the first ball. 文例⇩

しき 死去 ⇨しぼう².

しきょ 辞去 ¶辞去する《文》take *one's* leave (of *sb*); leave, go away (from).

しきょう¹ 市況 the tone [state, movements] of the market; the market ¶市況報告 a market report.

しきょう² 司教 a bishop ¶大司教 an archbishop / 司教管区 a diocese; a bishopric; a[an episcopal] see / 大司教管区にも用い / 司教職 bishopric; episcopate.

しきょう³ 試供 ¶試供する offer *sth* free as a promotion [for advertisement] / 試供品 a free (promotional) gift; a free sample;《米俗》a freebie.

しぎょう 始業 the start [《文》commencement] of work; opening ¶始業の鐘 the starting bell / 始業式 the opening ceremony. 文例⇩

じきょう¹ 自供 a confession ¶自供する confess / 自供させる get [《文》induce] *sb* to confess; get [《文》elicit] a confession (from *sb*) / 犯行を自供する confess to a crime; confess that *one* has committed a crime.

じきょう² 耳鏡《医》an otoscope.

じぎょう¹ 地形 ¶地形をならす level [prepare] the ground (of a building site).

じぎょう² 事業 an undertaking;《文》an enterprise; a project;《仕事》work; a task;《実業》business; an industry 《産業》;《業績》an achievement ¶事業を営む run [carry on] a business;《文》engage in business / 事業をおこす start an enterprise / 事業を拡張する expand the business / 事業に失敗する fail in business / 国家的事業 a state [national] undertaking / 事業家〈企業家〉an entrepreneur;〈実業家〉an industrialist; a businessman / 事業所得 a business income; the income from an enterprise / 事業所得税 the business tax / 事業年度 a business year. 文例⇩

しきよく 色欲《文》sexual [carnal] desire;《文》lust.

しきょく 支局 a branch (office).

じきょく 時局 the situation; the state of things [affairs] ¶困難な時局を収拾する settle [sort out, straighten out] a difficult situation / 時局

に処する deal [cope] with the situation / 時局にかんがみて in view of the situation.

じきょく² 磁極《物》a magnetic pole.

しきり 仕切り〈区画〉a partition; a compartment;(a) division;〈境界〉a boundary ¶仕切りをする partition; divide; close off ((a part of the hall)) / 仕切り壁 a partition wall / 仕切り状 an invoice.

しきりに 頻りに〈しばしば〉《文》frequently; repeatedly;〈絶えず〉incessantly; constantly; in succession;〈熱心に〉eagerly;〈切実に〉earnestly; strongly ¶しきりに行きたがる be eager [anxious] to go / しきりに顔を見る look [stare] hard at *sb* / しきりに勧める《推奨する》recommend [support] ((a course of action)) enthusiastically;《文》give *one's* hearty recommendation (to);〈強いる〉press (drink) on *sb* / しきりに反対する oppose (a proposal) strongly; make an active protest (against). 文例⇩

しきる 仕切る ¶しきり(仕切りをする)《相撲》toe the mark ¶部屋を2つに仕切る partition [divide] a room into two parts [compartments].

しきわら 敷き藁 litter ¶敷きわらを敷く litter (a stall) down; spread (a sty) with straw.

しきん¹ 至近 ¶至近距離で at close range; (at) point blank / 至近弾 a near hit [miss].

しきん² 資金 funds; a fund (基金); (a) capital (資本) ¶資金が充分ある be well funded / 資金が不足している be short of funds; be poorly funded / 資金を出す provide [《文》furnish] funds (for); fund; finance / 資金を調達する [集める] raise funds (for) / 資金集め a fund-raising campaign [building] fund / 運転[回転, 準備]資金 working [revolving, reserve] funds / 資金カンパ a fund-raising campaign [drive] / 資金ぐり financing / 資金難 financial difficulty; lack of funds.
⌐poem.
しぎん 詩吟 recitation (chanting) of a Chinese
しきんせき 試金石 a touchstone;〈試験〉a test (case). 文例⇩

しく¹ 詩句 a verse; a stanza; a line of a poem.

しく² 如く be equal (to); can compare ((with)). 文例⇩

しく³ 敷く spread; lay; cover (the floor with a carpet); pave ((a path with flagstones)) ¶布団を敷く lay out the *futon* [bedding]; make a bed / ござを敷く spread a mat / 座布団を敷いて座る sit on a cushion / 鉄道を敷く lay a railroad (line). 文例⇩

じく¹ 軸〈心棒〉an axis (*pl.* axes); an axle (車輪の);《機》a shaft; a spindle; a pivot;〈茎〉a stem; a stalk;〈掛け物〉a scroll; a *kakemono* ¶マッチの軸 a matchstick;《文》matchwood / ペン軸 a penholder / x 軸《数》the x-axis; the horizontal axis / y 軸《数》the y-axis; the vertical axis / 〈投手の〉軸足 ((a pitcher's)) pivoting foot. 文例⇩

---

hours are from 9 a.m. to 4 p.m.
じぎょう² 彼はなかなか事業家だ。He is very enterprising.
しきりに 彼はしきりに物を書いている。He is busily writing (away).
しきんせき この仕事は彼の手腕を試す試金石だ。This work is the touchstone of his ability.
しく² 用心するにしくはない。Caution is the best policy. | It is best to be cautious.
しく³ 往来には石が敷いてある。The streets are paved with stone. / さあお敷きになって下さい。Please take your seat on this cushion.
じく¹ 地球はその軸を中心として24時間に1回転する。The earth

じく² 字句 〈言葉〉 words and phrases; terms; 〈言い方〉 expressions; wording; 〈法律の〉 letter of the law ¶字句を修正する make some changes in the wording / 法律の字句に拘泥(㌧)する keep [stick, 《文》adhere] to the letter of the law. 文例◎

じくう 時空 〈物〉 space-time ¶時空の連続体 a space-time continuum (pl. -tinua).

じくうけ 軸受け 〈機〉 a (shaft) bearing; a ball bearing (玉軸受け); 〈台〉 a pillow block.

しぐさ 〈演技〉 acting; action; 〈身振り〉 one's gestures; 《文》 one's bearing [carriage]; 〈仕打ち〉 ⇒うち.

ジグザグ a zigzag ¶ジグザグに (walk) in zigzags / ジグザグコースを取る follow a zigzag course; zigzag (★ zigzagged, zigzagging と活用する) / (デモの)ジグザグ行進 (stage) a snake dance; snake dancing.

しくしく ¶しくしく泣く sob; weep / 腹がしくしく痛む have a griping pain in the stomach.

じくじく oozily ¶じくじくにじみ出る ooze out / じくじくした damp; soggy; boggy.

しくじる 〈失敗する〉 fail; (one's plans) fall through; 〈失策する〉 blunder; make a mistake [blunder]; 《文》 commit an error; 〈不手際なことをする〉 make a mess (of); make a bad job (of); bungle sth; botch.

じぐち 地口 a play on words; (make) a pun.

しくつ 試掘 prospecting; (a) trial digging [boring] ¶試掘する prospect (a mine); drill [bore] for (oil); drill an experimental ((oil, gas)) well / 試掘権 a prospecting right.

シグナル 〈信号〉 a signal.

しくはっく 四苦八苦 ¶四苦八苦する be in great trouble; 《口語》 be in a bad way; 《文》 be in dire distress; be hard pressed ((for money)).

じくばり 字配り the arrangement [positioning] of characters (in calligraphy).

しくみ 仕組み 〈仕掛け〉 《文》 a contrivance; a mechanism; a device; a plot (小説などの); 〈構造〉 structure; construction; (a) setup; 〈計画〉 a plan; 《文》 design; (an) arrangement.

しくむ 仕組む plan; 《文》 devise; 《文》 contrive; get up; 《文》 engineer ¶劇に仕組む make a play of ((an incident)); dramatize (a story) / 仕組んだ狂言 《口語》 a put-up job; 《口語》 a got-up affair.

シクラメン 〈植〉 a cyclamen.

しぐれ 時雨 drizzling rain [a shower] (in late autumn and early winter). 文例◎

しけ 〈暴風雨〉 stormy weather [seas]; a storm; 〈不漁〉 a poor catch [haul]; 〈不況〉 (a) business depression; a dull [dead] period (in trade) ¶しけにあう be overtaken by a storm / しけ続きである have a long spell of stormy weather [poor business]. 文例◎

しけい¹ 死刑 capital punishment; the death penalty ¶死刑を宣告する sentence [condemn] sb to death; pass a death sentence on sb / 死刑を執行する execute ((a criminal)) / 死刑に相当する罪 a capital offense [crime]; an offense punishable by death / 死刑に処する put sb to death / 死刑執行人 an executioner; a hangman (絞首刑の) / 死刑囚 a condemned criminal / 死刑囚監房 a condemned cell; 《米》 a death row [house].

しけい² 私刑 lynching; lynch law ⇒リンチ ★ ¶私刑を加える lynch (虐殺する); take the law into one's own hands.

しけい³ 紙型 a papier-mâché mold; a matrix ((pl. matrices, matrixes)) ¶紙型をとる make [take] a papier-mâché mold (of).

しけい⁴ 詩型 a verse form.

じけいだん 自警団 a vigilante group [corps] ¶自警団員 a vigilante.

しげき¹ 史劇 a historical play [drama]; a history play ¶シェークスピアの史劇 Shakespeare's histories.

しげき² 刺激 〈刺激(物)〉《文》 a stimulus ((pl. -li)); a spur; 《文》 an impetus; an incentive; 《文》 an impulse; 〈刺激すること〉 stimulation; incitement; encouragement (激励) / 刺激する stimulate; give an impulse (to); give [provide] an impetus [a stimulus] (to); excite; stir up; irritate (the skin) / 刺激となる serve as a stimulus (to) / 刺激性の《文》 stimulative; (文) incentive; irritant; excitant; excitative / 刺激的[の強い] exciting; thrilling; sensational / 刺激のない dull; boring; monotonous / 刺激剤 a stimulant; an irritant; an excitant. 文例◎

しげき³ 詩劇 a poetical drama; a play in verse.

しげしげ 繁々 〈しばしば〉 very often [《文》 frequently]; lots of times; 〈じっと〉 fixedly; narrowly; closely ¶しげしげと通う《文》 frequent (a place) / 人の顔をしげしげと眺める look ((文)) gaze, stare) hard at sb; look sb in the face; fix one's eyes [《文》 gaze] on sb.

しけつ 止血 〈医〉 hemostasis; arrest [stopping] of bleeding ¶止血する stop [check, arrest] bleeding / 止血剤 a hemostatic (agent); a styptic / 止血帯 a tourniquet.

じけつ 自決 〈民族の〉 self-determination ((for [of] the Cypriots)); 〈自殺〉 ⇒じさつ.

しげみ 茂み a thicket; a bush ¶雑草の茂み a growth of weeds.

しける¹ 湿気る be [get] damp; be moist [wet].

しける² get [《文》become] stormy; 〈海が〉《文》 rage; get choppy; 《文》 become turbulent; 〈不況になる〉 get [《文》become] dull [slack] ¶しけた顔をする look glum [blue]; pull a long face; 《口語》 be in the blues [dumps].

しげる 茂る 〈草木が主語〉 grow thick; be rank; 《文》 be luxuriant; be rampant; 〈場所が主語〉 be overgrown [densely covered] ((with)) / 木

---

turns on its axis once in twenty-four hours.

じく² 翻訳をするにはあまり原文の字句にとらわれていけない. In translation you must not adhere blindly to the original wording. / その手紙にはうまい字句が用いてある. The letter is well worded.

ジグザグ 道は丘をジグザグに横断していた. The road zigzagged [ran zigzag] across the hills.

しぐれ 今日は時雨模様のお天気でしょう. It will rain off and on today.

しけ (海は)しけ模様だ. It's going to be rough.

しげき² いやに神経を刺激する音

しけん¹ 私見 one's personal [private] views [opinion] ¶私見によれば in my (personal) opinion ; to my thinking.

しけん² 私権 《法》 a private right.

しけん³ 試験 an examination ; 《口語》an exam ; a test ; 《米》a quiz (*pl.* quizzes) ; 〈実験〉an experiment ; a trial ¶数学の試験 an exam in mathematics ; a math(s) exam / 〈試験を行う〉examine *sb* ; hold 《文》 conduct] an examination ; give *sb* an exam [a test] (in) ; 〈実験する〉 experiment (on) ; do [《文》 conduct] an experiment [a test] (on, in) ; test / 人物を試験する put *sb*'s character to the test / 試験の監督をする supervise [《米》 proctor, 《英》 invigilate] an exam / 試験を受ける take [sit for, go in for] an exam / 試験を受けて[受けずに]入学する enter a school through [without (going through)] an examination / 試験的に tentatively ; on trial [probation] ; experimentally / 学期末[中間]試験 a term-end [midterm] exam / 最終[学年末]試験 the final examination ; (the) finals / 試験科目 the subjects for [of] examination ; an exam subject / 試験官 an examiner / 試験管 a test tube / 試験管培養 a (test-)tube culture / 試験管ベビー a test-tube baby / 試験監督 〈事〉《米》the proctoring of an exam ; 〈英〉invigilation ; 〈人〉《米》a proctor ; 《英》an invigilator / (新方式などの)試験期間 a test [testing] period / 試験工場 a pilot plant / 試験紙 《化》 test [litmus] paper / 試験地獄 the ordeal of (entrance) exams / 試験場 an examination room [hall] ; 〈実験所,研究室〉a (hygienic) laboratory ; an 〈agricultural〉 experiment station ; 〈兵器・農法などの〉a testing [proving] ground / 試験済みの tried and tested [trusted] / 試験段階 the testing stage / 試験発射 test firing / 試験発射をする test-fire / 試験飛行 a test [trial] flight / 試験飛行を行なう test (an airplane) in flight ; flight-test (a plane) / 試験飛行士 a test pilot / 試験勉強をする prepare [cram] for an exam ; slog [grind] (away) at examination subjects / 試験問題 examination [exam] questions ; questions for an examination ; test problems ; an examination paper (用紙). 文例⇩

しげん¹ 至言 ¶至言である《文》It is well [truly, wisely, aptly] said that… ; 《文》There is much (truth) in the saying that….

しげん² 資源 a (natural) resource ; (natural) resources ¶資源の豊かな rich in natural resources / 資源を開発する exploit [develop, tap] natural resources / 有限な資源 finite resources / 資源供給[産出]国 resource-supplying[-producing] countries [nations] / 資源問題 the [a] resources problem / 資源有限時代 an era of limited natural resources.

じけん 事件 〈出来事〉an event ; a happening ; an incident ; 〈問題〉an affair ; a matter ; 〈訴訟の〉a case ; 〈ごたごた〉a trouble ¶殺人事件 a murder case / 事件記者 a news reporter on the police beat. 文例⇩

じげん¹ 次元 a dimension ⇒ さんじげん ¶次元が違う be on a different level [plane] / belong to a different category [order] / 次元の低い 《文》unworthy ; low-grade ; vulgar / 多次元の multi-dimensional.

じげん² 時限 〈時間の制限〉a time limit ; a deadline ; 〈授業の〉an hour ; a period ¶第3時限に in the third period / 時限爆弾 a time bomb.

しこ 四股 ¶四股を踏む stamp (on the ring for a warm-up).

しご¹ 死後 ¶死後(に) after one's death ; 《文》posthumously / 死後の 《文》posthumous (honors) ; postmortem (examinations) / 死後の世界 《文》the afterworld ; 《文》the life beyond [after death] / 死後硬直 (be stiff in) rigor mortis. 文例⇩

しご² 死語 a dead language (ラテン語など) ; an obsolete word.

しご³ 私語 whisper(ing) ; private talk ¶私語する whisper ; talk in whispers.

じこ¹ 自己 one's self ; oneself ¶自己の one's own ; personal ; private / 自己流の 《文》(a painting) after one's own style ; self-taught (sculptors) / 自己流に in one's own way ; 《文》after [in] one's own style / 自己暗示 autosuggestion / 自己暗示にかかる be subjected to autosuggestion / 自己意識 a sense [an awareness] of self ; self-identification / 自己犠牲 self-sacrifice ; self-deception / 自己欺瞞(ぎまん) self-deception / 自己嫌悪 《文》self-hate / 自己嫌悪に陥る yield to self-hatred / 自己顕示欲の強い self-assertive ; pushy ; aggressively [《文》excessively] self-confident ; 《文》obtrusive / 自己催眠にかかった self-hypnotized / 自己資本 owned capital / 自己紹介をする introduce oneself (as) / 自己宣伝 self-advertisement ; self-display / 自己宣伝をする advertise oneself ; seek publicity / 自己疎外 《哲》self-alienation / 自己中心[本位] 《文》egoism ; self-centeredness ; selfishness / 自己中心[本位]の人 a self-centered person ; an egotist ; 《文》an egoist / 自己調整 self-adjustment[-regulation] / 自己陶酔 narcissism / 自己批判 self-criticism / 自己弁護 《文》self-justification ; an excuse / 自己弁護する defend [justify] oneself / 自己放棄 《文》self-renunciation / 自己満足 self-satisfaction ; (self-)complacency.

じこ² 事故 〈不慮の〉an accident ; 〈故障〉a hitch ; a trouble ; 〈事件〉an incident ¶交通

文例

だ。 The sound gets [jars] on my nerves. / 煙が目を刺激した。 The smoke irritated my eyes.

しけん³ その問題はこの前の試験に出た。 The same question was asked in the last examination. / あの人を試験に使ってみて下さい。 Give him a trial. | Take him on trial.

じけん 大事件になりそうだ。 It is likely to assume serious proportions. / 私はこんなおかしな事件に出会ったことがない。 Never in my life have I experienced such a strange event.

しご¹ 死体は死後1週間経過したものと推定される。 The man is estimated to have been dead for

[鉄道]事故で死ぬ be killed in a traffic [railroad] accident / 事故多発地点 a [an accident] black spot. 文例⇩

じご¹ 事後 ¶事後の[に]《文》after the fact [event] / 事後検閲 post-censorship / 事後承諾を求める《文》ask for *ex post facto* approval.

じご² 持碁 a drawn game of go.

しこう¹ 私行 *one's* private activities [《文》conduct] ¶私行を暴く expose *sb's* private affairs [life].

しこう² 志向 《文》(an) inclination ¶《文》(an) orientation; (an) intention ¶機械志向の machine-oriented (people). 文例⇩

しこう³ 思考 thought; consideration ¶思考する think; consider; regard 《*sth* as》/ 思考力 ability to think 《文》thinking faculty [power].

しこう⁴ 施行 《文》enforcement; operation ¶施行する put into operation [effect]; enforce / 施行される come into force [operation]; go into effect; take effect; 《文》become effective; be enforced / 施行されている be in force [operation] / 施行規則[細則] enforcement regulations [detailed enforcement regulations].

しこう⁵ 指向 ¶指向する point 《to》/ 指向性《無線》directivity / 指向性アンテナ a directional antenna [aerial].

しこう⁶ 嗜好 (a) taste; (a) liking; *one's* likes and dislikes; a preference 《for》¶嗜好に合う be to *one's* taste [liking]; suit *one's* taste(s) / 一般の嗜好に投じる suit the public taste; catch [capture] the popular fancy / 嗜好品〈好きな食品〉*one's* favorite food; 〈茶・コーヒー・酒など〉nonessential [luxury] grocery items [foods].

じこう¹ 事項〈事柄〉《文実》matters; 《文実》facts; 〈項目〉《文》items ¶調査事項 matters for investigation / 事項索引〈図書館〉a subject index.

じこう² 時効《法》〈民法上の〉prescription (取得時効); limitation (of action(s)) (消滅時効); 〈刑法上の〉limitation of time ¶時効にかかる be barred by statute; be statute-barred / 時効になる the statute of limitations runs out. 文例⇩

じこう³ 時候〈季節〉the season; 〈天候〉the weather ¶時候のあいさつ《文》(exchange, offer) the compliments of the season; 《文》the season's greetings / 時候当たりする suffer from the weather / 時候はずれの《文》unseasonable / 時候はずれの暖かさ unseasonably warm weather.

じごう 次号 the next number [issue]. 文例⇩

しこうさくご 試行錯誤 《by, through》trial and error ¶試行錯誤法 a trial-and-error method [technique].

じごうじとく 自業自得 ¶自業自得だ be *one's* own fault; have brought it 《one's troubles》on oneself [*one's* own head]; it serves *one* right; 《口語》*one* asked for it; 《文》be the natural result [consequence] of *one's* own (mis)deeds [of what *one* has done]. 文例⇩

じごえ 地声 *one's* natural voice. 文例⇩

しごく¹ 扱く draw (a piece of cloth) through *one's* hands; strip off (leaves); stroke (*one's* beard); 〈激しく鍛える〉put *sb* through the mill; put *sb* to hard work (training).

しごく² 至極 very; 《文》most; extremely; 《文》exceedingly. 文例⇩

じこく¹ 自国 *one's* (own) country; 〈故国〉《文》*one's* native land; *one's* home country ¶自国の人々《文》*one's* fellow countrymen / 自国語《文》*one's* own language / 《文》*one's* mother tongue. 文例⇩

じこく² 時刻 a [the] time; 《文》the hour ⇨とき¹, じかん¹ ¶時刻表〈掲示・本〉a timetable; 《米》a (train) schedule; 〈本〉a train guide (時刻以外のいろいろな情報が載る). 文例⇩

じごく 地獄 hell; 《文》the pit (of hell); 《文》Hades; the inferno (*pl.* -s) ¶この世の地獄 a hell on earth / 地獄のような《文》infernal; hellish / 地獄に落ちる go to hell; land in hell / 地獄耳《have》a sharp ear; 《have》long ears. 文例⇩

しこしこ ¶しこしこした〈歯ざわりが〉firm.

しごせん 子午線 the meridian (line) ¶本初子午線 the prime [first] meridian.

しこたま a lot 《of》; plenty 《of》; 《口語》loads [pots] 《of》¶しこたまもうける make a big profit; make pots [piles] of money.

しごと 仕事 work; business; toil; labor; a job; 《文》a task; 〈職〉employment; 《文》an occupation; *one's* trade; 〈事業〉an undertaking; 〈任務〉《文》a mission; 《文》*one's* duties; 〈天職〉《文》a vocation ¶仕事がある have work to do [to attend to]; have a job; be in work [employment] / 仕事がない have nothing to do

---

a week. / すでに死後硬直の状態にあった. Rigor mortis had already set in.

じこ² その夜は何の事故もなくて済んだ. The night passed quietly [uneventfully].

しこう² 日本は輸出志向の国だと思っている人が多い. Many people believe Japan is an export-oriented country.

じこう² アメリカの法律では人身傷害を伴わない犯罪は10年で時効になる. According to American law, in crimes where there is no bloodshed the statute of limitations runs out after 10 years.

じこう³ 今は散歩によい時候だ. This is the best season for (going for) walks. / 毎年今頃は時候が悪い. This is an unhealthy time of year. / 時候の変わり目にはいつも具合がよくない. I am always off color at the turn of the season.

じごう 以下次号. To be continued. / 次号完結. To be concluded.

じごうじとく 自業自得だ. You have brought it on yourself. | You have brought it to blame. / 自業自得だから放っておきなさい. (It's his own fault.) Let him stew in his own juice. / 彼の貧乏は自業自得だ. His poverty is of his own making.

じごえ 声の大きいのは地声だから仕方がない. I cannot help having a loud voice.

しごく² 至極ごもっともです. You are quite right. | Quite so.

じこく¹ 彼は英語を自国語のように話す. He speaks English as if he were born to it [like a native (speaker)].

じこく² 彼はちょうどよい時刻にやって来た. He made his appearance at a good [the right] time.

しこな be jobless ; be out of work / 仕事が手につかない be unable to settle [get] down to work ; cannot concentrate on one's work / 仕事をする work ; do one's work [job] / 1 時間余分に仕事をする do an hour's extra work / 仕事をしている be working ; be at work / 仕事を休む have [take] a day off (from work) / 仕事にかかる start (one's) work ; get (down) to business ; set to work / 仕事に追われる be pressed [overloaded] with business ; be under great pressure in one's work / 1日の仕事 a day's work / 一生の仕事 one's life's work [lifework] / 仕事着 working clothes ; 〈職工の〉 overalls / 仕事場 a workshop ; one's place of work / 仕事率《物》power. 文例⇩

しこな 醜名 the professional name of a *sumo* wrestler.

しこみ 仕込み 〈教育・訓練〉training ; education ; teaching ; upbringing ; 〈仕入れ〉stocking ; laying in ; 〈食物の〉preparation ¶ 仕込みがいい be well educated [trained] ; be well-bred / パリ[フランス]仕込みの Paris-[French-]trained / パリ[フランス]で仕込む trained in Paris [France] / 仕込みつえ a sword stick [cane]. 文例⇩

しこむ 仕込む 〈訓練する〉train *sb* (to be an actor) ; 〈教える〉teach ; educate ; break (in) 〈動物を〉; 〈仕入れる〉stock 〈goods〉; lay in a stock 《of》; 〈醸造する〉prepare ; ferment ¶ 子供に商売を仕込む train [bring up] a child to a trade.

しこり ¶ しこりが出来る feel stiff [《文》have a stiffness] 《in the shoulders》/ しこりを残す leave an unpleasant feeling [aftertaste].

しこる go [get, 《文》become] stiff ; harden.

しこん 歯根 the root of a tooth.

しさ¹ 示唆 (a) suggestion ¶ 示唆する[を与える] suggest ; hint 《at》; give suggestions / 示唆に富む 《文》be (highly) suggestive.

しさ² 視差《天》(a) parallax ¶ 視差の[による] parallactic (motion).

しざ 視座 a vantage point ; a viewpoint ; a standpoint ; an outlook.

じさ 時差 a time difference [differential] ; (a) difference in time ¶ 時差出勤 《adopt, enforce》staggered working 《office, commuting》hours / 時差ぼけ (be suffering from) jet lag. 文例⇩

しさい¹ 子細 〈理由〉reasons ; 〈事情〉circumstances ; 〈詳細〉《文》particulars ; details ¶ 子細に in detail ;《文》minutely / 子細に語る give a detailed [full] account 《of》/ 子細に点検する make a close inspection 《of》/ 子細あって for some reason or other / 子細ありげに 〈訳ありげに〉《文》meaningfully ;《文》with a significant look ; 〈もったいぶって〉with an air of importance.

しさい² 司祭 a priest ; a pastor ¶ 司祭館 a parsonage.

しさい³ 市債 a municipal [city] loan [debt] ; 〈債券〉a municipal bond.

しさい¹ 私財 private funds [《文》means, property] ¶ 私財を投じる use [spend,《文》expend] one's own funds [fortune] 《on》/ 私財を投じて from [out of] one's own purse [pocket] ; at one's own expense.

しさい² 資材 (building) materials ;《軍》《フランス語》*materiel*.

じざい 自在 ⇒じゆう¹ ¶ 自在かぎ a pothook / 自在スパナ《米》a monkey wrench ;《英》an adjustable [a universal] spanner / (パイプなどの)自在接合部 a lobster joint / 自在継ぎ手《機》a universal joint [coupling] / 自在扉 a swing(-ing) door.

しさく¹ 思索 thinking ;《文》speculation ;《文》contemplation ;《文》meditation ¶ 思索する 《文》think reflectively ;《文》muse [meditate] 《on》;《文》speculate ;《文》contemplate / 思索にふける be lost [absorbed,《文》engrossed] in meditation [one's thoughts].

しさく² 施策《文》a measure ; a policy ¶ 国の施策 state measures / 施策を誤る take a wrong step [measure].

しさく³ 試作 〈製作〉trial manufacture ; 〈栽培〉trial rearing / 〈詩文の〉a study ;《フランス語》an *étude* ¶ 試作する manufacture [produce, cultivate, grow] *sth* by way of trial [experiment] / 試作車 an experimental car / 試作品 a trial piece.

じさく 自作 one's own work ¶ 自作の《文》of one's own making / 〈詩文など〉《poems》that one has written *oneself* ;《文》of one's own writing [composition] / 自作自演する play [perform, read] one's own work / 自作農 an independent farmer ; an owner farmer.

じざけ 地酒 (a) local wine [brew].

しさつ¹ 刺殺 ¶ 刺殺する stab *sb* dead [to

じごく 地獄のさたも金次第. Money (is the key that) opens all doors. | 砂漠で仏. An oasis in the desert. | A friend in need. / 彼は地獄で仏に会ったように感じた. He was greatly relieved to find such a friend in his distress.

しごと 彼は今仕事のことで大阪に行っています. His work has taken him to Osaka. / 仕事のことで彼女を訪ねたことがあります. I've visited her on [in the way of] business. / そこの大工は私の家の仕事をしている. That carpenter is working on my house. / 彼は仕事が早い. He is a quick worker. / 今日はうんと仕事をしたよ. I've done a day's work. / 長い間仕事から離れていたので,だいぶ時代遅れになっていた. I had been away from work a long time and I was considerably behind the times. / 魚釣りも仕事となると楽じゃない. Angling is no fun when you do it for a living. / そこまで行くのは一日仕事だよ. It will take you a whole day to get there. / 私はよく仕事を家に持ち帰って,夜家族の者が寝静まってからそれを続けます. I often take work home with me, and continue it at night after the rest of the family has gone to sleep. / ここでは仕事の話はやめよう. Let's not talk shop here.

しこみ あの人の英語はイギリス仕込みだ. He learned his English in England.

じさ 東京とロンドンとでは9時間の時差がある. There is a nine-hour time difference between Tokyo and London. | The time difference between Tokyo and London is nine hours.

death]; 〈野球で〉 put [throw] (a runner) out.
しさつ 視察 (an) inspection ¶視察する inspect; make an inspection (of a school); visit / 視察団 a group of inspectors; 〈実業の〉 a business mission (to the U.S.); 〈軍事施設などの〉 an observation team (to Laos) / 視察旅行に行く go on a tour of inspection [a fact-finding tour].
じさつ 自殺 (a) suicide ¶自殺する kill *oneself* (by taking poison); commit suicide; 《文》put an end to *one's* own life; 《文》take *one's* own life / 自殺(的)行為 a suicidal act / 自殺者 a suicide / 自殺未遂 (an) attempted suicide. [文例⇩]
しさん¹ 四散 ¶四散する scatter [(《文》disperse, be scattered] (in all directions).
しさん² 資産 property, a fortune; 《文》means; assets (会社の) / 資産と負債 assets and liabilities / あまり資産のない人 a person of modest means / 資産家 a man of property [means]; a wealthy [rich] person / 資産再評価 revaluation [reassessment] of property / 資産状態 *one's* financial standing.
しざん 死産 a stillbirth ¶死産の stillborn (babies) / 死産をする have a stillborn baby [a stillbirth]; *one's* baby is born dead.
じさん 持参 ¶持参する 〈持ってくる〉bring *sth* (with *one*); 〈持って行く〉take *sth* with *one*; carry / 持参金 a dowry / 持参人払い (a check) payable to (the) bearer. [文例⇩]
しさんひょう 試算表 《簿記》a trial balance (sheet).
しし¹ 四肢 《文》the limbs; the arms and legs.
しし² 死屍 ⇒したい¹. [文例⇩]
しし³ 志士 〈愛国者〉《文》a noble-minded patriot.
しし⁴ 孜々 ¶ししとして 《文》diligently; 《文》 assiduously; 《文》with untiring zeal; 《work》 hard.
しし⁵ 獅子 ⇨ライオン ¶獅子身中の虫 《文》a snake in *one's* bosom / 獅子奮迅の勢いで 《文》 with irresistible force; 《口語》like fury [mad] / 獅子吼(しく)する 《文》make an impassioned [eloquent] speech / 獅子座 《天》Leo; the Lion ⇨ざ五例.
しじ¹ 支持 support; backing ¶精神的支持 《give *sb*》moral support / 世論の支持 the backing of public opinion / 支持する support; stand by [behind] *sb*; back (up); 《文》espouse (a cause); 《文》uphold; be for [in favor of] (a proposition); take *one's* stand [《文》range *oneself* behind the Government) / 支持しがたい 《文》untenable (propositions) / 支持を受ける [得る] get [《文》receive, 《文》gain] (strong) support (from, among) / 支持者 a supporter; a backer. [文例⇩]
しじ² 私事 a personal [private] matter; private [personal] affairs ((文) concerns) ¶人の私事にわたる go (poke *one's* nose) into *sb's* private affairs; 《文》intrude on *sb's* privacy / 私事にわたって恐縮ですが Excuse me for being personal, but...
しじ³ 指示 ¶指示する 〈指図する〉instruct; direct; issue instructions to *sb*; 〈示す〉《文》indicate; show; 〈指摘する〉point out / 指示を待つ wait for instructions (from) / 指示に従う follow *sb's* instructions / 指示代名詞 《文法》a demonstrative pronoun / 指示物 《言語》a referent. [文例⇩]
しじ⁴ 師事 ¶師事する study under *sb*; have [take] *sb* as *one's* teacher; be [become] *sb's* pupil.
じじ 時事 current events [news]; the events [news] of the day ¶時事を論じる discuss current events / 時事英語 English for current topics [affairs] / 時事解説 comments on current news; (a) news commentary / 時事解説者 a news commentator / 時事問題 a current question; current topics.
じじい 爺 an old man.
じじこっこく 時々刻々 《vary》from hour to hour; from moment to moment; every moment ¶時々刻々に変わって行く光景 《文》an ever-changing scene.
ししそんそん 子々孫々 《文》posterity; *one's* descendants; 《文》*one's* offspring; 《文》*one's* children's children ¶子々孫々に至るまで to *one's* remotest descendants / 子々孫々に伝える [伝わる] hand [go] down to posterity.
しじつ¹ 私室 a private room; 《文》a boudoir (婦人の).
ししつ² 資質 《文》(*one's*) endowments; 《文》*one's* natural gifts; *one's* nature; 《文》(*one's*) innate disposition. [文例⇩]
しじつ 史実 a historical fact; historical evidence.
じしつ 自室 *one's* own room; (have) a room of *one's* own ¶自室に引きこもる keep to [stay in] *one's* room.
じじつ² 事実 a fact; 〈fiction に対して〉fact; a reality; 〈実情〉the case; 〈真実〉the truth ¶覆うべからざる事実 《文》an undeniable [unconcealable] fact / 事実をありのままに述べる tell the whole truth [story] / 《米口語》tell it like it is / 事実を曲げる 《文》falsify [misrepre-

---

しさつ これぐらいのことで自殺するやつがあるものか. This is nothing to kill yourself over. / そんな事をしたら自殺行為だ. That [To do that] would be suicidal.
じさん 印鑑をご持参ですか. Have you got your seal with you?
しし² 死屍累々たる有様だった. The bodies lay in heaps. | The ground was covered with the dead.
しじ¹ 彼は女性からかなりの支持を得た. He gained considerable support from women. / この新思想は徐々に支持者がふえていった. The new ideas slowly found wider support among the people.
しじ³ 直ちに帰国せよという指示が本社から電報で送られた. Telegraphic instructions were sent out from the head office that he should return home at once.
ししつ² 彼は医師としての資質に欠けている. He's not the stuff that doctors are made of. | He doesn't have it in him to be a doctor.
じじつ¹ それは事実ではない. That isn't true. / 君がいくら否定しても, 事実からするとそう考えられる. For all your denials, the facts point that way. / 予言が事実となった. The prediction has come

じじつ sent] the facts ;《文》pervert the truth / 事実を調査する inquire into the facts (of the case) / 事実上〈実際に〉actually ; in reality ;〈実の所〉as a matter of fact ; in point of fact ;〈実質上〉practically ; virtually /《文》factual ; actual ; real ; practical ;《文》virtual / 事実上の承認 (a) de facto recognition / 事実誤認《法》a mistake of fact / 事実調査 fact-finding / 事実無根の《文》groundless ; unfounded ; false. 文例⇩

じじつ² 時日〈日取り〉the date ; the day (of) ;〈時〉time ¶時日がかかる take [《文》require] considerable [a great deal of] time / 時日を定める fix [set] the date ;《文》appoint the day. 文例⇩

ししっぱな 獅子っ鼻 an upturned nose ; a pug [snub] nose.

しじみ〔貝〕a shijimi clam.

じじむさい frowzy ; slovenly ; seedy ¶じじむさくなる run to seed.

ししゅ¹ 支社 a branch (office).

ししゃ² 死者 a dead person ;《文》the deceased ;〈総称〉the dead ;《文》the killed ¶多数の死者 a heavy loss [《文》toll] of lives ; a large number of deaths. 文例⇩

ししゃ³ 使者 a messenger ;《文》an envoy.

ししゃ⁴ 試写 a private showing ; a (film) preview ; a trade première [show] (映画関係者だけに見せる)¶試写会を行なう give [hold] a preview (of).

ししゃ⁵ 試射 test [trial] firing ¶試射する test(-fire) (a gun) ; 試射場 a firing range / ミサイル試射場 a missile firing range ; a test-firing site for missiles.

ししゃく 子爵 a viscount ¶子爵夫人 a viscountess.

じしゃく 磁石 a magnet ;〈方位を測るための〉a (pocket) compass ¶棒[馬蹄形]磁石 a bar [horseshoe] magnet. 文例⇩

ししゃごにゅう 四捨五入 ¶四捨五入する round (off (to the nearest whole number) / 小数点第3位以下を四捨五入する round (5.362) off to two decimal places. 文例⇩

ししゃも〔魚〕a smelt.

ししゅ 死守 ¶死守する《文》defend to the last [to the death] ; defend desperately ; fight hard in defense (of) ;《文》die hard.

ししゅ 詩趣 ¶詩趣のある poetic(al) ; 詩趣に乏しい have no [hardly any] poetry (in it) ;《文》be prosaic.

じしゅ¹ 自主 ¶自主(的)の independent ;《文》autonomous ;〈主動的〉active / 自主的に independently ; of one's own free will ;《act》on one's own judgment / 自主的外交 an autonomous [independent] foreign policy / 自主管理 self-management / 自主規制 self-imposed control (on) ; self-regulation / 自主権 autonomy / 自主講座 a student-initiated course / 自主性 autonomy ;《文》independency ; (one's) independence (of mind) / 自主独立 (sovereign) independence / 自主防衛 autonomous defense.

じしゅ² 自首 ¶自首する give oneself up (to the police) ; surrender oneself (to the police).

ししゅう¹ 死臭 the smell of a dead body.

ししゅう² 刺繍 embroidery ; needlework ;〈模様〉an embroidered design [pattern] ¶刺繍する embroider 《a pattern on a dress, one's initials on a handkerchief》; do embroidery 《on》/ 手[機械]で刺繍をした hand-[machine-]embroidered / 金糸で花鳥を刺繍した帯 an obi embroidered with birds and flowers in gold thread / 刺繍糸 embroidery thread / 刺繍台[わく] an embroidery frame.

ししゅう³ 詩集 a collection of poems ; collected poems ; an anthology (名詩選)¶テニスン詩集〔書名〕(The) Poetical Works of Tennyson.

じしゅう¹ 四十 forty ¶第40 the fortieth / 40倍の[に]《文》fortyfold / 40代の人 a person in his forties / 四十七士 the forty-seven Ronin.

じしゅう² 始終 from beginning to end ; all the time [way] ;〈いつも〉always ;《文》at all times [hours] ;《口語》forever ;《文》ever ;〈たびたび〉very often ;《文》frequently ;〈絶えず〉constantly ; continually. 文例⇩

じしゅう 自習[修] private study ; self-teaching ¶自習[修]する study by [for] oneself ;〈予習する〉prepare one's lessons / 自習時間 (private) study hours / 自習室 a study room [hall] / 自修英文典〔書名〕English Grammar Self-Taught.

じじゅう¹ 自重 empty weight ; tare ; dead load ; one's [a vehicle's] own weight.

じじゅう² 侍従 a chamberlain ;《英》a gentleman in waiting ¶侍従長 the Grand Chamberlain.

しじゅうから〔鳥〕a (Japanese) great tit ; a tit.

しじゅうしょう[そう] 四重唱[奏]《音楽》a quartet(te).

しじゅうはって 四十八手〔相撲〕the forty-eight tricks of sumo wrestling ;〈一般的に〉all the tricks (of).

ししゅく 私淑 ¶私淑する《文》adore sb (in one's heart) ; look up to sb as one's model ; be

---

true. 科学者は1つの真理を獲得するためにできるだけたくさんの事実を収集する。The scientist collects as many facts as he can to get at a truth. | 彼は事実上その会社の社長である。He is virtually [practically] the head of the company. | He is the head of the company in all but name. | その改訂版は事実上、別の新しい本だと言ってよい。The revised edition is to all intents and purposes a new book. / 事実は小説よりも奇なり。Fact [Truth] is stranger than fiction. / 諺

じじつ² 時日が迫っている。We are pressed for time.

ししゃ² この事故で多数の死者を出した。Many lives were lost in the accident. / 死者50人以上を数えた。Fatalities numbered more than fifty.

じしゃく 磁石は鉄を引きつける。Magnets attract iron.

ししゃごにゅう 3.76 を小数点以下2桁で四捨五入すると 3.8 になる。3.76 rounded off to one decimal place is 3.8.

じしゅう² そうするように始終言って聞かしている。I keep telling him to do that. / 旅行中始終あの人が一緒だった。He accompanied me all through my journey.

しじゅく　strongly influenced 《by》.
しじゅく　私塾 《keep, run》 a private school.
じじゅく　自粛 self-imposed control 《on trade practices》; self-discipline[-control] ¶自粛する practice self-control; 《文》 voluntarily refrain 《from making exorbitant profits》 / 自粛値段 voluntarily regulated prices.
ししゅつ　支出 expenses; (an) outlay; 《文》 expenditure; outgoings ¶支出する pay; 《文》 defray; 《文》 disburse; 《文》 expend; put out / 支出高[額] the expenditure; 《文》 the amount expended [disbursed].
しじゅほうしょう　紫綬褒章 a Purple Ribbon Medal.
ししゅんき　思春期 puberty; adolescence ★ puberty は生殖が可能になる年齢を言う。米国では男は14歳, 女は12歳と法律で決めている州が多い。adolescence は puberty から成年までの期間を言う。¶思春期の adolescent; 《文》 pubescent / 思春期の少年 a boy at puberty / 思春期に達する reach 《文》 attain, arrive at》 puberty.　　　　　　　　　　　　「tion.
ししょ　支署[所] a branch (office); a substaししょ[2]　司書 a librarian　¶司書教育を受ける be trained in librarianship.
しじょ　子女 ⇒こども　¶良家の子女 children from good homes; children [young men and women] from [《文》 of] good [respectable] families.
じしょ[1]　地所 land; a piece [plot] of land; <宅地> a lot (of ground); <所有地> an estate (大地所); property in land　¶地所付き売り家 a house and lot for sale.
じしょ[2]　自署 ¶自署する sign (one's name); 《文》 autograph.
じしょ[3]　辞書 a dictionary　¶辞書を引く refer to [go to, 《文》 consult] a dictionary; look 《a word》 up in a dictionary. 文例⇩
じじょ[1]　次女 one's second daughter.
じじょ[2]　侍女 a waiting maid; a lady in waiting.
ししょう[1]　支障 《文》 a hindrance; an obstacle; 《文》 an impediment; a difficulty　¶支障をきたす hinder; 《文》 impede; obstruct; be [《文》 constitute] an obstacle 《to》.
ししょう[2]　私消 embezzlement [《文》 misappropriation] 《of public funds》　¶私消する embezzle [《文》 misappropriate] 《public property》.
ししょう[3]　師匠 a master; a mistress (女); <先生> a teacher; an instructor　¶踊りの師匠 a dancing master [mistress, teacher].
しじょう[1]　史上 ¶史上に名をとどめる go

down in history; 《文》 be immortalized in history ¶史上に例を見ない 《文》 be unparalleled [unexampled] in history.
しじょう[2]　市場 a market; a mart　¶市場を見付ける[開拓する] find 《文》 cultivate, open up] a market 《for one's products》 / 市場に出す put [《文》 place] 《goods》 on the market / 市場に出る[出ている] come onto [be on] the market / 外国[海外]市場 a foreign [an overseas] market / 国内市場 the home [domestic] market / 中央卸売り市場 the central wholesale market / 市場開発 market development; opening up new markets [the market] / 市場価格 a market price [rate] / 市場価値 market value / 市場経済 the market economy / 市場性 marketability / 市場性のある marketable / 市場占有率 a (market) share / 市場操作 market operations [manipulation] / 市場調査 market research (特に製品の販売前の); marketing research (広く市場開発のための) / 市場分析 (a) market analysis.
しじょう[3]　至上 ¶至上の supreme; highest / 至上命令 《口語》 (be) an absolute must; 《哲》 a categorical imperative.
しじょう[4]　至情 one's genuine [deep, sincere] feeling [《文》 sentiment]; sincerity　¶至情を吐露する 《文》 lay one's true heart bare; 《文》 express one's deep-felt sentiment [sincere opinion]. 文例⇩
しじょう[5]　私情 personal feelings [《文》 sentiment, 《文》 consideration]　¶私情にとらわれないで 《文》 regardless of [unbiased by] one's personal feelings; impartially.
しじょう[6]　紙上　¶紙上に[で] on paper; in print; <新聞で> in the newspaper / 紙上身の上相談欄 a personal advice column.
しじょう[7]　試乗 ¶試乗する have a test ride [trial run]; test (a car); give (a car) a test run (試運転).
しじょう[8]　詩情 《文》 poetic(al) sentiment ¶詩情をそそる 《文》 awaken one's lyre; 《文》 stir one's poetical imagination; appeal to the poet in one / 詩情豊かな (a person) full of poetic sentiment; 《a place》 which calls up in one's mind a host of poetical associations.
しじょう[9]　誌上 ¶誌上で in the magazine.
じしょう[1]　自称 ¶自称の self-appointed [《文》-styled]; 《文》 self-professed; would-be / 自称する call [《文》 style] oneself (a poet); 《文》 profess oneself 《to be》 / 自称詩人 a would-be poet / 自称哲学者 a self-styled philosopher. 文例⇩

じしょ[3] その単語は僕の辞書に出ていない。That word is not (given) in my dictionary.
しじょう[4] 彼らはいずれも愛国の至情に燃えていた。All of them were full of intense patriotic fervor.
じしょう[1] その名は自称松平であった。Matsudaira was the name he went by.
じじょう[1] 10の自乗は100である。The square of 10 is 100. | Ten squared is [makes] a hundred. / どんな数を自乗すると12,321になるか。What number multiplied by itself makes 12,321? / 引力は距離の自乗に比例して減少する。The force of gravity decreases [varies inversely] with the square of the distance.
じじょう[2] 元来, 河川にはかなりの自浄力がある。Under natural conditions, rivers have very considerable powers of self-cleansing.

じじょう[3] どういう事情で君は会社をやめたんですか。Why did you leave the company? / 家庭の事情でやむなく退学しなければならなかった。I had to leave school for family reasons. / 私が行くことは事情が許さない。Circumstances do not permit me to go. / 我が国では全く事情が違う。Conditions are [The situation is] quite different in this country.
ししょうしゃ 幸いに死傷者は一人

じしょう² 事象 《文》a phenomenon 《pl. -na》.
じじょう¹ 自乗［二乗］《数》a square 《a number》; multiply 《a number》by itself / 自乗根 a square root. 文例⇩

じじょう² 自浄 〖自然の自浄作用〗the self-cleansing action of nature;《生物》biological purification. 文例⇩

じじょう³ 事情 《文》circumstances; conditions; the situation ; the state of things [affairs]; reasons ¶ どんな事情があっても in any circumstances [event] / 事情の許す限り as far as circumstances permit / 事情を詳しく話す give [tell] all the details ; 《文》give a detailed account 《of an event》; put *sb* into the picture / 政界の事情に通じている be well informed on [about] political affairs / こういう事情だから in [under] these circumstances ;《文》such being the case ; things being what they are / 事情やむなく under unavoidable circumstances ; through force of circumstances / アメリカ事情 American affairs / 《文》things American / 住宅事情 the housing situation. 文例⇩

じじょうぎ 持将棋 a drawn game of *shogi*.
ししょうじ 指小辞 《文法》a diminutive.
じじょうじばく 自縄自縛 ¶ 自縄自縛に陥る be caught in *one's* own toil ;《文》lose *one's* freedom of action as a result of *one's* own actions.

ししょうしゃ 死傷者 casualties ; the killed and (the) wounded [injured] ¶ 多数の死傷者 《suffer》heavy [many] casualties / 死傷者名簿 a casualty list ; a list of casualties.
ししょうせつ 私小説 a novel [story] depicting the author's private life;《ドイツ語》an Ich-Roman ; an 'I novel '.
ししょく 試食 ¶ 試食する sample ; taste ; try / 試食会 a food tasting ; a sampling party.
じしょく 辞職 resignation ¶ 辞職する resign 《as president of the university》; resign 《from》 *one's* office [position]; go out of office / 辞職願い has been accepted.
じじょでん 自叙伝 an autobiography ⇒じてん.
ししょばこ 私書箱 a post-office box (略: P.O.B., POB).
シシリー Sicily (Island).
ししん¹ 私心 selfishness ;《文》a selfish motive ; 《文》self-interest (利己) ¶ 私心のない unselfish ;《文》disinterested ; fair ¶ 私心を捨てて from [driven by] unselfish [disinterested] motives.
ししん² 私信 a private note [letter].

ししん³ 使臣 an envoy ; an ambassador (大使); a minister (公使) ¶ 各国の使臣 the foreign representatives ;《外交団》the diplomatic corps.
ししん⁴ 指針 〈磁石の〉a compass needle ;〈計器の〉a needle ; an indicator ; a pointer ; an index ;〈手引き〉a guide 《to》;〈指導方針〉a guiding principle 《in *one's* life》; a guideline 《for governmental action》¶ 明日への指針 a guide into tomorrow.
じしん¹ 私人 a private individual [citizen] ¶ 一私人の資格で《文》in *one's* private [individual] capacity.
じしん² 詩人 a poet ; a poetess (女) ¶ 詩人肌である have something of the poet in *one* ; be something of a poet ; have [《文》be of] a poetic turn (of mind).
じしん¹ 自身 *one's* self; oneself; itself ;《文》self ¶ 自身で *oneself* ; by [for] *oneself* ; in person / 私自身の on my own. 文例⇩
じしん² 自信 self-confidence ¶ 自信がある, 自信を持つ be confident 《of, that...》; have confidence 《in oneself》; be sure 《of, that...》/ 自信がない have no confidence 《in oneself》; lack [have no] self-confidence; be not sure 《of, that...》/ 自信のある confident; self-confident; self-assured / 自信を得る［がつく］gain (self-)confidence / 《文》acquire confidence [faith] in *oneself* / 自信満々として with complete [abundant] self-confidence / 自信過剰 overconfidence 《in *one's* own ability》. 文例⇩
じしん³ 地震 an earthquake (shock); an earth tremor ¶ 海底地震 a submarine [an undersea] earthquake / 大地震 a big [《文》severe] earthquake / 地震学 seismology / 地震学者 a seismologist / 地震観測所 a seismological [seismograph] observatory ; a seismographic (warning) station / 地震計 a seismograph ; a seismometer ; an earthquake recorder / 地震国 a country with frequent earthquakes / 地震帯 an earthquake zone / 地震対策 anti-earthquake procedures [measures] / 地震地帯 a seismic zart [zone, belt] / 地震波 a seismic [an earthquake] wave. 文例⇩

しんけい 視神経 《解》the optic [visual] nerve.
しずい¹ 歯髄 《解》the dental pulp.
しずい² 雌蕊 《植》a pistil.
じすい 自炊 ¶ 自炊する cook *one's* own food ; do *one's* own cooking / 自炊設備 《a room with》cooking facilities.
しすう¹ 指数 《経済・数》an index (number);《数》an exponent ¶ 指数関数《数》an exponential

---

もなかった. Fortunately there were no casualties. / 列車が脱線して多くの死傷者を出した。 The train was derailed, causing a large number of casualties.
じしょく 彼は辞職を許された。 His resignation has been accepted.
じしん¹ 私自身はいやではないのです。 Personally I don't dislike it.
じしん² 彼はなかなか自信が強い。 He has great confidence [faith] in himself. / 私はあまり自信がない。 I am not too sure of myself. / 僕は水泳には自信がない。 I am not much of a [not a good] swimmer. / I am not much good at swimming. / 彼は自分の力に充分自信を持って試験に臨んだ。 He took the examination with every confidence in his own ability. / 今度の小説は彼の自信作であったが, 売れ行きはかんばしくなかった。 He was confident of the merits of his new novel, but it did not sell as well as he had expected.
じしん³ 地震が起こった［あった］. An earthquake occurred. / 今朝大きい地震があった。 We had [There was] a strong earthquake this morning. / 日本は地震が多い。 Earthquakes are frequent in Japan. / あのビルは去年の地震でひどく損壊した。 That building was badly damaged in the earthquake last year.

(function). [文例⇩]

しすう² 紙数 〈紙面〉 space ¶紙数に限りがあるので 《文》 owing to limited space ; for want [lack] of space.

しずか 静か ¶静かな quiet ; silent ; calm ; still ; 《文》 placid ; 《文》 serene ; peaceful ; 《文》 tranquil ; gentle ; soft ; slow / 静かな物腰 gentle [graceful] manners / 静かな口調で話す speak in a quiet [an unruffled, a calm, 《文》 an equable] (tone of) voice / 静かに quietly ; silently ; calmly ; still ; 《文》 serenely ; peacefully ; gently ; softly ; slowly / 静かにしている keep quiet [still] ; 《文》 be silent / 静かになる ⇨しずまる / 「静かに」という合図をする signal [make a signal] 《with *one's* hand》 for silence. [文例⇩]

しすぎる し過ぎる do too much ; overdo ; go too far [《文》 to excess] ; do *sth* more than is good for *one* ¶仕事をし過ぎる work too hard ; overwork (*oneself*) / 倹約し過ぎる carry [take] economy too far [《文》 to excess].

しずく 滴, 雫 a drop ¶滴が垂れる drip ; trickle ; fall in drops / 涙の滴 a tear(drop).

しずけさ 静けさ stillness ; silence ; quiet(-ness) ; calm ; peace ; 《文》 serenity ¶静けさを求めて山に登る 《文》 seek quiet on the mountain / 夜の静けさを破る break the stillness [silence] of the night. [文例⇩]

しずしずと 静々と quietly ; calmly ; 《文》 composedly ; slowly ; gracefully.

ジステンパー 〈犬の病気〉 (canine) distemper ¶ジステンパーの済んだ健康な小犬 a healthy puppy that is over distemper.

ジストマ 〔動〕 a fluke ; a distoma ¶肝臓ジストマ a liver fluke / ジストマ病 distomiasis ; fluke infestation.

ジスプロシウム 〔化〕 dysprosium.

じすべり 地滑り a landslide ; 《英》 a landslip ; (a) dislocation (断層) ¶総選挙での地滑り的勝利 《the Liberal Democrats'》 landslide victory [win] in the general election.

ジスマーク a JIS mark ★JIS は Japanese Industrial Standard (日本工業規格)の略.

しずまる 静[鎮]まる go [《文》 become] quiet [still] ; calm [quiet] down ; 《文》 be lulled (なぎる) ; 《文》 subside ; die down ; go down (波が) ; 《文》 abate (風・痛み・騒ぎなどが) ; 〈鎮圧される〉 be suppressed ; be put down ; 《文》 be quelled ¶静まり返る be [become] as silent as the grave.

しずむ 沈む sink ; 《文》 be submerged ; go down (to the bottom) ; go under ; 〈太陽が〉 set ; go down ; 〈地盤が〉 fall [cave] in ; 〈気分が〉 feel depressed [low, down] ; be in low spirits ; 《口語》 have the blues ; 《文》 be downcast ¶沈んだ 〈陰気な〉 《文》 melancholy ; gloomy ; glum ; 〈考え込んでいる〉 《文》 pensive ; 〈悄然とした〉 depressed ; downhearted ; crestfallen ; dejected ; downcast / 沈みかけた太陽 a declining [setting] sun / 沈む球 〔野球〕 a sinker. [文例⇩]

しずめる¹ 沈める sink ; send to the bottom (of the sea) ; put under water ; 《文》 submerge 《beneath the sea》 ¶船に穴をあけて沈める scuttle 《a vessel》.

しずめる² 静[鎮]める quiet ; 《文》 still ; calm ; soothe ; 《文》 appease ; pacify ; 〈痛みなどを〉 relieve ; 《文》 allay ; 《文》 alleviate ; 《文》 assuage ; 《文》 mitigate ; 〈鎮圧する〉 suppress ; put down ; quell ¶心を静める calm down ; settle [《文》 compose] *oneself*. [文例⇩]

しする 資する contribute [《文》 be contributory] to ; 《文》 be conducive to ; help ; be helpful to ; 《文》 be instrumental in ; make for. [文例⇩]

じする 辞する ⇨じきょ, じしょく, じたい⁴ ¶どんな犠牲も辞さない be prepared [ready, willing] to sacrifice anything.

しせい¹ 市制 city organization [system] ¶市制を敷く reorganize 《a town》 as a city.

しせい² 市政 municipal [city] government [administration].

しせい³ 至誠 sincerity ; 《文》 devotion ¶至誠をもって heart and soul ; with all *one's* heart ; 《文》 in all sincerity ; wholeheartedly ; 《文》 faithfully.

しせい⁴ 私製 ¶私製の private / 私製はがき an unofficial postcard ; a postcard ★postcard は絵葉書まで含めて官製・私製の区別なく使われる. 英国には官製葉書はあるが, あまり使われないので, postcard と言えば私製葉書のことと思うのがむしろ普通である.

しせい⁵ 施政 administration ; government ¶施政方針 an administrative policy ; 〈政党の〉 a party line / 施政方針演説 a speech on *one's* administrative policies / 沖縄施政権の日本への返還 return of the administrative rights over Okinawa to Japan.

しせい⁶ 姿勢 《文》 (a) posture ; a pose ; a position ; 〈態度〉 an attitude ¶姿勢がいい[悪い] have good [poor] posture / 楽な姿勢で座る sit in a comfortable position / 射撃の姿勢をとる take up the stance for firing the gun / 姿勢を正す straighten *oneself*. [文例⇩]

じせい¹ 自生 〔生物〕 natural [spontaneous] growth ¶自生する grow wild [naturally] / 自

しすう¹ たとえば 10,000 を 10^4 と書くように指数を用いて簡単な形に書き直せる数はごくわずかしかない. Very few numbers can be put into simple exponential form, as, for instance, 10^4 for 10,000.

しずか 静かに. Hush! | Keep quiet! / まあお静かに. Don't get so excited, please. | Please be quiet. / 帰省するたびに都会では味わえない静かな気分になる. Whenever I return home in the country, I enjoy a quietness which I can never find in town.

しずけさ 部屋はもとの静けさに帰った. Silence settled down once more upon the room.

しずむ 君は今日はばかに沈んでいるね. You look awfully miserable [《口語》 blue] today. / 彼は物思いに沈んでいた. He was deep in thought.

しずめる² 騒ぎをようようのことで鎮めた. We could barely manage to get them quiet [to calm them down] again.

しする この協約は世界の平和に資するところが大であろう. This agreement will contribute great-

生の native; indigenous.
じせい² 自制 self-control; 《文》self-restraint ¶自制する control [restrain] oneself; check oneself 《from doing》/ 自制力を失う lose (one's) self-control; lose control of oneself; let oneself go.
じせい³ 自省 〈反省〉⇒はんせい¹; 〈内省〉《文》introspection.
じせい⁴ 自製 ¶自製の homemade; 《a boat》made by oneself;《chairs》of one's own making.
じせい⁵ 時制《文法》a tense ¶時制の一致 sequence of tenses.
じせい⁶ 時勢 the trend [《文》tendency] of the times; 〈世相〉(the) conditions of life;《時代》the times;《文》the day;《文》the age ¶今の時勢に《文》in these times [days] / 時勢に遅れる[遅れている] fall [be] behind the times / 時勢に逆らう go against the times; swim [row, go] against the current / 時勢に伴って行く keep pace with [keep up with, keep abreast of] the times;《文》swim with the current. 文例⇩
じせい⁷ 辞世 a farewell poem composed on the eve of one's death; one's swan song.
じせい⁸ 磁性 magnetism; magnetic properties ¶磁性を与える magnetize / 磁性を帯びた magnetic 《steel rods》; magnetized / 磁性を失う lose its magnetism / 磁性を除く demagnetize.
しせいかつ 私生活 one's private life ¶私生活に立ち入る dig [nose] into sb's private life.
せいし[じ] 私生子[児] an illegitimate child;《文》a child born out of wedlock.
しせいだい 始生代［地質］the Archeozoic era.
しせき¹ 史跡 a historic spot [site]; a place of historic interest ¶史跡に富む《文》be rich in historic remains [associations].
しせき² 歯石［歯科］tartar; dental calculus ¶歯石を取る scrape [remove] tartar from sb's teeth; scale sb's teeth.
じせき¹ 次席〈すぐ下の位の官吏〉an official next in rank; 〈部課長に次ぐ役〉an assistant chief clerk; a deputy ¶次席にいる〈席順が〉sit next (to); 〈位が〉rank next (to).
じせき² 自責 self-reproach[-reproof] ¶自責の念にかられる have [suffer from] a guilty conscience; have twinges [pangs] of conscience;《文》feel remorse (for what one has done) / 自責点［野球］an earned run (略: e.r., er).
じせき³ 事績 an achievement;《文》a deed.
しせつ¹ 私設 ¶私設の private.
しせつ² 使節 an envoy; an ambassador; a delegate ¶使節として行く go on a mission / 使節団 a mission; a delegation.

しせつ³ 施設 an institution; an establishment; 〈孤児や老人などの〉a home; 〈設備〉equipment;《文》facilities; 〈生活を快適にする〉《文》amenities ¶施設の子供たち children living in a home; inmates of an orphanage / 〈孤児などが〉施設に収容される be placed in [sent to] a home 《for orphans》/ 軍事施設 military installations / 娯楽施設 facilities for recreation. 文例⇩
じせつ¹ 自説 one's own view [opinion] ¶自説をあくまで主張する[曲げない] persist in [stick to] one's views [opinion] / 自説を捨てる[曲げる] give up [change] one's views.
じせつ² 時節〈時代〉the times; 〈季節〉the season; the time of (the) year; 〈時機〉time; 《文》due time; 〈機会〉an opportunity; a chance ¶時節が来れば in (due) time;《文》in (due) course of time; when the time comes / 時節を待つ watch for a chance; bide one's time / 時節はずれの out of season;《文》unseasonable / 時節柄《文》in view of the times. 文例⇩
しせん¹ 支線〈鉄道の〉a branch line; a feeder (line).
しせん² 死線〈生死にかかわる危機〉a life-or-death crisis ¶死線を越える survive a life-or-death crisis. 文例⇩
しせん³ 私線〈鉄道〉a private [nongovernmental] (railroad) line.
しせん⁴ 視線 one's eyes [《文》gaze]; a glance; a look ¶視線を避ける avoid sb's eye [gaze] / 視線をそらす look away (from);《文》avert [turn] one's eyes (from) / 視線を向ける look (at); 《文》turn one's eyes [gaze] (on). 文例⇩
しぜん 自然 nature ¶自然の natural; native; wild; 〈生得の〉《文》inborn;《文》inherent; 〈自然発生の〉《文》spontaneous; 〈飾らない〉《文》unstudied; unaffected / 自然の法則 a law of nature / 自然の成り行きに任せる leave sth to take its own course; leave sth to chance / 自然を歌った詩 a nature poem; nature poetry / 自然に naturally; instinctively;《文》spontaneously; 〈自動的に〉automatically; 〈ひとりでに〉by itself; of its own accord / 自然に近い near-natural 《conditions》/ 自然に帰る return to nature / 自然に接して暮らす live close to nature / 自然に反する be unnatural; be against [《文》contrary to] nature / 大自然《文》(Mother) Nature / 自然愛好家 a nature lover / 自然界 (the world of) nature; the natural [physical] world / 自然界の均衡 the balance of nature / 自然科学 natural science; the natural sciences / 自然環境 the [a] natural [physical]

---

ly to the peace of the world.
しせい⁶ 姿勢が悪いよ、背筋を伸ばして！ Don't slouch! Sit up straight!
じせい⁶ 時勢のしからしむるところでやむを得なかった。There was no countering the trend of the times. / あの頃とは時勢が違う。Things are not what they used to be. / 時勢が変わった。Times have [are] changed.
しせつ³ 彼は幼くして孤児になり、施設に入れられた。He was left an orphan very young and placed in [put into] an institution.
じせつ² 時節到来した。The time has come (at last). / ベストを尽くして、あとは時節を待ちたまえ。Do your best and leave the rest to Heaven. / 時節が来ればどちらが正しいかわかる。Time will show which is right.
しせん² 幾度か死線を越えて来た人。He has been face to face with death several times.
しせん⁴ 2人の視線が合った。Their eyes met. / 全員の視線が私に集

environment / 自然現象 a natural phenomenon / 自然主義[主義者] naturalism [a naturalist] / 自然主義的 naturalistic / 自然状態で in *its* natural state / 自然状態では《文》in (a state of) nature ; under natural circumstances [conditions] / 自然承認 automatic approval / 自然食品 natural foods / 自然食品店 a natural food store / 自然人〘哲〙a natural man ;〘法〙a natural person / 自然数〘数〙a natural number / 自然崇拝 nature worship / 自然選択[淘汰]〘生物〙natural selection / 人口の自然増加率 a population's rate of natural increase / 自然増収 a natural increase in revenue / 自然治癒 self-healing / 自然地理学 physical geography / 自然破壊 destruction of nature / 自然発火[発生] spontaneous combustion [generation] / 自然描写 a description of nature / 自然法 (the) natural law / 自然保護 conservation [preservation] of nature ; protection of the natural environment ; wildlife conservation / 自然保護運動 a (nature-)conservation movement / 自然保護区 a wildlife sanctuary ; a nature reserve. [文例⇩]

じせん[1] 自選 ¶自選する select《the best》out of [from among] *one's* own works / 自選集 the author's (own) selection / 自選詩集を編む make a selection of *one's* own poems.

じせん[2] 自薦 ¶自薦する put *oneself* forward ; recommend [offer] *oneself*《for the post》. [文例⇩]

じぜん[1] 次善 the second best ¶次善の策 the second best policy.

じぜん[2] 事前 ¶事前の《文》before the fact ;《文》prior《notice》; advance《warning》/ 事前に in advance ; beforehand / (日米安全保障条約関係の)事前協議 prior consultation / 事前検閲 precensorship / 事前工作 preparatory operations / 選挙の事前運動 preelection campaigning ; precandidacy propaganda / 事前通告 (an) advance notice ; (a) previous notice.

じぜん[3] 慈善 charity ;《文》benevolence ¶慈善の, 慈善的 charitable ;《文》benevolent ;《文》philanthropic / 慈善を行なう give to charity ;《文》practice [perform an act of] charity ; do good / 貧しい人々に慈善を施す《文》render aid to the poor in charity ;《文》give alms to the poor / 慈善音楽会 a charity concert / 慈善家 a charitable [《文》benevolent] person ; a philanthropist / 慈善興行 a benefit (performance) / 慈善事業 charitable [《文》philanthropic] work ; charities / 慈善心《文》a charitable spirit / 慈善団体 a charitable institution [organization] ; (organized) charities / 慈善なべ a 'charity pot' (for collecting public contributions). [文例⇩]

しそ[1] 始祖 the founder ;《文》the originator ;《文》the father ;《文》the progenitor ¶人類の始祖 the progenitor of the human race. [文例⇩]

しそ[2]〘植〙a perilla ; a beefsteak plant.

しそう[1] 死相 [文例⇩]

しそう[2] 志操《文》《a man of》principle ;《文》constancy (節操) ¶志操堅固である《文》be faithful to *one's* principles ;《文》be firm of purpose.

しそう[3] 使嗾 ¶使嗾する ⇨ そそのかす.

しそう[4] 思想《文》thought ; an idea ; an ideology ¶思想の健全な《文》sound-thinking / 思想の自由 freedom of thought / 新旧思想の衝突 a conflict between new and old ideas / 思想家《文》a thinker ;《文》a man of thought / 思想界《文》the world of thought / 思想改造運動 a thought-reform campaign / 思想傾向《文》a tendency [trend] of thought / 思想史 the [a] history of ideas [thought] / 思想戦 ideological warfare / 思想取り締まり thought control ; censorship of ideas. [文例⇩]

しぞう 死蔵 ¶死蔵する hoard (up) ; keep *sth* idle.

しそうのうろう 歯槽膿漏〘歯科〙pyorrhea alveolaris ; pyorrhea / 歯槽膿漏の pyorrheal.

しそく 四則〘数〙the four (fundamental) rules of arithmetic.

しぞく[1] 士族 a descendant of a *samurai* ¶士族の商法 amateurish business methods.

しぞく[2] 氏族〘史〙a family ; a clan ;〈古代ローマの〉a gens《*pl.* gentes》¶氏族社会 a clan society [community].

じそく 時速 ¶時速 120 マイル《at》120 miles an hour [per hour] ; 120 mph [m.p.h.] / 時速 60 キロ《at》60 kilometers an hour [per hour] ; 60 km/h.

じぞく 持続 ¶持続する last ;《文》endure ; hold out [up] ;〈支える〉《文》maintain ; keep

---

まった. All eyes were turned [fixed] on me.

じぜん 東京からは自然が日に日に失われてゆく. Nature is being destroyed in Tokyo day by day. / こうなるのは自然だ. It was only natural that it should come to this. / 自然に振る舞うようにすればもっと人から好かれるのだが. If he would just be himself, he would be more popular. / 同法案は 6 月 19 日午前零時に国会で自然承認になった. The bill automatically passed through the Diet at midnight on June 18th.

じせん[2] そのポストには自薦他薦様々の候補者があった. There were several candidates for the post, some of whom had no recommendation but their own.

じぜん[3] 収益は慈善事業に寄付する予定だ. The proceeds are to be devoted to charity.

しそ[1] ヒポクラテスは医学の始祖といわれる. Hippocrates is called the father of medicine.

しそう[1] 彼の顔には死相が現われていた. The shadow of death was on his face.

しそう[4] 彼の思想はどうやら枯渇してしまった. His ideas have apparently dried up. / 彼の思想はその時代よりも 100 年進んでいた. His ideas were a century ahead of the times [his age]. / 彼らは直接あるいは間接に西欧思想の影響を受けた. They were under the direct or indirect influence of Western thought. / 白秋の詩には思想性がないと言う人もある. Some people say that Hakushu's poetry lacks depth (of thought).

じそんしん なぜもっと自尊心を持たないのか. Why do you hold yourself so cheap? | Why don't you have more self-respect? / 私にだって自尊心があります. I

しそくじゅう 四足獣 a quadruped; a four-footed animal.

しそくなし 仕損ない ⇨ しぞんじ.

しそちょう 始祖鳥 《古生物》 an archaeopteryx; an archaeornis.

しそん 子孫 a descendant; 《集合的》《文》posterity; 《文》offspring; 《文》progeny ¶ 子孫を残す 《survive and》leave offspring / 子孫に伝える hand [go] down to one's posterity / …の子孫である be descended from…; be a descendant of…; 《文》trace one's descent to…/ …の子孫と称する 《文》claim descent from….

しそんじ 仕損じ a failure; a blunder; 《文》an error; a miss; a slip.

しそんじる 仕損じる fail; make a mistake; blunder; bungle; make a mess [《米俗》a ball-up, 《英俗》a balls-up] (of the job); 《米俗》ball [《英俗》balls] sth up; do sth badly.

じそんしん 自尊心 self-respect; pride; 《文》self-esteem ¶ 自尊心のある self-respecting; proud / 自尊心を傷つける hurt [wound] sb's pride / 自尊心を抑える swallow [pocket] one's pride.

した¹ 下 〈下部〉the lower part; the bottom; the foot; the base ¶ 下の 《文》under; lower; 《文》subordinate 〈下位の〉/ 下の級 the lower classes / 下の部屋 a downstair(s) room / 下を見る[向く] look down / 下に[へ] under; 《文》beneath; below; 〈下方に〉down(ward) / 坂の下に at the foot of a slope / 階段の下に at the foot [bottom] of the stairs / 下に置く put [《文》lay] down / 《人の》下で働く work under sb / 下から5行目 the fifth line from the bottom / 下へ降りる go [come] down; go [come] downstairs 〈階下へ〉/ 下へも置かずにもてなす treat sb very courteously to sb; 《文》extend every courtesy to sb; 《文》receive sb with a hearty welcome / give sb a warm reception / (H₂O の ₂ のような) 下付き記号 《数字, 文字》a subscript. 文例❶

した² 舌 a tongue; 〈鈴や鐘の〉a clapper; 〈楽器の弁〉a reed ¶ 舌が回らない[もつれる] be tongue-tied; 《文》be unable to speak distinctly; one's speech is slurred (酔っている時な ど); have an impediment in one's speech (言語障害) / 舌の先 the tip of the tongue / 舌を出す put [《文》thrust] one's tongue out (at); loll (out) its tongue (犬が) / 舌を巻く be astonished (at, by); 《文》marvel (at); be speechless with admiration (at) / 〈発音がむずかしくて〉 舌をかみそうな 《口語》crackjaw 《medical words》; 《口語》jawbreaking 《foreign names》/ 回らぬ舌で言う slur (one's words); lisp (out) (子供が). 文例❶

しだ 〈植〉a fern ¶ しだの茂った ferny.

じた 自他 文例❶

したあご 下顎 the lower jaw; the underjaw.

したい¹ 死体 a dead body; a corpse; a cadaver (解剖用の); a carcass (動物の) ¶ 死体の(ような) 《文》cadaverous / 死体を遺棄[発掘]する abandon [exhume] a dead body / 死体となって発見される be found dead / 死体解剖 dissection of a dead body; necrotomy / 〈検死のための〉an autopsy; a post-mortem (examination) / 死体仮置場 a mortuary; a morgue. 文例❶

したい² 肢体 the arms and legs; 《文》the limbs; 《文》one's members ¶ 肢体不自由児 a physically handicapped child.

したい³ 姿態 〈姿〉a figure; a person; 〈身振り〉a pose.

-したい want [《文》wish] to do; would [should] like to do; be anxious [eager] to do ¶ …したいような気がする feel like doing; feel [be] inclined to do / なんでも自分のしたい放題にする have everything one's own way. 文例❶

しだい 次第 〈順序〉order; 〈事情〉《文》circumstances; the state of things; 〈即刻〉as soon as…; directly… ¶ 式次第 the order of [program for] the ceremony / ご都合つき次第 《文》at your earliest convenience / 天気になり次第 on the first fine day; as soon as it clears up / 到着次第 as soon as one arrives; 《文》on one's arrival / …次第である depend on (the weather); 《文》be dependent on; hang on; 《文》rest [lie] with / さような次第で 《文》such being the case / 次第に gradually; by degrees; little by little / 次第に暑くなる grow hotter and hotter. 文例❶

しだい² 私大 a private college [university].

じたい¹ 自体 〈自分〉oneself; 〈そのもの〉itself.

---

have my pride.

した¹ 下を見よ. 〈本などの注意書き〉See below. / 僕は下を向いたまま立っていた. I stood with my eyes cast down. / あの人は下であなたを待っています. He is downstairs waiting for you. / 犬はテーブルの下から出て来た. The dog came out from under the table. / 彼は僕よりも1級下でした. He was one [a] grade below me.

した² 舌が荒れている. My tongue is rough. / カレーの辛いのは舌をひりひりさせる. Hot curry burns your tongue. / 2度としまいと言ったのに, その舌の根もかわかぬうちに誓いを破った. His promise never to do it again was hardly out of his mouth when he broke it. / 君の博識には舌を巻くよ. Your erudition amazes me.

じた 氏が憲政の守り神であることは自他共に許すところである. He is universally recognized as a guardian of constitutionalism. / 彼が我が国一のゴルファーであることは, 自他共に許すところである. He is acknowledged (to be) the best golfer in this country.

したい¹ 死体の引取人がいない. No one has claimed the body. / 死体はまだ発見されない. The body has not been recovered yet.

-したい 僕らが向こうへ着くまでには晴れるようにしたい. I hope it will clear up before we get there. / 特にそうしたい訳ではない. I don't particularly want to do it.

しだい¹ 事の次第はこうです. This is how it happened. / まあざっとこんな次第です. There you have, in brief, the facts of the case. / 飛行機の便のあり次第立ちます. I'll take the first available flight. / 品物を受け取り次第金を払います. I will pay on receipt of the goods. / どんな仕事でもあり次

じたい² 字体 the form of a character; 〈活字の〉type; print ¶明瞭な字体で書く write clearly; print (the address) clearly ((in capital letters)) ★ print は筆記体でなく活字体で書くこと.

じたい³ 事態 the situation; (the state of) things [affairs] ¶容易ならぬ事態 a serious situation / 事態を改善する improve matters [the situation] / 事態を見てから see [find out] how the land lies. 文例▶

じたい⁴ 辞退 ¶辞退する 《文》decline 《an offer》; refuse to accept. 文例▶

じだい¹ 地代 (a) ground [land] rent. 文例▶

じだい² 次代 the next [(文) coming, rising] generation ¶次代の人々 the new [rising] generation of young men [of citizens] / 日本の次代を担う人々 《文》the rising generation who are to bear the destiny of Japan on their shoulders.

じだい³ 時代 〈時期〉a period; an epoch; an age; an era; 〈一代〉a generation; 〈時世〉the times ¶時代のついた old-looking; antique(-looking) / 時代をさかのぼる[くだる] go back [come down] in time / 時代を超越した timeless / 時代に逆行する swim against the current / 時代に先んじる be ahead ((in)) in advance] of one's time / 時代に遅れる, 時代遅れになる get [go] out of date; fall behind the times; become old-fashioned / 時代遅れのout-of-date; old-fashioned / 明治時代の the Meiji era / 徳川時代に in the Tokugawa period; in the days of the Tokugawa shogunate / 学校時代に in one's school days / 時代と共に進む keep up [pace] with the times; swim with the tide / 時代と共に変わる change with the times / 時代感覚 sensitivity to [a sense of] the times / 時代区分 the division (of history) into periods; periodization (in history) / 時代劇 a period drama [film] / 時代錯誤 an anachronism / 時代錯誤の anachronistic / 時代小説 a historical [period] novel / 時代色 a period flavor / 時代精神 the spirit of the times; 《ドイツ語》the Zeitgeist / 時代離れした生活をしている be out of touch with the times / 時代物の家具 antique furniture; a period piece of furniture. 文例▶

じだいしゅぎ 事大主義 《文》worship of the powerful; toadyism; flunk(e)yism ¶事大主義者 a toady; a flunk(e)y.

したう 慕う long for; 《文》yearn for [after]; be attached to; 《文》sigh [pine] for; 《文》love sb dearly; adore; 《文》make an idol of sb ¶亡き母を慕う 《文》sorely miss one's dead mother / 後を慕って...へ行く follow sb to 《France》. 文例▶

したうけ 下請け a subcontract ¶下請けする subcontract / 下請けに出す subcontract; sublet / 下請け工場 a subcontract factory / 下請け仕事 subcontracted work / 下請け人 a subcontractor.

したうち 舌打ち ¶舌打ちする click [cluck] one's tongue / 舌打ちの音 tut.

したえ 下絵 a rough [preliminary] sketch; 〈図案〉a design; 〈壁画などを描くための実物大の〉a cartoon ¶下絵を描く make a preliminary sketch [a cartoon] (of).

したおし 下押し 《相場》a sag; a drop; a fall ¶下押し気配 a downtrend; 《文》a downward tendency.

したおす 下押す 《相場》sag; drop; fall; decline; go down.

したおび 下帯 a loincloth; a waistcloth.

したがう 従う 〈服従する〉obey; 《文》be obedient to; 〈屈服する〉《文》yield [submit] to; give in to 《sb's view》; 《応じる》《文》comply with 《a request》; 《文》accede to 《a demand》; accept; 〈守る〉keep; 《文》observe; 《文》abide by 《the rule》; 《文》conform to 《the customs》; 〈随従する〉follow; 《文》be guided by; 〈忠告に〉take; act on [go by] 《sb's advice》 ¶時勢に従う go with the tide / 党の方針に従う follow [toe] the party line / 従わない disobey 《sb's orders》; 《文》be disobedient to 《one's superior》; defy 《the law》. 文例▶

したがえる 従える 〈伴う〉《文》be attended by; have sb with one; 〈征服する〉⇒ せいふく³.

したがき 下書き ¶下書きする make a draft [rough copy] of; draft / 文章に下書きしないで書く write offhand.

したがって 従って 〈だから〉《文》accordingly; 《文》consequently; 《文》hence; 《文》therefore; so (that); 〈...に準じて〉《文》according to [as]; 《文》in accordance with 《the regulations》; 《文》in compliance with 《sb's request》; 〈...するにつれて〉as; 《文》in proportion to [as] ¶文明が進むに従って as civilization progresses; with the progress of civilization / ...の言葉に従って at sb's suggestion [《文》instance].

-したがる want [《文》wish, 《文》desire, long] to do; be eager [anxious, impatient] to do ¶けんかをしたがる be eager [spoiling] for a fight / ...と交際したがる 《文》long for sb's companionship.

引き受けるよ. I'll undertake anything that comes my way. / 値段は品物次第です. The price varies with the quality. / 彼は細君の言いなり次第だ. He is tied to his wife's apron strings. / これを決定するのは君次第だ. The decision is up to you. | It is up to you to decide. / 生徒は教師次第である. A student is what a teacher makes him. / ご注文次第でいかようにもこしらえます. It will be made any way you wish [according to your instructions]. / 夜が次第に長くなる. The nights are gaining on the day.

じたい³ 事態が好転した. Things took a favorable turn. / 容易ならぬ事態になった. Things have come to a serious pass. / それで事態がはっきりした. Now we know where we are.

じたい⁴ せっかくのご親切ですがその仕事は辞退させて頂きとう存じます. Thank you for your kindness in offering me the job, but I must ask to be excused from it.

じだい¹ 彼には毎月地代の収入が3万円あった. He collected 30,000 yen in ground rent every month.

じだい³ 今は実力の時代だ. We live in an age where ability counts (for everything). / 彼らは

したぎ 下着 underwear; 《文》 underclothing; underclothes; 〈婦人の〉 lingerie; 《口語》 undies (★ 女性用語).
したく 支[仕]度 arrangements; 《文》 preparations; 〈身支度〉 (an) outfit; equipment; 《口語》 a getup ¶ 支度する 《文》 prepare 《for》; make arrangements [preparations] 《for》; get 《*oneself* [*sth*]》 ready; 〈身支度をする〉 get dressed; 《文》 dress (*oneself*) / 食事の支度をする get a meal ready / 支度金 an outfit allowance / 支度部屋 a dressing room (芝居などの); a retiring room. [文例⇩]
じたく 自宅 *one's* (own) house; *one's* home ¶ 自宅にいる be (at) home / 自宅にいない be not (at) home; be away from home; be out / 自宅で教授する give private lessons at *one's* home.
したくさ 下草 undergrowth.
したげいこ 下稽古 (a) rehearsal; a run-through ¶ 下稽古する rehearse; have a run-through [rehearsal] 《of a play》.
したけんぶん 下検分 ¶ 下検分する 《文》 make a preliminary examination [inspection] 《of》.
したごころ 下心 a secret intention [《文》 desire]; 《文》 an ulterior [underlying] motive ¶ 下心がある have [《文》 harbor] a secret intention; 《文》 have some private end in view; have an ax to grind.
したごしらえ 下拵え preparations; 《文》 preliminaries; 《文》 preliminary arrangements ¶ 下ごしらえをする make preparations; arrange [prepare] *sth* beforehand; pave the way 《for》.
したざわり 舌触り ¶ 舌触りがいい be soft and pleasant on [to] the tongue / 舌触りが悪い be rough and unpleasant on [to] the tongue.
したじ 下地 〈基礎〉 groundwork; foundations; 〈下準備〉 preparations; 《文》 prearrangements; 〈素養〉 a grounding; 〈素質〉 《文》 (an) inclination; the making(s); 〈下塗り〉 the undercoat(ing) ¶ 下地ができている 〈素養がある〉 《文》 be well grounded 《in》; have a good grounding 《in》.
しだし 仕出し 〈出前〉 (outside) catering; supplying food [dishes] to order; 〈映画などの「その他おおぜい」〉 walk-on parts [roles] ¶ 仕出しをする supply dishes to order; cater 《for a party》 / 仕出し屋 a [an outside] caterer (人); a caterer's shop (店).
したしい 親しい close; familiar; friendly; 《文》 intimate (★ intimate は「異性と性交渉を持つほどに親しい」の意味を表わすので注意を要する) ¶ 親しい友人 a close [great, bosom] friend; 《米口語》 a buddy / …と親しい, 親しくする be on good [friendly] terms with…; be friends with… / 親しくなる make friends 《with》; get [《文》 become] friendly [familiar] 《with》; become intimate 《with》. [文例⇩]
したじき 下敷き 〈机の上に置く〉 a desk pad; 〈ノートの〉 a celluloid sheet (laid under writing paper) ¶ 下敷きになる be buried [crushed, caught, held] under *sth* / …を下敷きにして 〈手本にして〉 《文》 on the model [pattern] of…; 《文》 after the model of….
したしみ 親しみ familiarity; friendship; 《文》 intimacy; 《文》 affection ¶ 親しみがある be attached 《to》; be familiar [《文》 acquainted] 《with》; be no stranger 《to》.
したしむ 親しむ 《文》 become [be] intimate [familiar] 《with》 ⇨ したしい ★; get to know *sb* better; 〈常用する〉 《文》 take 《wine》 habitually; 《文》 make a habitual use of 《a medicine》 ¶ 自然に親しむ 《文》 commune with nature / 藤村の文章に親しむ spend a lot of *one's* time reading Toson's works; be fond of reading Toson / 酒に親しむようになる take to drink [drinking] / 親しみやすい人 an amiable [approachable] person; an easy person [a person who is easy] to talk to [to get on with] / 親しみにくい人 a difficult person to talk to; a person who is not easy to talk to [to get on with]. [文例⇩]
したじゅんび 下準備 ¶ 下準備する 《文》 make preliminary arrangements 《for》; prepare for *sth* beforehand; pave the way 《for》.
したしらべ 下調べ ¶ 下調べをする 《文》 make a preliminary investigation [inquiry] 《into》; 《文》 examine beforehand / 明日の授業の下調べをする prepare [go over] *one's* lessons for tomorrow.
しだす し出す ⇨ はじめる.
したそうだん 下相談 ¶ 下相談をする 《文》 hold preliminary negotiations [talks] 《with》; arrange 《a matter》 beforehand; 《文》 make preliminary arrangements 《for》.
したたか 〈強く〉 severely; hard; 《beat》 soundly; 〈多く〉 《文》 much ⇨ たくさん [用法]; 《drink》 heavily ¶ したたか小言を食う be given a good telling-off [scolding] / したたかもの a real tough customer; 〈ずるい奴〉 a wily old fox; 〈悪人〉 a vicious man.
したためる 〈記す〉 write; put [《文》 take] down; draw [make] up 《a document》; 〈食べる〉 take; have; eat.
したたらず 舌足らず ¶ 舌足らずの 〈口のよく回らない〉 lisping 《children》; 〈不充分な〉 lame 《expressions》. [文例⇩]

時代の要求に応じることを忘れている. They are making no effort to meet the needs [demands] of the times. / こんな時代がこれから先長く続くだろうか. Will things go on like this much longer?
したう 彼は生徒から深く慕われている. He is the idol of his pupils.
したがう 彼らは上からの統制に容易には従わない連中です. They are not easily amenable to control from above.
したく 会の支度は全く整った. Everything is ready for the party. / 海外出張の支度金として 50 万円受け取った. I have been given 500,000 yen to fit myself out for my mission abroad.
したしい 2 人はとても親しい間柄です. They are close [great] friends. | They are very friendly with each other. / 親しき中にも礼儀あり. The courtesies matter, even between friends.
したしむ 野鳥に親しむ人の少ないのは残念なことだ. It is too bad that there are so few people who take an interest in wild birds.
したたらず 舌足らずの英語しか使

したたり 滴り dripping; a drop; a trickle; a dribble.

したたる 滴る drip; drop; trickle; dribble; fall in drops ¶水の滴る海水着 a dripping wet bathing suit / 緑滴るばかりの fresh green.

したつづみ 舌鼓 ¶舌鼓を打つ smack *one's* lips;《文》smack appreciative lips《over a dish》; enjoy《*one's* favorite dish》/ 舌鼓を打って食べる eat with great gusto [relish].

したっぱ 下っ端 an underling ¶下っ端役人 a petty [minor] official.

したづみ 下積み ¶下積みになっている〈荷物が〉be in the lower layer;〈人が〉《口語》be (at) the bottom of the heap [pile, pecking order]; live [《文》remain] in obscurity;《文》hold a lowly [an ignominious] position《in a firm》/ 下積みの生活から抜け出そうと努力する try hard to escape from *one's* life as an underling.

したて[1] 下手 ¶《囲碁・将棋で》下手を持つ play as an inferior player; give *sb* a handicap《of four stones》《in a game of go》/ 下手に出る《文》assume a humble [subservient] attitude toward *sb* / 下手投げ《相撲》an underarm throw;《野球》underhand throwing [delivery].

したて[2] 仕立て〈裁縫〉sewing; tailoring;〈仕立て方〉a cut ¶仕立てがいい[悪い]be well [badly, poorly,《文》ill] cut [tailored] / 特別仕立ての列車 a special train / 最新流行の仕立てである be in the latest style / 仕立てて物がする sew《a garment》; tailor《男物の》(★ただし, 女物でも上着や厚い生地のスカートなら tailor と言う) / 仕立しおろしの newly-made《suits》; brand-new / 仕立て屋〈洋服の〉a tailor;〈婦人服の〉a dressmaker. 文例₃

したてる 仕立てる〈裁縫する〉make《clothes》; tailor;〈仕立ててもらう〉have《*one's* coat》tailored; get《*one's* clothes》made;〈準備する〉《文》prepare;〈養成する〉train; bring up;〈差し向ける〉send;《文》dispatch;〈偽りの人物に〉pass *sb* off《as》¶列車を仕立てる form [dispatch] a train / 外交官[法律家]に仕立てる train *sb* for the diplomatic service (the legal profession) / 仕立て直す make [do] over《a coat》; alter [《文》renovate]《a garment》;〈人にしてもらう〉have《*one's* dress》renovated / 仕立て直しのドレス a made-over [《文》renovated] dress.

したどり 下取り trade-in; part exchange ¶下取りする take《a car》as a trade-in《on a new one》/ 下取りに出す trade《*one's* car》in《for a new one》/ 下取り価格 a trade-in price / 下取り品 a trade-in. 文例₃

したなめずり 舌舐めずり ¶舌なめずりする lick *one's* lips.

したぬり 下塗り ¶下塗りする put the undercoat(ing)《on》; give the first coat《of paint to》.

したば 下歯 the lower teeth.

したばえ 下生え undergrowth; underbrush.

したばき 下穿き underpants《男性用》; briefs《男女両用》; panties《女性用》.

じたばた ¶じたばたする(kick and) struggle; wriggle. 文例₃

したばたらき 下働き〈仕事〉《文》subordinate work;〈人〉《文》an underservant;《文》an underworker; an assistant ¶下働きをする work under *sb*.

したはら 下腹 the belly; the stomach;[解]the abdomen; the abdominal region.

したび 下火 ¶下火になる〈火事が〉be under control; burn low [down]; die down;〈衰える〉decline; go down. 文例₃

じたまご 地卵 eggs of local production.

したまち 下町 the traditional shopping, entertainment and residential districts《of Tokyo》★「下町」を downtown と訳すのは正しくない. downtown は米語で「市の中心部」である.「下町」はむしろ東京の一定の区域を称するなかば固有名詞とみなしていたほうがよい.

したまわる 下回る be less [lower] than; be [fall] below ¶《結果が》予想を下回る《文》fall short of *one's* expectation(s).

したみ 下見 ¶下見をする《文》make a preliminary inspection [examination]《of》; look *sth* over [examine *sth*] beforehand / 下見もせずに買う buy *sth* sight unseen.

したみ(いた) 下見(板) a clapboard; a weatherboard;〈集合的〉weatherboarding; clapboarding ¶下見を付けた weatherboarded《houses》.

したむき 下向き ¶下向きになる look down [downward]; lower *one's* eyes [《文》gaze];〈相場が〉begin to decline [go down];《文》show a downward tendency / 下向きに置く place《a cup》with the bottom up; turn《a glass》over [upside down].

したやく 下役 a minor employee; an underling;《文》a subordinate (official) ⇒したっぱ ¶下役である《文》hold a subordinate position; work [be placed] under *sb*.

したよみ 下読み preparation; a rehearsal《脚本の》¶下読みする prepare《*one's* lessons》; run through《a book》beforehand; rehearse《a play》.

じだらく 自堕落 ¶自堕落な sluttish《女が》;〈道徳的に〉《文》morally lax; debauched;〈だらしがない〉slovenly;《文》slatternly《女が》.

したりがお したり顔 ¶したり顔をする look triumphant [smug, pleased with *oneself*]/したり顔に triumphantly;《文》with a triumphant air; smugly.

しだれざくら 枝垂れ桜 a weeping cherry.

しだれやなぎ 枝垂れ柳 a weeping willow.

したわしい 慕わしい dear;《文》beloved.

したん[植]a red sandalwood.

しだん 師団 a division ¶師団長 a division(al) commander / 師団司令部 the division(al) headquarters.〔circles.

しだん 詩壇 the world of poetry; poetical

えない. I cannot express myself satisfactorily in English.

仕立て[2] この服の仕立てが気にくわない. I don't like the cut of this coat.

下取り テレビ一銘柄にかかわらず下取り致します.〈店頭の表示〉Any make of TV accepted for trade-in. / 車がさびていると, 下取り価格が下がります. If your car is rusty its trade-in value will fall [you won't get a good trade-in price for it].

じたばた 今さらじたばたしても始まらない. It is no use struggling

じだん 示談 settlement out of court; a private settlement ¶示談にする settle 《a case》 out of court; settle 《a matter》 without going to law; 《文》 bring 《a dispute》 to an amicable settlement / 示談金 a composition.
したんかい 試胆会 ⇨きも(きもだめし).
じだんだ 地団駄 ¶地団駄踏んで悔しがる stamp (*one's* feet) with frustration [《文》 vexation, 《文》 chagrin].
しち[1] 七 seven ¶第7 the seventh / 7倍 seven times; 《文》 septuple. [文例⇩]
しち[2] 死地 ¶死地に赴く[を脱する] go into [escape from] the jaws of death.
しち[3] 質 〈質物〉 a pawn; a pawned article; an article placed in pawn; a pledge ¶質を受け出す take [get] *sth* out of pawn; redeem [recover, take out] a pawned article / 質に入れる pawn 《a watch for 10,000 yen》; put *sth* in pawn; 《米口語》 hock 《*one's* watch》; 《米口語》 put *sth* in hock / 質に入っている be in pawn [《米口語》 in hock] / 質に取る take *sth* in pawn [as a pledge] / 質草 an article for pawning [to pawn] / 質権 《establish》 the right of pledge / 質流れになる 〈人が主語〉 have *one's* pawn forfeited; 〈物が主語〉 pass to a pawnbroker [be sold off] as unredeemed / 質流れ品 a forfeited [an unredeemed] article / 質札 a pawn ticket / 質屋 a pawnshop; 《米口語》 a hock shop; 〈人〉 a pawnbroker. [文例⇩]
じち 自治 self-government[-rule]; 《文》 autonomy ¶自治(団)体 a self-governing body; 〈地方自治体〉 ⇨ちほう / 学生自治会 a students' self-government association; a student council / 自治権 the right of self-government; 《acquire》 autonomy / 自治省[大臣] the Ministry [Minister] of Home Affairs / 自治能力 power of [capacity for] self-government; 《文》 autonomous ability / 自治領 a dominion.
しちがつ 七月 July (略: Jul.).
しちかっけい 七角形 a heptagon.
しちごさん 七五三 a festival for children of three, five and seven years of age.
しちごちょう 七五調 ¶七五調の 《a verse》 in seven-and-five syllable meter.
しちじゅう 七十 seventy; 〈寿命〉 《文》 threescore (years) and ten; 《文》 the Biblical span ★寿命についてのこれらの句は気取った言い方で, 普通には「70歳」は seventy でもちろんよい ¶第70 the seventieth / 70代の老人 a septuagenarian.
しちじゅうしょう[そう] 七重唱[奏] 〖音楽〗 a septet(te).
しちてんばっとう 七転八倒 ¶七転八倒の苦しみをする toss about [writhe] in agony [《文》 excruciating pain].
しちならべ 七並べ 〖トランプ〗 sevens 《単数扱い》; fan-tan.
しちふくじん 七福神 the Seven Deities [Gods] of Good Fortune [Luck].
しちみとうがらし 七味唐辛子 a mixture of red pepper and other spices.
しちめんちょう 七面鳥 a turkey. [文例⇩]
しちめんどう 七面倒 ⇨めんどう.
しちゃく 試着 ¶試着する try 《a suit》 on / 試着室 a fitting room.
しちゅう[1] 支柱 a prop; a strut; a stay; a support; a post ¶一家の支柱 《文》 the mainstay [prop and stay] of a family / 支柱を施す prop [shore] 《a house》 up; provide 《a structure》 with supports / 支柱や張り線をめぐらした strut-braced 《biplanes》.
しちゅう[2] 市中 ¶市中に in the city [streets] / 市中銀行 a city [commercial] bank.
しちゅう[3] 死中 ¶死中に活を求める find a way out of a fatal situation.
シチュー (a) stew ¶シチューにする stew / ビーフ[タン]シチュー beef [tongue] stew; stewed beef [tongue] / シチューなべ a stewpan; a casserole (土・ガラス製の).
しちょう[1] 支庁 a branch office.
しちょう[2] 市庁 a municipal [city] office ¶市庁舎 a city hall.
しちょう[3] 市長 a mayor ¶市長の職[任期] mayoralty / 京都市長 the Mayor of Kyoto / 市長選挙 a mayoral election.
しちょう[4] 思潮 《文》 a current [trend] of thought ¶近代文芸思潮 the trend of modern literature / 現代思潮 contemporary thought [ideas] / 時代思潮 the spirit of the times.
しちょう[5] 視聴 ¶視聴覚 the visual and auditory senses / 視聴覚教育[教材] audiovisual education [aids] / 視聴者 a (TV) viewer; 〈集合的〉 an audience / 視聴率 a program [an audience] rating / 視聴率調査 《make》 an audience rating survey; 〈営業としての〉 a television rating service / 視聴率の一番高いテレビ番組 the top-rated TV program.
しちょう[6] 試聴 an audition 《of new recordings》 ¶試聴室 an audition room / 試聴テストをする audition; give an audition 《to》.
しちょう[7] 輜重 ¶輜重兵[隊] a transport soldier [corps].
じちょう[1] 次長 a vice-director; a deputy chief.
じちょう[2] 自重 《文》 prudence; 《文》 caution ¶自重する 〈自愛する〉 take care of *oneself*; 〈慎む〉 《文》 be prudent; 《文》 be circumspect. [文例⇩]
じちょう[3] 自嘲 《文》 self-ridicule[-contempt] ¶自嘲的に 《文》 self-contemptuously; 《say *sth*》 as if *one* is [was, 《文》 were] laughing at *oneself*.
しちょうそん 市町村 cities, towns and villages; municipalities ¶市町村合併 merging [consolidation] of municipalities.
しちょく 司直 《文》 the judicial authorities; the court(s) ¶司直の手が伸びる 《文》 the arm of

---

now.
したび ボウリングの人気はすっかり下火になった. The popularity of bowling has died down.
しち[1] その利益は7分3分に分けよう. Let's split the profit seventy-thirty.
しち[3] 質はとうの昔に流れてしまったろう. That will have been sold off long ago as an unredeemed pledge [as unredeemed].
しちめんちょう 七面鳥が鳴くのを聞いた. I heard a turkey gobble.
じちょう[2] 今後いっそう自重しなくてはならない. We must be more

しちりん 七輪 a portable clay cooking stove.
じちん 自沈 ¶自沈する〈船が主語〉be scuttled; sink;〈人が主語〉sink [scuttle] 《one's own》boat).
じちんさい 地鎮祭 the Shinto ceremony of purifying a building site; a ceremony of laying the cornerstone (of).
しつ¹ 室 ⇨ へや ¶8号室 room (number) eight. 文例⇩
しつ² 質 quality ¶質がいい[悪い]《文》be of good [bad] quality;《文》be superior [inferior] in quality / 質を落とす lower [debase] the quality (of) / 質をよくする improve the quality (of) / 質を落として量を増す improve quantity at the expense of quality / 質的にも量的にも both in quality and in quantity. 文例⇩
じつ 実〈真実〉the truth; the reality;〈誠意〉sincerity;《文》fidelity; good faith;《文》faith;〈数〉a dividend〈被除数〉; a multiplicand〈乗数〉/ 実の〈本当の〉true; real / 実の息子 one's own son / 実のある sincere;《文》faithful;《文》truehearted / 実のない insincere;《文》faithless / 実をあげる〈実現する〉bring sth to fruition;《文》realize;〈実行する〉act up to (one's principles) / 実を捨てて実を取る ⇨しっ¹ /実に〈真に〉truly; really;《文》indeed;〈実際〉in fact;〈確かに〉surely; to be sure;〈甚だ〉very; (very) much / 実に,実を言えば really, in reality; to tell the truth; as a matter [《文》in point] of fact; the fact (of the matter) is....
しつい 失意〈失望〉disappointment; despair;《文》loss of hope; a broken heart;〈不遇〉bad [《文》hard] luck;〈文》ill fortune;〈文》adversity / 失意の境涯にある《文》be in adverse circumstances / 失意のどん底にある be in the depths of despair / 失意の人 a disappointed man / 失意の時代 one's dark days. 文例⇩
じついん 実印 one's registered [legal] seal.
しつうはったつ 四通八達 ¶四通八達している〈道路が主語〉run in all directions / 四通八達

の地 a key junction; the focus of the arteries of traffic; a center of traffic.
じつえき 実益〈実収〉an actual [a net] profit;〈実利〉practical [real] use;《文》utility; usefulness ¶実益がある be profitable; be useful. 文例⇩
じつえん 実演 (a) stage performance; a stage [live] show;〈実験・授業などの〉a (public) demonstration [presentation] ¶実演する act [perform] on the stage; give a demonstration (of).
しつおん 室温 (at) room temperature.
しっか 失火 an accidental fire. 文例⇩
じっか 実家 one's parents' home [house];《文》one's parental home.
じっかい 十戒 the ten commandments ¶モーゼの十戒 Moses' Ten Commandments.
じつがい 実害 actual harm; actual damage; real loss. 文例⇩
しつがいこつ 膝蓋骨〈解〉a kneecap; a kneepan; a patella (pl. -s, -lae).
しっかく 失格 ¶失格する be disqualified (from doing, for a post); be eliminated (out of, from); be put out of the race (競走で) / 失格者 a disqualified person; a nonqualifier (競技の).
じつがく 実学 practical science [learning].
じつかぶ 実株〈株式〉a real stock.
しっかり(と)〈堅く〉firmly; fast;〈文〉securely;〈strongly; tightly;〈はっきり〉definitely;《文》decidedly ¶しっかりつかまる hold on tight to sth / しっかり結ぶ tie [fasten] sth tightly; make (the rope) fast (to the ring) / しっかりした strong〈character〉; solid〈structure〉; firm〈foundations〉; steady〈steps〉;〈信頼できる〉reliable; trustworthy; hardheaded;〈判断の〉sound / 考えのしっかりした levelheaded;《文》sound-thinking / しっかり者 a person of strong [firm] character. 文例⇩
しっかん 疾患 a disease; an ailment (軽い); a (heart) complaint; (chest) trouble; a disorder.
じっかん 実感 a feeling of reality [that sth is real] ¶実感がわく〈事が主語〉seem real to one;〈人が主語〉feel that it [sth] is real [is really happening] / 実感を込めて with feeling. 文例⇩

prudent in the future. / 前途有望の君だ,大いに自重したまえ。You have a bright future before [ahead of] you. You must take good care of yourself.
しつ¹ (ホテルなどの)902号室におります。I'm in room 902. ★数字は nine o two のように棒読みにする。
しつ² あの店は経営者が変わったら料理の質がガタ落ちした。The quality of food at that restaurant has dropped sharply since it changed hands. / 量よりも質だ。Quality matters more than quantity.
じつ 実は彼の誤解であった。In

fact it was (all) a misunderstanding on his part. / 僕は実にばかなことをした。I did something very foolish.
しつい 彼は失意のうちに世を去った。He died a brokenhearted man.
しつうはったつ この地方は鉄道が四通八達している。There is a whole network of railroads in this district.
じつえき それは趣味と実益とを兼ねている。It is useful as well as beautiful. |《文》It combines utility [benefit] with beauty. / そんなものがはたして実益があるかどうかは疑わしい。I doubt if such

a thing is of any practical use.
しっか 火事は失火ではなく放火だった。The fire was not an accident, but an act of arson.
じつがい 別に実害はあるまい。Actually, it will do no harm.
しっかり(と) しっかりしろ!〈元気を出せ〉Cheer up! | Pull yourself together! |〈頑張れ〉Come on! | Play up! |〈気をつけろ〉Look out! | まあ,しっかりやりたまえ。君ならきっとうまくやるだろう。Well, keep your chin up. I'm sure you'll do a good job. / 酒に酔ってもしっかりしている。He keeps his head even after a few drinks. / 父は息を引き取るまで

しつかんせつ 膝関節 a knee joint.

しっき[1] 湿気 damp(ness); moisture; humidity ¶湿気の多い damp; moist; humid; moisture-laden ((air)) / 湿気のない dry; free from moisture / 湿気を取り除く dehumidify. 文例⇩

しっき[2] 漆器 lacquer(ed) [japan] ware; lacquer (work).

しつぎ 質疑 a question; an inquiry; 〈国会での〉an interpellation; 《英》a parliamentary question ¶質疑応答 questions and answers / (講演の後などの)質疑応答の時間 a question [discussion] period.

じつぎ 実技 practice; practical skill; 〈体育の〉physical culture.

しっきゃく 失脚 《文》a downfall; 《文》a fall ¶失脚する fall from power; lose one's position; be routed. 文例⇩

しつぎょう 失業 unemployment ¶失業している be unemployed; be out of work [《文》employment]; have no job / 失業する lose one's job [work, 《文》employment]; be thrown out of work / 失業者 an unemployed person; a jobless man; a person who has no job; out-of-work people; 〈総称〉the unemployed [jobless] / 失業対策 a measure against unemployment; a relief measure for the unemployed / 失業対策の道路修理計画 a make-work road repair program / 失業対策事業 a relief program for the unemployed / 失業手当 unemployment pay; an unemployment allowance; 《英口語》the dole / 失業手当を受ける[ている] get [be getting] unemployment benefit; 《英口語》go [be] on the dole / 失業保険 unemployment insurance / 失業問題 the unemployment problem / 失業率 the unemployment rate.

じっきょう 実況 the real [actual] situation [state of things] ¶実況放送 on-the-spot broadcasting; an outside broadcast [telecast (テレビ)]; a running commentary; a ball-by-ball [blow-by-blow, 《米》play-by-play] commentary [account] 《of a sporting event》/ スポーツの実況放送のアナウンサー a sports commentator / 実況放送をする broadcast on the spot; do a commentary 《on a baseball game [boxing match]》.

じつぎょう 実業 〈産業〉industry; 〈商業〉business ¶実業の〈産業の〉industrial; 〈商業の〉business; commercial / 実業につく go into [《文》enter] business / 実業家 a businessman; an industrialist / 実業界 the business world; business circles / 実業学校 a vocational [technical, business] school / 実業評論家 a business commentator.

しっきん 失禁 〖医〗incontinence 《of urine》.

しっく 疾駆 ⇨しっそう[2].

シック 《フランス語》chic; smart; stylish; 《文》tasteful.

しっくい 漆喰 mortar; plaster; stucco (化粧) ¶しっくいを塗る plaster; stucco.

つくす し尽くす do everything possible [imaginable]; 《文》exhaust the possibilities of... ¶ばかの限りをし尽くす do all sorts of stupid things; 《文》commit every sort of folly.

しっくり exactly; like a glove ¶しっくり合う fit nicely [《文》to a nicety, like a glove]; suit one to a T; be perfectly in tune 《with》. 文例⇩

じっくり 《文》without haste; 《文》deliberately; carefully ¶じっくり考える think 《it》over; ponder (on [over]) / じっくりやる take one's time 《over, at》; give oneself (plenty of) time to do [in doing].

しつけ[1] 仕付け 〈着物の〉tacks; tacking; basting ¶仕付けをする baste; tack / 仕付けをとる unbaste; untack / 仕付け糸 tacking thread; basting.

しつけ[2] 仕付け 〈育て方〉breeding; upbringing; rearing; 〈訓練〉training; discipline ¶しつけがいい[悪い] be well [badly] brought up; be well-[not well-, 《文》ill-]bred / 家庭のしつけ home discipline [training] / (幼児の)用便のしつけ toilet training. 文例⇩

しっけ 湿気 ⇨しっき[1].

しつけい 失敬 ¶失敬な rude; 《文》impolite; bad-[《文》ill-]mannered; disrespectful; 〈生意気な〉impudent; impertinent / 失敬な事を言う make insulting remarks 《about sb》/ 失敬する 〈いとまを告げる〉say good-bye 《to》; 《文》take one's leave 《of sb》; 〈盗む〉steal; filch; make off with sth; borrow (無断借用).

じっけい 実刑 《pass》a jail sentence 《on sb》;

しっかりしていました。My father remained lucid to the end. / あの男にはしっかりした所がない。He has no backbone. | He lacks firmness of character.

じっかん この絵は実感が出ていない。This picture is not realistic enough [does not do full justice to the model]. / その出来事の意味が彼にとってはなかなか実感にならなかった。It took time for the events to register in his mind. / 優勝の気持ちはいかがです。—まだ実感がわいてきません。What does it feel like to have won?—Well, it doesn't seem real yet.

しっき[1] 湿気厳禁.《包装表示》Keep dry. | Store in a dry place.

しっきゃく このために結局彼は失脚してしまった。This finally brought about his downfall [proved his undoing].

しっくり 原語の意味にしっくり合わない。It does not convey the exact meaning of the original word. / 2人の間がしっくりいかない。They don't get on [along] well with each other. | Things are not going very well between them. / その考えは僕にはどうもしっくりこない。I don't think much of that (for an) idea.

しつけ[2] 親のしつけ次第で子供はどうにでもなる。Children are what their parents make them. / ジムはいい子だ。家庭でのしつけの良さがわかる。Jim is a good boy. He shows his good home training.

しっけい (会などの後)昨日は失敬. That was a good party yesterday! / ちょっと失敬。Please excuse me (for a moment). / これは失敬。Oh! I beg your pardon. / 今度は失敬します。I wish to be excused this time. / 昨日はせっかく訪ねてくれたのに留守をして失敬した。I am sorry I was out when you came to see me yesterday. / そろそろ失敬しなければ。Well, I must be going now. / 失

imprisonment [penal servitude] without a stay of execution.
じつげつ 日月 〈日と月〉 the sun and the moon; 〈歳月〉 time; days (and months); years ¶長[短]日月 (for) a long [short] period of time. 文例⇩
しつける 仕付ける train; discipline; teach *sb* manners.
しっけん 執権 『日本史』a regent ¶執権政治 (the Hojo) regency.
しつげん 失言 a slip of the tongue ¶失言する make a slip of the tongue; (文) use improper language [words]; (口語) put *one's* foot in *one's* mouth [in it] / 失言を取り消す take back [(文) withdraw, (文) retract] *one's* words [what *one* said].
しつげん 湿原 a bog; a swamp; marshland ¶湿原植物 marsh grasses.
じっけん¹ 実権 (hold) real power(s) ¶実権のない社長 a president in name only. 文例⇩
じっけん² 実験 experimentation; laboratory work (実験室における操作); 〈1回の〉 an experiment; a test ¶実験をする experiment (on, in); do (carry out, make, (文) conduct) an experiment [a test] (on); put *sth* to the test / 実験的に experimentally; by way of experiment; on an experimental basis / 追実験 a check experiment / 動物実験 experiments with [on, using] animals / 実験劇場 (an) experimental theater / 実験工場 a pilot [demonstration] plant / 実験式〖化〗an empirical formula / 実験室 a laboratory / 被実験者 (an experimental) subject / 〈新兵器などの〉実験場 a proving ground; a test site / 実験装置 an experimental device; experimental equipment [gadgetry] / 〈ミサイルなどの〉実験地域 a testing area / 実験農場 a pilot [an experimental] farm / 実験材料 (a) material for experiments; (an) experimental material / 実験材料にされる be used as a guinea pig 《for a new treatment》 / 実験動物 an experimental animal. 文例⇩
じつげん 実現 (文) realization; (文) actualization; (文) materialization ¶実現する put (a plan) into practice; turn (the dream of flight) into reality; make (a dream) come true; (文) bring (an idea) to fruition; (文) realize; (文) actualize; (文) materialize / 〈計画したことが〉come off; materialize / 〈予言などが〉come true. 文例⇩

しつこい 〈執拗な〉 persistent; insistent; stubborn; 〈つきまとって離れない〉 clinging; gluey; 〈うるさい〉(文) importunate; pestering (children); 〈せんさく的な〉 inquisitive; (口語) nos(e)y; 〈濃厚な〉 too rich; over-rich; fatty; cloying (food) ¶しつこく persistently; (文) tenaciously; (文) importunately / しつこく質問する pester [plague] *sb* with questions. 文例⇩
しっこう¹ 失効 ¶失効する (文) lapse; (文) become null and void; lose (*its*) effect.
しっこう² 執行 (文) execution; (文) enforcement; (文) performance 〈遂行〉 ¶執行する carry out; (文) execute; (文) enforce; (文) perform; (文) conduct; (文) exercise; put into effect / 執行委員会[機関] an executive committee [organ] / 執行者 an executor / 執行部 the executives.
じっこう¹ 実行 〈実践〉(文) practice; action; 〈遂行〉(文) execution; (文) fulfillment〈履行〉¶実行しうる[しがたい] (文) practicable [impracticable]; (文) feasible [unfeasible] / 実行する practice; put (*one's* ideas) into practice; carry out (a plan); (文) translate (a program) into action; (文) execute / 主義を実行する act up to (*one's*) principles / 約束を実行する carry out [(文) fulfill] *one's* promise / 実行委員(会) an executive committee / 実行予算 the working budget / 実行力のある人 a man of action. 文例⇩
じっこう² 実効 (文) practical effect; (文) efficacy ¶実効を現わす prove (to be) effective (in practice); (文) produce material results.
しっこうゆうよ 執行猶予 a stay of execution; probation (保護観察) ¶執行猶予になる be granted a stay of execution; be given a suspended sentence 《of two years》. 文例⇩
しっこく¹ 桎梏 ¶しっこくを脱する (文) break [shake off] the fetters [bonds] (of); (文) throw off [break away from] the yoke (of).
しっこく² 漆黒 漆黒の jet-[coal-]black (hair); pitch-dark[-black] (night).
しつごしょう 失語症 〖医〗aphasia ¶失語症患者 an aphasic.
じっこん 昵懇 ¶昵懇な familiar; (文) intimate ⇒ したい ★ / 昵懇な間柄である be familiar [intimate] (with); be on familiar terms (with).
じっさい 実際 〈事実〉 the truth; a fact; 〈実地

敬なことを言うな. None of your cheek! / Watch your tongue!
じつげつ その完成に10年の長日月を要した. It took [required] ten long years to complete.
じっけん¹ あの会社の社長は飾り物で, 実権は副社長が握っている. The president of that firm is a mere figurehead; the business is actually under the control [management] of his son, the vice-president. / 実権は陸軍にあった. The real power rested with [resided in] the army.

じっけん² このシステムはアメリカではすでに実験的に使われています. This system is already in experimental use in the U.S. / それは今のところまだ実験段階です. At the moment it is still in the experimental stage. / 彼らは各種新兵器の実験台にされただけのことだ. They were apparently just used as guinea pigs to test new weapons on.
じつげん 彼の理想は実現されそうもない. His ideal is unlikely to be realized. / ついに彼の少年時代

の夢が実現した. His boyhood dream finally materialized [became (a) reality]. / 宇宙旅行は近く実現されるだろう. Manned space navigation will soon become an accomplished fact. / 夏にヨーロッパへ行くつもりだったが実現しなかった. I had planned to go to Europe for the summer, but it did not come off.
しつこい そんなにしつこく聞くものではない. Don't be so inquisitive. / 入党しろとしつこく言ってくる. He is always after me to

じつざい 実在 《文》 real existence; reality; 《文》 being;〈実在物〉a being ¶実在の real; actual; 《文》 existent ¶実在する (really) exist; be in (actual) existence; 《文》 have being / 実在しない 《文》 unreal; nonexistent / 実在論〖哲〗realism; externalism.

しっさく 失策 《文》 an error; a mistake; a slip (ちょっとした) ¶失策する make a mistake; commit a blunder [an error]; 《文》 err; take a false step. 文例⇩

しっし 嫉視 ¶嫉視する be jealous of sb;《文》regard sb with jealousy;《文》keep a jealous eye on sb.

しつじ 執事 a steward; a butler.

じっし¹ 実子 one's own [《文》true] child.

じっし² 実施 《文》 enforcement ¶実施する put [《文》carry] sth into effect;《文》enforce;《文》execute;《文》implement; put in [into] force; put into practice / 実施される take effect; come into force;《文》be enforced / 実施案 a working plan. 文例⇩

じつじかん 実時間〖コンピューター〗real time ¶実時間処理〖演算〗real-time operation.

じっしつ 実質〈本質〉《文》substance;《文》essence;〈素質〉quality;〈材料〉material ¶実質的な 《文》substantial;《文》essential;《文》material; real; solid / 実質的に, 実質上 《文》substantially; essentially; virtually; practically / 実質賃金 real wages.

じっしゃかい 実社会 the real [actual,《文》workaday,《文》sober] world ¶実社会に出る go out into the world.

じっしゅう 実習 practice 《in》; (an) exercise; (a) drill; training ¶実習する practice; have (practical) training / 実習生 a trainee; a student apprentice; 〈病院の〉an intern.

じっしゅう(にゅう) 実収(入) a real [an actual, a net] income; actual [net] receipts.

じっしゅきょうぎ 十種競技 the decathlon ¶十種競技の選手 a decathlete.

しつじゅん 湿潤 ¶湿潤な wet; damp; moist; humid.

しっしょう 失笑 ¶失笑する ⇨ふきだす.

じっしょう 実証 《文》(an) actual [empirical] proof;《文》corroborative evidence ¶実証する prove;《文》corroborate (a statement); establish (a fact) (by proof);《文》substantiate; verify;《文》demonstrate / 実証的に 《文》empirically / 実証主義〖哲〗positivism.

じつじょう 実情[状] the actual situation [condition(s), circumstances]; the real state of affairs; the true facts; the realities ¶実情は as things [matters] stand; the fact is (that…) /実情調査 fact-finding; a fact-finding inquiry /実情調査委員会 a fact-finding committee.

しっしょく 失職 ⇨しつぎょう.

しっしん¹ 失神 ¶失神する faint; fall unconscious;《文》fall into a swoon;《文》swoon.

しっしん² 湿疹〖医〗eczema.

じっしん 十進 ¶十進法 the decimal system /〈図書の〉十進分類法 the Dewey (decimal) classification.

じっすう 実数〈実際の数〉the actual number;〖数〗a real number.

しっする 失する ¶均衡を失する lose the balance (between supply and demand) / 厳格に失する be too [excessively] strict;《文》be severe to a fault / 時機を失する miss a chance.

しっせい¹ 失政 《文》misgovernment;《文》misrule;《文》maladministration;《文》misadministration.

しっせい² 湿性 ¶湿性の wet / 湿性肋膜炎 wet [moist] pleurisy; pleurisy with (serous) exudation.

じっせいかつ 実生活 real [actual] life; practical life; life in the real [《文》workaday] world.

しっせき 叱責 a scolding;〈口語〉a telling-off; a reprimand;《文》a reproach;《文》(a) reproof ¶叱責する scold;〈口語〉tell sb off;《文》reprove;《文》reproach;《文》berate;《文》castigate;《文》reprimand ⇨ しかる.

じっせき 実績 (actual) results; one's record

---

join his party.

じっこう¹ 彼は口先ばかりで実行力がない. He is all talk and no action.

しっこうゆうよ 彼は懲役2年執行猶予3年の判決を受けた. He was sentenced to two years in prison suspended for three years.

じっさい それは実際あった事です. It actually happened. / 彼はけちだという評判だが, 実際そうだ. He has a reputation as a miser, as indeed he is. / それは実際よりもずっと大きく見える. It appears much larger than life./ この絵は実際を描いたものだ. This picture is drawn from life./ 理論としてはまことに結構だが, 実際問題としてはうまく行くまい. It is all very well in theory, but it won't work out in practice.

しっさく あんな男を信用したのが失策だ. I made a mistake in trusting such a man. / 一塁手の失策で加藤は生還した. Kato reached home on the first baseman's error.

じっし² この法律は今でも実施されている. The law is still in force [effect].

じっしつ 外見よりも実質のよい物を選べ. Choose substance before [over] appearance. / 実質においては大差はない. It is essentially [substantially] the same. | It is the same in its essentials. | この5年間, 世界の木材価格は年々金額にして10.4 パーセント, 実質価格で3.9 パーセントの上昇を示している. During the last five years, the world price of lumber has been rising at an annual rate of

(of performance); achievements; past records ¶実績をあげる give [《文》achieve] satisfactory results; bear fruit / 昨年度の営業実績 business results [performance] for last year / 実績制 a merit system.

しつぜつ 湿舌〘気象〙a wet [moist] tongue.

じっせん[1] 実践 practice ¶実践する practice; put into practice / 実践主義 activism / 実践道徳 practical ethics [morality, morals]. [文例⇩]

じっせん[2] 実戦 actual warfare [fighting]; active service ¶実戦に参加する be in action [actual combat]; be under fire; take part in actual fighting.

じっせん[3] 実線 a solid line.

しっそ 質素 《文》simplicity; 〈倹約〉《文》frugality ¶質素な simple; 《文》austere; homely; plain; modest; 〈倹約な〉《文》frugal / 質素に暮らす live in a simple [small] way; live a simple [frugal] life.

しっそう[1] 失踪 disappearance; absconding (特に犯罪容疑者の) ¶失踪する disappear; run away; abscond; elope / 失踪者 a missing person; a runaway / 失踪宣告 the adjudication of *sb's* disappearance / 失踪届け a report of *sb's* disappearance; a missing person report.

しっそう[2] 疾走 ¶疾走する run at full speed; spank; scuttle; scamper; dash.

じっそう 実相 the facts; 《文》the aspects; the real state of affairs; actual circumstances; reality.

じつぞう 実像〘光〙a real image.

しっそく 失速〘航空〙a stall ¶失速する stall; be stalled; go into a stall.

じっそく 実測 (a) survey; (an) actual survey; (a) survey on the spot [ground]; actual measurement ¶実測する survey; make a survey of 《a forest》/ 実測図 a surveyed map; a measured drawing.

じつぞんしゅぎ 実存主義 existentialism ¶実存主義者 an existentialist.

しった 叱咤 ¶しったする 〈しかる〉 scold; 《文》berate; 〈激励する〉 encourage [spur] 《*sb* to *do*》; 《文》put [set] spurs to *sb* / 三軍をしったする command an army.

しったい 失態 〈失敗〉 a mistake; a blunder; 《文》an error; 《俗》a boo-boo; 《英俗》a boob; 〈不面目〉(a) disgrace; 《文》(an) ignominy ¶失態を演じる commit a blunder [《文》an indiscretion]; 《口語》come a cropper.

じったい[1] 実体〘哲〙substance; an entity ¶実体のある substantial; solid; physical / 実体のない unsubstantial / 実体化する make *sth* substantial; substantiate / 実体論〘哲〙substantialism; noumenalism.

じったい[2] 実態 ⇨じつじょう.

しったかぶり 知ったか振り ¶知ったか振りをする pretend to know (all the answers); act as if *one* knew; 《文》assume an air of wisdom / 知ったか振りをする人 a know-all; a know-it-all / 知ったか振りに《speak》knowingly.

しったつり 執達吏 a bailiff.

じつだん 実弾 〈小銃の〉 a live cartridge; live ammunition; 〈大砲の〉 a loaded shell; 〈比喩的に〉 money ¶実弾射撃 firing [target] practice with live shells [bullets]; 〈小銃の〉 ball-firing; 〈大砲の〉 live-shell shooting [firing].

しっち[1] 失地《the recovery of》(a) lost territory.

しっち[2] 湿地 damp [marshy] ground; a bog; (a) swamp; (a) swampland.

じっち 実地 practice; the practical side 《of a matter》; 〈実際〉 reality ¶実地に practically; in practice; personally / 実地に行なう practice; put *sth* into practice / 実地に経験する have practical experience 《in》/ 実地検証 an inspection of the scene 《of a murder》; an on-the-spot investigation / 実地試験 a practical [field] test / 実地調査[検分] an on-the-spot [on-site] survey; field work [research]; the firsthand investigation 《of social conditions》/ 実地練習[訓練] practice; practical training. [文例⇩]

じっちゅうはっく 十中八九 in nine cases out of ten; nine times out of ten; ten to one; in all probability [likelihood].

じっちょく 実直 ¶実直な steady; honest; trustworthy; 《文》faithful / 実直に steadily; honestly; 《文》faithfully. [文例⇩]

しっつい 失墜 ¶威信[面目]の失墜 loss of prestige / 失墜する 〈失う〉 lose 《*one's* credit with *sb*》; 《文》forfeit 《*sb's* confidence》; 〈落ちる〉 fall 《in public estimation》/ 権力を失墜する fall from power. [文例⇩]

じつづき 地続き ¶地続きの neighboring; 《文》adjoining; 《文》adjacent; 《文》contiguous. [文例⇩]

しつっこい ⇨しつこい.

じっていほう 実定法 the positive law; the law(s).

しつてん 質点〘物〙a material point; a (material) particle ¶質点力学 particle dynamics.

しってん 失点 points [runs] *one* allows *one's* opponent in a game; points lost; penalty points.

10.4% in money terms, and by 3.9% in real terms.

じっせん[1] 理論よりも実践. An ounce of practice is worth a pound of theory.

じっち 実地は理論ほど容易ではない. It isn't as easy in practice as in theory. / 私は実地に経験した事を話しているのです. I speak from experience. / このルールは簡単なようで, 実地に応用する段になるととてもそうではない. This rule may appear simple, but it is far from simple to put into effect.

じっちょく 彼は実直に勤めている. He is a loyal worker.

しっつい 米国は大いに威信を失墜した. The prestige of the United States suffered a severe setback.

じつづき 互いに地続きになっているヨーロッパの国々の気持ちは日本人にはなかなかわからない. It is hard for Japanese to understand the feelings of the Europeans whose countries are adjacent to each other.

しっと 彼は君の幸運をしっとしているのだ. He envies you your good fortune. / しっとに目がくらんで彼女は夫を刺した. Blinded by jealousy [In a fit of jealous rage] she stabbed her husband.

しつど 湿度は現在80. The humidity is 80 per cent at present.

じっと (カメラを向けて)そのまま

しってんばっとう 七転八倒 ⇨ しちてんばっとう.

しっと 嫉妬 《嫉妬心》jealousy; envy ¶ しっとする be jealous 《of, over》; envy sb; be envious 《of》/ しっと深い jealous; envious / しっと深い目つき a jealous look; 《文》《with》jealous eyes / しっとの余り from jealousy; out of envy / しっとに身を焼く 《文》be consumed with jealousy.

しつど 湿度 humidity ¶ 高い[低い]湿度 high [low] humidity / 湿度計 a hygrometer; a hygrograph 《自記の》. [文例↓]

じっと 《文》fixedly; firmly; 《忍耐して》patiently; 《静かに》still; quiet(ly) ¶ じっと動かないでいる stay put; sit tight / じっと見つめる 《文》gaze intently 《at》; look hard [fixedly] 《at》; 《文》rivet one's eyes [gaze] 《upon》/ じっと考え込む be lost [sunk] in thought / じっとしている keep [stand, sit] still; 《文》be [remain] motionless / じっとしていられない cannot stay [keep] still; be [feel] restless. [文例↓]

しっとう¹ 失投 《野球》a careless pitch [throw].

しっとう² 執刀 performance of an operation ¶ 執刀者 an operating surgeon. [文例↓]

じつどう 実働 ¶ 実働8時間 (have) an eight-hour day / 実働時間 actual working hours / 実働資本 《経済》working capital.

しっとり ¶ しっとりした damp(ish); wet / しっとり露にぬれた牧場 《文》a dewy [bedewed] meadow.

じっとり ¶ じっとりしている be damp; be moist; 《文》be dewy. [文例↓]

しつない 室内 ¶ 室内の indoor / 室内に[で] indoors; in [inside, within] a room / 室内アンテナ an indoor antenna [aerial] / 室内楽 chamber music / 室内管弦楽団 a chamber orchestra / 室内装飾 interior decoration [décor] / 室内装飾家 an interior decorator / 室内装飾を施す decorate a room / 室内遊戯 an indoor [a parlor] game.

しつねん 失念 ¶ 失念する 〈人が主語〉forget; 〈事が主語〉escape [slip from] one's memory.

ジッパー ⇨ ファスナー.

しっぱい 失敗 (a) failure; a mistake; a blunder; 《文》an error; 《口語》a flop; 《口語》a washout ¶ 失敗する fail (in); 《文》be unsuccessful (in); 《零落する》sink [come down] in the world; 《事が主語》fail; turn out a failure; fall through; go wrong [《文》amiss]; 《文》miscarry; 《文》come to grief [naught]; end [result] in failure / 失敗の 《文》unsuccessful 《attempts》/ 大失敗 a complete [an utter] failure; a bad mistake; a fiasco (pl. -(e)s) / 失敗者 a failure / 〈世間での〉a social failure. [文例↓]

じっぱひとからげ 十把一絡げ ¶ 十把一からげに 《文》in the lump; wholesale / 十把一からげにする[扱う] treat (everybody) alike; 《口語》lump (all the students) together 《in one's criticism》/ 十把一からげに批評する make a sweeping criticism.

しつはんしゃ 膝反射 《生理》a patellar reflex; a knee jerk.

しっぴ 失費 (useless) expenses; (unnecessary) expenditure.

じっぴ 実費 actual expense(s); 〈原価〉the cost price ¶ 実費で at cost. [文例↓]

しっぴつ 執筆 ¶ 執筆する write (for a magazine); contribute (to a weekly) / 執筆者 the writer; the contributor.

しっぷ 湿布 a wet cloth [compress]; a poultice 《薬を塗ったもの》¶ 湿布する apply a poultice (to); put a poultice [compress] (on) / 温湿布 a hot compress [poultice].

じっぷ 実父 one's real [own] father.

しっぷう 疾風 a gale; a strong wind; 《気象》a fresh breeze ¶ 疾風迅雷のごとく 《文》swiftly; as quick as lightning; like a whirlwind.

じつぶつ 実物 the real thing; an (actual) object; 〈問題になっているそのもの〉the thing in question; 〈本物〉a genuine article [thing]; 〈絵に対して〉life; 〈写真に対して〉the original ¶ 実物大の life-size(d) 《portraits》; full-size(d) 《samples》/ 実物教育 practical teaching / 実物取引 (a) spot transaction. [文例↓]

しっぺい 疾病 ⇨ びょうき.

しっぺがえし しっぺ返し retaliation; tit for tat; 〈口答え〉a retort; a (quick) piece of repartee ¶ しっぺ返しをする give tit for tat; pay sb back; retaliate (on, against); serve sb with the same sauce; make a riposte; retort; throw [《文》cast] (an accusation) (back) in sb's face; 《文》riposte in kind.

しっぽ 尻尾 the tail; 〈端〉the end (of a radish) ¶ しっぽをつかまえる pick up sb's slip [mistake]; catch sb out (in sth) / しっぽを出す show (oneself in) one's true colors; 《文》betray one's true self; give oneself away / しっぽを巻いて逃げる sneak away with one's tail between one's legs / 〈遁走する〉beat a hasty retreat / 《米俗》hightail (it). [文例↓]

じつぼ 実母 one's real [own] mother.

しつぼう 失望 loss of hope; despair; disap-

じっとして. Hold it, please! / 心配でじっとしていられなかった. I was so frightened I couldn't keep still. / 天気がいいので家にじっとしていられなかった. The weather was too fine for me to stay indoors. / 今の所じっとしていなさい. Stay just [right] where you are.

しっとう² 手術は北田博士執刀の下に行なわれた. The operation was perfomed by Dr. Kitada.

じっとり 背中にじっとり汗をかいていた. His back was clammy with perspiration.

しっぱい 彼の試みはことごとく失敗に終わった. His attempts have all met with failure [proved abortive]. / 失敗は成功のもと. Every failure is a stepping stone to success. | Failure teaches success.

じっぴ 売価は千円だから実費は600円ぐらいです. It sells for 1,000 yen, so its cost (price) will be about 600 yen.

じつぶつ この造花は実物のように見える. This artificial flower looks like a real [natural] one. / このりんごの絵は実物そっくりだ. This picture of an apple is quite lifelike. / 実物を見なければわからない. I can't tell unless I see the thing itself.

しっぽ あんな不正を働きながらよくしっぽを出さないでいられるも

しっぽうやき 〔失望〕 pointment ¶失望する be disappointed 《at, in, of》;《文》despair 《of》; lose heart [hope] / 失望して《文》dejectedly; in despair / 失望させる disappoint *sb*《文》*sb's* hopes》;《文》disillusion; let *sb* down.

しっぽうやき 七宝焼 *cloisonné* ware ¶七宝焼の花瓶 a *cloisonné* vase.

しつぼく 質朴 ¶質朴な simple (and honest);《文》simplehearted; unsophisticated.

しつむ 執務 ¶執務する work 《from 9 a.m. to 5 p.m.》;《文》attend to *one's* duties / 執務中である be at *one's* desk; be on duty / 執務時間 office [business, working] hours.

じつむ 実務 (practical) business; business practice ¶実務の経験がある be experienced in business / 実務の才能がある have a talent for business; have a lot of《文》considerable business ability / 実務を習う get a training in the practice of business / 実務につく go into business / 実務家 a man of business; a businessman.

しつめい 失明 loss of *one's* eyesight [sight] ¶失明する go blind;《文》become sightless;《文》lose *one's* eyesight; be blinded (外傷によって).

しつもん 質問 a question; a query; 〈国会の〉 an interpellation; 〈英〉 a parliamentary question ¶質問する ask *sb* a question; put a question to *sb*; ask a question of *sb*; 〈国会で〉 interpellate / 矢継ぎ早に質問する fire questions 《at》; discharge [fire off] a volley of questions 《at》; hurl [throw out] a question 《at》/ 質問を受け流す[そらす] turn a question aside; parry a question / 質問演説をする address an interpellation 《on a matter to a minister》/ 質問者 a questioner; an interpellator (国会の) / 質問書 a written inquiry; 〈アンケートの〉 a questionnaire / 質問責めに会う be pestered [persecuted] with questions; face a barrage of questions / 質問責めに会わせる bombard *sb* with questions; quiz *sb*. 文例⇩

しつよう 執拗 ¶執拗な obstinate; persistent; stubborn;《文》tenacious.

じつよう 実用 practical use;《文》utility ¶実用に供する put *sth* to practical use / 実用化する make 《a process》 practicable; make *sth* fit for practical use / 実用的な《文》utilitarian / 実用向きの for practical use / 実用性のある useful;《文》of practical use / 実用性のない of no practical use / 実用英語 practical English / 実用家具 utility furniture / 実用主義 pragmatism / 実用新案 a new design for practical use / 実用品 utility goods;〈必需品〉necessities / 実用本位の functional. 文例⇩

じづら 字面 〈見た目〉the appearance of written [printed] characters;〈表面の意味〉the apparent meaning of a word. 文例⇩

しつらえる 設える ⇨ よういʳ (用意する), せつび (設備する).

じつり 実利 〈有用性〉(actual) use;《文》utility;〈利益〉(an actual) profit;《文》material gain;《文》benefit ¶実利的な《文》utilitarian; practical / 実利主義 utilitarianism; commercialism (営利本位).

しつりょう 質量 〔物〕mass;〈質と量〉quality and quantity ¶質量数 a mass number / (原子の)質量単位 a mass unit / 質量不変[保存]の法則 the law of conservation of mass [matter] / 質量共に both in quality and quantity.

じつりょく 実力 real ability [power];《文》capability;《文》merit;〈言葉に対する行為〉(take) action;〈暴力〉(use) force ¶実力のある《文》able; capable / 英語の実力がある《文》be proficient in English /《文》a man of ability;《文》an able man / 実力を養う《文》make *oneself* proficient [improve *oneself*] (in English); improve (*one's* English) / 実力に応じて according to *one's* ability [merits] / 実力以上のことをやってのける surpass *oneself* / 実力行使 use of force; 〈ストライキ〉 a strike /〈労働者が〉実力行使を行なう[中止する] go on [call off a] strike / 実力試験 a test of working knowledge / 政界の実力者 a strong man [one of the dominant figures] in politics / 実力主義《米》the merit system. 文例⇩

しつれい 失礼《文》impoliteness; rudeness; 〈不作法〉bad manners;《文》a breach of etiquette ¶失礼な《文》impolite; rude;《文》discourteous;〈生意気な〉impertinent; impudent / 失礼なことを言うbe rude; say something rude; say rude things / 失礼なことをす

のだ. I wonder how he manages to get away with it when he has behaved so dishonestly. / 言葉になまりがあったばかりにしっぽをつかまれてしまった. His accent gave him away.

しつぼう 彼は失望のあまり自殺した. Despair drove him to suicide. / 失望するな. Keep your heart [chin] up! / 今度の英語の先生には失望した. I am disappointed in our new teacher of English.

しつもん 何か質問がありますか. Have you got any questions (to ask)? / 質問してよろしいですか. May I ask you a question? / 1つ質問がある. Let me ask you a question.

じつよう それは実用には役に立たない[実用向きでない]. It is of no practical use. / これは実用向きにできている. This is intended for practical use. / これは実用と装飾とを兼ねている. It is both useful [practical] and decorative.

じづら この2つの漢字を並べて書いては字面が悪い. If you write those two *kanji* next to each other, they will be rather offensive to the eye. / 字面からはそういう意味は読み取れなかった. I couldn't read that meaning into the characters.

じつりょく 今では肩書きよりも実力が重んじられる. People have come to value ability above titles. / 当社では実力本位で人を雇っています. 'Ability first' is our motto in employing people. / 彼は実力を示した. He proved himself to be really capable. / 彼は民衆の指導者になるだけの実力を持っている. He has it in him to be a leader of men.

しつれい この前の日曜は不在で失礼しました. I am sorry I was out when you called last Sunday. / 失礼ですがあなたは小田さんではありませんでしょうか. Excuse me, but aren't you Mr. Oda?

る be rude to *sb*; act rudely; 《文》 commit a breach of etiquette / 失礼ですが Excuse me, but... / 失礼ながら Perhaps I shouldn't say so [this], but... / 失礼を顧みず…する take the liberty of *doing* / お話中失礼ですが… Sorry to interrupt you, but.... [文例⇩]

じつれい 実例 an example; an instance; an illustration (例証); a case in point (適例); 〈前例〉 a precedent ¶実例を示す[あげる] give [《文》 cite] an example [instance] / 実例をあげて説明する illustrate by an example; 《文》 exemplify. [文例⇩]

しつれん 失恋 《文》 disappointed love; a broken heart; 〈片思いで〉 《文》 unrequited love ¶失恋する be disappointed in love / 失恋の悩み 《文》 agonies of a broken heart. [文例⇩]

じつろく 実録 a true [《文》 an authentic] record [history, account].

じつわ 実話 a true story; a real-life story; 《文》 an authentic account 《of》.

して 仕手 〈能の〉 a *shite*; the main character in a *Noh* drama; 〖株式〗 an operator; a speculator ¶(能で)仕手を演じる play the leading part / 仕手株 a speculative stock.

してい[1] 子弟 sons; children.

してい[2] 私邸 *one's* private house [《文》 residence].

してい[3] 指定 ¶指定する 《文》 designate; 《文》 specify; appoint; name; earmark 《for a specific purpose》 / 面会の場所[時刻]を指定する appoint [designate] the place [hour] for the meeting / 別に指定がなければ 《文》 unless otherwise specified / 指定の時間までに 《文》 by the appointed time / 指定席 a reserved seat / 指定旅館 an appointed hotel; a hotel designated 《by the school》. [文例⇩]

してい[4] 師弟 master and pupil; teacher and student ¶師弟の関係 the relationship between teacher and student. [文例⇩]

じてい 自邸 《文》 *one's* (own) residence; *one's* home.

しでかす 仕出かす ⇨ する[2] ¶大きなへまをしでかす make a terrible mess.

してき[1] 指摘 ¶指摘する point out; 《文》 indicate; put *one's* finger on.

してき[2] 史的 ¶史的現在 〖文法〗 the historical present / 史的唯物論 historical materialism.

してき[3] 私的 personal; private ¶私的なつながりがある be in personal contact 《with》.

してき[4] 詩的 poetic(al).

してつ 私鉄 a private [privately-owned] railroad [railway]; a railroad under private management; 〈会社〉 《米》 a railroad (corporation); 《英》 a railway (company) ¶私鉄労働組合 a private railroad workers' union.

じてっこう 磁鉄鉱 〖鉱〗 magnetite.

-しても ¶…としても if...; even if [though] ...; though [although]...; (even) granting [supposing] that... / それが事実にしても (even) granting [supposing] that it is true; 《文》 (even) granting [supposing] it to be true. [文例⇩]

してやる do *sth* for *sb*; 〈だます〉 outwit; take *sb* in; 《文》 deceive; 〈うまくやる〉 succeed 《in》; make a success [go] 《of》; get away with 《it》. [文例⇩]

してん[1] 支店 a branch; a branch office [store] ¶支店を出す open [establish] a branch (office) / 支店長 a branch manager; the manager of a branch office.

してん[2] 支点 〈てこの〉 a fulcrum 《*pl.* -s, -cra》.

してん[3] 視点 〈観点〉 a point of view; a viewpoint; 〈眼のつけ所〉 where *one's* eyes are aimed; 《文》 the point at which *one's* gaze is [eyes are] directed.

しでん 市電 a (municipal) streetcar; 《英》 a tram(car).

じてん[1] 次点 〈票数〉 the number of votes obtained by the runner-up; the largest number of votes obtained by an unsuccessful candidate; 〈人〉 the runner-up 《in a contest》.

じてん[2] 自転 rotation; the spin 《of the earth》 on 《its》 axis ¶自転する rotate [revolve, turn round] on *its* (own) axis / 地球の自転周期 the earth's rotation period.

じてん[3] 事典 an encyclop(a)edia 《of places》; a dictionary 《of psychology》.

じてん[4] 時点 a point of [in] time ¶今日の時点で as of today.

じてん[5] 辞典 ⇨ じしょ[3].

じでん 自伝 an autobiography ¶自伝を書く write *one's* life story [the story of *one's* own life] / 自伝小説 an autobiographical novel.

じてんしゃ 自転車 a bicycle; a cycle; 《口語》 a bike; 《英口語》 a pushbike (motorcycle に対し

[し]

これは失礼. I beg your pardon. | 《英》 Sorry. | 《米》 Excuse me. / ちょっと失礼します. Excuse me a moment. / もう失礼いたします. Well, I must be going now. | I'm afraid I must say good-bye now./ あなたの前でこう申しては失礼かもしれませんが, あの男は信用できませんよ. Perhaps I ought not to say this in front of you, but I'm afraid we cannot trust him.

じつれい 金持ちが必ずしも幸せでないことを示す実例は世間に少なくない. There are any number of instances which show that the rich are not always happy.

しつれん 彼はその女性に失恋した. His love for the girl was not returned [requited]. / ウエルテルはロッテに失恋してピストル自殺を遂げた. Werther put a bullet into his head out of disappointment in his love for Lotte.

してい[3] 彼は金曜日を会合の日に指定してきた. He set Friday as the day for our meeting. / 全席指定. 〖掲示〗 All Seats Reserved.

してい[4] 2人の間は師弟の関係である. The relationship between them is that of master and pupil.

-しても 1週間のうちに出来るとしても間に合うまい. Even if it is finished in a week, it will not be in time. / 相談がまとまるにしても急には行くまい. Even granted that it will be satisfactorily settled, it may take some time. / たとえ君の方が正しいとしても, あんな風に言うもんじゃない. Even if you are in the right, you shouldn't have put it like that. / その金は全部でないにしても半分以上は使ってしまった. He has spent more than half the money, if not all of it.

してやる その時はまさにしてやったりと思った. I really thought I'd done it then.

してんのう 四天王 《仏教》the Four Devas; 《比喩的》the big [best] four.

しと¹ 使途 ¶金の使途を明らかにする account for the money spent / 使途不明の金 (an) unaccounted-for expenditure.

しと² 使徒 an apostle; a disciple ¶十二使徒《キリスト教》the Twelve Apostles / 使徒行伝《聖書》The Acts of the Apostles /《略称》Acts.

しど¹ 示度 a reading; the degrees registered [recorded]. 文例◊

しど² 視度《気象・航空・海》visibility.

しとう¹ 死闘 a fight to the death; a desperate struggle;《文》(locked in) mortal combat ¶死闘する fight for one's life [desperately];《文》engage in a life-and-death struggle 《with》.

しとう² 至当 ¶至当な proper; right; fair;《文》just; reasonable. 文例◊

しどう¹ 私道 a private road [path].

しどう² 始動《機》starting ¶始動機 a starter. 文例◊

しどう³ 指導《文》guidance; leading; leadership;《文》direction; coaching (競技などの) ¶指導する guide; lead; direct; coach / …の指導の下に under the guidance [tuition, leadership] of… / 指導の任に当たる take on the job [《文》undertake the task] of teaching [coaching] / 指導を誤る lead [direct, guide] sb wrongly [《文》amiss]; 《文》misdirect / …に指導を求める turn to sb for guidance [leadership] / 指導的役割を演じる play a leading [prominent] part (in); play the part of the leader;《文》play a leadership role / 指導員 an instructor; an advisor / 指導原理[方針]《文》a guiding principle; guidelines / 指導者 a guide; a leader; a coach; a mastermind (黒幕) / 指導主事《教育》a supervisor; a (teachers') consultant / 指導的地位《文》a position of leadership;(the) leadership / 指導要領《教育》guidelines / 指導力 one's leadership 《over the group》;《文》(lack) leadership qualities;《文》(have) qualities of [the capacity for] leadership. 文例◊

じどう¹ 自動 ¶自動(式)の automatic / 自動的に automatically;《機械的に》mechanically ¶自動エレベーター an automatic elevator / 自動拳銃 an automatic (pistol) / 自動小銃 an automatic rifle / 自動ドア an automatic door; a self-operating door / 自動制御《機》automatic control; servomechanism (装置) / 自動操縦装置《航空》an automatic pilot; an autopilot; a gyropilot / 自動装置 an automaton (pl. -ta, -s) / 自動販売機 a vending [slot] machine; an automat (食物の) / タバコ自動販売機 a cigarette machine / 自動ピアノ a pianola; a player piano / 自動巻きの時計 an automatic [a self-winding] watch. 文例◊

じどう² 児童 a child;《総称》children; boys and girls ¶児童(向き)の children's (books);《文》juvenile;《drama》for young people / 児童憲章 the Children's Charter / 児童心理学 child psychology / 児童福祉法 the Child Welfare Act / 児童文学 juvenile literature.

じどうし 自動詞《文法》an intransitive verb (略: vi., v.i.).

じどうしゃ 自動車 a motorcar; a car; an automobile;《米口語》an auto (pl. -s); 〈各種のものの総称〉《文》a motor vehicle ¶自動車を走らせる drive a car / 自動車に乗る〈運転する〉drive a car; 〈他の人の運転で〉ride in a car / 自動車による輸送《文》motor transportation / 自動車で行く go by car / 自動車学校 a driving school / 自動車公害 automobile pollution / 自動車工業《米》the automobile industry;《英》the motor industry / 自動車競走 an auto race / 自動車事故 a motor(ing) [an auto] accident /《口語》a car crash [smash] / 自動車修理工 a car mechanic /《自家用》自動車常用者 a motorist / 自動車税 the automobile tax / 自動車製造業者 a car manufacturer / 自動車専用道路 an expressway;《米》a superhighway;《英》a motorway / 自動車損害賠償責任保険《自賠責》automobile third party liability insurance / 自動車泥棒〈人〉a car [an auto] thief;〈事〉a car [auto] theft / 自動車売買業者 a car [motor] dealer / 自動車パレード a motorcade; an autocade / 自動車保険 automobile insurance /

じてんしゃ 彼は自転車で自動車と競争した. He raced his bicycle against a motorcar.

しと¹ 金の使途を問われたが彼は返答に窮した. When questioned as to how the money had been spent, he was stuck [at a loss] for an answer.

しど¹ 台風24号の中心示度は895ミリバール. The registered central atmospheric pressure of Typhoon No. 24 is 895 millibars.

しとう² そうするのが至当だ. That is what you ought to do. | It is (right and) proper that you should do so.

しどう² エンジンがうなりを上げて始動した. The engine started (up) with a roar.

しどう³ よろしくご指導を願います. I look to you for guidance.

じどう¹ このドアの開閉は自動式になっている. This door opens and shuts automatically. / チューインガムの自動販売器があった. There was an automatic vending machine for chewing gum.

じどうしゃ 自動車で駅まで行った. I drove to the station. / 君の自動車に乗せてくれ. Give me a ride [lift] in your car. ★ a ride を使えば,乗心地はどうか「ちょっと乗らせてくれ」の意. これに対して a lift を使うと,どこそこまで「乗せて行ってくれ」の意になる. / この通りは朝8時から10

しどけない　slovenly ⇨ だらし(の)ない.
しとげる　し遂げる ⇨ なしとげる.
しとしと　gently; softly ¶しとしとと降る雨 drizzling rain; (a) drizzle. 文例↓
じとじと　じとじとする damp; wet.
シドニー　Sydney.
しとめる　仕留める kill; shoot 《a lion》 dead; bring down 《a flying bird》.
しとやか　淑やか ¶しとやかな modest; 《文》 graceful; gentle; polite; ladylike / 物腰がしとやかである《文》 bear *oneself* gracefully; 《文》 be graceful in manner.
じどり　地取り laying out; a ground plan; the layout ¶地取りをする lay out 《a garden》.
しどろもどろ　¶しどろもどろの faltering; confused; 《文》 disordered; 《文》 incoherent / しどろもどろになる《文》 be thrown into confusion; falter 《in *one*'s speech》 / しどろもどろに話を終える flounder through a speech / しどろもどろに弁解をする《文》 blunder out an apology.
シトロン　〈木・果実〉 a citron; 〈飲み物〉 citron water; lemonade.
しな¹　品 〈品物〉 a thing; 《文》 an article; goods; wares; stock(s) (在庫品); 〈品質〉 quality; a brand (品種) ¶あらゆる品 all sorts of goods; 《文》 goods of every description [all descriptions] / 品がいい[悪い] the quality of *sth* is good [poor]; 《文》 be of good [poor] quality / いろいろの品を[品数をたくさん]取りそろえておく keep a wide variety [large assortment] of goods in stock / 品不足 a shortage (of goods). 文例↓
しな²　〈嬌態〉 flirtatiousness; flirting; 《文》 coquetry ¶しなをつくる《文》 act flirtatiously [coquettishly]; flirt (with *sb*); be flirtatious; 《文》 be coquettish.
シナ　支那 China ⇨ ちゅうごく.
-しな　¶帰りしな on *one*'s [the] way home [back] ⇨ -がけ. 文例↓
しない¹　市内 ¶市内に[で] in the city; within the city limits / 市内通話 a local call / 市内電車 ⇨ しでん / 市内版 the city edition.
しない²　竹刀 a bamboo sword (for fencing practice).
しなう　撓う bend; be supple; be flexible; be springy; 《文》 be pliant ¶よくしなうつえ a springy cane. 文例↓
しなうす　品薄 (a) shortage [scarcity] of stock [goods] ¶品薄になる〈人・商店が主語〉 run short (of an item); 〈商品が主語〉 be in short supply; run short; get 《文》 become] scarce. 文例↓
しなおす　し直す ⇨ やりなおす.
しなぎれ　品切れ ¶品切れである[になる] be [run] out of stock; be sold out.
しなさだめ　品定め ¶品定めする《文》 discuss the (relative) merits 《of》; criticize; comment (on); size *sb* [*sth*] up; 《口語》 weigh *sb* [*sth*] (up).
しなびる　萎びる wither; shrivel; wilt; be shriveled up (by the frost) ¶しなびた shriveled; wizened (faces); dried-up.
しなもの　品物 《文》 an article; a thing; goods; wares; (a) stock (在庫品) ¶品物で払う pay in kind.
シナモン　〈香料〉 cinnamon.
しなやか　¶しなやかな《文》 pliant; supple; limber; flexible; elastic; 《文》 lithe(some) / しなやかな手 supple hands / しなやかな革 supple leather / しなやかな体 a lithe body; 《文》 a wiry physique / しなやかな指 wiry [flexible] fingers.
じならし　地均し ground leveling [breaking] ¶地ならしをする level [smooth, break] the ground; roll (the soil) (flat) / 新政策施行の地ならしをする pave [prepare] the way for a new policy / 地ならし機 a (road) leveler; a grader.
じなり　地鳴り a rumbling of the earth [ground]. 文例↓
シナリオ　a scenario (*pl.* -s); a filmscript; a screenplay ¶シナリオライター a scriptwriter; a scenario writer.
しなれる¹　死なれる have *sb* die; lose (*one*'s son); 《文》 be bereaved of (*one*'s mother); survive (*one*'s husband).
しなれる²　し慣れる be used [accustomed] 《to *sth*, to doing》; be experienced 《at *doing*, in》.
しなん¹　至難 ¶至難の most difficult; hardest.
しなん²　指南 ¶指南する teach; 《文》 instruct; coach; give lessons (in an art) / 指南番[役] an instructor; a coach; a teacher; a (fencing) master.
じなん　次男 *one*'s [a, the] second son.
しにいそぐ　死に急ぐ《文》 hasten to *one*'s death; 《文》 seek death prematurely.
しにおくれる　死に遅[後]れる outlive [survive] (*one*'s son).
しにがお　死に顔《文》 *sb*'s face in death ¶死に顔がいい《文》 look peaceful in death.

時まで自動車は通行止めです. This street is closed to motor vehicles from 8 to 10 a.m.
しとしと　雨がしとしと降っている. It is drizzling. | A gentle rain is falling.
しとやか　彼女は至っておしとやかにしていた. She was on her best behavior.
しな¹　これはそれより品が落ちる. This is (of) poorer quality than that. | This isn't such good quality as that. | 《文》 This is inferior to that. / 品を落とさずの値上げもしないのは見事だ. It is admirable [most commendable] of them to keep the quality up and the price down.
-しな　寝しなに物を食べるな. Don't eat anything just before you go to bed.
しなう　竹が雪でしなった. The bamboos bent [bowed] under (the weight of) the snow.
しなうす　品薄だ. The stocks are low. / サイズの大きいのが品薄だ. We are short of the larger sizes. / 大豆が品薄だ. We are low in [on] soybeans.
しなぎれ　品切れ. 《表示》 Sold out.
じなり　地鳴りがした. I heard an underground rumbling [the ground rumble].
しにいそぐ　何もそんなに死に急ぐことはないではないか. Why do you risk your life 《文》 court

しにがね 死に金 ¶死に金を使う throw one's money away 《on sth》; waste one's money 《on sth》; spend money to no [little] purpose.
しにがみ 死に神 《文》the god of death; 《文》Death ¶死に神に取りつかれる be in the grip of Death.
しにぎわ 死に際 ¶死に際に in one's last moments; on one's deathbed / 死に際の遺言 one's last [dying] words [《文》injunctions].
しにせ an old-[a long-]established store [shop]; a store of long standing.
しにそこない 死に損ない 〈人をあざけって〉a swine; a bastard; 〈老人をあざけって〉a dotard; a doddering old man.
しにたえる 死に絶える die out; become extinct; be exterminated.
しにはじ 死に恥 ¶死に恥をさらす die a shameful [an ignominious] death.
しにばしょ 死に場所 the place of sb's death; 〈死すべき所〉a place (for one) to die (in).
しにばな 死に花 [文例⇩]
しにみず 死に水 ¶死に水をとる attend sb's deathbed.
しにめ 死に目 ¶死に目に会う be with sb when he dies; be present at sb's death [deathbed]. [文例⇩]
しにものぐるい 死に物狂い ¶死に物狂いの desperate; frantic / 死にもの狂いの競争 (a) desperate [cutthroat] competition / 死にもの狂いで desperately; in [《文》with] desperation; frantically; 《口語》like mad [hell] / 死にもの狂いになる get [《文》become] desperate; 《文》make frantic efforts. [文例⇩]
しにわかれる 死に別れる 《文》be separated from 《one's mother》by death; lose 《one's parents》; 《文》be bereaved of 《one's husband》; have 《one's son》die. [文例⇩]
しにん 死人 a dead person; the dead; 〈事故などの〉the person [people] killed. [文例⇩]
じにん¹ 自任 ¶自任する flatter oneself (that one is..., to be); fancy [think] oneself (to be) (an expert); regard [look upon] oneself (as) (★ regard を consider としてもいいが, その場合はあとの as は省く). [文例⇩]
じにん² 自認 ¶自認する 《文》acknowledge [own] oneself (to be).
じにん³ 辞任 ⇨じしょく.
しぬ 死ぬ; pass away [on, over] (婉曲的に); 〈命を落とす〉《文》meet one's end [death]; be killed; 《文》expire; 〈野球で〉be put out ¶国のために死ぬ die [《文》lay down one's life] for one's country / 卒中で死ぬ die of apoplexy / 負傷して死ぬ die from [of] (one's) wounds / 死ぬまで for the rest of one's life; until one's death; 《文》to one's dying day / 死ぬまで戦う fight to the last [《文》to the last drop of one's blood] / 死ぬほど...したがる be dying (to do, for sth) / 死んでいる be dead; 〈生気がない〉《文》be lifeless; 《文》lack life / 死んで冷たくなっている 《口語》be as dead as mutton [a doornail] / (いっそ)死んでしまいたいと思う wish one were dead; 《文》wish death upon oneself / 死にかけている be dying; be on the point of death; be at death's door / 死んだ dead; deceased; 〈故〉the late 《Mrs. D》/ ずっと前に死んだ祖父 my long-dead grandfather / 死んだ子の年を数える count how old one's dead child would be if he [she] were alive / 死んだ振りをする a sham [《文》feign] death; pretend to be dead; 《口語》play dead / 死んても同然だ be as good as dead. [文例⇩]
じぬし 地主 a landlord; a landowner ¶地主階級 the landed class.
じねつ 地熱 the heat of the earth; terrestrial heat.
シネマスコープ 《商標名》CinemaScope.
シネラマ 《商標名》Cinerama.
シネラリヤ 〖植〗a cineraria.
じねんじょ 自然薯 a Japanese yam.
しの 篠 〖植〗a kind of very small bamboo ¶しのの突く雨 (a) pelting [driving, pouring] rain; a (torrential) downpour.
しのうこうしょう 士農工商 the classes of warriors, farmers, artisans and tradesmen.
しのぎ¹ 凌ぎ ¶しのぎがつかない be in a hopeless [desperate] position [situation]; be driven to the wall; be completely at a loss as to how to overcome one's problems [the problems facing one] / 空腹しのぎに 《文》just to allay one's hunger; to stave off hunger pains / 退屈しのぎに just to kill time.
しのぎ² 鎬 ¶しのぎを削って戦う fight des-

---

death] like that? | Why do you hold your life so cheap?
しにぞこない .この死に損ないめ. You bastard!
しにばな 何かひと仕事して死に花を咲かせたいものだ. I should like to do something great to adorn the last page of my life [to end my life with].
しにめ 帰宅が遅れて母の死に目に会えなかった. I got home too late to see my mother alive.
しにものぐるい 人間, 死に物狂いになるとどんなことでもやるものだ. A desperate man will go to any lengths [will stick at nothing].
しにわかれる 彼は5歳のときに両親に死に別れた. He was left an orphan when he was five (years old) / 彼女は早く夫に死に別れる運命にあった. She was destined for an early widowhood.
しにん 死人が多数出た. A large number of people were killed. | Many lives were lost. / この衝突でたくさんの死人が出た. The collision took a heavy toll of lives. / 死人に口なし. Dead men tell no tales. 《諺》 | The dead cannot speak in their own defense.
じにん¹ 氏は社会改良家をもって自任している. He regards [looks upon] himself as a social reform-er. / 彼はあれでもいっぱしのワイン通だと自任している. He fancies himself (as) something of a wine expert [connoisseur]. | He does make pretensions to an expert knowledge of wines.
しぬ 暑くて死にそうだ. The heat is killing me. / 彼は死んだものと思われていた. He has been given up for dead [lost]. / 結核で死んだ. He died of tuberculosis [T.B.]. / こんな苦しい思いをするくらいなら死んだ方がましだ. I would rather die than live and suffer like this. / 彼が死んでから3年になる. He has been dead (for) three years. / 死んだ子の年を数えてもしかたな

しのぐ 凌ぐ 〈耐える〉《文》endure; bear; stand; hold out 《against the attacks》; 〈防ぐ〉keep 《the cold》 out [off]; 〈切り抜ける〉get [pull] through; survive; 〈まさる〉《文》exceed; 《文》surpass; 《文》excel; outdo; outshine;《文》be superior to ¶木陰で雨をしのぐ shelter [take shelter] from the rain under a tree / 夏の暑さをしのぐ keep off [《文》temper] the summer heat / しのぎやすい be easy to bear / しのぎやすい冬 a mild winter. 文例⊕

しのこす し残す ¶(…を)し残す leave sth unfinished [half done].

しのごの 四の五の ¶四の五の言わずに without grumbling [complaining, arguing, 《文》complaint, 《文》argument]; with (a) good grace.

シノニム a synonym.

しのばせる 忍ばせる hide; 《文》conceal 《a knife in one's pocket》/ 足音を忍ばせて in a subdued voice; in a whisper; under one's breath; 《イタリア語》sotto voce.

しのび 忍び ¶忍びの者 ⇨ にんじゃ / 忍び足で stealthily; 《文》with stealthy [soft] steps; 《文》with noiseless footsteps; (walk) on tiptoe / 忍び込む steal [creep, sneak, slip] into; steal one's way into / 忍び泣く cry [《文》weep] in secret [silently]; 《文》shed silent tears / 忍び寄る steal [creep, sneak] up to 《a place》/ 忍び笑いする laugh up one's sleeve; laugh to oneself.

しのびがえし 忍び返し 《建》spikes.

しのぶ[1] 忍ぶ 〈たえる〉bear; 《文》endure 《hardships》; stand 《the pain》; put up with; 〈隠れる〉hide; 《文》conceal oneself; lie hidden; be in hiding ¶世を忍ぶ bury oneself in obscurity / 《文》live in seclusion / …するに忍びない do not have the heart to do; be reluctant [not willing] to do; cannot bring oneself to do / 忍び難い unbearable. 文例⊕

しのぶ[2] 偲ぶ think of; remember; recall; 《文》recollect ¶しのばせる remind one of; make one remember [think of] 《bygone days》.

しば[1] 芝 turf; 《a patch of》 grass ¶芝を植える plant grass [a lawn]; grass 《a piece of land》/ 芝を敷く turf a lawn / 芝刈機 a lawn mower.

しば[2] 柴 brushwood; firewood ¶柴を刈る cut [gather] firewood / 柴垣 a (woven) brushwood fence.

じば 磁場 a magnetic field.

しはい[1] 支配 〈管理〉control; 《文》superintendence; 〈統治〉rule; 《文》sway; government; 〈運営〉management; 〈指揮〉direction ¶支配する rule; govern; dominate; direct; manage; control / 白人の支配する社会 a white-dominated society / 境遇に支配される 《文》be at the mercy of one's circumstances / 自然の法則に支配される 《文》be subject to the laws of nature / …の支配を受ける be (put) under the control [《文》rule] of…; be ruled [controlled] by… / 支配下に置く keep [bring, place] sb [sth] under one's control [rule] / 支配階級 the ruling class; the governing class(es) / 支配者 a ruler / 支配人 a manager / 総[副]支配人 a general [an assistant] manager. 文例⊕

しはい[2] 紙背 ⇨ がんこう.

しはい[3] 賜杯 a trophy given by 《the Emperor》.

しばい 芝居 〈演劇〉a play; a drama; 《文》a (dramatic [theatrical]) performance; 〈狂言〉play-acting; a fake; 《口語》a put-up job ¶芝居を見に行く go to the theater; go to (see) a play / 芝居をやる perform [put on] a play / 《文》stage a dramatic performance / 〈役を演じる〉play [act] the part (of); 〈…の振りをする〉act (as if); pretend; 《文》feign / 芝居に仕組む dramatize 《an event》; make a play of sth / ひと芝居打つ play a trick; put on an act [show] / 芝居じみた[がかった] theatrical; pompous; affected / 芝居好き a theatergoer; a playgoer / 芝居熱に浮かされた stagestruck. 文例⊕

じばいせき 自賠責 ⇨ じどうしゃ (自動車損害賠償責任保険).

しばいひん 試売品 goods on trial sale.

しばえび 《動》a prawn.

じはく 自白 (a) confession ¶自白する confess (to); make a confession; own up (to an offense) / 犯行を自白する confess one's guilt; confess to a crime / 自白を強要する force [extract, wring] a confession (from a suspect).

じばく 自爆 ¶自爆する crash one's plane into the target.

しばし ⇨ しばらく.

しばしば ⇨ たびたび.

じはだ 地肌 〈きめ〉(a) texture; 〈地面〉(the surface of) the ground. 文例⊕

ない. It is no use crying over spilt milk. 《諺》/ 死ぬか生きるかの境だ. His life is hanging in the balance. | He is hovering between life and death. / それでは死んでも死に切れない. I can't bear to die, leaving things like this. / 人はいろんな死に方をするものだ. Death comes to people in different ways.

しのぐ 冬の寒さより夏の暑さの方が私にはしのぎよい. I can stand the heat of summer better than the cold of winter. / 横浜は人口が名古屋をしのいだ. Yokohama has overtaken [surpassed] Nagoya in population. / この点で彼をしのぐ者は1人もない. He has no rival [stands unrivaled] in this respect. / あの人は進歩が早いからじきに先輩をしのぐようになるだろう. His progress is so fast [rapid] that he'll soon outstrip his seniors.

しのぶ そんなことはするに忍びなかった. I hadn't the heart [could not find it in my heart] to do it.

しはい 当時この地域はポルトガル人ががっちりと支配していた. At that time the Portuguese were in firm control of this region. / 異様な静けさが全市を支配してい

た. A strange quiet rests over the entire city. / アイルランドではカトリックが支配的である. Catholicism is the predominant religion in Ireland.

しばい 私はあまり芝居へ行きません. I am not much of a one for the theater. | I am not much of a playgoer. / 本当に泣いているんじゃないよ. 芝居だよ. Those aren't real tears. She's putting it on [She's only (play-)acting]. / あの男は なかなか 芝居気がある. He is quite a showman.

じはだ 雪解けであちこちに地肌が見えてきた. The snow has be-

しばたたく 瞬く blink [wink] ((one's)) (eyes).

しはつ 始発 the first train [car] ¶始発駅 the starting station. 文例⇩

じはつてき 自発的 ¶自発的に (文) spontaneously; of one's own accord; voluntarily; on one's own initiative.

しばふ 芝生 a lawn; a grass plot ¶芝生を刈る mow the lawn.

じばら 自腹 ¶自腹を切る pay for sth out of one's own pocket / 自腹を切って at one's (own) expense; out of one's (own) pocket.

しはらい 支払い payment; 《文》defrayment; 《文》disbursement ¶支払いを延期する postpone [put off, delay] payment / 支払いを停止する stop [suspend] payment / 支払い期限 the time for payment / 支払い期日 the date of payment / 支払い高 the amount of payment; a payment / 支払い停止 suspension of payment; 〈非常の緊法令による〉a moratorium (pl. -ria, -s) /支払い伝票 a payment slip / 支払い人 a payer; a drawee (手形の) /支払い能力 solvency / 支払い保証小切手 a certified check.

しはらう 支払う pay (out); 《文》defray; 《文》disburse; clear (one's debts); settle (one's accounts); honor (a check).

しばらく 暫く 〈少しの間で〉for some time; (for) a (little) while; for a period of time; a minute; a moment; 〈当分〉for the present; for the time being; 〈長い間〉for a long time [while] ¶しばらくすれば in a short time; in a little while / しばらくしてから after a while; presently / 経費問題はしばらくおき apart from [setting aside] the question of expense. 文例⇩

しばる 縛る bind; tie; fasten; 〈拘束する〉restrict ¶きつく[固く, しっかり]縛る tie [bind] fast; fasten tightly / 縛って束にする tie into a bundle / 縛りつける tie (a horse) (to a post); bind sb to (a stake); fasten (a rope) to (a tree) / 規則に縛られる be bound by a rule / 時間に縛られいる be restricted by time; have very little time to call one's own / 仕事に縛られる be chained [tied down] to one's work [business].

しはん[1] 市販 ¶市販する market; put [place] (goods) on the market [on (public) sale] / 市販される come onto the market; on the market of... on the market / 市販品 goods on the market.

しはん[2] 師範 a teacher; a coach; a master; an instructor ¶剣道の師範 a fencing master.

しはん[3] 紫斑 a purple spot ¶紫斑病 【医】purpura.

じばん 地盤 〈土台〉the foundation; the base; 〈土地〉the ground; 〈地歩〉a footing (★ a is one に代えることはできない, 複数形にもしない); a foothold (★ 複数は通常用いられない); 〈勢力範囲〉《文》one's sphere of influence; 〈選挙区〉《nurse》one's constituency ¶地盤を固める〈土台を〉strengthen [solidify] the foundation; 〈地位を〉make one's position safe [secure] / 地盤を築く lay the foundation (for) / 〈選挙の〉build (up) a basis of support / 固い地盤 firm [solid] ground along / 柔らかい地盤 soft [flimsy] ground / 地盤沈下 (land) subsidence / 地盤沈下をひき起す cause subsidence; cause the land to sink. 文例⇩

ジバン ⇨じゅばん.

しはんき 四半期 a quarter (of the year) ¶第一四半期 the first quarter (of the year).

しひ 私費 ¶私費を投じる spend one's (own) money ((on)) / 私費で at one's own expense; at private expense /私費で留学する study abroad at one's own expense.

じひ[1] 自費 ¶自費で at one's own expense / 自費出版する publish (a book) privately [on one's own account].

じひ[2] 慈悲 〈情け〉《文》mercy; 〈恵み〉charity; 《文》benevolence; 〈哀れみ〉《文》compassion; pity ¶慈悲深い《文》benevolent; kindhearted; 《文》tenderhearted; 《文》merciful / 慈悲をかける show mercy ((to)); have mercy ((on)) / 〈仏に〉do an act of charity / お慈悲に for mercy's sake / 慈悲心 a merciful heart; mercy.

じびいんこうか 耳鼻咽喉科 otolaryngology; otorhinolaryngology ¶耳鼻咽喉科の医院 an ear, nose and throat hospital / 耳鼻咽喉科の医者 an otorhinolaryngologist; an ear, nose and throat [ENT] doctor.

じびき 字引き ⇨じしょ[3].

じびきあみ 地引き網 a beach [shore] seine; a long-haul seine ¶地引き網を引く draw a beach seine; haul ashore a seine.

じひつ 自筆 ¶自筆の《文》autograph(ic); written by oneself; of [written in] one's own handwriting / 自筆の原稿 an autograph manuscript / フランクリンの自筆で書かれた written in Franklin's own writing [《文》hand].

じひびき 地響き a rumbling of the ground ¶地響きを立てて倒れる fall with a heavy [an earth-shaking] thud / 〈戦車などが〉地響きを立てて進む rumble [thunder] along.

しひょう 指標 an index ((pl. -es, indices)); an indicator; a pointer.

しびょう 死病 a fatal [《文》mortal] disease ¶死病に取りつかれる suffer from [catch, 《文》contract] a fatal disease.

---

gun to thaw, so that the ground shows through here and there.
しはつ 始発は午前4時30分です。The first train leaves [is] at 4:30 am.
しばふ 芝生に入らないで下さい。[掲示] Keep off the grass.
しばらく 私はしばらく前から健康がすぐれません。I have been in poor health for some time past. /

しばらくでしたね。It's a long time [an age] since I saw you last. / まだしばらくは牛肉の値段は下がらないでしょう。It will be some time before the price of beef comes down. / しばらくして初めてそれが偽物だと知った。It wasn't for some time that [It was quite a while before] I discovered that it was a fake.

しばる 僕は何事にも縛られるのは嫌だ。I can't stand being tied down. /《文》I am impatient of any restriction.
じばん この辺は地盤が緩い。The ground around here is not firm.
じひ[1] その本は自費出版である。The book was printed privately.
じびょう 頭痛が私の持病だ。Headache is a chronic disease with

じひょう¹ 時評 comments on current events [on the topics of the day] ¶月間文芸時評 a monthly literary review / 時評担当者 a news commentator.

じひょう² 辞表 a [one's] resignation; a letter of resignation ¶辞表を受理[却下]する accept [refuse, reject,《文》decline] sb's resignation / 辞表を出す hand in [《文》tender, submit, present] one's resignation;/辞表を撤回する withdraw one's resignation.

じびょう 持病 a chronic disease; an old complaint.

しびれ 痺れ numbness;《口語》(have) pins and needles;〈病気の〉palsy; paralysis ¶〈待ちあぐんで〉しびれを切らす get [《文》grow] impatient; lose one's patience.

しびれえい 〖魚〗 an electric ray.

しびれる 痺れる go [《文》become] numb;《口語》have [get] pins and needles; go dead ¶しびれた足 one's dead [《文》benumbed] feet. 文例⇩

しびん a urine glass; a urinal; a (urine) bottle

しぶ¹ astringent juice;〈かきの渋〉persimmon tannin ¶渋を抜く remove the astringency of〈persimmons〉/ 渋をひく tan / 渋がき a sour persimmon / 渋好み《文》(have) a taste for things of austere elegance / 渋紙 tanned paper / 渋茶 bitter [over-stewed] tea; coarse tea.

しぶ² 支部 a branch (office); a chapter;《米》a local (of a labor union).

しぶ³ 四部 ¶四部合唱 a chorus in four parts / 四部合奏 a quartet(te).

じふ 自負 ¶自負(心) pride; self-confidence / …と自負する flatter oneself that…; feel proud that…. 文例⇩

しぶい 渋い 〈渋味のある〉《文》astringent; mouth-puckering, sour; bitter;〈気難しい〉glum; sour; sullen;〈雅趣のある〉quiet and simple;《文》tasteful;〈地味な〉sober;《文》austere;〈けちな〉stingy; parsimonious;《英》mean; tightfisted ¶渋いぶどう酒 rough wine / 渋い柄 a quiet pattern / 渋い顔をする look glum; frown (at, on);《文》grimace; pull [make] a wry [sour] face / 渋い声で歌う sing in a well-trained voice. 文例⇩

しぶかわ 渋皮 (an) astringent skin; the epidermis; the astringent coat (of a chestnut) ¶渋皮がむける〈あかぬけしてくる〉《文》become urbane [refined] / 渋皮のむけた女 a sophisticated woman.

しぶき spray; a splash ¶しぶきを飛ばす spray; splash; send [toss] up spray. 文例⇩

しぶく¹ 私服 plain clothes;〈軍服に対して〉civilian clothes;《口語》civvies ¶私服で[の]《〈an officer) in plain clothes [in mufti] / 私服巡査 a plainclothes policeman.

しぶく² 私腹 ¶私腹を肥やす line [fill, stuff] one's (own) pocket(s) [purse]; 《文》enrich oneself; feather one's nest.

しぶく³ 雌伏 ¶雌伏する lie low (awaiting one's (a) chance); bide one's time; pocket one's pride. 「(music).

ジプシー a gipsy; a gypsy ¶ジプシーの gipsy

しぶしぶ 渋々 reluctantly;《文》with reluctance; halfheartedly; unwillingly ¶渋々承知する[譲る] accept sth [give sth up,《文》yield sth] with (a) bad grace. 文例⇩

ジブチ Djibouti ¶ジブチの Djiboutian / ジブチ共和国 the Republic of Djibouti.

しぶちん 渋ちん a tightfisted person; a miser;《米口語》a tightwad.

しぶつ¹ 死物 a useless thing; deadwood ¶死物と化する become useless.

しぶつ² 私物 one's (private) property; one's personal belongings [《口》effects].

じぶつ 事物 things; affairs ¶日本の事物《文》things Japanese.

ジフテリヤ 〖医〗 diphtheria ¶ジフテリヤ血清 antidiphtheria serum.

しぶとい 《文》 tenacious;《文》unyielding;《文》persevering;《文》enduring; die-hard; tough; stubborn. 文例⇩

しぶみ 渋味 〈味の〉astringency;〈雅趣〉quiet taste;《文》elegant simplicity;《文》severe exquisiteness;《文》austere elegance.

ジブラルタル Gibraltar ¶ジブラルタル海峡 the Strait(s) of Gibraltar.

しぶる 渋る hang [hold] back; hesitate; be unwilling (to do);《文》demur ¶答えを渋る hesitate [be reluctant] to answer / 出し渋る grudge (money) / 腹が渋る have a griping pain but find it difficult to empty one's bowels.

しふん 私憤 ⇒しえん². 文例⇩

しふん 脂粉 cosmetics ¶脂粉の香り a (seductive) fragrance of cosmetics.

しぶん¹ 四分 ¶四分する divide [separate] sth into four parts; quarter / 4分の1[3] a quarter [three quarters]; one-fourth [three-fourths] / 四分円 a quadrant / 四分儀 a quadrant / 四分五裂する be torn apart [into pieces,《文》asunder]; be disrupted;《文》become (totally) disorganized.

しぶん² 死文 (become) a dead letter; a scrap of paper.

じぶん 自分 oneself; I; you; one ¶自分(自身)

---

me. | I am subject to headaches.
しびれる 足がしびれた。My legs have gone to sleep [gone numb]. | 〈ちくちくする〉I've got pins and needles in my legs. / 右半身全体しびれていた。My whole right side felt numb. / あの人の声を聞いただけでしびれちゃう。I only have to hear his voice for a thrill to go through me.

じふ 彼は なかなか 自負心が強い。He has a very high opinion [thinks very highly] of himself.
しぶい 彼は渋い文章を書く。He writes (in) a sober [an austere] style.
しぶき しぶきがかかった。I was caught in [got wet with] the spray. / 噴水が銀色のしぶきを上げていた。A fountain was throwing its silvery spray into the air.
しぶしぶ 彼は僕の忠告を渋々受け入れた。He took my advice with (a) bad grace.
しぶとい 何てしぶといやつだろう。He's a persistent devil. | You have to give him full marks for persistence [determination].
しぶる 筆が渋った。His pen faltered [slowed down].

の *one's* own ; personal ; private / 自分のために図る《文》pursue *one's* own interests / 自分の物にする〈物を〉make *sth one's* own ; 〈技術などを〉master ; get [《文》achieve] mastery of / 自分のことは考えないで unselfishly / 自分の物になる become *one's* (own) ; fall into *one's* hands ; 《文》come into *one's* possession / 自分(自身)で〈親しく〉personally ; in person ; 《文》in *one's* (own) person ; 〈1人で〉by *oneself* ; 〈自分のために, 独力で〉for *oneself* ; 〈勝手に〉of *one's* own accord [free will] ; 〈自前で〉on *one's* own account / 自分で調べる examine *sth* for *oneself* [at first hand] / 自分で言うのはおかしいけれど though I say it myself / 自分から《文》voluntarily / 自分としては for my part ; as for me [myself] ; I for one《think of it this way》/ 自分勝手な selfish ; 《文》self-seeking ; 《文》egoistic / 自分勝手に〈利己的に〉for selfish reasons [《文》ends] ; 〈思うままに〉《文》at will ; as *one* pleases [likes] ; 《文》at *one's* own pleasure ; 〈独断で〉at *one's* own discretion / 自分免許の self-styled《cooking experts》. [文例⇩]

じぶん[2] 時分 〈時刻〉time ; an hour ; 〈時節〉a season ; 《at this》time of (the) year ¶来[去]年の今時分 about this time next [last] year / (もう)今時分は by this (time) ; by now. [文例⇩]

しぶんしょ 私文書 《forgery of》a private document.

しべ 蕊〘植〙〈雄しべ〉a stamen《*pl.* -s, stamina》; 〈雌しべ〉a pistil.

しへい 紙幣 ⇨ さつ.

じへいしょう 自閉症 autism ¶自閉症の子供 an autistic child.

じべた 地べた ¶地べたに座る squat on the (bare) ground [earth].

しべつ 死別 ¶死別する lose《*one's* husband》; 《文》be bereaved of《a son》.

シベリア Siberia ¶シベリア横断の trans-Siberian《flights》/ シベリア鉄道 the Trans-Siberian Railroad.

しへん[1] 四辺 ¶四辺に on all sides ; all around.

しへん[2] 紙片 a piece [bit] of paper ; a slip [strip] of paper (細長い).

しへん[3] 詩篇〘聖書〙the (Book of) Psalms (略 : Ps., Psa.).

しべん[1] 支弁 ¶支弁する pay ; 《文》defray《expenses》; 《文》disburse《funds》.

しべん[2] 思弁 《文》speculation ¶思弁する speculate / 思弁哲学 (a) speculative philosophy.

じへん 事変 an incident ; a trouble.

じべん 自弁 ¶自弁する pay *one's* own expenses / 自弁で at *one's* own expense. [文例⇩]

しへんけい 四辺形〘数〙a quadrilateral ; a quadrangle ¶四辺形の quadrangular.

しほ 試補 a probationer ¶司法官試補 a probationary judicial officer ; a judicial officer on probation.

しぼ 思慕 (a) longing [《文》yearning]《for》; 《文》deep attachment《to》¶思慕する love *sb* dearly ; adore ; long for ; 《文》yearn after [for].

じぼ 字母 〈文字〉an alphabet ; a letter ; 〈活字の型〉a matrix《*pl.* matrices, matrixes》; a printing type.

しほう[1] 四方 ¶四方(八方)に on all sides ; on every side ; in all directions ; all around ; to all points of the compass / 四方八方から from all quarters ; from every direction / 10キロ四方に within a radius of ten kilometers. [文例⇩]

しほう[2] 司法 administration of justice ; judicature ¶司法官 a judicial officer [official] / 司法警察 the judicial police / 司法権《exercise》judicial [judicatory] power [rights] / 司法研修所 the Judicial Research and Training Institute / 司法試験 a state law examination / 司法書士 a judicial scrivener / 司法制度 the judicial system [arrangements] / 司法当局 the judiciary (authorities).

しほう[3] 至宝 the greatest [《文》a cherished] treasure ¶国家の至宝 a great national asset.

しほう[4] 私法〘法〙private law.

しぼう[1] 子房〘植〙an ovary ¶子房室 a cell.

しぼう[2] 死亡 death ; 《文》decease ; 《文》demise ¶死亡する die ; pass away (婉曲的に) ; 〈事故などで〉be killed / 死亡記事[欄] an obituary notice [column] / 死亡者《文》the deceased ; the dead ; deaths (事故などの) / 死亡診断[証明]書 a certificate of death ; a death certificate / 死亡統計 statistics of mortality ; mortality statistics / 死亡届け a notice of (*sb's*) death / 死亡率 a death rate ; 《infant》mortality / 胃がんの死亡率 the rate of deaths [the mortality] from stomach cancer / 結核の死亡率 the death rate from tuberculosis. [文例⇩]

しぼう[3] 志望 《文》a desire ; a wish ; 《文》an aspiration ; an ambition (大望) ; a choice (選択) ¶志望する《文》desire ; wish ; choose ; prefer / 外交官を志望する want to be a diplomat ; 《文》aspire to a diplomatic career / 志望を抱く harbor [cherish] a desire / 志望校 the school of *one's*《first, second》choice / 志望者 an applicant [a candidate]《for》/ 文学志望者 an aspiring writer [author].

じぶん[1] 自分も初めはそう思った. I thought so myself at first. / 自分のことは自分でせよ. Look after yourself. / 彼には自分の家がある. He has a house of his own. / 失敗したのは自分が悪いからだ. He has only himself to blame for his failure. / その文章を読んでいるうちに, 急にそれが自分のことのように思われてきた. All at once [Suddenly] the words of the passage seemed to apply to me personally. / あの娘はまだ若くて, 自分で自分の心がわからないのだ. She is still too young to know her own mind. / どうしてあんなことを言ったか自分ながらわかりません. I cannot imagine what made me say a thing like that. / そんな事をするのは自分勝手だ. It is selfish of you to behave that way.

じぶん[2] いつも今時分は天気が定まらない. We always have changeable weather at this time of (the) year. / 君が行く時分には会は始まっているでしょう. The meeting will already have started when you get there.

じべん 交通費は各自自弁のこと. Each to pay his own fare.

しほう[1] 6メートル四方ある. It is six meters square. / その山の頂

しほう⁴ 脂肪 fat; grease; lard(豚の); suet(牛・羊などの固い); blubber(鯨の) ¶脂肪がつく put on fat; run to fat / 脂肪を取る remove (surplus) fat; slim; 〈運動をして〉exercise fat off / 脂肪質の, 脂肪の多い fatty / 脂肪のない肉 lean [red] meat / 植物性[動物性]脂肪 vegetable [animal] fat(s) / 脂肪過多 obesity; excess of fat / 脂肪ぶとりの obese; fat; corpulent.

じほう 時報 a time signal ¶ラジオの時報に合わせる set (one's watch) by the radio (time signal).

じぼうじき 自暴自棄 desperation; despair; 《文》self-abandonment ¶自暴自棄のdesperate; 《文》abandoned ¶自暴自棄になる get [grow, 《文》become] desperate (at one's failure); give oneself up to despair.

じほく 磁北 magnetic north.

しぼむ 萎む wither; wilt; shrivel; 〈風船が〉deflate; get deflated.

しぼり 絞[搾]り 〈染め物の〉tie-dyed fabric; 《写真》a stop; an iris (pl. -es, irides) ¶絞りの〈染めが〉tie-dyed; white-spotted; dappled; parti-colored / 搾りかす strained lees; draff / (洗濯機の)絞り機 a (clothes) wringer / 絞り絵の具 tube colors; a tube paint.

しぼる 絞[搾]る wring; squeeze; press; 〈しかる〉《文》reprimand; scold; take sb to task ¶搾り上げる 〈人から金などを〉extort [squeeze, wring] (money from [out of] sb); 《口語》milk [bleed] sb / 絞り出す press [squeeze] (juice from [out of] a lemon); 絞って水気を取る wring sth dry [out] / 声を絞る strain one's voice / 知恵[頭]を絞る a rack (cudgel, beat) one's brains; split one's head; think hard / 議論を(要点だけに)絞る narrow an argument down (to one point) / レンズを絞る stop the lens down / 牛の乳を搾る milk a cow / 搾りたての牛乳 milk fresh from the cow.

しほん(きん) 資本(金) (a) capital; a fund ¶資本の蓄積 accumulation of capital / 資本の流出 capital outflow / 資本の流入 the influx [inflow] of capital / 資本が要る finance [provide capital for]《an enterprise》/ 資本を調達する raise capital / 資本を投入する[下ろす] invest [lay out] capital (in); put in capital / 資本を寝かせる let capital lie idle / …の資本で with a capital of (20 million yen) / 授権[固定, 公称]資本 authorized [fixed, nominal] capital / 資本家 a capitalist / 資本家階級 the capitalist class / 資本家と労働者 capital and labor / 資本化する capitalize / 資本金10億円の会社 a company capitalized at one billion yen / 資本構成 the capital structure 《of a firm》/ 資本財 capital goods / 資本主義 capitalism / 資本主義の[的] capitalistic; capitalistic / 資本主義経済 (a) capitalist(ic) economy / 資本主義国[陣営] a capitalist country [the capitalist camp] / 資本投資 capital investment / 資本力 the capital strength 《of an enterprise》/ 資本論《書名》Das Kapital; Capital. [文例В]

しま¹ 島 an island; 《文》an isle; an islet (小島) ¶島(状)の insular / 島の人 an islander; a native [an inhabitant] of an island / 島宇宙 an island universe / 島陰に under [in] the lee of an island / 島国 an island country [nation]; 《文》a seagirt country / 島国根性 insularity; the islander mentality; 《文》insularism / 島流しになる be exiled [banished] to an island / 島巡りをする make a tour of the islands / 島伝いに移動する island-hop (one's way); move [migrate] by island-hopping; move from island to island.

しま² 縞 stripes; 〈幅広の〉a band; 〈獣の毛皮や鳥の羽などの〉markings ¶しま(柄)の striped; 〈白と明るい色の〉candy-striped / ピンクと白のしまのズボン pink and white striped [candy-striped] trousers / 黄色と黒の鮮やかなしまをなした昆虫 an insect brightly banded with yellow and black.

しまい¹ 仕舞 〈能の〉a Noh dance in plain clothes.

しまい² 仕舞い 〈終わり〉an end; 《文》a conclusion ¶仕舞いの last; final; 《文》closing / 仕舞いに finally; at last [length]; in the end [long run] / 仕舞にする put an end to (a period, a full stop)《to》; make an end of《a foolish argument》; close; 《文》conclude / 仕舞いになる end; close; come to an end [a close]; be finished; be over / 仕舞いから2番目の the last but one / 仕舞いまで to the end [last] / 芝居を仕舞いまで見る sit out a play / 長いお説教を仕舞いまで聴く sit through a long sermon.

しまい³ 姉妹 sisters ¶姉妹会社 an affiliated company [corporation]; an affiliate / 姉妹船[都市] a sister ship [city] / 姉妹編 a companion [sister] volume《to》; 〈続編〉a sequel《to》.

しまいこむ 仕舞い込む put [stow] sth away; hide [tuck] sth away (in a box).

しまう 仕舞う 〈片づける〉put [lay, stow] 《goods》away; put back (元の場所に); 〈仕舞っておく〉keep; store (蓄える) ¶店を仕舞う 〈閉店する〉close one's store; 〈廃業する〉

上からは50キロ四方が見える. From the top of the mountain you can see for fifty kilometers in every direction.

しほう² この事故で多くの死亡者を出した. Many lives were lost in the accident. / この病気は死亡率が高い. This disease has a high mortality (rate).

しぼる ブランデーを水で割って, レモンをちょっと絞って入れてくれ. Give me brandy and water with a little lemon squeezed in it. / 交渉は一点に絞られてきた. The negotiations have narrowed down to one single issue.

しほん(きん) 彼の事業は資本が足らない. His enterprise is insufficiently capitalized [short of funds]. / 体だけが僕の資本だ. Health is the only asset I have.

しまい² しまいにはとうとうけんかになった. It ended in a quarrel. / その品はもうおしまいになりました. We've run out of that (item). | It's all gone. / さあこれで今日はおしまいだ. That's it [all] for today. | Let's knock off here today. | Let's call it a day. ★ この a day は必ずしも「きょう」の意味ではない. / 僕の言うことをしまいまで聞いて下さい. Hear me out, please! / 彼はしま

しまうま 縞馬 《動》a zebra.

じまえ 自前 ⇨ じぶん.

じまく 字幕 《映画》〈俳優名など字が映る部分〉credit titles; credits; a title; 〈せりふの〉subtitles.

しまつ 始末 〈次第〉circumstances; 《文》particulars; 〈処理〉management; 《文》disposal; 《文》settlement; 〈倹約〉《文》thrift; 《文》frugality; economy ¶始末する 〈処理する〉manage; deal with; dispose of; settle; 〈片づける〉put in order; put [stow] away; put back 〈元の所へ〉; 〈倹約する〉economize; save / 始末をつける settle 《one's accounts》; wind up 《a company》; liquidate [do away with] sb / 始末に負えない[困る] difficult to deal with; hard to manage [to do with]; unmanageable; unruly; 《文》refractory; 《文》intractable; 《文》ungovernable 〈人・事件などが〉始末に負えなくなる get out of control [《one's》 hand] / 始末書 a written explanation [apology]; a letter of apology / 始末屋 a frugal [thrifty] person. 文例⇩

しまった oh, dear!; 《俗》oh hell!; oh my God!; how stupid of me!

しまへび 《動》a Japanese striped snake.

しまり 締まり 〈口に締まりがない〉have a loose mouth; 《文》be lax in the mouth; 〈おしゃべりである〉have a loose tongue / 締まりのある firm; tight; compact / 締まりのない loose; slack; lax; slovenly; sloppy / 締まり屋 a tightfisted [《文》thrifty] person; a person who is careful with *his* money.

しまる 閉[締]まる 〈戸などが〉shut; close; 〈ぴんと張る〉tighten; 《文》become taut; 〈気持ちが〉become sober [steady]; pull *oneself* together; reform 〈改心する〉; 〈節約する〉《文》thrifty; 《文》be frugal; tighten [pull in] *one's* belt / 締まった compact; firm; well-set / 締まった口元 a firm mouth / 締まった体格 a well-knit[-set] frame; a firm build. 文例⇩

じまん 自慢 pride; a boast; 《文》self-praise ¶自慢する 〈口で〉boast 《of, that...》; be boastful; 〈心で〉be proud 《of, that...》; take pride 《in》; pride *oneself* 《on》; have a high opinion of *oneself* [*one's sth*] / 自慢そうに boastfully; proudly / 自慢ではないが… though I say it myself; 《文》without boasting [any boastfulness] I may say...; 《文》I flatter myself that... / 〈物を〉自慢して見せる make a display [show] of *sth*; show off 《*one's* new car》 / 力自慢をする boast about [of] *one's* strength / 自慢話 boastful talk; bragging; a brag / 自慢話をする blow *one's* own trumpet. 文例⇩

しみ¹ 染み a stain; a blot; a smear; a smudge; a spot ¶インキ[お茶]の染み an ink spot [a tea stain] / 雨漏りの染み a patch of damp / 染みが付く be stained; be smudged / 染みのある stained; smeared / 染みだらけの covered with stains [blots]; blotchy / 染みのない spotless; 《文》immaculate / 染みのつかない stain-resistant 《carpets》 / 染みを取る remove [take out] a stain 《from》 / 〈洗ったりふいたりして〉wash [wipe] out a stain. 文例⇩

しみ² 《昆》染みに付く〈衣類に付く〉a 《clothes》moth; 〈本に付く〉a bookworm ¶しみの食った worm-eaten 《books》.

じみ¹ 地味 地味な 〈簡素な〉plain; simple; 〈落ち着いた〉quiet; sober; 〈控え目の〉《文》restrained; modest; low-key(ed) 《campaigns》 / 〈保守的な〉conservative / 地味な人 《文》a modest and reserved [retiring] person / 地味な色 a sober color [hue] / 地味なネクタイ a quiet tie / 地味なデザイン a restrained design / 地味な服装をする be quietly [soberly] dressed / 地味に暮らす live in a quiet way. 文例⇩

じみ² 滋味 《文》tastefulness; 《文》exquisiteness ¶滋味掬(きく)すべきものがある 《文》have a subtle charm (that is to be quietly appreciated).

シミーズ ⇨ シュミーズ.

しみこむ 染み込む soak [sink] into; 《文》permeate 《a rock》; filter [seep] into 《the soil》 ¶〈思想・感情が〉染み込んでいる 《文》be deeply ingrained in 《*one's* thought and feeling》; 〈人が主語〉《文》be imbued with 《patriotism》; have 《the work habit》 in *one's* bones / 染み込ませる 《文》infiltrate 《water》 into *sth*; 《文》infiltrate [saturate] *sth* with 《water》; 《文》imbue [inspire] 《*sb* with an idea》; instill 《an idea into *sb*》. 文例⇩

いには彼女と結婚することになるだろう。He will end up by marrying her.

しまつ こんな始末になってしまって申し訳ありません。I'm sorry things have come to this.

しまる この戸はなかなか閉まらない。The door won't close. / 戸が閉まった。The door was closed [to]. / あの店は8時に閉まる。The store closes at eight o'clock. / 締まって行こうぜ.〈競技などで〉Let's all pull together. / Let's play it close [tight] this time. / 金は使っても締まる所はちゃんと締まる。He knows when to spend and when to save.

じまん そんな事は自慢にならない。That's nothing to be proud of. / この町の下水設備は自慢できる代物ではない。The state of the drains in this town is nothing we can be proud of. / 自慢のような話はしないでおきます。Modesty forbids me from talking about it. / 自慢じゃないが僕はこういうことにかけては人後に落ちません。I flatter myself that I am second to none at this sort of thing.

しみ¹ この染みはなかなか[洗っても]落ちませんよ。I'm afraid the stain won't come [wash] out. / 天井は雨漏りの染みができていた。The ceiling was patched with damp.

じみ¹ 彼女たちのブラウスは色も型もどちらかと言えば地味なものだった。Their blouses were relatively restrained in color and design. / このドレスは私には地味でしょうか。Is this dress too old for me? / 営業方法が地味だ。His business methods are rather conservative.

しみこむ 薬が背中の傷口に染み込んで思わずうめき声をあげた。He groaned in spite of himself, as

しみじみ 〈痛切に〉keenly; deeply; fully; 〈心から〉《文》heartily; 〈全く〉quite; thoroughly; 〈しんみり〉seriously / しみじみ感じる〈人が主語〉feel keenly / 〈事が主語〉come home to *one* / しみじみ話す have a quiet (heart-to-heart) talk ((with)).

しみず 清水 a spring; spring water ¶清水を飲む drink from a spring.

じみち 地道 ¶地道な〈真面目な〉honest; sober; 〈着実な〉steady; straightforward / 地道に in an honest way; soberly; steadily; step by step / 地道に暮らす make an honest living.

シミちょう 文例⇩

しみつく 染み付く be dyed ((in blue)); be stained ((with grease)).

しみったれ ⇨けち[1].

しみでる 染み出る ooze (out); 《文》exude. 文例⇩

しみとおる 染み透る seep [soak] through [into]; penetrate (through); 《文》permeate / 《文》infiltrate into.

シミュレーター a simulator.

しみる 染みる 〈液体が〉soak [sink] into; permeate; pierce; 《文》infiltrate; 〈ひりひりする〉smart ¶目に染みる〈感銘する〉sink deeply into *one*'s mind; come home to *one*; go straight to *one*'s heart; 〈寒さなどが〉be biting; be piercing; cut *one* to the bone / 身に染みて keenly; fully; 《文》heartily; deeply. 文例⇩

-じみる have a touch of; 〈...に似ている〉look like ¶田舎染みている look like a countryman; be countrified. 文例⇩

しみん 市民 〈個人〉a citizen; 〈集合的〉the citizens; the townsmen ¶京都市民 the citizens [people] of Kyoto / 市民運動 a citizens movement / 市民会館 a civic hall / 市民権を与える grant citizenship to *sb* / 市民権を獲得する《文》acquire [obtain] 《U.S.》citizenship / 市民社会 civil society / 市民生活 the civic life / 市民大会 a citizens' rally [mass meeting] / 市民団体 a citizens' civic group [organization].

しみんせいのうえん 嗜眠性脳炎〔医〕(lethargic) encephalitis; sleeping sickness.

じむ 事務 business (matters); affairs; office [clerical] work; an office job ¶事務を執る attend to *one*'s business; do office work / 事務的に in a businesslike manner; 〈機械的に〉mechanically; 《文》perfunctorily / 事務的才能がある have [《文》possess] business ability [talent] / 事務員 a clerk; an office worker [clerk]; 〈全員〉the staff of an office / 女事務員 an office girl / 事務官 a secretary / 事務局 a secretariat / 事務局長 a secretary-general (*pl.* secretaries-) / 事務系統の仕事 white-collar work; a clerical job / 事務次官 a permanent vice-minister [undersecretary] / 事務室[所] an office / 事務職員 a clerical employee / 事務折衝 negotiations at the level of government officials [at the official level]; 〈国連などでの〉negotiations [consultations] between permanent representatives [officials] / 事務総長 a secretary-general (*pl.* secretaries-) / 事務長 a head official; 〈船の〉a purser / 事務引き継ぎ taking over the work [the management of an office] ((from *one*'s predecessor)) / 事務用品 office supplies; 〈文房具〉stationery / 学長事務取扱 an acting president. 文例⇩

しむける 仕向ける 〈促す〉urge [《文》induce, tempt] *sb* ((*to do*)); 〈送る〉send; forward; dispatch; ship; 〈取り扱う〉treat *sb* ((well, badly)); do *sb* a (good) turn; act ((kindly, unkindly)) toward *sb* ¶仕向け港 the port of destination / 仕向け先[地] the destination. 文例⇩

しめ[1] 締め 〈束〉a bundle; 〈紙の〉a *shime*, a unit denoting 2,000 sheets of Japanese *hanshi* paper; a ream ((of paper)) ★ream は紙の一定の枚数, 通常 500 枚 ¶締めをする, 締め高 ⇨そうりょ[2].

しめ[2] ¶しめ(縄, 飾り) a (*Shinto*) straw festoon (decorated with cut paper).

しめい[1] 氏名 a (full) name ¶氏名を秘す《文》conceal [veil] *one*'s identity / 氏名不詳の unidentified.

しめい[2] 死命 ¶死命を制する have *sb*'s life in *one*'s hands; have a hold over *sb*; 《文》seal [decide] the fate of *sb*.

しめい[3] 使命 《文》a mission; 《文》an appointed task ¶使命を帯びる[帯びて行く] be entrusted with [go on] a mission / 使命を果たす perform [fulfill] *one*'s mission. 文例⇩

しめい[4] 指名 《文》nomination; 《文》designation ¶指名する name; 《文》nominate; 《文》designate; call on *sb* to *do*; pick (on) ((a student to answer the question)) / 議長に指名される be nominated (as) chairman / 指名された人 a nominee / 議長に指名された人 ¶まだ就任

---

the medicine worked into his wounded back. / 土壌が凍っているので, 水が地中に染み込まない. Because the soil is frozen, the water does not seep down into the earth. / その言葉は私の心に染み込んだ. The remark sank into my mind. / この世は苦界であるという仏教の考えが彼らの心の中に深く染み込んでいた. The Buddhist idea that this world is a place of universal suffering was deeply embedded in their minds.

シミちょう あの女, シミちょろだ. Her slip is showing.

しみでる その農薬が土から染み出て地下水に入ったのです. The agricultural chemicals seeped out of the soil into the ground water.

しみる 煙が染みて目が痛かった. My eyes smarted from the smoke. /煙が目に染みて涙が出た. The smoke made my eyes water. /今朝の寒さは身に染みる. It is bitterly cold this morning.

-じみる 彼は言語動作に気違いじみたところがある. He has a touch of insanity in his speech and behavior. / 言うことが坊主染みている. His talk smacks of a preacher.

じむ 2階の1室が事務を執る所になっている. One of the rooms on the second floor is used for office purposes. / あれはただの事務屋だ. He is no one except as a clerk. / 交渉はまだ事務折衝の段階だ. The negotiations are still at the stage of (preliminary) arrangements at the official level.

しむける 彼はいやでも応でも辞任しなければならないように仕向けられた. He was forced [compelled] to resign.

しめい[3] 彼の行動は強い使命感に基

じめい 自明 ¶自明の obvious;《文》self-evident;《文》axiomatic;《文》self-explanatory / 自明の理《文》a self-evident truth; a truism;《文》an axiom.　[⇒びじょ]
しめがね 締め金 a buckle; a clasp; a clamp
しめきり 締め切り closing; a close; a deadline ¶4月1日の締め切りまでに by the deadline, April 1 / 締め切り期日 the closing day; the deadline (date)《for》. 文例↓
しめきる 締[閉]め切る 〈戸を〉close [shut] up; keep (a door) shut [closed];〈受付を〉close《the subscription list》¶戸を閉め切って behind closed doors.
しめくくり 締めくくり〈決着をつけること〉《文》(a) conclusion; (a) settlement;〈要約〉a summing-up; a summary;〈最後〉the end; the finish; the last stage ¶締めくくりをつける finish sth (off); complete; put an end [a period] to; sum up.
しめくくる 締めくくる〈決着をつける〉settle; finish sth off;《文》bring sth to a conclusion; round off;〈固く縛る〉bind [tie] fast.
しめころす 絞め殺す strangle [throttle] sb (to death).
しめし 示し〈手本〉an example; a lesson;〈規律〉discipline ¶示しがつかない set a bad example《to》. 文例↓
しめしあわせる 示し合わせる arrange beforehand; conspire《with》¶示し合わせたように《文》as if by common [prior] consent / 示し合わせて《文》in collusion [concert]《with》;《文》by prearrangement / あらかじめ示し合わせたとおり as (previously) arranged;《文》according to a previous arrangement.
じめじめ ¶じめじめする be [feel] damp; be wet;〈土地が〉be marshy; be soggy;〈陰気で

ある〉be gloomy;《文》feel melancholy.
しめす[1] 示す show; give a sign《of sth》; point out;《文》indicate; tell;《文》set forth 模範を示す set an example / 実例を示す give an example; cite an instance / 実力を示す show [display] one's ability / 場所を示す point to a place / 承諾を示す身ぶり a gesture of [indicating] consent. 文例↓
しめす[2] 湿す wet; moisten; dampen.
しめた I've got it!; Good!; That's it! 〈発見して〉Eureka! ★Eureka は I have found it. の意のギリシャ語から.
しめだし 閉[締]め出し ¶閉[締]め出しを食う be shut out; be barred; be kept on the wrong side of the door / 閉[締]め出しを食わす shut the door on sb; shut sb out; bar sb;《文》exclude sb (from the discussion); lock out《workers》.
しめだす 閉[締]め出す ⇒しめだし.
しめつ 死滅《文》extinction;《文》annihilation; (a) death ¶死滅する die out; become extinct;《文》be annihilated;《文》perish / 死滅した extinct.
じめつ 自滅《文》self-destruction ¶自滅する destroy [ruin] oneself;《文》perish / 自滅的な《文》self-defeating《processes》; suicidal《behavior》.
しめつけ 締め付け a control;《口語》a squeeze ¶締め付けを強化する tighten one's control《of》;《口語》put the squeeze [screws]《on》.
しめつける 締め付ける〈縛る〉fasten [bind] sth tight;〈ぴんと張る〉tighten;〈圧迫する〉compress; squeeze;〈のどを〉throttle ¶〈心臓病などが〉胸を締めつけられるような感じがする feel a tightness [(a) constriction] in the [one's] chest. 文例↓
しめっぽい 湿っぽい damp; moist; wet; humid;〈陰気な〉gloomy; sad; depressing.
しめやかな quiet;《米》lonesome; gloomy ¶しめやかな雨 a soft [gentle] rain / しめやかな通夜《hold》a quiet and sorrowful vigil《over sb's body》/ しめやかに quietly; softly.
しめり 湿り〈湿気〉dampness; moisture;〈雨〉rain.
しめる[1] 占める《文》occupy; take (up); hold;

づくものであった. He was moved by a firm sense of mission.
しめい[4] 指名された方は起立して下さい. Those whose names are called [mentioned] are requested to rise. / ご指名によりまして、乾杯の音頭をとらせていただきます. Having been called upon by the toastmaster [Mr. —] I would ask you all to join me in raising your glasses.
しめきり 午前3時が朝刊の（原稿の）締め切りになっています. 3 a.m. is the deadline for the morning edition (of the paper). / 図案募集の締め切りは来る3月10日です. Competitors are requested to send in their designs not later than March 10th. / 予約締め切り

は本月30日です. The subscription list closes on the 30th of this month. / 締め切りに間に合わせようとして、できるだけ頑張った. I did my best to make [meet] the deadline.
しめし 親が不品行では子供に示しがつかない. If a parent behaves badly, he will lose all authority over his children. / 先生がそんなことをしては生徒に示しがつかない. That sort of conduct on the part of a teacher will affect [damage] school discipline. / いったん例外を認めると、示しがつかなくなる. One exception would lead to another. | Once we allow an exception, there will be no end to them.

しめす[1] 赤旗は危険を示す. A red flag means [is a sign of] danger. / 私の時計は8時3分を示していた. My watch said [showed] three minutes past eight. / 寒暖計は30度を示した. The thermometer registered [read, stood at] 30°. / 広い額は頭のよさを示すものとされている. A high forehead is regarded as a sign of intelligence. / この事実は彼の優しい心根を示すものである. This fact is evidence of his kindness. / この新政策はアメリカが自信を取り戻したことをよく示している. This new policy

しめる have; account for ¶第1位を占める rank first; hold [win] (the) first place; head the list ((of)) / クラスで首席を占める be (at the) top of *one's* class; be [stand] first in *one's* class / 鉄道事故の3割を占める account for [amount to] 30 per cent of all railroad accidents / 絶対多数を占める command an absolute majority (in the Diet).

しめる² 湿る get [((文)) become] damp [moist, wet]; dampen; moisten ¶湿った moist; damp; wet / 湿らないようにする keep ((powder)) dry.

しめる³ 締[絞,閉]める <ゆわえる> tie (up); bind; ぴんと張る pull *sth* tight [taut]; tighten; <絞める> throttle; strangle; <帯などを> put on; buckle; <閉じる> shut; close; <合計する> add up; total (the figures); <節約する> economize; ((文)) use economy (in); save; <厳しく扱う> be firm [strict] ((with)); ((文)) exercise rigid [strict] control [supervision] ((over)); tighten *one's* control ((of)); apply the screw to; ((口語)) put the screws [squeeze] on ((the students)); <しかる> ((口語)) tell *sb* off; ((文)) rebuke; ((文)) reprimand; ((文)) take [call] *sb* to task ¶戸を引いて閉める draw [pull] the door to / 戸をきちんと閉める shut the window tight(ly); pull the window tight shut / バイオリンの弦を締める tighten [screw up] the strings of a violin / 勘定を締める in; all told. 文例⇩

しめん¹ 四面 ((副詞的)) on all sides; on every side ¶四面海に囲まれた国 ((文)) a seagirt country; a country surrounded by sea [((文)) the seas] / 四面楚歌の声を聞く[の中にある] be forsaken by everybody; have the whole world against *one* / 四面体 a tetrahedron ((*pl.* -s, -dra)).

しめん² (page) space ¶紙面が許すならば ((文)) if space permits [allows]; if there is enough space / 紙面の都合で <紙面に限りがあるので> for want of space; ((文)) due to limitations of space / 紙面をさく[当てる] ((文)) devote space ((to)); allow space ((for)) / (多くの)紙面を取る take up [((文)) occupy] a lot of space. 文例⇩

じめん 地面 <表面> the surface of the earth; <土地> land; ground; <地所> a lot; a plot ¶広い地面 a large tract [piece] of land / 地面に座る squat on the ground.

しも¹ 下 ¶下の句 the second half of a *tanka* / 下の世話をする attend to all *sb's* personal needs / 下半期 the latter [second] half year. 文例⇩

しも² 霜 (hoar [white]) frost ¶ひどい霜 a severe frost / 霜の降りた frosted; frosty / 霜の花 frost flowers [ferns] / (髪が)霜を置いたる gray; grizzled / 霜を取る defrost ((a refrigerator)) / 霜取り装置 a defrosting device; a defroster / 霜柱 ice needles [columns]; frost columns [crystals] / 霜解けの季節 the thawing season / 霜夜 a frosty night / 霜よけをする shelter [protect] ((a tree)) from the frost. 文例⇩

しもがかった 下掛かった ((文)) improper; indecent; obscene; dirty; off-color.

しもがれ 霜枯れ ¶霜枯れの <霜害を受けた> frostbitten ((plants)); <冬枯れの> wintry; bleak / 霜枯れ時 the winter season; <不況期> the lean [off] season. 文例⇩

じもく 耳目 ¶世間の耳目を驚かす startle the world; create a sensation.

しもごえ 下肥 night soil.

しもざ 下座 ¶下座につく take a lower seat; give [((文)) cede] the seat of honor ((to *sb*)); sit at the foot of the table.

しもじも 下々 the common people; the masses; the lower classes.

しもたや しもた屋 a dwelling house (in a district composed mainly of shops).

しもて 下手 the lower part; <舞台の> the right stage; (the) stage right; the left of the stage (seen from the audience).

じもと 地元 ¶地元の local / 地元チーム a home [local] team / 地元民 local residents [inhabitants].

しもぶくれ 下脹れ ¶下ぶくれの full-cheeked.

しもふり 霜降り ¶霜降りの <服地の色> pepper-and-salt ((pattern)) / 霜降り肉 marbled beef.

しもべ a servant ¶((文)) a manservant ((*pl.* menservants)); ((文)) a menial.

しもやけ 霜焼け chilblains (軽度の); frostbite (重症の) ¶霜焼けにかかる have chilblains

---

is a good indication of America's renewed self-confidence.

しめた こうなったらもうしめたものだ。We've [I've] got them [him] (beaten) now.

じめつ 彼らは遠からず自滅するであろう。They will come to ruin sooner or later.

しめつける 彼女の話を聞くと胸が締めつけられるような気持ちだ。It wrings my heart to hear her story.

しめる¹ この国は鉄の産額において世界第3位を占めている。This country stands third in the world as regards the output of iron. / うちの会社はこのビルの3階と4階を占めております。Our office oc- cupies [has] the third and fourth floors of this building. / 奨学生は本学の在学生総数のほぼ5分の1を占めている。Scholarship students account for close to a fifth of the whole enrollment in our college.

しめる³ 後を閉めなさい。Shut the door after you. / 締めていくらになるかね。What is the total? | ((口語)) How much does it come to altogether? | ((口語)) What's the damage?

しめん² もっと詳しく述べたいが紙面に限りがあるのでやむを得ない。Lack of space prevents me from going into further detail.

しも¹ この川の2キロほど下に橋 がある。There is a bridge about two kilometers down this river.

しも² けさ霜が降りた。Frost formed this morning. / 草に霜が降りている。There is frost on the grass. / 霜が解けた。The frost has melted. / もう霜は降りますまい。I don't think we'll have any more frost. / 頭に霜を置き始めた。His hair is beginning to show white streaks [traces of pepper and salt]. / この道は午後になると霜解けでひどくぬかる。In the afternoon the road becomes muddy as it thaws.

しもがれ 手前どもの商売は今が霜枯れ時でございます。Our business is in the doldrums now.

しもん¹ 指紋 a fingerprint; a finger mark; a thumb print (親指の) ★口語では, 状況上意味が明らかなときは the suspect's prints のように省略して言うこともある. これは通常複数形で言う ¶指紋を残す leave one's (finger-)prints (on sth) / 指紋を採る take sb's (finger-)prints / 指紋を検出[確認]する detect [identify] fingerprints.

しもん² 試問 an interview; an examination ¶試問する interview sb; question sb; put a question to sb.

しもん³ 諮問 an inquiry ¶諮問する inquire; submit [refer] (a problem) to (a committee for deliberation); consult / 諮問機関 an advisory [a consultative] body.

じもんじとう 自問自答 《文》 a soliloquy; a monologue ¶自問自答する think aloud; ask oneself; answer one's own questions; wonder.

しや 視野 a field of vision; a view; an outlook (on sth); a visual [viewing] field; 《文》 one's mental [intellectual] horizon ¶視野が広い far-sighted; levelheaded / 《文》 discerning; 《文》 discriminating / 視野が狭い shortsighted; 《口語》 blinkered; prejudiced; bigoted; intolerant / 視野を広げる broaden [expand] one's horizons / 視野に入る come in sight [into view]; come within the range [sweep] (of a telescope) / 広い視野から物事を見る take a broad view of things; put [get, have] things in perspective. 文例⇩

しゃ¹ 紗 (silk) gauze.

しゃ² 斜 ¶斜に構える 〈からだを〉 assume an attitude with one's right [left] shoulder drawn back; 〈比喩的に〉 take 《文》 assume) a challenging attitude 《toward》.

じゃ 蛇 a (large) snake; a serpent ⇒へび.

じゃあ ⇒では. 文例⇩

ジャー a vacuum bottle [《英》flask]; 《商標名》a Thermos (flask [《米》bottle]).

じゃあく 邪悪 ¶邪悪な wicked; vicious; malicious; 《文》 black-hearted.

ジャーク 【重量挙げ】 the jerk ¶ジャークで155キロ挙げる lift 155 kilograms in the jerk.

しゃあしゃあ ¶しゃあしゃあと shamelessly; 《文》 unabashedly; brazenfacedly; 《文》 with (provoking) composure; coolly / しゃあしゃあしている do not turn a hair; look unruffled. 文例⇩

じゃーじゃー ¶水をじゃーじゃーかける pour 「water (on, over).

ジャーナリスト a journalist ¶ジャーナリストの文章 〈よい意味で, 簡潔な〉 journalistic style; 〈悪い意味で〉 journalese.

ジャーナリズム journalism.

シャープペンシル an automatic [a mechanical] pencil; 《英》a propelling pencil.

シャーベット sherbet.

しゃい 謝意 ¶謝意を表する 〈感謝の意を〉 《文》 express one's gratitude [thanks]; 〈わびる〉《文》 tender an apology (for); apologize (for).

ジャイロコンパス a gyrocompass; a gyro 《pl. -s》.

ジャイロスコープ a gyroscope; a gyro 《pl. -s》.

しゃいん 社員 a member (of the staff); an employe(e) (of a company); 《総称》the staff; the personnel (of a company) ¶社に入る join the staff (of a company) / 正社員 a regular member; a staff member (of a company) / 新入社員 a new employee [member of staff]; an incoming employee / 社員一同に代わって in the name of all the staff of our corporation / 社員食堂 the staff canteen / 社員割引で at the employees' rate; at a staff discount. 文例⇩

しゃえい 射影 【数】 a projection.

しゃおん 謝恩 ¶謝恩会 a thank-you party for the teachers; a testimonial dinner / 謝恩大売出し thank-you sales.

しゃか 釈迦 S(h)akyamuni; Gautama; Buddha.

ジャガー 【動】 a jaguar; an American leopard.

しゃかい 社会 a society; 《世間》the world; 〈大衆〉 the (general) public; 《共同社会》a community ¶一般社会 the general public; society at large; the public in general / 社会の[的] social / 反社会的[性] antisocial; 《文》 antisociality] / 社会に復帰させる 《文》 enable sb to return to society; rehabilitate sb (in society) / 社会的動物 a social animal / 社会的地位 one's social standing [position]; one's place in society / 社会的地位のある人 a person in a public position / 社会悪 social ills [evils] / 社会意識 social awareness / 社会意識の強いcommunity-[social-]minded; socially aware / 社会運動 a social movement; a public campaign; 〈社会主義の〉 a socialist movement / 社会科 social studies; civics / 社会改良 social reform [amelioration] / 社会科学 social sciences / 社会学 sociology / 社会学の[的] sociological / 社会契約説 the theory of social contract / 社会教育 social education / 社会史 social history / 社会事業 social work / 社会事業家 a social [welfare] worker; 社会主義 socialism (a socialist) / 社会主義的な socialist(ic) 《movements》 / 空想的社会主義 Utopian socialism / 国家社会主義 state socialism / 社会人 a (full-fledged) member of society / 社会人

しゃ 当時の私はまだ若くて, 物事を広い視野から見ることができなかった. I was still young then and wasn't able to get things in (their proper) perspective. / 彼は視野が広い[狭い]. His mental horizon is wide [limited].

じゃ 蛇の道はへび. Set a thief to catch a thief. 【諺】

しゃあしゃあ 彼はあんな事をしておきながらしゃあしゃあしている. He doesn't seem to care a bit [《口語》give a damn] about what he has done.

しゃい 細部にわたって御指導下されたヒギンズ教授に特に謝意を表します. My special thanks are due to Professor Higgins for guiding my work with detailed comments.

しゃいん 彼はうちの社員です. He works for our corporation. | He is on the staff of our company. / これらの会社の社員には英語のできる大学出が1人や2人はいるはずだ. Presumably these companies have one or two graduates

じゃがいも 543 じゃくでん

になる go out into the world; start one's adult life / 社会心理学 social psychology / 社会生活 social life《★「社交生活」「人との交際」の意味でも使う》; life in society [as a member of society]; community [communal] life / 社会性昆虫 social insects / 社会政策 (a) social policy / 社会制度 a social system / 社会組織[機構] the social structure [fabric, framework, machine] / 社会調査 social research / 社会福祉 the Socialist Party; the Socialists / 社会党大会 a Socialist Convention / 社会鍋 a (Salvation Army) collecting [charity] pot / 社会部〖新聞〗the local news section;《米》the city desk / 社会不安 (cause) social unrest / 社会福祉 social welfare / 社会奉仕 (do) social [public] service(s) / 社会保障 social security / 社会保障制度 the social security system / 社会民主主義 social democracy /（新聞の）社会面 the local [《米》city] news page / 社会問題 a social problem / 社会問題になる become an object of public concern. 文例⊘

じゃがいも じゃが芋 a potato《pl. -es》★米国ではスイートポテトと区別して a white potato; an Irish potato とも呼ぶ.

じゃかご 蛇籠〖土木〗a gabion.

じゃかすか ¶じゃかすか儲ける《口語》make money hand over fist.

しゃかっこう 斜滑降〖スキー〗traversing ¶斜滑降をする traverse《down a slope》; make a traverse.

しゃがむ sit down on one's heels; squat down ¶物陰にしゃがむ crouch for shelter.

ジャカルタ Djakarta.

しゃがれる 嗄れる ⇨ しわがれる.

しゃかん 舎監 a dormitory superintendent; a warden; the head of residence; a housemaster; a housemistress (女).

しゃかんきょり 車間距離 the space [distance] between a car and the one in front ¶車間距離をとる keep one's distance / 車間距離を充分にとる keep a safe distance between oneself and the car ahead. 文例⊘

しゃきしゃき ¶食べるとしゃきしゃきする〈物が主語〉be crisp (to eat) / しゃきしゃきした口調で in precise, clipped language.

じゃきょう 邪教 (a) heresy;《文》a false creed [religion].

しやく 試薬〖化〗a (chemical) reagent.

しゃく¹ 尺〈単位〉a shaku (=30.3 cm) ⇨ すんぽう. ¶fill sb's cup.

しゃく² 酌 ¶酌をする serve《sb with sake》.

しゃく³ 笏 a (wooden) mace; a scepter.

しゃく⁴ 癪 ¶しゃくの種 have an《文》a cause of annoyance;《口語》a peeve / しゃくな, しゃくにさわる annoying;《文》vexatious; irritating /

しゃくにさわる〈人が主語〉feel [be] vexed [annoyed]《with sb, about [at] sth》; be offended《at, by》;《文》be chagrined《at》;〈事が主語〉annoy; irritate; vex; hurt; gall; grate on one's nerves / しゃくにさわるほど落ち着いている be provokingly [maddeningly] cool. 文例⊘

じやく 持薬 a medicine that one uses regularly.

-じゃく …弱 a little less than [short of]; a little under ¶1割弱 a little less than 10 per cent.

しゃくい 爵位 peerage; a (noble) title; a title of the peerage ¶爵位のある titled.

じゃくおんき 弱音器〖音楽〗a mute; a damper.

じゃくさん 弱酸〖化〗a weak acid.

しゃくし 杓子 a dipper; a (wooden) ladle; a scoop ¶しゃくしですくう ladle; scoop (up [out]) with a dipper / しゃくし定規の人 a stickler (for the rules); a formalist / しゃくし定規でやる go by [stick to] the rules [the book].

じゃくし 弱視 weak [poor] eyesight;〖医〗amblyopia ¶弱視の weak-eyed[-sighted]; amblyopic.

じゃくしゃ 弱者 the weak ¶弱者に味方する side with [stand by] the weak; support [take the side of] the underdog.

しゃくしょ 市役所 a city [municipal] office;《米》a city hall;《英》a town hall.

しゃくじょう 錫杖 a priest's staff; a crosier (ビショップの持つ).

じゃくしょう 弱小 ¶弱小な small and weak / 弱小国 a lesser [minor] power.

じゃくしん 弱震 a slight earthquake shock; an [a faint] earth tremor. 文例⊘

しゃくぜん 釈然 ¶釈然としない be not satisfied [happy] with《sb's explanation [apology]》.

じゃくたい 弱体 ¶弱体の weak / 弱体化する（他のものを）weaken;（自分が）get [grow,《文》become] weak / 弱体内閣 a weak [frail] Cabinet.

しゃくち 借地 leased land; rented ground ¶借地権 a lease; a leasehold / 借地人 a leaseholder; a tenant; a renter;〖法〗a lessee / 借地料 (a) (land) rent.

じゃぐち 蛇口《米》a faucet;《英》a (water) tap ¶蛇口をひねって開ける[閉める] turn a tap on [off].

じゃくてん 弱点〈弱味〉a weakness; a weak [vulnerable] point;〈痛い所〉a sore [tender] spot;〈欠点〉a defect; shortcomings《★複数形で使うことが多い》¶人の弱点を突く touch sb on a sore spot;《文》find [hit] sb's Achilles(') heel.

じゃくでん 弱電 a weak (electric) current ¶弱電機器 a light electrical appliance.

---

on their staff who know some English.

しゃか 釈迦に説法. Don't try to teach your grandmother (how) to suck eggs.〖諺〗

しゃめん 社会の窓が開いているよ. Your flies are open.

しゃかんきょり 車間距離を充分にとっていなかったのが、追突の原因だ. He ran into the car in front because he was driving too close to it.

しゃく⁴ 彼の言う事が一々しゃくにさわった. Every word he uttered irritated [annoyed] me. / しゃくにさわる雨だな. Drat this rain! /

あいつに負けるのはしゃくだ. I just can't stand being beaten by that fellow.

しゃくし 物事はしゃくし定規にはいかないよ. It doesn't do to go by hard-and-fast rules.

じゃくしん 弱震があった. There was an earth tremor. | A slight

しゃくど 尺度 a (linear) measure; a (measuring) rule; a scale; 〈標準〉a standard; a yardstick; 《文》a criterion 《pl. -ria, -s》 ¶…の尺度になる be [《文》constitute] a measure [a barometer, an index] of…; be a yardstick for…. 文例も

しゃくどういろ 赤銅色 ¶赤銅色の bronze; brown; copper(-colored); 〈日焼けして〉bronzed; (sun)tanned; browned (by the sun).

しゃくとり(むし) 尺取(虫) a measuring worm; an inchworm; a looper (caterpillar).

しゃくなげ 【植】a rhododendron; 《米》a rosebay.

じゃくにくきょうしょく 弱肉強食 the law of the jungle ¶弱肉強食の世界 a world where the weak are victims of the strong; 《文》a world where the law of the jungle prevails.

しゃくねつ 灼熱 ¶灼熱の incandescent; red[white-]hot; baking (dry sand) /灼熱の太陽 a scorching sun /灼熱の砂漠 a sunbaked desert.

じゃくはい 若輩 a young fellow; a youngster; 〈未熟者〉a greenhorn.

しゃくはち 尺八 a (five-holed) vertical bamboo flute.

しゃくふく 折伏 ¶折伏する《文》convert sb by persistent argument [preaching].

しゃくほう 釈放 (a) release; (a) discharge; (an) acquittal ⇒かりしゃくほう ¶釈放する release; turn sb loose; let sb off; let sb out of prison; acquit; set sb free [at liberty].

しゃくめい 釈明 (an) explanation; (an) apology(わび); 《文》(a) vindication (弁明) ¶釈明する explain; apologize; 《文》vindicate (oneself).

しゃくや 借家 《live in》a rented house ¶借家する have [want] a house for rent /借家を捜す look for a house for rent [to let] (a house for rent は《米》, a house to let は《英》) /借家人 a tenant /家賃料 (a) (house) rent. 文例も

しゃくやく 【植】a peony.

しゃくよう 借用 ¶借用する borrow; have a [the] loan of /借用証書 a written acknowledgement of a debt [loan]; an IOU 《pl. -s, -'s》 (★ I owe you の略で,証書面には 'IOU £5' のように書かれる). 文例も

しゃくりあげる しゃくり上げる heave with sobs; sob (convulsively).

しゃくりょう 酌量 ¶酌量する consider; take sth into consideration [account]; make allowance(s) (for).

しゃけい 斜頸 【医】torticollis; a wryneck.

しゃげき 射撃 firing; shooting; gunshot; 〈術〉marksmanship ¶射撃する shoot; fire at sb; fire on (a fortress) /射撃の技量 marksmanship /射撃を開始する〈人が主語〉start firing; open fire (on); open (up) (with rifle and machine-gun fire on the enemy); 〈火器が主語〉open (on the enemy) /射撃がうまい be a good shot [marksman] /射撃に熟練している /射撃演習 field firing; shooting practice /射撃場 a firing range.

しゃけつ 瀉血 bloodletting; phlebotomy ¶瀉血する phlebotomize; let [draw] blood (from a patient).

ジャケツ [<jacket] a sweater.

ジャケット 〈本のカバー〉a (book) jacket [wrapper]; a dust cover; 〈レコードの〉a jacket (for a phonograph record); 《文》a jacket.

しゃけん 車検 〈自動車の定期検査〉an automobile inspection.

じゃけん 邪険 ¶邪険な hardhearted; cruel; unkind /邪険にする be hard on sb; be cruel [unkind] (to); ill-treat.

しゃこ[1] 車庫 〈自動車の〉a garage; a carport (屋根と柱だけの); 〈電車の〉a depot; 《米》a train [car] shed ¶車庫に入れる put (a car) into the garage.

しゃこ[2] 【動】a squilla 《pl. -s, -lae》.

しゃこ[3] 【鳥】a partridge.

しゃこう[1] 社交 social life [《文》intercourse] ¶社交的な sociable /社交家〈交際家〉a sociable person; 《口語》a good mixer; 〈社交界で活躍している人〉a society man [woman] /社交界 fashionable society [circles]; the fashionable world /社交界に出る make one's debut in society /社交性 sociability /非社交性 unsociability /社交ダンス (ballroom [social]) dancing; a (social) dance. 文例も

しゃこう[2] 遮光 ¶遮光する shield [shade] (the light) /(灯火管制用の)遮光幕 a blackout curtain; a shade (灯火のまわりの).

じゃこう 麝香 musk ¶じゃこうじか【動】a musk deer.

しゃこうしん 射幸心 (a) fondness for speculation [gambling] ¶射幸心をそそる[かき立てる] arouse [stir up] the passion for gambling.

しゃさい 社債 a debenture; a bond ¶長期[短期]社債 a long-[short-]term debenture /無記名社債券 a bearer bond /記名社債券 a registered debenture.

しゃざい 謝罪 (an) apology ¶謝罪する apologize (to sb for); beg sb's pardon (forgiveness); 《文》express one's regret (for) /謝罪を要求する demand an apology (from) /謝罪広告を出す publish an apology (in a newspaper).

しゃさつ 射殺 ¶射殺する shoot sb dead. 文例も

しゃし[1] 斜視 (a) squint; 【医】strabismus ¶斜視である have a squint [cast in the eye];

---

earthquake shock was felt.
しゃくど 詩人や美術家を他の人々と同じ尺度で測ることはできない. It is impossible to apply the same yardstick to poets and artists as to other people.
しゃくや いまだに借家住まいの身. I can't afford a house of my own yet. / なぜご自分の家をお持ちにならないで借家住まいをなさるのですか. Why do you pay rent instead of owning your own home?
しゃくよう 日本語には中国語や英語からの借用語はたくさんあるが,日本語から外国語に入った語はほんのわずかである. Though Japanese has borrowed heavily [a great deal] from Chinese and English, only a few Japanese words have entered other languages.
しゃこう[1] 彼は社交が嫌いだ. He is very unsociable.

be squint-eyed [cross-eyed (内斜視)], wall-eyed (外斜視)].
しゃし² 奢侈 ⇨ ぜいたく.
しゃじ 謝辞 ¶謝辞を述べる 《文》express *one's* gratitude;《文》give [make] an address of thanks;〈わびる〉apologize (for).
しゃじく 車軸 an axle. 文例⇩
しゃじつ 写実 ¶写実する representing things as they really are; realism ¶写実的な realistic;《文》graphic; true to life [nature] / 写実的に realistically;《文》graphically / 写実的に描写する give a realistic [graphic] description [《文》depiction,《文》representation](of) / 写実主義 realism / 写実主義者 a realist / 写実小説 a realistic novel. 文例⇩
じゃじゃうま じゃじゃ馬〈あばれ馬〉an unruly [a vicious, a restive] horse;〈言うことをきかない女〉an unmanageable [《文》a wayward, an unruly] girl.
しゃしゅ 射手 a marksman; a shot; an archer (弓の) ¶名射手 a master [crack] shot; a master bowman (弓の).
しゃしゅつ 射出 ¶射出する《文》emit; project; shoot out /《航空》eject (緊急時にパイロットを).
しゃしょう¹ 車掌《米》a conductor (英国ではバスの); a conductress (女);《英》a guard (列車の) ¶車掌区 a conductors' station [office] / 車掌室 a conductors' compartment.
しゃしょう² 捨象《哲》abstraction ¶捨象する abstract.
しゃしん 写真 a photograph;《口語》a photo 《pl. -s》; a picture;〈スナップ〉a snapshot, 《口語》a snap;〈術〉photography ¶写真を撮る〈自分で〉photograph; take a photograph [picture] (of);〈写してもらう〉have [get] *one's* photograph taken / 写真に写った顔 a face in a photograph / 写真入りの《a magazine》illustrated with [by] photographs / グループ写真 a group portrait [photograph] / 全身[半身]写真 a full-length [half-length] photograph / 写真画報 a pictorial [an illustrated] magazine / 写真機 a camera / 写真技術 a photographic technique / 写真ぎらいである be camera-shy; be a camera-hater / 写真植字《米》photocomposition,《米》phototypesetting /《英》filmsetting / 写真製版《印刷》a photomechanical process /《a》photo survey / 写真測量 photographic measurement [surveying] / 写真帳 a photograph album / 写真電送 phototelegraphy / 写真電送をする telephotograph; facsimile transmission / 写真版 a photo plate / 写真版《凸版》 a prototype / 写真凹版《凹版》 a photogravure / 写真班員 a (newspaper) cameraman / 写真判定 a photo finish / 写真複写機 a photo-

copying machine / 写真屋〈店〉a photo studio; 〈人〉a photographer / 写真屋で写してもらった写真 a studio portrait. 文例⇩
じゃしん 邪心 malice;《文》a wicked [black] heart; evil [《文》malicious] intentions;《文》an evil [a sinister] design.
ジャズ《音楽》jazz; jazz music ¶ジャズ風に演奏[編曲]する jazz up (a tune) / ホットジャズ hot jazz / ジャズバンド a jazz band.
じゃすい 邪推《文》a groundless [an unjust] suspicion; distrust ¶邪推する suspect *sb* without reason / 邪推深い suspicious;《be》given to suspicion; distrustful.
ジャスト ¶5時ジャスト just five o'clock ★ five o'clock just とは言わない.
ジャスミン《植》a jasmine; a jessamine;〈香水〉jasmine; jessamine ¶ジャスミン茶 jasmine tea.
しゃする 謝する〈礼を言う〉thank;《文》express *one's* gratitude;《文》tender *one's* thanks; 〈わびる〉apologize (to *sb* for); make an apology (for) ¶厚意を謝する thank *sb* for *his* kindness / 無礼を謝する apologize to *sb* for *one's* rudeness.
しゃせい 写生 ¶写生する sketch; paint [draw] from nature [life]; make a sketch of《a view》;〈描写する〉《文》portray;《文》depict; 《文》delineate / 写生に出かける go sketching / 写生画 a sketch /(モデルを使った)写生教室 a life class / 写生帳 a sketchbook / 写生文 a (literary) sketch.
しゃせい² 射精 ejaculation ¶射精する ejaculate; emit semen.
しゃせつ 社説 an editorial (article);《英》a leader;《米》a leading article. 文例⇩
しゃぜつ 謝絶 (a) refusal ¶謝絶する refuse; 《文》decline; turn down / 面会を謝絶する decline to see [receive] a visitor; be not at home to visitors. 文例⇩
しゃせん¹ 車線 a (traffic) lane ¶片側2車線の道路 a four-lane road [highway] / 車線区分線 a (painted) lane marking.
しゃせん² 社線 a private [nongovernmental] railroad line.
しゃせん³ 斜線 a diagonal [an oblique] line; a slanting line;〈and/or というような場合の〉a (diagonal [slanting]) stroke; a solidus《pl. -di》; a slash (mark) ★ 斜線で区切った番号の読み方は, 例えば673/26ならば six-seven-three-stroke [slash]-two-six のように言う.
しゃそう¹ 車窓 a car [train] window ¶車窓の景色 the scenery seen from a car [train] window.
しゃそう² 社葬《give *sb*》a company-sponsored funeral.

しゃさつ 脱走する者は射殺せよと命じられていた. Our orders were that, if we saw anyone trying to escape, we should shoot to kill.
しゃじく 車軸を流すような雨だった. It rained in torrents.
しゃじつ ティツィアーノはさまざまなものの質感を非常に写実的に描き分けた. Titian depicted a wide variety of textures with great realism.
しゃしん 写真を1枚下さいませんか. Please give me a photograph of yourself. | 彼女は写真顔がいい. She photographs well. | She's very photogenic. | She always comes out well in a photograph.
しゃせつ 朝日新聞は社説で, インフレ対策を最優先に考えるべきだと言っている. The *Asahi* editorial says that anti-inflation measures should be given top priority.
しゃぜつ 彼は重体で面会謝絶で

しゃぞう 写像 〖数〗mapping.
しゃたい 車体 the body ((of a car)); the frame ((自転車の)) ¶車体の低い自動車 a low-slung car.
しゃだい 車台 a chassis ((pl. -(es))).
しゃたく 社宅 a company(-owned) house ((for its employees)). 用例↓
しゃだつ 洒脱 〖洒脱な〗free and easy; unconventional; 〖文〗unconstrained.
しゃだん 遮断 ¶熱の遮断 heat insulation / 遮断する cut [shut, wall] off; insulate; intercept ((the enemy's retreat)) / 交通を遮断する block (up) ((a street)) / 遮断器〖電〗a (contact [circuit]) breaker / (踏切の)遮断機 a crossing gate.
しゃだんほうじん 社団法人 〖法〗a corporate juridical person; an incorporated body; a corporation.
しゃち 〖動〗a killer whale; a grampus.
しゃちほこ 鯱 a fabulous dolphinlike fish ¶しゃちほこ立ちする stand on one's head (and hands) / しゃちほこ立ちしても及ばない be far beyond one [〖文〗one's power].
しゃちほこばる be stiff (and formal); stand on ceremony ¶しゃち(ほ)こばって座る sit up rigidly.
しゃちゅう 車中 ¶車中で in [〖米〗on] a train; in a car / 車中談 an informal talk given ((by a politician)) in a train; a press interview aboard a train.
しゃちょう 社長 the president [head] ((of a company [firm])); a company president ¶副社長 a vice-president.
シャツ an undershirt; 〖英〗a vest ⇒したぎ ¶シャツ1枚になる[でいる] strip [be stripped] to one's undershirt.
しゃっかん 借款 a loan ¶借款を申し込む ask [apply] for a loan / 借款を供与する grant [〖文〗extend, give] credit ((to)) / 長期貿易借款 a long-term trade credit / 借款協定 a loan agreement.
じゃっかん¹ 若干 ¶若干の some; a number of; some [a certain] amount of; a few; a little; a sum of ((money)).
じゃっかん² 弱冠 用例↓
じゃっき 惹起 〖惹起する〗〖文〗bring about; cause; 〖文〗occasion; give rise to; lead to.
ジャッキ 〈起重機〉a jack ¶ジャッキで持ち上げる jack up ((a car)).
しゃっきん 借金 a debt; a loan ¶借金する borrow money ((from)); run [get, fall] into debt;

〖文〗contract [incur] a debt / 借金がある be (\$100) in debt ((to sb)); owe sb (¥8,000) / 借金を返す pay [clear] (off) one's debts / 借金を催促する press sb to pay a debt; dun sb for the payment of a debt / 借金を踏み倒す bilk sb of a debt ((of ¥5000)) / 借金で首が回らない be deeply [up to the ears] in debt / 借金取り a debt collector; a bill collector. 用例↓
ジャック 〖トランプ〗the jack; the knave ¶ハートのジャック the jack of hearts.
ジャックナイフ a jackknife ((pl. -knives)).
しゃっくり a hiccup ¶しゃっくりする hiccup; have the hiccups. 用例↓
ジャッグル 〖野球〗¶ジャッグルする juggle; fumble ((the ball)).
しゃっこつ 尺骨〖解〗the ulna.
シャッター 〈よろい戸〉a shutter; 〈カメラの〉a shutter; a shutter release button ((シャッターボタン)) ¶シャッターを降ろす pull down a shutter / (カメラの)シャッターを切る release the shutter; trigger a camera / 自動シャッター an automatic shutter / シャッター速度を決める set the shutter speed.
シャットアウト 〖スポーツ〗〖米〗a shutout (game); 〖口語〗a whitewash ¶シャットアウトする 〖米〗shut out [win a shutout victory over] ((the opposing team)); 〖口語〗whitewash ((the Giants)).
しゃてい 射程 range ¶射程内[外]に within [out of] range [shot]. 用例↓
しゃてき 射的 ⇒しゃげき ¶射的場〈遊戯の〉a shooting gallery.
しゃとう 斜塔 the Leaning Tower ((of Pisa)).
しゃどう 車道 a roadway; 〖英〗a carriageway.
じゃどう 邪道 〈悪行〉〖文〗a wrong [an evil] course; 〖文〗evil ways; 〖文〗vice. 用例↓
しゃない¹ 車内 the inside of a car ¶車内灯 an interior light.
しゃない² 社内 用例↓ ¶社内で in the firm [office] / 社内結婚 a marriage between two employees [with another employee] of the company / 社内報 a house organ [journal].
しゃなりしゃなり gracefully; 〖文〗affectedly; 〖文〗(walk) with a mincing gait.
しゃにくさい 謝肉祭 the carnival.
しゃにむに 〈むやみに〉recklessly; furiously; desperately; 〈夢中になって〉feverishly; 〖口語〗like mad; headlong; 〈無理に〉forcibly; by force ¶しゃにむに突進する push on furi-

---

す. He is so seriously ill that no one is allowed to see him [he is allowed no visitors].
しゃたく 社宅の家賃は極めて安いので、他へ移りしづらくなる家庭が多く出る. The rental for company(-owned) housing is so low that many families find it difficult to move away.
じゃっかん² 弱冠27歳で彼はそれを発明した. He invented it when he was only twenty-seven.
しゃっきん 一生懸命働いて何とか借金だけは免れた. He could only

manage to keep his head above water [keep out of debt, make both ends meet] by working as hard as he could. / 彼には古い借金がある. I owe him a debt of long standing. / 借金の返済はもう少しの間猶予してください. Please let me owe you the money a little longer.
しゃっくり しゃっくりがなかなか止まらなかった. The hiccups wouldn't stop. / I couldn't stop my hiccups.
しゃてい このライフルの射程は約

1.6キロだ. This rifle carries about 1.6 kilometers. / 蒙古勢の石弓は日本の弓よりずっと射程が長かった. The crossbows of the Mongols far outranged the Japanese bows.
じゃどう それは邪道だ. That's not the way you're supposed to do it. / That's not the proper [approved] way of doing it.
しゃない¹ (自動車について)当社の新型車の特徴の1つは車内が広々としていることでございます. The roominess of the interior is one

じゃねん 邪念 《文》an evil thought [desire, mind, design] ¶邪念を払う free *oneself* of evil thoughts; put all distracting thoughts out of *one's* mind.

じゃのめ 蛇の目 〈模様〉a double ring; a bull's eye; 〈傘〉a paper umbrella with a bull's-eye design.

しゃば¹ 車馬 horses and vehicles. 文例⇩

しゃば² 娑婆 this world; the outside (world) (囚人などが言う) ¶しゃば気を捨てる[が抜ける]《文》give up [outlive] worldly ambitions [desires].

じゃばら 蛇腹 〈写真機や引き伸ばし機の〉a bellows; 〈建〉a cornice.

ジャブ 〔ボクシング〕a jab ¶ジャブを出す jab (*one's opponent*) / 右[左]のジャブ a right(-hand) [left(-hand)] jab.

しゃぶしゃぶ *shabushabu*; thin slices of beef parboiled in hot soup.

じゃぶじゃぶ ¶水をじゃぶじゃぶさせる dabble in water (水いたずら) / 水の中をじゃぶじゃぶ歩く splash along in the water / ソースをじゃぶじゃぶかける drown (*one's hamburger*) in sauce; pour large quantities of sauce (over).

しゃふつ 煮沸 ¶煮沸する boil / 煮沸消毒する sterilize *sth* by boiling / 煮沸器 a scalder.

シャフト a shaft; a shaftway.

しゃぶる suck (*one's finger*); chew (a piece of candy) ¶乳をしゃぶらせる breast-feed (a baby); 《文》let (a baby) suck at the breast; suckle (a baby) / 骨までしゃぶる〈比喩的〉suck *sb* to the very marrow.

しゃへい 遮蔽 ¶遮蔽する cover; shelter; screen (*sth* from observation); shade (a light) / 遮蔽物 cover; shelter / 遮蔽幕 a blackout curtain; 《軍》に遮蔽幕をする black out a window.

しゃべる 喋る talk; chat; chatter; prattle (子供が片言で); 〈告げ口する〉tell (on *sb*); 〈漏らす〉let (*secrets*) out; 《文》divulge ¶しゃべらす〈誘いをかけて〉draw *sb* out / 〈人前に立たせて〉put *sb* up to speak / うっかりしゃべってしまう blurt out (a secret) / しゃべりたがらない close-lipped[-mouthed]; 《文》uncommunicative; 《文》reticent; 《文》reserved (in speech) / よくしゃべる人 a great talker; a chatterbox ⇒おしゃべり / しゃべり負かす outtalk *sb*; talk *sb* down / しゃべりまくる talk away; 《文》talk volubly; talk and talk; 〈口語〉talk *one's* head off / ひとりでしゃべりまくる do all the talking / しゃべり損 a waste of breath.

シャベル a spade; a shovel ★a spade は足で押して地面を掘るのにも使えるもの. a shovel は, 先端を除く3辺が上の方へ少し曲がっていて, 石炭・砂などをすくって移動するのが専用のシャベル ¶シャベルですくう shovel / シャベル1杯の砂 a shovelful of sand.

しゃへん 斜辺 〔数〕an oblique side; a hypotenuse (直角三角形の). 文例⇩

しゃほん 写本 《本》a manuscript (略: MS., *pl*. MSS.); a manuscript [handwritten] copy / 〈事〉transcription [copying] (*of a book*).

シャボン 〔<《ポルトガル語》*sabão*〕soap ¶シャボン玉 a soap bubble / シャボン玉を吹く blow (soap) bubbles.

じゃま 邪魔 〈障害〉an obstacle; 《文》a hindrance; an obstruction; 《文》an impediment; 〈妨害〉(a) disturbance; trouble; 〈干渉〉interference; (an) interruption; 《文》(an) intervention ¶邪魔な awkward; obstructive; 《文》hampering; 〈厄介な〉cumbersome; 《文》burdensome / 邪魔をする get in the way (*of*); be a nuisance; obstruct; hinder; check; hamper; disturb; interfere with; interrupt / 勉強[睡眠]の邪魔をする disturb *sb* [*sb in his*] studies [sleep] / 邪魔になる be [stand] in *sb's* way; 《文》be a hindrance [an encumbrance] (*to*); be a drag (*on*) / 邪魔物 an obstacle; 《文》a hindrance; a nuisance; a stumbling block / 〈足手まとい〉《文》an encumbrance; a drag / 邪魔(物)を除く remove [get rid of] an obstacle; get an obstacle out of the way / 老母を邪魔物扱いする treat *one's* old mother as a nuisance. 文例⇩

ジャマイカ Jamaica ¶ジャマイカ島[人]の Jamaican.

しゃみせん 三味線 (play) a *samisen*; a *shamisen*.

シャム Siam; Thailand (1949年よりの正式国名) ⇒タイ ¶シャム双生児 Siamese twins / シャム猫 a Siamese cat.

ジャム jam; preserve(s) ¶いちごジャム strawberry jam.

しゃむしょ 社務所 a shrine office.

ジャムセッション 〔ジャズ〕a jam session.

しゃめん¹ 斜面 a slope; an inclined plane ¶斜

---

of the outstanding features of our new model. / 車内でのおタバコはご遠慮下さい. Passengers are requested to refrain from smoking in the car.

しゃば¹ 車馬通行止. 《掲示》No thoroughfare for horses or vehicles.

しゃべる 彼は2時間立て続けにしゃべった. He rattled on for two hours on end. / 彼は平素あまりしゃべらない方だ. He is usually rather taciturn. / その晩彼はつにもなくしゃべった. That night he was unusually talkative. / この事はめったにしゃべってもらっては困るよ. Be sure and keep your mouth shut about this. / 彼は何でもしゃべってしまう. He gives everything away. | He is given to blabbing.

しゃへん 直角三角形の斜辺の2乗は他の2辺の2乗の和に等しい. The square of [on] the hypotenuse of a right(-angled) triangle is equal to the sum of the squares of [on] the other two sides.

じゃま それがこの国の科学の進歩の邪魔になった. It was a stumbling block to the progress of science in this country. / 邪魔するな. 〈うるさい〉Leave [Let] me alone. / 〈通行の〉Get out of my way. / お前なぞは邪魔だ. You are not wanted here. / ちょっとお邪魔します. Excuse me. / お邪魔になってすみません. Excuse me [I am sorry] for being in your way. / お邪魔さま. Excuse me for interrupting [disturbing] you. / たいへん長くお邪魔いたしました. I'm afraid I have taken up

しゃめん 面になっている form a slope / 急[緩]斜面 a steep [easy] slope.

しゃめん² 赦免 (a) pardon; (a) remission (of sentence); (an) amnesty (大赦) ¶赦免する pardon;《文》absolve (sb from [of]); remit (a punishment); let sb off (a penalty); /放免する《文》discharge;《文》liberate; set [let] sb free.

しゃも〈鳥〉[<Siam] a gamecock; a fighting cock.

しゃもじ 杓文字〈汁の〉a ladle; a large (wooden) spoon;〈飯の〉a rice scoop.

しゃよう¹ 社用 ¶社用で on company [one's firm's] business / 社用族 expense-account businessmen; businessmen wining and dining at their firms' expense.

しゃよう² 斜陽 the setting [《文》declining] sun ¶斜陽産業 a declining industry; an industry on the decline / 斜陽族 the new poor; the declining upper class; the impoverished aristocracy.

しゃらくさい 洒落臭い〈知ったかぶりの〉knowing;〈生意気な〉impertinent; saucy; impudent; cheeky.

じゃらじゃら〈音〉jingle-jangle; clitter-clatter (マージャンのパイをかき混ぜるときの) ¶じゃらじゃらいう jingle (coins).

じゃらす tease (a kitten); have fun with.

じゃり 砂利 gravel; (small) pebbles ¶砂利を敷く gravel (a road) / 砂利を敷いた道 a gravel(ed) road [path] / 砂利置場 a gravel yard / 砂利採取 gravel-digging / 砂利採取場 a gravel pit / じゃりトラ a gravel truck.

じゃりじゃり ¶じゃりじゃりする be crunchy / 砂でじゃりじゃりしている海水着 a sandy-feeling bathing suit.

しゃりょう 車両 vehicles; cars;〈客車〉a (railroad) coach;《米》a car;《英》a carriage;〈鉄道・運送会社の〉rolling stock ¶車両会社 a rolling stock (manufacturing) company. 文例

しゃりん 車輪 a wheel ¶(飛行機の)前車輪 a nosewheel.

しゃれ 洒落〈言葉の〉a witticism; a joke;《文》a jest;〈地口〉a pun; a word play; a play on words ¶うまいしゃれ a clever joke [pun] / 古臭いしゃれ a stale [an old,《口語》a corny] joke / しゃれがうまい be good at jokes; be a good punster. 文例

しゃれい 謝礼〈感謝〉thanks;〈報酬〉a reward;《文》a remuneration;〈医師・弁護士など〉a fee ¶謝礼する reward;《文》remunerate; pay a fee (to) / 謝礼のしるしに《文》in token of one's thanks [gratitude] (for).

しゃれこうべ ⇒されこうべ.

しゃれこむ 洒落こむ 文例

しゃれた 洒落た〈言うことが〉witty; humorous;〈服装などが〉stylish (appearance); smart; fancy (clothes);《文》tasteful; chic (女性について) ¶しゃれた料理 a fancy dish / しゃれた名前 a fanciful [an attractive] name.

しゃれ(っ)け 洒落っ気 〈言葉に〉a sense of humor;〈服装に〉a wish to look smart;《文》vanity in dress. 文例 「the last.

しゃれのめす 洒落のめす continue joking to

しゃれる 洒落る dress smartly [stylishly]; dress [smarten] oneself up; try to look smart [stylish]; be decked out.

じゃれる〈戯れる〉play with (a ball); fool about; be playful;《文》be frolicsome;〈はね回る〉frisk;《文》gambol ¶じゃれて playfully / じゃれている猫 a playful cat. 文例

ジャワ Java ¶ジャワの Javanese / ジャワの人 a Javanese.

シャワー a shower (bath) ¶シャワーを浴びる have [take] a shower (bath); shower / シャワーをひねって出す[止める] turn on [off] the shower / シャワー室 a shower stall [room].

ジャンク a (Chinese) junk.

ジャングル the jungle ★定冠詞をつけるのが普通 ¶ジャングルに覆われた jungle-covered (islands) / インドのジャングル the jungle(s) of India / ジャングルジム〈子供の体育用〉《米》a jungle gym;《英》a climbing frame / ジャングル地帯 a jungle area.

じゃんけん じゃん拳 the game of 'paper, stone and scissors'. ★英米では順番などを決めるとき、じゃんけんではなく、硬貨を投げ上げて、その表か裏かで決める。これを tossing a coin といい、日本語の「じゃんけんで決めよう」に相当するのは 'Let's toss (up) for it.'

じゃんじゃん〈鐘の音〉《文》clangor; ding-dong; jingle-jangle;〈大いに〉(do) ding-dong ¶じゃんじゃん鳴る jangle; clang / じゃんじゃん金をもうける make money hand over fist; (simply) rake it in.

シャンソン《フランス語》a chanson; a French popular song ¶シャンソン歌手 a chanson singer; a chansonnier.

シャンツェ [<《ドイツ語》Schanze]《スキー》a ski jump [slide].

---

too much of your time. / いずれそのうちお邪魔に上がります。I'll come and see you one of these days.

しゃめん¹ 彼はその谷の東向きの斜面を下って行った。He went down the east-facing slope of the valley. / 南向かいの丘の斜面には梅の花がさいている。Ume blossoms are coming out on the hillsides facing south.

しゃらくさい しゃらくさいことを言うな。None of your cheek!

じゃり 道に砂利が敷いてある。The road is graveled [covered with gravel].

しゃりょう 次の電車は車両故障のため10分ほど遅延の見込みです。Owing to a breakdown, the next train will be ten minutes late.

しゃれ 僕にはその洒落が分からない。I cannot see the point of the joke. / 彼にはさっぱりしゃれが通じなかった。My joke was lost [fell flat] on him.

しゃれこむ 正月はハワイ旅行としゃれこむか。Shall we treat ourselves to a holiday in Hawaii for the New Year?

しゃれ(っ)け あの娘は全くしゃれっ気がないね。That girl has no dress sense at all.

じゃれる 犬がボールに飛びついてじゃれていた。The dog was making dives at the ball.

しゃんと 頭は白くなっていたが、まだ背も曲がらずしゃんとしていた。Though his hair was white, he still stood erect.

シャンデリア a chandelier.
しゃんと ¶しゃんとしている be in shape [good condition] ; 《文》 be in full possession of oneself / しゃんとなる pull oneself together ; straighten oneself out ; brace oneself up / しゃんとして歩く 《文》 walk with a steady gait / 腰も曲がらず, しゃんとしている 《文》 be straight as a ramrod and full of dignity.
ジャンパー a jumper. ¶ジャンパースカート 《米》 a jumper ; 《英》 a pinafore dress.
シャンハイ 上海 Shanghai.
シャンパン ⇨ シャンペン.
ジャンプ a jump. ¶ジャンプする jump ; give a jump (over the bar) / スキーのジャンプ競技 a ski jumping contest.
シャンプー 〈髪洗い〉 a shampoo ; 〈洗髪剤〉 shampoo. ¶シャンプーで髪を洗う shampoo (one's hair) ; have a shampoo.
シャンペン champagne. ¶シャンペンの栓をポンと抜く pop open a bottle of champagne.
ジャンボ ジャンボジェット機 a jumbo jet.
ジャンボリー a jamboree.
ジャンル 《フランス語》 a genre ; a category ; a kind.
しゅ[1] 主 〈主人〉 one's master ; one's employer ; 〈主君〉 one's lord ; 〈神〉 the Lord ; 〈キリスト〉 our Lord ; 〈主体〉 the subject. ¶主たる main ; 《文》 chief ; primary ; principal / 主として mainly ; 《文》 chiefly ; for the most part (大部分) / 主の祈り the Lord's Prayer / 主になる lead (others in some enterprise) ; be the leader [head] (of) ; take the lead [initiative] (in doing). 文例↓
しゅ[2] 朱 cinnabar (red) ; vermilion. ¶朱塗りの vermilion-lacquered. 文例↓
しゅ[3] 種 a sort ; a type ; a class ; 《生物》 a species 《単複同形》 ¶種の 《生物》 specific / この種の articles of this kind / 種の起原 《書名》 *The Origin of Species*. 文例↓
しゅい[1] 首位 the first [top, premier] place ; the leading position ; 《文》 primacy. ¶首位争い a struggle for primacy / 首位を占める win [take, 《文》 occupy] the first place ; be first (in class) ; be at the top [head] (of) ; head the list (of) / 首位を譲る go up [《文》 yield] one's first place (to) / 首位から転落する lose one's (first) place ; 《文》 forfeit one's primacy / 首位打者 《野球》 the leading hitter. 文例↓
しゅい[2] 趣意 〈意味〉 《文》 the purport ; 《文》 the effect ; 〈要旨〉 the point ; the gist ; 〈目的〉 a purpose ; an aim ; 《文》 an object. ¶演説の趣意 《文》 the tenor [purport] of a speech / 談話の趣意 the drift [gist] of a discourse / 文の趣意 the meaning of a sentence / …という趣意の手紙 《文》 a letter to the effect that… / 趣意書 a prospectus.
しゅいん[1] 手淫 masturbation. ¶手いんをする masturbate ; practice masturbation.
しゅいん[2] 主因 the primary [principal, chief] cause ; the main [prime] factor.
しゆう[1] 私有 ¶私有の private ; privately-owned / 私有地[財産] private land [property] / 私有財産制度 the system of private ownership.
しゆう[2] 雌雄 male and female ; the two sexes. ¶雌雄を鑑別する determine the sex (of) ; sex (a chicken) / 雌雄を決する 《文》 fight a decisive battle (with) ; fight [battle] it out (with) ; come to a showdown / 雌雄を争う 《文》 strive [contend] for mastery [supremacy] ; 《文》 try conclusions (with).
しゅう[1] 州 〈大陸〉 a continent ; 〈行政区画上の〉 a province ; a state (米国の) ¶州になる 《米》 attain statehood / オハイオ州知事 the governor of the State of Ohio / 信州 the province of Shinano / 五大州 the Five Continents / (米国の)州立大学 a state university.
しゅう[2] 宗 〈宗派〉 a sect. ¶真言宗 the Shingon sect.
しゅう[3] 周 a circuit ; a lap ; 〈中国の古名〉 Chou. ¶3周する 〈トラックを〉 do [make] three laps [circuits, rounds] of (the track) ; 〈人工衛星が地球のまわりを〉 orbit (the earth) three times / 3周目に on one's third lap (トラックで) ; on one's third orbit (地球をまわって). ¶週35時間労働制に移行する go onto a 35-hour week. 文例↓
しゅう[4] 週 a week ⇨ しゅうかん[2]
しゅう[5] 衆 ¶衆を頼む rely on one's numbers [《文》 numerical superiority] / 衆を率いる lead a great number of people / 衆を率いて with a large troop under one / 衆に抜きん出た 《文》 preeminent ; distinguished ; superb ; 《文》 overtowering.
しゅう[6] 集 a collection. ¶第1集 the first series / 漱石書簡集 《書名》 *The Collected Letters of Soseki*.
しゅー ¶しゅーという hiss ; 〈むちなどが〉 swish ; 〈マッチなどが〉 whoosh ; 〈砲弾が〉 whiz(z) / しゅーという音 a hiss ; a hissing sound ; a swish ; a whoosh ; a whiz. 文例↓

しゅ[1] 彼らの旅行は遊びが主で見学の方は二の次だった。They made the journey not so much for information as for pleasure. / 私は主としてイギリスの劇を研究するつもりです。My chief object is to study English plays [drama]. / 主よ我らを哀れみたまえ。Lord, have mercy upon us.
しゅ[2] 満面に朱をそそいで怒った。He was flushed [red] with anger. | He went purple with rage. | 朱に交われば赤くなる。Evil communications corrupt good manners. 《聖書》| You cannot touch pitch without being defiled. 《諺》
しゅ[3] この種の人間も少なくない。There are quite a few people of this sort.
しゅい[1] アメリカは世界における経済上および政治上の首位の座を占める運命にあった。The primacy among nations, economic and political, was destined to go to the United States.
しゅい[2] 趣意に賛成して会員となった。I joined the society in support of its objectives.
しゅう[4] この部屋の部屋代は1週50ドルです。The rent of this room is 50 dollars a week. / 1, 2週あとの金曜日にまた彼女がやって来た。A Friday or two later, she called on me again. | この工場では週40時間5日制です。They are working a 40-hour, five-day week at this factory.
しゅー 風船がしゅーといってしぼ

じゆう 自由 freedom; liberty ¶言論[信仰,出版]の自由 freedom of speech [worship, the press] / 自由な free; unrestricted / 体の自由がきかない helpless 《old men》/ 自由の(ために戦う)闘士 a freedom fighter / 自由の身になる be set free [at liberty] / 自由の女神 ⇒めがみ / 自由を失う be deprived of one's liberty;〈身体が〉be disabled / …する自由を持たない《文》be not at liberty to do; be not allowed to do / 自由に as one likes [pleases]; freely;《文》at liberty;《文》at will;《文》without restraint / 自由自在に with perfect freedom; freely; with complete control / 自由にする〈勝手にする〉do as one pleases; make free with 《sb's possessions》;〈解放する〉《文》liberate; set 《a slave》free / 自由に使う make free use of sth / 自由にさせておく give sb a free hand; let sb have his own way / 自由にならない〈人が主語〉have no control 《of》;〈物が主語〉be beyond one's control / 人の自由にされる be at sb's mercy.

¶自由意志 free will / 自由業 a profession; the professions (総称) / 自由競争 free [open] competition; competition open to all / 自由経済 a free economy / 自由航行権《国際法》freedom of the seas / 自由国 a free state / 自由作文 an essay / 自由詩 free verse;《フランス語》vers libre / 自由時間〈団体旅行などの〉free time; time at leisure / 自由体操 自由種目 free exercises / 自由世界〈共産圏に対して〉the Free World / 自由席 an unreserved seat / 自由選択 free choice / 自由都市 a free city / 自由貿易 free trade / 自由貿易港 a free port / 自由放任 noninterference;《経済》laissez-[laisser-]faire/ 自由放任主義 the principle of laissez-faire / 自由民 a free citizen; free men /〈奴隷の身分から解放された〉a freedman / 自由民権運動 the Freedom and Popular Rights Movement (of the 1880s). ★ 自由化,自由形,自由行動,自由主義,自由民主党,自由訳は別見出し. 文例⇩

じゆう² 因 a cause; a reason のうに / 十 ten ¶第10 the tenth / 10分の1 one tenth; a tenth (part) / 何十回も dozens [scores] of times / 10倍 ten times;《文》tenfold / 10倍にする multiply 《a number》by ten [ten times].

じゆう² 柔 文例⇩ [ten times]. 文例⇩
じゆう³ 従 従の[たる] secondary;《文》subordinate;《法》accessory.
じゆう⁴ 銃 a gun; a rifle (小銃) ¶銃を構える hold one's gun at the ready / 銃を担う shoulder a gun / 銃を向ける point [level] a gun 《at》.
じゆう⁵ ¶じゆうじゆういう(油で揚げる時など) sizzle.

-じゆう¹ …中 (all) through 《the night》; all 《day》through; throughout 《the year》¶…中に during 《tomorrow》; in the course of 《next week》/ 一日中 all day long / 一年中 all the year round; throughout the year / 一晩中 all through the night; all night (long [through]) / 今週中に during this week; before the week is over / 東京中に [all over] Tokyo; everywhere in Tokyo / 冬中 all through the winter / 国中に知れ渡る be known throughout [all over] the country. 文例⇩

-じゆう² …重 ¶2重の《文》twofold; double / 2重に重ねる put one on top of [above] the other / 3重の《文》threefold; treble.

しゆうあく 醜悪 ¶醜悪な〈見るからに〉ugly;《文》unsightly; hideous; disgusting; horrible; grotesque;〈感じ・印象が〉《文》monstrous; filthy; abominable; repulsive; scandalous (affairs).

じゆうあつ 重圧 (heavy) pressure ¶重圧を加える put pressure on sb to do;《文》bring pressure (to bear) on sb to do / 経済的重圧を受ける undergo [be under] economic stress.

しゆうい 周囲 〈周辺〉the circumference; the girth;〈幾何〉the periphery;〈環境〉the surroundings; the environment; the circumstances;〈付近〉the neighborhood;《文》the environs ¶周囲の surrounding 《hills》;《文》encompassing 《mountain ranges》; neighboring 《villages》;《文》circumambient 《air》/ 周囲の人々 those around [close to] one;〈家族〉one's family;〈友人・知人〉one's friends and acquaintances / 周囲を見回す look around (one) / 周囲に around; round. 文例⇩

じゆうい¹ 重囲 a close siege ¶敵の重囲を脱する cut one's way through the besieging enemy / 重囲に陥る be closely besieged 《by》.

じゆうい² 獣医 a veterinarian; a veterinary (surgeon); a vet ¶獣医学 veterinary medicine [science] / 獣医学校[大学] a veterinary school [college].

じゆういち 十一 eleven ¶第11 the eleventh.
じゆういちがつ 十一月 November (略: Nov.).
しゆういつ 秀逸 ¶秀逸な excellent; superb; splendid; first-rate.
しゆうう 驟雨 a shower ¶驟雨にあう be caught in [overtaken by] a shower / 驟雨がち

んだ. The toy balloon deflated with a whoosh.
じゆう¹ 自由はややもすると放縦になる.Liberty often degenerates into lawlessness. / 行くか残るか,それは君の自由だ. You are free [at liberty] to go or stay. / わからないことは何でも自由に質問したまえ. Feel free [Don't hesitate] to ask me whatever you are in doubt about. / 家の中にあるものは何でもご自由にお使い下さい. Everything in this house is at your disposal. / 事の真相を語る自由を持たない. I am not in a position to tell the truth about it. / ご自由に召し上がって下さい. Help yourself, please. / 彼は英語を自由自在に操る. He has a perfect command of English. /(無料のパンフレットなど)ご自由にお取り下さい.《掲示》Free Literature. | Please take one.

じゆう² その病気で何十人もの人が死んだ. The disease killed people by the score [by scores].

じゆう² 柔よく剛を制す. Soft methods often get the better of brute force. | Persuasion is often more effective than force. | A smile can have a disarming effect.

-じゆう¹ 僕はひと夏追分にいた. I stayed at Oiwake all last summer. / 彼はほとんど日本中を旅行している. He has traveled almost all over Japan.

しゆうい その島の周囲はどのくらいですか. What is the circumference of that island? | How

しゅうえき¹ 収益 proceeds; profits; gains; earnings; returns ¶収益のある profitable;《文》lucrative / 収益をあげる make [《文》realize] a profit; make [fetch]《a million yen》/ 平均[純, 総, 予定]収益 average [net, gross, estimated] earnings / 収益逓減の法則 the law of diminishing returns.

しゅうえき² 就役 ¶就役する go [come] into commission [service]; be commissioned / 欧州航路に就役する go into service on the European line / 就役している be in commission / 就役させる put [place] (a ship) in [into] commission / 就役を解く remove (a ship) from service; decommission (a ship).

しゅうえん¹ 周縁 the fringe; the rim;《文》the periphery; the borders; the outskirts ¶周縁の《文》peripheral;《文》marginal.

しゅうえん² 終焉 ¶終焉の地 the place of sb's death / 終焉を告げる come; come to an end.

しゅうえん³ 終演 the end of a show. 文例⇩

じゅうおう 縦横 ¶縦横に〈たてよこに〉lengthwise and crosswise; vertically and horizontally;〈四方八方に〉in all directions; in every direction; throughout the length and breadth of 《the country》/ as one pleases;《文》at will / 縦横(無尽)に論じる talk freely 《on a subject》. 文例⇩

じゅうおく 十億 a billion ★英国では, これまで a billion は 10^{12} を意味したが, 最近では米国流に合わせて a billion を 10^9 の意味で使うことが一般化しつつある.

しゅうおん 集音 ¶集音機 a parabolic reflector / 集音マイク a highly directional microphone.

しゅうか 秀歌 an excellent [a superb] poem; a gem of a tanka.

しゅうか² 臭化《化》bromination ¶臭化銀 silver bromide / 臭化物 a bromide.

しゅうか³ 集荷 collection of cargo.

しゅうか⁴ 衆寡 ¶衆寡敵せず be (hopelessly) outnumbered. 文例⇩

じゆうか 自由化 liberalization [freeing] (of trade); removal of restrictions (on trade) ¶自由化する liberalize; free / 日本の貿易を90パーセントまで自由化する liberalize [remove restrictions on] 90 per cent of Japan's trade / 自由化商品 liberalized goods.

じゅうか 銃火 rifle fire; gunfire ¶銃火を浴びる come [be] under fire / 銃火を交える exchange fire 《with the enemy》.

しゅうかい 集会 a meeting;《文》a gathering; an assembly ¶集会する meet (together); gather; assemble; hold a meeting;《文》congregate / 集会所 a meeting place; an assembly hall; a clubhouse.

しゅうかいどう《植》a begonia.

しゅうかく¹ 収穫 a harvest; a crop; a yield; harvesting (行為);〈比喩的に〉《文》the fruit(s) (of one's labor) ¶収穫する harvest; gather [take] in; reap / 収穫が多い[少ない] have a good [poor] harvest [crop] / 1日の収穫 the (one's) day's take (of fish) [pick (of apples)] / 収穫期 the harvesting season; the harvest time / 収穫祭 a harvest festival / 収穫高 the yield; the crop / 予想収穫高 the estimated crop (of corn) / 収穫率の高い[低い] high- [low-]yield (varieties). 文例⇩

しゅうかく² 嗅覚 ⇨きゅうかく.

しゅうがく 就学 ¶就学する enter [go to, start (attending)] school / 就学させる send (a boy) to school / 就学児童 a schoolchild [preschool child] / 就学年齢 (reach) (the) school age / 就学率 the school attendance rate.

しゅうがくりょこう 修学旅行 (go on) a school excursion [trip]. 文例⇩

じゅうかさんぜい 重加算税 a heavy additional tax.

じゅうかぜい 従価税 an ad valorem duty.

じゆうがた 自由形《水泳》freestyle ¶百メートル自由形で1位になる finish [come in] first in the 100 meter freestyle (swimming) event / 自由形泳者 a freestyle swimmer.

じゅうがつ 十月 October (略: Oct.) ¶十月革命《世界史》the October Revolution.

しゅうかん¹ 週刊 weekly publication ¶週刊の (published) weekly / 週刊(雑)誌 a weekly (magazine).

しゅうかん² 週間 ⇨しゅう⁴ ¶2週間 two weeks; a fortnight / 3週間にわたって over [for] three weeks / 何週間も for weeks / 今日から3週間後に three weeks from today. 文例⇩

しゅうかん³ 習慣〈しきたり〉a custom;《文》(a) usage; (a) practice;〈癖〉(a) habit; a way ¶習慣がつく get [fall] into the habit (of); get [form,《文》acquire,《文》contract, pick up] the habit (of) /…する習慣がある have [be in] the habit of doing / 習慣の[的]《文》habitual; customary; usual; conventional / 習慣のとり

---

large round is that island? / この湖の周囲は20キロあります。This lake is twenty kilometers round [in circumference]. / その屋敷は周囲に高い塀を巡らしてある。The mansion is surrounded by a high wall.

しゅうえん³ 音楽会の収益は全部恵まれない子供たちの福祉のために当てられる。All the proceeds of the concert will be used for the benefit of children in special need.

しゅうえん³ 午後10時終演。The curtain falls at 10 p.m.

じゅうおう 鉄道が国中を縦横に走っている。A whole network of railroads crisscrosses the land. / 下水は市内を縦横に貫通している。Sewer pipes run in all directions through the city.

しゅうか⁴ 衆寡敵せずだ。There is no contending against such heavy odds.

しゅうかく¹ バナナは年2度の収穫がある。Bananas bear two crops a year. / 収穫が済んだ。The crops are in. / 本年の収穫は平年作以下の見込みである。This year's harvest is estimated to be below average. / 努力にもかかわらず彼にはあまり大した収穫はなかった。His efforts yielded him a poor harvest.

しゅうがくりょこう 彼らは明日京都へ修学旅行に出かける予定です。They are leaving tomorrow on a school trip to Kyoto.

しゅうかん² 5月10日から16日ま

じゅうかん ことなっている habit-[convention-]bound (people) / 習慣を捨てる break (off [up]) [shake off] a habit; give up [《文》discard, throw aside] the habit (of) / 悪い習慣を直す〈自分の〉get over [cure *oneself* of, get rid of] the (bad) habit (of);〈他人の〉break [cure] *sb* of a (bad) habit / 習慣で (*do*) from [by force of, out of] habit / 長い習慣で from [by] long habit / 習慣性の habit-forming [addictive] (drugs). 文例⇩

じゅうかん[1] 縦貫 ¶縦貫する run right across (the island); run through (the country) (lengthwise); cross (the island) (from one end to the other) ⇨ じゅうだん[2].

じゅうかん[2] 獣姦 bestiality.

じゅうがん 銃眼 a loophole; a port.

しゅうき[1] 周忌 the 《second》anniversary of *sb's* death.

しゅうき[2] 周期 a period; a cycle ¶景気の周期 a business cycle / 周期的 cyclical; periodic(al) / 周期的に periodically / 周期的に増減を繰返す have cyclic ups and downs / 周期性 periodicity / 周期律《化》the periodic law / 元素周期表《化》a periodic table (of the elements).

しゅうき[3] 臭気 a bad [《文》an offensive, 《文》an odious] smell; a bad odor; a stench; a stink ¶臭気のある bad-smelling; stinking / 臭気を放つ give off [send out] a bad smell;《文》emit a foul [filthy] odor / 臭気を消す deodorize; get rid of [destroy] the foul odor (of) / 臭気止め a deodorizer; a deodorant. 文例⇩

しゅうき[4] 秋季 autumn;《米》(the) fall ¶秋季運動会 an autumn athletic meet.

しゅうぎ[1] 祝儀〈祝賀〉a celebration; congratulations;〈祝い物〉《文》a congratulatory gift;〈心付け〉a tip;《文》a gratuity ¶祝儀をやる〈waiter に〉tip 《a waiter》; give a tip [《文》gratuity].

しゅうぎ[2] 衆議 ¶衆議一決する〈事が主語〉be unanimously decided [agreed on].

じゅうき 什器 《文》a utensil;《an article of》furniture;《office》fixtures.

しゅうぎいん 衆議院 the House of Representatives; the Lower House ¶衆議院議員[議長] a member [the Speaker] of the House of Representatives.

しゅうきゅう[1] 週休 a weekly day off [holiday] ¶週休2日制 the five-day-week system. 文例⇩

しゅうきゅう[2] 週給 weekly wages [pay] ¶週給200ドルである get 200 dollars a week (in) wages [wages of 200 dollars a week].

しゅうきゅう[3] 蹴球 ⇨ サッカー.

じゅうきょ 住居 a (dwelling) house;《文》a residence ¶住居を定める settle (down) (in);《文》fix *one's* residence (in the city);《文》establish residency / 住居跡《考古》a dwelling [habitation] site; the site of a (prehistoric) settlement.

しゅうきょう 宗教 (a) religion;《文》(a) (religious) faith ¶宗教的[上の] religious / 啓示[自然]宗教 (a) revealed [natural] religion / 宗教家 a man of religion / 宗教画 a religious picture; a picture of a sacred subject; a religious painting / 宗教界 religious circles; the religious world / 宗教改革 religious reformation;《史》the Reformation / 宗教学 science of religion / 宗教学の教授 a professor of religion / 比較宗教学 comparative religion / 宗教建築 religious architecture / 宗教裁判《史》the Inquisition / 宗教裁判所 a spiritual court;《史》the Inquisition / 宗教心 religious feelings [sentiment] / 宗教心のある religious(-minded); pious;《文》godly / 宗教心のない《文》irreligious;《文》impious;《文》godless; not religious / 宗教団体 a religious body [organization] / 宗教彫刻 religious sculpture / 宗教哲学 the philosophy of religion / 宗教美術 religious art. 文例⇩

しゅうぎょう[1] 修業 ¶修業する〈勉強する〉study; get *one's* education [training] (from);〈修了する〉complete [finish] a course of study / 修業年限 the term of study; the (minimum) period required for graduation [completing *one's* course of study]. 文例⇩

しゅうぎょう[2] 終業 finishing [the end of] work [school] ¶終業時間 finishing time;《口語》knocking-off time (工場などの);〈店の〉closing time / 終業式 the closing ceremony [exercises] / 終業日 breaking-up day; the last day of school. 文例⇩

しゅうぎょう[3] 就業 ¶就業する start [begin, set about] work / 就業している be at work; be on duty / 就業時間中 during working hours / 就業規則 office [shop, working] regulations / 就業契約をする give or take [at [with, to work for] a company] / 就業日数 days worked. 文例⇩

じゅうぎょういん 従業員〈1人〉an employee; a worker;〈総称〉men; the work force ¶従業員教育 the training of employees; employee education [training].

しゅうきょく[1] 終曲《音楽》the finale.

しゅうきょく[2] 終局 an end;《文》a close; a conclusion;《文》a denouement; a finale ¶終局の final;《文》ultimate; eventual / 終局を告げる come [be brought] to an end [a close, a conclusion];《文》be concluded. 文例⇩

では愛鳥週間である. Bird Week is observed [held] from May 10 to 16.

しゅうかん[3] いったんこの習慣がつくとなかなか抜けない. Once you get into this habit, you will find it hard to break [get out of] it. / 古い習慣は容易に廃れないものだ. Old habits die hard. / テレビを見ながら食事をするのが彼らの習慣なのだ. They are in the habit of watching television while they eat. / 習慣は国によって異なる. Each country has its own customs. | Social customs vary from country to country. / 習慣は第二の天性である. Habit is second nature. / この薬は習慣性になることがある. This drug can be addictive.

しゅうき[3] 悪臭が鼻をついた. The stench from the ditches assailed my nostrils.

しゅうきゅう[1] 我々は週休2日制だ. We are on [We work] a five-day week.

しゅうきゅう[2] あの会社は週給制をとっている. They are paid weekly in that company. / この工場では賃金は週給制です. In this factory the wages are paid on a weekly basis.

しゅうきょう ほとんどすべての宗

しゅうきょく[3] 褶曲 〘地質〙 a (crustal) fold; a bend 《in a stratum》 ¶ 褶曲山脈 folded mountains.

しゅうぎょとう 集魚灯 a fish-luring light.

しゅうきん 集金 ¶ 集金する collect money [bills] / 集金人 a money [bill] collector.

じゅうきんぞく 重金属 (a) heavy metal.

しゅうぐ 衆愚 《文》 the ignorant [vulgar] crowd; 《文》 the mob ¶ 衆愚政治 mobocracy; mob rule; 〘政〙 ochlocracy.

じゅうく 十九 nineteen ¶ 第19 the nineteenth.

ジュークボックス a jukebox.

シュークリーム [＜《フランス語》 *chou à la crème*] a cream puff.

じゅうクロムさん 重クロム酸 〘化〙 dichromic acid ¶ 重クロム酸ナトリウム sodium dichromate.

じゅうぐん 従軍 ¶ 従軍する go to the front; join the army; 《文》 serve in the war / 従軍記者 a war correspondent. ⌈total ⇨ ごうけい.

しゅうけい 集計 ¶ 集計する add [sum] up;

じゅうけい 重刑 a severe punishment; a heavy penalty ¶ 重刑を科する sentence *sb* to a severe punishment; 《文》 inflict a heavy penalty 《on》; punish *sb* severely.

しゅうげき 襲撃 an attack; an assault; a raid; a charge ¶ 襲撃する make an attack [a raid] 《on》; attack; assault; charge; storm; fall on; descend [swoop down] on 《an enemy》 / 不意に襲撃する take 《the enemy's camp》 by surprise; make a surprise attack 《on》; surprise / 襲撃して占領する take 《a fortress》 by assault [storm].

じゅうげき 銃撃 ¶ 銃撃する 〈小銃で〉 shoot a rifle 《at》; 〈機関銃で〉 machine-gun 《a factory》; strafe (飛行機から).

しゅうけつ[1] 終結 (a) conclusion; 《文》 termination; an end; 《文》 a close ¶ 終結する come [be brought] to an end [a close]; end; 《文》 close; 《文》 terminate; 《文》 be concluded / (議会で票決に入るために)討論を終結させる apply the closure [《米》 cloture] to a debate; invoke [declare] closure / 戦争終結の交渉を開始する begin negotiations for an end to the war.

しゅうけつ[2] 集結 concentration; 〈軍隊の〉 assembly; build-up ¶ 集結する 〈集める〉 concentrate; collect; gather; assemble; mass 《its troops》; build up; 〈集まる〉 be concentrated; be collected; gather; assemble; build 《themselves》 up / (軍隊の)集結地 an assembly place [area].

じゅうけつ 充血 〘医〙 congestion 《of the brain》; hyperemia ¶ 充血する be congested; be [become] engorged [suffused] with blood; 〈目が〉 be bloodshot.

じゅうけつきゅうちゅう 住血吸虫 a blood fluke; a schistosome ¶ 住血吸虫病 schistosomiasis; snail fever.

しゅうげん 祝言 ⇨ けっこん[2] (結婚式).

じゅうけん 銃剣 a bayonet ¶ 銃剣を付ける fix a bayonet 《to a rifle》 / 銃剣を突き付けて at the point of the bayonet / (銃から)銃剣を取る unfix a bayonet 《from a rifle》 / 銃剣で突く bayonet *sb*; stab *sb* [run *sb* through] with a bayonet / 銃剣術 bayonet drill [fencing] / 銃剣突撃 a bayonet charge.

じゅうご[1] 十五 fifteen ¶ 第15 the fifteenth / 15分 a quarter of an hour; fifteen minutes / 十五夜 a night with a full moon / 十五夜の月 a full moon; 〈秋分ごろの〉 the harvest moon.

じゅうご[2] 銃後 the home front.

しゅうこう[1] 周航 a journey round 《the world》; 《文》 (a) circumnavigation ¶ 周航する sail [cruise] round 《the world》; 《文》 circumnavigate 《the globe》.

しゅうこう[2] 修好[交] ¶ 修好条約 《conclude》 a treaty of amity [friendship].

しゅうこう[3] 就航 ¶ 就航する enter service; go [be placed] into commission [service]; be commissioned ⇨ しゅうえき[2].

しゅうこう[4] 集光 ¶ 集光器 a light-gathering instrument / 集光レンズ a condensing [collecting] lens; a condenser.

しゅうごう 集合 (a) gathering; (a) meeting; an assembly; 〘数〙 a set ¶ 集合する 〈集まる〉 gather; meet; collect; assemble; 《文》 throng; 《文》 flock; 《文》 rally; swarm; get together; 〈集める〉 gather (together); collect; assemble; summon; call [get, put] together; muster 《troops》 / 集合時間 the time appointed for meeting [assembling]; the time *one* is supposed to meet / 集合場所 the meeting-place; the rendezvous (point); the roll-call [assembly] point; 《文》 the appointed [designated] place / 集合名詞 〘文法〙 a collective noun / 集合論 〘数〙 set theory; the theory of sets. [文例⇩]

じゅうこう[1] 重厚 ¶ 重厚な 《文》 profound; deep; imposing. [文例⇩]

じゅうこう[2] 銃口 the muzzle 《of a rifle》 ¶ 銃口を向ける train *one's* gun on [point *one's* gun at] 《the enemy》 / 銃口を突き付けて[られて] at the point [end] of a gun; at gunpoint.

じゅうごう 重合 〘化〙 polymerization ¶ 重合する polymerize / 重合体 a polymer.

じゅうこうぎょう 重工業 heavy industry [in-

教は信仰を異にするものとの結婚に反対である. Practically all religions are opposed to marriage outside their faith. / この地方の人々の宗教はカトリックである. The people of this region are Catholic in [of the Catholic] faith.

しゅうぎょう[1] 本校の修業年限は4か年です. The course of study in our school extends over four years.

しゅうぎょう[2] 終業式は24日です. School will break up on the 24th.

しゅうぎょう[3] 就業中面会謝絶. 〘掲示〙 Interviews declined during working hours.

しゅうきょく[2] 争議も終局に近づいた. The dispute is drawing to a close.

しゅうごう 明朝7時に学校に集合することになっている. We are to meet at the school at seven tomorrow morning. / 彼は集合時間に20分遅れて来た. He arrived twenty minutes after [later than] the appointed time. | He came twenty minutes late for the meeting.

じゅうこう[1] 重厚な感じの人だ. He

じゆうこうどう 自由行動 free [unorganized] activities ¶自由行動をとる act for oneself [《文》at one's own discretion]; take one's own course.

じゆうこん 重婚 《commit》bigamy.

しゆうさ 収差 〔写真・光〕(an) aberration.

じゆうざ 銃座 a gun emplacement [position].

ジューサー a juice extractor; 《米》a juicer.

しゆうさい 秀才 a brilliant [bright] boy [student]. 文例⇩

じゆうざい 重罪 a serious crime [offense]; (a) felony ¶重罪犯人 a felon.

しゆうさく¹ 秀作 an excellent work [piece].

しゆうさく² 習作 a study; 《フランス語》an étude.

じゆうさつ 銃殺 ¶銃殺する shoot sb dead; execute 《a criminal》by shooting / 銃殺される be shot dead [to death]; face [《文》die before] a firing squad.

しゆうさつがかり 集札係 〔鉄道〕a ticket collector.

しゆうさん¹ 集散 ¶集散する collect [gather, receive] and distribute / 集散地 a distributing [trading] center; an entrepot.

しゆうさん² 蓚酸 〔化〕oxalic acid.

じゆうさん 十三 thirteen ¶第13 the thirteenth / 13を不吉とする迷信 (a) superstitious fear of the number thirteen. 文例⇩

しゆうし¹ 収支 income [revenue] and expenditure; earnings and expenses ¶収支の差引勘定をする settle an [one's] account; strike a balance / 収支を明らかにする account for receipts and disbursements / 収支を償わせる make both ends meet. 文例⇩

しゆうし² 宗旨 〈宗門の教義の趣旨〉the doctrines [《文》tenets] of a religious body; 〈宗教〉a religion; 〈宗派〉a denomination; a religious sect ¶宗旨を変える be converted to 《another sect》; abandon [《文》abjure] one's faith for 《another》; change one's church / 宗旨を同じくする 《文》a coreligionist. 文例⇩

しゆうし³ 修士 ¶文学修士〈学位〉Master of Arts《略：M.A.》/ 〈人〉a master of arts / 理学修士〈学位〉Master of Science《略：M.S., M. Sc.》/ 修士課程 the master's course 《in law》/ 修士号 the master's degree / 修士号をとる get [《文》receive, earn] a master's degree 《in political science from Harvard University》;

get one's master's [M.A.] 《in linguistics》/ 修士論文 a master's thesis 《in anthropology》. 文例⇩

しゆうし⁴ 終止 an end; a stop; 《文》termination; 《文》cessation ¶終止する stop; terminate; come to an end [《文》a close]; 《文》be brought to a conclusion; 《文》cease / 終止符を打つ put an end [a period] 《to》/ 終止符を打つ put an end [a period] 《to》.

しゆうし⁵ 終始 from beginning to end; from start to finish; all along; throughout; all the time; constantly ¶終始一貫した consistent / 終始一貫して consistently. 文例⇩

しゆうじ¹ 修辞 a figure of speech; rhetoric ¶修辞学[法] rhetoric / 修辞学者 a rhetorician / 修辞[学]上の rhetorical.

しゆうじ² 習字 penmanship; calligraphy ¶習字が上手[へた]だ be a good [poor] calligrapher / 習字の先生 a calligraphy teacher; a writing master / 習字のお手本のような字を書く 《文》write a copybook hand / 習字をする practice calligraphy [penmanship] / 英習字 English penmanship / 習字帳 a copybook; a writing book.

じゆうし¹ 十四 fourteen ¶第14 the fourteenth.

じゆうし² 重視 ¶重視する think [《文》consider] that sth is important; 《文》regard sth as important; 《文》set great store by sth [on doing]; 《文》attach importance to sth; think a great deal [《文》much] of sth.

じゆうじ 従事 ¶従事する〈仕事に〉《文》engage in 《business》; attend to 《one's work》; 〈職業に〉《文》pursue 《a calling》; 《文》follow 《a profession》/ 従事している《文》be engaged in 《atomic research》; be occupied in [busy with] 《some important work》; be at work 《on a new book》. 文例⇩

じゆうじか 十字架 a cross ¶十字架を負う bear one's cross / 十字架にかける crucify; put sb on the cross / 十字架上のキリスト像 a Crucifixion.

じゆうじぐん 十字軍 a crusade; the crusaders ¶十字軍の戦士 a crusader.

じゆうじ(けい) 十字(形) a cross ¶十字を切る cross oneself / 十字に crosswise / 十字形の cross-shaped; 《文》cruciform / (吊輪の)十字懸垂[体操] the crucifix.

じゆうしち 十七 seventeen ¶第17 the seventeenth / 十七条の憲法〔史〕(Prince Shotoku's)

---

impresses one as being a man of depth. | He has a lot of depth.

しゆうさい 彼は学校の秀才であった。He was the brightest boy in the (whole) school.

じゆうさん 13という数は西洋では不吉とされている。The number thirteen is regarded as unlucky in Western countries.

しゆうし¹ 収支が償わない。The income does not cover [meet] the expenses.

しゆうし² 彼は前にはテニスをやっていたが, 近頃はゴルフに宗旨変

えしている。He used to play tennis, but he has switched over to golf.

しゆうし³ 僕の修士論文はミルトンだった。I wrote a dissertation on Milton for my master's degree.

しゆうし⁵ 彼は社会主義者で終始した。He lived and died a socialist. / 我々は終始一貫してそれに反対してきた。We were against it from start to finish [from beginning to end].

じゆうじ 僕はブラジルに行って農

業に従事するつもりだ。I intend to go to Brazil and engage in agriculture [work as a farmer].

じゆうじつ 私は今の仕事にある程度の充実感を得ています。I find some fulfillment in my present work. / この本は内容が充実している。This book is very substantial.

しゆうじゃく 私は現在の地位に何ら執着していない。I have no attachment whatever to my present position. / だれでも人生に強い執着がある。Everyone has a

Constitution of Seventeen Articles.

しゅうじつ[1] 週日 a weekday.

しゅうじつ[2] 終日 all day (long); the whole day; all through the day; throughout the day; from morning till [to] night.

じゅうじつ 充実 ¶軍備の充実 military preparedness / 充実する enrich; make *sth* satisfactory [complete]; complete; perfect; 《口語》bring 《facilities》 up to scratch [up to the mark] / 充実した full; complete; 〈内容の〉substantial; solid / 充実した生活 a full [fulfilling] life / 最高に充実した生活を送る live life to the full(est). 文例↓

じゅうじほうか 十字砲火 crossfire ¶十字砲火を浴びせる pour crossfire 《on the enemy》.

じゅうしまつ 《鳥》a society finch.

じゅうしゃ 従者 a follower; an attendant; a valet.

しゅうじゃく 執着 attachment 《to, for》; 〈固執〉《文》persistence 《in》 ¶執着する be attached 《to》; stick 《to》 adhere, cling, hold fast 《to》 / 執着心 attachment 《to》; 《文》tenacity of purpose. 文例↓

しゅうしゅう[1] 収拾 ¶収拾する control; get *sth* under control; save; deal [cope] with; sort 《a problem》out; handle; manipulate; manage / 混乱を収拾する unsnarl [disentangle] the chaos / 難局を収拾する save [settle, straighten out, sort out] a difficult situation / 収拾がつかなくなる get out of hand [control]; become uncontrollable.

しゅうしゅう[2] 収集 (a) collection; gathering; 《文》(an) accumulation 《of phrases》 ¶収集する collect; gather; 《文》accumulate 《data》; make a collection of 《autographed photos》/ 収集家 a collector / 収集癖 a mania for 《stamp》 collecting; a collecting mania. 文例↓

しゅーしゅー しゅーしゅーいう hiss; fizz; whoosh 《風船などがしぼむとき》.

じゅうじゅう 重々 〈繰り返し〉repeatedly; 〈非常に〉very; extremely. 文例↓

じゅうじゅう[2] 〈(フライパンの中で焼ける肉などが)じゅうじゅういう sizzle / 焼き肉のじゅうじゅういう音 the sizzling (noise) of the meat in the pan [on the fire].

じゆうしゅぎ 自由主義 liberalism ¶自由主義経済 free economy / 自由主義国 a free nation / 自由主義者 a liberal (thinker).

しゅうしゅく 収縮 contraction; shrinking; 《文》constriction ¶収縮する contract; shrink; 《文》be constricted; 《文》deflate (排気して) / 収縮筋 《解》a constrictor; a contractor; a retractor / 収縮性 contractibility / 収縮力 contractile force [power].

しゅうじゅく 習熟 ⇒じゅくれん

じゅうじゅん 従順 ¶従順な obedient; 《文》submissive; meek; tame / 従順に obediently; 《文》submissively; meekly; tamely.

じゅうしょ 住所 one's address ¶住所を定める make one's home 《at》; 《文》take up residence 《at》/ 住所氏名 one's name and address / 住所不定の having no fixed [permanent] address [《文》abode, 《文》residence] / 住所変更通知 a change-of-address note / 住所変更届け a report of one's removal / 住所録 an address book. 文例↓

しゅうしょう 愁傷 《文》grief; sorrow; 《文》lamentation. 文例↓

じゅうしょう[1] 重症 a serious illness ⇒じゅうびょう, じゅうたい ¶重症患者 a patient with an advanced disease; a serious case (of cholera).

じゅうしょう[2] 重傷 a serious injury [wound] ¶重傷を負う receive a serious injury; be badly [seriously] injured [wounded] / 重傷を負わせる 《文》inflict a severe injury 《on》; injure *sb* seriously / 重傷者 a seriously injured person. 文例↓

じゅうしょう[3] 銃床 the stock of a rifle; a gunstock.

じゅうしょうしゅぎ 重商主義 《経済》mercantilism ¶重商主義者 a mercantilist.

しゅうしょうろうばい 周章狼狽 《文》consternation; bewilderment; (a) flurry ¶周章ろうばいする be confused; be flustered; be flurried; be panic-stricken; fall into a panic; be thrown into confusion; lose one's head [presence of mind] / 周章ろうばいして in confusion [《文》dismay, consternation]; (all) in a flurry [fluster]; helter-skelter.

しゅうしょく[1] 秋色 〈秋の景色〉《文》autumnal scenery; 〈秋の気配〉signs of autumn [fall]. 文例↓

しゅうしょく[2] 修飾 ¶修飾する 《文法》modify; qualify; 〈潤飾する〉《文》embellish; embroider / 修飾語 《文法》a modifier; a qualifier.

しゅうしょく[3] 就職 ¶就職する find work [《文》 employment, a job]; get [《文》secure, 《文》obtain] a position [job] 《with a firm》; 《文》enter 《industrial》employment; 《口語》sign on 《with a firm as a driver》/ 就職の機会 employment

---

strong instinctive hold on life. / 彼は金銭に執着している. His heart is set on moneymaking. / 彼には写真はきまって左側面をとってもらうという病的執着があった. He had a fixation about always being photographed from his left side. | He had an [a pathological] aversion to being photographed from his right side.

しゅうしゅう[2] 氏は人形の収集家として知られている. He is well known for his large collection of dolls. / 今ではその切手は収集家のねらう対象になっている. That stamp is now a collector's item.

じゅうじゅう[1] 重々恐れ入りました. A thousand pardons! | I am most terribly sorry. / 私の方が重重悪いのです. I am very much in the wrong. / 重々承知しております. I am well aware of it.

じゅうしょ ご住所はどちらですか. Would you give me your address? | What is your address, please? / あの人の住所がわからない. I haven't got his address. | I don't know where he lives. / 住所不明. 《表示》Address unknown.

しゅうしょう ご愁傷のほどお察し申し上げます. Please accept my sincere sympathy in your sad bereavement.

じゅうしょう[2] その事故で死者2名重傷者3名を出した. Two people were killed and three severely injured in the accident.

しゅうしょく[1] 秋色まさにたけなわである. The trees are aflame

じゅうしょく [job] opportunities / 就職の世話をする find [get] sb a job [position]; put sb in the way of a job [of making a living] / 就職を申し込む apply for a position [place, job]; submit a job application (to) / 就職運動 job hunting / 就職運動で忙しい be busy looking for a job [(文) seeking employment] / 就職係 〈学校の〉 an employment officer; a careers [vocational] advisor / 就職口 a job; a position; (文) a situation; an opening / 就職口を捜す look [hunt] for a job [position]; seek employment / 就職試験 an examination for employment; an employment exam / 就職難 the difficulty of finding employment [work]; a job shortage / 就職率 an employment rate. 文例🔽

じゅうしょく 住職 the chief [head] priest (of a Buddhist temple).

じゅうじろ 十字路 (be at) a crossroads.

しゅうしん¹ 修身 〈学科〉 morals; ethics; 〈修養〉 moral training [culture].

しゅうしん² 執心 enthusiasm; (文) ardor; infatuation 《with》(男女間の) ¶執心する set one's heart (on); be intent [(文) bent] (on moneymaking); 〈異性に〉 be infatuated 《with》; be head over heels [over head and ears] in love 《with a girl》; (口語) be gone on 《a girl》.

しゅうしん³ 終身 for life; all (through) one's life ¶終身の lifelong; for life / 終身会員 a life member / 終身官 an official appointed for life / 終身刑 (serve) a life sentence; (be sentenced to) imprisonment for life / 終身雇用制度 the lifetime [lifelong] employment system / 終身生命保険 whole [straight, ordinary] life insurance.

しゅうしん⁴ 就寝 ¶就寝する go to bed; turn in; (文) retire (to rest [to bed, for the night]) / 就寝時間 (one's) bedtime / 就寝中 while (one is) asleep [sleeping]; (while) in bed.

しゅうじん¹ 囚人 a prisoner; a convict; (口語) a jailbird; (俗) a con ¶囚人服 (a) prison uniform.

しゅうじん² 衆人 the people; the public ¶衆人の前で, 衆人環視の中で in public; in company; (文) in the presence of the whole company; (文) with all eyes fixed on one.

じゅうしん¹ 重心 《物》 the center of gravity; a center of balance ¶重心を失う lose one's balance / 重心を保つ keep [(文) maintain] one's [the] balance [equilibrium]; balance oneself (on one leg). 文例🔽

じゅうしん² 重臣 a chief [senior] vassal [retainer]; a senior statesman ¶重臣会議 a senior statesmen's conference. ¶barrel.

じゅうしん³ 銃身 the barrel (of a rifle); a gun

ジュース¹ 〈果汁〉 (orange, grape) juice.

ジュース² 〈競技〉 deuce ¶ジュースになる go to deuce.

じゅうすい 重水 《化》 heavy water; deuterium oxide.

じゅうすいそ 重水素 《化》 deuterium; heavy hydrogen.

しゅうせい¹ 修正 (文) (an) amendment; (a) revision; (a) modification; 〈誤りの〉 (a) correction; (文) (a) rectification; 〈写真の〉 a retouch; retouching ¶修正する (文) amend; revise; modify; correct; (文) rectify; 〈写真を〉 retouch / 字句を修正する alter [make some changes in] the wording / 修正案 〈草案〉 a draft amendment; a proposed amendment [revision]; 〈修正された議案〉 an amended [a revised] bill; an amendment / 修正資本主義 modified capitalism. / 修正主義(主義者) revisionism [a revisionist] / 修正申告 (file) a revised (income tax) return / 修正予算 a revised budget.

しゅうせい² 終生 all [till the end of] one's life; as long as one lives ¶終生変わらぬ友情 lifelong friendship / 終生の lifelong / 終生の事業 one's lifework. 文例🔽

しゅうせい³ 習性 a habit; living habits; one's way(s) ¶動物の習性 animal behavior ⇒くせ.

しゅうせい⁴ 集成 (a) compilation 《of historical materials》 ¶集成する collect; compile; gather (the facts) together (into a whole); codify.

しゅうぜい 収税 ¶収税する collect [gather] taxes / 収税官 a tax collector; a revenue officer.

じゅうせい¹ 銃声 the report of a gun [rifle]; (the sound of) gunfire.

じゅうせい² 獣性 (文) (man's) brutal [animal] nature; (文) the brute [beast] (in man); (文) brutishness.

じゅうぜい 重税 〈税金〉 a heavy tax [duty]; 〈課税〉 heavy [oppressive] taxation ¶重税に苦しむ groan under heavy taxes; suffer from heavy taxation / 重税を課す impose heavy taxes (on the people).

しゅうせき 集積 (an) accumulation ¶集積する accumulate; pile (up) / 集積回路 《電子工学》 an integrated circuit (略: IC) / 大規模集積回路 a large-scale integrated circuit (略: LSI).

じゅうせき 重責 (assume) a heavy responsibility; an important duty [(文) mission]. 文例🔽

しゅうせん¹ 周旋 〈斡旋(あっせん)〉 (文) good [kind] offices; 〈推薦〉 recommendation; 〈取り持ち〉 (文) mediation; (文) agency ¶周旋をする use

---

with autumn colors. | The autumnal tints are in full glory.

しゅうしょく² 学校教育とは, いいところに就職するための手段に過ぎないと心得ている人が多い. To many people school education is only a step to getting a good job. / こんにち我々が直面している最大の問題の1つは職のない多数の大学卒業者をいかにして就職させるかということである. One of the greatest problems facing us today is how to find employment for a large number of jobless university graduates.

じゅうしん¹ 彼は身体の重心を片方の足からもう一方の足に移した. He shifted his weight from one foot to the other.

しゅうせい² ご恩は終生忘れません. I shall never forget your kindness as long as I live.

じゅうせい¹ 銃声がとどろいた. Bang went a gun. | There was the loud report of a gun. / 遠くで銃声が1発聞こえた. I heard a shot [Gunfire could be heard] in

しゅうせん one's influence 《on behalf of》; 《文》exercise one's good offices 《with the employer on behalf of the workers》; recommend; 《文》mediate 《between》; 《文》intercede 《with A for B》/ 職を周旋する get [find] sb a position [job] / …の周旋で through the good offices of 《a friend》/ 周旋業 brokerage / 周旋人 an agent；周旋屋 a broker，a middleman；〈雇い人の〉an employment agent；〈土地・家屋の〉a land [house] broker [agent] / 周旋料 brokerage; a commission.

しゅうせん² 終戦 《at, since》the end of the war ¶終戦後の postwar / 終戦記念日 the anniversary of the end of the Pacific War.

しゅうぜん 修繕 repair(s); mending; a refit; an overhaul ⇨しゅうり ¶修繕する repair; mend; fix (up); 〈航海から帰った物を〉overhaul / 〈仮, 大, 小〉修繕を施す make temporary [large, small] repairs 《on》/ 修繕費 the cost of (the) repairs; repair costs / 修繕屋 a repairman / 修繕用具 repair tools. 文例⇩

しゅうそ 臭素《化》bromine.

しゅうぞう 収蔵 収蔵する house 《a collection of Rouault's paintings》; stock 《original editions of 18th-century poetry》/ 収蔵庫 a repository.

じゅうそう¹ 重曹《化》sodium bicarbonate; bicarbonate of soda; baking soda.

じゅうそう² 縦走 ⇨じゅうかん¹ ¶日本アルプスを縦走する climb the length of the Japan Alps.

しゅうそうれつじつ 秋霜烈日 秋霜烈日のごとき relentless; rigorous; severe; stern.

しゅうそく¹ 収束《数》convergence ¶収束する 〈乱れをまとめる〉settle (the dispute);《文》restore sth to its normal [an orderly] state;《数》converge / 収束級数《数》a convergent series.

しゅうそく² 集束《物》focusing ¶集束作用 focusing action / 集束能力 focusing ability [power].

しゅうぞく 習俗 manners and customs; usage(s);《社会》folkways;《社会》mores.

じゅうそく 充足《文》sufficiency ¶充足する fulfillment ¶充たす ⇨みたす / 自己充足的 self-sufficient; self-contained.

じゅうぞく 従属 subordination;《文》dependence ¶従属する《文》be subordinate (to); be dependent (on) / 従属的《文》subordinate;《文》dependent / 従属節[接続詞]《文法》a subordinate clause [conjunction].

しゅうたい 醜態〈行動〉disgraceful behavior;《文》shameful conduct;〈外観〉《文》an unseemly sight;〈状態〉a scandalous situation [state of affairs] ¶醜態を演じる[さらす] make a (sorry) display of oneself; cut a sorry [ridiculous, pitiable] figure;〈へまをする〉《口語》come a cropper.

じゅうたい¹ 重体[態] ¶重体に陥る〈病人が〉《文》fall into a critical condition;〈病気が〉take a serious turn / 重体である be seriously ill 《with cancer》/《文》be in a critical [serious] condition. 文例⇩

じゅうたい² 渋滞 (a) delay;〈交通の〉《文》congestion ¶渋滞する be delayed;《文》be retarded;〈道路が〉get choked [《文》become congested]《with traffic》/ 交通の渋滞 a traffic jam [snarl-up, back-up] / 交通の渋滞を解消する sort out [unsnarl] a (rush-hour) traffic jam / 渋滞なく smoothly; without a hitch; without delay / 事務に渋滞を来たす《文》cause delay in business. 文例⇩

じゅうたい³ 縦隊 a column; a file ¶1 [2] 列縦隊で in single [double] file / 4列縦隊 a column of fours.

じゅうだい¹ 十代 (be in) one's teens ¶10代の少年[少女] a teen-ager; boys [girls] in their teens; teenage boys [girls] ★「十代」といっても, teens, teen-ager は語尾に -teen の付く13～19の年齢で, 10～12という年齢は初め[終わり]の[に] in one's early [late] teens ★low-teens, high-teens は和製英語.

じゅうだい² 重大 重大な matters;《文》grave; important;《文》matters of great importance / 重大になる, 重大化する《文》become serious (in character);《文》assume serious proportions / 重大事件 a serious affair [case] / 重大性 seriousness;《文》gravity; importance / 重大視する take (a matter) seriously;《文》attach (great) importance (to); take a serious view 《of》/ 重大問題 a grave issue; a serious [vital] question;《文》a matter of grave concern. 文例⇩

しゅうたいせい 集大成 ¶集大成する compile (all the available data) into one book; make [give] a comprehensive [complete] survey of 《past studies on a subject》.

じゅうたく 住宅《文》a residence; a residential building;〈総称〉housing ¶住宅公団 the Housing Corporation / 住宅街 a residential street / 住宅金融公庫 the Housing Loan Corporation / 住宅建設 house building [construction] / 住宅地域 residential quarters [areas]; the residential sections [zones] 《of the city》/ 住宅手当 a housing allowance / 住宅難 (a) housing shortage [trouble] / 住宅費 housing costs [expenses] / 住宅問題 the housing problem. 文例⇩

---

the distance.
じゅうせき 私はそのような重責には耐えられない。I am not equal to such an important task.
しゅうぜん この靴は修繕が必要だ。These shoes need repairing. / 修繕費は3千円ぐらいです。The repairs will cost about 3,000 yen.
じゅうたい¹ 病気が重体になった。

His illness became very grave [serious].
じゅうたい² 環状7号線は高円寺付近で2キロにわたって渋滞しています。Loop 7 is congested [choked] with traffic for 2 kilometers near Koenji. / 雪が市圏に積もるにつれて交通が渋滞した。Traffic was snarled as snow

blanketed the metropolitan area.
じゅうだい² これは我々にとってきわめて重大な問題だ。It is a matter of vital importance to us.
じゅうたく まだ全部の人に行き渡るだけの住宅がない。There are still not enough houses to go round. / 日本の住宅事情は今でもひじょうに悪い。The housing sit-

しゅうだつ 収奪 plundering;《文》exploitation ¶収奪をする plunder;《文》exploit / 収奪的な《文》exploitative.

しゅうたん 愁嘆《文》lamentation;《文》grief; sorrow ¶愁嘆場 a pathetic [tragic] scene.

しゅうだん 集団 a group ¶集団を作る form a group / 集団で in a group; en masse / 集団的に collectively; as a group / 集団安全保障 collective security / 集団移民[欠勤] mass emigration [absenteeism] / 集団競技 a group game / 集団結婚 (a) group marriage / 集団検診 a mass examination [checkup]《for stomach cancer》/ 集団行動 group [collective] action; collective behavior / 集団志向の group-oriented《society》/ 集団指導制《be under》collective leadership / 集団住宅 group housing / 集団食中毒 mass food poisoning / 集団心理(学) group psychology / 集団生活 communal living [life] / 集団脱走をする run away [break out] en masse《from a reformatory》/ 集団農場 a collective farm;《ロシア語》a kolkhoz《pl. -zy, -khozes》/ 集団農場化 farm collectivization / 集団発生 a mass outbreak《of dysentery》/ 集団反応 (a) mass reaction / 集団暴行 mob violence;〈輪姦〉gang rape. 文例↓

じゅうたん 絨緞 a carpet; a rug (小型・粗毛の);〈総称〉carpeting ¶魔法のじゅうたん a magic carpet / じゅうたんを敷く spread a carpet; carpet《a floor, a room》/ じゅうたんを敷きつめたような一面のこけ a carpet of moss / ペルシャ[トルコ]じゅうたん a Persian [Turkish] carpet [rug] / (階段の)じゅうたん押え a carpet rod / じゅうたん掃除機 a carpet sweeper / じゅうたん爆撃 carpet bombing.

じゅうだん¹ 銃弾 a bullet.

じゅうだん² 縦断 ¶縦断する〈切断する〉cut [divide] vertically;〈場所を〉run through; travel down through《the Americas》/ travel the length of《Africa》/ 縦断面 a longitudinal [vertical] section.

じゅうたんさんソーダ 重炭酸ソーダ ⇒じゅうそう¹.

しゅうち¹ 周知 ¶周知の widely [《文》universally] known; well-known; known to everybody / 周知の事実 (a matter of) common knowledge; a well-known fact / …は周知の事実である It is common knowledge that… / 周知のように《文》as is generally [commonly] known; as everybody knows.

しゅうち² 羞恥 shyness; bashfulness;〈恥辱〉shame ¶羞恥を感じる feel [be] ashamed [《文》abashed] / 羞恥心 a sense of shame / 羞恥心がない have no sense of shame;《文》be lost [dead] to shame.

しゅうち³ 衆知 ¶衆知を集める ask a large number of people for their advice [opinion];《文》gather the wisdom of many; put (our) heads together (to see what should be done).

しゅうちゃく 執着 ⇒しゅうじゃく.

しゅうちゃくえき 終着駅 a terminus《pl. -ni, -nuses》; a terminal station ⇒しゅうてん.

しゅうちゅう 集中 concentration; centralization ¶過度の集中 overconcentration / 集中する〈集める〉concentrate; centralize; mass (troops);〈集まる〉concentrate; center (on); focus (on); converge (on, into) / 注意を集中する concentrate [focus] one's attention (on);《文》bring one's mind [attention] to bear on sth / 集中安打《野球》an avalanche [a rally] of hits / 集中豪雨 a localized torrential downpour / 集中講義 a closely-packed series of lectures; an intensive course (in linguistics) / 集中排除 decentralization / 集中砲火[射撃] converging [concentrated] fire / 集中力 (powers) of concentration; ability to concentrate. 文例↓

しゅうちょう 酋長 a (tribal) chief; a headman; a chieftain.

じゅうちん 重鎮《文》a person of influence [authority]; a prominent [leading] figure; an authority (学界の) ¶わが国英学界の重鎮 a leading scholar of [an authority on] English in this country.

しゅうてい 舟艇 a boat; a craft《単複同形》¶上陸用舟艇 a landing craft.

しゅうてん 終点 〈駅〉the terminus《pl. -ni, -nuses》; the rail terminal; the last stop; the railhead; the end of the line.

じゅうてん¹ 充填 filling up; plugging (虫歯などの) ¶充填する fill up; stop (up); plug.

じゅうてん² 重点 an important point ¶…に重点を置く put [《文》lay] emphasis [stress] on sth; emphasize;《文》attach importance to sth; give priority to sth;《文》accentuate / 重点主義 the principle of establishing clear priorities; a policy of concentrating (only) on (the) essentials / 重点政策 a policy with overriding priority / 重点的に (apply policies) selectively.

じゅうでん 充電 ¶充電する charge (a battery); give a charge of electricity《to a (storage) battery》/ 電池の充電 battery charging / 充電器 a battery charger / 充電式シェーバー a rechargeable shaver. 文例↓

しゅうでんしゃ 終電車 ⇒しゅうでん.

しゅうと 舅 a father-in-law《pl. fathers-》;〈しゅうとめ〉a mother-in-law《pl. mothers-》.

シュート ¶シュートする《バスケットボール》shoot;《野球》〈球が主語〉shoot《inside》/ シュ

---

uation is still very bad in Japan.
しゅうだん 日本人は集団意識が強い。The Japanese are group-oriented[-minded]. / 昨夜彼の会社に集団強盗が入った。Last night a gang of burglars broke into the offices of his firm. / 烏は様々な理由で集団生活をする。Birds form colonies for a variety of reasons.

しゅうちゅう 彼らの知能指数は120から150の間に集中している。Their I.Q.'s show a concentration between 120 and 150. / 彼は集中力がないから、何をやっても長続きしない。He has very little power of concentration, so he can't stick to anything.

じゅうでん この電気自動車は1回のバッテリー充電で100キロ走る。This electric automobile will go 100 kilometers on one battery charge.

しゅうとう 彼は事を図るにきわめて周到綿密であった。In working out his plans he was as cautious and circumspect as could be.

しゅうとく² 英語をそのような短

ートをきめる〖バスケットボール〗sink a shot; make a basket; 〖サッカー〗shoot a goal / シュートボール〖野球〗a shooter; a shoot ball; a screwball.

しゅうとう 周到 ¶周到な《文》scrupulous;《文》meticulous; careful;《文》circumspect; thorough(going) / 周到な計画 a carefully worked-out plan; a well-laid plan / 周到な準備をする make thoroughgoing [careful] preparations 《for》/ 周到に《文》meticulously; thoroughly;《文》scrupulously; carefully;《文》circumspectly. 文例⇩

しゅうどう 修道 ¶修道院 a religious house; an abbey; a monastery; a friary (托鉢修道士の); a convent (尼の) / 修道院長〈男〉an abbot; a prior;〈女〉an abbess; a prioress / 修道(院)生活 (lead) a monastic life; monasticism / 修道会[団] a monastic [religious] order / 修道士[僧] a monk; a friar (托鉢する) / 修道尼 a nun.

じゅうとう 充当 ¶充当する allot [assign]《to》; apply《to》;《文》appropriate (a sum of money for a purpose).

じゅうどう 柔道 ¶柔道をやる do [practice] judo; have a judo match (試合を) / 柔道家 a judo man [expert]; a judoka / 柔道着 a suit for judo practice / 柔道場 a judo hall.

しゅうとく¹ 拾得 ¶拾得する pick up; find / 拾得者 a finder / 拾得物 a find; something found /《文》a found article.

しゅうとく² 習[修]得 ¶習得する learn;《文》acquire (a skill); master (完全に). 文例⇩

しゅうとめ 姑 a mother-in-law (pl. mothers-).

じゅうなん 柔軟 ¶柔軟な soft;《文》pliant; pliable; flexible; supple; elastic;《文》limber / 柔軟性 softness; pliability; flexibility / 柔軟性のある (比喩的に) flexible; adaptable / 柔軟体操 setting-up exercises; calisthenics. 文例⇩

じゅうに 十二 twelve ¶第 12 番の twelfth / 12 時 twelve o'clock;〈正午〉noon /〈夜の〉midnight / 十二分に more than enough; to one's heart's content. 文例⇩

じゅうにおん 十二音 〖音楽〗 ¶十二音twelve-tone《music》; dodecaphonic《composers》/ 十二音音列 a twelve-tone row / 十二音方式 dodecaphonism.

じゅうにがつ 十二月 December (略: Dec.).

じゅうにきゅう 十二宮 〖天〗the twelve zodiacal signs; the 12 figures [signs] of the zodiac.

じゅうにし 十二支 〖暦法〗the twelve horary signs.

じゅうにしちょう 十二指腸 〖解〗the duodenum (pl. -s, -na) ¶十二指腸炎 duodenitis; inflammation of the duodenum / 十二指腸潰瘍(ょぅ) a duodenal ulcer / 十二指腸虫 a hookworm / 十二指腸虫症 ancylostomiasis; hookworm disease.

じゅうにしんほう 十二進法 the duodecimal system (of notation).

しゅうにゅう 収入 (an) income; earnings;〈歳入〉revenue(s);〈売り上げ〉proceeds; takings;〈入金〉receipts ¶収入がある earn [draw,《文》enjoy] an income《of》/ 収入を得る draw [《文》derive] one's income 《from》/ 文筆で相当の収入をあげる make a comfortable [steady,《文》handsome,《文》substantial] income from writing [《文》by one's pen] / 収入以上[以内で]生活をする live beyond [within] one's means [income] / 収入印紙 a revenue stamp / 収入役 a treasurer.

しゅうにん 就任 《文》assumption of office;《文》inauguration ¶就任する take [《文》assume] office (as); take up one's post (with a corporation); be installed (as); be sworn in (宣誓して) / 大統領に就任する be inaugurated as President / 就任の宣誓をする take the [one's] oath of office / 就任を受諾する accept an appointment / 就任を断わる refuse [《文》decline, turn down] an offer of a position / 就任演説 an inaugural (address) / 就任式 an inaugural ceremony; an inauguration / 大統領就任式の日 (米) Inauguration Day.

じゅうにん¹ 十人 ten people [《文》persons, men] ¶十人並みの ordinary; average; common; mediocre / 十人並み以上[以下]の above [below] the average [《文》ordinary]; above [below] mediocrity. 文例⇩

じゅうにん² 住人 an inhabitant; a resident.

じゅうにん³ 重任 〈責任〉a heavy responsibility;〈任務〉an important duty [《文》mission];〈地位〉a responsible post [position];〈再任〉reappointment ¶重任する be reappointed / 重任を引き受ける《文》take upon oneself an important task; shoulder a heavy responsibility / 重任を帯びている《文》be entrusted with an important mission.

しゅうねん¹ 周年 (all) the year round ¶周年の year-round (observations).

しゅうねん² 執念 〈執着〉《文》tenacity of purpose; a deep attachment (to);〈復讐心〉(a) spite;《文》vindictiveness;《文》vengefulness ¶...したいというのが執念である it is one's fixed idea to do / 執念深い〈しつこい〉(too) persistent;《文》tenacious;〈恨みを忘れない〉vindictive;《文》vengeful; spiteful / 執念深く persistently;《文》tenaciously;《文》with tenacity; vindictively.

-しゅうねん ...周年 an anniversary ¶5 周年(祭) the fifth anniversary 《of》.

じゅうねん 十年 ten years; a decade ¶1980

日月に習得することは不可能である。It is impossible to learn English in such a short time.

しゅうなん 彼は柔軟をしている。He is lithe in build. / 彼は法の解釈に柔軟性がない。He lacks flexibility [is too rigid] in his interpretation of the law.

じゅうに 昼[夜中]の 12 時にベルが鳴ることになっている。A bell will ring at twelve noon [midnight]. / 一同は十二分に満足して散会した。The party dispersed, fully [more than] satisfied. / ご馳走は十二分に頂戴しました。We have had quite enough, thank you.

しゅうにゅう あの人は著作で年に 700 万円の収入がある。His writing brings him ¥7,000,000 a year.

じゅうにん¹ 湖には何十人もの人が出てスケートをしていた。The skaters were out in dozens on the lake. / 十人十色。There are as many opinions as there are people. | So many men, so many

年代の10年間《for》the decade of the 1980s / 10年ごとの decennial / 10年ごとに every ten years; once a decade / 十年一日のごとく without a break for ten (long) years; tirelessly, year in year out; 《be》in a rut. [文例⇩]

しゅうのう 収納 〈金銭の〉《文》receipt 《of funds》 ¶収納する receive / 収納係り a receiver; 〈銀行の〉a receiving teller / 収納伝票 a receipt (voucher).

じゅうのう 十能 a fire shovel.

じゅうのうしゅぎ 重農主義 〘経済・史〙physiocracy ¶重農主義者 a physiocrat.

[し]

しゅうは[1] 周波 〘電〙a cycle ¶周波計 a frequency indicator [meter] / 周波数《radio, high, low》frequency / 周波帯 a frequency band.

しゅうは[2] 宗派 a denomination; a (religious) sect ★ sect は軽蔑的意味を含む故, 信徒が自派のことを sect とは呼ばない. [文例⇩]

しゅうは[3] 秋波 ¶秋波を送る make eyes at; ogle; 《口語》give 《a girl》the eye; 《文》cast amorous glances 《at》.

しゅうはい 集配 collection and delivery ¶集配人〈郵便の〉a postman; 《米》a mailman.

じゅうばこ 重箱 a nest of boxes ¶重箱のすみをほじくる split hairs; make a fuss about (minor) details [《文》about minutiae]; be fussy; 《文》be overnice.

じゅうはち 十八 eighteen ¶第18 the eighteenth / 18金 18-carat gold / 十八番〈おはこ〉*one's* forte; *one's* specialty; *one's* favorite trick; *one's* hobbyhorse (毎度のお話).

じゅうはん[1] 重版 〈重刷〉a second [another] impression [printing]; a reprint; 〈改訂版〉a second [revised] edition.

じゅうはん[2] 従犯 〘法〙participation in a crime ¶従犯者 an accessory 《to a crime》; an accomplice / 事前[事後]従犯 an accessory before [after] the fact.

しゅうばん(せん) 終盤(戦) 〈囲碁・将棋の〉an end game; 〈選挙などの〉the last phase [stage(s)] 《of an election campaign》.

しゅうび 愁眉 ¶愁眉を開く feel relieved; breathe freely [again]. [文例⇩]

じゅうひ 獣皮 a hide; a [an animal] skin; a fur.

じゅうびょう 重病 a serious illness [disease] ¶重病である[になる] be [get, fall, be taken] seriously ill / 重病患者 a serious case.

しゅうふく 修復 restoration 《of an ancient building》 ¶修復する (repair and) restore *sth* to *its* former condition [state, shape]; put *sth* back [restore *sth*] to the condition *it* was in.

じゅうふく 重複 ¶重複する overlap; be repeated ⇨ ちょうふく.

しゅうぶん[1] 秋分 the autumnal equinox ¶秋分の日 Autumnal Equinox Day.

しゅうぶん[2] 醜聞 (a) scandal; 《文》ill fame ¶醜聞が立たないようにする avoid scandal / 醜聞を流す create [give rise to] a scandal.

じゅうぶん 重文 〘文法〙a compound sentence.

じゅうぶん(に) 充[十]分(に) fully; thoroughly; 《文》sufficiently; well; enough; 〈豊富に〉《文》amply; 《文》plentifully; 〈存分〉satisfactorily; to *one's* heart's content ¶充分な plenty 《of》; 《文》sufficient; full; thorough; satisfactory; enough / 見る価値が充分ある be well worth seeing / 充分に食べる eat *one's* fill / 十分条件 〘論〙a sufficient condition ★「充分」というと反射的に enough とする傾向が強いが, enough は「…するに足りるほど」であって「ありあまるほど充分」を意味しない. [文例⇩]

しゅうへん 周辺 〈周囲〉the circumference; the periphery; 〈都会の〉the outskirts; 《文》the environs ¶東京及びその周辺に in and around Tokyo; in Tokyo and its outskirts [suburbs, environs] / 周辺の surrounding 《areas》; peripheral 《systems》; outlying 《islands》/ 台風の周辺部の風 the fringe winds of a typhoon.

しゅうほう 週報 〈新聞〉a weekly (paper); 〈公報〉a weekly (bulletin); 〈報告〉a weekly report.

しゅうぼう 衆望 popularity; 《文》public confidence [expectation] ¶衆望がある be popular [《文》enjoy popularity] 《among, with》. [文例⇩]

じゅうほう 銃砲 guns; firearms ¶銃砲店 a gunshop; a gun dealer (人).

シューマイ 焼売 a steamed Chinese pork dumpling wrapped in a thin flour-and-water pancake; a *shao-mai*.

しゅうまく 終幕 〈最後の1幕〉the final act 《of a play》; 〈終末〉an end; 《文》a close; a curtain fall (芝居の); a denouement (大団円) ¶終幕となる end; come to a close [an end].

しゅうまつ[1] 週末 a weekend ¶週末を箱根で過ごす spend the weekend at Hakone; stay at Hakone over the weekend / 週末旅行 a weekend trip.

しゅうまつ[2] 終末 ⇨ おわり, しゅうきょく[2] ¶終末論[観] 〘神学〙eschatology.

じゅうまん[1] 十万 a hundred thousand ¶十万億土 Paradise.

じゅうまん[2] 充満 ¶充満する be full 《of》; be filled 《with》; 《文》be replete 《with》. [文例⇩]

じゅうみん 住民 inhabitants; residents; 〈人

---

minds. 〘諺〙

じゅうねん 彼は十年一日のごとく職務に精励した. For many years he attended to his (routine) duties with unswerving fidelity. / 私は彼に初めて会ったときから十年の知己のように感じた. The first time I met him, I felt as if we were old friends. / 十年一昔. Ten years make an epoch [can bring a lot of changes].

しゅうは[2] お宅の宗派は何ですか. What denomination are you? | What is your religious affiliation?

しゅうび 病人が峠を越したので一同愁眉を開いた. We all felt greatly relieved to see that his illness had turned the corner.

じゅうぶん(に) 充分歓を尽くした. We enjoyed ourselves to the full. / 電車には充分間に合う. We are in plenty of time for the train. / もう充分頂戴しました. I have had quite enough. / ここから5キロは充分ある. It is a good five kilometers from here. / その仕上げは充分であるとは言えない. The finish leaves something to be desired.

しゅうぼう 彼は衆望を担って立候補した. He ran for the Diet with popular support.

じゆうみんしゅとう ロ> the population ¶住民運動 a local residents' campaign; concerted action by the residents (of the district) / 住民税 a resident tax / 住民投票 a local referendum; a poll of residents / 住民登録 resident registration / 住民票 a resident's card.

じゆうみんしゅとう 自由民主党 the Liberal Democratic Party (略: LDP); the Liberal Democrats.

しゅうめい¹ 醜名《文》an ill name;《文》infamy; notoriety; (a) scandal ¶醜名を得る get a bad name [reputation];《文》earn [fall into] bad repute; become notorious ((for)); cause [《文》give rise to] a scandal.

しゅうめい² 襲名 succession to *sb's* name ¶襲名する succeed to *sb's* (stage) name; succeed ((*one's* father)) to the name ((of Jusuke)) / 襲名式 *one's* name-taking ceremony.

じゅうめん 渋面 ¶渋面を作る make a wry face; give a scowl; frown;《文》grimace; look angry [《文》displeased] / 渋面を作って with a frown [wry face].

じゅうもう 絨毛《解·植》a villus (*pl*. villi).

しゅうもく 衆目 public attention ¶衆目の見る所…である《文》It is universally admitted that... / 衆目注視の的《文》the cynosure of all eyes [of the world].

しゅうもん 宗門 ⇒ しゅうは².

じゅうもんじ 十文字 a cross ¶十文字に in the shape of a cross / 十文字の cross-shaped;《文》cruciform. 文例⇩

しゅうや 終夜 all [the whole] night; through the night; all through [long] ¶終夜運転 an all-night service / 終夜営業の all-night (cafés)) / 終夜灯 an all-night lamp; ((寝室用)) a nightlight. 文例⇩

しゅうやく 集約 ¶集約する《文》epitomize; put together [in a nutshell]; abridge; condense; summarize / 集約的の intensive / エネルギー集約的 energy-intensive ((industries)) / 集約農業 intensive agriculture [farming].

じゅうやく 自由訳 (make, do) a free translation ¶自由訳する translate *sth* freely.

じゅうやく¹ 重役 a (company) director; 〈全体〉 the board of directors ¶重役会議 a directors' [board] meeting / 重役(会議)室 a boardroom.

じゅうやく² 重訳 (a) secondhand translation. 文例⇩

じゅうゆ 重油 heavy oil; crude [raw] petroleum ¶重油燃料船 an oil burner.

しゅうゆう 周遊 a (circular) tour; an excursion; a pleasure trip ¶周遊する make a tour; make [take] an excursion [a pleasure trip]; take a cruise ((海を)) / 周遊券 an excursion ticket.

しゅうよう¹ 収用《法》expropriation ¶収用する expropriate *sth* ((from *sb*)) ★「人の所有物を収用する」の意で expropriate *sb* の形で使うことも可能 / 土地収用権《法》(the right of) eminent domain / 土地収用法《法》the Compulsory Purchase of Land Act.

しゅうよう² 収容 ¶収容する《文》accommodate;《文》receive; seat; take in; admit; intern ((prisoners)); 〈救い上げる〉 pick up ((shipwrecked sailors)) / 受刑者2,000名を収容している刑務所 a 2,000-inmate prison / 〈養老院などの〉 inmates; residents; 〈敵国人収容所などの〉 ((civilian)) internees; 〈病院の〉 inpatients / 収容所 a home; an asylum; a (concentration) camp ((敵国人や捕虜などの)) / 収容力 〈劇場などの〉 (a) seating capacity ((of 500)); 〈ホテルなどの〉 sleeping accommodation(s) ((for 700 persons)) ⇒ しゅくはく. 文例⇩

しゅうよう³ 修養《文》moral [mental] culture;《文》cultivation of the mind; training ¶修養する《文》cultivate *one's* mind; improve *oneself* / 修養のできた人《文》a well-cultivated mind.

じゅうよう 重用 ¶重用する give *sb* an important position; appoint *sb* to a position of trust; promote *sb* to a responsible position / 重用される be taken into ((*one's* superior's)) confidence.

じゅうよう(せい) 重要(性) importance ¶重要な important;《文》of importance [consequence]; essential; 〈主要な〉 principal / 重要でない《文》of no importance; unimportant / …を重要視する regard [《文》look upon] *sth* as important;《文》attach importance to; set great store by;《文》think much of; take *sth* seriously / 重要性を帯びる take on [《文》acquire,《文》assume] importance / 重要産業 key industries / 重要事項 an important matter ; 《文》matters of weight / 重要証拠 material evidence / 重要書類 important documents [papers] / 重要人物 an important person; a strategic person ((問題の解決などに関係のある)); a key figure [man] / 重要物産 staple [key] products /重要文化財 important cultural properties [assets]. 文例⇩

じゅうよく 獣欲《文》animal appetites [desire(s), passion(s)]; lust.

しゅうらい 襲来 an invasion; an incursion; a raid; an attack ¶襲来する invade; attack;

じゅうまん² 有毒ガスが坑内に充満していた。The pit was filled with poisonous gas.

じゅうもんじ 椅子は十文字に切れていた。A cross-shaped slash had been cut [made] in the seat of the chair.

しゅうや 大みそかの晩には電車は終夜運転する。On New Year's Eve the trains run all night. / 終夜営業.《掲示》Open all night.

じゅうやく² 原文はスエーデン語で、これは英訳からの重訳だ。This is a retranslation of the English translation of the Swedish original.

しゅうよう² このホテルには約1,500人の客を収容できる。This hotel can accommodate [has accommodation(s) for] about 1,500 guests. / 講堂は千人は収容できる。The hall seats 1,000. | The auditorium has a seating capacity of 1,000.

じゅうよう(せい) それは我々にとって非常に重要な問題だ。That is a matter of great importance to us. / この問題を解決することは、現在、何にもまして重要である。It is of overriding importance today that we settle this question. / 我々の計画に必要な物を重要なものから順に並べるとこうな

じゅうらい 襲来 raid; make an incursion 《into》; descend [swoop down] on; 〈暴風が〉 strike; hit; 《文》 visit. 文例⇨

じゅうらい 従来 ¶従来の usual; past; 《文》former; old / 従来(は) 《文》 hitherto; up to now [this time]; so far / 従来どおり as usual; as in the past; as before [ever]. 文例⇨

しゅうらく 集落 〈人間の〉 a community; a settlement; a town; a village; 〈生物の〉 a colony.

じゅうらん 縦覧 (general) inspection; 〈読むこと〉 reading ¶縦覧する inspect; read; go over; visit / 縦覧に供する make (the list of electors) available for public inspection / 縦覧者 a visitor; a reader. 文例⇨

しゅうり 修理 repair(s); mending; a refit (特に船の); service ⇨ しゅうぜん ¶修理する repair; make repairs on (a house); mend; 《米口語》 fix; recondition (a car); refit (a ship); service (a motorcar) / 修理してもらう have [get] 《one's watch》 repaired [mended] 《by》 / 修理がきかない be beyond [past] repair / 修理が行き届いている[いない] be in good [bad] repair / 修理の必要がある be in need of repair; need repairs [repairing] / 修理に出す send sth to 《a shop》 for repair [to be mended] / 修理中である be under repair / 大修理をする make [do] thorough [large] repairs 《on》 / 修理工 a repairman / 修理工場 a repair shop. 文例⇨

しゅうりょう[1] 修了 《文》 completion (of a course) ¶修了する complete; finish / 3学年を修了する finish the third-year course / 修了証書 a certificate (of completion of a course).

しゅうりょう[2] 終了 an end; 《文》 a close; (a) conclusion; 《文》 (a) termination; 〈完了〉 《文》 completion; 〈期間の〉 《文》 expiration; 《文》 expiry ¶終了する end; be over; come to an end [a close]; 《文》 be concluded; 《文》 be terminated; 〈期限が〉 expire; 〈完了する〉 《文》 be brought to completion; be completed; be finished.

じゅうりょう 重量 weight ¶総[正味]重量 gross [net] weight / 重量制限 weight [load] limits / 重量超過[不足] overweight [short weight] / 重量トン a deadweight ton / 重量トン数 deadweight tonnage [capacity] / 重量分析 《化》 gravimetric analysis / 重量感がある be massive; look solid. 文例⇨

じゅうりょうあげ 重量挙げ 〈スポーツ〉 weight-lifting ¶重量挙げの3種目 the three divisions of weightlifting; press, snatch and jerk / 重量挙げの選手 a weightlifter / 重量挙げをやって体を強くする improve one's physique by weight training.

じゅうりょうぜい 従量税 a specific duty.

じゅうりょく 重力 (the pull [weight] of) gravity; gravitation ¶〈宇宙ステーション内の〉人工重力 artificial gravity. 文例⇨

じゅうりん 蹂躙 trampling down; 《文》 infringement; 《文》 violation ¶じゅうりんする trample on sth; trample sth underfoot; 〈荒す〉 lay (a village) waste; devastate; 〈犯す〉 《文》 infringe (on); 《文》 violate.

じゅうるい 獣類 beasts; the animals.

シュールレアリスム 《英》 surrealism ¶シュールレアリスムの surrealistic.

しゅうれい 秀麗 ¶秀麗な beautiful; 《文》 graceful.

しゅうれつ 収列 a column; a file.

しゅうれっしゃ 収列車 (miss, catch) the last train.

しゅうれん[1] 収斂 〈物・数〉 convergence ¶しゅうれんする converge / しゅうれん剤 an astringent / しゅうれん性 astringency / しゅうれん性の astringent / しゅうれんレンズ a converging [positive] lens.

しゅうれん[2] 収練 practice; training; exercise ⇨ くんれん, れんしゅう.

しゅうろう 就労 ¶就労する go to [start] work / 就労している be at work / 就労時間[日数] working hours [days].

じゅうろうどう 重労働 heavy [hard] labor ¶重労働3年の刑を言い渡される be sentenced to three years at hard labor [《英》 three years' hard labour].

しゅうろく 収[集]録 ¶収録する 〈集める〉 gather; collect / 〈記載する〉 《文》 contain; put (together) (in a book); mention; 〈記録する〉 record; put on tape ⇨ ろくおん, ろくが; 〈編集する〉 compile; edit.

じゅうろく 十六 sixteen ¶第16 the sixteenth / 16ミリ映画 a 16 mm (movie) film / 16ミリフィルムにとる photograph sth on 16 mm film / 十六むさし 〈遊戯〉 the game of fox and geese.

しゅうわい 収賄 《文》 acceptance of a bribe; corruption; 《米》 graft ¶収賄する take [accept] a bribe; 《口語》 take graft; 《米》 be on the take (常習) / 収賄事件 a bribery case; 《米》 a graft scandal / 収賄者 《文》 a recipient of a bribe; a bribe-taker.

しゅえい 守衛 〈見回り役〉 (a security) guard; 〈門衛〉 a doorkeeper; a gatekeeper; a porter; 《英》 a commissionaire (ホテルなどの); 〈議院の〉 a sergeant (at arms).

じゅえき 樹液 sap ¶樹液をとる tap (a tree).

じゅえきしゃ 受益者 《文》 a beneficiary; a person who is to benefit (by the improvement of

---

る. Here is a list of things necessary [needed] for our purpose, put in order of importance.

しゅうらい その地方は恐ろしい台風の襲来を受けた. The district was visited [hit] by a frightful typhoon. / 暴風襲来の恐れがある. There are signs of an approaching storm.

じゅうらい これは従来の型に比べて一段と進歩したものだ. This is a remarkable improvement on the current model.

じゅうらん 縦覧随意. 【揭示】 Visitors welcomed. / 縦覧謝絶. 【揭示】 No visitors.

しゅうり テープレコーダーを修理に出さなくてはならない. I'll have to take my tape-recorder to be repaired.

じゅうりょう 重量が3トンある. It weighs three tons. / 液体中において, 物体の重量はそれと等しい量の液体の重量だけ少なくなる. The weight of a body immersed in a fluid diminishes by an amount equal to the weight of

しゅえん¹ 主演 ¶主演する play the leading part [role] (in); star (in a play); head the cast 《of a film》/ チャップリン主演の映画 a picture starring Charlie Chaplin / 主演者 a star;〈男〉a leading actor [man];〈女〉a leading actress [lady].
しゅえん² 酒宴 a banquet; a feast; a drinking bout ¶酒宴を張る hold a banquet; give a feast / 夜通し酒宴を張る feast [drink] the night away.
しゅかい 首魁 the ringleader.
じゅかい¹ 受戒《仏教》receiving the commandments (of Buddhism); becoming a disciple of the Buddha; Buddhist confirmation.
じゅかい² 授戒《仏教》giving the commandments (of Buddhism); a Buddhist initiation ceremony ordaining sb priest [to the priesthood].
じゅかい³ 樹海《文》a sea of trees [leaves, foliage].
しゅかく¹ 主客 〈主人と客〉host and guest;〈主なるものと従なるもの〉《文》principal and subsidiary [auxiliary]. 文例8
しゅかく² 主格《文法》the nominative [subjective] case.
じゅがく 儒学 Confucianism ¶儒学者 a Confucian; a Confucian scholar.
しゅかん 主幹〈編集の〉the chief editor; the editor in chief.
しゅかん² 主管《文》superintendence; supervision; management;〈人〉a superintendent; a supervisor; a manager ¶主管する《文》superintend; supervise; manage; be in charge 《of》/ 主管事項 matters [affairs] in one's charge.
しゅかん³ 主観 subjectivity ¶主観的に subjectively / 主観的な subjective / 主観論[主義]《哲》subjectivism.
しゅがん(てん) 主眼(点)〈目的〉《文》the principal [primary, prime] object;《文》the chief aim [end]; the main purpose;〈要点〉the (main) point; the gist.
しゅき¹ 手記 a note; a memorandum《pl. -da, -dums》;〈回想録〉memoirs.
しゅき² 酒気 the smell [odor] of sake [liquor]; an alcoholic smell ¶酒気を帯びている be drunk;《文》be intoxicated; be under the influence of liquor;〈口語〉have had one [a few] too many;〈口語〉have had one over the eight / 酒気帯び運転 driving under the influence of liquor.
しゅぎ 主義 a principle;《文》a doctrine; an 'ism'; a cause;〈方針〉a line; a basis《pl. bases》¶営利主義の病院 a hospital run [operated] for profit / 主義を守る live [act] up to one's principles; be true [《文》faithful] to one's principles; stick [hold fast] to one's principles; stand by one's principles / 主義を曲げる sacrifice [make a compromise with] one's principles / 主義に殉じる die for [《文》be a martyr to] one's cause [principles] / 主義として on principle; as a matter of principle / …を主義とする make it a principle [point] to do; make a point of doing / 現金主義で《do business》on a cash basis. 「gear.
しゅきゃく 主脚〈飛行機の〉the main landing
じゅきゅう 需給 supply and demand ¶需給を調整する《文》adjust supply and demand; keep supply and demand in balance.
じゅきゅうしゃ 受給者 a recipient《of a pension》.
しゅきょう 主教《キリスト教》a bishop; a prelate.
しゅぎょう 修業[行]〈鍛練〉training;〈苦行〉《文》ascetic practices;〈勉学〉study ¶修業[行]する〈鍛練する〉《文》receive one's training [education] (from); train oneself (in); serve one's apprenticeship (under [with]);〈苦行を積む〉《文》practice asceticism;《文》lead an ascetic life;〈勉強する〉study《文》pursue learning《under》/ 修業が足りない be not sufficiently trained (in) / 修行中の僧 a trainee monk. 文例8
じゅきょう 儒教 Confucianism; the teaching of Confucius ¶儒教の経典 the Confucian classics.
じゅぎょう 授業 teaching; (a) class; a session; (school) lessons; school(work); classwork; instruction ¶授業する teach; give lessons [classes] / 授業を受ける take lessons (in); attend school [class] / 授業を休む do not attend [come to, go to] class; miss a lesson / 授業をさぼる play truant;《口語》cut classes [school, a lesson] / 英語の授業 an English class; a class in English / 授業計画 syllabus planning / 授業時間 school hours; hours of teaching [instruction] / 授業(時間)中に during school hours; in [during] class / 授業日数 the number of school days《in a year》/ 授業料 school fees; a school [course] fee; tuition (fees). 文例8
しゅぎょく 珠玉 a jewel; a gem;〈集合的〉jewelry ¶珠玉の文学作品 a literary gem.
じゅく 塾〈私立学校〉a private school;〈児童・生徒用の夜間などの〉a school [extra classes] run outside normal school hours; a crammer; cramming classes;〈予備校〉a crammer; a private prep(aratory) school ¶塾を開いてい

---

the fluid displaced. / この壁が建物の全重量を支えているのです。These thin walls are bearing the full load of the structure.
じゅうりょく 宇宙飛行士はロケット発射の際通常の8倍の重力が身体にかかるのに耐えねばならなかった。At the time of the blast-off of the rocket, the astronaut had to withstand eight times the normal gravitational pull on his body.
しゅかく¹ それは主客転倒だ。That is putting the cart before the horse. / たちまち主客転倒した。Very soon the tables were turned. | The tail immediately began to wag the dog.
しゅぎょう それには多年の修業が必要だ。It requires years of training.
じゅぎょう 授業は何時に始まるのですか。What time does school begin? / 今日は授業がない。We have no school today. / 生徒たちは今授業中です。The students are now in class. / 木村先生は授

しゅくい 祝意 ¶祝意を表わす《文》express [offer] one's congratulations [good wishes]; congratulate 《sb on sth》/…に祝意を表して in honor of sb;《文》in celebration of 《an event》.

しゅくえん¹ 祝宴 a banquet [feast]《given in honor of sb, held in celebration of an event》.

しゅくえん² 宿怨 (harbor) an old [a deep-seated] grudge 《against》;《文》a long-cherished enmity [resentment]《against》¶宿怨を晴らす pay off one's old scores 《with sb》.

しゅくえん³ 宿縁《文》karma;《文》(a) destiny;《文》fate ¶宿縁とあきらめる resign oneself to one's fate [lot].

しゅくが 祝賀 (a) celebration; congratulations;《文》felicitations; one's good wishes ¶祝賀する celebrate《an event》; congratulate 《sb on sth》/祝賀会を催す hold a celebration;〈祝宴を張る〉hold a banquet [feast] to celebrate《an event》.

しゅくがん 宿願 ⇒しゅくぼう².

じゅくご 熟語〈日本語の〉a pair [set, combination] of kanji;〈英語などの〉an idiomatic [a set] phrase; an idiom.

しゅくさいじつ 祝祭日 ⇒しゅくじつ.

しゅくさつ 縮刷 ¶縮刷する print in reduced size / 縮刷版 a reduced-size edition; a pocket edition.

しゅくじ 祝辞《文》a congratulatory address [speech]; (a message of) congratulations ¶祝辞を述べる deliver a congratulatory address 《at a ceremony》;《文》offer [extend] one's congratulations 《to sb》; congratulate 《sb on his success》.

じゅくし 熟柿 a ripe (and soft) persimmon ¶熟柿臭い息をしている one's breath smells of stale sake / 熟柿の落ちるのを待つ〈比喩的に〉bide one's time 《until》; wait until the time is ripe; wait for a good opportunity.

しゅくじつ 祝日 a festival (day); a national [public] holiday.

しゅくしゃ¹ 宿舎 lodgings; a lodging house; quarters;〈軍隊の〉a billet ¶宿舎の設備 (hotel) accommodation(s) ⇒しゅくはく ★ / 参加選手に宿舎を用意する provide accommodation for the participants (in the meet).

しゅくしゃ² 縮写 ¶縮写する make a reduced copy 《of》; copy [draw] on a smaller scale.

しゅくしゃく 縮尺 (a map on) a reduced scale ¶縮尺する scale sth down / 縮尺 5 万分の 1 の地図 a map with [drawn on] a scale of 1 to 50,000 / 縮尺 7 分の 1 の模型 a one-seventh scale model. 文例⇩

しゅくしゅ 宿主【生物】a host ¶…の宿主になる play host to… / 中間宿主 an intermediary host.

しゅくしゅくと 粛々と〈厳かに〉solemnly;《文》with (all) due solemnity;《文》in state;〈静かに〉silently;《文》in hushed silence.

しゅくじょ 淑女 a lady;《文》a gentlewoman ¶淑女らしいladylike;《文》(deportment) becoming a lady. 文例⇩

しゅくしょう 縮小 (a) reduction;《文》(a) curtailment;《文》(a) retrenchment; a cut; a scale-down; (a) contraction (短縮) ¶軍備の縮小 a reduction in armaments; a cutback in military strength / 縮小する〈削減する〉reduce; curtail; retrench; cut [scale] down;〈短縮する〉contract / 人員を縮小する cut [reduce] the personnel (of).

しゅくず 縮図 a reduced drawing; a miniature (copy);《文》a microcosm ¶アメリカの縮図 America in miniature [microcosm] / 人生の縮図《文》an epitome of life; the world in microcosm / 縮図にして表わす draw [represent] sth on a smaller scale / 縮図器 a pantograph.

じゅくすい 熟睡 a sound [deep] sleep ¶熟睡する sleep well [soundly]; sleep like a top [log]; fall into a deep sleep / 熟睡している be fast [sound] asleep. 文例⇩

じゅくする 熟する〈果物などが〉get [《文》become]ripe; ripen; mature;〈言葉が〉be in common use; come to sound natural ¶熟したripe; mature; mellow / 熟し過ぎた overripe / 熟さない unripe; green (fruit) / 機の熟するを待つ wait till the time is ripe (for). 文例⇩

しゅくせい¹ 粛正 ¶綱紀を粛正する enforce discipline 《among government officials》.

しゅくせい² 粛清 a purge; a cleanup;《文》(a) liquidation ¶粛清する purge; clean up;《文》liquidate; carry out [《文》effect, institute] a purge of 《revisionists》.

しゅくぜん 粛然 ¶粛然と〈静かに〉silently; quietly;〈厳かに〉solemnly;《文》in state / 粛然として襟を正す《文》be struck with awe / 粛然として襟を正さしめるような《文》awe-inspiring.

しゅくだい 宿題〈学校の〉homework;《米》an assignment;〈未決問題〉a pending [an open] question ¶宿題を課する set sb an assignment; give sb homework / 宿題をする do (one's) homework / 宿題をみてやる help sb

---

業中です。Mr. Kimura is teaching. / 彼のかくし芸には相当授業料がかかっている。He must have spent a good sum of money to learn that parlor trick.

じゅく 当時私は田中さんが自宅で開いていた英語の塾に通っていた。In those days I attended the English classes held by Mr. Tanaka at his home.

しゅくしゃく 地球を豆粒大に縮尺してみても、やはり宇宙の大きさは天文学的数字になる。Even when we scale the earth down to the size of a pea, the size of the universe is still immeasurably great. / 縮尺 5 万分の 1.〈地図に書いて〉Scale : $^1/_{50,000}$.

しゅくじょ あんな振舞いをするなんて淑女とは言えないね。It is not very ladylike of her to behave like that.

じゅくすい 昨夜はよく眠れましたか。―ええ、気持ちよく熟睡しました。Did you sleep well last night? ―Yes, I slept like a log.

じゅくする 時機運は熟した。The time is ripe (for it). / The opportunity has matured [ripened].

しゅくだい 物理の宿題を済ませた。I have finished my physics homework [《米》assignment]. / この問題は宿題にしておこう。Let's

じゅくたつ 熟達 ⇨ じゅくれん ¶英語に熟達している have a very good command of English; 《文》be proficient in English. 文例⑥

しゅくち 熟知 ¶熟知している be well aware (of); have a thorough [full, detailed] knowledge (of); be familiar (with); 《文》be well acquainted (with); know *sth* fully [very well]; be fully [well, thoroughly] posted 《on, about, concerning》; be at home with 《things Japanese》; be well up in [on]; have *sth* at *one's* fingertips.

しゅくちょく 宿直 night duty [watch] ¶宿直する be on night duty; keep night watch / 宿直員 a person on night duty; a night watchman / 宿直室 a night watchman's room / 宿直手当 a night-duty allowance.

しゅくてき 宿敵 an old enemy [《文》foe]; an enemy [rival] of long standing.

しゅくてん 祝典 a celebration; a festival; a commemoration (記念の) ¶祝典をあげる hold a celebration [festival] / 25 [50, 60]年祝典 the silver [golden, diamond] jubilee.

しゅくでん 祝電 a congratulatory [greetings] telegram; a cable of congratulations ¶祝電を打つ send a congratulatory [greetings] telegram 《to》; send *sb one's* congratulations by wire.

じゅくどく 熟読 ¶熟読する read thoroughly [carefully]; 《文》peruse / 熟読玩味する《文》read 《a poem》with appreciation. 文例⑥

しゅくば 宿場 a post town; a stage.

しゅくはい 祝杯 a toast; 《文》a celebratory drink ¶祝杯をあげる drink a toast 《for, to》; drink [toast] 《to》《*sb's* health [success]》; drink in celebration 《of an event》.

しゅくはく 宿泊 (a) lodging; 《軍隊の》billeting; quartering ¶宿泊する stay 《at, with》; take up 《*one's*》lodgings; stop [put up] 《at》; lodge 《at, in》;《軍隊が》be billeted 《on》; be quartered 《on, with》/ 友人の家に宿泊する stay with a friend; put up at a friend's house / 宿泊所 *one's* lodgings; *one's* quarters [billet]《軍人などの》/ 宿泊設備 accommodation(s) ★《米》では複数形を使うのが普通だが，《英》では単数でしか使わない./ 宿泊人 a lodger ⇨下宿人), とまり² (泊まり客) / 宿泊料 hotel charges [expenses]; lodging charges; a hotel bill.

しゅくふく 祝福 (a) blessing; 《文》(a) benediction ¶祝福する bless; give *sb one's* blessing / 前途を祝福する wish *sb* good luck; wish *sb* well / 祝福された《文》blessed.

しゅくほう 祝砲 ¶21発の祝砲を放つ give [fire] a twenty-one gun salute.

しゅくぼう¹ 宿坊 a hospice; a guesthouse (kept by a temple).

しゅくぼう² 宿望 《文》(realize) a long-cherished [-fostered] ambition [hope, desire];《文》*one's* heart's desire. 文例⑥

しゅくめい 宿命 《文》(a) destiny; fate;《文》*one's* (fated) lot;《文》karma ¶…する宿命にある《文》be fated [destined] to do / 宿命的《文》fatal;《文》predestined / 宿命論[論者] fatalism [a fatalist] / 宿命論的 fatalistic.

じゅくりょ 熟慮 ⇨ じゅっこう ¶熟慮断行する《文》be deliberate in council, (and) prompt [resolute] in action / 充分熟慮された計画 a well-thought-out plan.

じゅくれん 熟練 skill; experience;《文》dexterity;《文》proficiency ¶熟練する get [《文》become] skillful 《at, in》;《文》acquire skill;《文》attain proficiency; master 《an art》/ …に熟練している be practiced [experienced] in 《teaching》; be a good hand at 《the violin》; be (an) expert in [at] 《the abacus》; be at home [well up] in 《legal practice》/ 熟練した skilled; skillful; trained / 熟練していない, 不熟練の unskilled / 熟練を要する仕事 a skilled job [profession] / 熟練工 a skilled worker;〈総称〉skilled [trained] labor / 熟練家《文》a man of experience; an expert 《in, at》; a skilled hand. 文例⑥

しゅくん¹ 主君 *one's* lord; *one's* master.

しゅくん² 殊勲 《文》distinguished service(s); 《文》meritorious deeds ¶殊勲をたてる render distinguished service(s); distinguish *oneself*;《文》fight [play] with distinction / 殊勲賞《相撲》the outstanding performance award / 殊勲打《野球》a crucial [scoring] hit / 最高殊勲選手《野球》the most valuable player (略: MVP).

しゅけい 主計 an accountant;《文》a pay officer; a paymaster ¶主計局《大蔵省の》the Budget Bureau.

しゅげい 手芸 handicrafts; manual arts;〈くしゅう・編物〉fancywork ¶手芸品 a piece [an article] of fancywork.

じゅけいしゃ 受刑者 a convict; a prisoner serving a sentence.

しゅけん 主権 sovereignty ¶主権を侵犯[害]する violate [infringe on] the sovereignty 《of》/ 主権者 a sovereign; a supreme ruler. 文例⑥

じゅけん 受験 ¶受験する take an examination / 早稲田を受験する take the exam for

---

じゅくたつ 1学期やそこらで外国語に熟達できるものではない. One or two terms are altogether too short a time for you to master a foreign language.

じゅくどく この本は熟読に値する. This book is well worth careful reading.

しゅくはく この町では旅行者は比較的安い料金で宿泊できる. Travelers can find accommodation at moderate rates in this town. / あのホテルには600人宿泊[600人分の宿泊設備が ある]という ことだ. I am told that the hotel can provide [has] sleeping accommodations for 600 guests.

しゅくぼう² 彼は多年の宿望がかなって海外留学を命じられた. His long-cherished wish has materialized, and he has been sent to study abroad.

じゅくれん それには非常な熟練を要する. It requires a great deal of skill.

しゅけん 主権在民. Sovereignty resides in [rests with] the people.

しゅげんじゃ entrance to Waseda University; go in for the entrance examination for Waseda University / 受験勉強をする prepare (oneself) for an examination; study for (one's) exams / 受験科目 the subjects of the examination / 受験技術 exam(-taking) techniques / 受験参考書 《口語》 a crambook / 受験資格 qualifications of candidacy for an examination / 受験生 a candidate for an examination; an examinee / 受験写真 an exam photo; an examinee's photograph / 受験生 a student preparing (himself) for an examination / 受験番号 an examinee's (seat) number / 受験票 an admission ticket for an examination / 受験料 an examination fee.

しゅげんじゃ 修験者 a monk who leads an ascetic life in the mountains; a mountain ascetic.

しゅご¹ 主語 《文法》 the subject (word).

しゅご² 守護 protection; (safe)guard; defense ¶守護する protect; guard; keep (a place) safe (from); defend / 守護神 a guardian (tutelary) deity (god, spirit).

しゅこう¹ 首肯 ¶首肯する 〈納得する〉 be convinced (that, 《文》 of); be persuaded (that ...); understand; 〈同意する〉 《文》 assent (to); consent (to); agree (to sth, with sb); give one's approval (to).

しゅこう² 趣向 〈案〉 a plan; an idea; 〈工夫〉 《文》 a device; 〈意匠〉 《文》 a contrivance; a design; 〈筋〉 a scheme; a plot ¶うまい趣向 a good [《文》happy] idea; an ingenious plan / 趣向を変えて for a change; for variety's sake / 趣向を凝らす work out [think out, 《文》devise] an elaborate plan. 文例⇩

しゅごう 酒豪 a hard [heavy] drinker; a man who drinks like a fish.

じゅこう 受講 ¶受講する attend a lecture [class]; 〈実技の講習を〉 take part [participate] in a training session / 受講者 a member (of a class); 《文》 a participant; a trainee.

しゅこうぎょう 手工業 handicraft; handicraft manufacturing [industry] ¶手工業者 a handicraftsman.

ジュゴン 《動》 a dugong; a sea pig.

しゅさい¹ 主宰 ¶主宰する 《文》 preside over (a society); 《文》 superintend; run / 吉田氏の主宰する雑誌 a magazine edited by Mr. Yoshida / 主宰者 the president; the leader; the chairman.

しゅさい² 主催 ¶主催する sponsor / ...の主催で 《文》 under the auspices [sponsorship] (of); sponsored (by) / 主催国[団体] 《招待競技会などの》 the host nation [organization] / 主催者 the sponsor; the promoter.

しゅざい 取材 ¶取材する collect [gather] (news) materials [data] 《on, for》; /新聞記者が〉 cover (a meeting) / 取材記者 a (news) reporter; 《米》 a legman.

しゅざん 珠算 calculation on the abacus.

しゅし¹ 種子 a seed; 〈桃・あんずなどの〉 a stone; 《米》 a pit; 〈りんご・みかんなどくだものの〉 a pip ⇒たね.

しゅし² 趣[主]旨 〈要旨〉 the gist; the point; 《文》 the purport; 《文》 the effect; 〈意味〉 the meaning; 〈目的〉 《文》 an object; an aim; a purpose ⇒しゅい². 文例⇩

しゅじ 主事 a manager; a director; a superintendent ¶主事補 a deputy-manager[-director].

じゅし 樹脂 (a) resin ¶樹脂の resinous / 樹脂状の resinoid / 樹脂加工の resin-treated 《textiles》.

しゅじい 主治医 the physician in charge 《of》; 〈家庭の〉 one's (family) doctor.

しゅじく 主軸 the principal axis.

じゅしゃ 儒者 a Confucian (scholar); Confucianist.

しゅしゃ(せんたく) 取捨(選択) 《文》 selection; sorting out; choice; (an) option ¶取捨選択する sort out; choose; 《文》 select; make one's choice / 取捨に迷う be at a loss which to take [choose] 《from among》.

しゅじゅ 種々 ¶種々(雑多)の various; 《文》 diverse; 《文》 sundry; 《文》 manifold; 《文》 multifarious; all sorts of; all manner of; of every sort and kind; a variety of; a whole assortment of / 種々の理由で for various [many] reasons / 種々様々の意見 all shades of opinion / 種々相 《文》 various (diverse) aspects [phases] 《of》. 文例⇩

じゅじゅ 授受 ¶授受する give and receive; transfer / 政権の授受 transfer of political power. 文例⇩

しゅじゅう 主従 《the relationship of》 master and servant [《文》 man]; 《文》 lord and vassal (武士の).

しゅじゅつ 手術 an [a surgical] operation 《for tonsillitis》; surgery ¶手術をする do [perform, 《文》 conduct] an operation 《on sb for cancer》; operate 《on》 / 難しい手術をする perform delicate surgery (on the eye) / 手術を受ける have 《文》 undergo, go through》 an operation; be operated on 《for appendicitis》; 《口語》 be [go] under the knife / 蓄膿症で鼻を手術してもらう have one's nose operated on for sinusitis; undergo an operation on one's nose for sinusitis / 手術をこわがる be afraid [have a terror] of the surgeon's knife / 手術中に死ぬ die on the operating table / 手術前[後]の preoperative [postoperative] / 手術室[台, 衣] an operating room [table, gown] / (患者として)手術室に入る go into surgery [《英》 (the operating) theatre]. 文例⇩

じゅじゅつ 呪術 magic; 《文》 an occult art

しゅこう² うまい趣向が浮かんだ. A bright idea occurred to me. | I hit upon a happy idea.

しゅし² それでは法の趣旨に反する. That would run counter to the spirit of the law. / 私の趣旨 を徹底させることができなかった. I failed to make myself properly [completely] understood.

しゅじゅ この団体には種々雑多な会員がいる. This society has all sorts and conditions of people as its members.

じゅじゅ 「金銭の授受は行なわれなかった」と彼は明言した. He declared that no money had changed hands.

しゅじゅつ 手術はうまく行った.

しゅしょ

¶呪術・宗教的 magico-religious / 呪術の儀式 magic rituals; medicine rites / 感染[共感, 類感]呪術 contagious [sympathetic, homoeopathic] magic. 文例⇩

しゅしょ 朱書 ¶朱書する write in red (ink).

しゅしょう¹ 主将 the captain ¶主将を勤める captain (a team); 〈ボートの〉 skipper (a college eight).

しゅしょう² 主[首]唱 《文》advocacy;《文》promotion ¶主唱する《文》advocate; promote; suggest / …の主唱で《文》at the instance of…; on the suggestion of… / 主唱者《文》an advocate; a promoter;《文》the high priest (of modern education).

しゅしょう³ 首相 the prime minister; the premier;《英》the PM ¶首相の地位 premiership / 大平首相 Prime Minister Ohira / 第一副首相〈ソ連の〉 a first deputy premier.

しゅしょう⁴ 殊勝 ¶殊勝な《文》commendable;《文》laudable;《文》praiseworthy / 殊勝な心がけ《文》a creditable endeavor;《文》a commendable purpose. 文例⇩

しゅじょう 衆生《仏教》(save) mankind; the world ¶一切衆生《文》all sentient beings;《文》all creatures; all life.

じゅしょう¹ 受賞 ¶受賞する get [《文》receive] a prize [an award]; win [be awarded] a prize / 受賞作品 a prize-[an award-]winning work [novel] / 受賞作家 an award-winning writer / 受賞者 a prize winner.

じゅしょう² 授賞 ¶授賞する award a prize (to sb) / 授賞式 an award ceremony.

じゅじょう 樹上 ¶樹上の[に, で] in a tree.

しゅしょく¹ 主食 the staple [principal] food; a (diet) staple;《文》the chief article of food ¶米を主食とする live on rice.

しゅしょく² 酒色 ¶酒色にふける《文》be addicted to sensual pleasures;《文》abandon *oneself* to wine and women;《文》be debauched.

しゅしん 主審《スポーツ》the chief judge [umpire].

しゅじん 主人〈家長〉the master (of a house); the head (of the family [house]); the man of the house [family];〈客に対して〉the host; the hostess (女) /〈旅館・下宿の〉the landlord; the landlady (女) /〈店の〉the proprietor; a shopkeeper; the proprietress (女);〈雇い主〉the employer; the master;〈夫〉*one's* husband ¶主人公〈小説などの〉a hero (*pl.* -es); a heroine (女); the leading character;《文》the protagonist / 主人顔をする act [look] as if *one* owned the place;《文》assume [put on] a proprietary air / 主人役を勤める act as host [hostess]; play (the) host [hostess].

じゅしん 受信 ¶受信する receive a message [letter] / 受信回路 a receiving circuit / 受信機・受信装置 a receiver; a receiving set; receiv-

567

ing apparatus [equipment] / 受信局 a receiving station / 受信者 the addressee;《文》the recipient. 文例⇩

しゅす 繻子 satin.

じゅず 数珠 a (Buddhist) rosary; praying [prayer] beads ¶数珠をつまぐる tell [count] the beads (of a rosary) / 数珠つなぎにする link [rope] (prisoners) together; tie (them) in a row.

しゅすい 取水 ¶都の水道用に利根川から取水する take [《文》utilize] the waters of the Tone River for Tokyo's water supply.

しゅせい 守勢 a defensive attitude [position]; the defensive ¶守勢の defensive; passive / 守勢を脱する get off the defensive / 守勢をとる[に立つ] go on《文》assume, take] the defensive; be [stand, act] on the defensive / 守勢に立たせる put (the union) on the defensive.

しゅぜい 酒税 a liquor tax.

じゅせい 受[授]精《生物》fertilization; fecundation; insemination ¶授精する fertilize; fecundate; inseminate / 受精する be fertilized; be fecundated; be inseminated / 体内[外]受精 internal [external] fertilization / 受精卵 a fertilized egg.

しゅぜいきょく 主税局〈大蔵省の〉the Tax Bureau.

しゅせいぶん 主成分 the principal ingredient(s); the main component(s);《文》the chief element(s).

しゅせき¹ 首[主]席〈席〉the top seat;〈人〉the head; the chair;〈中国の〉the Chairman ¶級の首席を占めている be (at the) top of the class; be first in the class / 首席で卒業する graduate first on the list [at the top of the list] / N響のフルートの首席奏者 the first flutist of the NHK Symphony Orchestra / 首席代表 the chief delegate; the head of the delegation.

しゅせき² 酒席 a banquet; a feast; a drinking party.

しゅせきさん 酒石酸 tartaric acid.

しゅせつ 主節《文法》a main clause.

しゅせんど 守銭奴 a miser; a niggard.

しゅせんとうしゅ 主戦投手《野球》an ace pitcher [hurler].

しゅせんろん 主戦論 support for [《文》advocacy of] war ¶主戦論者《文》a war advocate; the pro-war party.

じゅそ 呪詛 ⇒ のろい¹.

しゅぞう 酒造 酒造《業》sake brewing (醸造);《whisky》distilling (蒸留) / 酒造家 a (sake) brewer; a《whisky》distiller / 酒造場 a brewery; a distillery.

じゅぞう 受像 ¶受像する receive (television) pictures / テレビ受像機 a television [TV] set / 受像面 a television screen; a telescreen.

しゅぞく 種族〈人種〉a race; a tribe;〈動物の〉

しゅぞく

The operation was a success. / 彼の手術は約30分かかった。He was under the knife for about half an hour.

じゅじゅつ このつぼのなぞのような文様には何か呪術的な意味があると思っていいだろう。The enigmatic patterns on the pot may well have some magical significance.

しゅしょう² 彼の主唱で寄付が募集されたのだ。It was at his sug-

gestion that the contributions were collected.

しゅしょう⁴ 彼は殊勝らしく勉強している。He is working hard like a good boy.

じゅしん その放送は普通の受信機

しゅたい　a family ; a species 《単複同形》　¶種族をふやす spread [produce more of] 《their》 kind ／ 種族間の intertribal ; interracial ／ 民族間の〉 種族保存の本能 the instinct of preservation of the species.

しゅたい　主体　〈哲〉the subject ; 〈中核〉the nucleus (pl. -cleuses, -clei)　¶大学生を主体とする団体 a group [an organization] mainly composed of college students ／ 主体性 《文》 autonomy ; independence ; identity ／ 主体性を確立する establish one's independence ／ 主体的 independent.

しゅだい　主題　〈主要題目〉the subject (matter) ; 〈音楽などの〉a theme　¶主題歌 a theme song (of a motion picture) ／ 〈図書館の〉主題目録 a subject catalog.

じゅたい　受胎　conception ; 《文》 impregnation　¶受胎する 《文》 conceive (a child) ; become pregnant ／ (聖母マリアの)受胎告知 the Annunciation ／ 受胎調節 birth control.

じゅたく　受託　¶受託する 《文》 be given sth in trust ; 《文》 be entrusted with sth ／ 受託収賄 the crime of accepting a bribe in return [consideration] for services promised.

じゅだく　受諾　《文》 acceptance　¶受諾する accept (an offer) ; agree to (the conditions) ; 《文》 assent [give one's assent] to (the terms offered).

しゅだん　手段　a means 《単複同形》 ; a way ; a measure ; a step ; 〈工夫〉 a device ; 〈便法〉 《文》 an expedient ; 《文》 a shift　¶手段が尽きる be at one's wits' end ; be at the end of one's resources ／ 手段をとる take a step ; take (appropriate) measures ／ 過激[極端]な手段をとる take [《文》 resort to] drastic [extreme] measures ／ 手段を誤る take a wrong step ／ あらゆる手段を尽くす try every means available ; take all possible steps ; 《文》 exhaust one's resources ; leave no stone unturned ／ 手段を選ばず by fair means or foul ; by hook or by crook ／ 一時の間に合わせの〉a makeshift ; 《文》 an expedient ／ 最後の手段として as a [in the] last resort. 文例目

しゅちしゅぎ　主知主義　《文芸・哲》intellectu-　「alism.
しゅちゅう　手中　¶…の手中にある to be in sb's hands [possession] ; be at the mercy [《文》 disposal] of… ／ 手中に納める get one's hands on sth ; 《文》 secure ; capture ; take [gain] possession of ／ …の手中に帰する 〈物が主語〉 fall [come] into sb's hands ; 《文》 pass into sb's possession (occupation).

じゅちゅう　受注　¶受注する receive an order.
しゅちょ　主著　one's main [chief] (literary) work.

しゅちょう¹　主張　《文》(an) assertion ; a claim ; 〈唱道〉advocacy ; 〈論点〉one's argument ; one's point ; 《文》one's contention ; 〈持論〉one's opinion　¶主張する 《文》assert ; maintain ; 《文》hold ; claim ; allege ; 《文》contend ; argue ; 《文》plead ; 《文》make a plea [case] ; make the point (that…) ; make a point of doing ; 〈言い張る〉insist (on, that) ; 〈唱道する〉advocate ; 〈強調する〉emphasize ; lay stress (on) ／ 権利を主張する assert one's rights ／ 無罪を主張する plead innocence [not guilty] ／ 主張を通す win [carry] one's point ／ 主張を曲げない stand firm (for) ; stick to one's position [guns]. 文例目

しゅちょう²　首長　a head ; a chief ; 〈アラブの〉a sheik(h)　¶首長国 a sheik(h)dom ／ 首長選挙 an election for the heads of local governments.

じゅつ　術　〈技術〉an art ; a technique ; 〈手段〉a way ; a means 《単複同形》 ; 〈たくらみ〉《文》an artifice ; a trick ; 〈魔術〉magic ; witchcraft　¶術を使う practice magic.

しゅつえん　出演　one's appearance (on the stage) ; a [one's] performance　¶出演する appear [come] on the stage ; play ; perform ; sing (歌う) ; take part in (a concert) ／ 初めて出演する one's debut [first appearance] (on the stage, on television) ／ 出演者 a performer ; 〈集合的〉the cast (of a play) ／ 出演料 a performing [an actor's, a singer's] fee.

しゅっか¹　出火　an outbreak of fire ; a fire　¶出火する a fire breaks out [《文》occurs, starts] (in a factory) ／ 出火の原因 the cause of the fire.

しゅっか²　出荷　forwarding ; shipment ; shipping　¶出荷する forward ; ship ; 《商》consign　★〈米〉では一般語として船・貨車・トラックなど輸送手段を問わず ship という.〈英〉ではこの意味の ship は商業用語 ／ 出荷先〈目的地〉the destination ; 〈荷受人〉the consignee ／ 出荷通知 a shipping [shipment] advice (note) ; a consignment note.

じゅっかい　述懐　recollection(s) ; reminiscence(s)　¶述懐する 《文》relate one's thoughts [reminiscences] ; 《文》speak reminiscently [reflectively] ; reminisce (about) ; recall (the past).

しゅっかん　出棺　文例目
しゅつがん　出願　(an) application　¶出願する apply [make an application] (to the government for an official sanction) ; file an application (with the Patent Office for a patent) ／ 出願者 an applicant.

しゅっきん¹　出金　〈支出〉payment ; 〈出資〉(an) investment ; 〈寄付〉(a) contribution　¶出金する pay ; invest [sink] money (in) ; contribute (to).

で受信できる. The radio transmission can be received on an ordinary set.
しゅほう そうするよりほかに手段がない. I can't think of any other way but that. ／ I can find no alternative to it. ／ 彼は目的を達するためには手段を選ばない男だ. He sticks at nothing [has no scruples about what he does] to achieve his aims. ／ 目的のためには手段を選ばずというのはよくない. The end does not justify the means.

しゅちょう¹　もし彼らの前に出て自分の立場を立派に主張することができれば, 嫌疑も晴れることだろう. If you can make (out) a really good case for yourself in front of them, you will be able to dispel their suspicions.

しゅっかん　出棺は午後1時です. The hearse will leave the house at 1 p.m.
しゅつがん²　専売特許出願中. 〈表示〉Patent pending [applied for].
しゅっきん³　僕は毎日電車で出勤

しゅっきん 出勤 attendance (at work) ¶出勤する go [come] to work [the office] / 出勤している be at work ; be present / 出勤時間 the time *one* starts ; the start [beginning] of office [working] hours / 出勤簿 an attendance book. 文例⇩

しゅっけ 出家 a priest ; a monk ; a bonze ¶出家する become a priest ; 《文》 renounce the world ; 《文》 retire [go] into religion.

しゅつげき 出撃 a sortie ; a sally ¶出撃する 《文》 sally forth ; make a sortie [sally].

しゅっけつ[1] 出欠 attendance (and [or] absence) ⇒ しゅっせき ¶出欠の記録 a record of 〈student〉 attendance / 出欠を通知する give notice whether *one* will attend 〈the meeting〉 or not / 出欠をとる call the roll.

しゅっけつ[2] 出血 bleeding ; loss of blood ; 〔医〕 hemorrhage ; 〈戦争などの犠牲〉 casualties ¶出血する bleed ; lose blood ; 〔医〕 hemorrhage / ひどく出血する bleed heavily / 出血を止める stop [stanch] the bleeding [flow of blood] / 出血多量のため死ぬ die from loss of blood 〔excessive bleeding〕 / 出血販売 a sacrifice [below-cost] sale / 出血販売をする sell 〈goods〉 below cost [at a sacrifice, 《口語》 at a giveaway price]. 文例⇩

しゅつげん 出現 appearance ; 《文》 emergence ; arrival ; 《文》 advent ¶出現する appear ; make *one's* appearance ; turn [show] up ; come in.

じゅつご[1] 述語 〔文法〕 a predicate ¶述語として用いてある be used predicatively [as a predicate].

じゅつご[2] 術語 a technical term ; 〈総称〉 《文》 terminology ; 《文》 nomenclature.

しゅっこう[1] 出向 loan (of an employee) ; 《英》 secondment ¶出向する go [be sent] on loan 〈to another department〉 ; 《英》 be seconded 〈to the Osaka branch〉 / 出向させる loan 〈personnel〉 ; send 〈an employee of one department〉 on loan 〈to another department〉 / 出向中である be on loan 〈to another agency〉 / 出向中の役員 a loaned executive ; an executive on loan.

しゅっこう[2] 出校 ¶出校する attend [go to] school.

しゅっこう[3] 出港 departure (from a port) ¶出港する leave port ; clear a port ; set sail 〈from〉 ; put out to sea ; sail [steam] out. 文例⇩

しゅっこう[4] 出講 ¶出講する give lectures 〈at〉 ; teach 〈at〉 ; be a part-time lecturer 〈at〉.

じゅっこう 熟考 (serious) consideration ; deliberation ; hard thinking ¶熟考する think (it) over ; consider (carefully) ; turn 〈a matter〉 over (and over in *one's* mind) ; 《文》 deliberate

〈what to do〉 ; ponder / 熟考の上 after due [careful, 《文》 mature] consideration.

しゅつごく 出獄 ¶出獄する be discharged [released] from prison ; leave prison ⇒ しゅっしょ / 出獄者 a released convict.

じゅっさく 術策 《文》 an artifice ;《文》 a stratagem ; a trick ; a ploy ; 《文》 wiles ¶術策をろうする resort to tricks / 術策に富むを be artful ; be full of resources ; be wily / …の術策に陥る play into the hands of....

しゅっさつ 出札 ¶出札係 《米》 a ticket clerk ; 《英》 a booking clerk / 出札口 a ticket window / 出札所 a ticket office ; 《英》 a booking office.

しゅっさん 出産 (a) childbirth ; (a) birth ; a delivery 〈分娩〉 ¶出産する give birth to 〈a child〉 ; 《文》 be delivered of 〈a baby〉 / 出産祝い a celebration of a birth ; congratulations on a birth (他からの) / 出産休暇 (a) maternity [confinement] leave / 出産手当 (a) maternity benefit / 出産予定日 the expected date of confinement.

しゅっし 出資 (an) investment ; financing ¶出資する invest (sink, lay out) money (in) ; finance 〈an enterprise〉 / 共同出資 a joint contribution ; 〈合弁〉 joint capital / 出資額 the amount (of money) invested ; the amount of the investment [contribution] / 出資金 money invested ; an investment / 出資者 an investor ; a financier ; a contributor ; a subscriber.

しゅっしゃ 出社 ¶出社する go [come] to the office ; go to work.

しゅっしょ 出所 〈出どころ〉 the origin ; the source ¶出所する 〈刑務所から〉 be released [discharged] from prison ; leave jail ; come out of prison / 仮出所する ⇒ かりしゃくほう / 出所の確かな 〈information〉 (obtained) from reliable sources ; authentic / 出所を明らかにする 〈引用文などの〉 indicate [name] the source (of) ; give chapter and verse (for). 文例⇩

しゅっしょう 出生 ⇒ しゅっせい[1].

しゅつじょう 出場 〈参加〉 ;《文》 participation ; 〈出演〉 *one's* appearance on the stage ¶出場する take part [《文》 participate] 〈in〉 ; enter (for an event) ; appear on the stage ; 〈競技に〉 take the field ; compete 〈in a game〉 / (申し込んだ競技の)出場をとりやめる withdraw from a race [competition] ; scratch / 出場者《文》 a participant ; an entrant ; a panelist (ラジオ・テレビのクイズ番組の) / 出場資格をとる qualify (for the finals) / 出場有資格者 a qualifier. 文例⇩

しゅっしょく 出色 ¶出色の prominent ; distinguished ;《文》 conspicuous ; preeminent ; outstanding ; remarkable.

します。I take the train to work every day.
しゅつげき 彼はジェット機の操縦士で, 朝鮮戦争中は出撃50回を越えた。He is a jet pilot, who flew more than fifty missions during the Korean war.
しゅっけつ[2] 出血がなかなか止まらなかった。The bleeding would

not stop.
しゅっこう[3] 悪天候のために, 船は出港できないでいた。Bad weather kept the boat in port.
しゅっしょ この句の出所はシェイクスピアです。This phrase is (a quotation) from Shakespeare. / このデマの出所を探ってみたらつまらぬうわさ話からであった。The

rumor has been traced to idle gossip.
しゅつじょう (競泳で)8名の決勝出場者全員頭をそろえてスタートした。The whole final field of eight got off in a bunch. / 35人の出場者の中でどうにか完走したのはわずか11人だった。Of the 35 starters, only 11 managed to

しゅっしょしんたい　出処進退 ⇨ **しんたい**³ 文例⇩

しゅっしん　出身 ¶東京大学の出身である be a graduate of Tokyo University / 九州出身である come [be, hail] from Kyushu / 出身校 《文》one's alma mater; the school one went to [graduated from] / 出身者〈学校の〉a graduate; (米) an alumnus (pl. -ni) (男); (米) an alumna (pl. -nae) (女) / 出身地 one's home; one's hometown; one's home city [village]; one's birthplace.

しゅつじん　出陣 ¶出陣する take the field; go to war [the front].

しゅっすい　出水 a flood; an inundation; a freshet (雪解けなどによる) ¶出水する〈川が主語〉overflow (its banks); 〈土地が主語〉be flooded; be inundated.

しゅっせ　出世 success [《文》advancement] in life; promotion (昇進) ¶出世する succeed [get on, make one's way] (in life); rise [go up, advance] in the world; make headway in life; rise to greatness [a high position]; get ahead in the (business) world; be promoted; make [win] a name for oneself / 出世した人 a successful man / 出世の秘訣 secrets of success [a successful life] / 出世魚 fishes that are called by different names as they grow larger / 出世街道を歩む《文》take the highroad to success [fame] / 出世頭 the most successful (of one's classmates) / 出世作 a work which has won [earned] the author distinction (as a novelist); a work by which the writer has made a name for himself / 出世第一主義 careerism. 文例⇩

しゅっせい¹　**出生** a birth ¶出生地 one's birthplace; one's place of birth / 出生届 a report [register] of a birth / 出生届を出す have [get] the birth (of one's child) registered / 出生年月日 one's date of birth (略: d.o.b.) / 出生率 a birthrate.

しゅっせい²　**出征** ¶出征する go to war [the front] / 出征している be at the front; be on campaign / 出征軍人 a soldier in active service [at the front, going to the front].

しゅっせき　出席 attendance; 《文》presence ¶出席する attend (a meeting); present oneself (at); put in an [make one's] appearance (顔を出す) / 出席している be present (at) / 出席が不規則である do not attend regularly; 《文》be irregular in attendance / 出席をとる call the roll; take the register (学校での) / (学生の) 出席カード an attendance card / 出席者 a person present; 《総称》the attendance; those present / 出席者数 the number of people present / 出席日数 the number of days [times] one has attended / 出席簿 a roll book / 出席率 the percentage of attendance.

しゅつだい　出題 ¶出題する set sb a problem (in mathematics); set questions (for an examination in English) out of (the textbook material); set [prepare] an examination paper / 出題者 a proposer (of a problem).

しゅったん　出炭 ¶出炭する produce [yield] coal / 出炭量[額] output of coal (from); coal output.

じゅっちゅう　術中 ¶術中に陥る play into the hands (of); fall into [be caught in] the trap (of); be taken in [《文》entrapped] (by).

しゅっちょう¹　**出張** a business trip; an official tour [trip]; a tour of duty ¶出張する travel on (official) business (to); go on a business trip; make an official trip (to) / 出張させる send [dispatch] sb (to Hokkaido) / 出張を命じられる be sent [ordered (to go)] to (Kyushu) on business / 出張教授する give lessons at one's pupil's home / 出張員〈役人〉a dispatched official; 〈代理人〉an agent / 出張所 an agency; a branch [local] office / 出張旅費 travel expenses; a travel(ing) allowance. 文例⇩

しゅっちょう²　**出超** an excess of exports over imports.

しゅってい　出廷 ¶出廷する appear in court; present oneself at the court / 出廷を命じられる be subpoenaed; receive a subpoena; be ordered to (appear in) court.

しゅってん　出典 the source; the authority ¶出典を示す name [indicate] the source (of); give an authority (for); 〈正確に〉give chapter and verse (for).

しゅつど　出土 [考古] ¶出土する〈物が主語〉be excavated [unearthed, exhumed] (at a site, from the ruins of...); be found (at); 〈場所が主語〉produce; yield / 出土地 the site [location] at which (an artifact) was found [excavated]; the find site / 出土品 an (important) archaeological find site; an unearthed [excavated] article.

しゅっとう　出頭 《文》presence; appearance; 《文》attendance ¶出頭する appear; attend; present oneself (at); make one's [put in an] appearance; turn [show] up; report personally

---

finish the course.

しゅっしんたいしょ 政治家の出処進退には常に充分な理由がなければならない. A politician must always have a good reason for every move he makes.

しゅっしん うちの社長は農家の出身です. The president of our company comes from a peasant family. / 新内閣の閣僚中5人までが官僚出身者である. As many as five members of the new Cabinet are former government officials.

しゅっせ あの調子だと彼は相当出世するぞ. At that rate he will go far. / 私の同窓には出世した者が多い. Many of my former schoolmates have risen to high positions.

しゅっせき 彼は出席が悪い. His record of attendance is bad. / これを祝ってお歴々が大ぜい出席した. A large number of dignitaries were on hand to celebrate the occasion. / ぜひご出席下さいますように. Kindly give us the pleasure of your company. / 会は出席者が多[少]かった. The meeting was well [poorly] attended. / 送別会には出席者が200名以上あった. The farewell meeting was attended by more than 200 persons.

しゅつだい 入試の化学の出題者は中野教授だということです. I hear that the chemistry paper in the entrance examination was set by Professor Nakano.

しゅつどう 出頭 [in person] [(to sb, at an office)] / 出頭しないときは if sb does [should] not attend ; 《文》in case of nonattendance ; 《文》in default of attendance / 法廷に出頭を命じられる be subpoenaed ; be ordered to court / 裁判所への出頭命令 a subpoena ; (issue) a summons to appear in court.

しゅつどう 出動 ¶出動する〈軍隊が〉take the field ; be sent out ; 〈艦隊が〉sail ; put to sea / 出動させる dispatch (troops) ; send ; 《jets》in action / 出動を命じられる be ordered to (the front) ; be called [ordered] out. 文例⇩

しゅつにゅう 出入 ¶出入する go [come] in and out ; enter and leave ; 〈しきりに通う〉frequent ; 自由に出入する 《文》have free access to (a house) / 出入する船舶 incoming and outgoing vessels / 出入国管理令 the Immigration Control Ordinance. 文例⇩

しゅつば 出馬 ¶出馬する〈選挙に〉come [put *oneself*] forward as a candidate (for) ; 《米》run [《英》stand] for (the Diet) ; 〈自分で出かける〉go in person.

しゅっぱつ 出発 starting ; 《文》(a) departure ¶出発する start (from) ; 《文》depart (from) ; leave 《Tokyo》; set out (from a place, on one's journey) ; take off (飛行機が) / 人生の出発を誤まる make a wrong start in life / 出発係〈競技の〉a starter / 出発時間 the starting [departure] time / 出発点 the starting point [place] ; a takeoff point / 出発点に立つ〈競技で〉be on the [one's] mark / (空港の)出発ロビー a departure lounge. 文例⇩

しゅっぱん[1] 出帆 (a) sailing ; 《文》(a) departure ¶出帆する sail (from) ; set sail (from) ; leave 《Yokohama for America》; put (out) to sea / 出帆日 the sailing date.

しゅっぱん[2] 出版 (a) publication ; publishing ¶出版する publish ; bring [put] out ; issue / 出版される be published (in book form) ; come out (in print) ; appear in print ; see the light (of day) / 出版されている be in print / 出版の自由 freedom of the press / 出版界 the publishing world ; publishing circles / 出版記念会 a party in honor of the publication of sb's book ; a publication party / 出版業 publishing ; the publishing business / 出版者[元] the publisher(s) / 出版社 a publisher ; a publishing company [firm, house] / 出版物 a publication / 出版目録 a catalog(ue) of publications. 文例⇩

しゅっぴ 出費 expenses ; expenditure ; (an) outlay ¶多額の出費をする make a great [heavy] outlay (for).

しゅっぴん 出品 ¶出品する exhibit ; show ; display ; put [place] on show [exhibition, display] ; 〈品評会に〉enter 《one's work in a competition》/ 展覧会に出品する send [《文》submit] 《one's picture》to an exhibition / 出品者 an exhibitor / 出品点数[目録] the number [a catalog(ue)] of exhibits / 出品物 an exhibit ; an article on exhibition [display].

しゅっぺい 出兵 ¶出兵する dispatch [send] troops [an expeditionary force] (to).

しゅつぼつ 出没 ¶出没する 《文》make frequent appearances ; 《文》frequent ; haunt ; infest / 海賊[潜水艦]の出没する海 a sea infested with pirates [submarines] ; pirate-[submarine-]infested seas.

しゅっぽん 出奔 ¶出奔する run away [off] ; 《文》abscond ; 《文》decamp ; 《口語》clear out ; make off ; elope (駆り落ちする).

しゅつらん 出藍 ¶出藍の誉れがある outstrip [《文》surpass, 《文》excel] *one's* teacher [master] (in).

しゅつりょう 出漁 ¶出漁する sail [go] out fishing (in Korean waters) / 銚子沖に出漁中の船 boats [vessels] fishing off Choshi / 出漁区域 a fishing area.

しゅつりょく 出力 output ; generating power ; power [energy] output ¶出力 300 馬力のエンジン a motor that develops [has a capacity of] 300 hp / 出力 25 万キロワットの発電所 a power plant that generates [has a generating capacity of] 250,000 kilowatts of electricity / 出力端子 an output terminal. 文例⇩

しゅつるい 出塁 ¶出塁する〈野球〉get to 《first (base)》/ 出塁している be on 《second》base.

しゅと 首都 a capital (city) ; 《文》a metropolis ¶首都の metropolitan / 首都圏 the Metropolitan area.

しゅとう 種痘 (a) vaccination ; (an) inoculation ¶種痘する vaccinate ; inoculate sb against smallpox / 種痘を受ける be vaccinated [inoculated] against smallpox / 種痘の跡 a vaccination scar.

しゅどう 手動 ¶手動の hand-powered ; manually operated / 手動機械 a hand-powered machine / 手動操縦(装置) manual control(s) / 手動(操縦)に切り換える go on (to) [over to] manual / 補助手動装置 a back-up manual

---

しゅっちょう[1] 彼は商用で大阪へ出張している。He is now in Osaka on business. | He has gone on a business trip to Osaka.

しゅつど これらの出土品によりこの地方の縄文文化以前のことが大分明らかになるであろう。 These new finds [discoveries] will throw considerable light on the pre-Jomon culture in this district.

しゅつどう 米国は第 7 艦隊をインド洋に出動させた。The United States moved the Seventh Fleet to the Indian Ocean. / 昨夜の火事で十数台の消防自動車が出動した。Some dozen fire engines turned out to fight the fire last night.

しゅつにゅう 楽屋への出入はご遠慮下さい。Kindly keep out of the dressing rooms. / あそこは学生の出入を禁じてある。The students are not allowed to go there. / 《米》The place is off limits to the students.

しゅっぱつ 私は明日米国へ向かって出発します。I leave for America tomorrow.

しゅっぱん[2] この本は出版されたばかりだ。The book is just off the press. / この小説は現在少なくとも 5 種類の版が出版されている。There are at least five in-print editions of this novel.

しゅつりょく ラジオの出力が弱かった。The output of the radio was weak. / ロケットを地上から打上げるには、1 分以内に出力ゼロから最大に達しうる性能が必要

じゅどう　572　じゅふん

system / 手動ブレーキ[ポンプ] a hand brake [pump].

じゅどう 受動 ¶受動的[の] passive / 受動態《文法》the passive voice. 文例◊

しゅどうけん 主導権 (take) the initiative [leadership] (in).

しゅとく 取得《文》(an) acquisition ¶取得する《文》acquire;《文》gain;《文》obtain; get / 取得者《文》an acquisitor / 取得物 an acquisition; a find.

しゅとして 主として mainly;《文》chiefly;《文》principally;《文》primarily; for the most part; in the main.

じゅなん 受難 ordeals; a severe trial; sufferings; ⟨キリストの⟩ the Passion ¶受難日《キリスト教》Good Friday / 受難曲《音楽》Passion music.

ジュニア a junior ¶ジュニアスタイル《洋裁》a junior [teen-age] style.

しゅにく 朱肉 cinnabar seal ink; a vermilion inkpad.

じゅにゅう 授乳 ¶授乳する suckle《a baby》; nurse;《文》give the breast to《a child》/ 授乳期 lactation; the lactation period.

しゅにん 主任 a chief; a head; a manager ¶3年の主任である be in charge of a third-year class / 編集主任 the managing editor / 主任技師 a chief engineer / 主任教授 the chairman [《英》head]《of the department of psychology》.

しゅのう 首脳 the head; the leader ¶首脳部 the top-level executives《of a company》/ 首脳会談[議] a top-level [summit] meeting [conference]; a talk [conference] at the highest level.

シュノーケル a snorkel.

しゅはん¹ 主犯 the principal (offender).

しゅはん² 首班 the head ¶内閣の首班 the head of a cabinet; the premier; the prime minister / 政府[一国]の首班 the head of government [state] / 政府の首班となる《文》assume [take over] the reins of government; head the cabinet / 首班に指名する name [designate] sb as premier.

じゅばん ⟨<《ポルトガル語》gibão⟩ an undershirt; underwear.

しゅび¹ 守備 (a) defense;《野球》fielding ¶鉄壁の[まずい]守備《野球》airtight [poor] fielding / 守備がうまい[まずい] be good [poor] at fielding; be a good [poor] fielder / 守備についている be on garrison duty;《野球》be in the field / 守備につく assume the defensive;《野球》take to the field / 守備をする defend; guard; garrison《a fort, a town》/ 守備隊 [守備兵[隊]] a garrison; guards / 守備率《野球》one's fielding average.

しゅび² 首尾 ⟨初めと終わり⟩ beginning and end; ⟨結果⟩ the result;《文》the issue; the outcome ¶首尾よく successfully; smoothly / 首尾よく…し succeed [《文》be successful] in doing; make a success of (it); carry sth off (successfully) / 首尾一貫した consistent / 首尾一貫して consistently.

じゅひ 樹皮 (tree) bark ¶樹皮をはぐ bark《a tree》.

しゅひぎむ 守秘義務 the duty of confidentiality《concerning private matters learned through one's business》 ¶守秘義務違反 (an) abuse of confidentiality.

しゅひつ¹ 主筆 the (chief) editor; the editor in chief ¶副主筆 an assistant editor; a sub-editor.

しゅひつ² 朱筆 ¶朱筆を加える correct《errors》;《口語》red-pencil《a book》; ⟨改訂する⟩ revise.

しゅびょう 種苗 seeds and saplings; seedlings ¶種苗会社 a nursery company.

じゅひょう 樹氷 trees covered with hoar frost [with ice]; (a silver birch hung with) frosticles and leaves of ice.

しゅひん 主賓 the guest of honor ¶…を主賓として晩餐会を催す give a dinner in honor of….

しゅふ¹ 主婦 a housewife; ⟨一家の女主人⟩《文》the woman [mistress] of the house ¶主婦の務め the duties of a housewife; a housewife's chores / 主婦連合会 the Housewives' Federation.

しゅふ² 首府 ⇨しゅと.

しゅぶ¹ 主部《文法》the subject; ⟨主要部⟩ the main [principal] part.

しゅぶ² 首部 ⟨ミサイルの⟩ a nose cone.

シュプール ⟨<《ドイツ語》Spur⟩《スキー》the track [lines] of skis in the snow.

シュプレ(ッ)ヒコール ⟨<《ドイツ語》Sprechchor⟩《演劇》choral speaking; choric speaking [speech]; ⟨デモ隊の⟩ yelling (a slogan) in chorus.

しゅぶん 主文 ⟨判決文の⟩ the text (of a judgment).

じゅふん 授[受]粉《植》pollination; fertiliza-

である. To get a rocket off the ground it must be able to go from zero to full power in less than a minute.

じゅどう 次の文を受動態に変えなさい. Put the following sentence into the passive.

しゅび² 万事首尾よく運んだ. Everything went smoothly [well] (for me). / 試験の首尾はいかがでしたか. How did you fare [《口語》make out] in the exam? / 首尾よく彼を味方に引き入れた. We succeeded in winning him over to our side. / 首尾よく行けばいいが. I do hope it comes off well.

しゅほうしゃ この暴動の首謀者はだれか. Who led [masterminded] the mutiny?

しゅみ あなたの趣味は何ですか. What are you interested in? | What do you do in your spare time? | What is your hobby? / 彼女の服装はとっても趣味がいい. She has excellent taste in clothes. | Her clothes are in very good taste [in the best of taste]. / これならすべての人の趣味に合うだろう. This should please [meet, suit] every taste [all tastes]. / 僕は少年時代から釣りに趣味をもっていた. Even as a child he was fond of angling. / こういうことには僕はあまり趣味を持たない. I have little interest in this sort of thing. / この本は趣味と実益とを兼ねている. This book is both interesting and useful.

じゅみょう つるは寿命が長い.

しゅへい 手兵 soldiers under *one's* command ; 《with》*one's* men.

しゅほ 酒保 a canteen ; a camp shop ; 《米》a post exchange (略 : PX).

しゅほう¹ 手法 a technique ; a style ; a method.

しゅほう² 主砲 the main [principal] gun 《of a warship》.

しゅぼうしゃ 首[主]謀者 a ringleader ; a leader ; a mastermind (黒幕). 文例⇩

しゅみ 趣味 (a) taste ; (an) interest ; 〈道楽〉a hobby ; *one's* outside interests ¶上品[俗悪] な趣味 refined [vulgar] taste / …に趣味がある have a taste (for) ; be interested [take an interest] (in) / 趣味がいい〈人が〉have good taste (in clothes) ; 〈物が〉be tasteful / 趣味の広い人 a person with a lot of interests [hobbies] / 趣味のいい人 a person who has good taste ; 《文》a person of (good [well-cultivated]) taste / 趣味の園芸 horticulture [gardening] for pleasure [as a pastime] / 趣味の問題 a matter of taste / 趣味にかなった to *one's* taste / 趣味豊かに飾られた部屋 a room decorated with (great) taste / 趣味と実用を兼ねた陶器《文》porcelain combining beauty and utility / 江戸趣味の図案 a design in the fashion of the Edo period. 文例⇩

シュミーズ [<chemise] a slip ; a petticoat ★ chemise は今はワンピースの1種.

じゅみょう 寿命 *one's* life ; *one's* life span ; 《文》the span of life ¶車[電池]の寿命 the life of a car [battery] / 寿命が長い《文》be long-lived ; have [《文》enjoy] a long life / 寿命が短い《文》be short-lived ; have a short life / 寿命を縮める shorten *one's* life / 〈事が主語〉take years off *one's* life / 《口語》drive [put] a nail in [into] *one's* coffin / 寿命が延びる take (on) [win] a new [fresh] lease of life / 寿命で死ぬ die a natural death. 文例⇩

しゅむ 主務 ¶主務大臣[官庁] the competent minister [authorities].

シュメール Sumer ¶シュメールの Sumerian 《culture》/ シュメール語 Sumerian / シュメール人 a Sumerian.

しゅもく¹ 種目 an item ; an event (競技の) ¶営業種目 items of business.

しゅもく² 撞木 a wooden bell hammer.

じゅもく 樹木 a tree ; 〈総称〉trees (and shrubs) ¶樹木の茂った wooded 〈hills〉; tree-covered 〈mountains〉; woody / 樹木のない bare 〈hilltops〉; 《文》〈plains〉bare of trees ; treeless.

じゅもん 呪文 a (magic) spell ; a charm ; an incantation ; a magic formula ; magic words ¶呪文を唱える cast [chant, make] a spell / 呪文を解く break a spell.

しゅやく 主役 〈役〉the leading [principal] part [role] ; 〈役者〉the leading actor [actress] ; a star ¶主役を勤める play the leading part ; star (in a play) ; head the cast.

じゅよ 授与 〈証書などの〉《文》conferment ; 《文》presentation ; 〈賞品の〉awarding ¶授与する give ; 《文》confer (a degree on *sb*) ; award (a prize to *sb*, *sb* with *sth*) / 〈勲章を〉decorate (*sb* with an order) / 卒業証書授与 the presentation of diplomas.

しゅよう¹ 腫瘍 《医》a tumor ¶悪性[良性]腫瘍 a malignant [benign] tumor / 腫瘍の発生 formation of a tumor.

しゅよう² 主要 ¶主要な main ; 《文》principal ; 《文》chief ; leading ; major ; (most) important / 主要産業 ⇨さんぎょう / 主要産物 staple products ; staples / 主要人物 〈劇や小説の〉the leading characters ; 〈事件などの〉the key figures.

じゅよう¹ 受容 ¶受容する accept / 感覚受容器 《動》a sense [sensory] receptor.

じゅよう² 需要 (a) demand ¶需要と供給の合致 the meeting of supply and demand / 需要がある be in demand ; be wanted / 需要を満たす [に応じる] supply [meet] a demand. 文例⇩

しゅよく 主翼 the wing 《of an airplane》.

しゅら 修羅 ¶修羅のちまた《文》a scene of carnage [bloodshed] / 修羅のちまたとなる become [be turned into] a (veritable) shambles.

ジュラき ジュラ紀 [地質] the Jurassic period.

ジュラルミン duralumin.

しゅらん 酒乱 〈事〉(a) drunken frenzy ; 〈人〉a fighting [violent] drunk.

じゅり 受理 ¶受理する accept ; 《文》receive. 文例⇩

しゅりけん 手裏剣 a throwing-knife ¶手裏剣を使う throw a knife (at).

じゅりつ 樹立 ¶樹立する establish ; found ; set up.

しゅりゅう 主流 the main current 《of American literature》; the mainstream ¶主流派 〈政党などの〉the faction in power ; the leading [mainstream, main-current] faction / 反主流派 the factions out of power ; an anti-mainstream group.

しゅりょう¹ 狩猟 hunting ; shooting ; 《文》the chase ¶狩猟に行く go shooting [hunting] / 狩

Cranes live to a great age. / 今は昔に比べて寿命が延びた. People live longer than they used to. / 医師は彼の寿命があと1年ぐらいのものだと言った. The doctor said he had only a year to live. / タバコを1本吸うごとに, 君は寿命を縮めているんだぞ. Every cigarette you smoke is a nail in your coffin, you know. / あの時の苦労で, 彼は寿命を縮めた. The trouble he went through then took years off his life. / 現内閣の寿命ももう知れている. The present Cabinet's days are numbered. / その倉庫が来て建て直さなければだめだった. The warehouse had done its term of service and had to be rebuilt. / これはもう寿命が来ていますね. It's had its day [It's on its last legs], I'm afraid. / この電池は寿命が来ています. This battery is almost dead.

じゅよう² これらの品は非常に需要がある. There is a big demand for these articles. | These articles are very much in [are in great] demand. / 需要が多くて供給がとても追いつかない. The demand far exceeds [outruns] the supply. / 産ば一般の需要を満たすに足りない. The output is not large enough to meet the demand from the public.

じゅり 10月10日以後の願書は受理しない. No application submit-

猟家 a hunter ; a sportsman / 狩猟期 the hunting [open] season / 狩猟許可証 a shooting [hunting] license / 狩猟禁止期 《米》the closed [《英》the close] season / (原始的な)狩猟採集経済 a hunter-gatherer [hunting-and-gathering] economy / 狩猟場 a hunting ground / 狩猟法 the game law(s) / 狩猟民族 hunting people.

しゅりょう² 首領 a chief ; a leader ; a head ; a chieftain ; a boss.

しゅりょう³ 酒量 one's drinking [alcohol] capacity ¶酒量が多い be a heavy drinker ; drink a great deal / 酒量が増える[減る] come to drink more [less] than before [one used to].

じゅりょう 受領 ¶受領する《文》receive ;《文》be in receipt (of) ; accept / 受領書[証] a receipt. 文例↓

しゅりょく 主力 the main force [strength, body] ¶主力を注ぐ concentrate [focus] one's efforts (on) ; devote oneself (to) / 主力株 leading [key] stocks [shares] / 主力艦隊 the main squadron [fleet] / 主力部隊 main-force units.

しゅるい 種類 a kind ; a sort ; a variety ; a species (単複同形) ; a type (型) ¶あらゆる種類のもの all kinds [sorts] of things ; all manner of things ;《文》things of every kind [description] / この種類の品 this sort of goods ; goods of this sort / こういう種類の犯罪 crimes of this nature / こういう種類の詐欺 this type [form] of swindling / 普通の種類の魚 the usual [common, ordinary] run of fish / 種類別[分け]にする classify ;《文》assort. 文例↓

じゅれい 樹齢 the age of a tree. 文例↓

シュレッダー a shredder.

しゅれん 手練 skill ;《文》dexterity ¶手練の早業 with the speed and precision of a trained hand.

しゅろ 〖植〗a hemp palm ¶しゅろ縄 (a) hemp-palm rope / しゅろの木[葉] a palm tree [leaf].

しゅわ 手話〈手で話す事〉talking with the hands [fingers] ;〈その言葉〉(the) manual sign language ; (the) finger language ; 〈use〉(deaf-and-dumb) sign language.

じゅわき 受話器〈電話の〉a (telephone) receiver ; an earpiece ; a handset 〈送話器もついている, 卓上電話の〉;〈交換手などの用いる, 頭にかける式の〉a headset ; (a pair of) headphones ;〈無線の〉radio earphones ¶受話器をとる pick up the receiver ; lift the phone [receiver] / 受話器を耳に当てる put the telephone [receiver] to one's ear / 受話器をかける [置く] hang up (the phone) ; put back《文》replace the receiver / 受話器を外したままにしておく leave the phone [receiver] off the rest [cradle] / 受話器に手をかぶせる cover the receiver with one's hand ; cup one's hand over the receiver.

しゅわん 手腕 ability ;《文》capability ;《文》competence ; (a) talent ; skill ;《文》a faculty ¶手腕のある able ; capable ; competent ; talented / 手腕のない incompetent ; inefficient / 手腕を振るう《文》exercise one's ability [skill] ; give full play to one's ability [abilities] / 手腕を見せる display [show] one's skill / 手腕家《文》a man of ability [abilities] ; an able man. 文例↓

しゅん 旬 the season ¶しゅんの野菜 vegetables in season ; in-season vegetables. 文例↓

じゅん¹ 順〈順序〉order ;〈輪番〉a turn ¶順が狂っている be out of order / 順を変える[繰り上げる] change [move up] the order / 順を追って in due order / 順に; 順々に, 順々に in turn ; in sequence ; one by one ; in order ; one after another ; successively ; by turns / 順に送る pass sth on / 滞在期間の古い順に in order of the length of time 《they》have stayed 《here》/ ABC順に並べる arrange in alphabetical order [alphabetically] / 順に回す pass around. 文例↓

じゅん² 純 ¶純(な)〈純粋な〉pure ; genuine ;《文》unalloyed ; unmixed ; natural〈自然の〉;〈無邪気な〉unspoilt ; innocent / 純日本風の《a garden》in a purely Japanese style ; completely Japanese in style [character] / 純文学 (the novel as) pure literature ;《フランス語》belles-lettres.

じゅん- 準… semi- ; quasi- ¶準会員[社員] an associate member / 準決勝 a semifinal (game) ; the semifinals / 準軍事的 paramilitary.

じゅんあい 純愛〈交じり気のない愛情〉pure [genuine] love ;〈純潔な愛〉《文》chaste [platonic] love.

じゅんい 順位 order ; ranking ; standing ; placing ¶(同点者間の)順位決定戦 a play-off ;〈跳躍競技の〉a jump-off ;〈射撃の〉a shoot-off.

じゅんえき 純益 net [pure] profit. 文例↓

じゅんえん 順延 ¶順延する postpone ; put off.

じゅんおくり 順送り ⇨じゅん¹.

しゅんか 春歌 a bawdy [lewd] song.

しゅんが 春画 an erotic [a pornographic] picture.

じゅんか 純化 ¶純化する purify ; refine.

じゅんかい 巡回 a round ; a tour ; a patrol ¶巡回する go round ; go [make] one's rounds ; make the rounds (of) ; patrol ; make [go on] a tour (of inspection) / 巡回区域 one's beat [round] / 巡回講演 a lecturing [lecture] tour / 巡回診療所 a traveling clinic / 巡回図書館 on mobile library ; a library on wheels ;《米》a

---

ted later than October 10th will be accepted.

じゅりょう 右正に受領致しました. Received with thanks. | 4月5日付のご書状正に受領致しました. Thank you for your letter of April 5th.

しゅるい 彼は色々な貝を千種類以上集めている. He has a collection of over 1,000 different types of shell. / 1種類3つずつもらいましょう. I'll take three of each sort.

じゅれい ここにある木の中には樹齢500年以上になるものがある. Some of the trees here are more than 500 years old.

しゅわん 彼が外交官としての手腕を振るう余地はほとんどない. There is little scope left for his diplomatic abilities.

しゅん かきは今がしゅんだ. Oysters are now in season. | It is the season for oysters now. / たけのこは毎年今頃しゅんになる. Bamboo sprouts come into season at this time of year.

bookmobile.
しゅんかしゅうとう 春夏秋冬 〈四季〉 the four seasons ; 〈一年中〉(at) all seasons of the year ; all the year round.
じゅんかつゆ 潤滑油 lubricating oil ; (a) lubricant ¶ 潤滑油の役目をする 〈比喩的に〉 help (to) smooth 《the progress of negotiations》; reduce the friction 《between》.
しゅんかん 瞬間 a moment ; a second ; an instant ¶ 瞬間に 《文》 instantaneously ; in an instant ; in a twinkling ; in a flash / 瞬間の[的] 《文》 instantaneous / 瞬間最大風速 the maximum instantaneous [momentary] wind velocity / 瞬間接着剤 (a tube of) instant glue ; 瞬間湯沸かし器 an instantaneous water heater. 文例▷
じゅんかん¹ 旬刊 ¶ 旬刊の (a magazine) published [issued] every ten days.
じゅんかん² 循環 circulation ; rotation ; a cycle ¶ 血液の循環 the circulation of the blood / 血液の循環がいい[悪い] have (a) good [bad] circulation / 循環する 《文》 recur ; go in cycles ; circulate 《through》; rotate / 循環器 a circulatory organ / 循環系(統)〈血液・リンパ液の〉 the circulatory system / 循環系統の病気 circulatory illness [troubles, ailments] / 循環小数 a recurring [repeating] decimal / 循環線 a loop (railroad) line / 循環論法〔論〕 a circular argument ; a vicious circle. 文例▷
しゅんき 春季 spring ; springtime.
しゅんぎく 春菊 a crown daisy.
しゅんきはつどうき 春機発動期 (the age of) puberty ; adolescence ⇨ ししゅんき.
じゅんきゅう 準急 a semi-express (train).
じゅんきょ 準拠 ¶ 準拠する a base (a decision) on ; 《文》 conform to ; follow / …に準拠して 《文》 in conformity to… ; 《文》 in accordance with… 文例▷
じゅんきょう 殉教 martyrdom ¶ 殉教者 a martyr / 殉教者となる be martyred ; 《文》 die a martyr (for one's faith).
じゅんきょう 順境 ¶ 順境にある 《文》 be in favorable [comfortable, prosperous, easy] circumstances ; be well (comfortably) off.
じゅんぎょう 巡業 ¶ 巡業する make [go on] a provincial tour ; take to [go on] the road ; 《米》 go on a barnstorming tour ; 《米》 barnstorm / 〈劇団が〉 大都市を巡業して回る play (in) the larger cities / 巡業中である be on tour ; be on the road / 巡業劇団 a strolling [traveling] company ; a touring theater.
じゅんきん 純金 pure [solid] gold.
じゅんぎん 純銀 pure [solid] silver.
じゅんぐり 順繰り ⇨ じゅん¹.

じゅんけつ 純潔 purity ; 《文》 chastity ¶ 純潔な pure ; clean ; 《文》 chaste ; 《文》 virginal (★男性にも言う) / 心の純潔な人 a purehearted person / 純潔教育 education in sexual morality.
じゅんけつ 純血 ¶ 純血のa thoroughbred ; a pure-blood ¶ 純血種の pure-[full-]blooded ; thoroughbred 〈馬・犬など〉; purebred ; pureblood.
じゅんけっしょう 準決勝 a semifinal (game [match, round]) ¶ 〈go on to〉 the semifinals ¶ 準決勝戦出場者 a semifinalist.
しゅんげん 峻厳 ¶ 峻厳な stern ; 《文》 rigorous ; strict ; severe ; rigid.
しゅんこう 竣工 《文》 completion ¶ 竣工する be completed ; be finished / 竣工式 a ceremony to celebrate the completion (of a bridge).
じゅんこう 巡航 a cruise ; cruising ; 〈飛行機の〉 cruise flight ¶ 巡航する cruise ; take a cruise 《to the Bahamas, in the South Pacific》/ 巡航中である be on a cruise / 巡航高度に達する reach [climb to] cruising altitude / 〈最大〉 巡航速度で (sail) at (full) cruising speed / 巡航ミサイル a cruise missile.
じゅんさ 巡査 a policeman ; a police officer ; a constable ; 《口語》 a cop ; a copper ; 《英口語》 a bobby ; police 〈総称〉 ¶ 巡査派出所 a police box / 巡査部長 a police sergeant.
しゅんさい 俊才 a brilliant boy [youth] ; a promising youth.
じゅんさい 〔楯〕 a water shield.
じゅんさつ 巡察 ⇨ じゅんし¹.
しゅんじ 瞬時 ⇨ しゅんかん ¶ 瞬時も (not) even for a moment.
じゅんし¹ 巡視 a tour [round] of inspection ; an inspection ¶ 巡視する make [go on] a tour of inspection ; inspect ; 〈持ち場を〉 patrol ; walk one's beat (巡査が) / 工場内を巡視する inspect [go over] a factory / 巡視船 a patrol boat.
じゅんし² 殉死 ¶ 殉死する 《文》 immolate oneself at the funeral 《of one's lord [master]》; 《文》 follow (one's lord [master]) to the grave.
じゅんじ 順次 ⇨ じゅん¹ (順に).
しゅんじゅう 春秋 〈春と秋〉 spring and autumn ; 〈年月〉 years ; 〈年齢〉 age ; 〈a girl of twenty〉 summers ; 《文》 (a gentleman of eighty) winters ¶ 春秋の筆法をもってすれば 《文》 as the ancient chroniclers of Lu would say / 春秋に富む be still young ; have a long future before [ahead of] one.
しゅんじゅん 逡巡 ⇨ ちゅうちょ.
じゅんじゅん¹ 順々 ⇨ じゅん¹.
じゅんじゅん² 諄々 ¶ じゅんじゅんと 《文》 earnestly ; repeatedly / じゅんじゅんと説く 《文》 inculcate 《sth in sb, sb with sth》; rea-

---

じゅん¹ ご期待に願います。In order, please！It is natural that a parent should die before his child. / 必ずしも順を追う必要はない。It is not always necessary to follow the order.
じゅんえき その取引で彼は100万円の純益を得た。He netted [cleared] a million yen in the transaction. | The transaction netted him a million yen.
しゅんかん それを見た瞬間彼女は真っ青になった。The moment [instant] she saw it, she turned pale [went as white as a sheet]. / ほんの一瞬間の出来事だった。It all happened in a moment [flash]. / 娘の顔を見つけた次の瞬間には、彼はもうしっかりと彼女を抱いていた。He found his daughter, and the next moment he was holding her tight.
じゅんかん² 景気不景気は循環する。Good and bad times follow each other.
じゅんきょ 準拠すべき規定がな

じゅんじゅんけっしょう 準々決勝 a quarter-final (game [match, round]); the quarterfinals ¶ 準々決勝戦出場者 a quarterfinalist.

じゅんじょ 順序 〈次第〉 (an) order; (a) sequence; 〈手続き〉 (a) procedure; 〈方法〉 a system; a method ¶ 順序のある, 順序だった orderly; systematic; methodical / 順序の(立た)ない disorderly; out of order; irregular; unsystematic; unmethodical / 順序よく[正しく](文) in (good [regular]) order; methodically; systematically / 順序を誤る fail to follow the right order / 順序を整える put sth in (the) correct [proper] order / 順序立てる put sth in order; arrange 《one's ideas》 (well); (文) systematize;《文》methodize / 順序不同に in random order. 文例⇩

じゅんじょう 純情 《文》 a pure heart; 《文》 naiveté; 《文》 naivety; naiveness ¶ 純情な unspoilt; unsophisticated; naive.

じゅんしょく¹ 殉職 ¶ 殉職する die at one's post;《文》be killed [lay down one's life] in the performance of one's duties; die in harness [on duty] / 《口語》die with one's boots on / 殉職警官 a policeman who died on duty / 殉職者 a person who has died at his post [in the performance of his duties].

じゅんしょく² 潤色《文》(an) embellishment;《文》ornamentation ¶ 潤色する《文》embellish; color; give color to 《one's account》; dress 《the facts》 up.

じゅんじる¹ 殉じる die 《for》; sacrifice oneself 《for one's country》; die a martyr 《for one's faith》.

じゅんじる² 準じる〈準用する〉apply similarly;〈比例する〉be proportionate [in proportion] to 《the population》;〈相応する〉correspond to;〈則る〉follow; be based on 《基づく》 ¶ …に準じて in proportion to 《one's years》; in proportion as 《one becomes older》; according to 《the amount of your work》;《文》according as 《your work is good or bad》.

じゅんしん 純真 ¶ 純真な unspoilt; innocent;《文》purehearted;《文》ingenuous; unsophisticated.

じゅんすい 純粋 ¶ 純粋の pure; genuine; real;〈交ざり物のない〉unalloyed; unadulterated / 純粋の江戸っ子 a trueborn Edokko / 純粋のポインター犬 a pointer of pure stock / 純粋培養する cultivate a pure culture 《of an organism》.

じゅんせい 準星 【天】 a quasar.

しゅんせつ 浚渫 dredging ¶ 浚渫する dredge 《a harbor》 / 浚渫機 a dredging machine; a dredge; a dredger / 浚渫作業 dredging operations / 浚渫船 a dredger.

じゅんぜん 純然 ¶ 純然たる pure (and simple); sheer; utter; absolute; thorough; out-and-out; complete; downright / 純然たる私事 a purely personal matter. 文例⇩

しゅんそく 俊足 ¶ 俊足の《文》fleet-[swift-]footed / 俊足である《文》be fleet [swift] of foot; be a fast runner.

じゅんたく 潤沢 ¶ 潤沢な《文》abundant;《文》plentiful; ample. 文例⇩

じゅんちょう 順調 ¶ 順調な satisfactory; fair; fine; favorable; smooth;《文》seasonable 《weather》 / 順調に smoothly; favorably; satisfactorily; (very) well; without a hitch / 順調に進む go (very) well [smoothly];《文》progress satisfactorily [favorably]; 〈人が主語〉have smooth sailing / 順調に売れる sell steadily;《文》enjoy a steady sale / 順調に行かない go wrong [《文》amiss]; be unsatisfactory. 文例⇩

しゅんと ¶ しゅんとなる be dejected;《文》be crestfallen; be dispirited; be disheartened; (suddenly) go [《文》become, fall] quiet.

じゅんど 純度 purity.

しゅんとう 春闘 the spring (labor) offensive.

しゅんどう 蠢動 ¶ しゅん動する 〈うごめく〉wriggle; writhe;〈策動する〉stir;〈策動する〉plan mischief / 不平分子のしゅん動 the (behind-the-scenes) maneuvering of discontented elements.

じゅんとう 順当 ¶ 順当な proper; normal; natural; reasonable / 順当に行けば in the ordinary course of things; in the natural course of events; if all [everything] goes well. 文例⇩

じゅんどうし 準動詞 【文法】 a verbal.

じゅんのう 順応 ¶ 順応する adapt [《文》accommodate oneself] 《to the new environment》; adjust 《to the prevailing atmosphere》; conform 《to the customs of the country》; get [《文》become acclimatized 《米》acclimated] 《to the changed circumstances》 / 時代に順応する go [swim] with the tide [current, times] / 環境に順応できない人 a misfit / 順応性[力] adaptability;《文》capacity for adaptation / 順応性のある adaptable; flexible; malleable.

じゅんぱく 純白 pure [snow] white;《文》immaculate whiteness ¶ 純白の pure-[snow-]white; immaculate 《shirts》 / 純白でない off-

---

い. We have no rule to go by.
じゅんじゅん² 彼は じゅん じゅんと説いて彼女の愚かしさを悟らせようとした. He tried patiently to talk her out of her silly ideas.
じゅんじょ 順序不同. No special order is observed. / 映画が私たちが映画館で見るときと同じ順序で撮影されることはない. A film is never photographed in the order in which you see it in the cinema. / まず彼の意向を聞くの

が順序だろう. It would be proper to ask him about his intentions first. / そういう結論に達した順序をお話し申しましょう. I'll show you how [the steps by which] I reached that conclusion.
じゅんぜん これは純然たる捏造だ. This is pure invention [an invention pure and simple].
じゅんたく 資金は潤沢である. We have ample funds.
じゅんちょう 万事順調に運んでい

る. Everything is going well [all right]. / 仕事は順調に行っています. I am getting along well with my work. / 病人の経過は順調です. The patient is making satisfactory progress. / 病人はすこぶる順調に回復した. The patient made a remarkably untroubled recovery. / 就任して半年の間, 国会は首相にとって万事が順調に運んだ. In his first six months in office, the Prime

じゅんばん 順番 ⇨じゅん¹ ¶順番(の来るの)を待つ wait for *one's* turn (to come around); be on the waiting list. 文例⇩

じゅんび 準備 〈用意〉preparation(s); (preliminary) arrangements; 〈予備〉a reserve 〈of money〉 ¶準備の 〈文〉preparatory; preliminary; 〈予備の〉reserve; spare / 準備する prepare (*oneself*) (for); arrange (for); make preparations [arrangements] (for); get ready (for); 〈備える〉provide for [against]; reserve 〈a fund〉 / 準備中である 〈人が主語〉be getting ready (for); 〈事が主語〉〈文〉be in (course of) preparation / 旅行の準備をする prepare (*oneself*) ready] for a journey / 会合のための部屋の準備をする get the room ready for a meeting / 準備委員会 a preparatory [an arrangements] committee (for founding a medical college) / 準備運動 warming [limbering] up; warming-up exercises / 準備金 a reserve fund / 準備室 a preparation room / 準備通貨 a reserve currency / 準備なしに 〈speak〉off the cuff; impromptu / 準備不足である be poorly 〈〈文〉ill] prepared. 文例⇩

しゅんびん 俊敏 ¶俊敏な smart; quick-[sharp-]witted.

じゅんぷう 順風 a favorable [〈文〉fair] wind ¶順風に帆を揚げて走る sail before [with] the wind. 文例⇩

しゅんぷうたいとう 春風駘蕩〈文〉balmy [genial] spring weather. 文例⇩

しゅんぶん 春分 the vernal [spring] equinox ¶春分の日 Vernal Equinox Day.

じゅんぶん 純分 〈金・銀の〉fineness; 〈通貨の〉metal content.

じゅんぽう¹ 旬報 a report issued every ten days; a ten-day report.

じゅんぽう² 順法 ¶順法精神がある be law-abiding / 順法闘争〖労〗a work-to-rule / 順法闘争戦術 work-to-rule tactics / 順法闘争をする work to rule.

じゅんぼく 純朴 ¶純朴な simple and honest; 〈文〉unspoilt; 〈風俗の〉homely; simple-mannered (people).

しゅんみん 春眠 文例⇩

しゅんめ 駿馬 a fine horse; 〈文〉a fleet steed.

じゅんめん 純綿 ¶純綿の all-cotton.

じゅんもう 純毛 pure wool ¶純毛の all-wool; pure-wool.

じゅんよう 準用 ¶準用する〈文〉apply (provisions) correspondingly 〈to other cases〉; 〈文〉apply 〈the law〉*mutatis mutandis* [with necessary modification] 〈to〉.

じゅんようかん 巡洋艦 a cruiser.

じゅんれい 巡礼 a pilgrim ¶巡礼する make [go on] a pilgrimage / 巡礼姿で〈文〉in a pilgrim's garb.

じゅんれき 巡歴 ¶巡歴する tour (round) (Europe); make a tour (of the country, round the world).

しゅんれつ 峻烈 ¶峻烈な〈非難など〉severe; sharp; 〈文〉unsparing; scathing; 〈態度など〉stern; 〈文〉rigorous.

じゅんれつ 順列〖数〗(a) permutation ¶順列(と)組合わせ permutations and combinations.

じゅんろ 順路 the suggested route (for visitors); the way round ¶順路を経て by the usual [suggested] route.

しょ 書〈書法, 書道〉penmanship; (Oriental) calligraphy; 〈筆跡〉handwriting; 〈書簡〉a letter; a note; 〈書物〉a book; 〈書いたもの〉〈文〉*sb's* writing(s).

しょ- 諸 ¶アジア諸国 the countries of Asia; the Asian nations ★「諸…」を various, different, diverse などと訳すと不適切になることが多い。上の句例のように the＋名詞の複数形で「諸…」の意味が表わせる。

じょ 序〈前書き〉a foreword; a preface ⇨じょぶん.

じょい 女医 a woman doctor (*pl.* women doctors); a lady [female] doctor.

しょいこむ 背負い込む be burdened [saddled, 〈文〉encumbered] (with debts).

しょいちねん 初一念 ¶初一念を貫く carry out *one's* original intention.

しょいなげ 背負い投げ ⇨せおいなげ ¶しょい投げを食わす 〈投げる〉throw *sb* over *one's* shoulder; 〈裏切る〉〈文〉betray *sb's* trust; go back on (a promise); 〈文〉play *sb* false / 〈事が主語〉fall short of *one's* expectations.

しょいん¹ 所員 a member of the staff; 〈総称〉the staff; the personnel.

しょいん² 書院 〈書斎〉a study; 〈客間〉a drawing room.

しよう 子葉〖植〗a cotyledon; a seed leaf.

しよう² 止揚〖哲〗sublation; 《ドイツ語》*Aufheben* ¶止揚する sublate.

しよう³ 仕様 a way; a method; a measure; 〈文〉a means〈単複同形〉¶仕様のない 〈やくざな〉good-for-nothing; worthless; 〈度し難い〉past praying for; 〈文〉beyond redemption; hopeless; 〈ひどい〉out-and-out 〈scoundrels〉; absolute; confirmed; regular; 〈文〉egregious / (…したくて)仕様がない ⇨たまらない / 仕様書

Minister had remarkably smooth sailing in the Diet. / 貿易が順調になった. Trade has got back to normal.
君がお父さんの後を継ぐのが順当だ. It is (right and) proper that you should succeed your father. / この陽気が順当です. This is normal weather.
じゅんばん ようやく彼の順番になった. At last his turn came (around). / 彼らは順番に試験された. They were examined in turn. / 順番でないに口をきいてはいけない. You must not speak out of (your) turn.
じゅんび 準備は すっかり出来た. Everything is ready. | We are all set (to go). / 準備は不充分であった. The preparations were incomplete. | 入用の金は手元に準備してある. I have the necessary sum ready to hand.
じゅんぷう 順風に乗って20ノットの航海を続けた. We had a fair wind [tailwind] all the time, making twenty knots.
しゅんぷうたいとう あの人はどことなく春風たいとうとした雰囲気がある. There is something sunny and genial about him.
しゅんみん 春眠暁を覚えず. In spring one sleeps a sleep that

しよう 《meet》 specifications. 文例⇩

しよう⁴ 私用 ¶私用の for *one's* private use; private / 私用で on private [personal] business.

しよう⁵ 使用 use; employment; 《文》application (応用) ¶使用する a use; put *sth* to use; make use of; 《文》employ; apply; 《文》appropriate; 《文》devote 《to》/ できるだけ有効に使用する make the best (possible) use of / たびたび使用する 《文》make frequent use of / 使用しない部屋 an unused room / 一般に使用されている [されるようになる] be in [come into] general use; be [come to be] widely used / 日常使用されている be in daily [everyday] use / 使用されていない機械 a machine that is not in use [is lying idle] / 使用されなくなる go [drop] out of use / 石油の使用を節約する economize in the use of oil / 長く使用に耐える stand long use / 使用可能な usable; workable; available / 使用者 a user; a consumer (消費者) / 雇い主 an employer / 使用人 an employee; a servant (召使い) / 使用法 how to use; use; directions (for use) (薬などの) / 使用料 a rental fee.

しよう⁶ 枝葉 ¶枝葉の minor; unessential; 《文》of minor importance / 枝葉の事柄[問題] a side issue; a mere detail (trifle) / 枝葉にわたる deviate [《文》digress] from the subject [the point, the main issue]; go [《文》make a digression] into unimportant [minor] details / 枝葉末節にとらわれる be concerned about unimportant details.

しよう⁷ 試用 ¶試用する try 《a drug》; give *sth* a trial.

しょう¹ 抄 ⇨ぱっすい.

しょう² 性 〈天性〉(a) nature; *one's* disposition; 〈気質〉(a) temperament; 〈性格〉(a) character; (a) personality ¶性の悪い《文》ill-natured; malicious; wicked; vicious / 性に合う agree with *one*; suit *one*; 《文》be congenial to *one*; come natural to *one* / 性に合わない be not in *one's* line; be not *one's* type; disagree with *one* (食物などが). 文例⇩

しょう³ 省 〈内閣の〉a department; a ministry; 〈中国の行政区画〉a province ¶各省間の interdepartmental.

しょう⁴ 将 a commander; a general; a leader. 文例⇩

しょう⁵ 称 ¶…の称がある be called…; be known [referred to] as…; go [be known] by the name of….

しょう⁶ 章 〈本の〉a chapter; 〈記章〉a badge; an emblem ¶第3章 the third chapter; Chapter 3 / 会員章 a membership badge.

しょう⁷ 商 〈数〉the quotient; 〈商人〉a merchant; a dealer ¶貴金属商 a bullion dealer; a dealer in precious metals; a jeweler.

しょう⁸ 笙 〈楽器〉a traditional Japanese wind instrument resembling panpipes.

しょう⁹ 勝 ⇨しょうり ¶3勝1敗 three victories [wins] and [to] one defeat.

しょう¹⁰ 賞 a prize; a reward ¶賞を懸ける offer a prize 《for》/ 賞を取る[受ける] win [be awarded] a prize / 賞をさらう carry off [away] a prize / 一等賞 the first prize. 文例⇩

しょう¹¹ 衝 ¶衝に当たる be in charge of; undertake.

しょう¹² 背負う carry *sth* on *one's* back; shoulder; 〈引き受ける〉take *sth* on *oneself*; undertake; 〈重荷を〉be burdened [saddled] 《with》 ¶荷物をしょって with a load on *one's* back / しょっている 〈うぬぼれている〉be conceited; think too much [highly] of *oneself*.

しょう-¹ 小… ¶小アジア Asia Minor / 小委員会 a subcommittee / 小劇場 a little theater. 文例⇩

しょう-² 正… ¶正5時に at five sharp; punctually [exactly, just] at five.

じよう 滋養 nourishment; nutrition ¶滋養物 nourishing [nutritious] food; nourishment / 滋養分 a nutritious [nutritive] element / 滋養になる, 滋養分の多い nutritious; nourishing / 滋養分の少ない (food) of poor nutritive value.

じょう¹ 上 〈上の〉〈上部の〉upper; 〈等級〉first; best; 〈文〉superior; excellent; 〈上巻〉the first volume / 上中下 the first, second and third classes [grades] / 上の上 the very best. 文例⇩

じょう² 条 〈箇条〉a provision; an article; 〈線〉a line; a stripe (素地とは違う色の) ¶前条 the preceding article / 第1条 Article 1 / 一条の煙 a wisp of smoke / 一条の光線 a ray of light / 一条の流れ a stream of running water. 文例⇩

じょう³ 乗 〈数〉¶2乗する square 《a number》; raise 《a number》to the second power / xの2乗 x squared / xの3乗 x cubed / xの4乗 the fourth power of x; x to the power four; x to the fourth. 文例⇩

---

knows no dawn.

しよう³ ほかに何とか仕様があったろうに. You could have done it some other way. / こうするよりほかに何とも仕様がない. There is no alternative for it. | There is nothing for it.

しよう⁵ この金はどうようともご随意にご使用下さい. This money is entirely at your disposal. / 蔵書はどれでもご自由にご使用下さい. You are welcome to any book in my library. / 使用中, (トイレ・浴室などの掲示)'Occupied.' |

'Engaged.'

しょう² ゴルフは僕の性に合わない. Golf isn't my cup of tea.

しょう⁴ 彼は人に将たるの器である. He has the makings of a leader (in him). / 将を射んと欲せば先ず馬を射よ. He that would the daughter win, must with the mother first begin. 《諺》

しょう¹⁰ 賞は皆川さんが獲得した. The prize went to Miss Minagawa. | Miss Minagawa won the prize.

しょう¹¹ だれがこの難局の衝に当たるか. Who will tackle this difficult job? | Who will bell the cat?

しょう-¹ 彼は小ハーキュリーズだ. He is a Hercules in miniature. / 高山きはいわば小京都だ. Takayama may be called a little Kyoto.

じょう¹ この品は上の部のだ. This is one of the best of its kind. / 彼の学校の成績は上の部です. He does rather well at school.

じょう² それは第3条第1項に規定してある. It is stipulated in Art. 3, paragraph 1.

じょう⁴ 城 ￭犬山城 Inuyama Castle / 城中に in [inside] the castle ; within the gates (of the castle).

じょう⁵ 情 〈感情〉feeling(s) ; (a) sentiment ; 〈情緒〉(an) emotion ; 〈愛情〉love ; affection ; 〈文〉heart ; 〈思いやり〉sympathy ￭親の情 parental affection / 情が移る become attached ((to sb)) ; begin to love sb / 情のある[深い] kindhearted ; 〈文〉tenderhearted ; warmhearted ; affectionate / 情の薄い[ない] hardhearted ; coldhearted ; 〈文〉unfeeling ; heartless ￭情を込めて with feeling ; affectionately ; passionately / …と情を通じる have an affair [a liaison] with sb / 情にもらい softhearted ; susceptible ; sentimental. 文例⇩

じょう⁶ 錠 〈錠前〉a lock ; a padlock (ナンキン錠) ; 〈錠剤〉a tablet ; a pill ￭錠が掛けてある be locked ; be kept under lock and key (物が保管されてある) / 錠を下ろす lock ((a door)) ; fasten a lock / 錠を外す[開ける] unlock / ビタミン錠 a vitamin tablet [pill].

じょう⁷ 嬢 〈少女〉a girl ; 〈若い女性〉a young lady ; 〈娘〉a daughter ￭川上嬢 Miss Kawakami ⇨ おじょうさん

-じょう¹ …上 〈…の点から見て〉《文》from the viewpoint of… ; in terms of… ; 〈…として〉as a matter of… ￭教育上 educationally ((harmful)) ; from the educational point of view / 歴史上 historically ￭歴史上の historical. 文例⇩

-じょう² …畳 ￭1 畳 a mat / 四畳半の部屋 a four-and-a-half-mat room. 文例⇩

じょうあい 情愛 《文》affection ; love ⇨ じょう⁵, あいじょう.

しょうあく 掌握 ￭掌握する hold ; 《文》seize ; grasp ; command / 政権を掌握する take (over) the reins of government ; come into power.

しょうい 小異 ￭小異を捨てて大同につく sink one's differences for the (sake of the) common good ; 《文》ignore [forget (about)] minor conflicts of opinion for the sake of greater common interests.

じょうい¹ 上位 a higher rank ￭上位にある rank higher ((than)) ; be above / 〈文〉superior to] sb in rank ; outrank sb ; 〈優先する〉take precedence ((over)) / 女性[男性]上位 ((a tradition of)) female [male] dominance / 上位力士 high-ranking *sumo* wrestlers. 文例⇩

じょうい² 譲位 abdication (of the throne) ￭譲位する abdicate the throne ((in favor of)).

じょうい³ 攘夷 antiforeign sentiment ; exclusionism ￭攘夷論者 an exclusionist.

しょういいんかい 小委員会 a subcommittee.

しょういぐんじん 傷痍軍人 a disabled ex-serviceman ; a wounded soldier ; 〈総称〉the war disabled.

しょういだん 焼夷弾 an incendiary (bomb [shell]) ; a fire bomb ￭焼夷弾を落とす drop incendiary bombs ((on a city)) ; fire-bomb ((a town)).

しょういん 勝因 the reason for (one's) victory [success].

じょういん¹ 上院 〈一般に〉the Upper House ; 〈英国の〉the House of Lords ; 〈米国その他の国の〉the Senate ￭上院議員 a member of the Upper House ; a Senator.

じょういん² 冗員 ￭冗員を減らす get rid of surplus staff.

じょういん³ 乗員 (a member of) the crew ; a crew member ; a crewman ★乗員全部を集合的に a crew という.

しょうう 小雨 slight rain ; a light [thin] rain. 文例⇩

しょううちゅう 小宇宙 《文》a microcosm ((of human society)) ; 〈星雲〉a galaxy.

じょうえい 上映 ￭上映する put (a movie) on the screen ; screen ; show ; run / 6 週間の上映 (close after) a run of 6 weeks / 近日上映の映画 a forthcoming film / 目下上映中の「ナイル殺人事件」*Death on the Nile* currently showing [on view] / 上映時間 the running time (of a movie). 文例⇩

しょうえん 荘園 a *shoen* ; a manor (in medieval Japan) ￭荘園制度 the manorial system ; manorialism.

じょうえん 上演 ￭上演する put [present] ((a play)) on the stage ; stage ((a drama)) ; mount ((a play)). 文例⇩

しょうおう 照応 《文》correspondence ; 《文》agreement ; 《文》coincidence ￭照応する correspond ((to)) ; agree [《文》accord] ((with)) ; coincide ((with)) ; 《文》be coincident ((with)).

じょうおん 常温 (a) normal temperature.

しょうおんき 消音器 〈ピストルの〉a silencer ; 〈自動車の〉《米》a muffler ; 《英》a silencer ￭消音器を取付けた銃 a gun fitted with a silencer ; a silenced gun / 消音器を外したスポーツカー an unmuffled sports car. 文例⇩

じょう³ すべての数の 0 乗は 1 になる. Any number to the power of zero [nought] equals 1.

じょう⁵ 猛獣にもやはり優しい情がある. Even a fierce brute has a tender spot in its heart. / そんなことは情において忍びない. I cannot find it in my heart to do such a thing.

-じょう¹ 水泳は子供の体育上非常に良い. Swimming is very good for the physical training of young people.

-じょう² あの座敷は何畳ですか. How many mats does that room have?

じょうい¹ この分野では女性上位だ. In this field women are placed [rated] above men. / 大昔の中国では音楽は紳士のたしなみとして必要な科目のうちで上位に置かれていた. In ancient China music was put high on the list of required subjects in the education of gentlemen.

しょうう 小雨決行.《掲示》Meet [Game] canceled only in case of heavy rain.

じょうえい その映画はまだ二流館で上映しています. The film is still on (show) at second-run theaters. / 上映時間は 3 時間です. The film runs for three hours.

じょうえん その劇は明治座で上演中だった. The play was running at the Meijiza. / この脚本は来月国立劇場で上演する. This play will be presented at the National Theater next month.

しょうおんき 一団の若者がオートバイの消音器を外して, 街を飛ばして行った. A group of youths

しょうか

しょうか¹ 昇華 〖化・心理〗 sublimation ¶昇華する[させる] sublimate ; 〖化〗 sublime.

しょうか² 消化 digestion ¶消化する digest ; 〈商品を〉consume ; 〈自分のものにする〉《文》assimilate / 消化しやすい[しにくい] be easy [hard] to digest ; be digestible [indigestible] / 消化を助ける help [《文》promote] the [one's] digestion ; 《文》assist the process of digestion / 消化を妨げる upset [disturb,《文》impair] the digestion / 消化液 digestive juices [fluid(s)] / 消化管 the alimentary canal [tract] ; a digestive tract / 消化器 a digestive organ / 消化系 the digestive [alimentary] system / 消化酵素 digestive enzymes / 消化剤 an anti-indigestion tablet [powder] / 消化不良 indigestion ; dyspepsia. 文例

しょうか³ 消火 fire fighting ¶消火に当たる fight a fire / 消火演習 a fire drill ; a fire-fighting exercise / 消火器 a fire extinguisher /〈泡立(ﾀﾞ)式の〉a foam extinguisher / 消火栓 a (fire) hydrant ; a fireplug / 消火バケツ a fire bucket / 消火ホース a fire hose.

しょうか⁴ 唱歌 〈歌〉a song ;〈歌う事〉singing ¶唱歌が上手[下手]だ be a good [poor, bad] singer ; be good [bad] at singing / 唱歌集 a collection of songs / 唱歌隊 a choir / 唱歌隊長 a choirmaster.

しょうか⁵ 商科 a commercial course [department] ¶商科の学生 a commerce student / 商科大学 a commercial college ; a college of commerce.

しょうか⁶ 商家 a tradesman ; the family [household] of a merchant.

しょうか⁷ 漿果 〖植〗a berry.

しょうか 〖植〗a ginger plant ;〈香料〉ginger ¶豚肉のしょうが焼き ginger-fried pork.

じょうか 浄化 purification ;《文》purgation ; a cleanup ¶浄化する purify ; purge ; clean up / 選挙の浄化運動 a "clean election" movement / 浄化設備〈下水の〉sewage disposal facilities / 浄化槽〈下水の〉a septic tank [for sewage] /〈飲料水の〉a water-purifier tank / 浄化装置 a purifier.

しょうかい¹ 哨戒 ¶哨戒する patrol / 哨戒している,哨戒中である be on patrol / 哨戒機[艇] a patrol plane [boat].

しょうかい² 紹介 (an) introduction ¶紹介する introduce ; present / 皆に紹介する introduce sb all round [《米》around] / …の紹介で with an introduction from... ; on the introduction of... / 紹介者 an introducer / 紹介状 a letter of introduction. 文例

しょうかい³ 商会 a commercial firm [concern] ; a trading company / 山田商会 Yamada & Co.

しょうかい⁴ 照会 an inquiry ; (a) reference ¶照会する inquire 《of sb about sth》; make inquiries 《as to》; apply [write, refer] 《to sb for information》/ 照会先〈身元・信用などの〉a reference / 照会状 a letter of inquiry. 文例

しょうかい⁵ 詳解 a detailed [《文》minute] explanation 《of》; a full commentary 《on》¶詳解する explain in detail [《文》minutely] ;《文》give a detailed account [explanation] 《of》;《文》provide copious annotations 《to a work》.

しょうがい¹ 生涯 a life ; a lifetime ; a career ¶生涯の事業 one's lifework / 生涯の友 one's lifelong friend / 幸せな生涯を送る live [lead] a happy life / 生涯を終える《文》end one's days [life] / これまでの生涯において in one's life / 生涯教育 lifelong education. 文例

しょうがい² 渉外 public relations ; liaison ¶渉外課 the liaison [public relations] section [division] / 渉外係 a public relations man ; a liaison officer.

しょうがい³ 傷害 (an) injury ; (bodily) harm ¶傷害を与える injure ;《文》inflict an injury on sb / 傷害致死で逮捕される be arrested on a charge of (bodily) injury resulting in death / 傷害保険 accident insurance.

しょうがい⁴ 障害 an obstacle ; an obstruction ; a barrier ;《文》an impediment ; a hindrance ; a difficulty ; a snag ; a hitch ;〈体の〉(a) trouble ; a disorder ;〖医〗a lesion〈組織・機能の〉¶障害を乗り越える get over [《文》surmount] an obstacle [a difficulty] / 多くの障害にあう run into [up against] a lot of difficulties [[口語]snags] ;《文》encounter many obstacles / 障害になる be an obstacle 《to》; hinder ; impede ; be [get] in the way 《of》/ 身体障害者 a disabled [physically handicapped] person / 障害飛越(ﾁｮｳ)〈競技〉〖馬術〗show jumping / 障害物 an obstacle ; a barrier / 障害物をとび越える〈馬術競技で〉clear a bar ; take a (clear) jump 《over》/ 障害物競走 a hurdle race (ハードルの); an obstacle race (運動会の); a steeplechase (競馬の). 文例

しょうがい 場外 ¶場外に[で] outside the hall [grounds, arena] / 場外馬券売り場 an off-course[-track] betting office [《英》shop] / 場外ホームラン a homer hit out of the park / 場外ホームランをかっ飛ばす hit [belt] a home run out of the (ball) park.

しょうかいは 小会派 〈議会の〉minor (political) parties.

しょうかく 昇格 ¶昇格する be promoted

---

roared along the street on motorcycles with the mufflers removed.
しょうか² これは消化がいい[悪い]. This is easy to digest [is rather indigestible]. / 暑さがひどいので消化不良を起こした. The severe heat has given me indigestion.
しょうかい² 友人小川氏をご紹介申し上げます. Let me introduce [present] my friend Mr. Ogawa. /

I'd like you to meet my friend Mr. Ogawa. |〈名刺に書くとき〉Introducing my friend Mr. Ogawa.
しょうかい⁴ 詳細は事務所あてにご照会下さい. For particulars apply to the office. / あなたのことはどなたに照会すればわかりますか[あなたの照会先は]. Who are your references? / 直接先方へ照会した

ほうがいい. You'd better write direct to him for information.
しょうがい¹ これが彼の生涯にまた新たな時期を画した. This marked another milestone in his life. / 35年という短い生涯のうちにモーツァルトは600曲以上の作品を書いた. In a brief life of 35 years Mozart wrote more than 600 works. / これは生涯忘れない

しょうがく¹ 小学 ¶小学教育 elementary education / 小学生 schoolchildren (総称); a schoolboy (男); a schoolgirl (女).

しょうがく² 少[小]額 ¶《文》petty sum [amount] / 少額の金 a small [petty] sum of money / 小額紙幣 a low-value bill [note]; a small-[low-]denomination note [bill].

しょうがく³ 商学 ¶商学部 the department of commercial science; the Business School / 商学士[博士] 〈人〉a bachelor [doctor] of commercial science; 〈学位〉Bachelor [Doctor] of Commercial Science (略: B.[D.]C.S.).

しょうがく⁴ 奨学 ¶〈返済を要しない〉a scholarship; (英) a (student) grant [bursary] / 〈返済を要する〉a student loan / 奨学金を受ける win [get, 《文》obtain] a scholarship (of ¥30,000) / 奨学金を出す[与える] offer [award] a scholarship / 奨学資金を設定する set up [establish, create] a scholarship fund / 奨学生 a scholarship student; a student on (a) scholarship. 文例⇩

じょうかく 城郭 a castle; 《文》a citadel.

しょうがつ 正月 〈1月〉January (略: Jan.); 〈新年〉the New Year; 〈元旦〉New Year's Day; 《米口語》New Year's.

しょうがっこう 小学校 a primary [an elementary] school; (米) a grade school ¶小学校教員 a primary [(米) grade] school teacher; a primary teacher; a schoolmaster (男); a schoolmistress (女). 文例⇩

しょうかほう 消夏法 a way of spending the summer [forgetting the summer heat].

じょうかまち 城下町 a castle town.

しょうかん¹ 召喚 《法》a summons (pl. -monses); a call ¶召喚する call; summon; (米) subpoena; serve sb with a summons; issue a summons (against sb); serve a subpo(e)na [summons] (on sb) / 召喚状 a subpoena; a (writ of) summons.

しょうかん² 召還 ¶召還する recall; call [order] sb back / 本国に召還される be summoned [ordered] home.

しょうかん³ 将官 〈陸軍〉a general (officer); 〈海軍〉a flag officer; an admiral.

しょうかん⁴ 償還 (a) repayment; a refund; redemption ¶償還する repay; refund; redeem 《national bonds》; pay off; amortize (年賦で) / 10年後に償還の債券 a bond redeemable in ten years / 償還期限 the term [period] of redemption; the date of maturity (満期日) / 償還期限になる fall [be] due for redemption. 文例⇩

しょうがん 賞玩 ¶賞玩する appreciate; admire; enjoy; 〈賞美する〉《文》prize.

じょうかん¹ 上官 a higher [senior] officer [official].

じょうかん² 情感 feeling ¶情感をこめてピアノをひく play the piano with (great) feeling.

しょうかんしゅう 商慣習 (according to) business [commercial] usage; (normal) business [commercial] practice.

しょうき¹ 正気 ¶正気の〈狂っていない〉sane; 〈しらふの〉sober / 正気を失う〈気絶する〉lose consciousness; faint; 〈発狂する〉lose one's senses [wits]; go mad / 正気に返る come to oneself; be oneself again; come to one's senses; recover one's wits / 正気である be in one's right mind; be (quite) right in the [one's] head ★ これらの表現は疑問文否定文で使う / 正気でない be out of one's senses [(right) mind]; be mad / 正気づかせる bring sb round [to (his) senses]. 文例⇩

しょうき² 商機 《miss, let slip, seize》a business opportunity [a chance to do business]. 文例⇩

しょうき³ 勝機 a chance of victory; a chance to win (the game).

しょうぎ¹ 床机 a (camp) stool.

しょうぎ² 省議 《refer a matter to》the departmental council.

しょうぎ³ 将棋 shogi; Japanese chess ¶将棋のこま a man; a piece / 将棋を指す play [have a game of] shogi (with) / 将棋盤 a shogi board / 将棋倒しになる fall down one after another; fall [be knocked] over like dominoes [ninepins].

じょうき¹ 上気 ¶上気する have a rush of blood to the head / 上気したほお flushed cheeks.

じょうき² 上記 ¶上記の《文》the above; 《文》the above-mentioned[-named]; 《文》the aforesaid / 上記のように《文》as stated above; 《文》as aforesaid.

じょうき³ 常軌 ¶常軌を逸した eccentric; 《文》deviant; abnormal; preposterous.

じょうき⁴ 蒸気 〈湯気〉steam; 〈水蒸気〉vapor ¶蒸気を起こる generate steam / 蒸気を上げる give off steam; steam / 蒸気を止める shut off the steam / 蒸気で動く〈駆動する〉steam-driven 《trains》; steam-powered 《generators》/ 蒸気圧[熱] the pressure [heat] of (the) steam; steam pressure [heat] / 蒸気機関 a steam engine / 蒸気機関車 a steam locomotive ★ この略の SL は和製英語, 英・米では通じない / 蒸気タービン a steam turbine / 蒸気暖房装置 a steam-heating system; a steam heater.

じょうぎ¹ 定規 a ruler; a rule; a square (直角

でしょう. I won't forget it for the rest of my life.

しょうがく³ 核保有国の増加は軍備撤廃への新たな障害となるであろう. An increase in the number of nuclear powers will place new hurdles on the road to disarmament.

しょうがく⁴ 彼は奨学金をもらってアメリカに留学中です. He is studying in the United States on a scholarship.

しょうがっこう うちの社長は小学校を出ただけだ. Our president has had only an elementary school education.

しょうかん⁴ 本公債の償還期限は1985年である. The bond matures [will be due for redemption] in 1985.

しょうき¹ 君は正気で言っているのか. Are you serious? | You can't mean it (seriously)! | 全く正気のさたではない. It's sheer madness.

しょうき² 彼は商機を見るに敏であった. He was always quick to

じょうぎ — しょうきょく

の）／¶定規で引いた線 a ruled line. 文例⇩

じょうぎ[2] 情義 (ties of) friendship; friendly feelings ¶情義に厚い be very friendly; 《文》 be cordial ((to a friend)).

じょうきげん 上機嫌 ¶上機嫌で in high [good] spirits; in a (high) good humor; (be) all smiles; cheerfully. 文例⇩

しょうきゃく[1] 焼却 ¶焼却する destroy sth by fire; 《文》 commit sth to the flames; burn sth (up); throw sth into the fire; incinerate ／焼却炉[器] an incinerator.

しょうきゃく[2] 償却 (a) repayment; redemption (公社債の); amortization (年賦による); 〈減価償却〉depreciation ¶償却する repay; pay [clear] off; redeem; amortize ／償却資金[積立金] a redemption fund; a sinking fund (減債).

じょうきゃく 乗客 a passenger ¶乗客専務 (車掌) 《米》a conductor, 《英》a guard (on a passenger train)／乗客名簿 a passenger list; a register [list] of passengers.

しょうきゅう[1] 昇級 (a) promotion; 《文》 advancement; 《文》 preferment ¶昇級する be promoted [raised] ((to a higher grade)); rise in rank／昇級が早い, どんどん昇級する get [《文》] obtain, win] rapid promotion.

しょうきゅう[2] 昇給 a rise [an increase, 《米》a raise] in salary [pay]; a pay rise [increase]; a rise; 《米》a raise ¶昇給する have one's salary raised; get a rise [《米》raise] in (one's) pay [salary]／昇給率 the rate of increase in salary.

じょうきゅう 上級 a high(er) rank; an upper [a higher] grade [level, class] ¶上級の upper(-class); higher(-grade); senior (officials); advanced (courses)／上級の学校 a school of higher grade／上級公務員 high-ranking government officials; 《文》 government officials in the upper echelon(s)／上級裁判所 a higher court／上級職についている have [be in] a senior position [post] (in the Finance Ministry)／上級生 an upper-class student, 《米》 an upperclassman (大学や高等学校の4年生または は3年生).

しょうきょ 消去 ¶消去する eliminate; cancel／消去法 《数》 (by) (a process of) elimination.

しょうきょう 商況 business [market] conditions; the business situation; (the state of) the market ¶商況不振 a dull [an inactive] market; (a) depression (in trade)／商況報告 a market report [bulletin].

しょうぎょう 商業 commerce; business; trade ¶商業の commercial; business; 《文》mercantile／商業の中心地 a center of commerce; a commercial [mercantile] center／商業上 commercially; from the commercial point of view／商業を営む 《文》 engage in business; carry on trade／商業化する commercialize; put sth on a commercial basis; put ((one's invention)) into commercial service／商業英語 business [commercial] English／商業界 the commercial world; business circles／商業高等学校 a commercial high school／商業国 a mercantile nation／商業主義 commercialism／商業地理［簿記] commercial geography [bookkeeping]／商業地区 the business area [sections, districts]／商業手形《商》a commercial [mercantile] bill; commercial paper (総称)／商業道徳 business morality／商業都市 a commercial [merchant] town [city]／商業美術 commercial art／商業文 business [commercial] correspondence／商業放送 commercial broadcasting／〈1回の〉a commercial [sponsored] broadcast [telecast, program]／商業放送を開始する begin broadcasting [telecasting] on a commercial basis／商業放送局 a commercial radio [TV] station. 文例⇩

じょうきょう[1] 上京 ¶上京する come [go] (up) to Tokyo／上京中である be (up) in Tokyo. 用法 首都が高いところにあるという観念は英語にもあり go up to London と言うが、一方で北が高く南が低いという感じがあり、そのために go down to London と言うこともよくある。

じょうきょう[2] 状［情]況 the state of affairs [things]; things; conditions; circumstances; a situation; a setting; 《文》 the context ¶目下の状況では in the present situation [state of things]; as the situation now stands; as things stand [are]; under the existing conditions／状況証拠 (a) circumstantial [indirect] evidence／状況判断 one's judgment [assessment] of the situation. 文例⇩

しょうきょく[1] 小曲 a short piece (of music).

しょうきょく[2] 消極 ¶消極的な not active enough; 《文》 passive; halfhearted; unenterprising; 《文》 negative ¶消極的に 《文》negatively; 《文》passively; (act) in a halfhearted way／消極主義 negativism／消極性 passivity／

---

seize a business opportunity.

じょうぎ[1] その文には 定規できちんと下線が引いてあった。There was a neat line ruled under the sentence.

じょうきげん だれも彼も誠に申し分ない上機嫌だった。Everybody was in the very best of spirits.／彼は上機嫌で家に帰った。He went home highly pleased [all smiles].

しょうぎょう これは現在の生産量ではまだ 商業的に成立しません。It is not yet being produced in commercial quantities [on a commercial scale].／札幌は北海道第一の商業都市である。Sapporo is the biggest commercial center [center of commerce] in Hokkaido.

じょうきょう[2] そちらの状況をお知らせ下さい。Please let me know how matters stand with you.／どんなに状況がいい時でもこの岩壁をよじ登るのには危険が伴う。Under the best of circumstances, climbing this rock face involves some danger.／目下の進捗状況では 今月中に完成は おぼつかない。Judging from the progress that has been made so far, there is little likelihood [hope] of its being completed in the course of this month.／情況が情況だったものだから、彼女と話している暇はなかった。Things being what they were, I didn't have time to talk to her.／状況証拠によると、君が容疑者ということになる。The circumstantial evidence points to you as a suspect.

しょうきょく[2] 君のやり方ではまだ 消極的だ。You still aren't going

しょうきん 消極政策 a negative policy／消極戦法 passive tactics. 文例↓

しょうきん 賞金 prize money; a prize; a (money [cash]) reward; a premium《奨励のための》 ¶賞金を出す[与える, 獲得する] offer [award, win] a prize／賞金かせぎ《口語》pot-hunting;〈人〉a pothunter. 文例↓

じょうきん 常勤 full-time employment ¶常勤の full-time〈workers〉／常勤者 a full-time [whole-time] employee; a full-timer.

しょうきんるい 渉禽類《鳥》wading birds.

じょうくう 上空《空》the sky; the skies《of Tokyo》;〈空の高い所〉the upper air ¶パリの上空を飛ぶ fly over Paris／500 メートルの上空で at a height [altitude] of 500 meters／はるか上空で far up in the sky.

しょうぐん 将軍 a general;〈武家時代の〉a shogun ¶乃木将軍 General Nogi／将軍家光の時代に in the shogunate of Iemitsu.

しょうくんきょく 賞勲局 the Decoration Bureau.

じょうげ 上下 top and bottom; the upper and lower sides [parts]; high and low;〈動き〉rise and fall ¶上下する go up and down; rise and fall;〈変動する〉《文》fluctuate; seesaw／上下の別なく《文》irrespective of rank or standing;《文》high and low alike／上下に up and down; above and below;〈高く低く〉high and low／〈鉄道の〉上下線 both up and down tracks [lines]／上下動 a vertical [an up-and-down] motion;〈地震の〉a vertical shock. 文例↓

しょうけい 小計 a subtotal ¶小計を出す do a partial sum.

じょうけい 情景 a scene; a sight; a view.

しょうけいもじ 象形文字〈古代エジプトなどの〉a hieroglyph; a hieroglyphic (character);〈中国・日本などの〉a pictograph.

しょうげき 衝撃 a shock; an impact; percussion ¶衝撃を与える shock; give sb a shock; make an impact《on》／衝撃に耐えうる shock-resistant／衝撃波《物》a shock wave. 文例↓

しょうけつ 猖獗 ¶猖獗を極める rage;《文》be rife;《文》be rampant.

しょうけん 証券 a bill; a bond;〈有価証券〉a security ¶証券会社 a stock [securities] company; a stock brokerage firm／証券業者 a stockbroker; a bill broker／証券市場 a security [stock] market.

しょうげん[1] 証言《法》testimony; (verbal) evidence;《文》witness ¶証言する give evidence; testify《to a fact, that...》; swear [depose]《to》; attest《to》／目撃者の証言《give》eyewitness evidence／証言台に立つ《米》take the witness stand;《英》enter the witness box.

しょうげん[2] 象限《数》a quadrant.

じょうけん 条件 a condition; terms; a qualification《制限的な》 ¶会員になるための条件 a membership requirement／条件を付ける make [set] conditions;《文》impose conditions《on》;《文》attach conditions《to》／無条件で⇒むじょうけん／…という条件で[の下に] on condition that...; provided that...;《文》under the condition that...／条件付きの conditional;《文》subject to conditions;《文》qualified〈consent〉／条件闘争 a limited struggle／条件反射[反応]《心理・生理》(develop) a conditioned reflex [response]／条件文[節]《文法》a conditional sentence [clause].

じょうげん[1] 上弦 ¶上弦の月 a young [an early crescent] moon.

じょうげん[2] 上限《put [set]》an upper limit《on [to] the size》; a maximum;《数》the supremum; the least upper bound《略: lub》.

しょうこ 証拠 evidence; (a) proof;《法》(a) testimony ¶証拠をあげる give [《文》adduce, produce, bring forward] evidence《to show that...》; cite sth as proof《of》／証拠を隠滅する destroy evidence《of, as to》／証拠を握る obtain [secure] proof／確か[わずか]な証拠に基づいて on reliable [slight] evidence／証拠立てる prove;《文》evidence;《文》testify to;《文》attest《to》; show (clearly); confirm; bear out／証拠不充分で on the ground of insufficient evidence／証拠固めをする gather [collect] evidence／証拠金 a deposit; deposit money／証拠書類 documentary evidence／証拠調べ the taking of evidence／証拠物(件) evidence; an exhibit. 文例↓

しょうご 正午 noon; midday ¶正午に at (twelve) noon; at midday.

じょうご[1] 上戸 a drinker; a tippler;《口語》a boozer ¶泣き[笑い]上戸 ⇒なきじょうご, わらいじょうご.

じょうご[2] 漏斗 a funnel ¶じょうご形の funnel-shaped.

しょうこう[1] 小康 a (temporary) lull; a breathing space;《米》breathing room ¶小康を得る get a breathing space.

---

far enough.

しょうきん 彼は1等に当選して10万円の賞金を得た。He won [carried off] the first prize of 100,000 yen.

じょうげ 東海道線は上下線とも不通になっている。The service of both up and down trains on the Tokaido Line is suspended.／昨夜の地震は上下動であった。The motion of the earthquake last night was vertical [an up-and-down].

しょうげき そのニュースを聞いて私は大きな衝撃を受けた。The news gave me a great shock.／I was terribly shocked at the news.

じょうけん 君にやってもいい。ただし, それには条件がある。You can have it, on certain conditions.／賛成は賛成だが条件つきで賛成だ。I do agree, but with qualifications.／2人の間に協定額以上の金を使わないという条件が定められた。It was agreed as a condition between us that neither of us should spend more than the agreed sum.

しょうこ あくびは面白くない証拠だ。Yawning is a sign that you are bored [not interested].／人を疑うのは常に心の弱い証拠だ。Suspicion is always indicative of a weak mind.／彼がそわそわしていたのが, 身にやましい所のある何よりの証拠だ。Nothing was better evidence of his guilty conscience than the fact that he looked ill at ease.／証拠が明らかだったので, 判事は有罪を宣告した。The evidence being clear against him, the judge declared him guilty.

しょうこう² 昇汞 【化】mercuric chloride; corrosive sublimate. ¶昇汞水 a solution of corrosive sublimate.

しょうこう³ 昇降 《文》ascent and descent; rise and fall; 〈変動〉fluctuations ¶昇降する go [move] up and down; rise and fall; fluctuate / 昇降口 an entrance; 〈船の〉hatch(way) /〈飛行機の〉昇降舵 an elevator.

しょうこう⁴ 将校 an [a commissioned] officer ¶陸軍将校 a military officer.

しょうこう⁵ 症候 a symptom ⇒しょうじょう² ¶症候群 【医】a syndrome.

しょうこう⁶ 商工 ¶商工会議所 the Chamber of Commerce and Industry / 商工業 commerce and industry.

しょうこう⁷ 焼香 ¶焼香する burn [offer] incense 《for the repose of a departed soul》.

しょうごう¹ 称号 a title; a name; a degree 〈学位〉.

しょうごう² 照合 (a) comparison; 《文》collation; checking; a check ¶照合する compare 《with》; collate sth 《with》; 《文》verify; check sth 《up》《against, with》.

じょうこう¹ 上皇 【史】a retired emperor.

じょうこう² 条項 articles; clauses; 〈各項・項目〉a provision; terms ¶契約書に…の旨の条項を加える add to the contract a clause to the effect that 《the principal shall be repaid in one year》.

じょうこう³ 乗降 getting on and off 《a train》; 《文》boarding and alighting ¶乗降客 passengers getting on and off 《a train》.

しょうこうい 商行為 a commercial [business] transaction.

しょうこうねつ 猩紅熱 【医】scarlet fever; scarlatina.

しょうこく 小国 a small country [nation]; a minor [lesser] power.

しょうこく² 生国 《文》one's native country; 《文》the country of one's birth.

じょうこく 上告 【法】a final appeal ¶上告する make a final appeal; appeal [make an appeal] to a final court / 上告を棄却する reject [dismiss] a final appeal / 上告裁判所 a court of final appeal; a court of last resort. 文例❽

しょうこり 性懲り ¶性懲りもなく《文》incorrigibly; in spite of one's bitter experience(s). 文例❽

しょうこん 商魂 commercial enthusiasm [《文》fervor]; 《aggressive》salesmanship ¶商魂たくましい be a shrewd salesman; be a smart businessman; be very business-minded[-conscious].

しょうさ 小差 ¶小差で《win》by a narrow [slim] margin.

じょうざ 上座 ⇒ かみざ.

しょうさい 商才 business ability [talent] ¶商才がある have a good head for business; have plenty of business sense. 文例❽

しょうさい² 詳細 details; 《文》particulars ¶詳細な detailed; 《文》minute; 《文》circumstantial / 詳細に in detail; 《文》minutely; at length; 《文》at large; fully; in full / 詳細にわたる, 詳細に述べる go 《文》enter] into details [《文》particulars]; give a full [circumstantial] account 《of》; enlarge [《文》expatiate] 《on》; 《文》relate in detail; 《文》detail the particulars 《of》. 文例❽　　　　　「a citadel.

じょうさい 城砦 a fortress; a stronghold; 《文》**じょうざい¹** 浄財 an offering of money; a subscription; a donation ¶浄財を集める collect voluntary subscriptions 《for》.

じょうざい² 錠剤 a tablet; a pill 〈丸薬〉.

じょうさく 上策 a good plan [idea]; the best policy. 文例❽

じょうさし 状差し a letter rack.

しょうさっし 小冊子 a booklet; a pamphlet; a brochure 〈観光案内など〉; a tract 〈宗教・政治関係の〉.

しょうさん¹ 消散 ¶消散する 《文》disperse; disappear; vanish; lift 〈もやなどが〉.

しょうさん² 硝酸 【化】nitric acid ¶硝酸塩 nitrate / 硝酸銀 silver nitrate; nitrate of silver.

しょうさん³ 勝算 a chance of success [winning]; 《文》prospects of victory ¶勝算がある[ない] stand a fair [no] chance of success; have (all) the odds in one's favor [against one]; be in [out of] the running. 文例❽

しょうさん⁴ 称[賞]賛 praise; applause; admiration ¶称賛する praise; admire; applaud; 《文》extol; speak highly [in high terms] of; put in a good word for sb / 口を極めて称賛する praise [extol] sb sky-high [to the skies] / 称

じょうこく 彼は最高裁判所に上告した。He appealed to the Supreme Court. / 上告の結果原判決は破棄された。On final appeal the judgment of the lower court was reversed.

しょうこり 性懲りもなくまた株に手を出している。He appears not to have learned his lesson; he has begun to dabble in stocks again. | He is an incorrigible fool to have begun dabbling in stocks again.

しょうさ 彼は浅田氏に500票の小差で勝った。He won his victory over Mr. Asada by the narrow margin of 500 votes.

しょうさい¹ あの男は商才にたけている。He is a shrewd businessman.

しょうさい² 氏の説明は詳細を極めたものであった。He explained everything down to the minutest details.

じょうさく それ以上の上策はない。It's the best thing you can do.

しょうさん³ 我々に勝算がある[ない]。The odds are in our favor [against us]. / 初めから勝算がなかった。It was a lost cause from the start.

しょうさん⁴ 将軍は部下の勇気を称賛した。The general praised his men for their bravery. / 世人は口を極めて彼を称賛した。People were loud in his praises. / 君がこれを独力でやりとげたのはことに称賛に値する。It is greatly to your credit that you have done it all by yourself. / クリスチャンと自称している彼からそのような小説を書いたと聞いて僕は驚いた。I was surprised to hear that he, who called himself a Christian, had found something good to say for such a novel as this.

しょうじ² その火事で13人の焼死者が出た。The fire killed thir-

じょうさん 賛すべき 《文》praiseworthy；《文》admirable；《文》laudable / 称賛を博する win [call forth] the admiration (of) / 称賛者 an admirer. 文例↓

じょうさん 蒸散 【植】transpiration ¶蒸散する transpire.

しょうし¹ 笑止 ¶笑止な〈笑うべき〉laughable；ridiculous；ludicrous；absurd；〈哀れむべき〉《文》pitiable；pitiful / 笑止千万である be highly ridiculous；be quite absurd.

しょうし² 焼死 ¶焼死する be burned to death；《文》perish in the flames / 焼死体 a charred body. 文例↓

しょうし³ 証紙 a certificate stamp.

しょうじ¹ 小事 a trifle；a small [trifling, trivial] matter ¶小事にこだわらない do not care [worry] about trifles.

しょうじ² 正時 ¶(毎)正時に (every hour) on the hour. 文例↓

しょうじ³ 障子 a shoji；a shoji screen；a paper sliding door ¶ガラス障子 a glass-fitted shoji.

じょうし¹ 上司 one's superior(s)；one's boss(-es)；《口語》the higher-ups in one's firm [office]；one's chief.

じょうし² 城址 the ruins of a castle；the site of an ancient castle.

じょうし³ 情死 ⇒ しんじゅう¹.

じょうじ¹ 情事 a love affair；an affair《with》；a romance；《文》an amour.

じょうじ² 常時 ⇒ ふだん、へいじょう¹ ¶常時運転 regular (bus) service / 常時利用者 a regular user (customer, visitor, passenger).

しょうじがいしゃ 商事会社 a trading company [firm].

しょうじき 正直 honesty；《文》uprightness；《文》integrity；《文》veracity；truthfulness ¶正直な〈行ないが正しい〉honest；straightforward；《文》upright；〈うそを言わない〉truthful / 正直に honestly；《文》faithfully；〈包まずに〉frankly；straightforwardly；truthfully / 正直に言えば to tell the truth；honestly；speaking truthfully；to be frank [honest] with you；candidly [frankly] speaking / 正直そうな honest-looking / 正直者 an honest person. 文例↓

じょうしき 常識 common sense；practical sense [《文》wisdom；《口語》horse sense；〈周知の事〉common knowledge ¶…は常識だ it is obvious that…；it goes without saying that…；it is taken for granted that… / 常識的な common-sense；sensible；practical；normal；ordinary；matter-of-fact；〈新味のない〉commonplace；trivial / 常識的に(は) in common-sense terms；ordinarily / 常識がある have (plenty of, a good deal of) common sense；be sensible / 常識がない have no [《文》lack] common sense；be senseless；《口語》be dumb / 常識を付ける increase one's general knowledge / 常識家 a sensible person / 常識試験(テスト) a general knowledge test；〈問題〉a general knowledge paper / 常識人 a straightforward [plain] common-sense man. 文例↓

しょうしつ¹ 消失 ⇒ きえる (消え失せる) ¶消失点《透視画法》a vanishing point.

しょうしつ² 焼失 ¶焼失する be destroyed by fire；be burned down；《文》be reduced to ashes；go up in smoke / 家財道具を焼失する lose all one's household goods in a fire / 焼失を免れる escape the fire / 焼失家屋 houses burned down / 焼失区域 the burned-out [《文》ravaged, devastated] district [area].

じょうしつ 上質 ¶上質の《文》《paper》of fine [choice] quality；high-quality [-grade] (protein).

じょうじつ 情実 《文》personal considerations [motives]；〈くえこひいき〉favoritism ¶情実に左右される[とらわれる] be influenced [swayed] by personal considerations / 情実人事 (the appointment (of sb to a position) through) favoritism. 文例↓

しょうしみん 小市民 a petty [petit] bourgeois；〈階級〉the petty bourgeoisie；the lower middle class.

しょうしゃ¹ 商社 a trading company [firm]；a business [trading] concern ¶商社マン a trading company employee.

しょうしゃ² 勝者 a winner；a victor；《文》a conqueror (征服者)；〈総称〉《文》the victorious.

しょうしゃ³ 照射 irradiation ¶照射する irradiate / エックス線を照射する X-ray (sb's leg)；apply X-rays to (sb's neck).

しょうしゃ⁴ 瀟洒 ¶しょうしゃな elegant；《文》tasteful；smart；neat；《文》refined；styl-

---

teen people. | Thirteen persons were trapped [killed] in the fire.

しょうじ¹ バスは30分間隔で、正時と30分に出ています。Buses leave at thirty-minute intervals, on the hour and at half past.

しょうじき 正直の話役はいささかびっくりしましたよ。I confess I was somewhat taken aback. / 君は言うことがいつも正直すぎるよ。You are always too truthful. / 正直者が損をする世の中だ。We are living in a world where honesty does not pay. / 正直の頭に神宿る。God is in an honest man's heart. | God dwells in an honest heart. / 正直は最善の策。Honesty is the best policy. 【諺】

じょうしき 今日では常識のようになっている考えで、かつては全くそうではなかったものがたくさんある。Many ideas that are taken for granted [seem obvious] today were once the very opposite. / そんなことは常識だ。Everybody knows that. | It is a matter of common knowledge. / そのぐらいの事は常識でわかるはずだ。Common sense ought to tell you as much. / 何も知らない私たちでも、放射能とその生物に及ぼす影響について常識程度の知識は持ち合わせている。Though we are not particularly well-informed, we have a layman's knowledge of radioactivity and its biological effects.

じょうじつ 公事に情実は禁物だ。Private [Personal] considerations must not enter into public affairs. / 彼は少しも情実に動かされない。He is unmoved by any private consideration whatsoever. / あの会社内ではだいぶ情

しょうじゃ 生者 [文例⇩]
じょうしゃ 乗車 ¶乗車する get on a train [bus]; get in a car /（タクシーが）乗車拒否をする refuse (to accept) passengers [customers] / 乗車口 the entrance to a platform / 乗車券 a train [bus, streetcar] ticket / 乗車券売場 a ticket window /（英）a booking office / 乗車賃 a fare /〈鉄道の〉a rail /（米）railroad,（英）railway / 電車などの a carfare.
しょうしゃく 照尺 （銃の）the sight(s); a gun-sight.
じょうしゅ[1] 城主 the lord (of a castle).
じょうしゅ[2] 情趣 〈感じ〉《文》a sentiment;〈雰囲気〉(an) atmosphere;〈趣〉an artistic effect (in a painting) ¶情趣に富んだ charming; appealing; quaint.
じょうじゅ 成就 《文》accomplishment;《文》achievement;〈実現〉《文》realization ¶成就する carry out (a plan);《文》accomplish (one's purpose);《文》achieve (an end);《文》attain (one's object); complete (a project);《文》realize (one's wishes); succeed (in doing).
しょうしゅう 召[招]集 a call; a summons (pl. -monses);〈軍隊・乗組員などの〉a muster;〈軍隊への〉a call-up;（米）a draft;〈会議の〉《文》convocation ¶召[招]集する〈会議を〉call (a committee) (into session); convene;《文》convoke; summon;〈軍隊を〉muster; call up;〈軍隊に〉call sb into the army;（米）draft sb (for service) / 軍隊に召集される be called into [up to] the armed forces; be called up for (military) service / 召集解除になる be demobilized /〈英口語〉be demobbed / 召集令 a draft (call) / 召集令状（米）a draft card /（英）one's call-up papers. [文例⇩]
しょうじゅう 小銃 a rifle ¶小銃弾 a bullet.
じょうしゅう 常習 ¶常習的の《文》habitual; customary; confirmed; regular / 常習的に…する be in the habit of doing / 常習犯 a habitual [confirmed] criminal;《文》a recidivist; a habitual offender (of the rules). [文例⇩]
しょうじゅつ 詳述 ⇨しょうせつ[3].
じょうじゅつ 上述 ⇨じょうき[2].
じょうしゅび 上首尾 a (great) success; a satisfactory [《文》happy] result ¶上首尾に successfully; satisfactorily. [文例⇩]
しょうじゅん 照準 ¶照準を合わせる aim (at); set [get] one's sights (on); take aim (at);（accurately）align a sight (at rifle); lay (a gun) / 照準器 a sighting device.
じょうじゅん 上旬 the first ten days [the early part] (of the month) ¶7月上旬に at the beginning of July; early in July / 来月上旬に early next month.
しょうしょ 証書 a bond; a deed; a paper; a document; an instrument; a certificate (証明書) ¶証書を作成する prepare [write out, draw out] a deed; execute a deed (法の規定どおり正式に) / 証書にする put (a contract) in writing; commit (an agreement) to writing.
しょうじょ 少女 a little [young] girl;《文》a maiden ¶少女らしい, 少女趣味の (school-)girlish (dresses) / 少女歌劇 a girls' opera / 少女時代 girlhood / 少女のための a story for young girls.
じょうしょ 情緒 ⇨じょうちょ.
しょうしょう 少々 ⇨すこし, ちょっと. [文例⇩]
しょうじょう[1] 小乗《仏教》Hinayana; Theravada; the Lesser Vehicle ¶小乗仏教 Hinayana [Theravada] Buddhism / 小乗的見地 a narrow-minded [shortsighted] view.
しょうじょう[2] 症状 〈徴候〉(disease) symptoms;〈容態〉the condition of a patient ¶流感の症状を呈する show [develop] symptoms of influenza.
しょうじょう[3] 猩々 ⇨オランウータン.
しょうじょう[4] 賞状 《award》a certificate of merit; a letter of commendation ((from the Governor)).
しょうじょう[5] 蕭条 ¶蕭条たる bleak; dreary, desolate; deserted; lonesome / 蕭条たる冬景色 a bleak wintry scene.
じょうしょう[1] 上昇 a rise (in altitude);《文》an ascent; an increase; an upturn ¶上昇する rise;《文》ascend; go up / 上昇しつつある be rising; be on the rise / 上昇曲線 an upward [a rising] curve / 上昇気流, an updraft; an up-current of air; a rising air current [draft] /《航空》a bump;〈温暖気流〉《気象》a thermal / 上昇気流に乗る ride an up-current of air; ride updrafts / 上昇傾向 an upward tendency; a rising trend / 上昇限度《航空》the (absolute) ceiling / 上昇速度《航空》a rate of climb /（飛行機の）上昇力 climbing power. [文例⇩]
じょうしょう[2] 常勝 ¶常勝の《文》ever-victorious;《文》invincible.
じょうじょう[1] 上々 ¶上々の very fine; the very best; superb. [文例⇩]
じょうじょう[2] 上場 〈上演する〉⇨じょうえん;《株式》list《stocks》/ 上場される

実が行なわれている. Favoritism is rife in that firm.
しょうじゃ 生者必滅. All that has life [All living things] must die.
じょうしゃ ご乗車の方はお急ぎ下さい. All aboard! / ご乗車の方は3列にお並び下さい. Would passengers boarding this train please line up in threes. / どなたも乗車券をお切らせ願います. All fares, please.
しょうしゅう 臨時国会が近く召集される. A special session of the Diet will soon be convened. / 昨日アメリカ陸軍は6万人に召集令を発した. Yesterday the U.S. Army issued a draft call for 60,000 men.
じょうしゅう 昔は海賊が瀬戸内海の船を常習的に襲ったものだった. In days gone by, pirates routinely preyed on merchantmen in the Inland Sea. / 彼は遅刻の常習犯だ. He is always late (for appointments). /〈学校などで〉He comes late for school all too often.
じょうしゅび 交渉の結果は上首尾だった. The negotiations were concluded very successfully [most satisfactorily].
しょうしょう 少々お待ち下さい. Please wait a moment. / 僕は少々不満だ. I am not quite [entirely] satisfied. / 少々御免下さい. Excuse me, please.

じょうじょう 【株式】 be listed ((on the Tokyo Stock Exchange)) / 上場[非上場]株 listed [unlisted] stocks [shares].

じょうじょう³ 情状 circumstances; conditions ¶情状を酌量する take the circumstances into consideration [account] ;《文》allow for *sb's* circumstances / 情状を酌量して《文》in consideration of the (extenuating [mitigating]) circumstances / 情状酌量を求める plead extenuating circumstances. 文例↓

しょうじょうばえ 【昆】 a drosophila (*pl.* -lae) ; a fruit fly.

しょうしょく 小[少]食 ¶小食である have a small appetite ; do not eat much ;《口語》eat like a bird ; be a small eater / 小食家 a light [poor] eater.

じょうしょく 常食 staple [daily] food ; a diet ¶米を常食とする live [subsist] on rice.

しょうじる 生じる 〈産出する〉produce ; yield ; create ;《文》generate ;〈できる〉come ((out of, from)) ; take shape [《文》form] ;〈引き起こす〉cause ;《文》bring about ;《文》give rise [birth] to ;《文》engender ;〈起こる〉happen ; take place ; come about ;〈発生する〉arise ((from)) ;《文》originate ((in, from)) ;《文》come into being [existence] ;《文》result ((from)) ;〈利子などが〉accrue ((from)) ¶火災によって生じた損害 the damage caused by fire. 文例↓

じょうじる 乗じる 〈つけ込む〉take advantage [《文》avail *oneself*] of (*sb's* weakness) ; seize (on) ((an opportunity)) ;《口語》cash in ((on)) ;《文》exploit ((the situation)) ;《数》multiply ¶…に乗じて taking advantage of… ; profiting by (*sb's* ignorance) ; under cover of ((darkness)).

しょうしん¹ 小心 小心な 〈憶病な〉timid ; cowardly ;《文》timorous ;《文》fainthearted ;《俗》chicken ; 〈用心深い〉《文》prudent ; cautious / 小心翼々として《文》scrupulously ; cautiously ;《文》with circumspection ; meticulously / 小心者 a timid person ; a coward.

しょうしん² 昇進 (a) promotion ;《文》advancement ;《文》(a) preferment ; a rise in rank ¶昇進する be promoted ((manager)) ; be promoted [《文》advanced] ((to manager, to the position of manager)) ; rise in rank ; get ahead ;《文》gain preferment / 昇進させる promote ; raise. 文例↓

しょうしん³ 傷心 a broken heart ;《文》grief ; sorrow ;《文》distress ¶傷心の brokenhearted ; heartbroken ;《文》grief-stricken ; downhearted.

しょうじん¹ 小人 a small-minded person ;《文》a man of small caliber. 文例↓

しょうじん² 精進 〈精励〉devotion ;《文》close application ; 〈菜食〉《文》abstinence from (eating) fish and meat ¶精進する〈精励する〉devote [apply] *oneself* ((to)) ; 〈菜食する〉《文》abstain from eating fish and meat ; practice vegetarianism / 精進揚げ fried vegetables / 精進日 a day of abstinence / 精進料理 a vegetarian diet [dish, meal].

じょうしん 上申 ¶上申する report ((to a higher official)) ; lay a report before ((the authorities)) ; submit a report ((to *one's* chief)) / 上申書 (submit) a (written) report [statement].

じょうじん 常人 an ordinary [average] person ¶常人と異なる be out of the common run of people ; be out of the ordinary ; be extraordinary. 文例↓

しょうしんじさつ 焼身自殺 burning *oneself* to death ; self-burning ;《文》self-immolation ¶焼身自殺する burn *oneself* to death ; commit suicide by fire ;《文》immolate *oneself*.

しょうしんしょうめい 正真正銘 ¶正真正銘の true ; genuine ; real ; authentic.

じょうず 上手 〈熟練〉skill ;《文》dexterity ; cleverness ;《文》proficiency ; 〈巧みな人〉an expert ¶上手な good ((at)) ; skillful ((in)) ;《文》dexterous ((in, at)) ;《文》proficient ((in)) ; clever ((workers, works)) ★「上手な」に相当する最も普通の英語は good ((at)) である。skillful がともすれば使われがちであるが, この語は「熟練した」「腕のある」の意で, その意味範囲はかなり限られており, 無条件に「上手な」=skillful としてはいけない。 / 上手なお世辞 a clever [《文》an adroit,《文》a well-turned] compliment / 泳ぎの上手な人 a good swimmer / 上手に well ; skillfully ; cleverly ;《文》with skill ;《文》dexterously ; tactfully (人に対して) / 上手になる get [《文》become] good ((at)) ;《文》acquire [attain] skill ; improve *oneself* ((in cooking)) ;《文》become proficient [skillful] ((in English)) ; master / 字[文章]を上手に書く write in a good hand [style] ★ in がないと《文》/ 絵が上手である draw well ; be a good painter / ドイツ語が上手である be good at German / お上手を言う flatter *sb* ; pay a compliment ; say nice things ((to *sb*)). 文例↓

しょうすい 憔悴 ¶憔悴する grow haggard ;《文》become emaciated ; be exhausted ; be worn out ; waste away ; wither / 憔悴した顔 a haggard face ; a worn-out look.

じょうすい¹ 上水 water supply ; 〈水〉service

じょうしょう¹ 経済は着実に上昇線をたどっているように思われた。The economy seemed to be on a steadily rising trend.

じょうじょう² コンディションは上々だ。I'm in the best of health [condition]. / 天気は上々であった。The weather was perfect. | The weather couldn't have been better.

じょうじょう³ 被告の残酷な所業は情状酌量の余地がない。There can be no extenuating circumstances for [Nothing can excuse] the cruelties committed by the accused. / 彼の不行跡は情状酌量の余地が全くない。Nothing can mitigate his misconduct.

しょうじる 無から有は生じない。Nothing comes out of nothing.

しょうしん² 彼は昇進が早かった。He won rapid [quick] promotion.

しょうじん¹ 小人閑居して不善をなす。The devil finds mischief for idle hands to do. 諺

じょうじん 彼はどこか常人と違った所がある。There is something out of the ordinary about him. / それはとうてい常人の全て及ぶ所ではない。It is quite beyond the power of ordinary mortals.

じょうず 彼はテニスが上手だ。He is a good tennis player. | He is good at tennis. / あの人はそろばんが上手だ。He is clever with the abacus. / 彼は話が上手でない。He

じょうすい [tap] water ¶上水道(設備) waterworks.
じょうすい² 浄水 ¶浄水場 a filtration (purification) plant / 浄水装置 a water-purifying device ; a water purification system ; a cleaning [filter] bed.
しょうすう¹ 小数 《数》 a decimal (fraction) ¶帯小数 a mixed decimal / 小数点 a decimal point / 小数点以下 3 位まで計算する calculate (a value) to three decimal places [three places of decimals, the third decimal place].
しょうすう² 少数 a small number ; a minority ¶少数の人々 a small number of persons ; a few people ; a handful of people / 少数意見 [民族] a minority opinion [race] / 少数派[党] a minority group [party] ; the minority. 文例⇩
じょうすう 乗数 《数》 a multiplier.
しょうする 称する call ; name ; 《呼ぶ》 style ; 《文》 designate ; 《偽る》 pretend ; 《文》 feign ; 《主張する》 claim ¶病気と称するpretend to be ill ;《文》 feign illness / 牧と称する男 a man who calls himself [goes under the name of] Maki / 彼が書いたと称する手紙《文》 a letter purporting to be written by him / …と称して《文》 on [under] the plea [pretext] of ; under (the) pretense of ; claiming to be 《《文》 representing oneself as ((a policeman)).
しょうせい¹ 招請 (an) invitation ¶招請する invite / 招請国 the host nation [country] / 招請状 (extend, issue, send) an invitation (to).
しょうせい² 笑声 (a peal of) laughter ; a laugh. 文例⇩
しょうせい³ 照星 〈銃の〉 the bead ; the foresight ; the front sight.
じょうせい¹ 上製 《文》 superior make ; 〈製本〉 superior binding [getup] ¶上製本 a deluxe edition.
じょうせい² 情[状]勢 the state of affairs [things] ; things ; the situation ; 《文》 conditions ; the picture ⇨じたい³, じょうきょう³ ¶世界の情勢 the world situation / 現在の情勢では as things stand now ; judging from the present state of things ; under the present circumstances / 一般情勢 the general drift of affairs (in Asia) ; the general context. 文例⇩
じょうせい³ 醸成 ¶醸成する〈醸す〉 brew ; 〈引き起こす〉 cause ; bring about.
しょうせき 硝石 《化》 saltpeter ; niter ; potassium nitrate.
じょうせき¹ 上席 ⇨かみざ ¶上席判事 a senior judge.
じょうせき² 定石[跡] 〈囲碁・将棋〉 the standard openings ((in the game of go [shogi]) ; set moves ((of the opening game)) ; 〈比喩的に〉 a (generally observed) formula ¶定石[跡]どおりに打つ[指す] play by the book / 〈物事を〉定石どおりにやる go [do] by the book.
しょうせつ¹ 小節 《音楽》 a bar ; a measure ¶第 1 小節 the first measure ; measure 1.
しょうせつ² 小説 a novel ; a story ; a piece ; a tale ; fiction 《総称》 ¶小説を書く write a novel / 小説にする make a novel [story] out of ((an affair)) ; 《文》 fictionalize / 小説的 romantic ; fictitious / 小説家 a novelist ; a story [fiction] writer / 短編小説 a short story / 長編小説 a novel / 中編小説 a novelette ; a short novel ; a long short story.
しょうせつ³ 詳説 a detailed [full] account [explanation] ¶詳説する explain [state] in detail [in full] ; give a detailed [full] account (of) ; 《文》 dwell [enlarge] on.
じょうせつ 常設 ¶常設の permanent ; standing.
じょうぜつ 冗舌 《文》 loquacity ; 《文》 garrulity ; talkativeness ¶冗舌な 《文》 loquacious ; 《文》 garrulous ; talkative / 冗舌家 a talkative man ; a great talker ; a loquacious man.
しょうせっかい 消石灰 slaked [slack, dead, hydrated] lime.
ジョーゼット 〈織物〉 georgette (crepe).
しょうせん¹ 商船 a merchant ship [vessel] ; a trading vessel ; 《文》 a merchantman (pl. -men) ; 〈総称〉 the merchant [mercantile, commercial] marine ((of a nation)) ¶商船隊 a merchant fleet / 商船大学[学校] a mercantile marine college [school].
しょうせん² 商戦 a sales battle ; a trade war.
しょうぜん 悄然 ¶悄然と 《文》 dispiritedly ; sadly ; despondently ; dejectedly ; 《文》 with a heavy heart / 悄然としている look depressed [cast down] ; 《文》 be crestfallen ; be down in the mouth.
じょうせん 乗船 embarkation ; boarding ¶乗船する go [get] aboard [on board] (a ship) ; take (a) ship [boat] ((at Yokohama for America)) ; embark ((at Niigata for Nakhodka)) / 乗船の予約をする be [been] engaged ((one's)) passage ((on a ship)) / 乗船券 a boat ticket ; a passage ticket. 文例⇩
しょうせんきょく 小選挙区 a small electoral district ; 〈1 区 1 人の〉 a single-member constituency ¶小選挙区制 the single-member constituency system.
しょうぜんてい 小前提 《論》 a minor premise.

is a poor storyteller. / 彼女は子供の面倒をみるのはあまり上手でない。 She is not much of a hand at looking after little children. / 上手の手から水が漏れる。 (Even) Homer sometimes nods. 【諺】
しょうすう² 我が社は 少数精鋭主義です。 Our personnel policy is 'Small numbers—exceptional talent'.
しょうする 当市の人口は 7 万と称されている。 The population of the city is given as [put at] 70,000. / ハワイはよく太平洋の楽園と称される。 Hawaii is often referred to as the Paradise of the Pacific.
しょうせい² 彼がこう言うとどっと笑声が起こった。 This utterance of his was greeted with bursts of laughter.
じょうせい² 情勢はどうか？ How do things stand? | What is the situation?/今日では情勢はすっかり変わってしまった。 Today the picture has completely changed. | The whole climate of the situation has changed.
じょうせん アメリカからイギリスへはフランスの船に乗船しました。 I sailed from America to England by a French steamer. / サンフランシスコ行きの貨客船に乗船の予約がしてある。 I have a passage booked on a cargo-passenger boat bound for San Francisco.

しょうそ 勝訴 〔勝訴になる〈人が主語〉win [gain] a [one's] case; 〈裁判が主語〉be decided in one's favor.

じょうそ 上訴 〖法〗an appeal ¶上訴する appeal (from a lower court to a higher court).

しょうそう¹ 少壮 ¶少壮の young; 《文》youthful / 少壮気鋭の young and spirited [energetic]; up-and-coming young (economists).

しょうそう² 尚早 ¶尚早の too early; premature. 文例⇩

しょうそう³ 焦躁 《文》fretfulness; irritation; impatience ¶焦躁を感じる fret [be in a fret] 《about》; feel impatient [restless].

しょうぞう 肖像 a portrait; 《文》a likeness ¶肖像を描いてもらう have one's portrait [likeness] painted [drawn] 《by a painter》; sit for one's portrait / 等身大[実物そっくり]の肖像 a life-size(d) [lifelike] portrait / 肖像画 a portrait 《in oils》 / 肖像画家 a portrait painter. 文例⇩

じょうそう¹ 上層 〈社会の〉the upper classes [social strata]; 《口語》the upper crust; 〈地層などの〉an upper layer [stratum]; 〈空の〉the upper air; 〈建築の〉the upper stories ¶上層階級 the upper classes / 上層気流 the upper air currents / 政府の上層部 the top-[high-] ranking government officials; the higher [highest] reaches of government. 文例⇩

じょうそう² 情操 《文》(a) sentiment; (good) taste ¶情操教育《文》cultivation of aesthetic sentiments; education in good taste.

じょうぞう 醸造 brewing ¶醸造する brew; distill (蒸留して) / 醸造酒 a liquor [an alcoholic beverage] made by fermentation / 醸造所〈ビールなどの〉a brewery; 〈ウイスキーなどの〉a distillery. 文例⇩

しょうそく 消息 ⇨ たより¹ ¶消息がある[ない] hear [hear nothing] from sb / 消息を聞く hear about sb; hear sb's news; hear [learn] the news about [of] sb / 消息を伝える bring [pass on] sb's news [the news about sb] 《to》 / …の消息に通じている be well-informed 《about, on》; be well posted 《in, on》; be well [fully] primed 《with》; be familiar [《文》conversant, 《文》acquainted] 《with》 / 消息筋 (well-)informed sources [circles, quarters] / 消息通 a well-informed person; a person in the know; an insider / 消息文 a personal letter. 文例⇩

しょうぞく 装束 costume; dress; 《文》attire; 《文》apparel ¶白装束の 《a woman》 (dressed) in white.

しょうぞくし 消息子 〖外科〗a probe.

しょうたい¹ 小隊 a platoon ¶小隊長 a platoon leader [commander].

しょうたい² 正体 one's true character [colors] ¶正体のわからぬ unidentifiable 《objects》 / 正体を現わす show one's true colors; show oneself in one's true colors; throw off one's mask; 〈心ならずも〉give oneself away / 正体を隠し wear [put on] a mask; disguise oneself / 正体を暴く unmask; 《口語》debunk / 正体なく眠る be fast [dead, sound] asleep; sleep like a log [top] / 正体なく酔う be [get] blind [dead] drunk; drink oneself into a stupor.

しょうたい³ 招待 (an) invitation ¶招待する invite; ask / 晩餐(ばん)に招待する invite [ask] sb to dinner / 招待を受ける get [《文》receive] an invitation / 招待に応じる accept an invitation / 招待を断わる《口語》turn an invitation down; do not accept an invitation; 《文》decline an invitation / …の招待で at the invitation of… / 〈展示会などの〉招待会 a trade show; a preview / 招待客 an invited guest / 招待券 an invitation card [ticket]; a complimentary ticket / 招待試合 an invitation(al) match / 招待状 a letter of invitation; an invitation (card); 《口語》an invite / 招待席 a seat reserved (for a guest).

じょうたい¹ 上体 the upper part of the body; the upper body.

じょうたい² 状態 the state 《of things》; a condition; the situation; 〈様子〉an appearance ⇨ じょうきょう², じょうせい² ¶目下の状態では as things [matters] stand; in the present state of things [affairs]; in the present circumstances. 文例⇩

じょうたい³ 常態 a normal state [condition]; an ordinary [a usual] state ¶常態に復する return [be restored] to normal [its normal condition].

しょうたく 沼沢 a marsh; a swamp; a bog ¶沼沢地 marshy ground; marshland; swampy areas / 沼沢地の植物 swamp plants.

しょうだく 承諾 consent; 《文》assent; agreement; 《文》acceptance ¶承諾する consent [agree, 《文》assent] 《to》; give one's consent [《文》assent] 《to》; 《文》comply 《with》; say yes 《to》; accept / 承諾を得て[得ずに] with [without] sb's consent / 承諾書 a letter of acceptance. 文例⇩

じょうたつ 上達 〈進歩〉progress; improvement; headway; 《文》advancement; 〈熟達〉proficiency ¶上達する make progress [headway] 《in》; improve 《in》; advance [《文》progress] 《in》; get better 《at》; get [《文》become]

しょうそう² 時機尚早である。It is still too early to do that. | The time is not ripe for it yet.

しょうぞう 彼は肖像権を主張した。He claimed the right to refuse to be photographed.

じょうそう¹ 《会社の》上層部で経営方針の変更が決められた。There has been a change of policy at the top.

じょうぞう ビールは大麦から醸造する。Beer is brewed from barley.

しょうそく 登山隊は10日に出発したまま消息がない。Nothing has been heard of the mountaineering party since its departure on the 10th. / 彼は裏面の消息に通じている。He has some inside knowledge. | He is in the know (about it). / このことからその間の消息が多少うかがわれると思う。I believe this throws some light on how it really happened [how things stood then].

じょうたい² その写本は今でもほとんど完全な状態で残っている。The manuscripts are still in almost perfect condition today. / 橋が今にも押し流されそうな状態になっている。The bridge is in danger of being swept [carried] away.

しょうだく そんな条件は承諾でき

good (at); become skillful 《in》. 文例⇩
しょうだん¹ 昇段 ¶昇段する be promoted 《to a higher grade》.
しょうだん² 商談 a business talk; 《交渉》negotiations ¶商談する have a business talk 《with》; talk business 《with》; negotiate 《with》/ 商談を取り決める close [strike] a bargain 《with》; close a deal 《with》/ 商談に応じる agree to [enter into] negotiations 《with》.
じょうたん 上端 the upper end; the top.
じょうだん¹ 上段 the upper row [tier, step] ¶上段の寝台 an upper berth / 刀を上段に構える raise [hold] *one's* sword over *one's* head.
じょうだん² 冗談 《戯言》a joke; 《文》a jest; a wisecrack (ぴりっと気のきいた);《からかい》chaff; banter;《文》badinage (冗談のやりとり);《戯れ》a prank; a joke ¶冗談を言う crack [make] a joke; joke / 冗談に in joke; for fun; in sport / 冗談半分に《文》half in jest; half as a joke; jestingly. 文例⇩
しょうち¹ 承知 〈承諾〉consent;《文》assent; agreement; an O.K.;〈承認〉《文》acknowledgment;〈知っていること〉knowledge ¶承知する〈承諾する〉agree to [《文》consent,《文》assent] to;《文》comply with 《sb's request》;〈承認する〉accept; acknowledge;〈知る〉know; be aware [《文》conscious] of;〈許可する〉permit; allow;〈勘弁する〉(not) forgive /〈説き伏せて〉承知させる persuade [《文》prevail upon] *sb* to *do*;〈思いとどまらせる〉persuade *sb* not to *do*;《文》dissuade *sb* from *doing* / 承知の上で deliberately; on purpose;《文》intentionally / 互いに承知の上で《文》by mutual consent [agreement] / ご承知のとおり as you know [are aware]. 文例⇩
しょうち² 招致 ¶招致する〈招く〉invite;〈呼び寄せる〉summon; send for.
じょうち¹ 常置 ¶常置する keep [《文》maintain] permanently / 常置委員 a standing committee.
じょうち² 情痴 infatuation ⇨ ちじょう².
しょうちゅう¹ 掌中 ¶掌中の[に] in *one's* hands / 掌中にある be in *one's* hands; be in *one's* power; be at the mercy 《of》/ 掌中の玉 the apple of *one's* eye;《文》*one's* treasure [jewel].
しょうちゅう² 焼酎 *shochu*; Japanese spirits distilled from sweet potatoes, rice, etc.
じょうちょ 情緒 emotion(s); feeling(s) ¶情緒的 emotional / 情緒障害児 an emotionally

disturbed child / 情緒不安定 emotional instability / 情緒不安定の emotionally unstable.
しょうちょう¹ 小腸【解】the small intestine ¶小腸炎 enteritis.
しょうちょう² 消長 prosperity and decline; rise and fall; ebb and flow; ups and downs;《文》vicissitudes (of fortune).
しょうちょう³ 象徴 a symbol; an emblem ¶象徴する symbolize;《文》be symbolic [emblematic] of / 象徴的 symbolic / 象徴主義 symbolism / 象徴主義運動 the symbolist movement / 象徴派 the symbolist school; the symbolists.
じょうちょう¹ 情調 an atmosphere; a mood; a tone ¶異国情調 an exotic atmosphere;《文》exoticism.
じょうちょう² 冗長 ¶冗長な lengthy (speeches);《文》verbose (writing);《文》diffuse (style) / 冗長性【コンピューター】redundancy.
しょうちん 消沈 ⇨ いき⁵ (意気消沈する).
じょうてい 上程 ¶上程する put [place] (a bill) on the agenda; lay (a bill) before the Diet (国会に);〈討議にかける〉bring (a bill) up for discussion.
しょうてき 小敵 a weak enemy [opponent,《文》adversary]. 文例⇩
じょうでき 上出来 a (great) success; a good job; good work ¶上出来である be very good; be well done [made]; be a success. 文例⇩
しょうてん¹ 昇天《文》ascension to heaven;〈キリストの〉the Ascension;〈聖母マリヤの〉the Assumption;〈死〉death ¶昇天する rise [go,《文》ascend] to heaven; die.
しょうてん² 消点【製図】a vanishing point.
しょうてん³ 商店《米》a store;《英》a shop ¶商店街 a shopping street; a shopping center [district]; a street of stores.
しょうてん⁴ 焦点 a focus (*pl*. -es, foci); a focal point ¶焦点が合っている [外れている] be in [out of] focus / 焦点の定まらない unfocused (eyes) / 焦点の 2 つある bifocal / 焦点を合わす focus 《*one's* glasses on an object》; adjust the focus of (a lens) / 焦点を変える change focus 《on an object》; focus on 《an object》; bring 《an object》into focus [to a focus] / 固定焦点【写真】a fixed focus / 虚[実]焦点 a virtual [real] focus / 焦点距離 the focal length [distance] / 焦点深度 the depth of focus / 二焦点レンズ a bifocal lens. 文例⇩

ない. I cannot accept such terms.
じょうたつ 君は近ごろ英会話がだいぶ上達した. You speak English much better than you used to. / 上達が早い者もあるし, 遅いものもある. Some make rapid progress, others don't. / Some people are quicker at learning than others.
じょうだん あれでなかなか気のきいた冗談を飛ばすこともある男である. He is sometimes very joky and bright. / まさかご冗談でしょ

う. You must [You've got to] be joking! | You don't mean it, do you? / 冗談言うなよ! Cut out the fooling! | Talk sensibly, won't you! / 冗談にもほどがある. You carry your joke too far. | It is beyond a joke. / あいつは冗談ばかり言っている. He is very fond of joking. / 冗談はさておいて午後は仕事をする. Joking aside [Now to be serious], what are we going to do in the afternoon? / 道楽に働いているんだろうだって? 冗談じゃ

ない. I'm working for the fun of it? Nothing of the sort! / まだ出来てないなんて, 冗談じゃない. Not ready yet? Come off it! [You can't be serious!]
しょうち 何としても同行することを承知しなかった. Nothing could prevail upon him to accompany me. / ご注文の品は本日ご送付申し上げましたからさようご承知願います. We have the pleasure to inform you that we have sent you today the articles you or-

しょうでん 小伝 a biographical sketch.
じょうてんき 上天気 fine [fair, beautiful] weather. 文例○
しょうど 焦土 ¶焦土と化する be burned to the ground; be reduced to ashes / 焦土戦術 scorched-earth strategy [tactics].
じょうと 譲渡 《法・商》transfer; conveyance; 〈証券の〉negotiation;〈領土の〉cession / 譲渡する hand [make] over (one's property to one's son); transfer (sth to sb); alienate (land to sb); negotiate (securities) ⇒ゆずる / 財産の譲渡 alienation of property / 譲渡禁止の nonnegotiable / 譲渡証書 a (deed of) transfer; a conveyance / 譲渡人 a transferer / 被譲渡人 a transferee.
じょうど 浄土《仏教》the Pure Land; Paradise ⇒ごくらく ¶西方浄土 the Pure Land in the West; Western Paradise / 浄土宗 the Jodo [Pure Land] sect.
しょうとう¹ 小党 a small [minor] (political) party; a splinter party (分離してできた). 文例○
しょうとう² 消灯 ¶消灯する put the lights out; switch the lights off / 消灯時間 lights-out (time). 文例○
しょうどう¹ 唱道 ¶唱道する《文》advocate; propose《文》advance, introduce] (a new doctrine); preach / 唱道者 an advocate;《文》a proponent.
しょうどう² 衝動《文》(an) impulse; (an) impetus; an urge;《心理》a drive ¶衝動的な impulsive / 衝動的に impulsively; on [from] impulse; on the spur of the moment / 一時の衝動に駆られる act on the spur [give way to the impulse] of the moment; act on impulse; feel [have] the urge (to do); have an urge [impulse] (to do) / 衝動買い impulse buying / 衝動買いをする buy sth on impulse / 衝動買いをする人 an impulse buyer.
しょうとう¹ 上等 ¶上等の first-class[-rate]; very good; fine; superior / 最上等の《文》of the highest [finest] quality; the best; prime 《beef》/ 上等品 a first-class article;《文》an article of superior [excellent] quality. 文例○
じょうとう² 上棟 ¶上棟式 the ceremony of putting up the ridge beam of a new house.
じょうとう³ 常套 ¶常套の conventional; commonplace / 常套を脱する break the routine; get out of the rut / 常套語 a hackneyed expression; a cliché / 常套手段 a well-worn device; an old trick [《口語》ploy].
じょうどう 常道《follow》a regular [normal] course; a beaten track; the practice (in business transaction); the normal way (of doing).
しょうどく 消毒 disinfecting; sterilization; pasteurization ★ disinfecting は最も日常的な意味での消毒。便所・どぶなどに石炭酸などをまくなどがこれに相当する。sterilization は医学用語: The nurse sterilized the surgical instruments. (看護婦は外科用器具を消毒した). pasteurization は主に牛乳などを高温処理でする消毒 ¶消毒する disinfect; sterilize; pasteurize; fumigate (いぶして) / 消毒した disinfected; sterilized; pasteurized / 消毒器 a sterilizer / 消毒薬 a disinfectant; an antiseptic.
しょうとつ 衝突 a collision;《口語》a bump; 《口語》a pileup (数台の車の);〈不一致〉a conflict; a clash;《文》a discord; a feud;〈戦闘〉an encounter; a skirmish (小さな) / (車体がめちゃくちゃになるような)激しい衝突 (have, be in) a smash(up) / 感情の衝突 an emotional clash; a clash of personalities [temperaments] / 利害の衝突 a conflict of interests / 衝突する collide [have a collision] (with); run (bump, smash) (into);《意見などが》《文》conflict (with); run counter (to); come in [into] conflict with sb;《文》be at variance (with);〈不和になる〉quarrel (with); be at odds (with); fall out (with);〈敵に〉meet;《文》encounter / 三重衝突 a three-way collision / 武力衝突 an armed conflict (with, between). 文例○
しょうとりひき 商取引《have》(a) commercial [business] transaction (with);《make》a business deal.
じょうない 場内 ¶場内で[に] in [within] the enclosure; on the premises; in the enclosure grounds;《会場内》in the hall / 《劇場の》場内照明 the houselights / 場内放送 (an announcement over) the public address [PA] system (in the stadium).
しょうに 小児 a little child; an infant ¶小児科《医》pediatrics / 小児科医 a pediatrician; a children's doctor / 小児科医院 a children's hospital / 小児語 a nursery [baby] word; baby talk; nursery language / 小児ぜんそく〈ぜんそく性気管支炎〉asthmatic bronchitis;〈気管支ぜんそく〉bronchial asthma / 小児病 children's [infantile] diseases;〈比喩的に〉《文》infantilism / 小児病的 infantilistic / 小児まひ in-

---

dered from us. / だれが何と言うとこのおれが絶対承知しない。I'm dead against it whatever anybody else may say. / おれの言うがおりにしろ。承知せんぞ。If you don't do as I tell you, you'll be sorry for it. | I'll have your neck if you don't do what you're told.
じょうちょう²手紙の文は冗長にならないほうがいい。Your letters should not be needlessly long.
しょうてき 小敵たりとも侮るなかれ。Don't despise a weak enemy.

じょうでき 上出来, 上出来! Well done! | Splendid! | Excellent! / あなたは初心者にしては上出来ですよ。You're doing very well for a beginner.
しょうてん⁴ この点に焦点をしぼって論じよう。Let's concentrate (our discussion) on this point.
じょうてんき すばらしい夕焼けだ。あしたもまた上天気だろう。What a marvelous sunset! We are going to have another fine day tomorrow.

しょうとう¹ 小党分立は議会政治にとってマイナスである。For political parties to break into small groups is bad for parliamentary government.
しょうとう² ここは9時消灯です。Lights go out at ['Lights-out' is] 9 p.m. here.
しょうとう¹ もっと上等のを見せてください。Show me a better one, please. / これより上等のはありません。This is the best we have.
しょうとつ その四つ角で自動車の

しょうにゅう fantile paralysis; poliomyelitis; polio. 文例⇩
しょうにゅうせき 鍾乳石 [地質] (a) stalactite, 鍾乳洞 a limestone cave [cavern].
しょうにん¹ 上[聖]人 a saint; a holy priest ¶日蓮上人 Saint Nichiren.
しょうにん² 昇任 promotion ¶昇任する be promoted [(文) advanced] (to); rise in rank.
しょうにん³ 承認 〈認可〉 (an) approval; (文) (a) recognition; (文) admission; (an) acknowledgment; 〈承諾〉 (文) consent; agreement; 〈口語〉 an O.K. [OK, okay] (pl. O.K.'s) ¶承認する approve; give one's approval (to); admit; recognize; acknowledge; (文) consent (to); 〈口語〉 give one's consent (to); 〈米口語〉 O.K. [okay] (★過去形や -ing の形で O.K.'d, O.K.'ing もあるが, okayed, okaying と書くことが多い) 〈正式に〉 refuse; deny; disapprove (of) /…に外交上の承認を与える accord 《a new government》 diplomatic recognition; extend (full) diplomatic recognition to 《a country》/承認を得る obtain sb's approval [consent]; receive recognition; get sb's [an] O.K. [agreement] 《to a proposal》/承認を求める ask for sb's approval / 承認状 a letter of approval; a written acknowledgment.
しょうにん⁴ 商人 a merchant; a trader; a dealer (in earthenware); a shopkeeper; 〈店主〉 a tradesman; 〈集合的に〉 tradespeople ¶商人根性 commercialism.
しょうにん⁵ 証人 [法] a witness; an attestor 〈証書作成の〉; a surety 〈保証人〉 ¶検事[被告]側の証人 a prosecution [defense] witness / 証人に立てる call sb as (a) witness / 証人となる 〈事件の〉 testify (to); bear witness (to, that…); 〈身元の〉 stand (go) surety for sb / 証人台[席] 〈米〉 the witness stand / 〈英〉 the witness box / 証人台に立つ take [go on] the (witness) stand. 文例⇩
じょうにん 常任 ¶常任 standing; permanent; regular / 常任委員 (a member of) a standing [permanent] committee / 国連の常任理事国 a permanent member of the (United Nations) Security Council.
しょうね 性根 〈根性〉 nature; (文) (a) disposition ¶性根の腐った corrupt; depraved / 性根の曲がった perverse; cross-grained; warped / 性根を入れ換える reform; mend one's ways; turn over a new leaf / 性根をたたき直す straighten 《a boy》 out.

じょうねつ 情熱 enthusiasm; passion; 《文》 zeal ¶情熱的な passionate / 情熱をかき立てる stir (fire) sb's enthusiasm / 情熱を傾ける put one's heart into 《one's work》/非常な情熱を示す be very enthusiastic (about) / 情熱に燃える burn [glow] with enthusiasm.
しょうねつじごく 焦熱地獄 a (burning) hell; an inferno (pl. -s); (文) Gehenna.
しょうねん 少年 a boy; a lad ¶少年院 a reformatory; a training school; 《英》 an approved school / 少年鑑別所 a juvenile (delinquent) classification home; 《米》 a detention home; 《英》 a remand home [centre] / 少年時代に when 《one was》 a boy; 《as》 a boy's boyhood / 少年雑誌 a boys' magazine / 少年審判所 the Juvenile Court / 少年団[団員] the Boy Scouts [a boy scout] / 少年犯罪 juvenile delinquency / 少年犯罪者 a juvenile delinquent [offender]. 文例⇩
しょうねんば 正念場 the crucial moment [point]; the moment of truth.
しょうのう¹ 小脳 [解] the cerebellum (pl. -s, -bella).
しょうのう² 小農 a small [petty] farmer; a peasant (proprietor); 〈集合的に〉 peasantry.
しょうのう³ 樟脳 camphor / 〈虫よけ用の玉〉 a mothball.
じょうば 乗馬 〈騎乗〉 horse [horseback] riding; 〈馬〉 a riding [saddle] horse; (文) one's mount ¶乗馬靴[ズボン] riding boots [breeches] / 乗馬クラブ a riding club / 乗馬服 riding clothes (dress, wear); a riding habit (婦人の).
しょうはい¹ 勝敗 victory or defeat; (文) the issue [outcome] (of a battle) ¶勝敗を決する fight it out; 〈口語〉 have [come to] a showdown (with); fight to the finish. 文例⇩
しょうはい² 賞杯 a (prize) cup; a trophy.
しょうばい 商売 〈商業〉 trade; business; commerce; 〈職業〉 one's business; (文) an occupation; (文) a calling; a trade (大工などの); a profession (専門的) ¶商売がうまい have a good head for business / 商売が繁盛する 〈人が主語〉 do [carry on] a good [thriving] business / 商売をする do 〈口語〉 engage in business; deal [trade] (in jewels) / 1か月に100万円の商売をする do a business of ¥1,000,000 a month; have a turnover [turn over] ¥1,000,000 a month / 商売を始める start a [one's] business; set up in business; begin [go into] business;

四重衝突があった. There was a pileup of four cars at the crossroads. / 彼は父と衝突して家を出た. He fell out with his father and left home.
しょうに 3歳の時に彼は小児まひにかかった. At the age of three he was stricken with polio.
しょうにん⁴ あいつは商人根性が強過ぎるから嫌いだ. I don't like him; he is too mercenary.
しょうにん⁵ 彼は明日証人に[として]喚問されることになっている. Tomorrow he is going to appear

in court as witness. | He is going to take the (witness) stand tomorrow.
しょうねん 彼は金沢で少年時代を過ごした. He spent [passed] his boyhood at Kanazawa. / 少年法は未成年者の保護を目的とし, 少年の非行を特別に扱っている. The Juveniles Act aims at the protection of persons under age by making special provisions for juvenile delinquency. / 少年老いやすく学成りがたし. Do as much learning as possible while you

are young, for memory soon grows feeble. | Art is long, time is fleeting.
しょうはい¹ 勝敗がまだ決しない. The issue is still undecided. / 勝敗を度外視して善戦するつもりだ. Win or lose, I mean to fight as well as I can. / 勝敗は時の運. Chance plays a part in deciding the issue of a battle.
しょうばい ご商売はいかがですか. How are you getting along in business? | How's business? / そんなことをされたら, こちらの商売

じょうはく 上膊 〖解〗⇒じょうわん.
しょうばつ 賞罰 reward and punishment ¶賞罰を行なう《文》mete out justice [reward and punishment] (to).
じょうはつ 蒸発 evaporation ; 〈人が姿を消すこと〉(a) mysterious disappearance ¶蒸発する evaporate ; escape as vapor ; 〈姿を消す〉disappear into thin air / 蒸発させる vaporize / 蒸発皿 an evaporating dish.
しょうばん 相伴 ⇒おしょうばん.
じょうはんしん 上半身 the upper half [part] of the body ; the bust ¶上半身を乗り出し lean [bend oneself] forward / 上半身裸体で naked from the waist up ; stripped (down) to the waist / 上半身写真 a photograph from the waist up [of the upper part of the body].
しょうひ 消費 consumption ¶消費する consume ; spend / 消費者 consumer products ; 〖経済〗consumer(s') [consumption] goods / 消費者 a consumer / 一般消費者〈総称〉the consuming public / 消費者運動 consumer movements / 消費者価格〖経済〗consumer(s') price / 消費者組合[団体] a consumer(s') union [group] / 消費者代表 consumer representatives / 消費者物価指数 the consumer(s') price index (略：CPI) / 消費社会 (a) consumer [consuming] society / 高度消費社会 (a) high-consumption society / 消費税 a consumption tax [duty] ; an excise tax / 消費生活 one's life as a consumer. 文例⇩
しょうび[1] 焦眉 ¶焦眉の urgent ; pressing ; 《文》impending / 焦眉の急 an urgent [a crying] need ; a pressing [burning] necessity / 焦眉の急に応じる《文》meet the exigencies of the moment / 焦眉の問題 a burning [an urgent] question ; 《文》an issue of burning concern.
しょうび[2] 賞美 ¶賞美する〈ほめる〉admire ; praise ; 〈珍重する〉prize ; 〈良さを認める〉appreciate.
じょうひ 冗費 unnecessary expenses [expenditure] ¶冗費を省く cut down (on) [curtail] unnecessary [wasteful] expenditure.
じょうび 常備 ¶常備の standing ; permanent ; regular / 常備する always have sth ready [available, on hand] / 常備軍[兵力] a standing army [force] / 家庭常備薬 a household medicine ; a (standard) medicine-chest item.
じょうびたき 〖鳥〗a Daurian redstart.
しょうひょう 商標 a trademark ; a brand ¶商標を盗用する pirate the trademark (of) / 商標権 the trademark right / 商標盗用 trademark piracy / 商標名 a brand name.
しょうびょうへい 傷病兵 (the) sick and wounded (soldiers) ; invalids.
しょうひん[1] 小品 a short piece 《of music [writing]》; a small(-sized) painting [sculpture].
しょうひん[2] 商品 a commodity ; an item on [for] sale ; a product (製品) ; 〈総称〉goods ; 《文》wares ; merchandise ¶商品イメージ the brand image / 商品化する produce sth on a commercial basis ; commercialize / 商品価値のある marketable ; salable / 《chemical compounds》of commercial value / 商品券 a gift certificate [token] / (デパートなどの)商品搬入口 a goods entrance / 商品見本 a trade sample / 商品名 a brand [trade] name / 商品目録 a catalog(ue). 文例⇩
しょうひん[3] 賞品 a prize ¶賞品を与える[もらう, さらう] award [win, carry off] a prize.
じょうひん 上品 ¶上品な refined ; 《文》elegant ; polished ; 《文》decorous ; polite ; graceful ; 〈女性が〉ladylike / 上品な言葉を使う use refined [respectable] language / 上品に《文》elegantly ; gracefully ; (eat) with good manners / 上品ぶる give oneself [put on] airs. 文例⇩
しょうふ 娼婦 a prostitute.
しょうぶ[1] 勝負 〈勝敗〉victory or defeat ; 〈試合〉a match ; a game ; a contest ; a bout ; 《play》a hand (トランプの1勝負) ¶勝負する play ; fight ; have a match [game, bout] / くのるかそるかやってみる〉try one's luck / 勝負をつける fight to the finish ; fight it out ; have a showdown ; play off (同点者の間で) ⇒けっせん[3] / 勝負に勝つ[敗ける] win [lose] a game / 勝

あがったりだ. That would make it impossible for me to make a living. / これは商売にならない. It doesn't pay. / It is not a paying proposition. / この店はちゃんと商売になっているんです. We've got a going concern in this store. / あの人の商売は何ですか. What line of business is he in? / What's his line? / 彼の商売は建築業です. He is a builder by trade. / 道楽に魚を釣っているのではなくて, 商売なんです. I don't go fishing for pleasure, but as a means of earning my bread. / 商売柄いつもネクタイをしていなければなりません. The nature of my job means that I have to wear a tie at all times. / 思わぬ商売気が出て, あんなことを言ってしまいました. The tradesman in me got the better of me and prompted me to say what I did.
しょうひ 現在の消費率で行けば石炭は 900 年はもつだろう. At the present rate of consumption [usage] coal could last for 900 years.
しょうひん[2] あの店ではこの種の商品は取り扱っていない. That store does not deal in this line of goods. / 同社が合成繊維を商品として生産を開始したのは 1939 年のことである. It was in 1939 that the company began producing synthetic fibers commercially [in commercial quantities]. / 商品見本. 〖郵便物表記〗Samples.
じょうひん 彼女は上品な服装をしている. Her dress is [She is dressed] in good taste. / 彼女はお上品だから, そんなことはしないよ. She is too much of a lady to

しょうぶ 〖植〗 an iris ; (a) (sweet) flag.

じょうふ¹ 情夫 a lover ; 〈文〉 a paramour.

じょうふ² 情婦 a mistress ; 〈文〉 a paramour (妻帯者の).

じょうぶ¹ 上部 the upper part ; the top [head] ((of the page)) ¶上部の upper / 上部構造 a superstructure.

じょうぶ² 丈夫 ¶丈夫な 〈堅牢な〉 strong ; solid ; firm ; 〈耐久性のある〉 durable ; 〈壮健な〉 healthy ; (well and) strong ; robust / 丈夫になる get [〈文〉become] fit [healthy] ; 〈文〉 improve in health ; one's health improves ; 〈回復する〉 get better ; get well (again) ; recover ; 〈文〉 regain [recover] one's health / 身体を丈夫にする build up one's health / (建物などが) 丈夫にできている be strongly [solidly] built / 身体が丈夫である be in good health. 文例⇩

しょうふく 承服 ¶承服する 〈同意する〉 agree [〈文〉consent] ((to)) ; 〈受け入れる〉 accept / 承服できない条件 unacceptable conditions [terms].

じょうふくろ 状袋 an envelope ⇒ふうとう.

しょうふだ 正札 a price mark [tag, label] ¶千円の正札がついている be marked [labeled] '¥1,000' / 正札をつける set [put, mark] a price on ((an article)) ; price ((all the goods in the store)). 文例⇩

じょうぶつ 成仏 ¶成仏する attain Buddhahood ; 〈死ぬ〉 die ((with one's mind at ease [peace])) ; 〈文〉 pass away. 文例⇩

しょうぶん 性分 〈文〉 (one's) natural disposition ; (one's) nature ; 〈気質〉 (one's) temperament ¶性分に合わない do not suit one ; go against the grain ((with)) ; 〈口語〉 be not one's cup of tea / 〈口語〉 be not in one's line. 文例⇩

じょうぶん 条文 〈全体〉 the text ((of the agreement)) ; 〈1箇条〉 a provision.

しょうへい¹ 招聘 ¶招聘する invite ; 〈依頼する〉 call on ((sb to do)) ; 招聘に応じる accept the offer of a position ; accept the appointment ((to the chair of physics)) ; accept the invitation ((to give a lecture)).

しょうへい² 将兵 officers and men.

しょうへい³ 傷兵 a wounded soldier ; 〈総称〉 the wounded.

しょうへき 障壁 a fence ; a wall ; a barrier ; an obstacle ¶障壁となる be an obstacle ((to)) ; be in the way ((of)) / 言語障壁 a language barrier / 障壁画 pictures on (room) partitions.

じょうへき 城壁 a castle wall ; (town) walls ; a rampart ¶城壁を巡らす surround ((a castle)) with a rampart ; wall (a town) ; build walls [ramparts] round ((a city)) / 城壁を巡らした町 a walled town.

しょうへん 小片 a small piece ; a fragment ; 〈口語〉 a bit.

しょうべん 小便 urine ; 〈卑〉 piss ; 〈小児語〉 pee ¶小便が近い have to urinate frequently / 小便をする urinate ; pass [make] water ; 〈卑〉 piss ; 〈小児語〉 pee / 小便を我慢する retain [hold] one's urine / 小便小僧 Manneken Pis ; Manikin Piss / 小便所 a urinal. 文例⇩

じょうほ 譲歩 a concession ; (a) compromise ¶譲歩する make a concession ; give way to sb ; compromise ; meet sb halfway / 少しも譲歩しない make no concessions at all ; do not yield a single point / …から譲歩を取りつける get [win, 〈文〉obtain, 〈文〉wrest] concessions from….

しょうほう¹ 商法 〈法律〉 commercial [mercantile] law (総称) ; the Commercial Law Act (狭義の「商法」) ; 〈商売の仕方〉 a business method.

しょうほう² 詳報 a detailed [full] report ¶詳報する report in detail [full] ; make a full report ((on, of)) ; give a full account ((of)).

しょうぼう 消防 fire fighting ¶消防に努める fight a fire / 消防訓練 a fire drill / 消防自動車 a fire engine [truck] / 消防署〈米〉a firehouse ; 〈英〉 a fire station / 消防隊 a fire brigade (company) ; a fire-fighting team / 消防庁〈自治省の外局の〉 the Fire Defense Agency / 〈東京消防庁〉 the Metropolitan Fire Department / 消防当局 the fire authorities / 消防ばしご a fire ladder ; an extension ladder (繰り出しできる) / 消防士 a fireman ; a fire fighter / 消防法〈法〉 the Fire Services Act ; the fire laws / 消防ポンプ a fire pump.

じょうほう¹ 上方 ¶上方の upper / 上方に above ; upward(s).

じょうほう² 乗法〈数〉multiplication.

じょうほう³ 情報 information ; a report ; news ¶…との情報がある It is reported that… / 情

---

do that.
しょうぶ 勝負あった。The game is over. | Game! / こちらが2点リードしているが，勝負はまだ安心できない。Our team is leading by two runs [points], but the game is still too close for comfort. / 彼は勝負強い。He has a knack [habit] of coming out best [on top] in the end. / とうとう勝負がつかなかった。They fought to a standstill. | The battle ended without a clear result. / この24時間が勝負です。(病気などで) The next twenty-four hours will tell [decide].
じょうぶ² 彼はいかにも丈夫そうだ。He looks very tough. / この布地は丈夫です。This cloth wears well. / 丈夫なことはお請け合います。I will answer for its durability.
しょうふだ たまたま正札がついたままになっていた。The label happened to have been left on.
じょうぶつ これではあの人も成仏

できないだろう。This will make him turn in his grave.
しょうぶん 私の性分としてそんな事はできません。It is not in my nature to do such a thing. / 僕の性分だから仕方がない。I can't help the way I am [the way I'm made].
しょうべん 小便無用。『掲示』No Urinating. / Commit no nuisance.
じょうほ この点は譲歩しかねる。We cannot concede [compromise on] this point. / 問題は双方の譲

しょうほん 抄本 an extract; an abstract; an abridged transcript.

じょうまえ 錠前 a lock ⇨ じょう⁶ ¶錠前屋 a locksmith.

じょうまん 冗漫 ¶冗漫な《文》diffuse; tedious;《文》verbose; wordy.

しょうみ¹ 正味 ¶正味の net; clear / 正味の目方[数量] the net weight [quantity] / 正味8時間働く work for eight clear [for a full eight] hours. 文例⇩

しょうみ² 賞味 ¶賞味する appreciate; eat with relish (gusto, pleasure); relish.

じょうみゃく 静脈 【解】a vein ¶大静脈 the main vein / 太い静脈が浮き出ている手 a heavily veined hand / 静脈の venous (venose)《血》/ 静脈注射 (an) intravenous injection / 静脈瘤(ﾘｭｳ) a varix (pl. varices) / 静脈瘤が出来ている have varicose veins.

じょうむ 常務 ¶常務取締役 a managing [an executive] director ★《英》では a managing director は「社長」

じょうむいん 乗務員 〈列車の〉a member of a train crew;〈総称〉a (train) crew; the crew of a train;〈市電の〉a carman;〈飛行機の〉a member of a (flight) crew; a crewman (軍用機の); a (flight) crew (総称) ¶乗務員室 the driver's [engineer's] cab [cabin];〈飛行機の〉crew space.

しょうめい¹ 証明 (a) proof; evidence; testimony (証言); (a) demonstration; corroboration; certification; verification ¶証明する prove; show;《文》attest (to) (a fact);《文》bear witness (to); confirm; certify (to); corroborate; verify / 定理を証明する demonstrate [prove] a theorem / 正直であることを証明する〈事が主語〉prove sb (to be) honest; show that sb is honest; testify to [《文》attest] sb's honesty / 誤りであることを証明する disprove sth / ここに…であることを証明する〈証明書の文句〉This is to certify that…; I hereby certify that… / 証明できないものである be unverifiable / 証明書(give, issue) a certificate; a testimonial (人物資格などの); a warrant (許可証). 文例⇩

しょうめい² 照明 lighting; illumination ¶照明する light (up); illuminate;《文》illumine / 照明のいい[悪い] well-[poorly-,《文》ill-]lit / 舞台照明 stage lighting / 照明係 an electrician; a lighting technician; a spotlightman / 照明効果 the lighting effects / 照明弾 a flare (bomb); a star shell.

しょうめつ 消滅〈絶滅〉《文》extinction;〈消失〉disappearance; passing (of a movement);《文》expiation (罪障の) ¶権利の消滅 the lapse of one's right / 消滅する〈死滅する〉《文》cease to exist [be]; die out; become extinct;〈消失する〉disappear; vanish;〈失効する〉lapse; become null and void;〈罪が〉《文》be expiated / 消滅させる extinguish (a mortgage); nullify (a right) / 自然消滅する die out [go out of existence] in course of time. 文例⇩

しょうめん 正面 the front; the facade (建物の) ¶正面から攻撃する make a frontal attack on (the enemy);〈正面切って〉attack sb openly / 正面から取り組む grapple squarely with (the problem) / 正面切って言う say sth openly (to sb) / 正面から見ると seen head-on / 正面から見た顔 a full face / …の正面に in front of… / 正面攻撃(open, deliver) a frontal attack (against) / 正面衝突 a head-on collision; a frontal clash・交渉など(で) / 正面衝突する collide [clash] head-on (with, against) (★ clash は車については使えない); run head-on into sth / 正面図 a front view / 正面跳び〈走り高跳びの〉a scissors jump. 文例⇩

しょうもう 消耗《文》consumption;《文》exhaustion; waste; wear and tear;〈やつれること〉《文》emaciation ¶消耗する《文》consume; use up;《文》exhaust; waste [《文》dissipate]《one's strength》/ 消耗した〈やつれた〉haggard;

歩で解決した. The affair was settled by mutual concessions. / 彼は我々に譲歩させようとしているのだ. He is trying to get concessions from us.

じょうほう³ その事に関しての情報が来ていない. No information has been received on that matter.

しょうみ¹ 種々の雑費を引いて正味 5 万円しか手に入らなかった. After (deducting) various expenses, I netted [cleared] only 50,000 yen.

しょうめい¹ この理論はまだ科学的に証明されていない. This theory is not yet scientifically established. / 医者の証明がなければこの薬は売れません. We can't sell this medicine without a doctor's prescription.

しょうめつ 方言の中には消滅しかかっているものがある. Some dialects are threatened with extinction. | Some dialects are in danger of dying out.

しょうめん 彼女は横顔はそれほどでもないが, 正面から見るとなかなか愛きょうがある. In full face she's very attractive, though less so in profile. / この問題は正面から行ったのではうまくないだろう. It won't do to approach this question direct. / 会期の延長をめぐって社会党と自民党の正面衝突が予想される. A frontal clash between the Socialists and the Liberal Democrats is expected over the extension of the Diet

じょうもの 《文》emaciated; 〈疲れ果てた〉exhausted; dog-tired / 消耗戦 a war of attrition / 消耗品 consumption articles; expendable supplies / 事務用消耗品 office supplies.

じょうもの 上物 an article of high quality; choice [(high-)quality] goods.

しょうもん 証文 ⇨ しょうしょ ¶証文を書く draw up [write out] a deed / 証文を入れる give sb a signed (and sealed) deed / 証文にする put 《a contract》in writing. 文例↓

じょうもん 定紋 a family crest.

じょうもん 城門 a castle gate.

じょうもんしき 縄文式 ¶縄文式土器 straw-rope pattern pottery; Jomon ware.

しょうやく¹ 生薬 crude drugs (of plant and animal origin); nature remedies.

しょうやく² 抄訳 ¶抄訳する translate selected passages [chapters] (from); make an abridged translation 《of》.

じょうやく 条約 a treaty; a pact; an agreement; a convention ¶条約を結ぶ conclude [enter into] a treaty 《with》/ 条約を改正[廃棄]する revise [abrogate, revoke] a treaty / 条約に調印する sign a treaty / 条約加盟国 signatory countries; the members of a treaty / 条約批准 the ratification of a treaty. 文例↓

じょうやど 定宿 one's regular [usual] hotel [inn]; the place [inn, hotel] where one usually stays. 文例↓

じょうやとう 常夜灯 a night [an all-night, a security] light.

しょうゆ 醤油 soy [soya] sauce; soy.

しょうゆうせい 小遊星 〖天〗⇨ しょうわくせい.

しょうよ 賞与 a bonus ¶年末賞与 a year-end bonus.

じょうよ 剰余 a surplus; the remainder; 〈差し引き〉a balance; what is left over 《of sth》⇨ よじょう ¶剰余価値〖経済〗surplus value / 剰余金 a surplus (fund) / 剰余定理〖数〗the remainder theorem.

しょうよう¹ 商用 ¶商用で on (commercial) business / 商用で訪れる pay a business call [visit] (to) / 商用文 a business letter; commercial correspondence / 商用旅行 a business trip.

しょうよう² 逍遙 ⇨ さんぽ.

しょうよう³ 称賞揚 ⇨ しょうさん⁴.

しょうよう⁴ 従容 ¶従容たる composed; calm / 従容として 《文》composedly; calmly.

じょうよう¹ 乗用 ¶乗用の for riding / 乗用(自動)車 a (passenger) car.

じょうよう² 常用 ¶常用の in common [ordinary, everyday] use; common / 常用する use regularly [《文》habitually]; make regular use of 《a medicine》/ 常用漢字 Chinese characters designated for daily use / 常用者 a constant [habitual] user; an 《opium》addict / 常用対数 common logarithms.

しょうようじゅりん 照葉樹林 an evergreen [a glossy-leaved] forest.

じょうよく 情欲 sexual desire; lust.

しょうらい¹ 招来 ¶招来する cause; give rise to; lead to; 《文》bring about; invite; 《文》incur.

しょうらい² 将来 〈未来〉the future; 〈前途の見込み〉(the future) prospects ¶将来は[に] in (the) future; in time to come; in the days [years] ahead / 将来いつか some time [day] (in the future) / 将来の future; prospective / 将来を戒める warn [caution] sb for the future / 将来を見通した行動 a farsighted action / 近い[遠い]将来において in the near [distant, far-off] future / あまり遠くない将来に in the not-too-distant future; before too long / 将来(性)のある promising; hopeful; with a bright [rosy] future (before one); 《文》(a youth) of great promise. 文例↓

じょうらん 上欄 〈一番上の欄〉the top column; 〈前の欄〉the preceding column.

しょうり 勝利 a victory; (a) triumph; 《文》(a) conquest; a success; a win (競技での) ¶勝利を得る[占める] win; win 《the match [war]》; 《文》carry [win] the day; win [《文》gain, 《口語》clinch] a victory 《over》; earn [score, chalk up] a win 《over》/ 勝利を手中にする have victory in one's grasp; have the game in one's hands / …の勝利に帰する end in (a) victory for… / 勝利者 a victor; a winner (競技の) / 勝利投手 the winning pitcher. 文例↓

じょうり¹ 条理 logical sequence; reason ¶条理のある[立った] reasonable; consistent; logical; 《文》tenable; justifiable / 条理の立たない unreasonable; absurd; illogical; 《文》untenable / 条理にかなう stand to reason; be reasonable.

じょうり² 情理 ¶情理を尽くして説く try to persuade sb by appealing both to his heart and head; reason with sb.

-じょうり …場裡 the arena 《of competition》¶国際場裡に活躍する be active in the international session.

しょうもん 今頃わびを入れたって証文の出し遅れだよ. Your apology comes too late. | It is too late for you to apologize.

じょうやく 講和条約が両国間に調印された. A peace treaty was concluded between the two countries.

じょうやど 京都ではホテル四条を定宿にしている. I always put up at the Hotel Shijo when I go to Kyoto.

じょうよう この薬は常用しなければ効果がない. This medicine has to be taken regularly to be effective.

しょうらい² これらの事は君らが将来世の中に出るとき大いに役立つだろう. These things will prove useful some day when you go out into the world. / 将来どんな事があるかわからない. There is no knowing what will happen in the future. | Nobody can tell what the future has in store [holds] for us. / 将来いつか人類が戦争を一切やめるときが来るであろうか. Will the time come when man will put a complete end to war? / 彼の第一作はかなり将来の楽しめるものであった. His first novel was a work of considerable promise. / 彼女は歌手として大いに将来性がある. She has a great future as a singer. / 彼女には, 言語学より心理学のほうが, 将来性があるように思えた. It seemed to her that there was more of a future in psychology than in linguistics.

しょうり 木谷投手は今シーズン14

じょうりく 上陸 ¶上陸する land 《in a country, at a port》; go ashore 《at Kobe》;《文》disembark;〈軍隊などが〉make [《文》effect] a landing;〈台風が〉strike [hit]《Kyushu》/ 上陸している be ashore ; be on shore ;〈水兵が〉be on shore leave / 上陸地 a landing [disembarkation] point / 上陸用舟艇《軍》a landing craft.

しょうりつ 勝率 the percentage of victories (to the total number of matches [games]); a winning average.

しょうりゃく 省略《文》(an) omission;《文法》(an) ellipsis (*pl.* -lipses);〈簡略化〉(an) abbreviation;《文》(an) abridg(e)ment ¶省略する《文》omit ; leave out ;〈短縮する〉abbreviate ; abridge / 省略語 an abbreviation;《言語》a clipped form [word] (★ doctor をつづめた doc のような) / 省略符号 an apostrophe / 省略文 an elliptical sentence / 省略法 ellipsis. 文例⇩

しょうりゃく² 商略 a business [commercial] policy.

じょうりゅう 上流 〈川の〉the upper stream [course, reaches] ¶上流へこぎ上る row upstream / 上流の生まれである《文》be of high birth ; be born with a silver spoon in *one's* mouth / 上流の人びと, 上流人士《文》people of high birth ; the elite of society / 上流社会 high [fashionable] society ; the upper classes ; the cream of society ;《口語》the upper crust / 上流地域[地方] an upriver district / 上流婦人 a fashionable [《文》high-born] lady , a lady of fashion ; a society woman. 文例⇩

じょうりゅう² 蒸留 distillation ¶蒸留する distill / 蒸留器 a still ; a distiller / 蒸留酒 spirits ;《米》liquors / 蒸留水 distilled water / 蒸留装置 distillation apparatus [equipment].

しょうりょ 焦慮 ¶焦慮する be impatient [to *do*] ; be anxious 《for *sb*, about *sth*》; worry 《oneself》《about》/ 焦慮の色 a worried look / 焦慮の色が見える look worried.

しょうりょう¹ 少[小]量 a small quantity [amount] 《of》; a (little) bit ; a little ; a small dose 《of morphine》.

しょうりょう² 渉猟 ¶渉猟する《文》read extensively / 広く文献を渉猟する range extensively over [dig deeply into] the literature 《concerning *sth*》.

しょうりょくか 省力化 labor saving ¶省力化に役立つ work-[labor-]saving 《machines》.

じょうりょくじゅ 常緑樹 an evergreen tree ; an evergreen.

しょうれい¹ 省令 a ministerial ordinance.

しょうれい² 症例 a case 《of cholera》.

しょうれい³ 奨励 encouragement ¶奨励する encourage ;〈助成する〉《文》promote ; put [place] a premium 《on》/ 奨励給 incentive wages / 奨励給方式 an incentive pay system / 奨励金 a bounty ; a bonus. 文例⇩

じょうれい 条例 regulations ; rules ; a law ; a by(e)law ; an act ¶市の条例 a municipal bylaw [ordinance].

じょうれん 常連 regular visitors [customers] ;《口語》regulars ;《文》frequenters ; a patron (1 人) ;〈ファン〉an enthusiast ; a fan. 文例⇩

しょうろ《植》a truffle.

じょ(う)ろ a watering can [pot].

しょうろう 鐘楼 a bell tower ; a belfry.

しょうろく 抄録 ⇨ばっすい.

しょうろん 詳論 ¶詳論する discuss 《a subject》in detail [at (full) length] ;《文》dwell on *sth* ; go into details.

しょうわ¹ 小話 a little story ; an anecdote.

しょうわ² 笑話 a funny [humorous] story ; a joke.

しょうわ³ 唱和 ¶唱和する sing [give cheers] in chorus ; join in (the chorus) ;〈宗教儀式で〉respond ; make responses.

しょうわくせい 小惑星 《天》a small planet ; an asteroid ; a planetoid ¶小惑星帯 the asteroid belt.

しょうわる 性悪 ¶性悪の wicked ; malicious.

じょうわん 上腕 the upper arm ;《解》a brachium (*pl.* brachia) ¶上腕骨《解》a humerus (*pl.* -meri).

しょえん 初演 the first (public) performance [showing] 《of the play in Japan》; the (world) premiere 《of》¶初演する put (a play) on for the first time ; give the first public performance [showing] 《of》; premiere 《a play in Tokyo》. 文例⇩

じょえん 助演 support ; supporting performance ¶助演する play a supporting role ; support [assist]《the leading actor》/ 助演者 a supporting actor [actress]. 文例⇩

ショー 《put on》a show ; a display ¶ショールーム a showroom.

じょおう 女王 a queen ¶女王あり a queen ant / 女王ばち a queen bee [wasp].

回目の勝利をおさめた. Pitcher Kitani scored [posted] his 14th win [victory] of the season. / 最後の勝利を得るのはいずれか. Who will come out best [on top] in the end? / 彼らが勝利を喜んだのもほんのつかの間のことであった. They enjoyed their triumph only briefly.

しょうりゃく¹ ビオロンチェロというのを省略してもっと簡便にチェロと呼ぶのが普通である. The word 'violoncello' is usually shortened to the more convenient 'cello'.

じょうりゅう¹ その滝は橋よりも少し上流です. The falls are some distance above the bridge. / その川をさらに5キロ上流へ行った所に小さな村がある. There is a small village five kilometers (farther) up the river.

しょうれい¹ それは英語研究の奨励となるであろう. It will serve as an incentive [give a stimulus] to the study of English. / そんなことをすれば詐欺を奨励するようなものじゃない. That would be offering a premium to fraud.

じょうれん 彼はここで開かれるパーティーには大概出席する常連の1人だ. He is a regular at most of the parties held here.

しょえん この劇の初演は1950年です. The play was first staged [was put on for the first time] in 1950.

じょえん 彼女は最優秀助演女優として, アカデミー賞を受けた. She

ショーウインドー a show [《米》store] window; a shopwindow ¶ショーウインドーの陳列品 window displays / ショーウインドーを飾る dress a shopwindow / ショーウインドーをのぞき歩く window-shop / go window-shopping / ショーウインドーに陳列されている be on display in a window.
ジョーカー 《トランプ》a joker.
ジョージア Georgia (略: Ga.) ¶ジョージア州 a Georgian.
ショーツ (a pair of) shorts.
ショート¹ 《野球》a shortstop ¶ショートを守る play shortstop.
ショート² 《電》a short circuit ¶ショートする[させる] short-circuit; short.
ショートケーキ (a strawberry) shortcake.
ショール (wear, put on) a shawl; a wrap.
ショールダーバッグ ⇒ ショルダーバッグ.
しょか¹ 初夏 (in) early summer; (at) the beginning of summer ¶初夏に early in summer.
しょか² 書架 a bookshelf (pl. -shelves); a bookcase; a (book) stack (図書館の).
しょか³ 書家 a calligrapher; a calligraphist; a penman.
しょが 書画 paintings [pictures] and calligraphic works ¶書画骨董(ﾄｳ) objets d'art and curios.
じょがい 除外 ¶除外する exclude; 《文》except; make an exception of; count sth out / 除外条項 an escape clause / 除外例 an exception.
しょがかり 諸掛かり (sundry) expenses.
しょがくしゃ 初学者 a beginner; a beginning student; a novice ¶初学者向きの (a book) (intended) for beginners.
じょがくせい 女学生 a girl student; a schoolgirl.
しょかつ 所轄 jurisdiction ⇒ かんかつ ¶所轄官庁 the authorities concerned.
じょがっこう 女学校 a girls' (high) school.
しょかん¹ 所感 impressions (of); give 《文》express one's opinion [view] (on). 文例⇩
しょかん² 所管 ⇒ かんかつ.
しょかん³ 書簡 a letter; 《文》an epistle; a note (略式の); 〈外交文書〉a note; 〈総称〉correspondence ¶書簡集 a collection of letters / 書簡体の (a story) in letter 《文》epistolary form.
じょかん 女官 a lady of the court; a lady-in-waiting (pl. ladies-).
しょき¹ 初期 the early days [years]; the beginning; 〈病気などの〉the first [《文》incipient] stage ¶初期の early; initial; 《文》incipient / 初期に early on / 15世紀の初期に in the early years [part] of the 15th century; early in the 15th century. 文例⇩

しょき² 所期 ¶所期の expected; 《文》anticipated ¶~よき. 文例⇩
しょき³ 書記 a clerk; a secretary; 《文》an amanuensis (pl. -enses) ¶書記官 a secretary / 書記局 a secretariat / 書記生 an embassy [a legation, a consulate] clerk / 書記長 a chief secretary; 〈政党の〉a secretary-general (pl. secretaries-).
しょき⁴ 暑気 the heat; hot weather ¶暑気あたりする be affected by the (summer) heat; 〈日射病にかかる〉get [have, be affected by] sunstroke [heatstroke] / 暑気払いに to forget [beat] the summer heat.
しょきゅう 初級 the junior class (in); the beginners' course (in) ¶初級フランス語 〈書名〉French for Beginners.
じょきゅう 女給 a waitress; a barmaid.
じょきょ 除去 removal; elimination ¶除去する remove; 《口語》get rid of; do away with; eliminate; weed out (選んで).
しょぎょう 諸行 文例⇩
じょきょういん 女教員 a woman teacher (pl. women teachers); a female teacher; a schoolmistress; 《口語》a schoolmarm.
じょきょうじゅ 助教授 an assistant professor; an associate professor (准教授).
じょきょく 序曲 an overture (to an opera); a prelude (to).
ジョギング jogging; a jog ¶ジョギングをする jog / ジョギングに行く go jogging; go 《to the park》 for a jog.
しよく 私欲 self-interest ¶私欲を満たす 《文》satisfy one's selfish desires / 私欲に走る 《文》pursue one's own self-interest.
しょく¹ 食 〈食事〉a meal; a [one's] diet; 〈食物〉food; foodstuff(s); 〈食欲〉appetite ¶食が進む[進まない] have a good [poor] appetite / 日に3食を摂る have [eat, take] three meals a day / 食前[後]に before [after] a meal / 食後の果物[菓子] a dessert / 食前酒 an aperitif / 食中毒 food poisoning. 文例⇩
しょく² 蝕 《天》an eclipse.
しょく³ 燭 ⇒ とうか¹, しょっこう¹.
しょく⁴ 職 〈仕事〉work; 《文》employment; a job; a post; 〈働き口〉a position; 《文》a situation; a place; an opening; 〈職務〉one's duties; one's job; 〈職業〉《文》an occupation; a calling; a profession; a trade; 〈官公職〉《文》an office; a post; 《文》service ¶職のない unemployed; jobless / 職を探す look for [hunt] a job; 《文》seek employment [work] / 職を見つけてやる find work [an opening] for sb; get sb a job; put sb in the way of making a living / 職を失う lose one's job; 《文》employment,

---

won an Academy Award [an Oscar] as Best Supporting Actress.
しょかん¹ この事について一言所感を述べさせて頂きたい。Let me say a few words about this.
しょき¹ これは近松の初期の作である。This is one of Chikamatsu's early works.
しょき² 辛抱がなくてはとうてい所

期の目的は 達せられない。You'll never get what you want unless you persevere.
しょぎょう 諸行無常。All things are in flux and nothing is permanent.
しょく¹ 食後30分に服用。〈薬の袋などに書かれた指示〉To be taken 30 minutes after meals [each

meal].
しょく⁴ 君はもう職がすっかり決まっているんでしょう。You've got a job all lined up, haven't you？ / 今日我々が当面する最大の問題の1つはいかにしてこれらの人々に職を与えるかということである。One of the greatest problems facing us today is how to

しょくあたり 職を転々と変える hop from one job to another / 職をやめる leave [give up, quit] one's job ; resign one's office / 職を解かれる be dismissed from [《文》relieved of] one's post / 職を代える change one's job [《文》employment] ;《口語》switch jobs / 職を与える give sb work [a job, something to do] ; employ ; hire / 職を覚える learn a trade / 職につく[を得る] take [secure] employment ; get a job ;《文》obtain a position / 職についている have [keep, hold] a job ; be in employment [《regular》work] / 職にとどまる stay [remain, continue] in office 《as》. 文例⇩

しょくあたり 食あたり ¶食あたりする get [suffer from] food poisoning ; <食物が主語> disagree with one. 文例⇩

しょくあん 職安 ⇨ しょくぎょう(公共職業安定所)

しょくいき 職域 (the scope of) one's work ;《文》one's walk in life.

しょくいん 職員 <総称> the staff ; the personnel ;《米》the faculty (学校の) ; <個人> a member of the staff ¶《学校の》職員会議 a staff meeting / 職員組合 an office [a clerical] workers' union ; a white-collar [staff] union / (学校の)職員室 the staff [teachers', 《米》faculty] room / 職員名簿 a staff list ; a personnel directory ; a roster 《of a firm》 / 職員録 a directory of government officials.

しょぐう 処遇 treatment ¶処遇する treat ; deal with.

しょくえん 食塩 (table) salt ¶一つまみの食塩 a pinch of salt / 食塩入れ a saltcellar / 食塩水 a solution of salt / 食塩注射 a saline injection.

しょくぎょう 職業 <一般の> a job ;《文》an occupation ;《文》a calling ; a vocation (聖職) ; <専門的な> a profession ; <商業及び手細工の> a trade ¶…を職業とする be 《a typist》 by occupation ; be 《a carpenter》 by trade ; be 《a lawyer》 by profession / …を職業として選ぶ choose 《farming》 as one's occupation ; take up 《dancing》 professionally / 職業上の秘密 a trade secret / 公共職業安定所 a public employment security office / 職業意識 pride in [《文》identification with] one's job ;《文》awareness of the responsibilities of one's profession / 職業化する《文》professionalize ; put 《an enterprise》 on a commercial basis / 職業教育 vocational education / 職業軍人 a professional [career] soldier / 職業訓練 job [work] training 《for the unskilled》 / 職業紹介所 an employment office [agency] / 職業病 an occupational disease / 職業婦人 a working woman ; an office girl ; <専門能力を持った> a career woman / 職業別に 《arrange》 by [according to] (the) occupation / 職業別組合 a craft [《米》horizontal] union / 職業別電話帳 a classified telephone directory ; the yellow pages / 職業補導 [教育] vocational guidance [training]. 文例⇩

しょくげん 食言 ¶食言する go back on one's word ; break [take back] one's promise.

しょくご 食後 ⇨ しょく¹.

しょくざい 贖罪《文》atonement for [expiation of] one's sin(s) ¶キリストの[による]贖罪 the Redemption ; the Atonement / 贖罪する make (amends) for [《文》atone for] one's sin(s) ;《文》expiate one's sin(s).

しょくし 食指 the index finger ; the forefinger ¶食指が動く have an itch [《文》a desire] 《for sth, to do》 ; be eager 《for sth, to do》 ; have a (great) mind 《to do》 ; want 《to do》.

しょくじ¹ 食事 a meal ; (a) dinner ⇨ ゆうしょく¹ 囲み ; <まかない> board ¶軽い[粗末な]食事 a light [simple] meal / 充分な食事 a good [big, square, substantial] meal / バランスの取れた食事 a balanced diet / 食事の用意をする <料理の> get a meal ready ;《文》prepare a meal ; <食卓を> set [lay,《文》prepare] the table / 食事の後片付けをする clear the table / 食事をする have [eat, take] a meal ; eat ; dine / 家で食事をする have one's meal(s) [dinner] at home ; eat in / 外で食事をする eat [dine] out / きまった時間に食事をする have regular mealtimes / 早目に[大急ぎで]食事をする have an early [a hurried] meal / 食事を抜かす miss [《口語》skip, do not take] a meal / 食事を制限する put 《a patient》 on a diet / やせるために食事を制限する go on a (reducing) diet / 食事に招かれる be invited [asked] to dinner / 食事中である be in the middle of [be having] a meal [lunch, dinner] / 食事中に at (the) table ; while 《one is》 eating / 食事ごとに at each meal / 食事時間 a mealtime / 食事制限をしている人 a dieter. 文例⇩

しょくじ² 植字 typesetting ; composing ¶植字する set (up) [compose] type / 植字機 a composing [typesetting] machine / 植字工 a compositor ; a typesetter.

しょくしゅ¹ 触手 a feeler ; a tentacle ; an antenna《pl. -nae》 ¶触手を伸ばす put out a feeler ; <取ろうとする> reach 《for》 ; try to get (hold of).

しょくしゅ² 職種 the sort [type] of occupation 《one is engaged in》 ; an occupational category ¶職種別に 《arrange》 by [according to] (the) occupation.

しょくじゅ 植樹 ¶植樹する plant trees / 植樹運動 a tree planting campaign [drive] / 植樹

---

employ these people. / 不況で多くの人が職を失った。The depression threw a large number of people out of work.

しょくあたり 何か食あたりをしたに違いない。Something you ate must have disagreed with you.

しょくぎょう 彼の職業は何ですか。What does he do? | What is his occupation? | What is he? | What business is he in? / 職業の安定と公正な賃金を得る道は組合活動以外にないと思っている労働者は多い。Many workers think that unionism is the only way to obtain job security and fair wages. / 私は職業上たびたび旅行しなければならない。My job [business] requires a good deal of traveling. / 職業に貴賤なし。All legitimate trades are equally honorable.

しょくじ¹ この部屋は食事つきで月8万円です。The rent of this room is 80,000 yen a month with board. / 食事が50人分用意された。Places were laid for fifty persons. / お食事の仕度ができまし

しょくじょ 祭《米》Arbor Day.
しょくじょ 織女《星》Vega.
しょくしょう¹ 食傷 ¶食傷する《文》be surfeited [satiated] 《with》;《文》be cloyed 《with》;《文》glut [sate] *oneself* 《on》; have had enough 《of》;《くうんざりする》be fed up with *sth* (★ be fed up with *sth* は現代英語では比喩的にしか使われない).
しょくしょう² 職掌 *one's* (official) duties ¶職掌上[柄] as a matter of duty; in view of *one's* (official) position;《文》in *one's* official capacity; officially. 文例①
しょくじりょうほう 食事[餌]療法 a diet [dietary] cure ¶食事療法をする go [be] on a (special [specially prescribed]) diet / 食事療法をさせる put 《a patient》on a diet.
しょくしん 触診《医》palpation; examination by touch ¶触診する palpate; examine with the hand.
しょくじんしゅ 食人種 a cannibal race; cannibals.
しょくせい 職制 〈機構〉the organization [set-up] of an office;〈管理職〉(members of) the management.
しょくせいかつ 食生活 ¶食生活の変化《文》a change of diet ; a change in *one's* eating《文》dietary] habits / 食生活を改善する improve *one's* diet [eating habits] / 食生活をより楽しくする add interest [variety] to what *one* eats [《文》*one's* diet];《文》enhance the pleasure of the table.
しょくせき 職責 the responsibilities of *one's* work [job]; *one's* duty ¶職責を果たす《文》perform [discharge, fulfill] *one's* duties. 文例①
しょくぜん¹ 食前 ⇨ しょく¹ ¶食前酒 an aperitif.
しょくぜん² 食膳 a (dining) table ⇨ しょくたく¹ ¶食膳に上る be served.
しょくだい 燭台 a candlestick; a candlestand.
しょくたく¹ 食卓 a (dining) table ¶食卓の用意をする set [lay, spread] the table / 食卓を離れる leave the table; get up [《文》rise] from the table / 食卓を片づける clear the table [dishes] / 食卓につく sit down at the table [for *one's* meal, for lunch] / 食卓塩 table salt / 食卓用ナイフ[ナプキン] a table knife [napkin].
しょくたく² 嘱託 a part-time employee ¶嘱託する《文》entrust [charge] 《*sb* with a job》; commission 《*sb* to do》/ 嘱託殺人 murder at the victim's request.
しょくちゅう 食虫 ¶食虫動物[植物] an insectivorous animal [plant]; an insectivore.
しょくちょう 職長 a foreman; an overseer.
しょくつう 食通 a gourmet.

しょくどう¹ 食堂 a dining room [hall];〈駅・列車内の〉a buffet; a refreshment room;〈軍隊・工場などの〉a messroom; a canteen;〈大学・修道院などの〉a refectory;〈店〉a restaurant; an eating house ¶軽食堂 a snack bar;《米》a lunch counter;《米》a lunchroom; a cafeteria （セルフサービスの）/ 食堂車 a dining《英》restaurant] car;《米》a diner. 文例①
しょくどう² 食道《解》the gullet; the esophagus (*pl.* -guses, -gi) ¶食道の esophageal / 食道がん cancer of the esophagus; esophageal cancer.
しょくどうらく 食道楽 ⇨ くいどうらく.
しょくにく 食肉 (edible) meat ¶食肉加工業者 a meat processor / 食肉用の牛〈集合的〉beef cattle / 食肉類《動》carnivorous [predatory] animals; carnivores.
しょくにん 職人 a craftsman;《文》an artisan ¶職人気質[根性] pride in *one's* craftsmanship; the artisan spirit [attitude]. 文例①
しょくのう 職能 a function ¶職能給 wages based on job evaluation / 職能代表 vocational [functional] representation.
しょくば 職場 *one's* place of work [《文》employment]; *one's* workplace; the office (where *one* works);〈工場〉a workshop ¶職場を守る stick to *one's* post / 職場を離れる[放棄する] desert [quit] *one's* post [job]; walk out (on *one's* job); walk off the [*one's*] job / 職場環境 *one's* work environment / 職場結婚 marriage between people who work in the same place / 職場大会を開く hold a shop floor meeting [rally] / (労働争議の)職場代表 a shop steward [deputy] / 職場放棄 a walkout; a strike. 文例①
しょくばい 触媒《化》a catalyst; a catalytic (agent) ¶触媒作用《bring about》catalysis; catalytic activity.
しょくはつ 触発 ¶触発する〈機雷などが〉detonate on [be detonated by] contact;〈事態を〉touch off; trigger; spark; provoke 《a crisis》.
しょくパン 食パン《a loaf of》bread.
しょくひ 食費 food expenses [costs]; (the charge for) board (下宿の). 文例①
しょくひじゅつ 植皮術《外科》skin grafting.
しょくひん 食品 food(s); foodstuffs;《文》an article [item] of diet ¶食品衛生[化学] food hygiene [chemistry] / 食品科学 food science / 食品工業 the food industry / 食品添加物 an [a food] additive.
しょくぶつ 植物 a plant;〈総称〉plant life; vegetation;〈一地帯の〉the flora (*pl.* -s, -rae); the botany (of Japan) ¶植物園 a botanical garden / 植物学 botany / 植物学者 a botanist / 植物学の botanical / 植物界 the vegetable

---

た. Dinner is ready [served].
しょくしょう² 彼は職掌柄 そのことはよく心得ている. His duties have made him familiar with it.
しょくせき 彼は首相としての国家に対する職責を充分に遂行することができなかった. He was unable to serve his country properly as Prime Minister.

しょくどう¹ この列車には食堂車がついている. This train has a dining car attached.
しょくにん あの理髪店では職人が足りない. That barbershop is short of staff.
しょくば 私たちは職場結婚だった. I met my wife [husband] at work. | I used to work in the

same place [office, firm] as my wife [husband].
しょくひ 食費は幾ら払っていますか. How much do you pay for your board? / 月々の予算では食費が一番高くつく. Food is the most expensive item in my monthly budget.
しょくぶつ 植物の成長には日光が

kingdom / 植物形態学 morphological botany / 植物採集 plant collecting ; botanization / 植物採集に出掛ける go plant collecting / 植物誌 a flora ; a herbal / 植物質 vegetable matter [material] / 植物状態 《be left in》 a vegetable-like state ; 《口語》 《be no more than》 a cabbage [vegetable] / 植物性[質]の vegetable 《oils》 / 植物性食品 plant [vegetable] foods / 植物生態学 plant ecology / 植物性繊維 (a) vegetable fiber / 植物繊維 (a) plant fiber / 植物人間になって生き続ける 《口語》 live as a cabbage [vegetable]; 《文》 keep alive at a vegetative level / 植物標本 a botanical specimen ; ‹集合的に› a herbarium 《*pl.* -s, -baria》 / 植物分類学 systematic botany. [文例⇩]

しょくぶん[1] 食分 〘天〙 a phase of an eclipse.

しょくぶん[2] 職分 *one's* duty ; *one's* job ¶ 職分を守る 《文》 be faithful [true] to *one's* duty / 職分を全うする do [《文》 discharge] *one's* duty (to the full) ; 《文》 fulfill *one's* duty.

しょくべに 食紅 food red ; 《be pigmented red with》 a food color.

しょくぼう 嘱望 ¶ 嘱望する fasten [hang, put, pin] *one's* hopes on *sb* ; expect a great deal of [from] *sb* / 嘱望すべき promising. [文例⇩]

しょくみん 植民 colonization ¶ 植民する colonize (in) 《a land》 ; settle 《in》 / 植民地 a colony / 植民地の colonial / 植民地化する colonialize / 非植民地化する decolonialize / 植民地支配 colonial rule / 植民地支配国 a colonial ruler / 植民地主義 colonialism / 反植民地主義 anticolonialism / 植民地政策 a colonial policy / 植民地保有国 a colonial power.

しょくむ 職務 a duty ; 《文》 an office ; 《文》 a function ¶ 職務を果たす do *one's* duty ; 《文》 discharge [perform] *one's* duties / 職務を怠る neglect [《文》 be negligent of] *one's* duties / 職務上の official / 職務給 ⇨ しょくのう (職能給) / 職務規程 office regulations / 職務質問 questioning ; a police checkup / 職務質問をする question [check up on] 《a criminal suspect》 / 職務手当 a service allowance. [文例⇩]

しょくめい 職名 ‹職業名› 《文》 (the name of) *one's* occupation ; a job name ; ‹役職名› 《文》 the title of *one's* office [position] ; *one's* official title.

しょくもく 嘱目 ¶ 嘱目する pay attention to ; expect a lot of [from].

しょくもつ 食物 food ; foodstuffs ; a diet (一定の) ; ‹糧食› provisions ⇨ **たべもの** ¶ 食物源 a food source / 食物連鎖 〘生態〙 a food chain.

しょくよう 食用 ¶ 食用の for food ; edible / 食用に適する be edible ; be fit to eat [for food] / 食用に栽培[飼育]する grow [raise] *sth* for food / 食用油 (vegetable) cooking fat ; cooking [edible] oil / 食用がえる an edible frog / 食用植物 a food plant.

しょくよく 食欲 (an) appetite ¶ 食欲がある have a good appetite / 食欲がない have no [a poor] appetite / 食欲を満たす satisfy [《文》 appease] *one's* appetite / 食欲を減退[増進]させる 《文》 diminish [increase] *one's* appetite / 食欲を起こさせる arouse [whet, stimulate, sharpen] *one's* appetite / 食欲制御中枢 the appetite-controlling center (of the brain) / 食欲抑制剤 an appetite-suppressant. [文例⇩]

しょくりょう[1] 食料 food ¶ 食料品 provisions ; groceries ; 《an article of》 food ; foodstuffs / 食料品商 a dealer in foodstuffs ; a grocer / 食料品店 《米》 a grocery (store) ; 《英》 a grocer's (shop).

しょくりょう[2] 食糧 provisions ; food ¶ 1日分の食糧 ‹兵士や登山隊員などの携行する› a day's ration(s) / 食糧生産 food production / 食糧不足 a food shortage / 食糧問題[事情] the food problem [situation]. [文例⇩]

しょくりん 植林 《文》 afforestation ; tree planting ¶ 植林する 《文》 afforest ; plant trees ; reforest (再び).

しょくれき 職歴 *one's* (business [professional]) experience [career] ; *one's* work experience.

しょくん 諸君 you ; ‹呼びかけ› Gentlemen ; My friends.

じょくん 叙勲 ¶ 叙勲する 《文》 confer a decoration 《on *sb*》 ; decorate / 叙勲を申請する recommend *sb* for a decoration.

しょけい[1] 処刑 ‹死刑執行› (an) execution ¶ 処刑する execute ; put *sb* to death ; send *sb* to the scaffold / 処刑台 a scaffold ; a gallows 《単複同形》.

しょけい[2] 書痙 writer's cramp ; 《文》 scrivener's palsy.

じょけい 叙景 (a) description of scenery ¶ 叙景文 a scenery sketch.

じょけつ 女傑 a brave [spirited, heroic] woman ; 《文》 a lady of firm character ; 《文》 an Amazon.

しょげる be disheartened ; be dispirited ; 《文》 be crestfallen ; look dejected [《口語》 blue] ; 《口語》 be down in the dumps ; be downcast ; be cast down ; be downhearted ; be in low spirits ; 《口語》 be down in [at] the mouth.

しょけん[1] 初見 seeing *sth* [*sb*] for the first time ¶ 初見で歌う[演奏する] sing [play] 《a piece of music》 at sight ; sight-read.

しょけん[2] 所見 *one's* view 《of, on》 ; *one's* opinion 《on, about》 ; *one's* impressions 《of》 ; what [something] *one* has to say 《about *sth*》 ¶ 所

必要である. Sunlight is needed for plant growth.

しょくぼう 彼はみんなに嘱望されている. Everyone's hopes rest on him. / 我々はこの青年たちの将来に大いに嘱望している. We place great hopes upon the future of these young men.

しょくむ 職務上でやることだから, 悪く思わないで欲しい. I'm doing this as a matter of duty. I hope you will not take it amiss. / 彼は職務怠慢のかどで解雇された. He was dismissed on the grounds of neglect of duty.

しょくよく 病人は食欲が衰えている. The patient has lost his appetite. / 少し運動すると食欲が出る. A little exercise will give you a good appetite.

しょくりょう[2] 旅行にはたくさんの食糧を持って行った. We took plenty of provisions on our journey. / 我々の食糧はまだ1か月はある. Our provisions will last [hold out] for another month. / 食糧が欠乏した. The provisions

じょけん 見を述べる give [《文》express] *one's* opinion [views] 《on》; give *one's* impressions 《of》/ …について二，三所見を述べる 《文》make a few observations 《on》; pass a few remarks 《on》.

じょけん 女権 women's [woman's] rights; the rights of women /《参政権》female suffrage ¶女権運動 the women's rights movement / 女権拡張 extension of women's rights / 女権(拡張)論者 a feminist.

じょげん 助言 (a piece of) advice; a suggestion;《口語》a tip;《文》counsel ¶助言する advise;《文》counsel; give *sb* advice [counsel]; suggest; give *sb* a suggestion / 助言を求める ask *sb* for (*his*) advice / 助言者 an adviser; a counselor. 文例⇩

しょこ 書庫 a library; a stack (room) (図書館の).

しょこう¹ 初校 the first proof (sheet).

しょこう² 諸侯 feudal lords.

しょこう³ 曙光 ¶文明の曙光 the dawn of civilization / 希望の曙光 a gleam [flash] of hope / 事件解決の曙光 the first ray of hope for the solution of the matter. 文例⇩

じょこう¹ 女工 a factory girl;《文》a female operative; a woman worker (*pl.* women workers).

じょこう² 徐行 ¶徐行する go slowly; go [drive] at a slow speed; slow down [up]; reduce speed / 徐行中の車 a slow-moving vehicle / (鉄道ストなどの)徐行戦術 go-slow tactics. 文例⇩

しょこく 諸国 countries / 海外諸国 foreign countries / 中近東諸国 the Middle and Near East countries.

しょこん 初婚 (*one's*) first marriage. 文例⇩

しょさ 所作 〈身のこなし〉the way (in which) *one* moves [carries *oneself*];《文》*one's* carriage; 〈芝居の〉posturing; acting /〈バレーの〉a *pas d'action* ¶所作事 a pantomime [posture] dance (in *kabuki*).

しょさい¹ 所載 ¶本巻に所載の《*one's* article》printed in this volume.

しょさい² 書斎 a study ¶書斎人 a man who spends a great deal of his time in his study; an armchair expert [critic].

しょざい 所在 〈人の〉*one's* whereabouts; 〈物の〉(the place) where *sth* is (kept); 〈位置〉the position; the location / 所在を突き止める locate 《the enemy's camp》; discover [find out] *sb's* whereabouts; find out where sth is / 所在をくらます 《文》conceal *one's* whereabouts; disappear; hide *oneself*; go into hiding / 責任の所在を明らかにする find out who is responsible [where the responsibility lies] / 所在ない have nothing to do; be [feel] bored / 所在なさ boredom;《文》tedium;《文》ennui / 県庁の所在地 the seat of a prefectural government. 文例⇩

じょさい 如才 ¶如才(の)ない〈抜け目のない〉smart; sharp; clever;〈巧妙な〉《文》adroit; skillful;〈調子のよい〉《口語》slick; affable / 如才なく立ち回る keep *one's* wits about *one*; play *one's* cards well.

しょさん 所産 a product;《文》fruit(s); an outcome; a result.

しょさんぷ 初産婦 《医》a primipara (*pl.* -ras, -rae); a woman bearing [expecting] her first child.

じょさんぷ 助産婦 a midwife (*pl.* -wives).

しょし 初志 *one's* original purpose [intention, aim,《文》object] ¶初志を貫く carry out *one's* original intention / 初志を翻す[翻さない] give up [abide by, stick to] *one's* original purpose.

しょじ 所持 ¶所持する possess; own; have 《cash》about [on, with] *one*; carry / 所持金 money [cash] carried in *one's* pocket 《on *one's* person》/《文》on *one's* person / 所持者 the possessor; the owner / 所持品 *one's* belongings [things]; *one's* personal effects. 文例⇩

じょし¹ 女子 〈婦人〉a woman (*pl.* women); a lady; 〈女児〉a girl; 〈娘〉a daughter ¶女子の female; women's; ladies'; girls' / 女子学生 a female [girl] student /《米口語》a co-ed (男女共学の大学の) / 女子教育 education of women [girls] / 女子大学 a women's college / 女子寮 a women's dormitory (《口語》dorm).

じょし² 女史 ¶田中女史 Mrs. [Miss, Ms.] Tanaka / 女史タイプの女 a highbrow-looking woman; 〈口語〉a schoolmarm.

じょし³ 助詞 《文法》a postpositional particle (of Japanese).

しょしがく 書誌学 bibliography ¶書誌学者 a bibliographer.

しょしき 書式 a 《prescribed, due》form ¶書式どおりに in the proper [《口語》in due] form /《文》according to the form prescribed. 文例⇩

じょしし 叙事詩 an epic (poem) ¶叙事詩の時代 the age of epic poetry / 英雄叙事詩 a heroic epic.

じょしつ 除湿 ¶除湿する dehumidify / 除湿剤 a dehumidifying agent.

しょじ(ばんたん) 諸事(万端) everything;《文》all matters [affairs].

しょしゃ 諸車 [《文》口語].

しょしゅ 諸種 ⇨ しゅじゅ.

じょしゅ 助手 an assistant 《to Prof.—》¶W大学化学研究室の助手 a chemistry assistant at W University / 運転助手 《英》the driver's

---

have run short. | We have run short of food. / ヨットは3日分の食糧を積んでいた。The yacht was provisioned for three days.

じょげん 途方に暮れていたが、そのとき河野さんの助言を仰ごうという考えが浮かんだ。I was at a loss what to do, when the idea of going [turning] to Mr. Kono for advice occurred to me.

しょこう³ まだ平和の曙光を見るに至らない。There is as yet no prospect of a return of peace.

じょこう² 列車は駅に近くなって徐行した。The train slowed down for the station. / 徐行。【掲示】Go slow.

しょこん 彼は38歳ですが初婚です。Though he is thirty-eight he has never been married before.

しょざい 常に所在を明らかにしておいてもらいたい。Keep me informed as to your whereabouts. / 所在なさに子供を相手に半日暮らした。I had to beguile my time by playing with the children half the day.

しょしゅう assistant [《口語》mate] ;《米》an assistant driver (自動車の) ;《米》an assistant motorman (電車の) /《運転》助手席 the passenger seat ; the assistant driver's seat.

しょしゅう¹ 初秋 early autumn [《米》fall] ; the beginning of autumn.

しょしゅう² 所収 ¶…所収の論文 an article published [carried, printed] in 《a journal》⇒しょさい¹.

じょしゅう 女囚 a female prisoner [convict].

じょじゅつ 叙述 (a) description ; an account ;《文》(a) depiction ;《文》narration ¶叙述する describe ; give an account of sth ; give a 《good》picture of sth ; narrate / 叙述的 descriptive ; narrative ;《文法》predicative.

しょしゅん 初春 early spring ; the beginning of spring.

しょじゅん 初旬 ⇒じょうじゅん.

しょじょ 処女 a virgin ;《文》a maiden ¶処女降誕《キリスト教》the Virgin Birth / 処女作《航海》a maiden work [the voyage] / 処女性 virginity ;《文》maidenhood ;《文》maidenhead / 処女生殖《動》virgin birth ;《reproduce by》parthenogenesis / 処女地 virgin soil ; (a) virgin territory / 処女飛行を行なう make its maiden flight / 処女膜【解】the hymen ;《文》the maidenhead.

しょじょう 書証【法】documentary evidence.

しょじょう 書状 ⇨てがみ.

じょじょう 叙情 description of feelings ; lyricism ¶叙情的 lyric(al) / 叙情詩 a lyric (poem) ; lyric poetry (総称) / 叙情詩人 a lyric poet.

じょじょうふ 女丈夫 ⇨じょうふ.

じょじょに 徐々に slowly ; gradually ;《by》(slow) degrees ; little by little ; step by step.

しょしん¹ 初心 ¶初心の inexperienced ;《口語》green (as grass) / 初心に返る remember what state of mind one was in at first ; remember one's original purpose / 初心者 a beginner ; a novice /《米口語》a greenhorn ;《文》a tyro 《pl. -s》/ 初心者向きの《books》for beginners /《自動車に貼る》初心者マーク the symbol of a newly-licensed driver. 文例⇩

しょしん² 初診 the first medical examination ¶初診の患者 a new patient / 初診料 the fee charged for a patient's first visit.

しょしん³ 所信 one's belief [《文》conviction] ; one's opinion [view] ¶所信を断行する force [push] one's decision through ; carry through [out] what one has decided [《文》determined on] / 所信を述べる give [express] one's opinion ;《文》voice one's conviction / 所信を曲げない be firm [unshaken] in one's convictions ; stick [hold fast] to one's view [belief].

じょすう¹ 序数 an ordinal (number).

じょすう² 除数【数】a divisor.

しょする 処する《処理する》manage ; deal with ; cope with ; dispose of ;《罰する》sentence [condemn]《sb to death》¶身を処する act ; behave ;《文》conduct [bear, carry, comport] oneself. 文例⇩

しょせい¹ 処世《文》conduct of life ¶処世訓 one's motto [guiding principle] in life / 処世法[術] how to get on in the world ; the secret of success in life / 処世術を心得ている know how to get on in life [how to swim with the current] / 処世術がへたである《文》be lacking in worldly wisdom.

しょせい² 書生《学生》a student ;《玄関番》a houseboy ⇒がくせい¹.

じょせい¹ 女声 a female voice ¶女声合唱 a female chorus.

じょせい² 女性 a woman 《pl. women》; womenfolk ;《総称》womankind ;《文》the fair [gentle, weaker, feeble] sex ;【文法】the feminine (gender) ¶女性的の feminine ;《文》womanly /《柔弱な》effeminate / 女性解放運動 the women's (liberation [《口語》lib]) movement / 女性差別 discrimination against women ; sexism / 女性上位 ⇨じょうい¹ / 女性美 feminine beauty.

じょせい³ 女婿 a [one's] son-in-law 《pl. sons-》.

じょせい⁴ 助成 ¶助成する《補助する》《文》assist ;《文》aid ;《促進する》《文》further ;《文》promote / 助成金 a subsidy ; a grant / 農業助成計画 a farm subsidy program.

じょせいと 女生徒 a schoolgirl ; a girl student.

しょせき 書籍 books ; publications ¶書籍愛好家《文》a bibliophile ; a lover of books ; a book lover / 書籍市 a book fair / 書籍商《人》a bookseller /《店》a bookstore ;《英》a bookshop / 書籍収集狂《事》bibliomania ;《人》a bibliomaniac.

じょせき 除籍 ¶除籍する remove 《sb's name》 from the register ; strike sb's name off the list ;《学校から》expel.

しょせつ¹ 所説 one's opinion [view].

しょせつ² 諸説 various views [opinions, theories] ;《風説》different rumors ¶諸説紛々としている opinion is divided 《on sth》.

じょせつ¹ 序説 an introduction 《to》⇨じょろん.

じょせつ² 除雪 ¶除雪する clear (away) (the) snow 《from the street》/ 除雪(機関)車 a snowplow.

しょせん 所詮 ⇨とうてい, けっきょく. 文例⇩

しょぞう 所蔵 ¶…の所蔵である be owned by… ;《文》be in sb's possession.

じょそう¹ 女装 ¶女装する disguise oneself as a woman ; wear female dress ;《俗》be in drag.

じょそう² 助走 a run-up ; an approach run

しょじ 所持金が千円しかない. I have only a thousand yen with [on] me. / 体を調べたらこの短刀を所持していた. This dagger was found on his person.

しょしき この請願は書式が違っている. This petition is not (written) in the proper form.

しょしゃ 諸車通行止.《掲示》Closed to vehicular traffic.

しょしん 初心忘るべからず. Keep your mind as open as when you began to learn the art.

しょする 彼は厳罰に処すべきだ. He deserves severe punishment. / 当時百姓は土地を離れることを禁じられ, 違反すれば厳罰に処せられた. In those days peasants were forbidden to leave their land un[under] pain of severe punishment. / あらゆる場合によく身を処するということはやさしいことではない. It is not easy to act properly on every occasion.

しょせん 所詮は彼の努力次第です. In the final analysis it depends on his own efforts. / 病人

《for the long jump》 ¶助走路 a runway ; an approach.

じょそう[3] 助奏 〔音楽〕《イタリア語》an *ob(b)ligato* 《pl. *-s, -ti*》.

じょそう[4] 序奏 〔音楽〕an introduction 《to》.

じょそう[5] 除草 ¶除草する weed 《a garden》/ 除草剤 a weed killer ; a herbicide.

じょそう[6] 除霜 ¶除霜する defrost ; deice / 除霜装置 a defroster.

しょぞく 所属 ¶…所属の belonging to… ; attached to… / 所属する belong [be attached] 《to》/ 所属させる attach ; assign ; put *sb* under the control [command] 《of》. 文例⇩

しょぞん 所存 ⇨かんがえ, つもり.

じょそんだんぴ 女尊男卑 respect for woman at the expense of man ; putting women above men. 文例⇩

しょたい[1] 所[世]帯 a household ; a home ¶所帯を構える[持つ] (get married and) set up [make] a new home ; make *one's* home 《at》; keep [set up] house / 所帯を畳む shut up *one's* house ; give up housekeeping / 所帯染みる be domesticated ; become domestic [housewifely] ; go [run] to seed (身なりなどに気を使わなくなる) / 大所帯 《have》 a large family ; 《文》《keep》 a large establishment / 所帯道具 household goods; furniture and kitchen utensils necessary for housekeeping / 所帯主 the head of a household [family] ; a householder / 所帯持ち a married man [woman] ; a family man / 所帯やつれする be [look] worn out by domestic [family] cares. 文例⇩

しょたい[2] 書体 a style of handwriting [penmanship] ; 〈活字の〉 a style of type ; a type face.

しょだい 初代 the founder ¶初代の the first / 初代団十郎 Danjuro I [the First].

じょたい 除隊 ¶除隊になる be discharged from military service / 満期除隊 an honorable discharge.

しょたいめん 初対面 *one's* first meeting [interview] 《with》; the first meeting 《between》. 文例⇩

しょだな 書棚 a bookshelf 《*pl.* -shelves》.

しょだん 初段 *shodan* ; the lowest [first] grade (of the senior class) 《in *judo*》. 文例⇩

しょち 処置 〈処理〉《文》disposition ; 《文》disposal ; management ; 〈手当〉 treatment ; 〈方策〉《文》a measure ; a step ⇨しょぶん ¶処置する 〈処理する〉 dispose of ; deal with ; manage ; 〈手当する〉 treat ; give medical treatment 《to》/ 適宜な処置をとる deal with *sth* as *one* thinks fit ; use *one's* discretion in dealing with *sth* / 処置を誤る take the wrong measures ; make a mistake in dealing with 《an affair》/ …の処置に窮する do not know what to do with … ; be at a loss how to deal with…. 文例⇩

しょちゅう 暑中 ⇨なつ, せいか[7] ¶暑中休暇 the summer vacation [holidays] / 暑中見舞を出す write to *sb* offering best wishes for (*his* health in) the hot season.

じょちゅう 女中 a maidservant ; a woman servant 《*pl.* women servants》; a housemaid ; a maid ¶女中を置く[使う] keep a maid.

じょちゅうぎく 除虫菊 〔植〕a Dalmatian pyrethrum ★日常語としては単に a pyrethrum で足りる.

じょちゅうざい 除虫剤 an insect repellent ; an insectifuge.

しょちょう[1] 初潮 〔生理〕menarche ; the beginning [establishment] of menstruation ¶初潮を見た時に at the onset of *one's* first menstruation.

しょちょう[2] 所長 the head [chief, manager] 《of an office, a factory》.

しょちょう[3] 署長 the head [chief, superintendent] ; 《米》a 《town, fire》 marshal (警察署·消防署の).

じょちょう 助長 《文》promotion ; 《文》furtherance ; encouragement ¶助長する 《文》promote ; encourage ; 《文》further ; 《文》foster ; 《文》be conducive to 《better mutual understanding》; make for 《national welfare》.

しょっかいせい 職階制 a job-ranking [job classification] system.

しょっかく[1] 触角 a feeler ; an antenna 《*pl.* -nae》; a tentacle ¶触角を伸ばす put out *its* feelers.

しょっかく[2] 触覚 the sense of touch ; 《文》(a) tactile sensation ; (a) feeling ¶触覚の 《文》tactile ; 《文》tactual / 触覚器官 a tactile [touch] organ.

しょっかん[1] 食間 《to be taken》 between meals.

しょっかん[2] 触感 the sense of touch ; the feel.

しょっき[1] 食器 tableware; 《文》eating utensils; a dinner [table] service (一揃い) ¶食器洗い 《米》dishwashing ; 《英》washing-up / 食器戸棚 a cupboard ; a sideboard.

しょっき[2] 織機 a loom.

ジョッキ a beer mug ; a tankard ; a stein (陶器製の) ★この外来語は jug に由来するが, jug は注ぎ口のある水さし, ミルク入れの類をいう ¶ジョッキ1杯のビール a mug of beer.

ショック a shock ¶ショックを与える give *sb* a shock ; shock / ショックを受ける be 《greatly》 shocked / ショック死 (a) death from shock / ショック療法 shock therapy [treatment].

しょっけん[1] 食券 a food [meal] ticket [cou-

は所詮助かるまい. I'm afraid he is past all hope of recovery.

しょぞく 私の所属はまだ決まっていない. I have not yet been assigned to a post.

じょそんだんぴ アメリカは女尊男卑の国だ. The United States of America is a women's paradise.

しょたい[1] あなたなら所帯持ちの上手な奥さんになられることでしょう. I'm sure you'll make a good housewife. / どことなく所帯染みた所のある女だ. There is something of the housewife about her. / 彼女はすっかり所帯染みてしまった. She is now every inch a housewife. / 息子もいよいよ所帯を持ちます. My son is going to settle down (and get married) at last.

しょたいめん あの方とはそのときが初対面でした. That was the first time I met him. | He had been a complete stranger to me until then.

しょだん あの人は柔道初段だ. He is a *shodan* [has reached the first grade] in *judo*.

しょち それは私が処置しておきます. I'll see to it. / 彼は断固たる

pon]; 《英》a luncheon voucher (従業員に支給する).

しょっけん[2] 職権 *one's* (official) authority ¶職権により《文》in [by] virtue of *one's* office; 《ラテン語》*ex officio* / 職権を行使[乱用]する《文》exercise [abuse] *one's* authority / 職権乱用 abuse of (*one's*) authority; 〘法〙misfeasance. [文例⇩]

しょっこう[1] 燭光 〘物〙candlepower (略: c.p.); candle ¶50燭光のバーナー a burner of 50 candlepower; a 50-candle burner / 8万燭光を出す produce 80,000 candlepower.

しょっこう[2] 職工 a workman; a worker; an operative; a factory hand; a mechanic (機械工) ¶職工長 a foreman; a supervisor / 職工服 working clothes; 《denim》overalls.

しょっちゅう 〈始終〉always; all the time; 《口語》forever; constantly; 《文》at all times; 〈しばしば〉very often. [文例⇩]

しょっぱい (too) salty; there is too much salt 《in the soup》.

ショッピング 《go, be out》shopping ¶ショッピングカー a shopping trolley / ショッピングセンター a shopping center [district] / ショッピングバッグ a shopping [《英》a carrier] bag.

しょてい 所定 ¶所定の《文》designated; 《文》stated 《hours》; 《文》prescribed 《form》/ 所定の場所[時間] the appointed [fixed, stated] place [time] / 所定の位置につく take [be in] *one's* place [position] / 机を所定の位置に置く put a desk in place.

じょてい 女帝 an empress.

しょてん 書店 a bookseller's; 《米》a bookstore; 《英》a bookshop.

じょてんいん 女店員 a saleswoman; a salesgirl; 《英》a shopgirl.

しょとう[1] 初冬 early winter; the beginning of winter ¶初冬に in (the) early winter; early in winter.

しょとう[2] 初等 ⇨しょほ ¶初等科 an elementary course; the beginners' class / 初等数学 elementary mathematics / 初等教育 elementary [primary] education.

しょとう[3] 初頭 ⇨はじめ.

しょとう[4] 蔗糖 cane sugar.

しょとう[5] 諸島 (a group of) islands; an archipelago 《*pl.* -(e)s》 ¶ハワイ諸島 the Hawaiian Islands.

しょどう 書道 (the art of) calligraphy; penmanship ¶書道の大家 a master [great] calligrapher; a calligraphy master.

じょどうし 助動詞 〘文法〙an auxiliary verb.

しょとく 所得 〈収入〉(an) income; 〈収益〉earnings; profits ¶年800万円の所得がある have a yearly income of ¥8,000,000 / 純[総]所得 net [gross] income / 所得額 (the amount of) *one's* income / 所得格差 income differentials [disparities] / 所得水準 the income level 《of the nation》/ 所得税 an income tax / 所得政策 an incomes policy / 所得層 《different》income groups / 最低所得層 the lowest income groups / 所得倍増案 the income doubling program / 所得配分 income distribution. [文例⇩]

しょなのか 初七日 (a religious service held on) the sixth day after *sb's* death.

じょなん 女難 《get into》trouble with women ¶女難の相がある have the sort of looks that ask for trouble in the way of women.

しょにち 初日 the first [opening] day [night]; the premiere.

しょにんきゅう 初任給 *one's* [the] starting [《文》initial] salary [pay]. [文例⇩]

しょねん 初年 〈第1年〉the first year; 〈初期〉the early years ¶明治の初年に in the early years of Meiji; early in the Meiji era.

じょのくち 序の口 (only) the beginning; the opening; the start; the first [initial] stage. [文例⇩]

しょばつ 処罰 punishment 《for a crime, of a criminal》; (a) penalty ¶処罰する punish 《*sb* for a crime》; 《文》inflict a penalty 《on *sb* for an offense》/ 処罰を免れる escape punishment; get away with it; get off scot-free.

しょはん[1] 初犯 〈罪〉the first offense; 〈人〉a first offender.

しょはん[2] 初版 《a copy of》the first edition.

じょばん 序盤 an opening [the opening moves] 《of a game of *go*》 ¶序盤の手 the opening moves. [文例⇩]

しょひょう 書評 a book review ¶書評をする review a book / 書評家 a book reviewer; a book critic; a book columnist 《for *The New Yorker*》/ 書評用の献本 a review copy.

じょひょう 除氷 ¶除氷する defrost; 〈航空機から〉deice / 除氷装置 a defroster; 〘航空〙a deicer.

しょぶん 処分 〈処置〉《文》disposal; 《文》disposition; dealing 《with a problem》; 《文》a measure; 〈処罰〉punishment ¶ごみの処分 garbage disposal / 処分する dispose of; deal with; make a clearance of 《shop-soiled goods》; 〈罰する〉punish / 古雑誌を処分する dispose of old magazines / 不当処分 《文》an improper [unwarrantable] proceeding [measure] / 処分品 clearance goods.

じょぶん 序文 a preface 《to》; a foreword 《to, for》; an introduction 《to》; a preamble 《to, of》(法令などの).

処置が取れないでいる. He cannot bring himself to take any decisive steps.

しょっけん[2] 議長の職権により退場を命じます. On my authority as chairman I order you to leave the room.

しょっちゅう 塩屋さんはしょっちゅう飼犬の話ばかりしている. Mr. Shioya is forever talking about his dog.

しょとく 普通定年まで大体30年間は働いて所得が得られる. The average worker has about thirty years of earning life until retirement.

しょにんきゅう 私の初任給は8万円だった. I started with [on] a salary of 80,000 yen.

じょのくち (感心している相手に) いや, まだ序の口だよ. Just wait till I [we] really get started. | You should see me [us] when I [we] really get going. | 《俗》You ain't seen nothin' yet!

じょばん 選挙はまだ序盤戦だ. The election campaign is still in

しょほ 初歩 the first step(s) (to, in); a beginners' course (in French); the rudiments (of); the elements (of); the ABC (of) ¶初歩の《文》rudimentary; elementary. 文例⇩

しょほう 諸方 ⇒ほうぼう.

じょほう 除法 【数】division.

しょほう(せん) 処方(箋) a (medical) prescription ¶処方箋を書く write (out) [make out] a prescription; prescribe (a medicine for a patient, for a complaint) / 処方どおりに as prescribed.

しょぼしょぼ ¶しょぼしょぼした目 bleary eyes / しょぼしょぼした目で見る look blearily (at).

じょまく 序幕 the opening [first] act [scene].

じょまくしき 除幕式 an unveiling (ceremony); (米) an unveiling exercise.

しょみん 庶民 <総称> the (common) people; 《文》the populace; 《文》the masses (米) common [ordinary] folks (《英》is folk); <平均的> the man in the street; <1人> a commoner ¶庶民の英雄 a popular [folk] hero / 庶民的everyday (dishes); 《文》unpretentious (tastes); popular; folksy (humor).

しょむ 庶務 general affairs ¶庶務課 the general affairs section.

しょめい¹ 書名 the title (of a book) ¶「歴史とは何か」という書名の本 a book entitled *What is History?* / 書名目録【図書館】a title catalog(ue).

しょめい² 署名 a signature; an autograph (自分の写真・作品などにするもの); <新聞・雑誌記事の執筆者の> a by-line ¶署名する sign *one's* name; sign (a contract); autograph; 《文》subscribe *one's* name to (a document) / ...の署名がある 《文》carry [bear] *sb's* signature / 署名を請う ask *sb* for *his* autograph / 百万人の署名を集める collect [get, 《文》obtain] one million signatures / 署名入りの記事 an article signed by the writer; an article under the writer's name [by-line] / 署名入りの写真 an autographed photo / 署名入りの絵 a picture signed by the artist / 署名運動 a signature-collecting campaign / 署名国 a signatory (power) / 署名者 a signer / 下記[上記]署名者 <文書などでいう> the undersigned [oversigned] / 署名捺印する sign and seal (a document) / 署名捺印のある (a bond) under *sb's* hand and seal.

じょめい¹ 助命 *sb's* life / 助命を請う appeal for mercy; ask for *sb's* life.

じょめい² 除名 《文》dismissal from membership; (an) expulsion ¶除名する strike [take] *sb's* name off the list; dismiss (*sb* from membership); expel [oust] (*sb* from the club). 文例⇩

しょめん 書面 <手紙> a letter; 《文書》a document ¶書面にする put *sth* in writing; 《文》commit *sth* to writing / 書面で in writing; by letter.

しょもう 所望 ¶所望する《文》desire; wish for; ask for; call on [upon] (*sb* to do) / 所望により 《文》in compliance with] *sb's* request.

しょもく 書目 a catalog(ue) of books.

しょもつ 書物 a book; a volume ⇒ほん.

しょや 初夜 <結婚の> the bridal [first] night.

じょや 除夜 New Year's Eve; 《文》the watch night ¶除夜の鐘 the watch-night bell; the bell ringing out [speeding] the old year.

じょやく 助役 <市の> a deputy mayor; <町村の> the headman's assistant; <駅の> an assistant [a deputy] stationmaster.

しょゆう 所有 《文》possession; ownership ¶所有する have; own; 《文》possess; hold; be the owner of; 《文》be in possession of / 所有となる come into *one's* hands; 《文》pass into *one's* possession / ...の所有の owned by...; belonging to... / 所有格【文法】the possessive [genitive] case / 所有権【法】(the right of) ownership [proprietorship]; proprietary rights; a right [title] (to *sth*) / 所有者 an owner; a possessor; 《文》a proprietor / 共同所有者 a joint [common] owner / 所有者のない ownerless / 所有高 <株などの> holdings / 所有地 *one's* land; the land that *one* owns / 所有物 *one's* possessions [property] / 所有欲 a desire for possessions / 所有欲の強い possessive; grasping; 《文》covetous. 文例⇩

じょゆう 女優 an actress.

しょよ 所与 ¶所与の《文》given / 所与の条件のもとで under the given condition(s).

しょよう¹ 所用 ⇒ようじ¹.

しょよう² 所要 ¶所要の necessary; (articles) needed; required / 所要時間 the necessary time; the time required [needed].

しょり 処理 management; 《文》disposition; 《文》disposal; dealing (with); 《文》conduct; processing; (a) (chemical) treatment (薬品などの) ¶処理する manage; deal with; dispose of; 《文》transact; 《文》conduct; <生産用原料などを> process; <薬品などを> treat / 予め処

しょほ 英文法の初歩も知らない。He doesn't know the first thing about [He does not have even a rudimentary knowledge of] English grammar. / 私たちの仕事はまだほんの初歩の段階です。Our work is still in its early stages [at an early stage].

じょまくしき 来月7日故アーノルド博士の銅像除幕式が行なわれる。The bronze statue of the late Dr. Arnold will be unveiled on the 7th next month.

じょめい² 彼らは党から除名された。They were expelled from the party.

しょゆう この土地は池田氏の所有だ。This land belongs to Mr. Ikeda.

しょり 私はその事件の処理を一任された。I was entrusted with bringing the affair to a (satisfactory) conclusion. | I was given the job of sorting things out. / その工場からの廃棄物がすべて、未処理のまま海へ流されていた。All the waste from the factory was passing untreated into the sea.

じょりょく 君の助力がなかったら成功しなかったろう。I could not have succeeded without your assistance. / 僕は君以外に助力を仰ぐ人がない。I have no one but you to turn to for aid.

しら 彼は知らぬ存ぜぬとしらを切っている。He persists in denying all knowledge of it.

じょりゅう 女流 ¶女流(の) lady; female / 女流作家 a woman writer (*pl.* women writers); a lady writer; an authoress.

じょりょく 助力 help; 《文》aid; 《文》assistance; cooperation (協力); backing (後援) ¶助力する help 《*sb* in work, (to) *do*》; 《文》assist [aid] 《in *sb's* work》; 《文》give aid [assistance] (to); cooperate 《with *sb* in *his* work》/ 助力を仰ぐ ask for *sb's* help; 《文》look to *sb* for assistance / 人の助力を受けないで 《文》unaided; by *oneself*; single-handed.

しょるい 書類 documents; papers ¶書類かばん a briefcase; an attaché case / 書類整理箱 a filing cabinet / 書類選考する draw up a short list on the basis of the candidates' documents [records] / 書類送検する send the papers pertaining to a (criminal) case to the Public Prosecutors Office / 書類ばさみ a file; a folder (厚紙を2つに折った).

ショルダーバッグ a shoulder bag.

じょれつ 序列 a rank; ranking; a grade; order (of precedence) ¶序列をつける 《文》rank (people) hierarchically.

しょろう 初老 ¶初老の middle-aged; elderly; aging ★ middle-aged は大体40・50代の人に用い, elderly はそれを越えた人に用いる.

じょろう 女郎 a prostitute ¶女郎屋 (visit) a brothel.

じょろん 序論 an introduction (to); 《文》introductory remarks.

しょんぼり ¶しょんぼりと (sit) looking miserable [《口語》blue]; 《文》dejectedly; by *oneself* with an unhappy look; 《文》despondently; downheartedly; 《文》crestfallen.

しら ¶しらをきる 《文》feign [affect] ignorance; pretend to know nothing (about); play (the) innocent; brazen [face] it out. 文例↓

じらい 地雷 a (land) mine ¶地雷を仕掛ける lay a mine; mine (a field) / 地雷探知機 a mine detector.

しらうお 白魚 a whitebait (単複同形); an icefish ¶白魚のような指 long [delicate] white fingers.

しらが 白髪 gray hair (半白); white hair (全白) ¶白髪になる 〈髪が主語〉 turn gray [white]; 〈人が主語〉 go gray [white]; one's hair goes gray [white] / 白髪頭の gray-haired; white-headed / 白髪交じりの streaked [shot] with gray; grizzled / 白髪染め a hair dye. 文例↓

しらかば 白樺 a white birch.

しらかべ 白壁 (a house with) a white [whitewashed] wall.

しらかわよふね 白河夜船 ¶白河夜船である be fast [sound] asleep 《while...》.

しらき 白木 plain [unvarnished, unpainted] wood ¶白木造りの 《a *Shinto* shrine》 built of plain wood.

しらくも 【医】tinea; ringworm ¶しらくも頭 a ringwormed scalp; a head infected with ringworm.

しらける have a chill cast over *it*; be spoiled ¶座をしらけさせる人 a kill-joy; a wet blanket. 文例↓

しらこ 白子 〈魚の〉 soft roe (食用の精巣); milt (魚精); 〈病気〉 albinism / 〈人間〉 an albino

しらさぎ 〔鳥〕 an [a white] egret. (*pl.* -s).

しらじらしい 白々しい ¶白々しいうそ a barefaced [shameless] lie / 白々しく with an air of innocence; 《文》with feigned ignorance; shamelessly.

しらす 〔魚〕 a whitebait (単複同形) ¶しらす干し dried young sardines.

-しらず ...知らず 文例↓

じらす 焦らす irritate; tease; 〈見せびらかして〉 tantalize; 〈気をもます〉 keep *sb* in suspense ¶子供をじらして泣かす tease a child into tears. 文例↓

しらずしらず 知らず知らず 《文》unwittingly; 《文》unawares; without knowing it ¶知らず知らず悪の道にはまる slip [drift] into evil ways.

しらせ 知らせ news; a notice; a report; information; 〈前兆〉 an omen; 《文》a portent. 文例↓

しらせる 知らせる let *sb* know; tell 《*sb* about *sth*》; 《文》inform (notify) 《*sb* of *sth*》; send [bring] word (to); report 《*sth* to *sb*》; give *sb* the news (that...); 《口語》let *sb* in on *sth*; get (a fact) across to *sb* ¶前もって知らせる give *sb* (previous) notice; warn [《文》forewarn] 《*sb* about *sth*》/ 知らせずにおく leave *sb* uninformed (about *sth*); keep *sth* (secret) from *sb*; keep *sth* to *oneself*. 文例↓

しらたき noodles made from devil's tongue starch.

しらたま 白玉 rice-flour dumplings.

しらなみ 白波 white-[foam-]crested waves; 〈砕け波〉 foaming [white-capped] breakers; whitecaps; 《文》white horses. 文例↓

しらが 少し白髪になり始めた. My hair is beginning to go [turn] gray [to show white streaks]. / 君は白髪があるね. You've got gray in your hair. / その友の人はこめかみに白髪がありました. The lady was gray at the temples. / 彼はすっかり白髪になった. His hair is completely white.

しらける 彼がつまらぬことを言ったので座がしらけてしまった. His stupid remarks cast a chill over the whole room. / 彼が顔を出したので楽しかったパーティーの空気がしらけてしまった. His appearance threw a wet blanket over the happy atmosphere of the party.

-しらず ここは暑さ知らずの所だ. This place is immune to [free from] the summer heat.

じらす じらさないで早く教えてくれ. Don't keep me in suspense; tell me right away [straightaway].

しらせ 船が座礁したという知らせが入った. Word [News] came in that the ship had run aground.

しらせる これはもっと世間に知らせる必要がある. That must be given wider publicity. / もっと早く知らせてくれりゃよかったのに. You might have let me know earlier.

しらなみ 白波が立っている. The sea is white with foam.

しらぬい sea fire; marine bioluminescence.
しらは 白羽 ¶白羽の矢が立つ be singled out; be chosen [selected] for 《a post》; be marked out 《for a mission》. 文例⇩
しらばくれる pretend not to know; play (the) innocent; 《文》feign ignorance; 《文》dissemble. 文例⇩
しらふ ¶しらふの sober; not drunk / 全くしらふである be stone cold sober.
シラブル a syllable ¶シラブルに切る syllabify [syllabicate] 《a word》.
しらべ 調べ 《調査》 (an) investigation; (an) examination; (an) inspection; a checkup; (an) inquiry; 〈調子〉(an) tune; a melody ¶調べを受ける be examined 《by》; 〈詰問される〉 be (cross-)questioned 《by》/ たえなる調べ sweet music; a sweet tune; 《文》an enchanting melody.
しらべもの 調べ物 ¶調べ物をする do research(es) 《on, into》; study [read up on] 《a subject》 ⇨ しらべる.
しらべる 調べる study; investigate; examine; survey; inquire [look] into; take a (close) look at; check up (on); check out 《a story》; look [go] over; find out 《what is wrong》; 〈細かく調べる〉comb over 《the papers》; go into 《the murder case》; 〈参考する〉refer to; 《文》consult; 〈下調べする〉《文》 prepare; 〈捜査する〉 search 《a room for the stolen money》; 〈尋問する〉(cross-)question; (cross-)examine; interrogate ¶徹底的に調べる investigate *sth* thoroughly; 《文》make a thorough investigation (of); 《口語》give *sth* a thorough going-over / 答案を調べる mark [grade, go over] examination papers / 荷物を調べる search *sb*'s baggage 《for a weapon》/ 人員[人数]を調べる call the roll; 《口語》count heads / 書類を調べる look over [through] papers / 経歴を調べる check [look up] *sb*'s past record / 電話番号を調べる look up [find] *sb*'s telephone number 《in the telephone book》/ 辞書で単語を調べる look up a word in a dictionary; 《文》consult a dictionary for the meaning [usage] of a word. 文例⇩
しらほ 白帆 (a boat with) a white sail.
しらみ a louse 《*pl.* lice》 ¶しらみがわく be infested with lice; become lousy / しらみだらけの lousy / しらみを駆除する rid 《the bedding》 of lice; delouse 《the bedding》/ しらみつぶしに one by one; thoroughly / しらみつぶしに調べる comb 《the files for a missing letter》; go through [over] 《a suspect's apartment》 with a fine-tooth(ed) comb; 《文》make a thorough investigation (of).
しらむ 白む grow light; turn gray ¶東の空が白むころに 《文》at the first gray of dawn; with the first daylight.
しられる 知られる be [《文》become] known 《to *sb*》; make *oneself* known; 〈有名になる〉 become famous [well known] ¶よく知られた famous; well-known.
しらんかお 知らん顔 ¶知らん顔をする 〈無関心〉look on *sth* with indifference [an unconcerned air]; take no notice 《of *sb*》; 〈知らぬ振り〉pretend [make believe] not to know [one does not know]; look the other way; 〈往来などで会って〉《口語》cut *sb* (dead); pretend not to recognize *sb* / 知らん顔をして as if nothing had happened (何事もなかったかのように); with an air of perfect innocence [nonchalance] (何くわぬ顔で). 文例⇩
しり¹ 尻 the hips; the buttocks; the haunches; 《口語》the backside; 《口語》the behind; 《米俗》the butt; 《米俗》the ass; 《英俗》the arse; 《小児語》the bottom; 〈ズボンの〉the seat; 〈下部の〉the bottom; the base; 〈席次〉the bottom; the tail end; 〈後方〉the back; the rear ⇨ 囲語 ¶尻が長い stay too long; outstay [overstay] *one*'s welcome (いやな顔をされる)/ 尻の大きい wide-[full-, fat-]hipped; heavy-bottomed / 尻の重い lazy; slow in doing / 尻を持って行く complain to 《*sb* about [of] *sth*》/ 尻をまくる take [《文》assume] a defiant attitude; 《口語》stick *one*'s chin out / 子供の尻をぶつ spank a child; give a child a spanking; smack a child's bottom (for him) / 尻を据えて(でんと)座り込む squat [sink back determinedly] on *one*'s haunches / 尻を落ち着ける settle down 《in a place》/ 女の尻を追い回す chase after [hang about] a girl / 尻に帆をかけて逃げる show a clean pair of heels; take to *one*'s heels / 女房の尻に敷かれる be under *one*'s wife's thumb; be henpecked / 亭主を尻に敷く keep *one*'s husband under *one*'s thumb / 馬の尻 the rump of a horse / なべの尻 the undersurface of a saucepan. 文例⇩
囲語 backside, buttocks, behind, bottom は「尻」のうしろの, 腰掛けたときに座席に接する部分をいうのだが, the hips は少し前からでも「横はば」をいう。したがって「彼女はでっかいお尻だ」は She has a fat backside. だが, hips を使えば She has broad hips. となる。He smacked the child's bottom. や He patted the girl's behind [backside]. の bottom, behind [backside] は hips に換えることはできない。

しらは 宇野氏に白羽の矢が立った。The choice fell on Mr. Uno.
しらばくれる しらばくれて聞いてみた。I asked him about it as if I did not know. / しらばくれちゃいけないよ，自分がどんなことをしたのか百も承知のくせに。Don't look [play] innocent. You know very well what you've done.
しらべる 始発は何時か調べてくれないか。Will you try and find out when the first train leaves? / 金は調べずに受け取った。I accepted the money without counting it. / 調べてみたら人違いだった。When I inquired [《文》On inquiry] I found that it was the wrong person. / よく調べてみると両者の間にわずかに時間のずれのあることがわかった。Close examination showed that there was a slight time lag between them. / 彼は自分の損害の程度をいちいち調べてみた。He made [took] an inventory of his losses.
しらんかお いいですか，あの人が何を言おうと，あなたは知らん顔しているんですよ。Be sure to [Mind you] take no notice of anything he says.
しり¹ 彼は下から5番だった。He came out fifth from (the) bottom.
しりあい どうして彼と知り合いに

しり² 私利 self-interest;《文》personal gain ¶私利を図る look to [after] one's (own) interests /《文》be self-seeking[-serving]; feather one's (own) nest.

シリア Syria ¶シリア・アラブ共和国 the Syrian Arab Republic / シリア(人)の Syrian / シリア人 a Syrian.

しりあい 知り合い an acquaintance ¶知り合いが多い[少ない] have a large [small] circle of acquaintances / 知り合いになる get to know sb; make sb's acquaintance; get [《文》become] acquainted (with); make friends (with). 用例あ「る」.

しりあう 知り合う ⇒しりあい (知り合いになる).

しりあがり 尻上がり ¶尻上がりの調子で〈言葉が〉with a rising intonation [tone, inflection]. 用例あ

しりあて 尻当て 〈ズボンなどの〉a seat.

シリーズ a series ¶ワールド[日本]シリーズ the World [Japan] Series / シリーズもの a serial.

しりうま 尻馬 ¶尻馬に乗る imitate [follow] sb blindly; follow suit.

しりおし 尻押し ⇒あとおし.

シリカ 《化》silica.

しりがる 尻軽 ¶尻軽な〈浮気な〉《口語》easy; loose;《文》wanton;《文》(a woman) of loose morals [easy virtue]. 用例あ

じりき¹ 自力 ⇒どくりょく ¶自力で《文》by one's own ability [efforts]; by oneself; single-handed;《文》unaided;《文》through one's own resources;《get along》on one's own / 自力でやっていかねばならなくなる be left to [thrown on] one's own resources / have to fend for oneself / 自力更生《文》regeneration by one's own efforts;《口語》pulling oneself up by one's own bootstraps; self-reliance.

じりき² 地力 ¶(show [reveal]) (one's) true [《文》intrinsic, real] ability [strength] ¶地力をつける get [《文》acquire] solid [stable] power [ability].

しりきれとんぼ 尻切れとんぼ ¶尻切れとんぼになる be left unfinished [half done]. 用例あ

シリコン 《化》silicon.

しりごみ 尻込み ¶尻込みする recoil [flinch,《文》shrink] (from); hesitate (at [《文》before]); balk (at). 用例あ

じりじり little by little; inch by inch; step by step;《文》by (slow) degrees; slowly and steadily; gradually ¶じりじりする ⇒じれる / じりじりと進む edge forward [ahead]; worm one's way (through, toward); inch along / じりじりと詰めよる draw closer (to); edge up

《to the enemy》/ じりじりと照りつける太陽 a scorching sun / 〈肉などを〉じりじり焼く frizzle. 用例あ

しりすぼまり 尻すぼまり ⇒しりつぼみ.

しりぞく 退く〈後へさがる〉move [go, step] backward;〈退却する〉retreat;《文》recede;〈退出する〉withdraw;〈引退する〉retire ¶1歩退く take a step backward / 一歩へ退く step [move] aside / 役職を退く retire from [resign] one's post / 理事の職を退く retire as director. 用例あ

しりぞける 退ける〈追い払う〉drive [turn] (the enemy) away [back];《文》beat; expel;〈拒絶する〉refuse; reject; turn down;〈負かす〉beat; defeat ¶攻撃を退ける beat off [《文》repulse, repel] an attack.

しりつ¹ 市立 ¶市立の municipal; city / 豊橋市立病院 the Toyohashi Municipal [City] Hospital.

しりつ² 私立 ¶私立の private; nongovernmental; independent / 私立学校 a private school; a nongovernmental school.

じりつ¹ 自立〈独立〉independence; self-reliance;〈自活〉self-support ¶自立する〈独立する〉become [be] independent; stand on one's own feet; set oneself up (in business);〈自活する〉support oneself.

じりつ² 自律 ¶自律的 autonomous / 自律神経《生理》an autonomic nerve / 自律神経失調症 autonomic ataxia [imbalance] / 自律神経系 the autonomic nervous system.

しりつくす 知り尽くす know sth thoroughly;《文》have full knowledge of sth; have sth at one's fingertips.

しりっぺた 尻っぺた (one of) the cheeks of one's buttocks [behind].

しりつぼみ 尻つぼみ ¶尻つぼみになる narrow toward the end; taper (off); fizzle out; end (up) in an anticlimax; trail off; peter out.

しりとり 尻取り ¶尻取りをする a cap (verses).

しりぬぐい 尻拭い ¶尻ぬぐいをする clear [wipe] up sb's mess; bear the consequences of sb's mistake [《文》failure,《文》error]; pay sb's debt (借金の).

しりびれ 尻鰭〈魚の〉an anal fin.

じりひん じり貧 ¶じり貧の a gradual decline;《文》dwindling ¶じり貧になる be driven to one's ruin by inches. 用例あ

しりふりダンス 尻振りダンス a hip-swaying dance;〈蜜蜂の〉a tail-wagging dance.

しりめ 尻目 ¶尻目にかける〈先んじる〉show a clean pair of heels to (the other competitors); outrun;《文》outrival;〈ばかにする〉

なりましたか. How did you come to know him?

しりあがり 株式相場は年末にかけて尻上がりになるであろう. The stock market will show a rising tendency toward the year-end.

しりがる 彼女は尻軽女だ. She's an easy lay. |《米俗》She's got round heels.

しりきれとんぼ せっかくまとまりかけた交渉が尻切れとんぼに終わった. The negotiations, which seemed to be near fruition, were abruptly broken off.

しりごみ いざとなると彼はいつも尻込みをする. He always draws [pulls] back at the last moment.

じりじり 気温はじりじりと40度に近づいた. The temperature edged on toward 40 degrees.

しりぞく こうなっては一歩も退かぬ決心だ. If it's come to this, I'm determined to hold my ground at any cost.

しりつ¹ この病院は市立です. This hospital is run by the City [is a municipal institution].

じりひん このままでは, じり貧だ. We shall go to the wall if we do nothing about it.

give *sb* a contemptuous glance; disregard; 《文》 set *sb* at naught. [文例⇩]

しりめつれつ 支離滅裂 ¶支離滅裂な 〈不条理な〉 incoherent; inconsistent; incongruous; 〈四分五裂の〉 chaotic / 支離滅裂になる lose *its* coherence; be thrown into confusion.

しりもち 尻餅 ¶尻もちをつく fall on *one's* behind [buttocks]; land on *one's* rear; 《米俗》 take a pratfall.

しりゅう 支流 a tributary; a feeder; a branch. [文例⇩]

じりゅう 時流 〈風潮〉 the current [trend] of the times; 〈流行〉 the fashion of the day ¶時流に乗る swim [row] with the tide [current]; catch the public fancy; 《口語》 jump [get] on the bandwagon / 時流を追う follow the fashion (of the day). [文例⇩]

[し]

しりょ 思慮 thought; 《文》 consideration; (good) sense; 《文》 prudence; 《文》 discretion ¶思慮のある thoughtful; sensible; 《文》 prudent; 《文》 discreet; 《文》 well-advised / 思慮のない thoughtless; 《文》 imprudent; 《文》 indiscreet; 《文》 ill-advised; senseless.

しりょう[1] 史料 historical material [records, sources, documents] ¶史料編纂官[員] a historiographer; an official historian / 史料編纂所 the Institute for the Compilation of Historical Material.

しりょう[2] 資料 material; data ★ material は「資料」の意味では単数形が普通. data は datum の複数. 《米》ではしばしば this data のように単数にも用いる ¶資料を集める[あさる] collect [hunt up] material [data] 《for》 / 一次資料 primary sources.

しりょう[3] 飼料 (livestock) feed; fodder; animal food; forage ¶飼料用穀類 feed grain(s).

しりょく[1] 死力 ¶死力を尽くす make desperate [frantic] efforts 《to *do*》 / 死力を尽くして desperately; 《文》 to the utmost of *one's* ability.

しりょく[2] 視力 (eye)sight; (acuteness of) vision; visual power [《文》 acuity] ¶視力が弱い *one's* (eye)sight is poor; have poor eyesight; be weak-sighted / 視力を失う[回復する] lose [recover] *one's* eyesight / 視力の optic(al) / 視力計[測定装置] an optometer / 視力検査 an eye(sight) test / 視力(検査)表 an eye(sight)-test chart. [文例⇩]

しりょく[3] 資力 means; funds; (financial) resources ¶資力が充分ある have plenty of funds 《for》 / 資力が続かない suffer from a lack of money [funds] / 資力のある[ない]人 a man of means [with no means]. [文例⇩]

じりょく 磁力 〘物〙 magnetic force [attraction, power]; magnetism ¶磁力の magnetic / 磁力(作用)で magnetically / 磁力計 a magnetometer / 磁力線 lines of magnetic force.

シリンダー 〘機〙 a cylinder; 〈エンジンの〉 a piston chamber ¶シリンダー錠 a cylinder lock.

しる[1] 汁 〈液〉 juice (果実の); sap (草木の); 〈食膳の〉 soup; broth ¶汁の多い juicy; 《文》 succulent; watery (水っぽい) / 汁を絞る squeeze [《文》 extract] juice 《from a lemon》 / 甘い汁を吸う 《口語》 be onto a good thing; 《口語》 make a good thing out of *sth*.

しる[2] 知る know; learn; 《文》 become aware 《of》; get [come] to know; 〈知り合う〉 get to know; be [get, 《文》 become] acquainted 《with》; 〈気づく〉 find; see; notice; 《文》 be conscious 《of》; realize; 〈経験する〉 experience ¶健康の有難みを知る 《文》 appreciate the blessing of health / 知っている know; have an idea 《of *sth*, that...》; 《文》 have a knowledge of 《Spanish》; be aware 《of》 / よく知っている know *sth* well; be familiar 《with》; be at home 《with》 ⇨ じゅくち / 私の知っている限りでは so far as I know; to (the best of) my knowledge / 名[顔]を知っている know *sb* by name [sight] / 知らん振り[知らん顔]をする ⇨ しらんかお / 知らない間に before *one* knows [is aware of it]; without *one's* knowledge; unnoticed; 〈潜行性の病気などが進む〉 《文》 insidiously / 知らずに without knowing 《it》; unconsciously; 《文》 unwittingly / 知った顔に会う come across [find] a familiar face / 知った風な顔をして knowingly; with a knowing look. [文例⇩]

シルエット a silhouette.

シルクハット a silk hat; a top hat.

シルクロード the Silk Road [Route].

しるこ 汁粉 adzuki-bean soup with rice cake.

ジルコニウム 〘化〙 zirconium.

ジルコン 〘鉱〙 zircon ¶ジルコン酸 zirconic acid.

しるし[1] 印 〈符号〉 a sign; a mark; 〈表徴〉 a symbol; 〈記章〉 an emblem; a badge; 〈証拠〉 (a) proof 《of》; evidence 《for, of》; 〈徴候〉 《文》 an indication; a symptom; 〈表われ〉 《文》 a manifestation; 〈商標〉 a trademark; a brand;

しりめ 同輩を尻目にかけて，彼一人出世して行った. He was the only one to rise in the world, rapidly outstripping his colleagues.

しりゅう アマゾン川には多くの支流がある. The Amazon is fed by a large number of tributaries.

じりゅう 彼の識見は常に時流に先んじている. His views are always ahead of the times.

しりょく[2] 視力が衰え始めた. My eyesight is beginning to fail.

しりょく[3] 彼にはそれを完成するだけの資力がなかった. He lacked the wherewithal to bring it to completion.

しる[2] 彼はフランス語も多少知っている. He has some knowledge of French, too. / それは私は全然知らない. I haven't got the slightest [faintest] idea about it. / 大抵は私の知らない人だった. Most of them were strangers to me. / 昨夜の地震を君は知っていたか. Did you feel the earthquake last night? / そいつは僕の知ったことじゃない. It's no concern of mine. | It's nothing to do with me. / 彼が賄賂をもらっていたことは僕がちゃんと知っている. He had, to my certain knowledge, been bribed. / あいつがどうなろうと，おれは知っちゃいないよ. I don't give [care] a damn what becomes of him. / 知らぬは亭主ばかりなり. The husband is always the last to find out [notice, know]. / 知らぬが仏. Where ignorance is bliss, 'tis folly to be wise. 〘諺〙 / 知るを知るとなし，知らざるを知らざるとなす，これ知

しるし <謝礼などの>《文》a token ¶Xの印のついた marked X;《文》bearing the mark 'X' / 印をつける mark; put a mark (on);<照合の> check; tick off / 星の印をつける mark sth with an asterisk; asterisk sth / …の印である be a sign [symbol] (of);<表象》《文》symbolize;《文》be symbolical [emblematical] (of) / お礼の印として in token [as a token] of one's gratitude / 印ばんてん (in) livery; a livery (coat). 文例⇩

しるし² 験 ⇨ ききめ、こうか².

しるす 記す <書きつける> write (note, take, set, put, jot) down; make [take] a note of;《文》inscribe (刻銘する);<記述する> give an account of; describe;<印をつける> mark. 文例⇩

しるべ 知るべ ⇨ しりあい、あんない、てびき.

シルリアき シルリア紀【地質】the Silurian period.

しれい¹ 司令 ¶司令官 a commander; a commandant / 司令長官 a Commander-in-Chief (pl. Commanders-) (略: C-in-C) / 司令塔 <飛行場の> a control tower;<潜水艦の> a conning tower / 司令部 the headquarters.

しれい² 指令 an order; a directive; instructions;《コンピューター》a command ¶指令を発する order (sb to do); issue an order (that…),《文》to the effect that…); give instructions / <宇宙船の>指令船 a command module (略: CM).

じれい¹ 事例 <例> an instance; an example; a case;<先例> a precedent ¶事例研究 (a) case study.

じれい² 辞令 a letter of appointment.

ジレー【洋裁】《フランス語》a gilet; a dickey.

しれた 知れた <分かりきった> obvious; (self-) evident;<高の知れた> trifling; negligible.

しれつ 熾烈 ¶熾烈な keen [severe, cutthroat] (competition); bitter (rivalry); hot [hard] (contests).

しれつきょうせい 歯列矯正 straightening of irregular teeth;<術> orthodontics (単数扱い); orthodontia.

じれったい <物事が> irritating;《文》vexing;<人が> impatient; irritated;《文》vexed. 文例⇩

-しれない ⇨ かもしれない.

しれる 知れる 《文》become known (to sb); come to sb's knowledge; come to light (真相などが); be discovered; be found out;《文》be disclosed;<…だと分かる> prove (turn out) (to be); be found (to be); be identified (as) (身元が) ¶知れないようにする keep sth secret from sb; keep sth in the dark 《about sth》/ 行方が知れない be missing / 広く知れ渡る become [be] widely [generally] known. 文例⇩

じれる fret (and fume); get impatient; be irritated (at);《文》chafe (at, under) ¶じれて fretfully; impatiently. 文例⇩

しれん 試練《文》a trial / an ordeal; a test ¶試練の場《文》a trial ground (for one's ability) / 試練を受ける be tried (by); be tested; be put to the test; go through《文》undergo) hardships [an ordeal] / 時の試練を経た well-tried;《文》time-tested; …that has stood [《文》withstood] the test of time / 多くの試練に耐えた well-tried; tried and tested.

ジレンマ (be (caught) in) a dilemma.

しろ¹ 白 white;<潔白> innocence ¶(囲碁で)白を持つ play white (in a game of go) / 白を黒と言いくるめる call white black / 白い<color; fair (肌の); gray (頭髪の); blank (何も書いてない) / 色が白い be fair; have a fair complexion; be light-skinned / 髪に白いものが交じる <髪が主語> show white streaks; be streaked [shot] with gray; get [go, become] grizzled [grizzly] / 白くする whiten; bleach (色抜きして) / (髪が)白くなる go [turn] gray [white] / 白く塗る <壁を> whitewash / 白っぽい whitish. 文例⇩

しろ² 城 a castle;<要塞>《文》a citadel; a fortress; a fort; a stronghold ¶城を築く build a castle / 城を囲む[落とす] besiege [take, capture] a castle [fortress] / 城跡 the ruins of a castle. 文例⇩

しろあり 白あり a termite; a white ant ¶白あり駆除 eradication of termites.

じろう 痔瘻 (an) anal fistula (pl. -s, -lae).

しろうと 素人 an amateur; a layman; a non-professional;<信徒> the laity (集合的);<初心者> a novice;<門外漢> an outsider ¶素人の[臭い] amateur(ish); untrained / 素人離れがしている be as good as professional /《文》be far from amateurish / 素人考え a layman's view [idea] / 素人下宿 a private boarding [lodging] house / 素人芝居 amateur theatricals;<出し物の1つ> an amateur dramatic performance / 素人目に to the untrained eye / 素人療法 ama-

---

るなり. To know that we know what we know, and that we do not know what we do not know, that is true knowledge.

しるし¹ お骨折り頂いた感謝のしるしに何かお礼を差上げたい. I would like to give you something in appreciation of your help.

しるす そのことはこの本には何も記されてない. There is no mention of it in this book.

しれた 知れた事さ That goes without saying. | It's a matter of course. / 彼の財産といっても知れたものだ. He has no property to speak of [worth mentioning].

じれったい ぐずぐずしていて本当にじれったいね. You're so slow that it really gets on my nerves [makes me impatient].

しれる 黙っていれば、だれにも知れずにすんだのに. If you had kept quiet, nobody would have noticed. / どんなに心配したか知れんぞ. You can't imagine how worried [anxious] I was about you.

じれる 今日は子供がじれてばかりいる. The child has been in a fret all day. / うまく行かなかったので彼は大いにじれた. His failure really irritated him.

しれん 同社は石油危機の時に最大の試練を受けた. The company was given its greatest test during the oil crisis.

しろ¹ あの男はどうやら白だ. It looks as if he is innocent [in the clear].

しろ² 城の跡は今は公園になっている. The site of the castle is

しろくじちゅう 四六時中 around [round] the clock ; day and night ; all the time.

しろくま 白くま a white [polar] bear.

しろくろ 白黒 ¶白黒の black and white / 白黒映画 a black-and-white movie ; a monochrome film / 白黒テレビ black-and-white television / 目を白黒させる be [look] bewildered [nonplussed, surprised].

しろざけ 白酒 sweet white *sake* (used as the celebratory drink for the Doll's Festival in March).

しろざとう 白砂糖 white [refined] sugar.

じろじろ ¶じろじろ見る look *sb* up and down ; eye *sb* 《suspiciously》.

シロップ 《米》sirup ; 《英》syrup.

しろながすくじら 白長須鯨 a blue whale ; a sulphur-bottom (whale).

しろなまず 白癜 《医》leucoderma ; vitiligo.

しろぬり 白塗り ¶白塗りの white-painted[-plastered] ; whitewashed / 白塗りにする paint [plaster] (a wall) white ; whitewash.

しろバイ 白バイ a motorcycle policeman ; 《米俗》a speed cop.

しろぼし 白星 《白点》a white dot ; 《勝ち星》a win ; a victory mark ¶白星をとる be a victor ; win a victory 《over》.

シロホン a xylophone.

しろみ 白身 《卵の》the white (of an egg) ; an egg white ; 《鶏肉・魚の》white meat [《文》flesh] ¶卵を黄身と白身に分ける separate an egg into yolk and white ; separate the yolk of an egg from the white.

しろむく 白無垢 ¶白無垢を着て (be) dressed (all) in white ; wearing a pure [《文》an immaculate] white *kimono* [dress].

しろめ 白目 the white of the [one's] eye ¶白目でにらむ fix *sb* with an icy stare ; look coldly (upon).

しろもの 代物 《物》a thing ; 《curious》stuff ; 《悪い意味で》《口語》nasty business ; 《口語》an affair ; an article (商品) ; 《人》a fellow ¶得体の知れない代物 a nondescript / 厄介な代物《人》《口語》an [awkward] customer ; 《人・事》a tough [touchy] proposition ; 《人・物》a nuisance / とんだ代物《口語》a terrible [nasty] business ; 《口語》an appalling affair. 文例⇩

じろり ¶じろりと見る give *sb* a sharp look ; throw [《文》cast, dart] a glance 《at》; 《文》throw *sb* a searching glance. 文例⇩

しろん¹ 試論 an essay (in, on) ¶試論の域を出ない 《文》be no more than a tentative assumption.

しろん² 詩論 an essay on poetry ; 〈詩学〉poetics (単数扱い).

じろん 持論 《文》*one's* cherished opinion [view] ; *one's* (pet) theory.

しわ 皺 wrinkles ; 《皮膚の》lines ; furrows ; 〈目尻の〉crow's-feet ; 〈物の〉creases ; folds ¶しわの寄った 《皮膚》wrinkled ; 《文》furrowed ; lined ; 〈布・紙など〉crinkled ; crumpled / 《生地が》しわの寄らない crease-resistant ; wrinkleproof ; wrinkle-free 《polyester clothing》/ 額にしわを寄せる 《文》knit *one's* brows ; frown / しわくちゃになる get [be] wrinkled [crumpled, crinkled] / しわくちゃばあさん a wrinkled [withered] old woman ; 《文》a [an old] crone / しわを伸ばす smooth (down) ; iron out the wrinkles [creases] 《from a shirt》; take creases 《out of the trousers》. 文例⇩

用困 布・衣服などの「しわ」で, wrinkles と creases の違いはその細かさによる. wrinkles はかなり細かくて, 数も多く, 生地の薄いものにできにくい. creases は, 背広・スカートなどやや厚い生地にできる「しわ」. ワイシャツなどはクシャクシャにしわがついていれば wrinkles だが, 数の少ない大き目の「しわ」なら creases. folds はだいたい人為的につけたもので,「しわ」というよりは「折り目」「ひだ」.

しわい ⇒けち.

しわがれる 嗄れる go [grow, 《文》become] hoarse ¶声がしわがれるほど しゃべる talk *oneself* hoarse / しわがれ声で hoarsely ; in a hoarse [husky] voice ; throatily.

しわけ 仕分け 《分類》sorting (out) ; 《文》classification ; 〈仕訳〉《簿記》journalizing ¶仕訳する《簿記》journalize / 仕訳帳 a journal.

しわける 仕分ける 《品物を》sort (out) ; divide (into different groups) ; 《文》assort ; classify.

しわざ 仕業 《文》an act ; 《文》a deed ; *sb's* doing [work] ; 《the Devil's》handiwork. 文例⇩

じわじわ gradually ; slowly ; 《口語》by slow degrees ¶じわじわと進む edge (*oneself*) (along) ; edge *one's* way (through, into). 文例⇩

しわす 師走 December (略: Dec.) ; the year-end.

しわよせ 皺寄せ ¶皺寄せする shift (the loss) on to (unprivileged people). 文例⇩

じわれ 地割れ a crack [an opening, a fissure] (in the ground). 文例⇩

---

now a park.

しろうと こういう事は僕はずぶの素人です. I am a complete beginner at this business. / ラジウムは素人が扱うと危険です. Radium is dangerous in untrained hands. / 素人にだってこんなことはわかる. You don't have to be an expert to see that.

しろもの とんだ代物をつかまされた. A fine thing I've been landed with here! | Here's a nice thing to be landed [stuck] with!

じろり 親父は突然僕をじろりと見た. My father suddenly fixed me with a piercing look [stare].

しわ 額に深いしわが寄っていた. Deep lines could be seen on his forehead. | His forehead was deeply lined [furrowed]. / 彼は年齢の割にしわが多い. His face is very lined for his age. / 彼女は枕のしわを伸ばした. She smoothed the wrinkles out of her pillow. / この生地はしわになりやすい. This material creases easily. / 鯨は脳にしわが多くて, 非常に知能が高いと言われる. The whale is said to be very intelligent, having, as it does, many folds on its brain.

しわざ どいつの仕業だ. Who the devil did it [this]?

じわじわ その間, 環境破壊がじわじわ進んだのだ. In the meantime, environmental disruption was proceeding in a creeping way.

しわよせ この案では経営の不手際

しん¹ 心 <こころ> a heart; a mind; spirit; <核心> the core [heart] (of the matter); the center; <ろうそくの> a wick; <帯などの> padding; <果物の> a core; <鉛筆の> lead; <骨髄> the marrow ¶心から sincerely; 《文》heartily; heart and soul / 心からかわいいと思う think the sun shines out of sb's eyes / 心から嫌になる get [grow] heartily sick of / 心のある飯 undercooked rice / 心まで (be rotten) to the core; (be chilled) to one's very bones [to the marrow] / ランプの心を出す[ひっこめる] turn the wick up [down] / ろうそくの心を切る snuff a candle / (シャープペンシルの)替え心 a lead; a spare [a refill, an extra] lead / (りんごの)心取り器 a [an apple-]corer. 文例⇩

しん² 真 (a) truth; (a) reality ¶真の true; real; 《文》veritable; genuine / 真のやみ pitch [《文》utter] darkness / 真に really; truly; 《文》in truth; 《文》indeed; 《文》in a true sense / 真に迫る be true to nature [life]; be lifelike / 真善美 goodness, truth and beauty; the true, the good and the beautiful. 文例⇩

しん³ 清 <中国の王朝> Ching ¶清朝 the Ching dynasty.

しん-¹ 新... ¶新大統領 the new President; <就任前の> the President-elect; the incoming President.

しん-² 親... pro- ¶親米[日]の pro-American[-Japanese]/ 親英主義(者) Anglophilism [an Anglophile].

じん¹ 仁 <儒教の> perfect virtue; <仁愛> benevolence; charity.

じん² 陣 <陣形> battle formation [《文》array]; <陣営> a camp; an encampment; <陣地> a position ¶陣を敷く take up a position / 陣を張る pitch a camp; 《文》encamp.

ジン <酒> gin ¶ジンフィ(ー)ズ (a) gin fizz.

しんあい 親愛 ¶親愛なる dear; 《文》beloved / 親愛の情を示す show affection 《for》.

じんあい 塵埃 dust; dirt.

しんあつ 針圧 <レコードの> stylus pressure; tracking force.

しんあん 新案 a new idea [design, device]; a novelty ¶新案の 《文》newly-devised; newly-designed; novel / 新案特許 a patent on a new device / 新案特許を申請する apply (to the Patent Bureau) for a patent on a new device [design].

しんい¹ 神意 God's [the divine] will; Providence.

しんい² 真意 <意図> one's real intention(s); what one really means; <動機> one's real motive; one's purpose; <意味> the true meaning. 文例⇩

じんい 人為 human work; 《文》artificiality ¶人為的(な) artificial; 《文》factitious; man-made / 人為的に artificially.

しんいき 神域 (in) the (holy) precincts 《of a Shinto shrine》.

しんいり 新入り a newcomer; 《文》an initiate.

しんいん¹ 心因 ¶心因性の psychogenic 《symptoms》.

しんいん² 真因 the true reason [cause, motive] 《for》.

じんいん 人員 <人数> the number of men; <職員> the staff; the personnel ¶人員が不足である be short of staff [labor]; be shorthanded; be understaffed / 人員を整理する reduce the work force [the staff] / 人員過剰である be overstaffed; be overmanned / 人員構成 personnel organization / 人員整理 a personnel cut [reduction].

じんう 腎盂 【解】the renal pelvis ¶腎盂炎 pyelitis.

しんうち 真打ち a main [principal] entertainer [performer]; 《米》a headliner ¶真打ちとして出る top the bill.

しんえい 新鋭 ¶新鋭の new and powerful 《weapons》; fresh 《troops》.

じんえい 陣営 a camp; quarters ¶保守陣営 the conservative camp / 東西両陣営 the East and West camps / 東西いずれの陣営にも属さない国 a nonaligned [an unaligned] nation. 文例⇩

しんえいたい 親衛隊 the 《President's》bodyguards; <歌手などの> 《俗》a groupie ★bodyguard は普通名詞としてだけでなく集合名詞としても使われる。その場合の扱いは単複両用: The President's bodyguard is [are] waiting there. 従って,「多数[少数]の親衛隊」は a large [small] number of bodyguards / his large [small] bodyguard のように2通りの言い方ができる。「of honor]。

しんえつ 親閲 (personal) inspection 《of a guard》

しんえん¹ 深淵 《文》an abyss; (out of) the depths.

しんえん² 深遠 ¶深遠な 《文》profound 《theories》; deep 《meanings》; 《文》abstruse 《ideas》; 《文》recondite; 《文》esoteric.

じんえん 腎炎 【医】nephritis.

のしわ寄せが自分たちだけに来るのではないかと労働者側は考えている。The workmen suspect that the plan is aimed at making them the sole sufferers of the incompetence of the management. / 現在の教育制度の無理が高等学校にしわ寄せされている。The high schools have to carry all the stresses [strain] of today's system of education.

じわれ 地割れ 地震で地割れが出来た。The earthquake caused cracks [fissures] in the ground.

しん¹ あいつは心はいい男だよ。At heart he's good [all right]. / きゃしゃな体つきだが心が強い。He looks delicate but at heart [bottom] he's tough. /おとなしいが心はしっかりした女だ。She is very gentle but there is a firm core to her character.

しん² 彼の戦争の話は真に迫っていた。He gave a graphic [vivid] account of the battle. / His account of the battle made me feel as if I were there myself.

しんい² 彼の真意がわからない。I can't make out what he's driving at. / I'm in some doubt as to his purpose. / I can't see what he really means.

じんえい 国連における今回の投票で西側の陣営を脱落した主要国は次のとおりである。Notable defectors from the Western alignment in the recent vote at the UN were as follows.

しんおう 震央 【地震】the epicenter.
しんおん¹ 心音 heart [cardiac] sound.
しんおん² 針音 〈レコード演奏時の〉needle scratch; surface noise.
しんか¹ 唇音 【音声】a labial.
しんか² 臣下 a subject; a vassal; a retainer ¶臣下の礼をとる pay homage to sb.
しんか³ 真価 the real [true, 《文》intrinsic] worth [value, 《文》merit] ¶真価を発揮する prove one's merits [worth]; give full play [do full justice] to one's talent [ability] / 真価を認める appreciate [recognize] the value [worth] (of). 文例⇩
しんか⁴ 進化 evolution ¶進化する evolve [develop] (from... into...) / 進化論 the theory of evolution; 《modern》evolutionary theory / 進化論者 an evolutionist.
じんか 人家 a house; 《文》(a) human habitation ¶人家の多い[少ない]所 a densely-[sparsely-] [populated place.
シンカー 【野球】a sinker.
シンガーソングライター a singer-songwriter.
しんかい 深海 the depths of the sea; ocean depths; 《文》an abyss ¶深海の 《文》abyssal; 《文》abysmal / 深海魚 a deep-sea fish / 深海漁業 deep-sea fishing [fishery].
しんがい¹ 心外 ¶心外な annoying; 《文》vexatious; outrageous ¶心外に思う be [feel] annoyed [vexed, mortified, offended, put out]; be not happy (with the result). 文例⇩
しんがい² 侵害 《文》(an) infringement; (a) violation ¶侵害する infringe (on); 《文》violate (sb's right); trespass [《文》encroach] (on sb's rights).
じんかい 塵芥 dust; dirt; rubbish; refuse; trash; litter; 《米》garbage (台所のごみ).
じんかいせんじゅつ 人海戦術 a human-wave attack [sweep].
しんかいち 新開地 a new [newly-opened] region [land]; a newly-peopled district [suburb] ¶経済的新開地 an economic frontier.
しんがお 新顔 〈新人〉a newcomer; a new face; 〈見知らぬ人〉a stranger. 文例⇩
しんがく¹ 神学 theology; divinity ¶神学校 a theological [divinity] school / 神学者 a theologian / 神学博士〈人〉a doctor of divinity / 〈学位〉Doctor of Divinity (略: D.D.).
しんがく² 進学 ¶進学する go on to [enter, 《文》proceed to] the next stage of education [a school of higher grade]; go on to (high school, university); go in for higher schooling / 進学志望者 students who wish to go (on) to the next stage of education / 進学率 the ratio of students who go on to the next stage of education.
じんかく 人格 character; personality ¶人格形成 character building [《文》formation]; /

formation of character; 《文》personality development [formation] / 人格者《文》a man [person] of character.
しんかくか 神格化 deification 《of Stalin》.
じんかさん 〈議員〉the rank and file (of a political party); a backbencher (個人).
しんがた 新型 a new style [fashion]; the latest model [design] ¶新型の帽子 a new-style hat.
シンガポール Singapore ¶シンガポールの Singaporean / シンガポール共和国 the Republic of Singapore / シンガポール人 a Singaporean.
しんがり 殿 the rear(guard); the tail end (of a procession) ¶しんがりにやって来る be the last to come / しんがりをつとめる bring up the rear.
しんかん¹ 神官 a Shinto priest ¶〈古代エジプトの〉神官文字 the hieratic (script).
しんかん² 信管 a fuse ¶信管を取り除く remove the fuse (from a bomb); defuse.
しんかん³ 森閑 ¶森閑とした quiet; still; hushed; silent. 文例⇩
しんかん⁴ 新刊 ¶新刊の newly-published[-issued]; new / 新刊書 a new book [publication] / 新刊紹介 a book review / 新刊目録 a list of new publications. 「nex (to a hotel).
しんかん⁵ 新館 a new building; 〈別館〉an annex
しんがん 心眼 (in) one's mind's eye ¶心眼で見る see in [with] one's mind's eye / 心眼に映じる《文》be visible to the eye of the mind.
しんかんせん 新幹線 the Shinkansen.
しんき¹ 心機 ¶心機一転する change one's mind; become a new man; turn over a new leaf.
しんき² 新奇 ¶新奇な novel; original / 新奇を追い求める seek the new; chase after [《文》crave] novelties.
しんき³ 新規 ¶新規の new; fresh / 新規にafresh, newly; 《文》anew / 新規まき直しにする begin [start] all over again; make [take] a fresh start.
しんぎ¹ 信義 faithfulness; loyalty; 《文》faith; 《文》fidelity ¶信義を守る[破る] 《文》keep [break] faith with sb; be loyal [disloyal] to sb; be true [untrue] to sb (配偶者・恋人に対して) / 信義を重んじる人《文》a man of honor / 信義にあついる faithful; loyal; 《文》true.
しんぎ² 真偽 truth (or falsehood); 《文》authenticity; genuineness ¶真偽を確める verify; confirm; 《文》ascertain the truth (of a statement). 文例⇩
しんぎ³ 審議 《文》deliberation; careful discussion; consideration ¶審議する discuss; consider; 《文》deliberate (on) / 審議中である〈会議体が主語〉be discussing (a proposal); be sitting (on a bill); 〈事が主語〉be under discus-

---

しんか² 芸術家で，同時代には真価を認められないでいて，のちの時代の人間に高く評価されることがよくあるのはなぜであろうか。Why is it that an artist is often unappreciated in his own times yet highly praised by following generations?
しんがい¹ 彼に協力を断わられたのは心外だ。It has upset me [put me out] that he has refused to help.
しんがお 4月に入って我が社にも新顔が大分ふえた。In April a number of new faces joined to the staff of our company.
しんかん³ 家の中は森閑としていた。Deep [Dead] silence reigned in the house.
しんぎ² 事の真偽は保証しかねる。I cannot vouch for the truth of

じんぎ [consideration] / 審議未了にする shelve [pigeonhole] (a bill) ; talk (a measure) out [to death] / 審議会 a (deliberative) council ; an inquiry commission / 教育[経済]審議会 an educational [economic] council. 文例↓

じんぎ 仁義 ⟨義理⟩ duty ; ⟨やくざなどのおきて⟩ a code of conduct ¶⟨やくざが⟩仁義を切る make the formal greeting (customary among members of *yakuza* groups).

しんげん 新紀元 ¶新紀元を画する mark an epoch [a new era] / 新紀元を画するできごと an epoch-making 《文》epochal) event.

しんこうしん 心悸亢進 《医》tachycardia ; accelerated heartbeat.

しんきじく 新機軸 a new device [《文》departure] ; originality ¶新機軸を出す strike out in a new direction ; make a new departure. 文例↓

ジンギスカン Genghis Khan ¶ジンギスカン鍋《料理》(a) Mongolian mutton barbecue.

しんきゅう¹ 進級 (a) promotion ¶進級する be promoted 《to a higher degree [position]》; move up to (the senior class).

しんきゅう² 新旧 ¶新旧の old and new ; incoming and outgoing 《ministers》. 文例↓

しんきょ 新居 one's new house [home] ¶新居を構える set up [make] a new home.

しんきょう¹ 心境 a state [frame] of mind ; a mental state [attitude] ¶心境の変化を have [《文》undergo] a change of mind [heart] / 心境を語る speak one's mind ; open one's heart 《to》; 《口語》unbosom oneself 《to》.

しんきょう² 進境 ⇨しんぽ ¶進境が著しい make remarkable progress ; 《文》show a marked improvement 《in》. 文例↓

しんきょう³ 新教 ⟨キリスト教の⟩ Protestantism ¶新教の Protestant / 新教徒 a Protestant.

しんきょく¹ 神曲 ⟨ダンテの⟩ *The Divine Comedy* ; *La (Divina) Commedia*.

しんきょく² 新曲 a new musical composition ; a new piece [tune] ; ⟨歌⟩ a new song.

しんきろう 蜃気楼 a mirage.

しんきろく 新記録 (make, establish) a new 《Japanese》record ; 《set》a new mark ¶世界新記録 a world record.

しんきん 心筋 《解》the myocardium (*pl.* -dia) ; the heart muscle ¶心筋梗塞(ざ) myocardial infarction / 《口語》a coronary (★ これは coronary thrombosis (冠状動脈血栓症) の略称で, 厳密には myocardial infarction とは別物だが, 俗に「心筋梗塞」の意味で使う).

しんぎん 呻吟 ¶呻吟する groan ; moan ; ⟨苦しむ⟩ be in distress ; suffer severely [《文》grievously] 《from poverty》/ 獄窓に呻吟する《文》languish in prison [behind bars] / …の圧制に呻吟する《文》groan under the tyranny of….

しんきんかん 親近感 《文》a sense of affinity ¶親近感を感じる《文》feel an [a strong] affinity 《for, to》; find something congenial 《in *sb*》.

しんく¹ 辛苦 ⟨困苦⟩ hardship(s) ; trials ; 《文》privation(s) ; labor ; trouble ; ⟨苦心⟩《文》toil ; 《文》pains ¶辛苦をなめる suffer [go through] hardships ; have a bitter experience ; 《口語》have a hard time ; 《口語》go through the mill.

しんく² 深紅 ¶深紅(の) deep (bright) red ; cardinal ; (of) a rich red color.

しんぐ 寝具 bedding ; bedclothes.

しんくう 真空 a vacuum ¶真空の evacuated 《vessels》/ 真空にする evacuate 《a flask》; form [create, make] a vacuum ¶真空になる be evacuated ; a vacuum forms [is created] / 真空管 a vacuum [an electron(ic)] tube ; 《米》a tube ; 《英》a valve / 真空掃除機 a vacuum cleaner (sweeper) ; 《英》《商標名》a Hoover ⇨でんき²(電気掃除機) / 真空内で in a vacuum / 真空パックによる貯蔵 vacuum storage / 真空包装する vacuum-seal 《frankfurters in a plastic package》.

じんぐう 神宮 a *Shinto* shrine ¶明治神宮 the Meiji Shrine / 神宮球場 the Jingu Stadium.

ジンクス 《口語》a jinx ¶…というジンクスがある There is a jinx [a popular belief] that … ★ There is a jinx that… とは言わない。英語では There seems to be a jinx on this room. (この部屋は縁起が悪い)という使い方しかない / ジンクスを破る break [smash] the jinx.

シングル 《野球》a single (hit) ; ⟨服の⟩ a single-breasted coat [jacket] ; ⟨ホテルの⟩ a single (room) ¶シングル盤 ⟨レコード⟩ a single / シングルヒットを打つ single (to left) ; hit a single ; make a one-base hit. 文例↓

シングルス 《テニス》singles 《matches》¶シングルスのテニス試合をやる play singles at tennis / 女子シングルス準決勝 a women's singles semifinal (match).

シンクロナイズドスイミング 《水泳》synchronized swimming.

しんぐん 進軍 a march ; marching ; (an) advance ¶進軍する march [advance] 《on a town, against the enemy》/ 進軍させる march 《a troop》/ 進軍ラッパを吹く sound (the bugle for) the march.

しんけい 神経 one's nerves ;《解》a nerve ¶神経が高ぶっている be nervous ;《口語》be edgy [on edge,《文》nervy] / 神経が太い be fearless ;《文》be undaunted ; have a lot of nerve / 神経の細かさ《文》delicacy / 神経の鋭い[鈍い] sensitive [insensitive] ; thin-[thick-]skinned / 神経をいらだたせる set *sb*'s nerves on edge ; make *sb* jittery [irritable, touchy] / (歯の)神経を抜く extract a nerve / 神経を静める quiet [soothe, tranquilize] one's nerves / 神経にこた

---

it. / この報告の真偽はまだ確かではない。This report remains to be confirmed.

しんぎ その法案は今日審議のために上程されている。The bill is up for consideration today.

しんきじく 彼はそれまでにないざましい新機軸のアニメーションを作り出した。He developed a style of animation that was a marked departure from anything that had been done before.

しんきゅう² 今は新旧交替の過渡期だ。We are now in a period of transition, the old giving way to the new.

シングル センターにシングルヒットを放って 2 者生還させた。He

じんけい えるbe a strain on [be trying to] one's nerves / 神経にさわる get [jar] on one's nerves / 神経科の医者 a neurologist / 神経過敏な oversensitive; hypersensitive;《口語》touchy;《英口語》nervy / 神経系 a nervous [neural] system / 神経細胞 a nerve cell; a neuron / 神経質な nervous; highly-strung; very sensitive / 神経終末《解》a nerve ending / 神経症 neurosis / 神経症の neurotic / 神経衰弱 a nervous breakdown; nervous prostration;〈トランプの〉memory; Pelmanism;《米》concentration / 神経戦 psychological warfare; a war of nerves / 神経中枢 the nerve center / 神経痛 neuralgia / 神経痛の neuralgic / 神経病 a nervous disease [disorder] / 神経病学 neurology / 神経網 a nerve network. 文例▣

じんけい 陣形 a formation.

しんげき¹ 進撃 (an) advance; a drive; a push; an attack (攻撃); a charge (突撃) ¶進撃する march [advance] (on, against); attack; make an attack (on); charge (at, on).

しんげき² 新劇 the Western-style drama newly developed in modern Japan.

しんけつ 心血 ¶心血を注ぐ put one's heart (and soul) [everything one has] (into one's work);《文》devote all one's energies (to).

しんげつ 新月 a new [young] moon; a crescent moon (三日月).

しんけん¹ 親権 (exercise) parental authority ¶親権者 a person in parental authority; a guardian (実の親以外の).

しんけん² 真剣《文》earnest; serious / 真剣に《文》in earnest; seriously / 真剣勝負〈本物の刀での勝負〉(have) a fight with real swords;〈本気の勝負〉a game played in earnest [《口語》for real,《口語》for keeps]. 文例▣

しんげん¹ 進言 (a piece [word] of) advice; a suggestion;《文》counsel ¶進言する advise; suggest; propose; put forward a suggestion;《文》counsel /《文》offer counsel to sb.

しんげん² 箴言《文》an aphorism; a maxim; a proverb;《文》an adage;『聖書』The Book of Proverbs (略: Prov.);〈略称〉Proverbs (単数扱い).

じんけん¹ 人絹 artificial silk; rayon.

じんけん² 人権 human rights; personal rights;《文》the rights of man; civil liberties / 基本的人権 fundamental human rights / 人権じゅうりん [侵害] (a) violation of human rights; an infringement on personal rights / 人権宣言 the Declaration of Human Rights [of the Rights of Man] / 人権問題 a question of personal rights / 人権擁護委員 a Commissioner for the Protection of Fundamental Human Rights.

しんげんち 震源地 the seismic center; the epicenter (震央). 文例▣

じんけんひ 人件費 labor costs; personnel expenses.

しんご 新語〈新造語〉a newly-coined word; a new coinage;《文》a neologism;〈教科書などの初出語〉a new word ¶新語を造る coin a new word.

じんご 人後 ¶人後に落ちない be second to none (in); be as good as anyone.

しんこう¹ 信仰 (religious) faith; belief;《文》a creed ¶信仰する believe [have faith] in 《God》/ 信仰の厚い pious /《文》devout; godly / 信仰のない unbelieving / 信仰の自由 freedom of religion [worship] / 信仰を捨てる abandon [《文》forsake,《文》abjure,《文》renounce] one's faith (in) / 稲荷信仰 the cult of Inari / 信仰箇条 the articles of faith [belief]; a creed;《文》a credo (pl. -s) / 信仰告白 (a) confession of faith;《文》the profession (of Christianity) / 信仰者 a believer / 信仰心 (religious) piety / 信仰生活 (lead, enter) a religious life / 信仰療法 faith healing. 文例▣

しんこう² 振興 promotion;《文》furtherance ¶振興する promote;《文》further; encourage / 産業の振興を図る promote the development of industry / 経済振興計画 a program of economic build-up / 振興策 measures for the encouragement [promotion,《文》furtherance] (of).

しんこう³ 進行 progress;《文》progression; (an) advance ¶進行する advance;《文》progress; make progress [headway];〈列車などが〉run; move / 予定どおり計画を進行させる proceed with the program as arranged / 議事を進行させる《文》expedite the proceedings / 進行が早い[遅い] make rapid [slow] progress / 進行を妨げる hinder [《文》impede] the progress (of) /〈病気の〉進行を阻止する arrest《tuberculosis》/ 進行中である be in progress; be going on; be under way / 進行中の列車 (jump off) a running [moving] train; a train in motion / 進行係 a person charged with expediting the proceedings (of a conference);〈司会者〉the master of ceremonies / 進行形《文法》the pro-

---

singled to center and knocked [drove] in two runs.

しんけい 神経がくたくたに疲れた. My nerves are in tatters. / 彼はその事で神経を悩ましている. He is worried about the affair. / お前の病気は全く神経さ. Your illness is simply imaginary. / 彼は借金を気に病んで神経衰弱になってしまった. He worried himself into a nervous breakdown over his debts.

しんけん もっと真剣にやれ. Put your heart into it.

しんげんち 震源地は大島付近の海底といわれる. It has been reported that the center of the shock was the sea floor near Oshima Island. | The epicenter of the tremor has been traced to the sea bottom off Oshima Island.

しんこう¹ 彼女は僕と信仰が同じです. She and I share the same religion. / 彼女は一生その信仰を捨てなかった. She retained [kept] her religious faith all through her life. / 信仰は山をも動かす. Faith can move [remove] mountains.

しんこう³ 工事は九分どおり進行した. The construction work is 90 per cent complete. / 仕事の進行はどうですか. How are you getting along with your work? / 仕事はどんどん進行している. The work is in full swing. / 列車の進行方向と反対の向きに座るのは嫌だ. For some reason [Somehow] I don't like sitting with my back

しんこう / 進行方向に in the direction of travel [of movement]. 文例⇩

しんこう⁴ 進講 ¶進講する give [deliver] a lecture 《on a subject》in the presence of 《the Emperor》.

しんこう⁵ 新興 ¶新興の rising; new / 新興国 a rising [developing] nation [country] / 新興アフリカ諸国 the emergent African countries / 新興宗教 a new [newly-risen] religion / 新興都市 a boom [new] town.

しんこう⁶ 親交 (a) friendship; friendly relations;《文》intimacy ¶親交がある be on friendly [close,《文》intimate] terms 《with》⇨したしい ★; be good friends 《with》/ 親交を結ぶ make friends 《with sb》; form [《文》contract] a (close) friendship 《with》/ 20年来の親交《break off》a friendship of twenty years' standing. 文例⇩

しんごう 信号 a signal;《事》signaling ¶信号する signal sb to do; make a signal / 信号を掲げる raise [hoist, put up] a signal / 信号[交通信号]を待つ wait for the signal [for the traffic lights to change] / 信号で救助を求める signal for rescue [assistance, help] / 危険[注意]信号 a danger [caution] signal / 呼出し信号 a call signal [sign] / 信号機 a semaphore / 〈腕木〉信号旗[所, 塔] a signal flag [station, tower] / 信号手 a signalman / 信号灯 a signal lamp [light]; a blinker (明滅方向指示灯など) / 信号無視を犯す ignore a red light;《口語》jump the lights (ドライバーが). 文例⇩

じんこう¹ 人口 (a) population ¶人口が多い[少ない] have a large [small] population / 人口が稠密(ちゅうみつ)である be densely [thickly] populated / 人口が希薄である be sparsely [thinly] populated / 人口の多い heavily populated;《文》populous / 農村人口の減少 rural depopulation / 人口7万人の都市 a city (with a population) of 70,000 (people) / 人口過剰 (suffer from) overpopulation / 人口構成 population composition /《口語》make-up) / 人口数 a population size / 人口政策 a population policy / 人口増加 (allow for) population increase ; a rise [an increase] in population / 人口増加率 a population growth rate / 人口調査を行なう take a census (of the population) / 人口統計 population statistics ; vital statistics (動態の) / 人口統計学 demography / 人口爆発 a population explosion / 人口問題 the《world, Japanese》population problem / 人口抑制 population control. 文例⇩

じんこう² 人工 human work [labor]; 〈技巧〉art; human skill;《文》artificiality ¶人工の美 man-made beauty; the beauty of art / 人工的 artificial;《文》unnatural; man-made / 人工的に artificially;《文》by the art [hand] of man / 人工衛星 a [an artificial] satellite / (乳児の)人工栄養 bottle-feeding / 人工栄養の bottle-fed 《babies》/ 人工甘味料 an artificial sweetener / 人工降雨[雨] artificial rain; 〈降らすこと〉rainmaking / 人工呼吸を施す practice [try] artificial respiration on sb; give the kiss of life to sb (水没しの) / 人工授精 artificial insemination [fertilization] / 人工頭脳 a mechanical brain.

しんこきゅう 深呼吸 ¶深呼吸をする breathe deeply; draw [take] a deep [full] breath; do deep breathing exercises.

しんこく¹ 申告 a report; a statement; a declaration; a return ¶申告する report;《文》notify; declare; state; make a return of《one's income》/ 所得税の申告 an income tax return / 所得税の申告をする declare 《one's earnings》for income tax; make [fill out] one's income tax return / 申告者 a reporter / 申告書を提出する return a report / 申告制 《税の》the return system; tax payment by self-assessment; 《関税などの》a declaration system / 申告税 a self-assessed tax / 申告納税 tax payment by self-assessment / 申告用紙 a return form. 文例⇩

しんこく² 深刻 ¶深刻な serious;《文》grave / 深刻な人生問題 a serious problem in one's life / 深刻な顔をする look serious [《文》grave] / 深刻になる, 深刻化する get [《文》become] worse; get [《文》become] more acute [strained]; be aggravated;《文》assume serious proportions. 文例⇩

しんこっちょう 真骨頂 ⇨ほんりょう.

しんこん 新婚 ¶新婚の夫婦 a newly-married couple;《口語》newlyweds / 新婚旅行をする go on 《one's》honeymoon 《to》; honeymoon 《in, at》/ 新婚生活 newly-married life. 文例⇩

しんさ 審査 (an) examination; 《調査》(an) investigation; 〈判定〉judgment ¶審査する judge; examine; inspect; investigate; screen (人を) / 審査委員会 a judging [screening] committee; a board of review; a jury / 審査官[員] a judge; an examiner; 〈総称〉a panel of judges. 文例⇩

しんさい 震災 an earthquake (disaster) ¶震

---

toward the engine.
しんこう⁶ 父は浅田氏と親交があった。My father enjoyed the friendship of Mr. Asada.
しんごう 信号のところで渡るんですよ。You must cross at the light. / いいかい, 青信号になったら渡るんだよ。Cross the road on the green light, mind you. / 赤信号が青になるまで待たなくてはいけない。You must wait until the (red) light changes to green.
じんこう¹ 東京の人口は1千万以上である。The population of Tokyo is more than 10,000,000. / 東京は人口が過密になって, 他の遊星に移住せねばならぬ時が来るかもしれない。The time might come when man will have to emigrate to some other planet because of population pressure on Earth.
しんこく¹ 彼は偽りの所得申告をした。He falsified [《口語》fiddled] his (income) tax return. / He made a false return of his income.
しんこく² 生活難はますます深刻になってきた。It is getting more and more difficult to make a living [to manage].
しんこん この家は新婚の夫婦にはおあつらえ向きだ。This house is ideal for newlyweds [a newly-married couple].
しんさ 私は, 昔, 近代社募集の懸賞小説の審査員をしたことがある。I was once judge in a competition held by Kindaisha to award

災に会う suffer from an earthquake / 震災地 an area devastated [damaged, affected] by an earthquake; a quake-stricken district.

じんさい 人災 a consequence of [a disaster caused by] human neglect ⇨ てんさい² 文例.

じんざい 人材 talent; 《文》 a man of talent; a talented person; a capable man ¶ 人材を登用する open positions to men of talent; promote the men on the basis of their talent [on their merits] / 人材銀行 an employment agency for (older) people with special talent or skills.

しんさつ 診察 (a) medical examination ¶ 診察する examine [see] 《a patient》 / 医者の診察を受ける see [《文》 consult] a doctor; take medical advice (from a doctor) / 診察券 a consultation ticket / 診察時間 consultation [《英》 surgery] hours / 診察室 a consultation [consulting] room / 診察日 a consultation day / 診察料 a doctor's fee; a fee for medical advice. [文例⇩]

しんさん 辛酸 hardship(s) ¶ 辛酸をなめる go through a lot of hardships [《口語》 the mill]; 《文》 suffer [undergo] all sorts of privations.

しんざん 新参 ¶ 新参の new; 《口語》 green (未熟の); newly-appointed (新任の) / 新参者 a newcomer; 〈未熟者〉 a new hand 《at》; 《口語》 a greenhorn; a novice.

しんざん(ゆうこく) 深山(幽谷) ¶ 深山(幽谷)に deep in the mountains.

しんし¹ 紳士 a gentleman; 〈総称〉 《文》 gentry; 《米》 gentlefolk(s) ¶ 紳士ぶる play the gentleman; pose as a gentleman / 紳士的(な) gentlemanly; gentlemanlike / 非紳士的 ungentlemanly / 紳士気取りの snobbish / 紳士気取りの俗物 a snob / 紳士協定 a gentleman's [gentlemen's] agreement / 紳士服 men's suits ★ 単数ならば a man's suit / 紳士録 a Who's Who; 《米》 a social register. [文例⇩]

しんし² 真摯 ⇨ まじめ.

じんじ 人事 〈人間同士の間のこと〉 human affairs; 〈会社などの〉 personnel affairs ¶ 人事を尽す 《文》 do all that is humanly possible; try every possible way 《of *doing*》 / 人事異動 personnel changes; a personnel reshuffle / 人事院 the National Personnel Authority / 人事部[課, 局] the personnel department [section, bureau] / 人事行政[管理] personnel administration [management]. [文例⇩]

しんしき¹ 神式 ¶ 神式で 《hold a ceremony》 with *Shinto* rites.

しんしき² 新式 a new style [type]; 〈方法〉 a new method ¶ 新式の new; new-style[-type]; 〈現代的〉 modern; up-to-date / 新式にする modernize.

シンジケート 《form》 a syndicate.

しんしつ¹ 心室 【解】 the 《right, left》 ventricle (of the heart).

しんしつ² 寝室 a bedroom ¶ 寝室兼居間 《英》 a bed-sitting room; 《英口語》 a bedsitter.

しんじつ 真実 truth; 〈実際に〉 really; truly; 《文》 in reality ¶ 真実の true; real; 《文》 veracious / 真実を述べる tell [speak] the truth / 真実性[味] the truth [《文》 veracity, authenticity] 《of a report》.

じんじふせい 人事不省 ¶ 人事不省になる[陥る] lose consciousness; fall [《文》 become] unconscious; lose *one's* senses; 《文》 become insensible; faint; 《文》 swoon.

しんしゃ 深謝 ¶ 深謝する 〈感謝する〉 thank *sb* warmly; 《文》 express *one's* heartfelt gratitude 《to》; 〈わびる〉 make a sincere apology.

しんじゃ 信者 a believer 《in》; 《文》 a devotee 《of》; a follower 《of》; 《文》 an adherent 《of》; 〈総称〉 《文》 the faithful.

じんじゃ 神社 a *Shinto* shrine ¶ 神社仏閣 (*Shinto*) shrines and (Buddhist) temples / 靖国神社 the Yasukuni Shrine.

ジンジャーエール ginger ale.

しんしゃく 斟酌 ¶ 斟酌する consider; take *sth* into consideration [account]; allow for; make allowance(s) for / …を斟酌して 《文》 in consideration of….

しんしゅ¹ 進取 ¶ 進取的な progressive; enterprising / 進取の気象 an enterprising [a go-ahead] spirit; 《have no》 enterprise.

しんしゅ² 新種 〈新しい種〉 a new species; 〈新発見の種〉 a newly-discovered species 《of orchid》; 〈変種〉 a new variety 《of tulip》.

しんじゅ 真珠 a pearl ¶ 真珠の養殖 cultivation of pearls; pearl cultivation / 真珠を採取する dive [fish] for pearls / 養殖真珠 a cultured pearl / 真珠色 pearl gray / 真珠貝 a pearl oyster [shell] / 真珠採り 〈採取〉 pearl fishery; pearling; 〈人〉 a pearl diver [fisher] / 真珠養殖場 a pearl farm [bed].

じんしゅ 人種 a race; an ethnic group ¶ 人種の[的] racial; ethnic / 人種間の racial 《tension》; 《文》 interracial 《understanding》 / 人種的反感 racial [race] antipathy / 人種的偏見 racial prejudice; racism; racialism / 白色[黄色]人種 the white [yellow] race(s) / 人種意識 racial [color] consciousness / 人種関係 《improve》 race relations / 人種差別 racial discrimination; 〈米国の黒人に対する〉 segregation; 〈南アフリカの〉 apartheid / 人種差別をする discriminate against colored people; segregate 《the blacks》 /

---

prizes for fiction.

しんさつ 僕だったら, 病院へ行って診察してもらうのだが. If I were you, I would go to the hospital for an examination.

しんし¹ 君の取った行動は紳士的だ. You acted like a (true) gentleman. / あまり紳士とは言えないね. He is hardly a gentleman. / そんなことをしたら紳士の体面にかかわるだろう. That would be beneath your dignity as a gentleman.

じんじ 人事を尽くして天命を待つ. Do your best and leave the rest to Providence.

しんしゅつ¹ そのデパートは新宿へ進出しようと計画している. That department store is planning to open a branch at Shinjuku. | The department store is thinking of extending its business to Shinjuku. / 今度の選挙では社会党の進出が目立った. The recent election was marked by a striking advance of [by the great gains scored by] the Socialists.

しんじょう¹ 彼らの気持ちは心情的に理解できるが, その行為は認めがたい. Emotionally I feel sym-

しんじゅう 心中 a double suicide; a joint suicide《with a woman》; a lovers' suicide ¶心中する[を図る] commit [attempt] a double suicide; commit [attempt] suicide with *sb*; die [attempt to die] together 《for love》/ 心中未遂 an attempted double suicide.

しんじゅう[2] 臣従 ¶臣従する serve 《a feudal lord》as a vassal; render homage and service 《to》.

しんしゅく 伸縮 expansion and contraction ¶伸縮する expand and contract; be elastic [flexible]/ 伸縮自在な《文》elastic; flexible; stretch《fabric》/ 伸縮性《文》elasticity; flexibility.

しんしゅつ[1] 進出 ¶進出する advance 《into》; gain ground; go [launch]《into》; find *one's* way into; 《文》forge ahead; 《文》debouch (軍隊などが狭い所から広い所へ) / 政界[映画界]に進出する go into politics [the movies] / 海外市場に進出する make inroads into foreign markets. 文例⇩

しんしゅつ[2] 滲[浸]出 ¶滲出する《文》exude; ooze (out); ooze *its* way through; seep out [through].

しんしゅつきぼつ 神出鬼没 ¶神出鬼没の appearing in unexpected places [at unexpected moments]; 《文》elusive.

しんしゅん 新春 the New Year.

しんじゅん 浸潤 ¶浸潤する《文》permeate through; soak [《文》infiltrate] 《into》.

しんしょ 信書 a letter; 《文》correspondence (総称) ¶信書の秘密を侵す violate the privacy of (personal) correspondence.

しんしょう[1] 心証 an impression; 〈判事の〉a strong belief; 《文》a conviction ¶心証を害する give *sb* an unfavorable impression; create a bad impression 《by doing》.

しんしょう[2] 心象 an image; a mental picture [image].

しんしょう[3] 身上 ⇨ しんだい.

しんしょう[4] 辛勝 ¶辛勝する win《a game》by a narrow [small] margin; 《口語》nose [edge] out.

しんじょう[1] 心情 *one's* feelings; 《文》*one's* sentiment; 《文》*one's* heart ¶心情を察する understand [sympathize with, appreciate] *sb's* feelings; 〈同情する〉feel for *sb*. 文例⇩

しんじょう[2] 身上〈取り柄〉an asset; a strong point; 《文》*one's* merit ¶身上調査書 a report card on *one's* family.

しんじょう[3] 信条〈主義〉a principle; a belief; 〈教条〉a creed; 《文》a credo (*pl.* -s); an article of faith ¶自分の生活信条 the principles by which *one* lives; *one's* principles. 文例⇩

しんじょう[4] 真情 *one's* real feelings; 《文》*one's* true (genuine) sentiments ¶真情を吐露する express *one's* true sentiments; speak from *one's* [the] heart.

じんじょう 尋常 ¶尋常な,尋常一様の ordinary; common; usual; 〈並の〉average; 〈平凡な〉commonplace; mediocre; 〈常の〉normal; 〈単純な〉plain; simple / 尋常に commonly; ordinarily; 〈正々堂々と〉fairly; honestly / 尋常でない uncommon; unusual; extraordinary / 尋常に勝負する play fair. 文例⇩

しんしょうしゃ 身障者 ⇨ したい[1] (身体障害者).

しんしょうぼうだい 針小棒大 (an) exaggeration ¶針小棒大の exaggerated; high-flown; 《文》bombastic / 針小棒大に言う exaggerate; overstate 《*one's* case》; make a mountain (out) of a molehill (問題・苦情などの).

しんしょく[1] 神職 Shinto priesthood ¶神職につく become a *Shinto* priest.

しんしょく[2] 浸食 erosion; corrosion ¶浸食する eat away; eat *its* way 《through solid rock》; erode; corrode.

しんしょく[3] 寝食 ¶寝食を忘れて看護する《文》nurse 《a sick person》devotedly ¶寝食を共にする live under the same roof 《as *sb*》; live with *sb* under the same roof. 文例⇩

しんじる 信じる〈本当だと思う〉believe; accept 《a report》as true; 《文》place credence 《in》; 〈信仰する〉believe in 《God》; 〈確信する〉be convinced [《文》persuaded]《of, that ...》; 〈信用する〉trust; believe [put *one's* trust] in *sb*; 〈信頼する〉rely [depend] on *sb* ¶人の言葉どおりに信じる take *sb* at *his* word; take *sb's* word for it / 固く信じている firmly believe《that...》; 《文》have a firm belief《that..., in》; be sure [convinced]《that..., of》/ 私の信じる所では to the best of my belief / ...と信じて believing [in the belief] that... / 信ずべき reliable; trustworthy; credible / 信じ難い unbelievable; incredible; doubtful / 信じやすい 《文》credulous; too ready to believe / 容易に信じない be incredulous 《about》; be skeptical 《about》. 文例⇩

しんしん[1] 心身 ¶心身共に健全である《文》be sound in mind and body; be mentally and

---

pathy with them, but I still cannot approve of their conduct.
しんしょう[2] それが あの男の身上だ. That's his sole merit. | That's all he has to recommend him.
しんしょう[3] それは僕の信条の1つだ. That is an article of my creed.
じんじょう 彼は尋常一様の学者ではない. He is no mean scholar.
しんしょく[3] 彼は寝食を忘れて貧民救済のために尽くした. He denied himself all the comforts of life and worked for the cause of the poor and needy.
しんじる 僕の言うことが信じられないのか. Don't you believe me? (★ believe in me とすると「私の人柄を信用しない」の意味になる) / 日本では塩には物を清める力があると信じられている. In Japan, salt is believed to have [is credited with] purifying powers. / この報道は信ずべき筋から出たものである. The news came from a reliable source. / 彼女は全く信じられないという顔つきでそれを見た. She looked at it with complete unbelief on her face. / 一般に信じられているのとは違って,彼は根は好人物であった. Con-

physically sound / 心身爽快になる《文》feel refreshed [bright] in mind and body ; 《英口語》be (all) bright-eyed and bushy-tailed / 心身を打ち込む《文》devote *oneself* entirely 《to》; lose *oneself* 《in》; 《文》give *oneself* body and soul 《to》/ 心身症 (a) psychosomatic disease.

しんしん[2] 新進 ¶新進の rising / 新進気鋭の young and energetic ; up-and-coming / 新進作家 a rising novelist.

しんしん[3] 深々 [文例⇩]

[し]

しんじん[1] 信心 faith ; belief ; 《文》piety ; 《文》devotion ¶信心する believe 《in》; worship / 信心深い《文》pious ; (deeply) religious ; 《文》godly ; 《文》devout / 信心のない《文》impious ; 《文》unbelieving ; 《文》godless / 信心家 a pious [religious] man.

しんじん[2] 新人 a newcomer ; a new figure [face] ; ‹芸能界の› a new face [star] ; 《scout for》new talent (集合的) ; ‹野球の› a recruit ; a rookie ¶新人王〘野球〙the rookie king / 新人賞 the Rookie of the Year award.

しんじん[3] 深甚 ¶深甚なる《文》profound ; deep.

じんしん[1] 人心 the feelings of the general public ; 《文》the popular mind ¶人心をまどわす mislead the public.

じんしん[2] 人身 ¶人身売買 traffic in human beings ; slave trade / 人身保護法〘法〙the Protection of Personal Liberty Act ; 〘英法〙the Habeas Corpus Act / 人身攻撃をする make a personal attack 《on》/ 議論で人身攻撃を始める bring personalities into [《口語》get personal in] an argument / 人身事故 an accident resulting in injury or death.

しんすい[1] 心酔 ¶心酔する be fascinated 《by》; be infatuated 《with》; be devoted 《to》; adore ; idolize / 心酔者 an ardent admirer ; 《文》an enthusiastic devotee.

しんすい[2] 浸水 ¶浸水する be flooded ; 《文》be inundated ; ‹船が› spring a leak ; leak / 浸水家屋 flooded houses ; houses under water / 浸水地域 the flooded [submerged, inundated] area. [文例⇩]

しんすい[3] 進水 ¶進水する ‹船を› launch ; ‹船が› be launched ; 《文》take the water / 進水式 a launching (ceremony) / 進水台 《leave, slide off》the launching platform [ways].

しんずい 真髄 《文》the essence ; 《文》the quintessence ; the spirit ; the soul ; 《文》the pith.

じんずうりき 神通力 ⇨ じんつうりき.

しんせい[1] 申請 (an) application ; (a) request ; (a) petition ¶申請する apply [make an application] 《to *sb* for *sth*》; 《文》petition 《for》/ 申請人[者] an applicant / 申請書 an [a written] application.

しんせい[2] 神性 《文》divine nature ; 《文》divinity ¶神性を帯びる be touched by [with] divinity.

しんせい[3] 真性 ¶真性の genuine ; true / 真性コレラ (a case of) genuine [true] cholera.

しんせい[4] 新制 a new system ¶新制の 《schools》under the new system 《of education》; new-system 《schools》.

しんせい[5] 新星〘天〙a nova 《*pl*. -s, -vae》.

しんせい[6] 神聖 ¶神聖な《文》sacred ; holy ; consecrated ; 《文》divine / 神聖を汚す desecrate ; 《文》profane / 神聖にして犯すべからざる《文》sacrosanct ; 《文》sacred and inviolable / 神聖にする make holy ; consecrate ; 《文》sanctify ; 《文》hallow / 神聖同盟〘西洋史〙the Holy Alliance / 神聖ローマ帝国 the Holy Roman Empire.

じんせい 人生 (*one's*) life ¶人生を悲観[楽観]する look on the dark [bright] side of life ; take a gloomy [cheerful] view of life / 人生観 *one's* view of life ; an outlook on life / 人生哲学 *one's* philosophy of life. [文例⇩]

しんせいかつ 新生活 a new life ¶新生活に入る begin [start] a new life ; turn over a new leaf.

しんせいじ 新生児 a newborn baby ; 〘医〙a neonate ¶新生児の neonatal 《death》/ 新生児黄疸(おうだん) neonatal jaundice.

しんせいだい 新生代〘地質〙the Cenozoic [Cainozoic] era [period].

しんせいめん 新生面 a new aspect [phase] ¶新生面を開く open (up) a new field 《in, for》; 《文》make a new departure 《in》; make [be] a breakthrough 《in》; 《文》innovate.

しんせかい 新世界 a new world ; ‹米大陸› the New World.

しんせき 親戚 ⇨ しんるい[2].

じんせき 人跡 ¶人跡まれな《文》unfrequented ; 《文》trackless ; 《文》《a place》away from the haunts of men / 人跡未踏の地《文》a region untrodden by men ; a region where no human being has ever set foot.

シンセサイザー a synthesizer.

しんせつ[1] 新設 ¶新設の newly-established[-organized] ; new / 新設する found ; establish ; organize ; create.

しんせつ[2] 新雪 fresh [new-fallen, 《文》virgin] snow.

しんせつ[3] 新説 ‹学説› a new theory ; ‹新見解› a new light [view] ¶新説を立てる put forward [《文》propound, 《文》advance] a new theory.

---

trary to general belief he was a good-natured man at heart.

しんしん[3] 夜はしんしんとふけていった. The night was getting far advanced. / 雪がしんしんと降っている. The snow is falling thick and fast.

しんすい[2] 船はたちまち浸水して沈没した. The ship immediately filled and sank.

じんせい 人生夢のごとし. Life is but an empty dream. / 人生わずか五十年と昔は言ったものだ. People used to say that man's span of life is but fifty years. / 僕は君とは人生観が違う. I don't view life in the same light as you (do). / あの人は人生経験が豊かだから, 話が面白い. His stories are interesting as he has seen a lot of the world.

しんせつ[4] ご親切なお言葉有り難うございます. It is very kind [nice] of you to say so. / 彼は色々親切にしてくれた. He was kind to me in various [all sorts of] ways. / 色色と親切にして下さって有り難う

しんせつ⁴ 親切 (a) kindness ; goodwill ; a favor ¶親切な kind ; good ; friendly ; obliging ; kind-hearted / 親切そうな kind(ly)-looking / 親切にも…する be kind [good] enough to do / 《文》 be so kind as to do ; have the kindness to do / 親切ごかしに under the mask [a show] of kindness [friendship] / 親切心から out of kindness.

しんせっき 新石器 【考古】 a neolith ; a neolithic stone implement ¶新石器時代 the Neolithic era [age] ; the New Stone Age.

しんせん 新鮮 ¶新鮮な fresh ; new ★fresh は「新鮮な」のほかに「加工・缶詰め・冷凍でない」の意もある / 新鮮さ freshness / 新鮮にする make fresh ; freshen ; refresh.

しんぜん¹ 神前 ¶神前に before the altar / 神前結婚 a wedding (ceremony) according to Shinto rites.

しんぜん² 親善 friendship ; friendly relations ; goodwill ; 《文》 amity ¶親善を strengthen the ties of friendship 《between our two countries》; 《文》 promote friendly relations 《between》/ 親善試合 a friendly (game) / 親善使節 a goodwill envoy ; a goodwill mission (使節団) / 親善訪問 a goodwill visit (to a country).

じんせん 人選 ¶人選する choose a person ; 《文》 select a suitable person (for). 文例⇩

しんそう¹ 真相 the truth ; the actual [real] facts ¶真相を明らかにする 《文》 disclose [reveal] the truth ; give a true account (of) / 真相を窮める find out the (real) truth of the affair ; inquire into the true state of things ; 《文》 get to the root [bottom] of the matter. 文例⇩

しんそう² 深窓 ¶深窓に育つ be brought up with tender care in a good family.

しんそう³ 深層 (one's emotional) depths ¶深層構造 〖言語〗 (at) deep structure / 深層心理学 depth psychology.

しんそう⁴ 新装 ¶新装を凝らす give a new look (to) ; refurnish ; reequip ; redecorate ; remodel (改造する) / 新装成った講堂 the refurbished auditorium.

しんぞう 心臓 〖解〗 the heart ; 〈図太さ〉 (a) cheek ; a nerve ¶心臓が強い have a strong [stout] heart ; 〈図太い〉 be cheeky ; be brazen(-faced) ; be thick-skinned / 心臓が弱い have a weak [bad] heart ; have heart trouble ; 〈気が弱い〉 be timid ; be shy / 心臓の鼓動な beating ; a heartbeat / 心臓の鼓動停止 cardiac arrest ; a heart stoppage / 心臓の働き heart action / 心臓部 the heart (of a city) / 心臓(部)の 〖解〗 cardiac / 心臓移植(手術) a heart transplant (operation) / 心臓外科 open-heart surgery / 心臓切開手術 an open-heart operation / 心臓障害 heart trouble / 心臓肥大 dilation of the heart ; cardiac hypertrophy ; megalocardia / 心臓病 a heart disease ; heart trouble / 心臓弁膜症 a valvular disease of the heart / 心臓マッサージ (do) (a) heart massage / 心臓まひ heart failure ; a heart attack ; cardiac paralysis. 文例⇩

じんぞう¹ 人造 ¶人造の artificial ; man-made ; 〈模造の〉 imitation ; 〈合成の〉 synthetic / (ダム建設などでできる)人造湖 a man-made [an artificial] lake / 人造ゴム synthetic rubber / 人造繊維 synthetic [man-made] fibers [textiles].

じんぞう² 腎臓 〖解〗 the kidney ¶人工腎臓 a [an artificial] kidney machine / 腎臓移植 a kidney transplant / 腎臓病 a kidney [renal] disease ; kidney trouble / 腎臓炎 ⇒じんえん / 腎臓結石 a renal calculus (pl. -li) ; kidney stones / 腎臓摘出 〖医〗 a nephrectomy.

しんぞく 親族 ⇒しんるい² ¶親族会議 a family conference [council] / 親族関係 kinship.

じんそく 迅速 ¶迅速な quick ; rapid ; 《文》 swift ; prompt / 迅速に quickly ; rapidly ; 《文》 swiftly ; promptly. 文例⇩

しんそこ 心底 ¶心底から from the bottom of one's heart ; sincerely ; 《文》 heartily ; with all one's heart / 心底からの sincere (devotion) ; deep-rooted (hatred) ; heartfelt (gratitude) ; 《文》 cordial (support).

しんそつ 新卒 a new [recent] graduate ¶本年度の新卒大学生 this year's university graduates.

しんたい¹ 身体 the body ; the person ¶身体の bodily ; physical ; 《文》 corporal / 身体の自由を失う become helpless ; 〈不具になる〉 be disabled / 身体各部 the parts of the body / 身体活動 physical [body] activity / 身体検査を受ける have 《文》 undergo a physical [medical] examination [checkup] ; 〈持ち物を調べられる〉 have one's person searched ; 《口語》 be frisked / 身体障害 (suffer from) a disability / 身体障害者 a physically handicapped person ; a disabled person ; the physically handicapped (総称).

しんたい² 神体 a shintai ; a Shinto object of worship.

しんたい³ 進退 ¶進退の自由を失う lose the [one's] freedom of movement ; 〈立往生する〉 be [get] stalled (in the mud) / 進退窮まる be in a fix [dilemma] ; be driven to the wall [into a tight corner] ; be (caught) in a cleft stick [between the devil and the deep sea] / 《文》 find oneself between Scylla and Charybdis /

ございました. Thank you for all you've done for me. / こちらの親切から仇となった. What I had done out of kindness turned out to be against [contrary to] his interests.

じんせん 目下人選中です. We are looking for a suitable man for the post. / 人選難だ. We're having difficulty (in) finding somebody [the right person] for the job.

しんそう¹ 少しずつ真相がわかってきた. Bit by bit the real situation dawned on me.

しんぞう 心臓がどきどきしている. My heart is beating fast [violently]. / 死因は心臓まひであった. She died of heart failure. / なんて心臓だ! What a nerve he's got! | What (a) cheek! / コーヒー1杯で2時間もねばる心臓は僕にはないねえ. I haven't got the nerve to make a cup of coffee stretch over two hours.

じんそく 彼の反応の迅速な事は驚くばかりだ. The swiftness [speed] of his reactions is amaz-

しんだい 進退を共にする《文》cast in *one's* lot with *sb*; act in line with *sb* / 進退を決する decide on *one's* course of action;《文》define [clarify] *one's* attitude / 進退よろしきを得た[を誤る] take the right [wrong] course of action; act properly [unwisely] / 進退伺いを出す submit an informal resignation. 文例□

しんだい¹ 身代 a fortune; *one's* property [《文》wealth] ¶身代を作る make *one's* [a] fortune [《口語》pile];《文》amass a fortune / 身代をつぶす《使い果たす》ruin *oneself*; run through [《文》dissipate] *one's* fortune / 身代限り ⇨ しさん.

しんだい² 寝台 a bed; a bedstead; 〈列車・船の〉a (sleeping) berth; 〈船の〉a bunk ¶〈寝台車の〉上[下]段の寝台 an upper [a lower] berth / 寝台料金[券] a berth charge [ticket] / 寝台車 a sleeping car;《口語》a sleeper.

じんたい¹ 人体 the human body [organism] ¶人体解剖学 human anatomy / 人体解剖図 an anatomical chart / 人体実験 an experiment on a human body; a living-body test; human experimentation / 人体模型 an anatomical model (of the human body).

じんたい² 靱帯《解》a ligament; a cord.

じんだい 甚大 甚大な very great; immense; tremendous; enormous; huge.

しんたく¹ 信託 trust ¶信託する trust *sb* with *sth*;《文》entrust *sth* to *sb* [*sb* with *sth*]; leave 《*one's* property》 in trust with 《a bank》/ 選挙民の信託を受ける get [《文》receive] a 《clear》 mandate from the voters [electorate] / 信託会社[銀行] a trust company [bank] / 信託者 a truster / 被信託者 a trustee / 国連の信託下に置く place [put] 《an island》 under a UN trusteeship / 信託統治領 a trust territory 《under the U.S.A.》/ 信託預金 money in trust.

しんたく² 神託 an oracle; a divine revelation [message]. 文例□

しんたん 心胆 ¶心胆を寒からしめる〈事が主語〉make *sb's* blood run cold; make *sb's* flesh creep; strike terror into *sb's* heart;《文》chill the heart of *sb*.

しんだん 診断 (a) diagnosis《pl. -noses》¶診断する diagnose; make a diagnosis (of); give *one's* diagnosis (of) / 診断を誤る make a wrong diagnosis / 診断を下す give [《文》pronounce] a [*one's*] diagnosis (of) / 診断技術[方法] a diagnostic technique [method] / 診断書 a medical certificate. 文例□

ing.

しんたい³ 進退これ窮まる. A precipice in front, a wolf behind. | A pond in front, and a stream behind.

しんたく² クロイソスに「汝は大帝国を滅ぼすであろう」というデルフォイの神託があった. The Delphic oracle told Croesus that he would 'destroy a great empire'.

しんだん 医者は私の病気を肋膜炎と診断した. The doctor diagnosed my illness as pleurisy.

じんち¹ 人知 human intelligence [knowledge,《文》intellect, understanding] ¶人知の及ばない beyond human knowledge [understanding];《文》beyond the wit of man. 文例□

じんち² 陣地 ⇨じん² ¶陣地を構築する build up a strong point.

しんちく 新築 ¶新築の newly-built; new / 新築する build;《文》construct / 新築中の建築 a house under [in course of] construction / 新築祝い〈建主が友人を招いて行なう〉(give) a housewarming (party) / 新築祝いに花びんを贈る give *sb* a vase as a housewarming present.

じんちく 人畜《文》men and [or] beasts;《文》man and beast; living creatures [things]. 文例□

しんちゃ 新茶 this year's tea; newly-picked tea.

しんちゃく 新着 newly-arrived (books) / 新着品 new stock; newly-arrived (items of) merchandise.

しんちゅう¹ 心中 ¶心中を察する share [《文》appreciate] *sb's* feelings; sympathize with *sb* / 心中を打ち明ける take *sb* into *one's* confidence / 心中に at heart; in *one's* heart (of hearts); inwardly.

しんちゅう² 真鍮 brass ¶真鍮(製, 色)の brass;《文》brazen / 真鍮のボタン a brass button / 真鍮磨き metal polish.

しんちゅう³ 進駐 ¶進駐する advance 《into》; make an (armed) entry 《into》; be stationed 《at》《駐留する》/ 進駐軍 the Occupation Army [Forces].

じんちゅう 陣中 ¶陣中の at the front; on the field (of battle) / 選挙の候補者への陣中見舞 《send in》 a present [a supply of secret funds] to encourage a candidate during an election campaign.

しんちょう¹ 身長 height;《文》stature ¶身長が伸びる grow (taller); grow [increase] in stature / 身長168センチ be 168 centimeters tall [in height, in stature]; stand 168 centimeters (tall) / 身長180センチに達する attain a stature of 180 centimeters / 身長を測る measure [take] *sb's* height / 身長順に並ぶ〈高い方から〉line up [stand] in (decreasing) order of height; 〈低い方から〉line up in order of increasing height. 文例□

しんちょう² 伸張 ¶伸張する extend; expand;《文》elongate / 伸張性がない have no stretch. 文例□

しんちょう³ 新調 ¶新調の newly-made; spick-

じんち¹ 人知の発達はとどまることがない. The advance of human knowledge will never cease.

じんちく 人畜に被害はなかった. No harm was done to men or cattle. / 人畜に無害.〈散布剤などの表示〉Harmless to men and animals.

しんちょう¹ 身長は幾らありますか. How tall are you? / 赤ん坊は身長58センチ, 体重4キロあった. The baby was 58 centimeters long and weighed 4 kilos. /〈競泳で〉千メートルのラップで彼は紺野に2身長遅れて[先んじて]いた. At the 1,000-meter mark he was two lengths behind [ahead of] Konno.

しんちょう² 人口が増加したからとて国力が伸張するというわけではない. A nation is not necessarily growing in power because it is increasing in population.

しんちょう³ これはデリケートな問題で, 慎重に扱わなくてはならない. This is a sensitive problem

しんちょう / しんどう

and-span; brand-new; new / 新調する have [get] (a dress) made; 《買う》buy oneself《a new bag》.

しんちょう⁴ 慎重 ¶慎重な《文》prudent; careful; 《文》circumspect; discreet; cautious; 《文》deliberate / 慎重な態度を取る tread warily 《in a matter》; 《口語》go easy on sth / 慎重に《文》prudently; carefully; discreetly; 《文》cautiously; 《文》deliberately; 《文》with caution [prudence, deliberation] / 物事を慎重にする be circumspect [wary, deliberate] in doing; use discretion 《in》; handle sth with kid gloves / 慎重審議する give careful consideration to《a matter》/ 慎重を期する deliberate carefully《on》/ 慎重論を唱える be against taking risks; insist on playing (it) safe. 用例⇩

じんちょうげ 《植》a daphne.

しんちょく 進捗 progress; (an) advance ¶進捗する make (good) progress; make headway; advance / 進捗している be in progress; be (well) under way / 進捗させる speed up; hasten; 《文》expedite.

しんちんたいしゃ 新陳代謝 《生物》metabolism; 〈比喩的〉《文》regeneration; replacing the old with the new ¶人体の新陳代謝 body metabolism / 新陳代謝の metabolic / 新陳代謝する replace the old with the new; be renewed; 《文》be regenerated. 用例⇩

しんつう 心痛 mental agony 《(an)》anguish; heartache ⇒ しんぱい / 心痛のあまり in anguish; in agony; in the [an] agony of despair.

じんつう 陣痛 labor (pains); the pains of childbirth. 用例⇩

じんつうりき 神通力 a supernatural [an occult] power; a divine power.

しんてい 進呈 ¶進呈する present [give] sth to sb; present sb with sth; make sb a present of sth; offer. 用例⇩

じんてい 人定 《法》confirmation of sb's identity ¶人定尋問 identity questioning; an identity interrogation.

しんてき 心的 mental 《attitude》; psychological ¶心的現象 a mental phenomenon.

じんてきしげん 人的資源 human [manpower] resources; manpower.

シンデレラ ¶シンデレラ物語〈比喩的に〉a Cinderella story.

しんてん¹ 進展 development; progress; advance ¶進展する develop; progress; advance.

しんてん² 親展 〈封筒の表書き〉Confidential

¶親展の confidential; personal; private.

しんでん 神殿 a temple; a shrine; a sanctuary ¶アポロの神殿 the Temple of Apollo.

しんでんず[けい] 心電図[計] 《医》an electrocardiogram [electrocardiograph].

しんてんち 新天地 ¶新天地を開拓する open up a new field of activity; break new ground.

しんと¹ 信徒 a believer; 《文》an adherent; a follower; 〈集合的に〉《文》the faithful; 《文》the flock (キリスト教の).

しんと² ¶しんとした still; silent (as the grave); quiet; 《文》hushed; 〈ひと気がない〉deserted. 用例⇩

しんど¹ 進度 progress ¶学科進度 the progress of classwork. 用例⇩

しんど² 深度 depth ¶深度を測る measure the depth (of); sound the sea, (the distance to the bottom) / 深度計 a depth gauge / 《自記》a depth recorder.

しんど³ 震度 〈地震の〉seismic intensity ⇨ マグニチュード ¶震度6の地震 a tremor with an intensity ★ 6 on the Japanese seven-stage scale ★ 日本の気象庁で定められる震度階と、外国で用いられるリヒタースケール (the Richter scale) は同じではない.

じんど ⇨ じんく.

しんどい 〈疲れた〉(be) tired [exhausted]; 〈つらい〉hard; exhausting ¶しんどい仕事 a tough job.

しんとう¹ 心頭 ¶怒り心頭に発する fly [get] into a rage [passion]; be in a towering rage. 用例⇩「a Shintoist.

しんとう² 神道 Shintoism; Shinto ¶神道家

しんとう³ 浸透 《文》permeation; penetration; 《文》infiltration; 《文》percolation; seepage; 《化・生理》osmosis ¶共産主義の浸透 the infiltration of communism (into a country) / 浸透する《文》permeate (全域に); spread itself (into, through(out)); percolate [seep] (through) (すき間・小穴を通して); infiltrate [penetrate] (into) (侵す) / 浸透圧 (an) osmotic pressure / 浸透作用 (an) osmotic action / 浸透性 osmosis; permeability. 用例⇩

しんとう⁴ 親等 《法》the degree of relationship [kinship] ¶2親等の親族 a relative in the second degree / 3親等内の親族 a relative within the third degree of relationship.

しんどう¹ 神童 a child prodigy; an infant genius. 用例⇩

しんどう² 振動 (an) oscillation 《of the needle

---

and requires careful handling. / 大いに慎重を期して仔細に調べた. I took great care to examine it minutely.

しんちんたいしゃ 新陳代謝は自然の法則である. It is the law of nature that the old give place to the new [the new take the place of the old]. / 体は常に新陳代謝する. Our bodies are subject to constant metabolism.

じんつう 陣痛が始まった. Her labor started. | She felt the be-

ginnings of labor. / 陣痛が激しくなった. Her labor pains have quickened. | She is in violent labor.

しんてい 見本無料進呈. 〈広告などで〉Write for free samples. | Samples sent free on request.

しんと² 場内はしんとした. A hush fell over the hall. / 家の中はしんと静まり返っていた. A profound silence reigned within the house.

しんど¹ クラスによって進度が違う. Progress differs from class to

class. | Some classes have got further [are further on] (in the course) than others.

しんとう¹ 心頭を滅却すれば火もまた涼し. Clear your mind of all mundane thoughts, and you will find even fire cool.

しんとう³ 水は地中に浸透して行くが、堅い岩は浸透できない. Water sinks into the ground [percolates downward through the soil], but cannot pass through hard rock.

しんどう¹ あの子は本当に神童だ.

しんどう on the dial); (a) vibration 《of the train》; a swing 《of the pendulum》 ¶空気の振動 air vibrations / 振動する oscillate; swing; vibrate; move to and fro / 振動計 a vibrometer; a vibroscope / 振動数 the number of vibrations; the frequency of vibration / 《ベルなどの》振動板【電】a trembler.

しんどう³ 震動 a shock; (a) vibration; a tremor; a quake; 〈エンジンなどの起こす〉 throbbing [throbs] 《of the engine》 ¶震動する shake; tremble; vibrate; throb / 震動時間 the duration of the shock [vibration]. 文例⇩

じんとう 陣頭 ¶陣頭に立つ be in the van(guard) [at the head] 《of an army》; take the lead 《in doing》/ 陣頭で指揮をする lead one's men by working (together) with them.

じんどう 人道 《人να》《文》 humanity ¶人道に背く[もとる] be contrary to humanity; be inhumane / 人道にかなった, 人道的な humane; humanitarian / 人道主義 humanitarianism / 人道主義者 a humanitarian / 人道的見地から 《criticize sth》 on humanitarian grounds; for humanitarian reasons / 人道問題 a question touching [affecting] humanity; a problem demanding a humanitarian solution.

じんとうぜい 人頭税 a poll (head, per capita) tax ¶人頭税を取る levy a poll tax.

じんとく 人徳 one's natural qualities [《文》 virtue]; one's personal reputation.

じんどる 陣取る 〈陣を敷く〉 take up one's position; encamp; 〈位置を占める〉 place [install] oneself 《at, in》; take one's stand 《at, in》; occupy 《a corner of the room》.

シンナー (a) (paint) thinner ¶シンナー遊びをする sniff glue; inhale paint thinner.

しんなり ¶しんなりした 《文》 pliant; pliable; flexible.

しんにち 親日 ¶親日の pro-Japanese / 親日家 a Japanophile; a sympathizer for Japan.

しんにゅう¹ 侵入 (an) invasion; inroads; a raid; 〈ちん入〉 (an) intrusion ¶侵入する 〈他国へ〉 invade; enter forcibly; make an invasion [a raid] 《into, on》; make inroads 《into enemy country》; 〈家などに〉 trespass 《on》; break into; force one's way into / 侵入軍 an invasion force / 侵入者 an invader; an intruder; a trespasser.

しんにゅう² 進入 ¶進入する enter; go [《文》 penetrate, march] into; find [make] one's way into / 〈空港の〉進入援助設備 approach aids / 進入旋回 【航空】 an approach turn / 進入灯 《航空・鉄道》 an approach light / 進入路 〈自動車道路の〉 an approach ramp.

しんにゅう³ 新入 ¶新入社員 a new [newly-hired] employee / 新入生 a new pupil [boy, girl]; a new [newly-enrolled] student; a [an incoming] freshman 《大学の》.

しんにゅう⁴ ¶しんにゅうをかけて言う exaggerate. 文例⇩

しんにん¹ 信任 confidence; trust ¶信任する trust; 《文》 place confidence [one's trust] in / 信任を得る, 信任される win [gain] the confidence (of); be trusted 《by》/ 信任を得ている have [《文》 enjoy] the confidence (of) / 信任状 《present one's》 credentials; a letter of credence / 信任投票 《win, lose》 a vote of confidence 《in the Diet, on a policy》; a confidence vote.

しんにん² 新任 ¶新任の newly-appointed / 新任の知事 《文》 a governor new to office / 新任の大使 the new ambassador; 〈就任前の〉 the incoming ambassador; the ambassador designate / 新任のあいさつを述べる make an inaugural address / 新任地 one's new post.

しんねりむっつり ¶しんねりむっつりした 〈無口な〉 《文》 taciturn; 〈不機嫌な〉 sullen.

しんねん¹ 信念 belief; faith; (a) conviction ¶信念を強める strengthen one's faith [belief]; 〈事が〉 confirm [《文》 corroborate] one's belief. 文例⇩

しんねん² 新年 the New Year; a new year; 〈元日〉 New Year's Day; 《米》 New Year's ¶新年を迎える greet the New Year; see the new year in / 旧年を送り新年を迎える see the Old Year out and the New Year in; 〈除夜の鐘と共に〉 ring out the old (year) and ring in the new / 新年早々 at the beginning of the New Year / 新年宴会 a New Year('s) party / 《雑誌の》新年号 a New Year issue. 文例⇩

しんのう 親王 an Imperial prince; a prince of the blood (royal).

しんぱ 新派 〈新しい流派〉 a new school; 〈新派劇〉 the Shimpa drama. 「traveler.

シンパ a 《communist》 sympathizer; a fellow

じんば 人馬 《文》 (both) man and horse. 文例⇩

しんぱい 心配 〈気がかり〉 anxiety; concern; 《文》 solicitude; apprehension(s); 〈不安〉 uneasiness; misgivings; (a) fear; suspense; alarm; 〈悩み〉 worry; care; trouble; 〈世話〉 《文》 good offices ¶心配する 〈憂慮する〉 be anxious [《文》 solicitous, concerned] 《about》; be alarmed; 〈不安に思う〉 fear; have misgivings 《about》; feel uneasy 《about》; be ill at ease 〈心を悩ます〉 be worried 《about》; trouble oneself

---

That child is really a phenomenon [wonder]. / 十で神童, 十五で才子, はたち過ぎればただの人. A prodigy at ten, a clever boy at fifteen, and a mediocrity at twenty.

しんどう³ この車は震動がひどい[少ない]. This car shakes horribly [runs smoothly]. / 昨夜微震あり, 震動時間数秒. Yesterday evening there was a slight earthquake, the vibration lasting a few seconds.

しんにゅう⁴ 田中も間抜けだが小野はそれにしんにゅうをかけたような大間抜けさ. Tanaka is certainly a dope, but Ono is another, with a capital D.

しんねん¹ 人々に嘲笑されるほどその使命を説く彼の信念はいっそう高まっていった. The more people laughed at him, the greater was his faith in his mission. / 彼は信念がぐらついた. His faith wavered [was shaken].

しんねん² 新年おめでとうございます. Happy New Year! | I wish you a happy New Year.

じんば 人馬もろともに倒れた. The horse fell with its rider. / 人馬一体となっていた. He sat on his horse as though he were part of it.

《about》; 〈世話する〉 look after ; 〈…を周旋する〉 find ; get / 心配して anxiously / 心配のあまり overcome with anxiety ; 《文》 in an excess of anxiety / 心配な anxious ; uneasy / 心配のない easy 《circumstances》; carefree 《life》/ 心配の種である[になる] be a worry to *one* ; 《文》 give cause for anxiety / 心配なく at ease ; free from care / 心配をかける 《文》 cause anxiety 《to》; give *sb* trouble ; trouble *sb* / 家庭の心配 family worries [cares] / 金の心配 financial troubles [worries] ; worries about money ; 〈金銭上の助力〉 financial help ; 《文》 pecuniary aid / 金の心配をしてやる help *sb* (to) raise money ; give financial help [pecuniary aid] 《to》/ 就職の心配をしてやる (try to) find *sb* a job [position] ; put *sb* in the way of making a living / 心配でたまらない be worried sick / 心配事 cares ; worries ; a trouble / 心配事がある have something to worry about ; have something [a weight] on *one's* mind / 心配性(の人) a (natural) worrier ; a person given to worrying ; an alarmist. [文例⇩]

しんばつ 神罰 divine punishment [judgment, 《文》 retribution] ; 《文》 Heaven's vengeance ¶ 神罰を被る 《文》 incur [be visited with] divine punishment ; be punished by God / …に神罰が下るように祈る 《文》 call down the vengeance of Heaven upon *sb*.

ジンバブエ Zimbabwe ¶ ジンバブエの Zimbabwean / ジンバブエ人 a Zimbabwean.

シンバル 〈楽器〉 cymbals ¶ シンバル奏者 a cymbalist ; a cymbals player.

しんぱん[1] 侵犯 〈権利の〉 (a) violation ; (an) infringement ; 〈領土の〉 (an) invasion ¶ 侵犯する violate ; infringe (on) 《*sb's* rights》; invade 《the territory》.

しんぱん[2] 新版 〈新刊〉 a new publication ; 〈改版〉 a new edition ¶ 新版の newly-published[-edited].

しんぱん[3] 審判 〈人〉 an umpire (野球の) ; a referee (ボクシング・フットボールなどの) ; 〈事〉 umpiring ; refereeing ; 〈判定〉 a decision ; (a) judgment ¶ 審判する[を務める] referee 《a game》; umpire; act as umpire [referee]; judge / 最後の審判 〖キリスト教〗 the Last Judgment ; the Great Assize / 最後の審判の日 (the) Judgment Day ; doomsday.

しんび 審美 ¶ 審美的 《文》 aesthetic(al) / 審美眼がある have an eye for [a good sense of] the beautiful ; have a sense of beauty.

しんぴ[1] 神秘 (a) mystery ¶ 神秘的な mysterious ; 《文》 mystic(al) ; 《文》 occult ; 《文》 enigmatic / 神秘のベールを剝ぐ strip *sth* of *its* aura of mystery ; demystify / 神秘をさぐる explore a mystery / 神秘を解く solve [unravel] a mystery / 神秘に包まれている 《文》 be shrouded in mystery / 神秘主義 mysticism / 神秘主義者 a mystic ; an occultist / 神秘性[感] 《文》 a mystique.

しんぴ[2] 真皮 〖解〗 the true [inner] skin ; the corium 《*pl.* -ria》; the derma.

しんぴつ 真筆 *one's* own handwriting ; an authentic writing. [文例⇩]

しんぴょうせい 信憑性 credibility; reliability; 《文》 authenticity ¶ 信憑性のある reliable ; authentic / 信憑性のない unreliable ; 《文》 unauthentic / 信憑性に欠ける have no [《文》 lack] credibility.

しんぴん 新品 ¶ 新品の new ; brand-new / 新品同様である look brand-new ; be [look] as good as new ; be virtually new.

じんぴん 人品 〈ふうさい〉 (personal) appearance ; 《文》 mien ; 〈人柄〉 character ; personality ¶ 人品卑しからぬ人 a respectable-looking person ; 《文》 a person of respectable appearance.

しんぷ[1] 神父 〈カトリックの〉 a priest; a Father ¶ ゴードン神父 Father [Fr.] Gordon.

しんぷ[2] 新婦 a bride.

しんぷ[3] 新譜 a newly-issued[-released] record.

しんぷう 新風 a new phase ¶ 新風を吹き込む mark [《文》 usher in] a new phase 《in East-West relations》; allow a fresh breeze to blow 《into the political situation》.

シンフォニー a symphony.

しんぷく[1] 心服 ¶ 心服する be devoted 《to》; 〈尊敬する〉 《文》 hold *sb* in high esteem ; have a high regard for *sb* / 友人から心服されている 《文》 enjoy the high esteem of *one's* friends.

しんぷく[2] 振幅 〖物〗 amplitude (of a swing).

しんふぜん 心不全 〖医〗 cardiac insufficiency ; heart failure.

じんぶつ 人物 〈人〉 a person ; a man ; a character (一風変わった) ; a figure (大立者) ; 《文》 a personage (大物) ; 〈人格者〉 《文》 a man of character ; 〈人材〉 an able [a talented] person ; 《文》 a person of ability ; 〈小説・劇の〉 a character ; 〈画中の〉 a human figure ; 〈人柄〉 character ; personality ¶ 偉大な人物 a great man [mind] / 人物画 a figure painting ; a portrait / 人物試験 a character test / 人物評 a character sketch ; personal criticism / 人物本位に考える judge *sb* chiefly by *his* personal character / 人物を造る mold [form] *sb's* character. [文例⇩]

しんぱい それは心配するほどの事ではない. It's nothing to worry about. / 僕のことでしたらご心配には及びません. You need not worry [trouble yourself] about *me*. / これで心配がなくなった. It's a load off my mind. / 心配しだしたらきりがない. Once you start worrying, there's no end to it. / 子供に一人旅をさせるのは心配だ. It worries me to send my child alone on a journey. / 人にかみつきはしないかと心配で, 彼は絶えずその犬から目が離せなかった. He had to keep an eye on the dog every minute for fear it would bite someone. / 彼女は心配事が多かった. She had a great deal on her mind [plenty to worry about]. / 僕は生まれつきの心配性でね. I'm a natural worrier. / それだけが心配の種だ. That is the only source of anxiety for me. / 心配ご無用! Don't worry! | Never mind! | 《俗》 No sweat!

しんぴつ これは真筆ですか, それとも偽筆ですか. Is this writing genuine or forged?

じんぶつ 彼はどんな人物ですか. What sort of person is he? / 彼の人物は僕が保証する. I will answer for his character. / あれは人物がよくない. He is a bad char-

しんぶん　新聞 a newspaper; a paper; the press (総称) ¶新聞をとる take a newspaper; subscribe to a paper / 新聞を配達する deliver newspapers / 新聞に…と出ている The paper says that…; It says in the paper that…; It is reported in the paper that… / 新聞に載る get into the paper [the papers] / 新聞で好評を得る have [enjoy] a good [favorable] press / 今日の朝日新聞 (in) today's (issue of the) *Asahi* / 新聞売り子 a newspaper-seller; a newsboy; 《米》a news vendor / 新聞界 the press / 新聞記事 a newspaper story [article, account] / 新聞記事の一節 a news paragraph / 新聞記者 a newspaperman (男); a newspaperwoman (女); 《英》a pressman; a (newspaper) reporter (探訪記者) / 新聞記者席 the press box [gallery] / 新聞広告 a newspaper advertisement; 《口語》classified ads (項目別になった広告欄の) / 新聞購読料 the subscription (for a paper); the (monthly) charge for newspapers / 新聞社 a newspaper publishing company; a newspaper office / 毎日新聞社に勤める be on (the staff of) the *Mainichi* / 新聞週間 Newspaper Week / 新聞小説 a serial story in a newspaper / 新聞種 news; a news item / 新聞取次店 a newspaper agency / 新聞配達人 a newsboy; a paper boy / 新聞売店 a newsstand; 《英》a news stall / 新聞販売店 《米》a news dealer's shop; 《英》a newsagent's shop / (官庁からの)新聞発表 (issue) a press release [handout (印刷した)] / 新聞用紙 newsprint. 文例⇩

じんぶん　人文 humanity; 〈文化〉civilization; culture ¶人文学 humanities; humane studies / 人文科学 the humanities / 人文地理 human geography / 人文主義(者) humanism [a humanist].

じんぷん　人糞 (human) feces; excrement ¶人糞肥料 human manure; 〈婉曲的に〉night soil.

しんぺい　新兵 a (fresh [raw]) recruit; 《口語》a rookie; a new conscript.

しんぺん　身辺 ¶身辺の整理をする put *one's* affairs in order / 身辺を気遣う worry [be anxious, be apprehensive] about *sb's* (personal) safety / 身辺を警戒する watch over *sb* to protect *him* from danger / 身辺小説 a novel depicting the author's personal life.

しんぽ　進歩 progress; (an) advance; (an) improvement ¶進歩する make progress [headway]; 《文》progress; 《文》advance; improve / 著しく進歩する make remarkable progress; 《文》make a marked advance / …より進歩している be ahead [in advance] of… / 進歩した国民 an advanced nation / 進歩的 progressive; liberal (★ 保守的·右傾的の反意語としてよく使う) / 進歩的な意見 《文》advanced [enlightened] views; a progressive idea / 進歩的な考えを持った progressive-minded; progressively-inclined / 進歩的文化人 an intellectual with progressive ideas; a liberal intellectual. 文例⇩

しんぼう¹　心房 〖解〗an atrium (of the heart) (*pl.* -ria) ¶右[左]心房 the right [left] atrium.

しんぼう²　心棒 〈車軸〉an axle; 〈機械の〉a shaft; 〈こまの〉a stem.

しんぼう³　辛抱 patience; endurance; perseverance ¶辛抱強い patient; persevering / 辛抱強く patiently; 《文》with great patience [perseverance] / 辛抱する be patient; persevere ⟨in, with *one's* task⟩; bear ⟨misfortune⟩; 《文》endure; stand; put up with; hold out. 文例⇩

しんぼう⁴　信望 popularity; confidence; prestige ¶信望がある 《文》enjoy the confidence ⟨of⟩; be popular ⟨with⟩ / 一般の信望を得る win public confidence / 信望を失う lose 《文》forfeit] the confidence ⟨of⟩.

しんぽう　信奉 ¶信奉する〈人を〉believe [have faith] in; follow ⟨Plato⟩; 〈主義·説を〉《文》espouse ⟨socialism⟩; adopt ⟨scientific methods⟩ / 信奉者 a believer ⟨in⟩; 《文》a devotee ⟨of⟩; an adherent ⟨of⟩. 文例⇩

じんぼう　人望 popularity ¶人望のある popular / 人望のない unpopular / 人望を得る win popularity; become popular / 人望を失う lose *one's* popularity; 〈政治家などが〉lose popular support (the support of the people]. 文例⇩

しんぼうえんりょ　深謀遠慮 ⇨しんりょ.

しんぼく¹　神木 a sacred tree.

しんぼく²　親睦 friendship; 《文》amity; friendliness ¶相互の親睦を図る 《文》cultivate [promote, enhance] mutual friendship / 親睦会 a social (gathering [party]); a convivial meeting; 《米》a get-together (meeting).

シンポジウム a symposium (*pl.* -ums, -sia).

シンボル a symbol; an emblem ¶…のシンボルである 《文》be symbolic of…; be a symbol of…; symbolize… / (選挙運動の)シンボルバッジ a campaign button / シンボルマーク an emblem; a logotype; a logo (*pl.* -s).

しんまい　新米 〈米〉new rice; 〈人〉a beginner; a novice; 《口語》a greenhorn; 〈職工な—

---

acter. / 人間の価値は財産よりもその人物にある。A man's worth lies not so much in what he has as in what he is. / あの会社には人物がいない。There are no men of ability on the staff of that company. / 私は党派にこだわらず人物本位で投票した。I cast my vote for a candidate whose personal character I approve of, regardless of which party he belongs to. / 結婚は人物本位にすべきだ。You should chose a husband [wife] on the basis of his [her] character. / 地方選挙は政策よりも人物中心になることが多い。Local elections often turn on personalities rather than issues.

しんぶん 我々は新聞で日々の出来事を知る。We depend on newspapers for the daily news. ¦ We learn from the newspapers what is going on in the world. / 新聞社の方ですね。You're from the press, aren't you? / こんな小さな事件は新聞に出まい。Such a minor incident is unlikely to find its way into the papers [the press]. / その汚れた靴は新聞紙で包みなさい。Wrap the dirty shoes in newspaper. / 私はそれを新聞で見た。I saw it in the paper. / それが新聞に出なければいいが。I hope it doesn't get into the papers. / まだ新聞辞令の域を出ない。His appointment has only been rumored in the papers.

しんぽ 君はだいぶ英語が進歩した。Your English has got much bet-

じんましん 蕁麻疹 nettle rash; hives. 文例⇩

しんみ[1] 新味 freshness; novelty ¶新味が薄れる the novelty wears off / 新味のある fresh; original; novel / 新味を出す strike a fresh note; ((文)) make a new departure; show ((a lot of)) originality ((in)).

しんみ[2] 親身 ¶親身になる feel warmly about *sb*; take *sb* to ((one's)) heart / 親身になって世話をする look after with tender care.

しんみつ 親密 ¶親密な ((文)) intimate; close; friendly ⇒したい ★ / 親密になる get on intimate terms ((with)); make friends ((with)); ((文)) develop [establish] a rapport ((with)) / 親密である be on intimate [friendly] terms ((with)); be very good friends ((with)) / 親密さ ((文)) intimacy; closeness. 文例⇩

じんみゃく 人脈 personal relationships [connections].

しんみょう 神妙 ¶神妙な docile; tame; ((文)) meek; gentle; unresisting / 神妙に meekly; without resistance [((文)) defiance] / 神妙にしている be on one's best behavior; behave oneself; ((文)) conduct *oneself* properly.

しんみり ¶しんみり(と) quietly; confidentially; (talk) heart to heart / しんみり話をする have a quiet [confidential, heart-to-heart] talk ((with)).

じんみん 人民 the people; the public; ((文)) the populace ¶人民の, 人民による, 人民のための政治 government of the people, by the people, for the people / 人民解放軍 the People's Liberation Army / 人民管理 popular [people's] control / (中国の)人民公社 a people's commune / 人民裁判 a people's trial [court] / 人民戦線 the popular [people's] front.

しんめ 新芽 a sprout; a bud; a shoot ¶新芽を出す sprout; put out [((文)) forth] leaves [buds]; bud; ((文)) burgeon. 文例⇩

しんめい 身命 ¶身命をとして at the risk of one's life.

じんめい[1] 人名 a person's name ¶人名辞典 a biographical dictionary / 人名簿 a roll; a list of names.

じんめい[2] 人命 (human) life ¶人命を尊重する respect (human) life; ((文)) hold life sacred / 多くの人命を犠牲にして with the loss [at the cost] of a great many lives; with great loss of life / 人命救助で表彰される be given public recognition for saving a life. 文例⇩

しんめんぼく 真面目 one's true self ¶真面目を発揮する ⟨真価を発揮する⟩ give full play [do full justice] to one's ability [gifts]; ⟨本性を現わす⟩ show [appear in] one's true colors.

しんもつ 進物 a present; a gift ¶進物用に包装した gift-wrapped ((packages)) / 進物用品 articles suitable as [for] presents.

しんもん 審問 a trial; a hearing; an inquiry; an examination ¶審問する try; hear [examine, inquire into] ((a case)).

じんもん[1] 人文 ⇒じんぶん.

じんもん[2] 尋問 questioning; (cross-)examination ¶尋問する question; (cross-)examine / きびしく尋問する press *sb* with questions; ((口語)) grill.

しんや 深夜 ¶深夜に in the middle of the night; at [in the] dead of night (★ midnight は一般に「夜中の12時」を意味する。したがって, at midnight は「夜中の12時に」であって, ばくぜんと「深夜に」「夜中に」ではない) / 深夜まで (till) very late at night; far [deep] into the night; until (long) after midnight / ((口語)) until the small hours / 深夜業 (late-)night work [labor] / 深夜放送 late-night [all-night] broadcasting; a night(time) broadcast [(radio) program] / 深夜料金 a late-night rate.

しんやくせいしょ 新約聖書 the New Testament.

しんゆう 親友 a close [great, good, ((文)) bosom] friend; one's best friend; ((口語)) a buddy ¶親友になる make great [very good] friends ((with)).

しんよう 信用 trust; credit; confidence; ((文)) reliance (信頼); one's reputation (信望) ¶信用する trust; put ((one's)) trust [faith] in; ((文)) place confidence [credence] in; rely on; give credit to / 人の言葉をそのままに信用する take *sb* at *his* word / …に信用がある be trusted (by); ((文)) have [enjoy] *sb's* confidence / 信用のできる[できない] trustworthy [untrustworthy]; reliable [unreliable]; credible [not credible] / 信用を得る gain credit ((with *sb*)) / 信用を得る win *sb's* confidence / 信用を落とす lose *sb's* confidence; lose credit ((with *sb*)); ((文)) fall into discredit ((with)) / 信用にかかわる affect one's credit; harm [damage, ((文)) compromise] one's reputation / 信用貸し a credit loan; a loan on credit / 信用貸しをする give [((文)) extend] *sb* (a) credit ((for 50,000 dollars)) / 信用金庫[組合] a credit association [union] / 信

---

ter [has improved a great deal]. / これは我が国の医学の一大進歩である. This marks a big step in the progress of medical science in this country. / オランダは教育が非常に進歩している. Education has reached a very high standard in the Netherlands.

しんぼう あの男はどんな仕事をやらせてみても辛抱が足りない. He cannot stick to any job for long. / もう辛抱しきれない. I can't stand it any more. | It is more than I can stand. | My patience is at an end. / もう少しの辛抱だ. We are almost there. | A little more patience and it will all be over. / もうあと3日の辛抱だ. We only have to wait three days. | It's only three days away.

しんぽう 彼女は大の自然食の信奉者である. She is a great believer in natural [macrobiotic] food.

じんぼう 彼は町内に人望がある. He is popular with his neighbors.

しんまい 私はこの仕事は新米です. I am new to this job.

じんましん またじんましんが出た. My nettle rash has broken out [erupted] again.

しんみつ 私たちの交際は年を追って親密の度を加えた. Our relationship has grown closer over the years [year by year].

しんめ 木々は一斉に新芽を吹いていた. The trees were coming [bursting] into leaf.

じんめい[2] それは人命にかかわる重

じんよう 用状 a letter of credit (略: L/C) / 信用状態 one's financial [credit] standing / 信用調査 an inquiry [investigation] into [concerning] the financial status [credit standing] (of) / 〈照会〉 a credit inquiry [research] / 信用取引 dealings on credit / 信用取引をする buy [sell] on credit. 文例⇩

じんよう 陣容 〈軍隊の〉 battle array [formation]; 〈野球チームや内閣の〉 a line-up ¶陣容を整える array (troops) for battle; put (troops) in battle formation / 〈比喩的に〉 arrange one's forces / 陣容を固める close ranks / 陣容をたて直す reorganize the battle line.

しんようじゅ 針葉樹 a coniferous tree; a conifer ¶針葉樹林 a coniferous forest.

しんらい 信頼 《文》 reliance (on); trust (in) ¶信頼する rely on; trust (in) / 信頼するに足る [し難い] trustworthy [untrustworthy]; reliable [unreliable] / 信頼して (follow sb) trustingly / …に信頼を置く put faith [confidence] in; 《文》 place (one's) trust in; give sb one's trust / 《文》 place reliance on / 信頼に答える prove worthy of sb's trust; live up to sb's expectation / 信頼に背く[を裏切る] betray sb's trust [confidence]; 《口語》 let sb down / 信頼関係 a relationship of mutual trust; 《法》 (a) fiduciary relation. 文例⇩

しんらつ 辛辣 ¶辛辣な pungent; bitter; acrid; sharp; harsh; cutting; 《文》 incisive; 《文》 vitriolic; caustic; tart; 《文》 trenchant; biting; stinging / 辛辣な皮肉 (with) cutting sarcasm; (in) bitter irony / 辛辣な人 a sharp-tongued person / 辛辣に sharply; severely / 辛辣にこきおろす criticize scathingly.

しんらばんしょう 森羅万象 the universe; all [the whole of] creation; all nature; 《文》 Nature.

しんり¹ 心理 〈状態〉 a state of mind; a mental state; psychology; mentality ¶心理的 mental; psychological / 心理的に mentally; psychologically / 心理的に悪い影響を与える be bad [harmful] in (its) psychological effect on (a child); have harmful psychological effects on (a child) / have a bad effect on the mind of (a child) / 実験[ゲシュタルト, 児童, 群集, 犯罪, 社会, 異常, 産業]心理学 experimental [Gestalt, child, mass, criminal, social, abnormal, industrial] psychology / 心理学者 a psychologist / 心理作戦 psychological tactics / 心理作用 a mental process / 心理小説 a psychological novel / 心理テスト a psychological test / 心理描写 (a) psychological description / 心理療法 psychotherapy.

しんり² 真理 (a) truth ¶真理の探求 a search for [《文》 the pursuit of] truth / 真理の探求者 《文》 a seeker after truth / 真理を求める 《文》 seek (after) truth / 真理値 (a) truth-value / 真理関数 《論》 a truth-function / 真理集合 《数・論》 a truth set / 真理(値)表 《論》 a truth table. 文例⇩

しんり³ 審理 (a) trial; (an) examination; (an) inquiry; (a) (legal) hearing ¶審理する try [examine, hear] (a case); inquire into (a case) / 再審理 (a) retrial; (a) rehearing; 《法》 a review / 審理中である be on trial; be pending; 《法》 be sub judice.

じんりきしゃ 人力車 a jinrikisha; a rickshaw.

しんりゃく 侵略 (an) invasion; (an) aggression; an incursion ¶侵略する invade; 《文》 aggress (against); conquer / 直接[間接]侵略 a direct [an indirect] invasion / 侵略行為 an act of aggression / 侵略国 an aggressor nation; an aggressor / 侵略者 an invader; an aggressor / 侵略主義 an aggressive policy / 侵略戦争 a war of aggression; an aggressive war.

しんりょ 深慮 thoughtfulness; deliberation ¶深慮遠謀の人 a far-sighted person / 深慮遠謀を巡らす work out [《文》 devise] a far-sighted scheme; take a long view (of).

しんりょう 診療 ⇨ しんさつ, ちりょう ¶診療時間 consultation [《英》 surgery] hours / 診療所 a clinic; a medical office.

しんりょく 新緑 tender [spring] green(ery); 《文》 fresh verdure ¶新緑の候 the season of fresh green.

じんりょく¹ 人力 human strength [power]; 〈工率の単位〉 a manpower (普通 10 分の 1 馬力) ¶人力では及ばない 《文》 be beyond human power; be humanly impossible / 人力飛行 (a) man-powered flight.

じんりょく² 尽力 (a) 《努力》 《文》 effort(s); exertion(s); 〈世話〉 《文》 good offices; 《文》 services ¶尽力する 《文》 endeavor; try hard to do; 《文》 strive; make efforts; exert oneself; 《文》 render services (to); use one's influence (for); 《文》 be instrumental in doing. 文例⇩

しんりん 森林 a forest; woods ★「森林」の意味では常に複数形で, There are some woods near the house. のように複数名詞としても扱う. There is a woods... のような使い方は 《米》 では見られるが 《英》 では不可 ¶森林の乱伐 reckless deforestation / 森林の生い茂った土地 a lushly forested land / 森林資源 forest [timber] resources / 森林地方[地帯] wooded country; a wooded region; woodland(s) (★ wood-

---

大事である. It is a serious matter since it affects people's lives. / 人命に別条はなかった. No lives were lost.

しんよう あの男の言うことはどこまで信用していいのかわからない. I don't know how far we should believe him. / 僕なら彼の言うことより彼女の方を信用したのだが. I should have taken her word against his. / あそこは信用のある店だ. That store has a high reputation. / 何も知らずに信用しきって, 契約に署名してしまったのです. I had signed the contract in blind faith. / そんなことをしたら世間にまるっきり信用がなくなるよ. That'll discredit you hopelessly with the public. / 今度こそうまくやらないと信用にかかわる. I must succeed this time, since my reputation is at stake.

しんらい 彼は社長からすっかり信頼されている. He enjoys the fullest confidence of the president. / 彼は信頼できる男だ. He is a man to be depended on. | He is a man we can trust.

しんり² 君の言う事は一面の真理がある. There is some truth in

じんりん 人倫 〈人道〉 humanity;〈道徳〉morality.

しんるい[1] 進塁 ¶進塁する〈野球〉advance [move on]《to second》.

しんるい[2] 親類 a relation; a relative;《文》a kinsman (男);《文》a kinswoman (女);〈総称〉kinfolk ¶近い[遠い]親類 a near [distant] relation [relative] / 親類同然の付き合いをしている associate with sb as if they were relatives;《口語》be just like family / 親類縁者《文》one's kith and kin; one's relatives by blood and marriage [《文》in blood and law]. 文例⇩

じんるい 人類 man; mankind; the human race [species]; humanity ¶人類の human; man's《future》;《the welfare》of mankind / 人類愛 love for humanity [mankind] / 人類学 anthropology / 文化[形質]人類学 cultural [physical] anthropology / 人類学者 an anthropologist / 人類史 the history of man.

しんれい[1] 心霊 spirit ¶心霊学 psychics / 心霊研究 psychic(al) research / 心霊現象 a psychic [spiritual] phenomenon.

しんれい[2] 振鈴 a (hand)bell ¶振鈴を鳴らす ring a bell / 10時の振鈴で at (the sound of) the ten o'clock bell.

しんれい[3] 新例 a new example [precedent] ¶新例を作る[開く]《文》create [establish] a precedent.

しんれき 新暦 the solar [Gregorian] calendar ¶新暦で according to the solar calendar / 新暦の12月22日 the 22nd of December, New Style.

しんろ[1] 針路 〈羅針盤の指示による〉a course;〈航空機の〉a flight path ¶針路を…へ向ける direct [set] one's course toward [for]; sail [head, make] for / 針路を変える turn [change, alter] one's course 《toward》/ 針路を北へとる take [beat] a northerly course; steer one's course northward / 針路をそれる swerve [deviate] from one's course; go [stray] off one's course; be driven [taken] off (one's) course《by a storm》/ 針路をそれないように船を進める hold one's ship on course / 針路修正 course correction [adjustment].

しんろ[2] 進路 a course; a way; a route (道順) ¶進路を開く open the way; turn (in life) / 進路を切り開く cut [《文》cleave] one's way 《through》/ 進路を妨げる block [stand in] sb's way / 後進のために進路を開く make way for one's juniors. 文例⇩

しんろう[1] 心労 ⇨ しんぱい。

しんろう[2] 新郎 a bridegroom; a groom ¶新郎新婦 the bride and (bride)groom; the contracting parties.

しんわ 神話 a myth; mythology〈総称〉¶国家誕生の神話 the birth-myth of a nation / ギリシャ神話 the Greek myths; Greek mythology / 神話の[的] mythical; mythological; fabulous / 神話の世界 a mythical world / 日本の神話によれば… according to Japanese myth;《文》Japanese mythology has it that… / 神話学者 a mythologist / 神話時代 the mythical age; the age of fables.

しんわりょく 親和力《化》affinity《of oxygen for hydrogen》.

す

す[1] 州 a sandbank; a shoal; a shallow; a (sand-)bar.

す[2] 巣 〈鳥の〉a nest;〈はちの〉a hornets' [wasps'] nest; a beehive (飼育蜜ばちの);〈くもの〉a cobweb;〈獣の〉a lair; a den ¶愛の巣《keep》a love nest / 悪の巣《文》a sink [cesspool] of iniquity; a hotbed of crime / 同じ巣の仲間 a nest-mate / 巣のある所 the nest site / 巣を造る build a nest; nest《in a tree》/〈くもが〉巣をかける spin [weave] a web / 〈雌鳥が〉巣につく brood; sit (on its eggs) / 巣穴〈小さなねどなど〉a burrow;〈小鳥の〉a nesting cavity / 巣棚 a nest ledge.

す[3] 酢 vinegar ¶酢の物 a vinegared dish / 酢に漬ける pickle《onions》in vinegar.

す[4] 〈大根などの〉a pore;〈鋳物の〉a (mold) cavity; a porosity ¶すの多い porous; full of pores.

す[5] 図 〈絵図〉a drawing; a picture;〈設計図〉a plan;〈図解〉a figure; a plate; an illustration (挿絵);〈図表〉a diagram; a chart; a graph;〈地図〉a map ¶図で説明する illustrate sth with a figure [by a diagram] / 図を引く draw a plan / 図に当たる work well; come off; hit the mark / 図に乗る《口語》push [《米》press] one's luck; get [be] carried away《by one's success》; be puffed up《with success》; get stuck-up / 第3図 figure [fig.] 3. 文例⇩

---

what you say. / 科学者は、1つの真理に到達するために、できるだけたくさんの事実を収集する。The scientist collects as many facts as he can to get at a single [a grain of] truth.

じんりょく 彼の尽力によって事が都合よく運んだ。Through his good offices the matter was brought to a successful conclusion. / Thanks to his efforts, everything turned out well. / 今にご尽力を願うようになりましょう。I think I will need your services very soon.

しんるい[2] あれは私の遠い親類です。He's a distant relation of mine. / He is distantly related [connected] to me. / 猫はとらの親類だ。The cat is kin [related] to the tiger.

しんろ[2] 台風は進路を東に転じつつある。The typhoon is shifting toward the east [turning its course eastward].

ず[5] 図に表わせば、この2つの力の強さと方向はどちらも線分の長さと方向で示すことができる。Diagrammatically the strength and direction of each of the two

ず²　頭 ¶頭が高い be proud ; be arrogant ; be haughty.

すあし　素足 bare feet ¶素足に靴をはく wear shoes without [but no] socks ; wear [put] shoes on *one's* stockingless feet / 素足で歩く walk barefoot(ed).

ずあん　図案 a design ; a sketch ¶図案を造る design ; draw a design (for) / 図案家 a designer / 図案化する make a design of ((flowers)).

すい¹　粋 〈精華〉 《文》 the essence ; 《文》 the quintessence ; the cream ; the pith ; the best ¶粋な 〈趣味のよい〉 refined ; elegant ; 《口語》 classy ; 《文》 (a person) of well-cultivated tastes ; 〈物分かりのいい〉 understanding ; 〈思いやりのある〉 considerate ; thoughtful / 粋をきかす 《文》 show delicacy (in) ; have the delicacy [consideration] ((to do)) ; be considerate ((toward the feelings of others)). 文例↓

すい²　酸い sour ; acid ; tart ; 〈酸っぱい味がする〉 taste sour ¶文例↓

ずい¹　蕊 【植】 〈雌〉 a pistil ; 〈雄〉 a stamen.

ずい²　髄 〈動物の〉 the marrow ; 〈植物の〉 the pith ¶骨の髄 the marrow of a bone / 骨の髄まで凍る be chilled to the marrow ; be frozen to the bone.

ずい³　隋 【中国史】 Sui.

すいあげ　吸い上げ suction.

すいあげる　吸い上げる suck [pump, draw] up. ¶吸い上げポンプ a suction pump.

すいあつ　水圧 water [hydraulic] pressure ¶水圧クレーン[ジャッキ, ブレーキ, ポンプ] a hydraulic crane [jack, brake, pump] / 水圧計 a water-pressure gauge / 水圧試験 a hydraulic test.

すいい¹　水位 the water level ¶水位標 a watermark. 文例↓

すいい²　推移 《文》 (a) transition ; (a) change ¶推移する change ; 《文》 undergo a change [transition] ; shift / 絶えず推移する everchanging[-shifting] / 時代の推移と共に[につれて] with the change of the times. 文例↓

ずいい　随意 ¶随意の optional ; free ; 【生理】 voluntary / 随意に freely ; as *one* pleases ; at *one's* pleasure / 随意に使える have the free use (of a telephone) / 人に随意にさせる let sb have *his* way ; put [《文》 place] ((the decision)) at *sb's* disposal ; leave *sth* up to *sb* / 随意科[科目] an optional [elective] course [subject] / 随意筋 【解】 a voluntary muscle / 随意選択 free choice. 文例↓

すいいき　水域 (in) the area (of the sea) ((designated for oil exploration)) ; ((in Japanese)) waters ; a body of water ¶200 カイリ経済水域 a 200-mile economic zone.

ずいいち　随一 ⇨ だいいち. 文例↓

スイートピー a sweet pea.

ずいいん　随員 ⇨ すいこう (随行員).

すいうん　水運 water transport ; transport by water ¶水運の便がある 〈川が主語〉 be navigable. 文例↓

すいうん　衰運 《文》 *one's* declining fortune(s) ¶衰運に向かう begin to decline [sink, wane] ; be going downhill ; be on the wane [decline].

すいえい　水泳 swimming ; a swim ; bathing ; 《英》 a bathe ¶水泳する swim ; have a swim ; go swimming ; 《英》 bathe ((in the sea)) ; 《英》 have a bathe ★ 競技としての「水泳」「水泳する」は swimming, swim だけで, それ以外は水浴・水遊びの類 / 水泳が上手[下手]である be a good [poor] swimmer ; be good [no good, poor] at swimming / 水泳のコーチ a swimming coach / 水泳に行く go swimming [for a swim] ; 《英》 go bathing [for a bathe] / 水泳教室 a swimming class / 水泳選手 a swimmer / 水泳大会 a swimming competition [《米》 meet] / 水泳パンツ swim(ming) trunks / 日本水泳連盟 the Japan Swimming Federation.

すいえき　膵液 【解】 pancreatic juice.

すいおん　水温 the temperature of the water ; water temperature.

すいか¹　水火 文例↓

すいか²　西瓜 a watermelon (果実) ; a watermelon plant.

すいがい　水害 damage from a flood [caused by flooding] ; flood damage ; 〈惨禍〉 a flood disaster ; 〈洪水〉 a flood ; an inundation ¶水害をこうむる suffer from flooding [a flood] ; 〈物が主語〉 be damaged by flooding [flood water, a flood] / 水害対策 〈防止の〉 a flood-control measure ; 〈救済の〉 a relief measure for flood victims / 水害地 a flooded [flood-stricken] district.

すいかずら 【植】 a Japanese honeysuckle.

すいがら　吸い殻 〈紙巻きの〉 a cigarette butt [end, stub] ; 《口語》 a fag end ; 《英口語》 a dog-end ; 〈葉巻きの〉 a cigar stub ¶吸い殻入れ an ashtray.

すいがん　酔眼 ¶酔眼もうろうとして with glazed [drunken] eyes ; with *one's* eyes blurred by [bleary from] drink ; dazed by liquor.

すいき　水気 〈むくみ〉 dropsy ¶水気がくる become dropsical [dropsied].

---

forces can be represented as the length and direction of a line segment. / どこまでも図に乗る男だ。 Give him an inch and he'll take a yard [mile]. / 彼が人がいいからといって図に乗ってはいけない。 You must not presume upon his good nature. / あんまり図に乗るな。 Don't push [press] your luck too far.

すい¹ この博物館の陳列品は日本美術の粋を集めたものである。 The exhibits at the museum are selected from the masterpieces of Japanese art.

すい² あの人は世の中の酸いも甘いもかみ分けた人だ。 He has tasted the sweets and bitters of life.

すいい¹ その日の隅田川の水位は高[低]かった。 The Sumida River was (flowing) high [low] on that day.

すいい² 現状で推移するのは得策でない。 It is not advisable to let things stand as they are.

ずいい この 'that' を略す略さないは書く人の随意である。 This 'that' may be included or not at the discretion of the writer. | The ' that ' here is optional. / 独仏いずれの語学を選ぶかも学生の随意である。 The students have the option of taking either German or French. / 行くも留まるも君の随意だ。 You may go or

ずいき 随喜 ¶随喜の涙を流す shed tears of joy; weep for joy.

すいきゅう 水球 water polo.

すいぎゅう 水牛 a (water) buffalo 《pl. -(e)s》 ★集合的に言うときは単複同形.

すいきょ 推挙 ⇒ **すいせん**³.

すいきょう 酔狂 a whim;《文》a vagary;《文》a freak;《文》a caprice; (an) eccentricity ¶酔狂な《文》whimsical;《文》capricious;《文》freakish; fanciful; fantastic; eccentric / 酔狂に[で] for fun;《文》out of (a) whim ;《文》whimsically.

すいきん 水禽 ⇒ みずとり.

すいぎん 水銀 mercury ¶水銀の mercurial; mercuric / 水銀寒暖計[晴雨計, 圧力計] a mercury thermometer [barometer, manometer] / 水銀柱 a column of mercury; a mercurial [mercury] column / 水銀中毒(症) mercurialism; mercurial [mercury] poisoning / 水銀灯 a mercury lamp; a mercury-vapor tube [light, lamp]. 文例回

すいくち 吸口 a mouthpiece.

すいくん 垂訓 a sermon;《文》a discourse; a lecture; teaching.

すいけい¹ 水系 a water [river] system; the drainage pattern 《of the North American continent》.

すいけい² 推計 estimating; (an) estimation ¶推計する estimate / 推計学 stochastics 《単数扱い》; inductive statistics 《単数扱い》.

すいげん 水源 the source (of a river); a headspring;〈水道の〉the source of water supply; the water source ¶川の水源を尋ねる trace a river to (as far as) its source / 水源地の catchment area [basin] (of the Tone River). 文例回

すいこう¹ 遂行 《文》accomplishment;《文》execution;《文》performance ¶遂行する carry out [through] 《one's task》;《文》execute (a plan);《文》accomplish 《one's purpose》;《文》effect 《one's design》/ 任務を遂行する perform [fulfill] one's duty / 戦争の遂行 the conduct of the war.

すいこう² 推敲 ¶推敲する work on one's manuscript [composition] to improve [revise] the wording; polish;《文》elaborate (on); improve.

すいごう¹ 水郷 a riverside [lakeside] district.

すいごう² 水濠〈障害物競争の〉a water jump.

ずいこう 随行 ¶随行する attend 《sb on a journey》; accompany; follow / …に随行して《文》in attendance upon sb; accompanying sb;《文》in sb's suite [retinue] / 随行員[者] a member of sb's suite [retinue]; an attendant; a staff in attendance (全体) / 大平首相及びその随行員 Prime Minister Ohira and his suite.

すいこうほう 水耕法 hydroponics; hydroponic [soilless] (plant) culture; water culture; tank farming; tray agriculture; aquiculture ¶水耕法の hydroponic.

すいこみ 吸い込み〈吸い入れること〉drawing; suction; intake;〈排水口〉a drainage hole. 文例回

すいこむ 吸い込む〈気体を〉breathe in; draw [suck] in;《文》inhale;〈液体を〉suck in [up]; 《文》imbibe;〈吸収する〉absorb; soak in [up];〈呑み込む〉swallow up; engulf; suck (a boat) down. 文例回

すいさい 水彩 ¶水彩絵の具 water colors / 水彩画 a water-color painting; a water-color; a picture in water-colors / 水彩画家 a water-color painter; a water-colorist.

すいさし 吸い差し〈タバコ〉a half-smoked cigarette [cigar];〈吸い殻〉a cigarette end [butt, stub]; a cigar butt.

すいさつ 推察 a guess;《文》(a) conjecture; 《文》(an) inference;《文》(a) surmise ¶推察する guess;《文》conjecture; infer (from); imagine; gather (from);《文》surmise / 人の気持を推察する enter into sb's feelings;〈同情する〉sympathize with sb; feel for sb / 僕の推察が正しければ if I guess right; if my guess is not wrong / 推察に任す leave sth to sb's conjecture. 文例回

すいさん 水産 ¶水産加工品 processed marine products / 水産業 the marine products industry; fisheries / 水産国 a fishing country; one of the nations that are richest in marine products / 水産試験所 a fisheries experimental station / 水産大学 a fisheries college / 水産庁 the Fisheries Agency / 水産物 marine [aquatic] products; sea food (食品).

すいさんか 水酸化 《化》hydration ¶水酸化カルシウム[マグネシウム] calcium [magnesium] hydroxide / 水酸化物 a hydroxide.

すいし 水死 ⇒ できし.

すいじ 炊事 cooking; kitchen work ¶炊事する cook / 炊事係 a cook / 炊事設備 cooking facilities / 炊事道具 cooking utensils; kitchenware / 炊事当番 (a soldier on) the cook's duty / 炊事場 a kitchen; a cookhouse (別棟になった); a galley (船の).

ずいじ 随時 (at) any time;《文》at all times;〈必要に応じて〉whenever (it is) necessary; as

---

stay at your pleasure [as you please].

ずいいち そこは北陸随一の景勝の地である. It is the most picturesque place in the Hokuriku region.

すいうん 大阪は水運の便が非常によい. Osaka enjoys excellent facilities for water transport.

すいか 彼女のためなら水の中もあえて辞さない. I would go through fire and water for her sake.

すいぎん 水銀柱は35度に達した. The mercury rose to 35 degrees.

すいげん この川の水源地はどこですか. 十和田湖です. Where does this river rise?—It originates in Lake Towada. / 東京都はその上水道の水源を利根川にも仰いでいる. Tokyo depends on the Tone River as well for its water supply.

すいこみ このストーブの煙突は吸い込みが悪い. The chimney of this stove does not draw well.

すいこむ 彼の姿は闇の中に吸い込まれていった. His figure was swallowed up in the darkness.

すいさつ 私の推察が当たった. I was right in my conjecture. / 彼の口振りから推察すると彼は生活に困っているらしい. I gather from his words that he is badly off. / あとは賢明なる読者の推察に任せよう. I will leave the rest

すいしつ 水質 the quality [(degree of) purity] of water ¶ 水質汚濁防止法 《法》the Water Pollution Prevention Act / 水質管理 water-purity control / 水質検査 (an) examination of water; 〈分析〉(a) water analysis.

すいしゃ 水車 a water [mill] wheel ¶ 水車小屋 a water mill.

すいじゃく 衰弱 weakening; 《文》debility; 《医》asthenia; emaciation (やせること) ¶ 衰弱する become weak [low, feeble]; weaken; 《文》be enervated; be worn out; be emaciated (異常にやせる) / 病気で衰弱する grow weak from illness / 全身衰弱 general prostration [debility]; total debilitation.

すいしゅ 水腫 《医》〈水腫症〉dropsy; 〈浮腫〉an edema (pl. -mata).

ずいじゅう 随従 ¶ 随従する follow sb's lead; 《口語》play second fiddle (to); toe the 《party》line.

すいじゅん 水準 a level; a standard ¶ 水準に達する reach [《文》attain] the level; come up to the standard / 水準に達しない[水準以下である] be below the level; fall short of the standard / …と同じ水準にある be on a level with …; be on the same level as [with]…; be on a par with… / 最高水準 the highest level; the peak; the high-water mark (of English poetry) / 水準器 a (spirit) level / 水準儀 《測量》a leveling instrument; a surveyor's level.

ずいしょ 随所 ¶ 随所に everywhere; at every turn. 文例

すいしょう¹ 水晶 (a) (rock) crystal; crystallized quartz ¶ 水晶のような crystalline; crystal(-clear) 《water》/ 水晶細工 crystal ware / 水晶体 《解》the (crystalline) lens / 水晶時計 a quartz(-crystal) clock [watch, chronometer].

すいしょう² 推奨 ¶ 推奨する 〈推薦する〉recommend; 《文》commend; endorse 《a product》《広告などで》; 〈ほめる〉admire; praise; 《文》pay (a) high tribute to / 推奨すべき 《文》admirable; 《文》commendable.

すいじょう 水上 ¶ 水上の aquatic; water-surface / 水上に on (the surface of) the water / 水上運送 water(-borne) transport; shipping by water / 水上競技 water [aquatic] sports / 水上競技大会 a swimming meet; an aquatic competition / 水上警察 the harbor [marine, river] police / 水上スキー 〈競技〉water-skiing; 〈道具〉water skis / 水上スキーをする water-ski / 水上スキーをしに行く go water-skiing / 水上生活 life on the water / 全日本水上選手権大会 an all-Japan aquatic championship meet / 水上バス a water-bus / 水上飛行機 a seaplane.

すいじょうき 水蒸気 (water) vapor; 〈湯気〉vapor; steam.

すいしん¹ 水深 〈sound〉the depth of (the) water ¶ 水深10メートルのところに at a [the] depth of 10 meters / 水深の深い港 a deep-water harbor / 水深図 a bathymetric map / 水深測量器 a depth sounder; a bathymeter / 水深測量法 bathymetry.

すいしん² 垂心 《幾何》an orthocenter.

すいしん³ 推進 ¶ 推進する propel; drive [push, 《文》thrust] forward; 〈促進する〉《文》promote; step up / 推進母体 a nucleus (pl. -clei) / 推進力 propulsive force; (a) driving force; a thrust. 文例

すいじん 粋人 《文》a man of refined [well-cultivated] tastes; a man about town.

スイス [<《フランス語》Suisse] Switzerland ¶ スイスの Swiss / スイス人 a Swiss; the Swiss (総称) / スイス連邦 the Swiss Confederation.

すいすい すいすいと lightly and quietly; 《do the job》with no trouble at all; 《文》〈carry on〉unhindered / すいすいと飛ぶ flit 《from flower to flower》.

すいせい¹ 水生 ¶ 水生の aquatic; 〈plants〉living in the water; water-dwelling / 半水生の semiaquatic / 水生動物 an aquatic animal / 水生植物 an aquatic [a water] plant; a hydrophyte / 水生生物 〈総称〉aquatic life; water creatures.

すいせい² 水性 ¶ 水性塗料 emulsion (paint); water paint; distemper / 水性乳剤 an aqueous emulsion.

すいせい³ 水星 《天》Mercury ¶ 水星の Mercurial.

すいせい⁴ 水勢 the force of water [a current].

すいせい⁵ 彗星 a comet ¶ ハレー彗星 Halley's comet / 彗星の尾 the tail of a comet / 彗星のごとく現われる 《文》come [be brought] into sudden prominence; 《文》make a meteoric rise from obscurity / 彗星のごとく現われ彗星のごとく消える disappear as suddenly as one appears / 彗星群 a comet group.

すいせいがん 水成岩 《地質》(an) aqueous [(a) sedimentary] rock.

すいせいむし 酔生夢死 ¶ 酔生夢死する live idly [to no purpose]; slumber [sleep, idle] one's life away / 酔生夢死の徒 《文》a lotus-eater.

すいせん¹ 水仙 《植》a narcissus (pl. -es, -cissi); a daffodil (らっぱ水仙); a jonquil (黄水仙).

すいせん² 垂線 《draw [drop]》a perpendicular (line).

すいせん³ 推薦 (a) recommendation ¶ 推薦す

---

to the sagacious reader's imagination.

ずいじ 本校は随時学生の入学を認める。Students are admitted at any time into this school.

すいしょ ミスプリントは随所にある。There are misprints on almost every page.

すいしん³ この運動の最大の推進力となったのは江口さんのグループだった。It was Miss Eguchi and her group who gave this movement its greatest forward push.

すいせん³ よろしかったら、うちのクラブ員にご推薦いたしましょう。I will put you up for [recommend you to] our club, if you like. / 彼なら安心して推薦できる。I can confidently recommend him.

すいそく それは単なる推測に過ぎません。It's no more than a guess. | It's guesswork [conjecture] (and nothing more). / ソ連が近く頂上会談を提案するだろうという推測がしきりに行なわれている。Speculation is rife

すいせんべんじょ 水洗便所 a flush toilet; a W.C. (★ water closet の略. ただし, water closet 自体は現在はあまり使われない).

すいそ 水素 【化】 hydrogen ¶水素と化合させる hydrogenate / 水素イオン a hydrogen ion / 水素爆弾 ⇨ すいばく.

すいそう¹ 水草 a water [an aquatic] plant.

すいそう² 水葬 water burial; burial at sea ¶水葬にする bury at sea.

すいそう³ 水槽 a (water) tank [cistern]; 〈魚を飼うための〉a fish tank; a glass tank (ガラス張りの) ¶実験用の水槽 a test tank.

すいそう⁴ 吹奏 ¶吹奏する blow (the trumpet); play (on) (the flute) / 吹奏楽 wind(-instrument) music / 吹奏楽団 a brass [military] band.

すいぞう 膵臓 【解】the pancreas; 〈食用としての牛・羊の〉a sweetbread (しばしば複数で) ¶膵臓の pancreatic / 膵臓炎 pancreatitis.

ずいそう 随想 occasional [stray, random] thoughts ¶随想録 stray notes; jottings; essays / モンテーニュ随想録《書名》 *The Essays (of Montaigne)*.

すいそく 推測 《文》(a) conjecture; 《文》(a) surmise; 《文》(an) inference; 《文》(a) supposition; 《文》(a) presumption; speculation ¶推測する guess; 《文》 infer (from); presume; gather (from); 《文》 conjecture; suppose; speculate / 推測が当たる[外れる] guess right [wrong]; be right [wrong] in *one's* conjecture / 推測に止まる remain (no more than) speculation; remain conjectural. 文例⇩

すいぞくかん 水族館 an aquarium (*pl.* -s, -ria).

すいたい 衰退 decline; decay ¶衰退する decline; decay; fall off / 衰退期にある be on the decline; be at a low ebb.

すいだし 吸出し 〈膏薬(こうやく)〉 a blister plaster.

すいだす 吸い出す suck [draw] out.

すいだん 推断 《文》(an) inference; (a) conclusion; 《文》(a) deduction ¶推断する 《文》 infer (from); 《文》 deduce (from); conclude; draw a conclusion the conclusion that....

すいちゅう 水中 ¶水中の underwater / 水中を航行する cruise underwater / 水中に潜って[入れて]water; below the surface of the water / 水中に飛び込む jump [plunge] into the water; 〈船から〉leap overboard / 水中に沈む[没する]sink under water [below the surface of the water]; 《文》 submerge; 《文》 be submerged / 水中で作業する work underwater / 水中から引き揚げる raise (a sunken ship) from the water / 水中花 a paper flower that opens when placed in a glass of water / 水中速力 〈潜水艦の〉 an underwater speed ((of 30 knots)) / 水中テレビカメラ an underwater TV camera / 水中聴音機 a hydrophone / 水中眼鏡 〈箱めがね〉 a water glass; 〈水泳用の〉 swimming goggles / 水中翼船 a hydrofoil (ship [vessel, craft]).

すいちょく 垂直 ¶垂直の perpendicular; vertical; plumb; sheer ((cliffs)) / 垂直に perpendicularly; vertically; plumb; (rise) sheer ((from the water)) / ...に垂直に線を引く draw a line perpendicular [at right angles] to ((a given line)) / 垂直安定板 【航空】 a vertical stabilizer / 垂直線[面] a vertical [perpendicular] line [plane] / 垂直離着陸機 a vertical takeoff and landing aircraft 【略】 VTOL; a vtol plane (★ vtol の発音は [víːtɔːl]).

すいつく 吸い付く stick [cling, 《文》adhere] ((to)) / 吸い付いて離れない stick fast ((to)); cling to *sb* like a leech. 文例⇩

すいつける 吸い付ける attract; draw to *itself*; 〈タバコを吸いなれる〉 be used to smoking ((cigars)).

スイッチ a switch ¶スイッチを入れる[切る] switch (the light) on [off] / 電気のスイッチ an electric [a light] switch / タイムスイッチ a time switch / スイッチヒッター 【野球】 a switch hitter. 文例⇩

すいてい¹ 水底 ¶水底に on the bottom; on the bottom of the pool [river, lake, etc.] / 水底深く deep in the water.

すいてい² 推定 《文》(a) presumption; an estimate; 《文》(an) inference; 《文》(an) estimation ¶推定する presume; assume; 《文》 infer; estimate / 推定価格 the estimated [presumed] value ((of an article)) / 推定相続人 【法】 an heir presumptive (*pl.* heirs presumptive) / 推定年齢 the estimated [probable] age ((of the victim)). 文例⇩

すいてき 水滴 a drop of water; a waterdrop.

すいでん 水田 a paddy field; a (rice) paddy; an irrigated rice field; a flooded paddy.

すいとう¹ 水筒 a canteen; a flask; 《英》 a water bottle.

---

that, before long, the Soviet Union will propose a summit conference.
すいつく 磁石のそばへ鉄を持って行くと吸い付く. A piece of iron, if placed near the magnet, will be attracted to it.
スイッチ これはひとりでにスイッチが切れるようになっている. It switches itself off. / スイッチひとつで, 現代人は住居の温度を一定に保つことができる. With the flick of a switch [At the flip of a switch] modern man can keep the temperature of his home the same all the time.
すいてい² この地域の人口は約50万人と推定されている. The population of this region is estimated to be about 500,000. | This region has an estimated population of approximately half a million. / その後彼は関西方面に高飛びしたものと警察では推定している. The police assume that, later, he escaped to somewhere in the Kansai. / この写本の年代は, 4世

すいとう² 水稲 paddy [wet-field] rice ¶水稲栽培 wet-rice cultivation [farming].
すいとう³ 出納 receipts and disbursements [expenses]; revenue and expenditure; incomings and outgoings ¶出納係 a cashier; ⦅米⦆ a teller (銀行の) / 出納簿 a cashbook; an account book; a ledger.
すいどう 水道 〈用水〉 tap [city, piped] water; 〈設備〉 waterworks; (a) water service [supply]; 〈導水路〉 an aqueduct; 〈海峡〉 a channel ¶水道の栓 a tap; ⦅米⦆ a faucet; a hydrant (消火栓) / 水道のメートル a water meter / 水道を引く have water pipes laid; have water laid on [supplied]; lay on water / 水道を止める[出す] turn the tap [⦅米⦆ faucet] off [on] / 水道局 the Waterworks Bureau; the (municipal) water department / 水道工事 waterworks / 水道橋 a raised aqueduct / 水道料金 water rates [charges] / 豊後水道 the Bungo Channel. [文例⇩]
すいとりがみ 吸取紙 blotting paper; a blotter ¶吸い取り紙で吸い取る blot ⦅the line⦆.
すいとる 吸い取る absorb; suck up; soak up; 〈搾取する〉 squeeze; sweat ⦅workers⦆.
すいとん flour dumplings boiled in soup.
すいなん 水難 ⇨できし, すいがい.
すいのみ 吸い飲み a feeding [spout] cup.
すいばく 水爆 a hydrogen [fusion, thermonuclear] bomb; an H-bomb ¶水爆実験 a thermonuclear [an H-bomb] test / 水爆弾頭 a hydrogen [thermonuclear] warhead / 水爆保有国 ⦅the latest member of⦆ the thermonuclear club.
すいばん 水盤 a basin; 〈生け花用の〉 a (shallow) flower container [bowl].
ずいはん 随伴 ⇨ずいこう ¶行政改革に随伴する諸問題 the problems accompanying [⦅文⦆ concomitant with] administrative reforms.
すいはんき 炊飯器 a rice cooker ¶電気[ガス]炊飯器 an electric [a gas] rice cooker.
すいび 衰微 a decline; ⦅文⦆ decay; ⦅文⦆ eclipse ¶衰微する decline; ⦅文⦆ decay; ⦅文⦆ fall into decay / 衰微しつつある be on the wane [decline].
ずいひつ 随筆 an essay; literary jottings ¶随筆家 an essayist.
すいふ 水夫 a sailor; a seaman ¶水夫になる become a sailor; go to sea / 水夫長 a boatswain.
すいぶん 水分 moisture (content); water; 〈液汁〉 juice; 〈樹液〉 sap ¶水分の多い watery; moist; ⦅文⦆ water-laden ⦅winds⦆; humid ⦅air⦆; juicy ⦅fruit⦆; succulent ⦅plants⦆ / 水分を取る[除く] dehydrate; 〈乾燥させる〉 ⦅文⦆ desiccate; dry (up) / 水分を補給する ⦅文⦆ rehydrate; restore moisture ⦅to⦆.
ずいぶん 随分 〈かなり〉 pretty; ⦅口語⦆ good and ⦅drunk⦆; 〈非常に〉 very ⦅expensive⦆; very much ⦅liked⦆; extremely. [文例⇩]
すいへい¹ 水平 ¶水平の level; horizontal / 水平に horizontally; on the level; on a level ⦅with⦆ / 地面と水平の[に] even [level] with the ground / 水平距離 a horizontal distance / (飛行機が)水平姿勢に移る level off; 〈急降下してから〉 flatten [pull] out / 水平線 a horizontal line; 〈水と空との境界〉 the horizon / はるかに水平線にまで続いている stretch as far as the horizon / 水平線下に没する sink beneath the horizon / 水平舵 〈潜水艦の〉 a diving rudder [plane] / 水平動 〈地震などの〉 a horizontal motion [vibration, shock] / 水平飛行 level flight / 水平尾翼〘航空〙 a tailplane; ⦅米⦆ a horizontal stabilizer / 水平面 a horizontal plane; a level [horizontal] surface / 水平面に対してななめになっている be slanted off the horizontal.
すいへい² 水兵 a seaman; a sailor; ⦅口語⦆ a bluejacket ¶水兵服 a seaman's uniform.
すいほう¹ 水泡 foam; a bubble ¶水泡に帰する come to nothing; ⦅文⦆ come [be brought] to naught; end [result] in failure.
すいほう² 水疱〘医〙 a (water) blister; a vesicle (小さな).
すいぼう¹ 水防 flood control; prevention of floods; defense against floods ¶水防訓練 a flood-fighting drill / 水防対策 measures to prevent floods.
すいぼう² 衰亡 a decline; a downfall; ⦅文⦆ a fall; ⦅文⦆ decay; ruin ¶衰亡する decline; be ruined; go to ruin; go down; fall / ローマ帝国衰亡史〘書名〙 *The Decline and Fall of the Roman Empire*.
すいぼくが 水墨画 ⇨すみ⁴ (墨絵).
すいぼつ 水没 ¶水没する ⦅文⦆ be submerged; go under water; sink out of sight.
すいま 睡魔 〈眠気〉 drowsiness; sleepiness; 〈おとぎ話などの〉 the sandman; 〈ギリシャ神話の〉 Morpheus ¶睡魔に襲われる get [⦅文⦆ become, feel] sleepy [drowsy] / 睡魔に悩まされる be troubled by sleep / 睡魔と闘う try to keep [stay] awake; try not to fall asleep. [文例⇩]
すいみつ(とう) 水蜜(桃) a peach.
すいみゃく 水脈 a water vein ¶水脈を掘り当てる strike [hit] water.
すいみん 睡眠 (a) sleep; ⦅文⦆ (a) slumber (軽い) ¶睡眠する sleep; ⦅文⦆ slumber; have a sleep / 充分睡眠をとる sleep well; take [have] a good sleep (1回の); get [have] enough [plenty of] sleep (一般に) / 睡眠をちゃんと取る sleep regular hours / 睡眠を妨げる disturb [interrupt] *sb's* sleep / 睡眠学習法 sleep-learning; hypnopedia / 睡眠時間 (*one's*) sleeping hours; hours of sleep / 睡眠不足 shortage [lack] of sleep / 睡眠療法 sleep therapy; a sleep cure /

紀から8世紀の間と推定されている. The date of the manuscript is placed somewhere between the fourth and eighth centuries A.D.
すいどう お宅は水道ですか井戸ですか. Do you use city or well water?
ずいぶん あの人のことはずいぶん話には聞いている. I've heard a good deal about him. / ずいぶん長いことかかっているじゃないの. You've been at it long enough, haven't you? / ずいぶんな人だ. 〈反語的に〉 What a charming fellow he is!
すいま 睡魔に襲われて眠ってしまった. He was overcome by [He could no longer fight off] sleep.

すいみんやく 睡眠薬 a sleeping drug [pill, tablet];《薬》a hypnotic ; a soporific. 文例⇩

すいめん 水面 (on) the surface of the water ; the water surface ¶ 水面から2メートル上[下] two meters above [below] the surface (of the water) / 水面から空中へ跳び上がる leap clear of the water / 水面に浮かび出る come up [rise] to the surface ; break (the) surface ; surface.

すいもの 吸い物 soup ¶ 吸い物わん a soup bowl.

すいもん 水門 a sluice (gate); a floodgate ; a water gate ; a lock gate (運河の).

すいようえき 水溶液 a solution.

すいようせい 水溶性 ¶ 水溶性の water-soluble (vitamin B).

すいようび 水曜日 Wednesday (略: Wed.) ⇨ にちようび 囲扉.

すいよく 水浴 ¶ 水浴する〈冷水浴する〉have [take] a cold bath ;〈水浴びする〉have [take, get] a bathe (in a river).

すいらい 水雷〈魚雷〉a torpedo《pl. -s》;〈機雷〉a mine ⇨ ぎょらい, きらい[1] ¶ 水雷艇 a torpedo boat.

すいり[1] 水利〈給水〉water supply ;〈かんがい〉irrigation ;〈舟運〉navigability《of a river》¶ 水利の便が悪いため owing to an unsatisfactory water supply / 水利のよい[悪い]地域 a well-[poorly-]watered area / 水利組合 an irrigation association / 水利権 water [irrigation] rights ; rights to the use of water.

すいり[2] 推理 reasoning ;《文》(an) inference ;《文》ratiocination ¶ 推理する《文》reason ;《文》infer (from) / 推理の過程 a reasoning process / 推理作家 a mystery writer / 推理小説 a detective [mystery, crime] story ; a mystery ;《口語》a whodunit / 推理力《文》reasoning powers [faculties] ;《文》deductive powers.

すいりく 水陸 land and water ¶ 水陸両生動物 an amphibian (animal) / 水陸両用[車生]の amphibian ; amphibious / 水陸両用自動車 an amphibian [amphibious] car [vehicle].

すいりゅう 水流 a (water) current ; a stream (of water).

すいりょう[1] 水量 the quantity [volume] of water ¶ 水量計 a water gauge [meter].

すいりょう[2] 推量 a guess ;《文》(a) conjecture ;《文》(a) supposition ;《文》(a) presumption ¶ 推量する a guess ;《文》conjecture ; presume ;《文》infer (from) ; have [make, venture, hazard] a guess ⇨ すいそく.

すいりょく[1] 水力 water [hydraulic] power ¶ 水力で動く water-powered ; hydraulic / 水力電気 hydroelectricity / 水力電気の hydroelectric / 水力発電 hydroelectric power generation ; water-power generation / 水力発電所 a hydroelectric power station [plant].

すいりょく[2] 推力〈ロケットなどの〉thrust ¶ 16,000キログラムの推力を出す produce [generate] 35,000 pounds of thrust.

すいれいしき 水冷式 ¶ 水冷式の water-cooled.

すいれん 睡蓮《植》a water [pond] lily.

すいろ 水路 a waterway ; a watercourse ; a water route ; a fairway (港口の) ; a channel ¶ 水路…へ行く go to《Beppu》by sea [water] / 水路測量 a hydrographical survey / 水路測量術 hydrography / 水路図 a hydrographic map / 水路標識 a beacon / 水路部 the Hydrographic Department (of the Maritime Safety Agency).

すいろん 推論 reasoning ;《文》(an) inference ;〈当然に導き出される〉《文》a corollary (argument) ;〈帰納〉《文》induction ;〈演繹〉deduction ¶ 推論する《文》reason ;《文》infer (from) ;《文》draw an inference (from) ;〈帰納する〉《文》induce ; make an induction (from) ;〈演繹する〉deduce ; make a deduction (from) / 理詰めの推論 by reasoned deduction.

スイング《音楽》swing (music) ;《スポーツ》a (long) swing ¶ スイングアウトの3振を喫する be whiffed.

すう[1] 数〈数字〉a number ; a figure ¶ 多い[少ない]数 a large [small] number / かなりの数の軍勢 a good-sized army / 勝敗の数 the result [《文》issue] of the battle / 数において勝る《文》exceed (the enemy) in number ;《文》be numerically superior (to) ; be stronger (than us) (in numbers) ; outnumber《us》. 文例⇩

すう[2] 吸う breathe in ;《文》inhale ;〈すする〉suck (blood) ;〈吸収する〉absorb ; suck in [up] ;〈吸い出す〉draw [suck] out ;〈タバコを〉smoke ; puff (at a pipe) ¶ タバコをぐっと吸う take a deep pull [draw,《口語》drag] at [on] a cigarette / 音を立てて吸う slurp (one's soup).

すう- 数… several ¶ 数日 several [a few] days/十数日 over [more than, upward(s) of] ten days ; ten-odd days / 数百[千, 万, 百万]の人々 hundreds [thousands, tens of thousands, millions] of people.

スウェーデン Sweden ¶ スウェーデン(人)の Swedish / スウェーデン語 Swedish / スウェーデン人 a Swede / スウェーデン体操 Swedish gymnastics.

すうかい 数回 several [a number of] times ¶ 数回にわたって掲載する publish serially [in serial form] ; serialize.

すうがく 数学 mathematics《単数扱い》;《米口語》math ;《英口語》maths ¶ 新しい数学 the new math [mathematics] / 数学の[的] mathematical / 数学上[的に] mathematically / 数学的正確さで with mathematical precision [exactitude] / 数学の問題 a mathematical problem ; a problem in mathematics / 数学者 a mathematician. 文例⇩

すいみん 6時間の睡眠で大丈夫ですか。Can you manage on six hours' sleep? / 4時間では睡眠が足りない。Four hours' sleep is not enough. / 君は睡眠不足だ。You are short of sleep. / 時々睡眠不足を取り戻す必要があった。Sometimes I had to catch up on my sleep.

すう[1] この式はnがどのような数であっても成り立つ。This equation holds for any number n.

すうがく 私は数学が苦手だ。I am very bad [poor] at mathematics. ; I am no mathematician. / ベティーはボブと同じくらい数学の知識があった。Betty knew as much mathematics as Bob.

すうき　数奇 ¶数奇な生涯 a checkered [varied] career / 数奇な運命をたどる lead a checkered life; have a lot of ups and downs (in *one's* life); 《文》pass through various vicissitudes of fortune.

すうききょう　枢機卿《カトリック》a cardinal.

すうこう　崇高 ¶崇高な《文》lofty;《文》sublime; noble.

すうし　数詞《文法》a numeral.

すうじ¹　数字 a figure; a numeral ¶数字で示す state [express] in figures / 数字記譜法《音楽》numerical notation. 文例⇩

すうじ²　数次 ⇨すうかい.

すうしき　数式 a numerical formula [expression].

すうじく　枢軸《機械の》a pivot; an axle; an axis (*pl.* axes);《中枢》a central point; the center ¶枢軸国《史》the Axis powers.

すうじつ　数日 (for) several [some, a few] days ¶この数日来 for the last [past] few days.

すうじゅう　数十 ¶数十の scores of 《men》; dozens of 《people》/ 数十年 (for) several decades.

すうすう ¶すうすういう音 a hissing [《文》sibilant] sound.

ずうずうしい　図々しい cheeky;《文》audacious; shameless; impudent; brazen; brazen-faced;《口語》pushy ¶ずうずうしく as bold as brass / ずうずうしさ impudence;《文》audacity; cheek　ずうずうしくも…する have the cheek [face, nerve, brass, impudence, effrontery] to *do*. 文例⇩

ずーずーべん　ずーずー弁《東北人の》(speak with) a 《strong》Tohoku accent.

すうせい　趨勢 a tendency; a trend; a drift ¶時代の趨勢 the trend [current] of the times / 時代の趨勢に従う[逆らう] go with [against] the current.

ずうたい　図体 a body;《文》a frame ⇨からだ ¶図体の大きな男 a bulky fellow; a hulk of a man. 文例⇩

スーダン　the Sudan ¶スーダンの Sudanese / スーダン人 a Sudanese.

すうち　数値 a numerical value ¶数値解析《数・統計》numerical analysis.

スーツ《婦人服》a suit.

スーツケース a suitcase.

ずうっと《初めから》all the time; all along;《まっすぐに》right down 《the corridor》;《keep》straight on; all the way 《to the end》

すうとう　数等 ⇨ずっと.

すうねん　数年 (for) several [some, a few] years; a number of years ¶ここ数年は for some years ahead [to come].

スーパー〈店〉a supermarket;〈字幕〉a subtitle; a superimposition.

スーパーマーケット a supermarket.

スーパーマン a superman ¶スーパーマン的 superhuman.

すうはい　崇拝《文》worship;《文》adoration; admiration; (a) cult 《集団の》¶崇拝する worship; admire; adore; idolize; make an idol of *sb*; make a cult of *sth* / 盲目的に崇拝する make a fetish of *sth*; be a blind adorer [devotee] of *sb*;《文》hold 《an animal》in reverence [veneration] / 崇拝の対象 an object of veneration / アポロ崇拝 the cult [worship] of Apollo / 崇拝者 a worshiper; an adorer; an admirer. 文例⇩

すうひょう　数表 a table 《of logarithms》.

スープ《vegetable》soup ¶濃い[澄んだ]スープ thick [clear] soup; potage [consommé] / スープを飲む drink [have, eat] soup ★昔は eat soup と言うのが正しいとされていたが, 今ではきざだとして避ける人が多い / 固形スープ a soup cube / スープのもと (a) soup stock / スープ皿 a soup plate; a soup bowl 《深い》.

ズームレンズ《写真》a zoom lens.

すうよう　枢要 ¶枢要の《文》pivotal; key; vital; important; principal;《文》cardinal; responsible《責任ある》/ 枢要の地位を占める occupy [hold] an important [a key, a vital] position.

すうり　数理 ¶数理的 mathematical / 数理的に mathematically / 数理経済[統計]学 mathematical economics [statistics] / 数理哲学 mathematical philosophy.

すうりょう　数量 (a) quantity; (an) amount ¶数量詞《文法》a quantifier.

すうれつ　数列《数》a progression.

すえ　末〈終わり〉the end;《文》the close;〈先端〉the end; the tip; the top;〈ささいな事〉trifles; trivialities;〈未来〉the future;〈子孫〉⇨しそん ¶末の問題 a mere trifle; a matter of almost no [《文》of the least] importance / 末(に)〈未来は〉in (the) future;〈結局〉in the long run; in the end;〈あげくに〉finally; at last / 4月の末に at the end of April / 3月の末頃に toward [about] the end of March / 多年努力の末 after many years' efforts / 末長く for a long time; for ever; for good / 末頼もしい青年 a young man with a great deal [a lot] of promise; a promising youth. 文例⇩

すうじ¹ 私は数字に弱い. I am no good at figures. | I have no head for figures. / 首相は演説の中でさかんに数字を並べ立てた. The prime minister flourished a lot of figures in his speech.

ずうずうしい あの人にそんなずうずうしいことは言えやしない. I haven't the nerve [face] to say such a thing to him. / ずうずうしいにもほどがあるぞ. That's quite enough of your cheek. | What a nerve (you've got)!

ずうたい 女は大きな図体を暖炉で暖めていた. She was warming her large bulk at the fire.

すうはい 彼はレーニンを心から崇拝している. He is an ardent admirer of Lenin. | He has an ardent admiration for Lenin.

すえ 口論の末なぐり合いになった. They proceeded from words to blows. / 子供がないので末の楽しみというものがない. Since we have no children, we have nothing to look forward to in life. / これをご縁に末長くご交際願います. I hope this will lead to a lasting relationship. / 末はどうなる事やら. I wonder what will become of him. / この子は恐ろしい子供だ. I wonder what he will grow up to be. /〈悪い意

スエード suede (leather) ¶スエードの手袋 suede gloves.

すえおき 据え置き ¶据え置きの unredeemable; deferred / 5年間据え置きの貸し付け金 a loan unredeemable for five years / 据え置き貯金 deferred savings. 文例⇩

すえおく 据え置く 〈事柄を〉leave sth as it is [stands]; 〈負債などを〉(a loan) unredeemed; 〈支払いを〉defer [delay, put off] ((the payment of a loan for three years)).

スエズ Suez ¶スエズ運河(地帯) the Suez Canal (Zone).

すえぜん 据え膳 a meal set before one. 文例⇩

すえつけ 据え付け installation; setting; fitting; mounting ¶据え付けの fixed; stationary ((engines)) / 据え付け工事 installation work / 機械の据え付け台数 the number of machines installed.

すえつける 据え付ける put [((文)) set] sth in place; put [((文)) place] sth in position; fix ((a statue on a pedestal)); install ((a machine)); set up ((a camera)); mount ((a gun)).

すえっこ 末っ子 the youngest child.

すえひろがり 末広がり ¶末広がりになる〈先が広がる〉widen [broaden] toward the end; 〈だんだん栄えてゆく〉get [grow, ((文)) become] more and more prosperous [((文)) enjoy increasing prosperity] as time goes on.

すえる¹ 据える put into position; fix; ((文)) set; ((文)) place; lay; 〈地位に〉install ⇨ すえつける ¶上座に据える give sb the seat of honor / 校長に据える appoint sb principal ((of)) / 腹を据える decide ((on doing, to do)); make up one's mind ((to do, to sth)); ((文)) determine ((to do)).

すえる² 饐える go bad; turn sour ¶すえたにおい a strong bad smell; a stink.

ず 図画 drawing; ((絵))a drawing; a picture ¶図画の先生 a drawing teacher / 図画を書く draw a picture ((of)).

スカート a skirt ¶スカートのひだ a pleat [gather] on a skirt / スカートをはく put one's skirt on / スカートを脱ぐ take one's skirt off; ((文)) remove one's skirt / ロングスカート a long skirt / 〈子供が〉スカートめくりをする lift ((a girl's)) skirt.

スカーフ a scarf ((pl. -s, scarves)).

ずかい 図解 an illustration ¶図解する illustrate [((文)) by] a diagram [picture] / 図解辞典 an illustrated [a pictorial, a picture] dictionary. 文例⇩

ずがい 頭蓋 ((解)) the cranium ((pl. -s, crania)); the brainpan; the braincase ¶頭蓋骨 the skull.

スカイダイビング skydiving ¶スカイダイビングをする skydive / スカイダイビングをする人 a skydiver.

スカイライン a skyline drive ((running along the high ridges for 20 kilometers)).

スカウト a scout ¶スカウトする scout (for) ((young talent)); recruit ((new members)).

すがお 素顔 a face with no [((文)) devoid of] make-up; an unpainted face. 文例⇩

ずがく 図学 graphics.

すかさず 〈直ちに〉without a moment's delay; instantly; promptly; at once; lose no time ((in doing)); 〈ためらわずに〉unhesitatingly; without hesitation.

すかし 透かし 〈紙の〉a watermark; 〈彫りなどの〉openwork ¶透かし入りの watermarked / 透かし編み〈細工〉openwork / 透かし封筒 a window envelope / 透かし彫り(の) openwork.

すかす¹ 透かす 〈間を置く〉leave a space [an opening] ((between)); space ((the lines)); thin (out); 〈透かして見る〉look through; hold sth (up) to the light ¶やみを透かして見る peer [look closely] into the darkness / 間を透かして at intervals; sparsely.

すかす² 賺す〈なだめる〉coax [cajole, wheedle] sb ((into doing, to do)); humor sb.

すかす³ 〈気取る〉try to look smart [clever]; show off. 文例⇩

ずかずか straight; directly; without (any) hesitation; 〈許可なく〉without permission [leave]; without so much as a by-your-leave; 〈不作法に〉rudely; unceremoniously. 文例⇩

すがすがしい refreshing; fresh; bracing; crisp ¶すがすがしい気分になる〈さわやかな〉feel refreshed; 〈清らかな〉((文)) feel oneself purified. [ennobled] ((by)).

すがた 姿 〈体付き〉a figure; a form; 〈形〉a shape; 〈姿勢〉((文)) a posture; a pose; 〈様相〉((文)) an aspect; 〈外見〉(personal) appearance; 〈有様〉a state ¶姿の美しさ((文)) ((her)) personal beauty / 姿の見えない invisible / 姿がいい have a good figure / 姿を現わす appear; show oneself; make one's appearance; turn [show] up; come in sight [into view] / 完全に姿を現わす come into full view / 姿を消す disappear; go [fade] away; vanish ((from sight [the scene])) / 姿をくらます hide [((文)) conceal] oneself / 姿を隠している be in hiding / 姿をやつす[変える] disguise oneself ((as a woman)) / みすぼらしい姿をしている

味で) He will come to no good [((口語)) will turn out a bad 'un]. | 〈良い意味で〉We'll hear more of him [He'll make a name for himself] some day. | He's got a bright [great] future ahead of him.

すえおき 公共料金は今後1年間据え置きとする。Public utility charges will be pegged for one year.

すえぜん 据え膳食わぬは男の恥。It's a poor sort of man who runs from a girl's advances.

すえる¹ 彼女は椅子を引っ張って暖炉の前に据えた。She pulled [towed] a chair into position before the fire.

ずかい 図解すれば次のようになる。It can be graphically shown as follows: ―.

すがお この写真より素顔の方がいい。This photo does not really do her justice.

すかさず 検事はそこをすかさず被告に畳みかけて質問を浴びせた。The prosecutor cleverly seized the opportunity to cross-question the accused.

すかす³ すかしてやがら。He's really showing off, isn't he?

ずかずか 僕たちが食事をしている所へずかずかやって来た。He

すがたみ 姿見 a full-length mirror; a large mirror [looking glass]; a cheval glass (わく付きで前後に倒せる大型の).

スカッシュ (lemon) squash.

すかっと ⇒すっきり ¶すかっとする feel completely satisfied; 〈お互いの間のわだかまりを除く〉clear the air / すかっとしない be not quite happy; be worried [in doubt]《about sth》

すがめ 眇 ⇨しゃし¹, やぶにらみ. [[sb]].

ずがら 図柄 a pattern; a design.

スカル a scull ¶スカルの選手 a sculler.

すがる 縋る 〈すがりつく〉cling to sb; hang on (to) 《sb's neck》; hold on to 《a rope》; 〈依頼する〉depend [rely] on; lean [hang] on; 〈哀願する〉《文》entreat; implore ¶慈悲にすがる appeal to sb for mercy / つえにすがって歩く walk with [leaning on] a stick / 人の肩にすがって泣く weep on sb's shoulder / 人にすがって助けを請う implore [turn to] sb for help. 文例⇩

ずかん 図鑑 a picture [pictorial] book; an illustrated reference book; an (insect) identification manual ¶鳥類図鑑 a bird guide / 日本植物図鑑《書名》An Illustrated [A Pictorial] Book of Japanese Flora.

スカンク《動》a skunk.

スカンジウム《化》scandium.

スカンジナビア Scandinavia ¶スカンジナビアの Scandinavian / スカンジナビア人 a Scandinavian.

ずかんそくねつ 頭寒足熱 keeping one's head cool and one's feet warm.

すかんぴん 素寒貧 of penniless;《文》impecunious; 素寒貧だ have no money;《口語》be (stony) broke;《俗》be cleaned [wiped] out;《英俗》be skint.

すかんぽ《植》a garden [cock] sorrel; a sour dock.

すき¹ 好き (a) liking; (a) fondness; (a) love ¶…が好きになる get [come, learn] to like sth; grow [get,《文》become] fond of; begin to love; take to; take a fancy to; get [《文》form] a liking for; 〈異性を〉fall in love with / 好きにさせる let sb have his own way [do as he pleases] / …が好きだ like; be fond of; care for (★ 否定文・疑問文でのみ使われる); love; have a liking [taste] for / A より B が好きである like B better than A; prefer B to [rather than, over] A;《文》have a preference for B to A / 好きなようにする do as one pleases [likes]; have everything one's own way / 好きな本[作家] one's favorite book [author] / 好きな道 one's weakness [passion] / 好きな趣味 one's hobby / 好きな時に when one feels like it [doing]; when the fancy takes one / 好き好んで by [from] choice; for preference; 〈面白くて〉for the fun [love] of it / 本好き ⇨-ずき. 文例⇩

すき² 透き, 隙 ¶〈すき間〉an opening;《文》an aperture; a gap; a chink;〈余暇〉space; room; 〈機会〉a chance; an opportunity;〈油断〉an unguarded moment ¶すきがない be always on the alert; be thoroughly on one's guard 《against》; 〈議論が〉hold water; be watertight / 〈身なりが〉一分のすきもないほど be impeccably dressed / すきを狙う watch for a [one's] chance (to do); try to catch sb off his guard; seek an opening / すきを見せる lay oneself open to attack; be off one's guard. 文例⇩

すき³ 数寄 ¶数寄を凝らした庭園[建物] a tastefully [an artistically,《文》an aesthetically] laid-out [designed] garden [building];《文》a garden [building] showing refined [well-cultivated] taste.

すき⁴ 鋤, 犁 〈人力による〉a spade; 〈牛馬に引かせる〉a (traction) plow;《英》a plough ¶牛に引かせるすき an ox plow.

すぎ 杉《植》a Japanese cedar; a cryptomeria.

-すぎ …過ぎ 〈時〉past; after; 〈度合〉over-; too (much) ¶10時20分過ぎ twenty minutes past《米》after] ten / 12時過ぎまで起きている sit up till after midnight / 食い過ぎ eating too much; overeating.

-ずき …好き a lover (of music); an enthusiast; a fan ¶本好き a lover of books; a book lover;《文》a bibliophile / 野球好き a baseball

---

barged in on us when we were eating dinner.

すがた この姿では人前へ出られない. I am not fit to be seen. | I can't go out looking like this. / 近頃さっぱり彼の姿を見ない. I have seen nothing of him lately. / きつねが美しい女の姿になった. The fox took on the form of a beautiful woman. / これが現代日本のありのままの姿である. This is a true picture of present-day Japan.

すがる 人にすがるような者は成功しない. No one who looks to others for assistance will succeed. / あなたのお力にすがるのが一番だと信じます. I'm afraid I can't do better than put myself under your wing.

すき¹ 兄は釣りが非常に好きになってしまいました. Angling has become a passion with my brother. / 泳いだり, 町を散歩したり, 好きなようにして一日を過ごした. He spent the whole day swimming, and walking about the streets as the fancy took him. / そのことでしたら, どうぞお好きなようになさって下さい. You can suit yourself about that. / この金は君の好きなようにしたまえ. This money is at your disposal. | You can do what you like with this money. / 彼は次男が特に好きらしい. He seems to be particularly fond of his second son. / 私はこれが一番好きです. This suits my taste best. / こういう音楽はだれでも好きだとは限らない. This sort of music is not to everybody's taste. | Not everyone is partial to this sort of music. / だれも好きこんでこんなアパートに住んでいるんじゃない. We are not living in this flat from choice. / 好きでなけりゃあんな仕事はできない. You can't do that sort of work unless you enjoy it. / もし何でも好きなことができるものなら宇宙船に乗ってみたい. If I could do anything [whatever] I chose, I should like, first of all, to travel in a spaceship. / レコードなら好きなものを好きなときに聞くことができるが, ラジオではそれができない. With records you can hear anything you like at any time of the day, which you can't with the radio. / 好きこそものの上手なれ. You become good at what you like by

スキー fan. 文例↓
スキー 〈滑走〉skiing;〈器具〉(a pair of) skis ¶スキーをする[で滑る] ski; go [slide] on skis / スキーに行く go skiing 《at Naeba》/ スキーウエア a ski suit [outfit] / スキー教師 a ski instructor / スキー靴[ズボン] (a pair of) ski boots [pants] / スキー場 a skiing ground; a ski area; a ski slope / スキー大会 a ski competition / スキー帽 a ski cap / スキーヤー a skier / スキーリフト a ski [chair] lift.
すきかえす 鋤き返す plow up 《roots》; turn 《the soil》over.　　　　　　　　　　　[に].
すきかって 好き勝手 ⇨じぶん¹ (自分勝手な).
すききらい 好き嫌い likes and dislikes; taste(s) ¶好き嫌いがある be fussy [particular, 《文》fastidious] 《about one's food》/ 食べ物に好き嫌いが多すぎる have too many likes and dislikes in [be too particular about] what one eats. 文例↓
すきぐし 梳き櫛 a fine-toothed comb (used for removing loose hairs).
すぎこしのいわい 過ぎ越しの祝い《ユダヤ教》the Passover.
ずきずき ¶ずきずきする《傷が》throb (with pain).
すきっぱら 空きっ腹《drink on》an empty stomach; hunger. 文例↓
すきとおる 透き通る be transparent; be clear; (can) be seen through ¶透き通った transparent; clear;《文》pellucid;《文》limpid;《文》crystal《water》.
-すぎない …過ぎない be nothing but…; be no more than…; merely…; only…. 文例↓
すきま 透き間 a crevice; a crack; a chink; a gap; an opening;《文》an aperture; (a) space ¶透き間なく closely; compactly; leaving [with] no space between 《them》/ 透き間風《米》a draft;《英》a draught / 透き間風の入るdrafty《rooms》/ 透き間風を防ぐ cut off [prevent]. 文例↓
スキムミルク skim [skimmed] milk.
すきや 数寄屋〈茶室〉a tea-ceremony room ¶数寄屋造り the *sukiya* style of building.
すきやき すき焼 *sukiyaki* ¶すき焼きなべ a *sukiyaki* pan.
スキャンダル a scandal.
すぎる 過ぎる〈通過する〉pass (by [through]); go [run] past;〈経過する〉pass (away);《文》elapse; go by [on]; wear away;〈期限が〉expire; be out;〈超過する〉《文》exceed; be above [over, more than]…;〈過度になる〉go too far [《文》to excess] ¶働き過ぎる overwork (oneself) / 食い過ぎる eat too much; eat more than is good for one / 1センチ長過ぎる be one centimeter too long / ひとり[ひとつ]多過ぎる be one too many / 冗談が過ぎる take [carry] a joke too far / 90歳を過ぎた人 a person past [over] ninety (years of age) / 10年過ぎて《文》the lapse of ten years; ten years later / 時が過ぎるに従って as time goes on [by] / 過ぎ去った日々 the long-ago days (of childhood). 文例↓
ずきん 頭巾 a hood.
スキンシップ《constant》physical contact (between mother and infant); togetherness.
ずきんずきん ⇨ずきずき. 文例↓
スキンダイビング skin diving ¶スキンダイビングをする a skin-dive; go skin-diving.
すく¹ 好く like; love; be fond of; have a liking [fancy] for; have a weakness [preference] for; care for (★疑問文・否定文でのみ使われる)¶好かれる be (well) liked [loved] (by); be popular《with, among》/ 好いて好かれる《文》love and be loved; be in love with each other / 人に好かれない unlik(e)able; unpopular;《文》unamiable《character》/ 好かない《文》distasteful; unpleasant / 好かないやつ an unpleasant [a disgusting] fellow. 文例↓
すく² 空く〈からになる〉empty; get [《文》become] empty;〈混雑しなくなる〉《文》become] less crowded ¶腹がすく feel hungry / 手がすいている be unoccupied; be free. 文例↓
すく³ 透く〈透き通る〉be transparent;〈まばらになる〉get [《文》become] sparse [thin];

ing. | What you like you will do well. / それは好きずきです。It is a matter of taste [individual preference].
すき² 逃れるすきがなかった。I had no chance of escape.
-ずき トニーは子供の頃から機械好きだった。Tony was mechanically inclined even as a boy.
すききらい だれでも好き嫌いはある。Everybody has his likes and dislikes. / 物を恵んでもらうのに好き嫌いは言えない。Beggars can't be choosers.《諺》
すきっぱら 空きっ腹にまずい物なし。Hunger is the best sauce.《諺》| Hunger makes any food palatable. / 空きっ腹で飲んだのですぐ回った。I drank on an empty stomach and it went straight to my head.
-すぎない 私はただなすべきことをなしたに過ぎない。I only did what I ought to. / 彼とは年賀状をやり取りするくらいの間柄に過ぎない。My relations with him are confined to the exchange of New Year's greetings. / それは口実に過ぎない。It is nothing but an excuse. | It is an excuse, and nothing more.
すきま 雪が戸の透き間から吹き込んだ。The snow sifted in through the door crevices. / ここは透き間風が来る。There is a draft here.
すぎる 彼女はもう30歳を幾つか[だいぶ]過ぎている。She is already some way [well] into her thirties. / あの人は40歳を過ぎている。He is on the wrong side of forty. | He has turned forty. / 冬

が過ぎて春になった。Winter is over and spring has come. / その一日も徐々に過ぎようとしていた。The day was wearing on. / 彼は世の中に出るにはまだ若過ぎる。He is still too young to go out into the world. / 喜びこれに過ぎるものはありません。Nothing could please me more. / 過ぎたことは仕方がない。What is done cannot be undone.《諺》| It's no use crying over spilt milk.《諺》/ 過ぎたるは及ばざるがごとし。Too much is as bad as too little.
ずきんずきん 頭がずきんずきんしだした。My head began to throb (with pain).
すく¹ 彼は人に好かれる性質だ。He is a very likable person.
すく² この電車はすいている。This

すく 〈すき間がある〉 leave [have] a gap [an opening] / 〈透いて見える〉 (can) be seen through/〈間が透いている〉 (some) space is left between....

すく⁴ 梳く 〈髪を〉 comb (out) ; 〈羊毛を〉 card.

すく⁵ 鋤く 《米》 plow ; 《英》 plough ; 《文》 till ; break up 《land》 ; turn 《the soil》 over.

すく⁶ 漉く ¶紙をすく make [《文》 manufacture] paper.

すぐ 直ぐ 〈直ちに〉 immediately ; at once ; straight-away ; instantly ; in a moment [minute] ; in no time ; on the spot ; right away [off] ; 〈間もなく〉 soon ; before long ; 〈容易に〉 easily ; 《文》 readily ; 〈ちょうど〉 just ; right ¶…するとすぐ as soon as... ; 《文》 no sooner... than... / 今すぐに this very instant ; right now / すぐ怒る be (very) quick to take offense ; be easily offended 〈薬などが〉すぐ効く work at once ; 《文》 take immediate effect / すぐ目の前で right in front of one ; right under one's nose / すぐ近くに close [near, 《文》 hard] by ; close at hand (手近に) / すぐ近くの nearby. 文例⇩

-ずく ¶…ずくで by means of [《文》 dint] of ; for the sake of / 腕ずくで by (sheer [brute]) force / 相談ずくで 《文》 by mutual agreement / 欲得ずくで 《文》 for the sake of gain ; for love of money.

すくい 救い (a) rescue ; relief ; 〈助力〉 help ; 《文》 aid ; 〈宗教上の〉 salvation ; 〈埋め合わせとなる取り柄〉《文》 the saving grace ¶救いようもない be past saving ; 《文》 be beyond salvation / 救いのない悲劇 《文》 an unrelieved tragedy / 救いの手を差し延べる extend a helping hand (to) / 救いを求める ask for help / 救いを得る 《文》 attain [achieve] salvation. 文例⇩

すくいあげる 掬い上げる dip [scoop] up ; pick up.

スクイズ 〈野球〉 a squeeze (play) ¶スクイズをする run [try] a squeeze.

すくいだす 掬い出す bail (water out of a boat).

すくう¹ 救う 〈危難から〉 rescue sb (from danger) ; save sb (from death) ; 〈困難から〉 help sb (out of a difficulty) ; 《文》 relieve (sb from (his) suffering, sb's suffering) ; 《文》 deliver sb (from a difficulty) ; 《文》 release sb (from pain) ; 〈罪より〉 save [reclaim, 《文》 redeem] sb (from a life of sin) / 難船した人を救う pick up a shipwrecked crew / 貧しい人々を救う 《文》 relieve [give relief to] the poor / 人命を救う save a man's life / 救いがたい hopeless ; past praying for ; 《文》 past redemption [salvation] / 救いがたい怠け者 an incurably lazy man / 救いに行く go to sb's rescue [《文》 aid] ; go to help sb.

すくう² 掬う scoop (up) ; dip (up) ; ladle out (杓子(しゃく)で) ; spoon up [out] (さじで) ; shovel (up) ¶手ですくって飲む drink 《water》 out of one's hands / 足をすくう trip sb (up) / 《波などに》 足をすくわれる be carried off one's feet.

すくう³ 巣食う 〈巣を造る〉 build a nest ; nest ; 〈比喩的に〉 haunt 《a place》 ; 《口語》 hang out (in, at) ; have one's den [《口語》 hangout] (in, at).

スクーター a (motor) scooter ¶スクーターに乗る ride a scooter ; have [take] a ride on a scooter / スクーターで行く go on a scooter.

スクーナー 〈船〉 a schooner.

スクープ 〈特種〉 《口語》 a scoop ¶スクープする scoop (rival papers for a piece of news) ; get a scoop ; 《口語》 pull a (big) scoop ★英語の scoop は scoop all the other papers のように「他社を出しぬく」の意で使われることが多い / 鮮やかなスクープ a clean beat.

スクーリング 〈教育〉 schooling.

スクエアダンス a square dance ¶スクエアダンスをする dance [take part in] a square dance ; square-dance.

すぐさま 直ぐさま ⇨ すぐ.

すくすく 〈どんどん〉 fast ; quickly ; rapidly ; 〈故障もなく〉 without mishap [a hitch].

すくない 少ない 〈数〉 do not have [there are not] many (trees) ; very few [not many] (people do) ; 《文》 have [there are] few (trees) ; 〈量〉 do not have [there is not] much (money) ; 《文》 have [there is] little (money) ; 〈限られた〉 be limited ; 〈まれな〉 be rare ; 《文》 be not frequent ; be few and far between ; 〈乏しい〉 be scarce ; be scanty ; 〈足りない〉 there is [are] not enough (sufficient)... ¶少なからぬ 《文》 not a few [little] ; 《文》 no small / 少なからず in no small way ; 《文》 to no small extent / 少なく見積もっても at the lowest estimate / 少なく(とも) at (the) least ; to say the least (of it) / 少なくなる get fewer [less] ; 《文》 decrease ; 《文》 diminish ; lessen. 文例⇩ 用法「木が少ない」を Trees are few. とは英語では言わない。同様に「お金が少ない」を Money is little. というのも英語ではない ⇨ おおい 用法. では, このような場合 There are few trees. とか I have little money. と言えばよいかというと, 確かに間違いではないが, 口語ではそうは言わないで, There are not many trees. | There are only a few trees. | There are very few trees. / I don't have much money. | I have only a little money. | I have very little money. のように言うのが普通。一般に「少ない」「少ししかない」は few, little, 「少しはある」を a few, a lit-

train is not crowded.

すぐ 今すぐという訳にはいきません。It can't be done at a moment's notice [《米》 in short order]. / 東京にお着きになったらすぐ電話を下さい。Please call me as soon as you arrive in Tokyo. / 僕を見るとすぐ逃げ出した。He ran off directly [immediately, the instant, the moment] he saw me. / 朝食の後すぐ出かけた。He left the house right after breakfast. / 職場に着くと, すぐ仕事にとりかかった。When he arrived at the office, he lost no time in setting to work. / もうすぐ夏休みだ。It'll soon be the summer vacation (holidays). / もうすぐクリスマスだ。Christmas is just around the corner. / もうすぐ3時だ。It will soon be three o'clock. | It's getting on for three. / もうすぐ40ですよ。I am close on [pushing] forty. / 早くしなさい。—今すぐ行きます。Be quick, please.—I'm just coming. / すぐ戻って来ます。I won't be a minute.

すくい ユーモアを解しうるのが彼の救いになっている。He has a

すくみあがる 竦み上がる ⇨ すくむ.

すくむ 竦む 〈勝る〉crouch; cower;《文》quail《at, before》; shrink [flinch]《at,《文》before, from》¶足がすくむ feel weak at the knees / 蛇を見てすくむ recoil [draw back] from [at the sight of] a snake.

-ずくめ ¶いいことずくめ unmixed blessings; one good thing after another / 規則ずくめの生活 a life all bound by rules and regulations / 黒ずくめの服装をしている be (dressed) all in black / 宝石ずくめである be covered [《口語》plastered] with jewels. 文例⇩

すくめる 竦める 〈首を〉duck《one's head》; 〈肩を〉shrug《one's shoulders》¶身体をすくめる shrink [recoil, flinch, draw back] from.

スクラップ scrap ¶スクラップにする scrap《an old car》/ スクラップにされる運命にある be destined for the scrap heap / スクラップとして売る sell《a dismantled ship》as [for] scrap.

スクラップブック a scrapbook.

スクラム 《ラグビー》a scrum(mage) ¶スクラムを組む form a scrum; scrum down;〈比喩的に〉join forces [hands]《to do》/ スクラムを組んで in a scrum.

スクランブル〈緊急発進〉(order) a scramble;《make》a scramble takeoff ¶スクランブルエッグ scrambled eggs / スクランブル交差点 a crossroads where traffic lights allow pedestrians to cross in any direction simultaneously.

スクリーン〈映写幕〉a screen;〈映画界〉the screen.

スクリプター a continuity clerk [man, girl] ★ scripter は和製英語. scriptwriter は「シナリオ作家」.

スクリプト a (TV) script ⇨ だいほん.

スクリュー a screw ¶スクリューで推進される be propelled by a screw.

すぐれる 優れる 〈勝る〉be better than《anybody else》; surpass《sb in skill》; be superior to《the others》;《文》excel《all of us》at tennis, as a tennis player》; outdo《one's opponent》;〈優秀である〉be excellent; shine《as a student, at tennis》¶優れた〈立派な〉excellent; superb; fine;〈傑出した〉prominent; outstanding;〈まさった〉《文》superior;《文》surpassing;《文》eminent / 優れて〈極めて〉extremely;《文》exceedingly;〈はるかに〉by far, far and away;〈並はずれて〉exceptionally;〈目だって〉remarkably;《文》conspicuously / 気分がすぐれない do not feel well;《文》feel unwell;《文》[be feel] off color ★ off color は「気分がすぐれない」ことで「顔色が悪い」ではない

い). 文例⇩

すげ 菅《植》a sedge ¶すげがさ a sedge hat.

ずけい 図形 a figure ¶平面[立体, 幾何学的]図形 a plane [solid, geometrical] figure / 図形認識 pattern recognition.

スケート skating;〈器具〉(a pair of) skates ¶スケートが上手[下手]だ be good [no good, poor] at skating; be a good [poor] skater / スケートをする skate《on the ice》; do《some, a lot of》skating / スケートに行く go skating《on a nearby pond》/ スピードスケート speed skating / フィギュアスケート ⇨ フィギュアスケート / スケート場[リンク] a skating [an ice] rink / スピードスケート選手権大会 a speed skating championship.

スケール〈規模〉a scale;〈人物の〉《文》(a) caliber ¶スケールの大きい[小さい] large-[small-]scale《projects》;《business》on a large [small] scale;《a man》of large [small] caliber.

すげかえる すげ替える ¶首をすげ替える shift personnel; replace《A》with《B》.

スケジュール a schedule; a program ¶ぎっちり詰まったスケジュール a crammed [crowded, heavy, tight] schedule / スケジュールどおりに as scheduled; according to schedule; on schedule / スケジュールを立てる make [map, lay] out a schedule《for, of》/ スケジュールを立て直す reschedule.

ずけずけ ¶ずけずけ言う do not mince matters [one's words]; say unpleasant things to sb's face; be (very) outspoken《in one's criticism of sb》; tell sb what one thinks of him; speak bluntly; speak one's mind;《口語》give sb a piece of one's mind.

すけそうだら《魚》a walleye [an Alaska] pollack.

すけだち 助太刀〈加勢〉help; assistance;《文》(an) aid;〈助力者〉a helper; a supporter; a backer ¶助太刀する help [lend a helping hand to] sb;《文》assist sb《in a fight》; back sb up; support.

スケッチ〈写生〉sketching;〈写生画〉a sketch ¶スケッチする sketch; make [do] a sketch of sth / スケッチブック a sketchbook; one's book of studies.

すけっと 助っ人 ⇨ すけだち.

すげない cold; curt《replies》; icy《tones》; flat; unhelpful; blunt; short ¶すげなくする treat sb coldly; give a cold [frosty] reception《to》;《口語》give sb the cold shoulder [《俗》the brush-off] / すげなく断わる give a flat [pointblank] refusal; turn down《an offer》bluntly.

すけべい 助平 a dirty-minded man; a dirty old man.

---

saving sense of humor.

すくない 100歳まで生きる人は少ない. Very few people live to be a hundred. / あの人は家にいることが少ない. He is rarely [seldom] at home. / こういう例は極めて少ない. Such instances are few and far between [are rarely to be met with]. / 氏の助力に負うところが少なくない. We owe a great deal to his assistance. | We have been aided by him to no small extent. / 彼は少なくとも1,000ドルは持っている. He has at least [not less than] 1,000 dollars.

-ずくめ 工業化が必ずしもいい事ずくめではないことは, もはや明白になった. The fact that industrialization is a mixed blessing has become all too apparent. / 人生はいいことずくめじゃないよ. Life isn't all fun. | Life is not a bed of roses. | You can't expect life to be roses (roses) all the way.

すぐれる 最近どうも気分が優れない. I have been rather off color

すける 透ける be transparent ¶透けて見える(can) be seen through ((one's dress)); show through ((衣服・紙などが)) be (semi)transparent / 肌が透けて見えるブラウス a see-through blouse. 文例⇩

すげる tie ((a thong to a *geta*)); fit ((a clog with a thong)).

スケルツオ 《音楽》 a scherzo (*pl.* -s, -zi).

スコア 〈競技の〉 a score; 〈楽譜〉 a (musical) score ¶スコアをとる keep the score ((of)) / 5対3で勝つ win (the game) by a score of 5 to 3 / スコアカード a scorecard / スコアブック a scorebook / スコアボード a scoreboard. 文例⇩

すごい 凄い 〈恐ろしい〉 terrible; dreadful; horrible; 〈気味悪い〉 uncanny; unearthly; weird; ghastly; gruesome; grim; 〈すばらしい〉 superb; fantastic; marvelous; wonderful; terrific; amazing; great; 〈非常な〉《口語》awful (liars); tremendous ¶すごい腕前 amazing [striking] ability ((in, for)) / すごい人出 a terrific [mammoth] turnout [crowd]; a terrible [an awful] crowd.

ずこう 図工 〈教科〉 drawing and manual arts ¶児童の図工作品 ((exhibits of)) children's art work.

すごうで 凄腕 ⇨ らつわん(辣腕家).

スコール a (sudden) shower (in the tropics) ★「スコール」は俗には「南洋のにわか雨」と解されているが、英語の squall は突然襲って来る「強風」で、雨を伴うことが多いが、単なる「にわか雨」ではない。

すごく very; 《口語》awfully; 《口語》terrifically; tremendously; really.

すこし 少し ⇨すくない 囲団 ¶少し(の)〈量〉a little; a (little) bit of; 《文》a small quantity of; 〈数〉a few; a small number of; 〈多少〉some; 〈度合〉rather; a little; a bit; a little bit; a shade; 《文》somewhat; a trifle; 《文》to some [a small] extent; 《文》in some measure; slightly; 〈時間〉a moment; a minute; a (little) while; 〈距離〉a little way; a short distance / 少しずつ little by little; gradually; by degrees; piecemeal; a bit at a time / 〈距離〉by inches; inch by inch / 少しはある have [there are] a few ((eggs)); have [there is] a little ((milk)) / 少ししかない have [there are] not many [only a few] ((eggs)); have [there is] not much [only a little] ((milk)) / もう少し(…するところだった) nearly; almost / 少したって in a little while; in a short time; shortly; soon; a little later / 少しの差で by a narrow [slim] margin; by a small majority (選挙などで) / 少しも (not) in the least; (not) at all; (not) the slightest; (not) a bit; 《文》(not) in any degree / 少しも構わない do not care a bit [a straw, 《文》an iota, a scrap, 《口語》a damn] ((about, whether…)); 《口語》couldn't care less ((if, whether)) / 少しも役に立たない be of no use at all; be completely useless. 文例⇩

すごす 過ごす spend; pass; go [get] through ((the evening)) ¶むなしく時を過ごす waste time; idle [dawdle] one's time away / 読書に時を過ごす spend one's time (in) reading / 酒を過ごす drink too much; have more to drink than is good for one. 文例⇩

すごすご ¶すごすごと dejectedly; 《文》in dejection; 《口語》abashed; disappointed; crestfallen.

スコッチ 〈ウイスキー〉 Scotch (whisky); 〈毛織〉 tweed ((suits)); 〈服〉(in) (Scotch) tweeds ¶スコッチテリア an Aberdeen (terrier); a Scotch [Scottish] terrier.

スコットランド Scotland ¶スコットランド(人)の Scottish / スコットランド人〈男〉a Scotsman / 〈女〉a Scotswoman / 〈総称〉the Scotch [Scottish] (people); the Scots ★スコットランド人は Scotch よりも Scottish 又は Scots を好む。

スコップ [〈(オランダ語)〉 *schop*] a spade; a shovel; 〈小型の〉 a scoop; a trowel (園芸用).

すこぶる 頗る ⇨ひじょう² (非常に).

すごみ 凄味 ¶凄味のある gruesome; grim; weird; dreadful / 凄味をきかせる 〈脅す〉threaten; intimidate; 〈凄文句を並べる〉《文》use menacing language.

すごむ 凄む 〈脅す〉threaten *sb* with violence; intimidate *sb*; 《文》use menacing language.

すごもり 巣籠り nesting ¶巣ごもりする, 巣ごもる nest.

すごもんく 凄文句 《文》threatening words [language] ¶凄文句を並べる make threatening remarks; 《文》use menacing language.

すこやか 健やか ¶健やかな healthy; sound / 健やかに育つ grow up in good health ⇨けんこう, そうけん⁴.

スコラ ¶スコラ哲学 Scholasticism / スコラ哲学の Scholastic / スコラ哲学者 a Scholastic.

---

lately.
すける 着物が薄くて腕が透けて見える。Her arms are visible through her thin dress.
すこし これは少しですがあなたにどうぞ。Here's something for you. / もう少しで電車に乗り遅れるところだった。I almost missed the train. / 猫はもう少しでひかれるところでした。The cat came very near (to) being run over. / The cat was nearly [almost] run over. / 我々はその点では彼らに少しも引けを取らない。We are not in the least inferior to them in that respect. / 彼は少しは詩も作る。He is a bit of a poet. / 少しでも良心があればそんな事はしない。If he has an ounce of conscience, he won't do a thing like that. / 車に乗ってばかりいないで、少しは歩きなさいよ。Do some walking, instead of driving all the time. / もう少しはやく歩けないか? Can't you walk any faster? / 矢はほんの少しのところで的に当たらなかった。The arrow missed the target by a hairsbreadth. / 少し行ったら川に出た。A little way on, we came to a river. / 少しでも早い方がいい。The sooner the better. / もう少ししてからおいでなさい。Come back a little later. / コニャックは少しずつ飲もうや、もう少しの1本しかないんだから。Let's go easy on the cognac—it's the last bottle!
すごす 帳簿調べでまる3時間を過ごした。I put in a good three hours on the account books.
すさまじい この本の売れ行きはす

すごろく 双六 *sugoroku*; a Japanese variety of parcheesi ¶双六をする play *sugoroku*.

すさまじい 凄まじい terrific; tremendous; fierce; terrible; dreadful; awesome; amazing. 文例⇩

すさむ 荒む ⟨心などが⟩ grow [get,《文》become] wild ⇒ **あれる** ¶すさんだ生活を送る lead [live] a wild [dissolute, dissipated] life.

ずさん 杜撰 ¶ずさんな careless; slipshod; slovenly; sloppy; loose ⟨thinking⟩ / ずさんな辞書 a carelessly compiled dictionary.

すし 鮨 *sushi*; fish on vinegared rice ¶すし屋 a *sushi* shop [bar].

すじ 筋 ⟨筋肉⟩ a muscle; ⟨腱(けん)⟩ a tendon; a sinew; ⟨繊維⟩ a fiber; a string; ⟨線⟩ ⟨draw⟩ a line; ⟨きめ⟩ grain; texture; ⟨条⟩ a stripe; a streak; ⟨劇の⟩ a plot; a story (line); ⟨条理⟩ reason; logic; ⟨脈絡⟩ the thread; 《文》 coherence; ⟨方面⟩ quarters; a source; circles; a channel; ⟨血統⟩ ⟨文⟩ lineage; 《文》descent; 《文》 stock; blood; ⟨素質⟩ makings; nature; 《文》 an aptitude ¶筋の込み入った[簡単な]小説 a novel with a complicated [simple] plot / ⟨物語の⟩筋の展開 plot development / 筋の通った[通らない] logical [illogical]; 《文》rational [irrational]; reasonable [unreasonable]; 《文》 just [unjust] / 筋がいい have an aptitude ⟨for tennis, for math⟩; have a head ⟨for figures, for languages⟩ / 筋を違える sprain ⟨one's back⟩; get [have] a strain ⟨in one's leg⟩; pull a muscle / 首の筋を違える get a crick in the neck; wrick one's neck / ⟨えんどうの筋を取る⟩ string ⟨peas⟩ / 信頼すべき筋 a reliable source / 筋だらけの sinewy; stringy. 文例⇩

ずし¹ 図示 illustration; graphic(al) representation ¶図示する illustrate; diagram; give a graphic representation of; map out.

ずし² 厨子 a [miniature] shrine.

すじあい 筋合い (a) reason; (a) right. 文例⇩

すじかい 筋交い ⟨斜めに入れる木材⟩ a diagonal beam; a strut; a brace ¶筋交いの diagonal / 筋交いに diagonally; 《文》obliquely; crosswise; crossways / 筋交い入り構造 ［木工］ a braced frame; a full frame.

すじがき 筋書き ⟨梗概⟩ a synopsis 《pl. -opses》; an outline; the argument ⟨of a drama⟩; a plot; the story; ⟨計画⟩ a program; a plan; a schedule ¶筋書きを述べる give a synopsis [summary] ⟨of⟩; outline; describe in outline; sketch (out) a plan ⟨of⟩; make a (rough) sketch ⟨of⟩ /

筋書きどおりに as planned [scheduled]; according to schedule.

すじがね 筋金 ¶筋金入りの tried (and tested) 《revolutionaries》; out-and-out; dyed-in-the-wool; 《英》staunch / 筋金入りの党員 party stalwarts / 筋金を入れる give (some) backbone 《to》; put steel into the spine of *sb.*

ずしき 図式 a diagram; a graph; 《文》a schema 《pl. schemata》; a figure ¶図式化する put into the form of a diagram [graph]; 《文》express schematically; 《文》schematize / 図式的に示す show schematically; 《文》give a schematic presentation [picture] of *sth.*

すじこ 筋子 salmon roe.

すじちがい 筋違い ¶筋違いの ⟨不条理な⟩ unreasonable; absurd; ⟨間違っている⟩ wrong; ⟨見当違いの⟩ irrelevant.

すしづめ すし詰め ¶すし詰めの packed like sardines (in a can); jam-packed ⟨cars⟩. 文例⇩

すじみち 筋道 reason; logic; the thread ⟨of *one's* argument⟩; ⟨系統⟩ a method; a system ¶筋道の立った[立たない] reasonable [unreasonable]; logical [illogical]; justifiable [unjustifiable]; 《文》coherent [incoherent]; consistent [inconsistent] / 筋道の立たない話をする talk incoherently; make disjointed remarks; ⟨不当な主張をする⟩ make 《文》lodge] an unjustified claim. 文例⇩

すじむかい[むこう] 筋向かい[向こう] ¶筋向かい[向こう]の[に] diagonally opposite ⟨to⟩; diagonally across 《the street》 from 《one's house》.

すじょう 素性 ⟨生まれ⟩ birth; 《文》lineage; origin; ⟨身元⟩ identity; ⟨経歴⟩ *one's* history; *one's* past career ¶素性がいい 《文》be of good birth; come from a 《文》be of] good family / 素性が卑しい 《文》be lowborn; 《文》be of humble origin [background] / 素性を調べる inquire [go] into *sb's* past life / 素性を暴く reveal [《文》disclose] *sb's* identity. 文例⇩

ずじょう 頭上 ¶頭上に over [above] *one's* [the] head; overhead / 頭上に落ちる fall on *one's* head / 頭上を飛ぶ fly overhead.

ずしりと ⟨feel, weigh⟩ heavy.

ずしんと with a thump [thud]; heavily.

すす 煤 soot ¶すすだらけの sooty; soot-covered; smoke-stained / すす払い house-[spring-]cleaning / すす払いをする sweep the soot off [away]; clean the house. 文例⇩

すず 鈴 a bell ¶鈴の音 the tinkle [tinkling]

さまじい. The sales of the book are [The way the book is selling is] simply amazing.

すじ 彼の帽子には白い筋が2本ついていた. His cap was banded with two white stripes. / 筋の通った要求ならいつでも入れる. I will grant any reasonable request. / 彼の議論には筋も何も通っていない. There is neither rhyme nor reason to his argument. / この議論は筋が通っている. There is logic in this argument. / その話は確かな筋から聞いた. I have the news from a reliable source. / I have been told so on very good authority.

すじあい 君にそんなことを言われる筋合いはない. You have no right to say that to me.

すじがき 万事筋書きどおりに運んだ. Everything went as scheduled [as arranged].

すしづめ 列車はすし詰めで, 席にありつけるどころか, 立っているのもやっとだった. The train was packed so tight with people that there was barely room on the floor, let alone on the seats.

すじみち 彼のやることには少しも筋道が立っていない. There is no method in his way of doing things.

すじょう 彼はどうしても素性を明かさなかった. He refused to tell us who and what he was. / 素性は争われないものだ. Blood will tell.

すす 煙突がすすでつまった. The

すず 《a bell/鈴を鳴らす ring [jingle, tinkle] a bell.
すず² 錫，スズ tin ¶スズ製の tin 《cups》; (made) of tin／スズはく tin foil.
すずかけ 鈴懸け〖植〗a plane tree; a platan; 《米》a sycamore.
すずき〖植〗(a) miscanthus; Japanese pampas grass; silver grass; zebra grass (たかのはすすき)¶枯れすすき a dead [withered] miscanthus／〈比喩的に〉(like) withered grass.
すずき〖魚〗a sea bass.
すすぐ 濯[漱，雪]ぐ wash; rinse ¶衣類をすすぐ rinse clothes (in clean water)／口をすすぐ rinse [wash] (out) *one's* mouth／汚名をすすぐ ⇒ おもい.
すすける 煤ける get [be,《文》become] sooty ¶すすけた ⇒ すす (すすだらけの).
すずしい 涼しい cool; refreshing ¶涼しい目 bright [clear, liquid] eyes／涼しい顔をして nonchalantly;《文》with studied unconcern [indifference]／涼しい顔をしている look unconcerned; be [《文》remain] unruffled／涼しさ the cool《of evening》; coolness. 文例⇩
すずなり 鈴なり ¶すずなりになる grow in clusters (on a tree);〈木が主語〉be heavy [《文》laden] with fruit;〈乗り物が人で〉be overflowing with passengers.
すずみ 涼み ¶涼みに出る go out to enjoy the cool of evening／涼み客 people (who are) out to enjoy the cool air／涼み台 a bench.
すすみでる 進み出る come [step] forward ¶1歩前へ進み出る take [make] a step forward.
すすむ 進む〈前進する〉《文》advance; go [step] forward [ahead]; make *one's* way (to);〈進歩する〉make progress [headway]; improve;〈はかどる〉get on [along] with 《*one's* studies》;〈時計が〉gain; run fast;〈昇級する〉be promoted [raised] 《to a higher position》¶時代と共に進む keep up with [keep abreast of] the times／時代より先に進む get [go] ahead of the times; be ahead of *one's* time／世の中が進むにつれて with the progress of the times／準決勝に進む go to the semifinals; get [win *one's* way] into the semifinals／大学へ進む go (on) to college [university]／進んだ思想[国]an advanced idea [country]／(時計が) 10分進んでいる be ten minutes fast／自分から進んで of *one's* own accord [free will]; willingly; voluntarily／気が進まない be reluctant [disinclined] to *do*; be not in the mood to *do* [for *sth*]; do not feel like *doing*.
すずむ 涼む cool *oneself*; cool off; enjoy the cool of evening [the cool evening air].

すすめ 薦[勧]め〈推薦〉(a) recommendation;〈助言〉(a) suggestion; (a piece of) advice;《文》(an) exhortation;〈奨励〉encouragement ¶…のすすめで〈推薦〉on the recommendation of *sb*;〈勧告〉on the advice of *sb*; at *sb's* suggestion. 文例⇩
すずめ 雀 a sparrow ¶すずめの涙ほどの a mere trace [particle] of; an atom [《文》a modicum] of. 文例⇩
すずめばち 雀蜂〖昆〗a hornet; a wasp.
すすめる¹ 進める〈前へ出す〉《文》advance; put [《文》set] forward;〈位を〉raise;《文》promote;《文》advance;〈助長する〉《文》promote; help on;〈先へ〉further;〈はかどらせる〉《文》hasten; speed (up) ¶交渉を進める go on [get on,《文》proceed] with the negotiations／時計(の針)を1時間進める put (the hands of) a clock forward (by) an hour.
すすめる² 薦[勧]める〈推薦する〉recommend;〈勧告する〉suggest《*doing*, that...》; advise;《文》counsel;《文》exhort;〈奨励する〉encourage; urge;〈差し出す〉offer;〈強いる〉press; force ¶勉強を勧める encourage *sb* to work hard;《文》exhort *sb* to diligence／座ぶとんを勧める offer *sb* a cushion／…に勧められて at [on] the suggestion of *sb*; on *sb's* advice; at the urging of *sb*. 文例⇩
すずらん 鈴蘭 a lily of the valley ¶鈴蘭の花 a lily bell [cup].
すずり 硯 an inkstone ¶すずり箱 an inkstone case.
すすりなき 啜り泣き sobbing; a sob.
すすりなく 啜り泣く sob.
すする 啜る〈お茶などを〉sip;〈音をたてて〉slurp《*one's* soup》; suck in《*one's* noodles》★欧米人は飲物を口に入れるのに，空気と共に音を立ててすすり込むことを一般にしない。sip は音をたてず少しずつちびりちびりと口へ入れることで，日本人とは飲み方が違う．
すそ 裾〈衣服の〉the hem《of a skirt》; the bottom [lower] edge《of a dress》; the bottom《of a *kimono*》;〈山の〉the foot; the base ¶すその線 the hemline《of a skirt》／すその広がった wide-based《mountains》／すそを引く trail the skirt《of *one's* gown》／すそを持つ hold up《a lady's》train／ズボンのすそをまくり上げていて wear the bottoms of *one's* trousers rolled up／裾板 a baseboard／すそ模様 (a formal *kimono* with) a design on the skirt.
ずぞう 図像 ¶図像学 iconography／図像(学)的 iconographic／図像(学)的に iconographically.

---

chimney is choked (up) with soot.
すずしい ここはとても涼しい. It is nice and cool here.
すすむ 前へ進め．〖号令〗Forward!｜March!／僕らは人込みを分けて進んで行った. We pushed [elbowed] our way through the crowd.／(教室で先生が)この前はどこまで進みましたか. How far did we get [Where did we get to] in our last lesson?／14ページの3行目まで進みました. We got (up) to page 14, line 3.／君は世間よりもずっと考えが進んでいる. You are way ahead of the times in your ideas.／私の時計は1日に2秒ずつ進みます. My watch gains two seconds a day.／彼らは進んで探検隊に加わった. They volunteered to join the expedition.／彼らの方が技術が我々より進んでいるかもしれない. They may be technologically further along than we are.／同級生が代数で四苦八苦している時に, 彼は高等数学に進んでしまっていた. He had gone on to higher math when his classmates were still struggling with basic algebra.
すすめ 医者の勧めで近頃ゴルフを始めた. On my doctor's advice I

すその 裾野 the skirts [the plains at the foot] of 《Mt. Fuji》.

スター a《movie》star ¶スターになる become a《movie》star; achieve stardom.

スタート a start;《口語》a getaway ¶スタートする start; make a start; get started / スタートがいい[悪い] start well [badly] / make a good [bad] start / スタートの合図 a starting signal / スタートを切る start; make a start; get off the mark / スタート係 a starter /《競泳の》スタート台 a starting box / スタートライン a starting line / スタートラインに立つ toe the line [mark].

スターリン Stalin ¶スターリン主義 Stalinism / 非スターリン化 de-Stalinization.

スタイル〈姿〉one's figure;〈様式・服装などの〉a《one's》style; a mode ¶スタイルブック a stylebook. 文例⇩

スタウト《ビール》stout.

すだく sing [chirp] together [in chorus].

スタグフレーション《経済》stagflation.

すたこら ¶すたこら逃げる take to one's heels; show a clean pair of heels 《to the enemy》; beat a hasty retreat; scamper [scurry] away《俗》beat it;《英俗》scarper.

スタジアム a stadium.

スタジオ a studio《pl. -s》;《米》a movie lot (映画の).

すたすた《walk》briskly; at a brisk pace; quickly;《文》in haste.

ずたずた ¶ずたずたに to pieces; into shreds / ずたずたに裂く tear sth to pieces [shreds, ribbons].

すだち 巣立ち ¶巣立ちする ⇨すだつ.

すだつ 巣立つ leave [fly from] the nest;〈社会に出る〉start (out) in life; go out into the world;〈独立する〉become independent; stand on one's own (two) feet.

スタッカート《音楽》¶スタッカートの[で] staccato.

スタッフ the staff ¶スタッフが足りない be short-staffed; be short of workers / スタッフのよく揃った well-staffed《laboratories》/ スタッフを入れ替える restaff. 文例⇩

ずだぶくろ 頭陀袋 a sack; a bag; a holdall.

スタミナ stamina (★英語では「精力」ではなく,「持久力」の意で使われる); staying power; strength ¶スタミナが切れる one's stamina runs out / スタミナをつける perk oneself up / give oneself new vigor [a lift] / スタミナ食 sustaining food.

すたる 廃る ⇨すたれる. 文例⇩

すだれ 簾 a reed screen; a bamboo [rattan] blind.

すたれる 廃れる go out of use; fall into disuse [《文》desuetude];〈言葉が〉become obsolete; die out;〈流行・習慣が〉go out of fashion [vogue, style]; be outmoded;〈古くさくなる〉be outdated; go out of date;〈廃止になる〉be done away with; be abolished;〈衰微する〉《文》decline; be on the decline [wane] ¶廃れた disused; out of fashion [date]; outmoded; antiquated; obsolete. 文例⇩

スタンス《野球・ゴルフ》a stance ¶スタンスを取る take one's stance / オープン[クロース]スタンス an open [a closed] stance.

スタンド〈観覧席〉the stands;《米》the bleachers (屋根なしの);〈ランプ〉a desk [bedside] lamp; a standard [floor] lamp (床に置く);〈売り場〉a《fruit》stand;《英》a stall ¶スタンドプレー a grandstand play / スタンドプレーをする play to the grandstand(s) [to the gallery].

スタントマン《映画》a stunt man.

スタンプ a stamp;〈日付印〉a datemark;〈郵便の消し印〉a postmark ¶スタンプを押す stamp; affix a stamp《on a card》/ 記念スタンプ a commemorative stamp / スタンプインク stamp ink.

スチーム〈蒸気〉steam;〈暖房〉steam [central] heating ¶スチームが通っている be steam-heated / スチーム暖房装置 a steam heater.

スチール¹《映画》a still (picture).

スチール²《野球》a steal ⇨とうるい¹.

スチール³〈鋼鉄〉steel ¶スチールギター a steel guitar.

スチュワーデス a stewardess; an air hostess.

スチロール《化》styrene ¶スチロール樹脂 polystyrene; styrene plastic.

-ずつ ¶少しずつ little by little / ひとり300円ずつ 300 yen each / (各人) 1 個ずつ与える give 《the boys》one each; give one to each / 1つずつ one by one; one at a time / 3人に1つずつ one to [among] every three persons / 毎週2度ずつ twice a week.

ずつう 頭痛 (a) headache ¶割れるような頭痛 a splitting [racking] headache / 少し[ひどく]頭痛がする have a slight [bad] headache / 頭痛の種 a cause [source] of anxiety [trouble]; a (real) headache《to one》; a worry; a thorn in the [one's] flesh / 頭痛を訴える complain of a headache / 頭痛を起こす get [《文》develop] a headache / 眠って頭痛を直す sleep off one's headache / 頭痛鉢巻である rack

---

took up golf recently.

すずめ すずめがさえずっている。Sparrows are chirping [twittering]. / すずめ百まで踊り忘れず. What is learned in the cradle is carried to the grave. | The child is father of the man.《諺》

すすめる² いやがるのを無理に勧めても仕方がない。It would be no use forcing it on him. / 彼は私に辛抱せよとしきりに勧めた.

He urged me to be patient. / 本日のおすすめは. 〈メニューに書いてある〉Chef's suggestions. | Today's special.

スタイル 彼女はスタイルがいい. She has a good [graceful] figure. / 彼はすらりとして, スタイルがよかった。He was tall and slim, with a good figure.

スタッフ 現在の20人というスタッフは1975年当時に比べてわずか

に3人ふえただけである。The present staff of 20 is only three more than in 1975.

すたる こんなことに一喜一憂していたんでは男がすたる. It should be beneath your dignity to trouble yourself over such trifles.

すたれる そんなスタイルはもう廃れた. That style is no longer in fashion [has gone out of fashion]. / 一時廃れてまたはやってき

すっからかん ¶すっからかんになる become (quite) penniless;《口語》go (stony) broke;《俗》be cleaned out.

すっかり all; quite; completely; utterly; thoroughly; entirely; perfectly;《文》in (its) entirety ¶すっかり準備を整える make all the preparations (for); be all set [ready] (for) / すっかり承知している know sth from A to Z / すっかり変わる change completely;《文》undergo a complete change.

すっきり ¶すっきりする〈気持ちが〉feel [be] refreshed; feel fine / すっきりした〈姿・形な〉neat; streamlined; clear-cut; elegant;〈文章など〉《文》lucid; clear / 非常にすっきりした形の式《文》a formula of great elegance. 文例⇩

ズック [く《オランダ語》doeck] canvas; duck ¶ズックの靴 canvas shoes.

すっくと ¶すっくと立ち上がる rise [jump, spring] to one's feet; rise to one's full height.

すづけ 酢漬け ¶酢漬けにする pickle sth (in vinegar).

ずっこける make a fool of oneself.

ずっしり ¶ずっしりした heavy (as lead); thick and heavy (本など).

すったもんだ ¶すったもんだのあげく after a lot of argument [fuss, quarreling] / すったもんだの騒ぎをする make a great fuss (about); kick up a row (with).

すってんころり ¶すってんころりと転ぶ fall plump. 文例⇩

すってんてん ¶すってんてんになる lose all one's money;《俗》be cleaned out;《俗》go clean broke.

すっと 〈真っ直ぐに〉straight;〈静かに〉quietly; gently; softly;〈素早く〉quickly; all of a sudden ¶胸がすっとする〈さっぱりする〉feel refreshed;〈満足する〉be pleased [satisfied] ((with, at));《文》be gratified (by) / すっと入る [出る] slip into [out of] (the room) / すっと着る [脱ぐ] slip (her dress) [on, off]; slip into [out of] (her dress). 文例⇩

ずっと 〈真っ直ぐ〉straight; direct;〈続けて〉all the time [way];《文》throughout; all along (the line);〈時〉for a long time;〈はるかに〉by far; far [out] and away;《口語》a sight ⇨ ずうっと ¶朝からずっと ever since morning / 10時からずっと all the time since 10 o'clock / ずっと以前に a long time [while] ago; long ago;〈ある出来事よりも〉long before (the event) / ずっと北下の方に a long way north [down] / ずっと遠くに far away; far in the distance. 文例⇩

すっとんきょう 素っ頓狂 ⇨ とんきょう.

すっぱい 酸っぱい sour; acid; tart ¶酸っぱい味がする taste sour / 酸っぱくなる go [turn] sour /《文》disclose; uncover; lay bare; reveal; unmask ¶人の秘密をすっぱ抜く betray [give away] sb's secrets.

すっぱだか 素っ裸 ¶素っ裸で stark-naked; in the nude; with nothing on.

すっぱぬき すっぱ抜き (an) exposure; (a) disclosure.

すっぱぬく すっぱ抜く give (a secret) away; expose;《文》disclose; uncover; lay bare; reveal; unmask ¶人の秘密をすっぱ抜く betray [give away] sb's secrets.

すっぱり ¶すっぱりと切る cut sth cleanly [with a single stroke] / すっぱりとやめる give up (smoking) once and for all.

すっぽかす ¶〈仕事を〉leave (a task) undone; neglect (one's duties);〈人を〉give sb the slip; let sb down ¶約束をすっぽかす break an appointment; cut an engagement;《口語》stand sb up (特にデートで). 文例⇩

すっぽぬける すっぽ抜ける come out suddenly (with a pop);〈野球で投手の投球が〉fly out of control (in the wrong direction) ¶すっぽ抜けたカーブ a hanging curve.

すっぽり entirely; clear; clean ¶すっぽりかぶせる cover (the cat's head) completely ((with a sack)) / 毛布にすっぽりくるまっている be snugly wrapped in a blanket.

すっぽん 《動》a soft-shelled turtle.

すで 素手 ¶素手で empty-handed; with empty hands;〈武器なしに〉with (one's) bare hands; barehanded; unarmed; (fight) with (one's) naked fists / 素手で魚を捕える catch a fish with one's bare hands / 素手で商売を始める start a business with practically no capital [《口語》from scratch,《口語》from

---

た. It went out for a time but it has now come back into fashion.

ずつう 一晩中ひどい頭痛で苦しみました. I suffered from a bad headache the whole night.

すっかり 彼女はもうすっかり大人になった. She has quite grown up. / すっかり夜が明けた. It is broad daylight now. / あの人にはすっかりごぶさたしています. I haven't been to see him for so long. / すっかり忘れていた. I'd clean forgotten it. / それには彼もすっかりびっくりしてしまった. It startled him no end. / すっかりお見限りですね. You are quite a stranger to me.

すっきり それはすっきりした答の出るような問題じゃない. It is not a question which has a neat and tidy answer [solution].

すってんころり すってんころりと転ばしてやった. I knocked him clean off his feet.

すっと 言いたいだけ言って気持ちがすっとした. I've said my say and I feel as if a load had been taken off my mind. / あー, すっとした. Ah, that's better. / はっかはすっとする. Peppermint is very refreshing.

ずっと ずっと以前から君には親しみを感じていた. I've always had an affection for you ever since I can remember. / この道をずっと行きますと駅に出ます. Go right down this street, and you'll come to the station. / (今まで)ずっと待っていたんですよ. I've been waiting all this while. / 熱海からずっと立ちん坊でした. I was kept standing all the way from Atami. / パリの方が東京よりずっと美しい. Paris is far more beautiful than Tokyo.

すっぱい そんなことはしてはいかんと口がすっぱくなるほど話してある. I have told him a thousand times not to do it.

すっぽかす 黙って行ってしまって

すていし 捨て石 《囲碁》a sacrifice ¶五目を捨て石にして先手をとる make a sacrifice of five stones to gain the initiative.

すてうり 捨て売り a sacrifice sale ¶捨て売りする sell at a sacrifice; sell dirt-cheap.

ステーキ (a) 《grilled》 steak; a beefsteak ¶ステーキハウス a steakhouse.

ステージ a stage ⇒ぶたい.

ステートメント a statement ¶ステートメントを発表する make [issue] a statement.

すておく 捨て置く 《放っておく》leave *sth* as *it* is [stands]; let [leave] *sb* alone; 《見逃す》⇒みのがす.

すてがね 捨て金 money thrown away; wasted money.

すてき ¶すてきな lovely 《主に女性用語》; 《俗》dreamy 《若い女性が使う》; 《美しい》beautiful; 《米》cute (かわいい); 《うれしい》《口語》great; 《口語》fantastic; 《英口語》marvelous; superb; splendid; 《俗》groovy; 《俗》cool; 《英俗》magic / すてきに fantastically; awfully; terrifically. 文例⇩

すてご 捨て子 《文》a foundling (拾った); an abandoned child ¶捨て子をする desert [abandon] *one's* child.

すてぜりふ 捨てぜりふ a parting shot [thrust] ¶捨てぜりふを言いながら with a parting shot. 文例⇩

ステッカー a sticker; a [an adhesive] label.

ステッキ a (walking) stick; a cane ⇒ つえ.

ステップ[1] a step; 《ダンスの》a step; 《バレーの》《フランス語》a *pas* (単複同形) 《★ 単数形は [pa:], 複数形は [pa:(z)] と発音する) ¶ステップを踏む dance; do [perform] dance steps.

ステップ[2] 《シベリアの草原》a steppe.

すててこ a type of men's underpants resembling loose Bermuda shorts.

すでに 《もはや》already; 《(not)》any longer; 《前に》previously; before ¶既に述べたように as previously stated. 文例⇩

すてね 捨て値 a giveaway price; 捨て値の dirt-cheap; ridiculously cheap / 捨て値で at a giveaway price; at a great sacrifice; far below cost; for a song.

すてば 捨て場 a dump 《for rubbish》; 《米》a garbage [《英》rubbish] dump; 《英》a (rubbish) tip ¶捨て場がない find no place to throw 《the rubbish》 into.

すてばち 捨て鉢 ¶捨て鉢な desperate; reckless / 捨て鉢になる be driven [abandon *oneself*] to despair; get [《文》become] desperate [reckless] / 捨て鉢になって in desperation; out of despair.

すてみ 捨て身 ¶捨て身で at the risk of *one's* life; in desperation / 捨て身になる get [《文》become] desperate; resort to *one's* last trick / 《背水の陣をしく》 burn *one's* boats [bridges] (behind *one*).

すてる 捨てる 《投げ捨てる》throw [fling, 《口語》chuck, 《文》cast] *sth* away; 《ごみなどを》dump; 《米口語》junk; 《放棄する》《文》renounce; 《文》relinquish; give up; discard; abandon; 《見捨てる》desert; leave; 《文》forsake; 《口語》throw over ¶命を捨てる 《文》 lay down *one's* life / 信仰を捨てる give up [renounce] *one's* faith / 世を捨てる renounce [forsake] the world. 文例⇩

ステレオ 《音響装置》a stereo (*pl.* -s); a stereo record player; stereophonic apparatus [equipment]; 《方式》the stereophonic sound (reproduction) system ¶ステレオで聞く listen 《to a recording of a symphony》on [in] stereo / ステレオ録音する make a stereo(phonic) recording of 《Strauss's *Salome*》; record (music) in stereo / ステレオ音響 stereo sound / ステレオテープ (a) stereotape / ブルーノ・ワルター指揮によるブラームスのステレオ盤 Brahms in stereo (conducted) by Bruno Walter / ステレオレコード a stereo(phonic) record [disc].

ステロイド 《生化》(a) steroid.

ステンドグラス stained glass.

ステンレス stainless steel.

スト a strike ⇒ストライキ ¶交通スト a traffic strike / スト規制法 an antistrike law; a strike regulation law / スト権 the right to strike / スト権を確立[行使]する 《文》establish [exercise] *one's* right to strike / スト破り a strikebreaker; 《口語》a scab; 《英口語》a blackleg. 文例⇩

ストア ¶ストア学派 the Stoic school; the Stoics / ストア学派の Stoic / ストア学派の人 a Stoic.

すてき 僕をあんなふうにすっぽかすなんて、ひどいよ君は. It was cruel of you to just walk away and leave me like that.

すてき パーティーはすてきに面白かった. We had a great time at the party. / あなた、その服装だとすてきだわ. You look great [How lovely you look] in that dress!

すてぜりふ 「今に覚えていろ」とその男は戸口のところで捨てぜりふを残して行った. As a parting shot, he called to me from the door: 'I warn you, you'll pay for this!'

すでに 時既に遅い. It is (already) too late. / 列車は既に出たあとだった. The train had already gone. / ダイヤはその時既にそこにはなかった. The diamond was gone by then. / その場所をたずねてみると、彼女は既にそこには住んでいなかった. I visited the place only to find her no longer living there. / この事が既に彼の無実を証明している. The very fact proves his innocence.

すてる 彼女は自分の命を捨てて子供を助けた. She saved her child at the cost of her own life. / その計画はいつでも捨てる用意がある. I'm quite ready to let this scheme go. / 名を揚げようという望みをきれいさっぱり捨ててしまった. He completely gave up all his hopes of making a name for himself. / それは金を捨てるようなものだ. It is a mere waste of money. / You might as well put your money down the drain. / まんざら捨てたものでもない. He is not altogether worthless. | 《物について》It may serve [answer] some purpose. / 捨てがたい風情がある. It is charming in its own way. / 捨てる神あれば助ける神あり. The world is as kind as it is cruel.

スト スト決行中. 《掲示》On Strike.

ストイック ¶ストイックな stoic(al).
すどおし 素通し ¶素通しの plain ((glass)); transparent ((glass doors)); unfrosted ((light bulbs)).
ストーブ a stove; a heater ¶ストーブをたく light a stove [heater]; make a fire (in the stove) / 薪(き)ストーブ a wood-burning stove / ストーブリーグ〘野球〙the trading of players in the off season. 文例

すどおり 素通り ¶素通りする pass through ((a place)) without stopping; pass ((sb's door)) without dropping in; pass by; bypass. 文例

ストール 〈肩掛け〉a ((fur)) stole ¶ストールをまとう put a stole around one's shoulders.
ストッキング ((a pair of)) stockings ¶ひざまでのストッキング knee-length stockings.
ストック¹〈在庫品〉(a) stock ¶ストックがある[ない]〈品物が主語〉be in [out of] stock;〈人が主語〉have ((some, one, etc.)) [have no more] in stock.
ストック² 〈<(ドイツ語) Stock〉〈スキーの〉a (ski) stick [pole].
ストックホルム Stockholm.
ストップ a stop ¶ストップする stop / ストップをかける call a halt to 〘((a)) moratorium on〙 ((nuclear tests)); put a stop to ((the experiment));〈トランプで〉call a halt / ストップモーション〘映画〙a freeze-frame / 〈自動車の〉ストップライト a stoplight; a brake light.
ストップウオッチ ((start)) a stop watch.
すどまり 素泊まり (a) bed without meals [board]; staying overnight [a night's stay] without meals [board].
ストライキ a strike; a walkout ¶ストライキをする go [come out] on strike; have [((文)) conduct] a strike; walk out / ストライキ中である be on strike / ストライキを中止する halt [call off] a strike. 文例

ストライク 〘野球〙a strike ¶高め[低め]いっぱいのストライク a strike at the letters [knees] / カウントノーストライク, スリーボールの時のバッター a batter with three balls and no strikes on him / ストライクをとる score a strike / ストライクゾーン ((pass through)) the strike zone. 文例

ストラックアウト 〘野球〙a strikeout ¶ストラックアウトにする strike ((the batter)) out / ストラックアウトになる be [get] struck out.
ずどり 図取り ¶図取りする draw a plan; sketch.
ストリキニーネ 〘薬〙strychnine.
ストリッパー a stripper.
ストリップ (a) striptease; a strip show ¶ストリップ劇場 a strip(-show) theater.
ストレート 〘ボクシング〙((give)) a straight (punch) ¶ストレートで勝つ win a straight victory ((over)); whitewash ((one's opponent)) / ストレートで負ける suffer a straight defeat ((from)); be whitewashed ((by)).
ストレス stress ¶ストレスがたまる stress builds up / ストレスの多い ((文)) stressful ((situations)) / ストレスを解消する get rid of stress ((by playing go)) / ストレス学説 the theory of stress / ストレス病 a stress disease.
ストレプトマイシン 〘薬〙streptomycin.
ストロー a (drinking) straw; ((米口語)) a sipper (紙製の) ¶ストローで ((suck lemonade)) through a straw.
ストローク a stroke ¶ワンストロークの差で勝つ win ((a competition)) by one stroke.
ストロボ 〘写真〙a stroboscope; a strobe ¶ストロボ電球 a strobe (light); a stroboscopic lamp.
ストロンチウム 〘化〙strontium.
ずどん 〈銃声〉a bang ¶ずどんと with a bang.
すとんと with a thump [thud, plump] ¶すとんと落ちる fall plump.
すな 砂 sand; grit (粗い); a grain of sand (1粒) ¶砂の多い sandy / 砂で磨く sand ((a metal bar)) / 砂遊び playing with [in the] sand / 砂遊びをする play in the sand / 〈動物の〉砂浴び a dust bath; dust bathing / 砂浴びする have a dust bath; bathe in dust / 砂嵐 a sandstorm / 砂地 a sandy place;〈土壌〉sandy soil / 砂時計 a sandglass; an hourglass; an egg timer (ゆで玉子用) / 砂場 (play in) a sandbox [((英)) a sandpit] / 砂浜 a sandy beach; the sands / 砂原 a sandy plain;((文)) the sands /〈鳥の〉砂袋 a gizzard / 砂風呂 a sand bath / 砂ぼこり〈煙〉((raise)) a cloud of dust / 砂まじりの風 a sand-laden wind / 砂山 a sand hill [mound]; a dune (砂丘).
すなお 素直 ¶素直な〈従順な〉obedient; ((文)) submissive; tame; ((文)) tractable; docile; unprotesting;〈温和な〉gentle; mild; meek / 素直に obediently; without protesting; meekly / 素直に意見をきく accept sb's advice at once [without argument] / 素直に白状する confess ((to sth)) frankly [with (a) good grace).
すなかぶり 砂かぶり 〘相撲〙a ringside seat.
スナック 〈軽食〉((have, eat)) a snack ¶スナックバー a snack bar [counter, stand].
スナッチ 〘重量挙げ〙the snatch (lift) ¶スナッチで120キロ挙げる lift 120 kilograms in the snatch.
スナップ 〈服の〉((米)) a snap fastener; ((英)) a press stud; 〈写真〉a snapshot ¶スナップ写真を撮る take a snapshot ((of)); snap ((the scenery)).
すなわち 即ち〈つまり〉((文)) namely; or; that

ストーブ ストーブが消えている. The stove is out.
すどおり 名古屋を素通りで大阪へ直行した. I went straight to Osaka without stopping (off) [breaking my journey] at Nagoya.
ストライキ O社のストライキは既に3か月近く続いている. The strike at the O Company has been on for nearly three months.
ストライク カウントはワンストライク, ツーボール. The (batter's) count is two balls, one strike.
ずどん ずどんと鉄砲が鳴った. Bang! went the gun. | The gun went off with a bang.
すな 目に砂が入った. I have got some [a few grains of] sand in my eye. / もうもうと砂ぼこりが立っていた. The air was full of flying grit. / 机に砂ぼこりがたまっていた. The desk was covered with grit.

is (to say);《文》viz. (*videlicet* の略);《文》i.e. (*id est* の略);〈まさしく〉just; precisely; exactly;〈取りも直さず〉nothing but; neither more nor less. [文例⇩]

[用法] 日本語の文章では, 先行の文を受けて,「すなわち」と新しい文を始めることがよくあるが, これを英語にしようとすると, かえって不自然な英文になることが多い. 英語ではこういう場合単刀直入に本論に入る. 例:「before は使い方が3つある. すなわち, 前置詞, 副詞, 接続詞として用いられる」*Before* can be used in three ways:—as preposition, adverb and conjunction.

ずぬけて 図抜けて ⇨ ずばぬけて.

すね 脛 the leg; the shank (★ 今でも馬について使うが, 人体に関しては古語); the shin (向こうずね) ¶ 親のすねをかじる sponge on [live off, be dependent on] *one's* parents / すねに傷持つ人 a person with a guilty conscience / すね当て leggings;〈競技用の〉shin guards; shin-pads.

すねる get [be,《文》become] sulky [peevish]; pout; sulk ¶ 世をすねる ⇨ よ[1] / すね者 a cross-grained fellow; a cynic (皮肉屋);《文》a misanthrope (人間嫌い);《文》a malcontent (不平家).

ずのう 頭脳 a head; brains ¶ 頭脳明晰である have a clear head; be clear-headed; be bright; have a brilliant [sharp] mind / 人工頭脳 a mechanical brain / 頭脳集団 a think tank [factory] / 頭脳線〘手相〙the line of Head / 頭脳流出 a brain drain / 頭脳労働[労働者] brainwork [a brainworker].

すのこ 簀の子〈台所の〉《米》a slatted drainboard [《英》draining board];〈風呂場などの〉duckboards.

スパーク a spark ¶ スパークする spark.

スパート 〘競技〙a spurt ¶ スパートする spurt; make [put on] a spurt; kick《for the line》. [文例⇩]

スパーリング 〘ボクシング〙sparring ¶ スパーリングパートナー *one's* sparring partner.

スパイ a spy; an [a secret] agent; an informer (密告者);《俗》a rat (仲間を裏切る) ¶ スパイする spy《into, on》; act as spy; spy out (探り出す) / スパイをつける set a spy on *sb* / 二重スパイ a double agent / スパイ映画[小説] a spy [an espionage] movie [novel] / スパイ活動[行為] spying;《文》espionage / スパイ飛行 aerial spying; a spy [an espionage] flight / スパイ団 a spy ring / スパイ網 an espionage chain; a network of spies / スパイ任務を帯びて on a spy mission.

スパイク 〈靴の金具〉a spike;〘バレーボール〙spiking; a spike ¶ スパイクする spike *sb*; injure *sb* with the spikes of *one's* shoes;〘バレーボール〙spike (the ball) / スパイク靴 spiked [track] shoes; spikes.

スパゲッティ spaghetti ¶ スパゲッティナポリタン spaghetti Napolitana / スパゲッティミートソース spaghetti with meat sauce; spaghetti Bolognese.

すばこ 巣箱 a nest [nesting] box;〈みつばちの〉a beehive.

すばし(っ)こい 〈動作が〉nimble; quick;《文》agile;〈性質が〉quick-witted; shrewd; sharp; smart ¶ すばしこく nimbly; quickly.

すぱすぱ ¶ すぱすぱ吸う puff (away)《at *one's* cigarette》.

ずばずば ¶ ずばずばやる be aggressive; act without worrying about other people's feelings / ずばずば言う say《what *one* feels》plainly [bluntly, without mincing (*one's*) words]; talk [speak] in plain language.

すはだ 素肌 bare skin ¶ 素肌につける wear《*one's* shirt》next to *one's* [the] skin / 素肌を見せる strip [《文》bare *oneself*]《to the waist》.

スパッツ 〈登山用などの〉spats.

スパナ 《米》a wrench;《英》a spanner ¶ 自在スパナ ⇨ じざい.

ずばぬけて ずば抜けて by far; far [out] and away;《口語》by miles;《文》preeminently;《文》exceptionally. [文例⇩]

すばやい nimble; quick;《文》agile ¶ すばやく quickly; swiftly; nimbly; quick as thought.

すばらしい wonderful; marvelous; magnificent; splendid; superb;《口語》fantastic;《口語》great;《口語》fabulous;《口語》terrific;《米口語》swell;《英俗》magic;〈めざましい〉outstanding; phenomenal; fantastic; amazing ¶ すばらしい景気 a great boom / すばらしい大成功 a phenomenal [dazzling] success / すばらしく marvelously; splendidly;〈非常に〉immensely; wonderfully;《口語》awfully. [文例⇩]

ずばり ¶ ずばりと〈思い切って〉《文》decisively;《文》decidedly; once and for all;〈はっきりと〉《文》unreservedly; frankly; (straight) from the shoulder / ずばりと言う say frankly; speak out; be outspoken; come directly to the point [the heart of the matter]; do not mince matters《in》;《口語》tell *sb* straight《that ...》/ ずばり言い当てる hit it [the mark]; guess right. [文例⇩]

すばる 昴〘天〙the Pleiades.

スパルタ Sparta ¶ スパルタ人 a Spartan / スパルタ(式)の Spartan《education》.

ずはん 図版 a plate; a figure; an illustration.

スピーカー a (loud)speaker ¶ スピーカーで呼び出す call *sb* over the loudspeaker [over the P.A.] ★ P.A. は public-address system の略.

スピード speed ¶ スピードを出す[上げる]

すなわち 議会は2院, すなわち参議院と衆議院より成る. The Diet consists of two Houses, namely the House of Councilors and the House of Representatives. / $NaHCO_3$ は重炭酸ソーダ, すなわちいわゆる重曹のことである. $NaHCO_3$ stands for sodium bicarbonate, or 'bicarb' as it is commonly called.

スパート ホームストレッチにかかるところで彼は猛然スパートしてトップに出た. He burst into the lead when he came around the curve into the homestretch.

ずばぬけて 彼はクラスでずば抜けてよく出来た. He was by far the best student in the class.

すばらしい すばらしいお天気ですなあ. What glorious weather! / 彼はすばらしく元気だった. He was in the highest of spirits.

ずばり 正にそのものずばりです. You've hit the mark! | That's

スピッツ

speed up; gather [get up, put on, pick up] speed; accelerate; 《文》increase the [one's] speed; 《口語》step on it / 時速300キロのスピードを出す get up to [develop] (a speed of) 300 kilometers an hour / スピードを落とす slow down / 《文》reduce [decrease] the [one's] speed / スピードを落として at reduced [lower, slower] speed / もっとスピードを出せと言う ask [tell] (the driver) to drive faster / スピードアップ speeding up; a speedup / スピードアップする speed up / 《文》expedite (the proceedings) / ものすごいスピードで at a terrific [furious, breakneck] speed / スピード違反をする break [go over, 《文》exceed] the speed limit / スピード違反で捕まる be caught speeding [going over the speed limit] / スピード違反者 a person guilty of exceeding the speed limit; a speeder / スピード違反取締まり警官 《俗》a speed-cop / スピード狂 a speed maniac [fiend, demon] / スピード検挙 a lightning arrest [roundup] / スピード時代 the age of speed.

スピッツ a spitz.

ずひょう 図表 a chart; a diagram; a graph ¶図表にする[で表わす] chart; put (figures) into the form of a diagram [graph]; represent (the trends) by a chart.

ずぶ ¶ずぶの utter; sheer ⇒まったく(全くの).

スフィンクス a sphinx.

スプートニク a sputnik.

スプール a (film) spool.

スプーン a spoon ¶スプーン1杯の砂糖 a spoonful of sugar / スプーンレース an egg-and-spoon race.

すぶた 酢豚 sweet-and-sour pork.

ずぶとい 図太い ⇒ずうずうしい.

ずぶぬれ ずぶ濡れ ¶ずぶぬれになる get wet [get soaked, be drenched] to the skin; get wet through; get dripping wet.

すぶり 素振り a practice swing;〈木刀・ゴルフなど〉a practice stroke ¶素振りをする swing (one's bat); practice one's swing; do a practice swing; cut the air 《with one's sword》. 文例⇩

ずぶり ¶ずぶりと刺す stab sb through; 《文》plunge (a knife into sb's breast); 《文》thrust (a dagger) home (into sb's chest) / ずぶりと針を刺す stick a needle (right into the skin).

スプリング 〈ばね〉a spring ¶スプリングコート a light overcoat; a topcoat / スプリングボード〈水泳〉a springboard.

スプリンクラー a (water) sprinkler.

スプリンター a sprinter.

スプレー 《hair》spray ¶スプレーの缶 a spray (can).

スプロール ¶(都市の)スプロール現象 urban sprawl.

すべ 術 《文》a means 《単複同形》; a way; how to do ¶施すすべを知らない be at a loss (as to) what to do; be at one's wits' end. 文例⇩

スペア a spare ¶スペアタイヤ a spare tire.

スペイン Spain ¶スペインの Spanish / スペイン語 Spanish / スペイン人 a Spaniard;〈総称〉the Spanish (people).

スペース (a) space; room ¶スペースを置く space (out) 《letters, words》/ スペースシャトル a space shuttle.

スペード 〈トランプ〉a spade ¶スペードのクイーン the queen of spades.

スペクタクル a spectacle ¶スペクタクル映画 a spectacular film.

スペクトル a spectrum 《pl. -tra, -s》¶太陽[音響, 線]スペクトル a solar [sound, line] spectrum / スペクトルグラフ a spectrograph / スペクトル写真 a spectrogram / スペクトル分析 (a) spectroscopic analysis.

すべすべ ¶すべすべした smooth; velvety; silky; sleek 《髪・毛皮など》.

すべっこい 滑っこい ⇒すべすべ.

すべて all; everything;〈全然〉all;《文》wholly; entirely; altogether ¶すべての all;《文》entire; whole; (each and) every / すべての点で in every way [《文》respect]; in all points / おのれのすべてをささげる devote [offer, give] oneself [one's self] entirely (to). 文例⇩

すべらす 滑らす let sth slip ¶足を滑らす miss one's footing; slip / 口を滑らす blurt out; come out with (a secret) inadvertently. 文例⇩

すべり 滑り sliding; slipping; a slide; a slip.

すべりおちる 滑り落ちる slip down (the stairs); slip off (the bed).

すべりこみ 滑り込み 《野球》sliding.

すべりこむ 滑り込む 《野球》slide (into second base);〈やっと間に合う〉arrive barely [only just] in time.

すべりだい 滑り台 a (playground) slide.

すべりだし 滑り出し ¶滑り出しがいい make a good start;《文》make a favorable beginning; get off to a good start / 滑り出しが悪い make a bad start; make an unpromising beginning. 文例⇩

すべりどめ 滑り止め a device to prevent slipping [skidding];〈靴の底に付ける〉creepers; cleats ¶滑り止めのしてある nonskid [skidproof] 《tires》/ 滑り止めにT大学を受験する take the entrance exam to T University as a safety measure [as an insurance (against failure at all the other universities)].

すべる 滑る slide; glide; skate 《スケートで》;〈つるつるする〉be slippery;〈足が〉slip ¶バ

---

the very thing! | That's exactly it! / ずばり言えよ. Stop beating [Don't beat] about the bush!

ずぶぬれ 雨でずぶぬれになった. We were wet through from the rain. / ずぶぬれだ. He hasn't got a dry thread on him.

すぶり 彼は素振りを何回かバッターボックスに入った. He entered the batter's box after (doing) a few practice swings.

すべもはやなすすべもない. There is nothing that can be done. | It's all up with [all over for] me.

すべて すべての点で彼がまさっている. He is better in all respects. / それが人生のすべてではない. That is not everything in life. / 彼女にとってはひとり息子がすべてであった. Her only son was everything to her.

すべらす ついうっかり口を滑らせてしまった. The word slipped out of my mouth.

ナナの皮を踏んで滑る slip on a banana skin / 試験に失敗する 《米口語》flunk] an examination / 滑るように glidingly / 滑って転ぶ slip and fall. 文例⇩

ずほう 図法 drawing; draftsmanship.

スポーク 〈車輪の〉a spoke ¶スポークのついた車輪 a spoked wheel.

スポークスマン a spokesman ((for, of)); a mouthpiece ((for, of)).

スポーツ sports; 〈その一つ〉a sport ¶何かスポーツをやる take up a sport / 見る[自分でやる]スポーツ a spectator [participant] sport / スポーツ医学 sports medicine / スポーツカー a sports car / スポーツ界 the sporting world / スポーツ活動〈go in for〉sporting activities / スポーツ着 sportswear; sports clothes / スポーツ雑誌 sports magazine / スポーツ新聞 a sport(s) paper [journal] / スポーツ精神 sportsmanship; (the) sporting spirit / スポーツニュース sports news / スポーツ評論家 a sports columnist / スポーツ放送 sportscasting; a sportscast / スポーツマン a sportsman; an athlete / スポーツマンらしい[らしくない] sportsmanlike [unsportsmanlike] / スポーツ用品 sporting goods / スポーツライター a sportswriter / スポーツ欄 a sports section [column].

スポーティ ¶スポーティな sporty.

ずぼし 図星 ¶図星を指す hit the mark; guess right; hit the nail on the head. 文例⇩

スポット ¶スポットニュース a news flash / スポット放送 a spot announcement / スポットライト a spotlight / スポットライトを当てる direct [turn] a spotlight on; spotlight.

すぼまる, すぼむ get [grow,《文》become] narrower; narrow ((into a strait)); contract ¶先がすぼまる taper off.

すぼめる make sth narrower;〈閉じる〉shut [fold] ((one's umbrella));〈肩をすぼめる〉shrug one's shoulders / 口をすぼめる pucker up one's mouth; purse (up) one's lips.

ずぼら ¶ずぼらな sloppy; slovenly;《文》negligent; slipshod / ずぼらな人 a slovenly person / ずぼらにやる do sth sloppily [in a sloppy way].

すぽん pop ¶すぽんと抜ける come out with a pop; pop out.

ズボン [〈《フランス語》jupon]《a pair of》trousers;《米》pants; slacks〈上着と対でない、緩いもの〉¶たっぷりした[細い]ズボン full [narrow] trousers / ズボンの脚 a trouser [pants] leg / ズボンのポケット a trouser(s) pocket / 〈前側の小さな〉a fob (pocket); 〈後側の〉a hip pocket / ズボンの前ボタン[ファスナー] a fly button [fastener] / ズボンのすその折り返し《米》

the cuffs [《英》the turn-ups] on trousers / ズボンをまくり上げる roll up one's trouser legs / ズボンに折り目をつける put a crease in one's trousers / 半ズボン ⇨はんズボン / ズボン下 undershorts;《商標名》《米》BVD's / ズボンつり《米》suspenders;《英》braces.

スポンサー 〈商業放送の〉a sponsor ¶スポンサーのついている sponsored 〈programs〉/ スポンサー[共同スポンサー]になる sponsor [cosponsor] 〈a TV program〉/ …のスポンサーになって下さいと頼む ask sb to sponsor…;《文》solicit sb's sponsorship for….

スポンジ (a) sponge ¶スポンジケーキ (a) sponge cake / スポンジゴム sponge rubber / スポンジボール a sponge ball.

スマート ¶スマートな〈肥満していない〉slim;《文》well-proportioned;〈くしゃれている〉smart; stylish; chic 〈女性についてしか使わない〉 ★smart には「肥満していない」の意味は全くない。文例⇩

すまい 住まい《文》a dwelling; a house;《文》a residence; a home; one's (home) address 〈所番地〉;〈居住すること〉living; life ¶住まいを定める settle ((in Tokyo));《文》take up residence ((in));《文》make [take up] one's abode; have [make] one's home. 文例⇩

すましじる 澄まし汁 clear soup.

すましや 澄まし屋 a smug(-looking) [an affected] person; a prude; a prim-looking girl.

すます[1] 済ます 〈片付ける〉finish; get [be] through with; get sth over (with); settle ;《文》conclude;〈払う、返す〉repay; pay back; clear;〈…で間に合わせる〉make do with sth ¶…なしですます do [manage, get along] without sth;《文》dispense with sth. 文例⇩

すます[2] 澄ます〈汁を〉clear; make clear; clarify ((cooking oil));〈動じない〉be [《文》remain] unruffled; look unconcerned [《文》nonchalant];〈まじめな顔をする〉look demure [grave]; look prim 〈女性が〉; keep a straight face [one's face straight]〈笑いをこらえて〉;〈知らん振りをする〉play the innocent;《文》affect [feign] ignorance [indifference];〈気取る〉be affected; put on airs ¶澄ました顔をして〈平気で〉with an indifferent [unconcerned] air;《文》composedly;《文》with composure;〈まじめくさって〉with a straight [serious] face;〈女性が〉prudishly; primly / つんと澄まして with one's nose in the air.

スマッシュ 〈球型〉a smash; smashing; an overhead (smash) ¶スマッシュする a smash (the ball).

スマトラ Sumatra ¶スマトラの Sumatran.

すまない 済まない ¶すまない(と思う) be [feel] sorry ((for)); regret; have no excuse ((for));

すべりだし 彼は大使として上乗の滑り出しである。He is off to a fine start as Ambassador.

すべる 凍った道が滑って危ない。The frozen street is slippery and dangerous to walk on.

ずぼし 図星だ。You've hit it! | You said it!

スマート きみはずいぶんスマートになったじゃないか。You've got quite slim, haven't you?

すまい お住まいはどちらですか。Where do you live? | What is your address, please?

すます[1] この辞書がなくては一日もすまされない。I cannot spare [do without] this dictionary even for a single day. / 忙しくて昼飯なしですませばならなかった。I was so busy that I had to go without lunch. / 卒業論文を他人の著書からのつぎはぎ細工ですますわけにはいかない。One cannot get away with a patch-

be conscience-stricken;《文》be penitent [contrite] (for).

すみ¹ 炭 charcoal ¶炭をつぐ put more charcoal 《on the fire》; feed 《the fire》 with charcoal / 炭を焼く burn charcoal / 炭になる be charred / 炭俵 a charcoal sack / 炭取り a charcoal scuttle / 炭火 (a) charcoal fire / 炭火をおこす make [build] a fire with charcoal / 炭屋 a charcoal dealer / 炭焼き〈人〉a charcoal burner / 魚の炭焼き〈料理〉charcoal-broiled [charbroiled] fish / 炭焼き窯 a charcoal kiln.

すみ² 済み〈書類などの分類表示〉Finished (完了); Settled (決裁ずみ); O.K.'d.

すみ³ 隅 a corner; 《文》a nook ¶隅に in a corner / 隅々まで in every corner 《of》; all over 《the world》 / 世界の隅々から from the four corners of the world [earth].

すみ⁴ 墨〈汁〉India(n) ink; Chinese ink;〈固形〉 sumi; an ink stick; an ink-cake ¶墨をする grind an ink-cake / 墨をたっぷり含ませた筆 an ink-filled [《文》ink-laden] brush /〈いかが〉墨を吹く spurt ink / 墨入れ《製図》inking / 墨入れする ink in [over] / 墨絵 (a) sumie; an Indian-ink drawing; a black-and-white painting / 墨染めの衣 a (Buddhist priest's) black robe / 墨つぼ《大工》an [a carpenter's] ink pad;〈墨汁入れ〉an inkpot; an ink bottle / 墨縄 an [a carpenter's] inking line [string].

すみか 住み処〈住居〉⇒ すまい;〈巣窟〉a den 《of criminals, of foxes》.

すみごこち 住み心地 ¶住み心地のいい comfortable (to live in); snug.

すみこみ 住み込み ¶住み込みの家政婦 a resident [live-in] housekeeper / 住み込みの口を見つける get a living-in position;《文》obtain a resident post. 文例⇩

すみこむ 住み込む live in (with *one's* employer); live with 《a family》.

すみつく 住み着く settle (in a place).

すみっこ 隅っこ ⇒ すみ³.

すみなれる 住み慣れる〈長く住む〉live (in the neighborhood) (for) a long time;〈住んで慣れる〉get used to 《a place》 ¶住み慣れた家 *one's* dear old house [home] / 住み慣れた土地 a place where *one* has lived for a long time. 文例⇩

すみやか 速やか ¶速やかな《文》rapid;《文》swift; speedy;《文》prompt; quick; fast; immediate / 速やかに promptly; speedily; immediately; at once; without delay;《米》in short order / 速やかに返事をする《文》make a prompt reply.

すみれ 菫《植》a violet ¶三色すみれ a pansy / すみれ色(の) violet.

すみわたる 澄み渡る be perfectly clear; clear up ¶澄み渡った空 a clear [《文》an azure] sky.

すむ¹ 住む live (in, at);《文》dwell [reside] (in, at); inhabit 《a place》 ¶人の住んでいない家 an unoccupied [untenanted] house; a vacant [deserted] house / 住むに適した〈適さない〉inhabitable [uninhabitable]; fit [unfit] to live in; livable [unlivable] / 住む家もない be homeless; have nowhere to live; have no house to live in / 大勢の人の住んでいる[あまり人の住んでいない]地方 a densely-[sparsely-]populated district; thickly-[thinly-]peopled country. 文例⇩

すむ² 済む〈終わる〉end; come to [be brought to] an end [《文》a close,《文》a conclusion]; be settled; be [get] finished; be over [done];〈なくてすませる〉do [manage, get along] without *sth*;《文》dispense with *sth*; can spare *sth* ¶しないですむ need not *do* / 無事に come off without a hitch; pass off quietly / すみませんが I'm sorry to trouble you, but...; Excuse me, but.... 文例⇩

すむ³ 澄む become clear; clear ¶澄んだ clear; transparent;《文》lucid;《文》limpid;《文》crystal / 青く澄んだ水 the clear-blue water / (月が)澄んでいる shine bright(ly) / 澄み切った心境で《文》with a serene mind; serenely. 文例⇩

スムーズ smooth ¶スムーズに smoothly; without a hitch [hindrance].

スメール ⇒ シュメール.

ずめん 図面 a drawing; a map;〈設計図〉a plan; a blueprint (青写真) ¶図面を引く draw a plan.

すもう 相撲 *sumo* (wrestling) ¶相撲を取る wrestle 《with》 / 相撲を見に行く go to watch *sumo* (wrestling) / 相撲にならない be no match 《for》; cannot be mentioned in the same

---

work of extracts from books for one's graduation thesis.
すまない 君にすまない事をした。I am sorry I have done you wrong. / すまないが, 水を1杯。A glass [Give me a glass] of water, please. / すまないがこの手紙をポストに入れてくれないか。May I trouble you to post this letter for me? | Do you mind posting this letter for me? | これを僕にくれるの, すまないね。This is for me? How kind [nice] of you! / すむもすまないもないじゃないか, 2人の中で。There is no need for apologies between us, is

there? / 忘れていたではすまないよ。To say 'I forgot it' will be no excuse.
すみ³ 僕はこの辺は隅から隅までよく知っている。I know every inch of this neighborhood. / 君はなかなか隅に置けないね。You are a smart [knowing] fellow.
すみこみ 今の給料は住み込みで月12万円です。My present wage is 120,000 yen a month (and) all found.
すみなれる 彼は長年住み慣れたおじの家を出た。He left his uncle's house which had been his home for many years. / 長年住み慣れた

家を手放すのはつらかった。It was hard for me to give up the house where I had lived for so long.
すむ¹ 人の住んでいる気配がなかった。There was no sign of human habitation. / 金持ちでなければこのあたりには住めないよ。You have to be a rich man to live in this area. / 住めば都。Home is where you make it. | You [One] can get used to [can come to like] living anywhere.
すむ² 試験がすむまで帰省できない。I cannot go home till after the examination. / すんだら私に

スモッグ / スリッパ

スモッグ smog ¶スモッグのかかった smoggy / スモッグに包まれた smog-bound 《Los Angeles》.

すもも 李 a Japanese plum; a plum (西洋すもも); a prune (干した).

スモンびょう スモン病 〖医〗SMON disease ★SMON は subacute myelo-optico-neuropathy の略.

すやき 素焼き unglazed pottery; biscuit (ware); bisque ¶素焼きの unglazed.

すやすや すやすやと眠る sleep peacefully [calmly]; sleep a peaceful [sound] sleep.

-すら ⇨ さえ².

スライダー 〖野球〗a slider.

スライディング 〖野球〗sliding ⇨ すべりこみ.

スライド a (photographic) slide; a filmstrip (フィルム状の); a transparency; 〈顕微鏡の〉a slide ¶スライドを映す show slides; project a slide on a screen / スライドを使って講演する illustrate a lecture with slides / カラースライド a color slide [transparency] / スライド映写機 a slide [filmstrip] projector / スライド制〈賃金などの〉indexing; indexation; index-linking; a sliding scale system.

ずらかる run away; escape; make one's escape [getaway]; 〈文〉flee; 〈文〉fly; 〈口語〉beat it; 〈米口語〉hightail (it); 〈俗〉skedaddle ¶早いとこずらかる make a quick getaway.

ずらす shift; move; 〈ずり落とす〉work down 《one's trousers》; 〈時間などを〉stagger 《office hours》. 文例⇩

すらすら 〈順調に〉smoothly; without a hitch; 〈文〉without let or hindrance; 〈よどみなく〉fluently; 〈容易に〉〈文〉with facility [ease]; easily ¶すらすら答える answer without hesitating. 文例⇩

スラックス slacks.

スラブ ¶スラブ語[の] Slavic; Slavonic / スラブ人 a Slav / スラブ民族 the Slavs.

スラム a slum ¶スラム街 slums; slum areas / スラムの一掃 slum clearance.

すらりと smoothly; without trouble [a hitch] ¶すらりとした slender; slim; 〈文〉svelte.

ずらりと in a row [line]. 文例⇩

スラローム 〖スキー〗the slalom.

スラング a slang word [expression]; 〈総称〉slang.

スランプ a slump; a (sudden) loss of form (スポーツ選手などの) ¶スランプに陥る hit [be in] a slump; lose form; cannot get down to one's work (受験勉強などの) / スランプから抜け出る come out of a slump; come back into form; recover one's form; get back into the mood for work.

すり¹ 刷り ⇨ いんさつ ¶刷りがいい[悪い] be well [badly] printed.

すり² 掏摸 a pickpocket ¶すりの集団 a gang of pickpockets / すりを働く pick sb's pocket / すりにやられる have one's pocket picked. 文例⇩

すりあがり 刷り上がり completion of printing ¶刷り上がりがいい[悪い] be well [badly] printed.

すりあがる 刷り上がる be off (the) press; be printed off ¶刷り上がったばかりの wet from [just off] the press(es).

すりあげる 刷り上げる finish printing; print [run] off 《3,000 copies》.

すりあし 摺り足 ¶すり足で歩く shuffle (along); slide one's feet (along).

すりえ 摺り餌 ground feed [food] 《for a bird》.

ずりおちる[さがる] ずり落ちる[下がる] slide [slip, glide] down. 文例⇩

すりかえる 摺り替える secretly change [《文》substitute] 《A for B》; 〈口語〉switch.

すりガラス 磨りガラス frosted [ground] glass.

すりきず 擦り傷 a graze; a scratch; 〖医〗an abrasion.

すりきれる 擦り切れる wear [be worn] out [off]; get [〈文〉become] threadbare ¶擦り切れた worn-out; threadbare / ヘリの擦り切れたカラー a frayed collar. 文例⇩

すりくだく 磨り砕く grind sth down [up]; rub sth fine [into powder]; bray.

すりこぎ 摺り粉木 a wooden pestle ¶すりこぎでする grind [bray] with a wooden pestle / (地球などの)すりこぎ運動 precession / すりこぎ運動をする precess.

すりこむ 擦り込む rub in [into].

すりたて 刷り立て ¶刷り立ての just off the press; wet [fresh] from the press.

スリッパ 《a pair of》(backless) slippers ★英

回して下さい. Pass it to me when you have done with it. / 金ですむことなら幾らでも出す. What's done is done [cannot be undone]. / そうすれば, わざわざ出なおさなくてすみます. It would save you the trouble of coming here again. / 罰金ですませて貰う. We let sb off with a fine. / 一言わびればすんだものを. One word of apology from you would have settled the matter. | If you had only said you were sorry first, there would have been none of this trouble. / お待たせしてすみませんでした. I am sorry to have kept you waiting. / 遅れてすみません. Excuse me for being [coming so] late.

すむ³ 水は底まで澄んでいる. The water is clear to the bottom.

すもう 相撲に勝って勝負に負けた. He was the better wrestler but lost the bout.

ずらす 僕は椅子を少しずつ後ろにずらして, 彼が拳骨を飛ばして来ても届かないようにした. I pushed my chair back far enough to be out of reach of his fist.

すらすら 彼女はすらすらと見事に全問題を解いた. She solved all the problems with such beautiful ease.

ずらりと 自動車がずらりと並んでいた. There was an array of motorcars. / 沿道には警官がずらりと並んでいた. The route was lined with policemen.

すり² すりにご用心. 〖掲示〗Beware of pickpockets.

ずりおちる 赤ちゃんのおむつは, ひざまでずり落ちていた. The baby's diapers had dragged down to its knees.

すりきれる じゅうたんが擦り切れ

スリップ 語の slippers は室内用の軽いヒールをつけてない靴.

スリップ 〈滑ること〉a slip; a skid (自動車の); 〈婦人の下着〉a slip; an underskirt (ウエストより下の). ¶スリップする slip; skid (横滑りする).

すりつぶす 磨り潰す〈砕く〉grind down; mash (potatoes) 〈磨滅させる〉rub out; deface (硬貨の面などを); 〈身代を〉run through 〔《文》dissipate〕《one's》fortune).

スリナム Suriname. ¶スリナム共和国 the Republic of Suriname.

すりぬける 擦り抜ける slip 〔get, manage to pass〕through; make *one's* way through 《the crowd》quickly.

すりばち 擂り鉢 an earthenware mortar ¶すり鉢する crush 〔pound〕in a mortar ¶すり鉢形の cone-shaped; conic(al) / すり鉢山 a conical hill; a sugar-loaf mountain.

すりへらす 磨り減らす wear away 〔down〕; rub off 〔down〕/ 靴のかかとをすり減らす wear the heels of *one's* shoes down; have *one's* shoes worn at the heels / 神経をすり減らす fray 〔wear out〕*one's* nerves.

すりみ 擂り身 ground fish meat.

すりむく 擦り剝く graze; bark 《*one's* shin》; skin 《*one's* knee》;《医》abrade.

すりもの 刷り物 printed matter 〔paper〕; a handout (研究会で配られる資料など) ⇨ いんさつ(印刷物).

すりよる 擦り寄る edge 〔sidle〕up 《to》; nestle up 《to》.

スリラー a thriller.

スリランカ Sri Lanka (旧名: Ceylon).

スリル a thrill ¶スリルのある thrilling; adventuresome (life) / スリルを感じる be thrilled (by) / get a thrill 〔《口語》kick〕(out of).

する¹ 刷る print; put (a book) into print; run 〔print, work〕off (1,000 copies) ¶きれいに刷れている be well 〔clearly〕printed. 文例⇩

する² 為る〈なす〉do; make (a discovery);《文》perform;〈試みる〉try;《文》attempt;〈遊ぶ〉play (a game);〈実行する〉practice;〈行動する〉act;〈従事する〉《文》engage 〔be engaged〕in;〈...にする〉make (her happy);〈...に変える〉change 〔turn, convert〕(goods into money);〈...を勤める〉act 〔《文》officiate, serve〕as (chairman);〈価する〉cost (2,000 yen); be worth ⇨ やる ¶する事がある〔たくさんある〕have nothing 〔a lot,《文》much〕to do / する事なす事 everything 〔whatever〕one does 〔tries〕/ 子供を医者にする make a physician of *one's* son; bring up *one's* boy for the medical profession / 2, 3年もすればin a few years; two or three years from now / …しようとしてin an effort 〔《文》endeavor〕to do; by way of doing / まさに…しようとしている be about 〔going〕to do; be on the point 〔verge〕of doing / …することにしている make it a rule 〔practice〕to do; make a point of doing. 文例⇩

用法「する」に相当する代表的英語は do であるが, 「約束をする」make a promise,「努力する」make efforts,「選択する」make a selection,「準備する」make preparations など,「する」に相当する連語が非常に多い. また,「…する」の「する」に相当する英語を求めるよりも, 全体で1語の動詞とする方が適切な場合も少なくない. 例えば,「努力する」は make efforts でもよいが try (to do) と言う方がいいかもしれないし,「勉強する」は work, study. 動名詞を do の目的語にして,「…する」を表わすこともよくあるが, この場合, 動名詞の前には何らかの限定詞が必要. 例えば,「買物をする」は do some shopping, do a lot of shopping, do my shopping のように言って, 単に do shopping とは言わない.

する³ 掏る pick *sb's* pocket 〈of a wallet〉⇨ り² ¶すられる have *one's* pocket picked; have 《a purse》picked from *one's* pocket; have 《*one's* watch》stolen.

する⁴ 擦〔磨〕る rub; chafe; file (やすりで); 〈すりつぶす〉grind; pound; crush;〈失う〉lose;《文》forfeit / マッチをする strike a match. 文例⇩

ずる 〈行為〉a (dirty 〔mean〕) trick; (a) foul play;〈人〉a cunning fellow; a shirker; a dodger ¶ずるを決めこむ dodge *one's* chores; shirk;《文》neglect *one's* duties;《文》be undutiful / ずるをする cheat; play foul.

ずるい dishonest; sly; cunning; crafty; slick; 〈不正な〉foul ¶ずるい事をする behave dishonestly 〔in an underhand way〕;〈競技で〉play foul; cheat (at cards) / ずるいやつ a cunning fellow; a sly dog / ずるそうな目付き shifty eyes. 文例⇩

ずるがしこい ずる賢い sly; cunning; crafty; (dishonestly) tricky.

ずるける shirk *one's* duties 〔job〕;〈学校を〉play truant 〔《米口語》hooky〕(from school).

するする ¶するする(と) smoothly; easily /〈車が〉するすると運ぶ go (on) smoothly 〔without a hitch〕/ するすると開ける glide (the door) open. 文例⇩

てきた. The carpets are showing a lot of wear.

する¹ 名刺を刷ってもらいたい. I want to have some visiting cards printed.

する² あの人はデパートの店員をしている. He is a salesman at a department store. / 彼女は青い眼をしている. She has blue eyes. / 今, y が x² に等しいとしよう. Let y equal x² [x squared] / 野山君を私たちの代表にしよう. Let's make Noyama our representative. / 歩きもしないうちから走ろうとするな. Don't try to run before you can walk. / 学生時代にはずいぶん旅行をした. I used to do a lot of traveling when I was a student. / この間の晩, 妙な経験をした. I had a strange experience the other night. / そこまでしないでこの問題を穏便に解決できないものだろうか. Can't we bring this matter to a peaceful settlement, without resorting to such measures? / これは幾らしたかね. How much did you give 〔pay〕for it? / 王子は目玉焼きにして下さい. I'd like my eggs fried 〔《米》sunny-side up〕. / 今日はいつもとどうかしているよ. He isn't himself today.

する⁴ 彼は賭博で有り金を全部すってしまった. He gambled away all his money. | He was cleaned out 〔lost all his money〕gambling.

ずるい それはずるいよ. That's not fair.

ずるずる ¶ずるずる滑る be slippery / ずるずる中へ落ちる slither [slide] down ((a tree)) / ずるずる引きずる drag ((a heavy box)); trail ((the skirt)) / ずるずると失敗に陥る drift into failure.

ずるずるべったり 文例⇩

すると and (just then); then; 《文》 thereupon; 《文》 hereupon.

するどい 鋭い sharp; keen; pointed (先のとがった); stinging 〔《文》 caustic, 《文》 pungent〕 (sarcasm); biting [cutting] (criticism); 《文》 acute (pain); 《文》 poignant 《satire》; 《文》 trenchant (wit); 〈眼力が〉piercing; 〈抜け目のない〉smart; shrewd ¶聴覚[嗅覚]が鋭い have acute hearing [a keen sense of smell] / 頭の鋭い男 a quick-witted man; 《文》 a man of keen intelligence / 鋭く sharply; keenly; 《文》 poignantly / 鋭くする[なる] sharpen / 鋭く攻撃する make hot [fierce] attacks ((on)); 〈口で〉 make cutting remarks ((about)). 文例⇩

するめ 鯣 dried cuttlefish.

ずるやすみ ずる休み ¶ずる休みする stay away ((from work)) without (a) good reason; play truant 《米口語》 hooky] ((from school)).

すり ¶すりと指の間から抜ける slip through *one*'s fingers / すりとはまる[外れる] slip in [out of] place / 指輪を指からすり抜く slip a ring off *one*'s finger.

ずれ 〈遅れ〉 a lag; 〈逸脱〉 aberration; 〈食い違い〉《文》 (a) divergence; 《文》 (a) discrepancy (in); 〈すきま〉 a gap ¶ 時間のずれ a time lag.

すれあう 擦れ合う rub [chafe] against each other; jostle ((with)). 文例⇩

スレート (a) (roofing) slate ¶スレートで屋根をふく slate a roof; roof ((a house)) with slates.

すれすれ 擦れ擦れ ¶すれすれに 〈距離的に〉 close to ((the rocks)); 〈miss〉 by a whisker; 《口語》 (manage) by the skin of *one*'s teeth; 〈やっと〉 barely; just / (飛行機が)海面すれすれに飛ぶ skim [buzz] the surface of the sea.

すれちがう 擦れ違う pass each other; meet (on the road); brush past.
[用法] 「すれちがう」の意味を表わす代表的な英語は pass であるが, We passed a lot of cars. は「たくさんの車とすれちがった」の意にもなれば「たくさんの車を追い越した」の意味にもなる。その間の混同が生じる可能性があるときは meet を使ってもいいが, たいていは文脈で明らかになる。

すれっからし 擦れっ枯らし a shameless person; a knowing [sophisticated, 《文》 worldly-wise] person; 〈女〉 a shameless [a brazen] hussy ¶すれっからしである 《文》 be lost to shame; be dead to all sense of shame; be blasé; be thick-skinned.

すれる 擦れる rub [scrape, chafe] ((against)); be rubbed; 〈磨滅する〉 wear; be worn; 〈悪擦れする〉 lose *one*'s simplicity (naïveté, modesty] ¶木の葉の擦れる音 rustling [a rustle] of leaves / 擦れて薄くなる wear thin. 文例⇩

ずれる slip (down, off); slip out of place; get out of position [line]; shift; slide ¶横にずれる be off to the side.

スローガン a slogan; a motto ((*pl.* -(e)s)); 《文》 a watchword ¶…というスローガンを掲げて under the slogan of ….

ズロース (a pair of) drawers; bloomers; underpants ★日本語で「ズロース」が今ではこっけいな感じがするのと同じように, drawers も bloomers もこっけいな感じを伴う。

スロープ a slope.

スローモー 〈人〉 a dull fellow; a slow-starter; 《口語》 a slowcoach ¶スローモーの slow-moving[-motioned].

スローモーション ¶スローモーション映画 a slow-motion picture.

ずろく 図録 a record in pictures; an illustrated book [history].

スロットル 〔機〕 a throttle.

すわ Good Heavens [God, gracious]! ¶すわというときは 《文》 in the hour [moment] of peril [danger]; in case of [in an] emergency.

スワジランド Swaziland ¶スワジランド王国 the Kingdom of Swaziland.

スワヒリご スワヒリ語 Swahili.

すわり 座り stability ¶座りのいい[悪い] stable [unstable, shaky, rickety] / 座り心地がいい be comfortable to sit in [on].

すわりこみ 座り込み a sit-in (protest); a sit-down (strike [demonstration]) ¶座り込みをする stage a sit-in ((at City Hall)); go on a sit-down (strike) / 座り込み戦術に出る use [go in for, 《文》 resort to] sit-in tactics.

すわりこむ 座り込む sit down (and refuse to move); plant *oneself* down.

すわる 座る sit [squat] down; 《文》 take a seat; 〈座っている〉 sit; 《文》 be seated; 〈動かない〉 be set ¶ちゃんと座る sit (up) straight; sit up / 椅子にどっかと座る sink [drop] into a chair / どしんと座る plump [plunk] *oneself* down / 足を折り曲げて(日本式に)座る sit with *one*'s legs under *one*; sit on *one*'s heels. 文例⇩

すん 寸 a *sun* (=3.03 cm); 〈寸法〉 ⇨ すんぽう ¶寸が足りない be (a little) too short ((for)).

するする 蛇がするすると土手をはい上がって行くところであった。A snake was gliding smoothly up the bank. / 旗がするすると上がった。The flag ran up the pole.

ずるずるべったり ほんの一晩泊めてやるとつもりだけだったのに, ずるずるべったりに今日まで居着いてしまったというわけだ。All I offered him was a bed for the night, but somehow he has stayed on with us ever since.

すると すると, 君の家はかかあ天下ってわけだね。That means that you are a hen-pecked husband, doesn't it?

するどい 彼は実に鋭い男だ。He is as sharp as a needle [razor].

すれあう 道は肩と肩とが擦れ合う程の混雑であった。The street was so crowded that people jostled against one another.

すれる 石段が擦れてすべすべになっている。The stone steps are worn smooth.

ずれる 彼の考えはどうしようもないほど今の時代からずれている。His ideas are hopelessly out of step [tune] with the times.

すわる 職業柄座ってばかりいる者にはこれがいい運動になる。This is good exercise for people in sedentary occupations. / お座りになりなさい。Won't you sit down [have a seat]? / お座り。〈犬に向かって言うとき〉Sit!

すんか 寸暇 a moment's leisure; a spare moment. 文例⇩

ずんぐり ¶ずんぐりした thickset; short and thick; fat and short; stocky; squat; dumpy; squab; chunkily built / ずんぐりした娘 a dumpling [pudding] of a girl / ずんぐりむっくりの roly-poly.

すんげき 寸劇 a short (comic) play; a tabloid play; a skit.

すんし 寸志 a little token of *one's* gratitude [appreciation]; a small present. 文例⇩

すんしゃくさぎ 寸借詐欺 swindling a petty sum of money out of sb by pretending to borrow it.

ずんずん 《文》rapidly; fast; by leaps and bounds (とんとん拍子に); steadily ¶ずんずん進む〈行く〉 go on and on; walk quickly away; 〈仕事が〉 make rapid progress [headway].

すんぜん 寸前 immediately [right, just] before ¶本塁寸前で刺される《野球》be tagged out just short of home.

すんだん 寸断 ¶寸断する cut [tear] sth to [into] pieces [shreds, ribbons]; 《文》fragment sth.

すんづまり 寸詰まり ¶寸詰まりの (too) short 《clothes》; undersized; sawed-off 《pants》.

すんてつ 寸鉄 〈武器〉a small weapon; 〈警句〉《文》an epigram; a terse, witty saying ¶身に寸鉄を帯びない carry no weapons; be quite unarmed.

すんでのことに[ところで] almost *did*; nearly *did*. 文例⇩

ずんどう ¶ずんどうである have no waist.

すんなり ¶〈議案が〉すんなり通る go through on the nod; pass with no objection ¶すんなりした〈すらりとした〉slim; slender; 《文》svelte; 〈しなやかな〉lithe; supple.

すんぴょう 寸評 a brief review 《of》; a brief comment 《on》.

すんぶん 寸分 ¶寸分たがわず accurately 《to an inch》; exactly the same 《as》; exactly [precisely, just] like….

すんぽう 寸法 measurements; 《文》dimensions; size ¶寸法をとる take *sb's* [*its*] measurements; measure the size 《of》; measure 《*sb* for a suit》 / 寸法を間違える take[get] the wrong measurements 《of, for》; get the dimensions [size] 《of *sth*》 wrong; make *sth* to the wrong measurements 《of》; for〉 / 寸法に合わせて作った made-to-measure 《suits》 / 寸法どおりに to 《precise》 measure; 〈計画どおりに〉as arranged; according to schedule / 寸法書 measurements. 文例⇩

せ

せ¹ 背 〈背中〉the back ⇨ せなか; 〈身長〉⇨ せい⁶ ¶本の背 the spine of a book / 椅子の背 the back of a chair / 背を伸ばす straighten one's back / 世間に背を向ける turn *one's* back on the world / 壁を背にして with *one's* back to [against] the wall.

せ² 瀬 〈早瀬〉rapids (in a river); 〈浅瀬〉shallows; a shoal.

ぜ 是 ¶是が非でも〈是非とも〉by some means or other; by fair means or foul; 〈否応なしに〉willy-nilly; whether one likes it or not / 是とする consider [think] (it) right; approve of (a plan); give *one's* approval to 《what he has done》/ 是を是とし非を非とする call what is right right, and wrong wrong; call a spade a spade.

せい¹ 正 〈正義〉justice; 《文》righteousness; 《文》(the) right; 〈資格の〉regular; full; 〈負に対して〉original; 〈負に対して〉plus; positive ¶正会員 a full [regular] member / 正教授 a full professor.

せい² 生 life; living; 《文》existence ¶生をうける〈生まれる〉be born; 《文》come into being; 《文》come into the [this] world; 〈生きている〉live; be alive / 生あるもの all living things; 《文》the living; life.

せい³ 性 〈男女の〉(a) sex; 《文法》gender; 〈本性〉nature; 〈品性〉character ¶性の《文》sexual / 性の目覚め sexual awakening / 性の問題 a sex [sexual] problem / 性に目覚める 《文》be sexually awakened / 性教育 sex education / 性知識 knowledge about sex; sexual information / 性転換 a change of sex; a sex change / 性道徳 sexual morality / 性犯罪 a sex crime / 性ホルモン[染色体] a sex hormone [chromosome] / 性本能 sex instinct. 文例⇩

すんか 彼は寸暇を惜しんで読書している。He devotes [gives] every spare moment to reading.

すんし 寸志.〈包みの上書き〉With compliments.

すんでのことに[ところで] もうすんでのところでトラックにひかれるところだった。I narrowly [just] missed being run over by a truck. | I was nearly [almost] knocked over by a truck. / すんでの所で溺死するところだった。I nearly [almost] drowned. | I came very near (to) drowning.

すんぽう そこへ僕が出て行くという寸法なんだ。It has been arranged that I will turn up just that moment.

せ¹ 彼はこちらに背を向けていたので、私がそばにいるのに気がつかなかった。As he had his back [As his back was] to me, he didn't know that I was standing near him. / 町は山を背にしている。The town has hills at the back. | The town is backed by mountains. / 背に腹は換えられない。Necessity [Need] knows [has] no law. 【諺】

せい² 人の性は善なり。All men are born good. | Man is naturally good.

せい³ 彼は自分の姓を捨てて妻の姓を継いでいる。He has dropped his own surname and taken that of his wife.

せい⁴ 姓 a family name; a surname; *one's* last name. 文例⇩

せい⁵ 制 〈制度〉a system; 〈組織〉an organization ¶〈労働の〉8 時間制 an eight-hour day / 町[市]制 the town [city] organization / 4 年制の大学 a four-year university [college].

せい⁶ 背 height;《文》stature ¶背が高い[低い] be tall [short];《文》be high [low, short, small] in stature / 背が伸びる grow taller /〈急に伸びる〉shoot up /〈水中で〉背がたつ can touch bottom; be in *one's* depth / 背の順に in order of height [stature] / 背を測る measure *sb's* height / 背比べする measure *oneself* against *sb*; compare heights [*one's* height with *sb's*]. 文例⇩

せい⁷ 聖 ⇨せいなる ¶聖ペテロ St. Peter ★ St. は Saint の略.

せい⁸ 精 〈精霊〉a spirit;〈精力〉energy; vigor ¶海の精 a sea nymph /《ギリシャ神話》a Nereid (*pl.* -(e)s) /空気の精 a sylph /地[土]の精 a gnome /火の精 a salamander /水の精 a water nymph [sprite];《ギリシャ神話》a naiad (*pl.* -(e)s) /森[木]の精 a wood nymph; a dryad (*pl.* -(e)s) /山の精 an oread / 精のつく nourishing; nutritious; invigorating; tonic 〈wine〉/ 精のつく薬 a tonic / 精を出す work hard; put *one's* heart into 《*one's* work》; put *oneself* out 《to do》; exert *oneself* 《to do》; apply *oneself* to 《*one's* studies》;《文》be diligent [assiduous] 《in *one's* occupation》; 精を出して 《try》hard; 《work》with a lot [a great deal] of effort /《文》diligently;《文》assiduously / 精一杯 ⇨せいいっぱい.

せい⁹ ¶…のせいにする blame *sb* [*sth*] for *sth*; blame *sth* on *sb* [*sth*]; put [pin] the blame on *sb* [*sth*]; put 《*one's* headache》 down to 《the weather》;《文》lay the fault [responsibility] at *sb's* door;《文》attribute [ascribe]《*one's* failure》to《bad luck》/ …のせいで because of…; owing to…;《be》due to…; on account of…. 文例⇩

-せい¹ …世 ¶ヘンリー八世 Henry VIII [the Eighth] /洪積世《地質》the Pleistocene epoch.

-せい² …製 ¶木製の made of wood; wooden / 外国製の foreign-made / ドイツ製の鉛筆 a German pencil; a pencil made in Germany; a German-made pencil /《文》a pencil of German make [manufacture] /ソ連製のミサイル a Soviet-built missile.

ぜい¹ 税 ⇨ぜいきん ¶税引きの[で] after tax(-es); after deduction [payment] of tax; net of tax(es); tax excluded / 税込みの[で] before tax; before deduction [payment] of tax; including [inclusive of] tax.

ぜい² 贅 ¶ぜいを尽くした behave [live] extravagantly;《文》indulge in the utmost luxury / ぜいを尽くした〈a house〉provided with every luxury imaginable; most luxurious.

せいあくせつ 性悪説 the view of human nature as fundamentally depraved.

せいあつ 制圧 ¶制圧する bring《the seas》under *one's* control;《文》gain ascendancy [supremacy, mastery] over《the enemy》.

せいあん 成案 a definite plan; a concrete program.

せいい 誠意 good faith ¶誠意のある〈心・性格が〉honest; straightforward; reliable; trustworthy;《口語》straight;《文》《a person》of good faith;〈言葉が〉sincere; honest / 誠意のない〈心・性格が〉unreliable; untrustworthy;《口語》shifty;《文》《people》lacking in good faith;〈言葉が〉insincere;《文》false / 誠意のない行動をする act in bad faith / 誠意を示す show *one's* good faith / 誠意を疑う doubt [question] *sb's* good faith [sincerity] / 誠意をもって in good faith; sincerely; with [in all] sincerity.

用法 「誠意」「誠実」を sincerity, 「誠意のある」「誠実な」を sincere と英訳する傾向が一般にあるが, sincerity は「言うことに偽わりのないこと」「口と心が一致していること」であって, 主として心のあり方を言う「誠意」「誠実」には必ずしも当たらない. sincere も「言うことが心で思っていることと一致している」「見せかけではない」の意で, 心のあり方や性格を述べるのには適語とは言えない.

せいいき¹ 声域 a range of voice;《音楽》a (voice) register.

せいいき² 聖域 sacred [holy] precincts; a sanctuary.

せいいく 生[成]育 ¶生[成]育する〈育てる〉grow; raise;〈育つ〉grow (up) / 生育期《植》the growing period [season].

せいいたいしょうぐん 征夷大将軍《日本史》the Barbarian-subduing[-suppressing] Generalissimo [Great General].

せいいっぱい 精一杯 as hard as possible [*one* can]; to the best of *one's* ability; with all *one's* might;《文》to the utmost (of *one's* ability) ¶精一杯やる do *one's* best; do everything in *one's* power / 精一杯働く work as hard as *one* can; work for all *one* is worth. 文例⇩

せいいん 成因 the origin 《of a volcano》.

せいう 晴雨 ¶晴雨にかかわらず rain or shine; wet or fine; whether it rains or not; in all

---

君の背はどの位ですか. How tall are you? / 僕の背は 169 センチです. I am 169 centimeters tall. / 彼は僕より 2 センチ背が高い. He is two centimeters taller than me. | He is taller than me by two centimeters. ⇨より⇩

用法 うちの坊やはまだあの棚の上のキャンデーの缶には背が届かない. My little boy is still not tall enough to get at the can of candy on the shelf. / そこはとても深くて, 私には背が立たなかった. The water there was so deep that I was out of my depth [I could not touch bottom]. / 背の立たない所へ行くな. Don't go out of your depth! / 背比べしてみよう. Let's see which of us is (the) taller.

せい⁹ 目のかすむのは過労のせいだ. Your dim sight comes from overwork. / それは君のせいじゃない. It isn't your fault. | You're not responsible [to blame] for it. / みんな私のせいだということにしておきなさい. Let it all be my fault. / だれでもない, 君が悪いのだ. It's nobody else's fault [nobody's fault but your own]. | You've only yourself to blame [thank] for it.

せいいっぱい 彼は自分一人食うだけが精一杯だった. It was all he could do to support himself. / これで私には精一杯です. This is

せいうけい 晴雨計 a barometer.
せいうち 【動】 a walrus.
せいうん¹ 青雲 ¶青雲の志を抱く have great ambitions;《文》have [entertain] a high [lofty] ambition.
せいうん² 星雲 a galaxy; a nebula《pl. -lae, -s》¶星雲(状)の nebular / 楕円星雲 an elliptical galaxy.
せいえい 精鋭 the best [pick]《of the airmen》;《文》the flower《of an army》; elite [choice] troops ¶精鋭な picked《members》; crack《troops》; highly efficient《troops》/ 精鋭5千 a troop 5,000 strong.
せいえき 精液 semen; sperm ¶精液の seminal; spermatic.
せいえん¹ 声援 (a shout of) encouragement; (vocal) support;〈競技の〉cheering;《米口語》rooting ¶声援する encourage; give *one's* (vocal) support (to);〈競技で〉cheer;《米口語》root (for a team) / 声援者《援助者》a supporter;〈競技の〉a cheerer;《米口語》a rooter. 文例⤵
せいえん² 製塩 salt manufacture [making] ¶製塩所 a saltworks; a saltern.
せいおう 西欧 Western Europe;〈西洋〉the West; the Occident ¶西欧化する be Westernized; go Western / 西欧諸国 West European countries / 西欧文明 Western civilization.
せいおん 静穏《文》serenity;《文》tranquillity; calmness; quiet(ness) ¶静穏な《文》serene;《文》tranquil; calm; quiet.
せいか¹ 正価 a (net) price ⇒ ていか².
せいか² 生家 the house where *one* was born; *one's* (parents') home.
せいか³ 正課[科]〈全体〉the regular curriculum [course];〈1科目〉a subject on the regular curriculum ¶柔道を正課にする include *judo* in the regular curriculum; place *judo* on the regular curriculum / 正課外の科目 an extracurricular subject.
せいか⁴ 成果 a result ¶a fruit; an outcome ¶努力の成果 the fruit [product, result] of *one's* labor [efforts] / 立派な成果をあげる〈事が主語〉get [《文》obtain, produce] excellent results; be rewarded with good results;《文》be crowned with great success. 文例⤵
せいか⁵ 声価 ⇒ ひょうばん, めいせい.
せいか⁶ 青果 ¶青果物 fruit and vegetables; greengrocery / 青果市場 a fruit and vegetable market.
せいか⁷ 盛夏 high summer;《in》the height of summer ⇒ まなつ.

せいか⁸ 聖火 the sacred fire [flame]; a sacred torch ¶オリンピックの聖火 the Olympic Flame [Torch] / 聖火走者 a flame-bearer / 聖火台 the flame holder / 聖火リレー an Olympic-torch[-fire] relay.
せいか⁹ 聖歌 a sacred song; a hymn ¶聖歌集 a hymnal; a hymnbook / 聖歌隊 a choir / 聖歌隊員 a chorister; a choir boy [girl] / 聖歌隊指揮者 a choirmaster.
せいか¹⁰ 精華《文》the essence;《文》the quintessence;《文》the flower; the cream ¶武士道の精華 the flower of *bushido* [chivalry].
せいか¹¹ 製菓 confectionery ¶製菓会社 a confectionery company / 製菓業者 a confectioner.
せいかい¹ 正解 the [a] right [correct] answer ¶正解する answer [solve]《the problem》correctly; give the [a] right [correct] answer [solution] / 正解者 a person who gives the [a] right [correct] answer.
せいかい² 政界 the political world; political circles ¶政界の大立物 a prominent [big] figure in politics; an important [a major] political leader / 政界に入る go [launch (out)] into politics / 政界を去る retire from political life; leave [quit] politics.
せいかい³ 盛会 a successful meeting. 文例⤵
せいかいけん 制海権 (the) mastery [control, command] of the sea; naval supremacy ¶制海権を握る《文》secure [lose] the mastery of the sea / 制海権を握っている have [hold] the mastery of the sea; command the sea.
せいかがく 生化学 biochemistry ¶生化学の[的] biochemical / 生化学者 a biochemist.
せいかく¹ 正確 ¶正確な exact《sizes》; accurate《information》; precise《statements》; correct《time》/ 正確に exactly; accurately; correctly; precisely;《文》with precision [exactness]; punctually (時間的に) / 時計のように正確に with clockwork precision / 正確に言えば to be exact; to put it more precisely / 時間を正確に守る be punctual (to the minute); be (always) on time. 文例⤵
せいかく² 性格 character; personality ¶強い[弱い]性格の人 a person with a [《文》of] strong [weak] character / 性格の不一致 personality clashes / …の性格を帯びる《文》take on the character of《ritual》/ 性格上の欠陥 a flaw [defect] in *one's* character / 性格俳優 a character actor [actress] / 性格破綻 a personality disorder / 性格描写 characterization; character drawing [《文》portrayal,《文》delineation]. 文例⤵
せいかく³ 製革 tanning; leather manufacture ¶製革業者 a tanner.

---

the best [as much as] I can do.
せいえん¹ 彼らは代表者たちに盛んな声援を送った. They gave enthusiastic encouragement to their representatives. / 君の声援を頼りにしている. I count on your support.
せいか⁴ 彼女をなびかせようとジョンはいろいろやってみたが, 結局何の成果もなかった. For all his attempts to win her affection John got nowhere. / 所期の成果を収め得なかった. The result fell short of our expectations.
せいかい³ 会は盛会だった. The meeting was a great success. ǀ The party was well attended.
せいかく¹ この時計は正確だ. This watch keeps good time [is very accurate]. / 正確には知らない. I don't know for certain.
せいかく² そこに彼の性格がよく表われている. His personality strongly asserts itself there. / 歩き方にまで性格が出ていた. His character showed even in the way he walked. ǀ《文》The very

せいがく 声楽 singing; vocal music ¶声楽を習う take singing [voice] lessons 《from sb》; study singing 《under sb》/ 声楽家 a vocalist / 声楽科 a singing [vocal music] course.

せいがく 税額 the amount of (a) tax ¶税額の査定 (a) tax assessment.

せいかぞく 聖家族 the Holy Family.

せいかつ 生活 (a) life 《pl. lives》; 〈生計〉(a) livelihood; (a) living(★複数にはしない) ¶生活する live; make a living; support oneself 《on 90,000 yen a month》/ 月給で生活する live on one's salary / どうにかこうにか生活して行く manage to keep body and soul together; pick up a scanty [bare] livelihood / live at subsistence level; subsist 《on》/ 生活が豊かである be well [comfortably] off; make a good living; 《文》 be in easy circumstances / 〈物質的に〉 improve one's standard of living; 〈精神的に〉 enrich one's life / 孤独な生活を送る lead [live] a lonely life / 生活に困る cannot make a living; find it hard to keep body and soul together [make ends meet]; be badly off / 生活改善運動 a movement for the improvement of living conditions / 生活環境 one's (living) environment / 生活機能 《生理》 vital functions / 生活給 pay [wages] calculated [paid] on the basis of need / 生活協同組合 ⇒せいきょう¹ / 生活記録 a human [life] document; an account [a record] of one's life 《during the war》/ 生活苦 the hardships of life / 生活空間 living space / 生活困窮者 a needy person; 《集合的》 the (poor) and needy / 生活資金 money to live on / 生活条件 living conditions / 生活水準 a living standard; a standard of living / 生活水準の向上[低下] an improvement [a fall, a drop, 《文》a deterioration] in the standard of living / 生活設計 a plan for one's life; life planning / 生活程度 ⇒ 水準 / 生活体験 experience in actual life / 生活難 the difficulty of living; 《struggle against》 hard living / 生活反応 《生理》 (a) vital reaction / 生活費 living expenses; the cost [price] of living; 《work for》 one's keep / 生活必需品 daily [living] necessities; (the) necessities [essentials] (for life) / 生活扶助 livelihood assistance / 生活物資 everyday goods [commodities] / 生活保護を受ける be getting 《文》be in receipt of) public assistance 《《英》 supplementary benefit》; 《米口語》 be on welfare [relief] / 生活保護法 the Daily Life Security Act; the Livelihood Protection Act / 生活様式 a way of life; a life-style; 《文》a mode of living / 生活力 one's earning power; one's ability to make [earn] one's living; 〈活力〉 《full of》 vitality. 文例⒝

せいかっこう 背恰好 ⇒ たいかく¹, からだ(からだつき).

せいかん¹ 生還 ¶生還する come back [return] alive [safe]; 《野球》⇒ホームイン(ホームインする) / (打者が走者を)生還させる send [bring] home 《a runner》/ 生還者 a survivor.

せいかん² 製缶 canning; can manufacturing ¶製缶業者 a canner / 製缶工場 a cannery; a canning factory.

せいかん³ 静観 ¶静観する watch [look on] calmly; wait and see / 静観主義 a wait-and-see policy / 静観的態度をとる take [《文》assume] a wait-and-see attitude 《toward》.

せいかん⁴ 精悍 ¶精悍な 《文》 intrepid; 《文》 dauntless; fearless.

せいがん 請願 a petition 《for》; an application 《for》 ¶請願する petition 《the government for sth》; present [submit, send in] a petition 《to》; file [lodge] a petition 《with the House of Representatives》; apply 《for》/ 請願者[人] a petitioner / 請願書 a (written) petition.

せいかん 税関 a customs house; 《主に米》 a customhouse; the customs ¶手荷物が税関を通る get one's baggage [luggage] through the customs / 税関申告書 a customs declaration / 税関手続き customs procedures [formalities] / 税関明細書 a customs specification / 税関吏 a customs officer [inspector].

用法 the customs は場所として考えるときは Where is the customs? のように単数扱いが普通で, 人として考えるときは The Japanese customs are very strict. のように複数扱い.

せいがんざい 制癌剤 an anticancer drug; a cancer-inhibiting drug.

せいがんしゃ 晴眼者 a sighted person.

せいき¹ 生気 life; vitality; vigor; verve ¶生気のある lively; 《文》 animated / 生気のない lifeless; dull; anemic / 生気のない顔 a face with no [《文》 lacking in, 《文》 devoid of] animation / 生気を取り戻す come to life; be revitalized / 生気はつらつたる vigorous; full of life [vivacity]. 文例⒝

せいき² 世紀 a century ¶20世紀 the twentieth [20th] century / 今世紀 this [the present] century / 前世紀 (the) last century / 19世紀の中ごろ (in) the mid-nineteenth century / 世紀末 the end of a century /《文芸》(フランス語) the fin de siècle (19世紀の)/ 世紀末的な decadent / 世紀末的不安[文学] fin-de-siècle unrest [literature] / 幾世紀にもわたる迫害 centuries of persecution; persecution over the centuries / 建てられてから2世紀たった家 a two-centuries-old house.

せいき³ 生起 ¶生起する take place; happen;

---

way that he walked bespoke the man. / 性格だからどうも仕方がない. I can't help my nature. ‖ I can't help being the way I am. / 主人公の性格がよく描けている. The character of the hero is skillfully described.

せいかつ 彼には生活の心配が全くない. He has no difficulty in making ends meet. / 彼女は昼間は生活のために働き, 夜は学校に通っている. She works for her living [keep] by day and goes to school by night. / 1人でも2人でも生活費は変わらないものだ. Two can live just as cheaply as

one. / 東京は生活費が高い. Tokyo is an expensive place to live in. / この土地は生活費のかからない所だ. Living is cheap here. / 彼は生活力が旺盛だ. He is full of vitality. ‖ His earning power is very high [good].

せいき¹ その頃の私は生気はつら

せいき⁴ 正規 ¶正規の〈正式の〉regular; formal; proper;〈合法的〉legitimate; legal / 正規の教育 regular [formal] school education / 正規の値段[運賃] the regular price [fare]; the full price [fare]（割引きのない）/ 正規のルート（through）the proper channels / 正規の手続きをふむ go through the regular procedure [proper formalities] / 正規軍 a regular army.

せいき⁵ 性器 (the) sex [genital] organs; the genitals.

せいぎ 正義 justice;《文》right;《文》righteousness ¶正義の just;《文》righteous / 正義の戦a just [《文》righteous] war / 正義のために戦う fight in the cause of justice / 正義感が強い have a strong sense of justice. 文例

せいきゅう¹ 性急 ⇒ せっかち.

せいきゅう² 請求 a demand; a request; a claim ¶損害賠償の請求 a claim for damages / 請求する ask [apply] for;《文》request; demand; claim; call on《sb to do》;〈代価・料金を〉charge sb《10 dollars for sth》; bill sb《for sth》; send a bill to sb / 請求があり次第 on demand [request, application] / 請求に応じる meet [go along with,《文》comply with] sb's request [demand] / 請求に応じて at sb's request / 請求権 a (right of) claim / 請求書 a bill; an account / 請求人 a claimant.

せいきゅうりょく 制球力 (lose) one's (pitching) control ¶制球力がある[ない] have good [poor] ball control.

せいきょ 逝去 ¶逝去する die; pass away（婉曲的に）⇒ しぬ.

せいぎょ 制御 control; management ¶制御する control; manage; bring [keep] under control / 制御しやすい[にくい] be easy [hard] to control / 制御し得ない uncontrollable; ungovernable; out of hand / 制御盤 a control console [board] / 制御棒〈原子炉の〉a control rod.

せいきょう¹ 生協 a cooperative society; a co-op ¶生協の売店 a co-op (store).

せいきょう² 政教 ¶政教一致 the unity [union] of religion and politics [Church and State] / 政教分離 (the principle of) separation of government and religion.

せいきょう³ 盛況 ¶盛況である be prosperous; be thriving; be flourishing;〈商人が〉be doing a flourishing business;〈会などが〉be a success; be very well attended. 文例

せいぎょう 正業《文》a legitimate occupation; an honest [a respectable] job [《文》calling];《文》honorable employment ¶正業を営む make an honest living / 正業につく take up an honest calling.

せいきょうかい 正教会 the Greek [Eastern] Orthodox Church.

せいきょうと 清教徒 a Puritan ¶清教徒的な puritanical; puritan.

せいきょく 政局 the political situation ¶政局の危機 a political crisis; a tense [serious,《文》grave] political situation / 政局を担当する be in [take] charge [control] of the government /《文》take [be at] the helm of state / 政局を安定[収拾]させる bring stability to the political situation / 政局を打開する break a political deadlock.

せいきん 精勤 hard [conscientious] work;《文》diligence;《文》industry;〈勤務者の〉good [regular] attendance ¶精勤する work hard;《文》be diligent; attend (the office) regularly / 精勤者 a worker with a good attendance record; a regular attender / 精勤賞 a prize for good [regular] attendance.

ぜいきん 税金 a tax; taxes;〈物品税〉a duty (on) ¶税金がかかる[かからない] be taxable [tax-free]; be subject to [free of] duty / 税金を課する impose a duty (on an article); levy a tax (on sb) / 税金を取り立てる collect taxes (from) / 税金を払う[逃れる] pay (evade, dodge) a tax / 税金でまかなわれている奨学金 a tax-supported grant. 文例

せいく 成句 a set phrase; an idiomatic phrase [expression].

せいくうけん 制空権 (the) mastery [command] of the air; air supremacy（完全な）¶制空権を握る[失う] secure [lose] the mastery of the air / 制空権を握っている have [hold] the mastery [command] of the air; command the air.

せいくん 請訓 ¶請訓する ask (one's home government) for instructions.

せいけい¹ 生計 (a) livelihood; a living（★複数にはしない）¶生計の資《文》a means of livelihood / 文筆で生計を立てる make [earn] a [one's] living [livelihood] by writing; live by one's pen / 生計費指数 the cost of living index.

せいけい² 西経 the west longitude ¶西経 18 度 18° West Longitude; Long. 18° W（★longitude eighteen degrees west と読む）.

せいけい³ 整形 plastic surgery; orthopedics / 整形外科 plastic surgery; orthopedics / 整形外科医 a plastic surgeon; an orthopedist / 整形外科病院 an orthopedic hospital / 整形手術を受ける undergo plastic surgery [an orthopedic operation].

せいけいがくぶ 政経学部 the politics and economics department.

つとしていた. I was in the full flush of my vigor in those days.
せいぎ 正義はついに勝つ. Right will prevail in the end. / 正義は我にあり. Right and justice are on our side. / 我々は正義のため暴力と戦っているのだ. We are fighting for justice against brute force.
せいきゅう² 先月買った本の代金を請求された. I have been asked to pay [They sent me a bill] for the books I bought last month.
せいきょう³ 店は押すな押すなの盛況. The shop is doing a roaring trade.
せいきょく 政局は意外な進展を見せた. The political situation has taken an unexpected turn.
ぜいきん 税金を払ったら幾らも残らないだろう. I won't have much (money) left after taxes. / 毎月3万円も月給から税金として差し引かれている. As much as 30,000 yen is deducted from my monthly pay for taxes.
せいけつ 清潔な衣服を着るようにしなければいけない. You must take care to be neatly dressed.
せいげん スピーチは1人15分に

せいけつ 清潔 cleanliness ; neatness ¶清潔な clean ; neat / 清潔にする clean ; make *sth* clean / 清潔にしておく keep (*oneself*) (neat and) clean. 文例⇩

せいけん¹ 政見 one's political views [opinions] ¶政見を発表する 《文》 state [set forth] one's political views / 政見発表演説会 a campaign meeting / 政見放送 an [a candidate's] election broadcast (on TV).

せいけん² 政権 (political) power [office] ¶政権の交替 a change of regime [government] / 政権を握る come to power ; take office ; 《文》 take the helm of state / 選挙に勝って政権を握る be elected to office / 政権を失う [離れる] lose office ; go out of power / 政権に復帰する return to power / 政権争奪(戦) a scramble for political power.

せいげん¹ 正弦 《数》 a sine 《of an angle》 (略: sin) ¶正弦曲線 a sine curve ; a sinusoid / 正弦法則 the law of sines.

せいげん² 制限 (a) restriction 《on》; a limit 《to, on》; (a) limitation 《on》; conditions 《資格の》 ¶制限する, 制限を加える restrict ; limit ; put [impose, 《文》] place, lay down] restrictions 《on》 / 数に制限がある there is a limit to the number 《of》; 《文》 be limited in number / 制限を緩める relax the restrictions 《on trade》 / 制限を撤廃する lift [《文》 remove, withdraw] restrictions / 制限なく without limit [limitation] ; freely ; 《文》 unrestrictedly / 制限内で [外に] within [beyond] the limits / 数量制限 quantitative restrictions / 電力(消費)制限 restrictions on power consumption / 制限速度 a speed limit ; the regulation speed. 文例⇩

ぜいげん 税源 a source of tax revenue ; 〈課税対象〉 an object of taxation.

せいげん³ 誓言 文例⇩

せいご¹ 生後 ¶生後3か月の幼児 a three-month-old baby / 生後1週間で死ぬ die a week after (*its*) birth.

せいご² 正誤 correction ¶正誤表 a list of errata [corrigenda] ; an errata (slip) / 完全な正誤表を掲げる give a full list of errata ★ errata は erratum の複数形であるが, erratum を使うことはまれで, list of errata が普通. an errata は, 人によっては正用法と認めない.

せいご³ 《魚》 a young sea bass.

せいこう¹ 性交 (sexual) intercourse ; 《医》 coitus ; 《医》 coition ¶性交する have (sexual) intercourse 《with》; 《口語》 have sex 《with》 ; make love 《to》 《婉曲的に》 / 性交不能 impotence.

せいこう² 性向 ⇒ せいしつ.

せいこう³ 生硬 ¶生硬な raw ; crude ; unrefined ; stiff.

せいこう⁴ 正鵠 ¶正鵠を得[射]る hit the nail on the head ; be to the point / 正鵠を失する be wide of [miss] the mark.

せいこう⁵ 成功 (a) success ¶成功する 〈事が主語〉 succeed ; come out well ; go well ; 〈人が主語〉 succeed ; be successful ; do well ; make good ; make one's mark (as a writer, in business), 《口語》 make a go of (it [one's attempt]) ; 〈出世する〉 succeed [rise] in the world ; get on in life [in the world] / 成功の秘訣 the secret of success ; the key to success / 大成功を収める be [have, 《文》 achieve] a great success ; 《口語》 make a (great) hit / 成功者 a successful man ; a success / 成功率 a success rate (of 47%). 文例⇩

せいこう⁶ 政綱 a political [party] program ; (米) a platform ; a policy ¶政綱の1項目 an item [a policy] in a political [party] program ; (米) a plank in the party platform.

せいこう⁷ 精巧 ¶精巧な elaborate 《design》 ; 《文》 exquisite 《workmanship》 ; delicate 《mechanism》. 文例⇩

せいこう⁸ 製鋼 steel manufacture ; steelmaking ¶製鋼業 the steel industry / 製鋼業者 a steelman ; a steelmaker / 製鋼所 a steel mill ; a steelworks ; a steelmaking plant.

せいごう 整合 adjustment ; coordination.

せいこうかい 聖公会 《米》 the Protestant Episcopal Church ; 《英》 the Anglican Church ¶聖公会員 《米》 an Episcopalian ; 《英》 an Anglican.

せいこうほう 正攻法 (employ, adopt) the regular tactics for attack ; (make) a frontal attack (正面攻撃).

せいこつ 整骨 ¶整骨療法 《医》 osteopathy / 整骨師 an osteopath.

せいこん 精魂[根] ¶精魂を傾ける put one's (whole) heart and soul 《into》 ; 《文》 devote all one's energy 《to doing [sth]》 ; 《文》 exert one's utmost strength 《in》 / 精根尽き果てるまで to the limits of one's strength.

せいざ¹ 正座 ¶正座する sit straight [upright] ; sit square (on one's seat).

せいざ² 星座 a constellation ¶星座早見図 a star chart ; a planisphere / 星座表 a table [catalog] of constellations.

せいさい¹ 正妻 one's legal [lawful] wife ; one's legally wedded wife.

せいさい² 制裁 sanctions ; punishment ¶制裁を加える take [apply] sanctions 《against》 ; punish / 道徳[経済, 社会, 軍事]的制裁 moral [economic, social, military] sanctions.

制限されていた. The speeches were limited to fifteen minutes each. / 会員の資格には男女及び年齢の制限はありません. Membership is open to persons of either sex and of any age.

ぜいげん³ 本書の真価についてはあえて贅言を要しない. There is no need to dwell upon [We need not emphasize] the value of this work.

せいこう⁵ 彼はする事なす事成功した. Everything he attempted succeeded [went well] for him. | He succeeded in everything he tried. / 企画が成功した. The project has proved successful. / 彼は実業家としては成功したが, 政治家としては失敗だった. He was a success as a businessman but a failure as a politician. / 会は大成功だった. The meeting was a great success. / 努力のかいあって彼は成功した. His efforts were crowned [rewarded] with success. / ご成功を祈る. I wish you success. | Good luck !

せいこう⁷ 細工は精巧を極めている. The workmanship is exquisite.

せいさい³ 精[生]彩〈光彩〉luster; (a) color; 〈生気〉life; vividness ¶精彩のある colorful; vivid; lively; spirited; animated / 精彩のない lifeless; spiritless; dull.

せいざい 製材 sawing; lumbering (主に米・カナダでの);〈材木〉sawn wood;《米》lumber;《英》timber ¶製材する saw (up)《logs into boards》/ 製材業者 a lumberer; a sawmiller / 製材所 a lumbermill; sawmill.

せいさく¹ 制作 ⇒せいさく³ ¶(絵などを)制作中である be at work 《on a picture》.

せいさく² 政策 ¶政策をたてる work out [frame,《文》formulate] a policy / 政策を決定する decide on a policy / 政策をとる adopt a policy / 政策を転換する change one's policy / 前内閣の政策を踏襲する take over [carry on with, make no changes in] the policy of the previous cabinet / 外交[対外]政策 a diplomatic [foreign] policy / アメリカの対日政策 American policy toward Japan / 政策立案者 a policy maker / 政策論争 an argument [a controversy] over policy.

せいさく³ 製作 ¶製作する《文》manufacture; make; produce; turn out / 製作者 a maker; a manufacturer /《映画》a producer / 製作所 a factory; a works; a plant / 製作費 production cost.

せいさつ 生殺 ¶生殺与奪の権を握っている have [hold,《文》possess] the power of life and death 《over》.

せいさん¹ 生産 production ¶生産する produce; make; turn out; put out / 生産を開始する bring [put] sth into production / 生産過剰 overproduction / 生産管理 production control / 生産技術 manufacturing technique(s) [know-how]; industrial technology / 生産財《経済》producers' [producer, capital] goods / 生産者価格 a producers' [producer] price / 生産性 productivity / 生産性を高める increase [raise] the productivity 《of》/ 生産制限 restriction [curtailment] of production / 生産設備 production [productive] facilities; plant and equipment / 生産高[額] (an) output; a yield / りんごの生産地 an apple-producing center [district] / 生産費 the cost(s) of production; production cost(s) / 生産物 a product; produce (農産物を集合的にいう) / 生産目標 a production target [goal] / 生産力 production [manufacturing] capacity [power] / 生産割当て a production quota.

せいさん² 正餐 a formal dinner.

せいさん³ 成算 ¶成算がある[ない] be confident [do not have much hope] of success [succeeding]. 文例↓

せいさん⁴ 青酸《化》hydrocyanic [prussic] acid; hydrogen cyanide ¶青酸ガス hydrocyanic acid gas / 青酸カリ potassium cyanide;《俗に》cyanide.

せいさん⁵ 凄惨 ¶凄惨な ghastly; gruesome; grim; appalling.

せいさん⁶ 清[精]算 liquidation;〈差引計算〉adjustment ¶清[精]算する〈会社などを〉liquidate; wind up;〈支払いを〉clear off [up]《one's debts》; balance [settle]《one's accounts》/ 〈運賃を〉pay (up) the difference on one's ticket / 過去を清算する bury [forget] the past / 過去を清算して新生活に入る bury the past and start one's life again / 清算会社 a company in liquidation / 精算書 a statement of accounts / 破産清算書 a statement of liquidation / 運賃精算所 a fare adjustment office / 清算人 a liquidator; a balancer.

せいざん 青山 文例↓

せいさんかくけい 正三角形 an equilateral [a regular] triangle.

せいさん(しき) 聖餐(式)《キリスト教》Holy Communion; the Lord's Supper; the Eucharist; the Sacrament ¶聖餐を受ける take [receive] the Sacrament [Eucharist] / 聖餐(式)用のパン[ぶどう酒] the sacramental wafer [wine].

せいし¹ 生死 life and [or] death; one's safety (安否); one's fate (運命) ¶生死の境をさまよう hover between life and death; linger on the brink [verge] of death; stare death in the face / 生死を共にする share one's fate 《with》; throw [《文》cast] in one's lot 《with》/ 生死にかかわる問題 a matter of life and [or] death; a vital question.

せいし² 正視 ¶正視する look sb in the face; look straight [squarely] 《at》. 文例↓

せいし³ 制止 (a) restraint; a check; control ¶制止する keep sb from 《doing》; check; hold sb in check; pull sb up; control; restrain; keep [hold]《the crowd》back / 制止がきかなくなる〈対象が主語〉get out of hand [《one's》control];〈人が主語〉lose control 《of》. 文例↓

せいし⁴ 精子《動・植》a spermatozoon (pl. -zoa); a sperm (通俗的に).

せいし⁵ 静止 stillness; (a) standstill; rest ¶静止している stand still; be at a standstill; be at rest / 静止衛星 a stationary satellite / 静止状態(in) a state of rest / 静止状態の stationary; static.

せいし⁶ 製糸 silk reeling ¶製糸業 the silk-reeling industry / 製糸工場 a silk mill; a filature.

せいし⁷ 製紙 paper manufacture; papermaking ¶製紙会社 a paper(-manufacturing) company / 製紙工場 a paper mill [factory] / 製紙パルプ用 paper pulp.

せいさん³ 君は成算があるのか。Are you quite sure that you will succeed? / だれだって成算のない事業に賛成できるものではない。No one can support an undertaking that offers no hope of success.

せいざん 人間いたる所青山あり。Fortune can be found everywhere. | There's room for us all [for all kinds of people] in the world.

せいし² それは正視するに忍びなかった。I could not bear to look at it. | It was too horrible to look at.

せいし³ 彼らは守衛の制止もきかずに建物の中へ入ろうとした。They tried to force their way into the building, defying the porter.

せいし² 彼らは政治意識が発達している。They are very politically-minded. / 校長はなかなかの政治家だ。The principal is something of a politician. / 彼の政治感覚は

せいじ[1] 青滋 celadon (porcelain [ware]) ¶ 青滋色 celadon (green); pale sea-green.

せいじ[2] 政治 politics; 〈行政〉 government; administration; 〈政治上の事〉 political affairs ¶ 政治を行なう govern (the country); 《文》 administer [conduct] the affairs of state; 《文》 take the reins of government; 《文》 take the helm of state / 政治を語る talk [discuss] politics / 政治に関係する take up [《文》 engage in] politics / 明るい[清潔な]政治 clean politics / 武断政治 military government; government by the military; 《文》 the rule of the bayonet / 政治的 political / 政治的手腕 political ability [skill]; 《文》 statecraft; 〈外交〉 diplomacy / 政治的に politically / 政治意識 political awareness / 政治運動 a political movement [campaign] / 政治家 a politician (時に悪い意味で); a statesman 《*pl.* -men》 ★ statesman は公正な見識と指導力を具えた人物に与えられる一種の尊称で, 政治家本人が自分について使う語ではない / 政治学 political science; politics; (the science of) government / 政治活動 a political activity (★複数形で使うことが多い) / 政治活動をする take part [《文》 engage] in politics [political activities] / 政治機構 political structure / 政治記者 a reporter [writer] on political affairs / 政治気違い 〈病〉 politicomania; 〈人〉 a politicomaniac / 政治局 〈ソ連の〉 the Politburo / 政治嫌い a person with an aversion to politics; 《戯語》 a politicophobe / 政治結社 a political organization [association] / 政治献金 a political contribution [donation] / 政治工作 political maneuvering; 《口語》 politicking / 政治裁判 a political trial / 政治史 (a) political history / 政治資金 political funds; money for political activities / 政治資金規正法 〖法〗 the Act for the Regulation of Political Funds / 政治思想 political ideas [thought] / 政治色抜きの unpolitical; unpoliticized / 政治責任 (*one's*) administrative responsibilities / 政治組織 a political system / 政治哲学 political philosophy / 政治道徳 political morality / 政治犯 a political offense; 〈人〉 a political offender; 〈囚人〉 a political prisoner / 政治評論家 a political commentator [journalist, columnist] / 政治問題 a political issue [problem] / 政治問題に発展する develop into a political issue / 政治力 *one's* political power [influence]. [文例⇩]

セイシェル the Seychelles; the Republic of Seychelles (正式国名).

せいしき 正式 ¶ 正式の formal 《procedure》; 《文》 due 《formality》; full-dress 《debates》; regular 《education》; proper / 正式に formally; 《文》 duly; 《文》 in due [proper] form; properly / 正式承認 (a) *de jure* recognition / 正式メンバー a regular [card-carrying] member.

せいしつ 性質 〈生まれつき〉 (a) nature; 《文》 (a) disposition; 〈気質〉 a temperament; 〈特性〉 (a) character; a property (物の); 《chemical》 behavior; 〈素質〉 a quality ¶ 性質の良い[悪い]人 a good-natured [an ill-natured] person / 温和な性質の人 a person with a gentle nature [《文》 of a mild disposition] / 問題の性質上 (considered) from the nature of the matter. [文例⇩]

せいじつ 誠実 good faith; reliability; 《文》 fidelity ¶ 誠実な reliable; faithful; trustworthy / 誠実に in good faith; faithfully; honestly / 誠実でない unreliable; untrustworthy; 〈言葉が〉 insincere ⇨ せいい [用法].

せいじゃ[1] 正邪 right and [or] wrong ¶ 正邪をわきまえる know [can tell] right from wrong; know the difference between right and wrong.

せいじゃ[2] 聖者 ⇨ せいじん[2].

せいじゃく 静寂 silence; 《文》 stillness; quiet; (a) hush ¶ 静寂な 《文》 still; silent; quiet; hushed / 静寂を破る break the silence.

ぜいじゃく 脆弱 ¶ 脆弱な weak; frail; fragile; delicate; brittle.

せいしゅ 清酒 *sake*.

ぜいしゅう(にゅう) 税収(入) tax revenue(s).

せいしゅく 静粛 ¶ 静粛な quiet; silent; 《文》 still / 静粛にする keep quiet; do not make any noise. [文例⇩]

せいじゅく 成熟 ripeness; maturity; full [complete] growth ¶ 成熟する ripen; get ripe; mature; reach [《文》 attain] full growth / 性的に成熟する become sexually mature; reach sexual maturity / 成熟した ripe; mature / 成熟期 (the period of) maturity / 成熟味を増す become more mature.

せいしゅん 青春 youth; 《文》 the springtime of life ¶ 青春の youthful / 青春の情熱 the passion of youth; 《文》 《burn with》 youthful ardor / 青春の血潮 《stir up》 *one's* young blood / 青春時代に in *one's* youth [young days]; when *one* was young.

せいじゅん 清純 ¶ 清純な pure (and innocent).

せいしょ[1] 清書 a fair [clean] copy ¶ 清書する make a fair copy 《of》; copy [write] out.

せいしょ[2] 聖書 the (Holy) Bible; 《文》 the Scriptures; 《文》 Holy Writ ¶ 聖書学者 a Biblical [Bible] scholar / 聖書台 a lectern.

せいじょ 整除 〖数〗 ¶ 整除できる[できない] be divisible [indivisible].

せいしょう 斉唱 ¶ 斉唱する sing in unison.

せいじょう[1] 正常 normality; 《米》 normalcy

少々狂っている. There is something wrong with his political sense.

せいしつ 兄弟でも性質はまるで違う. They are brothers, but their characters are entirely different. / この問題は委員会が決すべき性質のものだ. This question, by its nature, is one that should be decided by the committee. / もって生まれた性質は直らない. One cannot help one's nature. | The leopard cannot change his spots. 〖諺〗 / このような状態になると, 水素は金属のような性質を示す. In this state hydrogen behaves like a metal.

せいしゅく 議長は静粛にとテーブルをこつこつたたいた. The chairman rapped the table for order. / 静粛に願います. Be quiet, please. ★ quiet の代わりに silent を使うと「お黙り!」ということになって不穏当である. / 静粛. 〈図書館の

¶ 正常な normal / 正常でない abnormal; irregular / 正常化する 〈正常にする〉 normalize; 〈正常になる〉 be normalized / 正常に復する return [get back] to normal; get back [be restored] to normality [normalcy] / 正常位 a normal position [posture];《俗》the missionary position.

せいじょう² 政情 a political situation [condition]; political affairs ¶ 政情に通じている be familiar with 《《文》 conversant》 with political conditions (in Korea) [the political conditions 《of Korea》].

せいじょう³ 清浄 ¶ 清浄な pure; clean / 清浄野菜 clean vegetables.

せいじょうき 星条旗 the Stars and Stripes; the Star-Spangled Banner.

せいしょうねん 青少年 young people; youth; the younger generation; juveniles ¶ 青少年犯罪 juvenile delinquency.

せいしょく¹ 生色 ¶ 生色がない look as pale as death [as white as a sheet].

せいしょく² 生殖 reproduction; generation; procreation ¶ 生殖する reproduce; generate; procreate / 生殖器 sexual [reproductive, generative] organs; genitals / 生殖細胞〔生物〕a reproductive [germ, generative] cell / 生殖力 procreative [generative] power.

せいしょく³ 聖職 〈牧師〉a religious vocation; holy orders; the ministry; the clergy / 〈単なるサラリーマン稼業でない〉a vocation; a calling; a profession as a sacred calling ¶ 聖職につく〈牧師になる〉take [be admitted to] holy orders; enter the ministry; be ordained (to the priesthood).

せいしょほう 正書法 (an) orthography.

せいしん¹ 精神 spirit; mind (心); soul (魂); will (意志); a motive (動機) ¶ 精神の[的] mental; spiritual; moral / 精神的愛 platonic love / 精神的支持[圧迫] moral support [pressure] / 精神的打撃 a mental blow; a shock / 精神を打ち込む put *one*'s heart (and soul) into 《*one*'s work》; throw *oneself* wholeheartedly into 《the task》; do 《a job》 with (all *one*'s) heart and soul / 精神を集中する concentrate *one*'s attention on *sth* / 精神に異常をきたす be mentally deranged [unbalanced]; have a mental breakdown / 〈気が狂う〉go 《《文》become》 insane; go mad [out of *one*'s mind] / 精神安定剤 a tranquilizer / 精神異常 mental derangement [disorder]; psychosis / 精神衛生 mental health / 精神家 an idealist / 精神鑑定 a psychiatric test / 精神構造 *one*'s mental make-up [structure] / 精神修養をする discipline *one*'s mind / 精神主義 spiritualism; idealism / 精神主義者 a spiritualist; an idealist / 精神障害 a mental disability [disorder] / 精神状態 a mental condition; a state of mind; mentality / 精神身体医学 psychosomatic medicine; psychosomatics / 精神生活 spiritual [mental] life / 精神年齢 mental age / 精神薄弱 mental weakness; feeble-mindedness; low intelligence / 精神薄弱者 a feeble-minded [weak-minded] person; a mentally deficient person; 〈集合的〉the mentally handicapped; mentally retarded [backward] people / 精神病 (a) mental illness; a disease of the mind; a mental disease / 精神病医 a psychiatrist; a mental specialist / 精神病医学 psychiatry / 精神病院 a mental hospital;《口語》a madhouse (★ madhouse は冗談で使うことはあるが、実際の精神病院についていっていうことは極めてまれ) / 精神病患者 a mental [psychiatric] patient;《口語》a mental case / 精神病理学 psychopathology / 精神分析 psychoanalysis / 精神分析を受ける undergo analysis / 精神分析学者[医] a psychoanalyst / 精神分裂症〔医〕schizophrenia; split personality / 精神分裂病患者 a schizophrenic / 精神力 spiritual strength.

せいしん² 清新 ¶ 清新な fresh; new.

せいじん¹ 成人 an adult; a grown-up man [woman]; 〈子供からみた〉a grownup ¶ 成人する grow up to be a man [woman]; 《文》 attain [arrive at] manhood [womanhood]; come of age / 成人の日 Coming-of-Age Day / 成人映画 an adult film / 成人学校 an adults' school / 成人教育 adult education / 成人式 a coming-of-age ceremony; an initiation rite (未開社会の) / 成人病 diseases of adults.

せいじん² 聖人 《文》a sage; a saint ¶ 聖人のような saintlike; saintly.

せいしんせいい 誠心誠意 wholeheartedly; devotedly; faithfully; from (the bottom of) *one*'s heart ¶ 誠心誠意事に当たる deal with *sth* wholeheartedly; go heart and soul into *sth*; do *sth* with *one*'s whole heart.

せいず¹ 星図 a star map.

せいず² 製図 drafting; drawing ¶ 製図する draft; draw / 製図家 a draftsman / 製図器械 a drawing instrument / 製図室 a drafting room; a drawing office / 製図板 a drafting [drawing] board / 製図用具 a draftsman's outfit.

せいすい 盛衰 ups and downs; rise and fall [decline]; 《文》 vicissitudes.

せいずい 精髄 ⇒ しんずい.

せいすう¹ 正数〔数〕a positive number.

せいすう² 整数〔数〕an integer; a whole number ¶ 整数比 (be expressed as) the ratios of whole numbers / 整数論 the theory of numbers; number theory.

せいする 制する 〈支配する〉control; com-

掲示〉Silence (please).

せいしん 法の条文にこだわらず、その精神をとれ。Don't stick to the letter of the law but observe its spirit. / 彼はただもう精神力だけでもっていた。Only the sheer force of his will to live kept him alive. / 精神一到何事か成らざらん。Where there's a will, there's a way.〔諺〕

せいする 与党は参議院で過半数を制することができなかった。The Government party failed to command a majority in the House of Councilors.

せいせい 彼がいなくなってせいせいした。I was glad to be rid of him. / 借金を払ったらせいせいしたよ。The load is [It is a load] off my mind now that I have cleared (off) my debts.

せいせい mand;《制圧する》have the upper [whip] hand of;《得を》get the better of;《抑圧する》check; restrain; suppress / 怒りを制する suppress one's anger; hold back [down] one's (rising) anger / 制し難い uncontrollable; irresistible. 文例

せいせい¹ 生成 ¶生成する create;《文》generate; form / 生成文法 generative grammar.

せいせい² 精製 refining ¶精製する refine / 精製した refined《sugar, oil》/ 精製所 a refinery.

せいせい³ 清々 ¶せいせいする《さわやかになる》feel refreshed;《ほっとする》feel relieved. 文例

せいぜい 精々《たかだか》at (the) most; at best;《できるだけ》to the utmost; as far [much] as possible [one can] ¶精々1マイル a mile at the (very) outside / 精々10日 ten days at the longest / 精々骨折る do one's (level) best; make every effort (to do);《文》exert one's utmost strength. 文例

ぜいせい 税制 a system of taxation; a tax [taxation] system ¶税制改革 a reform of the taxation system; a tax reform [revision] / 税制調査会 the Tax Commission.

ぜいぜい ¶ぜいぜい言う wheeze (out); be wheezy.

せいせいどうどう 正々堂々 ¶正々堂々たる fair and square; open and aboveboard / 正々堂々と戦う play fair; play the game. 文例

せいせき 成績 a result; a record ¶成績がいい[悪い] do well [badly] (at school); have a good [poor] record in one's studies); have good [bad, poor] grades; give good [poor] (business) results / 成績のよい生徒 a high-achieving pupil / 学校の成績 one's school record / 営業成績 ⇒えいぎょう / 成績順に座る sit in (the) order of merit / 成績証明書《米》a transcript / 成績表《全体の》a list of the students' records;《個人の》a report card; a grade transcript. 文例

せいせつ 正接《数》a tangent (略: tan).

せいせっかい 生石灰 quicklime; unslaked lime.

せいせん¹ 生鮮 ¶生鮮食品 perishable food(s); perishables.

せいせん² 精選 ¶精選する select [sort out, pick out] carefully [with care] / 精選した choice; select; hand-picked / 夏物の精選品 a fine selection of summer goods.

せいぜん¹ 生前 ¶生前(の, に) during [in] one's lifetime; while [when] one was alive;《文》in life; before one's death.

せいぜん² 整然 ¶整然たる orderly; systematic; well-regulated / 整然と in (good [perfect]) order; systematically.

せいぜんせつ 性善説 the view of human nature as fundamentally good; belief in the innate goodness of man.

せいそ 清楚 ¶清楚な neat and clean; tidy; trim / 清楚な身なりをしている be neatly dressed.

せいそう¹ 正装 ¶正装する dress up; be in full dress [uniform].

せいそう² 政争 a political dispute [issue];《文》political strife ¶政争の具に供する make a political issue of sth.

せいそう³ 星霜 years; time ¶百年の星霜を経た建物《文》a building which has seen [been through] 100 winters.

せいそう⁴ 清掃 ¶清掃する clean / 清掃車《米》a garbage truck [wagon];《英》a dustcart / 清掃作業員《米》a garbage man [collector];《英》a dustman;《英》a dustbinman.

せいそう⁵ 盛装 ¶盛装する be dressed up; be (dressed) in one's (Sunday) best; be (all) decked out in one's finest clothes;《文》attire oneself [be attired] in rich clothes [apparel].

せいぞう¹ 聖像 a sacred image; an icon (特に正教の).

せいぞう² 製造《文》manufacture; production ¶製造する make;《文》manufacture; produce; turn out / 商品として製造を開始する start manufacturing sth on a commercial basis [scale] / 製造業 the manufacturing industry / 製造業者《文》the manufacturer; the maker / 製造工程 a manufacturing process / 製造所 a factory; a manufactory; a works, a mill / 製造番号 the (manufacturer's) serial number《on a camera》. 文例

せいそうけん 成層圏 (fly through) the stratosphere ¶成層圏の stratospheric / 成層圏飛行 a stratosphere [stratospheric] flight.

せいそく 生息 ¶生息する inhabit (a forest); live (in the water) / 生息地 a habitat; the home (of the tiger) / 生息動物 an inhabitant (of the forest).

せいぞろい 勢揃い ¶勢揃いする meet [get] together; assemble in full force; muster; line up.

せいぞん 生存 existence;《文》subsistence; life; survival (残存) ¶生存する exist; live;《生き残る》survive / 生存競争 the struggle for existence / 生存権 the right to live [life] / 生存者 a survivor / 生存中に in one's lifetime;《文》in life / 生存能力 viability / 生存本能 survival instincts / 生存率 a survival rate.

せいたい¹ 生体 a living body; an organism ¶生体解剖 vivisection / 生体解剖をする vivisect / 生体実験 medical experimentation [a medical experiment] on a living person.

せいたい² 生態 a mode of life; ecology ¶昆虫の生態 the ecology of insects / 落葉樹の生

せいぜい《売る時》精々勉強いたしましょう. I'll let you have it at my lowest possible price. / 借金せずにやって行くのが精々だ. It is as much as I can do [all I can do] to keep out of debt.
せいせいどうどう 正々堂々とやれ. Play fair! | Play the game!
せいせき 君の学校の成績はどうですか. How are you getting on at school? / 学校の成績はどんどん落ちた. His school work got steadily worse. / 彼は成績が良いのできっと奨学金をもらえるでしょう. His grades are so good that he's bound to win a scholarship. / 昇進は成績次第です. Promotion is by merit.
せいぞう² 彼はボール箱の製造販売をやっている. He makes and sells cardboard boxes.

態 the botany of deciduous trees / 現代女性の生態 the mode of life of today's women / スラム街の生態 the facts [truth] about slum life / 生態学 (animal, plant) ecology; bionomics / 生態学的 ecological; bionomic(al) / 生態系 an ecosystem; an ecological system.

せいたい³ 声帯 the vocal cords [chords] ¶声帯模写 vocal mimicry / 声帯模写をする mimic sb's voice [way of speaking, way of singing].

せいたい⁴ 政体 a form [system] of government ¶立憲[共和]政体 the constitutional [republican] system of government.

せいたい⁵ 聖体 《キリスト教》the Eucharist ⇒ せいさん(しき).

せいたい⁶ 臍帯 《解》the umbilical cord.

せいだい 盛大 ¶盛大な 〈繁盛している〉prosperous; flourishing; 〈堂々たる〉grand; magnificent; 〈首尾よい〉successful / 盛大な歓迎 a very warm welcome [reception] / 盛大に splendidly; pompously; in grand style; on a large scale / 盛大に見送る give sb a rousing send-off. 文例⇩

せいたく 請託 ¶請託する beg [implore, 《文》entreat] sb to exercise his influence 《in favor of》.

せいだく 清濁 ¶清濁あわせのむ be broadminded enough to show tolerance toward all sorts of men.

ぜいたく 贅沢 〈豪華〉(a) luxury; 〈乱費〉(an) extravagance ¶ぜいたくな 〈豪華な〉luxurious; expensive; 〈浪費的な〉extravagant; lavish / ぜいたくな食事 a sumptuous meal; a feast; 《文》(keep) a luxurious table / ぜいたくな生活 a luxurious [an extravagant] life; high living / ぜいたくに暮らす live [lead] a life of luxury [an extravagant life]; live in luxury; live [be] in the lap of luxury; live on the fat of the land (食生活で) / ぜいたくに使う use sth lavishly; make lavish [free] use of sth / ぜいたくを言う ask [expect] too much; ask [《文》wish] for more than one's due / ぜいたく品 luxury goods [wares]; luxuries. 文例⇩

せいだす 精出す ⇒ せい¹(精を出す).

せいたん 生誕 ⇒ たんじょう.

せいち¹ 生地 one's birthplace.

せいち² 聖地 a sacred [holy] place; holy ground; the Holy Land (パレスチナ) ¶聖地巡礼 《make》a pilgrimage to the Holy Land.

せいち³ 整地 〈建築のための〉leveling of ground; site preparation; 〈耕作のための〉soil preparation ¶整地する level the land 《for construction》; prepare the soil 《for planting》.

せいち⁴ 精緻 ¶精緻な 〈細かい〉minute; detailed; fine; 〈綱羅的な〉《文》exhaustive / 精緻な研究 a detailed study / 精緻な筆使い minute brushwork.

ぜいちく 筮竹 divining sticks.

せいちゃ 製茶 tea manufacture.

せいちゅう¹ 成虫 an imago (pl. -es, imagines); an adult (insect) ¶成虫の imaginal / 成虫期 the imago stage.

せいちゅう² 掣肘 (a) restraint; (a) restriction; (a) check; control ¶掣肘する restrain; restrict; check; control; hamper / 掣肘を受ける[受けない] be under [be free from] restraint.

せいちゅう³ 精虫 《動》a spermatozoon (pl. -zoa).

せいちょう¹ 正調 the orthodox [traditional] melody 《to [for] a folk song》.

せいちょう² 成[生]長 growth ¶成長する grow (up) / 成長するにつれて as one grows / 成長して大人になる grow (up) to be a man [woman]; grow into a man [woman] / 成長した full-grown; adult / 安定成長 stable [steady] growth / 成長過程 a growth process / 成長株 《株式》a growth stock / 成長期(間) a growth period; the growing season (植物の) / 成長曲線 a growth curve / 成長ホルモン a growth hormone / 年次経済成長目標 an annual economic growth target / 成長率 a growth rate / 経済成長率 the rate of economic growth; the rate of growth of the (Japanese) economy.

せいちょう³ 性徴 sex [sexual] characteristics ¶第2次[1次]性徴 the secondary [primary] sex characteristics.

せいちょう⁴ 清聴 文例⇩

せいちょう⁵ 整調 〈ボートの〉(a) stroke (oar) ¶整調する row [pull] stroke.

せいちょうざい 整腸剤 (a) medicine for intestinal disorders.

せいつう 精通 ¶…に精通する be well informed about…; 《文》be well [deeply] versed in…; have a thorough [detailed] knowledge of…; be at home in [on]…; be well posted on [in]…; be familiar [well acquainted] with…; have sth at one's fingertips. 文例⇩

せいてい 制定 enactment ¶制定する enact; lay down; establish / 法律を制定する enact [make] laws; legislate 《against, for》.

せいてき¹ 政敵 a political opponent [rival, 《文》antagonist, 《文》adversary].

せいてき² 性的 《文》sexual ¶性的魅力がある[ない] have a lot of [have no] sex appeal; 《文》be [be not] sexually attractive.

せいてき³ 静的 static.

せいてつ 製鉄 iron manufacture; 〈製鋼〉steel manufacture; steelmaking ¶製鉄会社 an iron-manufacturing company; a steel(-manufacturing) company / 製鉄業 the iron (and steel) industry; the steel industry / 製鉄所 a steelworks; an ironworks (製鋼設備のない).

せいてん¹ 青天 ¶青天白日の身となる have

せいだい 会は盛大であった. The meeting was very well attended [a great success]. / 盛大に商売をやっている. He is doing a thriving business.

ぜいたく 彼女はぜいたくな女だ. She is too prone to extravagance. / そんな服は私にはぜいたくだわ. That dress is an extravagance I can't afford. / 「ぜいたくよりまず必要品」ということを忘れないでくれたまえ. Keep this in your mind: necessities before luxuries. / これ以上望むのはぜいたくだ. You couldn't reasonably ask [wish] for more.

せいちょう⁴ ご清聴を感謝致します. Thank you for your kind attention.

せいつう 彼は中国の事情に精通している. He is well acquainted

せいてん one's innocence proved; be cleared of the charge (brought against one) / 青天のへきれき (like) a bolt from [out of] the blue. 文例[U]

せいてん² 晴天 fine [fair] weather; a bright [clear] sky ¶晴天続き a long spell of fine weather.

せいてん³ 聖典 a sacred [holy] book.

せいでんき 静電気 static electricity ¶静電気の electrostatic.

せいと 生徒 a schoolchild; a schoolboy; a schoolgirl; 《米》a student (特に高校の);a pupil (at [of, in] Minami Junior High School) ¶生徒会 <自治会> a student council; <生徒大会> a students' meeting.

せいど¹ 制度 a system; an institution; an organization ¶西洋から導入された諸制度 institutions imported from the West 《in the Meiji period》/ 制度を設ける frame [《文》formulate, build up] a system / 制度を施行する enforce a system; put a system in operation [practice] / 制度化する《文》institutionalize / 制度的に(は)《文》institutionally.

せいど² 精度 precision; accuracy ¶精度が高い be extremely precise [accurate]; 《文》be capable of extraordinary precision / 精度を高める improve the precision of sth.

せいとう¹ 正当 ¶正当な《文》just (cause); proper; right; 《文》rightful; reasonable 《doubt》; justifiable 《grounds》; <合法的な>《文》lawful; legal; legitimate / 正当な手段により by fair means / 正当な理由もなく without good [sufficient] reason / 正当な地位を得る come into one's own / 正当に justly; rightly; rightfully; <合法的に> lawfully; legally; legitimately / 正当に評価する do sb justice; do justice to sth; give sb his due;《文》duly appreciate 《sb's achievements》/ 正当化する justify / 正当防衛 (legitimate) self-defense / 正当防衛で 《kill a man》in self-defense. 文例[U]

せいとう² 正統 ¶正統の legitimate; orthodox / 正統政府 a de jure [legitimate] government.

せいとう³ 政党 a political party ¶政党間の interparty 《cooperation》/ 二大政党制 a two-party system / 政党員 a member of a political party; a party man / 政党政治 party politics [government] / 政党組織 party organization / 政党内閣 a party cabinet.

せいとう⁴ 製陶 pottery manufacture ¶製陶術 the ceramic art; ceramics / 製陶所 a pottery.

せいとう⁵ 精糖 sugar refining; <精糖した砂糖> refined sugar ¶精糖所 a sugar refinery [mill].

せいとう⁶ 製糖 sugar manufacture ¶製糖会社 a sugar-manufacturing company / 製糖業 the sugar-manufacturing industry.

せいどう¹ 正道《文》the path of righteousness [virtue]; the right path [track] ¶正道を踏む《文》tread on the path of righteousness;《口語》keep on the straight and narrow / 正道を踏み外す stray [《文》deviate] from the right path / 正道につかせる set sb on the right track / 正道に導く guide sb into the right path / 正道にもどる get back on the right track;《口語》go straight (犯罪者が).

せいどう² 制動 〖機〗braking;〖電〗damping;〖スキー〗stemming ¶制動回転〖スキー〗a stem turn (雪渓の制動滑降〖登山〗(make) a glissade / 制動機 a brake ⇒ブレーキ / 空気制動機 an air [a pneumatic] brake / 真空[自動]制動機 a vacuum [an automatic] brake / 制動手《鉄道》《米》a brakeman /《英》a brakesman / 二重制動装置 a dual braking system / 制動灯 a brake light; a stoplight.

せいどう³ 青銅 bronze ¶青銅器 bronze ware / 青銅器時代 the Bronze Age.

せいどう⁴ 聖堂 <孔子の> a temple [shrine] (of Confucius); <一般に> a church; a sanctuary.

せいとく 生得 ¶生得の《文》innate; inborn ¶生得観念〖哲〗innate ideas / 生得権 one's birthright / 生得性《文》innateness.

せいどく 精読 careful [close] reading;《文》perusal ¶精読する read sth carefully [with care];《文》peruse.

せいとん 整頓 tidying (up) ¶整頓する put sth in order; tidy up; put [set] (a room) to rights; arrange (one's belongings) properly [neatly] / 隊列を整頓させる dress the ranks; dress (the men) in line / 整頓した (neat and) tidy (rooms); in order; orderly / 整頓してない untidy; out of order; in disorder.

せいなる 聖なる holy;《文》sacred.

せいなん 西南 (the) southwest (略:SW) ¶西南の southwestern; southwesterly.

ぜいにく 贅肉 superfluous flesh; <脂肪> fat; <こぶ> an excrescence ¶贅肉がつく put on [pick up] extra flesh / ずいぶんと贅肉のついた男 a man with a lot of fat on him.

せいねん¹ 生年 the year of one's birth ¶生年月日 (one's) date of birth (略: d.o.b., D.o.B.); the date of one's birth; one's birth date.

せいねん² 成年 ¶成年に達する come of age; reach [《文》attain] one's majority / 成年者 an adult; a major;《文》a person of full age.

せいねん³ 青年 a youth, a young man; <総称> young people; the younger [《文》rising] generation;《文》the young ¶青年時代 (one's) youth; one's younger days / 青年団[会] a young men's association / 青年男女 young men and women.

せいのう 性能《文》capacity; efficiency; power; performance (機械などの); <特質> a property

---

with Chinese affairs. | He is an authority on things Chinese.

せいてん¹ その報道はまさに青天のへきれきであった。The news came like a bolt from the blue [as a great surprise to us].

せいてん² ただ今マイクの試験中。本日は晴天なり, 本日は晴天なり。One—two—three—four—testing! Testing! One—two—three—four—testing! Testing!

せいとう¹ 君の方が正当だとしても, そんな言い方をするもんじゃない。Though you may be right, you should not put it like that. / この問題を正当にしていたのにも彼には充分正当な理由があった。He was fully justified in doing nothing about [having nothing to do with] the matter. / 目的は必ずしも手段を正当化しない。The

¶…より性能がすぐれている outperform《the other machine》/ 性能のよい highly efficient ;《a machine》with a good [high] performance / 性能を高める improve *its* performance / 性能試験 a performance [an efficiency] test / 性能特性 a performance characteristic / 高性能爆薬 a high explosive.

せいは 制覇 ¶制覇する conquer ; dominate ;《文》gain supremacy [mastery]《over》; 〈競技で〉win [gain] the championship《of》/ 世界制覇 domination of the world ;《文》world hegemony.

せいばい 成敗 〈刑罰〉punishment ; 〈裁断〉judgment.

せいはく[1] 精白 ¶精白する polish《rice》; refine《sugar》/ 精白米 polished [cleaned] rice.

せいはく[2] 精薄 ⇨ せいしん[1] (精神薄弱者) ¶精薄児 a mentally-handicapped[-retarded] child ; a weak-minded child.

せいばつ 征伐 〈討伐〉《文》subjugation ;《文》conquest ; 〈鎮圧〉suppression ; 〈遠征〉an [a punitive] expedition ; 〈駆除〉extermination ¶征伐する《文》subjugate ; conquer ; punish ; suppress《a revolt》; 〈駆除する〉exterminate ; stamp out ; 〈懲らしめる〉《文》chastise ; punish / 征伐に行く go on an expedition《against》.

せいはん[1] 正犯 the principal [main] offense ¶正犯者 the principal [main] offender.

せいはん[2] 製版 〖印刷〗make-up ¶製版する make up.

せいはんたい 正反対 ¶正反対の方向に進む go [《文》proceed] just in the opposite direction / 正反対に in direct opposition《to》/ 正反対である be just the opposite《of》; be diametrically [directly] opposite [opposed]《to》; be the exact reverse《of》; be quite contrary《to》;《文》be antipodal《to》. [文例⇩]

せいひ 成否 success (or failure) ; the result ;《文》《decide》the issue ¶成否を度外視して regardless of the issue.

せいび 整備 preparation ; maintenance ; servicing ; 〈調整〉tuning up ;《口語》a tune-up ; 〈船の〉fitting-out ¶整備する service《an airplane》;《米》fix《a machine》; fit out《a ship》; equip《a factory》fully with《machinery》; provide《a laboratory》with all《the necessary equipment》/ グラウンドを整備する put the ground(s) in good condition ; tend [fix] the ground(s) / 整備しておく keep《a road》in repair / 整備の行き届いた車 a car kept in good repair / (地上)整備員〖航空〗〈個人〉a ground man ; 〈総称〉the ground crew / 整備工 a (car) mechanic / 整備上の必要事項 maintenance requirements. [文例⇩]

せいひょう 製氷 ice manufacture ¶製氷機 an ice machine ; an ice-maker / 製氷皿 〈冷蔵庫の〉an ice (cube) tray / 製氷所[会社] an ice plant [company] / 自動製氷装置 an automatic ice-maker.

せいびょう 性病 a venereal [sexual] disease (略 : V.D.) ;《米》a social disease.

せいひれい 正比例 ¶正比例する be in direct proportion [ratio]《to》; be directly proportional《to》.

せいひん[1] 清貧 ¶清貧に甘んじる《文》be contented with honest poverty.

せいひん[2] 製品 manufactured goods [articles] ; a product ¶絹製品 silk goods [products] / 国内製品 home products / 日本製品 Japanese(-made) goods ; products made in Japan.

せいふ 政府 a government ; the Government (一定の国の) ;《米》the Administration ; 〈内閣〉the cabinet ¶政府の所在地[首長] the seat [head] of government / 政府を樹立する establish [set up] a government / 政府を支持[打倒]する support [overthrow] the Government / 現政府 the present Government / 時の政府 〈当時の〉the then Government ; the Government of the day ; 〈現に支配している〉the Government in power / カーター政府 the Carter Administration / 日本政府 the Japanese Government / 政府(提出法)案 a Government bill [measure] / (国会の)政府委員 a government delegate / 政府機関 a government body [agency] / 政府筋 government [administrative] circles / 政府当局 the government authorities.

せいぶ 西部 the western part(s) ; the west ; 〈米国の〉the West ¶西部の western / 西部劇 〈映画の〉a western (film) ; a cowboy picture.

せいふく[1] 正副 〈書類の〉original and duplicate [copy] ¶正副2通作成する prepare [make out]《a document》in duplicate / 正副議長 the speaker and deputy speaker ; the chairman and vice-chairman.

せいふく[2] 制服 a uniform ¶制服の警官 a uniformed policeman ; a police officer in uniform / 制服組 uniformed personnel / 制服姿で[の] in uniform.

せいふく[3] 征服 defeat ;《文》conquest ;《文》subjugation ¶征服する defeat ; conquer ;《文》subjugate ;《文》gain [obtain] mastery over《the environment》/ 征服者 a conqueror ;《文》a vanquisher / 征服欲 lust [desire] for conquest.

せいぶつ[1] 生物 a living thing [creature, being, organism] ; a life form ; an organism ; life (総称) ¶高等な生物 a higher organism [form of life] / 生物のいる惑星 a life-bearing[-supporting] planet / 生物界 animals and plants ; the animate nature ; life / 生物学 biology / 生物学者 a biologist / 生物学的 biological《time》/ 生物学的に biologically.

せいぶつ[2] 静物 〖絵画〗still life ¶静物画 a still

---

end does not always justify the means.

せいはんたい 私とあなたは物の見方が正反対だ. You and I are poles apart in the way we look at things. / 彼は勉強家だが弟は正反対に怠け者だ. He is as hard-working as his younger brother is idle.

せいび この車は整備に出さなくてはいけない. This car needs to go to the garage. | This car is in need of repair.

せいぶん[2] それはアヘンが主成分になっている. It has opium as its main ingredient.

せいべつ[2] 性別による教育水準の統計によれば, 男性の方が女性よ

life《*pl.* still lifes》; a still-life painting.
せいふん 製粉 (flour) milling ¶製粉機[所] a (flour) mill.
せいぶん¹ 正文 the (official) text《of a treaty》.
せいぶん² 成分 an ingredient; a constituent; a component ¶主(要)成分 the main [chief, principal] ingredients / 副成分 an accessory ingredient. [文例⇩]
せいぶん³ 成文 ¶成文化する codify; put in statutory form / 成文憲法 a written constitution / 成文法 a statute; (a) written law; statute law (総称).
せいへき 性癖 *one's* nature;《文》*one's* natural disposition; an inclination;《文》a propensity.
せいべつ¹ 生別 a (lifelong) separation [parting]; 〈離婚〉(a) divorce ¶生別する part from *sb* (for ever [for life, never to meet again]).
せいべつ² 性別 the distinction of sex ¶性別に関係なく irrespective [without distinction] of sex / ひなの性別鑑定[鑑定者] chicken sexing [a chicken sexer]. [文例⇩]
せいへん 政変 a political change; a change of government; a coup d'état《*pl.* coups d'état》(武力による).
せいぼ¹ 生母 *one's* (real) mother.
せいぼ² 聖母 the Holy Mother; Our Lady ¶聖母像 a Madonna / 聖母マリア the Virgin Mary.
せいぼ³ 歳暮 the end of the year; the year-end; 〈進物〉a year-end present [gift] ¶歳暮の売出し a year-end sale.
せいほう¹ 西方 ¶西方の west; western / 西方へ《go》west; westward / 市の西方に (to the) west of the city.
せいほう² 製法 a manufacturing method [process]; 〈料理の〉a recipe《for》¶菓子の製法を教える teach *sb* how to make a cake; give *sb* a recipe for (making) a cake / 製法を見て作る make *sth* from a formula [recipe].
せいぼう¹ 声望 ⇨じんぼう.
せいぼう² 制帽 a regulation [uniform, school] cap.
ぜいほう 税法 〈法律〉the tax law; 〈課税方法〉a system of taxation.
せいほうけい 正方形 a square.
せいほく 西北 (the) northwest (略: NW) ¶西北の northwestern; northwesterly.
せいぼし 聖母子 the Virgin and [with] Child ¶聖母子像 a picture of the Virgin and [with] Child; a Madonna and Child.
せいほん¹ 正本 〈原本〉the original (copy [text]).
せいほん² 製本 bookbinding ¶丈夫な製本 (a) durable binding / 製本する bind《a book》/ 製本がよくできている be well bound / 製本中である be at the binder's; be binding / 製本所 a bookbindery / 製本屋 a bookbinder.
せいまい 精米 〈精白〉rice cleaning [polishing]; 〈米〉cleaned [polished] rice ¶精米所 a rice(-cleaning) mill.
せいまがいしゃ 製麻会社 a hemp-dressing company.
せいみつ 精密 ¶精密な〈詳細〉《文》minute; detailed; close; 〈正確〉precise; accurate / 精密な技術 precision techniques / 精密な地図 a detail(ed) map / 精密に〈詳細〉《文》minutely; closely; in detail; 〈正確〉precisely; accurately / 精密に検査する examine《a matter》closely; make a close investigation《into》/ 精密科学 an exact science / 精密機械 a precision machine / 精密器具 a precision instrument / 精密工業 the precision machinery industry. [文例⇩]
せいみょう 精妙 ¶精妙な《文》exquisite; fine;《文》subtle.
せいむ 政務 state [political] affairs; government business ¶政務を見る[執る] attend to government affairs;《文》administer the affairs of state / 政務次官 a parliamentary under-secretary [vice-minister] / 政務調査会〈政党の〉the Political Affairs Research Committee.
ぜいむ 税務 taxation business; tax matters ¶税務官 a revenue officer [official] / 税務署《the superintendent of》a tax [revenue] office / 税務署員 a tax(-office) clerk / 税務相談所 a tax information office.
せいめい¹ 生命 life; existence; 〈精髄〉the life; the soul《of》¶生命の長い[短い] long-[short-]lived / 生命を賭する risk *one's* life / 多くの生命を犠牲にして at the cost of many lives / 生命にかかわる fatal《diseases》;《文》mortal《wounds》/ 生命力のある〈赤ん坊などが〉viable / 生命維持装置 a life-support system / 生命感 a feeling of vitality; the sense of being alive / 生命線《guard》*one's* lifeline; 〈手相の〉the line of Life; the Lifeline / 生命力 life force; survival power [ability]; *one's* [*its*] hold on life; vitality. [文例⇩]
せいめい² 声明 a statement; a (public) declaration; an announcement; a proclamation ¶声明する declare; announce; proclaim; make [issue] a statement / 反対[賛成]を声明する declare *oneself* against [for, in favor of] *sth* / 公式声明を発表する issue [deliver] an official statement《on》/ 声明書 a (public) statement; a manifesto《*pl.* -(e)s》.
せいめい³ 姓名 *one's* (full) name ¶姓名を名乗る give *one's* name《as》/ 姓名判断 telling *sb's* fortune on the basis of *his* name; onomancy.
せいめいほけん 生命保険 life insurance;《英》life assurance ¶生命保険に入る insure *one's* life《for ¥20,000,000 with Fuji Insurance Company》; take out life insurance; have *one's* life insured / 生命保険に入っている have life

りも大学進学率が高い. According to the figures for educational level by sex, more men than women go (on) to university.
せいみつ 彼女たちは手先が器用だから, 精密作業にはもってこいである. Their nimble fingers make [《文》manual dexterity makes] the girls ideal for precision work./ これはかなり精密に分析できる. This can be analyzed with a fair degree of precision.
せいめい¹ この伝染病のために大勢の人の生命が奪い去られた. The epidemic took a heavy toll of lives. / その自動車事故で3人の若者の生命が失われた. The automobile accident claimed the lives

せいもん¹ 正門 the main [front] gate ; the main entrance.

せいもん² 声門 〚解〛the glottis ((pl. -es, -tides)) ; the vocal chink.

せいもん³ 声紋 a voiceprint.

せいもん⁴ 誓文 a written oath ¶五箇条の御誓文 the Imperial Covenant of Five Articles ; the Charter Oath (of the Emperor Meiji).

せいやく¹ 制約 a restriction ; a limitation ; 〈条件〉a condition ; a constraint ⇨ せいげん².

せいやく² 誓約 an oath ; 〚文〛a pledge ; 〚文〛a vow ¶誓約する swear ; 〚文〛vow ; make [take, swear] an oath ((that...)) ; 〚文〛pledge oneself ((to do)) ; give one's word (of honor) ((to do, that...)) ; 〚文〛make a vow ((to do, that...)) / 誓約を守る keep one's word [pledge, vow] ; be as good as one's word / 誓約を破る break one's oath [vow] ; 〚文〛violate one's pledge ; go back on one's promise [word] / 誓約どおりに faithful [true] to one's word [vow] ; 〚文〛in conformity with one's pledge [promise] / 誓約書 a written oath [pledge] ; a covenant.

せいやく³ 製薬 medicine [drug] manufacture ; pharmacy ¶製薬会社 a pharmaceutical [drug] company.

せいゆ 製油 oil manufacture ; 〈精油〉oil refining ¶製油業 the oil industry / 製油所 an oil factory [refinery].

せいゆう 声優 〈外国映画吹替えの〉an actor [actress] whose voice is used for dubbing ((Western films into Japanese)) ; 〈ラジオの〉a radio actor [actress] ; an actor [actress] in radio.

せいよう¹ 西洋 the West ; the Occident ; 〈諸国〉Western countries ¶西洋の Western ; European ; 〚文〛Occidental / 西洋人 a Westerner / 西洋化 Westernization / 西洋化する Westernize / 西洋かぶれ〈人〉an ultra-Westernized person [Japanese] / 西洋史 the history of the Western world / 西洋文明 Western civilization.

せいよう² 静養 (a) rest ; 〈病後の〉convalescence ; recuperation ¶静養する〈病後に〉convalesce ; recuperate ; 〈静かに休む〉take a rest ; rest quietly ; 静養のため for (the benefit of) one's health ; in order to recuperate.

せいよく 性欲 sexual desire ; sex drive ¶性欲の強い highly-sexed / 性欲倒錯 sexual perversion / 性欲倒錯者 a sexual pervert.

せいらい 生来 by nature ; naturally ; 〚文〛congenitally ¶生来の natural ; 〚文〛innate ; in-born ; born ; 〚文〛congenital / 生来身体が弱い have a weak constitution. 〚文例〛

せいり¹ 生理 ¶生理(学) physiology / 生理(学)的 physiological ((phenomena)) / 生理的要求 the needs of the body / 生理衛生 physiology and hygiene / 生理学者 a physiologist / 生理休暇 a menstrual leave ; a special monthly leave for women / 生理帯 a sanitary napkin / 生理痛 menstrual colic [〔米〕cramps] ; period pains / 生理日 one's menstrual period ; ((have)) one's period.

せいり² 整理 ¶整理する (re)arrange ; put ((a room, one's books)) in order ; (re)adjust ; 〈整理分類する〉pigeonhole ((data)) ; sort out ((the mess)) ; 〈会社などを〉reorganize ; liquidate ; 家財を整理する dispose of one's household goods and furniture / 交通を整理する regulate [control] traffic / (一家の)財政を整理する sort out [adjust] one's financial affairs / 残品を整理する clear off the unsold goods / 人員を整理する reduce [cut down] the staff [personnel] ; cut the number of employees / 整理棚 pigeonholes / 整理だんす a chest of drawers ; 整理箱 a filing cabinet / 整理番号 a reference number / 整理部〚新聞〛the make-up department ; the copy desk.

せいりきがく 静力学 statics.

せいりし 税理士 a licensed tax accountant.

せいりつ 成立 ¶成立する〈実現する〉materialize ; 〚文〛be realized ; 〚文〛be effected ; 〈組織される〉be formed ; be organized ; 〈協定などが〉come into effect ; 〚文〛be concluded ; 〈生まれる〉come [be brought] into being [existence] / 成立予算 the approved budget. 〚文例〛

ぜいりつ 税率 the rate of taxation ; a tax rate ; 〈関税の〉a tariff ¶税率を引き上げる[下げる] raise [lower] the tax rate.

せいりゃく 政略 political tactics ; a political maneuver [move] ; a policy ¶政略的 political / 政略結婚 a marriage of convenience [expediency] ; (a) marriage for political reasons. 〚文例〛

せいりゅう 整流 〚電〛rectification ; commutation ¶整流する rectify ; commute ; commutate / 整流(真空)管 a rectifying tube / 整流器 a rectifier / 整流子 a commutator.

せいりょう¹ 声量 the volume of one's voice ¶声量がある have a powerful [rich, full] voice.

せいりょう² 清涼 ¶清涼飲料水 a refreshing [cooling] drink ((〚文〛beverage)) ; a soft drink ; a carbonated drink ; ((a bottle of)) pop.

せいりょく¹ 勢力 power ; 〈権勢〉influence ; 〈力〉strength ; 〈物理的の〉energy ¶勢力が

---

of three young people. / 雑草は, しぶとい生命力があって, なかなか根絶やしにできない. The weeds are difficult to eradicate owing to their strong hold on life.

せいよう² 病気を直すためには静養しなければいけないと医者に言われた. The doctor prescribed a rest cure for my illness. / 1か月ほど自宅で静養すればすっかり元気になるだろう. He will be completely restored to health by recuperating at home for a month or so.

せいらい 日本人は生来潔癖である. Love of cleanliness is innate in the Japanese.

せいりつ 本年度の予算は昨夜成立した. The budget for the current fiscal year was given final approval by the Diet last night. / 両人の間に妥協が成立した. A compromise has been effected between them. / 両家の間に縁談が成立した. A marriage has been arranged between the two families. / そのような理論は成立し

せいりょく ある have (a great deal of) influence 《over, with》; carry weight 《with, among》 / 勢力のある powerful; influential / 勢力のない powerless; uninfluential / 勢力の均衡 the balance of power / 勢力を振るう《文》wield power [influence] / 勢力争い a power struggle; a struggle [contest] for power / 勢力範囲を広げる extend [expand] one's sphere of influence / widen [《文》enlarge] the scope of one's influence / 国会内の新勢力分野 the new power alignments in the House. 文例⬇

せいりょく² 精力 energy; vigor; vitality;《口語》go;《文》one's sexual capacity [powers];《文》potency; virility ¶ 精力的な energetic; vigorous;《口語》full of go / 精力を傾注する put [throw] all one's energies [into] / 精力を使い果たす run out of steam / 精力を発散する let [work] off steam [one's energy] / 精力家 an energetic man;《口語》a ball of fire / 精力絶倫の人《文》a man of unbounded [immense] virility [potency]. 文例⬇

せいるい 声涙 ¶ 声涙ともに下る speak with tears in one's eyes [rolling down one's cheeks].

せいれい¹ 政令 a government ordinance; a cabinet order ¶ 政令審査委員会 the Ordinance Review Committee.

せいれい² 聖霊《キリスト教》the Holy Ghost [Spirit] ¶ 聖霊降臨 the Descent of the Holy Spirit (on the Apostles) / 聖霊降臨日 Whitsunday.

せいれい³ 精励 hard work;《文》diligence;《文》industry ¶ 精励恪勤である《文》work hard;《文》be diligent; be industrious;《文》be assiduous (in one's work); apply oneself (to one's duties).

せいれい⁴ 精霊 〈霊魂〉the spirit; the soul; the ghost; 〈精〉a spirit; a sprite;《文》a genius (pl. genii).

せいれき 西暦 the Christian Era; Anno Domini (略: A.D., AD) ¶ 西暦 79 年に in A.D. 79; in 79 A.D. ★ A.D. を付けるは西暦紀元の初期の年号のみ。1066 年を A.D. 1066 とはしない。

せいれつ 整列 ¶ 整列する stand in a row; line [be lined] up; form (a line) / 3 列に整列する be drawn up in three lines / 整列させる dress (the men).

せいれん 精錬 ¶ 精錬する refine 《metals》; smelt 《copper》; reduce 《ores》 / 精錬所 a refinery; a smelting works.

せいれんけっぱく 清廉潔白 absolute honesty;《文》unsullied integrity ¶ 清廉潔白な honest;《文》upright / 清廉潔白の士 a man who is as straight as a die;《文》an upright man;《文》a man of integrity.

せいろ 蒸籠 a steaming basket; a basket steamer.

せいろん 正論 a sound [fair] argument. 文例⬇

セイロン Ceylon ⇨ スリランカ ¶ セイロンの Ceylon; Ceylonese / セイロン語 Sinhalese / セイロン紅茶 Ceylon tea / セイロン人 a Ceylonese (単複同形).

セーター a sweater;《英》a jersey; a pullover.

セーフ〖野球〗safe ¶ 一塁で危うくセーフ be narrowly safe on first (base).

セーフティーバント〖野球〗a safety bunt.

セーラーふく セーラー服 a sailor [middy] blouse; a middy blouse and skirt.

セールスマン a (book) salesman; a saleswoman;〈外交販売員〉a traveling salesman (in cosmetics); a commercial traveler;〈戸別訪問の〉a doorstep salesman ¶ 自動車のセールスマン a car salesman.

せおいなげ 背負い投げ a shoulder throw; throwing sb over one's shoulder.

せおう 背負う carry sth on one's back; shoulder (a heavy burden); be burdened with (an important duty); be saddled with (a debt) ¶ この国の将来を背負う若人たち young men who carry the future of this country on their shoulders.

せおおい 背覆い 〈椅子の〉an antimacassar;《米》a tidy.

せおよぎ 背泳ぎ the backstroke ¶ 背泳ぎをする swim the backstroke; swim on one's back / 背泳ぎの選手 a backstroke swimmer.

せかい 世界 the world;〈地球〉the earth;《文》the globe;〈宇宙〉the universe;〈世間〉the world;〈特殊な社会〉(movie) circles;〈領域〉《文》a realm ¶ 子供の世界 the world of children / 想像の世界 the world of (the) imagination / 理想の世界 an ideal world / 世界的[の] world; worldwide; international;《文》global; universal / 世界的に有名な world-famous;《文》of worldwide (global) fame / 世界の各地から from all over [all parts of] the world / 世界の果てまでも[すみずみまで] to the ends of [the four corners of] the earth / 世界を一周する go [take a trip] around [《英》round] the world; make a round-the-world trip;《文》circle the globe / 世界中に[の] all over [in all, throughout] the world; (all) the world over / 世界一である be the best [greatest] in the world; lead the world (in) / 世界一周旅行 a round-the-world trip; (go on) a world cruise (客船による) / 世界観 an outlook on [a view of] the world; a world view [outlook];《ドイツ語》a Weltanschauung / 世界記録 (establish, make) a world record (in) / 世界銀行 the World Bank; the International

---

いだろう. A theory of that sort will not stand up [hold water].

せいりゃく それは一時の政略から出た処置である. It is a measure dictated by political expediency.

せいりょう² 今の世の中にあのような人がいるとは一服の清涼剤だ. It is refreshing to meet a man like him these days.

せいりょく¹ 彼は省内でなかなか勢力がある. He wields a lot of power [influence] in the Ministry. / 台風は勢力を増してきている. The typhoon is increasing in strength. / 台風は勢力が衰えて温帯低気圧に変わった. The typhoon petered out [subsided] into an extratropical cyclone.

せいりょく² 年をとると精力が衰える. One's energy declines with age. / 彼は精力家だ. He has plenty of go in him. | He is a (real) bundle of energy.

せいろん 君のは確かに正論だ. I

Bank for Reconstruction and Development (正式名称) / 世界経済 the world [international] economy / 世界語 a world [an international] language / 世界選手権 a world [an international] championship [title] / 世界戦争 a world [global] war / 世界史 world history; the history of the world / 世界史的 world-historic (events) / 世界主義[主義者] cosmopolitanism [a cosmopolitan] / 世界人権宣言 the Universal Declaration of Human Rights / 第一[二]次世界大戦 the First [Second] World War; World War I [II] (★ローマ数字は one, two と読む) / 世界平和 world peace; the peace of the world / 世界保健機構 the World Health Organization (略: WHO) / 世界連邦 the World Federation of Nations / 世界連邦主義 World Federalism.

せかす 急かす hurry sb (up); rush; press; urge sb on ⇒いそぐ (急がせる). 文例⑩

せかせか ¶せかせかする be restless; be fidgety; be in a fidget; fidget / せかせかした restless; fidgety; bustling.

せがむ pester sb (for money) ⇒せびる. 文例⑩

せがれ 伜 〈自分の〉 my son; 〈一般に〉 a son; a boy.

せがわ 背革 ¶背革とじの 《books》 quarter-bound in leather.

セカンド 〖野球〗〈二塁〉 second base; 〈二塁手〉 a second baseman; 〖ボクシング〗 a second.

せき[1] 咳 a cough; coughing ¶せきが出る have a cough / せきをする cough / 猛烈にせきをする cough violently; cough one's lungs out [head off] / せきを止める stifle [suppress] a cough; 〈文〉 relieve a cough / せき払いをする clear one's throat; give a cough; hem; harrumph (重々しく) / せき止めドロップ cough drops / せき止めの薬[水薬] a cough medicine [syrup]. 文例⑩

せき[2] 席 a seat; one's place ¶席の暖まる暇もない be too busy to stay long in one place; be always on the move / 席を立つ get up [《文》 rise] from one's seat / 席を離れる leave [quit] one's seat / 席をけって去る fling [stalk] out of the room / 席を譲る offer [give up] one's seat to 《an old man》; make room for sb / 席を代える change one's seat; 〈人と〉 change seats with sb / 席を取る[予約する] keep [take, 《文》 secure] a seat 《for sb》; reserve [book] a seat 《for the play, on the train》 / 席に着く〈文〉 take one's seat; 〈文〉 seat oneself 《at the table》; sit down / 席に着いている be sitting [《文》 seated] 《at a table》 / 公開の席で in public / 婦人席 the ladies' seats; the seats for ladies. 文例⑩

せき[3] 隻 ¶4隻の船 four boats [ships].

せき[4] 堰 a dam; a sluice (水門つきの) ¶せきをする dam (up) 《a stream》; construct [build] a dam 《across a river》. 文例⑩

せき[5] 関 ⇒せきしょ ¶白河の関 the Shirakawa Barrier.

せき[6] 積 〖数〗 the product.

せき[7] 籍 〈戸籍〉 one's family register; 〈本籍〉 《文》 one's domicile; 〈団体の籍〉 membership ¶籍を入れる[抜く] have sb's name entered in [removed from] the family register / 籍を置く《会などに》 be a member 《of》; 〈学校に〉 be enrolled 《at a college》 / 英国籍の商船 a British-registered merchant ship.

せきうん 積雲 a cumulus (pl. -li); a cumulus cloud.

せきえい 石英 〖鉱〗 quartz ¶石英ガラス quartz [silica] glass.

せきがいせん 赤外線 〖物〗 infrared light [rays] ¶赤外線ランプ an infrared [a heat] lamp / 赤外線療法[写真] infrared therapy [photography].

せきがく 碩学 a great [《文》 an accomplished] scholar; 《文》 a man of erudition 《profound learning》; 《文》 a savant.

せきかっしょく 赤褐色 reddish brown.

せきぐん 赤軍 the Red Army.

せきこむ[1] 咳き込む have [be taken with] a fit of coughing.

せきこむ[2] 急き込む get [be] flurried [flustered, agitated]; 《文》 be in haste; get [《文》 become] impatient ¶急き込んで impatiently; 《文》 in haste; 《文》 impetuously.

せきさい 積載 ¶積載する load; carry; 〈船に〉 have 《cargo》 on board; take on [in] / 積載トン数 capacity [freight] tonnage / 積載能力 carrying [loading] capacity [power] / 積載排水量 《a ship of 5,000 tons》 load displacement / 積載量 loadage; load capacity.

せきざい 石材 (building) stone ¶石材商 a stone dealer.

せきじ 席次 〈学校の〉 the class order; the order of seats [places]; the seating order; 〈身分による〉 the order of precedence; ranking ¶〈学校の〉席次が5番上がる[下がる] go up [down] five places in class [in the class order].

せきじゅうじ 赤十字 ¶赤十字社 the Red Cross (Society) 《of Japan》 / 赤十字条約 the Red Cross Convention / 赤十字病院 a Red Cross hospital.

---

admit the justice [rightness] of your argument.

せかい 僕らはお互いに住む世界が違うのだ。 You and I live in different worlds. | We don't move in the same circles.

せがむ もっとお金をくれと母親にせがんだ。 He pestered his mother for more money.

せき[1] 近頃少しせきが出ます。 I've had a slight cough lately. | I have developed a slight cough recently.

せき[2] その会館には約3千の席があります。 The hall contains about 3,000 seats [can seat about 3,000 (people)]. / この席はどなたかいらっしゃいますか。 Is this seat taken [occupied]?

せき[4] せきを切ったように彼はしゃべり出した。 Words began to pour from [come out of] his lips as though a dam inside him had broken.

せきせつ 積雪 50 センチだった。 The snow lay fifty centimeters deep. / 積雪は平地で 23 センチあった。 The snowfall measured 23 centimeters on the level.

せきどう 赤道は地球上最も暑い所と思われがちだが、それは間違いだ。 It is often assumed that the equator is the hottest place on

せきしゅつ 析出 〖化〗eduction; extraction ¶析出する educe; extract / 析出物 an educt; an extract.

せきじゅん¹ 石筍 〖地質〗a stalagmite.

せきじゅん² 席順 ⇨ せきじ.

せきしょ 関所 《pass》a barrier (station); 《pass through》a checkpoint (検問所).

せきじょう 席上 ¶席上で 〈会合で〉at the meeting; 〈その時〉on the occasion ⇨ そくせき¹ / この席で here; on this occasion / 会議の席上で at the conference.

せきしょく 赤色 ¶赤色革命 (a) Red revolution.

せきずい 脊髄 〖解〗the spinal cord ¶脊髄炎 myelitis / 脊髄病 a spinal disease.

せきせいいんこ 〖鳥〗a budgerigar; a shell parrakeet [parrot].

せきせつ 積雪 (fallen) snow ¶〈列車が〉積雪のために立ち往生する be snowbound; be snowed up / 積雪計[標] a snow gauge / 積雪調査 a snow survey.

せきぞう¹ 石造 ¶石造の 《castles》built of stone; stone-built 《houses》; stone 《buildings》.

せきぞう² 石像 a stone statue [image].

せきたてる 急き立てる hurry (up); press; urge [goad, egg] *sb* on ¶仕事にせき立てられる be swamped with work.

せきたん 石炭 coal ¶石炭を燃やす[たく] burn coal / 燃えている石炭 live [red-hot] coals / 石炭入れ a (coal) scuttle / 石炭液化装置 coal liquefaction equipment / 石炭ガス coal gas / 石炭殻 (coal) cinders / 石炭紀 〖地質〗the Carboniferous period / 石炭酸 〖化〗carbolic acid; phenol / 石炭層 a coal bed.

せきちく 石竹 〖植〗a (China) pink.

せきちゅう 脊柱 〖解〗the spinal [vertebral] column; the spine; the backbone ¶脊柱湾曲 (a) spinal curvature.

せきちんけんさ 赤沈検査 a blood sedimentation [precipitation] test.

せきつい 脊椎 〖解〗the spinal [vertebral] column; the spine; the backbone ¶脊椎骨 a vertebra (*pl.* -brae, -s) / 脊椎動物 a vertebrate (animal) / 脊椎カリエス 〖医〗spinal caries.

せきてい 石庭 a rock [stone] garden (in the Ryoanji Temple).

せきてっこう 赤鉄鉱 〖鉱〗hematite.

せきとう 石塔 ⇨ せきひ.

せきどう 赤道 the equator; (cross) the line ¶赤道の equatorial / 赤道ギニア ⇨ ギニア / 赤道祭 the ceremony of crossing the equator [line] / 赤道地帯 the equatorial region / 赤道直下の[に, で] right on the equator / 赤道反流 the Equatorial Countercurrent / 赤道無風帯 the doldrums.

せきとめる 堰き止める 〈流れを〉dam (back) 《a stream》; 〈阻止する〉check.

せきとり 関取 a ranking *sumo* wrestler.

せきにん 責任 (a) responsibility; 〈法律上, 特に支払いの〉(a) liability; 〈義務〉one's duty; an obligation ¶責任は…にある 〈文〉the responsibility rests [lies] with…; 〈文〉the fault lies with… / 責任がある be responsible [answerable, accountable] (to sb, for what one does); must answer (to sb, for one's action); be to blame (for) / 責任ある回答 a responsible answer / 責任ある地位 a responsible post; a position of trust / 責任の分担 the division of responsibility / 責任を負う bear [take on, shoulder] (the) responsibility (for, of); hold *oneself* responsible 《for》; 〈文〉bear the onus 《of *doing*》 / 責任を負わせる put [〈文〉place] the responsibility 《for *doing*》on [upon] sb; 〈文〉put [lay] the onus 《of sth》on [upon] sb; 〈失態の責任を〉lay the blame on sb [at sb's door] / 責任を回避する avoid [evade, shirk] one's responsibility 《for》; 〈文〉avoid the onus 《of *doing*》 / 責任を転嫁する shift [shuffle] the responsibility (from onto sb) / 責任を取る admit that one is responsible 《for》; take the consequences / 責任を問う take sb to task (for); 〈文〉call sb to account / 責任を果たす fulfill one's responsibility [duty] / 責任を放棄する 〈文〉abdicate responsibility / 責任観念が強い have a strong sense of responsibility / 責任校了 〖印刷〗〈表示〉O.K. with corrections / 責任校了にする O.K. (a proof) with corrections / 責任者 a responsible person; a person in charge (of sth) / 責任内閣 a Cabinet responsible to the Diet [to Parliament] / 責任逃れ evasion of [shirking] (one's) responsibility; 〈口語〉passing the buck. 文例図

せきのやま 関の山 ⇨ せいいっぱい, せいぜい.

せきはい 惜敗 ¶惜敗する lose a close game; lose [〈文〉be defeated] by a narrow margin.

せきばく 寂寞 ¶寂寞たる lonely; lonesome; 〈文〉desolate; 〈文〉forlorn.

せきはん 赤飯 (glutinous) rice boiled with red beans; (festive) red rice.

せきばん¹ 石版 〈術〉lithography; 〈画〉a lithograph ¶石版印刷法 the lithographic process / 石版刷りにする lithograph.

せきばん² 石盤 a (writing) slate.

せきひ 石碑 〈記念碑〉a stone monument; 〈墓石〉a tombstone; a gravestone.

---

earth, but this is not true.

せきにん 君の安全については, 君のご両親に対して責任があるからね. I am responsible to your father and mother for your safety, you see. / 責任の大半は会社側にある. Most of the blame belongs with [should fall on] the firm. / …の責任は すべて政府にある. The government alone is to blame for this. / そんなことを言って, あなたはあとの責任が取れますか. It's all right saying [for you to say] that, but are you ready to take the consequences? / 責任の所在を明らかにする必要がある. It is necessary to see where the responsibility lies [rests]. / だれも自分が責任を持ってその仕事をやろうと言う者がない. No one will undertake the work on his own responsibility. / どうしてもやりたいと言うのなら, 自分の責任でやるがよい. If you insist on doing that, do it at your own risk. / 次の手をうつのは君の責任だよ. It is up to you to make the next move. / 男は自分の行動に自分で責任を持たなくてはならない. A man must be responsible to himself. / 学生食堂の責任者はだれか. Who is in charge of the school cafeteria?

せきひん 赤貧 extreme [grinding, 《文》dire, 《文》abject] poverty; 《文》penury; 《文》indigence ¶赤貧洗うがごとし be [live] in dire [abject] poverty; be reduced to extreme poverty; be as poor as a church mouse.

せきぶつ 石仏 a stone image [figure] of the Buddha.

せきぶん 積分 《数》integral calculus ¶積分する integrate / 積分の integral / 定[不定]積分 a definite [an indefinite] integral / 線積分 a curvilinear integral / 面積分 a surface integral / 積分定数 a constant of integration / 積分法 integration / 部分積分法 integration by parts / 積分方程式 an integral equation.

せきぼく 石墨 《鉱》graphite; black lead; plumbago.

せきむ 責務 〈義務〉(a) duty; an obligation; 〈責任〉(a) responsibility.

せきめん¹ 石綿 《鉱》asbestos.

せきめん² 赤面 a blush 《with [for] shame》; turn red [crimson]; 〈恥ずかしく思う〉feel ashamed 《of, for》/ 赤面させる put sb to shame 《《文》the blush》. 文例⇩

せきゆ 石油 petroleum; 〈灯油〉《米》kerosene; 《英》paraffin; 《米》coal oil ¶海底石油の採掘 offshore oil drilling / 石油会社 an oil company / 石油業者 an oilman / 石油化学 petrochemistry / 石油化学工業 the petrochemical industry / 石油化学工場 a petrochemical plant / 石油化学コンビナート a petrochemical complex / 石油化学製品 a petrochemical (product) / 石油危機 an oil crisis / 石油基地 an oil camp / 石油工業 the petroleum [oil] industry / 石油こんろ an oil cooking-stove / 石油採掘業者 an oil driller / 石油採掘やぐら an oil-drilling platform / 石油資源《develop [exploit]》 oil [petroleum] resources / 石油食品 petrofood; food produced from petroleum [oil] / 石油ストーブ an oil [《米》a kerosene, 《英》a paraffin] heater [stove] / 石油精錬所 a petroleum refinery / 石油輸出国機構 the Organization of Petroleum Exporting Countries (略: OPEC) / 石油輸送管 an oil pipe (1本の); an oil pipeline (輸送管路) / 石油ランプ an oil [《米》a kerosene] lamp [lantern].

せきらら 赤裸々 ¶赤裸々な〈率直な〉frank; plain; outspoken / 赤裸々な事実 a naked [bald] fact / 赤裸々な人生 life in the raw / 赤裸々に《文》率直に〉frankly; plainly; outspokenly;《文》without reserve. 文例⇩

せきらんうん 積乱雲《気象》a cumulonimbus (pl. -es, -bi); a cumulonimbus cloud.

せきり 赤痢 dysentery ¶赤痢患者 a dysentery patient; a case of dysentery / 赤痢菌 a dysentery bacillus / 赤痢症状 a dysentery symptom.

せきりょう¹ 席料 〈室代〉the charge for (the hire of) a room; 〈入場料〉an admission fee; 《口語》the admission.

せきりょう² 責了 ⇒ せきにん (責任校了).

せきりょう³ 寂寥 ⇒ せきばく.

せきりょく 斥力《物》repulsion; (a) repulsive force; a force of repulsion.

せきれい 《鳥》a (water) wagtail.

せく 急ぐ hurry; rush;《文》hasten;《文》make haste;〈待ち兼ねる〉be impatient《for》;〈せき立てる〉hurry [rush] sb; press; urge sb on;〈急ぐ〉be too eager《to do》. 文例⇩

セクショナリズム sectionalism.

セクション a section.

セクト a sect ¶セクト主義 sectarianism / セクト主義者 a sectarian.

せけん 世間 the world; the public; people; society ¶世間の手前 for appearance' [decency's] sake / 世間に出る go out into the world / 世間を騒がす create a sensation; make a splash; make a noise in the world / 世間並みの common; ordinary; average / 世間離れした〈変わった〉strange; uncommon; extraordinary;《超俗的》unworldly / 世間離れのした生活をしている live away from the world / 世間知らず a person who does not know [has not seen] much of the world; a person who is inexperienced in [《文》ignorant of] the ways of the world; a babe in arms; an innocent / 世間体を繕う keep up [patch up] appearances / 世間話をする chat [have a chat]《with a friend》; make small talk; have a gossip / 世間擦れのした sophisticated. 文例⇩

せこ¹ 世故 ¶世故にたけた《文》worldly-wise; wise in the ways of the world;《文》rich in worldly wisdom / 世故にたけている人 a man of the world; a man who has seen a great deal of life ⇒ せけん.

せこ² 勢子 a beater.

セコイア 《植》a sequoia; a redwood.

セコハン ⇒ ちゅうふる.

セコンド 〈秒〉a second;《ボクシング》a second ¶(時計が)セコンドを刻む ticktock; tick away [off] the time.

せせい 世才 worldly [practical] wisdom ⇒ せこ¹.

せざるをえない ⇒ -ざるをえない.

セし セ氏 centigrade [Celsius] (略: C.) ★科学・技術関係では Celsius を使っているが、一般人の間では centigrade が普通 ¶セ氏8度3分 (at) 8.3°C. ¶ eight point three degrees

---

せきめん² 誠に赤面の至りです。I am really ashamed of myself.

せきらら 彼は自分の過去の悪事を赤裸々に告白した。He made a clean breast of his past evil deeds.

せく せいては事を仕損じる。Haste makes [is] waste.《諺》

せけん 世間とはこうしたものさ。That's how it goes. | That's the way things are. |《口語》That's the way the cookie crumbles. / いや、世間はせまいもんだ。It's a small world, isn't it? / 彼はまだ世間に知られていないが、優れた才能を持った詩人である。He is a poet with a fine talent, though he is not yet in the public eye. | 世間から取り残されたくない一心でベストセラーを読む人が多い。Many people read best sellers merely because they are afraid of being left out of things. / 世間体などは構わなかった。He didn't care a bit [twopence] what people would say about him. / 大学教授ともなれば、世間体というも

centigrade と読む / セ氏寒暖計 a centigrade (thermometer) ; a Celsius thermometer / セ氏目盛りの《a thermometer》 with a centigrade scale ; 《a thermometer》 marked in degrees centigrade. [文例⇩]

せじ 世事 worldly affairs ; the ways of the world ⇨せこ[1] ¶ 世事にうとい《文》be ignorant [know little] of the world [the ways of the world]. [文例⇩]

セシウム〘化〙cesium.

せしめる get ; 《文》 obtain ; 《文》 secure ; extort [squeeze] 《money from *sb*》; swindle 《*sb* out of *his* money》; wheedle 《*sth* from *sb*》.

せしゅ 施主 a donor.

せしゅう 世襲 ¶ 世襲の hereditary ; 《文》 patrimonial / 世襲財産 hereditary property [estate] ; 《文》 a patrimony ; 《文》 a heritage.

せじょう[1] 世上 in the world ; among people.

せじょう[2] 世情 ⇨せじ, せこ[1] ¶ 世情に通じている know what is going on in the world.

せじん 世人 people ; the (general) public ; the world.

せすじ 背筋 ¶ 背筋を伸ばす straighten *one's* back [spine]. [文例⇩]

ゼスチャー 〈身振り〉《make》 a gesture ; 〈遊戯〉《play》 (a game of) charades.

[用法] gesture は, 日本語の「ゼスチャー」と同じように, 本気でやる気がないのに, かっこうだけして見せる「思わせぶりな言動」の意味でたしかに用いられる. He offered to help me, but I was sure it was only a gesture. (彼は「手伝おうか」と言ったが, それが単なるゼスチャーであることはわかりきっていた) しかし, 英語の gesture はそういう悪い意味だけでなく,「意思表示としての行為」の意味でも使われる. The Chinese government gave us a giant panda as a gesture of friendship. (中国政府は友好のしるしとして我々にパンダを贈ってくれた)

ぜせい 是正 correction ; revision ; 《文》 rectification ¶ 是正する correct ; set *sth* to rights ; put *sth* right ; straighten out 《the accounts》; 《文》 rectify / 国際収支の悪化を是正する redress the deteriorating international balance of payments.

せせこましい 〈狭い〉 (uncomfortably) narrow ; limited ; 《口語》 pok(e)y 《little rooms》; 〈気質が〉 fussy ; fidgety.

ぜぜひひ 是々非々 ⇨ぜ (是を是とし, 非を非とする) ¶ 是々非々主義である be impartial ; be unbiased.

せせらぎ 〈細流〉 a little stream ; 《文》 a brooklet ; 〈浅瀬〉 a shallow ; shallows ; 〈流れる音〉 murmuring 《of a stream》.

せせらわらう せせら笑う laugh at *sb* ; laugh [grin] derisively [mockingly, scornfully] 《at》; ridicule.

せそう 世相 a phase [an aspect] of life ; a sign of the times ; 《reflect》 social conditions.

せぞく 世俗 ¶ 世俗の common ; 〈俗界の〉《文》 worldly ; 《文》 secular ; 《文》 temporal / 世俗におもねる play down [cater] to the popular taste.

せたい 世帯 a household ⇨しょたい[1] ¶ 世帯主 the head of the household [family] ; a householder.

せだい 世代 a generation ¶ 若い世代 the younger [rising] generation / 世代のずれ a generation gap / 世代間の 《文》 (inter)generational 《conflict》 / 世代交代[番]〘生物〙(the) alternation of generations.

せたけ 背丈 ⇨しんちょう[1].

セダン 《米》 a sedan ; 《英》 a saloon (car).

せちがらい 世知辛い ¶ せち辛い世の中 a hard world (to live in). [文例⇩]

せつ[1] 節 〈時期〉 (a) time ; a season ; an occasion ; 〈文章の〉 a paragraph ; a passage ; 〈詩の〉 a stanza ; 〘文法〙 a clause ; 〈節操〉《文》 fidelity ; 《文》 constancy ; 《stand by》 *one's* principles ¶ その節は at that time ; on that occasion / お暇の節は when you are free [《文》 at (your) leisure, not engaged] ; when you have time to spare [nothing better to do] / 節を売る sell *one's* honor 《for money》; 《文》 prostitute *oneself* [*one's* talents] / 節を守る stick [hold] to *one's* principles. [文例⇩]

せつ[2] 説 〈意見〉 an opinion ; a view ; 〈学説〉 a theory ; a doctrine ; 〈風評〉 a rumor ; a report ¶ 説を唱える put forward [《文》 advance] a theory / 説を同じく[異に]する agree [disagree] 《with *sb*》; *one's* opinion is the same 《as *sb's*》 [is different from *sb's*] / 私の説は…だ In my opinion... ; 《文》 I am of the opinion that... / 別の説によれば according to another theory. [文例⇩]

せつ[3] 切 ¶ 切なる eager ; 《文》 earnest ; 《文》 ardent / 切なる思い[恋心] *one's* ardent love / 切なる願い *one's* fervent desire ; *one's* ardent hope / 切に eagerly ; 《文》 earnestly ; 《文》 ardently / 切に勧める urge [strongly advise] 《*sb* to *do*》.

せつえい 設営 ¶ 設営する 〈建てる〉 construct ; set up ; 〈準備する〉 arrange ; prepare / 設営隊 a construction party.

ぜつえん 絶縁 〘電〙 insulation ; isolation ¶ 絶縁する 〈縁を切る〉 break off relations 《with》; cut [《文》 sever] *one's* connections 《with》; put an end to *one's* relationship 《with》; 〘電〙 insulate ; isolate / 過去と絶縁する break [part] with *one's* past / 宗教と絶縁した科学 science divorced from religion / 電気絶縁性 electric

---

のがありますからね, めったな真似はできませんよ. When you are a university professor, you've got your reputation to think about, and you must be careful how you behave.

セし 室温はセ氏で今何度ですか. What is the room temperature in degrees centigrade [Celsius]?

せじ 学者は概して世事に疎いものだ. Most scholars are impractical as far as affairs of the world are concerned.

せすじ 背筋が寒くなった. A cold shiver ran [It sent a chill] down my spine. | I felt a chill go down my spine.

せちがらい せち辛い世の中だ. What a hard world we are living in! | Things are tough nowadays.

せつ[1] こちらへお出かけの節はぜひお立ち寄り下さい. Please drop in when you happen to come this way.

せつ[2] その点はお説のとおりです. I quite agree with you on that point.

non-conductance / 絶縁線 an insulated wire / 絶縁体 an insulator ; an isolator / (電線に巻く) 絶縁テープ《米》friction [《英》insulating] tape.

せっか 赤化 ¶赤化する turn [go] red ; go communist / 赤化を防ぐ check the spread of communism.

せっかい[1] 切開 ¶切開する〖医〗incise ; cut open [out]《the affected parts》; open《an abscess》; operate《on》/ 切開手術 a surgical operation.

せっかい[2] 石灰 lime ¶消石灰 slaked [slack, dead, hydrated] lime / 生石灰 quicklime ; unslaked lime / 石灰岩[石] limestone ; 〈露出した岩面〉(a) limestone rock / 石灰岩の洞穴 a limestone cave / 石灰水 limewater.

せ

せつがい 雪害 damage from [caused by] snow [a snowfall] ; snow damage.

ぜっかい 絶海 ¶絶海の孤島 a desert island ; a solitary island far off in the sea.

せっかく 〈骨折って〉with considerable trouble [effort] ;《文》at great pains ; 〈殊更に〉specially ;《文》expressly ; 〈親切に〉kindly ¶せっかくの 〈親切な〉kind《advice》; 〈待ち望んだ〉long-[eagerly-]awaited《holidays》; 〈貴重な〉precious ; valuable ; good. [文例⇩]

せっかち ¶せっかちな hasty ; impatient ; impetuous / せっかちなことをする act rashly [on impulse].

せっかん[1] 石棺 a stone coffin ; a sarcophagus《*pl.* -gi, -guses》.

せっかん[2] 折檻 ¶折檻する 〈懲らしめる〉punish ;《文》chastise ;《文》castigate ; 〈打ちたたく〉give *sb* a thrashing ; give [《文》administer] a whipping [flogging]《to *sb*》; spank《a naughty child》.

せつがん[1] 接岸 ¶接岸する come alongside the pier [quay, berth].

せつがん[2] 接眼 ¶接眼レンズ an eyepiece ; an eye lens ; an ocular.

ぜつがん 舌癌 cancer of the tongue.

せっき 石器〖考古〗a stone implement [tool] ¶打製石器 a chipped stone tool / 摩製石器 a polished stone tool / 石器時代 the Stone Age / 新[旧]石器時代 the Neolithic [Paleolithic] Age ; the New [Old] Stone Age / 石器時代人 Stone Age man (総称).

せっきゃくぎょう 接客業 a service trade.

せっきょう 説教 a sermon ; preaching ; 〈訓戒〉moralizing ;《文》a moralizing discourse [lecture] ¶説教する preach (a sermon) ; 〈訓戒する〉lecture《a child》; scold ;《文》remonstrate《with *sb* against [on] *sth*》;《文》admonish《*sb* for *sth*》/ 説教を聞かせる 〈訓戒する〉read *sb* a lecture [lesson] ; give *sb* a (good) scolding [《口語》telling-off] / 説教師 a preacher / 説教壇 a pulpit.

ぜっきょう 絶叫 ¶絶叫する shout [《文》exclaim] at the top of *one's* voice [lungs] ; cry out loudly.

せっきょく 積極 ¶積極的な positive ; active ; aggressive ; enterprising ; 〈熱心な〉keen《on *sth*》; enthusiastic / 積極的に positively ; actively ; aggressively ; enthusiastically ; on *one's* own initiative / 積極性 positiveness ; drive ;《口語》push ; enterprise ; enterprising spirit ; enthusiasm ; initiative / 積極政策 a positive policy.

せっきん 接近 (an) approach ;《文》access ; 〈国際間の〉《フランス語》*rapprochement* ; 〈密接な関係〉close relations ¶接近する approach ; draw [get] near ; come [get] close《to》; 〈艦船が〉close《another boat, the land》; 〈親しくなる〉get on better [closer,《文》more intimate] terms《with》/ 接近しやすい[し難い] be approachable [unapproachable] ; be easy [difficult] to approach ;《文》be easy [difficult] of access / 接近した[して] near (at hand) ; close [《文》hard] by / 一層接近させる《文》bring《A and B》into (a) closer relationship ;《文》establish greater intimacy《between》/ 接近経路 an access route / 接近戦 close combat ; close(-quarter) fighting《between》; in-fighting (特にボクシングの).

せっく 節句 a seasonal festival.

ぜっく 絶句 〈漢詩の〉a Chinese quatrain ¶絶句する 〈言葉に詰まる〉break off (short)《in *one's* speech》; be at a loss for words.

セックス sex ⇨せい[3] ¶セックスする《口語》have sex《with》; make love《to》(婉曲的に) / セックスアピール sex appeal ;《文》sexual attractiveness / セックスアピールがある have (a lot of) sex appeal ;《文》be sexually attractive.

せっくつ 石窟 a stone cave ¶石窟寺院 a cave temple [shrine] / 石窟彫刻 (a) cave sculpture.

せっけい[1] 雪渓 a snowy valley [ravine, gorge].

せっけい[2] 設計 a plan ; a design ¶設計する plan ; make a plan《for》; design ; work out a design《for》; 〈図取りをする〉lay out《a garden》; draw up a plan / 設計し直す redesign / …の設計で《build a house》(according) to the design [《文》after the plans] of… / 設計中の《a rocket》under design / 設計者 a designer / (建物などの)設計(明細)書 specifications / 設計図 a plan ; a blueprint / 設計変更 design changes. [文例⇩]

ぜっけい 絶景 a superb [marvelous] view ; a grand sight.

せっけっきゅう 赤血球〖解〗a red (blood) corpuscle ; a red (blood) cell ; an erythrocyte ¶赤血球数検査《do》a red cell count / 赤血球沈降速度検査 ⇨せきちんけんさ.

せっけん[1] 石鹸《a cake of》soap ¶せっけん

せっかく せっかくあれまでに骨を折って失敗するとはなんという気の毒なことだろう. What a pity that he should have failed after putting so much work [effort] into it! / せっかくためた金をなくしてしまってとんだ事をした. I was foolish enough to lose the money I had gone to such trouble to save. / せっかくのお勧めですからやってみましょう. Since you are so kind as to recommend it to me, I will give it a try. / せっかくのお招きですが, あいにく先約がありますので残念ながらお受けすることができません. Many thanks for your kind invitation, but a previous engagement unfortunately compels me to decline.

せっけい[2] そのビルディングはまだ

の泡 soap bubbles [froth]; (soap)suds; lather (きめの細かい) / せっけんで洗う wash with soap and water / 化粧せっけん toilet soap / 洗濯せっけん (a bar of) washing [laundry] soap / 粉せっけん soap powder / せっけん受け a soap dish / せっけん工場 a soap works / せっけん水 soapy water; <泡立った> soapsuds; suds / せっけん箱 a soap case.

せっけん² 席巻 ¶席巻する carry everything before one; sweep (over, across); conquer.

せつげん¹ 雪原 a snowfield; a frozen waste.

せつげん² 節減 (a) reduction; 《文》(a) retrenchment; economies; a cut; 《文》(a) curtailment ¶節減する reduce; 《文》retrench; 《文》curtail; cut (down) / 経費を節減する cut (down) expenses.

ゼッケン [<《ドイツ語》Decken] ¶ゼッケン番号 a number 《on an athlete's singlet》.

せっこう¹ 石工 a (stone)mason; a stonecutter.

せっこう² 斥候 ⇒ていさつ.

せっこう³ 石膏 【鉱】 gypsum; plaster (of Paris) (焼石膏) ¶石膏細工 plaster work; plastering / 石膏像 a plaster figure [bust] / 石膏模型 a plaster cast.

せつごう 接合 ¶接合する join; connect; unite; put together; splice (ロープ、フィルムなどを); 【医】inosculate (血管などを).

ぜっこう¹ 絶交 ¶絶交する break off one's friendship (with); break (with); cut one's connection (with); 《米》be done [through] with sb. 文例⇩

ぜっこう² 絶好 ¶絶好の perfect; splendid; the best; 《文》capital / 絶好の機会 a golden opportunity; a rare chance; (miss) the chance of a lifetime / 絶好調である be in the best possible condition; be in the pink (of condi-
せっこうさん ⇒ぜんしゅ(tion).

せっこつ 接骨 bonesetting ¶接骨する set (a bone, a broken leg) / 接骨医 a bonesetter.

せっさく 拙策 a poor [an inadequate, an unsatisfactory] policy [plan]; 《文》an imprudent [impolitic] measure.

せっさたくま 切磋琢磨 ¶切磋琢磨する 《文》apply oneself closely to 《one's study》; work [study] hard / 切磋琢磨し合う work hard together; be in friendly rivalry (with).

ぜっさん 絶賛 ¶絶賛する speak very highly of sb [sth]; 《文》speak of sb [sth] in the highest terms; praise [《文》laud] sb to the skies / 絶賛を博する win the highest praise (from); be praised sky-high (by).

せっし 摂氏 ⇒セし.

せつじ 接辞 【言語】an affix.

せつじつ 切実 ¶切実な <切なる>《文》earnest (wish); 《文》fervent (desire); <緊急な>urgent (need); pressing (problems) / 切実に <痛切に>

acutely; keenly; <心から>《文》heartily; sincerely.

せっしゃ 接写 close-up photography.

せっしゃくわん 切歯扼腕 ¶切歯扼腕する clench one's fists and grind one's teeth 《at the news》; 《文》feel [be] deeply chagrined 《at》.

せっしゅ¹ 接種 【医】(an) inoculation; (a) vaccination ¶接種する inoculate; vaccinate / 病菌を接種する inoculate sb with a virus.

せっしゅ² 摂取 ¶摂取する take (in); absorb; adopt (a foreign culture); 【生理】ingest (栄養物を); 《文》assimilate (同化する) / カロリーの摂取量 caloric intake.

せっしゅ³ 節酒 moderation in drinking; 《文》temperance (★「禁酒」の意味でも使うので要注意).

せっしゅう 接収 《文》seizure; requisitioning ¶接収する requisition; take over; commandeer / 接収解除する release.

せつじょ 切除 【医】excision; resection; (a) surgical removal ¶切除する excise; cut off; resect.

せっしょう¹ 折衝 negotiation(s); a parley ¶折衝する negotiate [parley] (with sb for sth).

せっしょう² 殺生 ¶殺生 the taking [destruction] of life ¶無益の殺生 wanton destruction of life; useless [pointless] cruelty / 殺生する destroy [take] life; kill animals / 殺生な cruel; heartless.

せっしょう³ 摂政 《事》regency; <人> a regent ¶摂政殿下 the Prince Regent.

ぜっしょう 絶唱 a superb song [poem].

せつじょうしゃ 雪上車 a snowmobile; a snow tractor [vehicle].

せっしょく¹ 接触 touch; contact; 【数】tangency ¶電流の接触 electrical contact / 個人的接触 personal contact / 接触する touch; come in [into] contact (with); <初めて> get in touch [into contact] (with); 《文》establish contact (with) / 接触を保つ[断つ] keep in [get out of] touch [contact] (with) / 接触感染 (spread by) contagion. 文例⇩

せっしょく² 節食 ¶節食する eat sparingly [in moderation]; 《文》practice temperance in eating.

せつじょく 雪辱 《文》vindication of one's honor; revenge ¶雪辱する 《文》vindicate one's honor; clear oneself of a disgrace; <仕返しをする> get revenge for one's defeat; 《口語》get even (with); square [settle] accounts [one's account] (with) / 雪辱戦 a return match [game].

ぜっしょく 絶食 ¶絶食する fast; go on a fast (of a week); 《文》abstain from food / 絶食して病気を直す fast an illness off / 絶食療法 a starvation cure.

設計中の段階だった。The building was still on the drawing board [in the design stage]. / 新図書館は若い建築家寺田氏の設計したものである。The plans for the new library building were drawn up by the young architect Mr. Terada.

ぜっこう¹ 君とはもう絶交だ。I will have nothing to do with you any longer. / I'm through [done] with you.

ぜっこう² 今日は絶好の野球日和だ。Today's weather is perfect [ideal] for baseball. / 僕は今絶好調だ。I couldn't be better. | I'm in perfect condition [top form].

せっしょく¹ 彼は商売柄色々な人と接触する。His business brings him into contact with all sorts of people. / (電気の)接触が悪い。

せっすい 節水 ¶節水する save water;《文》economize in water consumption.

せっする 接する 〈接触する〉touch; come in [into] contact [touch] (with);〈隣接する〉border [abut] on;《文》be adjacent to; adjoin;〈応接する〉see; give an interview to sb;《文》receive;〈店員が客に〉attend to; serve;〈受け取る〉《文》receive /〈計報(_ふ_)に接する〉hear [《文》receive news] of sb's death.

ぜっする 絶する ¶言語に絶する be beyond words [description];《文》beggar description / 古今に絶する have no equal in any age / 想像を絶する be unimaginable;《文》be beyond all imagination; you can hardly imagine (that…, how huge…).

せっせい[1] 摂生 ¶摂生する take care of one's health; observe the rules of health ⇒ようじょう[2].

せっせい[2] 節制 moderation;〈飲食の〉《文》temperance;《文》abstinence (from alcohol) ¶節制する be moderate (in);《文》be temperate (in);〈廃する〉give up (alcohol);《文》abstain from (smoking) / 節制家《文》a man of temperate habits.

ぜっせい 絶世 ¶絶世の《文》peerless;matchless; unequaled (in beauty) / 絶世の美人 a rare beauty; a woman of matchless [peerless] beauty.

せつせつ 切々 ¶せつせつと訴える《文》implore earnestly.

せっせと《文》diligently;《文》assiduously; hard;〈しばしば〉frequently ¶せっせと通う《文》frequent (a library); visit (a place) frequently / せっせと働く work hard; work [《口語》beaver] away; be hard at work; peg away (along, on).

せっせん[1] 接戦 〈近接戦〉a close [tight] battle; close combat;〈いい勝負〉a close game [race, match] ¶接戦する fight at close quarters / 接戦を演じる be in keen competition (with); have a close contest [game] (with); run neck and neck; run a close race (with, against).

せっせん[2] 接線《数》a tangent; a tangential line ¶…に対して接線の方向に tangential to….

せっせん[3] 雪線《地理》a snow line [limit].

ぜっせん 舌戦《文》verbal warfare; a heated discussion (with);a war of words ¶舌戦を交える have 《文》engage in a war of words [a heated discussion](with).

せっそう 節操《文》constancy;《文》fidelity;《文》integrity;〈貞操〉chastity ¶節操のない《文》inconstant; unprincipled / 節操のある人《文》a principled person; a man of principle / 節操を守る be [《文》remain] faithful to one's principles; keep [hold, live up] to one's principles / 節操を売る sell one's honor;《文》prostitute oneself.

せつぞく 接続 (a) connection; joining ¶接続する connect; join; link / 接続駅 a junction / 接続詞《文法》a conjunction.

せっそく(しゅぎ) 拙速(主義) a rough-and-ready method [rule].

せっそくどうぶつ 節足動物 an arthropod.

セッター〈犬〉a setter.

せったい 接待 (a) reception; a (warm) welcome ¶接待する attend to (a guest); welcome; entertain (one's guests with refreshments);《文》receive (a guest); serve (sb with coffee and cake) / 接待費 entertainment expenses; an entertainment allowance. 文例⇩

ぜったい 絶対 ¶絶対の[的] absolute / 絶対の真理 (an) absolute truth / 絶対に absolutely / 絶対安静 (a) complete [(an) absolute] rest / 絶対音感 (have) absolute [perfect] pitch / 絶対温度《物》the absolute temperature / 絶対権力 absolute authority [power] (over) / 絶対者《哲》the Absolute; the absolute being / 絶対主義 absolutism / 絶対値《数》the absolute value / 絶対反対である be positively [dead] against (a plan) / 絶対命令《哲》the categorical imperative / 絶対多数を占める get [win] an absolute majority / 絶対服従を要求する demand sb's absolute [unconditional] obedience. 文例⇩

ぜつだい 絶大 文例⇩

ぜったいぜつめい 絶体絶命 ¶絶体絶命になる be driven into a corner; have one's back to the wall; be cornered [at bay]; be in a (bad) fix [a desperate situation].

せつだん 切断 cutting; amputation (手足の) ¶切断する cut off;《文》sever; amputate /〈手術で〉足をひざから切断する have one's leg amputated [《口語》off] at the knee / 切断面 a section. 文例⇩

せっち 設置 establishment; foundation ¶設置する establish; found; set up; create / 大学の設置基準 the official requirements for the establishment of a college.

せっちゃくざい 接着剤 an adhesive (agent); a bonding agent.

The contact is bad. / タクシーが彼の車に接触した。A taxi scraped his car.
せっする まだ詳報に接していない。Particulars are not yet to hand. / 勝報に接してみんな歓声を上げた。We all exclaimed with joy at the news of victory.
せっせと「いや僕はごめんだね」と彼は、せっせとほうきを動かしながら答えた。'No,' he answered, busy with the broom, 'I don't want to.'
せつぞく この列車は新潟行に接続する。The train connects [makes a connection] with one for Niigata.
せったい 私は接待係です。I am on the reception committee.
ぜったい 真相は絶対秘密にされている。Absolute secrecy is being preserved as to the truth. / 絶対に教えるわけにはゆきません。I can't tell you for the life of me. / 絶対いやです。I won't do it for anything [all the world]. / うそではありません、絶対に。I'm not lying. Cross my heart! / 患者は絶対安静を要す。The patient must have absolute [complete] rest. / 在庫をいくらやり繰りしても絶対量の不足にはどうにもならない。Juggling with stock is useless in (the) face of the basic shortage.
ぜつだい 絶大なるご支援を賜わりたい。Please give me your full

せっちゅう 折衷 ¶折衷する arrange [work out] a compromise ((between)) / 折衷案 a compromise; a compromise plan [suggestion, proposal] / 折衷主義 eclecticism / 折衷派[主義]の eclectic.

ぜっちょう 絶頂 〈山の〉 the top; the summit; 〈頂点〉 the peak; the height; 《文》 the acme; 《文》 the zenith; 頂点を極める 〈山の〉 reach the summit / 〈頂点〉 reach the climax / 好景気の絶頂にある be at the peak of the boom / 人気の絶頂にある be at the height [《文》 zenith, crest] of one's popularity.

せっちんづめ 雪隠詰め ¶雪隠詰めにする corner; drive sb into a tight corner.

せっつく ⇨ せきたてる, さいそく[2].

せってい 設定 ¶設定する establish; 《文》 institute; set up (a fund); create (a right).

せってん 切[接]点 【数】a point of contact [tangency].

せつでん 節電 economy in (electric) power consumption; power saving ¶節電する economize (in) power; save electricity.

セット 〈組・そろい〉 a set (of); 〈映画の〉 a (film) set; a studio set; 〈パーマの〉 a set; 〈テニスの〉 a set / 〈パーマで〉 set sb's [one's] hair / 応接(間)セット a drawing-room suite / コーヒーセット a coffee set [service] / 3点セット a three-piece set [suite (家具)] / 3セットの試合 a three-set match / セットポイント a set point / セットポジション 〈野球〉 the (pitcher's) set position. 文例⇩

せつど 節度 ¶節度のない uncontrolled; unrestrained; loose; rampant / 節度を守る be moderate; 《文》 exercise moderation (in).

せっとう 窃盗 〈事〉 (a) theft; pilferage (小物を少しずつ); 【法】 larceny / 〈人〉 a thief (pl. thieves) ¶窃盗を働く 《文》 commit a theft; steal; pilfer; filch ★ steal は一般的に「盗む」の意. pilfer は「小さな物を何回にも分けて少しずつ盗む」, filch は pilfer に近いが「何回にも分けて」の意は含まず, 「こっそりと」「ひょいと」「すっと」といった感じを表わす.

せっとうじ 接頭辞 【文法】 a prefix (to).

せっとく 説得 persuasion ¶説得する persuade; 《文》 prevail on sb / 説得して…させる persuade [《文》 prevail on sb to do; persuade [《文》 reason, argue, talk] sb into doing / 説得してやめさす persuade [《文》 reason, talk] sb out of (doing, his foolish plans); 《文》 dissuade sb from doing / 説得して自説に引き入れる talk [bring] sb over [round] to one's point of view / 説得力がある[ない] be very [be not at all] persuasive; 〈人が主語〉 have strong powers [no power] of persuasion; 〈論点が主語〉 be convincing [unconvincing]; 《文》 have considerable [no] persuasive power. 文例⇩

せつな 刹那 ⇨ しゅんかん ¶せつな主義 the principle of living only for the pleasure of the moment.

せつない 切ない painful; trying; 《文》 heart-rending (sorrow).

せっぱく 切迫 ¶切迫する 《文》 draw near; be imminent; 《文》 be impending; 〈緊張する〉 be [grow, 《文》 become] tense [strained] / 切迫した urgent (problems); pressing (matters); imminent (danger); 《文》 impending (doom); 〈緊張した〉 tense; acute / 切迫感 a sense of urgency. 文例⇩

せっぱつまる 切羽詰まる be driven into a corner [to the wall]; be in a fix; be at one's wits' end; be at [《文》 be brought to] bay ¶切羽詰まって driven by [under the pressure of] necessity; as a last resort. 文例⇩

せっぱん 折半 ¶折半する halve; divide sth into halves; split sth in half; 《口語》 go halves (with sb, on sth) / 利益を折半する go fifty-fifty (with sb) on the profit(s); share [《口語》 split] the profit(s) fifty-fifty.

ぜっぱん 絶版 ¶絶版になる[である] go [be] out of print.

せつび 設備 facilities; equipment; (modern) conveniences; accommodation(s) (宿泊設備) ¶設備する equip [provide, 《文》 furnish] (with) / …の設備がある be equipped [provided, 《文》 furnished] with… / 設備の良い well-equipped[-furnished] / 設備投資 capital investment; investment in plant and equipment / 設備費 the cost of equipment. 文例⇩

せつびじ 接尾辞 【文法】 a suffix.

ぜっぴつ 絶筆 sb's last work [writing]. 文例⇩

ぜっぴん 絶品 a superb [《文》 an exquisite] piece of work; a unique article; a rarity.

せっぷく 切腹 ¶切腹する perform [commit] hara-kiri [seppuku].

せつぶん 節分 the day before the calendrical beginning of spring.

せっぷん 接吻 a kiss ⇨ キス ¶接吻する kiss (sb on the cheek).

ぜっぺき 絶壁 a precipice; 〈主として海岸の〉 a cliff; a sheer [《文》 precipitous] cliff. 文例⇩

せっぺん 雪片 a snowflake.

[total] support.

せつだん その柱の切断面は2フィート平方ある. The pillar is 2 feet square in section.

セット セットして下さい. I would like a set, please. / 〈映画で〉彼女は今お(の)セットに入っています. She is now on (the) set. / この3点でセットになっております. The three (pieces) make a set.

せっとく どんなに説得に努めてみても連中には通じない. No amount of reasoning has any effect on them.

せっぱく 試験の期日が切迫してきた. The examination is just around the corner [is almost on us].

せっぱつまる せっぱ詰まってやったのだ. He did it as a last resort. / 人はせっぱ詰まるまでめったに一生懸命にならないものだ. One seldom does one's best till one is forced to.

せつび この作業場の設備は不完全だ. The workshop is not properly [fully] equipped. / 寄宿舎の衛生設備は行き届いている. The sanitary arrangements of the dormitory are perfect.

ぜっぴつ その一文が氏の絶筆となった. The article was the last thing that he did [penned] before his death.

ぜっぺき 彼は絶壁頭だ. His head is flat at the back.

せつぼう 切望 《文》an earnest desire; an eager wish [hope]; (a) yearning (for) ¶切望する《文》desire *sth* earnestly; be anxious for *sth* [to *do*]; long for *sth*; crave (for) *sth*; hanker [yearn] for [after] *sth*.

せっぽう 説法 ⇒ せっきょう.

ぜつぼう 絶望 despair ¶絶望する give up all hope (of success); despair of 《*one's* future》; be driven to [thrown into] despair (by) / 絶望して in despair; despairingly / 絶望的 hopeless. 文例⇩

ぜつみょう 絶妙 ¶絶妙な《文》exquisite; superb.

ぜつむ 絶無 ⇒ かいむ. 文例⇩

せつめい 説明 (an) explanation; 《文》(an) exposition; an account ¶説明する explain 《*sth* to *sb*》; give an account of *sth*; 《文》elucidate; make *sth* clear; illustrate 《実例をあげて》; outline 《大体を》; account for 《わけを》/ …の説明として in explanation [illustration] of… / 説明の[的]《文》explanatory; 《文》elucidative / 説明のつかない inexplicable; unaccountable / 説明書 an explanatory leaflet; 《文》an exposition; a description 《品物などの》; 〈機械の扱い方などの〉an operating manual; an instruction book; (the) instructions 《for operating an audio system》. 文例⇩

ぜつめい 絶命 ¶絶命する die; 《文》expire; 《文》breathe *one's* last ⇒ しぬ.

ぜつめつ 絶滅 extermination; 《文》extirpation; annihilation; eradication ¶絶滅する〈絶やす〉exterminate; 《文》extirpate; eradicate; annihilate; stamp out; wipe out (of existence); 〈絶える〉become extinct; go out of existence; die out / …の絶滅を防ぐ protect…from extinction / 絶滅寸前である be on the verge [brink] of extinction; face extinction; be in danger of extinction [dying out]. 文例⇩

せつもん 設問 a question.

せつやく 節約 economy; saving; 〈倹約〉《文》frugality; thrift; 《文》husbandry ¶節約する save; economize on; 《文》be frugal of; 〈節減する〉curtail; cut (down) / 節約を行なう economize (on); 《文》practice [exercise] economy (in). 文例⇩

せつゆ 説諭 《文》(an) admonition; 《文》(a) reproof ¶説諭する《文》admonish; give *sb* a lecture (for being lazy); 《文》reprove; 《口語》have *sb* on the carpet.

せつり 摂理 (divine) providence ¶天の摂理《文》the wise providence of Heaven / 自然の巧みな摂理《文》a happy dispensation of Nature.

せつりつ 設立 《文》establishment; foundation; organization ¶設立する establish; found; set up; organize / 設立者 a founder; an organizer / 設立趣意書 a prospectus / 設立発起人 a promoter.

ぜつりん 絶倫 ¶絶倫の matchless; unequaled.

せつれつ 拙劣 ¶拙劣な ill-managed; blundering; botched; badly done; unskillful; poor.

せつわ 説話 a tale; a story; a narrative ¶説話的 narrative / 説話体の 《(a) novel》in narrative form / 説話文学 narrative [legendary] literature.

せと 瀬戸 a strait, straits ★単複両形が用いられるが, 英国では複数形が標準的 ¶音戸の瀬戸 the Strait(s) of Ondo.

せどうじんしん 世道人心 (be detrimental to) public morals [morality].

せとぎわ 瀬戸際 a critical [crucial] moment; a crisis (*pl.* crises) ¶瀬戸際になって at the last moment; at the eleventh hour / 大事の瀬戸際に at the critical [crucial] moment / …の瀬戸際にある be on the verge [brink] of 《ruin》/ 事態を戦争の瀬戸際まで押し進める push matters to the brink of war / 瀬戸際政策 (tactics of) brinkmanship (on, over). 文例⇩

せとないかい 瀬戸内海 the Inland Sea (of Japan).

せとびき 瀬戸引き ¶瀬戸引きの enameled / 瀬戸引きにする enamel.

せともの 瀬戸物 crockery; earthenware; china(ware); pottery ¶瀬戸物屋 a china store [shop].

せなか 背中 the back ¶背中が曲っている *one's* back is bent [stooped] / 背中をたたく pat *sb* on the back; pat *sb's* back; give *sb* a tap on the back; slap *sb's* back (親しげに) / 背中を向ける turn *one's* back (on, to) / (猫が)背中を立てる arch *its* back / 背中を丸くする a hunch (up) *one's* back / 敵に背中を見せる〈逃げる〉turn tail; beat a retreat / 背中合わせに 《sit》back to back 《with》.

ぜに 銭 ⇒ かね[1] ¶(自動販売機などの)銭入れ口 (drop a coin in) a slot / 銭箱 a cashbox; a money box.

ぜにあおい 【植】a mallow.

ぜにごけ 【植】liverwort.

ぜつぼう 必ずしも絶望ではない. There is still some hope. / おれを絶望させないでくれ. Don't let me down. / 全く絶望だ. All hope is gone.

ぜつむ そんな事は絶無と言ってよい. It is next to impossible that such a thing should happen.

せつめい あとのことは説明するまでもない. The rest is self-evident [needs no explanation]. / この説明は説明になっていない. This explanation does not explain anything. | This is no [no sort of an] explanation.

ぜつめつ その鳥は絶滅の一途をたどっている. That bird is on the way to extinction.

せつやく それは時間の節約になる. It saves time. / 水を節約して使わなくては. We have to go easy on water. / 燃費の節約が我々のセールスポイントだ. Our selling point is the saving in fuel bills.

せとぎわ 今が大事の瀬戸際だ. This is the critical moment.

ぜひ ぜひうんと言って下さい. Please say yes. / あの映画はぜひ見ておきなさい. You mustn't miss that picture. / ぜひ来たまえ. You *must* come! | Do [Be sure to] come. / ぜひやってみるつもりです. I will try it whatever happens [come what may]. / ぜひその理由を聞かせてもらいた

ぜにん 是認 approval ¶是認する approve of *sth*; give *one*'s approval to *sth*;〈文〉admit ★ approve は approve of と他動詞としても使われるが、その場合は「承認する」「認可する」の意味になる.

せぬき 背抜き ¶背抜きの unlined at the back;《a coat》with an unlined back.

セネガル (the Republic of) Senegal ¶セネガルの Senegalese / セネガル人 a Senegalese《単複同形》.

ゼネスト a general strike.

せのび 背伸び ¶背伸びする stand on tiptoe; stretch *oneself*;〈比喩的に〉overreach *oneself*; try to do something beyond *one*'s power;《口語》bite off more than *one* can chew.

セパード ⇒ シェパード.

せばまる 狭まる get [〈文〉become] narrow, narrow; contract.

せばめる 狭める narrow; reduce《the width》.

せばんごう 背番号 a player's number.

ぜひ 是非〈善悪〉right and [or] wrong;〈是否〉〈文〉the propriety《of》;〈ぜひとも〉by some means or other; at any cost; without fail ★「ぜひとも」の意味は, 副詞語句よりもむしろ, 助動詞 must に強勢を置いて表わすのが適切であることも多い ¶ぜひと言うなら if you insist;〈文〉if you will have it so / ぜひ欲しい want *sth* badly / ぜひもない inevitable; unavoidable; necessary. 文例⑪

セピア sepia.

せひょう 世評〈世論〉public opinion;〈評判〉(a) reputation;〈うわさ〉rumor ¶世評によれば People [They] say that…; It is said [reported, rumored] that…;〈文〉Rumor has it that… / 世評に上る be talked about; be the talk of the town. 文例⑪

せびる pester [press]《*sb* for money》; extort《money from *sb*》;《口語》put the squeeze [《米》bite] on *sb*.

せびろ 背広〈上着〉a jacket;〈上下〉a suit;〈軍人・警官などの平服〉(in) civilian [ordinary] clothes ★ 上着とズボンが同じ生地でできているものをすべて a suit というが, サラリーマンなどが職場で着ているようなやや地味なものを a business suit といい,《英》では a lounge suit ともいう ¶三つ揃いの背広 a (man's) three-piece suit / 背広の上着 a suit jacket / 背広を着た男 a man in a suit.

せぶみ 瀬踏み ¶瀬踏みをする〈やってみる〉try;《口語》have a try [go]《at *do*ing》;〈探りを入れる〉sound *sb* (out)《on a subject》;《米》fly [send up] a trial balloon / 瀬踏みに〈試し

に〉as [by way of] a trial;〈探りとして〉as [by way of] a feeler [《米》trial balloon].

せぼね 背骨 the backbone; the spine;〈脊柱(ちゅう)〉the spinal column ¶背骨が曲がっている have a curvature of the spine.

せまい 狭い〈幅が〉narrow;〈面積が〉small; cramped《living quarters》;〈限られた〉limited ¶視野の狭い shortsighted; nearsighted; (a man) with narrow [limited] views / 了見の狭い narrow-minded / 狭い町 a small town / 狭くする narrow (down) / 狭くなる become narrower; narrow. 文例⑪

せまきもん 狭き門〈文〉the strait gate《to Heaven》;〈大学など〉a highly competitive university [school]; a difficult college to enter [get into]. 文例⑪

せまくるしい 狭苦しい cramped; confined. 文例⑪

せまる 迫る〈強く求める〉press《*sb* for *sth*》; urge《*sb* to *do*》; push (on); force; compel;〈近づく〉approach;《文》draw near;〈文〉be (near [close]) at hand; be imminent ¶敵に迫る close in on [《口語》upon] the enemy / 必要に迫られて driven by [under the pressure of] necessity. 文例⑪

せみ[1] ⇒ かっせみ.

せみ[2]《昆》a cicada《*pl.* -s, -dae》; a balm cricket;《米》a locust ¶せみの抜け殻 the cast-off shell of a cicada / せみしぐれ the chirring of cicadas in chorus.

セミコロン《put》a semicolon《to》.

セミナー a seminar《on》.

ゼミナール《conduct, hold》a seminar《on public finance》.

セミファイナル〈準決勝〉semifinals.

セミプロ ¶セミプロの semiprofessional;《口語》semipro《actors》.

せむし a hunchback; a humpback ¶せむしの hunchbacked.

せめ[1] 攻め ⇒ こうげき ¶攻め手〈軍勢〉the attacking [《口語》assailant] force;〈攻撃の手段〉a means of attack /〈囲碁・将棋などの手〉an offensive move / 攻め道具 a weapon of attack; an offensive weapon.

せめ[2] 責め〈責任〉(a) responsibility;〈非難〉blame;〈文〉(a) censure; a charge ¶責めを負う hold *oneself* responsible (for); take the responsibility on *oneself*; answer (for); take [bear] the blame (for) / 責めを負わせる lay [put] the blame on *sb*; blame (a failure) on *sb*; hold *sb* responsible (for); hold *sb* to blame (for) / 責めをふさぐ carry out [〈文〉fulfill]

い. I must know your reason without fail. / ぜひ留学したいものです. I am dying to study abroad. / ぜひもないことだ. It can't be helped. | There's no help for it. / ぜひない事情で退学した. He left school through unavoidable circumstances.

せひょう 彼は世評などにはとんちゃくしない. He does not care what people say about him.

せまい 彼は交際が狭い. He has only a small circle of acquaintances. / 世間は狭い. It is a small world.

せまきもん オックスフォード大学は全く狭き門だ. It is very hard indeed to get into Oxford University.

せまくるしい ここはいささか狭苦しいね. We feel a bit cramped for room here.

せまる 山が左岸に迫っている. There is a mountain close to the left bank. | A mountain rises sheer from the left bank. / こちらはもう冬が迫っています. Winter is closing in on this part of the country. / 試験は3日後に迫っている. The examination is only three days off [away]. | There are only three days to the exam now. | 万感胸に迫って言葉が出

せめあぐむ 攻めあぐむ be at *one*'s wits' end because of [be completely frustrated by] the impregnable defenses (of the enemy); be at a loss how to renew *one*'s attack.

せめおとす 攻め落とす carry ((a fortress)); take ((a castle)) by storm [assault].

せめく 責め苦 (a) torture; 《文》torments; 《文》ordeals ¶責め苦に会う be tortured; 《文》be put to the torture.

セメダイン 《商標名》Cemedine;〈接着剤〉a glue; an adhesive.

せめたてる¹ 攻め立てる attack ((the enemy)) repeatedly [hotly]; 《文》make an incessant onslaught ((on));〈苦しめる〉persecute ((*sb* with questions)).

せめたてる² 責め立てる〈きびしく責める〉torture *sb* severely;〈詰問する〉(cross-)question *sb* closely;〈さいなむ〉grill;〈促す〉press [urge] ((*sb* to do)) ¶責め立てて白状させる squeeze [extort] a confession from *sb* / 債鬼に責め立てられる be persecuted [tormented] by an insistent creditor; be dunned.

せめて at least; at most; at best. 文例⇩

せめよせる 攻め寄せる 文例⇩

せめる¹ 攻める attack; make an attack [assault] ((on the enemy)); assault ((the fortress)); 《文》assail.

せめる² 責める〈非難する〉blame; reproach; denounce; 《文》censure; take [《文》call] *sb* to task;〈さいなむ〉torture; torment; persecute;〈督促する〉urge; press. 文例⇩

セメント cement ¶セメントを塗る[で固める] cover [coat, hold *sth* together] with cement / セメント工場 a cement plant [factory].

せもじ 背文字 the titling ((on the spine of a book)).

せもたれ 背凭れ the back ((of a chair)).

-せよ though; even if [though] ¶どんなに貧乏にせよ however [no matter how] poor *one* may be; 《文》be *one* ever so poor / 真偽いずれにもせよ whether it is true or not;〈酔っていたにせよ〉granting [granting] that ((he)) was drunk. 文例⇩

ゼラチン gelatin(e) ¶ゼラチン状の gelatinous.

ゼラニウム 《植》a geranium.

せり¹ 競り (an) auction ⇨ **きょうばい** ¶競りに出す put *sth* up for [《米》to] auction / 競りで売る sell by [《米》at] auction / 競り市 an auction sale;〈場所〉an auction room [house] / 競り手 a bidder.

せり² 《植》a dropwort; a Japanese parsley.

せりあい 競り合い competition ⇨ **きょうそう**¹.

せりあう 競り合う struggle (for); compete [《文》vie] ((with *sb* for *sth*)).

せりあげる 競り上げる bid ((the price)) up.

ゼリー jelly;〈菓子〉a jelly ¶ゼリー状になる[する] jellify; jelly.

セリウム 《化》cerium.

せりおとす 競り落とす〈競売人が〉knock *sth* down ((for 1,000 yen));〈買い手が〉make a successful bid ((for an article)).

せりだす 迫り出す〈押し出す〉push *sth* out;〈芝居の舞台で〉come up from below the stage.

せりふ (a) speech; words; *one*'s line(s) ¶せりふのない役をする do [have] a nonspeaking [walk-on] part /〈せりふを言う〉speak *one*'s part [lines] / せりふをとちる bungle [《口語》fluff] *one*'s lines [a line]. 文例⇩

せりもち 迫持ち《建》an arch.

せる 競る bid ((for an article)); make a bid ((for)).

セル serge.

セルフサービス self-service. 文例⇩

セルフタイマー a delayed-action (shutter release); a self-timer.

セルロイド celluloid.

セルロース 《化》cellulose.

セレナーデ, セレナード 《音楽》a serenade.

セレン 《化》selenium.

セロ ⇨ **チェロ**.

ゼロ zero (*pl.* -(e)s) (★ zero は文例の2番目の文のように「0の記号」の意味では可算名詞として扱う); nought; nothing; nil ★電話番号・部屋番号・飛行機の便番号などを伝えるときは0を[ou]と読む。ただし、アメリカ人にはzeroもしくはnoughtと読む人もいる。競技のスコアで0点は、nothingか《米》zero [《英》nil]が普通であるが、テニスではloveと言う。文例⇩

ゼロックス 《商標名》Xerox ¶ゼロックスで複写する xerox ((the page)).

セロテープ cellulose (adhesive) tape;《商標名》Sellotape;《商標名》Scotch tape ★《米》ではScotch tapeが、《英》ではSellotapeが、それぞれほとんど普通名詞のように使われる.

セロハン[ファン] cellophane ¶セロハン紙 (a sheet of) cellophane (paper).

なかった. My heart was too full for words.

せめ² 責めは彼にある. It is his fault. | He is to blame. | He is responsible for it. / その失敗の責めを引いて辞職した. He accepted the blame for the failure and resigned. / 知らなかったからと言ってその責めを免れられるものではない. You cannot escape the consequences because you did not know.

せめて せめてもう1日お泊まりなさい. Stay just one day longer. / せめて葉書の1枚くらいはこしてもよさそうなものだ. He might at least send [have sent] me a postcard. / それがせめてもの慰めです. That is my sole [only] consolation.

せめよせる 敵の大軍が攻め寄せて来た. The enemy closed in on us in vast numbers.

せめる² 自分を責めて人を責めるな. You should be severe with yourself but lenient with others.

-せよ どんな金持ちにせよ寝て食うのはよくない. However rich a man may be [《文》Be a man ever so rich], he ought not to live in idleness.

せりふ それは僕のせりふだよ. I'm the one who's supposed to say that! | Those are my lines!

セルフサービス セルフサービスでどうぞ. Please help [serve] your-

セロリ 〖植〗 celery.
せろん 世論 ⇨ よろん.
せわ 世話 〈めんどう〉 care; trouble; 〈助力〉 help; 《文》 aid; assistance; 〈とりもち〉《文》 good [kind] offices; (a) recommendation ¶世話する take care [charge] of; help; 《文》 aid; 《文》 give assistance ((to)) / 世話の焼ける troublesome / 子供の世話をする look after children / 就職の世話をする find [get] sb a job [position]; 《文》 put sb in the way of making a living / 病人の世話をする look after [take care of, 《文》 tend; attend on] a sick person / 世話を焼かす give [cause] sb a lot of trouble; put sb to a great deal of trouble / 余計な世話を焼く meddle in [with] 《sb's private affairs》; poke one's nose into 《sb's business》 / 世話になっている be under the care of 《sb》; be indebted to 《sb for sth》 / ...の世話で through the good offices of...; at the recommendation of... / 世話好きな obliging; kind / 世話人[役]〈周旋者〉 a go-between; a mediator; an agent / 〈発起人〉 an organizer; a sponsor; 〈面倒を見る人〉 a manager / 世話女房 a good [practical] housewife; a devoted wife / 世話物 〖劇〗 a drama dealing with common people's life / 世話焼き 〈お節介〉 an interfering [an officious, a meddlesome] person; a busybody. 文例⇩

せわしい 忙しい ⇨ いそがしい.
せわしない restless; fidgety; (be) in a hurry [rush] ¶このせわしない時代に in this hurry-scurry age / せわしなく hurriedly.

せん¹ 千 a thousand ¶千をもって数えられる be counted by the thousand [by (the) thousands] / 千に1つ one in [out of] a thousand / 3千 three thousand / 幾千の thousands of (people) / 千分の1 a [one] thousandth; one-thousandth / 千倍する increase sth (a) thousandfold; increase ((the number [quantity])) a thousand times. 文例⇩

せん² 先 ⇨ さき.

せん³ 栓 a stopper (びんなどの); a cork (コルク栓); a stopcock (水道・ガス管などの); a plug (穴をふさぐ); a tap (たるの); a bung (ボートの底穴などの); an earplug (耳の); 〈水道の蛇口〉《米》a faucet; 《英》a tap ¶コルクの栓をする[抜く] cork [uncork] ((a bottle)) / ガス[水道]の栓を開ける[閉める] turn the gas [water] on [off] / 水道の栓を一杯に開ける turn the faucet [tap] full on / 綿[指]で耳に栓をする stuff cotton [put one's fingers] in one's ears.

せん⁴ 腺 〖解〗a gland.
せん⁵ 線 a line; a route (経路・航路); a track (軌道); a wire (電線) ¶体の線 a [one's] figure / 線の太い政治家 a strong-nerved politician / 線を引く draw a line / ...の線に沿って行動する act in line with ((the party policy)) / 三番線 Platform Three; 《米》Track Three / 常磐線 the Joban line. 文例⇩

せん⁶ 選 (a) selection; (a) choice; 〈編集の〉compilation; editing ¶選をする select; choose / 選に入る be chosen; be selected; be accepted / 選に漏れる be rejected; be not accepted; be left out / 選者 a selector; a judge. 文例⇩

ぜん¹ 善 《文》(the) good; goodness; 《文》virtue; 〈善行〉a good deed ¶善をなす do good; 〈親切にする〉do sb a good turn.

ぜん² 禅 Zen (Buddhism) ¶禅宗 the Zen sect / 禅僧 a Zen priest [monk] / 禅寺 a Zen temple / 禅堂 a (Zen) meditation hall.

ぜん³ 膳 a small dining table; a tray ¶ぜんに着く sit down to a meal [to dinner, to table] / ぜんを据える set a meal (before sb); lay [set] the table (for dinner) / ぜんを片づける clear the table; take away [《文》remove] the cloth / はし1ぜん a pair of chopsticks / 飯1ぜん a bowl(ful) of rice.

ぜん-¹ 全... whole; entire; all; full; complete ¶窓を全開にする open the window to its full width / 全校 all the school; the whole school / 全国民 the whole nation / 全アジア会議 the Pan-Asiatic Conference / 全16巻の (an encyclopedia) complete in 16 volumes / 1ページ全面広告 a full-page advertisement (in a newspaper).

ぜん-² 前... former; ex-; previous ¶前総理大臣 the ex-Prime Minister / 前代議士 an ex-member of the Diet.

-ぜん ...然 ¶学者然としている be quite like a scholar; have a scholarly air about one.

ぜんあく 善悪 good and evil; 〈正邪〉right and wrong ¶善悪の区別を知る[わきまえる] know [can tell] good from evil; can distinguish right from wrong; see [know] the difference between right and wrong.

せんい¹ 船医 a (ship's) doctor.
せんい² 戦意 the will to fight; 〈闘志〉(a) fighting spirit; morale; fight ¶戦意がない have no will to fight; have no intention of fighting; have no fight (in one); have no stomach for a fight / 戦意を失う lose one's

---

selves.
ゼロ 僕の化学の知識はゼロに等しい。I know practically nothing about chemistry. / ある数の右にゼロがつくと、その数は10倍になる。A zero to the right of a number makes it ten times as large.
せわ 彼にはたいして世話になってはいない。We don't have much to be thankful to him for. / たいへんお世話になりました。Many thanks for your kindness [kind help]. / できることなら親父の世話になりたくないんだが。I would not be a burden upon my father, if I could help it. / 君に世話なんか焼いてもらいたくないね。I will thank you to leave my affairs alone. / 大きな[余計な]お世話だ。This is none of your business. / それが一番世話なしだろう。That would be the simplest plan.
せん¹ それらは何千という数に達する。They run [reach] into the thousands.
せん⁵ いい線を行っている。You are on the right track. / 彼女はまだからだの線がくずれていない。She hasn't lost her figure.
せん⁶ これは世間にありふれた著書とは選を異にしている。This cannot be classed with common, run-of-the-mill writings.
ぜん¹ 善は急げ。Good deeds should be done quickly [without hesitating]. | Strike while

せんい³ 繊維 a fiber ¶繊維性の fibrous (繊維の多い); fibroid (繊維からなる) / 繊維状の fibriform / 天然繊維 a natural fiber / 植物性繊維 a vegetable [an animal] fiber / 繊維ガラス fiber glass / 繊維工業 the textile [fiber] industry / 繊維工場 a textile mill / 繊維製品 textile goods / 繊維素〖生理〗fibrin;〖化〗cellulose.

ぜんい 善意 <好意> goodwill; good will; <よい意図> good intentions; <よい意味> (in) a favorable sense;〖法〗good faith;〖ラテン語〗 bona fides ¶善意の well-meant; well-intentioned / 善意の第三者 a third party (acting) in good faith / 善意の人々 people of good will / 善意に解釈する take (it) in a favorable sense [in good part] / <疑わしい場合> give sb the benefit of the doubt.

せんいき 戦域 a war area; a theater of war.

ぜんいき 全域 <領域> (through) the whole area ((of the Kansai)); (throughout) the length and breadth ((of the domain)); (in) all parts [every part] (of); the whole field ((of natural science)) ¶…全域にわたって throughout [all over] ((the Kansai)); ((the)) ranging over the whole [full] gamut of ((the spectrum)).

せんいつ 専一 ¶専一に <特に> exclusively; <熱心に> single-mindedly;〖文〗earnestly;〖文〗devotedly. 文例⇩

せんいん 船員 a sailor; a seaman; a mariner; a crewman; <集合的に> the crew; officers and men; the forecastle [fo'c's'le] (下級船員); the quarterdeck (高級船員) ¶(同じ船の)船員仲間 one's shipmates.

ぜんいん 全員 all the members; the entire staff; <船の> the full complement; the whole crew; all hands ¶全員一致の unanimous / 全員一致して unanimously. 文例⇩

せんうん 戦雲〖文〗war clouds ((hanging [gathering] over Europe)).

せんえい 先鋭 ¶先鋭な radical (急進的) / 先鋭分子 radicals; (the) extreme [radical] elements / 先鋭化する get [((become)) militant; <急進的になる> become more radical ((in one's ideas)).

ぜんえい 前衛 <軍の> an advance(d) guard; the van(guard); <競技の> a forward ¶前衛をつとめる play forward / 前衛派 an avant-gardist / 前衛美術[文学] avant-garde art [literature].

せんえき 戦役 ⇨ せんそう³.

せんえつ 僭越 ¶僭越な〖文〗presumptuous; arrogant;〖文〗audacious / 僭越なことをする go beyond one's powers; exceed one's authority; be presumptuous / 僭越ながら with your permission ((leave)). 文例⇩

せんおう 専横 ¶専横な domineering; high-handed;〖文〗arbitrary; despotic; tyrannical / 専横に振舞う〖文〗manage ((a matter)) arbitrarily; have one's own way; lord it ((over one's subordinates)).

ぜんおん 全音〖音楽〗a whole tone ¶全音階 the diatonic [whole-tone] scale / 全音程 a whole step [tone] / 全音符 a whole note;〖英〗a semibreve.

せんか¹ 戦火 ¶戦火から救う[守る] save ((a country)) from war; keep war from ((one's country)).

せんか² 戦果 (achieve brilliant) military results [gains]; ((have outstanding)) military achievements.

せんか³ 戦禍 the disasters [devastation,〖文〗ravages,〖文〗afflictions, horrors] of war; war damage ¶戦禍を被った〖文〗war-torn[-shattered, -racked] ((countries)).

せんか⁴ 選歌 <選ぶこと> the selection of poems [tanka]; <歌> a selected [chosen] poem [tanka].

せんが 線画 a line drawing (画); line drawing (描法).

ぜんか¹ 全科 all the courses (offered by a school); the full [whole] curriculum.

ぜんか² 前科 a previous offense [conviction] ¶前科がある have a criminal [police] record; be an ex-convict / 窃盗の前科のある男 a man with a past conviction for theft / 前科3犯の男 a man with three previous convictions / 前科者 an ex-convict;《俗》an ex-con;《俗》an old lag.

せんかい 旋回 a revolution; a turn; circling ¶旋回する turn; revolve; rotate; gyrate; whirl round / 東京上空を旋回する circle over the city of Tokyo / 旋回運動 a gyrating [rotating] movement / 旋回飛行 ((make)) a circular flight.

せんがい 選外 ¶選外の left out of the final selection [the prize list] / 選外となる be not chosen [accepted]; be left out of the final selection; be rejected / 選外佳作 a good work left out of the final selection / 選外佳作となる receive an honorable mention.

ぜんかい¹ 全会 ¶全会一致で unanimously;〖文〗with one [by common] consent.

ぜんかい² 全快 (a) complete recovery ((from (one's) illness)) ¶全快する recover completely ((from)); make a complete recovery ((from)); get [be] quite well again;〖文〗be completely restored to health. 文例⇩

ぜんかい³ 全開 ¶エンジンを全開にする take the engine to full power; give ((the plane)) full throttle; open the throttle wide.

ぜんかい⁴ 全壊 ¶全壊する be completely destroyed;〖文〗be razed to the ground.

---

the iron is hot.〖諺〗| What is worth doing is worth doing promptly.〖諺〗

せんいつ ご自愛専一に願います。Please take good care of yourself.

ぜんいん 今日は僕らのクラスは全員出席だ。Our class has one hundred percent attendance today.

せんえつ 僭越ながら私がその説明を致します。With your permission I will explain it.

ぜんかい² 全快までには半年はかかると医者は言っている。The doctor says it will be six months before he is completely well again.

せんがくひさい 浅学非才をかえりみず, 私が本学会の会長に立候補

ぜんかい[5] 前回 the last time [occasion, session] ¶前回の… the last…; 《文》the preceding… / 前々回の the last [meeting] but one.

ぜんがく[1] 全学 the whole college [school] ¶全学集会 an all-campus meeting.

ぜんがく[2] 全額 the (sum) total; the total [full] amount ¶全額を払う pay in full / 全額払い込み済みの fully paid-up 《stocks》.

せんかくしゃ 先覚者 a pioneer; a pathfinder; 《文》a precursor.

せんかくひさい 浅学非才 文例⇩

ぜんがく[2] 前額 the forehead ⇒ひたい.

ぜんがくれん 全学連 the National Federation of Students' Self-Government Associations.

せんかし 仙花紙 recycled paper.

せんかん 戦艦 a battleship.

せんかん 潜函 a caisson ¶潜函工法 the caisson method / 潜函病 the bends; caisson disease;《医》decompression sickness.

せんがん 洗眼 ¶洗眼する wash one's eyes / 洗眼してもらう have one's eyes washed / 洗眼薬 an eyewash; an eye lotion;《薬》a collyrium 《pl. -s, -ria》.

ぜんかん 全巻 ¶全巻を読み通す read 《the book》from cover to cover; read 《the book》through.

ぜんがんしょうじょう 前癌症状 《病理》a precancerous [precancer] condition.

せんカンブリアじだい 先カンブリア時代《地質》the Precambrian era.

せんき[1] 疝気 colic ¶人の疝気を頭痛に病む worry about other people's affairs [business].

せんき[2] 戦記 a record [an account] of (a) war; a military history ¶ガリア戦記《書名》Commentaries on the Gallic Wars.

せんき[3] 戦機 the time for opening hostilities. 文例⇩

せんぎ 詮議 ¶詮議する《審議する》consider;《文》deliberate over;〈取り調べる〉inquire into; examine; investigate / 詮議立て a thorough [《文》rigorous] investigation / 詮議立てする《文》make exhaustive inquiries 《into》;《文》carry out a thorough investigation 《of》.

ぜんき[1] 前記 ¶前記の《文》aforesaid;《文》above-mentioned; referred to above;《文》(the) said 《person》/ 前記の場所《文》the above address.

ぜんき[2] 前期〈1年を2期にわけて初めの〉the first term; the first half year;〈2学期制の大学などの〉the first semester;〈今期の前の〉the last [previous] term ¶前期繰越金 the balance carried over [brought forward] from the previous [preceding] term / 前期試験 the midyear examinations.

ぜんぎ 前戯 foreplay.

せんぎけん 先議権 the right to prior deliberation 《on a budget bill》.

せんきゃく[1] 先客 an earlier visitor. 文例⇩

せんきゃく[2] 船客 a passenger ¶1等船客 a first-class passenger / 2[3]等船客 a second-class [third-class, steerage] passenger / 船客名簿 a passenger list.

せんきゃくばんらい 千客万来 ¶千客万来である have a great number of [《文》be thronged with] visitors.

せんきゅうがん 選球眼《野球》¶選球眼がある[ない] have a good [poor] batting eye.

せんきょ[1] 占拠 occupation ¶占拠する occupy; take; capture; hold / 不法占拠 unlawful [illegal] occupation; squatting / 不法占拠者 an unlawful [illegal] occupant; a squatter.

せんきょ[2] 選挙 (an) election ¶選挙する elect; vote for;《英》return 《代議士を》/ 大統領[知事]選挙 a presidential [gubernatorial] election / 選挙違反 election offenses [irregularities, frauds]; an election law violation / 選挙運動 an election campaign; electioneering; canvassing (主に戸別訪問による) / 選挙運動員 an election campaigner / 選挙演説 a campaign speech; an election address (政見発表の) / 選挙応援演説 a vote-getting speech / 選挙干渉 (government) intervention [interference] in an election / 選挙管理委員会 an election administration commission / 選挙区 an electoral district; a constituency / 選挙区改正 redistricting / 大[中, 小]選挙区制 the large [medium, small] constituency system; the multi-member [single-member] constituency system (★ 選挙区の面積でなく, 議席数によって大・小を区別する言い方. 日本の「中選挙区制」は, 議員定数が複数だから multi-member の方を使う) / 選挙権 the suffrage; the franchise; the right to vote; voting rights / 選挙権のない voteless 《slaves》/ 選挙権を与える enfranchise; give the franchise 《to》/ 選挙権を奪う disfranchise / 選挙権取得年齢 (the) voting age / 選挙公報 the official gazette for elections / 選挙資金 an election campaign fund / 選挙事務所 a campaign office / 選挙事務局長《米》a campaign manager;《英》an election agent / 選挙立会人 a witness (at the polls);《英》a scrutineer (開票の) / 選挙人〈個人〉an elector; a constituent; a voter;〈総称〉the electorate / 選挙人名簿 a voting roll [register]; a pollbook; a voters' list / 選挙日 election [polling] day / 選挙費用 election expenses; expenses for an election campaign / 選挙法 election [electoral] law / 選挙妨害 election obstruction / 選挙民 the voters; the electorate.

せんぎょ 鮮魚 (fresh [raw]) fish.

せんきょう[1] 船橋 the bridge.

せんきょう[2] 戦況 the progress of a battle; the war situation ¶戦況を報告する report on the

---

する決心をしたのにはそれなりの理由があります。 I have my reasons for standing as a candidate for the presidency of our society, though I am well aware that I have no pretensions to learning or ability.

せんき[3] 戦機は熟した。 The time to strike has come.

せんきゃく[1] 今朝早く彼を訪ねたら既に先客があったのには驚いた。 When I called at his house early this morning, I was surprised to find that he already had a visitor.

せんきょ[2] 明朝10時ごろには選挙の結果が判明することでしょう。 The election results will be known by ten tomorrow morn-

せんぎょう military situation. 文例⤵

せんぎょう¹ 専業 《文》a principal occupation; a full-time job ¶…を専業とする《文》devote *oneself* (full-time) to 《writing》/ 専業農家 a full-time farmer.

せんぎょう² 賤業 《文》a dishonorable [discreditable] occupation.

せんぎょうし 宣教師 a missionary.

せんきょく 戦局 the war situation; the progress of the war. 文例⤵

ぜんきょく 全曲 ¶全曲演奏 a full-length performance 《of *Carmen*》.

せんぎり 千切り ¶千切りにする cut 《a radish》into fine [thin] strips.

せんきん¹ 千鈞 ¶千鈞の重みがある〈言葉などが〉《文》carry great weight.

せんきん² 千金 ¶千金の値打ちがある be priceless.

せんく 先駆 ¶先駆的 pioneering 《works》; pioneer 《physicists》/ 先駆者を pioneer; 《文》a precursor; 《文》a pathfinder / 原子核物理学の先駆者をつとめる break new ground [blaze the trail] in nuclear physics.

せんぐ 船具 ship's fittings; rigging 《索具》.

せんくち 先口 a previous engagement 《約束》; a previous application 《申し込み》.

ぜんくつ 前屈 《医》anteflexion 《of the uterus》.

ぜんぐん 全軍 the whole army [force].

せんぐんばんば 千軍万馬 ¶千軍万馬の古つわ者《文》a veteran of many battles.

せんけい 扇形 《幾何》a sector ¶扇形の fan[pie-]shaped / 扇形に fanwise / さらに扇形に広がる fan out; spread out in a wide fan.

ぜんけい¹ 全景 a complete [a general, an overall, a panoramic] view 《of》; a panorama 《of Paris》.

ぜんけい² 前掲 ¶前掲の《文》shown [cited] above [before]; 《文》above-mentioned; 《文》aforenamed; 《文》aforecited / 前掲書《ラテン語》*op. cit.* ★ *opus citatum* の略 / 前掲書中に《ラテン語》*op. cit.* ★ *opere citato* の略.

ぜんけい³ 前景 《in》the foreground.

せんけつ 鮮血 (fresh) blood.

せんげつ 先月 last month ¶先月 5 日 《on》the 5th (of) last month.

せんけつもんだい 先決問題 《文》the first consideration; 《文》a matter calling for prior settlement. 文例⤵

せんけん¹ 先見 foresight ¶先見の明のある farseeing; farsighted; longsighted / 先見の明を欠いた 《a politician》with no [《文》lacking] foresight; shortsighted.

せんけん² 先験 ¶先験的 《哲》transcendental; 《ラテン語》*a priori* / 先験哲学〈カントの〉transcendental philosophy; transcendentalism.

せんげん 宣言 a declaration; a proclamation; an announcement; a manifesto 《*pl.* -(e)s》; a statement ¶宣言する declare; 《文》proclaim; announce; 《文》make a declaration of 《*one's* ideas》/ 〈議長が〉開会を宣言する call a meeting to order / 中立[独立]を宣言する declare *one's* neutrality [independence] / ポツダム宣言 the Potsdam Declaration / 宣言書 a manifesto 《*pl.* -(e)s》; a declaration.

ぜんけん 全権 《文》full [plenary] power; 《文》carte blanche ¶全権を委任する《文》invest *sb* with full power 《to *do*》; 《文》give *sb* carte blanche 《to *do*》/ 全権大使 an ambassador plenipotentiary. 文例⤵

ぜんげん¹ 前言 《文》*one's* previous remarks [words, statement] ¶前言を取消す withdraw [take back] *one's* words [what *one* said]; 《文》retract *one's* word / 前言を翻す《文》retreat [withdraw] from *one's* previous commitment; go back on *one's* word; back down.

ぜんげん² 漸減 ¶漸減する《文》decrease [diminish] gradually / 漸減傾向にある be on the decrease.

せんこ 千古 ¶千古不滅の《文》eternal; everlasting; 《文》immortal.

せんご 戦後 ¶戦後の postwar; 《フランス語》*après guerre* / 戦後最大の危機 the worst crisis since the war / 戦後派の "*après guerre*" generation [school].

ぜんご 前後 〈前と後〉in front and behind; 《文》before and behind 《場所》; before and after 《時》; 〈順序〉order; sequence; 〈ごろ〉about; nearly; 《ten pages》or so ¶それと前後して about that time / 《文》前後の関係 the context / 前後の見さかいもなく《文》regardless of the consequences; recklessly; rashly / 前後を見回す look around [about] *one*; 《文》look before and after / 前後を忘れる be beside *oneself* 《with anger》; be extremely upset / 前後に敵を受ける be attacked both in front and in the rear / 前後に揺れる swing back and forth / 前後左右に揺れる〈船が〉pitch and roll / 前後不覚になる lose consciousness; 《文》become unconscious / 30 歳前後である be about [around] thirty; be thirty or so [thereabouts]. 文例⤵

せんこう¹ 先行 ¶先行する go [be] ahead 《of》; 《文》precede / 先行詞《文法》an antecedent /

---

ing. / 国民は参議院議員選挙のために投票した。The Japanese people went to the polls to elect a new House of Councilors.

せんきょう 戦況は思わしくない。The war is not going in our favor.

せんきょく そのために戦局が一変した。That turned the tide of the war.

せんけつもんだい この方が先決問題だ。This question must be settled first.

ぜんけん 彼は会社の全権を握っている。He holds absolute power in the company. / 彼は条約改正の全権を帯びて渡米した。He went to America with full power to revise the treaty.

ぜんご 彼とは前後 10 年間ほどのお付き合いです。I have known him for ten years altogether. / 2人は相前後して入って来た。The two of them came in, one on the heels of the other. / それはちょうど震災前後の出来事だった。It happened round about the time of [just before or after] the Great Earthquake of 1923. / これらの文章は前後の関係を無視して引用されている。These passages have been taken out of context.

せんこう¹ 2点先行されたのを跳ね

先行権 〈道路交通の〉《have》《the》right of way. 文例⇩

せんこう² 先攻 ¶先攻する 〖野球〗go to bat first ; bat first ; be at bat at the top. 文例⇩

せんこう³ 専攻 a special study ; one's (main) subject ; one's (academic) specialty [《英》speciality] ¶専攻する study 《a subject》specially ; make a specialty of ; specialize in ;《米》major in / 専攻科目 a subject of special study ;《米》a major. 文例⇩

せんこう⁴ 穿孔 perforation ; boring ; punching ¶穿孔機 a drill ; a boring [drilling] machine ; a key [card] punch (コンピューターカードの) / (コンピューター用の)穿孔テープ a punched [perforated] tape.

せんこう⁵ 閃光 a flash ; a glint [sudden gleam] of light ¶閃光を放つ flash / 閃光電球 a flash lamp [bulb, tube]; a photoflash (lamp).

せんこう⁶ 戦功 《文》meritorious [distinguished] services in war ¶戦功を立てる《文》distinguish oneself on the field of battle.

せんこう⁷ 選考 choice ; selection ; screening ¶選考する select ; screen / 選考に漏れる be not chosen ; be rejected ;《文》fail to be selected / 選考委員会 a selection [screening, nomination] committee / 選考基準《文》a criterion [the criteria] for selection.

せんこう⁸ 選鉱 ore dressing.

せんこう⁹ 潜行 ¶潜行する go underground ; travel incognito [in disguise] / 潜行活動 underground activities.

せんこう¹⁰ 線香 a joss [an incense] stick ¶線香をあげる offer incense sticks / 線香をたく burn incense / 線香立て an incense holder [burner].

せんこう¹¹ 潜航 an underwater cruise ; submarine navigation ¶潜航する go [cruise] underwater ; 〈水中に没する〉submerge / 潜航時間 underwater time.

ぜんこう¹ 全校 the whole school ¶全校生徒に演説する speak to [《文》address] the whole school.

ぜんこう² 前項《文》(in) the preceding clause ;《文》(in) the foregoing paragraph ;〖数・論〗the antecedent.

ぜんこう³ 善行《文》good conduct ;《文》a good deed.

ぜんごう 前号 the last [《文》preceding] issue [number]. 文例⇩

せんこうはなび 線香花火 a sparkler ¶線香花火のような short-lived ;《文》ephemeral ;《文》meteoric / 線香花火のように消える flicker [fizzle] out ; be a flash in the pan. 文例⇩

せんこく¹ 先刻 ⇨さっき, すでに. 文例⇩

せんこく² 宣告 a sentence ¶宣告する sentence ; pass sentence on sb ; adjudge《sb guilty》; condemn ; pronounce / 無罪を宣告する judge sb not guilty ; acquit 《the prisoner》of the charge / 10年の懲役を宣告される be sentenced to ten years' imprisonment with hard labor [penal servitude for ten years] / 死刑を宣告する pass [pronounce] a death sentence on sb ; sentence sb to death [capital punishment] / 死刑を宣告されている be under sentence of death / 破産を宣告する adjudicate sb to be bankrupt ; 有罪を宣告される be convicted / 不治を宣告される《文》be pronounced incurable [past all hope of recovery]. 文例⇩

ぜんこく 全国 the whole country ¶全国の[的]national ; nationwide ; countrywide / 全国を通じて[にわたって] all over [throughout] the country [《文》land] ;《文》across the nation / 全国区選出参議院議員 a member of the House of Councilors elected from the national constituency / 全国紙 a national paper ; a paper with a national circulation / 全国大会〈政党の〉a national convention ;〈スポーツの〉a national athletic meeting [competition,《米》meet] / 全国農業協同組合連合会 the National Federation of Agricultural Cooperative Associations / 全国放送 a broadcast on a national network [hookup] ; a national network broadcast.

せんごくじだい 戦国時代 〖日本史〗the Age of Civil [Provincial] Wars ;〖中国史〗the Age of the Warring States.

ぜんごさく 善後策 ¶善後策を講じる《文》devise [work out] remedial measures.

ぜんざ 前座 an opening performance ; 〈前座語り〉a minor performer [storyteller, artiste] (at a vaudeville theater).

せんさい¹ 先妻 one's former [divorced] wife ; one's late wife (亡妻). 文例⇩

せんさい² 戦災《suffer, escape》war damage ¶戦災孤児 a war orphan / 戦災者 war (-damage) sufferers ; bombed-out people / 戦災地 a war-damaged [-devastated] area.

せんさい³ 繊細 delicate ; fine. ¶繊細な delicate ; fine.

せんざい¹ 千載 ¶千載一遇の好機 a rare [golden] opportunity ; the chance of a lifetime.

せんざい² 洗剤 a cleanser ; a detergent ¶中性[合成]洗剤 a neutral [synthetic] detergent.

せんざい³ 潜在 ¶潜在する《文》be latent ;《文》be dormant / 潜在的《文》latent ;《文》potential ;《文》dormant / 潜在意識 subconsciousness ;《be in one's》subconscious / 潜在

返して試合に勝った. Our team fought back from two runs behind to win the game.

せんこう² 早稲田の先攻で試合が開始された. The game started, with Waseda going to bat first.

せんこう³ 大学では何をご専攻でしたか. What did you major in [What was your major] at the university?

ぜんごう 前号より続く. Continued from our last issue.

せんこうはなび その問題は線香花火のようにぱっと広がって, またぱっと消えてしまった. The issue flared up suddenly and disappeared as suddenly.

せんこく¹ 先刻承知だ. I'm well aware of that.

せんこく² 彼はあとひと月の命だと医者に宣告された. The doctor gave him only a month to live.

ぜんこく その会社は日本全国に支店がある. The company has branches in all parts of Japan. / 東京には全国からの学生が集まる. Students gather in Tokyo from all over the country.

せんさい¹ 彼には先妻の子供が3人ある. He has three children by

意識的[の] subconscious ; subliminal / 潜在意識の領域《文》the realm of the subconscious / 潜在失業 latent [invisible] unemployment / 潜在失業者 the hidden jobless / 潜在主権 residual sovereignty.

ぜんさい 前菜 an hors d'oeuvre《*pl.* -(s)》★複数形で使うことが多い.

せんさく 詮索 ¶詮索する inquire into ; investigate ;《文》scrutinize ; pry [delve] into / 詮索好きな inquisitive ; curious.

せんさばんべつ 千差万別 ¶千差万別の《文》multifarious ;《文》《insects》of infinite [endless] variety.

せんし[1] 先史 prehistory ¶先史時代 the prehistoric age ;《study》the prehistory《of Japan》/ 先史考古学 prehistoric archaeology / 先史時代の日本 prehistoric Japan.

せんし[2] 戦士 a soldier ;《文》a warrior.

せんし[3] 戦史 (a) military [war] history ; the history of a war.

せんし[4] 戦死 ¶戦死する be killed《in the war, in Vietnam》; be killed in action ;《文》fall [die] in battle ;《文》die on the battlefield / 名誉の戦死を遂げる《文》meet glorious death in action / 戦死者 a fallen soldier ; the war dead (総称).

せんじ 戦時 ¶戦時中 during the war ; in wartime / 戦時経済[財政] wartime economy [finance] / 戦時産業 industry in wartime / 戦時体制《establish, build up》a war regime ;《on》a war footing / 戦時内閣 a war cabinet / 戦時編成の《a division》at war [fighting] strength.

ぜんし 全市 the whole city [town] ¶全市を挙げての[にわたる] citywide.

ぜんじ 漸次 ¶漸次に gradually ;《文》by (slow) degrees ; step by step ; little by little.

せんじぐすり 煎じ薬 an infusion.

せんしつ 船室 a cabin ; the passengers' quarters (総称) ¶1等船室 a first-class cabin ; a saloon / 3等船室 the steerage.

せんじつ 先日 the other day ; some [a few] days ago ; recently ; not long ago ¶先日の recent / 先日から for some time past. [文例⇩]

ぜんじつ 前日 the day before ; the previous [《文》preceding] day ¶結婚式の前日に on the day before the wedding.

せんじつめる 煎じ詰める boil down (薬を) ¶せんじ詰めると〈比喩的に〉to put it in a nutshell ; in short ;《文》in the final analysis. [文例⇩]

せんしゃ[1] 洗車 ¶洗車する wash a car / 洗車場 a car wash.

せんしゃ[2] 戦車 a tank ¶重[軽, 豆]戦車 a heavy [light, midget] tank / 戦車隊 a tank corps [unit] / 戦車兵 a tankman.

ぜんしゃ[1] 前車 ¶前車の轍(てつ)を踏む repeat *one's* predecessor's mistakes.

ぜんしゃ[2] 前者《文》the former (the latter に対して) ;〔法〕the prior [antecedent] party. [文例⇩]

せんじゃく 繊弱 ¶繊弱な weak ; feeble ; frail ; fragile ; delicate.

せんしゅ[1] 先取 ¶3点先取する[先取(得)点をあげる]〔野球〕score three runs first / 先取特権〔法〕(the right of) priority ; a preferential right.

せんしゅ[2] 船主 a shipowner ¶船主協会 a shipowners' association.

せんしゅ[3] 船首 the bow ; the prow ; the head ¶船首から船尾まで from stem to stern / 船首飾り a figurehead.

せんしゅ[4] 選手〈代表選手〉a representative player [athlete] ;〈競技者〉a《tennis》player ★日本語の「選手」に当たる語は, 英語では多くの場合 a runner, a high-jumper, a swimmer a skier, a skater と, 動詞に -er を付けた形で言う. だいたい, a baseball [tennis] player のように game のときは player を使うが, それでも a golfer, a footballer のような例外も多いので,「選手」についてはそれぞれの競技・スポーツの項で確かめたほうがいい ¶選手村 athletes' quarters [dormitories]. [文例⇩]

せんしゅう[1] 先週 last week ¶先週の今日 this day last week ; a week ago today / 先週の金曜日 last Friday ;《文》《on》Friday last.

せんしゅう[2] 選集 a selection ; selected works ; an anthology (詩文選) ¶明治文学選集〔書名〕*Selected Masterpieces of Meiji Literature.*

ぜんしゅう 全集 the complete works《of Dickens》.

せんじゅうしゃ 専従者〔労〕a full-time union official.

せんじゅうみんぞく 先住民族 (the) aborigines ;〈個人〉an aboriginal ; an aborigine.

せんしゅうらく 千秋楽《文》a close ; an end ; the closing [last] day [night, evening]《of a show》¶千秋楽になる《文》conclude *its* run ;《the show, *its* run》closes [comes to an end].

せんしゅけん 選手権 a championship ; a title ¶選手権を失う lose the title / 選手権を取る win [《文》gain, capture] the championship / 選手権を守る〈防衛試合をする〉defend the title ;〈防衛に成功する〉keep *one's* [the] title ; retain the title / 選手権試合 a title match [bout (ボクシングなどの)] / 選手権大会 a championship series / 選手権保持者 a champion ; a championship holder ; a titleholder.

せんしゅつ 選出 election ¶選出する elect ;《英》return (代議士を) / 代議士に選出される

---

an earlier marriage [his first wife].

せんじつ 彼女は先日来ずっと病気で寝ています. She has been sick [ill] in bed for several days. / お手紙を差し上げて先日のお礼を申し上げたいと思っておりました. I have been meaning to write to say thank you for the other day.

せんじつめる せんじ詰めれば我々がアメリカの事情に甚だ疎かったということになる. It boils down to this : we were ill-informed as to American affairs. | The heart of the matter is that we were quite ignorant of the situation in America.

ぜんしゃ[2] 彼らは馬と牛を飼っている. 前者は乗用で, 後者は乳をとるためだ. They keep horses and cattle ; the former for riding, the latter for milking.

せんしゅ[4] 彼は大学では野球の選手だった. He played baseball for [He was on the baseball team of] his university.

せんしゅつ イタリア, チュニジア, アルゼンチンの3国が国連安全保

せんじゅつ 戦術 tactics ¶巧妙な戦術 a clever piece of tactics; sharp tactics / 戦術上の要点 a tactical point / 戦術用核兵器 a tactical nuclear weapon / 戦術で…に勝つ outmaneuver; outgeneral / 高等戦術 grand tactics / 戦術家 a tactician / 戦術転換 a change of tactics.

ぜんじゅつ 前述 ¶前述の《文》above-mentioned; 《文》aforesaid; 《文》(the) said [above] 《article》/ 前述のとおり《文》as mentioned [stated] above.

ぜんしょ 善処 ¶善処する《文》take the appropriate steps (in [concerning] a matter); cope with (a difficult situation); make the best of (a bad bargain).

せんしょう¹ 先勝 ¶先勝する win the first game; score the first point.

せんしょう² 戦勝 a victory; 《文》a triumph ¶戦勝を祝う[祈願する] celebrate one's [pray for] victory / 戦勝国《文》a victorious country; 《文》a victor nation.

せんしょう³ 戦傷 a war [《文》battle] wound ¶戦傷者《米》a wounded veteran; 《英》a wounded ex-serviceman; a wounded soldier [sailor, airman]; the war wounded (総称).

せんじょう¹ 千丈 文例⇩

せんじょう² 洗浄 ¶洗浄する wash; rinse (a bottle); rinse out (impurities); 【医】deterge (a wound) / 胃を洗浄する【医】carry out a lavage of sb's stomach; administer a stomach pump 《to sb》/ 洗浄器 a washer; a syringe / 洗浄薬 a wash; a lotion.

せんじょう³ 扇状 a fan form [shape] ¶扇状地【地質】an alluvial fan; a fan.

せんじょう⁴ 扇情 ¶扇情的な〈読者の感情をあおる〉sensational; 〈情欲を刺激する〉suggestive.

せんじょう⁵ 船上 ¶船上で[に] on board (a ship); aboard / 船上生活 life on board 《a ship》; shipboard life / 船上大学 a floating university.

せんじょう⁶ 戦場 a battlefield; a battleground; 《文》the seat [theater] of war; the front; a scene of battle [action] ¶戦場で on the battlefield / 《prove one's worth》in battle / 戦場と化する turn into a scene of battle.

ぜんしょう¹ 全称【論】¶全称命題[肯定, 否定] a universal proposition [affirmative, negative].

ぜんしょう² 全勝 ¶全勝する win a complete victory (over); win three [ten, etc.] games [matches] out of three [ten, etc.]; win all one's games; have a hundred-percent record; sweep the field.

ぜんしょう³ 全焼 ¶全焼する be completely [entirely] destroyed by fire; be burned down [to the ground].

ぜんしょう⁴ 前哨 an outpost; an advance(d) post ¶前哨戦 a (preliminary) skirmish; 〈比喩的に〉《文》a prelude (to the coming election); 《口語》a dry run.

ぜんじょう 前条《文》the preceding [foregoing] article ¶前条に述べたとおり《文》as mentioned in the preceding article.

ぜんしょうがい 全生涯 ¶全生涯を通じて throughout [all through] one's life.

せんしょく 染色 dyeing; 〈顕微鏡下〉staining ¶染色工場 a dye works / 染色体【生物】a chromosome / 染色体の構成 chromosomal composition (of male and female body cells) / 染色体数 a chromosomal number / 染色体地図 a chromosome map / 染色薄片 a stained [dyed] slice [section] 《of an onion root》/ 染色法〈顕微鏡下〉staining techniques [procedures].

せんじる 煎じる boil; make an infusion of; 【薬】make a decoction of; decoct.

せんしん¹ 専心 ¶専心して wholeheartedly; single-mindedly; 《文》with all one's heart and soul; 《文》devotedly / 専心…に当たる, …に専心する devote oneself [all one's energies] (to); concentrate (one's thoughts [energies]) (on); apply oneself closely (to); be intent (on).

せんしん² 線審『テニス・フットボール』a linesman.

せんじん 先陣 the van (of an army); the vanguard ¶先陣を承る lead [be in] the van / 先陣争い competition [rivalry] to be the first rider in a charge.

ぜんしん¹ 全身 the whole body ¶全身に all over (one's body) / 全身全霊をあげて with all one's heart and mind and strength ⇒ぜんりょく / 全身像 a full-length figure [portrait] / 全身像を描く paint sb full length / 全身不随 total paralysis / 全身麻酔 general anesthesia. 文例⇩

ぜんしん² 前身《文》one's antecedents; 《文》one's former [past] self ¶前身を洗う check up on sb's record [past (life)]; 《文》inquire into sb's antecedents. 文例⇩

ぜんしん³ 前進 an advance; a forward movement; progress ¶前進する advance; march forward; go ahead / 一歩前進する take a step forward / 前進基地 an advance base; an outpost / 前進命令 《give》orders for an advance; 《give the troops their》marching orders. 文例⇩

ぜんしん⁴ 漸進 ¶漸進的に gradually; progressively; step by step; 《文》by gradual

---

障理事会のメンバーとして選出された。Italy, Tunisia and Argentina were elected to seats on the UN Security Council.

せんじょう¹ 千丈の堤もありの一穴より崩る。A little leak will sink a great ship. | For want of a nail the rider was lost. ⇒あり 文例★

ぜんしん¹ 毒が全身に回った。The poison has pervaded his whole [passed into his] system. / 全身泥だらけだった。He was all over [was covered with] mud. / 寒さで全身が震えた。The cold made me shiver from top to toe. / 水泳は全身の運動になる。Swimming gives exercise to every part of your body.

ぜんしん² 彼は今の法政大学の前身である和仏法律学校に学んだ。He studied in the Japanese-French Law School, the predecessor of the present Hosei University.

ぜんしん³ 前進命令を待っていた。

ぜんじん 全人 ¶全人教育 education for the whole man.

せんしんこく 先進国 an advanced [a developed] nation [country] ¶工業先進国 an industrially advanced nation [country]. 文例⇩

せんしんどうこう 先進動向 a heading.

せんじんのたに 千尋の谷 《文》an abyssal [unfathomable] ravine;《文》an abyss.

ぜんじんみとう 前人未到 ¶前人未到の unexplored;《文》untrodden;《文》uncharted;《文》virgin 《forests》/ 前人未到の領域 a region no man has ever explored [ventured into].

せんす 扇子 a (folding) fan ¶扇子の骨[かなめ] the ribs [pivot] of a fan / 扇子を使う use a fan; fan oneself.

センス (good) sense; taste ¶センスがある[ない] have good [poor, no] taste / 洋服のセンスがある[ない] have a good [have no] dress sense; have good [poor] taste in clothes / 音楽のセンスがある[ない] have a good [have no] musical sense; have an [no] ear for music; have good [poor] taste in music.

ぜんず 全図 a complete map 《of Tokyo》.

せんすい¹ 泉水 〈池〉a (garden) pond; a miniature lake;〈泉〉a fountain.

せんすい² 潜水 diving ¶潜水する dive; go under water; submerge / 潜水工作員 a frogman / 潜水病 the bends; caisson disease / 潜水夫 a diver / 潜水服 a diving suit [dress]; diving gear / 潜水帽 a diving helmet.

せんすいかん 潜水艦 a submarine;《口語》a sub ¶潜水艦隊 a submarine [an underseas] fleet / 潜水艦探知機 an asdic; a sonar / 潜水艦から発射されるミサイル a submarine-launched missile / 潜水艦搭載のミサイル a submarine-borne missile.

せんすいぼかん 潜水母艦 a submarine tender [depot ship].

せんする 宣する 《文》declare;《文》proclaim; announce; call 《a recess》¶開会を宣する announce the opening of a meeting. 文例⇩

ぜんせ 前世 《文》one's previous [former] life [existence] ¶前世の約束《文》predestination; one's fate;《文》one's karma.

せんせい¹ 占星 (cast [work out]) a horoscope ★ a horoscope は「占星術」ではなく，1回の星うらない ¶占星術 astrology.

せんせい² 先生 〈教師〉a teacher; an instructor; a master;〈医師〉a doctor ★ teacher は職能を表わすのみで, 尊敬の念を含まないから，「先生」と呼びかけるのに teacher とは言わない. Mr. [Miss, Mrs., Prof.] Yamada のように名前を言う. 医師に呼びかける時は Doctor と言う ¶数学の先生 a teacher of mathematics; a mathematics teacher. 文例⇩

せんせい³ 宣誓 an oath ¶宣誓する swear; take [make, swear,《文》pronounce] an oath / 宣誓させる put sb on (his) oath / 就任の宣誓をする take the oath of office 《as》; be sworn in [into office] / 宣誓供述書 an affidavit / 宣誓式 the administration of an oath;〈就任の〉swearing-in ceremony / 宣誓書 a written oath. 文例⇩

せんせい⁴ 専制 despotism; autocracy; absolutism ¶専制的(な) despotic; autocratic; absolute; tyrannical / 専制君主 a despot; a despotic [an absolute] monarch; an autocrat / 専制政治 despotic government; autocracy.

ぜんせい¹ 全盛 ¶全盛を極める be at the height [《文》zenith] of its [one's] prosperity; be in the heyday of its [one's] power; be in (all) its glory / 全盛期 the golden age [days] (of English literature); the heyday;《文》the palmy days;〈人の〉sb's best days; the days of sb's glory. 文例⇩

ぜんせい² 善政 wise [good] government;《文》just rule ¶善政を施す[敷く] govern [rule] well [wisely].

ぜんせいき 前世紀 ¶前世紀の遺物 a relic from an earlier [《文》a former] age; a museum piece; an antediluvian ★ 日本語と同様に, 日常会話でおどけて使う.

せんせいこうげき 先制攻撃 a preemptive attack [strike] ¶先制攻撃を加える strike (the enemy) first [before (he) attacks one]; carry out a preemptive strike against 《the enemy's nuclear installations》.

せんせいりょく 潜勢力 potential;《文》potentiality;《文》latent force [power].

センセーショナル センセーショナルな sensational.

センセーション a sensation ¶センセーションを巻き起こす create [cause] a sensation 《stir》《in the medical world》.

ぜんせかい 全世界 ¶全世界の[に] all over [throughout] the world; across [around] the globe / 全世界を旅行する travel all over the world [round the world, world wide] / 全世界から〈come〉 from all parts [corners] of the world.

せんせき¹ 船籍 the nationality [registration]

They were waiting for the go-ahead.

せんしんこく ドイツはこの技術の分野では世界でも一番の先進国である. Germany leads the world in this field of technology.

せんする 審判は彼にアウトを宣した. The umpire gave him out.

せんせい 先生，母の容態はいかがでしょう. How is my mother, doctor? / お料理は姉を先生にして習いました. I learned cooking under my sister's tuition. / あの方は何の先生ですか. What is she a teacher [professor] of?

せんせい² メキシコの選手が,参加者を代表して,オリンピックの宣誓をした. A Mexican athlete, speaking for all the participants, pronounced the Olympic oath.

ぜんせい¹ ローマはオーガスタスの時代に全盛を極めた. Rome reached the acme of its prosperity in the age of Augustus. / 彼の全盛時代は過ぎた. He has seen his best days.

せんせん¹ 全線開通には1週間はかかる見込み. It will probably be a week before the line is completely reopened to service.

ぜんせん その計画は全然失敗であった. The project was a complete [an utter] failure. / 最近

せんせき 船籍 of a ship ¶ ギリシャ船籍の貨物船 a cargo ship sailing under the flag of Greece.
せんせき² 戦跡 a battle site.
せんせき³ 戦績 〈戦争の〉a war record; 〈競技の〉results; a record.
せんせん¹ 宣戦 a declaration of war ¶ 宣戦を布告する declare war 《on》.
せんせん² 戦線 (at) the front; (in) the battle line.
せんぜん 戦前 ¶ 戦前の prewar; before the war / 戦前の標準に達する[しない] reach [fail to reach] the [its] prewar level; come up to [fall short of] the prewar standard / 戦前には in prewar days [times]; before the war / 戦前派 《belong to》the prewar generation [school].
ぜんせん¹ 全線 ¶ 信越線全線にわたって all along [the whole length of] the Shin'etsu Line. 文例↓
ぜんせん² 前線 〈第一線〉the front (line); 〖気象〗a front ¶ 前線の発生〖気象〗frontogenesis / 前線に出る[出ている] go up to [be in] the front line / 前線で戦う fight in the front line / 寒冷[温暖]前線 a cold [warm] front / 前線基地 a frontline base.
ぜんせん³ 善戦 ¶ 善戦する fight well [bravely]; fight [put up] a good fight.
ぜんぜん 全然 (not) at all; utterly; simply; entirely; quite 《wrong》; completely. 文例↓
せんせんきょうきょう 戦々恐々 ¶ 戦々恐々として《文》in great fear; trembling with fear. 文例↓
せんせんげつ 先々月 the month before last.
せんぞ 先祖 an ancestor; a forefather ¶ 先祖の《文》ancestral / 先祖をたどる trace back one's ancestry / 先祖代々の墓 a family tomb / 先祖伝来の ancestral 《estates》 / 先祖返り〖生物〗(an) atavism; (a) reversion; (a) throwback / 先祖返りをする revert 《to》; throw back 《to》. 文例↓
せんそう¹ 船倉 the hold (of a ship) ¶ 船倉に積み込む stow [load] 《cargo in》the hold.
せんそう² 船窓 a porthole.
せんそう³ 戦争 (a) war; warfare ¶ 冷たい[熱い]戦争 a cold [hot] war / 戦争をする go to war 《with, against》; 《文》war 《against, with》; 《文》wage war 《against》; 《文》take up [resort to] arms 《against》; 《文》open hostilities 《against, with》 / 戦争中である be at war 《with》 / 戦争景気 a war [wartime] boom / 戦争犠牲者[未亡人, 映画, 小説] a war victim [widow, film, novel] / 戦争ごっこ playing soldiers / 戦争状態 (enter into, be in) a state of war / 戦争体験がある have war memories / 戦争成金 a war profiteer / 戦争犯罪 ⇨ せんぱん² / 戦争反対の運動 an anti-war movement / 戦争放棄《文》the renunciation of war / 戦争放棄の憲法[条項] a war-renouncing constitution [article]; a 'no-war' constitution [article] / 戦争屋[挑発者] a warmonger; a warmaker.

ぜんぞう 漸増 a gradual increase ¶ 漸増する increase gradually [little by little].
ぜんそうきょく 前奏曲〖音楽〗a prelude 《to》; an overture 《to》.
せんそく 船側 the side of a ship.
せんぞく 専属 ¶ 専属する《文》belong exclusively 《to》 / 専属女優 an actress under (exclusive) contract 《with》.
ぜんそく 喘息〖医〗asthma ¶ 喘息の発作 an asthma attack / 喘息患者 an asthmatic (patient).
ぜんそくりょく 全速力 ¶ 全速力で at full [top] speed; (at) full tilt; 〈飛行機・船などが〉at full power; 〈馬が〉at full gallop; 〈船が〉at [under] full steam / 全速力を出す develop [《人》] put forth, gather] full speed.
ぜんそん 全損〖保険〗total loss.
センター 〈施設〉a center; 〖野球〗(the) center field (中堅); a center fielder (中堅手) ¶ センターフライ a fly to center; a center fly / センターフライをあげる fly to center / センターライン 〈球技のコート・道路などの〉the center line [stripe].
せんたい¹ 船体 the hull, 〈船〉a ship.
せんたい² 船隊 ⇨ せんたん².
せんたい³ 蘚苔〖植〗moss(es) ¶ 蘚苔類 bryophytes.
せんだい 先代《文》[the [one's] predecessor (in the family line); sb's father ¶ 先代菊五郎 the last Kikugoro / 先々代菊五郎 the last Kikugoro but one.
ぜんたい¹ 全体 〈全部〉the whole; 《文》the totality ¶ 全体の whole; entire; general / 全体に wholly; entirely; generally / 全体にわたって all over [the land]; throughout 《the world》 / 全体で 〈全部で〉all together; in all; all told; 《文》in the aggregate / 全体として as a whole; collectively; in the aggregate / 全体から見ると on the whole; altogether; taken all together; all things considered; all in all; taken overall / 全体的な問題 an overall problem / 全体会議 a plenary session [meeting]; 〈総会〉a general meeting [assembly] / 全体集合〖数〗a universal set / 全体主義 totalitarianism / 全体主義国家 a totalitarian state. 文例↓
ぜんたい² 全隊 文例↓

彼女に全然会っていない。I have seen nothing of her lately. / それは全然違う。〈事実ではない〉That isn't true [so] at all. 〈異なる〉It is quite different. / あんな人は全然知らない。He is a complete stranger to me. / 彼の話はだれも全然信用しなかった。Nobody believed a word of his story. / 私の経験など、あなたのなさった苦労とは全然比較にもなりません。My experience does not (even) begin to compare with what you have gone through.
せんせんきょうきょう 彼は悪事の露顕を恐れて、戦々恐々としていた。He was in constant fear lest the scandal should come to light.

せんぞ 私の先祖はスコットランド人です。My ancestors came from Scotland. / I am of Scottish descent [ancestry].
ぜんたい¹ この組の生徒は全体に出来がよい。Generally speaking [All in all], the students of this class are very good.
ぜんたい² 全隊、止まれっ！〖号令〗Procession—halt !

ぜんだいみもん 前代未聞 ¶前代未聞の unheard-of; unprecedented; 《文》unparalleled (in history).

せんたく¹ 洗濯 washing; laundry; cleaning ¶洗濯する wash; launder / 洗濯がきく be washable; stand [bear] washing / 洗濯をする do one's washing [wash] / 命の洗濯をする《口語》recharge one's batteries / 洗濯でone's energy / 洗濯板 a washboard / 洗濯女 a washerwoman / 洗濯機 a washing machine; a clothes-washer / 洗濯代 laundry charges / 洗濯だらい a washtub / 洗濯場 a washhouse; a laundry / 洗濯ばさみ a clothespin; 《英》a clothes peg / 洗濯屋 a laundry; 《セルフサービスの》《米》a Laundromat; 《英》a Launderette (★《米》《英》とも登録商標だが、しばしば普通名詞扱いで、小文字でつづる);《人》a laundryman (男); a laundress (女); a dry cleaner / 洗濯物 washing; laundry (★「洗たく物１つ」は a piece of washing [laundry] / たくさん洗濯物がある have a lot of washing to do / 洗濯物を入れるかご a washing basket / 洗濯物を干す hang out (the) washing (to dry).

せんたく² 選択 selection; choice; (an) option ¶選択する choose;《文》select / 選択よろしきを得る make a good choice / 選択を誤る make a bad choice; make the wrong choice; choose the wrong thing / 人為［自然／強制］《生物》artificial [natural] selection / 選択科目 an optional course;《米》an elective (course);《英》an option / 選択肢《多項式選択法の》《six》choices / 選択飛び《飛込競技》an optional dive. 文例⇩

せんだつ 先達 〈開拓者〉a pioneer;〈先輩〉《文》a precursor;〈指導者〉a leader;〈案内〉a guide.

せんだって 先だって → せんじつ.

ぜんだて 膳立て setting [laying] the table (for dinner);〈準備〉preparations; arrangements ¶膳立てする set the table (for dinner);〈準備する〉arrange;《口語》set things up (for); make (the) arrangements [preparations] (for); pave the way (for). 文例⇩

ぜんだま 善玉《口語》a goody;《米口語》a good guy.

せんたん¹ 先端 the point; the tip; a pointed end [head] ¶時代の先端を行く set the trend [《文》be in the van] of the new era / 流行の先端を行く set [lead] the fashion / 時代[流行]の先端を行く人 a trendsetter / 先端的 ultra

modern; up-to-date;〈流行の〉ultrafashionable.

せんたん² 戦端 ¶戦端を開く《文》open hostilities 《with》;《文》take up arms 《against》.

せんだん¹ 専断《文》(an) arbitrary decision ¶専断で[に]《文》arbitrarily; at one's own discretion; on one's own authority.

せんだん² 船団 a fleet (of vessels) ¶出漁船団 a fishing fleet /《護衛艦つきの》輸送船団 a convoy of transport ships.

せんだん³《植》a Japanese bead tree. 文例⇩

ぜんだん¹ 全段〈新聞の〉a whole [an entire] page ¶全段抜きの大見出し〈外字新聞で〉a banner (headline).

ぜんだん² 前段〈前半〉the first half;〈前の部分〉the first part;〈前の段落〉《文》the preceding paragraph.

せんち 戦地 the front ¶戦地へ行く[にいる] go to [be at] the front / 戦地勤務 field service.

ぜんち 全治 ¶全治する be completely cured [recovered]; heal completely. 文例⇩

ぜんちし 前置詞《文法》a preposition ¶前置詞句 a prepositional phrase. 文例⇩

ぜんちぜんのう 全知全能 ¶全知全能の《文》omniscient and omnipotent / 全知全能の神 the Almighty; Almighty God.

センチ(メートル) a centimeter (略: cm).

センチメンタリズム sentimentalism.

センチメンタル ¶センチメンタルな sentimental.

せんちゃ 煎茶 green tea (of middle grade).

せんちゃく 先着 ¶先着順に in (the) order of arrival;《文》in (the) order of receipt (申込書などの); on a first-come-first-served basis. 文例⇩

せんちゅうは 戦中派 the war [wartime] generation.

せんちょう 船長 a captain; a skipper (漁船などの) ¶船長室 the captain's cabin.

ぜんちょう¹ 全長 the full [《文》total] length (of) ¶全長15メートルある have a total [an overall] length of 15 meters;〈船が〉be 15 meters long from stem to stern /…の全長にわたる stretch [run] the (full) length of....

ぜんちょう² 前兆 an omen; a warning; a sign;《文》a portent;《文》a premonition ¶よい[悪い]前兆 a good [a bad,《文》an ill] omen / 前兆となる[である]《文》augur [bode] 《well, badly, ill》;《文》be ominous of;《文》portend. 文例⇩

せんたく¹ インクの染みが洗濯してもおちない。The ink stain will not wash out. / この布は洗濯すると縮みますよ。This cloth will shrink in the wash. / シーツが洗濯しないので薄汚れていた。The sheets were gray [a little soiled] from want of washing.

せんたく² 学者になろうと公務員になろうとお前の選択に任せる。I leave it to you (to choose) whether you will be a scholar or a civil servant.

ぜんだて すっかり膳立てができている。It's all laid on.

せんだん³ せんだんは二葉より芳し。Genius displays itself even in childhood.

ぜんち 彼は全治3週間の負傷をした。He has had an injury which will take three weeks to heal completely.

ぜんちし この動詞の後にはどんな前置詞がつくか。What preposition follows [comes after] this verb?

せんちゃく 先着200名様に粗品呈上。Gifts presented to the first two hundred arrivals.

ぜんちょう² 物には必ず前兆というものがある。Coming events cast their shadows before. /〈諺〉このなぎはあらしの前兆だ。This calm is a sign of a storm coming on. / これは日本の将来にとってよい前兆だ。This augurs well for the future of Japan.

せんて 警察の先手を打って、彼は九州を高飛びしてしまった。He

せんて 先手 ‹機先› forestalling; the first [initial] move (囲碁などの) ¶先手を打つ[取る] forestall; get ahead [the start] of *sb*; take [get, seize] the initiative;《文》preempt (*sb's* action). 文例↓

せんてい¹ 剪定 ¶剪定する prune; trim / 剪定ばさみ (a pair of) pruning shears;《英》secateurs.

せんてい² 選定《文》selection; choice ¶選定する select; choose; make a selection (of) / 選定図書目録 a reading list; a reference (reading) list.

ぜんてい¹ 前庭 a front garden [《米》yard];《解·動》the vestibule.

ぜんてい² 前提《文》(a) presupposition;《論》a premise; ‹必要条件›《文》a prerequisite; ‹交渉の› preconditions ¶前提として挙げる *sth* forth as a premise; premise (that...) / ...を前提として《文》on the assumption [premise] that...; supposing...; on condition that...;《文》presupposing... / 大[小]前提 a major [minor] premise. 文例↓

せんてつ 銑鉄 pig iron.

せんてん 先天 ¶先天的(性)の inborn;《文》innate;《文》inherent;《文》native; congenital (deformity); hereditary (diseases); inherited (character);《哲》*a priori* / 先天的に by nature;《文》inherently;《文》innately / 先天的欠陥 a congenital defect / 先天性梅毒 congenital syphilis. 文例↓

せんでん 宣伝 propaganda; publicity; ‹広告› advertisement ¶宣伝する give publicity to; publicize; propagandize; ‹広告する› advertise;《口語》give *sb* [*sth*] a build-up; boost (ちょうちん持ちをする) / 誇大に宣伝する advertise *sth* with exaggerated praise;《口語》puff (a product) / 宣伝カー a loudspeaker van; a loudspeaker car; a sound car [truck] / 宣伝係 a public relations man; a publicity man / 宣伝活動 propaganda activities / 宣伝機関 ‹政府·国家の› a propaganda organ [machine]; propaganda machinery / 宣伝業者 a publicity agent / 宣伝効果 (a) propaganda effect / 宣伝工作 propaganda efforts [maneuvers] / 宣伝攻勢 a propaganda offensive [campaign] / 宣伝戦 a propaganda war [battle, contest] / 宣伝費 advertising [publicity] expenses / 宣伝ビラ a propaganda bill [leaflet]; a publicity handout; a handbill (散らし) / 宣伝部 a public [public relations] department / 宣伝文句 an advertisement; a sales message; an advertising statement / 宣伝屋 a propagandist. 文例↓

ぜんてんこう 全天候 ¶全天候機[カメラ] an all-weather plane [camera].

せんと 遷都 the transfer of the capital (to) ¶遷都する transfer [move] the capital 《from Kyoto to Tokyo》.

セント ‹米貨› a cent (略: c., 記号: ¢) ¶5 [10, 25, 50]セント貨 a nickel [dime, quarter, half dollar] / 1ドル75セント one dollar seventy-five cents;《口語》one [a] dollar seventy-five;《口語》one seventy-five; = $1.75.

せんど¹ 先途 ¶ここを先途と戦う fight desperately (to the last man); make a final [one's last] stand; make a stubborn resistance.

せんど² 鮮度 (the degree of) freshness ¶鮮度が落ちる lose (some of) *its* freshness / 鮮度が高い[低い] be very [not very] fresh.

ぜんと 前途 *one's* course; (*one's*) prospects ¶前途を誤る ‹事が主語› ruin [wreck] *one's* career [future] / 前途を祝う wish *sb* a happy future / 前途に横たわる lie ahead of *one* / 前途遼遠(りょう)である ‹人が主語› have a long way to go; ‹事が主語› be a long way off [in the future] / 前途有望である have a bright [rosy] future (in front of [《文》before] *one*) / 前途有望な青年 a promising youth; a young man (full) of promise.

ぜんど 全土 ¶全土にわたって all over the land; throughout the country.

せんとう¹ 尖塔 a spire; a steeple; a pinnacle (小尖塔); a minaret (回教寺院の).

せんとう² 尖頭 ¶尖頭アーチ a pointed arch; an ogive.

せんとう³ 先頭《文》the forefront; the front (position); the head; the lead; the top ¶先頭に立つをに at the head (of); take the lead (in); be in the front [van] (of the parade); spearhead (a campaign) / 先頭に立って歩く walk at the head (of a procession) / 先頭打者 ‹野球›‹メンバーの中の› a lead-off man; ‹その回の› the first batter. 文例↓

せんとう⁴ 戦闘 a battle; an action; an engagement; a fight; combat ¶戦闘に参加する take part in a battle; see combat [action] / 戦闘中の兵士 a soldier in combat / 戦闘的な militant (labor unionists) / 戦闘員 a combatant / 非戦闘員 a noncombatant / 戦闘機 a fighter / 戦闘隊形 (a) battle formation / 戦闘服 (a) combat uniform; ‹機動隊の› riot gear / 戦闘部隊 combat troops / 戦闘帽 a field cap /

---

anticipated the police by fleeing out of Kyushu. / この将棋はどちらが先手(番)だったのですか。Who had the first move in this game of *shogi*?

ぜんてい² 彼の議論は前提が間違っている。He argues from wrong [false] premises.

せんてん 彼の数学の才能は先天的だ。He was born with a talent [head] for mathematics.

せんでん 彼の提案にはだれがみても宣伝臭がある。His proposal has obvious propaganda overtones. / これは我々にとっていい宣伝になる。This will make good publicity [propaganda] for us.

ぜんと 前途は暗澹たるものだ。My prospects are really gloomy [bleak]. / 目標までは前途なお遠だ。We are still a long way from our object [goal]. / 宇宙船に乗って火星旅行ができるまでにはまだ前途遼遠だ。The day is still far off when we can take a trip to Mars in a spaceship. / 彼には洋々たる前途が開けている。A great career is open to him. | He has the whole world at his feet. / 我々の前途には幾多の困難が横たわっている。There are any number of difficulties in store for us. | Many difficulties lie ahead of us. / 彼の前途が案じられる。It's a bad lookout for him.

せんとう³ 彼はこの大運動の先頭に

戦闘力 fighting [combat] strength [power].
せんとう[5] 銭湯 ⇨ ふろ (風呂屋).
せんどう[1] 先導《文》guidance; leadership ¶ 先導する guide; lead (the way) / …の先導で《文》《inspect the school》conducted by [under the guidance of]《the principal》/ ガイドに先導されて led [《文》preceded] by a guide.
せんどう[2] 扇動 agitation; 《文》abetment; 《文》instigation; 《文》(an) incitement ¶ 扇動する fan; 《文》instigate; incite; egg on; stir up; 《文》abet / …に扇動されて incited by…; 《文》at *sb's* instigation / 扇動的な inflammatory; 《文》seditious / 大衆扇動家 a rabble-rouser / 扇動者《文》an instigator; an agitator; 《文》a provocateur; 〘法〙an abettor / 扇動政治家 a demagogic politician; a demagog(ue). [文例⇩]
せんどう[3] 船頭 a boatman; a waterman; a ferryman (渡し船の). [文例⇩]
ぜんどう[1] 善導 ¶ 善導する《文》guide *sb* onto the right path [in the right direction].
ぜんどう[2] 蠕動 writhing; 〘生理〙peristalsis《*pl.* -stalses》; vermiculation ¶ 蠕動する《文》move in a wormlike manner; writhe; 〘生理〙move peristaltically.
ぜんとうよう 前頭葉〘解〙a frontal lobe.
せんどきじだい 先土器時代〘考古〙the preceramic period [age].
セントクリストファー・ネビス Saint Christopher and Nevis.
セントビンセント ¶ セントビンセントおよびグレナディーン諸島〈国名〉St. Vincent and the Grenadines.
セントラルヒーティング central heating. [文例⇩]
セントルシア Saint Lucia.
ぜんなんぜんにょ 善男善女 pious people [folk].
ぜんにちせい 全日制 ¶ 全日制の full-time《high schools》.
ぜんにほん 全日本 ¶ 全日本の all-Japan / 全日本レスリングチーム the all-Japan wrestling team.
せんにゅう 潜入 ¶ 潜入する sneak [smuggle *oneself*] into; 《文》infiltrate into.
せんにゅうかん[しゅ] 先入観[主]《文》a preconception; 《文》a preoccupation; a prejudice; a bias ¶ 先入主となる〈事が主語〉preoccupy《*one, one's* mind》; 〈人が主語〉be preoccupied with《an idea》/ 先入主を捨てる get rid of *one's* prejudice《against》[preconceived ideas《about》].
せんにょ 仙女 a fairy; a nymph.
せんにん[1] 仙人 a mountain hermit; a wizard.
せんにん[2] 先任 ¶ 先任の senior; elder / 先任者 a senior official [member]; *one's* predecessor (前任者) / 先任順で in order of seniority.
せんにん[3] 専任 ¶ 専任の full-time《teachers》/ 専任講師 a full-time lecturer; 《米》an instructor (大学の).
せんにん[4] 選任 ¶ 選任する elect; nominate; 《文》assign《*sb* to a post》.
ぜんにん[1] 前任 ¶ 前任者 *one's* predecessor / 前任地 *one's* last [《文》former] post. [文例⇩]
ぜんにん[2] 善人 a good(-natured) man [person].
せんぬき 栓抜き a bottle opener; a corkscrew (コルク栓の).
せんねつ 潜熱〘物〙latent heat ¶ 蒸発[凝結]の際の潜熱 the latent heat of evaporation [condensation].
せんねん[1] 先年《文》formerly; some [a few] years ago; the other year.
せんねん[2] 専念 ⇨ せんしん.[1]
ぜんねん 前年 the year before; 《in》the previous [《文》preceding] year ¶ その前年 the year before / 開戦の前年 the year before the war broke out.
せんのう 洗脳 brainwashing ¶ 洗脳する brainwash *sb*《into believing》.
ぜんのう[1] 全能 ¶ 全能の《文》omnipotent; 《文》almighty ⇨ ぜんちぜんのう.
ぜんのう[2] 前納 payment in advance; prepayment ¶ 前納する pay《the rent》in advance; prepay.
ぜんば 前場〘相場〙the morning market [session]; the first session [call].
せんばい 専売 a monopoly ¶ 専売する have a monopoly (on the sale) of / 専売特許(権) a patent (right) / 専売特許を得る get a patent《on an article》/ 専売特許品 a patented article / 専売品《government》monopoly goods; monopolies / 日本専売公社 the Japan Tobacco & Salt Public Corporation.
せんぱい 先輩 *one's* senior ¶ 先輩風を吹かす act in a patronizing way; make much of [a great play with] *one's* seniority [senior status] / 先輩づらをする pose [give *oneself* airs] as *sb's* senior. [文例⇩]
[用法] 英語国では「先輩」「後輩」の関係はあまり重要視されず, これらの語にぴったり相当する英語はない.「あの人は僕の先輩です」を英語で言うには He entered the company [University] earlier than I did. とか He was at Hosei University (ten years) before me. などと言うのが一番自然であろう.
ぜんぱい[1] 全敗 ¶ 全敗する be completely [totally] defeated; lose all *one's* games [every game]; 《口語》be whitewashed.
ぜんぱい[2] 全廃 (total) abolition ¶ 全廃する abolish (completely); do away with.
せんぱく[1] 浅薄 ¶ 浅薄な shallow; superficial; half-baked《theorists》.
せんぱく[2] 船舶 a vessel; a ship; shipping (総称) ¶ 船舶解体 shipbreaking / 船舶修理 ship-repairing / 船舶設計 ship design / 船舶用ロープ marine rope.
せんばつ 選抜 ¶ 選抜する《文》select; choose;

立っている. He is in the vanguard of this great campaign.
せんどう[2] この紛争の背後にはだれか扇動者がいるに相違ない. Someone must be behind [at the bottom of] this disturbance.
せんどう[3] 船頭多くして舟山に上る. Too many cooks spoil the broth.〘諺〙
セントラルヒーティング 大多数の日本の家はセントラルヒーティングになっていない. Most homes in Japan are not centrally heated.
ぜんにん[1] あなたの前任者はだれでしたか. Who held the post before you?
せんぱい 彼は大学で私より2年先輩でした. He was my senior by two years at the university.
ぜんぶ[1] この百科事典は全部で24巻あります. This encyclopedia

せんぱつ pick [single] out / 選抜した picked; selected / 選抜委員会 a selection [screening] committee / 選抜試験 a selection examination / 選抜チーム a picked team; 《all-star》 selections.

せんぱつ¹ 先発 ¶先発する start first; 《文》start [go] in advance 《of》; go ahead 《of the others》/ 先発隊 an advance party / 先発投手 a starting pitcher; a starter.

せんぱつ² 洗髪 a shampoo; washing one's hair ¶洗髪する wash one's hair / 洗髪してもらう have a shampoo; have one's hair washed [shampooed].

せんばづる 千羽鶴 (a string of) a thousand origami [paper] cranes.

せんばん¹ 千万 〈大変〉《文》exceedingly; extremely; very much; indeed.

せんばん¹ 旋盤 【機】 a lathe ¶旋盤にかける shape [turn] 《a block of wood》on a lathe; lathe / 木工用旋盤 a wood-turning lathe / 旋盤工 a turner; a latheman / 旋盤工場 a turnery.

せんばん¹ 先般 some time ago; 〈先日〉 ⇨ せんじつ. 先般来 some time ago (past).

せんぱん¹ 戦犯 〈罪〉a war crime; 〈人〉a war criminal ¶戦犯法廷 a war crimes court.

ぜんはん[ぱん] 前半 the first half; 〈ラグビーなどの〉the first period.

ぜんぱん 全般 ¶全般の whole; general; overall / 全般的情況 the overall [《米》all-over] situation / 全般的に論じる make a general comment 《on》/ 全般にわたった all-round 《education》/ 全般にわたって generally; across the board / 科学全般にわたる cover the whole field of science.

せんび¹ 船尾 the stern ¶船尾に[の方へ]astern; aft / 船尾舵 a stern rudder.

せんび² 戦備 preparations for war; (military) preparedness ¶戦備を整える prepare for war.

せんび 戦費 war expenditure.

ぜんび 善美 ¶善美を尽くした 《文》exquisite; superb; gorgeous; 《文》 (be) as perfect as wealth and art can make (it) / 善美を尽くした宮殿 a sumptuously furnished palace.

ぜんぴ 前非 ¶前非を悔いる《文》repent of one's past folly [error, sin].

せんびょうし 戦病死 ¶戦病死する die from a disease contracted at the front.

せんびょうしつ 腺病質 ¶腺病質の delicate 《children》; (a girl) in delicate health.

ぜんびん 前便 (in) one's last letter.

せんぷ 先夫 one's former [divorced] husband; one's late husband (亡夫).

ぜんぶ¹ 全部 〈形容詞〉all; whole; entire; total; complete; every; 〈副詞〉wholly; entirely; completely; 《文》in its entirety; in full ¶全部で in all; all told; altogether. 文例◊

ぜんぶ² 前部 the front part; the forepart ¶最前部 the very front; 《文》the foremost part (of).

せんぷう 旋風 a whirlwind; a cyclone; a tornado 《pl. -(e)s》 ¶旋風を巻き起こす〈大評判になる〉create a furor [great sensation]; 《口語》make a splash.

せんぷうき 扇風機 an electric fan; 〈天井からつるした〉a ceiling fan ¶扇風機の風 a current of air sent by an electric fan; the draft [breeze] from an electric fan / 扇風機をかける[止める] turn [switch] an electric fan [on/off].

せんぷく¹ 船腹 the bottom of a ship; 〈船舶〉 《Japanese》bottoms; shipping (総称); 〈積載量〉tonnage; (freight) space ¶船腹不足 a shortage [scarcity] of bottoms.

せんぷく² 潜伏 ¶潜伏する《文》conceal oneself; lie [be] hidden; hide (out); 〈病気が〉be dormant; be latent / 潜伏期 the incubation [latent] period. 文例◊

ぜんぷく 全幅 ¶全幅の full; 《文》utmost; all; wholehearted 《sympathy》/ 全幅の信頼を寄せる《文》place full confidence in sb; trust sb completely.

せんぶん 線分 【数】 a line segment; a segment (of a line).

ぜんぶん¹ 全文 〈条約などの〉the full text 《of a treaty》 ¶全文を[にわたって]引用する quote 《a letter》in full [《文》in its entirety].

ぜんぶん² 前文 〈上記の文〉《文》the above (passage); 《文》the foregoing remark; 〈条約などの〉the preamble (to, of).

せんべい 煎餅 a rice cracker ¶せんべい布団 thinly stuffed bedding; a thin and hard coverlet.

せんべつ¹ 選別 ¶選別する sort (out); 《文》select / 選別機 a sorting machine.

せんべつ² 餞別 a good-by present; 《文》a parting [farewell] gift [present]. 文例◊

せんべん 先鞭 ¶先鞭をつける get a (head) start on [《米》of]; take the initiative; be the first to do.

ぜんぺん¹ 全編 ⇨ ぜんかん.

ぜんぺん² 前編 the first volume; the first part (of).

せんぺんいちりつ 千編一律 ¶千編一律の monotonous; stereotyped. 文例◊

せんぺんばんか 千変万化 ¶千変万化する change endlessly; 《文》undergo kaleidoscopic changes / 千変万化の ever-changing; 《文》kaleidoscopic.

せんぼう 羨望 ¶羨望する envy 《sb, sb his good fortune》; 《文》feel envy 《at》; be envious 《of》; look enviously 《at》/ 羨望の的になる be the envy 《of》/ 羨望の的 an object of envy 《among one's friends》.

せんぽう¹ 先方 〈相手〉the other party [side]; he [she]; they; 〈行先〉one's destination; the

is complete in 24 volumes. / 全部でそれだけですか。Is that all?/ 全部支払いました。I paid him in full. / この数字は全部の平均を表わすものである。This figure represents an overall average.

せんぷく 彼は都内のどこかに潜伏しているはずだ。He must be in hiding somewhere in Tokyo. / その病気は潜伏期が長い。The disease has a long incubation [latent] period.

せんべつ² ご餞別の印までに差し上げます。Kindly accept this as a token of my best wishes for your journey.

せんぺんいちりつ 彼の説く所は千編一律で何の変化も見られない。

せんぽう² 先鋒 the van; the vanguard; a spearhead ¶先鋒となる be in the van 《of the attack》; spearhead 《an operation》.

せんぽう³ 戦法 tactics; strategy.

ぜんぽう 全貌 ¶全貌を示す give sb the full [entire] picture 《of》; 《文》give sb the full particulars 《of》; 《口語》put sb in the picture / 全貌を現わす appear in 《C》 emerge into] full view. 文例↓

ぜんぽう 前方 in front of 《(the enemy) in front / 前方を見る look ahead / 前方に in front 《of》; ahead 《of》; forward / 100メートル前方に 100 meters ahead. 文例↓

せんぼうきょう 潜望鏡 a periscope.

ぜんぽうこう 全方向 ¶全方向アンテナ an omnidirectional antenna.

ぜんぽうこうえんふん 前方後円墳 an ancient burial mound, square at the front and rounded in the rear; a 'keyhole-shaped' tumulus.

せんぼつ 戦没 ⇨ せんし⁴ ¶戦没者《文》a fallen soldier; the war dead 《集合的》/ 戦没者記念碑 a war memorial. 「a royal fern.

ぜんまい¹《植》a flowering fern; an osmund.

ぜんまい²《ばね》a (coil [spiral]) spring ¶ぜんまいを巻く wind a spring / 大[主]ぜんまい a mainspring / ひげぜんまい a hairspring / ぜんまい仕掛けの clockwork(-driven) [spring-driven, windup] (toys) / ぜんまいばかり a spring balance. 文例↓

せんまいどおし 千枚通し an eyeleteer.

せんみん 選民 the chosen (people); 《文》the elect ¶選民意識 élitism.

せんむ 専務《取締役》a managing [an executive] director ¶専務車掌 a conductor; 《英》a guard.

せんめい 鮮明 ¶鮮明な clear; distinct; vivid; sharp; clear-cut / 鮮明な映像《テレビ》a clear [distinct] picture / 鮮明度《テレビ》definition.

ぜんめつ 全滅《文》annihilation; total [complete] destruction ¶全滅する be annihilated; be completely destroyed; be stamped [wiped] out.

せんめん 洗面 ¶毎朝の洗面 one's morning wash; 《文》one's morning toilet / 洗面する wash one's face; have a wash; 《米》wash up / 洗面器《米》a washbowl; 《英》a (washhand) basin; a washbasin / 洗面所〈手や顔を洗うための部屋〉a washroom; 〈トイレ〉⇨ トイレット) / 洗面台 a washstand; a washing stand / 洗面道具 toilet things; 〈旅行用の一式〉a toilet [shaving (男性用), make-up (女性用)] kit / 洗面道具入れ a toilet [shaving, make-up] bag.

ぜんめん¹ 全面 ¶全面にわたって研究する study 《a subject》in all 《its》aspects [from every angle》/ 全面的 all-out; overall; general / 全面的に改正する make an overall [a sweeping, a wholesale] revision 《of》/ 全面的に支持する give one's wholehearted [all-out] support 《to》/ 全面講和 an overall peace / 全面戦争 a full-scale war.

ぜんめん² 前面 the front; the façade (建物の) ¶前面の敵 the enemy in front / 前面に in front 《of》; ahead 《of》/ 前面に浮かび上がる〈顕著になる〉come to the fore.

せんもう 繊毛《動》a cilium (pl. cilia).

せんもん 専門《米》a specialty; 《英》a speciality; a special subject of study; a profession ¶…を専門にやる make a specialty of 《(importing liquors)》/ 専門に研究する make a special study 《of》; specialize 《in》/ 専門医 a medical specialist / 専門家 a specialist 《in》; an expert 《on》/ 〈アマチュアに対して〉a 《golf》professional / 専門学校 a college; a special [vocational] school / 専門科目 a special [specialized] subject / 専門教育 (a) professional [technical] education; professional [specialized] instruction / 専門語 a technical term; 〈集合的に〉technical terminology [nomenclature] / 専門雑誌 a technical journal [periodical, magazine] / 専門知識 expert [technical] knowledge; expertise / 専門店 a specialty store; a store specializing in 《cameras》/ 専門馬鹿《文》the ignorance of the learned; 〈人〉an expert ignoramus / 専門分野 a [one's] (special) field (of study); one's line.

ぜんもん 前門 文例↓

ぜんや 前夜《文》the previous night; the night before; the eve (祭りなどの) ¶…の前夜に on the evening before (the fire broke out); 〈比喩的に〉《文》on the eve of 《the revolution》/ 前夜祭 an eve.

せんやく 先約 a previous engagement [appointment].

ぜんやく 全訳 a complete translation 《of》¶全訳する translate the whole of 《Shakespeare》; translate 《Hamlet》completely 《into Japanese》.

せんゆう¹ 占有 occupation; possession; 【法】occupancy ¶占有する occupy; possess; take possession of; 【法】be seized of / 占有者 an occupant; 《文》a possessor; 【法】a seizer.

せんゆう² 専有 ¶専有する monopolize; take sole possession of / 専有権《法》a monopoly; an exclusive right / 専有者 a sole owner.

せんゆう³ 戦友 a comrade (in arms); a fellow soldier.

He always harps on the same string.

せんぽう¹ すべては先方の出方一つにかかっている。Everything depends on their [his, her] move. / 先方の女の声は、「ちょっとお待ち下さい」と言って、かなり長く私を電話口で待たせた。The woman at the other end asked me to wait a minute, and kept me waiting on the phone quite a long time.

ぜんぽう 事件の全貌はまだ明らかでない。We do not yet know everything about the matter. | All the details of the affair have not yet been brought to light.

ぜんぽう 事故の原因は運転手の前方不注意。The accident was due to inattention on the part of the driver.

ぜんまい² ぜんまいが緩んでいる。The spring has unwound. / このおもちゃはぜんまい仕掛けになっている。This toy works by clockwork [by a spring].

せんもん 数学は私の専門ではない。Mathematics is not in my line [is not my field]. / それは私の専門外だ。It is not in my line. | It is out of my line. | It is off my

せんよう 専用 ¶専用の exclusive; for (*one's*) private [exclusive] use / 専用機 a plane for *one's* personal use / 大統領専用機 a presidential plane / 専用線 an exclusive line.

ぜんよう 善用 ¶善用する make good use of; turn *sth* to good account.

ぜんら 全裸 ¶全裸の stark-naked; nude (pictures); 《a girl》in the nude; with nothing on.

せんらん 戦乱 the disturbances of war ¶戦乱の欧州《文》war-torn[-shattered] Europe / 戦乱のちまた the scene of war [a battle] /《文》a scene of deadly strife and carnage.

せんり 千里 文例⇩

せんりがん 千里眼 clairvoyance;《see *sth* by》second sight;《人》a clairvoyant (男); a clairvoyante (女) ¶千里眼の clairvoyant.

せんりつ¹ 旋律 (a) melody ¶旋律の美しい《文》melodious; tuneful.

せんりつ² 戦慄 a shiver; a shudder ¶戦慄する shudder; shiver; tremble with fear / 戦慄すべき horrible; shocking; bloodcurdling / 戦慄させる make *sb* shudder [shiver] /《口語》give *sb* the shivers [creeps]; freeze *sb's* blood. 文例⇩

ぜんりつせん 前立腺《解》the prostate (gland) ¶前立腺炎 prostatitis / 前立腺肥大症 enlargement of the prostate; prostatomegaly.

せんりひん 戦利品 a (war) trophy; booty;《文》the spoils of war.

せんりゃく 戦略 (a) strategy;《文》a stratagem ¶戦略を立てる work [map] out *one's* strategy; plot *one's* strategy;《文》devise a stratagem / 戦略をめぐらす elaborate [plan] a strategy / 戦略を用いて《文》by stratagem / 戦略上から見て from the strategical point of view; strategically / 戦略的 strategic / 戦略家 a strategist / 戦略空軍 a strategic air force / 戦略爆撃 strategic bombing / 戦略物資 strategic goods [materials] / 戦略兵器 strategic arms [weaponry] / 戦略目標 a strategic target.

ぜんりゃく 前略〈手紙の冒頭で〉Dispensing with the preliminaries, ... ★英米人の手紙は,まさに時候のあいさつなどの前置きなしに,直接用件に入るのを常とするから,前置きを省略の意味の「前略」に相当する表現は英語には実際にはない.

せんりょ¹ 千慮 ¶千慮の一失 an oversight [a slip] by a very careful [normally wise] man.

せんりょ² 浅慮 thoughtlessness;《文》imprudence;《文》indiscretion.

せんりょう¹ 占領 occupation; capture; possession ¶占領する capture; take; seize; occupy / 占領下にある[入る] be under [pass into]《American》occupation / 占領軍 the occupation army [forces] / 占領地 an occupied area. 文例⇩

せんりょう² 染料 dyestuffs; dyes; colors; stain.

ぜんりょう 善良 ¶善良な good(-natured); honest.

ぜんりょうせい 全寮制 ¶(学校の)全寮制である be residential; be a boarding school.

せんりょうやくしゃ 千両役者 a great actor.

せんりょく 戦力 war potential; fighting power [strength].

ぜんりょく 全力 ¶全力を尽くす do *one's* best [utmost]; do all *one* can; do everything in *one's* power;《文》exert *oneself* to the utmost;《口語》go all out / 全力を尽くして with *one's* full strength; with all *one's* might;《文》《try》with might and main; to the best of *one's* ability; for all *one* is worth / 全力を傾ける《文》devote all *one's* energies (to);《文》concentrate *one's* energies (on). 文例⇩

ぜんりん¹ 前輪 a front wheel ¶前輪駆動の車 a front-wheel-drive car.

ぜんりん² 善隣 ¶善隣関係 good (neighborly) relations《with》/ 善隣外交 a good-neighbor policy.

せんれい¹ 先例 a precedent;《文》a previous instance ¶先例のない unprecedented / 先例を作る create a precedent / 先例になる be [form] a precedent. 文例⇩

せんれい² 洗礼 baptism; christening (乳児の)洗礼の baptismal (water) / 洗礼を施す baptize *sb*;《文》administer baptism to *sb* / 洗礼を受ける be baptized; be christened / 洗礼を受けてキリスト教徒になる be baptized a Christian / 砲火の洗礼を受ける《文》receive [undergo] *one's* baptism of fire / 洗礼式 (a) baptism; (a) baptismal service / 洗礼者 a baptist / 洗礼名 *one's* Christian [baptismal] name.

ぜんれい 前例 ⇨ せんれい¹.

ぜんれき 前歴 *one's* past record; *one's* personal history;《文》*one's* antecedents ⇨ けいれき.

せんれつ 戦列 a line (of battle) ¶戦列を離れる leave [desert] the line of battle / 戦列に加わる join [go into] the line(s).

ぜんれつ 前列 (in) the front rank [row].

せんれん 洗練 ¶洗練する polish up; refine / 洗練された polished; refined; elegant; sophisticated / 洗練されない unpolished; coarse《manners》.

せんろ 線路 a railroad [railway] track; a track; a (railroad) line ¶線路を敷く lay a line [track] / 線路に横たわる lie [put *one's* neck]

---

beat. / これを充分に理解するためには原子物理学についての専門的知識が必要である. To understand it fully requires a special knowledge of nuclear physics.

せんもん これには前門のとら, 後門のおおかみだ. I'm caught between the devil and the deep blue sea [《文》between Scylla and Charybdis].

せんり 千里の道も1歩より始まる. A journey of a thousand miles starts with but a single step. | Step by step one goes a long way.

せんりつ² その有様を見たばかりで彼らは戦慄した. The very sight was enough to make their flesh creep.

せんりょう¹ 君はこの広い部屋を1人で占領しているのか. Do you have this large room (all) to yourself?

ぜんりょく 及ばずながら全力を尽くします. I will do my poor best. / 全力をあげて彼を援助すべきだ. We should go all out to help him.

せんれい¹ これには先例が全くない. There is no precedent for this. / これが先例になるのは考えものだ. It would not be wise for

ぜんわん 前腕【解】the forearm.

on a railroad track / 線路伝いに歩く follow [walk along] the track / 線路工夫 a lineman; a trackman; 《米》a section hand [man]; 〈総称〉《米》the section crew [gang].

そ

そ 祖 an ancestor; 《文》a forefather; 《文》a progenitor; 〈始祖〉《文》the father; the founder.
ソ 【音楽】sol; so.
そあく 粗悪 ¶粗悪な bad; coarse; crude / 粗悪品 poor quality goods; an inferior article; 《文》goods of inferior [poor] quality.
ソアラー a soarer; a sailplane.
そいそしょく 粗衣粗食 ¶粗衣粗食に甘んじる be content [happy] with plain living; 《文》be reconciled to a simple life.
そいね 添い寝 ¶添い寝する sleep [go to bed] 《with one's child》.
そいん¹ 素因 《文》a (causative) factor; 《文》a primary cause; 【医】a predisposition 《to tuberculosis》.
そいん² 訴因 【法】the cause of a legal action; a charge; a count. 文例↓
そう¹ 相 an aspect; a phase; 〈人相〉《文》physiognomy; 《文》a countenance; a look. 文例↓
そう² 装 よそおい.
そう³ 僧 a (Buddhist) priest; a clergyman; a monk; a bonze; 〈総称〉the clergy ¶僧になる become a priest [bonze]; 《文》be ordained priest; be ordained to the priesthood; 《文》take the tonsure; join a monastery (修道僧になる).
そう⁴ 想 an idea; 《文》a conception; a thought ¶想を練る think deeply; 《文》ponder 《over, on》; meditate 《on》; turn sth over in one's mind; (try to) put one's thoughts together / …から想を得る be inspired by….
そう⁵ 層 a layer; a stratum 《pl. -ta》 ¶層が厚い be thick-layered; 〈人材が豊富な〉have a large stock 《of players》 to draw on; the 《skating》 population is large / 層をなす be in layers [strata]; be stratified / 層状の stratiform; stratified.
そう⁶ 宋 【中国史】Sung.
そう⁷ 沿う ¶…に沿って along; by; parallel to [with] / 〈鉄道などが〉海岸に沿って走る skirt [run along] the coast / 〈道路などが〉川に沿って続く run parallel to [alongside] a river / 〈船が〉陸地に沿って航行する coast / アメリカの対外政策に沿って in line 《文》 alignment》 with the foreign policy of the U.S. / 川に沿った家 houses on [by] a river / 通りに沿った店 shops along [a shop fronting] a street.
そう⁸ 添う 〈同行する〉go (along) with; 《文》accompany / 《文》…の希望に添う go along with [meet, 《文》gratify, 《文》comply with] sb's wishes; satisfy sb / 目的に添う answer the purpose / 期待に添う live up to sb's expectations. 文例↓
そう⁹ 壮 ¶壮とする admire 《sb's courage》; approve of 《sb's noble enterprise》.
そう¹⁰ so; such; 〈問いに答えて〉Yes; No (否定疑問に対して); 〈そんなに〉so; like that; that way; 《文》thus; 〈大して〉(not) very (much); (not) so much [many] ¶そういう ⇨そういう / もしそうなれば if so; if that is the case; in that case / そうすると / そうでなければ if not (so); otherwise; or (else) / そうこうするうちに ⇨そうこう⁶ / それはそうとして by the way [by(e)]; incidentally. 文例↓
-そう 〈…らしい〉look (expensive, as if it is expensive); seem (to be); appear (to be); be likely to do; 〈…が当然〉ought to do; 〈今にも…しそう〉be going to do; be on the point

---

us to allow this to become a precedent.
そいん² 彼は起訴された4つの訴因全部について有罪と判定された. He was found guilty on all four counts.
そう¹ 彼は長命の相がある. His physiognomy indicates that he will enjoy long life.
そう⁸ 精一杯ご希望に添うように努めましょう. I will do my utmost to meet your wishes. / 常に親の期待に添うということは息子にとって楽なことではない. It is not easy for a son always to live up to the expectations of his parents.
そう¹⁰ そうですか. Really? | Is that so? | Yes? / そうですとも. So it is. | Quite so. | Certainly! | Indeed it is. / そうですね. 〈なめらって〉Well, let me see. / そうだ. 〈思いついて〉Oh, yes! | I've got it. / きのう山田さんに会いました.—そうでしょうね. 〈あいづちを打って〉Yes, I think so, too. / ローマへ着いたときにはすっかり疲れてしまっていました.—そうだろうね. When I arrived in Rome, I really felt tired.—I'll bet you did. / あれは 10万円以上もするそうだよ.—そうだろうね. I'm told it costs over 100,000 yen.—I can imagine. / そうとばかりは言えない. It is not always the case. / そう言えば, 彼女がそんな意味のことを言うのを聞いた覚えがあります. Now you come to mention it, I remember hearing her say something to that effect. / 自分のからそう申しては何ですが, あまり出来は悪くありません. My work is not so bad, though I say it myself. / そう急ぐにはあたらない. You need not be in such a hurry. / まさかそうなるとは思わなかった. That's the last thing I expected. / おれがばかならお前だってそうだ. If I am a fool, you are another.
-そう ミルクが吹きこぼれそうだ.

of *doing*; be about to *do*; threaten to *do*; 〈…の由〉 they [people] say; it is said; I hear; I am told; I understand ¶ 重そうな heavy-looking / あやうく…しそうになった almost [nearly] *did*; came near to *doing* / うれし[悲し]そうに with a happy [sad] look; happily [sadly, glumly] / 満足そうに with evident satisfaction / 物欲しそうに 《look at *sth*》 with longing in *one's* eyes; 《look》 wistfully 《at》 / 今にもほころびそうなつぼみ a bud just ready to burst [on the point of bursting]. [文例⇩]

ぞう[1] 象 〖動〗 an elephant ¶ 象の牙 an elephant('s) tusk / 象の鼻 a [an elephant's] trunk / 象狩り elephant hunting / 象使い an elephant trainer [driver]; 〈インドの〉 a mahout.

ぞう[2] 像 《文》 an image; a figure; a statue; 〈画像〉 a picture; a portrait ¶ (レンズを通して)像を結ぶ focus into an image 《of》; build up a picture / 大理石像 a marble statue / マリア像 an image of the Virgin Mary.

ぞうあざらし 〖動〗 an elephant seal.

そうあたり 総当たり ¶ 総当たり戦 a round robin (competition).

そうあん[1] 草案 a (rough) draft ¶ 草案を起草する[作る] prepare [make out] a draft 《for》; draft [draw up] 《a bill》.

そうあん[2] 創案 an original idea ¶ 創案者 the inventor; 《文》 the originator. [文例⇩]

そうい[1] 相違 (a) difference; 《文》 (a) disparity; 〈食い違い〉 a gap; 《文》 (a) discrepancy ¶ 相違する 《文》 differ 《from》; be different 《from》; vary 《from》; disagree 《with》; 《文》 be at variance 《with》 / …に相違ない It is certain that…; There is no doubt that …; I am sure that… / 相違なく certainly; surely; without fail / 案に相違して 《文》 contrary to *one's* expectations / 意見の相違 a difference of opinion [views] / 年齢の相違 (a) difference [disparity] in age / 相違点 a point of difference / A と B の相違点を明らかにする make it clear where A is different from B; 《文》 clarify the distinction between A and B. [文例⇩]

そうい[2] 創意 an original idea; 〈独創性〉 originality; 〈工夫の才〉 ingenuity ¶ 創意に富んだ original; inventive.

そうい[3] 総意 the collective [general] opinion [《文》 will] 《of the nation》; the consensus 《of the people》.

そういう 《things》 like that; that sort of 《person》; 《a thing》 of that sort; such 《people》 (★ この意味での such はやや 《文》) ¶ そういう訳で for that reason; 《文》 such being the case / そういう訳なら if that is the case; if so; then / そういう場合には in that case. [文例⇩]

そういん[1] 僧院 a monastery; 《文》 a cloister. ⇨ しゅうどう (修道院).

そういん[2] 総員 《文》 the whole personnel; 《文》 the entire [full] strength; all hands (船の) ¶ 総員 50 名 fifty people in all [all told].

ぞういん 増員 ¶ 増員する increase the number of staff; 《文》 augment the personnel 《of》.

そううつびょう 躁鬱病 〖医〗 manic-depressive [alternating] psychosis ¶ 躁鬱病患者 a manic-depressive.

そううん 層雲 a stratus 《*pl.* -ti》; a cloud bank.

ぞうえい 造営 ⇨ けんちく.

ぞうえいざい 造影剤 〖医〗 a contrast medium.

そうえん 蒼鉛 〖化〗 bismuth.

ぞうえん[1] 造園 landscape gardening ¶ 造園家 a landscape gardener; a garden designer.

ぞうえん[2] 増援 ¶ 増援する reinforce 《an army》 / 増援隊 reinforcements.

ぞうお 憎悪 hatred; 《文》 abhorrence; (an) animosity 《toward, against》 ¶ 憎悪する hate; 《文》 have a hatred 《for》; feel animosity 《toward, against》; detest; 《文》 abhor / 憎悪すべき hateful; detestable; 《文》 odious; 《文》 abhorrent.

そうおう 相応 ¶ 相応な 〈適した〉 suitable 《for》; fit 《for》; 《文》 suited 《to》; 〈似合わしい〉 《文》 becoming; 《文》 befitting; 〈妥当な〉 adequate; reasonable; proper; 〈分に合った〉 deserved 《reward》; 《文》 just 《deserts》 / 相応する 〈適する〉 be suitable 《for, to》; be suited 《to》; suit; 〈似合う〉 become; befit; be proper 《for》; 〈対応する〉 correspond 《to》 / 年相応に見える look *one's* age [years] / 身分相応[不相応]に暮らす live within [beyond] *one's* means.

The milk is going to boil over. / 雨が降りそうだ. It looks like rain. | We are going to have rain. / 今にも雨が降り出しそうだった. It was threatening to rain. / 病気になりそうだ. I'm going to be a sick man. / ロープが切れそうだ. The rope is in danger of breaking [giving way]. / 雨はやみそうにもありません. There is no sign of the rain stopping. / 彼女は今にも泣き出しそうだった. She looked as if she was going to burst into tears (at) any minute. | She was ready to cry. / この計画はうまく行きそうだ. This plan seems likely to succeed. / 僕にはできそうな気がする. I feel I can do it. / あいつのやりそうな事だ. That's like him. / 彼のいそうな所を全部捜した. I looked for him in every likely place. / 大学生なら知っていそうなものだ. A college student ought to know that. / 行く前にあいさつぐらいしてもよさそうなものだ. He might at least have come to say good-by.

そうあん[2] これは彼の創案です. The plan [idea] originated with him. | It's his idea.

そうい[1] 幻灯とテレビでは大変な相違だ. It is a far cry from a magic lantern to television. / 両者の見解は天地の相違がある. Their views are poles apart. / 右のとおり相違ありません. I affirm the above to be true and correct in every particular [respect]. / 見ると聞くとは雲泥の相違だ. There is all the difference in the world between seeing and hearing. / 途中で何事か起こったに相違ない. Something must have happened to him on the way.

そういう ではそういう風にしましょう. Well, then, let's do it that way. / そういう訳で私は黙っていた. That's why [For that reason] I kept silent. / 君は間違っているよ.—そういうことにしておきましょう. You are in the wrong.—I'm not going to argue with you about it.

そ

そうおん 騒音 (a) noise; (a) din ¶町の騒音 the din and bustle of a town; city sounds; street noises／騒音計 a noise [sound-level] meter／騒音公害 noise damage [pollution] ⇨ こうがい³ ★ ／騒音防止 prevention of noise; sound suppression／騒音防止条例 an antinoise ordinance.

ぞうか¹ 造化 〈万物〉creation; nature ¶造化の神 the Creator ⇨ ぞうぶつしゅ／《文》 造化の妙 (文) the wonder(s) of nature／造化の戯れ a freak of nature.

ぞうか² 造花 an artificial [an imitation] flower.

ぞうか³ 増加 (an) increase; (a) gain; (a) rise ¶増加する 〈ふえる〉increase; grow;〈ふやす〉increase;《文》augment; step up 《production》／数[人口]が増加する《文》increase in number [population]／増加しつつある be on the increase／自然増加 a natural increase [(《文》increment]／増加率 a rate of increase. 文例⇩

そうかい¹ 掃海 ¶掃海する drag [sweep] the sea for mines; clear the sea／掃海作業 minesweeping [sea-clearing] operations; minesweeping／掃海艇 a minesweeper.

そうかい² 総会 a general meeting [assembly]; a plenary session [meeting] ¶総会屋 a racketeer who extorts money from a company by threatening to cause trouble at the general meeting of the stockholders.

そうかい³ 爽快 ¶爽快な refreshing; exhilarating; invigorating; bracing; crisp 《autumn days》／爽快になる feel [be] refreshed. 文例⇩

そうがい¹ 窓外 ¶窓外を眺める look out of the window／窓外に outside the window.

そうがい² 霜害 damage by frost; frost damage ¶霜害を被る suffer from frost. 文例⇩

そうがかり 総掛かり ¶総掛かりで all together;《文》with united [combined] efforts.

そうがく¹ 奏楽 music; a musical performance ⇨ えんそう.

そうがく² 総額 ⇨ そうけい².

ぞうがく 増額 (an) increase ¶増額する increase; raise／予算の増額を要求する demand an increase in one's budget allocation／増額分 the increased amount.

そうかつ 総括 (a) summary; generalization;《文》a recapitulation ¶総括する summarize; sum up; generalize;《文》recapitulate;《口語》recap／総括して en masse; in the lump;《フランス語》en bloc; collectively／総括して言えば to sum up;《文》recapitulate, (《口語》recap)／generally speaking ／総括的 all-inclusive[-embracing]; overall; blanket; omnibus／総括的条項 a blanket clause／総括的議案 an omnibus [a blanket] bill／総括制御システム 〔鉄道〕the multiple-unit control system.

そうがわ 総革 ¶総革(製)の full-[whole-] bound in leather.

そうかん¹ 壮観 a grand [thrilling] sight; a magnificent sight [view, 《文》 spectacle] ¶ 壮観を呈する present a grand sight [《文》spectacle].

そうかん² 送還 ¶送還する send sb back; 〈本国に〉send sb home; repatriate; 〈外国人を強制的に〉deport／本国送還者 a returnee; a returnee.

そうかん³ 相関 ¶相関的《文》interrelated;《文》correlative;《文》mutually related／相関関係《文》mutual relation; (a) correlation;《文》(an) interrelation;《文》(an) interrelationship ／…と密接な相関関係がある《文》correlate closely with…／相関係数〔統計〕a correlation coefficient. 文例⇩

そうかん⁴ 創刊 ¶創刊する start 《a periodical》／創刊号 the first [inaugural, initial] number [issue]. 文例⇩

そうかん⁵ 総監 an inspector [a superintendent] general.

ぞうかん 増刊 ¶増刊(号) (publish) an extra [a special] number [issue] 《of a magazine》.

ぞうがん 象眼 ¶象眼する inlay 《sth with gold》／象眼した inlaid;《文》inwrought／象眼細工 inlaid work.

そうがんきょう 双眼鏡 (a pair of) binoculars; 〈屋外用〉field glasses; 〈劇場用〉opera glasses ¶双眼鏡を目に合わせる apply [adjust, set] one's [the] binoculars to suit one's eyes／双眼鏡で見る look through field glasses.

そうかんとく 総監督 a general manager.

そうき¹ 早期 an early stage ¶早期に発見する detect [find, spot] 《a disease》 in (its) early [earliest] stages; find [spot] 《a disease》 early (enough)／早期発見 early detection 《of cancer》. 文例⇩

そうき² 想起 ¶想起する remember; recollect; recall; call sth to mind.

そうぎ¹ 争議 〈紛争〉(a) trouble; a dispute; 〈労働者の〉a labor [an industrial] dispute; 《英》industrial action;〈ストライキ〉a strike; a walkout ¶争議を起こす start a dispute [《英》industrial action]／争議を解決する settle a dispute [strike]／争議権 the right to engage in labor disputes [《英》industrial action]／争議行為 a labor dispute; 《英》(an) industrial action／争議団 the strikers.

そうぎ² 葬儀 ⇨ そうしき ¶葬儀委員〈総称〉(the chairman of) a funeral (organizing) committee; 〈個人〉a funeral committeeman／葬儀代 funeral expenses／葬儀屋 an undertaker;《米》a mortician;〈店〉an undertaker's (office);《米》a funeral home [parlor].

ぞうき¹ 雑木 miscellaneous small trees ¶雑木林 a thicket; a copse; a coppice.

そうか² 本年度の同社の売上げは昨年に比して2割5分の増加を示している。 The company's turnover this year shows an increase of 25% over last year.
そうかい³ ひと晩ぐっすり寝たのでけさは気分爽快だ。I'm feeling bright this morning after a good night's sleep.
そうがい² 野菜の霜害がひどかった。The frost caused severe damage to the vegetable crop.
そうかん³ 創造性が豊かなことと知能指数が高いこととは、わずかな相関関係しかない。There is only a low correlation between creativity and high I.Q.
そうかん⁴ 1928年創刊.《表示》First

ぞうき² 臓器 internal organs; viscera ¶臓器移植 an organ transplant.

そうきかん 送気管 an air hose.

そうきゅう¹ 早急 ⇨ さっきゅう².

そうきゅう² 送球 ¶送球する pass [throw, toss] the ball (to).

そうきょ 壮挙 《文》 a grand undertaking [scheme]; a heroic [daring] attempt.

そうぎょう 早暁 ¶早暁に at dawn; early in the morning.

そうぎょう² 創業 《文》 inauguration (of an enterprise); 《文》 establishment; foundation ¶創業する start (business); found; establish / 創業者 the founder / 創業費 the initial expenditure [expenses]; the costs of starting up a business [an enterprise]. 文例⇩

そうぎょう³ 操業 operation; work ¶操業する operate (a mine); run (a factory); work (a mill) / 操業を短縮する reduce [《文》 curtail, cut down] operations / 完全操業 full operation / 操業休止 a shutdown / 操業短縮 reduction [《文》 curtailment] of operations; short-time working. 文例⇩

ぞうきょう 増強 (a) reinforcement; (an) increase; a 《military》 build-up ¶増強する reinforce (an army); increase; build up (the country's military strength) / 輸送力を増強する increase [《文》 augment] the carrying capacity (of the railroad).

そうきょういく 早教育 (receive) early education.

そうきょく 箏曲 (a piece of) koto music.

そうきょくせん 双曲線 《数》 a hyperbola (pl. -s, -lae); a hyperbolic curve.

そうきん 送金 (a) remittance ¶送金する remit [send] money (to); make (a) remittance 《to》 / 銀行[郵便]で為替で送金する remit [send] (10,000 yen) by bank draft [postal money order] / 送金先[受取人] the remittee; the payee / 送金手形[小切手] a remittance draft [check] / 送金人 the remitter.

ぞうきん 雑巾 a floorcloth; a mop (柄の付いた); a swab (主として船の甲板掃除用の) ¶雑巾をかける wipe (the walls) with a (damp) cloth; wash (the floor); mop; swab (the deck).

そうきんるい 走禽類 《鳥》 cursorial birds; the runners.

そうく 痩軀 つるのごとし be (as) lean as a rake.

そうぐ¹ 装具 〈人の〉 an outfit; equipment; 《文》 accoutrements; gear; 〈馬の〉 harness; trappings ¶装具を付ける fit sb [sth] out; equip; harness (a horse).

そうぐ² 葬具 a funeral outfit.

そうぐう 遭遇 ¶遭遇する 《文》 encounter (the enemy); meet with (an accident); come across / 遭遇戦 an encounter.

そうくずれ 総崩れ a rout; a collapse; a stampede; 《文》 a debacle ¶総崩れになる be routed; take to [be put to] flight; collapse completely ((under the pressure of)); stampede.

そうくつ 巣窟 a den; a haunt; a nest; 《口語》 a hangout (for criminals) ¶犯罪の巣窟 a hotbed of crime.

そうぐるみ 総ぐるみ altogether; all put [taken] together; 《文》 wholly; one and all; en masse.

そうけ 宗家 the head family [house] ¶観世流の宗家 the head of the Kanze school (of Noh drama).

ぞうげ 象牙 an elephant tusk; 〈材質〉 ivory ¶象牙の塔に閉じこもる stay in one's [an] ivory tower / 象牙色の ivory-white; ivory (skin) / 象牙細工 ivory work / (歯の)象牙質 dentin(e) / 象牙彫り ivory carving; 〈物〉 a carving in ivory; an ivory carving.

そうけい¹ 早計 ¶早計な premature; too hasty; overhasty; rash.

そうけい² 総計 the total; the total amount [sum]; the sum (grand, full) total (小計に対して) ¶総計する sum [add] up / 総計で in all; in total; all told / 総計で…に達する amount to; total (one million yen).

そうげい 送迎 ¶送迎デッキ a spectators' deck (at an airport) / 送迎用バス a pickup bus; an airport (a hotel, etc.) bus. 文例⇩

ぞうけい 造詣 ¶造詣が深い 《文》 have a great [detailed] knowledge (of); 《文》 be well versed (in); be familiar (with); be at home (in).

ぞうけいびじゅつ 造形美術 (the) plastic arts.

ぞうげかいがん 象牙海岸 the Ivory Coast ¶象牙海岸共和国 the Republic of the Ivory Coast.

そうけだつ 総毛立つ one's hair stands on end (at); have [get] goose flesh (all over); shudder (at).

ぞうけつ¹ 造[増]血 《生理》 blood formation; hematogenesis; hematosis ¶造血器官 a blood-forming organ / 増血剤 a blood-forming medicine; a hematic [hematinic] (drug) / 造血組織 [機能] hematogenous [blood-forming] tissues [functions].

ぞうけつ² 増結 ¶客車を2両増結する add two passenger cars [《英》 two coaches] to the train.

そうけっさん 総決算 the final settlement of accounts ⇨ けっさん.

そうけん¹ 双肩 one's shoulders ¶双肩にかかる fall [rest] on one's shoulders.

そうけん² 送検 ¶送検する 〈人を〉 commit sb for trial; 〈書類を〉 send ((the papers pertaining to a case)) to the public prosecutors office.

そうけん³ 創見 an original view [idea]; 〈独創性〉 originality ¶創見に富む have an origi-

---

published in 1928.

そうき¹ この種のがんも早期に発見されれば直る。This sort of cancer can be cured if it is discovered early enough [in its early stages]. / がんは早期診断がとても大切である。Early diagnosis is of great importance in cancer.

そうぎょう² 弊社は創業以来80年になります。It is eighty years since this company was established.

そうぎょう³ 工場はフルに操業している。The works is in full operation.

そうげい 駅は送迎の客でにぎわっていた。The station was crowded [alive] with people who had

そうけん 壮健 ¶壮健である be healthy; be well; be in [《文》enjoy] good [excellent] health; be fit (as a fiddle); 《文》be hale and hearty (老人が). 文例⇩

そうげん 草原 a grass-covered plain; grassland(s); a savanna(h) (熱帯・亜熱帯の); the prairie(s) (北米の); the pampas (南米の) ⇨ パンパス ★; a steppe (中央アジアの).

ぞうげん 増減 《文》increase and [or] decrease; fluctuate; 〈河川が〉rise and [or] fall; 〈変わる〉vary (in quantity) / 体重の増減 weight gain and loss. 文例⇩

そうこ 倉庫 a warehouse; a storehouse; a depot (building) ¶倉庫に預ける[入れる] store; warehouse; put [deposit] (goods) in storage [a warehouse] / 倉庫会社 a warehouse [warehousing] company / 倉庫係[番] a warehouseman; a storekeeper (管理人) / 倉庫業 warehousing; the warehousing industry / 倉庫業者 a warehouseman / 倉庫渡し《商》ex store [warehouse].

そうご 相互 ¶相互の mutual; 《文》reciprocal / 相互に each other; one another; 《文》mutually; 《文》reciprocally / each other と one another については ⇨ たがい 囲語 / 相互に助け合う help [《文》offer aid to] each other / 相互安全保障[防衛]条約 a mutual security [defense] pact [treaty] / 相互依存 interdependence; interdependency / 相互関係 (a) mutual relationship / 《文》(an) interrelationship / 相互銀行 a mutual bank / 相互作用 reciprocal [mutual] action; (an) interaction; an interplay / 相互参照 (同一書中の事項の相互参照) a cross-reference / 相互扶助 mutual aid / 相互保険会社 a mutual insurance company. 文例⇩

ぞうご 造語 a coined word; a coinage ¶漢字が持っている高度な造語力 the high word-building capacity [word-forming ability] of Chinese characters.

そうこう¹ 走行 traveling ¶走行距離 (a) distance covered (in a given time); (a) mil(e)age / 走行距離計 an odometer; (a) mileage indicator [recorder]; (英) a mil(e)ometer / (口語)(have) 1,000 kilometers on the clock / 走行車線 a slow [cruising] lane. 文例⇩

そうこう² 草稿 a (rough) draft; notes; a manuscript (略: MS) ★MSの複数形はMSS ¶草稿を作る make (out) a draft (of); prepare notes (for a lecture) / 草稿を見ながら話す speak from notes / 草稿を離れて話す depart [deviate] from one's prepared text [notes]. 文例⇩

そうこう³ 奏効 ¶奏効する《文》be effectual; be effective; be successful; 《文》bear fruit / 〈薬が〉take effect.

そうこう⁴ 装甲 ¶装甲を施した armored; armor-plated / ironclad.

そうこう⁵ 操行 《文》conduct; behavior.

そうこう⁶ ¶そうこうするうちに in the meantime; meanwhile.

そうこう¹ 相好 one's looks; 《文》features ¶相好を崩す be all smiles; beam [《文》be radiant] with joy; grin from ear to ear.

そうごう² 総合 《文》(a) synthesis 《pl. -theses》¶総合する synthesize; put [piece] together / 総合的 comprehensive; 《文》synthetic; 《文》composite; (米) all-(a)round / 個人[団体] 総合 [体操] individual [team] combined (exercises) / 総合芸術 a composite art / 総合雑誌 a (general) magazine / 総合商社 a general trading company / 総合所得税 a composite income tax / 総合大学 a university / 総合ビタミン剤 a vitamin complex preparation [pill]; a multivitamin pill / 総合病院 a polyclinic (hospital); a general hospital / 総合保険 comprehensive [umbrella] insurance.

そうこうかい 壮行会 (give) a send-off [farewell] party (for sb).

そうこうげき 総攻撃 an all-out attack; a full-scale offensive ¶総攻撃する launch [make, start, open] an all-out attack (on, against); attack (the enemy) in full force.

そうこうせい 走光性 《生物》(positive, negative) phototaxis.

そうこく 相克 (a) conflict; (a) rivalry; 《文》strife; friction ¶相克する《文》conflict 《with》; 《文》be at variance 《with》.

そうこん 早婚 (an) early marriage. 文例⇩

そうごん 荘厳 《文》solemnity; 《文》sublimity ¶荘厳な《文》solemn; 《文》majestic; solemn; impressive / 荘厳ミサ《カトリック》(a) High [Solemn] Mass; (ラテン語) Missa Solemnis.

そうさ¹ 走査《テレビ》scanning ¶走査線 a scanning line.

そうさ² 捜査 (a) criminal investigation; 〈捜索〉a search; a manhunt ¶捜査する investigate (a case); 〈捜索する〉search [make a search] (for the criminal) / 捜査を開始する start [《文》institute] a search / 捜査を打ち切る give up [abandon] the search / 科学捜査 scientific crime detection / 捜査課 the criminal investigation department (略: C.I.D.) / 捜査カード a 'wanted' card / 捜査主任 the chief investigator / 捜査本部 the investigation headquarters / 捜査網 (spread) a dragnet / 捜査令状 a search warrant. 文例⇩

---

come to meet friends or see them off.

そうけん⁴ ご壮健で何よりです. I am glad to find you so well [in good health].

ぞうげん 受験者数は年によって増減がある. The number of applicants varies from year to year.

そうご 会員相互の親睦を図るを もって目的とする. It is our aim to promote friendship among our members.

ぞうご この語はルイス・キャロルの造語である. This is a word coined by Lewis Carroll.

そうこう¹ この車は時速60キロで,1リッター当たりの走行距離は20キロである. This car gives 20 kilometers to the liter (traveling) at 60 km/h.

そうこう² 彼は草稿なしで演説した. He spoke without (referring to) notes.

そうこん 彼は早婚だった. He married young.

そうさ² ジムは警察の捜査網に引っ掛かった. Jim was caught in [by]

そうさ³ 操作 (an) operation;《文》(a) manipulation; management; handling ¶**操作する** operate [work] (a machine); manipulate ((the market)); handle ((people)); manage ((a tool)) / **人為的操作** artificial manipulation ((of prices)) / **市場[金融]操作** market [monetary] manipulation [operation] / **操作盤** a control board [panel]; a console.

そうさい¹ 相殺 ¶**相殺する** set ((the advantages)) off ((against the disadvantages)); cancel ((each other)) out; offset ((each other)); counterbalance / **相殺勘定** an offset account.

そうさい² 総裁 a president ¶**副総裁** a vice-president.

そうざい 総菜 an everyday (household) dish.

そうさく¹ 捜索 a search;《文》a quest; a manhunt ((犯人の)) ⇨ **そうさ²** ¶**捜索する** search [look, hunt] for; rummage ((in a room for sth)); drag ((a river for a dead body)) / **捜索願を出す** ask the police to search for sb / **捜索隊[艇, 機]** a search party [boat, plane] / **捜索令状** a search warrant. 文例⇩

そうさく² 創作《文》creation;〈制作〉production;〈小説を書くこと〉story [fiction] writing;〈創作品〉a creative [an original] work; a creation (of a great artist);〈小説〉a novel; fiction (総称) ¶**創作する** create; write a novel [story] / **創作的** creative; original /(**大学の)創作演習** practice in creative writing / **創作家** a novelist; a writer / **創作欲** a creative urge / **創作力** creative power.

ぞうさく 造作 fixtures ((of a house));〈建築〉building;〈顔の〉features ¶**造作を取り付ける** build [fit out] (the interior of a house).

ぞうさつ 増刷 reprinting ¶**増刷する** reprint ((a book)); do a reprint. 文例⇩

ぞうさない 造作ない easy; simple; straightforward ¶**造作なく** easily;《文》with ease; without any trouble [difficulty, effort]; effortlessly;(win) hands down.

そうさらい 総浚い〈復習〉a general review;〈一掃〉a cleanup;【演劇】(hold) a dress rehearsal ¶**総ざらいをする** make a general review of one's lessons.

そうざん 早産 premature delivery; a premature birth ¶**早産する** have one's [a] baby [child] prematurely;《文》be prematurely delivered of a child / **早産で生まれる** be born prematurely.

ぞうさん 増産 an increase [a step-up] in production; a production increase; increased production; an increased yield ((of rice)) ¶**増産する** increase [step up] production; increase the yield ((of rice)) / **木材の長期増産計画** a long-range program for increasing the output of lumber.

ぞうざん 造山【地質】¶**造山運動** mountain-building[-making] activity [movements] / **造山作用** orogeny; orogenesis; mountain-building[-making].

そうし 創始 ¶**創始する** found;《文》create; establish; start;《文》originate / **創始者** the founder [《文》father,《文》originator] ((of modern linguistics)).

そうじ¹ 相似 (a) resemblance; (a) similarity;【生物】(an) analogy ¶**相似の** similar ((to));《文》analogous ((to));《文》like ((faces)) / **相似器官**【生物】an analogous organ / **相似形**【数】similar [like] figures / **相似点** a point of likeness ((between)); a resemblance; a similarity / **相似性**《文》an analogy; a parallel. 文例⇩

そうじ² 掃除 cleaning;〈掃き掃除〉sweeping;〈ふき掃除〉dusting (棚のほこりなどの);scrubbing ¶**掃除をする** clean; sweep; dust; scrub / **きれいに掃除をする** clean up ((the room)) / **掃除の行き届いた** clean; tidy / **大掃除** ⇨ **おおそうじ** / (**電気)掃除機** a vacuum cleaner / **掃除道具** cleaning things / **掃除道具を入れる押入れ** a broom [mop, cleaners'(会社などで)] closet [《英》cupboard] / **掃除当番** one's turn for doing the sweeping [cleaning] / **掃除婦** a cleaning woman [lady]; a charwoman; a charlady. 文例⇩

ぞうし 増資 ¶**増資する** increase the [its, their] capital;〈株式会社が〉increase its [their] stock / **増資(新)株** newly issued stocks.

そうしき 葬式 a funeral (service);《文》burial [funeral] rites ¶**葬式の費用** funeral expenses / **葬式を営む** hold a funeral ((for)); perform a funeral service ((for)) / **葬式に参列する** attend [be present at] a funeral;《文》pay one's last respects ((to)) / **葬式に集まった人びと** the funeral party [group]. 文例⇩

そうじしょく 総辞職 (a) mass resignation; resignation in a body [en masse] ¶**総辞職する** resign in a body [en masse, en bloc].

そうしそうあい 相思相愛 ¶**相思相愛の仲である** be deeply in love with each other;《文》be strongly attached to each other.

そうしつ 喪失 loss;《文》forfeiture ¶**喪失する** lose;《文》forfeit;《文》be deprived ((of)).

そうして ⇨ **そして**.

そうじて 総じて ⇨ **がいして**.

そうしはいにん 総支配人 a general manager.

そうはい¹ 壮年 a man in the prime of life [in his prime] ¶**壮年をしのぐ** be as strong as a young man; be so vigorous that ((he)) puts young men to shame.

---

the police dragnet.
そうさく¹ 男は警察で捜索中の殺人犯であった。 The man turned out to be a culprit wanted by the police for murder. / 警察では犯人を捜索中である。 The police are after the culprit.
そうさつ この本は目下増刷中だ。 The book is at present reprinting.
そうじ¹ 魚類のえらは地上動物の肺の相似器官である。 The gills of fish are analogous to the lungs in terrestrial animals.
そうじ² この部屋をきれいに[よく]掃除してみなさない。 Give this room a good cleaning. / 今日は台所をきれいに掃除するつもりです。 I'm going to have a good cleanup of the kitchen today.
そうしき 長年付き合っていた友人の葬式に行ってきたところだ。 I have been at [to] the funeral of an old friend. / 父にはろくな葬式もしてあげられなくてつらい気持ちでした。 Sad to say, I couldn't give my father a good funeral.

そうしゃ² 走者 a runner;《野球》a (base) runner ¶走者を一掃する clear the bases (of runners) / 走者を出す send a runner (to) / 走者を2人置いて with two runners on [aboard].

そうしゃ³ 奏者 a player [performer]《on the harp》/ フルート奏者 a flute player; a flautist;《米》a flutist.

そうしゃ⁴ 掃射 ¶掃射する sweep [rake]《the enemy's position》with fire; mow《the enemy》down; machine-gun.

そうしゃ⁵ 操車《鉄道》marshaling ¶操車係 a train dispatcher / 操車場 a marshaling yard;《米》a switchyard.

そうしゅ 宗主 a suzerain ¶…の宗主権の下にある be under the suzerainty of … / 宗主国 a suzerain power [state]; a suzerain.

そうじゅう 操縦 steering; piloting; control; operation; handling; management ¶操縦する control; steer; pilot (飛行機を); drive (自動車を); operate; handle; work; manipulate; manage / 意のままに操縦する twist [turn] sb around one's little finger / 巧みに操縦して…させる maneuver sb into doing / 妻の意のままに操縦されている be tied to one's wife's apron strings; be under one's wife's thumb / 操縦の自由を失う lose control of (an airplane) / 操縦桿 a control stick [lever, column];《口語》a joystick / 操縦士 a pilot / 副操縦士 a copilot / 操縦席 a cockpit / 操縦装置 controls; controlling [steering] gear. 文例⇩

ぞうしゅう 増収 an increase in [of] revenue [receipts, income]; increased revenue [receipts, income]; ⟨収穫⟩ an increased yield. 文例⇩

ぞうしゅうわい 贈収賄 (a case of) bribery; (official) corruption; bribery and corruption (are rife).

そうじゅく 早熟《文》precocity;《文》premature development [growth] ¶早熟な precocious; premature;《文》prematurely developed / 早熟である be precocious; grow [mature, ripen] early. 文例⇩

そうじゅつ 槍術 (the martial art of) spearfighting; spearmanship ¶槍術家 a spearman; an expert with the spear.

そうしゅん 早春 early spring.

そうしょ¹ 双書 a series (単複同形); a library.

そうしょ² 草書 the cursive [running] style of writing Chinese characters; the 'grass' hand [style] ¶草書で書く write in sosho [in a running hand].

ぞうしょ 蔵書 a collection of books; one's (private) library ¶3万冊の蔵書がある own [have a library of] 30,000 books /《図書館が》house 30,000 books / 蔵書印 an ownership stamp [mark] / 蔵書家 a book collector / 蔵書票 a bookplate;《ラテン語》an ex libris (単複同形) / 蔵書目録 a library catalogue. 文例⇩

そうしょう¹ 宗匠 a master; a teacher.

そうしょう² 相称 symmetry ¶左右相称の (bilaterally) symmetrical.

そうしょう³ 総称 a general [generic] term ¶総称する《文》name generically;《文》give a generic name (to). 文例⇩

そうじょう¹ 相乗 ¶(薬などの)相乗効果 the synergistic [mutually potentiating] effect (of the two medicines).

そうじょう² 僧正 a bishop.

そうじょう³ 騒擾 ⇨そうどう ¶騒擾罪 the crime of rioting [riotous assembly] / 騒擾罪で起訴される be indicted for rioting.

ぞうしょう 蔵相 the Finance Minister.

そうしょく¹ 草食 ¶草食の herbivorous / 草食動物 a herbivorous animal; a herbivore (pl. -s, -vora); a grazer. 文例⇩

そうしょく² 装飾 (an) ornament; (a) decoration;《文》(an) adornment; (an) embellishment; décor ¶装飾する ornament;《文》adorn; decorate;《文》bedeck; deck out / 装飾の(的な) ornamental; decorative / 装飾のない ornament-free; unadorned / 装飾用の for decoration; for decorative [ornamental] purposes / 装飾用電球 a decorative light bulb / 装飾音《音楽》a grace note; grace (総称) / 装飾芸術 (a) decorative art / 装飾彫刻 ornamental carving; carved decorations / 装飾品 an ornament; a decoration.

そうしょく³ 僧職 the priesthood; the clerical profession ¶僧職につく become a bonze [priest]; take holy orders.

ぞうしょく 増殖 multiplication; increase;《文》proliferation;《文》propagation ¶増殖する increase; multiply;《文》propagate;《文》proliferate / 自己増殖 self-reproduction / 増殖(型)原子炉 a breeder (reactor).

そうしれいかん 総司令官 the supreme commander; the commander-in-chief (略: C. in C.).

そうしれいぶ 総司令部 the General Headquarters (略: GHQ).

そうしん 送信 transmission (of a message) ¶送信する transmit [dispatch] a message (to) / 送信機 a transmitter / 送信局[塔] a transmit-

---

そうじゅう この船は操縦しやすい。This ship is easy to steer [control]. / 彼らはすっかり彼女に操縦されていた。They were completely under her thumb. / 副操縦士が機長に代わって操縦桿を握った。The copilot relieved the pilot at the controls.

ぞうしゅう 米作は前年に比して約3パーセントの増収である。This year's rice crop shows an increase of about 3 per cent over last year.

そうじゅく 概して西洋人は日本人よりも早熟だ。Broadly speaking, Westerners mature earlier than Japanese.

ぞうしょ あの人は蔵書家だ。He owns a large library. | He is a great book collector. / 彼の蔵書は2万冊に上る。He has a library of about 20,000 books.

そうしょう³ これらを総称して「両生類」という。Amphibia is the general term for these animals. | These are known generally as Amphibia.

そうしょく¹ ゴリラは草食だ。Gorillas feed on plants.

ぞうすい 豪雨のため隅田川が2メートル増水した。As a result of the heavy rainfall, the Sumida River has risen (by) two meters.

ぞうしん 増進 (an) increase ; 《文》promotion ; 《文》furtherance ¶増進する increase ; 《文》promote ; 《文》further / 健康を増進する improve [build up] one's health / 実力を増進する improve one's ability / 社会福祉を増進する improve [《文》promote] social welfare / 社会福祉の増進 extension [《文》promotion] of social welfare / 能率を増進する increase [improve] efficiency.

そうしんぐ 装身具 personal ornaments [《文》adornments] ; accessories.

そうすい¹ 送水 ¶送水する《運ぶ》carry [《文》convey] water ((to)) ; 《供給する》supply water ((to)) ; supply ((a town)) with water / 送水管 a water pipe / 送水本管 a water [service] main.

そうすい² 総帥 the commander-in-chief ; the leader.

そうすい³ 増水 ¶増水する《川が》rise ; swell. 文例⇩

ぞうすい 雑炊 a porridge of rice and vegetables.

そうすう 総数 the total [《文》aggregate] (number). 文例⇩

そうすかん 総すかん ¶総すかんを食う lose all one's popularity [support] ; have not a friend left ; 《口語》get the cold shoulder [the brush-off, a frosty reception] from everybody.

そうする 奏する《演奏する》play ; perform ¶効を奏する ⇨ こう⁵.

そうすると 《それでは》 then ; in that case. 文例⇩

そうすれば if one does that ; if that happens ; in that case ; if so ; then. 文例⇩

そうせい 総勢 the whole force [army, number, party] ¶総勢100名 one hundred men in all [all told] ; (a party) 100 strong.

ぞうせい 造成《creation》¶《preparation (of a housing site)》¶造成する make 《new land》 ; 《文》create 《land》 ; prepare 《the ground for housing》 ; develop 《an area of land》.

ぞうぜい 増税 a tax increase [《米口語》hike] ; an increase in taxation ; increased taxation ¶増税する increase [raise] taxes / 増税案《提案》 a proposed tax increase ; 《法案》 a tax increase bill.

そうせいき 創世記『聖書』(The Book of) Genesis (略 : Gen.).

そうせいじ 双生児 ⇨ ふたご ¶一卵性双生児 identical twins / 二卵性双生児 fraternal twins.

そうせき 僧籍 ¶僧籍を離脱する leave holy orders [the religious life] ; 《文》renounce the cloth / 僧籍に入る become a bonze [priest] ; enter the priesthood ; take holy orders ; 《文》renounce the world.

そうせきうん 層積雲『気象』a stratocumulus (pl. -li) (略 : Sc).

そうせつ¹ 創設 ⇨ そうりつ.

そうせつ² 総説 ⇨ ぞうろん.

ぞうせつ 増設 ¶増設する increase ; establish more (schools) ; install more ((telephones)) ; extend ; enlarge / 支店を3か所増設する establish [set up] three more branches.

そうせん 操船 managing [maneuvering, controlling] a ship ¶操船余地『海』sea room.

そうぜん 騒然 ¶騒然たる noisy ; 《文》clamorous ; agitated ; confused ; 《文》tumultuous ; uproarious / 騒然と in an uproar ; 《文》tumultuously ; 《文》in a tumult ¶騒然となる be thrown into a commotion [an uproar]. 文例⇩

ぞうせん 造船 shipbuilding ; marine engineering (造船工学) ¶造船会社 a shipbuilding company / 造船技師 a shipbuilder ; a marine [naval] engineer [architect] / 造船業 the shipbuilding industry / 造船所 a shipyard ; a dockyard / 造船台 a shipway ; a slip(way) (傾斜した).

そうせんきょ 総選挙 a general election ¶総選挙を施行する call a general election ((on June 25)).

そうそう¹ 錚々 ¶錚々たる prominent ; 《文》eminent ; outstanding ; leading ; first-rate ; distinguished ; 《文》foremost ; 《口語》crack.

そうそう² 早々 ¶早々(に) early ; immediately ; 《いち早く》promptly ; quickly ; without delay ; 《急いで》hurriedly ; in a hurry ; hastily ; 《文》in haste / 帰国早々 immediately after one's return home / 来月早々 early next month / 早々に引き上げる beat a hasty retreat ; hurry away [off]. 文例⇩

そうそう³ 《たびたび》(not) so often. 文例⇩

そうそう⁴ 《思い出して》oh yes ; I remember. 文例⇩

ぞうぞう¹ 創造 《文》creation ¶創造する《文》create ; make / 天地創造の神話 a creation myth / 天地創造以来 since the creation of the world / 創造的 creative / 創造者 a creator ; the Creator (神) / 創造力《文》creative power [faculty] ; creativity ; 《独創性》originality ; inventiveness.

ぞうぞう² 想像 imagination ; (a) fancy ; 《仮定》(a) supposition ; 《推測》《文》(a) conjecture ; (a) guess ; (a) surmise ¶想像する imagine ;

そうすう 総数幾らになるか. How many do they come to altogether? / What do they amount to in all? / 総数100になる. The total is one hundred. / There are 100 in all. / They come to [total] a hundred.

そうすると そうすると僕は5時までにそこに行っていなければならないんですね. Am I to understand, then, that I must be there by five?

そうすれば こうやりなさい. そうすれば うまく行くでしょう. Do it this way [like this], and it'll work out well.

そうぜん そのために場内は騒然となった. It threw the audience into an uproar. / It caused quite a commotion in the hall.

そうそう² 新年早々風邪を引いてまだ治らない. I caught cold at the very beginning of the year, and haven't got rid of it yet.

そうそう³ そうそう彼に頼むわけにもいかない. I can't keep [be forever] asking him. / I can't ask him so often. / そうそう君の要求ばかり聞かれない. I can't grant every request you make.

そうそう⁴ そうそう, 去年の今頃だったなあ. Now I remember, it was about this time last year. /

そうそうこうしんきょく 葬送行進曲 a funeral [dead] march.
そうぞうしい 騒々しい noisy; loud;《文》clamorous; riotous; boisterous; uproarious;《口語》rip-roaring;〈言葉遣いなど〉loudmouthed ¶騒々しくする make a noise [din];《口語》raise [kick up] a racket. 文例⇩

そうそく 総則 general rules [provisions].
そうぞく 相続 succession; inheritance ¶相続する succeed to 《sb's estate》; inherit / 共同相続 joint inheritance [succession] / 相続争い a dispute about [a quarrel over] the succession / 相続権 heirship;《claim》(the right of) succession; one's inheritance rights / 相続財産 an inheritance; inherited property / 相続税 (an) inheritance [(a) succession] tax;《英》(a) death duty / 相続人 a successor; an heir (男); an heiress (女)〈▲日常語では「女相続人」でも heir と言う。heiress は「大資産家の女相続人」の意。法律用語としても「女相続人」は heir と呼ぶのが普通で、特に女性であることを強調する場合にのみ heiress と言う〉/ 法定相続人 a legal heir; an heir-at-law (pl. heirs-) / 推定[法定推定]相続人 an heir presumptive [apparent].
そうそふ 曾祖父 a great-grandfather.
そうそぼ 曾祖母 a great-grandmother.
そうそん 曾孫 a great-grandchild (pl. -children).
そうだ 操舵 steerage; steering ¶操舵機[装置] steering gear / 操舵室 a pilothouse; a wheelhouse; a control room / 操舵手 a steersman; a helmsman; a quartermaster / 操舵術 steersmanship; steering.
そうたい¹ 早退 ⇨ はやびけ.
そうたい² 相対 相対的 relative / 相対的に relatively / 相対性理論[原理]《物》the theory [principle] of relativity / 一般[特殊]相対性理論 the general [special] theory of relativity.
そうたい³ 総体 the whole; all ¶総体で in all;《文》in the aggregate; all told / 総体(的)に on the whole; all things considered; in general; generally (speaking).
そうだい¹ 総代 a representative; a deputy; a delegate ¶…の総代となる represent…/ …の総代として on behalf of…; representing….
そうだい² 壮大《文》grandeur;《文》magnificence ¶壮大な magnificent; grand; imposing;《文》majestic;《文》stately; spectacular.
ぞうだい 増大 ¶増大する〈大きくなる〉get [grow,《文》become] larger [bigger,《文》greater];〈大きくする〉make sth bigger [larger,《文》greater]; enlarge; increase;《文》augment / 新年増大号 the enlarged January number 《of》.
そうたいきゃく 総退却 (make) a general [full] retreat.
そうだいしょう 総大将〈総司令官〉a commander-in-chief (pl. commanders-);〈頭目〉a leader; a captain; a boss.
そうだち 総立ち ¶総立ちになる stand up all at once; stand up en masse. 文例⇩
そうたつ 送達 delivery;《文》conveyance;《文》dispatch ¶送達する send;《文》convey; deliver;《文》dispatch / 令状を送達する serve a writ on sb; serve sb with a writ.
そうだつ(せん) 争奪(戦) a scramble 《for》; a contest 《for》; a struggle 《for》; a competition 《for》 ¶争奪する scramble [struggle,《文》contest,《文》contend, fight] 《for》.
そうたん 操短 ⇨ そうぎょう³(操業短縮).
そうだん 相談 (a) consultation; a talk; (a) conference;《口語》a confab;《口語》a pow-wow;〈申し出〉an offer; a proposal;〈取り決め〉arrangements ¶相談する talk 《with sb over sth》; have a talk [hold a consultation] 《with》; discuss 《sth with sb》; consult 《with, together》;《文》take counsel together; confer [《文》confabulate] 《with sb over sth》;《口語》go into a huddle 《with》〈秘密の〉;〈助言を求める〉ask [take] sb's advice; consult 《a lawyer》;《文》take counsel 《with [of] sb》;〈交渉する〉negotiate 《with》;〈取り決める〉make arrangements 《with》/ 相談がまとまる come to terms [an agreement] 《with》/ 相談の上、相談ずくで by mutual agreement [consent] / あらかじめ相談しておいて《文》by prearrangement [advance arrangement] / 相談に行く go 《to sb》 for advice / 相談に乗る give advice [《文》counsel] 《to》;〈援助する〉give [lend] sb

---

それから、そうそう、葉書を 10 枚買って来て。And, oh yes, get me ten postcards.
そうぞう それはどんなものか想像がつかない。I haven't the faintest [have no] idea (of) what it is like. / 何とでも想像できる。It may be anything one chooses to imagine. / あとは読者のご想像にお任せする。What followed must be left to the imagination of the reader. / その大きさは想像を絶する。The size surpasses [defies] the imagination. / Its scale is almost beyond imagining.
そうぞうしい 騒々しくて私の声は伝わらなかった。My voice was drowned in the noise. / It was so noisy that I could not make myself heard.
そうだち 聴衆は総立ちとなった。The entire audience [house] rose to its feet.
そうだん そりゃあできない相談だ。That's an impossible proposition. / That's a very tall order. / 僕には相談相手がいない。I have no one to consult with [to turn to for advice].
そうち 自然に発火する装置になっている。It is contrived so as to ignite automatically.
そうちょう¹ 儀式はきわめて壮重に

a helping hand; reach out a helping hand ((to)); 〈申し出を受ける〉 accept sb's offer; agree to sb's proposal / 相談相手[役] an adviser; 〈腹心の友〉《文》a confidant (男); 《文》a confidante (女); 〈会社などの〉a counselor; a consultant (専門的な); 〈総称〉an advisory board [body] / 児童相談所 a child guidance clinic / 職業相談所 a vocational clinic / (新聞・雑誌の)相談欄 the advice column. 文例↓

そうち 装置 〈物〉a (mechanical) contrivance; a device; (an) apparatus 《pl. -(es)》; fittings; 〈備えつけること〉equipment; (an) installation ¶装置する equip [fit] 《with》; install. 文例↓

ぞうちく 増築 ¶増築する extend [enlarge, add to] a building; build an annex [extension] 《to the main building》 / 増築工事 extension work.

そうちゃく 装着 ⇒ とりつける.

そうちょう¹ 早朝 early morning ¶早朝に in the early morning; early in the morning / 明日[月曜]の早朝に early tomorrow [Monday] morning / こんなとんでもない早朝に (get up) at this unearthly hour (of the morning).

そうちょう² 総長 〈大学の〉《米》the president; 《英》the chancellor; 《英》the vice-chancellor ★《英》chancellor は儀式などで大学を代表する名誉職で, 王室その他の著名な人がそれに付くことが多い. 実際の大学の長は vice-chancellor である.

そうちょう³ 荘重 ¶荘重な solemn; 《文》sublime; impressive; 《文》grave / 荘重に solemnly; 《文》with solemnity; 《文》gravely; impressively. 文例↓

ぞうちょう 増長 ¶増長する be puffed up 《with pride》; 《口語》get stuck-up; 〈子供が〉get cheeky; grow impudent; be spoiled / わがままが増長する become more and more disobedient; get naughtier and naughtier. 文例↓

そうで 総出 ¶総出で all together; in full force.

そうてい¹ 装丁 binding ¶装丁する bind; get up.

そうてい² 想定 an assumption; 《文》a supposition; 《文》a hypothesis 《pl. -potheses》 ¶想定する suppose; assume; presume; imagine; 〈見積もる〉estimate / …という想定のもとに on the assumption (supposition, hypothesis) that….

ぞうてい 贈呈 ¶贈呈する give; 《文》present 《sb with sth, sth to sb》; make a present [gift] of sth / 贈呈式 the ceremony of the presentation 《of》/ 贈呈者《文》a giver; 《文》a donor / 贈呈品 a present; a gift / 贈呈本 a presentation (complimentary) copy.

そうてん¹ 争点 《文》the point at issue [in dispute]; 《文》an issue.

そうてん² 装塡 ¶装塡する load [charge] 《a gun with a cartridge》.

そうでん 送電 transmission of electricity; power [electric] transmission; electric [power] supply ¶送電する transmit electricity 《from…to…》; supply electric power 《to》 / 送電線 a (power-)transmission line [wire]; a power cable (高圧線) / 送電力 carrying capacity.

そうとう¹ 双頭 ¶双頭の double-[two-]headed / 双頭のわし a double-headed eagle.

そうとう² 相当 ¶相当な 〈かなりの〉considerable (success); good (results); sizable (income); quite a (price); 〈充分な〉enough (money); 《文》sufficient (funds); plenty of (courage) / それ相当の 〈妥当な〉appropriate (measures); suitable (replies); reasonable (attitude); 〈適合した〉fit (persons); fitting (responses); satisfactory (qualifications); the right (man); 《文》due (recompense); 〈相応な〉corresponding (rewards); proportionate (appropriate) (salary); (the wages) that one [the job] deserves / 相当な成功 a fair measure of success / 相当な理由 a good reason / 相当に pretty (bad); considerably (excited); 《口語》good and (drunk) / 相当する 〈適する〉suit; be suitable for; be suited to; be proper [fit] for; 〈ふさわしい〉be worthy of; 《文》become; befit; 〈等しい〉be equal [equivalent] to; correspond to [with] / 3 か月分の俸給に相当するボーナス a bonus equivalent to three months' pay / 子供に相当した仕事 a job fit for a child / 能力に相当した給料 a salary proportionate to one's ability / 収入に相当した生活をする live up to one's income. 文例↓

そうとう³ 掃討 ¶掃討する sweep; clear; stamp [wipe] out; mop [clean] up / 掃討(作)戦 a mopping-up (cleanup) operation; a sweep.

そうとう⁴ 総統 〈旧ドイツの〉the Führer.

そうどう 騒動 〈もめごと〉trouble; 《文》a dispute; 〈けんか〉a quarrel; a row; 〈なぐり合い〉a brawl; 《文》a fracas; 《口》fracases, 《英》fracas; 《英俗》a punch-up 〈混乱〉confusion; disorder; a commotion; 〈暴動〉a riot; an uprising; a rising; 〈騒ぎ〉(a) disturbance; (an) upheaval; (an) uproar; (an) agitation ¶騒動を起こす make [create] a disturbance;

執り行なわれた. The ceremony was conducted with all solemnity.

ぞうちょう 小言を言わずにいると彼はいい気になって増長する. If I don't nag him, he will get cheeky and start taking advantage (of me).

そうで 家中総出で道路の雪かきをやった. All the family were out to rake the snow off the road.

ぞうてい 贈呈.〈書物に署名して〉With the compliments of the author. / 退任する学長にりっぱな記念品が贈呈された. A handsome present was made to the outgoing president.

そうとう² 彼は相当に英語を話す. He speaks English pretty well. | He speaks fairly good English. / そこも相当暑い. It is hot enough there, too. / あいつは相当な悪だ. He is a real bad lot. / 今にこの分野では相当な人物になるだろう. I'm sure he'll be somebody in this field. / そいつは相当なものだ. That's something. / この罰は彼に相当している. He deserves the punishment. / それに相当する英語はない. There is no

ぞうとう　贈答 an exchange of presents [gifts] ¶贈答する exchange presents [with] / 贈答品 presents; gifts.

そうどういん　総動員 general mobilization ¶国家総動員 national mobilization.

そうとく　総督 a governor-general 《pl. governors》¶インド総督 〖史〗the Viceroy of India / 総督府 the government-general.

そうなめ　総嘗め ¶総なめにする win a sweeping victory (over); 《口語》beat (them) hollow; 《米》all hollow; 《口語》beat (them) all ends up; 〈火事などが〉make a clean sweep (of the street).

そうなん　遭難 a disaster; an accident; a mishap; 〈船の〉(a) shipwreck ¶遭難する meet with a disaster [an accident] / 〈船が〉be in distress (難破・沈没の危険にさらされている); be wrecked (難破している); 〈船員・船客が〉be shipwrecked / 遭難救助艇 a rescue boat; 〈航空機事故の〉a crash boat / 遭難現場 the scene of a disaster [an accident] / 遭難者 a victim; a sufferer / 遭難信号 a distress signal [call]; (send) an SOS / 遭難船 a ship in distress (遭難中の); a wrecked ship (難破した).

そうに　雑煮 rice cakes boiled with vegetables.

そうにゅう　挿入 《文》insertion ¶挿入する put sth in [between]; 《文》insert; 《文》interpolate (spurious passages in a book) / 挿入句 a parenthesis 《pl. -theses》.

そうねん¹　壮年 《文》(in one's) manhood; (in) the prime of life ¶壮年に達する reach manhood.

そうねん²　想念 an idea; a notion.

そうは¹　走破 ¶走破する run [cover] the whole distance (between).

そうは²　掻爬 〖医〗curettage ¶掻爬する curet(te); remove the fetus by scraping the uterus; perform [do] a D and C (★D and C は dilation and curettage の略).

そうば　相場 the going rate (of the yen); 〈市価〉the market price [value]; a quotation (on, for); 〈投機〉speculation; 〈評価〉estimation; an estimate ¶相場が上がる[下がる] rise [fall] in price / 相場の変動をつける quote (for an article); offer a price (for an article) / 〈幾らと〉相場をつける quote [for an article]; estimate [value] 《an article at 5,000 yen》/ 相場に手を出す dabble in [go in for] speculation; speculate [gamble] (in stocks); 《口語》play the market / 相場でもうける[損をする] make [lose] money in speculation / 公定[やみ, 名目]相場 an official [a black-market, a nominal] quotation / 小売[卸売]相場 the retail [wholesale] price / 相場師 a speculator / 相場表 a list of market prices [quotations]; a stock list (株や公債の). 文例▷

そうはい　増配 ¶増配する 〈配給を〉increase the (rice) ration; 〈株の配当を〉pay an increased [a larger] dividend. 文例▷

そうはく　蒼白 a 蒼白な pale; 《文》deathly white [pale]; 《文》pallid; (as) white as a sheet ⇒まっさお.

そうはせん　争覇戦 《文》a struggle for supremacy; 〈競技で〉a championship game [tournament]; 《米》a pennant race.

そうはつ　双発 ¶双発の《航空》twin-engine(d).

そうはつ　増発 ¶列車を増発する increase the number of trains (between); improve the railroad service / 臨時列車を増発する operate [run] a special train.

そうばな　総花 ¶総花的に to please everybody; 〈気前よく〉《文》with sweeping generosity; liberally / 総花主義 a please-everyone policy.

そうばん　早晩 sooner or later; by and by; in (the course of) time.

ぞうはん　造反 (a) revolt; a rebellion ¶造反する revolt (against one's ruler); start a rebellion; rise in rebellion.

そうび　装備 equipment; outfit; rigging (船の) ¶装備のいい[悪い] well-[poorly-, 《文》ill-]equipped / 完全装備の fully equipped (soldiers); 《200 men》with full equipment / 装備する equip 《oneself with》; fit out [《文》furnish] 《an expedition [a ship] with》; rig; mount (a gun) / 20インチ砲9門を装備している 〈軍艦が主語〉mount nine 20-inch guns.

ぞうひびょう　象皮病 〖医〗elephantiasis.

そうひょう　総評 〈日本労働組合総評議会〉the General Council of Trade Unions of Japan; Sohyo.

そうびょう　躁病 〖医〗mania ¶躁病患者 a maniac.

ぞうひょう　雑兵 common soldiers; the rank and file; 〈小もの〉small fry (集合的).

ぞうびん　増便 〈旅客機の〉an increase in the number of flights.

そうふ¹　送付 ¶送付する send; forward; remit (金を) / 送付先 the addressee.

そうふ²　総譜 〖音楽〗a full score.

ぞうふ　臓腑 ⇒はらわた.

そうふう　送風 ¶送風する send air (to); ventilate (a room) / 送風管 a blast pipe / 送風機 a [an air] blower; a ventilator; a fan.

ぞうふく　増幅 〖電〗amplification ¶増幅する amplify / 増幅器[装置] an amplifier.

ぞうぶつしゅ　造物主 the Creator; the Maker; the Great Artificer.

そうへい　僧兵 a monk soldier; a fighting [an armed] monk.

ぞうへいきょく　造幣局 the Mint (Bureau) ¶造幣局長 the Director [《米》Treasurer] of

そうへき 双璧 the two greatest authorities; the best two ¶現代日本画壇の双璧 the two master painters of contemporary Japan.

そうべつ 送別 a farewell; a send-off ¶送別会を開く give [hold] a farewell [seeing-off, send-off] party (for sb, in honor of sb).

そうほ 相補 ¶相補性《物》complementarity / 相補分布《言語》(a) complementary distribution.

ぞうほ 増補 ¶増補する enlarge; supplement; make an addition ((to a book)) / 改訂増補版 a revised and enlarged edition ((of)).

そうほう¹ 双方 both parties [sides] ¶双方の both; 《文》mutual; two-way (両方からの); 《文》bilateral (双務的な) / 双方のために《文》in (their) mutual interests; in the interest of both parties.

そうほう² 奏法《音楽》(a style of) rendition; execution; how to play ((the clarinet)).

そうぼうべん 僧帽弁《解》the mitral valve.

そうほん 草本 a herbaceous plant ¶草本の herbaceous.

そうほんけ 総本家 〈分家に対して〉the main [head] family; ¶元祖《文》the originator; the original maker.

そうほんざん 総本山 the head temple of a Buddhist sect.

そうほんてん 総本店 the main [head] office.

そうまくり 総捲り ¶総まくりする《文》do [carry out] a general [comprehensive] survey ((of)); 《文》make a sweeping review ((of)).

そうまとう 走馬灯 a revolving lantern ¶走馬灯のような《文》kaleidoscopic; 《文》ever-changing[-shifting].

そうむ¹ 双務 ¶双務的 bilateral; 《文》reciprocal / 双務契約 a bilateral [reciprocal] contract.

そうむ² 総務 〈仕事〉general affairs; 〈人〉a director; a manager ¶総務会(会長) (the Chairman of) the Executive Council [Board] / 総務長官 a director-general / 総務部 the general affairs department [bureau]; the executive section.

そうめい 聡明 intelligence; 《文》sagacity ¶聡明な intelligent; 《文》sagacious; wise.

そうめいきょく 奏鳴曲《音楽》a sonata.

そうめん 素麺 vermicelli; fine noodles.

そうもく 草木 trees and plants; plant life; vegetation.

そうもくろく 総目録 a complete catalog(ue) ((of)); a full list ((of)).

ぞうもつ 臓物 entrails; guts; 〈鳥の〉giblets; 〈動物の〉pluck (食用).

ぞうよ 贈与《文》donation; 《文》presentation ⇨そうてい ¶贈与税 a donation [gift] tax.

そうらん 騒乱 (a) disturbance; (a) commotion; a riot ⇨そうどう ¶騒乱罪を発動する [適用する] invoke [apply] the anti-riot law (against extremist rioters).

そうり 総理 〈総理大臣〉the Prime Minister; the Premier ¶副総理 the Deputy Prime Minister / 総理大臣の職[地位] the premiership / 総理大臣官房 the Prime Minister's Secretariat / 総理府(総務長官) (the Director-General of) the Prime Minister's Office.

ぞうり 草履 (Japanese) sandals; (a pair of) zori ¶草履をはく[はいている] wear [be in] sandals.

そうりつ 創立《文》establishment; founding; 《文》foundation; 《文》organization ¶創立する establish; found; organize; build; set up; start / 創立30周年を祝う celebrate the 30th anniversary of the founding ((of the school)) / 創立記念日 the anniversary of the founding [establishment] ((of the school)) / 創立者 the founder.

ぞうりむし《動》a paramecium (pl. -cia, -s); a slipper animalcule.

そうりょ 僧侶 a (Buddhist) priest; a bonze; a monk.

そうりょう¹ 送料 postage; carriage ¶小荷物の送料 the carriage on a parcel.

そうりょう² 総領 the eldest [oldest] son [child] ¶総領娘 the eldest [oldest] daughter. 文例⇩

そうりょうじ 総領事 a consul general (pl. consuls general) ¶総領事館 a consulate general.

そうりょく 総力《文》the aggregate power; all one's energy [strength] ¶総力をあげて with all one's strength [might]; 《文》with might and main; 《文》with concerted efforts / 総力をあげての all-out ((support)) / 総力戦 a total [(an) all-out] war.

ぞうりん 造林 afforestation; forestation ¶造林する afforest ((a valley)); plant trees.

ソウル¹《音楽》soul (music) ¶ソウルの soul (songs).

ソウル²〈韓国の首都〉Seoul.

そうるい¹ 走塁《野球》(base) running.

そうるい² 藻類《植》(the) algae (sing. alga); seaweeds; waterweeds ¶藻類学 algology.

そうれい 壮麗 magnificence; 《文》grandeur; splendor ¶壮麗な magnificent; grand; splendid; imposing; glorious; gorgeous.

そうれつ¹ 葬列 a funeral procession.

そうれつ² 壮烈 ¶壮烈な《文》heroic; brave; 《文》(moments) of high heroism / 壮烈な戦死を遂げる《文》meet a heroic death in action.

そうろ 走路 a track; a course.

そうろう¹ 早老 ¶早老の prematurely aged.

そうろう² 早漏 premature ejaculation.

そうろん 総論 general remarks; an outline ((of)); an introduction ((to)) ¶総論から各論に入る go [move] from the general to the particular; 《文》proceed from generalities into particulars. 文例⇩

とてもそんな相場では買えません。/ 夏は暑いものと相場は決まっている。People take it for granted that it is hot in summer. | Summer is, almost by definition, a hot season.

ぞうはい この会社は近く増配を発表するものと期待されている。The company is expected to declare an increased dividend.

そうりょう² 総領の甚六. First born, least clever.

そうろん 総論賛成, 各論反対. It is one thing to be liberal-minded

そうわ¹ 送話 transmission ¶〈電話の〉送話器 a mouthpiece.

そうわ² 挿話 an anecdote; a (little) story.

そうわ³ 総和 the sum total ⇒ そうけい².

ぞうわい 贈賄 bribery ¶贈賄する bribe *sb*; give *sb* a bribe / 贈賄の試み an attempt at bribery / 贈賄の話を持ちかける approach *sb* with the offer of a bribe / 贈賄罪に問われる be charged with bribery / 贈賄事件 a bribery case / 贈賄者 a briber.

そえがき 添え書き〈手紙の〉a postscript (略: P.S.);〈書画の〉a note explaining the origin [history, etc.] 《of a work of art》.

そえぎ 添え木 a splint ¶腕に添え木を当てる splint an arm; put a splint on *sb*'s arm.

そえもの 添え物《文》an adjunct (to); an addition (to);《文》an appendage (to);〈景品〉a premium (on);〈料理のつま〉(a) garnish;〈付録〉a supplement.

そえる 添える attach (to);《文》affix (to);《文》append (to);〈加える〉add (to);〈料理のつまを〉garnish《cutlets with vegetables》¶力を添える《文》lend *one*'s aid (to); give [lend] a helping hand (to); help; give (moral [financial]) support (to) / 一層の魅力を添える add to the charm (of); give additional appeal (to) / 言葉に身振りを添える accompany *one*'s speech with gestures / 口を添える put in a (good) word (for *sb*) / 教科書に添えるテープ tapes to go with the textbook.　文例⇩

そえん 疎遠《文》(an) estrangement;《文》alienation; a long silence〈無沙汰〉¶疎遠になる《文》become estranged [alienated] (from).　文例⇩

ソース sauce ¶ソースをかける put [pour] (some) sauce (on, over) / ホワイト[タルタル]ソース white [tartar(e)] sauce / ソース入れ a sauce bottle; a sauceboat〈舟型の〉.

ソーセージ (a) sausage ¶ウインナソーセージ a wienerwurst;《米》a wiener;《米口語》a weenie / フランクフルトソーセージ(a) frankfurter / レバーソーセージ (a) liver sausage;《米》(a) liverwurst.

ソーダ soda ¶洗濯ソーダ washing soda / ソーダ水 soda water [pop];〈1杯〉a soda (pop).

ソーラーハウス a solar house.

ゾーン a zone.

そかい¹ 租界 a concession; a settlement.

そかい² 疎開〈立ちのき〉(an) evacuation;〈散開〉dispersal ¶疎開する〈立ちのく〉evacuate; be evacuated〈戦争などで〉; move [flee] to (a place) for safety;〈散らばす〉disperse;〈取り除く〉remove; thin out / 強制疎開 forced [compulsory] removal [evacuation] / 集団疎開 an evacuation in a group [body] / 疎開児童 evacuated children; (child) evacuees / 疎開者 an evacuee.

そがい¹ 阻害 blocking; a check;《文》(a) hindrance;《文》an impediment;《文》obstruction;〈心理〉a blockage ¶阻害する block; check; hinder;《文》impede; obstruct;《文》hamper; prevent;〈遅らせる〉delay;《文》retard.

そがい² 疎外《文》(an) estrangement;《文》alienation ¶疎外する《文》estrange;《文》alienate; avoid [shun] *sb*'s company; give [show] *sb* the cold shoulder; keep *sb* at a distance [at arm's length] / 人間疎外 the alienation of man [human beings].

そかく 組閣 formation of a cabinet [ministry] ¶組閣する form [organize] a cabinet / 組閣本部 the cabinet organization [formation] headquarters.

そがん 訴願 a petition; an appeal ¶訴願する petition (for); appeal (to the authorities, for the repeal of an administrative measure) / 訴願委員会 the Petition Committee / 訴願人 a petitioner.

そぎばさみ 削ぎ鋏 thinning shears [scissors].

そきゅう 遡及 ¶遡及する《文》retroact (to);《文》be effective retroactive(ly) (to) ⇒ さかのぼる / 遡及力《文》retroactivity / 遡及力をもった retroactive. ¶pair(s) of shoes.

-そく …足 a pair (of socks) ¶靴2足 two

そぐ 削ぐ《文》〈削り取る〉chip; slice [cut] off;〈髪を〉thin;〈減殺する〉《文》diminish; reduce; take something from;《文》detract from; weaken; spoil; mar ¶感興をそぐ dampen [spoil, throw a wet blanket over] *one*'s enjoyment.

ぞく¹ 族〈生物〉a tribe;〈種族〉a race; a tribe ¶キクユ族 the Kikuyu tribe; the Kikuyu(s)〈1人〉a Kikuyu (tribesman) / 族長 a patriarch; the head of a family [clan] / 族長時代 the patriarchal age.

ぞく² 属〈生物〉a genus (*pl*. genera, genuses) ¶属名 a generic name / ハマダラカ属の蚊 mosquitoes of the genus *Anopheles*.

ぞく³ 賊〈賊徒〉a rebel;《文》an insurgent;〈盗賊〉a thief (*pl*. thieves); a burglar; a robber ¶賊軍 a rebel army; rebels.

ぞく⁴ 俗 ¶俗な〈通俗な〉common; popular;〈卑俗な〉vulgar; low / 俗に…と呼ばれている be commonly called…;《文》be called…in common parlance.

ぞくあく 俗悪 ¶俗悪な vulgar; coarse; low;《文》gross.

そくあつ 側圧 lateral pressure.

そくい 即位《文》accession to the throne; enthronement ¶即位する《文》ascend [accede to] the throne / 即位式 an enthronement ceremony; a coronation (ceremony) (戴冠式).

ぞくうけ 俗受け ¶俗受けする appeal to the

---

in talking about the general good and quite another to sacrifice one's own interests for it. | It is a good citizen who can make a sacrifice of his private interest for the general good.

そえる 願書に履歴書を添えて提出すること. Applications should be accompanied by a curriculum vitae.

そえん 2人はだんだん疎遠になっていった. They drifted farther and farther apart.

ぞくえん 好評によりさらに1週間続演される. The show will be retained for a further week in response to public demand.

そぐ その問題には即座に意見を述べかねた. Nobody could give an immediate opinion on the matter. / それを英語で何

ぞくえい [俗映] vulgar] taste; be popular with people with low [vulgar] tastes.

ぞくえい 続映 ¶続映する continue to show ⟪a movie⟫; run ⟪for three months on end⟫.

そくえん 測鉛 〘測量〙 ⟨cast⟩ a sounding lead; a plumb (bob); ⟨a lead⟩ plummet.

ぞくえん 続演 ¶続演する continue to stage [put on] ⟪a play⟫; run ⟪for two consecutive months⟫.

そくおう 即応 ¶即応する ⟪文⟫ conform to; adapt *oneself* to fit [suit] / 時代の要求に即応する meet the needs [demands] of the times / …に即応して in line with…, ⟪文⟫ alignment, ⟪文⟫ conformity] with…; in response to….

そくおん 促音 〘音声〙 a double [long] consonant.

そくおんき 足温器 a foot warmer.

ぞくがら 続柄 relationship; relation.

ぞくけ 俗気 ⇨ぞっけ.

ぞくご 俗語 ⟨卑語⟩ a slang word [expression] (★ a slang から slangs と言うのは誤り); slang (総称); ⟨口語⟩ a colloquial expression [word]; a colloquialism ¶俗語を使う use slang.

そくざ 即座 ¶即座に immediately; instantly; at once; promptly; ⟪文⟫ in short order; ⟪文⟫ with dispatch; (reject *sth*) out of hand; right away; ⟨即席に⟩ offhand; ⟨口語⟩ off the cuff; ⟪文⟫ extempore [extemporary]; on the spot / 即座の決定 an instantaneous [a snap] decision. 文例⇩

そくさい 息災 ⇨ぶじ.

そくし 即死 instant [⟪文⟫ instantaneous] death ¶即死する be killed instantly [on the spot].

そくじ 即時 instantly; immediately; straight- away; on the spot [⟪文⟫ instant]; in no time; at once; without delay ¶即時通話 direct distance [⟪英⟫ trunk] dialing / 即時払い spot [immediate] payment. 文例⇩

ぞくじ¹ 俗耳 ⟪文⟫ vulgar [profane] ears; the attention of the masses ¶俗耳に入りやすい simple enough to be understood by the masses.

ぞくじ² 俗事 worldly [mundane] affairs.

そくじつ 即日 on the same day ¶即日開票 ballot counting done on the day of voting / 即日速達 special delivery within the day.

そくしゃ 速射 firing in rapid succession; rapid fire ¶速射砲 a quick-firing gun; a rapid- fire[-firing] gun.

ぞくしゅう 俗臭 vulgarity ¶俗臭ふんぷんたる extremely vulgar; ⟪文⟫ gross; ⟪文⟫ world- ly-minded.

ぞくしゅつ 続出 ¶続出する appear [come out] one after another ⇨ぞくはつ. 文例⇩

ぞくしょう 俗称 a popular [familiar] name; ⟨学名に対して⟩ a common [⟪文⟫ vernacular] name ¶俗称を…という be commonly called

…; be popularly known as….

そくしん¹ 促進 ¶促進する ⟪文⟫ promote; ⟪文⟫ accelerate; ⟪文⟫ expedite; ⟪文⟫ facilitate; ⟪文⟫ give [lend] impetus to; ⟪文⟫ hasten; quicken; speed [step, gear] up; ⟪文⟫ further; help ⟪a movement⟫ forward [on].

そくしん² 測深 (depth) sounding ¶測深する measure the depth ⟪of⟫; sound; make sound- ings / 測深器 a (depth) sounder; a bathym- eter.

ぞくじん¹ 俗人 ⟨僧侶から見て⟩ a layman; a secular person; the laity (総称); ⟨理想家から 見て⟩ a philistine; a boor; a man with low tastes.

ぞくじん² 俗塵 ¶俗塵を避けて ⟪文⟫ far from the madding crowd; (live) away [⟪文⟫ se- cluded] from the world. 文例⇩

ぞくじんしゅぎ 属人主義 ⟨裁判の⟩ the per- sonal [nationality] principle; the principle of personal (privilege for) jurisdiction.

そくする 即する ⟨合致する⟩⟪文⟫ conform ⟪to⟫; agree ⟪with⟫; be adapted ⟪for, to⟫; be in line [⟪文⟫ alignment] ⟪with⟫; ⟨基づく⟩ be based [founded] ⟪on⟫ ¶時代に即した教育 educa- tion adapted to the times; education to meet the needs of the times / …に即して in line [⟪文⟫ (strict) conformity] with…. 文例⇩

ぞくする 属する ⟨所属する⟩ belong ⟪to, in, among, with⟫; ⟨分類項目上⟩ come [fall] under ⟪a heading⟫; ⟨人・会社などが⟩ be affiliated with ⟪the party⟫; ⟨内在している⟩⟪文⟫ be inherent in *sb* [*sth*]. 文例⇩

そくせい 速成 ¶速成科 a crash [short] course ⟪in English⟫ / 速成チーム a scratch team / 速成 法 a shortcut [⟪文⟫ royal road] ⟪to⟫; a quick way [method] ⟪of learning English⟫. 文例⇩

ぞくせい¹ 族生 ¶族生する grow in clusters.

ぞくせい² 属性 ⟪文⟫ an attribute; a property.

そくせいさいばい 促成栽培 forcing ¶促成栽 培する force ⟪strawberries⟫ / 促成栽培の野菜 forced vegetables / 速成栽培用の温室[温床] a forcing house [bed].

そくせき¹ 即席 ¶即席の ⟪文⟫ extempore; im- promptu; improvised; offhand; ⟨口語⟩ off- the-cuff; ad-lib / 即席に immediately; off- hand; ⟪文⟫ extempore; impromptu; ⟨口語⟩ off-the-cuff; ad-lib / 即席で…する *do* offhand [on the spot]; improvise ⟪a poem⟫; ad-lib ⟪a song⟫; ⟪文⟫ extemporize ⟪a speech⟫ / 即席料 理 a (light) quickly prepared dish.

そくせき² 足跡 a footprint; a footmark; an impression [imprint] of a foot ¶足跡を残す leave *one's* marks [⟪文⟫ impress] ⟪on *one's* age⟫ / ⟨旅行する⟩ travel; visit.

ぞくせけん 俗世間 the (workaday) world; ⟨聖 職者に対して⟩ secular society.

と言うか即座には出てこない. Right offhand I can't find the English for it.
そくじ この問題は即時解決を要する. The question calls for im- mediate solution.
そくしゅつ 苦情が続出した. We had a bumper crop of grievances.
ぞくじん² 彼は俗塵を避けて夏休 みの間山村で過ごした. He spent his summer holidays in a moun- tain village, away from the hus- tle and bustle of the world.
そくする この計画は現実に即して いない. This plan is quite unre- alistic [has little to do with the realities of the world].
ぞくする それらもこの部類に属す る. They come into this category [under this heading].
そくせい 彼は渡仏する前に 3 か月

ぞくせつ 俗説 a popular [《文》lay] view [account]; a popular version 《of an incident》; 〈伝説〉folklore; 《文》a tradition; a legend.
そくせん 側線 〈鉄道の〉a siding; 《米》a sidetrack; 〈魚類の〉a lateral line; 〈運動競技の〉a sideline; a touchline (フットボールの).
そくせんそっけつ 速戦即決 ¶速戦即決でやる strike while the iron is hot; act decisively on the basis of a quick decision.
ぞくぞく¹ 続々 one after another; in (rapid [close]) succession ¶続々来る[出る] pour [flow] in [out] / 続々詰めかけて来る[押し寄せる] rush on (a place). 文例⇩
ぞくぞく² ¶寒くて体がぞくぞくする feel a chill (creep over one); shiver with cold / ぞくぞくするほどうれしい feel like hugging oneself for joy; 《文》thrill with joy. 文例⇩
そくたつ 速達 ¶速達で (send a letter) by express [special delivery] / 速達郵便 express mail [《英》post]; 〈手紙〉a special delivery letter; 《英》an express letter / 速達料金 a special delivery fee.
そくだん 速断 ¶速断する 《文》make [form, draw] a rash conclusion; jump to a conclusion; jump to the conclusion that...; decide rashly [hastily].
そくち 測地 land surveying ¶測地学 geodesy; geodetics.
ぞくちしゅぎ 属地主義 〈裁判の〉the territorial principle; the principle of territorial jurisdiction.
ぞくっぽい 俗っぽい vulgar; in poor taste; (be) not in good taste; cheap; lowbrow 《books》.
そくてい 測定 measurement ⇨そくりょう ¶測定する measure; gauge; find / 正確に測定する take an accurate measurement of / 測定を誤る measure sth wrong(ly); make a mistake [an error] in measuring 《the depth》/ 測定器 a measuring instrument / 測定技術 measurement techniques / 測定装置 a measuring device / 測定値 a measured value.
そくど 速度 (a) speed; (a) rate; a pace; (a) velocity ¶速度を増す speed up; accelerate; gain [gather, put on, get up] speed; increase speed; one's speed rises [increases] / 速度を落とす slow down; 《文》decelerate; lose [《文》decrease, reduce] speed; one's speed drops [falls] / 1時間300キロの速度で at a speed of 300 kilometers an hour / 猛烈[非常]な速度で at (a) terrific [great] speed / 初[終]速度 the initial [final] velocity / 高[低]速度で at a high [low] speed / 速度違反に問われる be charged with speeding / 速度計 a speedometer (自動車の); a speed indicator / 速度制限 (set) a speed limit.
そくとう 即答 an immediate [a quick, 《文》ready] answer ¶即答する give an immediate [《文》a ready] answer; answer promptly; answer at once.
そくどく 速読 rapid [speed] reading.
ぞくねん 俗念 《文》worldly [earthly] thoughts [desires] ¶俗念を去る 《文》free oneself from earthly desires.
そくばい 即売 a spot sale ¶即売する sell on the spot / 展示即売会 an exhibition and sale 《of handicrafts》.
そくばく 束縛 (a) restraint; (a) restriction; 《文》shackles; 《文》trammels; 《文》fetters; 《文》a yoke ¶束縛する restrain; restrict; put [《文》impose] restraints [restrictions] 《on》; 《文》place [lay] sb under restraint; fetter; 《文》shackle; 《文》bind; 《文》enchain / 束縛を脱する free oneself from the restrictions 《of》; 《文》shake [cast, throw] off the fetters [shackles, trammels] 《of》; 《文》break away from the yoke 《of》. 文例⇩
ぞくはつ 続発 ¶続発する happen [《文》occur] in (quick [rapid]) succession; come out [crop up] one after another. 文例⇩
ぞくばなれ 俗離れ ¶俗離れしている〈俗事に超然としている〉《文》stand aloof from mundane affairs; 〈世事に疎い〉know (almost) nothing about / be quite ignorant of the world.
ぞくぶつ 俗物 a vulgar person; 《文》a philistine ¶俗物根性 《文》philistinism.
ぞくぶつてき 即物的 (a man) with a practical turn of mind; practical; matter-of-fact; realistic.
そくぶん 側[仄]聞 ¶側聞する learn by hearsay; hear say [《文》tell] 《of, that...》; 〈うわさである〉I hear [《文》am told] 《that...》; 〈了解している〉I understand 《that...》/ 側聞するところによれば from what I heard (by chance); I hear [《文》am told] 《that...》; somebody says....
ぞくへん 続編 a sequel 《to》; a continuation
そくほう 速報 a prompt report [announcement]; 〈ラジオ・テレビなどの〉a news flash;

のフランス語速成教授を受けた. Before he left for France, he took a three months' intensive course in French.
ぞくぞく¹ 注文が続々来た. Orders poured in. | We were flooded with orders. / 彼らは続々とホワイトハウスにやって来た. They came in a stream to the White House.
ぞくぞく² 体がぞくぞくして歯がかちかち鳴った. A shiver ran through me and my teeth chattered.
そくど 速度をおとせ. 《掲示》Slow (down). | Reduce speed. / 外部の力を受けない物体の速度は常に一定である. The velocity of a body not subject to external forces remains constant. / 台風は毎時8キロの速度で, ゆっくりと北上していた. The typhoon was advancing northward at a leisurely pace of 5 miles per hour.
そくばく 終日仕事に束縛されています. I am chained [tied down, pinned down] to my work all day. / 彼らは因襲に束縛されているために物を正しく見ることができない. They are so bound by the fetters of [are so blinkered by] conventionalism that they cannot look at things rationally.
そくはつ この1か月間の鉄道事故の続発はまことに嘆かわしい次第である. The rash of railroad accidents over the last month is quite deplorable.

spot news ¶速報する report promptly; make a quick report《on》/ 選挙速報 hour-by-hour reports of the election returns / 速報板 a bulletin board;《主に英》a newsboard.

ぞくみょう 俗名 〈戒名に対して〉a secular name;〈僧の出家前の名〉*one's* name as a layman.

ぞくめい 俗名 〈一般に使われている名称〉a [the] popular name《of a plant》;〈戒名に対して〉⇨ **ぞくみょう.**

そくめん 側面 the side; the flank;〈横顔〉a profile ¶側面から援助する help [《文》aid, 《文》assist] *sb* indirectly / 側面から見る[観察する] take a side view of / 側面を突く attack《the enemy》in the flank; launch [make] a flank attack《against, on》/ 側面を固める secure the flanks / 側面迂回 a flanking maneuver《of lions》/ 側面攻撃《make》a flank attack《on the enemy》/ 側面史 (an) anecdotal history《of》/ 側面図 a side [lateral] view.

ぞくよう 俗謡 a folk song; a ballad.

ソクラテス Socrates ¶ソクラテス的[流]の Socratic / ソクラテス以前の哲学 pre-Socratic philosophy.

そくりょう 測量 measurement; measuring; surveying; a survey; survey work;〈水深の〉sounding ¶測量する measure; survey; make [take] a survey [measurement]《of》; make [take] soundings of《the sea》/ 測量器 a surveying instrument / 測量技師 a (land) surveyor; a surveying engineer / 測量士 a surveyor registered / 測量図 a survey map;《英》an ordnance map (陸地測量部の) / 測量班 a surveying squad / 測量ポール a surveying [range] pole; a ranging pole [rod].

ぞくりょう 属領 〈領土〉a territory; a possession;〈属国〉a dependency.

そくりょく 速力 ⇨**そくど** ¶速力の早い[遅い] fast [slow] / 速力を出す[落とす] speed up [slow down]; increase [reduce] the speed / 最大速力…に達する reach [《文》attain] a maximum speed of… / 速力試験 a speed test. [文例⇩]

ぞくろん 俗論 a conventional [vulgar] view; a popular [《文》lay] opinion.

そぐわない do not match [suit, go well with] *sth* [*sb*];《文》be inappropriate《for, to》;《文》be unbecoming《to》; be out of character《with》; be out of keeping《with》;《文》consort ill《with》; be unsuitable《for》; be at odds《with》; be incongruous; be out of place.

そけい 鼠蹊〔解〕the groin ¶鼠蹊部[リンパ腺] the inguinal region [glands].

そげき 狙撃 ¶狙撃する shoot [fire] at; snipe (at) / 狙撃兵 a sniper; a marksman.

ソケット a socket ¶ソケットにはめる fit [screw]《a light bulb》into the socket; socket / 2また[3つまた]ソケット a two-[three-]way socket.

そげる 削げる split; be split; splinter ¶ほおのそげた with hollow [sunken] cheeks; hollow-cheeked.

そこ[1] 底 the bottom; the sole (靴の); the bed (川·池の) ¶底の知れない bottomless; unfathomable;〈なぞの〉mysterious;《文》enigmatic / 底をつく〈資源などが〉run out;《文》be exhausted;〈相場が〉reach the bottom; touch bottom; bottom out / 財布の底をはたく spend every penny *one* has [*one's* last penny] / …の底に in the bottom of《a cup》/ 底につく〈錨(いかり)が〉find bottom;〈足が〉touch bottom / 心の底から《thank *sb*》from (the bottom of) *one's* heart / 心の底では at bottom;《口語》deep down (inside); (deep) in *one's* heart; in *one's* heart of hearts;《文》in the depths of *one's* soul. [文例⇩]

そこ[2] ¶そこの[に] there; in that place / そこから from there;《文》thence / そこへ there;《文》thither; to that place / そこへ持ってきて in addition to that; on top of that; what is worse; to make matters worse; into the bargain;《文》moreover / そこまで《go》that [so] far; to that extent / そこまではいいのだが, … So far so good, but… / そこで there;〈それから〉then;《文》thereupon;〈それ故〉so; and (so);《文》accordingly;〈さて〉now / そこここに here and there / 10キロかそこら ten kilometers or so [thereabouts]; about [around, a matter of] ten kilometers / そこらじゅう all over the place; everywhere / どこかそこらあたり somewhere about there. [文例⇩]

そご[1] 祖語〔言語〕a parent language ¶印欧祖語 Proto-Indo-European.

そご[2] 齟齬 ⇨ **くいちがい, くいちがう.**

そこい 底意 an underlying [ulterior] motive; *one's* secret [true] intention ¶底意なく frankly; without reserve.

そこいじ 底意地 ¶底意地が悪い be a malicious [spiteful] person at bottom [heart].

そくりょく この列車は1時間180キロの速力だ. This train runs at a speed of 180 kilometers an hour.

そこ[1] 水はよく澄んでいて, 底まで見えた. The water was so clear that I could see the bottom. / 彼の謙遜(けんそん)もよくその底を割ってみれば, 一種のごうまんに過ぎないように思われる. When you get to the bottom of it, his humility is a type of pride. / 箱の底が抜けた[すっぽり抜けた]. The bottom came [fell clean] out of the box. / 株価が底なしに下落している. Stock prices have been going down and down with no sign of bottoming out.

そこ[2] そこまで一緒に行こう. I will go part of the way with you. / そこまでは考えなかった. I never thought of that. / そこまでは認める. That much I will admit. / その町の人口は3万かそこらあたりだ. The population of the town is in the neighborhood of 30,000. / そこが君の腕の見せどころだ. That's where you come in. / そこまでやったんだったら, 全部やってしまえばいいじゃないか. You've gone so far, so why not all the way? / そこへ行くと君などはのんきなものさ. You are quite carefree in that respect. / 2人が殴り合いを始めた, そこへ警官がやって来てすぐに2人を引き分けた. They had just come to blows, when a policeman appeared and at once

そこう 素行 behavior; 《文》conduct ¶素行が修らない lead a fast [《文》dissolute] life; 《文》be a person of loose morals [character] / 素行を改める mend one's ways; reform (oneself); turn over a new leaf.

そこうお 底魚 a bottom fish; a groundfish.

そこがわ 底革 《靴の》sole leather; a sole ¶靴の底革を付け替えてもらう have one's shoes resoled.

そこく 祖国 《文》one's fatherland [motherland, homeland]; 《文》one's mother [native] country ¶祖国愛 love of one's country; patriotism.

そこそこ only about; or so [thereabouts] ¶そこそこに hurriedly; in haste; 《文》in haste. 文例⇩

そこぢから 底力 《文》latent [potential] power ¶底力のある strong; powerful; energetic.

そこつ 粗忽 《不注意》carelessness; 《文》heedlessness;《軽率》rashness;《過失》a mistake;《文》an error ¶粗忽な careless;《文》heedless;〈うっかりした〉absent-minded;〈軽率な〉hasty; rash / 粗忽者 a careless fellow; 《口語》a scatterbrain.

そこつち 底土 subsoil.

そこづり 底釣り bottom fishing; ground angling.

そこなう 損なう harm; hurt;《文》injure;《文》vitiate; damage; do damage to sth;《文》spoil ¶感情を損なう hurt [offend] sb; hurt sb's feelings / 健康を損なう ruin [lose] one's health / 美観を損なう spoil 《文》mar] the beauty (of) / …し損なう fail to do; miss doing;〈危く…する〉almost [nearly] do; come near (to) doing / 言い損なう guess wrong / 言い損なう make a slip of the tongue / おぼれ損なう almost [nearly] drown; come near drowning. 文例⇩

そこに 底荷 ballast ¶《船が》底荷だけ積んでいる be in ballast / 底荷を積む ballast 《a ship》.

そこぬけ 底抜け ¶底抜けの〈底なしの〉bottomless;〈甚だしい〉《文》unbounded;〈締まりのない〉《文》imprudent;《文》indiscreet / 底抜けのばか a complete [《文》an egregious] fool; a perfect idiot / 底抜けのどんちゃん騒ぎ uninhibited merrymaking / 底抜け騒ぎをやる enjoy oneself rowdily [boisterously]; go [be] on the loose [spree]. 文例⇩

そこね 底値 the (rock-)bottom price.

そこねる 損ねる ⇨損なう.

-そこのけ ¶本職そこのけの腕前である (almost) outdo [outshine] a professional; can beat even an expert [the experts].

そこひ 《医》(a) cataract (白内障); amaurosis (黒内障); glaucoma (緑内障) ¶そこひにか

かった目 a cataracted eye.

そこびえ 底冷え ¶底冷えがする feel very chilly [cold]; be chilled to the bone [marrow].

そこびかり 底光り ¶底光りのする 《an eye》with a strange [an uncanny] luster;《silk cloth》with a quiet [subdued] gloss [sheen].

そこびきあみ 底引き網 a dragnet; a trawlnet (トロール網).

そこまめ 底豆 a blister (on the sole of one's foot); a (soft) corn.

そさい 蔬菜 vegetables; greens;《米》(garden) truck (市場向けの) ¶蔬菜園 a kitchen [market] garden;《米》a truck farm [garden] / 蔬菜造り kitchen [truck] gardening.

そざい 素材 (raw) material 《for one's book》;〈新聞記事などの〉copy ★ material is building materials (建築材料), raw materials (原料)のように「材料」の意味では複数形が可能であるが, writing material (執筆素材) など「素材」の意味では不可算名詞扱い. writing materials とすると, ペン・紙など「筆記用具」のことになる.

そざつ 粗雑 ¶粗雑な lax;《口語》sloppy; slipshod; loose; rough / 粗雑な頭の人 a loose [《口語》sloppy] thinker; a person who is incapable of close reasoning.

そし 阻止 ¶阻止する obstruct; stand in the way; stop; hinder; resist; oppose; interrupt; check; prevent;《文》hamper;《文》impede;《文》arrest 《the development》; hold [keep] back [in check].

そじ 素地 ⇨したじ.

ソジウム 《化》sodium.

そしき 組織 (an) organization;《文》formation;《系統》(a) system;《構成》《文》construction;《文》constitution;〈構造〉structure; a setup;〈生物の〉(a) tissue ¶組織する form; organize; set up; incorporate (会社を); set up an organization;《文》constitute;《文》construct / …で組織されている consist [be composed, be made up] of… / 社会の組織 the structure [fabric] of society / 現在の経済[産業]組織 the present economic [industrial] system / 組織の損傷 tissue damage / 組織的な systematic; methodical / 組織的に systematically; methodically / 組織委員会 an organizing [organization] committee / 組織化《文》systematization; organization / 組織化する《文》systematize; organize; structure / 高度に組織化された社会 a highly structured society / 組織学《医》histology / 組織者 an organizer / 組織体 an organism / 組織を《make》(a) tissue culture / 《選挙の》組織票 block votes 《of a labor union》/ 組織力 organizing ability / 組織労働

---

pulled them apart.

そこそこ 50円そこそこのものだった。It didn't cost much more than fifty yen. | 当時は 30 そこそこだった。I was not much over thirty then. | 私は朝飯もそこそこに飛び出した。I took [snatched] a hasty breakfast, and

went out.

そこなう 5時半の列車に乗りそこなった。I missed the 5:30 [five-thirty] train.

そこぬけ あの人は底抜けに金離れがいい。There is no limit to his generosity. | He is absurdly free with his money.

そしき 人体の組織は 7 年ごとに全く一新するという。It is said that the tissues of the human body are completely renewed every seven years.

そしつ 彼は指導者としての素質を備えている。He has the making(s) of a leader. | 彼には立派な劇

そしつ 素質 〈資質〉 the making(s); (a) nature; character; 〈体質〉《文》constitution; make-up / a predisposition 《to diabetes》; 〈傾向〉a tendency 《to, toward》¶ 文学的素質のある人 a person with a literary turn (of mind) / 遺伝的犯罪素質 inherited criminal tendencies. 文例⇩

そして and; then; 〈今や〉(and) now.

そしな 粗品 a small [little] gift [present]. 文例⇩

そしゃく¹ 咀嚼《文》mastication ¶ そしゃくする 〈かむ〉chew; 《文》masticate; 〈理解する〉understand; digest; take in / そしゃく力 〈かむ力〉one's chewing power; 〈理解力〉ability to understand [grasp] (a problem).

そしゃく² 租借 ¶ 租借する a lease; hold 《land》by [on (a)] lease / 租借権 a (99 years') lease; leasehold / 租借地 a leased territory.

そしょう 訴訟 a lawsuit; a suit; an action (at law) ¶ 訴訟する bring an action [a suit] (against sb for sth); sue (sb for sth); go to law 《with [against] sb over sth》/ 訴訟を起こす start [raise, institute] a lawsuit 《against》; take [bring, file, enter] an action 《against》; bring suit 《against》; go to court / 訴訟を取り下げる drop [discontinue] the suit 《against》/ abandon an action / 訴訟に勝つ [負ける] win [lose] a lawsuit [one's case] / 訴訟依頼人 a client / 訴訟事件 a (legal) case / 〈弁護士が〉訴訟事件を引き受ける take a brief / 訴訟事実 the cause of a legal action / 訴訟手続 legal procedure; 《take, institute》legal [judicial] proceedings; 《go through》(due) legal process / 訴訟人 〈原告〉a plaintiff; a suitor; 〈当事者〉a (party) litigant; 〈総称〉the parties litigant; the litigants / 訴訟費用 the costs of a lawsuit; court costs.

そしょく 粗食 a plain [simple] diet; a poor [《文》frugal] meal ¶ 粗食する eat [take] plain food; 《文》live on a frugal diet.

そしらぬふり[かお] 素知らぬ振り[顔] ¶ 素知らぬ振り[顔]をする pretend not to know [《文》to be ignorant of] (a fact); 〈見て見ぬ振りをする〉look the other way; 〈出会って〉cut sb; pretend not to recognize sb.

そしり 謗り (a) slander; 《文》disparagement; 《文》calumny; 《文》vilification; 〈非難〉blame; a charge; 《文》censure ¶ 世のそしりを招く incur public blame; bring public censure upon oneself; lay oneself open to public censure.

そしる 謗る slander; abuse; 《文》malign; disparage; 《文》vilify; 《文》speak ill of; 《文》censure; run sb down; fling [throw] mud at sb.

そすい 疎水 a canal ¶ 疎水工事 drainage works.

そすう 素数〈数〉a prime number; a prime.

そせい¹ 粗製 ¶ 粗製の coarse; crude / 粗製品 a crude article; an inferior [a poor-quality] article; 《文》an article of inferior quality / 粗製乱造 mass production of inferior goods / 粗製乱造する manufacture [produce] inferior articles in large quantities.

そせい² 組成 composition; 《文》formation; 《文》constitution; make-up ¶ 組成する compose; 《文》constitute; make [set] up; form.

そせい³ 蘇生 revival; 《文》resuscitation ¶ 蘇生する be restored [recalled, brought back] to life; come to (oneself [one's senses]); regain [recover] consciousness; revive; 《文》resuscitate / 蘇生させる bring sb back to life; bring sb around; restore sb to consciousness; revive sb; 《文》resuscitate sb / 蘇生の思いをする feel greatly relieved; breathe freely (again).

ぜい 租税 〈課税すること〉taxation; 〈税金〉taxes ⇨ ぜいきん, かぜい.

そせき 礎石 a foundation stone; a cornerstone; the foundation(s) (土台).

そせん 祖先 an ancestor; a forefather; 《文》a progenitor ¶ 現在の象の祖先である象の種 species of elephant ancestral to modern elephants / 祖先伝来の ancestral; hereditary / 祖先崇拝 ancestor worship. 文例⇩

そそ 楚々 ¶ 楚々たる〈美しい〉graceful; (pure and) beautiful; 〈きゃしゃな〉slim; slender.

そそう¹ 阻喪 ¶ 意気阻喪する be depressed; lose heart 《at》; be in low spirits; one's heart sinks (within one).

そそう² 粗相 〈不注意〉carelessness; an oversight; 〈失策〉a blunder ¶ 粗相する make a careless mistake; stupidly [carelessly] do ; 〈汚す〉soil 《the floor》in one's carelessness; 〈小便などを漏らす〉have a toilet accident; wet one's pants.

そぞう 塑像 a plastic image; a clay figure (statue).

そそぐ 注ぐ〈注入する〉pour into; 〈振りかける〉sprinkle; pour on; 〈川が〉flow into; empty (itself) into ¶ 注意を注ぐ pay attention (to); give one's mind (to); 《文》direct one's attention [mind] (to) / 全力を注ぐ focus [concentrate] one's efforts (on) / 目を注ぐ turn [fix, rivet] one's eyes (on). 文例⇩

そそくさ ¶ そそくさと hurriedly; 《文》in haste / そそくさと立ち去る hurry away [off].

そそっかしい careless; 《文》heedless; slapdash;

家になる素質がある. He has it in him to be a very good playwright. / 私は音楽の素質はない. I'm not cut out for music [to be a musician].

そしな 粗品贈呈. Gift presented to all customers.

そしょう 数年にわたる訴訟ののち原告に有利な判決があった. After several years of legal proceedings judgment has at last been given in favor of the plaintiff. / 莫大な訴訟費用がかかった. Vast sums were consumed in (legal) costs.

そしり 彼は怠慢のそしりを免れない. He cannot escape the charge of negligence. | He is open to criticism for being negligent.

そせん これは祖先伝来の宝物だ. This is a family heirloom.

そそぐ この湖にはいくつかの川が注いでいる. This lake is fed by several streams. / 信濃川は新潟で海に注ぐ. The Shinano River

そそのかす 唆す〈誘う〉tempt; entice;《文》allure;《文》inveigle《sb into doing》;《文》seduce;〈扇動する〉stir up;《文》instigate; incite; put *sb* up (to (commit) a crime); egg [set] *sb* on (to *do*, to *sth*).

そそりたつ そそり立つ rise (steeply [precipitously]); tower; soar. 文例⇩

そそる excite; incite; stimulate; arouse; tempt; stir up ¶ 好奇心をそそる arouse [excite] *one's* curiosity / 興味をそそる excite [arouse] *one's* interest (in) / 味覚をそそる whet [stimulate] *one's* appetite; give an edge to *one's* appetite.

そぞろ 漫ろ ¶そぞろに in spite of *oneself*; somehow; involuntarily / そぞろに涙を催す be moved to tears in spite of *oneself* / そぞろ歩き a stroll ⇨ さんぽ.

そだ 粗朶 sticks; brushwood; a fagot; twigs.

そだいごみ 粗大ごみ a large-sized discarded [unwanted] article.

そだち 育ち upbringing;《文》breeding;〈発育〉growth ¶ 育ちのいい[悪い] well [badly] brought up;《文》well-[ill-]bred;《文》(a man) of high [low] breeding / 都会[田舎]育ちの town-[country-]bred / 育ち盛りの子供 a growing child. 文例⇩

そだつ 育つ grow; be brought up;《文》be bred ¶ 育ち過ぎる be overgrown / 田舎[都会]で育った子供 a country-[city-]bred child / ミルク[母乳]で育った子供 a bottle-[breast-]fed child. 文例⇩

そだて 育て ¶育ての親 a [*one's*] foster parent [father, mother] / 育て方 (the method of) upbringing [raising, rearing]. 文例⇩

そだてる 育てる〈養育する〉bring up;〈飼養する〉breed; raise; rear;〈培養する〉cultivate; culture;〈教育する〉train; educate ¶ミルク[母乳]で育てる raise (a child) on the bottle [at the breast] / 後継者を育て上げる train up *one's* successors. 文例⇩

そち 措置《文》a measure; a step; action ¶ 措置を講じる take a step;《文》take measures; take action.

そちら〈相手のいる所〉there; your place [country];〈あなた〉you;〈ご家族〉your family;〈もう一方〉the other. 文例⇩

そつ ¶そつがない faultless; perfect;〈用心深い〉careful;《文》prudent;〈如才ない〉tactful. 文例⇩

そつい 訴追 ⇨きそ[1] ¶(議会の)訴追委員会 the Impeachment Committee.

そつう 疎通〈意思の〉understanding; communication ¶意思が疎通する《文》come to a mutual understanding; be understood (by) / 意思を疎通させる get (*oneself*) across; get *oneself* [*one's* ideas] over; communicate (*one's* thoughts clearly, with *sb*);《文》promote [facilitate] mutual understanding (between); make *oneself* fully understood (by).

ぞっか 俗化 vulgarization; popularization ¶俗化する be vulgarized; be popularized; get [《文》become] vulgar; be spoiled / 俗化していない土地 an unspoiled place [area]. 文例⇩

ぞっかい 俗界 the (workaday) world;《文》earthly [secular] life ¶俗界に超然としている《文》stand aloof from mundane affairs.

そっかん 速乾 ¶速乾性である dry quickly / 速乾ペイント a quick-drying paint.

ぞっかん 続刊 ¶続刊する continue the publication (of the magazine).

そっき(じゅつ) 速記(術) shorthand (writing); stenography ¶速記する do [write (in)] shorthand; take down (*sb's* speech) in shorthand / 速記を取る take shorthand notes (of) / 速記者 a stenographer; a shorthand writer [clerk] / 速記文字 a stenographic character / 速記録 stenographic records; shorthand notes.

ぞっきぼん ぞっき本 remaindered books; remainders.

そっきゅう 速球【野球】a fast ball ¶速球投手 a fast-ball pitcher.

そっきょう 即興 ¶即興の impromptu;《文》extempore; improvised;《文》extemporaneous; offhand; ad-lib / 即興的に impromptu;《文》extempore;《文》extemporaneously; offhand; ad-lib / 即興的に作る[歌う, 演奏する, 話す] improvise;《文》extemporize;《文》compose [sing, play, speak] extempore;《口語》ad-lib (特に役者などが) / 即興曲 an impromptu / 即興詩 an improvised poem / 即興詩人 an improviser.

そつぎょう 卒業 graduation; completion of a course (of study) ¶卒業する graduate from 《Yale》; complete a course; leave 《school》;〈比喩的に〉outgrow 《comic books》 / 中学を卒業する complete the junior high school course; leave junior high school ★ graduate は英国では大学 (university) を卒業するのに限られる。米国では, 各種学校や高校を卒業するのにもこの語が用いられる。なお, be graduated from... の形は今ではあまり使われ

---

drains into the sea at Niigata.

そそっかしい ネクタイを締め忘れるなんて, そそっかしい人ねえ。How careless of you [You should have known better than] to forget to put on a tie!

そそりたつ その岩は水面から垂直にそそり立っている。The rock rises sheer from the water.

そだち 育ちのいい娘さんだ。She is a well-brought-up girl. / この子は育ち盛りで, 日一日と大きくなっているようだ。He is growing so fast that he seems to be taller every day. / 育ちが物を言うね。Breeding will tell, you know.

そだつ 私は東京で生まれて東京で育った。I was born and bred in Tokyo.

そだて 子供は両親の育て方ひとつです。A child is what his parents make it.

そだてる 子供を育て上げてしまったら, 何か自分の勉強になるようなことをやってみたいと思っています。I think I will take up something to improve myself once my children are grown [off my hands].

そちら そちらはお変わりございま

ない／アルバイトをしながら大学を卒業する work one's way through college／代数を卒業して微積分に進む graduate from algebra to calculus／大学を卒業したての fresh from college／卒業後 after graduation [leaving school]／卒業(証書授与)式 a graduation ceremony；《米》graduation exercises；《米》the commencement (exercises)／卒業式の日《米》the commencement day；《英》the speech day〈高校以下の〉／卒業試験[論文] a graduation examination [thesis]／卒業証書 a diploma；a certificate (of the completion of a school course)／卒業生 a graduate；an ex-student；a school leaver〈小・中学の〉；《男》an alumnus (pl. -ni)；an old boy；《女》an alumna (pl. -nae)；an old girl ★ alumnus, alumna は主に《米》／昭和 57 年の早稲田大学法学部卒業生 a graduate of the law department, Waseda University, in the class of 1982／卒業生名簿 a list of graduates. 文例⇩

ぞっきょく 俗曲 a folk song [melody]；a ballad ¶俗曲吹き寄せ a medley [an assorted collection] of folk songs.

そっきん 即金〈現金〉(spot) cash；ready money；〈即金払い〉cash [spot] payment ¶即金で払う pay in cash；pay (cash) down／半額は即金で, 半額は月賦で (pay) half cash down and half in monthly installments.

そっきん² 側近 a close adviser (of the President)；those close to《the Prime Minister》¶大統領の側近筋によれば according to sources close to the President.

ソックス《a pair of》socks.

そっくり〈全部〉all；altogether；entirely；《文》in its entirety；wholly；completely ¶そっくりそのままにしておく leave sth intact [untouched, as it is]／そっくりである be just [exactly] like sb；be a ringer for sb；《俗》be a (dead) ringer for sb／〈2 人が主語〉be as like as two peas (in a pod)／レーガン大統領のそっくりさん President Reagan's look-alike；Mr. Look-Like President Reagan. 文例⇩

そっくりかえる そっくり返る throw one's chest out；hold one's head high；〈威張る〉lord it (over)／そっくり返って歩く swagger 《around, about》；walk swaggeringly.

そけ 俗気 俗気のある《文》worldly；《文》worldly-minded；《文》《a man》of vulgar [low] ambition.

そっけつ 即決 ¶即決する decide promptly [immediately, on the spot]／即決で〈会議などで〉without debate／即決裁判 a summary trial [decision]／即決裁判で判決を言い渡す pass an instant sentence on sb.

そっけない cold；short；curt；blunt；《文》brusque ¶そっけなく coldly；curtly；bluntly；《文》brusquely／そっけなく拒絶される meet with a curt [flat] refusal／そっけなくあしらう give [show] the cold shoulder《to》／〈言葉使いについて〉be short《with sb》.

そっこう¹ 即効《have, produce》an immediate effect《on》¶即効薬 a quick(-acting) remedy.

そっこう² 速攻 ¶速攻をかける launch a swift attack on [against]《the enemy》；lose no time in attacking《the enemy》.

ぞっこう¹ 続行 ¶続行する go [carry] on《with》；continue《to do, with the work》；keep on《doing》；《文》proceed《with》；〈再開する〉take up《one's work》where one left off；《文》resume.

ぞっこう² 続稿 manuscripts which form a sequel《to》.

そっこうじょ 測候所 a meteorological observatory [station]；a (local) weather bureau [station].

そっこうせい 速効性 ¶速効性がある work [take effect] at once；《文》be immediately potent.

そっこく 即刻 instantly；at once；immediately；on the spot；without delay；straight [right] away [off]；in no time.

ぞっこく 属国 a dependency；a subject [vassal] state [country].

ぞっこん ⇨ すっかり ¶ぞっこんほれ込む be deeply [over head and ears] in love《with》；be smitten《by》；《口語》be completely stuck [gone]《on a girl》.

そっせん 率先 ¶率先する take the lead [initiative]《in》／率先して…する be the first to do；set an example《of moderation to others》.

そっち〈方面〉in that direction；that way；〈物〉that (one)；〈他方〉the other (one) ¶そっちこっち here and there；in places. 文例⇩

そっちのけ ¶そっちのけにする neglect《one's family》；ignore；《文》slight；pay no attention《to》.

そっちゅう 卒中《医》apoplexy；(a) stroke；cerebral paralysis ¶卒中の発作 a stroke；an apoplectic fit／卒中にかかる have a stroke；have a fit [an attack] of apoplexy.

そっちょく 率直 ¶率直な honest；frank；candid；outspoken；plain；openhearted；straightforward／率直に honestly；frankly；candidly；outspokenly；plainly；openheartedly；straightforwardly；without mincing words／率直に言えば frankly (speaking)；to

---

せんか. How are you getting along?／そちらは 731 局の 0111 ではありませんか. Isn't this 731-0111?／そちらのを見せて下さい. Show me the other (one), please.

そつ 彼は何をさせてもそつがない. He does everything neatly.｜He does a good job of whatever he undertakes.

そっか 彼は俗界にあって俗化しない. He is in this world, but not of it.

そつぎょう 兄は法科を卒業しました. My brother graduated in law.／その学校はこれまでに 1 千人の卒業生を出した. That school has graduated [turned out] 1,000 boys [girls].

そっくり この子は父親にそっくりだ. The boy is the spitting image [very picture] of his father.／あのお嬢さんはお母さんそっくりになってきた. She is turning out to be her mother's daughter.／その犬は魚を骨ごとそっくり食べてしまった. The dog ate up the fish, bone and all.

そっち そっちへ行っていなさい. Go away.｜Don't bother me.

そっと put it bluntly; to be frank [plain] with you. そっと 〈静かに〉 softly; gently; quietly; 〈こっそりと〉 secretly; in secret [private]; stealthily; 《文》 by stealth; on the sly ¶そっと歩く walk softly / そっと触れる feel [touch] lightly / そっと見る look furtively 《at》; steal a glance 《at》/ そっと入る[出る] steal [slip] into [out of] 《a room》/ そっと金を握らせる slip money 《to sb, into sb's pocket》/ そっとしておく leave sth as it is; leave [let] sb alone.

ぞっと ¶ぞっとする 〈恐怖で〉shudder 《with fear》; shiver; 〈怪談を聞いて〉《文》feel a thrill 《of horror》; 〈嫌悪で〉be filled with horror 《at》; be disgusted [horrified] 《at, with, by》/ 背筋がぞっとする feel [get] shivers down one's spine / 聞いた[見た]だけでもぞっとする shudder at the mere mention [sight] 《of》/ 考えただけでもぞっとする shudder [be horrified] at the very thought [mere idea] 《of》/ ぞっとさせる 〈事が主語〉send a chill through one; make one shudder; give one the creeps; make one's flesh creep; freeze one's blood; make one's blood run cold / ぞっとするような 〈怖い〉bloodcurdling; spine-chilling; gruesome; hair-raising; 〈いやな〉disgusting; horrifying; revolting; repulsive; 〈口語〉creepy. 文例⇩

そっとう 卒倒 a faint; fainting; 《文》a swoon; 《文》swooning ¶卒倒する faint; 《文》swoon; fall unconscious.

そっぱ 反っ歯 a projecting [prominent] front tooth; a bucktooth 〈大きな〉.

そっぽ ¶そっぽを向く look the other way; turn [look] away.

そで 袖 a sleeve; an arm 〈洋服の〉; 〈建物・机の〉 a wing ¶そでを捕らえる hold sb by the sleeve / そでを引く pull [tug] sb's sleeve / そでをまくり上げる roll [tuck] one's sleeves up / 涙でそでを絞る 《文》shed copious tears; 《文》be moved to tears / そでを連ねて 《resign》 in a body [en bloc] / そでにする 〈女が男を〉jilt 《one's boyfriend》/ 〈冷遇する〉give [show] sb the cold shoulder; 〈見捨てる〉《口語》leave sb in the lurch; run [walk] out on sb; 〈願いを聴き入れない〉turn a deaf ear to 《sb's entreaties》/ そで無しの sleeveless / そで裏 the lining of a sleeve / そでカバー a sleeve protector / そで口 a cuff; a wristband 〈シャツの〉/ そでぐり a sleeve-hole; an armhole / そで丈 the length of a sleeve /〈上着の〉そで付け an armhole. 文例⇩

ソテー 《料理》a sauté ¶ポークソテー sautéed pork.

そてつ 〈植〉a cycad; a Japanese sago [fern] palm.

そでのした 袖の下 ⇨ わいろ.

そてん 素点 〈テストなどの〉an unadjusted [raw] score.

そと 外 the outside; 《文》the exterior ¶外の outer; outside; 《文》exterior; 《文》external; outward; outdoor / 窓の外を見る 〈窓から〉look out 《of》[look out] the window; 〈窓越しに〉look out through the window / 外に[で, は] out; outside; out of doors; in the open; 《文》without / 外で遊ぶ play outside [outdoors, in the open] / 外で食事をする eat [《文》dine] out / 外へ出る go out 《of doors》. 文例⇩

そとうみ 外海 the open sea; the ocean.

そとがまえ 外構え the outward [《文》external] appearance; the outside; 《文》the exterior.

そとがわ 外側 the outside; the outer side; 《文》the exterior ¶外側の outer; outside; 《文》exterior; 《文》external / 一番外側の outermost; 《文》outmost / 外側から from the outside; 《文》from without.

そとづら 外面 the outside is pleasant to everybody except one's family; be 《surly [bad-tempered] at home but》pleasant to outsiders.

そとのり 外法 the outside measurement(s) 《of》; 《文》the external dimensions.

そとば 卒塔婆 a stupa.

そとぼり 外堀 the outer moat.

そとまた 外股 ¶外またに歩く walk with one's toes turned out.

そとまわり 外回り 〈周囲〉the circumference; the perimeter; 〈環状線の〉the outer tracks ¶外回りをする 〈外勤〉work outside (the office).

そとわく 外枠 the outer [outside] frame.

ソナー sonar ★ sound navigation ranging からの頭字語.

そなえ 備え 〈準備〉preparation(s) 《for》; 《文》preparedness 《for, against》; 《文》provision 《for, against》; 〈設備〉equipment; 〈防備〉de-

---

ぞっと 考えただけでもぞっとする. The mere thought of it makes me shudder [sends a chill through me]. | It gives me the shivers [creeps] when I think of it. / 肉はあまりぞっとしない. I don't care much for meat. / 色がぞっとしない. The color is not much to my taste [fancy]. | The color leaves me cold.

そで 無いそでは振られぬ. You can't make something of nothing. / そで振り合うも他生の縁. Even a chance acquaintance is decreed [preordained] by destiny.

そと 外はとても寒い. It is very cold outside. / 彼はめったに外へ出ない. He never goes out. | He is a real stay-at-home.

そなえ 備えあれば憂いなし. Providing is preventing. 諺

そなえる お墓には花輪が供えられていた. A wreath was laid [There was a wreath] on the tomb.

そなわる 彼の学問好きは生まれつき彼に備わっていたものだ. His love of learning was bred in the bone.

そねむ やつらはそねんでそんなことを言うのだ. They say that sort of thing out of envy.

その² 10名合格して私もその1人でした. Ten of us passed the examination, myself among them.

そのうえ その特賞10万円の賞金までもらった. What is more, he was awarded a grand prize of ¥10,000.

そのうち ではまたそのうちに. See you again soon. | Well, goodbye until we meet again. / 10名負傷し, そのうち3名は重傷であった. Ten people were injured, three of them seriously.

そなえつけ 備え付け ¶備え付け器具 fittings; fixtures / 備え付けのベッド a fixed bed / 教員室に備え付けの図書 books kept in the teachers' room.

そなえつける 備え付ける equip (provide, fit, 《文》furnish) (with); install (a copying machine in the office) ¶電話を備え付ける have a telephone installed [fixed] (in *one's* room).

そなえもの 供え物 (make) an [《文》a votive] offering (to).

そなえる¹ 供える offer ((to a god)); make an offering ((to)) 《文》/ 花をお墓に供える offer [place] flowers on the tomb ((of)). 文例↓

そなえる² 備える 〈準備する〉 get [have, keep] sth ready [for]; prepare [make preparations] (for); provide [《文》make provision] (for, against); 〈蓄える〉 stock (a library with books); lay up [by]; 〈設備する〉 provide [《文》furnish] (with); equip [fit] (with); install; 〈具備する〉《文》possess; have; 《文》be endowed with ¶不時の出費に備える provide [《文》make provision] for unforeseen expenses; save (up) for a rainy day.

ソナタ 【音楽】a sonata ¶ソナタ形式 (in) sonata form.

ソナチネ 【音楽】a sonatina.

そなわる 備わる 〈人が主語〉《文》be possessed of; 《文》be endowed [gifted] with; possess; 〈物が主語〉《文》be inherent in ¶本来備わっている《文》inherent; 〈人に〉inborn; 《文》innate; inbuilt ((ability)) / 自然に備わっている品位 *one's* natural dignity. 文例↓

ソネット a sonnet.

そねみ 嫉み (a) jealousy; envy ⇒ねたみ, しっと.

そねむ 嫉む be jealous [envious] ((of *sb's* success)); envy *sb* ((*his* wealth)) ⇒ねたむ. 文例↓

その¹ 園 a garden ⇒にわ.

その² that; 〈前述の〉the same; ((the book)) in question; 〈強めて〉the very ((day)); 〈それの〉its. 文例↓

そのうえ その上 on top of that; in addition (to that); into the bargain; to crown it all; what is more; besides; 《文》moreover ¶その上困ったことには what is worse; to make matters worse.

そのうち ¶そのうちに 〈近いうちに〉before (very) long; one of these days; by and by; soon; sooner or later; 〈他日〉some day; 〈その間に〉in the meantime; meanwhile; 〈時が来れば〉in (due) course of time; in time. 文例↓

そのおり その折 on that occasion; at that time; then.

そのくせ その癖 and yet; still; for all that; though; all the same; nevertheless; none the less. 文例↓

そのくらい so [as] many [much]; that much; 《文》to that extent ((程度)). 文例↓

そのご その後 〈以後〉after that; afterward(s); 《文》thereafter; later (on); 《文》subsequently; 〈以来〉(ever) since; from that time on ¶その後の later; 《文》subsequent / その後になって later (on); at a later time / その後ずっと ever since. 文例↓

そのこと その事 that; the thing; the matter (in question). 文例↓

そのころ その頃 about [at] that time; then; in those days. 文例↓

ソノシート a flexible (phonograph) record.

そのすじ その筋 ¶その筋の命により by order of the authorities (concerned).

そのた その他 the others; the rest; 〈…など〉and others; et cetera ((略: etc.)); and so forth [on]; and the like; 《口語》and what not ¶…その他大勢 … and many others.

そのため その為 〈理由〉for that reason; 《文》accordingly; therefore; so; on that account [score]; 〈結果〉consequently; 〈目的〉for that purpose; 《文》to that end; for that. 文例↓

そのつど その都度 each [every] time ((*it* happens [《文》occurs])); 《文》on all such occasions.

そのとおり その通り just [quite] so; just like that. 文例↓

そのとき その時 at that time [moment]; then; on that occasion ¶その時の内閣 the then Cabinet. 文例↓

そのば その場 ¶その場で then and there;

そのくせ 彼は息子をずいぶんしかるけれど, その癖かわいくてたまらないのだ。He is forever scolding his son, but he loves him none the less.

そのくらい 本はそれだけじゃない, 2階にもまだそのくらいある。Those are not all the books I have. I have as many more upstairs. / そのくらいの借金でくよくよするにはあたらない。Such a trifling [small] debt is not worth worrying about. / そのくらいのことは知っている。I know that much.

そのご その後いかがですか。How have you been (getting along)? / 私はその後ずっとここにいる。I have been staying here ever since. / その後彼がどうなったかだれも知りません。Nobody knows what has become of him since.

そのこと そのことでしたら彼がよく知っていますよ。As for that, he knows all about it. / そのことにかけたら彼にかなう者はない。When it comes to that, no one can beat him. / そのことなんですよ。That's just what I was going to say.

そのころ その頃には私の仕事も終わっているでしょう。My work will have been finished by that time. / その頃としては大変な記録だった。It was a great record for those days.

そのため そのために彼の希望はいれられなかった。That's why [For that reason] his request was turned down.

そのとおり そのとおり。You are right. | That's right. | That's what it is. | You've said it !

そのとき 出かけようとしていたちょうどその時康夫から電話がか

そのはず その筈 [文例↓]

そのひ その日 (on) that day;〈強めて〉the very (same) day;(on) that particular day ¶その日のうちに before the day is over; by the end of the day / その日暮らしをする live from hand to mouth; earn a precarious living; scrape a living day by day. [文例↓]

そのひと その人 the (very) man; the person in question ¶社会党にその人ありと知られた A 氏 Mr. A, a leading [well-known] member of the Socialist Party.

そのへん その辺〈そこいら〉about [near] there;〈それくらい〉... or so; ... or thereabouts; in the neighborhood of... ¶どこかその辺に somewhere about there / その辺まで一緒に行こう go part of the way (with).

そのほう その方〈方角〉that direction (way);〈そちらの物〉that (one);〈その事〉that.

そのほか その外 the rest; the others ¶その外の other;〈それ以上の〉《文》additional;《文》further;〈その外たくさん[色々]の物〉many other things / その外に besides;《文》moreover; in addition; on top of that;《文》further. [文例↓]

そのまま ¶そのままにしておく leave [let] sth alone [rest there]; let (it) stand [go]; leave sth as it is [stands]; leave sth intact (untouched). [文例↓]

そのみち その道〈職業〉the line (of business); the profession; the trade;〈芸道〉the art;〈方面〉the field ¶その道の大家 an expert in the line [field] / その道の人の意見を聞く seek expert [professional] advice (on [about] sth).

そのもの その物 the very thing ¶真理その物を愛する love truth for its own sake / 正直その物を honesty itself. [文例↓]

そば¹ 側, 傍 a side;〈付近〉neighborhood; vicinity;《文》proximity ¶そばの neighboring;《文》adjacent; nearby;〈隣接する〉《文》contiguous ((to)); next ((to));《文》adjoining / そばを通る pass by sb [sth] / そばに〈傍らに〉by (the side of); at one's side; beside;〈近く〉near (by);《文》hard by; close by / そばに置く keep sth at hand / そばに寄る come [go,《文》draw] near (to).

そば² 蕎麦〔植〕buckwheat;〔食品〕soba; buckwheat noodles ¶そば粉 buckwheat (flour) / そば屋 a noodle restaurant [shop];〈人〉a noodle vendor.

そばかす a freckle;〔医〕a lentigo ((pl. -gines)) ¶そばかすのある freckled; sprinkled [peppered] with freckles.

そばだつ ⇒ そびえる.

そばだてる strain [prick (up)] (one's ears) ¶耳をそばだてて聞く listen with strained ears.

そばづえ 側杖 ¶そば杖を食う get a by-blow ((in their fight)).

ソビエト Soviet ¶ソビエト化する Sovietize / ソビエト社会主義共和国連邦 the Union of Soviet Socialist Republics (略: U.S.S.R.);〈略称〉the Soviet Union; Soviet Russia / ソビエト政府 the Soviet Government; the Kremlin.

そびえる 聳える rise; tower; soar ¶...の上にそびえる overtop...; / 雲にそびえる rise [tower] above the clouds; rise [soar] to the sky [skyward]. [文例↓]

そびやかす 聳やかす ¶肩をそびやかす raise [draw up] one's shoulders / 肩をそびやかして swaggeringly; with an air of triumph [superiority] / 肩をそびやかして歩く stalk [strut] about [along]; swagger about.

そびょう 素描 a (rough) sketch.

-そびれる fail to do; miss a chance [an opportunity] to do;〈恐れて〉dare not do.

そひん 粗品 ⇒ そしな.

そふ 祖父 a grandfather.

ソファー a sofa; a settee; a couch ¶ソファーベッド〈展開するとベッドになる〉a studio couch; a sofa bed;〈そのままベッドとしても使えるソファー〉a divan (bed).

ソフィア Sofia.

ソフト〈帽子〉(米) a soft hat; (英) a felt hat;〈つばびろの〉a slouch hat ¶ソフトな soft / ソフトウエア『コンピューター』software / ソフトカラー a soft collar / ソフトクリーム (a) soft ice cream /（ピアノの）ソフトペダル the soft pedal / ソフトボール (play) softball;〈ボール〉

かってきた. I was about to leave, when I had a call from Yasuo. / その時になってみなければわからない. We won't know [can't tell] till the time comes. / その時はその時さ. When the time comes, that will take care of itself. ｜ We'll think about it when the time comes. ｜ Let's cross that bridge [hurdle] when we come to it.

そのば その場にはだれも居合わさなかった. No one happened to be about [by]. / 彼の介入でその場は丸く収まった. His intervention settled the matter peacefully for the time being.

そのはず 彼女は彼と結婚するのはいやだと言ったが, それもそのはずずっと好きな人がいたのだ. She refused to marry him and no wonder. There was someone else that she was in love with.

そのひ その日のうちに帰京した. I returned to Tokyo the same day.

そのひと だれあろう学長その人であった. It was no less a person than the president. ｜ Who should it be but the president.

そのほか その外のことは何も知りません. I know nothing more. ｜ This is all I know.

そのまま 聞いた話をそのまま話した. I told [repeated] the story just as I had heard it. / そのままの方がいい. I like it better as it is. / 彼は家出をして, そのまま帰って来なかった. He ran away from home, never to return. / そのままそこにいなさい. Stay where you are. / この部屋は文豪の生前の状態そのままに保存されている. The room is preserved in just the state it was in during the great writer's lifetime.

そのもの その物が小図書館である. The book is really a small library in itself. / 君は健康その

a softball.

そふぼ 祖父母 grandparents.

ソプラノ 〖音楽〗soprano ¶ソプラノ歌手 a soprano (*pl.* -s); a soprano singer / ソプラノで歌う sing (in) soprano.

そぶり 素振り a manner; behavior;〈様子〉an air; a sign;〈顔つき〉a look ¶そぶりが怪しい *sb's* behavior is suspicious; be behaving suspiciously / 変なそぶりをする act [behave] strangely. 文例⇩

そぼ 祖母 a grandmother.

そほう 粗放 ¶粗放な careless; reckless / 粗放農業[農法] extensive agriculture [farming].

そぼう 粗暴 ¶粗暴な rough; rude; ill-mannered; boorish; unpolished; unrefined; uncouth; uncivilized;《文》uncivil / 粗暴な振舞をする act [behave] rudely; be rude (to *sb*).

そほうか 素封家 ⇨ ふごう³.

そぼく 素朴 simplicity;《文》naiveté;《文》artlessness ¶素朴な simple; unsophisticated; unaffected;《文》artless;《文》ingenuous.

そぼふる そぼ降る drizzle ¶そぼ降る雨 drizzling rain; a drizzle.

そぼろ powdered fish; (sugared) fish powder.

そまつ 粗末 ¶粗末な coarse; crude; inferior; shabby; humble; plain; poor / 粗末な品《口》an article of poor [inferior] quality / お粗末な理論 an ill-prepared theory / 粗末にする〈物を〉waste; spend (*one's money*) recklessly; use [handle] *sth* roughly; treat [handle] *sth* without due respect (神聖なものを);〈なおざりにする〉be careless about [《文》of]; neglect;〈人を〉treat *sb* unkindly [coldly];《文》slight;《文》make little of. 文例⇩

ソマリア Somalia ¶ソマリアの Somalian / ソマリア人 a Somalian / ソマリア民主共和国 the Somali Democratic Republic.

ソマリランド Somaliland ⇨ ソマリア.

そまる 染まる dye (well); be dyed (black); be tinged (with red) (薄く);〈感染する〉be tainted [infected, stained,《文》imbued] (with);《文》be steeped (in vice). 文例⇩

そむく 背く〈従わない〉disobey (*one's father*); defy (*public opinion*);〈違反する〉be [act] against (*one's principles*); be [act] contrary to (*sb's expectations*);《文》violate (a rule); break (the regulations); fly in the face of (convention);《文》contravene (the custom); offend [《文》transgress] against (the law);〈裏切る〉betray *sb*;《文》play *sb* false; be untrue to *sb*;〈反逆する〉rebel [revolt] against (*one's ruler*); turn traitor to (*one's country*) ¶法の精神に背く run counter to the spirit of the law / 約束に背く break [go back on] *one's* word (promise) / 規則に背いて against [(《文》in contravention of] the rule / 親の意に背いて against *one's* parents' wishes / 名に背かない be true to *one's* name [reputation]; be worthy of the name; live [act] up to *one's* reputation. 文例⇩

そむける 背ける ¶顔を背ける turn *one's* face away (from) / 目を背ける《文》avert *one's* eyes (from); look away (from).

そめ 染め dyeing ¶染めがいい[悪い] be well [badly] dyed.

そめもの 染物 dyeing goods; goods to be dyed ¶染物業 the textile dyeing industry / 染物工場 a dye-works《単複同形》/ 染物屋〈人〉a dyer;〈店〉a dyehouse.

そめもよう 染模様 a printed [dyed] pattern [design, figure].

そめる 染める〈染料で〉dye;〈彩色する〉color; paint (*one's face*); tinge (薄く) ¶黒く染める dye *sth* black / 血に染める stain (*one's hands*) with blood / 顔を赤く染める blush; turn red [crimson] / 染め返す redye / 緑に染め替える dye *sth* over green / 染め過ぎる overdye / 染め抜く leave (a pattern) undyed (on a field of red) / 染め分ける dye in different [various] colors.

そもう 梳毛 ¶梳(ﾞ)いた羊毛 combed wool;〈梳く羊毛〉combing [long] wool ¶梳毛糸 worsted yarn; worsted / 梳毛機 a combing [carding] machine.

そもそも 〈第一に〉in the first place; to begin with;〈一体〉《what [who, when, etc.]》on earth; at all. 文例⇩

そや 粗野 ¶粗野な《文》rustic; boorish; unpolished; unrefined; crude;《文》impolite; rough; coarse; vulgar / 粗野な趣味 unsophisticated《vulgar》taste / 粗野な態度をとる be impolite (to *sb*).

そよ 文例⇩

そよう 素養 (a) knowledge (of); a grounding

ものだ. You're [You look] the very picture of health!／(肖像を見て)浜田氏そのものじゃないかい. Isn't it Mr. Hamada to the life?

そば 坊や, そばを離れちゃいけないよ. Keep close to me, dear.／火のそばに寄るな. Keep away from the fire.／君などは彼のそばへも寄りつけないよ. You are no match for him.｜You [can't [aren't fit to] hold a candle to him.／私は教わるそばから忘れてしまう. I forget as soon as I learn.

そびえる 東京の西方に富士がそびえている. To the west of Tokyo rises the peak of Mt. Fuji.

そぶり 彼はぶっとおし12時間仕事をしているが, 疲れたそぶりも見せない. He has been at work for twelve hours on end but shows no sign of tiredness [of being tired].／不平などはおくびにさえ出さなかった. He did not betray his dissatisfaction either in his look or in his manner.

そまつ 自分の時間を粗末にする者は他人の時間をも粗末にしがちだ. Those who are careless about their own time are apt to make light of others'.

そまる この生地はよく染まる. This material takes dye well.

そむく ご信任に背かないようにいたします. I will try to be worthy of your trust.／これでは先例に背く. This is against all precedents.／彼は我々に背いてそんなことをした. He played us false in doing so.

そもそも そもそもそう考えてよいか問題がある. To begin with, the whole idea [the idea itself] is open to question.／そもそもどこでそれを手に入れたのか. Where on earth did you get them?

そよ 風がそよとも吹かなかった. There

そよかぜ そよ風 a gentle [light] breeze; a soft wind; a breath of air.

そよぐ 〈さらさら鳴る〉rustle; 〈動く〉stir; flutter; 〈揺らぐ〉sway; wave; 〈震える〉tremble; quiver. 文例↓

そよそよ gently; softly.

そら¹ 空 the sky; the air; 《文》the heavens; 《文》the firmament ¶空の旅 an air trip; travel by air [plane] / 空を飛ぶ fly in the air / 空から見ると, … (seen) from the air, … / 空飛ぶ円盤 a flying saucer / UFO 《pl. UFO's, UFOs》(★ unidentified flying object の略. 発音は [júːfou] または [jú(ː)fou]) / 空高く high up in the sky [air] / 《文》(soar) skyward (空の方へ) / そらで覚える [覚えている] learn [know] sth by heart / そらで読む recite 《a poem》from memory / 心もそらに くれしくて〉as if one was [were] treading on air; 〈ぼんやりして〉absent-mindedly / そらを使う pretend not to know, 《文》feign ignorance. 文例↓

そら² there!; here!; look! 文例↓

そらいろ 空色 ¶空色(の)sky-blue; 《文》azure.

そらうそぶく 空嘯く feign indifference; put on [assume] a nonchalant air [an air of unconcern] / そらうそぶいて with an indifferent [a nonchalant] air; nonchalantly.

そらおそろしい 空恐ろしい ⇨ おそろしい ¶そら恐ろしい気がする 《文》have an unfathomable fear [apprehension]; feel alarmed; feel gloomy (about the future).

そらす¹ 反らす bend; curve ¶身体を反らす bend oneself backward / 胸を反らす throw [stick] one's chest out; be inflated [puffed up] with pride [self-importance]. 文例↓

そらす² 逸らす turn sth aside [away]; 《文》 avert sth 《from》; divert [deflect] sth 《from》; 〈よける〉elude; dodge; evade ¶目をそらす turn one's eyes away 《from》/ 話をわきにそらす change [divert] the subject 《from, into》/ 人をそらさない friendly; affable / 《文》suave / 注意をそらす〈事が主語〉distract [divert] one's attention 《from》.

そらぞらしい 空々しい 〈虚偽の〉false; 《文》feigned; empty; 〈見えすいた〉thin; transparent; hypocritical ¶そらぞらしいうそをつく tell a transparent [《文》palpable] lie / そらぞらしいお世辞を言う pay hollow compliments 《to》.

そらだのみ 空頼み a vain [an empty] hope; hoping against hope ¶そら頼みする hope against hope (for sth, that…). 文例↓

そらとぼける 空惚ける feign ignorance; play [do] the innocent; pretend not to know [《文》to be ignorant 《of》].

そらなみだ 空涙 ¶そら涙を流す shed crocodile [false, sham] tears.

そらに 空似 an accidental resemblance (between strangers); a chance likeness. 文例↓

そらまめ 空豆 〖植〗a broad bean; a horsebean; a fava bean.

そらみみ 空耳 〈聞き違い〉mishearing. 文例↓

そらもよう 空模様 (the look of) the sky [weather] ¶この空模様では (judging from the look of) the sky.

そらんじる 諳じる ⇨ あんしょう¹(暗誦する), あんき²(暗記する).

そり¹ 橇 〈大形の馬・となかいなどが引く〉a sleigh; 〈小形の〉《米》a sled; 《英》a sledge ¶そりに乗る [で行く, で滑る] ride [go] in a sled [sledge]; sled [sleigh] (along, down the hill); travel by sleigh / そり犬 a sled dog.

そり² 反り a warp (板の); a curve; a bend; an arch (橋の) ¶反りが合わない do not [cannot] get along [on] 《with sb》; do not [cannot] hit it off 《with sb》; do not fit well 《with》/ 反り橋 an arch(ed) bridge.

---

was not a breath of air.

そよう 英語の素養がなくてはこの仕事は勤まらない. You cannot tackle this job without some knowledge of English.

そよぐ 樹木が風にそよいでいた. The trees were sighing [《文》soughing] in the wind.

そら¹ 空ににじが出た. A rainbow appeared across the sky. / ややもすれば心がそらになって, 先生の言うことを聞き漏らした. My thoughts wandered so much that I often missed what the teacher said.

そら² そらサイレンだ. There goes the siren. / そらご覧. There (you are)! What did I tell you? / そらここにあるよ. Here it is. | Here you are! / そらやるよ. There you are! | Here, take it!

そらす¹ 〈体操の号令〉はい次は, 足を開いて, からだを2回思いきりそらす! Next, stand with your legs apart and bend backward as far as you can twice.

そらだのみ 私の期待はそら頼みだった. My hopes were not fulfilled [did not materialize].

そらに 他人のそら似ということがある. There is such a thing as resemblance between people who are not related.

そらみみ それは君のそら耳だよ. You only fancy [imagine] you heard it. | It's only your fancy [imagination]. / 鉄砲の音がする. —それはそら耳だよ. I hear gunfire.—It's in your head [Your ears are playing tricks on you].

そらもよう 怪しい空模様だ. The weather [sky] looks threatening.

それ¹ よく撮れた写真だ, それはそれで結構な物である. A good photograph is a fine thing in its own right.

それ² ドアが開くと, 皆それっとばかり売り場に殺到した. The instant the door opened they all rushed to the counter as if at a signal. / 知らせを受けてそれっとばかりに皆避難現場に駆けつけた. The moment they received the news, they all rushed to the scene of the disaster.

それこそ それこそおあつらえ向きだ. That's just the thing. / それこそ我の求めていたものだ. That's the very thing I wanted. / あの男を怒らせたらそれこそ大変だ. If you provoke him [make him angry], there will be the devil to pay.

それぞれ 各人それぞれの理想がある. Everyone has his own ideal. / 物にはそれぞれ取り柄がある. Everything is useful in its own way. / x, y, z をそれぞれ 2, 3, 5 としてみよう. Let x, y and z be

そりあじ 剃り味 ¶そり味がいい〈かみそりが主語〉 shave (very) well.
そりかえる 反り返る〈曲がる〉 bend backward ; warp ; get warped ; 〈身体が〉 throw one's head back ; stick [throw] out one's chest ; 〈威張る〉 hold one's head high ¶縁の反り返った花びん a vase with a recurved rim / 爪先の反り返った靴 shoes (that are) turned up at the toes.
ソリスト〔音楽〕a soloist.
ソリッドステート ¶ソリッドステートの solid-state (circuitry).
そりみ 反り身 ¶反り身になる throw one's head [shoulders] back ; stick [throw] out one's chest.
そりゃく 粗略 ⇨ そまつ, ぞんざい.
そりゅうし 素粒子〔物〕an elementary [a subatomic, a fundamental] particle ¶素粒子物理学 particle physics / 素粒子論 the theory of elementary particles.
そる¹ 反る warp ; be warped ; curve ; be curved ; be arched〈橋などが〉; 〈身体・指などが〉bend backward [back].
そる² 剃る shave ; 〈そってもらう〉get [have] a shave ¶顔をそる shave (oneself) ; get (oneself) shaved〈そらせる〉/ そり落とす shave off《one's mustache》/ きれいにそった顔 a clean-shaven face.
それ¹ that ; it ¶それもそうだが It may be so, but... / それはそれとして setting it aside ; apart from that ;《文》be that as it may / それはそれで in its own way / それ以来 since (then). 文例⇩
それ² there! ; look (out)! 文例⇩
それかあらぬか I don't know whether it is because of that (or not), but....
それから〈そのあと〉after that ; 〈それ以来〉since (then) ; 〈そのついでに〉and (then) ; 〈そして〉and ¶それから 1 週間後に a week after [later] / それからそれと one after another / それからそれと用事がある have no end of business.

それくらい ⇨ そのくらい.
それこそ 文例⇩
それしきの so trifling ⇨ そのくらい.
それじたい それ自体 in itself ;《文》per se ; for its own sake.
それぞれ each ;《文》severally ; respectively ★ respectively は文例にみるように,「それぞれ, 今挙げた順に」の意を含む /《文》respective ;《文》several ; one's [its] own ; each. 文例⇩
それだから (and) so ; so that ; therefore ; for that reason ; accordingly ; consequently ; on that account [score]. 文例⇩
それだけ that [so] much ; as much ;《文》to that extent [degree] ; 〈そのことだけ〉only that ; that alone ; 〈それっきり〉no more than that ¶...すればするほど, それだけますますthe more..., the more.... 文例⇩
それだま 逸れ玉 a stray bullet.
それ(っ)きり 〈それだけ〉no more than that ; 〈それ以来〉since (then). 文例⇩
それで〈そこで〉and ; (and) then ; 〈それだから〉⇨ それだから.
それでいて ⇨ そのくせ.
それでこそ 文例⇩
それでは then ; if so ; if that is the case ; 〈別れる時〉well, ...
それでも but (still) ; and yet ; nevertheless ; still ; for all that ;《文》notwithstanding. 文例⇩
それどころか それ所か on the contrary ; far from that. 文例⇩
それとなく indirectly ; casually ; in a casual way [《文》manner] ;《文》as if not so intended ; as if by accident ¶それとなく言う hint (at) ; drop a hint ;《文》allude (to) ; insinuate / それとなく探りを入れる sound sb《about sth》.
それとも or ; (or) else.
それなのに ⇨ それでも.
それなりに in its own way ; after its fashion ; 〈そのままに〉as it is [stands]. 文例⇩
それに besides ; moreover ; into the bargain ⇨ そのうえ.

2, 3 and 5, respectively.
それだから それだからこそ友達もたくさんいるのだ. That is why he has so many friends.
それだけ 今日はそれだけにしよう. That's all [We'll leave it at that] for today. | Well, call it a day there [now]. / それだけか. Is that all? / それだけは真っ平だ. I will do anything but that. / 話はそれだけのことだ. That's all there is to it. / それだけでは詩にならない. That alone will not make a poem. / この子は体が弱いから, それだけによけいかわいいのです. I love this boy all the more because he is delicate. / よい事をすればそれだけの事がある. A good deed will have its reward. / 今出かければ, それだけ早く帰れるよ. If you start now, you will be back that much

sooner. / この種の建物は費用もかかるが, それだけに丈夫できる. A building of this sort is as strong as it is expensive. / 富はそれだけでは大したものではない. Wealth, as such, doesn't matter much.
それ(っ)きり それっきり彼に会わない. I haven't seen him since. | That was the last I saw of him. | I have seen no more of him. / そのとき別れて, それっきり再び会うことはついになかった. We parted then, never to meet again. / その話はそれっきりになった. There was no further development regarding the proposal.
それでこそ それでこそ男だ. That's worthy of a man. / それでこそ彼だよ. That's just like him. | That's typical of him.

それでも 随分勉強するのだが, それでも学校の成績はあまりかんばしくない. For all his hard work, he is still not doing well at school [his grades are still unsatisfactory]. / 確かにいろいろ欠点のある人ですけれども, それでもやはり私はあの人が好きなんです. It is true he has shortcomings, but I love him for all that.
それどころか それどころか食うや食わずのありさまだ. On the contrary, I can hardly make a living. / それどころか自分の仕事で忙しい. I am too busy with my work to care about that.
それなりに それなりに面白い. It is interesting in its own way. / 事件はそれなりになっている. The matter has been left as it was. | The matter remains unsettled.

それにしても ⇒ それでも. 文例↓
それにつけても 文例↓
それはそうと by the way; by the by(e); well; now, while you're at it, ...
それほど so; so [that] much; 〈否定〉(not) very [so]. 文例↓
それまで 〈その時まで〉till [until] then; till [up to, until] that time; 〈そんなに長く〉so long; 〈それほど〉⇒ それほど ¶それまでには by then [that time]. 文例↓
それも and that; at that. 文例↓
それゆえ それ故 ⇒ それだから.
それる 逸れる turn away [aside]; veer away (from); 〈話などが〉stray [deviate, 《文》digress] (from); 〈弾丸が〉miss; go astray [wild] ¶的をそれる miss the target; go wide of the mark / 〈話が〉わき道へそれる wander [《文》digress] from the subject [point].
ソれん ソ連 the Soviet Union; Soviet Russia ⇒ ソビエト ¶ソ連国旗 the hammer and sickle / ソ連人 a Russian.
ソロ 《音楽》(play) a solo (pl. -s).
ゾロアスターきょう ゾロアスター教 Zoroastrianism; Mazdaism ¶ゾロアスター教徒 a Zoroastrian.
そろい 揃い a set; a suit ⇒ おそろい ¶そろいの matching; 《文》uniform; of the same pattern / 家具ひとそろい a suite of furniture / 食器ひとそろい a table service / 茶器ひとそろい a set of tea-things / 馬具ひとそろい a suit of harness.
ソロイスト 《音楽》a soloist.
そろう¹ 疎漏 〈不注意〉carelessness; 《文》inadvertence; 〈見落とし〉an oversight ¶疎漏な careless; 《文》heedless; negligent; 《文》inadvertent. 文例↓
そろう² 揃う 〈完全になる〉be [《文》become] complete; 〈対になる〉make a pair [set]; 〈一様になる〉be equal [《文》uniform]; 〈集まる〉gather; meet; assemble; 〈釣り合う〉match ¶そろった 〈完全な〉complete; perfect; 〈等しい〉even; equal; 〈一様な〉《文》uniform; regular 《teeth》/ そろわない incomplete; unequal; uneven; irregular / そろって 〈一団となって〉in a body; en masse; *en bloc*; 〈皆一緒に〉all together; 〈皆一様に〉all alike / そろって出かける go all together / そろいもそろって every (last) one of them; one and all; without a single exception. 文例↓
そろえる 揃える 〈並べる〉arrange; put 《the books》in order; line up 《the equipment needed》; 〈一様にする〉make *sth* even [《文》uniform] ¶数をそろえる complete [make up] the number / 板の端をそろえる true up the edges of the boards / 家具をそろえる get a complete suite of furniture / 漱石の作品をそろえている have a complete set of Soseki [Soseki's works] / 色々な商品をそろえている keep a rich assortment of goods in stock.
そろそろ 〈ゆっくり〉slowly; leisurely; 〈静かに〉softly; gently; 〈だんだんに〉gradually; little by little; by (slow) degrees; 〈やがて〉by and by; soon ¶そろそろと歩く walk very slowly [at a snail's pace]. 文例↓
ぞろぞろ in great numbers; in a crowd; in droves; in succession ¶ぞろぞろ入って行く [出て行く] stream [file, troop] into [out of] 《a room》/ ぞろぞろやって来る come in a stream (*to*). 文例↓
そろばん 算盤 an [a Japanese] abacus (*pl.* -cuses, abaci) ¶そろばんが合う [合わない] pay [do not pay] / そろばんの取れる profitable; paying / そろばんをはじく use an abacus; 〈比喩的に〉act from selfish motives; be guided by self-interest (*in doing*) / そろばんで計算する count [reckon] on the abacus / そろばんずくの calculating; mercenary; 《文》(be) bent on gain; commercial(ly)-minded / そろばん玉 a counter; a bead (on an abacus). 文例↓
ソロモンしょとう ソロモン諸島 〈国名〉the Solomon Islands.
そわせる 添わせる match 《a man with a woman》; marry 《a girl to a man》; 《文》unite 《the lovers》in marriage.
そわそわ ¶そわそわする be [grow] restless; fidget; be fidgety; be nervous; be excited; be on tenterhooks. 文例↓

それにしても また山で3人死んだ. —そう, それにしても近頃山の遭難が多いわねえ. Three more people have died in the mountains.—Have they? There really seem to have been even more mountain tragedies than usual lately, don't there?

それにつけても それにつけても思い出されるのは死んだ兄だ. That reminds me of my late brother.

それほど それほどひどい病気でもない. It is not a very serious illness.

それまで それまでは無難だった. Up to that point [So far] everything had gone well (with us). / 病人はそれまで持つまい. I fear the patient may not live so long.

それも 彼は間違いをする, それもしょっちゅう. He makes mistakes, and very often at that. / あの店のコーヒーは 500 円もするし, それもあんまりうまくないコーヒーじゃない. They charge 500 yen for only a cup of coffee, and not a very good one at that.

それる 彼女は私を避けるかのように横町にそれてしまった. She ducked into an alley as if to avoid me. / 台風は東京をそれた. The typhoon swerved away from Tokyo.

そろう¹ 万事疎漏のないようにしなさい. See (to it) that everything is as it should be.

そろう² 皆そろったかね. Is everybody here? / もう1冊あると全部そろう. One more volume will complete the set. / あの人の所には中国の美術品がよくそろっている. He has a good collection of Chinese works of art. / そろいもそろってばかりだ. They are fools, every one of them. / うちの学校には立派な先生がそろっている. Our school has a good staff of teachers.

そろそろ そろそろ暗くなってきた. It is getting dark. / もうそろそろ蚊の出る頃だ. We'll soon have mosquitoes. / そろそろ出かけよう. Let's be going [moving, off]. / もうそろそろお昼だ. It is getting on for noon. / もうそろそろ桜んぼの季節だ. It is about the season for cherries.

ぞろぞろ 子供たちがぞろぞろサンドイッチマンの後について行った. A troop of children followed close on the heels of the sand-

そん 損 (a) loss；〈不利〉(a) disadvantage; a handicap；a drawback；〈損害〉damage ¶損な unprofitable；〈文〉disadvantageous; unfavorable / 損な目に会う have [get] a bad deal / 損をする lose (money) (over)；suffer [incur] a loss；be a loser / 損をかける〈文〉inflict a loss upon sb；cause sb a loss / 損をして得をする〈文〉sow loss and reap gain；gain by losing / 損を埋め合わせる make good [make up (for)] the loss / 損を補償する〈文〉cover [compensate for] the loss / 損として売る sell sth at a loss [below cost] / 損になる do not pay；〈文〉be to one's disadvantage. 文例↓

そんえき 損益 profit and loss ¶損益勘定 the profit-and-loss account / 損益計算書 a profit-and-loss statement.

そんかい 村会 a village assembly ¶村会議員 a member of a village assembly.

そんがい 損害 〈損傷〉damage；(an) injury；harm；〈損失〉(a) loss；〈死傷〉casualties ¶損害を与える damage；injure；〈文〉inflict a loss (on)；cause damage [losses] (to)；inflict damage (on the enemy) / 損害を被る〈to〉／損害を被る suffer [〈文〉sustain] a loss；suffer damage / 損害を賠償する make good [〈文〉repair] the loss [compensate [〈文〉indemnify] sb for his loss [losses, the damage] / 3百万円の損害 damage [a loss] of [amounting to] ¥3,000,000 / 大損害 a heavy loss / 損害高[額] the damage；the loss；the amount of the damage / 損害賠償 ⇒そんがいばいしょう / 損害保険 nonlife [property] insurance / 損害見込みの estimated damage [loss]. 文例↓

ぞんがい 存外 ⇒あんがい

そんがいばいしょう 損害賠償 【法】(a) compensation for damage [the loss]；reparation for injury；indemnity；〈賠償金〉damages ★ damage が複数形になるのはこの意味のときだけ．またこの意味では複数形が常 ¶損害賠償を請求する claim [demand] damages / 損害賠償の訴訟を起こす go to law (against sb) for damages；sue sb for damages / 損害賠償金(obtain) damages. 文例↓

そんきょ 蹲踞 ¶そんきょの姿勢をとる《相撲》assume the ritual squat (before a match).

そんけい 尊敬 respect；〈文〉esteem；(文)reverence ¶尊敬する respect；〈文〉esteem；honor；〈文〉hold sb in respect [esteem, honor]；have respect [a high regard] for；look up to；think much [highly] of；〈敬意を表わす〉show one's respect for / …を尊敬して out of respect for / 〈文〉in deference to / 大いに尊敬している[あまり尊敬していない] have great [do not have much] respect (for sb) / 尊敬すべき honorable / 〈文〉estimable；〈文〉worthy of respect [esteem] / 大政治家として尊敬される be looked up to as a great statesman / 尊敬を受けるに値する be respected (by) / 尊敬の respect (of)；〈文〉be held in high esteem (by). 文例↓

そんげん 尊厳 dignity；prestige ¶尊厳を傷つける[保つ]〈文〉impair [maintain] the dignity (of) / 人間の尊厳 the dignity of man.

そんざい 存在 existence；〈文〉being ¶存在する exist；be in existence [〈文〉being]；〈残存する〉remain；〈文〉be extant / 自分の存在を(人々に)意識させる make one's presence felt / 存在を認める recognize the existence (of) / 存在を認められる be recognized；win recognition / 存在理由〈文〉the [its, one's] raison d'être；its [one's] reason for existing [being]；its [one's] justification for existence / 存在論【哲】ontology. 文例↓

ぞんざい ¶ぞんざいな〈失礼な〉rude；〈文〉impolite；rough；〈不注意な〉careless；〈文〉negligent；〈雑な〉slovenly；slipshod；sloppy / 口のきき方がぞんざいである be rough [rude, short] in one's speech；be rough-spoken. 文例↓

そんしつ 損失 (a) loss ⇒そん, そんがい ¶損失を被る suffer [〈文〉sustain, have] a loss / 損失を与える cause a loss (to)；inflict a loss (on). 文例↓

そんしょう¹ 尊称 a title (of honor)；an honorific (title).

そんしょう² 損傷 (an) injury；damage ¶身体の内部の損傷 an internal injury / 損傷を与える damage；injure；impair；do harm [injury]

---

wich man.

そろばん 世の中はそろばんどおりには行かない．Few things in the world turn out as calculated.

そわそわ 彼女はそわそわしていた. She was in a fidget. / 彼はそわそわして, じっと椅子に座っていられなかった. He was very nervous and couldn't sit still in the chair.

そん それが6千円なら買っても損はない. It's not a bad bargain [deal] at 6,000 yen. / 道を間違えて30分以上損をしました. I took the wrong road, and wasted more than half an hour. / それは君のために損だ. It is against your interests. / それをほうっておくのは損だ. It is to your disadvantage to leave it as it is. / し そんなことをすると大変な損になるだろう. It would involve a big loss. / 彼は損になるような金は出さない男だ. He always gets value for his money. / そうしても損にはならないさ. You will lose nothing by doing so. | You would not be any the worse for it.

そんがい この台風でこれらの地方の稲作は大損害を受けた. The typhoon has done a lot of damage to the rice crop in these regions. / 損害は約5千万円の見込み. The damage [loss] is estimated [put] at about fifty million yen. / 損害高は2千万円だ. The damage comes [amounts] to twenty million yen.

そんがいばいしょう 就業中に片腕切断したことに対して, 彼は会社に1千万円の損害賠償を要求した. He claimed ¥10,000,000 damages [compensation] from his employers for the loss of an arm while at work.

そんけい エリオット氏に対する彼女の尊敬が高まった. Mr. Eliot rose in her esteem.

そんざい 彼はその小説で存在を認められるようになった. The novel won him public recognition.

ぞんざい 仕上げがぞんざいだ. The workmanship is slovenly [slipshod].

そんしつ 氏の亡くなられたことは史学界にとって大きな損失である. His death is a serious loss to the world of historical scholarship.

そんしょく 遜色 ((to)); (文) inflict injury ((on)) / 脳に損傷を受ける suffer brain damage / 損傷を被る be damaged; be injured; (文) sustain an injury; suffer a loss / 損傷を免れる escape damage.

そんしょく 遜色 ¶遜色がある be inferior ((to)) / 遜色がない bear [stand] comparison ((with)); be equal ((to)); compare favorably ((with)); (文) be by no means inferior ((to)). 文例⇩

そんじょそこら 文例⇩

そんじる 損じる 〈痛める〉 damage; injure; (文) impair; hurt; 〈痛む〉 be damaged; be injured; be spoiled; wear (out); 〈故障する〉 get out of order / 機嫌を損じる〈自分が〉 get out of humor; take offense ((at)); be offended ((by)); 〈人の〉 offend; hurt sb's feelings; (文) incur the disfavor [displeasure] of sb.

ぞんじる 存じる 〈知る〉 know; be aware ((of)); 〈思う〉 think.

そんする 存する 〈存在する〉 exist; live; 〈残存する〉 (文) remain (in existence); 〈保存する〉 keep; preserve; retain; 〈…にある〉 (文) lie [consist] in; (文) reside in; (文) rest with; 〈依存する〉 depend on.

そんぞく[1] 存続 continuation; (文) continuance; duration ¶存続する continue (to exist [be]); (文) endure; last / 存続させる continue; maintain; retain; keep up.

そんぞく[2] 尊属【法】 an ascendant ¶直系[傍系]尊属 a lineal [collateral] ascendant.

そんだい 尊大 haughtiness; arrogance; (文) imperiousness; hauteur ¶尊大な haughty; arrogant; self-important; overbearing; (文) imperious; supercilious; disdainful; (文) pompous; domineering / 尊大ぶる[に構える] behave haughtily; put on [give oneself] airs; assume an air of importance [superiority, hauteur]; lord [queen] it ((over)).

そんたく 忖度 ¶忖度する (文) surmise; guess; (文) conjecture.

そんち 存置 ¶存置する retain; maintain.

そんちょう[1] 村長 a village headman [chief].

そんちょう[2] 尊重 ¶尊重する (文) esteem; respect; have respect [a high regard] for sth; hold sth in high regard; prize; value; think highly [much] of; pay serious attention ((to)); give sth serious consideration / 尊重すべき (文) estimable; (文) worthy (of esteem).

ゾンデ【気象】 a sonde.

そんとく 損得 loss and gain; profit and loss; 〈利害〉 interests ¶損得を計算する calculate the loss and gain ((of)); 〈差し引き勘定をする〉 balance the profits and losses ((of)) / 損得ずくで for money [(文) mere gain]; (文) for mercenary reasons / 損得を離れて (文) from disinterested motives. 文例⇩

そんな such; like that; of that sort [kind] ¶そんな時には in a case like that; then; (文) on such an occasion / そんなに so; so much; like that; 〈格別〉 particularly; 〈否定〉 (not) very [as, so] / そんなにまで as much [far] as (all) that; (文) to such an extent; so [that, (文) thus] far [much] / そんな風に that way; in that manner / そんな訳で therefore; for that reason; (文) such being the case. 文例⇩

そんなこんなで (what) with [for, by] this thing and that [one thing and another]; with [for, owing to]…and what not.

そんのう 尊王 reverence for the Emperor ¶尊王家 a royalist. 文例⇩

そんぱい 存廃 (文) (the question of) maintenance (or abolition); existence.

そんぷうし 村夫子 a village schoolmaster; (文) a rustic moralist.

ぞんぶん 存分 ¶存分に to one's heart's content; as much as one likes [wants]; freely; (文) without reserve / 存分に食べる[飲む] eat [drink] one's fill ((of)) / 存分に才能を発揮する (文) give free scope [full play] to one's talent; let one's ability have full play.

そんぼう 存亡 life or death; existence; fate; (文) destiny ¶危急存亡 ➡ ききゅう[1].

そんみん 村民 the villagers; the village people [folk].

ぞんめい 存命 ¶存命中に (文) in life; while sb is [was] alive; in sb's lifetime.

そんらく 村落 a village; a hamlet (小さな) ¶村落共同体 a village community.

そんりつ 存立 ¶存立を危くする threaten the existence ((of)).

そんしょく この点においては日本は中国に比べてあえて遜色を見ない。In this regard Japan can stand comparison with China.

そんじょそこら これはそんじょそこらにある代物とは違うんだ。This isn't the sort you'll find on every corner.

そんとく 損得などどうでも構わん。I don't give a damn whether I gain or lose. / 双方損得なしで終わった。They finished by breaking even.

そんな そんなはずはない。That can't be right [so, true]. / そんなような事を言った。He said something to that effect. / そんなに使ったのか。Did you spend as much as that? / まあそんなとこだ。That's about it. / そんな事を言ったかもしれませんが、そんな言い方はしなかったはずです。I may have said something like that, but I can't have put it that way. / 私の欲しいのはそんなんじゃない。That isn't what I want. / おや, もうそんな時間ですか。Oh, dear! Is it as late as that? / 情勢がそんなに悪化しているとは知らなかった。I didn't realize the situation was that [quite so] bad. / そんなこともある。It sometimes happens like that.

そんのう 近代日本の到来を告げたスローガンが尊王攘夷であった。The battle cry that ushered in the modern era in Japan was 'Revere the Emperor and expel the barbarians'.

た

た[1] 田 a rice field ; 〈水田〉 a paddy field ; a (rice) paddy ¶田を耕す plow [till] a rice field / 田に水を引く irrigate [flood] a rice field.
た[2] 他 ⇨ほか, そのた. [文例⇩]
た[3] 多 ¶多とする appreciate ; be grateful [thankful] for ; think highly of.
だあ ¶だあとなる be dum(b)founded 《by the rebuke》.
ダークホース a dark horse.
ダース a dozen; 〈略字〉 doz. 《単複とも》 ¶ビール1ダース a dozen bottles of beer / ハンカチ5ダース five dozen handkerchiefs / 幾ダースも dozens of... ; ...by dozens / ダース売りする sell 《pencils》 by the dozen. [文例⇩]
[用法] dozen の用法は hundred, thousand の用法に準じる．すなわち，dozen の前に数詞及び a few, several, quite a few などが来るときは複数形の -s をつけない．some だけは例外で，some dozen eggs と言うと「約1ダースの卵」という意味になるので，some dozens of eggs と言わなければならない．しかし，この場合も several dozen eggs と言う方がいい．「鉛筆2ダース」は two dozen pencils で，two dozen of pencils とは言わないが，名詞(この例では pencils)の前に限定詞 (the, these, those など) があるときは of が用いられる．例 : two dozen of these pencils.
タートルネック ¶タートルネックのセーター a turtleneck [turtle-necked] sweater ; 《米》 a turtleneck ; 《英》 a polo-neck(ed) sweater.
ターバン 《wear》 a turban ¶ターバンを巻いた turbaned 《Pakistani》.
ダービー the Derby.
タービン a turbine ¶ガス[蒸気, 水力]タービン a gas [steam, water] turbine.
ターボジェット a turbojet (engine) ¶ターボジェット機 a turbojet.
ターボプロップ a turboprop (engine) ; a turbo-propeller engine ¶ターボプロップ機 a turbo-prop.
ターミナル a 《bus》 terminal ; 〈終着駅〉 a terminus 《*pl.* -es, -ni》 ¶ターミナルデパート a department store at a railroad terminal.
タール tar ¶タールを塗る tar ; put tar 《on *sth*》.
ターン 〘水泳・ダンス〙 a turn ¶ターンする turn ; make a 《quick》 turn.
ターンテーブル a turntable.
ターンパイク a turnpike (road).

たい[1] 他意 other intentions ; 《文》 an ulterior motive. [文例⇩]
たい[2] 体 ¶体をかわす dodge ; avoid ; get out of the way of 《*sb's* punch》 / 体をあずける〘相撲〙 lean on 《*one's* opponent》 with all *one's* weight ; put *one's* full weight on 《*one's* opponent》 / 体を成す take [get into] shape ; take form / 体を成さない be shapeless ; be out of shape / 体を引く draw back. [文例⇩]
たい[3] 対 〈互角〉 even ; equal ; 〈同点〉 a tie ⇨タイ[1] ; 〈対等〉 《on》 an equal footing 《with》 ; 〈...に対する...〉 versus (略 : v., vs.) ; against ; to ; with ¶2対1で勝つ win 《a game》 by (a score of) 2 to 1 ; win two-one / 対で勝負する play 《a game》 without handicaps [on equal terms] / 日本の対米政策 Japan's policy toward America / 対英貿易 trade with Britain / 労働者対資本家の闘争 a struggle of labor against capital / A 対 B の野球試合 a baseball game between A and B / 空対空[空対地, 地対空]ミサイル an air-to-air [an air-to-surface, a ground-to-air] missile. [文例⇩]
たい[4] 帯 a zone ; a belt ¶火山帯 a volcanic zone / 森林帯 a forest belt.
たい[5] 隊 a party ; a company ; 〈軍隊の〉 a body 《of troops》 ; a corps (★ 単複同形だが，発音は単数 [kɔː], 複数 [kɔːz]) ; a unit ; a squad (小人数の) ; 〈楽隊など〉 a band ¶隊を組む form a party ; 〈整列する〉 draw up in line ; line up / 隊を組んで行進する march in formation / 隊を解く disband [break up] (a party).
たい[6] 態 〘文法〙 voice.
たい[7] 鯛 a sea bream ¶たい焼き a fish-shaped pancake filled with bean jam.
タイ[1] 〈同点〉 a tie ¶タイにする tie the score / タイに終わる end in a 《2-2》 tie / タイ記録 an equal record / 世界タイ記録を出す equal [tie, match] the world mark [record] / タイスコア a tie [tied] score 《of 3 to 3》.
タイ[2] Thailand ¶タイ(国)の Thai / タイ語 Thai / タイ(国)人 a Thai.
-たい want [wish, 《文》 desire, long] to *do* ; would [should] like to *do* ; feel like *doing* ; be anxious [eager, impatient] to *do*. [文例⇩]
[用法] 日本語では「私はそうしたい」と言って，「私は

た[2] 彼をおいて他に人がない．He is irreplaceable. / 他は推して知るべし．The rest you can easily imagine. | I leave the rest to your imagination.
ダース 鉛筆を何ダース持っていますか．How many dozen pencils do you have?
たい[1] 別に他意はありません．I have no other purpose. | I've got no ulterior motive. | That's all there is to it.
たい[2] これは辞書の体をなしていない．This is a failure as a dictionary. / 土俵際で打っちゃりをかけたとき，まだ体があった[もう体がなかった]. When he tried to throw his opponent out sideways at the edge of the ring, he was still just keeping his balance [he was already completely off balance].
たい[3] 議案は300票対100票の賛成多数で衆議院を通過した．The bill passed the House of Representatives by a majority of 300 to 100. / タイガースは4対3でジャイアンツを破った．The Tigers beat the Giants four-three.
-たい 読んでみたいかね．Would you like to read it? / ぜひお供をしたいものです．I'd love to accompany you. / 僕まで泣きたくなった．I felt like crying, too. / しかしその後に起きたことを考えると彼があの時言ったことの真偽

そうしたがっている」とは言わず,「彼はそうしたがっている」「彼はそうしたいと言っている[思っている]」と言って,「彼はそうしたい」とは言わない.「したい」と「したがる」「したいと言う」の選択は主語によって制約されている.英語にはそういう制約はないので,「彼は行きたいと言っている」も,必ずしも He says he wants to go. ではなく He wants to go. でよい.また,一人称の場合,会話では I want... と言うよりも I would like... と言う方がいい.I want... はつっけんどんな感じを与えることが多いから.

だい[1] 大 ¶大なり小なり to a greater or lesser degree / 大の音楽好き a great lover of music / 大の男 a grown man; a man / 大の字に寝る lie at full length (with arms outstretched); lie spread-eagled《on the grass》/ 卵大のひょう egg-sized hailstones / 大事業 a great undertaking [enterprise] / 大出血 a great loss of blood; 〈損害〉 a heavy loss [casualty] / 大平原 a wide [vast] plain / 大問題 a big problem; a serious question. [文例⇩]

た

だい[2] 代 〈時代〉 a time; an age; 〈世代〉 a generation; 〈治世〉 a reign ¶代が変わる〈店などが〉 change hands; 〈家長が〉 be succeeded《by his son》/ 代々 for generations; through the ages; from generation to generation / 一代で in *one's* lifetime / 第15代の天皇 the fifteenth Emperor / 親の代に in *one's* father's day / 30代である be in *one's* thirties [30s, 30's] / 10代 ⇨じゅうだい[1], ティーンエージャー / 1960年代に in the 1960s [1960's] / 1850年代の半ばこのかた since the middle of the eighteen-fifties. [文例⇩]

だい[3] 代 〈代金〉 a price; 〈料金〉 a charge; a fee ¶タクシー代 a [*one's*] taxi fare / 部屋代 a room rent [charge].

だい[4] 台 a stand; a rack (台架); 〈支え台〉 a holder; a support; a pedestal (像などの); a setting (宝石などの); 〈壇〉 a platform; 〈足場〉 a stage; 〈数量の〉 a level ¶車5台 five cars / トラック3台分の荷物 three truckloads of freight / プラチナの台にはめ込む mount《a diamond》in a platinum setting / 千円台に達する reach [hit] the 1,000-yen mark.

だい[5] 題 a subject; a theme; 〈表題〉 a title ¶題を出す give [set] a theme [subject] / 「自由」と題する論文 an essay entitled 'Liberty'. [文例⇩]

たいあたり 体当たり ¶体当たりする dash *oneself*《against》; hurl *oneself*《at》; throw *one's* weight《against》. [文例⇩]

タイアップ a tie-up《between the two companies》 ¶タイアップする tie [link] up《with》; enter into partnership《with》.

たいあん 対案《make》a counterproposal;《work out》a countermeasure.

だいあん 代案 an alternative plan.

たいい[1] 大意 〈要旨〉 the gist;《文》the (main) purport; the substance; 〈大略〉 the general idea; an outline; 〈綱要〉 a summary; a synopsis《*pl.* -opses》; a résumé. [文例⇩]

たいい[2] 体位 〈体格〉 physique; 〈姿勢〉 a position; a posture ¶体位の向上を図る try to improve the physique《of young people》; try to improve [raise] the physical standard《of the younger generation》/ 楽な体位をとる take [《文》assume] a comfortable position [posture].

たいい[3] 退位 (an) abdication ¶退位する abdicate (the throne); step down from the throne《in favor of *one's* son》.

だいい 題意《miss》the point of a question.

たいいく 体育 physical training (略: P.T.); 〈科目〉 physical education (略: P.E.) ¶体育の先生 a physical education teacher / 体育の日 Physical Culture Day / 体育館 a gymnasium《*pl.* -ums, -sia》; a gym / 体育大会 an athletic meet.

だいいし 台石 a pedestal.

だいいち 第一 the first; number one (略: No. 1) ¶第1の first; primary;《文》foremost / 第一(に) first (of all); firstly; in the first place; to begin with / 第1に位する stand [rank] first / 第一にする put《*one's* family》first; give first place [priority] to《*one's* studies》/ 第1課 the first lesson; Lesson One / 第一義 the first principle [consideration] / 第一人者 the leading [best, greatest] person [expert]. [文例⇩]

だいいっせん 第一線 〈最前線〉 the forefront;《文》the vanguard;【軍】the front ¶第一線の実業家 a man actively at work in the business world / 第一線の兵士 a front-line soldier.

だいいっとう 第一党 the leading party《in the Diet》.

を疑いたくなる. But when I think of what happened later, I am inclined to doubt the truth of his remarks at the time. / 1年ぐらいパリへ行って来たいものだ. I wish I could go and spend a year in Paris. / 今度は及第させたいものだ. I (do) hope he succeeds this time.

だい[1] 大は小を兼ねる. The greater [larger] also serves for the lesser [smaller]. / それは葉書大の紙片に書かれていた. It was written on a piece of paper the size of a postcard. / 彼は堅実な営業ぶりで今日の大を成したのである. He owes his present success [position] to his sound business methods. / 大なり小なり欠点のない者はない. There is no one but has some faults. / 泣くな. 大の男がみっともない. Stop weeping, and behave like a man! | Aren't you ashamed of yourself, a grown man in tears!

だい[2] リンカーンは第16代のアメリカ大統領であった. Lincoln was the sixteenth President of the United States. / その家は代々医者である. They [That family] have been doctors for generations. / 彼はまだ20代を出ない. He isn't out of his twenties yet. / 彼は1960年代の初めに英文学研究のため英国に行った. In the early 1960s he went over to England in order to study English literature.

だい[5] 橋という題で作文を1つ作りなさい. Write an essay on the subject of 'Bridges'.

たいあたり 正に体当たり的演技だった. He really put everything he had into (playing) his part.

たいい[1] その理論の大意はこうである. In substance [outline], the theory is as follows [like this].

だいいっぽ 第一歩 the first step 《to, toward》 ¶第一歩を踏み出す take the first step; make a start.

たいいほう 対位法 〖音楽〗counterpoint ¶対位法の contrapuntal 《passages》.

たいいん¹ 退院 ¶退院的な leave (the) hospital; be discharged (from hospital) / 退院している be out of hospital.

たいいん² 隊員 a member 《of a fire brigade》.

だいいん 代印 ¶代印する affix one's seal to 《a paper》 as proxy [for sb].

たいいんれき 太陰暦 the lunar calendar.

たいえい 退嬰 ¶退嬰的な 《保守的な》 conservative; 《引っ込み思案の》 unenterprising.

たいえき¹ 体液 (a) body fluid.

たいえき² 退役 ¶退役する retire (from service) / 退役軍人 an ex-serviceman / 退役将校 a retired officer.

たいえん 大円 〖数〗a great circle.

たいおう 対応 correspondence ¶1対1の対応 〖数〗one-to-one correspondence / 対応する correspond 《to》; answer 《to》; be equivalent 《to》; 《対処する》 cope 《with》 / 対応策 ⇒たいさく². 文例⇩.

だいおう¹ 大王 a great king ¶フレデリック大王 Frederick the Great.

だいおう² 大黄 〖植〗(a) rhubarb.

ダイオード 〖電子工学〗a diode.

たいおん 体温 body temperature ¶体温が高い[低い] have a high [low] temperature / 体温を計る take the temperature 《of》/ 《薬などが》体温(の温度)で溶ける melt at body temperature / 体温計 a (clinical) thermometer / 体温表 a temperature [fever] chart. 文例⇩.

だいおんじょう 大音声 (in) a loud voice.

たいか¹ 大火 a big [great] fire; a conflagration.

たいか² 大家 a (great) master 《of, in, at》; a great expert 《on》; an authority 《on》 ¶老大家 a venerable authority 《on medieval literature》; an old master 《of calligraphy》.

たいか³ 大過 ¶大過なく without committing [free from] (any) serious mistakes [major blunders].

たいか⁴ 対価 value; 《支払う》 a price ¶充分の対価を受け取る get good value 《for》 / …の対価として in [by way of] compensation for….

たいか⁵ 耐火 ¶耐火の fireproof / 耐火建築 a fireproof [fire-resistant] building / 耐火煉瓦 a firebrick / 耐火性がある be able to resist fire. 文例⇩.

たいか⁶ 退化 〖生物・医〗degeneration; retrogression; 《器官などの》 atrophy ¶退化する degenerate; deteriorate; retrogress; 《器官などが》 atrophy; be atrophied / 退化した degenerate(d); degraded; atrophied.

たいか⁷ 滞貨 (an) accumulation of undelivered goods [cargo]; piles of dead stock (売れ残りの在庫品).

たいが 大河 a large [great] river ¶大河小説 《フランス語》 a *roman-fleuve* (pl. *romans-fleuves*); a long novel; an epic; a novel dealing with its subject over a long period of time.

だいか 代価 《価格, 値段》 (a) price; 《費用》 (a) cost; 《料金》 a charge ¶代価を払う pay the price 《for》; pay for 《an article》. 文例⇩.

たいかい¹ 大会 a mass [large] meeting; a rally; 《総会》 a general meeting; 《会議》 a plenary meeting [session] 《of a conference》; a convention; 《競技の》 a tournament; a meet.

たいかい² 大海 an ocean; a wide expanse of sea.

たいかい³ 退会 《文》 withdrawal; resignation ¶退会する withdraw [resign] from 《a society》; leave 《a society》; resign one's membership 《in a society》 / 退会届 a notice of withdrawal / 退会届を出す notify 《the secretary》 of one's withdrawal [resignation].

たいがい¹ 対外 ¶対外政策 a foreign [an external] policy / 対外貿易 foreign [overseas, international] trade.

たいがい² 大概 《一般に》 generally (speaking); in general; 《大部分》 mostly; for the most part; 《主として》 mainly; in the main; chiefly; 《ほとんど》 nearly; about; almost; 《たぶん》 probably; perhaps ¶たいがいの general; most; almost [nearly] all / たいがいにしておく 《文》 do not go to excess; keep within bounds. 文例⇩.

たいかく¹ 体格 physique; build ¶りっぱな体格の 《a man》 with a [《文》 of] strong [good] physique [build]; well-built[-constructed] / 引き締まった[ほっそりした]体格の 《a man》

だいいち まず第一に何をしようか. What shall we [are we going to] do first? / 第一に身体を大切にしなければならない. Before all else [Above all], you must be careful about your health. / そんなことを言っても無理だよ. 第一, 金がない. That's impossible. I haven't the money, to begin with [For one thing, I haven't the money]. / 彼は現代作家中の第一人者だ. He stands foremost among today's writers.

たいおう すべての分数の無限集合はすべての整数の無限集合に対応させることができる. The infinite set of all the fractions can be matched off against that of all the whole numbers.

たいおん 彼の体温は平熱より少し高い[低い]. His temperature is a little above [below] normal. / 彼女は体温が上がった[下がった]. Her temperature rose [fell]. / その椅子には前に座っていた人の体温がまだ残っていた. The chair was still warm from the person who had been sitting there before.

たいか⁵ この建築材料は耐火性が強い. This building material has high resistance to fire [is highly fire-resistant].

だいか この本の代価はまだ払ってない. This book is not paid for yet. / 農家はその生産物に対して適正な代価を受け取る権利がある. Farmers have the right to receive a reasonable price for the products that they produce.

たいがい² 学生はたいがいこの辞書を持っている. Most students have this dictionary. / 彼は明日はたいがい来るだろう. He will probably [I think he will] come tomorrow. / 酒もよいがたいがいにしておきなさい. You may drink, but don't drink too much

with a well-knit [slender] figure. 文例◊

たいかく² 対角 《幾何》the opposite angle ¶対角線 a diagonal (line) / 対角線の diagonal.

たいがく 退学 ¶退学する leave [give up, withdraw from] school / 退学させる take (a boy) out of school; withdraw [remove] (a boy) from school / 退学を命じられる be expelled [dismissed] from school / 退学届 a notice of quitting [leaving] school.

だいがく 大学 a university; a college ¶大学の学科目及び講義内容一覧 a university catalog; 《英》a university calendar / 大学へ行く go to college [university] / 大学を卒業する graduate from [《英》leave] college [university] / 大学で at college [university] / 大学構内で on campus / 大学時代に when one was at college [university]; in one's college days / 大学出の技術者 a university-trained [college-educated] engineer; an engineer with a college training / 大学教育 university education; college education [training] / 大学教授 a university [college] professor / 大学出身者 a university [college] graduate / 《英》a graduate / 大学生 a university [college] student; an undergraduate / 大学ノート a large-sized notebook / 大学病院 a university hospital.

[用法] university は大学院のある総合大学で、college は単科大学を指す。また、college は university に属する1つの学部(大学院を含まない)の意味で使うこともあり、大学以外の各種の職業専門学校でも college と呼ばれるものもある。「私は大学の学生です」と言う場合、《米》では特に university の学生であることを強調したときは別として、university の学生でも I'm at college. と言うのが普通だが、《英》では上記の区別のように I'm at university. と I'm at college. を使い分ける。

だいがくいん 大学院 a postgraduate course; 《米》a graduate school ¶大学院の学生[ゼミナール] a postgraduate [graduate] student [seminar] / 大学院のない大学 an undergraduate college.

だいかぞく 大家族 a big [large] family ¶大家族制度 an extended family system.

だいかつ 大喝 ¶大喝する shout (in a thunderous voice) (at); thunder (at). 文例◊

たいかん¹ 大官 a high-ranking official; a government dignitary.

たいかん² 大観 a general survey ¶大観する take a large view (of); make a general survey (of).

たいかん³ 体感 (a) bodily sensation ¶体感温度 effective temperature.

たいかん⁴ 退官 ¶退官する retire (from office [service]); resign.

たいかん⁵ 耐寒 ¶耐寒訓練 training for endurance in low temperatures / 耐寒性の cold-resistant[-resisting, -tolerant] (plants); (winter-)hardy (grasses).

たいがん 対岸 ¶対岸に on the other side; on the opposite bank [shore] / 対岸の火災視する look on 《sb's trouble》unconcernedly [with indifference]; regard (an incident) as having nothing to do with one [as a matter of no concern to one].

だいかん¹ 大寒 the coldest season [time of the year].

だいかん² 代官 《日本史》a local magistrate ¶代官所 a magistrate's office.

だいがん 大願 ¶大願成就《文》the attainment of one's cherished desire.

たいかんしき 戴冠式 a coronation (ceremony).

だいかんみんこく 大韓民国 the Republic of Korea ⇒かんこく².

たいき¹ 大気 the atmosphere; the air ¶大気の atmospheric / 大気中の酸素 atmospheric oxygen; oxygen in the atmosphere / 大気圧 the pressure of the atmosphere; atmospheric [air, barometric] pressure / 大気汚染 atmospheric [air] pollution / 大気圏 the atmosphere / 大気圏外 (from, into) outer space / 大気圏内の[で] in the atmosphere.

たいき² 大器《文》a person of real caliber; a man of great promise (前途有望な人) ¶未完の大器 a diamond in the rough. 文例◊

たいき³ 待機 ¶待機する watch (and wait) (for a chance); stand [wait] ready [in readiness] (for, to do); stand by / 待機命令を受けるbe ordered to be ready [to hold oneself in readiness] (for); be alerted (for). 文例◊

たいぎ¹ 大義 〈正義〉justice;《文》righteousness;〈目的〉a (great) cause ¶平和の大義のために in [for] the noble cause of peace / 大義名分が立たない cannot be justified; be not justifiable / (表向きは)…という大義名分で on the pretext of….

たいぎ² 大儀 ¶大儀である〈事がめんどうである〉be troublesome;〈疲れている〉be [feel] tired; be weary / 《文》feel languid / 大儀そうに wearily;《文》languidly; listlessly. 文例◊

だいぎ¹ 台木 〈接ぎ木の〉a stock; 〈木工の〉a block.

だいぎ² 代議 ¶代議制(度) a representative system [institution] / 代議政治 representative [parliamentary] government.

だいぎいん 代議員 a representative; a delegate ¶代議員団 a delegation.

だいぎし 代議士 a member of the House of Representatives; a Dietman; 《米》a Con-

---

[more than is good for you].

たいかく¹ 彼はりっぱな体格をしている。He is very well built. / He has a splendid physique.

だいかつ 彼は「ばか者」と大喝一声した。'You fool!' he bellowed.

たいき² 大器晩成。Great talents mature late [are slow in maturing].

たいき³ 洪水に備えて待機するようにとの命令を受けた。They were ordered to be on standby alert for possible flooding of the river.

たいぎ² 大儀であった。Well done! Thank you for your trouble.

だいきち おみくじは大吉と出た。The written oracle [fortune] said that I would have the best of luck.

たいきょ² 彼は24時間以内に国外に退去するよう命じられた。They gave him twenty-four hours to leave the country.

たいきょく¹ この一小事件が大局を決することになろうとはだれも夢にも思わなかった。No one

gressman; 《英》a member of Parliament; an M.P. ¶代議士になる be elected to the Diet; obtain a seat in the House / 婦人代議士 a Dietwoman.

だいきち 大吉 excellent [best] luck. 文例▽

だいきぼ 大規模 ⇨ きぼ.

たいきゃく 退却 (a) retreat ¶退却する retreat ((from, to)); make [beat] a retreat; withdraw / fall back / 予定の退却をする retreat as arranged beforehand; 《文》make a prearranged retreat [withdrawal].

たいぎゃく 大逆 ¶大逆事件 a case of high treason.

たいきゅう 耐久 endurance ¶耐久力[性]〈物の〉durability; 〈人の〉powers of endurance; staying power; stamina / 耐久力のある durable; lasting / 非常な耐久力がある[耐久力に乏しい] have considerable [not much] endurance / 耐久試験を行なう do [《文》subject sth to] an endurance test; test sth for endurance / 耐久消費財 consumer durables; durable consumer goods.

だいきゅう 代休 ((give, take)) a compensatory day off (for going to work on a holiday).

たいきょ¹ 大挙 ¶大挙して in a body; en masse; in great [full] force; in large [great] numbers.

たいきょ² 退去 ¶退去する leave; quit; go away [withdraw, 《文》depart] ((from)); evacuate / 退去を命じる order sb out of ((a place) [to quit ((a place))]; expel sb from ((a place)) / 退去命令 an expulsion order. 文例▽

たいぎょ 大魚 a big [large] fish. ¶大魚を逸する narrowly miss a great chance (of obtaining [winning] success).

たいきょう 胎教 the prenatal [antenatal] care of an unborn child through attention of a pregnant woman to her own mental health; prenatal influence of the mother on her child.

たいぎょう 怠業 work stoppage; a go-slow; 《米》a slowdown ¶怠業する start a slowdown [go-slow].

だいきょう 大凶 worst luck; the worst of ill fortune ⇨ だいきち.

たいきょく¹ 大局 the general [whole] situation. ¶大局的に見る take a broad [wide] view of ((the situation)); see ((a matter)) in perspective / 大局に重大な影響を及ぼす have an important effect on the whole situation. 文例▽ 「go with)).

たいきょく² 対局 ¶対局する play a game ((of だいきらい 大嫌い ¶大嫌いである detest; hate; loathe.

たいきん 大金 a large sum [amount] of money; a lot [great deal] of money; 《口語》big money. 文例▽

だいきん 代金 ⇨ だいか ¶代金取り立て手形 a bill for collection / 代金引換郵便《米》collect on delivery mail (略: C.O.D. mail); 《英》cash on delivery post (略: C.O.D. post) / 代金引換郵便で送る send sth C.O.D.

たいく 体軀 the body; 〈身長〉height; 《文》stature; 〈体格〉physique; build.

だいく 大工 a carpenter; 《英》a joiner ¶大工仕事 carpentry / 大工道具 carpenter's tools; a carpenter's outfit [kit] (1 そろい).

たいくう¹ 対空 ¶対空射撃 shooting at an aircraft (from the ground [from on board ship]) / 対空砲火 antiaircraft fire.

たいくう² 滞空 ¶滞空時間 the duration of a flight / 滞空飛行記録 an endurance flight record.

たいぐう¹ 対偶 〖数・論理〗contraposition ¶対偶命題 a contrapositive.

たいぐう² 待遇 treatment; 〈接待〉reception; 〈旅館などの〉service; 〈給料〉pay; salary ¶待遇する treat; receive; entertain; pay / 待遇がいい[悪い] be treated well [badly]; be [be not] well looked after; meet with a friendly [cold] reception; 〈給料〉be well [poorly] paid / 待遇のよい 〉hospitable; 〈給料の〉well-paid / 待遇をよくする give sb better treatment; increase sb's pay (増給する) / (労働者の)待遇改善 improvement of labor conditions.

たいくつ 退屈 tedium; 《文》ennui; boredom; dullness; 〈単調〉monotony ¶退屈な tedious; boring; 《文》wearisome; tiresome; dull; uninteresting; tame; 〈単調な〉monotonous; humdrum / 退屈な人[事, 物] a bore / 退屈する be bored ((by, with)); feel weary [tired] / 退屈させる bore / 退屈をしのぐ[まぎらす] kill time; relieve the tedium / 退屈しのぎに to kill time; by way of diversion / 退屈な時を過ごす to pass the tedious hours ((of one's convalescence)). 文例▽

たいぐん¹ 大軍 a large [big] army.

たいぐん² 大群 a large crowd [flock, herd, school, shoal] ((of)) ⇨ むれ.

たいけ 大家 〈金持ち〉a rich [wealthy] family; 〈名家〉《文》a distinguished [an illustrious] family.

たいけい¹ 大系 an outline (of history).

たいけい² 大計 a far-reaching [farsighted] policy ¶国家百年の大計をたてる make [lay (out)] a grand plan for the long-term future of the nation; establish [《文》formulate] a national policy on a long-range basis.

たいけい³ 体刑 〈体罰〉corporal punishment;

---

imagined that this little incident would bring about such a decisive change in the general situation.

たいきん 彼の懐に大金が転がり込んだのだと人々は思った。People thought he had (suddenly) come into a fortune.

たいぐう² あんなに親切な待遇を受けようとは思いもよらなかった。I little thought that I should meet with such a kind reception. / ホテルの待遇が大変よかった。They looked after [treated] us very well at the hotel.

たいくつ こんなお話を申し上げしては、さぞかしご退屈なさいますでしょう。I'm afraid you will be bored by a story like this. | You must find this story rather tiresome. / なんともはや実に退屈な女だった。She bored me stiff. | She was a crashing bore. / ひどく退屈な一日だった。We passed a very dull [slow] day. / 今ではうちの息子も童話では少々退屈するようだ。My son doesn't seem

たいけい〈懲役〉penal servitude; imprisonment with hard labor ¶体刑を加える《文》inflict corporal punishment ⟨on⟩ / 体刑に処する send *sb* to prison [jail]; sentence *sb* to ⟨five years'⟩ penal servitude.

たいけい⁴ 体形〈動物の〉a ⟨body⟩ form; a body plan.

たいけい⁵ 体系 a system; an organization ¶体系がない lack [have no] system / 体系をたてる develop [《文》formulate] a system ⟨of philosophy⟩ / 体系的な systematic / 体系的に systematically / 体系づける, 体系化する systematize / 法体系 a body of law. 文例⇩

たいけい⁶ 体型 ⇨たいかく¹.

たいけい⁷ 隊形 (a) formation; order ¶隊形を整える put the formation in good order.

だいけい 台形《数》《米》a trapezoid;《英》a trapezium (*pl.* -zia, -s) ¶台形の trapezoid(al).

たいけつ 対決 (a) confrontation;《口語》a showdown ¶対決する have [come to] a showdown ⟨with⟩ / 対決させる confront (the accused with his accuser). 文例⇩

たいけん¹ 大圏 ¶大圏コース《fly》the great-circle route.

たいけん² 体験 (personal) experience ¶体験する experience; go through; undergo / 体験を語る, 体験談を話す describe [[《文》relate, 《文》narrate, give an account of] *one's* own (personal) experience(s) ⟨of, in⟩.

たいげん¹ 体言〔国文法〕indeclinable parts of speech that can stand as the subject of a sentence.

たいげん² 体現《文》(an) embodiment ¶体現する《文》embody.

たいげんそうご 大言壮語 boasting; bragging; boasts; a loud boast; big talk ¶大言壮語する talk big [boastfully] ⟨about⟩; boast [brag] ⟨of, about⟩; make a great brag [boast] ⟨about, of⟩; blow *one's* own trumpet ¶大言壮語する人 a braggart; a boaster.

たいこ¹ 太古 ancient times;《文》remote ages [antiquity] ¶太古の ancient;《文》primeval / 太古の時代から《文》from time immemorial; from the earliest times.

たいこ² 太鼓 a drum ¶太鼓の皮 the head of a drum; a drumhead / 太鼓の連打 the roll of a drum; a drum roll / 太鼓を打つ beat [sound] a drum / 大[小]太鼓 a big [high] drum /⟨オーケストラ用の⟩a bass [side, snare] drum / 太鼓橋 an arched bridge / 太鼓腹 a paunch; a potbelly / 太鼓腹の potbellied; big-bellied; paunchy / 太鼓判を押す vouch for *sb* [*sth*];《文》give *one's* seal of approval ⟨to⟩.

たいご¹ 大悟 ¶大悟徹底する《文》attain perfect spiritual enlightenment.

たいご² 隊伍 the ranks; a line;〈行列〉a procession ¶隊伍を組む form ranks / 隊伍を組んで in line [formation, procession] / 隊伍を組んで行進する march in parade; parade / 隊伍を乱す break ranks / 隊伍を乱して in disorder; in disarray / 隊伍を乱さない stay in [keep] formation.

たいこう¹ 大公 a grand duke ¶大公国 a grand duchy.

たいこう² 大綱 general [fundamental] principles; main lines;〈概要〉an outline ¶大綱において意見が一致する《文》reach [be in] broad [substantial] agreement ⟨with⟩; agree ⟨with *sb*⟩ on the whole.

たいこう³ 対抗 ¶対抗する oppose; confront; face; stand up to; counter; meet; rival; cope with;《文》emulate; vie with / 対抗させる set [put, match] (A) against (B); oppose (A) to (B) / …に対抗して against…; in opposition to…; in rivalry with… / 対抗策[措置]a countermeasure; a countermove / 東西対抗試合 Kanto vs. Kansai (rugby, football) game / 対抗者 a rival; an opponent / 対抗馬 a rival horse (in a race) /〈選挙の〉a rival candidate. 文例⇩

たいこう⁴ 体腔 a body cavity.

たいこう⁵ 退行 ⇨たいか⁶.

たいこう⁶ 退校 ⇨たいがく.

たいごう 大剛 an exceptionally strong player [man];《文》a man [player] of exceptional strength.

だいこう¹ 代行 ¶代行する carry out [carry on,《文》execute] ⟨business⟩ for *sb* / 学長代行 an acting president / 代行機関 an agency / 代行者 an agent.

だいこう² 代講 ¶代講する teach [give a lecture] for [in place of] *sb*.

たいこうじあい 対抗試合 an interschool [intercollegiate] match [game].

たいこうしゃ 対向車 an oncoming car; oncoming traffic. 文例⇩

たいこうぼう 太公望 an angler ¶太公望を決め込む give *oneself* up to the pleasure of angling.

たいこく 大国〈強国〉a great [big] power [nation] ¶世界の大国としての地位を築く achieve the status of a world power.

だいこくばしら 大黒柱〈柱〉the central pillar;〈人〉the mainstay;《文》the prop (and stay) ¶一家の大黒柱 the breadwinner [supporter] of the family.

だいごみ 醍醐味 the (real [true]) pleasure ⟨of reading⟩; the (true) charm ⟨of music⟩.

だいこん 大根 a Chinese [Japanese] (white)

---

to enjoy fairy tales much any more.
たいけい⁵ 数学はサイエンスではなく、別個に存する独自の知識体系である。Mathematics is not a science, but is a separate body of knowledge in its own right.
たいけつ このために早晩米ソ間の対決が見られることであろう。Sooner or later this will probably lead to a showdown between the United States and the Soviet Union.
たいこ¹ 危険はない。太鼓判を押す。I (can) assure [promise] you there is no danger.

たいこう³ 彼にはとうてい対抗できない事を知った。I found I was no match for him. | I realized he was more than a match for me. / 彼はこの前の選挙に自民党のA氏に対抗して立候補した。He ran in the last election against Liberal Democrat Mr. A. / インドは中国

radish ¶大根脚 thick legs / 大根下ろし grated radish / 大根役者 a poor [bad] actor; 《口語》a ham.

たいさ 大差 a great [wide, big, vast] difference;《文》a great discrepancy [disparity] ¶大差がある be very different 《from》;《文》differ a great deal 《from》/ 大差がない do not make much difference; make little [no great] difference; be much the same / 大差をつける get a big [long] lead 《on, over》/ 大差をつけて勝つ beat sb easily; win (a victory 《over one's opponent》) by a large margin. 文例⇩

たいざ 対座 ¶対座する sit opposite 《each other, sb》; sit face to face 《with》.

だいざ 台座 a pedestal.

たいさい 大祭 a grand [high] festival.

たいざい 滞在 a stay;《文》a sojourn ¶滞在する stay [stop] 《at a place, with sb》; make a stay (at) / 久しく[ちょっと]滞在する make a long [short] stay / ロンドン滞在中 during one's (three-month) stay in London; while staying in London / 3日間滞在の予定で 《arrive in Tokyo》on a three-day visit 《to Japan》/ 滞在客 a guest; a long-time visitor / 滞在日数 the length of one's visit [stay]. 文例⇩

だいざい¹ 大罪 a serious [《文》heinous] crime; a deadly [mortal] sin ¶大罪 (地獄に落ちるという) 七つの大罪《キリスト教》the seven deadly sins.

だいざい² 題材 subject matter; material 《for a novel》.

たいさく¹ 大作 a monumental [great, major] work;《ラテン語》a *magnum opus*;《大型の》a large [long] work /《大部の》a voluminous work.

たいさく² 対策《文》a measure; a step; a countermeasure ¶対策を講じる take measures [steps] to meet [cope with] the (new) situation;《文》devise a countermeasure [対策を練る] work out countermeasures [a countermeasure]; study how to [try to find the best plan to] cope with the situation. 文例⇩
用法 countermeasure は人の取った策に対するものにしか言わない. たとえば"公害対策"は measures [policies] against pollution で, countermeasures against pollution ではない. measure; step は通例複数で使う.

だいさく 代作 ¶代作する write [compose] for sb; ghost (a speech); ghostwrite (a novel) / 代作者 a ghostwriter.

たいさつ 大冊 a big [bulky] volume; a big [bulky,《文》voluminous] book.

たいさん 退散 ¶退散する disperse; run away;《文》flee;《口語》clear off [out]; make off / 退散させる disperse; drive away; expel;《文》put to flight [rout].

たいさん 大山 文例⇩

だいさん¹ 代参 ¶代参する visit a shrine [temple] to do homage on behalf of sb; visit a shrine [temple] as proxy for sb.

だいさん² 第三 number three (略: No. 3); the third / 第3に third(ly); in the third place / 第三紀《地質》the Tertiary (period) / 第三者 a third person [party];〈局外者〉an outsider / 第三勢力 a third force / 第三世界 the Third World.

たいさんぼく 泰山木《植》an evergreen magnolia.

たいし 大志 ⇒たいもう. 文例⇩

たいし 大使 an ambassador / 駐英大使 an ambassador to Great Britain / 大使館 an embassy / 在米日本大使館 the Japanese Embassy in Washington / 大使館員 a member of the embassy staff / 大使級会談を開く hold a meeting [conference] at ambassadorial level; hold an ambassador-level meeting.

たいし³ 太子 the Crown Prince ¶聖徳太子 Prince Shotoku.

たいじ¹ 対峙 ¶対峙する stand face to face 《with》; confront; face;〈比喩的〉take a stand 《against》.

たいじ² 胎児 an unborn child [baby]; an embryo 《pl. -s》(妊娠3か月までの); a fetus (妊娠3か月以後の).

たいじ³ 退治〈撲滅〉《文》extirpation; extermination;〈征服〉《文》conquest;《文》subjugation; suppression ¶退治する exterminate; root [stamp, wipe, drive] out; clean up;《文》extirpate; eradicate; destroy; get rid of; subdue; conquer;《文》subjugate / 怪物を退治する kill [《文》slay] a monster / ごきぶりを退治する rid (the kitchen) of cockroaches.

たいじ⁴ 帯磁 ¶帯磁する be magnetized; become magnetic.

だいし 台紙 pasteboard;〈写真の〉a mount ¶台紙にはる mount (a photograph).

だいじ 大事 a great thing;〈大事業〉a great undertaking [《文》enterprise,《文》task];〈重大事〉a serious [《文》grave] matter [affair] ¶大事な〈重大な〉important; serious; critical;〈大切な〉precious;《文》highly esteemed [prized];《a picture》(that is) dear to one;《a project》close to one's heart; valuable / 大事なことから先にやる do [put] first things first / 大事をとる act cautiously;《文》act with prudence;〈危ないことを避ける〉do not take chances [risks]; be on the safe side; take (all) the necessary precautions / 大事にする prize; value; cherish; think a great deal of / 身体を大事にする take (good) care of oneself. 文例⇩

の対抗勢力である. India stands as a counterpoise to China.
たいこうしゃ 対向車に注意. Beware of cars coming toward you.
たいさ AとBとは大差がない. There is not much difference [not much to choose] between A and B. | A is virtually the same as B.
たいざい 彼はたまたまその地に滞在中だった. He happened to be there on a visit. / 1週間前から手前どもにご滞在でございます. The gentleman has been our guest since a week ago.
たいさく² これが最善の対策だ. This is the best way of dealing with it.
たいさん 大山鳴動してねずみ一匹. The mountains have brought forth a mouse.《諺》
たいし 少年よ, 大志をいだけ. Boys, be ambitious.
だいじ お大事に. Take (good) care

たいした 大した ⟨数量⟩ many; much; a great deal of; a lot of; immense; enormous; ⟨偉い⟩ great; ⟨重要な⟩ important; ⟨文⟩(affairs) of (some [considerable]) importance [consequence]; ⟨ゆゆしい⟩ serious; ⟨文⟩ grave ★ many と much は主に否定文・疑問文で用いる ⇒ たくさん 囲因 ¶大した人出 a huge [an immense, a fantastic] crowd of people / 大したものではないと思う have a bad [low, poor] opinion of; do not think much of. 文例⇩

だいじだいひ 大慈大悲 Buddha's great love and mercy (toward all living things).

たいしつ 体質 ⟨文⟩ one's (physical) constitution; one's ⟨遺伝的⟩ make-up; a predisposition ⟨to diabetes⟩ ¶虚弱体質である have a weak constitution / 体質的な constitutional / 体質的に constitutionally / 体質改善 improving one's physical condition / ⟨組織の⟩ (radical) reform; revamping. 文例⇩

たいして¹ 大して very; much; greatly; seriously ¶たいして危険でない be not very [so] dangerous. 文例⇩

たいして² 対して ⇒ **たいする¹** (対して).

たいしゃ¹ 大赦 (an) amnesty; a general [grand] amnesty ¶大赦を行なう grant an amnesty (to).

たいしゃ² 代謝 ⇒ **しんちんたいしゃ** ¶代謝異常 a metabolic disorder / 代謝作用[機能] metabolism / 代謝機能が弱い have a low metabolic rate.

たいしゃ³ 退社 ¶退社する ⟨退職する⟩ leave [retire from] (the company); ⟨帰宅する⟩ leave work [the office] / 退社時間 quitting time; clocking-off time (主に工場労働者の).

だいじゃ 大蛇 a big snake; a huge serpent.

たいしゃいろ 代赭色 burnt sienna; reddish brown; bronze.

たいしゃく 貸借 (a) loan; debit and credit (帳簿上の) ¶貸借対照表 (draw up) a balance sheet. 文例⇩

だいしゃりん 大車輪 ⟨機械体操の⟩ a giant swing ¶大車輪で働く work at high pressure; ⟨口語⟩ work [sweat] one's guts out. 文例⇩

たいしゅ 大酒 heavy [hard] drinking ¶大酒家 a heavy [hard] drinker ★ a heavy drinker は「アル中」に近く、酒で体をつぶすだろうという意味が強く入っている。a hard drinker の方は、「よく飲むがいくら飲んでもつぶれない人」の意で、ほめ言葉に近い。

たいじゅ 大樹 ⇒ **たいぼく**. 文例⇩

たいしゅう¹ 大衆 the mass of the people; ⟨文⟩ the masses; ⟨文⟩ the populace; ⟨文⟩ the multitude ¶大衆向きの for everybody; popular / 大衆値段の popular-priced / 大衆化する popularize / 大衆性 popular appeal; popularity / 大衆運動 ⟨launch⟩ a mass movement / 大衆場 a (cheap) bar [⟨米⟩ saloon]; ⟨英⟩ a pub (★ public house の略) / 大衆作家[雑誌] a popular writer [magazine] / 大衆車 a popular car / 大衆食堂 a cheap restaurant; an eating place [house] / 大衆政党 a mass party / 大衆団交 mass bargaining; a mass bargaining session / 大衆文学 popular [lowbrow] literature.

たいしゅう² 体臭 body odor; ⟨口語⟩ B.O. ⟨動物の⟩ body smell. 文例⇩

たいじゅう 体重 one's (body) weight ¶体重が60キロある weigh 60 kilograms / 体重を gain [put on] weight / 体重が2キロ増える[減る] gain [lose] two kilograms / 体重を量る weigh oneself / 右足に体重をかける get [rest] one's weight on one's right foot / 体重を減らす lose weight; take off weight; ⟨口語⟩ reduce / 体重計 a weighing machine; (the) scales / 体重検査 ⟨スポーツ⟩ a weigh-in. 文例⇩

たいしゅつ¹ 退出 ¶退出する leave (one's office); ⟨文⟩ retire [withdraw] ⟨from⟩ ⇒ **たいしゃ³**.

たいしゅつ² 帯出 ¶帯出する ⟨持ち出す⟩ carry [take] sth out; ⟨図書館の本を⟩ take (a book) out of (a library); borrow (a book) from (a library). 文例⇩

たいしょ¹ 対処 ¶対処する cope [deal] with; tackle; meet; counter (an epidemic). 文例⇩

たいしょ² 対蹠 ¶対蹠的 ⟨文⟩ antipodal ⟨to⟩; exactly [⟨文⟩ diametrically] opposite ⟨to⟩; (be) quite the opposite ⟨of⟩ / 対蹠地 the antipodes.

たいしょう¹ 大笑 ¶大笑する laugh heartily;

---

of yourself. | ⟨家族に病人のある人に⟩ I hope your mother [wife, daughter, etc.] gets better soon. / 何より身体が大事だ。Health comes before everything else. / 火事は大事に至らずに消し止められた。The fire was put out before it got serious. / 大事をとるに越したことはない。It is always best to err [be] on the safe side. / 大事は小事より起こる。Great things have small beginnings. / いわばそれは大事の前の小事だ。It is, so to speak, a small sacrifice in a great cause.

たいした 大した学者だ。He's a great scholar. / 大した学者じゃない。He's not much of a scholar. / 大したことにはなるまい。It won't come to much. / 病気は大したことはないでしょう。Your illness is nothing serious, I hope. / どっちにころんでも大したことはない。I don't care much which way it comes out. | It doesn't matter much who wins. / それだけの金では大したこともできまい。That much [That amount of money] won't go far [a long way]. / あの男、大したものになるぞ。He will (really) come to something. / 大した心臓だ。What a nerve (he's got)!

たいしつ これは僕の体質に合わない。This doesn't agree with me.

たいして¹ 雪はたいして降らなかった。It didn't snow much. | We didn't have much snow. / たいして見栄えのする家じゃない。It isn't an especially [a particularly] fine house to look at.

たいしゃく 私は彼と貸借関係はない。I have no accounts to settle with him. / これで君とは貸借関係はなくなった。We're quits now.

だいしゃりん 昨日は大車輪で働かねばならなかった。I was kept awfully busy yesterday.

たいじゅ 寄らば大樹の陰。Look for a big tree when you seek shelter. | If you must rely on someone, rely on someone powerful [strong].

たいしゅう² この作品には著者の体臭が感じられる。This work reflects the distinctive personality

roar with [burst into] laughter ; burst out laughing ; give a loud laugh.
たいしょう² 大将 〈陸軍〉a (full) general ; 〈海軍〉an [a full] admiral ; 〈首領〉a chief ; a (ring)leader ; a head ; a boss ¶お山の大将 the king of the castle ; the cock of the walk. 文例⬇
たいしょう³ 大勝 ¶大勝する gain [win] a great [sweeping] victory 《over》; beat sb easily [by a wide margin] ; 〈選挙で〉win in a landslide ; win a landslide victory 《over》.
たいしょう⁴ 対称 〈数〉symmetry ¶対称的な symmetrical / 対称的に symmetrically.
たいしょう⁵ 対象 a subject (of our investigation) ; 《文》an object (of study) ; a target (of criticism) ¶高校生を対象とする辞書 a dictionary (intended) for [aimed at] high-school students / 2千人の大学生を対象として政治意識調査を行なう conduct a survey of political awareness on 2,000 college students.
たいしょう⁶ 対照 (a) contrast ; 〈比較〉(a) comparison ; 〈照合〉《文》(a) collation ¶対照する contrast [compare] 《A with B》; make a comparison 《between A and B》; set [put] (A) against (B) ; 《文》collate 《A with B》/ 好対照をなす make a beautiful [an excellent] contrast 《with》; 〈AとBが〉set each other off well / …と著しい対照をなす be in striking [strong, 《文》marked] contrast 《to》; 《文》form [be, offer] a pronounced [remarkable] contrast 《with》; contrast sharply 《with》/ …と対照的に in contrast 《to》; 《文》contradistinction) to … ; 〈前文を受けて〉これとは対照的に By [In] contrast, … / 対照研究 contrastive study (of English and Japanese) / 対照実験 a control experiment. 文例⬇
たいしょう⁷ 隊商 a caravan ¶らくだを連れた隊商 a camel caravan.
たいじょう 退場 ¶退場する leave (the hall) ; go away 《from》; walk out 《of》; make one's exit 《from》/ …退場を命じる order sb out of (the hall) / …退場〈芝居のト書きを〉Exit… (1人の場合). Exeunt… (2人以上の場合).
だいしょう¹ 大小 〈大きさ〉size ; 〈大刀と脇差〉a pair of swords ¶大小の large and [or] small ; of all [various] sizes / 大小の差がある vary in size / 大小により見る see how large sth is / 大小により according to size. 文例⬇
だいしょう² 代償 a price ; compensation ¶…の代償として in return for…; in compensation for… / 手痛い代償を払う pay heavily [a painful price] 《for sth, for doing, to do》/ どんな代償を払っても at any price ; whatever the cost. 文例⬇
だいじょう 大乗 《仏教》Mahayana ; the Great Vehicle ¶大乗的見地から見る look at (the situation) from a broader viewpoint ; take an overall view of (the state of affairs).
だいじょうだん 大上段 ¶大上段に構える hold one's sword over one's head ; 〈比喩的〉take a highhanded attitude 《to, toward》.
だいじょうぶ 大丈夫 〈大丈夫な〉safe ; all right ; 《口語》O.K. ; 〈確かに〉surely ; certainly ; 《文》undoubtedly / 大丈夫と思う feel quite safe [sure] / 大丈夫…である 《文》You may depend upon it that…; 《口語》You can bet (your life) that…. 文例⬇
たいしょうりょうほう 対症療法 〈医〉symptomatic treatment ¶対症療法を行なう treat symptoms.
たいしょく¹ 大食 gluttony ¶大食する eat a lot [a great deal] / 大食の gluttonous / 大食漢 a great [big] eater ; a glutton.
たいしょく² 退色 ¶退色する fade ⇒ さめる³.
たいしょく³ 退職 〈定年の〉retirement ; 〈辞職〉resignation ¶退職する retire ; resign (one's position) ; leave [retire from] office (から) / 退職させる retire ; discharge / 退職金〈手当〉〈定年による〉a retirement allowance ; 〈解雇による〉a discharge allowance / 退職者 a retired person [employee] ; a retired official (公務員).
たいしょこうしょ 大所高所 ¶大所高所から見る take a wide [broad, long] view (of the situation).
だいしょにん 代書人 a scribe.
だいじり 台尻 the butt (of a gun).
たいしん 耐震 ¶耐震性の earthquake-proof[-resistant] (buildings).
たいじん¹ 大人 a great man. 文例⬇

---

of the author.
たいじゅう 君はどのくらい体重があるの. How much do you weigh? | What is your weight? / 彼の体重は僕の2倍はあるだろう. I think he weighs twice as much as me. ⇒ より² 用法 | I would guess that he's twice my weight./ 病人の体重は60キロから50キロに減った. The patient's weight fell from 60 kilograms to 50./鳥のひなの中には毎日自分の体重と同じだけの虫を食べるものもある. Some young birds eat their own weight in insects daily.
たいしゅつ² 帯出禁止. 〈ラベルの文言〉Not to be taken out. | Not to be removed (from the premises).
たいしょ¹ それは対処のしようがない. There is nothing that can be done about it.
たいしょう² あいつはお山の大将おれ一人と思っている. He thinks he's the king of the castle. | He thinks he's the monarch of all he surveys.
たいしょう⁶ 光と影の対照が彼の絵をとても効果的にしている. It is the contrast of light and shadow that makes his painting so effective. / ジョンの反応はトムのそれとは全く対照的であった. John's reaction was a complete contrast to Tom's.
だいしょう¹ それは大小種々ある. They come in [are of] various sizes. / 世界には大小合わせて100余国ある. There are more than one hundred countries, large and small, in the world.
だいしょう² 勝つには勝ったが代償が大きすぎた. We certainly won, but the price we paid (for it) was too high.
だいじょうぶ 大丈夫かね〈無事か〉Are you all right? | 〈自信があるか〉Are you quite sure? / 彼は大丈夫成功する. I assure you that he will succeed. | He is sure to succeed. / 病人はもう大丈夫だと医者は言った. The doctor declared that the patient was out of danger.
たいじん¹ 彼には大人の風格がある. He impresses us as a man of great character.

たいじん² 対陣 ¶対陣する〈一方が主語〉take up a position (800 meters away from the enemy);〈双方が主語〉be encamped facing each other.

たいじん³ 退陣 ¶退陣する retire (from a position); give up *one*'s position; step down; go out of office; resign / 近く退陣する首相 the outgoing premier.

だいしん 代診 a locum ((for)) ¶代診する examine [diagnose] (a patient) on [((米)) in] behalf of ((another doctor)).

だいじん 大臣 a minister (of state); a Cabinet minister ¶大臣の職[椅子] a portfolio (*pl.* -s) / 大臣になる become a Cabinet minister; be named to a Cabinet post.

たいじんかんけい 対人関係 personal relations [relationships]; relations with other people.

だいじんぶつ 大人物 a great man;((文)) a man of great stature [caliber].

ダイス〈さいころ〉dice ⇒ さい⁵ ★;〈工具〉a die (*pl.* -s) ¶ダイスで切る stamp out (leather) (with a die).

だいず 大豆 a soybean ¶大豆油 soybean oil / 大豆粕(⼄) a soybean cake.

たいすい 耐水 ¶耐水性の impervious to water; waterproof (cloth); water-resistant (完全防水ではない).

たいすう 対数〈数〉a logarithm ¶30 の対数 log. 30; the logarithm of 30 / 自然[常用]対数 a natural [common] logarithm / 対数関数[目盛] a logarithmic function [scale] / 対数表 a table of logarithms; a log table; log tables (1冊になっているもの).

だいすう(がく) 代数(学) algebra ¶代数の問題 an algebra problem / 代数で解く solve ((a problem)) algebraically / 代数方程式 an algebraic equation.

だいすき 大好き ¶…が大好きだ be very fond of…; have a great liking for… ⇒ すき¹.

たいする¹ 対する〈面する〉face; confront; be confronted with;〈応対する〉receive;〈対抗する〉oppose ¶(…)に対して〈向かって〉to; toward; for;〈関して〉((文)) concerning; ((文)) in regard to;〈対向して〉against; face to face with;〈敵対して〉against; in opposition to;〈用意して〉against; in preparation for;〈比例して〉per; to;〈比較して〉(as) against; (as) compared with;((文))whereas (前の文言を受けて) / 親に対する務め *one*'s duty to [by] *one*'s parents / 英文学に対する興味 an interest in English literature. 文例↓

たいする² 体する〈従う〉obey;((文)) comply with;〈留意する〉keep [bear] *sth* in mind.

たいせい¹ 大成 ¶大成する〈成功する〉((文)) be crowned with success;〈人格が〉((文)) attain greatness; mature. 文例↓

たいせい² 大勢 the general tendency [trend, drift] ((of the times)); the general situation ((of the world)) ¶大勢に順応[逆行]する swim [go] with [against] the tide [current]. 文例↓

たいせい³ 体制〈組織〉a system; an organization; a setup; (a) structure ¶体制側の新聞 the Establishment press / 体制側に属している belong to the Establishment / 経済体制 an economic structure / 政治体制 a political system; a regime / 反体制 ⇒ はんたいせい.

たいせい⁴ 体勢 a posture; a stance (立った) ¶(相撲などで)体勢が崩れる lose *one*'s balance / 体勢を立て直す recover [regain] *one*'s balance.

たいせい⁵ 耐性〈医・生物〉(a) tolerance ((to radioactivity)) ¶耐性がある be tolerant ((of, to)) / …に対して耐性ができる develop [((文)) acquire, build up] resistance to ((insecticides)).

たいせい⁶ 胎生 ¶胎生の viviparous. 文例↓

たいせい⁷ 退勢 ((文)) *one*'s declining fortunes ¶退勢を挽回する restore [retrieve] the declining fortunes ((of)); rally.

たいせい⁸ 態勢〈態度〉an attitude;〈準備〉((文)) preparedness;〈状態〉a condition ¶態勢を整える make preparations [arrangements] ((to do, for)); get ready ((for, to do)) / …する態勢にある be [((文)) stand] prepared [ready] ((to do, for)); be [stand] poised ((for)).

だいせいどう 大聖堂 a cathedral.

たいせいよう 大西洋 the Atlantic (Ocean) ¶大西洋の Atlantic / 大西洋横断飛行 a transatlantic flight / 大西洋憲章 the Atlantic Charter.

たいせき¹ 体積 (cubic) volume; cubic content(s).

たいせき² 対蹠 ⇒ たいしょ².

たいせき³ 退席 ¶退席する leave *one*'s seat [the room]; ((文)) retire; ((文)) withdraw.

たいせき⁴ 堆石〈地質〉a moraine.

たいせき⁵ 堆積 a pile; a heap; (an) accumulation; a build-up ¶堆積する be piled up; be heaped up; accumulate / 堆積岩 (a) sedimentary rock / 堆積層 a sedimentary layer [stratum] / 堆積物 a layer of sediment / 堆積物デポジット deposits; sediment(s).

たいせつ 大切 ¶大切な〈重要な〉important; ((文)) of importance; ((文)) weighty;〈貴重な〉valuable; valued; dear (to *one*); precious;〈重大な〉((文)) grave; serious / 大切に care-

---

たいする¹ 手数料は千円に対して50円です。We charge fifty yen as commission for every thousand. | We charge a commission of fifty yen per thousand. / どうしても私に対する彼の怒りを解くことができなかった。Nothing could calm his anger against [toward] me.

たいせい¹ あの男は大成しないだろう。He will never amount to much.

たいせい² 大勢はすでに決まった。The overall situation is no longer in doubt. | The final outcome is now certain. / 世論の大勢は彼に有利になってきた。The tide of public opinion has turned in his favor.

たいせい⁶ 蛇の中には胎生のものがある。There are some snakes that bear their young alive.

たいせつ 外国語を学ぶには不断の練習が一番大切だ。What is most important in learning a foreign language is constant practice. / 何をするにも身体が一番大切だ。In everything you do health should be your first consideration.

たいせん fully; with (great) care; with caution / 大切にする《注意する》take good care of; look after *sb* well;《尊重する》value;《文》prize; think a great deal of; cherish;《文》esteem (highly);《文》hold in high esteem《regard》/ 夫を大切にする take great care of *one's* husband; be devoted to *one's* husband / 親を大切にする look after *one's* parents well; be kind to《considerate toward》*one's* parents / 部下を大切にする treat *one's* subordinates kindly; always have *one's* subordinates' interests in mind. 文例⇩

たいせん¹ 大戦 a great war;〈世界大戦〉a world war. ⇨ せいたい (第一[二]次世界大戦).

たいせん² 対戦 ¶対戦する oppose [confront, fight]《the enemy》; compete《with》; play a match《against》; play《the Giants》/ 対戦成績 the win-loss records《between A and B》. 文例⇩

たいぜん 泰然 ¶泰然たる calm; cool;《文》composed; unruffled / 泰然(自若)として coolly; calmly;《文》composedly;《文》with (perfect) composure; with great presence of mind. 文例⇩

たいせんしゃほう 対戦車砲 an antitank gun.

たいせんしょうかいき 対潜哨戒機 an antisubmarine patrol plane.

たいそう¹ 大葬 the funeral services for the late Emperor.

たいそう² 体操 gymnastics; physical [gymnastic] exercises ¶頭の体操 mental gymnastics;《問題》a brain teaser / 体操の時間 a gymnastics hour [period] / 体操をする do gymnastics [gymnastic exercises] / 男子団体体操競技 the men's team gymnastics competition / 体操場〈雨天の〉a gymnasium (*pl.* -siums, -sia); a gym / 体操選手 a gymnast / 体操チーム a gymnastic team / 体操器具 gymnastic apparatus [appliances].

たいそう³ 大層〈非常に〉very; so;《文》exceedingly; greatly; highly; awfully; very much ¶たいそうな〈数〉a great [good] many; many a(★続く名詞は単数);〈量〉a great deal of;〈数量とも〉a lot of; plenty of; a large amount of;〈ぎょうぎょうしい〉exaggerated / たいそうらしく言う exaggerate; make a mountain out of a molehill.

だいそう 代走《野球》〈事〉running for *sb*;〈人〉a pinch runner.

だいそうじょう 大僧正 an archbishop.

だいそれた 大それた outrageous; monstrous; appalling;《文》inordinate ¶大それた望み an inordinate ambition / 大それた事をする commit an outrage; behave outrageously [very badly].

ただい 怠惰 idleness; laziness;《文》indolence ¶怠惰な idle; lazy;《文》indolent.

だいだ 代打《野球》¶代打(者)に立つ bat [pinch-hit]《for》/ 代打者 a pinch hitter.

だいたい¹ 大体〈概要〉the substance; the gist;〈あらまし〉an [a rough] outline;〈要点〉the main points ¶大体から言えば generally [roughly] speaking / 大体の〈一般の〉general;〈主要な〉main / 大体を述べる give an [a broad] outline 《of》/ 大体において《概して》generally;《文》in the main; on the whole; by and large;《よろそ》roughly; in the rough;〈大部分〉for the most part;〈ほとんど〉more or less. 文例⇩

だいたい² 大隊 a battalion.

だいたい³ 大腿 a thigh ¶大腿骨 a thighbone / 大腿部 the femur ((*pl.* -s, femora).

だいたい⁴ 代替 ⇨ だいよう ¶代替エネルギー資源 alternative energy resources.

だいだい 橙《植》a bitter [sour] orange ¶橙色 orange color.

だいだいてき 大々的 ¶大々的に on a large scale;《文》extensively;《口語》in a big way / 《新聞が》大々的に報道する give a great deal [a lot] of space 《to》; give prominent coverage 《to》. 文例⇩

だいたすう 大多数 the greater part 《of》; a large [great] majority ¶大多数は for the most part; mostly / 大多数の賛成を得る be supported by a large majority.

たいだん 対談 a talk; a conversation;《文》a tête-à-tête (talk); an interview《会見》¶対談する talk [《文》converse]《with》; have a talk [an interview]《with》.

だいたん 大胆 boldness; daring;《文》audacity ¶大胆な bold; daring;《文》dauntless; fearless;《文》audacious / 大胆な柄の着物 a *kimono* with a bold pattern / 大胆に boldly;《文》fearlessly; daringly;《文》dauntlessly;《文》audaciously / 大胆に…を試みる make a brave try at《*sth*, doing》. 文例⇩

だいち¹ 大地 the earth;〈stand on〉firm ground ¶母なる大地 Mother Earth.

だいち² 台地 a tableland; a plateau (*pl.* -s, -x); a height ★ height は複数形で使われることが多い。

たいちょ 大著《大部な本》《文》a voluminous work;〈力作〉a great work [book];《ラテン語》a *magnum opus*.

たいちょう¹ 体長〈動物の〉the (body) length ¶体長が2メートルある be two meters long /

たいせん² この両試合の勝者が明日対戦する The winners of these two games will meet tomorrow.

たいぜん そのような危険に直面しても彼は泰然自若としていた。He did not lose his presence of mind even in face of such (a) danger.

だいそれた 大それた事を申し上げるようですが…. I'm afraid it's rather forward of me to say this, but…. I know this is impertinent of me, but….

だいたい¹ 大体次のとおり。It may be summarized as follows. / 大体の話をしよう。I'll give you a rough idea of it. / 太陽系は今でもその創成当時と大体変わらないと考えられている。It is believed that the solar system has remained much the way it was created. / 大体からして君が間違っているんだ。You're wrong from the very beginning.

だいだいてき その事件は全世界各地で大々的に報道された。The incident made the headlines all over the world.

だいたん 彼は大胆にも1人でその敵に立ち向かった。He was bold

たいちょう　体長が最大3メートルに達する reach a maximum length of three meters.
たいちょう² 体調 one's physical condition ¶体調を整える get into (good) trim 《for the race》; get in shape 《for the contest》.
たいちょう³ 退庁 ¶退庁する leave the office / 退庁時刻 (the) closing time.
たいちょう⁴ 退潮 the ebb [ebbing] tide ¶〈物事が〉退潮を示す be declining; be on the decline; be on the ebb.
たいちょう⁵ 隊長 a captain; a leader; a commander.
だいちょう¹ 大腸 the colon; the large intestine ¶大腸炎 colitis / 大腸カタル catarrh of the colon / 大腸菌 a colon bacillus; 《ラテン語》 Escherichia coli (略: E. coli).
だいちょう² 台帳 a ledger.
たいちょうかく 対頂角 《幾何》 vertical angles.
タイツ tights ¶タイツ姿の女 a girl [woman] in tights.
たいてい¹ 大帝 a great emperor ¶ピョートル大帝 Peter the Great.
たいてい² 退廷 ¶退廷する leave (the) court.
たいてい³ 大抵 〈大部分〉 generally; mostly; for the most part; 〈通常〉 usually; as a rule; more often than not; most of the time; much [a great deal] of the time; 〈たぶん〉 probably; likely; 〈大体〉 more or less; 〈ほとんど皆〉 nearly [almost] all; 〈ほとんど〉 almost; nearly ¶たいていの general; most; usual. 文例⇩
たいてき 大敵 a powerful [《文》 formidable] enemy; 〈競争者〉 a great [formidable] rival [competitor] ¶人類の大敵 《文》 an archenemy [a deadly foe] of mankind.
たいでん 帯電 ¶帯電する take a [an electrical] charge / 正[負]に帯電する become positively [negatively] charged / 帯電している electrified; charged (with electricity); live 《wire》 / 帯電体 an electrified [electrically charged] body.
たいど 態度 an attitude; behavior; bearing; a manner ¶態度を決める[明らかにする] determine one's attitude 《toward》 / 態度を明らかにしない do not commit oneself 《on》; be noncommittal 《about》 / 強硬な態度をとる take [《文》 assume, 《文》 adopt] a firm attitude 《toward》; take a strong stand 《against sb [sth], on an issue》 / 決然たる態度で 《文》 determinedly; in a determined manner. 文例⇩
たいとう¹ 台頭 ¶台頭する raise one's [its]

head; become conspicuous; gain power.
たいとう² 対等 ¶対等の equal / 自分と対等の仲間[相手] one's equal / 対等に[で] on equal terms [on an equal footing] 《with》 / 対等である be on a level [an equal footing] 《with》.
たいどう 胎動 〈胎児の〉 the movements of the fetus; quickening (最初の); 〈徴候〉 signs; indications. 文例⇩
だいどう 大道 〈大通り〉 a highway; 〈街路〉 a street ¶大道で 《米》 on the street; 《英》 in the street / 大道芸人 a street performer.
だいどうしょうい 大同小異 ¶大同小異の[で] nearly [very much] alike; much [《文》 substantially, practically] the same. 文例⇩
だいどうみゃく 大動脈 《解》 the aorta (pl. -s, -tae); the main artery ¶大動脈の aortic; aortal. 文例⇩
だいとうりょう 大統領 the President 《of the United States》 ¶大統領の presidential / ルーズベルト大統領 President Roosevelt / 副大統領 a vice-president / 大統領官邸 an executive [a presidential] mansion; 《米国の》 the White House / 大統領候補者[選挙] a presidential candidate [election].
たいとく 体得 ¶体得する 《文》 acquire; learn (from experience); master.
たいどく 胎毒 eczema in newborn babies (popularly believed to be transmitted to the fetus by the mother).
だいどく 代読 ¶代読する read 《a message》 for [on behalf of] sb.
だいどころ 台所 a kitchen; 〈アパートの小さな〉 a kitchenette ¶台所仕事 kitchen work / 台所道具 kitchenware; kitchen utensils.
タイトスカート a tight [straight] skirt.
タイトル a title ¶タイトルを失う lose the title 《to sb》 / タイトルを獲得する win the title / タイトルバック 《映画・テレビ》 a title background; the background to the credits / タイトル防衛に成功する defend the title successfully; retain the title / タイトル保持者 the holder of the title; the champion / タイトルマッチ a title match.
たいない¹ 体内 ¶体内の[に] in the body [system]; 《文》 internal [internally] / 体内時計 《動》 a biological [an internal] clock.
たいない² 対内 ¶対内的 domestic; 《文》 internal / 対内政策 a domestic [home] policy; a policy for domestic consumption.

[brave] enough to engage the enemy all alone. / たった1人でそんなところへ行くとは大胆過ぎる。 How reckless you are to go to such a place alone!
たいてい³ この病気にかかるとたいてい死ぬ。 This disease usually [normally] proves fatal. / たいていいつも自分の自慢ばかりする人はあまり人気のないものだ。 More often than not [In general], a man who is always [forever] boasting about himself is not very popular. / これだけの家族を養うのはたいへいのことじゃありません。 It's no easy task to provide for this large family, you know!
たいど 目上の人にはもっと丁寧な態度をとらなければいけない。 You ought to be more polite to your superiors. / この問題に関してソビエトの態度がいくらかでも軟化する気配はない。 There is no indication of any softening of the Soviet position on this issue.

たいとう² これで対等になった。 Now we are quits. / この分野では日本は今日アメリカと対等の地位にある。 Japan has now achieved equality [now stands on a par] with the U.S. in this field.
たいどう 彼女ははじめて子供の胎動を感じた。 She felt the movements of her child for the first time. / The child quickened in her womb.
だいどうしょうい この2つは大同

たいない[3] 胎内 ¶胎内の[で] in the womb / 胎内感染 prenatal [antenatal] infection.

だいなし 台無し ¶台無しにする spoil ; ruin ; make a mess of ; 《口語》 mess [《米》 foul] *sth* up / 台無しになる be spoilt ; 〈無に帰する〉 come to nothing. [文例⇩]

ダイナマイト dynamite ¶ダイナマイト2本 two sticks of dynamite / ダイナマイトで岩をくずす dynamite a rock.

ダイナモ 〈発電機〉 a dynamo 《*pl.* -s》.

だいに 第二 number two (略 : No. 2) ; the second ¶第2の the second ; 〈もう一つの〉 a second ; another ; 〈重要さが〉 secondary ; 《文》 of secondary importance / 第2に second(ly) ; in the second place / 第2党 the second largest party. [文例⇩]

たいにん[1] 大任 《文》 a great task ; an important mission ¶大任を果たす perform [carry through] a great task ; carry out an important mission / 大任を負っている 《文》 be charged [entrusted] with an important task [duty].

たいにん[2] 退任 ⇨ たいしょく[3].

だいにん 代人 a proxy ; a deputy.

ダイニングキッチン a kitchen-(cum-)dining room ; 《米》 an eat-in kitchen ; 《英》 a breakfast(ing) kitchen.

たいねつ 耐熱 ¶…よりも耐熱性の点ですぐれている have greater heat-resistance than… / 耐熱ガラス heat-resistant glass / 耐熱試験 a heat-resistance test / 耐熱服 a heatproof suit.

たいのう 滞納 arrears 《of rent, taxes》 ; 《文》 delinquency in (making) payment ¶滞納する let 《*one's* taxes》 fall into arrears ; be in arrears with 《the rent》 ; fail to pay / 滞納金 arrears / 滞納者 a 《tax》 delinquent / 税の滞納処分をする make an attachment on *sb's* property for unpaid taxes ; take proceedings [institute a process] against *sb* for the recovery of taxes in arrears. [文例⇩]

だいのう 大脳 the cerebrum 《*pl.* -s, -bra》 ¶大脳皮質 the cerebral cortex.

たいは 大破 ¶大破する be badly [seriously] damaged.

たいはい[1] 大敗 ¶大敗する suffer [meet with] a crushing defeat ; be severely defeated 《by》 ; be routed.

たいはい[2] 退廃 《文》 decadence ¶道義の退廃 decadence ; 《文》 moral decay / 退廃的 decadent.

だいばかり 台秤 a platform scale.

たいばつ 体罰 ¶体罰を加える 《文》 inflict corporal [physical, bodily] punishment 《on》.

だいはっせい 大発生 an explosive increase 《in the number of pests》 ; an [a severe] outbreak 《of locusts》 ; an upsurge 《of harmful insects》 ¶大発生する increase explosively.

たいはん 大半 the greater [better] part 《of》 ; the great [large] portion 《of》 ; the (great) majority 《of》 ¶大半は mostly ; for the most part ; nearly all. [文例⇩]

たいばん 胎盤 〘解〙 the placenta 《*pl.* -s, -tae》.

たいひ[1] 対比 〈対照〉 contrast ; 〈比較〉 comparison ¶対比する contrast 《A with [and] B》 ; compare 《A with [and] B》 ; set 《A》 against 《B》.

たいひ[2] 待[退]避 ¶退避する take shelter 《in, under》 / 退避壕 a shelter ; a dugout ; a foxhole (たこつぼ式の) / (狭い道路で対向車を通すための)待避所 《米》 a turnout ; 《英》 a passing-place / 待避線 〘鉄道〙 a siding ; a sidetrack ; 《米》 a turnout.

たいひ[3] 堆肥 compost ; barnyard [farmyard] manure ¶堆肥を施す compost 《the land》 / 堆肥積み a compost pile [heap].

タイピスト a typist ¶タイピスト学校 a typing school.

だいひつ 代筆 ¶代筆する write 《a letter》 for *sb*.

たいびょう 大病 a serious illness ¶大病になる be taken seriously ill / 大病にかかっている be seriously ill ; be in a serious condition / 大病人 a patient in a serious condition ; a serious case.

だいひょう 代表 〈事〉 《文》 representation ; 〈人〉 a representative ; a delegate ; a delegation (団体) ¶代表する represent ; stand [act] for ; 〈…の典型である〉 be typical of ; 《文》 typify / 代表を送る send delegates [a delegation] 《to a conference》 / 代表的 representative ; typical (種類の) / …を代表して in [on] behalf of … / 代表作 the most important work 《of Maugham》 / 代表社員 a representative partner / 代表番号 〈電話の〉 the key [main] number. [文例⇩]

たいぶ 大部 ¶大部の big ; bulky ; 《文》 voluminous.

タイプ (a) type ; a pattern ¶同じタイプの人 a person of the same type. [文例⇩]

だいぶ 大分 〈非常に〉 very ; greatly ; 〈大いに〉 highly ; to a great degree ; 〈たくさん〉 much ; a good [great] deal ; 〈かなり〉 pretty ; well ; 〈多数〉 many ; a great [good] many ⇨ たくさん [用法] ¶だいぶ時間がある have plenty of time. [文例⇩]

小異だ. There is little to choose between the two.

だいどうみゃく 新幹線は関東と九州を結ぶ交通の大動脈だ. The Shinkansen line is the main artery between the Kanto (region) and Kyushu.

だいなし あんな帽子をかぶったのではせっかくの美貌が台無しだ. That hat spoils her good looks.

だいに 顔形は第2の問題だ. Physical beauty is of secondary importance.

たいのう 彼は月謝が10日間[3か月]滞納になっている. His tuition fees are 10 days overdue [three months in arrears].

たいはん 工事は大半出来上がった. The greater [best] part of the work is finished. | The work is virtually complete.

だいひょう 阿部博士は日本を代表して同会に列した. Dr. Abe represented Japan at the conference. / この会議に日本も代表を送るでしょう. Japan will be represented at the conference. / 彼はこの協議会の米国代表です. He is the American representative on the council.

タイプ 彼女は私の好きなタイプじゃない. She is not the type of woman (that) I like. | She is not my type.

だいぶ 病人はだいぶよくなった. The patient is much better. / 彼はそれにだいぶ金をかけている. He has spent a great deal of money on it. / このごろは学生の

たいふう 台風 a typhoon ¶台風の目 the eye of a typhoon / 台風に襲われる be struck [hit,《文》visited] by a typhoon / 台風圏内にある be within the typhoon area / 台風警報を発す issue [give] a typhoon warning. 文例⇩

だいぶつ 大仏 a great image [statue] of Buddha.

たいぶつレンズ 対物レンズ an object lens [glass]; an objective.

だいぶぶん 大部分 the greater part [of]; the majority [of]; most [of] ¶大部分は for the most part; mostly. 文例⇩

タイプ(ライター) a typewriter ¶タイプを打つ operate [use] a typewriter; typewrite / タイプに打つ type; typewrite / タイプに打った原稿 a typescript; a typed [typewritten] manuscript / 手紙をタイプライターで書く type a letter; write a letter on a typewriter / 和文タイプライター a Japanese-character typewriter.

たいぶんすう 帯分数《数》a mixed fraction.

たいへい 太[泰]平 (perfect) peace ¶太平の peaceful;《文》tranquil; quiet ¶太平をおうかする《文》enjoy the blessings of peace. 文例⇩

たいへいてんごく 太平天国 ¶太平天国の乱《中国史》the Taiping Rebellion.

たいへいよう 太平洋 the Pacific (Ocean) ¶太平洋横断飛行 a transpacific flight / 太平洋戦争 the Pacific War. 文例⇩

たいへいらく 太平楽 ¶太平楽を並べる talk without restraint; indulge in carefree talk.

たいべつ 大別 ¶大別する classify [divide] roughly [broadly] (into) / 2種に大別する divide broadly into two categories.

たいへん¹ 対辺《数》the opposite side. 文例⇩

たいへん² 大変 ¶大変な《重大な》serious;《文》grave;《おそろしい》terrible; awful; dreadful; horrible;《さんたんたる》disastrous;《たくさんの》enormous; immense;《皮肉の意味で》nice; fine / 大変な事 a serious matter [affair]; (be) no laughing matter; (be) no joke / 大変なことになる grow [get] serious;《文》assume alarming proportions / 大変に《非常に》very; greatly;《文》exceedingly; awfully; remarkably; frightfully;《たくさんに》in large numbers [quantities] / 「大変だ!」と叫ぶ cry out in alarm. 文例⇩

だいへん 代返 ¶代返する answer the roll for sb.

だいべん¹ 大便 feces; excrement; stools ¶大便をする defecate; empty [《文》evacuate] one's bowels.

だいべん² 代弁 ¶代弁する speak for sb / 代弁者 a spokesman.

たいほ¹ 退歩《文》retrogression; a step backward ¶退歩する go [move] backward; deteriorate; slip back;《文》retrogress.

たいほ² 逮捕 (an) arrest; (a) capture ¶逮捕する arrest; capture; seize; catch;《文》apprehend / まだ逮捕されていない be still at large / 逮捕状 an arrest warrant; a warrant for sb's arrest. 文例⇩

たいほう 大砲 (fire) a gun; an artillery gun [piece]; a cannon (旧式の).

たいぼう 待望 ¶待望する hope for; look forward to / 待望の hoped-for; long-[eagerly-]awaited;《文》long-sought.

たいぼうしき 戴帽式《看護婦の》the capping ceremony.

たいぼうせいかつ 耐乏生活《文》(a life of) austerity; belt-tightening ¶耐乏生活をする put up with [bear] a hard life; practice austerity; tighten one's belt.

たいほく 台北 Taipei.

たいぼく 大木 a big [large] tree.

だいほん 台本〈劇の〉a (play) script;〈映画の〉a scenario (pl. -s); a (film) script;〈歌劇の〉a libretto (pl. -tos, -ti).

たいま 大麻《植》hemp. ¶大麻(製)の hempen / インド大麻 Indian hemp; marihuana.

たいまい¹ 大枚 ⇒たいきん ¶大枚100万円 as much as [no less than] 1,000,000 yen;《pay out》to the tune of a million yen.

たいまい²《動》《海亀》a hawksbill (turtle).

たいまつ (flaming) torch ¶たいまつ行列《hold》a torchlight procession [parade].

たいまん 怠慢 negligence; neglect;《義務・職務の》(a) default;《不注意》inattention; carelessness ¶怠慢な negligent;《文》neglectful; inattentive; careless / 怠慢な学生 an idle [a lazy] student / 職務に怠慢である neglect [be remiss in] one's duty.

中に眼鏡を掛けている者がだいぶある. Nowadays a considerable percentage of students wear glasses. / 彼は60歳をだいぶ越している. He is well past sixty.

たいふう 台風が発生した. A typhoon formed [was born]. / 台風は急速に発達した. The typhoon developed quickly. / 台風24号の中心気圧は895ミリバル, 半径280キロ以内は秒速25メートル以上の暴風となっている. Typhoon No. 24 has a central atmospheric pressure of 895 millibars and winds of over 25 meters per second within its 280-kilometer radius. / 台風は本州に上陸せず, 太平洋上に去った. The typhoon did not hit Honshu, but passed by off the Pacific coast.

だいぶぶん 生徒の大部分は寮に入っている. Most [The majority] of the students of this school live in the dormitory.

タイプ(ライター) 彼はタイプライターで原稿を作っていた. He was preparing a manuscript on the typewriter. / タイプライターがぱたぱた鳴っていた.「Click, click, click」went the typewriter. / 向こうの部屋からぱたぱたいうタイプライターの音が聞こえてきた. From the room beyond came the rattle [clacking sound] of a typewriter. / これをタイプに打ってもらいたい. I want (to have) this typed.

たいへい 戦乱がおさまって後は太平の世が続いた. After the war the people enjoyed a long period of peace and tranquility.

たいへん¹ 直角三角形の直角の対辺を「斜辺」と言う. The side of a right-angled triangle which subtends [is opposite] the right angle is called the 'hypotenuse'.

たいへん² 大変だ. (Good) Heavens! / こりゃ大変だ. Now this is serious. / お母さんが大変なことになったんだ. Something

だいみょう 大名 a *daimyo*; a feudal lord ¶大名のような暮らしをする live like a lord [prince] / 大名旅行をする go on an expensive tour.

タイミング timing ¶タイミングのいい timely 《remarks》; well-timed 《responses》/ タイミングの悪い untimely 《visits》; mistimed 《actions》/ …とぴったりタイミングを合わせて in exact timing [in perfect synchronization] with….

タイム 〈時間〉 time; 〈試合を一時停止して協議する時間〉 a time-out ¶タイムをとる[計る] time; clock / …のタイムを出す, タイムは…である clock (10.3 seconds); be clocked in [at] (2:37.2); be timed (in) (1:04.2) / …のタイムで with a time of (54.6 seconds) / タイムカプセル a time capsule.

タイムリー ¶タイムリーな timely / タイムリーヒット a timely hit.

タイムレコーダー a time clock ¶タイムレコーダーを押す punch a time clock ;〈出勤して〉clock in [on];〈退社の時〉clock out [off] / 出勤時刻と退社時刻をタイムレコーダーで記録する clock on and off at work; have *one's* arrival and departure times recorded by a time clock.

たいめい 待命 ¶待命になる be ordered to await further instructions; be placed on the waiting list.

だいめい 題名 a title ¶『東京の夜』という題名の映画 a picture entitled 'A Night in Tokyo'.

だいめいし 代名詞 〖文法〗 a pronoun;〈比喩的〉a synonym 《for punctuality》¶代名詞の[的] pronominal.

たいめん 体面 〈名誉〉honor;〈名声〉(a) reputation;〈威厳〉dignity; prestige;〈面子(めんつ)〉face;〈体裁〉appearances ¶体面を保つ[維持する] keep up appearances; save 《*one's*》face / 体面を繕う keep up appearances /〈自分の〉体面を汚す disgrace *oneself* / lose face / 体面にかかわる〈事が主語〉affect *one's* honor; compromise [harm] *one* [*one's* reputation] / 体面上 for appearance' sake; for the sake of appearances. 文例⇩

たいめん[2] 対面 an interview ¶対面する see; meet; interview; have an interview with / 対面交通 walking so as to face the oncoming traffic. 文例⇩

たいもう 大望 (an) ambition;〖文〗(an) aspiration ¶大望ある ambitious; aspiring ¶大望を抱く [〖文〗harbor] an ambition 《to do》. 文例⇩

だいもく 題目 ⇒だい[5], ひょうだい ¶『階級なき社会』という, 共産主義のお題目を唱える reiterate the Communist theme of 'a classless society '. 〖for *sb's* death.

たいや 逮夜 the eve of the (third) anniversary

タイヤ a tire;《英》a tyre ¶自動車のタイヤ an automobile [a car] tire / タイヤの跡 a tiremark; the imprint of a tire (tread) / タイヤを取り替える change a tire; fix [fit] a new tire (on the wheel) / タイヤに空気を入れる pump up [inflate] a tire.

ダイヤ[1] [<diagram] 〈列車の〉a (railroad) schedule [timetable] ¶ダイヤどおりに on schedule. 文例⇩

ダイヤ[2] (a) diamond ¶(トランプの)ダイヤのキング the king of diamonds.

たいやく[1] 大厄 〈不幸〉a great calamity [disaster, misfortune];〈厄年〉a 'grand climacteric'; the most critical year in a person's life (thought to be age 42 for men and 33 for women).

たいやく[2] 大役 〈任務〉an important duty [〖文〗task];〈役割〉an important part [role];〈使命〉a great mission ¶大役を仰せつかる be given [〖文〗be charged with] an important task [mission] / 大役を果たす carry out [〖文〗discharge, 〖文〗perform] an important duty.

たいやく[3] 対訳 a translation (of *Hamlet*) with (its) (Japanese) translation (printed) on the opposite page; a translation printed side by side with the original text. 文例⇩

だいやく 代役 a substitute;〖劇〗an understudy;〖映画〗a stand-in ¶代役を勤める play the part for *sb*; stand in 《for》; understudy 《the leading actor》; act as a substitute 《for》.

ダイヤモンド 〖鉱〗(a) diamond;〖野球〗the diamond ¶工業用ダイヤモンド (an) industrial diamond / ダイヤモンドゲーム Chinese checkers.

---

awful has happened to your mother. | 大変な男だね. What a man! / 大変おもしろかった. I had a very good time. / 病人は大変によくなった. The patient's condition has very much improved. / この知識を得るのは大変だった. This knowledge was hard won. / 群衆を抑えるのに警官は大変だった. The police had a difficult job keeping the mob back. / 大変な一日だったわ』と彼女はあえぎながら言った. 'It has been quite a day,' said she, gasping for breath. / 君は大変なことをしてくれたねえ.〈皮肉に〉A nice [fine] mess you've made of it!

たいほ[2] 彼に逮捕状が出ている. There is a warrant out for his arrest. | There is an arrest warrant out against [for] him.

だいほん 台本なしのテレビインタビューは台本のあるものよりずっと面白い. Unscripted TV interviews are far more interesting than scripted ones.

タイム 僕がタイムを計ってやろう. I'll time you. / タイムアップ. Time's up.

たいめん 彼の体面にかかわることだ. It is a point of honor with him. / そんなことをするとあなたの体面にかかわりますよ. It should be beneath you [your dignity] to do things like that. / 彼は学校の体面を汚すやつだ. He is a disgrace to the school.

たいめん[2] 20年ぶりで親子が対面した. Father and son met after twenty years' separation.

たいもう 彼は大望を抱いてむなしく死んだ. He died without realizing his ambition.

ダイヤ[1] ダイヤが乱れている. The trains are not running on schedule. |〈ひどく〉The schedule has gone haywire.

たいやく[3] この双書は英和対訳になっている. In this series the English original has its Japanese

ダイヤル a dial ¶ダイヤルを回す dial 《a certain number》/ ダイヤルを回して電話をかける dial a call 《to》/ ラジオのダイヤルを第一放送に合わせる turn on [tune in to] the First Program.

たいよ 貸与 ¶貸与する lend; give the loan of *sth*; loan / 貸与を請う ask for the loan 《of》.

たいよう¹ 大洋 an ocean ¶大洋の of oceanic / 大洋の真中で[に] in the middle of the ocean; in mid-ocean [mid-sea] / 大洋を航海する sail the ocean.

たいよう² 大要 ⇨ たいりゃく.

たいよう³ 太陽 the sun ¶太陽の solar / 太陽の光線 the rays of the sun; sunbeams / 太陽の光 sunlight / 太陽に照らされたベランダ a sunlit verandah / 太陽系 the solar system / 太陽黒点 a sunspot / 太陽神 the sun god (goddess) / 太陽神話 a solar [sun] myth / 太陽電池 a solar cell [battery] / 太陽灯 a sunlamp; a sunray lamp / 太陽灯治療を受ける take sunray [artificial sunlight] treatment; lie under a sunlamp / 太陽熱 solar heat / 太陽熱利用の温水プール a solar-heated swimming pool / 太陽風 (the) solar wind / 太陽暦 the solar calendar.

だいよう 代用 ¶代用する substitute [use] 《B》for《A》/ …の代用として in place of…; (in substitution), for… / 代用品 a substitute 《for》.

たいようしゅう 大洋州 Oceania ¶大洋州の Oceanian.

たいようねんすう 耐用年数 the life 《of a building》¶耐用年数は6年である last six years; do not [be unlikely to] last more than six years.

たいよく 大欲 avarice; greed. 文例⇩

たいら¹ 平〈山中の平地〉a plain; a flat ¶松本平 the Matsumoto Plain.

たいら² 平ら ¶平らな〈偏平な〉flat;〈平滑な〉even; smooth;〈水平な〉level; horizontal / 平らにする level (down, up, off); flatten; make *sth* even [smooth]; smooth; roll 《金属などを》/ 地面を平らにする level the ground / 平らでない uneven; rugged.

たいらげる 平らげる〈平定する〉put down;《文》subjugate; suppress;〈飲食する〉eat [drink] up; finish up (the dinner); put away; make a clean sweep of 《a pound of beef》.

だいり 代理《文》proxy,《文》agency;〈特に医者や牧師の〉a locum tenens 《*pl.* locum tenentes》;〈口語〉a locum ¶代理する act for [in behalf of]; represent; substitute for / …

の代理として in [on] behalf of… / 代理で by proxy / 校長代理 an acting principal / 代理公使 a chargé d'affaires 《*pl.* chargés d'affaires》/ 代理戦争 a war by proxy / 代理店 an agency / 代理人 a deputy; an agent; an attorney; a substitute. 文例⇩

だいりき 大力 ¶大力の《文》of great [enormous] strength / 大力無双の《文》of unparalleled physical strength.

たいりく 大陸 a continent ¶大陸の[的] continental / 大陸性的気候 a continental climate / アジア[ヨーロッパ]大陸 the Continent of Asia [Europe]; the Asian [European] continent / 大陸移動説〔地理〕the continental-drift theory / 大陸横断の transcontinental / 大陸間弾道弾 an intercontinental ballistic missile (略: ICBM) / 大陸棚 a continental shelf.

だいりせき 大理石 marble ¶大理石の彫像 a marble statue; a statue in marble.

たいりつ 対立 (a) confrontation 《between A and B》¶対立する a confront; be opposed 《to》/ …に[と]対立して in opposition to…; in rivalry with… / 対立意見 an opposing [a rival] opinion / …の対立候補として選挙に打って出る《米》run for《President》against…;《英》stand for《Parliament》against….

たいりゃく 大略〈摘要〉a summary; the gist;《文》an epitome; a résumé;〈概略〉an outline;〈ほぼ〉almost; about; nearly; roughly [broadly] (speaking); in broad outline; on the whole;〈一般に〉generally; in general ¶大略を述べる give an outline [a summary] 《of》; sum up; summarize; outline. 文例⇩

たいりゅう¹ 対流〔物〕a convection current ¶対流させる circulate (warm air) by convection / 対流圏〔気象〕the troposphere.

たいりゅう² 滞留 ⇨ たいざい.

たいりょう¹ 大量 a large [great] quantity 《of》; a lot 《of》¶大量に in large quantities; in (great) volume; on a massive [large] scale / 大量生産 mass production; production on a large scale / 大量生産する mass-produce; produce on a large scale / 大量解雇[検挙] a mass discharge [arrest].

たいりょう² 大漁[猟] a large [big] catch [take];〈大漁〉a good [rich] haul;〈大猟〉a big [good] bag. 文例⇩

たいりょく 体力 physical [bodily] strength ¶体力を養う develop [build up] *one's* (physical) strength / 体力テスト a test of physical strength. 文例⇩

たいりん 大輪 ¶大輪の large-flowered; big-

---

translation on the opposite page.

たいよく 大欲は無欲に似たり. Grasp all, lose all. 諺

たいら 平らぞお平らに. Please make yourself comfortable [at home].

だいり 私が主人の代理を致します. I will act for my husband. / 父が病気ですから私が代理にお得意を回っています. My father is ill; so I have to go round seeing customers on his behalf.

たいりゃく 大略左のごとし. It may be summarized [summed up] as follows. / 実情は大略このようである. Roughly [Broadly] speaking, that is the (true) situation.

たいりょう² 今日はいわしが大漁だった. We had a successful [rich] haul of sardines today. / 大漁を祈る! Good fishing!

たいりょく 彼にはそれをするだけの体力が充分ある. He is strong enough for it.

たえがたい 東京の夏の暑さは耐え難い. I cannot bear [stand] the heat of summer in Tokyo.

たえだえ 彼は息も絶え絶えだった. I found him breathing feebly. / やがて笛の音も絶え絶えとなり、ついに消えた. Then the notes of the flute grew fainter

タイル a tile ¶陶製タイル a ceramic tile / タイルを張る tile 《the bathroom》; cover [face] 《the floor》 with tiles; lay tiles 《on》 / タイル張りの tiled 《floors》.

ダイレクトメール direct mail ¶ダイレクトメールによる広告 direct-mail advertising; advertising by direct mail.

たいれつ 隊列 ⇒たいご².

たいろ 退路 one's (path of) retreat ¶退路を断つ intercept [cut off] sb's retreat / 退路を断たれる have one's retreat cut off.

だいろっかん 第六感 a sixth sense.

たいわ 対話 (a) conversation; (《文》) (a) colloquy; a dialogue ¶対話をする talk [《文》converse]《with》; have [hold] a talk [conversation]《with》/ 対話形式の written in dialogue / プラトンの対話篇 the Dialogues of Plato.

たいわん 台湾 Taiwan ¶台湾の Taiwanese / 台湾海峡 the Taiwan Strait / 台湾人 a Taiwanese 《単複同形》.

ダウ ¶ダウ平均株価 the Dow-Jones average (price of stocks)《on the Tokyo Stock Exchange》.

たうえ 田植え rice-planting ¶田植えをする transplant rice seedlings; set out rice plants; plant rice / 田植え時 the rice-planting season.

ダウン ¶ダウンする〈倒す〉knock down;《口語》floor;〈倒される〉be knocked down; be floored.

たえいる 絶え入る ¶絶え入るばかりに《weep》as if one's heart would break.

たえがたい 耐え難い〈我慢できない〉unbearable; intolerable;《文》unendurable;〈圧倒的な〉overpowering; overwhelming;〈抵抗できない〉irresistible. 文例↓

だえき 唾液 saliva; sputum ¶唾液腺 a salivary gland.

たえしのぶ 耐え忍ぶ ⇒たえる¹.

たえず 絶えず constantly; incessantly;《文》ceaselessly; continually; continuously;《without interruption》《文》cease, a break》;〈常に〉always; all the time;〈永久に〉perpetually ¶絶えず見張る keep a constant watch《over》.

たえだえ 絶え絶え ¶息も絶え絶えに言う gasp out《that...》. 文例↓

たえま 絶え間 an interval; a pause; a break; a gap ¶雲の絶え間から through a break [gap, rift, rent, cleft] in the clouds / 絶え間なく ⇒たえず. 文例↓

たえる¹ 耐[堪]える〈我慢する〉endure; bear; stand; put up with;〈抵抗する〉stand up to; withstand; hold (out);〈適する〉be fit [good]《for》; be equal《to》;《文》be competent《to do》¶あらしに耐える weather (out) a storm / どんな天候にも耐える be proof against all weathers / 不幸に耐える bear up under misfortune / 誘惑に耐える resist temptation / 任に堪える[堪えない] be equal [unequal] to the task / 重荷に耐えかねる give way under the burden / ...は遺憾に堪える《文》It is much to be regretted that...; It is a great pity that.... 文例↓

たえる² 絶える〈消滅する〉《文》cease to exist; become extinct; go out of existence; die (out);〈止む〉《文》cease; be discontinued;〈終る〉end; come to an end;〈泉の水などが〉fail ¶息が絶える《文》expire;《文》breathe [gasp] one's last / 供給が絶える《人が主語》be cut off from supplies [the supply]《of》/ 絶えざる《文》incessant; ceaseless; constant; continual;《文》unfailing; perpetual / 絶えて...しない never; not...at all.

だえん 楕円 an ellipse; an [a regular] oval ¶楕円(形)の elliptic(al); oval.

たおす 倒す〈転倒させる〉knock [push, throw, bring] sth down;〈吹き倒す〉blow sth down;〈切り倒す〉cut [fell] down; fell;〈取りこわす〉pull down; demolish;〈地震などが〉destroy;〈勘定を〉fail to pay;〈負かす〉beat; defeat;〈殺す〉kill;〈滅ぼす〉overthrow; ruin; topple ¶政府を倒す overthrow [topple] the government / 家を倒す demolish [wreck, destroy, pull down] a house. 文例↓

たおやか ¶たおやかな graceful; willowy.

たおる 手折る break [snap] off《a twig》; pluck《a flower》; nip off《a leaf》.

タオル a towel ¶タオルで拭く towel《oneself》; wipe [dry]《one's hands》with [on] a towel / タオル地 toweling.

たおれる 倒れる fall (down); come down; collapse;〈病気などで〉break down; give way [《文》succumb];〈下に〉be down (with); be laid low《by》;〈死ぬ〉die《of, from》; be killed;〈滅びる〉be ruined; go to ruin;《文》perish;〈崩壊する〉be overthrown;〈破産する〉go《文》become》bankrupt; fail;《口語》go bust / 前[後]に倒れる fall forward [backward] / 疲れ切って倒れる break down from exhaustion / 倒れかかっている be on the point of falling; be on the verge [brink] of collapse [bankruptcy] / 戦場に倒れる be killed in action; fall in battle / 倒れて後やむ die fighting; fight to the death. 文例↓

and fainter, and at last died [faded] away.

たえま この通りは車の絶え間がありません。There is a ceaseless stream of traffic in this street. / 彼は心配の絶え間がない。He always has something worrying him.|He is never free from cares.

たえる¹ それは私には耐えられない事だ。It is more than I can bear.｜It is too much for me. / もうこれ以上耐えられない。I can't stand it any more. / まだまだ君は幾多の試練に耐えなければならない。You still have more trials to go through. / 彼はこの職に耐え得る年ではない。He is too old for the post. / たとえ回復しても激務にはえられないだろう。Even if he recovered, he would never be fit for hard work. / このジェット機は 4 g の加速度に耐えるように作られている。This jet plane is built to withstand four g.

たえる² キリマンジャロの頂上には年中雪が絶えない。There is snow on the summit of Mt. Kilimanjaro all the year round.

たおす 独裁者を倒せ。Down with the dictator!

たおれる この柱があるので家が倒れないのだ。This post is all that

たか¹ 高 〈量〉(a) quantity; volume; an amount;〈数〉a number;〈金額〉a sum ¶高が only; merely; at best; at most; no more than; after all / 高の知れた trifling; trivial; inconsiderable; insignificant / 高をくくる make light [nothing] of; belittle; minimize; underrate; underestimate. 文例④

たか² 鷹〖鳥〗a hawk; a falcon (たか狩用の) ¶たか狩 falconry / たか狩をする hunt with a falcon / たか匠 a falconer / たか派(の人) a hawk.

たが 箍 a hoop ¶たがをかける hoop; put a hoop on; bind (a barrel) with hoops / たがをはずす unhoop; take the hoops off (a barrel). 文例④

だが but; however; yet; nevertheless; for all that; still;〈一方では〉on the other hand ¶なるほど…だが… It is true [To be sure], but…; indeed…, but…. 文例④

たかあしがに〖動〗a giant crab; a Japanese spider crab.

たかい¹ 他界 ¶他界する ⇒しぬ.

たかい² 高い high; tall;〈文〉lofty;〈文〉exalted;〈文〉elevated;〈高貴な〉noble;〈音量が〉loud;〈高価な〉dear; expensive; costly ¶高い望み a high ambition / 身分の高い人〈地位が〉a person with a [〈文〉of] high position [status];〈生まれが〉〈文〉a person of high [noble] birth; 調子の高い〈声の〉high-pitched; shrill;〈堂々とした〉〈文〉(a work) written in an exalted style / 高い声で loudly; in a loud voice;〈かん高く〉in a shrill voice / 高そうな expensive-looking / 高く high;〈文〉aloft;〈高価に〉dear; (buy) at a high price / 高くする raise;〈文〉elevate;〈増す〉increase;〈値上げする〉raise the price (of) / 高くなる be raised;〈文〉be elevated; get [grow,〈文〉become] taller (丈が); go up [increase] in price (値段が) / お高くとまる be supercilious; be haughty; look down on sb / 高くつく cost one a great deal [a lot]; be [〖口語〗come] expensive / 高くても at (the) most; at the highest / 空高く high up in the air (sky). 文例④

たがい 互い ¶互いの〈文〉mutual;〈文〉reciprocal; each other's; one another's / 互いに mutually; (with) each other [one another] / 互いに話合い[相談]の上で〈文〉by mutual consent / 互いに助け合う help each other [one another]. 文例④

用法 each other は2人[2つのもの]について, one another は3人以上[3つ以上のもの]について使うことにしている人もあるが, この原則は守られないことが多い.

だかい 打開 a breakthrough; a break; a solution ¶局面を打開する achieve a breakthrough; resolve the situation / 難局を打開する find a way out of the difficulties / 行き詰まりを打開する break the deadlock.

たがいせん 互い先〖囲碁〗¶互い先で打つ make the first move in alternate games; play on an equal footing.

たがいちがい 互い違い ¶互い違いに alternately / 互い違いにする[なる] alternate 《with》.

たかいびき 高鼾 a loud snore ¶高いびきをかく snore loudly.

たがう 違う〈異なる〉〈文〉differ 《from》; be different 《from》;〈違反する〉break;〈文〉violate;〈文〉infringe; offend 《against》; run counter 《to》; go back on (one's word);〈そむく〉deviate 《from》; go against (human nature); be contrary to (humanity) / 名声にたがわない live [act] up to one's reputation / (約束などの) 時間に1分とたがわない be punctual to the minute / 寸分たがわずに without the least difference; exactly.

たがえる 違える break [fail to keep] (one's word) ¶1分と時間をたがえない be punctual to the minute / 約束をたがえない keep [fulfill] one's promise; be as good as [true to] one's word.

たかく 多角 ¶多角的 many-sided; multilateral / 多角形 a polygon / 多角経営 diversified business (operations) / 多角貿易 multilateral trade.

たがく 多額 ¶多額の a lot of; a large sum [amount] of (money); a great deal of (money); (not) much; large (funds); considerable (profits) / 多額の欠損 a heavy loss of money; heavy losses / 多額納税者 a high [an upper-bracket] taxpayer.

---

keeps the house from falling down. / 風でたくさんの木が倒れた. The wind brought [blew] down a large number of trees. / この地震で何軒かの家が倒れた. Several houses were destroyed by the earthquake. / 彼も流感に倒れた. He, too, came down [was laid up] with influenza. / その疫病で数千の人々が倒れた. The plague carried off thousands of people [took a toll of thousands of lives].

たか¹ 高が数分の遅れでそうかんかんになって怒ることはないじゃないか. What's the use of getting so angry over a mere few minutes' delay? / 僕の財産なんて高の知れたものだ. My property is nothing to speak of. / 高が千円ばかりのものだ. It is worth no more than a thousand yen. / 高の知れたものさ. It's a mere trifle. | It's nothing much. / 落第することはあるまいと彼は高をくくっていた. He didn't really take the possibility of failing seriously.

たが たががはずれた. The hoops have come off. / たががゆるんでいる. The hoops have got loose. / あの男もそろそろたががゆるんできた. He has lost some of the intellectual power [strength of character] that he used to have. だが 学者は学者だが, 彼は常識がない. He is a good scholar, to be sure, but he is lacking in common sense. / だが君は行ったほうがいいよ. Still, you'd better go.

たかい² 彼は僕よりも3センチ高い. He is three centimeters taller than I am. | He is taller than me by three centimeters. ⇒より² 用法 彼の望みは高すぎる. He sets his sights too high. | He is too ambitious. / 降る雪を見ながら, どのくらい高い所から降っているのかしらと思った. She stared at the snowflakes and wondered how high up they were falling from. / 何もかも高くなった. Everything has gone up [risen] in price.

たかぐもり 高曇り overcast 〈weather〉 with high cloud.

たかさ 高さ height ;《文》(an) altitude ; loudness (音量の); (a) pitch (音高の) ¶高さが3メートルある be three meters high [in height]/(樹木などが)非常な高さになる grow to a great height / 2千メートルの高さを飛ぶ fly at a height [an altitude] of 2,000 meters. 文例⇩

だがし 駄菓子 cheap cakes [confectionery].

たかしお 高潮 a flood [high] tide. 文例⇩

たかだい 高台 a hill ;《文》an eminence ; a height ;《文》an elevation ;《文》elevated ground ★ height は複数形で用いられることが多い.

たかだか 高々 at (the) most ; at the highest [greatest, largest] ; at best ; no more than ; merely ; only ;《文》but ¶高々と high ;《文》aloft / 声高々と in a loud voice ; loudly. 文例⇩

だがっき 打楽器 a percussion instrument ;《ジャズ》traps.

たかとび[1] 高飛び ¶高飛びする run away ;《口語》flee ;《文》decamp ; make off ; abscond.

たかとび[2] 高跳び the high jump ¶走り高跳び the running high jump / 棒高跳び ⇨ぼうたかとび.

たかとびこみ 高飛び込み high [platform] diving ; a high dive ¶女子10メートル高飛び込み women's ten-meter high diving / 高飛び込み競技 a high-diving event / 高飛び込み選手 a high diver.

たかな 高菜 leaf mustard.

たかなり 高鳴り 〈胸の〉fast beating ; violent throbbing [palpitation].

たかなる 高鳴る 〈潮が〉roar ; 〈胸が〉throb violently ; beat fast.

たかね[1] 高値 ¶高値で at a high price / 高値で売れる sell for [fetch] a high price.

たかね[2] 高嶺 a high [《文》lofty] peak ¶高嶺の花 a prize beyond one's reach ; an unattainable object. 文例⇩

たがね 鑽 〈彫刻の〉a graver ; a burin ; 〈鉄切り用の〉a cold chisel.

たかのぞみ 高望み ¶高望みする hope for what one cannot be reasonably expected to obtain ; aim too high ; be overambitious ; be too [《文》inordinately] ambitious.

たかびしゃ 高飛車 ¶高飛車に出る act [speak] overbearingly [highhandedly] ; adopt highhanded methods [measures] ; take a highhanded approach.

たかぶり 高ぶり ⇨こうふん[2] ¶感情の高ぶりを感じる get [grow] excited (at) ; feel excitement 《文》an upsurge of emotion (at).

たかぶる 高ぶる 〈いばる〉be proud ; be haughty ; be arrogant ; be puffed up ; 〈えらそうにする〉put on airs ;《口語》be uppish [uppity] ; assume an air of importance ¶感情が高ぶる grow [get] excited (at) ; be worked up (about) ⇨ たかぶり (高ぶりを感じる) / 高ぶった proud ; haughty ; arrogant ; patronizing. 文例⇩

たかまくら 高枕 ¶高枕で眠る sleep in peace ; live free from care.

たかまり 高まり a rise ; a build-up (of pressure) ;《文》an upsurge (of emotion) ¶緊張の高まり a rise in tension ; increasing tension.

たかまる 高まる rise ; be raised ;《文》be elevated ; increase ; mount ¶名声が高まる rise in fame [popularity]. 文例⇩

たかみ 高み a height ;《文》an eminence ★ height はしばしば複数形で用いられる ¶高みの見物をする stand by idly ; look on with folded arms ; watch as an idle [《文》a disinterested] spectator.

たかめ 高目 ¶高めの球 a high ball / (野球で)投球が高めに外れてボールになる〈ピッチャーが主語〉pitch a little too high and have it called a ball / (値段などが)どちらかと言えば高めである be on the high side.

たがめ 【昆】a giant water bug.

たかめる 高める raise ; lift ; heighten ;《文》elevate ;《文》exalt ;《文》enhance ; boost 《morale》; improve ; 〈助長する〉promote ; 〈高尚にする〉《文》ennoble (one's character) ¶趣味を高める refine [cultivate] one's taste / 価値を高める enhance [increase, heighten] the value (of). 文例⇩

たがやす 耕す cultivate ; till ; turn over 《the soil》;《米》plow ;《英》plough.

たから 宝 a treasure ; a precious thing ¶(先祖からの)家の宝 an [a family] heirloom / 地

たがい 彼らは互いに顔を見合わせた. They looked at each other [each other's faces]. / お互いに相手の都合など念頭にない様子だった. Neither of them seemed to be concerned about the convenience of the other. | They even appeared to be acting with no concern for the other's convenience. ★ このように other が each から離れて the other となる. / お互いさまです / 《私もそうです》That makes two of us. | So am I.

たかさ この木は高さが20メートルぐらいになる. This tree grows to (a height of) about 20 meters. / この山は高さが3千メートルある. The mountain is 3,000 meters high [in height]. / そのような高さの所では空気がきわめて希薄である. At those altitudes the air is extremely thin.

たかしお 台風は神戸港を襲い, 高潮が岸壁を越えた. The typhoon hit the port of Kobe, sweeping high tides across the wharves.

たかだか その取引の利益は高々1万円だった. The profit from the transaction was only 10,000 yen. | All we got out of the deal was a miserable 10,000 yen.

たかね[2] 彼女は高嶺の花だ. She is as unattainable as the stars [moon].

たかびしゃ そんな高飛車な態度はよしてちょうだい. Don't take that high and mighty tone with me.

たかぶる His nerves are (all) on edge. / 成功したからといっておごり高ぶってはいけない. You mustn't get puffed up with your success.

たかまる その知らせを受けて我々の希望は高まった. Our hopes mounted [rose high] at the news.

たかめる 新しい機械を入れたので, 我が社の製品の品質は大いに高められた. The installation of the new machine has greatly improved the quality of our

だから so; therefore; (and) consequently; for that reason ¶…だから because…; because of *sth*; as…; since…; on account of *sth*; owing to *sth*; now that…; seeing that…. 〔文例⇩〕

たからか 高らか ¶高らかに loudly; in a loud [ringing] voice.

たからがい 宝貝 a cowry; a cowrie.

たからくじ 宝籤 a public lottery. ¶宝くじを買う buy a lottery ticket / 宝くじで1等に当たる win the first prize in a public lottery.

たからもの 宝物 ⇨たから.

たかり 〈行為〉 sponging; extortion; 〈人〉 a sponger.

たかる 〈集まる〉 swarm; crowd; gather; flock; be infested with (場所が主語); 〈せびる〉 squeeze [extort] 〈money from *sb*〉; sponge on 〈*sb* for *sth*〉. 〔文例⇩〕

-たがる want [wish, long, 《文》 desire] to *do*; be eager [anxious] to *do*; be curious to 〈know〉; 〈…しがちである〉 be apt [liable] to *do*. 〔文例⇩〕

たかわらい 高笑い a loud [boisterous] laugh; loud laughter; a guffaw; a horselaugh ¶高笑いする laugh loudly [boisterously]; roar with [burst into a roar of] laughter; guffaw.

たかん 多感 ¶多感な 〈感じやすい〉 sensitive; susceptible; 〈感傷的〉 sentimental; 〈多情多感の〉 passionate.

だかんけん 兌換券 a convertible note.

たき¹ 多岐 ¶多岐にわたる 〈色々のことを含む〉 include many (different) things; 〈色々のことを取り上げる〉 take [bring] up various topics (for discussion).

たき² 滝 a waterfall; a cascade (別れ滝); a cataract (大きな). ¶華厳(ごん)の滝 the Kegon Falls / 幾段にもなって落ちる滝 a waterfall dropping down a series of cascades / 滝に打たれる stand under a waterfall (offering prayers to a deity) / (さけるごとく)滝を登る climb up a waterfall / 滝つぼ the basin [plunge pool] of a waterfall. 〔文例⇩〕

だき 唾棄 ¶唾棄すべき 〈不快な〉 detestable; disgusting; revolting; 〈いやしむべき〉 despicable.

だきあう 抱き合う hug [《文》 embrace] each other; go [fall] into each other's arms.

だきあげる 抱き上げる take 《a child》 (up) in one's arms.

だきあわせ 抱き合わせ ¶抱き合わせ販売 tie-in sale.

だきおこす 抱き起こす raise *sb* in one's arms.

だきかかえる 抱き抱える hold [carry] 《a child》 in one's arms.

たきぎ 薪 firewood; wood for fuel; 〈束ねた〉 a fag(g)ot ¶たきぎを拾う gather [collect] firewood / たきぎをくべる put [lay] more wood (on the fire) / たきぎ小屋 a woodshed.

たきぐち 焚き口 the (fire) door (of a furnace).

だきこむ 抱き込む 〈誘う〉 win [bring] *sb* over (to one's side).

タキシード 《米》 a tuxedo (*pl*. -s); 《主に英》 a dinner jacket.

だきしめる 抱き締める hug [《文》 embrace] *sb* close; hold *sb* tight; give *sb* a tight hug; press 《a baby》 to one's breast ¶抱きしめたくなるような女の子 a cuddlesome [cuddly] little girl.

だきすくめる 抱きすくめる hold *sb* firmly in one's arms so that *he* is unable to move; hug *sb* fast; hold [get] *sb* in a bear hug.

たきだし 炊き出し ¶炊き出しをする distribute boiled rice.

だきつく 抱き付く cling to *sb*; fly [throw oneself] into *sb's* arms; throw [fold] one's arms around [about] *sb*.

たきつけ 焚き付け kindling (wood) ¶たきつけによい be good for lighting [starting] a fire with. 〔文例⇩〕

たきつける 焚き付ける 〈火を〉 light; kindle; make [start] a fire; 〈扇動する〉 put *sb* up 《to (commit) a crime》; incite; agitate; egg *sb* on 《to *do*, to *sth*》; instigate; 《法》abet 《*sb* in a crime》 ¶ストーブに火をたきつける make a fire in a stove; start a stove / 人にかをたきつける fan [stir up] a quarrel / 人にたきつけられて…する《文》 do at *sb's* instigation.

だきとめる 抱き止める stop *sb* by throwing one's arms around *him*; catch 《a child》 in one's arms; hold *sb* back.

たきび 焚き火 a bonfire ¶焚き火をする make [build] a fire [bonfire] / 木を燃やして小さな焚き火をする make a small wood fire.

たきもの 焚き物 fuel (for a fire); something to make a fire with ⇨たきぎ.

だきょう 妥協 (a) compromise ¶妥協する compromise; come to terms [an understanding] 《with》; reach a compromise [an agree-

---

products.

たから 彼は我が社の宝である。He is a great asset to our company.

だから だから病気になったのだ。That is why you got [fell] ill. / だからといって行かずにもいられない。Even so [For all that], I must go. / やつはけちだ、だからみんなに嫌われる。He is stingy; that's why everyone hates him.

たかる 床にこぼした砂糖にありがたかっている。Ants are swarming on the sugar that someone spilled on the floor. / あの梅の木に毛虫がいっぱいたかっている。That *ume* tree is swarming with caterpillars. / 交番のまわりに大勢人がたかっていた。There was a big crowd of people around the police box.

-たがる 彼は修学旅行に行きたがっていたが、急に風邪を引いて参加できなかった。He was very keen to go on the school trip [He wanted to go on the school trip very much], but unfortunately caught (a) cold and could not take part. / 女というものはとかくぜいたくをしたがるものだ。Women love to go to extravagance.

たき² 滝がけっぷちから流れ落ちていた。A waterfall was rushing [streaming] over the edge of the precipice. / 雨が滝のように降っている。The rain is coming down in torrents. / 汗が彼の顔を滝のように流れた。Sweat poured down his face.

たきつけ たきつけに使えるよ。They can be used for lighting fires.

たきょく 多極 ¶多極化した世界政治 multi-polarized world politics.

だきよせる 抱き寄せる draw sb closer to one(-self) [《文》 one's breast].

たぎる boil; be on the boil; seethe.

たく¹ 宅 a home; a house; a residence / 夫 my husband;〈われわれ〉we ⇨ **おたく**/宅扱い (direct) door-to-door service.

たく² 卓 a table; a desk ¶卓を囲む sit (a)round a table / 卓をたたく bang [hit] (one's fist on) the table /《文》strike the table /〈続けて激しく〉pound [beat] the table.

たく³ 焚[炊]く 〈燃やす〉burn; kindle; make [light, build] (a fire);〈煮る〉boil; cook ¶ふろをたく heat (the) water for a bath; heat [make] a bath / ボイラーをたく stoke a boiler / 何もたくものがない have nothing to make a fire with; have no fuel.

だく 抱く hold [take] (a baby) in one's arms;《文》embrace; hug;〈鳥が卵を〉sit (on eggs); brood (eggs) ¶肩を抱く take [hold] sb round the shoulders / 抱いている have [carry] (a baby) in one's arms. [文例⇩]

たくあん 沢庵 pickled radish.

たぐい 類い ⇨ **しゅるい** ¶たぐいない《文》matchless;《文》peerless; unique; unequaled;《文》unparalleled /たぐいまれである《文》be rare; be rarely (to be) met with /〈他に例を見ない〉be unique; stand unparalleled [unequalled] (in).

たくえつ 卓越 excellence;《文》preeminence;《文》primacy; superiority ¶卓越する《文》excel (in),《文》surpass (in); be distinguished /卓越した excellent; eminent; superb;《文》paramount;《文》preeminent; distinguished /卓越した偉人《文》a person of outstanding stature [greatness].

だくおん 濁音 a voiced sound.

たくさん 沢山 ¶〈量〉much; a large quantity 《of》; a great [good] deal 《of》;〈数〉(a great) many; many a (★続く名詞は単数); a large number 《of》;〈量・数ともに〉a lot 《of》; lots 《of》;〈充分な〉plenty 《of》; sufficient ¶たくさん(に) plentifully; in plenty; abundantly; 〈量〉in large quantities;〈数〉in (large) numbers /たくさんある〈その物が主語〉there is plenty of (food);《文》be abundant;《文》be plentiful /〈物のあり場所が主語〉be full of /《文》abound in [with] / 朝食をたくさん食べる have a large [big] breakfast. [文例⇩]

[用法] 日常語では much や many は肯定文の中で単独に名詞の前につけて使われることはほとんどなくなっている。He has much money. や He has many books. などの much や many は a lot of; a great deal of; a large number of; a great many など, 本項に挙げた, 口語的な句で言い換えられる。He doesn't have much money. や Does he have many books? のような否定文や疑問文では much, many を使う。

たくしあげる たくし上げる tuck [roll] up.

タクシー a taxi; a taxicab; a cab ¶流しのタクシー a cruising taxi /タクシーの運転手 a taxi driver; a cabman;《口語》a cabby / タクシーを呼ぶ call [hail] a taxi / タクシーを拾う pick up a taxi / タクシーで行く go by taxi (to); take a taxi (to) / タクシー会社 a taxi [taxicab] company / (駅前などの)タクシー乗り場 a taxi stand;《英》a taxi rank. [文例⇩]

たくじしょ 託児所 a day nursery; a day-care center;《英》a crèche.

たくじょう 卓上 ¶卓上の[に] on the table [desk] /卓上用の desk [dictionaries] /卓上電話 a desk telephone.

たくす 託す ¶卓上の[に]《文》entrust 《sth to sb, sb with sth》; 《文》charge 《sb with a task, to do》; place sth in [under] sb's charge; place sth under sb's care [in sb's hands]; leave [commit] sth to sb's care. [文例⇩]

たくせつ 卓説 a remarkable opinion; a far-sighted [sound and sensible] view.

たくぜつ 卓絶 ⇨ **たくえつ**.

たくせん 託宣 ⇨ **ごたくせん, しんたく²**.

たくそう 託送 ¶託送する send sth by [through, with, under the care of] sb; consign 《goods to a forwarding agency》.

だくだく ¶だくだく流れる flow in streams; gush out.

たくち 宅地 land for housing; a housing site; a house [building] lot (普通1軒分の);〈既に家のある〉residential land ¶宅地を造成する prepare a housing site; turn (the land) into housing lots / 宅地造成 residential development.

だくてん 濁点 a sonant mark.

タクト [<《ドイツ語》*Taktstock*]〈指揮棒〉a baton ¶タクトをとる[振る] conduct [direct]

だきょう 両者の間に妥協が成立した。A compromise was reached between them. / 妥協の余地はない。There is no room for compromise. |《文》It admits of no compromise.

だく 赤ん坊は母親に抱かれて眠っている。The baby is sleeping in its mother's arms. / 子供が甘えて, 抱っこ。Carry me. Carry me.

たぐい それは空中に楼閣を築くのたぐいだ。That is like building castles in the air.

たくさん まだ言いたいことがたくさんある。There's a lot more I'd like to say. / この川には魚がたくさんいる。This river is full of [《文》abounds with] fish. / まだ時間がたくさんある。There is plenty of time yet. / 彼女は着物をたくさん持っている。She has a lot of clothes [《文》a large wardrobe]. / 1万円もあればたくさんです。Ten thousand yen will do. / もうたくさんです。Thank you, (but) I've had enough. / そんな話はもうたくさんだ。I'm fed up with that sort of story.

タクシー タクシーを止めて乗り込んだ。She halted [flagged down] a taxi and stepped in.

たくす 彼は名刺を私に託して行った。He has left his card with me. / 彼は大事を託するにたりる。He is worthy of a heavy trust.

だくだく 汗がだくだく出た。Sweat poured off him.

たくはつ 托鉢 religious mendicancy ¶たくはつする go about asking for alms / たくはつ僧 a begging bonze ; a mendicant (friar).

だくひ 諾否 yes or no ; 《文》consent or refusal. 文例⇩

たくほん 拓本 a rubbed copy (of) ; a [an ink] rubbing ¶拓本を取る do a rubbing (of) ; take an ink rubbing (from).

たくましい 逞しい sturdy ; 《文》stalwart ; robust ; strong ; powerful ; 《精神の》strong-minded ¶体つきのたくましい strongly-[stoutly-]built ; 《文》(a man) of sturdy [strong] build / たくましく vigorously ; powerfully / 想像をたくましくする give free rein [full play] to *one's* imagination. 文例⇩

タグマッチ ⇨ タッグマッチ.

たくまない 巧まない natural ; 《文》artless ; 《文》guileless ; 《文》ingenuous ; unintentional.

たくみ 巧み ¶巧みな skillful ; 《文》adroit ; dexterous ; ingenious ; clever / 巧みな答弁 a clever [slick] reply / 巧みに skillfully ; 《文》adroitly ; dexterously ; ingeniously ; cleverly.

たくらみ 企み a plot ; a scheme ; a trick ; a conspiracy ; an intrigue ; 《文》a design ¶深い企み a deep-laid plot.

たくらむ 企む plot ; scheme ; plan ; contrive ; 《文》design ; think [work] out (a plan) ; devise ; conspire. 文例⇩

だくりゅう 濁流 a muddy stream ; 《文》turbid waters (of a river).

たぐる 手繰る pull [haul] in (hand over hand) ; draw [reel] in.

たくわえ 蓄え 〈貯蔵〉a store ; a stock ; 〈予備〉(a) reserve ; 〈補給品〉supplies ; 〈商品・材料などの〉(a) stock ; 〈貯金〉savings ¶多少の蓄えがある have some savings ; have some money saved.

たくわえる 蓄える 〈金などを〉save ; lay [set, put] aside ; put [lay] by ; 〈貯蔵する〉store ; lay in (a stock of) ; stock up (with [on]) 《food》; 〈置く〉keep ¶蓄えてある 〈物が主語〉be (kept) in store [stock] ; 〈人が主語〉have *sth* in store / 大いに精力を蓄えている have great reserves [a great reserve] of energy.

たけ[1] 丈 〈身長〉height ; 《文》stature ; 〈長さ〉length ¶丈が高い[低い] be tall [short] / 身の丈が1メートル80センチある be 1.8 meters tall [in height, 《文》in stature] / 思いの丈を述べる unburden *oneself* ; 《文》disclose [lay bare] *one's* (inmost) heart. 文例⇩

たけ[2] 竹 (a) bamboo ¶竹の皮[節] a bamboo sheath [joint] / 竹を割ったような straightforward ; openhearted ; 《a man》with a [《文》of] frank disposition / 木に竹を継いだような quite incongruous ¶竹垣 a bamboo fence / 竹細工 bamboo ware [work] / 竹竿(ぼうき) a bamboo pole [broom] / 竹藪 a bamboo thicket [grove] / 竹槍 a sharpened bamboo ; a bamboo spear.

-だけ 〈…ばかり、のみ〉only ; alone ; merely ; nothing but ; 〈限度、範囲〉as many [much] as ; so far as ; 〈相当するだけ〉enough ; ('ten dollars') worth ; 〈少なくとも〉at least ; 〈過不足の程度〉by ¶1回だけ only once / 東京だけにおいて in Tokyo / 東京だけで in Tokyo alone ; only in Tokyo / 私だけは as [so] far as I am concerned ; as for me / できるだけ as much [far] as possible [one can] ⇨ できる / 文明が進めば進むだけ (in proportion) as civilization advances / 1つだけ余る be one too many. 文例⇩

たげい 多芸 ¶多芸な versatile ; all-round ; 《米》all-around.

たけうま 竹馬 (walk on) stilts. 文例⇩

だげき 打撃 a blow ; a knock ; 〈野球〉batting ; 〈精神的な〉a shock ¶打撃を与える strike ; hit ; knock ; give [deliver] a blow (to) ; deal *sb* a blow / 〈精神的に〉shock ; give *sb* a shock / 大打撃を受ける be hard [severely] hit ; suffer a telling blow / 打撃戦 〈野球〉a game with

---

だくひ 諾否ご一報下さい. Please let us have an answer one way or the other. | Please inform us whether or not this is acceptable (to you).

たくましい 彼女は彼のたくましい肩に頭を当てて長い間すすり泣いていた. She sobbed for a long time, with her head resting on his manly shoulder. / いくら想像をたくましくしても彼がそれを成し遂げた方法は私には分からない. By no stretch of the imagination can I see [visualize] how he accomplished it.

たくらむ このけんかは前もってくらんだ狂言だった. The quarrel was a put-up job. / お前は何をたくらんでいるのか. What are you up to? / 彼らは僕をおとしいれようと前からたくらんでいたらしい. They seem to have been plotting to trap me for a long time.

たけ[1] このオーバーは僕には丈が短かすぎる. This overcoat is too short [long] for me. / 小麦のこの新しい品種は在来のものよりもずっと丈が低い. This new variety of wheat is much shorter in height than the traditional ones.

-だけ 彼は金のある時だけ元気だ. He is happy only when he has money. / ネクタイをしているのは彼だけだった. He was the only one wearing a tie. / 頼りにするのは君だけだ. You are the only man I can depend on. / ニューヨークだけで2万人以上の日本人がいるそうだ. I have heard that there are more than 20,000 Japanese in New York alone. / そのあざらしの子は乳だけを飲んで2週間で体重が2倍になった. The seal pup doubled its weight in two weeks on a straight diet of milk. / それだけではなく、夜も働かなければならない. Besides that, I must work at night [《口語》work nights]. / 見ただけで気持ちが悪くなる. The mere sight of it sickens me. / それだけはごめんだ. I will do anything but that. / 私はただ自分の義務を果たしただけです. I have done nothing but my duty. / あの男に聞きたいのはそれだけだ. That is all I want to ask him about. / 彼は稼いだだけためる. He saves everything [every cent] he earns. / あなたのためにできるだけの事を致します. I will do what [all] I can for you. / 私だって食べるだけの収入は必要です. Even I must have enough to live on. / 松島は行ってみるだけの価値があります. Matsushima is worth visiting [a visit]. / さすがは東京だけあっ

たけだけしい 猛々しい fierce(-looking); ferocious ¶盗人たけだけしい feel no compunction 《about [in] *doing*》; be shameless 《about *one's* wrongdoing》.

だけつ 妥結 (seek) a (compromise) settlement; 〈協定〉an agreement ¶妥結する come to terms 《with》; reach an agreement 《with》; make a compromise agreement 《with》; settle 《with》/妥結の条件 terms of agreement. 文例⇩

たけつしつ 多血質 ¶多血質の《文》(a man) of sanguine temperament.

たけなわ 酣 ¶たけなわである be at *its* height; be in full swing; 《口語》be going (at) full blast / 戦いたけなわの時に in the thick [midst] of the battle. 文例⇩

たけのこ 竹の子 a bamboo shoot [sprout] ¶雨後の竹の子のように出る ⇨ご.

たける[1] 長ける ¶たけている《文》excel 《in》; be at home [well up] 《in》; be versed [proficient] 《in》/奸知(かんち)にたけている be cunning; be crafty; be wily; be a sly old fox.

たける[2] 猛ける become furious; rage; be fierce ¶たけり狂う rush about in a frenzy [rage]; rave; go [be] on the [a wild] rampage; run amuck [amok]. 「be well on.

たける[3] 闌ける wear on;《文》be far advanced /

たげん[1] 多元 ¶多元的 plural; pluralist / 多元論《哲》pluralism.

たげん[2] 多言 ¶多言を要しない there is no need to dwell on [《文》upon]《the subject》.

だけん 駄犬 a mongrel; a cur.

たこ[1] 凧 a kite ¶たこの尾 a kite tail / たこをあげる fly a kite ; 〈糸をゆるめて〉let out a kite / たこをおろす draw [reel] in a kite / たこ糸 a kite string ; twine [(a) string] for a kite.

たこ[2] 蛸《動》an octopus (*pl.* -puses, -pi) ¶たこつぼ an octopus trap ;〈退避壕〉a foxhole / たこ配(当) a bogus dividend.

たこ[3]〈手足などにできる〉a callus; a corn (主に足の) ¶耳にたこが出来るほど聞く hear more than enough of *sth*; be sick (and tired) of hearing *sth*;《俗》have had a bellyful of *sth* / たこになる get [《文》become] callused; thicken into callus. 文例⇩

たこう[1] 多孔 ¶多孔質の porous / 多孔性 porosity.

たこう[2] 多幸 ¶多幸な fortunate; lucky;《文》happy;《文》blessed. 文例⇩

だこう 蛇行 ¶蛇行する meander; wind *its* way《through》.

たこうしき 多項式《数》a polynomial (expression).

たこく 他国〈外国〉a foreign country ; a strange [《文》an alien] land ; 〈同国内の〉another province ¶他国の foreign ; alien / 他国人 〈見知らぬ人〉a stranger ; 〈外国人〉a foreigner ; an alien.

たこくせききぎょう 多国籍企業 a multinational corporation [company]; a multinational.

タコグラフ a tachograph.

たこのき たこの木《植》a pandanus.

タコメーター a tachometer ;《英口語》a rev counter.

たごん 他言 ¶他言する tell others ; betray [confide] (a secret) to others ; let *sth* out ; disclose ;《文》divulge ; give *sth* away / 他言しない keep *sth* (a) secret ; keep 《a secret》to *oneself*. 文例⇩

たさい[1] 多才 versatility ¶多才な versatile; many-talented.

たさい[2] 多彩 ¶多彩な colorful; multicolored;《文》varicolored; variegated.

たさく 多作 ¶多作な《文》prolific / 多作家 a prolific [productive] writer.

ださく 駄作 a poor work; poor [worthless] stuff; trash.

たさつ 他殺 murder. 文例⇩

たさん 多産 ¶多産の《文》prolific;《文》fecund. 文例⇩

ださん 打算 calculation ¶打算する calculate / 打算的な calculating; selfish / 非打算的な《文》disinterested; unselfish. 文例⇩

たざんのいし 他山の石 ¶他山の石とする let

て, いい本屋がたくさんある. As you'd expect of a big city like Tokyo, there are lots of good bookstores. / 苦労したけっして, なかなか辛抱強い人だ. As might be expected of someone who has gone through so many hardships [who has had such a hard life], he is a man of admirable perseverance. / 私は子供に高等学校だけはやらせるつもりだ. I will give my boy a high school education at least. / 品物は高ければ高いほどよくなると思いがちだ. People are apt to think that the more expensive something is, the better it is. / その旅行は快適なだけに金もかかった. The journey was as expensive as it was comfortable. / さおの長さが1メートルだけ足りない. The pole is one meter too short. | The pole is too short by one meter.

たけうま ずいぶん高い竹馬だなあ. These stilts are quite high off the ground, aren't they!

だげき 米国チームは日本チームよりも打撃において勝っていた. The American team outhit the Japanese.

だけつ 交渉は円満に妥結した. The negotiations reached a peaceful and satisfactory settlement.

たけなわ 春はまさにたけなわである. Spring is really here. / 秋色まさにたけなわである. Autumn is well advanced. | The autumnal tints can now be seen in all their glory.

たこ[1] 足の親指にたこが出来た. I've got a callus on my big toe./ 書き物のために彼は中指にペンだこが出来ていた. His middle finger was callused from writing.

たこう[2] ご多幸を祈ります. I wish you every happiness (and prosperity).

たごん これは他言をはばかる事です. This is confidential. / 他言は無用です. Say nothing of it to anyone. / 他言しないと約束します. I promise that it will go no farther.

たさつ 彼が死体となって発見されたときは他殺の疑いがもたれた. When he was found dead, murder [foul play] was suspected.

たさん 彼女の家は多産系だ. She comes from a prolific family.

ださん あの男のすることは何でも打算的だ. He always has his own interests in mind. |《口語》He always has an eye to the main chance.

sth be a [an object] lesson to *one*; draw a lesson from *sth*; profit by ⟪*sb's* experience of *sth*⟫. [文例⇩]

たし 足し ¶足しにする make up (for); supplement; help / 内職をして収入の足しにする supplement *one's* income with a side job / 足しになる go (far [a long way]) toward; help; be of use. [文例⇩]

たじ 多事 ⇨たじたたん.

だし[1] 出し〈煮出し汁〉(soup) stock;〈口実〉a pretext; an excuse ¶出しを取る prepare [brew] stock / (人を)だしに使う〈言い訳などで〉involve *sb* [use *sb's* name] in ⟪*one's* excuses⟫.

だし[2]〈祭礼の時などの〉a float.

だしあう 出し合う club (up [together]) ⟪to *do*⟫; pool ⟪their money⟫. [文例⇩]

だしいれ 出し入れ taking [putting] in and out;〈貯金の〉depositing and withdrawing [drawing]. [文例⇩]

だしおしみ 出し惜しみ ¶出し惜しみする grudge; be unwilling to give [pay].

たしか 確か〈たぶん〉maybe; probably; if I remember right [rightly]; if I am not mistaken ¶確かな〈確実な〉sure; certain; positive;〈疑いのない〉undoubted; unquestionable; ⟪文⟫ indubitable;〈確定した〉definite; decisive;〈正確な〉accurate; correct; exact;〈信頼すべき〉reliable; trustworthy;〈出所の明らかな〉authentic;〈強固な〉sound; firm;〈安全な〉safe; secure;〈純粋な〉genuine;〈腕の〉⟪文⟫ able; competent / 確かな事実 a positive fact / 確かな返事 a definite answer / 確かな筋から聞く hear from a reliable source; have ⟪the news⟫ on good authority / 確かに〈確実に〉certainly; surely; for certain; to be sure; definitely;〈誓って〉upon *one's* word [honor];〈疑いなく〉no doubt; undoubtedly; beyond [without] doubt; decidedly; ⟪文⟫ indubitably;〈間違いなく〉without fail / 確か(なもの)にする〈立証する〉confirm; ⟪文⟫ corroborate; verify; ⟪文⟫ substantiate;〈確立する〉put *sth* on a firm basis [footing]; establish;〈裏書きする〉endorse. [文例⇩]

たしかめる 確かめる ⟪文⟫ ascertain ⟪that..., whether...⟫; make sure [certain] ⟪of⟫; see if [whether]...;〈確証する〉confirm; ⟪文⟫ corroborate; verify; check (照合して) ¶念を入れて確かめる make doubly sure [certain] ⟪that...⟫. [文例⇩]

たしざん 足し算 addition ¶足し算をする add up ⟪figures⟫.

たしせいせい 多士済々 [文例⇩]

たじたじ ¶たじたじと staggeringly; totteringly; falteringly / たじたじとなる〈よろめく〉stagger; totter;〈ひるむ〉flinch ⇨たじろぐ. [文例⇩]

たじたたん 多事多端 ¶多事多端な eventful;〈多忙な〉busy. [文例⇩]

たじつ 他日 some [another] day; some other time;〈近日中に〉one of these days;〈将来〉(at some time) in the future; at some future date ¶他日の用に当てる set *sth* aside for future use.

だしっぱなし 出しっ放し ¶出しっ放しにしておく leave ⟪the water⟫ flowing [running]; leave ⟪a tap⟫ on; leave ⟪books⟫ lying about.

たしなみ 嗜み〈好み〉(a) taste;〈慎み〉modesty; decency;〈心遣い〉delicacy;〈行儀〉etiquette;〈芸事などの心得〉⟪文⟫ accomplishments ¶女のたしなみ feminine modesty; female accomplishments / 音楽のたしなみがある have some knowledge of [have a taste for] music / たしなみのいい well-bred[-mannered]; refined; ⟪文⟫ ⟪a lady⟫ of refined manners and well-cultivated taste. [文例⇩]

たしなむ 嗜む〈好む〉have a taste for; relish; like; love; be fond of ¶タバコをたしなむ smoke; be a smoker / 酒をたしなまない do not drink.

たしなめる〈しかる〉⟪文⟫ reprove; reproach; ⟪文⟫ reprimand; rebuke;〈訓戒する〉⟪文⟫ admonish; warn ¶不注意をたしなめる reprove *sb* for *his* carelessness.

だしぬく 出し抜く forestall; get a start on; outwit.

たざんのいし もって他山の石とすべし. Let this be an object lesson to you. | A valuable lesson can be learned from this.

たし 将来何かの足しになりましょう. I hope it will be of some use in the future. / そんなことでは汚染防止には大して足しにならないのではないだろうか. I'm afraid that will not be (of) much use in [will go only a short way toward] preventing pollution.

だしあう 費用は各自出し合った. Everyone paid his own share of the expenses. / 2人の少年が出し合って5,000円こしらえた. The two boys raised 5,000 yen between them. / 皆で金を出し合って車を買った. We clubbed together [We all chipped in] to buy a car.

だしいれ この財布は金の出し入れに不便だ. This wallet is inconvenient for getting money in and out.

たしか 彼が来たのは確か先月の12日でしたろう. If I remember correctly, it was on the 12th of last month that he called on me. / それは確かだよ. There is no doubt about it.|You can take my word for it. | I'm sure [certain] of it. | I know it for certain. / 僕は確かなよりどころがあってそう言うのだ. I say so on good authority. / あの男は確かかね. Is he to be trusted [relied on]? / あの男の射撃の腕は確かなものだ. He is a very accurate [good] shot. / 確かに魚は好きだけれど, 今夜はステーキの方がいいな. I like fish all right, but I (would) prefer (to have) steak tonight. / この報道はまだ確かではない. The report has yet to be confirmed. / 確かに戸締まりはしてあったのですね. Are you sure that the door was locked? / 確かに70にはなっている. He is seventy (years old) if he's a day.

たしかめる 真偽を確かめてみよう. Let's see if it is true or not./ その報告に誤りのないことを確かめた. I have satisfied myself of the truth of the report.

たしせいせい 当社は多士済々です. We have a large number of talented men.

たじたじ たじたじになって弁解した. He was driven into a corner and had to come up with an excuse. / その質問に彼はたじたじの体であった. He seemed to find

だしぬけ 出し抜け ¶出し抜けの訪問 a surprise visit 《from sb》/ 出し抜けに 《突然に》suddenly ; all at once ; all of a sudden ; 《知らない間に》unawares ; 《思い掛けなく》unexpectedly ; out of the blue ; out of nowhere ; 《予告なく》without notice.

たしまえ 足し前 ⇨たし.

だしもの 出し物 《当日の全部の》a program ; 《1つの》a number ; a piece ; 《英》a turn (寄席などの) ¶主な出し物 the principal feature 《of the evening》; the highlight 《of the program》. 文例 ⇩

だしゃ 打者 《野球》a batter ¶3割打者 a .300 hitter ★a three hundred hitter と読む.

だじゃれ 駄洒落 ¶駄じゃれを言う make a (poor) pun ; crack a (poor) joke ; make a (poor) play on words.

だしゅ 舵手 a helmsman ; a steersman ; 《ボートの》a coxswain ; a cox.

たしゅたよう 多種多様 ¶多種多様の various ; 《文》diverse ; 《文》multifarious ; a great [wide] variety of.

たしゅみ 多趣味 ¶多趣味な人 a person with a wide range of interests ; a person of varied interests ; 《文》a person with catholic tastes / 多趣味である be interested in a large number of things ; 《文》be catholic in *one*'s tastes [interests].

だじゅん 打順 《野球》a batting order. 文例 ⇩

たしょう 多少 《数》the number ; 《量》the quantity ; 《額》the amount ; 《幾分》a little ; some ; somewhat ; slightly ; to some [a certain] extent ; in some degree ; in a way [manner, 《文》measure] ¶多少名の知れた《文》(a man) of some note / 多少英語が話せる speak English a little / …の多少によって according to the number [amount, quantity] of.... 文例 ⇩

たじょう 多情 ¶多情な《文》wanton ; flighty ; 《文》(a woman) of loose morals / 多情多感な passionate ; sentimental ; emotional / 多情多恨の一生を送る live a life full of tears and regrets.

たじろぐ draw [fall, shrink] back ; flinch 《from》; wince 《under bitter criticism》; falter [waver, hesitate] 《in》.

たしん 多神 ¶多神教[論] polytheism / 多神論の polytheistic / 多神論者 a polytheist.

だしん 打診 ¶打診する 《医者が》examine 《the patient's chest》by percussion ; 《探る》sound 《sb on sth》; feel out 《sb about sth》/ 意見を打診する sound [tap] *sb*'s opinion.

たす 足す 《加える》add 《A to B》; 《補う》make up (for) ; make good ; supply ; supplement ¶用を足す よう⇩. 文例 ⇩

タス 《ソ連の通信社》Tass.

だす 出す put out ; 《伸ばす》stretch [hold, reach] out ; 《押し出す》push out ; 《取り出す》take out ; 《速力・力などを》put out [《文》forth] ; 《水・ガスなどを》turn on (栓をひねって) ; 《声を》《文》utter ; let out (a loud roar) ; 《露出する》expose ; show ; bare ; 《出て行かせる》let [put] 《a cat》out ; 《出品する》exhibit ; place on display ; 《送る》send ; forward (荷を) ; 《発行する》publish ; issue ; bring [put] out ; 《掲載する》carry ; print ; 《掲げる》hoist ; set [put] up ; display ; 《提出する》submit ; turn in ; 《提示する》show ; produce ; 《課する》set [give] 《a question》; 《食物などを》serve ; set out ¶手を出す hold out one's hand ; 《比喩的に》⇨ て 13 / 窓から首を出す lean out of the window / ポケットから財布を出す take *one*'s wallet out of *one*'s pocket / 《祭礼などで》ちょうちんを出す hang out a lantern / 力を出す exert [《文》put forth] *one*'s strength / 高い声を出す shout ; raise *one*'s voice / 金を出す pay [put up] money ; supply sb with money / 展覧会へ出す exhibit 《a picture》at a show / 手紙を出す 《書く》write (a letter) to sb ; 《送る》send [《米》mail, 《英》post] a letter to sb / 小説を雑誌に出す publish a story in a periodical / 切符を出す show [produce] one's ticket / 願書を出す submit [send in] an application / 答案を出す give in one's (examination) paper / お茶を出す serve tea ; offer sb a cup of tea / 店を出す open [start] a store. 文例 ⇩

-だす ...出す start [begin] doing [to do] ¶笑

---

it hard to hold his ground when that question was put to him.

たしたたん 内外多事多端である. We are having eventful days [It is an eventful period] both at home and abroad.

たしなみ 彼女はたしなみよくその事には触れなかった. She had the good taste not to mention it. / 彼が紳士のたしなみを身につけたのはその当時のことなのである. It was in that period of his life that he learned all that a gentleman should know.

だしもの 来月の帝劇の出し物は何ですか. What's on [What's the program] at the Imperial Theater next month? / 今, 第一劇場の出し物は何だろう? What's on [playing] at the Daiichi Theater? / 来月の歌舞伎座の出し物は忠臣蔵です. The Kabukiza will stage 'Chushingura' next month. / 今夜の出し物はいくつあるのですか. How many numbers [《英》turns] are there on the program tonight?

だじゅん この回には打順が良く[悪く]1番[7番]バッターからだ. For this inning the stronger [weaker] batters come to bat, starting with number 1 [7].

たしょう 多少にかかわらずご寄付願います. All contributions gratefully accepted. / 多少にかかわらず注文には迅速に応じさせていただきます. All orders, large or small, will be promptly executed. / 多少物足りないところがある. It leaves something to be desired. / その報告は多少事実と相違していることがわかった. It turned out that the report was not quite faithful to the facts.

たじろぐ それにはさすがの彼もたじろいだ. Brave as he was, he flinched before it.

たす 2足す4は6. Two and four make [are] six. / Two plus four is six. / 3にいくつ足すと10になるか. What do you have to add [What must be added] to 3 to get 10? | 3 and what make 10? / この数字を足してそこに出ている合計に間違いがないかどうか確かめて下さい. Add up these figures and see if the total given there is correct.

だす その火事に私は何も出さなかった. I saved nothing from the fire. / 夜は子供を外へ出してはいけない. Don't allow the children to go out at night. / 家々に国旗

たすう - ダスターコート

い出す burst out laughing; burst into laughter / 急に走り出す break into a run.

たすう 多数 ¶多数の many; many a 《man》; a great many; a lot of; a (large) number of; numerous ⇨ たくさん 囲圧/圧倒的[a two-thirds] 多数で by an overwhelming [a two-thirds] majority / 多数を頼りに by [relying on] force of numbers / 多数(を頼んで)の横暴 tyranny of the majority / 多数を占める command [win, get, have, hold] a 《House》majority / 多数意見[案] a majority opinion [proposal] / 多数決にする decide by majority / 多数決に従う accept a majority decision / 多数決に従わない defy majority rule / 多数党 a majority party. 文例⇩

だすう 打数 文例⇩

たすかる 助かる be saved; be rescued; survive 《a disaster》; escape 《death》;〈労力などが省ける〉be saved;〈物事が助けとなる〉be of help [use,《文》service]; be helpful (in); go 《far, a long way》toward ¶危い所を助かる have a narrow escape (from danger) / 助かった人々 the survivors / 助かりそうもないものとあきらめる give sb [oneself] up for lost. 文例⇩

たすき 襷 ¶たすきを掛ける tuck [《文》gird] up one's sleeves with a sash [cord] / たすきがけで with one's sleeves tucked up.

たすけ 助け 〈援助〉help;《文》aid; assistance;〈救助〉(a) rescue;〈救済〉relief;〈後援〉support ¶助けとなる be a help (to);《文》be of assistance (to);〈...に資する〉contribute to;〈...〉go 《far, a long way》toward / 助けを求める seek help (from sb); ask sb for help; turn [look] to sb for help / 助けを呼ぶ cry [call] for help / ...の助けをかりて with [by] the assistance [《文》aid] of.../ 助けに行く go to sb's rescue. 文例⇩

たすけあい 助け合い《文》mutual aid [help]; cooperation ¶助け合いの精神 charity; a spirit of cooperation;《文》(a spirit of) mutual helpfulness / 歳末助け合い運動 a year-end charity drive.

たすけあう 助け合う help each other [one another]; cooperate 《with》.

たすけあげる 助け上げる rescue; pick sb up (船へ); bring sb safe to land (陸へ).

たすけおこす 助け起こす help sb to his feet; help sb up.

たすけだす 助け出す help sb out of 《a burning house》;《文》deliver sb out of 《the jaws of death》.

たすけぶね 助け船 〈救助船〉a lifeboat; a rescue boat ¶助け船を出す launch a life-boat; 〈比喩的に〉come [go] to sb's rescue; put in a word [a few words] to help sb out.

たすける 助ける 〈援助する〉help;《文》assist; 《文》aid; give [lend] a helping hand (to); stand by;〈救助する〉save; rescue;《文》deliver; relieve;〈助命する〉spare sb's life /〈後援する〉support; give support to; back sb up / 〈増進する〉promote;〈資する〉contribute to ¶仕事を助ける help sb in [with] his work / 弱きを助け強きをくじく support [side with] the weak against the strong / おぼれようとするところを助ける rescue [save] sb from drowning / 「助けてくれ」と叫ぶ cry, 'Help, help!'; cry for help / 消化を助ける《文》aid [promote] (the) digestion / 乗る[降りる]のを助ける help sb into [out of] 《a car》; help sb onto [off] 《a bus》. 文例⇩

たずさえる 携える take [have, carry] sth along [with one];〈手に〉carry [have] sth in one's hand / 1つえを携えて with a stick in one's hand.

たずさわる 携わる 〈与(す)かる〉take part [《文》participate] in; be a party to; have a hand in; be concerned [involved] in; have something to do with;〈手を出す〉meddle [deal] with [in]; be concerned [concern oneself] with. 文例⇩

ダスターコート《米》a duster;《英》a dust-coat.

が出されていた. The national flag was flown over every door. / ひどいことで船が出せない. It is too stormy to put out a boat. / そんなまをすると新聞に出されるぞ. If you do that sort of thing, you'll be in [get into, find yourself in] the papers. / 本県では大臣を2人出した. This prefecture has produced two Cabinet ministers. / この時計にいくら出しましたか. How much did you pay [What did you give] for this watch? / この事故で死者10人を出した. The accident resulted in ten dead [took a toll of ten lives].

たすう この森にはシカが多数生息している. A large number of deer inhabit this forest. | Deer are found in great numbers in this forest. / 議案は120票対70票の賛成多数で通過した. The bill was carried [passed] by a majority of 120 to 70. / その動議は通過に必要な3分の2の多数を16票の差で得られず否決された. The motion fell 16 votes short of the two-thirds majority required (for passage). / 本委員会の運営は多数決による. This commission operates under majority rule.

だすう 6打数でヒット2本だった. He was six times at bat and hit two singles.

たすかる この事故で助かったのは彼1人だった. He was the only survivor of the accident. | He was the only one to survive the accident. / あの人はもう助かりません. He is past all hope of recovery. | There's no hope [chance] that he will recover. | It is all over for [all up with] him. / とても助からないと思った. We had given up all hope of surviving. / 助手が来たので大いに助かる. My new assistant saves me a great deal of trouble. / こう忙しくちゃ助かりません. Such a busy life as this is almost more than I can take [almost too much for me].

たすけ あとで何かの助けになるだろうと思ってこの土地を買いました. I bought this land because I thought it would stand me in good stead later. / 1万円くらいの金では何の助けにもならない. A mere ten thousand yen is no help at all.

たすける ぜひ助けて欲しいというときに彼は助けてくれなかった. When I was in real need of his help, he let me down. / 助けると思ってこの願いを聞いて下さい. Grant me my request for mercy's sake.

たずさわる 彼は政治には携わろうとしなかった. He stood aloof

ダストシュート a trash [refuse, rubbish] (disposal) chute.

たずねびと 尋ね人 a missing person.

たずねる¹ 訪ねる 〈訪問する〉visit; call 《on sb, at sb's house》; go [come] to [and] see sb; pay a visit [call] 《to sb》; 《口語》look sb up; 《米》visit with sb; 〈見物する〉visit; 《米口語》take in 《a place》; 〈立ち寄る〉drop [look] in 《on sb, at sb's house》‖ 朝早く訪ねる make an early call 《at, on》; pay a morning call 《to》. 文例⇩

たずねる² 尋ねる 〈問う〉ask 《sb a question》; inquire 《of sb about sth》; question; put a question to sb; demand 《sb's name》; 〈捜す〉look [search, hunt] for; make a search for; 《文》seek; 〈求める〉《文》seek; look for ‖ 道を尋ねる ask sb the way 《to》; 容体を尋ねる inquire after sb [sb's health] / うるさく尋ねる annoy sb with repeated questions; pester [plague] him with questions / …を尋ねて 《start》 in search of…. 文例⇩

だする 堕する degenerate 《into》; become degraded 《into》.

たぜい 多勢 ‖ 多勢に無勢である be outnumbered / 多勢をたのんで relying on [trusting to] numbers.

だせい 惰性 ⇒だりょく². 文例⇩

だせき 打席 〔野球〕‖ 打席につく have a turn at bat [the plate]; go to bat / 打席についている be at bat ⇒だする.

だせん 打線 〔野球〕a 《powerful》 batting lineup ‖ 相手チームの打線を沈黙させる keep the opposing team's bats silent.

たそがれ dusk; twilight ‖ たそがれどきに at dusk; at twilight; in the (evening) twilight / 人生のたそがれどきに in the twilight years of one's life; in the twilight of life; in [at] the evening of one's life.

だそく 蛇足 《文》a superfluity ‖ 蛇足の superfluous / 蛇足を加える make an unnecessary addition 《to》. 文例⇩

ただ 多々 文例⇩

ただ 唯, 只 merely; simply; 《文》solely; only ‖ ただ…しさえすればよい only have [need] to do; need only do; all one has to do is (to) do; have only to do / ただの〈わずか〉mere; sole; 〈普通の〉ordinary; common; plain; 〈無料の〉free / ただで for nothing; free (of charge); gratis / ただ1人で (all) alone; by oneself / ただ1度 just [only, 《文》but] once / ただの1日でも even for a day / ただの人 a common [an ordinary] man; a man in the street / ただの水 plain water / ただならぬ uncommon; extraordinary; unusual; serious / ただならぬ物音 an alarming sound / たださえ困っているところへ to make matters worse; to add to one's misery / ただ事でない be no joke; be not a trifling [trivial] matter. 文例⇩

だだ 駄々 ‖ 駄々をこねる a fret; be fretful; throw a tantrum / 駄々っ子 a spoilt [fretful] child.

ただい 多大 ‖ 多大の great; considerable; a great deal of / 多大の損害をこうむる suffer a heavy loss; 《文》sustain a serious [severe] loss / 多大の労力を要する require considerable labor.

だたい 堕胎 (an) abortion ⇒ちゅうぜつ ‖ 堕胎罪 criminal abortion.

ただいま 只今 〈現在〉now; at present; 〈たった今〉just [right] now; 〈すぐに〉soon; presently; in a minute ‖ ただいまのところ〈当分〉for the present; for the time being / 〈現在〉at present / ただいままでのところでは until [till] now; up to this time [the present]; so [thus] far / ただいまでは now; nowadays. 文例⇩

たたえる¹ 称える praise; give high praise to; 《文》extol(l); admire ‖ 勇気をたたえる praise sb for his courage.

たたえる² 湛える 〈充たす〉fill 《with》; 〈あふれる〉be filled 《with》; brim 《with》‖ 笑みをたたえる smile; wear a smile; beam / 口元にほほえみをたたえながら with a smile (playing) on one's lips / 両の目に涙を一杯にたたえながら

---

from politics.

たずねる¹ まだ 2, 3 軒訪ねる所がある. I have a few more visits to make. / 今朝彼が訪ねて来た. I had a visit from him this morning. / 故郷に帰った私は親戚や近所の人たちを訪ねて楽しく過ごした. I went to my hometown, and had a good time staying with my relatives and neighbors.

たずねる² 少々お尋ねしたいことがあるのですが. May I ask you some questions? | I have some questions to ask you. / お詳しいことは青木氏にお尋ね願います. For further particulars, I refer you [please apply] to Mr. Aoki. / 方々尋ね回って, やっとその有栖堂という骨董屋にたどり着いた. I found the curio store named Yurakudo after a great deal of asking around.

たぜい 多勢に無勢でとうていかなわない. There is no contending against such heavy odds.

だせい 惰性でついそうしてしまったのです. I did it simply by [from] force of habit.

だそく それは蛇足だ. That's quite unnecessary to add.|That's like putting a fifth wheel on a coach.| That's gilding the lily.

たた 多々ますます弁ず. The more, the better.

ただ それには誤りがただの1つもない. There is not a single mistake in it. / 彼が来ない日はただの1日もなかった. Never a day passed without his coming to see me. / 彼女はただ泣くばかりだった. She did nothing but cry. / 君は僕のただ1人の友人だ. You are the only friend (that) I have. / ただでもいらない. I wouldn't have it even as a gift. / ただより高いものはない. Nothing is as costly as a free gift. | The obligation incurred in accepting something free is often more burdensome than paying for it would have been. / ただお聞きしてみただけです. I just wanted to know. / ただで入場できますか. Is admission free? / ただ同様で買った. I bought it for almost nothing.

ただいま 〈帰宅のあいさつ〉Hullo [Hi], mother [father, dear]. ★英米には, 帰宅のときの「ただいま」に相当する表現はない. 'Hello' 'Hi' と言う場合もあるし, 'Hello, I'm back.' とも言う. 家に人がいるかはっきりしないときは, 'Is anyone in [at home]?' と言うこともある. / はいただいま. 〈呼ばれて〉Yes, I'm coming. | 〈料理店で〉Coming

たたかい 戦い 〈戦闘〉a fight; a battle; an encounter; an engagement; an action; 〈戦争〉(a) war; warfare; 〈一騎打ち〉(a) combat; 〈争闘〉a struggle; a conflict; 《文》strife; 〈試合〉a contest; 〈運動〉a campaign ((for, against)) ¶がんとの戦い〈個人の〉a battle against cancer; 〈医学界全体の〉the war against cancer / 戦いを宣する declare war ((on, against)) / 戦いをいどむ challenge sb to a battle [game]; 〈文〉throw [fling] down the gauntlet to sb / 戦いを交える ⇒たたかう / 戦いに出る go to war; go to the front; go into battle.

たたかいぬく 戦い抜く fight it out; battle [win] through.

たたかう 戦う fight ((with, against)); fight a battle; 《文》join [engage in, do] battle ((with)); battle sb; 〈一騎討ちする〉《文》do combat ((with)); 〈戦争する〉make war ((on)); 《文》wage [go to] war ((against, on, with)); 〈困難・運命などと〉struggle ((against)); grapple ((with)); 《文》contend ((with)); 《文》strive ((against fate)); 《文》battle [war] ((against poverty)); 〈試合をする〉play a game ((with)) ¶最後[あく]まで戦う ⇒たたかいぬく / 四つに組んで戦うbe locked in battle [combat] ((with)); 〈正々堂々と〉fight a pitched battle ((with)) / 自由のために戦う fight for liberty / 誘惑と戦う struggle [wrestle] with temptation; resist (a) temptation / 戦わんかなという気構えである be in a fighting mood. 文例

たたかわす 戦わす set (A) to fight with (B); match (A) with [against] (B); fight ((cocks)) ¶議論を戦わす argue ((with sb over sth)); have an argument [a discussion] ((with sb about sth)); discuss ((sth with sb)).

たたき 〈土間〉a concrete floor; (a) concrete facing; 〈肉の〉minced meat ¶あじのたたきfinely chopped horse mackerel / かつおのたたき lightly roasted bonito / たたきにする pave; cover [face] with cement; cement; 〈肉を〉mince.

たたきあげる 叩き上げる work [struggle] one's way up ((from an office boy)) ¶自分の腕一本でたたき上げた人 a self-made man.

たたきおこす 叩き起こす rouse sb out of bed; 《英》knock sb up ★《米》での knock ((a woman)) up は卑語で「妊娠させてしまう」の意.

たたきおとす 叩き落とす knock [《文》strike] sth down [off]; knock sth from [out of] ((sb's hand)).

たたききる 叩き切る hack; chop (off).

たたきこむ 叩き込む 〈打ち込む〉drive [《文》strike, hammer] sth in [into]; 〈教える〉hammer [beat] ((an idea)) into sb's head; indoctrinate sb ((with an idea, in a principle)) ¶牢屋へ叩き込む fling [throw, 《文》cast] sb into prison [jail]; put sb in prison; imprison sb.

たたきころす 叩き殺す beat [flog] sb to death; beat the life out of sb.

たたきこわす 叩き壊す knock sth to pieces; smash (up); shatter; wreck ((a building)); break [batter, tear] down ((a house)).

たたきだい 叩き台 ¶叩き台として試案を提出する present a tentative plan as a basis for discussion.

たたきだいく 叩き大工 a clumsy [an unskillful] carpenter; a jerry-builder.

たたきだす 叩き出す 〈追い出す〉turn [throw, kick] sb out (of doors [the room)); 〈解雇する〉dismiss; 《文》discharge; 《口語》fire; 《口語》sack; 《口語》give sb the sack; 〈得点を〉drive in ((the tying run)); 〈ヒットを〉bang out ((a hit)); collect ((5 hits off a pitcher)); 〈タイプライターで〉type out ((a letter)); 〈ピアノで〉hammer [pound, beat] out ((a tune on the piano)).

たたきつける 叩き付ける 〈たたきのめす〉knock sb down; floor; 〈投げつける〉throw [hurl, fling] sth at [against] ¶辞表をたたきつける fling down one's resignation; leave one's job [post] in anger / たたきつけるような雨 (a) pelting [drumming] rain / たたきつけるような風 a pounding wind. 文例

たたきつぶす 叩き潰す shatter; smash (up); knock sth to pieces; 〈計画などを〉upset; 〈破る〉crush; beat. 「out of ((a boy)).

たたきなおす 叩き直す flog [beat] ((laziness)

たたきのめす, たたきふせる 叩きのめす, 叩き伏せる knock sb down [out]; floor sb with a blow; 〈屈服させる〉subdue; defeat; crush.

たたきわる 叩き割る smash (up); break [smash] sth into pieces; shatter.

たたく 叩く 〈打つ〉hit; 《文》strike; beat; knock ((on [at] the door)); rap ((on) the table)); 〈平手で〉slap; 〈軽く〉pat ((a dog, sb on the arm)); tap ((on the window, sb on the shoulder)); 〈強く〉bang ((on [at] the door)); beat [《俗》paste] sb; 《俗》give sb a pasting; pound ((the

---

right up, sir.

たたえる² 彼女は満面に喜色をたたえて僕を迎えた. She came out to meet me beaming with joy. / 彼は口もとに微笑みをたたえていた. A smile played about his lips.

たたかい 戦いはこれからだ. Real war is yet to come. / 賤が岳の戦いで彼はその勇名をとどろかせたのであった. It was at the Battle of Shizugatake that he distinguished himself by his valor.

たたかう ドイツは当時フランスと戦っていた. At that time Germany was at war with France. / 探検隊は寒気しながら進んだ. The expedition party marched on, struggling against the cold.

たたきつける 雨がたたきつけるように降っていた. The rain was pelting down. | It was pelting with rain.

たたく 彼は僕の肩を軽くたたいた. He patted me on the shoulder. / ぴしゃりと顔をたたかれた. He got [received] a nice slap in the face. / 風にたたかれ, 雨にたたかれながら彼らは夜も彼らは前進を続けた. By night and day, whipped by wind and lashed by rain, on they marched. ただし よし, この10万円は君に上げよう. ただし, これ以上はさわりだよ. All right. I'll give you this 100,000 yen, but [only] don't come asking me for any more. / 委員の任期は3年とする. ただし補充の委員は前任者が残した任期

ただし (繰返し);〈非難する〉attack; criticize;《文》censure ¶人の頭をたたく hit [pat] sb on the head/手をたたく clap one's hands; clap hands (人を呼ぶとき)/(人の)意見をたたく ask sb's opinion (about sth);consult《an expert》for advice/値段をたたく beat down the price (of)/新聞でたたかれる be attacked [severely criticized] in the newspapers,《口語》take a beating [《俗》pasting] in the press/敵陣をたたく pound the enemy position (by sea and air); give the enemy a beating. 文例⇩

ただし 但し but; however; only;〈条件〉provided (that)…; on condition that… ¶ただし書き a proviso (pl. -(e)s); a conditional [provisory] clause/…というただし書きをつけて with the proviso that….

ただしい 正しい〈正当な〉right;《文》rightful;〈正義の〉《文》righteous,《文》just;〈正直な〉honest;《文》upright;〈真実な〉true; truthful;〈本来の〉proper;〈誤のない〉correct;〈正確な〉accurate; exact;〈合法の〉《文》lawful; legal; legitimate ¶心の正しい upright; right-minded/正しいことをする do the right thing; do what is right; do right/正しい答 a correct [the right] answer ¶正しく rightly; rightfully; by right(s); properly;《文》justly;《文》lawfully; honestly; correctly; accurately/正しくない〈不正な〉unjust; dishonest;〈真実でない〉untrue; untruthful;〈不当な〉improper;〈誤った〉incorrect;〈不法な〉《文》unlawful; illegal ¶アメリカ, 正しくはアメリカ合衆国 America, or more accurately, the United States of America. 文例⇩

ただす[1] 正す〈訂正する〉correct;《文》rectify;〈調整する〉adjust;〈矯正する〉reform; set [put] right [to rights];《文》amend ¶姿勢を正す straighten oneself/誤った考えを正す put sb right in his ideas;《口語》put [set] sb straight; undeceive sb (of his misconception). 文例⇩

ただす[2] 質す〈質問する〉ask; demand; put a question《to》; inquire《of sb about sth》;〈調査する〉inquire [investigate, look] into;〈確かめる〉ascertain; make sure of; verify ¶専門家にただす consult an expert/事の起こりをただす trace the origin of《a custom》/身元をただす look [inquire] into sb's background [personal history]/元をただせば originally;《文》primarily.

たたずまい (an) appearance; (a) shape.
たたずむ 佇む stand (still); linger;《口語》hang around ¶軒下にたたずむ stand under the eaves.
たたせる 立たせる make sb stand (up); lift [help] sb to his feet;〈奮起させる〉rouse [stir] sb to action. 文例⇩
ただただ 唯々〈全く〉quite; utterly; absolutely;〈実に〉really; indeed. 文例⇩
ただちに 直ちに at once; immediately; without delay; instantly;《米》right away [off]; directly; in no time;〈即座に〉on the spot;《stop》in one's tracks. 文例⇩
だだっぴろい だだっ広い needlessly large; unnecessarily wide.
ただなか 直中 ¶ただ中に (right) in the middle of《a raging river》; in the thick of《a battle》.
ただのり 只乗り ¶只乗りする steal a ride (on a train); pinch a free ride.
ただばたらき 只働き free service ¶只働きをする work for nothing.
たたみ 畳 (a) tatami; a tatami mat. ¶畳を敷く lay tatami; cover《a room》with tatami/畳を替える renew [reface] the tatami/畳の上で死ぬ die in one's bed; die a natural death/畳表 tatami facing/畳敷きの部屋 a tatami-floored room/畳屋 a tatami maker.
たたみかける 畳み掛ける ¶畳みかけて尋ねる press sb hard for an answer; fire (off) question after question at sb; rain [shower] questions on sb.
たたみこむ 畳み込む fold in [up];〈三脚などを〉telescope.
たたむ 畳む〈折る〉fold (up);〈閉じる〉shut; close ¶紙を4つに畳む fold a sheet of paper into four/ふとんを畳む fold up the bedding;〈片付ける〉put away the bedding/帆を畳む take in sail/店を畳む close down [shut up] one's store; give up one's business.
ただよう 漂う float (about); be adrift;〈浮く〉float; be afloat;〈空中に〉hang in the air ¶波のまにまに漂う drift about at the mercy of the waves/顔に憂いの色を漂わせて with one's face clouded with sorrow/口元に微笑を漂わせながら with a smile on [playing about] one's lips. 文例⇩
たたり 祟り《文》an evil consequence;《文》divine punishment [vengeance];〈わざわい〉a curse ¶たたりを受ける《文》incur divine

---

閒在任するものとする. The term of office of members of the Commission shall be three years, provided that a member filling a vacancy shall remain in office during what remains of the term of his predecessor.
ただしい 彼らの要求は決して正しいとは言えない. Their demands are far from reasonable [just]./君の言うことは正しい[正しくない]. You are in the right [wrong]./どちらの側が正しいのか調べてみよう. Let us find out on which side the right lies.
ただす[1] 次の文中に誤りがあれば正しなさい. Correct errors, if any, in the following sentences.
たたせる 雨の中に長い間立たせた. I was kept standing in the rain for hours.
ただただ 忘れっぽいのに自分がいらだたしくあきれるばかりだ. I am really [utterly] disgusted with myself for my short memory./その至芸には恐れ入って, た

だただ賛嘆するばかりだった. I had no comments to make on his superb performance; I just sat silent in admiration and wonder.
ただちに 直ちにご返事は致しかねます. I cannot give you an immediate answer./帰京すると直ちに彼の家へかけつけた. As soon as I returned to Tokyo I hurried to his home./われわれは直ちに彼の救助にかけつけた. We lost no time in running to his rescue.
ただよう あたりにかすかな春の気

たたる 祟る 《文》 bring evil [a curse] upon; cast an evil spell on; haunt 〈怨霊などが〉; 《苦しめる》 torment; harass ¶たたられた 《文》 accursed; 《文》 ill-fated. 文例↓

ただれ 爛れ 〈傷・腫れ物の〉 a sore; inflammation; 〈かいよう〉 ulceration ¶ただれ目 a sore eye.

ただれる 爛れる be sore; be inflamed; 〈化膿する〉 fester; 〈潰瘍(%)化する〉 ulcerate ¶ただれた sore; inflamed; festered; ulcerated.

たたん 多端 ¶用務多端である be pressed with business / 公務多端のため owing to the pressure of official business.

ただしきだん 多段式 ¶多段式ロケット a multi-stage rocket.

たち[1] 太刀 a sword; a katana ⇨ かたな ¶太刀持ち a sword-bearer.

たち[2] 質 〈性質〉 nature; character; 〈品質〉 quality; 〈気質〉《文》(a) disposition; (a) temperament; 〈傾向〉 an inclination ¶たちのいい 〈気質が〉 good-natured; 〈品質が〉 good [high] quality 《goods》; 〈病気が〉 benign / たちの悪い 〈気質・性質が〉《文》 ill-natured; wicked; vicious; 《口語》 nasty; 〈品質が〉 poor [inferior] quality 《goods》; 〈病気が〉 bad; malignant / たちの悪い風邪 a bad [nasty] cold. 文例↓

-たち …達 ¶子供たち children / 農民たち farmers / 浜田たち Hamada and others.

たちあい 立会[合]い 〈出席〉《文》 presence; 《文》 attendance; 〈取引所の〉 a session; a call; 〈相撲の〉 standing up to wrestle ¶関係者立会いの上で in the presence of the parties concerned / 立会いを求める request [ask for] sb's presence 《at》 / 〈選挙の〉立会い演説会 a joint meeting for campaign speeches by rival candidates / 立会い人 an observer; 〈証人〉 a witness.

たちあう 立ち会う 〈出席する〉 attend 《an operation》; be present 《at》; 〈証人として〉 witness; be (a) witness 《to》. 文例↓

たちあおい 〖植〗 a hollyhock.

たちあがる 立ち上がる stand [get] up; 《文》 rise; rise [get] to one's feet; 〈比喩的に〉 stand up and take action; rise (up) 《against》 ¶椅子から立ち上がる rise from one's chair [seat] / さっと立ち上がる jump [spring] to one's feet / よろよろ[のっそり]と立ち上がる stagger [lumber] to one's feet / ようやくの思いで立ち上がる scramble [climb] to one's feet. 文例↓

たちい 立ち居 ¶立ち居が不自由である have difficulty in moving about / 立ち居振る舞い manners; behavior; 《文》 demeanor; 《文》 bearing / 立居振る舞いがしとやかで have graceful manners; 《文》 have a graceful carriage.

たちいた 裁ち板 a cutting [tailor's] board.

たちいり 立ち入り entrance; entry ¶立ち入りを禁止する forbid sb to enter 《a place》 / 「立ち入り禁止」の立て札を立てる put up a Keep Out sign / 立ち入り検査をする enter and inspect 《a factory》. 文例↓

たちいる 立ち入る enter 《a place》; go into; 〈侵入する〉 trespass 《on》; 〈干渉する〉 meddle with [in]; interfere in ¶私事に立ち入る [go] into sb's private [personal] affairs / 立ち入ったことを聞く ask a personal question. 文例↓

たちうお 太刀魚 a hairtail; a scabbard [cutlass] fish.

たちうち 太刀打ち ¶太刀打ちする 〈対抗する〉 rival; compete 《文》 contend, 《文》 vie 《with》 / とうてい太刀打ちできない[充分に太刀打ちできる] be no [a good] match 《for》.

たちえり 立ち襟 a stand-up collar.

たちおうじょう 立ち往生 ¶立ち往生する 〈立ち止まる〉 be brought to a standstill [halt]; be stalled; be held up; be stuck; be stranded 〈当惑する〉 be at [brought to] one's wits' end; be in a dilemma [fix]. 文例↓

たちおくれる 立ち後れる lag [fall] behind sb 《in sth》; 〈出発が〉 make a belated start. 文例↓

たちおよぎ 立ち泳ぎ ¶立ち泳ぎする tread water.

たちかえる 立ち返る come [go] back 《to》; re-

が漂っている。 There is a faint suggestion of spring in the air. / 彼の詩には甘い哀愁が漂っている。 His poems have a touch of sweet melancholy.

たたり 後のたたりが恐ろしいぞ。 There will be the devil to pay. ! You'll pay dearly for this! / あの家には何かたたりがあるらしい。 There seems to be a curse on that family.

たたる 僕はこの病気に一生たたられるだろう。 This disease will torment me all my life. / 過労がたたったらしい。 It seems that the strain of overwork has begun to tell on him.

たち[2] 船酔いするたちでなかったら船で行く方がいい。 You had better take a boat unless you are prone [subject] to seasickness [as long as you are not liable to get seasick]. / 彼はそんなことをするたちではない。 It is not in his nature [He is not the kind of man] to do such a thing. / 僕はそういうたちなんだ。 I am born [made] that way.

たちあう 外科医を呼んで立ち会ってもらった。 A surgeon was called in for a joint consultation.

たちあがる 現在の東京は灰燼の中から立ち上がったのだ。 It was from the ashes that the present Tokyo rose. / ドイツ軍の侵略に対して彼らは武器を取って立ち上がった。 They took up [rose up in] arms against the German aggression.

たちいり 立ち入り禁止。 〖掲示〗 Private. / 無用の者の立ち入りを禁ず。〖掲示〗 No admittance except on business.

たちいる 芝生に立ち入るべからず。〖掲示〗 Keep off the grass. / 立ち入ったことをお伺いするようですが…. Excuse me if I am too personal, but…. / 立ち入った話になっていった。 Their conversation was taking a personal turn.

たちおうじょう 列車は大雪のために立ち往生した。 The train was snowed up. / 先生はその質問に立ち往生した。 The teacher stood silent for a while, not knowing how to answer the question.

たちおくれる 日本はこの方面ではアメリカにはるかに立ち後れている。 Japan is far behind the United States in this field.

たちかた 裁ち方 a cut; cutting; how to cut.
たちがれ 立ち枯れ ¶立ち枯れする stand decayed [dead].
たちき 立ち木 a living [standing, growing] tree; standing timber (木材としての).
たちぎえ 立ち消え ¶立ち消えになる〈炭などが〉go [die] out;〈物事が〉go up in smoke; come to nothing; be dropped; be discontinued; flicker [fizzle] out. 文例⇩
たちぎき 立ち聞き overhearing; eavesdropping ¶立ち聞きする overhear; eavesdrop 《on sb's talk》.
たちきる 断[裁]ち切る cut off;《文》sever ⇒ たつ⁴.
たちぐい 立ち食い a stand-up meal ¶立ち食いする〈屋台などで〉take a stand-up meal;〈行儀悪く〉eat while one is standing (up); eat without sitting at table.
たちぐされ 立ち腐れ ¶立ち腐れになる be dilapidated; fall into decay [ruin].
たちくず 裁ち屑 waste pieces (of cut cloth); offcuts (of cloth); cuttings; scraps.
たちくらみ 立ち暗み ¶立ちくらみする feel [get] dizzy [giddy] on standing up. 文例⇩
たちげいこ 立ち稽古 a rehearsal.
たちこめる 立ちこめる hang over; envelop;《文》shroud ¶朝霧の立ちこめた村々 villages veiled [enveloped] in a morning mist. 文例⇩
たちさる 立ち去る leave; go off [away]《from》; depart《from》; quit ¶黙って立ち去る take French leave / 立ち去れと命じる order sb away. 文例⇩
たちしょうべん 立ち小便 ¶立ち小便する urinate outdoors [by the roadside]. 文例⇩
たちすがた 立ち姿 one's standing posture [figure].
たちすくむ 立ち竦む be petrified《with terror》; stand paralyzed; be unable to move (on); be [stand] riveted [transfixed] on 《the spot》.
たちつくす 立ち尽くす keep [remain] standing till the end《of sth》. 文例⇩
たちどおし 立ち通し 文例⇩
たちどころに 立ち所に〈すぐに〉at once; in an instant [a moment]; instantly; immediately;〈その場で〉then and there; on the spot.
たちどまる 立ち止まる stop; halt; pause; come to a stop [stand, standstill] ¶急に立ち止まる stop short [suddenly]; come to a sudden stop. 文例⇩
たちなおる 立ち直る recover (oneself); regain one's footing; make a comeback; get back on one's feet; get back on the right track (正道に戻る);〈相場などが〉rally; pick up. 文例⇩
たちならぶ 立ち並ぶ stand in a row; line (a street).
たちのき 立ち退き〈移転〉removal; quitting;〈明け渡し〉evacuation ¶立ちのきを要求する demand that sb [tell sb to] leave 《the house》/ 立ちのきを命じる order sb out / 立ちのき先 one's place of refuge;《立て札の文句》Temporary address: ... / 立ちのき料 compensation for one's forced removal.
たちのく 立ち退く〈去る〉quit; leave;〈転居する〉move [clear] out; remove;〈撤退する〉《文》evacuate;《文》vacate; withdraw《from》;〈避難する〉take refuge《at》¶立ちのかせる eject; evict;《文》evacuate; order sb out (命令を出して).
たちのぼる 立ち上る go up; rise; ascend.
たちのみ 立ち飲み ¶立ち飲みする drink (sake) standing [without sitting down].
たちば 立場〈立脚地〉a footing; one's ground; a standpoint;〈観点〉a point of view; a viewpoint;〈境遇〉a position; a situation ¶立場を変えて見る look at sth from a different standpoint [angle] / ...について強い立場を取る take a strong stand on sth / 中間の立場を取る take a middle position; take the middle ground / ...の立場になって考える put oneself in sb's place [shoes] / 外交上の立場から from a diplomatic standpoint [point of view] / 対等の立場で on an equal footing《with》. 文例⇩
たちはだかる 立ちはだかる〈面と向かう〉con-

たちぎえ その計画は簡単に立ち消えになった。The project soon fizzled out.
たちくらみ あまり急に立ち上がったので立ちくらみした。I stood up so suddenly [quickly] that my vision blurred for a moment.
たちこめる 室内にはタバコの煙がもうもうと立ちこめていた。The room was heavy with cigarette smoke. / 霧がロンドンに立ちこめていた。A fog blanketed London. / 太平洋沿岸には霧が立ちこめていた。A fog lay along the Pacific coast. / やみが立ちこめてきた。The dark closed in on us. / The (evening) dusk gathered.
たちさる 客はいつとはなしに2人、3人と立ち去って行った。The guests drifted away in [by] twos and threes.
たちしょうべん 彼はその塀に向かって立ち小便をした。He urinated against the wall.
たちつくす 彼女は彼の後ろ姿が見えなくなるまでその場に立ち尽くしていた。She stood there, without moving, until he went out of sight.
たちどおし 電車がこんで静岡まで立ち通しだった。The train was very crowded and I was kept standing all the way to [I couldn't get a seat until we reached] Shizuoka.
たちどまる〈群衆などに〉立ち止まらないでください。Move on [along], please.
たちなおる 景気はまだなかなか立ち直るまい。It will be a long time before business recovers from this depression. / 夫を失った痛手から容易に立ち直れなかった。She found it hard to get over the loss of her husband. / 長い間の失意からようやくにして立ち直った。At last he pulled himself together after the long period of despondency.
たちば 僕の立場からははっきりしたことは言えない。I am not in a position to tell you anything definite (about it). / 彼の立場は苦しく[むずかしく]なっていた。He found himself in an awkward [a delicate] position. / 自分の置かれている立場を知ろうとした。I tried to see where I stood [how I was placed]. / 僕が君の立場に

たちはたらく 立ち働く work; go about one's work ⇨ はたらく.

たちばなし 立ち話 ¶立ち話をする stand chatting [talking]; talk without sitting down.

たちばん 立ち番 〈事〉(a) watch; 〈番人〉a guard; a watchman ¶立ち番をする stand guard (duty); keep watch [guard].

たちふさがる 立ち塞がる block [bar, stand in] sb's way.

たちまち 忽ち 〈一瞬のうちに〉in a moment [an instant, a flash]; instantly; 〈すぐに〉(all) at once; immediately; on the spot; in short order; 〈口語〉before you can say Jack Robinson; 〈急に〉suddenly; all of a sudden. 文例⇩

たちまわり 立ち回り 〈格闘〉fighting; a scuffle; a fight; 〈芝居の〉a fighting scene.

たちまわる 立ち回る 〈動く〉move about; maneuver; 〈演じる〉act; play one's part; 〈行く〉go (to); ¶じょうずに立ち回る play one's part [cards] well; …よりも上手に立ち回る outmaneuver sb. 文例⇩

たちみ 立ち見 ¶立ち見する stand to watch 《a play》; see 《a movie》standing / 立ち見客 a standee; 〈総称〉the gallery / 立ち見席 (see a play from) the gallery.

たちむかう 立ち向かう 〈直面する〉face; confront; stand face to face with; 〈戦う〉fight (against); pit oneself against; 〈反対する〉stand [rise] against; oppose ¶〈…に敢然と[正面から]立ち向かう face up squarely to 《a problem》; take [bear] the full brunt 《of an attack》.

たちもどる 立ち戻る return 《to》; go [come] back 《to》; 〈もと来た道を戻る〉retrace one's steps; go back [return] the way one has come.

たちもの 断ち物 ¶断ち物をする〈文〉abstain from some particular article of food.

たちゆく 立ち行く 〈店などが〉can be kept going; 〈暮らしが〉can get along; can make a living; can make both ends meet. 文例⇩

だちょう 駝鳥 an ostrich ¶だちょうの卵 an ostrich egg.

たちよみ 立ち読み stand-up reading; browsing ¶本屋で立ち読みする stand reading in a bookstore.

たちよる 立ち寄る call (in) at 《sb's house》; stop at [in] 《a place》; 〈通りがかりに〉drop [look] in 《on sb, at sb's house》; stop by; 〈船が〉call [touch] at 《a port》 ¶途中名古屋に立ち寄る stop (over) [break one's journey] at Nagoya / 京都に2日立ち寄る stop [stay] two days at Kyoto.

たちわざ 立ち技 〈柔道などの〉standing techniques.

だちん 駄賃 a reward; a tip.

たちんぼう 立ちん坊 文例⇩

たつ¹ 辰 〈十二支の〉《the Year of》the Dragon.

たつ² 起,立つ 〈立ちあがる〉stand up;〈文〉rise; get [rise] to one's feet; 〈立ちのぼる〉rise; go up; 〈建設される〉be built;〈文〉be erected; be set up; go up; 〈設立される〉be established; be founded; 〈奮起する〉rouse oneself (to action); rise (to the occasion); 〈店などが維持される〉be maintained; 〈出発する〉start; leave; set out [off]; 〈鳥が〉fly off; 〈とげなどが〉run into; stick; 〈波が〉run high; 〈理屈が〉hold up [good, water]; stand up [to reason]; 〈選挙に〉⇨ りっこうほ ¶立っている be standing / 神戸へたつ start [leave] for Kobe / 東京をたつ leave [depart from] Tokyo. 文例⇩

たつ³ 経つ pass; pass by [away]; 〈文〉elapse; go by [on]; 〈早く〉fly; 〈だんだんに〉wear away [on]; 〈知らない間に〉glide on [by]; slip by [away] ¶もう少したってから later a little later; later on / 〈それから〉3日たって (から)three days later [after that]; after a [the] lapse of three days / 1時間たてば in an hour [hour's time] / 時がたつに従って as time passes [goes by] / 時のたつのを忘れる be unaware [unconscious] of the passage of time / ひと月もたたないうちに in less than a month / 1週間たつかたたないうちに A week had hardly passed when…. 文例⇩

たつ⁴ 断,絶,裁つ 〈切断する〉〈文〉sever; cut (off); break off; 〈へりを〉trim; 〈遮断する〉cut off; shut off; interrupt; intercept; 〈物断ちする〉〈文〉abstain from 《alcoholic drinks》; give up 《smoking》;〈根絶やする〉exterminate;〈文〉extirpate;〈文〉eradicate; root up [out]; stamp out ¶2つに断つ cut in two [into halves] / 連絡を絶つ cut off communications 《with》/ 関係を断つ sever [break off] one's relationship [relations, connections] with sb; break [part] with sb; have done [be through]

あったとしたらやはり同じようにしただろう. In your place, I'd probably have done the same thing. / それでは私の立場がないじゃないか. That would mean a complete loss of face for me, wouldn't it?

たちはだかる 彼の前に突然1人のがっしりした男が立ちはだかった. All of a sudden a burly man came and stood there, feet planted apart, facing him.

たちまち 彼はたちまち英語がうまくなった. He made rapid progress in English. / それを見るとたちまち気が変わった. He changed his mind the moment he saw it.

たちまわる 彼は友人の家へ立ち回ったところを張り込み中の刑事に捕えられた. When he turned up at his friend's house, he was arrested by a waiting detective.

たちゆく 生徒が減って学校が立ち行かなくなった. The fall in the number of students made it difficult to keep the school going. / 広告がないとこの雑誌は立ち行かない. Without advertisements this magazine cannot pay its way.

たちんぼう (列車内で)3時間立ちん坊をした. I was kept standing for three hours.

たつ² 立て!〈号令〉Stand up! | On your feet! / 一日中立ったままアイロン掛けをするなんて私には無理だわ. I'm afraid I can't stand on my feet and iron all day. / 彼は立ったまま居眠りしていた. I found him asleep on his feet. / この間中ずっと立ち通しだった. She was kept standing all this

だつ- with sb / 禍根を断つ eliminate [remove] the root of an evil ; eradicate an evil / 上着を寸法に合わせて裁つ cut a coat to measure.

だつ- 脱... ¶脱イオン deionization / 脱サラリーマン志向 a wish to quit [extricate oneself from] the life of a white-collar worker.

たつい 達意 ¶達意の clear ; easy to understand ; lucid / 達意の文を書く express oneself clearly (in writing) ; write in such a style that the meaning is clearly understood.

だつい 脱衣 ¶脱衣する take off one's clothes ; undress / 脱衣所 a dressing [changing] room.

だつえん 脱塩 ¶脱塩する desalinize ; desalinate ; desalt / (海水を真水に変える)脱塩工場 a desalination plant.

だっかい¹ 脱会 ¶脱会する leave [resign from] an association ; a society, a club).

だっかい² 奪回 ⇒ だっかん.

たっかん 達観 ¶達観する 〈見通す〉 take a long view (of) ; 〈諦観(κ)をもって見る〉 regard [consider] 《a matter》 philosophically / 将来を達観する see far into the future (of).

だっかん 奪還 ¶奪還する recover ; regain ; recapture.

だっきゃく 脱却 ¶脱却する grow out of ; slough off ; shake oneself free (from).

たっきゅう 卓球 table tennis ; ping-pong ¶卓球の選手 a table-tennis [ping-pong] player / 卓球のボール a ping-pong ball / 卓球をする play table tennis / 卓球台 a table-tennis table.

だっきゅう 脱臼 dislocation ¶脱臼する be dislocated ; be put out of joint.

ダッグアウト a dugout.

ダックスフント 〈犬〉 a dachshund.

タッグマッチ a tag-team (wrestling) match.

タックル 《球技》 a tackle ¶タックルする tackle.

たっけん 卓見 〈先見の明〉 far-sightedness ; 《文》 penetration ; 〈名案〉 a fine [an excellent] idea [view, opinion].

だっこう¹ 脱肛 prolapse of the anus.

だっこう² 脱稿 ¶脱稿する complete 《a novel》 ; finish writing 《an article》.

だっこく 脱穀 ¶脱穀する thresh ; thrash / 脱穀機 a threshing [thrashing] machine.

だつごく 脱獄 a jailbreak ; prison-breaking ¶脱獄する escape (from) prison ; break (out of) prison / 脱獄囚 an escaped convict ; a prison breaker.

たっし 達し an official notice ; a notification ¶達しを出す issue an official notice 《to》; inform 《(を) notify》《sb of sth》.

だっし 脱脂 ¶脱脂する remove grease [fat] (from) / 脱脂乳 skim [skimmed, nonfat] milk / 脱脂綿 absorbent [sanitary] cotton ; cotton wool [《米》 batting].

たっしゃ 達者 ¶達者な 〈健康な〉 healthy ; well ; robust ; strong ; hale and hearty (老人が) ; 〈巧みな〉 skillful (in) ; 《文》 proficient (in) ; at home (in) ; expert [《文》 adept] (in, at) ; good [clever] (at) / 達者に skillfully ; well ; 〈すらすらと〉 《文》 with facility ; fluently / 達者でいる be quite well ; be (as) fit as a fiddle ; be in [《文》 enjoy] good health / 口が達者である be a glib talker ; have a glib tongue. 文例4

だっしゅ 奪取 ¶奪取する capture ; 《文》 carry ; seize ; grab.

ダッシュ¹ 《符号》 a dash ¶〈伏せ字の個所の〉 a blank ¶ダッシュをつける put a dash (after a word) / b ダッシュ (b') /《数》b prime / 《英》 b dash / b ツー [スリー] ダッシュ (b'', b''') b double [triple] prime.

ダッシュ² 《突進》 a dash ¶ダッシュする dash ; make a dash (at, for).

だっしゅう 脱臭 ¶脱臭する deodorize ; remove [kill] the odor (of) / 脱臭剤 a deodorant.

だっしゅつ 脱出 ¶脱出する escape (from) ; get out of / (地球などの引力圏から宇宙船が)脱出速度に達する[にまで加速される] achieve [be boosted to] escape velocity.

だっしょく 脱色 ¶脱色する remove (the) color (from) ; bleach / 脱色剤 a bleaching agent ; a bleach.

たつじん 達人 a master (of) ; a past master 《at, in, of》; an expert 《at, in》; 《文》 an adept 《in, at》 ¶…にかけては達人である be a master of... ; be at home in... ; be clever at....

だっすい 脱水 ¶脱水する dehydrate ; desiccate ; dry / 脱水機 a drier / (人体の)脱水症状 [状態] dehydration / (人が)脱水状態になっている be dehydrated.

たっする 達する 〈到達する〉 reach ; arrive at [in] ; get to [at] ; gain ; 〈数量が〉 amount to ; run up to ; 〈達成する〉 reach [《文》 attain, gain] 《one's objective》 ; achieve [《文》 accomplish] 《one's purpose》 ; 《文》 realize ; carry out [through] ; 〈通達する〉 notify [inform] 《sb of

---

while. / 明日の国会では社会党からK氏が質問演説に立つ。 Mr. K of the Socialist Party will rise in the House tomorrow to make an interpellation. / 立つ鳥跡を濁さず。 A bird does not foul the nest that it is about to leave. | On leaving a place one should see that everything is in good order before one goes.

たつ³ 結婚してからこれで10年たつ。 Ten years have passed [It is ten years] since they got married. | They have been married (for) ten years. / なにしろこう時がたっているとはっきり思い出せません。 I cannot recollect it clearly at this distance in time. / 時がたてばわかる。 Time will tell. / この木は少なくとも100年はたっている。 This tree is at least a hundred years old. / 1時間たったらまたいらっしゃい。 Come back in an hour. / 時がたつのが早いこと。 How time flies! / その1日のたつのが長かった。 The day dragged on. | I thought the day would never end. / 1週間もたたないうちに彼は旅行からもう帰って来た。 It was not a week before he returned from his journey. / 年月がたつにつれて、問題はこじれてきた。 With the passing of the years, the problem became more and more complicated.

たっしゃ ありがとう、達者です。 I'm very well, thank you. / 足さえ達者なら徒歩旅行にもそれなりの面白みがある。 To a good walker, traveling on foot has a charm of its own. / 彼はフランス

だっする 脱する get out of ; escape from ; find one's way out of. 文例⇩

たつせ 立つ瀬 文例⇩

たっせい 達成 (文) achievement ; (文) attainment ; (文) accomplishment ¶達成する achieve ; (文) attain ; (文) accomplish ; (文) realize ; carry out [through].

だつぜい 脱税 evasion of taxes ; tax evasion ¶脱税する evade (a) tax.

だっせん 脱線 〈鉄道の〉 derailment ; 〈話の〉 (文)(a) digression (from) ; an excursion (into) ¶脱線する 〈車が〉 be [get] derailed ; run off the rails [track] ; 〈行動が〉 go astray ; be eccentric ; 〈話・議論などが〉 (文) digress (from the subject) ; make a digression ; wander (in one's talk).

だっそう 脱走 (an) escape ; (a) flight ; 〈軍隊からの〉 desertion ¶脱走する escape ; (文) flee ; run away ; 〈軍人が〉 desert (barracks) / 脱走者 an escapee ; a runaway / 脱走兵 a deserter.

だつぞく 脱俗 (文)脱俗的な (文) detached from worldly things ; (文) unworldly.

たった only ; merely ; (文) but ; no more than ; just ¶たった3日間で for three days / たった今 just ; just now ; a moment ago ; this moment ; this very minute ★just is He has just arrived. のように現在完了時制と共に, just now は He went out just now. のように過去時制と共に使うのが普通であるが, 《米》では just を過去時制でも用いる. a moment ago は過去時制で, this moment と this very minute は現在完了時制で用いる / たった1人で all alone ; by oneself. 文例⇩

だったい 脱退 (文) secession ; (文) withdrawal ¶脱退する withdraw ((文)) secede) from ; leave.

タッチ 〈音楽・絵画・野球〉 a touch ¶タッチする 〈野球〉 touch ((a runner) with the ball) ; 〈仕事などに〉 touch on ; concern oneself [be concerned] (in, with) ; have a hand (in) ; be a party (to) / (競泳で)ゴールにタッチする touch the finish wall / タッチの差で破る defeat ((one's opponent)) by a touch ; touch ((another swimmer)) out / タッチアウトにする tag ((a runner)) out / タッチアップする 〖野球〗 tag up / タッチダウン 〖ラグビー〗《make》 a touchdown.

だっちょう 脱腸 (abdominal) hernia ¶脱腸になる have a [be affected with] hernia / 脱腸帯 a hernia belt ; a truss.

たって 〈しきりと〉(文) earnestly ; urgently ; pressingly ; (文) importunately ; 〈無理に〉 forcibly ¶たっての earnest ; urgent ; pressing ; (文) importunate / たってのたのみで at sb's earnest [earnest] request / たってのお望みなら if you particularly wish it ; if you insist (on it). 文例⇩

たって 〈なぜなら〉 because ; for ; 〈だが〉 but ; though ; 〈やはり〉 still. 文例⇩

-だって 〈…でも, すら〉 even ; 〈…もまた〉 also ; too ; 〈…だという〉 I hear… ; they say. 文例⇩

だっと 脱兎 ¶脱兎のごとく with lightning speed ; as fast as one can / 脱兎のごとく走り去る run off like a hare / 〈英口語〉 hare off.

たとい 尊[貴]い ⇨ とうとい.

だっとう 脱党 ¶脱党する leave [withdraw from] a party.

たっとぶ 尊[貴]ぶ ⇨ とうとぶ.

たづな 手綱 reins ¶手綱を取る hold [lead] ((a horse)) by the bridle ; hold [take over] the reins ((of)) / 手綱を引き締める tighten [pull up, draw in] the reins ; rein in ((a horse)) / 手綱を引いて馬を止める rein in [back] one's horse / 手綱を緩める loosen [slacken, let out] the reins ; give ((a horse)) its head ; give the reins to ((a horse)). 文例⇩

たつのおとしご 竜の落とし子 a sea horse.

たつび 脱皮 〖動〗 molting ; (a) molt ¶脱皮する shed [slough, cast (off)] its skin ; molt (into an adult) / 旧態を脱皮する break with convention ; (文) outgrow one's former self.

たっぴつ 達筆 good handwriting ¶達筆である have good handwriting ; (文) write a good hand ; (文) be an excellent penman / 達筆で書かれている be well [beautifully] written ; (文) be written in a good hand.

タップダンサー a tap dancer.

語を達者に話す. He speaks good French. | He speaks French fluently. | He has a good command of French.

だっする もうこれで危険を脱した. Now we are out of danger.

たつせ それじゃ僕の立つ瀬がない. Then, where does that leave me [do I come in?] | That would put me in an awkward position.| That would make my position untenable.

たっせい 音よりも早く飛ぶということは人力では達成できないと長い間考えられていた. Flying faster than sound was long thought to be beyond human achievement.

たった たった1分のところで列車に間に合わなかった. I missed the train by just one minute. / たった1人の旅人がその山道を行くのが見えた. The figure of one lone traveler was seen walking along the mountain path.

タッチ 彼女のピアノはタッチがとても確かだ. Her touch on the piano is very sure.

たって その気がないならたっては言わない. I will not press you, if you don't really feel like doing it.

だって なぜ来なかった?―だってお腹が痛かったんだもの. Why didn't you come?―Because I had a stomachache.

-だって ぼくがばかだって君たちはばかだ. If I am a fool, you are another. / あの男が正直者だって? (Do) you say he's [Do you call him] an honest man? / そうだって. So they say. | So he says.

たづな 手綱をしっかり両手に握っていた. He kept the reins tightly in his hands. / 手綱を引いて

タップダンス a tap dance ¶タップダンスをする man a tap-dancer.

たっぷり 〈充分〉fully;《文》amply;〈たくさん〉《文》plentifully; abundantly; generously; in plenty;〈全く〉quite ¶たっぷり15分 a good [full] quarter of an hour / たっぷり10キロ a good ten kilometers / 金がたっぷりある have money (enough and) to spare / たっぷり食べる have [eat] one's fill (of); have a meal; eat to one's heart's content [as much as one wants] / バターをたっぷり塗る spread butter thick(ly) (on a slice of bread). 文例⇩

だつぼう 脱帽 ¶脱帽する take off one's cap [hat]; uncover one's head.

だっぽうこうい 脱法行為 (an) evasion of the law.

たつまき 竜巻 a whirlwind; a tornado (pl. -(e)s);〈海上の〉a waterspout.

だつもう 脱毛〈抜けること〉loss of hair;〈抜くこと〉removal of hair; depilation ¶脱毛クリーム depilatory cream.

だつらく 脱落 ¶脱落する〈漏れる〉be left out;《文》be omitted;〈落後する〉fall away [behind]; drop out.

だつりゅう 脱硫 ¶脱硫装置 desulfurization equipment.

だつりょくかん 脱力感《文》(a feeling of) lassitude.

たて¹ 盾 a shield;《史》a buckler (丸い小型の) ¶盾にとる use (a tree) as a shield (against bullets); shield oneself behind sth; hide [shelter] (oneself) behind sth / 法律を盾にとって on the strength [authority] of the law / 病気を盾に on the pretext [plea] of illness / 盾を突く ⇨たてつく / 盾の半面しか見ない look only at [at only] one side (of a question); take a partial [biased] view (of). 文例⇩

たて² 殺陣 演劇 a sword battle; a fight (scene) ¶たて師 a man who teaches actors how to use swords.

たて³ 縦〈長さ〉(a) length;〈高さ〉(a) height ¶縦30センチ横20センチ高さ10センチのブロック a block 30 by 20 by 10 centimeters / 縦の《文》longitudinal; lengthwise;〈垂直の〉vertical; perpendicular /（クロスワードの）縦の1番 number one down / 縦に lengthwise; lengthways;《文》longitudinally;〈垂直に〉perpendicularly; vertically / 縦に並べる arrange (the blocks) lengthways [lengthwise]; place (the desks) one behind another [the other] / 縦に線を引く draw a perpendicular [vertical] line / 首を縦に振る agree; nod one's agreement;《文》nod (in) assent;《文》give one's consent (to) / 縦から見ても横から見ても (be) every inch (a gentleman); to all appearance(s) / 縦社会 a vertically-structured society. 文例⇩

-たて just; fresh [green] from ¶大学を出たての青年 a young man fresh from college / パリから帰りたての画家 a painter just returned from Paris / 焼きたてのパン bread hot from the oven / 刷りたての校正刷り proof wet [damp] from the press / 買いたての帽子 a new [brand-new] hat / 生みたての卵 a new-laid egg. 文例⇩

たで 〖植〗(a) smartweed; (a) water pepper.

だて ¶だてに for show; for appearance' sake / だて男 a dandy. 文例⇩

-だて …建[立]て ¶9階建てのビル a nine-story [-storied] building / 円[ドル]建ての〈bonds〉denominated in yen [dollars]; yen-[dollar-]denominated (bills) / 2本立て〈映画〉a double bill / 2頭立ての馬車 a carriage and pair. 文例⇩

たてあな 縦穴 a pit ¶縦穴住居〖考古〗a pit dwelling.

たていた 立て板 ¶立て板に水を流すように very fluently;《文》with great fluency; glibly.

たていと 縦糸 warp; a warp thread [yarn] (一本).

たてうり 建売り ¶建売りする sell a ready-built house / 建売り住宅 a (private) house built for sale; ready-built housing;《英》speculative [《口語》spec] housing.

たてえり 立て襟 a stiff [stand-up] collar.

たてかえ 立て替え payment on sb's behalf [for sb];〈前払い〉payment in advance;〈前渡し金〉an advance.

たてかえる¹ 立て替える〈前貸しする〉advance; pay in advance;〈代わって払う〉stand (the bill for sb); defray (sb's expenses); pay (for sb, on sb's behalf).

たてかえる² 建て替える rebuild; reconstruct.

たてがき 縦書き ¶縦書きにする write vertically [in vertical lines].

馬を止めた。He reined up his horse. / 君は部下の者たちに対してもっと手綱をゆるめて自由にやらせるべきだ。You should ease up on the reins and allow your men more freedom.

たっぷり 歩いてたっぷり2日かかる。It is a full [good] two days' journey on foot. /（狙っている獲物までは）たっぷり300メートルはあると思った。I judged the range to be fully [all of] three hundred meters. / 朝飯をたっぷり食べた。I ate a big [large] breakfast.

だつぼう 脱帽! Hats off! | Off caps! | 彼の勇気には脱帽した。I had to take my hat off to him for his courage.

たて¹ 盾を持って帰れ, しからずんば盾に乗りて帰れ。Return [Come back] with your shield or upon it. / 盾には両面がある。There's always another side to the coin. | Everything has its two sides.

たて³ これは縦が3メートルある。It is three meters long. | It measures three meters in length. / 縦から見ても横から見ても軍人だ。He looks every inch a soldier.

-たて まだ入りたてですので, 社内の事情はよく分かりません。I'm quite new to this company, so I don't really know (much about) how matters stand here.

たで たで食う虫も好き好き。There is no accounting for tastes. | Every man to his taste. | Tastes differ.

だて だてに英語を勉強してはいない。I didn't learn English for nothing.

-だて けさの毎日新聞は30ページ建てだ。There are 30 pages to this morning's issue of the Mai-

たてかける 立て掛ける lean [rest, stand, set, 《文》place] *sth* (against).

たてかた 建て方 〈様式〉a style of building; 《Renaissance》architecture; 〈方法〉a method of construction; how to build (houses); 〈構造〉structure; construction.

たてがみ 鬣 a mane ¶たてがみのある maned (lions).

たてかんばん 立て看板 a standing signboard.

たてきる 立て切る close [shut] up (*fusuma*).

たてぐ 建具 fittings such as sliding doors, *fusuma*, *shoji*, etc., used for partitioning off a house ¶建具をとりつける fit up 《a room》/ 建具屋 a joiner.

たてこう 縦坑 〈鉱山〉a (mine) shaft.

たてごと 竪琴 a harp.

たてこむ¹ 立て込む 〈場所が〉be crowded [《文》thronged, packed]《with》; 〈仕事が〉be pressed 《with business》; have *one's* hands full 《with》; be busy 《with, in》 ¶仕事が立て込んでいるにもかかわらず despite the pressure of *one's* duties.

たてこむ² 建て込む be crowded with houses ¶建て込んでいる地域 a heavily built-up area. 文例⇩

たてこもる 立て籠もる barricade *oneself* 《in a fort》; hold 《a castle》; entrench *oneself* 《in a castle》.

たてじく 縦軸 a vertical axis;《数》the y-axis; the vertical axis (グラフの).

たてじま 縦縞 a vertical stripe ¶縦じまの vertical-striped.

たてじわ 縦皺 a vertical line (between the eyebrows).

たてつく 盾突く disobey; oppose; defy;《文》bid defiance to; rebel [set *oneself*] against ¶公然と盾突いている《文》be in open defiance (against).

たてつけ 立て付け ¶立てつけが悪い do not open and shut smoothly / 立てつけのよい[悪い] well-[badly-, poorly-,《文》ill-]fitting (doors); well-[badly-, poorly-,《文》ill-]fitted (windows).

たてつづけ 立て続け ¶たて続けに in (rapid [quick]) succession; on end; at a stretch;《口語》on the trot ¶たて続けに3日間 [working] for three days together [running] / たて続けに2週間 for two consecutive weeks; for two weeks on end [in succession].

たてつぼ 建坪 floor space ¶建坪が200平方メートルある have a floor space of 200 square meters.

たてなおし 建て直し rebuilding; reconstruction;〈組織の〉reorganization;〈政策・陣容などの〉reshuffle ¶内閣の建て直し a Cabinet reshuffle.

たてなおす¹ 立て直す recover; restore; retrieve 《*one's* fortunes》;〈勢いを〉pull *oneself* together; rally;〈組織・政策などを〉rearrange; reorganize; reshuffle ¶計画を立て直す revise the plan.

たてなおす² 建て直す rebuild; reconstruct.

たてなが 縦長 縦長の (a sheet of paper) longer than 〈it〉is wide / 紙を縦長に use the sheet of paper with the shorter side at the top. 文例⇩

たてね 建値〈公定相場〉an official quotation;〈為替相場〉an exchange rate;〈市価〉a market price.

たてひざ 立て膝 ¶立てひざをする sit with one knee drawn up.

たてふだ 立て札 a notice; a board ¶立て札を立てる put up a notice (reading...). 文例⇩

たてまえ¹ 建て前〈主義・方針〉a principle; a rule;〈本音に対して〉*one's* words; *one's* public [《文》professed] position ¶...を立て前とする make a point of *do*ing; make it a principle to *do*. 文例⇩

たてまえ² 建て前〈棟(む)上げ〉(the ceremony of) the erection of the framework 《of a house》.

たてまし 建て増し extension of a building;〈建て増した部分〉an extension (to a building); an annex;《米》an addition ¶建て増しする extend [add to] (a building); build an annex to (a house); make an extension to (a house); enlarge (a house) / 2間(ま)建て増しする have two rooms added [build two rooms on] to *one's* house; add on two rooms.

たてまつる 奉る〈捧呈する〉offer; present;《文》tender;〈あがめる〉revere; look up to;〈祭り上げる〉put *sb* on a pedestal.

たてむすび 縦結び ¶縦結びにする tie 《a bow》in a granny knot.

たてもの 建物 a building; a structure;《文》an edifice (大きな). 文例⇩

たてやくしゃ 立て役者 the leading actor [player]; a star;〈中心人物〉a leader; a central figure ¶《ある情況下で》立て役者になる play

---

たてかける 君の傘は壁に立てかけてあります。Your umbrella is against the wall.

たてこむ² 僕たちの遊び場だった原っぱも今はすっかり建て込んでしまった。The field where we used to play is quite built up now.

たてなが この四角形は縦長に見える。This square looks taller than it is broad.

たてふだ「芝生に入るべからず」という立て札が立ててある。There is a notice [A notice has been put up] reading 'Keep off the grass'.

たてまえ¹ 建て前と本音は別だ。There are differences between people's stated principles and their real intentions. / あの人は建て前と本音が全く違う。There's a big gap [difference] between what he says and what he is really thinking [between his words and his real intentions, between his public position and his private intentions].

たてもの 駅はルネッサンス風のりっぱな建物です。The station is a fine specimen of Renaissance architecture. / 新校舎はがっしりした建物です。The new school building is a very solid construction.

たてやくしゃ 氏は当時の政界の立て役者であった。He was playing a leading part on the political stage at that time.

たてる 彼は新しい家を建てた。He has had a new house built. | He has built himself a new house. / テレビ放送局が各地に建てられつつある。New TV stations are going up all over the country.

a leading part; hold the center of the stage. 文例⇩

たてゆれ 縦揺れ 〈船・航空機の〉 pitching; (fore-and-aft) pitch.

たてよこ 縦横 length and breadth ¶縦横に lengthwise and breadthwise; crosswise; crossways.

-だてら ¶女だてらに woman as [though] she is.

たてる 立[建]てる raise; set [put] up; stand; plant (柱などを); 〈建造する〉build; 《文》 erect; set [put] up; throw up (急いで); 〈設定する〉set up; establish, found, organize; lay down 《rules》; 《文》 institute; create; 〈計画を〉draw up; form; make; map out (a program); shape (a course); 〈説などを〉set up; put forward 《an argument》; 《文》 advance; 《文》 formulate (a theory); frame; 〈戸を〉shut [close] (a door); 〈あがめる〉look up to sb (as); hold sb in high esteem; respect ¶ろうそくを立てる stand a candle / 卵を立てる stand [put] an egg on (its) end / 〈いを立てる set [put] a stake in the ground / 耳を立てる prick up one's ears / 銅像を建てる erect [set up] a bronze statue / 学校を建てる found [set up] a school / 候補者を立てる put up a candidate (for) / 人生の方針を立てる lay down the course of one's life / 政策を立てる shape [frame, establish] a policy / 暮らしを立てる earn one's living [livelihood] / 身を立てる establish oneself [set oneself up] (as a physician) / 声を立てる（叫ぶ）give a cry; 〈話す〉speak; ほこりを立てる raise [kick up] dust / 大きな音を立てる make a loud noise / 夫を夫として立てる treat one's husband with due respect; give one's husband his proper place in the family. 文例⇩

だてん 打点 〈野球〉 a run batted in (略: r.b.i.).

だでん 打電 ¶打電する telegraph; send a telegram [wire] 《to》; wire 《to》.

だとう¹ ⇒たとえ².

だとう¹ 打倒 ¶打倒する overthrow. 文例⇩

だとう² 妥当 ¶妥当な proper; appropriate; adequate; 《文》 pertinent / 妥当でない 《文》 improper; inappropriate; inadequate / 妥当する apply (in the case); hold good [water].

だとうか 多党化 ¶(議会が)多党化する be split into many different parties.

たどうし 他動詞 《文法》 a transitive verb (略: vt., v.t.).

たとえ¹ 譬え 〈隠喩〉 a metaphor; 〈直喩〉 a simile; 〈風喩〉 an allegory; 〈寓話〉 a fable; 〈ことわざ〉 a proverb; a saying; 〈例〉 an example (人の); an instance (事柄の); an illustration (例証); 〈比較〉 a comparison ¶たとえに言うように as the proverb says; as the saying goes [runs] / たとえ話 a fable; a parable; an allegory. 文例⇩

たとえ² 〈仮に〉 (even) if [though]; although; (even) admitting [granting, supposing] that... ¶たとえ冗談でも even as a joke; even in fun / たとえそうであっても even so / たとえどれほどの金持ちにせよ however [no matter how] rich one may be / たとえどんな事があっても whatever [no matter what] may happen; come what may. 文例⇩

たとえば 例えば for instance; for example; e.g. (★ ラテン語 exempli gratia の略); such as; as; (let us) say. 文例⇩

たとえる 例える 〈なぞらえる〉 compare (to); 《文》 liken (to); 〈比喩を用いる〉 use a metaphor [simile]; 〈例証する〉 take an illustration ¶たとえて言うと figuratively [metaphorically] speaking / たとえようもないほど incomparably; 〈名状しがたいほど〉 indescribably; 《文》 ineffably / 何にたとえようもない be (beautiful) beyond comparison [description]; beggar [baffle] description. 文例⇩

たどく 多読 《文》 extensive reading ¶多読する read widely [extensively] / 多読家 《文》 an extensive reader; a well-[widely-]read person. 文例⇩

たどたどしい 辿々しい faltering; tottering; unsteady ¶たどたどしい英語で書いた手紙 a letter written in shaky [halting] English / たどたどしい口調で言う falter out 《that...》 / たどたどしい足取りで歩く totter (along) / たどたどしく totteringly; falteringly; with unsteady steps [《文》 an unsteady gait]; with difficulty.

たどる 辿る pursue (a course); follow (a road); trace (a path); follow up (a clue) ¶山道をたどる trudge [toil] along a mountain path / 青春の思い出をたどる retrace [recollect, go over again in memory] the experiences of

---

僕は今度の休暇を長崎で過ごす計画を立てています。 I'm planning to spend the coming holidays at Nagasaki. / あちら立てればこちらが立たずで困ったものだ。 I'm in a dilemma, quite unable to satisfy both sides.

だとう² 打倒軍国主義! Down with militarism!

たとえ¹ 「壁に耳あり」 というたとえもある。 There is [We have] a proverb which says 'Walls have ears'.

たとえ² たとえそれが事実としたところでどうだと言うのだ。 Even if it should be [Even if it were]

true, what would it matter? / 彼はそんな所へたとえ行くことがあってもごくまれだ。 He seldom, if ever, goes to such places. / 立ち木はたとえあるとしてもごくわずかだ。 There are very few trees, if any. / たとえそれが本当にしてもやはり君の方が間違っている。 Granting it to be true [Granted that it is true], you are still in the wrong.

たとえば たとえばたかやわしのような猛禽はくちばしが曲がっている。 Birds of prey, such as the hawk and the eagle, have hooked bills. / たとえばロダンなどそのよ

い例である。 Rodin is a case in point. / 過去の事件(たとえばフランス革命)に対する是非の価値判断はすべてこの仮定の上に基づいている。 Every historical approval or condemnation, say of the French Revolution, is based on this assumption.

たとえる 人生はしばしば航海にたとえられる。 Life is often compared [likened] to a voyage. / その景色はたとえようもないほど美しい。 The scenery is beautiful beyond (all) description.

たどく 彼は多読家である。 He is very well read.

たどん 764 たね

one's youth / 一字一字文字をたどりながら読む spell out (a sentence) / たどり着く arrive at [reach] ((one's) destination) at last ; find one's way (to a place). 文例▷

たどん 炭団 a charcoal ball ; a small round briquet(te).

たな 棚 a shelf ((pl. shelves)) ; a rack (網だな) ; a trellis(藤やぶどうなどの) ¶棚をつる put up [hang] a shelf ; fix a shelf (to the wall) / 自分の事を棚にあげる shut one's eyes to [be blind to] one's own faults [blemishes] ; 《文》 do not see the beam in one's own eye.

たなあげ 棚上げ ¶棚上げする 〈議案などを〉 shelve ; pigeonhole. 文例▷

たなおろし 棚卸し 〈商店の〉 stocktaking ; 〈あら捜し〉 faultfinding ¶棚卸しする take stock (of) ; make [take, draw up] an inventory (of) ; 〈あら捜しをする〉 criticize ; find fault with / 棚卸し表 〈draw up〉an inventory (of).

たなご 〔魚〕 a Japanese bitterling.

たなざらえ 棚浚え clearance ¶棚ざらえ大売り出し a clearance sale.

たなざらし 店晒し dead stock ; 《口語》 a shelf warmer ¶たなざらしの shopworn ; shop-soiled. 文例▷

たなばた 七夕 the Festival of the Weaver [Star Vega] ; the Star Festival.

たなびく 棚引く trail ; hang [lie] over ¶たなびく煙 trailing smoke.

たなぼた 棚ぼた a windfall ; a godsend. 文例▷

たなん 多難 ¶多難 full of troubles [difficulties] ; eventful / この多難の時代に in these difficult times / 多難な道 a thorny path / 国家多難の時 (in) a national crisis.

たに 谷 a valley ; 〈峡谷〉 a ravine ; a gorge ; 〈気圧・音波などの〉 a trough ¶両側の切り立った谷 a steep-walled valley / 川の流れている谷 a river [stream] valley / 谷の斜面 valley walls [sides] / 〈川が〉谷をうがつ cut a valley [gorge] / 山を越え谷を越えて up hill and down dale / 谷川 a mountain stream [torrent] / 谷底 the bottom of a ravine [gorge] ; the valley floor / 谷間 a ravine ; a gorge / ビルの谷間 a valley between tall buildings.

囲底 両岸の切り立った深い渓谷は ravine 又は gorge と言い, その規模の大きなものを特に 《米》 では canyon と言う. 前に steep-walled などのような形容詞を付けずに単に valley と言えば両側の斜面が緩やかなものを指す.

だに 〔動〕 a tick ; a mite.

たにくしょくぶつ 多肉植物 a fleshy [succulent] plant ; a succulent.

たにし 田螺 a mud [pond] snail.

たにん 他人 〈他の人〉 another person ; others ; 〈未知の人〉 a stranger ; 〈血縁のない人〉 an unrelated person ; 〈局外者〉 an outsider ¶他人行儀にする stand on ceremony ; be distant (toward). 文例▷

たにんずう 多人数 a great many [a large number of] people ⇨ おおぜい.

たぬき 狸 a raccoon dog ; 〈比喩的に〉 a sly dog ; an old fox ¶たぬき親父 a sly [cunning] old man / たぬき寝入りをする a sham [《文》 feign] sleep ; pretend to be asleep. 文例▷

たね 種 〈果実の〉 a seed ; a stone (堅核) ; a kernel (核) ; a pip (みかんなどの) ; 〈品質〉 quality ; 〈話などの〉 a subject ; a topic ; 〈仕掛け〉 a (secret) device ; a trick ; 〈原因・みなもと〉 a cause ; a source ; 〈材料〉 material ; 〈get〉 copy (新聞などの) ¶ぶどう[かき]の種 a grape [persimmon] seed / 桃[梅]の種 a peach [an ume] stone / 涙の種 a cause for tears / 悩みの種 what worries one ; a thorn in one's flesh [side] (特に人について言う) / 書く種がない have nothing to write about / 話の種がない have no end of things [topics] to talk about / 〈牛馬が〉種がいい be of (a) good stock ; be of a fine breed / 種をまく 《a garden》 ; sow seeds (in) ; 〈比喩的に〉 sow the seeds (of discord) ; give rise to 《a quarrel》 / …のたねを宿す be going to be the mother of sb's child ; be pregnant by sb / 種を生じる seed ; bear seeds / 種を取る 〈まくために〉 gather the seeds ; 〈取り除く〉 remove the pips [seeds] (from) ; 〈grapes〉 / 種を明かす reveal the trick 《to sb》 ; show sb the secret ; let sb into the secret.

たどる このような遺伝的特徴は何世代も前までたどることができる. These genetic traits can be traced back many generations. / 家業を継げば父と同じ運命をたどることになろう. If I carry on my father's business, I'll be in for the same fate as him. / より² 囲底 / その会社は破産の道をたどった. The firm headed for bankruptcy.

たな それは自分のことは棚に上げて人のことを言うようなものだ. That's a case of [That's like] the pot calling the kettle black. / 棚からぼたもちは落ちて来ない. You must sow before you can reap.

たなあげ この問題はいつまでも棚上げにしておくわけにはいかない. This problem cannot be left on the shelf indefinitely.

たなざらし 品物がたなざらしになっている. The goods are lying unsold on the shelf. | The goods are on the shelves as dead stock.

たなびく 野に山にかすみがたなびいている. There is a haze hanging over the hills and fields.

たなぼた たなぼた式に 200 万円ももうけた. We realized a windfall profit of two million yen.

たにん 他人とは思えない親切ぶりだった. He was kinder to me than I could ever have expected from a stranger. / この家を他人の手に渡すようなことは絶対しない. I shall never let this house fall into strange hands. / 他人より身内. Blood is thicker than water. 〔諺〕

たぬき 取らぬたぬきの皮算用. You should never count your chickens before they are hatched.

たね¹ この種からとったすいかはおいしい. The watermelons raised from this seed are sweet. / あのすし屋は種がいい. They use good materials at that sushi shop. / これはいい話の種が出来た. This will make a good topic for conversation. / 話の種に見ておこう. I'll have a look at it, so that I can say that I've seen it. / 彼女の小説の種になった. It made copy for her story. | It found its way into her story. / それを種に劇を書いた. He wrote a drama out of it. / すべて私どものことには種も仕掛けもございません. There is no kind of trick whatever behind anything we do. / 今が麦の種まきどきです. Now is the time for sowing the

たねん

¶ 種油 rape(seed) oil / 種いも a seed potato / 種牛 a stud bull / 種馬 a stallion at stud ; a stud / 種牛 a stallion / 種切れになる be [run] out of stock ; run out of 《sugar》 ; 〈物を主語に〉 run out ;《文》 be [become] exhausted / たね違いの兄弟［姉妹］ a half brother [sister] / 種付け《畜産》mating ; a service / 種無しの seedless 《grapes》 / 種本 a source book / 種まき時 seed-time ; the planting season / 種まき機 a sowing [seeding] machine / 種屋〈人〉a seed(s)man ; 〈店〉a seed store. 文例⇩

たねん 多年 many years ¶ 多年の努力 years of effort ; one's many years' efforts / 多年の希望を達する《文》realize a long-cherished desire / 多年にわたって for (many) years ; over a period of years / 多年生植物 a perennial (plant).

-だの and ; or ; and the like ; and so forth [on] ¶ 牛だの羊だの cows, sheep, and the like [and so forth].

たのう 多能 ⇨ たさい¹

たのしい 楽しい 〈パーティーなどが〉pleasant ; happy ; enjoyable ; delightful ; merry ;《文》joyful ;《文》joyous ;〈人・表情などが〉happy ; cheerful ; joyful ¶ 楽しい我が家 one's happy home / 楽しい思いをする have a good [a pleasant, an enjoyable] time / 一生に一度の［この上なく］楽しい思いをする have the time of one's life / 楽しく, 楽しげに pleasantly ; delightfully ; with delight ; merrily ; cheerfully ; joyfully / 楽しく暮らす live [lead] a happy life ; live happily. 文例⇩

たのしませる 楽しませる delight ; please ; amuse ; give [《文》afford] pleasure [delight] to ; entertain (歓待する) ;《文》regale (花や音楽などが) ¶ 目を楽しませる〈人が主語〉feast one's eyes 《on》 ;〈事物が主語〉delight the eye. 文例⇩

たのしみ 楽しみ 〈愉快〉pleasure ; joy ; enjoyment ; delight ; fun ;〈幸福〉happiness ;〈娯楽〉(an) amusement ; a diversion ;〈慰め〉comfort ;〈趣味〉a hobby ¶ 読書の楽しみ the pleasure of reading / 楽しみに《write》for pleasure ; by way of amusement ; as a hobby [pastime] / …を楽しみにして待つ look forward to《the New Year》(with pleasure) / …を楽しみにして in anticipation [expectation] of… 文例⇩

たのしむ 楽しむ《文》take [find] pleasure [delight] in 《music》 ; enjoy 《an evening》 ; enjoy [amuse] oneself 《with sth, by doing》 ; gain enjoyment 《from》 ; have fun ¶ 花を見て楽しむ feast one's eyes on the flowers. 文例⇩

たのみ 頼み 〈依頼〉(a) request ;〈信頼〉《文》reliance ; confidence ; trust ¶ 頼みがある have a favor to ask (of) sb / 頼みになる reliable ; trustworthy ; dependable ; to be relied [depended] on / 頼みにならぬ unreliable ; untrustworthy ; undependable / 頼みにする rely [depend] on ; lean [count] on ; trust in ; place one's faith in ; look [turn] to 《sb for help》 / 頼みを聞く［に応じる］do sb a favor ; grant [《文》comply with] sb's request / …の頼みで［によって］at the request of… / 頼みの綱 one's only hope ; one's last resort ; one's mainstay. 文例⇩

たのむ 頼む 〈依頼する, 願う〉ask ; beg ;《文》request ; ask a favor of sb ;〈懇願する〉《文》entreat ; implore ;《文》solicit ;《文》beseech ; appeal (to) ;《文》supplicate ;〈委託する〉trust [entrust] sb with sth ;《文》charge sb to do ; place sth under sb's charge [care] ; commit 《one's child》 to sb's care ; commission sb to do ;〈注文する〉call for 《a jug of beer》 ;〈雇う〉engage ; hire ; take on ;〈頼る〉rely [depend, lean, count] on ; look [turn] to 《sb for help》 ; trust to sb ¶ 演説を頼む ask [call on] sb for [to make] a speech / 手をついて頼む implore [《文》supplicate] 《sb for help》 on one's knees ; go down on one's knees to beg 《sb for sth, sb to do》 / 伝言を頼む《文》charge sb with a message / 医者を頼む call in a doctor / 家庭教師を頼む engage [get] a tutor (for one's child) / 自らを頼む rely on oneself ; be self-reliant / 数を頼む rely on [put one's trust in] numbers / 頼むに足りる reliable ; to be relied on ; trustworthy / 頼む所〈手段〉《文》one's resort [recourse] ;〈希望〉

---

wheat.

たねん この著作は氏の多年にわたる研究の成果である。This work of his is the fruit of many years' study.

-だの 世間では私の事をなんだのかんだのという。People are always saying this or that about me.|People say all sorts of things about me.

たのしい 釣りは実に楽しいものだ。Angling is great fun. / 実に楽しかった。I had a very good time. | We really enjoyed ourselves. / これを見ると楽しい昔を思い出す。This reminds me of the good old days. / 結婚生活は楽しいことばかりではない。Married life isn't all beer and skittles [isn't roses all the way].

たのしませる 快い音楽が彼らの耳を楽しませてくれた。Delightful music regaled their ears.

たのしみ 読書の他に彼はあまり楽しみはなかった。Besides reading, there were very few things in which he took pleasure. | He had few diversions apart from reading. / 人の楽しみのじゃまをするな。Don't stand in the way of my pleasures. / あとのお楽しみ。Wait and see. /〈テレビ番組などで〉あとはこの次のお楽しみ。Don't miss our next installment./あの人はいったい何が楽しみで生きているんだろう。What does he live for, I wonder? / その子は彼の両親の唯一の末の楽しみでした。The boy was his parents' only hope. / この子は将来が実に楽しみだ。The boy has a great future [shows great promise for the future].

たのしむ 楽しめる時に楽しめ。Take your fun where you can find it. |〈若いうちに〉Gather ye rosebuds while you may. 《諺》| Make hay while the sun shines. 《諺》

たのみ 君に一つ頼みがあるんだが。I have a favor to ask (of) you.| Will you do me a favor? / 頼みとあれば行かないものでもない。I may as well go if you want me to. / もう彼を頼みに思えない。I don't feel that I can rely on him any more. / いよいよという時になると頼みになる友人は少ないものだ。Real friends in need are scarce indeed. / 頼みの綱が切れた。I've lost my last prop. | My last hope is gone. / 彼女は頼み少ない身の上です。She has very

たのもしい

one's hope; 〈支え〉one's prop [support, mainstay, strength] / …に頼んで through (the courtesy of) sb / …を頼んで on the strength of (sb's promise); relying on… / 人に頼まれて at sb's request / 頼まれもしないのに 《文》 gratuitously; without being asked; unasked. 文例⇩

たのもしい 頼もしい 〈頼むになる〉reliable; trustworthy; 〈望みある〉hopeful; promising ¶頼もしからぬ unreliable; untrustworthy; not to be depended upon / 末頼もしい人 a promising person; a person of promise; a person with a rosy [bright] future (ahead of him) / …を大いに頼もしく思う expect [hope for] a great deal 《from》; put 《《文》place》great trust [confidence] 《in sb》.

たば 束 a bundle 《of straw》; a bunch; 〈稲や書類などの〉a sheaf (pl. sheaves); a fag(g)ot ¶束にする bundle; tie up in [make up] a bundle; sheave (穀物などを) / 束にして[なって] in a bundle [bunch] / 束になってかかる attack sb all at a time [all at once].

だは 打破 ¶打破する break down; overthrow; abolish / 因習を打破する do away with conventionalities.

だば 駄馬 〈荷馬〉a packhorse; a draft [cart] horse; a workhorse; 〈やくざ馬〉a horse of an inferior breed.

タバコ 煙草 [<《ポルトガル語》tabaco] a cigarette; 〈原料〉tobacco; 〈植〉a tobacco plant ¶タバコ1箱 a pack 《英》packet] of cigarettes / 火の消えたタバコ a dead cigarette / タバコの煙 tobacco [cigarette] smoke; the smoke from one's cigarette / タバコの煙を輪に吹く make [puff (out)] smoke rings [a smoke ring] / タバコの灰 cigarette ash; the ash on a cigarette (タバコの先についている) / タバコの火を貸す give sb a light / タバコの火を消す put one's cigarette out / タバコの火をもみ消す crush [stub] one's cigarette out / タバコを吸う[のむ] smoke (a cigarette [pipe]) / タバコを一服吸う have a smoke / タバコをすぱすぱ吸う puff away (at) one's pipe [cigar, cigarette] / タバコを深く吸い込む draw deeply on [pull deeply at] one's cigarette / 隠れてタバコを吸い始める start smoking on the sly [sneaking smokes] / タバコをやめる give up [stop, 《米》quit] smoking / タバコを吸わない do not smoke; be a nonsmoker / タバコに火をつける light a cigarette / タバコでやに色になった歯 tobacco-stained teeth.

¶噛みタバコ chewing tobacco; a plug (1本) / 紙巻きタバコ a cigarette / パイプタバコ pipe [smoking] tobacco / 葉タバコ leaf tobacco / 長巻きのタバコ a king-size(d) cigarette / タバコ好き a heavy smoker / タバコ銭 cigarette money / タバコ畑 a tobacco plantation / タバコ屋〈店〉《米》a cigar store; 《英》a tobacconist's (shop); 〈人〉a tobacconist. 文例⇩
[用法] 英語国でタバコを買うとき、国によって頼み方が違う。「…を1つ[2つ]下さい」はアメリカ・カナダなどでは (Give me) a pack [two packs] of (Chesterfields), please. にるよる。イギリスでは10本入りの箱もあるので、(Can I have) ten [twenty] 《Embassy》 please. という。

たはた 田畑 fields of rice and other crops; farms.

たはつ 多発 ¶多発する 〈事故などが〉happen [《文》occur] often [frequently]; 《文》be of frequent occurrence; 〈病気が〉occur in many places [localities]; 〈症状が〉occur [be met with] in many cases.

たばねる 束ねる ⇒たば (束にする) ¶髪を束ねる do (up) one's hair in a bun [knot].

たび¹ 足袋 (a pair of) tabi ¶足袋はだしになっている be [go about] in tabi / 足袋屋〈店〉a tabi store [shop]; 〈人〉a tabi maker.

たび² 度 ¶幾たびも any number of times; many times; often ⇒いくど / …するたびごとに whenever [every time]… / たび重なる repeated 《failures》. 文例⇩

たび³ 旅 traveling; travel(s); a journey; a tour (漫遊); a trip (短期の) ¶3日の旅 a trip of three days; a three-day tour / 汽車の旅 a railroad journey; rail travel / 船旅 a voyage; a journey by sea; sea travel / 空の旅 a flight; a trip by air / 人生の旅《文》life's journey / 旅の道連れ a traveling companion; a fellow

few people to turn to. / 神こそはわが頼み。God is my strength [castle].

たのむ 君にちょっと頼みたいことがある。I have a favor to ask (of) you. / 頼むから放っといてくれ。Do me a favor, will you, and let [leave] me alone. / 万事よろしく頼む。I leave everything to you [in your hands]. / 彼に頼んでやってもらう。Get him to [Have him] do it for you. / 万事手落ちのないように頼む。Make sure [See to it] that nothing is amiss. / 大工に頼んで修繕させなければいけない。We must have a carpenter repair it. | We must get a carpenter to repair it. / We must get it fixed by a carpenter. / 君をおいて他に頼む人がいないのだ。I have no one but you to look [turn] to for assistance.

タバコ タバコを吸いますか。Do you smoke? / タバコを一服吸おうと思ってホールを出た。I went out of the hall for a smoke. / 部屋の中にはタバコの煙がもうもうとこもっていた。The air in the room was gray [blue] with cigarette smoke. / タバコに火をつけて、ゆっくりと鼻から煙を出した。He lit a cigarette, and blew the smoke out [expelled the smoke] slowly through his nostrils. / タバコを1本振り出して、それをひょいと口にくわえた。He shook a cigarette out of the pack and stuck [popped] it between his lips [in the corner of his mouth]. / 彼は吸いさしで新しいタバコに火をつけた。He lit a fresh cigarette from the butt of the one he was smoking. / あの男は口からタバコを離すことがない。He is a chain smoker. / タバコを吸ったらよろしいでしょうか。Do you mind if I smoke? / タバコはご遠慮ください。[揭示] Kindly refrain from smoking. / 紙巻きタバコは身体の害になります。Cigarette smoking is hazardous [injurious] to your health.

たび² 彼らは顔を合わせるたびにけんかをする。They never meet without quarreling. | They quarrel every time they meet.

たび³ このような所が東京からわずか数時間の旅で行けるところに今なお存在しているということは信じ難いことである。It is almost

traveler / 旅をする travel; go on a journey [trip]; make a journey [trip] / 旅に出る, 旅立ちする start [set out] on a journey / 旅に出ている be away (from home) on a journey.
¶旅商人() a peddler; a traveling merchant / 旅がらす a wanderer; 《文》a bird of passage / 旅先〔行き先〕 a destination; 〈滞在地〉the place where one is staying while on a journey / 旅先で while traveling; on one's journey / 旅支度をする get ready [prepare, make preparations] for a journey; fit oneself out for a journey / 旅慣れた人 a seasoned traveler; a much-traveled person / 旅日記 a travel diary / 旅人 《文》a wayfarer / (劇団などが)旅回りをしている be on the road; be on tour / 旅回りの一座 a touring [traveling, strolling] company / 旅役者 a strolling [《文》an itinerant] player. 文例⇩

だび 荼毘 ¶だびに付する cremate ((the body remains)).

たびたび 度々 often; lots of [many] times; frequently; repeatedly; again [time] and again ¶たびたびの frequent; repeated. 文例⇩

ダビット 〖海〗a davit.

たびょう 多病 ¶多病な weak; infirm; sickly; ⎱of delicate health.
タフ 多病な tough.

タブー (a) taboo ¶タブーになっている be taboo; be under (a) taboo.

だぶだぶ ¶だぶだぶする 〈衣類などが〉be baggy; be loose; 〈水などが〉slosh [slop] about; tumble (in a vessel) / だぶだぷの[した] loose(-fitting) (clothes); baggy (trousers). 文例⇩

だぶつく 〈大きすぎる〉be too large (for); 〈あり余る〉there is a glut ((of government bonds)) (on the market); 《文》be overabundant. 文例⇩

だふや だふ屋 《米》a (ticket) scalper; 《英》a ticket tout. 文例⇩

たぶらかす 〈ばかす〉bewitch; enchant; 〈だます〉cheat; deceive; take in.

ダブリン Dublin ¶ダブリン市民 a Dubliner.

ダブる 〈重なり合う〉overlap; 〈二重になる〉be doubled.

ダブル double ¶ダブルの上着 a double-breasted coat / ダブルスチール 〖野球〗a double steal / ダブル幅の double-width ((cloth)).

ダブルス 〖球技〗(play) doubles; a doubles match ¶混合ダブルス mixed doubles.

ダブルプレー 〖野球〗a double play ¶ダブルプレーを食わす make a double play; get two runners out at once / ゴロを打ってダブルプレーを喫する ground into a double play.

ダブルヘッダー 〖野球〗a double-header ¶ダブルヘッダーで星を分ける split a double-header ((with)) / ダブルヘッダーをストレートで勝つ take [sweep] both ends of a double-header ((from the opposing team)).

タブロイド ¶タブロイド判の新聞 a tabloid (newspaper) / タブロイド判の週刊誌 a weekly in tabloid form.

たぶん¹ 多分 ¶多分の 《文》much; a lot of; a great deal of / 多分に (very) much; greatly; highly; 《文》exceedingly; to a great extent; 《文》in great [large] measure. 文例⇩

たぶん² 多分 〈たいてい〉probably; perhaps; maybe; (very) likely; in all likelihood [probability]. 文例⇩

だぶん 駄文 poor writing. 文例⇩

たべあきる 食べ飽きる be tired of eating; have enough (of). 文例⇩

たべあわせ 食べ合わせ ⇒ くいあわせ.

たべかけ 食べ掛け ⇒ たべのこし ¶食べかけのみかん a half-eaten orange.

たべかた 食べ方 how to eat; 〈作法〉table manners; 〈調理法〉how to cook.

たべごろ 食べ頃 ¶食べ頃である be ready [ripe enough] to eat; be in season.

たべざかり 食べ盛り

たべずぎらい 食べず嫌い ¶食べず嫌いである dislike (cheese) without having tried (it). 文例⇩
⎱eat.
たべすぎる 食べ過ぎる eat too much; over-

たべのこし 食べ残し leftovers; leavings (at the table) ¶食べ残しの leftover; half-eaten.

たべのこす 食べ残す leave ((an apple)) half [partially] eaten; leave ((a dish)) unfinished.

たべほうだい 食べ放題 ¶食べ放題の eating as much as one likes / 食べ放題の食堂 a res-

---

unbelievable that such a place still exists only a few hours' journey from Tokyo. 旅は道連れ世は情け. In traveling, companionship, in life, kindness. / 旅の恥はかき捨て. One tosses all one's inhibitions [all sense of shame] (when one is) away from home.
たびたび 今年はたびたび地震があった. Earthquakes have been very frequent this year. / たびたびお手を掛けて済みません. I am sorry to trouble you so often.
タブー その部族では狩猟中に物を言うことはタブーになっている. Among those tribesmen speech is taboo while hunting.
だぶだぶ 彼の洋服は借り着みたいにだぶだぶだった. His suit hung loosely about [sat loosely on] him as if it had been meant for someone else.
だぶつく 市場には養殖真珠がだぶついている. The market is glutted with cultured pearls.
だふや 彼女の演奏会の切符は何倍もの値段でだふ屋が売っていた. The tickets to her concert were being scalped [sold on the black market] for many times their face value.
たぶん¹ その懸念が多分にある. That is very much to be feared. / 彼には多分に詩人肌な所がある. He has a good deal of the poet in him.
たぶん² 多分来られないでしょう. He probably won't be able to come. / 多分彼は失敗するでしょ
う. The chances [odds] are that he will fail. / 多分彼は 22 歳ぐらい. My guess is (that) he's about twenty-two. / 多分そうでしょう. Maybe so. | I suppose so.
だぶん 文章とは全く素人の私だが, 編集長の要請で, あえて駄文をろうすることにした. Though I am far from being a professional at writing [a professional writer], I have decided to do this article at the request of the editor.
たべあきる これはもう食べ飽きた. I have had enough of this.
たべざかり あの年頃の子供は食べ盛りである. Boys of his age have such good appetites.
たべずぎらい 食べず嫌いだが, これだけはどうも. I've never tried it, but I don't think it will suit me.

たべもの 食べ物 food;〈食事〉(a) diet;〈糧食〉provisions ¶何か温かい[冷たい]食べ物 something hot [cold] to eat / 食べ物がいい[悪い]〈栄養が〉be well-[badly-, poorly-,〈文〉ill-]fed;〈ホテルなどが〉the food is good [poor] [at];serve good [poor] food / 食べ物をやる feed / 食べ物屋 a restaurant; an eating house. 文例⇩

たべる 食べる eat; have; take;〈生活する〉live (on);《文》subsist (on) ⇒くう² ¶食べてみる try《the dish》; taste; sample / …を食べている〈常食とする〉live [subsist] on《rice》;〈動物が〉feed on《grass》/ 食べさせる〈食物を〉feed《a child》;〈手伝って〉help《a little boy》to eat;〈養う〉support; keep; provide for《one's family》/ 食べつける, 食べ慣れた be used [《文》accustomed] to《eating》/ 食べられる〈有毒でない〉edible; fit to eat;〈そうまずくない〉eatable /〈うまい〉good to eat / 食べられない〈本質的に食用にならない〉unfit [not fit] to eat;〈有害で, 又はかめないほど固くて〉inedible;〈まずくて〉uneatable. 文例⇩

だべる 駄弁る chatter; chat《with》; talk idly《with》;《俗》chew the fat《with》.

たべん 多弁 talkative;《文》loquacious; garrulous.

だべん 駄弁 empty [idle] talk; nonsense ¶駄弁をろうする talk rubbish; indulge in idle talk. 文例⇩

たへんけい 多辺形 a polygon.

だほ 拿捕 ¶拿捕する capture; seize.

たほう 他方 the other side [party] ¶他方においては on the other hand [side]; while.

たぼう 多忙 ¶多忙な busy / 多忙である be busy; have a lot [a great deal] of work; have very many things to do / 多忙をきわめる be very busy; be pressed by business [work] / 多忙のため owing to pressure of business [work]. 文例⇩

だほう 打法〈野球〉a style [way] of batting ¶一本足打法 flamingo-style batting.

だぼう 打棒 ¶打棒を封じる〈野球〉throttle the bats《of the opposing team》. 文例⇩

たほうめん 多方面 ¶多方面の various; varied;《文》multifarious《activities》;〈趣味の〉many-sided; versatile / 多方面に in many directions [fields] / 多方面に交友がある have a wide [varied] circle of acquaintances.

だぼくしょう 打撲傷 ¶打撲傷を受ける get a bruise《on the arm》; be bruised《all over》.

だぼはぜ だぼ鯊 a small goby (regarded as worthless, being unfit to eat).

だぼら 駄法螺 big talk; a tall story ⇒ほら¹.

たま¹ 玉, 球, 弾〈球〉a ball;〈球形(球形をしたもの)〉a globe;〈電球・寒暖計などの〉a bulb;〈数珠・そろばんの〉a bead;〈露などの〉a drop;〈宝石〉a gem;〈a jewel〉;〈弾丸〉a ball;〈銃弾〉a bullet;〈散弾〉shot;〈砲弾〉a shell ¶電気の球 an electric bulb [globe (大形の)] / 眼鏡の玉 a lens; a glass /〈野球などで〉いい球 a good throw / 弾の来る所にいる be in the《enemy's》line of fire / 弾の届く〈かぬ〉所に within [out of] gunshot [range]《of》/ 玉を投げる〈受ける, ころがる, 打つ〉throw [catch, roll, hit] a ball / 弾を込める load《a gun》/ 弾を抜く unload《a gun》/ 玉をころがすような声で《sing》in a silvery voice / 玉にきず a fly in the ointment / 弾で打ち抜く send [fire] a bullet through《a wall》/ 弾傷 a bullet [gunshot] wound /〈曲芸の〉玉乗り balancing on a rolling ball / 球拾いをする collect balls (for the [other] players); act as ball boy / 弾よけの bulletproof.

たま² 偶 ¶たまの occasional; rare;(be) few and far between / たまに occasionally; at times; now and then; once in a while / ごくたまに on rare occasions; at rare intervals; once in a long [great] while. 文例⇩

だま a [an unmixed-in] lump of flour ¶だまの多い lumpy《batter》.

たまいし 玉石 a boulder.

たまう 賜う grant; give;《文》bestow; award; honor《sb with a visit》;《文》confer《a title

---

たべほうだい 食べ放題だ. You may eat as much as you like. / 千円, 食べ放題〈掲示〉All you can eat for ¥1,000.

たべもの 私は食べ物はなにも欲しくない. I don't want anything to eat. / 彼は食べ物が難しい. He is very particular about his food. | He is a fussy eater. / この土地では食べ物に困ることはない. People living here always have a sufficient supply of food [have no food problems]. / いなごはいい食べ物になる. Locust makes good eating.

たべる ほかに何も食べる物がない. We have nothing else to eat. / 私は一日中なにも食べなかった. I didn't touch food [have a bite to eat] all day. | I had nothing to eat all day. / 何でも勝手に取って食べて下さい. Help yourself to anything on the table. / この子は何てかわいいんでしょう. 食べてしまいたい程だわ. What a cute child! He looks good enough to eat.

だべん このことにつきましては, 皆様すでによくご存じでございますので, これ以上私が駄弁をろうすることはないと存じます. Since you already know all [a great deal] about this, I think it will be a waste of time if I attempt to say anything more about it.

たぼう ご多忙のところおじゃましてすみません. I am sorry to trespass [intrude] on your precious time. |〈別れ際に〉I am sorry to have taken so much of your valuable time. / 今日は一日中多忙だった. I've been [kept] busy all day.

だぼう W大学チームは打棒大いに振った[はなはだ振わなかった]. W University team batted very well [badly].

たま¹ 彼は額に玉の汗を浮かべていた. Beads of sweat [perspiration] stood (out) on his forehead. | The sweat beaded [stood in beads] on his forehead. / 弾がビュンと音を立ててかすめた. Bullets sang past us. / 彼は手首に弾を受けた. He got [received] a bullet in the wrist. / 弾が彼の腕にあたって止まっている. A bullet has lodged in his arm. / 彼は優柔不断なのが玉にきずだ. Irresolution is a defect in his otherwise perfect character. | Indecisiveness is his only fault. / すばらしい本だが, 誤植がやや多いことだけが玉にきずだ. This is an excellent book; the only fly in the ointment is that there are

たまぐし 玉串 《offer》a sprig of the sacred tree (to).
たまげる 魂消る ⇒びっくり.
たまご 卵 〈鶏などの〉an egg ; 〈魚や蛙が生んだ〉spawn ; 〈魚の体内の〉roe ¶生みたての卵 a new-laid egg / 〈店頭の表示〉fresh eggs / 生卵 (a) raw egg / ゆで卵 a boiled egg ; 〈堅ゆでの〉a hard-boiled egg ; 〈半熟の〉a soft-boiled [half-boiled] egg / かき[落とし]卵 scrambled [poached] eggs / 腐った卵 a bad [a rotten, an addled] egg / 医者の卵 a doctor in the making / 卵の殻 an eggshell / 腐った卵のようなにおい a smell like rotten eggs ; a rotten-egg smell / 卵を生む lay an egg ; 〈魚が〉spawn ; discharge *its* spawn / 卵を抱く sit on eggs ; brood / 卵を抱かせる set 《a hen》《on eggs》/ 卵からかえす hatch an egg / 卵を割る break an egg 《into a bowl》/ 卵形の egg-shaped ; oval ; ovoid / 卵酒 eggnog / 卵立て an eggcup / 卵とじ egg soup / 卵焼き an omelet. 文例⇩

たましい 魂 a soul ; a spirit ; a ghost ¶魂のない soulless ; 〈生気のない〉lifeless / 魂を吹き込む[入れる] breathe life 《into》; 《文》inspire a soul 《into》/ 魂を入れ替える reform 《oneself》; turn over a new leaf / 魂を打ち込む put [throw] *one's* whole soul 《into》/ 魂を打ち込んで with all *one's* heart ; 《go》heart and soul 《into one's work》/ 魂を奪う bewitch ; fascinate ; charm ; captivate / 魂を揺すぶるような音楽 soul-stirring music. 文例⇩

だましうち 騙討ち a surprise [《文》perfidious] attack ; foul play ¶だまし討ちにする play *sb* foul ; make a surprise attack 《on, against》; defeat *sb* by underhand means [《文》an unfair stratagem].

だます 騙す 〈あざむく〉deceive ; cheat ; impose on *sb* ; take *sb* in ; 〈裏切る〉play *sb* false ; betray ¶だまして…させる trick [cheat] *sb* into *doing* / だまされやすい gullible ; credulous. 文例⇩

ダマスカス Damascus.

たまたま 偶々〈偶然〉by chance ; by accident ; accidentally ; 〈まれに〉⇒たま² (たまに) ¶たまたま…する happen [chance] to *do*. 文例⇩

たまつき 玉突き 《play》billiards ¶玉突きのゲーム取り a billiard marker / 玉突き台 a billiard table / 玉突き場 a billiard room [saloon, hall]. 文例⇩

たまてばこ 玉手箱 Urashima's casket ; Pandora's box.

たまねぎ 玉葱 an onion ¶玉ねぎの皮 the skin of an onion.

たまのこし 玉の輿 ¶玉の輿に乗る marry into a wealthy family ; 《文》marry a man of wealth [high birth] ; 《口語》marry into money.

たまむしいろ 玉虫色 ¶玉虫色の iridescent ; 〈あいまいな〉deliberately ambiguous 《statements》.

たまもの 賜物 a present ; a gift ; 《文》a boon ; 〈天の〉a blessing ¶努力の賜物 the result [《文》fruit(s)] of *one's* efforts. 文例⇩

だまらせる 黙らせる silence ; make *sb* hold *his* tongue ; hush *sb* (up).

たまらない 堪らない〈耐えられない〉cannot stand 《it》; be unable to bear [put up with] ; be unbearable ; be unendurable ; 〈押え切れない〉cannot help *doing* ; cannot (help) but *do* ; 《文》cannot [can hardly] refrain from *doing* ; 〈余りである〉be too much for *one* ¶暑くてたまらない be unbearably hot ; cannot stand the heat 《of》/ 心配でたまらない be racked with anxiety ; be worried to death / 悲しくてたまらない be overwhelmed with grief / うれしくてたまらない cannot contain *oneself* for joy / …したくてたまらない cannot wait to *do* ; be anxious [eager, impatient] to *do* ; have a great mind to *do* / 行きたくてたまらない be anxious [dying] to go ; be impatient [all eagerness] to go / 会いたくてたまらない be dying to see *sb* ; miss *sb* a great deal / たまらなく unbearably ; unendurably ; 《文》beyond endurance ; irresistibly. 文例⇩

たまりかねる 堪り兼ねる ⇒たまらない.

だまりこくる 黙りこくる keep [《文》remain]

---

rather too many misprints. / 玉磨かざれば光なし. An uncut gem does not sparkle. / 玉を抱いて罪あり. Opportunity makes the thief. 《諺》

たま² 客はたまにしかない. We rarely have visitors. / たまには訪ねて来てくれてもいいだろう. You might come and see us once in a while. / たまにしか来ないのだから、今回は少しゆっくりして行きたまえ. Stay a little longer this time, since you don't come often. / たまの休日ぐらいはゆっくり家で休ませてくれ. I only get a holiday once in a while [I don't get many holidays], so you might at least let me take it easy [have a good rest] at home when I do have one.

たまご 卵がかえった. The eggs have hatched. / この鶏はよく卵を生む. This hen is a good layer. / 卵の生み具合はどうかね. How are the chickens laying?

たましい 魂のない肖像だ. This portrait lacks life [soul].

だます まんまとだまされた. I was completely [fairly] taken in. / おとなしそうな様子にだまされた. His quiet manner deceived [fooled] me. / あなたはあの男にだまされているのよ. You're deceived by him. / 人にだまされるような男ではない. He's nobody's fool. / そんな甘い言葉にはだまされない. I won't fall for such honeyed words. / その男は僕の金を半分だまし取った. The man cheated me out of half my money. / だまされると思ってこの薬を一度のんで見たまえ. Just trust me [Take me at my word for] this once and try this medicine. / 彼は損傷を受けた彼の飛行機をだましだまし操縦して、ついに着陸に成功した. He nursed his damaged plane to a successful landing.

たまたま たまたま彼がその場に居合わした. He happened [chanced] to be there [to be by].

たまつき 東名高速道路で事故があり、5台の車が次々に玉突き衝突をした. There was a multiple pileup on the Tomei Expressway, involving five cars one after the other.

たまもの わが社の今日の繁栄は前社長A氏の努力の賜物であります. This concern owes its present prosperity to the efforts of Mr. A, the former president.

たまらない そんなことが本当にあってたまるものか. I'll be

だまりこむ 黙り込む fall silent ; lapse [retreat] into silence ; say nothing more ¶再び黙り込んでしまう relapse into silence.
たまり(ば) 溜り(場) 〈待合室〉a waiting room ; 〈よく集まる所〉a haunt 〈of taxi drivers〉.
たまりみず 溜り水 stagnant [standing] water.
たまる 溜まる 〈集まる〉collect ; gather ; 〈積もる〉accumulate ; be accumulated ; build up ; heap ; 〈金が〉be saved ; 〈支払いが〉be in arrears ; be overdue. 文例❶
だまる 黙る fall [become] silent ; 《口語》shut up ; hold *one*'s tongue ; stop talking ¶黙って 〈無言で〉 in silence ; silently ; without a word ; 〈文句を言わずに〉without protest ; 〈無断で〉without leave [permission] / 黙っている 《文》remain silent ; keep silence ; 《口語》keep *one*'s mouth shut / 黙って言い付けを聞く obey *sb* without asking questions 〈無用の question〉/ 黙ってさせておく allow [leave] *sb to do*; leave *sb* to *himself* ; let *sb* alone [be]. 文例❸
たまわる 賜わる be given ; be granted ; be awarded ; be honored with 《an imperial message》.
たみ 民 〈人民〉the people ; 〈臣民〉subjects ; 〈国民〉a nation ; a people ¶自由の民 children [sons] of liberty / 遊牧の民 a nomadic race.
だみごえ 濁声 〈in〉a thick voice.
だみん 惰眠 ¶惰眠をむさぼる live in idleness ; idle *one*'s time away.
たみんぞくこっか 多民族国家 a multiracial nation [country].
ダム a dam 《on the Tenryu River》 ¶ダムを造る build a dam 《across a river》; dam 《a river》/ 発電用ダム a hydroelectric [power] dam / ダムサイト a site for a dam ; a damsite.
たむけ 手向け an offering ; a tribute.
たむける 手向ける offer ; lay 《flowers》.
たむし 〈医〉ringworm.

たむろ 屯 ¶たむろする be stationed ; be quartered ; encamp ; 〈集まる〉gather ; assemble.
ため 為 〈利益〉good ; advantage ; benefit ; profit ; interest(s) ; welfare ¶芸術のための芸術 art for art's sake / 議論のための議論をする argue for argument's sake / 自分のためを図る work [look out] for *one*'s own interests / …のために 〈文〉for ; for the sake [benefit, good] of ; in [on] *sb*'s behalf ; in [on] behalf of ; in the interest(s) of ; in favor of ; 〈目的〉to *do* ; in order to [that…may] *do* ; so as to *do* ; for ; for the purpose of ; 《文》to the end that… ; with a view *to doing* ; with the object of ; 〈so that… may *do*〉; 〈原因, 理由〉because of ; on account of ; owing [due] to ; for ; from ; through ; by ; 〈結果〉as a result of ; in consequence of / ためになる benefit ; be to *one*'s advantage ; be profitable [《文》beneficial, 《文》advantageous] 〈to〉; do *sb* good ; be good 〈for〉/ 〈教訓になる〉《文》be instructive 〈to〉/ ためにならぬ 《文》do *sb* no good ; 〈損である〉be against *sb*'s interests ; 〈害になる〉do *sb* harm ; 《文》be harmful [injurious] 〈to〉; be bad 〈for〉/ 正義のために 〈fight〉in the cause of justice / 戒めのために by way of warning / 病気のために because of illness / 飢えのために死ぬ die of [from] hunger / ためにする所がある have an ulterior motive [purpose] ; have an axe to grind.
だめ 駄目 ¶だめな 〈be〉no good ; 〈役に立たない〉useless ; 〈of〉no use ; 〈無駄な〉futile ; 《文》to no purpose ; 〈望みのない〉hopeless ; 〈不可能な〉impossible / だめにする spoil ; ruin ; waste / だめになる be spoilt ; be ruined ; fail ; end in failure ; go wrong / だめとあきらめる give up *sth* as hopeless [in despair] / だめを押す make sure ; make *sth* doubly sure ; 《文》make assurance double sure ; tell *sb* twice / だめ押しの1点 〈野球〉〈score〉an insurance run / だめ親父 a failure as a father ; a failed father. 文例❸
ためいき 溜め息 a sigh ¶ため息をつく sigh

damned [hanged] if it's true. / これではとてもたまらない。This is more than I can bear. / こう寒くてはとてもたまらない。I cannot stand this cold. | It is too cold for me. / 東京へ行きたくてたまらなかった。I felt an irresistible yearning for Tokyo.
たまる 部屋のすみにほこりがたまっていた。Dust has collected in the corner of the room. / 机にほこりがいっぱいたまっていた。Dust lay [was] thick on the desk. / ここは雨上がりになると水がたまる。Puddles form here after rain. / 道路にところどころ水がたまっている。There are puddles on the road. / 大分金がたまったろう。You have saved a good deal, I suppose. / 家賃の支払いが半年分たまっている。I'm six months behindhand [in arrears] with my rent. / (月賦で)

ピアノの払いが3回分たまっている。I'm three payments behind on my piano. / 彼は借金が100万円もたまっている。He is in debt to the extent of one million yen. / 本屋の払いが大分たまった。I have run up a big [long] bill at the bookstore. / うんと仕事がたまっている。I have a lot of work on my hands.
だまる 黙れ!Shut up !|Hold your tongue! | Silence ! / そのことについては黙っているほうがいい。You had better keep quiet about it. / なぜ今まで私に黙っていたのだ。Why haven't you told me before (now)? | Why have you kept it from me? / 彼はそれっきり黙ってしまった。He said nothing more. / 黙って外出してはいけない。You must not go out without telling me. / 侮辱されて黙ってはいないぞ。I'm not going

to [You needn't think I will] take insults lying down.
ため 君のためを思えばこそ言うのだ。I say this only because I have your best interests at heart. / このことは覚えておいたらためになるぞ。What I say will prove useful if you keep it in mind. / そんな事をしてはためにならないよ。You are acting against your own interests. / 彼のために送別会を開いた。We gave a farewell dinner in his honor. | We gave him a farewell dinner. / 君はなんのためにここへ来たのだ。What have you come here for? | What has brought you here? / 彼は英文学研究のために英国へ渡った。He went to England for the purpose of [with a view to] studying English literature. / 人は食うために生きるのではなく, 生きるために食うのだ。Man does not live

ためいけ 溜め池 a (holding) reservoir; an irrigation pond; a farm pond.

ためこむ 貯め込む hoard; amass; save up (金を); store up (物を). 例文⇩

ためし¹ 例し an instance; an example; 〈場合〉a case; 〈先例〉a precedent ¶ためしのない unprecedented; unheard-of. 例文⇩

ためし² 試し a trial; a try; an attempt; an experiment; a test ¶試しに by way of experiment [trial]; as a test [an experiment]; as a trial; on trial; tentatively / 試しにやってみる try; have a try (at); give sth a trial [try] / 《文》engage sb on probation / 試しに雇う take sb on for a trial period / 試しに着て[かぶって]みる try (a dress, a hat) on / 試しに食べる[飲む] try; taste; sample. 例文⇩

ためす 試す have a try (at); make a trial (of); 〈試験する〉test; put sth to the test; 〈実験する〉experiment [make an experiment] 《on, with, in》; 〈試食[飲]する〉try; taste; sample ¶知識[能力]を試す test sb on his knowledge 《of》 [ability 《to do》]. 例文⇩

ためつすがめつ ¶ためつすがめつ見る 《文》scrutinize; take a good look 《at》; look closely 《at》.

ためらう hesitate 《over, about, to do》; waver 《between》; think twice 《about》; flinch [wince, shrink] 《from》 ¶ためらわずに without hesitation; unhesitatingly.

ためる¹ 溜[貯]める 〈蓄積する〉accumulate; heap [pile] up; amass; 〈集める〉collect; gather; 〈たくわえる〉save; lay [put, set] by [aside]; hoard; store ¶水をためる collect [store] water (in a reservoir) / 勘定をためる be behind in one's payments; run up a (big) bill / ためた金 one's savings. 例文⇩

ためる² 矯める 〈曲げる〉bend; 〈まっすぐにする〉straighten; make sth straight; 〈矯正する〉correct; reform; 《文》remedy; cure; put [set] to rights.

ためん¹ 他面 the other side; 〈一方〉on the other hand; while; whereas.

ためん² 多面 ¶多面的な many-sided; versatile; multilateral / 問題の多面的な研究 a many-faceted attack on the problem / 多面体 《数》a polyhedron (pl. -s, -dra).

たも 〈網〉a landing [scoop] net.

たもうさく 多毛作 multiple cropping.

たもくてき 多目的 ¶多目的ダム a multipurpose dam.

たもつ 保つ 〈保持する, 維持する〉keep (up); 《文》preserve; retain; maintain; 〈支える〉support ¶秩序を保つ maintain [keep, preserve] good order / 若さを保つ keep [《文》retain] one's youth; stay young.

たもと 袂 a sleeve ¶たもとに入れる put sth in one's pocket [kimono sleeve] / たもとをわかつ part from [with]; part company with; break with / たもとを連ねて 《resign》 in a body; all together; en masse / 橋のたもとで at the foot of a bridge; near the approach to a bridge.

たやす 絶やす 〈絶滅させる〉root [wipe] out; uproot; put an end to; exterminate; 《文》extirpate; eradicate; let 《the species》 die out; 〈切らす〉run [be] out of; exhaust ¶火を絶やす let the fire go out. 例文⇩

たやすい easy; simple ¶たやすく readily; easily; 《文》with ease; without difficulty [trouble] / たやすくする make sth easy; 《文》facilitate; 〈簡単にする〉simplify.

たゆむ 弛む ⇒うむ² (うまずたゆまず).

たよう¹ 多用 ⇒たぼう.

たよう² 多様 ¶多様な various; 《文》diverse; 《文》multifarious / 多様化する diversify / 多様性 diversity; variety.

たより¹ 便り 〈消息〉news; 《文》tidings; 〈情報〉information; 〈文通〉correspondence; 〈手

---

to eat, but eats to live. / 病気のために会に出られなかった。I could not attend the meeting as I was ill. | Illness kept me from attending the meeting. / それは気候のためだ。The climate accounts [is responsible] for it. / 彼が尽力してくれたために予期しない成功を納めた。Thanks to his efforts, we achieved greater success than we had expected.

だめ このナイフはだめだ。This knife won't do [is no good]. | 僕はもうだめだ[万事休した]。I am done for. | It's all up [over] with me. / あの男は教師としてはだめだ。As a teacher, he is a failure./ 試験はだめだとあきらめている。I've resigned myself to failure in the examination. | I've given up (all) hope of passing the examination. / この間の暴風で今年の米作はだめになった。The recent storm has spoilt this year's rice crop. / 今は教育がなくてはだめだ。Nowadays education is everything. / やってみたがだめだった。I tried, but in vain. / 彼は将来は社長に, それがだめでも, 少なくとも重役にはなるだろうと思われていた。He had been expected to become the president of the company in future or, failing that, at least to get a seat on the board of directors. / よく考えなくちゃだめだよ。You must think carefully.

ためこむ あの男はまず1千万円はため込んでいるだろう。I dare say he's salted away ten million yen.

ためし¹ 彼は他人を褒めた例しがない。He was never known to speak well of others. / いつ行っても家にいた例しがない。I've never yet found him at home when I called.

ためし² 物は試しだ。You'll never know unless you try. | Nothing venture, nothing win. 【諺】

ためす 彼はこの新薬を動物に試してみた。He conducted experiments with the new medicine on animals.

ためる ここへくずをためてはいけない。Don't pile up rubbish here. / わずかの給料の中から, 故郷の村へ帰る汽車賃をやっとためた。Out of his scanty wages he managed to save enough for the railroad fare to his home village./ だいぶ仕事をためてしまった。I've fallen [got] a long way behind in my work.

たやす 火を絶やさないように頼む。See that the fire is kept burning [alive].

たやすい 彼はたやすくは承知してくれまい。I'm afraid he won't consent readily.

たより

紙》a letter ¶便りがある hear [get a letter] from sb / …の便りを全く聞かないでいる hear nothing of sb; have no news of sb / 便りをする write (a letter)《to》; drop sb a line. 文例⇩

たより² 頼り《依頼》reliance; dependence;《信頼》trust; confidence ⇨たよる / 頼りにする人《文》one's prop (and stay) / 誰も頼りにする人がない have no one to depend on; have no one to turn [look] to (for help) / 頼りになる reliable; trustworthy;《a person》to be relied [depended] on / つえを頼りに歩く walk leaning on one's stick / 頼りない unreliable; untrustworthy / 頼りない返事 a vague [an unsatisfactory] answer.

たよる 頼る rely [depend, reckon, count] on; trust to; look [turn] to sb (for help) /《訴える》《文》resort [have recourse] to / 息子に頼る depend on one's son for support; lean on one's son / 過去の経験に頼る draw on one's past experience.

たら 鱈《魚》a cod《単複同形》; a codfish《単複同形》¶たら子 cod roe.

-たら 《もし…したら》if;《…したら》and (then); 《…の時は》when ⇨ もし ¶雨が降ったら if it rains; in case of rain. 文例⇩

たらい 盥 a washtub; a tub.

たらいまわし 盥回し《政権などの》rotation (of office) ¶たらい回しで《hold office》in [by] rotation / 政権をたらい回しする hand over the reins of government by prearrangement to a colleague in one's own party / 役所の窓口をたらい回しにされる be sent around from one window [office] to another. 文例⇩

ダライラマ 《ラマ教主》the Dalai Lama.

だらかん だら幹 a corrupt (labor) leader.

だらく 堕落《文》depravity; corruption ¶堕落する go to the bad; be corrupted;《文》become depraved / 堕落する学生 a degenerate student; a student who has gone to the bad / 堕落した役人 a corrupt official / 堕落させる lead sb astray.

-だらけ full of《misprints》; covered with《dust》¶岩だらけの谷 a rock-strewn valley / 借金だらけである have a lot of debts;《口語》be up to one's ears [neck] in debt. 文例⇩

だらけ be lazy; be slack;《体が》feel dull [《文》languid, listless] ¶だらけた生活 a lazy [an idle] life. 文例⇩

だらしな(が)ない slovenly; loose; lax; slack;《不身持な》loose;《口語》easy;《服装など》untidy;《仕事など》careless; sloppy; slipshod ¶だらしない服装をする be untidily dressed / だらしなく slovenly; untidily; carelessly. 文例⇩

たらしこむ 誑し込む snare [inveigle]《sb into doing》; cajole《sb to do [into doing]》; coax《sb to do, money out of sb》.

たらす 垂らす《したたらす》drop; drip; let sth fall;《こぼす》spill《water》;《つるす》trail; hang (down);《文》suspend ¶髪を背に垂らしている have one's hair hanging down one's back.

-たらず …足らず《より少ない》(a little) less than; something under; (just) short [inside] of ¶1キロ足らず inside [a little short] of a kilometer; less than a kilometer. 文例⇩

たらたら in drops; dripping ¶たらたら垂れる drip [trickle]《from》/ 汗をたらたら流して《be》dripping with sweat; with streams of perspiration pouring《off one》/ 不平たらたらである complain [grumble] bitterly [incessantly]《of, about, at》/ お世辞たらたらである be full of empty [《文》honeyed] compliments; be lavish with [《文》profuse in] one's compliments.

だらだら《水滴などが》in drops; tricklingly; 《ぐずぐず》sluggishly; lazily; slowly; at a snail's pace ¶《血などが》だらだら出る ooze out / だらだら長引く drag on / だらだら坂 a gentle slope / 仕事をだらだらやっている be slow at [in] one's work; dawdle along with one's work.

タラップ [《オランダ語》trap] a movable flight of steps;《船の》a gangway; an accommodation ladder;《飛行機の》a ramp; landing steps ¶タラップを上がる [降りる] go [step] up [down] the ladder [ramp].

たらばがに《動》a king crab.

たより¹ たまにはお便りをください. Drop [Write] me a line once in a while. / その後まだ１回も便りがない. I have not heard from him [He has not been heard from] since. / 便りのないのは良い便り. No news is good news.

たより² 彼は年老いた母の唯一の頼りだった. He was the sole support of his aged mother. / 彼にはすっかり自分を頼りにしている老母があった. He had an aged mother who was entirely dependent on him. / あの男はいざというときには頼りになるよ. I'm afraid he will let you down [fail you] in your hour [time] of need. / 彼こそは頼りになる人だと思った. We found him a tower of strength. / 頼りになる証拠がほとんどない. There is little evidence to go on.

たよる 彼女は自分自身の力に頼らなければならなくなった. She was thrown back onto her own resources. | Now she had to fend for herself. / 日本では高校生になってもまだ母親に頼り切っている男の子が多い. Many Japanese high-school boys are still tied to their mothers' apron strings.

-たら 行けたらいいだろうなあ. I wish I could go. / 本があいたら返してくれ. Let me have the book back when you have done with it. / 問い合わせてみたら誤報だと分かった. Upon inquiry, the report proved false. / もうおよしったら. Have done with it, I tell you! / あの女のおしゃべりったらない. How she goes on [prattles]! / 役に立たないったらありゃしない. What a good-for-nothing!

たらいまわし その患者はどの病院でも受け入れてもらえず、たらい回しにされて救急車の中で死亡した. The patient was not accepted by any of the hospitals, and died in the ambulance while doing the rounds.

だらく 意志の弱い青年はいろいろの誘惑のために堕落する. Weak-minded youths go to the bad as a result of various temptations.

-だらけ 頭から足の先まで泥だらけになった. I was covered with mud from head to foot. / 仲間に取り残されて、私は怖いことだらけだった. When I was left be-

たらふく to *one's* heart's content ¶たらふく食う〈充分に〉have [eat] *one's* fill (of); take [make] a hearty meal;〈うんざりするほど〉be fed up 《with》; have more than enough (of);〈俗〉have a bellyful (of).

だらり(と)〈文〉languidly ¶だらりと下がる dangle; hang down limply /〈犬などが〉だらりと舌を出している loll out *its* tongue / だらりの帯 a dangling *obi*.

タランテラ〔舞曲・舞踏〕the tarantella.

‐たり…たり now…now [and then]…; what by [with]…what by [with]…; by turns; alternately; sometimes…sometimes… ¶降ったり止んだりする rain off and on / 行ったり来たりする come and go; travel to and fro; walk up and down (the room);〈文〉ply 《between》.

ダリア〔植〕a dahlia.

タリウム〔化〕thallium.

たりき 他力〈文〉help from without ¶他力本願〔宗教〕salvation [justification] by faith (alone);〈依頼心〉reliance upon others.

たりつ 他律 heteronomy ¶他律的行動 heteronomous behavior; behavior subject to external controls [not originating in *one's* own free will].

だりつ 打率《野球》*one's* batting average (略: bat. avg.).

たりゅう 他流 another [a different] school ¶他流試合をする try *one's* skill against a member of another school;〈比喩的に〉polish *one's* research by laying its results open for the criticism of rivals; have a game (of *go*) with a stranger.

たりょう 多量 ¶多量の a large quantity of; plenty of; much;〈文〉abundant; a great volume of; a great deal of ⇒たくさん 囲込 / 多量の出血 copious [profuse] bleeding; a serious loss of blood / 多量の睡眠薬を飲む take a large dose of a sleeping drug; take a large quantity of sleeping pills / 多量のぶどう糖を注射する give *sb* massive [generous] injections of dextrose / 多量に in large quantities; in plenty;〈文〉in abundance / ビタミンBを多量に含んでいる be rich [high] in vitamin B.

だりょく¹ 打力《野球》batting [hitting] power.

だりょく² 惰力 inertia; momentum; force of habit ¶惰力で走る run by inertia.

たりる 足りる〈充分である〉be enough;〈文〉be sufficient;〈文〉suffice;〈間に合う〉serve; answer; do;〈…に値する〉be worth;〈文〉be worthy of; deserve;〈満足する〉be content(ed)《with》¶…と言えば足りよう〈文〉Suffice it to say that… / 足りない〈不足である〉be not enough;〈文〉be insufficient;〈文〉lack; be lacking (in experience); be short (of);〈価値がない〉be not worth (it);〈文〉be unworthy of; be below (contempt); be beneath (notice);〈頭が〉be stupid; be dull;〈口語〉be soft [weak] in the head / 数学の力が足りないを見ると no good at bad, weak in, poor at] mathematics / 千円足りないな be 1,000 yen short / 食糧が足りなくなる run short of [go short on] provisions.

だりん 舵輪 a steering wheel ¶舵輪を握る take [be at] the wheel.

たる 樽 a barrel; a cask; a butt (大だる); a keg (小だる) ¶ビール2たる two casks [barrels] of beer / たるの口をあける broach [tap] a cask (of *ale*) / たるに入れる[詰める] put (*beer*) in a barrel; barrel / たるから酒を出す draw *sake* from a cask / たる詰めの barreled (*beer*).

だるい 怠い (feel) weary [〈文〉languid, listless];《he》(be) dull [heavy] ¶だるそうにしている〈文〉languidly.

たるき 垂木〔建〕a rafter.

タルク〔薬〕talc.

だるま〔達磨(ぼう)〕大師〕Bodhidharma;〔玩具〕a tumbler ¶だるまストーブ a potbellied stove.

たるみ 弛み〈ゆるみ〉slack; slackening; a sag;〈商況などの〉dullness; a slackening (in sales);〈目の下の皮膚の〉bags ¶(張った綱などに)たるみを出す slacken off (the stretched rope).

たるむ 弛む slacken; sag;〈心が〉slack (off) (in *one's* studies) ¶たるんだ slack; loose; sagging / たるんだ皮膚 flabby skin / ひざがた

---

hind by the members of our party, I had all sorts of fears.

だらけ 君は近県だらけているじゃないか。You are not working as hard as you ought to be these days, aren't you?

だらしが)ない 彼は何をやらしてもだらしがない。He does everything in a slovenly way [manner]. / ソファーの上でだらしなく眠りこけていた。He was sleeping untidily on the sofa. / だらしのない負け方をしたものだ。What a humiliating defeat !

‐たらず 寄付金は合計100万円足らずだった。The subscriptions came to a little less than a million yen.

‐たり…たり あの電灯は赤くなったり青くなったりする。Those lights become red and green by turns. / 釣りに出かけたり、ゴルフをしたりで、仕事の方は遅々としてはかどらなかった。What with [Between] fishing and golfing, the progress of my work was extremely slow.

たりき 彼はいつも他力本願だ。He relies upon others for everything. | He always turns to others for help.

だりつ 彼は打率3割2分だ。He has a batting average of .320. | He is now hitting .320. ★ .320 は three twenty と読む。.300 ならば three hundred と読む。

たりる 5千円ほどもあれば足ります。Five thousand yen or so will do [〈文〉suffice]. / このセットはまだ1冊足りない。One volume is still needed [required] to complete the set. / 規定の寸法に2センチ足りない。It is two centimeters short of the regulation length. / 1万円では旅費にも足りない。Ten thousand yen will not cover even the traveling expenses. / 一日の苦労は一日にて足れり。《聖書》Sufficient unto the day is the evil thereof. / あんなに勉強するのだから入試に合格しても怪しむに足りない。No wonder [Small wonder that] he passed the entrance examination; he works so hard. / あの男は少々足りない。He's a little weak in the head.

だるい 暑いので身体がだるい。The heat makes me feel listless. / 足がだるい。My legs feel heavy.

るんでいるズボン trousers that bag [are baggy] at the knees / たるませる loosen; slacken; slack off. 文例⇩

たれ 垂れ 〈かけ汁〉 sauce; gravy (肉汁); 〈ポケットの〉 a flap ¶垂れ汁〈肉の〉 dripping / 垂れ幕〈劇〉 a drop curtain / (犬などの)垂れ耳 a drooping ear; a lop-ear / 垂れ耳の lop-eared.

だれ 誰 ¶だれが who / だれの whose / だれを, だれに who; whom / だれか someone; somebody / だれでも, だれも 〈肯定〉 anyone; anybody; whoever; 〈否定〉 no one; nobody; none / だれでも皆 everybody; all; everybody / だれが見ても to any eye / 英語ではだれにも負けない be second to none in English / 友人のだれかれに相談する consult with various friends [this and that friend] (of mine) / だれかれの区別なく 《文》 irrespective of persons / だれそれさん Mr. [Mrs., Miss] So-and-so. 文例⇩

用法 日常会話では whom はほとんど使われなくなっていて, 文章でもごく改まったもの以外では who がだんだんと whom に取って代わりつつある. 会話では From whom did you get it? などは非常に不自然で, ほとんどの人は Who did you get it from? という.

たれこめる 垂れこめる 〈かすみなどが〉 hang [lie] (low) (over) ¶低く垂れこめた雲 low-hanging clouds / 雲の垂れこめた山 a cloud-draped mountain.

たれさがる 垂れ下がる ⇨ たれる.

たれながし 垂れ流し ¶垂れ流しである 《文》 be incontinent; dirty one's clothes. 文例⇩

たれる 垂れる 〈滴る〉 drip; drop; fall in drops; trickle; 〈下げる〉 hang (down); droop; lower (one's head); drop; let [pull] down (the blind); 〈垂れ下がる〉 hang (down); dangle (ぶらんと); droop ¶尾を垂れる droop its tail / 足をだらりと垂れて with one's legs dangling / 範を垂れる set an example (to) / 教えを垂れる teach; 《文》 admonish; preach; lecture. 文例⇩

だれる 〈人が〉 get [《文》 become] bored; be [get] tired of; lose one's enthusiasm (for); 〈物事から〉 flag; get [《文》 become] dull [flat]; slacken; become less active. 文例⇩

タレント a personality; 〈集合的〉《young》 talent ¶テレビタレント a TV personality.

タロいも a taro (pl. -s).

-だろう 〈…であろう〉 I think; I suppose; I reckon; 《米》 I guess; 〈恐らく…だろう〉 perhaps; probably; maybe. 文例⇩

たわい(も)ない 〈ばかげた〉 silly; foolish; absurd; idle (chatter); nonsensical; 〈取るに足りない〉 trifling; trivial; petty; frivolous; 〈無邪気な〉 childish; simple; innocent; 〈容易な〉 easy ¶たわいもないを言う say silly things; talk nonsense [rubbish] / たわい(も)なく 〈容易に〉 easily; without effort [difficulty]; 〈無邪気に〉 childishly; innocently; 〈下らなく〉 uselessly; foolishly.

たわけた 戯けた foolish; silly; idiotic; stupid ¶たわけた事を言う talk nonsense [rubbish].

たわけもの 戯け者 a fool; an idiot.

たわごと 戯言 silly talk; nonsense; rubbish ¶たわ言を言う talk nonsense; say silly things.

たわし 束子 〈床の〉 a scrubbing brush; 〈台所の〉 a (pot) scourer; a pot cleaner.

たわむ 撓む bend.

たわむれ 戯れ 〈遊戯〉 play; 《文》 sport; 〈冗談〉 fun; (a) joke; 《文》 (a) jest; 〈男女の〉 flirtation; 〈気紛れ〉 a whim; 《文》 a caprice ¶戯れに for fun; in play; out of mere caprice. 文例⇩

たわむれる 戯れる 〈遊戯する〉 play; 《文》 sport; toy (with sth); 〈跳ね回る〉 frolic; frisk; caper; gambol; 〈冗談を言う〉 joke; 《文》 jest; 〈男女が〉 flirt [《文》 dally] (with); 〈ちょうが〉 花に戯れる flit from flower to flower.

たわめる 撓める bend.

たわら 俵 a straw bag ¶米俵 a straw ricebag.

たわわ 文例⇩

たん¹ 反 〈土地の〉 a tan (=約 1,000 m²); 〈反物の〉 a roll (of cloth) (=約 10.6 m) ¶反別 the area 《of a farm》; acreage.

だるくて働くのがいやだ. I feel too lazy to work.

たるむ 彼女は 40 も 1, 2 歳過ぎて, 目の下のたるみが気になっていた. She was one or two years past forty, with bags [pouches] under her eyes. / 昔はぽってりと太っていた彼女だが, 今では肉がたるんでしまった. She was plump once but has now run to flab. / お前, たるんでるぞ. You should put more of your heart into your business.

だれ 僕がだれだか分かるかね. Can you tell who I am? / Can you place me? / だれがしたと君は思うか. Who do you think did it? / これはだれの鉛筆ですか. Whose is this pencil? / だれを待っているのか. Who are you waiting for? / だれかと思ったら父だった. Who should it be but my father. / It was no less a person than my father. / 彼は友人に頼まれてそうしたのですと言ったが, だれかれという名は出さなかった. He said he did it at the request of a friend, but he didn't tell us his name. / その人がだれであるかはテレビのニュースでは明らかにされなかった. His identity was not disclosed in the TV news. / 真っ暗やみの中で, だれがだれだか分からなかった. I couldn't tell them apart in the total darkness. / その家を化物屋敷と言うようになった. Somehow or other it has come to be known as a haunted house. / だれでも欠点のない人はない. No one is free from faults. / だれにも言ってはならない. You must not tell anybody. / だれもこの規則を犯したものは罰せられる. Anybody who violates these regulations will be punished. / だれでも君の好きな人にそれをやってよい. You may give it to anyone you like. / 戦争がすんでだれ一人として喜ばない者はなかった. Everyone was glad that the war was over.

たれながし その工場はカドミウムを含んだ廃水を川に垂れ流しにしていた. The factory had been discharging its untreated cadmium-containing waste water into the river.

たれる 雨垂れが軒から垂れていた. The rain was dripping from the eaves. / 戸口に幕が垂れていた. The door was hung with a curtain. / 雲が低く垂れている. Clouds are hanging low.

だれる 会議はだれ気味だった. The conference went somewhat

たん² 短 〈欠点〉a fault; a shortcoming; a weak point ⇨ ⇨ **たんちょう** 短 ¶ 短三度《音楽》a minor [flat] third.

たん³ 痰 phlegm; 〈たんつば〉(a) sputum《pl. -ta》¶ たんを吐く cough out [bring up] phlegm; spit phlegm out / たんを切る clear *one*'s throat (of phlegm) / たんつぼ a spittoon;《米》a cuspidor.

たん⁴ 端 ¶ 端を発する start [rise,《文》arise]《from》; originate《in, from》;《文》have *its* origin [inception]《in》.

タン 《料理》(a) tongue ¶ タンシチュー stewed tongue; tongue stew.

だん¹ 団 a body; a group; a party; 〈一座〉a company; a troupe ¶ 観光団 a group of tourists; a tourist party / 一団となって in a body.

だん² 段 〈階段〉a step (of the stairs); 〈欄〉a column; 〈文の区切り〉a paragraph; a passage ¶ はしごの段 a rung of a ladder / 上から2番目の段 the next to the top stair / 階段を数段降りる go down several steps of the stairs / 1度に2段ずつ階段を上る go up the steps (taking them) two at a time / 幾段にもなったケーキ a many-layered[-tiered] cake / 段が違う be not in the same class《as》; stand on different levels / 〈かなわない〉be outclassed《by》; be no match《for》/ 4段抜きの広告 a four-column advertisement / (ロケットの)第1段 the first stage. 文例⇩

だん³ 断 ¶ 断を下す give *one*'s [make a] decision.

だん⁴ 暖 ¶ 暖を取る warm *oneself* (at the fire).

だん⁵ 談 〈話〉(a) talk; 〈conversation〉;〈物語〉a story; a tale; an account ¶ 沢村氏談 Mr. Sawamura says… / 車中談 informal talk (of a politician) in a railroad train; a press interview aboard a train / 冒険談 a story of adventure / 旅行談 an account of *one*'s tour.

だん⁶ 壇 a platform; a stage (舞台); a rostrum (演壇); 〈…界〉《literary》circles; the (artists') world.

all political activity》/ 弾圧的な oppressive; highhanded.

たんい 単位 a unit; a denomination (貨幣の); 《教育》《米》a credit ¶ フランス語を2単位とる take French for two credits / 1週2時間, 30週の講義で4単位与える give four credits for [to] a lecture of two hours per week for a term of thirty weeks / 卒業に必要な数の単位をとる earn [《文》obtain,《文》acquire] enough credits to graduate / 単位を間違える get the unit wrong; mistake the unit / 単位面積[質量]当り per unit area [mass] / 単位制度 the accrediting [credit] system. 文例⇩

たんいつ 単一 a single; sole; 〈個々の〉individual / 単一化する simplify; unify (統一する) / 単一民族国家 a racially homogeneous nation.

だんいん 団員 a member《of an association》.

たんか¹ 担架 a stretcher ¶ 担架で運ぶ carry *sb* on a stretcher. 文例⇩

たんか² 単価 a unit price [cost] ¶ 単価50円で at 50 yen apiece [each]. 文例⇩

たんか³ 炭化《化》carbonization ¶ 炭化する carbonize / 炭化カルシウム calcium carbide / 炭化水素 a hydrocarbon / 炭化物 a carbide.

たんか⁴ 啖呵 ¶ たんかを切る bluster (out); bluff;《文》hurl defiance《at》.

たんか⁵ 短歌 a *tanka*; a Japanese poem of thirty-one syllables.

だんか 檀家 a supporter of a Buddhist temple; a parishioner.

タンカー a tanker ¶ オイル[マンモス]タンカー an oil [a mammoth] tanker.

だんかい 段階 a stage; a grade; a step ¶ 段階的な phased《withdrawals of troops》/ 1段階先へ進める carry (the investigation) a stage further. 文例⇩

だんがい¹ 断崖 a precipice; a cliff ¶ 断崖絶壁 a precipitous cliff; a sheer precipice.

だんがい² 弾劾 impeachment; accusation; 《文》censure ¶ 弾劾する impeach《*sb* of [with] a crime》; accuse《*sb* of misdemeanor》;《文》

---

slowly.

-だろう 彼はあす来るだろう。He will probably come tomorrow. / 今日は波が荒いだろう。I am afraid [I fear] the waves will be high today. / 私はじきに直るだろう。I expect I'll be better soon. / あいつ、きっと腹がへってるんだろう。He must be hungry. / 彼はなんで来なかったのだろう。I wonder why he didn't come. / 君は来るだろうと思った。I expected you (to come). | I thought you would come.

たわむれ それはほんの戯れにしたことだった。He did it just for fun [from mere caprice].

たわわ 枝もたわわに実がなっている。The branches bent low [were heavy] with fruit. | The fruit was weighing down the branches.

たん³ たんがのどにからまった。The phlegm stuck in my throat.

たん⁴ その争議は解雇問題に端を発したのだ。The dispute arose from the dismissal of some employees.

だん² いざ机に向かって筆をとる段になると何も頭に浮かんで来ない。Now that I sit at my desk to write, my mind is a (complete) blank. / 日本に関する段になると彼らは全く別の見方をしているようである。When it comes to the case of Japan, they appear to take quite a different point of view. / あの人は私とは段違いだ。I am no match for him. / 氏の新作は前作に比べて数段落ちる。His new work is several cuts below his previous one. / 彼は柔道6段だ。He is a sixth *dan* in judo.

たんい 君の計算は単位が違っている。You are calculating in the wrong units. / この表の人口は千単位。The population in the table is shown [expressed] in thousands. / この表の数字は千単位。The numbers in the table have been rounded off to the nearest thousand. / 株は1,000株単位で売買されている。Stocks are now sold in blocks of 1,000. / 彼が取得した単位数は卒業のためには2単位不足だった。The number of credits he had earned was two short of the requirement for graduation.

たんか¹ 担架で運ばなければならない患者がたくさんいた。There were a large number of stretcher cases.

たんか² それは単価50円です。They cost 50 yen apiece.

だんかい 現代の科学はその過程の基礎的段階を明らかにした。Mod-

censure / 弾劾裁判所 a Court of Impeachment.
たんかだいがく 単科大学 a college.
たんがら 炭殼 (coal) cinders.
たんがん 単眼 《昆虫の》a simple eye.
たんがん² 嘆願 a petition; 《文》(an) entreaty; (an) appeal; 《文》(a) supplication ¶嘆願する 《文》entreat (*sb* for mercy); 《文》supplicate; implore; petition (the government); appeal 《to》/ 嘆願書を提出する present [submit, hand in, send in] a (written) petition (to). 文例↓
だんがん 弾丸 〈小銃の〉a bullet; 〈砲弾〉a shell.
たんき¹ 単記 《投票の》単記制 a single ballot [vote] system / 単記無記名投票 secret vote [ballot] with single entry. 文例↓
たんき² 短気 a quick [hot, short] temper; hot-headedness; 《性急》impatience; 《文》impetuosity ¶短気な quick-[hot-]tempered; 〈怒りっぽい〉irritable; touchy; 《文》irascible; petulant; testy; 《性急な》impetuous; impatient / 短気を起こす lose *one's* temper; become impatient; 《口語》lose *one's* cool / 短気を起こして losing patience / 短気を起こさないようにする keep [control, restrain] *one's* temper; 《口語》keep *one's* cool. 文例↓
たんき³ 短期 a short term [period] ¶短期の brief; short; 《文》of short duration; short-term / 短期貸付 a short-term loan / 短期大学 a junior college / 短期手形 a short bill.
だんき 暖気 warmth; warm weather.
たんきかん 短期間 a short period (of time); a short space of time ¶短期間の滞在 a short stay.
たんきゅう 探求[究] 〈追求〉(a) search; 《文》a quest; 〈研究〉research; (an) investigation; (an) inquiry; (a) study ¶真理の探究 《文》the pursuit of truth / 探究する investigate; do research (in); search (for); inquire (into); study / 《文》pursue (truth) / 探究心 the spirit of inquiry; (have) an inquiring [a questing] mind.
だんきゅう 段丘 a terrace ¶海[河]岸段丘 a marine [river] terrace.
たんきょり 短距離 a short distance; (a) short [close] range (射撃の) ¶短距離で at a short distance; at close range / 短距離競走 a short-distance race; a sprint (race) / 短距離 a dash / 短距離選手 a sprinter / 短距離輸送 short-haul transportation.
タンク 〈戦車〉a tank; 〈ガス・油などの〉a tank; 〈水槽〉a water tank; a cistern / 球形のタンク a spherical tank / 高圧タンク a (high-)pressure tank [vessel] / 石油タンク an oil tank / 〈鉄道の〉タンク車 a tank car / タンクローリー a tanker / 《米》a tank truck / 《英》a tank lorry.

タングステン 《化》tungsten.
たんぐつ 短靴 《a pair of》shoes; 《米》low shoes.
たんげい 端倪 ¶端倪すべからざるものがある 《文》be inscrutable; 《文》defy conjecture; be beyond all imagination.
だんけつ 団結 solidarity; unity; 《文》union ¶団結する unite; stand together / 団結して in a body / 《労働者の》団結権 the right to organize / 団結心 cooperative spirit; 《文》(an) esprit de corps.
たんけん¹ 探検 (an) exploration; an expedition ¶探検する explore; make an exploration 《of, into》/ 探検に出かける go on an 《Arctic》expedition / 探検家 an explorer / 探検隊 an expedition (team); an expeditionary [exploration] party / 探検飛行 an exploratory flight 《over the Antarctic continent》/ 探検隊長 the leader [chief] of an expedition.
たんけん² 短剣 a short sword; a dagger (匕首(短刀)).
だんげん 単元 《教育》a unit ⇨ たんい.
だんげん 断言 (an) assertion; (a) declaration; a positive [definite] statement ¶断言する 《文》assert; declare; state positively. 文例↓
たんご 単語 a word ¶単語をたくさん知っている have a rich [large] vocabulary 《of English》/ 基礎単語 a basic word / 単語集 a collection of 《everyday》words; a wordbook.
タンゴ 《dance》the tango 《*pl.* -s》. 文例↓
だんこ 断固 ¶断固たる firm; 《文》resolute; decisive; positive / 断固たる処置をとる take decisive measures; take strong action / 断固として 《文》resolutely; decisively; 《文》with decision; positively / 断固として主張を曲げない stick to *one's* opinion and will not yield / 断固として否定する deny *sth* emphatically.
だんご 団子 a dumpling ¶団子鼻 a button(-shaped) nose.
たんこう¹ 炭坑 a coal mine; 〈坑道〉a (coal) pit ¶炭坑夫 a coal miner; a collier.
たんこう² 炭鉱 a coal mine; a colliery ¶炭鉱会社 a colliery [mining] company / 炭鉱業 the coal-mining industry / 炭鉱地帯 a coal-mining area [region].
たんこう³ 探鉱 prospecting.
だんこう¹ 団交 ⇨ だんたい¹ (団体交渉).
だんこう² 断行 ¶断行する carry out 《*one's* plan》(resolutely) / 所信を断行する act according to *one's* convictions. 文例↓
だんこう³ 断交 ¶断交する break off relations 《with》/ 経済断交 a rupture of economic relations.

---

ern science has thrown light on the basic steps of the process. / その計画はまだ実験段階を出ない The project is still in an experimental stage.
たんがん² 彼は妻の嘆願で釈放された. He was released on the petition of his wife.

たんき¹ 投票は単記で行ないます. 《議長の言葉》The vote is to be taken on the single ballot system.
たんき² こんなことで短気を起こしてはいけない. Don't let such a thing ruffle your temper. / 短気は損気. Nothing is to be gained by losing your temper.

だんけつ 我々は団結して彼らに当たらなければならない. We must unite against them.
だんげん これが事実であると私は断言してはばからない. I have no hesitation in saying that this is the truth.

だんごう 談合 (illegal) collusion 《between contractors》; an illegal [improper] agreement 《to fix prices》 ¶談合する conspire to agree on prices (before tendering); form a (price-fixing) ring.

たんこうしき 単項式 〖数〗 a monomial (expression).

たんこうしょく¹ 淡紅色 ¶淡紅色の pink; salmon(-pink).

たんこうしょく² 淡黄色 ¶淡黄色の light-[lemon-]yellow.

たんこうぼん 単行本 a book; a separate volume ¶単行本として 《publish》 in book form.

たんこぶ ⇨こぶ³ ¶目の上のたんこぶ a person standing in *one's* way; a superior who obstructs *one's* freedom of action.

だんこん¹ 男根 〈いんけい〉 ¶男根崇拝 a phallic cult; phallus worship; phallicism.

だんこん² 弾痕 a bullet mark [hole].

たんさ 探査 (an) inquiry; (an) investigation ¶探査する investigate; inquire [look] into.

たんざ¹ 単座 ¶単座戦闘機 a single-seater[-seated] fighter (plane).

たんざ² 端座 ¶端座する sit straight [upright].

だんさ 段差 〈段位の〉 a difference in grade; 〈道路などの〉 a difference in level; 《英》 a ramp. 文例石

ダンサー a (stage) dancer; a dancing girl.

たんさい 淡彩 ¶淡彩の light-colored (drawings) / 淡彩を施す apply thin coloring (to).

たんさいほう 単細胞 ¶単細胞の 〖生物〗 single-[one-]celled (animals); unicellular (microorganisms) / 単細胞的な考え方 a simple, one-track-minded way of thinking.

たんさく¹ 単作 〖農〗 a single crop ¶単作地帯 a one-crop area / 単作農業 single-crop farming.

たんさく² 探索 〈捜索〉 a search; a hunt; 《文》 a quest; 〈調査〉 (an) inquiry; (an) investigation; (a) research ¶探索する 〈捜索する〉 search (for); look [seek] for; hunt for; 〈調査する〉 inquire [make inquiries] into; look into; investigate (into).

たんざく 短冊 a strip of fancy paper (for writing a *tanka* [*haiku*] on).

タンザニア (the United Republic of) Tanzania ¶タンザニアの Tanzanian / タンザニア人 a Tanzanian.

たんさん¹ 単産 an [a single-industry] industrial union.

たんさん² 炭酸 〖化〗 carbonic acid ¶炭酸ガス carbon dioxide (gas); carbonic acid gas / 炭酸カリ[カルシウム] potassium [calcium] carbonate / 炭酸水 aerated [carbonated] water; soda (water); (soda) pop / 炭酸ソーダ sodium carbonate; carbonate of soda.

たんし¹ 短資 a short-term loan.
たんし² 短詩 a short poem [verse].
たんし³ 端子 〖電〗 a terminal.

だんし 男子 〈男の子〉 a boy; a son; 〈女子に対して〉 a male ¶男子高校 a boys' high school / 男子事務員 a male clerk. 文例石

タンジェント 〖数〗 a tangent (略: tan).

だんじき 断食 a fast; fasting ⇨じぜん ¶断食する fast; observe a fast / 断食療法 a fasting [starvation, hunger] cure.

たんしきぼき 単式簿記 single-entry bookkeeping.

だんじこむ 談じ込む protest strongly 《against *sb's* act》; 《文》 lodge a strong protest 《with *sb* against [about] *sth*》.

たんじじつ 短時日 ¶短時日に in a short (space [period] of) time.

だんじて 断じて 《文》 decidedly; absolutely; positively; (up)on my word [honor]; 〈否定〉 never; by no means.

たんしゃ 単車 a two-wheeled vehicle with a motor; a motorcycle.

だんしゃく 男爵 a baron ¶K男爵 Baron K / 男爵夫人 a baroness.

だんしゅ 断種 castration; sterilization.

たんじゅう¹ 胆汁 bile; gall ¶胆汁質の人 《文》 a person of bilious temperament.

たんじゅう² 短銃 ⇨けんじゅう.

たんしゅく 短縮 shortening; 《文》 curtailment; reduction ¶短縮する shorten; cut (down); reduce; curtail / 夏休みを2週間短縮する shorten [cut down] the summer vacation by two weeks / 労働時間の短縮を要求する demand [clamor for] shorter working hours. 文例石

たんじゅん 単純 ¶単純な simple; 〈頭が〉 simple-minded / 単純化 simplification / 単純化する simplify / 単純さ simplicity.

たんしょ 短所 a fault; a shortcoming; 《文》 a defect; a weak point; a weakness ¶短所を補う make up for *one's* [*sb's*] shortcomings / 短所を直す 《文》 remedy *one's* defects.

だんじょ 男女 man and woman; men and women; both [the] sexes ¶男女の関係 a man-woman relationship; relations between the sexes / 男女の差別 sex discrimination / 男女の三つ子 mixed triplets / 男女の役割 sex roles; male and female roles / 男女を問わず regardless [without distinction] of sex / 男女共学 coeducation / 男女共学の学校 a coeducational 《米口語》 co-ed, 《英》 mixed-sex] school / 男女共学制 the coeducational method [system]; coeducationalism / 男女同権 equal rights for both sexes [for men and women]; (the) equality of the sexes.

たんしょう¹ 探勝 sightseeing ¶紅葉の奥入

たんご 僕の知っている英語の単語はいくらでもない。 My vocabulary of English is very small.

だんこう² 私は飽くまで所信を実行するつもりだ。 I will carry out my intention to the last.

だんさ この先に段差あり。〖掲示〗 Sharp drop in road level ahead. / 《英》 Beware ramp!

だんし 男子の一言だ。 間違いない。 I have given you my word of honor. There can be no going back on it.

たんしゅく この急行列車の所要時間は去年よりも2時間の短縮になっている。 This express train covers the distance in two hours less than it did last year. / 今日は30分の短縮授業を行なう。 The school hours will be cut (by) 30 minutes today. / 飛行機は世界の距離を短縮した。 Airplanes have made the world smaller.

たんしょう 瀬(せ)渓谷を探勝する visit the Oirase Valley to see the beautiful autumnal tints.

たんしょう³ 短小 ¶短小な little; small; stunted.

たんしょう³ 嘆賞 admiration; praise ¶嘆賞する admire; praise; applaud;《文》extol(l); speak highly [admiringly] of. 文例⇩

たんしょう⁴ 単勝《競馬》¶単勝で賭ける bet 《10,000 yen on Shinzan》to win.

たんじょう 誕生 (a) birth ¶誕生する be born; come into the world;《事柄・作品などが》see the light of day / 誕生日 a birthday / 誕生日を迎える reach *one's* (fiftieth) birthday / 誕生日を祝う celebrate *sb's* birthday / 誕生日の贈り物 a birthday present [gift] / 誕生地 *one's* birthplace / 誕生祝いを贈る present *sb* with a gift [send *sb* a gift] in celebration of the birth of 《*his* son》/ 誕生石 a birthstone. 文例⇩

だんしょう¹ 男娼 a male prostitute.

だんしょう² 談笑 a pleasant chat ¶談笑する chat 《with》; have a pleasant talk ¶談笑する a chat 《with》; have a pleasant talk ¶談笑する chat cheerfully 《with》. 文例⇩

たんしようしょくぶつ 単子葉植物 a monocotyledonous plant; a monocotyledon; a monocot.

たんしょく 単色 ¶単色の monochromatic; one-color (light) ¶単色で in one [a single] color; in monochrome / 単色画 a monochrome.

だんしょく 男色 ⇒ どうせい²(同性愛).

だんしょく 暖色 a warm color.

たんじる 嘆じる ⇒ なげく.

だんじる 談じる〈語る〉talk 《about》;〈論じる〉discuss *sth* ¶ have a discussion 《with *sb*》.

たんしん¹ 単身 ¶単身で (all) alone; by *oneself*; single-handed;《文》unattended / 単身赴任する (go to) take up a post (in London) without *one's* family [by *oneself*, alone].

たんしん² 短針〈時計の〉the hour [short] hand.

たんじん 炭塵 coal dust ¶炭塵爆発 an explosion of coal dust.

たんす 箪笥 a chest of drawers; a chest;《米》a bureau (*pl*. -s, -x)(通例鏡つきの).

ダンス a dance; dancing ¶ダンスの教師 a dancing instructor;《英》a dancing-master / ダンスをする dance; have a dance 《with》; perform a dance / ダンスパーティー a ball; a dance / 〈高校・大学での〉《米》a prom.

たんすい 淡水 fresh water ¶淡水魚 [湖] a freshwater fish [lake].

だんすい 断水 suspension of water supply

¶断水する cut off (the) water (supply); stop the supply of water. 文例⇩

たんすいかぶつ 炭水化物《化》a carbohydrate ★日常会話では複数で使うのが普通 ¶炭水化物の少ない食事 a low-carbohydrate diet; a diet low in carbohydrates.

たんすう 単数《文法》the singular number ¶単数の singular / 単数で使う use 《a word》in the singular. 文例⇩

たんせい¹ 丹精〈努力〉《文》exertion; efforts; labors;〈勤勉〉《文》diligence; industry;〈苦心〉pains; (great) care ¶丹精する《文》exert *oneself*; take pains; apply *oneself* (closely) to / 丹精して育てる cultivate [raise] with loving care / 永年の丹精の結果《文》the fruit of years of effort [painstaking work] / 丹精をこらす spare no pains; make every effort / 丹精をこらした [こめた] painstaking; elaborate. 文例⇩

たんせい² 嘆声 ¶嘆声を漏らす〈嘆く〉sigh (over); heave [breathe,《文》utter] a sigh of grief; deplore; grieve [《文》lament] 《for, over》;《感嘆する》let out [utter] a cry of admiration.

たんせい³ 端正 ¶端正な《文》noble;《文》decorous;《文》seemly; decent; proper;〈顔立ちの〉clear-cut.

だんせい¹ 男声 a male voice ¶男声合唱 a male chorus; a male-voice choir /〈曲〉a chorus for male voices.

だんせい² 男性 the male (sex); a man;《文法》the masculine gender ¶男性の male / 男性的 manly; masculine / 男性美 masculine beauty. 文例⇩

だんせい³ 弾性 elasticity ¶弾性体 an elastic body.

たんせいせいしょく 単性生殖《生物》parthenogenesis.

たんせき 旦夕 ¶命旦夕に迫る《文》be [lie] at death's door; be on the brink of death.

だんせき 胆石 a gallstone.

だんぜつ 断絶〈絶えること〉extinction;〈中絶〉《文》discontinuation; (an) interruption;〈決裂〉《文》(a) rupture ¶断絶する《文》cease to exist; become extinct;〈断つ〉break [cut] off;〈断たれる〉be broken [cut] off;〈決裂する〉come to a rupture / 世代間の断絶 a generation gap / 断絶の時代 the age of discontinuity. 文例⇩

たんしょう³ 氏の学識は世界の人々の嘆賞するところである。His scholarship commands the admiration of the world.

たんじょう 今日は彼女の30回目の誕生日です。Today is her thirtieth birthday. / 僕の誕生日は8月8日です。My birthday is (on) August 8. / お誕生日おめでとうございます。I wish you many happy returns of the day. | Many happy returns!

だんしょう² 問題は談笑のうちに解決された。The question was settled by friendly talk.

だんすい 水道管工事のため次の地域は明日午前9時から12時まで断水になります。Owing to repair work on the service pipe, water supply will be cut off from 9 a.m. to 12 noon in the following areas.

たんすう この単語は単数です。This word is in the singular.

たんせい¹ これまでするには丹精が大変だったでしょう。I can see it must have cost you tremendous efforts [a great deal of labor] to bring it to this stage.

だんせい² 彼には男性的なところがない。He lacks manliness.

だんぜつ 一家断絶した。The family (line) has died out. / 世代間の断絶が起きている。Communication between generations is breaking down.

たんせん 目下その区間は単線運転中です。Single-track operation is in effect on that section of the line.

だんぜん 僕は断然タバコを止めた。I have given up smoking

たんせん 単線 《鉄道》a single (railroad) line [track] ¶ 単線の鉄道 a single-track railroad / 単線運転 single-track operation. 文例↓

たんぜん¹ 丹前 ⇨ どてら.

たんぜん² 端然 ¶ 端然たる neat; proper / 端然と neatly; properly / 端然と座る sit straight [upright].

だんせん 断線 the snapping [breaking down] of a wire ¶ 断線する 〈線が主語〉snap; come down; break (down).

だんぜん 断然 positively; resolutely; decidedly; 《はるかに》by far (the best); far and away 《better》¶ 断然拒否する refuse flatly / 断然否定する deny sth emphatically. 文例↓

たんそ 炭素 《化》carbon ¶ 炭素と化合させる carbonize.

たんそう 炭層 a coal seam [bed].

たんぞう 鍛造 forging ¶ 鍛造する forge.

だんそう¹ 男装 ¶ 男装する disguise oneself as [be dressed like] a man; wear [be in] men's clothes.

だんそう² 断層 《地質》a dislocation; a [an earth] fault; 〈考え方などの〉a gap (between) ¶ 断層地震 a dislocation earthquake / 断層写真《医》a tomogram.

だんそう³ 弾奏 ¶ 弾奏する play (the piano).

だんそう⁴ 弾倉 a magazine. └perform.

たんそく¹ 探測 sounding; probing ¶ 探測機 a sounding device; a probe / 探測気球 a sounding balloon.

たんそく² 嘆息 a sigh ¶ 〈嘆き〉grief ¶ 嘆息する〈ため息をつく〉sigh (over); heave a sigh (of grief); 〈嘆く〉grieve (about, for); deplore / 嘆息しながら with a sigh of grief; sighing. 文例↓

だんぞく 断続 ¶ 断続する be intermittent / 断続的に intermittently; off and on.

だんそんじょひ 男尊女卑 domination of men over women; subjection of women. ¶ 男尊女卑の社会 a male-dominated society.

たんだ 単打 《野球》a single (hit) ¶ 単打する single (to left field).

たんだい 短大 a junior college.

だんたい¹ 団体 a body; a party; a group ¶ 《競技で》団体で2位になる place second as a team / 旅館の団体客 a party of tourists / 団体競技 team competition; a team event / 団体交渉《労》collective bargaining / 団体交渉をする bargain collectively 《with》/ 団体行動を とる act as a group [together] / 団体生活 a group life; corporate life / 団体精神 a group [corporate] spirit; 《文》(an) esprit de corps / 団体保険 collective insurance; 〈生命保険〉group (life) insurance / 団体旅行をする make a group tour. 文例↓

だんたい² 暖帯 the warm temperate zone ¶ 暖帯林 a warm-temperate forest.

だんだら 段だら 《red and white》stripes.

タンタル 《化》tantalum.

たんたん¹ 坦々 ¶ 坦々たる 〈平坦な〉level; even; 〈単調な〉monotonous; 〈無事な〉uneventful; peaceful / 坦々たる大道 a broad level highway / 坦々たる生活 an uneventful life.

たんたん² 淡々 ¶ 淡々たる 〈われ関せずの〉unconcerned; 〈無頓着な〉indifferent; 〈私心のない〉disinterested; 〈冷静な〉cool; calm; 〈悟り切った〉philosophic(al); 〈味・色の〉plain; light / 淡々たる心境 a serene state of mind.

だんだん(と) 段々(と) 〈徐々に〉gradually; by degrees; little by little; 〈次々に〉one after another; 〈ますます〉more and more (増す時); less and less (減る時) ¶ だんだん増す go on increasing; be on the increase. 文例↓

だんだんばたけ 段々畑 terraced [layered] fields; (farming) terraces. 文例↓

たんち 探知 detection ¶ 探知する detect; learn (by inquiry); get wind of 《an affair》; monitor 《radio communications》/ 探知機 a detector / 〈核実験などの〉探知所 a monitoring station / 探知装置 a detection [monitoring, sensing] device.

だんち 団地 a housing [an apartment] development [complex]; 《英》a housing estate ¶ 団地のアパート a housing-development apartment / 団地族 dwellers in modern apartments.

だんちがい 段違い ⇨ だん(段が違う) ¶ 段違い平行棒 《器具》uneven (parallel) bars; 〈種目〉the uneven (parallel) bars.

たんちょ 端緒 〈初め〉the beginning; the start; 〈第一歩〉the first step; 〈手掛かり〉a clue 《to, for》¶ 端緒をつかむ get [find] a clue 《to, for》/ 端緒を開く begin; start; 《文》commence / …を端緒とする originate in [with]…; date from …; 《文》have its origin in…. 文例↓

たんちょう¹ 丹頂 《鳥》a Japanese crane.

たんちょう² 単調 monotony ¶ 単調な monot-

once and for all. / 私より彼の方が断然上手だ. He is far more skillful than me [I am]. ⇨ より¹ 用法 / 断然そうするつもりだ. I am determined to do it. | I am set on (doing) it. / これは真に重要な発見なのだろうかという問に対する答は断然「然り」である. To the question of whether this is really an important discovery, the answer is a decided " Yes ".

たんそく² この悲報に一同深く嘆息した. The sad news drew deep sighs of grief from everyone present.

だんたい¹ われわれは 20 名の団体で京都見物に出かけた. Twenty of us made up a party and went on a sightseeing trip to Kyoto. / M 石油会社は N 保険会社に従業員の団体保険をかけている. M Oil Company carries a group policy on its employees with N Insurance Company.

だんだん(と) だんだん寒くなってくる. It is growing [getting] colder and colder. / 彼はだんだん勉強しなくなった. He became less and less interested in his studies. / 客がだんだん帰って行く. The guests are leaving one after another. / だんだん聞いてみるとその子は孤児であった. On further inquiry I learned that the child was an orphan.

だんだんばたけ 丘はぶどうの段々畑になっていた. The hillside was terraced with vineyards.

たんちょ まだ問題解決の端緒が見出されない. No clue has yet been found which might lead to a solution of the problem. / これ

たんちょう monotonous; dull; humdrum; flat / 単調を破る [和らげる] break [relieve] the monotony 《of》/ 単調に monotonously. 文例⇩

たんちょう³ 短調 《音楽》a minor (key) ¶ ハ短調 (in) C minor.

だんちょう¹ 団長 the leader 《of a party》 ¶ …を団長として headed [led] by ….

だんちょう² 断腸 ¶ 断腸の思いである feel as if one's heart would break.

たんてい 探偵 a detective; an investigator ¶ 探偵をする spy 《on sb, into a secret》; investigate [inquire into] 《an affair》/ 探偵につけられる be shadowed by a detective / 探偵をつける set [put] a detective on sb / 私立[素人]探偵 a private [an amateur] detective / 私立探偵社 a private detective agency [firm] / 探偵小説 a detective [mystery] story.

だんてい 断定 a conclusion; 《決定》a decision ¶ 断定する conclude; come to [arrive at] a conclusion; make up one's mind 《that…》.

たんてき 端的 ¶ 端的な direct; straightforward; frank; plain; point-blank / 端的に directly; straightforwardly; frankly; plainly; point-blank / 端的に言う speak frankly [plainly]; talk straight; go right to the point / 端的に言うと plainly speaking; to be frank with you.

たんでき 耽溺 《文》indulgence; addiction ¶ 耽溺する indulge in; be addicted [given up] to; give oneself up [abandon oneself] to.

たんでん 炭田 a coalfield.

たんと ⇨たくさん.

たんとう¹ 担当 ⇨たんにん ¶ 担当する take [have] charge of; be in charge 《of》; take sth under one's charge / 担当させる put [place] sb in charge 《of》/ この科目の担当教授 the professor who teaches this subject / 担当業務 the business for which one is responsible; the business in one's charge / 担当者 the person in charge 《of》.

たんとう² 短刀 a short sword; 《ヒ首(あいくち)》a dagger.

たんとう³ 短頭 《人類》brachycephalism; brachycephaly; ¶ 短頭の shortheaded / 短頭の人 a brachycephalic; short-headed / 短頭の人 a brachycephalic; a shorthead.

だんとう¹ 弾頭 a warhead ¶ 核[水爆]弾頭 a nuclear [hydrogen] warhead.

だんとう² 暖冬 a mild winter. 文例⇩

だんどう 弾道 a trajectory; a line of fire ¶ 弾道を描いて飛ぶ follow a ballistic course / 弾道弾 a ballistic missile.

だんとうだい 断頭台 a guillotine (フランスの); 《史》the block ¶ 断頭台の露と消える be guillotined; die on the block.

たんとうちょくにゅう 単刀直入 ⇨たんてき. 文例⇩

たんとうるい 単糖類 《化》simple sugars.

たんどく¹ 丹毒 《医》erysipelas.

たんどく² 単独 ¶ 単独の 《独立の》independent; 《個々の》individual; 《ひとりの》single; sole; 《文》lone; 《別々の》separate; 《独力の》single-handed / 単独で [に] 《独立で》independently; 《個々に》individually; separately; 《ひとりで》alone; by oneself / 《独力で》single-handed / 単独会見 (have) an exclusive interview 《with》/ 単独内閣 a one-party cabinet / 単独犯 an offense committed alone [without accomplices] / 単独行動をとる take independent action; act independently / 単独飛行をする make a solo flight; fly solo.

たんどく³ 耽読 ¶ 耽読する be absorbed [engrossed] in (reading); pore over; devour 《a book》. 文例⇩

だんどり 段取り a plan; a program; 《手はず》a course of action; arrangements ¶ 段取りを決める work out a plan; make arrangements; arrange 《for》.

だんな 旦那 《主人》a master; 《夫》a husband; 《敬称》sir.

たんなる 単なる mere; simple.

たんに 単に only; merely; just; simply; 《文》solely; alone ¶ 単に…のみでなく not only [merely]… 《but also》…). 文例⇩

たんにん 担任 ¶ 担任する take [have, be in] charge of; take 《a class》under one's charge / 2年の英語を担任する teach English in the second-year class [to the second year] / 担任させる put [《文》place] sb in charge of 《a class》/ 担任のクラス the class in [under] one's charge; one's class / 担任教師 a class [《米》homeroom] teacher; a teacher in charge 《of a class》. 文例⇩

タンニン 《化》tannin ¶ タンニン酸 tannic acid; tannin.

だんねつざい 断熱材 a heat insulator; (heat [thermal]) insulating material.

たんねん 丹念 ¶ 丹念な painstaking; careful; elaborate / 丹念に painstakingly; carefully;

が犯人逮捕の端緒となった. This (clue) led to the arrest of the culprit.

たんちょう² 景色は単調だ. The scene lacks variety. / 単調な毎日であった. One day was very much like another.

だんてい にわかに断定はできない. We must not jump to conclusions.

だんとう² 今年は暖冬異変だった. We have had an abnormally warm winter this year.

たんとうちょくにゅう 単刀直入に話したまえ. Come straight [right] to the point.

たんどく³ 私も若い頃はトルストイのものを耽読したものです. I, too, was a great lover of Tolstoy's works when I was young.

だんどり まだそこまでの段取りはできていない. The arrangements have not yet reached that stage [haven't got that far]. / どんな段取りでやるのかね. How are we going to set about it? / 仕事

は来月から開始の段取りだ. We are to start the work next month.

たんに それは単に模倣に過ぎない. It is no more than an imitation. / それは単に私 1 人のみならず, 私の家族全体のためにもなります. It will benefit not only myself, but also all my family.

たんにん このクラスは長谷川先生の担任です. This is Mr. Hasegawa's class. / Mr. Hasegawa is in charge of this class.

だんねん あの計画はまだ断念しな

だんねん 断念 ¶断念する give up (the idea of *do*ing); abandon / 断念させる persuade *sb* to abandon [give up] (the idea of *do*ing);《文》dissuade *sb* from 《*do*ing》. [文例⇩]

たんのう¹ 胆嚢〖解〗the gallbladder ¶胆嚢炎 inflammation of the gallbladder.

たんのう² 堪能 ¶堪能である be skilled [skillful] 《in, at》; be good 《at》;《文》be well versed 《in》;《文》be proficient 《in》; be at home 《in, on》/ 英語に堪能である be proficient in English; have a good command of English / ピアノに堪能である be a good [an accomplished] pianist / 堪能する be satisfied [《文》satiated] 《with》; have *one's* fill 《of》; have (more than) enough 《of》/ 堪能するまで [ほど] to *one's* heart's content;《文》to satiety.

たんぱ 短波 a short wave ¶短波で送信する transmit 《a message》 on short wave / 波長20メートルの短波で放送する broadcast on a (short) wavelength of 20 meters / 短波放送 short-wave broadcasting / 短波送[受]信機 a short-wave transmitter [receiver].

たんぱく 淡泊 ¶淡泊な〈性格の〉candid; frank; openhearted;〈あっさりした〉indifferent 《to, about》;〈味・色の〉light; simple; plain / 淡泊な食物 plain [light] food / 淡泊に candidly; frankly; openheartedly. [文例⇩]

たんぱくしつ 蛋白(質)〖生化〗protein;〈動物・野菜などに含まれている〉albumin ¶蛋白質に富む[乏しい]食品 high-[low-]protein foods; protein-rich[-poor] foods / 上質の蛋白質を含む食品 high-quality protein foods / 動物[植物]性蛋白 (an) animal [(a) vegetable] protein / 蛋白(質)源 a source of protein(s); a protein source.

たんぱくせき 蛋白石 opal.

だんぱつ 断髪 bobbed hair; a bob ¶断髪にしている wear *one's* hair bobbed; wear bobbed hair.

タンバリン a tambourine.

だんぱん 談判 (a) negotiation; talks; bargaining ¶談判する negotiate 《with》; have talks 《with》; bargain 《with》/ 談判がまとまる come to terms [an agreement] 《with》. [文例⇩]

たんび 耽美 ¶耽美的 (a)esthetic / 耽美主義 (a)estheticism / 耽美主義者 an (a)esthete.

たんぴょう 短評 a short criticism [comment] ¶短評を加える make a brief comment 《on》.

たんぴれい 単比例 simple proportion.

ダンピング〖商〗dumping ¶ダンピングする dump 《goods》.

ダンパー a dump truck [《英》lorry]; a dumper.

タンブラー〈コップ〉a tumbler.

タンブリング〖体操〗tumbling.

たんぶん¹ 単文〖文法〗a simple sentence.

たんぶん² 短文 a short sentence;〈作品〉a short composition [piece]. [文例⇩]

たんぺいきゅう 短兵急 ¶短兵急な impetuous;《文》precipitate; rash; headlong / 短兵急に impetuously;《文》precipitately; abruptly. [文例⇩]

たんぺん 短編〈小説〉a short story [piece]; a sketch;〈映画〉a short film ¶短編小説家 a short-story writer / 短編集 a collection of short stories; collected short stories 《of Hemingway》.

だんぺん¹ 断片 a fragment; a piece; a scrap; odds and ends ¶断片的 fragmentary 《knowledge》/ fragmented 《information》/ 断片的に in fragments.

だんぺん² 弾片 a shell splinter; a fragment of shell.

たんぼ 田んぼ a rice field;〈水田〉a paddy field; a (rice) paddy ¶たんぼ道 a path [lane] through rice fields. [文例⇩]

たんぽ 担保 (a) security; a mortgage; a guarantee;〈見返り担保〉(a) collateral (security) ¶担保に入れる give [offer] *sth* in [as] security 《for》; mortgage; take out [raise] a mortgage on 《*one's* property》/ …を担保にとっている hold a mortgage on 《the house》/ …を担保に金を借りる borrow money on (the) security of *sth* / 十分な担保をとって金を貸す lend money on good [ample] security / 担保付き貸付 a secured loan; a loan secured on 《the land》.

たんぽう 探訪 ¶探訪する inquire [make inquiries] into *sth* / 探訪記事 a report / 探訪記者 a (newspaper) reporter.

だんぼう 暖房 heating ¶暖房装置 a heating system / 暖房用の油 heating oil / 暖房用器具 a heating apparatus; a heater. [文例⇩]

だんボール 段ボール corrugated cardboard ¶段ボール箱 a corrugated carton.

たんぽぽ〖植〗a dandelion.

タンポン a tampon.

だんまく 弾幕 a [an artillery] barrage ¶弾幕を張る put up a barrage.

い. I still have hope for that project.

たんぱく 一般に学者は金銭に淡泊だ. Generally speaking, scholars are not really interested in money.

たんぱく(しつ) 尿から多量の蛋白が検出された. A large quantity of albumin was found in urine.

だんぱん 地主に談判して地代を下げさせよう. I will negotiate with the landlord for a reduction in the rent. / 談判が決裂した. The negotiations broke down.

たんぶん² 次の語句を用いて短文を作れ. Make short sentences using the following words and phrases.

たんぺいきゅう そう短兵急にやろうとしてはだめだ. It won't do to try to rush it through like that.

たんぼ 2, 3年前まではこの辺は一面のたんぼだった. Only a few years ago there was nothing but paddy fields in this neighborhood.

たんぽ 僕の家は800万円の担保に入っている. There is a mortgage of eight million yen on my house. | My house is mortgaged for eight million yen. / 何を担保になさいますか. What security can you offer [put up] for it? / 僕の家をその金の担保に入れてある. My house has been mortgaged to him for the money.

だんぼう この部屋は電気で暖房されている. This room is heated

たんまつ 端末 《コンピューター》 a terminal.
だんまつま 断末魔 one's last moments;《文》 the [one's] hour of death ¶断末魔の苦しみ《文》 the agonies of death; death throes.
たんまり ⇒たくさん. 文例⇩
だんまり《無言》silence; reticence;《文》taciturnity;《劇》a dumb show ¶だんまり屋 a person of few words;《文》a taciturn person.
たんめい 短命 a short life ¶短命の short-lived;《文》ephemeral / 短命に終わる die young. 文例⇩
だんめん 断面 a section ¶断面図 a cross section (of); a sectioned drawing [diagram] / 部分断面図 a partial cross section / 断面図で示す show sth in section. 文例⇩
たんもの 反物 piece goods;《米》dry [soft] goods;《英》drapery;〈織物〉cloth; (textile) fabrics.
だんやく 弾薬 ammunition; munitions.
だんゆう 男優 an actor.
たんようひこうき 単葉飛行機 a monoplane.
たんらく 短絡《電》a short circuit; a short ¶短絡する[させる] short-circuit; short. 文例⇩
だんらく 段落〈文章の〉the end of a paragraph;〈段階〉a stage.
だんらん 団欒 ¶一家団欒の楽しみ the pleasures of a happy home.

たんり 単利《at》simple interest.
だんりゅう 暖流 a warm current.
たんりょ 短慮 ⇒たんき², けいぞつ.
たんりょく 胆力 ⇒どきょう.
だんりょく(せい) 弾力(性) elasticity; spring; resilience; bounce; give;《融通性》flexibility ¶弾力のある elastic; springy; resilient / 弾力のない nonelastic / 弾力性のある態度をとる take a flexible attitude / 弾力性のない計画 an inflexible program.
たんれい 端麗 ¶端麗な fine-looking; handsome; graceful; elegant; personable; comely ⇒ようし⁴.
たんれん 鍛練[錬]〈鉄などの〉temper;《心身の》discipline; training ¶精神の鍛練 mental training / 鍛練[錬]する〈鉄を〉temper; forge;《心身を》discipline; drill; train.
だんろ 暖炉 a stove; a fireplace ¶暖炉をたく light a stove; make a fire in the stove / 暖炉にあたる warm oneself at a stove.
だんろん 談論 ¶談論風発する have [carry on] a very lively [animated] conversation 《with》.
だんわ 談話 (a) talk; (a) conversation ¶談話する[《文》converse, speak]《with》/ have a talk [conversation, chat]《with》/ 談話の形式で発表する publish [announce] in the form of an informal talk / 談話室 a common [conversation] room.

ち

ち¹ 血 blood ¶血が出る bleed《at the nose》/ 血がつながっている be related by blood;《文》be of the same blood / 血の雨を降らす《文》create a scene of carnage / 血のかたまり a clot of blood / 血の付いた[血みどろの, 血染めの] bloodstained; bloody; gory / 血の気の多い hot-blooded / 血の巡りの悪い人 a slow-witted person / 血のにじむような努力をする sweat blood《over sth》/ 血を出す[取る] draw [let] blood / 血を止める stop [《文》arrest] the bleeding; stanch blood / 血を流す spill [shed] blood / 血を吐く〈喀血〉cough blood;〈吐血〉vomit blood / 血を引く be descended 《from》; descend 《from》/ 血に飢えた bloodthirsty / 血で血を洗う quarrel with one's own flesh and blood / 血も涙もない cold-blooded; unfeeling / 血もあり涙もある warmhearted; kind and sympathetic; 血だらけの covered [smeared] with blood / 血生臭い bloody;《文》sanguinary / 血ぬられた blood-smeared /〈目が〉血走っている be bloodshot / 血沸き肉躍る stirring; thrilling. 文例⇩
ち² 地《大地》the earth;〈地面〉the ground;〈陸地〉land;〈土壌〉soil;〈場所〉a place ¶地の中の[に] underground; in the earth / 地の利を占める have the advantage of the terrain [land]; occupy a vantage ground / 日本の地を踏む set foot on Japanese soil / 足が地に着いている〈着実である〉have one's feet on the ground; be down to earth. 文例⇩
ちあん 治安 public peace (and order); (public) security ¶治安がいい[悪い] be a safe [dangerous] place [city, country, etc.] / 治安を維持する[乱す] maintain [disturb] public order.

---

by electricity. | This room has electric heating. / この建物は暖房がない。There is [We have] no heat in this building.
たんまり 彼はその取り引きでたんまりもうけた。He made a large profit on the transaction.
たんめい 新内閣は短命に終わるであろう。The new Cabinet will be short-lived [will not last long].
だんめん その装置は次ページの断面図に見られるように, 非常に複雑なものである。The device is a very complicated one, as is seen in section on the next page. / この新聞記事はアメリカ社会の一断面を示している。This news story reveals a cross section of American society.
たんらく この2つの出来事を短絡して, 両者の間に因果関係ありとするのはよくない。It won't do to connect these two events hastily in your mind and suppose that there is a cause-and-effect relationship between them.
ち¹ 彼にはフランス人の血が混じっている。He has some French blood (in his veins). / 彼らは血を分けた兄弟だ。They are full brothers. / 顔から血の気が引いた。He went [became] pale. | He blanched. / そのため私は血を吐く思いをした。I had a dreadful [terrible] experience. / 血は水よりも濃い。Blood is thicker than

ちい¹ 地衣 〖植〗lichen.
ちい² 地位 〈位置, 職〉a position ; a situation ; a rank 〈階級〉; 〈身分〉(one's) status ; (social) standing ; 《文》one's station (in life) ¶女性の地位 the place of women (in Japanese society); 《raise》 the (social) status of women / 社会的地位 one's social standing [position] / 地位が上がる rise in (social) standing; improve one's position / 地位(高[低]い have [《文》be of] high [low] (social) standing / 地位の象徴 a status symbol ; a symbol [sign] of status / 地位の上の者から下の者へ順に in descending order of status / 地位のある 《文》a person of position [rank] / 地位を得る gain [《文》 attain, win] a position / 地位を占める occupy [hold] a position / 地位を失う lose one's position [《文》 station, place].

ちいき 地域 a region ; an area ; a zone ¶地域的 local ; regional / 地域的に locally ; regionally / 地域によって違う differ from place to place ; vary according to the locality [in different localities] / 地域差をなくす iron out regional differences / 地域社会に尽くす work for the good of the (local) community / 地域研究 area studies / 〈一研究〉 an area study.

ちいく 知育 ¶知育に偏する overemphasize intellectual education [training].

チーク 〈木〉a teak (tree); 〈材〉 teak.

チークダンス cheek-to-cheek dancing.

ちいさい 小さい small ; little ; tiny ; 〈微細な〉fine ; 〈ささいな〉small ; unimportant ; trivial ; trifling ; 《文》petty ¶小さい事柄 a small affair ; a trivial matter ; a triviality / 小さい人物 a person with very little to [about] him ; 《文》a person of small caliber ; a small-minded person / 小さい時 when (one was) a small [little] child ; in one's childhood / 小さい声で in a low voice ; 〈声をひそめて〉under one's breath ; in whispers / 小さくなる 〈形が〉get [《文》become] smaller ; shrink (in size) ; 〈音が〉get [《文》become] lower ; fade, 〈遠ざかして〉make oneself small ; 〈怖くて〉cower (before, at) / 小さくする make sth smaller ; reduce / ラジオの音を小さくする turn the radio down / 小さく切る cut sth small [fine] ; cut sth into small pieces / 小さくなったズボン 《my brother's》 outgrown pants.

チーズ cheese ¶くさび形[三角]のチーズ a wedge of cheese / チーズバーガー a cheeseburger.

チータ 〖動〗a cheetah.

チーム a team ¶チームの一員である be a member of the team ; be in [《米》on] the (football) team / チーム打率 〖野球〗a team batting average / チームワーク teamwork.

ちえ 知恵 wisdom ; wits ; intelligence ¶知恵が付く grow wise [intelligent] ; 〈赤ん坊が〉begin to show signs of intelligence / 知恵の輪 a puzzle ring ; a wire puzzle / 知恵のある wise ; intelligent / 《口語》brainy / 知恵のない unwise ; stupid / 知恵を貸す give advice [《文》counsel] (to) / 知恵を絞る think hard (about a difficult problem) ; rack [cudgel] one's brains / 知恵を付ける give sb a hint [suggestion] ; put an idea into sb's head ; 〈そそのかす〉instigate (sb to do) / 知恵遅れの子供 a (mentally) retarded child / 知恵比べ a competition in ingenuity / 知恵比べをする match [pit one's] wits against sb ; try and see who is the cleverest / 知恵者 a resourceful person / 知恵熱 (a) teething fever. 文例⇩

チェーン a chain ¶チェーンストア a chain store ; 《英》a multiple (store) / チェーンソー a chain saw / チェーンブロック a chain block. 文例⇩

チェコスロバキア Czechoslovakia ¶チェコスロバキア社会主義共和国 the Czechoslovak Socialist Republic / チェコスロバキアの Czechoslovakian / チェコスロバキア人 a Czechoslovakian.

チェス 〈西洋将棋〉《play》chess ¶チェスの盤 a chessboard / チェスのこま a chessman 《pl. -men》.

ちぇっ Oh, damn [drat]!

チェック ¶チェックをする a check ; check sth up ; check up on sth ; 〈レ印をつける〉tick [《米》check] sth off ; put a tick against sth ; mark (off).

チェロ 〖楽器〗a cello 《pl. -s》 ¶チェロ奏者 a cellist.

ちえん 遅延 (a) delay ¶遅延する delay ; be delayed ; get late.

チェンジアップ 〖野球〗a change of pace ; a change-up.

ちか¹ 地下 ¶地下の[に] underground ; under the ground ; 〈墓の中に〉《文》in the grave / 地下にもぐる go underground / 地下10メートルのところに (at) ten meters underground [below ground] / 地下100メートルまで掘る dig (in the ground) to a depth of 100 meters / 地下街 an underground shopping area [complex] / 地下核実験 an underground nuclear test / 地下茎 〖植〗an underground [a subterranean] stem / 地下運動 underground activities / 地下資源

---

water. 〖諺〗
ち² 名声が地に落ちた. He has entirely lost his reputation. / あの人たちのする事は足が地に着いている. They keep their feet firmly on the ground.

ちい² 会社での彼の地位は私より高い. He is higher (up) in the company than me [than I am]. ⇨品⇩

ちいさい この帽子は私には小さい. This hat is too small for me. / 太郎はズボンが小さくなった. Taro has outgrown [grown out of] his trousers. / 小さいながら独立して店をやっています. I keep a store on my own account, though it's only in a small way. / 私は彼を小さい時から知っている. I have known him since he was a child [since (his) childhood]. / 何もそんなに小さくなっているには及ばない. You need not feel so small. / この大聖堂の前では人間はひどく小さく見える. A man is dwarfed by the cathedral.

ちえ 彼は少し知恵が足りない. He hasn't much (is rather short on) sense. / それは知恵のないやり方だ. That is a stupid [not a very sensible] way of doing it. / それくらいの知恵はあるだろう. I think he has that much sense.

チェーン その車はチェーンを付けていた. The car had chains on.

ちか² 地価 the price [value] of land; land value.
ちかい¹ 地階 the basement.
ちかい² 誓い 《文》an oath;《文》a vow ¶誓いを立てる ⇨ ちかう／誓いを守る[破る] keep [break] *one's* vow／必ず誓いを守ると約束させる《文》pledge *sb* to keep *his* oath.
ちかい³ 近い 〈時間が〉near; immediate;《文》at hand／〈距離が〉near／〈場所が〉close [near,《文》hard] by; not far off／〈ほとんど同様〉nearly; close to;《文》hard upon;〈似ている〉be like; resemble;《文》be akin to ¶近い親戚 a near relation／近いうちに in the near future; (pretty) soon; in a short time; one of these days; before very long／近い将来に in the near future; at an early date／〈年齢が〉50 近いに be going [close] on fifty; be getting on toward [《英》for] fifty. 文例↓
ちがい 違い (a) difference; (a) distinction〈区別〉(a) disparity ¶年齢の違い (a) difference in age; an age difference／3分の違いで電車に乗り損なう miss the train by three minutes.
ちがいだな 違い棚 (fancy) alcove shelves.
ちがいない 違いない 〈確信〉I am sure; certainly; surely;〈推測〉must 〈be〉.
ちがいほうけん 治外法権 extraterritorial rights; extraterritoriality.
ちかう 誓う swear;《文》take an oath;《文》make a vow; give《文》pledge *one's* word; promise 《to do》 ¶神に誓う swear by God／禁酒を誓う swear off drinking; take the pledge (おどけて言うことも多い)／誓って on [《文》upon] my word [honor]. 文例↓
ちがう 違う differ 《from》; be different 《from》;〈種々に〉vary 《from》;〈間違う〉be mistaken; go [be] wrong;〈一致しない〉disagree 《with》 ¶違った, 違っている〈異なる〉different;〈別の〉distinct; another;〈間違った〉wrong; mistaken／まるで[全く]違う be completely [entirely] different 《from》;《文》differ entirely 《from》; be a far cry 《from》／見本と違う be not the same as the sample; do not come up to (the) sample／寸分違わないbe quite the same; be exactly alike. 文例↓
ちがえる 違える 〈変更する〉change; alter;〈間違える〉make a mistake;〈関節を〉put 《*one's* elbow》out of joint; sprain 《*one's* ankle》;〈筋を〉strain; pull 《a muscle》¶言い方を違える otherwise; rephrase 《a statement》／薬を飲み違える take the wrong medicine／道を違えて行く go by another [a different] route.
ちかく¹ 地殻 the earth's crust ¶地殻運動 tectonic [crustal] movements／地殻変動 diastrophism.
ちかく² 知覚〈認識〉《文》(sense) perception;〈意識〉consciousness ¶知覚する《文》perceive; be conscious of; feel／知覚を失う lose consciousness;《文》fall insensible／知覚神経 a sensory nerve／知覚動詞《文法》a verb of perception／知覚力 (powers of) perception;《文》ability to perceive.
ちかく³ 近く〈近々〉shortly; before long; in a short time; in the near future;〈ほとんど〉almost; nearly ¶100 名近く nearly [little less than] one hundred persons／夕暮れに近く toward evening／近くなる《文》be near [close] at hand; draw near／近くに near; close (by [to]); in the neighborhood 《of》／学校のすぐ近くに住む live near [just by] the school／近くで見る see *sth* at close range [《口語》up close]. 文例↓
ちがく 地学 earth science.
ちかごろ 近頃〈近来〉lately;《文》of late; recently;〈当節〉nowadays; these days; now; today ¶recently は過去時制・現在完了時制の文で使われるもので, 単純現在時制の文ではあまり使わない。また, lately, of late は現在完了時制の文で, 主に疑問文・否定文で使われる ¶近頃の recent; modern (近代の)／近頃の出来事 a recent event／《文》an event of recent occurrence／近頃にない大地震 the severest earthquake in (recent) years [《英》for years]／近頃まで until lately [recently]. 文例↓
ちかしい 近しい close; friendly ¶…と親し

ちかい³ 学年末が近い. The end of the school year is not far away [nearly on us].／近いうちに桜も咲くでしょう. It won't be long before the cherry blossoms are out.／郵便局はここから近い. The post office is only a little way from here.／It isn't far to the post office.／この道を行こう. そのほうが近い. Let's take this way. It's shorter.／解決は近いところにある. We won't have to look far for a solution.／猿のうちでゴリラが人間に一番近いという人もある. Some people say that of the apes the gorilla comes closest [nearest] to being human.／月は地球にもっとも近い天体である. The moon is the heavenly body nearest (to) the earth.／もう夕暮れに近い. It is nearly dusk.／彼の倹約はりんしょくに近い. His frugality verges [borders] on stinginess.／彼は 100 万円近い金をなくしてしまった. He lost a sum in the neighborhood of one million yen.

ちかい 田中君は私と 5 つ違いの年上[年下]だ. Tanaka is five years older [younger] than me. ⇨ より² 用法.

ちがいない 彼は試験に落ちたに違いない. He must have failed the examination.／いい方法には違いないが, 実行が困難だ. It is a good method, to be sure, but it will be difficult to put into practice.

ちかう この事は絶対に他人には言いません, 誓います. I give you my word (of honor) that I shan't tell anyone about this.／助け合うことを誓った. We promised to stand by each other.

ちがう 私の考えは違う. I don't share that opinion.／I don't think so [that way].／He どこか違うか. How else [In what other respects] are they different?／あの人は常人と違った所がある. There is something extraordinary about him.／《文》He is not as other men are.／僕と違って弟は勉強家だ. Unlike me my

ちかちか　　　　　　　　　　　　　　　　　　　　　　　　　　　　　　　　　ちぎ

い仲である be close to...; be friendly with...; be good friends with...; be on friendly terms with....
ちかちか ¶ちかちかする glitter; flicker.
ちかぢか 近々 ⇨ ちかく³.
ちかづき 近付き〈交際〉friendship;《文》acquaintance;〈知人〉an acquaintance ¶全然近付きのない人 an utter stranger / 近付きになる ⇨ ちかづく. [文例]
ちかづく 近付く〈自分・対象が〉approach; draw [come] near;〈知り合いになる〉get [《文》become] acquainted (with); make sb's acquaintance ¶終わりに近付く draw to a close / 完成に近付く《文》be near [nearing] completion / 近付きやすい〈人が〉approachable;〈場所が〉accessible;《文》easy of approach [access] / 近付き難い〈人が〉unapproachable;〈場所が〉inaccessible;《文》difficult of approach [access]. [文例]
ちかづける 近付ける bring [put] sth close (to); bring (A) near (to) (B);〈接近を許す〉allow sb to come near;〈交わる〉associate with; keep company with ¶近付けない keep sb away [at arm's length]; avoid (sb's company).
ちかてつ 地下鉄 an underground railway;《米》a subway;《英》the underground (Underground); the Tube (ロンドンの);〈パリなどの〉the Metro ¶地下鉄に乗る take a subway train [the Underground] / 地下鉄で行く go by subway [underground]. [文例]
ちかみち 近道 a shorter way; a shortcut ¶経済的安定を得る近道 a shortcut to economic stability / 近道をする take a shortcut [a shorter way] (to).
ちかよる 近寄る ⇨ ちかづく.
ちから 力〈体力〉(physical) strength;《文》might;〈物の力〉force; power;〈働き〉《文》agency;〈語勢〉stress; emphasis;〈努力〉effort; exertion;〈助力〉assistance; support;〈能力〉ability;《文》capacity;〈資力〉means; resources / 蒸気の力 the power of steam / 語学の力 one's linguistic ability / 力がある〈強い〉be strong;《文》be mighty / 力がない be weak; be feeble; do not have much strength / 力が付く gain strength / 力が抜ける lose (all) one's strength / 力の及ぶ限り as hard as one can; to the best [《文》utmost] of one's ability / 力を合わせる cooperate; join forces [hands] / 力を入れて言う emphasize [lay stress on] (one's words); 《文》emphasize...; lay stress on... / 子供の教育に力を入れる regard the education of one's children as important [《文》as of importance] / その言葉に力を得る be encouraged by those words / 力を落とす be disappointed; be discouraged; lose courage [heart] / 力を出す bring one's ability into (full) play;《文》put forth one's strength / 力を付ける cheer sb up; encourage / 力にする, 力と頼む rely [depend, count] on (《文》upon) / 力を貸す help; assist;《文》give [be of] assistance to; stand by / 力に及ばない [余る] be more than one can do; be beyond [not in] one's power / 力に任せる by (main) force; with all one's might [strength] / 力一杯 with all one's strength [《文》might]; 《文》with might and main / 力一杯やる do one's best [《文》utmost] / 力なく, 力なげに helplessly / 力関係 a power relationship / 力関係で according to (their) relative strength / ...に力こぶを入れる put [《文》lay] emphasis on...; give importance to...; show enthusiasm [《文》zeal] for...;〈後援する〉back up (a project) with enthusiasm / 力こぶを作る flex one's muscles; flex one's arm to make the muscle stand out / 力仕事 physical labor; a job that requires muscle power; heavy physical work / 力ずくで by force; by sheer strength;《文》by main force / 力試し〈腕力の〉a trial of (one's) strength;〈能力〉a test of one's ability / 力強い〈強力な〉powerful;《文》mighty; strong;〈議論など〉forceful;〈気強い〉reassuring / 力持ち a powerful man; a man with [《文》of] great (physical) strength / 力わざ a feat of strength. [文例]
ちかん¹ 弛緩 ⇨ しかん⁴.
ちかん² 痴漢 a molester of women;《口語》a groper (人混みの中などの); a (would-be) rapist.
ちかん³ 置換《数》permutation.
ちき 知己 ⇨ ちじん, しりあい.
ちぎ 千木 ornamental crossbeams on the gable of a *Shinto* shrine.

---

brother is a hard worker. / 習慣は国によって違う。Customs differ from country to country../ Different countries have different customs. / これは道が違いはしないか。Haven't we taken the wrong way? / それは違う。It isn't true. / 今年のジャイアンツは去年のジャイアンツとは違う。The Giants of this year are not what they were last year.

ちかく 私は近く渡米します。I am going over to America shortly. / 休暇もいよいよ近くなった。The vacation is drawing to its end. / この近くに文房具店はありませんか。Is there a stationer's around [near] here?

ちかごろ あのような正直者は近頃珍しい。It's rare to meet such an honest man nowadays. / つい此頃の事です。It happened quite recently.

ちかづき お近付きになれてうれしいです。I am very glad to have met you. | I am very pleased to make your acquaintance. / あの方とは戦後にお近付きになったのです。I had the pleasure of getting to know him after the war.

ちかづく 春休みが近付いた。The spring vacation is approaching [is close at hand, is (just) around the corner]. / 波が荒くて我々は遭難船に近付けなかった。The high seas prevented us from approaching the distressed ship. / あんな連中には近付くな。Keep away from them.

ちかてつ 僕は地下鉄に乗って家へ帰るところだった。I was going home on the subway. / 地下鉄で３つ先の動物園駅まで行った。I took the subway three stops to the Zoo station.

ちから 力が出ない。I haven't the strength (for it). / 彼は非常に衰弱して歩く力もなかった。He was so weak that he had not got the strength to walk. / こうなっては力には力で対抗するほかない。We must meet force with force now. / 僕らの学校は運動競技に力を入れている。Sports are en-

ちきゅう 地球 the earth [Earth]; 《文》the globe ¶地球の terrestrial; 《文》earthly / 地球の反対側で half the globe [world] away / 地球以外の場所に生物が存在する可能性 the possibility of extraterrestrial life / 地球上で on earth; on the face of the earth / 地球儀 a (terrestrial) globe / 地球人 an earthling; an earthman / 地球物理学 geophysics.

ちぎょ 稚魚 fry; the young of fish ★ fry も young も単複同形．構文上はいずれも複数扱いが普通 ¶さけの稚魚 salmon fry.

ちきょう 地峡 an isthmus; a neck of land ¶パナマ[スエズ]地峡 the Isthmus of Panama [Suez].

ちきょうだい 乳兄弟[姉妹] a foster brother [sister].

ちぎり 契り 《文》a pledge; 《文》a vow.

ちぎる¹ 千切る 〈寸断する〉tear (to pieces); 〈もぎとる〉tear off; pluck off; pick.

ちぎる² 契る 《文》〈誓う〉pledge (oneself to do); 《文》vow /〈約束する〉promise.

ちぎれぐも 千切れ雲 broken [scattered] clouds.

ちぎれる 千切れる be torn off; come off ¶ちぎれた torn-off; tattered; broken. 文例⇩

チキン chicken ¶チキンカツ a chicken cutlet / チキンライス rice fried with chicken.

ちく 地区 a district; an area; a zone; a region ¶京浜地区 the Tokyo-Yokohama area [district].

ちくいち 逐一 〈詳しく〉minutely; in detail; fully;〈一々〉one by one ¶逐一報告する make a detailed report (of) / 逐一承知している know all [everything] (about).

ちくおんき 蓄音器 a gramophone; 《米》a phonograph.

ちくご 逐語 ¶逐語的に word for word;《文》verbatim; literally / 逐語訳 (a) word-for-word [literal] translation [《文》rendering].

ちくざい 蓄財 ¶蓄財する《文》accumulate [amass] wealth.

ちくさん 畜産 ¶畜産業 stock raising [farming]; stockbreeding; the livestock industry / 畜産業者 a stock raiser [farmer]; a stockbreeder / 畜産物 stock farm products.

ちくじ 逐次 〈一つずつ〉one by one;〈次々に〉one after another; successively.

ちくしょう 畜生 〈けだもの〉a dumb animal; a beast; a brute;〈ののしり〉Damn it!; Hang it (all)!; Blast (it [you])! ¶畜生同然の人間 a brute (of a man).

ちくじょう 逐条 ¶逐条審議する discuss 《a bill》article by article; go through 《a plan》 item by item.

ちくじょう² 築城 castle construction [building] ¶築城する construct a castle; fortify 《a hill》.

ちくせき 蓄積 《文》accumulation; storage ¶蓄積する accumulate;《文》amass; store (up) / 長期にわたる農薬の体内蓄積 a long-term accumulation [build-up] of agricultural chemicals in the body. 文例⇩

ちくたく 〈時計の音〉ticktock.

ちくちく ¶ちくちくする prick; prickle / 針でちくちく刺す prick sb with a needle / ちくちくする毛糸の下着 itchy woolen underwear.

ちくてい 築堤 embankment.

ちくでん 逐電 ¶逐電する run away;《文》decamp;《俗》beat it;《英俗》scarper.

ちくでん² 蓄電 ¶蓄電器 a [an electric] condenser / 蓄電池 a storage battery [cell];《英》an accumulator.

ちくのうしょう 蓄膿症 ozena.

ちくば 竹馬 ¶竹馬の友 a childhood friend; an old playmate.

ちぐはぐ ¶ちぐはぐの odd; irregular / ちぐはぐの靴 an odd pair of shoes / ちぐはぐである be not properly paired;〈話が〉be confused;《口語》be all mixed up; be incoherent; be (talking (arguing)) at cross-purposes (互いの議論や行動に). 文例⇩

ちくび 乳首〈動物の〉a teat (★哺乳びんの先につけるものも teat).

ちくり ⇨ちくちく ¶ちくりちくりとやる質問 a needling question / ちくりと痛いことを言う make a cutting remark (at); needle sb.

チグリス(がわ) チグリス(川) the Tigris (River) ¶チグリス・ユーフラテスの流域 the Tigris-Euphrates Valley.

チクロ 《化》(sodium) cyclamate.

ちくわ 竹輪 a fish paste cake in the form of a tube.

ちけい 地形 the lay [lie] of the land; geographical [natural] features; topography ¶地形図 a topographical [terrain] map; a contour map (等高線を示した); a relief map (等高線だけでなく，陰影・色彩その他の方法を用いた). 文例⇩

ちけん 知見 knowledge; information ¶知見を広める extend one's knowledge; add to one's stock of information.

ちこう 地溝 〖地質〗a rift valley.

ちこく 遅刻 ¶遅刻する be late (for); (to work) late; be behind time / 学校を遅刻する be late for school / 遅刻回数 the number

---

couraged in our school. / お互いに力になりましょう．Let us help each other. / 自分の力の足りない事は承知です．I am well aware of my lack of ability. / この仕事は私の力に及ばない．This work is too much for me. | 《文》I am not equal [am unequal] to this task. / 私には家を建てるだけの力がない．I can't afford [haven't enough money] to have a house of my own. / それは人間の力ではどうする事もできない．It is beyond human power. | It is humanly impossible. / 彼の英語の力は素晴らしい．His command of English is marvelous. | He has a wonderful command of English. / さぞお力落としでございましょう．I can well imagine how grieved you must be. / 力比べをしよう．Let us see which of us is the strongest. / その企ては力こぶを入れる程のものではない．The project is not worth much effort.

ちぎれる 寒くて耳がちぎれそうだ．My ears are tingling with the cold.

ちくせき 我々は蓄積効果不明の様様な化学物質を食物を通じて体内に取り入れている．With our food we are taking in various chemical substances whose cu-

ちこつ 恥骨 〖解〗the pubis (*pl.* -bes); the pubic bone.

ちし 地誌 a topography; a geographical description.

ちじ 知事 a (prefectural) governor ¶京都府知事原田氏 Mr. Harada, Governor of Kyoto Prefecture / 知事候補[選挙] a gubernatorial candidate [election].

ちしき 知識 knowledge; 〈見聞〉information; 〈実際の経験に対して〉book learning; theory ¶知識を広める[増す] widen *one's* knowledge; enlarge [add to] *one's* stock of knowledge / 知識階級 the educated class(es); intellectuals; the intelligentsia / 知識人 an intellectual / 知識体系 a body of knowledge / 知識欲が盛んである have a strong desire to learn. 文例②

ちじき 地磁気 terrestrial magnetism.

ちじく 地軸 the earth's axis ¶地軸を揺るがすようなとどろき a deep, earthshaking rumble.

ちしつ 地質 geological features;〈土質〉the nature of the soil ¶地質学 geology / 地質学者 a geologist / 地質年代〈地質学的記録しかない古い時代〉the geological age; geologic time;〈地質学上の一時代〉a geological era [age].

ちしま(れっとう) 千島(列島) the Kuril [Kurile] Islands.

ちしゃ 〖植〗(a) lettuce.

ちじょう¹ 地上 on the ground; surface《winds》/ 地上に[で] on the ground; on (the) earth / 地上での温度 temperature at ground [earth] level / 地上 300 メートルの所に at 300 meters above (the) ground / 地上性の terrestrial《animals》; ground-dwelling[-living]《monkeys》; ground《birds》/ 地上8階地下2階のビル a building with eight stories above ground and two below / 地上権 superficies / 地上施設 ground facilities / 地上誘導着陸方式〖航空〗ground control(led) approach (略: GCA) / 地上部隊〖兵力〗ground forces [strength]; land forces.

ちじょう² 痴情 ¶痴情による犯罪 a crime of passion.

ちじょく 恥辱 ⇒はじ.

ちしりょう 致死量 a fatal [lethal] dose.

ちじん 知人 an acquaintance; a friend ¶知人が多い have a wide [large] circle of acquaintances / 私の知人のイギリス人 an Englishman (that) I know; an English acquaintance of mine.

ちず 地図 a map;〈地図書〉an atlas ¶簡単な地図 a rough map / 5万分の1の地図 a map (drawn) on a scale of 1 to 50,000 / ボタンを押すと豆電球がつく地図 a push-button map / 地図の見方を教わる take lessons in map reading / 地図の見方をよく知っている be good at reading maps; be a good map-reader / まだ地図のない地域 a still uncharted [unmapped] area / 地図を書きかえる remap (Europe) / 地図を頼りに with the aid [help] of a map / 地図に出ている be on a map / 地図で探す look up (a place) on a map / 掛け[白, 道路]地図 a wall [blank, road] map.

ちすい 治水 river improvement; flood control ¶治水工事 flood prevention works.

ちすじ 血筋〈血統〉《文》lineage; descent;《文》stock;〈血縁〉blood relationship ¶...の血筋を引いている〈子孫である〉be descended from...;〈血族関係である〉be related by blood to.... 文例②

ちせい¹ 地勢 the lay [lie] of the land; geographical [natural] features; topography.

ちせい² 治世 a reign; a rule; a regime ¶...の治世中に in [during] the reign of....

ちせい³ 知性《文》intellect; intelligence ¶知性的な intellectual.

ちせつ 稚拙 ¶稚拙な naive; artless.

ちそう 地層 a (geologic) stratum (*pl.* -ta); a layer ¶地層図 a strata map.

ちたい¹ 地帯 a zone; a region ¶工場地帯 an industrial area.

ちたい² 遅滞 (a) delay ¶遅滞する delay;〈滞る〉be overdue; be in arrears;《文》be delinquent《納税などが》/ 遅滞なく without delay.

チタン, チタニウム 〖化〗titanium.

ちち¹ 父 a father ¶父の, 父らしい fatherly; fatherlike; paternal / 父の日 Father's Day / 父方の on *one's* father's [the paternal] side / 父方の祖母 *one's* paternal grandmother.

ちち² 乳 milk;《文》the breast《母乳》;〈乳房〉a breast ¶乳のような, 乳色の milky / 乳をしぼる milk《a cow》/〈子に〉乳を飲ませる suckle《a child》《on *one's* breast》; give the breast to《a baby》; feed [nurse] (an infant) (at the breast) /〈子が〉乳を飲む suckle; take *one's* milk; nurse /〈牛が〉よく乳を出す milk well / 乳を出さなくなった牛 a cow that has stopped giving milk; a dry cow / 乳臭い smelling of milk /〈小児らしい〉babyish;〈未熟な〉green《youths》/ 乳しぼり milking / 乳離れ ⇒ちばなれ.

ちち³ 遅々 ¶遅々たる slow;《文》tardy /〈工事などが〉遅々として進まない make very slow progress; progress at a snail's pace.

---

mulative effects are unknown.

ちぐさ これらの考えは, 人種的偏見なんかない, と言った彼女の前の宣言とはちぐはぐだ. It is hard to square these views with her earlier declaration that she has no racial prejudice.

ちけい 道路は, 地形的に可能な限り, まっすぐに造られていた. The road was as straight as the lay [lie] of the land permitted.

ちしき 彼は多少園芸の知識がある. He has some knowledge of gardening. / あの人は世間的知識が乏しい. He knows nothing of the world. / 知識は力なり. Knowledge is power. / 人間知識だけでは実際の役に立たない. Book learning is not enough to make you an able man in practice. | Theory without practice is not much use.

ちじょう¹ 地上はまだ雪で覆われている. The ground is still covered with snow.

ちすじ 血筋は争えないものだ. Blood will tell. / あの人は血筋がいい. He comes of good stock.

ちち² うちで飼っている牛の中では, これが一番よく乳を出します.

ちち⁴ ¶ちちと鳴く chirp; chirrup.
ちちに ¶千々に ¶千々に心を砕く think [worry] about this, that, and the other [about a thousand and one things]. 文例⇩
ちちまる 縮まる ⇨ ちぢむ.
ちぢみ 縮み cotton crepe ¶縮みのシャツ a crepe undershirt / 縮み止めのしてある preshrunk; 《商標名》Sanforized.
ちぢみあがる 縮み上がる shrink (up); 〈恐れて〉quail [cower] (before, at). 文例⇩
ちぢむ 縮む shrink; dwindle; contract; 《文》diminish (in size); 〈しわがよる〉wrinkle; shrivel. 文例⇩
ちぢめる 縮める〈短縮する〉shorten; shrink; reduce; lessen; 〈省略する〉abridge; 〈衣服を〉take in ¶足を縮める draw in one's legs / ベルトを3センチ縮める take in [shorten] a belt by three centimeters / 記録を縮める improve on [break] the (previous [existing]) record / 首を縮める 〈物の下をくぐる時〉duck one's head; 〈身振り〉shrug one's shoulders. 文例⇩
ちちゅう 地中 ¶地中の underground / 地中に in the earth [ground].
ちちゅうかい 地中海 the Mediterranean (Sea).
ちぢらす 縮らす crisp; 〈髪を〉curl; wave; crimp [frizzle] (one's hair) (細かく); 〈しわにする〉wrinkle; shrink.
ちぢれげ 縮れ毛 curly [wavy] hair; curls; frizzled [crimpy] hair (細かく縮れた) ¶縮れ毛の curly-haired[-headed]; wavy-[frizzly-]haired.
ちぢれる 縮れる〈髪などが〉be wavy; curl; be curled; 〈しわになる〉be shrunk ¶縮れた〈巻き毛に〉curled; curly; 〈波形に〉wavy; 〈細かく〉frizzled; crinkly / 縮れた木の葉 a crinkled leaf. 文例⇩
ちつ 膣〔解〕the vagina.
チッキ ¶手荷物をチッキにする have one's baggage sent separately by rail; 《米》have one's baggage checked.
ちっきょ 蟄居 ¶蟄居する stay in [do not leave] the house; shut oneself up in one's house.
チック 〈<《フランス語》cosmétique〉hair oil [cream] (in stick form).
ちっこう 築港 harbor construction [improvement] ¶築港する construct [improve] a harbor / 築港工事 harbor works.
ちつじょ 秩序 order; 〈組織〉(a) system; 〈規律〉discipline ¶秩序ある orderly; systematic / 秩序が乱れている be in disorder; be out of order / 秩序のない disorderly; unsystematic; confused / 社会の秩序を保つ[乱す] maintain [disturb] public order / 秩序整然たる well-ordered / 秩序整然としている be in good [perfect] order / 秩序立てる put sth in order; 《文》systematize.

ちっそ 窒素 《化》nitrogen ¶窒素を含んだ, 窒素(性)の nitrogenous / 空中窒素 atmospheric nitrogen / 窒素固定(法) nitrogen fixation / 窒素肥料 (a) nitrogen fertilizer.
ちっそく 窒息 suffocation ¶窒息する suffocate; choke; be suffocated; be choked; be smothered / 窒息して死ぬ suffocate; be suffocated; choke [be choked, be smothered] to death.
ちっちゃい tiny; little ⇨ ちいさい ¶赤ん坊のちっちゃい指 a baby's tiny fingers.
ちっと ⇨ ちょっと ¶(not) a bit; (not) at all; (not) a bit; (not) in the least; 〈少しの時間も〉(not) for a moment. 文例⇩
チップ¹ 〈茶代・祝儀〉a tip; 《文》a gratuity ¶チップを置く leave a tip (on the plate) / チップをやる tip (the waitress a dollar); give sb a tip / チップをはずむ客 a high-tipping customer; a good [generous] tipper.
チップ² 〔野球〕¶チップしてファウルになる tip the ball foul.
ちっぽけ ¶ちっぽけな very small; tiny; 〈くだらない〉《口語》footling; petty.
ちてい 地底 the bottom (of a hole in the ground [of a cave]) ¶地底から from deep under the ground.
ちてき 知的 intellectual; mental ¶知的生活[職業] an intellectual life [occupation] / 知的能力 《文》one's intellectual powers; 《文》one's mental faculties.
ちてん 地点 a spot; a place.
ちどうせつ 地動説 the heliocentric [Copernican] theory.
ちどめ(ぐすり) 血止め(薬) a styptic.
ちどり 千鳥 a plover ¶千鳥足で歩く walk drunkenly; reel along; weave one's way (along).
ちなむ 因む be connected [associated] (with) ¶…にちなんで名付ける name (a child) after (his) grandfather) / ちなみに by the way; in passing; in this connection; incidentally.
ちねつ 地熱 terrestrial [geothermal] heat ¶地熱発電所 a geothermal (generating) plant.
ちのう 知能 intelligence; 《文》intellect; 《文》intellectual [mental] faculties ¶知能の遅れ mental retardation / 知能の遅れた子供 a mentally retarded child / 知能の発達 intellectual growth / 知能の優れた子供 an intellectually gifted child / 知能検査 an intelligence test / 知能指数 an intelligence quotient (略: IQ, I.Q.) / 知能犯 an intellectual offense [crime]; 〈人〉a thinking (《口語》smart) criminal.
ちのみご 乳飲み子 a babe [a baby, a child, an

Of the cows we keep, this one is the best milker.
ちちに 心が千々に乱れた. My heart was torn with conflicting emotions.
ちぢみあがる それは縮み上がるほどの痛みだった. I felt a wrenching pain.
ちぢむ これは洗っても縮まない. This won't shrink in the wash.
ちぢめる 彼は身を縮めてその間を通った. He squeezed himself through. / 彼は200メートルの平泳ぎで世界記録を1.2秒縮めた. He bettered the world record for the 200-meter breaststroke by 1.2 seconds.
ちぢれる その紙片はちりちりと縮れて燃え上がった. The piece of paper crinkled into flame.
ちっと 腹はすかないかい？ いいえ, ちっとも. Aren't you hungry?—No, not in the least. / 君がここにいるとはちっとも知らな

ちはい 遅配 ¶給料の遅配 delayed payment of wages / 郵便の遅配 delay in mail delivery.

ちばなれ 乳離れ ⇨ りにゅう ¶乳離れさせる wean / 乳離れした[しない]子供 a weaned [an unweaned] child. 文例⬇

ちび 〈小さい人〉《口語》a shrimp;《口語》a pipsqueak;〈子供〉a kid ¶ちびである be very short [small]; be undersized.

ちひょう 地表 the surface of the earth; the earth's surface ¶地表温度 ground temperature; temperature at ground level.

ちび(り)ちび(り) little by little; bit by bit ¶酒をちびりちびり飲む sip (at one's) sake; drink one's liquor in thimblefuls [in dribs and drabs] / 金をちびちび使う use one's money in driblets [in dribs and drabs].

ちびる 禿びる wear away [out] ¶ちびた筆 a worn-out writing brush / ちびた鉛筆 a stubby pencil.

ちぶ 恥部 the genitals;〈婉曲的に〉the private parts; the privates. 文例⬇

ちぶさ 乳房 a breast; the breasts ¶乳房をふくませる《文》give the breast (to one's baby).

チフス 〈腸チフス〉typhoid (fever); enteric fever;〈発疹チフス〉typhus.

ちへいせん 地平線 the horizon ¶地平線上に above the horizon; on the horizon (接して) / 地平線下に below the horizon.

チベット Tibet ¶チベットの Tibetan / チベット語 Tibetan / チベット人 a Tibetan.

ちほ 地歩 one's stand; a footing; a position ¶地歩を占める take one's stand; get [gain] a footing (in society) / 地歩を失う lose one's footing; lose ground / 社会的地歩を築く build up one's social position. 文例⬇

ちほう 地方 〈地域〉a region; a district; a locality;〈首都に対して〉the provinces;〈いなか〉the country;〈...付近〉neighborhood; vicinity ¶地方的[の] provincial; local; regional / 関西地方 the Kansai region / 京都地方 Kyoto and its neighborhood / 地方の中心都市 a district [provincial] capital / この地方に[では] in these parts; in this part of the country / 地方に行く go into [down to] the country / (セールスマンなどが)地方回りをしている be on the road / 地方行政 local administration / 地方公務員 a local government employee [worker] / 地方裁判所 a district court / 地方自治体 a local government;《英》a local authority;《米》the State (County, City, etc.) government;《英》the local [county, city] council;〈市〉a municipality ★ local self-governing body などと直訳すると英米では通じないおそれがあるので避けるべきである / 地方色 local color / 地方税 a local tax;《英》the rates / 地方政治 local politics [government] / 地方版 a local-news section [page] / 地方分権 decentralization of power [authority].

ちまき 粽 a cake wrapped in bamboo leaves.

ちまた 巷 a street ¶戦火のちまた a scene of battle / ちまたのうわさでは according to what people say; according to the rumors going around (the town).

ちまなこ 血眼 ¶血眼になって捜す look for sth frantically [in a frenzy]; make a frantic search for sth.

ちまみれ 血塗れ ¶血まみれになる be covered [smeared] with blood; get bloodied / 血まみれの bloodstained.

ちまめ 血豆 a blood blister.

ちまよう 血迷う lose one's head; lose control of oneself; forget oneself; run [go] mad; go wild; be in a frenzy ¶血迷った frenzied.

ちみ 地味 the fertility of the soil. 文例⬇

ちみち 血道 ¶血道をあげる〈異性に〉be head over heels in love (with); be besotted (by); be completely infatuated (with, by);《口語》be (dead) gone on (a woman);〈遊び事に〉be obsessed with [give oneself up to] (gambling).

ちみつ 緻密 ¶緻密な〈精密な〉minute; fine;〈精確な〉accurate;〈精巧な〉elaborate / 緻密な観察 (a) careful [close] observation / 緻密な計画 a carefully thought-out plan / 綿密に練った計画 a finely worked-out plan / 緻密な頭の人 a person capable of precise thinking / 緻密に minutely; accurately; elaborately.

ちめい¹ 地名 the name of a place; a place name ¶地名辞典 a geographical dictionary; a gazetteer.

ちめい² 知名 ¶知名の well-known; noted / 知名度によって人を評価する judge sb by how widely he is known.

ちめい³ 致命 ¶致命的 fatal; lethal; deadly / 致命的打撃を与える deal sb a fatal blow [deathblow] / 致命傷 a fatal [《文》mortal] wound / 致命傷を受ける[負う] be fatally wounded; suffer a mortal wound. 文例⬇

ちゃ 茶 〈木〉a tea plant [bush];〈飲料〉tea ⇨ おちゃ ¶濃い[薄い] 強い strong [weak] tea / 茶の木 a tea plant [bush] / 茶の支度をする get the tea ready;《文》prepare the tea / 茶を1杯飲む have a cup of tea / 茶を摘む pick tea / 茶を入れる make (a cup [pot] of) tea / 茶を入れ替える make a fresh pot of tea / 茶を入れるために湯を沸かす boil water for tea / (茶の湯の)茶を立てる perform the tea ceremony / 茶を飲みながら話す talk over (a cup of) tea /〈客に〉茶を出す serve tea / 茶を飲む drink tea / 茶菓子 cakes served at [with] tea / 茶釜 a teakettle; a

---

かった. I had no idea (at all) that you were here. / 彼の言う事は何の事だかちっとも分からない. I can make (absolutely) nothing of what he says.

ちばなれ 太郎はもう乳離れしました. Taro is weaned now. / 彼はまだ(精神的に)乳離れしていない. He's still tied to his mother's apron strings.

ちぶ この地域は我が国の恥部である. We are ashamed to have such an area as this in our country.

ちほ 彼は実業家としての地歩を固めた. He established himself as a businessman.

ちみ 地味が肥えて[やせて]いる. The soil is fertile [infertile]. / 地味が米作に適さない. The soil is not suitable for [suited to] the cultivation of rice.

ちめい³ その傷が致命傷となった. The wound proved fatal. / それは日本の海外貿易にとって致命的

kettle / 茶殼 used tea leaves / 茶さじ a teaspoon / 茶室 a tea-ceremony room [house] / 茶筅(෭) a tea whisk [stirrer] / 茶托 a saucer / 茶つぼ[筒] a tea canister [caddy] / 茶道具, 茶器 tea-things ; 〈一組の〉a tea set [service] / 茶飲み話 a chat (over tea); gossip / 茶箱 a tea chest / 茶畑[園] a tea plantation [estate]. 文例⇩

チャーター chartering ¶チャーターする charter 《a ship》/ チャーター機 a chartered plane / (飛行場の)チャーター便 a charter flight.

チャーハン 炒飯 (Chinese) fried rice (with eggs, shrimps, etc.).

チャイム a chime ; 〈連続して鳴る〉chimes. 文例⇩

ちゃいろ 茶色 brown (color).

ちゃかす 茶化す make fun of ; poke fun at.

ちゃかっしょく 茶褐色 dark brown.

ちゃきちゃき ¶ちゃきちゃきの〈純粋の〉pure ; genuine ; thoroughbred ; full-blooded ; 〈一流の〉first-class ; leading ¶江戸っ子のちゃきちゃき a true [hundred-percent] Edokko.

-ちゃく …着 ⇨とうちゃく ¶洋服1着 a suit of clothes / ズボン1着 a pair of trousers / 最近着の『タイム』the latest [most recent] issue of *Time* (to arrive) / 5時上野着の列車 the train due (to arrive) at Ueno at 5 / 第1[2]着になる come in first [second]. 文例⇩

ちゃくい 着衣 ¶着衣のまま with *one's* clothes on / 着衣の人像 a clothed [draped] figure.

ちゃくえき 着駅 the destination station.

ちゃくがん 着眼 ¶着眼する〈ねらう〉aim at ; 〈留意する〉turn *one's* attention to / 着眼点《文》the point to which *one* has directed *one's* attention ; the point aimed at / 着眼点がいい know where to look ; be perceptive ; have a sure eye (for). 文例⇩

ちゃくじつ 着実 ¶着実な steady ; sure and steady ; sound / 着実な営業振り sound business methods / 着実に steadily.

ちゃくしゅ 着手 ¶着手する start (on) *sth* [to *do, doing*] ; 《米》start in on *sth* [to *do*] ; set about *sth* [*doing*] ; undertake *sth* ; begin (on) *sth* [to *do, doing*] ; make a start on *sth* ; put *sth* in hand ¶仕事に着手する set [get] to work ; set about *one's* business. 文例⇩

ちゃくじゅん 着順 the order of arrival.

ちゃくしょく 着色 coloration ; coloring ¶着色する color ; paint ; stain / 着色ガラス colored glass / 着色剤[材料] a coloring agent [material] ; a colorant / 食品[人工]着色料 (a) food [(an) artificial] coloring.

ちゃくすい 着水 ¶着水する land [《文》alight] on the water ; 〈宇宙船が〉splash down.

ちゃくせき 着席 ¶着席する《文》take *one's* seat ; sit down / 着席している《文》be seated / 着席順に in the order of seats / 着席券 a 'seat ticket' ; a ticket entitling a passenger to a seat in a non-reserved-seat train. 文例⇩

ちゃくそう 着想 an idea ; a conception ¶着想が浮かぶ an idea occurs to *one* ; 〈人が主語〉hit on an idea / 着想がよい《文》be cleverly conceived ; be good.

ちゃくだつ 着脱 ¶着脱に便利である be easy to put on and take off (quickly) [to get on and off] ; can be easily put on and taken off.

ちゃくち 着地〈体操などの〉landing ¶着地する land 《on a mat》/ うまく着地する[着地に失敗する] make a good [poor] landing.

ちゃくちゃく 着々 steadily ; step by step ¶着々進行する make steady [good] progress [headway] ; 《文》progress steadily.

ちゃくにん 着任 ¶着任する arrive at *one's* post.

ちゃくふく 着服 ¶着服する embezzle ; 《口語》pocket.

ちゃくよう 着用 ¶着用する wear ; have 《a morning suit》on.

ちゃくりく 着陸 (a) landing ; touchdown (滑走路に車輪が着く) ¶着陸する land ; make a landing ; touch down / 〈飛行機が〉着陸のために進入してくる come in for a landing / 着陸の失敗で大破する crash on landing / 強制着陸をさせる force [make] down / 着陸場 a landing field [strip] / (宇宙探査用)着陸船 a landing module / 着陸装置 landing gear ; an undercarriage / 着陸地点 a touchdown point [spot]. 文例⇩

チャコ (a piece of) French [tailor's] chalk.

ちゃだい 茶代 ⇨チップ[1].

ちゃだんす 茶箪笥 a cupboard (for tea-things).

ちゃち ¶ちゃちな cheap ; small ; insignificant ; 〈造りが〉flimsy ; poorly-made ; 〈建物が〉jerry-built.

ちゃっかり ¶ちゃっかりした shrewd ; calculating ; 《米口語》nervy ; 《英口語》cheeky. 文例⇩

ちゃっかん 着艦 ¶着艦する〈飛行機が〉land

打撃であった. It was a deathblow to Japan's foreign trade.
ちゃ 茶さじに1杯の砂糖を入れなさい. Put a teaspoonful of sugar in it. / 茶柱が立つのは縁起がいい. It is a sign of good luck to have a tea stalk floating erect in one's tea.
チャイム 玄関のチャイムが鳴った. The door chimes rang.
ちゃく 彼はレースで何着でしたか. —3着でした. How [Where] did he finish [come in] in the race?—He was [finished, came in] third.
ちゃくがん (論文などについて)彼は着眼がいい. He is well advised in his approach to the subject. / 君と僕とは着眼点が違うようだ. We seem to be directing our attention to different points.
ちゃくしゅ 何から着手しようか. What shall we begin with? | Where shall we start? | What shall we do first? / 我々はさっそく調査に着手した. We immediately set about making inquiries. / 工事は未着手です. No start has been made with the work yet.
ちゃくしょく 人工着色料含有.〈食品の表示〉Contains artificial colorants.
ちゃくすい 宇宙船は太平洋に無事着水した. The spaceship made a safe splashdown [splashed down safely] in the Pacific.
ちゃくせき 皆さん, ご着席を. Please be seated, ladies and gentlemen.
ちゃくそう その経験から素晴らしい着想が浮かんだ. From that ex-

チャック a zip fastener; a zipper; a zip ¶チャックを掛ける zip (up); do up a zipper / チャックを外す unzip; undo a zipper / かばんのチャックを開ける zip a bag open / チャック付きの zippered 《bags》; zipper 《jackets》.
[文例⇩]

ちゃづけ 茶漬け boiled rice with tea (poured on it); tea on rice; 〈簡単な食事〉a simple meal.

ちゃっこう 着工 ¶着工する start (construction) work.

チャド Chad ¶チャドの Chadian / チャド共和国 the Republic of Chad / チャド人 a Chadian.

チャドル 〈回教婦人の〉a chador.

ちゃのま 茶の間 a living room; 《米》a parlor; 《英》a sitting room.

ちゃのゆ 茶の湯 the tea ceremony.

ちゃばん 茶番 〈play〉a farce ¶茶番的 farcical; ridiculous; absurd.

ちゃぶだい ちゃぶ台 a low dining [tea] table.

ちゃぼ 〈鶏〉a bantam.

ちやほや ¶ちやほやする make a fuss of; pamper; indulge; spoil 《a child》.

ちゃみせ 茶店 ⇨ちゃや.

ちゃめ 茶目 〈いたずら〉mischief; 〈いたずらもの〉a scamp ¶茶目な 〈こっけいな〉playful; full of play [fun]; 〈いたずらな〉mischievous; 〈人〉puckish / 茶目な顔付き an arch look / 茶目をする play pranks.

ちゃや 茶屋 〈茶商〉a tea store [shop]; a tea dealer 〈人〉; 〈茶店〉a teahouse.

ちゃらちゃら ¶ちゃらちゃら音がする[させる] jingle.

ちゃらんぽらん ¶ちゃらんぽらんを言う say irresponsible things; talk irresponsibly.

チャリティーショー a charity show.

ちゃりん a clink ¶ちゃりんという clink.

チャルメラ 〈<《ポルトガル語》*charamela*〉a street vendor's flute.

ちゃわいい 〈可愛い〉=さわかい.

ちゃわん 茶碗 〈食事用〉a (rice) bowl; 〈湯飲み〉a teacup ¶茶わんに1杯 a bowlful [bowl] (of rice).

チャンス a chance; an opportunity ¶絶好のチャンス a golden [perfect] opportunity; a chance not to be missed / 少しでもチャンスがあれば given [if one gets] half a chance / チャンスをうかがう wait for an [one's] opportunity / チャンスをつかむ seize a chance [an opportunity] / チャンスをつかんで...する seize the chance to *do*; seize *one's* chance and *do* / チャンスを逃がす lose *one's* [the] chance; miss the [*one's*] opportunity.

ちゃんちゃんこ a padded sleeveless *kimono* jacket.

ちゃんちゃらおかしい laughable; ridiculous; 《口語》(be) a (big) joke.

ちゃんと 〈正しく〉properly; correctly; 《文》duly / 〈整然と〉neatly; tidily; in good order ¶ちゃんとした職業 a proper [steady] job; a regular occupation / ちゃんとした a decent [an upstanding] person / ちゃんとした服装をしている be tidily [neatly] dressed / ちゃんと座る sit properly; sit up straight / ちゃんと知っている know *sth* perfectly well; know *sth* for certain [for a fact]; be well aware 《of》/ ちゃんとした暮らしをする lead a decent life.
[文例⇩]

チャンネル a channel ¶NHKテレビ第1チャンネル NHK TV Channel 1 / チャンネルを選ぶ select channels / チャンネルを切り替える change the channel / 第6チャンネルにする turn to Channel 6 / チャンネル争い a dispute over which television program (they) should watch / 8チャンネルのテープレコーダー an eight-track tape recorder.

ちゃんばら a sword battle ¶ちゃんばら映画 a *samurai* picture (with plenty of sword-fights).

チャンピオン a champion.

ちゃんぽん 〈長崎料理〉*champon*; a dish of noodles with seafood, vegetables, etc. ¶ちゃんぽんに (all) together; mixed up / ちゃんぽんに飲む mix *one's* drinks ★ mix a drink と言えば「カクテルを作る」の意 / 酒とビールをちゃんぽんに飲む mix beer and *sake*.

ちゆ 治癒 〈文〉healing; recovery ¶治癒する 〈文〉heal; recover; be cured / 治癒し得る curable / 自然治癒 spontaneous recovery / 治癒率 a cure rate.

ちゅう¹ 中 ¶中ぐらいの middling; medium; mediocre / 中以上になる[以下に下がる] rise above [fall below] the average.

ちゅう² 宙 〈空間〉space; 〈大空〉the air; 〈中空〉midair ¶宙にぶら下がる hang [be suspended] in midair / 宙を踏んで歩くような気持ちである be [feel as if one is] walking on air / 宙に浮いている be floating in the air;

---

perience he came up with an excellent idea.

ちゃくよう 登校の際は制服着用のこと。Students must attend school in uniform. | 当日は礼服着用のこと。《案内状などで》Evening dress. | Dress: Formal.

ちゃくりく 次の着陸予定地はサンフランシスコだった。The next scheduled stop was San Francisco.

ちゃっかり あいつ、ちゃっかりしてるなあ。He's got a nerve [《英》cheek].

チャック その上着はボタン式ですかチャック式ですか。Does the jacket button or zip?

ちゃのま 色々のものがテレビを通じて直接茶の間に入りこむ。A lot of things come straight into your living room via television.

ちゃんと 部屋はちゃんと片づいている。The room is (kept) very tidy. / 用意はちゃんと出来ている。Everything is ready. / 切符はちゃんと買ってある。I've got my ticket all right. / ちゃんと机の上に置いたんだ。I am sure I put it on the desk. / 彼は家賃を月々ちゃんと払う。He pays his rent regularly every month. / あの男は家庭生活がちゃんとしていない。His home life isn't all that it ought to be.

チャンネル 第3チャンネルで何かいい番組をやっているそうだ。I hear there's something good on Channel 3. / そのチャンネルははっきり出なかった。Reception of that channel was poor. / うちでは子供がチャンネル権を握って

〈問題などが〉 be (still) up in the air ; be (still) undecided ; 〈議論·交渉などが〉 be inconclusive. [文例⇩]

ちゅう[3] 注 notes ⇨ ちゅうしゃく.

ちゅう- 駐… (accredited) to ; resident in ¶ 駐米日本大使 the Japanese ambassador to [in] the United States [at Washington] / 駐ソイタリア大使 the Italian ambassador to the Soviet Union [to the Kremlin].

-ちゅう …中 〈…の中で[の, に]〉 in ; within (以内) ; among (中でも) ; 〈…の間〉 during ; in (the course of) ; while ; 〈進行中〉 under 《investigation》 ¶ 食事中である be (just) eating ; be in the middle of dinner [breakfast, lunch, etc.] ; 《文》 be at table / 十中八九 in nine cases out of ten ; ten to one / 不在中 《文》 during [in] *one's* absence ; while *one* is away / 授業中 in class. [文例⇩]

ちゅうい 注意 〈留意·注目〉 attention ; notice ; 《文》 heed ; 〈用心〉 care ; caution ; precaution ; 〈助言〉 《a piece of》 advice ; 〈警告〉 (a) warning ¶ 注意する 〈心を留める〉 pay [give] attention 《to》 ; take notice [account] 《of》 ; 《文》 pay [give] heed 《to》 ; 《文》 heed ; 〈気を付ける〉 mind ; take care [be careful] 《of》 ; 〈用心する〉 beware 《of》 ; be cautious 《about》 ; look out 《for》 ; 〈忠告する〉 advise ; give advice 《to》 ; 〈警告する〉 warn ; give (a) warning ; caution 《*sb* against *sth*》 ; 〈指摘する〉 point out ; 〈思い出させる〉 remind 《*sb* of *sth*》 / 健康に注意する take care of *oneself* ; be careful about *one's* health / 食物に注意する be careful about what *one* eats / 注意が足りない[を怠る] be careless ; be inattentive ; 《文》 be negligent / 注意を促す call [draw] *sb's* attention 《to *sth*》 / 注意を引く attract (*sb's*) attention / 注意をそらす distract (*sb's*) attention 《from》 / 注意を向ける turn [《文》 direct] *one's* attention [mind] 《to》 / 注意すべき事実 a noteworthy fact / 注意すべき点 a point to notice / 注意深い careful ; cautious ; discreet / 注意して carefully ; attentively ; 《文》 with care [attention] ; cautiously / 注意事項 matters to be attended to ; hints ; 〈書物などに書く略語〉 N.B. (★ ラテン語 *nota bene* の略) / (薬などの)注意書 directions / 注意人物 a person on the black list ; a suspicious character / 注意報 〘気象〙 a 《storm》 warning / 注意力 attentiveness. [文例⇩]

チューインガム chewing gum ; 〈1 枚〉 a stick of (chewing) gum ¶ チューインガムをかむ chew gum.

ちゅうおう[1] 中央 the center ; the middle ¶ 中央の central ; middle / …の中央に at [in] the center of… ; in the middle of… / 町の中央にある be (situated) in the center of the town / 中央アジア Central Asia / 中央気象台 the Central Meteorological Observatory / 中央教育審議会 the Central Education Council / 中央銀行 a central bank / 中央集権 centralization (of administrative power) / 中央政府 the central [national] government / 中央突破 a frontal breakthrough / 中央部 the central part ; the midsection / 中央労働委員会 the Central Labor Relations Committee.

ちゅうおう[2] 中欧 Central Europe.

ちゅうおうアフリカきょうわこく 中央アフリカ共和国 the Central African Republic.

ちゅうおんぶきごう 中音部記号 〘音楽〙 the alto clef.

ちゅうか 中華 ⇨ ちゅうごく ¶ 中華人民共和国 the People's Republic of China / 中華そば Chinese noodles / 中華民国 the Republic of China / 中華料理 Chinese food ; 〈料理法〉 Chinese cuisine [cooking] / 中華料理店 a Chinese restaurant.

ちゅうかい[1] 仲介 mediation ¶ 仲介する 《文》 mediate 《between》 ; 《文》 offer *one's* good offices 《in the dispute between, in the matter of》 ; 〈執り成す〉 intercede 《with A for B》 / 仲介の労を取る act as go-between [intermediary] / K 氏の仲介で 《文》 through the good offices of Mr. K / 仲介者 a mediator ; a go-between ; 〈周旋人〉 an agent ; a middleman.

ちゅうかい[2] 注解 ⇨ ちゅうしゃく.

ちゅうがい 虫害 damage from [done by] insects ¶ 虫害を受ける be damaged by insects / 虫害による不作 a crop failure due to an insect plague.

ちゅうがえり 宙返り a somersault ; 〈飛行機の〉 a loop ¶ 宙返りする turn [throw] a somersault ; 〈飛行機で〉 loop the loop / 宙返り飛行 a loop-the-loop flight.

ちゅうかく 中核 the kernel ; the core.

ちゅうがく 中学 a junior high school ; a middle school ¶ 中学を卒業する finish [graduate from] (a) junior high school ; complete the junior high school course / 中学に入る enter junior high (school) / 中学生 a junior high school student [boy, girl] / 私の中学時代に in my junior high school days ; when I was in junior high (school).

ちゅうがた 中形[型] ¶ 中形[型]の medium-

いる. The children have [hold] a monopoly of the TV channels in our family. / この機械では 9 チャンネルの特殊なテープが用いられている. This machine uses a special nine-track tape.

ちゅう[2] 彼は宙を飛んで帰った. He flew home [back].

-ちゅう 会は来月中に開かれる. The meeting will be held some time next month. / 今試験中です. An examination is in progress [is going on now].

ちゅうい 足元に注意なさい. Watch your step. / それは注意が足りないからだ. You should be more careful. | It happened because you didn't take enough care. / 子供にけがのないように注意して下さい. See [Take care] that the child does not get hurt./ この品の取り扱いは注意の上にも注意を要する. This article must be handled with the utmost care.| Extreme care must be used in handling this article. / ご注意ありがとう. Thank you for your kind advice [suggestion, warning]. / 火のそばへ行かないようにって, 何度注意したらわかるの. How often do I have to tell you to keep away from the fire? / 人は大抵衛生に関する注意が足りないから伝染病にかかる. People catch contagious diseases mainly through lack of attention to

ちゅうかん [middle-]sized ;《文》of medium size.

ちゅうかん¹ 中間 the middle ; in-between (groups) ; medium (中位の) / 中間的[の]立場をとる take a middle position 《between》/ 中間に midway [halfway] 《between》/ 中間駅 an intermediate station / 中間業者 a middleman / 中間色 neutral tints ; a color between 《blue and green》/ 中間搾取 intermediary exploitation / 中間試験 a midterm examination / 中間選挙〈米国の〉a midterm [an off-year] election / 中間報告 an interim report.

ちゅうかん² 昼間 (in) the daytime ; day ¶昼間人口 the daytime population 《of downtown Tokyo》. 文例⇩

ちゅうかんし 中間子〔物〕a meson.

ちゅうき¹ 中気 palsy ; paralysis ¶中気になる be paralyzed / 中気の[にかかった] be stricken with paralysis/be paralytic.

ちゅうき² 中期 the middle period ¶平安朝中期に in the middle of the Heian era.

ちゅうぎ 忠義 loyalty ;《文》devotion ¶忠義な loyal ; faithful ; devoted / 忠義を尽くす be faithful [devoted] to 《one's master》.

ちゅうきゅう 中級 中級の medium ;《文》of the middle class [intermediate rank] / 中級英文法〈書名〉An English Grammar for Intermediate Students / 中級ドイツ語〈書名〉Intermediate German.

ちゅうきょり 中距離 ¶中距離走 a middle-distance race / 中距離走者 a middle-distance runner.

ちゅうきん 忠勤《文》loyal [faithful] service ¶忠勤を励む《文》be a faithful servant (to) ; serve 《one's master》faithfully.

ちゅうきんとう 中近東 the Middle and Near East.

ちゅうくう 中空 ¶中空の〈うつろの〉hollow / 中空に in midair ; in the air.

ちゅうくらい 中位 ¶中位の medium ; middling ;〈大きさが〉middle-[medium-]sized ;《文》of medium size ;〈品質が〉《文》of medium quality. 文例⇩

ちゅうけい 中継 relay ¶中継する relay / 実況中継 a relay from the spot / 中継局 a relay station / 中継車 an outside broadcast van / (通信や競走の)中継点 a relay point / 中継放送 outside [relay] broadcasting ;〈番組〉an outside broadcast / 全国に中継放送する broadcast over a nationwide hookup.

ちゅうけん¹ 中堅 the backbone ; the mainstay ¶中堅作家 a writer of middle [medium] standing / 中堅手〔野球〕a center fielder. 文例⇩

ちゅうけん² 忠犬 a faithful dog.

ちゅうげん 中元 ¶中元の贈り物 a midyear present [gift] / 中元売出し a midyear sale.

ちゅうこ 中古 ¶中古の《文》¶中古車 a used car / 中古品 a secondhand article ; secondhand goods.

ちゅうこう¹ 中項〔数〕the middle term ¶比例中項 a mean proportional.

ちゅうこう² 忠孝 loyalty and filial piety.

ちゅうこうせい 昼行性 ¶昼行性の動物 a diurnal animal ; an animal of diurnal habit(s).

ちゅうこく 忠告 〈助言〉(a piece of) advice ;《文》counsel ;〈いさめ〉《文》(an) admonition ;〈警告〉(a) warning ; a caution ¶忠告する advise ; give sb (one's) advice ;《文》counsel sb (to do) ;〈戒める〉《文》admonish ; warn ; caution / 忠告を無視する take no notice of [《文》pay no heed to] sb's advice / 忠告に従う follow [take] sb's advice / 忠告者 an adviser. 文例⇩

ちゅうごく 中国 China ⇒ちゅうか ¶中国の Chinese / 中国語 Chinese ; the Chinese language / 中国共産党 the Chinese Communist Party / 中国人 a Chinese.

ちゅうごくちほう 中国地方 the Chugoku region.

ちゅうごし 中腰 ¶中腰で in a half-sitting posture ; half-sitting ; half-rising.

ちゅうざ 中座 ¶中座する leave before (the meeting) is over ; leave (the room) while (the party) is going on ; leave halfway through [in the middle of] 《dinner》.

ちゅうさい 仲裁 mediation ; peacemaking ;〔法〕(binding) arbitration ¶仲裁する mediate 《between》; arbitrate ; act as arbitrator [(a) peacemaker] / けんかを仲裁する settle [make up] a quarrel / 仲裁を頼む ask for arbitration/ 仲裁裁判所 a court of arbitration / 仲裁裁定 an arbitration award / 仲裁人[者] an arbitrator ; a mediator (調停者).

ちゅうざい 駐在 ¶駐在の《文》resident 《at, in》/ 駐在する《文》reside 《at, in》/ 駐在所 a police substation [box].

ちゅうさんかいきゅう 中産階級 the middle class(es) ; people in the middle-income brackets (of society) ; the bourgeoisie ; a bourgeois (一人).

ちゅうし¹ 中止 suspension ; cancellation ; stoppage ;《文》discontinuance ;〈延期〉postponement ¶中止する stop ; discontinue ; cancel

---

hygiene. / この家は採光に注意して建ててある。This house has been built with special attention paid to lighting. / この参考書を諸君に勧めるについては、ひと言注意しておかねばならない。A word of caution is necessary in recommending this book to you./ すりに注意。〔掲示〕Beware of pickpockets./ 信号は「注意」になっていた。The signal was at 'Caution'. / 警察は彼を注意人物にしている。The police have him under surveillance (observation). | The police have got their eye on him.

ちゅうかん 豊橋は東京と大阪の中間にある。Toyohashi lies halfway between Tokyo and Osaka.

ちゅうくらい 彼は高校2年の時は、やっと中位の成績だった。In his second year of high school, he was just managing to get average grades.

ちゅうけん 中産階級は国家の中堅である。The middle class forms the backbone of the nation.

ちゅうこく 彼は医者の忠告に従ってタバコをやめた。He gave up smoking on his doctor's advice./ 彼は私の忠告を全く耳に入れなかった。He turned a deaf ear to my advice.

ちゅうざい 同市には日本商社の駐在員が数人いる。There are a few representatives of Japanese firms

ちゅうし (a meeting); leave off 《work》; call off 《a strike》; give up 《doing》. 文例⇩

ちゅうし² 注視 ¶注視する observe *sth* closely; watch [look at] *sth* carefully; fix *one's* eyes on *sth* / 注視の的になる become the center of attention; have every eye fixed on one ⇨ ちゅうもく.

ちゅうじ 中耳 the middle ear; the tympanum 《*pl.* -na, -nums》¶中耳炎 otitis media; tympanitis; inflammation of the middle ear.

ちゅうじく 中軸 the axis; 〈中心人物〉 the central [leading] figure; a key [pivotal] man ¶中軸打線〔野球〕the leading hitters (of a team).

ちゅうじつ 忠実 faithfulness; 《文》fidelity ¶忠実な faithful; devoted; 《文》true; loyal / 忠実に faithfully; devotedly; loyally; 〈綿密に〉conscientiously / 職務に忠実である be faithful to *one's* duties; 《文》discharge *one's* duties faithfully / 〔再生装置の〕忠実度 fidelity.

ちゅうしゃ¹ 注射 (an) injection; 〔口語〕a shot; 〔口語〕a jab ¶注射する inject (a drug into *sb's* arm [*sb* with penicillin]); give *sb* an injection [a shot] / 注射をしてもらう get [receive] an injection / 注射液 an injection / 注射器 a syringe; a hypodermic (syringe); 〔皮下注射用〕an injector. 文例⇩

ちゅうしゃ² 駐車 ¶駐車する park (a car) / 駐車違反をする violate the parking regulations; get [pick up] a parking ticket 〈呼び出しカードを貼られる〉/ 駐車場 a car park; 〈米〉a parking lot; 〈建物〉a (five-story) parking garage / 駐車計 a parking meter / 駐車料金 a parking fee. 文例⇩

ちゅうしゃく 注釈 (explanatory) notes; 《文》(an) annotation ¶注釈する write notes (on a book);《文》annotate / 注釈付きの with notes;《文》annotated / 注釈者 an annotator / 注釈書 an annotated edition (of *Hamlet*).

ちゅうしゅう 中秋 ¶中秋の名月 the harvest moon.

ちゅうしゅつ 抽出 ¶抽出する extract (metal from ore); sample 《a population》/ 抽出検査 (a) sampling inspection; a spot check / 蒸留抽出物 a distilled extract (of).

ちゅうじゅん 中旬 the middle [second] ten days (of a month) ¶10月中旬に in mid-October; about [in] the middle of October.

ちゅうしょう¹ 中傷 (a) slander; a slur; 《文》aspersions ¶中傷する slander;《文》malign;《文》speak ill of; injure *sb's* reputation; cast a slur on *sb's* good name;《文》cast aspersions on [upon] *sb* [*sb's* honor]; stab *sb* in the back / 中傷的な libelous; slanderous.

ちゅうしょう² 抽象 abstraction ¶抽象的 abstract / 抽象的な思考をする think in the abstract [in abstractions] / 抽象画 an abstract painting / 抽象派〔美術〕abstractionism;〈人〉an abstractionist / 抽象美術 abstract art / 抽象名詞〔文法〕an abstract noun / 抽象論 an abstract argument; generalities. 文例⇩

ちゅうしょうきぎょう 中小企業 small and medium-sized enterprises; smaller businesses. 文例⇩

ちゅうしょく 昼食 lunch ⇨ **ゆうしょく¹** 用例 ¶昼食をとる have [eat] lunch / 昼食会 a luncheon / 昼食時に at lunchtime; in the lunch hour.

ちゅうしん¹ 中心 〈真中〉the center; the middle;〈焦点〉the focus;〈中核〉the core ¶中心となる take a leading part (in a project); play a central role (in a movement) / 中心の central; middle / 身体の中心をとる balance *oneself*; keep *one's* balance / 中心思想 the central idea / 中心示度〔気象〕the central pressure / 中心人物 the central [leading] figure / 中心勢力 the main strength 《of the Party》/ 工業の中心地 an industrial center / 中心点 the center; the central [center] point / 中心部 the central part; the heart (of a city) / 台風の中心部の風 the center wind of a typhoon. 文例⇩

ちゅうしん² 忠臣 a loyal [faithful] retainer [vassal, subject].

ちゅうしん³ 衷心 ¶衷心から《文》heartily; from (the bottom of) *one's* heart; with all *one's* heart / 衷心からの《文》hearty; heartfelt (gratitude).

ちゅうしんせい 中新世〔地質〕the Miocene epoch [period]; the Miocene.

ちゅうすい¹ 虫垂〔解〕the vermiform appendix ¶虫垂炎 appendicitis / 虫垂炎切除 (an) appendectomy.

ちゅうすい² 注水 ¶注水する pour water (into).

ちゅうすう 中枢 the center; the pivot; the hub ¶中枢産業 a pivotal [key] industry / 中枢神経系 the central nervous system (略: CNS, C.N.S.).

ちゅうせい¹ 中世 the Middle Ages; the medieval period ¶中世史 the medieval history.

ちゅうせい² 中性〔文法〕the neuter gender;《化》neutrality ¶中性の〔文法〕neuter;〔化〕

---

in the city.
ちゅうし 試合は中止〔雨で中止〕になった。The match was called off [rained out]. / 私は外国行きを中止した。I have given up the idea of going abroad. / これまでに進んだ仕事を中止するのは実に惜しい。What a shame [pity] it is to discontinue a job that has got so far!

ちゅうじく 小林氏を中軸としてこの仕事は推進されてきた。This work has been carried out with Mr. Kobayashi holding the key [central] position.

ちゅうしゃ¹ 痛み止めの注射をしてもらった。I had an injection to relieve the pain. / その病人は注射でもっていた。The patient was barely kept alive by injections.

ちゅうしゃ² その通りには駐車する場所がなかった。There was no parking place [space] along the street. / 駐車禁止。〔掲示〕No parking.

ちゅうしょう² 君の言う事はあまりに抽象的だ。You speak in too general terms.

ちゅうしょうきぎょう 父は中小企業の経営者でした。My father ran [owned] a small [medium-sized] business.

ちゅうしょく 我々は昼食を共にしながらそのことについて話し合った。We talked about it over

ちゅうせい neutral / 中性化した女性 a sexless woman / 中性子《物》a neutron / 中性微子《物》a neutrino 《pl. -s》.

ちゅうせい³ 忠誠 ¶忠誠を誓う《文》pledge one's[take the oath of] loyalty[allegiance]《to》.

ちゅうせい 中背 ¶中背の be of medium [middle] height; medium tall / 中背である be of medium height ⇨ちゅうにくちゅうぜい.

ちゅうせいだい 中生代《地質》the Mesozoic (Era).

ちゅうせいぶ 中西部《米国の》the Midwest; the Middle West ¶中西部の Midwest; Midwestern; Middle Western.

ちゅうせき 沖積 ¶沖積期 the alluvial epoch/ 沖積層 an alluvium 《pl. -ums, -via》/ 沖積土 alluvial soil

ちゅうぜつ 中絶《文》discontinuation;《文》discontinuance; stoppage; suspension; interruption ¶中絶する discontinue; suspend; interrupt /《事業などを》break off / 妊娠中絶 ⇨にんしん.

ちゅうせん 抽選 drawing lots; a lottery ¶抽選する draw lots; drawing lots; by lottery / 回転式抽選器 a lottery wheel / 抽選券 a lottery ticket. 文例↓

ちゅうソ 中ソ Sino-Soviet (relations).

ちゅうぞう 鋳造 casting; founding;《貨幣の》minting ¶鋳造する cast; found;《貨幣を》coin; mint; strike.

ちゅうたい¹ 中退 ⇨ちゅうと(中途退学する).

ちゅうたい² 中隊《軍》a company ¶中隊長 a company commander.

ちゅうだん 中段《階段の》the middle of the stairs; halfway up [down] the stairs;《寝台の》the middle bunk.

ちゅうだん² 中断《文》discontinuation;《文》discontinuance; interruption ¶中断される be discontinued; be interrupted; be suspended.

ちゅーちゅー ¶ちゅーちゅー鳴く《すずめなどが》twitter; chirp;《ねずみなどが》squeak.

ちゅうちょ 躊躇《ためらい》hesitation;《不決断》indecision ¶ちゅうちょする hesitate; waver;《文》be irresolute / ちゅうちょして[しながら]hesitatingly;《文》irresolutely / ちゅうちょなく, ちゅうちょせずに hesitation / ちゅうちょせずに…する do not hesitate to do; have no hesitation about [in] doing. 文例↓

ちゅうづり 宙吊り ¶宙づりになる hang [dangle, be suspended] in midair. 文例↓

ちゅうてつ 鋳鉄 cast iron.

ちゅうてん 中点《数》the middle point [median (point)]《between A and B》; the midpoint.

ちゅうと 中途 ¶中途に[で]halfway; midway / 坂の中途で halfway up [down] the hill / 橋の中途で halfway [part way] across the bridge / 中途から引返す turn back halfway / 中途退学する leave school without completing the course; leave college before graduation / 中途半端な halfway; half-finished; unsatisfactory / 中途半端な手段 half measures / 中途半端なやり方をする do by halves; leave sth half done. 文例↓

ちゅうとう¹ 中東 the Middle East.

ちゅうとう² 中等《等級》the middle class; the second grade;《質》medium quality;《中位, 並》mediocrity ¶中等の middle(-class); medium; middling / 中等学校 a secondary school / 中等教育 secondary education.

ちゅうとう³ 柱頭《建》a capital;《植》a stigma.

ちゅうどう 中道 ¶中道を歩む《文》take the golden mean; take [choose] a moderate course / 中道派 middle-of-the-roaders / 中道右[左]寄り (be) right [left] of center.

ちゅうどく 中毒 poisoning;《麻薬などの》(drug) addiction ¶中毒する be [get] poisoned 《by fish》/ 中毒になる get [《文》become] addicted《to narcotics》/《俗》get hooked《on heroin》/ 中毒症状を呈する develop [present] symptoms of poisoning. 文例↓

ちゅうとん 駐屯 ¶駐屯する be stationed《at, in》/ 駐屯地 a post; an army post; a garrison / 駐屯軍《守備の》a garrison;《占領地の》occupation forces.

チュートン ¶チュートンの Teutonic; Teuton / チュートン民族 the Teutonic race.

チューナー《ラジオ・テレビの》a tuner.

ちゅうなんべい 中南米 South and Central America; Latin America.

ちゅうにかい 中二階 the mezzanine (floor); 《フランス語》the entresol.

ちゅうにくちゅうぜい 中肉中背 ¶中肉中背の人 a person of medium [average] height and build; a middle-sized person.

ちゅうにち 中日《彼岸の》the day of the equinox.

ちゅうにゅう 注入 ¶注入する《物を》pour [put, pump] into;《薬液を》inject into; infuse 《考えを》instill《an idea》into《sb's mind》/ 注入液《医》an infusion(食塩水 など).

---

lunch.

ちゅうしん¹ 君の議論は中心を外している。Your argument is beside the point [wide of the mark]. / 原氏を中心としてフランス文学研究会が組織された。A society has been organized for the study of French literature, with Mr. Hara as leader [under the leadership of Mr. Hara].

ちゅうせん 抽選で僕の番号が当たった。Mine was a winning number in the lottery. / 準決勝の組み合わせの抽選は明日行なわれる。The draw for the semifinals will be made tomorrow.

ちゅうちょ その危険の大きさが私をちゅうちょさせた。The danger was so great that I hesitated. / それを買うのはだれでもちゅうちょするだろう。Anyone would think twice before he bought it.

ちゅうづり 登山者の一人が岩場からちゅうづりになっているのが見えた。One of the climbers was seen dangling on a rope from a ledge.

ちゅうと 本を読んでいると中途で他の本が読みたくなることがある。While reading a book I often feel like laying it down halfway through and starting on another./ 洋子は何事も中途半端にしない。Yoko does nothing by halves. / 今から出かけても時間が中途半端だ。If we start now, we shall arrive there at an awkward time.

ちゅうどく 一酸化炭素中毒はこわい。Carbon monoxide poisoning

ちゅうねん 中年 middle age; *one's* middle years ¶中年の男 a middle-aged man; a man in his middle life [years] / 中年を過ぎた人々 people past [over] middle age / 中年で死ぬ die in middle age / 中年ぶとりになる develop (a) middle-aged spread.

ちゅうは 中波 〖通信〗 a medium wave.

チューバ 〖楽器〗 a tuba.

ちゅうばいか 虫媒花 an insect-pollinated [entomophilous] flower.

ちゅうばんせん 中盤戦 〈囲碁・将棋〉 the middle game; 〈選挙などの〉 the middle phase 《of an election campaign》.

ちゅうび 中火 a medium flame [heat] ¶中火にする 〈ガス[電気]こんろを〉 turn the heat [flame, gas] (down [up]) to 'medium'; 〈オーブンを〉 set the oven at 'medium' / 中火で煮る〈ガス[電気]こんろで〉 cook over [on] a medium flame [heat]; cook with the gas turned [set] to 'medium'; 〈オーブンで〉 cook with the oven on medium [heat]; cook with the oven on [turned to] 'medium.'

ちゅうヒール 中ヒール 〈婦人靴の〉 a medium-high heel; a Cuban heel.

ちゅうぶ 中部 the central [middle] part; the midsection 《of a country》 ¶《日本の》中部地方 the Chubu region.

チューブ a tube; 〈タイヤの〉 an inner tube ¶チューブから絵の具を絞り出す squeeze paint from a tube / チューブ入り絵の具 tube colors.

ちゅうぶう 中風 ⇒ちゅうぶ¹.

ちゅうふく 中腹 ¶丘[山]の中腹に halfway up [down] a hill [mountain]; on a hillside [mountainside]. 文例⇩

ちゅうぶらりん 宙ぶらりん ¶宙ぶらりんになっている be left up in the air; be left half done; be pending.

ちゅうこ 古古 ¶中古の used; secondhand/中古で買う buy *sth* secondhand.

ちゅうべい 中米 Central America.

ちゅうへん 中編 〈小説〉 a short novel; a novelette.

ちゅうぼそ 中細 ¶中細の medium-point(ed) 《pen》; medium-fine 《woolen yarn》.

ちゅうみつ 稠密 ¶人口が稠密である〈場所が主語〉 be densely populated; have a high population density.

ちゅうもく 注目 attention; notice ¶注目する pay attention 《to》; watch; keep *one's* eye(s) 《on》; take notice 《of》/注目すべき notable; noteworthy / 注目される attract [draw] *sb's* attention; be watched / 多くの人々の注目を引く attract a great deal of [considerable] attention; be widely noticed. 文例⇩

ちゅうもん 注文 〈あつらえ〉 an order; 〈要求〉 a request; a demand ¶注文する order 《an article from a firm》; give [put in] an order 《for an article to a firm》/ 注文を取る take [accept] orders / 注文をつける make a special request; lay down [make] (specific) conditions / 注文に応じて作る make *sth* to order / 注文書 a written order; an order form 《書式》/ 注文取り a salesman / 注文品 an article on order; an article made to order (でき上がった). 文例⇩

ちゅうや 昼夜 day and night ¶1 昼夜 (for) twenty-four hours / 2 昼夜 two days and (two) nights / 昼夜兼行で働く work night and day / 昼夜交代で (work) in night and day shifts. 文例⇩

ちゅうゆ 注油 oiling; lubrication ¶注油する oil 《an engine》; lubricate / 注油を受ける be lubricated; receive lubrication.

ちゅうよう 中庸 moderation; 〖文〗 the (golden) mean; a [the] middle course [way]; 〈経書の〉 the Doctrine of the Mean ¶中庸を得た moderate; 中庸を得る be moderate; use [〖文〗 exercise] moderation; follow the golden mean; strike a happy mean.

ちゅうりつ 中立 ¶中立の neutral; independent (議員など) / 厳正中立の態度を崩さない 〖文〗 maintain an attitude of strict neutrality / 中立の立場で on neutral ground / 中立を守る observe [〖文〗 maintain] neutrality; stand neutral / 中立を侵す[尊重する] violate [respect] (a country's) neutrality / 中立国 a neutral power [country] / 非武装中立主義 unarmed neutralism / 中立(主義)政策 a neutrality [neutralist] policy / 中立地帯 a neutral zone.

チューリップ a tulip.

ちゅうりゃく 中略 an omission of a middle part 《of a sentence [passage]》 ¶中略の印に点々を打つ put suspension periods [points] 《between the two words》 ★この点々は three spaced periods (...) だ.

ちゅうりゅう¹ 中流 〈川の〉 the middle reaches [courses] (上流・下流に対して); midstream (川幅の中央)/ 〈階級の〉 the middle class ¶中流階級の人々 middle-class people; the middle classes. 文例⇩

ちゅうりゅう² 駐留 ¶駐留する be stationed

---

is very dangerous.

ちゅうふく その山の中腹にほこらがある. There is a small shrine halfway up the mountain. / 富士の中腹以上は雲に包まれていた. The upper half of Mt. Fuji was enveloped in clouds.

ちゅうもく 彼らがそのような運動に参加したことは注目すべきことである. It is worthy of notice that they took part in such a movement. / 彼の態度は多大の興味を以て注目されている. His attitude is being watched with keen interest. / 彼の新理論はあまり注目されなかった. His new theory did not receive much attention. / その新型自動車は世間の注目の的となった. The new model of that car has attracted a great deal of public attention. / こちらを見て下さい. May I have your attention, please.

ちゅうもん 私は新刊書を数冊英国へ注文した. I have ordered some new books from England. / こういう品はいつも注文が多い. There is always a great demand for this sort of product. / これは注文した靴です. These shoes were made to order. / ご注文は承りましたでしょうか. 〈ウェーターの言葉〉 Are you being served, sir? / 〈レストランで〉ウェーターが来て注文を聞いて行った. A waiter came up and took our orders. /

ちゅうろう (at, in); garrison 《a town》 / 在日アメリカ駐留軍 the U.S. forces (stationed) in Japan. 【文例⇩】

ちゅうろう 柱廊 a pillared corridor.

ちゅうわ 中和《化》neutralization; ⟨counteraction⟩ / 〈毒などの〉 a neutralize; 〈毒などを〉 counteract / 酸を塩基で中和する neutralize an acid with a base / 毒性を中和する neutralize a poison; counteract (the effects of) a poison.

チュニジア Tunisia ¶チュニジアの Tunisian / チュニジア共和国 the Republic of Tunisia / チュニジア人 a Tunisian.

チュニス Tunis.

ちょ¹ 著 a work ¶田中博士著 ...(written) by Dr. Tanaka.

ちょ² 緒 ¶緒につく be [get] started; be fairly under way; 〈計画など〉begin to take shape.

ちょいちょい 〈折々〉 (every) now and then;《口語》off and on; (just) occasionally; from time to time;〈しばしば〉often; frequently; 《文》at frequent intervals.

ちょう¹ ちょこ 〈はさみ 1 丁〉a pair of scissors.

ちょう² 兆 〈数の〉《米》a trillion;《英》a billion ⇨ おく 《囲炉》;〈兆候〉⇨ちょうこう² ¶何兆もの millions of millions of 《years》; billions upon trillions of 《molecules》.

ちょう³ 長 〈かしら〉the head; the chief; the leader; 〈長所〉《文》a merit; a strong point ¶一家の長 the head of a family / 長3度《音楽》a major third / 長を取り短を捨てる take what is good and leave what is bad / 人の長を取って己れの短を補う improve oneself by following the good example of others / 人に長たる器でない《文》be not competent to lead [stand above] others. 【文例⇩】

ちょう⁴ 朝 〈王朝〉a dynasty;〈治世〉a reign; 〈時代〉a period; an epoch ¶平安朝 the Heian era [period].

ちょう⁵ 腸 (the) bowels; the intestines ¶腸が悪い have bowel trouble [a bowel disease] / 腸液 intestinal fluids [juices] / 腸炎 inflammation of the 《small, large》 intestine; enteritis / 腸カタル intestinal catarrh / 腸内バクテリア intestinal bacteria / 腸捻転 volvulus; twisting of the intestines / 腸閉塞(そく) obstruction [constriction] of the intestines; an intestinal blockage / 腸壁 the intestinal wall.

ちょう⁶ 調 〈調子〉a pitch; a tone; 〈拍子〉time; a tempo (pl. -pos, -pi); 〈詩の〉 a meter; 〈音楽〉a 《major, minor》key ¶ ニ長調 (in) D major [minor] / 七五調 (in) the 7-5 syllable meter.

ちょう⁷ 蝶 a butterfly ¶ 蝶よ花よと育てる bring up 《one's daughter》 with tender care and affection.

ちょう- 超... ultra-; super- ¶超自然的 supernatural / 超国家主義 ultranationalism / 超大国 〈米国・ソ連のような〉a superpower.

ちょうあい 寵愛 ¶寵愛する a favor; make a favorite of; love sb tenderly; think the sun shines out of sb's eyes / 寵愛を受ける be in sb's favor; be the apple of sb's eye / 寵愛を失う lose sb's favor; fall out of favor [《文》into disfavor] with sb / 寵愛を得る win sb's favor.

ちょうい¹ 弔意 ¶弔意を表する offer [《文》tender] one's condolences 《to》; express one's sympathy 《with》.

ちょうい² 潮位 a tide level.

ちょういきん 弔慰金 condolence money.

ちょういん 調印 signature; signing ¶調印する sign 《a treaty》; affix one's seal 《to a document》/ 記名調印する sign and seal 《a note》/ 調印国 a signatory (power) / 調印式 a signing ceremony.

ちょうえき 懲役 penal servitude; imprisonment with hard labor ¶ 5年間の懲役に処せられる be sentenced to five years' penal servitude [to five years at hard labor] / 2年間の懲役に服する serve a sentence of two years' penal servitude; serve a two-year prison term.

ちょうえつ 超越《文》transcendency ¶超越する transcend; rise above; stand aloof 《from》/ 現世を超越する rise above the world / 超越主義《哲》transcendentalism / 超越神 a transcendental deity. 【文例⇩】

ちょうえん 長円 ⇨だえん.

ちょうおん 長音《音声》a long vowel [sound].

ちょうおんそく 超音速 supersonic ¶超音速で飛ぶ fly at supersonic speed / 超音速飛行 (a) supersonic flight; supersonic aviation / 超音速旅客機 a supersonic transport (略: SST).

ちょうおんぱ 超音波 ultrasonic waves ¶超音波発生装置 an ultrasonic generator.

ちょうか 超過 ¶超過する be more than...; be above [over]...;《文》exceed;《文》be in excess 《of》/ 超過額 a surplus; an excess 《of》 / 超過勤務 overtime work; extra duties / 超過勤務をする work overtime; do 《two hours'》 overtime / 超過勤務手当 an overtime allowance. 【文例⇩】

ご注文の品は入念に調製致します. Your order will receive our best attention. / 君の注文どおりに行けばうまいが. If things turn out as you wish, all well and good. / 別に何の注文もつけません. I make no conditions. / それは難しい注文だ. That's asking too much. / それはどんな人にとってもいささか無理な注文だ. That's rather a tall [large] order for anyone.

ちゅうわ 少年は病床にあって, 母親の昼夜を分かたぬ看護を受けていた. The boy lay ill in bed, under the day-and-night care of his mother.

ちゅうりゅう¹ 中流は川底が深い. The river is deep in midstream.

ちゅうりゅう² その国ではなお引き続き米軍の駐留が必要とされよう. Some continuing U.S. military presence will be required in that country.

ちょう³ 人の長を採っておのれの短を補え. Use others' merits to compensate [make up] for your (own) deficiencies. / この分野では彼は私に対して一日の長がある. He has a bit more experience than me in that line. ⇨ より² 【用法】

ちょうえつ あの人は中々超越している. He is quite a philosopher.

ちょうか 応募者は募集人員を超過した. There were more appli-

ちょうかい¹ 町会 〈町議会〉a town assembly [council]; 〈町内会〉a neighborhood association ¶町会議員 a member of a town assembly; 《米》a town councilman [assemblyman]; 《英》a town councillor.

ちょうかい² 懲戒 an official reprimand; a disciplinary punishment ¶懲戒する《文》reprimand; discipline; 《文》reprove / 懲戒免職 a disciplinary dismissal [discharge] / 懲戒処分を受ける《文》be subjected to disciplinary action.

ちょうかく 聴覚 (the sense of) hearing; 《文》auditory sense ¶聴覚が鋭い have a keen sense of hearing; have keen [acute] hearing / 聴覚を失う lose one's hearing / 聴覚に訴える appeal to the ear / 聴覚型〈記憶の〉the auditory type / 聴覚中枢 the auditory [hearing] centers 《of the brain》/ 聴覚障害 hearing impairments [difficulties] / 聴覚神経 the auditory nerve(s).

ちょうかん¹ 長官 a chief (officer); a director; a governor / 〈米国の〉国務長官 the Secretary of State.

ちょうかん² 朝刊 a morning edition [issue]《of the Asahi》¶今日の「毎日」の朝刊 this morning's Mainichi.

ちょうかんず 鳥瞰[瞰]図 a bird's-eye view [picture].

ちょうき¹ 弔旗 ¶弔旗を掲げる hang [hoist] a flag at half-mast; hang [put out] a flag draped in black.

ちょうき² 長期 a long term [time] ¶長期の long; long-term〈contracts〉/ 長期的には in the long run [term]; on a long-term basis / 長期にわたる《文》extend over a long period of time / 長期にわたった干魃(ばつ) (during) an extended drought / 長期計画 a long-range[-term] plan / 長期欠席 a long absence / 長期興行 a long run / 長期政策 a long-range[-term] policy / 長期戦 a long-drawn-out《文》protracted war [contest].

ちょうきょう 調教 ¶調教する break (in) 〈a wild horse〉; train 〈a horse〉/ 調教師 a 〈horse〉trainer; a 〈lion〉tamer.

ちょうきょり 長距離 a long [great] distance; (a) long range〈射程の〉¶長距離電話 a long-distance call; 《英》a trunk call / 長距離電話をかける make a long-distance call; telephone [talk to] sb long distance / 長距離トラックの運転手 a long-haul [long-distance] truck driver / 長距離飛行 a long(-range) flight / 長距離輸送 long-distance transportation [transport, haulage] / 長距離ランナー[レース] a (long-)distance runner [race] / 長距離列車 a long-distance train.

ちょうけい 長兄 one's eldest brother ⇒あに 囲及.

ちょうけし 帳消し ¶帳消しにする offset.

ちょうげんじつしゅぎ 超現実主義 ⇒シュールレアリスム.

ちょうげんぼう 長元坊〖鳥〗a kestrel.

ちょうこう¹ 長考 ¶長考する think for a long time《about what move to make》.

ちょうこう² 徴[兆]候〈病気の〉a symptom; 〈一般の〉a sign; an indication ¶肺炎の徴候を示す develop symptoms of pneumonia / あらゆる徴候から見て by all indications / 良い[悪い]徴候である《文》augur [bode] well [ill] 《for》. 文例R

ちょうこう³ 聴講《文》attendance (at a lecture) ¶聴講する attend (a lecture); 《米》audit 〈a course at a university〉/ 聴講生 a special student; 〈大学の〉《米》an auditor; 《英》an occasional student. 文例R

ちょうごう 調合 ¶調合する mix; make up; prepare.

ちょうこうぜつ 長広舌 a long talk; a long-winded speech ¶長広舌を振るう give a long talk; make a long-winded speech.

ちょうこく 彫刻〈事〉sculpture; engraving; 〈物〉a sculpture; an engraving; a statue (彫像) / 動く彫刻 kinetic sculpture; a mobile (針金・鉄板・木片などで作った) ★ これと区別して普通の動かない彫刻は static sculpture といい, mobile に対応する動かない抽象彫刻は stabile という / 彫刻する carve; sculpture; sculpt; engrave / 金属板に像を彫刻する engrave figures on a metal plate / 彫刻的な sculptural / 彫刻家[師] an engraver; a carver; a sculptor (塑像などの) / 彫刻刀 a chisel; an engraving knife.

ちょうこつ 腸骨〖解〗the ilium《pl. -ia》.

ちょうさ 調査 (an) investigation; (an) examination; (an) inquiry; 〈踏査〉(an) exploration ¶調査する investigate (into); examine; inquire [delve] into; go into〈a problem〉; check on sth; find out; 〈検査する〉inspect; 〈未知の地を〉explore / 徹底的に調査する make a thorough [《文》an exhaustive, an intensive] investigation (into); investigate sth thoroughly / 調査委員会 an investigative [a fact-finding] committee / 調査員 an investigator; an examiner / 調査結果 findings / 調査団 an inquiry commission; a research group / 調査報告 a report (of an investigation); an investigation

---

cants than required. / 工員たちは超過勤務を拒否している. The workers are refusing to do overtime.

ちょうこう² 天候は回復の徴候を見せなかった. The weather showed no sign of improvement. / 状勢は悪化する徴候がある. There are indications [The indications are] that the situation will get worse. / そのカニは危険な徴候を感じるや否や急いで穴に潜ってしまう. The crab runs into its burrow at the first sign of danger.

ちょうこう³ 多数の聴講者があった. There was a large audience [attendance].

ちょうこく 絵を買う人は多いが彫刻を買う人は少ない. Lots of people buy paintings but not many buy sculpture.

ちょうさ その事件は目下調査中である. The matter is under investigation. / 当局は事故の原因調査を始めた. The authorities have started to investigate the cause of the accident. / 調査の結果エンジンに異常があったことが判明した. On investigation it was found that the engine was out of order.

ちょうし 私はそんな高い調子では歌えない. I cannot sing at such

ちょうざい [investigative] report / 調査用紙 a questionnaire. 文例↓
ちょうざい 調剤 ¶調剤する prepare [make up] a medicine; fill [make up] a prescription (処方に従って).
ちょうざめ 蝶鮫 a (green) sturgeon.
ちょうし 調子 〈音調〉a tune; a tone; a note; a pitch (高低の); 〈絵の明暗の〉the values; 〈具合〉a way; 〈文〉a manner ¶調子のいい harmonious; 〈文〉melodious; rhythmical; 〈言うことが〉too smooth [《文》suave]; smooth-tongued; 〈文〉unctuous / 調子の高い[低い] high-[low-]pitched / 調子外れの out of tune; off-key / 調子が合っている[いない] be in [out of] tune / 調子が出る warm up 《to one's work》; get into one's stride / (体の調子がよい) be in good health; be well; be doing well /〈選手などが〉be in fine shape; be in form [trim] /こういう調子に in this way [manner] / この調子では at this rate; if we [things] go on at this rate / (事が)調子よく進む[運ぶ] go well [smoothly] / 調子を上[下]げる raise [lower] the pitch; 〈文章などの〉raise [lower] the tone / 調子を合わせる〈楽器の〉tune (up); 〈人に〉be in tune《with sb》; keep in step《with sb》/ (選手が)調子を崩さないようにする keep in training [trim] / (選手が)調子を取り戻す regain one's form / 調子をのみこむ learn how to do smoothly; get the hang [knack] 《of sth doing》/ 調子に乗る be [get] carried away; be elated 《with success》; be (too) excited; 〈得意になって限度を忘れる〉push [《米》press] one's luck; 〈子供などが〉show off. 文例↓
ちょうじ¹ 丁字 〈植〉a clove (tree); 〈香辛料〉clove.
ちょうじ² 弔辞 a message of condolence; 〈葬儀での〉a memorial [funeral] address ¶弔辞を述べる express one's condolences; make a memorial address / 弔辞を読む read one's message of condolence.
ちょうじ³ 寵児 ¶運命の寵児 Fortune's favorite / 時代の寵児 a hero of the times.
ちょうじかん 長時間 (for) a long time; (for) many hours ¶長時間の long;《文》long-sustained.
ちょうじく 長軸 〈数〉〈楕円(だえん)の〉the major [long] axis.
ちょうしゃ 庁舎 a government office building.
ちょうしゅ 聴取 ¶聴取する〈聞く〉listen to; hear; 〈ラジオを〉listen (in) to / ラジオ聴取者 a (radio) listener / B.B.C. の聴取者 a listener to the B.B.C.

ちょうじゅ 長寿 (a) long life;《文》longevity ¶長寿を保つ live long; enjoy longevity; live to a great age / 長寿法 the secret of longevity.
ちょうしゅう¹ 徴収 collection;《文》imposition; levying ¶徴収する collect; levy; impose; charge.
ちょうしゅう² 聴衆 an audience; hearers ¶多数[少数]の聴衆 a large [small] audience / 約3千人の聴衆 an audience of about 3,000. 文例↓
ちょうじゅう 鳥獣 birds and beasts;《文》fur and feather ¶鳥獣店 a pet store [shop] / 鳥獣保護区 a wildlife sanctuary.
ちょうしょ¹ 長所 a strong point; a good point;《文》a merit; 〈利点〉an advantage ¶長所も短所もある have both good and bad points [《文》merits and demerits]. 文例↓
ちょうしょ² 調書 a record ¶調書に取る put sth on record.
ちょうじょ 長女 the [one's] eldest daughter; 〈娘2人の時〉one's elder daughter ⇒あに 因縁
ちょうしょう 嘲笑 scornful [derisive] laughter; 〈あざけり〉ridicule; a gibe ¶嘲笑する laugh [jeer] 《at》; scoff 《at》/ 嘲笑のまとにする make a laughingstock of sb; hold sb up to ridicule [derision] / 嘲笑を浴びせる pour [《文》cast] ridicule [scorn] 《upon》;《文》laugh sb to scorn / 嘲笑を買う〈招く〉《文》incur ridicule; draw ridicule upon oneself.
ちょうじょう 頂上 〈山の〉the top; the summit; 〈極点〉《文》the zenith; the peak; the highest point ¶頂上を極める《文》gain [the summit / …の頂上で[に] at [on] the top of… / 暑さの頂上 the hottest time of the year; the height of summer / (国家首脳間の)頂上会談 a summit conference [meeting]. 文例↓
ちょうしょく 朝食 breakfast ¶朝食の時に at breakfast / 朝食をとる have [eat] breakfast / トーストとコーヒーの朝食をとる have toast and coffee for breakfast; breakfast on toast and coffee / 朝食後に after breakfast.
ちょうじり 帳尻 the balance (of accounts) ¶帳尻を合わす make the accounts balance / 帳尻をごまかす falsify [《口語》fiddle] the accounts /《英口語》cook the books.
ちょうしん¹ 長身 ¶長身の tall.
ちょうしん² 長針 〈時計の〉the minute [long] hand.
ちょうじん 超人 a superman ¶超人的努力 a superhuman [《文》herculean] effort.
ちょうしんき 聴診器 a stethoscope.

---

a high pitch. / 原文の調子を翻訳に持たせるのは難しい。It is difficult to retain the tone of the original in a translation. / あの調子, その調子! That's it [the way]! / 調子はどうだい。〈物事が〉How's everything? / 〈病人に〉How are you feeling today? / 彼は人とうまく調子を合わせていく。He gets on well with other people. / この運動をすれば体の調子がよくなります。This exercise will tone up your body. / あの調子では彼はılara いに慣れない。If he goes [carries] on like that, he will never amount to much. / あんまり調子に乗らないで! Don't push your luck! / 〈はしゃぐ子供に〉Calm [Quiet] down! / Don't show off!
ちょうしゅう 聴衆が多かった[少

なかった]. There was a large [small] audience. / The attendance was good [poor].
ちょうしょ¹ 彼の寛大なのは長所であって同時にまた短所である。His generosity is both his strength and his weakness. / この機械の長所は取扱いが簡便な点にある。The advantage of this machine is that it is easy to handle.
ちょうじょう その山の頂上にほこ

ちょうしんけい 聴神経 the auditory [acoustic] nerve.

ちょうする 徴する 〈徴集する〉collect;〈求める〉《文》seek ¶意見を徴する seek sb's opinion; ask for sb's advice / 従来の結果に徴すれば judging from the results so far obtained. 文例↓

ちょうせい¹ 調製《製作》《文》manufacture; preparation ¶調製する 〈こしらえる〉make;《文》prepare;〈作成する〉draw up; compile. 文例↓

ちょうせい² 調整 adjustment; coordination ¶調整する 〈価格などを〉adjust;〈各部分の間を〉coordinate;〈音調などを〉modulate.

ちょうぜい 徴税 collection of taxes ⇨ かぜい ¶徴税する collect taxes 《from》/ 徴税令書 a tax bill; tax papers.

ちょうせき¹ 長石《鉱》feldspar.

ちょうせき² 潮汐〈干満〉ebb and flow;〈潮〉a tide ¶潮汐表 a tide table.

ちょうせつ 調節 regulation; adjustment; control;〈ラジオの〉tuning in;〈目の水晶体の〉accommodation ¶調節する regulate 《prices》; adjust 《a telescope》; control 《a mechanism》/ ラジオを調節する tune in the radio / 調節弁 a control valve.

ちょうぜつ 超絶《文》transcendence ⇨ ちょうえつ ¶超絶的《文》transcendent《techniques》.

ちょうせん¹ 挑戦 a challenge; defiance ¶挑戦する challenge 《sb to a fight》; make [give] a challenge 《to sb》; defy / 挑戦に応じる accept a challenge; take [accept] a dare /〈口〉take [pick] up the gauntlet / 挑戦的態度に出る take《文》assume a defiant attitude / 挑戦者 a challenger / 挑戦状を送る send a challenge 《to sb》. 文例↓

ちょうせん² 朝鮮 Korea ¶朝鮮の Korean / 北[南]朝鮮 North [South] Korea / 朝鮮人 a Korean / 朝鮮海峡 the Korea Strait / 朝鮮語 Korean / 朝鮮にんじん (a) ginseng / 朝鮮民主主義人民共和国 the Democratic People's Republic of Korea.

ちょうぜん 超然 ¶超然たる《文》transcendental /…から超然としている hold oneself [stand, keep] aloof from…; rise above 《the world》.

ちょうそ 彫塑〈彫刻と塑像〉carvings and sculptures;〈造形美術〉the plastic arts.

ちょうぞう 彫像 a (carved) statue; a sculptured figure ¶アインシュタインの彫像 a (portrait) statue of Einstein.

ちょうそく 長足 ¶長足の進歩をする make rapid [great, remarkable] progress; make great [rapid] strides.

ちょうそん 町村 towns and villages.

ちょうだ¹ 長打《野球》a long hit ¶長打を放つ make a long hit; hit a long ball / 長打者 a long hitter.

ちょうだ² 長蛇 ¶長蛇の列を作る make [stand in] a long line [《英》queue] / 長蛇を逸する miss a big prize [chance]; have 《one's enemy》at bay but [yet] fail to defeat 《him》. 文例↓

ちょうだい 長大 ¶長大な山系 a long and massive mountain system / 長大な小説 a very long novel;《文》a novel of great length.

ちょうだい 頂戴 〈下さい〉Please give me; I would like (to have); Can [May] I have…? ¶…してちょうだい Please do; Would you mind doing?; Will you be so kind as to do? / 頂戴する 〈もらう〉《文》receive; be given; be presented with sth;〈飲食する〉have; take / 有り難く頂戴する accept sth with thanks / お小言を頂戴する get scolded (by) / 頂戴物 a present; a gift. 文例↓

ちょうたつ 調達 supply;《文》procurement;〈金の〉raising ¶調達する supply; provide;《文》procure; raise 《capital》.

ちょうたん 長短 〈長さ〉(relative) length;〈長所と短所〉strong and weak points;《文》merits and demerits;〈得失〉relative merits [importance]. 文例↓

ちょうたんぱ 超短波 ultrashort waves ¶超短波受信器 an ultrashort wave receiver.

ちょうちょう¹ 町長 the mayor (of a town).

ちょうちょう² 長調《音楽》a major key ¶ト長調 (in) G major.

ちょうちん 提燈 a (paper) lantern ¶ちょうちんを持つ[つける] carry [light] a lantern / ちょうちん行列 a lantern procession [parade] / ちょうちん持ちをする sing sb's praises;《口語》give sb a (big) build-up / ちょうちん屋 a lantern maker.

ちょうつがい 蝶番い a hinge. 文例↓

ちょうてい¹ 朝廷 the (Imperial) Court.

ちょうてい² 調停 mediation; arbitration; intervention;《法》conciliation ¶調停する mediate 《between two persons》; arbitrate 《in》a case》; intervene 《in an affair》;〈落着させる〉settle 《a dispute》/ 調停に付する refer [submit] 《a dispute》to arbitration / 調停裁判所 a court of arbitration / 調停者 a mediator; an arbitrator;〈仲裁者〉a peacemaker;〈仲介者〉

らが立っている。A small shrine stands at the top of the hill. / 頂上の眺めはえも言われぬ程です。The view from the summit is indescribably beautiful.

ちょうする この事業が失敗に終わる事は過去の経験に徴して明らかである。In the light of past experience, it is obvious that this enterprise will fail.

ちょうせい¹ 本剤は精選した原料で調製したものであります。This medicine is prepared from the best materials.

ちょうせん¹ 彼はこの挑戦を受けて立った。He rose to the challenge. / 彼はいつでも挑戦試合に応じる用意があると言った。He said he was open, any time, to a challenge match.

ちょうだ² その劇場の入口まで長蛇の列が続いていた。A long queue was snaking [winding] its way to the entrance of the theater.

ちょうだい² これを頂戴できましょうか。May [Can] I have this? / 先日は結構な物を頂戴して誠に有り難う。Many thanks for the nice present you gave me the other day. / たいそうおいしく頂戴致しました。I have enjoyed my dinner very much, thank you.

ちょうたん 両者を組み合わせれば長短相補ってうまく行くだろう。

ちょうてん 頂点 the top; the summit; the peak;《文》the zenith; the climax;《幾何》the apex (*pl.* apexes, apices); the vertex (*pl.* -tices, -texes) ★ 山などの頂点の意味では the top; the summit; the peak を用いるが、比喩的な意味で言うときは the top から the climax までのどの語も使える ¶三角形の頂点 the vertex [apex] of a triangle / 頂点に達する reach the summit [peak] (of);〈危険など が〉come to a head.

ちょうでん 弔電 ¶弔電を打つ send a telegram of condolence [sympathy] (to).

ちょうど¹ 丁度 just; exactly; precisely;〈あたかも〉(just) as if [though] ¶ちょうど1時間 just [exactly] an hour / 〈端数のない与り〉1マイルのちょうど an even mile / ちょうど5時に just [exactly] at five o'clock; at five o'clock sharp / ちょうどよい時に just in time.

ちょうど² 調度 supplies;〈家具〉furniture; furnishings ¶調度の整った座敷《文》a well-appointed room.

ちょうとう 長頭《人類》dolichocephalism; dolichocephaly; a longhead ¶長頭の dolichocephalic; long-headed / 長頭の人 a dolichocephalic; a longhead.

ちょうとうは 超党派 ¶超党派の nonpartisan 《diplomacy》.

ちょうどきゅう 超弩級 ¶超弩級の extraordinary;《文》far superior (to others) / 超弩級の選手 an outstanding player; a player outclassing (the) others; a player who is head and shoulders above the others. 用例⇩

ちょうとくさく 超特作 a super-colossal film; a superfilm.

ちょうとっきゅう 超特急 a superexpress (train); a bullet train.

ちょうない 町内 the street; the neighborhood; 〈全町〉the whole town.

ちょうなん 長男 the first-born son; the [one's] eldest son;〈息子2人の時〉one's elder son ⇒ あに 用法. 用例⇩

ちょうにん 町人 tradesmen and artisans;〈町の人〉a townsman; townspeople (総称).

ちょうは 長波《電》a long wave.

ちょうば¹ 帳場〈店の〉the counter;〈宿屋の〉the office;《米》the (front) desk;《英》the (reception) desk ¶貴重品を帳場に預ける check [《英》deposit] one's valuables at the desk (for safekeeping).

ちょうば² 跳馬《体操》〈種目〉the long horse (vault);〈器具〉a long [vaulting] horse.

ちょうはつ¹ 長髪 ¶長髪の long-haired;《a young man》with long hair / 長髪にしている wear one's hair long.

ちょうはつ² 挑発 provocation ¶挑発する arouse; excite; stir up; incite / 挑発的な provocative; suggestive (性的に).

ちょうはつ³ 徴発 ¶徴発する commandeer; requisition.

ちょうはつ⁴ 調髪 ⇒ りはつ².

ちょうばつ 懲罰 discipline; punishment;《文》chastisement ¶懲罰する punish; discipline;《文》chastise / 懲罰委員会に付する refer (a case) to the Disciplinary Committee.

ちょうふく 重複 repetition (繰り返し);《文》redundancy (よけい); duplication (二重); (an) overlap (部分的);《修辞》(a) tautology; (a) pleonasm ¶重複する be repeated;《文》be redundant; duplicate; overlap / 重複した repeated; redundant; overlapping;《修辞》tautological; pleonastic.

ちょうぶん 長文 a long sentence; a long passage (文章); a long article (記事·論文) ¶長文の lengthy; long / 長文の読解力テスト a comprehension test using a passage of substantial length; a long-passage reading-ability test.

ちょうへい 徴兵 conscription; enlistment;《米》the (military) draft; compulsory draft;《英》the call-up ¶徴兵を忌避する evade conscription / 徴兵にとられる be enlisted; be enrolled;《米》be drafted;《米》be inducted (into the U.S.Army);《英》be called up / 徴兵忌避者《米》a draft dodger / 徴兵年齢 (lower) the draft age.

ちょうへん 長編 a long piece [article];〈小説〉a long story; a (full-length) novel;〈映画〉a long film; a feature (film) ¶長編漫画映画 a feature-length cartoon film.

ちょうぼ¹ 帳簿 a book ¶帳簿をつける keep accounts [books] / 帳簿をごまかす falsify [juggle] accounts /《英口語》cook the books / 帳簿に記入する enter《an item》in a book; make an entry (in).

ちょうぼ² 徴募 ¶徴募する enlist; recruit.

ちょうほう¹ 重宝 ¶重宝な convenient; useful; handy / 重宝な辞書 a useful [handy] dictionary / 重宝がる[する] find *sth* useful. 用例⇩

ちょうほう² 諜報 intelligence ¶諜報員 an intelligence operative [man]; a spy / 諜報機関 a secret service; an intelligence organiza-

---

They will make a happy combination, the good points of each making up for the defects of the other.

ちょうつがい 戸のちょうつがいが外れている。The door is off its hinges. / この戸はちょうつがいで開く。This door turns [opens] on hinges.

ちょうど¹ ちょうど出掛けようとする所へ田中が来た。I was on the point of going out, when Tanaka came to see me. / この仕事にちょうどいい人がなくて困っている。We can't find the right [a suitable] person for this job. / その帽子は君にちょうどいい。That hat is a perfect fit for you. / 〈値段などを〉ちょうどにしておきなさい。Make it a round sum.

ちょうどきゅう 「戦争と平和」は超弩級の文学作品の一つである。*War and Peace* is one of literature's towering achievements.

ちょうなん 彼は町一番の財産家の長男として生まれた。He was born first son to the wealthiest man in the town.

ちょうほう¹ そういう場合にそれは重宝なのだ。That's where it comes in handy [useful]. / あの男はどこへ行っても重宝がられる。He makes himself useful wherever he goes. / 頂戴物は誠に重宝しています。We find your present very handy [valuable].

ちょうほう 諜報 /諜報網 an intelligence [espionage] network.
ちょうぼう 眺望〈展望〉a view;《文》a prospect;〈景色〉scenery;〈全景〉a panorama (of Paris).
ちょうほうけい 長方形 a rectangle; an oblong ¶長方形の rectangular; oblong.
ちょうほんにん 張本人 the very man (who did sth);《文》the author (of a plot).
ちょうまんいん 超満員 ¶超満員の filled to overflowing;《口語》(a bus) bursting at the seams / 超満員の観衆 an overflowing audience.
ちょうみ 調味 ¶調味する season; flavor; give flavor to / 調味料 a seasoning; a condiment; a flavor enhancer /(食卓に置く)調味料入れの台 a cruet stand.
ちょうみん 町民〈1人〉a townsman;〈全体〉townspeople.
ちょうむすび 蝶結び a bow; a bowknot ¶蝶結びにする tie in a bow; make a bowknot.
ちょうめい¹ 町名 the name of a town;〈市街の〉the name of a street.
ちょうめい² 長命 ⇒ちょうじゅ.
ちょうめん 帳面〈帳簿〉a book; an account book;〈雑記帳〉a notebook;〈掛け売りの〉a passbook; a charge account (勘定) ¶帳面を付ける keep accounts [books] / 帳面に付ける enter in the book; make an entry / 帳面で買う buy sth on credit / 帳面づらを合わせる make the accounts balance;〈不正に〉falsify (《口語》fiddle) the accounts;《英口語》cook the books / 帳面づらだけのもうけ paper profits. 文例⬇
ちょうもん 弔問 ¶弔問する make a call to express one's condolence [sympathy] / 弔問者 [客] a person calling to express his sympathy.
ちょうもんかい 聴聞会 a hearing.
ちょうやく 跳躍 a jump; a leap; a spring ¶跳躍する jump; leap; spring /(競技の)跳躍種目 a jumping event. 文例⬇
ちょうらく 凋落《文》decay;《文》a decline ¶凋落する decline; go downhill.
ちょうり 調理 ⇨りょうり ¶調理師 a licensed cook / 調理台 a dresser.
ちょうりつ¹ 町立 ¶町立の established by a town / 町立高等学校 a town [municipal] high school.
ちょうりつ² 調律 tuning ¶調律する tune (a piano) / 調律の悪いピアノ a badly tuned piano / 調律師 a (piano) tuner.

ちょうりゅう 潮流 a tide; a (tidal) current ¶時代の潮流に従う[逆らう] swim with [against] the stream [current of the times]. 文例⬇
ちょうりょく¹ 張力 tension; tensile strength.
ちょうりょく² 潮力 tidal energy ¶潮力発電所 a tidal-powered electric plant.
ちょうりょく³ 聴力 (the power of) hearing; hearing ability;《文》auditory capacity ¶聴力を失う lose one's hearing / 聴力検査 a hearing test.
ちょうるい 鳥類 birds; fowls; bird [《文》avian] life ¶鳥類学 ornithology / 鳥類学者 an ornithologist.
ちょうれい 朝礼 a morning assembly.
ちょうろう¹ 長老〈年とった人〉an elder; a senior;〈団体の〉a senior member;《文》a doyen;《文》a dean ¶長老教会 the Presbyterian Church.
ちょうろう² 嘲弄 ridicule; derision; mockery ¶嘲弄する laugh at; ridicule; deride; scoff at; make a fool of.
ちょうわ 調和 harmony ¶調和する harmonize; be in harmony [keeping]《with》; go《with》; match / 調和した harmonious; well-matched / 調和しない lack harmony /《文》be inharmonious; be out of keeping《with》. 文例⬇
チョーク chalk ¶チョーク1本 a piece [stick] of chalk / チョークの粉 chalk dust / チョークで書く write with [in] chalk; chalk (sth on the blackboard) / 色チョーク colored chalk.
ちよがみ 千代紙 paper with colored figures.
ちょきちょき〈はさみで切る音〉snip, snip ¶ちょきちょき切る snip (with a pair of scissors).
ちょきん¹ 貯金 savings;〈事〉saving (money) ¶貯金する save money; lay [put] money by;〈預ける〉deposit money (in a bank) / 貯金を引き出す draw one's savings out [of (from) the bank]; draw [withdraw] one's savings / 貯金通帳 a savings [deposit] passbook / 貯金箱《米》a savings bank,《英》a moneybox;〈陶器の〉a piggy bank. 文例⬇
用法 savings は常に複数形で, あとに続く動詞も All my savings are in this bank.（僕の貯金はすべてこの銀行に預けてある）のように複数形になるが, それでいながら many savings と言わず, I took out as much savings as I had.（ありったけの貯金をおろした）と不可算名詞のような使い方をする.
ちょきん² 〈はさみで切る音〉snip (off).
ちょくえい 直営 ¶直営する manage [operate]

──────────

ちょうぼう その山頂は眺望が良い. The view from the top of the mountain is superb. | The summit commands a fine view.
ちょうめん 帳面に付けておいて下さい. Please charge it to my account.
ちょうやく ライオンは跳躍力が強い. The lion is a powerful jumper.
ちょうりゅう 時代の潮流には逆らえない. There is no fighting (against) the trend of the times.
ちょうわ このじゅうたんは壁紙と調和しない. This carpet does not match [go with] the wallpaper.
ちょきん 僕は銀行に10万円貯金している. I have 100,000 yen (deposited) in the bank. | I have a bank account of 100,000 yen. / 小学生には貯金は貯蓄を奨励することだ. Elementary school children should be encouraged in [to form] the habit of saving. / 彼は一生かかってためた貯金をだまし取られた. He was swindled out of his life savings. / 僕は床屋は私の頭の後ろのところを数回ちょきんちょきんとやった. The barber made a few snips at the back of my head.
ちょくげき インフレで直撃を受けるのは年金生活者だ. Pensioners are the hardest hit by inflation.
ちょくせつ それが彼の失敗の直接原因であった. That was the im-

ちょくげき 直撃 a direct hit ¶直撃に会う〈比喩的に〉be hard hit 《by》/ 直撃弾 a direct hit 《on *sth*》/ 直撃弾を受ける be hit directly 《by a bomb [shell]》. 文例↓

ちょくげん 直言 ¶直言する speak plainly [frankly,《文》without reserve].

ちょくご 直後 ¶…の直後の〈時〉immediately [right] after…;〈場所〉just behind [at the back of] … / 終戦直後に just [directly, immediately] after the end of the war.

ちょくさい 直截 ¶直截な direct; plain; frank; straightforward / 直截に directly; plainly; frankly; straightforwardly.

ちょくし 直視 ¶直視する look *sb* [*sth*] in the face; look squarely [straight] 《at》.

ちょくしゃ 直射 ¶直射する shine [fall] directly on / 直射日光の当たる所に置く put *sth* in direct sunshine [in full sunlight] / 直射日光を避ける[受ける] avoid [be exposed to] direct sunlight.

ちょくじょうけいこう 直情径行 ¶直情径行である be of a straightforward disposition; be honest in *one*'s actions.

ちょくしん 直進 ¶直進する go straight on [ahead].

ちょくせつ 直接 ¶直接の direct; immediate / 直接に direct(ly); straight;〈自分で〉personally; in person;〈人を経ずに〉《hear》at first hand / 直接行動 (a) direct action / 直接税 a direct tax / 直接話法《文法》《米》direct discourse;《英》direct speech. 文例↓

ちょくせつほう 直説法《文法》the indicative mood.

ちょくせん 直線 a straight line ¶一直線 ⇨ いっちょくせん / 直線運動 (a) straight-line motion / 直線コース〈一本の〉a straight course /〈環式コースの直線部〉the straight. 文例↓

ちょくぜん 直前 ¶…の直前に just [immediately, directly] before… / 試験の直前に just before the examination.

ちょくそう 直送 direct shipment [delivery] ¶直送する send direct(ly) 《to》/ 産地直送の野菜 vegetables direct [fresh] from the farm.

ちょくぞく 直属 ¶直属の under the immediate [direct] control 《of》; (working) under *one*'s direct orders.

ちょくちょう 直腸《解》the rectum.

ちょくちょく ⇨ ちょいちょい.

ちょくつう 直通 ¶直通する〈乗物が〉go directly 《to》;〈道路が〉lead directly 《to》/ 直通電話 a direct line; a telephone for direct communication 《with, between》/ 直通列車 a through train. 文例↓

ちょくばい 直売 ¶直売する sell direct(ly) 《to》/ 産地直売のりんご apples sold directly by the producers / 直売店 a direct sales store.

ちょくめん 直面 ¶直面する face; come up against (a problem); be confronted with [by]; look *sb* [*sth*] in the face / 死に直面する be confronted by death; face [confront] death / 困難な問題に直面して in (the) face of a difficult problem.

ちょくやく 直訳 (a) literal [word-for-word] translation ¶直訳する translate 《a passage》 literally [word for word].

ちょくゆにゅう 直輸入 direct import [importation] ¶直輸入する import *sth* direct(ly) 《from》.

ちょくりつ 直立 ¶直立している stand upright [《文》erect];《文》be in an upright stance / 直立の straight; upright;《文》erect / 直立歩行する walk erect [upright]. 文例↓

ちょくりゅう 直流《電》direct current (略: DC) ¶直流回路 a direct current circuit.

ちょくれつ 直列《電》¶直列につなぐ connect [join up] (batteries) in series / 直列変圧器[回路] a series transformer [circuit].

ちょこ 猪口 a *sake* cup ¶〈傘が〉おちょこになる be blown inside out.

ちょこざい 猪口才 ¶ちょこざいな presumptuous; impertinent;《口語》fresh;《英口語》cheeky.

ちょこちょこ 〈落ち着かずに〉restlessly;〈歩きぶり〉with short steps ¶ちょこちょこ歩く walk with short steps /〈小児が〉toddle about [along] / ちょこちょこ走る run with short, quick steps; scurry; scuttle.

ちょこなんと looking small and quiet. 文例↓

ちょこまか ¶ちょこまかする move about restlessly ⇨ ちょこちょこ.

チョコレート (a) chocolate; a bar [stick] of chocolate ¶チョコレート色の chocolate-colored / チョコレート1箱 a box of chocolates.

ちょさく 著作 ⇨ ちょじゅつ ¶著作権侵害 ⇨ はんけん² / 著作権法 the copyright law. 文例↓

ちょしゃ 著者 a writer; an author.

ちょじゅつ 著述〈書くこと〉writing;〈書いたもの〉a 《literary》 work; *one*'s writings ¶著述する write a book / 著述で生活する live by

---

mediate cause of [directly responsible for] his failure. / あの人には直接間接に色々お陰を被っている. I am indebted to him in many ways, directly and indirectly.

ちょくせん ここから東京までは直線距離にして約500キロる. Tokyo is about 500 kilometers away from here in a straight line [as the crow flies]. / 両地間の直線距離は5キロだ. The distance between the two places is five linear kilometers.

ちょくぞく 田中氏が私の直属の上役だ. I am directly responsible to Mr. Tanaka.

ちょくつう 両市間に直通列車が通じた. A direct train service has been started between the two cities.

ちょくりつ その岩は水面から5メートルの高さに直立している. The rock rises for five meters sheer out of the water.

ちょこなんと かえるがはすの葉の上にちょこなんと乗っているのが見えた. I saw a little frog sitting quietly on a lotus leaf. / そのお寺の本堂に小坊主が一人ちょこなんと座っていた. In the main hall of the temple sitting primly and all alone was a young novice priest.

ちょさく 氏には建築に関する著作が多数ある. He has written wide-

ちょしょ writing [《文》the pen] / 著述家 an author; a writer / 著述業 the literary profession. 文例⇩

ちょしょ 著書 a 《literary》 work, a book; *one's* writings. 文例⇩

ちょすい 貯水 storage of water; 〈たくわえる水〉 stored(-up) water ¶貯水池 a reservoir / 貯水槽 a water tank.

ちょぞう 貯蔵 storage; storing ¶貯蔵する store; lay [put] up [by] / 貯蔵してある be held in storage / 貯蔵の利く storable 《products》 / 貯蔵庫 a storehouse / 貯蔵室 a storeroom / 貯蔵所 a store(-place) / (a) storage space / 貯蔵物[品] stores; stock.

ちょちく 貯蓄 〈蓄えること〉 saving ¶貯蓄する save (up); lay by [aside]; put [set] by / 貯蓄銀行[債券] a savings bank [bond] / 貯蓄心のある thrifty; 《文》 provident / 貯蓄率 a rate of savings.

ちょっか 直下 directly [just, right] under *sth* ¶直下型地震 a (strong) local earthquake.

ちょっかい ちょっかいを出す meddle in 《*sb's* business》; poke *one's* nose into 《*sb's* affairs》.

ちょっかく 直角 a right angle ¶直角の right-angled 《corners》 / 直角をなす make a right angle 《with》 / …と直角に at right angles to…; perpendicular to… / 直角に交わる cross [meet] at right angles / 直角に方向転換をする make a right-angled turn / 直角三角形 《米》 a right triangle / 《英》 a right-angled triangle.

ちょっかく² 直覚 ⇨ ちょっかん.

ちょっかつ 直轄 direct control ¶文部省直轄の施設 an institution under the direct control of the Ministry of Education.

ちょっかっこう 直滑降 《スキー》 a straight descent; (downhill run); schussing; a schuss ¶直滑降する schuss 《a slope》; make a schuss 《down a slope》.

ちょっかん 直感[観] intuition ¶直感する know by intuition [《文》intuitively]; feel *sth* in *one's* bones / 直感的《文》 intuitive / 直視力 intuition; 《文》 intuitive power.

チョッキ 《米》 a vest; 《英》 a waistcoat.

ちょっきゅう 直球 《野球》 a straight ball [pitch] ¶直球を投げる throw [pitch] a straight ball.

ちょっけい¹ 直系 a direct line (of descent) ¶直系の子孫 a direct [《文》lineal] descendant / …の直系の子孫である be descended in a direct line from…; come down in straight descent from… / 直系会社 a directly affiliated concern.

ちょっけい² 直径 a diameter; the distance across ¶直径が3メートルある be three meters across [in diameter]; have a diameter of three meters / 直径を計る measure across 《a wheel》 / 直径2センチの管 a pipe with a diameter of two centimeters. 文例⇩

ちょっけつ 直結 direct connection; 《電》 direct coupling ¶…に直結している be connected directly with…; 〈比喩的に〉 have a direct bearing on….

ちょっこう¹ 直行 ¶直行する go straight [direct] 《to》; run through 《to》 《電車に》 / …へ直行で行く go by [take a] through train to…; go through to… / 直行列車 a through train.

ちょっこう² 直航 ¶直航する 〈船が〉 sail direct [straight] 《to》; 〈飛行機が〉 fly direct 《to》; make a nonstop flight 《to》. 文例⇩

ちょっと 〈しばし〉 for a moment [a while, a short time]; briefly; 〈わずか, 少し〉 a little; a bit; just; slightly; 〈かなり〉 rather; pretty ¶ちょっとの間に in a minute [moment]; in the twinkling of an eye / ちょっとした親切 a little act of kindness / ちょっとした風邪 a slight cold / ちょっとした機会さえあれば given [if *one* had] half a chance / ちょっとした料理店 (be) not a bad-looking (little) restaurant / ちょっと見る take a (casual) glance 《at》 / ちょっと見ると[考えると] at first sight [thought] / ちょっとばかり預金がある 〈わずかな〉 have only a little money in the bank; 〈かなりの〉 have a nice little bank account. 文例⇩

---

ly on the subject of architecture. / 著作権所有 《本の奥付け》. All rights reserved. | Copyright.

ちょじゅつ これはあの人の著述です. This book was written by him. / 大学講師として数年を過ごした後, 彼はユニアに転じた. After spending several years as a college lecturer, he turned to full-time writing.

ちょしょ あの人には著書が多い. He has written a large number of books. | He is a prolific author.

ちょっけい² これは直径幾らあるか. How wide across is it? / 大多数の木の幹は先が細くなっているが, ココやしの幹は上までほとんど直径が変わらない. While most tree trunks taper toward the top, the coconut's is the same diameter almost all the way up. / 地球の赤道面の直径は両極間の

直径より 40 キロ余り長い. The earth is thicker through the equator than through the poles by 40-odd kilometers.

ちょっこう¹ この列車は新潟まで直行だ. This train goes through to Niigata. / 彼はロンドンから直行で来た. He came straight from London.

ちょっこう² この船はホンコン直航です. This ship is bound direct for Hongkong.

ちょっと ちょっと待ってくれ. Wait a minute [moment]! / ちょっと木戸さんにお目にかかりたい. I would like to see Mr. Kido for a few minutes. / 君だということがちょっと分からなかった. I didn't recognize you for the moment. / だれだかちょっと行って見てきてくれないか. Just go and see who it is, will you? / 僕

は途中ちょっと名古屋へ寄った. I paid a short visit to Nagoya on the way. / 彼はその楽器をちょっといじれるようになった. He gained the rudiments of skill on the instrument. / このような例はちょっと見にはよくわからない. That sort of case is not obvious to the casual eye [on casual observation]. / ちょっと聞くと変だ. It sounds strange at first. / 僕はちょっとのところで電車に乗り遅れた. I missed the train by a minute. / 彼はもうちょっとで死ぬ所だった. He was within a hairsbreadth of death. / それはちょっとできない事だ. It is no easy thing to do. / おれの大工の腕前, ちょっとしたものだろう. I'm something of [quite] a carpenter, aren't I? / 昔はちょっとした映画俳優だった. He was once a film

ちょっぴり a tiny [wee] bit ⇨ すこし. 文例⬇
ちょとつもうしん 猪突盲進 〖猪突盲進する〗 rush recklessly; make a headlong rush 《at》. 文例⬇
ちょびひげ ちょび髭 (wear) a small mustache.
ちょほくじょう 貯木場 a timber yard.
ちょめい 著名 ⇨ ゆうめい¹.
ちょうい easy; simple. 文例⬇
ちょろちょろ 〖ちょろちょろ流れる〗 trickle / 〈ねずみなどが〉ちょろちょろ走り回る scamper about.
ちょろまかす 〈くすねる〉 filch; pilfer; 〈着服する〉 embezzle; 〈だまし取る〉 cheat sb out of sth.
ちょんぎる ちょん切る chop [nip, snip] off.
ちょんまげ a topknot (hairstyle).
ちらかす 散らかす scatter (about); mess up (a room); (文) put (a room) in disorder; make a mess (in a room); throw (a room) into a mess 〖部屋に紙くずを散らかす litter a room with scraps of paper / 物を散らかしておく leave things lying about. 文例⬇
ちらかる 散らかる 〈物が〉 be in a mess; (文) be in disorder; be [lie] scattered [(文) in disarray] (about the room, on the floor); 〈部屋などが〉 be untidy; be (in) a mess; be littered [scattered] (with scraps of paper).
ちらし 散らし 〈ビラ〉 a [an advertising] leaflet; a handbill 〖ちらしをまく distribute handbills.
ちらしずし 散らし鮨 unrolled *sushi* (served in a box or bowl).
ちらす 散らす 〈花などを〉 scatter; 〈まき散らす〉 strew; sprinkle; 〈群衆などを〉 disperse; 〈追い払う〉 dispel; 〈はれ物などを〉 resolve 〖散らし薬 a resolvent.
ちらちら 〖ちらちらする〈明滅する〉 flicker; 〈きらきらする〉 glitter; twinkle / 目がちらちらする〈人が主語〉 be dazzled; be dazed. 文例⬇
ちらつかせる let sth be seen for a moment (as if by chance); show off; flash.

ちらつく 〈物が〉 flicker; flit; 〈目が〉 be dazzled.
ちらばり 散らばり 〖散らばりぐあい the way (in which) (stones) are scattered. 文例⬇
ちらばる 散らばる ⇨ ちる. ちらかる.
ちらほら 〈そちこちに〉 here and there; 〈少しずつ〉 in [by] twos and threes; 〈まばらに〉 sparsely; thinly. 文例⬇
ちらり 〖ちらりと見る glance [cast a glance] 《at》; take a brief look 《at》 / ちらりと見える get [catch] a (momentary) glimpse 《of》; 〈が主語〉 show fleetingly [for the twinkling of an eye] / ちらりと聞く hear by chance. 文例⬇
ちり¹ 地理 〈地勢〉 geographical features; topography; 〈地理学〉 geography 〖地理的 geographic(al); topographic(al) / 地理上 geographically; topographically / 地理学者 a geographer / 地理書 a geography book; a geography (of China). 文例⬇
ちり² 塵 〈ほこり〉 dust; 〈ごみ〉 dirt; trash 〖ちりを払う dust (off) (one's coat) / ちりほども気にかけない do not care a bit [straw] 《about sth, if...》 / 〈人を〉ちりあくたのように扱う treat sb like dirt. 文例⬇
チリ Chile 〖チリの Chilean / チリ共和国 the Republic of Chile / チリ硝石 Chile saltpeter / チリ人 a Chilean.
ちりがみ 塵紙 tissue paper.
ちりしく 散り敷く 〈物が主語〉 lie scattered; 〈場所が主語〉 be scattered [(文) strewn] 《with》. 文例⬇
ちりぢり 散り散り 〖ちりじりに〈ばらばらに〉(文) asunder; scatteringly; scattered(ly); 〈別々に〉 separately; 〈四方に〉 in all directions / ちりぢりばらばらになる disperse; scatter; 〈離散する〉 break up; go (their) separate ways.
ちりとり 塵取り a dustpan.
ちりばめる 散りばめる inlay; set; stud 〖金銀を散りばめる inlay with gold and silver / ダイヤモンドを散りばめた王冠 a crown set with diamonds / 宝石を散りばめたような星空 (文)

---

actor of a sort. / ちょっと. 〈呼びかけ〉 Just a minute! | Excuse me! | Look here! | (米) Say! | (英) I say!
ちょっぴり それにはちょっぴり勇気がいる. It needs [takes] a bit of courage (guts).
ちょとつもうしん 彼は猪突盲進型だ. He is the type that goes headlong at [feet first into] what(ever) he has decided to do.
ちょうい 試験はちょろかった. The exam was a cinch.
ちらかす 部屋を散らかしっぱなしにしてはいけない. Don't leave your room untidy [in a mess].
ちらちら 雪がちらちら降っている. A light snow is falling. / 遠くに灯がちらちら光っていた. I saw a flickering of light in the distance. / 目がちらちらする. My eyes are dazzled.

ちらつく 彼の面影がまだ目の前にちらついている. The memory of his face [appearance] still haunts me.
ちらばり 散らばりぐあいはだいたい平均している. The scatter is more or less uniform.
ちらほら 桜がちらほら咲き始めた. Cherry blossoms are coming out here and there. | A few cherry blossoms are beginning to come out. / 聴衆の中にはなじみの顔もちらほら見うけられた. There was a fair sprinkling of familiar faces in the audience.
ちらり 彼の後姿がちらりと見えた. I caught a glimpse of his back.
ちり¹ 彼はロンドンの地理に明るい. He knows his way about London. / 彼はこの辺の地理に明るい. He is quite familiar [well

acquainted] with this neighborhood. / 私はこの辺の地理に暗い. I am a stranger here.
ちり² 家の中にはちり一つない. There is not a speck of dust in the whole house. / 机の上にはうっすらとちりが積もっていた. The desk was filmed with dust. / あの男に良心なんかちりほどもない. He hasn't an ounce [a particle] of conscience in him. / ちりも積もれば山となる. Many a little makes a mickle. 《諺》 | Many drops make a shower [flood]. 《諺》
ちりしく 森の小道には落ち葉が散лев敷いていた. The path in the wood was strewn with fallen leaves.
ちりぢり 戦争で一家はちりぢりになった. The household was scattered [torn apart] by the war. / 行きは一緒だったが帰りはちりぢ

ちりめん 縮緬 (silk) crepe ¶ちりめんじわ fine wrinkles.

ちりょう 治療 (medical) treatment ¶治療する〈手当をする〉treat;〈なおす〉cure;/目を治療してもらう have *one's* eyes treated / 治療せずにほうっておく leave (a decayed tooth) untreated / 治療の仕様のない病気 an untreatable disease / 治療を受ける have [((文)) receive, ((文)) undergo] (medical) treatment / 治療を受けに行く go to ((a doctor)) for treatment / 治療中である be under (medical) treatment; be under the doctor / 再治療 retreatment / 治療効果 ((文))(a medicine with) a curative effect; ((have)) therapeutic value / 治療師 a healer / 治療費 a doctor's fee [bill] / 治療法 a remedy; a cure. 文例⇩

ちりょく 知力 intellectual [mental] power(s); intellect.

ちりんちりん tinkle-tinkle; ting-a-ling ¶ちりんちりん鳴る tinkle; clink; jingle.

ちる 散る〈花・葉などが〉fall; scatter;〈群衆が〉disperse; break up;〈雲・霧などが〉break up [away]; ((文)) be dispelled; lift (霧が);〈くずれ物が〉resolve;〈にじむ〉spread; run; blur ¶散っている be [lie] scattered. 文例⇩

ちん 狆 a Japanese spaniel.

ちんあげ 賃上げ a raise ((in *one's*)) wages; a boost in salary ¶賃上げを要求する demand a raise [((英)) rise] in (*one's*) wages; demand higher wages / 賃上げスト[闘争] a strike [struggle] for higher wages.

ちんあつ 鎮圧 suppression; repression; ((文)) subjugation ¶鎮圧する bring [get] (the mob) under control; suppress, repress; put down; stamp out; crush; quash.

ちんか[1] 沈下 ¶沈下する sink; subside.

ちんか[2] 鎮火 ¶鎮火する be put out; ((文)) be extinguished; be brought under control; be got under (control); die down.

ちんがし 賃貸し ⇒ちんたい[2].

ちんがり 賃借り ⇒ちんしゃく.

ちんき 珍奇 ¶珍奇な curious; rare;〈奇異な〉quaint; queer; strange; funny; fantastic.

ちんきゃく 珍客 ((文)) a least-expected visitor; a welcome guest.

ちんぎん 賃金 wages; pay ¶1日4千円の賃金で働く work at a wage [for wages] of 4,000 yen a day / 食って行けるだけの賃金が取れる職を得る get a job with a living wage / 賃金格差 a wage differential / 賃金カット a cut in wages; a wage cut; (a) wage reduction / 賃金水準を押えておく hold [keep] down the wage level [the level of wages] / 賃金生活者[労働者] a wage earner; ((米)) a wageworker.

ちんこう 沈降 ¶沈降する precipitate; subside; settle (down) / 赤血球沈降速度[試験] a blood sedimentation rate [test].

ちんこんきょく 鎮魂曲 a requiem.

ちんざ 鎮座 ¶鎮座する be enshrined.

ちんじ 珍事 a strange [((文)) singular] incident; an unexpected [a rare] event.

ちんしごと 賃仕事 a job (of work); job work;〈出来高払いの〉piecework;〈時間払いの〉timework ¶賃仕事をする work on a job; work at piece rates.

ちんしもっこう 沈思黙考 ¶沈思黙考する meditate; sit in silent thought; muse; ((文)) be in a brown study.

ちんしゃ 陳謝 an apology ¶陳謝する apologize ((to *sb* for *sth*)); beg *sb's* pardon (for); ((文)) express *one's* regret ((for)) / 陳謝を要求する demand an apology ((from *sb*)).

ちんしゃく 賃借 lease ¶賃借する lease (land); rent (a house) / 賃借人 a hirer (a), a lessee (a); a leaseholder.

ちんじゅ 鎮守 ¶鎮守の社(やしろ) a village [tutelary] shrine; 鎮守の森 the grove of the village shrine.

ちんじゅつ 陳述 a statement ¶陳述する state; make [give] a statement; ((文)) set forth / 陳述書を提出する send [hand] in a statement.

ちんじょう 陳情 a petition; an appeal ¶陳情する〈請願する〉petition (the authorities); appeal ((to the mayor));〈苦情を言う〉complain ((about, of)) / 陳情者 a petitioner / 陳情書を提出する send in a petition; file a petition (with the government) / (国会への)陳情団 a group of lobbyists.

ちんせい 鎮静 ¶鎮静させる calm; quiet;〈苦痛などを〉appease; soothe / 薬を与えて患者を鎮静させる put a patient under sedation / 鎮静剤 a sedative (drug); a tranquilizer.

ちんたい[1] 沈滞 ((文)) stagnation; dullness; slackness; inactivity ¶沈滞している ((文)) be stagnant; be slack; be inactive.

ちんたい[2] 賃貸 lease; letting out (on hire) ¶賃貸する lease (the land); rent (a house); let out (on hire) / 賃貸人 a lessor / 賃貸料 a rent.

ちんたいしゃく 賃貸借 ¶賃貸借契約 a lease contract.

ちんだん 珍談 a funny [an amusing, an intriguing] story.

ちんちくりん ¶ちんちくりんな undersized; very short; dwarfish / ちんちくりんな着物 a *kimono* too short for *sb*.

ちんちゃく 沈着 ((文)) composure; self-possession; presence of mind ¶沈着な self-pos-

---

りだった. They set off together, but returned separately.
ちりょう 彼は宮田博士の治療で全快した. He completely recovered under the treatment of Dr. Miyata. / 治療法のない病気がまだたくさんある. For many diseases there is still no cure.
ちる 桜はもう散ってしまったろう. The cherry blossoms must have fallen by now. / 木の葉が風で散った. The leaves were scattered by the wind. / 彼らの話し声で気が散った. Their voices distracted me [my attention].
ちんちゃく 実に沈着な態度であった. He showed wonderful presence of mind. / 沈着さを失ってはいけない. Don't lose your presence of mind.
ちんつうざい モルヒネやコデインは今でも鎮痛剤として処方される. Morphine and codeine are still prescribed for pain.

ちんちょう

sessed; composed; calm; cool / 沈着な態度 a calm attitude / 沈着に calmly; coolly; 《文》 composedly; 《文》《act》with composure. 文例⇩

ちんちょう 珍重 ¶珍重する think much of; value; prize; treasure.

ちんちん ¶ちんちん鳴る〈鈴などが〉tinkle; jingle /〈犬が〉ちんちんをする sit up (and beg).

ちんつう 沈痛 ¶沈痛な〈文〉grave; sad / 沈痛な口調[面持ち]で in a grave tone [with a sad look].

ちんつうざい 鎮痛剤 a painkiller; an analgesic (drug); a pain-reliever; an anodyne. 文例⇩

ちんでい 沈泥 silt ¶沈泥層 a silt bed. 文例⇩

ちんでん 沈殿 precipitation; deposition ¶沈殿する be precipitated; be deposited; settle (out) / 不純物を沈殿させて取り除く precipitate [settle] impurities out of 《the water》/ 溶液から分離して沈殿する settle out (of solution) / 沈殿池[槽] a settling basin [tank] / 沈殿物 a precipitate; a deposit; a sediment.

ちんどんや ちんどん屋 brightly-dressed musicians playing in the street for advertising purposes.

ちんにゅう 闖入 ¶闖入する break [force one's way] into / 闖入者 an intruder; a gatecrasher (パーティーなどの).

ちんば ⇨ びっこ.

チンパンジー a chimpanzee; 《口語》a chimp.

ちんぴら a young hooligan; 《米》a (young) punk.

ちんぴん 珍品 a rare article; a rarity; a curiosity.

ちんぷ 陳腐 ¶陳腐な old-fashioned; commonplace; trite; stale / 陳腐な句 a hackneyed phrase /〈決まり文句〉a cliché / 陳腐なしゃれ a stale [《口語》corny] joke.

ちんぷんかんぷん unintelligible language [speech]; gibberish;《英口語》double Dutch. 文例⇩

ちんぼつ 沈没 ¶沈没する sink; go down; go to the bottom / 沈没船 a sunken ship.

ちんぽん 珍本 a rare book.

ちんまり ¶ちんまりした snug; compact.

ちんみ 珍味〈食品〉a dainty; a delicacy; a (delicate) tidbit;〈味〉a delicate flavor [taste].

ちんみょう 珍妙 ¶珍妙な funny; queer; quaint; odd; fantastic.

ちんむるい 珍無類 ¶珍無類の queerest; strangest; 《文》(most) singular.

ちんもく 沈黙 silence ¶重苦しい沈黙 a heavy silence / 沈黙する fall [《文》become] silent; say nothing / 沈黙した silent / 沈黙して[のうちに] in silence / 沈黙させる silence; put sb to silence / 沈黙を守る keep silent [silence]; hold one's tongue / 沈黙を破る break silence. 文例⇩

ちんれつ 陳列 ¶陳列する exhibit; display; put [《文》place] sth on show [exhibition, view] / 陳列室 a show room / 陳列台 a display stand [counter] / 陳列棚 a showcase; an exhibit [a display] case / 陳列品 an exhibit; an article on show [display] / 陳列窓 a show window.

つ

-つ ¶行きつ戻りつする go to and fro; walk back and forth [up and down] / 浮きつ沈みつ《文》now sinking, now rising.

ツアー (go on) a tour (of Europe).

つい¹ 対〈一双〉a pair; a couple;〈一組〉a set;〈対の一方〉a companion (piece) (to) /〈対になる双方が〉make a pair; pair up;〈一方のものに対して〉be a companion (piece) (to); form a counterpart 《to》.

つい²〈ほんのちょっと〉just; only;〈うっかり, ふと〉carelessly; by mistake; by accident [chance];《文》inadvertently; unintentionally;〈思わずか〉in spite of oneself; against one's better judgment (いけないと思いながら) ¶つい今しがた only a moment ago; just now / つい近くに quite near《the station》; just by《the house》/ ついしゃべってしまう blurt out 《a secret》inadvertently; reveal 《a secret》in an unguarded moment / つい忘れる〈事が主語〉slip from one's memory; slip one's mind;〈人が主語〉carelessly forget (to do). 文例⇩

ついえる 潰える〈つぶれる〉collapse; go under;〈負けと〉be defeated.

ついおく 追憶 ⇨ ついそう.

ついか 追加 (an) addition; a supplement ¶追加する add (A to B); make an addition (to); supplement /〈宴会などで〉酒を追加する order more sake / 追加予算 a supplementary budget / 追加料金 additional charges; an additional fee.

ついかんばん 椎間板 ¶椎間板ヘルニア (suffer from) a slipped disk.

ついき 追記〈追伸〉a postscript (略: P.S.) ¶追記する add a postscript (to); add (to).

ついきゅう¹ 追及 ¶追及する pursue the ques-

ちんでい 運ばれて来た沈泥で水路がふさがってしまった。The flow of water has silted up the channel. / この池にはどんどん沈泥がたまっている。This pond is silting up fast.

ちんぷんかんぷん そんなことは僕には全然ちんぷんかんぷんだ。It's (all) Greek to me.

ちんもく 1発の銃声が沈黙を破った。The report of a gun broke the silence. / 彼らはあくまで沈黙を守っていた。They kept strict silence to the last. / 部屋はまた沈黙に戻った。Silence settled down once more upon the room.

つい² ついうっかりしておりました。I am sorry I was so careless. / こういう場合にはついそう考えたくなるものだ。Under these circumstances we are tempted to think so. / あれほど用心していたのについつい彼らのわなにかかってしまった。For all my cau-

ついきゅう　追求 《文》 pursuit ¶幸福の追求 the pursuit of happiness ¶追求する pursue; follow [《文》seek] after / …を追求する 《文》 pursue [search, quest] of….

ついきゅう　追究 (a) close inquiry; (a) thorough investigation ¶追究する inquire [go] into 《a matter》 closely; investigate 《a matter》 thoroughly; 《文》 carry out a thorough investigation (of an incident).

ついく　対句 an antithesis (pl. -theses); a couplet ¶対句をなす make [form] an antithesis [a couplet].

ついげき　追撃 《文》 pursuit; chase ¶追撃する run after; 《文》 pursue; chase; give chase to / 敵を激しく追撃中である 《文》 be in hot pursuit of the enemy / 追撃をやめる give up the chase (for); 《文》 start in pursuit [chase] of (the fleeing enemy) / 追撃戦 a pursuit battle.

ついこつ　椎骨 《解》 a vertebra (pl. -brae).

ついし¹　追試 〈実験結果の〉 a double check ¶追試する double-check (the findings).

ついし²　墜死 ¶墜死する a fall to one's death (from the scaffold, off the frozen ridge of a mountain).

ついしけん　追試験 〈学校の試験の〉《米》a make-up; 《英》 a resit ¶追試験を受ける retake 《英》resit] an [one's] examination (because of illness [failure] on an earlier occasion); 《米》 take a make-up.

ついじゅう　追従 ⇒ついしょう.

ついしょう　追従 (a) flattery; 《文》 adulation ⇒おべっか, へつらい ¶追従笑い a sycophantic smile.

ついしん　追伸 a postscript (略: P.S.).

ついずい　追随 ¶追随する follow (in the wake of) / 他の追随を許さない 《文》 be peerless; be without a peer; have no equal; be unrivaled; outclass [outdistance, outstrip] others / 追随者 a follower.

ついせき　追跡 《文》 pursuit; chase ¶追跡する 《文》 pursue; chase; give chase to; run [be] after / 追跡中である 《文》 be in pursuit [chase] of (the offender); be on the track of (a criminal) / 〈人工衛星などに対する追跡装置〉 a tracking station [device] / 追跡元素 《化・生理》 a tracer element / 追跡者 a pursuer; a chaser / 追跡調査を行なう conduct a follow-up (study) (of).

ついぜん　追善 ¶追善供養を営む hold memorial services (for, in honor of) / 追善興行 a memorial performance; a performance in memory of sb.

ついそ　追訴 (bring) a supplementary suit [action] (against).

ついぞ　never; not…at all. 文例⇩

ついそう　追想 reminiscence; recollection; 《文》 (a) retrospection ¶追想する recollect; look back on; recall 《to one's memory》; go over (the past) in one's mind / 昔を追想させる〈事が主語〉 remind sb of [take sb back to] the old days; make sb remember the past / 追想談 [録] reminiscences; memoirs.

ついたいけん　追体験 ¶追体験する experience for oneself what sb has gone through.

ついたち　一日　the first day (of a month) ¶5月1日 the 1st of May; May 1.

ついたて　衝立 a screen.

ついちょう　追徴 ¶追徴する collect (a sum of money) in addition; make an additional collection (of ¥10,000); 〈罰として〉fine; impose a penalty (of ¥10,000) on sb / 追徴金 money paid [collected] in addition (to); 〈罰〉a forfeit; a penalty. 文例⇩

ついて　〈関して〉as to; as for; 《文》 concerning; regarding; 《文》 with regard [reference] to; as regards; relating to; of; about; on; over; 〈したがって〉 after; 〈…に沿うて〉 along; 〈…とともに〉(along) with; 〈…の下に〉under; with; 〈ごとに〉a; per; for ¶教師について勉強する study (English) under a teacher / 1ダースについて 400円 400 yen a [per] dozen / この問題について on [concerning] this subject / ついては in this connection; so; therefore / …のすぐあとについて immediately behind [after] sb; on the heels of sb. 文例⇩

ついで¹　序で ¶ついでに by the way; incidentally; 《文》 (mention sth) in passing; 《文》 (say) in parenthesis ▶ by the way と incidentally は会話で使えるが, そのあとの2つは書いた文章でしか使えない / おついでの節に〈都合〉at your convenience; 〈機会〉when you have an opportunity [a chance] (to do, of doing) / ついでがあり次第 〈機会〉 on the first opportunity (of doing); 〈都合〉《文》at one's earliest convenience / 金沢へ行くついでに

---

tion I went and fell into the trap that they had set.

ついきゅう¹　更に追及されて, 彼は自分がやったことを告げた. In response to further interrogation he admitted that he had done it.

ついきゅう²　警察は脱走した犯人の行方を全力を挙げて追求している. The police are in full cry after the escaped convict.

ついずい　日本はただアメリカに追随しているだけではだめだ. It will not do for Japan just to follow in the footsteps of the U.S.

ついぞ　彼はついぞうそなどついたことがない. He has never been known to tell a lie.

ついちょう　裁判所は彼に100万円の追徴金を納めるよう命令した. The court ordered him to forfeit 1,000,000 yen.

ついて　その事についてはご安心下さい. Please don't worry about it. / だれをリーダーにするかという事について争っていた. They were quarreling about who should be the leader.

ついで¹　おついでの時にお立ち寄り下さい. Please call on me when you are around this way. / 彼の家族のことをついでに一言しないわけにはいかない. I cannot finish [close] without a word about [a passing reference to] his family. / 話のついでだが地震と言えば昨夜も1つあったよ. Talking of earthquakes, we felt one last night.

ついてくる　彼のような授業のやり方では生徒はついてこない. The way he handles his classes, he cannot hold the attention of his

ついで 〈途中〉on the [one's] way to Kanazawa / ついでながら申し上げますが I take this occasion [opportunity] to say that....

ついで² 次いで ⇨つぐ¹.

ついてくる 付いて来る follow；〈一緒に来る〉come along with one；〈忠実に従う〉《文》adhere to；be faithful to. 文例⇩

ついてまわる 付いて回る pursue；〈尾行する〉dog；shadow. 文例⇩

ついてゆく 付いて行く follow；follow (close) on the heels of sb；〈尾行する〉dog；shadow；〈遅れずに〉keep up [pace]《with》；〈一緒に行く〉go along《with》，accompany；〈忠実に従う〉《文》adhere to《a policy》；be faithful to 《sb, sb's teachings》. 文例⇩

ついとう 追悼 mourning ⇨ ついぜん ¶追悼する mourn (for the dead, over sb's death)；pay a [one's] tribute to the memory of sb / 追悼の辞を述べる give a memorial address (for sb's soul).

ついとつ 追突 a rear-end collision ¶追突する collide with [run into]《a car》from behind；bump into the rear of《a truck》. 文例⇩

ついに 遂に at (long) last；at length；finally；eventually；in the end；in the long run. 文例⇩

ついにん 追認 《law》ratification；confirmation ¶追認する ratify；confirm《a telegraphic order》.

ついばむ 啄む pick (at)；peck (at).

ついひ 追肥 additional [supplementary] fertilizer.

ついび 追尾 ¶追尾する follow；pursue /《ミサイルの》自動追尾装置 a homing device.

ついほう 追放 〈流刑〉《文》banishment；exile；〈一定の場所・組織などからの〉expulsion；eviction；《米》ouster；deportation (国外への)；a purge (粛正) ¶追放する banish；exile；send sb into exile；deport；oust《from public life》；evict《from the premises》；expel《from the Party》/ 国外に追放する banish [deport, expel] sb from the country；〈祖国から〉expatriate / 追放の刑に処せられる be banished；be punished with banishment / 追放令 a deportation order；an expulsion decree.

ついやす 費やす spend；《文》expend；lay out；〈浪費する〉waste；throw away；squander；〈消費する〉《文》consume ¶100万円を費やして at a cost of 1,000,000 yen. 文例⇩

ついらく 墜落 a fall；a crash (飛行機の) ¶墜落する fall；drop；go down；crash / 海中に墜落する crash [go down] into the sea / 猛烈な早さで墜落して地面に激突する hurtle down and crash into the ground. 文例⇩

ツイン 〈ホテルの〉a twin (room) ¶ツインベッド a twin bed.

つう 通 an expert (in, at)；a connoisseur《of antiques》¶通がる pretend to know everything《about》/ 通を振り回す make a show [display] of one's knowledge《of》；parade one's expertise《about, on, concerning》/ 通である be well informed《about, on,《文》concerning》；be well up《in, on》；《文》be conversant《with》；《文》be (well) versed (in).

ツー ¶ツーと言えばカーだ be very responsive；be quick to take a hint；《口語》be quick on the uptake.

-つう …通 ¶1通の手紙 a letter；a note / 書類3通 three documents；three copies of a document (同じもの).

つういん¹ 通院 ¶通院する attend a hospital (as an outpatient)；go to hospital.

つういん² 痛飲 ¶痛飲する drink a great deal；drink heavily [hard]；《文》carouse.

つううん 通運 transportation；transport ¶通運会社 a forwarding agency；《米》an express company；《英》a transport company.

つうか¹ 通貨 currency ¶通貨の安定 stabilization of the currency / 通貨の安定を乱すturb the stability of the currency / 通貨の膨張[収縮] inflation [deflation] / 国際通貨危機 an international monetary crisis / 通貨制度 a monetary system / 通貨制度の改革 (a) monetary reform.

つうか² 通過 (a) passage ¶通過する pass (through)；go [get] through；be carried (議案が)/ 通過する見込みのなさそうな法案 a bill that appears to have little chance of passage [passing《the Diet》] / 駅を通過する pass a station without stopping / トンネルを通過する pass through a tunnel / 大阪の上空を通過する pass over [fly over, overfly] Osaka / 議案を通過させる pass [get] a bill through the Diet / 強引に[大急ぎで]議案を通過させる ram [rush] a bill through the House / 通過駅 a station at which the train does not stop / 通過儀礼《人類》a rite of passage. 文例⇩

つうかい 痛快 ¶痛快な〈愉快な〉quite de-

---

students.

ついてまわる 我々にはどこまでも不運がついて回った. Misfortune dogged our steps right to the end.

ついてゆく その講義は難し過ぎて私にはついて行けなかった. The lecture was too difficult for me to follow. / 彼女は彼の考えにはついて行けないと言った. She refused to go along with his idea.

ついとつ 彼は追突されてむち打ち症になった. He got a whiplash injury when his car was run into from behind.

ついに 二人はついに離婚した. Their marriage ended in divorce. / 彼女はついに神経がまいってしまった. She wound [ended] up with a nervous breakdown.

ついやす 彼は毎日1時間をバッティングの練習に費やした. He put in one hour a day improving his batting. / 午前中一杯手紙書きに費やした. I have given all the morning to writing letters. / 彼はこの本を書くのに5年かかい努力を費やした. This book cost him five years' continuous effort. / この寺を建てるのに10年の歳月を費やした. It took ten years to build the temple.

ついらく この飛行機の墜落事故で乗客及び乗組員全員が死亡した. All the passengers and crew were killed in the plane crash.

つう 彼は中国通だ. He knows everything about China. | He is an authority on Chinese affairs. |《文》He is well acquainted with [versed in] things Chinese.

つうか² 法案は満場一致で衆議院を通過した. The House of Representatives passed the bill unan-

つうかく 痛覚 a sense [《文》sensation] of pain ¶痛覚がある[ない] feel a [no] pain / 痛覚中枢 the pain center.

つうがく 通学 ¶通学する attend [go to] school. 文例⇩

つうかん¹ 通関 clearance 《of goods》 through the customs; customs clearance 《of goods》 ¶通関する clear 《goods》 through (the) customs; pass the customs; clear 《a ship》 / 通関手続をすます go through the customs formalities.

つうかん² 通観 ¶通観する survey; take [make] a general survey of.

つうかん³ 痛感する ⇒つうせつ² (痛切に感じる).

つうき 通気 ⇒かんき², つうふう¹ ¶通気管 an air pipe / 通気孔 a [an air] vent; an air hole / 通気坑 a ventilation shaft / 《養魚槽などの》通気装置 an aeration system.

つうぎょう 通暁 ¶通暁している be well acquainted 《with》; 《文》 be well versed 《in》; be well up 《in, on》; have a thorough knowledge 《of》; be at home 《in, with》.

つうきん 通勤 ¶通勤する travel to work; commute; attend 《at》 the [one's] office; 《住み込みに対して》 live out / 毎日電車で通勤する take the train daily to work / 通勤時間 《時刻》 《at》 commuter time; 《at》 rush hour(s) ⇒ラッシュ / 《所要時間》 (the) time spent in commuting / 通勤者 a commuter / 通勤線 a commuter line [railroad] / 通勤手当 a commuting [《米》commutation] allowance; a travel allowance / 通勤電[列]車 a commuter train.

つうげき 痛撃 《deal sb》 a hard [severe] blow.

つうこう 通行 passing; 《文》 transit; 《文》 traffic ¶通行する pass (through); go through [along] / 通行をさまたげる obstruct [《文》impede] the traffic; bar the thoroughfare; stand [get] in sb's way; block sb's passage / 通行できる passable / 通行できない impassable / 通行止めになっている 《道路が主語》 be closed (to traffic) / 通行人 a passer-by 《pl. passers-by》; 《歩行者》 a pedestrian. 文例⇩

つうこく 通告 notice; 《文》 notification; (a) warning ⇒つうち ¶通告する 《文》 notify sb 《of sth, that...》; give sb notice 《of sth, that...》; send word 《that...》; warn sb 《of sth, that...》.

つうこん 痛恨 great sorrow [regret] ¶…は痛恨にたえない 《文》 It is greatly to be regretted that... / 痛恨事 《文》 a matter for deep [great] regret; a most deplorable [regrettable] fact.

つうさん¹ 通産 ¶通産省 the Ministry of International Trade and Industry (略: MITI) ★普通 [miti] と発音する / 通産大臣 the Minister of International Trade and Industry.

つうさん² 通算 ¶通算する sum [add] up; total; 《含める》 include / 通算して…になる 《(300 tons)》 aggregate (300 tons); amount to (10,000 yen) (in all [in the aggregate]) / 《選手生活を通じての》通算平均打率《野球》 one's career batting average.

つうじ 通じ a motion; a (bowel) movement; a passage ¶ べんつう ¶通じがきちんとある have regular motions / 通じがない have no motions; be constipated / 《薬で通じをつける》 loosen the bowels / 通じ薬 〈緩下剤〉 a laxative; an aperient.

つうじて 通じて 〈…を経て〉 through; via; 〈…中〉 throughout; all over / 安藤氏を通じて through (the good offices of) Mr. Ando / テレビとラジオを通じて through [via] TV and radio / 一生を通じて throughout (one's) life; all one's life / 一年を通じて all the year round; throughout the year / 全国を通じて throughout [all over] the country; in the whole country / あらゆる階級を通じて in every class of society.

つうしょう¹ 通称 the name a person is commonly known by ¶中村熊五郎, 通称「熊」 Kumagoro Nakamura, who goes by the name of [is commonly called] 'Kuma'.

つうしょう² 通商 commerce; trade ¶通商する trade 《with》 / 通商を始める open trade [commerce] 《with a country》 / 通商産業省 ⇒つうさん¹ (通産省) / 通商条約を結ぶ enter into a treaty of commerce 《with》 / 在日ソ連通商代表部 the Soviet Trade Representative in Japan / 通商貿易 trade and commerce.

つうじょう(は) 通常(は) usually; generally; commonly; normally; as a general rule; under normal conditions ¶通常の ordinary; common; usual; customary; regular / 通常国会 an ordinary session of the Diet / 通常総会 an ordinary general meeting / 通常兵器 a conventional weapon.

つうじる 通じる 〈交通機関などが〉 run; be laid 《鉄道の線路が》; 〈開通する〉 be opened to traffic; 〈道などが〉 lead (to, into); open (into a room); 《文》 communicate 《with》; 〈電気などが〉 transmit; 〈通暁する〉 be well up 《in, on》; be familiar [《文》conversant] 《with》; be at

つうしん home 《in, with》; be well informed 《about, on》; 《文》be 《well》versed 《in》; 〈意志・言葉などが〉be understood 《by》; 〈電話が〉get connected 《to the Embassy》; get through 《to sb》; 〈内応する〉communicate secretly 《with》; keep [be] in touch 《with》; 〈通知する〉inform 《sb about [of] a fact》; 《文》communicate 《a matter to sb》/ 海岸に通じる道 a road leading to the seashore / 廊下へ通じるドア a door that opens into the corridor / 6ヵ国語に通じている have a good knowledge of six languages / 中国問題に通じている be an authority on Chinese affairs / 意味を(相手に)通じさせる make *oneself* understood; get *one*'s meaning across. 文例⇩

つうしん 通信 〈交通〉correspondence; 〈連絡〉《文》communication; 〈報道〉news; a report; 〈情報〉information; 《文》intelligence ¶通信する correspond 《with》; 《文》communicate 《with》; report (for a paper) / 通信を始める[続ける] get into [keep in] communication 《with》/ ロンドンからの通信によれば according to a dispatch from London / 通信衛星 a communications satellite / 通信機関 communications media / 通信工学 communication engineering / 通信講座 a correspondence course (in French) / 通信社 a news agency / 共同通信社 the Kyodo News Service / 通信手段 a means of communication / 通信装置 communications equipment / 通信販売 mail-order business / 通信販売で売る sell (goods) by mail; sell *sth* to a mail-order customer / 通信販売で買う buy *sth* by mail (order); buy (clothes) from a mail-order house [firm] / 通信費 postage; communication expenses / 通信簿 a report book [card] / 通信網 a communications network [system] / (絵葉書などの)通信欄 the space for correspondence. 文例⇩

つうじん 通人 a man about town.

つうせい 通性 a common property [quality]; 《文法》the common gender.

つうせき 痛惜 a 痛惜する《文》regret deeply; 《文》deplore; 《文》grieve [lament] (at, over) / 痛惜の念にたえない《文》It is much to be regretted that …; It is a thousand pities that ….

つうせつ[1] 通説 a commonly accepted theory; a popular opinion; a common view.

つうせつ[2] 痛切 ¶痛切な keen; 《文》acute / 痛切に keenly; 《文》acutely / 痛切に感じる feel [realize] keenly [acutely]; take *sth* to heart. 文例⇩

つうそく 通則 a general [common] rule.

つうぞく 通俗 ¶通俗の[的な] popular; common / 通俗的に in plain language; 《文》in common parlance / 通俗化する (write) in a popular style / 通俗化する popularize; vulgarize / 通俗科学書 a popular [nonspecialist] book on science / 通俗小説 a popular [lowbrow] novel.

つうだ 痛打 a telling [crushing] blow ¶痛打する 〈野球〉make a telling hit (to left field) / 痛打を与える give *sb* a telling [crushing] blow.

つうたつ 通達 (a) notification; a circular (note) ⇒つうち.

つうたん 痛嘆 《文》deep regret [lamentation]; 《文》bitter grief ¶痛嘆する grieve [《文》lament] deeply [bitterly]; deplore / 痛嘆すべき deplorable; 《文》lamentable / 痛嘆にたえない It is deplorable [《文》much to be regretted] that….

つうち 通知 〈通告〉(a) notice; (a) notification; 〈報知〉information; 〈通信〉(a) communication; 〈商業上の〉an advice ¶通知する give *sb* notice (of, that…); 《文》notify *sb* (of, that…); inform [《文》apprise] *sb* (of, that…); let *sb* know (of, that…); 《文》communicate (a matter to sb) / 通知を受ける have [receive] notice (of, that…); be notified [informed] (of, that…) / 通知状 a notice; a letter of advice / 通知預金 a deposit at notice. 文例⇩

つうちょう[1] 通帳 a passbook; a bankbook (銀行の).

つうちょう[2] 通牒 a note; a notification; a circular ¶通牒を発する send [issue] a notification; 《文》notify *sb* (of, that…); give *sb* notice (of, that…).

つうどく 通読 ¶通読する read (a book) through; read (a book) from cover to cover; go through (a book). 文例⇩

ツートンカラー two-tone coloring ¶ツートンカラーの two-tone (shoes).

つうねん 通念 a common [generally accepted] idea.

つうば 痛罵 (a) denunciation 《of》; 《文》a diatribe (against); 〈酷評〉(a) harsh [bitter] criticism ¶痛罵する denounce; 《文》inveigh against; rail at; 《文》excoriate; criticize severely; level (a) scathing [(an) incisive] criticism at.

ツーピース a two-piece dress [suit].

つうふう[1] 通風 ventilation (部屋などの); a draft (ボイラーの) ¶通風のよい[悪い] well-[badly-]ventilated / 通風孔 a [an air] vent / 通風装置 a ventilation apparatus [device].

---

on the phone. / I couldn't get through to Mr. Smith. / 私のフランス語では通じなかった. I couldn't make myself understood with my French. / なぞを彼には通じなかった. My hint was lost on him.

つうしん そのころのアメリカでは農家の主婦は通信販売のカタログを見て物を買うか, 村の雑貨屋で買物をしたのだった. In the United States of those days the farmer's wife shopped out of a mail-order catalogue, or at a village general store.

つうせつ[2] トムはフランスを旅行してみて, 高校で習ったフランス語がどんなに役に立たないものかを痛切に感じた. Tom's trip to France brought home to him how useless his high-school French was.

つうち 着いたらすぐ通知して下さい. Please write to me as soon as you get there. / 変更の都度ご通知します. We will let you know whenever there is an alteration.

つうどく 1回通読しただけではこの文章は理解できなかった. I could not understand this passage the first time through.

つうふう² 痛風 gout. ¶痛風の gouty.
つうぶん 通分 《数》 通分する reduce (fractions) to a common denominator.
つうへい 通弊 a common abuse; 《文》 evil. 文例↓
つうほう 通報 a report; information ⇨つうち.
つうぼう 痛棒 ¶痛棒を加える deal *sb* a hard [severe] blow; 〈散々な目にあわせる〉 beat *sb* hollow; 〈批判する〉 criticize *sb* severely [harshly].
つうやく 通訳 〈事〉 interpreting; interpretation; 〈人〉 an interpreter ¶通訳をする interpret; act [serve] as interpreter (for) / 通訳を通して話す speak through an interpreter / 通訳官 an official interpreter.
つうゆう 通有 ¶通有の common (to). 文例↓
つうよう¹ 通用 ¶通用する pass (for); circulate; be current; 〈切符などが〉 be available; be good; be valid; 〈規則などが〉 hold good [true] / 切符の通用期間 the term for which a ticket is valid / 通用口[門] a side entrance [door]; 〈使用人や出入り商人などのための〉 a service entrance [door].
つうよう² 痛痒 ¶少しも痛痒を感じない be not at all [in the least] affected (by); do not care at all [a bit] (about). 文例↓
つうらん 通覧 a survey; a general [an overall] survey; an overview ¶通覧する survey; take a (general) survey of; look [glance] over; 〈通読する〉 read through.
ツーリスト a tourist ¶〈旅客機や客船の〉ツーリストクラスの乗客 a tourist(-class) passenger / ツーリストクラスで旅行する travel tourist (class).
つうれい 通例 ¶通例 usually; commonly; ordinarily; generally; as a rule / 通例の usual; common; ordinary; general; customary.
つうれつ 痛烈 ¶痛烈な sharp; cutting; scathing; 《文》 incisive; biting / 痛烈に批判する criticize severely; 《文》 deliver incisive [blistering] criticism (on).
つうろ 通路 a passage; a passageway; a way; a path; a pathway; 〈車内・劇場などの〉 an aisle ¶通路側の席 an aisle seat.
つうろん 通論 an outline (of); an introduction (to).
つうわ 通話 a telephone call ¶3通話 three (telephone) calls / 通話口 the mouthpiece / 通話料 the charge [rate] for a (telephone) call. 文例↓

つえ 杖 a cane; a (walking) stick; a staff;〈支え〉a prop; a stay ¶つえをついて[つかずに] with [without] the help of a stick / つえをついて歩く walk with a cane [stick] / つえを携える carry a cane / つえにすがる lean on one's stick / つえとも柱とも頼む lean on *sb* as the only [sole] support (of one's family). 文例↓
ツェツェばえ ツェツェ蠅 《昆》 a tsetse fly; a tsetse 《*pl.* -(s)》.
つか¹ 柄 the hilt 《of a sword》; the haft 《of a dagger》; the handle 《of a knife》 ¶刀の柄に手をかける put one's hand on the hilt of one's sword; be about to unsheathe one's sword / 柄も通れと刺す stab *sb* to the hilt; thrust a dagger home.
つか² 塚 a [an earth] mound; 〈古墳〉 a tumulus 《*pl.* -li》; a barrow ¶塚を築く build a mound.
つが 栂 《植》 a Japanese hemlock.
つかい 使い 〈用件〉 an errand; 〈使者〉 a messenger; 〈特に秘密の〉 an emissary; 〈神様の〉 a [an animal] familiar; 〈持参者〉 the bearer ¶使いをする[に行く] do [run] an errand; go on an errand / 使いにやる send *sb* on an errand / 手紙を使いに持たせてやる send a letter by (a) messenger [《文》by an emissary, by hand] / 使いに物を取りに[人を呼びに]やる send for [*sb*] / 象使い an elephant handler / ライオン使い a lion tamer. 文例↓
つがい 番い 〈1対〉 a pair; 〈雌雄〉 a couple;《文》a brace 《単複同形》 ¶番いになる pair (up [off]) / 番いで in pairs.
つかいかた 使い方 how to use [handle, operate] ¶前置詞の使い方 the use of prepositions / 使い方を誤る misuse (a word); make a wrong use of (statistics) / 部下の使い方を知らない do not know how to treat [handle] one's men.
つかいきる 使い切る 〈充分に利用する〉 make full use of; get all the use out of; 《文》 utilize *sth* to the fullest; 〈使い果たす〉 ⇨つかいはたす.
つかいこなす 使いこなす use *sth* efficiently; know how to handle *sth* ¶英語を完全に使いこなす have a perfect command of English; have English at one's command / 電動タイプライターを使いこなせるようになった become skilled in the use of [《文》proficient on] the electric typewriter.
つかいこみ 使い込み embezzlement; misappropriation.
つかいこむ 使い込む 〈横領する〉 embezzle;

つうへい 他人の成功をうらやむのは人間の通弊である. It is a common weakness of human nature to envy others for their success.
つうゆう それは日本人の通有性である. That is a characteristic [trait] common to [shared by] all Japanese.
つうよう¹ 彼のこの言葉は今日でも立派に通用する. This remark of his holds good [true] in our day. / この用語はごく最近一般に通用するようになったものだ. This is a term that has only recently gained general currency. / 通用は当日限り.《表示》Good [Valid] for day of issue only.
つうよう² 僕は少しも痛痒を感じない. It doesn't matter at all to me.
つうわ 1通話3分間の料金は10円です. The charge is ten yen for (each conversation of) three minutes.
つえ 彼女は老後のつえとも柱とも頼んだ一人息子に死なれてしまった. She lost her only son, on whom she had depended as the prop and stay for her old age.
つかい 使いの者にご返事を下さい. Please let me have an answer by the bearer (of this). / 横浜まで使いにやるのだが, この子に使い賃をどれくらいやったらいいだろうか. How much should I give the boy for going to Yokohama on an errand? / きつねはおいなりさまのお使いだ. The fox is the familiar [messenger] of

つかいすぎ　使い過ぎ 〈頻度〉 use (one's car) too much ; 〈数量〉 use too many (long words) ; use too much (sugar) ; 〈人〉 work sb too hard ; overwork (one's eyes) ; overtax (one's throat) ¶ 金を使い過ぎる spend one's money too freely ; spend too much money (on) / 身体を使い過ぎる work too hard ; overwork.

つかいすて　使い捨て ¶ 使い捨ての disposable (towels) ; throwaway (ball pens) ; (paper cups) to be thrown away after use / 使い捨てにする 〈1 回で〉 use sth once and then throw it away ; 〈使えるだけ使って〉 get all the use out of sth and then discard it / 使い捨て主義 the throw-away principle.

つかいだて　使い立て 文例⇩

つかいて　使い手 ¶〈使用者〉 a user ; 〈消費者〉 a consumer ; 〈雇い主〉 an employer ¶ やりの使い手 a master spearsman. 文例⇩

つかいで　使いで ¶ 使いでがある 〈品物が〉 last a long time ; last long (疑問文・否定文で) ; 〈金が〉 go a long way ; go far (疑問文・否定文で). 文例⇩

つかいならす　使い慣らす use sth for a long time ; train sb ; break in (a horse).

つかいなれる　使い慣れる be [get] accustomed to using [to use] sth ; get used [accustomed] to sth ¶ 使い慣れた familiar ; old.

つかいのこし　使い残し 《文》 the remainder ; the leftover(s) ; 《文》 the remnant ¶ 使い残しの 《文》 remnant ; left over (from).

つかいばしり　使い走り ¶ 使い走りする run [go on] errands (for sb).

つかいはたす　使い果たす use up ; 《文》 exhaust ; spend all (one's money) ; go [run] through (one's fortune) ¶ 精力を使い果たす exhaust [use up, be drained of] (all) one's energy / 資源を使い果たす drain (a country) of (its) resources / 貯金を使い果たす use up one's savings. 文例⇩

つかいふるす　使い古す wear sth out (by use) ¶ 使い古した worn-out ; well-worn ; 〈陳腐な〉 hackneyed (phrases) ; threadbare (expressions).

つかいまわす　使い回す ⇨ こくし (酷使する).

つかいみち　使い道 ¶ 使い道がある be useful [《文》serviceable (《文》of use) (for) ; can be used (as) ; be usable [《文》utilizable] (as) / 使い道がない be useless ; be of no use ; be good for nothing / 使い道が広い 《文》 be of wide [extensive] use. 文例⇩

つかいもの¹　使い物 ¶ 使い物になる be useful [《文》of use] (for) ; be usable [《文》utilizable] (as) / 使い物にならない be no good [useless, 《文》of no use] (for) ; be good for nothing. 文例⇩

つかいもの²　遣い物 〈贈り物〉 a present ; a gift (★ gift は present よりもやや改まった語) ; 〈わいろ〉 a bribe ¶ …を遣い物にする make a present [gift] of sth / 遣い物をする send a present [gift] (to sb) ; 〈人を贈る〉 bribe sb ; offer [give] a bribe (to sb).

つかいよう　使い様 ⇨ つかいかた 文例⇩

つかいわける　使い分ける put (each thing) to (its) proper use ¶ わかりやすいように掲示の色を使い分ける use different colors in signs to make them easier to follow / 聴衆に応じて言葉を使い分ける choose one's words to suit [according to] one's audience / 3 か国語を使い分ける use three different languages without getting them mixed up [confused] / あめとむちとをうまく使い分ける use the stick and the carrot appropriately.

つかう　使う 〈使用する〉 use ; 《文》 make use of ; 《文》 employ ; 〈取り扱う〉 handle (a tool) ; operate [work] (a machine) ; manage [handle, treat] (people) ; 〈雇う〉 employ ; take sb into one's service ; keep (a servant) ; 〈消費する〉 spend (money), consume (electricity) ; 〈術・法を〉 《文》 practice ; use ¶ 新兵器を使う use a new weapon ; bring a newly devised weapon into action / 本に金を使う spend money on books / 手品を使う do conjuring tricks / 人形を使う manipulate a puppet / 使われている 〈物、言葉などが〉 be in use ; 〈人が〉《文》 be in sb's employ [service] / 一般に[日常]使われている be in general [daily] use / 現在使われている言葉 words in current use [usage] / 使われるようになる come to be used ; come into use / 実際に[普通に, 広く, 段々多く]使われるようになる come into real [common, widespread, increasing] use / 使われなくなる drop out of use ; 《文》 fall into disuse ; 《文》 cease to

---

the god Inari.

つかいこむ 彼は僕が預けておいた金を使い込んでしまった. He has taken liberties with the money I gave him to look after. / この道具は使い込むほど味が出る. These tools improve with use.

つかいだて お使い立てしてすみませんか. I'm sorry to trouble you, but would you mind mailing this letter for me?

つかいて あんな男は使い手があるまい. No one will employ a man like that.

つかいで 今の1万円はあまり使いでがない. Ten thousand yen doesn't go very far today.

つかいなれる この万年筆は使い慣れると具合よくなります. The longer you use this pen, the more smoothly it will write.

つかいはたす 彼はこの仕事で彼はすっかり精力を使い果たした. He has spent all his energy on this work. | This work has sapped all his energy.

つかいみち 物にはそれぞれ使い道がある. Everything has its use [is useful in its own way]. / そんなものは使い道がない. There's no use for such a thing.

つかいもの¹ この機械はもはや使いものにならない. This machine is no longer usable. / その装置はまだ効率が悪くて使い物にならない. The apparatus is still so inefficient that it is useless. | The apparatus is still too inefficient to be any use.

つかいよう 千円でも使いようで1万円になる. A thousand yen well

つがう 番う mate 《with》;〈鳥など〉pair 《with》; cover (獣の雄が雌に).

つかえる¹ 支える be choked [blocked, obstructed] 《by, with》;〈ひっかかる〉stick [get caught] 《in》;〈言葉が〉be at a loss 《what to say》; falter; be stuck for words ¶〈骨などがのどにつかえる〈食物が主語〉stick [get caught, get stuck] in *one's* throat;〈人が主語〉get *sth* stuck in *one's* throat / 胸がつかえる lie heavy on *one's* stomach (食物が主語) ; *one's* stomach feels heavy / つかえながら話す speak in a halting way; stumble through *one's* speech. 文例⇩

つかえる² 仕える《文》serve *sb*;《文》be in *sb's* service; work under *sb*; work for *sb*;〈かしずく〉attend [wait] on *sb*.

つかえる³ 使える be usable [《文》utilizable] 《as》; be useful [《文》serviceable,《文》of use] 《for》; be fit for use ¶つかいみち〈…に使える〉serve for [the purpose of];〈目的に〉be employed for;〈言葉を話せる〉can speak《German》¶広く使える be useful in a variety of ways ; be of wide [extensive] use / フランス語を自由に使える have a perfect command of French / 使える男 a useful [capable] man. 文例⇩

つがえる 番える〈矢を〉fit 《an arrow on [to] the bowstring》.

つかさどる 司る〈治める〉rule; govern; administer;〈担任する〉take [have, be in] charge of;〈管理する〉《文》conduct; manage; direct; preside over ¶人間の運命をつかさどる神々 the gods who preside over men's destinies.

つかつか straight; without hesitation; boldly ¶つかつかと歩み寄る walk [go] directly [straight] up to *sb* [*sth*].

つかぬこと つかぬ事 ¶つかぬことをお尋ねいたしますが This may be a foolish [an abrupt] question, but….

つかねる 束ねる bundle; bunch ¶手をつかねて見ている look on with folded arms; just watch idly without doing anything about 《it》.

つかのま 束の間《for》a brief space of time; a passing moment ¶つかの間の brief; momentary; passing;《文》transient;《文》ephemeral;《文》transitory;《文》fleeting;《文》evanescent / つかの間も even for a moment. 文例⇩

つかまえどころ 掴まえ所 a hold; a grip;〈要点〉a point ¶つかまえ所のない slippery; elusive; evasive;《文》subtle;〈あいまいな〉vague; intangible / つかまえ所のない返事をする give an evasive answer.

つかまえる 掴まえる catch; take [get, catch, lay] hold of; seize; lay 《*one's*》 hands on;〈握る〉grasp;〈逮捕する〉arrest; capture ¶そでをつかまえる catch [seize] by the sleeve / つかまえて放さない keep fast hold of ;〈帰ろうとする人を〉detain; keep [prevent] *sb* from leaving / つかまえようとする catch [grasp] at ; make a grab [clutch] 《at》. 文例⇩

つかませる 掴ませる〈物を〉make *sb* catch hold of *sth*; let *sb* grasp *sth*;〈わいろを〉bribe;《俗》grease *sb's* palm;〈にせ物などを〉palm *sth* off on *sb*; fob *sth* off on *sb*; fob *sb* off with *sth*; foist *sth* off on *sb* ¶つかませて口止めする bribe *sb* into silence; buy *sb's* silence.

つかまる 捕まる〈捕えられる〉be caught; be arrested;《文》be apprehended; be captured; fall into the clutches of ;〈つかまえる〉catch [take, get] hold of ;〈すがる〉hold (fast) to; hold [hang] on to. 文例⇩

つかみ 掴み【機】a grip.

つかみあい 掴み合い grasping (at) each other; scrimmaging; a tussle; a scuffle ¶つかみ合いをする come to grips 《with》; grapple [scuffle] 《with》. 文例⇩

つかみあう ⇒ つかみあい (つかみ合いをする).

つかみかかる 掴み掛かる catch [grasp, clutch,

---

spent is worth ten thousand. つかう それはあまり小さいので顕微鏡を使わないと見えません。It is too tiny to see without using [without the use of] a microscope. / 私の事務所を使いなさいと言ってくれた。He offered me the use of his office. / 1 カ月に砂糖をどのぐらい使いますか。How much sugar do you use [consume] a month? / 彼はその 100 万円のお金をあっけなく使ってしまった。He went [ran] through that one million yen all too fast. / 彼は立派な英語を使う。His English is good. | He speaks English well. | 彼はフランス語を楽に使えるようになった。He acquired a fluent command of French.

つかえる¹ 〈のどに〉声がつかえてしまった。My voice caught in my throat. / 餅がのどにつかえてしまった。He choked on a piece of rice cake. / 僕はまだ仕事がつかえている。I have more work (on my hands) than I can handle. | My hands are full.

つかえる³ 彼は右手が使えなくなった。He lost the use of his right hand. / あの男はなかなか使えますよ。You will find him quite useful. / いつでも使えるようになっています。They are ready for use.

つかのま 喜びもつかの間であった。His joy was short-lived.

つかまる 牧の意見を聞こうと思って、彼のいそうな所へあちこち電話してみたのですが、つかまえることができませんでした。I wanted to hear Maki's opinion and phoned several likely places, but I couldn't get hold of [get in touch with] him.

つかまる しっかりつかまっておいで。Hold (on) tight! / 手長猿は巧みに枝につかまった。The gibbon caught itself skillfully on a branch. / 子じかは生まれて数週間すると、もうすばしこくて人間にはつかまらない。When only a few weeks old, a fawn is agile enough to evade capture by man. / とうとう警察につかまってしまった。The law caught up with him at last. / 犯人はまだつかまらない。The culprit is still at large. / 彼につかまってしまって なかなか来られなかったのさ。I was held up by him and couldn't come earlier.

つかみあい 口論の果てはつかみ合いになった。They progressed [went] from words to blows.

つかむ 少年は両手で枝をつかんで木にぶら下がっていた。The boy hung on to a tree with his hands gripping a branch. / しっかりつかんで放すな。Don't let go your

つかみだす 掴み出す 〈物を〉take *sth* out 《of *one's* pocket》; take a handful of 《money out of...》; 〈追い出す〉turn *sb* out 《of the room》.

つかみどころ 掴み所 ⇨ つかまえどころ.

つかみどり 掴み取り ¶つかみ取りをする get as much 《rice》[many 《coins》] as *one* can grasp in one handful.

つかむ 掴む seize; catch; 〈握る〉grasp; grip; grab; hold; take [catch] hold of; lay (*one's*) hands on ¶しっかりつかむ grasp [hold] tightly; get a secure grasp 《of, on》; have a sure [fast] grip 《on》/ しっかりつかんで放さない keep a tight grasp 《on》/ つかもうとする grab [grasp, catch] at; clutch [make a grab] at / 手をつかむ grasp [seize] *sb's* hand; grasp [seize] *sb* by the hand / つかみそこなう fail to grasp; miss *one's* [a] hold / 〈手を伸ばせば〉つかめる所に 《lie》within grasping distance / 真意をつかむ grasp what *sb* really means / 真相をつかむ get at [find out] the truth. 文例⇩

つかる 漬かる 〈ひたる〉be soaked 《in》; be steeped 《in》; 〈浸水する〉be flooded; 〈漬物が〉be well pickled ¶風呂につかる soak in the bath(tub) / 〈海水浴で〉ちょっと海につかる have a dip / 〈英〉bathe / 川の水に胸までつかって歩いて渡る wade chest-deep across a stream. 文例⇩

つかれ 疲れ tiredness; 〈文〉fatigue; weariness; exhaustion ¶体[心]の疲れ physical [mental] fatigue / 読書の疲れ fatigue from reading / 神経の疲れ nervous strain / 目の疲れ eyestrain / 疲れが出る feel tired [〈文〉fatigued] / 疲れが取れる recover from [get over] *one's* fatigue / 疲れを休める rest *oneself* / 疲れを取る relieve *one's* fatigue / 眠って疲れを取る sleep off *one's* fatigue / 疲れの色を見せる show signs of fatigue. 文例⇩

つかれさせる 疲れさせる tire; weary; 〈文〉fatigue; 〈くたくたに〉tire [wear] *sb* out; exhaust; 〈過労させる〉strain; overtax.

つかれる¹ 疲れる be [get] tired; tire; grow weary; 〈文〉become fatigued ¶綿のように疲れる, 疲れ切[果]てる be [get] tired [worn] out; be quite [dead] tired; be exhausted; 〈口語〉get dog-tired; 〈米俗〉be pooped; 〈英俗〉be knackered / 歩き疲れる be tired from walking / 疲れてもの も言えない be too tired to speak.

つかれる² 憑かれる 〈物の怪(け)に〉be possessed 《by, with》; 〈観念に〉be obsessed 《by, with》¶憑かれた人のように 《work》like one possessed.

つき¹ 月 the moon; 〈暦の〉a month ¶二十日(はつか)の月 a moon twenty days old / 月の lunar / 月のない夜 a moonless night / 月の光 moonlight ⇨ げっこう¹ / 月の光を浴びた moonlit / 月の光で浴びて in the moonlight / 月の照り渡る空〈文〉a moon-filled sky / 月の出 moonrise; the rise of the moon / 月の入り moonset; 〈米〉moondown / 月の裏側 the other [dark, hidden] side of the moon / 月のかさ a halo [ring] round the moon / 〈ロケットなどによる〉月の探索 a moon [lunar] probe / 月への着陸 (a) lunar landing / 月とすっぽんほど違う be as different as light and darkness [chalk and cheese, day and night] / 月に3万円 30,000 yen per [a] month / 月1回 once a month; monthly / 月2回の twice a month; semi-monthly / 月がわりで 〈英〉fortnightly / 〈英〉once a fortnight / 月が変わると next month; at the beginning [〈文〉with the coming] of the next month / 月着陸船 a lunar module; a moon-landing craft / 月ロケット a moon rocket. 文例⇩

つき² 付き〈運〉luck ¶付きがいい[悪い]〈インクの〉take well [badly] (to paper); print well [badly] / 〈火の〉be quick [slow] to kindle / 付きが変わるのを待つ wait for *one's* luck to change. 文例⇩

つき² 突き a thrust; a pass; a lunge;〈フェンシング〉a pass ¶一突きに at a stroke; with a

---

hold [grip] on it. / 彼はその虫をさっとつかんで捕えた. He caught the insect with a swift grab of his hand. / 彼は自分に割り当てられた役割をしっかりつかんでいる[いない]. He has a sure grip [has only a shaky grip] on the role assigned to him.

つかる 屋根[床]まで水につかってしまった. My house was flooded roof-[floor-]deep. / 村は過去20年間にこの川のはんらんで2度も水につかった. The village has been under water twice in the last twenty years when the river has overflowed.

つかれ 1杯のコーヒーで疲れも直った. A cup of coffee took away my tiredness [fatigue]. / A cup of coffee livened [perked] me up again. / そのような長旅の疲れにはとても耐え得ないように思われます. I am afraid I wouldn't be able to bear such a long and tiring journey. / どうやら旅の疲れが出てきたらしい. It seems the strain of traveling has begun to tell on me.

つかれる 彼はまだ体が弱っていてすぐ疲れる. He is still weak and tires quickly [and soon gets tired]. / この仕事は大変疲れる. This work is very fatiguing [wears me out]. / 薄暗いところで読書をすると当然目が疲れる. Reading in a poor light taxes your eyes. / あれにはすっかり神経が疲れました. That was a great strain on my nerves.

つき¹ 月が出た. The moon rose [came up]. / 月が沈んだ. The moon set [went down]. / 月も欠けはする. The moon waxes and wanes. / 月が低くかかっている. The moon is (hanging) low in the sky. / 今夜はまあなんて明るい月だこと. What a bright moon we have tonight! / 明るい月の光を浴びながら彼女と散歩をした. I took a walk with her in the bright moonlight. / 何月の月ですか. How old is the moon? / 今夜は月が出ていますか. Is there a moon tonight? / 今夜は月が出ていません. There is no moon tonight. / その晩にはどんな月が出ていましたか. What phase was the moon in (on) that night? / 月の石は地球上のどんな岩石とも全く違ったものであることがわかった. The moon rocks proved to be totally different from any found on earth. / 彼女は月が満ちて女の子を生んだ. At full term she gave birth to a girl.

つき² 付きが回ってきた. My luck has turned in [is in]. / その時にはえらく付きが続いていた. We were then having a remarkable

thrust / 一突き突く give sb a thrust; lunge at; give sb a stab (in the back).

つき⁴ 就き 《...ごとに》 per; for; 《...ゆえに》 on account of; owing to; because of; as; since ¶ 1ダースにつき 1,000円 1000 yen a [per] dozen / 病気につき on account of [owing to] (one's) illness; as [because, since] one is ill.

-つき …付き with…; including…; …included ¶ 朝食[2食]付きで breakfast [two meals] included / 5分利付き公債 a public bond bearing 5 per cent interest. 文例⇩

つき¹ 次 ¶次の of the next; following; 《文》ensuing; 《文》succeeding; coming; 《第2位の》 second / 次の間 the next [《文》 adjoining] room; 《控え室》 an anteroom / 次の間つきの部屋 a 《hotel》 suite / 次の日 the next [following] day; the day after / この次の日曜日 next Sunday / 次の次の日曜日 the next [following] Sunday / 次の次の日曜日に 《今日から数えて》 on Sunday after next; 《過去や未来のある日から数えて》 two Sundays later [after that] / 次に next; secondly; 《その後で》 (and) then / …の次に next to…; after… / この次に next [another] time / 一つおいて次に next but one (to) / …の次に位する be [rank] next [second] to… / 次から次へと one after another; in succession; successively / 東海道五十三次 the fifty-three stages on the Tokaido Highway. 文例⇩

つぎ² 継ぎ 《補布》a patch ¶ 継ぎを当てる patch 《a jacket》; put a patch 《on》/ 継ぎだらけの covered with patches; 《文》 much-patched 《trousers》. 文例⇩

-づき …付 attached 《to》 ¶ 大使館付武官 a military [naval] attaché to an embassy / 連隊付中尉 a lieutenant serving with a regiment.

つきあい 付き合い 《交際》 association ⇒こうさい³ ¶ 付き合いが広い know a lot of people; have a wide [large] circle of acquaintances / 付き合いが狭い do not know many people; do not have many acquaintances / 付き合いのいい[悪い]人 a sociable [an unsociable] person; 《口語》 a good [bad] mixer / お付き合いに[で] for company; for the sake of friendship. 文例⇩

つきあう 付き合う 《友達として》 associate with; go around [about] with; mix with 《多数の相手と》, go about [around] with; 《口語》 go steady with; 《男女のカップルが》 go around together; 《一緒に行く》 go with sb; 《一緒にいてやる》 keep sb company ¶ 対等に付き合う 《be》 associate (with sb) on equal terms / …と親しく付き合っている be on friendly terms with… / 仲よく付き合う get along [on] (well) (with sb) / 人と付き合っていくうちを嫌う be unsociable; prefer one's own company / 付き合いやすい[難い]人 a person who is easy [hard] to get along [on] with / 付き合っていくうちに as one gets to know sb better; 《文》 on further acquaintance. 文例⇩

つきあかり 月明かり moonlight / 月明かりのある晩 a moonlight night / 月明かりのさしている庭 a moonlight [moonlit] garden / 月明かりで道を見分ける make out one's way by moonlight.

つきあげる 突き上げる push [《文》 thrust] up; toss 《組合員などから》 突き上げられて under pressure (from); 《文》 at the insistence [demand] (of); goaded (by).

つきあたり 突き当たり 《終端》 the end [bottom] 《of a street》 ¶ 廊下の突き当たりに at the (other [far]) end of the passage [corridor].

つきあたる 突き当たる 《衝突する》 run [bump, clash] against [into]; collide with; 《行き止まる》 come to the end [bottom] of 《a road》 / 路地を突き当たって左に曲がる turn to the left at the end of the lane.

つきあわせる 突き合わせる 《対決させる》 confront (A) with (B); 《向かい合わせに》 put (A) opposite (B); 《照合する》 compare [check, 《文》 collate] (A) with (B) ¶ 顔を突き合わせる come [be] face to face (with) / ひざを突き合わせて話をする talk face to face (with).

つぎあわせる 継ぎ合わせる join [piece] 《scraps of cloth》 together ⇒つなぎあわせる.

つきおくれ 月遅れ ¶ 月遅れの雑誌 a back number 《of a magazine》; a magazine a month [a few months] old.

つきおとす 突き落とす push [knock] down; push [shove] off; 《文》 thrust down [off] 《強く》 ¶ 列車[列車]から突き落とす push sb over a cliff [off a train].

つきかえす 突き返す give sb a poke [《文》 thrust] in return; 《商品などを》 send back; refuse to accept; 《提案などを》 reject; turn down.

つきかかる 突きかかる lunge [jab, 《文》 thrust (out)] at sb 《with a knife》.

つきかげ 月影 moonlight ¶ 月影さやかな夜

---

run of luck.

-つき 庭付き1戸建ての家に前から住みたいと思っていた。 I've always wanted to live in a detached house with a garden. / バス・トイレ付きの部屋がありますか。 Have you got a room with bath and toilet? / 1泊2食付きで 8,000円です。 We charge 8,000 yen a night, including two meals [with dinner and breakfast included].

つぎ¹ それはまたこの次にしよう。 Let us leave that for another time. / 次に来たのは田中氏です。 Mr. Tanaka was the next (one) to arrive. / 氏の論ずるところは次のごとくであった。 His arguments were as follows [like this]. / 出席者中には次の人びとがあった。 Among those present were the following. / 今朝は次から次へと客があった。 This morning we have had one visitor after another. / We have had a constant stream of visitors this morning. / 次から次へと奇妙な事件が持ち上がった。 A series of strange incidents took place in quick [rapid] succession.

つぎ² 彼はしりに継ぎの当たったズボンをはいていた。 He wore a pair of trousers which were patched in the seat.

つきあい 途中までお付き合いしましょう。 I will keep you company part of the way. / 僕たちは長い付き合いです。 We have been friends for many years. / 私の酒はほんのお付き合い程度です。 I drink just to be sociable.

つきあう ちょっと付き合ってくれ

つきがけ a bright moonlight night.

つきかけ 月掛け ¶月掛けで by monthly installments ⇨ げっぷ¹ / 月掛け貯金 a monthly installment deposit.

つきかためる 突き固める tamp (down); ram down 《the soil》; pack sth tightly by striking it.

つぎき 接ぎ木 〈方法〉 grafting; 〈木〉 a grafted tree ¶接ぎ木する graft (a tree into [on] another); put a graft in [on] 《a stock》.

つききず 突き傷 a stab 《wound》.

つきぎめ 月極め ¶月極め monthly 《subscribers》/ 月極めで by the month.

つきくだく 搗き砕く pound [crush] up; grind down.

つきごと 月ごと ¶月ごとに monthly; every [each] month.

つぎこむ 注ぎ込む 〈注ぐ〉 pour in [into]; 〈金を〉 sink [lay out] 《money》in; invest 《capital》in; put [pour] 《money》into. 文例⇩

つきころす 突き殺す stab sb to death; 〈牛が角で〉 gore sb to death.

つぎざお 継ぎ竿〈釣りざお〉 a jointed fishing rod; 〈三味線の〉 a jointed stem.

つきささる 突き刺さる stick in [into]; pierce. 文例⇩

つきさす 突き刺す pierce; stab ¶留め針を突き刺す stick [put] a pin into / やりで突き刺す pierce 《sb's side》with a spear [lance] / 短刀で突き刺す stab sb with a dagger; plunge [《文》thrust, run] a dagger into 《sb's chest》. 文例⇩

つきしたがう 付き従う 〈下僕をする〉 follow;《文》accompany; 〈部下として働く〉 serve sb; work under sb; 〈服従する〉《文》submit [yield] to.

つきずえ 月末 (at) the end of the month.

つきすすむ 突き進む push [plunge] on [forward]; 《文》push one's way (to).

つきそい 付き添い 〈付き添うこと〉《文》 attendance; 〈従者〉 an attendant; 《文》 a suite 《随員全員》; 〈護衛〉 an escort; 〈病人・子供の〉 a nurse; 〈花嫁の〉 a bridesmaid; 〈花婿の〉 a best man ¶付き添い看護婦 a nurse attending [in attendance on] a patient.

つきそう 付き添う attend [wait] on; 《文》 be in attendance upon;《文》accompany; escort ¶父親に付き添われて出席する present oneself accompanied by one's father. 文例⇩

つきたおす 突き倒す knock [push] down.

つきだし 突き出し 《料理》(an) hors d'oeuvre 《pl. hors d'oeuvre(s)》.

つきだす 突き出す stick [push,《文》thrust] sth out; stretch [put]《one's arm》 out ¶窓から首を突き出す stick [poke] one's head out of [《米》 out] the window / 警察に突き出す hand 《a culprit》over to the police; turn sb in.

つぎたす 注ぎ足す pour more (water) in [into]; replenish 《a glass with wine》; fill up 《one's [sb's] cup》again 《with coffee》.

つぎたす 継ぎ足す add (to); have (two rooms) added to 《one's house》; attach 《extra material》to 《a skirt》.

つきたてる 突き立てる 〈刺す〉 stab;《文》thrust; 〈立てる〉 plant 《a stick》in 《the ground》.

つきたらず 月足らず ¶月足らずの子 a premature baby / 月足らずで生まれる be born prematurely [before its time].

つきづき 月々 every [each] month ¶月々の monthly.

つぎつぎ 次々 ⇨ つぎ¹《次から次へと》.

つきっきり 付きっ切り ¶付きっ切りで看護する《文》be in constant attendance on 《a patient》; never leave 《the patient's》bedside / 付きっ切りで勉強をみてやる sit by 《a boy》 and help 《him》with 《his》studies.

つきつける 突き付ける put [place,《文》 thrust] sth under sb's nose;《文》thrust sth before sb ¶ピストルを突き付ける point a revolver at sb / 銃を突き付けて at the point of a gun / 動かぬ証拠を突き付ける confront sb with irrefutable evidence;《文》thrust [put] indubitable evidence before sb. 文例⇩

つきつめる 突き詰める 〈究明する〉 investigate [look into] sth thoroughly; make a thorough investigation of; get to the bottom of ¶突き詰めると in the final [last] analysis ⇨ けっきょく / 突き詰めて考える take 《a matter》 too seriously; take 《a matter》too much to heart.

つきでる 突き出る stick [jut] out; project ¶突き出た projecting; protruding / 海に長く突き出ている岬 a cape jutting out a long way into the sea.

つきとおす 突き通す ⇨つきさす.

つきとばす 突き飛ばす push [hurl, shove, 《文》thrust] sb away; send sb flying.

つきとめる 突き止める 〈確かめる〉《文》ascertain; make sure [certain] (of); assure oneself

---

ませんか. Won't you give me your company for a moment. / 今晩食事を付き合ってくれませんか. Would you please have dinner with me this evening? / 当時彼はよくプロボクサーたちと付き合っていた. In those days he went about with professional boxers a great deal. / あの女とは付き合わない方がいい. You had better avoid [keep away from] her.

つぎこむ 僕は莫大な金と時間とをこの計画に注ぎ込んできたのだ. I've put a great deal of time and money into this project.

つきささる タイヤにくぎが突き刺さっていた. I found a nail stuck into the tire.

つきさす もずは木の枝に獲物を突き刺しておくことがある. Butcher-birds sometimes keep their victims impaled on a twig of a tree.

つきそう 彼は体が弱く, 外出の時はいつも妻が付き添っていた. He was weak in health, and when he went out his wife was in constant attendance.

つきつける 彼は, さあどうだと突き付けられるまで, 自分の説の弱点に全く気付かなかった. He never saw the weak points of his theory until they were pressed on his attention [thrust under his nose].

つきでる 小さな半島が湖の真中まで突き出ている. A little peninsula runs out to the middle of the lake. / 岩が頭上にぐっと突き出ていた. The rock bulged out above us in an overhang. / 一連

つきなみ 月並み ¶月並みな conventional; commonplace; stale; trite; hackneyed; 《文》platitudinous; stereotyped.

つきぬく 突き抜く pierce [shoot, run, 《文》thrust] through; penetrate.

つきぬける 突き抜ける go through ★つきぬくの項の動詞を主語とすれば「突き抜ける」の意味ですべて使える。 文例 ↓

つきのける 突き除ける push [《文》thrust, shove] sb aside [out of the way]; elbow sb aside (ひじで).

つきのわ 月の輪 《くまの》 the white breast marking; the white V on the chest ¶月の輪ぐま a Japanese bear.

つきはぎ 継ぎ接ぎ patching (and darning) ¶継ぎはぎする patch (up); patch and darn / 継ぎはぎ細工 (a) patchwork / 継ぎはぎだらけの covered with [in] patches; full of patches.

つきはじめ 月初め ¶月初めに at the beginning of the month; early in the month.

つきはなす 突き放す throw [《文》thrust, push] sb off; 《見捨てる》 forsake; desert; abandon; 《競技で相手方を》 widen the lead (again).

つきばらい 月払い ⇨ げっぷ¹. 文例 ↓

つきひ 月日 ¶ time; days ¶月日のたつにつれて as time passes [goes on]; with the lapse [passage] of time ⇨ −とれて ★ / いたずらに月日を送る idle [dawdle] one's time away. 文例 ↓

つきびと 付き人 an attendant (on a performing artist).

つぎほ 接ぎ穂 a graft; a scion ¶話の接ぎ穂を失う be unable to keep up the conversation [to keep the ball rolling].

つきまぜる 搗き混ぜる 《一緒にしてつく》 pound together; 《混ぜる》 mix together.

つきまとう 付き纏う follow sb [around]; hang around [about] 《a girl》; 《尾行する》 shadow; 《口語》 tail; dog sb's footsteps. 文例 ↓

つきみ 月見 ¶月見をする enjoy the moonlight; view the moon.

つきみそう 月見草 《植》 an evening primrose.

つぎめ 継ぎ目 a joint (in a rail); a join; a seam (縫い目) ¶継ぎ目なしの jointless; seamless / 継ぎ目なしのレール a welded rail.

つきもの¹ 付き物 an inevitable [the usual] accompaniment to [《文》 concomitant of] sth ¶付き物である be commonly associated (with); be inseparable (from).

つきもの² つき物 ¶つき物がついている be possessed by 《a devil》 / つき物が落ちる come to one's senses. 「pierce.

つきやぶる 突き破る break [crash] through;
つきやま 築山 an artificial [a miniature] hill (in a landscape garden).

つきゆび 突き指 ¶突き指をする stub one's finger (with a ball).

つきよ 月夜 a moonlight [moonlit] night ¶月夜に on a moonlight night. 文例 ↓

つきる 尽きる be used up; run out; 《文》 be exhausted; 《文》 be consumed; give out; fail; 《終わる》 end; come to an end; 《文》 terminate; be up; be out ¶手段が尽きる be at the end of one's resources; have tried everything [all the means] that one can think of / 尽きない 《文》 inexhaustible; 《文》 never-failing; never-ending. 文例 ↓

つきわり 月割り ¶月割りで in [by] monthly installments ⇨ げっぷ¹.

つく¹ 突く 《どんと押す》 poke; give sb a push; 《突き刺す》 pierce; stab (刃物で); prick (針などで); 《き・きばで》 gore; 《頭で》 butt; 《攻撃する》 attack ¶敵の背後を突く attack [take] the enemy in the rear / 横腹を軽く突く give sb a jog [slight push] in the ribs / 《牛に》角で

の海底火山が太平洋上に突き出てハワイ諸島を形成している。A chain of sea-bottom volcanoes pokes up out of the Pacific, forming the Hawaiian Islands.

つきぬける 弾丸が彼の心臓を突き抜けた。A bullet went through his heart. | He was shot through the heart. | 彼はシャツを脱いで弾が抜けたところを示した。He took off his undershirt and showed where the bullet had gone in one side and out the other.

つきはなす 彼の態度には、そんなことは大した問題ではないといった、冷然と突き放したところがある。There is a touch of cold aloofness in his attitude, as though he considers the matter of little importance.

つきひ 月日のたつのは早いものだ。Doesn't time fly! | How quickly time flies! | 彼はその小島で寂しい月日を送った。He led a lonely life on the islet.

つきまとう どんなにがいても貧乏がつきまとった。For all his struggles, poverty dogged his steps.

つぎめ このテーブルの板には継ぎ目が1つも見えない。There's not a join to be seen in this table top.

つきもの¹ 日本画では梅にうぐいすは付き物です。In Japanese pictures the ume tree and the bush warbler always go [are always found] together. | 学者には貧乏は付き物だ。Scholars cannot escape poverty.

つきよ 実にいい月夜だ。The moon is very beautiful tonight! | その夜は月夜だった。There was a bright moon that night.

つきる 食糧が尽きた。Our provisions have run [given] out. | We have run out of provisions. / 1時間ほど歩くと林は尽きた。About an hour's walk brought us to the other side of the wood. / 手持ちの原料がだんだん尽きてきた。Our stock of raw materials has begun to run out [is running low]. / 金が尽きた。I have run through all my money. / 彼の詩は壮麗と言うに尽きる。'Sublime' is the only word to describe his poetry.

つく¹ 異様な臭気が鼻をついた。An offensive smell assailed my nostrils. / 列車は夜のやみをついて走った。The train sped through the darkness of the night. / 言葉がとうとうと口をついて出た。Words poured from his lips.

つく² 汚ない手で食べ物に触ってはいけません。ばい菌がつきます。Don't touch food with dirty hands. Germs will get on it. /

つく 突かれる be gored ((by a bull)); take a goring / 風雨をついて in spite of [in the teeth of] wind and rain. 文例↓

つく² 付着,就,点 〈付着する〉 stick (to); 〈文〉 adhere (to); 〈汚れる〉 be smeared [stained] ((with)); 〈接触する〉 touch; reach; 〈到着する〉 arrive at [in]; reach; get to; 〈従事する〉 engage in; 〈始める〉 set about ((one's work)); 〈師事する〉 study under [with] ((a tutor)); 〈随従する〉 wait [〈文〉 attend] on; 〈同伴する〉〈文〉 accompany; go with; follow; 〈従属する〉 belong to; be attached to; 〈味方する〉 take sides [a side] with; side ((with)); 〈連結する〉 be joined [connected] ((with)); 〈火が付く〉 catch ((fire)); 〈文〉 be ignited; 〈灯火が〉 be lighted; be kindled; burn ¶しっかり付く stick fast ((to)) / 歯が3本付いている頭骨の化石 a fossil of a skull with three teeth in place / インクが付いている be stained [smeared] with ink / (頭などが) 天井に着く touch the ceiling / 5分の利息が付く bear 5 per cent interest / 看護婦が付いている be attended by a nurse / 運がついている be lucky; be in luck / 運がついていない be unlucky; be out of luck / 地位に就く take up a position ((of, as)); be appointed to the position ((of)) / 所定の位置に就く take up one's appointed place / 王位に就く come to [〈文〉 ascend, 〈文〉 accede to] the throne / 世界漫遊の途に就く start [set out] on a (round-the-)world tour / 根が付く take [strike] root. 文例↓

つく³ 搗く pound; 〈脱穀する〉 hull; husk; 〈精米する〉 polish.

つく⁴ 憑く possess; obsess; haunt ¶きつねがつく 〈人が主語〉 be possessed [obsessed] by a demon [an evil spirit].

つぐ¹ 次ぐ rank [come, be] next [second] to; come [rank] after ¶ロンドンに次ぐ大都会 the next largest city to [after] London (in population) / 次いで 〈次に〉 next; secondly; in the second place; 〈その後に〉 after that; soon after; (and) then; 〈文〉 subsequently / 次いで起こる follow; 〈文〉 ensue. 文例↓

つぐ² 注ぐ pour (out, in) ((a cup with coffee)); put ((water in a bowl)) ¶グラスに半分ワインをつぐ pour [fill] a glass half full of wine.

つぐ³ 接ぐ 〈接合する〉 join (A to B); piece [put] together; 〈接ぎ木する〉 ⇨つぎき ¶2個の木材を接ぐ splice two pieces of wood / 骨を接ぐ set a broken bone.

つぐ⁴ 継ぐ 〈継承する〉 succeed ((sb to the property)); inherit ((the property)); come [succeed] to ((the throne)); 〈後に続く〉 follow; 〈文〉 ensue; 〈継ぎを当てる〉 patch; put a patch ((on)). 文例↓

つくえ 机 a desk ¶机に向かう sit at a desk / 机に向かってする仕事 desk work. 文例↓

つくし 〈植〉 a reproductive shoot of the field horsetail.

つくす 尽くす 〈ことごとく用いる〉 use up; 〈文〉 exhaust; 〈尽力する〉 do one's best [utmost]; 〈文〉 render ((service)); make efforts; exert oneself ¶手[手段]を尽くす try everything ((by every means)) ((in one's power)); leave no stone unturned / 食べ尽くす eat up / 論じ尽くす discuss ((a subject)) fully from every point / 検討し尽くす consider all angles of ((a question)) / 国家のために尽くす do one's best for [〈文〉 render good service to] one's country; serve one's country to the best of one's ability / 一言にしてこれを尽くすならば to put it in a nutshell; in a word. 文例↓

つくだに 佃煮 food boiled down in soy.

つくづく 〈全く〉 thoroughly; entirely; quite; 〈大いに〉 greatly; 〈深く〉 deeply; 〈じっと〉 intently; 〈痛切に〉 keenly; severely ¶つくづく眺める look hard ((at)); 〈文〉 gaze intently ((at, on)); watch; study / つくづくいやになる be [get] quite sick of; be utterly [profoundly] disgusted with / つくづく考える think ((a matter)) over (and over); ponder ((on [over])) ((a question)); reflect [〈文〉 muse] on. 文例↓

の列車には食堂車が付いている. There is a dining car attached to this train. / 大抵の名詞は複数形には -s がつく. Most nouns take -s in the plural. / 水が畳までつく. The water reached floor level. / 手が床に着くまで体を前に曲げなさい. Bend (your body) forward so as to touch the floor with your hands. / 彼は明日ここに着くはずだ. He is due (to arrive) here tomorrow. / さあ, 着いたぞ. Here we are! / 私の後に付いて言って下さい. Repeat after me. / 彼らは帰途に就いた. They started for home. / 移植した皮膚は着かなかった. The skin graft did not take. / 電球はつかなかった. The bulb did not light. / 電灯がついている. The light is on. / 通りの明かりがついた. The lights in the street came [went] on. / そのバーナーはサーモスタットでついたり消えたりする. The burner is switched on and off by a thermostat. / 50,000円に付いた. It cost me 50,000 yen. / 彼はついていた. He was lucky [in luck]. / Luck was with him [on his side]. / 私はずっとついていた. I had a run of luck.

つぐ¹ 日本の医学生にとって英語に次いでもっとも重要な外国語はドイツ語である. For Japanese medical students the most important foreign language after English is German. / 水素とヘリウムに次いで, 星間ガスに最も多くある成分は酸素である. Following hydrogen and helium, the most common component of interstellar gas is oxygen.

つぐ² コーヒーをもう1杯つぎましょうか. Will you have another cup of coffee? / 彼はもう1杯ついてくれと杯を差し出した. He held out his cup for a refill.

つぐ⁴ 彼は父の職業を継ぎたくなかった. He was unwilling to succeed to his father's profession. / 彼は父のあとを継いで医者になった. He succeeded his father as doctor. / He followed his father into the medical profession.

つくえ 私は机の上の書類を片付けた. I cleared the papers from [off] the top of my desk.

つくす 彼には僕としても尽くせるだけのことは尽くしてきた. I've done all [everything] I can for him. / 彼女は私のためによく尽くしてくれた. She did everything I asked of her. / She went out of her way on my behalf. / 彼女はただ一筋に夫のために尽くした. She devoted herself single-mindedly to her husband.

つくづく このような期待がいかにむなしいものかつくづくと悟っ

つぐない 償い 〈報償〉(a) compensation; 《文》(a) recompense; amends; 〈賠償〉(an) indemnity, reparation(s); 〈贖罪〉《文》atonement; 《文》expiation ¶…の償いに in compensation [《文》atonement, 《文》reparation] for…; in expiation [recompense] of….
つぐなう 償う 〈埋め合わせる〉make up (for); make good 《the loss》; make amends (for); recompense; compensate (for); 〈弁償する〉pay reparations [indemnity] (for); 〈罪を〉《文》atone for [《文》expiate] 《one's sin》. 文例④
つくねる 捏ねる knead; mold.
つくねんと 〈ぼんやり〉vacantly; absent-mindedly; 〈何もしないで〉idly.
つくばい 蹲い a washbasin (usually made of stone) set in a Japanese garden.
つぐみ 〔鳥〕 a thrush.
つぐむ 噤む shut [close] (one's mouth) ¶口をつぐんで語らない hold one's tongue; keep silent (about); keep one's mouth shut; keep one's lips tight.
つくり¹ 作[造]り 〈構造〉(a) make; make-up; structure; (a) construction; 〈体の〉physique; build; 〈細工〉workmanship; 〈栽培〉culture; cultivation ¶菊作り the growing of chrysanthemums / 黄金作りの太刀 a gold-mounted sword. 文例④
つくり² 旁 the right-hand portion of a Chinese character.
つくりあげる 作[造]り上げる make [draw] up 《a document》; build up 《a dike》; work up 《a block of wood into a mask》; 〈完成する〉complete; finish; 《文》accomplish; 〈でっちあげる〉fabricate; concoct; invent; 《口語》cook up.
つくりかえる 作り替える make sth again [afresh, 《文》anew]; remake; remodel; revamp; 〈再び〉rebuild; reconstruct; convert 《A into B》; 〈改作する〉adapt ¶小説を劇に作り替える dramatize a novel; adapt a novel for the stage.
つくりかた 作[造]り方 how to make sth; how sth is made; 〈料理の〉a recipe (for); 〈建築などの〉《a》style 《樣式》; structure 《構造》.
つくりごえ 作り声 a disguised [《文》feigned] voice ¶作り声で with [in] a feigned voice; in an affected tone / 作り声する disguise one's voice; imitate 《文》feign sb's voice.
つくりごと 作り事 a fabrication; an invention; a fake; a put-up job [affair]; 〈作り話〉a (made-up) story; a fiction ¶作り事を言う invent [make up] a story 《about》.

つくりざかや 造り酒屋 〈人〉a sake brewer; 〈醸造所〉a sake brewery.
つくりだす 作[造]り出す produce; make; 《文》manufacture; turn [put] out; 〈創造する〉create; 〈工夫する〉devise; hammer out 《a plan》; 〈発明する〉invent.
つくりつけ 作り付け ¶作り付けの fixed; built-in 《bookshelves》.
つくりなおす 造[作]り直す remake; redo ⇒かいぞう¹, つくりかえる ¶文章を作り直す rewrite a composition.
つくりばなし 作り話 a (made-up) story ⇒つくりごと. 文例④
つくりもの 作り物 〈人工物〉an artificial product; 〈にせ物〉a sham; a fake; 〈能舞台に据える〉stage properties.
つくりわらい 作り笑い a forced [strained, 《文》feigned] laugh [smile] ¶作り笑いをする[浮かべる] force a smile [laugh]; smile a forced smile.
つくる 作[造]る make; 《文》manufacture; 〈産出する〉produce; turn out; 〈創造する〉create; 〈書類などを〉draw up; make out; 〈詩文を〉compose [write] 《a poem》; 〈建造する〉build; 《文》construct; 〈栽培する〉raise; cultivate; grow; 〈醸造する〉brew; 〈料理を〉cook (煮炊きして); prepare 《sashimi》; get 《a meal》(ready); 〈鋳造する〉cast; coin; 〈組織する〉organize; form 《a new Cabinet》; 〈でっちあげる〉invent; concoct; fabricate; 〈化粧する〉make up; 〈身なりを〉《口語》get oneself up ¶粘土で花瓶(かびん)を作る make [《文》fashion] a vase from clay / 〈建造物などが〉木で作られている be built [constructed] of wood / 新語を造る coin a new word / 企画を作る draw up [map out, 《文》formulate] a plan [program] / 草稿を作る prepare [make] a draft / 列を作る form a line / 米を作る grow [raise] rice / 会を作る organize a society / 靴を造らせる get [have] one's shoes made (by) / 上手に作られた道具 a well-made tool. 文例④
つくろい 繕い 〈修理〉repair(s); mending; patching up (着物などの); darning (靴下などの) ¶繕いがきく be mendable; be repairable / 繕いがきかない be beyond [past] repair / 繕い物 things to be mended; mending; darning.
つくろう 繕う 〈修理する〉repair; mend; 《米》fix; 〈継ぎをあてる〉patch; 〈靴下などを〉darn ¶繕ってもらう get sb to mend sth; have sth mended [repaired] (by) / 人間[体裁]を繕う keep up appearances.

つけ 付け 〈勘定書〉a bill; 《米》a check; 〈勘

た. It was brought home to me only too keenly how futile my hopes were.
つぐなう 私の努力は十二分に償われたように思っている. I feel more than recompensed for my efforts. / 謝礼を受けとるといっても費用をかろうじて償う程度のものです. My fee barely covers my expenses. / その利益はほとんど損失を償うに至らなかった.

The gains hardly offset the loss.
つくり¹ この家は造りがしっかりしている. This house is stoutly built. / このシガレットケースはすばらしい作りだ. The workmanship of this cigarette case is excellent. | This cigarette case is superbly made.
つくりばなし あの男はいつもいい加減な作り話ばかり言っている. He's always making things up

[inventing things].
つくる そこで出土した道具らしいものは人間の作ったものかどうか疑わしい. It is doubtful whether the toollike object excavated there was of human manufacture [origin]. / 当市には特に子供のために造られた動物園があります. This city has a zoo designed especially for children.
つけ 新規のお客さまには付けでお

つげ ...

定〉 an [a credit] account ¶…の付けにする charge *sth* to *sb's* account ; put *sth* down on *sb's* bill [to *sb's* account] ; (口語) chalk *sth* up to *sb* / 付けで買う buy [get] *sth* on credit [using a charge account, (英口語) on tick] ; charge *sth* (to *one's* account) / 付けで売る sell *sth* on credit [(英口語) on tick] ; give [extend] credit to *sb*.

つげ 《植》 a box tree ; 〈つげ材〉 box(wood) ¶(将棋の)つげのこま a boxwood chessman.

-づけ …付け ¶8月5日付けの手紙 a letter dated [of] the 5th of August. 文例⇩

つけあがる 付け上がる 〈口語〉 get (big) ideas ; 〈口語〉 get [be] too clever by half ; be too big for *one's* boots [(米) britches] ; get above *oneself* ; be [get] stuck up ; put on airs ; grow impudent (insolent).

つけあわせ 付け合わせ 〈料理の〉 trimmings ; fixings ; a garnish ; a relish.

つけあわせる 付け合わせる add 《mashed potatoes and spinach》 as trimmings to 《a dish》; garnish 《a dish》 with 《parsley》.

つけいる 付け入る ⇨つけこむ.

つけおとし 付け落とし an omission (in a bill).

つけおとす 付け落とす fail to enter 《a sum against *sb's* account》.

つけかえる 付け替える renew ; replace (A with B) ; change 《an electric bulb for a new one》 ¶表紙を付け替える re-cover 《a book》; have 《*one's* book》 re-covered.

つけぐすり 付け薬 〈外用薬〉 a medicine for external use [application] ; 〈軟膏(なんこう)〉 (an) ointment.

つげぐち 告げ口 ¶告げ口する inform [(口語) tell] on (you) ; (口語) let on (to your teacher about, that…). 文例⇩

つけくわえ 付け加え an addition ; a supplement (補足).

つけくわえる 付け加える add [(文) append] 《(to)》;〈補足する〉(文) supplement 《A with B》. 文例⇩

つけげんき 付け元気 false [sham] courage ; Dutch courage (特に酒の力による) ; a show of courage [animation].

つけこむ 付け込む 〈付け入る〉 take (a mean) advantage of ; presume on ; capitalize on ; trade [cash in] on 《*sb's* credulity》;〈記入する〉 enter [make an entry] (in a book) ; put down 《an item on a bill》 ¶人のいいのにつけ込む presume on *sb's* good nature. 文例⇩

つけたし 付け足し ⇨つけたり.

つけたす 付け足す ⇨つけくわえる.

つけたり 付けたり an addition ; an accessory ; a supplement ; an appendix (*pl*. -dixes, -dices) ¶付けたりの additional ; (文) accessory, supplementary ; subsidiary.

つけつけ 付け付け ⇨ずけずけ.

つけとどけ 付け届け a present ; a gift ; 〈わいろ〉 a bribe ¶付け届けをする make [send] *sb* a present [gift] of *sth* ; 〈わいろを送る〉 offer [give] a bribe to *sb*.

つけな 漬け菜 〈漬け物用の野菜〉 greens for pickling [salting] ; 〈漬けた野菜〉 pickled [salted] greens.

つけね[1] 付け根 the root [base] (of) ¶親指の付け根 the base [root] of the thumb / ももの付け根 the groin / 腕の付け根 the shoulder joint / 右腕を付け根から切断される have *one's* right arm amputated [cut off] at the shoulder.

つけね[2] 付け値 a price offered ; an offer ; a bid.

つけねらう 付け狙う follow (after) ; dog ; shadow ; keep watch [*one's* eyes] on ¶命をつけねらう seek *sb's* life / すりにつけねらわれる be followed by a pickpocket.

つけび 付け火 ⇨ほうか[1].

つけひげ 付け髭 (wear) a false mustache [beard].

つけびと 付け人 an attendant (on a high-ranking *sumo* wrestler).

つけぼくろ 付け黒子 a beauty spot.

つけまつげ 付け睫 false eyelashes.

つけまわす 付け回す follow *sb* about ; 〈尾行する〉 shadow ; dog.

つけめ 付け目 文例⇩

つけもの 漬物 pickles ; pickled [salted] vegetables ¶漬物おけ a pickle tub / 漬物屋 〈店〉 a pickle store ; 〈人〉 a dealer in pickles.

つけやき 付け焼き ¶付け焼きの (fish) broiled with soy sauce / 付け焼きにする broil 《fish》 with soy sauce.

つけやきば 付け焼き刃 a superficial polish ; a veneer (of civilization) ; (文) (in) borrowed plumes ¶付け焼き刃の教養[教育] a thin veneer of culture [education].

つける[1] 付着,点じる join [fix, attach, fasten, (文) append, (文) affix] 《A to B》; put 《A on B》; stick *sth* (on, to) ; sew 《a button》 on (縫い付ける) ; 〈添加する〉 add 《A to B》;〈着用する〉 wear ; put on ; 〈記入する〉 enter 《an item in a book》; put down 《an item on a bill》; make an entry of 《an item in a book》;〈値段を〉 put [mark] a price (on *sth*) ; 〈競売などで〉 offer

---

売りはできません。No credit can be extended to new customers.

-づけ 本規則は10月20日付けをもって施行された。The rule took effect on [as of] the 20th of October.

つけあがる ああいう男にはおとなしくしていると付け上がるよ。He's the sort of man that'll presume on your patience. / ああいった手合いは少し優しくするとどこまでも付け上がってくる。Give that kind an inch and he'll take a yard [mile].

つげぐち 僕がタバコをすっている所をみつけたなんて母に告げ口しないで下さい。Don't let on to mother that you caught me smoking.

つけくわえる 「確かですよ」と彼は付け加えた。He added that he was sure of it. / 念のため一言付け加えておきます。Let me add a few more words for caution's

sake. / この件につきましては、なお一言付け加えておく必要があるかと存じます。I feel that a few more words are called for on this subject.

つけこむ こちらの無知につけ込んであの男は粗悪な品を売り付けた。Taking advantage of our ignorance, he palmed inferior goods off on us.

つけめ そこが彼らの付け目だ。That's what they are trying to

つける [bid] (¥10,000 for *sth*); 〈塗布する〉 put (paint) on; 〈文〉 apply; 〈後を追う〉 follow; shadow; dog; tail; 〈点火する〉 light (up); kindle; 〈電灯を〉 turn [switch] on; 〈備える〉 install; have ((a telephone)) installed ¶パンにバターを付ける spread butter on bread; spread bread with butter / 髪に油を付ける grease *one's* hair; apply hair oil to *one's* hair / 手紙を付けて送る send *sb* ((a book)) with a letter / 本に索引を付ける append an index to a book / 列車に機関車を付ける couple an engine to a train / 船をさん橋に着ける bring a ship alongside a quay / ボートを岸に着ける put a boat ashore / 自動車を玄関に着ける pull ((drive a car)) up to the door [entrance, porch] / 見張りを付ける keep [place] *sb* under guard; place a guard at [keep guard over] ((a place)) / 弁護士を付ける provide ((the defendant)) with a lawyer / 元気を付ける encourage *sb*; give *sb* courage / 目を付けている keep *one's* eye(s) on *sb*; 〈文〉 have an eye to *sth* / 日記[帳簿]を付ける keep a diary [books, accounts]. 文例↓

つける 漬ける 〈水に〉 soak [steep, souse] ((in)); 〈漬物を〉 pickle [salt] ((vegetables)) ¶ホルマリンに漬ける preserve [pickle] *sth* in formalin / 一晩水に漬けておく soak *sth* [let *sth* soak] overnight in water.

-つける ¶ ...しつける be [get] used ((accustomed)) to doing; be in the habit of doing / しつけた [しつけない] 仕事 familiar [unfamiliar] work. 文例↓

つげる 告げる 〈知らせる〉 tell *sb* ((about *sth*, that...)); let *sb* know; 〈文〉 inform *sb* ((of *sth*, that...)); 〈文〉 intimate ((*sth* to *sb*, that...)); 〈公告する〉 announce; 〈文〉 proclaim; 〈命じる〉 bid; order ¶名を告げる give *one's* name / 暁を告げる鐘の音 the temple bell telling the hour of dawn.

つごう 都合 〈事情〉 circumstances; 〈便宜〉 convenience; 〈合計〉 in all; all told ¶都合する arrange [manage] ((to do)); 〈金を〉〈文〉 accommodate ((*sb* with a loan)); lend; loan; 〈調達する〉 raise ((money)) / 都合がよければ if circumstances permit; if (it is) convenient for *one*; if it suits *one* [*one's* convenience] / 都合のいい convenient; 〈文〉 opportune / 都合のいい時に at *one's* convenience; when (it is) convenient for *one* / ご都合のつき次第に 〈文〉 at your earliest convenience / 都合のいいこと

だけを覚えている have a convenient memory / 都合の悪い inconvenient; 〈文〉 inopportune / 自分の都合を図る follow *one's* own convenience / 都合により for certain reasons; for reasons of *one's* own; owing to circumstances / 都合よく conveniently; luckily; satisfactorily / 都合よく行く go well. 文例↓

つじ 辻 〈十字路〉 a crossroads; a crossing; 〈街路〉 a street; 〈街角〉 a street corner ¶つじつじに at every street corner / つじ説法 street preaching.

つじうら 辻占 a slip of paper telling *one's* fortune.

つじつま 辻褄 ¶つじつまの合った 〈文〉 coherent; consistent; 〈論理的な〉 logical / つじつまの合わない (self-)contradictory; incoherent; inconsistent / つじつまの合わない言いわけ ((offer)) a lame apology / つじつまの合わない事を言う be incoherent; talk illogically [incoherently] / つじつまを合わせようとする try to make ((*one's* story)) sound plausible; try to give *sth* a show of truth. 文例↓

つた 蔦 〈植〉 ivy ¶つたにおおわれた covered with ivy; ivied ((walls)).

-づたい ...伝い 塀[線路]伝いに ((go)) along the wall [railroad tracks] / 屋根伝いに from roof to roof.

つたえきく 伝え聞く hear ((from others)); be told ((about)); learn by hearsay [at second hand]; hear tell ((of)).

つたえる 伝える 〈伝達する〉 tell ((*sb* that...)); report ((*sth* to *sb*, that...)); 〈文〉 communicate; bring word ((to *sb* that...)); 〈文〉 convey ((news to *sb*)); 〈知らせる〉 let *sb* know; make *sth* known ((to)); 〈文〉 notify *sb* ((of a matter)) / 分からせる get across; 〈宣伝する〉 〈文〉 propagate; 〈文〉 disseminate; publicize; 〈残す〉 hand [pass] down; 〈文〉 bequeath; 〈光・熱などを〉 transmit; conduct; 〈外国へ〉 introduce ((into)) ¶伝えられる所によれば I hear [It is said, They say] that... ; A rumor [report] has it that... ; There is a rumor ((abroad)) that... ; reportedly; allegedly / 新聞の伝える所によれば according to the newspaper reports; it is reported in the newspapers that... / 〈口語〉 it says in the paper that... / 知識を伝える pass on [〈文〉 impart] *one's* knowledge to ((the next generation)) / 秘訣を伝える initiate *sb* into the secrets ((of)) / 後世に伝えられる be handed

---

capitalize [trade] on.

つける¹ 彼は上着の胸に花を付けている。 He is wearing a flower in his buttonhole. / その勘定は僕に付けといてください。 Charge it [Put it down, Chalk it up] to my account, please. / いくらに値を付けましたか。 How much did you bid [offer for it]? / 〈競売場で〉 だれか5万円と付ける人はありませんか。 Who'll say 50,000 yen?

-つける 食べつけないものを食べると当たるぞ。 Food that you are not used to (eating) will disagree

with you.

つごう 今日は都合が悪いから明日来て下さい。 I'm not free today; please come tomorrow. / 1時よりも2時の方が私には都合がいいと思います。 Two o'clock will suit me better [is more convenient] than one. / いつでも都合のいい時に来てよろしい。 You may come any time that [whenever] it suits you. / あの人の家はバス停に近くて都合がいい。 Her house is conveniently near the bus stop. / ご都合のいいところでお

会いしましょう。 I will meet you anywhere you like. / 明日の会にはなんとか都合して出席してくれませんか。 Couldn't you arrange [manage] to attend the meeting tomorrow? / なんとか都合しましょう。 I will see to it, somehow or other. / 万事都合よく行きましょ。 Everything went well for me. / ご都合のよい時で結構です。 Please choose your own time. / 時間の都合がつきません。 I can't make time for it.

つじつま 彼の最初の報告と2度目

つたない

[passed] down to posterity / 名を永遠に伝える《業績が主語》 immortalize *sb's* name.

つたない 拙い ⇨ へた¹.

つたわる 伝わる be transmitted ;《文》be conveyed ; be passed along ;〈伝承される〉be handed down ; come [go] down (to) ;〈光・熱などが〉be conducted ;〈広がる〉spread ;〈うわさが〉get abroad [about] ; circulate 《through the town》;〈伝来する〉be introduced 《into》; be brought (to) /〈手から手に〉伝わる pass from hand to hand [mouth to mouth] / 屋根を伝わって歩く go from roof to roof / 木を伝わって降りる climb down a tree (to the ground). 文例

つち¹ 土〈土壌〉earth ; soil ;〈地面〉the ground ;〈泥〉mud ;〈粘土〉clay ¶1塊の土 a clod of earth / 土のにおい the smell of earth ; an earthy smell / 異郷の土となる《文》return [go back] to dust ; die / …の土を踏む set foot 《in, on》; land 《in, on》/ 土がつく《相撲》be beaten ; be defeated ; suffer a defeat / 顔色が土のようになる turn ghastly [deadly] pale ; go [turn] as pale as ashes [as white as a sheet]. 文例

つち² 槌 a hammer (金属製の) ; a mallet (木の) ; a sledge(hammer) (両手で使う) ; a gavel (議長が持つ) ¶つちで打つ hammer 《a nail》; hit *sth* with a hammer.

つちいじり 土いじり gardening (for pleasure) ; messing [《米》puttering,《英》pottering] about in the garden.

つちいろ 土色 the color of the earth ; (an) earthlike color ¶(顔などが)土色の deadly [ghastly] pale ; ashy ;《文》cadaverous.

つちかう 培う cultivate ; foster.

つちくさい 土臭い earth-smelling ; (an) earthy (smell) ;〈田舎臭い〉《文》rustic ; countrified ; unrefined.

つちくれ 土塊 a clod [lump] of earth.

つちけいろ 土気色 ⇨ つち¹ (顔色が土のようになる).

つちけむり 土煙 (raise) a cloud of dust. 文例

つちつかず 土付かず ¶土付かずである have a clean record ; have not suffered a defeat 《for 12 days》.

つちふまず 土踏まず〈足の裏の〉the arch of the foot.

つちぼこり 土埃 ⇨ つちけむり.

つちろう 土牢 a dungeon.

つつ 筒 a pipe ; a tube ; a cylinder (円い) ¶筒形の cylindrical ; cylinder-shaped.

-つつ〈…しつつある〉be *do*ing ; be in the process [in course] of *do*ing / 酒を飲みつつ語り合う talk over a drink / 悪い事と知りつつする do though *one* knows it is wrong to do so ; act against *one's* better judgment.

つつうらうら 津々浦々 ¶津々浦々に throughout [all over] the country ;《文》throughout the length and breadth of the land ; in every corner of the country ;〈広く〉far and wide.

つっかい(ぼう) 突っ支い(棒) a prop ; a stay ; a strut ; a shore ; a support ¶つっかいをする prop [shore] up (a pillar) ; support (a wall) / 戸につっかいをして開けておく prop a door open ; keep a door propped open.

つっかえす 突っ返す ⇨ つきかえす.

つっかかる 突っ掛かる turn on ; fly at ; pick a quarrel with ;《文》assume a defiant [an aggressive] attitude against.

つっかける 突っ掛ける slip on (a pair of sandals) ; putts *one's* feet into (*one's* slippers) ¶(将棋で)歩を突っかける threaten to take (a piece) with *one's* pawn.

つつがなく 恙無く safely ; in safety ; safe and sound ; without mishap ;《文》misadventure.

つつがむし 恙虫《動》a tsutsugamushi mite ; a harvest mite ; a chigger ¶つつが虫病 tsutsugamushi disease.

つづき 続き (a) continuation ;《文》continuance ;〈話の〉a sequel (to an earlier story) ¶日照り続き a long spell of dry weather / 不幸続き a series of misfortunes / 不作続き (have) a series of bad harvests. 文例

つづきがら 続き柄 (family) relationship.

つつきだす つつき出す peck [poke] out.

つつきまわす つつき回す poke around [about].

つづきもの 続きもの a serial (story) ¶続き物として in serial form ; serially. 文例

つっきる 突っ切る cross ; get [run, dash, cut] across ; make [force] *one's* way across.

つつく pick (at) ; peck (at) (鳥が) ;〈そそのかす〉incite ; egg *sb* on ; instigate《*sb* to *do*》; stimulate ;〈調べる〉look [inquire] into ;〈あら捜しをする〉find fault with ;〈いじめる〉tease ;

のとはつじつまが合わない。His first and second reports do not hang together.

-づたい 土手づたいに散歩した。We took a walk along the bank.

つたえる 遊びに来るように彼に伝えて下さい。Please tell him to come and see me. / よろしくお伝え下さい。Please give him my (best) regards. | Please remember me to him. / 絶対反対を彼が表明したと伝えられている。He is reported as saying [He reportedly said] that he is dead set against it. / これは乾山の作と伝えられている。This is by tradition the work of Kenzan. | Tradition has it that this was made by Kenzan. / 銅は熱をよく伝える。Copper conducts heat well. | Copper is a good conductor of heat.

つたわる 音は空気中を毎秒約340メートルの早さで伝わる。Sound travels through the air at about 340 meters per second. / 猿が木の枝から枝を伝わって動き回っていた。Monkeys were climbing about among the branches of the trees.

つち¹ 彼はイギリスの土を踏んだ

つづく

最初の日本人だった。He was the first Japanese to set foot on British soil. / 要するに人間はただ一塊の土に過ぎない。After all, man is but a lump of clay.

つちけむり 土煙がもうもうと立った。A cloud of dust boiled high into the air.

つづき これは5ページからの続きです。This is continued from page 5. / この話にはまだ続きがあるんだ。That isn't the whole story. | There's more to follow.

つづきもの この話は続き物として「朝日」に載るはずです。The sto-

harass. 文例⇩

つづく 〈継続する〉continue; go [keep] on; 〈後続する〉follow; succeed; 〈持続する〉last [hold] (out); 〈隣接する〉《文》adjoin; 〈通じる〉lead (to, into) ¶続いて ⇒つづけて (続けて, 続けざまに) / …の後にすぐ続いて (close) on the heels of…. 文例⇩

つづける 続ける continue sth; keep up; go [keep] on (with); proceed (with) ¶話を続ける go on [proceed] with one's story / 話し続ける go on talking; talk on / 歌い続ける sing on / 続けて, 続けざまに continuously; consecutively; without a break; one after another; in succession; successively; on end; running / 5日間を続けて for five days running [on end]; for five consecutive [straight] days / 3度続けて three times in succession [in a row]. 文例⇩

つっけんどん ¶つっけんどんな curt; 《文》brusque; blunt / つっけんどんに curtly; 《文》brusquely; bluntly.

つっこみ 突っ込み digging into (a matter).

つっこむ 突っ込む 〈物を〉stick [cram, pack, thrust, stuff] sth into; 〈自分が〉plunge [strike] into; 〈衝突する〉ram [bump, run] into; run [clash] against; 〈水中に〉dive ¶敵陣に突っ込む charge the enemy (position) / (船が)波浪の中へ突っ込んで行く drive [push, slam] into a rough sea / …に首を突っこむ poke one's nose into…; meddle [dabble] in… / ポケットに手を突っこむ thrust [stick] one's hand into one's pocket / 突っこんだ研究をする delve [dig] into (a matter) / make a thorough investigation of (a matter) / 突っこんだ質問(ask) a penetrating [sharp] question / 突っ込んだ討論 a discussion in depth. 文例⇩

つっさき 筒先 〈銃口〉the muzzle; 〈ホースの〉the nozzle ¶筒先を向ける point [level] a gun [hose] (at, toward).

つつじ 〔植〕an azalea.

つつしみ 慎み 〈謙そん〉modesty; 〈思慮〉discretion; 《文》prudence; 〈抑制〉self-control; self-restraint; 〈節制〉temperance; moderation; 〈禁欲〉《文》continence ¶慎みのない《文》immodest; brazen / 慎み深い modest; discreet; prudent; cautious.

つつしむ 慎む 〈用心する〉be discreet; be careful; be prudent; 《文》be circumspect; 〈控える〉keep [《文》abstain, 《文》refrain] from (drinking); 〈節制する〉be moderate 《文》use moderation (in smoking); 〈色欲を〉《文》be continent; 《文》practice continence ¶行ないを慎む behave (oneself) / 言葉を慎む mind [be careful about] one's language / 謹んで respectfully; reverently; humbly. 文例⇩

つつそで 筒袖 a tight sleeve ¶筒そでの着物 a tight-sleeved kimono.

つったつ 突っ立つ stand up ¶突っ立っているstand erect; 〈ぼんやりしている〉be standing around [about].

つつぬけ 筒抜け ¶筒抜けに聞こえる be clearly [distinctly] heard [audible] / (秘密が)筒抜けになる be leaked (outright) (to sb); leak out completely 《to》. 文例⇩

つっぱしる 突っ走る run at full speed; dash; rush; sprint (hard); dart; scud; tear. 文例⇩

つっぱねる 突っぱねる 〈拒絶する〉reject; refuse; turn down; spurn; snub.

つっぱり 突っ張り 〈支柱〉a prop; a strut; a support; 〈戸の〉a bar; 〔相撲〕a thrust ¶つっ張りかう prop [brace] sth up; support sth by a prop / つっ張り合い〔相撲〕an exchange of thrusts.

つっぱる 突っ張る stretch (an arm against the wall); square (one's elbows); 〔相撲〕thrust. 文例⇩

つっぷす 突っ伏す fall on one's face; fall prostrate. 文例⇩

つつましい 慎ましい 〈謙遜(牧)な〉modest; humble; reserved; 〈倹約した〉《文》frugal ¶つましい ¶つつましい婦人 a modest woman / つつましく modestly; humbly / つつましく暮す live carefully [《文》frugally] / つつましさ modesty.

つづまる 約まる ⇒ちぢむ. 文例⇩

---

ry is to be serialized in the Asahi.
つつく 鳥は虫をとろうとして木の皮をくちばしでつついて穴をあける。Hunting for grubs, birds peck holes in the bark of trees with their bills.
つづく 次号に続く。To be continued (in our next number). / 次ページに続く。Continued on the following page. / 裏面に続く。Please turn over (P.T.O.). / このお天気もあまり長くは続かないでしょう。This fine weather won't last much longer. / この不景気は1年ぐらい続くらしい。The present (business) recession is likely to last for about a year. / 毎年宝塚では2度は2回ある。Every year there are two shows at Takarazuka [running for] a month and a half each. / そのはっきりした足跡はなおもその先遠くまで続いていた。The clearly-defined footprints continued on into the distance. / 悪いことは続くものだ。Misfortunes never come singly. 〔諺〕洪水の後に続いて疫病が発生した。Pestilence followed on the heels of the flood. / この後にありとあらゆる災いが続いた。This brought all sorts of evil in its train. / 続いて起こった出来事は私が正しかったことを証明した。Subsequent events [The events that followed] showed that I was right.
つづける 彼は3時間続けて演説した。He spoke for three hours at a stretch. / あくまでも平和解決への努力を続けるつもりです。We will persevere with our efforts to settle it amicably. / 彼は観測に続けて理論的研究を行なった。He followed up his observations with a theoretical study.
つっこみ この論文は問題に対する突っ込みが足りない。The writer of this paper does not dig [go] deep(ly) enough into the subject.
つっこむ 片手はベルトに突っ込み, もう一方の手はステッキを握っていた。One hand was stuck into his belt, and the other grasped a stick. / 彼はポケットに手を突っ込んで10円玉を1枚とり出した。He thrust his hand into his pocket and took out a ten-yen piece. / 一般的なことを話し合っただけでその問題について突っ込んだ話はしなかった。We just talked about generalities and did not go into the matter

つつみ¹ 包み a bundle; a package; 〈小包〉a packet; a parcel ¶包みにする make a bundle [package] of ⇨ つつむ / 衣類ひと包み a bundle of clothes / 包み紙 wrapping [brown] paper; a wrapper.

つつみ² 堤 a bank; an embankment; a dike; ていぼう.

つつみ 鼓 a hand drum (used in traditional Japanese music).

つつみかくし 包み隠し ¶包み隠しのない plain; straightforward; candid; frank; outspoken; open-hearted.

つつみかくす 包み隠す hide 《a fact》from sb; keep 《a matter》secret from sb; conceal; hold back 《a fact》; wrap sth up ¶包み隠さずに unreservedly; outspokenly; frankly; openly / 包み隠さず言う be open [frank, plain-spoken] with sb; make a clean breast of 《one's secret》; lay bare one's heart to sb; tell sb the plain truth.

つつみなおす 包み直す wrap sth (over) again; rewrap; remake 《a parcel》.

つつむ 包む 〈くるむ〉wrap; pack 《goods》; bundle 《clothes》;〈おおう〉《文》envelop (in); 《文》veil (in); cover (with); 〈隠す〉conceal; hide ¶紙に包む do [wrap] sth up in paper / 炎に包まれる be engulfed in flames / なぞ〔霧〕に包まれている be veiled [enveloped] in mystery [mist] / 包み切れぬ喜び《文》(an) irrepressible joy / 包まずに ⇨ つつみかくす(包み隠さずに). 文例⇩

つづめる 約める ⇨ ちぢめる ¶つづめて言えば in short; in brief; to cut a long story short; to sum up.

つづら 葛籠 a wicker basket (for storing clothes in).

つづらおり つづら折り ¶つづら折りの winding; zigzag; meandering.

つづり 綴り 〈字の〉(a) spelling; orthography (正字法) ¶つづりを間違える misspell 《a word》/ 一つづりの便箋(びんせん) a writing pad.

つづりかた 綴り方 〈作文〉(a) composition; a theme.

つづる 綴る 〈語を〉spell; 〈文章を〉write; compose;〈縫う〉sew;〈とじる〉bind; file (書類などを) ⇨ とじる². 文例⇩

つづれ 綴れ ⇨ ほろ ¶つづれ織り (the) tapestry weave / つづれ錦 figured [handwoven] brocade; tapestry.

つて 〈縁故〉a connection;〈引き〉influence; 《口語》(a) pull;《口語》(have) an in (with); 〈世話〉《文》good offices ¶つてを求める hunt for connections [an in (an in with, to)]; try to get in touch with a person who will use his influence for one / …のつてで through the influence [good offices] of…. 文例⇩

つと suddenly; abruptly.

つど 都度 every [each] time; whenever; as often as ¶そのつど ⇨ そのつど.

つどい 集い a meeting; a gathering; a get-together.

つどう 集う ⇨ あつまる.

つとまる 勤まる be fit [《文》competent] for 《a post》; be equal to 《a task》 ¶勤まらない be unfit [《文》incompetent] for; be unequal to. 文例⇩

つとめ 務[勤]め 〈任務, 義務〉duty;〈職務〉duties; service; business; work;〈勤行〉religious [divine] service(s) ¶勤めをやめる resign [quit] one's post; retire (from office) / 務めを果たす《文》discharge one's duties; do one's share [party, duty] / 勤めを終えて after work / 勤めに出る〈出勤する〉go to work; go to the office; leave home for work;〈勤め人になる〉start to work for 《a firm》. 文例⇩

つとめあげる 勤め上げる serve out one's time [apprenticeship]; complete one's (six-year) service (as).

つとめぐち 勤め口 a position; a place;《文》a situation; an opening (明き); 〈仕事〉a job; work ¶勤め口を捜す look for [try to find] work [a job]; hunt for a job. 文例⇩

つとめさき 勤め先 one's place of work [《文》employment]; one's office ¶勤め先をしくじ

---

deeply.

つつしむ 謹んで新年のお慶びを申し上げます。 I wish you a happy New Year. / 謹んでご全快をお祝い申し上げます。Please accept my sincere congratulations on your recovery.

つつぬけ あの男には気をつけな。あの男に話したら何でも筒抜けだぞ。 Be careful (about) what you say to him. He's a regular sieve.

つっぱしる みんなが慎重に構えていた時に、彼1人だけが過激な行動に突っ走ったのだった。 While everybody else remained cautious, he alone rushed headlong into violent action.

つっぱな チムニーというのは山の岩壁の細い裂け目で、両足で突っ張って登るところのことだ。 A chimney is a narrow cleft in the face of a mountain which allows a climber to go up by pushing out with both feet.

つっぷす 彼は机に突っ伏して寝込んでしまった。 He fell asleep, with his head in his arms on the desk.

つづまる 'Won't' は 'will not' のつづまった形である。'Won't' is the contracted form [a contraction] of 'will not'.

つつむ これをきちんと包んで下さい。 Please make a neat parcel of them for me. / 彼はそれを新聞紙に包んで持ってきた。 He brought it wrapped (up) in newspaper. / 建物はすでに火炎に包まれていた。 The building was already enveloped in flames. / それ以上は包み切れず、彼はすべてを自白した。 Unable to hold out any longer, he confessed everything.

つづる お名前はどうつづるのですか。 How do you spell your name?

つて あの会社には特にこれといったつてもない。 I have no particular pull in [connection with] that firm.

つど 上京の都度彼は私のところに泊まります。 Every time [Whenever] he comes up to Tokyo he stays with us.

つとまる あの男ならどんな役目だって勤まる。 He can fill any position. | He is equal to any task.

つとめ これも教師の務めの一つです。 This is one of the things required of a schoolteacher. / 務めを大事にしなさい。 You must attend to your duties faithfully.

つとめぐち もっといい勤め口を捜してあげよう。 I'll find you a better job.

つとめにん 勤め人 an office worker; a salaried man; a white-collar worker.

つとめる 勤[務,務]める 〈勤務する〉 be employed (at, by, in); work (for a firm); 〈文〉 be in the service (of); 〈文〉 serve (in);〈勤めはじめる〉 start work [working] (for); 〈文〉 enter [go into] the service (of);〈努力する〉 exert oneself; make efforts [an effort];〈文〉 endeavor; try [strive] (hard);〈役割を〉 play [act, perform] (a part) / いい所に勤めている have a good job; be working for a good employer / 案内役を務める act as (a) guide / 主人役を務める play [act as] host (at a party, to a conference) / 仕事に努める attend to one's work faithfully;〈文〉 be assiduous in one's business / 努めて〈なるたけ〉 as much [hard] as possible [one can];〈努力して〉 to the best of one's ability; hard;〈文〉 assiduously;〈文〉 diligently; studiously.

つな 綱 〈一般の〉 a rope; a line;〈細い〉 a cord; a string;〈鉄の〉 a cable ¶命の綱 a [one's] lifeline / 綱を張る stretch a rope; rope (off an area) / 綱を繰り出す let out a rope;〈海〉 pay out a rope. 文例⇩

つながり 繋がり 〈連結〉 a connection; a link;〈関係〉 a relation; a relationship ¶つながりがある be related ((to)); be connected ((with)); have something to do ((with)) / 密接なつながりを保つ maintain close ties ((with the U.S.)).

つながる 繋がる 〈連結を作る〉 make a connection ((with));〈結ばれる〉 be connected [linked] ((with)); be bound up ((with)); be tied [fastened] ((to));〈関連する〉 be related ((to));〈電話が〉 get [be put] through ((to)) / 電話がつながらない〈人が主語〉 cannot get through ((to)) / 血がつながっている be related by blood (ties) ((to)); be a blood relative ((of)). 文例⇩

つなぎ 繋ぎ 〈連結〉 a connection; a link; a tie;〈代勤など〉 a stopgap ¶(時間の)つなぎにto fill up the time [gap].

つなぎあわせる 繋ぎ合わせる connect; join [link] together; tie together (糸などを).

つなぎとめる 繋ぎ止める ¶生命をつなぎ止める〈薬などが主語〉 save sb's life;〈自分が主語〉 (narrowly) escape death.

つなぎめ 繋ぎ目 a joint [join] ((between, of)).

つなぐ 繋ぐ tie (up); fasten; chain; tether (馬などを); moor (船を); keep on a leash (犬などに);〈連結する〉 connect; link; join;〈電話を〉 make a (telephone) connection (for sb); put sb through ((to));〈生命を〉〈文〉 sustain (one's life) ¶馬をつなぐ tie [hitch, tether] a horse (to a hitching post); put [harness] a horse (to a wagon) / テープレコーダーをラジオにつなぐ hook up [connect] a tape recorder to a radio / 電話をつないでもらう have a call put through ((to)). 文例⇩

つなひき 綱引き (have) a tug of war ((pl. tugs of war)).

つなみ 津波 a tsunami; a tsunami wave; a seismic sea wave;〈通俗に〉 a tidal wave ¶津波をひき起こす cause [set up] a tsunami. 文例⇩

つなわたり 綱渡り tightrope walking [dancing]; a high-wire act;〈ゆるんだ綱の〉 slack-rope walking ¶綱渡りをする walk a tightrope; walk the wire / 綱渡りをする軽業師 a tightrope walker [dancer]; a high-wire acrobat [artist, performer]; a slack-rope walker / 危ない綱渡りをやる run a risk; make a risky attempt; walk on thin ice; engage in a touch-and-go business. 文例⇩

つね 常 〈常態〉 the usual state of things; the ordinary course of events;〈常習〉 one's habit ¶常の usual; ordinary; normal; common;〈常習的〉 customary;〈文〉 habitual / 常のごとく as usual / 常に,常々〈いつも〉 always; at all times;〈通例〉 ordinarily; commonly; usually;〈常習的に〉〈文〉 habitually;〈文〉 customarily / 常の〈(in) ordinary〉ならば under normal conditions; in ordinary circumstances; at an ordinary time / …するのを常とする be in the habit of doing; have a habit of doing; make it a rule to do / …の常として as is usual [customary] with... / 常なき〈文〉 inconstant; changeable / 常ならぬ unusual; uncommon; extraordinary. 文例⇩

つねる 抓る pinch; give sb a ((sharp)) pinch ¶夢ではないかとわが身をつねる pinch oneself to make sure one is not dreaming [to see if it is real].

つの 角 〈しかの〉 a horn;〈しかの〉 an antler;〈触角〉 an antenna ((pl. -nae); a feeler ¶中空の[ねじれた,節のある,丸く曲がった]角 a hollow [cork-

---

つとめる 彼はこの学校で18年間も司書として勤めている。For eighteen years he has filled the post of librarian in this college. / 彼女は多年その会社に勤めているということだ。I hear she has been employed in that company for years. / 30年間大阪のM社に勤めて退職した。He retired after thirty years' service with the M Co. of Osaka. / あの人のためにはずいぶん尽くしてきたつもりだ。I think I have done a great deal for him. / 彼女には努めてよくしてあげた。I went out of my way to be nice to her. / 努めて冷静にしていた。I made every effort to restrain myself.

つな 入口に綱を張って警察は群衆を入らせなかった。The police roped off the entrance to keep the crowd back. / (これで)頼みの綱も切れ果てた。My last hope is gone.

つながる そのような不注意は死につながるかもしれぬ。Such carelessness could lead to [end up in] a fatal accident.

つなぐ 内線の260番につないで下さい。Extension 260, please. | Would you give me [put me through to] extension 260, please. | Can you connect me to [May I have] extension 260, please.

つなみ 三陸海岸に津波が襲来した。A tsunami struck [swept] the Sanriku coast.

つなわたり (比喩的に)彼がこの綱渡りをどんなふうにやりとげるかはおそらく見ものだろう。It will be quite interesting to see

screw, ridged, curling〉 horn / 角が生える〈動物が主語〉 sprout horns / 角のある horned / 角のない hornless / 立派な角を生やした magnificently horned 《antelopes》; splendidly antlered 《deer》 / 角で突く butt with *its* horns; gore; horn / 角で突かれる be gored [horned] 《by》; take a goring / 〈牛が〉角にかけてほうり上げる toss 《a man》 / 角隠し a bride's hood 《worn at a wedding in Japan》 / 角細工 antler work / 角樽 a horned *sake* cask / 角笛 a horn.

つのつきあい 角突き合い ¶角突き合いをしている be at odds [variance] 《with》.

つのる 募る 〈募集する〉 raise 《funds》; collect 《subscriptions》; invite 《applications》; advertise 《for》; recruit 《factory hands》; 〈勢いが〉 grow [get] worse [serious, violent]; 〈文〉 be aggravated; grow [gain] on one 《感情・癖などが》 / 寄付を募る raise [collect, 〈文〉 solicit] contributions 《for, to》. 文例⇩

つば¹ 唾 ⇨ つばき¹.

つば² 鍔 〈刀の〉 a handguard; the guard 《on a sword》; 〈帽子の〉 a brim ¶つばの広い帽子 a broad-brimmed hat / つばぜり合い a close contest [game]; keen [hot] competition.

つばき¹ 唾 spit; spittle; saliva ¶乾いた[吐いたばかりの] dry [fresh] spit / つばきを吐く spit 《at》 / つばきを飛ばす sputter; splutter / つばきを飛ばして語る splutter [sputter] 《the words》 out / 手につばきする spit on one's hands 《比喩的に》 brace *oneself* 《up》. 文例⇩

つばき² 椿 〈植〉 a camellia ¶つばき油 camellia oil.

つばさ 翼 a wing ¶翼のある winged / 翼を広げる[うつ] spread [flap] *its* wings / 〈飛べないように〉翼を切る clip 〈a chicken's〉 wings; pinion 〈a bird〉 / 翼を伸ばす spread *its* wings / 〈才能を発揮する〉 give full play to *one's* ability [talent]. 文例⇩

つばめ 燕 〈鳥〉 a swallow ¶つばめの巣 a swallow's nest; 〈中国料理〉 an edible bird's nest.

ツバル Tuvalu.

つぶ 粒 〈穀物・砂などの〉 a grain; 〈しずく〉 a drop ¶粒がそろっている be all of a size; be well matched; 〈文〉 be of even ability 《能力が》; 〈文〉 be of even quality 《質が》 / 一粒の米 a grain of rice / 申し分なく粒のそろった真珠 perfectly matched pearls / 粒よりの picked; choice; the best; the choicest / 粒よりのデリシャス the pick of the Delicious apples.

つぶさに 具さに minutely; in detail; at great length ¶つぶさに語る give a detailed account of; 〈文〉 enlarge on 《a subject》 / つぶさに世の辛酸をなめる go through all sorts of hardships; 〈口語〉 go through the mill.

つぶし 潰し ¶つぶしがきく 〈品物が〉 sell for the price of the material [metal]; 〈人が〉 be useful [good] for some other work / つぶしにする demolish [break up] and scrap; melt down 〈a gold vase〉; pulp 〈books〉 / つぶし値で売る sell 〈a machine〉 as scrap [junk, old metal]; 〈安く売る〉 sell dirt-cheap.

つぶす 潰す 〈粉砕する〉 crush; smash; squash; mash 〈potatoes〉; 〈つぶしにする〉 scrap; junk; melt down; pulp 〈books〉; 〈計画などを〉〈文〉 frustrate; baffle; foil; 〈身代を〉 ruin 《*oneself*》; squander [〈文〉] dissipate 〈a fortune〉; 〈時間を〉 pass; kill; while away 〈殺す〉 kill 〈a hen〉; butcher 〈cattle〉 ¶賭博(とばく)で身代をつぶす gamble away *one's* fortune / ぶらぶらして時間をつぶす idle [dawdle] away *one's* time / 時間つぶしに to kill time. 文例⇩

つぶて 礫 a stone [〈口語〉 a rock] 《thrown at *sb*》.

つぶやき 呟き a murmur; a mutter; murmuring.

つぶやく 呟く mutter; murmur 《at》; 〈不平を言う〉 grumble 《at, about, over》 ¶独りつぶやく mutter to *oneself*.

つぶらな 円らな round 《beady》 〈eyes〉.

つぶる shut 〈*one's* eyes〉; close ⇨ め¹.

つぶれる 潰れる be crushed; be smashed; be destroyed; collapse; 〈破滅する〉 be ruined; go to ruin [pieces]; 〈破産する〉 go [become] bankrupt; fail; 〈破滅する〉 be worn down; be effaced ¶雪の重みでつぶれる collapse [give way] under the weight of the snow / 声がつぶれる lose *one's* voice / 目がつぶれる lose *one's* sight [eyesight]; go [〈文〉 become] blind. 文例⇩

つべこべ ¶つべこべ言う 〈反対する〉 raise 〈trivial〉 objections 《to, against》; 〈口返答する〉 answer back; 〈苦情・不平を言う〉 complain 《about, of》; grumble 《at, over》; make complaints 《against, about》. 文例⇩

ツベルクリン 〈医〉 tuberculin ¶ツベルクリン反応 a tuberculin reaction / ツベルクリン反応検査 a tuberculin test / ツベルクリン検査を受ける be tuberculin-tested. 文例⇩

---

how he walks this tightrope.
つね これが世の常だ。This is the way of the world. / 学生の頃は遅くまで起きているのが常であった。When I was at college, I regularly stayed up (till) late at night. / 辞書を常に引いてみなければいけない。You must make constant use of your dictionary. / 男の子の常として彼もまた冒険物語を聴くのが好きだった。As is usual with boys, he liked to hear tales of adventure.
つのる 新会員をつのる。《掲示》

New members invited.
つばき¹ それを見たのちで彼女の口につばきがたまった。Her mouth watered just at [at the very] sight of it.
つばさ そのわしは翼を広げると約2メートルある。The eagle has a wingspan of about two meters.
つぶす 電車の待ち時間をつぶすために僕は喫茶店に入った。To fill in [pass] the time while I was waiting for my train, I went into a coffee shop. / その実験のためにひどく時間がつぶされた。

The experiment took up a great deal of my time.
つぶれる 昨日の地震でたくさんの家がつぶれた。A large number of houses were destroyed by yesterday's earthquake. / 不景気であの店はつぶれてしまった。Owing to the depression, that store has folded up [gone under].
つべこべ つべこべ言うな。Shut up! | Hold your tongue!
ツベルクリン ツベルクリン反応は僕は陽[陰]性でした。My tuberculin reaction was positive [nega-

つぼ¹ 坪 a tsubo (=約 3.3 m²) ¶坪数 acreage; area.

つぼ² 壺 a jar 〈土製・ガラス製の〉; a pot 〈土製・金属製などの〉; 〈灸(きゅう)の〉 an effective point for applying moxa; 〈指圧の〉 a pressure point ¶〈古代ギリシャの〉つぼ絵 a vase painting. 文例

つぼまる get [《文》become] narrower; 〈先細になる〉 taper off ⇒つぼむ.

つぼみ 蕾 a bud ¶つぼみが出る, つぼみを持つ put [shoot] out buds; bud / つぼみが出ている be in bud / 花もつぼみの乙女 《文》 a young maiden; a budding beauty. 文例

つぼむ 蕾む close; shut.

つぼめる 蕾める shut; close; make narrower; 〈先細にする〉 taper off ⇒つぼむ.

つま¹ 妻 a wife (pl. wives) ¶夫思いの妻 a devoted wife / 妻の務め 《文》 wifely duties / 妻をめとる take [get] a wife; marry / 妻にする make 《a woman》 one's wife; take 《a woman》 to wife; marry [get married to] 《a girl》 / 妻問(つまどい)婚 【人類】 uxorilocal [husband-visiting-wife] marriage.

つま² 〈料理の〉 a garnish; trimmings. 「beads.

つまぐる 爪繰る ¶数珠をつまぐる tell one's

つまさき 爪先 the tip of a toe; 〈靴・靴下などの〉 the toe ¶〈女性用の〉つま先の開いた靴 open-toed shoes / つま先の角ばった[丸い]靴 square-[round-]toed shoes / つま先で歩く walk on tiptoe; tiptoe / つま先で立つ stand on tiptoe.

つまされる be touched [moved] (by); feel deeply for sb ¶身につまされる みよ.

つましい 倹しい frugal; thrifty; careful (with one's money) ⇒つつましい ¶つましく 《文》 frugally; thriftily; economically / つましくする be careful (with one's money); 《文》 practice economy.

つまずき 躓き stumbling; a stumble; 〈失敗〉 a failure; a setback ¶躓きの石 a stumbling block (to). 文例

つまずく 躓く stumble (over, against); trip (over, on); lose one's footing; 〈失敗する〉 have [suffer, 《文》experience] a setback [failure] ¶石につまずいて転ぶ stumble over a stone / つまずきながら行く[進む] stumble along [forward].

つまだつ 爪立つ stand on tiptoe.

つまはじき 爪弾き ¶つまはじきする 〈排斥する〉 refuse to have anything to do with sb; shun; 〈村八分にする〉 send sb to Coventry; 《文》 ostracize. 文例

つまびき 爪弾き ¶つま弾きする play 《a samisen》 with one's fingers; pick [strum (on)] 《a guitar》.

つまびらか 詳らか ⇒あきらか, くわしい ¶つまびらかにする 《文》 ascertain; make clear.

つまみ 摘まみ 〈取っ手〉a knob; 〈スイッチを〉 a switch; 〈レバー〉 a lever; 〈酒の〉 a relish; (an) hors d'oeuvre (pl. hors d'oeuvre(s)) ¶一つまみの塩 a pinch of salt.

つまみあげる 摘まみ上げる pick 《a worm》 up in one's fingers; take a pinch of 《salt》.

つまみあらい 摘まみ洗い ¶つまみ洗いをする wash the soiled part 《of a dress》.

つまみぐい 摘まみ食い ¶つまみ食いする pick up food (with one's fingers) and eat it without waiting for the meal to start; 〈公金などを〉 embezzle; 《文》 appropriate for one's own use; 〈口語〉 help oneself to 《public money》; pocket. 文例

つまみだす 摘まみ出す 〈つまんで出す〉 pick out; 〈人を〉 drag out (引きずり出す); turn [throw, 《口語》chuck] out (追い出す).

つまむ 摘まむ take sth [pick sth up] with [between] one's fingers [chopsticks]. 文例

つまようじ 爪楊枝 a toothpick.

つまらない 〈取るに足りない〉 trifling; trivial; petty; insignificant; 〈無価値の〉 worthless; valueless; 《文》 of little importance; 《文》 of small account; poor; 〈ばかげた〉 silly; foolish; 〈役に立たない〉 useless; 〈面白くない〉 unintersting; dull; unexciting; 〈浮き立たない〉 cheerless ¶つまらない事[物] a trivial [trifling] thing; a trifle; trash; rubbish / つまらないやつ a worthless fellow; a good-for-nothing; 〈退屈な人〉 a bore / つまらない事を言う talk nonsense [rubbish]; say silly things / つまらない事に騒ぎ立てる make a fuss about trifles / つまらなく金を使う spend one's money on worthless things [to no purpose]; waste [fritter away] one's money / つまらなそうに with a disappointed look. 文例

つまり 〈結局〉 after all; in the long run; 〈要するに〉 to sum up; in short; 《文》 in brief; in a word; 〈すなわち〉 that is (to say); 《文》 namely; in other words. 文例

つまる 詰まる 〈ふさがる〉 be blocked; be stopped up; be choked; be closed; be stuffed; 〈一杯になる〉 get [《文》become] full; be packed; 〈短くなる〉 get [[《文》become] shorter; be shortened; 〈縮む〉 shrink; con-

---

つぼ² 計画がつぼにはまった. The plan worked. | The stratagem proved a success.

つぼみ 梅はつぼみが大きくふくらんでいる. Ume trees are in fat bud. / つぼみが大きくふくらんで今にもほころびようとしている. The buds were swollen to bursting. / 桜のつぼみはまだ固い. The buds of the cherry trees are still tight.

つまずき ちょっとしたつまずきから一生を棒に振った. A minor [trifling] mistake early in his career ruined his life [led to his fall].

つまはじき 彼はこの近所のつまはじき者だ. He is regarded as a nuisance [pest] by everybody in this neighborhood.

つまむ その著者の名はつまびらかではない. The name of the author is unknown.

つまみぐい (子供に向かって)つまみ食いはいけません. Wait until you're served.

つむ どうぞおつまみ下さい. Please help yourself (to it).

つまらない (人に物を贈る時)これはつまらないものですが. This is a small present for you. | Here's something for you. / あの本は僕には全くつまらなかった. I couldn't work up any interest in that book. | That book bored me

つみ￨tract ; 〈窮乏する〉 run short 《of food》;《口語》be hard up 《for money》¶車の詰まっている車線 a lane blocked with vehicles / 言葉に詰まる be at a loss for words [what to say] / ぎっしり字の詰まったページ a closely printed page / 声を詰まらせて in a choked [choking] voice / ぎっしり詰まった日程 a tight [close-packed] schedule. 文例⇩

つみ[1] 罪 〈法律上の〉 a crime ; an offense ; guilt ; 〈宗教・道徳上の〉 (a) sin ; 〈過誤〉 a fault ; 〈とがめ〉 blame ; a charge ; 〈罰〉 (a) punishment ¶罪な sinful ; guilty ; 〈残酷な〉 cruel ; heartless / 罪のない innocent ;《文》guiltless ; blameless ; harmless (害のない) / 罪のないうそ a white lie / 罪のない顔をする look innocent / 罪の意識 a sense of guilt [sin] ;《文》an awareness of one's sinfulness / 罪の意識に悩まされている人々 guilt-ridden people / 罪を犯す commit a crime [sin] ; sin 《against God》; be guilty of 《murder》/ 罪を着せる put [pin] the guilt on sb ; lay the blame at sb's door / 罪を着る take the blame 《on oneself》《for》; hold oneself responsible [to blame] 《for》/ 罪を免れる escape [《文》elude] punishment ; be acquitted of the charge [blame] / 罪を認める plead guilty 《to a crime》/ 罪に問う accuse sb of 《murder》; charge sb with 《theft》; bring a charge of 《theft》against sb / 罪におとしいれる incriminate sb. 文例⇩

つみ[2] 詰み《将棋》checkmate ; mate. 文例⇩

-づみ[2] …積み ¶9トン積みの貨車 a nine-ton freight car / 100トン積みの船 a ship of 100 tons burden.

つみあげる 積み上げる pile [heap]《boxes》up ; pile 《one thing》on top of 《another》.

つみいれる 積み入れる ⇨つみこ.

つみおろし 積み下ろし loading and unloading ; shipping and discharging ; 〈荷役〉 cargo work ¶積み下ろしをする load and unload 《a ship》.

つみかえ 積み替[換]え 〈貨物の〉 transshipment ; reshipment.

つみかえる 積み替[換]える 〈再び積み上げる〉 pile 《up》over again ; 〈他の貨車などに〉 transship ; reship ; transfer《the goods from the ship to a truck》.

つみかさなる 積み重なる be [lie] heaped [piled] up ; be piled on top of one another ; accumulate.

つみかさね 積み重ね a pile ; a heap ; 〈蓄積〉《文》(an) accumulation 《of knowledge》¶積み重ねによって学習すべき科目 a sequentially based [organized] subject. 文例⇩

つみかさねる 積み重ねる pile [heap] up ; accumulate ; put [lay] 《one thing》on 《top of》《another》¶山のように積み重ねてある be piled up mountain-high ; lie in a huge pile.

つみき 積み木 a (toy) building block ; a brick ¶積み木遊びをする play with building blocks.

つみくさ 摘み草 ¶摘み草をする gather herbs [edible grass].

つみこみ 積み込み loading ; 〈特に船舶への〉 shipping ; shipment.

つみこむ 積み込む load 《a truck with goods》; put [place] 《goods》on board ; 〈船に〉 ship 《a cargo》; 〈船が〉 take in 《a cargo》¶船倉に貨物を積み込む stow cargo in the hold ; stow the hold with cargo. 文例⇩

つみだし 積み出し shipment ; forwarding ¶積み出しを待っている荷物 goods awaiting shipment / 積み出し港 a port of shipment ; an embarkation port.

つみだす 積み出す forward ; send off ; ship off (特に船で).

つみたて 積み立て ¶積み立て金 a reserve (fund) ; a deposit / 積み立て貯金 installment [regular] savings.

つみたてる 積み立てる lay [put] by [aside] ; reserve ; save 《money for sth》; 〈保証金を〉 deposit 《money with sb as security》.

つみつくり 罪作り ¶罪作りな sinful ; cruel ; heartless.

つみとり 積み取り loading.

つみとる[1] 摘み取る pick ; pluck ; nip [pinch, trim] off ¶陰謀の芽をつみ取る nip a plot in the bud.

つみとる[2] 積み取る load ; take on board ; take aboard.

つみなおす 積み直す reload ; load over again ; 〈重ね直す〉 pile up again.

つみに 積み荷 〈貨物〉 a load ; freight ; (a) cargo (pl. -(e)s) (船の) ; 〈積み込み〉 loading ¶積み荷をする load 《a truck with goods》; ship 《goods》; put 《goods》on board / 積み荷をおろす discharge [unload] goods 《from a truck》; unload 《a ship》/ 積荷保険 cargo insurance. 文例⇩

つみのこし, つみのこり 積み残し, 積み残り 〈事〉 short shipment ; 〈荷〉 (a) left-off cargo ; left-off goods.

つみぶかい 罪深い sinful ;《文》ungodly.

---

stiff [was of no interest to me].

つまり つまりはだれが悪いのでもないということさ. The long and short of it is that nobody is to blame.

つまる 鼻が詰まってにおいが分らない. My nose is stuffed [bunged] up, and I cannot smell anything. / 煙突がすすで詰まっている. The chimney is clogged [choked] (up) with soot.

つみ[1] だれの罪か. Whose fault is it? | Where does the blame lie? | Who is to blame for it? / 罪は私にはない. It is not my fault. | I am not to blame. / 彼には罪のないことが証明された. He was proved innocent of the crime.

つみ[2] ここで詰みがある. A (check)mate is possible here.

つみかさね 人間は, ほかの動物と違って, すべての事を自分で発見し直していく必要はなく, 過去の世代が得た知識をもとにしてその上に積み重ねをして行くことができる. Unlike other animals, man does not have to rediscover everything again for himself, but can build on the knowledge acquired by earlier generations.

つみこむ 船は綿を積み込んだ. The ship took on a cargo of cotton. / チェーンとロープを積み込んだ方がいい. You had better load up chains and a rope.

つみに 僕ははしけに積み荷が下ろされるのを見ていた. I watched the unloading of a cargo into a lighter.

つみほろぼし 罪滅ぼし 《文》atonement for one's sin(s) ¶罪滅ぼしをする 《文》make amends for one's sin;《文》expiate [atone for] one's sin; pay the penalty of one's sin / …の罪滅ぼしに《文》in atonement for…;《文》in expiation of…;《補償》in [by way of] compensation for….

つみもどす 積み戻す load [ship] back.
つみれ 摘れ a fish ball.
つむ[1] 錘 a spindle.
つむ[2] 詰む《将棋》be checkmated; be mated ¶目の詰んだ close; fine.
つむ[3] 摘む pick; pluck;〈はさみなどで〉trim; clip; snip;〈採集する〉gather ¶芽をつむ nip [snip] a bud 〈off a stem〉/〈比喩的に〉nip 〈a plot〉in the bud / 茶[花]をつむ pick tea [flowers].
つむ[4] 積む pile [heap] (up); lay; stack 《boxes》;〈積載する〉load;〈船に〉ship; put 《goods》on board;〈船が主語〉take 〈a cargo〉on board;〈蓄積する〉accumulate;〈貯える〉lay [put] by; save ¶れんがを積む lay bricks / トラックに材木を積む load a truck with lumber; load lumber on a truck 〈船などに〉荷を積み過ぎる overload 〈a ship〉/ 今にも倒れそうに丸太を高く積んだトラック a truck loaded precariously high with logs. 文例↓
つむぎ 紬 pongee. into yarn.
つむぐ 紡ぐ spin ¶糸に紡ぐ spin 《cotton》
つむじ a hair whorl (on the head) ¶つむじを曲げる get [《文》become] cross 《at sth with sb》/ つむじの曲がった〈ねじけた〉perverse; cross-grained;〈かたくなな〉pigheaded;《英口語》bloody-minded / つむじ曲がり a perverse fellow.
つむじかぜ 旋風 a whirlwind.
つめ[1] 爪 a nail (人の); a claw (獣・鳥などの); a talon (わし・たか類の);〈琴などの〉a pick; a plectrum (pl. -trums, -tra) ¶手のつめ a fingernail / 足の爪 a toenail / つめのある clawed; taloned; nailed / つめの手入れをする manicure [do] one's nails / つめのあか the dirt in [under] the (finger)nails / つめをのばす let one's nails grow long; have long nails / つめを切る cut [trim, pare] one's nails / つめを赤く染める paint one's nails red [with red polish] /〈猫などが〉つめをとぐ sharpen [whet] its claws /〈猫などが〉つめを隠す draw in its claws /〈猫などが〉つめを立てる fasten [bury, plunge] its claws 《into sth》/ つめにあかをためる have dirty nails / つめに火をともすbe excessively mean; live stingily / つめに火をともすようなけちなせいかつ a skinflint / つめで引っかく scratch sb [sth] with one's nails;〈動物が〉claw (at) / つめあと a nail [claw] mark;〈引っかき傷〉a scratch / つめ切り a nail clipper; nail clippers /〈はさみ〉nail scissors / つめやすり a nail file. 文例↓
つめ[2] 詰め〈詰めること〉stuffing; packing;〈将棋などの〉moves for checkmating; an ending (寄せ)¶詰め碁[将棋] a go [chess] problem.
-づめ …詰め ¶箱詰めの 《articles》packed in a case; boxed 《biscuits》/ びん詰めの bottled 《beer》/ りんご100個詰め 1 箱 a box of [containing] one hundred apples / 本店詰めである[になる] work at [be transferred to] the head office / 警視庁詰めの記者 a reporter accredited to the Metropolitan Police Office.
つめあわせ 詰め合わせ〈取り合わせ〉an assortment ¶詰め合わせの assorted 《biscuits》.
つめあわせる 詰め合わせる pack an assortment of 《cookies》; pack together 《with sth》.
つめえり 詰め襟 a stand-up collar;〈服〉a jacket with a stand-up collar.
つめかえる 詰め替える refill; restuff; repack (荷物を); rebottle (びん詰めを).
つめかける 詰め掛ける crowd 《a house, into a house》;《文》throng 《to》; besiege 《a place》. 文例↓
つめきる 詰め切る be always on hand; do not leave one's post ¶事務所に一日詰め切る spend a whole day at one's office.
つめくさ〈植〉a pearlwort.
つめこみ 詰め込み〈勉強〉cramming ¶詰め込み勉強をする cram up 《history》;《英》swot up 《one's physics》;《米俗》bone up on 《algebra》. 文例↓
つめこむ 詰め込む cram 《things into a drawer》; stuff; jam; squeeze; pack;〈人を〉crowd 《people into a room》¶かばんに詰め込む

つむ[4] 机のかたわらに本がたくさん積んである. A lot of books are piled up beside the desk. / もっと練習を積まなければだめだよ. You need more practice. / 金を山ほど積んでも幸福は買えるものではない. No amount of money can buy happiness. / この船は米を積んでいる. The boat has a cargo of rice on board.

つめ[1] つめの先に黒くあかがたまっていた. His nails had black edges to them. / あの人のつめのあかでもせんじて飲んだらどうだ. You ought to pray to God that you may have a thousandth part of his virtue. / 彼の話にはつめのあかほどの真実もない. There's not an atom [ounce] of truth in what he said. / まだ台風のつめ跡が残っていた. The scars left by the typhoon were still visible.

つめかける 野球ファンが早朝から詰めかけることだろう. Baseball fans will be arriving in droves from early in the morning. / ホールにはあふれるほどの人が詰めかけていた. The hall was jammed [packed] to the doors with people.

つめこみ 試験で盛んに詰め込み勉強をやっている. He's busily cramming for the exam. / 詰め込み主義の教育はむしろ有害だ. Cramming does more harm than good.

つめたい 風はぴりっとするほど冷たかった. There was a nip in the air. / 彼女は冷たい女だ. She is a cold(-hearted) woman. / She is cold at heart. / 彼女は僕を冷たく見すてた. She gave me a stony [chilling] stare. / 彼はその人々から冷たくあしらわれた. He was treated coldly by [got the cold shoulder from] those people.

つめよる 彼女は詰め寄って返事をせまた. She pressed him hard for a reply.

つめる もう少しお詰め下さい. Please sit a little closer. / 小型車に詰めた. We packed (ourselves) into a small car. / このクッションには羽が詰めてある.

pack up a bag ; pack 《things》 into a bag ／腹一杯詰め込む eat one's fill ; gorge 《oneself》 《on, with》; stuff [cram] oneself [one's stomach] with food ／腹の皮がつっぱるまで詰め込む gorge to bursting-point ／知識を詰め込む cram knowledge into one's head ; cram [stuff] one's head with information.

つめしょ 詰め所 a post ; a station ; an office ; 〈番人の〉a guardroom ; a guardhouse.

つめたい 冷たい cold ; chilly ¶氷のように冷たい icy ; as cold as ice ; ice-cold ／体を刺すように[痛いほど]冷たい biting 《achingly》 cold ／心の冷たい cold-hearted ／冷たい戦争 a cold war ／冷たい態度 a cold [an unfriendly] attitude ／冷たく in a chilly [frigid] manner ; coldly ／冷たくなる get cold ; cool down [off] ; 〈死ぬ〉die ／冷たさ coldness.

つめて 詰め手 〈荷物を詰める人〉a packer ; 〈将棋の〉moves for checkmating ; an ending (寄し).

つめなおす 詰め直す repack ; pack over again ; rebottle (瓶に).

つめばら 詰め腹 ¶詰め腹を切らせる force sb to commit harakiri ／〈比喩的に〉force sb to resign his post.

つめもの 詰め物 〈はく製・料理の〉stuffing ; 〈歯などの〉(a) filling ; 〈穴などの〉a plug ; stopping ; 〈椅子などの〉padding ; 〈布団などの〉wadding ; 〈荷造りの〉packing ¶詰め物をする pack [stuff] 《sth with》.

つめよる, つめよせる 詰め寄る, 詰め寄せる press 《close》 on ; draw near ; draw close to. 文例↓

つめる 詰める 〈一杯に入れる〉fill ; stuff ; pack ; 〈席をつめる〉sit close [closer] ; 〈文を〉write close(ly) ; 〈短縮する〉shorten ; cut down ; curtail ; 〈勤務する〉be on duty ; be at one's post ; be stationed 《at》; 〈将棋〉checkmate ; time ¶穴に綿をつめる stop [plug] a hole with cotton ／トランクに着物を詰める pack one's clothes into a suitcase ; pack a suitcase with one's clothes ／瓶に詰める fill a bottle with 《water》; bottle 《milk》／ドレスのウエストを詰める take a dress in at the waist ; take in the waist of a dress ／指を詰める cut off the tip of one's 《little》 finger ／4時間の仕事を2時間に詰めてやる pack four hours' work into two hours ／パイプのタバコを詰める fill one's pipe 《with tobacco》／息を詰める hold one's breath ／息を詰めて without breathing ／終日働き詰める keep working all day (long). 文例↓

つめわた 詰め綿 wadding ; a wad ; padding ; a pad.

つもり 積もり 〈意図〉an intention ; 〈考え〉(a) thought ; an idea ; 〈目的〉a purpose ; 〈信念〉a belief ; 〈動機〉a motive ; 〈予期〉expectation(s) ; anticipation ; hope(s) ¶…するつもりで with the intention [object, aim] of doing ; with a [the] view to [of] doing ; for the purpose of doing ; in the hope of doing ／…するつもりである be going to do ; will do ; intend to do ; have a mind to do ; mean to do. 文例↓

つもる 積もる heap [pile] up ; accumulate ; 〈雪などが〉lie 《on》: be covered with 《snow》(場所が主語) ¶積もる話がある have old scores to settle 《with sb》／積もる話がある have a great deal to talk about ／落ち葉の積もった小道 a path drifted with leaves.

つや¹ 通夜 an all-night watch [a vigil] over the body of a dead person ; 《米, アイルランド》a wake ¶お通夜のような気分 a funereal gloom ／通夜をする keep vigil 《over sb's body》; sit up all night 《by sb's body》; hold a wake 《over》. 文例↓

つや² 艶 gloss ; luster ; polish ; sheen ¶つやが消える lose its luster ／つやのある. つやつやした glossy ; shiny ; lustrous ; bright ／つやのある声 a mellow voice ／つやのない dull ; lusterless ／つやのない肌 a sallow [muddy] complexion ／つやを出す make sth glossy ; give luster 《to》; burnish ; polish up 《磨いて》／つやを消す ⇒つやけし.

つやけし 艶消し matting ; frosting ; graying (写真の) ¶つや消しにする 〈ガラス・金属を〉frost ; mat ;【写真】gray ／つや消しの mat ; frosted 《glass》; ground 《surfaces》; grayed 《photographs》. 文例↓

つやだし 艶出し polishing ; burnishing ; calendering (紙の) ⇒つや²(つやを出す) ¶つや出し仕上げの glacé 《gloves》／つや出しラッ

る. This cushion is stuffed with feathers. ／そのベルトを5センチほど詰めてもらった. I had the belt shortened a couple of inches.
つもり 僕は休暇を京都で過ごすもりです. I am planning to spend the holidays in Kyoto. ／日本にどのくらい滞在なさるおつもりですか. How long are you going to stay in Japan? ／僕には規則を破るつもりは全くありません. I have no [don't have any] intention of breaking the rules. ／こんな事に使うつもりで建てたのではありません. The building was not intended for this sort of purpose. ／そんなつもりで言ったのではありません. I didn't mean it that way. ／これは英語のつもりか. Do you call this English? | Is this meant to be English? ／冗談のつもりだった. I said it as a joke. | It was meant to be a joke. ／彼は彼女に手を貸すつもりでそうしたのだ. He did so by way of helping her.
つもる 雪が2メートル積もった. The snow lay two meters deep. ／机の上にほこりが厚く積もっていた. Thick dust lay on the desk. ／毎日の観察記録が積もり積もって貴重な学問的データになった. The record of his daily observations added up to valuable scientific data.

つや¹ ごく近しかったわずかの人々だけが集まって, しめやかに通夜が営まれた. The vigil over his body was held quietly, attended only by the small number of people who had been closest to him. ／まるでお通夜みたいなパーティーだね. This party is about as much fun as a funeral. ／彼が来るまではパーティーは通夜のようだった. The party was dying until he came.
つやけし 彼女は顔立ちはいいのだが脚の太いのがつや消しだ. She's good looking all right, but it's spoilt by [it's a pity about] her thick legs.

つやっぽい 艶っぽい erotic; suggestive;《文》coquettish; flirtatious;《口語》sexy;《文》amorous ¶つやっぽい話 a love story; an erotic [a suggestive] story.

つやぶき 艶拭き ¶艶拭きする rub and polish.

つゆ¹ 汁 〈スープ〉soup; 〈肉汁〉gravy; 〈果物の〉juice; 〈樹液〉sap.

つゆ² 露 dew; a dewdrop (露の玉) ¶露が結ぶ dew forms; dewdrops form / 露を帯びた dewy; wet [moist] with dew / 露にぬれた wet with dew; dew-covered (grass) / 露ほども (not) in the least; (not) in the slightest (degree) / …とは露知らず not knowing [having no idea] (at all) that…; little dreaming that…. 文例⇩

つゆ³ 梅雨 the long spell of rainy weather in early summer; the rainy [wet] season ¶つゆ明け the end of the rainy season. 文例⇩

つゆはらい 露払い 〈前駆〉an outrider (for a procession); an advance man; 〈相撲の〉the wrestler who enters the ring first at the yokozuna's entrance ceremony.

つよい 強い 〈強力な〉strong; powerful;《文》mighty; 〈強健な〉《文》robust; stout; strong; 〈強烈な〉violent; hard; severe; intense; strong; 〈堅牢(ｹﾝﾛｳ)な〉durable ¶体が強い be strong; be strongly [sturdily] built / 強い酒 a strong [stiff, hard] drink / 強い光 strong [intense] light / 酒に強い hold [take] one's drink well / 数学に強い be good at mathematics / 強く strongly; powerfully; firmly; intensely / 激しく hard; severely; keenly; violently; emphatically (強調して) / 強く打つ strike hard / 強くする ⇒つよめる / 強く出る ⇒つよごし (強腰に出る) / 強くなる ⇒つよまる / 強さ strength; power;《文》might; toughness; intensity. 文例⇩

つよがり 強がり a show of courage; a bluff (はったり) ¶強がりを言う〈見せる〉try to hide one's weakness; put on a bold front;《口語》talk tough; 〈はったりをかける〉bluff.

つよき 強気 〈強腰〉⇒つよごし; 〈株式〉a bullish tone [sentiment] ¶強気の bullish; firm (しっかりした) / 強気である, 強気買いに出る be [go] long; be [go] on the long side of the market.

つよごし 強腰 a firm attitude [stand] ¶強腰に出る take [《文》assume] a strong [an aggressive,《文》a resolute] attitude《toward》; take a strong line《toward, against》; take a firm [determined] stand《against》.

つよび 強火 《料理》a strong fire ¶強火にする make the fire stronger / 強火で煮る cook over a strong fire; boil at high heat.

つよまる 強まる grow [get,《文》become] strong [powerful, intense]; grow [get,《文》become] stronger [more powerful, intenser]; increase in force [strength, violence];《文》intensify; 〈感情が〉grow on 《one》. 文例⇩

つよみ 強味 a strong point; one's forte; one's strength; an advantage. 文例⇩

つよめる 強める make sth stronger; strengthen; build up;《文》intensify (度を); 〈所信などを〉confirm; 〈強調する〉emphasize; lay [put] stress [emphasis] 《on》; underscore; underline; 〈増す〉increase. 文例⇩

つら 面 〈顔〉a face;《俗》a mug ⇒かお; 〈ずうずうしさ〉face; 〈表面〉the surface ¶学者面をする pose as [set oneself up as] a scholar / 面の皮の厚い shameless; brazen-faced; cheeky; impudent ⇒てつめんぴ, ずうずうしい. 文例⇩

つらあて 面当て a spiteful act; an action intended to annoy [injure] sb ¶面当てを言う say spiteful things《to, about》/ 面当てをする vent one's spite on sb; annoy; injure; hurt / 面当てに out of spite; from spite; to spite sb.

つらい 辛い trying; hard; painful; bitter; tough; cruel; heart-breaking ¶つらい思いをする, つらい目にあう go through hardships; have a hard [tough] time (of it); have a bitter experience / つらく当たる treat sb harshly; be hard (on sb);《口語》give sb a hard time [a raw deal] / つらくする make it tough [rough] (for sb) / つらさ pain; distress; bitterness. 文例⇩

つらがまえ 面構え a look;《文》a countenance ¶鬼のような面構えをしている have a forbidding look on one's face; look like an ogre.

つらなる 連なる range; lie [stand, run, stretch] in a row [line]; be strung out; 〈参列する〉attend (a dinner); be present 《at》. 文例⇩

つゆ² 草に露が宿っていた。There were dewdrops on the grass. / 露の玉を宿して, 草の葉が朝の光にきらきら光っていた。Beaded with dew, the blades of grass were sparkling in the morning sun. / ワインの冷たいびんは露を結んでいた。There were beads of moisture on the cold wine bottle.

つゆ³ 梅雨に入った[が明けた]。The rainy season has set in [is over]. / 梅雨は6月からです。The rainy season in Japan starts in June.

つよい それは日本の円が滅法強いからさ。It's because the Japanese yen is extremely strong. / 彼は米国の経済政策を強い言葉で批判した。He made a strongly-worded criticism of the United States' economic policy. / このプラスチックは熱に強い。These plastics are heat-resistant. / この木は公害に強い。These trees are tolerant of [have a high resistance to] pollution.

つよまる 望郷の念がだんだん強まってついにたえがたいものとなった。The longing for home grew on him until it became insupportable.

つよみ 彼の強味はその大きな財力だけだ。His only strong point is his immense wealth. / 何よりも安いのがその強味だった。Above all, it had the advantage of cheapness.

つよめる 心の優しさが何よりも大切であると彼は語気を強めて語った。He asserted with emphasis [was emphatic in his assertion] that kindheartedness was more important than anything else.

つら いい面の皮だ。What a nice position I'm in! / いくら面の皮が厚いからといって彼にそんなことは言えないよ。Even I haven't the cheek [nerve] to say such a thing to him. | How can I have the face to tell him that?

つらい 僕はつらい立場にある。I am in a difficult position. / 貧乏はつらいものだ。Poverty is hard

つらにくい 面憎い ⟨いやな⟩ disgusting; detestable; hateful; ⟨いまいましい⟩ infuriating; provoking; exasperating; cursed ¶面憎いほど落ち着いて with infuriating [provoking] coolness.

つらぬく 貫く ⟨貫通する⟩ pierce; go [run, shoot] through; penetrate; ⟨貫徹する⟩ carry through [out]. 文例⇩

つらねる 連ねる link; join; put [⟨文⟩ place] ⟨things⟩ in a row [line] ¶名を連ねる enter one's name (in); allow one's name to be added ⟨to the list⟩ / 自動車を連ねて in a fleet of cars; ⟨パレードで⟩ in a procession of cars; ⟨米⟩ in a ⟨twenty-five-car⟩ motorcade.

つらよごし 面汚し a disgrace ⟨to⟩; a stain ⟨on⟩; a shame ⟨on⟩ ¶面汚しな shameful; disgraceful; discreditable / …の面汚しである[になる] be a disgrace to ⟨one's family⟩; bring disgrace on ⟨one's name⟩.

つらら an icicle ¶つららの下がった軒 icicle-hung eaves. 文例⇩

つり[1] 釣り ⟨魚釣り⟩ angling; (line-)fishing ¶釣りがうまい be a good angler / 釣りの雑誌 an anglers' journal / 釣りに行く go fishing [angling] / ますを釣りに行く go trout-fishing / 釣りをする a fish [angle] ⟨(in) a stream⟩ / 1日釣りを楽しむ have [enjoy] a good day's fishing / 釣り糸 a fishing line / 釣り糸をたれる cast [drop] one's line ⟨in a river⟩ / 釣り具店 a fishing-tackle store / 釣り竿 a fishing rod; a fishing pole / 釣り師 an angler; a fisherman / 釣り道具 fishing tackle; a rod and line / 釣り場 a fishing place / 釣り針 a fishhook; a hook; ⟨蚊針⟩ a fly / 釣り船[堀] a fishing boat [pond] / 釣り宿 an anglers' [a fishermen's] hotel; a lodging for anglers. 文例⇩

つり[2] 釣り ⟨釣り銭⟩ change ¶釣りをもらう get (the) change / 釣りを出す give (fifty yen) change to sb / 釣りをごまかす shortchange sb; give sb short change / 釣りを確かめる examine one's change ⟨before leaving the counter⟩. 文例⇩

つりあい 釣り合い ⟨平均⟩ balance; ⟨均衡⟩ equilibrium; ⟨対比⟩ proportion; ⟨均整⟩ symmetry; ⟨調和⟩ harmony ¶釣り合いのとれた[悪い] well-[badly-]balanced; balanced [unbalanced]; well-[ill-]matched; well-[poorly-]proportioned; harmonious ⟨out of harmony⟩ ⟨with⟩ / 釣り合いの取れた物の見方をする see things in (proper) perspective / 釣り合いをとる balance ⟨(A)⟩ with [by, against] ⟨(B)⟩; bring ⟨(A)⟩ into harmony with ⟨(B)⟩; harmonize ⟨(A)⟩ with ⟨(B)⟩; ⟨体の⟩ balance [poise] oneself. 文例⇩

つりあう 釣り合う balance; be in harmony [in keeping] ⟨with⟩; suit; be in proportion ⟨to⟩; match ⟨with⟩; go (well) ⟨with⟩. 文例⇩

つりあがる 釣り上がる ¶目尻の釣り上がった almond-eyed; slant-eyed; with eyes slanting upward.

つりあげる 釣り上げる ⟨魚を⟩ land ⟨a fish⟩; fish out [up]; ⟨値段を⟩ raise; boost (up); pull up ¶目を釣り上げて with a fierce look in one's eyes.

ツリウム 〖化〗thulium.

つりおとす 釣り落とす fail to land ⟨a fish⟩; let ⟨a fish⟩ get away. 文例⇩

つりがね 釣り鐘 ⟨strike, toll⟩ a hanging [temple] bell ¶釣鐘堂 a bell house.

つりがねそう 釣鐘草〖植〗a (dotted) bellflower; a campanula.

つりかわ 吊り革 a strap ¶つり革につかまる hold (on to) a strap; hang on to a strap.

つりこむ 釣り込む draw into; attract; entice [⟨文⟩ allure, lure, tempt] into ¶話に釣り込まれる ⟨面白さに⟩ be charmed [carried away] by sb's story; ⟨約束などに⟩ be tempted by sb's promise [assurance(s)]. 文例⇩

つりさがる 吊り下がる hang [be hung] (down) (from); be suspended (from); dangle (from) ⟨だらりと⟩.

つりさげる 吊り下げる hang; suspend; dangle.

つりせん 釣り銭 change ⇒つり[2]. 文例⇩

つりだす[1] 吊り出す〖相撲〗carry ⟨one's opponent⟩ out of the ring.

つりだす[2] 釣り出す entice [lure] sb out.

つりにがす 釣り逃がす ⇒つりおとす.

つりばし 吊り橋 a suspension bridge ¶吊り

---

to bear. / あの男は貧乏のつらさを知らない。He doesn't know what it is to be poor. / 男はつらいよ。Life is hard [rough] on a man!

つらなる その山脈は南北に連なっていた。The mountain range extended [stretched, ran] north and south. / 遠く連なる峰々は雪を頂いていた。The distant range of mountains was crowned with snow.

つらぬく 弾丸は左のももを貫いた。The bullet went through his left thigh. / どんな犠牲を払っても初志を貫く覚悟です。I am determined to carry out my original intention at any cost.

つらら 軒につららが出来た。Icicles have formed under the eaves.

つり[1] この川は釣りに良いところです。This river has [provides] good fishing.

つり[2] お釣りでございます。Here's your change. / 釣りはいらないよ。Keep [You can keep] the change. | Never mind the change. / 1万円札でお釣りがもらえますか。Can you give me change for a 10,000-yen note? / それは千円札で釣りが来ます。You can get it for less than 1,000 yen.

つりあい 彼はタバコをベンチの縁にうまく釣り合いをとっていた。He balanced his cigarette delicately on the edge of the bench.

つりあう そのネクタイは服とは釣り合わないんじゃない。I'm afraid that necktie doesn't go with your coat. / 家具が部屋に釣り合わない。The furniture is out of keeping [doesn't go well] with the room.

つりおとす 釣り落とした魚を大きく話すのは釣り師の常である。Anglers are notorious for their exaggerated tales of the one that got away [the fish they almost caught]. / 釣り落とした魚は大きい。It is the fish you fail to land that is the biggest.

つりこむ 彼の微笑にみな釣り込まれて笑った。His smile evoked responsive smiles from us all. | His smile was quite infectious.

つりせん 釣り銭のいらないように願います。Pay the exact amount.

つりほうたい

橋をかける construct [throw] a suspension bridge ((over a river)); suspend [hang] a bridge ((over a gorge)).

つりほうたい 吊り包帯 a sling ¶つり包帯で腕をつっている have one's arm in a sling.

つりわ 吊り輪 《体操》 (flying) rings ¶つり輪で金メダルを取る win the gold medal in [on] the rings.

つる¹ 弦 〈弓の〉a bowstring; 〈楽器の〉a string; 〈どびんなどの〉a handle ¶つるを張る[はず す] string [unstring] ((a bow)) / つるを鳴らす twang ((one's fiddle)).

つる² 蔓 〈ぶどうなどの〉a vine; 〈巻きひげ〉a tendril; 〈いもなどの〉a runner; 〈眼鏡の〉a sidepiece.

つる³ 鶴 a crane ¶つるの舞 the (courtship) dance of cranes / つるの一声 a word from the top; a voice of authority. 文例⇩

つる⁴ 釣[吊]る 〈魚を〉fish ((for carp)); angle (for fish); 〈吊り下げる〉hang sth (down); sling; 《文》suspend; dangle (だらりと); wear (a saber); 〈あざむく〉lure; entice; take in; attract ¶くさりでつる hang sth on a chain / 首をつる hang oneself / 包帯で腕をつっている have one's arm in a sling. 文例⇩

つる⁵ 攣る ⇨つる².

つるくさ 蔓草 a creeper; a climber; a vine.

つるし 吊るし 《既製服》 ready-made clothes; off-the-peg clothes ¶つるしを買う buy ((a suit)) off the peg.

つるしあげ 吊るし上げ a kangaroo court ¶つるし上げを食う be subjected to [hauled before] a kangaroo court / つるし上げる subject sb to [haul sb before] a kangaroo court.

つるす 吊るす ⇨つる⁴.

つるつる ¶つるつるした slippery; smooth; slick; greasy (油で) / つるつるにはげている be (as) bald as a billiard ball [an egg].

つるはし 鶴嘴 a pickax(e); a pick.

つるばら 蔓薔薇 a climbing rose; a rambler; a rambling rose.

つるべ 釣瓶 a (well) bucket ¶つるべ落としの秋の日 the fast-sinking autumn sun / つるべ打ちに撃つ blaze away ¶うちまくる.

つるり ⇨つるつる ¶つるりとすべる slide; slip / つるりとぬける slip through ((one's fingers)).

つれ 連れ 〈1人〉a companion; 〈総称〉company; 〈能の〉a tsure; the second supporting character in a Noh drama ¶旅の連れ a fellow traveler; a traveling companion / 連れになる fall in with sb; fall into company ((with))/ 2人[3人]連れで in a couple [a party of three]. 文例⇩

つれあい 連れ合い 〈夫〉one's husband; 〈妻〉one's wife.

つれこ 連れ子 a child of one's wife by her former marriage; a stepchild.

つれこむ 連れ込む take [bring] sb into ((an inn)) ¶連れ込み宿 a hotel especially for couples; a 'love hotel.'

つれそう 連れ添う be [become] man and wife; marry; be married to sb ¶末長く連れ添う be sb's companion for [through] life.

つれだす 連れ出す take sb out; 〈だまして〉entice [《文》allure, lure] sb out; abduct ((a woman)).

つれだつ 連れ立つ go together; go (along) with sb; go in company with sb ¶...と連れ立って (in company) with...; 《文》accompanied by... / 2人3人と連れ立って in twos and threes. 文例⇩

-つれて ¶...につれて as...; with...; in proportion to... / 音楽につれて (dance) to the music / 日本経済の発展につれて as the Japanese economy developed; (along) with the development of the Japanese economy / 時がたつにつれて as time goes on; with the lapse [passage] of time ★後の2例のような場合, 'as+S+V' の型の方が 'with+抽象名詞' の型よりも普通に使われる.

つれない unkind; unsympathetic; heartless; cold-hearted; hard-hearted; 〈残酷な〉cruel ¶つれなく unkindly; heartlessly; coldly; harshly; cruelly / つれなくする treat sb coldly; be unkind to sb.

つれる¹ 連れる take [bring] ((sb with one)); 《文》be accompanied ((by)); 〈供を〉《文》be attended ((by)); be followed ((by)) ¶...を連れて (in company) with...; accompanied [attended] by... / 連れて行く 〈一緒に行く〉take [bring] sb along [with one]; take sb over to... (遠い所へ); 〈連れ去る〉take [lead] sb away / 連れて帰る take [bring] sb home [back] / 連れに行く go for sb; go to fetch sb; go and collect sb. 文例⇩

つれる² 攣れる 〈筋が〉get [have] (a) cramp ((in the leg)) ★ cramp は 《米》では不定冠詞をつけ,《英》では無冠詞で用いる. なお, cramps は 《米》で '急激な腹痛又は生理痛' の意.

つわもの 兵 《軍人》a soldier; a warrior; 〈猛者(もさ)〉a man of courage; a plucky [daring] fellow.

つわり 悪阻 morning sickness ¶つわりがひどい have bad morning sickness.

ツングース a Tungus ((pl. -(es))).

つんざく 劈く tear; break; split; pierce; 《文》rend ¶耳をつんざくような earsplitting; deafening. 文例⇩ 「too short.

つんつるてん ¶つんつるてんの very short;

つんつん ¶つんつんしている be cross ((with sb, at sth)); be bad-tempered.

つる³ 社長のつるの一声で方針が決まった. A word from the president settled the course of action (to be followed).

つる⁴ この辺はますがよく釣れます. Good trout fishing may be had [There's good trout fishing] in this part of the river. / 彼はだれと連れだって行ってもいつも一番たくさん釣って来る. He almost always outfishes any companions he has with him. / 今日はたくさん釣れた. I have had a good catch today.

つれ たまたま横浜駅でロイド氏と連れになったのである. I came across Mr. Lloyd at Yokohama Station and went the rest of the way with him.

つれそう 夫婦は 50 年間幸せに連れ添ってきた. The couple have

つんと〈すまして〉primly ; standoffishly ; with *one's* nose in the air ;〈においが〉pungently ¶つんとする〈すます〉look prim [prissy] ;〈気どる〉《口語》be stuck up ; be snobbish ; put on airs / つんとする薬のにおい a sharp odor of medicine / つんとくる be pungent ;《文》assail *one's* nostrils.

つんどく 積ん読 ¶積ん読をやっている buy books and just keep them without reading.

ツンドラ a tundra.

つんのめる fall forward ¶つんのめって川に落ちる go pitching forward into the river.

つんぼ 聾 deafness ;〈人〉a deaf person ; the deaf (総称) ¶つんぼになる go [《文》become] deaf ; lose *one's* hearing / つんぼである be deaf ; be hard of hearing (難聴) / つんぼさじき the upper gallery / つんぼさじきに置かれる be kept completely uninformed 《about, of》; be shut out 《from》.

て

て 手 **1.**〈上肢〉a hand ; an arm (腕) ; a paw (動物の) ¶手が早い be quick in snatching ; be a quick worker / 手のひら[甲] the palm [back] of *one's* hand / 手の届く所[届かない所]にある be within [beyond] *one's* reach [grasp] ; be [placed] where *one* can [cannot] get at it / 手の舞い足の踏むところを知らない dance about for joy / 手を挙げる put [hold] *one's* hand(s) up ; raise *one's* hand(s) ;〈なぐろうとして〉lift *one's* hand (against) ;〈降参する〉throw in *one's* hand ; give in ;〈断念する〉give up / 手を掛ける〈触れる〉put [《文》lay] *one's* hand on ; touch ;〈なぐる〉lay hands on ;《文》strike / 手をかざす shade *one's* eyes with *one's* hand / 手をこまねいて〈sit back〉with folded arms / 手を差し出す hold [stretch] out *one's* hand / 手をたたく clap *one's* hands / 手をつかむ seize *sb* by the hand / 手を取る take *sb's* hands into *one's* (own) / 手を握る〈自分の〉clasp *one's* hands ; clench *one's* fists (こぶしを作る) ;〈人の手を〉grasp *sb's* hand ;〈握手する〉shake hands 《with》;〈提携する〉join hands [go hand in hand] 《with》/ 手を延ばす stretch [put out] *one's* hand ; reach (for, after) / 手を伸ばして物を渡す reach *sb sth* / 手を放す let go (of) *sth* ; loose [let go] *one's* hold (on, of) / 手を引く lead *sb* by the hand / 手を広げる〈両腕を〉spread [open] *one's* arms (wide) ;〈手の平を〉open *one's* hand ; spread out the palm of *one's* hand / 手を振る wave *one's* hand / 手に汗を握って in breathless suspense / 手に渡す hand *sth* over to *sb* / 手に取って (go) hand in hand 《with》/ 本を手にして with a book in *one's* hand / 手に手に小旗を持って each carrying a small flag in his hand / 手取り足取りつかまえて holding *sb* by the hands and feet ;《lift *sb* up》bodily ;〈ていねいに〉giving every possible help 《to *sb* in learning *sth*》;《tutor *sb*》very attentively.

2.〈人手〉《文》a hand ; a worker ; staff ¶手が足りない[足りなくなる] be [become] short-handed [short-staffed] ; be [run] short of staff [workers] / 手を貸す help ; give [lend] *sb* a helping hand / 手を貸してコートを着せ脱がせてやる help *sb* on [off] with *his* coat / 手を借りる get *sb's* help ;《文》be aided 《by *sb*》.

3.〈筆跡〉handwriting ;《文》a hand.

4.〈仕事〉¶手があいている be free ; be not busy ;《文》be disengaged ; be at leisure ; have no work to do [on hand] / 手がふさがっている be busy [occupied] (in, with) ; have *one's* hands full ;《文》be engaged / (何かをしようとして, 又は途中で)手を止める stop doing ;《文》stay *one's* hand / 仕事が手につかない cannot settle to (*one's*) work ; be in no mood for work.

5.〈柄〉a handle.

6.〈手段〉《文》a means (単複同形) ; a way ;〈工夫〉a device ;〈策略〉a trick ;〈将棋などの〉a move ;〈相撲の〉a trick ;〈トランプの〉a hand ¶いい手 a good [clever] move / 相撲の四十八手 all the tricks in *sumo* wrestling / 手の内を見せる ⇨ てのうち / 手のつけられない hopeless ; incorrigible / 手のつけようがない be at a loss what to do with *sth* [*sb*] ; there is nothing to be done with *sb* [*sth*] ; do not know where to begin / 手を打つ take a measure [step] ; make a (clever) move / 手を変える try (resort to) some other means ; change *one's* plan [strategy] / 手を変え品を変えて by all possible means ; in every conceivable way / 手を尽くす try every possible means ; do everything possible ; do all *one* can ; leave no stone unturned ; use [try] every trick of the trade / 手に乗る fall [be lured] into a trap [snare] 《set by *sb*》; be taken in 《by》.

7.〈技量〉skill ; ability ¶手が上がる *one's* skill improves ; get better [more skillful] 《at》; show greater skill 《than before》;〈酒量が〉*one's* capacity for alcohol increases / 手が下

---

lived happily together in wedlock for fifty years.

つれだつ 2人連れだって歩いているところを見ました。I saw them walking together.

つれる¹ 連れて行って下さい。Let me go [Take me] with you, please. / 毎朝彼は羊を牧場に連れて行った。Every morning he led the sheep to the pasture.

つんざく 女の悲鳴があたりの静けさをつんざいて聞こえた。A woman's cries pierced the still air.

つんつるてん 春にはちょうどよかったジョニー坊やのズボンが秋にはつんつるてんになっていた。The pants that fitted little Johnnie in the spring were up above his ankles in the fall.

がる lose *one's* skill; *one's* skill goes [《文》 deteriorates]; get out of practice (練習せずにいて).

8. 〈種類〉 a kind; a line ¶この手の品 this sort [type] of article; an article of this sort [description]; this line of goods (集合的).

9. 〈方向・側〉 ¶右手に at [on, to] the right 《of》; to *one's* right.

10. 〈手数〉 trouble; labor; 〈世話〉 care ¶手が省ける 〈事が主語〉 save (*one*) trouble [work] / 手が回る 〈行き届く〉 see to [look after] 《*one's* guests [business]》 properly; be attentive 《to *sb*》; 〈警察の〉 be on *sb's* track / 手の掛かる laborious 《tasks》; troublesome 《work》 / 手の込んだ elaborate 《designs》; sophisticated 《instruments》 / 手を入れる 〈修正する〉 correct; touch up; 〈修繕する〉 repair; mend; 〈きれいにする〉 smarten [do] 《*one's* room》 up / 手を掛ける work carefully 《on *sth*》; take (great) pains 《over *sth* [to *do*]》 / 手を抜く scamp [cut corners in] *one's* work / 手に掛ける 〈世話をする〉 take care of; look after; 〈養育する〉 bring up 《a child》 under *one's* care ⇨ **てがける** / …の手に掛かって死ぬ be killed by *sb*; 《文》 die at the hands of *sb*.

11. 〈制御〉 ¶手に余る[負えない] be out of hand [control]; be unmanageable; be too much for *one*; be more than *one* can manage; be beyond [《文》 exceed] *one's* power.

12. 〈所有〉 ¶…の手にある 《文》 be in the possession [grasp] of… / 手に入れる get; 《口語》 get hold of; 《文》 obtain; come by; secure; win; take [get] possession of / 賞品を手に入れる win [carry off] a prize / 手に入る 〈物が主語〉 come into *one's* possession; fall into [come to] *one's* hands; be obtainable; can be had / 手に渡る pass [fall] into the hands of *sb* / 手から手へと渡る pass from hand to hand.

13. 〈関係・干渉〉 ¶…と手を切る cut [《文》 sever] *one's* connection(s) with; break with / 手を染める 〈始める〉 start; set about; take up 《golf》; 〈関係する〉 have a hand in; get [be] involved 《in》; meddle with; 〈試みる〉 try *one's* hand 《at》 / 手を出す turn *one's* hand to; attempt; dabble in / 手を付ける 〈触れる〉 touch; lay *one's* hand on; 〈着手する〉 set about; set [put] *one's* hand to / 手を控える hold back from 《*sth*, *doing*》; 《文》 refrain from 《*doing*》 / 手を引く wash *one's* hands of; pull out of / 商売の手を拡げる extend [expand] (the scope of) *one's* business.

14. 〈転義〉 ¶手の裏を返すように 〈たちまち〉 all of a sudden; 〈平気で〉 without turning a hair; 《文》 without scruple / 手の切れるような 1 万円札 a crisp 10,000-yen note / 手を打つ 〈値段が折り合う〉 strike [close] a bargain 《with》 / 手を焼く be at a loss 《what to do with it》; be put out 《by》; be unable to control [manage] *sth*; find *sb* a tough customer / 手を離れる become independent of 《*one's* parents》; be off *one's* hands / 手に取るように quite clearly [distinctly] / 手も足も出ない 〈途方に暮れる〉 be at *one's* wits' end; be at a loss what to do; 〈動きがとれない〉 be stuck; 《英口語》 be snookered; be quite helpless / 手もなく easily; with ease; 《yield》 without resistance; without any difficulty [trouble]. [文例⇩]

で[1] 出 〈出現〉 an appearance; 〈人出〉 a turnout; 〈出身〉 *one's* origin; 〈流出〉 flow; 〈出発〉 a start; 〈初め〉 a beginning ¶月の出 moonrise / 農民の出の 《a politician》 with a peasant background [《文》 of peasant origin] / (役者が)出を待つ wait for *one's* turn to appear on the stage. [文例⇩]

で[2] 〈それで〉 and; and so; 〈そういう訳で〉 that

て 手を触れるべからず. 〖掲示〗 Do not touch! | Hands off! / できるだけ高く上に手を伸ばしなさい. Reach up as high as you can. / それが人の手で作られた道具であることは明らかである. It is evident that it is a tool made by the hand of man [by human hand(s)]. / その鳥はひどく弱っていて, 手で拾い上げても逃げようともしなかった. The bird was so exhausted that it did not make so much as an attempt to escape when I picked it up in my hand. / 帽子に手をやらなければならないほど風が強かった. The wind was so strong that he had to hold on to his hat. / ちょっとの間手が明けられますか. Can you spare a few minutes? / 忙しくて, そんな細かい事までは手が回りかねる. I'm too busy to attend to such details. / 新計画作成の仕事で彼は手がふさがっている. His hands are full with the job of making a new plan. / 今大事な用事で手が放せません. I'm sorry I'm held up over some important business. / 係が 3 人では手が回らない. We are very shorthanded with only three people on the staff. / あらゆる手を使ってみた. He tried every possible expedient. / その手には乗らんぞ! You won't catch me that way [with that one]! | It's no use trying that sort of trick with [on] me. / そっちがその手なら, こっちも負けないぞ. Two can play at that game. | That's a game that two can play. / 手の下しようがない. It can't be helped. | There's no help for it. | I can't do anything about it. | There's nothing to be done about it. / あの患者はもう医者の手に負えません. The patient is past medical help. / この仕事は私の手にあまる. This job is beyond me. | I am not equal to this job. / その曲の彼の演奏は手に入ったものだった. He played it with perfect mastery. | He was quite at home with the piece. / そうなれば大分手が省けましょう. That would save me a great deal of trouble. / 子供たちも, もうあまり手が掛からなくなりました. My children no longer need much care and attention. / 彼はもう父親の手を離れてもいい頃だ. He is old enough to be independent of his father. | It is time he was independent of his father. / どちらが先に手を出したのか. Who started it [the fight]? | Who struck the first blow? / あの男は手八丁口八丁だ. He is not only eloquent but also very efficient. | He's both a good talker and a good worker. / あまりいろんなことに手を出すな. Don't try to have too many irons in the fire. / 建て売り住宅はますます一般の人には手の届かないものになっている. Commercially constructed private homes are getting beyond the financial reach of more and more people. / 100 万

-で in 《a room》; at 《the office》; on 《a street corner》; 〈時間〉in 《a week》; 〈年齢〉at 《(the age of) fifteen》; in 《one's forties》; 〈価格〉at 《¥800》; 〈代価〉for 《$10》; 〈割合〉by / 〈原因〉from; 〈文〉owing to; because of; 〈…を原料として〉from; 〈材料〉of; 〈…を手段として〉by; with; by means of ¶日本で為す Japan / 徒歩で on foot / 列車で by train [rail] / 浅間丸で by [on board] the Asama-maru / 手紙[電報]で by letter [telegraph] / リットルで売る sell by the liter / 金で買う buy *sth* with money / 2,000円で買う[売る] buy [sell] *sth* for 2,000 yen / 英語で書く write in English / 鉛筆で書く write with a pencil [in pencil] / 杖でなぐる beat *sb* with a stick / 顔色で知る know *sth* from *sb*'s look / 湯で手を洗う wash one's hands in hot water / エプロンで手をふく wipe [dry] one's hands on one's apron / 心臓まひで死ぬ die of [from] heart failure / 風邪で寝ている be in bed with a cold / 望遠鏡で見る look 《at a planet》through a telescope / 朝日新聞で見ると according to the *Asahi*; the *Asahi* says [reports] that…. 文例↓

てあい 手合い ⇨れんちゅう. 文例↓
てあい 出会い an encounter.
であう 出会[合]う 〈行き会う〉meet; happen to meet; come across [upon]; run across [into]; 〈会合する〉meet 《together》.
てあか 手垢 dirt from the hands ¶手あかをつける soil *sth* [make *sth* dirty] by handling it.
てあし 手足 one's hands and feet; 〈文〉the limbs ¶手足を縛る bind *sb* hand and foot / 手足をひろげて (lie) spread-eagled / …の手足となって働く be at *sb*'s beck and call.
てあし 出足 ¶出足が早い[遅い] start quickly [slowly]; 〈自動車・走者などが〉be quick [slow] off the mark / 出足がよい[悪い]〈出発が〉make a good [bad] start / 〈出席者などが〉there is a good [poor] turnout 《of people》/ 出足の早い自動車 a car with a fast pickup.
てあたりしだい 手当たり次第 ¶手当たり次第に at random; haphazardly / 手当たり次第に読む read whatever *one* can lay hands on; read at random. 文例↓
てあつい 手厚い warm;〈文〉cordial; courteous ¶手厚い看護を受ける be carefully nursed [attended to] / 手厚くもてなす receive *sb* warmly [〈文〉cordially]; give *sb* a warm [cordial] reception; be very hospitable 《to》.
てあて 手当 〈金銭の〉an allowance; a benefit (給付); 〈治療〉(a) (medical) treatment; (medical) care; dressing (傷の); 〈用意〉《文》provision; preparation(s) ¶月々５万円の手当を与える give *sb* a monthly allowance of 50,000 yen; allow *sb* 50,000 yen a month / 手当をする treat 《a patient》; give medical treatment [attention] 《to》/ 傷の手当をする treat [dress, bind up] a wound. 文例↓
てあみ¹ 手網 〈魚釣りの時の〉a landing net.
てあみ² 手編み ¶手編みの hand-knitted; knitted by hand.
てあら 手荒 ¶手荒な rough; rude; harsh; 〈乱暴な〉violent / 手荒に扱う handle *sth* roughly; 〈人を〉treat *sb* roughly [rudely]; manhandle *sb*; 〈文〉maltreat *sb*.
てあらい 手洗い ⇨トイレ(ット).
であるく 出歩く go out; gad about.
てあわせ 手合わせ 〈勝負〉a game; a contest; a bout ¶手合わせをする have [play] a game 《with》; have a bout 《with》.
てい¹ 体 ¶体よく断る 〈文〉decline politely / 体よく引きさがる bow out 《of an affair》/ 体のいい詐欺 nothing but [no more than] a fraud / 体のいい泥棒 〈事〉virtual robbery;

円では手が出ない. One million yen is a prohibitive price. / 彼はもう間もなく60に手が届く. He's getting on for [toward] sixty. / He's rising [pushing] sixty. / He's close on [to] sixty. / 30に手が届く頃になるまで結婚しなかった. She didn't marry until she was almost thirty [until her late twenties].
で¹ 今年はいちごの出が早い. Strawberries have appeared on the market [have come in] earlier this year. / この万年筆はインクの出が悪い. The ink doesn't flow properly [smoothly] from this pen. / あの人は名門の出です. He comes from [〈文〉of] a noble family. / あの人は盛岡の出だ. He is from Morioka. / シテの出が見ものだ. The main actor's entrance is something worth seeing.
で² で, 君は辞職したいというんだね. And so you wish to resign?
-で それは１か月で出来ます. It will be finished in a month. / 私はこの４月で日本にちょうど３年になります. I'll have been living [I shall have lived] in Japan just three years next April. / 君の時計で何時ですか. What time is it by your watch? / What time do you make it? / 最近 NHK で星の進化に関するテレビ番組があった. There was a television program on NHK recently about the evolution of stars. / このくぎは１キロで500本あります. There are 500 of these nails in one kilogram. / なまりで正体がばれた. His accent gave him away. / 昨夜は車の音で少しも眠れなかった. I couldn't sleep at all last night for the noise of traffic. / The noise of traffic kept me awake all last night. / 私は病気で学校を欠席した. I took the day off school because I was ill. / 酒は米で作る. *Sake* is made from rice. / 花は英語で何と言うか. What is the English for '*hana*'?

てあい 私たちの最初の出会いは３年前の夏のことでした. We first made each other's acquaintance in summer three years ago. / 出会いがしらに２人はどんとぶつかった. They knocked [bumped] into each other as they met.
であう 彼に公園でひょっくり出会った. I came across [upon] him in the park. / 私たちは駅で出会うはずです. We are to meet at the station. / 私たちはその後１度も出会わなかった. Our paths never crossed again.
てあたりしだい コモド大とかげは肉食で手当たり次第に食欲に食う. The Komodo dragon is a voracious and undiscriminating carnivore.
てあて この病気は早速手当をする必要がある. The disease calls for prompt treatment. / 手当がよければ助かるかもしれない. If properly cared for, the patient may live.
てあら 手荒なことはするなよ. Be

〈人〉《be》virtually a thief [robber]; a virtual thief / 満足の体である look pleased [satisfied] (with *oneself*). 文例⇩

てい² 邸 ⇨やしき ¶ジョンソン氏邸《文》Mr. Johnson's residence;《米》the Johnson house / 邸内に侵入する trespass on *sb's* premises.

ていあつ 低圧 low pressure;【電】low tension [voltage] ¶《空気などの》低圧帯 a low-pressure area / 低圧回路 a low-tension circuit / 低圧電流 a low-voltage current.

ていあん 提案 a proposal; a proposition; a suggestion; a motion; an offer ¶提案する propose; make a proposal [proposition]; suggest; put forward a suggestion; offer [《文》advance] a suggestion; come up with 《a new theory》; propose a motion; move 《for》; make an offer / 反対提案 a counterproposal / 提案者 a proposer.

ていい 定位【動・心理】orientation ¶定位する orient (*oneself*).

ティー¹〈紅茶〉tea ¶ティーバッグ a tea bag / ティーポット a teapot.

ティー²【ゴルフ】a tee ¶ティーショット a tee shot.

ディーケー ¶3DKのアパート an apartment [《英》flat] of three rooms plus a dining-kitchen.

ティーシャツ a T-shirt; a tee shirt.

ディーゼル ¶ディーゼルエンジン a diesel engine / ディーゼルエンジンを動力とした船 a diesel-powered[-driven] vessel / ディーゼル機関車 a diesel-electric locomotive [engine].

ていいち 定位置 the position ¶定位置に就く take *one's* place; get in(to) [put *oneself* in] position.

ディーディーティー DDT (dichloro*di*phenyl*t*richloroethane の略).

ディーピーイー【写真】film processing; 〈店〉a film-processing shop ★DPE は Developing, Printing, Enlarging の頭文字を連ねた和製英語.

ていいん 定員 the fixed [《文》prescribed, full] number (of the regular personnel); the (full) strength;〈乗り物の〉the 《seating》capacity ¶定員500名の劇場 a theater with a seating capacity of 500 [capable of seating 500]. 文例⇩

ティーンエージャー a teen-ager; a boy [girl] in his [her] teens; a teen-age(d) boy [girl] ★語尾に -teen のつく, 13歳から19歳までの人の意味で日本語の「十代」とは違うことに注意.

ていえん 庭園 a garden; a park 〈広大な〉⇨にわ.

ていおう 帝王 an emperor; a king ¶帝王切開【医】(perform) a Caesarean section;〈have〉a Caesarean (通俗に) / 帝王切開分娩 by Caesarean birth. 文例⇩

ていおん¹ 低音 a low tone; a low-pitched sound; 〈声〉(in) a low voice;【音楽】bass ¶低音の魅力 the spell of 《his》deep voice / 低音で〈sing〉in bass; on the lower keys / 低音部 the bass register / 低音部記号 a bass clef; an F clef.

ていおん² 低温 (a) low temperature ¶低温学 cryogenics / 低温殺菌 pasteurization at (a) low temperature.

ていおん³ 定温 (a) fixed temperature.

ていか¹ 低下 a fall;《文》a decline; a drop; 〈品質の〉deterioration;〈価値の〉《文》(a) depreciation ¶生活水準の低下 a decline in the standard of living / 道徳の低下《文》moral degeneracy / 能率の低下 a lowering of [drop in] efficiency / 低下する fall; drop; sink; lower; go down; deteriorate / 低下させる reduce; lower. 文例⇩

ていか² 定価 the list [marked, labeled] price ¶定価を上げる raise [put up] the price (of) / 定価を下げる reduce [lower, cut] the price / 定価を付ける put a price (on); set a price (on) / 定価の2割引きで at a 20 percent discount off the list [marked] price / 定価表[票] a price list [tag]. 文例⇩

ていかいはつ 低開発 ¶低開発の underdeveloped (countries, areas).

ていがく¹ 低額 a low 《prices》; small 《savings》/ 低額所得者 a person with a small income; 〈集合的〉people in the low(er)-income brackets.

ていがく² 定額 a fixed amount [sum] ¶定額に達する[達しない] come up to [fall short of] the required amount / 定額貯金 fixed amount savings.

ていがく³ 停学 suspension (from school [university]);《英》rustication (大学の) ¶停学を命じる[にする] suspend 《a student》(from school [university]).

ていがくねん 低学年 the lower classes [grades, forms].

ていかん¹ 定款 the articles of association.

ていかん² 諦観《文》resignation ¶諦観する resign *oneself*《to *one's* fate》; endure 《*one's* misfortune》philosophically.

ていかんし 定冠詞【文法】a definite article.

ていき¹ 定期 ¶定期の regular;《文》periodic(al) / 定期に periodically; regularly; at regular [periodic] intervals / 定期刊行物 a periodical (publication) / 定期(乗車)券 a season ticket;《米》a commutation [commuter] ticket;《英口語》a season / 定期券で通う commute / 定期券で通う乗客 a season-ticket holder; a

---

gentle with him.

てい¹ 彼らは体よく部屋から追い出された。They were politely shown the door. / 出発の体にして旅行に出かけた。He went on what was ostensibly a business trip. / あの男の仕事と称するのは、体のいい言い方で実はお遊びだ。His so-called work is nothing but a euphemism for enjoying himself [having a good time].

ていいん このバスは定員以上乗せている。This bus is overloaded.

ていおう あのふたごは帝王切開で生まれた。The twins were delivered by Caesarean section.

ていか¹ 目立って学生の学力が低下している。There is a marked decline in the students' scholastic performance.

ていか² これは定価は2千円となっていますがお安くしておきましょう。This is priced at two thousand yen, but I will let you have it for less.

ていぎ¹ 定義によれば, 哺乳類とは子を乳で育てる動物である。By

ていき commuter; 《米》a commutation passenger / 定期(券)入れ a commutation-ticket holder / 定期券購入証明書 a commuter's certificate / 定期検査 a periodic(al) inspection / 定期航空路 an airway / 定期試験 a regular [periodic] examination / 定期便 a regular service [run, flight]; a scheduled flight / 定期旅客機 an airliner / 定期預金 a fixed [time] deposit.

ていき² 提起 ¶提起する bring up [forward]《a proposal》; raise 《a question》; pose 《a problem》; propose.

ていぎ¹ 定義 a definition ¶辞書の定義 a dictionary definition / 定義を下す give [lay down] a definition 《of》; define 《as》 / 定義しにくい be difficult to define; 《文》be elusive of definition. 文例ід

ていぎ² 提議 ⇨ていあん.

ていきあつ 低気圧 low (atmospheric) pressure; an atmospheric depression; a depression; a low pressure area (低気圧域) ¶優勢な低気圧 the dominant low / 低気圧の中心 the center of a low pressure area. 文例ід

ていきゅう¹ 低級 ¶低級な low-grade; lowbrow; low-class; inferior; low; vulgar (俗悪な).

ていきゅう² 庭球 ⇨ テニス.

ていきゅうび 定休日 a regular holiday [day off] ¶月曜が定休日である〈店など〉be closed every Monday [on Mondays].

ていきょう 提供 an offer ¶提供する offer; present; supply; 《文》furnish; provide; sponsor 《a TV program》 / (移植のために)臓器を提供する donate [provide] an organ / 提供者 a 《blood》 donor. 文例ід

ていきんり 低金利 ¶低金利で at low interest; at a low rate of interest / 低金利政策 a cheap [an easy] money policy.

ていくう 低空 ¶低空を飛ぶ fly at 《a》 low altitude; fly low / 低空を飛行中の航空機 a low-flying aircraft / 低空飛行 (a) low-altitude flight.

ていけい¹ 定形[型] a fixed [regular] form ¶定形[定形外]郵便物 standard-size [nonstandard-size] mail / 定型詩 a fixed form of verse.

ていけい² 梯形 ⇨ だいけい.

ていけい³ 提携 cooperation ¶提携する cooperate 《with》; go hand in hand 《with》; join hands 《with》; 《文》be aligned 《with》 / …と提携して in cooperation 《with》, 《文》concert, 《文》alignment 《with》… / 提携して共同の敵に当たる be leagued together against the common enemy / 技術提携 technical cooperation; a technical tie-up 《between》. 文例ід

ていけつ 締結 conclusion ¶締結する conclude 《a treaty with》; enter into 《a treaty with》.

ていけつあつ 低血圧 《have》low blood pressure ¶低血圧症 hypotension.

ていけん 定見 ¶定見がある have a definite [fixed] opinion [view] / 定見がない have no definite opinion [view] of one's own.

ていげん 逓減 《文》gradual decrease ¶収穫逓減の法則 the law of diminishing returns.

ていこ 艇庫 a boathouse.

ていこう 抵抗 resistance; opposition (反対) ¶最後の抵抗 a last [final] stand; last-ditch resistance / 抵抗する resist; offer [put up] resistance 《to》; oppose; defy; stand 《struggle, hold out》against; withstand; make a stand against / 頑強に抵抗する offer 《a》 stubborn [tenacious, firm] resistance 《to》 / 権威に抵抗する make a strong stand 《against》 / 権威に抵抗する resist [revolt against] authority / 運命に抵抗する 《文》strive against fate / 抵抗し難い irresistible / …するのに抵抗を感じる be reluctant to do; do not feel like doing / 抵抗にあう meet [《文》encounter 《with》, run into] resistance / 抵抗器 《電》a resistor / 抵抗計 an ohmmeter / 抵抗コイル a resistance coil / 熱に対する抵抗性 heat-resistant properties 《of molybdenum》 / 抵抗力 power(s) of resistance 《to》; resistance; resisting power / 抵抗力がある be 《highly》 resistant 《to》; 《医》have a tolerance 《to, of》 / 抵抗力を失う[減ずる, 増す] lose [lower, increase] one's resistance [the power of resistance] 《to》 / 抵抗力をつける 《文》acquire resistance 《to》. 文例ід

ていこく¹ 定刻 ¶定刻に at the fixed [《文》appointed] time [hour]; punctually 《時刻表の》on [according to] schedule; on time / 定刻に遅れる be 《ten minutes》 behind time [schedule]; be 《five minutes》 late; arrive 《twenty minutes》 after [later than] the appointed time.

ていこく² 帝国 an empire ¶帝国の imperial; of an empire / 帝国主義 imperialism / 帝国主義者 an imperialist / 帝国主義的 imperialistic; imperialist 《exploitation》 / 反帝国主義 anti-imperialism / 反帝国主義者 an anti-imperialist.

ていさい 体裁 〈外見〉 an appearance; (a) form; (a) style; 〈こしらえ〉 a get-up ¶体裁が悪い do not look nice; be unsightly; 〈きまりが悪い〉 feel awkward / 体裁のいい 《文》 seemly; presentable; respectable / 体裁の悪い 《文》 unseemly; disreputable; awkward / 体裁を飾る[繕う] save [keep up] appearances / 体裁に[上]for appearance'[decency's] sake; for show; 〈世間体のため〉to keep up apearances / 体裁

---

definition, mammals are animals that nurse their young.

ていきあつ 低気圧は東南に進んでいる. The low pressure area is moving southeast. / 今日は課長が低気圧だぜ. The boss is out of sorts [in a bad temper] today.

ていきょう セラミックの提供でお送りいたしました. This program has been brought to you by Japan Ceramic.

ていけい 我が国は米国との密接な提携を崩すべきではないと彼は主張した. He insisted that this country should remain closely aligned with the U.S. / この薬は我が社とB社との技術提携によって開発された. This medicine has been developed under a technical tie-up between ourselves and B Company.

ていこう 人は一般に最も抵抗の少ない行き方を選ぶ. People generally choose the line of least resistance. / 昆虫の中には農薬に対する抵抗力ができてくるものがある. Some insects develop [build up] resistance to agricultural chemicals.

ていさつ 偵察 scouting; reconnaissance ¶偵察する scout; reconnoiter / 偵察に行く go scouting / 偵察衛星 a reconnaissance [spy] satellite / 偵察機 a reconnaissance plane / 偵察飛行 a reconnaissance [an intelligence] flight / 偵察飛行をする fly on a reconnaissance mission.

ていし 停止 a stop; 〈中止〉suspension; 〈禁止〉a ban; 〈止まること〉a standstill; 〈停頓〉(a) deadlock; 〈中絶〉(an) interruption ¶停止する〈止まる〉《文》cease; come to a standstill [a stop, an end]; 〈止める〉stop; put an end to; make an end of; suspend; interrupt; 〈禁止する〉ban; place [put] (a paper) under a ban; place [put] a ban on *sth* / 営業を停止する suspend business / 停止している be at a standstill;《文》be at rest; be stopped; be suspended ★ be stopping は「停止しかけている」で,「停止している」にはならない / 停止信号〈一般に〉a stop signal;〈道路の〉a stoplight.

ていじ[1] 丁字 ¶丁字形の T-shaped / 丁字帯 a T bandage / 丁字路 a T-junction.

ていじ[2] 提示 ¶提示する present; indicate; bring up;《文》cite; come up with (an idea).

ていじ[3] 定時 ¶定時の regular;《文》periodical / 定時に regularly; periodically; at the stated [fixed] time; at fixed [regular] intervals; on schedule / 定時制高校 a part-time high school / 定時番組 a regular program. 文例↓

ていしせい 低姿勢 ¶低姿勢をとる《文》assume a low posture (toward); take [《文》adopt] a modest attitude (toward) / 低姿勢でいる《文》maintain a low posture.

ていしゃ 停車 stopping; a stop ¶停車する stop [halt] (at a station); make a stop; come to a halt / 事故のために停車する be held up by an accident / 停車させる stop (a train); bring (a train) to a stop [halt] / 5分間停車する a five minutes' stop / 停車時間 stoppage time / 停車信号 a stop signal. 文例↓

ていしゅ 亭主 〈夫〉one's husband; 〈客に対して〉the host ¶亭主役を務める act as host; play the host.

ていじゅう 定住 ¶定住する settle (down);《文》reside permanently (at, in) / 定住地 one's fixed [permanent] dwelling place. 文例↓

ていしゅうにゅう 定収入 a regular income.

ていしゅうは 低周波〖無線〗low frequency (略: LF).

ていしゅく 貞淑 ¶貞淑な《文》chaste;《文》virtuous; modest ⇨ていせつ[2].

ていしゅつ 提出 ¶提出する〈議案などを〉present; introduce; submit; bring [lay] (a bill before the Diet); 〈意見を〉offer; 〈文》advance; 〈抗議を〉《文》lodge; file (a petition with the authorities concerned); 〈辞表を〉hand in;《文》tender; 〈証拠を〉bring forward; 〈問題を〉pose (a problem); moot (a question) (★ moot は通常受動態で使われる); 〈願書・答案を〉hand [send] in (an examination paper); turn in (a report). 文例↓

ていしょう 提唱 ¶提唱する put forward (a new doctrine); propose;《文》advance;《文》advocate / 提唱者《文》a proponent;《文》an advocate.

ていじょう 定常 ¶定常の regular; stationary; steady / 定常状態〖物〗a steady state; (an) equilibrium / 定常波〖物〗a standing [stationary] wave.

ていじょうぎ 丁定規 a T-square.

ていしょく[1] 定食〈料理店の〉a set meal [lunch, dinner]; a meal from the set [fixed] menu; a *table d'hôte* meal.

ていしょく[2] 抵触 〈衝突〉(a) conflict; (a) collision;〈矛盾〉《文》(a) contradiction;〈違反〉《文》(an) infringement;《文》(a) contravention ¶抵触する〈衝突する〉conflict [clash, collide] with; run counter to; 〈矛盾する〉be contrary to;《文》be incompatible with; 〈違背する〉infringe on / 法律に抵触している be against the law;《文》be in contravention of [be contrary to] the law. 文例↓

ていしょく[3] 定職 《文》a regular occupation;《文》(a) fixed employment; a steady job ¶定職がない have no regular occupation [employment] / 定職につく get [find] a regular job / 定職についている be in regular work; have [be in] a steady job.

ていしょく[4] 停職 《文》suspension from office [duty] ¶停職になる be suspended from *one's* duties.

ていしん[1] 挺身 ¶挺身する volunteer; offer *oneself*; come forward / 挺身して難局に当たる volunteer to undertake the difficult task; come forward to meet the critical situation.

ていしん[2] 艇身 a (boat's) length ¶2 [半]艇身の差で勝つ win (the race) by two lengths [half a length].

でいすい 泥酔 ¶泥酔する get dead [《俗》stinking] drunk;《俗》get smashed;《俗》get plas-

---

ていさい こんな格好では体裁が悪い. I am not fit to be seen. / 体裁など構わないから丈夫でこしらえてもらいたい. I don't care how it looks, as long as it's durable. / 本箱はただ体裁のためです. The bookcase is just an ornament. / 学問をてらうのは体裁のよいものじゃない. It is bad form to [It looks bad to] make a display of one's learning. / 体裁が悪くても彼に金の無心など言えたものじゃない. I haven't got the gall [face] to ask him for money.

ていじ[3] 定時退庁〖社〗.〖掲示〗No overtime. / 列車は定時に到着した. The train arrived on schedule [time].

ていしゃ この列車は静岡まで停車いたしません. This train goes nonstop to Shizuoka. / 電車が急に停車した. The train came to a sudden stop. / 列車はまだホームに停車している. The train is still standing at the platform. ★ standing be stopping とするのは不可. / この列車は当駅で5分間停車いたします. This train makes a five-minute stop at this station.

ていしゅ 彼は亭主関白だ. He is a very domineering husband. | He thinks the man should be the boss in the house [should wear the pants].

ていじゅう ここに定住するつもりだ. I'm going to settle down here

てすう / 泥酔者 a drunken person;《口語》a drunk; a drunkard.

ていすう 定数 〈一定の数〉a fixed number;《数・物・化》a constant; an invariable;〈定足数〉⇒ていそくすう.

ディスカウント a discount ¶ディスカウントする give *sb* a (10 percent) discount ((on *sth*)) / ディスカウントセール (discount) sale.

ディスクジョッキー a disc jockey.

ディスコ(テーク) a disco (*pl.* -s); a discotheque.

ていする 呈する 〈贈る〉present; offer;〈示す〉show;《文》exhibit;《文》display;《文》assume / 褐色を呈する turn [be, look] brown / 惨状を呈する be horrible to look at;《文》present a tragic sight / 重大な様相を呈する《文》assume [take on] a serious aspect.

ていせい[1] 訂正 (a) correction; (a) revision ¶訂正する correct; put *sth* [*sb*] right [straight];《文》rectify; revise / A を B と訂正する correct A to B / 訂正版 a revised edition. 文例⇩

ていせい[2] 帝政 imperial government [rule, regime];〈ロシヤの〉Czarism ¶帝政時代 the monarchical period;〈ロシヤの〉the Czarist era [period] / 帝政ロシヤ Czarist Russia; Russia under the Czarist regime.

ていせいぶんせき 定性分析《化》qualitative analysis.

ていせつ[1] 定説 〈学理上の〉an established theory;〈一般の〉an accepted opinion.

ていせつ[2] 貞節 faithfulness;《文》constancy;《文》fidelity;〈貞操〉《文》chastity ¶貞節な faithful; true (to *one's* husband);《文》constant;《文》virtuous;《文》chaste.

ていせん[1] 停船 stoppage (of a ship) ¶停船する 〈船が〉stop; heave to;〈船を〉bring (a ship) to / 霧のために停船する be held up in a fog.

ていせん[2] 停戦 a cease-fire; a truce;《文》cessation [suspension] of hostilities; an armistice ¶停戦する suspend [《文》cease] hostilities; cease fire; make a truce (with) / 停戦協定 a cease-fire agreement.

ていそ 提訴 ¶提訴する bring a case before (the court); present a case to (the court); file an action (in the court against *sb*); appeal to (the International Court of Justice).

ていそう 貞操《文》chastity;《文》(feminine) virtue;《文》honor;《文》constancy ¶貞操の正しい《文》chaste;《文》virtuous; faithful;《文》constant;《文》true / 貞操観念の薄い女 a woman of loose morals [of easy virtue] / 貞操を守る defend *one's* virtue [oneself]; remain faithful [true] to (*one's* husband).

ていそく 低速 ¶低速にする slow down / 低速で at a low speed; in low gear.

ていぞく 低俗 ¶低俗な low (tastes); vulgar;《文》of vulgar [uncultivated] taste; lowbrow (literature).

ていそくすう 定足数 a quorum ¶定足数に達する form [be enough for] a quorum / 定足数に満たない lack [fail to meet] a quorum; do not come up to [be short of] a quorum. 文例⇩

ていたい[1] 停滞 〈沈滞〉stagnation;〈貨物の〉(an) accumulation;〈延引〉delay ¶停滞する be stagnant; pile up; accumulate; be delayed;《文》be retarded / 停滞前線《気象》a stationary front. 文例⇩

ていたい[2] 手痛い severe; hard ¶手痛く severely; hard.

ていたく 邸宅 a house;《文》a residence; a mansion.

ていたらく 体たらく ⇒ありさま.

ていだん 鼎談 a three-man [tripartite] talk.

でいたん 泥炭 peat ¶泥炭層 a peat bed.

ていち 低地 low(-lying) ground [land]; lowlands;〈川沿いの〉《米》bottomland(s).

ていちあみ 定置網 a fixed net ¶定置網漁業 fixed netting.

ていちゃく 定着 fixing;《文》fixation ¶定着する fix; become established; establish *itself*;〈植物が、また、新しい風習などが〉take [strike] root / 〈写真の〉定着液 a fixing solution / 定着剤 a fixative; a fixing agent / 社員の定着率を改善する improve [increase] the stability of the work force.

ていちょう[1] 艇長 〈ボートの〉a coxswain;《口語》a cox; a skipper;〈水雷艇などの〉a captain.

ていちょう[2] 丁重 ¶丁重な polite; courteous; respectful ¶丁重に politely; courteously; respectfully / 丁重に葬る bury (*sb's* remains) with due ceremony.

ていちょう[3] 低調 ¶低調な low-toned; inactive; dull;《文》inanimate; sluggish. 文例⇩

ていちんぎん 低賃金 low wages ¶低賃金の仕事 a low-paying job / 低賃金労働者 〈個人〉a low-paid worker; a low-wage earner;〈集合的〉cheap labor.

ティッシュペーパー tissue paper;〈化粧用〉(facial [face]) tissues.

ていっぱい 手一杯 ¶手一杯仕事がある have *one's* hands full; be fully occupied / 手一杯

---

for good.

ていしゅつ 彼は最近論文を提出して工学博士の学位を得た. Recently he presented [submitted] his thesis and obtained the degree of Doctor of Engineering.

ていしょく 私は法律に抵触するような事はなにもしていない. I have done nothing contrary to the law.

ていせい 読者各位には正誤表によりご訂正下さい. Readers are requested to make the corrections given in the errata. (正誤表で) 'break' は 'brake' と訂正. For 'break' read 'brake'.

ていそくすう 議員定足数に満たず散会した. The House was adjourned for want of a quorum. / 会員の過半数をもって定足数とする. A quorum shall consist of a majority of the members.

ていたい[1] 事務がひどく停滞している. We are very much behind [behindhand] with our work.

ていち 豪雨のため県下の低地が浸水した. As a result of the heavy rain, the lower-lying districts of the prefecture were flooded.

ていちゃく この新しい習慣は日本人の生活にすっかり定着した. This new custom has taken a firm hold on the Japanese lifestyle.

ていちょう[3] 国会の討論は低調をきわめた. The debates in the

ていてつ 蹄鉄 a horseshoe; a shoe ¶蹄鉄を打つ shoe (a horse).

ていてん 定点 【数】 a fixed [definite] point ¶定点観測【気象】 fixed point observation / 定点観測船 a ship weather station.

ていでん 停電〈事故による〉(a) power failure;〈一般に〉a power cut; an interruption of [a break in] the power supply; (a) power stoppage ¶停電のため because of a power cut [the failure of the (electric) power supply]. 文例◊

ていど 程度〈度合〉a degree; an extent;〈標準〉a grade; a standard; a level;〈限度〉a limit ¶損害の程度 the extent of damage [loss] / ある程度(まで) to a certain extent; to some degree / ある程度の a (certain) measure of 《success》 / どの程度まで to what extent [degree]; how far / 程度の差はあっても to [in] greater or lesser degrees; to [in] varying degrees / 大学程度の講座 a course at (the) college level / 文明の程度が低い be [stand] at a low level of civilization / 程度問題 a matter [question] of degree. 文例◊

ていとう 抵当 (a) mortgage; (a) security ⇨ てんぽ ¶抵当にする[入れる] give sth as security; mortgage 《one's house》;《文》lay [put] sth in pledge / 抵当に取る take [accept] sth as security (for a loan) / 一番[二番, 二重]抵当 a first [second, double] mortgage / 抵当権者 a mortgagee / 抵当権設定者 a mortgagor / 抵当流れ foreclosure / 抵当流れになる be foreclosed / 抵当物 a collateral; a security; a pledge; a mortgage / …の抵当物に担保権を行使する foreclose on sb.

ていとく 提督 an admiral.

ていとん 停頓 a standstill; a deadlock; a stalemate ¶停頓する come to a standstill; get [be] stalled; be held up / 停頓している be in a stalemate [deadlock]; be deadlocked; be at a standstill.

ていねい 丁寧 ¶丁寧な polite; courteous; civil;〈うやうやしい〉respectful;〈周到な〉careful; conscientious; thorough; close;《文》 minute / 丁寧な口をきく use polite language / 丁寧に politely; courteously; civilly;《文》with civility [respect]; respectfully; carefully;《文》scrupulously;《文》with care;《文》minutely / 丁寧に過ぎる be polite to a fault / 仕事を丁寧にする be thorough [conscientious] in one's work. 文例◊

ていねん 定[停]年 retiring age; the (compulsory) retirement age ¶定年に達する reach retiring age / 定年で退職する retire; leave one's job [employment] on reaching retiring age / 定年制 an age-limit system. 文例◊

ていのう 低能 mental deficiency; feeblemindedness; imbecility;〈人〉a mentally deficient person; a fool ¶低能な feeble-minded; mentally deficient [retarded]; imbecile; backward (知能の発達が遅れた).

ていはく 停泊 anchorage; mooring ¶停泊する anchor; lie at anchor; take up moorings (at Buoy No. 2);〈いかりを下ろす〉drop anchor;〈寄港する〉stop [call, put in] at 《Kobe》/ 停泊している be [lie, ride] at anchor; be [stay] in port [harbor]; be berthed; be moored (at the pier) / 停泊地[所] an anchorage (area); a moorage; a roadstead. 文例◊

ていはつ 剃髪《文》tonsure ¶剃髪する have one's head shaved;《文》take the tonsure / 剃髪した《文》tonsured; shaven-headed.

でいばんがん 泥板岩 shale.

ていひょう 定評 an established reputation; a fixed opinion ¶定評ある《a novelist》with an [《文》of] established reputation; acknowledged; recognized;《文》proverbial. 文例◊

ていへん 底辺【幾何】the base ¶社会の底辺の人々 people at the bottom of the social pyramid [scale].

ていぼう 堤防 a bank; an embankment; a dike [dyke]; a levee; a causeway (土手道) ¶堤防を築く construct [build] a bank; put up a (confining) levee. 文例◊

ていぼく 低木 a shrub ¶低木林 scrub; a scrub thicket.

ていほん[1] 定本 the standard text [edition] 《of》.

ていほん[2] 底本 the original text; a source book (原典).

ていめい 低迷 ¶低迷する《dark clouds》hang low (over); hover around《the 120-yen level》.

ていめん 底面 the base.

ていめんせき 底面積 the area of the base 《of a cone》.

ていやく 定訳 a standard translation; a generally accepted translation.

ていらく 低落 ⇨ていか[1], げらく.

ていり[1] 低利 ¶低利で at low interest; at a low rate of interest / 低利資金 low-interest funds; cheap [easy] money.

ていり[2] 定理 【数】a theorem.

Diet were extremely dull. / いっぱい 現在の仕事で手一杯です. My time is completely taken up with the work I have on hand. | The work I already have is as much as I can manage.

ていでん 予告もなく停電になった. The electricity was cut off without warning. / 昨夜は2時間も停電した. Last night the (electric) power was off as long as two hours. / 地下鉄が30分停電した. The subway stopped running for half an hour because of a power cut.

ていど 誤差ははなはだしい程度に達しないうちに自動的に修正される. The errors are corrected automatically before they reach serious proportions. / こんな文章を読むと著者の頭の程度が知れる. These remarks show the measure of the author's intelligence. / 彼の報告はある程度当たっている. There is a certain amount [a modicum] of truth in his report. / この課程は大学[高校]程度です. This course is of college [high school] level. / 彼は1千万円程度の年収がある. His income is on [of] the order of 10 million yen a year. ★ on は《米》, of は《英》. / 物には程度がある. There is a limit to everything. | Everything has its limit(s).|Moderation in all things.

でいり 出入り ⟨人の⟩ going in and out; 《文》 entrance and exit; comings and goings; ⟨収支⟩ income and expenditure; receipts and expenditures ★ 日・英順序が逆になる点に注意 ¶出入りする《文》frequent; visit | 出入りの商人 a tradesman who regularly comes to one's house / 車[人]の出入りの激しい所 a place with a lot of traffic [people coming and going] / 出入りを許されている《文》have access to ⟨a house⟩ / 出入りを差し止める bar sb from [forbid sb] the house / 出入口 a gateway; a doorway.

ていりつ[1] 定率 a fixed rate.

ていりつ[2] 低率 a low rate ¶低率の low(-rate).

ていりゅう 底流 an undercurrent ¶…の底流をなしている underlie ⟨the U.S. foreign policy⟩; lie beneath [behind] ⟨his conduct⟩.

でいりゅう 泥流 a (volcanic) mud flow.

ていりゅうじょ 停留所 a (bus) stop. 文例⇩

ていりょう 定量 a fixed [《文》determinate] quantity ⟨of⟩; ⟨服薬の⟩ a dose ¶定量する《文》determine the quantity ⟨of⟩ / 定量分析 《化》quantitative analysis.

ていれ 手入れ ⟨修繕⟩ repair(s); mending; ⟨整備⟩ maintenance; ⟨世話⟩ care; attention; trimming ⟨庭木・髪などの⟩; ⟨警察の⟩ a (police) raid; a crackdown; a roundup (一斉の) ¶手入れが行き届いている[いない] be in good [poor] repair; be well [poorly] looked after / 手入れの行き届いた庭 a well-kept[-groomed, -cared-for] garden / 手入れをする repair ⟨a house⟩; mend ⟨shoes⟩; take care of ⟨one's hair⟩; maintain ⟨a car⟩; trim ⟨a tree⟩; ⟨警察が⟩ raid [make a raid on] ⟨a gambling den⟩; make a roundup ⟨of gangsters⟩ / つめの手入れをする manicure [do] one's nails. 文例⇩

ていれい 定例 ¶定例の regular; ordinary / 定例に従って according to usage / 定例閣議 an ordinary [a regular] Cabinet meeting.

ディレクター a director.

ていれつ 低劣 ¶低劣な low; 《文》mean; 《文》base; despicable; contemptible.

ディレッタント a dilettante.

ていれん 低廉 ¶低廉な cheap; low-priced; inexpensive ⇒やすい[1].

ティンパニー a kettledrum; timpani (★ timpano の複数形であり, 単数としても用いる) ¶ティンパニー奏者 a timpanist.

てうえ 手植え ¶…お手植えの planted in person by….

てうす 手薄 ¶手薄な ⟨人手が足りない⟩ short-handed; undermanned; ⟨防御などが⟩ weak. 文例⇩

てうち 手打ち ¶手打ちの ⟨手製の⟩ handmade (noodles) / 手打ちにする ⟨自分の刀にかける⟩ put sb to death with one's sword; ⟨取引きを決める⟩ strike [close] a bargain [deal]; ⟨和解する⟩《文》be reconciled ⟨with⟩.

テーゼ [<《ドイツ語》These] 【論】 a thesis (pl. theses); ⟨共産党の⟩ a program.

データ data ★ datum の複数だが this data のように単数としても用いる ¶データ処理 data processing / データ処理装置 a data processor; a data-processing device [machine] / データ通信装置 data communication(s) equipment.

デート a date ¶デートする《米》date ⟨a girl⟩; 《米》date ⟨with⟩; have [make] a date ⟨with⟩ / デートの相手《米》one's date; the girl [boy] one has a date [one is going out] with / デートを申し込む ask sb for a date. 文例⇩

テープ a tape; a paper streamer (見送り用の) ¶何も録音してないテープ a blank tape / テープを切る ⟨ゴールインのとき⟩ break [《文》breast] the tape / テープを投げる throw a (paper) streamer / テープに鋏(はさ)を入れる cut the ribbon (to open an exhibition) / テープに録音する record (music) on tape; tape; put [take down] (the speech) on tape; tape-record / テープで接着する tape ⟨A to B⟩ / テープデッキ a tape deck / テープレコーダー a tape recorder / テープ録音 tape recording. 文例⇩

テーブル a table ⇒しょくたく[1] ¶テーブルをはさんで相対する ⟨2人が主語⟩ sit across a table; ⟨一方が主語⟩ sit across ⟨from sb⟩ at a table / テーブル掛け a tablecloth; a table cover / テーブルスピーチ an after-dinner speech ★西洋ではスピーチは食事のあとにする. その習慣のない日本ではただ a speech と言うのが無難. table speech は和製英語 / テーブルマナー table manners.

テーマ [<《ドイツ語》Thema] a theme; subject matter ¶研究テーマ a subject of study [research] / テーマ音楽 theme music; a signature tune / テーマソング a theme [title] song.

テールボード a tailboard.

テールライト a taillight.

ておい 手負い ¶手負いの wounded (lions).

ておくれ 手遅[後]れ ¶手遅れである be too late (for); ⟨病気が⟩ be past cure / 手遅れにな

ていねい どうもご丁寧に. That is very thoughtful [kind] of you. ★このようなお礼の言葉に polite を使ってはいけない. polite は外見上のことで, 心のあり方を言うことにならないからである.

ていねん 彼は今年で定年だ. He is due to retire this year.

ていはく この湾は船舶の停泊に便利だ. The bay provides [affords] a good anchorage. / ブリストル沖に停泊した. We anchored [dropped anchor] off Bristol.

ていひょう 彼の紙切りのうまさには定評がある. He enjoys an established reputation for his skill in silhouette cutting.

ていほう 堤防が切れた. The dike has broken. | The embankment has collapsed.

ていりゅうじょ 次の停留所はどこですか. What is our next stop? | Where does the car [bus] stop next?

ていれ 家を手入れしなければならない. My house needs repairing [attention]. / 庭は手入れしないままになっている. The garden is uncared for [has been neglected].

てうす デモ隊の人数に比べて警察力ははなはだ手薄だった. Compared with the number of demonstrators, the police were very thin on the ground.

デート メリーはデートに出かけている. Mary is out on a date.

テープ すべてのデータはテープにとられて記憶装置に入れられる. All data go on tape for storage.

ておけ 手桶 a pail; a bucket ¶手おけ1杯の水 a pailful [bucketful] of water.

ておしぐるま 手押し車 a handcart; a pushcart; a barrow; a wheelbarrow (ねこ車).

ておち 手落ち 《文》an omission; a slip; *one's* fault; an oversight; 《文》neglect; 〈失策〉《文》an error; a mistake ¶手落ちなく thoroughly; perfectly; carefully.

ておどり 手踊り (posture) dancing.

ておの 手斧 a hand ax(e); a hatchet; an adz(e) (ちょうな).

ており 手織り ¶手織りの handwoven; handloomed; homespun.

でかい ⇒ おおきい

てかがみ 手鏡 a hand glass.

てがかり 手掛かり 〈つかみ所〉a handhold; a hold; 〈事件の〉a clue; a key; 〈こん跡〉a trail; a track; a scent ¶手掛かりを得る〈事件の〉find [hit on] a clue (to); 〈犯人の〉find traces (of); get on the track [scent] (of) / これを手掛かりに with this clue to go on. 文例↓

てかぎ 手鉤 a hook ¶手かぎで引っかける hook up. 文例↓

てがき 手書き ¶手書きの handwritten 《manuscripts》; 〈製図で器具を使わない〉freehand 《sketches》/ 手書きの本 a hand-lettered book / 手書きで宛名が書かれている封筒 a hand-addressed envelope.

でがけ 出掛け ¶出がけに when *one* is (on the point of) going out [leaving the house]. 文例↓

てがける 手掛ける 〈取り扱う〉handle; undertake; manage; deal with; 〈経験がある〉have experience in [with]; 〈養育する〉bring up; rear; 〈世話をする〉look after; take care of ¶たびたび手がけたことのある仕事 work *one* is used [《文》accustomed] to / 手がけた事のない unfamiliar; 《文》unaccustomed; new.

でかける 出掛ける 〈外出する〉go out; leave the house; 〈出発する〉start (off); set out ¶散歩に出かける go out for a walk / 旅行に出かける start [set] out [off] on a trip [journey]. 文例↓

てかげん 手加減〈手ごころ〉allowance(s); consideration; 〈こつ〉skill; a knack ¶手加減する make allowance(s) 《for》/ 手加減を覚える get the knack [hang] (of).

てかず 手数 《囲碁・将棋》the number of moves ⇒ てすう.

てかす 《する》do; 〈仕遂げる〉carry out; succeed (in *doing*); 《文》achieve; 《文》accomplish.

てかせ 手枷 handcuffs ¶手枷足枷をはめられている〈比喩的に〉be in fetters.

でかせぎ 出稼ぎ ¶出稼ぎする work away from home; 〈移住する〉emigrate 《to》/ 大阪へ出稼ぎに行く go to Osaka to work / 出稼ぎ労働者 migrant workers.

てがた 手形 a bill; a note; 〈手で押した形〉a hand print ¶手形を振り出す draw a bill (for ¥1,000,000 on *sb*) / 手形を現金に替える cash a bill / 〈替えてもらう〉have a bill cashed / 手形を書き換える renew a bill / 手形を落とす [不渡りにしない] honor [dishonor] a bill / 手形を割り引く discount a bill / 〈割り引いてもらう〉get a bill discounted / 手形で払う pay by draft / 手形交換所 a clearing house.

てかた 出方 〈態度〉*one's* attitude; 〈やり方〉a move; 〈劇場の〉a theater attendant. 文例↓

てがたい 手堅い 〈着実な〉sound; safe; 〈信用できる〉trustworthy; reliable; 〈相場などが〉steady; firm ¶手堅く 《do business》on a sound [steady] basis; 〈慎重に〉《文》prudently; cautiously.

てがたな 手刀 ¶(相撲で)手刀を切る make chopping motions at the prize with a hand by way of courtesy before receiving it.

てかてか ¶てかてかの shiny; glossy / てかてかのはげ頭 a shining bald head / てかてかに bright(ly). 文例↓

でかでかと in huge letters; conspicuously ¶新聞にでかでかかと書き立てられる make the headlines; be played up in the newspapers.

てがみ 手紙 a letter; a note (簡単な); 〈集合的〉mail ¶…という趣旨の手紙 a letter saying [to the effect] that... / 彼女とやり取りした手紙 letters to and from her / 20日付の手紙 a letter dated [of] the twentieth / 手紙のやり取り[往復] an exchange of letters 《with》; 《文》correspondence 《with》/ 手紙のやり取りをしている be writing (to *sb*, to each other); exchange letters 《with》; 《文》be corresponding [in correspondence] with *sb* / 手紙の形で 《write an article》in the form of a letter [《文》in letter form] / (人に)手紙を書く write

---

ておくれ がんも手遅れにさえならなければ直ることもある。Some cancers can be cured if they are discovered [treated] in time.

ておち それは僕の手落ちだ。It was an oversight on my part. | It is my fault. | I am to blame. | 手落ちのないように頼む。See (to it) that nothing is amiss [things are all as they should be].

てがかり どこにいるのかまだいっこうに手掛かりがつかめない。No clue has yet been found to his whereabouts. / 何か手掛かりが見つかったかね。Have you found anything [any clue] to go on? / 彼の持っていた傘が手掛かりになったそうだ。I hear that it was the umbrella he carried that put the police on the scent.

てかぎ 手かぎ無用。《包装表示》Use No Hooks.

でがけ 出がけに友人に来られた。Just as I was about to go out, a friend came to see me.

でかける お出かけですか。Are you going out? | Are you off? | 母は買物に出かけました。Mother is out shopping. / そろそろ出かけなければならない。We must be off [moving].

でかす 出かした! Well done! | Good for you!

でかた 先方の出方をみよう。Let's wait and see what move they make.

てかてか 彼の髪は油でてかてかしていた。His hair shone with grease.

てがみ あちらへお着きになったらお手紙を下さい。Please write me a letter [drop me a line] when you get there. / 彼女は国元へ長い手紙を書いた。She wrote a long letter home. / 漱石はなかな

てがら (to) *sb* ; write [send] *sb* a letter / 手紙を受け取る get [(文) receive, have] a letter (from) / 手紙で知らせる[言ってやる] write to [to tell] *sb* that…; (文) inform (*sb* of *sth*) by letter / 手紙で返事をする write back; answer by letter. 文例⇩

てがら 手柄 an exploit; a feat; a great [(文) high, glorious) achievement; (文) merit ¶手柄を立てる (文) render distinguished services; perform great exploits [feats] / 自分の手柄にする take the credit (for) / 手柄顔で with a triumphant look [air]; looking as if *one* has done something great / 手柄話をする brag [talk] about *one*'s exploits.

でがらし 出がらし ¶出がらしの茶 thin tea (made from used leaves).

てがる 手軽 ¶〈手軽で容易な〉easy; (文) facile; 〈簡単な〉simple; light; 〈略式の〉informal; 〈即席の〉offhand; 〈安値の〉cheap; inexpensive / 手軽に〈容易に〉easily; (文) with ease; 〈喜んで〉willingly; readily; 〈簡単に〉simply; 〈略式で〉informally; 〈即席の〉offhand; 〈安値で〉(buy) cheap(ly).

デカルト René Descartes ¶デカルト座標 Cartesian coordinates.

てき an enemy; (文) a foe; 〈相手〉an [*one*'s] opponent; (文) an adversary; (文) an antagonist; 〈競争者〉a rival; a competitor; 〈匹敵者〉a match; *one*'s equal / …の目を逃れる escape from *one*'s enemy / …を敵とする[に回す] have *sb* for an enemy; make an enemy of *sb*; antagonize / …を敵として戦う fight against *sb* / …の敵でない be no match (for) / 敵側につく on the enemy's side / 敵側につく go over [defect] to the enemy; side with the enemy / 敵味方に分かれる be divided into friends and enemies [foes] / 敵味方ともに friend and enemy [foe] alike; both sides. 文例⇩

-てき[1] …的 ¶政治的にも歴史的にも地理的にも both historically and geographically; in terms of history and geography.

-てき[2] …滴 ¶2,3滴たらす let fall a few drops / ほおを伝わる 1滴の涙 a tear running down the cheek.

でき 出来 〈出来ぐあい〉make; workmanship; craftsmanship; finish; cut (服などの); 〈収穫〉a crop; a yield; 〈成績〉(a) result ¶出来のよい[悪い]〈品物の〉well-[poorly-]made; (文) of fine [poor] make; 〈学業の〉(a boy who is) doing well [badly] at school / 出来不出来 success or failure; (good or poor) results. 文例⇩

できあい[1] 出来合い ¶出来合いの ready-made (clothes); ready-to-wear (suits); (a jacket) (bought) off the rack (英) peg; (米) store-bought (dresses) / 出来合いのサイズ a stock size.

できあい[2] 溺愛 blind love ¶溺愛する dote on (*one*'s child).

できあがり 出来上がり (文) completion; finish.

できあがる 出来上がる be ready; be finished; be completed / (酒で)出来上がっている (口語) be stoked up; (文) be well away. 文例⇩

てきい 敵意 hostile feelings; hostility; (文) enmity; (文) animosity; 〈悪意〉malice; ill will; spite; 〈恨み〉(a) grudge ¶敵意のある hostile; (文) antagonistic / 敵意を抱く have [(文) harbor, (文) entertain] hostile feelings (against); be hostile (to); bear a grudge (against); feel malice (toward).

てきおう 適応 (an) adaptation ¶環境に対する適応 (an) environmental adaptation / 適応する be (well) adapted (to); adjust [adapt, (文) accommodate] *oneself* (to); be suitable (for); fit; suit; get [(文) become] acclimatized (to) / 〈風土に〉適応させる adapt *sth* (to); adjust; (文) accommodate; fit [suit] *sth* (to) / 環境に適応できない人 a maladjusted person / 適応症 a disease which is susceptible to treatment (by a particular medicine) / 適応性 adaptability; flexibility / 適応性のある adaptable; (文) adaptive; flexible.

てきおん 適温 (keep foods at) a suitable temperature.

てきがいしん 敵愾心 hostility; (文) animosity; (文) enmity; hostile feelings ¶敵がい心をあおる[起こさせる] excite [provoke, arouse] *sb*'s hostility toward (*his* adversary); (文) inflame [stir up] *sb*'s animosity against.

てきかく[1] 的確 ¶的確な precise; accurate; exact / 的確に precisely; accurately; exactly.

てきかく[2] 適格 ¶適格の qualified; competent; eligible / 適格者 a competent [qualified] person; a person qualified [eligible] (for).

てきかん 敵艦 an enemy ship.

か手紙を書くのがうまかった。Soseki was a good letter-writer. / 手紙では彼は近くドイツへ立つということだ。He says in his letter that he is leaving for Germany before long. / 今日は僕に手紙が来ておりませんか。Any letters [mail] for me today? / うちへは毎日たくさん手紙が来る。I get a lot of mail every day. / この手紙は幾らで行きますか。What's the postage on this letter?

てがら それは全く彼の手柄だ。The credit is his alone. | It is all to his credit. / そんな事をしたところで大した手柄にもならない。That's nothing to be proud of. / お手柄お手柄。Bravo! | Well done!

てがる それが一番手軽なやり方だと思います。I think that is the easiest way to do it.

てき 彼には味方もあるが敵もある。He's got enemies as well as friends, you know. / ああいう人は女性の敵だです。A man like him is an enemy to womankind. / 彼は味方にすれば頼もしいが敵に回せば恐ろしい男だ。He is a good friend but a bad enemy. / 彼が敵なのか味方なのかわからなかった。We couldn't tell whether he was friend or foe. / 敵ながら天晴れだ。Our admiration goes out to him, though he is our enemy. / They certainly gave us a good match [fight]. / 敵は本能寺だ。This is not our real objective.

でき 僕は数学は出来が悪かった。In mathematics I did badly. / 今年は米の出来がいい[よくない]。We have a good [poor] crop of rice this year.

できあがる その本は9月2日に出来上がる。The book will be ready

てき 適宜 ¶適宜の suitable; proper; appropriate; fit / 適宜の処置をとる do as one thinks fit; take (what one regards as) appropriate measures; take proper steps / 適宜に suitably; properly; 《文》fittingly; 〈自分の裁量で〉at one's (own) discretion; as one thinks fit [proper].

てきぐん 敵軍 the enemy force; enemy troops; the hostile army.

てきご 適語 an apt [the right] word.

てきごう 適合 〈一致〉《文》conformity; agreement; 〈適応〉adaptation ¶適合する suit; fit (into); fit in (well) (with); be fit [fitted] (for); be suitable (to); 《文》conform (to); 《文》be in conformity (with); 〈適応する〉adapt (oneself) (to); be adapted (for); get [(文) become] acclimatized (to) (風土に) / 目的に適合する serve [suit] one's purpose.

てきこく 敵国 a hostile [an enemy] country [nation].

できごころ 出来心 an impulse; 《文》a caprice ¶一時[その場]の出来心で…をする act from [on] impulse and《commit a theft》; do on a whim [an impulse]. 文例◊

できごと 出来事 an event; a happening; 《文》an occurrence; an incident (事件); an accident (事故). 文例◊

てきざい 適材 the right person for the job; a person fit for the post ¶適材を適所に置く put the right person in the right post [place] / 適材適所である be just the man for the job [position]. 文例◊

テキサス 〈州名〉Texas (略:Tex.) ¶テキサス州の人 a Texan / テキサス(ヒット)《野球》a Texas leaguer.

てきし 敵視 ¶敵視する look on sb as an enemy; be hostile (to); 《文》regard sb with hostility; 《文》be at enmity (with).

てきじ 適時 timely; opportune.

できし 溺死 ¶溺死する be drowned; die by drowning; drown / 溺死者 a drowned person / 溺死体 the body of a drowned person. 文例◊

てきしゃせいぞん 適者生存 ¶適者生存の法則 (the law of) the survival of the fittest.

てきしゅつ 摘出 removal; 《文》extraction ¶摘出する remove; extract; take [pick] out.

てきじょう 敵情 《reconnoiter》the movements of the enemy.

てきじん 敵陣 the enemy's camp [position]; the enemy('s) lines ¶敵陣を突破する break through the enemy lines.

てきず 手傷 an injury; a wound ¶手傷を負う be injured; be wounded.

できすぎ 出来過ぎ 文例◊

テキスト 〈本文〉《a》text;〈教科書〉a textbook ¶英語のテキスト an English textbook.

てきする¹ 適する fit; suit; agree (with one's constitution); be fit (for);《文》be fitted (for); be suited (to); be suitable (for); 〈適応する〉be adapted (for, to); 〈適任である〉be competent [qualified] (for, to do); 使用に適する be fit to use [《文》for use] / 食用[健康]に適する be good to eat [for the health] / 初心者に適した本 a book suitable for beginners / 適しない ⇒ ふてきとう. 文例◊

用法 be fit for... は肯定平叙文では普通言えない. 代わりに be suited to... を使う. Is he fit for that job? (彼はその仕事に適しているか) / He's not fit for such responsibility. (彼にはこのような重職には適していない) / He's suited to the post. (彼はこの職務に適している).

てきする² 敵する 〈敵対する〉turn [fight] against; stand [《文》contend] against; 〈匹敵する〉be a match for; be one's match; be equal to.

てきせい 適正 ¶適正な proper; right; appropriate / 《文》just / 適正価格 a reasonable price.

てきせいけんさ 適性検査 an aptitude test.

てきせつ 適切 ¶適切な fit; suitable; (well-) suited; appropriate; adequate; proper; apt; 《文》apposite;《文》happy;〈時宜を得た〉timely; opportune; seasonable / 適切な言葉 an apt [《文》a happy] remark / 適切な例 ⇒ てきれい / 適切に suitably; to the point; 《文》happily; 《文》opportunely / 適切でない inadequate; inappropriate; out of place; out of order. 文例◊

てきぜん 敵前 ¶敵前で in the face of the enemy / 敵前上陸をする land [《文》effect a landing] in the face of the enemy.

できそこない 出来損い a failure; 《口語》a dead loss; 《口語》a washout; 〈人〉a good-for-nothing (fellow) / 出来損いの defective; good-for-nothing / 出来損いの子供 a child not properly brought up.

てきたい 敵対 ¶敵対する turn [fight] against; stand [《文》contend] against; oppose; be at war with / 敵対行為 a hostile act; hostile operations [activities].

できだか 出来高 〈収穫〉a crop; a yield; 〈生産高〉output; 《口語》(a) turnover; total transactions ¶出来高払い payment at piece rates; payment by results / 出来高払いで (work) at piece rates; (be paid) on a piece-work basis.

できたて 出来立て ¶出来立ての new; newly

---

on September 2.

できごころ 一時の出来心でやったのです. She did it on the spur of the moment.

できごと それはいつの出来事ですか. When did it happen? / 我々は新聞で世界の出来事を知る. We can tell from the newspapers what is going on in the world.

てきざい 彼では適材適所というわけにはとてもいかない. He is a square peg in a round hole. | He is quite unfitted for the post.

できし 溺死者数名を出した. Several people were drowned.

できすぎ 太郎君, 君にしては出来過ぎだよ. You surpass yourself, Taro.

てきする¹ 彼は実業家には適していない. He isn't suited to be a businessman. | He has no aptitude [isn't cut out] for a business career. / この雑誌の編集の仕事は彼には正に適していると思う. I think editing this magazine will be just the (right) job for him.

てきせつ 彼の提案はこの際まことに適切だ. His proposal is certainly pertinent at this juncture.

てきとう Please do as you think [see] fit. | I leave it to your discretion. / まあ適当にやるさ. Take

てきだん 敵弾 the enemy's bullets [shells].

てきち 敵地 enemy [hostile] country (★ an enemy country は「敵国」); the enemy's land [territory].

てきちゅう 的中 ¶的中する hit (the mark); go home; 《口》 tell; hit the nail on the head; be (right) to the point; 〈予言などが〉 come [prove, turn out] true; 〈推測が〉 guess right / 的中しない miss [be wide of] the mark; guess wrong.

てきど 適度 ¶適度の moderate; 《文》 temperate / 適度の運動 moderate [a proper amount of] exercise / 適度に moderately; 《文》 temperately / 適度に…する be moderate in *doing*; use moderation in….

てきとう 適当 ¶適当な fit; suitable; 《文》 befitting; adequate; apt; 《文》 apposite; appropriate; right; 〈文〉 competent [qualified] ((for, to *do*)); 〈妥当な〉 reasonable; 〈時宜にかなった〉 timely; 《文》 opportune; seasonable / 適当な条件で on fair [reasonable] terms / 適当な言葉がないので for want of a better word / 適当に suitably; as *one* thinks fit [right].

てきにん 適任 ¶適任である be fit [suitable] ((for the post)); be suited ((to the job)) ⇨ てきする 《口例》; 〈資格がある〉 be competent [well qualified] ((for)) / 適任者 a fit [competent] person for the job [post]; a well-qualified person.

できばえ 出来ばえ workmanship; make; 〈結果〉 the result / みごとな出来ばえの[出来ばえの悪い]品 a beautifully-[poorly-]made article; 《文》 an article of excellent [poor] workmanship.

てきぱき ¶てきぱきした brisk; prompt; quick; businesslike / てきぱきと briskly; promptly, quickly; 《文》 with dispatch; in a businesslike way; 《文》 with expedition and accuracy.

てきはつ 摘発 ¶摘発する expose; unmask; 《文》 lay bare [open]; uncover.

てきひ 適否 〈事の〉《文》 propriety / 〈人・物の〉 suitability (or otherwise); fitness; 〈適性〉 aptitude.

てきびしい 手厳しい severe; harsh; hard ¶手厳しい批評 (a) scathing [harsh] criticism / 手厳しく severely; harshly; in an unrelenting manner. 文例⇩

てきひょう 適評 (an) apt criticism; an appropriate comment ¶適評を下す make an apt criticism ((of)); make an appropriate comment ((on)). 文例⇩

てきふてき 適不適 ⇨ てきひ. 文例⇩

てきへい 敵兵 an enemy (soldier); 〈全体〉 the enemy.

てきほう 適法 ¶適法の lawful; legal; legitimate.

てきめん ¶てきめんに利く work [take effect] instantly [immediately]; have [produce] an immediate effect ((on)). 文例⇩

できもの 出来物 a swelling; a boil; a rash. 文例⇩

てきや てき屋 a racketeer.

てきやく¹ 適役 a suitable post [position, office]; 〈芝居の〉 a well-cast role [part]. 文例⇩

てきやく² 適訳 a good [happy, nice] translation; (give) an exact [a good] rendering ((of)). 文例⇩

てきよう¹ 適用 application ¶適用する apply ((a rule to a case)) / 適用し得る[し難い] 《文》 applicable [inapplicable] ((to)) / 適用を誤る misapply; make a wrong application ((of the law)) / 適用範囲が広い can be widely applied; 《文》 be (capable) of wide application.

てきよう² 摘要 a summary; a synopsis (*pl.* -nopses); a résumé; 《文》 an epitome; 〈概要〉 an outline; 〈抜粋〉 an abstract; 〈備考〉 remarks ¶摘要欄 the remarks column.

てきりょう 適量 a proper quantity; 〈薬の〉 a proper dose / 適量を過ごす take too much ((of)); 《文》 drink ((whisky)) to excess.

できる 出来る 〈出来上がる〉 be done; be finished; be ready; 〈造られる〉 be made; 〈発生する〉《文》 come into being [existence]; 〈形成される〉 form; 《文》 take shape [form]; 〈産出する〉 be produced; 〈…し得る〉 can *do*; be able to *do*; 〈…しても差支えない〉 may *do*; 〈成績がよい〉 do well; 〈熟達している〉 be good ((at)); be skillful ((at, in)); 《文》 be proficient ((in)) ¶英語ができる be good at English / 学問ができる be a good scholar / 出来かかった half-formed 《ideas》 / よく出来た人 a person of well-balanced character / (よく)できる生徒 an able [a clever, a bright] boy [girl] / できない cannot *do*; be unable to *do*; 〈不可能である〉 be impossible / 〈学問が〉 be backward; be dull / できない事[相談] an impossibility; an impracticable thing [proposal]; a tall order / できれば if possible; if *one* can / できるだけ as much [far] as *one* can; as much [far] as possible; all *one* can / できるだけ早く as

---

it easy; you don't have to be perfect.

てきにん 彼こそ適任者だ。He is just the man for it.

てきぱき 彼はてきぱきと命令を下していた。He was giving orders decisively.

てきびしい 彼はそのことを非常に手厳しく批判した。He criticized it with great severity.

てきひょう 正に適評だ。His comments are entirely to the point.

てきふてき 職業を選ぶにはその適不適をよく考えなければいけない。In selecting your occupation, you must consider whether it suits you or not.

てきめん この薬を飲むと頭痛がてきめんに止まる。This medicine will get rid of your headache like magic.

できもの 足にできものができた。 I have got a boil on my foot.

てきやく¹ その役は彼には適役だった。He was well cast in the role.

てきやく² この語の適訳が日本語にはない。There is no exact Japanese equivalent for this word.

てきよう¹ どんな場合にもこの規則が適用できるというわけではない。This rule does not apply to every case. | This rule does not

てきれい 適例 a good example; 《文》an apt instance; a case in point.

てきれいき 適齢期 〈結婚の〉(reach [《文》attain]) marriageable age.

てぎれきん 手切れ金 consolation money.

てぎわ 手際 〈巧みさ〉skill;《文》dexterity;《文》finesse;〈細工〉workmanship;〈かけひき〉tact ¶ 手際よく skillfully;《文》dexterously; cleverly; neatly; tactfully / 手際がよい[悪い] be skillful [awkward, clumsy] (in doing, at);〈事が主語〉be finely [poorly] made;《文》be of excellent [inferior] workmanship / 手際を見せる show [display] one's skill; show finesse (in dealing with people). 文例⇩

てきん 手金 ⇨ てつけん.

でく 木偶〈人形〉a wooden figure [doll]; a puppet ¶ でくの坊 a good-for-nothing (fellow); a blockhead.

てぐす 天蚕糸 (fishing) gut.

てぐすね 手ぐすね ¶ 手ぐすね引いて待つ be more than ready (for the encounter); wait expectantly (for an opportunity); wait eagerly (for).

てくせ 手癖 ¶ 手癖が悪い be light-[《口語》sticky-]fingered; be given to thievery.

てくだ 手管《文》wiles; a trick;《文》a sly artifice.

てぐち 手口 a method (employed in a crime); a criminal technique; a trick ¶ いつもの手口 the same old game [trick].

でぐち 出口 a way out; an exit;〈高速道路の〉an exit ramp. 文例⇩

てくてく てくてく歩く go on foot; walk;《口語》foot it;《俗》hoof it;〈とぼとぼ歩く〉trudge; plod.

テクニカルノックアウト《ボクシング》a technical knockout (略: T.K.O.) ¶ テクニカルノックアウトで勝つ win by [score] a T.K.O. (over one's opponent).

テクニシャン a skilled operator; a person with good technique.

テクニック a technique.

テクネチウム《化》technetium.

てくび 手首 a wrist ¶ 手首の骨 the carpal bones / 手首を押える seize [take] sb by the wrist.

てくらがり 手暗がり (be troubled by) the shadow of one's own hand.

でくわす 出くわす ⇨ であう.

てこ 挺子 a lever ¶ てこの支点 a fulcrum (pl. -crums, -cra) / てこで持ち上げる lever sth up; raise sth with a lever / てこでも動かない do not budge an inch; persist [stand firm] (in) / てこ入れする prop [shore, jack] up; bolster; support / てこ作用 leverage.

てごころ 手心 ¶ 手心を加える〈裁量する〉use one's discretion;〈酌量する〉make allowance(s) (for);〈追及を控えめにする〉tone down (one's criticism of sb); treat sb [sth] tolerantly;《口語》pull one's punches (in doing) (★ 主に否定の形で使う。)

てこずる do not know what to do with sb [sth]; have trouble in controlling sb [sth]; be put out (with); have a hard time (with) ¶ てこずらせる put sb out; drive sb to his wits' end; give sb a lot of trouble.

てごたえ 手答[応]え〈反応〉a response; a reaction;〈抵抗〉(a) resistance;〈効果〉(an) effect; (a) result ¶ 手答えがある tell (on); take [have] effect (on) / 手答えのある相手 a tough opponent;《文》a worthy antagonist / 手答えのない〈反応のない〉unresponsive; impassive;〈逆らわぬ〉unresisting. 文例⇩

でこぼこ irregularities ¶ でこぼこの uneven; bumpy; rough; rugged; irregular / でこぼこのない even; level; smooth / でこぼこ道 a bumpy road.

デコレーション (a) decoration ¶ デコレーションケーキ a party [decorated] cake.

てごろ 手頃 ¶ 手ごろな handy;〈丁度いい〉suitable (for); fit (for) ⇨ てきする¹ 囲⇩;〈便利な〉convenient (for);〈値段の〉reasonable ; 手頃な大きさの convenient-sized; handy-sized.

てごわい 手強い tough;《文》formidable; stubborn;《文》redoubtable ¶ 手ごわい相手 a formidable adversary; a strong antagonist;《口語》a tough customer.

デザート dessert. 文例⇩

てざいく 手細工 handwork; handiwork; a handicraft (★ 複数形で使われることが多い).

デザイナー a (dress) designer.

---

hold (true) in all cases.

できる 食事ができた. Dinner is ready. / できた事は仕方がない. What is done cannot be undone. / このテーブルはたいそうよくできている. This table is very well made. / この辺にだいぶ家ができた. Lots of houses have been built in this neighborhood. / こうしてアメリカ合衆国はできたのである. This is how the United States of America came into being. / 2人の間に男の子ができた. A son was born to them. / 雨あがりで所々に水たまりができた. Pools formed here and there after the rain. / 富士山は一夜にしてできたのだという伝説がある. Legend has it that Mt. Fuji rose in one night. / この地方では米がたくさんできる. This part of the country yields a great deal of rice. / ちょっと用事ができたので私は行けなかった. Some business turned up and I could not go. / 私にできる事なら何でもいたします. I will do anything in my power. / だれでも俳句を1つ2つ作るぐらいのことはできる. Everyone has it in him to compose a haiku or two. / そのような約束はできません. I am not in a position to make promises of that sort. / そんなことは私には我慢できない. It is more than I can bear. / できれば喜んでするのですが. I would gladly do it if I could. / 私はその問題ができなかった. I could not solve the problem. /《料理店で》サンドイッチは3種類できます. We can give you three kinds of sandwiches. / 私にはなんぜいたくはできない. I cannot afford such luxury. / 彼は学校はよくできる. He does well at school. / 彼らの条件をのむことはできない. We cannot accept their terms. /

デザイン a design ¶ デザインする design / デザイン料 a design fee. 文例↓

でさかり 出盛り the season 《for cherries》; the best time 《for》. 文例↓

てさき 手先 〈指〉the fingers; 〈お先棒〉a tool; a cat's-paw; an agent ¶ 手先の器用[不器用]な ⇨ きよう³, ぶきよう / 手先の仕事 handwork; handiwork ¶ 手先に使う make a cat's-paw [tool] of *sb*; use *sb* as a tool [an agent] / 手先になる act as an agent 《for》; work as *sb*'s instrument.

てさき 出先 ¶ 出先で at the place where *one* is staying; when *one* is away from home 《the office》; 〈途中で〉on the way / 出先から 〈telephone〉 from the place where *one* is [is staying] / 出先機関 a local agency 《of the government》; a branch office 《of a company》.

てさぐり 手探り ¶ 手探りする grope [feel, fumble] 《for, after》/ 手探りで行く feel [grope] *one's* way 《in the dark》; go feeling [grope] 《along the wall》/ かぎを手探りで探す feel [grope] for a key. 文例↓

てさげ 手提げ 〈婦人用の〉a handbag; a hand basket 〈かご〉/ 手提げかばん a briefcase; an attaché case / 手提げ金庫 a portable safe.

てざわり 手触り (a) feel 《★複数にはしない》; touch ¶ 手触りがいい feel smooth [nice]; have a pleasant feel; be pleasant to the touch [feel]. 文例↓

でし 弟子 〈門弟〉a pupil; a disciple; 〈徒弟〉an apprentice ¶ 弟子を取る take pupils / 弟子になる, 弟子入りする become *sb*'s (private) pupil; be apprenticed to 《a carpenter》.

てしお 手塩 ¶ 手塩にかけて育てる bring up 《a child》 under *one's* own care [with tender care].

てしごと 手仕事 handwork; handiwork; manual work.

てした 手下 an underling; a follower; a subordinate; 〈総称〉*one's* men ¶ 手下が大勢いる have a large following / 手下になって働く work under *sb*.

デジタル ¶ デジタルコンピューター[時計] a digital computer [watch, clock].

てじな 手品 a conjuring trick; sleight of hand; magic ¶ トランプの手品 a card trick / 手品の材料店 a magic store / 手品のようにすばやく with sleight-of-hand quickness / 手品をつかう do [perform] a conjuring trick; do magic; 〈だます〉play a trick on *sb* / 手品師 a conjurer; a magician.

デシベル a decibel (略: dB, db).

デシメートル a decimeter (略: dm).

でしゃく 手酌 ¶ 手酌で飲む help *oneself* to sake.

でしゃばり 〈出すぎること〉《文》self-assertiveness; forwardness; 《口語》pushiness; 〈おせっかい〉meddling; interfering; 〈出すぎたことをする人〉a self-assertive [forward, 《口語》pushy] person; 《口語》a showoff; 〈おせっかいな人〉a busybody; a meddler.

でしゃばる 〈出すぎる〉《文》assert *oneself* excessively [too much]; 《口語》be self-assertive; be forward; 《口語》show off; 《口語》be pushy; 〈おせっかいを焼く〉meddle [interfere] 《in *sb*'s affairs》; 《口語》stick *one's* nose 《in *sb*'s business》; 《口語》butt in. 文例↓

てじゅん 手順 〈工程〉a process; 〈手続〉procedure; 〈順序〉an order; 〈やり方〉a method, a way [《文》manner] of 《doing》; 〈手はず〉a plan; a program ¶ 手順を定める plan 《*one's* course of action》; arrange [make arrangements] 《for》/ 手順よく methodically; systematically; smoothly; without a hitch. 文例↓

てじょう 手錠 (a pair of) handcuffs; 《口語》cuffs ¶ 手錠をかける handcuff; put [place] handcuffs on *sb*. 文例↓

デシリットル a deciliter (略: dl).

てすう 手数 〈面倒〉trouble; 〈骨折り〉《文》pains; 〈囲碁・将棋〉the number of moves ¶ 手数のかかる troublesome / 手数がかかる be troublesome; take [be] a lot of trouble; be a bother [nuisance] / 手数をかける put *sb* to trouble; give [cause] (a lot of) trouble to *sb*; 〈面倒を起こす〉make trouble / …する手数を省く save *sb* the trouble (of) / お手数ですが… I am sorry to trouble you, but…; May I trouble you to do? / 手数料 〈口銭〉a commission; a percentage; brokerage (中立ちの); 〈料金〉a fee; a charge.

てずから 手ずから in person; personally; 《do》*oneself*.

It is impossible for us to accept their terms. | Their terms are impossible for us to accept.

てぎわ 手際はざっとこんなものさ. See how well I have done it. / 大工さんが家の屋根の修理を手際よくやってくれた. The carpenter did a good job of fixing the roof of my house.

でぐち 出口がわからない. I can't find my way out. / 出口はこちらです. This way out.

てごたえ 弾丸は確かに手答えがあった. I almost felt the bullet strike home. / その皮肉は彼にはなんの手答えもなかった. The sarcasm was lost [had no effect] on him.

デザート デザートにはシャーベットが出た. Sherbet was served as dessert.

デザイン このじゅうたんは工藤氏のデザインによるものです. This carpet has been made to Mr. Kudo's design.

でさかり 今はりんごの出盛りだ. Apples are now in season. / 今は銀座は人の出盛りだ. The Ginza is most crowded [is at its busiest] at this time of day.

てさぐり 万事手探りでしなければならなかった. I had to do everything by feel [by touch].

てざわり 手触りで絹だということがわかる. You can tell by the feel that this is silk. / どんな手触りですか. What does it feel like? / この紙は手触りが荒い. This paper feels rough (to the touch).

でしゃばる でしゃばるな. Mind your own business.

てじゅん 彼が病気になったので手順が狂った. His illness upset our plan.

てじょう 彼は手錠をかけられていた. He was in handcuffs. / 彼の手首にはさっと[ぱちんと]手錠がはめられた. Handcuffs were slipped [snapped] onto his wrists.

てすう そうすればだいぶ手数が省

てすき¹ 手隙 ¶手すきである be free; be not busy [engaged]; 《文》be at leisure; have nothing particular to do; have time to spare.

てすき² 手漉き ¶手漉きの handmade 《paper》.

てすぎる 出過ぎる ⇨でしゃばる.

デスク 〈机〉a desk;《新聞》a copy editor; a subeditor;《米》a deskman.

てすじ 手筋 ¶手筋がいい have a natural aptitude for 《the samisen》.

テスター《電》a (circuit) tester.

テスト a test; a tryout (★複数はなく a の代わりに one は使えない) / テストする test; give sb a test; put sth to the test / テストの成績 one's test score [record] / テストを受ける take [《文》undergo] a test / テストに合格する pass a test / テストケース a test case / テストパターン a test pattern. 文例⇩

デスマスク a death mask.

てすり 手摺り a handrail; a guardrail; a railing; banisters (階段の) ¶手すりにもたれる lean on the railing.

てずり 手刷り ¶手刷りの hand-printed.

てせい 手製 ¶手製の handmade; homemade; of one's own making. 文例⇩

てぜま 手狭 ¶手狭な narrow; confined; small.

てそう 手相 (the lines on) one's palm ¶手相がいい[悪い] have lucky [ominous] lines in one's hand / 手相を見る read sb's hand; tell sb's fortune by the lines on his palm; practice palmistry / 手相を見てもらう have one's palm read (by); consult a palmist / 手相見 a palmist. 文例⇩

でぞめしき 出初め式 the New Year's parade of fire brigades.

でそろう 出揃う be all present [out].

てだし 手出し ¶手出しする meddle with;《口語》put one's oar in;〈関係する〉have a hand in; concern oneself [be concerned] with;〈試みる〉try;《文》attempt; turn one's hand to;〈打ちかかる〉(try to) strike a blow; start a quarrel. 文例⇩

でだし 出だし ¶出だしがいい[悪い] make a good [bad] start; begin well [badly].

てだすけ 手助け help; assistance;《文》aid ¶手助けする help sb (out);《文》assist;《文》aid; lend sb a (helping) hand / 手助けになる be helpful (to); be a help (to); be of service [help, assistance] (to).

てだて 手立て ⇨しゅだん.

てだま 手玉 ¶手玉に取る lead sb by the nose; twist sb around [round] one's (little) finger (特に女が男を).

でたらめ nonsense; an irresponsible remark [act] ¶でたらめの nonsensical; irresponsible; random; haphazard;《文》unsystematic / でたらめに at random; irresponsibly; without system [a plan] / でたらめを言う talk nonsense [rubbish].

てぢか 手近 ¶手近な〈卑近な〉familiar;〈便利な〉handy;〈近くの〉《a police box》close-by; nearby / 手近に close by; nearby; close [near] at hand; (be near) at hand; be within (one's) reach / 手近に置いておく have [keep] 《a dictionary》handy [close at hand, at one's elbow, where one can reach (it)]. 文例⇩

てちがい 手違い ¶手違いになる go wrong [《文》amiss] / 何かの手違いで owing to [because of] some mistake [accident].

てちょう 手帳 a (pocket) notebook; a pocketbook ¶手帳に書き留める[つける] write [take, put, jot] 《sb's address》down in one's notebook.

てつ 鉄 iron ¶鉄の iron; ferrous / 鉄の意志 an iron will / 鉄のカーテン the Iron Curtain / 鉄の肺 an iron lung / 鉄製の iron; (made) of iron / 鉄亜鈴 (a pair of) dumbbells / 鉄くず iron [steel] scrap; iron filings (粉) / 鉄材 iron [steel] material / 鉄びん an iron kettle / 鉄棒 an iron (a steel) bar /《体操》a horizontal bar / (オリンピックの)鉄棒の優勝者 the gold medalist on the horizontal bar. 文例⇩

てっかい 撤回 (a) withdrawal;《文》(a) retraction; (a) repeal ¶撤回する withdraw; take back;《文》retract / …の撤回を要求する demand a retraction of….

てつがく 哲学 philosophy ¶哲学的 philosophical / 哲学する philosophize;《文》speculate 《about sth》in a philosophical manner / 哲学史 the history of philosophy /〈書物などの場合〉a history of philosophy / 哲学者 a philosopher / 哲学書 a philosophy book / 哲学体系 a philosophical system; a body of philosophy.

てつかず 手付かず ¶手付かずの untouched; unused / 手付かずにしておく leave [keep] sth untouched [intact, as it is]. 文例⇩

ける. That would save us a lot of trouble.

テスト この気体が二酸化炭素を含んでいるかどうかテストしてみたまえ. Test this gas for carbon dioxide.

てせい これはあなたのお手製ですか. Did you make this yourself? | Is this of your own making?

てぜま 生徒数が増えたので校舎が手狭になった. The schoolhouse is too small for the increased number of students. / 手狭で困っています. We are cramped [pressed, pinched] for room here.

てそう その易者は机に「手相, 見料千五百円」と書いた札を下げていた. The fortuneteller had a piece of paper tacked to his desk, on which was written: 'Have your Fortune Told. Palms Read, ¥1,500.'

てだし 私は自信のない仕事には決して手出しをしない. I never turn [put] my hand to anything I don't feel I'm equal to. / この問題には手出しをしたくない. I don't want to get mixed up in this affair. | I want to stay out of this affair. / どちらが先に手出しをしたのか. Who struck the first blow?

てちか 問題の解決は手近なところにある. We don't have to look far for the solution of the problem.

てつ 鉄は熱いうちに打て. Strike while the iron is hot.《諺》| You can't teach an old dog new tricks. / 彼は鉄棒で 9.80 の得点をあげた. He scored 9.80 points in the horizontal bar exercise.

てつかぶと 鉄兜 a steel helmet.

てづかみ 手摑み ¶手づかみにする grasp; grab; take *sth* in *one's* hand; catch ⦅a fish⦆ by hand / 手づかみで ⦅eat⦆ with *one's* fingers.

てつき 手付き ¶慣れた手つきで with practiced hand / 変な手つきで awkwardly; clumsily.

てっき[1] 鉄器 ironware; hardware ¶鉄器時代 the Iron Age.

てっき[2] 敵機 an enemy plane.

デッキ ⦅船の⦆ the deck; ⦅列車の⦆⦅米⦆ the vestibule ★ vestibule に対応する⦅英⦆はない ¶⦅空港の⦆送迎デッキ an observation deck / デッキチェア a deck chair.

てっきょ 撤去 ⦅文⦆(a) withdrawal; removal (除去) ¶撤去する withdraw; ⦅除去する⦆ remove; take away; dismantle (装備などを) / 障害物を撤去する clear ⦅the passage⦆ of obstacles.

てっきょう 鉄橋 a railroad [railway] bridge.

てっきり surely; certainly; beyond doubt. 文例⇩

てっきん[1] 鉄琴 a glockenspiel.

てっきん[2] 鉄筋 a reinforcing bar [rod] ¶鉄筋コンクリートの建物 a reinforced concrete [ferroconcrete] building.

てづくり 手作り ¶手作りの handmade; handcrafted ⦅chairs⦆; of *one's* own making [growing]; ⦅自家製の⦆ homemade; ⦅自家栽培の⦆ homegrown.

てつけきん 手付け金 a deposit; ⦅法⦆ earnest money ¶手付け金を払う put down [pay, make] a deposit ⦅of 100,000 yen on an antique⦆.

てっけん 鉄拳 a (clenched) fist ¶鉄拳をくらわせる hit [⦅文⦆ strike] *sb* with *one's* fist.

てっこう[1] 鉄鉱 iron ore.

てっこう[2] 鉄鋼 (iron and) steel ¶鉄鋼業 the steel industry.

てつごうし 鉄格子 ¶鉄格子の grilled; iron-barred / 鉄格子のしてある窓 an iron-barred window.

てっこうじょ 鉄工所 an ironworks ⦅単複同形⦆.

てっこつ 鉄骨 a steel [an iron] frame ¶鉄骨建築 ⦅a building of⦆ steel-frame construction.

てっさく[1] 鉄柵 an iron railing [fence].

てっさく[2] 鉄索 a wire rope; a cable; a cableway (運搬用の).

デッサン [<⦅フランス語⦆ *dessin*] a (rough) sketch; ⦅do⦆ a preliminary sketch; a preparatory drawing; ⦅実物大の⦆ a cartoon. 文例⇩

てっしゅう 撤収 ⦅文⦆(a) withdrawal; ⦅文⦆ removal ¶撤収する withdraw ⦅from⦆; remove ⦅from⦆; pull ⦅troops⦆ out of ⦅a region⦆.

てつじょうもう 鉄条網 barbed-wire entanglements ¶鉄条網を張りめぐらす set [stretch] barbed wire around ⦅a place⦆.

てつじん 哲人 a philosopher; a wise man.

てっする 徹する ⇨てってい (徹底する) ¶骨身に徹する go [come] home to *one*; sink deep into *one's* mind / 夜を徹する sit up all night / 金もうけに徹する put *one's* heart and soul into ⦅⦅文⦆ devote *oneself* wholly to⦆ moneymaking.

てっせん 鉄線 iron [steel] wire.

てっそく 鉄則 ⦅lay down⦆ a hard-and-fast rule [regulation]; ⦅文⦆ an invariable principle; ⦅文⦆ an iron [ironbound] law.

てったい 撤退 ⦅文⦆(a) withdrawal; (an) evacuation; (a) pullout ¶撤退する withdraw ⦅from⦆; evacuate ⦅a place⦆; pull [get] out ⦅of⦆ / 撤退命令 an evacuation order.

てつだい 手伝い ⦅事⦆ help; assistance; ⦅文⦆ aid; ⦅人⦆ a helper; a help; an assistant ¶お手伝いさん a housekeeper; a daily help (通勤の) ⇨じょちゅう. 文例⇩

てつだう 手伝う help ⦅*sb* with *sth*, *sb* (to) do⦆; ⦅文⦆ assist ⦅*sb* in doing⦆; give *sb* a helping hand; lend a (helping) hand ⦅to⦆ ¶宿題を手伝う help ⦅a child⦆ with ⦅his⦆ home work / 手伝って着物を着せる [脱がせる] help *sb* on [off] with *his* clothes. 文例⇩

でっち 丁稚 an apprentice.

でっちあげ でっち上げ ⦅口語⦆ a put-up job; a trumped-up story; ⦅口語⦆ a frame-up (特に犯罪の).

でっちあげる でっち上げる invent; make [⦅口語⦆ cook, trump] up ⦅a story⦆.

てっつい 鉄槌 an iron hammer ¶鉄ついを下す crack down (on racketeers); give [deal] a hard [crushing] blow ⦅to⦆.

てつづき 手続き formalities; ⦅文⦆ procedures; ⦅措置⦆ steps ¶手続きをする⦅ふむ,経る⦆ follow the necessary procedures ⦅for⦆; go through the formalities; take (the necessary) steps ⦅in a matter⦆ / 輸出手続き export procedures / 手続き上の ⦅文⦆ procedural / 手続き法 ⦅法⦆ an adjective law. 文例⇩

てつかず 問題は今もってほとんど手つかずのままになっている。The problem has as yet been scarcely dealt with. / Even now scarcely anything has been done about the problem.

てっきり てっきりそうに違いないと思った。I thought it must be so. / I was sure there was no doubt about it. / てっきり木村君の仕事だとばかり思いこんでいた。I took for granted that it was Kimura's work (and nobody else's).

デッサン この絵はデッサンがしっかりしていると思う。The preparatory drawing for this picture must have been well done. / この絵はデッサンが狂っている。The drawing in this picture is all wrong. / ドガは油絵を描く前に何時間もかけて幾枚ものデッサンをした。Degas spent hours drawing and redrawing his subjects before painting them.

てつだい 何かお手伝いすることがありますか。Can I do anything to help (you)?

てつだう 君に手伝ってもらわねばならない。I need your help. / 彼が手伝おうと言ったが僕は断わった。He offered me his help, but I declined it. / その他種々の原因が手伝ってこの結果になったのです。Many other factors contributed to this result. / 彼女は過労の上に心労が手伝って病気になった。Mental stress, in addition to overworking, made her ill.

てつづき 入会手続きはご存じですか。Do you know how one joins

でづっぱり 出突っぱり ¶出突っぱりである appear in every scene ((of a show)); be on stage throughout ((a play)).

てってい 徹底 ¶徹底的な, 徹底した thorough; thoroughgoing; ((文)) exhaustive; complete; perfect; utter; downright; ((口語)) all-out; ((根本的な)) radical; drastic / 徹底した利己主義者 an out-and-out egoist; an egoist through-and-through / 徹底する be thorough; be complete; be painstaking; ((文)) spare no pains ((in doing)) / 話を徹底させる have *oneself* fully understood ((by)) / 徹底的研究 an exhaustive study / 徹底的変革 a sweeping [complete] change / 徹底的に thoroughly; completely; through and through; all-out; to the hilt / 徹底的に話し合う have it out with *sb*; have a frank talk with *sb* / 徹底的に調査する a investigate [go into] *sth* thoroughly / ((文)) make a thorough investigation ((of)); probe ((a matter)) to the bottom [in depth]. 文例⇩

てっとう 鉄塔 a steel tower.

てつどう 鉄道 ((米)) a railroad; ((英)) a railway; a rail line ¶鉄道を敷く construct [lay, build] a railroad (line) / 鉄道を利用する take the train ((to Tokyo, to get there)); go ((to a place)) by train [by rail]; use the train service / 鉄道で運ばれる貨物 rail-borne goods / 鉄道で結ばれている be linked by rail ((with)) / 鉄道案内所 ((米)) a railroad information bureau; ((英)) a railway enquiry office / 鉄道運賃 ((人の)) a rail(-road) fare; ((貨物の)) freight rates / 鉄道会社 ((米)) a railroad corporation; ((英)) a railway company / 鉄道公安官 a railroad security officer; a railroad policeman; ((集合的に)) the railroad police / 鉄道連絡 rail communications ((with)) / 鉄道工事 railroad (construction) work / 鉄道事故 a railroad accident / 鉄道自殺をする a throw [commit suicide by throwing] *oneself* under a train / 鉄道(従業)員 ((米)) a railroad worker [man, employee]; ((英)) a railwayman / 鉄道線路 a railroad track; a railroad [rail] line / 鉄道便で送る send *sth* by rail [by train] / 鉄道網 a railroad system [network] / 鉄道渋谷 rail [railroad] transport [transportation, transit]; transport by rail.

てっとうてつび 徹頭徹尾 thoroughly; out and out; through and through; ((どの点から見ても)) every inch; from every point of view; ((終始)) from first to last; from beginning to end; all the way [time]. 文例⇩

デッドヒート a close contest; a blistering race ¶デッドヒートを演じる run neck and neck.

デッドボール 『野球』 a pitch that hits the batter ¶デッドボールを食う be hit by a pitched ball; be struck by a pitch / デッドボールで一塁に出る get to first hit by a pitched ball / デッドボールで出塁した打者 a hit batsman.

てっとりばやい 手っ取り早い quick; ((文)) prompt; rough and ready ¶手っ取り早く quickly; smartly; promptly; ((文)) with dispatch / 手っ取り早く片づける make short work of *sth* / 手っ取り早く言えば to make [cut] a long story short; in short; ((文)) in brief; in a word; to put it briefly.

でっぱ 出っ歯 projecting teeth; buckteeth ¶出っ歯の buck-toothed.

てっぱい 撤廃 abolition; ((文)) removal ¶撤廃する cancel; withdraw ((a measure)); abolish ((a provision)); remove; repeal ((a law)); do away with; lift ((the ban)).

でっぱる 出っ張る project; protrude; stick [jut] out.

てっぱん 鉄板 an iron [a steel] plate; a sheet of steel; sheet steel; ⟨料理用の⟩ a hot plate ¶鉄板焼き meat roasted on a hot plate.

てっぴつ 鉄筆 ⟨謄写版用の⟩ a stylus (*pl.* -luses, -li); a steel pen ¶鉄筆で原紙を切る cut a stencil with a stylus.

でっぷり ¶でっぷりした stout; fat; ((文)) corpulent; ((文)) portly; ((a man)) with a lot of fat on ((him)).

てつぶん 鉄分 iron (content).

てっぷん 鉄粉 iron powder [filings] ¶細かい鉄粉 finely ground iron.

てっぺい ((文)) 撤兵 ((a)) troop withdrawal ¶撤兵する withdraw ((one's [the] troops)) ((from)); pull troops out ((of a place)); evacuate ((a town)).

てっぺき 鉄壁 ¶鉄壁の impregnable / 鉄壁の防御態勢を築く build up impregnable defenses.

てっぺん 天辺 the top; the summit ⟨山の⟩ ¶頭の天辺 the top of the head; the crown of *one's* head.

てっぽう 鉄砲 a gun; ⟨総称⟩ firearms ¶鉄砲水 a flash flood.

てづまり 手詰まり ¶手詰まりになる ⟨行き詰まる⟩ reach (a) deadlock; ⟨囲碁・将棋で⟩ be unable to find an effective move.

てつめんぴ 鉄面皮 ¶鉄面皮な shameless; thick-skinned; unblushing; brazen-faced / 鉄面皮にも…する have the cheek [gall, face,

---

the club [what one does to become a member]?

てってい 彼のすることは万事徹底している。 He is thorough about everything he does. | He never leaves anything half done. | 彼は徹底した進歩主義者だ。 He is a progressive to the core.

てっとうてつび 我々はこの計画には徹頭徹尾反対してきた。 We have been dead set against this project from the very beginning.

てっとりばやい 語学は手っ取り早く学べるものではない。 There's no short cut to learning a foreign language, you know. | There is no other way of mastering foreign languages but to learn them step by step. | 電気技師になるならこの学校へ入るのが一番手っ取り早い。 The quickest way to become an electrician is to enter this school.

てつや 僕は徹夜で試験勉強をした。 I sat up all night preparing for the examination.

てづる あの会社なら手づるがある。 I know some men in that company who will use their influence for me. | あの会社には格別の手づるもない。 I've no particular pull in that company.

でどころ その出所を教えてくれ。 Tell me where you got [found] it. | その金の出所を知りたいものだ。 I'd like to know where the

てつや 徹夜 ¶徹夜する sit [be, stay] up all night / 〈文〉keep an all-night vigil / 徹夜で会議をする have an all-night conference / 徹夜で看護する sit up all night with ((an invalid)); keep an all-night vigil over ((a sick child)). 文例⇩

てつり 哲理 philosophy; philosophical principles. 文例⇩

てづり 手釣 handline fishing [angling]; handlining ¶手釣をする handline.

てづる 手づる connections; contacts; 〈引き〉(a) pull; 〈あっ旋〉〈文〉good offices ¶手づるを求める hunt up connections / …の手づるで through the influence [good offices] of…. 文例⇩

てつわん 鉄腕 ¶鉄腕投手 an iron man.

でどころ 出所 the source; the origin. 文例⇩

テトラポット a tetrapod ★日本では「テトラポッド」は商標名.

てどり 手取り 〈給料〉take-home pay [wages]; one's salary after tax (and deductions); 〈純領収高〉net receipts; 〈純益〉a net profit [income]. 文例⇩

テナー 《音楽》tenor; 〈人〉a tenor (singer).

でないと ⇨ でなければ.

てなおし 手直し (an) adjustment; 《文》(a) readjustment ¶手直しする adjust (afterward); 〈文〉readjust; rework; touch up.

てなおす 出直す come [go, call] again; 〈やり直す〉start afresh [over again]; make a fresh start.

てながざる 手長猿〖動〗a. long-armed ape; a gibbon.

でなければ 文例⇩

てなずける 手なずける 〈動物を〉tame; domesticate; 〈人を〉win [〈文〉gain] sb over (to one's side); bring sb round.

てなみ 手並 〈技量〉skill; 《文》dexterity; 〈実力〉ability; 〈演技[奏]〉(a) (fine) performance ¶手並を示す show [display] one's skill.

てならい 手習い ⇨ しゅうじ². 文例⇩

てならし 手慣〔馴〕らし practice; an exercise; training ¶手慣らしをする go into training; get some practice; get one's hand in.

てなれる 手慣れる ¶手慣れている be quite at home (in, with) / 10年来手慣れた仕事 the job one has got [《文》become] used to over the last ten years. 文例⇩

デニール 〈糸の太さの単位〉a denier ¶30デニールの糸 (a) 30-denier yarn.

テニス tennis ¶テニスをする play tennis / ローンテニス lawn tennis / テニスコート a tennis court / テニス選手 a tennis player / テニス試合[大会] a tennis match [tournament].

デニム denim ¶デニムのズボン denim trousers; denims.

てにもつ 手荷物 (hand) baggage [luggage]; 〈所持品〉《文》personal effects ¶手荷物を預ける check one's baggage; have one's baggage checked / 手荷物1個 a piece of baggage / 手荷物一時預かり所 《米》a baggage room; 《英》a left-luggage office; 〈コート・帽子などの〉《米》a checkroom; 《英》a cloakroom. 文例⇩

てにをは particles; postpositions. 文例⇩

てぬい 手縫い ¶手縫いの hand-sewn; hand-sewed.

てぬかり 手抜かり ⇨ おち.

てぬき 手抜き corner-cutting; 《文》(intentional) negligence ¶手抜きをする cut corners; skimp 〈one's job〉/ 手抜き工事 construction work done with some [a lot of] corner-cutting; jerry-building; 《文》unconscientious work.

てぬぐい 手拭 a (hand) towel; a facecloth; 《米》a washcloth ¶手ぬぐいでふく wipe [rub] with a towel; dry 〈one's hands〉on a towel / 手ぬぐいを絞る wring a towel (dry [out]) / 手ぬぐい掛 a towel rack.

てぬるい 手ぬるい lenient; lax; lukewarm; mild; not strict [severe] enough.

テネシー Tennessee (略: Tenn.) ¶テネシー州の人 a Tennessean.

てのうち 手の内 one's intention 〈★この意味でのintentionは複数形で使うのが普通〉; a (secret) plan ¶手の内を見せる show one's cards [hand]; put [lay] one's cards on the table; 〈うっかりと〉《口語》tip one's hand ((to sb)).

テノール ⇨ テナー.

デノミ(ネーション) a change in [redesignation of] the denominations of monetary units; redenomination ★denomination は「通貨単位の呼称」であって、その変更を意味しない ¶デノミを実施する carry out currency redenomination; redenominate ((the yen)).

てば 手羽 a chicken wing.

-てば 文例⇩

では then; well; well then; if so; in that case. 文例⇩

-では 〈…においては〉in; at; to; as for; in the case of; 〈…から判断すると〉judging by

---

money came from [who supplied the money].

てどり この仕事は税引きで手取り月8万5千円になります. This job will bring [fetch] you 85,000 yen net a month after tax.

でなければ でなければ喜んでお招きに応じたのですが. Otherwise I would have accepted your invitation with pleasure.

てならい 六十の手習い. It is never too late to learn.

てなれる 名工の評判にたがわず, 氏の材料の扱いは手慣れたものである. True to his reputation as a master craftsman, his handling of the material bespeaks the skill he has acquired through long experience.

てにもつ これは20キロの重量制限内の手荷物として扱うわけにいかない. This cannot be counted as part of the 20-kilogram baggage allowance.

てにをは これはてにをはが合っていない. The way you have used these particles is ungrammatical.

-てば いいってば. You needn't do it, I tell you. / 来いってば. Do come! / あなたってば, ひどい人ね. You heartless man!! Oh, you are awful!

では では君はパスしたのだね. So [Then, can I take it that] you have passed? / ではまた明日お電

デパート a department store.

てはい 手配 〈準備・用意〉 arrangement(s); preparations; 〈警察の〉 (a) search ¶手配する arrange [prepare] (for); make arrangements [preparations] ((for)); take (the necessary) steps ((for, to *do*)); 〈警察が〉 begin [((文))] institute] a search ((for)); cast a dragnet ((for)) / 手配師 a recruiter of day laborers / 〈警察の〉手配書 search instructions. 文例⇩

てはいり 出入り ⇨ でいり ¶出入りする go in and out; 〈しばしば〉 be a regular visitor ((to)); ((文)) frequent ((a house)).

てばこ 手箱 a box; a case; a casket (宝石などを入れる).

てはじめ 手始め ¶手始めに at the beginning [((文)) outset]; to begin [start] with; ((口語)) for [as] a starter; ((英口語)) for starters ¶手始めに…をする begin [((文)) commence, start] with [by] *doing*. 文例⇩

ではじめ 出始め 梨(½)の出始め early pears; pears just in.

ではじめる 出始める begin to appear; 〈市場に〉 begin to come in.

てはず 手筈 〈計画〉 a program; a plan; 〈手配〉 ⇨ てはい ¶手はずを整える make [map out] a plan ((for, of)); lay out [draw up] a schedule; ((文)) formulate a program; make (the) arrangements ((for)) / 手はずどおりに as scheduled [prearranged]; according to schedule / 手はずが狂わなければ if the plan does not miscarry [fall through]; if things go according to plan. 文例⇩

ではずれ 出外れ the end [edge] ((of a village)).

てばた 手旗 a semaphore flag ¶手旗信号 flag semaphore [signaling] / 手旗信号を送る signal [semaphore] with flags.

てばな 手鼻 ¶手鼻をかむ blow *one's* nose between *one's* fingers.

でばな 出鼻をくじく spoil [mess up] *sb's* start; dampen *sb's* early [first] enthusiasm ((for)).

てばなし 手放し ¶手放しの楽観 blind optimism / 手放しで without holding *sth* with *one's* hand; 〈露骨に〉 openly; broadly; freely; 〈抑制せずに〉 without check; 〈無批判に〉 uncritically; blindly / 手放しで自転車に乗る ride a bicycle with no hands / 手放しで息子の自慢をする brag freely [shamelessly] about *one's* own son.

てばなす 手放す 〈持った手を〉 ⇨ てl (手を放す); 〈仕事などを〉 leave [abandon] *one's* work; 〈持ち物などを〉 part with; dispose of; dispense with; spare; 〈子供などを〉 send away. 文例⇩

でばぼうちょう 出刃包丁 a kitchen knife.

てばやい 手早い quick; nimble; agile ¶手早く quickly; rapidly; promptly; ((文)) expeditiously; ((文)) with dispatch / 手早く片づける finish (off) ((one's work)) quickly; make short work of ((sb, sth)); dispatch ((one's work)) quickly.

てはらう 出払う be all out; have none [nothing] left. 文例⇩

でばん 出番 *one's* turn; *one's* time ((to go on stage)).

てびかえる 手控える ((文)) refrain ((from)); hold *one's* hand; do not go all out ((in *doing*)).

てびき 手引き 〈指導〉 ((文)) guidance; lead; 〈紹介〉 an introduction ((to)); 〈人〉 a guide; a coach; 〈案内書〉 a guide book; a guide ((to)); a handbook ((to, of)); a [an instruction] manual; a primer (入門書) ¶手びきをする guide; lead; coach; initiate ((sb into the world of ceramics)) (初心者を) / 手びきを受ける get advice ((from)); receive guidance ((from)) / …の手びきで ((文)) through the introduction [good offices] of…

デビスカップ ¶デビスカップ戦 the Davis Cup (tournament).

てひどい 手酷い severe; harsh; ((文)) scathing; ((文)) merciless; cruel ¶手ひどい打撃を受ける suffer a heavy blow; suffer [((文)) sustain] serious damage; be hard hit / 手ひどく severely; harshly; ((文)) scathingly; mercilessly; cruelly / 手ひどく扱う treat *sb* harshly [mercilessly]; be hard on *sb*.

デビュー a debut ¶デビューする make *one's* debut ((on the stage)); debut.

てびょうし 手拍子 ¶手拍子をとる beat time with *one's* hand(s); keep time ((to the music)) by clapping / 手拍子で悪手を指す make a bad move on the spur of the moment.

てびろい 手広い 〈家など〉 roomy; ((文)) spacious; ((文)) commodious; 〈仕事など〉 ((文)) extensive; wide; large ¶手広く ((文)) extensively; widely; on a large scale / 手広く商売をする do business in a big way.

でぶ a fat [((文)) an obese] person ¶でぶでぶの

話いたします。Well, (then,) I'll call again tomorrow.

-てば 歌では彼はだれにも負けない。When it comes to singing there isn't anyone who can beat him. / あの容態では明日まで持つまい。Judging from his present condition, he may not last the night. / 私の知る限りでは彼は外国へ行ったことはない。He has never been abroad, so far as I know.

てはい すぐに手配したけれども、彼の居所はわからなかった。A search was started at once, but he could not be found anywhere [he was nowhere to be found]. / 逮捕の手配は出来上がっている。Arrangements have been made for his arrest.

てはじめ 手始めにこの本から読みましょう。We'll begin with this book.

てはず このお険ですっかり手はずが狂ってしまった。This upset our plans completely.

てばなす その家は2千万円で手放された。The house went for twenty million yen. / この辞書は手放せない。I cannot do [I'd be lost] without this dictionary. / もうあの子は手放しても大丈夫だ。The child is old enough to look after himself. / 今のところ彼を手放すわけにはゆかない。I cannot spare him just now.

ではらう みんな出払って事務所はがらんとしていた。The office was

デフォルメ fat; obese.

デフォルメ [<《フランス語》*déformer*] deformation ¶デフォルメする deform.

てふき 手拭き 〈手ぬぐい〉a towel; 〈ハンカチ〉a (pocket) handkerchief; 〈ナプキン〉a (table) napkin; a serviette.

てぶくろ 手袋 (a pair of) gloves; 〈男性用の長手袋〉gauntlets; 〈親指だけが分かれているもの, 又は手の甲と手の平を覆うだけで指のないもの〉mittens ¶ゴム手袋 rubber gloves / 手袋をはめる put [pull] (*one's*) gloves on; wear gloves / 手袋をとる take [pull] *one's* gloves off.

でぶしょう 出不精 stay-at-home ¶出不精の人 a stay-at-home.

てぶそく 手不足 (a) shortage of staff [manpower] ¶手不足である be shorthanded; be short of staff; be undermanned.

てふだ 手札 〈トランプの〉a hand ¶手札を引く draw a hand / 手札を捨てる discard / 引きやすいように手札をそろえる arrange *one's* hand / 手札型写真 a card-size photograph.

でふね 出船 an outgoing vessel ¶出船入船 ships entering and leaving port.

てぶら 手ぶら ¶手ぶらで empty-handed; with *one's* hands empty; without taking a present (with *one*). 文例⇩

てぶり 手振り a gesture of *one's* hand; a hand movement [gesture]; 《文》a manual gesture ⇒てつき, てまね ¶手振りおもしろく踊る dance with expressive hand movements.

デフレ(ーション) deflation ¶デフレ政策 a deflationary policy.

テフロン 〔商標名〕Teflon ¶テフロン加工の Teflon-lined.

でべそ 出べそ (a) protruding navel.

テヘラン Tehran; Teheran.

てべんとう 手弁当 ¶手弁当で働く work (for *sb*) without pay.

てほどき 手ほどき 《文》initiation; introduction; 〈初歩〉the first step (in); 《文》the rudiments [elements] (of); the A.B.C. (of) ¶手ほどきをする initiate *sb* into 《the mysteries of an art》; give *sb* elementary lessons 《in flower arrangement》/ 手ほどきを受ける learn the basics [first principles, rudiments] (of dressmaking) from [under] *sb*; take rudimentary lessons (in the piano) from *sb*. 文例⇩

てぼり¹ 手彫り ¶手彫りの hand-carved.

てぼり² 手掘り ¶手掘りのトンネル a hand-cut[-dug] tunnel.

てほん 手本 〈習字の〉a copy; a copybook (本); 〈ひな形〉a model; a copy; 〈規範〉a model; an example ¶手本のとおりに書く copy out writing from a copybook / よい手本を示す set a good example (to) / 手本にする model 《it》on [after, according to] *sth*; model *oneself* on *sb*; copy *sth*; follow *sb's* example; take *sth* as a model; learn (from); imitate / 手本になる行ない《文》exemplary conduct. 文例⇩

デボンき デボン紀 『地質』the Devonian period.

てま 手間 〈時間〉time; 〈労力〉labor; trouble ¶手間が省ける save *one* trouble / 手間仕事 〈手間のかかる仕事〉a time-consuming job; 〈手間賃を取っての仕事〉piecework; a job / 手間賃 the charge [wages] for *one's* labor / 手間賃を払う pay *sb* for *his* labor [work]. 文例⇩

デマ [<《ドイツ語》*Demagogie*] a false [groundless] rumor [story] ¶デマを飛ばす circulate a false rumor.

てまえ 手前 this side ¶交番の100メートルほど手前 about 100 meters (on) this side of the police box / …の手前(があるから) out of regard (consideration, respect) for…; for the sake of… / 子供の手前 in front of [《文》in the presence of] the children; when *one* thinks of *one's* children / 世間の手前 for decency's [appearance's] sake. 文例⇩

でまえ 出前 ¶出前をする do outside catering; deliver [send out] dishes to order / 出前持ち a delivery man.

てまえがって 手前勝手 ¶手前勝手な selfish; self-seeking; 《文》egoistic; 《文》egotistic / 手前勝手なことをする act selfishly; have *one's* own way (in) ⇒かって².

てまえども 手前共 we ¶手前共の our / 手前共を[に] us.

てまえみそ 手前味噌 ¶手前味噌を言う [並べる] sing *one's* own praises; blow *one's* own trumpet [《米》horn].

でまかせ 出任せ ¶出まかせを言う say the first thing that comes into *one's* head; make irresponsible remarks / 出まかせの返答をする answer without thinking.

てまき 手巻き ¶手巻きの hand-rolled (cigarettes).

てまくら 手枕 ¶手枕をする pillow [rest] *one's* head on *one's* arm.

でまど 出窓 a bay [bow] window.

てまどる 手間取る take time; be a long time 《(in) coming》; be delayed; be 《not》 kept

---

empty, with all the staff gone out. / この手の品は出払いました。We are right out of [We have completely sold out] this line.

でばん そこで君の出番だ。That is where you come in.

てぶら 初めて訪ねるのに手ぶらでも行かれない。This is my first visit to him. I think I must take a present (of some sort).

てほどき 私はあの人からラテン語の手ほどきを受けました。I took lessons in elementary Latin from him.

てほん あの人がいいお手本だ。He is a good example for you. / 彼は役者のお手本だ。He is the embodiment of what an actor ought to be. / He is everything that you would expect of an actor. / この制度は現在アメリカで行なわれているものを手本としたものだ。The system is modeled on the one now in use in America.

てま お手間は取らせません。I will not keep you long. / 大工の手間は1日2万円です。We pay our carpenter 20,000 yen a day. / この仕事は大分手間がかかる。This work takes [requires] a great deal of time.

てまえ レバーを手前に引け。Pull the lever forward [toward you]. / その家は警察の先ですか手前ですか。Is the house on the far side of the police station or this side of it? / その崖のずっと手前で車を止めた。We stopped our car well short of the cliff.

てまね 手真似 a gesture;《文》(a) gesticulation; signs ¶手まねをする make signs; gesture; make a gesture; gesticulate / 手まねで話す speak by signs [gesture]; talk in sign language ⇒ しゅわ / 手まねで座れと言う motion sb to sit down.

てまねき 手招き ¶手招きする beckon 《to》/ 手招きして呼び入れる beckon sb into 《the room》.

てまめ 手まめ ⇒ まめ³ (まめな).

てまわし 手回し preparations; arrangements ¶手回しがいい be fully prepared 《for sth》《beforehand》/ 手回しの 《a coffee-mill》 worked by hand. 文例⇩

でまわり 出回り arrivals on the market; movement 《of commodities》; supply 《of goods》.

てまわりひん 手回り品 《所持品》《文》personal effects; one's things [belongings] / 《手荷物》 baggage; luggage.

でまわる 出回る arrive [appear] on the market; 《果物・野菜・魚などが》 be in season.

てみじか 手短 ¶手短な brief; short / 手短に shortly; briefly;《文》in brief [short] / 手短に言えば《文》in brief [short]; to put it briefly; to cut [make] a long story short.

でみせ 出店 a branch 《store》 ¶出店を出す start [open] a branch 《store》《at, in》.

デミタス a demitasse.

てみやげ 手土産 a present ¶手土産を持って訪問する call on sb with a present.

てむかい 手向かい resistance; opposition ¶手向かいする resist; oppose; rise [stand] against; turn on.

てむかう 手向かう ⇒ てむかい.

でむかえ 出迎え meeting;《文》reception 《要人などの》 ¶駅へ出迎えに行く go to the station to meet sb / 《要人などの》出迎えの列車 《diplomatic》 receiving [reception] line. 文例⇩

でむかえる 出迎える go [come] (out) and [to] meet;《文》receive; meet. 文例⇩

でむく 出向く go [proceed] to.

テムズ(がわ) テムズ(川) the (River) Thames.

でめ 出目 bulging [protruding] eyes ¶出目の popeyed / 出目金 a telescope goldfish.

-ても but; however; though; (even) if ¶どれほど金があっても however [no matter how] rich one may be / 雨が降っても even if it rains.

でも ⇒ しかし. 文例⇩

デモ a demonstration ¶デモをやる demonstrate 《against raising the railroad fares》; hold [stage] a demonstration / デモを解散させる disperse a demonstration / デモ行進 a demonstration march [parade] / デモ隊 demonstrators.

-でも 〈…ですら〉 even; 〈…もまた〉 also; as well;〈たとえ…でも〉though; (even) if ¶雨天でも even if it rains [should rain] / うそでもほんとうでも whether it's true or not;《文》whether or not it be true / どんな難事でも however hard the task may be. 文例⇩

デモクラシー democracy ⇒ みんしゅ (民主主義).

てもち 手持ち ¶手持ち外貨《Japan's》foreign currency holdings [reserve(s)] / 手持ち資材 materials on hand / 手持ち品 holdings; reserve supplies; goods in stock [store]; stock.

てもちぶさた 手持ちぶさた ¶手持ちぶさたである have nothing to do; be bored. 文例⇩

てもと 手元 ¶手もとに 《in [on] hand; with one》;〈手ぢかに〉at [to] hand;〈家に〉at home;〈監督下に〉under one's care / 手もとにある金 the money [cash] one has with one / 手もとにあるものを何でも武器として使う use as a weapon whatever lies ready to hand / 手もとに置く keep sth handy [at hand] / 手もとが狂う miss one's aim [the mark]. 文例⇩

でもどり 出戻り a divorced woman (back at her parents' home).

でもの 出物 《売物》an article on sale;《古物》a secondhand [used] article.

デモンストレーション 〈実演・街頭デモ〉demonstration;〈自己宣伝〉showing off; parading ★「自己宣伝」の意味では demonstration と言わない.

デュエット《音楽》a duet.

でよう 出様 ⇒ でかた.

てら 寺 a Buddhist temple ¶寺男 a sexton / 寺参りする visit a temple.

てまどる 途中でひどく手間取ってしまった. I was badly held up [seriously delayed] on the way. / どうして手間取っているんだろう. I wonder what is keeping him so long.

てまわし ずいぶん手回しがいいね. You are awfully thorough in your preparations, aren't you!

でむかえ 弟が駅まで出迎えに来てくれるはずになっていた. My brother was supposed to [was to] meet me at the station.

でむかえる 主人が親しく玄関まで出迎えた. The master of the house came out in person to greet me at the door.

-ても あってもなくても同じ事だ. It doesn't matter [It makes no difference] whether I have it or not. / あんなに努力しても結果は思わしくなかった. For all his efforts, he could not get the results he wanted.

でも でも私に話してくれればよかったのに. I wish you had told me, though. / でもこのあたりの眺めは悪くない. For all that, the view from around here is not bad.

-でも 深い所でも1メートルほどしかない. The water measures no more than a meter at the deepest part. / 人はいくら金持ちでも遊んでいてはならない. No matter how rich a man may be, he must not live in idleness. / それをやるのは明日でもいい. You can do it tomorrow just as well. / 私はこれでもクリスチャンだ. I am a Christian, such as I am. / どんな紙でもよろしい. Any paper will do. / 日曜にでも行きましょう. Let's go there, on Sunday, say. / 空気は元素でも化合物でもない. Air is neither an element nor a compound.

てもちぶさた 編み物のお陰で手持ちぶさたにならずにすみました. Knitting helped me pass away my otherwise tedious hours. / タバコをやめてから人と話をする時何となく手持ちぶさただ. I feel

てらい 衒い 《文》(an) affectation; 《文》pretension(s) ¶何のてらいもなく quite unpretentiously.

てらう 衒う 〈誇示する〉show off; make a show [display] of; 〈装う〉pretend; 《文》affect ¶学問をてらう make a display [a parade, 《文》an affectation] of *one*'s learning / てらうことなく unaffectedly.

デラウェア Delaware (略: Del.) ¶デラウェア州の人 a Delawarean.

テラコッタ terra cotta ¶テラコッタの terracotta (figurines).

てらこや 寺子屋 a 'temple school'; a private elementary school (in the Edo period).

てらしあわせる 照らし合わせる ⇒ しょうごう (照合する).

てらす 照らす 〈光などが〉shine (on); throw [《文》shed] light (on, over); light (up); 《文》illumine; illuminate; 〈比較する〉compare (with); 〈照合する〉check (with); 《文》collate (with); refer (to) ¶…に照らして〈比較する〉in comparison with…; when [as] compared with…; 〈したがって〉according to (the regulations); 〈参照して〉《文》in (the) light of (these facts); in view of ((the gravity of the situation)) / 論理的に構成した理論を客観的事実に照らして見る subject a logically constructed theory to the light of objective facts.

テラス a terrace.

てらせん 寺銭 the rent of a gambling house; the house cut.

デラックス ¶デラックスな deluxe.

てらてら ¶てらてらした (a face) with a greasy luster; shiny; glossy; 《文》lustrous.

テラマイシン 《薬》《商標名》Terramycin.

てり 照り sunshine; 〈ひでり〉dry weather; a drought; 〈光沢〉gloss; luster ★ gloss と luster は を つけることはできるが, 複数形では用いない.

てりかえし 照り返し 〈反射〉reflection; 〈反射熱[光]〉reflected heat [light] ¶照り返しで暑い be very warm because of the reflected heat of the sun.

てりかえす 照り返す reflect; throw back light.

てりかがやく 照り輝く shine brilliantly.

デリカシー delicacy; sensitivity; tact ¶デリカシーに欠ける be insensitive; be tactless.

デリケート ¶デリケートな delicate; subtle.

てりつける 照り付ける shine [blaze, beat] (down) on ¶じりじりと照りつける太陽 ((under)) a burning [scorching] sun. 文例↓

テリヤ 〈犬〉a terrier.

てりやき 照り焼き fish broiled with soy sauce.

てりゅうだん 手榴弾 a hand grenade.

てりょうり 手料理 a homemade dish ¶妻の手料理 food prepared by *one*'s wife.

てる 照る shine; blaze (日が激しく); 〈晴天である〉be fine ¶照る月 a bright moon / 照っても降っても rain or shine; in all weathers ⇒ てんき¹ ★.

でる 出る 〈外へ出る〉go [come] out; find *one*'s way out (of the cave); 〈出席する〉be present (at); attend (a meeting); 〈参加する〉join; take part in (a quiz show); enter [go in for] (a beauty contest); 〈現われる〉come out [《文》forth]; appear; 〈昇る〉rise; 〈露(露)われる〉show *itself*; 《文》be revealed; 〈見つかる〉be found; 〈膳・料理などが〉be brought; be served; 〈出版される〉be published; be out; 〈産出される〉be found; be produced; 〈出発する〉start; leave; 〈由来する〉come (from); 《文》originate (in, from); 《文》be derived ((from)); 〈船が〉set sail; sail (for); 〈風が〉rise; get up; 〈川などが〉《文》arise; come (from); 〈突き出る〉jut out; 〈茶が〉draw (well); 《文》infuse (properly); 〈超える〉be more than; 《文》exceed ((\$200)) ¶庭へは出る go out into the garden / 部屋から出る go out of a room / 大学を出る graduate from (a) university / 大学を出たばかりの (young men) fresh from college ⇒ そつぎょう / そっと出て行く go away stealthily; 《口語》make *oneself* scarce / 役所[会社]へ出る go [come] to the office; go to work / 出ている be out / 市役所に出ている work in the Municipal Office / 舞台に出ている be on the stage / 出ると負けだ be a constant loser; lose every game / 出たとご勝負で行く leave ((a matter)) to chance; take *one*'s chance. 文例↓

デルタ a delta ¶ナイル川のデルタ the Nile

---

somewhat ill at ease talking with people, now that I've given up smoking.

てもと あの本は今手もとにありません. I haven't got the book by me now.

でもの 出物はれ物ところ嫌わず. Necessity [Need] has [knows] no law. 《諺》

てらす 月が家々の屋根を青白く照らしていた. The moon cast a pale light on the roofs of the houses. / 街はネオンの光で明るく照らされていた. The street was brightly lit by the light of the neon signs.

てりつける 日が彼女の顔にまともに照りつけていた. The sun was beating full into [directly on to] her face.

でる 出て行け! Get out! | Go away! | Clear off! / 私はいつも7時半に家を出て7時42分の列車に乗る. As a rule I leave the house at half past seven and take the 7:42 train. / 彼は6週間も部屋から出なかった. He kept to his room for as long [many] as six weeks. / 部屋から半分ほどかかって立ち止まった. He stopped halfin, half-out of the room. / 間もなく湖へ出た. Soon I came to a lake. / 昨日は人がずいぶん出た. There was an enormous turnout of people yesterday. / 昨日は学校へ出なかった. I did not attend [go to] school yesterday. / 彼はある新聞社に出ています. He is on the staff of a certain newspaper. / 出るところへ出て話をつけよう. Let's have it settled before the proper authorities. / 性格が外見に出ることはよくある. Character often shows through. / 盗まれた本はついに出なかった. The stolen book never turned up. / (テレビの)つまみを引けば画が出る. You pull (out) the knob and the picture comes on. / やがて料理が出た. Presently dinner was served. / (ディナーで)魚の次にステーキが出た. The fish was followed by a beefsteak. / さいころを振ったら4が出た. I

Delta / デルタ地帯 a delta area / (飛行機の)デルタ翼 a delta wing.
てるてるぼうず 照る照る坊主 a paper doll to which Japanese children pray for fine weather.
テルビウム 〖化〗terbium.
テルル 〖化〗tellurium.
てれかくし 照れ隠し ¶照れ隠しに to cover *one's* confusion; to hide 《文》conceal *one's* embarrassment.
てれくさい 照れ臭い be embarrassed;《文》feel abashed ¶照れ臭さそうに self-consciously. 文例⇩
テレタイプ a teleprinter;《米》a teletype-writer;〖商標名〗a Teletype ¶テレタイプで送信する teletype; send 《a message》 by tele-printer 《via teletypewriter》.
テレックス 〈システム〉telex;〈通信文〉a telex.
でれでれ ¶でれでれする〈だらしない〉be slovenly; behave lackadaisically /〈女に〉be moonstruck; behave like a moonstruck calf;《英口語》be sloppy 《on a girl》.
テレパシー 《communicate by》telepathy ¶テレパシーを行なう人 a telepathist.
テレビ(ジョン) television (略:TV);《英口語》(the) telly;《米俗》a boob tube;《英口語》the box;〈受像機〉a television [TV] set ¶テレビの取材班 a television crew / テレビをつける [切る] turn the television on [off] / テレビを見る watch [look at] television / テレビを長時間見る人 a heavy TV watcher / テレビに出演する appear [be, go] on television / テレビで見る watch 《a baseball game》 on television / テレビで放送する televise / カラー [教育, 工業用, 閉回路] テレビ color [educational, industrial, closed-circuit] television / テレビ映画 [カメラ] a television [TV] film [camera] / テレビ局 a television [TV] station / テレビ視聴者 a (television) viewer;〈集合的に〉the TV audience / テレビ電話 a TV phone; a video-phone; a videotelephone / テレビ塔 a television [TV] tower / テレビドラマ a television drama [play]; a teledrama / テレビニュース television [TV] news / テレビ放送 a television [TV] broadcast; a telecast. 文例⇩

テレピンゆ テレピン油 turpentine;《口語》turps.
テレメーター a telemeter ¶テレメーターで伝える telemeter 《the data》 / テレメーター法 telemetry.
てれる 照れる be [feel] shy [awkward, embarrassed,《文》abashed]; get [《文》become] self-conscious ¶照れ屋だ be shy; be a very shy person. 文例⇩
てれんてくだ 手練手管 techniques 《of winning an election》;《文》wiles 《of a coquette》.
テロップ 〖テレビ〗a telop.
テロリスト a terrorist.
テロ(リズム) terrorism ¶テロ行為 terrorism; a terrorist act / テロ集団 a terror group / テロ戦術 terrorist tactics / テロ組織 a terrorist organization.
てわけ 手分け ¶手分けする〈分業する〉divide 《the work among us》 / 手分けして捜す split up [go out in several parties] to search for *sb* [*sth*].
てわたし 手渡し ¶手渡しする ⇨てわたす.
てわたす 手渡す deliver *sth* personally [in person]; hand *sth* (over) to *sb*. 文例⇩
てん¹ 天 〈空〉the sky;《文》the heavens;〈天国〉Heaven; paradise;《文》Providence;《文》Heaven's [divine] will;〈神〉God ¶天の heavenly / 天の底が抜けたかと思えるような大雨《文》a cataclysmic rainstorm / 天に向かって《文》heavenward; skyward / 天にも昇る心地がする be in (the) seventh heaven / 天を仰ぐ gaze up [raise *one's* face] to the sky; turn *one's* face skyward / 天を摩する sky-scraping 《buildings》;《文》cloud-[heaven-]kissing 《peaks》 / 天から降ってくる fall from the sky; drop out of the clouds / 天と地の出会う所に《文》where earth meets sky / 天から授かった heaven-sent; divine 《inspiration》 /〈生まれついた〉《文》innate;《文》inborn; natural / 天まで届く reach the sky [heavens]. 文例⇩
てん² 点 a point; a dot;〈斑点〉a spot; a speck; a speckle;〈成績〉a mark;《米》a grade;〈競技の〉a point; a score 《of 5 to 3》;〈品物〉a piece; an item;〈事〉a respect;

threw a dice, and a four came [turned] up. / I threw a four. / それは新聞に出ています。It is in the papers. / この単語は僕の辞書に出ていない。This word is not given [listed] in my dictionary. / 試験の発表を見に行ったら僕の番号も出ていた。I went to see the announcement of the examination results and found that my number was up. / 彼の新著は来月出ます。His new work will be [come] out next month. / 古い本だがまだ出ている。It is an old book but it is still in print. / 近所にコレラ患者が出た。A case of cholera has occurred in our neighborhood. / (電話に)僕が出

るよ。I'll take [get] it. / お出になりました。〈電話交換手の言葉〉Your party is on the line. / この県からは偉い人がたくさん出た。This prefecture has produced a large number of great men. / この報道は信ずべき筋から出ている。This report comes from a reliable source. / 平家は桓武天皇から出た。The Taira family was descended from the Emperor Kammu. / 茶が出すぎた。The tea is stewed. / 費用は5千円を出ては困る。The expenses must not exceed 5,000 yen. / 彼女は30を1つ2つ出ていた。She was a year or two on the wrong [other] side of thirty. / 出るくいは打たれる。

The stake that sticks out gets hammered in. | The best policy is [It is always safest] to keep your head down.
てれくさい 人前でスピーチをするのは照れ臭い。It's embarrassing to make a speech in public.
テレックス 今, ニューヨークからテレックスが入った。A telex has just arrived from New York.
テレビ 昨日テレビで君のお父さんを見たよ。I saw your father on television yesterday.
てれる 「彼と僕とは同窓でしてね」と彼は少々照れながらこう言った。'He and I were at the same school,' said he a little self-consciously. / 彼女はひどく照れ

てん a way;〈見地〉a standpoint; a point of view ¶〈文中の省略を示す〉点々々 (...) the points of suspension／英文では3つ (three dots) 打つのが普通／点が良い[悪い] have good [bad] marks [grades]《for English》; get [《文》obtain] high [low] marks (in algebra)／点が甘い[辛い] be generous [severe] in marking [giving marks]／点をつける give marks (to);《米》grade;《米》rate／〈競技で〉5点入れる score five points／シングルヒット4本で2点あげる earn [score] two runs on four singles／その点において in that respect [regard]; on that point; for that matter／その他の点では《文》in other respects;《文》otherwise／…の点では as regards...;《文》in point [respect] of...; in terms of...;《文》so far as...is [are] concerned／ある点では in some ways／どの点まで how far;《文》to what extent／すべての点で《文》in all respects;《文》in every respect; on all counts／商業上の点から見て from a commercial point of view [viewpoint]; in commercial terms／この点から言うと from this standpoint [angle]／衣類数点 several pieces [items] of clothing／家具2点 two articles [pieces] of furniture. 文例⇩

囲碁 100点満点の試験の成績が75点だったとすると 75 marks (out of 100) とか 75 per cent と言う。また, mark を点数の単位としてではなく, 1回のテストの「成績」の意味で a mark of 75 とも言うので, 「きのうはフランス語でいい点を取った」は I got good marks for [in] French yesterday. とも I got a good mark.... とも言える。《米》では, mark の代わりに grade も使われるが, grade は a grade of 75 という言い方しかできない。mark には good, poor, fair, bad, high, low などの形容詞のいずれをつけてもよいが, grade には high, low をつけることはあまりない。「優」「良」「可」で示す成績は an A grade [mark] または a grade [mark] of A の形で言う。スポーツ・競技では, フットボール・テニスのように客観的な基準によるものは point(s), スケート・体操などのように審査員の主観的評価によるものは mark(s) と言うが, ボクシングの判定だけは point(s) を使う。

てん[3]〈動〉a marten; a sable (黒); an ermine (白).

でん 伝〈伝記〉a life; a biography ¶いつもの伝で as usual; as often happens;《文》as is often the case; as is sb's way;《文》as sb is wont to do／ナポレオン伝 a life of Napoleon／伝宗達《a painting》attributed to Sotatsu.

でんあつ 電圧 (a) voltage ¶100 ボルトの電圧〈have〉a voltage of 100／高い[低い]電圧 high [low] voltage／電圧が高い[低い] be high [low] in voltage／電圧を上げる[下げる] increase [drop] the voltage／電圧計 a voltmeter.

てんい 転移 (a) change;《文》transference;〈病巣の〉spread〈of a disease〉from its original site to another part of the body;〈医〉metastasis (pl. -tases); implantation ¶転移する metastasize; spread by metastasis.

でんい 電位 (an) electrical potential ★複数にはしない, また an の代りに one を用いることもしない ¶電位差 a potential difference (略: p.d.); a difference of (electric) potential.

てんいむほう 天衣無縫 ¶天衣無縫である〈詩歌などが〉《文》be flawlessly composed, with no labored expressions;〈人が〉be quite free and easy.

てんいん 店員《米》a (store) clerk;《米》a salesclerk; a salesperson; a salesman; a saleswoman (女);《英》a shop assistant;《英》a shopgirl (女).

でんえん 田園 the country; the rural districts ¶田園の《文》rural;《文》pastoral／田園生活をする lead a rural life; live in the country／田園都市 a garden city.

てんおうせい 天王星〈天〉Uranus.

てんか[1] **天下** 〈一国〉the whole country; the State;〈世界〉the world; the earth;〈世間〉the public;〈政権〉《文》the reins of government ¶天下を取る〈征服する〉conquer [take control of] the (whole) country;〈君臨する〉rule over the whole land;〈政権を握る〉come into power;《文》take [hold] the reins of government;《文》assume [take] the helm of the ship of state／天下に under the sun; in the world; on earth／天下一品の〈比類ない〉《文》peerless;《文》unrivaled;《文》unequaled;《文》unparalleled;〈卓絶した〉《文》unsurpassed; superb; supreme;〈独特の〉unique／天下分け目の戦い a decisive battle. 文例⇩

て両手で顔を覆った。She covered her face with her hands in great embarrassment.

てわたす この手紙を彼に手渡して下さい。Please hand him this letter yourself.

てん[1] 天から降ったか地から湧いたか忽然として1人の老人が現われた。There suddenly appeared an old man as if he had dropped out of the clouds.／天は自ら助くるものを助く。Heaven helps those who help themselves.／意気正に天を突くの概があった。His spirits soared to heaven [the skies].

てん[2] 空には一点の雲もなかった。There was not a speck of cloud in the sky.／彼はそこに住みたくないわけを一点一点あげて説明した。He explained, point by point, why he hated living there.／しかし, 1つの点ではみんな似ている。But they are all alike in one way.／そこが困難な点です。That is where the difficulty lies.／能力の点では両者は比較にならない。In ability [Where ability is concerned] there is no comparison between the two.／その点はご安心下さい。You needn't have any anxiety on that score.／物理の点は良だった。I got [was given] a B (grade) in physics.／彼女はフランス語で最高点をとった。She received the highest [best] marks in French.

てんか[1] ここは私1人の天下だ。Here I am absolutely my own boss [master].／今は自民党の天下だ。The Liberal Democrats are now in power.／天下は彼の手に帰した。The whole country came under his rule.／これは天下一品だ。There is nothing like this in the whole world.／天下泰平だ。Peace reigns in the land.／そんなことを言っていられるのは天下泰平の証拠だ。That you can say that sort of thing is proof [proves] that you have nothing serious to worry about.／関が原の戦は天下分け目の戦であった。The battle of Sekigahara was one

てんか² 点火 ignition ¶点火する《文》ignite; light (up); fire (up); kindle / 点火しやすい easy to ignite; easily ignited / 点火装置 an ignition system; a firing mechanism; 〈エンジンの〉the ignition / (内燃機関の)点火プラグ《口語》a plug; a spark plug;《英》a sparking plug.

てんか³ 転化〈変化〉(a) change;《文》(a) transformation ¶転化する change;《文》be transformed.

てんか⁴ 添加 addition ¶食品添加物 an [a food] additive. 文例⇩

てんか⁵ 転科 ¶転科する be [get] enrolled in another [a different] course.

てんか⁶ 転訛 ⇨なまり¹ ¶転訛する be [get] corrupted (from, into) ⇨なまる¹.

てんか⁷ 転嫁 ¶転嫁する shift [shuffle off] (the responsibility for *sth*) onto *sb*; lay [throw] (the blame) on *sb*;《文》impute [ascribe] (the failure) to *sb*.

てんが 典雅 ¶典雅な refined; elegant; graceful.

でんか¹ 伝家 ¶伝家の宝刀 (be) one's last resort; (play) one's trump card.

でんか² 殿下 His [Her, Your] Highness ¶三笠宮殿下 His Highness Prince Mikasa / 高松宮同妃両殿下 Their Highnesses Prince and Princess Takamatsu / 英国皇太子殿下 His Royal Highness the Prince of Wales ★ His [Her] Highness, Their Highnesses は第三人称, Your Highness は第二人称, ただしこれに伴う動詞はみな第三人称.

でんか³ 電化 electrification ¶電化する electrify (a railroad); install electrical appliances 《in *one*'s house》.

でんか⁴ 電荷 (an) electrical charge ¶正[負]の電荷を有する carry a positive [negative] charge / 正[負]の電荷を帯びる become positively [negatively] charged.

てんかい¹ 展開 development; unfolding;〈軍隊の〉deployment ¶展開する〈進展する〉develop; unfold;《文》evolve; roll out;〈拡大する〉spread [open] (out);〈軍隊が〉deploy; fan out;〈数〉expand; multiply out (掛け合わせて) / 新局面を展開する take a new turn. 文例⇩

てんかい² 転回 revolution; rotation;〈転向〉《文》a volte-face;〈転倒〉《文》inversion ¶転回する revolve; turn / 急転回する take a sudden turn 《from, to》 / 180度の転回をする make a complete volte-face [reversal of *one*'s position]; turn (the other way) around.

てんがい 天蓋 a canopy.

でんかい 電解《化》electrolysis ¶電解する electrolyze / 電解質 an electrolyte.

でんがく 田楽 bean curd baked and coated with *miso* ¶田楽刺しにする pierce through.

てんかふん 天花粉 talcum powder.

てんから 天から ⇨てんで.

てんかん¹ 転換 (a) conversion; a changeover; (a) switchover;〈注意の〉diversion ¶転換する a convert; change; switch (from...to...); turn; divert / 百八十度の転換をする do a complete about-face;《文》make a complete volte-face / 歴史的な転換をとげる go through a historic change / 転換期 a turning point;《文》a transition period [stage];《文》a period of transition.

てんかん² 癲癇《医》epilepsy ¶てんかんを起こす have an epileptic seizure [fit] / てんかん持ち an epileptic.

てんがん 点眼 ¶点眼する apply eyewash (to);《文》administer eye drops / 点眼器 an eyedropper.

てんがんきょう 天眼鏡 a (physiognomist's) magnifying glass.

てんき¹ 天気〈天候〉weather;〈晴天〉fine [fair] weather ¶いい天気 (in) good [《文》favorable] weather / 悪い天気 bad [nasty] weather / 定まらぬ[変わりやすい]天気 unsettled [changeable] weather / 天気がよければ if it is fine; weather permitting / 天気がよくても悪くても rain or shine; whatever the weather; in all weathers (★ in all weathers は未来については使えない. They marched in all weathers. あるいは Boy scouts go camping in all weathers. とは言えるが The match [garden party] will be held in all weathers. とは言えない) / 天気を見る look at the weather / こんな天気では in weather like this / 天気概況 the general weather; 〈概報〉《give》a meteorological summary / 天気図 a weather [meteorological] chart [map] / 天気相談所 a weather information bureau / 天気模様 the weather (conditions) / 天気予報 a weather forecast / 明日の天気予報 the weather forecast for tomorrow / 天気予報官 a weather forecaster / (テレビなどの)天気予報担当者 a weatherman.

てんき² 転記 ¶転記する《簿記》transfer (an entry to another account); post (an item from the daybook to a ledger).

てんき³ 転機 a turning point;《文》a point of change.

てんぎ 転義 a transferred [figurative] meaning.

でんき¹ 伝記 a life (story); a biography ¶伝記

---

which was to decide who would rule Japan [the country].

てんか⁴ いろいろな食品添加物が問題になった. Additives in foods became an issue.

てんかい¹ この事件は今後いかに展開するだろうか. What future developments will there be in this affair? / 事態がどう展開するか静観しよう. Let's wait and see how things shape up.

てんき¹ 天気がいい. It is fine (weather). | The weather is fine. / 今日は天気がいい. We have fine weather today. / 今日の天気はどうかね. How is the weather today? / 遠方の人に電話で今そちらはどんなお天気ですか. What kind of weather are you having right now? / 天気が崩れた. The fine weather has broken. / 天気は持ち直しそうです. The weather is likely to improve. | There are signs of the weather getting better. / この天気はもう1週間は続くでしょう. This weather would hold for another week. / 天気が定まった. The weather has settled. / 秋は天気が変わりやすい. The weather is changeable in autumn. / 明日は降るまい. From [Judging from] the look of the sky, it will

でんき / でんこう

でんき² 電気 electricity ¶電気の electric(al) / 電気のメーター an electric meter / 電気を起こす generate [make] electricity / 電気をつける[消す] switch [turn, put] the (electric) light on [off] / 電気かみそり an eletric razor ; a shaver ; 《英》a dry shaver / 電気機関車 an electric locomotive / 電気器具 an electrical appliance ; electrical apparatus (実験・工業用の) / 電気技師 an electrical engineer ; an electrician / 電気くらげ a Portuguese man-of-war / 電気系統 an electrical system / 電気工学 electrical engineering ; electrotechnology / 電気こんろ an electric heater / 電気座ぶとん a heating pad / 電気仕掛けの electrical (toys) ; (a device) worked [operated] by electricity / 電気刺激 electrical stimulation / 電気自動車 an electrically-powered car ; an electric car / 電気スタンド a desk lamp / 電気ストーブ an electric heater [radiator] / 電気製品の会社, 電気製品[appliances] firm / 電気洗濯機 a washing machine ; a washer / 電気掃除機 a vacuum cleaner / 電気掃除機で掃除する clean (the floor) with a vacuum cleaner; vacuum(-clean) ((the room)) ; 《英》hoover ((a room)) / 電気装置 an electrical device; electrical equipment / 電気時計 an electric clock / 電気のこぎり an electrically-powered [a power] saw / 電気分解 ⇨ でんきぶんかい / 電気メス《外科》a radio knife / 電気屋 an electrical (appliances) store / 電気料金 electricity charges; power rates / 電気冷蔵庫 《英口語》a fridge. 文例⇩

でんきしょうせつ 伝奇小説 a romance.

でんきゅう 電球 an electric [a light] bulb; an electric-light bulb ¶切れた電球 a burnt-out light bulb.

てんきゅうぎ 天球儀 a celestial [an astronomical] globe.

てんきょ¹ 典拠 an authority; a source ¶ちゃんとした典拠のある based on a sound [proper] authority; having a definite [proper] source / 典拠を挙げる give the authority ((for)) ; mention [quote] one's authority [authorities] ((for)) ; indicate the source ((of)). 文例⇩

てんきょ² 転居 a move; a change of address ¶転居する move ((to, into)); move house 《文》one's residence)) / 《文》change one's place of residence / 転居先 one's new address / 転居通知 a change of address notice [announcement]. 文例⇩

てんぎょう 転業 a job change ¶転業する change one's trade [《文》occupation]; change [switch] jobs.

でんきょく 電極 an electrode.

てんきん¹ 天金《製本》gilt tops [top edges] ¶天金の ((a book)) with top edges gilt (略: TEG).

てんきん² 転勤 ¶転勤する[になる] be transferred to ((the Nagoya branch)).

てんぐ 天狗 a long-nosed goblin [genie]; 〈自慢家〉a braggart; a boaster ¶天狗の[になった] (self-)conceited; vain / 天狗になる be puffed (up); get [《文》become] vain [conceited] ((about)); pride oneself ((on)).

てんぐさ《植》an agar weed; Gelidium amansii.

デングねつ デング熱 dengue.

でんぐりがえし でんぐり返し ¶でんぐり返しをする do a forward [backward] roll; turn a somersault.

でんぐりがえる でんぐり返る ⇨ ひっくりかえる.

てんけい¹ 天啓 a (divine) revelation ⇨ けいじ⁴.

てんけい² 典型 a type; a model; a pattern ¶典型的な typical; representative; model; ideal / 日本人の典型 a typical Japanese.

でんげき 電撃〈衝撃〉an electric shock;〈治療〉an electroshock ¶電撃作戦 blitz tactics / 電撃療法 electroshock therapy [treatment].

てんけん 点検 (an) inspection ¶点検する inspect; make an inspection of; examine; check / 人員を点検する call the roll; take a roll call ((of)).

でんげん 電源 a power source;〈水源〉a waterhead ¶電源を切る cut the power supply; shut off the power / 電源開発 development of power resources. 文例⇩

てんこ 点呼 a roll call ¶点呼する call the roll; make a roll call ((of)).

てんこう¹ 天候 ⇨ てんき¹. 文例⇩

てんこう² 転向 (a) conversion ¶転向する (a) turn [shift] ((to)); be converted ((to)); abandon 《communism》 / 百八十度の転向をする do a complete about-face; 《文》make a complete volte-face / 銀行員から教師に転向した人 a bank clerk turned schoolteacher.

てんこう³ 転校 ¶転校する change [transfer] to another school; change one's school / 転校生 a transfer student.

でんこう 電光 (a flash of) lightning ¶電光形

---

not rain tomorrow. / 天気予報では明日は晴れです。The weather forecast says it will be fine tomorrow.

でんき² この機械は家庭用の電気で動きます。This machine operates on domestic current [voltage]. / この針金には電気が通じている。This wire is live.

てんきょ¹ 古代ギリシャには, 市民が機械を使う職業に従事することを禁じた都市国家があったということを, 我々はソクラテスを典拠として知っている。We have it on the authority of Socrates that some city-states in ancient Greece forbade their citizens to engage in occupations using machinery.

てんきょ² このたび左記に転居いたしました。I have recently moved to the address given below.

てんけん つぶさに点検してみたら, びょうが1本ゆるんでいることがわかった。It was found, on close inspection, that a rivet was loose.

でんげん このシェーバーの電源は乾電池です。This shaver runs [operates] on batteries. / This shaver is powered by batteries.

てんこう¹ 当たり前の話だが, 宇宙

てんこく の zigzag / 電光ニュース an illuminated sign spelling out news items / 電光石火のごとく (as) quick as lightning; 《文》 with lightning speed [swiftness].

てんこく 篆刻 seal-engraving ¶篆刻する engrave a seal / 篆刻家 a seal-engraver.

てんごく 天国 Heaven; Paradise; 《文》 the Kingdom of Heaven [God]; 《文》 the Celestial City ¶天国の(ような) heavenly; 《文》 celestial; 《文》 paradisiac(al) / 天国に行く[行っている] go to [be in] Heaven / 地上の天国 《文》 an earthly [a terrestrial] paradise; a heaven on earth / 労働者の天国 a paradise for workers.

でんごん 伝言 a (verbal) message ¶伝言する give sb a message; leave a message for sb; send sb word 《that...》 / 伝言を依頼する leave a message with sb / 伝言をもたらす bring word; deliver a message (to) / よろしくと伝言する send one's regards (to) / 伝言板 a message board. 文例⇩

てんさ 点差 a gap; 〈勝っている側からみて〉 a lead.

てんさい¹ 天才 〈才能〉 genius (for); a natural gift [talent] (for); 〈人〉 a genius; 《文》 a man of genius ¶天才的〈人が〉 gifted; talented; 〈能力が〉 outstanding (ability); 〈知力が〉 prodigious (intelligence) / 天才教育 (the) education of gifted children / 天才児 an infant prodigy; a child genius / 天才ぶりを見せる show one's genius (as a pianist). 文例⇩

てんさい² 天災 a natural calamity [disaster]; an act of God (不可抗力) ¶天災に見舞われる be struck [《文》 visited] by a natural calamity. 文例⇩

てんさい³ 甜菜 《植》 a sugar beet ¶甜菜糖 beet sugar.

てんさい 転載 ¶転載する reproduce [reprint] (from).

てんざい 点在 ¶点在する 〈場所が主語〉 be dotted [studded, spattered, 《文》 interspersed] with 《cottages》 / 〈物が主語〉 be scattered [dotted] about 《the countryside》.

てんさく 添削 correction ¶添削する correct; touch up / 添削してもらう have (one's composition) corrected (by) / 通信添削 a service by mail which provides corrections and comments on students' answers given in a correspondence course / 添削料 a correction fee.

でんさんき 電算機 ⇨ コンピューター ¶小型電算機 a minicomputer.

てんさんぶつ 天産物 natural products.

てんし 天使 an angel; a cherub (pl. -ubim, -ubs) ¶天使のような angelic; an angel of a (lady) / 大天使 an archangel.

てんじ¹ 点字 Braille; braille ¶点字を読む read Braille / 点字本 a book in braille (type) / 点字印刷物 〈郵便の上書き〉 literature for the blind.

てんじ² 展示 exhibition; display ¶展示する exhibit; put 《文》 place》 sth on display [exhibit, show] / 展示される go [《文》 be placed] on (public) display / 展示している be on display [show] / 展示会 an exhibition; a (kimono) show / 展示場 an exhibition hall [room, area] / 展示即売会 an exhibition and sale (of paintings) / 展示品 an exhibit; exhibition (総称) / 展示用見本 a sample for display.

でんし 電子 an electron ¶電子の electronic / 電子音楽 electronic music / 電子計算機 ⇨ コンピューター / 電子顕微鏡 an electron microscope / 電子工学 electronics / 電子工学製品 electronic products [goods] / 電子工学製品の会社 an electronics firm / 電子装置 an electronic device [apparatus]; electronic equipment / 電子レンジ a microwave oven.

でんじ 電磁 《物》 ¶電磁気 electromagnetism / 電磁波 an electromagnetic wave; a radio wave / 電磁場 an electromagnetic field / 電磁誘導 electromagnetic induction.

でんじしゃく 電磁石 an electromagnet.

てんしゃ 転写 ¶転写する transcribe; copy.

でんしゃ 電車 〈連結の〉 an electric train (★ ただし, 汽車などの区別する必要のあるときは, 単に train と言えばよい ⇨ れっしゃ); 〈市街電車〉《米》 a streetcar; 《英》 a tram [tramcar] ¶電車の便がいい be convenient for (taking) the train / 電車の駅 a railroad station / 市街電車の停留場 a streetcar stop / 電車で行く go by train; take a train (to) / 電車に乗る get on a train / 〈交通手段として〉 take a train (to Shibuya) / 電車を降りる get off [leave] the train / 郊外電車 a suburban train / 電車賃 a (railroad) fare / 電車通り a street with a car track. 文例⇩

てんしゅ 店主 《米》 a storekeeper; 《英》 a shopkeeper; the proprietor [proprietress (女)] (of

---

船の内部には天候というものはない. Naturally, there's no weather inside a spaceship.

でんごん あす行くと伝言しておいた. I have sent him word that I am coming tomorrow. / 彼なら伝言を頼んでも大丈夫だ. He can be trusted with a message [to pass a message on]. / これをあなたに伝言してくれと頼まれました. Here's a message for you.

てんさい¹ 彼は音楽の天才だ. He has a genius [great talent] for music. / スチーブンソンは機械については生まれつき天才的才能があった. Stephenson had an innate genius with machines. / 彼は日本の生んだ最大の数学の天才である. He is the greatest mathematical genius that Japan has ever produced. / 彼はその少年に天才的なものを感じ取った. He sensed genius in the boy. / エジソンは天才とは「1%のインスピレーションと99%の汗」である と言った. Edison defined genius as '1% inspiration and 99% perspiration'.

てんさい² それは天災ではなくて人災だ. It was not a natural disaster but a man-made one. / 天災だからしかたがない. There is no help for it; it's an act of God.

てんさい⁴ 禁転載. 《版権表示》 All rights reserved.

でんしゃ ここから湯本まで電車がある. Trains run from here to Yumoto. | There is a train service between here and Yumoto. / その町まで電車で行ける. Trains are available as far as the town. / うちは郊外にあるが, 電車の便はいい. Though I live in the suburbs, there is a station not far

てんじゅ 天寿《文》one's natural term of existence;《文》one's natural span of life ¶天寿をまっとうする《文》live out the whole of one's allotted span of life; die a natural death / 天寿をまっとうせずして死ぬ die early;《文》die prematurely [before one's time].
でんじゅ 伝授 ¶伝授する《文》give instruction (in);《文》initiate sb into (the secrets of an art).
てんしゅかく 天守閣 a castle tower [keep]; a donjon.
てんしゅつ 転出 ¶転出する move out ((to Taito Ward))／転出届 a moving-out notification.
てんしょ 篆書 the seal-engraving style of writing Chinese characters.
てんじょう¹ 天上 ⇨てん¹ ¶天上の heavenly;《文》celestial.
てんじょう² 天井 the ceiling; the roof ((of a cave)); 〈物価などの〉the peak; the top [ceiling] (price) ¶天井の高い[低い]部屋 a high-[low-]ceilinged room／天井を張る hang [put up] a ceiling; provide [《文》furnish] a room with a ceiling／天井板 a ceiling board／天井画 a painting on the ceiling／天井さじき the upper gallery／(車・トンネルなどの)天井灯 a ceiling lamp [light]. 文例⇩
でんしょう 伝承〈伝説〉《文》(an) oral tradition; (a) word-of-mouth tradition;〈口碑〉folklore ⇨でんせつ ¶伝承する hand down orally; pass ((a story)) down (from generation to generation) by [through] oral tradition／伝承叙事詩 an oral epic／伝承文学 oral [traditional] literature.
てんじょういん 添乗員 a courier ((to a party of tourists)); a tour conductor [manager].
てんしょく 天職 a vocation;《文》a calling; a mission (in life) ¶自分の天職を見出だす find [discover] one's vocation. 文例⇩
てんしょく² 転職 ⇨てんきょう.
でんしょばと 伝書鳩 a carrier [homing] pigeon ¶伝書鳩を放つ fly [release] a carrier pigeon.
てんじる 転じる〈変える〉turn; shift; alter ¶心を転じる divert [distract] one's mind ((from))／目を転じる turn one's eyes ((to, from)). 文例⇩
てんしん¹ 転身 ¶転身する take up a new course of life; turn over a new leaf.
てんしん² 転進 ¶転進する change (one's) course; go in a different direction; turn ((northward)).
でんしん 電信〈電報〉a telegram; a wire;〈電信術〉telegraphy ¶電信を替 a telegraphic transfer [remittance]／電信係 a telegraph operator／電信機 a telegraph; a telegraphic instrument／電信局 a telegraph station [office]／電信柱 a telegraph pole. 文例⇩
てんじんひげ 天神ひげ a handlebar mustache.
てんしんらんまん 天真爛漫 ¶天真爛漫な naive;《文》artless; innocent; simple(-hearted); unsophisticated.
てんすい 天水 rainwater ¶天水桶 a rain barrel [tub]; a rainwater cistern.
てんすう 点数〈評点〉marks;〈成績〉〈米〉a grade;〈競技の〉a score; points; runs (野球の);〈品物の〉the number of articles ⇨てん² 囲碁 ¶点数をかせぐ〈比喩的に〉《文》ingratiate oneself ((with sb));《口語》earn Brownie points; curry favor ((with sb))／点数制 a point(s) system.
てんせい¹ 天性〈性質〉one's nature;《文》one's innate character;〈生来〉by nature; naturally ⇨うまれつき ★ ¶天性の natural; born;《文》innate.
てんせい² 展性 malleability ¶展性に富む malleable.
てんせき 転籍 ¶転籍する《文》transfer one's domicile ((from, to)).
でんせつ 伝説 a tradition; a legend;〈民間伝承〉folklore; a folk tale [story] ¶伝説的な traditional (chronicles);《文》legendary (events);《文》fabulous (heroes)／半[半]伝説的な semi-[half-]legendary (early emperors)／伝説によれば according to legend [tradition]／伝説で名高い be famous in legend;《文》((monsters)) of legend [fable]. 文例⇩
てんせん¹ 点線 (draw) a dotted line; a perforation (切り取り線).
てんせん² 転戦 ¶(競技の選手などが)各地を転戦する play (games) in one place after another [at various places].
でんせん¹ 伝染〈医〉infection (間接); contagion (接触) ¶伝染する〈人が主語〉be infected ((with)); catch;〈病気が主語〉infect／伝染力 virulence.

---

from my house.／電車で2時間の距離の所で. It is two hours away [from here] by train.
てんじょう² 天井に蛾が止まっている. There is a moth on the ceiling.／天井裏でねずみがあばれている. Rats are running about in the roof-space.／物価は天井知らずだ. Prices are sky-rocketing.／Prices are going sky-high [through the roof].
てんしょく¹ これが私の天職である. I have a vocation for this work.／I feel that God has called me to this work.

てんじる 彼は学界から身を転じてジャーナリストになった. He left the academic world and turned journalist [switched to journalism].
でんしん 電信が不通になった. Telegraphic communications are suspended.
てんせい¹ 最小の努力で最大の利益を得ようとするのは人の天性である. It is human nature to want to gain the greatest profit by the smallest effort.／習慣は第二の天性である. Habit is second nature.／彼は天性の詩人だった. He was a born poet.

でんせつ バイキングはコロンブスの約500年前にアメリカを発見したという伝説がある. Legend has it [says] that the Vikings discovered America some 500 years before Columbus.／これは伝説に過ぎないかもしれない. This may be only legend.／これらの物語の真相は伝説の霧に包まれている. The truth about these stories is shrouded in (the mists of) legend.
でんせん¹ 彼の病気は子供から伝染した. He caught [contracted] the disease from his child.

でんせん² 伝線 〈靴下の〉《米》a run;《英》a ladder ¶伝線しない靴下 runproof [ladderproof] stockings. 文例⇩
でんせん³ 電線 (an) electric(al) wire; an electric cord; a power line; a cable ¶電線を張る string [lay] electric wires. 文例⇩
でんせんびょう 伝染病 an infectious ¶a contagious (接触による)] disease; an infectious illness; an epidemic ¶伝染病患者 a case of infectious disease / 伝染病病院 an isolation hospital / 伝染病流行地 an infected area. 文例⇩
てんそう 転送 ¶転送する《文》transmit; send on;〈郵便物などを〉forward; send on [forward] / 転送先 a forwarding address.
でんそう 電送 electrical [wireless] transmission (of pictures) ¶電送する transmit〈a picture〉by telephotography / 電送写真 a telephotograph;《口語》a telephoto(pl. -s).
てんそく 纏足 bound [compressed] feet.
てんたい 天体 a heavenly [a celestial, an astronomical] body; a celestial [an astronomical] object ¶天体観測 an astronomical [a celestial] observation / 天体物理学 astrophysics / 天体望遠鏡 an astronomical telescope / 天体力学 celestial mechanics; dynamical astronomy.
てんたいしゃく 転貸借 subletting.
でんたく 電卓 a pocket [desk] calculator; a desk-top computer.
でんたつ 伝達 ¶《文》transmission;《文》communication;《文》notification ¶伝達する transmit;《文》communicate;《文》notify. 文例⇩
てんたん 恬淡 ¶恬淡な《文》disinterested; unselfish;《文》indifferent (to fame).
てんち¹ 天地 heaven and earth; 〈宇宙〉the universe; 〈自然〉nature; 〈場所〉a land; a world;《文》a realm; 〈上下〉top and bottom ¶自由の天地 a land of freedom / 天地の差がある be poles [worlds] apart (in opinion) / 天地の創造以来 since the beginning of creation; since the Creation.
てんち² 転地 ¶転地する go 《to the country》 for a change of air [climate]; take [get] a change of air (for one's health) / 転地療養 treatment by a change of air.
でんち¹ 田地 rice land (owned by sb).

でんち² 電池 a battery; a dry cell (乾電池) ¶(機械などが)電池で働く work on [by] batteries. 文例⇩
でんちゅう 電柱 a telegraph pole.
てんちょう¹ 天頂 the zenith.
てんちょう² 転調 【音楽】modulation; a change of key ¶転調する modulate; change (the) key.
てんで《not》at all; altogether; entirely ⇒まるで, まったく. 文例⇩
てんてき¹ 天敵 【生物】a natural enemy; a natural check (on rats).
てんてき² 点滴 falling drops of water; 【医】a [an intravenous] drip ¶点滴をする administer [give] an intravenous drip injection to sb; put sb on a 〈glucose〉 drip. 文例⇩
てんてこまい てんてこ舞い ¶てんてこ舞いである be tremendously busy (in) doing; be rushed off one's feet; never stop moving.
てんてつ 転轍 ¶転轍器《米》a (railroad) switch;《英》points / 転轍手《米》a switchman;《英》a pointsman.
でんてつ 電鉄 an electric railroad.
てんでに ⇨ めいめい².
てんてん¹ 点々 ¶点々と here and there; scattered / 点々として散在する 〈物が主語〉lie scattered (about); 〈場所が主語〉be dotted 《文》interspersed》(with). 文例⇩
てんてん² 転々 ¶転々する〈持ち主が変わる〉pass from hand to hand; change hands; 〈ころがる〉roll; go rolling; 〈さまよう〉wander [roam] about [from place to place] / 転々を変える often change one's job 《文》occupation).
でんでんこうしゃ 電電公社 the Nippon Telegraph and Telephone Public Corporation.
てんでんばらばら ¶てんでんばらばらな far from united; badly organized; uncoordinated. 文例⇩
テント a tent ¶テントの支柱 a tent pole / テントを張る pitch [put up] a tent; set up camp / テントをたたむ strike [pull down] a tent / テント生活をする camp (out).
でんと heavily;《文》imposingly;《文》in a dignified manner. 文例⇩
てんとう¹ 店頭《店》《米》a store;《英》a shop; 〈店先〉《米》a storefront;《英》a shop front ¶店頭に飾る[飾られている] display [be on

---

でんせん² 彼女の靴下は伝線している. There is a run in her stocking. / 伝線が大きくなった. The run went farther.
でんせん³ 台風が去ったあと, 数か所で電線が切れていた. When the typhoon had passed, electric cables were down in several places. / そのロケットエンジンには総計100キロメートルの電線が使われている. The rocket engine contains 100 kilometers of electrical wiring altogether.
でんせんびょう あの国では各地に種々の伝染病が流行している. All sorts of infectious diseases are prevalent in several parts of that country.
でんたつ その指令は口頭で伝達された. The directive was given by word of mouth.
てんち¹ 両者の間には天地の差がある. There is a world of difference [all the difference in the world] between them. / 天地無用.《標示用》This side up.
でんち² 電池が切れている. The batteries are dead.
てんで それはてんで問題にならない. It is altogether out of the question. / 君の言う事はてんで話にならん. What you say is quite [perfectly] absurd. / てんで見込みがない. There is no chance whatever. / なんの事やらてんでわかりません. I can't make head or tail of it. | I haven't got the slightest idea what it's all about. / てんで条件に合わない. It doesn't begin to meet our requirements.
てんてき² 点滴石をもうがつ. Constant dripping wears away a stone.《諺》
てんてん¹ この地図の点々をつけ

てんとう display] in the shopwindow / 店頭に出す put 《goods》on sale / 店頭で《be sold》over the counter / 《米》at the store / 《英》in the shop / 〈器具・家具などの〉店頭見本 a display [《米》floor] model. 文例⇩

てんとう² 点灯 ¶点灯する light a lamp; turn [switch] on a light.

てんとう³ 転倒 ¶転倒する〈ころぶ〉fall [tumble] down; have a fall; topple (down) / 〈逆にする〉《文》invert; reverse / 気が転倒する ⇨ き³ / 上下を転倒する turn *sth* upside down. 文例⇩

でんとう¹ 伝統 (a) tradition; (a) convention ¶伝統を誇る学校 a school with a proud history [with proud traditions] / 50 年の伝統を有する学校 a school with fifty years' tradition / 伝統を固executive [逸脱]する cling to [《文》deviate from] tradition / 伝統を破る break with tradition ;《文》make a departure from tradition / 伝統にしばられた《文》tradition-bound《artisans》/ 伝統的[の] traditional; conventional / 伝統主義《文》traditionalism;《文》conventionalism. 文例⇩

でんとう² 電灯 a [an electric] light [lamp] ¶電灯をつける[消す] switch [turn] a light on [off] / 電灯をつけっ放しにしておく leave a light on [burning]. 文例⇩

でんどう¹ 伝道 mission work ¶伝道する《文》preach the gospel;《文》engage in mission work / 伝道者 an evangelist; a missionary.

でんどう² 伝導 conduction (熱・電気の); transmission (光・音の) ¶伝導する conduct; transmit / 伝導体 a conductor; a transmitter / 伝導率[力, 性] conductivity.

でんどう³ 電動 ¶電動の electrically-powered[-driven, -run]《machines》; electric《typewriters》.

でんどう⁴ 殿堂〈御殿〉a palace;《文》an edifice; 〈神殿〉a temple; a shrine ¶学問の殿堂《文》a sanctuary of learning.

てんどうせつ 天動説 the Ptolemaic [geocentric] system [theory].

でんどうそうち 伝動装置〈自動車の〉(a) transmission.

てんとうむし てんとう虫 a ladybird;《米》a ladybug.

てんとりむし 点取り虫《米口語》a grind;《英口語》a swot.

てんどん 天丼 a bowl of rice topped with fried fish.

てんにゅう 転入 ¶転入する move in [into] / 転入生 a transfer student / 転入届 a moving-in notification.

てんにょ 天女《文》a heavenly maiden;《文》a nymph of paradise.

てんにん¹ 天人《文》a heavenly [celestial] being; an angel.

てんにん² 転任 a change of post [assignment] ¶転任する[になる] be transferred《from, to》/ 転任地[先] *one's* new post.

でんねつ 電熱 electric heat ¶電熱器 an electric range [stove].

てんねん 天然 nature ¶天然の natural;《文》native (金属などの); spontaneous (自生の); wild (野生の) / 天然に naturally; spontaneously / 天然ガス[資源] natural gas [recources] / 天然記念物 a natural monument [treasure]. 文例⇩

てんねんとう 天然痘 smallpox.

てんのう 天皇 an emperor; the Emperor of Japan ¶天皇陛下 His Majesty [H.M.] the Emperor / 明治天皇 the Emperor Meiji / 天皇杯 the Emperor's Trophy / 天皇制 the *Tenno* system / 天皇誕生日 the Emperor's Birthday. 用法 上記の「明治天皇」について. 英語では「チャールズ国王」は King Charles だが,「チューダー王朝の国王」は the Tudor Kings となる. 日本の場合, 孝明天皇までは天皇の名と年号は別であったので, the Emperor Komei でよいが, 明治天皇, 大正天皇の「明治」「大正」は天皇の名ではなく, 年号であるから, the Meiji Emperor, the Taisho Emperor とすべきだという考えが, 欧米の日本研究者の間に広く行なわれている. しかし, 専門家の書いたもの以外では, the Emperor Meiji というのが普通である.

でんば 電場〔物〕an electric(al) field.

でんぱ¹ 伝播《文》propagation; spread;〔人類・社会〕〈文化などの〉diffusion ¶伝播する《文》be propagated; spread.

でんぱ² 電波 a radio wave ¶電波に乗る be broadcast; go on the air (waves) / 電波管理委員会 the Radio Regulatory Commission / 電波天文学 radio astronomy / 電波望遠鏡 a radio telescope / 電波妨害 jamming.

てんばい 転売 (a) resale ¶転売する resell.

てんばつ 天罰 divine punishment [retribution];《文》Heaven's vengeance [judgment];《文》nemesis ¶天罰を受ける《文》be punished by Heaven;《文》incur the wrath of God;《文》provoke nemesis.

た部分は海抜 1 メートル以下の地域です. On this map the stippled area is less than one meter above sea level. / 海には白帆が点々と見えた. The sea was dotted with white sails. / 空には星が点々と瞬いている. The sky is studded [strewn] with twinkling stars.

てんでんばらばら 彼らはてんでんばらばらに行動した. They all acted just as they liked [They each went their own way], with no coordination between them.

でんと テーブルの上に鉢植えがでんと据えてあった. A flowerpot was placed ostentatiously on the table.

てんとう¹ 店頭に今年の水着が飾られている. The store has this year's swimming costumes on display in the window. / この本はもう 2, 3 日すれば店頭に出るでしょう. The book will be ready for sale in a few days.

てんとう² 今や彼らの地位は転倒した. Their positions are now reversed.

でんとう¹ そのワルツはウィーンの伝統に従って演奏された. The waltz was played in [according to] the best Viennese tradition.

でんとう² 電灯が突然消えた. The light suddenly went out.

てんねん この物質は天然には存在しない. This substance does not occur in nature. / 昔は染料はすべて天然のものだった. Formerly all dyes came from nature. / カモシカは昭和 30 年に特別天然記念物に指定された. The Japanese serow was designated as a special natural treasure in 1955.

てんばつ 疫病は昔は人間の罪に対する天罰だと考えられた. Plague

てんぴ[1] 天日 the sun; sunlight ¶天日にさらす expose *sth* to the sun / 天日で乾かす dry *sth* in the sun / 天日で干した sun-dried ((raisins)).

てんぴ[2] 天火 an oven.

てんびき 天引き ¶天引きする deduct ((a sum from *sb's* salary)); subtract; knock off / 天引き貯金 savings deducted from *one's* pay [salary]. 文例⇩

てんびょう 点描 a sketch; ‹横顔› a profile ((of)) ¶点描画法 pointillism; stippling / 点描画家スーラ the pointillist Seurat.

でんぴょう 伝票 a voucher; a payment slip ¶伝票を切る issue a voucher.

てんびん 天秤 a balance; (a pair of) scales; ‹さおばかり› a steelyard ¶てんびんにかける weigh *sth* on a scale, with a steelyard]; ‹比喩的に› weigh (A) against (B); compare (A) with (B) / 天秤座 《天》Libra; the Balance ⇨ ざ 文例 / てんびん棒 a (carrying) pole / てんびん棒でかつぐ carry *sth* on a pole.

てんぶ 転部 ¶転部する change departments; transfer [be transferred] to a different department.

てんぷ 天賦 ¶天賦の natural; ((文)) inborn; ((文)) inherent; ((文)) innate / 天賦の才能 a natural gift [((文)) endowment]; an innate talent.

てんぷ 添付 ¶添付する attach (A to B); ((文)) append; ((文)) annex / …が添付される ((文)) be accompanied by… / …を添付して (together) with… / 添付書類 attached papers.

でんぶ[1] 田麩 mashed and seasoned fish.

でんぶ[2] 臀部 the buttocks; the haunches.

てんぷく 転覆 ((文)) an overthrow; a downfall; a capsize (船の) ¶転覆する ‹ひっくり返る› overthrow; ((文)) subvert; overturn; upset; capsize (船を); ‹ひっくり返る› be overthrown; be overturned; be upset; capsize (船が) / 列車の転覆を図る attempt to wreck [derail] a train / 政府の転覆を計る plot against the government; scheme for the overthrow of the government. 文例⇩

てんぷら tempura ¶えびのてんぷら prawns fried in batter / てんぷらそば buckwheat noodles topped with *tempura*.

てんぶん 天分 *one's* natural gifts [talent(s), ((文)) endowments] ¶天分のある資質; talented / 天分の豊かな人 a highly-gifted person; ((文)) a person richly endowed by nature / …の天分を備えている have an aptitude for… / 天分を充分に発揮する give full play to *one's* natural talent.

でんぶん[1] 伝聞 ⇨ またぎき ¶伝聞証拠 hearsay evidence.

でんぶん[2] 電文 a telegraphic message; (the wording of) a telegram.

でんぷん 澱粉 starch ¶澱粉質の starchy; farinaceous.

テンペラ ‹絵の具› (paint in) tempera; ‹画› a tempera.

てんぺんちい 天変地異 ((文)) a convulsion of nature; ((文)) an extraordinary natural phenomenon; ((文)) a cataclysm.

てんぽ 店舗 ((米)) a store; ((英)) a shop ¶店舗用の建物 a store building.

てんぽ 填補 ¶填補する ‹充填する› fill up; ‹補償する› compensate [make up] for; make good (the loss); cover; ‹補足する› supply; replenish.

テンポ (a) tempo (*pl*. -pos, -pi); speed ¶速いテンポで, 急テンポで in quick tempo; rapidly / テンポの早い rapid; speedy; fast-moving[-paced] / テンポののろい slow-moving[-paced] / …のテンポに合わせる keep pace with (the tempo) of….

てんぼう[1] 点棒 ‹マージャンなどの› a chip; a counter.

てんぼう[2] 展望 a view; ((文)) a prospect ¶展望する view; survey; have [take, get] a view of; have a look round [over] / 展望がきく give a fine view (of); ((文)) afford a fine prospect (of); ((文)) have [command] an extensive view ((of)) / 展望を妨げる obstruct the view ((of)) / 展望車[台] an observation car [platform] / (潜水艦の)展望塔 the conning tower. 文例⇩

でんぽう 電報 a telegram; a wire; a telegraphic message; ‹無電› a wireless (telegram) ¶電報の配達係 a telegraph messenger / 電報を打つ send a telegram [((口語)) a wire] (to); telegraph [wire] (*sb*, to *sb*) / 電報で by telegraph [telegram, wire, cable]; telegraphically / 電報為替 ⇨ でんしん(電信為替) / 電報取扱局 a telegraph office / 電報料 a telegram fee [charge]. 文例⇩

デンマーク Denmark ¶デンマークの Danish / デンマーク王国 the Kingdom of Denmark / デンマーク語 Danish / デンマーク人 a Dane.

てんまく 天幕 a tent ⇨ テント.

てんません 伝馬船 a lighter.

てんまつ 顛末 ‹事情› the circumstances; ‹委細› the particulars; the details ¶事故のてんまつ used to be regarded as a visitation of God for the people's sins. / 天罰てきめんだった. Retribution swiftly overtook him.

てんびき 5分の利息を天引きしてその金を渡した. He subtracted 5% interest before handing over the money.

てんぷく 船はあらしにあって転覆した. The ship capsized in the storm.

てんぼう[2] 展望をよくするために木を少し切りましょう. Let's cut down some of the trees so that we can have a better view.

でんぽう 結果を電報で知らせて下さい. Please wire me the result. / 駅に迎えに来てくれと電報で言ってきた. He wired me [asked me by wire] to meet him at the station.

てんまつ 彼は加藤君遭難の顛末を語ってくれた. He told us [gave us a full account of] how Kato had met his tragic death.

てんめい そうなったのも天命だ. It has been ordained by Providence.

てんもう 天網かいかい疎にして漏らさず. The meshes of Heaven's net are as wide as the sea but let nothing through. | The mills of God grind slowly, yet they grind exceeding small.

てんやわんや 彼が踏み込んで来たら, てんやわんやになったことだろう. It would have been a pretty kettle of fish if he had stepped in.

てんまど 天窓 a skylight.

てんめい 天命 God's;《文》Heaven's] will;《文》Providence;《文》a mandate from Heaven;《運命》fate; destiny ¶天命とあきらめる resign *oneself* to *one's* fate. 文例⇩

てんめつ 点滅 点滅する〈くつけたり消したりする〉turn [switch, blink] [lights] on and off;〈ついたり消えたりする〉go [flash] on and off.

てんもう 天網

てんもん 天文 ¶天文学 astronomy / 天文学者 an astronomer / 天文学的数になる run into astronomical figures [numbers] / 天文航法《航空・海》celestial navigation / 天文台 an (astronomical) observatory / 天文年表 an astronomical chronology.

てんやく 点訳 ¶点訳する transcribe《a book》into Braille.

てんやもの 店屋物 food ordered from a caterer; sent-in food.

てんやわんや ¶てんやわんやである be in utter confusion; be in a mess; be at sixes and sevens. 文例⇩

てんゆう 天佑《文》《by》the grace of Heaven [God];《文》《by》the Providence of God.

てんよ 天与 ⇒てん¹（天から授かった）.

てんよう 転用 diversion ¶転用する divert [[文》appropriate]《*sth* to some other purpose》.

てんらい 天来 ¶天来の heavenly; heaven-sent;《文》divine.

でんらい 伝来《文》transmission（祖先からの）;《文》introduction（外国からの）¶伝来の〈祖先から〉《文》ancestral; hereditary（世襲の）; traditional（昔からの）;〈外来の〉imported / 伝来する〈伝わる〉be handed down;〈渡来する〉be imported; be introduced《from, into》. 文例⇩

てんらく 転落 a fall; a downfall ¶転落する fall; roll [tumble] down;《堕落する》《文》be degraded《to》;《文》degrade《to》/ 3位に転落する slide down to third place.

てんらん 展覧 ⇒てんじ² ¶展覧する、展覧に供する exhibit; display; put [place] *sth* on display [exhibition]; show / 展覧会 an [a public] exhibition; a show / 展覧会を開く[見に行く] hold [visit] an exhibition / 展覧会場 an exhibition room [hall].

でんりそう 電離層 the ionosphere.

でんりゅう 電流 an electric(al) current; a current of electricity ¶電流の通じている針金 a live [an electrified] wire / 電流を通じる turn the power [electricity] on; send an electric current《to》; pass an electric current《through》/ 電流計 an ammeter.

てんりょう 天領『日本史』〈朝廷の〉an Imperial demesne;〈徳川将軍の〉*bakufu* lands; a *shogun's* demesne.

でんりょく 電力 electric(al) power ¶電力会社 a [an electric] power company / 電力計 a wattmeter / 電力資源[需要]《electric-》power resources [needs] / 電力生産《electric-》power production / 電力不足 a power shortage / 電力不足の power-short《areas》/ 電力料金 power rates.

でんれい 伝令 a runner; a messenger;『軍』an orderly.

でんわ 電話 a telephone;《口語》a phone ¶《内線》33 番の電話 extension 33 / あとでまた電話する call *sb* again [back] / 電話がかかる have [get] a telephone call《from》/ 電話の声 a voice heard over the telephone / 電話で話す talk by telephone; talk over [on] the telephone / 電話に出ている be on the phone [line] / 電話に出る answer the phone;〈話中に交換手が〉come on the line《to say...》/ 電話口に呼び出す call [get] *sb* to the phone / 電話をかける telephone; phone; ring up; make [place] a telephone call《to》; put in [through] a（phone）call《to》/ 電話をかけ違える misdial; dial the wrong number / 電話を入れる put in a call / 電話を受ける have [get, 《文》receive] a telephone call《from》/ 電話を切る ring off; hang up (the receiver);《文》replace the receiver / 電話を引く have a telephone installed /（玩具の）糸電話 a string telephone / 電話線 a telephone wire / 電話帳 a telephone directory;《口語》a (tele)phone book / 電話帳に出て[載って]いる be (listed) in the phone book / 電話ニュース a telephone news service / 電話番号 a (tele)phone number / 電話ボックス a (tele)phone booth《英》box》/ 電話魔 a habitual dialer / 電話料 telephone charges [rates] / 電話料の請求書 a telephone bill / 絶えず電話連絡をとる《文》keep in constant telephone communication《with》. 文例⇩

でんらい 仏教がはじめて日本に伝来したのは千余年前のことである. It was more than 1,000 years ago that Buddhism found its way [was first introduced] into Japan. / それは彼の家の先祖伝来の秘法であった. It was a secret recipe that had come down in his family.

でんわ 君のうちには電話があるか. Do you have a telephone? / Are you on the phone? / 電話を借してくれませんか. May I use your telephone? / 鈴木さん、電話ですよ. Mr. Suzuki, you are wanted on the phone. / 田中さんが電話に出ている. Mr. Tanaka is on the line. /（内線で）中村は只今会議室におります. そちらへ電話をお回しいたしましょうか. Nakamura is in the conference room now. May I transfer you? / 彼は会議中だったが急用だからといって電話をつないでもらった. He was in conference, but I had the call put through to him as urgent. / 2, 3か所電話をかける所がある. I have a few phone calls to make. / なぜ電話をくれなかったのだ. Why didn't you give me a (phone) call? / 君に電話したら外出中だった. I tried to get you on the phone but you were out. / 耳が遠いですよ. もう少し大きい声でお願いします. Please speak a little louder. I can't hear you. / 突然電話が切れた. The telephone suddenly went dead. / 電話が通じない.

と

と¹ 戸 〈とびら〉a door; 〈引き戸〉a sliding door, 〈くよお い戸〉a shutter ¶表[裏]の戸 the front [back] door / 戸をたたく knock at [on] the door / 戸を開ける[閉める] open [shut, close] a door / 戸をちゃんと閉める shut a door properly / 人が入れないように[入ろうとする目の前で]戸を閉める close the door on *sb* [in *sb's* face] / 入って[出て]戸を閉める shut the door behind one. 文例⇩

と² 都 the Metropolis (of Tokyo) ¶都の Metropolitan / 都会議員 a member of the Metropolitan Assembly / 都議会 the Metropolitan Assembly / 都知事 the Governor of Tokyo / 都庁 the (Tokyo) Metropolitan Government (Office) / 都電（車）a (Tokyo) streetcar; 〈運行〉the Metropolitan streetcar service.

ト《音楽》G ¶ト長[短]調 (in) G major [minor].

-と and; 〈ともに〉(together) with; 〈…に対して〉《struggle》against; 〈もし…すれば〉if; 〈…すると〉when; 〈…のたびに〉whenever; 〈たとえ…でも〉even if [though] ¶だれがそう言おうと whoever [no matter who] may say so / 事実であろうとなかろうと (no matter) whether it is true or not. 文例⇩

ど 度〈角度・温度・経緯度〉a degree; 〈尺度〉a measure; 〈程度〉a degree; an extent; 〈限度〉a limit; 〈適度〉moderation; 〈回数〉a time ¶45度の角 an angle of 45 degrees / セ氏プラス[マイナス]3度《at》three degrees C. [centigrade] above [below] zero / 38度線で at the 38th parallel (of latitude) / 度の強い眼鏡 powerful spectacles; thick glasses (近limits の) / 度を失う lose *one's* head [presence of mind]; be flurried / 度を過ごす go too far (in); carry things too far; 《文》do to excess; overdo *sth*; 《文》be immoderate [intemperate] (in) / 度を過ごさない keep within bounds; be moderate; 《文》be temperate / 1, 2度 once or twice. 文例⇩

ド《音楽》do.

ドア a door ¶ドアの取っ手(握り) a doorknob / ドアチェーン a door chain / ドアチェック a door check [closer]. 文例⇩

どあい 度合 (a) degree; (an) extent; a rate (割合).

とあみ 投網 a cast [casting] net ¶投網を打つ cast a net.

とある a; a certain ¶とあるレストランで in a (certain) restaurant.

とい¹ 問い a question; an inquiry ¶問いをかける[発する] put a question to *sb*; ask *sb* a question;《文》ask a question of *sb* / 問いに答える answer a question.

とい² 樋〈横樋〉a gutter; 〈竪樋〉a drainpipe; a rainwater pipe;《米》a downspout;《英》a downpipe.

といあわせ 問い合わせ (an) inquiry [enquiry] ¶問い合わせの手紙 a letter of inquiry / (電話局の)問い合わせ係 an information operator / (身元などの)問い合わせ先 a reference.

といあわせる 問い合わせる inquire (from [(《文》of] *sb* about *sth*); make inquiries (at an office about *sth*); send inquiries (to *sb* about *sth*). 文例⇩

といかえす 問い返す〈再び〉ask again; 〈反問する〉ask back.

といかける 問い掛ける question; ask *sb* a question; put a question to *sb*; shoot a question at *sb*; 〈問い始める〉begin to ask.

といし 砥石 a whetstone; a grindstone ¶砥石でとぐ sharpen (a knife) on a whetstone; whet; hone (a razor).

といた 戸板 ¶戸板に載せて運ぶ carry *sb* (feet foremost) on a door ★ feet foremost をつけるのは死体の時.

といただす 問い質す question *sb* about *sth*; ask *sb* a question.

ドイツ Germany ¶ドイツの German / ドイ

The telephone is out of order. / 5台の電話が鳴りっぱなしだった. The five phones were going constantly. / 一体これはどうしたことなのかという電話が住民から新聞社や役所に殺到した. The residents swamped newspaper and government offices with anxious calls. / 伊藤さんを電話口までお願いします. Would you please call Mr. Ito to the phone? / 彼の番号は電話帳に載せていない.《米》He has an unlisted phone number. |《英》He has an ex-directory phone number.

と¹ 裏の戸から出て行った. He went out by [at] the back door. / この戸を開けると庭へ出る. This door opens into the garden.

-と それは本当だと思った. I thought (that) it was true. / 君の歌を聞くと, 人は君を本物の歌手だと思うだろう. Hearing [To hear] you sing, people would think you were a professional singer.

ど フクロウは頭をほとんど360度の全方向に回すことができる. Owls can twist their heads through nearly a full 360°. / 大半のトカゲは体温が40度から47度になると熱射病にかかる. Most lizards suffer heat prostration if their body temperature reaches 40 to 47 degrees. / 核融合反応は6千万度から7千万度にわたる熱を発生する. Nuclear fusion reactions generate temperatures in the 60 to 70 million degree range. / 倹約も度を越すとけちになる. Frugality, if carried too far, becomes miserliness.

ドア 閉まるドアを押さないで下さい.〈駅のアナウンス〉Don't prevent the doors from closing. / 閉まるドアにご注意下さい.〈駅のアナウンス〉Mind the doors!

といあわせ 問い合わせてみたらそれは誤報だった. On inquiry, the report turned out to be false. / 佐藤さんの所へ行って問い合わせてみなさいと言われた. I was referred to Miss Sato for information.

-といって 物質的に恵まれているからといって, それで何の心配もないということにはならない.

ツ語 German / ドイツ人 a German 《*pl.* -s》 / 西ドイツ West Germany /〈正式呼称〉the Federal Republic of Germany / 東ドイツ East Germany ;〈正式呼称（ドイツ民主共和国）〉the German Democratic Republic.

-といって〈理由〉because...; as... ¶ たとえ…だといっても (even) if...; (even) though... / どんなに…だといっても however...; no matter how...; whatever...; no matter what....

といつめる 問い詰める question closely; press *sb* for an answer. 文例⇩

トイレ(ット) a lavatory; a toilet; a W.C. (★ water closet の略) ;〈英口語〉a loo ;〈米俗〉a john ;〈軍隊・学校などの〉a latrine ;〈銀行・会社・駅などの〉a men's [ladies'] room ;〈婉曲に〉〈米〉a rest room ;〈英〉a convenience ; a gents' (★ gentlemen's lavatory の略) ; a ladies' (★ ladies' lavatory の略) ¶ トイレに行く go to the lavatory [toilet] ;〈婉曲に〉go to wash *one's* hands; use the bathroom (家庭で) / トイレに行っている be in the lavatory [toilet] / トイレットペーパー (a roll of) toilet paper [tissue]; a toilet roll / トイレットペーパーをちぎる tear off a length of toilet paper. 用法 a toilet は1人分の区画を意味する．したがってそれがいくつかある公衆便所では toilets となる．同じことは a lavatory についても言える．

とう¹ 当 ¶ 当の〈その〉that ;《文》the said ;〈問題の〉in question; at issue / 当の本人 the person in question / 当を得た〈正当な〉right ;《文》just; fair ;〈適切な〉proper; suitable / 当を得ない [失した]《文》unjust; unfair ;《文》improper / 当不当〈正否〉right or wrong ;〈適否〉《文》propriety. 文例⇩

とう² 党 a party ; 〈仲間, 徒党〉a clique ;《文》a coterie ¶ 党を組織する form a party / 党に入る join a party / 党中党をたてる form a faction within a party / 自民[社会]党 the Liberal Democratic [the Socialist] Party / 党員 a member (of a party) / 党規[則] party regulations [rules] / 党大会〈米〉(hold) a party convention ;〈英〉a

party conference / 党役員 a party officer. 文例⇩

とう³ 塔 a tower ; a pagoda (仏寺などの) ; steeple (尖塔).

とう⁴ 糖 sugar ¶ 血液中の糖 blood sugar.

とう⁵ 薹〈花軸〉a flower stalk ¶ とうが立つ run [go] to seed ; (lettuces) bolt ;〈盛りを過ぎる〉have passed [be past] *one's* prime ;《文》have lost the first bloom of *one's* youth.

とう⁶ 籐 cane; rattan ¶ 座る所が籐で出来ている椅子 a chair with a cane [rattan] seat ; a cane-bottomed chair / 籐椅子 a wicker(work) [cane, rattan] chair / 籐細工 wickerwork ; canework; rattan work.

とう⁷ 唐〈中国王朝の名〉Tang.

とう⁸ 問う〈尋ねる〉ask (*sb sth*) ; question ; put a question to *sb* ; inquire (about *sth*) ; demand (詰問する) ;〈気にかける〉care (about) ¶ 罪に問う charge (*sb* with a crime) ; accuse (*sb* of a crime) ; bring a charge ((of murder against *sb*)) / 殺人罪に問われる be accused of [charged with] murder / 殺人罪に問われて (be tried) on a charge of murder / …を問わず irrespective [regardless] of ;《文》without regard to ;《文》without distinction of ; no matter 《how, what, which》/ 時と場所を問わず at any time and place ;《文》(alike) in all ages and places. 文例⇩

-とう¹ 等〈など〉and so on [forth] ; and what not ; etc. ¶ 1 [2] 等 the first [second] class [grade] / 1 [2] 等で行く go [travel] first [second] class / 5等星 a fifth-magnitude star. 文例⇩

-とう² …頭 a head (単複同形) ★ 特に牛を数えるのに使う ¶ 牛5頭 five (head of) cattle / 馬5頭 five horses.

どう¹ 胴〈身体の〉the trunk; the body ;〈太鼓の〉the frame ;〈バイオリンなどの〉the body ¶ (身体の)胴が長い[短い] have a long [short] trunk / 胴が太い be fat around the waist / 胴が細い have a slim waist; be slim-waisted.

どう² 堂 ¶ 堂に入る be (a) master of (the art) ; be quite at home 《with》; be in *one's* element.

(Just) because you are materially well off, it doesn't follow that you are free from all cares. / どんなに蔵書が多いからといって, 整理されていなければ役に立たない. However large it may be, a library will not be of much use unless it is kept in order.

といつめる 問い詰められて, とうとう, それは自分がやりましたと白状した. Driven into a corner by their questioning, he finally admitted that he had done it.

トイレ トイレはどこですか.〈家庭で〉Where is the bathrooom? /〈女性が〉Where can I go and powder my nose? /〈デパートなどで〉Where are the toilets, please?

とう¹ 今, そのようなことを問題にするのは当を得たものではない. It is not proper to call such matters into question at this juncture. / It is unhelpful to raise points like that at this stage. / この提案はまことに当を得ている. This proposal is quite in place. / 当の本人は全く平気だった. He himself was quite undisturbed.

とう² 彼は社会党から立候補した.〈米〉He ran under the Socialist label [on the Socialist ticket]. /〈英〉He stood as a Socialist (candidate). / 民社党は当地で党大会を開くことになっている. The Democratic Socialists are to hold their party convention here.

とう⁴ 尿に糖が出た. Sugar was found in my urine.

とう⁵ 彼女もそろそろとうが立ってきた. なにしろもう30近いから. She's getting on. She's nearing thirty.

とう⁸ 今問われているのは, ヨーロッパ文化が築かれてきた社会的基盤全体である. What is in question now is the whole social foundation upon which European culture has been built. / このようなことを問うのはやさしいがそれに答えるのはむずかしい. This sort of question is more easily asked than answered. / 勝敗は問うところではない. It doesn't matter whether we win or not. / 能率さえ上がるなら費用は問わない. We don't care about the expense [cost], if it increases efficiency.

-とう¹ 何等で行きますか. What class do you travel [go]?

どう³ 銅 copper ¶銅製の copper; made of copper / 銅鉱 copper ore / 銅山 a copper mine / 銅線 (a) copper wire / 銅板 sheet copper / 銅版画 a copperplate print.

どう⁴ how; what ¶どうあっても[あろうと] in any case; under any circumstances; at any price [cost]; at all costs; whatever happens [may happen]; by all means / どうにかこうにか ⇒ どうにか, どうか (どうかこうか) / どういう what kind [sort] of / どう見ても to all appearances; whichever way you look at (it); from every point of view; in every respect. 文例↓

どう⁵ 〈馬に〉 whoa!

どう- 同… 〈同上の〉 the same;《文》the said;〈問題になっている〉(the project) in question;《文》(the question) at issue ¶同日 (on) the same day / 同社 the said corporation.

どうあげ 胴上げ ¶胴上げする toss sb into the air.

とうあつせん 等圧線【気象】an isobar.

とうあん 答案 an answer ¶答案を出す hand [turn] in one's (answer) paper / 答案を調べる grade [mark] examination papers (in English composition) / 答案用紙 a (blank) answer paper.

とうい 等位 ¶等位節[接続詞]【文法】a coordinate clause [conjunction].

どうい 同意 〈一致〉agreement;〈承諾〉consent;《文》assent; approval ¶同意する《文》consent to; agree with [in, to, on];《文》subscribe to 《(an agreement, a plan)》/ 同意を得る get [《文》obtain] sb's consent. 文例↓

どういう ⇒ どう⁴, どんな ¶どういうふうに how; in what way / どういうわけで why;《文》for what reason / どういうわけ[もの]か somehow; for some reason or other.

どういげんそ 同位元素【物】an isotope.

どういご 同意語 a synonym (for). 文例↓

とういじょう 糖衣錠 a sugar-coated pill [tablet].

とういそくみょう 当意即妙 ¶当意即妙に答える quickly make [come back with] a (sharp) witty reply [answer]; make a witty riposte; make repartee.

とういつ 統一 unity; unification;〈標準化〉standardization ¶統一する unify;〈精神を〉gather 《one's thoughts》;〈標準化する〉standardize;〈統御する〉《文》bring under one's sway / 統一国家 a unified nation / …に対して統一戦線を張る form [present] a united front to [against]…. 文例↓

どういつ 同一 ¶同一の the same (as); identical 《with》; one and the same ¶AとBとを同一視する regard A in the same light as B; place [put] A and B in the same class [category] / 同一水準にある be on a [the same] level 《with》/ 同一性《文》identity;《文》oneness; sameness.

とういん¹ 登院 ¶登院する attend the House.

とういん² 頭韻【詩】alliteration ¶頭韻をふんだ alliterative 《verses》.

どういん 動員 mobilization ¶動員する〈人を〉mobilize 《(an army)》; call out 《500 policemen》;〈物を〉bring sth into play; call [press] sth into service. 文例↓

とうえい 投影〈影〉a (cast) shadow;〈投影図〉a projection;〈図法〉projection ¶投影する project; reflect; cast a reflection 《on, in》.

どうおん 同音 the same sound ¶同音異義語 a homonym; a homophone.

とうおんせん 等温線【気象】an isotherm.

とうか¹ 灯火 a light; a lamplight ¶灯火管制 a blackout. 文例↓

とうか² 投下 投下する throw down; drop;〈資本を〉invest [sink] (in) / 投下資本 invested [investment] capital; capital outlay.

とうか³ 透過 permeation; penetration ¶透過する permeate 《through》; penetrate; filter (out) /透過性 permeability /透過性の膜 a permeable membrane.

とうか⁴ 等価 (an) equal value;〈原子の〉【化】equivalence / 等価の《文》of equal value /【化】equivalent.

とうか⁵ 糖化【化】saccharification ¶糖化する convert (starch) into sugar.

どうか¹ 同化《文》assimilation ¶同化する assimilate / 同化作用【生物・生理・地質】

どう⁴ どうしたのだ. What is the matter (with you)? (★ What is the matter? はごく日常的に「どうしたのですか」の意味で使う. これに対して What is the matter with you? は,相手が病気だとか,悲しんでいるとか,はっきり見てとれて,その訳を知りたいときに使う. 又は,その悲しみ方や怒り方が度が過ぎているという批判をこめて言うこともある. 病人に対して, matter に強勢を置き, with you を弱く言えば「どうしたのですか」という普通の意味になる. 要するに, What is the matter with you? は病人に対して(それも強勢の位置に気をつけた上で)しか使わない方が無難である) / 機械がどうした. Something is wrong [the matter] with the machine. / 〈問い返して〉それがどうした. So what? / さてどうしたものだろう. What shall I [am I going to] do? / それはどう言う意味なのか. What do you mean by that? / 君はあの男をどう思う. What do you think of him? / 失敗したらどうする. What will you do if you fail? | What would you do if you failed[should fail]? / その小説はどうです. How do you find the novel? / 鳥料理はどうです. What do you say to (having) chicken (for dinner)? / どうとも好きにしたまえ. Do what you like [as you please]. / そうなったら僕らはどうなるんだろう. Then what will happen to us? / 食べ物はどうしました. たくさん缶詰を持って行きましたよ. What did you do for food? — I took a lot of canned goods along. / うまく行くだろうか — さあ, どうかな. Will it go all right? — Well, I don't know. / どうとも言えない. I am not certain [sure]. | I can't say for certain. / 君はこの前,私に見せた写真をどうした? What did you do with the photo you showed me the other day? / その後, 君の仕事はどうなっているかね. How is your work coming along [on]? / その後どうしていましたか. How have you been doing [getting on, making out] since? / どう見ても日本の住宅はお粗末だ. Any way [No

どうか² 銅貨 a copper coin.
どうか³ ⟨どうぞ⟩ please ; ⟨…かどうか⟩ whether (…or not) ; if ¶ どうかして somehow or other ; in one way or another ; in some way ; ⟨ぜひとも⟩ by all means / どうかする ⟨方法を講じとも⟩ do something (in order to …) ; 《文》 take some measures ; manage ((to do)) somehow / どうかすると sometimes ; at times ; in some way / どうかこうか ((manage to do)) somehow (in some way) (or other) ; by some means or other ; ⟨かろうじて⟩ barely. 文例⇩
どうが 動画 an animated cartoon ; a cartoon ; an animation.
とうかい 倒壊 collapse ¶ 倒壊する collapse ; fall [come] down ; be destroyed / 倒壊家屋 collapsed houses.
とうがい 当該 ¶ 当該官庁 the authorities concerned ; the competent [proper] authorities / 当該期間中に 《文》 during the said period.
とうがい² 凍害 frost damage.
とうがい³ 等外 a failure ; ⟨競技の⟩ an also-ran ¶ 等外の ⟨競技で⟩ unplaced ; ⟨品質が⟩ off-grade ; substandard / 等外に落ちる be [run] unplaced ; fail to win a prize ; be eliminated (予選で) ; be judged to be below standard (品評会などで).
とうかく¹ 倒閣 overthrowing the Cabinet ¶ 倒閣運動 a movement to overthrow the Cabinet.
とうかく² 等角 《数》 ¶ 等角の equiangular / 等角三角形 an equiangular triangle.
とうかく³ 頭角 ¶ 頭角を現わす 《文》 cut [make] a conspicuous [brilliant] figure (in) ; distinguish *oneself* ; stand out.
どうかく 同格 the same rank ; 《文法》 apposition ¶ 自分と同格の人 one's equal ; 《文》 one's peer / …と同格である be [stand] on an equal footing with… ; be on a par with… ; rank with… ; 《文法》 be in apposition to… / 同格名詞 a noun in apposition.
どうがく 同額 ¶ 同額の 《文》 of the same amount.
どうかせん 導火線 a fuse ; a train (of powder) ; ⟨誘因⟩ a cause ¶ 導火線に点火する light the fuse ((of)) / 導火線になる cause ; touch off ; spark.
とうかつ 統轄 ¶ 統轄する control ; 《文》 exercise control over ; supervise ; govern ; be in charge of.
どうかつ 恫喝 a threat ; intimidation ; blackmail ¶ 恫喝する threaten ; intimidate ; blackmail.
とうがらし 唐辛子 〖植〗 a pepper ; a capsicum ; ⟨果実⟩ a chili (*pl.* chilies) ; ⟨香辛料⟩ red [cayenne] pepper ; chili (powder).
とうかん¹ 投函 ¶ 投函する drop (a letter) into a mailbox ; 《米》 mail ; 《英》 post.
とうかん² 等閑 ¶ 等閑に付する neglect ; make light of ; 《文》 slight ; disregard.
とうがん 冬瓜 〖植〗 a wax gourd ; a white gourd (melon).
どうかん¹ 同感 ¶ 同感である sympathize ((with)) ; feel the same way ; share *sb*'s feelings ; ⟨同意する⟩ agree ((with)). 文例⇩
どうかん² 導管 ⟨導水管⟩ a conduit ; 〖解・動〗 a duct ; 〖植〗 a conducting [water, sap] vessel.
どうがん 童顔 a boyish face ¶ 童顔の baby-faced ; boyish-looking.
とうかんかく 等間隔 ¶ 等間隔に at even [regular] intervals.
どうかんすう 導関数 〖数〗 a derived function ; a derivative.
とうき¹ 冬季[期] the winter season ; winter ; wintertime ¶ 冬季には in winter ; during the winter months / 冬期用に (preserve) for winter use / 冬季休暇 the winter vacation (holidays).
とうき² 当期 this [the current, the present] term [period] ¶ 当期損益 the profits and losses for this term.
とうき³ 投棄 ¶ 投棄する throw [《文》 cast] *sth* away ; dump ((waste into a river)).
とうき⁴ 投機 (a) speculation ; a venture ¶ 投機をやる speculate (in) ; gamble (in) / 投機に手を出す dabble in speculation / 投機的 speculative ; risky / 投機心 a speculative streak [《文》 disposition] / 投機熱 a craze [mania] for

---

matter how] you look at it, Japanese housing is poor. / いえどう致しまして. Not at all. / I Don't mention it. / You're welcome. / Oh, that's all right.
どうい この点は同意できかねる. I cannot agree with you on this point. / 未成年者が結婚するには, 親の同意を得なければならぬ. Marriage between minors requires parental consent. / その案には僕は同意できない. I cannot approve of the plan.
どういご happy はかつては lucky と同意語であった. 'Happy' used to be synonymous with 'lucky'.
とういつ 党は内部の統一を欠いている. The party is divided against itself.
どういん この映画は10万人の観客を動員した. The film drew audiences totaling 100,000 people. / その研究を促進するために高性能のコンピューターが動員された. They had recourse to high-efficiency computers in order to push forward their research.
とうか 灯火親しむべき候となった. Autumn has arrived, with its long cool evenings, so conducive to reading.
どうか³ 彼はどうかして逃げようとした. He tried to find some means of escape. / どうかしなければならない. Something has to be done. / あの人はどうかしている. Something is wrong [the matter] with him. / 彼はどうかこうか学校の課程だけは終えた. He got through his school course somehow or other. / それはどうかと思うよ. I doubt the wisdom of it.
とうかい 地震のため200戸の家屋が倒壊した. Two hundred houses were destroyed by the earthquake.
どうかせん 1人の警官の発砲が一大騒動の導火線となった. A shot fired by a policeman sparked [triggered] off a great riot.
どうかん¹ 彼の意見に対して, 同僚の多くが同感だというわけではない. It is not that many of his colleagues share [are in agreement with] his view. / その点は私もあなたと全く同感です. I quite agree [I see eye to eye]

とうき speculation.

とうき⁵ 党紀 party discipline ¶党紀を乱す《文》infringe [offend against] party discipline.

とうき⁶ 陶器 earthenware; (a piece of) china; chinaware; ceramics; crockery; pottery ¶陶器の ceramic; china《vases》/ 陶器商《店》a china shop;〈人〉a dealer in china [crockery].

とうき⁷ 登記 registration ¶登記する register; have [get] sth registered / 登記所 a registry (office) / 登記簿 a register / 登記料 a registration fee.

とうき⁸ 騰貴 a rise (in prices) ¶騰貴する〈物価が〉rise; go [run] up.

とうぎ⁵ 党議 a party decision;〈会議〉a party conference ¶党議にかける refer《a matter》to a party conference / 党議によって決まる be decided at a party conference.

とうぎ⁶ 討議 (a) discussion; (a) debate;《文》(a) deliberation ¶討議する discuss (★「…について討議する」は discuss であって、discuss about sth は誤り); debate on [about];《文》deliberate on / 討議を始める begin [open] a discussion [debate] (on); enter into discussion (about) / 討議を打ち切る close [break off] a discussion [debate] / 討議にかける bring [take] up《a matter》for discussion / 討議中である be under discussion [consideration].

どうき¹ 同期 the same period ¶同期生 a classmate; graduates in the same class ¶(be) one's contemporary at college. 文例⇩

どうき² 動悸 palpitation; beating [thumping, throbbing] of the heart; heartbeats ¶動悸がする[を打つ] throb; beat; palpitate. 文例⇩

どうき³ 動機 a motive (of, for);《文》an inducement (to do);【音楽】a motif ¶不純な動機《from》an ulterior motive / …が動機となって motivated by… / 動機付け motivation. 文例⇩

どうき⁴ 銅器 a copper [bronze] utensil; copperware.

どうぎ¹ 胴着 a singlet; an undergarment; a vest.

どうぎ² 動議 a motion ¶動議を提出する move《that…》; make [move, bring forward] a motion / 動議を支持する second a motion / 動議を採択する adopt a motion. 文例⇩

どうぎ³ 道義 morality;《文》moral principles ¶道義上 morally《unpardonable》; for ethical reasons ¶上…しなければならない be (in) honor bound to do / 道義に反する be immoral;《文》offend against [be contrary to] morality [good morals] / 道義心 moral sense.

どうぎご 同義語 ⇒ どういご.

とうきゅう¹ 投球〈投手の〉delivery; pitching;〈野手の〉throwing; a throw ¶投球する pitch [hurl, throw] a ball; make a throw《to second》. 文例⇩

とうきゅう² 等級 a class; a grade; an order; a rank; a degree; magnitude《星の》¶等級をつける classify; grade / 等級別の graduated《admission fees》.

とうぎゅう 闘牛 a bullfight; bullfighting;〈牛〉a fighting bull / 闘牛士 a bullfighter; a matador / 闘牛場 a bull ring.

どうきゅう 同級 the same class [《米》grade,《英》form]　★ form はアメリカでも私立学校で使っているところがある ¶同級生 a classmate.

とうぎょ¹ 統御〈統治〉rule;〈制御〉control ¶統御する rule over; govern; control; manage.

とうぎょ² 闘魚 a (Siamese) fighting fish.

どうきょ 同居 ¶同居する live together; live [stay] with《a family》/ 同居人を take in a lodger [《米》a roomer]; rent a room (in one's house) to someone.

とうきょう 東京 ¶東京駅 Tokyo Station / 東京大学 the University of Tokyo; Tokyo University (略称)/ 東京都 (the Metropolis of) Tokyo ⇒ と² / 東京都民 a citizen of Tokyo / 東京都立大学 Tokyo Metropolitan University / 東京湾 the Bay of Tokyo; Tokyo Bay.

どうきょう¹ 同郷 the same district [province] ¶同郷のよしみで (just) because sb is from the same part of the country as one / 同郷人 a person from the same province [part of the country]. 文例⇩

どうきょう² 道教 Taoism.

どうぎょう 同業 the same trade [profession] ¶同業の田中氏 Mr. Tanaka, who is in the same line of business as ours / 同業組合 a trade association / 同業者《総称》the profession (医者・弁護士らの); the trade [craft] (商人・職人の);〈個人〉a person in the same trade as one. 文例⇩

とうきょく(しゃ) 当局(者) the authorities (concerned) ¶学校当局 the school authorities [administration].

とうきょり 等距離 an equal distance ¶等距離の《文》equidistant; equally distant / 等距離の所にある be at equal distances《from》; be equally distant《from》; be equidistant《from》/ 等距離外交 an evenhanded ['equidistant'] foreign policy.

どうぐ 道具 a tool;《文》a utensil; an instrument;〈装置〉an apparatus ¶道具箱 a tool-

---

with you on that point.

どうき¹ 僕たちは同期の出身です。We were in the same class at school.

どうき² 動悸が激しかった。My heart throbbed violently [beat fast].

どうき³ 彼の行動の動機はりっぱだ。His motives were most praiseworthy. / ちょっとした事件が戦争を引き起こす動機となることもある。A quite trivial incident may trigger off a war.

どうぎ² その動議は10票対50票で成立しなかった。The motion was defeated [lost] by ten votes to fifty.

とうきゅう¹ キャッチャーがその投球をすくい上げて1塁にトスした。The catcher scooped the throw up from the ground and tossed to first.

どうきゅう 私は彼と同級です。I am in the same class with him.

どうきょう¹ 彼は僕と同郷人だ。He is from the same province as me [I am]. ⇒ と² 用法

どうぎょう この商売は同業者が多すぎる。This (line of) business is overcrowded.

どうぐ 最古の原人もすでに道具を使用していた。The earliest man was already using tools [had al-

とうぐう 東宮 the Crown Prince ⇨ こうたいし ¶ 東宮御所 the Crown Prince's Palace.
どうぐだて 道具立て preparations; preliminary arrangements ¶ 道具立てをする make preparations 《for》; pave the way 《for》. 文例⇩
とうくつ 盗掘 ¶ 盗掘する rob a grave [tomb, burial mound].
どうくつ 洞窟 a cavern; a cave; a grotto 《pl. -(e)s》 ¶ 洞窟(絵)画 a cave painting [drawing, picture] / 洞窟魚 a cave fish.
とうげ 峠 the highest point on a mountain road; a (mountain) pass; 〈危機〉a crisis 《pl. crises》; a critical point [stage]; the worst; 〈絶頂〉the height; the crest; the peak ¶ 峠を越す cross a ridge; 〈危機を過ぎる〉pass the crisis [critical point]; 《口語》be over the hump; turn the corner (病気などが) 碓氷峠 the Usui Pass. 文例⇩
どうけ 道化《事》clowning; buffoonery;《文》drollery; antics;〈人〉⇨ 道化師 ¶ 道化た clownish; funny;《文》droll; facetious / 道化師 a clown; a buffoon; a fool / 道化役を演じる play the fool [clown].
とうけい¹ 東経 the east longitude ¶ 東経20度15分20秒 20 degrees 15 minutes of east longitude; long. 20°15′E ⇨ ほうい 文例.
とうけい² 統計 statistics《複数扱い》¶ 統計(学)的 statistical / 統計(学)上 statistically / 統計を取る take [collect, gather, prepare, compile] statistics 《of》/ 統計学 (the science of) statistics《単数扱い》/ 統計学者 a statistician / 統計図表[表] a statistical chart [table].
とうけい³ 闘鶏 a cockfight; cockfighting;〈鶏〉a gamecock ¶ 闘鶏場 a cockpit.
とうげい 陶芸 ceramics (the art of) pottery; ceramic art ¶ 陶芸家 a (craft) potter; a ceramic artist.
どうけい¹ 同形 ¶ 同形の of the same shape.
どうけい² 同系 ¶ 同系の of the same stock; affiliated 《concerns》;《文》cognate 《sciences》.
とうけつ 凍結 ¶ 凍結する freeze / 凍結資産 frozen assets / 賃金凍結政策 a wage-freeze policy / 凍結防止剤 (an) antifreeze.
とうけん¹ 刀剣 swords.
とうけん² 闘犬 a dogfight;〈犬〉a fighting dog.
どうけん¹ 同県 the same prefecture. 文例⇩
どうけん² 同権 ⇨ だんじょ (男女同権).
とうげんきょう 桃源郷《文》an earthly paradise;《文》Shangri-La.
とうこう 投降 (a) surrender ¶ 投降する surrender 《to the enemy》.
とうこう² 投稿 a contribution ¶ 投稿する contribute ((an article) to a paper); write 《for a magazine》/ 投稿者 a contributor. 文例⇩
とうこう³ 陶工 a potter.
とうこう⁴ 登校 ¶ 登校する go to school; attend school / 登校拒否(症) refusal to go to school (as a neurotic symptom).
どうごう¹ 等号【数】an equal sign.
どうごう² 統合《文》integration; unification; unity ¶ 統合する《文》integrate; combine; unite; unify; put together / 国民統合の象徴 the symbol of the unity of the people / (米国)統合参謀本部 the Joint Chiefs of Staff (略: J.C.S.).
どうこう¹ 同好 ¶ 同好の士 people interested in the same subject; people sharing the same interest / 釣同好会 an (amateur) anglers' club.
どうこう² 同行 ¶ 同行する go (along) with;《文》accompany; travel together with / 警察へ同行を求める ask sb to come [to accompany one] to the police station / 同行者 a (traveling) companion / 同行者の1人 one of the party.
どうこう³ 動向 a tendency; a trend ¶ 世論の動向に注意する watch the trend of public opinion.
どうこう⁴ 瞳孔 the pupil (of the eye) ¶ 瞳孔散大 [縮小] dilation [contraction] of the pupil.
どうこう⁵
どうこういきょく 同工異曲 ¶ 同工異曲である be practically the same;《口語》be six of one and half a dozen of the other. 文例⇩
とうこうき 投光器 a floodlight.
とうこうせん 等高線 a contour (line) ¶ 等高線であらわす contour; represent in contour / 等高線地図 a contour map.
とうごく 投獄 imprisonment ¶ 投獄する imprison; throw sb into prison [jail]; put sb in prison [jail]; send [《文》commit] sb to prison.
どうこく 同国 the same country ¶ 同国人 a (fellow) countryman;《文》a compatriot;〈同郷の人〉a person from the same province.
とうこつ 頭骨 skull [cranial] bones.
とうごろん 統語論【言語】syntax.
とうさ 踏査 a survey; (an) exploration;【土木】reconnaissance ¶ 踏査する survey; make a survey of; explore; make explorations into.
とうざ 当座 ¶ 当座は for the present; for the time being; for a time; temporarily / 当座の 〈今の〉immediate; present;〈一時の〉temporary / 当座のしのぎに as a temporary mea-

---

ready developed the use of tools].
どうぐだて 道具立ては整った。Everything's ready.
とうくつ そのピラミッドは再三盗掘されて財宝はほとんど残っていなかった。The pyramid was found to have been repeatedly robbed of its treasures so that almost nothing remained.
とうげ この仕事も峠を越した。The hardest part of this job is over. | We are over the hump

with this job. / この24時間が峠でしょう。《文の言》The next twenty-four hours will be critical. | We shall know one way or the other in the next 24 hours.
どうけん² 彼は私と同県人です。He comes [hails] from the same prefecture as me [I do]. ⇨ より² 用法
とうこう² 彼はよくこの雑誌に投稿します。He is a frequent contributor to this magazine.

どうこう⁵ どうこう言うわけではありませんが、ここはもうちょっと何とかなりませんか。I don't want to be fussy, but isn't there any room for improvement here?/ 私は何もしていないのですから、どうこう言う資格はありません。Since I've done nothing, I don't have any say at all.
どうこういきょく この2つは同工異曲だ。There is little to choose between the two.

どうさ 動作 action; movement(s); motion(s); 〈振舞い〉behavior; 《文》demeanor ¶動作が敏速である[鈍い] one's movements are quick [slow]; be quick [slow] in one's movements [actions] / 穴を掘る動作をやってみせる go through the motions of digging a hole.

とうさい¹ 当歳 ¶当歳の one-year-old; yearling / 当歳の動物 a yearling.

とうさい² 搭載 ¶搭載する load / 搭載している have 《heavy guns》on board; be loaded [《文》laden] with 《goods》. 文例⇩

とうざい 東西〈東と西〉east and west;〈東洋と西洋〉the East and the West;《文》the Orient and the Occident;〈共産圏諸国と資本主義諸国〉the East and the West ¶東西間の関係 East-West relations / 東西に広がっている extend east and west / 東西南北 north, south, east and west; the four points of the compass; the four cardinal points. 文例⇩

どうざい 同罪 ¶同罪である be equally guilty [to blame].

とうさきゅうすう 等差級数 an arithmetical series ⇒とうひきゅうすう.

とうさく¹ 倒錯《医》perversion ¶性欲倒錯者 a (sexual) pervert.

とうさく² 盗作〈行為〉plagiarism;〈作品〉a plagiarism; a crib ¶盗作する plagiarize / 盗作者 a plagiarist.

どうさつ 洞察 insight;《文》discernment ¶洞察《文》discern; penetrate [see] into; see through / 洞察力 insight;《文》penetration / 洞察力のある《文》discerning; penetrating. 文例⇩

とうさん 倒産 bankruptcy; insolvency; a (company) failure ¶倒産する go [《文》become] bankrupt [insolvent]; go under. 文例⇩

どうさん 動産 movable property; movables.

とうし¹ 投資 investment ¶多額の投資 a large investment / 投資する invest (in); sink [lay out] (money in an enterprise) / 投資で多額の収益を得る get a good return on an investment / 再投資 reinvestment / 一般投資家 the investing public / 投資者 an investor / 投資信託 (an) investment trust.

とうし² 凍死 ¶凍死する freeze [be frozen] to death; die of [from] cold.

とうし³ 透視 ¶透視する see through;〈エックス線を〉look at 《sb's chest》through the fluoroscope / 透視画法で描く draw in perspective / (エックス線の)透視検査 fluoroscopy.

とうし⁴ 闘士 a fighter;《文》a champion ¶自由の闘士 a fighter for freedom; a champion of liberty.

とうし⁵ 闘志 fighting spirit;《show》fight ¶闘志満々である be full of fight; be game 《enough to do》. 文例⇩

とうじ¹ 冬至 the winter solstice.

とうじ² 当時 at the [that] time; in those days [times]; then (★この意味の then は文や節の終わりに置く. 文頭に置いた then は「それから」「そして」の意味になる) ¶当時の《文》then; of those days / 当時の首相 the then Prime Minister / 当時の大学生 university students of those days / 当時はまだ新しかった特効薬ペニシリン the then-new wonder drug, penicillin. 文例⇩

とうじ³ 湯治 a hot-spring cure ¶湯治する take the baths (at Shima) for medical purposes / 湯治に行く go (to Kusatsu) for a hot-spring cure / 湯治客 a person staying at a spa to cure a disease / 湯治場 a spa; a watering place.

とうじ⁴ 答辞 ¶答辞を読む[述べる] make [deliver] an address in reply ★英米には卒業式などに答辞を読むという習慣はない. アメリカでは首席の卒業生 (the valedictorian) が別れの演説 (a valedictory speech [oration]) をすることがある.

どうし¹ 同士 a fellow ¶学生同士で with one's fellow students / 気の合った同士《文》congenial spirits / 男同士の共感 fellow-feeling between men / 同士打ちをする fight (by mistake) among 《themselves》. 文例⇩

とうざ ここに来た当座はすべてのものが私には面白かった. When I came here, I found everything new and interesting for a while. | これだけあれば当座のしのぎがつく. This sum will be enough for our immediate needs. | This will do for the present.

とうさい² この軍艦は12インチ砲10門を搭載している. The warship carries ten 12-inch guns. | 翼の縦横比は一定量の燃料を搭載した場合飛行機がどのくらい遠くまで飛べるかを知る目安になる. Wing aspect ratio helps determine how far a plane can fly with a given fuel load.

とうざい その広場から, 4本の道が東西南北に走っている. Four streets radiate to the four points of the compass from the plaza.

どうさつ 彼は人間性に対する洞察力がなかった. He had no insight into human nature. / 一瞬の洞察力のひらめきで問題の解決方法がわかった. In a single flash of insight he saw how to solve the problem.

とうさん 昨年はこの町だけで20余りの企業が倒産した. Last year there were more than twenty bankruptcies in this city alone.

とうし⁵ 相手のごうまんな態度を見て, 彼の闘志は高まった. His opponent's arrogant attitude increased his fighting spirit. / 彼はまだ闘志満々である. He is still full of fight. | He has plenty of fight left in him. / ジョンは闘志を失っていた. There was no longer any fight (left) in John. | All the fight had gone out of John. / 彼も若い頃は闘志満々だったよ. He was quite a fighter [He was a real fighter] in his younger days.

とうじ² 当時の彼にとっては1万円は大金だった. In those days 10,000 yen was a big amount for him.

どうし¹ 仲間同士でけんかするのはよくない. You should not quarrel among [between] yourselves. / 2人はかたき同士だった.

どうし² 同志 a comrade; a person fighting [working] for the same cause 《with one》/ a kindred spirit ¶同志をつのる rally [appeal to] like-minded people / (共産社会で)同志 K Comrade K.

どうし³ 動詞【文法】a verb ¶ドイツ語の動詞の変化を覚える learn the conjugations of German verbs. 文例↓

どうじ 同時 ¶同時に at the same time; simultaneously;〈一時に〉at a time; at once;〈一方で〉while; on the other hand / 同時性《文》simultaneity / 同時録音 synchronous recording. 文例↓

とうしき 等式【数】an equation.

とうじき 陶磁器 china and porcelain; pottery; ceramics.

どうじく 同軸 ¶同軸ケーブル a coaxial cable.

とうじしゃ 当事者 the person [《文》party] concerned;《文》an interested party; a party《to a suit》¶当事者能力を欠く lack the qualifications to deal (responsibly) with 《the union》.

どうじだい 同時代 ¶同時代の《文》of the same age [period] /《文》contemporary《with》/ 同時代の人 a contemporary / 同時代に in the same age [period].

とうしつ 等質《文》homogeneity ¶等質の《文》homogeneous.

とうじつ 当日 the [that] day;〈定めの日〉《文》the appointed day ¶当日限り有効の切符 a day ticket / (芝居などの)当日売りの切符 a ticket sold on the day of the performance. 文例↓

どうしつ¹ 同室 ¶同室の share a room《with sb》;《口語》room with sb;《文》occupy the same room (as sb) / 同室者 a roommate.

どうしつ² 同質 ¶同質の《文》of the same quality /《文》homogeneous.

どうじつ 同日 the same day [date] ¶…とは同日の談ではない (A) is not worthy to be named in the same breath with 《B》.

どうじつうやく 同時通訳 ¶〈事〉(carry out) simultaneous interpreting;〈provide〉a simultaneous translation /〈人〉a simultaneous interpreter.

どうして how;《文》in what way [manner];《文》by what means;〈なぜ〉why;《文》for what reason;〈それどころか〉on the contrary; far from that ¶どうしても at any cost; by any means;〈手段をえらばず〉by hook or by crook;〈必ず〉surely; without fail;〈とにかく〉anyhow; at any rate;〈決して…でない [...しない]〉by no means; never;〈いやでもおうでも〉whatever one wants to do; whether one is willing or not; willy-nilly;〈結局〉in the end; after all. 文例↓

とうしゃ¹ 投射【数】projection;【物】incidence ¶投射する project 《on》/ 投射影 a projection / 投射角 an angle of incidence.

とうしゃ² 透写 ¶透写する trace 《a drawing》/ 透写紙 (a sheet of) tracing paper.

とうしゃ³ 謄写 ¶謄写する copy; transcribe; mimeograph / 謄写版 a copying machine; a mimeograph / 謄写版刷り a mimeographed copy.

とうしゅ¹ 投手【野球】a pitcher ⇨ピッチャー ¶勝ち[負け]投手 a winning [losing] pitcher / 投手陣 the pitching staff / 投手戦 a pitching duel; a pitchers' battle / 投手力 the pitching strength 《of a team》.

とうしゅ² 党首 the leader [head] of a political party ¶3党首会談 a conference [talk] among the leaders of three political parties.

どうしゅ 同種 ¶同種の of the same kind [sort].

とうしゅう 踏襲 ¶踏襲する follow in sb's footsteps; follow suit; follow 《the policy of the former Cabinet》.

とうしゅく 投宿 ¶投宿する put up at 《a hotel》; check into 《a hotel》; lodge 《at a hotel, with a family》/ 投宿者 a guest (registered at a hotel).

どうしゅく 同宿 ¶同宿する stay at the same hotel; lodge in the same house / 同宿者 a fellow lodger [boarder]. 文例↓

とうしょ¹ 投書 a contribution; a letter from a reader [to the editor] (読者の);〈密告〉(an anonymous letter) ¶投書する contribute (an article)《to》; write (a letter)《to the Asahi》/ 投書家 a contributor / 投書箱 a suggestion [complaints] box / 投書欄 a readers' column.

The two of them were enemies.
どうし³ この類の動詞は同じように変化する. The verbs of this class are conjugated in the same way.
どうじ この本は面白いし、また同時に多くの知識を与えてくれる. This book is both interesting and informative. / ヨットは愉快でもあるが同時に危険も伴う. Yachting is a pleasant sport, but it is not without danger.
とうじつ 通用当日限り.〈切符の標示〉Valid for the day of issue only.
どうして あの人とどうして知り合いになったのですか. How did you come to know him? / どうしてこんなに同じ間違いが多いのか. Why is it that [《口語》How come] there are so many mistakes of the same sort? / どうしていいか私は途方にくれた. I was at a loss what to do. / 私に向かってどうしてそんな事が言えるのか. How can you say such a thing to me? / もうすんだかね. ―どうしてて, 今始めたばかりだ. Have you finished it yet?—Why, I have only just begun. / ウエーターはどうしてチップを取らなかった. The waiter absolutely refused to accept the tip. / 彼はどうしても費用を予算の範囲内にとどめなければいけないと思った. He felt honor bound to keep the expenses within the budget. / やってみたがどうしてもできなかった. Try as I might, I couldn't do it. / 彼はどうしても帰ると言ってきかなかった. He insisted on returning home. / 僕にはその吊り橋はどうしても渡れなかった. I was completely unable to negotiate the suspension bridge. / どうしてもその人の名を思い出せなかった. I couldn't, for the life of me, recollect his name. / この奇妙な音楽を聞くと, どんな楽器が使われたのかをどうしても尋ねたくなるでしょう. When you hear this strange music, you will inevitably feel like asking what kinds of instruments were used. / この戸はどうしても締まらない. This door just will not shut.
どうしゅく 彼はとりあえず僕と同宿することになりました. He is to

とうしょ²　頭書　¶頭書の《文》《the proposition》above；《文》the above-mentioned.

どうしょ¹　同所　the same place ¶《出所を示すとき》同所より《ラテン語》loc. cit.　★ loco citato の略. 文例⇩

どうしょ²　同書　the same book ¶《出所を示すとき》同書より《ラテン語》ib.; ibid.　★共に ibidem の略.

とうしょう　凍傷　frostbite (on the fingers); chilblains (frostbite より軽い) ¶凍傷になる be [get] frostbitten; get chilblains (on one's hands) / 耳が凍傷にかかる get one's ears frostbitten. 文例⇩

とうじょう¹　搭乗　board [get on] ((a plane); go [get] on board ((the aircraft)) / 搭乗員 the crew (総称); a crew member (1人) / 搭乗券 a boarding card / 搭乗手続きを終える complete boarding procedures / 《空港の》搭乗待合室 a departure lounge.

とうじょう²　登場　enter the stage; come onstage; appear (on television); make an entrance; 《出現する》appear (on the scene); make an appearance; enter the field / ハムレット登場〈ト書き〉Enter Hamlet / 登場人物 the characters (in a play); 《ラテン語》the dramatis personae. 文例⇩

どうじょう¹　同上　《文》as above; the same as (the) above; 《文》ditto (略: do.).

どうじょう²　同乗　¶同乗する ride together; ride with (sb in the same carriage); share a car 《with》《自動車に》/ 同乗者 a fellow passenger.

どうじょう³　同情　sympathy; 《文》compassion ¶同情する sympathize (with); feel [have] sympathy (for); pity sb ; feel pity (compassion) for sb ; feel for sb / 同情(心)のある sympathetic; warm-hearted / 同情(心)のない《文》unfeeling; cold-hearted / 同情すべき《文》pathetic; 《文》pitiable / 同情を示す[示さない] show one's [no] sympathy for sb / 同情の意を表する《文》express one's sympathy (for) / 同情を引く《文》engage sb's sympathy《文》/ 同情を寄せる《文》extend one's sympathy (to) / 同情に訴える appeal to sb's sympathy / 同情者 a sympathizer / 同情スト (go on) a sympathy [sympathetic] strike / 同情票を集める collect sympathy votes. 文例⇩

囲碁 上の「同情する」の英語は，いずれも相手に対する気持ちを表わしたもの. このうちで, feel pity [compassion] for sb の代わりに have [take] pity [compassion] on sb と言うと, 相手に手をさしのべてあげたいという意味が含まれてきて, I took pity on him and lent him 5,000 yen. といった文脈でよく使われる. また, I sympathize with you. と言えば相手に感謝されるだろうが I pity you. と言うと, I don't want your pity. といった反発を招きかねない.

どうじょう⁴　道場　an exercise [a training] hall ¶柔道の道場 a judo school / 道場破りをする make a challenge at a《kendo》hall and bring its members to their knees.

どうしょくぶつ　動植物　animals and plants ¶《ある地域または時代の》動植物相 the fauna and flora 《of Africa》.

とうじる　投じる　《投げる》throw; 《文》cast; 〈乗り出す〉plunge [launch] into《politics》; 《文》embark on《an enterprise》;〈仲間になる〉join; 〈資本などを〉invest 《in》; spend 《one's money on》 ¶一票を投じる cast a vote / 大金を投じて…を求める pay [give] a large sum for sth .

どうじる　動じる　be upset; be perturbed; be moved; be shaken ¶動じない be [《文》remain] unperturbed [unruffled]. 文例⇩

とうしん¹　刀身　the blade of a sword.

とうしん²　灯心　(a) wick.

とうしん³　投身　⇨みなげ. 文例⇩

とうしん⁴　答申　¶答申(書) a report / 答申する submit a report; report (back) the findings 《of the committee》to《the Prime Minister》.

とうしん⁵　等身　¶等身(大)の life-size(d); as large as life / 等身大よりも大きい銅像 a larger-than-life bronze statue.

とうじん　党人　a party man [member].

どうしん　童心　the mind [heart] of a child ¶童心を傷つける disillusion a child / 童心に帰る《文》retrieve one's childish innocence.

どうじん　同人　a member; 〈仲間〉《文》a coterie ¶同人雑誌 a (literary) coterie magazine.

どうしんえん　同心円　a concentric circle.

とうすい¹　陶酔　(intoxication; 《文》rapture ¶陶酔する be intoxicated [《文》enraptured] 《with》; be fascinated [carried away, transported] 《by》; be in [thrown into] ecstasies 《over》.

とうすい²　統帥　⇨とうそつ.

どうすいかん　導水管　an aqueduct.

---

stay with me for the present.

どうしょ¹ お手紙は同所あてに願います. Please direct your letters to the above address.

とうしょう 彼は顔をひどい凍傷にやられていた. He was suffering from a severe attack of frostbite on his face.

とうじょう² これがその小説に登場する女性たちです. These are the women who figure in the novel. | These are the female characters in the novel. | 老人学は比較的新しく登場した学問である. Gerontology is a fairly new arrival [is something of a newcomer] in the scientific field.

どうじょう³ 彼に心から同情した. He had my heartfelt sympathy. | My heart went out to him. | 彼女に同情が集まった. Everybody sympathized with her. | 彼はあまり同情されない. He doesn't get much sympathy. | 同情すべき人たちだ. They deserve our sympathy [pity]. | 我々は彼に大いに同情している. Our sympathy is very much with him.

どうじる 彼は何事にも動じなかった. Nothing rattled him.

とうしん³ 彼女はあの橋から投身自殺を図ったのです. She attempted to kill herself by jumping off [from] that bridge.

どうせ 彼はどうせ失敗するにきまっている. I'm sure that he'll fail. / どうせ助からないものならなんでも好きな物を食べさせるがいい. Let him eat what he likes, if there is no hope for his life [recovery]. / どうせ私は馬鹿ですよ. I know I am a fool; you don't have to tell me that.

とうせい¹ 当時, 政府のさまざまな経済統制が行なわれた. At that time, various government [governmental, state] controls were placed on the economy.

とうすう 頭数 the number (of head) (of livestock).

どうすう 同数 ¶同数の as many ((as)); 《文》of the same number.

とうすみとんぼ 〖昆〗 a damselfly.

どうせ 〈とにかく〉anyhow; at any rate; in any case; 〈結局〉after all; 〈精々〉at best; at most; 〈いやしくも〉at all ¶どうせ…するくらいなら if you do at all. 文例⇩

とうせい¹ 党勢 the strength [size] of a party ¶党勢を拡大する expand the party strength; 《文》enhance the party prestige.

とうせい² 陶製 ¶陶製の earthenware; 《文》earthen; ceramic.

とうせい³ 統制 control; regulation ¶統制する control; place sth under (government) control; 《文》exercise control over; regulate / (隊員などが)よく統制がとれている be well under control; be well disciplined / 統制を強化する tighten (the) control(s) (over) / 統制を緩和する relax [loosen, 《文》alleviate] (the) control(s) (over) / 統制を撤廃する lift [remove] the control(s) (over) / 統制価格[経済] controlled prices [economy]. 文例⇩

どうせい¹ 同姓 the same surname ¶同姓同名の人 a person with the same family and personal name.

どうせい² 同性 ¶同性の of the same sex / 同性愛 homosexual love; homosexuality; lesbianism (女性の).

どうせい³ 同棲 《文》cohabitation ¶同棲する live together; 《文》cohabit; 〈1人が主語〉live [cohabit] with sb.

どうせい⁴ 動静 movements (of the enemy); one's doings.

とうせき¹ 投石 ¶投石する throw [hurl, 《文》cast] a stone [rock] (at).

とうせき² 透析 〖化〗dialysis ¶透析治療 hemodialysis; extracorporeal dialysis.

とうせき³ 党籍 ¶党籍にある belong to [be a member of] a party; be on the list of party members / 党籍を離脱する leave 《文》secede from] the party; 《文》disaffiliate (oneself) from the party.

どうせき 同席 ¶同席する sit with sb; 〈レストランなどで〉share a table with sb / 同席の人 《文》those present. 文例⇩

とうせん¹ 当選 ¶当選する be elected; win the election; be returned ((to the Diet)); be voted into office / 当選の見込みがある[当選圏内に入っている] be in the running; have a fair chance of success / 当選確実である be sure to be [of being] elected / 当選者 a successful candidate; an elected person; those elected / 当選小説 a prize novel. 文例⇩

とうせん² 当籤 ¶当せんする win a prize; draw a winning [lucky] number / 1等に当せんする win first prize / 当せん者 a prize winner / 当せん番号 a winning [lucky] number.

とうぜん¹ ¶(酒に酔って)陶然となる get tipsy [pleasantly drunk, mellow] / 陶然として音楽を聞く listen enchantedly to music; be fascinated by the music.

とうぜん² 当然 ¶当然(に) naturally; justly; by rights; rightfully; as a matter of course; in the nature of things / 当然…だと思う take it for granted that… / 当然の natural; just; right; rightful; 〈当然受くべき〉deserved; due / 当然の事 a matter of course / 当然の結果 a natural [logical] result [outcome]; a foregone [logical] conclusion. 文例⇩

どうせん¹ 同船 ¶同船する take the same ship; be on [in] the same ship.

どうせん² 導線 a lead.

どうぜん 同然 ⇨ どうよう³. 文例⇩

どうぞ please; kindly; 〈ぜひ〉by all means; 〈たのまれたものを渡すとき〉Here you are. 文例⇩

とうそう¹ 逃走 《文》(a) flight; (an) escape ¶逃走する run away ((from, to)); escape; 《文》flee; make one's escape [getaway]; 《文》take to flight; make off / 逃走中である be on the run / 逃走用の車 a getaway car / 逃走者 a runaway; 《文》a fugitive.

とうそう² 闘争 《文》strife; a fight; (a) combat; 《文》a conflict; a struggle; 〈ストライキ〉a strike ⇨ ストライキ / 闘争委員会 a struggle [strike] committee / 闘争資金 a strike [fighting] fund / 闘争心 《文》combative spirit / 闘争本能をかき立てる arouse sb's fighting instincts [instinct for combat] / 闘争本部 the strikers' headquarters. 文例⇩

どうせい⁴ ご動静お知らせ下さい。Let me know how you are getting on.

とうせき 党籍というものには大きな意味をもつものと私は思っている。I believe that the party label means a great deal to the voters.

どうせき 私も同席した。I was (one of those) present.

とうせん¹ 山田さんがこの選挙区の衆議院議員に当選しました。Mr. Yamada was returned to the House of Representatives for [from] this constituency.

とうぜん² その財産は当然君のものだ。The property is of course yours. / そんなことは当然おわかりのはずだと思っていました。I took it for granted that you understood that. / 君が彼らを恐れるのは当然だ。It is natural that you should be afraid of them. / この名誉は当然あなたのものです。The credit is due to you. / あなたがそうおっしゃるのも当然です。You may well say so. / 彼には当然の罰だ。He deserves the punishment.

どうぜん それでは拒絶も同然だ。That amounts to a refusal. / 事は解決したも同然だ。The matter is as good as settled. / あんな奴に金をやるのは捨てるも同然だ。You might as well throw your money away as give it to a fellow like him. / 乞食同然の姿だった。He looked no [little] better than a beggar.

どうぞ ちょっとナイフを貸して下さい。—はい、どうぞ。Please lend me your knife.—Here you are [Yes, certainly]. / どうぞ戸を閉めて下さい。May I trouble you to shut the door? / 遊びに伺ってもよろしゅうございますか。—どうぞどうぞ。May I come and see you?—Yes, of course. [Yes, please do!]

とうそう² その時、彼は闘争的な気分になっていた。At that mo-

どうそう 同窓 ¶同窓である graduated from the same school ; 〈同期〉 was in school 《with》; 《英》 was at school 《with》; were at the same school / 同窓生 a schoolmate ; 〈卒業生〉 a graduate ; an old boy ; 《米》 an alumnus (*pl. -ni*) (男), 《米》 an alumna (*pl. -nae*) (女) / 同窓会〈組織〉《米》an alumni association ; 《英》an old boys' [girls'] association ; 〈会合〉a class reunion〈同年次の〉; 《米》an alumni meeting / 同窓会名簿 the membership list of an alumni association. 文例▷

どうぞう 銅像 a bronze statue.

とうそく 党則 the party rules [regulations].

とうぞく 盗賊 〈窃盗〉a thief ; 〈夜盗〉a burglar ¶とうぞくかもめ〖鳥〗a jaeger ; a skua.

どうぞく 同族 〈同種族〉the same race [tribe] ; 〈同家族〉the same family ¶同族会社〈家族の〉a family concern [firm] ; 〈同系の〉an affiliated concern / 同族目的語〖文法〗a cognate object.

どうそじん 道祖神 a roadside god.

とうそつ 統率 ¶統率する command ; lead ; direct ; take [《文》assume] the leadership of ; be in command [《文》at the head] of 《an army》/ 黒田将軍の統率する軍 the army under the command of General Kuroda / 統率者 a leader ; a commander / 統率力 (show good) generalship.

とうた 淘汰 〖生物〗selection ; 〈削減〉a cut(-back) (in staff) ; 《文》curtailment ¶淘汰する select ; weed out ; screen ; sift ; 〈削減する〉reduce the personnel of an office) ; curtail.

とうだい 灯台 a lighthouse ¶灯台船 a lightship / 灯台守 a lighthouse keeper. 文例▷

どうたい¹ 同体 ¶同体に落ちる fall down together.

どうたい² 胴体 the body ; the trunk ; 〈飛行機の〉the body ; the fuselage ¶胴体着陸をする make a belly landing ; belly-land.

どうたい³ 動態 movement (of the population).

どうたい⁴ 導体 a conductor (of heat [electricity]) ¶導体にする give conductivity 《to》.

どうたく 銅鐸 〖考古〗a bell-shaped bronze vessel of the Yayoi period, supposed to have been put to some ceremonial use.

とうたつ 到達 arrival ; 〈達成〉《文》attainment ¶到達する arrive at [in] ; reach ; get to ; 〈達成する〉《文》attain ; 《文》realize. 文例▷

とうだん 登壇 ¶登壇する take [《文》ascend, go on] the platform.

とうち¹ 当地 this place [district, city] ; here ¶ご当地の your place ; your part of the country.

とうち² 倒置 〖文法〗inversion ¶倒置文 an inverted sentence.

とうち³ 統治 rule ; 《文》reign ; government ¶統治する rule [《文》reign] (over) ; govern / …の統治下にある be under the rule of… / 統治者 the ruler ; 《文》the sovereign.

とうちゃく 到着 arrival ¶到着する arrive at [in] ; reach ; get to ; 〈手紙・荷物などが〉come to hand / 到着時刻 the arrival time / 到着次第 as soon as *one* arrives ; on arrival / 到着順に in order of arrival / 到着列車 an arriving train / 到着ホーム an arriving plaftform. 文例▷

どうちゃく¹ 同着 《文》simultaneous arrival ¶同着である arrive at the same time 《with》; reach [hit] the goal on the same instant.

どうちゃく² 撞着 ⇒ むじゅん.

とうちゅう 頭注 a headnote.

とうちょう¹ 盗聴 wire tapping ; a wiretap ¶盗聴する tap (a telephone wire) ; listen in (on the enemy's communications line) / 盗聴器 a listening microphone ; 《口語》a bug.

とうちょう² 登庁 ¶登庁する attend the office ; go to the office ; go to work.

とうちょう³ 登頂 ¶登頂する reach [get to] the summit [top] (of Mt. Everest).

どうちょう 同調 〖電〗tuning ¶同調する follow suit ; side 《with》; fall in 《with》; come into line 《with》/ (共産党の)同調者 a fellow traveler ; a sympathizer.

とうちょく 当直 ¶当直する be on (night) duty ; 〈海員が〉keep [be on] watch / 当直を交代する relieve the watch / (救急病院の)当直医 a duty doctor / 当直員 a person on duty [watch].

とうつう 疼痛 a pain ; an ache ⇒ いたみ.

とうてい 到底 《cannot》possibly ; (not) at all ; 〈全く〉utterly ; absolutely ⇒ とても. 文例▷

どうてい 童貞 virginity ; 〈人〉a virgin ¶童貞を守る keep [《文》preserve] *one's* virginity.

どうてき 動的 dynamic ; kinetic.

とうてききょうぎ 投擲競技 a throwing event.

---

ment, he was in a fighting mood.
どうそう 私たちは同窓です. We were at school together.
とうだい 灯台下暗し. We are apt to overlook important things that lie near at hand.
とうたつ このミサイルの最高到達距離は 4,500 キロメートルである. These missiles have ranges of up to 4,500 kilometers.
とうちゃく 彼は来月 10 日に到着します. He is expected here on the tenth of next month. / 彼は夕方の列車で到着します. He'll arrive on the evening train. / 列車の到着は午後 3 時です. The train is due in at 3 p.m.
どうちょう (映画・テレビで)音声と画面が同調していなかった. The sound and the picture were out of sync(h) [were poorly synchronized]. ★ sync(h) [siŋk] は synchronization の略.
とうてい それはとうてい不可能だ. It is absolutely [quite] impossible. / とうてい私の力では及ばないことだ. It is far beyond my powers. / その服はとうてい彼には合わない. That suit doesn't even begin to fit him.
どうでも 彼は人の言うことなどはどうでもいいと思っている. He doesn't care (about) what people say. / 彼の気に入ろうが入るまいがそんな事はどうでもいい. It makes no difference to me [I couldn't care less] whether it pleases him or not. / その後任を K 氏にするか M 氏にするかという問題に対して彼はどうでもいいという態度をとった. He took an indifferent attitude to the question of whether to choose Mr. K or Mr. M to fill the vacancy.
どうてん 試験の点数は田中君と同

とうてつ 透徹 ¶透徹した clear; penetrating;《文》lucid.
どうでも any way; anyhow; as one likes [pleases];〈ぜひとも〉⇒どうして(どうしても) ¶どうでもいい〈人が主語〉do not care (a bit [a straw]);〈about, if〉《口語》do not give a damn〈事が主語〉do not matter; be all the same《to one》. 文例⇩
とうてん 当店 this [our] store [shop]; we.
どうてん 同点 a tie;〈引き分け〉a draw ¶…と同点になる tie with…; tie [even] the score with…/同点に持ち込む gain a tie /〈野球で〉score the tying run / 同点で引き分けになる draw (with) / 3対3の同点で終わる finish [end] in a tie, 3 to 3; end as [in] a 3-all draw. 文例⇩
とうど 陶土 china clay; kaolin.
とうとい 尊[貴]い〈高貴な〉noble;《文》exalted;〈神聖な〉holy; sacred;〈貴重な〉precious; valuable.
とうとう¹ 滔々 ¶とうとうたる〈流水の〉rushing; rapid; swift;〈弁舌の〉eloquent; fluent / とうとうと swiftly;〈流暢の〉eloquently; fluently;《文》with fluency [eloquence] / とうとうとまくし立てる speak eloquently [fluently]; pour forth a flood of words / とうとうと流れている川 a river in flood.
とうとう² 到頭〈ついに〉at last [length]; finally;〈結局〉in the end; after all.
-とうとう …等々《文》etc., etc.; and so on; and so forth.
どうとう 同等 equality ¶同等の equal / 高等学校卒業または同等以上の学力ある者 a person with attainments equal to or higher than high-school graduates / 同等に equally; on an equal footing; on equal terms / 同等に扱う treat (them) equally; do not discriminate [make distinctions]《between》.
どうどう¹ 堂々 ¶堂々たる《文》stately; grand; magnificent;《文》majestic;〈正々堂々とした〉fair and square / 堂々たる邸宅を構えている live in an imposing house /《文》in a dignified manner /《文》majestically /〈あつかましくも〉shamelessly / 堂々たるすがた a dignified [an imposing] appearance / 堂々と戦う play fair.
どうどう² どうどうという音を立てて with a great [thunderous] roar; thunderingly.

どうどうめぐり 堂々巡り ¶堂々めぐりをする〈議論や話が〉go round in circles (and get nowhere);〈議会で〉file round to vote (in the Diet). 文例⇩
どうとく 道徳 morality; morals;《文》virtue ¶道徳的 moral;〈有徳の〉《文》virtuous / 道徳上 morally; from the moral point of view / 道徳観念 a moral sense / 道徳教育 moral education / 道徳律 a moral code.
とうとつ 唐突 ¶唐突な abrupt; sudden; unexpected /唐突に abruptly; suddenly; unexpectedly ⇒だしぬけ, とつぜん.
とうぶ 尊[貴]ぶ〈尊敬する〉respect; honor;《文》revere;〈尊重する〉value; prize;《文》esteem;《文》hold sth [sb] in high estimation.
とうどり 頭取 a president ¶銀行頭取の職を退く retire from the bank presidency.
とうない 党内 ¶党内の in [within] the party / 党内事情のため for party considerations.
どうなか 胴中 the trunk (of the body); one's middle. 「torsoed.
どうなが 胴長 ¶胴長の long-bodied; longとうなす 唐なす〈植〉a pumpkin.
とうなん¹ 東南 (the) southeast (略: SE) ¶東南の southeast; southeastern; southeasterly / 東南アジア Southeast Asia / 東南アジアの人々 Southeast Asians / 東南アジア諸国連合 the Association of Southeast Asian Nations (略: ASEAN) / 東南東 (the) east-southeast (略: ESE).
とうなん² 盗難 (a) robbery; (a) theft (こそ泥); (a) burglary (夜間の) ¶盗難にあう〈物が主語〉be stolen;〈家が主語〉be robbed; be burglarized /〈商店などの〉盗難による損失 pilferage (loss) / 盗難事件 a case of theft [burglary] / 盗難届を出す report a burglary [theft] to the police / 盗難品 a stolen article [object]; stolen goods / 盗難防止錠 an antitheft lock / 盗難保険 theft insurance / 盗難よけの antitheft (devices); burglarproof (doors). 文例⇩
とうに 疾うに ⇒とっくに.
どうにか《manage to do》somehow [in some way] (or other) ¶どうにかこうにか ⇒どうか(どうかこうか). 文例⇩
どうにも(こうにも) in any way (whatever);〈否定〉in no way.
とうにゅう¹ 投入 ¶投入する throw [《文》cast] sth in [into];〈資本を〉invest [sink] (money)

点だった. I got the same marks as Tanaka in the exam. | 第4位はジム, トム, マイクの3者が同点で分かち合った. There was a three-way tie for fourth place between Jim, Tom and Mike. / 彼は他の5選手と同点で第6位であった. He tied with five others for sixth place.
とうとう² 彼の帰りを待っているうちにとうとう夜が白み始めた. She sat waiting for his return, until the day began to break.
どうどう¹ 毛沢東は堂々とした感じの人だった. Mao Zedong had

considerable presence. | Mao Zedong was a man of great presence. / あの人は若いけれど, もう堂々たる重役です. Young as he is, he is already a director of a company in his own right. / 免許もないのに堂々と医者の看板を出していた. He had no license, but he hung out his shingle as a doctor, bold as brass.
どうどうめぐり 考えが堂々めぐりするばかりだった. I was just thinking in circles (and getting nowhere). / 議論は堂々めぐりになってらちがあかなかった. The

argument kept doubling back on itself and got nowhere.
とうなん² 昨夜彼女の家が盗難に遭った. There was a burglary at her house last night. | Her house was burglarized last night.
どうにか 親父の車を使ってもいいという許可をどうにか取りつけた. I got round my father and got him to let me use his car.
どうにも(こうにも) There is no help for it. / さすがのナポレオンでもそれはどうにもならなかった. Even Napoleon had no control over

とうにゅう¹ …… in ((factory equipment)). 文例⇩
とうにゅう² 豆乳 soymilk.
どうにゅう 導入 《文》 introduction; importation ¶導入する introduce; import / 外資の導入 introduction of foreign capital / 導入部《音楽》 the introduction; the introductory part.
とうにょうびょう 糖尿病《医》 diabetes ¶糖尿病患者 a diabetic.
とうにん 当人 ⇒ ほんにん.
とうねん 当年 〈本年〉 this year. 文例⇩
どうねん 同年 the same year; 〈年齢〉 the same age ⇒ おないどし ¶同年に in the same year; 〈その年に〉 in that year.
どうねんぱい 同年輩 ¶同年輩の仲間 a friend of about one's age / 同年輩である be about the same age (as).
とうは¹ 党派 a party; a faction (党中の) a clique (閥) ¶党派を組む form a faction [clique]; band together / 党派に関係なく[を問わず] regardless of party affiliation / 党派心[根性] party feeling [spirit]; partisan spirit; partisanship. 文例⇩
とうは² 踏破 ¶踏破する travel ((2,000 kilometers)) (completely on foot); traverse.
とうば 塔婆 a wooden symbol of a Buddhist stupa (set up behind a tomb).
どうはい 同輩 one's equal;《文》a peer; a colleague / one's contemporary (同年輩).
とうはつ 頭髪 the hair (of the [one's] head); one's (head) hair ⇒ かみ⁴.
とうばつ¹ 討伐《文》subjugation ¶討伐する《文》subjugate; put down.
とうばつ² 盗伐 ¶盗伐する cut down somebody else's trees.
とうはん 登攀 ¶登攀する climb (up); scale;《文》make the [an] ascent of.
とうばん¹ 当番 duty; watch; 〈人〉 a person on duty [watch] ¶当番である be on duty [watch]; be on a shift (交替制の). 文例⇩
とうばん² 登板 ¶登板する《野球》take the plate [mound]; go to the mound.
どうはん 同伴 ¶同伴する 〈…を伴う〉 have [let] sb go with one;《文》be accompanied by sb; 〈…といっしょに行く〉 go with sb;《文》accompany sb / 妻を同伴して with [accompanied by] one's wife / 同伴者 one's companion; one's partner.
どうばん 銅版 a copperplate; 〈画〉 a copperplate print ¶銅版彫刻 copperplate engraving.

とうひ¹ 当否 〈是非〉 right or wrong; justice / 〈適否〉《文》propriety; fitness ¶その措置の当否を論じる discuss whether the step should have been taken or not; argue about [over] the propriety of the measure.
とうひ² 逃避 (an) escape;《文》(a) flight ¶資本の逃避 a flight of capital / 逃避する escape; flee / 逃避主義 escapism / 逃避主義者 an escapist / 逃避文学 escapist literature.
とうひ³ 党費 〈党の出費〉 party expenses (expenditure); 〈党員として納入する〉 a party membership fee.
とうひきゅうすう 等比級数【数】a geometric(al) series ¶等比級数的に増加する increase in (a) geometric progression; 〈通俗に〉 increase geometrically. 文例⇩
とうひょう 投票 voting; ballot(ing); a poll; 〈票〉 a vote; a (paper) ballot ¶投票する vote (for, against); ballot; cast a ballot / Y 氏に投票する vote [cast one's vote] for [in favor of] Mr. Y; give one's vote to Mr. Y / 社会党[保守党]に投票する vote Socialist [Conservative] / 投票の結果 the voting results / 投票に付する[かける] put (a bill) to the vote;《文》submit (a question) to a ballot; take a vote [ballot] (on a question) / 投票で定める decide by vote [ballot] / 投票権 the right to vote; (exercise) one's voting power / 投票者 a voter / 投票所 a polling place [station];《米》(go to) the polls / 投票総数 the total number of votes cast / 投票立会人 a voting witness / 投票箱 a ballot box / 投票日 a voting day / 投票用紙 a ballot (paper); a voting paper / 投票率 the voting rate ((of women, among the young)). 文例⇩
とうびょう¹ 投錨 ¶投錨する anchor; drop [cast] anchor; come to anchor / 投錨している lie [be] at anchor / 投錨地 an anchorage.
とうびょう² 闘病 a fight [struggle] against a disease ¶闘病生活をする live fighting [carry on a struggle] against one's disease ((for ten years)); live under medical treatment.
どうひょう 道標 a signpost; a guidepost ¶道標の完備したハイキングコース a well-signposted hiking trail. 文例⇩
どうびょう 同病
とうひん 盗品 a stolen article; stolen goods.
とうふ 豆腐 tofu; soybean [bean] curd; a bean-

---

it. / 腹が空いてどうにもこうにもならない. I am so hungry I don't know what to do. / ひどいぶちこわしな事を言ってしまったからには, 彼はもうどうにも取り返しがつかなかった. Once he had made that devastating remark, the matter was completely past mending, past recall. / あの男は怠け者でどうにもならない. He is hopelessly lazy.
とうにゅう¹ アメリカはその戦闘に5個師団を投入した. The U.S. committed five divisions to the battle.
とうねん 彼女は当年とって 20 歳です. She is twenty (years old) this year.
とうは¹ その案は党派を越えた広い支持を得た. The proposal gained wide support that crossed party lines.
とうばん¹ 明日は君の当番だ. It's your shift [your turn to be on duty] tomorrow.
とうひきゅうすう マルサスによれば人口は等比級数的にふえるが, 生活資財は等差級数的にしかふえない. According to Malthus, whereas population tends to increase in geometric progression, its means of subsistence increases only in arithmetical progression.
とうひょう 投票の結果賛成 20 反対 15 だった. The vote was 20 ayes and 15 noes. / 彼らはこぞって社会党に投票した. They voted solid Socialist. / 会員は平等な投票権を持っている. Each member has an equal vote. / 彼は投票数の4分の1を得たに過ぎなかった.

とうぶ¹ 東部 the eastern part; the east;〈米国の〉the East ¶東部の eastern.

とうぶ² 頭部 the head; the head area (of a worm) ¶頭部に負傷する be wounded in the head.

どうふう 同封 ¶同封する enclose《a letter》/ 同封の書類 the enclosed papers / 同封物 enclosures / 同封で under the same cover. 文例⇩

どうぶつ 動物 an animal; a beast (獣) ¶動物的な brutal;《文》bestial / 動物性蛋白質 (an) animal protein / 動物愛護協会 the Society for the Prevention of Cruelty to Animals / 動物園 a zoo; zoological gardens / 動物園長 a zoo director / 動物園の虎 a tiger in a zoo / 動物画 an animal painting / 動物学 zoology / 動物学者 a zoologist / 動物界 the animal kingdom / 動物行動学 ethology / 動物質 animal matter / 動物実験 experiments on [with, using] animals / 動物相 the fauna《of Africa》/ 動物地理学 zoogeography; animal geography. 文例⇩

とうぶん¹ 等分 ¶等分する divide equally [in equal parts]; share (the profits) equally《with》/ 2等分する ⇒ にとうぶん / 3等分する ⇒ さんとうぶん / 4等分する divide into quarters.

とうぶん² 糖分 (the amount of) sugar; sugar content ¶糖分の多い食べ物 sugar-rich foods / 糖分の少ないぶどう grapes low in sugar. 文例⇩

とうぶん³ 当分 〈今の所〉for the present; for the time being;〈しばらくの間〉for some time (to come); for a while [time];〈一時〉temporarily. 文例⇩

どうぶん 同文 《with》the same wording; 《of》an identical text ¶同文の手紙を2通出す send a letter in duplicate. 文例⇩

とうへき 盗癖 (have) thievish habits;《口語》(have) sticky fingers;〈病気〉kleptomania ¶盗癖のある人 a kleptomaniac.

とうへん 等辺《数》¶等辺の equilateral《polygons》.

とうべん 答弁 a reply; an answer; an explanation (弁明); a defense (被告の) ¶答弁する reply; answer; make a reply; give an answer;〈弁護する〉defend [explain] oneself;《文》speak in defense《of》/ …に対する答弁として in answer to… / 答弁を求める demand an explanation《from sb》/ 答弁をしひかえる《文》reserve one's answer《on》.

とうへんぼく 唐変木 an insensitive fellow; a blockhead.

とうほう¹ 当方 I; we ¶当方の my; our; on my [our] part / 当方の手落ちで《文》my error;《文》an oversight on our part.

とうほう² 東方 the east ¶東方の east; eastern; easterly / 東方に to the east 《of》/ 東方へ toward the east; eastward. 文例⇩

とうほう 逃亡 (an) escape;《文》(a) flight ⇒ とうそう¹ ¶逃亡する《文》flee; fly; run away; escape [《文》abscond]《from》/ 逃亡者 a runaway;《文》a fugitive; an escapee.

どうほう 同胞 a (fellow) countryman; a compatriot.

とうほく 東北 (the) northeast (略：NE) ¶東北の northeast; northeastern; northeasterly / 東北地方 the Tohoku region / 東北東 (the) east-northeast (略：ENE).

とうぼく 倒木 a fallen tree.

とうほん 謄本 a (certified) copy; a transcript; a duplicate.

とうほんせいそう 東奔西走 ¶東奔西走する busy oneself《about sth》; be (constantly) on the move. 文例⇩

どうまき 胴巻き a money belt.

どうまごえ 胴間声 a thick harsh voice ¶胴間声を張り上げる raise one's voice loud and raucously.

どうまわり 胴回り《文》one's girth; one's waist measurement ¶胴回りが太くなる grow fat round the middle / 胴回りが70センチある measure 70 centimeters around the waist [in girth].

とうみつ 糖蜜 syrup (純粋); golden syrup (純度がやや低い);〈低純度〉《米》molasses《単数扱い》;《英》(black) treacle.

どうみゃく 動脈 an artery ¶動脈血 arterial blood / 動脈硬化 arteriosclerosis; hardening [sclerosis] of the arteries / 動脈瘤 an aneurysm. 文例⇩

とうみょう 灯明 a votive light ¶灯明を上げる offer a light《before the altar》.

とうみん¹ 冬眠 hibernation ¶冬眠する hibernate / 冬眠している be hibernating; be in hibernation / 冬眠に入る go [enter] into hibernation / 冬眠からさめる come out of hibernation.

He polled only a quarter of the votes cast.

どうひょう 道標があって、「左筑波山」と書いてあった。There was a signpost which read: 'Turn left for Mt. Tsukuba'.

どうびょう 同病相憐れむ。Fellow sufferers pity one another.

どうふう 200ドルの小切手を同封します。We are enclosing [Enclosed please find] a check for two hundred dollars.

どうぶつ 人間は社会的動物である。Man is a social animal.

とうぶん² ぶどう糖が体に糖分が欠乏したときに疲労回復に役立つ。Dextrose helps to overcome fatigue when one's body sugar is low.

とうぶん³ 当分それで間に合う。That will do for the present. / ここ当分雨はあるまい。It will not rain for some time.

どうぶん ぶん同文 wording thereafter [for the rest].

とうほう² その山は市の東方30キロのところにある。The mountain stands thirty kilometers (to the) east of the city.

とうほんせいそう 町長は工場誘致のため東奔西走している。The mayor is busy going here and there, visiting people, trying to persuade an industrial company to set up its plant in the town.

どうみゃく 国鉄はわが国産業の動脈とされていた。The national railways were regarded as the industrial arteries of the country. / 市政は動脈硬化に陥っていた。The city administration has become too inflexible [too set in

とうみん² 島民 an inhabitant [a native] of an island; an islander ¶小笠原諸島の島民 the inhabitants of the Ogasawara Islands.

とうめい 透明 transparency;《文》pellucidity ¶透明な transparent; clear;《文》limpid;《文》pellucid;《文》lucid / 湖水の透明度を計る measure the clarity of the water in the lake / 透明人間 an invisible man.

どうめい¹ 同名 the same name ¶同名の人 a person with [《文》of] the same name; one's namesake. 文例⇩

どうめい² 同盟 〈条約〉an alliance;〈連合〉union; a league ¶同盟する [を結ぶ] form [《文》enter into] an alliance《with》;《文》be allied《with》; unite / 同盟国 an ally; an allied power. 文例⇩

どうめいし 動名詞《文法》a gerund.

とうめん 当面 for the present; for the moment; for the time being / 当面の〈現在の〉present;〈差し迫った〉urgent; pressing / 当面の急務 an urgent [a burning, a pressing] question; the question that confronts one;《文》a problem calling for immediate solution [attention] / 当面の問題 the question of the moment [《文》hour]; the matter [question] in hand.

どうも 文例⇩

どうもう 獰猛 ¶どうもうな fierce; ferocious; savage / どうもうな顔付きをしている look fierce.

とうもく 頭目 a chief; a leader; a boss;〈悪事の〉a ringleader.

とうもろこし【植】maize; Indian corn;《米》corn ¶とうもろこしの皮 cornhusk / とうもろこしの毛 corn silk [floss] / とうもろこしの穂軸 a corncob; a cob / とうもろこしを栽培する cultivate corn (plants) / とうもろこし畑 a cornfield.

どうもん 同門 ¶同門の弟子 a fellow pupil.

とうやく 投薬 ¶投薬する give [《文》administer] (a dose of) medicine to 《a patient》;〈処方を与える〉prescribe (a medicine) for 《a disease》/ 過剰投薬 excessive dosing [medication]; overdosage / 過剰投薬する overdose.

どうやら ⇨どうか³(どうかこうか), たぶん². 文例⇩

とうゆ 灯油《米》kerosene;《英》paraffin (oil).

とうよ 投与 ⇨とうやく.

とうよう¹ 当用 ¶当用漢字 Chinese characters (designated) for daily use / 当用日記 a diary.

とうよう² 東洋 the East;《文》the Orient ¶ の Eastern; Oriental; of the East [Orient] / 東洋学 Oriental studies / 東洋学者 an Orientalist / 東洋区【生物】the Oriental region [realm] / 東洋史 Oriental history / 東洋人 Oriental / 東洋文明 Oriental civilization / 東洋風の Oriental / 東洋風にする Orientalize.

とうよう³ 盗用 embezzlement;《文》misappropriation;〈特許の〉theft;《文》illegal use ¶盗用する〈金銭を〉appropriate 《public money to one's own use》; embezzle;〈物を〉steal; make (a) fraudulent use of 《sb's registered design》.

とうよう⁴ 登用〔任用〕 (an) appointment;《文》(an) assignment;〈昇任〉(a) promotion ¶登用する appoint [《文》assign] 《sb to a position》;〈昇任させる〉promote 《sb to a higher position》.

どうよう¹ 動揺 shaking; trembling;《文》quaking;〈船の〉roll; rolling (よこゆれ); pitching (たてゆれ);〈不安〉unrest; restlessness;〈騒ぎ〉a stir; (a) disturbance ¶動揺する shake; tremble; quake; stir; jolt (車が); pitch and roll (船が);〈心が〉be unsettled; be agitated;〈決心が〉waver;〈迷う〉《文》vacillate《between》;〈世間が〉be disturbed / 動揺を来たす〈事が〉cause [create] unrest;〈人が〉get [《文》become] restless; get shaken.

どうよう² 童謡 a children's song; a nursery song ¶マザーグース童謡集 Mother Goose's Nursery Rhymes.

どうよう³ 同様 ¶同様の the same; similar《to》;《文》like (examples); of the same kind [sort] / 同様に similarly;《文》likewise; alike; equally; in the same way《as》;〈...もまた〉also; too / 新品同様である be as good as new / 兄弟同様にする treat sb like a brother. 文例⇩

とうらい 到来 ¶到来する come; arrive;〈機会が〉present [offer] itself / 時節の到来を待つ wait for an opportunity; bide one's time / 到来物 a present; a gift. 文例⇩

とうらく¹ 当落 one's electoral fortunes; success (or defeat) in an election; the result of an election. 文例⇩

とうらく² 騰落 rise and fall; fluctuations.

どうらく 道楽〈趣味〉a hobby; a pastime;

---

its ways].

どうめい¹ その人は同名異人とわかりました. It turned out to be a different person of the same name.

どうめい² 日本はかつて英国と同盟国でした. Japan and England used to be allies.

どうも どうもよく降るねえ. How it rains!／この間はどうも. Thank you for the other day.／どうもありがとう. Thank you very much.／Thanks a lot.／かばんをお持ちしましょう.—やあ, どうもすみません. Let me carry your bag.— Oh, thank you.／どうもあいつのしわざらしい. It does seem to be his doing.／It appears that he did it.／どうも会ったことのある人だと思った. I was sure I had met him somewhere before.／どうも英語はむずかしい. English is really very difficult for me to learn.／どうもそんなふうに思われて仕方がないんです. I don't know why, but I can't help thinking that way.

どうやら どうやら晴れそうだ. The weather seems likely to clear up.／どうやらあいつは金を持っているらしい. Something tells me that he's got some money.

どうよう 私は九州の人間です.—私も同様です. I am [come] from Kyushu.—So am [do] I.／君は酒をやらないんだね. 僕もご同様なんだ. You don't drink? Neither do I.／姉は猫がきらいなのですが, 私も同様です. My sister doesn't like cats, and I don't, either.／その点, 彼も同様だ. That goes for him, too.／The same thing can be said of him.／私もご同様の境遇です. I am in a similar situation.／他の恒星の

どうらん one's favorite amusement [diversion]; 〈熱狂〉 a mania; 〈好事〉《文》dilettantism; 〈放蕩〉《文》dissipation ¶道楽をする lead a dissipated [fast] life;《口語》sow one's wild oats (若い時に); have some fun / 道楽に《do》as a hobby [for mere pleasure] / 道楽者 a fast liver; a playboy. 文例⇩

どうらん 〈植物採集の〉a botanical [collecting] case.

どうらん[1] 胴乱 a disturbance; a riot; an upheaval; 〈戦争〉a war ¶動乱を起こす rise in riot / 動乱の中東《文》the strife-torn Middle East.

とうり 党利 party interests ¶党利党略を事とする政治 partisan politics / 党利党略に走る be overinfluenced by party interests; pursue party interests (at the expense of those of the nation).

どうり 道理 reason (条理); justice (正義);《文》right (正当); truth (真理) ¶道理の[にかなった]《文》reasonable; right / 道理を聞き分けない《文》be impervious to reason / 道理にかなう stand to reason; be reasonable / 道理にかなわない be unreasonable; be against [《文》contrary to] reason / 道理で《なるほど》indeed; no wonder. 文例⇩

どうりきがく 動力学 dynamics; kinetics.

とうりつ 倒立 ⇒さかだち ¶倒立飛び込み《水上競技》a handstand dive; handstand diving.

とうりゃく 党略 ⇒とうり (党利党略).

とうりゅう 逗留 ⇒たいざい.

とうりゅうもん 登竜門 a gateway to success (in a career);《文》a narrow opening to highly-prized membership (of a profession). 文例⇩

とうりょう[1] 当量 《物・化》an equivalent ¶化学当量 a chemical equivalent / 熱の仕事当量 the mechanical equivalent of heat.

とうりょう[2] 投了 《囲碁・将棋》¶投了する resign; give up the game for lost.

とうりょう[3] 棟梁 a master builder [carpenter].

とうりょう[4] 等量 the same [equal] quantity ¶等量の the same quantity of…;《文》of the same quantity;《文》equal in quantity.

とうりょう[5] 頭領 a chief; a leader; a boss; a chieftain.

どうりょう 同僚 a colleague; a fellow worker.

どうりょく 動力 (motive) power ¶動力の供給 supply of power / …に動力を供給する supply power 《to》; power 《a factory》/ 動力で動く道具 a power(-driven) tool / 動力計 a dynamometer / 動力源 a source of power; a power source / 動力線 a power line.

どうりん 動輪 a driving [drive] wheel; a driver.

とうるい[1] 盗塁 《野球》base stealing ¶盗塁する steal a base / 三塁に盗塁する steal third / (スコアブックの記入)盗塁33 stolen bases (略: s.b. 3).

とうるい[2] 糖類 《化》a saccharide.

どうるい 同類 the same kind [class, category]; 〈共謀者〉an accomplice ¶同類の《文》of the same class; similar / 同類項《数》like [similar] terms. 文例⇩

とうれい 答礼 a return salute ¶答礼する return a salute.

どうれつ 同列 the same rank [file] ¶同列に置く deal with 《A》on the same basis as 《B》.

どうろ 道路 a road; 〈街路〉a street; 〈大通り〉《文》a thoroughfare; a highway ¶道路建設 road construction [building] / 道路工事 road works [repairs, repair work]; street improvement / 道路交通法 the Road Traffic Act / 道路地図 a road [highway] map / 道路標識 a road [traffic] sign.

とうろう 灯籠 a (garden) lantern ¶灯籠流し sending off the spirits of the dead on lanterns floated on the waters of a river or the sea (on the last day of the Bon Festival).

とうろく 登録 registration; entry ¶登録する register; enter; put on record; enroll oneself (in a class) / 登録意匠 a registered design / 登録商標 a registered trademark / 登録制する istration system / 登録番号 a registration number / 登録簿 a register / 登録料 a registration fee.

とうろん 討論 (a) debate; (a) discussion ¶活発な討論 a lively discussion; a hot debate / 討論をする debate (a question with sb, about sth); discuss (a question with sb, what to do, how to do);《文》dispute 《about》; hold a debate (on a subject) / 盛んに討論された問題 a much-debated question / 討論に付する put (a question) to debate / 討論を打ち切る close the debate / 討論会 a debate; a (panel) discussion / 5党首テレビ討論会 a TV debate between the heads of the five political parties.

どうわ 童話 〈おとぎ話〉a fairy [nursery] tale; 〈子供のための物語〉a childrens' [juvenile]

面温度も同様にして計測された. The surface temperatures of other stars were also measured in a similar way [by similar methods]. / 僕も君と同様無経験だ. I have no more experience than you. / 2人は兄弟と同様だ. The two are like brothers.

とうらい いよいよ時節到来だ. The time has come at last.

とうらく 氏の当着は京都市部の票で決まる. His election [Whether he will win the election or not] depends on the votes in the Kyoto City area.

どうらく この仕事は道楽でやっているのではありません、生活のためです. I'm not doing this job for fun; it's my living.

どうり あの男に道理をわからせようとしても無駄だ. It's no use trying to make him see reason. / だからといって学校を休んでよいという道理はない. That isn't [doesn't have] sufficient reason to stay away from school. / 彼が驚いたのも道理だ. It is natural that he should have been surprised. / 道理で君は彼を弁護すると思った. Now I see why you spoke in favor of him.

とうりゅうもん このコンクールは多くの音楽家の登竜門となってきた. Success in this contest has been the first step to a successful career for a number of musicians.

どうるい 彼らはみんなあいつと同類だ. They are none of them any different from him.

どうろ この辺は道路事情が悪い. The roads are bad around here.

とうろく 登録済.【標記】Registered. / その意匠は特許局に登録されている. The design is registered with the Patent Office.

とうわく 当惑 perplexity;《文》embarrassment ¶当惑する be perplexed;《文》be embarrassed; be puzzled; be baffled; be put out; be in a fix [dilemma]; be (put) in a difficult position; be at a loss 《as to》what to do); be at *one's* wits' end / 当惑させる《文》embarrass; puzzle; perplex / 当惑した様子で with a perplexed [bewildered] look [air]. 文例⇩

とえ 十重 tenfold.

とえい 都営 ¶都営住宅 a municipally owned house / 都営バス a metropolitan bus.

どえらい ど偉い immense; enormous; awesome; terrific.

とお 十 ten ¶10ぐらいの男の子 a boy about ten years old.

とおあさ 遠浅 ¶遠浅になっている be shallow to a considerable distance from the shore; slope gently away from the water's edge.

とおい 遠い far;《文》distant;《文》remote; faraway; far-off ★肯定平叙文では far は《文》なので、その代わりに a long way と言うことが多い。It is quite a long way. (かなり遠い) / Is it far? (遠いですか) / It isn't far. (遠くはない) / 遠い国 a faraway country; a distant province / 遠い所に, 遠くに far away [off]; a long way off;《文》afar; in the distance / ここからほど遠からぬ所に not far from here / 遠くから from far [a long way] away;《文》from afar /《文》from a great distance / 遠い昔《文》remote antiquity; the old far-off days / 遠い遠い昔から《文》from time immemorial / 遠い親類 a distant [remote] relative / 遠い将来 in the remote [far-off] future / もっと遠い将来に farther in the future / 遠く及ばない《文》be greatly [far] inferior (to). 文例⇩

トーイン〘自動車〙toe-in.

とおえん 遠縁《文》a distant [remote] relationship ¶遠縁の人 a distant relative;《文》a remote kinsman / 遠縁に当たる be distantly related to *one*.

とおか 十日 〈10日目〉the tenth day; 〈10日間〉(for) ten days.

とおからず(して) 遠からず(して) soon; shortly; before long; in the near future. 文例⇩

とおく 遠く ⇨とおい.

トーゴ (the Republic of) Togo.

とおざかる 遠ざかる go away (from); withdraw (from);《文》recede (from); 〈音が〉die away; grow faint; 〈近寄らない〉keep away (from); 〈文〉hold [stand, keep] aloof (from); 〈疎遠になる〉《文》be [become] estranged [alienated] (from); drift apart (from each other). 文例⇩

とおざける 遠ざける 〈近づけない〉keep *sb* at a distance [at arm's length]; keep clear of; shun;《文》〈節制する〉abstain from (drinking); 〈超然とする〉《文》hold *oneself* aloof (from) ¶人を遠ざけて密談をする have a talk behind closed doors / 悪友を遠ざける avoid [keep away from] bad company.

とおし 通し ¶通しの through / 通し切符 a through ticket / 通し番号 serial numbers.

-どおし …通し ¶しゃべり通しにしゃべる keep talking all the time. 文例⇩

トーシューズ〘バレー〙blocked (ballet) shoes;〘米〙toe shoes.

とおす 通〈徹, 透〉す 〈通らせる〉let *sb* pass [pass, allow] *sth* through; 〈入れる〉let *sb* in; admit; 〈案内する〉show [usher, conduct] *sb* in [into (a room)]; 〈貫通する〉put (a needle) through; pierce; penetrate; 〈浸透する〉permeate; 〈濾過(か)する〉filter; 〈貫徹する〉carry *sth* through [out]; keep [stick, hold fast] to 《*one's* principles》; force 《*one's* opinion》through (the meeting); 〈続ける〉keep *doing*; continue 《at, to do》; remain (状態を); 〈振りをする〉pose 《as》; pass *oneself* off 《for, as》¶道を開けて通す make way [room] for *sb* / 管に水を通す let [run] water through a pipe / 水を通さない be waterproof; be watertight /〈物が〉可視光線を通す[通さない] be transparent [opaque] to visible light / 独身で通す remain single all *one's* life / 1枚の着物で通す wear the same clothes (all through the year) / 一晩中泣き通す do not stop crying all night; keep crying all night / 3日通して for three

---

とうわく なんと言って返事したらよいのか彼はすっかり当惑してしまった。He was completely at a loss for a (suitable) reply. / これには彼も当惑した。He was stumped by this.

とえ その周囲には十重二十重の人垣が出来ていてとても近寄れなかった。I was fenced off from it by a thick wall of spectators.

とおい 乙女座の星団はアンドロメダ星雲の16.5倍も遠い。The Virgo cluster is 16.5 times as far away [as distant] as the Andromeda Nebula. / その町の遠く北に1つの山が見える。A mountain is visible far to the north of the town. / 明かりが遠くに見えた。A light was [could be] seen in the distance. / その爆発音は遠くまで聞こえた。The explosion could be heard a long way off. / ここからは遠く大島が見える。We can get a distant view of Oshima Island from here. / 遠く離れた空港から都心までは長時間電車に乗らなければならない。It requires a long train ride to get to the heart of the city from the outlying airport. / この法律が廃止されるのも遠い先のことではあるまい。It will not be very long before this law is abolished. / 遠い親類より近い他人。A good neighbor is better than a brother far off.

とおからず(して) テレビ電話が日常使うようになる日も遠からず来るだろう。The day is not far distant when the TV phone will come into daily use. / 彼の病気も遠からず全快するだろう。He will recover before long. / It will not be long before he gets well.

とおざかる 遠ざかる馬の蹄の音に彼はじっと耳を傾けていた。He stood listening to the sound of the hoofs as it faded away into the night.

-どおし 電車がこんでずっと立ち通しでした。The train was so crowded that I had to stand all the way.

とおす (お客様を)お通ししなさい。Show [Send] him in. / ビーズ玉が10個金線に通してある。Ten beads are threaded on (to) a wire. / この壁は熱を

days running [on end] / …の手を通して through *sb*. [文例⇩]

トースター a toaster ¶自動トースター an automatic [a pop-up] toaster.

トースト toast ¶何もつけてないトースト dry toast / トースト2枚 two slices of toast / トーストにする toast《bread》/ バタートースト buttered toast.

とおせんぼう 通せん坊 ¶通せん坊をする bar *sb's* way ; stand [get] in *sb's* way.

トーダンス a toe dance ; toe-dancing.

トーチ a torch ¶金属切断用トーチ a metal-cutting torch / 溶接用トーチランプ a welding torch.

とおで 遠出 ¶遠出する go a long way ;《文》go to a distant place ; go for an outing.

トーテム〘人類〙a totem ¶トーテムポール a totem pole.

ドーナ(ッ)ツ a doughnut.

トーナメント a《lawn tennis》tournament ¶トーナメントに優勝する win a tournament.

とおのく 遠のく《文》become distant ; go off [《文》recede] into the distance ; 〈音が〉die away in the distance ¶足が遠のく come [visit] less often [《文》frequently] (than before) ; 〈近寄らない〉keep away《from》/ 遠のける keep *sb* at a distance [at arm's length] ; give *sb* a wide berth. [文例⇩]

とおのり 遠乗り ¶遠乗りする have a long drive [ride] ; drive [ride] a long way.

とおぼえ 遠吠え howling ; a howl (ひと吠え) ¶遠吠えする howl. [文例⇩]

とおまき 遠巻き ¶遠巻きにする make a wide circle around *sb* [*sth*] ; surround《the enemy》at a distance.

とおまわし 遠回し ¶遠回しな indirect ; roundabout / 遠回しに言う hint《at》; suggest ; drop *sb* a hint ; say *sth* in a roundabout way ;《文》allude [make an allusion]《to》; refer indirectly《to》; beat about the bush ;《文》use circumlocution.

とおまわり 遠回り a roundabout way ; a detour ¶遠回りする go a long way round ; take [go by] a roundabout way ; make a detour ;《文》take a circuitous route. [文例⇩]

とおみ 遠見 〈遠景〉a distant view ¶遠見がきく〈場所が〉《文》command a wide view [prospect] ; 〈人が〉⇨とおめ.

ドーム a dome.

とおめ 遠目 ¶遠目がきく be able to see a long way [far into the distance] / 遠目には (when viewed [looked at]) from a distance. [文例⇩]

ドーラン [<《ドイツ語》*Dohran*(会社名)] grease paint.

とおり[1] 通り 〈街路〉a street ;《文》a thoroughfare ; 〈道路〉a road ; 〈空気などの〉passage ; 〈種類〉a kind ; a sort ; a variety ; 〈方法〉a way ; a manner ¶通りがいい〈ことばが〉be more understandable ; 〈管などが〉draw well ; 〈水はけが〉drain well / 通りを通る go along [walk down] a street / 通りで《米》on the street ;《英》in the street. [文例⇩]

とおり[2] 通り ¶(…の)とおりの like ; the same…《as》/ …どおりに as ; like ; 〈…の仕方で〉《文》in the way [manner] of ; 〈…にしたがって〉according to ; 〈…にならって〉after / いつものとおり as usual / ご承知[ご覧]のとおり as you know [see] / 約束どおり as promised ; true to *one's* promise / 予定どおりに as scheduled ; according to schedule / 時間どおりに on time ; punctually / 予想どおりになる come [measure] up to *one's* expectations / 言葉どおりに信じる take *sb* at *his* word / 言われたとおりにする do as *one* is told ; follow *sb's* advice ; go along [《文》comply] with *sb's* request ; obey *sb's* order(s). [文例⇩]

とおりあめ 通り雨 a passing rain ; a shower.

とおりあわせる 通り合わせる ⇨**とおりかかる**.

とおりいっぺん 通り一遍 ¶通り一遍の passing ; casual ; 〈形式的〉formal ; 〈お役目だけの〉perfunctory ; 〈おきまりの〉conventional / 通り一遍の観察 (a) superficial [casual] observation / 通り一遍の客 a chance [stray] customer / 通り一遍の視察 a perfunctory inspection. [文例⇩]

とおりがかり 通り掛かり ¶通りがかりに as *one* passes / 通りがかりの人 a passer-by《*pl.* passers-by》/ お通りがかりの節は when you

---

通さない. This wall keeps out heat. / だれもかれも反対したけれども, 彼は最後まで頑張り通した. Everybody was against him, but he refused to budge an inch, right to the end. / 芝居は40日間通して上演された. The play ran for [had a run of] forty days. / この書類は副社長を通さなくてはいけない. These papers must be routed through the vice-president.

とおのく 船の姿がだんだん遠のいていった. The ship gradually receded from view.

とおぼえ 犬の遠吠えが聞こえた. I heard a dog howling in the distance. / そんなことを言っていても犬の遠吠えで始まらない. じかに行って談判したらいいじゃないか. It's no good complaining like a dog whining in a corner. Why not go straight to him and have it out with him?

とおまわり ずいぶん遠回りをした. We have come a very long way round. / それでは遠回りになる. That's a long way round [a roundabout route]. | It's farther (if you go) that way.

とおめ ここの景色は遠目には美しく見えるのだ. It's the distance that makes the view so attractive. / ワシやタカの類は驚くほど遠目がきく. Eagles and hawks can see for amazing distances.

とおり[1] 僕のパイプは通りが悪くなった. My pipe has begun to draw badly. / やり方が2通りある. There are two ways of doing it.

とおり[2] 冗談に言ったのがとうとうそのとおりになった. What I said as a joke ended up coming true. / 全くそのとおりです. You are quite right. / どうだい, 僕の言ったとおりだろう. Didn't I tell you so? / 私が期待したとおりだった. It was just as I had expected.

とおりいっぺん 彼の演説はほんの通り一遍のことを述べたにとどまった. His speech contained little more than platitudes. / その件についてはまだ通り一遍の話しか聞いていません. I haven't yet heard anything more than a rough outline of the case.

とおりかかる 通り掛かる happen [chance] to pass (by); come along.
とおりこす 通り越す go [walk] beyond [past]; pass (a place). 文例↓
とおりすがり 通りすがり ¶通りすがりの passing; (men) that happen to pass by [come along] / 通りすがりの人 a passer-by 《pl. passers-by》/ 通りすがりに when passing.
とおりすぎる 通り過ぎる go past [by]; pass (a place). 文例↓
とおりそうば 通り相場 an accepted price [standard].
とおりぬける 通り抜ける go [pass, get] through; trespass through 《sb's property》(不法に); 〈横断する〉cut across (a place). 文例↓
とおりま 通り魔 a phantom killer (robber); a man who wantonly knifes a passer-by.
とおりみち 通り道 a path; a passage; a route; a way; 〈動物の〉a trail ¶学校へ行く通り道にある be [(文)lie] on one's way to school / 通り道に立つ[のじゃまをする] stand [get] in sb's way.
とおる 通る 〈通行する〉go along [through, past]; pass (by, along, through); 〈通用する〉pass (as, for); be known (as); 〈意見,願望などが〉be heard; 《文》be realized; be granted; 〈貫く〉pierce; penetrate; pass through ¶家の前を通る pass [go past] a house / 右側を通る keep to the right / 試験に通る pass an examination / …の名で通る go under the name of... / カナダを通ってイギリスへ行く go to England via [by way of] Canada / よく通る声で in a far-carrying voice / 水の通らない waterproof (clothing); watertight (containers) / 光が通る[通らない] be transparent [opaque] / 通れない impassable; blocked. 文例↓
トおんきごう ト音記号 《音楽》a G [treble] clef.
とか 都下 ¶都下の in the capital; in the outer area of Tokyo.
-とか ¶尾形とか(なんとか)いう人 a person called Ogata or something (similar); a person called [with a name] something like Ogata / 地図とか磁石とかその他いろいろな物 a map, a compass, and what not [various other things]. 文例↓

とが 咎 〈過ち〉a fault; blame; 〈罪科〉a charge; an offense ¶とがのない innocent; 《文》blameless. 文例↓
とかい 都会 a city; a town ¶大都会 a large [big] city / 東京という大都会 the big urban complex called Tokyo / 都会風の urban; 〈洗練された〉urbane / 都会化する urbanize / 都会人 a city dweller; a townsman / 都会生活 urban [city] life / 都会育ち town-[city-]bred.
どがいし 度外視 ¶度外視する ignore; disregard; do not take sth into [leave sth out of] consideration; take no account of.
トがき ト書き 《劇》stage directions.
とかく ¶とかく…しがちだ be apt [liable, prone] to do; be given to doing / とかくする うちに in the meantime; meanwhile. 文例↓
とかげ 《動》a lizard ¶とかげのしっぽ切り a lizard's casting off of its tail (to escape); 〈比喩的に〉sacrificing a member so that the organization can survive (the scandal); 《口語》making somebody else [one of one's inferiors] carry the can (for one) / とかげ類の動物 a saurian.
とかす¹ 梳かす comb (one's hair).
とかす² 溶かす 〈熱で〉melt (ice); 〈固体の中で〉dissolve; 〈液化させる〉liquefy; 〈金属を〉melt; fuse; smelt 《ore》¶水に溶かす dissolve (salt) in water.
どかす 退かす move [get, shift] sth out of the [one's] way; remove; make sb leave the place; force sb to make way (for one).
どかた 土方 a construction laborer; a workman; 〈英〉navvy.
どかどか 〈足音荒く〉with loud footsteps; noisily; 〈いっしょに〉all together; 〈大勢で〉in large numbers; in crowds.
どかべん ど弁 《carry》a meal packed in an outsize lunch-box.
とがめる 咎める blame; 《文》censure; 《文》rebuke; 《文》(a) reproof ¶神様のおとがめ divine punishment / 良心のとがめ 《文》the pangs [prick, qualms] of conscience. 文例↓
とがめだて 咎め立て faultfinding ¶とがめ立てする ⇒ とがめる.
とがめる 咎める 〈あら捜しする〉find fault

とおりこす そんなのは馬鹿を通り越して気違いざただよ. Foolish is not the [is too good a] word for it; it's absolute madness.
とおりすがり 彼女の所には通りがかりに立ち寄ってみただけのことだ. I just dropped in to see her as I was going past her house.
とおりすぎる 台風も間もなく通り過ぎるだろう. The typhoon will soon pass over.
とおりそうば 人生70が通り相場なら, 僕はまだまだ生きられる. If I may take it that man's span of life is threescore (years) and ten, I am still a long way off the grave.
とおりぬける この路地は通り抜けられません. This is a blind alley. / 通り抜け禁止. 《交通標識》No thoroughfare.
とおる どの道を通って帰ろうか. Which way shall we go home? / この道路は大型トラックは通れない. This road will not take large trucks. / そんなごまかしは今では通らない. You couldn't get away with trickery like that these days. / そんな言い訳は通らない. Such an excuse will not do [be accepted]. / 法律は知らなかったでは通らない. Ignorance of the law is no excuse [not accepted as an excuse]. / このレインコートはすぐ雨が通る. This raincoat

lets the rain straight through. / 彼の声はよく通る. His voice carries a long way.
-とか 彼は今エジプトにいるとかいう話だ. I hear [They say, It is rumored] that he is now in Egypt.
とが だれの咎でもない, 私が悪いのだ. I have nobody to blame but myself. It's all my fault. / No one is to blame but me. / 失敗の咎を彼におかぶせた. They laid the blame for the failure on him [at his door].
とかく 我々はとかくそういうふうに考えがちである. We are apt [prone] to think that way. | We are given to looking at things

with sb；〈責める〉blame；《文》reproach；《文》rebuke；《文》censure；《文》reprove；call sb to account；take [call] sb to task；〈腫れ物を〉get [《文》become] inflamed；〈傷を〉aggravate《a wound》；〈過ちを〉blame [reprove] sb for his error / 警官にとがめられる be questioned by a policeman. 文例③

とがらす 尖らす sharpen ¶やすりで先をとがらす file (a piece of wire) to a point / 口をとがらす pout (out) [purse (up)] one's lips / (すねて)口をとがらしている have [be in] the pouts / 神経をとがらす get nervous；〈ある事が〉set one's nerves on edge.

とがる 尖る get [《文》become] pointed [sharp]；taper (off) to a point；〈不興である〉be [look] sour [displeased] ¶とがった pointed；sharp；peaked；〈先細の〉tapering / 先のとがった sharp-pointed / 爪先のとがった靴 (a pair of) pointed shoes / とがった声 a shrill [harsh, sharp] voice. 文例③

どかん¹ 土管 an earthenware pipe.

どかん² ¶どかんと破裂する go off with a bang.

とき¹ 時 〈時間・時刻〉time；an hour；a moment；〈場合〉a case；〈時期〉a season；〈機会〉(an) opportunity；(a) chance；〈時代〉the time(s)；the day；〈時制〉(a) tense ¶あの時 at that [the] time；then / 時がたてば in (the course of) time / 時が立つにつれて as time goes on；《文》with the passing [passage] of time；《文》with the passing [passage] of time / 時のたつのを忘れている《文》be unconscious of [oblivious to] the passage [lapse, flight] of time / 時の記念日 Time Day / 時を移さず immediately；at once；without a moment's delay；in no time / 時を移さず…する lose no time in doing / 時を違えず〈時間に正確に〉on time；punctually；〈間に合って〉in time / 時をかせぐ buy [play for] time；stall / 時をかせぐ give [allow] sb [sth] time / 〈雄鶏が〉時をつくる crow；proclaim the dawn / 時を待つ wait for one's [an] opportunity；bide one's time / …の時 when…；〈while…〉/ 妻の出産の時に when my wife was having her [our] first baby / 《文》at the time of my wife's first confinement / ちょうどいい時に just at the right moment / …と時を同じくして concurrently [simultaneously] with / 時を得顔に proudly；triumphantly / 時ならず untimely；out of season / 〈急な〉sudden；〈意外な〉unexpected / 時として，時には sometimes；in some cases；on occasion / …の時は in time [case, the event] of / その時は in that case；then / どんな時にも，時を選ばず《文》under all circumstances；at any time；at all times / 時と場合によっては《文》according to the time and circumstances；《文》should time and circumstances permit；《文》as the occasion demands [calls for] / 時の政府 the government of the day / 時の流行 the current fashion；the (latest) thing (in ties) / 時の人 the man [woman] in the news / 時に〈ついでながら〉by the way [bye]；incidentally / 〈ときどき〉⇒ときどき.

とき² 〈鳥〉a Japanese crested ibis；*Nipponia nippon*.

どき 土器 earthenware；an earthen vessel ¶(遺跡から出土する)土器片 a potsherd；a sherd；a shard.

ときあかす 説き明かす ⇒ かいめい².

ときいろ とき色 pink ¶とき色の pink.

ときおこす 説き起こす begin one's explanation [argument, story, narration] (at, with)；start (with).

ときおよぶ 説き及ぶ touch on；refer to；speak [《文》make mention of] ；mention.

ときおり 時折 ⇒ ときどき.

ときかわ 研ぎ革 a strop ¶研ぎ革で研ぐ strop (a razor).

とききかせる 説き聞かせる 〈説明する〉explain；〈理を説く〉reason (with sb)；〈教える〉teach；〈さとす〉《文》admonish.

ときじる 磨ぎ汁 (米の) the water in which rice has been washed.

ときすます 研ぎ澄ます sharpen [whet] well；〈磨いて〉polish [burnish] well ¶研ぎすましたナイフ a well-sharpened knife / 研ぎすまされた知性《文》a well-honed intellect.

ときたま 時たま (only) occasionally；at long intervals；once in a (long) while ¶ほんの時たま rarely；on rare occasions.

どぎつい garish；gaudy；heavy 《make-up》；loud 《colors》；shocking 《language》.

---

that way. / とかく女はそうしたもの. That is how [the way] women are. | That is the way it is with women. / あの人にはとかくのうわさがある. There are unsavory rumors about him.

とがめる 彼らはその美しい自然環境を破壊することに心のとがめを感じてはいないようだ. They seem to feel no compunction about destroying the beautiful natural environment.

とがめる 親の墓参りにこの10年行ってなくて, 気がとがめる. I feel guilty at [I feel bad about] never having visited my parents' grave for ten years.

とがる 一日中忙しかったので, 彼は神経がとがっていた. He had been very busy all day, and his nerves were on edge.

とき¹ いよいよ出発の時がやってきた. The time has come for us to leave. / 時がたってみなければわかりません. Only time will show. | Time alone can tell. / 時のたつのは早いものだ. How time flies! / こんど会う時は連れていってあげよう. I'll take you along the next time I go. / 僕は自分の好きな時に行くよ. I'll go there in my own time. / もうこの問題を考えなければならない時だ. It's high time that this question were gone into. / そんな気持ちになる時もあります. There are times when I feel that way. / こんなような時に, たったひとりでいると, とてもこわいんです. I'm really frightened [afraid] when I'm alone at times like this. / 時としてこの規則の当てはまらないこともある. There are occasions when [some cases where] this rule does not apply. / 時として役に立つこともある. It is useful [comes in handy] on occasion. / 万一行かれない時はご勘弁下さい. If by any chance I should be unable to come, please excuse me. / 花は時を得顔に咲き誇って

ときつける 説き付ける ⇨ ときふせる.
どきっと ¶どきっとする be startled; get a start; be taken aback; be shocked; feel a shock. 文例⇩
ときどき 時々 sometimes; at times; off and on [on and off]; (every) now and then [again]; occasionally; on occasion; ⟨ときたま⟩ once in a while; ⟨間を置いて⟩ at intervals; ⟨たびたび⟩ from time to time; often; frequently. 文例⇩
どきどき ¶(心臓が)どきどきする throb; beat (fast); go pit-a-pat. 文例⇩
ときのこえ 鬨の声 (raise) a war [battle] cry.
ときはなす 解き放つ untie; set free; let loose.
ときふせる 説き伏せる argue [talk] sb down; argue [talk] (sb into doing); 《文》prevail upon (sb to do); persuade (sb to do); 《思いとどまらせる》《文》dissuade (sb from doing). 文例⇩
ときほぐす¹ 溶きほぐす scramble (an egg).
ときほぐす² 解きほぐす disentangle (the snarled threads); unravel (the difficulty).
どぎまぎ ¶どぎまぎする be [get] flurried; be upset; get nervous; lose one's presence of mind. 文例⇩
ときめかす 文例⇩
ときめき palpitation; throbbing.
ときめく¹ 時めく be prosperous; prosper; flourish; 《文》enjoy great prosperity ¶今を時めく K 首相 Premier K who is now in a position of great fame and influence [who is at the pinnacle of his glory].
ときめく² ⟨胸が⟩ throb; flutter; palpitate; beat fast.
どぎも 度胆 ¶度胆を抜く scare sb out of his wits; dum[b]found; appall; stagger.
ドキュメンタリー a documentary ¶ドキュメンタリー映画 a documentary (film).
どきょう 度胸 courage; pluck; nerve; grit; 《口語》guts ¶度胸のある[いい] brave; bold; daring; plucky; 《文》courageous / 度胸のない timid; cowardly; 《文》white-livered; chicken-hearted / 度胸をすえる pluck up [gather] one's courage.
どきりと ⇨ どきっと.
とぎれ a break; a pause ¶とぎれとぎれの intermittent; disconnected; broken / とぎれとぎれに disconnectedly; at intervals; off and on; in [by] snatches; intermittently. 文例⇩
とぎれる break (off); pause; be interrupted ¶とぎれた broken; interrupted; disconnected / とぎれない unbroken; uninterrupted; continuous / とぎれずに without a break [pause]; continuously. 文例⇩
どきんと ⇨ どきっと ¶どきんと胸にこたえる strike home; tell; come home (to one).

とく¹ 得 ⟨利潤⟩(a) profit; gain; ⟨有利・便益⟩ advantage; benefit ¶得な profitable; 《文》advantageous; 《文》beneficial; economical / (経済的な)得をする profit [gain, benefit] (by, from) / 得になる 《文》be of benefit (to); 《文》be to one's benefit; 《文》be [prove] advantageous (to). 文例⇩
とく² 徳 《文》(a) virtue; 《文》a merit; goodness ¶徳の高い 《文》virtuous / 徳の高い人 《文》a man of virtue.
とく³ 溶く ⇨ かす².
とく⁴ 解く ⟨ほどく⟩ untie; undo; unbind; loosen; unfasten; unpack; ⟨髪を⟩comb ((one's) hair); ⟨解決する⟩ solve (a problem); work out (a puzzle); ⟨疑いなどを⟩ dispel; remove; clear up; ⟨解除する⟩ remove [lift] (a prohibition) ¶結び目を解く untie [undo] a knot / 包みを解く undo a bundle; unpack a parcel / 怒りを解く appease sb's anger / 禁制を解く lift the ban (on) / 誤解を解く remove [《文》dispel] sb's misunderstanding / 職を解く relieve sb of his post / 独力で考えて難問を解く think one's way through a difficult problem. 文例⇩
とく⁵ 説く ⟨説明する⟩ explain; 《文》expound (a doctrine); ⟨述べる⟩ state; mention; 《文》set forth [out]; 《文》maintain; 《文》assert; ⟨言

いた. The flowers were in their full glory. / 時は金なり. Time is money. 【諺】
どきっと その知らせを聞いてどきっとした. I was startled at the news. | The news gave me quite a turn. / 足音を聞いて彼女はどきっとした. Her heart jolted at the sound of footsteps.
ときどき 〈天気予報で〉今夜は時々小雨があるでしょう. There will be occasional showers tonight.
どきどき それを見て胸がどきどきした. My heart beat quickly at the sight. / 胸をどきどきさせながら見ていた. I watched it with my heart beating fast [pounding against my chest].
ときふせる 彼を説き伏せて味方に引き入れた. I succeeded in talking him over to our side. / 彼を説き伏せてその計画を止めさせた. I talked him out of his plan.

どぎまぎ 彼は女性の前に出るとどぎまぎする. He gets nervous [cannot behave naturally] in the presence of women.
ときめかす 彼女は明日は彼に会えると思って胸をときめかしていた. Her heart fluttered with excitement at the thought that she would be able to see him the next day.
どきょう とても度胸のいい男だ. He's a man with [who has] plenty of guts. / 私にはやってみるだけの度胸がない. I haven't the nerve to try it. / そこに座っている間にだんだん度胸がすわってくるらしかった. He seemed to gather courage as he sat there. / 度胸だめしにやらせてみたのだ. I made him do it to test (the strength of) his nerve.
とぎれ 彼らの話がとぎれとぎれに聞こえてきた. I could hear snatches of their conversation.
とぎれる 話がちょっととぎれた. There was a momentary pause [break] in the conversation. / 日記はそこでとぎれている. His diary breaks off there.
どきんと 彼の言葉に、さては彼は前々から私の秘密を知っていたのかと気が付いてどきんとした. At his words, I realized with a shock that he had in fact been on to my secret for a long time.
とく¹ うそをついたところで僕はなんの得にもならない. I have nothing to gain by lying. / 仲間に入った方が得だぜ. You'll find it in your interest [to your benefit] to join us. / 結局それは彼の得になった. It turned out to his advantage. / どっちへころんでも君の得だ. In either case, you will come off the gainer. / どっちが得かは知っている. I know which

及する〉 refer to ; touch on ; 〈詳述する〉《文》elaborate on ; 〈明らかにする〉make 《a matter》clear ; 〈解釈する〉interpret ; elucidate ; 〈説教する〉preach ; 〈唱道する〉《文》advocate ; advance ; 〈勧めて...させる〉prevail upon 《sb to do》; persuade [urge] 《sb to do》. 文例⇩

とぐ 研ぐ 〈砥石(いし)で〉whet ; grind ; sharpen ; 〈皮砥(がわ)で〉strop ; 〈米を〉wash / 砥石で研ぐ sharpen a knife on a whetstone.

どく¹ 毒 (a) poison ; venom (動物の) ; 〈害毒〉harm / 毒を為す a poison ; do sb harm ; corrupt / 毒の(ある) poisonous ; venomous 《snakes》/ 有害な harmful ; 《文》injurious ; noxious / 毒のない venomless 《snakes》; harmless ; innocuous ; innocent / 毒になる prove poisonous ; do sb harm ; be bad for 《one's health》/ 毒を仰ぐ take poison / 毒を盛る give [《文》administer] poison (to) ; poison sb / 毒を入れた [塗った] poisoned / 毒を以て毒を制す fight one evil with another / 毒にも薬にもならない do neither harm nor good. 文例⇩

どく² 退く get out of the [sb's] way ; clear the way (for) ; make room (for) ; step [move] aside. 文例⇩

とくい¹ 得意 〈失意に対して〉《文》prosperity ; 〈自慢〉pride ; triumph ; 〈得手〉one's strong point ; 《文》one's forte ; one's specialty ; 〈顧客〉a customer ; a client ; 《文》custom (総称) / 得意の時代には when one is enjoying one's greatest success ; 《文》in one's palmy days / 得意になって, 得意満面で with a triumphant air ; proudly ; in triumph ; triumphantly ; with a proud look ; (self-)complacently ; elatedly / ...が得意である, ...を得意とする be good [skillful] at ; be clever [at home] in ; be in one's line / 得意がる[になる] take pride 《in》; be proud 《of》; pride oneself 《on》; 《文》be puffed up with pride / 得意先 a customer ; a client ; 〈集合的に〉《文》custom ; one's clientele. 文例⇩

とくい² 特異 / 特異の《文》singular ; 《文》peculiar ; unique / 特異性《文》singularity ; 《文》peculiarity ; an idiosyncrasy / 特異体質〈異常敏感性〉(have) an allergy (to) ; an idiosyncracy. 文例⇩

どぐう 土偶 a clay figure [doll] ; a clay figurine (小さい).

どくえい 独泳 swimming alone ; 〈競泳で他の泳者を引き離しての〉swimming far ahead of the others.

どくえん 独演 a solo performance ; a recital / 独演会〈音楽の〉a solo recital ; 〈落語などの〉a one-man show.

どくが¹ 毒牙 a venom [poison(ed)] fang / 毒牙にかかる fall a victim [prey] (to a rogue) ; fall [get] into the claws [clutches] (of).

どくが² 毒蛾 〖昆〗an Oriental tussock moth.

とくがく 篤学 a love of learning ; devotion to one's studies / 篤学の士《文》a great lover of learning ; 《文》a diligent [devoted] scholar [student].

どくがく 独学 self-education / 独学する teach [educate] oneself ; study by oneself [on one's own] / 独学の self-educated[-taught] (men) ; 《文》unschooled (experts). 文例⇩

どくガス 毒ガス poison gas.

とくぎ¹ 特技 one's special ability [talent, gift] ; one's specialty.

とくぎ² 徳義 ⇒ どうぎ³.

どくけ 毒気 毒気を含んだ malicious ; spiteful / 毒気に当てられる be overwhelmed (by) / 毒気を抜かれる be taken aback ; be dum(b)founded.

どくけし 毒消し a medicine (for) ; 〈解毒剤〉an antidote.

どくごかん 読後感 one's impressions of a book [an article, etc.].

とくさ 〖植〗a scouring rush.

どくさい 独裁 dictatorship ; despotism ; autocracy / 独裁的 dictatorial ; despotic ; autocratic / 独裁国家 a dictatorship ; a despotism / 独裁者 a dictator ; a despot ; an autocrat / 独

---

side my bread is buttered.

とく⁴ この方程式を解いてxの価を求めなさい. Solve this equation for x [to find the value of x].

とく⁵ 彼は彼女を説いて退学を思いとどまらせた. He persuaded her not to leave school. / 彼に諄々(じゅんじゅん)と道理を説いてその会下を放棄させた. We reasoned him out of [into giving up] his scheme. / 遊びの必要を彼に説いてやった. I explained to him how necessary recreation is. / 彼は睡眠の大切な事を説いた. He pointed out the importance of sleep.

どく¹ 毒が回った. The poison has taken effect [passed into his system]. / 長い間には毒になる. It is a slow poison. / 彼女の声は毒を含んでいる. There was venom in her voice. / 毒を以て毒を制す. Set a thief to catch a thief. 〖諺〗/ 毒を食わば皿まで. In for a penny, in for a pound. 〖諺〗/ You might as well be hanged [hung] for a sheep as a lamb. 〖諺〗

どく² どいてくれ. Get out of the [my] way. | Don't stand in my way. / ちょっとどいてくれませんか. Won't you just move off, please? / どけ! 自動車が来るぞ. Get back! A car's coming.

とくい¹ 大統領と握手したときは彼の得意の瞬間であった. It was a proud moment for him when he shook hands with the President. / 彼は成功して大いに得意になっていた. He is highly elated by his success. / 当時彼は得意の絶頂にあった. At the time he was on [riding] the crest of the wave. / そんなことでは彼女は決して得意にならなかった. It did not turn her head at all. / そこが彼の得意とするところだ. That is where he is at his strongest. / 僕はダンスはあまり得意じゃない. I'm not much of a one for dancing. | Dancing is not my forte. / 英語は僕はあまり得意でありません. English is not much in my line. / あの店のお得意さは金持ちのご婦人方です. That store is patronized by wealthy ladies.

とくい² この 2つの特徴があるので, ベンゼンは 5つの基本的な炭化水素の中で他のものとなっている. These two characteristics lend benzene its distinction among the five basic hydrocarbons.

どくがく 彼のフランス語は独学です. He learned French without a teacher. / ジェイムズ・マレーは独学で, しかも事業不振の商人の家に生まれたというハンディキャップを負いながら学者になった. James Murray reached academic distinction by solitary

とくさく 得策 a good [wise] policy [plan] ¶得策な advisable; wise; 《文》expedient; 《文》well-advised. 文例⇩

どくさつ 毒殺 ¶毒殺する poison; kill with poison.

とくさん 特産 a specialty; a special product.

とくし 特使 《dispatch》a special envoy 《to》¶首相特使 the Prime Minister's personal envoy.

どくじ 独自 ¶独自の original; 《文》peculiar; of one's own; unique / 独自の立場から from an independent standpoint / 独自に on one's own terms; in one's own right / 独自性 individuality; originality; uniqueness / 民族としての独自性 ethnic identity. 文例⇩

とくしか 篤志家 a charitable [《文》benevolent] person; 《文》a philanthropist; 〈奉仕活動家〉a volunteer; 〈後援者〉a supporter.

とくしつ[1] 特質 ⇨とくせい[1].

とくしつ[2] 得失 advantages and disadvantages; 《文》merits and demerits; the relative merits [advantages] of 《A and B》¶得失を考量する weigh the merits 《of sth》against its demerits).

とくじつ 篤実 ¶篤実な 《文》faithful; honest; sincere; solid.

とくしゃ 特赦 (an) amnesty; a special amnesty; a special pardon (個人に対する). ¶特赦で出獄する be released from prison under an amnesty / 特赦を行なう grant [give] an amnesty 《to》/ 特赦を及ぼす extend amnesties 《to》.

どくしゃ 読者 a reader 《of》; 〈購読者〉a subscriber 《to a magazine》; 〈読書界〉the reading public ¶〈専門家でない〉一般読者のための本 a book (written) for the general reader / N誌の読者層を調査する investigate what kind of people are reading N magazine / 読者欄 a readers' column.

どくじゃ 毒蛇 a poisonous [venomous] snake.

とくしゅ 特殊 ¶特殊な special; 《文》peculiar; particular; unique (類のない) / 特殊な地位を占める hold a unique position / 特殊化する specialize; 《文》differentiate / 特殊鋼 special steel / 特殊撮影〈映画〉shooting for special effect(s); trick shooting / 特殊事情 special circumstances / 特殊性 (a) peculiarity; special characteristics.

とくじゅ 特需 special procurements; special procurement demands [orders].

とくしゅう 特集 ¶特集号《prepare》a special number [issue] / フランス料理特集号 a special number featuring articles on French cuisine.

どくしゅう 独習 ¶独習する teach oneself; learn [practice] by oneself ⇨ どくがく / スペイン語独習〈書名〉Teach Yourself Spanish; Spanish Self-Taught.

どくしょ 読書 reading ¶読書する read (books) / 読書家 an avid [《文》extensive] reader; a well-read person / 読書会 a reading circle / 読書室 a reading room / 読書人 a booklover; a bookman / 読書力を養う improve [《文》cultivate] one's reading ability / 読書用の眼鏡 reading glasses.

とくしょう 特賞 a special prize.

とくじょう 特上 ¶特上の superfine; the choicest.

どくしょう 独唱 a (vocal) solo 《pl. -s》¶独唱をする give [sing] a solo / 独唱会 a (vocal) recital / 独唱者 a soloist. 文例⇩

とくしょく 特色 a distinctive feature; 《文》a distinguishing characteristic [quality].

とくしん[1] 特進 ¶2階級特進になる be specially promoted two ranks 《after one's death in the line of duty》.

とくしん[2] 得心 ⇨ なっとく.

どくしん 独身 ¶独身の single; unmarried / 独身で暮らす stay [《文》remain, live] single; 《文》remain unmarried; lead a bachelor's life / (離婚して)再び独身になる《文》return to single status / 独身アパートに住んでいる live in a bachelor apartment / 独身貴族 a well-off unattached young man / 独身者 an unmarried person; 〈男〉a bachelor; 〈女〉a spinster; a bachelor girl / 独身生活 a bachelor [single] life.

どくしんじゅつ[1] 読心術 mind reading.

どくしんじゅつ[2] 読唇術 lip reading.

とくせい[1] 特性 a special quality; 《文》a specific [peculiar] characteristic [character]; 〈個性〉individuality; a peculiarity; a (special) property; an idiosyncracy. 文例⇩

とくせい[2] 特製 ¶特製の specially made [manufactured]; 《文》of special make; 〈製本の〉specially bound; 〈豪華な〉deluxe / 特製品 a specially made article.

とくせい[3] 徳性 moral character.

とくせい[4] 徳政〈日本史〉a (debt) moratorium 《pl. -riums, -ria》.

---

study and in spite of a family background of unsuccessful businessmen.

とくさく その方が得策だ。You had better do so. | It would be wiser to do that.

どくじ やがて彼ら独自のやり方で事業を始めた。Then they started business in a fashion unique to themselves.

どくしゃ 井上氏の小説は多くの読者を持っている。Mr. Inoue's novels are widely read. / 佐木氏の小説は外国で読者を獲得した。Mr. Sasaki has won an international audience for his novels.

とくしゅう NHKで「花言葉特集」を放映した。The NHK broadcast a special TV program on 'The Language of Flowers'.

どくしょう 次の番は A の独唱だ。The next number is a solo by A. / 日比谷公会堂へ K の独唱を聞きに行った。I went to the Hibiya Public Hall to hear K sing.

とくしょく この映画の最大の特色は音楽がきれいなことである。The most striking feature of this movie is its beautiful music.

とくせい 無生物のように見えるウイルスが, 侵入できる細胞に出会うと生物としての特性を帯びる。An apparently inert virus assumes the properties of life when it encounters cells it can invade.

どくぜつ 彼はフランスきっての毒舌家だ。He has the sharpest tongue in France.

どくせん[2] 僕はこの大きい部屋を独

どくせい 毒性 toxicity; virulence ¶毒性のある poisonous; toxic; virulent / 毒性のない nonpoisonous; nontoxic; nonvirulent.

とくせつ 特設 ¶特設する set up [establish, install] specially / 特設電話 a specially installed telephone.

どくぜつ 毒舌 a malicious [venomous] tongue ¶毒舌をふるう speak acrimoniously [《文》with acrimony] 《about》; make blistering remarks 《about, on》; give sb a tongue-lashing. 文例⇩

とくせん 特選 ¶特選になる win a special commendation 《at an art exhibition》/ 特選品 choice goods.

どくせん¹ 毒腺 《動》a venom [poison] gland.

どくせん² 独占 a monopoly; exclusive possession ¶独占する monopolize; have [keep] sth to oneself / 東京の食肉市場を独占している have a monopoly on the Tokyo meat market / 独占禁止法 the Antimonopoly [Antitrust] Act / 独占事業 a monopolistic enterprise [undertaking]; a monopoly / 独占資本 monopolistic capital / 独占資本の支配する産業 monopoly-controlled industries / 独占欲 a desire to have entire possession 《of》.

どくぜん 独善 《文》self-righteousness ¶独善的 《文》self-righteous; self-opinionated / 独善的な考えで行動する《文》act self-righteously; follow (only) one's own advice.

どくそ 毒素 a toxin; poisonous matter.

どくそう¹ 毒草 a poisonous herb [weed].

どくそう² 独走 running alone;《楽勝》a runaway (victory); a walkover. 文例⇩

どくそう³ 独奏 a recital; a solo 《pl. -s》; a solo performance ¶独奏する play [give] a solo / ピアノ独奏 a piano solo / 独奏会 a recital / 独奏者 a soloist.

どくそう⁴ 独創 originality ¶独創的 original; creative / 目ざましい独創的な作品 a strikingly original work / 《文》a work of striking originality / 独創力がある[ない] have [lack] creative power [talent].

とくそく 督促 ¶督促する urge sb (on) (to do); press 《sb for》; dun 《sb for the payment of a debt》/ 督促状 a reminder / 《借金の》a dunning letter.

ドクター a doctor ⇨ はくし². 文例⇩

とくだい 特大 ¶特大の extra-big [-large]; outsize; oversize;《口語》king-size(d) /《雑誌の》特大号 a special enlarged [bumper] issue.

とくたいせい 特待生 a scholarship student ¶特待生になる get [《文》obtain] a scholarship.

とくだね 特種 a scoop; an exclusive (story) ¶特種を取って他紙を出し抜く scoop [get a scoop on] rival papers ⇨ スクープ.

どくだわら 得俵 《相撲》the markers at the four enlarged places of the sumo ring.

どくだん 独断 (an) arbitrary decision;《文》dogmatism (学説の) ¶独断の arbitrary; dogmatic / 独断で on one's own judgment; at one's own discretion; (act) on one's own authority [responsibility].

どくだんじょう 独壇場 文例⇩

とぐち 戸口 the door; the doorway; the entrance ¶戸口に立つ stand at the door; stand in the doorway (ドアが開いている) / 戸口から戸口までのサービス《運送》door-to-door service.

とくちゅう 特注 ¶特注する place a special order《for an article of a specified size》/ 特注品 an article specially made to order; a made-to-measure [custom-made] article.

とくちょう¹ 特長 a strong point; a merit; a forte.

とくちょう² 特徴 a special [distinctive] feature; a (distinguishing) characteristic; a peculiarity;《文》a trait ¶特徴のある characteristic; distinctive; peculiar / 特徴のない featureless; common / (平凡で)何の特徴もない顔 a face without any character / 特徴づける《文》characterize; mark; distinguish; give sth a distinction. 文例⇩

どくづく 毒突く revile; rail at; call sb (bad) names; make blistering remarks《about》.

とくてい 特定 ¶特定の specific; specified; particular;〈特別の〉special / 特定する specify; identify; pin sth down.

とくてん¹ 特典 a privilege; a special favor. 文例⇩

とくてん² 得点〈点を取ること〉scoring;〈点〉the points [marks] obtained,《野球》the (number of) runs scored;〈全体〉the score ⇨ スコア ¶得点する score [earn, gain, obtain]《5》points [runs] / …より多く得点する score higher than sb; outpoint sb / 個人[団体]得点 one's individual [team] score / 得点表 a points table; a score book (帳);〈野球の〉a score sheet;〈ボクシングの〉a scorecard. 文例⇩

とくでん 特電 a special telegram [dispatch].

とくと 篤と thoroughly; fully; carefully ¶篤と考える ⇨ よく³(よく考える).

占している. I have this big room all to myself. / 800メートルのレースでは1位から4位までアメリカ選手が独占した. The American athletes swept the first four places in the 800-meter race.

どくそう² こんどの選挙は前田氏の独走と言ってよいだろう. Mr. Maeda will be elected virtually unopposed this time. / 最後の1周は彼の独走があった. He left all the other runners far behind on the last lap.

ドクター そこで試合はドクターストップがかかった. The doctor stopped the fight then.

どくだんじょう ショパンの演奏は彼女の独壇場である. She holds an unchallenged position [is unrivaled, has no peers] as an interpreter of Chopin.

とくちょう² 簡素なのが彼の文章の特徴だ. His style is characterized by simplicity. / この色調は正に彼の絵の特徴だ. This tone is indeed characteristic of his paintings. / この木は特徴的な形をしている. This tree has a distinctive shape.

とくてん¹ 彼は研究所の図書室に自由に出入りできる特典を与えられた. He was granted [given] the privilege of free use of the Institute's library.

とくてん² 得点はどうなっていますか? What is the score? / 得点は7対3で山田の勝ちでした. Yamada won the game 7:3 [7 to 3]. / 国連は問題解決の場という

とくど 得度 ¶得度する enter the Buddhist priesthood [nunhood]; enter religion; 《文》 take the tonsure.

とくとう¹ 禿頭 a bald head [《文》pate]; 〈状態〉 baldness ¶禿頭の bald(-headed) / 禿頭病 〖医〗alopecia.

とくとう² 特等 a special grade [class] ¶(くじで)特等が当たる win a special prize / (客船の)特等室 a stateroom / 特等席 a special seat; a box (seat) (劇場の).

とくとく 得々 ¶得々と(して) proudly; triumphantly; in triumph; with a triumphant [complacent] air; 《文》self-complacently; 《do》to show off / 得々としている be highly elated (about, over, with); be puffed up (with pride, with praise); pride [plume, preen] oneself (on sth); be struttingly proud ((of sth)).

どくとく 独特 ¶独特の 《文》peculiar (to); of one's own; characteristic (of); unique (to). 用例⇩

どくどく in continuous gushes; gushingly; copiously; profusely.

どくどくしい 毒々しい lurid; repulsive ¶毒々しいまでに濃い口紅をつけた女 a woman wearing revoltingly heavy lipstick.

とくに 特に specially; 《文》expressly; 〈ことさら〉especially; particularly; in particular ¶特にこれという理由もなく for no particular reason / 特にその日に限って on that particular day. 用例⇩

とくのうか 篤農家 a progressive, innovative farmer.

とくは 特派 ¶特派する send [dispatch] specially / (新聞社の)特派員 a (special) correspondent (at Washington) / 特派使節 a special envoy; an envoy extraordinary.

どくは 読破 ¶読破する read (through) (a book); go through (a volume).

とくばい 特売 a special [bargain] sale ¶特売する sell at a special [specially reduced] price / 特売場[日] a bargain counter [day] / 特売品 an article offered at a bargain (price); sale goods [merchandise]. 用例⇩

どくはく 独白 a monologue; a soliloquy.

とくひつ 特筆 ¶特筆する mention [write, refer to] specially / 《文》make special mention of; 〈新聞などが〉give (special) prominence to; lay special stress on / 特筆(大書)すべき 《文》deserving [worthy of] special mention;

(highly) important; remarkable / 宮部氏の新著の中で特筆大書されているエトルリアの彫刻 the Etruscan sculpture which features large in Mr. Miyabe's new book.

とくひょう 得票 ¶得票する get [gain, win] (10,800) votes; 《文》the number of votes obtained [polled] / 法定得票数 《obtain》 the legally required minimum number of votes. 用例⇩

どくぶ 独舞 〖バレー〗a solo dance; 《dance》a solo (pl. -s); 〈フランス語〉a pas seul (pl. pas seuls).

どくぶつ 毒物 a toxic substance [material] ¶毒物学 toxicology.

どくぶん 独文 〈ドイツ語〉German; 〈文学〉German literature ¶独文を専攻する major in German literature / (大学の)独文科 the department of German literature.

とくべつ 特別 ¶特別の special; 《文》especial; express; 〈特定の〉particular; 〈固有の〉peculiar; 〈並はずれた〉extraordinary; 〈余分の〉extra; 〈例外の〉exceptional / 特別に specially; 《文》especially; particularly; in particular; extraordinarily; exceptionally / 特別に注意を払う take [use] special care ((over, in doing)); pay special attention (to) / 特別扱いをする give [《文》accord] sb special treatment; make an exception in favor of sb / 特別機で来日する come to Japan by special plane / (客船の)特別室 a deluxe suite / 特別上等の extra-fine; superfine; choice / 特別号 a special [an extra (増刊)] number [issue]; a special / 特別席 a special seat / 2時間にわたるテレビの特別番組 a 2-hour TV special / 特別予算 a special [an extraordinary] budget. 用例⇩

とくほう 特報 a news special; a news flash ¶特報する flash (the news).

どくぼう 独房 a (solitary) cell; a prison cell ¶独房に監禁される be kept in solitary confinement.

とくほん 読本 a reader.

どくみ 毒味 ¶毒味をする taste (food) for poison; act as a taster (of the 《Shogun's》 food).

どくむし 毒虫 a poisonous insect.

とくめい¹ 特命 ¶特命全権大[公]使 an ambassador [a minister] extraordinary and plenipotentiary.

とくめい² 匿名 〈名前を隠していること〉《文》

よりも, 国際宣伝戦の得点稼ぎの場となってしまった。The United Nations has become an arena for international propaganda point-scoring rather than for the settlement of problems.

どくとく それには彼独特のやり方がある。He has his own way of doing it.

とくに これは特に本紙のために松田博士から寄せられたものであります。This was written by Dr. Matsuda specially for our paper. / 特にこのために上京しました. I have come up to town for this express purpose. / 特にこれという仕事もない. I have nothing particular to do. / 特にだれのことを言っているわけでもありません. I am not referring [alluding] to anyone in particular.

とくばい あの店でいまブーツの特売をやっている. The store is having a sale on boots. / このネクタイは特売で安く買ったのです. I got this tie cheap in a sale [《米》on sale]. / 定価5千円, 特売価格2千円. 〖表示〗Regular price ¥3,000, sale price ¥2,000.

とくひょう 彼の得票はS氏よりも5千票以上も多かった. He obtained over 5,000 votes more than Mr. S. / 得票数の差はわずかではあったが, N氏が勝った. The voting was close, but Mr. N won. / 自民党はそれまで数年間得票数が減り続けていた. The Liberal Democratic Party had been losing votes for some years.

とくべつ 特別にやってくれたまえ. Attend to it with special care. / 私に特別やさしくしてくれ

どくや 毒矢 a poisoned arrow; a poison-tipped dart.

とくやく 特約 ¶特約する make [《文》enter into] a special contract [agreement] 《with》/ …と特約する have a special contract with… / 特約を結ぶ make a special arrangement 《with》/ 特約(販売)店 a special agent.

どくやく 毒薬 a poison (drug).

とくゆう 特有 ¶特有の 《文》characteristic 《of》; special 《to》; 《文》peculiar [proper] 《to》. 文例⇩

とくよう 徳用 ¶徳用な economical / 徳用型 an economy size / 徳用品 an economical article.

とくり 利利 ⇨ とっくり¹.

どくりつ 独立 independence 《from》; 〈分離〉 separation ¶独立の independent; self-supporting; free / 独立する be [become] independent 《of》; set up 《as a carpenter》《on one's own》/ 独立して independently 《of》; oneself; alone / 独立の生計を営む support oneself / 独立の生計を営む earn one's own living / 独立させる set sb up in business 《on his own》; establish sb 《on his own》/ 《米国の》独立記念日 Independence Day; the Fourth of July / 独立国 an independent country; a sovereign state / 独立国家の地位を獲得する gain independent statehood / 独立採算制で on a self-paying basis / 独立心 a spirit of independence; 《文》a desire to be independent [for independence] / 独立心のある independent-minded 《women》/ 《米国の》独立宣言 the Declaration of Independence / 《米国の》独立戦争 the American Revolutionary War; the War of Independence. 文例⇩

どくりょく 独力 ¶独力で 《文》unaided; by one's own efforts; on one's own account; for [by] oneself / 独力でやる do unaided [single-handed]; 《口語》go it alone.

とぐるま 戸車 a door wheel.

とくれい¹ 特例 a special case [example]; 〈例外〉an exception ¶特例を設ける make an exception 《in favor of》/ 特例として as an exception.

とくれい² 督励 encouragement ¶督励する encourage sb 《to do》; urge [spur] sb 《on》《to do》.

とぐろ ¶とぐろを巻く coil itself (up); coil on itself; 〈ぶらぶらしている〉loaf; lounge / とぐろを巻いている lie in a coil / 酒場でとぐろを巻いている連中 bar-loungers.

どくろ 髑髏 a skull.

とげ 刺, 棘 〈バラなどの〉a thorn; 〈草の葉などの〉a prickle; 〈木・竹などの細片〉a splinter; 〈動植物の〉a spine ¶刺の多い[ある] thorny; 《文》thorned; spiny; prickly; 〈言葉などの〉cutting; stinging; biting; barbed 《questions》/ 刺を立てる run a thorn [splinter] into 《one's finger》/ 刺を抜く pick a thorn out of 《one's finger》/ 刺抜き (a pair of) tweezers. 文例⇩

とけあう¹ 溶け合う melt [fade] into each other. 文例⇩

とけあう² 解け合う 〈和解する〉come to an [《文》a mutual] understanding; 《文》be reconciled (to each other). 文例⇩

とけい 時計 《文》a timepiece; 〈壁(掛け)時計〉a (wall) clock; 〈置時計〉a (table) clock; 〈懐中時計〉a (pocket) watch; 〈腕時計〉a (wrist) watch ¶時計の針 the hands of a watch [clock]; a watch [clock] hand / 時計の番号 the number on the watchcase / 時計を進める put a clock [watch] on [forward, ahead] / 時計を遅らせる put a clock [watch] back / 時計を巻く wind (up) a watch [clock] / 時計をしている wear [be wearing] a watch; have a watch on / 時計をはずす take off [unstrap] one's watch / 時計を見る look at [consult] one's watch / 時計を修繕[掃除]してもらう have one's watch mended [cleaned] (by) / 時計を合わせる put one's watch right / 時計をラジオの時報に合わせる set one's watch by [with] the radio time signal / 薄型の時計 a thin-model watch / 自動巻き時計 a self-winding watch / 中3針時計 a watch with a sweep-[center-]second hand / 8日巻き時計 an eight-day clock / 時計仕掛け (by) clockwork / 時計台 a clock tower [turret, stand] / 時計方向[逆(時計)方向]に回転する rotate clockwise [《米》counterclockwise, 《英》anticlockwise] / 時計屋 〈人〉a watchmaker; a jeweler; 〈店〉a jewelry store; 《米》a watch store; 《英》a watchmaker's. 文例⇩

とけこむ 溶[融]け込む melt [dissolve] into;

女性が何人かあった. Several women put themselves out [went out of their way] to be nice to me.

とくゆう オレンジにはオレンジ特有の香りがある. The orange has a scent all [of] its own.

どくりつ インドは1947年に英国から独立した. India gained independence from Britain in 1947. / 彼は独立して商売をしている. He has set up in [is doing] business on his own. / マダガスカル島のアイアイは非常に変わっているので分類学者はこれを独立した科とした. The aye-aye of Madagascar is so aberrant that taxonomists have assigned it a family all its own.

とげ 彼の言葉にはいつも棘がある. He has a sharp tongue. | He is prone to making cutting [sarcastic] remarks. / 小指に棘がある. I've got a splinter [thorn] in my little finger.

とけあう¹ 離れて見るといろいろな色が溶けあって一つに見える. The distance melts the varied colors into one.

とけあう² 年ごとにお互いの心が解け合うようになった. Every year brought us closer together.

とけい 時計をお持ちですか. Have you got the time on you? / 君の時計は何時ですか. What time is it by your watch? | What time do you make it? /《米》What time do you have? / 君の時計は正確ですか. Does your watch keep good time? / あの時計合っているだろうか. Is that the right time? / 時計が1時を打った. The clock

どけざ 土下座 ¶土下座する kneel (down) on the ground ((as the Shogun's procession goes by)).

とけつ 吐血 〖医〗 hematemesis ¶吐血する vomit blood.

とげとげしい 刺々しい sharp; harsh; biting; stinging; cutting; barbed ((words)).

とける[1] 溶ける 〈熱で〉melt; 〈固体が液体の中で〉dissolve; thaw (雪・霜などが) ¶溶けやすい easily soluble / 溶けにくい (nearly) insoluble. 文例↓

とける[2] 解ける 〈ほどける〉get [come] loose; come untied [undone]; 〈問題が〉be solved; 〈疑いが〉《文》be dispelled; be removed; be cleared; 〈怒りが〉《文》be allayed; 《文》be appeased ¶解ける問題 a solvable [《文》soluble] problem / 解けない問題 an unsolvable [《文》insoluble] problem / なかなか解けない問題 an obstinate problem. 文例↓

とげる 遂げる 《文》accomplish; achieve; 《文》attain; 《文》realize; effect; carry out ¶思いを遂げる realize [attain] one's desire / 目的を遂げる attain one's object; achieve one's purpose / 自殺を遂げる commit suicide / 遂げられない 《文》unrealizable; 《文》unattainable. 文例↓

どける 退ける remove; dislodge; put [get] sth out of the way ⇒ どかす.

どけんぎょう 土建業 the civil engineering and construction business ¶土建業者 a civil engineering constructor.

とこ 床 〈寝具〉a bed ¶床を離れる get up (from bed); get out of bed; 〈病床から〉leave one's sickbed; be up and about / 床を敷く[取る]〈日本式に〉prepare a bed; lay out the bedding; 〈西洋式に〉make a bed / 床を上げる put away the bedding / 床につく go to bed; 《文》retire (to bed); (口語) turn in / 床についている be in bed; 〈病気で〉be laid up ((with a cold)); be ill in bed / 床につかせる put (children) to bed. 文例↓

どこ 何処 ¶どこに[へ] where / 《文》in [to] what place / どこに[で]も anywhere; everywhere; 〈否定〉nowhere / どこから where ... from; from where; 《文》whence / どこからともなく from [out of] nowhere; from God knows where / どこにか, どこか somewhere; 〈ある点で〉in some respects; in some way / どこまで how far; 《文》to what extent / どこまでも 〈どこへでも〉anywhere; to the end of the world; 〈あらゆる点で〉in every point [respect]; thoroughly; 〈最後まで〉to the end [last] / どこまでも反対する oppose stubbornly [to the last] / どこからどこまで all over ((the place)); throughout ((the country)); 〈すみずみまで〉every inch (of the town) / どこもかしこも everywhere; all over ((the place)) / どことなく somehow. 文例↓

とこあげ 床上げ 〈病気の全快〉《文》recovery from illness; 〈全快祝い〉《文》celebration of one's recovery (from illness) ¶床上げする leave one's sickbed; recover (from one's illness) / 床上げの祝いをする celebrate one's recovery (from illness).

---

struck one. / 僕の時計は少し進む[遅れる]. My watch gains [loses] a little. / 僕の時計は 10 分遅れて[進んで]いた. My watch was ten minutes fast [slow]. / 時計は 11 時半を指していた. The clock showed [pointed to] half past eleven. / My watch showed [gave] the time as 11:30. / 時計がカチカチ動いていた. 'Tick-tock, tick-tock' went the clock. / The clock was ticking away. / 時計は直しにやってある. I've sent my watch to be mended. / My watch has gone to be fixed. / 時計が止まった. My watch has stopped [run down]. / まるで時計の針が百年返されたようだった. It was as if the clock had been turned back a hundred years.

とける[1] この種のプラスチックは氏 205 度以下では溶けない. This type of plastic resists melting up to 205° C. / 海水中には多くの塩類が溶けている. Sea water contains many salts in solution.

とける[2] この問題は普通の代数では解けない. This problem does not yield to [is not soluble by means of] ordinary algebra. / 彼はまだ君に対して気持ちが解けていない. He still holds hard feelings for you.

とげる やっと私の願いも遂げられた. At last I've got my wish.

とこ 床に入ってから本を読むのは目によくない. Reading in bed is bad for the (one's) eyes. / この月末までには床を離れて動けるようになるでしょう. I will be up and about by the end of the month.

どこ 休暇中どこへ行きますか. Where do you plan to go during the vacation? / (列車などで)ここはどこですか. Where are we now? / あの車はどこのだ. 通行のじゃまになる. Whose car is that? It's blocking the traffic. / この色分け地図は日本で何がどこに生えているかを示したものです. This colored map shows what grows where in Japan. / 彼はどこそこでこれこれこういう人に会ったと話した. He told me he had met such and such a person at such and such a place. / あの男のどこがいいのか. What (good) do you see in him? / どこと言って別に取柄はない. He has nothing much to recommend him. / どことなく上品なところがある. There is something refined about him. / この町ならどこからどこまで知っている. I know every inch of this town. / これだけ立派に書けていればどこへ出しても恥ずかしくない. It is so well written that it will do credit to its writer anywhere it may be presented. / 彼はどこかこの辺に住んでいる. He lives somewhere around [near] here. / (教室で)この前はどこまで進んだかね. Where did we get to [How far did we go] last time? / ところで, どこまで話したっけ? Now where was I [were we]? / あの男のどこまで本当かわからない. I wonder how far I can believe him. / I don't know if he was serious about everything he said. / 彼はどこからどこまで英国紳士だ. He is every inch an English gentleman. / He is an English gentleman to his fingertips. / 鯨が魚と違うところは他にもあります. それがどこかわかりますか. Whales are different from fish in other ways. Can you tell what they are?

とこう 渡航 a voyage; 《文》a passage ¶渡航する make a voyage [passage] ((to)); go over [cross] ((to)); make an overseas journey / 渡航者 a passenger; 《旅行者》a visitor [traveler] ((to)) / 渡航手続をする go through the formalities for *one's* trip [journey] ((to America)).

どごう 怒号 a [an angry] roar ¶怒号する roar (in anger); bellow; howl (with rage).

とこずれ 床擦れ 《have》bedsores.

とことこ ¶とことこ走る run with short steps; trot.

とことん ¶とことんまで《終わりまで》to the finish [last]; 《徹底的に》thoroughly; through and through; (up) to the hilt / とことんまで考える think *sth* through / とことんまでやる go the whole way [《口語》hog]; 《米口語》shoot the works / とことんまで戦う fight to the finish; fight it out / 力の続く限りとことんまで働かされる be forced to work to the last atom of *one's* strength / とことんまで話し合って決める have it [things] out with *sb*.

とこなつ 常夏 ¶常夏の国《文》a land of everlasting summer.

とこのま 床の間 a *tokonoma*; an alcove.

とこばしら 床柱 an alcove post.

とこばなれ 床離れ ¶床離れが悪い be slow in getting [be reluctant to get] out of bed; waste time in bed (in the morning).

とこはる 常春 ¶常春の国《文》a land of everlasting spring.

とこぶし 〘貝〙an abalone.

とこや 床屋 《人》a barber; 《店》《米》a barbershop; 《英》a barber's (shop) ¶床屋の看板 a barber's pole.

とこやま 床山 a hairdresser for *sumo* wrestlers.

ところ 所, 処〈場所〉a place; a spot〈狭い〉; a scene〈現場〉; a seat〈所在地〉;〈所番地〉an address;〈地方〉a locality; a district; an area;〈家〉*one's* house [home];〈点〉a point;〈文章の中の〉a passage;〈部分〉a part ¶行きたい [住みたい]所 the place *one* wants to go (to) [live (in)] ★このように, place に続く, 不定詞を含む句では前置詞 to, in は省略できる / 人のいる所で in the presence of others; in company; in public / 人殺しのあった所 the scene of a murder / お城のあった所に on the site of the castle / 叔母の所にいる stay [live] with *one's* aunt / 所かまわず吸殻を捨てる throw away *one's* cigarette butts wherever *one* happens to be / …するところを be going to *do*; be (just) about to *do*; be on the point of *doing* / …したところだ have just *done* / ここのところ《文》of late; lately / 今のところは at present / 今までのところでは so [《文》thus] far; up to now [the present] / 所を得る gain [《文》attain] a proper place [position] ((for *one's* abitities)); fall into place. 文例⇩

-どころ …所 ¶茶所 tea-growing country; a tea-growing[-producing] district; a place famous for its (production of) tea. 文例⇩

ところが but; however; and yet; on the contrary; as it is [was] ★仮定法の文のあとに用いて,「ところが実際には」と直説法に切換える). 文例⇩

-どころか far from; not at all;〈…は言うに及ばず〉not to speak of; to say nothing of; let alone ¶それどころか far from it; on the contrary. 文例⇩

ところで〈時に〉now; well;〈ついでながら〉by the way; incidentally.

ところ 所もあろうにこんな所でお目にかかろうとは思いもよりませんでした. Fancy meeting you here, of all places! / 所きらわず彼を殴った. They beat him all over. / 座る所がない. There is nowhere to sit. | There is no room to sit down. / 所狭しとばかりに絵が掛けてあった. The wall was hung full to overcrowding with paintings. / 僕の所は家族が多い. I have a large family. / ブリッジをやりに私の所へ来ませんか. Won't you come over to my place for a game of bridge? / 私は上記の所でタイピストとして働いております. I'm employed at the above address as a typist. / ここが一番注意しなければならない所だ. This is the point to which we must pay particular attention. / パンダのからだには対照的に黒と白い所がある. The giant panda has a coat with contrasting areas of black and white. / この所は色々に意味がとれる. This passage may be read in several ways. / 僕たちは今着いたところです. We have (only) just arrived. / いいところへ来てくれた. You have come at the right moment. / 彼がため息をついている所を見ました. I saw him sighing. / すんでの事に溺死するところだった. I (was) nearly [almost] drowned. | I came near being drowned. / 出掛けようとしているところへ彼がやって来た. I was leaving when he came. / 彼にはどこか村の学校の校長先生といった所がある. There is something of the village schoolmaster about him. / 彼女には女らしい所がない. There is nothing feminine[womanly] about her. / 彼女の言葉にももっともな所があった. There was something in what she said. / 彼女の声にはちょっと意地悪そうな所があった. There was a touch of bitterness in her voice. / 彼の言葉にはどこか東北なまりを思わせる所がある. There is a suggestion of Tohoku accent in his speech. / これは我々の予期したところだ. This is what we expected. / 来ないところをみると何か急用も出来たのだろう. Seeing that he has not come, some urgent business may have turned up. / 国民の勤労意欲を殺ぐというところが増税の望ましからぬ点である. Increasing taxes is undesirable in that it discourages people from working harder. / ここは赤で書くべき所でした. This part should have been written in red. / 所変われば品変わる. Different places have different customs.

-どころ ここが我慢のしどころだ. This is where we must grin and bear it. / 仕事はまだ完成どころではなかった. The job was nowhere near [was far from being] finished. / 旅行どころ(の騒ぎ)ではない. Going on a pleasure trip is quite out of the question.

ところが 暇があれば行っただろう. ところがその日は一日中忙しかったのだ. If I had had time to spare, I would have gone there. As it was, I was quite busy all that day. / うまく行くだろうと思っていたところが, 失敗したよ. It failed, contrary to my expectation.

-どころか 彼はフランス語どころか英語も知らない. He knows no English, to say nothing of

-ところで ⟨...としても⟩ (even) if [though]...; granting that.... 文例↓

ところてん gelidium jelly (made into thin strips and eaten with vinegar) ¶ところてん式に ⟨順番に⟩ in turn; one after another; ⟨文⟩ successively; ⟨機械的に⟩ mechanically; automatically.

ところどころ 所々 here and there; in places. 文例↓

ところばんち 所番地 one's address ⇨ じゅうしょ. 文例↓

とざい 吐剤 an emetic.

とさか a cockscomb; a (head) crest.

どさくさ confusion; turmoil ¶どさくさに紛れて逃げ出す take advantage of the confusion to make one's escape.

とざす 閉ざす shut; close; bolt ⟨かんぬきなどで門を⟩; lock ⟨錠を下ろして⟩; block (up) (the street).

とさつ 屠殺 slaughter; butchery ¶屠殺する slaughter; butcher / 屠殺者 a butcher / 屠殺場 a slaughterhouse; an abattoir.

どさっと ⇨ どさり.

とざま 外様 ¶外様の outer [outside] (groups) / 外様大名 an 'outside' *daimyo* [feudal lord] (who was not a hereditary vassal of the Tokugawa family). 文例↓

どさまわり どさ回り ¶どさ回りの一座 a theatrical company on the road; a barnstorming troupe / どさ回りをやる be on the road; go on tour; ⟨米⟩ barnstorm. 文例↓

どさり どさりと with a thud; (fall) in a heap.

とざん 登山 mountain climbing; mountaineering ¶登山する climb [⟨文⟩ ascend, scale, go up] a mountain; ⟨文⟩ make an ascent of a mountain; go mountain-climbing / 登山家 a mountaineer; an alpinist / 登山靴 (a pair of) (mountain-)climbing boots / 登山者 a mountain climber / 登山隊 a mountaineering [climbing] party; a team of (mountain) climbers / ヒマラヤ登山隊 a Himalayan expedition / 登山鉄道 a mountain railway / 登山帽 an alpine hat. 文例↓

どさん ⇨ どさり.

とし¹ 年 a year; ⟨年齢⟩ age; ⟨文⟩ (one's) years ¶年が経つと [経つうちに] as (the) years pass [go] by; in the course of years; with (the passing of) the years / 年が明けるとすぐに early in the New Year [in January] / 年のいかない young / 年の市 a year-end fair / 年の功 ((possess)) the wisdom of age / 年の瀬 the last days of the year / 年を越す see the old year out; ⟨植物などが⟩ keep over the winter / 新しい年を迎える greet [welcome] the New Year / 年を取る grow older; age; ⟨文⟩ get on in years; ⟨口語⟩ get on; ⟨老人になる⟩ get [grow, ⟨文⟩ become] old; ⟨文⟩ advance in age [years]; ⟨ふける⟩ age / 10 年年を取る get [⟨文⟩ become] ten years older; put on ten years / 年を取った old; ⟨文⟩ aged / 大分年を食っている ⟨文⟩ be well along in years / 年の割に若い [老けている] look young [old] for one's age [⟨文⟩ years] / 年を経た大蛇(おろち) a huge serpent that has survived many a winter / 年ほどに見えない do not look one's age [as old as one really is] / この年になって at my age [time of life] / 年は50である be fifty years old [of age] / 年は若いけれども though young, ⟨文⟩ though young in years; ⟨文⟩ young though [as] one is / 彼と同じくらいの年の人 a man (about) his age / 年相応のことをする act one's age. 文例↓

とし² 都市 a city ¶都市の ⟨文⟩ urban / 都市の発達 the growth of cities; urban growth / 大都市 a large [big, great] city / 中小都市 small towns / 都市化 urbanization / 都市ガス town gas / 都市計画 urban [city] planning / 都市交通 urban transport [transportation, transit] / 都市国家 ⟨史⟩ a city-state / 都市生活 city [⟨文⟩ urban] life / 都市生活者 a city dweller; a townsman; ⟨複数⟩ city people; townsfolk / 都市対抗野球 the National Intercity Nonpro-

---

French. / 清流どころかまるでどぶ川だった. Far from being a clear stream, it was little better than an open sewer. / そんなことをしたら信用を得るどころか, 人から見下げられるよ. If you do that sort of thing, instead of giving you credit for it, people will simply despise you.

-ところで ぐずぐず言ったところで仕方がない. It is no use complaining. / 僕の代わりに君が行ったところで, 彼に面会はできないだろう. Even if you go in my place, I doubt if you will be able to see him.

ところてん この学校に入って4年すれば, ところてん式に卒業する仕組だ. The setup is that if you get into this school and put in four years, you'll graduate in belt-conveyor fashion.

ところどころ 毛布にところどころ穴があいていた. There were some [several] holes in the blanket. / ペンキがところどころはげていた. The paint was off in places.

ところばんち 手紙を書こうにも彼の所番地さえ知らないんです. I don't even know where to write to him.

どさくさ 引っ越しのどさくさでそのことは全く忘れていた. I had clean forgotten about it in the bustle and confusion of the move.

とざす 港は流氷ですっかり閉ざされてしまった. The harbor was blocked in by masses of floating ice. / 村は冬の間はずっと雪に閉ざされてしまう. The village is cut off by snow [is snowed in] right through [throughout] the winter.

とざま 我々は外様だ. We are outsiders. We're on the outside looking in.

どさまわり 彼はかつては一流の人気歌手だったが, 今では落ちぶれてもっぱらどさ回りをやっている. He was once a top-class popular singer but now he is down and out and only appears in small local theaters.

とざん この山には登山路が3つある. There are three trails leading to the top of this mountain.

とし¹ どうやって年を越すのかしら. I wonder how he is going to pull through into the new year. / お年は幾つですか. How old are you? | What is your age? / 67 という年にしては若く見える. She looks younger than her 67 years. / 彼は年はとっても若々しい. He carries [wears] his age well. / さすがの彼も年には勝てなかった. Age [The years] began to tell on

とじ 〈本などの〉binding ⇨ そうい¹; 〈衣服などの〉sewing ¶〈本の〉綴じがいい[悪い] be well[badly] bound / 〈本の〉綴じ糸 a binding thread / 綴じ目 a seam.

どじ ¶どじを踏む blunder; make[commit] a blunder; bungle;《口語》put one's foot in it;《英口語》make a bloomer.

とじあわせる 綴じ合わせる bind[stitch] together; sew up.

としうえ 年上 ¶年上の older; elder; senior / 3つ上である be three years older than sb;《文》be sb's senior by three years;《文》be three years sb's senior / 年上の人 one's senior. 文例⇩

としおとこ 年男 a lucky-bean scatterer at the setsubun rites.

としがい 年甲斐 ¶年がいもない be thoughtless for one's age;《文》be unworthy of one's years. 文例⇩

としがたい 度し難い 〈救い難い〉《be》past praying for;〈直しようのない〉incorrigible.

としかっこう 年格好 ¶30くらいの年格好の女 a woman (of) about thirty (years of age); a thirtyish-looking woman. 文例⇩

としご 年子 a child born within a year of another; children born in two successive years. 文例⇩

としこし 年越し ¶年越しする see the old year out (and the New Year in) / 年越しの晩 New Year's Eve / 年越しそば the buckwheat noodles eaten on New Year's Eve. 〚歳〛.

としごと 年ごと ¶年ごとに ⇨ ねん¹ (年々歳

とじこみ 綴じ込み a (newspaper) file ¶綴じ込みになっている新聞 newspapers kept on file / 〈雑誌の〉綴じ込み付録 a bound-in supplement (to a magazine).

とじこむ 綴じ込む 〈つづっておく〉file; keep 《newspapers》on file; 〈中に入れてとじる〉bind up 《a chart》between 《the pages》.

とじこめる 閉じ込める shut[lock] in[up]; coop[cage] up[in]; pen(up);《文》confine ¶雪に閉じ込められる be snowed up[in]. 文例⇩

とじこもる 閉じこもる shut[lock] oneself up [in];《文》confine oneself to[be confined in] 《a room》; stay[remain] indoors; stay cooped up《in a room》¶終日部屋に閉じこもる keep to one's room all day long / 病気で閉じこもっている be confined indoors[to one's bed] with illness / 自分の中に閉じこもる withdraw into oneself;《文》retire within oneself.

としごろ 年頃 〈年配〉age;〈婚期〉marriageable age;〈思春期〉adolescence; puberty ¶大人とも子供ともつかない年頃 the awkward age / 年頃の marriageable;《文》nubile; adolescent / 同じ年頃の 《children》of (about) the same age / 年頃になる reach [《文》attain, arrive at] a marriageable age [the age of puberty]; become adolescent. 文例⇩

用法 以上に挙げた語のうち, adolescence は子供から大人になる時期 (上の the awkward age) で, 身体と精神の発達のアンバランスなどいろいろの問題を含む年頃, puberty はその始まりで, 生理的に生殖が可能となる時を言う. nubile は女性についてだけ使う語で, 結婚適齢期という意味だが性的魅力があるという意味合いを含んでいる.

としした 年下 ¶年下の younger; junior / 3つ下である be three years younger than sb;《文》be sb's junior by three years;《文》be three years sb's junior / 年下の人 one's junior. 文例⇩

どしつ 土質 the nature of the soil ¶土質試験 a soil test.

としつき 年月 years; time ⇨ とし¹ ¶長い年月の間 for a long period of time / 長い年月を経て after (a lapse of) many years.

-として as; by way of; 〈…の〉in the capacity of; 〈…のしるしとして〉in token [as a token] of ¶通訳として as [in the capacity of] (an) interpreter / 学者として通用する

him at last. / 年のせいで少し腰が曲がっている. He stoops a little with age. / いつまでも年をとらないというわけにはいかない. You cannot stay the same age forever. / 年が年だから仕方がない. It can't be helped, considering his age. / はたちという年は二度とやって来ないのだよ. You'll never see twenty again. / 私ももう年だよ. I'm not as young as I was. / 花子, お前もそろそろ年だから, もう結婚した方がいいよ. You ought to get married, Hanako. You're not getting any younger. / It's about time you were married, Hanako. / 彼は年は30くらいだが, He looks [appears to be] about thirty. / こんなものはこの年になって初めて見た. I've lived all these years and I've never seen a thing like this. / 年はまだ30だが, 物の考え方はまことに円熟している. He is only thirty, but he is very mature in his way of thinking. / 年に不足はなかった. 〈ある役職に〉He was old[mature] enough for it. | 〈死んだ人について〉He had a (long) and full life. / このくらいの事はわかってもいい年だ. You are old enough to know that. / さすがに年の功だ. He has not lived all these years in vain [for nothing]. / 男よりも女の方が年を食う. Women age quicker than men. / 女には目もくれないなどという年でもあるまい. You aren't past looking at a woman, are you? / 彼は父親ほども年の違う金持ちの老人と結婚した. She married a wealthy man who was old enough to be her father.

としうえ お姉さんはあなたよりいくつ年上ですか. How much older is your sister than you?

としがい 何です, 年がいもない. Be[Act] your age! | You ought to know better at your age.

としかっこう 彼はちょうどそのくらいの年格好だ. He looks just about that age.

としご あの兄弟は年子だ. The brothers were born within a year of each other.

とじこめる 彼は(係員に)うっかり鍵をかけられ, 図書室に閉じ込められてしまった. He was locked into the library by mistake.

としごろ 彼は君と同じ年頃に結婚した. He got married when he was about your age. / 彼らは大体同じ年頃だ. They are about the same age.

としした 神田君は僕より2つ年下です. Kanda is two years my junior [two years younger than me]. ⇨ より² 用法

pass for [as] a scholar / 埋め合わせ[前置き]として by way of compensation [introduction] / それはそれとして leaving that aside ; apart from that / 女としては for a woman ; as women go / 私としては as for me ; I for one (think...) ; for my part ; as far as I am concerned. 文例⇩
-としても ⇨ -しても (...としても).
どしどし 《多数で》 in large numbers ; 〈絶え間なく〉 constantly ; one after another ; in rapid succession ; 〈急速に〉 rapidly ; 〈遠慮なく〉 freely. 文例⇩
としなみ 年波 age ; years ¶寄る年波に 《(bent, bowed) with age. 文例⇩
としは 年端 ¶年端も行かぬ very young ; 《文》 (a girl) of tender years.
としま 年増 a middle-aged woman ; 《文》 a woman of mature age ; 《文》 a woman past her first youth ¶年増盛りである be in the prime of [《文》 in full] womanhood.
とじまり 戸締まり ¶戸締まりする lock up 《for the night》; fasten [bolt, lock] the door(s) / 戸締まりを厳重にする lock up [fasten the doors] securely [carefully]. 文例⇩
としまわり 年回り ¶年回りがいい[悪い] the year is lucky [unlucky] for one.
としゃ 吐瀉 ¶吐瀉する suffer from diarrhea and vomiting / 吐瀉物 vomit and excreta.
どしゃ 土砂 earth and sand ¶土砂崩れ a landslide ; a soil avalanche.
どしゃぶり 土砂降り (a) pouring [pelting, heavy] rain ; a downpour ¶土砂降りに降る pour down ; rain in torrents. 文例⇩
としゅ 斗酒 ¶斗酒なお辞せず be ready to drink sake by the keg [like a fish].
としゅたいそう 徒手体操 gymnastic exercises without using apparatus ; 〈競技種目〉 free standing exercises.
としょ 図書 books ¶莫(ば)大な数の図書を集める collect a vast number of books ; assemble an immense library / 図書券 《米》 a book token (for 5,000 yen) / 《英》 a book token (for 5,000 yen) / 図書目録 a catalogue [《米》 catalog] of books [publications] / 図書室 a library.
としょう 徒渉 ¶徒渉する wade (across) (a stream) ; ford (a river).
とじょう 途上 ⇨ とちゅう ¶(発展)途上国 ⇨ はってん.

どじょう¹ 土壌 soil ¶土壌改良剤 a soil conditioner / 土壌学 soil science / 土壌微生物 soil microbes.
どじょう² 《魚》 a loach ¶どじょうひげ a thin mustache.
どしょうぼね 土性骨 the backbone ¶土性骨の太いやつ a man with plenty of guts.
としょかん 図書館 a library ¶図書館の本 a library book / 学校[公共]図書館 a school [public] library / 図書館員 a library clerk ; a librarian (司書) / 図書館学 library science ; 《米》 librarianship / 図書館長 the director [curator] of a library ; the chief [head] librarian.
としより 年寄り an old [《文》 aged] person ; an old man [woman] / 〈総称〉 the old ; 《文》 the aged ; 〈相撲〉 a manager ¶年寄りの old ; aged / 年寄りになる be old ; age / 年寄りじみている be old before one's time. 文例⇩
とじる¹ 閉じる shut ; close ⇨ しめる³ ¶会を閉じる close a meeting ; bring a meeting to a close / 目を固く閉じたまま with one's eyes shut tight.
とじる² 綴じる bind ; file ; 〈縫い合わせる〉 sew up ¶綴じておく keep (newspapers) on file.
としん 都心 the heart [center] (of Tokyo) ; (in) the downtown area.
とじん 都塵 ¶都塵を避けて郊外に住む live in a suburb avoiding [away from] the dust and noise of the city.
どしんと with a thud [thump] ; heavily ¶どしんと落ちる fall heavily / どしんとぶつかる bump (into sb, against the wall).
トス a toss ; tossing ¶トスする toss (a ball) / トスバッティング 《野球》 a pepper game. 文例⇩
どす 〈短刀〉 a dagger ¶どすの利いた声で in a deep, threatening voice ; with menace in one's voice.
どすう 度数 (the number of) times ; 《文》 frequency ; 〈角度・温度などの〉 a degree ¶(電話の)度数制 the message-[call-]rate system.
どすぐろい どす黒い darkish (-colored) ; dusky. 文例⇩
とする 賭する ¶職を賭して 《do》 at the risk of (losing) one's position.
-とする regard (A as B) ; consider [assume] (A to be B) ; treat (A as B) ¶《数学で》...を x とする let x be [stand for]... / n をゼロとする

-として 彼はその金を, 全部ではないとしても, 大部分は使ってしまった. He has spent most of the money, if not all of it. / 報酬としては何ももらっていない. We have received nothing as [in the way of] recompense. / 大学を出ての新人としては, なかなかよくやったよ. He's done a good job, considering he is [for someone who is] fresh from college and hasn't much experience.
どしどし 子供には本をどしどし読ませるのがよい. You should let children read as many books as they can. / 先生は生徒にどしどし質問しなさいと言った. The teacher said to the pupils, 'Ask me anything you like.'
としなみ 彼も寄る年波には勝てず, 目がかすんできた. The years began to tell on him ; his eyesight became weaker.
とじまり 戸締まりに気をつけて下さいね. See that all the doors are locked, will you?
どしゃぶり どしゃ降りだった. It rained in torrents. | The rain poured down. | It was pouring with rain. / その晩はどしゃ降り

だった. It was a pouring wet night. / 土砂降りになりそうだぞ. It's going to come down in buckets, you hear?
としより 年寄りの冷や水だ. Why don't you [doesn't he] admit that you are [he is] too old for that sort of thing?
としん ここは住宅地としてはいい所とは言えないが, 都心に出るのには便利だ. You couldn't call this [This cannot be called] a good residential area but it is convenient for the city center.
どしんと 2人は暗闇でどしんとぶつ

とせい 都政 the administration of Tokyo ¶ 都政を預かる administer the municipal affairs of Tokyo ;《文》assume the reins of Tokyo city government.
どせい 土星 Saturn ¶ 土星の環 Saturn's rings.
どせきりゅう 土石流 an avalanche of earth and rocks ; a debris-avalanche.
とぜつ 途絶 a stoppage ; a break ; (an) interruption ; (a) suspension (中絶) ¶ 途絶する be stopped ; be interrupted ; be disrupted ; be cut off ; be tied [held] up. 文例⇩
とそ 屠蘇 spiced *sake* ¶ とそ機嫌で tipsy from drinking the New Year in ★ see the New year in (新年を迎える ⇨ としこし) という表現からの変形.
とそう 塗装 painting ; coating (プラスチックなども含めて) ¶ 塗装する coat with paint ; paint / 塗装し直す repaint / 塗装してない unpainted (walls) / 塗装工 a painter / 塗装吹き付け機 a paint spray (gun).
どそう 土葬 《文》interment ; burial ¶ 土葬にする《文》inter ; bury in the ground.
どぞう 土蔵 a storehouse ; a warehouse.
どそく 土足 ¶ 土足で (enter the house) with *one's* shoes on. 文例⇩
どぞく 土俗 local customs ¶ 土俗作家 a folk writer.
どだい¹ 土台 a foundation ; a base ; a basis《*pl.* bases》; groundwork ¶ 土台をすえる lay the foundation(s) / 成功の土台を築く lay the groundwork [pave the way] for *one's* success. 文例⇩
どだい² 〈元々〉in the first place ; to begin with ; 〈全く〉utterly ; entirely ; altogether. 文例⇩
とだえる 途絶える stop ;《文》cease ; come to an end [a halt] ; break off ; 〈絶える〉die out. 文例⇩
とだな 戸棚 a cupboard ;〈衣服などの〉a closet ; a wardrobe.
どたばた ¶ どたばたと noisily ; bustlingly / どたばたする make a noise ;〈もがく〉(kick and) struggle ;〈はね回る〉romp about / どたばた歩く walk noisily ; stomp (along the corridor) / どたばた喜劇 a slapstick (knockabout) comedy ; a noisy farce / どたばた調の《a farce》of a naive, knockabout kind.
どたり ¶ どたりと heavily ; with a thud ;《fall》

in a heap.
とたん 途端 ¶ とたんに just at the moment ; just as... ; (the) very moment... / そのとたんに just then [at that moment]. 文例⇩
トタン [<《ポルトガル語》*tutanaga*] galvanized iron ¶ トタン板《a》galvanized iron sheet / トタン屋根 a tin [an iron] roof.
どたん ⇨ どたり.
どたんば 土壇場 ¶ 土壇場に追い込まれる be driven [brought] to bay ; have *one's* back against the wall / 土壇場で at the last moment ; at the eleventh hour / 土壇場で逃げる make *one's* escape in the nick of time ; make a last-minute exit.
とち 土地 〈地面〉(a piece of) land ;〈地所〉a lot ; a plot ; (a piece of) real estate ;〈地味〉soil ;〈地方〉a locality ; a region ; a district ; a part of the country ; a place ¶ 土地の native ; local / 土地の人 a native (of) / 土地を借りる lease [rent] a lot / 土地を持たない人 a landless person / 土地を売買する deal in real estate / 土地家屋 land and houses ; real estate / 土地柄 (nature of) the locality / 土地勘がある know [《文》be acquainted with] the place ; have the feel of the place / 土地収用 expropriation of land / 土地収用法《法》the Compulsory Purchase of Land Act / 土地所有権 landownership / 土地所有者 a landowner / 土地登記簿 [台帳] a land register ; a cadaster / この土地不足の国で in this land-short country / 土地面積 land area. 文例⇩
とちのき 栃の木 a Japanese horse chestnut.
どちゃく 土着 ¶ 土着の native (to) ;《文》indigenous (to) / 土着の人 a native.
とちゅう 途中 ¶ 途中で on the [one's] way ;《文》en route (for, to) ; 〈中途で〉halfway / 学校へ行く[から帰る]途中で on *one's* way to [from] school / 家に帰る途中で on *one's* way home / 途中でよす[から引き返す]give up [turn back] halfway / 食事の途中で in the middle of [halfway through] a meal / 途中まで車に乗せる give *sb* a lift [drive *sb*] part of the way / 映画を途中から見る see a movie from halfway [《米》partway] through / 途中下車 a stopover / 途中下車のできる切符 a stopover ticket / 途中下車する break *one's* (railroad) journey (at) ; stop off (at) ;《米》stop over (at) / 途中計時〈計時すること〉clocking part-

---

つかった. They collided bodily with each other in the darkness.
トス (バレーボールで)いいトスが上がった. That's a nice toss !
どすぐろい 床にどす黒く血がたまっていた. There on the floor was a pool of blackish blood.
-ても 1978年の推定ではその地方の人口数は約 30 万人とされている. A 1978 estimate places the population of the region at approximately 300,000.
とぜつ 吹雪で交通が途絶した. Traffic was paralyzed by the snowstorm. / その町とは電信電

話による連絡が全く途絶してしまっている. Telephone and telegraph communications with the town have been completely cut off [have completely broken down].
どそく 土足厳禁.〔掲示〕No outdoor [street] shoes allowed.
どだい¹ この家は土台がしっかりしている. This house is built on firm foundations.
どだい² どだい君が間違っていたんだ. You were wrong in the first place. / そいつぁどだい無理だよ. That's simply impossible. /

どだい話にならん. It's downright nonsense.
とだえる 雪が積もって人の往来も途絶えた. The snow piled deep and the street was absolutely deserted.
とたん 私が入って行ったとたんに彼は逃げ出した. He ran away the (very) moment I came in.
とち 彼は家を建てるつもりでその土地を買った. He bought the land for the purpose of building on it. / 農民は土地から離れられない. The peasant is bound [tied] to the land. / この土地はメロン

どちょう　way times [lap times] 《in a race》; 〈計った時間〉 times clocked partway 《in a race》; lap times / 1,000メートル途中計時 the time at 1,000 meters. 文例⇩

どちょう　怒張　overswelling 《of a blood vessel》.

どちら〈どれ〉which; 〈どこ〉where ¶どちらかと言えば if anything; on balance / どちらにしても in either case; either way / どちらへ[に] where (to); 《文》 in what direction. 文例⇩

とちる　make an error [a slip] ¶せりふをとちる fluff *one*'s lines.

とつおいつ　hesitatingly;《文》irresolutely ¶とつおいつする hesitate; be unable to make a quick decision; waver [《文》vacillate] 《between two courses of action》.

とっか　特価 a special [bargain] price ¶特価販売 a bargain sale / 特価品 an article offered at a special [specially reduced] price.

トッカータ〖音楽〗a toccata.

どっかいりょく　読解力 ability to read and understand ¶読解力をテストする give *sb* a reading comprehension test.

とっかかり ⇨てがかり.

どっかと ¶椅子にどっかと腰をおろす plump [flop] into a chair;《文》ensconce *oneself* in a chair（★《文》であるが, おどけて使うことも多い）.

とっかん　突貫 ⇨とつげき ¶突貫工事 a rush job; rush work.

とっき¹　突起 a projection;《文》a protuberance; a swelling;〖解・生物〗a process ¶突起する stick out; project;《文》protrude.

とっき²　特記 ⇨とくひつ.

どっき　毒気 ⇨とくけ.

とっきゅう¹　特急 a limited [special] express (train).

とっきゅう²　特級 a special grade ¶特級酒 super-high grade *sake*; *sake* of superfine quality.

とっきょ　特許 a special permission [license];〈発明・考案の〉a patent;〈採掘・敷設権などの〉a concession ¶特許を申請する apply for a patent; file a patent 《for》/ 特許を取る obtain [get, take out] a patent 《for, on》; be awarded [granted] a patent; have *sth* patented /特許権〈buy〉a patent (right) /特許権を侵害する infringe the patent 《on an invention》/ 特許権で守られている have patent protection / 特許権所有者 a patentee /特許庁 the Patent Office /特許法〖法〗the Patent Act /特許料〈特許申請のための〉a patent fee;〈特許権使用料〉a royalty /特許(使用)料をとる collect royalties 《on *one*'s invention from several countries》. 文例⇩

ドッキング〈宇宙船の〉docking ¶ドッキングさせる dock 《two spaceships》/ ドッキング操作を行なう perform a 《successful》docking maneuver.

とつぐ　嫁ぐ marry *sb*; be [get] married 《to *sb*, into a family》¶嫁がせる marry 《*one*'s daughter》(off)《to *sb*》.

ドック a (dry) dock; a dockyard〈造船及び修理ドック〉★英語の dock は船の修理だけでなく荷物の積み下ろしなどをする船付場の意味にも使われる ¶ドックに入る (go into) dock / ドックに入れる dock (a ship); put (a ship) into dock.

とっくに〈ずっと以前に〉long ago [《口語》since]; a long time ago;《口語》ages ago;〈既に〉already. 文例⇩

とっくあい　取っ組み合い a grapple; a scuffle ¶取っ組み合いになる come to grips 《with》.

とっくむ　取っ組む〈組み合う〉wrestle [grapple, scuffle]《with》;〈問題などと〉tackle《a task》; grapple [cope] with《difficulties》.

とっくり¹　徳利 a [an earthenware] *sake* bottle ¶とっくり(の)セーター a turtleneck (sweater);《英》a polo-neck sweater.

とっくり² ⇨とくと.

とっくん　特訓 special training; intensive training (to get quick results); a crash course ¶特訓中である be undergoing [receiving] special training; be training intensively.

とっけいかんぜい　特恵関税 preferential duties.

とつげき　突撃 a charge; a rush; a dash ¶突撃する charge 《at, on》; rush [dash]《at》; make a dash 《at》.

とっけん　特権 a privilege; a special [an ex-

の栽培に適している. The soil is suited to the cultivation of melons.

とちゅう　途中までお供しましょう. I will go some [part] of the way with you. / 途中までご案内しましょう. I'll put [set] you on your way. / 途中のどこかで何かあったに違いない. Something must have happened somewhere along the way. / お話の途中ですが, お飲み物は何にいたしましょう. Excuse me for interrupting, but what would you like to drink? / 途中下車無効.《表示》No stopover permitted.

どちら　伊藤さんはお国はどちらですか. Where [What part of the country] do you come from, Mr. Ito? / 光と音とどちらが速いか. Which travels faster, light or sound? / 彼はどちらかと言えば歌はうまいほうであった. He was, if anything, a good singer. / その事業はどちらかと言えば損になった. On balance, they lost rather than gained from the project. / 1つくれたまえ, どちらでもいいよ. Give me one, please; either will do. / この本はどちらも面白い. Both these books are interesting. / 私はどちらも知らない. I don't know either [I know neither] of them. / どちら様ですか. May I have your name, please?

とっきょ　特許出願中.《表示》Patent applied for. | Patent pending.

とっくに　とっくに起きる時間ですよ. It's more than time you got [were] up.

どっこい　どっこい, そうはいかない. Hold it (a minute)! We can't have that! / 2人の碁の力はどっこいどっこいだ. There's not much to choose between them at go.

どっこいしょ　父は「どっこいしょ」と言って立ち上がった. Father stood up, saying, 'Well, here

どっこい／とってかわる

clusive] right;《文》a prerogative ¶特権を与える grant [《文》accord] a privilege《to sb》;《文》confer a privilege 《on sb》/ 特権を行使する exercise *one*'s privilege / 特権階級 the privileged classes / 少数特権階級 the privileged few [minority].

どっこい 文例⇩

どっこいしょ《掛け声》oof! ¶どっこいしょと持ち上げる lift *sth* with an effort / どっこいしょと腰を下ろす plump down 《into a chair》.

とっこう 特効《文》special [miraculous] virtue [efficacy] (for) ¶特効がある be specially good [《文》efficacious] (for) / 特効薬 a specific (medicine) (for);《文》a sovereign remedy (for); a wonder drug.

どっこうせん 独航船 an independent fishing boat.

とっこうたい 特攻隊 a special attack corps; a suicide [*kamikaze*] squad.

とっさ ¶とっさの instantaneous; prompt; momentary / とっさに at once; instantly; in an instant; in the twinkling of an eye; on the spur of the moment; quick as thought; promptly; on the spot; then and there. 文例⇩

どっさり ¶たくさん.

ドッジボール dodge ball.

とっしゅつ 突出 projection;《文》protrusion ¶突出する project; jut [stick] out / 突出している projecting;《文》protuberant / 突出部 a projection;《文》a protrusion. 文例⇩

とつじょ 突如 ⇨ とつぜん.

どっしり ¶どっしりした〈物が〉massive; solid;〈体格が〉heavily-built; heavy-set;〈威厳のある〉dignified; imposing / どっしりした書物 a substantial [heavy] volume. 文例⇩

とっしん 突進 a rush; a dash; a charge; an onrush ¶突進する rush [charge] 《at》; make a dash 《at》; plunge 《into》.

とつぜん 突然 ¶突然(に) suddenly; all of a sudden; unexpectedly; all at once; without notice [warning]; out of the blue / 突然の sudden; abrupt; unexpected /〈考えが〉突然心に浮かぶ burst on *one*; flash into [through] *one*'s mind / 突然訪問する pay *sb* a surprise visit / 突然変異《生物》(a) mutation. 文例⇩

とったん 突端 a point; a tip; an end.

どっち ⇨ どちら ¶どっち道 ⇨ どの²(どの道) / どっちつかずの neutral; noncommittal (answers).

とっちめる 取っちめる〈叱る〉scold; take *sb* to task; call [bring] *sb* to account; teach *sb* a lesson; haul *sb* over the coals;〈いじめる〉be hard on *sb* ¶うんと取っちめてやる give *sb* a good scolding [talking-to] / 取っちめられるを be on the carpet; catch it (hot) (from *sb*);《文》be reprimanded severely (for what *one* has done, for *doing*);《口語》be told off [get a good telling-off] (for).

とっつき 取っ付き〈はじめ〉the beginning ¶取っ付きの first (room you come to) /〈人柄が〉取っ付きやすい be approachable; be affable; be easy to approach [talk to] / 取っ付きにくい be unapproachable; be cold and aloof; be difficult to approach [talk to].

とって 取っ手 a handle (柄); a grip (器物の); a knob (ドアの); a pull (引き手); an ear (水差しの).

-とって ¶…にとって(は) for; to. 文例⇩

とってい 突堤 a pier; a jetty; a breakwater (防波堤).

とっておき 取って置き ¶取って置きのreserve(d); spare;〈大切な〉《文》much-valued; treasured;〈とびきり〉best / 取って置きの手《play》a trump card / 取って置きの手がある have a plan [card] up *one*'s sleeve / 取って置きの着物を着て(dressed) in *one*'s Sunday best. 文例⇩

とっておく 取って置く〈保存する〉keep;《文》preserve;〈別にして〉put *sth* on one side; set [lay] aside; put [lay] by;〈貯える〉save (up); hoard;〈予約する〉reserve; book ¶座席を取って置く book a seat in advance; reserve a seat (for *one*).

とってかえす 取って返す return; turn back [turn and go back] (the way *one* has come); retrace *one*'s steps / 急いで取って返す hurry [dash] back.

とってかわる 取って代わる take the place of; replace;《文》supplant;《文》supersede;

---

goes!'
とっさ 彼はとっさにハンドルを左に切って衝突を免れた。He wheeled the car to the left almost without thinking and avoided a crash. / とっさの間に判断を下す能力が飛行機のパイロットには必要だ。The ability to make quick decisions in critical moments is required of the pilot of an airplane.

とっしゅつ その岬は弧を描いて南東に突出している。The cape juts [runs] out southeastward in an arc.

どっしり このブロンズ像の極端にやせたからだはそのどっしりした丸い頭部と著しい対照をなしている。The excessively thin figure of this bronze statue is in striking contrast with the solidly rounded head.

とつぜん 突然大きな滝が見えてきた。A large waterfall burst into view [into sight, on our sight].

どっち どっちがどっちか見分けがつかない。I can't tell which is which [tell them apart]. / どっちもどっちだ。It's six of one and half a dozen of the other. | There is little to choose between them. | They are both to blame. | One is as bad as the other.

-とって 彼らにとっては死活の問題だ。It means life or death to them. / 私にとっては便利です。That is convenient for me. / あの人にとっては酒は薬なのです。To him *sake* is a medicine.

とっておき 彼は取って置きの手品をやって見せてくれた。He entertained us with the conjuring tricks that he had kept secret and never performed before.

とっておく 金曜の午後は会議のためにいつも取っておいて下さい。Please keep (your) Friday afternoons free for meetings. / 帽子を置いてその席を取っておいた。I saved (myself) a seat by putting my hat on it. / I left my cap on the seat to claim it. / よかったら、取っておきたまえ。You may have [keep] it (for yourself), if

とってくる 取って来る go and get *sth*; collect; fetch; go for *sth* and bring it back.

とってつけたような 取って付けた ような unnatural; artificial;《文》strained 《interpretations》; forced ¶取って付けたようなほほ笑み a forced smile.

どっと 〈にわかに〉all of a sudden; suddenly; 〈一度に〉all at once; all together;〈turn out〉 in force ¶どっと出て来る rush [pour] out / どっと笑い出す burst out laughing; burst into laughter /観客をどっと笑わせる set the audience roaring with laughter. 文例⇩

とつとつ 訥々 ¶とつとつと語る speak in a halting way; tell 〈the story of one's life〉haltingly [《文》ineloquently].

とっとと 〈早く〉quickly; hurriedly; 〈すぐ〉 at once; 〈足早に〉at a brisk pace; at a trot. 文例⇩

とつにゅう 突入 ¶突入する rush [dash, break, run] in [into]; storm into 《the palace》;〈開始する〉plunge 《into》/ ストライキに突入する come [go] out on strike; rush into a strike.

とっぱ 突破 (a) breakthrough ¶突破する break through; burst [smash] through; 〈困難などを〉乗り越える〉《文》surmount; overcome; get over 《it》;〈越える〉pass;《文》exceed; rise above /入試の難関を突破する(successfully) pass a difficult entrance examination 《to a college》/ 突破口を作る open the way 《for resuming negotiations》. 文例⇩

トッパー a (woman's) short topcoat; a car coat.

とっぱつ 突発 (an) outbreak ¶突発する break out; happen [《文》occur] suddenly /突発事件 an unforeseen [unexpected] incident; an accident / 突発的(な) sudden; unexpected.

とっぱんいんさつ 凸版印刷 letterpress; relief printing.

とっぴ ¶とっぴな unusual; extraordinary; wild; extravagant; odd; fantastic; 《something》out of the common (run);〈向こう見ずな〉reckless /〈風変わりな〉eccentric / とっぴなことをする act recklessly / とっぴな考え a wild [fantastic] idea; an eccentric notion.

とっぴょうし 突拍子 ¶突拍子もない crazy 《ideas》; exorbitant 《prices》⇒ とんきょう, とっぴ, ほうがい.

トップ ¶トップを切る[行く] lead 《the field》; be in the lead 《in》; be the first 《to do》; be at the top [head] 《of》/ トップを行く W 大チーム the front-running W University team / トップに出る take [move into] the lead /トッ プ会談 a summit meeting [conference] /トップ 記事〈新聞第一面の〉the lead (story);〈週 刊誌などの〉a feature / トップクラスの first-rate; top-class;《口語》top-notch; top-flight; top-ranking; leading; foremost. 文例⇩

とっぷう 突風 a (sudden) gust of wind; a squall; a blast of wind ¶突風の多い gusty 《March》.

ドップラー ¶ドップラー効果《物》the Doppler effect.

とっぷり completely; entirely. 文例⇩

どっぷり ¶筆に墨をどっぷりと含ませる take up a full [generous] brushful of ink / 風呂に どっぷりと漬かる soak (for a long time) in a bath / …にどっぷり漬かっている be immersed in 《water》. 文例⇩

とつべん 訥弁 ¶とつ弁である be a poor [an awkward] speaker;《文》be ineloquent; do not have a glib tongue. 文例⇩

とつめん 凸面 a convex surface ¶凸面の convex / 凸面をなしている be convexly curved / 凸面鏡 a convex mirror.

とつレンズ 凸レンズ a convex lens.

-とて ⇒ -といって.

どて 土手 a bank; an embankment ¶土手を 築く build a bank.

とてい 徒弟 an apprentice ¶徒弟期間 one's apprenticeship / 徒弟制度 an apprentice system.

どてっぱら 土手っ腹 文例⇩

とてつもない ⇒ とほう (途方もない).

とても 〈まったく〉quite; utterly; absolutely; 〈非常に〉very;《文》exceedingly; awfully; terribly; badly ¶とても…ない by no means; not at all; not…possibly; hardly; not nearly 《so…as》/ とても助からない cannot possibly be saved; be past all help; be quite beyond recovery / とてもかなわない be no match

---

you like it.
とってかわる 新しい制度が古い制度に取って代わろうとしていた. The old system was giving way to the new.
どっと 明治維新後西洋の文化が どっと入って来た. After the Meiji Restoration Western culture flooded [rushed] into the country. /寒暖計が 26.7 度に達す ると、ビール党がどっと繰出す. When the thermometer hits 26 or 27 degrees centigrade, beer drinkers turn out in force.
とっとと とっとと歩いて行ってし まった. He trotted away. | He went away at a trot. / とっとと 出て行け. Get out at once!

とっぱ 志願者は千人を突破した. The number of applicants exceeded 1,000.
トップ 今朝が今朝の「毎日」の トップ記事だった. This morning's *Mainichi* led with that story.
とっぷり そのうちに日はとっぷり と暮れた. Meanwhile night had fallen [closed in] completely.
どっぷり 彼らは日常性の中にどっ ぷり漬かっている. They are totally immersed in their everyday concerns. | They have no time for [no interest in] anything but the humdrum business of their everyday lives.
とつべん 田中は小川に比べれば訥

弁だった. Tanaka was not as eloquent as Ogawa. | Tanaka's speech was less fluent than Ogawa's.
どてっぱら 土手っ腹に風穴を開け てやるぞ. Do you want a gutful [bellyful] of lead?
とても とても望みはない. There is no hope at all. / そんなこと はとても期待できない. Such a thing is hardly to be expected. / とてもそんな大金は持ったことも ありません. I have never had such a large amount of money in my whole life. / 頭が働くという 点で彼は兄にはとても及ばない. He is not half as clever as his brother. / とてもいい人ですよ.

どてら a padded *kimono*.
とど 【動】 a Steller's sea lion.
ととう 徒党 a faction; a clique ¶徒党を組む form a faction; band together; conspire《with》/ 徒党根性の強い cliquey.
どとう 怒濤 〈文〉 raging billows; angry waves. 文例↓
とどうふけん 都道府県 prefectures; the largest administrative divisions [units] of Japan.
とどく 届く 〈達する〉 reach; 〈手が〉〈かなう〉〈文〉 be attained; 〈到着する〉 reach; arrive at [in]; get to; 《文》 be received (手紙・品物などが) ¶手の届く[届かない]所に within [beyond, out of] *one*'s reach; where *one* can [can't] get at 《it》/ すぐ手の届く所に within easy reach; be within reach; near [close] at hand / 天井まで届く本棚 bookshelves (reaching) up to the ceiling / 遠くまで届く《a voice》that carries a long way; far-reaching 《cries》/ 的に届かない undershoot the target; fall short of the mark. 文例↓
とどけ 届《書》 a report; 〈文〉 a notification; a notice ¶届けを出す report 《*sth* to》; 〈文〉 notify 《the police of the damage》/ 転居届を出す give [send, hand] in a notice of *one*'s change of address / 届け先〈送り先〉the destination; the receiver's address; 〈荷受け人〉 a consignee.
とどけでる 届け出る ⇒とどけ（届を出す), とどける.
とどける 届ける 〈報告する〉 report; 《文》 notify; 《文》 give notice 《to》; 〈送る〉 forward; send; deliver (★自動詞ではない) ¶警察へ届ける report 《a fact》 to the police (★「警察へ届ける」 は「警察へ出頭する」); notify the police 《of the damage》/ 道に落ちていた札入れを交番に届ける take the wallet *one* has found on the street to a police box.
とどこおり 滞り 〈停滞〉 〈文〉 stagnation; 〈故障〉 a hindrance; 〈遅滞〉 (a) delay; 〈支払いの〉 arrears ¶家賃[地代]の滞り arrears of rent; back rent / 滞りなく smoothly; 《文》 duly; without delay (遅れずに) / 滞りなく済

む go off all right [without a hitch]. 文例↓
とどこおる 滞る 〈停滞する〉〈文〉stagnate; be left undone; 〈支払いが〉 fall into arrears 《with the rent》; be overdue; be left unpaid; 〈遅延する〉 be delayed; 《文》 be retarded; be behind [behindhand] 《with *one*'s work》¶家賃が滞っている be behind [behindhand, in arrears] with *one*'s rent. 文例↓
ととのう 整調う 〈用意が〉 be done; be made; be ready; 〈整頓してある〉 be (put) in (good) order [trim]; 〈調整される〉 be adjusted; 《文》 be regulated; 〈まとまる〉 be settled; be completed 〈整った〉 orderly; well-ordered; in good order [trim]; 〈服装など〉 neat; tidy; 〈顔立ちなど〉 regular 《features》/ 服装が整っている be neatly dressed / 用意が整っている be ready; be arranged; be prepared; the preparations [arrangements] 《for *sth*》 are complete.
ととのえる 整調える 〈用意する〉 prepare *sth*《for》; make 《preparations [arrangements]》; complete 《the preparations [arrangements] for》; make [get] *sth* ready; 〈調達する〉 raise 《money》; supply 《an article to》; 〈整頓する〉 put 《things》 in order; set 《things》 to rights; trim; 〈調整する〉 regulate; adjust; 〈米〉 fix; 〈まとめる〉 arrange; settle; 〈買う〉 buy; get / 夕食を整える get dinner ready; prepare supper / 注文の品を調える make up *sb*'s order; get the ordered article ready (for shipment) / 服装を整える straighten *one*'s clothes [《文》 dress]; tidy *oneself* (up) / 必要な金額を調える raise the necessary money; make up the sum needed /《英口語》 raise the wind.
とどのつまり ⇒けっきょく.
とどまる 止まる 〈残留する〉 stay; 《文》 remain; 〈限られる〉 be limited [confined] 《to》¶…するにとどまった went no further than *do*ing; did no more than *do*. 文例↓
とどめ 止め 〈最後の〉 a finishing blow [stroke]; 《フランス語》 a *coup de grace* ¶とどめを刺す put an end to *sb*'s life; 〈口語〉 finish *sb* off; 〈文〉 administer [deliver] the *coup de grace* to *sb* / 議論にとどめを刺す clinch the argument. 文例↓
どどめ 土留[止]め a retaining wall.

He is such a nice [good] man. / 彼はとても金に困っていた。He was badly in need of money. / とても金がかかった。It cost me a lot [no end] of money. / とても面白かった。We really enjoyed ourselves. |《口語》 We had a great [《米》 swell] time.
どとう 敵は怒濤のように押し寄せて来た。The enemy surged [poured] toward us.
とどく その縄では半分しか届かなかった。That rope reached only halfway. / 梯子をかけなければ届かない。I can't get at it without a ladder. / 彼女は腰まで長い髪をしていた。Her hair was so long that it came down to her waist. / 彼の声より僕の声の方が遠くまで届くはずだ。I'm sure my voice carries further than his. / 本は届きましたか。Has the book reached you? | Have you received the book?
とどこおり 彼は滞りなく支払いをすませた。He made his payment punctually.
とどこおる 仕事の滞ったのを片付けなければならない。I have some unfinished work to dispose of. | I have a backlog of work to get through. / 彼は家賃が半年も滞っていた。He was six months behind [in arrears] with his rent. / His rent was six months in arrears. / どうにか家賃を滞らせないでい

た。I managed to keep up with my rent payments [to carry on paying my rent].
とどまる ぜひ我々の側にとどまっていてほしい。I sincerely hope you will stick with us. / 彼がした事はこれだけにとどまらない。This is not all he has done. / この習慣は我が国だけにとどまるものではない。The custom is not confined to this country. / 単に私の希望を述べたにとどまります。All I did was express my wishes.
とどめ 彼にとってこれが最後のとどめになった。For him this was the last straw [finishing blow]. / ガリレオの実験はアリストテレス

とどめる 止める〈やめる〉stop;《文》cease;〈終らせる〉put an end [a stop] to;〈残す〉leave. 文例⇩

とどろき 轟き a roar; a peal; a rumble; booming;〈胸の〉beating; pounding; throbbing ¶遠雷のとどろき a roll of distant thunder / 砲声のとどろき the roar [booming] of guns.

とどろく 轟く roar; peal; thunder; roll; boom;〈反響する〉reverberate; resound;〈胸が〉beat; pound; throb ¶天地にとどろくような大声をあげて in a thundering [《文》stentorian] voice / 胸をとどろかして with a beating [throbbing] heart.

となえる¹ 称える ⇨ しょうする.

となえる² 唱える〈朗唱する〉recite; chant; intone;〈叫ぶ〉cry;〈唱道する〉《文》advocate; preach;〈相場が〉quote ¶万歳を唱える shout 'Banzai'; give three cheers [for] / 新説を唱える《文》advance [set forth] a new doctrine [theory] / …の必要を唱える《文》urge the necessity of… / 不平を唱える《文》voice one's discontent / 高値[安値]を唱える be quoted high [low].

となかい〈動〉〈ヨーロッパ産〉a reindeer(単複同形);〈北米産〉a caribou(pl. -(s)).

どなた ⇨ だれ. 文例⇩

どなべ 土鍋 an earthenware pot.

となり 隣〈隣家〉the house next door;〈人〉one's (next-door) neighbor; the people [family] next door (to one) / 隣の next (to one); next-door; neighboring;《文》adjoining (houses);《文》adjacent / 隣に住んでいる live next door to one [one's house] / 1軒置いて隣に住んでいる live next door but one to [two doors away from] one [one's house] / 隣合ってすわる sit side by side; rub elbows (with) / 隣り合わせに住んでいる live next door to each other / 右隣 one's neighbor [the next-door house] on the right / 右隣の人 one's right-hand neighbor / 隣近所 the neighborhood;〈人〉the neighbors / 隣座敷 the next [adjoining] room / 隣町 a neighboring [an adjacent] town. 文例⇩

どなる 怒鳴る shout; cry (loudly); roar; yell (out) ¶どなり込む storm into 《sb's house》 in a rage; go to 《sb's house》 to make a violent protest / どなりつける shout 《at sb》; roar (at); thunder (at); browbeat 《sb into doing》.

とにかく ⇨ ともかく(も). 文例⇩

どの¹ 殿 Mister (略: Mr.);〈英〉Esquire (略: Esq.) ¶小田太郎殿 Mr. Taro Oda;〈英〉Taro Oda, Esq. ★Esq. は私用の手紙に書くことはまだあるが、すたれつつあるし、気取っているといっていやがる人もいる。日本人の書く手紙は英米ともに Mr. でよい。

どの² which; what;〈どの…でも〉whichever; any; every;〈否定〉none ¶どのくらい〈距離〉how far;〈時間〉how long; how soon;〈数〉how many;〈量〉how much;〈大小・高低など〉how big [large](大きさ); how deep(深さ); how high(高さ); how wide(広さ); how thick(厚さ);〈程度〉どんな / どの道 anyhow; anyway; in any [either] case; at any rate / どのよう ⇨ どんな.

どのう 土嚢 a sandbag ¶堤防に土のうを積む sandbag a bank.

とのこ 砥の粉 polishing powder.

とのさま 殿様 a (feudal) lord ¶殿様のような lordly.

とのさまがえる 殿様蛙 a leopard frog.

とのさまばった 殿様ばった〈昆〉a migratory locust.

-とは〈…とは〉as; for;〈それほどは〉so much;〈意外〉how [why] should…;〈遺憾〉I am sorry that…; It is a pity [《文》to be regretted] that… ¶…とは言え though; although;〈young〉as 《he is》. 文例⇩

トパーズ (a) topaz.

とはいうものの とは言うものの but; however; still; nevertheless; and yet.

とばく 賭博 gambling; gaming ⇨ ばくち ¶賭博場 a gambling [gaming] house [room]; a

---

の物理学にとどめをさすものであった。Galileo's demonstration killed Aristotelian physics. / コーヒーならブルーマウンテンにとどめをさす。Of all brands of coffee 'Blue Mountain' is the best. ¦ There is no coffee like [as good as] 'Blue Mountain'.

とどめる ここでは大略を述べるにとどめたい。I will only give an outline here. / 今日はこのぐらいにとどめておきましょう。Let's leave it at that for today. ¦《口語》Let's call it a day.

とどろく 彼の名声は全世界にとどろいている。His name resounds [is known] throughout the world. / 彼は胸をとどろかした。His heart beat fast.

どなた どなたですか〈ドア越しに〉Who is it? /〈取り次ぐとき〉What name shall I say? ¦〈窓口で〉May I have your name, please? ¦〈電話で〉Who's speaking, please? / 昨日どなたか男の方がお見えになりました。A gentleman came to see you yesterday. /〈話しかけられて〉失礼ですが, どなたでしたっけ。Excuse me, but I forget your name.

となり 昨晩お隣へ晩ご飯によばれました。Last night we were invited next door for dinner. / ねえ、お隣の奥さんがまたご主人が帰ってこないよと言ってこぼしているわよ。Listen! The woman next door is complaining again that her husband hasn't come home. / 隣の家に行って, その奥さんに, 田中さんたちはお留守かのですかと聞いてみた。She went in next door and asked the lady there if the Tanakas had gone out. / このあたりつつある人たちはいつも放射能の危険と隣り合わせに暮らしているのです。People around here are living cheek by jowl with the danger of radiation.

どなる 「だれだっ」と彼は大声でどなった。'Who's there?' he bellowed.

どの² どの車にお乗りですか。Which car will you take? / 本郷はどの辺にお住まいですか。What part of Hongo do you live in? / この中のどの方法を取ってもいい。You may choose any (one) of these plans. / どの新聞もその事件を報道している。The affair is (reported) in all the newspapers. / どの道を行っても一つ所へ出る。Whichever road you take, you will come to the same place. / ここからどのくらいありますか。How far is it [What distance is it] from here? / 英語をお始めになってからどのくらいになりますか。How long have you been studying English? / それはどの

どばし

gambling den (秘密の).

どばし 土橋 a bridge covered with rammed earth.

とばす 飛ばす fly; let fly;〈吹き飛ばす〉blow off;〈紙片などを〉scatter;〈水などを〉spatter; splash;〈ピッチをあげる〉speed up;〈省略する〉skip (over); leave [miss] *sth* out;《文》omit ¶球を飛ばす send a ball flying / 飛行機を飛ばす fly an airplane / 自動車を飛ばす drive fast ((to)); hurry ((to a place)) in a motorcar / ピカピカの新車でさっそうと高速道路を飛ばす breeze along an expressway in a shiny new car / 檄を飛ばす issue [fire off] a manifesto / 数ページ飛ばす skip (over) a few pages / 10 ページから 15 ページまで飛ばして読む skip from page 10 to page 15 / 風に帽子を飛ばされる have *one*'s hat blown off.

とばっちり〈しぶき〉a splash; (a) spray;〈とばずえ〉a stray [chance] blow ¶とばっちりを食う be struck by a chance blow; be embroiled [caught up] in (a quarrel).

どばと 土鳩 a domesticated pigeon.

とばり a curtain; hangings. 文例②

とび《鳥》a kite;〈とび職〉⇒ とびしょく. 文例②

とびあがる 飛[跳]び上がる〈飛揚する〉fly up;〈飛行機や鳥が〉take off; take (to) the air;《文》take wing;〈はね上がる〉spring [jump] up;〈ぴょんと立ち上がる〉jump [start, leap] to *one*'s feet;〈びっくりして跳び上がる〉jump out of *one*'s skin / 跳び上がらんばかりに喜ぶ jump [dance] for joy. 文例②

とびあるく 跳[飛]び歩く gad about; run [bustle] about.

とびいし 飛び石 steppingstones ¶飛び石伝いに行く step from stone to stone; cross ((a stream in a garden)) by the steppingstones / 飛び石連休 a series of holidays separated by one or two workdays (in between).

とびいた 飛び板《水泳》a springboard; a diving board ¶飛び板飛び込み springboard diving / 飛び板飛び込みの選手 a springboard diver / 女子3メートル飛び板飛び込み競技 the women's three-meter springboard (diving) event [competition].

とびいり 飛び入り ¶飛び入りする take part [《文》participate] ((in a contest)) without submitting *one*'s entry beforehand / 飛び入り勝手の open to all comers [everyone]; free-for-all;《文》unrestricted as to entries.

とびいろ 鳶色 dark brown ¶とび色の dark-brown.

とびうお 飛び魚《魚》a flying fish. 文例②

とびうつる 飛[跳]び移る fly [flit, hop, leap] ((to)) ¶別のボートに跳び移る jump into another boat.

とびおきる 跳び起きる〈寝床から〉jump out of bed;〈跳び上がる〉jump [leap, spring] (up) to *one*'s feet.

とびおりる 跳[飛]び降[下]りる jump [leap, spring] down; jump [leap] off [from] ¶電車から跳び降りる jump [jump] off ((out of)) a moving train / 飛び下り自殺をする kill *oneself*《文》end *one*'s life] by leaping ((from a ninth-floor window)); plunge to *one*'s death ((from a high building)).

とびかう 飛び交う fly [flutter, flit] about [around]; fly past each other ¶木から木へ飛び交う小鳥 birds flitting from tree to tree.

とびかかる 飛[跳]び掛かる spring [leap, jump, pounce] on; fly [jump] at; turn on; fling [throw] *oneself* on.

とびきり 飛び切り《文》exceptionally; far and away; by far ¶飛び切り上等の of the very best quality; extra-fine; superfine;《文》choicest / 飛び切り安く買う buy ((an article)) dirt cheap.

とびぐち 鳶口 a fire hook.

とびこえる 跳[飛]び越える ⇒ とびこす.

とびこす 跳[飛]び越す jump [leap, spring] over; vault (over); clear ((a fence)). 文例②

とびこみ 飛び込み a plunge;〈水上競技の〉diving; a dive ¶飛び込み競技 a diving event;

くらいで出来上がりますか。How soon can you have it ready (for me)? / この山は海抜どのくらいありますか。How high is this mountain above sea level? / 私はどの道をそしなくてはならないのだ。I must do it sooner or later. / 僕の意見などはどの彼女の耳には届かないだろう。My opinion wouldn't reach his ears in any case.

-とは ここから上野まで1時間とはかからない。It takes less than [does not take] an hour to go to Ueno from here. / 事ここに至るとは実に嘆かわしいことである。That things should come to this pass! / 彼が学長になるとはね。Just think of his being our new president. | That he should be our new president! / こんな事をするとは、あの男、気でも狂ったのだろうか。He must be out of his mind to do a thing like this. / 長いこと病床にあるとはいえ、彼はまだ気を落としてはいなかった。Though he had been ill in bed for a long time, he had not let it get him down. / 彼はまだとても一人前の学者とは言えない。He is far from being a full-fledged scholar. / ここであなたにお会いしようとは思いませんでした。This is the last place I expected to meet you. / そのかっこうなら、だれも君だとは気がつかないだろう。Nobody will recognize you looking like that [《口語》in that get-up].

とはいうものの と言うものの彼は偉人に違いない。For all that, he is certainly a great man.

とばり 町に夜のとばりが降りた。Night fell [closed in] on the town. | Darkness came down on the city.

とび とびが「ぴーひょろろ」と鳴いた。The kite called "pee-hyor-r-r-r."

とびあがる 跳び上がるほど痛かった。I almost jumped with pain. / 彼女はその知らせを聞いて跳び上がらんばかりに喜んだ。Her heart leaped up with joy when she heard the news.

とびうお とびうおの群が水面から飛び上がった。A school of flying fish broke the surface [leaped into the air].

とびうつる 1匹の猿が木から木へ飛び移って行くのが見えた。I saw a monkey swinging through the trees [jumping from one tree to another].

とびきり あの男は僕が知っているうちでは飛び切りの秀才だ。He's far and away the cleverest man I know.

とびこす 彼は私を飛び越して昇進

とびこむ 飛び込む fancy diving / 飛び込み自殺をする kill *oneself* by jumping in front of a [an oncoming] train / 飛び込み台〔飛び板〕a diving board; a springboard; 〈高飛び込みの〉a diving platform.

とびこむ 飛び込む jump [spring, plunge, leap] in [into *sth*]; 〈水中に〉dive into; 〈鳥が〉fly into 〈the room〉; 〈突然入って来る〉dash [rush] in [into *sth*]; 〈家が〉burst [bounce] into 〈a room〉. 文例⇩

とびさる 飛び去る fly away [off].

とびしょく 鳶職 a steeplejack.

とびだす 飛[跳]び出す fly out [away]; 〈走り出る〉run [dash, rush] out; 〈跳び出る〉jump [leap] out; 〈おりなどから〉break 《out of》; 〈突出する〉《文》protrude; project; jut [stick] out; 〈現われる〉appear; make *one's* appearance ¶通りへ跳び出す rush out into the street / 家を飛び出す dash out of the house; 〈家出す る〉run away from home.

とびたつ 飛び立つ 〈鳥などが〉take wing; take flight; fly away / 〈飛行機などが〉take off; take the air.

とびちる 飛び散る fly about [off]; scatter; 〈水などが〉splash. 文例⇩

とびつく 飛[跳]び付く fly [spring, leap, jump] at 〈餌に飛びつく〉〈魚が〉rise to [snap at] the bait / 提案に飛びつく jump at *sb's* offer; seize on *sb's* proposal.

トピック a topic; a subject 《of conversation》.

とびでる 飛[跳]び出る ⇨ とびだす.

とびどうぐ 飛び道具 a projectile (weapon); firearms (火器).

とびとび 飛び飛び ¶とびとびに〈間を置いて〉at intervals; 〈ここここに〉here and there / とびとびに読む read 〈a book〉skipping here and there; scan; skim through 〈a newspaper〉.

とびぬけて 飛び抜けて by far 〈the best〉⇨ とびきり, ずばぬけて.

とびのく 跳[飛]び退く〈後ろへ〉jump [leap] back; 〈傍に〉jump aside.

とびのる 跳[飛]び乗る jump onto 〈a moving truck〉; jump on 〈a horse〉. 文例⇩

とびばこ 跳び箱 《体操》a vaulting horse.

とびはなれて 飛び離れて far; by far; far and away ⇨ ずばぬけて.

とびはねる 跳びはねる jump up and down; hop; 〈跳ね回る〉frisk; romp; gambol about.

とびび 飛び火 flying sparks; leaping flames; 〈皮膚病〉impetigo ¶飛び火する flames leap 《to, across》. 文例⇩

とびまわる 飛[跳]び回る 〈空中を〉fly about; flutter about (ひらひらと); 〈跳ね回る〉jump about; romp; gambol about; frisk; 〈駆け回 る〉rush [bustle] about; rush from place to place.

どひょう 土俵 a sumo ring ¶土俵で in [on] the ring / 土俵を割る be pushed out of the ring / 土俵入り the ceremony of entering the ring / 土俵際に追いつめられる be driven to the edge of the ring / 土俵際で踏ん張る make a stand 《against *one's* opponent》at the edge of the ring / 〈比喩的に〉make a last-ditch effort.

とびら 扉〈戸〉a door ⇨ と¹; 〈本の〉a title page; a front page.

どびん 土瓶 a [an earthenware] teapot ¶土瓶敷き a teapot rest.

とふ 塗布 ¶塗布する apply 《an ointment to》.

とぶ 飛ぶ fly; flit (ちょうなどが); flutter (ひらひらと); 〈風に吹かれて〉be blown off; 〈間を抜かす〉skip 《over》; 〈はね上がる〉jump; leap; spring; bound; hop; skip ¶高く[低く] 飛ぶ fly high [low] / 高い所を飛んでいる飛行機 a high-flying airplane / 飛んでいるところをつかまえる catch 《a bird》on the wing / 飛ぶように swiftly; 飛ぶようにうれる sell like hot cakes / 10 ページから 15 ページへ飛ぶ skip from page 10 to page 15 / 〈だちょうのように〉飛べない鳥 a flightless bird. 文例⇩

どぶ 溝 a ditch; 〈排水用〉a drain; a gutter ¶どぶをさらう clear 《out》a ditch / どぶ板 a board cover for a ditch / どぶ泥 ditch mud / どぶねずみ a brown [water, wharf] rat. 文例⇩

とぶくろ 戸袋 a shutter case.

どぶつ 吐物 vomited matter; vomit.

どぶろく unrefined *sake*; home-brewed *sake*.

どぶん ¶どぶんと落ちる drop into 《the water》with a plop (a dull splash).

とべい 渡米 ¶渡米する visit [go to] America.

どべい 土塀 a mud wall; an earthen wall.

とほ 徒歩 ¶徒歩で on foot / 徒歩で行く go [travel] on foot; walk 《to》/ 徒歩旅行 a walk-

---

した. He has been promoted over my head.

とびこむ 加藤さんの家へトラックが飛び込んだそうだ. I hear that a truck has plowed into Mr. Kato's house.

とびだす この通りは子供の飛び出し事故が多いので運転には注意しなさい. Drive carefully along this street, for there have been quite a few accidents to children suddenly rushing out in front of cars.

とびちる 突風で戸が倒れ, ガラスの破片が外へ飛び散った. A sudden blast of wind knocked down the door and sent fragments of broken glass flying all over the floor.

とびつく 飛びつきたいような話だった. The proposal was very attractive [tempting].

とびのる 彼は動いている貨物列車に跳び乗った. He jumped onto [aboard] a moving freight train.

とびび 通りの向こう側の家へ飛び火した. Flying sparks started another fire on the other side of the street. / 事件は意外な方向に飛び火した. The latest revelations involved people in quite unexpected quarters.

とぶ 飛行機は太平洋岸沿いに飛んでいた. The plane was flying [winging its way] along the Pacific coast. / 戦闘機は音速の 2 倍以上で飛んだ. The fighter plane streaked along at more than twice the speed of sound. / 鶏は飛ぶのは下手だ. The domestic fowl is a poor flier. / 2 メートル 20 を跳んで走り高跳ビで金メダルをとった. He cleared the bar at 2.20 meters to win the high jump (event). / 2 メートル 15 を跳んで銀メダルを獲得した. He won the silver medal with a jump of 2.15 meters. / 彼は当時飛ぶ鳥を落とす勢いであった. He was then at

とほう 途方 ¶途方もない extraordinary; outrageous; preposterous; wild;《くだけた》absurd; ridiculous; ludicrous;《規模の》gigantic;《文》untold《wealth》/《文》途方もない要求《文》an unconscionable [exorbitant] demand / 途方もなく高い値段 an outrageous [an exorbitant,《口語》a whopping,《文》a prohibitive, a steep] price / 途方もないやつ an impossible fellow / 途方もなく安い be ridiculously cheap; be dirt cheap / 途方に暮れる be bewildered; be at a loss; be at one's wits' end; be all at sea. 文例↓

どぼく 土木 ¶土木機械 an earth-moving machine / 土木建築業者 ⇨ どけんぎょう (土建業者) / 土木工事 civil engineering / 土木技師 a civil engineer.

とぼける 〈しらを切る〉play the innocent;《文》feign [affect] ignorance;〈おどける〉play the fool ¶とぼけた顔をする look innocent [blank].

とぼしい 乏しい 〈少ない〉scanty; scarce; meager;《文》exiguous;〈欠けている〉《文》deficient (in); lacking [《文》wanting] (in) ¶資金が乏しい lack funds; be short of [low on] funds / 鉱産物の乏しい国 a country poor in minerals / 経験に乏しい do not have much experience (in) /（高所の空気などが）酸素に乏しい be low in oxygen / 資力に乏しい《a man》of slender means / 乏しくなる〈物が主語〉run low; run short;〈人が主語〉run short (of oil).

とぼとぼ ¶とぼとぼ歩く trudge along (one's weary way); plod wearily along [on]. 文例↓

どぼん ⇨ どぶん.

どま 土間 an earth floor;《米》a dirt floor;〈劇場の〉the pit.

トマト a tomato (pl. -es) ¶トマトケチャップ tomato ketchup /《米》catsup / トマトピューレ tomato puree.

とまどう 戸惑う be bewildered; be perplexed; be flurried; be at a loss (which to choose).

とまり¹ 止まり 〈停止〉a stop; stoppage;〈終止〉an end;《文》(a) termination.

とまり² 泊まり 〈宿泊〉lodging; stopping;〈滞在〉a stay;〈一夜の〉a sojourn;〈宿直〉night duty ¶泊まり合わせる〈人と〉stay at the same hotel (as sb); be fellow lodgers (at);〈宿に〉

happen to be staying《at the inn where the murder was committed》/ 泊まりがけで旅行をする go on an overnight trip (to) (1晩;《to Kyushu》for a few days / 泊まり客 a guest [visitor]《at a hotel, staying with us》/〈1晩の〉an overnight guest;〈短期間の〉a transient (guest);〈長期間の〉a resident (guest); a permanent guest / 泊まり賃 ⇨ やど (宿賃). 文例↓

とまりぎ 止まり木 a perch; a roost;〈バーなどの〉《perch on》a high stool.

とまる¹ 止[留]まる stop; halt; come to a stop [halt, standstill]; stand still; draw [pull] up （馬・車などが）; heave to (船が); run down (動力などが);〈止む〉《文》cease;〈中絶する〉be interrupted; be suspended;〈ふさがる〉be stopped up;〈鳥・虫が〉perch [alight, settle, sit] (on) ¶止まっている be at a standstill; be standing《at a bus stop》(★ be stopping は「止まりかけている」の意になる) / すーっと止まる come to a smooth stop / 駅に止まる stop at a station /（機械装置が）自動的に止まる shut *itself* off. 文例↓

とまる² 泊まる stop (at); stay (at, with);〈投宿する〉put up (at) ¶1晩泊まる stay overnight; stay [stop, get accommodation] for the night; stay the night; take a lodging for the night / 泊まる所がない do not have a place to stay /〈ところ〉⇨. 文例↓

どまんじゅう 土饅頭 an earthen mound; a burial [grave] mound.

どまんなか ど真ん中 ¶...のどまんなかに at the very center of...; right [《口語》bang,《口語》slap-bang] in the middle of...

とみ 富 riches; wealth; a fortune ¶富を成す make [amass, pile up, build up] a fortune; grow rich.

とみくじ 富籤 a lottery; a raffle ⇨ くじ.

ドミニカ ¶ドミニカの Dominican / ドミニカ共和国 the Dominican Republic / ドミニカ国 the Commonwealth of Dominica / ドミニカ人 a Dominican.

とみん 都民 a citizen of Tokyo.

とむ 富む be [grow, get,《文》become] wealthy [rich];〈豊富である〉be rich (in);《文》abound (in, with) ¶創意に富む頭脳《文》a brain fertile in ideas / 富んだ rich; wealthy;《文》opu-

---

the zenith of his power. / 飛んで火に入る夏の虫だ. It is like a moth flying into the flame.

どぶ どぶが詰まっている. The street drain is choked.

とべい 渡米するのは今度が初めてだ. This is my first visit to America.

とほう 彼女はどうしてよいやら途方に暮れていた. She was at her wits' end. | いや, これは途方に暮れるなあ. Well, this leaves me completely at a loss.

とぼとぼ 彼はとぼとぼと家路をたどって行った. He went home with heavy [weary] feet.

とまり² 今晩は泊まりだ. I'm going to stay the night. |〈旅館に泊まる〉I'm going to put up at a hotel for the night. |〈宿直だ〉I am on duty tonight.

とまる¹ 時計が止まった. The clock has stopped [run down (ぜんまいが緩んで)]. / 離陸直後に右のエンジンが止まった. The starboard engine cut out immediately after take-off. / 出血がなかなか止まらない. The blood will not stop flowing. / 脈が止まった. His pulse has stopped beating. / 痛みは止まりましたか. Is the pain gone? | Has the pain left you? / 洪

水のために電車が止まった. The flood interrupted [paralyzed] the train service. / 1羽の鳥がその枝に止まった. A bird alighted [perched] on a branch of the tree. / 天井にはえが止まっている. There is a fly on the ceiling.

とまる² 今晩はお泊まりになっていらっしゃいませんか. Can't you stay the night [over till the morning]? / あのホテルなら気持ちよくお泊まりになれますよ. You'll find good accommodation at that hotel, I assure you. / そのホテルには500名の客が泊まれる. The hotel can accom-

とむらい

lent ; 《文》 affluent / 天然資源に富んだ国 《文》 a country abounding in [with an abundance of] natural resources.

とむらい 弔い a funeral ; a burial (埋葬) ¶弔いに行く attend a funeral / 弔いを出す hold a funeral (for) / 弔い合戦 an avenging battle.

とむらう 弔う 〈弔意を表する〉mourn for[over] 《the dead》 ; 〈葬式・法事を営む〉hold a funeral [memorial service] (for).

とめがね 留め金 a clasp ; a latch ; a catch ¶留め金で止める fasten with a clasp [latch] / 留め金を外す unclasp 《a box》; unlatch 《a door》.

とめだて 留め立て ¶留め立てする stop ; check ; persuade sb not to do ; 《文》dissuade sb from doing ; 〈帰るのをひきとめる〉《文》 detain.

とめど 止めど ¶止めどなく endlessly ; unceasingly ; interminably.

とめる¹ 止[留]める stop ; bring to a stop [halt, standstill] ; pull [draw] up (車や馬を) ; 〈離れないように〉fasten ; 〈固定させる〉fix ; hold sth in place ; 〈抑える〉hold back ; check ; curb ; arrest ; 〈引き留める〉《文》detain ; keep ; 〈禁止する〉forbid 《sb to do》 ; prohibit 《sb from doing》 ; 〈説いて思い切らせる〉《文》dissuade 《sb from doing》 / 交通を止める interrupt [hold up] the traffic / 流れを止める stop [stem] a stream ; check a current / 痛みを止める kill [remove] the pain / 争を止める prevent [stop, keep] 《iron》from rusting / けんかを止める stop a quarrel / ガスを止める turn [shut] off the gas / テレビを止める turn [switch] off the TV / 電気を止める cut off the power supply / 息を止める hold [catch] one's breath / 絵を壁に留める tack [pin up] a picture on the wall / 止めるのも聞かずに without listening to sb ; in spite [《文》 defiance] of sb's warnings.

とめる² 泊める put sb up ; 《文》 lodge sb ; take sb in ¶1 晩泊める put sb up for the night ; give sb a night's lodging.

とも¹ 友 a friend ; 〈伴侶〉a mate ; a companion ; 〈交友〉company ¶生涯の友 a lifelong friend ; a companion for life / …を友とする associate [keep company] with… / 自然を友として暮らす《文》live in communion with nature ; 《文》live in the bosom of nature.

とも² 供 〈従者〉an attendant ; a servant ; 〈同行者〉a companion ; 〈随行全員〉《文》a suite ; 《文》a retinue ¶供をする《文》attend on 《one's master》 ; 〈同行する〉go with ; 《文》accompany.

とも³ 艫 the stern ¶ともの方に aft ; astern ; abaft.

-**とも¹** …共 ⇒ともに.

-**とも²** どこへ行こうとも wherever [no matter where] you may go ; 《文》go where you may / 多くとも at (the) most / A氏ともあろうものが Mr. A, of all men.

-**ども** …共 ¶悪人ども (those) rascals ; the wicked (ones) / あの偽善者ども that bunch of hypocrites.

-**ども²** 行けども行けども no matter how far you (may) push your way 《across the desert》.

ともあれ ⇒ともかく(も).

ともえ 巴 a comma-shaped heraldic design ¶巴投げ《柔道》an overhead [a circle] throw.

ともかく(も) 〈いずれにしても〉at any rate ; at all events ; in any case [event] ; anyway ; anyhow ¶…はともかくも setting …aside ; aside [apart] from… ; let alone… ; not to mention [speak of]… ; to say nothing of… / それはともかくも however that may be ; 《文》be that as it may / 費用の問題はともかくも setting aside [apart from] the question of expense / 平生はともかくも whatever may be the case in normal times.

ともかせぎ 共稼ぎ ⇒ともばたらき.

ともぎれ 共切れ (a bit of) spare [the same] cloth.

ともぐい 共食い cannibalism ¶共食いする feed on [devour] one another ; eat its own kind / 共食い的競争 (a) dog-eat-dog [《文》(a) mutually destructive] competition.

ともしび 灯し火 a light.

ともしらが 共白髪 living together to [into] old age.

ともす 点す burn ; light (up) 《a lamp》; turn [switch] on 《a light》.

ともすれば ¶ともすれば…しやすい [し勝ち

---

modate [has accommodations for] 500 guests.

とむ 牛肉は蛋白質に富む. Beef is rich in protein.

とめど 彼は話し出すと止めどのない人間だった. I found him an interminable talker. / 涙が止めどなく流れて仕方がなかった. Try as I might, I could not hold [keep] back my tears.

とも¹ 池田君という良き友を得た. I found a good friend in Ikeda. / 人はその交わる友によって知られる. A man is known by the company he keeps.

とも² 途中までお供をいたしましょう. I will go some [part] of the way with you. / 彼には大勢のお供がついていた. He was accompanied by a train of followers.

-**とも¹** 代金送料とも2千円. Price ¥2,000 including postage [postage included].

-**とも²** そうですとも. That's [You're] right! | Yes, indeed. / (何かを頼まれて)いいですとも. Certainly. | With pleasure. / 大丈夫かね.--ええ, 大丈夫ですとも. Is it safe?--Sure [Of course], it's safe. / 彼は来るとも来ないとも言いませんでした. He didn't say whether he would come or not. / さようならとも言わずに部屋を出て行った. He left the room without even [so much as] saying good-bye. / 生は死の初めとも言うことができる. Birth is, so to speak [in a sense], the beginning of death.

-**ども²** 押せども引けども戸は開かなかった. For all my shoving and tugging the door would not open.

ともかく(も) ともかくやってみます. At any rate I'll try. / ともかくまず電車で神田まで行こう. Anyhow let's go to Kanda by train first. / 冗談はともかく, 君はそれをどうするつもりなのか. Joking aside [apart], what are you going to do about it? / ほかの人はともかく, 加藤君だけは絶対信用できる. You can place absolute confidence in Kato, if not in the oth-

ともだおれ 共倒れ ¶共倒れになる fall [go down, sink] together; come to grief [be ruined] together.

ともだち 友達 a friend;《口語》a pal;〈伴侶〉a companion;〈交友〉company ¶昔からの友達 an old friend / B君の友達の友達 a friend of a friend of B's / 友達がいがない be not quite reliable as a friend; be not much of a friend / 友達がいい[悪い] keep good [bad] company / 友達が出来る make a friend / 友達を選ぶ choose one's company; select one's friends / 友達になる make friends (with); strike up [《文》form,《文》contract] a friendship (with) / 友達である, 友達づきあいをしている be friends [on friendly terms] (with);《口語》be pally (with) / 友達づきあいを止める break off [《文》renounce] one's friendship (with); break (with); have nothing more to do (with) (絶交する) / 友達がいに for friendship's sake / マージャン友達 a mahjong(-playing) friend. 文例⇩

ともづな 纜 a stern line ¶ともづなを解く〈人が主語〉unmoor (a ship); cast off;〈船が主語〉unmoor; cast off.

ともづり 友釣り 〈あゆを〉fish [angle] for (ayu) with a live decoy.

ともどもに 共々に ⇨ともに.

ともなう 伴う ¶〈…に伴う〉《文》accompany;《文》attend; follow; go with;〈…を伴う〉be accompanied [attended] by [with] ¶技術の進歩に伴って as technology advances; with the advance of technology ⇨-つれて ★. 文例⇩

ともに 共に 〈両方共〉both; neither (否定);〈同様に〉alike; equally;〈一緒に〉together ¶…と共に〈一緒に〉(along [together]) with…; in company with…;〈含めて〉including;《文》inclusive of;〈について〉as; with / 兄弟共に both (the) brothers / 夫婦共に both husband and wife / 男女共に men and women alike ¶ irrespective [regardless] of sex / 共に暮らす live together [under the same roof]; live with sb / 共に働く work together; work with sb / 年を取ると共に as one grows older; 《文》with one's increasing [advancing] years / 共に語るに足らない《文》be not worthy of one's friendship; be not fit [《文》be unfit] to be one's friend [comrade] / 喜びを共にする《文》share in each other's joys.

ともばたらき 共働き ¶共働きの家庭 a two-income family. 文例⇩

どもり 吃り 〈どもる事〉stammering; stuttering;〈どもる人〉a man with a stammer [stutter]; a stammerer; a stutterer ¶どもりを治す cure sb's stammer.

ともる 点る burn; be [come] on ¶ともっている be alight; be burning. 文例⇩

どもる 吃る stammer; stutter ¶どもりながら stammering(ly); stuttering(ly) / どもり, どもり言う stammer [stutter] (out) (an apology). 文例⇩

ドモルガン ¶ドモルガンの法則〔数・論〕De Morgan's laws [theorems].

とや 鳥屋 a coop;〈鶏の〉a hencoop; a henhouse;〈鳥のねぐら〉a roost ¶鳥屋につく roost; go to roost;〈卵を抱く〉sit on its eggs; brood.

どやがい どや街 flophouse [slum] quarters; a street of flophouses.

とやかく ¶とやかく言う say this and that; talk (about); say things (about);〈難癖をつける〉criticize; find fault with;〈反対する〉object (to); make [raise] objections (to);〈苦情を言う〉bring a complaint (against);〈干渉する〉meddle [interfere] (in a matter, with sb). 文例⇩

どやす 〈たたく〉beat; thump;〈しかる〉scold; roar [thunder] (at).

どやどや 〈大勢一緒に〉in a crowd;〈騒々しく〉noisily ¶どやどやと入る crowd [《文》throng] into (a room).

どよう 土用 the hottest period of summer;《文》(the) dog days ¶土用干し summer airing (of clothes) / 土用干しする air (one's clothes) / 土用波 high waves in high summer.

どようび 土曜日 Saturday (略: Sat.) ⇨どよう(び) 用法.

どよめき a stir;《文》(a) tumult; (a) commotion.

どよめく〈鳴り響く〉《文》resound; reverberate;〈騒ぐ〉stir. 文例⇩

---

ers. / 林さんの考えはともかくとして, 僕はそれには不賛成だ. I'm against it, whatever Mr. Hayashi says [regardless of Mr. Hayashi's opinion] about it. / ともかくも, この計画を捨てるわけにはゆかない. I must stick to this plan whatever happens.

ともだち メアリーは友達が少なかった. Mary didn't have many friends. | Mary was a girl with few friends. / その事件のあと, トムと友達になっていた. After the incident, Tom gave me his friendship. / 僕は友達運がよかった. I was lucky in my friends.

ともなう 財産ができるということには色々な心配が伴うものだ. Wealth brings with it a number of anxieties. / 理論と実際とは相伴って行くべきものだ. Theory and practice should go together [hand in hand]. / 宇宙旅行には大きな危険が伴う. Traveling in space involves great risks. / 戦争に伴う困難の1つは食糧の不足であった. One of the difficulties resulting from the war was the food shortage. / 戦争にはさまざまな不幸が伴うものである. War brings all sorts of miseries in its train. / 権力には責任が伴うものだ. Power has its responsibilities. | When you come into power, you must take on the responsibilities that go with it.

ともばたらき あの夫婦は共働きをしている. They both go out to work. / 私たちは共働きで月収30万円です. Between us, we earn 300,000 yen a month.

ともる 小屋にはランプが薄暗くともっていた. The hut was dimly lit by a lamp.

どもる 彼は少しどもる. He has a slight stammer [stutter].

とやかく 彼女は人にとやかく言われるような事をしたことがない. She has never got herself talked about.

どよめく 彼が登場すると聴衆はどよめいた. There was a stir in the audience at his appearance.

とら 虎 a tiger; a tigress (雌); 〈十二支の寅〉《the Year of》 the Tiger ¶とらの子 a tiger cub / とらの子のように大事にする keep *sth* as the apple of *one's* eye; treasure / とらの威を借るきつね《文》an ass in a lion's skin / とらになる get (disgustingly) drunk / とら猫 a tabby (cat); a striped [brindled] cat / とらの巻 a crib [key]《to》; 《米口語》a pony; 《米口語》a trot. [文例⇩]

どら 銅鑼 a gong.

とらい 渡来 ¶渡来する come from abroad; visit《this country》; 〈伝来する〉 be introduced《into》; be brought over《from》/ 仏教の渡来 the introduction of Buddhism into Japan.

トライ 〖ラグビー〗 a try ¶トライをあげる score a try / トライで4点あげる score four points with a try.

ドライ ¶ドライな 〈非情な〉 unsentimental; 《口語》hard-boiled; 〈現実的な〉 realistic; businesslike; 《米俗》hard-nosed; down-to-earth.

と

ドライアイス dry ice.

トライアングル a triangle ¶トライアングルを鳴らす sound [tinkle] a triangle.

ドライクリーニング dry cleaning ¶ドライクリーニングする dry-clean / ドライクリーニング屋 〈人〉 a dry cleaner; 〈店〉 a dry cleaner's.

ドライバー 〈運転者〉 a driver; a motorist; 〈ねじ回し〉 a screwdriver.

ドライブ a drive; motoring ¶ドライブする[に行く] have [go for] a drive / ドライブイン 〈街道沿いの飲食店〉 a roadside restaurant; 〈車から降りないで用の足せる施設〉 a drive-in.

ドライヤー a drier; a dryer ¶(美容院で)ドライヤーをかぶる sit under a hair dryer.

とらえる 捕らえる catch; 《文》seize; get; grasp; take [catch, 《文》lay] hold of; 《文》lay (*one's*) hands on; 〈捕虜にする〉 capture; take *sb* prisoner; 〈逮捕する〉 arrest; 《文》apprehend ¶手を捕える catch [seize] *sb* by the hand / 文章の真意を捕らえる grasp [get, catch] the real meaning of the sentence / 捕らえどころのない slippery; 〈あいまいな〉 vague. [文例⇩]

とらがり 虎刈り 〈頭髪の〉 an unevenly cropped head. [文例⇩]

トラクター a tractor.

どらごえ どら声 《in》 a hoarse [gruff] voice.

トラコーマ 〖医〗 trachoma.

トラスト 〈企業合同〉 a trust ¶トラスト禁止法 an antitrust law.

トラック[1] 〈貨物自動車〉 a truck; 《英》a lorry ¶トラック3台分の荷物 three truckloads of goods / トラックの運転手 a truck driver / トラックで輸送する transport《goods》by truck; truck / 長距離トラック a long-haul truck / トラック運送業者 a trucker / トラック輸送 trucking.

トラック[2] 〈競走路〉 a (running) track ¶トラック競技 a track event [race] / トラック競技の走者 a track man.

どらねこ どら猫 a stray [an alley] cat.

トラバース 〖登山〗《make》 a traverse.

トラベラーズチェック a traveler's check.

トラホーム ⇨ **トラコーマ**.

ドラマ a drama. [文例⇩]

ドラマー a drummer.

ドラム 〈太鼓〉 a drum; 〈機械の〉 a drum; a cylinder ¶ドラム缶 an oil drum.

どらむすこ どら息子 *one's* good-for-nothing son; a spoiled [《文》prodigal] son.

とらわれ 捕らわれ ¶捕らわれの身《文》a captive; a prisoner / 捕らわれの身となる《文》be in bonds [fetters]; 《文》be held in captivity; 〈入牢する〉 be put in prison; be imprisoned; 〈捕虜になる〉 be taken prisoner [captive].

とらわれる 捕らわれる be caught; be captured; be arrested; 〈こだわる〉 stick [《文》adhere]《to a tradition》; 《文》be shackled《by old customs》 ¶感情に捕らわれる《文》be swayed by passion / 恐怖に捕らわれる be seized with fear; be panic-stricken; 《文》fall (a) prey to fear / 捕らわれた考え a conventional idea; a biased [prejudiced] opinion [view]; a prejudice. [文例⇩]

トランキライザー 〖薬〗 a tranquil(l)izer; a tranquilizing drug [pill (錠剤)].

トランク 〈大型の〉 a trunk; 〈小型の〉 a suitcase; 〈自動車の〉《米》a trunk; 《英》a boot.

トランシーバー a transceiver.

トランジスター a transistor ¶トランジスターラジオ a transistor radio.

トランス 〖電〗 a (power) transformer. [文例⇩]

トランプ [<trump (切札)] (playing) cards; cardplaying (トランプ遊び) ¶トランプをする play cards / トランプをしている be at cards / (占いで)トランプを並べる lay cards / トランプで占う tell *sb's* fortune with (playing) cards / トランプ1組 a pack [《米》deck] of cards.

とら 虎の子にしていた志野の茶碗がなくなっていた. He found his most prized possession, his Shino ware teacup, gone.

とらえる 彼の彫刻は今も何百万人もの人々の心を強く捕らえている. His sculptures still continue to exert a powerful hold on millions of people. / あの劇には本当に心を捕らえられました. The play was really gripping.

とらがり 彼の頭は虎刈りだ. His head is cropped badly, in ridges.

ドラマ 国際政治の舞台で興味しんしんたるドラマが展開された. An exciting drama unfolded on the international political stage.

とらわれる 彼はあまり目先の利益にとらわれ過ぎている. He is swayed too much by the thought of immediate gain. / 彼らはまだ伝統にとらわれている. They are still bound by tradition.

トランス トランスが焼けた. The transformer burned out.

とり 鳥なき里のこうもり. In the country of the blind the one-eyed man is king. 〖諺〗

とりあう 2人は手を取り合って泣いた. They took each other's hands and wept. / あんなやつに取り合うな. Have nothing to do with him.

とりあえず その知らせを受けるや, 彼は取るものも取りあえず現場に急行した. The moment he heard the news, he hurried to the spot. / 左記の事実, 取りあえずお知らせ申し上げます. We hasten to inform you of the following facts.

とりあげる それは特に取り上げて

トランペット a trumpet ¶トランペットを吹く play [blow] the trumpet / トランペット奏者 a trumpeter.
トランポリン a trampoline ¶トランポリンをやる bounce on a trampoline.
とり 鳥 a bird;〈鶏〉a hen (雌); a cock [《米》rooster] (雄); a chicken (ひな);〈食用〉a fowl; poultry (総称);〈鶏の肉〉chicken;〈十二支の酉〉(the Year of) the Rooster ¶(料理した)鶏(とり)の足 drumstick / 鳥の声 bird cries; birdsong / (動物園などの) 鳥の檻(おり) an aviary / 鳥籠 a (bird) cage / 鶏合 a hencoop (家畜用の) / 鳥小屋 a henhouse / 鳥鍋 chicken boiled in a shallow pan with bean curd and vegetables / 鳥もち birdlime / 鳥寄せをする attract birds by making birdcalls. 文例⇩
とりあい 取り合い〈争う〉a scramble ¶取り合いをする scramble [struggle] (for); squabble (over);《文》vie with each other to get possession of sth.
とりあう 取り合う〈奪い合う〉scramble [struggle] for sth;〈取り上げる〉pay attention to sth; listen to sth ¶取り合わない disregard; take no notice of / pay no attention 《文》heed) to《sb's request》; turn a deaf ear to《sb's warnings》.
とりあえず 取り敢えず〈さしあたり〉for the time being; for the present;〈直ちに, 急いで〉at once; in a hurry; without delay;〈何よりも先に〉first of all ¶取りあえず…する《文》hasten to do; lose no time in doing. 文例⇩
とりあげる 取[採]り上げる〈手に取る〉take [pick] up;〈採用する〉adopt; take up (a proposal);〈聞き入れる〉accept; listen to《sb's request》;〈奪う〉take away;《文》deprive (dispossess)《sb of sth》;〈没収する〉confiscate;〈徴発する〉requisition;〈お産で赤ん坊を〉deliver《a child》; deliver《a woman》of a child; assist《a woman》in childbirth ¶問題を取り上げる take up a problem [a subject for discussion] / 免状を取り上げる cancel sb's license; disqualify sb / 採り上げない ignore; put aside; reject; turn down; turn a deaf ear to《sb's request》.
とりあつかい 取り扱い〈人の〉treatment;〈客の〉service;〈物の〉handling;〈事務の〉management ¶ひどい取り扱いを受ける be ill-treated;《口語》have [get, be given] a raw deal / 取扱店 a store dealing in (this brand of tea) / 局長事務取扱い an acting director of a bureau.
とりあつかう 取り扱う〈遇する〉treat;〈処理する〉deal with sth; manage;〈手で扱う〉handle; manipulate; work [operate]《a machine》;〈行う〉carry on;《文》conduct;《文》transact;〈売買する〉deal in sth;〈受け付ける〉accept《telegrams》¶取り扱いやすい[にくい] easy [hard] to deal with; manageable [unmanageable] / 少年犯罪の問題を取り扱った本 the book concerned [dealing] with the problem of juvenile delinquency. 文例⇩
とりあわせ 取り合わせ〈商品などの〉an assortment;〈配合〉(a) combination;〈対照〉contrast ⇒はいごう ¶取り合わせのいい[悪い] well-[poorly-,《文》ill-]assorted / ビスケット各種取り合わせ assorted biscuits. 文例⇩
とりあわせる 取り合わせる《文》assort; combine; mix; group; match (colors).
ドリアン《植》a durian (fruit).
とりい 鳥居 a torii; a gateway at the entrance to a Shinto shrine.
とりいそぐ 取り急ぐ ⇒いそぐ. 文例⇩
とりいる 取り入る curry favor with sb; try to gain sb's favor;《文》insinuate oneself into sb's favor;《文》ingratiate oneself with sb; play [make] up to sb;〈へつらう〉flatter; toady.
とりいれ 取り入れ a harvest; harvesting ⇒しゅうかく[1] ¶取り入れ時the harvesttime;《at》(the) harvest / (ジェットエンジンの)空気取り入れ口 an air intake. 文例⇩
とりいれる 取り入れる〈農作物を〉harvest; gather (in);〈説などを〉accept; adopt;〈導入する〉borrow《sth from》; introduce《sth into》¶フランス語から英語に取り入れられた言葉 a word introduced into English from French.
とりうちぼう 鳥打帽 ⇒ハンチング. 文例⇩
トリウム《化》thorium.
とりえ 取り柄〈価値〉《文》worth; value;《文》(a) merit;〈長所〉a good [strong] point;《文》a forte;〈埋め合わせ〉a redeeming feature; a saving grace ¶多少取りえがある have something to recommend one [it] / 取りえのない worthless; good-for-nothing;《a man [a product]》with nothing to recommend《him [it]》. 文例⇩
トリオ a trio (pl. -s).
とりおこなう 執り行なう ⇒おこなう, しっこう[2] (執行する).

言うほどの事ではない. It is not worth mentioning specially. / このことは新聞に大きく取り上げられた. This was given a big headline in the papers. / 政府は私たちの手から選択権を全く取り上げてしまったのです. The government has taken the choice out of our hands altogether.
とりあつかい あのホテルは客の取り扱いが行き届いている. They look after their guests well at that hotel. | The service at that hotel is excellent. / 取扱注意. 《包装表記》Handle with care.
とりあつかう もっと丁寧に彼を取り扱うべきです. You should treat [deal with] him more politely. / 本書は問題を実際面から取り扱っている. The book deals with the problem from a practical angle.
とりあわせ 白に赤は良い取り合わせがいい. White goes well with red.
とりいそぐ 本件取り急ぎご通知申し上げます. I hasten to inform you of this matter.
とりいれ 農家は作物の取り入れに忙しい. The farmers are busy harvesting [gathering in] their crop. / 取り入れが済んだ. The harvest is in.
とりいれる あなたのお考えはこの計画の中に採り入れられています. Your idea has been incorporated into this project. / これらの言葉はまだ英語として採り入れられていない. These words are not yet naturalized as English.
とりえ あの男にはなんの取り柄もない. He has nothing to recommend him. / あの男でも少くとも

とりおさえる 取り押さえる 〈現場を〉catch 《sb doing》; arrest 《sb in the act》; 〈差し押える〉《文》seize; take; capture; 〈馬などを〉quiet.

とりおとす 取り落とす let sth fall [slip]; drop.

とりがい 鳥貝【貝】a cockle.

とりかえ 取り替え a change; an exchange; 《口語》a swap [swop] ¶〈不注意による〉病院での赤ん坊の取り替え a baby mix-up at a hospital.

とりかえし 取り返し recovery ¶取り返しがつかない there is no mending 《one's mistake》 [going back on 《one's promise》]; be beyond recall [《文》retrieval]; be irrevocable; 《文》be irreparable; 《文》be irretrievable; 《文》be irredeemable; 《文》be irremediable. 文例⇩

とりかえす 取り返す 〈取り戻す〉get [take] sth back; 《文》regain; recover; 〈埋め合わす〉make good [make up for] (the loss); 〈受け戻す〉《文》redeem. 文例⇩

とりかえっこ 取り替えっこ (an) exchange; 《口語》a swap [swop] ¶取り替えっこをする exchange [swap] 《A for B》.

とりかえる 取り替える 〈交換する〉exchange [change, switch] 《A for B》; 《口語》swap [swop] 《A for B》; 〈新たにする〉renew; 〈代わりを入れる〉replace 《A by [with] B》. 文例⇩

とりかかる 取り掛かる begin; set about; start (in) ¶仕事に取りかかろかから get [go, proceed] to work; set oneself to work [on a job]; get started on one's work / 今取りかかっている仕事 the work in hand.

とりかこむ 取り囲む ⇨かこむ.

とりかじ 取舵 ¶取舵にする port the helm. 文例⇩

とりかぶと【植】an aconite; a wolfsbane.

とりかわす 取り交わす exchange 《greetings, papers》.

とりきめ 取り決め 〈協定〉an arrangement; an agreement; 〈決定〉(a) decision; 《文》(a) settlement.

とりきめる 取り決める 〈協定する〉arrange; agree 《on a matter》; 〈決定する〉settle; decide on; fix (on) ¶契約を取り決める make [close] a contract 《with》; enter into [《文》conclude] an agreement 《with》.

とりくみ 取組 〈相撲などの〉a match; a bout; 〈取組表〉a program of bouts [matches].

とりくむ 取り組む wrestle 〈grapple〉《with》; come to grips 《with》; 〈試合で〉be matched 《with》; be pitted 《against》¶難問題と取り組む tackle [grapple with, come to grips with] a difficult problem. 文例⇩

とりけし 取り消し (a) cancellation; (a) revocation 《of a treaty》; 《文》withdrawal; 〈法律などの〉a repeal; 〈契約などの〉annulment.

とりけす 取り消す cancel; 〈撤回する〉withdraw; 〈ことばを〉《文》retract; take back; 〈法律などを〉repeal; 〈命令・契約などを〉annul (a contract); revoke 《a command》¶前言を取り消す withdraw [retract] one's statement; take back what one has said / 注文を取り消す cancel an order. 文例⇩

とりこ 虜 《a captive; a prisoner; 〈比喩的に〉a victim; a slave ¶とりこにする capture; take sb prisoner; 〈迷わす〉captivate; charm; 《文》enthrall / とりこになる be taken prisoner; 《文》be held captive; 〈比喩的に〉fall a victim [be a slave] 《to her charms》; be enslaved [enthralled, captivated] 《by her beauty》.

とりこしぐろう 取り越し苦労 ¶取り越し苦労をする worry (oneself) needlessly about the future; cross one's bridges before one comes to them; be overanxious [《文》oversolicitous] 《about》; meet trouble halfway / 取り越し苦労かもしれないが… I may be worrying unduly, but…. 文例⇩

トリコット tricot.

とりこぼし 取りこぼし (suffer) an unexpected defeat (through carelessness).

とりこみ 取り込み 〈混雑〉(a) bustle (★複数にはしない); confusion; disorder; 〈不幸〉a misfortune ¶取り込み詐欺 (play) a confidence trick [《米》game] 《on》/ 取り込み詐欺師 a confidence trickster [man]; 《口語》a con man. 文例⇩

とりこむ 取り込む 〈取り入れる〉take in 《the washing》; 〈混雑する〉be in confusion; 〈忙しい〉be busy [occupied] 《with》. 文例⇩

とりころす 取り殺す haunt [torment] sb to his death.

とりこわし 取り壊し demolition; pulling down; destruction; 〈施設などの〉dismantling ¶建築物取壊し業者《米》a (house) wrecker;

この程度の取り柄はあるのさ. At least this much can be said in his favor. / 〈美人ではないが〉彼女にはつつましさという取り柄があるる. She has the saving grace of being modest. / 簡単に出来ている所がこの器具の取り柄です. The good thing about [The good point of] this apparatus is that it is very simply constructed.

とりかえし すんだことは取り返しがつかない. What is done can't be undone. / We can't change the past. / うっかりしゃべってしまって取り返しのつかぬことをした. I made an irreparable error in blurting it out.

とりかえす 遅れを取り返さなければばらない. I must make up for lost time. / 失われた青春時代をだれが取り返すことができよう. Who can restore the lost years of his youth?

とりかえる 〈ホテルで〉部屋を取り替えてもらえますか. Can I have a different room? / この品がお気に召さない場合にはお取り替えいたします. This article can be changed [exchanged] if you find it unsatisfactory.

とりかじ 取舵.「号令」Port (the helm)!/《米》Left! / 取舵いっぱい! Hard aport! /《米》Left full rudder!

とりくむ 彼は直ちにその仕事に敢然と取り組んだ. He flung himself into the work with determination.

とりけす 彼は勝手に約束を取り消すことができると考えているらしい. It seems that he feels free to forget his promise.

とりこしぐろう そりゃ取り越し苦労だ. Don't cross your bridges till you come to them.

とりこみ 浅井さんの家では何か取り込みがある様子だ. Something unusual must have happened at

とりこわす 取り壊す pull [take, tear] down; demolish; destroy 《a house》; break up [down] 《文》 raze 《a building》(to the ground); 〈施設など〉 dismantle.

とりさげる 取り下げる withdraw; drop; call off 《a prosecution》.

とりざた 取り沙汰 ⇨ うわさ.

とりさる 取り去る take away; remove ⇨ とりのぞく, てっきょ.

とりしきる 取り仕切る manage (all by *oneself*); run 《the store》.

とりしまり 取り締まり 〈制御〉 control; 《文》 regulation; a crackdown 《on drunken driving》; 〈管理〉 management; 〈規律〉 discipline; 〈監督〉 supervision; 《文》 superintendence; 〈監督者〉 a supervisor; a superintendent; an overseer ¶取り締まりが行き届いている be well controlled / 取り締まりを厳重にする tighten (the) control 《of, over》/ 取締規則 regulations / 取締役 a director / 取締役会 the board of directors.

とりしまる 取り締まる manage; control; superintend; supervise; oversee; keep control over; keep 《the school》 in order ¶厳重に取り締まる 《文》 exercise strict control over; control *sth* [*sb*] strictly; crack down on 《gamblers》.

とりしらべ 取り調べ (an) investigation; (an) examination; (an) inquiry ¶取り調べ中である be being investigated; 《文》 be under investigation [examination] / 〈警察の〉取り調べ室 an interrogation room. 文例⇩

とりしらべる 取り調べる investigate; examine; inquire [look] into ¶厳重に取り調べる 《文》 subject *sb* to close examination / 徹底的に取り調べる make a thorough investigation 《of》. 文例⇩

とりすがる 取り縋る cling to; hold on to; hang on (to).

とりすます 取り澄ます ⇨ すます².

とりそこなう 取り損なう miss; fail to get [catch, win].

とりそろえる 取り揃える put together; gather; 《文》 assort (各種の品を) ⇨ そろえる. 文例⇩

とりだす 取り出す take [pull, bring] *sth* out; produce; 〈火事で〉 save; rescue ¶さっと取り出す whip out 《a pistol》.

とりたて¹ 取り立て 〈集金〉《文》 collection; 〈徴集〉 levying; 〈任用〉《文》 appointment; 〈登用〉 promotion; 〈ひいき〉《文》 patronage ¶…の取り立てによって under the patronage of… / 取立人 a (bill) collector.

とりたて² 取り立て ¶取り立ての fresh-caught 《trout》; freshly-picked 《strawberries》/ 〈a pear〉 just picked / 取り立ての果物 (a) fruit fresh from the field [orchard] / 取り立ての魚 a fish fresh from the sea [river, lake]. 文例⇩

とりたてて 取り立てて particularly; in particular ¶取り立てて言うほどの worth mentioning; (nothing) to speak of. 文例⇩

とりたてる 取り立てる 〈金を〉 collect; extort [《文》 exact] 《money from *sb*》; levy (税金を); 〈任用する〉 appoint; 〈昇進させる〉 promote; 〈ひいきする〉 patronize; 《文》 give *one*'s patronage to ¶やかましく借金を取り立てる dun *sb* for the payment of a debt; 《口語》 put the screws on *sb* to pay back a debt.

とりちがえる 取り違える 〈間違える〉 mistake (A for B); take (A for B); 〈誤解する〉 misunderstand; misinterpret; 《文》 misconstrue.

とりちらかす 取り散らかす scatter 《papers》 about; 《口語》 mess up 《the room》 ¶取り散らかしてある be in an untidy state; 《口語》 be in a mess; 《文》 be in disorder. 文例⇩

とりつ 都立 都立の metropolitan; under the direct control of the Tokyo Metropolitan government / 都立高校 a metropolitan high school.

とりつぎ 取り次ぎ 〈仲介〉 agency; 〈仲介人〉 an agent; 〈玄関などの〉 an usher; a doorkeeper ¶取り次ぎに出る answer the door 《knock, bell》/ 取次店 an agent [agency] 《for the *Asahi*》/ 取次販売 sale on commission / 取次販売店 a distributing agent [agency]; a distributor. 文例⇩

とりつく 取り付く 〈すがる〉 hold fast [on] to; cling [hang on] to; 〈憑(つ)く〉《文》 possess; haunt ¶取りつく島もない be left utterly helpless; have no one to turn to / 病気に取りつかれる be taken ill; 《口語》 fall a victim to a disease / 悪霊に取りつかれる be possessed by an evil spirit. 文例⇩

トリック a trick ¶トリックを用いる use [《文》

Mr. Asai's.

とりこむ 只今取り込んでおりますので、お目にかかれません。I'm afraid I can't see you because I am awfully busy just at the moment.

とりしらべ 彼は警察の取り調べを受けた。He was investigated by the police.

とりそろえる ゴルフ用品を色々取りそろえております。We have a large assortment of golfing equipment (for you to choose from).

とりたて² 私の運転免許はまだ取り立てです。It is only very recently that I got [obtained] my driving license.

とりたてて 取り立てて言うほどのことでもない。It is not worth mentioning specially. | It's nothing to write home about. / 彼には取り立てて言うほどの財産もない。He has no property to speak of [worthy of the name].

とりちらかす テーブルには食べ物の散りがいっぱい取り散らかしてあった。The table was littered with remnants of food. / 取り散らかしておりまして申し訳ありません。Please excuse the mess [untidiness].

とりつぎ ご伝言がございましたら、私がお取り次ぎいたします。If you have a message, please leave it with me. / 取り次ぎに出た秘書に名刺を渡した。I handed my card to the secretary who came out in answer to my ring.

とりつく 私は途方もない考えに取りつかれてしまいました。A fantastic notion took hold of me. / 当時私は、ほどなく死ぬかもしれない、という恐怖にとりつかれていた。At that time I was obsessed with the fear of approaching death. / 近頃彼は写真熱に取りつかれているらしい。《口語》 He

とりつぐ / **とりひき**

resort to] trickery / トリックにかかる be tricked [cheated] (into, out of); be taken in / トリック撮影 a trick shot.

とりつぐ 取り次ぐ〈仲介する〉act as an agent [intermediary];〈来客を〉answer the door [knock, bell]; announce ((a visitor));〈伝達する〉pass *sth* on;《文》transmit;《文》convey.

とりつくす 取り尽くす take [gather] all ((the mushrooms in the area));《文》exhaust ((a lake of its fish)).

とりつくろう 取り繕う smooth [gloss] over; patch ((things)) up ¶体裁を取り繕う keep up [save] appearances.

とりつけ 取り付け〈銀行の〉a run ((on a bank));〈設備〉installation;《文》furnishing. 文例⇩

とりつける 取り付ける fit (up);《文》furnish; install; lay on ((gas)) ¶電話を取り付けさせる install a telephone; have a telephone installed / 同意を取りつける (manage to) get *sb*'s agreement [《文》obtain *sb*'s consent]. 文例⇩

ドリップ ¶ドリップコーヒー drip coffee / (コーヒーをいれるときの)ドリップ式 (make coffee by) the drip [filter] method.

とりで 砦 a fort; a fortress; a stronghold; a ((mountain)) fastness.

とりとめ 取り留め ¶取りとめのない wandering; rambling; incoherent;《文》desultory; vague / 取りとめのない事を言う say incoherent things; make pointless remarks. 文例⇩

とりとめる 取り留める ¶一命を取りとめる escape [be saved from] death. 文例⇩

とりどり 取り取り ¶とりどりの various; diverse. 文例⇩

とりなおし 撮り直し〈写真の〉a retake.

とりなおす[1] 取り直す〈武器などを〉get a firmer hold of;〈筆を〉take up ((*one*'s brush)) again;〈相撲を〉wrestle the bout again;〈針路を〉reset ((*one*'s course)) ¶気を取り直す ⇒き[3].

とりなおす[2] 撮り直す retake; reshoot; photograph again.

とりなし 執り成し mediation;《文》intercession; intervention;《文》good offices ¶彼のとりなしで through his good offices [mediation, intercession].

とりなす 執り成す mediate ((in, between));《文》intercede ((with A for B));〈推薦する〉recommend; say [put in] a good word for *sb* ((with).

とりにいく 取りに行く go for *sth*; collect *sth*; fetch *sth*.

とりにがす 取り逃がす fail to catch; miss; let ((a thief)) escape [get away] ¶機会を取り逃がす let an opportunity go [slip]; miss a [*one*'s] chance. 文例⇩

とりにく 鳥肉 chicken; fowl.

トリニダードトバゴ (the Republic of) Trinidad and Tobago.

とりにやる 取りにやる send for *sth*; send *sb* for [to get] *sth*.

とりのける 取り除ける〈除去する〉remove; take [clear] away; get rid of;〈別にして置く〉put [《文》lay] *sth* aside; set *sth* apart [aside]; reserve;〈例外にする〉except *sth* ((from)); make an exception of *sth* ¶邪魔物を取りのける clear *sth* out of *one*'s way; clear ((a road)) of obstacles.

とりのこす 取り残す leave (behind) ¶時代の進歩から取り残される fall [be left] behind the times. 文例⇩

とりのぞく 取り除く remove; take [clear] away; get rid of.

とりはからい 取り計らい《文》management;《文》arrangement; disposal ¶…の取り計らいで《文》through *sb*'s arrangement; at *sb*'s (own) discretion. 文例⇩

とりはからう 取り計らう manage; arrange; deal with; dispose of; settle ¶しかるべく取り計らう settle [deal with] ((a matter)) as *one* thinks fit [at *one*'s (own) discretion]. 文例⇩

とりはずし 取り外し〈付属品・部品などの〉removal;〈設備の〉dismantling ¶取り外しのできる movable; removable; detachable / 取り外しのできない unmovable; fixed.

とりはずす 取り外す remove; take *sth* off [away];《文》detach; dismantle ((a plant of part of its equipment)).

とりはだ 鳥肌 gooseflesh; goose pimples [(米) bumps] ¶鳥肌が立つ have [get, feel] gooseflesh. 文例⇩

とりはらう 取り払う remove; take [clear] away;〈口語〉get rid of *sth*; get *sth* out of the way;〈取り壊す〉pull [take] down; demolish ¶道路の障害物を取り払う clear the road of obstacles.

とりひき 取り引き (a) transaction; dealings; business ¶取り引きする trade ((in cotton with)); have dealings ((with)); do [《文》transact] business ((with)); deal ((with)); make a deal ((with)) / 取り引きを結ぶ drive [strike] a bargain ((with)) / 取り引きを開始する start deal-

---

seems to have got [been bitten by] the photography bug. |(口語) He seems to be heavily into photography now.

とりつけ 銀行が取り付けに会った。There was a run on the bank.

とりつける 引出しには全部頑丈な錠前が付け付けてあります。All the drawers are fitted with strong locks.

とりとめ 考えに取りとめがなくなってしまった。My mind wandered.

とりとめる 彼はなかなかの重傷だったが一命は取りとめると医者が言った。The doctor said he would live [come through], though his wound was by no means a light one.

とりどり それについては世評はとりどりです。Public opinion is divided about the matter. | 人々はとりどりの服装で集まった。People gathered there wearing various types of clothes.

とりにがす 網が破れて魚を大半取り逃した。The net broke and most of the fish escaped.

とりのこす 彼はただ一人取り残された。He was left (all) alone.

とりはからい 万事お取り計らいにお任せします。I will leave the matter entirely to your discretion.

とりはからう なんとか取り計らいましょう。I will see what I can do (about it). | I will see about it.

とりはだ 彼女の腕に鳥肌が立った。Goose pimples came out on

とりふだ 取り札 〈カルタの〉cards for taking.
ドリブル 〖球技〗a dribble ¶ドリブルする dribble.
トリプルプレー 〖野球〗a triple play.
とりぶん 取り分 one's share [portion].
トリポリ Tripoli.
とりまぎれる 取り紛れる 〈ごっちゃになる〉get confused; 〈心が紛れる〉be distracted ¶用事に取り紛れて under pressure of business. 文例⇩

とりまき(れん) 取り巻き(連) followers; henchmen; 《文》adherents; hangers-on.
とりまく 取り巻く surround; encircle; hem sb in; ring sb about; gather [《文》throng, crowd] around sb.
とりまくる 撮りまくる 〈写真を〉take a great number of pictures; snap away.
とりまぜる 取り混ぜる mix; put together; 〈取り合わせる〉《文》assort ¶取り混ぜて all together; altogether; in all / 大小取り混ぜて売る sell big ones and small ones all mixed together.
とりまとめる 取りまとめる ⇨まとめる.
とりみだす 取り乱す 〈乱雑にする〉put sth in disorder; 〈口語〉mess [《米》muss] sth up; 〈姿, 形などを〉be disheveled; be in disarray; 〈あわてる〉be flurried; be agitated; be confused; be upset; lose one's presence of mind [《文》one's composure]; 〈自制を失う〉lose one's self-control; go to pieces ¶取り乱して in disorder; in confusion; distractedly;《文》confusedly / 取り乱した様子もなく calmly; 《文》without losing one's composure; 《文》composedly.
トリミング 〖写真〗trimming ¶トリミングする trim (a picture).
とりむすぶ 取り結ぶ ⇨むすぶ ¶ごきげんを取り結ぶ curry favor 《with》; 《文》ingratiate oneself 《with》; play up 《to》.
とりめ 鳥目 ⇨ やもうしょう.

とりもち 取り持ち 〈接待〉entertainment; 《文》reception; 〈媒介〉《文》mediation; 〈推薦〉recommendation ¶取り持ちをする act as an intermediary [a go-between] 《for》/ 友人の取り持ちで through the kindness [《文》good offices] of a [one's] friend; 《文》through the mediation of a [one's] friend.
とりもつ 取り持つ 〈周旋する〉《文》mediate; act as a go-between [an intermediary] 《for》; 〈歓待する〉receive; entertain; treat.
とりもどす 取り戻す take [win, get] sth back; regain; recover; 《文》redeem; retrieve ¶睡眠不足を取り戻す catch up on one's sleep / 取り戻したいと思う want sth back.
とりもなおさず 取りも直さず 《文》namely; in other words; that is (to say) ⇨ すなわち.
とりもの 捕り物 an arrest ¶大捕り物 an arrest (of a criminal) made by a large turnout of police; a roundup (of a big group of gangsters) / 捕物xx a detective story / 右門捕物帳 〖書名〗The Memoirs [Casebook] of Umon.
とりやめ 取り止め ⇨ ちゅうし[1].
とりょう 塗料 paint; coating(s) ¶塗料店 a paint store.
どりょう 度量 《文》magnanimity; generosity ¶度量の広い generous; big-hearted; big / 度量の狭い narrow-[small-]minded.
どりょうこう 度量衡 weights and measures ¶度量衡器 measuring instruments.
どりょく 努力 (an) effort; 《文》(an) exertion; 《文》(an) endeavor ¶努力する make efforts [an effort]; 《文》endeavor; exert oneself; 《文》strive / できるだけ努力する do one's best [utmost]; make all possible efforts; 《文》exert oneself to the utmost /…を実現しようと努力する 《文》strive [labor] for… / 努力家 a hardworking [an industrious] person / 努力賞 a prize (awarded) for effort. 文例⇩
とりよせる 取り寄せる get; 《文》obtain; 〈使いで〉send for; 〈手紙で〉write for; 〈注文する〉order (a book from England).
トリル 〖音楽〗a trill.
ドリル 〈穴あけ機〉a drill; 〈訓練〉(a) drill (in English sentence structures) ¶ドリルで穴をあける drill a hole (in) / 歯科用無痛ドリル a painless dental drill.
とりわけ 取り分け 《文》especially; above all; first of all; in particular. 文例⇩
とりわける 取り分ける divide; separate; 〈配分する〉distribute; deal out; 〈類別する〉sort;

---

her arms. / そのことを考えると全身に鳥肌が立った。I got gooseflesh all over me when I thought of it.
とりひき 直接その会社と取り引きするようになった。We have started dealing directly with the firm. / 同社の月間取引高は4億ドルを上回っている。The company is doing monthly business in excess of $ 400 million. / その法案をめぐって、自民党は社会党と取り引きをしようとしている。The Liberal Democrats are trying to make a deal with the Socialists over the proposed bill.
とりまぎれる 仕事に取り紛れて昼食をすっかり忘れていた。Under pressure of work I forgot to take lunch. / I had so much work to do that I forgot to have lunch.
とりみだす 室内はひどく取り乱してあった。The room was in complete disorder [an absolute mess]. / 彼は少しも取り乱さなかった。He remained calm [quite unruffled]. / 取り乱すなよ。Keep your head!
どりょく その計画には多くの努力が注がれた。A great deal of effort went [was put] into the project. / 努力したかいがあった。My efforts were rewarded. / 彼は自分の努力が実るのを見ることなく世を去った。He did not live to see the fruits of his labor.
とりわけ 私はこの丘からの眺めが好きです。とりわけ春の景色が。I like the view from this hill, es-

《文》assort ¶ 〈料理を〉鍋から椀に取り分ける serve into the bowls from a pot.

とる 〈取|捕, 採, 執〉 ¶〈手に〉take 《up, in one's hand》; pick sth up; 〈つかむ〉hold; 《文》seize; get [《文》take, 《文》lay] hold of; 〈得る〉get; obtain; secure; win; 〈受ける〉《文》receive; accept; 〈採用する〉adopt; take 《workers》on; 《文》engage; 〈態度を〉《文》assume; take; 〈選ぶ〉choose; prefer; 〈買う〉get; buy; 〈採集する〉pick; gather; 〈摘出する〉extract; 〈除く〉remove; strike off [out]; take off [out]; 〈捕える〉catch; capture; 〈食べる〉take; eat; have; 〈料金を〉charge; 〈事務などを〉manage; 《文》conduct; 〈解する〉take; interpret; understand; 《文》construe; make out; 〈奪う〉deprive [rob] sb of sth; 〈盗む〉steal; 〈予約する〉book; reserve; keep; 〈新聞などを〉take; subscribe (to); 〈費やす, 要する〉take; 《文》require; need; 〈場所などを〉take up 《a lot of space》 ¶ 自分で取って食べる help oneself to sth / 取ろうとする try to get [take, get hold of]; grab for sth; reach for sth 〈手を伸ばして〉/ 1等賞を取る win [carry away] the first prize / 3点取る score three points / 洋食屋からハンバーグを取る order a hamburger from a restaurant / しみを取る remove [take out] a stain; get a blot out / ふたを取る uncover 《a box》; take the lid off / 帽子を取る take one's hat off; remove [lift] one's hat / 事務を執る be [attend to] business / 〈学校で〉スペイン語を取る take Spanish [a Spanish course] / 強硬な態度をとる take [《文》assume] a firm attitude 《toward》/ よく〈悪く〉取る take sth well [badly]; take sth in good part [amiss] / 採るべき手段がない there is nothing one can do; 《文》have no means to use [resort to]. 文例 ⇩

ドル a dollar (記号: $) ★ たとえば4ドル30セントは, もちろん four dollars and thirty cents と言うが, 金額を列挙するときなどに, つづけて言うときは four dollars thirty あるいは four thirty のように言う ¶ ドル相場 the exchange rate of the dollar / ドル箱 a source of big profits; a moneymaker; 〈人〉a milch cow / ドル箱スター a star with a high box-office value.

トルエン 【化】toluene; 〈工業用〉toluol.

トルコ Turkey ¶ トルコの Turkish / トルコ語 Turkish / トルコ行進曲 a Turkish march / トルコ人 a Turk / トルコ玉 a turquoise / トルコ風呂 a Turkish bath / 〈風俗営業の〉sauna and massage / トルコ帽 a fez ((pl. fezzes)).

トルソー 【美術】a torso ((pl. -sos, torsi)).

とるにたらない 取るに足らない insignificant; 《文》negligible; trivial; trifling; unimportant; 《a matter》of no importance [account, consequence] ¶ 取るに足らない事[物] trifles / 取るに足らない人間 a person of no importance [account]; a person who is not worth bothering about; a nobody.

どれ 〈どちら〉which; 〈さあ〉come; well; now ¶ どれでも any; any one; whichever / どれくらい, どれほど ⇒どの² (どの位) / どれか any; some; either 《2つの中で》/ どれも any; all; every; 〈否定〉none; no. 文例 ⇩

どれい 奴隷 a slave; 〈境遇〉slavery; 《文》bondage ¶ 奴隷のように働く work like a slave; slave (away) / 奴隷に売られる be sold into slavery / 奴隷的な slavish / 奴隷解放 emancipation of slaves / 奴隷解放宣言【史】the Emancipation Proclamation / 奴隷制度 (abolish) slavery. 文例 ⇩

トレード ¶ トレードする 〈プロ野球などで〉trade 《a player》for 《another》; 《英》transfer 《a soccer player》/ トレードマーク a trademark / トレードマネー money paid for a 《baseball》player.

トレーナー a trainer.

トレーニング training ¶ 〈選手が〉トレーニングを受けている be (in) training (for the coming Olympics) / ハードトレーニング hard training / トレーニングウエア 《米》a sweat suit; 《英》a track suit.

トレーラー a trailer.

ドレス a dress ¶ ドレスを着た婦人 a lady in a dress / ドレスメーカー a dressmaker.

とれだか 取れ高 〈漁獲高〉a catch; a take; 〈収穫高〉a yield; a harvest; a crop.

ドレッシー ¶ ドレッシーな dressy.

ドレッシング (a) dressing ¶ サラダにドレッシングをかける put dressing on a salad; dress a salad.

トレパン 《米》sweat pants; 《英》track suit trousers ★ training pants はおしめから普通の下着に変わる時期の幼児用の下着パンツ.

---

pecially in spring.

とる 塩を取って下さい. Please pass me the salt. / あなたの上の本を取っていただけませんか. Would you reach me that book on the shelf? / 台の上にパンフレットがご自由にお取りください と置いてあった. There were pamphlets piled up on the stand, free for the taking. / 賞金は馬場さんが取りました. The prize went to Mrs. Baba. / 採り得る道は2つあった. There were two courses [alternatives] open to us. / 500人の志願者の中から60人しか採らなかった. Only sixty of the five hundred applicants were hired. / 美貌と知性のどちらを採りますか. Which do you prefer, good looks or intelligence? / このテレビの修理には1万円取られました. Having this TV repaired cost me 10,000 yen. / I gave [paid] 10,000 yen to get this TV repaired. / このインクの染みがなかなか取れません. This ink spot will not come out. / この湖のわかさぎは300年前から盛んに捕えられている. The smelt in this lake have been heavily fished for 300 years. / 家では朝日を取っている. We take [subscribe to] the Asahi.

とるにたらない 取るに足らない連中だ. They count for nothing. | They don't count for anything. / 彼の意見など取るに足らない. His opinion is not worth serious consideration.

どれ どれが欲しいのか. Which do you want? / どれから始めようか. Which shall I begin with? / この色の中のどれでもいい. Any of these colors will do. / この中から, どれでもいいから1つ選びなさい. Pick out any one of these. / この中からどれでもお好きなものを差し上げましょう. I'll

ドレミファ the (musical) scale; 《音名》the sol-fa syllables; do, re, mi, fa, sol, la, and si.

トレモロ 《音楽》(play with) a tremolo (*pl.* -s).

とれる 取捕, 撮れる 〈離れる〉come [be] off; come out; 〈除去される〉be taken off; be removed; 〈得られる〉be got; be had; 《文》be obtained; 〈産出する〉be produced; 《文》be yielded; 〈捕獲される〉be caught; 〈解釈される〉be interpreted; read ¶いく通りにも取れる文 a sentence that reads [can be interpreted in] several ways. 文例⇩

トレンチコート a trench coat.

とろ¹ 淀 a pool (in a river).

とろ² 吐露 ¶吐露する express [put] 《one's view》; 《文》set forth 《one's opinion》; speak 《one's mind》; 《文》give vent to 《one's feelings》; pour out 《文》lay bare 《one's heart》.

とろ³ 〈まぐろの〉the fatty meat of tuna. 文例⇩

どろ 泥 mud; dirt; 《文》mire ¶泥だらけの muddy; 《文》miry / 泥だらけになる be covered with mud; get muddy / 顔に泥を塗る 〈比喩的〉disgrace; bring disgrace on *sb*; 《文》sully *sb's* reputation / 泥を吐く confess 《one's crime》; own up; 《口語》come clean.

トロイ Troy ¶トロイ戦争 the Trojan War.

トロイカ 〈《ロシア語》〉a troika.

とろう 徒労 wasted [《文》fruitless, 《文》vain] effort ¶徒労に帰する come to [go for] nothing; 《文》be in vain; be [labor, work] to no purpose [《文》avail]; get nowhere; 《文》prove fruitless. 文例⇩

どろえのぐ 泥絵の具 color wash; 《英》distemper.

トローチ 《薬》a troche.

トロール ¶トロール網 a trawl / トロール漁業 trawling / トロール船 a trawler.

とろかす 蕩かす 〈溶かす〉⇒ とかす²; 〈うっとりさせる〉charm; bewitch; fascinate; enchant.

どろくさい 泥臭い 〈泥のにおいがする〉smell of mud; have a muddy odor; 〈洗練されていない〉《文》be unrefined; 《文》be unpolished.

とろける 蕩ける 〈溶ける〉⇒ とける¹; 〈うっとりとなる〉be enchanted [《文》enraptured] 《with, by》.

どろじあい 泥仕合 mudslinging at each other; 〈将棋などの〉a confused, long-drawn-out game ¶泥仕合をする sling [fling] mud at each other.

トロツキー Trotsky ¶トロツキー主義 Trotskyism.

トロツキスト a Trotskyist.

トロッコ a truck; a trolley.

ドロップ 〈菓子〉drops.

とろとろ ¶とろとろする 〈眠る〉doze [nod] off; drop off into a doze / とろとろ煮る cook (for a long time) over (a) low heat; simmer; boil gently / とろとろになるまで煮る boil *sth* to a pulp; reduce *sth* to (a) pulp by boiling.

どろどろ ¶どろどろの 〈泥で〉muddy 《roads》; 〈雪どけで〉slushy 《roads》; 〈泥状の〉pulpy; 〈濃い〉thick 《soup》/ どろどろになる 〈道が〉become muddy; 〈固形物が〉be reduced to (a) pulp; 〈煮物などが〉be reduced to jelly / 太鼓をどろどろと鳴らす give a roll on a drum. 文例⇩

どろなわ 泥縄 ¶泥縄式である be like locking the stable door after the horse has bolted ⇒ どろぼう.

どろぬま 泥沼 a bog; 《文》a quagmire; 〈比喩的〉a morass (of difficulties) ¶〈道が〉泥沼のようになる turn into a morass / 泥沼に落ちこむ 〈比喩的にも〉bog down; get bogged down / 泥沼から抜け出す 〈比喩的に〉find a way out of the swamp.

とび とろ火 a low flame [heat, gas] ⇒ よわび

どろぼう 泥棒 a robber; 〈こそどろ〉a thief (*pl.* thieves); 〈夜盗〉a burglar; 〈押し込み強盗〉a housebreaker ¶泥棒する steal *sth* from *sb*; rob *sb* of *sth* / 泥棒に入る break into a house; rob 《an orchard》; burgle 《米》burglarize a house / 泥棒を捕えて縄をなう lock the stable door after the horse has bolted; 《文》make belated efforts ⇒ どろなわ. 文例⇩

どろみず 泥水 muddy water.

どろよけ 泥除け 〈自転車の〉《米》a fender; 《英》a mudguard.

とろり ¶とろりとした thick 《liquid》.

トロリーバス a trolley bus.

とろろ grated yam ¶とろろいも a yam / とろろ昆布 shavings of tangle 《used in soup》.

とろん ¶とろんとした sleepy [dull, heavy,

---

give you whichever you like (of these). / この中のどれかちょうだいできましょうか. Can you spare me one of these? / この写真はどれも気に入った[気に入らない]. I like all [I don't like any of] these pictures. / どれ, ひとつやってみよう. Well, I'll try. / どれ, 何があるか見てもらおう. Let's see what you've got.

どれい 金銭の奴隷となってはいけない. You must not become a slave to money.

とれる 上着のボタンが1つ取れた. A button has come off my coat. / 痛みが取れた. The pain has gone [disappeared]. / 背中の痛みはじきに取れた. I was soon relieved of the pain in my back. / この山からウラニウムがとれる. Uranium is found in this mountain. / この文章は色々な意味に取れる. This passage can be interpreted in several ways [admits of several interpretations]. / 昔はこのあたりでにしんがたくさん捕れた. There used to be a great catch of herrings in these waters. / 写真はよく撮れた. The photo has come out well.

とろ³ まぐろの中とろがいい. 大とろは私には油っこすぎる. I like my tuna medium fatty; the marbled white one is too rich for me.

とろう その洪水で我々の努力はすべて徒労に帰した. The flood brought all our efforts to nothing. / この半年間の労苦はすべて徒労であった. My six months' hard work has all gone for nothing. / I have worked hard for six months, all to no purpose.

どろどろ どろどろと太鼓が鳴った. The drums rolled. / I heard a roll of drums.

どろぼう 泥棒! Stop, thief! / 昨日僕の家に泥棒が入った. My house was [I had my house] bro-

どろん [drowsy] ((eyes)) / 目がとろんとしている be dull-[heavy-]eyed ; look sleepy [drowsy].

どろん ¶どろんをきめる disappear ; 《口語》 pull a vanishing act ; get away ; make off.

ドロンゲーム a drawn game ; a draw.

どろんこ 泥んこ ¶泥んこ遊びをする play with mud ; make mud pies / 泥んこになる get muddy / 泥んこ道 a muddy road.

トロンボーン a trombone ¶トロンボーンを吹く[奏する] play [blow] the trombone / トロンボーン奏者 a trombonist.

とわずがたり 問わず語り 文例⇩

どわすれ 度忘れ a lapse [slip] of memory ¶度忘れする〈人が主語〉forget (for the moment) ;〈事が主語〉have slipped one's mind ; escape one. 文例⇩

トン a ton ; tonnage (トン数) ¶5千トンの汽船 a steamer of 5,000 tons / 8トン積みの貨車 an eight-ton freight car / 総[登簿]トン数 gross [registered] tonnage.

どん〈砲声〉a boom ;〈銃声〉a bang ¶どんとぶつかる bump against 《a wall》; bump into 《a man》.

トンガ (the Kingdom of) Tonga ¶トンガの Tongan.

どんか 鈍化 ¶鈍化する get [go,《文》become] dull ;〈遅くなる〉slow (down).

どんかく 鈍角 an obtuse angle ¶鈍角三角形 an obtuse triangle.

とんカツ 豚カツ a breaded pork cutlet.

とんがりぼうし とんがり帽子 a steeple-crowned cap.

とんがる 尖る ⇨とがる.

どんかん 鈍感 ¶鈍感な insensitive ; unresponsive ; dull ;《文》stolid.

どんき 鈍器 a blunt instrument [weapon]. 文例⇩

ドンキホーテ Don Quixote ¶ドンキホーテ流の quixotic.

とんきょう 頓狂 ¶頓狂な wild ; crazy ; madcap / 頓狂な声を出す screech ; shriek.

どんぐり an acorn ¶どんぐりまなこ big, round eyes ; bulbous eyes. 文例⇩

どんこう 鈍行 ¶鈍行列車 a slow train ; a local train ; a local.

とんざ 頓挫 ¶頓挫する be frustrated ; be held up ; be checked ; be deadlocked ;《文》be in an impasse.

どんさい 鈍才 a dull person.

とんし 頓死 a sudden [an unexpected] death ¶頓死する die suddenly ; die a sudden death.

どんじゅう 鈍重 ¶鈍重な slow-[dull-]witted ; stolid ;《文》bovine.

どんじり どん尻 the tail end ¶どんじりのチーム the team at the bottom [《口語》in the cellar] / どんじりに at the very end [last].

とんそう 遁走 ⇨とうそう¹ / 遁走曲 ⇨フーガ.

どんぞこ どん底 the bottom ; the depths ¶不幸のどん底にある《文》be at the nadir of adversity / 貧乏のどん底にいる be in the depths of poverty / どん底生活《文》a life of extreme poverty / どん底生活をしている be so poor that one doesn't know where one's next meal is coming from ;《口語》be (living) on [below] the breadline ; be living at [below] subsistence level. 文例⇩

とんだ ⇨とんでもない ¶とんだ目に会う have a terrible experience.

とんち 頓知 (a quick [《文》ready]) wit ¶頓知のある quick-witted ; witty / 頓知の利く人 a man with a quick [《文》ready] wit.

とんちゃく 頓着 ¶頓着する mind ;《文》pay regard to ; care [worry, bother] about ; trouble [concern] oneself about / 頓着しない be careless [unconcerned] about ; feel no concern (for) ; be indifferent 《to, about》;《文》pay no heed (to) / 費用には頓着なく regardless of [with no regard to] expense. 文例⇩

どんちゃんさわぎ どんちゃん騒ぎ a spree ; boisterous merrymaking ;《文》high jinks ¶どんちゃん騒ぎをやる go on a spree ;《口語》be [go] on the razzle ;《口語》paint the town red.

どんちょう 緞帳 a thick curtain ;〈垂れ幕〉a drop curtain.

とんちんかん ¶とんちんかんな〈見当違いの〉beside the point [question] ; out of place ; irrelevant ;《口語》off (the) beam ; off the track ;〈つじつまの合わない〉inconsistent ; incoherent ; incongruous ;〈食い違った〉at cross pur-

---

ken into yesterday.

ドロンゲーム ドロンゲームになった. The game ended in [as] a draw.

とわずがたり 彼は問わず語りに自分の生い立ちを語った. He told me about his early days, though I didn't ask him to.

どわすれ あの人の名前を度忘れした. His name escapes me [has slipped my mind]. | I forget [have forgotten] his name for the moment.

トン この船は何トンですか. What is the tonnage of this ship?

どん どんと鉄砲が鳴った. Bang! went the gun.

どんき 被害者の頭部には鈍器で数回強打された跡があった. Marks on the victim's head indicated that he had been struck several hard blows with a blunt instrument.

どんぐり どんぐりの背比べだ. They are all much of a muchness [all alike]. | There is nothing much to choose between them.

どんぞこ 今は不景気のどん底だ. We are [Business is] now at the bottom of a depression. | The times are now as bad as they can get.

とんだ これはとんだご迷惑をおかけいたしました. I am terribly sorry to have given you so much trouble. / とんだことになったね. This is a fine mess (we're in)!

とんちゃく 人が何を言おうと私は頓着しません. I don't mind [care] what people say (about me).

とんちんかん どうも話がとんちんかんだった. We were not talking on the same wavelength. / とんちんかんな返事が返って来た. His answer was completely off beam.

とんでもない とんでもない. What an (outrageous) idea ! |《口語》No way ! | It's quite out of the question. | Perish the thought ! | 何とお礼を申し上げてよいのやらわかりません.—いや、とんでもない. I don't know how to thank you.—Oh, don't mention it. / あの方はなかなかの学者ですからねえ.—学者だって、とんでもない. He's quite a scholar, you know.—

どんつう 鈍痛 a dull pain.

とんでもない 〈法外な〉 extraordinary; preposterous; outrageous; exorbitant (fees); 〈意外な〉 unexpected; fantastic; 〈恐ろしい〉 shocking; awful; terrible; terrific; appalling; 〈驚くべき〉 surprising; 〈非常な〉 tremendous; serious; 《文》 gross; glaring (mistakes) ¶とんでもない考え an absurd idea / とんでもない値段 an outrageous (exorbitant) price / とんでもない間違い a terrible [very serious] mistake; a big [an awful] error / とんでもない要求 a preposterous [《文》 an unconscionable] demand. 文例⇩

どんてん 曇天 a clouded sky; cloudy weather.

どんでんがえし どんでん返し a (sudden) complete reversal (of the plot); an unexpected twist (at the end of the story).

とんと 〈…ない〈少しも〉 never; (not) at all; (not) in the least; 〈全く〉 entirely (forgotten); absolutely 《impossible》; altogether (out of the question).

とんとん 〈たたく音〉 a knock; a rap; a tap ¶とんとん戸をたたく knock [rap] at [on] the door / とんとん拍子に without a hitch; 《by rapid strides》; swimmingly / とんとん拍子に出世する rise rapidly in the world; go from success to success / とん・とん・つー 〈モールス信号の…〉 dot dot dash / とんとんになる be quits [even] 《with sb》; break even. 文例⇩

どんどん 〈太鼓の音〉 rub-a-dub; 〈戸などをたたく音〉 rat-tat(-tat); 〈銃砲声〉 bang, bang!; 〈盛んに〉 ⇨ どしどし ¶どんどん戸を knock at 《the door》; pound 《the table》 / どんどん太鼓を打つ beat a drum loudly / どんどん進む go ahead [《文》 advance] rapidly; 《文》 make rapid progress / どんどん金をもうける make money hand over fist.

どんな what (book); what kind [sort] of (book) ★口語では What kind of a book is it? のように冠詞をつけて言うこともよくある ¶どんなに 〈どれほど〉 how; how much; 〈どれほど…than〉 however; 〈いかように でも〉 anyway; 〈どんな人でも〉 anybody; everybody; 〈否定〉 nobody / どんな事があっても whatever [no matter what] may happen; under [in] any circumstances; 〈決して…ない〉 (not) for all the world; (not) for anything (in the world); on no account / どんなに金があっても however rich [no matter how rich] you may be. 文例⇩

トンネル a tunnel ¶トンネルを掘る dig [cut, bore, build] a tunnel 《through a mountain》; tunnel 《a hill》 / (列車が)トンネルに入る[を通る] go into [go through] a tunnel / トンネルをやる 『野球』 let a grounder pass between one's legs / トンネル会社 a dummy company.

とんび 〈鳥〉 a kite ¶とんびに油揚げをさらわれる have something (nice) snatched away from under one's nose [from before one's very eyes] / とんびに油揚げをさらわれたような顔をして with a stupid look of surprise.

どんぴしゃり ¶どんぴしゃりで 〈答が〉 be exactly [quite] right; be quite to the point; really hit the bull's eye; 〈適合している〉 fit (the role) to a T; be tailor-made 《for the need》.

ドンファン 〈女たらし〉 《口語》 a womanizer; a Don Juan; 《文》 a libertine.

とんぷく(やく) 頓服(薬) a dose of medicine to be taken only once.

どんぶり 丼 a china bowl ¶どんぶり飯 rice served in a bowl. 文例⇩

とんぼ 〈昆〉 a dragonfly.

とんぼがえり とんぼ返り a handspring; a cartwheel (横向きの); a somersault ¶とんぼ返りをする do [turn, throw] a handspring; turn head over heels / 逆とんぼ返り a back [backward] handspring / とんぼ返り運転 driving 《a truck》 back without resting at the turnaround point. 文例⇩

とんま 頓馬 a silly [stupid] fellow; an ass ⇨ ばか.

とんや 問屋 〈人〉 a wholesale dealer [mer-

You call that a scholar? Huh!
とんと とんと存じません. I know nothing at all [absolutely nothing]. / 彼はどこへ行ってしまったのかとんとわからない. I haven't the faintest idea where he has gone. / とんと考えつかなかった. I never thought of that. / That never occurred to me.

とんとん とんとん拍子に運んだ. Everything went swimmingly. / すべてとんとん拍子というわけには行かなかった. It wasn't all plain sailing. / それでとんとんになる. That evens things up. / 《口語》 We're quits now. / That puts us all square. / 損得とんとんだ. The profits and losses even out.

どんどん 太鼓が どんどん, どんどんと鳴っていた. I heard a roll of drums. / 水がどんどん増してくる. The water is rising fast.

どんな どんな方か. What is he like? / What sort of (a) man is he? / 翻訳機械とはどんな物ですか. What is a translating machine like? / (教室で生徒に)海とはどんなものか考えてみよう. Let's think about the sea. / こんな風にやったらどんなものでしょう. Suppose you do it this way. / どんな事になるかわからない. There is no knowing what may happen. / どんな事があろうとも私は覚悟ができている. Whatever may happen [Come what may], I am prepared for it. / どんな事情があっても約束は守らなければならない. You must keep your promise under any circumstances. / どんな事をしてでもそれはやり遂げる決心だ. I am determined to accomplish it at all costs. / どんな代償を払ってもそれをしたかった. I would have given anything to (be able to) do it. / どんなにかお力落としでしょう. I can well imagine how grieved you must be (over your loss). / 彼は得意そうに, 「どんなもんだい」と言った. He said proudly, 'How about that, then?' / 彼はどんなにほめてもほめたりない. No praise is too much for what he has done.

どんぶり あの店の経営はどんぶり勘定だ. That store is run without proper bookkeeping.

とんぼがえり 大阪からとんぼ返りで帰って来た. I have been to

どんよく 〈貪欲〉《文》avarice; greed; 《文》covetousness ¶**どん欲な**《文》avaricious; greedy; 《文》covetous / **どん欲な読書家** an avid reader.

どんより ¶**どんよりした空** a heavy [an overcast, 《文》a leaden] sky; dull weather / **どんよりした目** glazed [dull, 《文》lackluster] eyes. 文例↓

chant]; a wholesaler; 〈店〉a wholesale store [house] ¶**問屋業** wholesale business. 文例↓

な

な¹ 名 〈名称〉a name; 〈肩書き・表題〉a title; 〈氏名〉one's name; 〈略さない正式の〉one's full name; 〈名字〉one's surname; one's family name; 〈名字に対して〉one's personal [given] name; 〈名声〉fame; 《文》renown ¶**名のある** ⇨ 文例↓ / **次郎という名の少年** a boy called [by the name of] Jiro / **名を言う** tell [give] sb one's name / **名を偽る** assume a false name; give a wrong name / **名をつける** name 《the baby Taro》 / **うまい[まずい]名をつける** give a good [poor] name 《to the new device》 / **名を呼ぶ** call sb by name / **名をあげる[成す]** become famous; 《文》win fame; make one's [a] name [reputation]; make one's mark / **名を残す** leave one's name 《on the history of...》 / **名を汚す** disgrace one's name [reputation] / **名を捨てて実を取る** would rather be down-to-earth than care about name; choose real achievement rather than empty reputation / **名にそむかない** be worthy of the name; be true to one's [its] name / **...の名で** 〈名をかりて〉in [under] the name of...; 〈口実として〉on [under] the pretext of 《social reform》 / **名もない** 〈無名の〉unknown; obscure; 〈つまらない〉worthless / **名ばかりの**〈名目だけの〉in name only; nominal; 〈申し訳程度の〉nominal 《fees》; token 《concessions》. 文例↓

な² 菜 〈青物〉greens; 〈菜種の菜〉rape ¶**菜の花** rape blossoms.

な³ 〈幾分念を押すようにして〉詠嘆を表わす〉

-な 〈禁止〉not. 文例↓   ⇨ なあ, ね⁶.

なあ 〈呼びかけ〉《米》say; 《英》I say; 〈そう思われる〉I should say; 〈願望〉I wish...; 〈そうでしょう〉you know ⇨ ね⁶, ね

え. 文例↓

なあて 名宛て ⇨ あて ¶**名あて人** an addressee.

なあなあ ¶**...となあなあでやっていく** do on a live-and-let-live basis.

ない 〈否定〉not; 〈存在しない〉there is [are] no...; 〈見当たらない〉be gone; be missing; cannot be found; 〈所有しない〉do not have; have no...; be without...; 〈欠く〉《文》want; lack; 《文》be devoid [bare] 《of》¶**欠点[誤り]がない** be free from [of] faults [mistakes] / **する事がない** have nothing to do / **...がない場合には** in the absence [《文》in default] of 《the article》 / **...がないので** for want [lack] of 《a better word》; in the absence of 《further information》 / **ないものとあきらめる** give sb [sth] up for lost / **少しも...でない** not...at all; not...in the least / **なくてはならない物** things indispensable 《for, to》; necessities / **ない物ねだり** asking for things which are unobtainable; crying for the moon ⇨ -なかったら. 文例↓

ないい 内意 〈意中〉one's intention; 〈私見〉one's private [personal] opinion ¶**内意を受けて** by secret order 《of》; under secret instructions 《from》 / **内意を伝える** let sb know [tell sb] one's wishes [intention(s)]; make one's wishes [intention(s)] known 《to》.

ナイーブ ¶**ナイーブな** unspoiled; naive ★英語の naive は今では「考え方の幼稚な」という悪い意味で使う。

ないえん 内縁 ¶**内縁の妻** a common-law wife; a wife not legally married / **内縁関係を結ぶ** make 《《文》contract》 a common-law [de facto] marriage 《with》.

ないか 内科 〈病院の〉the internal depart-

Osaka on a flying visit. **とんや** そうは問屋がおろさない. 〈その手は食わない〉You won't catch me with that one! | You can't catch old birds with chaff! | That won't wash! | 〈それではうまく行かぬ〉You won't get away with that. | 〈君の思うようにはならぬ〉That's expecting [asking] too much.
どんより その日はどんより曇っていた. The day was dull and cloudy.
な¹ その人の名なら知って[聞いて]いる. I know him by name. / そんな名の人は知らない. I do not know anyone of [with] that name. / 彼はその本で名をあげた. The book won him a reputation. / 社長とは名ばかりだ. He is President only in name. / その人の名は出さないでおくことにいたします. The person shall be [remain] nameless. / 彼は「ラッパ」の名で通っている. He goes by the name of 'Trumpeter.' / その子は祖父の名をとって大作と名づけられた. The boy was named Daisaku after [《米》for] his grandfather. / 名は体を表わす. Names and natures often agree. 【諺】

-な 来るなと言いなさい. Tell him not to come. / 決してうそをつくな. Never tell a lie.
なあ それは少し行き過ぎのようですなあ. That's going a little too far, I should say. / きれいだなあ! How beautiful (it is)! / 金がありさえすればなあ. If only I had money! / もう一度若くなれたらなあ. I wish I were young again! / なにしろ気難しい人ですからなあ. You know, he is very hard to please.
ない 机1つ, 腰掛け1個以外この部屋には家具が何もない. The room is bare of furniture except

ないかい 内海 an inland sea ¶瀬戸内海 the Inland Sea (of Japan).

ないがい 内外 〈内と外〉the inside and outside; 〈およそ〉some; about; around; or so ¶2千円内外 some [about] two thousand yen; two thousand yen or so / 内外の internal and external; 〈国内と外国の〉home [domestic] and foreign 《affairs》/ 内外に in and out; inside and outside 《the house》;《文》within and without; 〈国内と外国に〉at home and abroad / 市の内外に in and about [around] the city / 大学の内外で inside [within] the university and outside 《it》/ 国連の内外で within and outside the United Nations. 文例⇩

ないかく¹ 内角 《幾何》an interior angle;《野球》the inside ¶内角球 an inside ball; an insider. 文例⇩

ないかく² 内閣 〈政府〉the government ¶陰の内閣 the shadow cabinet / 内閣を組織する form [organize] a Cabinet / 内閣に入る join the Cabinet; become a Cabinet Minister 〈a member of the Cabinet〉/ 池田内閣 the Ikeda Cabinet / 内閣改造 the reorganization [reshuffling] of the Cabinet / 内閣官房長官 the Chief Cabinet Secretary / 内閣総理大臣 the Prime Minister; the Premier.

ないがしろ 蔑ろ ¶ないがしろにする make light of; despise; slight; neglect.

ないき 内規 (customary) rules; bylaws ¶…と内規に定められている be provided [laid down] in the rules 《of the school》 that….

ないきん 内勤 indoor service; office [desk] work ¶内勤である work inside [in the office] / 内勤員 an office [a desk, an indoor] worker.

ないくう 内宮 the Inner Shrine of Ise.

ないけい 内径 the internal [inside] diameter; the caliber; the bore.

ないこう¹ 内向 《心理》introversion ¶内向する turn in upon *oneself* / 内向的[性]の introverted / 内向的な[型の]人 an introverted person; an introvert.

ないこう² 内攻 《医》retrocession ¶内攻性疾患 a retrocessive [retrocedent] disease.

ないこう³ 内項 《数》internal terms.

ないこく 内国 ¶内国の home; domestic; internal / 内国為替 domestic exchange / 内国郵便 domestic mail.

ないさい¹ 内済 ¶内済にする settle 《a matter》 privately [out of court].

ないさい² 内債 ¶内債を起こす raise [float] a domestic loan.

ないざい 内在 《哲》immanence ¶内在的 immanent; indwelling.

ないし 乃至 〈…より…まで〉from …to…; between…and…;〈または〉or ¶甲ないし乙 A or B / 700 ないし千円 《anywhere from》¥700 to ¥1,000; between 700 and 1,000 yen. 文例⇩

ないじ¹ 内示 (an) unofficial announcement [《文》notification] ¶内示する announce unofficially 《that…》;《文》notify *sb* in private 《that…》.

ないじ² 内耳 《解》the inner ear ¶内耳炎 otitis interna; inflammation of the inner ear.

ナイジェリア Nigeria ¶ナイジェリア人 Nigerian / ナイジェリア〈人〉の Nigerian / ナイジェリア連邦共和国 the Federal Republic of Nigeria.

ないしきょう 内視鏡 《医》an endoscope.

ないじつ 内実 ¶内実は in fact; in reality; really / 内実は…である The truth [fact] is that….

ないじゅ 内需 domestic demand; home consumption.

ないしゅっけつ 内出血 internal bleeding [hemorrhage] ¶内出血する bleed [hemorrhage] internally.

ないしょ 内証 ¶内証の secret; private; confidential / 内証にする keep *sth* secret from *sb*; keep *sth* dark [to *oneself*] / 内証は我々の間だけの between ourselves [you and me] / 内証で secretly; privately; confidentially; in secret [private, confidence] / 内証事 a secret; a private matter [affair] / 内証事を打ち明ける confide a secret to *sb*; take *sb* into *one's* confidence / 内証話をする talk in whispers 《with》; have a private [confidential] talk 《with》. 文例⇩

ないじょ 内助 ¶内助の功によって thanks to

---

for a desk and a chair. / 成功の望みがないでもない. 《文》There is some hope of his success. | His prospects are not entirely hopeless. / この品は日本にはない. This is not available [cannot be obtained] in Japan. / この植物は日本にも中国にもない. This plant is found neither in Japan nor in China. / こんなものでもないよりはましだ. Such as it is, it is better than nothing. / 彼の失敗を聞いて驚かない者はなかった. Everybody was surprised at his failure. / おかしいなんてものじゃない. It's more than just funny. | Funny isn't the word for it. | 家康じゃないが鳴くまで待つことにしよう. Let's wait and see, as Ieyasu (would) put it. / そりゃないでしょう. I'm not happy about that ! | Oh, that doesn't stand up [won't hold water, won't wash]!

ないがい 彼の名は内外に知れわたっている. His name is well known both at home and abroad. / 費用は1万円内外でしょう. The outlay will be about [in the neighborhood of] ten thousand yen.

ないかく² 三角形の内角の和は二直角に等しい. The three (interior) angles of a triangle add up to [are equal to] two right angles.

ないし 費用は3万円ないし4万円でしょう. The outlay will be between thirty and forty thousand yen. / 月収は平均7万ないし8万というところです. Their average monthly income ranges [varies] from 70,000 to 80,000 yen.

ないしょ いいね, これは内証にしておいてくれたまえ. Don't let it go further, mind you. / これは絶対に内証だよ. This is strictly

ないしょう 内証 ⇨ ないしょ.

ないじょう 内情 〈内部事情〉 (the) inside affairs;《文》(the) internal conditions;〈実情〉 the real state of affairs ¶内情に明るい have a good inside knowledge 《of》; be familiar [well up] in the (internal) affairs 《of》.

ないしょく 内職 a side job; side work; homework; a sideline (兼業) ¶内職をする do a side job.

ないしん¹ 内心 〈心中〉《文》one's inmost heart;〈真意〉 one's real intention;【数】the inner center ¶内心(で)は at heart; at bottom; in one's heart (of hearts); inwardly.

ないしん² 内申 a confidential report ¶内申する report confidentially 《to》/ 内申書 a school report.

ないじん 内陣 the inner temple [shrine]; the chancel (キリスト教会の).

ないしんのう 内親王 an Imperial [a Royal] princess.

ないせい¹ 内政 domestic [home] administration ¶内政に干渉する interfere [intervene] in the domestic [internal] affairs 《of Japan》. 文例⇩

ないせい² 内省《文》introspection; reflection ¶内省する reflect on oneself / 内省的《文》introspective; reflective.

ないせつ 内接【幾何】¶内接する touch internally / 内接円 an inscribed circle.

ないせん¹ 内戦 a civil [an internal] war; domestic [internal] warfare.

ないせん² 内線〈電気の〉 indoor [internal, interior] wiring;〈電話の〉 an extension (略: ext.) ¶内線電話 an extension telephone / 内線番号 an extension number. 文例⇩

ないそう 内装 interior decoration [furnishings];〈自動車の〉 upholstery.

ないぞう¹ 内蔵 ¶セルフタイマー内蔵のカメラ a camera with a built-in self-timer.

ないぞう² 内臓《文》the internal organs;《文》the viscera ¶内臓の《文》visceral / 内臓の飛び出した disemboweled;《文》eviscerated.

ナイター a night game.

ないだく 内諾 an informal agreement [consent]. 文例⇩

ないだん 内談 ¶内談する talk privately 《with》; have a private talk [word] 《with》.

ないち 内地〈国の内部〉 the interior (of a country); inland;〈本国〉 home; homeland;

〈本土〉 mainland;〈北海道に対して〉 Honshu ¶内地の interior; inland; internal; domestic (consumption); home (products) / 内地勤務 home service / 内地産の馬 a homebred horse / 内地人 people at home [in Honshu] / 内地米 domestically-grown rice.

ないつう 内通《文》secret communication;〈裏切り〉(a) betrayal ¶内通する hold [be in] secret communication with 《the enemy》.

ないてい¹ 内定 (an) informal [unofficial] decision ¶内定する decide informally [unofficially]. 文例⇩

ないてい² 内偵 ¶内偵する make private [secret] inquiries into sth; investigate sth secretly [in secret].

ないてき 内的 internal; inner;〈心の〉 mental ¶内的独白《文芸》an inner monologue.

ナイト a knight ¶ナイトの位 knighthood.

ナイトクラブ a nightclub.

ないない 内々 ¶内々の〈内密の〉 secret; private; confidential;〈非公式の〉 informal; unofficial / 内々で〈内密に〉 secretly; in secret; privately; confidentially;〈非公式に〉 informally; unofficially / 内々にする keep sth secret; hush sth up. 文例⇩

ないねんきかん 内燃機関 an internal-combustion engine.

ナイフ a knife (pl. knives);〈小刀〉 a pocketknife;〈食卓用の〉 a table knife ¶ナイフで人を刺す stab sb with a knife; stick [run, plunge] a knife into sb; knife sb / ナイフを開く[たたむ] open [close] (the blade of) a knife / 折りたたみナイフ a clasp knife;〈ジャックナイフ〉 a jackknife;〈小型の〉 a pocketknife;〈ごく小型の〉 a penknife / 七つ道具つきナイフ an all-purpose knife.

ないぶ 内部 the inside; the interior; the inner part ¶身体の内部 the internal parts of the body / 〈機械などの〉内部が見えるように描いた説明図 a cutaway drawing / 内部の inside; internal; interior; domestic (国内の, 家内の) / 内部のもの a person on the inside; an insider / 内部の事情に詳しい have a good inside knowledge 《of》; be well up in the internal affairs 《of》/ 内部に inside; within / 身体の内部に傷を受ける receive an internal injury; be hurt internally / 内部から from within [the inside] / 内部構造〈物の〉(an) inner [internal, interior] structure ;〈動物の体の〉 internal anatomy.

ないふく 内服 ⇨ ないよう¹ ¶内服薬 an inter-

---

confidential.

ないじょ 彼の出世は内助の功によるところが大きい. His success is due, in no small measure, to his wife. | He owes much of his success to his wife.

ないしょく 何か内職が欲しい. I want some work that I can do at home. | 彼は内職にタバコ屋をしている. He keeps [runs] a cigar store as a sideline [on the side].

ないせい¹ 我が国は中国の内政には干渉しないと首相は述べた. The Prime Minister said that Japan would not interfere in China's internal affairs.

ないせん 内線105番をお願いします. Could I have extension 105? | (Give me) extension 105, please.

ないだく これについては既に成田氏の内諾を得ている. We have already obtained Mr. Narita's private consent to this. | Mr.

Narita has already given us his private consent to this.

ないてい 式は来月行なわれることに内定している. It has been informally arranged that the ceremony should be held next month. | M社から採用内定の通知が来た. The M Company have notified me of their decision, though not yet official, to hire me.

ないない 内々で君に話したいこと

ないふん 内紛 (an) internal trouble [conflict]; 《文》internal strife; 《文》domestic discord ¶政党の内紛 internal troubles [strife] in a political party; (an) intraparty conflict / (組織や団体の)内紛で割れている be torn by internal [factional] strife.

ないぶん 内聞 ¶内聞にする keep *sth* secret; hush *sth* up. 文例⬇

ないぶんぴ 内分泌 internal secretion ¶内分泌腺 an endocrine gland.

ないほう¹ 内報 a secret [confidential] report; secret information; 《口語》a tip-off ¶内報する report unofficially [secretly]; tell in private; 《口語》tip *sb* off about [on] *sth*.

ないほう² 内包 《論》a connotation ¶内包する involve; 《論》connote.

ないまぜ ない交ぜ ¶ないまぜにする blend [intertwine] 《fact and fiction into a story》.

ないみつ 内密 ⇨ないない, ないしょ.

ないめい 内命 informal [secret] instructions [orders].

ないめん 内面 the inside; the interior ¶内面的 internal / 内面的に internally / 内面生活 *one's* inner life / 内面描写 《文芸》(a) description of the workings of 《a character's》mind.

ないや 内野 《野球》the infield ¶内野手 an infielder / 内野席 the infield stands; the infield bleachers (屋根なしの) / 内野フライ[安打] an infield fly [hit]. 文例⬇

ナイヤガラ ¶ナイヤガラの滝 Niagara Falls 《単数扱い》.

ないやく 内約 ¶内約する make a private contract [agreement] 《with》.

ないゆう 内憂 domestic [internal] troubles ¶内憂外患こもごも至る be beset with troubles both at home and abroad.

ないよう¹ 内用 ¶内用する use 《a medicine》internally; take 《a pill》 ⇨ないふく.

ないよう² 内容 〈中味〉content(s); 〈意味〉《文》import; substance; matter ¶事件の内容 the details of a case / 手紙の内容 the text of a letter / 話の内容 what *sb* said; what was said; the gist [import] of the story [of what was said] / (話などに)内容がある[ない] be rich [poor] in content [substance] / 胃の内容物を調べる examine the stomach contents 《of a dead animal》 / (本の)内容見本 specimen pages / 内容証明郵便 contents-certified mail.
囲い「本の内容」と言う場合、その「内容」が充実しているとか、貧弱であるとかいうように、本の「内容」を全体としてとらえたり、あるいは抽象的に考えている時には、単数形の content を用い、本の目次などに記載されているような種々の項目を念頭に置いて言う場合、言いかえると「内容」を具体的にとらえて言う時には、複数形の contents を用いる。

ないらん¹ 内乱 (a) civil war; 《文》civil strife; internal disturbances. 文例⬇

ないらん² 内覧 a preview 《of an exhibition》; (a) preliminary inspection [examination] ¶内覧会 〈デパートの〉 a private view [show] 《of winter fashions》.

ないりく 内陸 the interior of a country; inland ¶上海から500キロ内陸に 500 kilometers inland [upcountry] from Shanghai / 内陸地方 inland provinces.

ナイル(がわ) ナイル(川) the Nile.

ナイロン nylon ¶ナイロンの靴下 nylon stockings [socks]; (a pair of) nylons (婦人用).

ナイン the 《Waseda》 nine; a baseball team.

なう 綯う twist (together); twine ¶縄をなう make a rope.

なうて 名うて ⇨なだかい, ゆうめい¹. 「elephant.

ナウマンぞう ナウマン象 《古生物》a Naumann

ナウル (the Republic of) Nauru.

なえ 苗 〈種から育てた〉a seedling; 〈苗木〉a young plant; a nursery tree ¶稲の苗 a young rice plant / 苗床 a seed bed; a nursery (bed).

なえる 萎える 〈麻痺する〉be paralyzed; go [get, 《文》become] numb; 《文》be benumbed; 〈しおれる〉wither; droop.

なお 尚 〈更に〉more; further; still [much] more; 〈否定〉less; still [much] less; 〈まだ〉still; yet ¶なおかつ and yet / なおまた besides; in addition to 《it》; on top of 《that》; furthermore; moreover / なお良い[悪い, 大切な]事は what is better [worse, more important]. 文例⬇

なおさら 尚更 ⇨なお. 文例⬇

なおざり ¶なおざりする 〈注意を払わない〉neglect; disregard; 《文》pay little heed 《to》; 〈軽視する〉make light of; slight.

なおし 直し (a) correction; 〈改正〉(an) alteration; 〈修繕〉mending; repair(s) ¶時計を直しに出す take *one's* watch 《to a watch repairer》to be mended / 直しがきかない 直し物 mending.

なおす 直[治]す 〈修繕する〉mend; repair; 《米》fix; 〈整える〉set *sth* to rights; put *sth* right; 〈矯正する〉reform; mend; 〈除去する〉get rid of; 〈復旧する〉restore; 〈訂正する〉

がある. I want to have a private talk with you. | I'd like to have a word with you in private. / こ の事は内々に願います. Please keep this secret [to yourself].

ないぶ その建物は火事で内部が完全に焼失した. The building was gutted by the fire. / 警察は内部のものの仕業だとにらんだ. The police suspected (that it was) an inside job.

ないぶん これはご内聞に願いま

す. I would like you to keep this secret [to yourself].

ないや 田中は3塁へ内野フライを打ち上げてアウト. Tanaka popped out to the third baseman.

ないらん 内乱が起こった. A civil war broke out.

なお 彼は手術してなお悪くなった. He is even worse since the operation. / 英語をうまく話すことはむずかしいが, りっぱな英語を書くことはなおむずかしい. It

is hard enough to speak English well, but writing it well is still harder. / 日本の畜産業はなお発展の余地がある. There is room for the further development of Japan's livestock industry. / なんでもなおお余りあるやつだ. Hate is too mild a word for how I feel about him.

なおさら 地震は不意に来るからなおさら恐ろしい. Earthquakes are all the more frightening be-

なおる

correct; revise; amend; 〈改善する〉better; improve; 《文》remedy; 〈変更する〉change; alter; 〈治療する〉cure; heal; 〈換算する〉convert; 〈翻訳する〉translate [turn, 《文》render, put] (English into Japanese) ¶病気を治す cure [heal] sb's [sb of his] disease / 悪い癖を直す get over [break oneself of, get rid of] a bad habit / ネクタイを直す straighten one's tie / ドルを円に直す convert dollars into yen / 時計を直してもらう get sb to mend one's watch; have [get] one's watch mended (by) / 直[治]しようのない incorrigible (habits); 《文》irremediable (defects) ⇒ なおし (直しがきかない). 文例⇩

用法 mendとrepairの違いは,mendの方がrepairよりやや口語的で,「直す」と「修理する」の違いに近い. fixはmendの類(米).

なおる 直[治]る 〈修繕される〉be mended; (米) be fixed; 〈治癒される〉get well [better]; be cured of 《a disease》; recover from 《a disease》; 〈傷などが〉be healed; heal (up); 〈訂正される〉be corrected; 〈矯正される〉be reformed; 〈〈人を主語にして〉癖などが〉get rid [be cured] of 《a vice》; get over [break oneself of] 《a bad habit》; 〈復旧する〉be restored ¶治りかけの病人 a convalescent. 文例⇩

なおれ 名折れ (a) disgrace; (a) discredit; (a) dishonor ¶名折れになる bring disgrace on 《the family》; reflect discredit on 《the party》; be a dishonor [disgrace] to 《the city》.

なか¹ 中 〈内部〉the inside; the interior; 〈平均〉the mean ¶中をとる〈中庸を選ぶ〉take the mean;〈相手の主張に〉半ば歩み寄る meet sb halfway; 〈値段の交渉で〉split the difference / 雨の中を外出する go out in the rain / 中を通って〈go, flow〉through 《the town》/ 中に[で]〈内部〉inside; in; 《文》within; 〈中間〉between; among ⇒ あいだ 用法; midway (between) (中途); 〈まん中〉in the middle [center] (of); 《文》amid(st) / …を中に置いて with … between 《them》/ …の中へ into… / …の中から from within…; out of…; from among… / 中からかぎをかける lock 《the door》on the inside / 中1日置いて at [after] one day's interval. 文例⇩

なか² 仲 relations; relationship ¶仲がいい[悪い] be on good [bad] terms 《with》/ …との仲がうまくいく get on [along] well with… / 仲のよい友人 a good [a close, an intimate, a bosom] friend / 仲を裂く come between 《A and B》; part 《the lovers》; 《文》alienate 《A from B》; 《文》estrange 《A and B》. 文例⇩

ながあめ 長雨 a long rain; a long spell of rainy weather.

ながい¹ 長居 ¶長居をする stay (too) long; 〈他の人より〉outstay sb / 長居をして嫌われる outstay [overstay] one's welcome.

ながい² 長[永]い long; lengthy ¶長い間,長いこと ⇒ながく / 長い間の交際 a friendship of long standing / 長い目で見る take the long(-term) [a long-range] view (of) / 長い目で見れば in [if one takes] the long view. 文例⇩

ながいき 長生き a long life; 《文》longevity ¶長生きする live long; live to a great [ripe old] age; 〈他人より〉outlive sb / 長生きのlong-lived.

ながいす 長椅子 a sofa; a couch; 〈ベンチ〉a bench.

ながいも 長薯 a Chinese yam.

なかいり 中入り (米) an intermission; (英) an interval.

ながえ 轅 〈馬車・牛車の〉shafts ★そのうちの1本をさす時はもちろんa shaft となる.

なかおれ(ぼう) 中折れ(帽) a soft [felt] hat ¶中折れの山 the (creased) crown of a soft hat.

なかがい 仲買(業) brokerage; 〈人〉a broker; a middleman; a commission merchant [agent] ¶仲買をする act as broker / 仲買手数料 bro-

---

cause they are unexpected.

なおす どうかこの作文を直して下さいませんか. Would you be kind enough to look over this essay and correct my mistakes there may be? / 今家を直しているところです. Our house is under repair now. / その箱はどうにも直しようがないほどに壊れてしまった. The box was broken beyond repair. / 1マイルをキロメートルに直すといくらになりますか. How many kilometers are there in a mile? [What is a mile in kilometers?] / 早く病気を治して出動できるようになることを祈っています. We hope you will get well as early as possible and work with us again. / 彼らはがんを治す薬を開発している. They are developing a medicine for fighting cancer.

なおる それで彼の機嫌も直った. That put him in a better mood. / 傷は治るのに思いのほか日数がかかった. The wound took longer to heal than it should. / 余病さえ出なければ,すぐ治りますよ. Unless complications develop, you will soon be all right (again). / この薬で治るはずです. This medicine should bring about a cure. / もう1日遅れたらとうてい治らなかったと医者は言った. The doctor said that another day's delay would have made a cure hopeless. / 持って生まれた性質は直らない. One cannot change one's nature. [One's nature cannot be helped.] / 〈他人の欠点について言う時〉 A leopard cannot change his spots. 【諺】 直れ!【号令】As you were!

なか¹ これはたくさんある中のほんの1部だ. This is just [《文》but] one instance out of many. / この中からでも2つ選びなさい. Choose any two from (among) these. / 彼はクラスの中で一番よく出来る. He is the brightest boy in the class. / 戸は中から開いた. The door opened from within. / 中には何がはいっていますか. What does it contain? [What's inside (it)? / 中には良い本も悪いもある. Some books are good and some bad. / 窓を通して彼女の部屋の中が見えた. I could see through the window into her room. / ビフテキは外側はよく焼けて中が生の方が好きだ. I like beefsteak well done on the outside but rare on the inside.

なか² 2人は血を分けた仲だ. They are related by blood. / 彼らはとても仲がいい. They are great friends. / 彼らは仲がよくない. They don't get along too well.

ながい² 英語に熟達するには長い年月がかかる. It takes a long

ながく

kerage 《on bills》.

ながく 長く [永] ／〈長い間〉for a long time ; for long ; for ages [an age] ;〈永遠に〉for ever ★ for long と long は疑問文, 否定文に限られ, 肯定平叙文では for a long time が用いられる ¶長くなる get [〈文〉become, grow] longer ; be lengthened ;〈寝そべる〉lie down ; lie at full length ／〈長くする[延ばす]〉make sth longer ; lengthen ;〈時間について, また数学で直線などを〉prolong ／長く続いた long ;〈文〉long-continued ／長くかかる take a long time ／長くて3日 three days at the longest [most, outside]. 用例↓

ながぐつ 長靴 high [long] boots ;〈ゴム製の〉rubber boots.

なかごろ 中頃 ⇒なかば.

ながさ 長さ length ¶長さが同じである be (of) the same length ; be as long as.... 用例↓

ながされる 流される 〈風浪に〉be carried [washed] away ; be driven out [along] ;〈漂流する〉drift ;〈流罪になる〉be banished [exiled, deported]《to Siberia》. 用例↓

ながし 流し 〈台所の〉a sink ;〈ふろ場などの〉a draining floor ¶流しのギター弾き a strolling guitarist ／流しのタクシー a cruising taxi ; a cruiser ／流しの水切り台《米》a drainboard ;《英》a draining board.

ながしあみ 流し網 a drift net.

ながしうち 流し打ち 〈野球〉hitting to opposite field.

なかじきり 中仕切り a partition (wall).

ながしこむ 流し込む 〈型などに〉pour [lead] into 《a mold》;〈食べ物をのどに〉wash sth down.

ながしめ 流し目 ¶流し目に見る look sideways [〈文〉aslant]《at》; cast [give] a sidelong glance 《at》; look 《at sb》out of the corner of one's eye(s).

なかす¹ 中州 ⇒す¹.

なかす² 泣かす ⇒なかせる ¶泣かされる〈涙を流す〉be moved to tears ;〈苦労する〉suffer greatly《from》.

ながす 流す 〈注ぐ〉pour ;〈流れさせる〉let 《water》flow [run out] ;〈汚水を〉drain ; empty 《the bath》;〈浮流させる〉float ; set sth adrift ;〈洗い去る〉wash sth away [off] ;〈抵当などを〉forfeit (金の借り主が主語) ; foreclose (金の貸し主が主語) ;〈うわさを〉spread《rumors》;〈放送する〉broadcast ; beam ;〈タクシーが〉cruise (for fares) ¶川に流す throw sth into a river ／下水管に流す flush《sewage》down the drain ／水に流す ⇒みず 用例 ／背中を流す wash [rub down] sb's back ／試合を流す call off a game ／ギター弾きながら町を流して歩く go around《the bars of Shinjuku》performing at one place and another.

なかせる 泣かせる make sb cry ;〈感動させて〉move sb to tears ;〈厄介をかける〉give sb a lot [great deal] of trouble ¶赤ん坊を泣かせる start a baby (off) crying ; set a baby crying ／泣かせる話 a touching [pathetic] story.

なかぞら 中空 ⇒ちゅうくう. 用例↓

なかだか 中高 ¶中高の convex.

なかたがい 仲違い a quarrel ; disagreement ;《文》discord ;《文》dissension ¶仲たがいする quarrel [fall out] 《with》; break 《with》;《文》be estranged [alienated] 《from》/ 仲たがいしている be on bad terms 《with》. 用例↓

なかだち 仲持ち〈仲介〉mediation ;〈媒酌(ばいしゃく)〉matchmaking ;〈仲介人〉an intermediary ;〈周旋人〉an agent ; a middleman ;〈媒酌人〉a go-between ; a matchmaker ¶仲立ちをする act as go-between [intermediary] ; mediate《between》/ ...の仲立ちで《文》through the mediation [good offices] of....

ながたらしい 長たらしい long-winded ; overlong ; lengthy ;〈飽き飽きする〉tedious ¶長たらしい演説 a long and boring speech. 用例↓

なかだるみ 中弛み a slump ; 中だるみ(状態に)なる fall into a slump ; become less ac-

---

time to master English. ／彼はかなり長い間そこに座っていた. He sat there for quite a long while [for quite some time]. ／長いことこちらにいらっしゃるんですか. Have you been here long? ／彼はもう長いことはあるまい. I'm afraid he hasn't long to live. ／彼の長い日々は数えられている. 長い目で見れば君の努力は無意味でないだろう. If you take the long view [In the long run you will find that] your efforts will not have been wasted. ／長いものにはまかれろ. Don't kick against the pricks.《諺》／ If you can't beat 'em, join 'em. ★ 'em は them のこと. ／あんなに長いことやったことはない. I have never put in such a long day in my life. ／3センチばかり長過ぎる. It is about three centimeters too long.

ながいき 彼は長生きしないだろう. He will not live long. ／これでもう10年は長生きするぞ. This will add ten more years to my life. ／私がこのように健康で長生きできたのは一つには長年の海上生活のお陰です. One reason that I have been able to reach this age is because I have spent a good part of my life at sea. ／何ておめでたいやつだとお前は. 長生きするよ. They say that fools live to a ripe old age, so you should be all right !

ながく 長くかかりますか. Will it take you a long time to finish it? ／Will you be long? ／少しずつ夜が長くなる. The nights grow longer little by little.

ながさ 長さはどの位ですか. How long is it? ／ What is its length? ／長さは3メートルです. It is three meters long [in length]. ／今年はフランスの女性はどのくらいの長さのスカートをはいていますか. How long are French women wearing their skirts this season?

ながされる ボートは強風で沖へ流された. The boat was driven out to sea by the gale. ／そこでは野鳥の声のテープが流されていた. A tape recording of bird songs was kept playing there.

なかす² あの男のわがままにはずいぶん泣かされた. I was plagued to death by his wayward behavior.

なかせる 泣かせる話だなあ. What a moving [touching] story !／不孝者は親を泣かせる. A bad son will break his parents' hearts.

なかたがい 何で2人は仲違いしたのか. What has come between them? ／《文》What has estranged them from each other?

なかたらしい ひどく長たらしい言葉だ. It's a terrible [real] mouthful.

ながだんぎ 長談義 a long talk [speech]; a tedious [boring] lecture.

なかつぎ 中継ぎ ¶中継港 a transit port / 中継ぎ貿易 transit [entrepôt] trade.

-なかったら 《…がなければ》if it were not for; if it had not been for;《文》were it not for;《文》had it not been for; but for; without;《…でなければ》if … not; except; but. 文例↓

ながっちり 長っ尻 文例↓

なかつづき 長続き ¶長続きする last (for) a long time;《do not》last long. ⇒ながく ★ /…より長続きする last longer than…; outlast…. 文例↓

なかなおり 仲直り (a) reconciliation; peacemaking ¶仲直りする make peace 《with》; make it up 《with》; be [《文》become] reconciled 《with》/ 仲直りさせる《文》reconcile 《A and B》;《文》bring about a reconciliation 《between》; act as peacemaker 《between》. 文例↓

なかなか 《すこぶる》very; quite; exceedingly; highly; considerably; 《かなり》rather; pretty; fairly;《容易には》(not) easily;《(not) readily;《…どころでない》far from; not nearly ¶なかなか容易でない be far from easy. 文例↓

ながなが 長々 ¶長々と very long;《長たらしく》at great length;《冗長に》tediously;《長い間》for a long time [while] / 長々と横になる lie at full length《with》/ 長々と述べる dwell on sth at (great) length; go on and on about sth /《文》expatiate on sth.

なかにわ 中庭 a courtyard; a [an inner] court; a quadrangle.

なかね 中値 《平均値》an average price;《中央の値》a middle [medium] price.

ながねん 長年 (for) a long time;《文》for many years ¶長年の long; of long standing / 長年の研究の結果 the result /《文》fruit, product] of (one's) long years of research [study]. 文例↓

ながの 長の long; eternal ¶長の別れ parting for ever / 長のわずらい ⇒ながわずらい. 文例↓

なかば 半ば 《半分》half;《中央》the middle;《ある程度》partly; in part ¶半ば無意識に half unconsciously / 半ば口を開いたままで with one's mouth half-open / 半ば病気のためである be partly due to one's illness / 半ば商用半ば遊山で partly on business and partly for pleasure / 月の半ばに in the middle of the month / 1970年代の半ばに in the mid-1970s / 試験半ばに when the examinations are half over; halfway through the examinations / 演説の半ばに in the middle [《文》midst] of one's speech / 学業半ばで (when one is) halfway through school [college] /《年齢が》50代の半ばである be in one's middle fifties. 文例↓

ながばなし 長話 ¶長話をする have a long talk [chat]《with》; keep chatting《with sb》for a long time. 文例↓

ながびく 長引く《文》be prolonged;《文》be protracted;《だらだらと》drag on;《遅れる》be delayed ¶長引かす《文》prolong;《文》protract; delay. 文例↓

なかほど 中程 ⇒なかば, ちゅうかん[1] ¶…の中程で[に] in [at, about] the middle of…; halfway between… / 坂の中程にある be [stand] halfway up [down] the hill.

なかま 仲間《連中》a group; a company; a party; a set; a circle; a gang (主に若者や悪党の);《連れ》a companion;《同僚》a colleague; an associate;《同輩》a fellow; a mate;《同志》a comrade;《会友》a fellow member;《同業者》a fellow trader;《共謀者》a confederate; an accomplice ¶仲間に入る, 仲間入りする join《others》in sth; take part [《文》participate] in sth / 仲間に入れる take sb into the circle [party]; let sb join in sth / 仲間意識 fellow feeling / 仲間値段 a trade price / 仲間はずれになる be left out of《the game》; be excluded from《the group》/《のけ者にされる》《文》be ostracized / 仲間褒めをする speak highly of the work [achievement] of one's friend [colleague] /《口語》logroll /《口語》go in for logrolling /《口語》scratch each other's backs / 仲間割れ a split among friends / 仲間割れの, 仲間げんかの internal discord / 仲間割れをする, 仲間げんかをする quarrel [fall out] with each other;《3人以上が》quarrel

---

-なかったら 氏の財政的援助がなかったら, この事業は失敗していたであろう. But [Had it not been] for his financial aid, I should have failed in this undertaking. / こんなに忙しくなかったら行ってみるのだが. I would go there if I weren't so busy. / 大金持ちでなかったらそんなことは考えない. Only a very rich man would dream up a thing like that.

ながっちり 彼は長っちりでよく人に嫌われる. He often irritates people by [makes the mistake of] outstaying his welcome.

ながつづき この晴天は長続きする[はしない]だろう. This spell of fine weather will hold [soon break]. / 彼は何をやらせても長続きしない. He can't stick at anything. | He lacks staying power [perseverance].

なかなおり 仲直りしよう. Let us shake hands (and be friends again).

なかなか バスはなかなか来なかった. The bus was a long time (in) coming. / 彼はなかなかうんと言うまい. I doubt if he will consent readily. | I think you'll have difficulty in persuading him to agree. / 彼はなかなかの外交家だ. He is quite a diplomat.

ながなが 長々お世話になりました. Thank you for your kindness to me during my long stay.

ながねん 長年の苦労の末にやっと完成した. He accomplished it after many years' labor.

ながの これが長の別れとなるかもしれない. This may be our last meeting. / それが長の別れとなった. We parted never to meet again. / 彼女とそれが長の別れとなった. It was (to be) the last I saw of her.

なかば 仕事はもう半ば出来上がった. The work is already half finished [halfway to completion]. / 仕事はまだ半ばしか出来上がっていない. The work is only half finished. / 学期半ばで退学した. He left school in midterm.

ながばなし たいそう長話をいたしました. I am sorry to have

なかみ 中身(味) ⇨ ないよう.

なかみせ 中店, 仲見世 the *nakamise*; shops lining a passageway in the precincts of a *Shinto* shrine [Buddhist temple].

ながめ[1] 長め ¶長めの longish; rather [fairly, quite, 《文》somewhat] long / バットを長めに持つ hold the [one's] bat by the end of its handle.

ながめ[2] 眺め 〈景色を〉a view; a scene; 〈見晴らし〉a prospect / 春の眺め spring scenery / 眺めのいいハイウエー a scenic highway / 眺めのいい部屋 a room with a view. 文例⇩

ながめる 眺める look at; watch; 〈みつめる〉gaze at [on]; stare at; 〈傍観する〉look on; 〈見渡す〉view; take [get] a view of ¶ゆっくり眺める take a long look (at) / 一心に眺める gaze intently [fixedly] (at).

ながもち[1] 長持ち ¶長持ちする last [keep] a long time; 《do not》 last [keep] long [well]; 〈病人などが〉live a long time; 《do not》 live long ⇨ ながく 用法; 〈衣類が〉wear well; 〈道具などが〉stand long use.

ながもち[2] 長持 a *nagamochi*; a large oblong chest (for clothing, personal effects, etc.).

ながや 長屋 terrace(d) houses; houses in a row ¶三軒長屋 a house partitioned (lengthways) into three units.

なかやみ 中休み ⇨ きゅうけい ¶中休みをhave [take] a rest [break, breather]; have 《ten minutes'》 breathing space.

ながゆ 長湯 a long bath.

なかゆび 中指 the middle [second] finger.

なかよく 仲良く ¶仲よくする become friendly 《with》; make [be good] friends 《with》; get on [along] well 《with》 / 仲よく暮らす live together happily; get on [along] well 《with》. 文例⇩

なかよし 仲良し a bosom [a close, an intimate] friend; 《米口語》a buddy ¶子供時代の仲よし a childhood friend / 仲よしになる become friendly 《with》; make friends 《with》; chum up 《with》. 文例⇩

-ながら 〈…する間に〉while; as; with; 〈…であるとは言え〉while; although; 〈けれど〉but; yet; 〈にもかかわらず〉in spite of; for [with] all…; 〈ともに〉both; 〈いずれも〉all ¶歩きながら読む read 《a book》 as *one* walks; walk reading / 一杯やりながら話す drink *sake* while talking; talk over a bottle of *sake* / 泣きながら[涙ながらに]語る tell 《a story》 between *one's* sobs [with tears in *one's* eyes] / 貧乏ながら though I am poor; poor as I am / 金がありながら for all *one's* wealth / いやいやながら against *one's* will; reluctantly / 残念ながら I am sorry, but…; I'm afraid (that)…; to my regret / AとBと2つながら both A and B / ながら族 young people who listen to the radio or watch TV while working. 文例⇩

用法 日本語では「AをしながらBをする」という時, Aが従でBが主たる行為であることが多い. これに対して英語では, One does A while one does [while doing] B. というように, 主たる行為Bが while の後に来る. たとえば「彼はピーナツを食べながら映画を見た」は, He ate peanuts while he watched the movie. となる.

ながらえる 長[永]らえる 〈命が続く〉live on; 〈長生きする〉have a long life; 《do not》live long ⇨ ながく ★; 〈他の人より〉outlive [survive] *sb*.

ながらく 長らく ⇨ ながく. 文例⇩

ながれ 流れ 〈水流〉a stream; a current; 〈流派〉a school; 〈血統〉descent; lineage ¶水[溶岩]の流れ the flow of water [lava] / 車の流れ the flow of traffic / 時の流れ〈経過〉the passage [lapse] of time; 〈時勢〉the current [trend] of the times / 流れの速い[ゆるやかな]川 a fast-flowing [slow-moving] river / 流れを下る[上る] go down [up] the river; go downstream [upstream] / …の流れをくむ 血筋が〉be descended from…; 〈流派が〉belong to the school of… / 流れに従う[逆らう] swim with [against] the stream [current] / 流れ解散する disperse on arrival at *one's* destination without holding a closing ceremony / 流れ作業 an assembly-line system / 流れ弾(なま) a stray bullet [shot] / 流れ星 a shooting star; a meteor. 文例⇩

---

stayed talking for so long.

ながびく 彼の病気は長引いた. He took a long time to recover from his illness. / 滞在が2, 3日長引いた. I stayed there a few days longer.

なかほど 中程へお進み下さい. 〈車内のアナウンス〉Move along (the car), please. | (Pass) right down, please.

なかま 彼も入って来て話の仲間に加わった. He came in and joined in our talk. / 君もその仲間だろう. I suppose you are one of them [the group]. / 記者の仲間入りをした. He was admitted into the brotherhood of reporters.

ながめ 城から見た津軽平野の眺めは美しい. The castle commands a fine view of the Tsugaru plains. / 幾度見ても飽かぬ眺めは富士だ. I never tire of looking at Mt. Fuji.

ながもち[1] この天気は長持ちするでしょうか. Do you think this fine weather will hold [last (long)]? / 今の政府は長持ちしますまい. I don't think the present government will remain in power long.

なかよく 仲よく別れよう. Let us part (as) friends. / 2人はとても仲よく暮らしている. They live together in perfect harmony.

なかよし 彼らは大の仲よしだ. They are great friends.

-ながら 彼は新聞を読みながら電車を待った. He read a paper while he waited for the train. / 体に悪いと知りながらタバコはやめられません. I can't give up smoking, knowing though I do that it is bad for my health. / 失礼ながらお幾つでいらっしゃいますか. Excuse me for asking, but how old are you? / そう言いながら彼は部屋から出て行った. So saying [With this] he went out of the room.

ながらく 長らくご無沙汰いたしました. 〈手紙で〉Excuse me for my long silence.

ながれ 近代産業は流れ作業による大量生産の原則に基づいている. Modern industry is based on the principle of mass production on the assembly line. / 行く

ながれる 流れる 〈水などが〉 stream; flow; run; 〈流失する〉 be carried [washed] away; 〈浮流する〉 float; drift; 〈計画などが〉 be given up; 〈試合などが〉 be called off; 〈悪い方向に〉傾く run to 〈extravagance〉; lapse into 〈luxury〉; 〈質物が〉 be forfeited ¶流れ出す[出る] flow [stream, run, pour] out; gush out [《文》forth] (勢いよく); 〈材木などが〉 drift [be carried] away / 流れ込む flow in [into]; pour [run, stream] in [into]; 〈漂泊して〉 drift [wander] into 《a place》/ 流れ着く〈漂流して〉 drift to; 〈岸に打ち上げられる〉 be washed ashore. 文例⇩

ながわずらい 長患い a long [《文》protracted] illness ¶長患いをする suffer from a long illness; be ill [sick] for a long time. 文例⇩

なかんずく ⇨ことに, とりわけ.

なき¹ 泣き ¶〈芸に〉泣きがはいる《文》acquire great (technical) skill after years of discipline [hard training] / 泣きの涙で別れる part (from one's sweetheart) in tears / 泣きを入れる beg [《文》implore] sb for mercy.

なき² 亡き 〈the deceased; the late ¶亡き母 one's deceased mother / 今は亡き福田氏 the late Mr. Fukuda / 今は亡き小沢博士 Dr. Ozawa of happy memory / 亡き後 after one's death; when one is gone / 亡き数に入る be numbered among the dead. 文例⇩

なぎ 凪ぎ a calm ¶大なぎ a dead calm / 小なぎ a lull. 文例⇩

なきあかす 泣き明かす cry [《文》weep] all night (long); 《文》weep the night out [through].

なきおとす 泣き落とす get one's way 《from [with] sb》by crying; 《文》obtain sb's consent by force of tears / 泣き落とす win sb over by entreaties.

なきがお 泣き顔 a tear-stained [tearful] face.

なきがら 泣き骸 sb's remains; the corpse; the (dead) body.

なきくずれる 泣き崩れる break down (crying [in tears]); burst [dissolve] into tears.

なきくらす 泣き暮らす spend one's days in tears.

なきごえ¹ 泣き声 a tearful [《口語》weepy] voice; a cry.

なきごえ² 鳴き声 〈猛獣の〉a roar; 〈鳥獣の〉a cry; a call; 〈小鳥の〉a song; a note; a chirp; a twitter で なく².

なきごと 泣き言 ¶泣き言を言う make complaints to sb about sth; complain (about, of); grumble [whine] (about).

なぎさ 渚 the water's edge; 〈浜辺〉the beach, the shore.

なきさけぶ 泣き叫ぶ cry; scream; howl.

なきじゃくる 泣きじゃくる sob ¶泣きじゃくりながら言う sob out; say sth between sobs.

なきじょうご 泣き上戸 a crying drunk; a maudlin drinker.

なぎたおす なぎ倒す 〈草などを〉cut [mow] down; 〈負かす〉mow down; beat; defeat.

なきだす 泣き出す begin to weep; 〈わっと〉burst into tears; burst out crying ¶今にも泣き出しそうである be on the verge of tears / 今にも泣き出しそうな空模様 a threatening sky. 文例⇩

なきつく 泣き付く beg [《文》entreat, 《文》implore] sb to do [for sth]; throw oneself on sb's mercy.

なき(っ)つら 泣き(っ)面 ⇨なきがお ¶泣き面にはちで to make matters worse. 文例⇩

なきどころ 泣き所 a weak [vulnerable] point ¶弁慶の泣き所 one's Achilles(') heel.

なぎなた 長刀 a partisan; a pole sword.

なきねいり 泣き寝入り ¶泣き寝入りする〈寝る〉cry oneself to sleep; 〈忍ぶ〉bear sth silently; accept sth meekly. 文例⇩

なきはらう なぎ払う cut [mow] off ⇨なぎむし.

なきはらす 泣き晴らす ¶目を泣きはらす one's eyes are swollen with crying.

なきふす 泣き伏す throw oneself down in tears [crying].

なきほくろ 泣きぼくろ a mole under one's eye.

なきまね 泣きまね ¶泣きまねする pretend to be crying [《文》weeping]; 《文》feign tears.

なきむし 泣き虫 a crybaby.

なきやむ 泣きやむ stop crying [weeping]; cry oneself out.

なきりほうちょう 菜切り包丁 a kitchen knife (for cutting vegetables); a (broad-bladed) vegetable knife.

なきわかれ 泣き別れ ¶泣き別れをする part from sb in tears.

川の流れは絶えずして,しかもも との水にあらず. Ceaselessly the river flows, and yet the water is never the same.

ながれる 涙が彼女のほおを伝って流れた. Tears trickled down her cheeks. / 川上から桃がどんぶらこ,どんぶらこと流れて来た. A peach came floating down the stream, rolling over and over as it came. / 川が市中を流れている. A river flows [runs] through the city. / 群衆は広場から流れ出た. The crowd streamed out of the plaza.

ながわずらい 彼は長わずらいの後に死んだ. He died after a long illness.

なき² 亡き妻に捧ぐ.〈著者の献辞〉To the memory of my beloved wife.

なぎ 今日はいい凪だ. The sea is very calm today. / 凪になった. The wind has dropped [died away].

なきごと 彼の泣き言を辛抱強く聞いてやった. I listened patiently to his tale of woe.

なきだす 今にも泣き出しそうな空模様だ. It is threatening to rain. | It looks like rain.

なき(っ)つら これでは泣きっ面にはちだ. This is adding insult to injury!

なきねいり 泣き寝入りは禁物. If you don't ask, you won't get!

なく¹ 泣いても笑ってもこれが最後だよ. This is your very last chance, mind you. / 泣き泣き立ち去った. She went away weeping. / もうこれ以上は泣けません. We can't bring our price down any lower.

なぐ¹ 昼頃になって風が少し凪いだ. The wind let up a little toward noon.

なぐさみ うまく行ったらお慰みだね. I very much doubt if you

なきわらい 泣き笑い ¶泣き笑いする smile through one's tears / 泣き笑いの人生《文》a life with many a joy and sorrow; a life full of tears and laughter.

なく¹ 泣く 〈声を出して〉cry; 〈涙を流して〉weep; shed tears; 〈すすり泣く〉sob; 〈嘆き悲しむ〉wail; moan; 〈値段を割り引く〉⇨わりびく(割り引する) ¶大声で泣く cry loudly; howl; bawl; squall / 思い切り泣く have a good cry / 胸が張りさけるほど泣く cry one's heart out / 両手に顔を埋めて泣く cry into one's hands [with one's head (buried) in one's hands] / 乳が欲しくて泣く cry for milk / 痛くて泣く cry with pain / 泣きたい気がする feel like crying / 泣く泣く tearfully; with [in] tears; weeping; crying / 泣き泣き言う say sth between sobs [with tears in one's eyes]; sob out / 泣き泣き頼む beg《文》implore sb in tears to do [for sth]. 文例⇩.

なく² 鳴く 〈吠える〉howl; roar; 〈犬が〉bark (わんわん); whine (きゃんきゃん); yelp (子犬が); 〈猫が〉mew; meow; 〈牛が〉low; moo; 〈馬が〉neigh; whinny; 〈ろばが〉bray; 〈羊・やぎが〉bleat; 〈豚が〉grunt (ぶうぶう); squeal (きーきー); 〈ねずみが〉squeak; 〈猿が〉gibber; chatter; 〈鹿が〉bell; 〈おんどりが〉crow; 〈めんどりが〉cackle; cluck; 〈ひよこが〉peep / 〈小鳥が〉sing; chirp; twitter; 〈からすが〉caw; 〈はとが〉coo; 〈ふくろうが〉hoot; 〈あひるが〉quack; 〈蛙が〉croak; 〈虫が〉sing; chirp; chirrup ¶鳴かず飛ばずでいる 〈目立たぬようにしている〉lie low; keep one's head down; avoid the limelight / くすぶっている stay《文》remain obscure [inactive].

なぐ¹ 凪ぐ become calm; calm down; 〈風が〉die down; drop; abate. 文例⇩.

なぐ² 薙ぐ mow; cut down.

なぐさみ 慰み 〈娯楽〉(an) amusement; a pastime; pleasure; 〈気ばらし〉(a) diversion; (a) recreation ¶慰みに for pleasure [fun]; as a [by way of] pastime; to amuse《文》divert oneself / 慰み半分に (partly) for fun [pleasure] / 慰み物にする make a plaything (of). 文例⇩.

なぐさめ 慰め (a) comfort; (a) consolation;《文》(a) solace; (a) diversion 〈気ばらし〉¶慰めを求める seek solace [consolation]《in》; take comfort《in, from》/ 慰め顔に consolingly.

なぐさめる 慰める comfort; give comfort to; console; 〈和らげる〉soothe; 〈気を晴らす〉divert; 〈廃止する〉do away with; 〈楽しませる〉amuse ¶人の悲しみを慰める console sb in his sorrow / 目[耳]を慰める feast one's eyes [ears]《on》.

なくす 無[亡]くす 〈失う〉lose; be deprived [《文》bereft] of; 〈除去する〉get rid of; remove; 〈廃止する〉do away with; 〈使い果す〉run out of ¶子供を亡くした母親 a mother whose child has died; a bereaved mother.

なくて 〈…なしで〉without; 〈ないために〉for want [lack] of; 〈…でなくて…〉not...but...; instead of... ¶金がなくて困る be hard up for [be badly in need of] money / なくてならない 〈人が主語〉cannot do without sth;〈物が主語〉be indispensable (to); be necessary (to, for) / なくてもいい 〈人が主語〉can do without sth;〈物が主語〉be unnecessary (for, to) / なくて済ます do without sth; dispense with sth. 文例⇩.

なくなす 無[亡]くなす ⇨なくす.

なくなる 無[亡]くなる 〈紛失する〉be [get] lost; be missing; 〈切れる〉run short [out]; be used up; 〈消える〉disappear; vanish; be gone; 〈死ぬ〉die; pass away (蜘蛛田に) ¶無くなった本 a lost [missing] book / 無くなっているのに気がつく miss sth. 文例⇩.

なぐりあい 殴り合い an exchange of blows; 〈けんか〉fighting; a (fist)fight;《英俗》a punch-up ¶なぐり合いになる begin to fight; come to blows《with》/ なぐり合いをしている be fighting《with》. 文例⇩.　　　　「《with》.

なぐりあう 殴り合う exchange blows [punches]

なぐりかえす 殴り返す hit [punch] sb back; return sb's blow [punch].

なぐりかかる 殴り掛かる hit [strike] (out) at sb.

なぐりがき なぐり書き ¶なぐり書きする write hastily [carelessly]; scribble; scrawl.

なぐりこみ 殴り込み ¶なぐり込みをかける make a raid (on); storm (a house).

なぐりころす 殴り殺す beat sb to death; strike sb dead.

---

can pull it off.

なぐさめ パリからの彼女の便りが私の唯一の慰めだ. Her letters from Paris are my only comfort. | I find my only consolation in her letters from Paris.

なぐさめる 何事も運命だと思って自らを慰めた. I consoled myself with the thought that there was no point in struggling against fate. | なんとか母を慰めようとした. I tried hard to cheer my mother up.

なくす 片腕をなくして帰って来た. He came back minus an arm. / 東京からスモッグをなくしてしまえたらなあ. If only we could get rid of [do away with] the smog in Tokyo! / 彼は愛児を亡くしてあきらめきれないでいる. He cannot get over the loss of his beloved son.

なくて 彼がなくて彼の細君がやって来た. It was his wife, not he, that came. / 米は日本人にはなくてはならぬ食料だ. Rice is an indispensable food for the Japanese. / 無くて七癖. Every man has his peculiarities [peculiar habits].

なくなる 僕の時計が無くなった. I've lost my watch. | My watch is missing. / 便箋が無くなった. We have run out of writing [letter] paper. / 燃料が無くなりかけている. The fuel supply is low. / 熱は無くなった. My temperature has come down (to normal). | The fever has left me. / そうなれば僕が上京する必要が無くなるのだが. That would make it unnecessary for me to go up to Tokyo. / T先生が亡くなられたと聞いてびっくりしました. I was shocked at the news of Prof. T's death.

なぐりあい 口論しているうちにかっとなって2人は危なくなぐり

なぐりたおす 殴り倒す knock [strike] *sb* down.
なぐりつける 殴り付ける ⇒ なぐる.
なぐる 殴る hit; beat; thump; punch; 《文》strike; knock; give [deal] *sb* a blow; slap (平手で) ¶頭をなぐる strike [beat] *sb* on the head / 顔をなぐる hit [strike] *sb* in [across] the face / 思い切りなぐる give *sb* a good beating / ぼかぼかなぐる rain blows [punches] on *sb*.
なげ 投げ 《相撲などの》 a throw; 《放棄》giving up; 《投了》resigning.
なげあげる 投げ上げる throw [toss, fling] up.
なげいれ 投げ入れ 《生け花》 free-style flower arrangement.
なげいれる 投げ入れる ⇒ なげこむ.
なげうつ 擲つ throw [fling] away; give up ¶仕事をなげうつ give up [abandon] *one's* job / 生命をなげうつ sacrifice 《文》 lay down] *one's* life (for) / 地位をなげうつ resign (from) *one's* position / 一命をなげうって at the cost [sacrifice] of *one's* life.
なげうり 投げ売り a sacrifice sale; 《蔵払い》a clearance sale ¶投げ売りする sell *sth* at a loss [sacrifice].
なげかえす 投げ返す throw [hurl] back.
なげかける 投げ掛ける throw [hurl] 《at》¶光を投げ掛ける throw light (on, over) / 疑問を投げ掛ける throw (some) doubt on 《*sb's* theory》.
なげかわしい 嘆かわしい regrettable; deplorable; sad; 《文》 lamentable ¶嘆かわしい事 a matter for regret / 嘆かわしい事態 a deplorable [sad] situation. 文例⇩
なげき 嘆き 《文》 grief; sorrow; 《文》 lamentation ¶嘆きのあまり頭がおかしくなる go nearly mad with grief / (エルサレムにある)嘆きの壁 the Wailing Wall (of the Jews) / 嘆きの種 a cause of (constant) grief / 嘆きに沈む be lost [sunk] in grief. 文例⇩
なげく 嘆く 《嘆息する》 sigh 《over》; heave a sigh; 《慨嘆する》 deplore; 《惜しむ》 regret; 《悲しむ》 grieve 《over》;《文》lament 《for, over》;《泣き悲しむ》 weep [mourn] 《over》 ¶死を嘆く mourn [lament] *sb's* death / 嘆き暮らす spend *one's* days in grief.
なげこむ 投げ込む throw [fling, 《文》 cast] in [into] ¶(船から)海に投げ込む throw *sth* overboard.

なげすてる 投げ捨てる throw [cast, fling] *sth* away.
なげたおす 投げ倒す throw *sb* down.
なげだす 投げ出す 《放り出す》 throw [《文》 cast] *sth* out (of the window);《地面などに》throw [fling] *sth* down (on the floor);《放棄する》 abandon; give [throw] up ¶足を投げ出す stretch out *one's* legs / 命を投げ出す sacrifice [《文》lay down] *one's* life (for) / 仕事を投げ出す give [throw] up *one's* job. 文例⇩
なげつける 投げ付ける throw [fling, hurl] 《at》;《投げ倒す》 throw *sb* down ¶腹立ちまぎれに花瓶を壁に投げつける dash a vase against the wall in anger.
なげとばす 投げ飛ばす fling [hurl] away [off].
なけなし 無けなし ¶なけなしの金 what (little) money *one* has.
なげなわ 投げ縄 a lasso 《*pl.* -(e)s》; a lariat ¶投げ縄で捕える catch 《a giraffe》 with a lasso; lasso 《a steer》.
なげに 投げ荷《物》 jettisoned cargo; 《行為》 jettison.
なげや 投げ矢 《遊び》 darts 《単数扱い》;《矢》 a (toy) dart.
なげやり[1] 投げ遣り negligence; neglect ¶投げやりな careless; slovenly; slipshod / 投げやりに carelessly; in a slipshod manner / 投げやりにする 《怠る》 neglect; be negligent [neglectful] about [《文》of];《ぞんざいにする》 do in a slovenly way / 《中途でほったらかす》 leave 《*one's* work》 unfinished. 文例⇩
なげやり[2] 投げ槍 a javelin ⇒ やり.
なける 泣ける ⇒ なかす (泣かされる), なかせる (泣かせる話).
なげる 投げる 《ほおる》 throw; hurl; pitch; cast; fling; toss 《軽く》;《倒す》 throw down;《断念する》 give [throw] up; throw away; abandon ¶石を投げる throw a stone 《at》/ 身を投げる drown *oneself* (in the river); jump 《from the roof》 to *one's* death / 勝負を投げる give [throw] up the game; resign.
-なければ ⇒ -なかった ¶勉強しなければ if *one* does not work hard; unless *one* works hard. 文例⇩
なこうど 仲人 《人》 a go-between; a matchmaker;《事》matchmaking ¶仲人をする act as go-between; arrange a marriage 《between A and B》/ 仲人口をきく say all sorts of nice

合いを始めるところだった. Their argument [quarrel] got so heated that they almost [nearly] came to blows.
なげかわしい 彼がまた同じ失敗を繰り返したのは実に嘆かわしいことだ. It is most regrettable [a matter for great regret] that he should have committed the same error again.
なげき 彼の行状が両親の嘆きの種であった. His behavior was a great grief to his parents.
なげだす 彼女は編み物を投げ出して外へ出た. She left off her knitting and went out.
なげやり[1] 彼はどんな仕事も投げやりにはしない. He never does a slovenly job.
なげる 犬に骨を投げてやった. I threw a bone to the dog. / 男子砲丸投げで 16.71 メートルを投げて日本新記録を樹立した. He established a new Japanese record in the men's shot-put event with a throw of 16.71 meters.
-なければ この本でなければだめだ. It must be [It has got to be] this book. | No book but this will do.

なごむ この音楽を聴くと心がなごむ. This music gives me peace of mind.
なごり これがお名残りになるかもしれません. I may not see you again. | This may be our last meeting. / 昔の栄華は今やまったくその名残りをとどめていない. Of its former glory not a trace [vestige] remains. / 石碑が小泉八雲の旧居の名残りをとどめているに過ぎない. A stone monument is all that is left to tell where once Lafcadio Hearn lived.

なごむ 和む become friendly; calm down. 文例⇩
なごやかな 和やかな 〈静かな〉quiet; 〈平和な〉peaceful; 《文》harmonious; 〈友好的な〉friendly; amicable; 〈穏やかな〉mild; calm; gentle; 〈にこやかな〉friendly; warm; 《文》amiable; 《文》genial ¶和やかな家庭 a happy [harmonious] family / 和やかに amicably; 《文》genially; peacefully.
なごり 名残り 〈痕跡〉remains; traces; 《文》vestiges; 〈余波〉⇨よば ¶名残りの last; farewell; remaining; lingering / お名残り公演 a farewell [one's last] appearance [performance] / 名残りをとどめない leave no trace / 名残りを惜しむ be reluctant [《文》feel loath] to part from sb [to leave 《a place》] / 名残りに as a keepsake [memento] / 名残り惜しげに reluctantly. 文例⇩
ナサ 〈アメリカ航空宇宙局〉NASA (the National Aeronautics and Space Administration の略).
なさけ 情け 〈同情〉sympathy; 〈哀れみ〉pity; 〈親切〉kindness; 〈慈悲〉charity; mercy; 《文》compassion; 〈仁慈〉《文》benevolence; 〈愛情〉love ¶情けのある, 情け深い〈同情的な〉sympathetic; 〈親切な〉kind; 〈思いやりのある〉tenderhearted; 〈思いやりのある〉thoughtful; considerate; 〈慈悲深い〉《文》merciful; charitable; 〈仁慈な〉《文》benevolent / 情けを知らぬ, 情け知らずの heartless; coldhearted; merciless; unfeeling / 情けを掛ける be kind to sb; show sb sympathy; take pity [《文》have compassion] on sb / 情けをこう 《文》implore sb for mercy / 情けにすがる throw oneself on sb's mercy; place oneself under sb's wing / お情けですから for pity's [mercy's] sake / 情け容赦もなく mercilessly; unmercifully; uncharitably; relentlessly. 文例⇩
なさけない 情けない 〈哀れな〉pitiable; pitiful; 〈惨めな〉miserable; wretched; sad; 〈恥ずべき〉shameful; 〈残念な〉regrettable ¶情けない死に方をする 〈恥ずべき〉die a disgraceful [《文》an ignominious] death; 〈惨めな〉die a dog's death [like a dog] / 情けないほど投げやりにされている be sadly [deplorably, 《文》grievously] neglected / 情けなくなる feel

miserable [wretched]. 文例⇩
なさす 名指す name; call [mention] sb by name; 〈任命する〉《文》designate; 《文》nominate ¶名指しで頼む name sb to do.
なさそう do not appear [seem]; be unlikely [not likely]; be improbable.
なさぬなか 生さぬ仲 ¶生さぬ仲である be not one's own [real] parent [child].
なし 梨 a pear ¶なしの木 a pear tree. 文例⇩
なしくずし 済し崩し ¶なし崩しで[に]《pay》by [in] installments; 《buy》on the installment plan; 《offer for sale》on the easy-payment[-purchase] system; 《do》little by little [a little at a time].
-なしで …無しで without…; with no… ¶…なしで済ます［やってゆく］manage [do] without…; dispense with….
なしとげる 成し遂げる accomplish; 《文》achieve; carry 《one's project》through; carry out 《a plan》; pull sth off; bring sth off.
なじみ 馴染み 〈状態〉familiarity; 〈人〉an old acquaintance [friend] ¶なじみの familiar; close / なじみになる ⇨なじむ / なじみ客 an old [a regular] customer. 文例⇩
なじむ 馴染む 〈親しくなる〉become familiar [friendly, acquainted] 《with》; 〈慣れる〉get used [grow accustomed] 《to》; 〈順応する〉adapt oneself 《to the new surroundings》; 〈風土に〉get acclimatized [《米》acclimated] 《to》; 〈なつく〉become attached 《to》; take 《to》; 〈靴などが〉get to fit one. 文例⇩
なじる 詰る 〈しかる〉scold; 《口語》tell sb off; 《文》rebuke 《sb for sth》; 《文》reprove; 《文》reproach; 〈とがめる〉take sb to task; 〈非難する〉《文》censure.
なす¹ 〈植〉an eggplant; an aubergine.
なす² 成す 〈形成する〉form; make; 〈構成する〉《文》constitute ¶財を成す make a fortune [《口語》pile]; 《文》amass riches / 円をなして in a circle. 文例⇩
なす³ 為す 〈する〉do; make; perform; 〈試みる〉try; attempt; 〈仕遂げる〉carry out [through]; 《文》accomplish; 《文》achieve ¶害[益]をなす do sb harm [good] / なす所を知らない do not know what to do. 文例⇩
なずな 〈植〉a shepherd's purse.
なする 擦る 〈塗りつける〉rub 《in, into》;

なさけ 君の情けがかえって彼のあだとなった. Your kindness proved his ruin. / 彼は先生のお情けで及第した. He only passed thanks to the mercy of his teacher [by his teacher's special favor]. / 情けは人のためならず. One good turn deserves another. 〖諺〗
なさけない 本当に情けない. Oh! How miserable I am !／カンニングをしたのか. 何て情けないやつだ. You cheated in the examination? I'm ashamed of you!
なさそう 彼はこの種の仕事をした経験は余りなさそうだ. He does not appear to have much experience at [of] this kind of job. / 彼がこの提案を拒絶することはまずなさそうだ. It is hardly probable [It isn't likely] that he will decline this offer.
なし 以来彼からは全くなしのつぶてだ. I have heard absolutely nothing from him since.
-なしで 彼なしではとてもやっていけない. We cannot do without him. / He cannot be dispensed with.
なじみ 私はこの町にはまだなじ

みが浅い. I am still [as yet] a virtual stranger in this town.
なじむ 2年目になって, 彼はようやく学校になじんできた. By his second year he began to feel at home in the school. / 靴ははいているうちに足になじんでくるものだ. Shoes get to fit one's feet through [with] wearing.
なす² これは意味を成さない. This does not make sense.
なす³ 当時アテネはスパルタのなすがままになっていた. At that time Athens was at the mercy of Sparta.

spread 《over》⇒ぬる ¶罪[責任]をなすりつける put [lay, fix] the blame on *sb*; lay the blame at *sb*'s door.

なぜ why?; how?; 《文》for what reason [purpose]?; 《口語》what...for? ¶なぜならば because; for / なぜだか分からないが I don't know why, but...; somehow; for some unknown reason. 文例⇩

なぞ 謎 a riddle; a puzzle; 《文》an enigma; 〈神秘〉a mystery; 〈暗示〉a hint ¶なぞの人 a mystery man / なぞを掛ける set [give] *sb* a puzzle; 〈暗示する〉hint at *sth*; drop *sb* a hint / なぞを解く solve a riddle [mystery] / なぞを悟る take the hint / なぞなぞ遊びをする exchange riddles 《with》. 文例⇩

なぞらえる 〈たとえる〉compare [《文》liken] 《A》to 《B》; 〈まねする〉imitate; model *sth* on [after] 《a pattern》. 文例⇩

なぞる trace; follow.

なた 鉈 a hatchet.

なだ 灘 an open sea ¶遠州なだ the Sea of Enshu.

なだい 名代 ⇒なだかい.

なだかい 名高い famous; well-known; 《文》noted; 《文》celebrated; 《文》renowned; notorious (悪い意味で) ¶歌や物語で名高い 《文》famed in song and story / 名高くなる become famous 《for》; win fame [《文》renown] 《for》. 文例⇩

なだたる 名だたる ⇒なだかい.

なたね 菜種 rape seed ¶菜種油 rape(-seed) [colza] oil.

なたまめ 鉈豆 a sword bean.

なだめる 宥める soothe; calm *sb* (down); 《文》allay; 《文》appease; pacify ¶怒りをなだめる calm [allay] *sb*'s anger [《文》wrath] / なだめすかす soothe and humor.

なだらか ¶なだらかな〈傾斜の〉gently-sloping 〈hills〉; gentle [easy] 〈slopes〉; 〈摩擦のない〉smooth / なだらかに gently; smoothly.

なだれ 雪崩 an avalanche; a snowslide ¶なだれに押し流される be carried away by an avalanche / なだれを打つ群衆 a surging crowd / (動物の群れなどが)なだれを打って逃げる stampede / 表層なだれ a surface snowslide [avalanche].

なだれこむ なだれ込む rush [surge] into 《a hall》. 文例⇩

ナチ(ス) 〈政党〉the Nazis; 〈主義〉Nazism ¶ナチス党員 a Nazi.

なつ 夏 summer; summertime; the summer season ¶夏のある日 one summer day; one day in summer / 夏の初め[終わり]に in early [late] summer; early [late] in summer / 夏の盛りに in [at] the height of summer; in midsummer / 夏を過ごす spend the summer 《at Karuizawa》/ 夏風邪 a summer [hot weather] cold / 夏枯れ時 the slack summer season / 夏時間(米) daylight saving time; 《英》summer time / (大相撲の)夏場所 the summer *sumo* tournament / 夏服 summer clothes; a summer suit; clothes (a suit, a dress, a garment) for summer wear / 夏負けする suffer from [《文》succumb to] the summer heat / 夏みかん a Watson pomelo; a thick-skinned grapefruit-like fruit / 夏向きの for summer use; 〈衣服〉for summer wear / 夏物 summer goods; 〈衣服〉⇒夏服 / 夏休み the summer holidays [vacation] / 夏やせする lose weight in summer / 夏山〈夏の山〉mountains in summer; 〈登山〉summer mountaineering. 文例⇩

なついん 捺印 ¶捺印する seal; put *one*'s seal on [《文》affix *one*'s seal to] 《a paper》.

なつかしい 懐かしい dear (old) 〈friends〉; 《文》fondly-remembered 〈scenes〉; 〈people〉that *one* thinks of [recalls] with affection [nostalgia] ¶懐かしい思い出 happy [sweet, fond] memories; memories (that are) dear to *one* / 懐かしく思う, 懐かしがる long for; 《文》yearn after [for]; feel a longing for; miss [yearn for] / 懐かしそうに longingly; wistfully / 懐かしそうに見る gaze fondly 《at》; fix *one*'s eyes wistfully 《on》. 文例⇩

なつく 懐く get [《文》become] attached 《to》; take 《to》; come to love; be tamed (動物が) ¶なついている be attached 《to》; be *one*'s great friend. 文例⇩

ナックルボール 〈野球〉a knuckle ball.

なづけおや 名付け親 〈洗礼名を与えられた子

なぜ なぜあんなことをやったんだ. What made you behave like that? | What did you do a thing like that for? / なぜパーティに行きたくないの. Why don't you [Why is it (that) you don't] want to go to the party? / なぜっていうこともないさ. There's no particular reason (for it).

なぞ 辞職しろというなぞですか. Is that a hint that you want me to resign? / やっと君のなぞが読めた. Now I see what you are hinting. / エジプト人のピラミッド建設の技術の中には今なお解けないなぞとなっているものがある. Some of the Egyptians' pyramid-building techniques still remain mysteries. / その旅客機の爆発は今なおなぞに包まれている. Mystery still cloaks the explosion of the airliner. / なぞなぞなあに. Riddle me a riddle, what's this?

なぞらえる 人は神の姿になぞらえて造られたものである. Man is created in the image of God.

なだかい 九十九湾は景色がいいので名高い. Tsukumo Bay is noted [widely known] for its beautiful scenery. / その町は避暑地として名高い. The town is famous [has a name] as a summer resort.

なだれこむ 群衆は我先きにと会場へなだれ込んだ. The crowd rushed [poured] into the hall.

なつ うちの学校は7月21日から夏休みに入ります. Our school breaks up for the summer on the 21st of July.

なつかしい 自分の故郷を懐かしく思わないものはない. There is no one who doesn't yearn for [feel nostalgic about] his hometown.

なつく その子は私になかなかなつきませんでした. The child didn't take easily to me. / 子供たちはすっかり彼女になついてしまった. The children have become very fond of her. / She has completely won the hearts of the children. / この犬は僕にすっ

なつける 933 なに

なつける 懐ける〈子供などを〉make《a child》attached to one;《文》gain sb's affection;《文》win sb's heart; win [gain] sb over (to one's side);〈動物を〉tame.

なづける 名付ける name《a satellite Osumi》; christen 《洗礼名を与える》 ⇨ な¹ (名をつける), めいめい¹ (命名する). 文例⇩

なっせん 捺染 (textile) printing.

なつっこい 懐っこい affectionate; affable. 文例⇩

なって(い)ない be no good; be a (complete) failure.

-なっている ⇨ はず. 文例⇩

ナット【機】a nut ¶ボルトをナットで締める fix [attach] a bolt with a nut.

なっとう 納豆 fermented soybeans.

なっとく 納得〈承諾〉agreement;《文》consent;〈了解〉understanding ¶納得する〈承諾する〉agree (to);《文》consent [give one's consent] 《to》;〈了解する〉understand,〈得心する〉be convinced (of, that...); satisfy oneself (of, that...); accept (that...) / 納得させる make sb consent (to); talk sb round; persuade sb to do [into doing]; convince sb of sth; bring sth home to sb / 納得ずくで with mutual consent; with sb's consent. 文例⇩

なっぱ 菜っ葉 ⇨ な² ¶菜っ葉服 overalls; a workman's blouse.

ナップザック a knapsack; a (small) rucksack.

なつめ 棗【植】a jujube tree;〈実〉a jujube;〈茶道具〉a (lacquered) tea caddy.

なつメロ 懐メロ a well-loved old song;《口語》a golden oldie.

なであげる 撫で上げる comb [brush] back.

なでおろす 撫で下ろす stroke down ¶ほっと胸をなで下ろす give [heave] a (deep) sigh of relief; feel (greatly) relieved.

なでがた 撫で肩 sloping shoulders.

なでぎり 撫で斬り ¶なでぎりにする cut [mow] down; make a clean sweep of 《one's opponents》.

なでしこ【植】a (fringed) pink.

なでつける 撫で付ける〈髪を〉smooth [comb] down 《one's hair》¶ (水油などで)髪をなでつける slick down one's hair.

なでる 撫でる stroke 《one's beard》; pass one's hand (over, across); comb [smooth] down 《one's hair》.

-など ...等 and so forth [on]; and [or] the like; and what not; et cetera (略: &c., etc.). ¶私などのような者には for the likes of me / 絵画彫刻などの美術品 works of art, such as paintings and sculptures. 文例⇩

ナトー〈北大西洋条約機構〉NATO (the North Atlantic Treaty Organizationの略) ★NATO は [néitou] と発音する.

ナトリウム【化】sodium.

ななかまど【植】a mountain ash; a rowan (tree).

ななくさ 七草〈春の〉the seven spring herbs;〈秋の〉the seven autumn flowers;〈正月の七日〉the Seventh of January.

ななころびやおき 七転び八起き tenacity of purpose;〈有為転変〉the vicissitudes of fortune; the ups and downs of life. 文例⇩

ななし 名無し ¶名なしの nameless; anonymous; unknown / 名なしの権兵衛《戯》a Mr. Unknown.

ななつ 七つ seven ¶7つ目の the seventh / 七つ道具 paraphernalia.

ななふしぎ 七不思議 the seven wonders (of the world).

ななめ 斜め ¶斜めの slanting; oblique;〈対角の〉diagonal / 斜めに obliquely; slantwise; aslant; diagonally / 斜めに引いた線 a line drawn at [on] a slant / 斜めに見る give sb [sth] a sidelong glance / 斜めにする[なる] incline; slant / (風が)斜め後ろから吹く blow obliquely from behind / ご機嫌斜めである be in a bad [be not in a good] mood [temper] / ご機嫌斜めならず be [look] highly pleased; be in a good mood. 文例⇩

なに 何 what? ¶何が何でも by any [all possible] means; whatever happens; by some means or other; at any cost; by hook or by

---

かわいがっている. This dog is a great friend of mine.

なづける その旧石器文化はその遺物の出土したフランスの地名オーリニャックの名を取ってオーリニャック文化と名付けられた. That paleolithic culture was named the Aurignacian from Aurignac, in France, where its remains were first discovered.

なつっこい この犬は懐っこい. This dog will take to anybody.

-なっている 旅館ということになっているけれど, 滞在客があるなんて聞いたことがない. It calls itself [claims to be] a hotel, but I have never heard of anyone staying there. / ここでは禁煙と

いうことになっているのです. Smoking is supposed to be forbidden here.

なっとく 彼が間違っているのだということを納得させることができなかった. I couldn't convince him that he was wrong. / そんなばかなことはやめると彼をうまく納得させた. I succeeded in persuading him to give up such a stupid idea. / 私の説明で納得が行きましたか. Are you completely satisfied with my explanation? / みんな納得したかね. Is everybody happy now?

-など 君に外交員などやれるかい. Could you work as a door-to-door salesman or something like

that? / 彼女を怒らせたりなどしなかったろうね. I hope you didn't offend her or anything. / 彼はうそなど言ったことはなかった. He was never known to tell a lie. / 日曜などによく釣りに出かけたものです. I used to go out fishing on Sundays. / 私などのような者にはとてもできません. That is quite impossible for the likes of me.

ななころびやおき 人生は七転び八起きだ. Life is full of ups and downs.

ななめ 船は川を斜めに横切って行った. The boat moved diagonally across the river.

なにか crook / 何はさておき, 何をおいても first of all ; above all ; before everything (else) / 何は ともあれ in any case ; at all events / 何をす るにも in doing anything ; in everything / 何 から何まで (anything and) everything ; all (about *sth*). 文例⇩

なにか 何か〈肯定〉some ; something ; 〈否定・ 疑問〉any ; anything ¶なにか何か a pot or something (of the sort [kind]) / 何か食べる[飲む]物 something to eat [drink] / 何か訳が あって for some reason (or other) / 何かかに か this or that ; something or other ; one thing or another / 何かしら somehow (or other) ; I don't know why, but… / 何かと, 何かにつけ in various ways ; one way or another ;〈機会 あるごとに〉whenever opportunity offers. 文例⇩

なにがし 某 a certain person ; Mr. So-and-so ¶なにがしかの金 some [a certain sum of] money / 木村なにがしという人 a (certain) Mr. Kimura.

なにくそ 何糞 文例⇩

なにくれと(なく) 何くれと(なく) ⇨なにか(何かと).

なにくわぬかお 何食わぬ顔 ¶何食わぬ顔で 〈平気と〉unconcernedly ; nonchalantly ; with an air of perfect nonchalance ;〈知らぬ顔を して〉pretending not to know ;《文》affecting [feigning] ignorance ; as if nothing had happened / 何食わぬ顔をする look innocent ; 《文》feign ignorance ;《文》assume a nonchalant air.

なにげない 何気ない〈何心ない〉casual ;〈平 然とした〉unconcerned ¶何気ない風をする 〈平然としている〉look unconcerned [nonchalant] ;〈しらを切る〉look innocent ;《文》 feign ignorance / 何気ない様子で in a casual manner ; as if nothing had been the matter with one / 何気なく unintentionally ; casually ;《pick *sth* up》without much attention ;《say *sth*》without much thought / 何気なく言った言葉 a casual remark. 文例⇩

なにごと 何事〈疑問〉what? ;〈何かあること〉 something ¶何事にも in everything ; in anything one does / 何事もなく quietly ; uneventfully ; smoothly ; without a hitch ; without accident [mishap]. 文例⇩

なにしろ 何しろ〈とにかく〉anyhow ; at any rate ;〈なぜなら〉for ; because ;〈ご承知のよ うに〉as you know [see]. 文例⇩

なにせ 何せ ⇨なにしろ.

なに(っ) 何(っ) what! ; why! 文例⇩

なにとぞ ⇨どうぞ.

なにぶん 何分〈ともかく〉anyway ; anyhow ; 〈ご承知[ご覧]のように〉as you know [see] ; 〈どうか〉please ¶何分天気が悪いので since the weather is bad, as you see [know].

なにほど 何程 how many [much]? ⇨いくら, どの²(どのくらい). 文例⇩

なにも 何も no ; nothing ; not...anything ; not ...any ¶何もかも (anything and) everything / 何もかも承知している know everything [all] (about) / 何もかも話す tell everything (about) ; tell the whole story (of) ;〈白 状する〉make a clean breast of *sth* ; own up. 文例⇩

なにもの¹ 何者 who? ¶何者も〈だれでも〉 whoever ;〈否定〉nobody ; no one / 何者かが somebody. 文例⇩

なにもの² 何物 ⇨なに. 文例⇩

なにやかや 何やかや ¶何やかやと ⇨なにか (何かにか, 何かと). 文例⇩

なにゆえ 何故 ⇨なぜ.

なにより 何より ¶何よりな[の] most… ; best / …が何よりだ Nothing is better than … ; You can't [Nothing can] beat… ; …is the most important thing / 何よりも above all ; more than anything else ; before everything else ; first of all ; of all things / 何より悪いこ とには The worst of [The worst thing about] it is that…. 文例⇩

なぬし 名主《日本史》the headman (of a village).

なのか 七日 seven days ;〈日付〉the seventh (of July).

なのり 名乗り ¶名乗りをあげる give *one's* name 《as》;〈立候補する〉announce *one's*

なに 君は何しに来たのか. What have you come here for? | What has brought you here? / そんなことをおぼえて何になる. What is the use [good] of learning that? / 話していたところで何になるものか. It's no (earthly) use talking to him! / 何から話してよいやら. I don't know [I'm quite at a loss] what to tell you first [where to begin]. / シェイクスピアの何をお読みになりましたか. Which of Shakespeare's works have you read? / 何よりも健康が一番だ. Health must be your first consideration in whatever you do. / 何をおいても それをしなければいけない. You must do it before anything else. / 何が何だかさっぱり分からない. I don't know what's what. | I can't make out what it's all about. | I am all in a muddle. / 何が何でもやり抜くんだ. Go through with it at any cost! / 何が何でもそれを手放すわけにはいかない. I won't part with it for anything in [for all] the world.

なにか 何かお役に立てば仕合わせです. I shall be happy if I can be of any help [service] to you. / 何かご用ですか. What can I do for you? / 子供たちはまた何かいたずらをたくらんでいる. The children are up to some mischief again. / 電車に乗り遅れたか何かしたらしいです. It's because he missed his train or something, I guess.

なにくそ 何くそ負けるものか. Oh! [Ha!] So they think they've got me beaten, do they?

なにげない 彼は何気なく空を見上げた. He glanced up casually at the sky. / 何気ない様子で座についた. He took his place as if nothing had happened to him.

なにごと あの音は何事だろう. What could [can] that noise be? / 何事が起こったのかと外へ飛び出してみた. I ran out to see what was the matter. / その日は何事もなく過ぎた. The day passed quietly.

なにしろ それぐらいの金は何でもないよ. 何しろ彼は金持ちなんだから. That much is nothing to him, for he is a very rich man.

なに(っ) 何訳はないさ. Why,

なのる 名乗る give one's name [introduce oneself] 《as Kimura》 ¶互いに名乗り合う exchange names 《with》.

ナパームだん ナパーム弾 a napalm bomb.

なびかせる 靡かせる 〈翻す〉fly; flutter; 〈意に従わせる〉win sb over; 〈女性の〉win 《a girl's》 heart [love]; 〈征服する〉《文》conquer; subdue ¶旗を風になびかせながら with a flag fluttering [flapping] in the wind /〈女性の〉長い髪を風になびかせて with one's hair streaming out [floating] in the wind [breeze] /金の力でなびかせる win sb over to one's side with money.

なびく 靡く 〈翻る〉wave; flutter; stream; 〈曲がる〉bend; 〈屈服する〉bow 《to》; yield [submit] 《to》; be won over to sb's side; 〈女が〉give one's heart 《to》 ¶風になびく稲などが〉 bend before the wind; 〈旗などが〉fly [flutter] in the wind /金の力になびく be won over with money; be bribed 《to do, into doing》;《口語》 be bought. 文例⇩

ナプキン a 《table》 napkin; 《主に英》 a serviette ¶ひざにナプキンを掛ける lay [spread] one's [a] napkin across [over] one's lap /紙ナプキン a paper napkin [serviette].

ナフサ《化》naphtha.

なふだ 名札〈表札〉a nameplate; a doorplate;〈席の〉a place card;〈胸などにつける〉a name card;〈荷物・迷子の〉an identification label [tag].

ナフタリン naphthalene.

ナフトール《化》naphthol.

なぶりごろし 嬲り殺し ¶なぶり殺しにする torture sb to death; kill sb by inches.

なぶりもの なぶり物 ¶なぶり物にする make fun [《文》sport] of sb; make a laughingstock of sb; mock at sb; torment sb.

なぶる 嬲る 〈愚弄(ぐろう)する〉make fun [sport] of sb;〈嘲弄する〉jeer 《at》sb; mock at sb;〈いじる〉⇨いじる.

なべ 鍋 a pan (浅い); a pot (深い) ¶なべで煮る boil 《fish》 in a pan /なべかま pots and kettles /なべ墨 kettle soot /なべ底景気 a chronic [prolonged] recession /なべづる[ぶた] a pot bail [lid] /なべ物 a hot-pot (cooked at the table) /なべ焼きうどん noodles served hot in a pot.

ナポリ Naples ¶ナポリの Neapolitan.

ナポレオン Napoleon ¶ナポレオン戦争《西洋史》the Napoleonic wars.

なま 生 ¶生の〈料理しない〉raw《meat》; uncooked《cabbage》;〈熟していない〉unripe《fruit》; green《bananas》/〈生焼け・生煮えの〉half-done; underdone;〈未加工の〉raw; crude;〈経験の浅い〉inexperienced;《口語》green /生の音楽 live music /生の情報 first-hand information /生の統計 raw statistics /生で食べる eat《fish》raw /〈暗号でなく〉生で送信する send《a message》in (the) clear /生菓子 (a) cake /生皮 rawhide; undressed hide /生ごみ kitchen refuse /生ゴム crude rubber /生卵 a raw egg /生煮えの half-cooked[-done]; underdone /生フィルム raw film /生焼けの half-roasted《meat》; half-baked《bread》; underdone; half-raw /生水 unboiled water /生物《腐敗しやすいもの》 uncooked food; perishables /生野菜 fresh vegetables /生ワクチン live《polio》vaccine.

なまあくび 生あくび ¶生あくびをかみ殺す stifle [suppress] a yawn.

なまあたたかい 生暖かい (disagreeably) warm.

なまいき 生意気〈うぬぼれ〉(self-)conceit;〈出過ぎたこと〉impertinence; cheek ¶生意気な〈うぬぼれた〉conceited;〈出過ぎた〉forward; impertinent;〈こしゃくな〉insolent; cocky; brash; pert (主に女性について);〈厚かましい〉impudent; audacious; cheeky /生意気なやつ an impertinent [insolent] fellow /生意気に impertinently; impudently /生意気にも...する have the cheek [audacity] to do; be impertinent enough to do; dare to do /生意気盛りだ be at a cheeky age. 文例⇩

なまえ 名前 ⇨な[1] ¶名前を呼ぶ[知っている] call [know] sb by name. 文例⇩

なまかじり 生嚙り ¶生かじりの superficial; shallow; half-understood[-learnt] /〈知識が〉生かじりだ have a superficial knowledge《of》;

---

nothing is easier. /何負けるもんか. No, I won't give in. /何構うもんか. All right! See if I care!

なにぶん その件は何分よろしくお願いします. I leave it entirely to your discretion [kind consideration]. / 2, 3 日中に何分のご返事を願います. Please let me have an answer one way or the other in a few days.

なにほど 利益は何程でもない. The profit is trifling [very small]. /何程のこともあるまい. I don't think it counts for anything [much].

なにも もう何も言うことはない. I have no more [I've said all I have] to say to you. /何もしないのにしかられた. I was scolded for nothing [without any reason]. /彼女とは何も関係がありません. I have nothing to do with her. /何もそんなに急ぐことはない. There is no need (whatever) to rush [hurry] like that. /それは何も日本人に限ったことではない. It is in no way peculiar to the Japanese. /何もかも手違いだらけだ. Everything has gone wrong for me.

なにもの[1] 何者も彼に抗し得なかった. Nobody [No one] could resist him. /何者の仕業だろうか. Who can have done it? | Who did this?

なにもの[2] 正に狂気以外の何物でもない. Madness is the only word for it. | It's nothing but madness. | It's sheer madness.

なにやかや 何やかやと出費が多い. There are a lot of demands on my purse.

なによりも 皆さまお元気で何よりです. I'm so glad that you are all well. /こういう寒い日には熱燗が何よりですね. You can't beat [Nothing can touch] a hot cup of sake on such a cold day. /何よりもまずその歯を治さなければいけない. You ought to get that tooth treated first of all [before you do anything else].

なびく 稲穂が風になびいていた. The rice plants were bending [swaying] before [in] the breeze.

なまいき 生意気言うな. None of your cheek [impudence]!

なまえ お名前は. May I have your name, please? | What's the name, please? /〈取り次ぐとき〉What

なまがわき 生乾き ¶生乾きの not fully [properly] dried; half-dried.

なまき 生木 〈立ち木〉 a live tree; 〈木材〉 raw wood, unseasoned wood [timber]; 〈まき〉 green wood; 〈血なまぐさく〉 separate 《(a loving couple)》; part 《(a child)》 from 《(its mother)》. 文例⇩

なまきず 生傷 a fresh wound; 〈打ち傷〉 a fresh bruise. 文例⇩

なまぐさい 生臭い 〈魚臭い〉 fishy(-smelling); smelling of fish; 〈血なまぐさい〉 bloody; smelling of blood. ¶生臭い物 fish and meat.

なまぐさぼうず 生臭坊主 〈品行の悪い僧〉 a depraved monk; a corrupt priest; 〈俗っぽい僧〉 a worldly priest.

なまくび 生首 a freshly severed head.

なまくら 鈍ら 〈なまくらな〉 dull 《(blades)》; blunt 《(swords)》. 文例⇩

なまけぐせ 怠け癖 ¶怠け癖がつく get [grow] lazy; 〈文〉 form [fall into] habits of laziness [indolence].

なまけもの[1] 怠け者 an idle [a lazy] fellow; an idler.

なまけもの[2] 〈動〉 a sloth.

なまける 怠ける be idle; be [get] lazy; 〈ゆるがせにする〉 neglect 《(one's lessons)》; 〈文〉 be neglectful of 《(one's duty)》; 〈故意に仕事などを〉 slow down ¶学課[仕事]を怠ける neglect [be lazy in] one's studies [work] / 学校を怠けて遊ぶ play truant (from school); 《米口語》 play hooky / 怠けて暮らす live in idleness; idle away one's time. 文例⇩

なまこ 〈動〉 a trepang; a sea cucumber [slug] ¶なまこ板 a corrugated iron sheet.

なまごろし 生殺し ¶生殺しにしておく 〈比喩的に〉 keep sb in anguish [agony].

なまじ(っか) 〈いい加減に〉 in a halfhearted way [fashion, manner]; 〈中途半端に〉 by halves; 〈軽率に〉 rashly; thoughtlessly; unwisely; 《文》 ill-advisedly; 〈少しでも〉 at all. 文例⇩

なまじろい 生白い ⇒なまっちろい.

なます a dish of raw fish and vegetables seasoned in vinegar.

なまず[1] 癜 〈医〉 leukoderma.

なまず[2] 鯰 〈魚〉 a catfish.

なまっちろい 生っ白い pale; 《文》 wan; pale-[《文》 wan-]looking.

なまつば 生唾 saliva (in one's mouth) ¶生つばを飲み込む swallow one's saliva.

なまづめ 生爪 ¶生づめをはがす have a nail torn off.

なまなましい 生々しい fresh; vivid ¶生々しい記憶 a fresh recollection 《(of)》 / 生々しい描写 a vivid [graphic] description.

なまぬるい 生温い 〈温度が〉 lukewarm; tepid; 〈中途半端な〉 halfway 《(measures)》; 〈いい加減な〉 halfhearted; lukewarm; 〈穏やか過ぎる〉 too mild [lenient] ¶生ぬるい態度 a lukewarm attitude / 生ぬるい湯 tepid [lukewarm] water. 文例⇩

なまはんか 生半可 ¶生半可の superficial; shallow ⇒ちゅうと(中途半端な), なまかじり. 文例⇩

なまビール 生ビール 〈びん・缶詰めでない〉 draft 《(英)》 draught] beer; beer on draft [tap]; 〈熱処理などされていない〉 live beer.

なまびょうほう 生兵法 文例⇩

なまへんじ 生返事 〈あいまいな〉 a vague [a noncommittal, an evasive] answer; 〈不承不承の〉 a reluctant [halfhearted] answer.

なまほうそう 生放送 ¶1回の〉 a live broadcast ¶生放送する broadcast 《(a drama)》 live; carry [cover] 《(an event)》 live on radio [television].

なまぼし 生干し ¶生干しの half-dried / 生干しにする half-dry 《(fish)》.

なまみ 生身 a living body [man]; flesh and blood.

なまめかしい 艶めかしい 〈あだっぽい〉 《文》 coquettish; 〈色っぽい〉 sexy; 〈魅力のある〉 charming; alluring; seductive; 《文》 captivating.

なまやさしい 生易しい easy; simple ⇒やさしい[1].

なまよい 生酔い ¶生酔いの half-drunk; half-tipsy.

---

name shall I say? / そのアンケートの回答者は、1人1人、名前は出さないことを保証された。Every person who answered the questionnaire was assured of anonymity. / あれは社長といっても名前だけさ. He is president in name only. / 僕は人の名前をよく忘れるんだ. I have a bad [poor] memory for names.

なまき 生木を裂くようなことは私にはできません. I can't be so cruel as to force them apart.

なまきず うちの子は手足に生傷の絶え間がありません. My son always has some unhealed cuts and bruises on his arms and legs.

なまくら この刀はなまくらだ. This sword is blunt [dull].

なまける 怠けてはいられない. I cannot afford to be idle.

なまじ(っか) なまじっかなことをしてはいけない. Never do things by halves. / なまじっかなお稽古なら始めからやらない方がいい. If you aren't serious about (taking) the lessons, you had better not begin at all.

なまぬるい そんなことでは生ぬるいよ. You ought to be harder on [more strict with] him. / 今は生ぬるい手段なんか取っていられない. This is no time for half measures.

なまはんか 1つの事を深く知ることは多くの事を生半可に知るよりましだ. To know one thing thoroughly is better than knowing many things by halves. | To know everything of something is better than to know something of everything.

なまびょうほう 生兵法は大けがのもと. A little learning is a dangerous thing.

なまみ お互いに生身の体なんだからいつどんな病気にかかるいとも限らない. Since we are but flesh and blood, we never know when some disease or other may befall us.

なまやさしい そんな生易しいものではないよ. It's not as simple as that [as you think].

なまり[1] 彼女の言葉にはあまりなまりはない. She doesn't have much of an accent. / 少しも関西なまりが残らないようにつとめた. He tried not to allow any

なまり¹ 訛り an accent; 〈方言〉a dialect; 〈転訛(か)〉a corruption; a corrupted form ¶なまりのないフランス語を話す speak French without an accent; speak accentless French / 仙台なまり丸出しで話す speak in a broad [strong] Sendai accent / 田舎なまり a provincial accent. 文例↓

なまり² 鉛 lead ¶鉛のような《文》leaden / 鉛色の lead-colored; lead-gray; leaden (skies). 文例↓

なまりぶし なまり節 half-dried bonito.

なまる¹ 訛る speak with an [a provincial] accent; 〈転訛(か)する〉be [get] corrupted. 文例↓

なまる² 鈍る get blunt(ed); become dull ¶腕がなまる lose one's touch [skill]; 〈練習しないでに〉get out of practice 《on the piano》.

なみ¹ 波 a wave; 〈大波〉a billow; 〈うねり〉(a) swell; 〈寄せ波〉surf; 〈砕け波〉a breaker; 〈さざ波〉a ripple ¶波にのまれる be swallowed up [carried away] by the waves / 波を打つ undulate; 《文》undulate; 〈髪などが〉be wavy / 〈船が〉波をかぶる ship a wave / 波をけって進む plow through [breast] the waves / 波に削られた崖 a wave-cut cliff / 波に乗る ride on the waves / 人気の波に乗る ride on a wave of popularity / 波打ち際 the water's edge / 波頭(がしら) the crest of a wave / 波形の wavy; wavelike / 波立つ 〈the seas〉run high; be choppy / 波間に浮かぶ float on the waves / 波よけ ⇒ぼうはてい. 文例↓

なみ² 並(み) 〈並(み)の〉〈普通の〉common; ordinary; mediocre; 〈平均の〉average / 並みはずれた, 並々ならぬ uncommon; 〈並以上の〉above (the) average / 並み大抵でない be no easy matter [task] / 並み足で at (a) walking pace; at a walk / 並型の ordinary-sized; average-sized; standard / 並製の 〈an article〉of medium quality. 文例↓

なみいる 並み居る ¶並み居る人びと those present.

なみかぜ 波風 ⇒ふうは ¶波風の絶え間ない家庭《文》a family in constant discord / 世間の波風にもまれる have a hard life; 《文》be tossed about in the storms of life; go through a lot of hardships in life. 文例↓

なみき 並木 a row of trees; roadside trees ¶並木道 an avenue; a boulevard (大通り); a tree-lined road [street]; a road lined [edged] with (rows of) trees.

なみすう 並数 〈統計〉the mode.

なみだ 涙 a tear ¶涙を流す cry; 《文》shed tears; 《文》weep / 涙を流しながら, 涙ながらに in tears; through one's tears / 涙を押える keep [fight] back one's tears; restrain one's tears / 涙を飲む swallow [pocket] an insult / 涙をふるって steeling oneself; 《文》hardening one's heart / 涙をふく wipe (the) tears from one's eyes [cheeks] 《with a handkerchief》 / 涙を催させる 〈お主語〉bring tears to one's eyes / 涙にむせぶ be choked with tears / 涙金 (a small sum of) consolation money / 涙声で in a tearful voice; with tears in one's voice / 涙ぐむ be (nearly) in tears; 《文》be moved to tears / 涙ぐましい touching; pathetic / お涙頂戴もの a tear-jerker; a sob [tear-milking] story [program] / 涙もろい be easily moved to tears; be sentimental; be maudlin.

なみなみ ¶コップになみなみとビールを注ぐ fill a glass to the brim with beer; pour a glass full of beer.

なみのり 波乗り ⇒サーフィン ¶波乗りをする ride on a surfboard; surf; surfboard / 波乗りに行く go surfing / 波乗り板 a surfboard.

ナミビア Namibia ¶ナミビア人 a Namibian.

なめくじ 〈動〉a slug.

なめしがわ 鞣皮 tanned hide; leather.

なめす 鞣す tan 〈hide into leather〉; dress ¶なめしてない untanned [raw] 〈hide〉.

なめらか 滑らか ¶滑らかな 〈すべすべした〉smooth; 〈柔らかな〉soft; velvety / 滑らかな弁舌 (have) a fluent tongue / 滑らかに smoothly; without a hitch / 滑らかにする smooth; make 〈the surface〉smooth.

なめる 舐める 〈舌で〉lick; 〈味わう〉taste; 〈経験する〉experience; 〈侮る〉make a fool

---

Kansai accent to remain in his speech. / 彼の英語には少しドイツなまりがある。He speaks English with a slight German accent. | There is a trace of (a) German accent in his English.

なまり² 翌朝目覚めたら手足が鉛のように重かった。In the morning I woke up feeling that my limbs were as heavy as lead.

なまる¹ Yes がなまって Yah となる。'Yah' is a corrupted form of 'Yes.'

なまる² この包丁はすぐになまってしまう。This knife goes blunt [dull] quickly in use.

なみ¹ 波が高い。The waves are high. | The seas are running high. / 日本は好況の波に乗っている。Japan is riding [is on] the crest of a boom. / 海は波立っていた。The sea was choppy.

なみ² 彼は並みの学生じゃない。He is different from the common [ordinary, average] run of students. / この仕事は並み大抵のことではない。This is no easy task. | This job is by no means easy. / 台風並みの激しい風になった。The wind attained typhoon force.

なみかぜ 彼の家では波風の絶え間がなかった。There were constant troubles in his family.

なみだ 彼女の目に涙が宿った。Tears stood [formed, gathered] in her eyes. / その煙で涙が出た。The smoke made my eyes water. / 涙が出そうになった。He was near (to) [on the verge of] tears. / 大粒の涙がぼろぼろと彼女のほおを伝ってこぼれた。Large tears trickled [rolled, coursed] down her cheeks. / 涙が込み上げた。Tears welled up in my eyes. / 彼女は涙を流して彼に嘆願した。She implored him with tears in her eyes. / 涙ながらにこう語った。Tears stood in his eyes as he told me. / だれ一人涙を流さないものはなかった。No one had dry eyes. | 〈ややおどけて言うとき〉There wasn't a dry eye in the house. / 思い出すも涙の種だ。Just thinking of it brings tears to my eyes. | I cannot recall it without bitter remorse. / 彼女は涙声になった。Her voice broke with emotion.

なや [《口語》monkey] of *sb*; 《口語》mess [fool] around with *sb*; treat *sb* with contempt; make light of / 飴をなめる eat candy / 鉛筆をなめる moisten the point of a pencil on *one's* tongue / 世の辛酸をなめる taste the hardships of life / なめるようにかわいがる dote on *sb*; fondle (手で撫でて) / なめたようにきれいに食べる lick 《the bowl》 clean / なめ回す run *one's* tongue over *sth*. 文例◊

なや 納屋 a barn; a shed.

なやましい 悩ましい 〈誘惑的な〉seductive; teasing; 〈ゆううつな〉《文》 melancholy; 〈けだるい〉 lackadaisical; 《文》 languid.

なやます 悩ます 〈苦しめる〉 torment; harass; 《文》 distress; 〈文》 cause *sb* pain [distress]; 〈困らせる〉 cause *sb* trouble; trouble; worry; vex; put *sb* out ¶頭を悩ます〈考えて〉rack [cudgel] *one's* brains 《over, about》; puzzle 《over, about》 / 心を悩ます worry [be worried, 《文》 be distressed] 《about, over》 / 質問で悩ます pester [harass] *sb* with questions / 悩まされる ⇒なやむ. 文例◊

なやみ 悩み trouble(s); worry; 《文》 distress; 〈ひどい〉 agony; 《文》 anguish; 〈問題〉 a problem ¶心の悩み anguish of heart / 生活の悩み troubles [worries] of life / 悩みがあるhave worries; be in trouble ¶悩みの種である〈事が主語〉be a (cause of) trouble [《文》 distress] to *one*; 《文》 often cause *one* great distress.

なやむ 悩む be troubled 《with, by》; be worried 《about》; 《文》 be distressed 《by》; 〈病気に〉suffer 《from》; 《文》 be afflicted 《with》¶物価の急騰に悩む suffer from a sudden rise in prices / 恋に悩む女〈恋に焦がれて〉a lovesick girl / 〈失恋して〉《文》 a lovelorn girl / 悩んでいる be worried [《文》 distressed]; be in trouble [《文》 distress, anguish].

なよなよ ¶なよなよとした 〈ほっそりした〉 slender; delicate; 〈しなやかな〉 supple; pliant.

なら 楢 《植》 a Japanese oak.

ならい 習い 〈習慣〉a habit; 〈慣習〉a custom; the (usual) way ¶世の習い the way of the world / 世の習いで as is (so) often the case in life. 文例◊

ならう¹ 習う 〈覚える〉learn; 〈教わる〉be taught 《by》; take lessons in 《French》; 〈研究する〉 study; 〈練習する〉 practice; get training in 《English pronunciation》 ¶...について英語を習う study English under [learn English from] *sb*. 文例◊

ならう² 倣う 〈まねる〉imitate; copy; 〈先例に従う〉follow 《a precedent》; 《お手本に》be modeled 《on》 ¶...にならって in imitation of ...; after the example [model] of.... 文例◊

ならく 奈落 〈地獄〉Hell; 《文》 the abyss; 〈芝居の〉 a trap cellar ¶奈落の底に落ちる fall into the bottomless pit.

ならし 均し ⇒へいきん.

ならす¹ 生らす cause 《a tree》 to bear fruit.

ならす² 均す 〈平らにする〉level (off); smooth (off); make even; even out; 〈平均する〉average ¶ローラーでならす smooth [level] 《the ground》 with a roller; roll 《the court》 / ならしで on (an [the]) average.

ならす³ 鳴らす 〈音を出す〉ring 《a bell》; sound 《a trumpet》; beat 《a drum》; clang 《a gong》; jingle 《coins》; clap 《*one's* hands》; blow 《a whistle》; 〈評判が高い〉be popular; be well [widely] known; be famous ¶呼び鈴を鳴らす 《玄関の》 ring the doorbell; 《人を呼ぶ時》ring for 《*one's* secretary》 / 自動車の警笛を鳴らす sound [honk] the [*one's*] horn. 文例◊

ならす⁴ 馴[慣]らす 〈飼い馴らす〉tame; domesticate; 〈訓練する〉 train 《a dog》; break in 《a horse》; 〈習慣をつける〉get [make] *sb* used [accustomed] to 《*sth, doing*》; 《文》 accustom *sb* to 《*sth, doing*》 ¶体を寒さに慣らす accustom [《文》 inure] *oneself* to the cold / 犬をならして色々な芸をさせる train a dog to do a number of tricks / 上からの命令に服従するよう慣らされた国民 a people accustomed [conditioned] to accepting orders from above. 文例◊

ならずもの ならず者 a blackguard; a scoundrel.

-ならでは 《none, nothing》 but; except; 〈くなしでは〉 without; but for. 文例◊

なめる 昨夜の火事がその辺一帯をなめ尽くした. The fire last night completely destroyed [swept right through] the area where he lives.

なやます 色々な心配事に彼は心を悩ましている. Cares and anxieties weigh heavily on him [his mind]. / 彼らは紅海で炎熱に悩まされた. They had a most trying time on the Red Sea on account of the scorching heat.

ならい 艱難は世の習いだ. It is man's lot to suffer. / 習い性となる. Habit is (a) second nature. 《諺》

ならう¹ 習うより慣れよ. Practice makes perfect. 《諺》

ならう² 右へ[前へ]ならえ! 《号令》 Right [Forward] dress! / 英国が賛成すれば他の欧州諸国もこれにならうだろう. If Britain agrees, other European nations will follow suit.

ならう³ 彼は当時野球選手として鳴らしたものだ. He was a famous baseball player at the time.

ならう⁴ イギリス映画は英語に耳を慣らすのによい. English movies give you good practice in understanding spoken English.

-ならでは 彼ならではとてもこの仕事は扱えない. He is the only person who can handle this job. / 《文》 No one but he would be equal to this task.

-ならない 家を修繕しなければならない. The house must be repaired. | The house needs repairing. / すぐ行かなければならなかった. I had to go at once. / 人は寝るときはいやでも横にならなければならない. Humans have got to [have no choice but to] lie down when they sleep. / どうもそう思われてならない. I can't help thinking that way. / 他人の悪口を言ってはならない. You should not speak badly about other people [《文》 ill of others]. / 君が行かなくてはならなかったのだ. You ought to have gone there.

-なら(ば) 私が鳥なら飛んでも行くが. If I were a bird, I would

-ならない 〈必要〉must *do*; have (got) to *do*; need to *do*; 〈禁止〉must not *do*; 〈道理上,義務上〉ought to *do*; should *do* ⇒ **いけない** 用因. 文例⇩.

-なら(ば) if; in case; suppose; supposing; provided (that...); 〈...に関しては〉as for; for ¶できる事[必要]なら if possible [necessary] / その事ならso far as that matter. 文例⇩.

ならび 並び 〈列〉a row; a line; 〈側〉a side ¶ひと並びの家 a row of houses / 並びない unrivaled; unequaled; 《文》matchless ¶ 世に並びない美人 a woman of matchless beauty / ...と並び称せられる rank [be classed] with... .

ならびに 並びに and (also); both...and; as well as.

ならぶ 並ぶ 〈列を作る〉form [stand in] a line; line [《英》queue] up; 〈並行する〉be [run] parallel (to, with); 〈匹敵がする〉rank (with); rival; equal; be a match (for) ¶ずらりと本の並んでいるK氏の書斎 Mr. K's book-lined study / 並ぶ者がない have no equal [《文》peer]; stand unrivaled / 並んで座る sit side by side / 並んで歩く 〈横に〉walk side by side [abreast]; walk alongside *sb* / 〈縦に〉walk one behind another. 文例⇩.

ならべる 並べる 〈配列する〉line 《things》up; put 《things》side by side; place 《A》beside [by the side of] 《B》; arrange; 〈整頓する〉put [place] 《things》in order; 〈陳列する〉display; 〈列挙する〉list; 《文》enumerate ¶2列に並べる arrange [place, set out] 《desks》in two rows; draw 《men》up in two lines / 食卓に料理を並べる set dishes on the table / 文句[不平]を並べる make complaints 《to *sb* about *sth*》/ 並べてある 〈陳列されている〉be displayed; be exhibited; be on display [show] / ...と並べれば as compared with...; by the side of...; alongside 《of》... / 並べ替える rearrange / 欠点を並べ立てる enumerate *sb*'s faults / 例を幾つも並べ立てる cite a large number of instances / 功績を並べ立てる itemize *sb*'s contributions 《to science》/ 並べ方 arrangement.

ならわし 習わし a custom ⇒ **ならい**. 文例⇩.

なり¹ 鳴り ¶鳴りがいい sound clear; ring well / 鳴りをひそめる〈静かになる〉fall [be] silent; 《文》be hushed; 〈活動しない〉be inactive; lie low / 鳴りをひそめて listen to *sb* with breathless [hushed] attention. 文例⇩.

なり² 〈形状〉(a) shape; a form; 〈外見〉(personal) appearance; 〈服装〉dress; 〈身長〉height; 《文》stature ¶なりが大きい[小さい] be big [small] (in stature) / 男のなりをして in the guise [disguise] of a man. 文例⇩.

なりあがり(もの) 成り上がり(者) an upstart; 《文》a parvenu ¶成り上がりの政治家 an upstart politician.

なりあがる 成り上がる 〈卑しい身分から〉《文》rise above *one*'s (proper) station; be an upstart; come up from the gutter (where *one* belongs); 〈成金になる〉suddenly become rich.

なりかわる 成り代わる take *sb*'s place; replace *sb* ¶成り代わって for; on behalf of; in the place of. 文例⇩.

なりきる 成り切る ¶保守主義者に成り切る become a dyed-in-the-wool conservative; become a conservative through and through / 〈演じる〉役に成り切る get right into *one*'s part [role].

なりきん 成金 《フランス語》a nouveau riche (pl. nouveaux riches); the newly rich (集合的) ¶成金になる suddenly 《文》become rich / 戦争成金 a war profiteer.

なりさがる 成り下がる be reduced to (beggary); be degraded to (a lower position).

なりすます 成り済ます successfully impersonate 《a painter》; pass *oneself* off as 《a policeman》; set *oneself* up as 《a professor》.

なりそこなう 成り損う fail to become 《an artist》; miss being 《a rich man》.

なりたち 成り立ち 〈歴史〉history; 〈起原〉origin; 〈組織〉organization; setup; 〈構造〉structure; mechanism; 〈要素〉elements.

なりたつ 成り立つ 〈構成される〉be made up of; consist of; be composed of; 〈実現される〉materialize; 《文》be realized; 〈締結される〉be concluded. 文例⇩.

---

fly to you. / この人ならという男性にまだお目にかかったことがありません。I've not yet met the right man for me. / こういう場合君ならどうするかね。What would you do in a case like this? / 酒をよすならこんどだけは許してやろう。I will forgive you (for) this once provided [on condition] that you give up drinking.

ならび それはこの並びの角から5軒目の家です。It is the fifth house from the corner on this side.

ならぶ 日食や月食は太陽と月と地球が一線に並んだ時に起こる。Solar and lunar eclipses occur when the sun, earth, and moon are in line. / 通りの両側には宏壮な建物が並んでいる。Magnificent buildings stand on both sides of the street. | The street is lined on both sides with fine buildings.

ならわし こういう場合はそうするのがこの国の習わしなのだ。It is customary in this country to do so on occasions like this.

なり¹ この2, 3年まったく鳴りをひそめている。He has been quite inactive [has kept very quiet] these last few years.

なり² そんななりで出かけると笑われるぞ。If you go out in that outfit [dressed like that], people will laugh at you.

なりかわる 父に成り代わってお礼申し上げます。I should like to thank you on behalf of my father.

なりたつ 日本は大小無数の島から成り立っている。Japan consists of innumerable islands, large and small. / 金持ちだから幸福だという理屈は成り立たない。If a man is rich, it does not follow that he is happy. / 君の説はこの場合は成り立たない。Your theory does not hold good in this case. / こんな所へホテルを立てても経済的に成り立たないだろう。It would not be economically feasible to run a hotel in such a place as this. | A hotel

なりて 為り手 文例⇩
-なりと(も) even 〖1分間なりと(も) even for a minute／どこへなりと anywhere; wherever. 文例⇩
-なりに 〖自分[それ]なりに in one's [its] own way; after one's [its] kind.
なりはてる 成り果てる be reduced to (beggary); become (a beggar).
なりひびく 鳴り響く 〈鳴る〉ring (out);〈鳴り渡る〉echo;《文》resound; reverberate;〈反響する〉(re-)echo.
なりふり 形振り ⇨なり² 〖なりふりを構う[構わない]be particular about [careless about, 《文》indifferent to] one's personal appearance; care [do not care] about how one looks.
なりもの 鳴り物 a musical instrument 〖鳴り物入りで with a flourish of trumpets; with a fanfare／鳴り物入りで宣伝する make a great to-do [loud noises] about 《a new invention》.
なりゆき 成り行き 〈経過〉the course (of events); the development [progress] (of an affair);〈転換〉the turn (of events);〈結果〉the outcome (of a matter);《文》the issue (of a contest) 〖成り行きを待つ[見る]watch the development [course] of events; wait for the turn of events; wait and see how things will turn out; see which way the wind blows／成り行きに任せる let (a matter) take (its) own course; let things ride; leave things [leave it, trust] to chance／今の成り行きでは the way things are going now.
なりわたる 鳴り渡る ⇨なりひびく.
なる¹ 生る 〈実が主語〉grow (on a tree);〈木が主語〉bear (fruit) 〖実(³)がよく生る〈木が主語〉bear well; bear a lot of [abundant] fruit; fruit well. 文例⇩
なる² 成[為]る 〈身分・地位・状態などが〉become; get; grow; be;〈季節がめぐってくる〉come (round);〈雨季が始まる〉set in;〈経過する〉pass;《文》elapse;〈し始める〉begin to do;〈…するにいたる〉come [get] to do;〈変わる〉turn [change] into;〈達する〉amount [measure up] to;〈年齢が〉《文》attain; reach; turn;〈結局…になる〉end [result] in; prove; turn out;〈ふんする〉play (the part of (Faust));〈成り立つ〉consist [be made up] of;〈成就する〉《文》be accomplished;〈成功する〉succeed ※ become は会話では主に名詞の前にしか使わない. 形容詞―過去分詞を含む―の前には get がくる場合が多い. 従って become angry は《文》の方が会話では普通である. grow はだんだん或る状態になることを表わす語で, たとえば, すでに或る程度暗くなりつつあるときに, だんだん暗さが加わる時, grow dark(er) という 〖音楽家になりたい wish [want] to be a musician／好きになる begin [get, come] to like 《sth, sb》; take a fancy to [for] 《sth, sb》／合わさって1つになる join 《文》unite, 《文》be united) into one／こわれて粉々になる break [be smashed] into fragments／本当になる come (out) true／致命傷になる prove fatal／よく[悪く]なる get better [worse]／病気などが〉take a turn for the better [worse]／春になると when spring comes (round); in spring／おとなになる grow up (into [to be] a man)／成年になる come of age;《文》attain one's majority／病気になる fall [be taken] ill／盲目になる go blind; lose one's sight／事が成る succeed in one's attempt. 文例⇩
なる³ 鳴る 〈響く〉sound; ring;〈反響する〉resound; echo;〈とどろく〉roar; thunder; rumble;〈きしむ〉creak;〈時計が〉strike 〖頭ががんがん鳴る have a pounding in one's

in a place like this would hardly pay its way.
なりて 委員になり手がなかった. No one was willing [volunteered] to sit on the committee.
-なりと(も) 何なりとお命じになって下さい. お言い付けどおりにいたします. I shall obey whatever orders you give me.／何なりとお好きなものをお選び下さい. Take anything you would like (to have).
なりひびく 彼の声は部屋中に鳴り響いた. The room rang with his voice.｜His voice rang through the room.／彼の名声は全国に鳴り響いた. The country resounded with his fame.｜His name rang through the land.
なる¹ 今年はなしがよく生った. Pear trees bore well this year.／りんごが少し生っている. There are a few apples on the tree.／庭の梅の木に実が生っている. The ume tree in my garden is now in fruit.／金の生る木などない. Money does not grow on trees.

なる² 君は何になる積もりか. What are you going [do you want] to be?／毛虫が蝶になった. Caterpillars change [turn] into butterflies.／風邪から肺炎になった. The cold developed into pneumonia.／聞いているうちに彼女の顔は赤くなったり青くなったりした. Her color came and went as she listened.／いつからお酒を飲むようになったの? When did you start drinking?／試合は味方の勝利となった. The game ended in victory for us [our side].／最後に受けた傷が致命傷となった. The last wound he received proved fatal.／景色は絵になる. This scenery will make a good picture.／あの娘さんはきっと良いお嫁さんになるだろう. I'm sure she will make him a good wife.／このつえは武器になる. This stick will serve as a weapon.／あの子はどうなったかしら. I wonder what has become of her.／世の中は一体どうなるのかわからない. One doesn't know what the world is coming to.／じきに泳げるようになりますよ. You will soon learn to swim.／梅雨になった. The rainy season has set in.／暖かくなると家畜は牧場へ出ます. When the warmer weather comes, the cattle go out to grass.／結局そうはならなかった. Things didn't work out that way.／なるようにならねば.〈打っちゃっておけ〉Leave things to take their own course.｜〈あきらめろ〉Take things as they are.／なるようになるさ. Things will take care of themselves.／2に3を足すと5になる. Two and three is [are, make(s)] five.／合わせて5千円になる. The total comes [amounts] to 5,000 yen.／費用は1人あたり2千円になる. The expenses work out at 2,000 yen a [per] head.／これを東京で売れば5万円にはなるよ. This will bring you at least 50,000 yen in Tokyo.／あの人が田舎へ行ってから6年になります. It is six years [Six years have passed] since he went to the country.／

なるこ 急に鳴り出す break [go off] into sound. 文例⇩

なるこ 鳴子 a clapper; a noisemaker.

ナルシシズム 〖心理〗narcissism.

なるたけ 成る丈 ⇨なるべく.

なるべく 成るべく as...as possible; as...as one can [may] ¶なるべくなら if possible; if circumstances allow.

なるほど 成る程〈分かりました〉I see!;〈確かに〉really!; indeed; to be sure ¶なるほど...だが, しかし... It is true..., but... / なるほど確かに...だが, しかし admittedly, ..., but / なるほどと思わせる convince sb of sth. 文例⇩

なれ 慣れ practice; experience ¶慣れで by practice; from experience.

なれあい 馴れ合い〈文〉collusion; (a) conspiracy ¶...となれ合いで〈口語〉in cahoots with ...;〈文〉in collusion [conspiracy] with ... / なれ合い仕事 a put-up job.

なれあう 馴れ合う〈共謀する〉〈文〉collude 《with》; conspire 《with》; plot (together) 《with》;〈密通する〉have [〈文〉engage in] a secret [〈文〉an illicit] love affair 《with》.

ナレーション (a) narration.

ナレーター a narrator ¶ナレーターの声 a voice-over.

なれそめ 馴れ初め 文例⇩

なれなれしい over-familiar ¶なれなれしく familiarly; unceremoniously;いやになれなれしく with too much [undue, irritating] familiarity / なれなれしくする take liberties [be too free] with 《a woman》;〈口語〉get fresh with 《a girl》. 文例⇩

なれのはて 成れの果て the wreck of one's former self; the ruin of what one was.

なれる 慣れる〈習慣づけられる〉get used to 《sth, doing》; grow [be] accustomed to 《sth, doing》; be [become] inured to 《sth, doing》;〈経験を積む〉〈文〉enrich [add to] one's experience 《in》; be richly experienced 《in》;〈動物が〉tame; become tame; be domesticated;〈熟する〉mature;〈打ち解け過ぎる〉get [〈文〉become] too familiar 《with》¶暑さに慣れる get [〈文〉become] used [accustomed] to the heat 《in Tokyo》/ 新しい環境に慣れる be acclimatized [〈米〉acclimated] to one's new environment / 慣れた〈経験を積んだ〉experienced; practiced;〈馴染みのある〉familiar;〈(動物など)人になれた〉tame; domesticated / 慣れた手つきで with a practiced hand; skillfully / 慣れない〈経験の浅い〉inexperienced; green;〈なじみのない〉unfamiliar; new;〈野生そのままの〉wild; untamed / 慣れない手つきではしを使う use chopsticks awkwardly; be awkward in using chopsticks.

なわ 縄 (a) rope; (a) cord 〈細引〉¶縄をかける tie sb up; bind sb with (a) rope;〈罪人に〉arrest / 縄を解く untie;〈罪人などの〉release; set 《a prisoner》free / 縄をなう make a rope / 縄を張る stretch a rope 《around a place》/ 縄張りをするために rope off 《a place》/ 縄のれん〈のれん〉a rope curtain;〈居酒屋〉a bar;〈米〉a saloon;〈英〉a pub / 縄ばしご a rope ladder.

なわしろ 苗代 a rice nursery; a bed for rice seedlings.

なわつき 縄付き a criminal. 文例⇩

なわとび 縄跳び〈縄を回してする〉(rope) skipping;〈縄を張ってする〉rope jumping ¶縄跳びをする skip / 縄跳びの縄を回す turn the skipping rope 《for the girls》/ 縄跳び競走

3月が4月になり, 4月が5月になっても父からの便りはなかった. March moved into April and April into May, and still nothing was heard from my father. / 東京に来てからもうどのくらいになりますか. How long have you been in Tokyo? / もう3カ月で5年になります. In three months I will have lived here for five years. / この8月で彼が死んでから3年になる. He will have been dead for three years this August. / ちょうど20歳になったばかりです. He has just turned twenty. / 彼は今度の誕生日で19歳になる. He will be nineteen (years old) next birthday. / 国会は2院からなる. The Diet consists of two Houses. / 成るも成らぬも君の努力しだいだ. Whether you succeed or not depends entirely on your efforts.

なる³ ほらサイレンが鳴っている. There goes the siren. / もう6時が鳴っている. It is striking six now. / 夕べの鐘が鳴る. The evening bell is tolling. / 靴が鳴る. My shoes creak. / 腕が鳴るよ. I'm burning [itching] to try my hand at it.

なるべく なるべく早くご返事をいただきたい. Let me have your answer as soon as possible [you can]. / なるべくお伺いするようにします. I'll try to come. / なるべくなら明日出発したい. If possible [If circumstances allow], I'd like to start tomorrow.

なるほど なるほどそれで彼が嫌いなんだね. I see! That's why you dislike him. / So that's why you don't like him! / なるほど僕が悪かった. I admit [acknowledge] that I was wrong. / なるほどいい案だが実行が難しかろう. That's a good plan, to be sure, but I'm afraid it is hardly practicable. / なるほど彼は利口だが, しかし誠実味に欠ける所がある. It is true that he is clever, but he is lacking in sincerity. / なるほど確かに彼は誠実味には欠ける所があるが, 有能な男ではある. Admittedly, he is lacking in sincerity, but he is an able man.

なれそめ そもそものなれそめは加藤氏宅でのダンスパーティーであった. Their romance began at the dance held at Mr. Kato's house.

なれなれしい なれなれしく近付いてくるよそのその人には用心するように子供には言ってある. I have warned my child about too friendly approaches by a stranger.

なれる 外国の婦人方と話をするのは慣れていません. I'm not used to talking with foreign ladies. / 目が暗がりに慣れるのにしばらくかかった. His eyes took a little time to accustom themselves to the gloom. / この猫は私によくなれています. This cat is quite tame with me. / This cat is a great friend of mine. / 豹は人になれません. Leopards cannot be tamed. / Leopards are untamable. / 彼は校正にも慣れたものです. He is an old hand at proofreading. / He is a veteran proofreader.

なわつき 彼の家から縄付きを出した. One of his family committed a crime and was arrested.

なわばり 縄張り〈縄を張ること〉stretching a rope; roping off;〈勢力範囲〉《文》one's sphere of influence; one's territory;《文》one's domain; one's pitch〈露天商人などの〉★動物学上で「縄張り」という時には，英語では常に territory を用いる ¶縄張りする stretch a rope (around a place) /〈遮断するために〉rope off (a place) / 縄張りを荒らす break [intrude] into sb's domain; encroach on sb's territory / 縄張り争い rivalry over territory;《文》a territorial dispute [conflict]; 〈官庁の〉a jurisdictional dispute. 文例↓

なん¹ 難〈困難〉(a) difficulty; hardship(s); 〈厄介〉(a) trouble;〈災難〉an accident; a mishap; a disaster; a calamity;〈危険〉danger; 〈欠点〉《文》a blemish; a fault;〈文〉a defect; 〈非難〉(a) criticism;《文》a charge ¶難を免れる escape danger / 難を避ける《文》take refuge (in a place) /《文》seek refuge [with sb] / 難に会う meet (with) an accident [a mishap] / 難に当たる face (up to) a difficulty; tackle a difficult situation / 難なく without difficulty; easily; with ease; hands down. 文例↓

なん² 何 ¶そう言っては何ですが if I may say so; though I say it myself.

なん- 何… ¶30何冊 thirty-odd copies / 1年と何か月 one year and some months / 午後4時何分かの列車 the four-something p.m. train / 彼が70何歳かの時の in his seventy-somethingth year / 何十[百, 千, 万, 十万, 百万]人もの人 dozens [hundreds, thousands, tens of thousands, hundreds of thousands, millions] of people / 何冊 how many copies [books]. 文例↓

なんア 南ア ⇨みなみ(南アフリカ共和国).

なんい¹ 南緯 the south latitude (略: S.L.) ¶北緯15度に in 15°S. lat.; in lat. 15°S. / 南緯20度10分に at 20°10'S. lat.; at lat. 20°10'S. ⇨くい.

なんい² 難易 (relative) difficulty; 《文》hardness or ease. 文例↓

なんおう 南欧 Southern Europe.

なんか¹ 南下 ¶南下する go [advance] south(-ward).

なんか² 軟化 ¶軟化する soften; weaken; 〈態度などが〉get soft [《文》conciliatory, less aggressive].

-なんか ⇨-など. 文例↓

なんが 南画〈流派〉the Southern school of Chinese painting;〈絵〉a painting in the Nanga style.

なんかい¹ 難解 ¶難解な difficult [hard] (to understand [solve]); knotty ((problems)). 文例↓

なんかい² 南海〈南太平洋〉the South Seas.

なんかげつ 何か月 how many months?; how long?

なんがつ 何月 ¶何月に in what month (of the year)? 「long?

なんかねん 何か年 how many years?; how

なんかん 難関 a [《文》an insurmountable] barrier; a difficult [tricky] problem; an obstacle; a difficulty ¶入学試験の難関 the barrier of an entrance examination / 難関を切り抜ける [乗り越える] get over [overcome,《文》surmount] a difficulty.

なんぎ 難儀〈困難〉hardship(s); (a) difficulty; difficulties;〈めんどう〉trouble;〈苦労〉《文》distress;〈苦悩〉suffering(s) ¶難儀な difficult; hard; tricky; trying; troublesome;《文》distressing / 難儀な仕事 a hard job;《文》onerous duties / 難儀する be in trouble [distress]; have a hard time (of it); go through hardships / 金がなくて難儀する be hard up for money; be in financial difficulties / 病気で難儀する suffer from illness / 難儀を救う help sb out of (his) difficulties / 難儀をかける give sb trouble.

なんきつ 難詰 ¶難詰する《文》censure; take [call] sb to task 《for sth, over sth》.

なんきゅう¹ 軟球 a rubber ball.

なんきゅう² 難球〈野球〉(make) a difficult [tricky] catch;（catch) a difficult [tricky] ball.

なんぎょうくぎょう 難行苦行 ¶難行苦行をする《文》do penance;《文》practice religious austerities;〈色々な困難にあう〉go through all sorts of hardships.

なんきょく¹ 難曲 a difficult [hard] piece (of music).

なんきょく² 難局 a serious [difficult,《文》grave] situation; a difficulty (★しばしば複数); 〈危機〉a crisis (pl. crises) ¶難局を乗り越える

なわばり 新宿はおれの縄張りだ. Shinjuku is within my territory [is an old stamping-ground of mine]. / 多くの鳥は巣の回りに縄張りを持っている. Many birds hold territory around the nest.

なん¹ しいて難と言えば彼女は背が少し低い. Her only defect is that she is rather short. / 難なく賊を取り押えた. I had no difficulty in seizing [collaring] the thief. / 難なく勝った. We beat them hands down.

なん- レコードは何枚持っていますか. How many records do you have? / 英語の本は何冊も持っていません. I don't have many [I only have a few] English books.

なんい¹ 報酬は仕事の難易により ます. The remuneration is according to the difficulty of the job. | The pay depends on how hard your job is.

-なんか 幽霊なんかいるもんか. Ghosts? Don't be ridiculous! | How could anyone believe in ghosts!

なんかい この詰将棋は僕には難解すぎる. This chess problem is too difficult for me. / メレディスは難解な作家だ. Meredith is a difficult author. | Meredith's novels are difficult [don't make easy] reading.

なんきょく² 彼はいかなる難局にも処しうる男だ. He is equal to any occasion.

なんきん¹ 彼は自宅に軟禁されている. He is under house arrest.

なんこう ソ連との交渉は難航している. Difficulties are being experienced in the negotiations with Soviet Russia. | The negotiations with Soviet Russia are going far from smoothly.

なんざん 組閣はなかなかの難産だった. The formation of the new Cabinet was attended with

なんきょく

[切り抜ける] get over a difficulty [crisis] / 難局に当たる deal [cope] with the difficult situation / 難局に立つ be in a difficult situation; find *oneself* in a fix [tight place]. 文例↓

なんきょく³ 南極 the South Pole ¶南極海[圏] the Antarctic Ocean [Circle] / 南極観測[探検]隊 an Antarctic expedition (team) / 南極光 the southern lights; an aurora australis ((*pl.* aurorae australes)) / 南極大陸 the Antarctic Continent; Antarctica.

なんきん¹ 軟禁 ¶軟禁する place *sb* under house arrest; confine *sb* in 《a room》; keep *sb* in *his* own custody. 文例↓

なんきん² 南京 Nanking ¶南京錠 a padlock / 南京錠をおろす padlock 《the door》/ 南京袋 a gunny sack / 南京豆 ⇒らっかせい / 南京虫 a bedbug.

なんくせ 難癖 ¶難癖をつける find fault 《with》; pick holes 《in》; criticize *sb* for one thing or another.

なんこう¹ 軟膏 (an) ointment;《文》salve ¶軟膏を塗る apply ointment 《to》.

なんこう² 難航 ¶難航する have a rough passage;〈比喩的に〉have [face] hard [rough] going. 文例↓

なんこうがい 軟口蓋 [解] the soft palate.

なんこうふらく 難攻不落 ¶難攻不落の要さい an impregnable fortress.

なんこつ 軟骨 [解] (a) cartilage;[料理] gristle.

なんさい 何歳 ⇒いくつ. 　　　　ttle.

なんざん 難産 a hard [difficult] labor [delivery] ¶難産する have a hard [difficult] labor; have a hard time in labor;《文》be delivered of a child with difficulty; have a hard time (in) giving birth to a child.

なんじ¹ 何時 when?; what time? ¶何時に (at) what time? / 何時までに by what time? / 何時からも till all hours.

なんじ² 難治 難治の hard to cure; almost incurable.

なんじ³ 難事 a difficult thing; a difficulty; a hard task; a tough job ¶難事に当たる tackle [grapple with] a difficulty.

なんじ⁴ 汝 thou; you ¶なんじの thy; your / なんじのもの thine; yours / なんじに[を] thee; you / なんじ自身 thyself; yourself / なんじら(に, を) you / なんじらの your / なんじ

らのもの yours / なんじら自身 yourselves ★ thou, thy, thee, thine, thyself は古語. 文例↓

なんじかん 何時間 how many hours?; how long? ¶何時間も for hours / 何時間も続けて for hours together [on end]. 文例↓

なんしき 軟式 ¶軟式庭球 soft-ball tennis / 軟式野球 a Japanese version of baseball played with a rubber ball.

なんじゃく 軟弱 ¶軟弱な weak; soft;〈心の弱い〉weak-kneed; spineless;〈女性的な〉effeminate;〈相場が〉bearish / 軟弱なグラウンド soft ground / …に対して軟弱である be soft on…/ 軟弱外交 weak-kneed diplomacy.

なんじゅう 難渋 ⇒なぎ.

なんしょ 難所 a dangerous spot;〈山道〉a difficult [《文》perilous] pass ¶最大の難所 the hardest part (of); the most difficult stage (of). 文例↓

なんしょく 難色 ¶難色を示す jib at《doing》; be against *sth*; be opposed 《to》;《文》show [express] disapproval 《of》.

なんしん 南進 ¶南進する advance [march, push] southward.

なんすい 軟水 soft water.

なんせい 南西 (the) southwest (略:SW) ¶南西の southwest(ern) / 南西の風 a southwesterly wind / 南西に[へ] southwest; southwestward / 南南西 (the) south-southwest (略:SSW) / 西南西 (the) west-southwest (略:WSW).

ナンセンス nonsense; rubbish ¶ナンセンスの nonsensical; ridiculous. 文例↓

なんだ 何だ what!; why! ¶何だかんだと言って on some pretext or other. 文例↓

なんだい 難題 ⇒なんもん(代);難題 ¶難題を持ち込む[吹っかける] ask too much of *sb*;《文》make an unreasonable request of *sb*;《文》make an unconscionable demand upon *sb*. 文例↓

なんたいどうぶつ 軟体動物 a mollusc.

なんだいめ 何代目 ⇒代目.

なんだか 何だか〈少々〉a little;《文》somewhat;《口語》kind [sort] of;〈何となく〉somehow (or other).

なんだったら 何だったら〈お好きなら〉if you like [wish];〈できれば〉if possible;〈必要なら〉if necessary;〈あなたの都合で〉if it

---

considerable difficulty.

なんじ¹ 今何時ですか. What time is it (now)? | Do you have the time? | What time do you have? | What is the time? / 何時の列車にしましょうか. What [Which] train shall we take? / 明日, 何時頃おいででしょうか. What time shall [should] we expect you tomorrow?

なんじ⁴ 汝自身を知れ. Know thyself.

なんじかん それをするのには何時間もかかるよ. It will take a good many hours to do that.

なんしょ 工事は最大の難所にか

かっている. The construction work is at its most difficult stage.

ナンセンス そいつは全くナンセンスだ. That's absolute nonsense [rubbish]! | That's utterly nonsensical!

なんだ 雨くらい何だ. Who cares if it rains? / 何だ君か. Oh, it's you, is it? / はて何だっけ.〈考え出そうとして〉Let me see. / 何だか忙しい. I am busy with one thing or another. / 何だかんだで金がいる. I need money for this or that. | There's always something that needs paying

for.

なんだい それは難題というもんです. That's asking too much. | That's rather a tall order. / 僕にはとても難題です. It's too much [difficult] for me.

なんだいめ リンカーンは何代目のアメリカの大統領ですか―16代目です. How many presidents were there before Lincoln?—Fifteen. | Whereabouts is Lincoln [does Lincoln come] in the list [order] of American Presidents?—The sixteenth.

なんだか 何だかあいつは好きになれない. I don't know why,

なんたん 南端 the southern extremity [tip, end]. 文例⇩

なんちゃくりく 軟着陸 (a) soft landing ¶軟着陸する make a soft landing 《on the moon》; soft-land 《on》.

なんちょう¹ 軟調 《取引》 a bearish tone [mood]; 《写真》 a soft tone.

なんちょう² 難聴 ¶難聴の hard of hearing / 難聴区域 《ラジオの》 a fringe area (where reception is poor).

なんて 何て how…!; what…! 文例⇩

なんで 何で ⇨なぜ. 文例⇩

なんでも 何でも ＜どれでも＞ any; anything; ＜ことごとく＞ everything; all; whatever; ＜うわさである＞ I hear; I am told; they say ¶何でも好きなものを選ぶ choose anything [whatever] one likes / 何でも読むを be an omnivorous reader 《of science fiction》 / 何でもか(ん)でも ＜すべてのもの＞ (anything and) everything; all sorts of things; ＜是が非でも＞ by all means; at any cost / 何でもない ＜容易な＞ easy; ＜取るにたらない＞ trifling / 何でも屋 a jack-of-all-trades (pl. jacks-); an all-rounder. 文例⇩

なんてん¹ 南天 《植》 a nandin(a); a sacred bamboo.

なんてん² 難点 the trouble 《with sth》; a drawback; a disadvantage; a fault; a flaw. 文例⇩

なんと 何と ＜疑問＞ what?; ＜感嘆＞ what…!; why!; how…! ¶何としても at any risk [cost]; by any means; come what may / 何と言っても when all is said and done; after all / 人が何と言おうと whatever others [people] may say 《about, of》. 文例⇩

なんど¹ 何度 ＜幾度＞ how many times?; how often?; ＜度盛り＞ how many degrees? ¶何度やってみても however often one may try / 何度も(何度も) any number of times; (very) often; frequently; over and over (again); again [time] and again; repeatedly; 《文》 times without number. 文例⇩

なんど² 納戸 a closet ¶納戸色 grayish blue.

なんとう 南東 (the) southeast (略：SW) ¶南東の southeast(ern) / 南東の風 a southeasterly wind / 南東へ[に] southeast; southeastward / 南南東 (the) south-southeast (略：SSW).

なんとか 何とか somehow [in some way] (or other); anyhow; one way or another ¶何とかいう人 Mr. So-and-so; Mr. What's-his-name / 何とかやっていく muddle through [along] / 何とかかんとか言って on some pretext or other / 何とかして手に入るものならば if it is to be had by fair means or foul.

なんとなく 何となく somehow; in some way; I don't know why, but…. 文例⇩

---

but I dislike him. / 何だか疲れたよ. I feel a little tired. | 《口語》 I'm kind [sort] of tired.

なんだったら 何だったら 明日お伺いしましょう. If necessary [you wish] I will come again tomorrow. / 何だったら君は行かなくてもいい. You don't have to go, if you don't want to. / 何だったら2, 3日中にまた訪ねて来て下さい. Please come and see me again in a few days, if you can. / 何だったらお供しましょう. I'll come with you, if you like [if you don't mind].

なんたん その学校はこの町の南端にあります. The school stands in the southernmost part [on the southern edge] of the town. / 白浜は房総半島の南端にある. Shirahama is on the southern tip [at the southern extremity] of the Boso Peninsula.

なんて 何てきれいな花なんだろう. How beautiful this flower is! | What a beautiful flower this is! / 何てずうずうしいんでしょう. What cheek [impudence, a nerve]! | What a nerve he's got! / ほんのかすり傷でこんな大騒ぎをするなんて何て弱虫なんでしょう. What a softie you are to make such a fuss over a mere scratch!

なんで そんな所へ行ったのだ. What did you go there for? / 何でそんなばかなことをしたのだ. What made you do such a stupid thing [do anything so foolish]?

なんでも 赤い花なら何でもよろしい. Any red flower will do. / I don't mind what flower it is, as long as it's red. / 彼はナイロビに向かって出発した時には, 「何でも見てやろう」という気持ちだった. When he left for Nairobi, he was determined to see all there was to be seen [to see]. / 何でもいいから一緒に来たまえ. Do come with me at any rate. / Don't ask questions. Just come with me. / 人が泳ぐのを見ると何でもないようだろう. To see people swim, you would think it quite easy. / 私なら負かすことなんか何でもないよ. I can beat him with one hand tied behind my back. / どうしたの. 一別に何でもないよ. What's wrong with you? — Nothing serious. / あいつなら1万円ぐらい何でもないよ. Ten thousand yen is nothing to him. / 彼は何でも近く辞任するという話だ. I don't know for certain, but they say he is going to resign.

なんてん² この計画の唯一の難点は経費がかかり過ぎることだ. The only drawback to this project is that it will cost too much.

なんと この木は英語で何と言いますか. What do you call this tree in English? / 保守, 反動その他の何と呼ばれようと平気です. I don't care what they call me—conservative, reactionary, or whatever [or what you will]. / 何とでも言わせておきなさい. Let her say what she likes. / 何と頼んでも彼は承知してくれなかった. Nothing could induce him to give his consent. / 相場に手を出すなんて何というばかなんだろう. What a fool [How silly] he is to dabble in speculation! / そのとき部屋に入ってきたのが何と妻だったのです. Who should then enter the room but my wife! / The woman who then entered the room was none other than my wife.

なんど¹ 寒暖計は何度ですか. What temperature is it by [on, according to] the thermometer? / What does the thermometer say? / 部屋の温度は何度ですか. What is the temperature in the room? / N大学に何度受験してみてもいつも失敗ばかりした. Every time he sat for the entrance examination of N University he failed. / あなたは何度中国へ行きましたか. How often have you been to China? / そこへ何度も行ったことがある. I have been there a good many times. / 何度も失敗した後成功した. He succeeded at last after a series of failures. / 何度も呼び鈴を押したがだれも出てこなかっ

なんとなれば 何となれば because ; for.

なんとも 何とも〈全く〉quite ;〈少しも…ない〉nothing ; not at all ¶何とも思わない〈平気である〉make [think] nothing of 《sth, doing》;〈ためらわない〉do not hesitate to do ; do not stick at 《sth, doing》;〈文〉make no scruple of doing ;〈無関心である〉be indifferent (to) ;〈厭うならない〉do not care a bit [straw] (about) / 何とも言えない〈言語に絶する〉unspeakable (ひどい), indescribable (ひどい, 漠とした), indefinable (漠とした) ;〈予見できない〉unpredictable ;〈断言できない〉there is no telling... ; who knows? ; nobody can tell.

なんなら 何なら ⇨**なんだったら**.

なんなりと 何なりと ⇨**なんでも**.

なんなんとする 垂んとする be close [hard] on 《seventy》; be near 《eighty》; be coming up to [approaching] 《ninety》. 文例↓

なんにち 何日〈何日間〉how many days? ; how long? ;〈何日に〉on what day? ¶何日も for days. 文例↓

なんにん 何人 how many people [《文》persons]? 文例↓

なんねん 何年〈何年間〉how many years? ; how long? ;〈何年に〉in what year? ¶何年も for years. 文例↓

なんの 何の〈疑問〉what? ; what kind [sort] of? ;〈否定〉no... (whatever) ; not at all ¶何のために why? ; what...for? ; for what purpose? / 何の役にも立たない be good for nothing ; it is no good [use] 《(doing, to do)》/ 何のか(ん)のと言って on some pretext or other / 何のか(ん)のと言っても after all ; when all is said and done ⇨**けっきょく** 囲碁 / 何の気なしに ⇨**なにげない**(何気なく) / 何のことはない…である be nothing but [no better than, no less than]... ; be nothing short of... 文例↓

なんぱ 軟派〈不良〉《口語》a skirt chaser.

なんぱ² 難破 (a) shipwreck ¶難破する be wrecked / 難破船 a wrecked ship ; a wreck ; a ship in distress.

ナンバー 〈数・番号〉a number ¶〈自動車の〉ナンバープレート a license [number] plate / ナンバーワン number one (略 : No. 1) ; an ace ¶ ナンバーワンのゴルファー the top [No. 1, number one] golfer ; an ace golfer.

ナンバリング a numbering machine.

なんばん¹ 何番〈番号〉what number? ;〈大きさ〉what size? 文例↓

なんばん² 南蛮〈南方の蛮人〉southern barbarians ;〈西洋人〉Europeans [Westerners] who visited Japan in the 15th, 16th, and 17th centuries ¶南蛮文学 early Christian literature (in Japan).

なんびょう 難病 an incurable disease ; a serious [an obstinate] case.

た. I rang and rang, but nobody answered.

なんとか 何とかしてあげよう. I will see what I can do for you. / 何とかしなければいけない. Something must be done about it. / 何とかやってみたまえ. Try and do it somehow or other. / イギリスの学者ジェームズ・マレーは 25 か国語以上を何とか読めると言っている. James Murray, a British scholar, said he could read in a sort of way 25 or more languages. / 10 時までに何とかしてお伺いいたしましょう. I will manage [try by all means] to be over by ten o'clock. / 問題はまだ何とかなる段階です. The problem is still at a manageable stage. / 中村何とかといったっけ. I remember he gave his name as Nakamura something-or-other. / このブライスとか何とかいう男はどこに住んでいるんだろう. Where does this Bryce or whatever he's called live?

なんとなく 何となく恐ろしい. I don't know why, but I feel so frightened by [of] it. / 彼女には何となく人を引き付ける所がある. There is something attractive about her.

なんとも 医者は何ともないと言っている. The doctor says there is nothing the matter with me. / 承諾する以外何とも致し方がなかった. I had no choice [alternative] but to accept it. / 何ともお礼の申しようもありません. I can never thank you enough. | I don't know how to thank you for it. / 何ともいまいましいことだ. It's really annoying. / 何とも言えない美しさだ. It is beautiful beyond description. | Its beauty beggars description. | 彼が勝つかどうか何とも言えません. There is no telling whether he will win or not. / その問題については何とも申し上げられません. I cannot say anything definite on the matter.

なんなんとする 工事の開始以来 5 年に**なんなん**としている. It is almost [nearly, close on] five years since the construction work was started.

なんにち 京都には何日ご滞在の予定ですか. How long are you going to stay in Kyoto? / 今日は何日ですか. What day of the month is it today? | What's the date today? / 何日でもお待ちします. I'll wait any number of days.

なんにん さて何人申し込むかな. How many people will apply (for it), I wonder? / 何人でも来ただけ使ってやる. I'll take on as many as come. / 何人でも結構. Any number (of people) will do. / 同じ間違いをした人が何人もある. Quite a few people have made the same mistake. / その試験に合格した人は何人もない. Hardly anybody passed the examination. / 僕はイギリス人を何人か知っている. I know several Englishmen.

なんねん 新憲法は何年[昭和何年]に公布されたか. When [In what year of Showa] was the new Constitution promulgated? / 彼はアメリカに何年もいなかった. He didn't stay long [many years] in America.

なんの 今日は何の試験かね. What examination do you have today? / 何のばちでこんなに苦しまなければならないのだろう. I wonder what I have done to deserve such misery. / 11 月 3 日は何の日ですか. What day is the third of November? / 何のためにそんなことをしたのかね. What have you done such a thing for? / 何のことはない, 詐欺も同然じゃないか. It's nothing short of a fraud. | It's a downright swindle. / 何のことはない, お前がばかだと言っているようなものじゃないか. It practically amounts to saying that you are a fool.

なんばん¹ 何番ですか.〈交換手が〉Number, please? / お宅の電話は何番ですか. What is your telephone number? / 君の座席は何番ですか. What is your seat number? / 君の成績はクラスで何番かね. Where are you in

なんぶ 南部 the south(ern) part;〈一定の国の〉the South ¶南部の人〈米国の〉a Southerner / 南部諸州〈米国の〉the Southern States.

なんぷう 軟風 a (gentle) breeze; a light [soft] wind ¶海[陸]軟風 a sea [land] breeze.

なんぶつ 難物〈事物〉a thing [matter] that is awkward to handle;《口語》a teaser;〈人〉a person who is hard to deal with;《口語》an ugly [awkward] customer.

なんべい 南米 South America ¶南米の South American.

なんべん ⇨なんど[1]. 文例⇩

なんぽう 南方 the south;〈南洋〉the South Seas ¶南方の south; southern / 南方に south; southward; to the south (of).

なんぼく 南北 north and south ¶南北に走る run from north to south; run north and south / 南北に走るハイウエイ a north-south highway / 南北問題 the North-South problem; the problem of disparity in income levels between developed and developing countries; 南北両アメリカ North and South America; both Americas; the American continent / 南北戦争〈米国の〉the Civil War.

なんみん 難民〈罹(り)災者〉sufferers;〈戦禍からの避難者〉refugees; displaced persons (戦争などで国を追われた) ¶難民収容所 a refugee camp.

なんもん(だい) 難問(題) a difficult [hard, knotty] problem; a poser;《口語》a hard nut to crack ¶難問を提出するput a hard question to *sb*; set a poser for *sb*.

なんよう 南洋 the South Seas ¶南洋諸島 the South Sea Islands.

なんら 何ら what; whatever;(not) any;(not) in any way ¶何らの関係もない have nothing to do (with);〈文〉have no relation whatever [at all] (with);〈文〉be not in any way related (to, with) / 何らの危険もなく without the slightest [least] danger / 何らかの理由で for some reason or other. 文例⇩

に

に[1] 二 two ¶第2 the second.

に[2] 荷〈積み荷〉a load;〈船荷〉(a) cargo (《*pl*. -(e)s》;〈鉄道の貨物〉freight;《主に英》goods;〈重荷〉a burden ¶荷を下ろす unload (a ship, a cart); unpack (a horse);〈船が主語〉discharge *its* cargo / 荷を軽くする lighten the load / 馬に荷をつける load a horse (with) / 荷を積む load (a cart);〈船が主語〉take on cargo / 荷になる be a burden to *one*. 文例⇩

＝《音楽》D ¶二長[短]調 (in) D major [minor].

-に〈時〉at (時刻); on (日); in (月,年,週);〈年齢〉at;〈場所〉at; in; on;〈ほとりに〉on;〈方位〉in; to;〈目的〉to; for (向かって);〈割合〉at; to; per ¶5時20分に at twenty (minutes) past five; at 5:20 [five-twenty] / 1962年に in 1962 / 午前[午後]に in the morning [afternoon] / 夕方に in the evening / 日曜日の夕方に on Sunday evening / 6日の朝に on the morning of the 6th / 6歳の時に at (the age of) six; when *one* was six years old [《文》of age] / ドイツに向かう leave for Germany / 目的地[東京]に着く arrive at *one*'s destination [in Tokyo] / 富久町19番地に住む live at No. 19, Tomihisa-cho / 窓に at [in] the window / 戸口に at the door / 壁にもたれる lean against the wall / つり革にぶら下がる hang on [by] the strap / 1日に2回 twice a day / 3日に1度 (once) every three days [third day] / 100円に5円の手数料 a commission of 5 yen per (one) hundred yen. 文例⇩

にあい 似合い ¶似合いの well-matched;《文》becoming; suitable / 似合いの夫婦 a well-matched couple.

にあう 似合う suit;《文》become;《文》befit;〈釣り合う〉match well; be in keeping (with); go well (with) ¶似合った[似合わない]《文》becoming [unbecoming]; well-[ill-]matched;〈…らしい〉(it is) like [not like, unlike] (Tom). 文例⇩

にあげ 荷揚げ unloading; landing; discharge ¶荷揚げする unload (a ship);〈船が主語〉discharge *its* cargo;〈陸に〉land (goods) / 荷揚げ港 a port of discharge [delivery] / 荷揚げ人足 a stevedore; a longshoreman / 荷揚げ場 a landing place [stage] / 荷揚げ料 landing

---

your class? / あなたのお父さんは左から何番目ですか。Where is your father from the left? / 何番目の引出しですか。Which drawer is it? / 名古屋は日本で何番目の大都市ですか。Where does Nagoya rank in population [come in order of size] among Japanese cities?

なんべん 何遍でもやってみなさい。Try as often as you can [like].

なんら 何ら疑わしい所はない。There is not a shadow of doubt about it. / 両者の間に何らかの相違をお認めなりますか。Do you see any difference between them?

に[2] 肩の荷が軽くなったように感じた。I felt as if a load had been taken off my shoulders. / この仕事は私には荷が勝ち過ぎる。I am not equal to the task [not up to the job]. | The job is too much for me. / 会員のうち3人に1人がその計画に反対だった。One in three of the members was against the plan.

-に あなたに手紙が来ています。There is a letter for you. / 君にお願いしたいことがあるんです。I have a favor to ask (of) you. / 規定の長さに2センチ足りない。It is two centimeters short of the regulation length.

にあう そのネクタイは君の服によ

にあつかい 荷扱い freight [cargo] handling ¶荷扱い所[人] a freight [goods, transport] office [agent].

ニアミス a near miss.

にい 二位 ＜席次＞(the) second place; ＜人＞ a runner-up (競技での) ¶2位である hold (the) second place; be rank[ed] second; stand [be, be placed] second on the list / 2位になる come off second best; ＜競技で＞finish [come in] second.

にいさん 兄さん one's (elder) brother ⇒あに[1] 囲и.

にいん 二院 ¶二院制度 the bicameral [two-chamber] system.

にうけ 荷受け receipt of goods ¶荷受人 a consignee.

にうごき 荷動き movement(s) of goods.

ニウム ➡アルミ(ニウム).

にえかえる 煮え返る boil; seethe.

にえきらない 煮え切らない ＜不決断の＞indecisive;《文》irresolute; ＜気乗りしない＞half-hearted; ＜あいまいな＞vague; noncommittal; ＜なまぬるい＞lukewarm.

にえくりかえる 煮え繰り返る ⇒にえかえる. 文例↓

にえこぼれる 煮えこぼれる boil over.

にえたつ 煮え立つ boil (up); come to a [the] boil ¶煮え立っている be boiling; be on the boil.

にえゆ 煮え湯 boiling water ¶煮え湯を飲まされる be (badly) let down; be betrayed; be badly burned.

にえる 煮える boil; be boiled; be cooked ¶よく煮えた[煮えない] well-done [underdone]. 文例↓

におい 匂[臭]い (a) smell; an odor; (a) scent; ＜芳香＞perfume;《文》fragrance;《文》aroma; ＜悪臭＞《文》stench;《口語》stink ¶いいにおい a sweet [a pleasant, an agreeable] smell [odor] / いやなにおい a bad [a foul, an offensive] smell [odor] / …のにおいがする smell [have a smell] of 《fish》; ＜いやな＞ stink of 《oil》; reek of 《garlic》 / …のようなにおいがする smell like 《bananas》 / いいにおいのする sweet-smelling; fragrant; aromatic / いやなにおいのする foul-smelling; smelly / においの強い strong-smelling 《herbs》 / においのない odorless; scentless / いやなにおいを取る get rid of [《文》remove] an unpleasant odor 《from》; deodorize / においけし ⇒だっしゅう(脱臭剤, 防␣ざい).

におう[1] 仁王 the two Deva Kings; the guardian gods of a temple gate ¶仁王立ちになる draw oneself up to one's full height / 仁王門 a Deva gate.

におう[2] 匂[臭]う smell (of); give out [off] a smell (an odor) (of); ＜香気が＞be fragrant; ＜悪臭が＞stink (of oil); reek (of garlic) ¶朝日に匂う山桜花 the wild cherry flowers catching the rays [light] of the morning sun.

ニオブ《化》niobium ¶ニオブ酸 niobic acid.

におろし 荷卸し ⇒あげ.

におわせる 匂わせる ＜かおりを発する＞ give out [off] an odor [a scent] (of); ＜暗示する＞hint (at); drop [give] a hint; insinuate. 文例↓

にか 二価 ¶二価の《化・生物》bivalent; divalent;《化》diatomic.

にかい[1] 二回 twice ¶1日2回 twice a day / 第2回の the second.

にかい[2] 二階 the upper [second] story [《英》storey];《米》the second floor;《英》the first floor ⇒かい[2] ¶2階の部屋 a room on the second floor; an upstairs room / 2階へ上がる[から下りる] go upstairs [downstairs] / 二階(建て)の a double-decker (bus) / 二階家 a two-storied[-story] house; a house with two stories. 文例↓

にがい 苦い (be, taste) bitter ¶苦い顔をする frown (at); scowl (at); make a sour [《文》wry] face / 苦い経験をする have [go through] a bitter [trying] experience.

にかえす 煮返す reboil; boil [cook] again.

にがお(え) 似顔(絵) a portrait; a likeness ¶似顔を描く paint [draw] sb's portrait [likeness] / 似顔をかかせる have one's portrait [likeness] painted [drawn]《by》 / 似顔(絵)画家 a portrait painter; ＜街頭の＞a street artist; a lightning sketch artist (早がきの).

にがす 逃がす ＜放してやる＞ let sb go [off]; set sb free; ＜逃げられる＞let sb escape [get away]; be given the slip 《by》; lose; ＜機会などを＞let 《an opportunity》slip; miss. 文例↓

にかた 煮方 how to cook sth. 文例↓

にがつ 二月 February (略: Feb.).

にがて 苦手 ＜人＞a person [subject] that is hard to deal with; ＜不得意＞a weak point ¶苦手である ＜扱いにくい相手＞be difficult for one to deal with; ＜不得意＞be bad [no good, poor] (at); be weak (in). 文例↓

く似合っている. The tie suits your coat well. | The tie goes well with your coat. / そんなことをするなんて君にも似合わないな. It's not like you to do a thing like that. / 彼は今度はいつもに似合わずうまくやった. This time he has done unusually well for him.

にえくりかえる 腹の中が煮えくり返るような思いだった. My blood boiled with anger. / 彼は彼女の言葉に煮えくり返るような思いをしていた. He was seething at her words.

にえる よく煮えていますか. Is it (properly) cooked?

におい これはいいにおいがする. This smells nice. / 確かにガスのにおいだ. I'm sure I smell gas.

におう[2] また飲んできたわね. におうわよ. You've been drinking again, haven't you? I can smell it on you. / このどぶはいやにおうね. Doesn't this ditch stink!

におわせる やめるかもしれないとにおわせておいた. I dropped him a hint that I might resign.

にかい[1] 2階に寝室が3つあります. There are three bedrooms upstairs. / 彼女は2階で寝ていますよ. She is upstairs in bed.

にがす 逃がした魚は大きい. The one that got away is always bigger.

にかた それは煮方が悪いからです. It's because you didn't cook it right [the right way].

にがて 英語は苦手だ. I am very

にがにがしい 苦々しい 〈不快な〉 unpleasant; disgusting; 〈恥ずべき〉 shameful ¶苦々しげに disgustedly; 《文》 with displeasure [a displeased look]. 文例◊

にがみ 苦み A bitter taste; bitterness ¶苦みがある be [taste] bitter / 苦みばしった顔 a stern and handsome face; 《文》 an imposing countenance.

にがむし 苦虫 ¶苦虫をかみつぶしたような顔をする ⇒にがい (苦い顔をする), にがにがしい (苦々しげに).

にかよう 似通う ⇒にる¹.

にがよもぎ 苦よもぎ 〖植〗 wormwood.

ニカラグア Nicaragua ¶ニカラグアのNicaraguan / ニカラグア人 a Nicaraguan.

にがり 苦り bittern.

にがりきる 苦り切る look sour [disgusted] (at); scowl [frown] (at); make a wry [sour] face (at).

にかわ 膠 glue ¶にかわでつける glue 《A》 to 《B》; fasten with glue.

にがわせ(てがた) 荷為替(手形) a documentary draft [bill].

にがわらい 苦笑い ¶苦笑いする smile [give] a wry [sour] smile.

にがん 二眼 ¶二眼レフ a twin-lens reflex camera / 二眼レンズ twin lenses.

にきび a pimple; acne (総称) ¶にきびの跡 an acne scar / にきびのある, にきびだらけの pimpled; pimply; 《英》 spotty / にきびをつぶす squeeze a pimple. 文例◊

にぎやか 賑やか 〈陽気な〉 lively; gay; 〈雑踏した〉 bustling; busy; crowded; 〈繁盛した〉 prosperous; flourishing / にぎやかな通り a crowded [busy] street / にぎやかな人 a lively [gay] person / にぎやかな笑い声 a gay [merry] laughter.

にぎらせる 握らせる let sb take hold of 《one's hand》; 〈金を〉 slip (money) into sb's hand [pocket]; slip 《sb a 10,000-yen note》; 心づけを〈ポーターに〉 tip 《a porter》; 〈わいろを〉 bribe; 《口語》 grease [oil] sb's palm. 文例◊

にぎり 握り ¶〈把握〉 a grip; a grasp; 〈取っ手〉 a handle; 〈扉などの丸い取っ手〉 a knob ¶ひと握りの米 a handful of rice / 握りこぶし a (clenched) fist / 握りずし hand-rolled[-shaped] sushi / 握り飯 a rice ball / 握り屋 a close-fisted [tightfisted, stingy] person; a miser.

にぎりしめる 握り締める grip [grasp] tightly [hard]; clasp; squeeze ¶手を握り締める squeeze sb's hand; give sb's hand a squeeze. 文例◊

にぎりつぶす 握り潰す crush sth in one's hand; 〈法案などを〉 shelve; kill; pigeonhole; 《米》 lay (a bill) on the table; 《米》 table.

にぎる 握る grasp; clasp; seize; take [get] hold of ¶固く[ぎゅっと]握る take fast [firm] hold of 《sb's hand》; clasp [grip] sth tightly / 手を握る 〈こぶしをつくる〉 clench one's fist; 〈人の手をつかむ〉 clasp sb's hand; 〈握手する〉 shake hands 《with》 / 秘密を握る hold [keep] sb's secret / 権力を握る[握っている] come into [be in] power / 覇権を握る hold the supremacy (in); 〈スポーツで〉 win the (wrestling) championship. 文例◊

にぎわい 賑わい 〈繁栄〉 prosperity; 〈雑踏〉 bustle; activity; 〈人出〉 a crowd; a (good, poor) turnout ★ turnout は形容詞なしで用いられることはまれ.

にぎわう 賑わう 〈繁盛する〉 prosper; flourish; do (a) good [thriving] business; 〈人が出る(場所が主語)〉 be crowded [thronged] with people; be in great bustle.

にぎわす 賑わす 〈繁盛させる〉 make prosperous; 〈活気をつける〉 enliven.

にく 肉 〈体の〉 flesh; 〈食用の〉 meat; 〈印肉〉 sealing ink; an ink pad (ケースに入った); 〈肉体〉 the flesh ¶ほほの肉 the flesh of the cheeks / 肉がつく[落ちる] put on [lose] flesh / 肉がついている 〈人間が〉 have plenty of flesh on one; 〈動物などが〉 have plenty of meat on it; be well fleshed out / 肉の厚い thick; 〈野菜などの〉 succulent / 肉の薄い thin / 肉の多い fleshy; 〈太った〉 fat / 肉のしまった muscular; brawny; well-knit / 肉のない fleshless; 〈やせた〉 thin / 肉牛 〈1頭〉 a beef cow; 〈集合的〉 beef cattle / 肉汁 meat juice; gravy / 肉質 fleshy substance; flesh; 〈果肉〉 pulpy substance; pulp / 肉団子 a meatball / 肉池(⁵) an ink-pad case / 肉片 a piece [cut (切った)] of meat / 肉屋 〈人〉 a butcher; 〈店〉 a meat [butcher] shop; 《米》 a meat store; 《英》 a butcher's / 肉料理 meat cookery [dishes]; 〈一品〉 a meat dish / 肉類 (various types of) meat / 肉色の flesh-colored / 肉切り包丁 〈食卓用の〉 a carving knife; 〈肉屋用の〉 a butcher's knife; a cleaver / 肉ひき機 a mincing machine; a mincer. 文例◊

にくい 憎い 〈いやな〉 hateful; detestable; horrible; 〈意地の悪い〉 spiteful; 〈腹の立つ〉 provocative; provoking ¶憎いことを言う say something uncappable [devastating] / 憎からず思う love; care for; feel affectionate toward; have a soft spot for.

-にくい hard; difficult ¶扱いにくい be hard

bad [no good] at English. | 〈教科としての〉 English is one of my poorest [weakest] subjects.

にがにがしい そんな事がまかり通るとは苦々しい限りだ. It's unforgivable that such things should be possible!

にきび 額にニキビができた. Pimples came[broke] out on his forehead. / それは僕のにきび華やかなりし頃だった. I was at the 'acne age' then.

にぎらせる 運転手に握らせて秘密を聞いた. I tipped my chauffeur and got him to tell me the secret. | I persuaded my chauffeur to tell me the secret by slipping him some money.

にぎりしめる 彼は両手を固く握りしめて, さあ来いと身構えた. He stood up, ready to fight, with his hands tightly clenched.

にぎる 彼は手を握ったり開いたりした. He clenched and unclenched his fist.

にぎわい 展覧会は大変なにぎわいだった. There was a great turnout (of people) at the exhibition.

にぎわす この問題は最近ずいぶんと新聞をにぎわした. This prob-

にくが to handle / 答えにくい質問 an awkward [a difficult, a tricky] question. 文例⇩

にくが 肉芽 〖医〗(a) granulation.

にくがん 肉眼 the naked [unaided] eye ¶肉眼で見る[見える] see with [be visible to] the naked eye.

にくげ 憎げ ¶憎げのない disarming;〈無邪気な〉artless / 憎げに ⇨にくらしい (憎らしげに).

にくさ 憎さ 〈憎らしさ〉hatefulness;〈憎悪〉hatred; hate.

にくしみ 憎しみ hatred;《文》enmity ¶憎しみから out of hatred (for) / 憎しみを受ける be hated;《文》incur sb's hatred.

にくしゅ 肉腫 〖医〗a sarcoma (pl. -s, -mata).

にくしょく 肉食 〈食べること〉meat-eating (人が); flesh-eating (動物が);〈食事〉a meat diet ¶肉食する〈人が〉eat meat;〈動物が〉eat flesh / 肉食獣 a carnivorous [flesh-eating] animal; a carnivore.

にくしん 肉親 〈人〉a blood relation [relative]; one's (own) flesh and blood;〈関係〉(a) blood relationship.

にくずく 肉ずく〈香料〉nutmeg;〈木〉a nutmeg tree.

にくずれ 荷崩れ load shifting; a load shift;〈船荷の〉cargo shifting; a cargo shift.

にくせい 肉声 a [one's] (natural) voice.

にくたい 肉体《文》the flesh; the body ¶肉体の《文》fleshly;《文》bodily; physical / 肉体関係 sexual relations / 肉体美 physical beauty;《文》the beauty of the body [the human form]/ 肉体労働 physical [muscular] labor.

にくたらしい 憎たらしい ⇨にくらしい.

にくづき 肉付き ¶肉付きのよい fleshy;〈太っとった〉fat;《文》corpulent / 肉付きのわるい fleshless;〈やせた〉thin; lean.

にくづけ 肉付け〈彫刻の〉modeling ¶肉付けする give body and substance (to); flesh out.

にくにくしい 憎々しい ⇨にくい, にくらしい.

にくはく 肉薄 ¶肉薄する〈戦争で〉close in on《the enemy》; press《the enemy》hard;〈競技で〉run《a competitor》close [hard].

にくばなれ 肉離れ ¶肉離れを起こす tear a muscle (in one's leg); have one's muscle torn.

にくひつ 肉筆 one's own handwriting; an autograph ¶肉筆で in one's own handwriting / 肉筆の手紙〈印刷に対して〉a handwritten letter;〈自筆の〉a letter in one's own handwriting; an autograph letter (文化財的価値を持った有名人の) / 肉筆画 an original painting [drawing].

にくぶと 肉太 ¶肉太の bold-faced《type》/ 肉太に書く write thick [《文》in a bold hand].

にくぼそ 肉細 ¶肉細の light-faced《type》.

にくまれぐち 憎まれ口 ¶憎まれ口をきく say spiteful things (to); throw [hurl] insults [brickbats] (at).

にくまれっこ 憎まれっ子 a bad [naughty] boy.

にくまれやく 憎まれ役 the part of the villain [《口語》the bad guy];〈損な役割〉a thankless role.

にくむ 憎む hate; detest; have a hatred for [of] ¶憎むべき hateful; detestable;《文》cursed; damnable / …を憎む余り out of hatred for….

にくよく 肉欲 lust;《文》carnal desire;《文》sexual appetite ¶肉欲にふける indulge in carnal pleasures / 肉欲を満たす gratify one's lust.

にぐら 荷鞍 a packsaddle.

にくらしい 憎らしい hateful; odious; detestable;《文》cursed ¶憎らしげに hatefully; in a hateful manner; with (obvious) hatred. 文例⇩

にぐるま 荷車〈手車〉a cart;〈主に英〉a handcart;〈荷馬車〉a wagon;〈英〉a cart ¶荷車に荷を積む load a cart [wagon] (with goods) / 荷車 1 台分の家具 a cartload of furniture.

ニグロ ニグロ くぐろん.

ニクロムせん ニクロム線 〖商標名〗Nichrome wire.

にぐん 二軍〈一般に〉the second team;〈野球の〉a farm team.

にげ 逃げ ¶逃げを打つ〈逃亡を図る〉try to escape [get away] (from);〈約束・義務などから〉try to back out of《one's promise》; try to excuse oneself (from); try to dodge [shirk]《one's duty》/ 逃げ馬〖競馬〗a front-runner.

にげあし 逃げ足 ¶逃げ足が速い be quick at running away [《文》at flight].

にげうせる 逃げ失せる run [get] away ⇨にげる.

にげおおせる 逃げおおせる make good [《文》effect] one's escape; make one's getaway.

にげおくれる 逃げ遅れる fail to escape.

にげかくれ 逃げ隠れ 文例⇩

にげぐち 逃げ口 a way of escape; a way out; an outlet.

にげこうじょう 逃げ口上 an excuse; an evasive answer;《文》a subterfuge ¶逃げ口上を言う〈言い抜けを言う〉find [cook up] an excuse;〈あいまいなことを言う〉give an evasive answer. 文例⇩

にげごし 逃げ腰 ¶逃げ腰になる〈逃げ出す用意をする〉get [make] ready to run away [back

---

lem has been in the newspapers a lot [a great deal] lately.

にく 君はもっと肉がつかなければいけない。You need more flesh on you.

-にくい 彼の思想は手短には説明しにくい。His ideas cannot be explained in a few words. / 彼の前ではどうも切り出しにくかった。I found it hard to mention it in his presence.

にくまれっこ 憎まれっ子世にはばかる。Ill weeds grow apace [fast]. 〖諺〗

にくらしい 憎らしい雨だな。How annoying this rain is! / 彼は憎らしいほど落ち着いていた。He remained provokingly cool. / 彼は憎らしいほど文章がうまい。I wish I could write as well as he does.

にげかくれ 逃げ隠れは決していたしません。I have no intention of trying to escape justice. | I'm quite ready to surrender myself to justice.

にげこうじょう 君のこの釈明は逃げ口上にすぎない。This explanation of yours is nothing but an excuse.

にげこむ 逃げ込む run 《into》; take refuge 《in》; seek [find] shelter 《in, under》; take [seek] sanctuary 《in》. 文例↓

にげじたく 逃げ支度 ¶逃げ支度する prepare to run away; make ready to back out.

にげそこなう 逃げ損う fail to escape.

にげだす 逃げ出す break into a run; run away; make off; 《文》flee; 《文》take (to) flight; take to *one's* heels.

にげのびる 逃げ延びる get away; make good [《文》effect] *one's* escape.

にげば 逃げ場 ¶逃げ場を失う have *one's* escape cut off; be driven [brought] to bay; be trapped 《in a burning building》. 文例↓

にげまどう 逃げ惑う run about [around] trying to escape; run this way and that to make *one's* escape.

にげまわる 逃げ回る 〈逃げ惑う〉⇒にげまどう; 〈比喩的に〉try [use every possible pretext] to avoid 《taking on a job》; fight shy of 《being named (the) chairman of the committee》.

にげみち 逃げ道 an escape route; 〈方法〉a way [means] of escape; 〈困難などからの〉a way out; an escape ¶逃げ道を断つ cut off *sb's* retreat / あらかじめ逃げ道を用意しておく provide for *one's* retreat; prepare *one's* escape [excuse] in advance.

にげる 逃げる run away [off]; get away; escape; 《文》flee; 《文》take (to) flight; take to *one's* heels; make *one's* escape [getaway]; 〈おりなどから〉break out [loose]; fly away 〈鳥が〉; 〈回避する〉shirk [dodge] 《*one's* duty》; back out of 《*one's* promise》¶…を持って逃げる run away [make off] with 《*sb's* money》/ 妻に逃げられた be deserted by *one's* wife; *one's* wife leaves *one*. 文例↓

にげん 二元 《哲》duality ¶二元的 dual / 二元論 dualism.

にこう 二項《数》¶二項の binomial / 二項式 a binomial expression [formula] / 二項定理 the binomial theorem / 二項方程式 a binomial equation.

にこごり 煮凝り jelly.

にごしらえ 荷ごしらえ packing ¶荷ごしらえする pack (up). 文例↓

にごす 濁す 〈濁らせる〉make *sth* muddy [《文》turbid]; 〈ことばを〉speak evasively; do not commit *oneself* ¶返事を濁す give a vague [a noncommittal, an evasive] answer.

ニコチン nicotine ¶ニコチンを除いた[のない] denicotinized [nicotineless] 《cigarettes》/ ニコチン中毒 nicotine poisoning; nicotinism. 文例↓

にこにこ smilingly; beamingly; with a smile ¶にこにこ笑う[する] smile (radiantly) 《at》; smile a sweet smile; beam (on); look happy / にこにこ迎える smile *sb* a welcome / 大にこにこで with a big smile on *one's* face / にこにこ顔 a smiling [beaming] face. 文例↓

にこみ 煮込み (a) stew.

にこむ 煮込む 〈よく煮る〉boil well; stew; 〈混ぜて煮る〉cook together.

にこやか にこやかな 〈もの柔らかな〉《文》benign; genial-looking; 〈にこにこした〉smiling; happy ⇒にこにこ ¶にこやかな顔 a smiling [beaming] face; a benign countenance.

にこり ⇒にこにこ ¶にこりともしないで unsmilingly; with a straight face.

にごり 濁り 〈混濁〉muddiness; 〈不純〉impurity; 〈濁音〉a voiced sound; 〈濁点〉the dot mark of a voiced sound ¶濁りをうつ[濁点をつける] write the dot mark of a voiced sound 《alongside a letter》.

にごる 濁る 〈水が〉get [《文》become] muddy [《文》turbid]; 〈飲み物が〉get [《文》become] cloudy; 〈音が〉be voiced; 〈不純になる〉《文》become impure ¶濁った muddy; 《文》turbid; 《文》impure; 〈空気などの〉foul; 〈飲み物の〉cloudy; 〈声の〉thick; 〈発音の〉voiced / 濁らせる ⇒にごす.

にごん 二言 ⇒ふし 文例.

にざかな 煮魚 boiled fish.

にさばき 荷さばき disposal of goods; (a) sale.

にさん 二、三 ¶2, 3 の two or three; a couple of / 2, 3 日中に in a day or two; in a couple of days / 二、三流の小説家 a minor novelist.

にさんか 二酸化《化》二酸化物 (a) dioxide / 二酸化炭素[窒素] carbon [nitrogen] dioxide.

にし 西 (the) west ¶西の west; western /西の〈西部の〉in the west; 〈西方に〉to the west; 〈西側に〉on the west / 西へ west; westward; to [toward] the west / 西に傾く太陽 the declining [setting,《詩》westering] sun / 西に向かう go [《文》proceed] west [westward] / 西向きの家 a house facing west; a house with a west [westerly] exposure / 西日のさす部屋 a room exposed to the afternoon sun / 西風 a west [westerly] wind / 西側 the west [western] side / 〈東西両陣営の〉the West. 文例↓

にじ 二次 ¶二次の secondary; second / 二次感染 secondary infection / 二次方程式《数》a quadratic equation / 二次方程式の根を解く

にげこむ 女は東慶寺に逃げ込んだ。 The woman sought [found] sanctuary in the Tokeiji Temple. / 雨に降られてその教会に逃げ込んだ。 We were caught in a shower and ran into the church for shelter.

にげば 賊は逃げ場を失ってとうとうつかまった。 The thief was at last driven into a corner and caught.

にげる とても逃げられない。 There is no getting out of it. | I am in for it. / 彼は急用があると言ってうまくその場を逃げてしまった。 He made a clever escape by saying that he had some urgent business.

にごしらえ 彼は直ちに荷ごしらえして宿を引き払った。 He packed up at once and left his lodgings.

ニコチン 彼はニコチン中毒だ。 He is addicted to smoking. | He is a tobacco addict.

にこにこ 彼はにこにこ顔だった。 He was all smiles. | His face was wreathed in smiles.

にごる 雨上がりで川の水は濁っていた。 The river was muddy [《文》turbid] after the rain.

にし はるか西に富士山がそびえている。 Far to the west towers Mt. Fuji. / 西も東もわからない。 I've no idea where I am.

にじ 虹が出た[空にかかっていた]。 A rainbow appeared [hung

にじ 951 **にたにた**

公式 the quadratic formula / 第二次吉田内閣 the second Yoshida Cabinet / 二次林 a second-growth forest.

にじ² 虹 a rainbow ¶虹のような気炎を吐く talk big / 虹色の rainbow-colored; iridescent. 文例⇩

にしインドしょとう 西インド諸島 the West Indies ¶西インド諸島の West Indian / 西インド諸島人 a West Indian.

ニジェール Niger ¶ニジェールの Nigerien / ニジェール共和国 the Republic of the Niger.

にじかい 二次会 a party after a party ¶二次会を開く have another [carry on the] party at another place.

にしき 錦 Japanese brocade ¶錦の御旗 the Imperial standard (made of gold brocade); 〈比喩的〉(文) a sacred [worthy] cause / 故郷に錦を飾る return home loaded with honors / 錦絵 a color [colored woodblock] print.

にしきごい 錦鯉 a varicolored [golden] carp.

にしきへび 錦蛇〖動〗a python.

にしサモア 西サモア〈国名〉Western Samoa.

-にしては for; considering. 文例⇩

-にしても ⇨-しても.

にじます 虹鱒〖魚〗a rainbow trout.

にじみでる 滲み出る ooze [seep] out. 文例⇩

にじむ 滲む 〈インクなどが〉run; spread; 〈ぼんやりする〉blur; be blurred ¶血のにじんだ bloodstained (cloth). 文例⇩

にしめ 煮染め vegetables [fish] stewed in soy

にしめる 煮染める stew (vegetables in soy sauce) ¶しょうゆで煮込したような手ぬぐい a horribly dirty towel.

にしゃたくいつ 二者択一 a (straight) choice between two things [alternatives].

にじゅう¹ 二十 twenty ¶第20 the twentieth / 20代の青年 a young man in his twenties.

にじゅう² 二重 ¶二重の double; (文) twofold; 〈二元的〉dual / 二重の利益がある be of double advantage (to) / 二重に doubly; twice; over again / 二重にする[になる] double (酔ったりなどして)二重に見える 〈いろいろの物が〉see [be seeing] double / 〈ある特定の物が〉see two of 《you》/ 二重に払う pay for *sth* twice / 二重国籍者 a person with dual nationality / 二重唱[奏]〖音楽〗a duet / 二重人格〖心理〗a split [double] personality / 二重生活 a double life; (文) a dual existence / 二重底の double-[false-]bottomed / 二重母音 a diphthong / 二重窓 a double-paned window / 二重丸 a double circle / 二重焼付け〖映画〗super-imposition.

にじょう 二乗〖数〗⇨じじょう¹.

にじょうき 二畳紀〖地質〗the Permian (period).

にしょく¹ 二色 ¶二色刷り two-color printing / 二色塗りの two-tone(d) (motorcars).

にしょく² 二食 《taking》two meals a day.

にじりでる にじり出る crawl out 《of a place》on *one's* knees.

にじりよる にじり寄る crawl up 《to a place》on *one's* knees; sidle [edge] up (to).

にしる, じしる 煮汁 (fish, meat) stock.

-にしろ ¶どんな金持ちにしろ however rich [no matter how rich] *one* may be / 本当にしろ, うそにしろ whether *it* is true or not.

にしん 鰊〖魚〗a herring (*pl.* -(s)).

にしんほう 二進法〖数〗the binary system [notation].

ニス varnish ¶ニスを塗る varnish (over) 《the surface》; apply varnish (to).

にせ 偽〈模造品〉an imitation; a sham; a fake; 〈贋造(ぞう)品〉a counterfeit; a forgery ¶にせ(もの)の false; sham; forged; fake(d) / にせ金 counterfeit money; 〈硬貨〉a false coin / にせ金造り a counterfeiter / にせ刑事[学生] a bogus detective [student] / にせ手紙 a forged letter.

にせアカシア〖植〗a black locust; a false acacia.

にせい 二世〈日系米人〉a *Nisei* (*pl.* -(s)); a Japanese American; an American-born Japanese ¶ヘンリー二世 Henry Ⅱ ★Ⅱ は the second と読む / ジョン・スミス二世〈父と同名の息子〉《米》John Smith, Jr. ★Jr. は junior と読む. 文例⇩

にせる 似せる 〈まねて造る〉imitate; copy; model (A) on [after] (B); 〈贋造(ぞう)する〉counterfeit; forge. 文例⇩

にそう 尼僧 a nun ⇨あま¹ ¶尼僧院 a convent; a nunnery.

にそくさんもん 二束三文 ¶二束三文で売る sell *sth* for a song; sell *sth* dirt cheap.

にだい 荷台 the bed (of a truck); a roof rack (for a car); the carrier (of a motorcycle).

にたき 煮炊き cooking ¶煮炊きする cook / 自分で煮炊きする do *one's* own cooking; cook for *oneself*; prepare *one's* own meals.

にだしじる 煮出し汁 (meat, fish) stock; broth.

にだす 煮出す extract (the flavor) by boiling; (文) decoct.

にたつ 煮立つ ⇨にえたつ.

にたてる 煮立てる boil up.

にたにた にたにた ¶にたにた笑う smirk (at);

---

in the sky].

にじかい どこか二次会に行かないか. Are we going on somewhere afterward?

-にしては 7月にしては涼しい. It is cool for July. / あの人は80歳にしては若い. He has very good eyesight considering that he is eighty years of age.

にじみでる 血がシャツからにじみ出た. Blood came oozing through his shirt. / 彼の額に玉の汗がにじみ出ていた. Beads of sweat stood on his forehead. / 手紙の文面には娘に対する彼の深い愛情がにじみ出ていた. His deep affection for his daughter permeated his letter.

にじむ このインクはどんな紙に書いてもにじみません. This ink does not run on any paper. / 包帯が血でにじんでいた. The bandage was red with blood. / 天井はところどころ雨でにじんでいた. The ceiling was stained here and there by rain.

にせい 永田君に二世が生まれた. Nagata's wife gave him [provided him with] a son.

にせる この建物は帝国ホテルに似せてある. This building is modeled after [on] the Imperial Hotel.

にそくさんもん そんな物を売っても二束三文だよ. That wouldn't bring [fetch] you anything much. | You wouldn't get much

にたりと　⇒にたに.

にたりよったり　似たり寄ったり　¶似たり寄ったりである be much [nearly] the same; be much of a muchness. 文例⇩

にだん　二段　¶二段構えで交渉に臨む start negotiations armed with a fall-back proposal; present one's terms while keeping an alternative up one's sleeve / 二段ベッド a bunk [double-deck] bed.

にちい　日伊　¶日伊の Italo-Japanese.

にちいん　日印　¶日印の Indo-Japanese.

にちえい　日英　¶日英の Anglo-Japanese.

にちげん　日限　⇒きじつ, きげん³.

にちじ　日時　the date (and time); the time.

にちじょう　日常　〈毎日〉every day; daily; 〈日ごろ〉usually　¶日常の daily; 〈普通の〉everyday; usual; ordinary / 日常の仕事 (one's) daily work [business]; 〈きまりきった〉routine work / 日常の出来事, 日常茶飯事 nothing out of the ordinary; a daily occurrence [happening]; an everyday affair / 日常生活 daily [everyday] life. 文例⇩

にちどく　日独　¶日独の Japanese-German.

にちふつ　日仏　¶日仏の Franco-Japanese.

にちべい　日米　¶日米の Japanese-American, U.S.-Japanese / 日米関係 relations between the United States and Japan; Japanese-American relations / 日米安全保障条約 the U.S.-Japan Security Treaty.

にちぼつ　日没　日没に at sunset [sundown]; at nightfall / 日没後[前] after [before] sunset / 日没ごろ (at) about sunset; toward sundown.

にちや　日夜　〈昼も夜も〉day and night; night and day; 〈常に〉always; constantly.

にちゃく　二着　〈順位〉the second place; 〈人〉a runner-up ⇒にい.

にちゃにちゃ　¶にちゃにちゃする sticky; greasy (油で).

にちよう　日用　¶日用の for daily [everyday] use / 日用品 daily necessities [necessaries].

にちよう(び)　日曜(日)　Sunday (略: Sun.)　¶日曜日に on Sunday; 〈いつも〉on Sundays; 〈米〉Sundays　⇒用法　次に[この前の]日曜日に next [last] Sunday; 〈文〉on Sunday next [last] / 日曜画家 a Sunday [weekend] painter / 日曜学校 a Sunday school / 日曜大工〈事〉home carpentry; 〈英〉D.I.Y.; 〈人〉a Sunday [weekend] carpenter [handyman]; 〈口語〉a do-it-yourselfer / 日曜礼拝 Sunday service(s). 用法 He will come on Sunday. の on Sunday は「次の日曜日に」の意. このように, on Sunday は話し手と聞き手の間でいつの日曜日か了解されている場合に用いられる. They never fail to meet on Sundays. の on Sundays は「日曜日にはいつも」の意. He died on a Sunday. の on a Sunday は「ある日曜日に」で, 父が亡くなったのがたまたま日曜日のことだったということ.

にちろせんそう　日露戦争　the Russo-Japanese War (of 1904-1905).

にっか　日課　〈授業〉a daily lesson; 〈仕事〉daily task; daily work; daily routine (きまりきった); 〈雑用〉daily chores　¶日課表 a (school) timetable; a daily schedule (of training). 文例⇩

にっかん　肉塊　a lump of flesh [meat].

につかわしい　似つかわしい　〈文〉becoming; suitable ⇒にあう (似合った).

にっかん¹　日刊　daily publication [issue]　¶日刊の published daily; daily / 日刊新聞 a daily (newspaper). 文例⇩

にっかん²　肉感　¶肉感をそそる〈事が主語〉arouse [excite] one's lust [〈文〉carnal desire] / 肉感的 sensual; voluptuous.

にっかん³　日韓　¶日韓の Japan-Korea; Japanese-Korean; 《trade》between Japan and Korea.

にっき　肉桂　⇒にっけい².

にっき(ちょう)　日記(帳)　a diary; a journal; 〈主に簿記で〉a daybook (略: d.b.)　¶日記をつける keep [write] a diary / 日記に書く record [make an entry of]《a matter》in one's diary / 日記文学 diaries (as a branch of literature).

にっきゅう　日給　daily wages [pay]　¶日給で働く work by the day. 文例⇩

にっきょうそ　日教組　〈日本教職員組合〉the Japan Teachers Union.

にづくり　荷造り　packing　¶荷造りする pack (up) / 荷造りをとく unpack / 荷造り費 packing charges. 文例⇩

につけ　煮付け　fish [vegetables] boiled with soy sauce (and sugar).

にっけい¹　日系　¶日系アメリカ人 an American of Japanese descent [extraction, parentage]; a Japanese American.

にっけい²　肉桂　〈香料〉cinnamon; 〈木〉a cinnamon tree.

にっけいひょう　日計表　〖簿記〗a daily trial balance sheet.

---

for that. / 彼は土地建物を二束三文で売り払わなければならなかった. He had to sell his property for a small fraction of its value.

にたりよったり　その点ではこの両者は似たり寄ったりです. There is not much to choose between them in that respect.

にちじょう　当時はそういう恐ろしいことが日常的に行なわれていた. Horrible things of that sort were being done routinely in those days.

にちよう(び)　日曜もなしに働いています. We work even on Sundays. / 日曜ごとに彼女の子供たちにピアノを教えてあげた. I gave piano lessons to her children every Sunday.

にっか　彼は毎朝散歩するのを日課としている. He makes a point of taking a walk every morning.

にっかん¹　それは日刊ですか週刊ですか. Is it a daily or a weekly?

にっきゅう　日給8千円をもらっています. They pay me [I get] 8,000 yen a day.

にづくり　荷造りが悪い. It isn't properly packed.

にっこう　日光が雲間からさしている. Sunlight is pouring down through rifts in the clouds.

にっさん²　この工場は日産200台の自動車を生産することができる. The factory can put [turn] out 200 cars a day.

にっけいれん 日経連 〈日本経営者団体連盟〉 the Japan Federation of Employers' Association.

につける 煮付ける boil 《fish》 with soy sauce (and sugar).

ニッケル nickel ¶ニッケルの nickel; 〈ニッケルめっきの〉 nickel-plated 《watches》; nickeled 《steel》.

にっこう 日光 sunlight; sunshine; 〈光線〉 the rays of the sun; sunbeams ¶激しい日光 a glaring [hard] sunlight; the strong sun / 日光でかわかす dry sth in the sun / 日光にさらす expose sth to the sun; sun / 日光消毒をする disinfect sth by sunlight [by airing in the sun] / 日光浴をする sunbathe; bathe in the sun. 文例↓

にっこり ⇨ にこに こ.

にっさん[1] 日参 ¶日参する pay a daily visit 《to》; visit 《a place》 daily [every day].

にっさん[2] 日産 daily production; (a) daily output ⇨ げっさん. 文例↓

にっし 日誌 ⇨ にっき(ちょう).

にっしゃびょう 日射病 sunstroke ¶日射病にかかる have [suffer from] sunstroke.

にっしょう 日照 sunshine ¶日照時間 hours of sunlight / 日照権 the right to sunlight; the right to light in 《one's home》.

にっしょうき 日章旗 the Rising-Sun flag.

にっしょく 日食 an eclipse of the sun; a solar eclipse. 文例↓

にっしんげっぽ 日進月歩 rapid progress [《文》advance] ¶日進月歩の rapidly-advancing; 《文》 ever-progressing.

にっしんせんそう 日清戦争 the Sino-Japanese War (of 1894-5).

にっすう 日数 the number of days ¶多くの日数がかかる take a great number of days [a long time] / 日数がたつにつれて as days pass [go by]. 文例↓

にっソ 日ソ ¶日ソの Soviet-Japanese; Japanese-Soviet / 日ソ漁業条約 the Japanese-Soviet Fisheries Treaty.

にっちもさっちも ¶にっちもさっちも行かない be in a fix [predicament, quandary]; have [see] no way out; be in deep trouble.

にっちゅう[1] 日中 in the daytime; by day; 〈日盛りに〉 during [in] the heat of the day. 文例↓

にっちゅう[2] 日中 ¶日中の Japanese-Chinese; Sino-Japanese / 日中関係 Sino-Japanese relations; relations between Japan and China.

にっちょく 日直 ¶日直である be on day duty.

にってい 日程 the day's program [schedule]; 〈議事順序〉 the day's agenda; the order of the day ¶ぎっしり詰まった日程 a crowded [crammed] schedule / 日程を変更する alter the day's schedule / 日程に入る proceed with the order of the day / 日程に載せる place [put] 《an item》 on the day's agenda / 日程に載っている事項 the items on the day's agenda. 文例↓

にっと ¶にっと笑う grin.

ニット ¶ニットの knitted [knit] 《clothing》.

にっとう 日当 a daily allowance; 〈日給〉 daily wages ¶日当いくらで働く work by the day [for so much a day].

にっぽう 日報 a daily report [bulletin]; 〈新聞〉 a daily (newspaper).

にっぽん 日本 ⇨ にほん.

につまる 煮詰まる be boiled down; boil down.

にづみ 荷積み loading ¶荷積みする load 《a truck》 (with goods).

につめる 煮詰める boil down.

にと 二兎 文例↓

にど 二度 twice; 〈再び〉 again ¶1週に2度 twice a week / 2度目の妻 one's second wife / 2度目に for the second time / 二度とない好機 the chance [opportunity] of a lifetime / ペンキを2度塗りする give 《the door》 two coats of paint / 2度咲き reblooming; (a) second blooming; a second flush (of roses).

にとう 二等 the second class; 〈船の〉 the cabin class ¶2等の切符 a second-class ticket / 2等になる finish [come off] second; get [win] second place / 2等で行く travel second-class / 〈口語〉 go second / 二等国 a second-rate power; a nation of the second rank / 2等車 a second-class car [carriage] / 2等賞 the second prize / 2等品 a second-grade[-rate] article.

にとうきん 二頭筋 〈解〉 the biceps (of the arm) ★ biceps は単複同形.

にとうぶん 二等分 ¶二等分する divide sth into two equal parts [two exact halves]; 《文》 bisect 《a line》 / 二等分線 a bisector.

にとうへんさんかくけい 二等辺三角形 〈数〉 an isosceles triangle.

にとうりゅう 二刀流 two-sword fencing.

ニトログリセリン nitroglycerin(e). 文例↓

になう 担う 〈肩でかつぐ〉 carry 《a load》 on one's shoulder; shoulder 《a gun》; 〈身に引き受ける〉 bear 《a burden》; take 《a job》 on oneself ¶栄誉を担う have [《文》 be bestowed] the honor 《of》. 文例↓

にっしゃびょう この人は長いこと日にさらされていたことで日射病にかかったのです. His is a case of sunstroke caused by long exposure to the sun.

にっしょく 今月10日に日食がある. A solar eclipse will occur [be seen] on the tenth of this month.

にっすう それをするのにどのくらい日数がかかりますか. How long [many days] will it take to do it?

にっちゅう[1] 日中は休んで夜歩く ことにした. We decided to rest by day and walk by night.

にってい 今日のご日程は. What is your schedule [program] for today?

につまる 問題は費用を100万円以内に抑えるかどうかという一点にまで煮詰まった. The problem boiled down to one point: whether or not to restrict the expenses to one million yen.

にと 二兎を追うものは一兎をも得 ず. He who runs after two hares will catch neither. | Grasp all, lose all. 〈諺〉

にど あんな所へは二度と行くもんか. I will never go there again. / 二度あることは三度ある. What happens twice will happen thrice. / ここへ来るのはこれで2度目だ. This is my second visit here.

になう 彼は学校を代表してその会に出席する栄誉を担った. He had

にんん

にんん 二人 ⇨ふたり ¶2人組 a pair 《of criminals》;《口語》a twosome;《俗》a duo《pl. -s》/ 二人三脚 a three-legged race.

にぬし 荷主〈持ち主〉the owner (of the goods);〈送り主〉the consignor.

にぬり 丹塗り ¶丹塗りの鳥居 a red(-painted) torii.

にねん 二年 two years ¶2年のクラス the second-year class;〈大学の〉《米》the sophomore class / 2年生 a second-year pupil [student];〈小学校の〉《米》a second-grade pupil, a pupil in the second grade;〈中学の〉《米》an eighth-grade pupil;〈高校の〉《米》an eleventh-grade student;〈大学の〉《米》a sophomore / 2年生植物 a biennial (plant).

にのあし 二の足 ¶二の足を踏む have second thoughts (about); hesitate (at, over, to *do*); jib [balk] (at); recoil [flinch] (from).

にのうで 二の腕 the upper arm.

にのく 二の句 ¶二の句がつげない be dum(b)-founded; be struck dumb. 文例⇩

にのつぎ 二の次 ¶二の次の secondary;《文》of secondary importance.

にのまい 二の舞 ¶二の舞を演じる repeat *sb*'s mistake [failure,《文》folly]; fall into the same trap (as *sb*);《文》commit the same error as *sb*.

にばい 二倍 twice; double ¶2倍長い[重い] be twice as long [heavy] as *sth* / 2倍の twice; double / 2倍(に)する double《the profit》⇨ばい. 文例⇩

にばこ 荷箱 a packing box [case].

にばしゃ 荷馬車 a (freight) wagon; a cart; a dray.

にばん 二番〈序列〉the second; number two; No. 2;〈2着の〉the runner-up (競走での) ¶2番目の兄 *one*'s second eldest brother / 末から2番目の弟 *one*'s youngest brother but one / 世界で2番目に高い山 the second highest mountain in the world / 二番せんじ〈茶〉the second brew of tea;〈比喩的に〉a pale [《文》pallid] imitation. 文例⇩

にひゃくとうか 二百十日 the 210th day (from the first day of spring according to the lunar calendar).

ニヒリスト a nihilist.

ニヒリズム nihilism.

ニヒル ニヒルな nihilistic.

にぶ 二部〈2つの部分〉two parts;〈2冊〉two copies [volumes];〈第2部〉the second part;〈夜間部〉a night school [class] ¶二部合唱をする sing《a piece of music》in two parts.

にぶい 鈍い〈人の性質などの〉dull; slow;〈刃物などの〉blunt;〈色・光の〉dim;〈音の〉dull ¶頭の鈍い slow (to learn [《文》in understanding]); dull; slow-witted / 動作が鈍い be slow-moving.

にふだ 荷札 a (tie-on) label; a (shipping) tag ¶荷札をつける fasten [attach] a label [tag]《to》; tag [label]《one's baggage》.

にぶらせる 鈍らせる; blunt ¶決意を鈍らせる weaken *sb*'s determination; shake [dampen] *sb*'s resolve [《文》resolution]; discourage *sb* from doing.

にぶる 鈍る〈鋭くなくなる〉grow [《文》become] dull;〈刃物が〉get [go,《文》become] blunt [dull]; dull ¶決心が鈍る *one*'s determination weakens [falters, wavers, is weakened]; have *one*'s resolve [《文》resolution] shaken; be shaken in *one*'s resolve [《文》resolution]. 文例⇩

にぶん 二分 ¶二分する divide *sth* in two [into two parts]; halve; bisect《a line》/ 2分の1 one [a] half / 二分法【論】dichotomy.

にべもなく ¶にべもなく断わる refuse [reject] flatly [bluntly, pointblank]; turn *sb* down flat; give *sb* a flat refusal.

にぼし 煮干し small dried sardines.

にほどき 荷解き ¶荷ほどきする unpack.

にほん 日本 Japan ¶日本の Japanese. 日本化する Japanize / 日本画 a picture [painting] in Japanese style; a Japanese-style painting / 日本海 the Sea of Japan / 日本学 Japanology / 日本髪に結う do up *one*'s hair in Japanese style / 日本銀行 the Bank of Japan / 日本犬 a Japanese dog / 日本語 Japanese; the Japanese language / 日本三景 the three great views [the scenic trio] of Japan; the three most famous scenic places in Japan / 日本史 Japanese history; the history of Japan;〈本〉a history of Japan / 日本酒 *sake* / 日本人 a Japanese《単複同形》;〈総称〉the Japanese (people) / 日本製の made in Japan; of Japanese make / 日本刀 a Japanese sword; a *katana* / 日本脳炎 Japanese encephalitis; sleeping [sleepy] sickness / 日本晴れ〈天気〉ideal [glorious] weather;〈空〉a clear and cloudless sky / 日本びいき〈人〉a Japanophile / 日本間 ⇨ わしつ / 日本料理 Japanese food [cooking, cuisine];〈一品〉a Japanese-style dish. 文例⇩

にほんだて 二本立て a double feature ¶二本立ての映画を見に行く go to a double-feature movie.

にまい 二枚 two sheets [pieces]《of paper》¶二枚貝【生物】a bivalve / 二枚舌を使う be double-tongued[-faced];〈約束を破る〉go

---

the honor of representing his school at the meeting. / 皆さんは次代に引き継ぐべき文化の担い手なのです。You are torchbearers of the culture which is to be transmitted to the next generation.

にのく それにはあきれて二の句がつげなかった。I was dum(b)-founded at that.

にばい A は B の2倍の大きさです。A is twice [double] the size of B. | A is twice as large as B. / 3と4を足してから、それを2倍する、という意味を示すには (3+4) ×2と書く。If we want to convey that 3 is added to 4, and the whole result is to be multiplied by 2, we write 2×(3+4).

にばん 2番目に来たのは武藤さんでした。Mr. Muto was the second (person) to arrive.

にぶる 彼の決心は鈍ったようだった。His resolution seemed to have faltered [been shaken].

にほん アメリカの名高い日本学者F教授が昨日奈良時代の日本美術について講演をされた。Prof. F, a well-known American Japanologist, gave a talk on Japanese

にまめ 煮豆 boiled [cooked] beans.

-にも 〈…にもまた〉 also; too; 〈さえも〉 even / 不幸にも unfortunately.

にもうさく 二毛作 raising [growing] two crops

にもつ 荷物 〈背負い荷, 車馬の荷〉 a burden; a load; 〈手荷物〉 (hand) baggage [luggage]; 〈貨物〉 freight; 《主に英》 baggage; 《米》 cargo 《pl. -(e)s》; 〈手回り品〉 one's things [belongings] ⇨ に², てにもつ / 荷物を預ける check one's baggage / 荷物をまとめる pack up. 文例⇩

にもの 煮物 〈料理〉 cooking; 〈煮た物〉 cooked food ¶煮物をする cook.

にゃあ 《猫が》にゃあと鳴く mew; miaow.

にやく 荷役 〈事〉 loading and unloading; 〈人〉 ⇨ おきなかし ¶荷役施設 loading facilities.

にやけた 〈気取った〉 foppish; 〈女々しい〉 effeminate ¶にやけた男 〈気取り屋〉 a fop; 〈女々しい男〉 an effeminate man; a sissy.

にやっかい 荷厄介 ¶荷厄介な burdensome; troublesome / 荷厄介になる be a burden [an encumbrance] to one; become a nuisance to one.

にやにや, にやり ¶にやにやする, にやりと笑う 〈歯を見せて〉 grin (at); 〈間が抜けたように〉 simper (at); 〈やや得意そうに〉 smirk.

ニュアンス a nuance; a (delicate) shade of meaning.

にゅういん 入院 ¶入院する enter [go into, be admitted to] hospital; be hospitalized / 入院させる 〈家族・友人が病人を〉 get [have] sb admitted to hospital; hospitalize; 〈医者が患者を〉 admit sb to hospital / 入院中である 《米》 be in (the) hospital; 《英》 be in hospital / 入院を申し込む apply for admission to (a) hospital / 入院患者 〈外来患者に対して〉 an inpatient / 入院料 hospital charges. 文例⇩

ニューイングランド New England ¶ニューイングランドの住民 a New Englander.

にゅうえい 入営 enrollment; enlistment ¶入営する join [enlist in] the army.

にゅうえき 乳液 〈化粧用の〉 (a) milky lotion; 〈植物の〉 latex.

にゅうか¹ 入荷 arrival [《文》 receipt] of goods ¶入荷する arrive; be received.

にゅうか² 乳化 ¶乳化する emulsify.

にゅうかい 入会 admission ¶入会する enter [join] 《a club》; become a member 《of a society》; be admitted 《to a circle》 / 入会を許す admit sb to 《the club》 / 入会金 an entrance [enrollment] fee / 新入会者 a new member.

にゅうかく 入閣 ¶入閣する join the Cabinet; become a Cabinet member.

にゅうがく 入学 entrance into [admission to] a school; matriculation (大学への) ¶入学する enter a school [a university]; be admitted to a school; 〈大学に〉 matriculate [be matriculated] 《in a university》 / 入学願書を出す send in an application for admission 《to a school》 / 入学金 an entrance [enrollment] fee / 入学志願者 a candidate [an applicant] for admission / 入学式 an entrance ceremony / 入学試験を受ける take [sit for] an entrance examination 《for [of] a school》 / 入学手続き entrance formalities. 文例⇩

にゅうがん 乳癌 cancer of the breast; breast [mammary] cancer.

ニューギニア 〈島〉 New Guinea ⇨ パプアニューギニア ¶ニューギニアの New Guinean / ニューギニア人 a New Guinean.

にゅうぎゅう 乳牛 a milk [milking, 《文》 milch] cow; 〈集合的〉 dairy cattle.

にゅうきょ¹ 入居 ¶入居する move into 《an apartment》 / 入居者 a tenant.

にゅうきょ² 入渠 ¶入渠する enter [go into] dock / 入渠中である be in dock.

にゅうぎょう 乳業 the dairy industry [business].

にゅうきん 入金 〈受領〉 receipt of money; 〈支払い〉 payment; paying in; 〈受取金〉 money received [paid in]; receipts; 〈内金〉 part payment; payment on account ¶入金する receive [pay (in)] 《50,000 yen》; 〈内金として払う〉 pay a part payment 《of 10 pounds》; pay 《100 dollars》 on account / 《銀行の》 入金伝票 a deposit [paying-in] slip.

にゅうこ 入庫 〈商品を〉 stock; warehouse; 〈商品が〉 be stocked; be put in storage; 〈電車が〉 enter the (car) shed.

にゅうこう¹ 入港 ¶入港する enter [put into] port; arrive 《in a port》 / 入港中である be in port [harbor] / 入港税 port [harbor] dues.

にゅうこう² 乳香 frankincense. 文例⇩

にゅうこく 入国 entry [entrance] into a country; 〈移民の〉 immigration ¶入国する enter [be admitted to] a country; 〈移民が〉 immigrate into a country / 入国を許可する admit sb to the country / 入国を拒絶する refuse sb entry into the country / 入国許可書 an entry permit / 入国手続き entry formalities.

にゅうざい 乳剤 (an) emulsion.

にゅうさつ 入札 a bid; a tender ¶入札する

---

art in the Nara period yesterday.

-にも 私にもできる。 I can do it, too. | I also can do it. / 払いたいにも金がない。 I want to pay, only I have no money. / 彼は親切にもその金を貸してくれた。 He was so kind as [was good enough] to lend me the money. / うかつにもそれに気付かなかった。 It was careless of me not to notice it.

にもつ 彼は僕たちのお荷物じゃしないかな。 I'm afraid he will be a burden to us.

にゅういん 入院させて治療する必要がある。 He must be put into the hospital for treatment.

にゅうがく トムはオックスフォード大学に入学できた。 Tom got into Oxford. / あの大学の入学試験科目は英語と数学と国語だ。 The entrance examination for that university is in English, mathematics, and Japanese. / 彼は目下入学試験の準備で忙しい。 He is now busy preparing for the entrance examination.

にゅうこう¹ 本船は明日午前7時神戸に入港する。 Our ship will put into Kobe at seven tomor-

にゅうさん

tender [bid] ((for)); offer [put in] *one's* bid [tender] ((for *sth* to the government)) / 入札を募る invite tenders ((for)) / 入札による put *sth* out to tender / 一般入札 an open tender ; 競争入札 a public tender; competitive bidding / 入札者 a tenderer ; a bidder. 文例⇩

にゅうさん 乳酸 〖化〗 lactic acid ¶乳酸飲料 a lactic acid drink ; 乳酸菌 a lactic acid bacterium ; a lactobacillus (*pl.* -li).

にゅうし¹ 入試 ⇨にゅうがく (入学試験を受ける).

にゅうし² 乳歯 a milk [baby] tooth. 文例⇩

にゅうじ 乳児 an infant ; a baby (at the breast) ¶乳児食 baby food.

ニュージーランド New Zealand ¶ニュージーランド人 a New Zealander.

にゅうしゃ¹ 入社 ¶入社する enter [join] a company; (文) obtain a position in a concern / 入社試験 an entrance [employment] examination (for, of) ; a test for employment (in a firm).

にゅうしゃ² 入射(物) incidence ¶入射角 an angle of incidence / 入射光線 a ray of light incident on ((the surface)); an incident [incoming] ray.

ニュージャージー New Jersey (略: N.J.) ¶ニュージャージー州の人 a New Jerseyite.

にゅうじゃく 柔弱 ¶柔弱な weak; effeminate.

にゅうしゅ 入手 ¶入手する ⟨得る⟩ get; (文) obtain; (文) procure; come by ; ⟨受け取る人⟩ (文) receive ; ⟨物が主語⟩ come to hand / 入手難である be hard to obtain.

にゅうしょ 入所 ¶入所する enter [be admitted to] ((an institution)); ⟨刑務所へ⟩ be put into [sent to] prison [jail]; be imprisoned / 入所中である be in prison [jail].

にゅうしょう 入賞 ¶入賞する win [(文) receive] a prize; get a place ((in a contest)) / 1等に入賞する win (the) first prize / 入賞者 a prize winner.

にゅうじょう¹ 入城 an [triumphal] entry into a fortress [city] ¶入城する make a triumphal entry into a fortress [city]; enter a city triumphantly [in triumph].

にゅうじょう² 入場 entrance ; ⟨見物人の⟩ admission ¶入場する enter; ⟨見物人の⟩ be admitted ((to)) / 一般の入場が許されている be open to the public / 入場券 an admission ticket; ⟨駅の⟩ a platform ticket / 入場券売場 a ticket office [counter]; (英) a booking office / 入場式 an opening ceremony / (開会式などで) 入場行進する march in / 入場者 visitors; spectators; ⟨総称⟩ an attendance ((of 1,000)) / 有料入場者 paying customers [visitors] ; ⟨総称⟩

(a) paid attendance / 入場料 an entrance [admission] fee [charge]. 文例⇩ sified.

にゅうじょう³ 乳状 ¶乳状の milky; emulsified.

にゅうしょく 入植 ¶入植する settle ((in Hokkaido)); colonize ((Canada)); immigrate ((into Brazil)) / 入植者 a settler ; a colonist ; an immigrant.

にゅうしん¹ 入信 ¶入信する come to believe in ((Buddha)); be converted to ((Christianity)).

にゅうしん² 入神 ¶入神の技 divine skill. 文例⇩

ニュース news ★単数として扱い, 不定冠詞をつけない。「1個の」という場合には a piece of news とする。発音は英語では [njuːz] となることに注意 ¶(ラジオ・テレビの) ニュースの時間 the news (hour) / ニュースになる make [become] news / ニュース映画 a newsreel ; a news film / ニュース映画館 a newsreel theater / ニュース解説 (radio, TV) news commentary / ニュース解説者 a news commentator [analyst] / ニュースカメラマン a news photographer / ニュースキャスター a newscaster; ⟨ニュース番組の総合司会者⟩ an anchor man / ニュース速報 a news flash / ニュースバリューがある be newsworthy / ニュース放送 newscasting ; ⟨一回の⟩ a news broadcast ; a newscast ; a news show (テレビで中継・対談などの入る). 文例⇩

にゅうせいひん 乳製品 dairy products.

にゅうせき 入籍 ¶入籍する have ((*one's* wife's name)) entered in the family register.

にゅうせん¹ 入選 ¶入選する be accepted / 入選者 a winner; a successful competitor / 入選論文 a winning essay. 文例⇩

にゅうせん² 乳腺 〖解〗 the mammary gland.

にゅうたい 入隊 ⇨にゅうえい.

ニュータウン a new town ¶多摩ニュータウン Tama New Town.

にゅうだん 入団 ¶入団する join ; enter; enroll in ((the Boy Scouts)).

にゅうちょう 入超 (an) excess of imports over exports; an unfavorable balance of trade. 文例⇩ [the courtroom.

にゅうてい 入廷 ¶入廷する enter [appear in]

ニューデリー New Delhi.

にゅうでん 入電 a telegram received ((from)) ¶...よりの入電によれば according to a telegram from ((London)), a telegram from ((New York)) says [reports] ((that...)).

にゅうとう¹ 入党 ¶入党する join ((the Socialist Party)). [teat.

にゅうとう² 乳頭 〖解〗 a (mammary) nipple ;

にゅうとう³ 乳糖 〖生化〗 lactose ; milk sugar.

---

row morning.

にゅうさつ 右入札希望者は1週間以内に申し出ること。Any person who wishes to tender for the above shall apply within a week.

にゅうし² 子供は普通 6 歳で乳歯が抜け始める。A child normally begins to lose his first teeth at six years of age.

にゅうじょう² この切符1枚で2名入場できる。This ticket admits two persons to the hall. / お子様のご入場お断わり。 Children not admitted. / 入場無料。〖掲示〗 Admission free. / 入場料はいくらですか。 What is the admission? | How much do you charge for admission?

にゅうしん² 彼の演奏はまさに入神の域に達していた。His performance was simply divine.

ニュース そんなことはニュースにならない。 That's hardly news! / 9時のテレビニュースで後報があった。 There was a further report (on it) on the nine o'clock TV news.

にゅうせん¹ 彼の絵は今年の日展に入選した。His painting was accepted [selected] for this year's

にゅうどう 入道 a lay priest; 《化物》a tonsured monster ¶大入道 a huge monster; a giant (of a man) / 入道雲 a towering thundercloud; a cumulonimbus (cloud).

にゅうねん 入念 ⇨ねんいり.

にゅうばい 入梅 (the beginning of) the rainy [wet] season. 文例⬇

にゅうはくしょく 乳白色 ¶乳白色の milky-white; opal.

にゅうばち 乳鉢 a mortar.

ニューハンプシャー New Hampshire (略: N.H.) ¶ニューハンプシャー州の人 a New Hampshireman.

にゅうひ 入費 ⇨ひよう.

にゅうぶ 入部 ¶入部する enter [become a member of] (a club).

ニューフェース a new face 《in the entertaining world》; a new name 《among the actors, in Hollywood》.

にゅうぼう 乳棒 a pestle.

ニューメキシコ New Mexico (略: N.Mex., N.M.) ¶ニューメキシコ州の人 a New Mexican.

にゅうもん 入門 〈弟子入り〉 entrance into [admission to] a private school; 〈入門書〉 a guide [an introduction] (to); a primer 《of》 ¶入門する 〈弟子になる〉 become a disciple [pupil] (of); 〈学び始める〉 be initiated 《into》/ 地質学入門 a primer of geology / 文学入門 an introduction to (the study of) literature.

にゅうよう 入用 need; want; necessity ¶入用な necessary; 《文》 needful; needed; indispensable / 入用である 〈人が主語〉 want; need; be in need of sth; 〈物が主語〉 be necessary [indispensable] (to, for). 《dren》.

にゅうようじ 乳幼児 babies (and little chil-

ニューヨーク New York (City) ¶ニューヨーク州 New York (略: N.Y.) / ニューヨークっ子 a New Yorker.

にゅうよく 入浴 bathing; a bath ¶入浴する have [take] a bath; bathe; 《英》 bath / 入浴させる give (a baby) a bath; bathe (a baby).

にゅうりょく 入力 (an) input ★ 1回の入力の意味では an input という. one input とは言わない. また, 複数にはしない.

ニュールック a new look ¶ニュールックの帽子 a new-look hat.

にゅうわ 柔和 ¶柔和な gentle; tender; 《文》 meek / 柔和な目をした牛 a meek-eyed cow.

にょっと ⇨ぬっと.

によう 二様 ¶二様に in two ways / 二様の意味 a double [《文》 twofold] meaning. 文例⬇

にょう 尿 urine ¶尿を検査する examine [test] sb's urine / カテーテルで尿を取る take [draw off] sb's urine by catheter.

にょうい 尿意 ¶尿意を催す《文》have a desire to urinate.

にょうかん 尿管 the ureter.

にょうさん 尿酸《化》uric acid.

にょうそ 尿素《化》urea.

にょうどう 尿道《解》the urethra (《pl.》 -s, -thrae) ¶尿道炎 urethritis; inflammation of the urethra / 尿道鏡 a urethroscope.

にょうどくしょう 尿毒症《医》uremia; urine poisoning.

にょうぼう 女房 a wife (《pl.》 wives) ⇨つま[1] ¶女房のしりに敷かれる be dominated by one's wife; be (completely) under one's wife's thumb; be tied to one's wife's apron strings / 女房のしりに敷かれた夫 a hen-pecked husband / 女房孝行の[女房に甘い] 夫 a doting [《文》an uxorious] husband / 女房持ち a married man / 女房運が悪い〈悪妻に悩む〉 be cursed with a bad wife; 〈妻に何度も先立たれたりする〉 have no luck with wives / 女房役 one's right-hand man.

にょきにょき〈つぎつぎに〉one after another; 〈あちこちに〉here and there; 〈一面に〉all over 《the place》. 文例⬇

にじつ 如実 ¶如実に〈忠実に〉truly; faithfully; 〈生き生きと〉vividly; graphically; 〈写実的に〉realistically; true to life / 人生を如実に描く depict life just as it is / 如実に物語る〈話す〉give a true [an accurate, a vivid, a graphic] account 《of》; 〈性格などを暴露する〉show 《sb's nature》 in (its) true colors; be a good sign (of); mirror 《sb's personality》.

にょにんきんせい 女人禁制 文例⬇

にょらい 如来《梵》a tathagata; a person who has attained Buddhahood.

により 似寄り ¶似寄りの similar; like.

にょろにょろ ¶にょろにょろ動く wriggle along; squirm around 《about》.

にら 韮《植》a leek.

にらみ 睨み ¶にらみが利く have authority 《over, with》; have (a) great influence 《with, among》. 文例⬇

にらみあい 睨み合い ⇨にらむ (にらみ合う).

にらむ 睨む stare (at); 〈監視する〉 keep [have] an eye (on); watch; 〈疑いをかける〉 suspect ¶こわい目でにらむ glare (fiercely) (at); look sharply [menacingly] (at); look daggers (at) / じっとにらむ stare fixedly [hard] (at) / にらまれる〈不興を買う〉incur sb's displeasure / にらみ合う〈目と目で〉 glare at each other; 〈反目する〉 be at daggers drawn; 《文》 be at feud / …をにらみ合わせて in the light of 《these facts》; considering 《that...》 / にらみ返

Nitten Exhibition.

にゅうちょう 昨年度の貿易尻は1億ドルの入超だった. The balance of foreign trade for the last year showed an excess of imports of one hundred million dollars. | The total of foreign trade for the last year showed an unfavorable balance of one hundred million dollars.

にゅうばい 当地では入梅は6月です. In these parts the rainy season starts [sets in] in June.

にゅうわ 小田さんはしごく柔和な人です. Mr. Oda is as gentle [meek] as a lamb.

によう このところは二様に解釈できる. This passage can be read in two ways. | 《文》 This passage admits of two different interpretations.

にょきにょき 町のそのあたりには煙突がにょきにょき立っていた. That part of the town bristled with chimneys.

にょにんきんせい このお寺はもと女人禁制だった. The temple used to be closed to women. | No women were admitted to the temple in former days.

にらみ 僕はうちの子供たちにも少しもにらみがきかないんだ. I've no authority even with [over] my own

にらめっこ 睨めっこ a staring-out[-down]
にりつはいはん 二律背反《哲》antinomy.
にりゅう 二流 ¶二流の second-rate[-class]; 〈群小の〉minor / 二流の人物 a second-rater.
にりゅうか 二硫化《化》¶二硫化炭素 carbon bisulfide / 二硫化鉄 iron disulfide / 二硫化物 (a) disulfide; (a) bisulfide.
にりん 二輪 ¶二輪咲きの twin-flowered / 二輪車 a two-wheeled vehicle; a two-wheeler; a bicycle.
にる[1] 似る be [look] like sb [sth]; 《文》resemble; be similar to sb [sth]; take after 《one's father》; be alike (2つの物[人]が) / 少しも似ていない[ほんの少し似ている] be nothing [slightly] like sb [sth]; bear no [a remote] resemblance to sb [sth] / 似た《文》like 《ideas》; similar; 《文》analogous / よく似ている bear a close resemblance 《to》; be [look] very much like sb [sth] / 少し似た所がある have some resemblance 《to》; 〈共通点が〉have something in common 《with》/ 似ても似つかない do not bear the slightest resemblance 《to》; be quite different from sb [sth]; 《文》be quite unlike sb [sth] / 似て非なる false; sham. 文例↓
にる[2] 煮る boil; cook ¶煮過ぎる boil too much [long] / 煮直す reboil; cook over again / 煮たての hot from the pot. 文例↓
にるい 二塁《野球》second base; second ¶二塁に進む advance to second base; get to second / 二塁手 a second baseman / 二塁打 a two-base hit; 《口語》a two-bagger.
にれ《植》an elm (tree).
にれつ 二列 two rows; a double line (横); a double file (縦) ¶2列になって進む march in double file; walk two abreast / 2列に並ぶ form two rows [a double row]; be drawn up in two lines; stand two deep (along the road).
にわ 庭〈庭園〉a garden / 〈中庭〉a courtyard ¶庭の草むしりをする weed a garden / 庭の手入れをする tidy (up) a garden / 庭を作る make [lay out] a garden / 庭で in the garden / 庭石 a garden rock / 庭木 a garden tree [plant] / 庭木戸 a garden gate / 庭師 a (landscape) gardener; a garden designer. 文例↓
にわか 俄か ¶にわかの〈突然の〉sudden; abrupt; 〈予期しない〉unexpected; unlooked-for / にわかに〈突然〉suddenly; on [of] a sudden; abruptly; 〈思いがけず〉unexpectedly; 〈簡単に〉《文》readily; 〈あわてて〉hastily / にわか雨 a (sudden) shower / にわか雨にあう be caught in [overtaken by] a shower / にわか景気 a boom / にわか仕込みの hastily acquired [《英俗》mugged up] / にわか仕立ての improvised / にわか仕立てのチーム a scratch team / 日本史のにわか勉強をする cram (up) Japanese history 《for an examination》. 文例↓
にわとこ《植》an elder (tree); an elderberry.
にわとり 鶏 a domestic fowl; a chicken; a hen (雌); a cock (雄); a rooster (雄); a chick (ひな) / 産卵用の鶏 a laying hen / 鶏が先か卵が先かという問題 the question of which came first, the chicken or the egg; a chicken-or-egg question / 鶏小屋 a hen house; a hencoop.
にん 任〈職〉a post; a position; 〈任務〉a task; 〈責任〉responsibility; 〈使命〉a mission ¶任を果たす fulfill [carry out] one's duty [mission] / 任に当たる undertake the responsibility 《of doing, for sth》; take [be in] charge (of); take a job on oneself; take on a job / 任に就く take up one's post; take office / 任にある be in office; hold the post (of) / 任に堪える be equal to the task; be up to the job.
-にん …人 ¶3人前食べる eat enough for three / 10人分の仕事 the work of 10 men; work enough for ten men.
にんい 任意《文》option ¶任意の any; optional; voluntary / 任意の2点 any two points (on the circumference) / 任意に at will; as one pleases [chooses]; voluntarily; of one's own accord [free will]; at one's discretion [《文》option] / 任意出頭を求める ask for [request] sb's voluntary appearance (at the police station); summon sb to appear voluntarily 《at》/ 自白の任意性 the voluntariness of one's confession / 任意抽出法《統計》random sampling. 文例↓
にんか 認可 approval, permission;《文》license; authorization ¶認可する approve; permit;《文》give license [sanction] 《to》; authorize / 認可を得る get authorization 《《文》sanction》《from》; get 《《文》obtain》a license [permit] 《from》; be authorized [sanctioned]

---

children.
にらむ 彼ににらまれて生徒たちは皆黙ってしまった。He stared his pupils into silence. / 彼は社長ににらまれている。The president is prejudiced against him. |《口語》He is in the president's bad books. |《米口語》He is in bad with the president. / 彼女はものすごい顔で私をにらみつけた。She gave me a fierce look. | She scowled fiercely at me.
にる[1] それは何に似ていますか。What is it like? / どんなところが[どんな風に]似ているのですか。How are they alike? / 彼は

お父さんにとてもよく似ている。He is the very picture of his father. / 2人とも性格が似ている。Their characters are very similar [very much alike]. / 私も似た話を聞いたことがある。I have also heard a similar story. / 彼と彼の弟は少しも似ていない。I see no likeness whatever between him and his brother. / この2つは全然似て非なるものです。The two are as like as chalk and cheese.
にる[2] 煮ても焼いても食えないやつだ。He is as crafty [shrewd] as anything. / I really don't know

how to deal with him. / おれのものを煮て食おうと焼いて食おうとおれの勝手だ。I'm free to do what I like with my own possessions, aren't I?
にわ その家には広い庭がある。The house has a large garden (to it).
にわか その提案にはにわかに賛同はできない。I cannot readily consent to the proposal. / にわかにそうとは断言できない。You can't say so for certain.
にんい 任意は任意で英語, ドイツ語のいずれかを選ぶことができる。It is at the option of the ap-

にんかん 任官 (an) appointment; 〈将校の〉(a) commission ¶任官する be appointed 《to an office》; be commissioned.

にんき¹ 人気 〈評判〉popularity; public [popular] favor; 〈その地方の気風〉the character of the people ¶人気がある be popular《with, among》; be a favorite《with》/ 人気がない be unpopular《with, among》/ 人気が増す[落ちる] rise [fall] in popularity / 人気を取る become popular; win popularity; catch on《with》/ 人気を落とす lose one's popularity; become unpopular / 人気作家 a popular writer / 人気スター a star at the height of his [her] popularity / 人気投票 a popularity vote / 人気取りをする seek popularity; court [make efforts to win] public favor; 《口語》play to the gallery (スタンドプレイをする) / 人気取り政策 (a) vote-catching policy / 人気者 a popular person. 文例⇩

にんき² 任期 one's term of office [service]; 《文》one's tenure (of office) ¶任期を勤めあげる serve out one's term. 文例⇩

にんぎょ 人魚 a mermaid.

にんきょう 任侠 (a) chivalrous spirit; chivalry.

にんぎょう 人形 a doll / 〈あやつり人形〉a puppet; a marionette ¶人形を使う manipulate [operate] a puppet; handle a doll / …の身代わりにその人形を火あぶり[首つり]にする burn [hang] sb in effigy / 人形遊びをする play《with》dolls / 人形劇 a puppet show / 人形使い a puppeteer; a puppet manipulator.

にんく 忍苦 endurance; 《文》stoicism ¶忍苦の生涯《文》a life of stoicism [hardships bravely endured].

にんげん 人間 a human being; a human; people; 〈いつかは死ぬべきものとしての〉a mortal; 〈人類〉man; mankind; humanity ¶人間の human; mortal / 人間以上の超human / 人間以下の subhuman / 人間関係 human relations / 人間嫌い〈性質〉《文》misanthropy / 〈人〉《文》a misanthrope / 人間形成 character building [《文》formation] / 人間工学 human engineering / 人間国宝 a living national treasure / 人間性 human nature; humanity / 人間性を奪う dehumanize / 人間尊重 respect for man's life and dignity / 人間中心的な man-centered / 《文》anthropocentric / 人間ドックに入る go into a hospital [be hospitalized] for a complete physical examination [clinical survey] / 犬を人間並みに扱う treat one's dog like [as if it were] a man / 人間味 humanity; a [the] human touch; 〈人情味〉humaneness / 人間業ではない be almost miraculous; be beyond human power; be humanly impossible. 文例⇩

にんさんぷ 妊産婦 expectant and nursing mothers.

にんしき 認識〈認めること〉《文》perception; awareness; 《文》cognition; recognition; 〈理解〉understanding ¶認識する《文》perceive; recognize; understand; realize; see; 〈知る〉know; become aware《of, that…》; 《文》take cognizance《of》/ 認識が浅い have only a a superficial understanding《of》/ 認識を新たにする see sth in a new [fresh] light; find a new meaning《in》/ 認識不足である have little understanding《of》; be ignorant《of》/ 認識論『哲』epistemology. 文例⇩

にんじゃ 忍者 a ninja; a professional spy (in feudal Japan) highly trained in stealth and secrecy.

にんじゅう 忍従 submission; subservience ¶忍従する submit《to》; lie down《under》.

にんじゅつ 忍術 the skills of stealth and secrecy practiced by the ninja.

にんしょう¹ 人称《文法》person ¶1 [2, 3]人称 (in) the first [second, third] person / 人称代名詞 a personal pronoun.

にんしょう² 認証 ¶認証する《文》attest; certify; authenticate; confirm / 認証官 a government official whose appointment requires the Emperor's attestation / 認証式 an attestation [investiture] ceremony. 文例⇩

にんじょう 人情〈人間的感情〉human feelings;〈人間性〉human nature; humanity;〈暖かい感情〉humane feelings ¶人情のある[厚い] humane; kind; warmhearted / 人情のない[薄い] unfeeling; coldhearted; heartless / 人情の暖かさ the milk of human kindness / 人情の機微 the secrets [subtleties] of human nature / 人情風俗 customs and manners. 文例⇩

plicant [examinee] to take either English or German.

にんき¹ 彼は生徒に人気がある。He is popular with the students. / この地方の音楽には近年若者の間で大変な人気を得た。Music of this kind has achieved great popularity among young people in recent years. / 歌舞伎は現代の日本でも依然として人気が高い。Kabuki still has great appeal in modern Japan. / あの事件以来大統領は人気が落ちた。The President's popularity has dropped since that incident.

にんき² 大統領の任期は4年です。 The President's tenure of office is four years.

にんげん 人間は万物の霊長である。Man is the lord of creation. / 人間の手でこれ以上のことはできない。No man living could do better. / 彼は決してわれわれを裏切るような人間じゃない。He is the last person to betray us. / 私ってそんな人間なのよ。That's how I am. | I'm like that. | 到底人間業とは思えない。I can't believe that it's humanly possible. | It is little short of a miracle.

にんしき これはわが国の現状に対する彼の認識不足を示している。

This proves that he has little understanding of the present situation in Japan. / その書物の価値は300年間認識されなかった。The value of the book went unrecognized for 300 years.

にんしょう² 皇居で内閣の認証式が行なわれた。The Cabinet was formally invested (in ceremonies held) at the Imperial Palace.

にんじょう そんな事は人情としてできない。I can't find it in my heart to do that. / そう思うのが人情だ。It is only human that you should think that way. / 人情はどこでも同じだ。Human na-

にんじょうざた ― ぬいめ

にんじょうざた 刃傷沙汰 ¶刃傷沙汰になる 〈事が主語〉end 《《文》result》in bloodshed.
にんじる 任じる 〈任命する〉appoint; 〈将校を〉commission; 〈自任する〉claim [《文》profess]《to be》; 〈自任する〉fancy *oneself* 《to be》.
にんしん 妊娠 pregnancy; conception (受胎) ¶妊娠する get [《文》become] pregnant; 《文》conceive 《a child》/ 妊娠させる make 《a girl》pregnant / 妊娠している be pregnant; be going to have a baby; 〈婉曲に〉be in the family way / 妊娠3カ月である be in the third month of pregnancy; be three months pregnant / 妊娠中(に) during (the period of) pregnancy / 妊娠中絶 (an) abortion.
にんじん 人参 a carrot.
にんずう 人数 the number of people [persons] ¶人数の多い家庭 a large [big] family / 人数をそろえる get (together) the required [necessary] number of people 《《文》persons》; make up the number(s) / 人数を減らす reduce the personnel [number of men].
にんそう 人相 《文》physiognomy; 《文》facial features; looks ¶人相のよくない evil-looking; sinister(-looking) / 人相を見る read [judge] *sb*'s character by *his* face; tell *sb*'s fortune by physiognomy / 人相書き *sb*'s description / 人相書きどおりの人物 a person answering [fitting, meeting] the description / 人相見 a physiognomist.
にんたい 忍耐 perseverance; 〈辛抱〉patience; 〈忍苦〉endurance ¶忍耐する persevere 《in》; be patient 《with》; endure; bear; stand; put up with / 忍耐強い persevering; patient / 忍耐力のない《a man》with no [lacking (in)] staying power [perseverance]; impatient. 文例↓
にんち¹ 任地 *one's* post. 文例↓

にんち² 認知 (legal) acknowledgment; recognition; 〈認識〉cognition ¶認知する acknowledge [recognize]《a child》as *one's* own; admit paternity / 認知心理学 cognitive psychology.
にんてい 認定 〈認知〉acknowledgment; 〈承認〉approval; 〈認可〉authorization ¶認定する acknowledge; approve; authorize / 認定講習会 a course of lectures for qualifying (teachers).
にんどう 〖植〗a honeysuckle.
にんとうぜい 人頭税 poll tax.
にんにく 〖植〗a garlic; 〈香料〉garlic ¶(料理に使う)にんにくの1かけら a clove of garlic.
にんぴ 認否 approval or disapproval; 〈訴因の〉arraignment.
にんぴにん 人非人 a brute (of a man).
にんぷ¹ 人夫 a workman; 《英》a navvy; 〈運搬人〉a porter; a carrier ¶人夫頭 a foreman.
にんぷ² 妊婦 a pregnant woman; an expectant mother ¶妊婦服 a maternity dress.
にんまり ¶にんまり笑う[する] smile complacently [in a satisfied sort of way]; smile a smile of satisfaction.
にんむ 任務 *one's* duty; an office; a task; a mission (使命) ¶任務を果たす fulfill [carry out] *one's* duty [mission]; do *one's* part / 任務を与える assign *sb* to a task [job] / 特別任務を帯びて on a special mission.
にんめい 任命 (an) appointment ¶任命する appoint *sb* to 《a post》; name [nominate] *sb* for 《a position》. 文例↓
にんめん 任免 appointment and dismissal [removal] ¶任免権 the power to appoint and dismiss [remove]《Cabinet ministers》.
にんよう¹ 任用 (an) appointment ⇒にんめい.
にんよう² 認容 ⇒ようにん.

ぬ

ぬい 縫い 〈裁縫〉sewing; 〈刺繡(しゅう)〉embroidery ¶手[機械]縫いの hand-[machine-]sewn / ひと縫い a stitch.
ぬいあわせる 縫い合わせる sew [stitch] together [up] ¶傷口を縫い合わせる sew [stitch] up a wound; suture an incision.
ぬいいと 縫い糸 sewing thread; 〖外科〗suture.
ぬいぐるみ 縫いぐるみ 〈人形〉a stuffed toy [doll]; 〈芝居で役者が着る動物の衣装〉an animal costume ¶熊(\$)の縫いぐるみを着る wear a bear costume / パンダの縫いぐるみで遊ぶ play with a stuffed panda.

ぬいこみ 縫い込み a tuck ¶縫い込みを出す let out a tuck.
ぬいこむ 縫い込む sew [stitch] *sth* in [into].
ぬいしろ 縫い代 a margin to sew up ¶縫い代が少ない leave [allow] only a slim margin to sew up.
ぬいつける 縫い付ける sew 《a button》on.
ぬいとり 縫い取り embroidery ¶縫い取りをする embroider 《a pattern on a handkerchief, a handkerchief with a figure》.
ぬいばり 縫い針 a (sewing) needle.
ぬいめ 縫い目 a seam; 〈傷の〉a suture ¶縫

---

ture is the same everywhere.
にんじる 彼は庶務課長に任じられた. He was appointed chief of the general affairs section. / 彼は米国通をもって自ら任じている. He claims [professes] to be well versed in things American.
にんたい 近頃の若い者は忍耐力がないね, すぐに音をあげるんだから. Young men nowadays have no staying power: they give up too easily.
にんち¹ 彼は新しい任地ロンドンに向かって昨夜出発した. Last night he left for his new post in London.

にんめい 矢野氏が駐英大使に任命された. Mr. Yano was appointed Ambassador to the United Kingdom.
ぬいもの 彼女は縫い物の手を休めて顔を上げた. She looked up from her sewing.
ぬか ぬかにくぎだよ. It is quite

ぬいもの　縫い物　sewing; needlework ⇒ さいほう.

ぬう　縫う　sew; stitch ¶手で[ミシンで]縫う sew *sth* by hand [with a machine]; hand-[machine-]stitch *sth* / 傷口を縫う suture [sew up] a wound [an incision (手術後に)] / 傷を3針縫う put three stitches in a wound; close a wound with three stitches / 人込みの中を縫って歩く thread [weave] *one's* way through a crowd (of people).

ヌード　(the) nude ¶ヌードで (pose) in the nude / ヌード写真 a nude picture [photo] / ヌードモデル a nude model.

ヌートリア　a nutria; 〈毛皮〉nutria.

ぬえ　鵺　a fabulous night bird ¶ぬえ的人物 an enigma; a man of mystery.

ぬか　糠　rice bran ¶ぬか雨 (a) drizzle; a drizzling rain / ぬかみそ salted rice-bran paste for pickling / ぬか(みそ)づけ vegetables pickled in rice-bran paste / ぬか喜び premature joy. 文例⇩

ヌガー　(a piece of) nougat.

ぬかす¹　吐かす　say; have the impudence [cheek] to say.

ぬかす²　抜かす　〈省く〉leave *sth* out;《文》omit;〈飛ばす〉skip.

ぬかずく　額ずく　bow (low); make a deep [profound] bow; prostrate *oneself*《before the altar》.

ぬがせる　脱がせる　strip [《文》divest] *sb* of 《*his* clothes》; take [strip] *sb's*《clothes》off; undress *sb*;〈手を貸して〉help *sb* off with [out of]《*his* overcoat》.

ぬかり　抜かり　〈失策〉a slip; a blunder;〈見落とし〉an oversight ¶する事に抜かりがない know what *one* is doing [about] / 抜かりなく cautiously; shrewdly;〈必ず〉without fail.

ぬかる¹　抜かる　make a slip [blunder]; commit an oversight. 文例⇩

ぬかる²　〈泥で〉be muddy;〈雪解けで〉be slushy.

ぬかるみ　a muddy place 《in a road》; mud; mire; a quagmire ¶ぬかるみで足をとられる[にはまって動けなくなる] slip and fall [get stuck] in the mud.

ぬき¹　抜き ¶…を抜きにする〈省略する〉leave [cut] *sth* out;《文》omit;〈なしでする〉do [go] without; dispense with / 5人抜きする beat five opponents in succession [in a row] / 夕飯抜きで without 《*one's*》supper; without having 《*one's*》supper / 冗談は抜きにして joking apart. 文例⇩

ぬき²　貫き　a batten.

ぬきあしさしあし　抜き足差し足 ¶抜き足差し足で stealthily; with stealthy steps;〈つま先で〉on tiptoe / 抜き足差し足で行く walk stealthily; steal [tiptoe]《away from the scene, into a room》.

ぬきうち　抜き打ち ¶抜き打ちにする draw *one's* sword and slash [cut] 《at *one's* adversary》in the same movement / 抜き打ち的に without (previous) notice [warning] / 抜き打ち検査 (make) a surprise inspection;《do》a spot check.

ぬきがき　抜き書き　an extract; an excerpt ¶抜き書きをする extract passages《from》; make extracts [excerpts]《from》.

ぬきさし　抜き差し ¶抜き差しならぬ羽目に陥る find *oneself* in a (pretty) fix [in the mire,《文》on the horns of a dilemma].

ぬぎすてる　脱ぎ捨てる　throw [fling,《文》cast]《*one's* coat》off;《文》shed 《*one's* clothes》; kick 《*one's* slippers》off.

ぬきずり　抜き刷り　an offprint《from a journal》¶抜き刷りをする offprint《an article》.

ぬきだす　抜き出す　〈引き出す〉pull [《文》draw] out;《文》extract;〈選び出す〉pick [single, sort] out; select.

ぬきて　抜き手 ¶抜き手を切る swim overarm.

ぬきとり　抜き取り ⇒ ぬきとる ¶抜き取り検査 (a) sampling inspection; sampling.

ぬきとる　抜き取る　pull [《文》draw] out;《文》extract;〈盗み取る〉filch; steal ¶為替を抜き取る steal a money order《from an envelope》.

ぬきみ　抜き身　a drawn [naked] sword.

ぬきんでる　抜きん出る　〈すぐれる〉《文》excel 《in [at] *sth*》; surpass《others in *sth*》;〈異彩を放つ〉cut a prominent figure《among》¶忠勤をぬきんでる serve《*one's* master》most faithfully / ぬきんでた eminent; prominent; distinguished; outstanding; conspicuous. 文例⇩

ぬく　抜く　〈引き抜く〉pull [《文》draw] out;《文》extract;〈除去する〉take out; remove;〈省略する〉leave out;《文》omit;〈抜粋する〉extract;〈引用する〉quote《from》;〈追い越す〉overtake; get [move] ahead of《*one's* opponent》; get a lead on《*one's* rival》;〈卓越する〉be far better than《others》;《文》excel《in [at] *sth*》; surpass《others in *sth*》¶シャンペンを抜く open [uncork] a bottle of champagne / 刀を抜く draw [unsheathe] a sword / 手を抜く〈仕事を〉skimp [scamp] *one's* work / 染みを抜く remove [take out] a stain / 昼食を抜く go without 《*one's*》lunch / 空気を抜く release air from《a balloon》; deflate《a tire》/ 群を抜く tower above the rest /

---

useless. | It will have no effect. / 私の忠告も彼にはぬかにくぎだった。My advice slid off him like water off a duck's back. / ぬか雨が降っている。It is drizzling.

ぬかる¹　Keep your wits about you! | Don't relax your guard!

ぬき¹　詳細は抜きにしてすぐ結論に入ります。I will omit the details and come to the conclusion at once.

ぬきんでる　クラスでは矢野が断然抜きんでいた。Yano was by far the best student in the class. / 数学では彼が断然抜きんでいる。In mathematics he is in a class by himself [of his own]. / 彼はギリシャの古典研究では我が国で断然抜きんでた存在である。He is a towering [the outstanding] figure in the study of Greek classics in this country.

-ぬく 抜かれる〈競技で〉lose the lead to ((one's opponent)).
-ぬく …抜く ¶困り抜く be in great difficulty [((文)) distress] / 苦労し抜く go through all sorts of hardships / 戦い抜く fight to the end, fight it out.
ぬぐ 脱ぐ take [pull] ((one's coat)) off; remove ((one's hat)); strip; divest oneself of ((one's)) undershirt); ¶着物を脱ぐ get undressed; undress [((文)) unclothe] oneself; shed [get out of] one's clothes.
ぬぐう 拭う ⇒ふく ¶靴の泥をぬぐい落とす wipe the mud off one's shoes / ぬぐうべからざる恥辱 ((文)) an indelible disgrace; ((文)) an ineffaceable humiliation.
ぬくぬく ¶ぬくぬくとした snug (and comfortable); comfortably warm / ぬくぬくとしている〈暖かくしている〉keep oneself comfortably warm;〈安楽である〉be comfortably off; 〈煩いがない〉be carefree.
ぬくみ, ぬくもり 温み, 温もり (slight) warmth ⇒ あたたかみ. 文例↓
ぬけあな 抜け穴 〈秘密の通路〉a secret passage; 〈地下道〉an underground passage; 〈法律などの逃げ道〉a loophole.
ぬけがけ 抜け駆け ¶抜け駆けをする steal a march on sb; forestall;〈新聞が〉get a scoop on ((rival papers)); scoop ((a news story)).
ぬけがら 抜け殻 a cast-off skin ¶せみの抜け殻 a cicada's shell / 蛇の抜け殻 the cast-off skin of a snake; a slough / 魂の抜け殻 a mere shadow of one's true self.
ぬけかわる 抜け替わる〈羽・毛が〉molt; 〈殻などが〉slough. 文例↓
ぬけげ 脱け毛 (a) fallen hair; hair left on the comb (くしについている).
ぬけだす, ぬけでる 抜け出す, 抜け出る get [go, steal, slip] out of ((a room)); sneak away ((from)); 〈動物が〉break loose.
ぬけぬけ brazenly; brazenfacedly; unashamedly ¶ぬけぬけと…する have the face [cheek] to do; have no scruples about doing.
ぬけみち 抜け道 〈裏通り〉a byroad; a byway; 〈秘密の通路〉a secret passage [path]; 〈法律などの〉a loophole ¶抜け道を通る go by a secret path.
ぬけめ 抜け目 ¶抜け目のない shrewd; sharp;

smart; canny; knowing; 〈注意深い〉careful; cautious / 抜け目がない商売人 a shrewd [canny] businessman / 抜け目なく shrewdly; cautiously. 文例↓
ぬける 抜[脱]ける〈脱落する〉come [fall] out [off]; 〈通る〉go by [through]; 〈脱出する〉escape; get away; 〈脱漏する〉be left out; 〈文〉be omitted; 〈力などが〉be gone; 〈物や部分が欠けている〉be missing; ((文)) be wanting; 〈脱退する〉leave; quit; withdraw from; pull [drop] out ((of an undertaking)) ¶縄を抜ける wriggle out of [oneself free from] one's bonds / 色が抜けるように白い be as fair as (fair) can be. 文例↓
ぬげる 脱げる come off; slip off [down]. 文例↓
ぬし 主 〈所有者〉the owner; the proprietor; 〈池などの〉the guardian spirit (of the lake); ((文)) the genius (of the river); 〈古手〉((口語)) an old-timer; ((英口語)) an old-stager ¶手紙の主 the writer [author] of the letter / 主のない ownerless; ((a dog)) belonging to nobody.
ぬすびと 盗人 ⇒ どろぼう. 文例↓
ぬすみ 盗み stealing; (a) theft; (a) larceny; pilfering (ちょろまかし) ¶盗みを働く steal; commit theft [larceny]; pilfer (少しずつちょろまかす).
ぬすみぎき 盗み聞き ¶盗み聞きする listen secretly [stealthily] to ((a talk)); eavesdrop on sb; overhear ((a chat)); 〈電話などを〉tap ((a telephone wire)); listen in on ((a telephone conversation)).
ぬすみぐい 盗み食い ¶盗み食いする eat sth on the sly; ((口語)) snitch [pinch] food [something to eat].
ぬすみみる 盗み見る steal a glance ((at)); sneak a look ((at)); look [glance] furtively ((at)).
ぬすみよみ 盗み読み ¶盗み読みする read ((sb's letter)) surreptitiously [((文)) by stealth].
ぬすむ 盗む steal ((sth from sb)); ((口語)) pinch; ((口語)) snitch; ((口語)) lift; 〈目立たぬように少量ずつくすねる〉pilfer; 〈他人の文章などを〉plagiarize ★「盗む」という行為を表わす英語としては steal が最も普通. ((口語)) の pinch, snitch, lift は, 日本語の「ちょいと失敬して来た」という場合の「失敬する」に当たる語で, 自分の罪の行為を軽く見せようとする意識が働いている ⇒ せっとう★ ¶盗まれる〈物が

ぬく この歯を抜いていただきたいのです. I would like to have this tooth out [extracted, pulled out]. / 決勝点近くで彼に抜かれた. I lost the lead to [was overtaken by] him near the finish line. / セントラルリーグでは巨人が中日を抜いて首位になった. / The Giants moved past the Dragons into top place in the Central League. / レースは最後まで抜きつ抜かれつの接戦だった. The race was nip and tuck until the last moment.
ぬぐ 靴は脱がなくてもけっこうです. You may keep your shoes on.

ぬくもり いすの上に脱ぎすてられていた彼女の服には彼女の肌のぬくもりがまだかすかに残っていた. The dress she had thrown off on the chair was still slightly warm from her body.
ぬけかわる 小鳥の羽が抜け替わってきた. The birds are starting to molt. / 動物の毛は春になると抜け替わる. Animals shed their coats in spring.
ぬけめ あの男は抜け目のない男だよ. He's nobody's fool.
ぬける 底が抜けた. The bottom came [fell] out. / ズボンのひざが抜けていた. His trousers were

out at the knees. / 力がすっかり脱けてしまった. All my strength was gone. / このビールは気が抜けている. This beer is flat. / 風邪がなかなか抜けない. I can't shake off [get rid of] my cold. / 5, 6ページ抜けている. There are several pages missing. / あの男は少し抜けている. He is a bit soft in the head.
ぬげる 靴がなかなか脱げない. My boots won't come off. / I can't get [take] my boots off.
ぬすびと 盗人にも三分の理. Even an evil-doer has his reasons.
ぬすみ 彼は勤め先のスーパーで

ぬた (a) fish salad.

ぬっと suddenly; abruptly; unexpectedly.

ぬの 布 cloth ¶布切れ a piece of cloth / 布目のあらい[細かい] coarse-[close-]textured; 《文》of coarse [fine] texture.

ぬま 沼 (a) marsh; (a) swamp; a bog; a tarn (山の湖水) ¶沼地 a marshy [swampy] place; bogland; marshland.

ぬめり slime; sliminess ¶ぬめりのある slimy.

ぬらす 濡らす wet; moisten; dampen; 〈浸す〉soak; drench; dip ¶手を水にぬらす get one's hands wet / 〈水につける〉dip one's hands into water / ぬらさない keep sth dry / 手もぬらさずに〈容易に〉easily; effortlessly; 《文》without effort.

ぬらぬら ⇒ぬるぬる.

ぬらりくらり ¶ぬらりくらりとしてつかまえ所がない be as slippery as an eel.

ぬり 塗り coating; 〈うるしの〉lacquering; 〈ニスの〉varnishing; 〈ペンキの〉painting; 〈しっくいの〉plastering ¶下[中, 上]塗り the first [second, last] coat / 二度塗りする give sth two coats of 《paint, lacquer》/ 黒塗りの箱 a black-lacquered box / 白塗りの壁 a white-plastered [whitewashed] wall / 塗りばし[下駄] lacquered chopsticks [geta].

ぬりえ 塗り絵 a line drawing for coloring-in ¶ぬり絵の本 a coloring book.

ぬりかえる 塗り替える repaint; recoat; paint [plaster]《a wall》afresh; give a new coat of 《paint》to《a door》¶ヨーロッパの地図を塗り替える[remake] the map of Europe.

ぬりぐすり 塗り薬 (an) ointment.

ぬりたて 塗り立て ¶塗り立ての freshly-painted[-plastered]. 文例⇩

ぬりたてる 塗り立てる paint (and powder) 《one's face》heavily [thick]; use (too) much make-up.

ぬりつける 塗り付ける ⇒ぬる.

ぬりつぶす 塗り潰す paint out《a letter》; cover《a wall》(completely)《with paint》.

ぬりもの 塗り物 lacquer ware ¶塗物師 a lacquer(-ware) artist.

ぬる 塗る give sth a coat of《lacquer, paint》; 〈ペンキを〉paint; 〈ニスを〉varnish; 〈うるしを〉lacquer; 〈しっくいを〉plaster ¶バターを塗る butter《a slice of toast》; spread butter on《bread》; spread《bread》with butter / 緑色に塗る paint sth green / エナメルを2度塗る give sth two coats of enamel / 地図に色を塗る color (in) a map / 壁に泥を塗る daub a wall with mud / 顔に墨を塗る smear one's face with ink / 油薬を塗る put ointment 《on》; 《文》apply ointment《to》. 文例⇩

ぬるい 温い 〈微温の〉tepid; lukewarm; 〈ゆるやかな〉soft ⇒てぬるい. 文例⇩

ぬるで 〘植〙a sumac(h).

ぬるぬる ¶ぬるぬるした slippery; 〈泥などで〉slimy; 〈脂で〉greasy. 文例⇩

ぬるまゆ ぬるま湯 tepid [lukewarm] water ¶ぬるま湯につかっている〈比喩的に〉be complacent; be having an easy [a soft] time of it (and have no wish to change [bestir oneself]).

ぬるむ get [《文》become] tepid [lukewarm]; get [《文》become] less hot [cold] ⇒いぶき 文例.

ぬるりと ⇒ぬるぬる.

ぬれえん 濡れ縁 an open veranda(h).

ぬれぎぬ 濡れ衣 a false charge [accusation] ¶ぬれぎぬを着せる accuse sb of《theft》falsely [unjustly]; make a false charge《of espionage》against sb;《口語》frame sb / ぬれぎぬを着せられる be wrongly [falsely, unjustly] accused《of stealing》.

ぬれて 濡れ手 a wet hand ¶ぬれ手で粟(を)つかむ make easy money [profits];《口語》rake it in;《口語》rake in the money [profits].

ぬれねずみ 濡れ鼠 ¶ぬれねずみになる be [get] soaked to the skin; be drenched; be [get] dripping wet. 文例⇩

ぬれば 濡れ場 a love [romantic] scene.

ぬれる 濡れる get [be] wet; be drenched; 〈湿る〉be [get] damp ¶雨[露]にぬれる get [be] wet with rain [dew] / びっしょり[ずぶぬれに]ぬれる get soaked to the skin; get dripping wet / ぬれた wet; 〈湿った〉moist; damp. 文例⇩

みを働いて首になった. He was fired for pilfering from the super-market where he worked.

ぬすむ 店に泥棒が入ってテレビを10台盗んで行った. Burglars broke into our store and took away ten TV sets. / その男の子がうちの果樹園からりんごを盗もうとしているところを見つけた. I caught the boy pinching [snitching] apples from our orchard. / スーツケースを盗まれてしまった. My suitcase was stolen when I was chatting with her.

ぬり このお盆は塗りがいい. This tray is excellently [beautifully] lacquered.

ぬりたて ペンキ塗り立て.《掲示》《米》Fresh paint.《英》Wet paint.

ぬりたてる こてこて塗り立てて部屋から出て来た. She came out of her room, all painted up.

ぬる ドアには新しくニスが塗ってあった. There was a fresh coat of varnish on the door. / 顔におしろいをこってり塗っていた. She was wearing heavy make-up. | She was heavily made up.

ぬるい お風呂はぬるくないですか. Is the bath hot enough?

ぬるぬる さわるとぬるぬるした. It was slimy to the touch.

ぬれねずみ ぬれねずみだった. He looked like a drowned rat.

ぬれる 荷物がぬれないようにビニールをかけた. We covered the goods with a vinyl sheet to keep them dry. / 彼女の目は涙でぬれていた. Her eyes were wet with tears. / 庭の草花が雨にぬれてしなだれていた. The flowers in the garden were drooping from the weight of the rain.

ね

ね¹ 子 〈十二支の〉(the Year of) the Rat.

ね² 音 〈響き〉(a) sound;〈楽音〉a tone; a tune; 〈小鳥などの鳴き声〉a note; a chirp ¶音がよい[悪い] have [make] a pleasant [an unpleasant] sound;〈楽音〉sound sweet [harsh] / 音をあげる give in [up]; admit *one's* defeat.

ね³ 根 〈草木の〉a root;〈根源〉the origin; the source ¶髪の根 the root of hair / はれ物の根 the core [root] of a boil / 根は正直である be honest by nature; be an honest person at heart [bottom] / 根がつく, 根を下ろす take [strike] root; root / 根を抜く pull up (a tree) by the [*its*] roots; root (a tree) up /〈指でつまんで〉pluck (a plant) by the [*its*] roots / 犯罪の根を絶つ eradicate [root out] the causes of crime / 根に持つ have [hold, 《文》harbor] a grudge against *sb* /〈否定文で〉根も (no) ill will / 根も葉もない groundless《rumors》; unfounded《reports》. 文例⇩

ね⁴ 値〈代価〉a price;〈元値〉(a) cost ¶値が上がる rise [go up] in price / 値が下がる fall [go down] in price / 値の高い[張る] dear; expensive; costly;《文》high-priced /〈文〉値の安い[張らない] cheap;《文》inexpensive;《文》low-priced / 値をつける put [set] a price on *sth* / よい値に売れる bring [fetch, sell for] a good price. 文例⇩

ね⁵ 寝 ¶寝が足りない do not get [have] enough sleep; sleep badly ⇨ねぶそく.

ね⁶ 〈…だろうと思う〉I believe; I suppose; I should think; I dare say;〈そうではないか〉isn't it?; doesn't it?; don't you?;〈ご承知のとおり〉you know; you see;〈呼びかけ〉I say;《米》say; look here. 文例⇩

ねあがり 値上がり 〈値段の〉a rise in price;《米口語》a price hike;〈価値の〉(an) increase in value ¶大変な値上がり a big jump in price / 諸物価の急激な値上がり a sudden [sharp] rise in prices / 値上がりする ⇨ね⁴ (値が上がる).

ねあげ 値上げ 〈物価の〉raising the price 《of》; 《米口語》a price hike;〈賃金の〉a rise [《米》a raise] in salary [wages];《米口語》a wage hike ¶値上げする raise the price [rates, fare] / 賃金の値上げを要求する[叫ぶ] demand [clamor for] higher wages.

ねあせ 寝汗 ¶寝汗をかく sweat at night.

ネアンデルタールじん ネアンデルタール人《人類》(a) Neanderthal man.

ねいき 寝息 the breathing of a sleeping person ¶寝息をうかがう make sure that *sb* is fast asleep. 文例⇩

ねいす 寝椅子 a sofa; a couch.

ねいりばな 寝入り端 ¶寝入りばなに in *one's* first sleep; when *one* has just fallen asleep.

ねいる 寝入る fall asleep; go [drop off] to sleep ¶ぐっすり寝入る fall fast asleep.

ねいろ 音色 tone quality; a tone color; timbre;〈音〉a tone.

ねうち 値打ち value; worth;《文》merit;〈世間の評価〉《文》public estimation ¶人の値打ち (a) man's worth / 値打ちが上がる rise [go up] in value [public estimation] / 値打ちが下がる fall [drop, go down] in value [public estimation] / 1千万円の値打ちがある be worth ten million yen /《文》値打ちのある valuable;《文》of value / 値打ちのない valueless; worthless; 《文》of no value. 文例⇩

ねえ ⇨ね⁶. 文例⇩

ねえさん 〈姉〉⇨あね;〈料理屋の女中〉a waitress;〈呼びかけ〉Miss!

ネーブル an [a navel] orange.

ネーム *one's* name ¶ネームバリューのある作家 a novelist with an established reputation; a writer who has made his name ★ name value は和製英語 / ネームプレート a nameplate.

ねおおい 根覆い mulching; a mulch ¶根覆いをする mulch《a plant》.

ねおき 寝起き ¶寝起きする live《under the

ね³ 仏教は日本の国土に深く根をおろした。Buddhism took deep root [planted its roots deeply] in Japanese soil. / 彼はいまだにあの事を根に持っている。He still bears me a grudge over that matter.

ね⁴ これに幾らの値をおつけになりますか。How much will you offer [give me] for this? / もちろんこの方が品物はよろしいのですが, ぐっと値が張ります。This is better, of course, but it is a good deal more expensive.

ね⁶ 今日は6月5日でしたね。Today is the fifth of June, isn't it? / 本当じゃないんだろうね。It isn't true, is it? / いいかね。Now, listen. / ずいぶん疲れただろうね。You must be [I expect you're] very tired. / 彼は多分遅れるでしょうね。He will be late, I dare say. / ずいぶん妙なことをお聞きになるのね。Well, that's an odd question, I must say. / ね, あの人はずいぶんと気難しい人でしょう。You know, he is very hard to please. | He is very hard to please, you see.

ねいき 妻の静かな寝息が聞こえた。I heard my sleeping wife breathing quietly.

ねうち 大した値打ちはない。It is not worth much [of much value]. / この本は読む値打ちがある。It is worth your while to read this book. | This book is worth reading. / そんな事をすると君の値打ちが下がるよ。It should be beneath you [your dignity] to do such a thing. / 何と言っても昨日見た車が一番値打ち物だよ。There's no question that the car we saw yesterday is the best value for (the) money.

ねえ ねえ, 加藤君。I say [Look here], Kato.

ねがい(ごと) 私の願いはそれだけです。That is all I wish [pray] for. / あなたに1つお願いがあるのです。I have a favor to ask (of)

ねおし

same roof) / 寝起きがよい wake in a good mood ; be a good riser / 寝起きが悪い wake in a bad temper [mood] ; be a poor riser.

ねおし 寝押し ¶寝押しをする press 《*one's* trousers》under *one's* mattress [bedding].

ネオジム 《化》neodymium.

ネオン 《化》neon. ¶ネオンで明るい通り a neon-lit street / ネオンサイン a neon sign.

ネガ 《写真》a (photographic) negative.

ねがい(ごと) 願い(事) 〈願望〉《文》a desire ; a wish ; a hope ; 〈懇願〉《文》(an) entreaty ; 〈要請〉(a) request ; 〈出願〉(an) application ; 〈祈願〉(a) prayer ¶願いがかなう have *one's* wish granted ; have *one's* request heard ; 願いを聞く grant [《文》comply with] *sb's* request / 願いを退ける refuse [turn down] *sb's* request / 願いを出す apply 《to the office for *sth*》; file [hand in, send in] an application《for》/ お願いだから please ; I implore [entreat] you to *do* ; for God's [mercy's] sake. 文例⇩

ねがいさげ 願い下げ 文例⇩

ねがいでる 願い出る 〈願いを出す〉 ¶辞職を願い出る tender [send in] *one's* resignation.

ねがう 願う 〈願望する〉《文》desire ; wish ; hope ; 〈依頼する〉request ; ask《for》; 〈懇願する〉beg ; implore ;《文》entreat ; 〈祈願する〉pray《for》; 神に願う pray to God《for *sth*》/ 願わしい[しくない] be desirable [undesirable] / 願わくは I pray ; I wish [If only]《I could…》; I hope ;《文》It is to be hoped [desired]《that…》. 文例⇩

ねがえり 寝返り ¶寝返りを打つ〈床の中で〉toss about in bed《1 回》; turn over in *one's* sleep《1 回》; 〈裏切る〉betray ;《文》play *sb* false ;《口語》double-cross《*one's* confederates》; go over《to the enemy》; defect《to the other side》; turn《*one's*》coat. 文例⇩

ねがお 寝顔 *one's* sleeping face. 文例⇩

ねがさかぶ 値嵩株 high-priced stock(s).

ねかしつける 寝かし付ける ⇨ ねかせる.

ねかせる 寝かせる 〈眠らせる〉put 《a child》to bed [sleep] ; 〈横にする〉lay *sb* down ; lay *sb* on *its* side ; 〈商品などを〉let 《money, goods》lie idle ; 〈麹(こうじ)などを〉ferment 《rice malt》

965

ねこ

¶歌を歌って寝かせる sing《a baby》to sleep / 寝かせてある商品 dead stock ; unsold goods ; goods remaining on the shelf for a long period.

ねぎ 〈白ねぎ〉a leek ; 〈青ねぎ〉a spring onion.

ねぎらう 労う ¶労をねぎらう thank *sb* for *his* trouble ; 〈ほうびを与える〉reward *sb* for *his* services.

ねきりむし 根切り虫 a cutworm.

ねぎる 値切る beat [knock] down the price ; bargain [haggle]《with a storekeeper》over the price ¶千円に値切る beat down the price to 1,000 yen / ひどく値切る drive a hard bargain《with a merchant》.

ねぎわ 値際 ⇨ ねじな.

ねくずれ 値崩れ ¶値崩れする (a sudden, sharp) drop [decline] in price《caused by oversupply》.

ねぐせ 寝癖 ¶寝癖がつく (a part of) *one's* hair gets bent the wrong way while *one* is in bed.

ネクタイ a tie ;《米》a necktie ¶ネクタイを着ける wear [put on] a tie / ネクタイを結ぶ tie a necktie / ネクタイを直す[ほどく] straighten [untie] *one's* necktie / ちょうネクタイ a bow (tie) / ちりめのネクタイ a string tie / ネクタイピン a tiepin ; a tie clasp. 文例⇩

ねくび 寝首 ¶寝首をかく murder a sleeping person ; kill *sb* in *his* sleep ;《比喩的に》betray ;《文》play *sb* foul ;《口語》play a dirty trick on *sb*.

ねぐら 塒 a (night) roost ¶ねぐらに着く go to roost ; roost / ねぐらに着いている be roosting [at roost] / ねぐらに帰る fly home to roost.

ネグリジェ a negligee.

ねぐるしい 寝苦しい cannot sleep well ; pass a bad [sleepless, wakeful] night ; sleep badly. 文例⇩

ねこ 猫 《動》a cat ; 〈愛称〉a puss(y) ¶猫の(ような) feline / 猫の額ほどの土地 a tiny plot of land / 猫の目のように変わる be as changeable [fickle] as a chameleon [weathercock] / 猫をかぶる play the hypocrite ;《文》pretend [feign] innocence ; look as if butter would not melt in *one's* mouth / 猫も杓子(しゃく)も everyone ; (anybody and) everybody ; (every) Tom, Dick and Harry / 雄猫 a tom(cat) / 子猫 a kitten / 《小児語》a kitty / 雌猫 a tabby (cat). 文例⇩

---

you. | Will you do me a favor [do something for me]? / 彼は願いによって本官を免ぜられた. He was relieved of his post at his own request.

ねがいさげ そんな話はこちらから願い下げだ. I must ask to be excused from such an undertaking.

ねがう 明朝お出で願えましょうか. May [Might] I ask you to come tomorrow morning? / お願いしたいことがあります. There is something I want to ask you.| I have a favor to ask (of) you. / 山田さんをお願いしたいのですが.〈電話で〉May I speak to Miss Yamada, please? | Would you

mind calling[Would you be kind enough to call] Miss Yamada to the phone? / そうさせていただければ願ったりかなったりです[もてないこと]です. Nothing would suit me better (than that). | I could wish for nothing better. / 神よ幸うばこの哀れな乙女に哀れみをたれたまえ. May God have mercy on this poor girl! | Have mercy on this poor girl, O God!

ねがえり 彼は床に就いたが眠れずに何度も寝返りを打った. He went to bed, but he couldn't get to sleep and turned from side to side.

ねがお ねえ, あなた. この子の寝顔はなんてかわいらしいんでしょう. Darling, how cute our boy looks when he's asleep!

ねかしつける 子供をなだめて寝かし付けてきたところです. I've just settled my son down for the night.

ネクタイ ネクタイが曲がって[ゆがんで]いるわよ. Your tie is crooked.

ねぐるしい 夏の夜は寝苦しい. A hot summer night often keeps [prevents] us from sleeping.

ねこ 猫は顔を洗っていた. The cat was cleaning its whiskers. / 小さな家と猫の額ほどの庭があ

ねこいらず 猫入らず rat poison; ratsbane.
ねこかぶり 猫かぶり 《事》 hypocrisy; feigned innocence; 《人》a hypocrite ⇒ ねこ(猫をかぶる).
ねこかわいがり 猫可愛がり ¶猫かわいがりにかわいがる dote on 《one's grandchild》.
ねこぎ 根扱ぎ ¶根こぎにする ⇒ ねこそぎ(根こそぎにする).
ねごこち 寝心地 ¶寝心地のよい床 a comfortable bed.
ねこじた 猫舌 ¶猫舌である have a tongue too sensitive to heat; cannot stand [be unable to eat] very hot food.
ねこぜ 猫背 ¶(have) a stoop ¶猫背の round-shouldered; with stooped shoulders; stooped.
ねこそぎ 根こそぎ all; completely; entirely; 《文》root and branch [all] ¶根こそぎにする 〈抜き取る〉 uproot; root 《a tree》up; pull [dig] 《a plant》up by the roots; 〈絶やしにする〉 exterminate *sth* root and branch; eradicate. 文例⇩
ねごと 寝言 ¶寝言を言う talk in *one's* sleep; 〈くだらぬことを言う〉talk nonsense [rubbish, 《英》rot].
ねこなでごえ 猫撫で声 ¶猫なで声で in an insinuating [a coaxing] voice [tone].
ねこばば 猫ばば ¶猫ばばをきめる embezzle; 《口語》pocket; 《文》peculate.
ねこみ 寝込み ¶寝込みを襲う surprise *sb* in *his* sleep; storm *sb's* house when *he* is asleep.
ねこむ 寝込む 〈寝入る〉fall asleep; go [drop off] to sleep; 〈病気で〉be down with (influenza); be ill [sick] in bed; be confined to *one's* bed ¶ぐっすり寝込んでいる be fast asleep; be in a deep sleep [《文》slumber].
ねこめいし 猫目石 〖鉱〗cat's-eye.
ねこやなぎ 猫柳 (a) pussy willow.
ねごろ 値頃 a reasonable [moderate] price. 文例⇩
ねころがる, ねころぶ 寝転がる, 寝転ぶ lie [throw *oneself*] down (on the grass).
ねさがり 値下がり a fall [drop] in price; depreciation (価値の) ¶値下がりする fall [drop, go down] in price.
ねさげ 値下げ a cut [reduction] in price; a price cut [reduction] ¶運賃の値下げ a cut [reduction] in (the) fare / 値下げする cut [lower, reduce] the price. 文例⇩
ねざけ 寝酒 ¶寝酒を飲む have a drink just before bedtime; have a nightcap.
ねざす 根ざす 〈植物が〉take [strike] root; 〈原因する〉arise [come, spring, stem] 《from》; 《文》originate 《in》¶…に深く根ざしている

have *its* roots deep in… / 深く根ざした deep-rooted[-seated].
ねざめ 寝覚め ¶寝覚めが悪い 《文》feel remorse 《for》; have a guilty conscience 《over, about》; be conscience-stricken.
ねざや 値鞘 a margin.
ねじ a screw ¶ねじの頭 the head of a screw; a screwhead / ねじを締める drive a screw in [home]; tighten a screw / ねじを固く締める drive a screw in tightly / ねじを巻く wind 《a watch》; 〈比喩的に〉rouse *sb* 《to, into》/ ねじを回す turn a screw / ねじを戻す unscrew / ねじを緩める loosen [slacken] a screw / ねじで締१ける screw *sth* up [down] / ねじ切り a (screw-)thread cutter / ねじこぶた a screw cap [top] / ねじ回し a screwdriver / ねじ山 the thread (of a screw). 文例⇩
ねじあげる 捩じ上げる screw [twist] 《*sb's* arm》hard.
ねじおる 捩じ折る twist [wrench] *sth* off; break *sth* off by twisting *it*.
ねじきる 捩じ切る wrench [twist] *sth* off.
ねじける 拗ける 〈ゆがむ〉be [get] distorted [twisted, warped]; 〈ひねくれる〉grow [get, 《文》become] perverse ¶心のねじけた cross-grained; perverse.
ねじこむ 捩じ込む 〈押し込む〉push [thrust] 《into》; 〈抗議する〉protest 《to *sb* about *sth*》; file [lodge] a protest 《with *sb* about *sth*》; demand an explanation [apology] (from *sb*).
ねしずまる 寝静まる fall [be] fast asleep; be lost [buried] in sleep [《文》slumber]. 文例⇩
ねしな 寝しな ¶寝しなに just before going to bed; 《文》when retiring; at bedtime.
ねじふせる 捩じ伏せる get *sb* under [down].
ねじまげる 捩じ曲げる bend *sth* by twisting; twist.
ねしょうがつ 寝正月 New Year holidays spent doing nothing.
ねしょうべん 寝小便 bed-wetting ¶寝小便をする wet one's bed.
ねじとる 捩じり取る wrench off; 《文》wrest 《a weapon》from 《*sb's* hand》.
ねじ(り)はちまき 捩じ(り)鉢巻き a twisted towel worn around *one's* head (while *one* is at work) ¶ねじ(り)はち巻きで with a twisted towel worn around *one's* head; 〈一生懸命に〉with all *one's* might; as hard as *one* can; wholeheartedly.
ねじる 捩じる twist; wrench; screw; 〈ゆがめる〉distort; warp ¶瓶の蓋をねじってあける[しめる] screw off [on] the cover of a jar.
ねじれる 捩じれる be [get] twisted; 〈ゆがむ〉

る. We have a small house, and *a garden the size of a postage stamp.* / それは猫に小判だよ. That's like casting pearls before swine.
ねこそぎ 泥棒が入って現金を根こそぎ持っていってしまった. A burglar broke in and took all the cash [every cent] I had in the house.

ねごろ どの辺の値頃の品をお望みでございますか. What price range are you interested in?
ねさげ ただ今店内全商品5割の値下げになっています. All the goods in our store are marked down by 50 per cent [to half price] now.
ねじ このねじは緩んでいる. This screw is loose. / ねじを巻いてや

る必要がある. He needs a kick in the pants.
ねしずまる 火事は皆が寝静まった時分に起こった. The fire broke out when everyone was fast asleep.
ねすぎる 30分寝過ごしたため学校に遅れてしまった. I slept half an hour too long [overslept by half an hour] and was late for

ねじろ 根城 〈根拠地〉 a base (of operations); 〈本拠〉 headquarters ¶…を根城にして with …as one's base of operations.

ねず 〘植〙 a needle juniper (tree).

ねすごす 寝過ごす oversleep. 文例⇩

ねずのばん 寝ずの番 〈事〉(an) all-night watch [vigil]; 〈人〉a night watchman ¶寝ずの番をする keep (all-)night watch [vigil] (against thieves).

ねずみ a rat; 〈小形の〉 a mouse (pl. mice) ★日本の家庭で出没するねずみは rat だが, 英米の家庭に出没するのは, rat より小形の mouse が普通 ¶ねずみの多いビル a rat-infested building / ねずみ入らず a cupboard / ねずみ色(の) dark gray / ねずみ捕り a rattrap; 〈警察の〉 a (police) speed-trap / ねずみ算で増える increase in geometrical progression. 文例⇩

ねぞう 寝相 ¶寝相が悪い be an untidy sleeper.

ねそびれる 寝そびれる fail to get to sleep; lie [stay] awake (in bed).

ねそべる 寝そべる lie [throw oneself] down; sprawl ¶寝そべっている lie sprawled [at full length].

ネタ 〈新聞の〉a news item; 〈小説などの〉 copy; material(s); 〈すしなどの〉(raw) material(s); 〈証拠〉(a) proof; evidence ¶いいネタになる make good copy / 新聞などの〉be big news / ネタがあがる 〈人が主語〉find [gather] evidence (against, for). 文例⇩

ねだ 根太 a joist.

ねたきり 寝たきり ¶寝たきりになる be bedridden; be confined to one's bed for a long time / 寝たきり老人 a bedridden old man [woman].

ねたましい 妬ましい enviable ¶ねたましく思う be [feel] envious [jealous] (of) ⇨ ねたむ.

ねたみ 妬み jealousy; envy ¶ねたみ深い jealous; envious / ねたみから from [out of] jealousy [envy].

ねたむ 妬む be [feel] jealous [envious] (of); envy ¶成功をねたむ envy sb his success; envy [feel envy at] sb's success / ねたみで from [out of] jealousy [envy].

ねだやし 根絶やし ⇨ こんぜつ.

ねだる (try to) wheedle sb into doing; pester [press, 《文》 importune] sb (for sth, to do); 《文》ask sb importunately (for sth, to do). 文例⇩

ねだん 値段 a price ¶値段が高い the price (of sth) is high; 〈品物が主語〉 be dear [expensive, 《文》 high in price] / 値段が安い the price (of sth) is low; 〈品物が主語〉 be cheap [《文》 inexpensive, 《文》 low in price] ⇨ やすい¹ / 値段が上がる the price (of sth) rises [goes up]; 〈品物が主語〉 rise [go up] in price / 値段が下がる the price (of sth) falls [goes down]; 〈品物が主語〉 fall [go down] in price / 値段を上げる[下げる] raise [lower] the price / 値段をつける 〈買い値を言う〉 make an offer (of 1,000 yen for an article); name one's price; 〈品物に〉 set [put] a price on (an article); price (an article); mark (an article) with (its) price / 値段を掛け合う haggle [bargain] over the price (of sth) with sb / 値段書き be a price list. 文例⇩

ねちがえる 寝違える twist [wrench, crick] (one's neck) in one's sleep; get a crick (in one's neck) while asleep. 文例⇩

ねつ 熱 heat; 〈体温〉(a) temperature; 〈高熱〉(a) fever; 〈流行〉 enthusiasm (for); a craze (for); a mania (for) ¶熱がある have a temperature; have (a) fever; be feverish / 熱が出る run a temperature [fever]; become feverish / 熱が高い have a (high) temperature; have a fever / 熱がない have no enthusiasm (for); 《文》 show [manifest] no zeal (for); be indifferent (to) / 熱が入っている warm to (one's work) / 熱のこもった演説 a fiery [an impassioned] speech / 熱のない話しぶり a lackadaisical way of talking / 熱を加える heat; apply heat (to) / 熱を発散する radiate [give off] heat / 熱をさます 〈事が主語〉 dampen [chill] one's enthusiasm [《文》 zeal] (for) / 熱を計る take one's temperature / 熱を上げる be enthusiastic (about, over, for); 《米口語》 enthuse (about, over); be mad (about, after, over); lose one's head over (a girl) / 勝手な熱を吹く say what one likes / 熱に浮かされる 〈うわごとを言う〉 be delirious because of violent fever / 運動熱 enthusiasm for sports / 太陽熱 solar heat / 文学熱 a craze [mania] for literature / 熱イオン a thermion / 熱エネルギー heat energy / 熱効率 thermal efficiency / 熱源 a source of heat / 熱さまし ⇨ げねつ (解熱剤) / 熱磁気 thermomagnetism / 熱単位 a heat [thermal] unit / 熱電気 thermoelectricity / 熱電池 a thermoelectric battery; a thermobattery / 熱電対 a thermocouple / 熱伝導(率) thermal conduction (conductivity) / 熱分解 pyrolysis / 熱容量 heat [thermal] capacity / 熱力学 thermodynamics.

ねつあい 熱愛 ¶熱愛する love passionately; 《文》 be an ardent lover (of); be madly [pas-

---

school.

ねずみ ねずみがちゅうちゅう鳴いた. A rat squeaked. / あの男はただのねずみじゃない. He is no ordinary rat.

ネタ ネタはちゃんとあがっているんだ. The evidence against you is clear.

ねだる お父さんにねだって買ってもらいなさい. Persuade your father to buy it for you.

ねだん その値段なら高い[安い]. It's dear [cheap] at that price. / 値段はいくらですか. How much (is it)? / What is the price?

ねちがえる 寝違えて首が回らない. I've twisted [wrenched] my neck in the night [in bed], and can't turn my head (either way).

ねつ (病人に向かって医者が)熱はありません. 脈も正常です. You have no temperature, and your pulse is normal. / 熱が上がった. My temperature rose [went up]./ 熱が下がった. My temperature dropped [went down]. / 熱が引いた. The fever abated [subsided, left me]. / 私は夕方になると熱が出る. I get a temperature in the evenings. / 起きた時、のどが痛く

ねつい 熱意 enthusiasm;《文》zeal ⇒ねつ
¶熱意のある enthusiastic;《文》zealous / 熱意を失わせる chill *sb's* zeal ; take the heart out of *sb* / 熱意を示す show [manifest] zeal《for》; display great [a great deal of] enthusiasm《for》.

ねつえん 熱演 an impassioned performance ¶熱演する play [perform] enthusiastically [with a lot of verve]; put a lot of spirit into *one's* performance.

ねつかく- 熱核… ¶熱核戦争 (a) thermonuclear war / 核反応 (a) thermonuclear reaction.

ネッカチーフ a neckerchief.

ねっから《生まれつき》by nature;《全然》(not) at all; (not) a bit [《文》whit]; 《(not)》in the least ¶根っからの正直者である be an honest man by nature / 根っからの商人である be born a merchant; be a born merchant / 根っからだめだ be no good《for》; be utterly impossible [useless] / 根っから知らない know nothing at all《about》; do not have the haziest idea《of》.

ねつき 寝付き ¶寝付きがいい[悪い] find it easy [difficult] to get to sleep; get [do not get] to sleep easily.

ねっき 熱気《熱い空気》a blast of [《文》hot air;《雰囲気》a heated atmosphere;《暑熱》heat.

ねつぎ[1] 根接ぎ ¶根接ぎをする graft《a rose》at the root.

ねつぎ[2] 根継ぎ ¶根継ぎをする splice《a post》at the base; underpin《a building》.

ねっきょう 熱狂《熱心》enthusiasm;《熱中》a rage;《興奮》excitement ¶熱狂する《興奮する》get [go] wild with excitement《at, by, over》; get [go] wild with excitement《over》;《夢中になる》be enthusiastic《over》;《米口語》enthuse《about, over》; be crazy《for, about》/ 熱狂的 enthusiastic; wild; mad; frantic / 熱狂者 a great fan《of the Beatles》; an《audio》enthusiast;《宗教や政治の》a《religious, political》fanatic. 文例⇨

ねつく 寝付く get [go] to sleep; fall asleep ¶病気で寝付いている be ill [sick] in bed. 文例⇨

ねづく 根付く take [strike] root《into the soil》; get [gain] a roothold《in the soil》.

ネックレス a necklace.

ねっけつ 熱血 hot [warm] blood;《文》ardor ¶熱血漢 a hot-blooded man;《文》a fervent soul.

ねっこ 根っ子《根》a root;《切り株》a stump.

ねっしゃびょう 熱射病 heat stroke [exhaustion, prostration].

ねつじょう 熱情 ⇒じょうねつ.

ねっしょり 熱処理 heat treatment ¶熱処理をする heat-treat.

ねっしん 熱心 eagerness; enthusiasm;《文》zeal ¶熱心な eager; enthusiastic;《文》zealous; ardent / 熱心に eagerly; enthusiastically; 《文》zealously;《文》with zeal [ardor] / 熱心である be eager《about, for, to *do*》; be intent [keen]《on》; be devoted《to》; be enthusiastic《in》. 文例⇨

ねっする 熱する《加熱する》make *sth* hot; heat;《熱くなる》get [《文》become] heated; 《激する》become hot; get excited ¶熱しやすい excitable. 文例⇨

ねっせい 熱誠 earnestness; enthusiasm; devotion（献身） ¶熱誠のこもった earnest; enthusiastic; devoted / 熱誠をこめて warmly; earnestly; enthusiastically; devotedly;《文》with zeal. 文例⇨

ねっせん[1] 熱戦 a hard fight;《競技》a hot contest; a close [tough] game.

ねっせん[2] 熱線《物》heat [thermic] rays.

ねつぞう 捏造 (a) fabrication; (an) invention ¶捏造する forge; invent;《文》fabricate; make [《口語》cook] up.

ねったい 熱帯 the tropics; the torrid zone ¶熱帯植物[魚] a tropical plant [fish] / 熱帯多雨[降雨]林 a tropical rain forest / 熱帯地方 the tropics; tropical regions / 熱帯低気圧 a tropical cyclone.

ねっちゅう 熱中 enthusiasm;《文》zeal; a craze ¶熱中する be enthusiastic《for, over, about》;《米口語》enthuse《about, over》; have a craze [rage]《for》; be crazy [mad]《about, over》; be engrossed [absorbed]《in》; devote *oneself*《to》; be keen《on》. 文例⇨

ねっぽい 熱っぽい《熱がある》feverish;《情熱的な》enthusiastic;《文》fervent ¶熱っぽい調子で語る speak warmly [enthusiastically]《about, of》; tell《a story》in an excited《tone of》voice.

ネット a net ¶球にネットする put the ball into the net; net the ball / 髪にネットをする wear a hair net / ネットを張る put up a《tennis》net / ネット裏から from behind the backstop / ネットプレーをする play close to the net.

ねっとう 熱湯 boiling water ¶熱湯でやけどをする be scalded with boiling water; get a scald from boiling water / 熱湯消毒をする dis-

---

て, 熱があった. I awoke with a sore throat and a temperature. / 汗をかいたので熱がとれた. The fever was sweated out of me. / 今若い人びとの間にスキー熱が盛んです. There is a lot of enthusiasm for skiing [Skiing has become all the rage] among young people. / 彼の態度を見てその計画に対するわれわれの熱もさめてしまった. His attitude has cooled down our interest in the project.

ねっきょう 全観衆はこの一戦に熱狂した. The whole stadium got excited over this one game. / 彼は熱狂的歓迎を受けた. He was given an enthusiastic welcome.

ねつく 昨夜は遅くまで寝つけなかった. Sleep did not come to me [I lay awake in bed] till late last night.

ねっしん 彼はスポーツにとても熱心だ. He is very keen on sports. | He is a real sports enthusiast. | 時折彼は熱心のあまりに行き過ぎをやった. He was occasionally carried away by his enthusiasm.

ねっする 日本人は熱しやすくさめやすい. The Japanese are easily excited but quick to cool down

ねっとり ¶ねっとりした sticky; viscous.
ネットワーク a (TV) network.
ねっぱ 熱波 a heat wave.
ねつびょう 熱病 a fever ¶熱病にかかる catch [suffer from] a fever.
ねっぷう 熱風 a hot wind [blast]; (a blast of) hot air.
ねつべん 熱弁 ¶熱弁をふるう make [deliver] an impassioned [a fiery] speech; 《文》speak with fervor; harangue [《文》declaim] (against, for).
ねつぼう 熱望 《文》an ardent [a fervent] wish; 《文》an eager desire ¶熱望する be eager [anxious] (for *sth*, to *do*); 《文》eagerly desire to *do*; be dying to *do*. 文例⇩
ねづよい 根強い deep-rooted; firmly-rooted ¶根強い偏見 a deep-rooted prejudice / 根強く firmly; tenaciously.
ねつらい 熱雷 《気象》a heat thunderstorm.
ねつりょう 熱量 quantity of heat; 〈発熱量〉calorific value; 〈カロリー〉(a) calorie ¶熱量の多い[少ない] high [low] in calorific value / 熱量計 a calorimeter / 熱量測定(法) calorimetry.
ねつれつ 熱烈 ¶熱烈な passionate; impassioned; 《文》ardent; 《文》fervent / 熱烈に passionately; 《文》ardently; 《文》fervently; 《文》with ardor [fervor].
ねどこ 寝床 a bed; 〈船などの〉a berth ¶寝床に入る go to bed; turn in / 寝床を離れる[から飛び起きる] get [jump] out of bed / 寝床で本を読む read in bed.
ねとねと ¶ねとねとした sticky; clammy.
ねとまり 寝泊まり ¶寝泊まりする stay [live, lodge] (with *sb*, at *sb*'s house).
ねなしぐさ 根無し草 〈浮き草〉duckweed; 〈人〉a rootless individual.
ネパール Nepal ¶ネパールの Nepalese / ネパール王国 the Kingdom of Nepal / ネパール語 Nepali / ネパール人 a Nepalese (単複同形).
ネバダ Nevada (略: Nev.) ¶ネバダ州の人 a Nevadan.
ねばっこい 粘っこい〈ねばねばした〉⇨ねばば;〈しつっこい〉persistent; persevering;《文》pertinacious.
-ねばならない ⇨いけない.
ねばねば ¶ねばねばした sticky;《文》glutinous; clammy.
ねはば 値幅 ⇨ねびらき.
ねばり(け) 粘り(気) 〈粘着性〉stickiness;《文》viscosity; 〈執着〉tenacity;《文》pertinacity ¶粘り気がある be sticky; be glutinous / 粘り強い be tenacious; be persevering.
ねばりつく 粘り付く stick [《文》adhere] (to).
ねばる 粘る 〈粘着性がある〉be sticky;《文》be adhesive; be glutinous; 〈執着する〉be tenacious; persevere (in); stick [《文》adhere] (to one's principles); 《口語》hold out (for one's demands); 《口語》stick to *one*'s guns ¶頑強に粘る adhere [stick] to *sth* with great tenacity / コーヒー1杯で3時間も粘る stay as long as three hours (in a tearoom) over a cup of coffee.
ねはん 涅槃 Nirvana ¶ねはんに入る enter [pass into] Nirvana; attain Buddhahood [supreme enlightenment].
ねびえ 寝冷え ¶寝冷えする get chilled while asleep [in bed].
ねびき 値引き (a) reduction in price; (a) discount ⇨わりびき ¶(売り手の)値引き競争 a price war. 「prices.
ねびらき 値開き a margin; (a) difference in
ねぶかい 根深い deep-rooted[-seated]; ingrained;〈とても直らない〉《文》inveterate; incurable ¶根深い習慣 an ingrained [inveterate] habit.
ねぶくろ 寝袋 a sleeping bag.
ねぶそく 寝不足 ¶寝不足で from [for] lack of sleep;《文》owing to insufficient sleep. 文例⇩
ネプツニウム 《化》neptunium.
ねぶと 根太 〈腫れ物〉a boil; a furuncle.
ねぶみ 値踏み 〈価格をつけること〉valuation; appraisal (特に課税のため);〈見積もり〉an estimate ¶値踏みする value [price, appraise] *sth* (at 2 million yen); put [set] a price (of 1,000 dollars) on *sth*;〈見積もる〉estimate (the cost at 5,000 dollars). 文例⇩
ネブラスカ Nebraska (略: Neb., Nebr.) ¶ネブラスカ州の人 a Nebraskan.
ねぼう 寝坊 〈人〉a late riser; 〈事〉getting up late;《文》late rising ¶寝坊する rise [get up] late;〈寝過ごす〉oversleep. 文例⇩
ねぼけまなこ 寝惚け眼 sleepy eyes; a drowsy look ¶寝ぼけ眼の sleepy-eyed[-faced] / 寝ぼけ眼をこする rub the sleep from *one*'s eyes.
ねぼける 寝惚ける be half asleep; be still only half awake. 文例⇩
ねほりはほり 根掘り葉掘り ¶根掘り葉掘り聞く[尋ねる] ask [《文》inquire of] *sb* about every detail of *sth*;《文》be inquisitive (about).
ねまき 寝巻き, 寝間着 nightwear; night clothes; 〈パジャマ〉《米》pajamas;《英》pyjamas ⇨パジャマ;〈婦人・子供用の〉a nightdress; a nightgown;《口語》a nighty;〈男子用の〉a nightshirt.

ねっせい 一字一句に氏の熱誠がこもっている。Every word breathes his ardor.
ねっちゅう 彼は物事に熱中するたちだ。He is the sort of person who puts all his efforts into anything he takes on.
ねつぼう アーノルド先生, 僕たちは皆クラス会に先生のご出席を熱望しております。Mr. Arnold, we are all very keen that you should attend our class meeting.
ねぶそく どうも最近は寝不足気味で, 仕事中についうとうとしてしまう。I haven't had [been getting] enough sleep lately, so I keep nodding off at work.
ねぶみ 家を買う前に値踏みはしておいた方がいい。You should have a valuation done before you buy a house. / 彼が持っているルノワールの絵を5千万と値踏みした。I put [estimated] his Renoir at fifty million yen.
ねぼう 寝坊して電車に乗り遅れてしまった。I overslept and missed my train.
ねぼける 寝ぼけてそんなことを言ったんだよ。He must have

ねまわし 根回し ¶根回しをする dig around the roots of a tree (before transplanting); 〈比喩的〉lay the groundwork 《for *sth*》.

ねみだれがみ 寝乱れ髪 hair that is disheveled [disordered] from sleeping; sleep-[bed-] tousled hair.

ねみみ 寝耳 ¶寝耳に水の出来事 a great surprise; a bolt from the blue.

ねむい 眠い be [feel] sleepy; be drowsy ¶眠い講義 a dull lecture / 眠い目をこする rub *one's* drowsy eyes / 眠くなる get [《文》become] sleepy [drowsy].

ねむけ 眠気 sleepiness; drowsiness ¶眠気がさす[を催す] become [feel] sleepy [drowsy] / 目をこすって眠気を覚ます wipe [rub] the sleep from *one's* eyes / 濃いコーヒーを飲んで眠気を払う drink strong coffee in order to keep awake /《文》to banish sleep]/眠気覚ましに to shake off sleepiness; to keep (*oneself*) awake. 文例①

ねむたい 眠たい ⇨ ねむい.

ねむ(た)そう 眠(た)そう ¶眠(た)そうな sleepy(-looking); drowsy / 眠(た)そうをした sleepy-eyed / 眠(た)そうな顔[目つき]をする look sleepy [drowsy]/眠(た)そうに sleepily; drowsily.

ねむのき 〘植〙 a silk tree.

ねむらせる 眠らせる put *sb* to sleep; 〈殺す〉kill; murder; 〈打totalsdlagrund〉knock *sb* out.

ねむり 眠り (a) sleep;《文》(a) slumber ¶眠りが浅い sleep badly [poorly]; be a light sleeper / 眠りが深い sleep soundly [deeply]; be a good [sound, heavy] sleeper / 眠りに落ちる fall asleep; drop off to [into] sleep / 眠りにつく get to sleep / 眠りから覚める awake from (*one's*) sleep [slumber] / 永遠の眠り ⇨ えいみん / 眠り薬 a sleeping drug [pill,《文》potion] ⇨ さいみん (催眠剤).

ねむりびょう 眠り病 sleeping sickness.

ねむる 眠る 〈睡眠する〉sleep; have [get] a sleep;《文》slumber; 〈寝入る〉fall asleep; go to sleep / よく[ぐっすり]眠る sleep well [soundly, deeply]; have a sound sleep [deep slumber]; sleep like a top [log] / 立ったまま眠る sleep on *his* [*its*] feet / 本を読みながら眠ってしまう read *oneself* to sleep / ぐっすり眠っている be fast asleep / 銀行に眠っている金 money lying idle at the bank / 眠れない sleep badly [poorly]; have a bad [wakeful] night;〈全然〉have a sleepless night;〈寝つかれない〉cannot get to sleep.

ねもと 根元[本] the base 《of a tree》; the part near the root ¶木を根元から切り倒す cut down a tree at the base (close to the roots).

ねものがたり 寝物語 a talk in bed;〈睦言〉sweet nothings.

ねやすかぶ 値安株 low-priced stock(s).

ねゆき 根雪 snow cover; lying snow.

ねらい 狙い aim;〈目的〉an aim; an end; an object ¶ねらいが外れる miss *one's* aim [the mark]; go wide of the target [mark] / ねらいを定める take aim (at); set *one's* sights (on); sight ((on) *sth*) / よくねらいをつける have a good [careful, accurate] aim (at) / 銃のねらいをつける take aim with *one's* rifle (at); level [point] *one's* gun (at). 文例①

ねらいうち 狙い撃[打]ち sharpshooting;〘野球〙place hitting ¶ねらい撃ちする snipe[shoot, fire] (at); pick off (*one's* pursuers).

ねらう 狙う 〈銃などで〉aim [take aim] (at); sight (a target); 〈うかがう〉watch for; 〈付けねらう〉be [go] after;〈目をつける〉have an eye (on); 〈志望する〉hope (to *do*, for *sth*);《文》aspire (to, after) ¶脱走の機会をねらう watch for a chance to run away (from) / 賞金をねらう be after [have an eye on] a reward / 高い地位をねらう aspire to a high position.

ねり 練り 〈絹の〉gloss; 〈粉などの〉kneading ¶練り絹 glossed silk / 練り薬 an ointment [a medicine in paste form / 練り粉 dough.

ねりあるく 練り歩く parade 《the streets》; go [walk] in procession.

ねりあわせる 練り合わせる knead 《the flour and fat》 together; mix 《the ingredients》 by kneading (them).

ねる¹ 寝る 〈横になる〉lie down; 〈床につく〉go [get] to bed;《文》retire (to bed); 〈口語〉turn in; 〈寝入る〉go [get] to sleep; fall asleep; 〈同衾する〉sleep (with); 〈病気で〉be laid up [be down] with 《influenza》; be ill [sick] in bed;〈商品などが〉lie idle ¶寝転がる lie down to sleep / 寝る時刻 bedtime / 早く寝て早く[遅く寝て遅く]起きる go to bed early [late] and get up early [late];《文》keep early [late] hours (★ 主に寝る時刻について言う) / 寝てもさめても waking or sleeping; awake or asleep / 寝ている商品 dead stock; unsold goods; goods lying idle on the shelf / 寝ずにいる〈床を離れて〉sit [stay] up 《till late into the night》;〈眠れずに〉lie awake (in bed). 文例①

ねる² 練る 〈粉を〉knead; 〈絹を〉gloss; 〈金属を〉temper;〈錬磨する〉train;〈文章を〉polish (up);〈計画を〉ponder (over, of on);《文》elaborate (a scheme) ¶〈計画などを〉充

---

been half asleep when he said it.

ねむけ 眠けがさしてきた. Sleepiness came [crept] over me. ¶ I started to feel drowsy [sleepy].

ねむる 昨夜はよく眠れましたか. Did you sleep well last night? ¶ Did you have a good night? / 町はまだ眠っていた. The town still lay wrapped in sleep. / 昨夜は遅くまで眠らずに起きていた. I sat [stayed] up late last night./

その夜は暑くてだれも眠れなかった. The night was so hot that there was no sleep for anyone.

ねらい 弾丸はねらいたがわず熊の月の輪に命中した. The bullet struck the bear square in its white collar. /あいつのねらいは一体なんだろう. What (on earth) is he driving at, I wonder? / この広告はねらいがいい. This advertisement makes its point very

well [is very apt].

ねる¹ 彼はしばらく草の上に寝ていた. He was lying on the grass for a while. / 寝る時間だ. It is time for bed [to go to bed]. / 1 晩寝えればまた元気になるよ. A night's sleep will set you right. / 僕はいつも 10 時に寝ます. My regular bedtime is 10 o'clock. / お茶を飲みすぎて寝られなかった. Too much tea kept me awake.

ネル flannel.

ねわけ 根分け ¶根分けする divide [part] the roots 《of a plant》 (for transplanting).

ねわざ 寝技[業] 〈柔道などの〉 groundwork techniques ¶寝業師 a person skilled in the secret manipulation (of others).

ねわら 寝藁 litter ¶寝わらを敷く litter down (a stable, a horse).

ねん¹ 年 a year;〈学年〉《米》a grade ⇨ がくねん ¶中学2年の時に in *one's* second year of [at] junior high school / 年に1度 once a year; annually / 年に1度[回]の yearly; annual / 年に2度の half-yearly; twice-yearly; semiannual; biannual / 2年に1回 once in two years; biennially / 年に4回の quarterly / 1976年に in (the year) 1976 / 年5分の利子 interest of five per cent a year [《文》per annum] / 年から年中 ⇨ ねんじゅう / 年々(歳々) year by year; year after year; year in, year out; every year; yearly; annually ★ year by year は物事が年と共に変化していく時に用い、year after year 及び year in, year out は年ごとに変わることなく同じことが繰り返される意を表わす. 用法 「中学2年の時に」という時, 《米》では when *one* was in the eighth grade [an eighth grader] というが, これは grade が小・中・高校生を通じての数え方である所からくる.

ねん² 念 〈観念〉a sense; an idea;〈思考〉thought;〈感情〉a feeling;〈願望〉《文》a desire; (a) wish;〈懸念〉concern;〈注意〉attention; care; caution ¶不安の念 a sense [feeling] of uneasiness / 感謝の念 (a feeling of) gratitude / 念のため〈確実にするため〉to make sure 《of it》; to make 《it》 doubly sure /《文》 to make assurance double sure /〈用心のため〉《文》by way of precaution / 念の入った間違いをしでかす pile up [《文》 compound *one's*] errors; make a mistake worse by another mistake / 念を入れる pay attention 《to》; be careful (in doing); be conscientious (in *one's* work) / ねんいり / 念を押す〈注意を促す〉 call *sb's* attention (to); remind *sb* of *sth*; make sure (of, that...); 〈強く言う〉 tell *sb* emphatically (of, about); emphasize. 文例⇩

ねんいり 念入り ¶念入りな careful; elaborate; conscientious / 念入りに carefully; elaborately; conscientiously;《文》with care.

ねんえき 粘液 mucus; viscous liquid ¶粘液質の mucous;《文》(《気質》の) phlegmatic / 粘液便 mucous feces [stool].

ねんが 年賀 New Year('s) greetings; a New Year('s) call [visit] ¶年賀の客 New Year's caller / 年賀のあいさつをかわす wish each other a happy New Year; exchange New Year's greetings / 年賀に行く pay a New Year's call [visit] (to) / 年賀状を出す send *sb* a New Year card [New Year's greetings] / 年賀郵便 New Year's mail.

ねんがく 年額 an annual [a yearly] amount ¶年額1千万円の利益 an annual profit of ten million yen; a profit amounting to ten million yen a year [《文》per annum].

ねんがっぴ 年月日 a date ¶年月日の入れてない undated / 年月日を入れる date [attach a date to] (a paper).

ねんかん¹ 年刊 ¶年刊の published once a year; annual (bulletins); yearly (magazines).

ねんかん² 年間 ¶5年間 for five years / 年間を通じて throughout the year / 大正年間に during the Taisho era. 文例⇩

ねんかん³ 年鑑 a yearbook; an almanac.

ねんがん 念願 《文》*one's* dearest wish; *one's* heart's desire ¶多年の念願 something that *one* has wanted [《文》wished] to do for a long time;《文》*one's* long-cherished desire.

ねんき¹ 年忌 ⇨ かいき[].

ねんき² 年季 *one's* term (of service);〈年季奉公〉apprenticeship ¶年季を入れる have [get] long experience (of); put in a great deal of time (*doing*); put a lot of time into (*doing*); go through a long (period of) training (in); 《文》apply *oneself* to (the acquisition of a skill) over many years [over a long period (of time)] / 年季を入れた practiced; experienced; trained / 年季奉公をする[に行く] be apprenticed [apprentice *oneself*] (to).

ねんきん 年金 a pension ¶年金をもらう get [《文》receive,《文》be in receipt of] a pension / 年金をもらって退職する retire on a pension; be pensioned off / 年金で生活する live on *one's* pension / 年金受給者 a pensioner.

ねんぐ 年貢 〈地租〉land tax;〈小作料〉farm [ground] rent. 文例⇩

ねんげつ 年月 years (and months); time ¶年月がたつにつれて as (the) years go by; with the passage [lapse] of (the) time; with the years. 文例⇩

ねんげん 年限 a term; a period ¶年限を勤め

この部屋は4人寝られる. This room sleeps four. / 寝た子を起したくなかったからさ. It's because I thought I'd better let sleeping dogs lie.

ねん¹ 今年は昭和何年ですか. What year of Showa is this? / 昭和58年です. It is the 58th year of Showa. | It's Showa 58. / 1年は365日だ. Three hundred and sixty-five days make a year. | There are 365 days in a year. / 父が亡くなったのは私が小学校6年の時でした. I was in the sixth grade [I was a sixth grader] when my father died. / 就職は年々むずかしくなる. Every year it becomes more and more difficult to get employment.

ねん² 念のためもう一度部屋中捜してみた. I searched the room all over again (just) to satisfy myself. / ご念には及びません. Please leave it to me, sir [mad-am]. | Don't trouble yourself about it. / 念には念を入れよ.《文》Make assurance double sure. | One cannot be too careful.

ねんかん² わが国の対米輸出額は年間400億ドルに達する. Japan's exports to the U.S. amount to forty billion dollars a year.

ねんぐ 年貢の納めどきが来た. My time has come. | My hour has struck.

ねんげつ この辞書の編集には長い

ねんこう 年功《勤続》long(-continued) service; 《経験》years' [long] experience ¶年功を積む work for [over] many years (for a firm); 《文》have long experience 《in》/ 年功で[により] through [in consideration of] one's long service / 年功序列制度 the seniority system.

ねんごう 年号 the name [designation] of an era; an era name.

ねんごろ 懇ろ ¶懇ろな〈丁寧な〉polite; courteous;〈親切な〉kind; considerate;〈暖かい〉warm(hearted);〈心からの〉《文》cordial; hearty / 懇ろに politely; courteously; 《文》cordially; kindly; warmly / 懇ろに葬る bury 《sb's remains》with due ceremony / 懇ろにもてなす give sb a hearty welcome [warm reception]; receive sb cordially / 懇ろになる become close friends 《with》; become close 《to》; get friendly 《with》;〈特に異性と〉get on intimate terms 《with》.

ねんざ 捻挫 a sprain ¶ねんざする sprain [twist, turn] (one's ankle); have (one's wrist) sprained.

-ねんさい …年祭 an anniversary《of the death [birth] of sb, of the founding of a school》¶三十年祭 the thirtieth anniversary / 百年祭 the centenary; the centennial / 二百年祭 the bicentenary;《主に米》the bicentennial; the two-hundredth anniversary / 千年祭 the millenary; the millennial.

ねんさん 年産 yearly production; (an) annual output ⇒ げっさん.

ねんし 年始〈年の始め〉the beginning of the year;〈元旦〉New Year's Day;〈年賀〉⇒ ねんが ¶年始回り (go on, make) a round of New Year's calls.

ねんじ 年次 ¶年次計画 a yearly [an annual] program / 1983会計年度の年次計画 a program for fiscal 1983 / 年次報告 an annual report.

ねんしき 年式〈自動車の〉¶1980年式の 《cars》made in 1980; 1980 (model) 《Fords》.

ねんしゅう 年収 an annual [a yearly] income. 用例．

ねんじゅう 年中〈1年中〉all the year round; throughout the year;〈毎年毎年〉year in, year out;〈常に〉all the time; always ¶年中行事 an annual function; a yearly event.

ねんしゅつ 捻出 ¶捻出する〈案を〉devise; think [work] out;〈金を〉(manage to) raise 《funds》.

ねんしょ 年書 ⇒ おぼえがき.

ねんしょう¹ 年少 ¶年少の young; juvenile / 年少の故をもって on account [《文》in consideration] of sb's youth [minority] / 年少者〈若い人〉a youth; young people;〈年下の者〉

one's junior;〈未成年者〉a minor / クラス[3人の中の]最年少者 the youngest in the class [of the three].

ねんしょう² 年商 the yearly [annual] turnover ¶年商10億円になる〈商品が主語〉account for one billion yen of business a year.

ねんしょう³ 燃焼 burning; combustion ¶燃焼する burn / 燃焼しやすい, 燃焼性の combustible; flammable.

ねんじる 念じる pray 《to God for the safety of one's husband》.

ねんすう 年数 (the number of) years ⇒ とし¹.

ねんだい 年代〈時代〉an age;《文》an epoch; a period;〈時期〉the date 《of a battle》¶年代が紀元前1700年から1300年にわたる楔形文字による記録 cuneiform documents ranging in date from 1700 to 1300 B.C. / 年代を経た建物《文》a building which has seen many years [winters] / 年代を測定する date 《the fossils to the Pliocene》/ 年代を決める establish the date 《of》/ …の年代を1630年と推定する place [set] the date of…at 1630 / 1930年代に in the nineteen-thirties; in the 1930s [1930's] / 年代記 a chronicle; annals / 年代順に chronologically; in chronological order. 用例．

ねんちゃく 粘着 ¶粘着する stick 《文》adhere, be glued》《to》/ 粘着力《文》adhesive power / 粘着力のある, 粘着性の sticky;《文》adhesive.

ねんちょう 年長 seniority ¶年長の older; elder; senior / 年長者 a senior; an elder. 用例．

ねんど¹ 年度 ¶営業年度 a business year / 会計年度 a fiscal [《英》financial] year / 本年度 the current year / 1982会計年度 the 1982 fiscal year; fiscal 1982 / 1982年度の予算案 the budget for fiscal 1982 / 年度末[替わり]に at the end [change] of the fiscal year.

ねんど² 粘土 clay;〈塑像用の〉《商標名》Plasticine ¶粘土(製)の clay 《figures》/ 粘土のような, 粘土質の clayey.

ねんとう¹ 年頭 (at) the beginning of the year ¶《米国大統領の》年頭教書 the President's annual State of the Union message to Congress.

ねんとう² 念頭 ¶念頭を去らない〈事が主語〉be always in one's mind;《文》be ever present in one's mind [thoughts];〈人が主語〉be unable to forget; cannot put sth out of one's mind / 先ず第一に念頭にある be in the forefront of one's mind; be uppermost in one's mind / 念頭に置く〈忘れないで〉bear [keep, have] sth in mind;〈考慮に入れる〉take sth into consideration [account] / …を念頭に置いて with 《this problem》in mind / 念頭に置かない do not care 《about》;《文》give [pay] no heed 《to》; take no notice [thought] 《of》;《文》

年月を費やした. It took us quite a number of years to compile this dictionary. / こんなに年月がたってもその価値には少しも変わりがない. It is as valuable as ever even after this lapse of time.

ねんしゅう 彼の年収は600万円だ. His income is [He makes] six million yen a year.

ねんだい この化石の年代は始新世にさかのぼる. These fossils date back [go back chronologically] to the Eocene.

ねんちょう 彼は私より2歳年長で

す. He is two years older than me. | He is my senior by two years. | He is two years my senior. ⇒ より¹ 囲因.

ねんとう² この事を念頭第一におくべきだ. This should be your first [primary] concern. | This should

ねんない 年内 within the year; before the year is out.

ねんねこ a short coat worn to protect the baby on *one's* back.

ねんねん 年々 ⇨ ねん¹.

ねんぱい 年配[輩] age; years ¶かなりの年配の人 an elderly person;《文》a person well on [advanced] in years. 文例⇩

ねんばんがん 粘板岩 (clay) slate.

ねんぴ 燃費 fuel expenses; the cost of fuel ¶低燃費の車 an economical car; a vehicle which is economical with [on] fuel.

ねんぴょう 年表 a chronological table 《of Japanese history》.

ねんぷ¹ 年賦 ¶年賦で by [in] yearly [annual] installments / 5年の年賦で払う pay by [in] yearly installments over a period of five years / 年賦償還 redemption by annual installments.

ねんぷ² 年譜 a chronological record 《of *sb's* career, of the development of an event》.

ねんぶつ 念仏 a prayer to Amida Buddha [the Buddha] ¶念仏を唱える pray to Amida Buddha; say [chant] a prayer to the Buddha.

ねんぽう¹ 年俸 an annual salary; a yearly stipend.

ねんぽう² 年報 an annual report [bulletin]; an annual.

ねんまく 粘膜《解》(a) mucous membrane.

ねんまつ 年末 the end [close] of the year; the year-end ¶年末に at the end of the year / 年末までに by year's end / 年末調整 the year-end adjustment.

ねんらい 年来 for (some) years (past); these several [many] years ¶年来の希望《文》*one's* long-cherished desire / 年来の計画 a plan of long standing / 10年来の友人 a friend of ten years' standing / 20年来の大雪 the heaviest snowfall in [for] twenty years 《★ in は《米》, for は《英》》; the heaviest snowfall that we [they] have had in the past twenty years. 文例⇩

ねんり 年利 annual interest ¶年利6分で 《give *sb* a loan》at six per cent a year / 年利5 分になる bear [draw] interest of five per cent a year.

ねんりき 念力 the power of the will; will; faith.

ねんりょう 燃料 fuel ¶燃料を補給する refuel 《an airplane》/ 燃料油 fuel oil / 燃料タンク a fuel tank / 燃料電池 a fuel cell / 燃料費 fuel expenses; the cost of fuel.

ねんりん 年輪 a growth ring ¶木の年輪を数える count the (growth) rings of a tree.

ねんれい 年齢 age;《文》years ⇨ とし¹ ¶年齢順に in (descending) order of age / 年齢層 an age bracket [group] / 彼と同じ年齢層の人々 people in his age bracket / 年齢制限 the age limit(s).

の

の 野 a field;〈田野〉the fields;〈平野〉a plain ¶野の花 a wild flower / 野に出て働く work in the fields / 武蔵野 the Musashi Plain. 文例⇩

-の〈所有・所属〉-'s; of; belonging to;〈…に関する〉on; in;〈場所〉in; at; on;〈…に対する〉for;〈…による〉by;〈材料〉(made) of; in ⇨ 用例 ¶兄の本 my brother's book / 妹の友人 my sister's friend; a friend of my sister's / 今日の新聞 today's newspaper / 4時間の睡眠 four hours' [four hours of] sleep / その時代の人々 men of that time; men in those days / 化学の本 a chemistry book; a book on chemistry / 英語の試験 an English examination; an examination in English / フランス語の手紙 a letter (written) in French / 東京のおじ *one's* uncle (who lives) in Tokyo / 京都大学の教授 a professor at Kyoto University / ロンドンの冬 the winter in London / 本郷の古本屋 a secondhand bookstore at Hongo /

このたなの本 a book on [from, that belongs to] this shelf / 多摩川の花火大会 a fireworks show on the Tama (River) / 頭痛の薬 (a) headache medicine; (a) medicine for headache / 船酔いの薬 a seasickness drug; a drug against [for] seasickness / 5千円の商品券 a 5,000-yen gift token; a gift token for 5,000 yen / マチスの絵 a picture (painted) by Matisse; a Matisse (picture) / 漱石の小説 a novel (written) by Soseki / 彼女の手を取る take her by the hand / 黄金の杯 a gold cup;《文》a cup of gold / 大理石の像 a marble statue;《文》a statue in marble 《★ a statue in marble と言う時, この im は大理石が特に「表現の手段」であること(例えば, carved in wood; painted in oils) を表わしている》/ にじの橋 a rainbow bridge / 成功の秘訣 the key to success in life. 文例⇩

用法 「AのB」を英語ではBof Aと言う他に, 名詞をそのまま限定用法の形容詞のように用いて, 単に

---

be uppermost in your mind.

ねんぱい 彼は私と同年配です。He is about my age.

ねんらい 我々は20年来の友人です。We have been friends these twenty years.

ねんりき 念力岩をも通す。Where there's a will, there's a way. 〖諺〗

ねんりょう 伊丹で燃料を補給して飛行を続けた。They refueled at Itami and flew on.

の やはり野に置けれんげ草。Leave wild flowers in the fields where they belong.

-の 彼は難民の恩人とあがめられるにいたった。He came to be looked up to as a benefactor to the refugees. / 木村博士は生物学の権威だ。Dr. Kimura is an authority on biology. / 彼には先妻の子供が2人いる。He has two

ABと言ってすます方が自然である場合が多い．例えば「歴史の教師」は a teacher of history とも a history teacher とも言える．

ノア Noah ¶ノアの箱舟 Noah's ark／ノアの洪水 the Flood; Noah's flood; the Deluge.

ノイローゼ [＜《ドイツ語》Neurose] (a) neurosis 《pl. -roses》; (a) nervous breakdown ¶ノイローゼに悩む suffer from neurosis／ノイローゼ患者 a neurotic.

のう[1] 能〈能力, 機能〉⇒のうりょく, さいのう, きのう;〈能楽〉Noh; the Noh play [drama]; a Noh play (個々の) ¶能がない, 能なしだ be good for nothing;《俗》be a dead loss／能狂言 a Noh farce／能舞台〔役者〕a Noh stage [player]／能面 a Noh mask. 文例⇩

のう[2] 脳 the brain;〈脳みそ〉the brains;〈知力〉brains／脳の cerebral／脳溢血[出血] cerebral hemorrhage／脳炎 encephalitis／脳幹 the brainstem／脳外科脳 [cerebral] surgery／脳細胞 a brain cell／脳死 brain death／脳充血 congestion of the brain; cerebral hyperemia／脳神経 a cranial [cerebral] nerve／脳震盪(とう) concussion (of the brain)／脳水腫 hydrocephalus; water on the brain／脳脊髄液 cerebrospinal fluid／脳脊髄膜炎 cerebrospinal meningitis／脳軟化症 softening of the brain／脳波 brain waves／脳波計〔図〕an electroencephalograph [electroencephalogram]／脳梅毒 syphilis of the brain／脳貧血 anemia of the brain; cerebral anemia／脳膜 ⇒うまく.

のう[3] 農 ⇒のうぎょう.

のう[4] 膿 ⇒うみ. ¶膿盆 a kidney basin [dish].

のうえん[1] 農園 a farm; a plantation (大規模な) ¶農園を経営する run [keep] a farm／農園で働く work on a farm.

のうえん[2] 濃艶 ¶濃艶な glamorous; voluptuous.

のうか 農家〈家〉a farmhouse;〈家庭〉a farm [farming] household; a farm family;〈人〉a farmer.

のうかい 納会 the last meeting of the year;〈取引所の〉the last [closing] session of the month.

のうがき 能書き〈薬の効能書き〉a statement of the virtues of a medicine;〈自己宣伝〉self-advertisement ¶能書きを並べる sing the praises 〔of〕; dwell on [enumerate] the virtues [merits] (of).

のうがく[1] 能楽 ⇒のう[1] ¶能楽堂 a Noh theater.

のうがく[2] 農学 (the science of) agriculture ¶農学部 the department of agriculture／農学士[博士]〈人〉a bachelor [doctor] of agriculture;〈学位〉Bachelor [Doctor] of Agriculture (略：B.[D.]Agr.).

のうかすいたい 脳下垂体【解】the pituitary gland [body].

のうがっこう 農学校 an agricultural school.

のうかん 納棺 ¶納棺する place [put]《sb's body》in a coffin.

のうかんき 農閑期 the off-season [quiet season] for farmers; the agricultural off-season. 文例⇩

のうき 納期 the date [time] of payment [delivery].

のうきぐ 農機具 agricultural machines and implements; farm(ing) appliances.

のうぎょう 農業 agriculture; farming ¶農業の agricultural; farming／農業機械 a farm [an agricultural] machine／《総称》agricultural [farm] machinery／農業技術 agricultural technology; farming techniques／農業協同組合 an agricultural cooperative (association)／農業国 an agricultural country [nation]／農業生産 agricultural [farm] production [output]／農業大学 an agricultural college. 文例⇩

のうきん 納金〈支払い〉payment of money;〈支払うべき金〉money due;〈支払い済みの金〉money paid.

のうぐ 農具 a farm [an agricultural] implement; a farm(ing) tool.

のうげい 農芸〈農業と園芸〉agriculture and horticulture; farming and gardening;〈農業技術〉agricultural technology ¶農芸化学 agricultural chemistry.

のうこう[1] 農耕 agriculture; farming ¶農耕の agricultural; farming／農耕用トラクター an agricultural (motor) tractor／農耕時代【史】the Agricultural Age／農耕民族 an agricultural tribe [people].

のうこう[2] 濃厚 ¶濃厚な thick; dense; heavy; rich (味・香りが); strong (味・色が); deep (色が)／濃厚に thickly; heavily／濃厚になる thicken;〈凝縮する〉get [《文》become] denser; condense;〈深まる〉deepen. 文例⇩

のうこつどう 納骨堂 a building to house the ashes of the dead.

のうこん 濃紺 dark blue; navy blue.

のうさぎ 野兎 a hare.

のうさぎょう 農作業 farmwork.

のうさく 農作 ⇒のうこう[1] ¶農作物 farm produce [products]; the crops. 文例⇩

のうさつ 悩殺 ¶悩殺する charm; bewitch／人を悩殺するような魅力《口》irresistible charm／悩殺するような目つきで見る throw [cast] seductive glances [a seductive glance]《at》;《口語》give sb the (glad) eye.

---

children by his former wife.／トムは先生のお気に入りです．Tom is his teacher's pet.／Tom is a favorite with his teacher.

のう[1] 飲み食いばかりが能じゃない．There is more to life than eating and drinking.／あいつは飲むよりほかに能のない男だ．All he can do is drink.／金をもうけるばかりが商人の能ではない．Merchants should not be concerned only with moneymaking.／学者は本を読むばかりが能ではない．よく考えることもまた大切である．For scholars reading is not everything; it is also important for them to think.／あたまはつめを隠す．A talented person doesn't need to show off.／Still waters run deep.《諺》

のうかんき 農閑期に入ると彼らの大半は東京に出かせぎに行く．When they are free from farm work, most of them go off to temporary jobs in Tokyo.

のうぎょう 近年日本の農業人口は減少している．The farming [agricultural] population of Japan has been declining in recent years.

のうこう[2] そのために彼の嫌疑が

のうさんぶつ 農産物 ⇨ のうさく (農作物).
のうじ¹ 能事 ¶能事終われりとする consider one's work [duty] done.
のうじ² 農事 agriculture; farming ¶農事試験場 an agricultural experiment [《英》test(ing)] station.
のうしゅく 濃縮 ¶濃縮する concentrate; condense; enrich / 濃縮ウラン enriched [concentrated] uranium / 濃縮オレンジジュース orange juice concentrate; concentrated orange juice.
のうしょう 脳漿 ⇨ のう² (脳脊髄液).
のうじょう 農場 ⇨ のうえん¹ ¶共同[実験]農場 a collective [an experimental] farm.
のうずい 脳髄 the brain ⇨ のう².
のうせい¹ 脳性 ¶脳性麻痺 cerebral palsy.
のうせい² 農政 agricultural administration.
のうぜい 納税 payment of taxes ¶納税する pay one's taxes / 納税の義務 a legal obligation to pay (one's) taxes / 納税額 the amount of one's taxes [of taxes that one has to pay] / 納税期日 the date on which taxes are due (for payment); the due date / 納税者 a taxpayer / 納税通知書 a tax notice.
のうぜんかずら 〖植〗a trumpet creeper.
のうそん 農村 a farm(ing) [an agricultural] village;〈小農〉a rural [an agricultural] district ¶農村の疲弊 impoverishment of rural communities / 農村問題 an agrarian problem.
のうたん 濃淡 light and shade ¶濃淡をつける shade《a drawing》/ 濃淡法 (a sketch in) chiaroscuro. 文例⇩
のうち 農地 agricultural [farming] land; farmland ¶農地改革 an agrarian [agricultural land] reform / 農地開発 development of farmland / 農地法 the Agricultural Land Act.
のうてん 脳天 the crown of the head.
のうど¹ 農奴〈人〉a serf;〈身分〉serfdom ¶農奴解放 emancipation of serfs.
のうど² 濃度 density; thickness;〖化〗concentration ¶海水中の塩分の濃度 the concentration of salt in sea water.
のうどう 能動 ¶能動的な active / 能動態《文法》the active voice.
のうにゅう 納入 ¶納入する pay (one's taxes); deliver (goods); supply (an office with typewriters) / 納入品 supplies; goods for supply.
のうのうと 納納と〈気楽に〉free from care; at (one's) ease;〈安楽に〉comfortably ¶のうのうと暮らしている be comfortably off;《文》live in easy circumstances.
のうはんき 農繁期 the (busy) farming season.
のうひん 納品〈事〉delivery of goods;〈品物〉

delivered goods ¶納品する deliver goods ((to)).
のうふ¹ 納付 ¶納付する deliver ((goods)); pay ((taxes)).
のうふ² 農夫〈自作農〉a farmer;〈小農〉a peasant;〈作男〉a farm hand [laborer].
のうべん 能弁《文》eloquence; glibness (舌がよく回ること) ¶能弁な eloquent; glib-tongued (軽蔑的) / 能弁である have a fluent tongue; have a glib [well-oiled] tongue (軽蔑的) / 能弁家 an eloquent speaker; a good orator.
のうほう 膿疱〖医〗a pustule.
のうほん 納本 ¶納本する deliver books [copies of a book]((to)).
のうまく 脳膜〖医〗the meninges ★ meninges は meninx の複数形 ¶脳膜炎 meningitis.
のうみそ 脳味噌〈灰白質〉the brains; gray matter;〈知力〉brains ⇨ のう² ¶脳みそを絞って考える rack [beat, cudgel] one's brains.
のうみん 農民 a farmer;〈小農〉a peasant; peasantry (総称) ¶農民組合 a farmers' association / 農民生活[文学, 芸術] peasant life [literature, art].
のうむ 濃霧 (a) dense [thick] fog. 文例⇩
のうやく 農薬 an agricultural chemical.
のうり 脳裏 ¶脳裏に描く picture sth in one's mind; imagine / 脳裏に浮かぶ cross [come across] one's mind; occur to one / 脳裏を去らない haunt one's memory; be always [《文》ever] present in one's mind.
のうりつ 能率 efficiency ¶能率の上がる, 能率的な efficient / 能率の上がらぬ, 非能率的な inefficient / 能率を上下[げ]する raise [lower] efficiency;《文》increase [decrease] efficiency / 能率給 efficiency wages. 文例⇩
のうりょう 納涼 ¶納涼のために to enjoy the cool of the evening / 納涼客 people out to enjoy the cool breezes of the evening.
のうりょく 能力 ability,《文》capacity; power(s);《文》competence;《文》a faculty ¶…する能力がある be able [competent] to do; be capable of doing / 能力をのばす develop one's faculties / 全能力をあげて to the limit [best] of one's ability [abilities] / 生産能力 productive capacity; productivity.
のうりょくしょく 濃緑色 dark green.
のうりん 農林 ¶農林水産省[大臣] the Ministry [Minister] of Agriculture, Forestry and Fisheries.
ノー no ¶ノーと言う[答える] say 'no' ((to));《文》answer [reply] in the negative.
ノーカウント no count ¶ノーカウントになる be called no count.
ノーコメント no comment. 文例⇩

一層濃厚になった. It served to increase their [people's] suspicion about [of] him.
のうさく この日照りが長く続くと農作物に大きな被害があることだろう. If this drought lasts long, the crops will suffer severe damage.
のうたん 紙に描いた円は, 円でしかないが, これに濃淡を施すと, 同じ円が球のように見えてくる. A circle drawn on a piece of paper is just a circle, but if shading is applied the circle begins to look like a sphere.
のうむ 濃霧がたちこめて来た. A thick fog came down. / 濃霧のため交通は陸上海上ともに麻痺した. The traffic on land and sea was paralyzed by heavy fog.
のうりつ 人数が多いのに仕事の能率が上がらなかった. In spite of the large number of workers, efficiency did not rise. / 行政事務の能率をはかるにはこれが必要である. This is necessary for the efficient prosecution of administrative affairs.
ノーコメント その問題については ノーコメントだ. I don't want to

ノースカロライナ North Carolina (略: N.C.) ¶ノースカロライナ州の人 a North Carolinian.

ノースダコタ North Dakota (略: N.D., N.Dak.) ¶ノースダコタ州の人 a North Dakotan.

ノート 〈ノートブック〉 a notebook ¶ノートを取る note [write, put, jot] down; take [make] notes of [on] ((a lecture)) (★ notes を a note とすると「メモする」というぐらいの意味になる).

ノーベリウム 【化】nobelium.

ノーベルしょう ノーベル賞 a Nobel prize ((for medicine)) ¶ノーベル賞受賞者 a Nobel prize winner; a Nobel laureate. 文例⇩

のがす 逃がす ⇨にがす.

のがれる 逃れる 〈逃げる〉 escape; get away [off]; make *one*'s escape; 〈逃げ込む〉 take [《文》seek] sanctuary [refuge] ((in)); 〈避ける〉 avoid; dodge 〈にげる〉¶危険を逃れる escape [get out of] danger / 危うく逃れる have a narrow [hairbreadth] escape; escape narrowly / 責任を逃れる shirk *one*'s responsibilities / 追手から逃れる shake off [escape, 《文》elude] *one*'s pursuers / 逃れられない unavoidable; inevitable. 文例⇩

のき 軒 the eaves ¶軒を並べる[つらねる] stand side by side; stand in a row / 軒下に[で] under the eaves / 軒並みに at every door / 軒並みに訪問する call from door to door / すぐ軒先に just in front of the house / 軒伝いに along the eaves. 文例⇩

のぎ 芒 〈麦などの〉 a beard; an awn.

のぎく 野菊 a wild chrysanthemum.

ノギス 【機】(a pair of) vernier calipers; a vernier micrometer.

のく 退く 〈わきによける〉 step aside; get out of the way; make way ((for)); 〈立ち去る〉 leave; quit.

ノクターン 【音楽】a nocturne.

のけぞる のけ反る bend backward; bend *one*self back.

のけもの 除け者 ¶のけ者にする leave *sb* out (in the cold); shun; 〈社会的に〉 ostracize.

のける 退[除]ける 〈どかす〉 remove; take [put] away; 〈邪魔にならないように〉 put *sth* out of the way; 〈除く〉 get rid of; 〈省く〉《文》 omit; leave *sth* out. 文例⇩

のこぎり 鋸 a saw ¶のこぎりの目立てをする

set (the teeth of) a saw / のこぎりで引く saw

のこぎりざめ 《魚》 a saw shark. 〈wood).

のこす 残す leave (behind); 〈節約して〉 save; 〈予備に〉 set aside; reserve; 〈遺産として〉 leave [《文》bequeath] ((money to *sb*)); 〈相撲で〉 hold on; stay in the ring ¶金を残す 〈貯蓄する〉 save money; 〈産を成す〉 make [amass] a fortune; 〈口語〉 make *one*'s pile; 〈死後に〉 leave [bequeath] a fortune ((to)) / 仕事を残しておく leave *one*'s work unfinished [half-done]; leave the job over (till the next week) / (学校などで) 残される be kept after school / 後に残された家族 the bereaved family. 文例⇩

のこのこ 〈厚かましく〉 shamelessly; brazen-facedly; 〈平気で〉 nonchalantly. 文例⇩

のこらず 残らず all; entirely; completely; without exception ¶一人[一滴]残らず to the last man [drop]. 文例⇩

のこり 残り what is left; 《文》the remainder; the rest; 《文》the remnant; 〈剰余〉 the surplus; 〈残金〉 the balance ¶借金の残り what is left [the remainder] of *one*'s debt ((to)) / 残りの remaining ((days)); surplus ((produce)) / 残り少なくなる 〈物が〉 run short [low]; 〈期間が〉 draw to an end [《文》a close]. 文例⇩

のこりおしい 残り惜しい 〈事が主語〉 be regrettable; 《文》 be much [greatly] regretted; 〈人が主語〉 feel regret; be reluctant.

のこりもの 残り物 leftovers; leavings; what was left of ((yesterday's evening meal)); unsold stock (売れ残り) ¶残り物のお菓子 leftover cakes / 残り物で料理を作る prepare a dish from leftovers.

のこる 残る remain; 〈留まる〉 stay; stop; 〈残される〉 be left over [behind]; 〈生き残る〉 survive; 〈残存する〉 linger ¶残るくまなく thoroughly; throughout; all over / 残るくまなく捜す comb ((a room)) for *sth*. 文例⇩

のさばる 〈出しゃばる〉 push *one*self forward; 〈いばる〉 put on airs; act important; 《文》 assume an air of importance; 〈いばり散らす〉 throw *one*'s weight about ((around)).

のざらし 野晒し ¶野ざらしの weather-beaten / 野ざらしにする expose *sth* to the weather [rain and wind].

---

make any comment [I have no comment to make] on the matter.

ノーベルしょう 湯川博士は 1949 年度のノーベル物理学賞を受賞した. Dr. Yukawa won [was awarded] the Nobel prize for physics in 1949.

のがれる 彼はうまく逃れた. He got away successfully. | He made good his escape. / 彼は逃れられぬ運命とあきらめた. He resigned himself to his fate.

のき すずめが軒でさえずっていた. Sparrows were twittering in the eaves.

のける その椅子を少しわきへのけてくれませんか. Will you please

move that chair a little to one [the] side?

のこす 彼は 1 億円残して死んだ. He died worth a hundred million yen. / 1 円も残さず使ってしまった. I spent all the money I had. | I spent my last cent.

のこのこ このこのこやって来たよ. なんて厚かましいんだろう. Look! There he comes. What cheek he has!

のこらず 君の知っていることを残らず聞かしてくれ. Tell me all you know about it.

のこり 費用を払ったら、残りは僅か 50 ドルしかなかった. After expenses, she only had 50 dollars left over.

のこりもの 昼の残り物で晩飯を作った. She made supper from the leftovers from lunch. / 残り物には福がある. There is luck in the last helping.

のこる 遠い山々に雪が残っていた. The snow still lies on the distant mountains. / 10 から 4 引くと 6 残る. Four from ten leaves six. / 23 を 7 で割ると、3 が立って、2 が残る. Seven into twenty-three goes three times and two over. / この風習は地方へ行くとまだ残っている. The custom still survives [lingers on] in the countryside. / その芳香は しばらくまで残っていた. The fragrance hung around for a while.

のし

のし ¶のしをつけて上げる make a (free) gift [present] of *sth*. 文例↓

のしあがる 伸し上がる rise in the world; be promoted [《文》advanced] to 《a higher position》 ¶2位にのし上がる move into second place.

のしかかる 伸し掛かる lean on [forward]; bend over ¶〈責任などが〉重くのし掛かる lie [weigh, bear] heavily [hard] on *one*. 文例↓

のしもち 伸し餅 flat rice cake.

のじゅく 野宿 ¶野宿する sleep in the open; sleep rough; camp out; bivouac.

のす 伸す〈伸ばす〉⇒のばす;〈なぐり倒す〉knock *sb* out [down, groggy]; floor.

ノスタルジア nostalgia ⇒ きょうしゅう¹.

のせる 乗[載]せる〈運ぶ〉carry;〈乗車させる〉take in;〈乗船させる〉take *sb* on board;〈途中で人を〉pick up;〈荷物を積む〉load;〈置く〉put [《文》place, lay, set] *sth* on 《a shelf》;〈掲載する〉carry; print;〈記事を〉report; mention;〈参加させる〉let *sb* take part [have a share] in 《a scheme》;〈だます〉take *sb* in; impose [put] on *sb* ¶乗せてやる〈乗物に〉give *sb* a lift [ride] 《in *one*'s car》; give *sb* 《a》passage 《on *one*'s boat》;〈手を貸して〉help *sb* into 《a car》/〈人の車に〉乗せてもらう get a ride [lift] in 《*sb*'s car》; hitch [thumb] a ride 《on a truck》/ 記録に載せる place [put] *sth* on record; record / 新聞に広告を載せる put [《文》insert] an advertisement in a newspaper. 文例↓

のぞき 覗き ¶のぞき穴 a peephole / のぞき窓〈ドアなどについている〉an observation window;〈機械の内部などを見るための〉an observation hatch.

のぞく¹ 除く〈取りのける〉take off; put [take] away; remove;〈除外する〉《文》exclude;《文》except;〈省く〉leave out;《文》omit;〈除する〉abolish; do away with;〈免れる〉get rid of ¶邪魔にならぬように障害物を除く clear the way of obstacles; move obstacles out of the way / 名前を名簿から除く cross [strike] *sb*'s name off the list / …を除いて except…; with the exception of…; but…; except for…/ 他に特別の規定のある場合を除いては unless otherwise provided. 文例↓
用法〈(…を)除いて〉に当たる最も普通の英語は except. but no; all; anything; everywhere などの後にしか用いられない. except for は not... except ... の意で, この句には肯定文が先行するのが普通. 例:「彼ら2人を除いて教室にはだれもいなかった」There was no one in the classroom except [but] them. | The classroom was empty except for them.

のぞく² 覗く look 《in at, out of》; peep [peek 《into a room, through a hole》]; get [have, take] a look [peep, peek] 《at》;〈立ち寄る〉drop [look] in 《on *sb*, at *sb*'s house》/ 窓からのぞく〈外を〉look out of the window,〈内を〉look in at the window / かぎ穴からのぞく look [peep] through a keyhole / 本をのぞく glance over [dip into] a book / 店をのぞいてみる look in at a store / 人の顔をのぞき込む look into *sb*'s face / ポケットから赤いハンカチをのぞかせて with a red handkerchief peeping from [out of] *one*'s pocket. 文例↓

のそだち 野育ち ¶野育ちの wild;〈行儀の悪い〉ill-mannered[-bred].

のそのそ slowly; sluggishly; in a sluggish way 《文》manner).

のぞましい 望ましい be desirable;《文》it is to be desired 《that…》;〈当を得ている〉be advisable ¶望ましからぬ undesirable; unwelcome. 文例↓

のぞみ 望み〈願望〉《文》a desire; a wish;〈期待〉(a) hope; expectation(s);〈抱負〉ambition(s);《文》aspiration(s);〈見込み〉a chance; a prospect; a likelihood ¶一縷(いちる)の望み a ray [gleam] of hope / 望みのある hopeful; promising / 望みのない hopeless; unpromising / 望みの大きい少年 an ambitious boy / 望みを遂げる,望みがかなう *one*'s wish is granted;《文》realize *one*'s desire [wish] / 望みをかなえてやる fulfill *sb*'s wish; gratify [satisfy] *sb*'s desire / 望みを掛ける set *one*'s hope(s) on *sth*; expect a great deal [《文》expect much] of *sb* / 望みを抱く have an ambition 《to do》;《文》have [cherish] a desire 《to do, for *sth*》/ 望みを捨てる give up [abandon] *one*'s hopes; despair of *sth* / 望みにより at *sb*'s request. 文例↓

のぞむ¹ 望む〈願望する〉《文》desire; wish;〈…を欲しがる〉want; crave [wish] for;《文》as-

---

のし のしをつけてやると言っても要らないよ. I wouldn't take it (even) as a gift. | I wouldn't give it houseroom.

のしかかる それが彼女の心に何よりも重くのし掛かっていた. It was that which weighed most heavily on her heart.

のせる まんまとのせられた. I was completely taken in.

のぞく¹ 2人を除き他の閣僚は全員この政策に賛成した. All the cabinet members but two [with two exceptions] have approved this policy. | 日曜を除いて彼はめったに家にいることがない. He is rarely at home except on Sundays. / 君の英作文はこの間違いを除いてはなかなかよく書けている. Your English composition is very well written except for this error.

のぞく² 昨日 二科展をちょっとのぞいて見ました. I had a look at the Nikakai Art Exhibition yesterday. / 月が木の間からのぞかせた. The moon peeped through the trees.

のぞましい 君がひとりで行くことが望ましい. It is desirable that you should go by yourself.

のぞみ これで望みの綱も切れた. My hopes have all been dashed to the ground [crushed to pieces]. / 結果は望みどおりに行った. The results turned out as we wished. | The results came [measured] up to our expectations. / あいにくお望みの品はございません. I'm afraid we don't have what you want. / 君は望みがかなうだろう. You will have your wish. | 《文》Your desire will be realized [satisfied]. / 千円でお望みの品を差し上げます. You may have your choice for a thousand yen. / 彼は成功の望みがあるだろうか. Is there any hope [chance] of success for him? / 彼が受諾する望みは薄い. There is little likelihood of his accepting our offer. | The prospects for his consenting to it are dim. / 私はもう何の望みもない男だ. I am a man

のぞむ¹ pire to [after]；〈関心を持つ〉care for《★ 主に否定・疑問の形で使われる》；expect；hope 《that..., for sth》；look forward to；〈好む〉like；choose；prefer；〈見渡す(場所が主語)〉command a view of 《a hill》；overlook 《the sea》 ¶…を望んで〈希望して〉hoping 《that...》；in the hope 《of doing, that...》；〈期待して〉in anticipation of... / お望みなら if you wish / 遠く筑波山を望む〈場所が主語〉command a distant view of Mt. Tsukuba. 文例⇩

のぞむ² 臨む 〈面する〉look onto [out on] 《the garden》；face 《onto, on》；front 《onto, on》；〈当面する〉meet；face；be confronted 《by》；〈臨席する〉attend 《a ceremony》；be present 《at a meeting》 ¶海に臨む家 a house facing [fronting] 《onto》the sea / 危険に臨んで in face [the presence] of danger / 死に臨んで on one's deathbed / 別れに臨んで at [on] parting. 文例⇩

のたうつ wriggle；writhe；squirm ¶苦しさのあまりのたうち回る writhe in agony / 高熱でのたうち回る thrash about in bed with a high fever.

のたくる 〈のたうつ〉⇨ のたうつ；〈下手[乱暴]に書く〉scrawl.

のだて 野点 an open-air tea ceremony.

のたれじに 野垂れ死に ¶野垂れ死にする die by the roadside [on the road, in the gutter, in a ditch].

のち 後 ¶後の later；〈未来の〉future / 後の世〈来世〉the next world；《文》the hereafter；〈後の時代〉coming [future] ages / 後に〈…のあとで〉after；following；〈後刻, 後日〉afterward(s)；later (on)；《文》subsequently；〈将来〉in future / 4日後に four days after [later]；after four days / 〈今から〉in four days；four days from now；《文》four days hence / その後 since then；《文》thereafter / 後々のため for the sake of the future. 文例⇩

のちほど 後程 later (on)；afterward.

のっかる 乗っかる ⇨ のる.

ノッキング 〈内燃機関の〉knocking.

ノック a knock；knocking ¶ドアをノックする knock on [at] the door. 文例⇩

ノックアウト a knockout 《略：KO, K.O.》 ¶ノックアウトする knock out / ノックアウトで勝つ win by knockout / ノックアウト勝ちでタイトルを防衛する defend [retain] the title by a knockout win 《over the contender》.

ノックダウン a knockdown ¶ノックダウンする knock sb down；floor.

ノックバッティング 〈野球〉batting for fielding practice；fungo (hitting). 「-es」

ノックバット 〈野球〉a fungo bat；a fungo 《pl.

のっしのっし ¶のっしのっしと歩く walk heavily (and clumsily) [with heavy strides]；lumber 《along》 (特に象などが).

のっそり slowly (and clumsily)；stolidly.

ノット a knot ¶20ノットを出す make [do, develop, log] 20 knots.

のっとり 乗っ取り a take-over 《of a firm》；(a) hijacking 《of an airplane》 ¶〈飛行機の〉乗っ取り犯人 a hijacker.

のっとる¹ 則る 〈従う〉follow 《a precedent》；act on [go by] 《a principle》；《文》conform to 《a rule》；〈倣(なら)う〉model sth after [on] 《a pattern》 ¶この規定にのっとって in conformity with this regulation.

のっとる² 乗っ取る 〈占有する〉take possession of；〈横領する〉《文》usurp；〈陣地などを〉capture [carry] 《a fort》；〈会社などを〉take over 《a firm》；〈飛行機などを〉hijack 《an airplane》.

のっぴきならない 退っ引きならない 〈人が主語〉be committed to 《a course》；be in for sth；〈事柄が主語〉be unavoidable；be inevitable ¶のっぴきならない事情のため 《文》owing to unavoidable circumstances. 文例⇩

のっぺらぼう 〈化け物〉a goblin with a blank face without features ¶のっぺらぼうな演説 a monotonous address.

のっぺり ¶のっぺりした顔 a smooth expressionless [blank] face.

のっぽ a tall, lanky [gangling] person.

-ので as；because 《of》；since；owing to；on account of；《文》by reason of. 文例⇩

のてん 野天 ⇨ ろてん¹ / 野天の open-air；out-

without anything left to hope for.

のぞむ¹ 名利は少しも望むところではない. I don't care a bit [I have no ambition] for fame or wealth. / 彼に多くは望めない. You cannot expect much of him. / 彼女は自分から望んで彼と結婚したのだ. She married him of her own choice. / 関西方面, 望めるなら神戸に職が欲しい. I want to get a position in the Kansai region, preferably in Kobe.

のぞむ² 彼は自若として死に臨んだ. He met his death calmly.

のち 晴, 後曇り. Fine, cloudy later. / この都市が後に世界の歴史にひじょうに大きな役割りを演じることになる. This city was to play a great part in world history.

のちほど また後程. See you later.

ノック ドアをノックしても返事がなかった. There was no answer to my knock. | No one answered the door.

のっぴきならない 今となってはもうのっぴきならない. There is no getting away from it now. | We are in for it now.

-ので 息子はまだ小さいので手がかかる. As my son is still very young, he needs looking after. / 彼は体が弱いので激しい筋肉労働はできない. He cannot do hard physical labor because of his delicate health [because he is in poor health]. / 彼は背が高いので「ノッポのトム」と呼ばれている. He is known as "Long Tom" because of his great height. / 彼が病気になったので約束はほごになった. The arrangement was canceled on account [by reason] of his illness. / 庭が暗いので手探りで歩かなければならなかった. The yard was so dark that I had to grope my way.

のど やたらにのどが渇く. I am parched. / 彼女は心配で食事がのどを通らない. She is so worried that she has lost her [has no] appetite. / 薬でものどを通らない. Even medicine wouldn't go down his throat. | He couldn't even get his medicine down. / 例の言葉がのどまで出かかっていたのだ. The word was on the [very] tip of my tongue. / のどもと過ぎれば熱さを忘れる. The danger [river] past and God forgotten. 〔諺〕

のどか のどかな一日であった.

door / 野天で in the open (air); outdoors / 野天興行 an open-air show / 野天風呂 an open-air bath.

のど the throat; 〈声〉a voice ¶のどが痛い have a sore throat / のどが渇く be thirsty; feel [be] dry / のどがいい have a sweet voice / のどにつかえる[ひっかかる] get [have (got)] sth stuck [caught] in one's throat / 物がのどに catch [stick] in one's throat / のどを痛める 〈風邪などで〉have a sore throat; 〈声をからす〉be [make oneself] hoarse / のどを潤す relieve [《文》allay] one's thirst / のどを締める grip [squeeze] sb's throat; strangle [throttle] sb / 《猫などが》のどをごろごろ鳴らす purr / のど自慢《人》a person who is proud of his (singing) voice / 素人ののど自慢大会 an amateur singing contest;《番組名》Amateur Singers on the Air / のどちんこ the uvula (*pl.* -las, -lae) / のどぼとけ the Adam's apple / のど笛 the windpipe.

のどか ¶のどかな《文》tranquil; calm; quiet; peaceful;《文》serene / のどかな春の日 a mild day in spring; a balmy spring day / のどかな海 a calm [placid] sea / のどかな空 a serene sky / のどかな心 a tranquil mind. 文例⇩

のどわ 喉輪 ¶喉輪で攻める attack [go for] (one's opponent's) throat.

のなか 野中 ¶野中の[に] in the field / 野中の一本杉 a lone [solitary] cedar in the middle of the field.

-のに[1]〈…にもかかわらず〉although; (even) though; in spite of (doing, the fact that…); when; 〈一方では〉while; 〈願望〉if only…; I wish…; 〈強勢・催促など〉I tell you; why don't [didn't] you do; should [ought to] have (done). 文例⇩

-のに[2]〈…のために〉to do; in order to do; for (sb, doing). 文例⇩

のねずみ 野鼠 a field [meadow] mouse.

ののしり 罵り abuse ¶ののしりの言葉 abusive language; a term of abuse.

ののしる 罵る abuse;《文》speak ill [evil] of sb; call sb names;《文》revile. 文例⇩

のばす 伸[延]ばす〈長くする〉make sth longer; lengthen; extend; 〈まっすぐに〉stretch; unbend; 〈しわなどを〉smooth out; 〈延期する〉put sth off; postpone; defer; 〈遅らせる〉delay; 〈延長する〉extend; prolong; 〈薄める・薄く〉thin; make sth thinner; dilute; 〈なぐり倒す〉knock sb out [down]; floor ¶ロープを2メートル伸ばす make a rope two meters longer; lengthen a rope by two meters / 体を伸ばす stretch [unbend] oneself / 手を伸ばす reach (for); hold out [《文》extend] one's arm [hand] (to) / 一日一日と延ばす put off from day to day / 期限を延ばす extend the term ((from… to…)) / 滞在を2週間延ばす extend [extend] one's stay for two weeks / 天賦の才能を伸ばす develop one's natural abilities / 髪を長く伸ばしている wear one's hair long. 文例⇩

のばなし 野放し ¶野放しにする〈鎖などを解く〉turn [let] (a dog) loose; 〈放任する〉let sb do as he pleases [chooses]; leave sb to take care of himself; leave sth to take its own course.

のはら 野原 〈野〉a field / 〈平野〉a plain ⇨ の.

のばら 野ばら《植》a wild rose; a brier.

のび[1] 伸[延]び ¶伸びをする stretch (oneself) / 伸びがよい〈生長が〉grow well; 〈塗料などが〉spread well / 伸びが早い grow fast [rapidly] / 生産の伸び率 a production growth rate.

のび[2] 野火 a grass [field, brush,《米》prairie] fire.

のびあがる 伸び上がる〈つま先で立つ〉stand on tiptoe.

のびちぢみ 伸び縮み ¶伸び縮みする expand and contract; 〈弾性がある〉be elastic; be stretchy.

のびなやむ 伸び悩む 文例⇩

のびのび[1] 伸び伸び ¶のびのびする feel relaxed; feel at (one's) ease / のびのびした文章を書く《文》write with a ready [vivacious] pen; write in a free and easy style / のびのびと横になる lie stretched ((on the lawn)).

のびのび[2] 延び延び ¶のびのびになる be put off from day to day; be delayed for a long time.

The day passed peacefully.

-のに[1] 雨が降っているのに出かけて行った。 He went out in spite of the rain. / He went out, (even) though it was raining. / 試験が近いのに彼は939んでばかりいる。 He does no work, even though the examination is almost upon him. / He wastes his time despite [in spite of] the approach of the examination. / (せっかく)誘ったのになぜ来ないの。 Why didn't you come, when I (specifically) told you to? / 歩けばいいのにタクシーに乗る。 He goes by taxi when he might walk. / 私の方は使いたいにも金がないというのに、君の方は金があっても使いたいものがないと言う。 While I have no money to spend, you have nothing to spend your money on. / 弟の方は勉強家だというのに彼の方は（その反対に）怠け者だ。 He is a very idle boy, whereas [while] his brother is very hardworking. / He is as idle as his brother is hardworking. / この部屋はもう少し広ければいいのに。 If only [I wish] this room were a little larger. / もっと勉強すればよかったのに。 You ought to have [should have] worked harder. / Why didn't you study harder! / ちょっと知らせてくれればよかったのに。 You might have just let me know. / 早く行けというのに。 Why don't you go quickly! / I tell you, Go quick(ly).

-のに[2] 新宿へ出るのに地下鉄で行った。 I took the subway to get to Shinjuku. / 本を読むのに眼鏡がいる。 I need spectacles for reading. / それを切るのにナイフが必要なんです。 I want a knife to cut it with. / この本は君のに買って来たんだ。 I have bought this book for you.

ののしる 彼はジョンをさんざんにののしった。 He heaped all sorts of abuse on John. | He cursed John to high heaven.

のばす 今日できることを明日に延ばすな。 Never put off till tomorrow what you can do today.

のびなやむ 今回の選挙でも社会党は伸び悩んだ。 In the recent election, the Socialist Party failed again to increase its Diet membership as much as expected. / 株価は需要が不足で伸び悩んでいる。 Stock prices are held in check [are unable to rise] for lack of sufficient demand.

のびやかな 伸びやかな free and easy;《文》unconstrained;《feel》relaxed.

のびる 伸[延]びる〈長くなる〉get [《文》become] longer; lengthen;〈広がる〉spread;〈続く, 達する〉extend; stretch;〈日延べになる〉be put off; be postponed;〈期間が〉be extended; be prolonged;〈遅れる〉be delayed;〈生長する〉grow;〈進歩発展する〉make progress;《文》advance; expand;〈ぐったりする〉be exhausted; get [go] groggy;《口語》be all in;《口語》flake out;〈意識を失う〉lose consciousness;《口語》pass out ¶背が伸びる grow taller / (塗料などが)よく伸びる spread well / 長く伸ばしたつめ long nails / (根などが)土の中に伸びていく grow down into the soil. 文例↓

のべ 延べ ¶延べ坪数 the total floor space (in *tsubo*) / 延べ日数 the total number of working days. 文例↓

のべつ（まくなしに）〈べつ（幕無しに）〉《文》ceaselessly; incessantly; all the time ¶のべつ幕なしにしゃべる《文》talk without ceasing; talk nineteen to the dozen.

のべばらい 延べ払い deferred payment ¶延べ払い方式で on a deferred payment basis.

のべぼう 延べ棒 a (metal) bar ¶金の延べ棒 a gold bar [ingot].

のべる[1] 述べる〈言い表わす, 物語る〉tell;〈話す〉relate; give an account (of);〈陳述する〉state;〈触れる〉mention; refer to;《文》touch upon;〈説明する〉explain ¶意見を述べる give [offer] one's opinion(s) (on); air [set forth] one's views (on) / 目に見えるように述べる give a graphic account [vivid description] (of) / 詳しく述べる give a full [detailed] account (of) /《文》give the particulars (of); go [《文》enter] into the details (of) / はっきり述べる state [explain] clearly [explicitly]; spell out / 先に述べたとおり《文》as mentioned [stated, described] above. 文例↓

のべる[2] 伸[延]べる ⇒のばす ¶床を延べる make [《文》prepare] a bed.

のほうず 野放図 ¶野放図な wild;《文》unbridled.

のぼす 上す ¶食膳(しょく)に上す serve [《文》set]《a dish》on the table / 舞台に上す put《a play》on the stage; stage《a play》/ 議題に上す put [《文》place] sth on the agenda; bring up sth for discussion.

のぼせしょう のぼせ性 liable to have a rush of blood to the head; easily excitable.

のぼせあがる ⇒のぼせる.

のぼせる〈上気する〉have a rush of blood to the head;〈めまいがする〉feel [be] dizzy;〈興奮する〉get excited;〈夢中になる〉be crazy [mad]《about》; be infatuated《with》;〈得意になる〉get [《文》become] (self-)conceited; be puffed up with pride; have a swelled head ¶女にのぼせる be infatuated with [have a crush on, be soft on] a girl. 文例↓

のほほん ¶のほほんと《文》unconcernedly; nonchalantly / のほほんとしている care nothing《about》; remain unconcerned [nonchalant]《about a matter, at the news》.

のぼり[1] 上[登, 昇]り ¶上り道[坂] an uphill road; an upslope / 上り列車[線路] an up train [line]. 文例↓

のぼり[2] 幟〈旗〉a banner;〈吹き流し〉a streamer.

のぼる 上[登, 昇]る〈高い所に〉go up; climb;《文》ascend; rise (上昇する);〈達する〉reach; amount《to》; come [add] up (to);〈昇進する〉be promoted [《文》advanced] (to); rise (to) ¶山に登る climb [go up] a mountain;《文》ascend [make an ascent of] a mountain / がけを登る scale [clamber up] a cliff / 演壇に登る go on [mount] the platform / 屋根に登る get on the roof / うわさに上る be talked about / その日の議題に上る be placed on the day's agenda. 文例↓

のませる 飲ませる make sb drink; give sb a drink《of wine》;〈薬を〉give sb《a medicine》;《文》administer《a dose of medicine》to sb;〈牛馬に水を〉water《cattle》¶無理に飲ませる force [compel] sb to drink《wine》; force《water》down sb's throat.

のまれる 飲まれる be swallowed (up)《by》;〈威圧される〉be overawed《by》; cower《before sb》. 文例↓

のみ[1] 蚤〔昆〕a flea ¶のみの夫婦 a little man with a big wife / のみの市 a flea market / のみに食われる be bitten by a flea / のみに食われた跡 a fleabite / のみ取り粉 flea powder / のみ取りまなこで with eager [sharp] eyes; very eagerly.

のみ[2] 鑿 a chisel ¶のみで彫る chisel.

のびる 木の枝は日の照る方に伸びる. The boughs of trees reach out toward the sunlight [in the direction of the sun]. / 日本の貿易はまだまだ伸びる. Japan's foreign trade is capable of further growth [expansion]. / ウィスキーを飲んで伸びてしまった. He had so much whisky that he passed out.

のべ 作業は延べ人員5千人[延べ5千時間]を要した. The work required 5,000 man-days [man-hours].

のべる[1] この事については後でまた述べます. I will come back to this later.

のぼせる ストーブにあたるとのぼせやすい. Sitting close to a stove can cause a rush of the blood to the head. / この成功でのぼせてしまった. The success has turned [gone to] his head.

のぼり[1] 道はずっと上りになっている. The road runs [is] uphill all the way. / この家まで緩やかな上りになっていた. The road led up a slight gradient to the house. / この道は5度の上り勾配になっている. The road rises with a slope of five degrees. / 上り坂に差しかかった. We came to a rise in the road. / そこからとても急な登りであった. From there we had a very steep climb.

のぼる 昨日は水銀柱が30度に上った. The thermometer rose [went up] to 30° yesterday. / 天にも昇る心地であった. I felt as if I were treading on air. / その子なら栗の木に登っている. The boy is up in the chestnut tree.

のませる あの店ではいいワインを飲ませる. That restaurant serves good wine. | They serve good wine in that restaurant.

-のみ ⇨ -だけ, -ばかり. 文例

のみあかす 飲み明かす drink all night long; drink the night away.

のみかけ 飲みかけ ⇨ のみさし.

のみくい 飲み食い ⇨ いんしょく.

のみぐすり 飲み薬 a medicine (for internal use).

のみくだす 飲み下す ⇨ のみこむ.

のみぐち 飲み口 《たるの》a tap;《主に米》a faucet.

のみこみ 飲み込み《理解》understanding;《文》apprehension ¶飲み込みがいい[悪い] be quick-[dull-]witted; be quick [slow] on the uptake [to understand],《文》of understanding] / 飲み込み顔で knowingly; with a knowing air.

のみこむ 飲み込む《飲み下す》swallow; down;《理解する》understand; grasp; take in; catch on to《the job》¶一息に飲み込む swallow《the pills》at one gulp / 無理に飲み込む force sth down one's throat / ごくごくのどを鳴らして飲み込む gulp《water》down / こつを飲み込む get the hang [knack]《of》/ 万事飲み込んでいる know what one is about [doing].

のみさし 飲みさし《酒の》liquor left in the glass; heeltap《酒の底の》;《タバコの》a half-smoked cigar [cigarette]; a cigarette end [butt, stub] ¶酒を飲みさしにする leave one's drink unfinished.

のみしろ 飲み代 drink(ing) money.

のみすぎ 飲み過ぎ drinking too much;《文》excessive drinking;《文》intemperance.

のみすぎる 飲み過ぎる drink too much [《文》to excess];《タバコを》smoke too much;《薬を》take an overdose (of a medicine).

のみすけ 飲み助 a hard [heavy] drinker; a tippler;《俗》a boozer.

のみち 野道 a track [path] across a field; a field path.

のみつぶす 飲み潰す《相手を》《口語》drink sb under the table;《身代を》drink [booze] away one's fortune [property].

のみつぶれる 飲み潰れる be [get] dead drunk.

のみともだち 飲み友達 a drinking companion.

のみならず not only [merely] ...but (also); besides; moreover. 文例

のみほす 飲み干す finish off《one's drink》; drink up《one's beer》; drain《a cup》¶一滴も残さず飲み干す drink [《文》drain]《a bottle of brandy》to the dregs [to the last drop]. 文例

のみみず 飲み水 drinking water; water (fit) to drink.

のみもの 飲み物 something to drink; a drink;《文》a beverage;《酒類》(a) liquor. 文例

のみや 飲み屋 a bar; a drinking shop;《米》a saloon;《英》a pub.

のむ 飲む《飲用する》drink; take; have;《のみ下す》swallow; take down;《ごくりごくり》gulp down;《がぶがぶ》guzzle; swill;《文》quaff;《軽視する》make light [think nothing] of;《受諾する》accept (an offer);《口調》swallow (a proposal);《英口語》wear (an argument) ¶薬を飲む take (a) medicine / 泉の水を飲む drink from a spring / 杯で飲む drink out of a cup /《波が》船を飲む swallow up [engulf] a boat / 一口[一息]に飲む swallow《one's medicine》at one gulp; drink《a glass of beer》in one go / 水を1口飲む have [take] a drink [gulp] of water《from, out of》/ 涙を飲む hold [keep] back one's tears / 恨みを飲む《文》suppress one's bitter feelings (against); swallow an insult / 匕首(xin)を飲む have a dagger hidden [《文》concealed] under one's clothes / お茶を飲みながらおしゃべりをする chat over a cup of tea / 飲める《飲料に適する》be good to drink; 酒を飲める》drink / 飲めや歌えの大騒ぎ a noisy [rowdy] drinking party; a drunken party [《文》revel]. 文例

のめりこむ のめり込む go into (one's work) heart and soul; get [be] into (one's work); give oneself up to (a job).

のめる 《前に》fall [tumble] forward; pitch over.

のやま 野山 hills and fields (dales).

のら 野良 a field ¶野良犬 a stray [an ownerless] dog / 野良着 farm [working] clothes; peasant clothing / 野良仕事 farm work / 野良猫 a homeless [stray] cat; an alley cat. 文例

のらくらと idly; lazily; aimlessly ¶のらくらする lead an idle life; idle one's time away; laze about; loaf;《うろつく》hang about [around]; loiter (about) / のらくらする者 an idler.

のり¹ 海苔 laver ¶焼き[味つけ]のり toasted [toasted and seasoned] laver / のり巻き vinegared rice rolled in laver.

のり² 乗り ¶乗りがよい《顔料などの》spread

のまれる 彼の堂々たる様子にすっかり飲まれてしまった. I allowed myself to be overawed by his (imposing) presence.

-のみ それをなし得る者はひとり彼なのみだ. No one but he can do it. | He is the only man that can do it.

のみならず それは経済的であるのみならずからだにもよいのだ. It is not only economical but also good for you. | のみならず彼は私の恩人だ. Moreover [Besides], he is my benefactor.

のみほす ぐっと飲み干して下さい. Drink it up, please. | Bottoms up!

のみみず この井戸の水は飲み水にならない. The water from [in] this well is not fit to drink [is not drinkable].

のみもの 飲み物は何になさいますか. What will you have [What would you like] to drink? / 何か暖かい[冷たい]飲み物がほしい. I'd like something hot [cold] to drink. | May I have a hot [cold] drink?

のむ 君は何を飲む. 紅茶それともコーヒー. Which will you have, tea or coffee? / 3日間飲まず食わずで海上を漂流した. He drifted over the sea for three days with nothing to eat or drink. / 酒は飲んでも飲まれるな. You may drink, but don't let the drink take over. | Don't drink unless you can hold your liquor. / 飲むと陽気な男だ. He is always cheerful when he's had a drink (or two). / この酒は飲めるよ. This sake is good [very drinkable].

のら 父は野良仕事に出ています. Father is working out in the fields.

のり³ 糊 paste;〈衣服用の〉starch ¶のりをつける starch 《a shirt》/のりで張る paste; stick sth with paste / 裏にのりのつけてあるラベル a gummed [sticky] label / のりのきいた well-starched / のりでぴんとしている be starched stiff / のりとはさみで作ったもの a product of scissors and paste / のりとはさみででっちあげた研究 a scissors-and-paste piece of research.

-のり …乗り ¶1人[2人]乗りの飛行機 a single-[two-]seater (plane) / 5人乗りの自動車 a five-seater (automobile).

のりあいじどうしゃ 乗合自動車 a (motor)bus; an omnibus ⇒ バス¹.

のりあげる 乗り上げる 〈浅瀬に〉run aground [ashore]; be stranded;〈暗礁などに〉hit [《文》strike, run onto] 《a sunken rock》¶〈自動車などが〉歩道に乗り上げる run on to the sidewalk.

のりあわせる 乗り合わせる happen to ride in the same carriage [car, boat] 《as, with》; share the car [carriage, boat] 《with》¶乗り合わせた人々 fellow passengers.

のりいれる 乗り入れる 〈馬を〉ride 《one's horse》into;〈車を〉drive 《one's car》into;〈鉄道などを延長して〉extend 《the railroad, the bus service》into.

のりうつる 乗り移る ¶ボートに乗り移る (leave one's ship and) take to a boat / 悪霊が乗り移る〈が主語〉be possessed by an evil spirit [the devil].

のりおくれる 乗り遅れる miss 《one's train》; fail to catch 《the 9:30 train》.

のりおり 乗り降り ¶乗り降りする get on and off [in and out].

のりかえ 乗り換え a change (of cars) ¶乗り換え駅 a station for changing trains; a junction (station) / 乗り換え切符 a transfer (ticket). 文例⇩

のりかえる 乗り換える change (cars, from one train to another); transfer (to another car);〈主義主張などを〉cross [change] over (to the other side);〈株などを〉switch (from A to B) ¶お茶の水で千葉行き[総武線]に乗り換える change at Ochanomizu for Chiba (to the Sobu line) / 電車を3度乗り換える change (trains) three times. 文例⇩

のりかかる 乗り掛かる 〈乗ろうとする〉be about to get on (the bus);〈着手する〉begin (to do); start (doing, to do); set about (doing, to do).

のりき 乗り気 ¶乗り気になる be keen to do; show 《great》 interest (in);《文》display 《great》 enthusiasm 《for》/ 乗り気になって eagerly; 《文》with eagerness / 乗り気な仕事をする work with a will; put one's heart and soul into one's job. 文例⇩

のりきる 乗り切る 〈原野や海を〉ride [sail] across;〈困難などを〉get over 《a crisis》; overcome [《文》surmount] 《difficulties》; ride out (the trouble).

のりくみいん 乗組員〈全員〉a crew;〈1人〉a member of a crew; a crewman. 文例⇩

のりくむ 乗り組む get [be] on board 《a vessel》; join 《a ship》; crew 《a fighter》¶操縦者が2人乗り組んだ飛行機 an airplane manned by two pilots.

のりこえる 乗り越える get [climb] over 《a wall》;〈困難などを〉overcome [《文》surmount, negotiate] 《obstacles》; get over 《a crisis》. 文例⇩

のりごこち 乗り心地 ¶乗り心地がいい[悪い] be comfortable (uncomfortable) to ride in.

のりこし 乗り越し ¶乗り越し切符 a fare-adjustment card / 乗り越し料金 an excess fare.

のりこす 乗り越す 乗り越し 乗り過ごす be carried beyond) one's stop [destination]. 文例⇩

のりこなす 乗りこなす manage 《a horse》.

のりこむ 乗り込む 〈乗り物に〉board 《a ship, a train》; go [come] on board [aboard] 《a ship》;《文》embark on [in] 《a steamer》; get into [on] 《a car》;〈乗り込む〉 march [ride] into 《a place》 ¶単身敵地に乗り込む venture into the enemy's territory alone.

のりしろ 糊代 a tab for sticking.

のりすてる 乗り捨てる〈下りる〉get off [out of]《a car》; leave;〈遺棄する〉abandon [leave]《a ship》to《her》fate.

のりだす 乗り出す〈出発する〉start; set out;〈出帆する〉sail; set sail;〈着手する〉《文》embark on 《an enterprise》; set about 《doing, to do》;〈出馬する〉come forward (as a candidate for Presidency);〈からだを〉lean forward; lean out of 《a window》¶大胆にあらしの海に乗り出す venture out on a stormy sea / 政界に乗り出す launch [go] into politics;《文》enter on a political career / 半身を乗り出して with one's body thrust forward.

のりづけ 糊付け ¶のり付けする〈紙に〉paste;〈衣服に〉starch / のり付けがよい[悪い] be not] well [properly] pasted [starched].

のりつける 乗り付ける〈乗って着く〉ride [drive 《one's car》] up to 《the porch》; draw [pull 《one's car》] up at 《the station entrance》;〈乗り慣れる〉get [be] used to rid-

---

のりかえ 終点, どなたもお乗り換えでございます。Terminus, all change! / 千葉行きは当駅乗り換え。[掲示] Change [Transfer] here for Chiba.

のりかえる 日比谷で乗り換えたほうが早い。It takes (you) less time if you [It is quicker to] change at Hibiya.

のりかかる 乗りかかった船で, 今さら後へは引かれない。Having set about [started on] the job, I can't back out of it now. | I've come too far to retreat [go back].

のりき 悪いけれど大して乗り気になれなかった。〈いやいやした時〉I'm sorry but I didn't feel half as enthusiastic (over it) as I ought. |〈実際に乗手しなかった時〉I'm sorry but it didn't appeal to me enough.

のりくみいん その船の乗組員は何名か。What is the size of her crew? / 乗組員は50名である。The ship has a crew of 50.

のりこえる 彼はその不屈の精神でこれらの障害を乗り越えた。His indefatigable spirit carried him over the obstacles.

のりこす 乗って来てみたら駅を3つも乗り越していた。I awoke to find that I had gone [been carried] three stops past [beyond]

のりつぶす 乗り潰す ride 《a horse》 down [to death]; ride 《a horse》 [drive 《a car》] into the ground; drive 《a car》 too hard and put 《it》 out of commission.

のりて 乗り手 〈馬の〉 a rider; 〈乗客〉 a passenger.

のりと 祝詞 a *Shinto* prayer.

のりならす 乗り慣らす break in 《a horse》.

のりにげ 乗り逃げ ¶乗り逃げする〈料金を払わない〉 run away without paying *one's* fare; 〈車を盗む〉 ride away with [drive off in] 《*sb's* car》.

のりば 乗り場 〈停留所〉 a (car, bus) stop; a (bus) depot; 〈プラットホーム〉 a platform ¶タクシー乗り場 a taxi stand [rank].

のりまわす 乗り回す 〈馬を〉 ride 《a horse》 around [about]; 〈自動車を〉 drive 《a car》 about [around].

のりもの 乗り物 a vehicle; 〈交通機関〉 (a means of) transport; 《文》 a (public) conveyance. 文例↓

のる 乗[載]る 〈乗り物に〉 take 《a bus, a plane》; ride 《a horse, a bicycle》; 〈乗り込む〉 get on [into] 《a train》; get into 《a car》; board 《a bus》; go [get] aboard [on board] 《a ship》; 〈物の上に〉 get [step] on; mount; 〈記載される〉 appear; be mentioned; be printed; be reported; be recorded; 〈だまされる〉 be taken in 《by》; 〈加わる〉 take part 《in》; participate in 《a scheme》 ¶自動車に乗る take [take a ride] in an automobile / 〈運転する〉 drive a car / 列車に乗る take a train / 乗っている車に 《a car, a train》; be aboard [on board] 《a ship》 / 列車[バス]に乗って行く go (to Atami) by rail [bus] / take a train [bus] 《to the airport》 / 馬に乗って行く ride 《go on horseback》 《to the village》 / 自転車に乗って行く go by [on a] bicycle / 船に乗って行く go by ship [boat] / 飛行機に乗って行く 《travel》 《to San Francisco》 by air [plane]; fly 《to Hawaii》 / エレベーターに乗って上り下りする go up and down in an elevator / 風に乗って運ばれる be borne [《文》] [wafted] on the breeze; be carried on the wind / 話に乗ってくる be drawn into conversation / たなの上に載る 《sit, lie》 on a shelf / 新聞に載る get into a newspaper / ブラックリストに載る be put [placed] on a blacklist.

ノルウェー Norway ¶ノルウェーの Norwegian / ノルウェー王国 the Kingdom of Norway / ノルウェー語 Norwegian; 〈古代の〉(Old) Norse / ノルウェー人 a Norwegian.

のるかそるか 伸るか反るか sink or swim; for better or worse; come what may; make or break [《文》] mar ¶のるかそるかの決断 a make-or-break decision. 文例↓

ノルマ [<《ロシヤ語》*norma*] a work (production) quota ¶ノルマを果たす fulfill *one's* (work) quota; finish the work assigned to *one*.

のれん 暖簾 〈店先に張る布〉 a curtain; 〈店の信用〉 credit; reputation; 〈店・商売の株〉 goodwill ¶のれんを売る sell the goodwill (of a store); sell out *one's* business / のれんを分ける set 《an employee》 up in *one's* own business / 店ののれんにかかわる[を汚す] affect [harm] the credit [good name] of the store. 文例↓

のろい 呪い a curse ¶のろいをかける curse; put [place] a curse 《on》.

のろい 鈍い 〈遅い〉 slow; 《文》 tardy; sluggish; slack; 〈にぶい〉 dull; dull-[slow-]witted; 〈甘い〉 indulgent; doting ¶足がのろい be slow-footed / 《文》 be slow of foot / 仕事がのろい be slow at [in] *one's* work; be a slow worker / 細君にのろい夫 a doting [《文》] an uxorious husband.

のろう 呪う curse; put [place] a curse on *sb* ¶のろうべき, のろわれた cursed; 《文》 accursed / 運命にのろわれた doomed; ill-fated.

のろけ ¶のろけを言う ⇨ のろける. 文例↓

のろける talk about *one's* (own) love affairs; speak fondly of 《*one's*》 wife》.

のろし a signal fire [flare]; a beacon; a rocket ¶のろしを上げる light a signal fire; send up a rocket as a signal / 倒閣運動ののろしを上げる start [launch into] an anti-government campaign / のろしで知らせる signal 《to *sb*》 by beacon.

のろのろ slowly; sluggishly; 《walk》 draggingly; in a leisurely fashion ¶のろのろ進む proceed at a slow [snail's] pace; make *one's* way with slow steps / のろのろした slow(-moving); sluggish.

のろま a dull [stupid] fellow; a slowcoach ¶のろまの stupid; dull(-witted).

のんき 暢気 ¶のんきな 〈楽な〉 easy; 〈やかましく考えない〉 easygoing; 〈屈託のない〉 carefree; 〈楽天的な〉 optimistic; 〈行き当たりばったりの〉 happy-go-lucky; 〈ゆっくりした〉 leisurely; 〈不注意な〉 careless; 〈考えなしの〉 thoughtless / のんきに暮らす live in ease and comfort; 〈金に困らない〉 be comfortably off / のんきに考える[構える] take things [it] easy. 文例↓

---

my destination.
のりもの 駅からはどんな乗り物がありますか. What transport is there from the station?
のる 君はジェット機に乗ったことがありますか. Have you ever been on a jet (plane)? / あの船には客は乗っていない. The steamer has no passengers on board. / その男は彼女に「車に乗りませんか」と言った. The man asked her if she would like a lift. / その手には乗りませんよ. That trick won't work with me. | You won't catch me with that one. / その語は辞書に載っていない. That word is not (given) in this dictionary. / そこは地図にも載っていない小さな山村である. It is a little mountain village not shown on the map. / 今日の朝日新聞にその事件が載っている. Today's *Asahi* carries an account of the incident.
のるかそるか のるか反るかだ. Let's give it a try, sink or swim [for better or worse]. | This is a make-or-break decision.
のれん のれんに腕押しだ. It is (like) beating the air [wind].
のろう 人をのろわば穴二つ. Curses, like chickens, come home to roost. 《諺》
のんき 彼は全くのんきそうだっ

ノンストップ nonstop 《flights》 ¶ノンストップで飛ぶ fly nonstop 《to New York》. 文例⑥

のんだくれ 飲んだくれ ⇒ のみすけ.

のんびり ¶のんびりする feel easy [at (one's) ease]; take it easy; make oneself at home / のんびりした 〈穏やかな〉 calm; 《文》 tranquil; peaceful; 〈のんきな〉 free and easy; carefree ¶何不自由なく育つ grow up [be brought up] free from all care / のんびりと隠居生活をする live in quiet retirement.

ノンフィクション nonfiction.

ノンプロ ¶ノンプロの nonprofessional; 《米口語》 nonpro / ノンプロの選手 a nonprofessional (player); 《米口語》 a nonpro (pl. -s).

のんべえ 飲み兵衛 ⇒ のみすけ.

のんべんだらりと doing nothing; idly ¶のんべんだらりと過ごす lead an idle life; idle [dawdle] one's time away.

ノンポリ ¶ノンポリ学生 an apolitical student.

は

は¹ 刃 an edge; a cutting [working] edge ¶鋭い刃 a keen [sharp] edge / 鈍い刃 a dull [blunt] edge / 刃が欠けたナイフ a knife with a nicked edge / 刃をつける put an edge (on); give an edge (to).

は² 派 〈団体〉 a group; 〈党派〉 a party; a faction; 〈学派, 流派〉 a school; 〈宗派〉 a sect ¶狩野派 the Kano school / 真宗大谷派 the Otani sect of Shinshu / 自民党の福田派 the Fukuda faction of the Liberal Democratic Party. 文例⑥

は³ 歯 〈口の中の〉 a tooth (pl. teeth); 〈下駄の〉 a support; 〈歯車の〉 a cog; (a) tooth (pl. teeth) ¶くし [のこぎり] の歯 the teeth of a comb [saw] / 歯が痛い have (a) toothache / 歯が浮く 〈ぐらぐらする〉 one's tooth feels loose; 〈酸っぱい物を食べた時など〉 one's teeth are (set) on edge / 歯が生える a tooth develops (comes through); 〈人が主語〉 cut a tooth; teethe (赤ん坊が) / 歯がいい [悪い] have good [bad] teeth / 歯の dental / 歯の浮くようなお世辞 (a piece of) nauseating flattery / 歯のない toothless / 歯を食いしばる clench [set] one's teeth / 歯を食いしばって我慢する bear sth with clenched teeth / 歯を抜く 〈人の歯を〉 extract a tooth; pull a tooth (out); 〈抜いてもらう〉 have one's tooth pulled (out) / 歯を磨く clean [brush] one's teeth / 白い歯を見せてにやにや笑う grin; smile a toothy smile / 歯にきぬ着せずに言う do not mince matters [one's words].

は⁴ 葉 a leaf (pl. leaves); a needle (針葉); a frond (しだなどの); foliage (総称) ¶葉が出る [出ている] the leaves come [are] out; 〈木が主語〉 come into [be in] leaf / 葉が落ちる the leaves fall; 〈木が主語〉 be stripped [become bare] of leaves / 葉の多い [茂った] leafy. 文例⑥

は⁵ 覇 ¶覇を争う 《文》 contend [vie] for supremacy / 覇を唱える 《文》 hold sway (over); 《文》 assume the hegemony (of).

は⁶ 〈応答〉 ⇒ はあ; 〈疑問〉 I (beg your) pardon? (★ 尻上がりの音調で言う).

ハ 《音楽》 C ¶ハ長 [短] 調 (in) C major [minor].

ば 〈場所〉 a place; 〈余地〉 space; room; 〈座席〉 a seat; 〈場面〉 a scene; 〈活動範囲〉 a field; 〈取引市場の〉 a session ¶その場 ⇒ そのば / 重力の場 a gravitational field / 力の場 the field of force / 場を外す leave [《文》 retire from] the room; 《口語》 make oneself scarce; slip away (そっと) / 場をふさぐ occupy too much space; take up a lot of room.

はあ 〈応答〉 yes; indeed; well; I see (なるほど); 〈驚き〉 ha!

ばあ 〈驚かす時〉 boo!; 〈あやす時〉 peekaboo!

バー 〈酒場〉 a bar(room); a bar parlor; 《米》 a saloon; 《英口語》 a pub; 《英》 a public house; 〈横木, 金属棒〉 a bar ¶バーの女 a bar hostess; 《米》 a bar girl.

パー 〈バーで〉〈同等で〉 on a par (with); 〈額面で〉 at par / パー以上 [以下] で above [below] par.

ばあい 場合 〈事例〉 a case; 〈時〉 an occasion; a time; a moment; 〈事情〉《文》 circumstances ¶今の場合は as things [matters] stand now; 《文》 in the present circumstances / こんな場合には in such a case; in [under] these circumstances / …の場合には if …; 《文》 should …; when …; in case of 〈trouble, rain〉; in the

---

た. He looked perfectly carefree. It looked as if he hadn't a care [worry] in the world. / 試験が近づいたのではのんきにしてもいられない. I cannot take it [things] easy with the examination in sight. / 非番の時は, みんなすこぶるのんきに過ごした. We had a wonderfully easy time of it when we were not on duty.
ノンストップ この便は東京からロサンゼルスまでノンストップで

行きます. This flight goes from Tokyo to Los Angeles nonstop.
は² 彼は社長派だった. He was one of the supporters of the president. / 中井氏は早稲田派の作家だ. Mr. Nakai is a writer of the Waseda group.
は³ 歯が1本抜けた. One of my teeth came [fell] out. / I lost a tooth. / 私は歯の治療に歯科医院へ行った. I went to the dentist to get my teeth seen to [treated]. /

犬は歯をむき出してうなった. The dog showed his teeth and snarled at me. / こわくて歯の根も合わなかった. My teeth chattered with terror [rattled with fear]. / この仕事は私には歯が立たない. This task is beyond me. / I'm not equal to this job. / 歯にきぬを着せずにいえば, あの男は愚物だ. Not to put too fine a point on it, he's a fool.
は⁴ 葉が出た. The leaves are out.

パーキング parking ¶パーキングメーター a parking meter.

はあく 把握 ¶把握する grasp 《the meaning》; get hold of 《the subject》. 文例⇩

ハーグ The Hague.

バークリウム 〖化〗berkelium.

ハーケン [くドイツ語〉Haken] 〖登山〗a piton; a mountain climber's spike.

バーゲンセール a bargain sale.

パーゴラ a pergola.

パーコレーター a percolator.

パーサー 〈旅客機などの〉a purser.

バージニア Virginia (略: Va.) ¶バージニアの Virginian / バージニア州の人 a Virginian.

パーセンテージ a percentage.

パーセント per cent [percent] (記号: %) ¶35パーセント 35 per cent; 35% / 5パーセントの増加 an increase by five per cent; a five percent increase.

バーター barter ¶バーター制 the barter system.

ばあたり 場当たり ¶場当たりの ad hoc 《decisions》; spur-of-the-moment 《answers》; 《policies》to fit [answer] the needs of the moment / 場当たりを ねらう play to the gallery / 場当たり[的]に 《decide》 on the spur of the moment; 《manage a firm》 on a day-to-day [patchwork] basis.

パーティー a party ¶《登山などの》パーティーを組む form a party / パーティーを開く give [have, hold, 《口語》throw] a party.

バーテン 《米》a bartender; 《英》a barman; 《米》a barkeep(er) (★バーのマスターをも意味する).

ハート 〈心臓, 心〉the heart; 〈トランプの〉a heart ¶ハートの女王 the queen of hearts / ハート形の heart-shaped.

ハードウエア 〖コンピューター〗hardware.

ハードカバー 〈表紙〉hard covers ¶ハードカバーの本 a hardback [hardcover] book; a hardback.

パートタイム ¶パートタイムの従業員 a part-time worker; a part-timer / パートタイムで働く work part-time.

ハードトップ 〈自動車〉a hardtop.

ハードトレーニング hard training ¶ハードトレーニングをする train hard. 文例⇩

パートナー a partner.

ハードル 〖競技〗〈障害物〉a hurdle; 〈競走〉a hurdle race; the hurdles ¶ハードルの選手 a hurdler / ハードルを跳び越す jump [leap] over a hurdle; hurdle / ハードルで1位になる come first [win first place] in the hurdles / ロー[ハイ]ハードル the low [high] hurdles.

はあはあ ¶《息を切らして》はあはあいう gasp; pant; puff and blow. 文例⇩

ハーフ ⇨こんけつ.

ハープ a harp ¶ハープを弾く play the harp / ハープ奏者 a harpist.

ハープシコード a harpsichord.

ハーフタイム 〖スポーツ〗half time.

ハーフバック 〖蹴球・ホッケー〗a halfback ¶ハーフバックをやる play (at) halfback.

バーベキュー a barbecue ¶バーベキューにする barbecue 《beef》.

バーベル 〖重量挙げ〗a barbell.

パーマ(ネント) a permanent wave; 《口語》a perm ¶パーマ(ネント)をかける have one's hair permed [permanently waved]; have [get] a perm.

バーミューダ 〈島の名〉Bermuda; 〈ズボンの一種〉Bermuda shorts; Bermudas ¶バーミューダの Bermudian / バーミューダ島民 a Bermudian.

ハーモニカ a harmonica; a mouth organ.

バーモント Vermont (略: Vt.) ¶バーモント州の人 a Vermonter.

ばあや an old housekeeper; an elderly maid.

はあり 羽蟻 〖昆〗a winged ant.

バーレーン (the State of) Bahrain.

ばあん ¶《警策で》肩をばあんと打つ give 《a monk sitting in Zen meditation》a resounding whack on the shoulder.

はい¹ 灰 ash(es) ¶タバコの灰を落とす knock [tap] the ash off one's cigarette 《into an ashtray》 / 焼けて灰になる be reduced [burnt] to ashes / 灰色 ⇨はいいろ / 灰神楽(ぬ゚)を上げる raise a cloud of ashes / 灰皿 an ashtray; a smoking stand (床上用の). 文例⇩

雑木林もすっかり葉が落ちた. The woods have all shed their leaves.

ばあい ぜひともそうしなければならない場合がよくある. It often happens that it is essential to do so. / この規則が当てはまらない場合もある. There are some cases where this rule does not apply. / このようなやり方も場合によっては有効であろう. Depending on the circumstances measures like this may prove effective. / それは場合による. That depends. / 今はぐずぐずしている場合でない. This is no time for shilly-shallying. / 今の場合私は物見遊山に出かけたりしてはいられない. As things are, I am not in a position to go off on a pleasure trip.

はあく 彼らは日本文化の本質を明確に把握してはいないと思う. I don't think they have a clear [an accurate] grasp of the essence of Japanese culture.

ハードトレーニング 大会に備えてハードトレーニングをしている. We are training hard for the competition.

はあはあ 彼ははあはあいって駆けて来た. He came running up, quite out of breath. / 私たちは, はあはあ言いながら山を登った. We huffed and puffed up the mountain.

はい¹ 浅間山が噴火したので軽井沢に多量の灰が降った. Large quantities of ash fell on Karui-

はい² 杯 a cup; a glass (コップ) ⇨ さかずき ¶お茶2杯 two cups of tea; two teas / ビール1杯 a glass of beer; a beer.

はい³ 胚《動・植》an embryo (pl. -s); a germ.

はい⁴ 肺 the lungs ¶右[左]の肺 the right [left] lung / 肺が悪い have a weak chest; have [suffer from] lung [pulmonary] trouble / 肺動[静]脈 the pulmonary artery [vein].

はい⁵ 蠅 ⇨ はえ².

はい⁶《応答の声》yes; certainly; all right; very well;《出席の答》here, sir!; present, sir! 文例⇩

ばい 倍 ¶2倍 double; twice; two times;《文》twofold / …の2倍 twice as much as…; 《数》twice as many as… / …の2倍の大きさ[長さ]の twice as large [long] as…; twice the size [length] of… / …の1.5倍の one and a half times as many [much, long, etc.] as…; half as many [much, long, etc.] again as… / 3倍 three times…《文》threefold / …の1.5倍の高さの塔 a tower one-and-a-half times as high as…; a tower half as tall again as… / 千五百倍の顕微鏡 a microscope of 1,500 magnifications; a 1,500-power microscope (★ 1,500-power は fifteen-hundred power とよむ) / 倍(に)する a double / 倍になる be doubled / 数[量]を10倍にする increase the number [quantity] by ten times / 倍大号 a double number / 倍額 double the amount [price, charge, fee]. 文例⇩

用法「…倍」を英語では「1倍」,「2倍」の時を除いては, …times というのが最も普通.「…の3倍の数量」は three times as many [much, heavy, etc.] as…; three times its amount [weight, etc.] のように言う.「この土地の地価は購入価格の3倍になっている」を英語では, This land is now worth three times what [as much as] we paid for it. | The value of this land has increased threefold [has shown a threefold increase] since we bought it. と言うように,「…倍」-fold で表わすことも可能であるが, -fold は …times と比べるとかなり《文》的であるのと, 上例でもうちがえるように, 副詞として単独に使われたり, 形容詞として名詞の直前に置かれる点が, …times との用法上の主な違いである.

ばい 牌《マージャンの》a tile; a piece.

パイ¹《菓子》a pie ¶パイの皮 the shell of a pie; piecrust / パイ図表 a pie chart.

パイ²《数》pi (記号: π).

はいあがる 這い上がる crawl [creep] up.

はいあん 廃案 a discarded [scrapped] plan [proposal, bill].

はいいろ 灰色《米》gray;《英》grey ¶灰色の《米》gray;《英》grey / 灰色の獄窓生活 the gray monotony of prison life / 灰色がかった grayish. 文例⇩

はいいん 敗因 a cause of defeat.

ばいう 梅雨 ⇨ つゆ³ ¶梅雨前線 a seasonal rain front.

はいえい 背泳 ⇨ せおよぎ.

はいえき 廃液 liquid waste; waste fluid ¶工場廃液 effluent(s) [liquid waste(s)] from a factory; (industrial) effluent(s); industrial waste(s).

ハイエナ《動》a hyena.

はいえん 肺炎 pneumonia.

ばいえん 煤煙 soot and smoke.

パイオニア a pioneer; a trailblazer.

バイオリズム (a) biorhythm.

バイオリン a violin;《口語》a fiddle ¶バイオリン奏者 a violinist. 文例⇩

はいか 配下 one's subordinates; one's men; one's followers ¶…の配下となって働く serve [work] under sb.

はいが¹ 胚芽《植》an embryo bud; a germ ¶はいが米 whole rice; rice with embryo buds.

はいが² 俳画 a haiku picture.

ばいか 倍加 ⇨ ばい(倍(に)する, 倍になる) ¶魅力たるを倍加する make sth doubly [far more] attractive.

ハイカー a hiker.

はいかい¹ 俳諧 ⇨ はいく ¶俳諧師 a haiku poet.

はいかい² 徘徊 ¶はいかいする〈歩き回る〉wander [roam] about;〈うろつき歩く〉loiter (about);《口語》hang around.

はいがい 排外 ¶排外思想 antiforeign feeling [《文》sentiment];《文》chauvinism.

ばいかい《文》媒介《文》mediation;《文》good offices (周旋) ¶媒介する mediate《between two parties》; act as (a) go-between;〈伝染病を〉transmit 《disease》, carry 《germs》/ …の媒介により《文》through the good offices of … / 媒介者 a mediator; a middleman / 媒介物 a medium (pl. media);〈病菌の〉a carrier; a vector (虫に).

はいかつりょう 肺活量 the air capacity of the lungs; lung capacity ¶肺活量計 a spirometer. 文例⇩

ハイカラ ¶ハイカラな〈おしゃれな〉《文》foppish;〈粋な〉smart; chic; stylish; fashionable /ハイカラにする smarten up.

バイカルこ バイカル湖 Lake Baikal.

はいかん¹ 拝観 ¶拝観する see;《文》have the honor of seeing;〈行って見る〉visit / 拝観を

---

zawa, as a result of the eruption of Mt. Asama. / パイプの灰を落とした. He knocked the ashes from his pipe.
はい⁶ はい, かしこまりました. Yes, sir. | Certainly, sir. /《物を渡す時》はい (ここにあります). Here you are. | Here it is.
ばい そうすると金が倍かかる. It would cost twice as much [cost as much again] (as that). / 彼は以前に倍して努力した. He re-

doubled his efforts. | He worked twice as hard as before. / 3の2倍は6. Twice 3 is 6. / 3を何倍すると60になりますか. What times 3 is 60? / 偶数は何倍しても偶数になる. An even number multiplied any number of times gives an even number. / それは長さの方が幅の1.5倍ある It is one-and-a-half times as long as it is wide. / 1等は2等運賃の倍額です. The first-class fare is

double [twice] the second-class. / 彼は父親似の理財家ではなかったが, 学者としては父に倍するものを持っていた. He was not quite the financier his father had been, but he was twice the scholar.
はいいろ 彼はさらに6年間の灰色の日々をその町で過ごした. He lived six more gray years in that town.
バイオリン オイストラフのバイ

はいかん 許される be allowed to visit [see] / 拝観者 a visitor / 拝観料 an admission [entrance] fee.

はいかん² 配管 laying pipes; plumbing ¶配管工 a plumber; a pipelayer.

はいかん³ 廃刊 《文》discontinuance (of publication) ¶廃刊になる 《文》be discontinued; go out of existence; 《口語》fold. 文例⇩

はいがん 肺癌 lung cancer; cancer of the lung.

はいき¹ 排気 exhaust ¶〈赤ん坊に授乳後〉排気させる burp 《a baby》/ 排気ガス exhaust (fumes); (engine) exhaust / 自動車の排気ガス car fumes / 排気管 an exhaust (pipe) / 排気装置 a device for exhausting gases; an exhauster / 排気弁 an exhaust valve / 排気量 1,800 cc の車 a car of 1,800 cc displacement.

はいき² 廃棄 abandonment; 《文》〈法令などの〉abrogation; repeal ¶廃棄する do away with; abolish; abandon; abrogate 《a treaty》; repeal 《a law》; scrap / 条約の廃棄通告 the renunciation of a treaty / 産業廃棄物 industrial waste(s) / 〈原子炉の〉廃棄処理 the disposal of radioactive waste.

ばいきゃく 売却 sale ⇨ うる¹.

はいきゅう¹ 配給 distribution; supply; 〈統制品の〉rationing ¶配給する distribute (among, to); supply 《sb with sth》; 〈統制品を〉ration / 配給機構 a distribution system / 配給所 a distributing [supply] station / 配給所 [station, ration] point [center] / 配給通帳 a ration book / 配給米 rationed rice / 配給ルート a distribution channel [route].

はいきゅう² 配球 《野球》a combination of pitches [deliveries] ¶配球が巧みである be clever at varying (the combination of) one's pitches [deliveries].

はいきゅう³ 排球 ⇨ バレー(ボール).

ばいきゅう 倍旧 ¶倍旧の 《文》redoubled 《efforts》; increased 《patronage》.

はいきょ 廃墟 ruins ¶トロイの廃墟 the ruins [remains] of Troy / 廃墟になる be ruined; fall in ruins [into ruin(s)] / 廃墟になっている be [lie] in ruins.

はいぎょ 肺魚 《魚》a lungfish (pl. -(es)).

はいきょう 背教 the abandonment of one's (religious) faith; apostasy ¶背教者 an apostate.

はいぎょう 廃業 ¶廃業する 〈商売をやめる〉close [give up] one's business; 〈店・工場などが主語〉close down; 〈医師・弁護士などが〉give up one's practice; 〈引退する〉retire from business; 〈役者や力士が〉retire from [《口語》quit] the stage [ring].

ばいきん 黴菌 ⇨ さいきん¹.

ハイキング hiking; a hike ¶ハイキングに行く go on a hike; go hiking (in Tanzawa) / ハイキングコース a hiking trail; a trail for hikers.

バイキング《西洋史》a Viking ¶バイキング料理〈北欧料理の〉smorgasbord; 〈一般に〉a restaurant meal in which people help themselves to as much food as they wish for a fixed price.

はいきんしゅぎ 拝金主義 worship of money [《文》mammon].

はいく 俳句 a haiku

バイク a motor bicycle; a motorbike.

はいぐう 配偶 ¶配偶者《文》one's spouse; one's mate / 〈書類の欄などで〉配偶者の有無 one's marital status / 配偶子《生物》a gamete.

はいぐん 敗軍 a defeated army; 〈敗戦〉(a) defeat. 文例⇩

はいけい¹ 拝啓 Dear Sir; Dear Mr....; 〈婦人あてに〉Dear Madam; Dear Miss [Mrs.]...; 〈会社などに〉Dear Sirs; 《米》Gentlemen / 〈婦人団体に〉Mesdames.
用法 Dear Sir [Madam] は Dear Mr.... などと違い、はじめてその相手に手紙を出す場合に限って使用される。

はいけい² 背景 〈後景〉a background; 〈舞台の〉scenery; a setting; a scene ¶山を背景にして写真を撮る photograph sth [sb] with a hill for a [the] background / 〈舞台の〉背景を描く paint a scene / 背景幕 a backdrop; 《英》a backcloth. 文例⇩

はいげき 排撃 ¶排撃する denounce; 《文》show strong disapproval of; reject; drive out.

はいけっかく 肺結核 tuberculosis [TB] of the lungs; pulmonary tuberculosis ¶肺結核患者 a tuberculosis [TB] patient.

はいけつしょう 敗血症 blood poisoning; septicemia.

はいけん 拝見 ¶拝見する 《文》have the honor of seeing; see; look [have a look] at. 文例⇩

はいご¹ 背後 〈背後に[の]〉behind; in [at] the rear (of); at the back (of); 《米》(in) back (of) / 敵の背後をつく attack the enemy in the rear [from behind] / 事件の背後関係を調べる inquire into the background of a case [the (hidden) circumstances that led up to the case]; 〈黒幕を〉investigate [find out] who is pulling the wires. 文例⇩

オリンでベートーベンのバイオリン協奏曲を聞いた。I heard Beethoven's violin concerto with Oistrakh on the violin.

ばいかい マラリアは蚊の媒介によって伝染する。Malaria is carried by mosquitoes. / Mosquitoes transmit malaria.

はいかつりょう 私の肺活量は 3,500 です。My lung capacity is 3,500 cc. / 女性の方が男性よりも肺活量が大きいと聞いています。I've heard that women have a greater lung capacity than men.

はいかん³ その新聞はわずか1年で廃刊になった。The paper only lasted [survived for] a year.

はいぐん 敗軍の将兵を語らず。A defeated general should not talk of battles. / It is not for the loser to talk about tactics.

はいけい² ブルゴーニュの風景がその肖像画の背景になっていた。A landscape of Burgundy formed the backdrop for the portrait. / 美しい富士の姿が青空を背景にしてくっきりと見える。The graceful figure of Mt. Fuji stands out clear against the blue sky. / 彼にはなんら政治的背景はない。He has no political backing.

はいけん ちょっと拝見。Let me have a look. / Show me, please.

はいご¹ 彼の背後に大金持がいる。He is backed by a wealthy man [has a rich friend behind

はいご² 廃語 an obsolete word. 文例⇩

はいこう¹ 廃鉱[坑] an abandoned [a disused] mine [pit].

はいこう² 廃校 ¶廃校にする close (down) a school / 廃校になる the school is closed (down).

はいごう 配合 〈取り合わせ〉combination; arrangement; 〈混合〉mixture ¶配合する combine; arrange; 〈混ぜる〉mix / 配合肥料 (a) compound fertilizer. 文例⇩

はいこうせい 背光性 【生物】negative phototropism; apheliotropism.

ばいこく 売国 ¶売国的行為 an act of treachery (against one's country); 《文》a traitorous act / 売国奴 a traitor to [《文》a betrayer of] one's country.

はいざい 配剤 ¶天の配剤 (God's) dispensation; 《文》(divine) Providence.

はいざん¹ 敗残 ¶敗残の defeated / 敗残兵 remnants of a defeated army [troop]; stragglers.

はいざん² 廃残 ¶廃残の ruined / 廃残の身 a failure; a [the] (mere) wreck of one's former self; the ruin of what one was.

はいし¹ 廃止 abolition; 《文》disuse; 《文》discontinuance; 〈法令などの〉repeal ¶廃止する do away with; abolish; discontinue; phase out (逐次, 段階的に); 〈法令などを〉repeal; abrogate / 廃止になる be abolished; go out of use [existence] / fall into disuse.

はいし² 〈馬に〉Gee-up!; Giddy-up!

はいしつ 廃疾 (a) disability ¶廃疾となる be disabled; be crippled (for life) / 廃疾者 a disabled person; a person crippled for life.

ばいしつ 媒質 【物】a medium (pl. media, -s).

はいしゃ¹ 配車 the allocation of buses [freight cars] ¶配車する allocate (send out, dispatch) buses [freight cars] / 配車係 a dispatcher.

はいしゃ² 敗者 a loser; a defeated person [player]; 《文》the defeated; 《文》the vanquished ¶(競技会の)敗者戦 a consolation match [race, round] / 敗者復活戦 a repechage.

はいしゃ³ 廃車 a scrapped car; a car [bus] out of service ¶廃車にする scrap a car; put a car [bus] out of service.

はいしゃ⁴ 歯医者 a dentist; a dental surgeon ¶歯医者にかかる consult [(go and) see] a dentist; have one's tooth [teeth] treated by a dentist. 文例⇩

はいしゃく 拝借 ⇨かりる. 文例⇩

ばいしゃく 媒酌 matchmaking ¶媒酌する arrange a match 《between》; act as (a) go-between / ...の媒酌で 《文》through the good offices of... / 媒酌人 a matchmaker.

ハイジャック a (plane) hijacking ¶ハイジャックする hijack 《an airplane》/ ハイジャックの犯人 a hijacker.

はいしゅ 胚珠 【植】an ovule.

ばいしゅう 買収 〈買い取り〉purchase; 〈わいろを使っての〉bribery; buying ¶買収する buy up; purchase; 〈わいろで〉bribe; win sb over by bribery; buy sb (off). 文例⇩

はいしゅつ¹ 排出 ⇨はいせつ ¶排出する discharge.

はいしゅつ² 輩出 ¶輩出する appear one after another [in succession, in large numbers]. 文例⇩

ばいしゅん 売春 prostitution ¶売春婦 a prostitute; 《米俗》a hooker / 売春宿 a brothel.

はいじょ 排除 removal; 《文》exclusion ¶排除する remove; 《文》exclude; 《文》eliminate; put sb out of the way.

ばいしょう 賠償 《文》reparation; 《文》(an) indemnity; compensation ¶賠償する pay for 《damage》; compensate [make reparation] for 《damage》; indemnify sb for 《damage》/ 現物賠償 reparations in kind / 賠償金 compensation; reparations (特に戦争の); an indemnity; 〈損害の〉damages / 賠償協定 a reparations treaty / 賠償責任保険 liability insurance.

はいしょく¹ 配色 a color scheme; the arrangement of colors.

はいしょく² 敗色 signs of defeat. 文例⇩

はいしん 背信 a breach of faith; an abuse of trust; 《文》betrayal; 《文》infidelity ¶背信行為 《文》an act of disloyalty.

はいじん¹ 俳人 a haiku poet.

はいじん² 廃人 a disabled person; a person who is maimed [crippled] for life. 文例⇩

ばいしん 陪審 ¶陪審員 a juryman; a juror; a jury (総称) / 陪審員になる serve [sit] on a jury / 陪審裁判 (a) trial by jury / 陪審制度 the jury system.

はいしんじゅん 肺浸潤 infiltration of the lungs.

はいすい¹ 配水 ¶配水する distribute [supply] water / 配水管 a conduit (pipe); a water pipe.

はいすい² 排水 〈水を外に吐き出させること〉draining; drainage; 〈水に浮かんだ物体がその重さで水を押しのけること〉displacement ¶排水する 〈吐き出させる〉drain (off); pump out (ポンプで); 〈自分の重さで水を押しのける〉displace / 排水がよい[悪い] the drainage (of the field) is good [bad, poor]; be well [badly] drained; drain well [badly, poorly] / 排水管 a

---

はいご² これらの語は今では廃語になっている。These words are no longer in use.

はいごう これは色の配合が良い。This is an attractive color scheme [combination of colors]. | These colors go together well.

はいしゃ⁴ ちょうどその時私は歯医者で治療を受けていた。Right at that moment I was sitting in a dentist's chair.

はいしゃく この本を2, 3日拝借できませんか。May I have this book for a few days? / 電話をちょっと拝借したいのですが？ Might I use your phone for a minute?

ばいしゅう 政府はその土地を買収した。The Government has bought the land. / 金で買収されるものか。Money can't buy me.

はいしゅつ² その町からは英才が多数輩出した。The town has produced many men of talent [has turned out a great many talented men].

はいしょく¹ 配色がよい。The colors go together well.

はいしょく² 敗色が濃い。Defeat

はいすいのじん 背水の陣 ¶背水の陣を敷く burn one's boats; burn one's bridges (behind one).

ばいすう 倍数 a multiple. 文例⇩

はいする¹ 拝する 〈拝む〉worship;《文》do obeisance ((to));〈見る〉see;〈受ける〉receive (a command); get (one's orders).

はいする² 配する 〈配置する〉arrange;〈対にする,めあわせる〉pair ((A)) with ((B));〈配属する〉put [《文》place] ((A)) under ((B)).

はいする³ 排する 〈退ける〉reject;〈押しのける〉push aside.

はいする⁴ 廃する ⇒はいし¹.

はいずる 這いずる ⇒はう ¶はいずり回る はいまわる.

はいせき 排斥 《文》expulsion ¶排斥する drive out;《文》expel; oust. 文例⇩

ばいせき 陪席 ¶陪席裁判官 an associate judge.

はいせつ 排泄《生理》excretion; discharge ¶排泄する excrete; discharge; evacuate / 排泄器官 an excretory organ / 排泄物 excreta; excretion(s); body wastes.

はいせん¹ 肺尖《解》the apex of a lung ¶肺尖カタル catarrh of the (pulmonary) apex.

はいせん² 配線 (electrical) wiring ¶配線する wire (a house) / 配線のミスが原因で due to [because of] faulty wiring.

はいせん³ 敗戦 a lost battle; (a) defeat ¶敗戦国 a defeated [vanquished] nation / 敗戦投手 a losing pitcher.

はいせん⁴ 廃船 a scrapped ship [vessel]; a ship that is out of service.

はいぜん 配膳 ¶配膳する lay [set] the table (for dinner); 〈dinner〉on the table /(ホテルなどの)配膳室 a service room.

はいそ 敗訴 a lost case ¶敗訴になる the case goes [turns out] against ((the plaintiff)); judgment is given against ((the defendant));〈人が主語〉lose one's [the] suit [case].

はいそう¹ 敗走《文》(a) rout;《文》flight ¶敗走する be routed; be put to rout;《文》flee; take to flight;《文》rout ((the enemy));《文》put ((the enemy)) to rout; have [get] ((the enemy)) on the run. 文例⇩

はいそう² 配送 ⇒はいたつ ¶配送センター a distribution [delivery] center.

はいぞう 肺臓 ⇒はい⁴.

ばいぞう 倍増《文》a twofold increase; (a) doubling ¶倍増する〈ふやす〉double ((one's income));〈ふえる〉increase to twice its amount [size]; become twice as much [many, large, etc.] as....

はいぞく 配属 ¶配属する assign [attach] sb ((to a department)).

はいた¹ 排他 ¶排他的 exclusive / 排他主義《文》exclusivism;《文》exclusionism.

はいた² 歯痛 (have) (a) toothache.

はいたい¹ 胚胎 ¶胚胎する《文》arise ((from));《文》originate ((in)).

はいたい² 敗退 ¶敗退する〈退却する〉retreat;〈負ける〉be beaten;《文》be defeated;《文》suffer a defeat; lose (a game).

ばいたい 媒体 a medium (pl. media, -s); a vehicle (of sound).

はいだす 這い出す ⇒はいでる.

はいたつ 配達 delivery ¶配達する deliver / 新聞[牛乳]を配達する deliver [carry] newspapers [milk] (from house to house) / 配達先 the destination; the receiver's address;〈受取人〉the addressee; the receiver /配達人 a delivery-man;〈郵便の〉a postman;《米》a mailman; a mail carrier;《文》a milkman /〈新聞の〉a newsboy / 配達不能の手紙 a dead letter / 配達料 a delivery charge. 文例⇩

はいち 配置 arrangement;《文》disposition ¶配置する arrange;〈部署に〉《文》dispose; post; station; put (missiles) in position / 配置につく take up one's [a] position / 配置転換 the redeployment of labor [the labor force] within the company [between different companies in the same group (to avoid redundancies)];〈一個人の〉a transfer (to a different department). 文例⇩

ハイチ Haiti ¶ハイチの Haitian / ハイチ共和国 the Republic of Haiti / ハイチ人 a Haitian.

はいちょう 拝聴 ⇒きく³.

はいつくばう go down on all fours [on one's hands and knees]; grovel.

ハイティーン ¶ハイティーンの娘 a girl in her late teens.

はいでる 這い出る crawl [creep] out.

はいてん 配点 the allotment [allocation] of marks ¶配点する allot (20 points) to (a question).

はいでん¹ 拝殿 a front shrine.

はいでん² 配電 power supply [distribution]; supply of electric power ¶配電する supply electricity; distribute power / 配電会社 a power distribution company / 配電線 a [an electricity] main; a main(s) cable; a service wire / 配電盤 a switchboard; a panel board.

---

seems certain.
はいじん² アルコール中毒で廃人同様になった. His alcoholism has destroyed him completely.
はいすい² 今度できた船は排水量が 3 万トンある. The new ship has a displacement of 30,000 tons [displaces 30,000 tons].
ばいすう 4 と 6 は 2 の倍数である. 4 and 6 are multiples of 2.
はいせき 学長排斥運動が起こっている. A movement is afoot to oust [drive out] the president.
はいそう¹ 敵は敗走中. The enemy is on the run.
はいたつ その手紙は間違って配達された. The letter was delivered to the wrong address. / 市内は配達無料です. Goods are delivered free within the city limits. / 配達料を 500 円取られた. They charged 500 yen for delivery.
はいち 庭石の配置がよい. The stones in this garden are tastefully placed. / 警官が沿道に配置された. The police were stationed along the route. / 彼は配置転換をむしろ望んでいた. He was if anything hoping for a

ばいてん 売店 a stand; a kiosk; a stall; a booth ¶駅の売店 a station stall / 新聞の売店《米》a newsstand《英》a news(paper) stall.

バイト¹《コンピューター》a byte.

バイト²《機》a tool.

バイト³ ⇨アルバイト.

はいとう 配当《割当》(an) allotment;《分け前》a share;《株の》a dividend;《保険の》a disbursement (to a policyholder) ¶配当する allot (to); divide ((the profits among the stockholders));《配当金を》pay a dividend ((of 10 per cent on the stocks)) / 利益の配当を受ける share in the profits / 配当落ち ex dividend (略: ex div.); 配当付き cum dividend (略: cum div.);《米》dividend on.

はいとく 背徳 immorality;《文》a lapse from virtue ¶背徳者《文》an immoral [a depraved] person.

はいどく 拝読 ⇨よむ.

ばいどく 梅毒 syphilis ¶梅毒にかかる get [《文》contract] syphilis / 梅毒患者 a syphilitic (person).

パイナップル a pineapple ¶パイナップルの缶詰 canned pineapple.

はいにゅう 胚乳《植》endosperm.

はいにょう 排尿 urination ¶排尿する pass [discharge] urine; urinate.

はいにん 背任 ¶背任罪に問われる be charged with malfeasance [breach of trust].

ハイネック ¶ハイネックのセーター a high-necked sweater.

はいのう 背嚢 a knapsack; a rucksack.

はいはい ¶(赤ん坊が)はいはいする crawl.

ばいばい 売買 buying and selling;《文》purchase and sale;《取引》trade; dealing; a bargain ¶売買する buy [《文》purchase] and sell; deal [trade] in *sth* / 売買価格 the sale [selling] price / 売買契約 a contract for [of] sale. 文例↓

バイバイ《口語》bye-bye.

バイパス a by-pass.

はいび 配備 ⇨はいち ¶軍隊の配備 the disposition of troops; military dispositions.

ハイヒール high-heeled shoes; high heels.

ハイビスカス《植》a hibiscus.

はいびょう 肺病 a lung [pulmonary] disease; chest trouble ⇨はいけっかく.

はいひん 廃品 ⇨はいぶつ ¶廃品回収 collection [reclamation] of unwanted [waste] articles [materials] / 廃品回収業者 a ragman; a junk dealer.

はいふ¹ 肺腑《肺臓》⇨はい¹;《心の奥底》《文》 *one's* inmost heart ¶肺腑をえぐる《文》touch *one's* heart deeply; sting *one* to the quick; come [be brought] home to *one*.

はいふ² 配付 distribution ¶配付する distribute (among, to); deal [pass] out.

はいふ³ 配布 ¶配布する distribute widely ((among)).

はいぶ 背部 the back ⇨せ¹, せなか.

パイプ《管》a pipe; a tube;《タバコの》a (tobacco) pipe (刻みタバコの); a cigarette holder (紙巻きタバコの) ¶パイプのモール a pipe cleaner / パイプに火をつける light *one's* pipe / タバコをパイプにはさむ fit a cigarette into the holder / パイプをはたく tap [knock] *one's* pipe out; knock the ashes from *one's* pipe / パイプをくわえて[くわえたまま] with a pipe in *one's* mouth [between *one's* teeth];《文》 pipe in mouth / パイプ用のタバコ pipe [《文》 smoking] tobacco / パイプオルガン a pipe organ / パイプカットを受ける have a vasectomy / 石油をパイプ輸送する pipe petroleum (to).

ハイファイ〈装置〉a hi-fi (system) ¶ハイファイの hi-fi; high-fidelity.

はいぶつ 廃物 a useless [discarded] article; 〈くず〉waste materials; refuse;《米》trash; 《英》rubbish ¶廃物になる become useless / 廃物利用[の再利用] the reuse [recycling] of discarded articles [waste materials].

はいぶつきしゃく 排仏毀釈《日本史》the anti-Buddhist movement in the Meiji era that led to the destruction of Buddhist temples.

バイブル the Bible ⇨せいしょ² ¶釣り人のバイブル an angler's bible (★このような比喩的な用法では小文字で書く).

ハイフン a hyphen ¶ハイフンでつなぐ join [connect] ((words)) with a hyphen; hyphenate.

はいぶん 配分 distribution ¶配分する distribute (to, among); divide ((among)); allot (to); 《文》apportion (to).

はいべん 排便 ¶排便する empty [《文》evacuate] the bowels / 排便のしつけ toilet training.

ハイボール《米》a highball;《英》(a) whisky and soda.

はいぼく 敗北 (a) defeat ¶敗北する《文》be defeated; be beaten; lose (a battle [game]); 《文》suffer a defeat / ...の敗北に帰する end in

---

change of job.

ばいばい これは1トンいくらで売買される. It is sold at so much a ton. / 彼は宝石の売買をやっている. He deals in jewels.

はいぼく スペインの無敵艦隊はイギリス海軍に手ひどい敗北を喫した. The Spanish Armada suffered [met] a severe defeat at the hands of the British navy.

ばいやく¹ 「売約済み」の札がはってある. It is labeled 'Sold'.

ばいりつ 君の顕微鏡の倍率はどのくらいですか. What is the magnification of your microscope? / 倍率は1500です. It has a magnification [magnifying power] of 1,500.

はいりょ よろしくご配慮います. I hope you will kindly see to it. / ご配慮に預かりまして有り難うございます. I am much [greatly] obliged to you for your trouble.

はいる 入ってもよろしいでしょうか. May I come in? / 入りたまえ. Come in. | 〈気さくに〉Come on in. / どうぞお入り下さいと言った. He asked me (to come) in. / 入ると右手に切符売場があった. The ticket office was on the right as we entered [came in]. / 列車が入って来た. The train came [pulled] in. / 風が入るように窓を開けなさい. Open the window to let in the fresh air. / 村田君はアルコールが入ると気が大きくなる. Murata gets bolder when he takes in alcohol [when he's had

はいほん

(a) defeat for... / 敗北主義 defeatism. 文例⬇

はいほん 配本 ¶配本する distribute books [copies of a book] /「世界文学全集」の第1回配本 the first volume of the "World's Literature Series" (to be) distributed.

はいまわる 這い回る creep [crawl] about.

ばいめい 売名 self-advertisement ¶売名の徒 a publicity seeker [hunter] /売名を事とする seek [court, 〈文〉strive for] publicity /売名行為〈文〉an act of self-advertisement.

はいめん 背面 the back ¶背面攻撃 a rear attack /〈走高跳の〉背面跳び a backward jump; the Fosbury flop /背面飛行 an inverted flight.

はいもん 肺門 〖解〗the hilum of the 《right, left》 lung; the pulmonary hilum.

ハイヤー a hired car; an automobile on hire.

バイヤー a buyer.

はいやく 配役 a cast (of characters) ¶配役を決める cast [〈文〉assign] the parts 《of a play to the actors》.

ばいやく¹ 売約 a contract for [of] sale ¶売約する make [〈文〉conclude] a sales contract 《with》; make a bargain 《with》. 文例⬇

ばいやく² 売薬 a patent medicine; a drug.

はいゆ 廃油 waste oil ¶廃油ボール a waste-oil ball.

はいゆう 俳優 an actor (男); an actress (女) ¶俳優になる become an actor [actress]; go on the stage /俳優学校 a school of acting.

はいよう¹ 肺葉 〖解〗a lobe of the lung.

はいよう² 胚葉 〖生〗germ [germinal, embryonic] layers ¶外胚葉 an ectoderm; an exoderm /中胚葉 a mesoderm /内胚葉 an endoderm.

ばいよう 培養 cultivation; culture (細菌などの) ¶培養する cultivate; culture; raise /培養基 a (culture) medium /培養皿 a culture dish [plate] /培養試験[検査] a culture test /培養土 potting compost.

はいらん 排卵 ovulation ¶排卵促進剤 an ovulation stimulant; a fertility drug (通俗に).

はいりこむ 入り込む get [come, step] in [into] ⇒はいる.

ばいりつ 倍率 〖光〗(a) magnification ¶倍率8の双眼鏡 8-power binoculars; field glasses of eight magnifications /倍率の高い[低い]望遠鏡 a high-[low-]powered telescope /(入試などで)倍率が高い be highly competitive; competition is very keen. 文例⬇

はえぬき

はいりょ 配慮 〈思いやり〉consideration; 〈心配〉care; concern; 〈尽力〉trouble ¶配慮する 〈考慮する〉consider; take sth into consideration; 〈手配する〉make arrangements (for); 〈世(を то it) 《that》…〉; 〈尽力する〉take the trouble (to do) /…のご配慮により 〈文〉through sb's good offices. 文例⬇

ばいりん 梅林 an ume grove.

はいる 入る 〈内へ〉come [go, get, step] in [into]; 〈文〉enter; find one's way into; 〈押し入る〉force one's way into; break into (かぎなどをこわして); 〈加入する〉join; 〈含まれる〉be contained; be (counted) among; 〈収容し得る〉can accommodate [seat]; 〈始まる〉begin; set in ¶そっと入る steal into 《a room》 /玄関から入る go [come] in by [at] the front door /窓から入る enter by a window /会社に入る enter [find a position in] a business firm /学校に入る enter a school; be admitted to a school /クラブに入る join a club; be enrolled in a club /月に20万円入る have an income of 200,000 yen a month /9月に入ってすぐ early in September. 文例⬇

はいれい 拝礼 ⇒れいはい¹.

はいれつ 配列 arrangement ¶配列する arrange; 〈文〉dispose; put in order.

パイロット a pilot ¶パイロットランプ a pilot lamp [light].

バインダー (文房具, 農機) a binder.

はう 這う crawl; creep ¶(草木を)はわせる train 《roses against a wall》 /はって歩く crawl about; 〈四つんばいで〉go on all fours; crawl on (one's) hands and knees. 文例⬇

ハウツーもの ハウツー物 a how-to book.

バウンド ¶バウンドする bound; bounce /ワンバウンドでボールを取る catch the ball on the first bounce [bound].

パウンドケーキ (a) pound cake.

はえ¹ 栄え ¶栄えある glorious; splendid.

はえ² 蠅 a fly ¶はえのふんの染み a flyspeck /はえたたき a fly swatter /はえ取り紙 flypaper.

はえぎわ 生え際 the (receding) hairline.

はえそろう 生え揃う all come out; be all out.

はえなわ はえ縄 a longline ¶はえ縄漁業 longline fishing; long-lining.

はえぬき 生え抜き ¶生え抜きの外交官 a career diplomat /生え抜きの国鉄[早稲田]マン a person who has spent all his life [career] with J.N.R. [at Waseda] /生え抜きのニュー

---

a drink (or two)) /この切符を持って行けば入れる. This ticket will get you in. /それは本道から少し入った所だ. It is a little way off the main road. /あの家にはまだ人が入っていない. That house is still unoccupied [empty]. /私の後任にだれが入って来ましたか. Who has succeeded to my post? /この広間には500人は入る. This hall can accommodate 500 people. /この財布には3千円入っています. This wallet has 3,000 yen in it. /このびんは2リットル入る. This bottle holds two liters. /雑費も勘定に入っている. The miscellaneous expenses have been included in the account. /私もその中に入っていた. I was among [one of] them. /今月に入ってから非常に寒い. The weather has been extremely cold since the beginning of this month. /(サッカーで)後半に入って間もなく同点になった. The score was tied a short way into the second half. /入るか, 入るか, 入りました. ホームランです. It's going! It's going! It's gone! It's a home run.

はいれつ ABC順に配列せよ. Arrange them in alphabetical order [alphabetically].

はう 窓の上に朝顔をはわせてある. Some morning glories are trained up over the window.

はえ² 自分の頭のはえを追え. Mind your own business!

ヨークっ子 a native-born [trueborn] New Yorker; a New Yorker born and bred.

はえる¹ 生える〈成育する〉grow;〈伸びて出る〉come out;〈芽を出す〉spring up; sprout ¶羽が生える grow wings /〈角⦿などが〉生え変わる be shed and regrown [replaced by new growth]. 文例⇩

はえる² 映える〈光に照らされて輝く〉shine; glow;〈見ばえがする〉look attractive [better,《文》to advantage] ¶夕日に映える西の空 the western sky glowing with the splendor of the setting sun / 映えない unattractive; dull. 文例⇩

はおと 羽音 the flapping [whirring] of wings;〈虫の〉the hum [buzz(ing)]《of an insect》¶羽音をたてる〈鳥が〉flap [beat] *its* wings;〈虫の〉hum; buzz.

はおり 羽織 a *haori*; a short coat for formal wear ¶羽織袴で in *haori* and *hakama*; formally dressed;《文》in formal (Japanese) attire.

はおる 羽織る put [slip]《a *haori*》on.

はか¹ 捗 ¶はかが行く ⇨ はかどる.

はか² 墓 a grave; a tomb ¶墓を建てる raise a tomb; erect a tombstone / 墓を掘る dig a grave / 墓穴 a grave (pit) / 墓石 a gravestone; a tombstone / 墓場 a graveyard; a cemetery / 墓掘り a gravedigger / 墓参りをする visit *sb's* grave.

ばか〈ばか者〉a fool; a simpleton; a stupid person; a blockhead;〈白痴〉an idiot;〈愚かな事〉《文》(a) folly; foolishness; stupidity ¶ばかな foolish; silly; stupid; dull-witted; idiotic ⇨ 用法 / ばからしい, ばかげた, ばかばかしい silly; absurd; ridiculous; nonsensical / ばかな[ばかげた]考え a foolish idea / ばか事[真似]をする do something foolish [stupid, silly]; play [act] the fool; make a fool of *oneself* / ばかな事を言う talk nonsense [rubbish] / ばかを見る make a fool of *oneself* / ばかに〈ひどく〉terribly; awfully;《文》exceedingly;〈法外に〉unreasonably; ridiculously;《文》absurdly / ばかに寒い be terribly cold / ばかに高い be absurdly dear / ばかにする〈か

らかう〉make fun [a fool] of *sb*;〈侮る〉《文》hold *sb* [*sth*] cheap [in contempt];《文》make little of *sb* [*sth*] / ばかになる〈しびれて〉go numb [dead];《文》get benumbed;〈ねじなどが〉lose *its* grip; do not work [《文》function] /〈からしなどが〉lose *its* bite [sharpness] / 大ばか a big [damned] fool; an idiot / ばか騒ぎをやる go on the spree; indulge in (inane) horseplay / ばか正直である be honest to a fault / ばか力がある have prodigious [enormous] strength / ばか丁寧な excessively polite;〈念を入れすぎた〉too thorough / ばか値 a fantastic price / ばかばやし festival music / ばか笑いする laugh boisterously; give a horse-laugh. 文例⇩

用法「ばかな」を表わす英語として, silly は相手に与える感じが柔らかであるのに反して, stupid は相手の愚鈍さを指摘しているから, 感情を害する恐れがある. foolish と absurd は共に「道理又は常識に反した」の意であって, 主に発言や行為に関して使われる.

はかい¹ 破戒 violation [transgression] of the《Buddhist》commandments ¶破戒僧 a depraved monk [priest].

はかい² 破壊 destruction; demolition ¶破壊する destroy; break; demolish / 家庭を破壊する disrupt *one's* family / 破壊的 destructive; subversive / 破壊活動防止法 the Anti-Subversive Activities Act / 大量破壊兵器 a weapon of mass destruction / 破壊分子 a subversive (element) / 破壊力 destructive power.

はがいじめ 羽交い締め ¶羽交い締めにする pinion.

ばかがい 馬鹿貝 a surf clam.

はがき 葉書《米》a postal card (官製); a postcard (私製);《英》a postcard (官製・私製とも) ¶葉書で by postcard / 葉書を出す send [drop] a (postal) card (to).

はかく 破格 an exception;〈語法違反〉a solecism ¶破格の〈例外的〉exceptional; unprecedented; special;〈変則的〉irregular;〈語法違反の〉solecistic. 文例⇩

はがす 剝がす ⇨ はぐ¹.

はえる¹ 庭には草がぼうぼうと生えている. The garden is overgrown with weeds.

はえる² 桜の花が朝日に映えている. The cherry blossoms are shining in the rising sun. / 新しく植えた松のおかげで庭が一層映える. The newly planted pine tree lends even more charm to the garden.

はか² お墓に花が供えてあった. There were flowers on the grave.

ばか そんなことを言うとはあの男もずいぶんばかだ. It is very silly of him to say such a thing. / 彼はそんな事をするほどばかじゃない. He knows better than to do something [a thing] like that. / ばか言え! Nonsense! | Get along [away] with you! / ばかにもほど

がある. How can you be so silly? / こんな辞書を作るなんて, ばかにならなきゃできやしない. You've got to be crazy to make a dictionary like this. / ばかばかしくて話にならない. It is too absurd to be taken seriously. / 10円 20円の金でもばかにはならない. / 1年たてば相当な額になる. Don't make light of pennies and dimes; they may add up to something by the end of the year. / ばかに安く買った. I bought them at an absurdly low price. / 風邪を引いて鼻がばかになっている. I've got a cold and can't smell a thing. / ばかにつける薬はない. No medicine can cure a fool. / ばかは死ななきゃ直らない. He who is born a fool is never cured. 諺 /

ばかほどこわいものはない. A fool may go to any extremes. / ばかとはさみは使いようで切れる. Praise a fool, and you may make him useful. / ばかの一つ覚え. A fool's memory sticks to one thing. | He that knows little often repeats it. 諺 / このばかやろう! You bloody [damn(ed)] fool!

はかく 君のは破格の昇進だ. Yours is an exceptional promotion.

はかどる 仕事ははかどっていますか. Are you getting along [doing well] with your work? / 建築工事はあまりはかどっていない. The construction work is progressing at a snail's pace.

はかない すべてこの世の幸福はは

ばかす 化かす bewitch; enchant.
ばかず 場数 ¶場数を踏む gain [add to *one's*] experience / 場数を踏んでいる have long [a lot of] experience 《of, in》.
はかせ 博士 ⇨ はくし².
はがた 歯形 a tooth mark.
はかどる 捗る 《文》 advance; 《文》 progress; make (good) progress ¶なかなかはかどらない make slow [do not make much] progress / はかどらせる speed up; 《文》 hasten; 《文》 expedite. 文例△
はかない short-lived; 《文》 fleeting; 《文》 transient; 《空虚な》《文》 vain; hopeless 《望みのない》; 《もろい》 fragile; frail ¶はかない人生 《文》 transient [ephemeral] life / はかない望みをいだく 《文》 entertain a vain hope《that...》; hope against hope 《that...》 / はかない夢 an empty dream. 文例△
はかなむ despair 《of the world》; lose all hope 《in life》.
はがね 鋼 steel ¶鋼色 steel blue.
ばかばか clip-clop; clippety-clop. 文例△
はかばかしい 《迅速な》 rapid; quick; 《満足な》 satisfactory ¶はかばかしい do not make much progress; be not doing well. 文例△
はかぶ 端株 odd-[broken-]lot stocks; an odd [a broken] lot.
はかま 《衣服の》 a *hakama*; a (Japanese) skirt for formal wear; 《徳利の》 a (bottle) stand.
はがみ 歯がみ ⇨ はぎしり.
はがゆい 歯がゆい 《人が主語》 feel impatient 《at》; lose 《one's》 patience 《with》; 《事が主語》 be irritating.
はからい 計らい 《処置》 management; arrangement; 《世話》《文》 good offices; 《裁量》 discretion ¶...の計らいで 《世話》 through the good offices of...; 《裁量》 at *sb's* (own) discretion. 文例△
はからう 計らう 《処置する》 manage; 《あんばいする》 arrange; 《処分する》 dispose of; 《なんとかする》 see to *sth* ¶いいように計らう arrange *sth* as *one* thinks best [fit]; see (to it) that everything is all right.

はからずも 図らずも unexpectedly; by chance [accident] ¶図らずも ...する happen [《文》 chance] to *do*.
はかり¹ 計[量]り measure (量); weight (重さ) ¶計りをよく [さく] する give good [short] measure [weight].
はかり² 秤 〈天秤(ﾋﾝ)〉 a balance; (a pair of) scales; 〈さおばかり〉 a steelyard; 〈ぜんまいばかり〉 a spring balance; 〈自動ばかり〉 a dial scale; 〈台ばかり〉 a platform scale; 〈大型計器器〉 a weighing machine ¶はかりのさお a balance beam / はかりの皿 the scales of a balance; a scale pan / はかりにかける weigh *sth* (in the balance [on the scales]) / 〈比較考量する〉 weigh 《A》 with [against] 《B》.
-ばかり 〈およそ〉 about; some; 《米》 around; ...or so [thereabouts]; 〈...のみ〉 only; 〈ただ〉 (a) mere; alone; 〈ほとんど〉 almost; all but; 〈事実上〉 practically; 〈...して間もない〉 just now; 〈...せんとして〉 be about to *do*; 《be》 on the point of *doing* ¶1週間ばかり a week or so / 30年ばかり以前 some [about] thirty years ago / ...であるばかりに only [simply] because...; simply on account of... / ...ばかりでなく...も not only 《A》 but (also) 《B》; 《B》 as well as 《A》 / 生きていると言っても名ばかりである be practically [all but] dead; be as good as dead / ...と言わぬばかりに as much as to say (that...) / 泣いてばかりいる keep crying; do nothing but cry; be always crying / これほばかりの金 such a small sum / こればかりの事[物] such a trifle. 用例△ 「A ばかりでなく B も」を英語で as well as を使って言う時、B as well as A の形もないではあるが、近年は A as well as B の形もかなり一般的になってきた。John came as well as Mary. は今でも明らかに「Mary ばかりか John までやってきた」の意であるが、John as well as Mary came. となると、「John も Mary もやってきた」程度の意味で、「Mary ばかりでなく John までやってきた」の意味を明確に持っているとは言い難くなっている。
はかりうり 量[計]り売り ¶量り売りする sell *sth* by measure [weight].
はかりごと 〈計画〉 a plan; 《文》 a design; a scheme; 〈計略〉 a trick; a snare; 《文》 a strat-

---

ことにはかないものである。How transient all happiness is in this world! / 人生ははかないものだ。Life is but an empty dream.
ばかぱか 彼はばかばかと馬を走らせて行った。His horse clip-clopped off down the road.
はかばかしい 彼の病気ははかばかしくありません。He has not been making any noticeable recovery. / His condition shows very little improvement. / 商売がはかばかしくない。The business is not doing well.
はからい 君の計らいでいいようにしてくれたまえ。You can do with it as you think fit [best]. / これはお任せします。I leave it to your discretion.
-ばかり 私ばかりが悪いのではない。I am not the only one to blame. / 金もうけばかりが人生の目的ではない。Moneymaking is not the sole end and aim of life. / そればかりではない。That is not all. / 学問ばかりでは成功できない。Mere scholarship will not win success for you. / 彼女は泣くばかりだった。She did nothing but cry. / テレビばかり見ているわけではない。I don't give all my time to watching TV. / I don't spend all my time watching TV. / そういう悩みは君ばかりではない。You are not the only one that is troubled by that sort of thing. / この時ばかりは彼が憎らしかった。For this once [On this occasion] I found him detestable. / 何でもあげるがこの時

計ばかりはあげられない。I will give you anything but this watch. / 彼は英語ばかりでなくフランス語も話す。He speaks French as well as English. / Besides English, he speaks French. / 彼は親に心配ばかりかけている。He is a constant source of anxiety to his parents. / 物価は上がるばかりだ。Prices go [keep] on rising. / 今日の勉強をやっと今終わったばかりだ。I have just finished my work for today. / 今朝着いたばかりです。I arrived here this morning. / 2人はなぐり合いを始めたばかりであった。They were on the point of coming to blows. / ふるえあがって腰を抜かさんばかりだった。He was virtually para-

はかる agem ; 〈陰謀〉 a plot. 文例⇩

はかる¹ 計量, 測る 〈度・量を〉 measure ; 〈相方を〉 weigh ; 〈測定する〉 survey ; 〈深さなどを〉 sound ; 〈算定する〉 calculate ; 〈評価する〉 estimate ¶身長を計る measure sb's height / 体温を計る take one's temperature / 体重を計る weigh oneself [sb] / 測りがたい 〈数・量の〉《文》 immeasurable ; 《文》 incalculable / 〈値段が〉 inestimable ; 《文》 《水深が》《文》 unfathomable / 計り知れない 〈不可解な〉 mysterious ; 《文》 unfathomable ; 《文》 inscrutable.

はかる² 謀[計, 図]る 〈画策する〉 plan sth ; 《文》 design ; scheme ; plot ; 〈欺く〉 deceive ; take sb in ; 〈努める〉 strive for ¶自殺を図る attempt suicide / 殺害を謀る plot sb's murder ; make an attempt on sb's life. 文例⇩

はかる³ 諮る 〈相談する〉 consult (with) sb ; confer with sb ; ask sb's opinion ; 〈会議にかける〉 refer (a plan) to a conference.

はがれる 剥がれる come [peel] off.

はがんいっしょう 破顔一笑 ¶破顔一笑する break into a broad smile.

バカンス [〈(フランス語) vacances〉] (米) a vacation ; (英) holidays ⇒ きゅうか².

はき¹ 破棄 〈無効にする事〉 annulment ; 〈取り消し〉 cancellation ; breach (約束の) ; abrogation (条約の) ; reversal (判決の) ¶破棄する annul ((an agreement)) ; cancel ((a contract)) ; break ((a promise)) ; abrogate ((a lease)) ; (口語) scrap ((a treaty)) ; reverse ((a sentence)) / 原判決を破棄する quash [reverse] the original judgment [decision].

はき² 覇気 〈意気〉 spirit ; 〈野心〉 ambition ; 《文》 aspirations ¶覇気のある full of spirit ; ambitious.

はぎ¹ 脛 ⇒すね.

はぎ² 萩 [植] a hagi ; a Japanese bush clover.

はぎ³ 接ぎ ⇒つぎ².

はきけ 吐き気 nausea ; a sickly feeling ¶吐き気を催す feel like vomiting ; feel sick [nausea] ; retch / 吐き気を催させる cause nausea ; make one sick (at the stomach) ; turn one's stomaching / 吐き気を催させるような光景 a nauseating [sickening] sight / 吐き気止めの(薬) an anti-nausea drug. 文例⇩

はぎしり 歯ぎしり ¶歯ぎしりする grind [gnash] one's teeth ((with vexation, while one is asleep)).

パキスタン Pakistan ¶パキスタンの Pakistani / パキスタン回教共和国 the Islamic Republic of Pakistan / パキスタン人 a Pakistani.

はきそうじ 掃き掃除 ¶掃き掃除をする sweep and clean ; sweep up.

はきだす¹ 吐き出す 〈吐く〉 vomit (up [out]) ; spew (up [out]) ; 《文》 disgorge ; 《俗》 throw up ; 〈息を〉 breathe out ; 《文》 exhale ; 〈煙などを〉 belch ; puff out ; 《文》 emit ; send up [out, 《文》 forth] ¶吐き出すように言う spit [rap] out. 文例⇩

はきだす² 掃き出す sweep out ((the dust)) ; sweep up ((a room)).

はきだめ 掃き溜め a dump ; a rubbish heap ¶はきだめに鶴 a jewel in a dunghill.

はきちがえる 履き違える 〈履き物を〉 wear somebody else's shoes [geta] ; put one's shoes on the wrong feet (左右を) ; 〈考え違いする〉 mistake [take] (A) for (B) ; have a wrong [mistaken] idea of ((democracy)). 文例⇩

はきつぶす 履きつぶす wear out ((through)) ((two pairs of shoes)).

はぎとる はぎ取る 〈はがす〉 strip [take, tear] sth off ((away)) ; 〈強奪する〉 rob sb of ((his clothes)).

はきはき 〈きびきびと〉 briskly ; 〈歯切れよく〉 crisply ; 〈はっきりと〉 smartly ¶はきはき返事をする answer clearly and crisply. 文例⇩

はきもの 履き物 footwear.

ばきゃく 馬脚 ¶馬脚をあらわす betray oneself ; give oneself away. 文例⇩

はきゅう 波及 ¶波及する 〈…に及ぶ〉 spread (to) ; 《文》 extend (to) ; 〈影響する〉 influence ; affect ; have repercussions. 文例⇩

はきょく 破局 a catastrophe ; a collapse ¶破局的の catastrophic.

はぎれ 歯切れ ¶歯切れがいい 〈言葉が〉 be crisp ; 〈人が〉 have a clear and crisp way of speaking / 歯切れが悪い 〈言葉が〉 be inarticulate ; 〈人が〉 slur one's words ; do not make oneself quite clear [《文》 explicit] (はっきりしたことを言わない).

はく¹ 泊 ¶1泊 ⇒いっぱく / 2, 3泊する stay for two or three nights / 4泊5日の旅行 a trip of five days and four nights.

はく² 箔 foil ; leaf ¶はくがつく gain prestige [a reputation] ((as a politician)) / はくを置く[塗る] put (silver) leaf ((over)) ; 〈金の〉 cover sth with (gold) leaf / はくをつける make oneself look more important ; add to its value.

---

lyzed with terror. / 飯は炊くばかりになっている。The rice only needs boiling. | The rice is ready for cooking.

はかりごと はかりごとは密なるを良しとす。Secrecy is the soul of [is essential to] strategy.

はかる¹ この紙の長さと幅とを計ってみて下さい。Please measure the length and width of this piece of paper. | Please find out how long and wide this sheet of paper is.

はかる² 産業を盛んにして国家の繁栄を図らねばならない。We should develop our industries for the sake of national prosperity. / 事を図るは人にあり, 事を成すは天にあり。Man proposes ; God disposes.

はきけ それを見ただけで吐き気がした。The very sight of it made me feel sick. | My stomach turned at the mere sight of it.

はきだす¹「勝手にしろ, 僕は知らないよ」と彼は吐き出すように言った。He spat [rapped] out, 'Do it your own way. I don't care.' / 毎日何万という乗客がこの駅から吐き出される。Tens of thousands of passengers get off the trains at [pour out of] this station every day. / 植物は炭酸ガスを吸って酸素を吐き出す。Plants breathe in carbon dioxide and breathe out oxygen.

はきちがえる だれかが僕の靴を履き違えて行った。Someone has gone out in my shoes by mistake. / 彼は自由と放縦を履きちがえている。He is confusing freedom with license.

はく³ 吐く〈吐き出す〉spew (up [out]); spit (out);〈嘔吐する〉vomit;《俗》throw up;〈噴出する〉belch;《文》emit; send up [out,《文》forth];〈息を〉breathe out ¶血を吐く ⇨ち¹/意见を吐く give [express] *one's* opinion《on, about》. 文例⊕

はく⁴ 掃く sweep ((the floor)) ¶まゆを掃く pencil *one's* eyebrows / 掃き寄せる[集める] sweep together.

はく⁵ 履く put on;〈履いている〉wear; have on ¶履いてみる〈a try (the shoes) on / 履き替える change ((*one's* socks)). 文例⊕

はぐ¹ 剝ぐ tear [peel, strip] off;〈皮を〉skin;〈奪う〉strip ((*sb of his* clothes)) ¶木の皮をはぐ peel [strip] the bark from a tree; bark a tree.

はぐ² 接ぐ ⇨つぐ³.

ばく¹《動》a tapir.

ばく² 漠 ⇨ばくぜん.

ばぐ 馬具 harness; horse [riding] gear ¶馬具をつける[はずす] harness [unharness] ((a horse)) / 馬具屋 a harness maker; a saddler.

はくあ 白亜 chalk ¶白亜紀《地質》the Cretaceous (period) / 白亜質の chalky.

はくあい 博愛《文》philanthropy ¶博愛主義《文》philanthropism.

はくい 白衣 a white robe [dress];〈医者などの〉a white coat ¶白衣の天使 an angel in white; a nurse.

ばくおん 爆音 buzzing; a whirr; a roar ¶爆音を立てて飛ぶ fly with a whirr. 文例⊕

ばくが 麦芽 malt ¶麦芽糖 maltose.

はくがい 迫害 persecution; oppression ¶迫害する persecute; oppress / 迫害を受ける be persecuted;《文》suffer persecution / 迫害者 a persecutor; an oppressor.

はくがく 博学《文》erudition;《文》extensive learning; wide knowledge ¶博学の《文》erudite;《文》learned.

はくがんし 白眼視 ¶白眼視する look coldly on; look askance at; have [take] a prejudiced view of / 世の中を白眼視する take refuge in cynicism;《文》affect a detached irony; turn *one's* back on the world.

はぐき 歯茎 the gums.

はぐくむ 育む〈子を〉bring up; rear; foster;〈学問などを〉promote; encourage.

ばくげき 爆撃 (aerial) bombing [bombardment] ¶爆撃する bomb; drop bombs ((on a city)) / 爆撃機 a bomber.

はくげきほう 迫撃砲 a trench mortar.

はくさい 白菜 a Chinese cabbage.

はくし¹ 白紙 white paper; a blank sheet of paper ¶白紙の答案を出す hand [turn] in a blank (answer) paper / 白紙に返す get back to where *one* was at the start;《英》go back to square one; start afresh [from scratch] / 白紙で臨む meet sb with an open mind;《文》do without preconceived ideas / 白紙委任する give *sb* carte blanche ((in a matter)) / 白紙委任状 a blank power of attorney; a carte blanche《pl. cartes blanches》.

はくし² 博士 a doctor ¶湯川博士 Dr. Yukawa / 博士課程 a doctoral course (in history) / 博士課程の学生 a doctoral student / 博士号をとる take [get,《文》obtain] a doctorate (in economics) / 博士論文 a thesis for a doctorate [doctor's degree]; a doctoral thesis [dissertation].

はくじ 白磁 white porcelain.

ばくし 爆死 ¶爆死する be killed by a bomb.

はくしき 博識 wide ((文)) extensive) knowledge;〈博学〉erudition ¶博識な〈博学な〉《文》learned;《文》erudite;〈物知りの〉well-informed; well-read.

はくじつ 白日 ¶白日のもとにさらされる be brought to light; be exposed to the light of day [to the public eye] / 白日夢 ⇨はくちゅう¹ (白昼夢).

はくしゃ¹ 拍車 a spur ¶馬に拍車を入れる spur (on) ((馬)) put spurs to) *one's* horse / インフレ傾向に拍車をかける spur on the inflationary tendency / 学生運動に拍車をかける give (an) impetus to the student movement.

はくしゃ² 薄謝 a small token of *one's* gratitude; a small reward;〈袋の上書き〉With compliments.

はくしゃく 伯爵 a count;《英》an earl ¶伯爵夫人 a countess ★イギリスの伯爵 (earl) の夫人のみ countess という.

はくじゃく 薄弱 ¶薄弱な weak; feeble; frail;《文》infirm / 意志薄弱である ⇨いし³ (意志が弱い). 文例⊕

はくしゅ 拍手 a handclap; (a) clapping of hands ¶あらしのような[割れるような]拍手 thunderous [a storm of] applause / 拍手する clap *one's* hands (in applause) /《口語》give *sb* a (big) hand / 立ち上がって拍手する give *sb* a

---

はぎとる 彼は着物をはぎ取られた. He was stripped of his clothes.

はきはき 彼ははきはきしない男だ. He is dull [slow].

ばきゃく あんなことを言ったので馬脚が現われた. He gave himself away by blurting it out.

はきゅう この事件は政界に波及する所が大であった. This affair has greatly affected [has had great repercussions in] the political world.

はく¹ (ホテルの予約係が)何泊のご予定でいらっしゃいますか. How long are you going to stay, sir?

はく³ 彼は指を3本のどに突っ込んで吐こうとした. He stuck three fingers down his throat to make himself vomit. / 彼は食べた物をみな吐いてしまう. He cannot keep anything down. / はるかかなたに浅間山が煙を吐いていた. Far away Mt. Asama could be seen, belching [sending up] smoke from its summit.

はく⁵ 彼は長靴を履いている. He has long boots on. / そのズボンはまだ履ける. Those trousers are still wearable.

ばくおん 飛行機の爆音が聞こえた. The sound of airplane engines was heard.

はくし² 彼は東京大学で法学博士の学位を取った. He took the degree of Doctor of Laws [his doctorate in law] at Tokyo University.

はくしゃ² お知らせ下さった方に薄謝を呈します. A reward is offered for any information.

はくじゃく その主張は根拠薄弱

はくしょ

standing ovation / 盛んな拍手を受ける receive warm [loud] applause (from); 《口語》get a big hand / 拍手で迎える clap *sb* in; welcome [greet] *sb* with a clapping of hands / 拍手かっさい cheers; applause. 文例⇩

はくしょ 白書 a white paper ¶経済白書を出す issue [publish] an economic white paper.

はくじょう¹ 白状 (a) confession ¶白状する confess ((that…, to a crime)); own up ((to *one's* misdeed, to having *done*)) / 一切を白状する make a full confession; make a clean breast of ((*one's* secret)); 《口語》come clean about ((what *one* has done)).

はくじょう² 薄情 ¶薄情な《文》unfeeling; heartless; cold-hearted; cruel / 薄情なことをする treat *sb* cruelly; be unkind to *sb*; be hard on *sb*.

ばくしょう 爆笑 ¶爆笑する burst out laughing; burst into [roar with] laughter.

はくしょく 白色 white ¶白色の white / 白色人種 ⇒はくじん.

はくしょん atchoo!; atishoo!

はくしん 迫真《文》verisimilitude ¶迫真性のある true to life; realistic / 迫真的に《文》with 《great》verisimilitude. 文例⇩

はくじん 白人 a white man; a Caucasian; 〈人種〉the white race(s) ¶白人による支配 white rule [domination] (in Africa).

はくしん(ち) 爆心(地) the center of the explosion; 〈原爆の〉the hypocenter; ground zero.

はくする 博する ¶かっさいを博する win [be greeted with] applause / 巨利を博する get [earn] a big profit / 信用を博する win *sb's* confidence; gain credit with *sb*.

はくせい 剝製 a stuffed animal [bird] ¶剝製にする stuff [mount] ((a bird)) / 剝製師 a taxidermist / 剝製術 taxidermy.

はくせん 白線 a white line; 〈駅のプラットフォームの〉a warning [white] line. 文例⇩

ばくぜん 漠然 ¶漠然とした vague; obscure; dim; indistinct; ambiguous (あいまいな) / 漠然としかわからない have only a vague idea of *sth*. 文例⇩

はくそ 歯くそ (dental [bacterial]) plaque.

ばくだい 莫大 ¶莫大な vast; huge; immense; enormous / 莫大な金額 a huge [vast] sum (of money) / 莫大な損害 a tremendous [an enormous] loss / 莫大な富 immense [colossal] wealth.

はくだつ 剝奪 ¶剝奪する strip [《文》deprive] *sb* of ((*his* office)); 《文》divest *sb* of ((*his* rank)).

バクダッド Bag(h)dad.

ばくだん 爆弾 a bomb; a bombshell ¶爆弾を投下する drop [throw] bombs ((on a town)) / 爆弾宣言をする《口語》drop a bombshell; a bombshell announcement / 爆弾動議を出す move [present] a snap [surprise] motion ((in the Diet)).

はくち 白痴 〈状態〉idiocy; 〈人〉an idiot.

ばくち 博奕 gambling ¶ばくちを打つ gamble; play for money [stakes] / 大ばくちを打つ play for high stakes; gamble heavily / ばくちで身上をつぶす gamble *oneself* out of house and home; gamble away *one's* fortune / ばくち打ち a gambler.

ばくちく 爆竹 a (fire)cracker ¶爆竹を鳴らす set off firecrackers.

はくちゅう¹ 白昼 ¶白昼に in broad daylight; in the daytime / 白昼堂々と openly [unashamedly] in broad daylight / 白昼夢 a daydream; daydreaming.

はくちゅう² 伯仲 ¶伯仲する be equal (to); be on a par ((with)); be evenly matched. 文例⇩

はくちょう 白鳥 a swan ¶白鳥の子 a young swan; a cygnet / 白鳥の湖〈バレー〉*Swan Lake* / 大白鳥〈日本で見る普通の種類〉a whooper [hooper] swan.

ばくつく 〈ぱくぱく食べる〉eat ((*one's* food)) in big mouthfuls; take quick [greedy] bites ((of, at, out of)); 〈くらそうに〉eat ((*one's* food)) with relish.

バクテリア a bacterium ((*pl*. -teria)).

はくとう 白桃 a white peach.

はくどう 白銅 nickel ¶白銅貨 a nickel coin ★《米》では単に a nickel というと「5セント貨」の意.

はくないしょう 白内障【医】cataract.

はくねつ 白熱 white heat; incandescence ¶白熱する become white-hot; be incandescent / 白熱的討議 a heated discussion [debate] / 白熱戦 a close contest; a blistering [thrilling] race.

ばくは 爆破 ¶爆破する blow up; blast.

バグパイプ 〈楽器〉(play) the [a set of] bagpipes.

ばくばく ⇒ばくつく.

はくはつ 白髪 ⇒しらが.

ばくはつ 爆発 an explosion; detonation; blowing up; 〈火山の〉(an) eruption ¶爆発する explode; blow up; burst; 〈火山が〉erupt / 爆発寸前である be close to (the) explosion point / 人口の爆発的増加 a population explosion; an explosive increase of population / 爆発物 an explosive. 文例⇩

だ. The claim is based on flimsy [tenuous] grounds.

はくしゅ 拍手が止んだ[まばらになった]. The clapping died down [thinned out]. / 氏が姿を現わすと割れるような拍手が起こった. A storm of clapping greeted his appearance. / あらしのような拍手のうちに演説を終えた. He finished his speech amidst a storm of applause.

はくじょう² 私にはそんな薄情な事はできない. I haven't the heart to be so cruel.

はくしん 彼のガンジーは迫真の演技だった. On the stage he was Gandhi to the life. / His portrayal of Gandhi carried complete conviction.

はくせん 白線の内側にお下がり下さい. 〈駅のアナウンス〉Please stand behind [《米》back of] the white line.

ばくぜん この説明はあまりに漠然としている. This explanation is too vague.

はくちゅう² 両チームは技術面でほとんど伯仲していた. The opposing teams were nearly equal in skill.

ばくばく 弁当をばくばく食べた. He wolfed [gobbled] his lunch down. / 鯉がばくばくえさを食べ

はくび 白眉 the finest example 《of》; the best 《of》 ¶英国短編小説の白眉 one of the best British short stories.

はくひょう¹ 白票 〈白紙のままの〉《cast》a blank ballot [vote]; 〈国会での〉a white ballot (indicating 'aye').

はくひょう² 薄氷 thin ice ¶薄氷を踏む思いである feel as if one were treading [skating] on thin ice.

ばくふ 幕府 the shogunate ¶徳川幕府時代に in the days of the Tokugawa shogunate [regime].

ばくふう 爆風 (a) bomb blast; (a) blast (from an explosion).

はくぶつ(がく) 博物(学) natural history ¶博物学者 a naturalist; a natural historian / 博物標本 a natural history specimen.

はくぶつかん 博物館 a museum ¶自然博物館 a natural history museum. 文例↓

はくへいせん 白兵戦 hand-to-hand fighting; close [hand-to-hand] combat.

はくぼ 薄暮 ⇒ ゆうぐれ, たそがれ.

はくぼく 白墨 ⇒ チョーク.

はくまい 白米 cleaned rice.

ばくまつ 幕末 ¶幕末の[に] in the last [closing] days of the Tokugawa shogunate [regime].

はくめい¹ 薄命《文》a sad [hapless] fate ¶薄命の unfortunate; unlucky;《文》ill-fated[-starred].

はくめい² 薄明 twilight; faint [dim] light.

はくや 白夜 ⇒ びゃくや.

ばくやく 爆薬 an explosive ¶爆薬を仕掛ける set [lay] an explosive (charge).

はくらい 舶来 ¶舶来の imported (from abroad); foreign-made / 舶来品 an imported [a foreign-made] article.

ばくらい 爆雷 a depth charge.

はぐらかす ¶〈連れをまく〉give sb the slip;〈質問などを〉dodge (duck, evade) (a question).

はくらんかい 博覧会 an exhibition;《米》an exposition;《米》a fair ¶博覧会場 exhibition grounds;《米》fairgrounds.

はくらんきょうき 博覧強記 ¶博覧強記の人《文》a learned man with a retentive memory.

はくり 薄利 a small profit ¶薄利多売 small profits and quick returns.

ぱくり ぱっくり ¶ぱくりと食いつく[口に入れる] snap at [up] (a piece of meat).

はくりきこ 薄力粉 weak flour.

ばくりょう 幕僚 a member of the staff; a staff officer; the staff (総称).

はくりょく 迫力 force; power;《口語》punch ¶迫力がある be powerful; be moving; appeal strongly (to). 文例↓

はぐるま 歯車 a cogwheel; a gear wheel; a cog; a toothed wheel ¶歯車装置 a gear. 文例↓

はぐれる get [go] astray; lose sight of [《文》stray from] (one's companions).

ばくろ 暴露《文》disclosure;《文》exposure ¶暴露する〈さらけ出す〉reveal; expose;《文》disclose; bring (a matter) to light;《口語》rake (up) the muck (about);〈露見する〉be discovered;《文》be disclosed; be exposed; be betrayed; come [be brought] to light / 自分の無知を暴露する betray one's ignorance / 暴露記事 an exposé / 暴露戦術 exposure [《米口語》muckraking] tactics. 文例↓

ばくろう 博労 a horse dealer.

はくろうびょう 白蠟病 pseudo-Raynaud's disease; a vibration syndrome (occurring in users of chain saws and similar machinery).

はけ¹ 刷毛 a brush ¶ブラシ ¶ペンキ用のはけ a paintbrush.

はけ² 捌け 〈排水〉drainage; draining;〈売れ行き〉sale; demand (需要) ¶はけがよい[悪い] ⇒ はける.

はげ 禿 baldness;〈はげた所〉a bald patch [spot] ¶はげを隠す hide one's baldness 《with a hat》/ はげ頭 a bald head /〈人〉a baldheaded person / はげ山 a bare [treeless] hill.

はげいとう《植》a tampala.

はけぐち 捌け口 〈水などの〉an outlet (for);〈商品の〉a market (for);〈感情の〉(a) vent (for) ¶うっ積した感情のはけ口を見出す find vent for one's pent-up feelings. 文例↓

はげしい 激しい violent; strong;〈文〉vehement; fierce; furious;〈熱烈な〉《文》ardent;《文》fervent ¶激しい暑さ intense heat / 激しい痛み an acute [a sharp] pain / 激しい気性 a violent [fiery] temper / 激しい議論 a hot [heated] argument / 激しい競争 keen [stiff] competition / 激しく violently;《文》vehemently; hard; furiously / 激しさ violence; intensity. 文例↓

はげたか《鳥》a vulture.

バケツ a bucket ¶バケツ1杯の水 a bucketful of water.

ばけのかわ 化けの皮 ¶化けの皮がはげる reveal one's true character; give oneself away /

ていた. The carp were snapping eagerly at the meat.

ばくはつ すさまじい音を立てて爆発した. It blew up with a terrific bang.

ばくふう あの花火工場が爆発してもここまで爆風が来ようとは予想もしなかった. I never thought the blast would reach this far even if that fireworks plant exploded.

はくぶつかん 全く博物館行きの代物だ. That's an absolute museum piece.

はくりょく 彼の言葉には迫力があった. There was plenty of punch in his remarks.

はぐるま 歯車がかみ合わなかった. The gears didn't [failed to] mesh. / ここで働いていると, 自分は歯車の歯の1つに過ぎないと思えてくる. Working here, I am made to feel a mere cog in a machine.

ばくろ その会社の内情が暴露された. The real condition of the company was disclosed [brought to light].

はけぐち 彼は精力のはけ口がなくて, 部屋の中をただぐるぐる歩き回っていた. He was walking around and around the room, unable to work off his energy.

はげしい 2人は激しい競争をしている. There is keen competition between the two of them. / 雨が

はげます 化けの皮をはぐ unmask.
はげます 励ます encourage; urge; cheer up ¶自分の心を励ます brace *oneself* 《to do, for a task》/ 声を励ます raise [lift] *one's* voice / 励まして…させる encourage *sb* to *do*.
はげみ 励み encouragement ¶励みになる(ような) encouraging. 文例⇩
はげむ 励む 《文》 strive 《for, to *do*》; make efforts 《to *do*》; apply [devote] *oneself* to 《a task》 ¶学業に励む work hard at *one's* lessons. 文例⇩
ばけもの 化け物 《妖怪》 a bog(e)y; a (hob-)goblin; 《怪物》 a monster; 《幽霊》 a ghost; a phantom; a specter ¶化け物みたいに大きなりんご a monster 《of an》 apple / 化け物屋敷 a haunted house. 文例⇩
はける 捌ける 《水が》 drain; flow off; run out; 《売れる》 sell; be in demand ¶《商品が》よくはける[はけない] sell well [do not sell]; find a ready [no] sale [market]; be in good [poor] demand / 水がはける[はけない] drain well [poorly, badly].
はげる¹ 剝げる 《塗りなどが》 come [peel] off; be worn off; 《色が》 fade; discolor ¶はげない[はげやすい]色 a fast [non-fast, 《文》 fugitive] color / 色のはげた faded; discolored / 洗ってもはげない stand washing [the wash]; wash well. 文例⇩
はげる² 禿げる 《頭が》 go [《文》 become] bald; 《山などが》 become bare ¶頭がはげかかっている人 a man who is going bald; a balding man / 頭のてっぺんのはげた with a bald patch on the crown of *one's* head. 文例⇩
ばける 化ける 《変化する》 take the shape 《of》; turn [change, transform] *itself* 《into》 / 《変装する》 disguise *oneself* 《as》. 文例⇩
はげわし 《鳥》 a vulture.
はけん¹ 派遣 派遣する send; dispatch 《a representative》; detail 《troops》 / 派遣団 a delegation; a contingent.
はけん² 覇権 《文》 hegemony ¶覇権を握る hold supremacy 《in》; gain the hegemony 《of》; 《競技で》 win a championship / 海上の覇権を握る dominate [rule] the seas.
ばけん 馬券 a betting ticket [slip] 《on a horse》 ¶馬券売場 a betting booth; a ticket window [office].
はこ 箱 a box; a case; 《ひつ》 a chest ¶りんご 1 箱 a box of apples / 箱に入れる[詰める] put [pack] *sth* in a box [case] / 箱詰めの packed in a case; boxed ¶箱入り娘 a girl brought up with tender care 《in a good family》; an innocent girl who knows nothing of the world / 箱庭 a miniature garden.
はごいた 羽子板 a battledore.
はごたえ 歯ごたえ ¶歯ごたえがある be hard to chew; be tough 《硬い》/ 柔らかすぎて歯ごたえがない be too soft.
はこび 運び 《進捗》 progress; 《進展》 development; 《段階》 a stage; 《手はず》 arrangements ¶足の運びが遅い walk at a slow pace. 文例⇩
はこぶ 運ぶ carry; 《文》 convey; transport; take [bring] *sth* to 《a place》; 《はかどる》 make (good) progress; go 《on》 well; be well under way ¶手[車]で運ぶ carry *sth* 《to a place》 by hand [car] / 列車[航空機]で運ぶ transport 《goods》 by train [air] / 運び出す[込む] carry *sth* out of [into] 《a room》 / 運び去る carry [take] *sth* away. 文例⇩
はこべ 《植》 chickweed.
はこやなぎ 《植》 an [a Japanese] aspen; a poplar.
はごろも 羽衣 a robe of feathers ¶天人の羽衣 《文》 the celestial raiment [robe] of an angel.
バザー a bazaar.
はざかいき 端境期 the preharvest month(s).
はざくら 葉桜 a cherry tree whose blossoms have fallen(, revealing the fresh green leaves).
はさばさ rustlingly; with a rustle ¶《葉が》ばさばさ音を立てる rustle 《in the wind》. 文例⇩
はさまる 挟まる ¶はさまれる be caught in; get jammed in; 《間にある》 lie [get] between; be sandwiched between ¶歯にはさまったものを取る remove *sth* lodged [stuck] between *one's* teeth. 文例⇩
はさみ 《a pair of》 scissors; shears 《大型の》; clippers 《髪やつめを切る》; 《かにの》 claws; nippers 《切符の》 a punch ★scissors, shears はいずれも複数扱い ¶はさみ 1 丁 a pair of scissors / はさみで切る cut *sth* with scissors; shear; clip / 《かにが》はさみではさむ nip *sth* with *its* claws / はさみを入れる cut *sth* with scissors; 《文》 put scissors to 《a tape》; trim 《a

---

激しく降った. It rained heavily [hard].
はげみ これっぱかりのボーナスをもらったって, 何の励みにもならない. Such a small bonus provides no 《sort of》 incentive.
はげむ 彼らは職務に熱心に励んだ. They attended to their duties with enthusiasm.
ばけもの 化け物が正体を現わした. The apparition revealed its true shape.
はげる³ この色は洗ったらはげるだろう. This color will not wash well. / 壁のしっくいがところどころはげていた. The whitewash on the wall had flaked off in patches.
はげる² 前[後ろ]の方がはげてきた. I am bald in front [at the back]. / 彼は額がはげ上がっている. He has a receding hairline.
ばける きつねが女に化けた. The fox took the shape of a woman.
はこび この鉄道は 7 月には開通の運びになるだろう. This railroad line will be opened in July. / 条約はまだ批准の運びに至らない. The treaty has not yet reached the stage of ratification./ 原稿はまだ印刷の運びに至らない. The manuscripts are not yet ready for printing [the press].
はこぶ 事がすらすら運んだ. The affair went smoothly. / 事はまだそこまで運んでいません. The matter has not advanced as far as that yet. ¦ Things haven't yet reached that stage.
ばさばさ 髪がばさばさだよ. Your hair is dry and dishevelled.
はさまる 指が戸に挟まった. My fingers were caught in the door. / 私は双方の間に挟まって困っている. I am in an awkward position, caught between the two interested parties.

はさみうち 挟み撃ち an attack on both sides [flanks]; a pincer movement ¶敵を挟み撃ちにする attack the enemy from both sides / 挟み撃ちになる be caught between two fires.

はさみきる 挟み切る snip; clip.

はさみむし [昆] an earwig.

はさむ 挟む 〈間に置く〉put [hold] sth between (one's knees), 〈挿入する〉insert; 〈つまむ〉nip ¶本の間にしおりを挟む put a marker between the leaves of a book / 指を戸に挟む catch one's finger [get one's finger caught] in the door / 言葉を挟む put [throw] in (a word); break [cut] in (with a remark).

ばさりと with a (loud) crash. 文例

はさん 破産 (a) bankruptcy; a (financial) failure; insolvency ¶破産する go [(文)become] bankrupt; 《口語》go broke; fail / 破産者 a bankrupt / 事実上破産状態である be in virtual bankruptcy. 文例

はし¹ 箸 chopsticks ¶はし 1 ぜん a pair of chopsticks / はしを使う use [handle] chopsticks / はしをつける touch (the dish) / 先に eating (one's food) / はしをつけない leave (one's food) untouched / はしを置く 〈休める〉put one's chopsticks down (on the table); 〈食べ終わる〉stop eating; finish one's meal [dinner, lunch] / はしにも棒にもかからない incorrigible; be past praying for / はし置き a chopstick rest / はし箱[立て] a chopstick case [stand]. 文例

はし² 端(末端) an end; a tip; 《文》the extremity; 〈縁〉the edge; the border; 《文》the brink; 《文》the verge ¶端から端まで from end to end; from one end (of sth) to the other; 《walk》the whole length (of the corridor).

はし³ 橋 a bridge ¶橋のたもと the foot of a bridge / 橋をかける build [throw, 《文》construct] a bridge across [over] (a river); 《文》span (a river) with a bridge / 橋を渡る cross a bridge; cross a river by a bridge / 橋げた[くい] a bridge girder [pile].

はじ 恥 (a) shame; (a) disgrace; (an) embarrassment ★ shame も disgrace も不定冠詞を付けることはあるが複数形にはしない ¶恥をかく be embarrassed; be humiliated / 恥をさらす disgrace oneself in public; bring shame on oneself / 恥を忍ぶ pocket one's pride / 恥を知らない be shameless; have no sense of shame [honor] / 恥を知らない be shameless; have no shame; 《文》be lost [dead] to (all sense of) shame / 恥を注ぐ 《文》vindicate one's honor; clear one's name / 恥知らず a shameless person. 文例

はじいる 恥じ入る ⇒はじる。

はしか 麻疹 (the) measles ¶はしかにかかる catch [get, have] (the) measles. 文例

はしがき 端書き an introductory remark; a foreword; a preface; a prefatory note.

はじきだす 弾き出す 〈指で〉flick (a marble) out; 〈数値を〉calculate [work out] (the approximate value) ¶仲間からはじき出される be forced out of [expelled from] one's group.

はじく 弾く 〈指などで〉snap; flick ¶そろばん玉をはじく work the beads (on an [one's] abacus) / はじかれたように立ち上がる jump to one's feet. 文例

はしくれ 端くれ ¶役人の端くれ a petty [minor] official.

はしけ 艀 a lighter; a barge ¶はしけの船頭 a lighterman; a bargeman / はしけ賃 lighterage.

はじける 弾ける burst open; split open.

はしご 梯子 a ladder ¶はしごの段 a rung / はしごを登る climb (up) [go up] a ladder / はしごを降りる climb [come] down a ladder / 塀にはしごをかける lean a ladder up against the wall; place [rest] a ladder against the wall / はしご段〈1 段〉a step; a stair; 〈階段〉(a flight of) stairs; a staircase / はしご車〈消防の〉(a hook and) ladder truck; an aerial ladder truck / はしご乗り〈事〉acrobatic performances on a ladder / 〈人〉an acrobatic performer on a ladder / はしご酒 stopping for a drink at a series of bars in one evening; 《米》barhopping; 《英》pub-crawling; a pub crawl. 文例

はした 端た a fraction; an odd sum (金額) ¶はしたを切り捨てる omit [round off] fractions / はした金 a small [paltry] sum (of money); a (mere) pittance. 文例

はしたない 端たない 〈慎みのない〉《文》im-

はさみ 僕のはさみはどこ? Where are my scissors?

はさむ テーブルを間に挟んで彼女に向かい合って腰を下ろした。I sat down in the chair across the table from her.

ばさりと 木がばさりと倒れた。The tree came crashing down.

はさん その計画はさんざんな失敗となり, 彼は破産寸前の状態に追い込まれた。The project proved a disaster and pushed him to the brink of bankruptcy. / そんなにお小遣いをねだられては, お父さん破産してしまうよ。My finances will be ruined, son, if I give you such a large allowance.

はし¹ 彼は私のはしの上げ下ろしにまで文句をつける。He finds a fault or two in every little thing I do.

はし² その川には橋が 2 つかかっている。There are two bridges across the river.

はじ 恥を知れ。Shame on you! / 君がそんな事をすれば僕らの恥になる。You will bring shame on us, if you do that sort of thing. / そんなことをするのは男の恥だ。A real man would be ashamed of doing that.

はしか うちの子は皆もうはしかがすんだ。All my children have had the measles.

はじく このレインコートはよく水をはじく。This raincoat sheds water well.

はしくれ これでも画家の端くれのつもりです。I regard myself as a painter, if not much of one. / あれでも彼は大学教授の端くれだ。He teaches in a university, though he is not much of a scholar.

はしご 屋根にはしごが掛けてある。A ladder is leaning against the roof. / 僕が登っている間, はしごを押さえていてくれ。Steady the ladder while I'm on it.

はした はしたの 30 円は結構です。Never mind the odd thirty yen.

はし(っ)こい smart; shrewd; clever; agile.

ばじとうふう 馬耳東風 ¶馬耳東風と聞き流す turn a deaf ear [pay no attention] to 《sb's advice》.

はしなくも 端なくも by chance; unexpectedly ¶はしなくも…する happen [《文》chance] to do.

はしばみ《植》a hazel ¶はしばみの実 a hazelnut.

はじまる 始まる〈開始する〉begin; start;《文》commence; open; be opened〈開始される〉; set in〈季節が〉; break out〈戦争・暴動などが〉;〈起源する〉originate〈in〉;《文》arise〈from〉¶始まっている have started; be (going) on; be under way; be in session〈会議が〉. 文例⇩

はじめ 初[始]め〈開始〉the beginning;《文》the commencement; the opening;〈発端〉a start;《文》the outset;〈起源〉the origin ¶始めから終りまで from beginning to end; from start to finish; from first to last; right [all the way] through 《the match》/ 初めからやり直す do all over again; make a fresh start; start afresh [《米》over] / 初めの〈最初の〉first;《文》initial; early〈初期の〉;〈もとの〉original / 初めに in the beginning; at the beginning [start, outset]; first(ly) / 今月の初めに at the beginning of this month / 20世紀の初めに early [in the early years of; at the opening of] the 20th century / 初めて for the first time; first / 初めは よ り at the start;〈もとは〉originally /首相始め各閣僚 the Premier and his Cabinet colleagues. 文例⇩

はじめる 始める begin 《the game, to do, doing》; start 《one's work, to do, doing》;《文》commence 《one's explanation, to do, doing》;〈口語〉start in 《to do, on sth》 ¶第1章[50 ページ]から始める begin with the first chapter [at page 50] / 仕事を始める set [set about] one's work; set to work / 事業を始める start [get launched] on an enterprise / 新たに始める start afresh; make a fresh [new] start / 新しい本を書き始める begin [start] writing [to write] a new book; begin [start] on a new book. 文例⇩

はしゃ 覇者 a supreme ruler;〈競技の〉a champion.

ばしゃ 馬車 a carriage; a coach;〈荷馬車〉a (horse) wagon; a cart ¶馬車に乗る ride in [《米》on] a carriage / 馬車馬 a carriage [cart] horse / 馬車馬のように働く work like a horse [slave].

はしゃぐ《文》make merry; frolic ¶大はしゃぎの子供《文》a very frolicsome child; a boy who is in high spirits.

パジャマ《米》pajamas;《英》pyjamas ¶パジャマ1着 a pair of pajamas / パジャマの上着 a pajama jacket.

ばしゃんと, ぱしゃんと with a splash.

はしゅつ 派出 ¶派出する send out [off]; dispatch / 派出所 a police box / 派出婦 a visiting housekeeper [maid]; a charwoman.

ばじゅつ 馬術 (horseback) riding; horsemanship ¶馬術が上手である be a good horseman [horsewoman] / 馬術を教わる take lessons in riding / 馬術競技 an equestrian event.

ばしょ 場所〈ところ〉a place; a spot;〈土地〉a place;《文》a locality;〈地面〉a lot;〈位置〉《文》a location; a position;〈現場〉a scene;〈座席, 所在地〉a seat;〈敷地, 所在地〉a site;〈空間〉room; space ¶火事のあった場所 the scene of a fire / 場所をつきとめる locate / 場所を取っておく book [reserve] a seat / 場所をふさぐ take up a lot of [too much] room; occupy a great deal of space / 場所を譲る yield one's place to sb / 場所によって異なる vary from place to place / 場所柄もわきまえずに regardless of where one is [of the occasion] / 大相撲初場所 the New Year's grand sumo

---

はしたない 花子, そんなはしたないことをして. Aren't you forgetting your manners, Hanako?

ばじとうふう いくら言っても馬耳東風だった. He turned a deaf ear to my repeated advice. / Everything I said was lost on him.

はじまる 博覧会は来月1日から始まる. The exposition opens [will be opened] on the first of next month. / 梅雨はたいてい6月の半ば頃に始まる. The rainy season generally sets in about the middle of June. / この本は田園生活の話から始まっている. This book begins [opens] with an account of country life. / あと5分で映画が始まる. The picture comes on in five minutes. / この習慣は近代《平安時代》に始まったものだ. This custom is of modern origin [dates from the Heian Era]. / 今さらそんな事を言っても始まらない. What is the use of saying that at this stage? / 今に始まったことではない. This is an old story. / そら,《いつもの癖が》また始まった. There you go again!

はじめ 初めが大事. A good beginning makes a good ending.《諺》/ これが初めでまた終わりだ. This is the first and the last. / 初めはそうするつもりではなかった. That was not my original intention. / 初めは会員はたった5人だった. We had only five members to start with. / 外国人として富士に登ったのは彼が初めだ. He was the first foreigner to make an ascent of Mt. Fuji. / 演壇に立ったのはこれが初めてです. This is the first time that I have ever stood on the platform. / 健康を失って初めてその有り難味がわかる. You only realize the value of health when [You don't realize the blessing of health until] you have lost it. / 数日たって初めて僕はその真相を知った. It was not until a few days later that I learned the truth. / あいつが山師だということは初めから知っていた. I knew all along [from the start] that he was a fraud. / 金子氏始め5人が委員に選ばれた. Mr. Kaneko and four others were elected to the commitee. / 首相を始めとして, 日本の指導的な人々は概して親米的である. Japanese leaders, from the Premier down, are generally pro-American.

はじめる 君はいつドイツ語を始めたのか. When did you start (learning) German? / 何から始

はじょう 波状 a wavelike; wavy; undulating / 波状攻撃 an attack in waves / 波状スト a piston strike.

ばしょう 〖植〗a Japanese banana (plant).

ばじょう 馬上 ¶馬上で[の] on horseback.

はしょうふう 破傷風 tetanus; lockjaw.

はしょる 端折る〈くすそを〉tuck up [in]《one's skirt》;〈省く〉cut short; abridge.

はしら 柱〈建築の〉a pillar; a column (円柱);〈直立材〉a post; a pole;〈支柱〉a support; a prop ¶柱を立てる set up [raise] a pillar / 柱時計 a wall clock.

はじらう 恥じらう be [feel] shy; be bashful; blush (赤面する) ¶花も恥じらう麗しい乙女《文》a girl who outblooms the lovely-colored rose.

はしらせる 走らせる run; let sth run;〈使いを〉send; rush (急いで);〈車を〉drive ¶筆を走らせる drive a pen.

はしり 走り ¶はしりの果物 early fruit / ひと走り走る have [go for] a run. 文例⇩

はしりがき 走り書き ¶走り書きする write hurriedly; scribble.

はしりたかとび 走り高跳び the running high jump.

はしりづかい 走り使い ¶走り使いをする run errands《for sb》.

はしりよみ 走り読み ¶走り読みする run one's eyes over [through]《a book》; skim [run] through《a book》.

はしる 走る run; rush; dash; race ¶矢のように走る run like a shot from a gun / 寝返って敵側に走る defect [go over] to the enemy / 走って帰る run back; come running back; come back at a run / 走り出す begin to run; start running;〈歩いていて〉break [burst] into a run / 走り出る run out [in] / 走り回る run about / 走り去る run away [off] / 走り過ぎる run by [past] / 走り抜ける run through《a place》/ 走り寄る run up to sb. 文例⇩

はじる 恥じる be ashamed (of);《文》feel shame《at》¶自分を恥じる be ashamed of oneself / 恥じて顔を赤らめる blush [flush] with shame / 紳士たるに恥じない《文》be worthy of a gentleman / その名に恥じない be true to its name.

はしわたし 橋渡し《文》mediation;《文》good offices ⇒ ちゅうかい¹.

ばしん 馬身 a (horse's) length ¶半[2]馬身の差で勝つ win by a half (length) [two lengths].

はす¹ 蓮〖植〗a lotus ¶はすの花 a lotus flower / はす池 a lotus pond.

はす² 斜 ⇒ ななめ.

はず 筈 ¶…のはずである〈当然〉ought to do; should do;〈推測〉must (be);〈予定〉be expected to do; be to do; be due to do / …のはずがない cannot (be); it is hardly possible that…. 文例⇩

バス¹〈乗物〉a bus ¶バスの停留所 a bus stop / バスの発着所 a bus [《英》coach] station / バスの出る時間 the bus time / バスに乗る get on [board] a bus; take a ride in a bus; take a bus《to Kanda》/ バスに乗り遅れる miss a bus;〈比喩的に〉miss the bus / バスで行く go《to a place》by bus; get [take] a bus《to a place》/ 長距離バス a long-distance bus;《英》a coach / スクールバス a school bus / バスガール a (bus) conductress / バス会社 a bus company / バス専用車線 a bus lane / バスターミナル a bus [《英》coach] station;〈大規模な〉a bus [《英》coach] terminal / バス代 a bus fare / バス優先レーン a lane on which buses have priority / バス旅行 a bus [《英》coach] tour.

バス²〈ふろ〉a bath ⇒ ふろ ¶バスタオル a bath towel / (ホテルの)バストイレ付きの部屋 a room with (private) bath and toilet.

バス³〖音楽〗bass;〈人〉a bass (singer) ★bass の発音は [beis].

パス〈送球〉a pass;〈無料の入場券・乗車券〉a (free) pass; a free ticket;〈定期券〉《米》a commutation ticket;《英》a season ticket ⇒ ていき¹ ¶パスする〈試験に〉pass《an exami-

---

ましょう. What shall I do first [to begin with]? / 私がギターを始めたのは11歳の時です. It was when I was eleven years old that I took up the guitar. / 雨が降り始めた. It began [started] raining [to rain]. / 初めまして. How do you do? ★ これに対しては How do you do? と答える.

ばしょ 学校は便利な場所にある. The school is conveniently situated. / 座る場所がわからない. I don't know where to sit. / ここが新しい病院の建つ場所です. This is the site for the new hospital. / まだ君ら2人が入る場所はある. There is enough room [space] for you two. / (映画館などで)ちょっと席を立ちますせんか. I am going out for a little while; please keep [save] my place, will you?

はしり どれ一走り行って取って来よう. Well, I will just run and fetch it.

はしる 駅まで走って5分だ. It is five minutes' run to the station. / 急行列車は15分でその距離を走った. The express train covered the distance in fifteen minutes. / これは古い車だがまだ走る. This car is old, but it's still in running condition. / この船は20ノットの速力で走っている. This ship is doing [making] twenty knots. / 道は北に真っ直ぐに走っている. The road runs straight to the north.

はじる 僕のした事は天地に恥じない. I have done right in the sight of God and man.

はず あの人は今日来るはずです. He is expected (to come) today. / ライトがついているんだから, バッテリーが上がったはずがない. The battery can't be dead [can't have gone flat], because the lights are on. / それぐらいは君だって知っているはずだ. You ought to know that much. / それでは彼が怒るはずだ. It is quite natural that he should have been offended. / 彼は今頃はもう向こうに着いているはずだ. He ought to have arrived there by this time. / 僕の伯父は昨日東京へ行くはずだった. My uncle was to have gone up to Tokyo yesterday. / 僕は確かそう言ったはずだ. I'm sure I said so.

バス¹ そこまではバスが行ってるよ. A bus service is available as far as there. / ここならバスで行けます. You can get there by bus. / ここはバスが通りますか. Is this a bus route? | Do

はすう　端数　a fraction ⇒はした.
バズーカほう　バズーカ砲　a bazooka.
バスーン　〈楽器〉a bassoon.
ばすえ　場末　a place far away from the business center ((of a city)); the outskirts ((of a town)); a suburb ¶場末の suburban; ((a pub)) a long way from the city center.
はずかしい　恥ずかしい　〈恥ずべき〉disgraceful; shameful; 〈きまりが悪い〉be ashamed ((of)); be embarrassed ((by, about)) ¶お恥ずかしいことですが... I am ashamed to say that ...; 〈文〉To my shame I must confess that ... / 恥ずかしい思いをさせる make sb feel ashamed; shame sb / 恥ずかしそうに bashfully; shyly; 〈文〉shamefacedly / 恥ずかしそうな顔をする look shy [embarrassed, abashed] / 恥ずかしからぬ〈文〉worthy; 〈文〉honorable; decent / 恥ずかしからぬ身なりをしている be decently dressed / 恥ずかしがる〈恥じる〉be ashamed ((of)); 〈気が引ける〉feel small; 〈はにかむ〉be [feel] shy; be bashful; be abashed / 恥ずかしげもなく unashamedly; unabashedly; brazenly / 恥ずかしさ shame; 〈文〉shamefulness. 文例⇩
はずかしめ　辱しめ　〈恥辱〉shame; an insult; (a) humiliation; 〈強姦〉rape ¶辱しめを受ける〈恥をかかされる〉be insulted; be shamed; 〈強姦される〉be raped.
はずかしめる　辱しめる　〈恥をかかせる〉humiliate; disgrace; bring disgrace on sb; insult; put sb to shame; 〈強姦する〉rape.
ハスキー　¶ハスキーな声で in a husky voice.
バスケット　a (hand) basket; a hamper (ピクニック用の).
バスケットボール　basketball ¶バスケットボールの選手 a basketball player; 〈米口語〉a cager / バスケットボールをする play basketball.
はずす　外す　〈取り外す〉take off; remove; 〈解く, 離す〉unfasten; undo; put sth out of place; 〈逸する〉miss; let go; 〈よける〉avoid; dodge (身をかわして) ¶障子を外す take a shoji out [off] / 鎖を外す undo the chain; unchain / 席を外す leave [quit] one's seat; slip away ((from)) (そっと) / 受話器を外しておく leave the (telephone) receiver off its [the] rest [hook].
はすっぱ　蓮っ葉 ¶はすっぱな frivolous; flippant / はすっぱ娘 a flirt.
パステル　pastel ¶パステル画 a pastel (drawing); a drawing in pastels / パステル画家 a pastel artist / パステルカラー pastel shades [colors] / パステルカラーのキャビネット a pastel-colored cabinet. 文例⇩
バスト　〈胸まわり〉one's bust (measurement).
パスポート　a passport ¶パスポート. 文例⇩
パスボール　〈野球〉a passed ball. 文例⇩
はずみ　弾み　〈はね返ること〉(a) (re)bound; 〈勢い〉momentum; 〈刺激〉(an) impetus; 〈機会〉a chance ¶はずみがつく gain [gather] momentum; 〈人が〉get [(〈文〉become] more (and more) animated; warm up / 時のはずみで on the spur of the moment / ちょっとしたはずみで by mere chance / ふとしたはずみで言った言葉 a chance [casual] remark / はずみ車 a flywheel. 文例⇩
はずむ　弾む　〈はねかえる〉spring; bound; bounce; 〈調子づく〉be stimulated; be encouraged; get [(〈文〉become] lively [animated, 〈文〉enlivened]; 〈奮発する〉treat oneself to ((a gold watch)); 〈口語〉splurge on ((a beefsteak)) ¶チップをはずむ tip ((a waiter)) generously / 息をはずませる pant; gasp (for breath); breathe hard; puff and pant [blow] / 心をはずませて cheerfully; 〈文〉buoyantly; with keen interest. 文例⇩
パズル　a puzzle ¶パズルを解く[やる] solve [do] a puzzle.
はずれ　外れ　〈端〉the end; 〈文〉the extremity; the outskirts ((of a town)); 〈失敗〉a miss; (a) failure; 〈くじの〉⇒からくじ ¶外れのない〈文〉unerring; infallible / 町の外れに on [at] the outskirts of the town.
はずれる　外れる　be [come] off (sth); be [get] out of place; run off ((the rails)); 〈骨などが〉be put out of joint; be dislocated; 〈当たらない〉miss; go wild; 〈失敗する〉fail; go wrong; 〈反する〉〈文〉be contrary to; be against ¶的から大きくはずれる fall [go] wide of the mark / 規則にはずれている be against the rules / 道理にはずれている be contrary to [against all] reason. 文例⇩

---

buses run along this road?
はずかしい　君はそんな事をして恥ずかしくないのか. Aren't you ashamed of having done such a thing? / それは専門家の作といっても恥ずかしくない. It would do credit to a professional. / こんな事を申し上げねばならないとは, 何ともお恥ずかしい次第です. I am deeply ashamed to have to tell you this. / ジェーンはとっても恥ずかしがり屋なのよ. Jane is very shy.
はずす　眼鏡を外すとこわい目付きをしている. Without (his) spectacles, his eyes look fierce. / 背中のホック[ボタン]を外してくださらない. Undo me behind, will you? / 彼は今ちょうど席を外しています. He is not at his desk now. | He is out right now. / 根本君, すまないがちょっとこの席を外してくれませんか. Would you mind excusing yourself, Mr. Nemoto?
バスト　彼女はバスト82センチ, ウエスト56センチ, ヒップ86センチだ. Her dimensions [〈口語〉vital statistics] are 82-56-86 in centimeters.
パスポート　有名大学の卒業証書こそ出世のパスポートだと思っている日本人は多い. Many Japanese regard the diploma of a prestigious university as the essential passport to success [advancement].
パスボール　キャッチャー森のパスボールで二塁に進塁した. He ran to second on a passed ball charged to catcher Mori.
はずみ　彼は自転車を避けようとしたはずみに転んだ. He began trying to dodge a bicycle. / どうしたはずみか機械の具合が悪くなった. For some reason the machine stopped working properly.
はずむ　ボールがはずまなくなっ

パスワーク 〖球技〗passing ; (ball-)handling.

はぜ 〖魚〗a goby.

はせい 派生 《文》derivation ¶派生する《文》derive [be derived]《from》/ 派生的《文》derivative ; secondary (二次的) / 派生語 a derivative.

はせさんじる 馳せ参じる rush [《文》hasten] to 《a place》; rally round *sb*.

はぜのき 〖植〗a wax tree ; a sumac(h).

パセリ 〖植〗parsley.

はせる 馳せる ¶名声をはせる《文》win fame ; become famous / 名声を世界にはせる become known all over the world ; 《文》win [achieve] global fame.

はぜる 〈はじける〉burst open ; 〈はじけ飛ぶ〉pop ; 〈裂ける〉split.

はせん¹ 波線 (〰) a wavy line ¶下に波線を引いた語 a word underscored with a wavy line.

はせん² 破線 (----) a broken line.

ばぞく 馬賊 mounted bandits.

パソコン a personal computer.

はそん 破損 damage ¶破損する be damaged ; be broken (down) ; be destroyed / 破損している be broken ;《文》be out of repair / 破損しやすい easy to break ; fragile / 破損箇所 a damaged [broken] part [section] ;〈堤防などの〉a breach.

はた¹ 旗 a flag ; a pennant (細長い三角旗) ;〈軍旗〉a standard ;〈文〉a banner ; an ensign (艦船旗) ¶…の旗の下に馳せ参じる《文》flock to [rally around] the banner of… / 旗を掲げる〈上に〉hoist [raise] a flag ;〈旗竿に〉run a flag up a flagpole ;〈出す〉display [hang out] a flag / 旗を下ろす take down a flag ; lower a flag / 旗を振る wave a flag / 旗を振って止める flag down 《a train》/ 旗行列 a procession with flags flying / 旗ざお a flagstaff ; a flagpole / 旗日 a national holiday. 文例⇩

はた² 端 ⇨ ふち², そば¹ ¶端の人たち bystanders ; outsiders / 端から見ると, 端の者の目には (seen) from the outside ; (as it appears) to outsiders.

はた³ 機 a loom ¶機を織る work [weave] at the loom ; weave ⇨ はたおり.

はだ 肌, 膚 the skin ¶肌がきれいだ have a clear [a smooth ;《文》an unblemished] skin / 肌が荒れている have a rough skin / 肌が合う [合わない] get [don't get] on well (with) / 肌の色 skin color / 肌を刺すような寒さ biting [cutting] cold / 肌を脱ぐ strip (*oneself*) to the waist / 学者肌の人《文》be of a scholarly turn of mind / 肌色の flesh-colored. 文例⇩

バター(ー) butter ¶バタ臭い《西欧風の》European ; Western ;〈異国風の〉exotic ;《文》alien / バタ臭い日本人 foreign-sounding [unnatural] Japanese / パンにバターを付ける butter *one's* bread ; spread butter on *one's* bread / バターナイフ a butter knife.

はだあい 肌合 a turn of mind ;《文》a disposition ; a temperament. 文例⇩

はたあげ 旗揚げ ¶旗揚げする start [launch] (out) on an enterprise.

ばたあし ばた足 〖水泳〗the flutter (kick) ; the thrash.

ばだい 場代 〈席料〉the price [charge] for a seat [room] ;〈入場料〉an admission fee.

はたいろ 旗色 〈戦況〉《文》the tide [fortunes] of war ;〈形勢〉the outlook ; the situation ¶旗色を見る sit on the fence ; (wait to) see which way the cat jumps. 文例⇩

はたおり 機織り 〈事〉weaving ;〈人〉a weaver.

はだか 裸 a naked body ; a nude (★見て楽しむための) ¶裸の naked ; bare ; nude / 裸の王様〈童話の題名〉*The Emperor's New Clothes* / 裸にする strip *sb* naked [of *his* clothes] / 〈木を〉strip 〈a tree〉of leaves / 〈されるbe stripped naked / 〈文なしにされる〉be robbed [fleeced] of all *one's* money / 裸になる undress ; strip *oneself* naked ; strip *one's* clothes off ;〈無一文になる〉become penniless / 裸になって話し合う have a heart-to-heart [completely candid] talk with each other ; have it out with each other / 裸で naked ; with nothing on / 裸一貫で 《start》from nothing [《口語》scratch] ; with empty pockets ; 《make *one's* fortune》without anything to start with / 裸岩 a bare rock / 裸馬 an unsaddled [a barebacked] horse / 裸馬に乗る ride bareback / 裸線 (a) bare wire / 裸電球 [ろうそく] a naked [an unshaded] bulb [candle] / 裸祭り a festival in which the participants go naked. 文例⇩

た. The ball has lost its bounce. / 話がはずんだ. The conversation grew lively. / 息子が息をはずませて自分の名前が合格者名簿に出ていたと私に告げた. My son told me in an excited voice that his name was on the list of successful candidates.

はずれ 私の8畳の間の南側は廊下になっていて, その西はずれに納戸がある. A verandah runs along the south side of my eight-mat room and leads into the utility room at its western end.

障子がはずれた. The *shoji* is off its groove. / たががはずれて水が流れ出した. The hoop broke and the water ran out. / 彼の家はその通りからはずれた所にある. His house is some way off the street. / する事なす事みんなはずれた. I failed in everything I did. | Everything I set my hand to went wrong.

はた¹ 旗が風にへんぽんと翻っていた. A flag was waving [fluttering] in the wind. / 旗が上がった. The flag went up (the pole).

はた² 端で見るほど楽ではない. It's not as easy as it might seem to outsiders.

はだ あの男は肌に始終木綿を着けている. He always wears cotton next to his skin. / 彼女は肌がきれいだった. She had a smooth [fine] skin. / その店で働きながら彼は商売のこつを肌に吸収していった. Working at the store, he got the knack of business by soaking it up through his pores. / 彼は芸術家肌の人だ. He is cut out for an artist. | He has something of the artist in him.

はだあい 彼は私と肌合いが違う. He is a man of different stamp from me.

はたいろ 彼の方が旗色がいい [悪い]. The odds are in his favor [against him].

はだか 彼は時々裸に近い格好でそこらを歩き回る. He often goes

はだかむぎ 裸麦 rye.
はたき a 《feather》 duster ¶はたきをかける dust 《a room》.
はだぎ 肌着 underwear;〈シャツ〉《米》an undershirt;《英》a vest.
はたく 叩く 〈ほこりを〉dust;〈打つ〉beat;《文》strike; slap (平手で) ¶財布をはたく empty *one's* purse.
はたけ 畑 a field; a farm;〈野菜の〉《米》a truck farm;《英》a market garden; a kitchen garden (家庭用); a plantation (大規模の);〈専門〉*one's* specialty [field] ¶畑を耕す plow [《文》till] a field [the soil] / 畑に麦を作る plant [sow] a field with barley / いちご畑 a strawberry field [patch (小規模の)] / コーヒー畑 a coffee plantation / じゃがいも畑 a potato plot [field] / 出版畑の人 a person experienced in the publishing trade / 畑違いである be not *one's* specialty [field]; be out of *one's* line. 文例↓
はだける bare [expose] 《*one's* chest》.
はださむい 肌寒い chilly;《文》chill.
はだざわり 肌触り a texture ¶肌触りがいい have a pleasant feel [texture]; feel pleasant [《文》agreeable] (to the touch); feel soft [nice] / 肌触りが悪い have a harsh [an unpleasant] texture; feel harsh [unpleasant] (to the touch) / 肌触りの柔らかな人《文》a gentle-mannered [an affable and courteous] person.
はだし ¶はだしの barefoot(ed) / はだしで barefoot; with [in one's] bare feet; without *one's* shoes (on) / 玄人(ミネミ)はだしである (almost) outdo [outshine] a professional. 文例↓
はたしあい 果たし合い ⇒ けっとう³.
はたして 果たして sure enough; just as one thought; as expected;〈本当に〉really. 文例↓
はたじるし 旗印 〈旗につける紋所〉the emblem [insignia] on a flag;〈目標〉a slogan; a motto (*pl.* -(e)s) ¶...を旗印として under the slogan of....
はたす 果たす〈し遂げる〉carry out;《文》accomplish;《文》achieve;《文》attain; finish;〈行なう〉do;《文》execute;〈履行する〉《文》discharge; keep;《文》perform ¶義務を果たす discharge [fulfill] *one's* duty / 使命を果たす perform [carry out] *one's* mission / 望みを果たす《文》realize *one's* wishes / 約束を果たす keep [make good] *one's* promise; be as good as [live up to] *one's* word. 文例↓
はたち 二十 twenty (years of age); *one's*

twentieth year. 文例↓
はたと 〈急に〉suddenly;〈全く〉completely ¶はたとひざを打つ slap *one's* knee / はたと思い当たる hit on 《an idea》/ はたと当惑する come to [be at] *one's* wits' end; be at a loss what to do / はたとにらむ ⇒ はったと.
はたはた fluttering(ly). 文例↓
ばたばた ¶ばたばたする〈旗などが〉flap;〈もがく〉(kick and) struggle;〈忙しく立ち回る〉bustle about / ばたばた走る run noisily /〈鳥が〉ばたばた羽ばたきする flap [beat] *its* wings. 文例↓
ぱたぱた〈足音・雨音など〉pattering; pitter-patter; pit-a-pat;〈翼などの音〉flap-flap ¶廊下をぱたぱた走る run pit-a-pat down [up] the corridor / 翼をぱたぱたさせる flap [flutter] *its* wings / ズボンをぱたぱた払う beat the dust off 《*one's* trousers》/ 雨が屋根をぱたぱた打つ音 the pattering [pitter-pat(ter)] of rain on the roof.
バタフライ【水泳】the butterfly stroke ¶バタフライ泳者 a butterfly swimmer.
はだみ 肌身 ¶肌身離さず持つ《文》carry *sth* about *one*; always keep *sth* on *one* [《文》*one's* person].
はため 傍目 ⇒ よそめ.
はためいわく 傍迷惑 (be) a nuisance to people around *one*.
はためく flutter (in the wind).
はたもと 旗本【日本史】a direct retainer [vassal] of the *shogun*.
はたや 機屋〈工場〉a weaving shop;〈人〉a weaver.
はたらかせる 働かせる make *sb* work; work; set *sb* to work;〈使用する〉use;《文》exercise (能力など);〈活動させる〉bring 《*one's* skill》into action [play] ¶機械を働かせる work [operate] a machine / 頭[知恵]を働かせる use *one's* head [brains]; exercise [use, work] *one's* wits. 文例↓
はたらき 働き 〈労働〉work; labor;〈作用〉《文》action;〈役〉a function;〈運用〉《文》operation;〈活動〉activity;〈才能〉《文》ability;〈功績〉《文》service ¶心の働き the workings of the mind / 働きのある[ない]人〈能力〉an able [a shiftless] person;〈稼ぎ〉a good [poor] provider / 頭の働きを敏活にする《文》increase [improve] the quickness [agility] of *one's* brain / 働きあり[ばち] a worker ant [bee]; a worker / 働き盛りである be in the prime of life / 働き手 a worker;〈一家の〉the bread-

---

around with very little [next to nothing] on.
はたけ 農夫の人たちが畑に出て働いている. Farmers are working out in the fields. / それは僕の畑じゃない. It is not in my line.
はだし みごとだね, 商売人はだしじゃないか. Excellent! A professional wouldn't be ashamed of it.
はたして 彼は果たして失敗した. He failed, as I had feared he

would. / 果たして事実だった. It proved to be true. / 果たして再び会えるだろうか. Will we ever meet again? / 果たしてそうだろうか. Can it really be so? / Are you sure of [about] it?
はたち 彼はまだ二十前だ. He is still in his teens.
はたはた 旗がはたはたとはためいていた. A flag was fluttering in the wind.
ばたばた 帆がマストに当たってば

たばた音を立てていた. The sails were flapping against the masts. / 5, 6 人の者が相次いでばたばた倒れた. Five or six men fell down in rapid succession (one after another).
ばたばた カーテンが風にばたばたあおられている. The curtain is flapping in the wind.
はたらかせる 水泳はほとんど全身の筋肉を働かせる. Swimming brings nearly all the muscles of

はたらきかける　働き掛ける　work on; make approaches to; appeal to.

はたらく　働く　〈労働する〉work; labor; 〈勤務する〉work (for); serve (at); 〈文〉be in the service [employ] (of); 〈機能する〉《文》function; operate; 〈作用する〉act on; 〈活動する〉come into play ¶働いている be working; be at work / 働きすぎる work too hard; overwork (oneself) / 忙しく働く busy oneself (at, in doing) / 悪事を働く commit a crime. 文例⇩

ばたりと, ばたんと　with a bang (戸などが); with a thud (flop) (どさりと) ¶ばたんと戸を閉める slam the door to [shut] ; shut the door with a bang / ばたりと倒れる flop down《on the floor》; fall down with a thud.

はたん　破綻　〈失敗〉(a) failure; 〈破産〉bankruptcy; 〈決裂〉《文》a rupture; a breakdown ¶破綻をきたす, 破綻を来たす〈失敗する〉fail; break down; come to grief ; 〈行き詰まる〉《文》reach an impasse; 〈破産する〉fail; go [《文》become] bankrupt; be ruined.

はだん　破談　¶破談になる be broken off; be canceled.

はたんきょう　[植] an almond (tree).

ばたんと　with a bang ; smartly　¶ばたんと戸を閉める slam the door to [shut]. 文例⇩

はち¹　八　eight　¶第8 the eighth / 額に八の字を寄せる frown; 《文》knit one's brows / 8分の1 one-eighth / 八重唱(奏)(曲) (an) octet(te)(t) / 8ミリ映画 (カメラ, 映写機) an 8-millimeter movie (cinecamera, projector).

はち²　鉢　〈どんぶり〉a bowl; 〈植木鉢〉a (flower) pot; 〈水盤〉a basin ¶鉢の開いた頭 a flat-crowned head / 鉢植えa potted plant; a house plant (室内用).

はち³　蜂　a (honey)bee (みつばち); a wasp (黄ばち) ¶はちの子 a wasp larva / はちの巣 a (honey)comb; a (bee)hive (巣箱) / はちの巣のようになる〈穴だらけになる〉be honeycombed; be riddled《with shots》/ はちの巣をつついたような騒ぎになる be thrown into utter confusion / はちに刺される be stung by a wasp [bee] / はち蜜(ミツ) honey. 文例⇩

ばち¹　罰　《文》divine punishment [retribution]; a curse (のろい) ¶罰が当たる incur divine punishment; be punished by Heaven; pay dearly for (one's sins) / 罰当たりの cursed; 《文》accursed; 《文》damned. 文例⇩

ばち²　撥　〈三味線などの〉a plectrum《pl. -s, plectra》; 〈太鼓の〉a (drum)stick.

はちあわせ　鉢合わせ　¶鉢合わせする〈頭を〉knock [bump] one's head against sb's; bump heads together; 〈衝突する〉clash [collide]《with》; 〈出会う〉run into sb.

ばちがい　場違い　¶場違いの〈その場にふさわしくない〉(be) out of place; 〈本場物でない〉not from the place where the best kind is produced.

はちがつ　八月　August (略: Aug.).

バチカン　〈ローマ法王庁〉the Vatican　¶バチカン市 Vatican City.

はちきれる　はち切れる　¶大入り満員ではち切れそうである be bursting with people / はち切れそうに詰まっている be filled to bursting / はち切れそうな元気である be full of vigor [energy]. 文例⇩

はちく　破竹　¶破竹の勢いで進む《文》advance unresisted [unopposed]; carry everything before one.

ぱちくり　¶目をぱちくりさせる blink one's eyes.

はちじゅう　八十　eighty　¶第80 the eightieth / 80代の人 an octogenarian.

バチスカーフ　〈深海潜水艇〉a bathyscaphe.

ぱちっと　with a crack ⇨ぱちぱち.

はちどり　蜂鳥　a hummingbird.

ぱちぱち　〈カメラのシャッターなどの音〉click-click-click ¶ぱちぱち鳴る[音を立てる] crackle ; crack; sputter; splutter / 小銃のぱちぱちいう音 the crackle [crackling] of rifle fire / 手をぱちぱちたたく clap one's hands / 写真をぱちぱち撮る snap [shoot] off pictures (one after another).

はちまき　鉢巻き　¶手ぬぐいで鉢巻きをする wear [tie] a towel around one's head.

はちめんたい　八面体　an octahedron《pl. -s, -hedra》.

ばちゃばちゃ　¶ばちゃばちゃさせる splash [dabble] (one's hands in the water) / 泥んこ道をばちゃばちゃさせながら歩く splash [slosh] along in slush [mud].

ばちゃん　¶ばちゃぱちゃする[させる] splash; plash / ばちゃぱちゃ音を立てて跳ねている魚 a fish splashing about in the water.

ばちゃんと　with a splash ⇨ぽちゃん.

はちゅうるい　爬虫類　reptiles ¶爬虫類学 herpetology / 爬虫類時代 [地質] the age of reptiles; the reptilian age.

---

the body into play.

はたらき　昇進は働き次第です。If you do well, you will be promoted. / 彼は働き口が見付かった。He has found a position [job].

はたらく　彼女は頑張って生活のために働かなければならなかった。She had to work hard for her living. / 働かざる者食うべからず。No work, no dinner. | The man who will not work shall not eat. / 頭が働かなくなった。My brain stopped working [ceased to work].

ばたんと　ばたんと戸が閉まった。The door banged to [shut with a bang]. / 彼はその辞書をぱたんと閉じた。He slammed the dictionary shut.

はち³　はちがぶんぶんいっている。Bees are buzzing [humming]. / はちの巣をつついたような騒ぎだった。The place was like an overturned anthill.

ばち¹　そんなことをすると罰が当たるぞ。Heaven will punish you for it. | You will pay dearly for it. / これも親不孝の罰だ。This is a judgment on me for not looking after my parents properly. / 英語を教えてるそうだね。—(冗談に答えて)何かの罰でね。You're teaching English, I hear.— Yes, for my sins. / この罰当たりめ！You ungrateful swine！

はちきれる　おなかがはち切れそうだ。I have had more than enough. | I have eaten my fill.

ぱちぱち　火はぱちぱちと燃えていた。The fire crackled cheerfully.

はちょう 波長 (a) wavelength ¶波長が違うbe on a different wavelength 《from》/ 波長を合わせる tune in to 《the second program of the NHK》.

はちりと ⇨ぱちんと ¶ぱちりと写真を撮る snap [take a snapshot of] *sb* [*sth*].

バチルス a bacillus (*pl.* bacilli).

パチンコ 〈遊戯〉a pinball game;〈玩具〉《米》a slingshot;《英》a catapult ¶パチンコの機械 a pinball machine / パチンコをやる play pinball / パチンコ屋 a pinball saloon [parlor].

ぱちんと with a snap [click] ¶ぱちんとしめる snap 《*one's* purse》to [shut] / ぱちんとしまる snap to [shut]. 文例⬇

はつ 初 ¶初の first; new / 初に for the first time. / 初飛行 the maiden flight 《of an aircraft》.

-はつ …発〈出発〉leaving...; from...;〈弾数〉a round; a shot 〈小銃の〉; a shell 〈大砲の〉 ¶6時20分発の列車 the 6:20 train; the train leaving [due out] at 6:20 (★6:20 は six-twenty とよむ)/ 上野発の急行 an express (train) from Ueno / 5月9日発の電信 the cable dated May 9th / パリ発の報道 a news report under a Paris dateline; a news report datelined Paris / 5発撃った five rounds [shots]. 文例⬇

ばつ¹ 罰 (a) punishment; (a) penalty (法律上の);《文》retribution (因果応報)¶罰を受ける be punished;《文》suffer punishment. 文例⬇

ばつ² 閥 a clique; a faction ¶閥を作る form a clique.

ばつ³ ¶ばつが悪い feel awkward [embarrassed] / ばつを合わせる say *sth* to suit the occasion;〈相づちを打つ〉chime in with *sb*.

はつあん 発案 a suggestion; a proposition; a proposal; an idea ¶発案する〈提案する〉suggest; make a suggestion; propose;〈考え出す〉invent;《文》devise / 金子氏の発案で at the suggestion of Mr. Kaneko / 発案権 the right to submit a bill to the Diet / 発案者 the original proposer; the originator.

はついく 発育 growth; development ¶発育する grow; develop / 発育がいい be well grown / 発育が悪い be undergrown;〈人が〉be underdeveloped / 発育の遅い子供 a (physically) retarded child / 発育盛りの子供 a growing child.

はつえき 発駅 the starting station.

はつえんとう 発煙筒 a smoke candle.

はつおん 発音 (a) pronunciation ¶発音する pronounce / 発音がいい[悪い] *one's* pronunciation is good [poor, bad] / 発音の明確[不明確]な clearly-[poorly-]pronounced [《文》articulated] / 発音を誤る mispronounce 《a word》/ 発音記号 a phonetic symbol [sign, alphabet] / 米語発音辞典 a pronouncing dictionary of American English. 文例⬇

はつか 二十日〈日数〉twenty days;〈第20日〉the twentieth [20th] 《of March》.

はっか¹ 発火〈引火〉ignition;〈燃焼〉combustion ¶発火する catch [take] fire;《文》ignite / 発火させる set fire to (the fuel);《文》ignite / 発火しやすい《文》ignitable;《文》combustible / 発火装置 an ignition device / 発火点 the ignition point;〈油の〉the firing [burning] point;〈紛争の〉the flash point. 文例⬇

はっか²【植】Japanese mint; peppermint (西洋はっか)¶はっか入りのガム peppermint [spearmint] gum / はっか入りのタバコ a mentholated cigarette.

はつが 発芽 germination; sprouting; budding ¶発芽する germinate; sprout; bud; put out [《文》forth] buds / 発芽期 a germinating period.

はっかい 発会 the opening of a meeting;〈取引所の〉the first meeting 《of the year》¶発会式 an opening [inaugural] ceremony.

はっかく 発覚 ¶発覚する《文》be detected; be found out; come [be brought] to light.

はっかくけい 八角形 an octagon ¶八角形の octagonal.

はつかねずみ【動】a mouse (*pl.* mice).

はっかん¹ 発刊 publication; issue ¶発刊する publish; issue;〈創刊する〉start 《a magazine》.

はっかん² 発汗 ¶発汗する perspire; sweat / 発汗剤 a diaphoretic; a sudorific / 発汗作用 perspiration; sweating.

はつがん 発癌 ¶発がん性の carcinogenic; cancer-causing[-producing] / 発がん物質 a carcinogen; a carcinogenic substance.

はっき 発揮 ¶発揮する〈表示〉display;《文》exhibit; show / 能力を充分に発揮する give full play 《to *one's* ability》; bring *one's* ability into full play.

はつぎ 発議〈提案〉a proposal; a suggestion;〈動議〉a motion ¶発議する propose; suggest; move / 神田氏の発議で《文》at the instance of Mr. Kanda; at Mr. Kanda's suggestion / 発議権《政治》the initiative.

はっきゅう 薄給 a small [low] salary; low wages ¶薄給の low-salaried; poorly paid.

はっきょう 発狂 ¶発狂する go mad; go [《文》become] insane [crazy]; lose *one's* mind

---

ぱちんと ハンドバッグをぱちんとしめた. She snapped her bag shut.

-はつ この手紙はロンドン発10月10日の日付になっている. This letter is dated October 10th, from London.

ばつ¹ 再犯からは罰が重くなる. Penalties go up [become heavier] after the first offense.

はつおん 僕はlとrの発音が正しくできるように努力した. I tried hard to get the pronunciation [sounds] of *l* and *r* right.

はっか¹ 両国間の緊張はまさに発火点に達しようとしている. The tension between the two countries is running so high it may erupt into a shooting war at any moment.

はっきり 頭がはっきりしてきた. My head is beginning to clear. / この写真ははっきり写っていない. This photograph has not come out clear. / 僕はそれをはっきり覚えている. I remember it very clearly [well]. | I have a vivid recollection of it. / 彼は何時に出発するかはっきりした事は言わなかった. He did not tell me the exact time of his departure. / はっきり言いなさい. Speak out！/ はっきり言えばインチキだ. To put it bluntly [baldly], it is phoney. / シェークスピアの若い頃のことははっきりと

[senses] / 発狂させる drive sb mad [crazy].
はっきり 〈明瞭に〉clearly; distinctly; vividly; plainly;〈明確に〉exactly; definitely ¶はっきり返事をする give a definite answer / はっきり言う tell sb sth frankly [definitely]; 〈発音を〉speak distinctly;《文》articulate / はっきり言えば to be frank (with you), … ; to put it bluntly, baldly], … / はっきりした clear; distinct; vivid; definite / はっきりした声で in a clear voice / はっきりしない vague;《文》indistinct;《文》inarticulate / はっきりする become clear [plain]; clear / はっきりさせる《文》clarify; make sth clear [plain]. 文例⇩
はっきん¹ 白金 platinum.
はっきん² 発禁 ⇨ はっぱい (発売禁止).
ばっきん 罰金 a fine; a penalty (違約の) ¶罰金を課する fine;《文》impose a fine (on); punish sb with [by] a fine;《文》lay [inflict] a penalty (on) / 罰金を取られる be fined (1,000 yen for doing); be punished with [by] a fine (of 3,000 yen) / 罰金を払う pay a fine [penalty] (of 5,000 yen).
パッキング packing; a gasket.
バック 〈うしろ〉the back;〈背景〉the background;〈後援者〉a supporter;〈庭球の〉backhand ¶バックする back; go back / バックさせる reverse [back] (up) (one's car) / バックアップする back sb up; support / バックストレッチ《米》the backstretch《英》the back straight / バックナンバー a back number / バックネット〖野球〗the backstop / バックボーン (the) backbone / バックミラー a rear-view mirror.
バッグ a bag.
パック¹ 〈化粧用〉a pack.
パック² 〖アイスホッケー〗a puck.
バックグラウンド the background ¶バックグラウンドミュージック background music.
バックスキン buckskin.
はっくつ 発掘 excavation; a dig; exhumation (死体の) ¶発掘する dig (out, up); excavate; unearth;〈死体を〉exhume / 古墳を発掘する excavate an ancient tomb / タレントを発掘する scout for [pick out] talent.
バックハンド 〖テニス〗a backhand (stroke) ¶バックハンドで打つ hit 《the ball》 backhand.
ぱっくり ¶ぱっくり口をあける gape; open one's mouth wide;〈地面が割れて〉yawn / 口をぱっくりあけて with one's mouth agape [wide open].

バックル a buckle.
はづくろい 羽づくろい ¶(鳥が)羽づくろいする preen (itself [its feathers]).
ばつぐん 抜群 ¶抜群の outstanding;《文》pre-eminent;《文》distinguished;《文》conspicuous / 抜群の功を立てる render distinguished services 《to》 / 抜群の成績で卒業する graduate (from a school) with honors. 文例⇩
はっけ 八卦 ⇨ うらない 文例⇩
はっけいろじん 白系露人 a Russian émigré.
パッケージ 〈容器〉a package ¶パッケージツアー a package tour.
はっけっきゅう 白血球 a white blood cell; a white corpuscle; a leukocyte ¶白血球数 the number of leukocytes; a [one's] white cell count.
はっけつびょう 白血病 leukemia.
はっけん¹ 発見 (a) discovery ¶発見する discover; make a discovery; find (out) ⇨ わかる 囲遇; detect; turn sth up;〈偶然に〉chance on; come across / 遺体が発見される be found dead / 発見時代〖西洋史〗the Age of Discovery / 発見者 a discoverer.
はっけん² 発券 the issue of banknotes ¶発券高 the amount of notes issued.
はつげん 発言 a statement;《文》(an) utterance;〈提案〉a proposal ¶発言する speak;《文》utter; open one's mouth;〈提言する〉propose; 発言を許されるbe allowed to speak;《米》be recognized (会議で) / 発言権 the right to speak; a voice / 発言者 a speaker / 大衆に政治的発言力を与える give a political voice to the masses. 文例⇩
はつこい 初恋 one's first love.
はっこう¹ 発行 publication; issue ¶発行する publish; issue; bring out; put 《silver coins》 into circulation; float 《a loan》 / 発行されたばかりの新聞 a copy of newspaper damp from the presses / 毎日[毎月]発行の published daily [monthly] / 発行者 the publisher / 発行所 a publishing office /（公債などの）発行高 the amount of issue / 発行停止 suspension of publication / 新聞の発行停止を解除する cancel the suspension of a newspaper / 発行日 the date of issue [publication] /（新聞・雑誌の）発行部数 a circulation. 文例⇩
はっこう² 発光 luminescence ¶発光する emit [give forth] light / 発光体 a luminous object / 発光塗料 luminous [luminescent] paint.
はっこう³ 発効 ¶発効する come [go] into effect [force];《文》become effective.

は知られていない. Nothing definite is known about Shakespeare's early life. / はっきりは存じません. I don't know for certain. / 天気がはっきりしない. The weather is unsettled. / 病気は相変わらずはっきりしません. I don't seem to be getting any better.
ばつぐん 彼は今度の試験で抜群の成績だった. He really distinguished himself in the last examination.
はっけ 当たるも八卦, 当たらぬも八卦. The prediction may or may not come true. / Fortunetelling is a hit-or-miss affair.
はっけん¹ それは医学史上最大の発見の１つである. It is one of the greatest discoveries in medical history.
はつげん 彼は会議中一言も発言しなかった. He remained quite silent [He said nothing] throughout the conference. / 僕はその事については発言権がない. I have no voice [say] in the matter. / 私は彼と対等の発言権を要求する. I claim [demand] an equal voice with him.
はっこう¹ Kタイムズが発行停止を食った. The publication of the K Times was placed under [subjected to] suspension (by the authorities). / この新聞は発行部数が多い. This paper has a large

はっこう⁴ 発酵 fermentation ¶発酵する ferment / 発酵させる ferment / 発酵している be fermenting; be in ferment.
はっこう⁵ 薄幸 ⇨ はくめい¹.
はっこつ 白骨 a bleached white bone. 文例↓
ばっさい 伐採 (tree) felling ¶伐採する cut [hew] down; fell / 伐採跡地 a cutover area.
ばっさり ¶予算をばっさり削る make a drastic cut in the budget; slash the budget.
はっさん 発散 〈蒸気・臭気などの〉《文》exhalation; 〈光などの〉《文》emanation; 〈数・物〉divergence ¶発散する give [send] out 《文》forth; 《文》emit; 《文》exhale; 《文》emanate; 〈数・物〉diverge (to infinity).
ばっし¹ 抜糸 ¶抜糸する take out [remove] the stitches; 〈抜いてもらう〉have one's stitches out [removed].
ばっし² 抜歯 ¶抜歯する pull out [extract] a tooth; 〈抜いてもらう〉have one's tooth out.
バッジ a badge ¶バッジをつける[つけている] put on [wear] a badge.
はっしと ¶はっしと打つ hit [《文》strike] sb with a sharp, loud sound [with all one's might].
はっしゃ¹ 発車 ¶発車する start [《文》depart] 《from》; leave (the station); pull out (of the station) / 発車信号 a starting signal; a signal for departure / 発車ホーム a departure platform. 文例↓
はっしゃ² 発射 〈発砲〉firing; 《文》discharge; 〈ロケットなどの打上げ〉launching; (a) blastoff ¶発射する fire (off); shoot; let off; 《文》discharge; 〈ロケットなどを〉launch; blast off / (ロケットなどの発射場[台]) a launching site [pad] / 発射装置 a launcher 《for a guided missile》.
はつじょう 発情 ¶発情する 〈雄が〉go [come] into rut; rut; 〈雌が〉go [come] into [《英》on] heat] / 発情している 〈雄が〉be in rut; be rutting; 〈雌が〉be in [《英》on] heat / 発情期 the mating season.
ばっしょう 跋渉 ¶山野を跋渉する 《文》range [roam] over hill and dale.
はっしょうち 発祥地 《文》the place of origin; 《文》the cradle (of civilization); the birthplace 《of jazz music》; where sth started.
はっしょく 発色 文例↓
はっしん¹ 発信 ¶発信する send (a letter, a telegraph); 《文》dispatch (a message) / 発信局 the sending office / 発信地 the place of dispatch / 発信人 the sender (of a telegram).
はっしん² 発疹 〈医〉eruption; 〈吹き出物〉a rash ¶発疹チフス typhus (fever). 文例↓

はっしん³ 発進 《文》departure; takeoff (航空機の) ¶発進する 《文》depart (from); leave 《Yokosuka》; take off (航空機が) / 緊急発進 ⇨ きんきゅう.
はっすい 抜粋 an extract; a selection (選集) ¶ワーズワースの詩の抜粋 extracts [selections] from Wordsworth's poety / 抜粋する extract; select.
はっする 発する give out [off]; 《文》emit (火・煙・光などを); radiate (光・熱などを); 〈出す〉issue; give; 〈与える〉give [《文》utter] (a cry); 〈源を〉《文》originate (in); arise [stem] (from). 文例↓
ハッスル [<《米》hustle] ¶ハッスルする be full of energy (vigor, 《口語》beans); 《口語》be an eager beaver [a live wire].
ばっする 罰する punish; penalize; 《文》subject sb to punishment [a penalty]; 《文》discipline ⇨ ばっ¹.
はっせい¹ 発生 《文》an occurrence; an outbreak; 〈誕生〉birth; 〈電気などの〉generation; production ¶コレラの発生 an outbreak of cholera / 発生する 〈事件などが〉happen; 〈事故などが〉break out; 〈生じる〉spring (from); 〈生まれる〉《文》come into existence [being]; 〈繁殖する〉breed; 〈電気などが〉be generated / 蚊の発生を防ぐ prevent the breeding of mosquitoes / 発生学 embryology / (病気などの)発生率 a rate of incidence; the (high) incidence (of stomach cancer). 文例↓
はっせい² 発声 ¶発声する produce [utter] a (speech) sound / 発声器官 the vocal organs / 発声順に in the order of speaking / 発声法《音楽》vocalization. 文例↓
ばっせき 末席 ⇨ まっせき.
はっそう¹ 発走 〈競馬などの〉the start (of a race).
はっそう² 発送 ¶発送する send out; forward; dispatch; ship (off).
はっそう³ 発想 an idea ¶…から発想を得る get an [the] idea (for one's work) from…; 《文》draw one's inspiration from…; 《文》be inspired by… / 日本人的発想 the Japanese way of thinking / 発想記号《音楽》an expression mark. 文例↓
はっそく 発足 ⇨ ほっそく.
ばっそく 罰則 penal regulations.
ばった〔昆〕a grasshopper.
バッター〔野球〕a batter ⇨ だしゃ / 右[左]バッター a right-[left-]handed batter / バッターボックス a batter's box / バッターボック

---

circulation.
はっこつ 死体はすでに白骨化していた。The body had been reduced almost to a skeleton.
はっしゃ¹ 発車いたします。〈駅のアナウンス〉All aboard!/その列車は午後5時に発車する。The train leaves [is due out] at 5 p.m. / 私は発車間際に駅に着いた。I got to the station just as the train was going to leave.

はっしゃ² 警官はその男に向かって拳銃を発射した。The policeman fired his revolver at the man.
はっしょく このフィルムは発色がいい。Colors come out well on this film.
はっしん¹ 胸に奇妙な発疹が出た。A mysterious rash appeared [came out] on his chest.
はっする 彼は一言も発しなかっ

た。He uttered not a single word [syllable]. / 淀川は源を琵琶湖に発する。The Yodo rises in Lake Biwa.
はっせい¹ 神戸にコレラが発生した。Cholera has broken out in Kobe.
はっせい² 多田氏の発声で万歳を三唱した。They gave three cheers, led by Mr. Tada.
はっそう¹ (競輪などで)第3レ

はったつ 発達 development; growth; 《進歩》progress; 《文》advance(ment) ¶発達する develop; grow; make progress; 《文》advance; 《文》evolve / 発達させた develop; 《文》advance / よく発達した highly-[well-]developed /…の発達を助ける[妨げる] 《文》promote [arrest] the development [growth] of… / 著しい[急速な]発達を遂げる make remarkable [rapid] progress [growth] / 発達心理学 developmental [genetic] psychology / 発達段階 a developmental stage. 文例↓

はっと ¶はっとにらむ glare [look fiercely] 《at》/ cast a fierce glance 《at》.

はったり (a) bluff ¶はったりをかける bluff / はったり屋 a bluffer.

ばったり ¶《音》with a thud; 〈突然〉⇒ばったり ¶ばったり倒れる fall down with a thud / ばったり出会う run into sb; come on [across] sb.

ばったり 〈突然〉suddenly; abruptly ¶ばったり止まる stop suddenly [short]; come to a dead stop. 文例↓

ハッチ 〈海〉a hatch; a hatchway.

はっちゃく 発着 arrival and departure ¶列車の発着時刻 arrival and departure times of trains / 発着時刻表 a timetable; 《米》a schedule / 汽船発着所 a landing place for steamers.

はっちゅう 発注 ¶発注する place an order 《with sb for an article》; order 《an article from England》; give sb an order 《for an article》.

ばっちり ¶ばっちりかせぐ make money in a sure way.

ばっちり ¶ばっちりした目 bright, clear eyes.

バッティング¹ 〈野球〉batting ¶バッティングの姿勢 one's batting stance / バッティングケージ a batting cage.

バッティング² 〈ボクシング〉butting; (illegal) use of the head ¶バッティングをやる butt 《one's opponent》; use one's head.

ばってき 抜擢 ¶抜擢する select [choose, pick out] sb 《from among many》 《for an important position》.

バッテリー 〈蓄電池〉a battery; 〈野球〉a battery / バッテリーが上がる the battery goes flat / バッテリー間のサイン signals between pitcher and catcher.

はってん 発展 development; growth; expansion; 《文》evolution ¶発展する develop; grow; expand; evolve / 海外へ発展する expand overseas; extend its activities overseas / (都市が)郊外へ発展する expand over the surrounding country / 発展途上国 a developing country [nation]. 文例↓

はつでん 発電 (electric) power generation; generation of electricity ¶発電する generate electricity / 発電機 a generator; a [an electric] dynamo 《pl. -s》 / 発電所 a [an electric] power plant [station].

ばってん 罰点 ¶罰点を付ける mark with a cross [an X]; mark an X 《on》.

はっと ¶はっとする be startled; be surprised; be taken aback; 《文》start; get a start / はっとして With a start; in surprise / ...と思わせる take sb's breath away; give sb a start; startle. 文例↓

バット 〈野球〉a bat ¶投球をバットの心でとらえる hit the ball solidly / バットを振る swing one's bat.

ぱっと suddenly; in a flash ¶ぱっと照らす flash a light 《on》 / ぱっと明るくなる light up suddenly / ぱっと燃え上がる burst into flame(s); flare [flame] up / ぱっと顔を赤らめる blush; flush (up) / ぱっとしない〈目立たない〉《文》undistinguished; inconspicuous; 〈はなばなしくない〉《文》unprepossessing; 〈文〉unspectacular; 〈思わしくない〉unsatisfactory / ぱっとしない学生 an undistinguished [a dull] boy.

パット 〈ゴルフ〉a putt ¶パットする putt.

パッド 〈洋服の肩などに入れる詰め物〉a pad; 〈ブラジャー〉a padded brassière; 《口語》falsies ¶パッドをたくさん入れた heavily padded 《shoulders》.

はつどう 発動 ¶発動する 〈動く〉move; 〈動かす〉《文》put [set] in motion; 〈行使する〉《文》exercise; 《文》invoke 《法・規約などを》 / 強権を発動する ⇒ きょうけん³.

ばっとう 抜刀 ¶抜刀する draw [unsheathe] one's sword / 抜刀して with a drawn sword (in one's hand).

はつどうき 発動機 a motor; an engine.

はっとうしん 八頭身 ¶八頭身の美人 a beautiful well-proportioned woman.

はづな 端綱 a halter.

はつに 初荷 the first cargo [consignment] of the New Year.

はつねつ 発熱 ¶発熱する〈熱を発生させる〉generate heat; 〈体温が高くなる〉run a temperature; become feverish; develop a fever / 発熱している have [be running] a temperature; be feverish; have a fever.

はっぱ 発破 ¶発破をかける〈ダイナマイトで爆破する〉blast sth [blow sth up] with dynamite; 〈気合いをかける〉urge sb to do.

は午後2時発走。The third (race) is [starts] at 2 p.m.

はっそう 英語と日本語とでは発想法が違う。Things are conceived differently in English and Japanese [in English from the way they are in Japanese].

はったつ 科学は近代になって急速に発達した。Science has made rapid progress [The advance of science has been very rapid] in modern times. / 象牙彫りは中国で最高度の発達を遂げた。Ivory carving reached [achieved] its highest development [sophistication] in China.

ばったり その後彼からは音信がばったりとだえてしまった。I've heard nothing from him since.

ばっちり 今日の試験はばっちりだ。Today's exam was a cinch. | 《米口語》I did great in today's exam.

はってん 形勢は有利に発展した。The situation has developed in our favor.

はっと その音に彼ははっとした。He started at [He was alarmed by] the sound.

ぱっと うわさがぱっと広がった。The rumor got about in a flash. / うまい考えがぱっとひらめいた。A bright [《文》happy] idea flashed

はつばい 発売 ¶発売する sell; put *sth* on the market / 発売になる be on sale; go on the market / 発売中である be on sale / 発売禁止 prohibition of sale / 発売元 a sales [selling] agency.

ぱっぱと 〈煙などを吐くさま〉 in puffs; puff-puff; 〈惜しげなく〉 freely; lavishly; 《文》 unsparingly; 《文》 ungrudgingly; 〈向こうみずに〉 recklessly ¶ぱっぱとタバコを吹かす puff (away) at *one's* cigarette [cigar, pipe] / ぱっぱと金を使う spend money like water [lavishly]; squander money (on).

はつはる 初春 〈春の初め〉 early spring; 〈新年〉 the New Year.

はっぴ 法被 a *happi* (coat); a (workman's) livery coat.

ハッピーエンド a happy end [ending] ¶ハッピーエンドになる have a happy ending; come to a happy end.

はつひので 初日の出 the sunrise on New Year's Day.

はつびょう 発病 ¶発病する be taken ill; fall [(become)] ill [(米) sick]; come down with [《文》 contract] a disease / 〈潜伏期を過ぎて〉 show [present] the symptoms of a disease.

はっぴょう 発表 an announcement; publication ¶発表する announce; publish; 《文》 make *sth* known [public] / 〈生徒が〉調べたことをクラスで発表する present the results of *one's* research to the class; read *one's* report to the class. 文例⇩

ばつびょう 抜錨する 〈いかりを上げる〉 weigh anchor; 〈船出する〉 set sail (from).

はっぷ 発布 promulgation ⇨こうふ².

はつぶたい 初舞台 *one's* first appearance on the stage; *one's* début ¶初舞台を踏む make *one's* début.

はっぷん 発奮[憤] ¶発奮する be stimulated 《by》; be roused (to action) 《by》; 《文》 make a new resolve 《to *do*》.

はっぽう¹ 八方 しほう¹(四方(八方)に, 四方八方から) ¶八方破れの構えをとる stand at open guard. 文例⇩

はっぽう² 発泡 foaming ⇨あわ¹ ¶発泡剤 a foaming agent ¶発泡スチロール expanded polystyrene; styrene foam.

はっぽう³ 発砲 ¶発砲する fire [open fire] (on); fire (off) [《文》 discharge] a gun. 文例⇩

ばっぽんてき 抜本的 《文》 radical; drastic.

はつみみ 初耳.

はつめい 発明 (an) invention ¶発明する invent / 発明の才がある have a genius for invention / 発明者[家] an inventor / 発明品 an invention.

はつもうで 初詣 *one's* first visit of the year to a shrine [temple] (made during the New Year).

はつもの 初物 the first (product) of the season ¶初物 early 《mushrooms》.

はつゆき 初雪 the first snow(fall) of the season.

はつゆめ 初夢 *one's* first dream of the New Year.

はつらつ 潑剌 ¶はつらつとした lively; sprightly / 生気はつらつとしている be full of vigor [vitality, life].

はつれい 発令 an official announcement; a proclamation ¶発令する announce 《*sb's* appointment》 officially; issue 《regulations, a warning》.

はつろ 発露 (an) expression; 《文》(a) manifestation.

はて 果て 〈終わり〉 the end; 《文》 the extremity; 〈際限〉 the limit(s); 〈結末〉 the result ¶旅路の果て [*one's*] journey's end / 世界の果てから from the other side of the world / 世界の果てまで to the ends of the earth (★ the end of the earth とすると, 「この世の終わり」「地球の滅亡の時」の意になる) / 果ては in the end; on top of that / 果てしない endless; 〈広さが〉 《文》 boundless; 〈時から〉 《文》 eternal; everlasting / 果てしなく endlessly; 《文》 eternally / …には果てしがない There is no end to.... 文例⇩

はで 派手 ¶派手な flamboyant; gay; showy; gaudy; loud / 派手なネクタイ a gaudy [loud(-colored)] shirt / 派手な生活をする live in (grand) style / 派手な服装をしている be flamboyantly [gaily] dressed / 派手好きである be fond of display [show]. 文例⇩

パテ putty ¶パテを塗る putty (up); apply putty (to).

ばてい¹ 馬丁 a groom; a horsekeeper.

ばてい² 馬蹄 a horse's hoof; 〈馬のひづめに打つ鉄〉 a horseshoe ¶馬蹄形磁石 a horseshoe magnet.

はて(な) 〈驚き・疑い〉 what!; why!; 〈考える時〉 let me see; well. 文例⇩

はてる 果てる 〈終わる〉 end; be finished;

---

across my mind. / 彼が話しかけると彼女はぱっと顔を赤くした. She flushed up [went bright red] when he spoke to her.

はつばい その雑誌は発売禁止になった. The sale of the magazine was prohibited [forbidden]. | The magazine was banned.

はっぴょう それについては彼は意見の発表を差し控えた. He refrained from expressing his opinion [making comments] on it. / 試験の成績が発表された. The results of the examination have been announced.

はっぽう¹ 彼は八方美人だ. He tries to please everybody. / 占いによると今年は僕は八方ふさがりだそうだ. A fortuneteller told me that everything will go against me this year.

はっぽう³ もし発砲されたら発砲せよと命令されていた. They were under orders to fire if fired upon.

はつみみ それは初耳です. That's news to me. | That's the first I've heard of it.

はて 彼女は彼を追って北海道の果てまで旅をした. She wanted to get in touch with him and traveled to the remotest part of Hokkaido.

はで 色が派手過ぎる. The colors are too bright [loud]. / 私には彼女には派手でしょう. I'm afraid that dress is too young for her.

はて(な) はて, どうしたものかしらん. Well, what am I to do now? / はて, どこへ置いたのかな. Let me see—where did I put it? / はてさて妙なことがあるものだ. How very odd!

はてる 彼のスピーチはいつ果てるともわからなかった. There was

はてんこう 破天荒 ¶破天荒の record-breaking; unprecedented; unheard-of.
はと 鳩 a pigeon (特に野ばと); a dove (特に野ばと) ¶はとが豆鉄砲を食ったような顔をしている look blank [puzzled] / はと小屋 a dovecot(e); a pigeon house / はと時計 a cuckoo clock / はと派 the doves; ⟨1人⟩ a dove / はと便で by carrier pigeon / はと胸の pigeon-chested.
はどう 波動 a wave motion; undulation ¶波動する move in waves; undulate / 光の波動説 the wave [undulatory] theory of light.
ばとう 罵倒 ⇨ ののしる, ののしる.
パトカー ⇨ パトロール (パトロールカー).
パドック a paddock.
はとば 波止場 a wharf (《pl.》 wharves, -s); a landing stage; a quay (岸壁); a pier (突堤).
バドミントン badminton.
はとめ 鳩目 an eyelet.
はどめ 歯止め a drag [skid] (for retarding the motion of a cart wheel); ⟨ブレーキ⟩ a brake ¶歯止めをかける put the brakes on (the rise in prices).
パトロール patrol ¶パトロールする go on patrol (duty); patrol (an area) / パトロール中の警官 a policeman on patrol (duty); a patrolman / パトロールカー a police car; a (police) patrol car; (米) a squad [cruise, prowl] car.
パトロン ⟨男⟩ a patron; ⟨女⟩ a patroness.
ハトロンし ハトロン紙 brown [kraft] paper.
バトン a baton ¶バトンを渡す pass [hand over] the baton (to); ⟨仕事などを⟩ hand over (one's duties to) / バトンを受け継ぐ accept [receive] the baton (from); ⟨仕事などを⟩ take over (sb's duties) / バトンガール [トワラー] a (female) baton twirler; a drum majorette / バトンタッチ a baton pass; a handover.
はな¹ 花, 華 ⟨草木の⟩ a flower; 《文》 a bloom; a blossom (特に果樹の); ⟨桜の花⟩ a cherry blossom; ⟨精粋⟩《文》 the essence;《文》 the flower ¶社交界の花 [華]《文》 the belle of society / 職場の花 a beauty in the office; a female employee who is (expected to be) decorative rather than useful [functional] / 武士道の華 the flower of chivalry / 花の floral / 花の咲いている木 a blossoming [flowering] tree; a tree in flower / 花の都パリ the gay [fine] city of Paris / 花を生ける arrange flowers; put flowers in (a vase) / 花を切る cut a flower / ⟨草や木が⟩花をつける flower; come into flower /《文》 bear flowers / 花を作る grow flowers / 花を摘む pick [gather] flowers / 議論 [話] に花を咲かす《口》《文》 engage in a heated discussion [in animated conversation] / 花を持たせる let sb have the credit for ⟨the success⟩ / 花売り a flower vendor / 花売り娘 a flower girl / 花言葉 the language of flowers / 花畑 a field of flowers; a flower garden. 用例⇩

はな² 洟 snivel ¶はなをかむ blow one's nose (with [into] one's handkerchief) / はなをチーンとかむ blow one's nose with a loud trumpeting noise / はなをすする sniff; sniffle / はなを垂らす one's nose runs; run at the nose / はなを垂らしている子供 a child with a running nose / はなも引っかけない ignore sb [sth] completely. 用例⇩

はな³ 鼻 a nose; ⟨犬・馬などの⟩ a muzzle; ⟨象の⟩ a trunk ¶はなをかむ a prominent [high-bridged] nose; a long nose / 低い鼻 a flat nose / 上を向いた鼻 a turned-up nose / 鼻があぐらをかいている have a wide [broad] nose / 鼻が利く have a sharp [keen] nose / 鼻が高い have a prominent [long] nose; ⟨誇る⟩ be proud (of) / 鼻の穴 the nostrils / 鼻の差で勝つ ⟨競馬⟩ win by a nose / すぐ鼻の先で right under one's nose / 鼻をほじる pick one's nose / 鼻をつまむ hold one's nose / くんくん鼻を鳴らす sniff / 鼻を高くする《文》 be puffed up (with pride); be elated ⟨over⟩ / 鼻をあかす outwit sb / ⟨高慢の⟩鼻を折る《文》 humble sb [sb's pride]; put sb's nose out of joint; ⟨口語⟩ take sb down a peg (or two) / 鼻につく ⟨においが⟩《文》 be offensive to the nose [smell]; stink; ⟨うんざりする⟩ be disgusted [fed up] ⟨with⟩; be (sick and) tired ⟨of⟩ / 鼻にかける be proud (of); pride oneself ⟨on⟩; take a pride (in) / 鼻で息をする breathe through one's nose / 鼻であしらう treat sb with contempt [scorn]; snub; ⟨口語⟩ high-hat / 鼻高々と proudly; triumphantly. 用例⇩

はな⁴ 端 ⟨初め⟩ ⇨ はじめ, ⟨末端⟩ ⇨ はし².
はないき 鼻息 ¶鼻息が荒い breathe hard through one's nose; ⟨比喩的に⟩ be arrogant;

---

no knowing when his speech would come to an end.
はと とがえぐうと鳴いていた. Pigeons were cooing. / はとは平和の象徴だ. The dove is the symbol of peace.

はな¹ 花はいかがですか. Flowers for sale! / 花が咲いている. The flowers are out. / The tree is in flower [bloom]. / 花が散った. The flowers have fallen [are over]. / 彼もあのころが花だった. Those were his best days. / 秀吉が天下を握っていた時に桃山時代の美術がその花を開いた. Hideyoshi's rule saw the flowering of the art of the Momoyama Period. | During Hideyoshi's rule Momoyama art came to flower. / 花より団子. Dumplings are better [more use] than cherry blossoms. | People would rather have rice dumplings than cherry blossoms. / 花言葉では赤いばらはどういう意味ですか. What does the red rose mean in the language of flowers?

はな² 洟が垂れているよ. Your nose is running [dripping]. / はなをかまなければいけないよ. Your nose wants blowing. / はなを強くかみすぎてはいけないよ. Don't blow your nose too hard. / 彼は鼻の穴を片方ずつ押えて, はなをかんだ. He blew his nose closing each nostril in turn.

はな³ 鼻が詰まった. My nose is stuffed [stopped] up. / あの人の言葉は少し鼻にかかる. He speaks rather through his nose. / 部屋へ入ると臭気が鼻を突いた. A nasty smell assailed my nose as I entered. / さぞお父様も鼻が高いでしょう. You are certainly doing your father proud. / 真の教

はないけ

はないけ 花生け a (flower) vase.
はなうた 鼻歌 ¶鼻歌を歌う hum a tune.
はなお 鼻緒 a (geta) thong; straps (of a geta) ¶鼻緒をすげる fix a thong 《on a geta》.
はなかご 花籠 a flower basket.
はなかぜ 鼻風邪 a cold in the head [nose].
はながた 花形 〈花模様〉a floral [flower] pattern; 〈人気者〉a star ¶花形株〔商〕leading stocks / 花形選手 a star player.
はながみ 鼻紙 (tissue) paper for wiping the nose.
はなぐすり 鼻薬 〈わいろ〉a bribe ¶鼻薬をかがせる bribe; 〈口語〉grease sb's palm.
はなくそ 鼻くそ nasal mucus; 〈俗〉snot.
はなぐもり 花曇り a hazy sky in the cherry-blossom season.
はなげ 鼻毛 the hairs of [in] the nostrils ¶鼻毛を抜く pull hairs out of one's nostrils / 鼻毛を抜かれる be outwitted.
はなごえ 鼻声 a nasal (tone of) voice; a (nasal) twang ¶鼻声を出す speak through one's nose [with a twang].
はなざかり 花盛り ¶花盛りである be at 〈their〉best; be in full bloom.
はなし 話 〈談話〉(a) talk; (a) conversation; a chat; 〈演説〉a speech; 〈講話〉a lecture; 〈言辞〉what one says; a remark; a statement; 〈物語〉a story; a tale; 〈事実談〉〈文〉an account; 〈うわさ〉a rumor; 〈相談〉〈文〉(a) consultation; 〈交渉〉negotiation(s) ¶話がつく [まとまる] come to an understanding 《with》; arrive at [come to] an agreement 《with》; come to terms 《with》/ 話の種 a topic for [of] conversation / 話の上手 [下手] な人 a good [poor] talker / 話のついでに by the way; in passing ⇨ついで〔ついでに★〕/ 話のつぎ穂がなくなる be stuck for something to say; run out of topics of conversation / 話の仲間入りをする join [take part in] 〈their〉conversation / 話をする 〈会話する〉speak 《to sb, about [〈文〉of] sth》; talk 《to sb, about sth》; have a talk [chat] 《with》; 〈話題を作って〉make conversation 《with》; 〈物語る〉tell a story; 〈文〉give an account of; 〈聴衆に向かって〉make a speech [give an address] 《on a subject, to the audience》/ 戦争の話をする talk about (the) war; give an account of a battle / 話を変える change the subject [topic] of conversation / 話をそらす change the subject; turn the conversation to a different subject 《〈文〉other matters》/ 話をつける arrange 《with sb, for [about] sth》; have it out 《with》/ 話を始める 〈会話〉begin to talk; start a conversation; get [fall] into conversation; 〈物語を〉begin (to tell) a story / 話を元に戻す 〈話題を〉go [get] back to the original topic [subject]; 〈段々と〉work the conversation back (to) / 話を元に戻して… As I was saying, … / 話にならないを be out of the question; 〈文〉be beneath one's notice / 話に花を咲かせる 〈文〉engage in animated conversation; have a lively discussion / 話に持ち出す bring (a topic) into the conversation / 小説の話で思い出したが talking of novels / ここだけの話だが between you and me; between ourselves; 〈文〉変わっていの meantime; meanwhile; on the other hand / 話相手 someone to talk to; a companion / 話相手になる keep sb company / 話言葉 spoken language; a colloquial expression / 話好きな talkative; chatty / 話半分に聞く 〈文〉discount sb's statement; take sb's story with a grain [pinch] of salt / 話半分としても even allowing for exaggeration. 文例⇩

はなしあい 話し合い 〈相談〉〈文〉(a) consultation; (a) conference; 〈交渉〉negotiation(s) ¶話し合いの上で 〈相談〉after consultation; 〈合意〉by common [mutual] consent / 話し合いがつく ⇨はなし〔話がつく〕.
はなしあう 話し合う 〈会話する〉talk 《to, with》; 〈相談する〉discuss 《sth with sb》; 〈文〉consult 《with sb》¶徹底的に話し合う talk sth out 《with》; have it out 《with》. 文例⇩
バナジウム 〔化〕vanadium.
はなしがい 放し飼い ¶放し飼いにする 〈放牧する〉pasture [graze] 《cattle》; put 《cattle》to grass; 〈犬などを〉leave 《a dog》 loose; give 《a dog》free run of 《one's house》.

養人は学問を鼻にかけるようなことはしないものだ. A truly educated man ought to carry his learning lightly.

はないき 金が出来たのであの男は近ごろ鼻息が荒くなった. Having acquired a fortune, he has grown quite arrogant lately.

はなし お話で〔電話〕〔米〕The line's busy. | 〔英〕The number's engaged. / 電話をかけたらブーッ・ブーッと〔英〕「お話中」の信号が聞こえた. The telephone gave a busy signal 〔英〕an engaged tone]. / お話中失礼ですが, Excuse my [me for] interrupting you, but…. / 案外話のわかる人だった. He was more sensible than I expected. / ちょっと君に話がある. I want to speak to you a moment. | I would like a word with you. / 話というのは何ですか. What do you want to say? / その話はもうやめにしましょう. Let's drop the subject. | We'll say no more about it. / 人によって話が違う. Accounts vary. そうなればまた話が違う. That's another question [story]. / それでは話が違う. 〈約束と違う〉That was not how I [we] understood it. / いつまでも話の種が尽きなかった. We never stopped talking. | We had an endless supply of topics for conversation. / 話が一層はずんだ. The conversation became even livelier [more animated]. / 話は現代の社会制度に及んだ. The talk turned to the social system of the present day. / 武井君の話で思い出したことがある. The mention of Takei reminds me of something. / ばかな話じゃないか. How stupid [ridiculous]! / その混雑ったら何ともお話にならなかった. The congestion was beyond description. / それは話がうますぎる. That (story) sounds too good to be true. / みんなの話ではなかなかの学者らしい. According to what people say, he is a good scholar. | They say that he is a good scholar. / そういう話だ. So That's [what] they say. | So I am told. / 何とか話がつかないものかね. Can't you come to some

はなしがい

はなしかける 話し掛ける speak [talk] to *sb*; start a conversation with *sb*;《文》address *sb*;〈知らない人に〉《文》accost *sb*.

はなしこむ 話し込む have a long talk 《with》¶ 話し込んでいる be deep in conversation 《with》.

はなしょうぶ 〖植〗 an iris.

はなじろむ 鼻白む look embarrassed; be disappointed.

はなす¹ 放す let *sth* [*sb*] go [off, loose];〈解放する〉set *sb* free; release ¶〈つかまえた〉手を放す let go (*one's* hold) 《of》/ 牛を牧場に放す turn cattle out to graze. 文例⇩

はなす² 話す talk《of》; have a talk [chat]《with》;〈告げる〉tell *sb*; speak (about, of);〈述べる〉《文》state; mention;〈物語る〉narrate ¶ 英語で話す speak in English / 英語を流暢(りゅうちょう)に話す speak English fluently; be a fluent speaker of English. 文例⇩

はなす³ 離す〈分ける〉《文》part; separate; divide;〈引き離す〉detach; keep (A) from (B) ¶ 木を2メートル離して植える plant trees two meters apart (2本またはそれ以上); plant trees at intervals of two meters (3本以上). 文例⇩

はなすじ 鼻筋 ¶ 鼻筋の通った美人 a beautiful woman with a shapely nose.

はなせる 話せる 《be》 (very) understanding ¶ 話せる男 a sensible man;《文》a man of sense. 文例⇩

はなぞの 花園 a flower garden.

はなたて 花立て a (flower) vase; a flower stand.

はなたば 花束 a bunch of flowers; a bouquet.

はなだより 花便り news about the cherry blossoms (from various parts of Japan).

はなぢ 鼻血 a nosebleed ¶ 鼻血が出る *one's* nose bleeds; bleed at [from] the nose. 文例⇩

はなつ 放つ 〈解き放す〉set *sb* free; let *sb* go (free);《文》release;〈発射する〉shoot (an arrow); loose (off) (an arrow); fire [discharge] (a gun);〈香気・光などを〉give out [off]; send [put] out [《文》forth];《文》emit ¶ 犬を放つ set [loose] a dog (on an escaping convict) / 火を放つ set fire to (a shed); set (a house) on fire / 芳香を放つ send forth fragrance; smell sweet.

はなっぱし(ら) 鼻っぱし(ら) ¶ 鼻っぱし(ら)の強い男 an aggressive [an overconfident,《文》a self-assertive] fellow / 鼻っぱしらをへし折る ⇨ はな³ (鼻を折る).

はなつまみ 鼻摘まみ a disgusting [detestable] fellow; a nuisance;《文》a rat;《口語》a (mean) stinker;《口語》a skunk.

はなづら 鼻面 〈動物の〉the muzzle.

はなどき 花時 cherry blossom time; the cherry blossom season.

バナナ a banana ¶ バナナの木[皮] a banana plant [skin].

はなばさみ 花鋏 scissors used in flower arrangement.

はなばしら 鼻柱 the bridge of the nose ¶ 鼻柱の高い high-bridged (noses).

はなはだ 甚だ very;《文》greatly;《文》highly; very much; awfully; terribly;〈過度に〉《文》exceedingly;《文》excessively.

はなはだしい 甚だしい extreme;《文》excessive ¶ はなはだしい暑さ intense [terrible] heat / はなはだしい誤り a glaring [gross] mistake;《文》a flagrant error / はなはだしい損・a heavy loss / はなはだしく ⇨ なはだ / はなはだしきに至っては in an extreme instance [case]; worst of all; to crown (it) all. 文例⇩

はなばなしい 華々しい splendid; brilliant; glorious; spectacular ¶ はなばなしい最期を遂げる《文》die a glorious [heroic] death (in the battle) / はなばなしく splendidly; brilliantly;《口語》in a big way.

はなび 花火 fireworks ¶ 花火を上げる display [set off] fireworks / 花火工場 a fireworks factory / 花火師 a pyrotechnist; a pyrotechnician / 花火大会 a display of fireworks; a firework(s) [pyrotechnic] display. 文例⇩

はなびら 花びら a petal ⇨ かべん.

はなふぶき 花吹雪 a shower of cherry blossoms; cherry blossoms falling in the wind.

パナマ Panama ¶ パナマの Panamanian / パナマ運河 the Panama Canal / パナマ共和国 the Republic of Panama / パナマ人 a Panama-

---

understanding? / あの話しぶりでは彼は何もかも承知らしい. From his manner of speaking [By the way he talks], he seems to know everything about it. / 隣の部屋で人の話声が聞こえた. I heard several voices talking in the next room.

はなしあう この問題について徹底的に話し合おうじゃないか. Let's talk this problem out [through].

はなす¹ すっぽんはかみついたら雷が鳴るまで放さない. When a snapping turtle bites you, he won't let loose until it thunders.

はなす² この方が先日お話しした岡田さんです. This is the Mr. Okada I mentioned to you the other day. / どんな本でもちょっと話して下さい. Just give me an idea of the book. / 君に話したい事がある. I have something to tell you. / これは君だけに話すのだ. This is for your ear alone. / これは二人の間の話だ. This is between the two of us. / 話せば長いことさ. It's a long story.

はなす³ この辞書は片時も離せない. I'd be lost without this dictionary. / This dictionary is indispensable to me. / 彼は仕事中で手が離せない. He is engaged [busy]. / 彼はいつも本を離さずおく. He is never without a book. / (けんかしないように) 犬を離しておけ. Keep the dogs apart [away from each other]. / 子供から目を離すな. Never take your eyes off the child. / Keep an eye on the child. / 彼はめったにパイプを口から離したことがない. The pipe is rarely out of his mouth.

はなせる 君も賛成だっていうのか? そいつは話せるなあ. Did you say you are for it, too? That shows you've some sense [That's grand].

はなぢ 彼はひどく鼻血を出した. He had a bad [severe] nosebleed. / His nose bled profusely.

はなはだしい 当時は就職難が今よりはなはだしかった. The difficulty of securing employment was felt more keenly then than now. / 人を愚弄するのもはなはだしい. You carry your joke too far.

はなび そら, 花火が上がった! There go the fireworks! / 今夕多摩川で花火大会がある. There

はなまつり 花祭り the Buddha's birthday festival; the Flower Festival.

はなみ 花見 cherry blossom viewing ¶花見に行く go to see the cherry blossoms 《at》/ 花見時 the cherry-blossom season. 文例⇩

はなみち 花道 an elevated passageway running from the stage to the dressing room at the rear of the theater; a 'flower way'.

はなむこ 花婿 a bridegroom.

はなめがね 鼻眼鏡 (a pair of) pince-nez.

はなもち 鼻持ち ¶鼻持ちならない〈においが〉smell bad [nasty, unpleasant]; stink; 〈人が〉be disgusting; be detestable; be offensive ⇒ はなつまみ.

はなもよう 花模様 a floral [flower] pattern [design].

はなや 花屋 〈人〉a florist; 〈店〉a flower shop; a florist's; a flower stall (屋台店).

はなやか 華やか ¶はなやかな flowery; flamboyant; gay; brilliant / はなやかな生活 a gay life / 政治家としてはなやかな生涯を送る have a brilliant career as a statesman / 武士道はなやかなりしころ〈文〉in the gallant days of chivalry;《文》when knighthood was in flower.

はなよめ 花嫁 a bride ¶花嫁学校 a finishing school; a school for domestic training / 花嫁修業 training for homemaking; domestic training / 花子の花嫁姿 Hanako in bridal dress.

はならび 歯並び ¶歯並びがいい[悪い]have regular [irregular] teeth; one's teeth are even [uneven].

はなれ 離れ 〈離れ家〉a cottage separate from the main building; 〈離れ座敷〉a detached room; an annex.

ばなれ 場馴れ ¶場馴れのした experienced; veteran / 場馴れがする get used to the stage [platform] / 場馴れがしている be at home 《in speech-making, on the platform》.

はなれじま 離れ島 a solitary [remote] island; a desert island (南洋の).

はなればなれ 離れ離れ ¶離れ離れの separated; scattered / 離れ離れに〈別れて〉separately; apart; 〈それぞれ〉independently / 離れ離れになる get separated 《from each other》;《文》be dispersed.

はなれる 離れる 〈分かれる〉separate;《文》part from [with]; fall apart; 〈とれる〉come off; 〈去る〉leave;《文》depart《from》; go away《from》¶《列車が》駅を離れる leave the station / 職を離れる quit one's job / 列を離れる fall out of (the) line / 離れた separated; detached; 〈孤立した〉isolated; 〈遠くの〉《文》distant; far; remote / 離れられない《文》inseparable; close《relationships》/ 離れて away from;《文》apart《from》; at a distance; 〈孤立して〉isolated; by itself; 離れ離れに〉separately《from》/ 2メートルずつ離れて at intervals of two meters / 遠く離れて《文》at a long [great] distance; a long way away [off]; far away《from》/ …から4マイル離れている be four miles away from…. 文例⇩

はなれわざ 離れ業 a feat; a stunt ¶離れ業を演じる do [perform] a feat [stunt].

はなわ¹ 花輪 a (floral) wreath; a (floral) garland.

はなわ² 鼻輪 a nose ring.

はにかむ be bashful; be shy ¶はにかんで bashfully; shyly.

はにく 歯肉 ⇒ はぐき.

ばにく 馬肉 horsemeat; horseflesh.

バニシングクリーム vanishing cream.

パニック a panic ⇒ きょうこう².

バニラ vanilla ¶バニラエッセンス vanilla essence [flavoring].

はにわ 埴輪 a clay [terra-cotta] image《of a man, of an animal》; a burial mound figurine.

バヌアツ Vanuatu ¶バヌアツの Vanuatuan / バヌアツ共和国 the Republic of Vanuatu.

はね¹ 羽 〈羽毛〉a feather; a plume (特に帽子などにつける、長いもの); plumage (総称); down (わた毛); 〈翼〉a wing ¶羽が生える fledge; grow wings (羽が) / 羽が生えて飛ぶように売れる sell like hot cakes / 羽のある feathered; winged / 羽を広げる[畳む]spread [fold] its wings / 羽を伸ばす have a good time; go on the loose [spree] / 羽布団 a down [feather] quilt. 文例⇩

はね² 羽 a shuttlecock ¶羽根をつく play battledore and shuttlecock.

はね³ 跳ね 〈泥などの〉splashes (of mud); 〈芝居などの〉the close ¶着物にはねを上げる have one's clothes spattered [splattered] with mud. 文例⇩

ばね 〈弾力性〉spring ¶ばねのある歩き方 a springy (foot)step / ばね仕掛けの worked by a spring; spring-loaded (locks). 文例⇩

はねあがる 跳ね上がる leap [jump, spring] up; 〈相場が〉rise suddenly; make a jump.

はねおきる 跳ね起きる 〈立つ〉jump [spring] up; spring [leap] to one's feet; 〈寝床から〉jump out of [spring from] (one's) bed.

---

will be a display of fireworks on the Tama this evening.

はなみ 上野公園には花見客が集まって陽気に騒いでいる。Ueno Park is full of cherry-blossom-viewing parties [of people come to view the cherry blossoms] who are having a fine old time.

はなめがね 眼鏡がずり落ちて鼻眼鏡になっている。His glasses have slipped down low on his nose.

はなれる 離れずについておいで. Keep close to me. / あの子は母親のそばを離れない。That child is always at his mother's side. / 時々町を離れるのも悪くないね。It's a good idea to get away from town from time to time. / 彼は私の家から少し離れた所に住んでいる. He lives (at) some way [distance] from my house. / 離れて見ると何でもきれいに見えるものだ。From a distance everything looks [shows] to advantage. | It's distance that lends charm to the view.

はね¹ あの鳥の羽はきれいだ. That bird has pretty feathers [beautiful plumage].

はね³ ズボンにはねが上がっている。The trousers were splashed [bespattered] with mud.

ばね 年はとっても歩き方にはまだ

はねかえす 跳ね返す drive 《the enemy》back ; 《文》repel ; 《文》repulse.

はねかえり 跳ね返り 〈はずんで返ること〉 rebounding ; 〈影響〉 repercussions ; 〈おてんば〉 ⇒ おてんば ¶運賃値上げの物価への跳ね返り the repercussions [effects] of a raise in railroad fares on price levels [the cost of living].

はねかえる 跳ね返る spring 《back》; rebound ; boomerang ¶…に当って跳ね返る bounce off 《the wall》. 文例⇩

はねかける 跳ね掛ける splash ; spatter ; 《文》 bespatter ¶泥[水]を跳ねかける splash *sb* [*sth*] with mud [water].

はねぐるま 羽根車 〈タービンなどの〉 a vaned [bladed] wheel.

はねつける はね付ける turn down; refuse; reject 《*sb's* request》; rebuff *sb*; wave 《*sb's* objection》aside.

はねつるべ a (well) sweep.

はねとばす 跳ね飛ばす send 《a stone》flying ¶はね飛ばされる be knocked over [down, flying] 《by a car》; be knocked off 《one's bicycle》.

はねのける はね除ける push [《文》thrust, brush] aside.

はねばし 跳ね橋 a drawbridge.

はねまわる 跳ね回る jump [skip, romp] about ¶跳ね回って遊ぶ gambol ; frolic.

ハネムーン a honeymoon ⇒ しんこん(新婚旅行をする).

はねる¹ 刎ねる ¶首をはねる cut *sb's* head off ; behead *sb*.

はねる² 跳ねる 〈跳び上がる〉 leap ; spring (up); jump ; hop ; 〈馬が〉 prance ; 〈水・泥が〉 spatter ; splash ; 〈終演になる〉 close ; be over ; break up. 文例⇩

はねる³ 撥ねる 〈はじく〉 flip ; 〈除く〉 reject ; eliminate ¶車にはねられる be hit [knocked down] by a car / 試験ではねられる fail [be eliminated] in an examination.

パネル a panel ¶パネルディスカッション a panel discussion / パネルヒーター an oil-filled electric radiator.

ハノイ Hanoi.

パノラマ a panorama ¶パノラマのような景色 a panoramic view.

はは 母 a mother ¶母の, 母らしい 《文》 maternal ; motherly ; motherlike / 母の愛 maternal affection [love] / 母の日 Mother's Day / 母のない motherless / 母方の親類 a relative on one's mother's [《文》the distaff] side / 母方の祖母 one's maternal grandmother / 母鳥 a mother bird. 文例⇩

はば 幅 〈横の長さ〉 width ; breadth ; 〈規則なくのゆとり〉 latitude ; 〈羽振り〉 influence ; 〈値段の差〉 a difference 《between two prices》; a margin 《of profit》 ¶幅が4メートルある be four meters wide [in width] / 村で幅が利く have influence with the villagers [in the village] / 幅の広い wide ; broad ; 〈船が〉 broad-beamed 《ships》 / 幅の狭い narrow / 幅を広げる widen ; broaden / 幅を利かせる make *one's* influence [authority] felt. 文例⇩

ばば 馬場 a riding track ; a racetrack.

パパ pa ; pop ; dad(dy) ; papa ¶おとうさん ★.

ははあ well ; indeed ; I see.

パパイヤ a papaya.

はばかり 憚り 〈ためらい〉 hesitation ; 〈気のとがめ〉 scruples ; 〈遠慮〉《文》reserve ; 〈便所〉 ⇒ トイレ(1) ¶はばかりながら 《文》I venture to say… ; Excuse me, but (I think)…. 文例⇩

はばかる 憚る hesitate 《to do》; have scruples about 《doing》; be afraid [shy] 《of》 ¶はばかる所なく 〈ためらいなく〉 without reserve [《文》scruple] ; 〈人前で〉 in public ; openly / 人前をはばかって for fear of being seen by others.

はばたき 羽ばたき the flap [flutter] of wings ; a wingbeat ; a wing stroke ¶羽ばたきする flap [beat, flutter] *its* wings.

はばたく 羽ばたく (羽ばたきする). ⇒

はばつ 派閥 a faction ¶派閥争い a factional dispute ; 《文》 factional strife ; rivalry between factions / 派閥解消 the elimination of factions [factionalism] / 派閥主義 factionalism. 文例⇩

はばとび 幅跳[飛]び the long jump ¶走り[立] 幅跳び the running [standing] long jump ★「幅跳び」を以前は《米》では the broad jump と言っていたが, 今は英米ともに the long jump が普通.

ハバナ Havana.

ばばぬき ばば抜き 《トランプ》(play) Old Maid.

バハマ 〈諸島〉 the Bahama Islands ; the Bahamas ; 〈連邦〉 the Commonwealth of Bahamas ¶バハマ人 a Bahamian.

はばむ 阻む keep [stop]《*sb* from *doing*》; prevent ; check ; hinder ; obstruct ¶敵の進撃を阻む check the advance of the enemy.

はばよせ 幅寄せ moving one's car sideways ; jockeying one's car back and forward.

ババリア Bavaria ¶ババリアの Bavarian / ババリア人 a Bavarian.

ババロア Bavarian cream ; bavarois.

ばねがある. Though he is an old man, there is still [he still has] a spring in his step.

はねかえる そういう無理を部下にしいれば我が身に跳ね返ってくるものだ. If you make such unreasonable demands on your men, it will rebound on you later.

はねる² 幕は10時にはねた. The curtain fell at 10 p.m.

はは 彼女は3人の子の母になっている. She is a mother of three. | She is the mother of three children.

はば この川の幅はどのくらいですか. How wide is this river? / 幅は 10メートルある. It is ten meters across [wide]. / 彼は近ごろ芸に幅が出てきた. His performances have gained in depth. / 委員会の方針決定に当たって彼に多少の幅を持たせる必要があろう. We should allow him some latitude in determining the course of the committee's action. / 彼は党員の間に影響が利かない. He has no influence among the members of the party.

はばかり はばかりながら人様に借金なぞはびた一文もありません. Let me remind you that I do not owe a (single) penny to anybody.

はばつ どの政党にも派閥が横行し

はびこる 〈広がる〉 spread; 〈草木が〉 grow thickly 《文》 luxuriantly, 《文》 rank; 〈のさばる〉《文》be rampant; thrive.
パピルス 【植】a papyrus (pl. -es, papyri); a papyrus plant [reed].
バビロニア Babylonia ¶バビロニアの Babylonian / バビロニア人 a Babylonian.
バビロン Babylon.
はふ 破風 【建】a gable.
はぶ 《動》a habu; a venomous pit viper of the Ryukyus.
パフ a powder puff.
パプア Papua (ニューギニア島の一部) ¶パプアの Papuan / パプア人 a Papuan / パプアニューギニア 〈国名〉 Papua New Guinea / パプアニューギニア人 a Papuan.
パフェ a parfait.
はぶく 省く 〈除く〉leave [miss] out; 《文》omit; 《文》exclude; 〈節約する〉save; 〈減じる〉《文》reduce, cut down; 《口語》cut down on *sth* ¶無用の形式を省く dispense [do away] with useless formalities / 手間を省く save labor. 文例◊
ばふさぎ 場塞ぎ ⇨ば(場をふさぐ). 文例◊
ばふだ 場札 〈トランプなどの〉the cards on the board.
はぶたえ 羽二重 *habutae*; a smooth, glossy silk cloth with a fine weave.
ハフニウム 【化】hafnium.
はブラシ 歯ブラシ a toothbrush.
はぶり 羽振り ¶羽振りがいい be prosperous; be doing quite well / 羽振りを利かせるに be influential; have a great deal of influence (with, over).
パプリカ paprika.
ばふん 馬糞 horse manure [dung, droppings]; stable manure.
はへい 派兵 ¶派兵する send [dispatch] troops (to).
バベルのとう バベルの塔 【聖書】the Tower of Babel.
はへん 破片 a broken piece; a fragment; a splinter; 〈土器などの〉《文》a shard; 《文》a potsherd ¶陶器皿の破片 a fragment of a china plate / 砲弾の破片 a shell splinter.
はぼたん 【植】a kale.
はほん 端本 〈欠本のある1組〉an incomplete set; 〈1 冊〉an odd volume.
はま 浜 the beach; the shore; 〈海岸〉the seashore; 〈砂浜〉the sands ¶〈船が〉浜に乗り上げる beach / 浜へ出る go [come] down to [out on] the beach / 浜伝いに along the beach.
はまき 葉巻き a cigar.
はまぐり 蛤 a clam ¶はまぐりの殻 a clamshell / 焼きはまぐり a baked clam.
はまち 《魚》a young yellowtail.
はまべ 浜辺 ⇨はま.
はまや 破魔矢 a decorative arrow supposed to ward off evil.
はまゆう 浜木綿 【植】a crinum.
はまりやく はまり役 a well-fitting role; a part in character ¶はまり役である〈俳優が〉be suited to (the part); be typecast for (the role); 〈仕事などに〉be the very person for (the post); be cut out for (the job).
はまる 〈入る〉get [go] into; 〈合う〉fit (in, into); be suited to; be fit for 〈疑問文・否定文で〉⇨できる¹ 囲語 ; 〈陥る〉fall into ¶敵の計略にはまる fall into the snare [trap] set by the enemy / 泥の中にはまり込む get [be] caught [stuck] in the mud. 文例◊
はみ 〈馬具の〉a bit ¶はみをかむ champ at the bit.
パミール(こうげん) パミール(高原) the Pamirs.
はみがき 歯磨き 〈練り歯磨き〉toothpaste; dental cream; 〈歯磨き粉〉tooth powder.
はみだす はみ出す, はみ出る 〈突き出る〉stick [jut] out; 《文》project; 〈押し出される〉be forced out; 〈満員で〉be crowded out.
バミューダ ⇨バーミューダ.
ハミング humming ¶ハミングする[で歌う] hum (a tune).
ハム¹ 〈肉〉ham ¶ハムエッグ(ス) ham and eggs / ハムサラダ a ham salad; ham and salad.
ハム² 〈アマチュア無線家〉a (radio) ham.
はむかう 歯[刃]向かう 〈手向かう〉turn on; rise against; 〈抵抗する〉defy; resist.
ハムスター 《動》a hamster.
はめ 羽目 【建】〈羽目板〉a panel (board); 〈腰羽目〉a wainscot ¶羽目をはずして騒ぐ make

---

ている. All the political parties are faction-ridden.
はぶく そのようにすれば費用が省けるでしょう. That way you will be able to cut down your expenses. / この機械のお陰でたいそう手間が省ける. This machine saves us a lot of time and labor. / 細かい事は報告から省いてよい. You may omit the details from the report.
ばふさぎ この本箱をここに置いては場ふさぎだ. This bookcase takes up [occupies] too much space here.
はまる このふすまははまらない. This sliding door will not fit [go] in.
はめ 僕の忠告を聞いていたらこんな羽目にはならなかったのに. If you had listened to my advice, you would not have been in [been reduced to] such a fix.
はめつ それが身の破滅になった. It proved [led to] his undoing. / あの男のお陰でみんなが破滅してしまう. He will be the ruin of us all.
はもん¹ その魚が水中に姿を消したあとに波紋が広がって行った. The fish sank down, leaving widening rings on the water. / 池に石を投げたら, 波紋が四方に広がった. I threw a stone into the pond, and ripples spread in all directions.
はや 僕が上京してからはや10年になる. It is now ten years since I came up to Tokyo.
はやい まだ早いよ. It's still early. | You've got plenty of time. / 〈時期尚早だ〉It's too early (for that) yet. / 早いほどいい. The sooner, the better. / 1日待っても飛行機で行った方が早いよ. You'll make better time by plane, even if you have to wait until tomorrow. / 彼はその知らせを聞くが早いか飛び出して行った. He had hardly heard the news before he rushed out. / 早

はめきざいく 嵌木細工 inlaid woodwork; wooden mosaic.

はめこむ 嵌め込む fit [set, let] *sth* in [into]; inlay ⇨ はめる.

はめつ 破滅 ruin; destruction;《文》fall ¶破滅する[に陥る]《文》go to ruin; be ruined / 破滅を招く[来たす]《文》bring ruin on *oneself*; ruin *oneself* / 破滅にひんする be on the brink [verge] of ruin. 文例⇩

はめて はめ手《囲碁・将棋》(fall into) a trap (set by *one*'s opponent).

はめる <指輪などを> put (a ring) on; <挿入する> put [get, fit, fix] *sth* in [into]; <充塡(てん)する> fill in; <陥れる> entrap; <だます> cheat; take in ¶障子にガラスをはめる fit a pane into a *shoji* / 手袋をはめる pull [draw] on *one*'s gloves / 指輪をはめている have [wear] a ring (on *one*'s finger).

ばめん 場面 <劇の> a scene;<場所を>a place;《文》the locale (of a novel) ¶(劇中の)場面の転換 a (quick) set change.

はもの[1] 刃物 an edged tool; cutlery (総称).

はもの[2] 端物 <はんぱになった1組> an odd [incomplete] set; <はんぱのもの> an odd piece; a remnant (反物などの残りぎれ).

はもん 波紋 a ripple ¶波紋を描く ripple; ripple out (in waves) (広がる) / 波紋を投げかける create a stir [a sensation];《文》have (major) repercussions. 文例⇩

はもん[2] 破門《宗教上の》excommunication;<師弟間の> expulsion ¶破門する excommunicate;<弟子を>expel.

ハモンドオルガン《商標名》a Hammond organ.

はや 早 <既に> already;<今や>now;<今頃は> by this time;<こんなに早くに> so soon. 文例⇩

はやあし 早足 a quick pace;《軍》a quick march;《馬術》a trot ¶早足で(walk) fast; at a fast walk; at a quick [brisk] pace; with quick steps;《馬術》at a trot.

はやい 速[早]い <速度が> quick; fast;《文》swift; speedy; rapid;《敏活な》brisk; prompt;<時間が>early; premature (尚早の) ¶仕事が早い be quick at (*one*'s) work / 進歩が早い make rapid progress / 速い電車 a fast train / 早い電車 an early train / …するが早いか no sooner… than…;《文》hardly [scarcely]…when [before]… / 早い話が to cut [make] a long story short; in short; in a word. 文例⇩

はやおき 早起き early rising ¶早起きする rise [get up] early. 文例⇩

はやが(っ)てん 早合点 ¶早合点する jump to conclusions;《文》draw [form] a hasty conclusion.

はやがね 早鐘 a fire bell; an alarm bell ¶早鐘をつく sound [ring] an alarm bell.

はやがわり 早変わり <芸人の> a quick change (of costume);《魔術の》a magical transformation ¶早変わりする make a quick change; transform *oneself* quickly (into) / 早変わりをやる芸人 a quick-change artist.

はやく[1] 破約 (a) cancellation of a contract ¶破約する cancel an agreement [a contract]. 文例⇩

はやく[2] 端役 a small [minor] part [role];《米口語》a bit part ¶端役をやる play a minor part;《米口語》be a bit player.

はやく[3] 速[早]く quickly; fast;《文》swiftly; rapidly;《敏活に》promptly;《急いで》hastily;<早い時に>early;<すぐ>instantly; soon ¶一刻も早く…する lose no time (in) *doing* / 早くとも at the earliest; at the soonest / できるだけ早く as soon [quickly] as possible. 文例⇩

はやくち 早口 ¶早口に話す speak [talk] fast [rapidly] / 早口言葉 a tongue twister. 文例⇩

はやければ 早ければ at the earliest;<順調に行けば> if things go well. 文例⇩

はやさ 速さ <速いこと> quickness;《文》swiftness;《文》rapidity;<速力>speed; velocity ¶潮の速さを計る measure the speed of the current; see how fast the current is running.

はやざき 早咲き ¶早咲きの菊 early chrysanthemums.

い者勝ち. First come, first served.〖諺〗

はやおき 彼は早起きだ. He always gets up early. | He is an early riser. / 早起きは三文の得. The early bird catches the worm.〖諺〗

はやがわり 彼の胸は早鐘を打った. His heart beat fast.

はやく[1] 押売りを断わったら、その男はピストル強盗に早変わりした. The man was trying to sell me something, and when I refused he suddenly produced a gun and held me up.

はやく[1] その契約はついに破約になった. The contract was eventually canceled.

はやく[3] こういう病人は早く手当をしなければならない. A case of this sort requires prompt attention. / かくて5年は早くも過ぎ去った. Thus passed five swift years. / 早くしろ! Hurry up! | Be quick! / 早く帰って来てね. Don't be long! / 一刻も早く! There is not a moment to lose. / できるだけ早くやりましょう. I'll do it as soon as possible. | I'll do it the first chance I get [have]. / 早くそう言えばよかったのに. You should have said so before [long ago]. / 早く試験の結果が知りたい. I am anxious to know the result of the examination. / どうやら冬が早くやって来そうだ. I'm afraid we're in for an early winter. / 早くお正月になればいいんだがなあ. I wish the New Year would come soon. / 車輪は人類史上かなり早くに発明された. The wheel was invented fairly early on in human history. / 早くても2日はかかるでしょう. It'll take two days at the soonest.

はやくち 彼はあまり早口で言う事がよく聞き取れない. He speaks so fast that I can't follow him.

はやければ 早ければ20日には出来上がっているでしょう. It

はやさし 早指し 〖将棋〗a quick game of *shogi*.
はやし 林 〈小さい森〉a wood (⇒しんりん★); woods; 〈木立ち〉a grove; 〈雑木の〉a copse ¶松林 a pine wood.
はやし 囃子 (a) musical accompaniment ¶おはやし入りで with (a) musical accompaniment / はやし方 an accompanist / はやし言葉 a (nonsense) refrain.
はやじに 早死に an early [〖文〗a premature, 〖文〗an untimely] death ¶早死にする die young [at an early age, before *one's* time].
はやじまい 早仕舞 ¶早仕舞の日 an early-closing day / 早仕舞にする leave work early; close the store earlier than usual.
ハヤシライス rice with hashed meat.
はやす¹ 生やす grow ¶口ひげを生やす[生やしている] grow [wear] a mustache.
はやす² 囃す 〈伴奏する〉accompany; play an accompaniment (for); 〈拍子を取る〉beat time (with the hands); 〈あざける〉jeer (at); hoot (at).
はやせ 早瀬 a swift current; rapids.
はやて 疾風 a gale.
はやで 早出 〖文〗(*one's* turn for) early attendance (at the office) ¶早出する arrive [turn up] early [before time] for work; 〖文〗attend the office early.
はやてまわし 早手回し ¶早手回しに beforehand; 〖文〗in anticipation / 早手回しをする make preparations in good time; 〈先回りする〉〖文〗anticipate [forestall] ((the enemy's) move).
はやとちり 早とちり ¶はやとちりする jump to conclusions [a wrong conclusion] (about); 〖口語〗jump the gun; 〖口語〗go off half-cocked [at half-cock].
はやとりしゃしん 早撮り写真 an instant [automatic] photograph.
はやね 早寝 ¶早寝する go to bed early / 早寝早起き early to bed and early to rise / 早寝早起きする go to bed early and get up early ★ keep early hours は早寝のみを意味し、早起きは含まないし、やや古くさい表現でもある。
はやのみこみ 早呑み込み ⇒はやが(っ)てん.
はやばまい 早場米 early rice; an early crop of rice.
はやばや 早々 ¶早々と 〈早い時期に〉early; 〈すぐに〉quickly. 文例⇩
はやばん 早番 the first [early] shift ¶早番の人たち (workers on) the first [early] shift.
はやびけ 早引け ¶早引けする 〈授業を〉leave school [(the) class] early; 〈勤めを〉leave work [the office] earlier than usual [before time].
はやぶさ 〖鳥〗a peregrine (falcon).
はやまる 早まる be hasty; be rash ¶早まって overhastily; 〖文〗without due consideration / 早まった決定 a hasty [an overhasty,〖文〗a premature] decision / 早まった事をする do something rash; act rashly.
はやみち 早道 a shortcut (to a place, to success).
はやみひょう 早見表 a chart; a table ¶(利息などの)計算早見表 a ready reckoner.
はやみみ 早耳 ¶早耳の (a person) with quick [sharp] hearing.
はやめに 早めに a little early [earlier]; ahead of time; in good time ¶早めに夕食をとる have an early supper. 文例⇩
はやめる 速[早]める 〖文〗hasten; quicken; 〖文〗expedite ¶足を速める quicken *one's* pace / 期日を早める bring the date forward; advance the date (of). 文例⇩
はやり 流行 ⇒りゅうこう. 文例⇩
はやる¹ 流行る be in fashion [〖文〗vogue]; be fashionable; 〈人気がある〉be popular; 〈繁盛する〉prosper; flourish; 〈得意が多い〉be doing well; 〖文〗have a large custom; have a large practice (弁護士・医者が); 〈病気などが〉be going around; be about ⇒りゅうこう(流行する) ¶はやる店 a flourishing store / よくはやる医者 a doctor with a large practice / はやってくる, はやり出す come into fashion [〖文〗vogue]; grow in popularity / はやらなくなる go out of fashion [〖文〗vogue]. 文例⇩
はやる² 逸る ¶心がはやる be impatient (to do); はやる心を抑える restrain *oneself* [*one's* impatience].
はやわかり 早分かり 〈理解が早いこと〉quick understanding; 〈手引き〉a handbook (of); a guide (to) ¶早分かりする 〈人が〉〖口語〗be quick on the uptake; 〖文〗be quick of understanding; 〈本などが〉be easy to understand.
はやわざ 早業 quick work; 〈手品での〉(by) sleight of hand; a juggler's trick ¶電光石火の早業 (do, perform) a lightning trick.
はら¹ 原 a field; 〈平原〉a plain.
はら² 腹 the stomach; 〖口語〗*one's* tummy; 〈腹部〉the belly; 〖解〗the abdomen; 〈ナイフの〉the flat; 〈心中〉〖文〗*one's* mind; *one's* intention(s); 〈胆力〉courage; spirit ¶指の腹 the finger cushion / 徳利の腹 the belly of a *sake* bottle / 腹一杯食べる eat *one's*

---

should be ready by the 20th, if things go smoothly [well].
はやばや 早々とお見舞いを頂き有り難うございました。幸い浸水は免れました。ご安心下さい。Thank you very much for your kind inquiry. I am happy to tell you that the flood did not reach our house.
はやめに 彼はいつもより少し早目に家を出た。He left home a bit earlier than usual.
はやめる 不摂生が彼の死期を早めた。His intemperance hastened his death.
はやり この品にははやり廃りがない。This article is unaffected by changes in fashion.
はやる¹ 大阪では流感が非常にはやっている。Influenza is raging in Osaka. / またはやり出した。It has come back into fashion.

はら² 昨夜のえびで腹を壊した。The lobster last night upset me. / もう腹が一杯だ。I've had enough. / My stomach is full. / たくさん食べたので腹の皮がつっぱっていた。My belly was tight (with food). / 腹がへってはいくさができぬ。An army travels on its belly. | You cannot work on an empty stomach. / あんなことを言われては腹の虫が治らな

ばら fill ; gorge *oneself* 《with meat》/ 腹八分にしておく do not overeat [eat too much] ; 《文》 eat in moderation / 腹が痛む have (a) stomachache ; feel a pain in the stomach / 腹が下る have [suffer from] diarrhea / 腹が減る get [feel] hungry / 腹が張る *one's* stomach feels heavy ; 〈ガスがたまる〉 have gas on the stomach / 腹がふくれる have a big belly ; have a potbelly [paunch] ; be potbellied / 腹ができている 《文》 be resolute ; be prepared (for anything) / 腹が大きい be big-hearted ; be generous / 《文》 be magnanimous / 腹の皮をよじる be convulsed with laughter ; laugh *oneself* into convulsions ; split [burst] *one's* sides (with) laughing / 腹の中は at heart ; at bottom / 腹の中を見せない conceal *one's* real intentions / 腹の中で笑う laugh [smile] to *oneself* [up *one's* sleeve] / 腹をくちくする satisfy *one's* appetite ; 《文》 appease *one's* hunger / 腹をかかえて笑う hold *one's* sides with laughter / 腹をこわす have [get] stomach trouble / 腹を立てる get angry (at sth, with sb) / lose *one's* temper (with sb for sth) ; take offense (at) / 腹を決める decide [《文》 make a resolve] 《to do》; make up *one's* mind 《to do, to do》/ 腹を探る probe [try to find out] sb's real intentions ; sound sb (out) 《on sth》; try to fathom sb's thoughts 《on sth》/ 痛くもない腹を探られる be suspected when one is innocent ; 《文》 incur groundless suspicion / 腹を割って話す speak frankly [《文》 unreservedly] ; be frank 《with sb》; have a heart-to-heart talk 《with sb》/ 自分の腹を痛めた子 *one's* own child / 〈食物が〉腹にもたれる weigh [be] heavy on the stomach / 腹に据えかねる cannot put up with 《sb's impertinence》; cannot stomach 《sb's affronts》. 文例↓

ばら[1]《植》 a rose ; a rose bush (木) ¶ばらのとげ a rose thorn / ばら色の rosy ; rose-colored. 文例↓

ばら[2] ¶ばらで売る sell 《oranges》 loose ; sell (parts of a dinner service) separately / ばらで持ち歩く carry 《coins》 loose (in *one's* pocket).

バラード《詩学・音楽》 a ballade.

はらい[1] 払い 〈支払い〉 (a) payment ; 〈勘定〉 an account ; a bill ¶払いがいい[よくない] pay 《*one's* bills》 punctually [late] ; be punctual [behind] in paying 《*one's*》 bills / 払いをする make payment ; pay [meet] *one's* bills. 文例↓

はらい[2] 祓い purification ; exorcism ¶地鎮祭 のお祓いをしてもらう have the site (for a new factory) purified 《by a *Shinto* priest》.

はらいおとす 払い落とす shake down ; brush 《dust》 off 《*one's* coat》.

はらいこむ 払い込む pay 《funds》 in ; pay up (株金を).

はらいさげ 払い下げ disposal ; (a) sale ¶払い下げ品 articles disposed of [sold off] by the government.

はらいさげる 払い下げる sell 《government property》; dispose of.

はらいせ 腹癒せ ¶腹いせに by way of revenge ; 《文》 to vent *one's* anger / 腹いせをする get *one's* revenge (on sb) ; 《文》 revenge *oneself* (on sb for sth) ; 《文》 vent *one's* anger [spite] 《on》; settle [pay off] old scores 《with sb》.

はらいのける 払い除ける brush sb [sth] aside ; sweep off [aside] ; 〈追い払う〉 drive away ¶〈頭を振って〉目にかかる髪を払いのける toss back *one's* hair from *one's* eyes.

はらいもどし 払い戻し (a) refund ; (a) repayment ¶税の払い戻しを請求する claim a refund [rebate] on *one's* tax.

はらいもどす 払い戻す pay back ; repay ; refund (the cost) ; reimburse (sb, the cost). 文例↓

はらいもの 払い物 things to dispose of.

はらう[1] 払う 〈きれいにする〉 sweep (away, off) ; brush off ; 〈支払う〉 pay ; 〈処分する〉 dispose of ; 〈追い払う〉 drive away ¶ズボンをたたいて雪をはらう brush the snow from *one's* trousers / 天井のくもの巣をはらう clear cobwebs from the ceiling / 代金を払う pay for (an article) / 勘定を払う pay a bill / 注意を払う ⇨ちゅうい (注意する). 文例↓

はらう[2] 祓う purify ; exorcise.

はらおび 腹帯 〈妊婦の〉 a [an obstetrical] binder ; 〈馬の〉 a (saddle) girth ; 《米》 a cinch.

はらぐあい 腹具合 ¶腹具合が悪い have stomach 《口語》 tummy] trouble.

パラグアイ Paraguay ¶パラグアイの Paraguayan / パラグアイ共和国 the Republic of Paraguay / パラグアイ人 a Paraguayan.

はらくだし 腹下し ⇨げり.

はらぐろい 腹黒い 《文》 black-hearted ; wicked ; crafty ; 《文》 scheming.

はらげい 腹芸 ¶腹芸で by force of [the force of *one's*] personality.

はらごしらえ 腹ごしらえ ¶腹ごしらえをする have a meal [something to eat] 《before

---

い. I can't take insults like that lying down. / 彼は腹の中は正直な男だ. He is an honest man at heart. / 彼の口と腹とは違う. He says one thing, and means another. / 万一そうでなかったら腹を切る I'll bet [stake] my life on it [that it's true]. / ぜひ君に話したいんだ. 物言わざれば腹ふくるるわざというからね. I've got to tell you, because if I don't tell somebody I'll burst. / 彼は重役の平氏を失脚させようという腹に違いありません. I'm sure he's planning [he intends] to force Mr. Taira off the Board (of Directors).

ばら[1] ばらにとげあり. There is no rose without a thorn.

はらい[1] あの人はいつも払いが遅れる. He is always behind with his payments. / 賃金は1週間払いです. We pay wages weekly.

はらいもどす 予約金は全額払い戻 してもらえますか. Can I have a full refund on [a full repayment of] the deposit?

はらう[1] その帽子を買うのに幾ら払ったのですか. How much did you pay for that hat? / この服はまだ代金を払っていない. I haven't paid for this suit yet. / 酒屋の勘定はまだ払ってなかった. His bill at the liquor store was still unpaid. / 彼女は立ち止まって着物の雪を払った. She

はらごなし 腹ごなし 〖文例⇩〗
パラジウム 〖化〗palladium.
パラシュート a parachute ⇨ らっかさん.
はらす[1] 晴らす ¶愛さを晴らす〈事が主語〉《文》dispel *one*'s gloom / 疑いを晴らす clear *oneself* of the charge ((of theft))；〈事が主語〉《文》dispel *one*'s doubts / 恨みを晴らす ⇨ うらみ[1].
はらす[2] 腫らす make *sth* [cause *sth* to] swell.
ばらす 〈あばく〉《口語》blow ((a secret)) wide open；expose；《英口語》blow the gaff ((on))；lay ((a secret)) bare；〈ばらばらにする〉take ((a watch)) to pieces；〈殺す〉kill；do away with；liquidate；〈売り払う〉dispose of.
ばらせん ばら銭 loose coins；(small) change.
パラソル a parasol；a sunshade.
はらだたしい 腹立たしい annoying；maddening；exasperating；《口語》aggravating.
はらだち 腹立ち ¶腹立ちまぎれに in a fit of anger [pique].
はらちがい 腹違い ¶腹違いの born of a different mother / 腹違いの姉妹[兄弟] *one*'s half sister [brother].
パラチフス 〖医〗paratyphoid (fever).
ばらつき 〖統計〗(a) scatter(ing)；dispersion ¶ばらつきが大きい vary widely.
バラック a temporary shelter；a hut；a shack ★「バラック」のもとになった barracks は兵舎などを言う.
はらっぱ 原っぱ an open field；an empty lot.
ばらづみ ばら積み (stowing) [stowing] ((coal)) in bulk ¶ばら積み輸送 bulk shipment.
はらどけい 腹時計 〖文例⇩〗
パラドックス a paradox ⇨ ぎゃくせつ.
ばらにく ばら肉 boned rib (of pork).
はらばい 腹這い ¶腹ばいになる lie on *one*'s stomach [belly] / 腹ばいで進む creep [move] on *one*'s stomach [belly].
はらはら ¶はらはら落ちる〈木の葉が〉flutter down；〈涙が〉roll [stream] down (*one*'s cheeks)／はらはらさせる be kept on tenterhooks [in suspense] ((in case...,《文》lest...))；feel [be] nervous [on edge]；be afraid ((that..., of *sth*))／はらはらしながら〈不安で〉in (great) suspense；on tenterhooks；〈wait〉with *one*'s heart in *one*'s mouth；〈興味で〉with breathless interest；(wait) with bated breath／はらはらさせるような exciting；thrilling；《口語》nail-biting ((drama))；suspenseful. 〖文例⇩〗

ばらばら ¶ばらばらの loose；disconnected ((parts))；in pieces／豆をばらばらまく scatter a shower of beans／ばらばらになる〈壊れる〉come apart；fall in [to] pieces／〈四方に散る〉be scattered；《文》disperse／ばらばらにされた死体 a dismembered body／ばらばら事件 a mutilation murder case. 〖文例⇩〗

ばらばら in (large) drops；pattering ¶(雨が)ばらばら降る patter；sprinkle／塩をばらばらとまく sprinkle salt ((on))；sprinkle *sth* with salt／本をばらばらめくる riffle [flip] through a book. 〖文例⇩〗

パラフィン 《米》paraffin；《英》(paraffin) wax ¶パラフィン紙 《米》paraffin paper；《英》wax(ed) paper.
パラボラアンテナ a parabolic antenna.
はらまき 腹巻 a stomach band.
ばらまく scatter；broadcast；〈金を〉spend (money) recklessly.
はらむ 孕む 〈みごもる〉《文》conceive；get [《文》become] pregnant ⇨ にんしん ¶(帆が)風をはらむ fill [be swollen] with the wind ／雨をはらんだ風 a rain-bearing wind. 〖文例⇩〗
バラモン a Brahman；a Brahmin ¶バラモン教 Brahmanism；Brahminism.
バラライカ a balalaika.
はらわた 腸 the intestines；《文》the bowels；〈内臓〉the entrails；the guts (特に動物の) ¶はらわたの腐った男 a corrupt [depraved] man／はらわたが煮えくり返る boil (over) with anger [indignation]／魚のはらわたを抜く gut a fish；remove the guts from a fish／鳥のはらわたを抜く draw a fowl.
はらん 波乱 ¶波乱に富んだ生涯 a checkered career；an eventful life／波乱を巻き起こす raise a disturbance；cause trouble／波乱万丈の full of ups and downs；《文》with many vicissitudes. 〖文例⇩〗
バランス balance ⇨ つりあい ¶バランスのとれた well-balanced／バランスのとれない badly-[《文》ill-]balanced；unbalanced／バランスシート a balance sheet.
はり[1] 針 〈縫い針〉a needle；〈留め針〉a pin；〈釣り針〉a hook；〈計器の〉a pointer；〈魚の〉a prickle；〈虫の〉a sting；〈縫いの〉a stitch；〈時計の〉a hand；〈レコード用〉a needle；a stylus (*pl*. -es, -li) ¶針のあな the eye of a needle／針のむしろ ⇨ むしろ[1]／針を含んだ言葉 sharp [stinging] words；a biting [scathing] remark／針に糸を通す thread a needle／針にえさをつける bait a hook／針で刺す prick (*one*'s finger) with a needle；(虫が) sting／

---

paused and brushed the snow from her clothes.
はらごなし 腹ごなしに散歩しよう. Let us take a walk to help our dinner to settle [our digestion].
はらどけい 腹時計ではもうそろそろ 12 時だ. My stomach tells me it's getting on for noon.
はらはら どうなることかとはらはらした. I trembled to think how it would end.／この物語にははらはらさせる場面がたくさんある. This story is full of suspense.
ばらばら 列は乱れた [in disorder]. The ranks are broken [in disorder]．／彼らは行きは一緒だったが帰りはばらばらに帰った. They went all together and came home separately.
ばらばら 雨がばらばら降ってきた. It began to sprinkle with rain. | The rain came pattering on the ground [roofs].

はらむ 船は順風に帆をはらませてぐんぐん走った. The ship sped on before a fair wind, with her sails swelling.／情勢はあらしをはらんでいる. The situation is critical [potentially explosive].
はらわた それを聞いてはらわたをかきむしられる思いがした. The news has rent [wrung] my heart.
はらん 政界はひと波乱ありそうな形勢だ. There are indications of a rather stormy political season.

はり¹ 針 a needle; 傷口を3針縫う put three stitches in the wound / 針ほどの事を棒ほどに言う ⇨ しんしょうぼうだい / 針供養 a requiem service for broken needles. 文例⬇

はり² 梁 a beam; a girder (鋼鉄の); a cross-beam (横げた).

はり³ 鍼 a needle; 〈治療〉acupuncture ¶ はりをする treat *sb* with acupuncture; acupuncture / はり医 an acupuncturator / はり麻酔 anesthesia by acupuncture.

はり⁴ 張り 〈張力〉tension; 〈心の〉will power; spirit ¶ 張りのある[ない]声 a voice full [devoid] of life / 張りの強い弓 a stiff bow. 文例⬇

ばり 罵言 abuse ¶ ばり雑言(ぞうごん)を浴びせる call *sb* names [all (the) names under the sun]; 《文》heap abuse on *sb*.

-ばり …張り トルストイ張りの小説 a novel written in the style of Tolstoy.

パリ Paris ¶パリの Parisian / パリっ子 a Parisian / パリ祭 the Fourteenth of July.

はりあい 張り合い 〈敵対〉rivalry; 〈競争〉competition ¶ 張り合いのない discouraging; 《文》unresponsive; dull / 張り合いがある be worth (*one's*) while; be worth doing [the trouble] / 働く張り合いがある be worth working for / 張り合いが抜ける be discouraged; lose interest (in); lose enthusiasm (for). 文例⬇

はりあう 張り合う rival (each other); compete [《文》vie, 《文》contend] with (each other). 文例⬇

はりあげる 張り上げる ¶ 声を張り上げる raise [lift] *one's* voice / あらん限りの声を張り上げて at the top of *one's* voice [lungs].

バリウム 【化】barium ¶ 胃のレントゲン検査のためにバリウムを飲ませる give *sb* a barium meal before a stomach X-ray; administer barium sulfate to *sb* in preparation for a radiological examination of *his* stomach.

はりかえる 張り替える repaper (a screen); re-cover (an umbrella); reupholster (a chair); put a new plaster on (a cut).

はりがね 針金 (a) wire.

はりがみ 張り紙 〈はりつけた紙〉a patch of paper (pasted) (on *sth*); (a) paper backing (裏打ち); 〈掲示の〉a bill; a poster; a placard. 文例⬇

バリカン [<*Bariquand et Marre* (フランスの会社名)] (a pair of) hair clippers.

ばりき 馬力 horsepower (略: h.p., hp); 〈体力〉(animal) energy ¶ 馬力をかける exert oneself [《文》*one's* energies] / 10馬力出す produce [deliver] 10 horsepower / 10馬力のある自動車 a high-powered car / 100馬力の発動機 a 100-horsepower motor; a motor of 100 h.p. 文例⬇

はりきる 張り切る 〈元気一杯である〉be in high spirits; be full of vigor; 〈意気込む〉be enthusiastic (about, for, over); be eager (to do) ¶ 張り切って働く work enthusiastically [《文》with zeal].

バリケード a barricade ¶ バリケードを築く set up a barricade (across a street) / バリケードで封鎖する block (the entrance of a building) with a barricade; barricade (a place).

ハリケーン a hurricane.

はりこ¹ 針子 a seamstress.

はりこ² 張り子 papier-mâché ¶ 張り子のとら a paper [papier-mâché] tiger. 文例⬇

はりこむ 張り込む 〈見張る〉keep watch (for, against, on); be on the watch [lookout] (for); 〈待ち伏せする〉lie in ambush (for); 〈奮発して買う〉treat *oneself* to (an expensive meal); 《口語》splash (out) [splurge] on (a gold watch) ¶ 張り込み中の刑事 a waiting detective; 《米口語》a cop on a stakeout.

はりさける 張り裂ける burst (open); break; split ¶ 胸も張り裂けるような heartbreaking; 《文》heart-rending / 胸も張り裂けんばかりに泣く cry [weep] *one's* heart out. 文例⬇

はりさし 針刺し a pincushion.

はりしごと 針仕事 needlework; sewing ⇨さいほう. 文例⬇〈打つ〉slap.

はりたおす 張り倒す knock *sb* down; 〈平手で打つ〉slap.

はりだし 張り出し ¶ 張り出し舞台 an apron stage / 張り出し窓 a bay [bow] window / 張り出し横綱 an additional *yokozuna*.

はりだす 張り出す post [put up] (a notice).

はりつけ crucifixion ¶ はりつけにする crucify.

はりつける 張り付ける paste [stick] (a bill on the wall) ⇨ はる².

ぱりっと ¶ ぱりっとしている look very smart (in *one's* well-tailored[-pressed] suit) / ぱりっとした背広 a well-tailored[-pressed] suit.

ぱりっと ぱりっとした smart; stylish; spruce; dapper.

はりつめる 張り詰める strain; stretch ¶ 気を張り詰める strain *one's* mind [nerves]; grow tense / 全神経を張り詰めて with *one's* nerves (stretched) taut / 氷が張り詰めている be frozen all over. 文例⬇

はり¹ 針で刺すように足が痛んだ. I had a stinging [sharp] pain in my leg.

はり⁴ 息子を亡くして, すっかり生きる張りがなくなりました. I have nothing left to live for, now that I have lost my son.

はりあい 子供のない生活は張り合いがない. Having no children, I must lead a dull life. / 勉強する張り合いが抜けた. I have lost enthusiasm for my work.

はりあう 両社はいつも互いに張り合っていた. The two firms were always vying with each other. ¶ There was constant rivalry between the two companies.

はりがみ 張り紙無用. 《掲示》Stick no bills here.

ばりき その発動機は200馬力ある. The motor develops 200 h.p.

はりこ² 米帝国主義は張り子の虎に過ぎない, と彼は言った. He said that American imperialism was no more than a paper tiger. / 張り子の虎じゃあるまいし, 濡れても平気だよ. I don't care if I get wet. I'm not made of sugar.

はりさける 胸も張り裂けそうな気持ちです. My heart is ready to break.

はりしごと 彼女は日なたで針仕事をしている. She is sitting at her needlework in the sun.

はりつめる 彼の声を聞くと彼女の張り詰めた気持ちが一時に緩ん

はりて 張り手《相撲》slapping.

パリティー《経》parity ¶パリティー価格 a parity price / パリティー方式で on the parity basis.

はりとばす 張り飛ばす ⇨ はりたおす.

バリトン《音楽》baritone ¶バリトン歌手 a baritone (singer).

はりねずみ《動》a hedgehog.

はりばこ 針箱 a workbox; a needlework box.

ばりばり ¶ばりばりかむ crunch / ばりばり裂く tear up / ばりばり働く work energetically《furiously, like blazes, like a demon》.

ぱりぱり ¶江戸っ子のぱりぱり a trueborn [genuine] Edokko; a Tokyoite born and bred / 大学出のぱりぱり a bright young university graduate / ぱりぱり食べる crunch (crackers) / ぱりぱりの紙幣 a crisp bank note.

はりばん 張り番《事》watch; lookout;《人》a watchman; a guard ⇨ みはり.

はりふだ 張り札《広告などの》a bill; a poster; a placard /《付け札》a label; a sticker ¶張り札をする stick [post] a bill (on a wall). 文例⇩

はりめぐらす 張り巡らす put [stretch] (a fence) around (a vacant lot) ¶全国に捜査網を張り巡らす spread a (police) dragnet over the (whole) country.

はる¹ 春 spring; springtime ¶人生の春《文》the springtime of life / 春の訪れ;《文》vernal / 春先に at the beginning of spring; in early spring / 春めく show signs of (the coming of) spring; become springlike / 春一番 the first strong south winds of the year (signaling the beginning of spring); the first spring storm / 春風 a spring wind [breeze] / 春雨 spring rain (drizzle);《食品》bean-starch vermicelli / 春休み a spring vacation. 文例⇩

はる² 張る《紙などを》stick; paste; put;《文》affix /《障子などを》paper /《伸ばす》stretch;《広げる》spread;《緊張させる》strain;《値が》be [《口語》come] expensive; cost too much /《平手で打つ》slap ¶切手を張る put [stick] a stamp on (an envelope) / こう薬を張る put [stick] a plaster (on a cut) / テントを張る pitch [set up] a tent / ネットを張る put up a net / 胸を張る throw out one's chest /《草木が》根を張る be deep-rooted; have spreading roots / たらい[風呂]に水を張る fill a tub [bath] with water / 弓に弦を張る string a bow /《池などが》水が張っている be frozen over / 店を張っている keep [run] a store / 勢力を張る extend [establish] one's influence (over a district). 文例⇩

はるか(に) 遙か(に)《距離が隔って》《文》far; far away [off]; in the distance /《時間が隔って》long ago [before];《段違いに》far; by far; far and away ¶はるかに富士を望む《人が》see Mt. Fuji in the distance /《場所が》command a distant view of Mt. Fuji / はるかに昔をしのぶ think of [look back on] the days long past. 文例⇩

用法 「A は B よりはるかに大きい」という時、英語では、A is far bigger than B. というのが最も普通. A is bigger by far than B. | A is bigger than B by far. はやや《文》. A is far and away bigger than B. は最も意味が強くなる.

バルカン バルカンの Balkan / バルカン半島[諸国] the Balkan Peninsula [States].

バルコニー a balcony ¶バルコニーへ出る go out on the balcony.

バルトかい バルト海 the Baltic (Sea).

バルバドス Barbados.

はるばる《文》from afar; over a great distance; all the way ¶はるばる九州からやって来る come all the way from Kyushu.

バルブ¹《カメラの》a bulb.

バルブ²《弁, 真空管》a valve.

パルプ (wood) pulp ¶パルプにする reduce (wood) to pulp; pulp / パルプ工場 a pulp mill / パルプ材 pulpwood.

はるまき 春巻《中国料理》《米》an egg roll;《英》a (crispy) spring roll.

はれ¹ 晴れ《晴天》clear [fair, fine] weather ¶晴れの場所で in a public place; on a formal [gala] occasion / 晴れの身となる have one's innocence established; be cleared of the charge. 文例⇩

はれ² 腫れ a swelling ¶はれを引かせる bring [take] the swelling down [away]. 文例⇩

はれあがる 晴れ上がる clear up.

はれあがる 腫れ上がる swell up.

ばれいしょ 馬鈴薯 ⇨ じゃがいも.

バレー ballet ¶古典[モダン]バレー classical [modern] ballet / バレー団 a ballet company; a ballet / バレー団の団長 a ballet master [mistress] / バレーダンサー a (male, female) ballet dancer; a ballerina (女).

ハレーション《写真》halation ¶ハレーションでぼやける be fogged by halation.

パレード a parade.

バレー(ボール) volleyball ¶バレーボールの選手 a volleyball player / バレーボールをする play volleyball.

はれがましい 晴れがましい formal;《文》gala.

はれぎ 晴れ着 one's best clothes; one's (Sunday) best;《文》a gala dress ¶晴れ着を着て

だ. On hearing his voice her strained nerves relaxed immediately.

はりふだ 「無用の者入るべからず」という張り札がある. There is a notice up, saying, 'No admission except on business.'

はる¹ 先月から見るとだいぶ春めいてきた. The weather is much more springlike than it was last month.

はる² その手紙には切手が張ってありますか. Is there a stamp on that letter? / あまり強く張ると切れる. If you strain it too hard, it will break. / 薄氷が張った. A thin sheet [coat] of ice has formed on the water.

はるか(に) 海上ははるかに白帆が見える. A white sail can be seen far out on the sea. / 2人のうち彼の方がはるかに学力が優れている. He is by far the better scholar of the two.

はれ¹ 西の風, 晴れ. Fair, with westerly winds. / その日は晴れになった. The day had cleared up. / 列席の人々は皆晴れと着飾っていた. Everyone present was gaily dressed.

パレスチナ Palestine ¶パレスチナの Palestine; Palestinian / パレスチナの住民 a Palestinian.

はれつ 破裂 (an) explosion ¶破裂する burst; explode; blow up / 破裂音《音声》a plosive; an explosive.

パレット a palette ¶パレットナイフ a palette knife.

はれて 晴れて openly; publicly; in public.

はればれ 晴れ晴れ ¶はればれした顔色 a bright [cheerful] look / 気がはればれする feel cheerful [refreshed] / 気分がはればれしない be in low spirits; feel depressed.

はれぼったい 腫れぼったい puffy; rather swollen ¶はれぼったい目をした puffy-eyed. 文例⇩

はれま 晴れ間 an interval of clear weather ¶雨の晴れ間を待つ wait for a lull [《口語》letup] in the rain.

ハレム a harem.

はれもの 腫れ物 a swelling; a boil ¶はれ物に触るように very cautiously [gingerly];《文》with great caution. 文例⇩

はれやか 晴れやか ¶晴れやかな bright; cheerful;《文》radiant; gay / 晴れやかに brightly; cheerfully;《文》radiantly; gaily.

バレリーナ a ballerina; a (female) ballet dancer.

はれる¹ 晴れる〈空が〉clear (up);〈霧が〉clear off [away]; lift;〈疑惑が〉be dispelled;〈気分が〉be [feel] refreshed ¶晴れ渡った空 a cloudless [clear] sky. 文例⇩

はれる² 腫れる swell; get [《文》become] swollen ¶リンパせんがはれる develop swollen lymphatic glands / 足がはれている have a swollen foot; one's foot is swollen.

ばれる come [be] out; come to light; be discovered; be found out. 文例⇩

バレル 《容量単位》a barrel.

ハレルヤ hallelujah.

バレンタイン ¶バレンタインカード a Valentine (card) / バレンタインデー St. Valentine's Day.

はれんち 破廉恥 ¶破廉恥な shameless;《文》infamous;《文》dead [lost] to all (sense of) shame / 破廉恥罪 an infamous crime [offense].

はろう 波浪 ¶《大波》a billow ¶波浪注意報 a high sea warning.

ハロゲン 《化》halogen.

バロック ¶バロック建築[音楽] baroque architecture [music].

バロメーター a barometer.

ハワイ Hawaii ¶ハワイの Hawaiian / ハワイ諸島 the Hawaiian Islands / ハワイ人 a Hawaiian.

はわたり 刃渡り the length of a blade ¶刃渡り三尺の大刀 a yard-long sword / (曲芸で)剣の刃渡りをする walk the edge of a sword.

はん¹ 半〈半分〉a half; semi-;〈奇数〉an odd number ¶9時半 half past [《米》after] nine / 1時間半 an hour and a half; one and a half hours / 2マイル半 two and a half miles; two miles and a half / 半ポンド half a pound;《米》a half pound / 半永久的 semipermanent. 文例⇩

はん² 判〈印判〉a stamp; a seal;〈印影〉a seal (mark) ¶神田氏の判が押してある bear the (personal) seal of Mr. Kanda / 判を押す seal;《文》affix a seal (to a bond) / 判を彫ってもらう have one's seal cut [by sb] / 判で押したように invariably; without exception. 文例⇩

はん³ 版〈印刷版〉a plate;〈印刷〉printing; print;〈本の〉an edition; an impression ¶第2版 the second edition (★改訂・増補をしたもの。単なる重版は the second impression と言う。the second impression は, 正確には「第2刷」と言うべきであるが, これも「第2版」と言うことが多い) / (本が)版を重ねる go through [run into] several impressions.

はん⁴ 班 a squad; a group ¶班長 a squad [group] leader.

はん⁵ 煩 trouble ¶煩をいとわない do not mind taking the trouble (to do);《文》spare no pains (to do) / 煩に耐えない find it too much trouble [too troublesome] to do.

はん⁶ 範 an example; a model ¶範を示す[垂れる] set [give] an example《to》/ 米国の制度に範をとる be modeled on [after] the American system.

はん⁷ 藩 a feudal domain (fief) ¶加賀藩 the domain [fief] of Kaga.

はん-¹ 反… anti- ¶反体制の anti-Establishment / 反陽子 an antiproton.

はん-² 汎… pan- ¶汎アメリカ主義 Pan-Americanism / 汎アラブ主義 Pan-Arabism / 汎神論 pantheism.

ばん¹ 万 ¶万やむを得なければ if absolutely necessary; when it is really unavoidable [inevitable].

ばん² 判〈紙などの大きさ〉size;〈書物などの〉a format ¶大[中]判のけい紙 large-[medium-]sized ruled paper / B 6 [A 5]判 B6 [A5] size.

はれ² はれが引いた. The swelling went down.
はれつ ボイラーが破裂して3人けがをした. The boiler burst, injuring three people.
はれぼったい 目のまわりのはれぼったさは取れていた. The puffiness around her eyes was gone.
はれもの 首にはれ物ができた. A swelling has come out on my neck.

はれる¹ 天気は晴れるだろう. It is going to be fine. / 明日は晴れるでしょう. [The weather] will clear tomorrow. / 君の言葉で疑いがすっかり晴れた. Your statement has got rid of [dispelled] all my doubts. / これで無実の罪が晴れた. This cleared me of the charge. / 散歩すると気が晴れるよ. A walk will cheer you up.
ばれる 筆跡でばれた. His handwriting gave him away.
はん¹ 何となく5時から5時半になり, やがて6時になった. Somehow it was five, then half-past, then six.
はん² 皆判で押したように同じ返事をした. They gave us exactly the same answer, every one of

ばん³ 晩 (an) evening; (a) night;《文》nightfall(日暮れ) ★ evening は就寝時間までを言う。¶晩の9時ごろに about nine in the evening [at night] / 日曜日の晩に on Sunday evening / 晩方に toward evening. 文例⇩

ばん⁴ 番 〈見張り〉watch;《文》vigil; guard; lookout;〈番人〉a keeper;〈番号〉a number;〈順番〉turn; order;〈交替制になっている仕事の〉a (work) shift ¶番をする watch《over》; keep watch《over》; stand [keep] guard《at, over》/ 番を待つ wait (for) *one's* turn / 番に当たる have *one's* turn; *one's* turn comes / 5番の部屋 room No. 5 / 右から3番目の男 the third man from the right ⇒ なんばん¹, いちばん.

ばん⁵ 盤 a board;〈円盤〉a disk; a disc ¶盤を使ってするゲーム a board game.

ばん⁶【鳥】a moorhen.

パン[<《ポルトガル語》pão]〈食パン〉bread;〈菓子パン〉a bun ¶1塊のパン a loaf of bread / 1切れのパン a slice [piece] of bread / 軽い[白い]パン light [white] bread / ジャム[バター]つきのパン bread and jam [butter] / パンの木 a bread(fruit) tree / パンのために働く work for *one's* bread / パンを焼く bake bread (in an oven); bake (flour) into bread /〈トーストにする〉toast bread / パンにジャムを塗る spread jam on bread / パンにバターを塗る バター / ジャム[クリーム]パン a jam [cream] bun / ぶどうパン raisin bread / パン粉〈小麦粉〉flour;〈パンくず〉bread crumbs / パン種 yeast;〈パン屋〈人〉a baker;〈店〉a bakery / パン焼きかまど a bread [bake] oven / パン類 baked goods. 文例⇩

バンアレン ¶バンアレン放射能帯 the Van Allen (radiation) belts.

はんい¹ 犯意【法】criminal intent; malice.

はんい² 範囲 an extent; a scope; a range; limits;《文》a sphere;《文》bounds ¶活動の範囲 the [*one's*] sphere [field] of activity / …の範囲内[外]に within [beyond] the limits [scope] of… / 交際範囲が広い[狭い]have a wide [small] circle of friends [acquaintances]. 文例⇩

はんいご 反意語 an antonym.

はんえい¹ 反英 ¶反英感情 anti-British feeling [《文》sentiment].

はんえい² 反映 reflection ¶反映する reflect; be reflected. 文例⇩

はんえい³ 繁栄 prosperity ¶繁栄する prosper; thrive; flourish.

はんえん 半円 a semicircle; a half circle ¶半円形の semicircular.

はんおん 半音【音楽】a semitone; a half tone [step] ¶半音上げる[下げる] sharp [flat]《a tone》/ …より半音高い[低い] be a half tone higher [lower] than…; be higher [lower] in pitch by a half tone than… / 半音階 a chromatic scale.

はんか¹ 反歌 an envoy.

はんか² 繁華 ¶繁華な町 a flourishing [thriving] town / 繁華街〈人通りの多い通り〉a bustling [busy] street;〈商店街〉business [shopping] quarters;《米》a downtown area;〈歓楽街〉an amusement center.

はんが 版画 〈木版画〉a woodcut; a (woodblock) print;〈銅版画〉a copperplate engraving;〈エッチング〉an etching;〈石版画〉a lithograph ¶版画家 a printmaker;〈木版の〉a woodblock artist;〈銅版の〉a copperplate engraver;〈エッチングの〉an etcher;〈石版の〉a lithographer.

ばんか¹ 挽歌 an elegy; a dirge.

ばんか² 晩夏 late summer ¶晩夏の頃に toward the end of summer; late in summer.

ハンガー a (coat) hanger.

バンカー〈ゴルフ〉a bunker; a sand trap.

ハンガーストライキ ⇒ ハンスト.

はんかい¹ 半開 ¶半開の partly open /〈花が〉半開である be half out [in bloom].

はんかい² 半壊 ¶半壊の家 a partially destroyed house.

ばんかい 挽回 recover ¶挽回する recover; retrieve / 退勢を挽回する recover from the discouraging situation / 挽回策 a measure for retrieving (*one's* lost credit).

ばんがい 番外 ¶番外の演奏 an extra performance. 文例⇩

はんがく 半額 half the amount [sum, price, fare] ¶半額の[で] at half the price [fare]; at half-price / 乗車賃半額で《travel》(at [for]) half-fare.

ばんがく 晩学 learning late in life. 文例⇩

はんかくめい 反革命 a counterrevolution.

ばんがさ 番傘 a coarse oilpaper umbrella.

ハンカチ(ーフ) a handkerchief ¶麻のハンカチ a linen handkerchief / 胸ポケットにのぞかせるハンカチ a pocket handkerchief / ハンカチを目に当てる hold a handkerchief to *one's* eyes / ハンカチを押し当てて泣く cry into *one's* handkerchief.

はんかつう 半可通 superficial knowledge; a

---

them, without a single exception.

ばん³ じきに晩になった. It was not long before night fell [evening set in].

ばん⁴ 今度は僕が見張りをする番だ. Now it is my turn to keep watch. / 彼の番になった. His turn came. | It came to his turn. / 番が狂った. The order went wrong. / しょっちゅう弟の番をしているわけじゃあるまいし, どこ へ行ったか知らないよ. I'm not my brother's keeper. / I don't know where he's gone. / 彼はクラスで2番です. He is second in his class.

パン 人はパンのみにて生くるものにあらず.【聖書】Man shall not live by bread alone.

はんい² 彼の読書の範囲は広い. He reads very widely [extensively]. / それは狭い範囲内に限られている. It is confined within narrow limits. / 私の知る範囲ではこれが最良の方法です. This is the best method so far as I know [so far as my knowledge goes]. / 試験の範囲は(どこから)どこまでですか. What's going to be in the exam?

はんえい² 世論はなかなか国会には反映されない. It takes time for public opinion to be reflected in the Diet. / 新聞は世相を反映する. The press is the mirror of society.

ばんカラ smattering; 〈人〉a smatterer ¶半可通を振り回す parade one's superficial knowledge.
ばんカラ 蛮カラ 〖蛮カラな (affectedly) careless about [《文》indifferent to] one's personal appearance; rough and uncouth.
ハンガリー Hungary ¶ハンガリーの Hungarian / ハンガリー語 Hungarian; Magyar / ハンガリー人 a Hungarian; a Magyar / ハンガリー人民共和国 the Hungarian People's Republic.
バンガロー a bungalow.
はんかん 反感 ill feeling; 《文》(an) antipathy ¶反感をいだく harbor ill feeling 《toward》; feel an antipathy 《against》/ 反感を買う arouse [provoke] sb's antipathy; incur sb's ill feeling / 反感をそそるような provoking.
ばんかん 万感 《文》a commingling of emotions. 文例⇩
はんがんびいき 判官びいき ⇨ほうがんびいき.
はんき[1] 反旗 a standard [banner] of revolt ¶反旗を翻す raise the standard of revolt; rise in revolt 《against》; take up arms 《against》.
はんき[2] 半期 ¶半期の half-yearly; semiannual / 半期ごとに half-yearly; semiannually.
はんき[3] 半旗 ¶半旗を掲げる fly [hoist] a flag at half-mast[-staff].
はんぎ 版木 a (printing) block; a woodcut.
はんぎゃく 反逆 (high) treason; treachery; (a) rebellion; (a) revolt ¶反逆する turn traitor; revolt [rebel] 《against》; rise in revolt [mutiny] / 反逆的 rebellious (elements); treasonable (activities); 《文》treasonous (intentions) / 反逆罪で処刑される be executed for treason / 反逆者 a traitor; a rebel.
はんきゅう[1] 半弓 a small bow.
はんきゅう[2] 半休 a half-holiday.
はんきゅう[3] 半球 a hemisphere ¶東[西, 北, 南]半球 the Eastern [Western, Northern, Southern] hemisphere.
はんきょう[1] 反共 ¶反共の anti-Communist / 反共戦線 the anti-Communist front.
はんきょう[2] 反響 〈こだま〉an echo 《pl. -es》; 《文》reverberation(s) 《★ 通常複数形で使う》; 〈影響〉influence; repercussions; 〈反応〉(a) reaction; a response ¶反響する echo; reecho; 《文》resound; 《文》reverberate / 反響がある, 反響を呼ぶ be echoed; 《文》call forth an echo [a response]; 〈世間に〉have [meet with] a public response / 一大反響を引き起こす create a sensation.

はんきょうらん 半狂乱 half madness ¶半狂乱になって as if one is half-crazed; half mad; frantically. 文例⇩
はんぎょく 半玉 an apprentice geisha.
パンク a blowout; a puncture (小あな) ¶パンクする〈タイヤが主語〉go flat; blow out; be [get] punctured;〈自動車・人が主語〉have [get] a blowout [flat (tire)] / パンクを直す mend [《米》fix] a puncture [a flat tire].
バンクーバー Vancouver.
ハンググライダー a hang glider ¶ハンググライダー飛行 hang gliding.
ばんぐみ 番組 a program ¶(新聞などでの)今日のテレビ番組 a list of today's TV programs / 番組を作る〈編成する〉get [draw] up a program;〈制作する〉make [produce] a program / 番組に載っているを be on the program. 文例⇩
バングラデシュ Bangladesh ¶バングラデシュ人 a Bangladeshi / バングラデシュ人民共和国 the People's Republic of Bangladesh.
ばんくるわせ 番狂わせ a surprise; an upset ¶番狂わせをやる spring an upset [a surprise] / 番狂わせで勝つ bring off [manage, 《文》achieve] an unexpected win / 大番狂わせ a big upset [surprise].
はんけい 半径 a radius 《pl. -dii》¶半径5センチの円を描く describe a circle with the radius of 5 centimeters; draw a circle of 5-centimeter radius.
はんげき 反撃 a counterattack; a counteroffensive; a counterblow;〈競技の〉a rally ¶反撃する counterattack; strike back 《at》; fight back 《against》; rally /(競技で)見事な反撃を見せる stage a magnificent rally (in the last inning) / 反撃に出る launch a counterattack 《on, against》; mount a counteroffensive 《against》.
はんけつ 判決 (a) judgment; a judicial decision; (a) decision (of the court) ¶判決する[を下す] decide 《on a case》; pass judgment [sentence] 《on a case》/ 判決を言い渡す deliver judgment 《on a prisoner》; pass [pronounce] sentence 《on the accused》/ hand down a decision / 判決に服する accept the decision / 判決日 the judgment day / 判決文を読みあげる read out the decision / 判決理由 reasons for judgment. 文例⇩
はんげつ 半月 a half moon ¶半月形 a semicircle / 半月形の semicircular. 文例⇩
はんけん[1] 半券 the stub (of a ticket).

ばんがい 高田君は番外だ。Takada is an exception. | Takada cannot be measured by the common yardstick. | The normal rules don't apply to Takada.
はんがく 12歳未満の子供は半額だ。Children under twelve are half price [fare (乗り物)].
はんかく 彼は晩学だ。He started learning late in life.
ばんかん 万感こもごも至る。A thousand emotions are crowding into my mind. / 万感胸に迫って言葉がなかった。My heart was too full for words.
はんきょう その番組は視聴者から少しも反響がなかった。The program provoked no response from the viewers. | There was no viewer response to the program.
はんきょうらん 息子が殺されたと聞いて彼女は半狂乱の体だった。She was quite frantic when she heard that her son had been killed.
ばんぐみ 番組の第1番は2年生の合唱です。The first item [number] on the program is a chorus by the second-year pupils.
はんけつ 判決は原告の敗[勝]訴となった。The case was decided against [in favor of] the plaintiff. / 彼は有罪[無罪]の判決を受けた。He was found guilty [not guilty].
はんげつ 今晩は半月だ。It's a half

はんけん² 版権 copyright ¶版権のある本 a copyrighted book / 版権を獲得する acquire [obtain] the copyright ((for a book)) / 版権を所有している own [hold] the copyright ((of [on] a book)) / 版権所有者 a copyright holder / 版権侵害 (an) infringement of copyright; (literary) piracy. 文例⇩

はんげん 半減 a 50 percent reduction [cut] ¶半減する〈半分にする〉reduce [cut] by half, 〈半分になる〉be cut [be reduced, 《文》diminish] by half /(放射性元素の)半減期 a half-life. 文例⇩

ばんけん 番犬 a watchdog.

はんこ 判こ ⇒はんこ² ¶判こ屋 a seal-cutter.

はんご 反語〈修辞的疑問〉a rhetorical question; 〈皮肉〉irony ¶反語的に ironically. 文例⇩

はんこう¹ 反抗〈手向かい〉opposition; 〈抵抗〉resistance; 〈挑戦〉《文》defiance; 〈不服従〉disobedience; 〈反逆〉rebellion; revolt ¶反抗する oppose; resist; disobey; defy; rebel 《against》/ 反抗的に rebelliously; defiantly / 反抗的な態度をとる take a defiant attitude (toward) / 第１[２]次反抗期 the first [second] period of rebelliousness (in one's life) / 反抗心 (a) rebellious spirit.

はんこう² 反攻 ⇒はんげき ¶反攻基地 a retaliation base.

はんこう³ 犯行 a criminal act; a crime; an offense ¶犯行を認める confess to the crime; plead guilty (法廷で) / 犯行を否認する deny having committed the crime; plead not guilty (法廷で).

はんごう 飯盒 a messtin.

ばんこう 蛮行《文》a barbarous act; an atrocity;《文》a barbarity;《文》a brutality.

ばんごう 番号 a number ¶番号を打つ[付ける] number; give [《文》assign] a number (to) / 番号を呼ぶ call out sb's number / 番号順に並ぶ line up in numerical order / 番号札 a number ticket [check (下足などの)].

ばんこく 万国 all nations; all (the) countries on earth ⇒せかい, こくさい² ¶万国旗 the flags of all nations; 〈装飾用の〉bunting (総称) / 万国博(覧会) a world's fair; an international exposition.

バンコク Bangkok.

ばんこや 番小屋 a watchman's box.

はんごろし 半殺し ¶半殺しにされる[の目にあう] be nearly killed; be beaten nearly to death [within an inch of one's life].

ばんこん 晩婚 (a) late marriage. 文例⇩

はんさ 煩瑣 ¶煩瑣な〈煩わしい〉troublesome;〈複雑な〉complicated;〈細かすぎる〉too detailed [《文》minute].

はんざい 犯罪 an offense; a crime ¶犯罪を犯す[構成する] commit [constitute] a crime / 少年犯罪 ⇒しょうねん ¶犯罪学 criminology / 犯罪行為 a criminal act [offense] / 犯罪者[人] a criminal; a culprit (未決の).

ばんざい 万歳 banzai; cheers ¶万歳を三唱する shout banzai three times; give three cheers ((for)). 文例⇩

ばんさく 万策 ¶万策尽きる be at the end of one's resources [tether].

はんざつ 繁[煩]雑 ¶繁雑な〈込み入った〉complicated; intricate; 〈厄介な〉troublesome.

ハンザどうめい ハンザ同盟《西洋史》the Hanseatic League ¶ハンザ同盟都市 a Hanseatic town.

はんさよう 反作用 (a) reaction ¶反作用を及ぼす react ((on)) / 反作用の原理《物》the principle of reaction / ⇒さよう¹ 文例⇩

ばんさん 晩餐 dinner; supper ⇒ゆうしょく¹ [用法] ¶晩餐会 ((give, hold)) a dinner party.

はんし 半紙 a (35 by 25 cm) sheet of plain paper ((for calligraphy)).

はんじ 判事 a judge; a justice; the bench (総称) ⇒さいばん (裁判官). 文例⇩

ばんじ 万事 everything; 《文》all things [affairs]; all ¶万事を切り回す manage [take control of] everything / 万事に in all things; 〈どの点からも〉in every respect; in all respects.

パンジー [植] a pansy.

はんしはんしょう 半死半生 ¶半死半生の more dead than alive; all but dead; half-dead.

はんじもの 判じ物 a puzzle; a riddle.

はんしゃ 反射 reflection ¶反射する reflect / 反射的 reflective; reflexive / 反射的に reflexively; by reflex action / 反射運動 a reflex movement [motion] / 反射角 the angle of reflection / 反射鏡 a reflecting mirror / 反射光[熱] reflected light [heat] / 反射作用 (a) reflex action; a reflex / 反射望遠鏡 a reflecting telescope / 反射炉 a reverberatory furnace [kiln]; a reverberator. 文例⇩

はんしゃかいてき 反社会的 antisocial.

ばんしゃく 晩酌 ¶晩酌をやる have a drink with one's dinner.

ばんじゃく 盤石 ¶盤石のごとき as firm as a rock (不動の);《文》adamantine (堅固な).

はんしゅう 半周 ¶半周する go half round ((the globe)).

---

moon tonight.
はんけん 版権所有.《表示》All rights reserved. | Copyright.
はんげん 価値が半減した. It's only worth half what it was. | It has lost half its value. | このアイソトープの半減期は23分だ. This isotope has a half-life of twenty-three minutes.
はんご 彼が「どうしたのだ」と言ったのは反語で, 「なんでもないじゃないか」ということなのだ. 'What of it?' was a rhetorical question; what he really meant was 'Don't complain!'
ばんごう 番号! [号令] Number [Count] off! / 本には皆番号が付いている. All the books are labeled and numbered. / ケースには１から150までの番号が振ってある. The cases are numbered 1 to 150.
ばんこん 彼は晩婚だった. He married late (in life).
ばんざい 天皇陛下万歳! Long live the Emperor! / 田中君万歳! Three cheers for Tanaka!
はんじ 近藤判事係りで開廷された. The court was opened, presided over by Justice Kondo.

ばんしゅう 晩秋 late autumn [《米》fall] ¶晩秋に late in autumn; in the latter part of autumn.

はんじゅく 半熟 ¶半熟の玉子 a soft-boiled egg / 半熟にする soft-boil 《an egg》; boil 《an egg》soft.

ばんじゅく 晩熟 ¶晩熟の late-maturing[-ripening].

はんしゅつ 搬出 ¶搬出する carry [take] sth out.

はんしゅん 晩春 late spring ¶晩春に late in spring; in the latter part of spring.

はんしょ 板書 ¶板書する write on the blackboard.

はんしょう¹ 反証 (a) proof to the contrary; 《文》counterevidence ¶反証を挙げる produce counterevidence; produce evidence against 《the theory》. 文例⇩

はんしょう² 半焼 ¶半焼する be partially destroyed (by fire).

はんしょう³ 半鐘 a fire bell. 文例⇩

はんじょう 半畳 〈畳の〉 half a mat; a half mat ¶半畳を入れる give a jeer 《at》; hoot 《at》.

はんじょう 繁盛[昌] prosperity ¶繁盛する prosper; flourish; be prosperous; 〈医師・弁護士など〉 have a large practice.

ばんしょう 万障 文例⇩

バンジョー a banjo 《pl. -(e)s》.

はんしょく 繁殖 breeding; reproduction; propagation ¶繁殖する breed; reproduce [propagate] itself / 繁殖期 a breeding season / 繁殖地 breeding grounds / 繁殖率 a reproductive rate; a rate of breeding / 繁殖力 reproductive [procreative] power; fertility.

はんじる 判じる 〈判断する〉 judge; 〈解く〉 solve; puzzle out; decipher (暗号などを).

はんしん 半身 〈上下に分けて〉 half the body; 〈左右に分けて〉 one side of the body ¶〈写真で〉半身を撮ってもらう get oneself taken in half-figure / 上[下]半身 the upper [lower] half of the body / 左[右]半身 the left [right] side of the body / 半身像 a half-length statue [portrait]; a bust.

はんしんはんぎ 半信半疑 ¶半信半疑で half in doubt; doubtfully; dubiously; suspiciously.

はんしんふずい 半身不随 paralysis of one side of the body ¶半身不随になる be paralyzed on one side.

はんしんろん 汎神論 pantheism ¶汎神論的 pantheistic / 汎神論者 a pantheist.

はんすう¹ 反芻 rumination ¶反芻する ruminate; chew the cud / 反芻動物 a ru-

minant.

はんすう² 半数 half the number; half 《of the members》.

ハンスト a hunger strike ¶ハンストをやる go on hunger strike.

パンスト ⇨ パンティー (パンティーストッキング).

はんズボン 半ズボン short pants [trousers]; knee trousers [pants].

はんする 反する go [be] against; 〈…の反対である〉 be opposed to; 〈文〉 be contrary to; 《文》 run counter to; 〈違反する〉《文》 violate; 《文》 infringe ¶規則に反する be against the rules; 《文》 violate [infringe] a rule / …に反して against…; 《文》 contrary to… / 希望[予期]に反して against [contrary to] one's wishes [expectation(s)] / これに反して on the contrary; on the other hand. 文例⇩

はんせい¹ 反省 《文》 self-examination; searching one's conscience ¶反省する think sth over; 《文》 reflect on one's past conduct; search [examine] one's conscience / 反省を促す call on sb to reflect on his past conduct / 反省会 a meeting for reviewing 《the past activities of the club》. 文例⇩

はんせい² 半生 half one's life.

ばんせい 蛮声 ¶蛮声を張り上げて歌う sing in a loud [raucous] voice.

はんせいひん 半製品 semi-[half-]finished goods.

はんせん¹ 反戦 ¶反戦を叫ぶ cry against war / 反戦運動 an antiwar movement / 反戦論[論者] pacifism [a pacifist].

はんせん² 帆船 a sailing ship [《文》 vessel, boat]; a sailboat.

はんぜん 判然 ¶判然と clearly; distinctly; plainly / 判然とする 〈はっきりする〉 become clear [《文》 distinct]; 〈確認される〉《文》 be ascertained; be made sure. 文例⇩

ばんぜん 万全 ¶万全の策をとる 《文》 take all possible measures to ensure 《the success of a project》; adopt the safest policy [most prudent course] / 万全を期するため《文》 to make assurance double sure.

ハンセンびょう ハンセン病 Hansen's disease; leprosy.

はんソ 反ソ ¶反ソの anti-Soviet.

はんそう 帆走 ¶帆走する sail.

ばんそう 伴奏 an accompaniment ¶伴奏する accompany sb 《on the piano》; play sb's accompaniment 《on the piano》 / ピアノの伴奏で歌う sing to a piano accompaniment / 伴奏なしで歌う sing without instrumental accom-

---

ばんじ 万事好都合だ. All goes well. / 僕もこれで万事休すだ. It's all over for [up with] me now. / 万事心得ているよ. I know what is what. | I know what I am doing [about]. / 万事よろしく頼む. See that everything is O.K. [all right]. / 万事君に任せる. I will leave everything to you [your discretion].

はんしゃ 月は太陽の光を反射して光る. The moon shines by the reflected light of the sun.

はんしょう¹ それに対する反証がない. There is no evidence to disprove it.

はんしょう³ そら半鐘が鳴っている. There goes the fire bell!

ばんしょう 万障お繰り合わせの上おいで下さい. We request the pleasure of your company.

はんする 太郎の不勉強に反して, 次郎は勉強家だ. Jiro is hardworking [diligent], while Taro is idle. / 彼らの利害は相反する. Their interests clash.

はんせい¹ 君は自分の行為を反省すべきだ. You should reflect on your past conduct.

はんぜん 彼の居所はまだ判然とし

ばんそうこう paniment / 伴奏者 an accompanist / 無伴奏バイオリンソナタ an unaccompanied violin sonata.

ばんそうこう 絆創膏 a sticking [an adhesive] plaster ¶絆創膏をはる apply an adhesive plaster (to the wound).

はんそく 反則 breaking the rules; 《文》 infringement [violation] of (the) rules; 《競技》 a foul ¶反則をする[犯す] break [《文》violate, 《文》infringe, act against] the rules; foul; play foul; commit a foul. 文例⇩

ばんぞく 蛮族 a savage tribe.

はんそで 半袖 ¶半そでのシャツ a short-sleeved undershirt; a T [tee] shirt (丸首の).

はんだ solder ¶はんだ付けする solder ¶はんだごて a soldering iron.

パンダ《動》a panda ¶大(^{おお})パンダ a giant panda / 小(^こ)パンダ a lesser panda.

はんたい 反対 ⟨反抗⟩ opposition; ⟨異論⟩ (an) objection; ⟨対照⟩ contrast; ⟨逆⟩ the reverse; the opposite; 《文》 the contrary ¶反対する oppose; be opposed ((to)); be [stand] against; object ((to)); take exception (to) / 反対の opposite (direction); the reverse (side); 《文》 contrary (opinions) / 反対の意志を表明する declare oneself (to be) against ((a policy)); come out against ((a proposal)) / 反対を受ける meet with [run into] opposition; meet [face] opposition ((from)); be opposed ((by)) / 反対を唱える object to ((a policy)); take objection [exception] to ((a plan)) / 反対に[逆方向に] the other [wrong] way; in the opposite direction; [これに反して] on the contrary / (合議法廷で,多数意見で決まった判決に対する) 反対意見《法》a dissenting opinion / 反対運動 a movement [campaign] against ((a measure)) / 反対給付 a consideration / 反対尋問 (a) cross-examination / 反対者 an opponent; a dissenter; an objector / 反対色 an antagonistic [opposing] color / 反対勢力 counterforce / 反対党 an opposition party; a party in opposition / 反対派 an opposition faction / 反対論 an argument against ((a proposal)); an opposite opinion [view].

はんたいせい 反体制 ¶反体制運動 an anti-Establishment movement / 反体制派 people who are against the Establishment; anti-Establishment groups.

はんだくおん 半濁音 the p-sound in the kana syllabary.

パンタグラフ a pantograph; a current collector.

バンタムきゅう バンタム級 the bantamweight class ¶バンタム級の選手 a bantamweight.

パンタロン pantaloons.

はんだん 判断 ⟨判定⟩《文》(a) judgment; (a) decision; 《文》(an) inference; ⟨結論⟩ a conclusion ¶判断する judge; 《文》 infer; conclude; ⟨夢などを⟩ interpret; read / …で[から]判断すると judging [to judge] from [by] … / …空模様から判断すると (judging) from the look of the sky / 私の判断では in my view [opinion, judgment]; 《文》 it is my judgment that… / 判断を誤る judge wrongly; make an error of [《文》err in one's] judgment / 判断力 discernment. 文例⇩

ばんたん 万端 everything;《文》all. 文例⇩

ばんち 番地 a house number (各戸の); a lot number (1区画の) ¶戸山町 14 番地 11 Toyama-cho / 同じ番地に住む live at the same (lot) number. 文例⇩

パンチ ⟨ボクシング⟩ a punch; ⟨はさみ⟩ a punch; (a pair of) cancels (切符切り用); ⟨迫力⟩ punch ¶壮烈なパンチの応酬 a fierce [vicious] exchange of punches / パンチのきいた言葉 a remark with punch (in it) / あごにパンチを見舞う punch sb on the jaw; land a punch on sb's jaw / パンチを利かせる put (more) punch ((into)) / 切符にパンチを入れる punch a ticket / パンチカード a punch(ed) card. 文例⇩

ばんちゃ 番茶 coarse tea.

はんちゅう 範疇 a category ¶…の範疇に入る belong to [fall under] the category ((of)).

ばんちょう 番長 the leader of a group of juvenile delinquents.

ハンチング a cloth [tweed, flat] cap ★hunting cap は乗馬用のもので,「鳥打帽」とは異なる.

パンツ ⟨下着⟩ short pants; briefs; underpants; trunks; ⟨ズボン⟩ trousers; pants.

はんつき 半月 half a month; 《米》a half month ¶半月ごとに twice a month;《文》semi-monthly.

はんつきまい 半搗き米 half-cleaned rice.

ばんづけ 番付 ⟨順位表⟩ a ranking [graded] list (of sumo wrestlers); ⟨番組⟩ a program ¶長者番付 a ranking list of millionaires.

はんてい 判定《文》(a) judgment; (a) decision ¶判定する judge; decide / 判定を下す《文》pass judgment ((on)); give a decision ((against, for, in favor of)) / (競技で)判定で勝つ, 判定勝ちする win [score] a decision ((over)); defeat ((one's opponent)) on points [by a decision] / 判定で負ける lose a decision ((to)); lose (a

---

ない. His whereabouts has [have] not been ascertained yet. / 意味が判然としません. I cannot get (at) its exact meaning.

はんそく それは明らかに反則だ. That is a clear [flagrant] breach of the rules. / (フットボールなどで)反則をして退場を命じられた. He was sent off the field for a foul. | 《米》He fouled out of the game.

はんたい 反対のご意見がございますか. Have you anything to say against it? / 彼の両親はその計画に大反対だ. His parents are strongly opposed to the plan. / その提案は労組の強硬な反対にあった. The proposal ran into strong opposition from the labor union. / 事実はその反対だ. The reverse is the case.

はんだん 一切の事実が判明するまでは判断を差し控えるべきである. You should suspend [withhold, reserve] judgment until all the facts are known.

ばんたん 用意万端整った. Everything is ready [《口語》O.K.].

ばんち 私の家は西片町3番地5号です. I live at 3-5, Nishikatamachi. / この手紙は番地が違っている. This letter is wrongly addressed [has the wrong house-

パンティー panties ¶パンティーストッキング《a pair of》panty hose《複数扱い》;《英》《a pair of》tights.

ハンデ(ィキャップ) a handicap ¶ハンディキャップをつける handicap /〈競走のとき前へ出してやる〉give sb (a) (2 meters') start / ハンデ20のゴルファー a 20-handicap player; a 20-handicapper. 文例⇩

はんてん¹ 反転 ¶反転する〈ひっくり返る〉turn over;〈逆に向く〉be reversed; turn the other way round;〈引き返す〉reverse one's [its] course; turn around (and go back).

はんてん² 半纏 a short coat;〈仕着せの〉a livery coat.

はんてん³ 斑点 a spot; a speck; a speckle;〈鳥獣の皮・毛างなどの〉marking(s) ¶斑点のある spotted; specked; speckled.

バント〖野球〗bunting; a bunt ¶バントする bunt; lay down a bunt / バントの構えをする take the bunting position [stance] / 送りバント a bunt for advancing a runner / スリーバント a two-strike bunt / ドラッグバント a drag bunt.

バンド¹〈ズボンの〉a belt;〈腕時計の〉a watch bracelet [strap];〈帽子の〉a hatband ¶バンドを締める[緩める] tighten [loosen] one's belt / ズボンのバンド通し the belt loops of one's trousers.

バンド²〖楽隊〗a band ¶バンドマン a band(s)-man.

はんドア 半ドア ¶半ドアで走る drive《one's car》with a door not properly closed.

はんとう¹ 反党 ¶反党の antiparty《elements, activities》.

はんとう² 半島 a peninsula ¶半島の peninsular / 伊豆半島 the Izu Peninsula.

はんどう 反動 (a) reaction;〈銃などの〉recoil; kick ¶反動として as a reaction / 反動的 reactionary《elements》/ 反動主義者 a reactionary.

ばんとう¹ 晩冬 late winter ¶晩冬に late in winter.

ばんとう² 番頭 〈店の〉a clerk;〈銭湯の〉a bath attendant ¶大番頭 the head clerk.

はんどうたい 半導体 〖物〗a semiconductor.

はんとうめい 半透明 ¶半透明の semitransparent; translucent.

バンドエイド 〖商標名〗《米》a Band-Aid;《英》《a piece of》Elastoplast ¶バンドエイドをはる put a Band-Aid《on a cut》.

はんどく 判読 reading;〈暗号などの〉decoding;《文》decipherment ¶判読する read; make out; decipher / 判読し難い illegible; undecipherable; hard to make out. 文例⇩

はんとし 半年 half a year;《米》a half year ¶半年ごとに every half year; semiannually.

パントテンさん パントテン酸 〖生化〗pantothenic acid.

ハンドバッグ a handbag; one's bag;《米》a pocketbook;《米》a purse.

ハンドボール 〖競技〗handball.

パントマイム a pantomime; a dumb show ¶パントマイムの pantomimic / パントマイムの俳優[作者] a pantomime artist / パントマイムで演じる[表わす] pantomime《an act》; represent sth by pantomime [by dumb show].

ハンドル a handle;〈自転車の〉handlebars;〈自動車の〉a (steering) wheel ¶(自動車の)ハンドルをとる be [sit] at the wheel; take the wheel.

はんドン 半ドン a half-holiday.

ばんなん 万難 ¶万難を排して at all costs; whatever the risk(s); by some means or other.

はんにえ 半煮え ¶半煮えの half-boiled; half-cooked; half-done.

はんにち¹ 反日 ¶反日感情 anti-Japanese feeling [《文》sentiment] / 反日政策 an anti-Japanese policy.

はんにち² 半日 half a day; a half day. 文例⇩

はんにゃ 般若 ¶般若の面 a mask of a female demon.

はんにゅう 搬入 ¶搬入する carry [bring] sth in; send sth in /（美術展覧会などの）搬入日 the days [period]《文》designated) for the sending in of exhibits.

はんにん 犯人 a criminal; a culprit; an offender. 文例⇩

ばんにん¹ 万人 ¶万人向きである suit [meet] all tastes [everyone's taste].

ばんにん² 番人〈守る人〉a guard; a keeper;〈見張り〉a watchman;〈留守居〉a caretaker ¶番人を付ける put [《文》place, keep] a guard《over the prisoners》; put [《文》place, keep]《a house》under guard.

はんね 半値 ¶半値で at half-price; at half the (usual) price; at a discount of 50 per cent / 半値に負ける take off half the price; give sb a 50% discount.

ばんねん 晩年 ¶晩年に late in life;《文》in one's last [closing] years.

はんのう 反応 〖化〗(a) reaction;〈反響〉a response;〈効果〉an effect ¶反応する react《to, on》; respond《to》;《文》be responsive《to》/ 反応がない show no reaction; be im-

---

number on it].
パンチ 彼のせりふはあまりパンチが利いていない。There is not much punch in his remarks.
はんてい レフリー全員一致の判定で勝った。He scored a unanimous decision over his opponent. | He won the match by a unanimous decision.| 審判員の判定は、3人が彼の勝ち、2人は彼の負けと分かれた。It was a 3-2 (split) decision in his favor.

ハンデ(ィキャップ) 学歴のないことが1つのハンディキャップになっている。He is handicapped by his lack of formal education.
はんどく この字の判読に苦しんだ。I found it hard to read [make out] the handwriting.
はんにち² 明日は半日休みです。We have a half-holiday tomorrow. / 昨日は半日読書で過ごした。Yesterday I spent half the day reading.

はんにん 犯人はまだつかまっていない。The criminal [culprit] is still at large. / この窓ガラスを壊したのはだれです。―「トムが犯人です。」'Who broke this window?'―'Tom did it.' ['It was Tom.'] / 放火事件の犯人は精神異常者だった。The perpetrator of the arson was insane.

ばんのう passive; have no effect 《on》/ 反応が鈍い be slow to react [respond] / 反応を起こさせる produce a response; act 《on》/ アルカリ性の反応を呈する show an alkaline reaction. 用例↓

ばんのう 万能 ¶万能の 《文》almighty; 《文》omnipotent / 万能の神 almighty God; the Almighty / 万能選手 an all-rounder; an all-round [《米》all-around] player [athlete] / 万能ナイフ an all-purpose knife / (どんなポジションもこなせる)万能補欠選手 a utility man [player] / 万能薬 a cure-all; 《文》a panacea.

はんのき 《植》an alder.

はんば 飯場 a workmen's shack; workers' (temporary) living quarters; 《米》a bunk-house.

はんぱ 半端 〈物〉a fragment; an odd item [article, piece]; 〈端数〉a fraction; an odd sum ¶半端 odd; 《文》fragmentary; 〈不完全な〉incomplete.

ばんば 輓馬 a draft horse.

ハンバーガー a hamburger (in a bun).

ハンバーグ(ステーキ) a hamburger; a hamburg(er) steak.

はんばい 販売 (a) sale; selling; marketing ¶販売する sell; deal in; handle / 販売されている be on sale; be on the market / 販売価格 the selling price / 販売係 《男》a salesman; 《女》a saleswoman / 販売政策 a sales policy / 販売促進 sales promotion.

はんばく 反駁 《文》(a) refutation ⇨ はんろん ¶反駁する refute; 《文》confute; rebut.

パンパス 〈アルゼンチンの〉the pampas ★ pampas は単複同様に扱う. また《米》ではそういう草原の1つをさす時は the pampa とも言う.

はんぱつ 反発 ¶反発する 〈人の発言・行為などに対して〉be offended 《by》; have (a lot of) bad feeling 《toward》; turn *one*'s back 《on》; 〈跳ね返る〉bound [spring] back; rebound; 〈相場に〉rally; recover / 反発力 〈はね返す力〉force of repulsion; 〈跳ね返る力〉elasticity; resilience. 用例↓

はんばり 半張り 〈靴の〉a half sole.

はんはん 半々 ¶半々に half-and-half; in half [halves] / 半々にする divide *sth* into halves; halve; share (the profits) equally 《between》; go halves; split *sth* fifty-fifty / 塩と砂糖を半半に入れる add [mix] equal amounts of sugar and salt.

ばんのう 万々〈充分〉very well; fully;〈確かに〉certainly; surely;〈否定〉never; by no means;《not》possibly. 用例↓

はんびょうにん 半病人 a semi-invalid; a sickly person ¶半病人の状態である be in poor health / 半病人になる become very weak (almost ill).

はんびらき 半開き ¶半開きの half-open; partly open.

はんぴれい 反比例 inverse proportion ¶反比例する be in inverse proportion 《to》; be inversely proportional 《to》. 用例↓

はんぷ 頒布 ¶頒布する distribute.

はんぷく 反復 repetition;《文》reiteration ¶反復する do *sth* over again; repeat;《文》reiterate / 反復して repeatedly; over (and over) again; again and again. 用例↓

パンプス 《a pair of》pumps.

ばんぶつ 万物 everything [《文》all things] (under the sun); creation. 用例↓

ハンブル ⇨ ファンブル

パンフレット a pamphlet; a brochure.

はんぶん 半分 (a) half ¶遊び [冗談]半分に ⇨ あそび, じょうだん² / 半分にする halve;〈分ける〉divide *sth* into halves;〈切る〉cut *sth* in half;〈減らす〉reduce *sth* to half / 半分に切ったグレープフルーツ a half grapefruit; a grapefruit half / 半分ずつ分ける go halves [shares]; share *sth* half-and-half《with *sb*》/ 半分済む [済ませる] be half through 《with》《*one*'s work》.

はんべい 反米 ¶反米感情 anti-American feeling [《文》sentiment].

ばんぺい 番兵 a guard; a sentry;《文》a sentinel ¶番兵を置く post [place] a guard [sentry]; keep guard / 捕虜に番兵をつける set a guard over the prisoners; place the prisoners under guard / 番兵に立つ stand guard; do [go on] sentry duty.

はんべつ 判別 distinction;《文》discrimination ¶判別する tell (A) from (B) [(A) and (B) apart]; distinguish 《between A and B》;《文》discriminate 《between A and B》/ 判別式《数》a discriminant. 用例↓

はんぼいん 半母音《音声》a semivowel.

ハンマー a hammer ¶ハンマー投げ《競技》the hammer throw(ing) / ハンマー投げの選手 a hammer thrower.

はんのう 我々の訴えに対して彼らからは何の反応もなかった. We got no response to our appeal from them. | They didn't respond to our appeal at all.

はんぱ その品は半端では売りません. We can't break the set.

はんぱつ 同一磁極は相反発する. Like magnetic poles repel each other.

ばんばん そんな事は万々あるまい. It is virtually [next to] impossible. | It's most unlikely.

はんぴれい 恒温では気体の体積は圧力に反比例して変化する. At constant temperature the volume of a gas is inversely proportional to [varies inversely with] the pressure. / 引力は距離の自乗に反比例する. The force of gravitation varies in inverse proportion to the square of the distance [in proportion to the inverse square of the distance].

はんぷく 反復練習することは学生たちに最も肝要だ. Repeated practice is of the first importance to students. / この本は反復熟読する価値がある. This book is worth reading over and over again.

ばんぶつ 万物は流転す. All things are in (a state of) flux. | Everything is constantly changing. / 人は万物の霊長である. Man is the lord of creation.

はんぶん 君の大きさは普通の馬の半分しかない. It is only half the size of an ordinary horse. / 茶わんに半分下さい. Just half a bowl, please. / 費用はお互い半分持ちこう. We will go halves in the ex-

はんまい 飯米 (a farmer's) rice for private [home] consumption.
はんみ 半身 ¶半身に構える take an oblique stance ((against *one*'s opponent)).
はんめい 判明 ¶判明する〈はっきりする〉become clear [plain]; 〈確認される〉《文》be ascertained; 〈知れる〉be known; 〈…と分かる〉prove [turn out] (to be) (false); be identified as…. 文例⇩
ばんめし 晩飯 ⇨ ゆうしょく¹.
はんめん¹ 反面 the other side; the reverse ¶反面 on the other hand / 反面教師 a person who serves as an example of how not to behave.
はんめん² 半面 〈顔の〉half the face; 〈事物の〉one side ¶他の半面 the other side / 半面だけの真理 a half-truth. 文例⇩
はんも 繁茂 ¶繁茂する grow thickly [《文》luxuriantly, 《文》rank]; flourish / 繁茂した thick; 《文》rank; 《文》luxuriant. 文例⇩
はんもく 反目 antagonism; hostility; 《文》enmity ¶反目する be at odds [《文》variance] ((with)); 《文》be at feud [enmity] ((with)); feud ((with)) / 仲間同士で反目し合う feud among ((themselves)).
ハンモック a hammock ¶ハンモックをつる[はずす] sling [unsling] a hammock / ハンモックで眠る sleep in a hammock.
はんもん¹ 反問 ¶反問する ask a question in return; cross-question sb (反対尋問で).
はんもん² 斑紋 ⇨ はんてん³.
はんもん³ 煩悶 worry; 《文》anguish; agony ¶煩悶する worry (*oneself*) [be worried] ((about, over)); be troubled (in *one*'s mind) ((about, over)); be in agony [anguish].
パンヤ [<《ポルトガル語》*pañha*] 〈植〉a kapok tree; 〈繊維〉kapok.
ばんゆう 蛮勇 ¶蛮勇を振るって…する take

drastic measures ((to cure the bad practice)).
ばんゆういんりょく 万有引力 universal gravitation ¶万有引力の法則 the law of universal gravitation.
ばんらい 万雷 ¶万雷の拍手を浴びる be given [greeted with] thunderous [a thunder of] applause.
はんらく 反落 《相場》a reactionary fall ((in stock prices)) ¶反落する fall [drop] in reaction.
はんらたい 半裸体 ¶半裸体の half-naked; seminude.
はんらん¹ 反乱 a rebellion; a revolt; an uprising (蜂起) ¶反乱を起こす rebel [revolt, rise] against; rise in revolt / 反乱軍 a rebel army; 《文》insurgent troops.
はんらん² 氾濫 〈あふれること〉flooding; 《文》inundation; 〈洪水〉a flood; 〈供給過剰〉a flood; oversupply ¶はんらんする flow over (*its* banks); overflow; flood; 《文》inundate / はんらんしている be in flood. 文例⇩
ばんりのちょうじょう 万里の長城 the Great Wall of China.
はんりょ 伴侶 a partner; a companion ¶生涯の伴侶 《文》one's life partner; *one*'s companion for life; 《文》one's spouse.
はんれい¹ 凡例 explanatory notes; a legend (図表などにつけた).
はんれい² 判例 a (judicial) precedent.
はんろ 販路 a market (for goods); an outlet ¶小売りの販路 a retail outlet / 販路を拡張する extend [enlarge] the market ((for)) / 販路を開く[開拓する] open [find] a market ((for)). 文例⇩
はんろん 反論 a counterargument; 《文》(a) refutation ⇨ はんぱく ¶反論する bring [put, set] forward [《文》forth] a counterargument; refute.

ひ

ひ¹ 日, 陽 〈太陽〉the sun; 〈暦日〉a day; 〈日付〉a date ¶ある日 one day / 日があたる catch [get] the sun / 日が出る[昇る] the sun rises / 日が傾く the sun goes down [《文》declines] / 日が沈む the sun sets [goes down, sinks] / 日が暮れる night falls; 《文》the day is declining / 日が落ちて with the sun down / 日が暮れてから after dark / 日が長く[短かく]

penses. | Let's share the expenses half-and-half. / その町は東京から京都までの大体半分の所だ。The town is situated nearly halfway between Tokyo and Kyoto. / これで道のりの半分だ。We have covered half the distance [come half the way]. / その値段の半分でも高い。It would be expensive at half that price. / 私はまだ半分しか読んでいません。I have read only half [am only half through with] the book. / 彼は戸口から半分出かかって足を止めた。He stopped at the door,

half in, half out of the room.
はんべつ 両者の判別に苦しみます。I cannot tell one from the other. / ちょっと両者の判別はつきますまい。You will not notice the difference between the two at first sight.
はんめい 彼の所在はまだ判明しない。His whereabouts is [are] still unknown. / 亡くなられた方々のうちで、まだ2人の身元が判明しておりません。Two of the dead have not yet been identified.
はんめん² 彼は問題の半面だけを見ている。He is only looking at

one side of the question. / それは真理の半面にすぎない。That is only half the truth.
はんも その山には樹木が繁茂している。The hill is thickly wooded [covered with trees].
はんらん² 利根川がはんらんした。The Tone has overflowed its banks. / 書店に漫画がはんらんしている。The bookstores are flooded with comics.
はんろ この手の品は販路が広い。There is a good market for these articles.

ひ¹ なる the days grow long(er) [short(er)] / 日のあたる[あたらぬ]所に in a sunny [sunless] place ; in [out of] the sun / 日の沈まぬうちに before the sun sets ; before dark ; while it is still light / 日の目を見ない〈屋内にいる〉 stay indoors ;〈場所が〉get no sunshine ;〈世の中に現われない〉do not see the light of day / 日を改めて another [some other] day / 日を定めて fix a date 《for a meeting》/ 日を経る〈重ねる〉に従って as (the) days go by / 日に日に, 日一日と day by day ; every day ;《文》with each succeeding day / 日に焼ける ⇒ひやけ. 文例↓

ひ² 火 fire ;〈火事又は炉などの〉a fire ;〈火炎〉(a) flame ; (a) blaze ;〈火熱〉heat ¶〈家などに〉火がつく[移る] catch [take] fire /〈赤ん坊が〉火がついたように泣く cry wildly / 目から火が出る see stars / 火のつきやすい (in)flammable /《文》fiery ; blazing ; burning / 火を使う use fire / 火をつける light 《a cigarette in a match》; set 《a piece of paper》alight ; set fire to sth ;〈発火させる〉《文》ignite ;〈燃やす〉burn ;〈比喩的に〉touch off 《a disturbance》/ 家に火をつける set fire to a house ; set a house on fire / 火をいける bank up the fire / 火を起こす make [build (up), start] a fire ; get a fire going / 火を吹いて出す blow on [at] the fire ; fan the fire with one's breath / 火をかき立てる stir the fire / 火を消す put out the fire / 火をかく breathe [emit] fire /〈銃砲が〉fire / 火を見るより明らかである be as clear as day ; be as plain as daylight / 火を通す heat (up) 《food》; cook / 火にあたる warm oneself at the fire / 火にかける[くべる] put sth over [into] a fire / 一面の火となる become a sheet of fire. 文例↓

ひ³ 比〈割合〉a ratio 《pl. -s》;〈比較〉(a) comparison ;〈匹敵するもの〉an equal ; a match ¶AとBとの比 the ratio of A to B ; the ratio A:B / その比を見ない be unique ; be unrivaled ;《文》be unparalleled ;《文》be without parallel / …の比ではない be no match for…. 文例↓

ひ⁴ 灯 a light ¶灯をつける[入れる] light a lamp ; put [turn, switch] the light on / 灯を消す put the light out ; turn [switch] the light off / 灯ともし頃に at nightfall ; toward evening.

ひ⁵ 否 no 《pl. noes》. 文例↓

ひ⁶ 妃 a princess ; a consort.

ひ⁷ 非〈欠点〉a fault ;〈非道〉(an) injustice ;《文》(a) wrong ¶〈形勢が〉非である《文》be adverse ; be unfavorable / 一点非の打ち所がない be faultless ; be flawless ;《文》be free from blemishes / 非を悟る《文》realize [be convinced of] one's error / 非を鳴らす denounce sb 《as a traitor》;《文》censure sb 《for his neglect of duty》/ 非を認める《文》admit one's error ; admit that one was wrong [mistaken]. 文例↓

ひ⁸ 緋 scarlet ¶緋の衣 a scarlet robe.

ひ⁹ 碑〈墓碑〉a tombstone ; a gravestone ;〈記念碑〉a monument ¶碑を立てる put up [raise, erect] a monument 《to the memory of…》/ 碑文[銘] an epitaph ; an inscription on a monument [tombstone].

ひ-¹ 非… non-… ; un-… ¶非営利事業 a nonprofit(-making) [noncommercial] undertaking / 非科学的な unscientific / 非芸術的な《文》inartistic / 非論理的な illogical / 非米活動 un-American activities.

ひ-² 被¹ ¶被験者 a (test) subject ; a testee / 被支配者 the ruled.

-ひ …費 ⇒ひよう ¶営業費 business expenses / 建築費 the cost of construction.

び¹ 美 beauty ;《文》the beautiful ¶自然の美 the beauty of the natural scenery ; natural beauty.

び² 微 ¶微に入り細にわたって説く give a detailed [《文》minute] account [explanation] 《of》; discuss 《a matter》in great detail [《文》exhaustively].

ひあい 悲哀《文》sorrow ; sadness ;《文》grief ¶人生の悲哀 the sorrows of life / 悲哀を感じる feel sad [sorrow] / 悲哀に満ちた《文》sorrowful ; full of sadness [sorrow].

ひあがる 干上がる dry up ¶口が干上がる lose one's livelihood. 文例↓

ひあそび 火遊び playing with fire ★この英語は子供が火をいじって遊ぶことにも, 比喩的な意味での大人のあやうい「火遊び」にも用いられる.

ひあたり 日当たり ¶日当たりがいい get a lot of sunshine / 日当たりが悪い do not get much sunshine / 日当たりのいい[悪い]部屋 a sunny [sunless] room.

ピアニスト a pianist ; a piano player.

ひ¹ めっきり日が短くなった. The days are noticeably shorter. / 日暮れて道遠し. The night is falling, and the way is long. | Alas! My goal is still a long way off. / 部屋に日が差し込む. The sun shines [comes] into the room. | The sunlight pours [streams] into the room. / 窓に日があたっている. The sun was on the window. / その部屋は南向きだから冬でも日があたる. As it faces south, the room catches the sun even in winter. / 彼と知り合いになってからまだ日が浅い. I haven't known him long. | It is not long since I got to know him. / 試験まで日がいくらもない. We have only a few days left before the examinations. / 暑さが日一日と加わってくる. It is growing warmer [hotter] every day.

ひ² 火は納屋から出た. The fire started in the barn. / 私は顔から火が出る思いだった. I felt as if my face was burning with shame. / まだ火がよく起こらない. The fire is not burning [going] properly yet. / ちょっと火を借して下さい. May I have a light? / ジャイアンツの打線が火を噴いた. The Giants' bats struck fire. / 飛んで火に入る夏の虫だ. It is like a moth flying into the flame. / その町は火の消えたように寂しかった. The town looked as if it had been completely deserted. / 火の用心! Look out for fire! | Take care not to start a fire. / 火のない所に煙は立たない. There's no smoke without fire. /《諺》 Where there's smoke, there's fire.

ひ³ 世界にその比を見ない. It is

ピアノ a piano《*pl.* -s》 ¶ピアノを弾く[練習する] play [practice on] the piano / ピアノを勉強する study the piano / グランドピアノ a grand piano / たて型ピアノ an upright piano / ピアノ線 piano wire / ピアノ用腰掛け a piano stool. [文例⇩]
ひあぶり 火あぶり ¶火あぶりにする burn *sb* (to death) at the stake / 火あぶりになる die at the stake; be burned alive [to death].
ひい- ¶ひいじいさん[ばあさん] a great-grandfather[-grandmother] / ひいまご ⇨ **ひまご**.
ピーアール public relations (略: PR).
ビーカー a beaker.
ひいき 〈愛顧〉《文》favor; 《文》patronage; 〈えこひいき〉favoritism; 《文》partiality ¶ひいきする favor; show favor《to》; 《文》show partiality《to》/ ひいきの関取 *one's* favorite *sumo* wrestler / ひいきの引き倒しをする do *sb* a disservice by showing *him* too much partiality / ひいきを受ける enjoy *sb's* favor [patronage]; be patronized《by》/ ひいき目に見る see *sth* in a favorable light / いくらひいき目に見ても (even) seen in the most favorable light; to say the most of it; at best / 日本びいき(の人) a friend [sympathizer] of Japan; a Japanophile / ひいき客 a patron (商店・芸人などの); a customer (商店の). [文例⇩]
ピーク a peak ¶ピーク時 peak hours.
ビーコン a beacon.
ビーシージー BCG (vaccine).
ビーズ a bead.
ヒーター a heater.
ビーチパラソル a beach umbrella.
ピーティーエー a PTA; a Parent-Teacher Association.
ひいては 延いては [文例⇩]
ひいでる 秀でる 〈勝る〉outshine [《文》surpass]《others in [at] *sth*》; 〈上手になる〉《文》come to excel《at, in》; get [《文》become] outstandingly good [skillful]《at *sth*》; 《文》attain great skill [proficiency]《in》 ¶秀でた outstanding; distinguished; 《文》pre-eminent / 秀でている be pre-eminent over《*one's* rivals》; surpass [tower above]《*one's* fellows》.
ビート a beat ¶強烈なビートのロックを演奏する perform rock music with a strong [powerful, violent] beat / ビート板〘水泳〙《米》a flutterboard; 《英》a float.
ビーナス〘ローマ神話〙Venus.
ピーナツ a peanut ⇨ **らっかせい** ¶ピーナツバター peanut butter.
ビーバー〘動〙a beaver.
ぴーぴー 〈鳥の〉peep, peep; 〈信号の〉bleep, bleep ¶ぴーぴー鳴く peep; chirp / ぴーぴー鳴る[鳴らす] whistle; pipe.
ぴいぴい ¶年中ぴいぴいしている be always hard up (for money).
ピーピーエム ppm ★parts per million の略.
ピーマン [<《フランス語》*piment*] a sweet [green, bell] pepper; a pim(i)ento《*pl.* -s》; a Spanish paprika.
ひいらぎ〘植〙a holly (tree).
ビール beer; ale ¶ビールの泡 froth [bubbles] on beer; the head on beer / ビールを1杯やる have a (glass of) beer / ビール醸造所 a (beer) brewery / ビール瓶 a beer bottle.
ビールス ⇨ **ウイルス**.
ひいれ 火入れ 〈溶鉱炉の〉lighting; 〈原子炉の〉igniting ¶火入れ式 a lighting [an igniting] ceremony.
ヒーロー a hero《*pl.* -es》.
ひうちいし 火打ち石 (a) flint.
ひうん 非運 ⇨ **ふうん**.
ひえ[1] 冷え the cold; chill.
ひえ[2] 稗 Japanese (barnyard) millet.
ひえこむ 冷え込む it gets [grows] cold; it is chilly.
ひえしょう 冷え性 ¶冷え性の女 a woman who cannot stand [whose health is affected by] the cold.
ひえびえ 冷え冷え ¶冷え冷えする feel [it is] chilly [very cold].
ひえる 冷える get [grow] cold; get chilly; cool down; 〈冷たく感じる〉feel cold [chilly] ¶体が冷え切ってしまう be chilled to the bone; be (absolutely) frozen. [文例⇩]
ピエロ a pierrot; a clown; a pierrette (女).
ひおおい 日覆い ⇨ **ひよけ**.
ビオラ a viola.
びおん 鼻音 a nasal (sound).
びおんてき 微温的 lukewarm; tepid.
ひか 皮下 ¶皮下注射 (a) hypodermic injection / 皮下注射をする inject《a drug》under the skin; give *sb* a subcutaneous [hypodermic] injection / 皮下脂肪 subcutaneous fat.
びか 美化 beautification ¶美化する beau-

[ひ]

---

unique in the world. / 東京の雑踏から見ればロンドンなどはその比でない. The traffic congestion in London is nothing to that in Tokyo.
ひ[4] 否とするもの3名, 可とするもの10名であった. There were ten ayes to [against] three noes. / 否とするものが多数であった. The noes had it.
ひ[6] 形勢はいよいよ非である. The situation is going from bad to worse. / 彼はまだ自分の非を悟っていないようだ. He does not seem to be convinced of his error yet.
ひあがる この長い日照りで池の水が干上がってしまった. The pond has dried up on account of the long drought. | The long drought has dried up the pond. / せっせと働かなくては口が干上がってしまう. I'll starve if I don't work hard.
ピアノ ピアノが鳴っている家のそばを通り過ぎた. We passed a house where a piano was playing.
ひいき 君は若乃花びいきか. Is Wakanohana your favorite (wrestler)? / 毎度ごひいきに預かりまして. I thank you for your (continued) patronage. / そこまでやったらかえってひいきの引き倒しになるだろう. That will do him more harm than good.
ひいては そうすればあなた御自身のためにも, ひいては町のためにもなることでしょう. It will be good for you. Not only for you, but also for the town. | It will benefit you, and will be to the good of the town as well.
ひえる 足が冷えて眠れない. My feet are so cold (that) I can't sleep. / 冷えないうちに召し上が

ひがい 被害 damage; harm; injury (主として人の) ¶被害を与える damage; do damage [harm] (to); injure sb / 被害を被る be damaged (by); suffer damage (from a flood) / 被害を免れる be undamaged; 〈人が〉 escape injury / 被害額 the amount [extent] of damage; the damage / 被害者〈災害・犯罪の〉 a sufferer; a victim / 〈負傷者〉 the injured (person) / 被害地 the stricken area / 〈文〉 the stricken district / 被害妄想狂〈病気〉 persecution mania; paranoia (通俗に); 〈人〉 a person suffering from persecution mania [paranoia]; 〈通俗に〉 a (person who is) paranoid. 文例⇩

ぴかいち ぴかー an ace; a star ¶ぴかーのNo.1; A 1; ace; topnotch.

ひかえ 控え〈覚え書き〉 a note; a memorandum (pl. -dums, -da) /〈写し〉 a copy; a duplicate; 〈手形・受取証などを切り離したままに残る〉 a counterfoil (of) / 〈英〉 a stub / 〈予備〉 a reserve ¶控えをとる take [make, prepare] a copy [duplicate] (of) / 控えをとっておく make a copy (of) / 控え所[室] a waiting room / 控え力士 a sumo wrestler waiting at the ringside.

ひかえめ 控えめ〈適度の〉 moderate; 〈文〉 temperate (主に飲酒の); 〈慎ましい〉 modest; self-effacing; 〈内輪の〉 conservative ¶控えめに moderately; in moderation; modestly (慎ましく) / 控えめにする be moderate (in); 〈文〉 be temperate ((in eating)) / 控えめに言う put it mildly; 〈文〉 speak with restraint; understate / ごく控えめに言っても say the least of it. 文例⇩

ひがえり 日帰り ¶日帰りの旅行 a day trip / 日帰り客 a day tripper; a visitor for the day / 日帰りする go and return in one day; make a day trip (to).

ひかえる 控える〈抑制する〉 keep [〈文〉refrain] from (doing); restrain oneself from (doing); 〈文〉 abstain from (wine) / 〈節制する〉 do in moderation; do moderately; be moderate [〈文〉 temperate] (in doing); 〈書き留める〉 write [put, jot] sth down; take [make] a note of 〈sb's address〉; 〈待つ〉 wait (in another room) ¶食物を控える eat less than one usually does;〈食べ過ぎない〉 do not eat too much; eat moderately; 〈文〉 practice moderation in eating. 文例⇩

ひかがみ the hollow [back] of the knee.

ひかく¹ 比較 (a) comparison ¶比較する compare (the two, A with B); make a comparison (between); 〈対照する〉 contrast (A with B) /…と比較して[すると] (as) compared with…; in comparison with [to]… / 比較し得る comparable / 比較すべきものがない〈文〉 be unparalleled;〈人が〉 stand unrivaled; be unique / 比較にならない cannot compare (bear comparison) (with) / 比較的に comparatively; relatively / 比較研究する make a comparative study (of); study (a subject) by the comparative method / 〈文学や言語の〉 比較研究者 a comparativist; a comparatist / 比較級〈文法〉 the comparative degree / 比較対照表 a comparative table / 比較多数〈米〉 a plurality ;〈英〉 a relative majority / 比較文学[言語学] comparative literature [linguistics]. 文例⇩

ひかく² 皮革 hides (and skins); leather ¶皮革工業 the leather industry / 皮革製品 leather goods.

ひかく³ 非核 ¶非核三原則 the three antinuclear principles.

びがく 美学 aesthetics ¶美学者 an aesthetician.

ひかげ 日陰 the shade ¶日陰に置く keep sth in the shade [out of the sun] / 日陰に入る go into the shade; get out of the sun / 〈樹木などが〉 日陰を作る 〈文〉 afford shade / 日陰者 〈やましい所のある人〉 a person with a shady past; 〈前科者〉 an ex-convict; 〈お尋ね者〉 a person who is on the run (from the police); 〈文〉 a fugitive from justice; 〈妾(めかけ)〉 a kept woman.

ひがけ 日掛け payment by [in] daily installments ¶日掛け貯金 savings by daily deposit.

ひかげん 火加減 ¶火加減を見る look to the fire; see if it is properly heated.

ひがさ 日傘 a parasol; a sunshade ¶日傘をさす put up a parasol.

ひかされる 引かされる be drawn (by); be moved (by).

ひがし¹ 干菓子 higashi; a type of dry Japanese candy.

れ. Eat it before it gets cold. / このビールはよく冷えていない. This beer is not properly cooled.

ひがい 暴風雨で米作に被害がありましたか.—いえ, だいぶありました. Did the storm do any damage to the rice crop?—Yes, a great deal of damage has been done. / その地震では東京の被害が最も甚だしかった. Tokyo suffered most from the earthquake. / だれもそのために大して被害を受けるわけではない. No one is much the worse for it.

ひかえめ 万事控えめにするよう忠告してやった. I advised him to do everything in moderation [to be moderate in everything].

ひがえり そこは電車で行って帰りができる. You can get there and back in a day by train.

ひかえる 私はその事を今まで控えて言わずにいたのです. I have refrained from saying anything about it until now. / その地は北に筑波山を控えている. The place faces Mt. Tsukuba on the north. / 試験を目の前に控えて学生はやけに忙しそうだ. With the examinations near at hand [just around the corner], the students seem to be very busy. / 彼の背後には大金持ちが控えている. He has a millionaire as his backer [behind him].

ひかく¹ 私は翻訳を原文と比較してみた. I have compared the translation with the original. / このほうが比較にならないほど上等だ. This one is incomparably better than that. / 本年度の収入は昨年度に比較して100万円の減少. This year's earnings show a drop of one million yen as compared with last. / 確かに沖縄も暑いがインドとは比較にならない. It is true that the heat in Okinawa is very intense, but it bears no comparison with that in India. / うちの庭なんかお宅とは全然比較になりません. Our gar-

ひがし 東 (the) east ¶東の east; eastern; easterly 《風などが》/ 東(の方)へ行く go east [eastward] / 東に《東面に》the east; 《東方に》to the east; 《東側に》on the east / 東風 an east [easterly] wind / 東側 the east [eastern] side; 《東西両陣営の》the East. 文例⇩

ひかず 日数 ⇒ にっすう.

ひかぜい 非課税 ¶非課税の tax-exempt 《bonds》; tax-free 《articles》.

ひがた 干潟 tidal [mud] flats;《米》tideland.

びカタル 鼻カタル nasal catarrh.

ぴかぴか ¶ぴかぴか光る sparkle; glitter; flash;《星が》twinkle / ぴかぴかした glittering; glistening; shiny. 文例⇩

ひがみ 僻み envy; jealousy;《劣等感》(an) inferiority complex ¶ひがみを起こす ⇒ ひがむ. 文例⇩

ひがむ 僻む imagine [fancy] that *one* has been wronged [unfairly treated]; be oversensitive; be too sensitive; grow jealous 《of》; become prejudiced 《against》;《文》take a jaundiced view 《of》.

ひがめ 僻目 《偏見》(a) prejudice; (a) bias;《誤解》(a) misunderstanding. 文例⇩

ひがら 日柄 ¶日柄を選ぶ choose a lucky [《文》an auspicious] day.

ひからす 光らす make *sth* shine [bright];《文》give luster 《to》; polish 《磨いて》 ¶目を光らしている keep a sharp [close] watch 《over, on》.

ひからびる 干からびる dry up; be dried up; shrivel ¶干からびた dried up; shriveled, withered.

ひかり 光《光明》(a) light;《光線》a ray; a beam;《閃光》a flash; a gleam (やみの中の); a twinkle (星などの);《かすかな光》a glimmer;《輝き》brightness; brilliance;《つや》shine; gloss;《文》luster ¶星の光 starlight / 蛍の光 the glow of a firefly / 親の光 the influence of *one's* parents / 光を通さない lightproof 《curtains》/ 光を放つ give out [《文》emit] light; send out rays of light.

ぴかりと ¶ぴかりと光る flash.

ひかる 光る shine; be bright; be brilliant; be luminous; glitter 《ガラス・宝石・金銀などが》; glisten (特にぬれたものなどが); twinkle (星などが); sparkle (宝石などが); glimmer (かすかに); gleam (暗がりで); flash (ぴかりと). 文例⇩

ひかん¹ 悲観 pessimism;《落胆》disappointment ¶悲観する be pessimistic《about》; give up hope;《落胆する》be disappointed; lose heart / 人生を悲観する take a pessimistic [gloomy] view of life / 悲観的な pessimistic / 悲観的に pessimistically / 悲観論 a pessimistic view;《一般》pessimism / 悲観論者 a pessimist. 文例⇩

ひかん² 避寒《文》wintering ¶避寒する spend [pass] the winter 《at, in》;《文》winter 《at, in》/ 避寒に行く go to《Zushi》for the winter / 避寒地 a winter resort.

ひがん¹ 彼岸 the equinoctial week ¶彼岸の入り the first day of the equinoctial week / 春[秋]の彼岸の中日 the spring [autumn] equinox.

ひがん² 悲願《心の底からの願い》*one's* dearest [《文》earnest] wish;《仏教》Buddha's vow to save mankind.

びかん 美観 a fine [beautiful] sight [spectacle] ¶美観を増す add to the beauty 《of》/ 街(み)の美観を損なう spoil [《文》mar] the appearance of the streets.

びがんじゅつ 美顔術 facial treatment;《口語》a facial; beauty culture (美容術).

びがんすい 美顔水 (a) beauty lotion.

ひき¹ 引き《愛顧》《文》patronage;《文》favor;《後援》backing; support;《勢力》influence; (a) pull;《釣の》a tug ¶よい引きがある have good backing [pull].

ひき² 悲喜 ¶悲喜こもごも至る《文》have a mingled feeling of joy and sorrow.

-ひき …匹 ¶5 匹の子猫 five kittens.

-びき …引き ¶5 分引きで at 5% discount; 5% off / ゴム引きの coated with india rubber; rubber-coated.

ひきあい 引き合い《参考》reference;《取り引きの》an inquiry ¶引き合いに出す mention; refer to; cite *sth* as an example 《to support *one's* case》/《取り引きで》引き合いがたくさんある receive a lot of inquiries 《for》.

ひきあう 引き合う《互いに引く》pull against each other;《利益になる》pay; be profitable ¶引き合う商売 a paying business / 引き合う

---

den doesn't begin to compare with yours.

ひかされる 友情に引かされてしたのだ. He did it out of affection for his friend. / He did it for friendship's sake.

ひかむ² 太陽は東から出て西に沈む. The sun rises in the east and sets in the west. / 東の空が白みはじめた. The eastern sky is becoming light. / 日本は東は太平洋に面している. Japan faces the Pacific on the east. / この島は本土から東へ5キロの東にある. This island is [lies] about five kilometers east of the mainland.

ぴかぴか 空に星がぴかぴか光って

いる. The stars are twinkling in the sky.

ひがみ 貧乏するとひがみ根性が出る. Poverty warps one's character [distorts one's view of the world].

ひがめ それは君のひが目だ. You are biased if that's what you think.

ひかる 木の葉に露がきらきら光っている. The dewdrops are sparkling on the leaves. / ネクタイの結び目の所がすれて光った. His tie was worn shiny at the knot. / あの人は同僚の中でも光っている. He outshines [shines among] his colleagues. / 光るも

のすべてが金ではない. All that glitters is not gold.

ひかん¹ そんなに悲観しないでまあせいぜいのんきにしましょう. Don't look so gloomy! Hope for the best, my friend! / この成績では悲観するよ. I am disappointed at the result. / 彼らは悲観的になった. They took a pessimistic view of things [the future].

ひかん¹ 暑さ寒さも彼岸まで. Neither heat nor cold lasts beyond the equinox.

ひき¹ 彼は昔の友達の引きで外務省に入った. He obtained a position in the Foreign Office through the influence of [through

ひきあげ 引き上[揚]げ 〈引っぱって上げること〉pulling [drawing] up;〈帰国〉repatriation; one's return home;〈撤退〉evacuation; (a) withdrawal; a pullback; a pullout;〈沈没船の〉refloating;《文》refloatation; salvage;〈値段の〉raising; a raise ¶引き揚げ作業 salvage work / 引き揚げ者 a repatriate / 引き揚げ船〈帰国船〉a repatriation ship;〈撤収者を乗せた〉an evacuation boat.

ひきあげる 引き上[揚]げる 〈引っぱって上げる〉pull [draw] up;〈値段を〉increase; raise;〈船を〉refloat;〈撤退する〉withdraw (from); pull out 《of a place》; leave [《文》evacuate] 《a place》;〈外国から〉return home; be repatriated.

ひきあてきん 引当金 a reserve fund 《to cover an expected loss》.

ひきあてる 引き当てる ¶当りくじを引き当てる draw the winning number.

ひきあわせ 引き合わせ 〈紹介〉(an) introduction;〈対照〉(a) comparison;〈照合〉《文》collation; checking. 文例↓

ひきあわせる 引き合わせる 〈引き寄せて合わせる〉draw 《them》 together;〈紹介する〉introduce; present;〈対照する〉compare 《A with B》;〈照合する〉《文》collate 《A with B》; check (up) ¶原簿と引き合わせる check (it) with [against] the ledger.

ひきいる 率いる lead 《a party》; command 《an army》; be in command of 《an army》.

ひきいれる 引き入れる 〈引き込む〉draw [pull] in [into];〈導き入れる〉lead sb in [into];〈連れ込む〉take sb into 《a room》;〈誘い入れる〉win sb over (to); tempt [entice] sb in [into] ¶味方に引き入れる win sb over to one's side.

ひきうけ 引き受け 〈負担〉undertaking;〈受諾〉acceptance (手形の); underwriting (株式・社債・公債の);〈保証〉(a) guarantee ¶引受人〈保証人〉a guarantor;〈手形の〉an acceptor.

ひきうける 引き受ける 〈仕事などを〉undertake; take on 《a job》; take 《a job》 on oneself;〈責任を負う〉answer for; take responsibility for;〈保証する〉guarantee;〈手形を〉accept;〈担当する〉take charge of;〈引き取る〉take over;〈応じる〉accept; agree [《文》consent] to ¶業務を引き受ける take over sb's business.

ひきうす 碾[挽]き臼 a (hand)mill; a quern.

ひきうつす 引き写す trace; copy 《a diagram》 by tracing.

ひきおこす 引き起こす 〈上げる〉raise [lift] sth up;〈事件などを〉cause; bring about [on]; lead to; give rise to ¶倒れた人を引き起こす help sb (to) get up; lift [《文》raise] sb / 戦争を引き起こす cause [give rise to] a war.

ひきおろす 引き下ろす pull [drag, draw] down;〈旗などを〉take [haul] down.

ひきかえ 引き替え 〈交換〉exchange;〈兌(ﾀﾞ)換〉conversion ¶…と引き替えに in exchange for… / 品物と引き替えに金を払う pay (for the goods) on delivery.

ひきかえす 引き返す turn [come] back; return ¶途中から引き返す turn back halfway / 来た道を引き返す turn back the way one has come; retrace one's steps. 文例↓

ひきかえる 引き替[換]える exchange 《goods for money》 ¶小切手を現金に引き替える cash a check / …に引き替えて(て) while…;《文》whereas…. 文例↓

ひきがえる《動》a toad.

ひきがたり 弾き語り ¶弾き語りをする recite [chant]《the Chanson de Roland》to one's own accompaniment (on the lute); recite [chant] 《the Heike》accompanying oneself (on the biwa).

ひきがね 引き金 a trigger ¶引き金を引く [press, squeeze] the trigger; trigger 《a rifle》. 文例↓

ひきぎわ 引き際 ⇨ ひけぎわ 文例.

ひきげき 悲喜劇 (a) tragicomedy.

ひきこみせん 引き込み線 ⇨ ひっこみせん.

ひきこむ 引き込む ⇨ ひきいれる.

ひきこもる 引き籠る stay [keep] indoors; stay at home ¶病気で引きこもる keep [be confined] to one's bed; be laid up with 《(influenza)》 / いなかに引きこもる retire into the country;《文》live in a rural retreat. 文例↓

ひきころす 轢き殺す knock sb down [run sb over] and kill him ¶列車にひき殺される be (run over and) killed by a train.

ひきさがる 引き下がる retire [《文》withdraw] 《from》; leave.

ひきさく 引き裂く tear up [off]; tear [pull] to pieces; rip up;〈仲を〉separate;《文》estrange ¶手紙を引き裂く tear up a letter; tear a letter to [in] pieces.

ひきさげ 引き下げ lowering; (a) reduction; a cut ¶賃金の引き下げ (a) reduction in wages; a wage cut.

---

his pull with] an old friend. / 〈釣りで〉引きがあった. There was a tug on the line.

ひきあう それでは引き合わない. It won't pay. / その機械を入れるのには金がかかるが, じきに引き合うようになる. The machine, though expensive, will pay for itself in a short time. / その企画で引き合うかどうかだ. The question is whether the project can be made to pay.

ひきあわせ これも神様のお引き合わせだ. It is divine will that has brought us thus together.

ひきうける 君が損をした時は僕が引き受ける. I'll answer [make up] for your possible losses. / 資金の調達は引き受ける. I'll see (to it) that the funds are raised. | I'll undertake to raise the funds. / 宣伝は僕が引き受けた. I will take it on myself to give publicity to it.

ひきかえす 激しい雨で山小屋まで引き返した. Since it was raining so hard we turned back to the hut.

ひきかえる 彼はあんなに勉強家だが, それに引き替え弟はいつも怠けている. His younger brother is always idle, while he himself is such a hardworking man.

ひきがね これが暴動の引き金となった. This triggered the riot.

ひきこもる その日は風邪で一日中引きこもっていた. A cold kept me at home the whole day.

ひきしお 今は引き潮だ. The tide

ひきさげる 引き下げる lower ; bring *sth* down ; 〈価格・賃金などを〉 reduce ; cut (down) ¶賃金を500円引き下げる cut [reduce] *sb's* wages by 500 yen / 値段を500円に引き下げる reduce [lower] the price to 500 yen.

ひきざん 引き算 subtraction ¶引き算する do subtraction ⇒ひく¹.

ひきしお 引き潮 (an) ebb tide ¶引き潮(時)に at low tide [water] / 引き潮になる (begin to) ebb. 文例⇩

ひきしぼる 引き絞る ⇒しぼる ¶弓を引き絞る draw a bow to the full / 声を引き絞る strain *one's* voice.

ひきしまる 引き締まる 〈物が〉get [〈文〉become] tight [tense] ; tighten ; be tightened ; 〈気分が〉be braced up ¶引き締まった tightened ; tight ; tense ; compact / 引き締まった顔だち firm features / 引き締まった体つき a compact [well-knit] figure / 引き締まった文章 a compact style.

ひきしめる 引き締める tighten ; strain ¶気持ちを引き締める brace *oneself* (up) / 金融を引き締める tighten the money market.

ひぎしゃ 被疑者 ⇒ようぎしゃ (容疑者).

ひきずる 引きずる drag ; trail ¶すそを引きずって歩く walk with *one's* skirt trailing / 足を引きずって歩く drag *oneself* along ; shuffle (*one's* feet) along / 疲れた足を引きずる 〈文〉drag *one's* weary feet / 引きずり上げる [下ろす] drag [pull] *sth* up [down] / 引きずり込む drag [pull] *sb* in [into] / 引きずり出す drag [pull] *sb* out (of the house) / 戦争に引きずり込まれる be drawn into a war / 引きずり回す drag *sb* about.

ひきたおす¹ 引き倒す pull *sth* down.

ひきたおす² 轢き倒す knock [run] *sb* down.

ひきだし 引き出し 〈机などの〉a drawer ; 〈預金の〉(a) withdrawal ; drawing out ¶引き出しを開ける[閉める] open [shut] a drawer / 引き出しに一杯の手紙 a drawerful of letters. 文例⇩

ひきだす 引き出す 〈引っぱって出す〉pull [〈文〉draw] *sth* out ; 〈取り出す〉take [get] *sth* out ; 〈抽出する〉〈文〉extract ; 〈預金などを〉withdraw [draw] (5,000 yen from *one's* (bank) account) ¶預金を引き出す withdraw *one's* deposit 《from the bank》 / 子供の隠れた才能を引き出す bring out the hidden talent in a boy.

ひきたつ 引き立つ 〈見映えする〉look better [〈文〉to advantage〉 ¶気分が引き立つ cheer ; take heart / 気分が引き立たない feel [be] depressed ; be in low spirits. 文例⇩

ひきたて 引き立て 〈愛顧〉a favor ; 〈文〉favor ; 〈文〉patronage ; 〈後援〉backing (up) ; support ¶引き立てを受ける 〈文〉be patronized 《by》; 〈文〉receive [enjoy] *sb's* favor [patronage] ; find favor 《with》/ 引き立て役になる serve as a foil 《for, to》.

ひきたてる 引き立てる 〈連れて行く〉take [drag, haul] *sb* off ; 〈ひいきにする〉〈文〉favor ; patronize ; 〈後援する〉support ; back (up) ; 〈見映えさす〉set *sb* [*sth*] off (to advantage) ; bring (the color) out [into prominence] ¶気を引き立てる cheer *sb* up.

ひきちぎる 引きちぎる tear [wrench] off.

ひきちゃ 挽茶 powdered tea.

ひきつぎ 引き継ぎ 〈事務の〉taking over 《*sb's* duties》(受け継ぎ) ; handing over 《*one's* duties》(引き渡し)／〈リレーの〉a pass ¶引き継ぎを失敗する 〈リレーで〉bungle a pass.

ひきつぐ 引き継ぐ 〈受け継ぐ〉take over 《*sb's* duties》; 〈引き渡す〉hand over 《*one's* duties》to *sb* ; 〈継承する〉succeed 《to》; inherit. 文例⇩

ひきつけ 引き付け ⇒けいれん.

ひきつける 引き付ける 〈引き寄せる〉draw ; attract ; 〈魅する〉charm ; fascinate ; 〈けいれんを起こす〉have convulsions ; have a (convulsive) fit ¶人を引き付ける所のある attractive ; charming ; engaging / 人の心を引き付ける微笑 a charming [winning] smile.

ひきつづき, ひきつづいて 引き続き, 引き続いて continuously ; uninterruptedly ; without a break ; in succession ; one after another (続々) ¶その日から引き続いて from that day on / 3日間引き続いて for three days running [on end]. 文例⇩

ひきづな 引き綱 〈船の〉a towline ; a towrope ; a towing rope.

ひきつり 引きつり 〈やけどなどのあと〉a scar ; 〈けいれん〉a cramp ; a twitch. 文例⇩

ひきつる 引きつる have a cramp ; be cramped ; twitch ¶右足が引きつる have a cramp [be cramped] in the right leg. 文例⇩

ひきつれる 引き連れる take [bring, have] 《*one's* men》along [with *one*] ; 〈文〉be accompanied 《by》. 文例⇩

ひきて¹ 引き手 〈戸などの〉a handle ; a knob

---

is ebbing [on the ebb].

ひきだし 彼女は引き出しをすっと閉めた。 She slid the drawer shut.

ひきたつ あの襟のドレスで彼は引き立って見える。 She looks better in that purple dress. | That purple dress sets her off to advantage.

ひきたて 毎度お引き立てをいただきましてありがとうございます。 Thank you very much for your continued favor [patronage]. / 彼は加納氏の引き立てによってぐんぐん出世した。 He got on rapidly in his career under Mr. Kano's patronage.

ひきつぐ (リレーで)彼は相手を大きく[約2メートル]抜いて次の走者に引き継いだ。 He handed over a good lead [an advantage of about two meters] to the next runner.

ひきつける 彼にはどこか人を引き付ける所がある。 There is something attractive about him.

ひきつづき, ひきつづいて 引き続き総会があった。 Then followed the general meeting. / 昨年に引き続き今年も優勝した。 He has won the championship for the second straight year [the second year running].

ひきつり 彼は若い時にけがをして左のほおにひどい引きつりがある。 On his left cheek he has an ugly scar from a wound received in his youth.

ひきつる 苦痛のあまり顔が引きつった。 His face twitched with pain.

ひきつれる 彼は家族を引き連れてブラジルへ移住した。 He emi-

(球形の).

ひきて² 弾き手 a player; a performer.

ひきでもの 引き出物 a present; a gift.

ひきど 引き戸 a sliding door.

ひきとめる 引き留[止]める 〈客などを〉(try to) prevent *sb* from leaving;《文》detain;〈阻止する〉keep *sth* back; check ¶〈辞職しようとする人の〉引き留め策を講じる take measures to persuade *sb* to stay in office. 文例あ

ひきとりて[にん] 引き取り手[人] 〈死体などの〉a claimant;〈孤児などの〉a caretaker ¶引き取り人のない死体 an unclaimed body.

ひきとる 引き取る 〈引き継ぐ〉take over;〈世話する〉look after; take care of;〈受け取る〉receive;〈預けた物などを〉collect; claim;〈退く〉《文》withdraw (from); leave ¶身柄を引き取る take *sb* along to *one*'s home; take *sb* in.

ひきなおす 引き直す〈線などを〉redraw; draw (a line) over again ¶風邪を引き直す catch cold again.

ビキニ a bikini ¶ビキニ姿の女 a woman in a bikini.

ひきにく 挽き肉 minced [ground] meat.

ひきにげ 轢き逃げ ¶ひき逃げする knock *sb* down and run away / ひき逃げ事件[運転手] a hit-and-run case [driver].

ひきぬく 引き抜く 〈引いて抜く〉pull [draw, pluck] *sth* out;《文》extract;〈選ぶ〉pick (the best specimen) out; select;〈他の会社などから人を〉lure [poach] (an actor from his company).

ひきのばし 引き伸[延]ばし 〈延長〉《文》extension;《文》prolongation;〈拡大〉enlargement 〈時間をかせぐための〉引き延ばし策 a delaying [《文》dilatory] measure /〈審議などの〉引き延ばし戦術 delaying [stalling] tactics /〈議会での〉審議引き延ばしのための長時間演説《米》a filibuster / 引き伸ばし写真 an enlarged photograph; an enlargement 《of a snapshot》.

ひきのばす 引き伸[延]ばす 〈引っ張って伸ばす〉draw [stretch] out;〈延長する〉extend;《文》prolong;〈写真を〉enlarge;〈延期する〉put (an appointment) off; postpone ¶写真を等身大に引き伸ばす make a life-size enlargement of a photograph / 文を無意味に引き延ばす pad out a sentence with useless words.

ひきはなす 引き離す 〈間をあける〉draw [pull] apart;〈競走で〉run ahead 《of *one*'s competitors》; get [have] a 《good》 lead 《on》; outdistance.

ひきはらう 引き払う leave; clear [move] out.

ひきふね 引き船 a tug(boat); a tow boat ¶引き船をする take (a ship) in tow; tow 《a boat》/ 〈運河などの〉引き船道 a towpath.

ひきまわす 引き回す 〈幕などを〉draw 《the curtain》 around;〈連れ回す〉take *sb* around [about];〈指導する〉lead ¶〈人を〉自由に引き回す lead *sb* by the nose.

ひきもきらず 引きも切らず ⇒ひっきりなしに.

ひきもどす 引き戻す 〈引っ張り戻す〉pull back;〈連れ帰る〉bring *sb* back [home];〈元に戻す〉restore.

ひきゃく 飛脚 an express messenger; a courier.

ひきゅう 飛球《野球》⇒フライ².

ひきょう¹ 卑怯 〈おくびょう〉cowardice;〈卑劣〉《文》meanness ¶卑怯な 〈おくびょうな〉cowardly;《口語》chicken;〈男らしくない〉unmanly;〈卑劣な〉《文》mean;〈不正な〉foul; unfair / 卑怯な振る舞いをする act in a cowardly way;〈競技で〉play foul; hit 《*one*'s opponent》 below the belt / 卑怯者 a coward. 文例あ

ひきょう² 秘境 an unexplored region; one of the most secluded regions 《of central Japan》.

ひきよせる 引き寄せる 〈近くへ引く〉pull [《文》draw] *sb* [*sth*] near [toward] *one*;〈客などを〉draw; attract.

ひきわけ 引き分け a drawn match [game]; a draw; a tie ¶引き分けになる end in a draw. 文例あ

ひきわける 引き分ける 〈引いて離す〉pull [《文》draw] apart;〈競技で〉fight [end in] a draw 《with》.

ひきわたし 引き渡し handing [turning] over; delivery; transfer ¶《国際間で》犯罪者の引き渡しを要求する ask for the extradition of a criminal.

ひきわたす 引き渡す 〈人・物を〉hand [turn] over; deliver;〈権利などを〉give [《文》deliver] up; transfer;〈外国の逃亡犯罪人などを〉extradite.

ひきわり(むぎ) 碾[挽]き割り(麦) cracked barley.

ひきん 卑近 ¶卑近な familiar; common / 卑近な例をあげる give [cite] a familiar example.

ひきんぞく¹ 非金属《化》a nonmetal ¶非金属

---

grated to Brazil with his whole family.

ひきとめる 長くお引き留めはしません。I won't keep you long.

ひきはなす 経済戦争では西ドイツはフランスを大きく引き離している。West Germany has a long lead in its [her] economic contest with France.

ひきょう¹ 敵に後ろを見せるとは卑怯だ。It is cowardly of you to turn your back on the enemy [not to take up the challenge]. / 卑怯な振舞いをして家の名誉を傷つけるな。Do not disgrace your family by an act of cowardice. / 卑怯にも彼は逃げ出した。He was timid [chicken] enough to run away.

ひきよせる 暖炉のそばへ椅子を引き寄せたまえ。Draw your chair up to the fire.

ひきわけ 今シーズンの我がチームの成績は4勝3敗2引き分けだ。Our team has had four wins, three defeats and two draws this season. / 田中と佐藤のレスリング試合は引き分けになった。Tanaka and Sato wrestled to a draw.

ひく¹ その家には水道もガスも電灯も引いてある。Water, gas and electricity are laid on in that house. / どの部屋にもみな電話が引いてある。A telephone is installed in each room. / ちょっと辞書を引いてみよう。I'll just look it up in my dictionary. / 辞書の引き方を知らない。He does not know how to use a dictionary. / 幾らか引けませんか。Can't you take something off 《the price》? / 10引く2は8。Two from

元素 a nonmetallic element.
ひきんぞく² 卑金属 a base metal.
ひく¹ 引く ¶〈引っぱる〉pull;《文》draw; haul; tug;〈引きずる〉drag; trail〈すそなどを〉;〈注意などを〉attract;〈導く〉lead;〈引用する〉cite; quote;〈減じる〉subtract;〈値段を〉reduce; cut down;〈後退する〉retreat; fall back;〈離れる〉leave;〈職から〉withdraw (from);〈職を〉resign;〈減退する〉go [die] down; subside ¶そでを引くtug (at) sb's sleeve; pull sb by the sleeve / 老人の手を引く lead an old man by the hand / 線を引く draw a line / 車を引く pull [draw] a cart / 辞書を引く look at [use,《文》consult] a dictionary; look up 《a word》 in a dictionary / 油を引く oil / テニソンから引いた句 a line quoted from Tennyson / 5から3を引く take [subtract] 3 from 5 / 同情を引く draw [win] sb's sympathy / 系統を引く be descended (from) / 舞台を引く retire from [leave,《口語》quit] the stage. 文例⬇
ひく² 挽く碾く〈のこぎりで〉saw;〈うすで〉grind ¶粉にひく grind 《wheat》 into flour.
ひく³ 弾く play ¶ピアノを弾く play the piano / 琴を上手に弾く be a good *koto* player / 弾き間違える play a wrong note.
ひく⁴ 轢く run sb over; knock sb down ¶車にひかれる be hit [run over, knocked down] by a car.
びく 魚籠 a (wicker) basket used for carrying fish; a creel.
ひくい 低い〈高さが〉low ¶低くする lower; bring sth down;〈音・声を〉drop / 低くなる fall; go [get,《文》become] low; go [come] down /〈声・調子が〉drop /〈日が〉decline / 声を低くして in a low [subdued] voice. 文例⬇
ひくいどり 火食い鳥 a cassowary.
ひくく 低く low ¶低くする lower; bring sth down;〈音・声を〉drop / 低くなる fall; go [get,《文》become] low; go [come] down /〈声・調子が〉drop /〈日が〉decline / 声を低くして in a low [subdued] voice. 文例⬇

びくしょう 微苦笑 ¶微苦笑する give a wry little smile; force a faint smile.
ひくつ 卑屈 ¶卑屈な《文》mean;《文》servile.
びくつく ⇨ びくびく (びくびくする), びくっと (びくっとする).
びくっと ¶びくっとする《文》start; give a start (at);びくっとさせる be startled / びくっとさせる give sb a start; startle.
ひくて 引く手 ¶引く手あまたである be very popular; be in great demand; be very much sought after.
びくとも ¶びくともしない do not turn a hair; remain calm [unperturbed]; be not daunted at all / びくともせずに without flinching;《文》undauntedly;《文》dauntlessly.
ピクニック (have) a picnic ¶ピクニックに出かける go on a picnic; go picnicking / ピクニックに行く〈来た〉人 a picnicker.
ひくひく ¶ひくひくする twitch; move convulsively.
びくびく ¶びくびくする be afraid 《of》; be in fear; be nervous; tremble with [for] fear / びくびくしながら timidly; fearfully; nervously.
ぴくぴく ¶ぴくぴく動く[させる]jerk; twitch. 文例⬇
ひぐま 《動》a brown bear.
ひくめ 低目 ¶低めの rather low; lowish / 低めの直球 a low, straight ball.
ひぐらし 《昆》a *higurashi* cicada.
ピクルス 《料理》pickles ¶きゅうりのピクルス pickled gherkins [cucumbers].
ひぐれ 日暮れ ⇨ にちぼつ, ゆうがた.
ひけ 引け ¶引けを取る be beaten 《by》; be outdone 《by》; be inferior (to);《文》compare unfavorably 《with》/ ...にも引けを取らない yield to nobody; be second to none; can hold one's own with anyone / 引け時 (the) closing time.
ひげ¹ 卑下 ¶卑下する belittle [《文》humble] oneself /《文》speak [think] depreciatingly of oneself / 卑下して humbly; modestly.
ひげ² 髭〈あごひげ〉a beard;〈口ひげ〉《米》a mustache;《英》a moustache;〈ほおひげ、猫・とらなどの〉whiskers ★「口ひげ」「ほおひげ」などの区別なしに、単に「ひげ」と言う時、英語では a beard と言う ¶濃い[薄い]ひげ a

---

ten leaves [is] eight. | Ten minus two equals [is equal to] eight. / もう一歩もあとへは引かない。 I will not budge an inch. / アメリカはベルリン問題では一歩も引かないと言った。 The United States refused to back down on Berlin. / 引くに引けなくなった。 I can't pull out now. / I have gone too far to retreat. / 私はその件から手を引きました。 I have washed my hands of that affair. / 〈洪水の〉水が引いた。 The water subsided [went down]. / 熱はすっかり引きました。 The fever has entirely left me. / はれが引いた。 The swelling has gone down.
ひくい 水は低きにつく。 Water seeks the lowest possible level. | Water always flows downhill.
ひくく 枝が低く垂れている。 The branches hang low down.
びくとも この建物は今度の地震にはびくともしなかった。 The building withstood the last earthquake perfectly well. / その暴徒を前にして彼はびくともしなかった。 He stood facing the riot-

ers without turning a hair.
びくびく 彼は首になりはしまいかとびくびくしている。 He is terribly afraid of being fired. / その晩は水が出やしないかとびくびくものですごした。 We passed the night in great fear of a flood.
ぴくぴく 彼は顔をぴくぴくさせていた。 I saw his face twitching [working].
ひけ 彼女は英語ではクラスのだれにも引けを取らない。 She is second to nobody [She is as good as anyone else] in our class in

dense [sparse] beard; a thick [thin] mustache / ひげのある bearded; mustached; whiskered / ひげのない beardless; clean-shaven / ひげの伸びた顔 a face with a stubbly beard; an unshaven face / ひげを生やす grow [cultivate] a beard [mustache] / 〈生やしている〉 have [wear] a beard [mustache] / ひげをそる〈自分で〉 shave (oneself); have a shave; 〈床屋で〉 get [have] a shave / ひげそり道具 shaving things / ひげそり用のブラシ[鏡] a shaving brush [mirror] / ひげ面(㊥) a bearded face; an unshaven face (無精した).

ピケ a picket ¶ピケを張る[置く] put [《文》place, post, station] pickets (in front of a factory); picket (a place) / ピケライン a picket line.

ひげき 悲劇 (a) tragedy ¶悲劇的事件 a tragic affair; a tragedy.

ひけぎわ 引け際 〖文例⇩〗

ひけしゃく 火消し役〈もめ事の〉a peacemaker; 〈救援投手〉a fireman. 〖文例⇩〗

ひけつ¹ 否決 (a) rejection ¶否決する reject; vote [decide] against (a bill); vote (a motion) down. 〖文例⇩〗

ひけつ² 秘訣 a secret (of); a key (to) ¶成功の秘訣 the secret of [a key to] success.

ひけめ 引け目 ¶引け目を感じる feel small (in sb's presence); feel inferior (to sb).

ひけらかす show off 《one's learning》; make a display [show] of 《one's wealth》.

ひける 引ける 〈終わる〉close; be over; 〈解散になる〉break up / 気が引ける ⇒き⁸.

ひげんじつてき 非現実的 unrealistic; 〈実行困難な〉impracticable; 《文》unfeasible.

ひけんしゃ 被験者 a (test) subject; a testee.

ひご¹ 庇護 ⇒ほご² ¶…の庇護のもとに under the protection [wing, 《文》patronage] of....

ひご² 卑語 a vulgar word [expression]; a vulgarism.

ひごい 緋鯉 a red carp.

ひこう¹ 非行 (a) misdeed; 《文》an evil deed / 《文》misconduct; delinquency ¶未成年者の非行 juvenile delinquency / 非行を暴く bring sb's misconduct [crime] to light / 非行少年 a juvenile delinquent / 非行性 (an inclination toward) delinquency.

ひこう² 飛行 (a) flight; flying; 〈航空術〉aviation ⇒こうくう³ ¶飛行する fly (in the air); make a flight; travel by air / 飛行中に while flying [in flight] / 《航空母艦の》飛行甲板 a flight deck / 飛行経路 a flight path / 飛行士 ⇒ひこうか / 飛行時間 flying hours; flight time / 飛行速度 (an) air speed / 飛行速度計 an air-speed indicator / 飛行船 an airship / 飛行艇 a flying boat / 飛行服 a flying suit / 飛行帽 an aviation cap. 〖文例⇩〗

ひごう 非業 ¶非業の死を遂げる die an unnatural death; meet (with) a violent end.

びこう¹ 尾行 ¶尾行する follow; 《口語》shadow; 《口語》tail / 尾行をまく 《口語》give one's tail the slip; shake off a shadow.

びこう² 備考 a note; a remark; 〈注記〉N.B. (★《ラテン語》*nota bene* (=note well) の略) ¶備考欄 remarks [reference] column.

びこう³ 鼻孔 a nostril.

ひこうか 飛行家 a flier; a flyer; an aviator; an airman; a pilot ¶飛行家になる become an aviator; 《文》take to the air.

ひこうかい 非公開 ¶非公開の not open to the public; private; secret.

ひこうき 飛行機 a plane; 《米》an airplane; 《英》an aeroplane; an aircraft (単複同形) ¶飛行機に乗る go [have a ride] in an airplane; take an airplane; 〈乗り込む〉get into [aboard] an airplane; board a plane / 《文》emplane / 飛行機に酔う get [《文》become] airsick / 飛行機で行く go by plane [by air, in an airplane]; fly (to Europe) / 飛行機で送る send sth by air; fly sth (to a place) / 軽飛行機 a light (air-) plane / 飛行機雲 a vapor [condensation] trail / 飛行機旅行 air air trip. 〖文例⇩〗

ひこうしき 非公式 ¶非公式の informal; unofficial; off the record (発言など) / 非公式に informally; unofficially; off the record (発言など) / 非公式会談 《外交》a [an informal] conversation.

ひこうじょう 飛行場 an airfield; a flying field [ground]; an airport (空港).

ひごうほう 非合法 ¶非合法の illegal; 《文》unlawful / 非合法化する make sth illegal; outlaw / 非合法すれすれのことをする do something just barely legal; act on the borderline between legality and illegality / 非合法活動 illegal activities.

ひこく 被告 《民事の》a defendant; 《刑事の》the accused ¶被告席 the dock.

ひこくみん 非国民 an unpatriotic person; an un-Japanese [un-American, etc.] person; 〈裏切り者〉a traitor.

ひこつ 腓骨 《解》a fibula (*pl.* -s, -lae).

ひごと 日ごと ⇒ひび¹, まいにち. 〖文例⇩〗

ひこばえ a sucker; a sprout 《from the stump of a tree》.

ひごろ 日頃 〈平生〉usually; 〈常々〉always;

English.
ひげぎわ 人間引けぎわが大切だ. It is important to know when to quit.

ひけしやく 火消し役を買って出るつもりかい. Are you going to offer yourself as peacemaker in this affair? / 火消し役に野村が登板した. Nomura went to the mound as fireman.

ひけつ¹ その動議は 40 対 10 で否決になった The motion was voted down, 40 to 10. | The motion was rejected by 40 votes to 10.

ひける 役所は 4 時に引けます. The office closes at four (o'clock). / 学校は 3 時に引ける. School finishes at three. / 少し値を幾らか引けますか. Can you take something off the price?

ひこう² 彼は飛行経験 5,000 時間のベテラン操縦士である. He is a veteran pilot with 5,000 hours' flying time.

ひこうき 飛行機に乗ったことがありますか. Have you ever traveled by air [in an airplane]?

ひごと 日ごとに情勢が悪化していった. Things grew worse with each passing day.

ひざ ズボンのひざがふくらんで[光って]いる. My trousers are

ひざ 膝 〈ひざがしら〉 the knee；〈すわったときに水平になる腰からひざがしらまでの部分〉 one's lap ¶ひざを進める draw closer ((to)) / ひざをつく fall [go down] on one's knees; kneel down / ひざを崩す sit at (one's) ease / ひざを立てる draw one's knees up / ひざを曲げる運動《体操》 a knee bend / ひざを交えて語る have a heart-to-heart talk [((文)) a tête-à-tête] ((with)) / ひざに乗せている have [hold] sth in [on] one's lap / (雪などが)ひざである[ひざを没する] be [be more than] knee-deep / ひざ掛け ((米)) a lap robe; ((英)) a (travelling-)rug / ひざの皿 the kneecap; the kneepan; the patella / ひざげりを食わせる knee sb (in the crotch) / ひざ小僧を出す show [expose] one's knees / ひざ詰め談判をする negotiate personally ((with)) / ひざ枕をする pillow one's head on [in] sb's lap / 親のひざ元を離れる live away from one's parents / ((文)) leave one's [the] parental home. 文例⇩

ピザ ⇨さしよう¹.

ピサ Pisa ¶ピサの斜塔 the Leaning Tower of Pisa.

ピザ 《料理》(a) pizza ¶ピザの店 a pizza parlor; a pizzeria.

ひさい¹ 非才 ⇨せんがくひさい ¶非才を顧みず[の身をもって] incapable [incompetent] as I am. 文例⇩

ひさい² 被災 ¶被災する suffer from ((a flood)); fall a victim to ((a calamity)); be struck [hit] by ((an earthquake)); be visited by ((a typhoon)) / 被災者 the sufferers ((from)); the victims ((of)) / 被災地 the (disaster-)stricken area.

びさい 微細 ¶微細な 〈極小の〉 minute; fine; microscopic;〈細密な〉((文)) minute; detailed;〈微妙な〉((文)) nice; subtle / 微細な点まで調べる investigate ((a matter)) down to the minutest details / 微細に in detail; minutely; fully.

ひざい 微罪 a petty [minor] offense.

ひざかり 日盛り high noon;((文)) noontide ¶暑い日盛りに in the heat of the day; in the noon heat.

ひさし 庇〈軒(%)の〉the eaves;〈帽子の〉 a peak ¶ひさしのついた帽子 a peaked cap.

ひざし 日差し the rays of the sun; sunlight ¶日差しを浴びる bathe in the sun. 文例⇩

ひさしい 久しい long; ((文)) long-continued

¶久しい以前に long ago; a long time ago / 久しく for a long time; ((文)) long.

ひさしぶり 久しぶり ¶久しぶりに[で] after a long time [interval, silence, absence, separation] / 久しぶりの好天気 fine weather after a long spell of rain; the first fine weather in quite a while. 文例⇩

ひさびさ 久々 ⇨ひさしぶり.

ひざまずく 跪く ¶ひざまずく kneel (down); fall [go down] on one's knees / ひざまずいて懇願する ((文)) implore sb on one's (bended) knees.

ひさめ 氷雨 a freezing rain.

ひさん¹ 砒酸《化》arsenic acid ¶砒酸鉛 lead arsenate.

ひさん² 飛散 ¶飛散する scatter; fly in all directions.

ひさん³ 悲惨 ¶悲惨な ((文)) wretchedness ¶悲惨な miserable; wretched; pitiful;((文)) pitiable; horrible (ぞっとするような) / 悲惨な出来事 a tragic accident; a tragedy; a disaster / 悲惨な最後を遂げる die tragically;((文)) meet (with) a tragic death [end]. 文例⇩

ビザンチン ¶ビザンチン式建築 Byzantine architecture / ビザンチン帝国《史》the Byzantine Empire / ビザンチン美術 Byzantine art.

ひし 菱 ¶a water chestnut [caltrop] ¶ひし形 a diamond (shape);((文)) a lozenge ⇨りょうけい¹ / ひし形の diamond-[lozenge-]shaped / ひし形に diamond-wise.

ひじ 肘 an elbow ¶ひじの関節 an elbow joint / ひじを枕にして横になる lie down with one's head on one's arm / ひじを張る square one's elbows; spread [bend] out one's elbows / ひじで突く poke [nudge] sb with one's elbow / ひじで押しのける elbow sb aside / ひじ鉄砲を食わせる refuse [reject] bluntly; snub; rebuff; give sb a rebuff / ひじ掛け椅子 an armchair. 文例⇩

びじ 美辞 flowery words [language] ¶美辞麗句を連ねる string together all sorts of flowery words.

ひししょくぶつ 被子植物 an angiosperm.

ひしつ 皮質《解》the cortex ((pl. -tices, -texes)).

びしてき 微視的 microscopic ¶微視的に microscopically / 微視的分析《経》(a) microscopic analysis.

ひしと firmly; tight(ly); fast. 文例⇩

ビジネス business ¶ビジネスマン a businessman / ビジネスライクに in a businesslike way.

びしびし severely; relentlessly; without mercy (容赦なく) ¶びしびし処罰する punish sb severely / びしびし取り締まる enforce strict

---

baggy [shiny] at the knees. / 男は女のひざ枕で眠った。He went to sleep with his head on her lap.

ひさい¹ 非才を顧みず本の職をお引き受けすることに致しました。I accepted the appointment, though I was afraid I hardly deserved [merited] it.

ひざし 日差しが薄らいだ。The sun grew less strong [weakened]. / 日差しで5時頃だとわかった。I knew from (the angle of) the sun's rays that it was about five o'clock.

ひさしぶり 久しぶりですね。I haven't seen you for a long time. / It is a long time since I saw you last. / 久しぶりで北海道へ行った。I went to Hokkaido after a long interval. / 久しぶりで雨が降った。It rained for the first time [We had the first rain] in many days.

ひさん³ その光景は実に悲惨であった。It was a really horrible [pitiful] sight (to see).

ひじ 上着の右ひじがすり切れた。My coat is worn through at the right elbow. / 人込みでひじで押し分けなければ通れなかった。We had to elbow our way through the crowd.

ひしと 彼女は赤ん坊をひしと抱き

ひしひしと ¶ひしひしと身にこたえる〈事が主語〉strike [go] home ; sting one to the quick.
ひしめく jostle ((each other)) ; crowd [press] ((against the gate)).
ひしゃく 柄杓 a ladle ; a dipper ¶ひしゃくで水をくむ ladle [dip up] water / ひしゃくで汁をわんによそう ladle soup into a bowl.
びじゃく 微弱 ¶微弱な feeble ; weak ; faint / 微弱な脈拍 a faint [feeble] pulse.
ひしゃげる be crushed (out of shape) ; be flattened out.
ひしゃこうてき 非社交的 unsociable ¶非社交的な人 an unsociable person ; 〈口語〉a bad mixer.
ひしゃたい 被写体 a subject.
びしゃりと, びしゃんと ¶びしゃりと戸を閉める slam [bang] a door to ; shut a door with a bang / びしゃりと打つ slap sb ((in the face)); give sb a slap ((on the back)) / 子供のおしりをびしゃりと打つ spank a child / 要求をびしゃりとはねつける refuse sb's request flatly ; turn sb down (pointblank).
ひじゅう 比重 〖物〗specific gravity ; 〈重要さ〉relative importance ¶比重を計る measure the specific gravity 《of》 / 比重計 a gravimeter ; a hydrometer (液体比重計). 文例↓
びしゅう 美醜 beauty (or ugliness).
ひじゅつ 秘術 a secret art ; the mysteries of an art ¶秘術を尽くして戦う fight to the best of one's skill ; use every trick one knows in a fight [game].
びじゅつ 美術 fine arts ; art ¶美術の artistic / 美術的に artistically / 美術愛好家[批評家] an art lover [critic] / 美術界の art world ; art circles / 美術学校 a school of fine arts ; an art school / 美術館 an art gallery [museum] ; a museum of art [fine art(s)] / 美術工芸 arts and crafts ; fine and applied arts / 美術史 history of art ; art history / 美術書[商, 展] an art book [dealer, exhibition] / 美術品 a work of art ; an art object.
ひじゅん 批准 ratification ¶批准する ratify 《a treaty》 / 批准書 an instrument of ratification / 批准書を交換する exchange instruments of ratification.
ひしょ 秘書 a (private) secretary 《to the president》 ¶秘書学校[科] a secretarial school [course] / 秘書課 the secretarial section / 秘書官 a secretary 《to the Foreign Minister》.
ひしょ² 避暑 ¶避暑に行く go to 《Nasu》 for the summer / 避暑客 a summer visitor 避暑地 a summer resort. 文例↓
びじょ 美女 ⇨びじん.
ひしょう 費消 ⇨こうきん¹(公金費消).

ひじょう¹ 非情 ¶非情の〈人情のない〉〈文〉unfeeling ; heartless ; 〈生命を持たない〉inanimate ; 〈無感覚の〉〈文〉insentient / 非情派〖文学〗the hard-boiled school.
ひじょう² 非常 〈変事〉an emergency ; 《文》a contingency ; 〈災害〉a disaster ; a calamity ¶非常な (very) great ; uncommon ; unusual ; extraordinary ; remarkable / 非常の場合には in an [in case of] emergency ; should an emergency arise / 非常の場合に備える provide against emergencies ; prepare for the worst / 非常に very (much) ; greatly ; 《文》exceedingly ; extremely / 非常口 an emergency exit [door] ; a fire exit / 非常呼集 an emergency call / 非常事態宣言を行なう declare a state of emergency / 非常手段を取る[講じる] take [resort to] extreme measures. 文例↓
ひしょう² 微小[少] ¶微小[少]の〈小さい〉minute ; microscopic ; infinitesimal (極微の) ; 〈少ない〉very little.
びしょう² 微笑 a smile ¶かすかな微笑 a faint smile / 微笑する smile ; give a 《friendly》 smile / 微笑を浮かべて with a smile ; smilingly / 顔に微笑を浮かべる[浮かべている] have [wear] a smile on one's face. 文例↓
びじょう² 尾錠 a buckle ; a clasp ¶尾錠で留める buckle ; clasp.
ひじょうきん 非常勤 ¶非常勤の part-time / 非常勤で働く work part time [on a part-time basis] ; be a part-timer / 非常勤講師 a part-time instructor.
ひじょうじ 非常時 an emergency ; a crisis (pl. crises).
ひじょうしき 非常識 lack of common sense ¶非常識な thoughtless ; senseless ; absurd. 文例↓
ひじょうすう 被乗数 〖数〗a multiplicand.
ひじょうせん 非常線 a (police) cordon ; 〈火事の〉fire lines ¶非常線を張る form a (police) cordon ; throw a cordon 《around a building》 / 非常線を突破する break through a cordon / 非常線で遮断する cordon off 《a block》.
びしょく 美食 〈食物〉dainty [delicious] food ; 《文》a rich [luxurious] diet ; 〈事〉《文》epicurism ¶美食する eat dainty food / 《文》keep a good table / 美食家 a gourmet ; 《文》an epicure.
ひじょすう 被除数 〖数〗a dividend.
びしょぬれ ¶びしょぬれになる be [get] wet through ; be wet [drenched] to the skin. 文例↓
びしょびしょ ⇨びしょぬれ.
ビジョン vision ¶ビジョンがある be a man of vision.
びしりと ⇨びしゃりと.
びしん 微震 a slight (earthquake) shock ; a

しめた. She pressed her baby tightly to her bosom.
ひじゅう 大学の教養課程で外国語の占める比重は大きい. The study of foreign languages is given considerable weight in the universities' general education courses.

ひしょ² これから軽井沢へ避暑に出かけます. We are leaving for Karuizawa to avoid the heat of the summer in Tokyo.
ひじょう² それを聞いて彼は非常に喜んだ. He was highly [greatly] delighted to hear it. / 転地が私には非常に利いた. The change

of air has done me a world of good.
びしょう² 彼は口元に微笑を浮かべながら答えた. He replied with a smile on [playing about] his lips. / 微笑が顔から消えた. The smile died from her face.
ひじょうしき あの男は非常識だ.

feeble earth tremor ¶微震計 a microseismometer; a microseismograph.

びじん 美人 a beautiful woman [girl]; a beauty ¶美人コンクール a beauty contest.

ひす 秘す

ひすい 翡翠 jade ¶ひすい色 jade green.

ビスケット 《米》a cookie;《米》a cracker;《英》a biscuit.

ヒステリー 〈病気〉hysteria;〈その発作〉hysterics ★hystericsは単数扱い ¶ヒステリーを起こす get [《文》become, be] hysterical; go into hysterics; have an attack of hysteria. 文例⇩

ヒステリック ¶ヒステリックな笑い hysterical laughter / ヒステリックになる get [《文》become] hysterical.

ピストル ⇨けんじゅう ¶ピストルのホルスター a revolver holster / ピストルをホルスターから引き抜く draw [pull] one's gun (from the holster) / ピストル強盗 a robber [holdup man] armed with a pistol; a gunman / ピストル強盗事件 an armed robbery [holdup] / ピストル競技 the pistol shooting event.

ピストン a piston ¶ピストン棒[リング] a piston rod [ring] / ピストン輸送 transport by a shuttle service; shuttle.

ビスマス 《化》bismuth.

ひずみ 歪み 《物》(a) strain;〈一般に〉(a) distortion; a warp.

びせい 美声 a sweet [beautiful] voice.

ひせいさんてき 非生産的 unproductive.

びせいぶつ 微生物 a microbe; a microorganism ¶微生物学 microbiology.

びせきぶん(がく) 微積分(学) 《数》(differential and integral) calculus.

ひぜに 日銭 daily income in cash.

ひぜん 皮癬 ⇨かいせん⁵.

ひせんきょけん 被選挙権 eligibility for election ¶国会議員の被選挙権がある be eligible for election as a Dietman [to the Diet]; be qualified to run for the Diet.

ひせんとういん 非戦闘員 〈軍医・主計兵など〉a noncombatant;〈民間人〉a civilian.

ひせんろん 非戦論 pacifism ¶非戦論者 a pacifist.

ヒソ ヒ素 《化》arsenic ¶ヒ素中毒 arsenic poisoning.

ひそう¹ 皮相 ¶皮相な superficial; shallow. 文例⇩

ひそう² 悲壮 ¶悲壮な決意《文》a tragic resolution;《文》a heroic resolve / 悲壮な最期を遂げる《文》die a hero's death;《文》meet (with) a tragic end.

ひぞう¹ 秘蔵 ¶秘蔵する treasure;《文》prize; 《文》cherish / 秘蔵の〈愛蔵の〉treasured; prized;〈愛する〉favorite; pet / 秘蔵の品 a treasure; a treasured article.

ひぞう² 脾臓 《解》the spleen.

ひそかに 密かに secretly; in secret; stealthily;《文》by stealth;《口語》on the sly ¶心ひそかに in one's heart; inwardly.

ひぞく¹ 卑俗 ¶卑俗な low (jokes); vulgar; coarse.

ひぞく² 卑属 a descendant ¶直系[傍系]卑属 a lineal [collateral] descendant.

びそく(ど) 微速(度) very slow speed ¶微速度撮影の映画 a time-lapse motion picture; a slow-motion film.

ひそひそ 〈こっそり〉secretly; in secret;〈小声で〉in a low voice; in whispers; in an undertone;〈ささやいて〉under one's breath ¶ひそひそ話 a whispered talk.

ひそみ 顰 ¶…のひそみにならって in imitation of sb; following sb's example.

ひそむ 潜む 〈潜在する〉lurk (in);《文》be latent;〈隠れている〉lie concealed [hidden]; lie up.

ひそめる¹ 潜める 〈隠す〉《文》conceal; hide; 〈声を〉lower; drop ¶身を潜める hide [conceal] (oneself); lie low (in, behind, under); lie low / 声を潜めて ⇨ひそひそ.

ひそめる² 顰める ¶まゆをひそめる《文》contract [knit, gather] one's brows; frown / まゆをひそめて《文》with knitted brows; with a frown.

ひだ 襞 a fold; a pleat ¶山のひだ the folds on [of] a mountain / ひだをとる[付ける] fold; pleat. 文例⇩

ひたい 額 the forehead;《文》the brow ¶額の広い[狭い] high-[low-]browed / 額を集めて相談する put 《their》 heads together;《口語》go into [be in] a huddle / 額に汗して働く live by the sweat of one's brow.

ひだい 肥大 《医》hypertrophy; dilatation ¶肥大した swollen; enlarged / 心臓肥大 ⇨しんぞう.

びたいちもん びた一文 ¶びた一文もない be penniless; do not have a penny [red cent] in the world. 文例⇩

ひたおし ひた押し ¶ひた押しに押す press [push] hard.

ピタゴラス Pythagoras ¶ピタゴラスの定理 Pythagoras' theorem; the Pythagorean theorem.

ひたす 浸す 《文》immerse (in);〈ちょっとの間水につける〉dip;《米口語》dunk 《a doughnut into one's coffee》;〈しばらくの間水につけておく〉soak [steep] (in).

ひたすら(に) single-mindedly; intently;《文》

He has no [is short of] common sense. | 非常識なことを言うものではない. Don't be absurd [ridiculous]. | Don't talk rubbish.

びしょぬれ 君は服がびしょぬれだ. Your clothes are dripping [soaking] wet.

ひす 本人の希望により特に名を秘す. His name has been withheld at his request. | He asked us not to identify him.

ヒステリー 彼女はヒステリーを起こして髪をかきむしった. She tore her hair in a fit of hysterics [hysteria].

ひそう¹ 君は事物の皮相だけを見ている. You only look on the surface of things. | Your views are superficial.

ひそむ その事件の裏に何か犯罪が潜んでいないとは言えまい. It may well be that there is some crime at the bottom of the affair.

ひだ スカートのひだが取れてしまっていた. The pleats on the skirt had come out.

びたいちもん あの男にはびた一文

ひだち 肥立ち 《回復》 convalescence 《after childbirth》;《成長》 growth 《of a baby》 ¶産後の肥立ちがよい[悪い] be doing well [badly] after one's confinement.

ひだね 火種 kindling [live] charcoal [coal] (to build [make] a fire with).

ひたばしり ひた走り ¶ひた走りに走る run without stopping; run for all one is worth; run and run.

ひたひた ¶(波が)ひたひたと舟べりを打つ lap against the sides of a boat / (波が)ひたひたと岸辺を洗う lap the shore gently.

ひだまり 日だまり a sunny spot [place].

ビタミン a vitamin ¶ビタミンAに富む be rich in vitamin A / ビタミン欠乏症 a vitamin deficiency disease;《医》avitaminosis / ビタミン剤《錠剤》a vitamin tablet.

ひたむき ¶ひたむきな《文》earnest; single-minded / ひたむきな努力 untiring efforts / ひたむきな情熱《文》passionate devotion (to).

ひだり 左 (the) left /左の left(-hand) /一番左の leftmost /左の側[方] the left (side) /〈車・馬の〉 the near side /君の左の方に on your left /左を見る look (to the) left /左に曲がる[向きを変える] turn (to the) left /左利きの人 a left-handed person /〈酒飲み〉 a drinker /左投げの投手 a left-handed pitcher /《米口語》 a southpaw /左うちわで暮らす《口語》(be able to) take it [things] easy;《口語》have things easy;《文》be in easy circumstances; live in clover /左前に着る wear (a kimono) with the right side under the left /〈暮らし向きが〉左前である be badly off;《文》be in straitened circumstances /左巻きに《米》counterclockwise;《英》anticlockwise /頭が左巻きである be crazy /《米俗》be a screwball /左寄りの政党 a left-leaning party /髪を左分けにする part one's hair on the left. 左例8

ぴたり 〈急に〉 suddenly;〈完全に〉 completely ⇒ぴったり ¶ぴたりと止まる〈急に〉 stop suddenly [short];〈完全に〉 come to a dead stop.

ひたる 浸る 〈つかる〉 be soaked [(文) immersed] (in);〈ふける〉 indulge (in) ¶楽しい雰囲気に浸る《文》 steep oneself in the happy [pleasant] atmosphere.

ひだるま 火達磨 ¶火だるまになる be covered with [《文》enveloped in] flames.

ひたん 悲嘆《文》grief; sorrow;《文》anguish

¶悲嘆に暮れる abandon oneself to grief; be grieved (at); be heartbroken (at);《口語》eat one's heart out.

びだん 美談 an admirable story; a fine [laudable] anecdote.

びだんし 美男子 a handsome [good-looking] man.

ピチカート ¶ピチカートで《音楽》pizzicato.

びちく 備蓄 ¶備蓄する store, reserve 《petroleum for [against] emergencies》/石油備蓄基地 an oil stockpiling base.

ひちしゃ 被治者 the ruled; the governed.

ぴちっと ⇒ぴったり.

ぴちぴち ¶ぴちぴちした娘 a young and healthy [lively] girl.

びちゃびちゃ ⇒ぴちゃぴちゃ.

ぴちゃぴちゃ ¶(波が)ぴちゃぴちゃ岸を洗う lap (against) the shore gently /ぬかるみの中をぴちゃぴちゃ歩く splash through the mud /ぴちゃぴちゃ音を立ててスープを吸う slurp one's soup.

ひちゅうのひ 秘中の秘《文》the secret of secrets.

ひちょう 飛鳥 ¶飛鳥のように(素早く)(as) quick as lightning; like an arrow.

びちょうせい 微調整 (a) fine adjustment;〈ラジオ・テレビの〉fine tuning.

ひつ 櫃 a chest.

ひつう 悲痛 ¶悲痛な sad;《文》grievous;《文》sorrowful; touching;《文》heart-rending.

ひっかかり 引っ掛かり 〈a〉 connection; (a) relationship;《文》(a) relation;〈手のかかる所〉 a (hand)hold (on) ¶引っ掛かりがある have (something) to do (with); be connected (with); be related (to).

ひっかかる 引っ掛かる 〈物に〉 catch; be caught (in, by);〈だまされる〉 be cheated (by); be taken in (by);〈関係する〉 be involved (in); get entangled (with) ¶くもの巣に引っ掛かる be caught in a cobweb /検閲に引っ掛かる be objected to by a censor. 左例8

ひっかきまわす 引っ掻き回す ⇒かきまわす.

ひっかく 引っ掻く scratch;〈猫などが〉claw ¶顔を引っかかれる be scratched on the face.

ひっかける 引っ掛ける 〈つるす〉 hang [《文》suspend] sth on (a peg);〈かぎなどに〉hook; 〈陥れる〉trap;〈だます〉entrap;〈だます〉cheat; take in ¶上着を引っ掛ける slip [throw] one's coat on /セーターを肩に引っ掛ける throw one's sweater over one's shoulders /一杯引っ掛ける have a drink; have a shot [drop] (of whisky).

ひつき 火付き ¶火付きがいい burn [kindle]

も借りはない。I don't owe him a red cent.

ひたすら(に) 彼はひたすら英文学の研究に没頭した。He devoted himself single-mindedly to the study of English literature. /彼はただひたすら逃れようとあがいた。His sole concern was how to make his escape.

ひだり 左向け左! Left turn [face]! /右へ曲がって左側の3軒目です。Turn right and (then) it's the third house on the left. | It is the third house on the left after you've turned to the right.

ひっかかる 服がくぎに引っ掛かった。Her dress caught on a nail. | The nail caught her dress. /たこが木に引っ掛かった。The kite got caught in a tree. /このペンは引っ掛かってだめだ。This pen won't dig; it scratches. /この話は僕にはどうも引っ掛かるな。I don't much like the sound of that. | I am a bit suspicious of this story. | This story just won't wash (with me).

ひっきりなしに その晩は犬が引っ切りなしにほえた。The dog kept barking all through the night. /通りを自動車が引っ切りなしに通っていた。There was a constant stream of cars along the street.

びっくり その知らせを聞いた時にはびっくりしたよ。I was sur

ひっき 筆記 ¶筆記する take notes 《of》; write [note] down / 筆記具 pens and [or] pencils; writing materials [things] / 筆記試験 a written examination / 筆記体 (in) script.

ひつぎ 柩 a coffin;《米》a casket.

ひっきりなしに incessantly;《文》unceasingly; continuously; without interruption; without a break. 文例⇩

ピックアップ a (phonograph) pickup.

びっくり ¶びっくりする be surprised [astonished, alarmed, startled]《at》; take alarm [fright]《at》/ びっくりするような surprising; amazing; startling / びっくりして in surprise; in astonishment; in amazement / びっくりさせる surprise; startle / びっくり仰天する be absolutely astonished [amazed, astounded, staggered,《口語》flabbergasted]《at》; be taken aback / びっくり箱 a jack-in-the-box《pl. -boxes》. 文例⇩

ひっくりかえす 引っくり返す 〈覆す〉upset; overturn;〈倒す〉turn [knock] *sth* over; knock *sth* down;〈逆さまにする〉turn (a picture) upside down (上下に);《文》invert (順序などを);〈裏返す〉turn (a coat) inside out; turn up (a card);〈逆転する〉reverse (the original decision).

ひっくりかえる 引っくり返る〈覆る〉be overturned; be upset;〈船が〉capsize; turn turtle;〈倒れる〉fall over [down]; tumble down;〈あおむけに寝る〉lie down on *one's* back;〈逆転する〉be reversed ¶引っくり返るような騒ぎである be in utter confusion.

ひっくるめる 引っくるめる ⇨くるめる.

ひづけ 日付 a date; dating ¶日付のない手紙 an undated letter / 日付を書く date (a letter) / 日付印 a date stamp / 日付変更線 the (international) date line. 文例⇩

ひっけい 必携 a handbook; a manual.

ひつけやく 火付け役〈ごたごたを起こす人〉a troublemaker;〈扇動者〉an instigator.

ピッケル a pickel; an ice ax(e).

びっこ〈状態〉lameness;〈人〉a lame person ¶びっこを引く be lame (in the right leg); crippled;〈不ぞろいの〉wrongly paired; odd / ひどいびっこである be badly [severely] lame [crippled] / びっこになる go [get,《文》become] lame; be crippled / びっこをひいて歩く limp along; walk lame [with a limp]. 文例⇩

ひっこう 筆耕〈事〉copying (for hire);〈人〉a copyist.

ひっこし 引っ越し a move;(a) removal ⇨いてん ¶引っ越し荷物 (the) furniture [property] to be moved (out of *one's* house, into a new house).

ひっこす 引っ越す move《to, into》; remove《to, into》¶田舎へ引っ越す move into the country / 住んでいる家から引っ越す move out of *one's* house.

ひっこみ 引っ込み (a) retreat;〈撤退〉(a) withdrawal;〈退場〉an exit ¶引っ込みがつかない have gone too far to retreat; cannot back out 《of *one's* engagement》/ (飛行機の) 引っ込み脚 (retractable) landing gear / 引っ込み思案の diffident; shy; retiring; withdrawn; unenterprising. 文例⇩

ひっこみせん 引っ込み線〈電気の〉a service wire [line];〈電話・テレビなどの〉a lead-in (wire); a down-lead;〈鉄道の〉a (railroad) siding;《米》a sidetrack ¶列車を引っ込み線に入れる pull a train into a siding;《米》sidetrack a train.

ひっこむ 引っ込む〈退く〉draw back; withdraw;《文》retire;〈隠れる〉disappear;〈へこむ〉fall in; sink ¶(人が, 表面に出ずに)引っ込んでいる stay [《文》remain, keep] in the background / 田舎へ引っ込む move [retire] into the country / 家に引っ込んでいる stay [keep] indoors; stay at home.

ひっこめる 引っ込める〈引き入れる〉draw [take, pull] in;《文》retract;〈後へ下げる〉put [pull, move] back;〈撤回する〉take《*one's* promise》back; withdraw; back down on《*one's* words》;《文》retract ¶手を引っ込める put back *one's* hands (かたつむりが)引っ込める retract [draw in] *its* horns / 各節の1行目を引っ込める indent the first line of each paragraph / 辞表を引っ込める withdraw *one's* resignation. 文例⇩

ヒッコリー【植】a hickory (tree);〈材木〉hickory (wood).

ピッコロ a piccolo《pl. -s》.

ひっさげる 引っ提げる carry [have] *sth* in *one's* hand ¶老軀(ゝ)を引っさげて in spite of *one's* (old) age.

ひっさん 筆算 doing sums on paper.

ひっし¹ 必死 ¶必死の desperate; frantic / 必死の努力をする make desperate [frantic] efforts / 必死になって for *one's* life; for dear life; desperately.

---

prised at [to hear] the news. | The news gave me a turn [start] when I heard it. / 犬がほえたので泥棒はびっくりして逃げた. The burglar was frightened away by the barking of the dog.

ひづけ その手紙は8月5日の日付であった. The letter was dated Aug. 5.

びっこ 彼は少しびっこをひいている. He is limping slightly. | He walks with [has] a slight limp.

ひっこす よかったら私の家へ引っ越して来なさい. Just move in (here) with us, if you like. / 引っ越したばかりで荷物がまだ大半は荷造りのままになっていた. Most of the luggage from their recent move was still to be unpacked.

ひっこみ 彼女には引っ込み思案な所があった. She was rather shy and retiring in her ways.

ひっこむ 彼はまだ弱っていて家の中にばかり引っ込んでいます. He is still weak and spends nearly all his time indoors. / その家は道路から引っ込んでいる. The house stands [is set] back from the road. / お前は引っ込んでいろ. You stay out of this! | Mind your own business!! Don't intrude where you are not wanted.

ひっこめる かめが首を引っ込めた. The turtle drew its head in. | The neck of the tortoise disappeared into its shell.

ひっし¹ 彼は必死になって泳いだ. He swam for his life [for dear life].

ひっし² 必至 ¶必至の inevitable / 必至であるbe inevitable ; be unavoidable / (文) be destined ((for defeat, to fail)). 文例⇩

ひつじ 羊 a sheep ((単複同形)) ; a ram (雄) ; a ewe (雌) ; 〈十二支の未〉 (the Year of) the Ram ¶羊の群れ a flock of sheep / 羊の肉 mutton / 羊の囲い a sheepfold / 子羊 a lamb / 羊飼い a shepherd ; a shepherdess (女).

ひっしゃ¹ 筆写 ¶筆写する copy ; transcribe.

ひっしゃ² 筆者 (作者) the writer ; the author ; 〈書の〉 the calligrapher ; (作者が自分を指して言う時) (文) the present writer ; (文) this writer. 文例⇩

ひっしゅうかもく 必修科目 a compulsory [an obligatory] subject ; (米) a required subject. 文例⇩

ひつじゅひん 必需品 necessities ; (文) necessaries ¶生活必需品 the necessities [necessaries] of life.

ひつじゅん 筆順 the stroke order ((of a Chinese character)).

ひっしょう 必勝 ¶必勝の信念を持って (fight) confident that one will win in the end ; (fight) with a firm conviction of ultimate victory [success] / 必勝を期する〈自信〉 be sure [certain] of (one's) victory [success] ; 〈決意〉 be determined [((文)) resolve] to secure [win] victory at any cost.

びしょ 必書 ⇒ びしょぬれ. 文例⇩

びっしょり 〈すきまなく〉 closely ; tightly ; 〈充分に〉 fully ¶びっしり詰まっている be closely [tightly] packed ((with)).

ひっす 必須 ¶必須の indispensable ; essential ; necessary ; (文) requisite.

ひっせき 筆跡 handwriting ; (文) a hand ¶男[女]の筆跡 a masculine [feminine] hand / 筆跡をまねる copy sb's hand(writing) / 筆跡鑑定人 a handwriting expert.

ひつぜつ 筆舌 ¶筆舌に尽くし難い (文) be beyond description ; (文) beggar (all) description ; (文) words cannot [fail to] describe ((the beauty of...)).

ひつぜん 必然 ¶必然の inevitable ; (文) necessary / 必然的に (文) of necessity ; (文) necessarily ; inevitably / 必然性 (文) inevitability ; (文) necessity. 文例⇩

ひっそり ¶ひっそりしている be quiet ; be still ; be silent ; look deserted. 文例⇩

ひったくり 引ったくり 〈事〉 bag-[purse-]snatching ; 〈人〉 a bag-[purse-]snatcher.

ひったくる 引ったくる snatch sth (away) ((from)) ; take sth by force ; tear sth from sb.

ひったてる 引っ立てる walk [march] sb off ((to the police station)).

ぴったり 〈密着して〉 tight(ly) ; close(ly) ; 〈きちんと〉 exactly ¶5時ぴったりに exactly at five ; at five sharp / 壁にぴったり体をつっけている keep up against the wall / ぴったり合う〈着物などが〉 fit one perfectly [to a T, (文) to a nicety] ; 〈計算などが〉 be perfectly correct ; 〈一般に〉 fit right in ((with)) / ぴったり合った上着 a well-fitting coat / ぴったりした言葉 an apt remark ; the right word ((for)) / 戸をぴったりと閉める shut the door tight(ly). 文例⇩

ひつだん 筆談 ¶筆談する make [carry on a] conversation by means of writing. 文例⇩

ピッチ 〈ボートなどの〉 a stroke ; 〈音の〉 a pitch ¶ピッチの高い声 a high-pitched voice / (ボートレースで) 37 のピッチを出す put in thirty-seven strokes per minute ; row 37 (strokes) to the minute / ピッチを上げる [落とす] quicken [slacken] one's pace ; speed up [slow down] / 急ピッチで at a high pace ; rapidly.

ヒッチハイカー a hitchhiker.

ヒッチハイク hitchhiking ¶ヒッチハイクする hitchhike ((to)) ; (口語) thumb a ride [lift] ((to)).

ピッチャー 【野球】 a pitcher ⇒ とうしゅ¹ ¶ピッチャープレート the pitcher's plate.

ひっちゅう 必中 ¶いっぱつ(一発必中を期する).

ぴっちり ⇒ ぴったり.

ピッチング pitching ⇒ とうきゅう¹ ¶ピッチングマシーン a pitching machine.

ひっつかむ 引っ摑む snatch ¶引っつかもうとする snatch at [for] sth.

ひっつめ(がみ) 引っ詰め(髪) hair drawn back into a bun [drawn back from the forehead and tied in a knot].

ひってき 匹敵 ¶匹敵する be a match for ; match ; be equal to ; equal ; rival ; compare with ; rank with (位などが) / 匹敵するものがない have no equal [match] ; be unrivaled. 文例⇩

ヒット 【野球】 a hit ; a safe hit ; a single (hit) (単打) ; 〈大当たり〉 a hit ; a (great) success ¶ヒットする hit ; make a hit ; 〈成功する〉 have [be, (文) win] a success ; be a hit / センターにヒットを放つ hit safely to center / ヒット3本で2点挙げる score two runs on three hits / ヒット5本を奪う collect five hits ((off the pitcher)) / ヒット3本に押える limit the opposing team to three hits ; pitch a three-

---

ひっし² 彼の没落は必至である. His downfall is inevitable [unavoidable]. | He is doomed.

ひっしゃ この文の筆者は女性である. This is a woman's writing. | This was written by a woman.

ひっしゅうかもく フランス語は必修科目ですか. Is French compulsory [required of all students]?

びっしょり シャツが汗でびっしょりだ. My shirt is wringing wet with sweat.

びっしり 彼の書斎にはびっしりと本が並んでいた. His study was [The walls of his study were] lined with books.

ひっせき 見事な筆跡だ. He writes an excellent hand.

ひつぜん 必然の結果としてそうなる. It follows as a logical [natural] consequence. / それは歴史の必然だ. That is one of the inevitabilities of history.

ひっそり 町はひっそりしている. All is still [hushed] in the streets. / 家の中はひっそりとしていた. Perfect silence reigned within the house.

ぴったり この帽子は僕の頭にぴったりだ. This hat fits me perfectly. | This hat is a perfect [an exact] fit (for me). / ぴったり当たった. You've guessed right.

ビット 1047 ひと

hitter / ヒットエンドラン a hit-and-run play / ヒットソング a hit song.
ビット 《コンピューター》a bit.
ひっとう 筆頭 ¶筆頭である be (the) first on the list; head the list / …の筆頭 at the head of… / 戸籍筆頭人 the head of a family.
ひつどく 必読 ¶学生の必読書 a book which every student must [should] read; an essential [《口語》a must] book for students.
ひっぱく 逼迫 pressure 《for money》; tightness 《on the money market》 ¶逼迫する 《金融などが》be tight; 《文》get stringent; 《関係が》be strained.
ひっぱたく ひっぱたく ⇨ たたく, はたく.
ひっぱりだこ 引っ張り凧 ¶引っ張りだこである be very popular; be in great demand; 《口語》be all the rage; be much [eagerly] sought after.
ひっぱる 引っ張る pull; draw; drag; tug 《強く》 ¶綱を引っ張る pull (at [on]) a rope / ぐいと引っ張る a jerk; give sth a jerk / 強く引っ張る give sth a strong pull / 引っ張って来る bring; fetch / 警察へ引っ張られる be taken to the police station / 引っ張り込む pull in; drag in. 文例⇩
ヒッピー a hippie.
ヒップ 〈腰〉the hips; 〈尻〉the buttocks; 《口語》the backside ⇨ しり[1] 用法. 文例⇩
ひっぽう 筆法 〈筆の運び方〉a style of penmanship; 〈言い回し〉a turn of expression; 〈やり方〉a manner; a way.
ひづめ 蹄 (pl. -s, hooves) ¶割れたひづめ a cloven hoof / ひづめのある hoofed / ひづめの跡 hoof prints [tracks] / ひづめの音 the sound [clatter] of hoofs; hoofbeats / ひづめにかける trample sth underfoot [down].
ひつめい 筆名 a pen name; 《文》a nom de plume (pl. noms de plume).
ひつよう 必要 《文》necessity; need ¶必要な necessary; needed; required; indispensable / …する必要がある it is necessary to do; must do; have to do / …する必要がない it is not necessary [is unnecessary] to do; there is no need [necessity] to do; there is no call for doing; need not do; don't have to do / 必要のない unnecessary; needless / 必要の場合には if need be; 《文》in case of need; if [when] necessary / …を必要とする need…; be [《文》stand] in need of…; call for… / 必要にして充分な条件 necessary and sufficient conditions / 必要に迫られて out of necessity; driven by necessity; under the pressure of necessity /

必要悪 a necessary evil / 必要条件 a necessary [an essential] condition; a requirement; 《ラテン語》a sine qua non (pl. sine qua nons) / 必要品[物] a necessity; 《文》a requisite; 《文》a necessary.
ひつりょく 筆力 〈運筆の勢い〉the power [strength] of the [one's] brush stroke(s); 〈文章力〉the ability to write.
ひてい 否定 (a) denial; 《文》(a) negation; 〈否認〉《文》(a) disavowal ¶否定する deny / 否定し難い undeniable / 否定的 negative / 否定文 a negative sentence. 文例⇩
びていこつ 尾骶骨 《解》the coccyx (pl. coccyges, -es).
ビデオ video ¶ビデオテープレコーダー a video tape recorder (略: VTR) / ビデオテープに録画する record (a TV program) on video tape / ビデオテープ録画 (a) video tape recording (略: VTR).
ピテカントロプス 《人類》a pithecanthropus (pl. -pi); a pithecanthrope.
びてき 美的 《文》aesthetic; 《文》esthetic ¶美的感覚[生活] an aesthetic sense [life].
ひてつきんぞく 非鉄金属 a nonferrous metal.
ひでり 日照り dry weather; (a) drought 〈旱ばつ〉 ¶日照り続き a spell of dry weather; a long drought.
ひでん 秘伝 a secret; 《文》the mysteries ¶秘伝の妙薬 a medicine secretly handed down (in the family) / 秘伝を授ける initiate sb into the mysteries 《of an art》.
びてん 美点 《文》a merit; a good point [quality].
ひでんか 妃殿下 Her Highness (the Princess [the Consort]).
ひと 人 〈人類〉man; mankind; 〈個人〉a man; a human being; a person; one; 〈他人〉(other) people; others; 〈世人〉people; 〈人材〉a person of talent [ability]; a talented [a capable, a competent, an able] person; 〈性格・性質〉character; personality; nature ¶伊藤という人 a man called Ito; a Mr. Ito; one Ito / 人々 ⇨ ひとびと / 人は知らず自分は as [so] far as I am concerned; as for me [myself] / 人が変わる《文》undergo a personality change; become another person / 人がいい be good-natured[-humored] / 人が悪い《口語》be a hard customer to deal with; 《文》be mischievous / 人の言うこと what people [others] say / 人を得る[見つける] get [find] a competent person [for a job] / 人を食った返事 a brazen-faced [contemptuously nonchalant] reply / 人を見る明がある

ひつだん 人に聞かれないように話は筆談で済ませた. We wrote down what we wanted to say, so as not to be overheard.
ひってき 彼の体重は我々3人に匹敵する. He is equal to three of us in weight. / 堅さではダイヤモンドに匹敵する物はない. Nothing can compare with diamond for hardness.
ひっぱる 木村君を引っ張って来た

まえ. Bring Kimura with you.
ヒップ すごいヒップだなあ. What a big backside (she's got)!
ひつよう 僕は今は金の必要がない. I have no need for [I am in no need of] money now. / 急ぐ必要はありません. There is no need to hurry. | You don't have to hurry. | You need not hurry. / 彼は必要に迫られてそのような手段を採るに至った. Necessity

drove him to take such a step. / そうした施設の必要が痛切に感じられる. The need for such an institution is keenly felt. / 必要は発明の母. Necessity is the mother of invention. 《諺》
ひてい 当局ははっきりこの報道を否定している. The authorities are quite emphatic in denying the report. / 彼がすぐれた指導者だったということは否定できない.

ひとあし be a good judge of (people's) character. 文例⇩
囲書 一般に「人」の意味で使う one は自分を必ず含んでいる。もしそうでない時は a man, people, they, etc. を用いる。

ひとあし 一足 a step. 文例⇩

ひとあじ 一味 ¶一味違う be a bit different 《from》; be something new to *one* / 一味違った所のある(*miso*) with a difference.

ひとあせ 一汗 ¶一汗かく 《go jogging and》 have a good sweat; take some good [light] exercise.

ひとあたり 人当たり ¶人当たりの柔らかい人 an affable person.

ひとあめ 一雨 a shower; a rainfall. 文例⇩

ひとあれ 一荒れ a storm. 文例⇩

ひとあわ 一泡 ¶一泡吹かせる frustrate sb 《in his plans》; upset 《sb's plans》.

ひどい 〈悪い〉bad; 〈残酷な〉cruel; harsh; hard; merciless; 〈無法な〉unfair; unreasonable; 〈激しい〉severe; violent; serious; heavy; 〈恐ろしい〉terrible; dreadful; awful ¶ひどい誤り a serious [bad, 《文》grave, 《文》gross] mistake / ひどい近眼の人 a very nearsighted person / ひどい寒さ severe [intense, bitter] cold / ひどい降り heavy rain; a heavy rainfall; a downpour / ひどい道 a bad road / ひどい目にあう have a terrible [dreadful] experience; have a hard [rough] time (of it) / ひどい目にあわせる treat sb cruelly; do sb a bad turn. 文例⇩

ひといき 一息 ¶一息に at a breath; 〈一口に〉at a [one] draft; 〈一気に〉at a stretch; at a (single) bound / 一息に飲み干す empty 《the glass》 at a single draft [in one gulp] / 一息する[つく] take [have] a rest [breather].

ひといきれ 人いきれ ¶人いきれがする be stuffy; be close.

ひといちばい 人一倍 more than others; uncommonly ¶人一倍働く work (much) harder than other people [than anybody else]; work twice as hard as anyone else.

ひどう 非道 ¶非道な 《文》unjust; atrocious; inhuman ⇨ごくあく.

びとう 尾灯 a taillight.

びどう 微動 a slight movement; a stir ¶微動だもしない do not move [budge, stir] an inch; stand as firm as a rock.

ひとうち 一打ち ¶一打ちに at a [one] stroke; with a single blow.

ひどうめい 非同盟 nonalignment ¶非同盟国 a nonaligned nation [country] / 非同盟政策 a policy of nonalignment.

ひとえ 一重 ¶一重の single / 一重の花 a single-petaled flower / 壁一重隔てて向こうに on the other side of the wall / 一重まぶた an eyelid with an epicanthic [a Mongolian] fold (so that it does not fold over itself when opened); a smooth [an Oriental] eyelid.

ひとえに 偏に 〈ひたすらに〉《文》earnestly; 〈全く〉simply; 《文》solely; entirely; 〈卑下して〉humbly.

ひとえもの 単物 an unlined *kimono* (for summer wear).

ひとおし 一押し ¶一押しする give a push (to). 文例⇩

ひとおじ 人怖じ ¶人おじする 〈幼児などが〉be afraid of [fear] strangers.

ひとおもいに 一思いに without more ado; once (and) for all.

ひとかかえ 一抱え ¶一抱えもある木 a tree around whose trunk one can barely put one's arms.

ひとがき 人垣 a crowd [《文》throng] (of people) ¶人垣を築く crowd [《文》throng] 《the street》. 文例⇩

ひとかげ 人影 〈姿〉a (human) figure; 〈影〉the

We cannot deny [There is no gainsaying] that he was a great leader.

ひと 彼は名古屋の人だ。He comes [is] from Nagoya. / 人によってはそれを嫌う人もある。Some people dislike it. / 人は正直にしなければならない。One [We, You] should be honest. / 彼はうそを言うような人ではない。He is not the sort of man to tell a lie. / 今度の先生はどんな人だ。What sort of (a) man is your new teacher? / 彼は人を人とも思わない。He cares nothing for anybody (else). | He thinks he's a cut above everybody else. / 人が何と言うだろう。What will people say? / 人もあろうに君がそんなことを言うとは！To think that you, of all people, should say such a thing! / ここに人の人たるゆえんがある。This is what makes man worthy of the name. / 人の口には戸は立てられない。People will talk. / 人のうわさも七十五日。A wonder lasts but nine days. / 人のふり見てわがふり直せ。Correct your conduct by observing that of others. / 人は一代名は末代。A man dies, but his name lives on. / 人は見かけによらぬもの。A man should not be judged by his looks [appearance]. / 人は見かけによらぬ物と思え。Appearances can be deceiving. / 人を見たら泥棒と思え。Don't be too ready to trust a stranger. / 人をのろわば穴二つ。Curses, like chickens, come home to roost. 《諺》/ 人を見て法を説け。Suit [Adapt] your speech to your audience.

ひとあし そこまではほんの一足です。It is no distance to the place. | It's just around the corner. / ほんの一足違いで会えなかった。I missed him by a second. | I just missed meeting him. / 一足お先に失礼します。I'll go on ahead, if that's all right.

ひとあめ 一雨来そうだ。It looks like rain. | It is threatening to rain. / 一雨ごとに暖かくなる。It's getting warmer each time it rains.

ひとあれ この空模様では一荒れ来そうだ。From the look of the sky, we are going to have a storm.

ひどい そんな事を言うなんて, ひどい女だ。It was mean [very unkind] of her to say things like that. / こんな事をしたらにはひどい目にあわせてやる。You will have to pay dearly for this. / 雨が降ったのでひどい目にあった。It rained, so we had a terrible time. / ひどい天気だった。We have had dreadful weather. / ひどい暑さだ。It is awfully [terribly] hot.

ひといき もう一息で仕事が済む。Just one more effort, and our job [task] is over. / いい文章だが今一息のところがある。This is a good composition; I just feel that it lacks a finishing touch.

ひとおし もう一押しすればその木

ひとかた 一方 ¶一方ならぬ great; extraordinary; unusual; uncommon / 一方ならず greatly; 《文》 not a little; very much; unusually. 文例◊

ひとかど 一廉 ¶一かどの tolerable; respectable / 一かどの学者 《文》 a scholar of some reputation [of no mean order] / 一かどの人間になる make something of *oneself* / 一かどの役に立つ be of some use [service]; be useful enough.

ひとがら 人柄 〈性質〉 (*one's*) (personal) character; personality; 〈風さい〉 personal appearance ¶人柄がよい have a pleasant personality; have gentle manners / 人柄のよい good-natured. 文例◊

ひとぎき 人聞き ¶人聞きの悪い harmful to *one's* reputation.

ひときれ 一切れ a piece 《of meat》; 〈薄い〉 a slice 《of bread》.

ひときわ 一際 〈一層〉 still more; further; 〈目立って〉 remarkably; strikingly; noticeably; 〈特に〉 specially; 《文》 especially ¶一際目立つ 《文》 stand out conspicuously.

ひどく 〈残酷に〉 cruelly; harshly; hard; 〈激しく〉 severely; violently; heavily; badly; 〈甚だしく〉 terribly; dreadfully; awfully; extremely ¶ひどく頭が痛い have a bad [terrible] headache / ひどくしかられる be severely scolded; get a good telling-off. 文例◊

びとく 美徳 a virtue.

ひとくい 人食い ¶人食いざめ[ライオン]a man-eating shark [lion]; a man-eater / 人食い人種 cannibals; a cannibalistic tribe; man-eaters.

ひとくさり 一くさり 〈物語の〉 a passage; 〈歌の〉 a snatch ¶一くさり話をする 《文》 tell a story of some length.

ひとくせ 一癖 a peculiarity ¶一癖ありそうな男 a sinister-looking man / 一癖ある男 a man who is hard to deal with; an ugly [awkward] customer.

ひとくち 一口 ¶一口に (eat *sth*) at a [in one] mouthful; 〈一飲みに〉 《drink beer》 at [in] one draft; at [in] one gulp; in one swallow / 一口に言えば in short; in a word / 一口ほお張る cram *sth* into *one's* mouth; take a big mouthful 《of》 / もう一口食べる take another bite [munch] 《of》 / 一口飲む take a sip 《of wine》 / 一口カツ a bite-size(d) cutlet / 一口ばなし a very short (comic) story.

ひとけ 人気 ¶人気のない deserted; empty.

ひどけい 日時計 a sundial.

ひとこいしい 人恋しい feel lonely; feel in need of company.

ひとこえ 一声 a voice; a cry ¶一声叫ぶ give 〔《文》utter〕 a cry.

ひとごえ 人声 the sound of (people's) voices. 文例◊

ひとごこち 人心地 ¶人心地がつく feel relieved.

ひとこと 一言 a word ⇨いちごん ¶一言言う speak briefly [say a word] 《about》; 〈人のために〉 say a (good) word 《for *sb*》 / 一言で言えば in a word; to sum up / 一言も言わずに without (saying) a word; in silence / 一言のあいさつもしないで without having the courtesy [politeness] to say anything [something]; 《leave》 without so much as saying good-bye; 〈許可を乞わずに〉 without asking permission 〔《文》 leave〕. 文例◊

ひとごと 人事 other people's affairs. 文例◊

ひとこま 一齣 〈フィルムの〉 a frame ¶歴史の一こま a page [scene] of history.

ひとごみ 人込み a crowd (of people) ¶人込みを避ける avoid crowds / 人込みに紛れて見

は倒れます. One more push, and the tree will be down on the ground. / もう一押しすれば相手も折れたのに. If you had pushed a little more, he would have given in.

ひとがき 道端に人垣が出来ていた. The street was lined with people.

ひとかげ 浜辺には全く人影が見えなかった. Not a soul was to be seen on the beach. | The beach was completely deserted.

ひとかた 一方ならぬご厚意に預かり有り難く御礼申し上げます. I offer you my heartfelt thanks for your kind ness. / あの人には一方ならず世話になった. I owe him a great deal [a heavy debt of gratitude].

ひとかど この努力を続ければ君もやがてはひとかどの人物になるだろう. If you would carry on working as hard as you are now, you would become somebody in the future.

ひとがら どんな人柄の人ですか. What sort [kind] of (a) man is he?

ひとぎき そんな事を言うなよ. 人聞きが悪いじゃないか. Don't say things like that. What will people think?

ひどく 昨夜はひどく霜がおりた. There was a heavy frost [We had a hard frost] last night. / 彼はインフルエンザでひどくやられて いる. He is suffering from a severe attack of influenza. / 家はひどくいたんでいる. The house is in very bad [in a terrible state of] repair.

ひとくち 今日は一口も食べていません. I haven't had a bite to eat all day. / 一口に俳優といっても色々ある. There are all sorts of actors. / 一口乗りませんか? Won't you take part in it? | What about joining us [me]?

ひとごえ 遠くで人声が聞こえた. Voices could be heard in the distance.

ひとごこち やっと人心地がついた. At last I feel myself again.

ひとこと 家内は英語は一言も話せません. My wife cannot speak a single word of English. / 彼はどうもいつも一言多い. He must always say one word too many. | He always has to have the last word. / 守衛に一言言って, 中へ入れてもらいなさい. Have a word with the porter and have him let you in. / 一言ごあいさつ申し上げます. Ladies and gentlemen, may I just say a few words by way of greeting. / 会議の席では彼は一言も発言しなかった. He did not utter a word [kept absolute silence] throughout the conference.

ひとごと 人事とは思われなかった. I felt as if it were my own affair. / まるで人事のような事を言っている. He talks as if it were no business of his [as if it had nothing to do with him]. / 人事ではありません. 〈警告〉 It ought

ひところ 一頃 once; at one time. 文例↓

ひところし 人殺し (a) murder; homicide; 〈事件〉a murder case; 〈人〉a murderer; a murderess (女); a homicide ¶人殺しをする commit murder / 「人殺し!」と叫ぶ声 a cry of 'Murder!'

ひとさしゆび 人差(指)し指 the forefinger; the index finger; the first finger.

ひとさと 人里 a village; 〈文〉a human habitation ¶人里離れた remote; out-of-the-way; far from human habitation.

ひとさらい 人さらい 〈事〉kidnapping; 〈人〉a kidnapper.

ひとさわがせ 人騒がせ ¶人騒がせをする give [raise] a false alarm; cry wolf. 文例↓

ひとしい 等しい equal (to); equivalent (to); similar (to); (be) alike; 〈同然の〉(be) as good as (dead); (be) no better than (a beggar) ¶全く相等しい be identical (with); be exactly alike ¶等しく equally; evenly (一様に); 〈同様に〉alike; similarly; 〈…の様に〉(just) like; 〈…もまた〉also; too / 等しくする make equal; equalize; even up / 等しく分ける divide (money) equally. 文例↓

ひとしお ⇒いっそ¹. 文例↓

ひとしきり for a time [while]. 文例↓

ひとじち 人質 a hostage ¶人質になる be taken [held] as hostage.

ひとじに 人死に loss of life; a death.

ひとしれず 人知れず secretly; in secret; inwardly.

ひとしれぬ 人知れぬ unknown to other people; secret; 〈内心の〉inward.

ひとずき 人好き ¶人好きのする friendly; affable; pleasing; attractive; lik(e)able.

ひとすじ 一筋 ¶一筋に 〈一直線に〉in a straight line; 〈いちずに〉〈文〉earnestly; intently; single-mindedly / 一筋道 a road without a branch; a straight road / 一筋縄ではいかない男 a man who is very hard to deal with; an awkward [ugly] customer. 文例↓

ひとずれ 人擦れ ¶人擦れする get sophisticated; lose one's simplicity [naiveté] / 人擦れ のした sophisticated / 人擦れのしない unsophisticated; unspoiled.

ひとぞろい 一揃い 〈道具の〉a set; 〈衣服の〉a suit ¶化粧品1そろい a toilet set.

ひとだかり 人だかり ¶人だかりをする people gather (around, in front of); 〈場所が主語〉be crowded with people. 文例↓

ひとだすけ 人助け (a) kindness; 〈文〉a kind deed; an act of charity [kindness] ¶人助け をする help sb in trouble [〈文〉distress]; lend [give] sb a helping hand.

ひとだのみ 人頼み ¶人頼みする depend [rely] on others; ask [turn to] others for help. 文例↓

ひとたび 一度 ⇒いちど.

ひとだま 人魂 the spirit of a dead person; 〈鬼火〉a will-o'-the-wisp.

ひとたまり 一たまり ¶一たまりもなく easily; without any [the least] resistance; helplessly.

ひとちがい 人違い ¶人違いする mistake [take] 《A》for《B》; 〈話しかける〉speak to the wrong person.

ひとつ 一つ 〈数の1〉one; 〈統一体〉a unity; 〈1回〉once; 〈ちょっと〉just ¶1つの 〈1個の〉one; a (single); 〈同一の〉the same / 1つずつ one by one; separately / 1つ50円 50 yen each [apiece] / 一つになる〈文〉become one; 〈文〉unite into one; be unified / パンツ一つになる strip oneself down to one's underpants / 一つには家のため, 一つには国のため partly for one's family, and partly for one's country. 文例↓

ひとつあな 一つ穴 the same hole. 文例↓

ひとつおき 一つ置き ¶1つ置きの alternate; every other / 1つ置きに alternately.

ひとつおぼえ 一つ覚え ⇒ばか 文例. 文例↓

ひとつかい 人使い ¶人使いが荒い work one's men hard; be a hard master.

ひとつかみ 一掴み 〈量〉a handful (of salt); 〈つかむこと〉a grasp; a grip ¶一つかみにする take sth in one handful; 〈わしづかみに〉 clutch; grab.

ひとづきあい 人付き合い ¶人付き合いがい

---

to be a warning to you, too. | 〈同情〉I sympathize with you.

ひところ それはひところ流行したものだ. There was a time when it was in fashion. / ひところはずいぶん話題になった. It was talked about a great deal at one time.

ひとさわがせ とんだ人騒がせをして相済みません. I am very sorry for alarming [upsetting] you.

ひとしい 面積の点では日本はフランスに等しい. In size Japan is equal to France. / 彼の要求はほとんど脅迫に等しかった. His demand practically amounted to a threat. / 彼もなをそれを希望している. He too is hoping for that.

ひとしお 三保の松原から眺めると白雪を頂いた富士の姿がひとしお 美しい. When seen from Miho-no-Matsubara the snow-capped view of Mt. Fuji is especially fine.

ひとしきり 雨が一しきり降って止んだ. After a short shower it cleared up.

ひとじに その事故でたくさんの人死にがあった. Many lives were lost [There were a great number of deaths] in the accident.

ひとしれず 彼女はトイレの中で人知れず幾度も泣いた. She often wept, unseen, in the toilet.

ひとすじ ただ一筋に学問に専念してきた人だ. He has been constant in his devotion to learning. / 彼は一筋縄ではいかない. He is very hard to deal with.

ひとだかり 何かあったらしく町角 に人だかりがしていた. Something seemed to have happened at the corner of the street, for a crowd of people had gathered there. / 地下の特売場は大変な人だかりだった. The bargain basement drew [attracted] a large crowd.

ひとだすけ それは大いに人助けになる. It will be a great help to others.

ひとだのみ 人頼みではだめだ. You must not rely [count] on other people's help.

ひとたまり 木造家屋は猛火に一たまりもなかった. The wooden houses fell easy victims to the furious flames.

ひとつ もう一つの方は80円です. The other is 80 yen. / この作文

ひとつこと **be** sociable [unsociable]; be a good [bad] mixer.
ひとつこと 一つ事 (one and) the same thing ¶一つ事を繰り返して言う say the same thing again and again; harp on *sth*.
ひとっこひとり 人っ子一人 [文例↓]
ひとづて 人づて hearsay ¶人づての話 a piece of hearsay [of information acquired at second hand] / 人づてに聞く hear from someone; get [come] to know by hearsay [at second hand]; hear tell [say] ((of a matter). [文例↓]
ひとつばなし 一つ話 a favorite topic of conversation; 《文》an often-repeated anecdote. [文例↓]
ひとつぶ 一粒 a grain ((of barley)); a drop ((of rain)) ¶一粒種 the only child ((of Mr. A)).
ひとづま 人妻 〈既婚婦人〉a married woman; 〈他人の妻〉another man's wife ¶人妻になる get married.
ひとつまみ 一つまみ a pinch ((of salt)).
ひとつめこぞう 一つ目小僧 a one-eyed goblin.
ひとで[1] 人手 〈他人の手〉someone else's [《文》another's] hand; 〈働き手〉a worker; 〈助力〉help ¶人手を借りる be helped [《文》assisted] by someone else; get help [《文》assistance] from somebody; ask for other people's help / 人手に渡る《文》pass into someone else's possession; change hands. [文例↓]
ひとで[2] 人出 a crowd ((of people)); a turnout.
ひとで[3] 《動》a starfish. [文例↓]
ひとでなし 人でなし a brute ((of a man)); a monster ((of cruelty)).
ひととおり 一通り 〈大体〉in a general way; in the main; 〈ざっと〉briefly ¶一通りの〈普通の〉general; ordinary; usual; 〈かなりの〉fair / 一通りの教育 ordinary education / 一通りの知識 a general [fair] knowledge ((of music)) / 一通りでない unusual; exceptional / 一通り目を通す look [run *one's* eyes] over; run through. [文例↓]
ひとどおり 人通り (pedestrian) traffic ¶人通りの多い[少ない]通り a busy [quiet] street. [文例↓]

ひととき 一時 a short time; a while ⇒ ひところ ¶憩いの一時 a breathing space; a breather / 一時の間 for a time [while].
ひととなり 人となり *one's* nature [《文》disposition]; *one's* personality.
ひととび ひと跳び ¶ひと跳びで in a single bound [leap, jump].
ひとなか 人中 ¶人中で in public; in company / 人中へ出る appear in public / 人中へ出ない keep *oneself*; keep *one's* own company.
ひとなつっこい 人懐っこい love company; be sociable; 〈動物が〉take kindly to men.
ひとなみ[1] 人並み ¶人並みの common; normal; ordinary; average / 人並みに like others [other people] / 人並みに暮らす make a decent living / 人並み優れた above the average; outstanding; 《文》surpassing ((ability)); matchless ((beauty)) / 人並み外れた uncommon; extraordinary; 《文》singular; out of [different from] the common run. [文例↓]
ひとなみ[2] 人波 a surging [milling] crowd ((of people)) ¶人波にもまれる be jostled in the crowd.
ひとにぎり 一握り a handful ((of rice)).
ひとねいり[ねむり] 一寝入り[眠り] ¶一寝入り[眠り]する have [take] a nap [short sleep].
ひとばしら 人柱 a human sacrifice.
ひとばしり 一走り a run; a spin (乗物での) ¶車で一走りする have a spin [ride] in a car / 町へ一走り行って来る take a run to town.
ひとはた 一旗 ¶一旗揚げる have [achieve, 《文》attain] some success in the world; try *one's* luck [《文》seek *one's* fortune] ((in another part of the country)) / 一旗組 fortune-seekers.
ひとはだ[1] 一肌 ¶一肌脱ぐ lend *sb* a helping hand; use *one's* influence for *sb*.
ひとはだ[2] 人肌 ¶人肌のお燗(ｶﾝ) sake warmed to body temperature.
ひとばらい 人払い ¶人払いする have the room to ((themselves)); order ((other people))

には一つの間違いもない. There is not a single mistake in this composition. / 見る物聞く物一つとして珍しくないものはなかった. Everything I saw or heard was strange [new] to me. / 彼は手紙一つ満足に書けない. He cannot so much as write a letter properly. / 一つやってみよう. I'll just give it a try. / I will have a go at it.
ひとつあな 彼らは一つ穴のむじなだ. They are all of a gang.
ひとつおぼえ あれは彼が宴会のたびに言う一つ覚えの冗談さ. That is the one and only joke he tells at every party.
ひとっこひとり 深夜の通りには人っ子一人見えなかった. Not a soul was to be seen on the street in the middle of the night.

ひとづて これは人づてに聞いた話なのです. I'm only passing on what I've heard. / I am speaking from hearsay.
ひとつばなし いっしょに集まると, その話は我々の間ではいまだに一つ話になっている. We still talk about the episode whenever we meet.
ひとで[1] 人手が足りなくて困っている. We are terribly short-handed [short of workers]. / 人手を借りずにやれないかね. Can't you do it by yourself?
ひとで[2] 銀座は非常な人出であった. The Ginza was very crowded.
ひととおり 私は生け花を一通りは習いました. I have learned the basics of the art of flower arrangement. / 僕は彼に事件のいきさつを一通り話した. I gave him an outline of the matter. / 一通り簡単に彼にどう起こったかを述べた. I explained briefly to him how it happened. / 一通りの心配ではなかった. I was extremely [more than] anxious about it.
ひとどおり その辺りは人通りが少なかった. Not many people were on the streets. / There were very few people about. / 駅の近くに来ると人通りが激しくなってきた. The streets became more crowded as we got near the station.
ひとなみ[1] 僕も人並みに風邪を引いたよ. I've caught a cold, like other people. / あの人たちは人並み以上の努力をしたからこそ成功したのだ. Their success has been attained as the result of more than ordinary efforts.
ひとばしり 一走り行って取って来ます. I will run for [and fetch] it.

ひとばん 一晩 a night ; one evening ¶一晩中 all night (long) ; all through the night / 昨夜一晩 all last night / 一晩で in a [one] night / 一晩泊る stay overnight ; put up for the night / 一晩寝て考える sleep on (a question). 文例↓

ひとびと 人々 people ; men ¶いろんな人々 all sorts of people [men] ⇒ひと.

ひとふき 一吹き a blow ; 〈強い〉a blast ; a gust ; 〈軽い〉a puff ; a whiff.

ひとふで 一筆 ¶一筆で with one stroke (of the pen [brush]) / 一筆書き a picture drawn with a single stroke of the brush.

ひとまえ 人前 ¶人前で in the presence of other people ; in public ; in company / 人前をはばかって from a sense of decency ; for decency's sake / 人前に出ることを嫌う avoid [《文》shun] company / 人前に出られない be not fit to be seen ; be not presentable.

ひとまかせ 人任せ ¶人任せにする leave sth to other people.

ひとまく 一幕 〈芝居の〉one act ; 〈1場面を〉a scene ¶一幕もの a one-act play.

ひとまず 一先ず for the time being ; for the present ; for a while. 文例↓

ひとまちがお 人待ち顔 ¶人待ち顔である appear to be [look as if one is] waiting for someone.

ひとまとめ 一まとめ ¶一まとめにする put [lump] together / 一まとめにして in a lump ; all together.

ひとまね 人まね mimicry ¶人まねする mimic (★ mimicked, mimicking と変化する) ; imitate ; ape. 文例↓

ひとまわり 一回り ¶一回りする go around ; make a circuit 《of a place》/ 〈持ち場を〉do [make] one's rounds / 池を1回りする go around [《英》round] the pond / 博物館の中を1回りする go [look] around [round] the museum / 一回り大きい be a size larger 《than》/ 一回り年下である be 12 years younger 《than》.

ひとみ 瞳 the pupil (of the eye) ¶ひとみを凝らす strain one's eyes (to see) ; fix [rivet] one's eyes 《on》 ; look closely [hard] 《at》 ; peer 《at》.

ひとみごくう 人身御供 〈事〉《practice》 human sacrifice ; 〈人〉《offer》 a human sacrifice ; a victim 《of, to》.

ひとみしり 人見知り ¶人見知りする be afraid [shy] of strangers ; be bashful ; be timid / 人見知りして泣く cry at the sight of a stranger.

ひとむかし 一昔 ¶一昔前に an age [a decade] ago. 文例↓

ひとめ[1] 一目 ¶一目で at a glance / 一目見て at first sight / 一目に(the) first glance / …を一目見たい wish to have a look at… ; long for the sight of… / 一目惚れする fall in love with 《a girl》at first sight. 文例↓

ひとめ[2] 人目 ¶人目を避ける《文》avoid public notice [the eyes of others] ; shun the public eye / 人目を忍んで secretly ; in secret ;《文》by stealth / 人目を忍んで会う have a secret [《文》clandestine] meeting 《with》/ 人目につく[をひく] attract (public) attention ; be conspicuous / 人目にとまらない escape notice [observation].

ひともじ 人文字 文例↓

ひとやく 一役 ¶一役買う accept a part 《in》; help sb out.

ひとやすみ 一休み ¶一休みする take [have] a (short) rest ; take [have] a breather.

ひとやま 一山 ¶一山500円 500 yen a heap [pile, trayful] / 一山当てる make a hit ; strike oil.

ひとよせ 人寄せ an attraction ; a draw.

ひとり 一人, 独り one person ¶一人で alone ; by oneself (単身で) ; for oneself (独力で) / 一人で笑っている smile (chuckle) to oneself / 〈他人に頼らず〉一人でやって行く be independent ; rely on [get along by] one's own efforts ; 《口語》paddle one's own canoe / 一人ずつ one at a time ; one by one / 一人残らず every (last) one 《of them》;《be killed》to a [to the last] man / 一人当たり for each person ; per head ;《文》per capita / 一人息子[娘] an [the] only son [daughter]. 文例↓

ひどり 日取り ¶日取りを決める fix [set] the date / 前もって日取りを決めて会う meet by appointment. 文例↓

ひとりあるき 一人歩き ¶一人[独り]歩きする〈歩行する〉go alone [(all) by oneself] ; walk by oneself ; walk without help (子供や病人が) ; 〈独立する〉⇒ひとりだち.

ひとりうらない 独り占い self-divination ; 〈トランプの〉solitaire ;《英》patience ¶(トランプで)独り占いをする play solitaire ; lay out a hand of solitaire [patience].

ひとりが(っ)てん 独り合点 ¶独り合点する〈当然と思い込む〉assume 《that…》; take it for granted 《that…》; 〈早合点する〉⇒はやが(っ)てん.

ひとりぎめ 独り決め ⇒どくだん ¶独り決めする decide by oneself ;〈勝手に思い込む〉take it for granted 《that…》/ 独り決めでやる do on one's own authority ; take it on oneself to do.

ひとばん 一晩泊まりで水戸へ行った. I made an overnight trip to Mito. / そこのホテルで一晩泊まろう. Let us spend a night at the hotel there.

ひとまず まずこれで終わりにしましょう. Let's stop here for the present.

ひとまね 彼はなかなか人まねがうまい. He is a great mimic.

ひとむかし 十年一昔. Ten years make(s) an epoch.

ひとめ[1] その丘からは町が一目に見下ろせる. From that hill you can see [get a view of] the whole city. / 僕はその場の様子を一目で見て取った. I took in the scene with a single glance. / 行く前に彼に一目会いたい. I'd like to have a chance of meeting him before I go.

ひともじ スタンドの学生が TO-KYO と人文字を書いた. The students in the stands spelled out the letters 'T-O-K-Y-O'.

ひとり 私はただ一人で行った. I went there all by myself. / 一人一人聞いてみた. I asked them one after another. / 合格者は20名で, 私もその一人だった. Twenty passed the examination, including myself. / その知らせを喜ばない者は一人もなかった. The news

ひとりぐらし 一人[独り]暮らし ¶一人暮らしをする live alone [by *oneself*]; lead a bachelor's life.

ひとりごと 独り言 ¶独り言を言う talk to *oneself*; think aloud ★say to *oneself* は「心の中で考える」の意味になるのが普通で,「独り言を言う」の意味で使われることはまれ / ぶつぶつ独り言を言う mutter [mumble] to *oneself*.

ひとりじめ 独り占め ¶どくせん².

ひとりずもう 独り相撲 ¶独り相撲をとる fight [tilt at] windmills.

ひとりだち 独り立ち ¶独り立ちする stand on *one's* own (two) feet; become independent 《of *one's* parents》; live [be] on *one's* own.

ひとりたび 一人[独り]旅 ¶一人旅をする travel alone [by *oneself*, without a companion].

ひとりっこ 一人っ子 an [the] only child [son, daughter].

ひとりでに 独りでに by 《(文)》 of *itself*; of *its* own accord; spontaneously; automatically (自動的に).

ひとりぶたい 独り舞台 ¶独り舞台である 〈独演する〉play alone [by *oneself*]; 〈演技が他を圧する〉outshine all the other actors; 〈競争者がない〉be 《(文)》 stand unrivaled.

ひとりぼっち 独りぼっち lonely; solitary; ¶独りぼっちになる be left alone [to *oneself*].

ひとりもの 独り者 ⇨どくしん.

ひとりよがり 独り善がり (self-)complacency ¶独りよがりの self-satisfied; complacent.

ひとわたり 一渡り ⇨ひととおり.

ひな 雛 〈鳥の〉a chicken; a chick; a young bird; a fledg(e)ling; 〈ひな人形〉a doll (displayed at the Girls' Festival) ¶ひなをかえす hatch chickens / おひな様を飾る display dolls 《on a tiered stand》 / ひな祭り the Girls' [Doll's] Festival.

ひなか 日中 ⇨にっちゅう¹.

ひなが 日長[永] ¶春の日長に on a mild spring day; in springtime when the days are long.

ひながた 雛型〈模型〉a pattern; a model;〈見本〉a sample;〈書式〉a form ¶…をひな型にして on [after] the model of….

ひなぎく〔植〕a daisy.

ひなげし〔植〕a red [corn, field] poppy.

ひなた 日向 ¶日なたで in the sun 〈sunshine〉; in a sunny place / 日なたに出る go out in the sun / 日なたに置かないようにする keep *sth* out of the sun [in the shade] / 日なたぼっこをする bask [sit, laze] in the sun.

ひなだん 雛壇 〈ひな祭りの〉a tiered stand (carpeted in red) for displaying dolls;〈国会の〉the state ministers' gallery ¶ひな壇式に in tiers.

ひなにんぎょう 雛人形 ⇨ひな.

ひなびた 鄙びた countrified; rustic; rural.

ひなわじゅう 火縄銃 a matchlock (gun).

ひなん¹ 非難 (a) criticism; blame;《文》(an) adverse criticism; blame;《文》(a) censure;《文》strictures; 〈攻撃〉an attack ¶非難する criticize (unfavorably [《文》adversely]);《文》censure; blame; disparage; attack / 非難すべき blameworthy /《文》reproachable / 非難の的となる become the focus [target] of criticism / 非難の余地がない be irreproachable; be above [beyond] reproach; have no fault to find with / 非難を免れない be open to censure [criticism].

ひなん² 避難 ¶避難する take [seek] refuge 《in》; take [find] shelter 《in》;《文》flee (to a place) for safety / 避難所 a (safe) shelter; a (place of) refuge;《文》a haven / 避難者[民] a refugee; an evacuee (疎開者) / (洪水の際など の)避難命令 an evacuation order. 用例⇩

びなん 美男 ⇨びだんし.

ビニール vinyl ¶ビニールのハンドバッグ a vinyl handbag.

ひにく 皮肉 sarcasm; irony (反語的); cynicism (冷笑) ¶運命の皮肉 the irony of fate / 人生の皮肉 life's ironies / 皮肉な sarcastic; ironical; cynical / 皮肉を言う,皮肉る make sarcastic [ironical] remarks; talk cynically 《about》 / 皮肉にも ironically (enough); as irony would have it / 皮肉屋 a sarcastic person. 用例⇩

ひにょうき 泌尿器 the urinary organs ¶泌尿器科 urology.

ひにん¹ 否認 (a) denial;《文》negation; nonrecognition ¶否認する say no 《to》; deny;《文》disavow; disown; disclaim.

ひにん² 避妊 contraception; 〈産児制限〉birth control ¶避妊する prevent conception; practice contraception [birth control] / 避妊具 a contraceptive device / 避妊薬 a contraceptive (pill); the pill.

ひにんしょう 非人称〔文法〕¶非人称の impersonal / 非人称動詞〔構文〕an impersonal verb [construction].

ひにんじょう 非人情 ¶非人情な〈人情のない〉⇨ふにんじょう;〈人情から超然とした〉《文》transcending human emotions.

ひねくれる get [《文》become] twisted [warped, perverse] ¶ひねくれた性質 a twisted [warped] personality / ひねくれた見方 a dis-

---

gladdened everybody. / 独りで考えてご覧なさい. Try thinking [working] it out for yourself. / 打っちゃっておけば独りで帰って来ますよ. Let him alone, and he will return of his own accord. / 一人口は養えないが二人口は養える. Two can live as cheaply as one. | It doesn't cost any more to feed two than one.

ひどり 僕たちの結婚式の日取りが決まった. The date has been set [fixed] for our wedding.

ひなん¹ 彼の行動は世間の非難を招いた. His conduct laid him open to public criticism. | He incurred public censure by his conduct. / その処置に対しては非難の声が高い. The measure is receiving a great deal of (vocal) criticism. / 彼は首相を非難する演説を行なった. He made a speech denouncing the prime minister.

ひなん² 洪水の危険があるので町民に避難命令が出された. In view of the danger of flood, the people of the town were ordered to evacuate their homes.

ひにく 彼のスピーチには皮肉が交じっていた. There was a touch [tinge] of irony in his speech. / 彼はイギリス一の皮肉屋である.

ひねた ①ひねた子供 an old-young [a precocious] child; a grownup-looking boy.

ひねつ 比熱 《物》specific heat.

びねつ 微熱 ①微熱がある have a slight temperature [fever].

ひねり 捻り 〈一つまみ〉a pinch; 〈一ひねり〉a twist.

ひねる 捻る 〈指先で〉twist; twirl; wrench (きつく); 〈体を〉bend; 〈つねる〉pinch; tweak; 〈負かす〉defeat; beat ¶栓をひねってガスを出す[止める] turn the gas on [off] / 首をひねって考える rack one's brains; think hard 《of, about》; puzzle 《over a question》/ ひねり出す squeeze out; 〈工夫する〉《文》devise (a scheme); work out (a plan); 〈金を〉raise money; ひねりつぶす crush (a flea) with one's fingernails.

ひのいり 日の入り sunset; 《米》sundown ⇒にちぼつ

ひのうみ 火の海 a sea of flames; a blazing inferno. [文例⇩]

ひのき 檜 〔植〕a hinoki; a (Japanese) cypress ¶ひのき舞台を踏む〈俳優が〉appear on the stage of [perform in] a first-class theater; 〈比喩的に〉be in the limelight.

ひのくるま 火の車 ¶火の車である be short of money; 《口語》be very hard up; 《俗》be strapped (for cash); 《文》be in straitened circumstances.

ひのけ 火の気 ¶火の気のない部屋 an unheated room.

ひのこ 火の粉 sparks (of fire). [文例⇩]

ひのたま 火の玉 a ball of fire; a fireball; 〈鬼火〉a will-o'-the-wisp.

ひので 火の手 a fire; flame(s) ¶火の手が上がる burst into flame(s); blaze up. [文例⇩]

ひので 日の出 sunrise; 《米》sunup ¶日の出の勢いである 《文》one's star is in the ascendant / 日の出に at sunrise / 日の出と共に起きる get up [rise] with the sun.

ひのべ 日延べ putting off; (a) postponement; 〈延会〉(an) adjournment ⇒〈期間延長〉an extension of the term ⇒えんき[1] ¶日延べする put off; postpone; extend (the term of payment).

ひのまる(のはた) 日の丸(の旗) the rising-sun flag.

ひのみやぐら 火の見櫓 a fire tower.

ビバーク 〔登山〕(a) bivouac; bivouacking.

ひばいひん 非売品 an article not for sale; 〔表示〕Not for sale.

ひばく 被爆 ¶被爆する be bombed / 原爆の被爆者 a victim of radiation sickness caused by an atomic bomb / 被爆地区 a bombed area; a bomb site.

ひばし 火箸 metal chopsticks (for handling charcoal).

ひばしら 火柱 a pillar of fire. [文例⇩]

ひばち 火鉢 a hibachi; a (charcoal) brazier ¶火鉢に当たる[手をかざす] warm oneself [one's hands] at [over] a hibachi.

ひばな 火花 a spark ¶火花が散る spark; sparks fly / 火花を散らす spark; give out [off] sparks; throw off [《文》emit] sparks / 火花を散らす論戦 a heated [hot] discussion [controversy].

ひばり 〔鳥〕a skylark; a lark ¶ひばりが上がる[さえずる] a lark soars [trills].

ひはん 批判 (a) criticism; (a) comment ¶批判する criticize; comment 《on》; pass judgment 《on》/ 批判の余地がない be above criticism; give no grounds for criticism / 批判的な critical / 批判的な態度を取る take 《文》assume] a critical attitude 《to, toward》/ 批判的に critically / …に批判的である be critical of …; have a poor opinion of… / 批判者 a critic / 批判力 critical power [ability] / 純粋[実践]理性批判〔書名〕Critique of Pure [Practical] Reason.

ひばん 非番 ¶非番の警官 a policeman off duty / 非番に当たる[なる] be [go] off duty.

ひひ 〔動〕a baboon. [文例⇩]

ひび[1] 日々 every day; daily; day after [by] day ¶日々の出来事 a daily happening 《《の》 occurrence》/ 日々の生活 everyday [daily] life / 日々の生活記録 a day-by-day account of one's life.

ひび[2] 〈割れ目〉a crack; 《文》a fissure; 〈皮膚の〉chaps ¶ひびが切れる be [get, 《文》become] chapped / ひびが入る, ひび割れる crack; be cracked / ひび焼き陶器 crackleware. [文例⇩]

びび 微々たる 〈小さい〉small; 〈取るに足りない〉insignificant; trifling.

ひびき 響き a sound; a peal (鈴・雷などの); a boom (鐘などの); a clash (金属の); a clang (剣などの); 《文》a report (銃砲の); an explosion (爆音); 〈反響〉an echo (pl. -es); 《文》reverberations (振動》a shock; 〈振動する》vibration; 〈影響》an effect 《on》; an influence 《on》 ¶馬蹄の響き the clatter [sound] of a horse's hoofs; a hoofbeat.

ひびく 響く 〈鳴る〉sound; ring; 〈反響する〉echo; 《文》reverberate; 〈振動する〉vibrate; 〈影響する〉affect; have an effect 《on》 ¶神

He has the bitterest tongue in Britain.
ひねり あんな相手は一ひねりだ。I can beat him hands down.
ひのうみ 気がついてみたら一面火の海だった。When I awoke, I found myself in an inferno.
ひのこ 火の粉が屋根に振りかかった。Sparks fell on the roof.
ひので わが家はたちまち火の手に包まれた。Very soon my house was in flames. / 政府攻撃の火の手が上がった。An attack was launched against the administration.
ひので 日の出が早い[遅い]。The sun rises early [late] (in the morning).
ひばしら 火柱が立った。A pillar of fire shot up.

ひばん 今日は非番だ。This is my day off. | I am off duty today.
ひび その事件で2人の友情にひびが入った。The affair has impaired [caused a crack in] their friendship.
ひびき その表現は響きがよくない。The expression does not sound well.
ひびく 物価の騰貴は暮らしに響

ひひょう 批評 (a) criticism; a critical essay; 〈論評〉(a) comment; 〈新刊書などの〉a review; a notice 〈短評〉¶ 批評する criticize; comment 《on》; review 《a book》/〈新聞などで〉好意的な批評を受ける get a good [favorable] review 《from》; get a good press / 批評に値しない be beneath criticism [notice] / 批評家 a critic; a reviewer / 文芸[美術]批評家 a literary [an art] critic / 批評眼がある have a critical eye.

びびる 《文》quail 《at, before》; 《文》be daunted 《by》; become nervous.

びひん 備品 equipment; fixtures; furnishings; furniture ¶ 事務室の1備品 a piece of office equipment / 備品台帳 a list of equipment; an inventory.

ひふ 皮膚 the skin ¶ 皮膚が弱い[強い, 荒れている] have a delicate [strong, rough] skin / 皮膚の cutaneous / 皮膚科医 a dermatologist / 皮膚科学 dermatology / 皮膚癌(がん) cancer of the skin; skin [cutaneous] cancer / 皮膚呼吸 cutaneous respiration / 皮膚病 a skin disease.

ひぶ 日歩 daily interest per 100 yen ¶ 日歩3銭払う pay interest of three sen a day per 100 yen.

びふう¹ 美風 a fine [good] custom.

びふう² 微風 a breeze; a gentle [light] wind.

ひふく 被覆 covering; coating ¶ 被覆銅線 coated [insulated] copper wire.

ひぶくれ 火脹れ a blister ¶ 火ぶくれができる blisters form 《on the skin》; blister. [文例⇩]

ひぶそう 非武装 ¶ 非武装の unarmed; demilitarized / 非武装化 demilitarization / 非武装地帯 a demilitarized zone / 非武装都市 an open city.

ひぶた 火蓋 ¶ 火ぶたを切る〈砲撃の〉start firing; open fire 《on》; 〈始める〉start; begin; 《文》commence / 攻撃の火ぶたを切る open [launch, mount] an attack 《on, against》.

ビフテキ ⑪ beefsteak.

ひふん 悲憤 indignation; resentment ¶ 悲憤の涙を流す shed tears of indignation / 悲憤慷慨(こうがい)する deplore; resent; be indignant 《at》.

びぶん¹ 美文 a literary composition full of flowery rhetoric; elegant prose. [文例⇩]

びぶん² 微分 《数》differential calculus ¶ 微分する differentiate / 微分関数 a differential function / 微分方程式 a differential equation.

ひへい 疲弊 《文》impoverishment; 《文》exhaustion ¶ 土壌の疲弊 the exhaustion of the soil / 疲弊する be [《文》become] impoverished [exhausted]. [文例⇩]

ピペット a pipette.

ひほう¹ 秘法[方]〈方法〉a secret process [method]; 〈処方〉a secret recipe.

ひほう² 悲報 (a piece of) sad news.

ひほう 誹謗 slander; abuse; a libel ¶ ひほうする speak ill of; slander; abuse; libel.
[用法] 正確には slander は口頭による「ひぼう」で, libel は文書によるものだが, 実際にはかなり混同して使われている. なお slander も libel も「ひぼう」の内容が事実に反するものであるのに対して, abuse は真実である場合もある.

びぼう 美貌 good [attractive] looks; beauty ¶ 美貌の good-looking; beautiful / まれに見る美貌の持ち主 《文》a person of rare personal beauty.

びほうさく 弥縫策 a makeshift; a temporary [stopgap] measure.

びぼうろく 備忘録 a memorandum 《pl. -s, -da》; a memo 《pl. -s》.

ひほけんしゃ 被保険者 the (person) insured.

ひほごしゃ 被保護者 a ward.

ひぼし 干[日]乾し ¶ 干ぼしになる be starved (to death); die from lack of food / 日ぼしにする dry sth in the sun / 日ぼしれんが a sun-dried brick; adobe.

ひぼん 非凡 ¶ 非凡な unusual; out of the ordinary; 《文》uncommon; extraordinary; remarkable; 《文》prodigious / 非凡な人 a remarkable man; 《文》a man of unusual [uncommon] ability; a prodigy / 非凡な腕前 rare [unusual] skill. [文例⇩]

ひま¹ 暇 〈時間〉time; 〈余暇〉spare time; leisure (hours); time to spare; a spare moment; 〈休暇〉leave (of absence); 〈解雇〉《文》dismissal; 《文》discharge ¶ 暇がない have no time (to do); cannot find time (to do); be too busy (to do); have no leisure [no time to spare]; be engaged / 暇がかかる take (up) time (to do) / お暇なら if you are free [not engaged]; if you have time to spare [nothing better to do] / 暇をこしらえる make time (to do) / 暇を出す fire; 《文》dismiss; 《文》discharge; sack; give sb the sack / 暇をつぶす ⇨ ひまつぶし / 暇をもらう ask for [get] 《three days'》leave / 暇に飽かせて taking advantage 《文》availing oneself] of all the time that one has at one's disposal / 暇にあかせて...する give ample time to doing / 暇である be free [not engaged]; 〈商売が〉be dull [slack] / 暇々に at odd moments; when one has [finds] time. [文例⇩]

ひま² 《植》a castor-oil plant.

く. The rise in prices affects our cost of living. / 彼の足音が廊下中に響いた. His footsteps sounded (right) through the corridor. | The hallway echoed with his footsteps.

ひぶくれ やけどで右手に火ぶくれができた. I burnt my right hand and got a blister on it. | I got my right hand blistered from a burn.

びぶん¹ (皮肉に)えらい美文だね. What a style! | What exquisite use of language!

ひへい 当時は農村が著しく疲弊していた. In those days farm villages were extremely impoverished.

ひぼん 彼にはどこか非凡な所がある. There is something special about him [something out of the ordinary in him].

ひま¹ 手紙を書く暇がない. I have no time to write a letter. / お暇は取らせません. I will not keep you long. | It won't take much of your time. / 大変お暇を取らせて相済みません. I am sorry to have taken up so much of your time. / ほかの者が遊んでいる暇に彼は一生懸命に頑張った. He

ひまご 曾孫 a great-grandchild 《*pl.* -children》.

ひまし 日増し ¶日増しに day by day; daily; every day. 文例⇩

ひましゆ ひまし油 castor oil.

ひまじん 暇人 a man of leisure; a leisured person; an idler (遊んでいる人).

ひまつ 飛沫 ⇨ しぶき.

ひまつぶし 暇つぶし ¶暇つぶしをする kill time; while away the time / 暇つぶしに to kill time; by way of killing time; to while away the time. 文例⇩

ひまどる 暇取る take (a lot of) time;〈遅れる〉 be delayed《on the way》. 文例⇩

ヒマラヤ ヒマラヤ山脈 the Himalayas; the Himalaya Mountains / ヒマラヤ杉 a Himalayan cedar; a deodar.

ひまわり a sunflower.

ひまん 肥満 ¶肥満する get fat; grow [《文》 become] stout / 肥満した fat; stout;《文》 corpulent; portly / 肥満型の人 a corpulent person / 肥満児 an obese [a fat] child.

びみ 美味〈うまさ〉a good flavor;《文》relish;《文》deliciousness;〈うまい物〉a dainty; a delicacy.

ひみつ 秘密〈状態〉secrecy; confidentiality;〈その内容〉a secret; a mystery; a confidence ¶よく守られた秘密 a well-kept secret / 公然の秘密 an open secret / 信書の秘密 the confidentiality [privacy] of correspondence / 秘密の secret; private; confidential; hidden; classified (公文書など) / 秘密の会合 a secret [《文》clandestine] meeting / 秘密の情報 secret [confidential, classified] information / 秘密の宝 a secret [hidden] treasure / 秘密を守る keep a secret;《文》maintain secrecy / 秘密を漏らす betray [give away, let out,《文》reveal] a secret; let the cat out of the bag (ついうっかり) / 秘密を明かす confide a secret to *sb*; let *sb* into the secret / 秘密に secretly; privately; in secret; in private; on the sly / 秘密にする [しない] make a [no] secret of *sth* / 秘密にしておく keep *sth* secret [private]; keep *sth* from *sb* / 秘密会議 a secret conference; a closed-door session / 秘密結社 a secret society / 秘密書類 a confidential [classified] document / 秘密探偵 a secret (service) agent / 秘密投票 a secret ballot; secret voting / 秘密兵器 a secret weapon / 秘密命令 sealed [secret] orders. 文例⇩

びみょう 微妙 ¶微妙な delicate; subtle;《文》 nice; fine / 微妙な区別 a fine [《文》] distinction / 微妙な情況 a delicate [ticklish] situation / 微妙な点《文》a nice point;《文》a point of nicety.

ひめ 姫 a princess;《文》a young lady of gentle [noble] birth ¶一姫二太郎 ⇨ いちひめ.

ひめい 悲鳴 a shriek; a scream ¶悲鳴を上げる shriek; utter a shriek; scream.

びめい 美名 a good [《文》fair] name ¶…の美名に隠れて under the pretext of 《charity》.

ひめゆり 姫百合【植】a (red) star lily.

ひめる 秘める ⇨ ひみつ (秘密にする) ¶胸に秘める keep *sth* to oneself.

ひめん 罷免 ⇨ めんしょく ¶首相の閣員罷免権 the prime minister's right to dismiss the members of his cabinet.

ひも 紐 (a) string; (a) cord;〈組みひも, 打ちひも〉a lace; (a) tape (さなだひも, 平打ちひも);〈皮ひも〉a thong;〈袋の口を締めるひも〉a drawstring;〈靴の〉a (shoe)lace; a bootlace;〈売春婦の〉a prostitute's protector; a man who lives off a prostitute's earnings; a pimp (客引きもする) ¶ひもを結ぶ[ほどく] tie [untie] the strings / 靴のひもを結ぶ[解く] lace [unlace] *one*'s shoes / ひもで結ぶ tie with a string / ひも付きの[の付かない]恩恵 a favor with strings [no strings] attached. 文例⇩

ひもかわ(うどん) noodles made in flat strips.

ひもく 費目 an item of expenditure.

ひもじい be hungry ¶ひもじい思いをする feel [be, go] hungry / ひもじくて死にそうである be dying of [from] hunger; be starving. 文例⇩

ひもと 火元 the origin [source] of a fire. 文例⇩

ひもとく 繙く read;《文》peruse.

ひもの 干物 dried fish / 干物にする dry 《a fish》.

ひや 冷や〈水〉cold water;〈酒〉cold *sake* ¶酒を冷やで飲む drink *sake* cold.

ひやあせ 冷や汗 ¶冷や汗をかく[かいている] break into [be in] a cold sweat.

ビヤガーデン a beer garden.

---

worked hard while the others were idling. / 暇をかけられるよ. You will be able to do it if you give it plenty of time. / もしお暇でしたら野球でも見に行きませんか. If you are not doing anything, how about going to see the baseball? / お暇の折にはいつでも遊びにおいで下さい. Come and see me when you have nothing better to do. / 暇な時にしなさい. Do it when you have time to spare. | Do it at your leisure. / 暇が出来次第取りかかりましょう. I'll start on it the first free moment I have. / 暇があり過ぎて困った. Time hung heavy on my hands.

ひまし 日増しに暖かくなります. It is getting warmer day by day [with every passing day].

ひまつぶし これ以上君と議論をしても暇つぶしになるばかりだ. It is a mere waste of time to argue any further with you.

ひまどる その家を捜すのにだいぶ暇取った. It took me a long time to find the house.

ひみつ 秘密が漏れた. The secret leaked [got] out. / この秘密は厳重に守らなければならない. This secret must be strictly kept. / 君に対して何も秘密はない. I keep nothing from you. / 彼らは秘密の会合を開いた. They met behind closed doors.

ひも 靴のひもが解けた. My (shoe)laces came untied [loose]. / これは純粋の援助で, 何のひもも付いていない. This is aid, pure and simple, with no strings attached (to it).

ひもじい 子供たちにひもじい思いはさせない. My children shall not go hungry. / ひもじい思いをしないためには働かなければならない. We must work in order to keep the wolf from the door.

ひもと 火元は風呂屋だった. The fire started [originated] in a bathhouse.

ひやかし 冷やかし〈冷笑〉derision; ridicule ¶冷やかし半分に partly for fun / 冷やかし客 a visitor just walking through the store; a window-shopper. 文例⇩
ひやかす 冷やかす〈からかう〉tease; poke fun at; bait;《口語》rib;〈店を〉just look at the goods (and go away).
ひやく¹ 秘薬 a secret medicine.
ひやく² 飛躍 a leap; a jump ¶論理の飛躍 a jump of logic; a logical leap / 飛躍する leap; jump / 政界に飛躍する play an active part in political life; make one's name in the political world / 飛躍的発展を遂げる make rapid progress; make great strides. 文例⇩
ひゃく 百 a [one] hundred ¶…を百も承知で in the full knowledge《of, that...》/ 第 100 the hundredth / 何百という人 hundreds of people / 100倍 one [a] hundred times / 100倍する multiply《a number》by one hundred; increase《a number》a hundred times [《文》a hundredfold] / 100 分の 20 twenty-hundredths; 20 per cent / 百八十度の転換をする make a complete change (in one's policy); make a complete about-face;《文》make a volte-face / 効果百パーセントである be 100 per cent [completely] effective [《文》efficacious]; work perfectly. 文例⇩
びやく 媚薬 a love potion; an aphrodisiac.
ひゃくさい 百歳 a hundred years of age ¶100歳の老人 a centenarian.
ひゃくしょう 百姓 a farmer (農業経営者); a peasant (小作農民); a farm laborer [hand] (作男);《総称》peasantry ¶百姓をする engage in farming; be a farmer [peasant] / 百姓一揆 a peasant uprising; a peasants' rising [revolt] / 百姓仕事 farming; farm work / 百姓家(ゃ) a peasant's cottage; a farmhouse.
びゃくしん〘植〙a Chinese juniper.
ひゃくせん 百戦 ¶百戦して百勝する win every battle (that is fought);《文》be ever-victorious / 百戦練磨の士 a veteran; an old-timer.
びゃくだん〘植〙a sandalwood tree;〈木材〉sandalwood; sandal.
ひゃくてん 百点 a [one] hundred points;〈満点〉full marks ⇒まんてん² ¶100点満点で成績を評価する grade the students out of a hundred.
ひゃくにち 百日 a [one] hundred days ¶百日ぜき whooping cough / 百日草 a zinnia. 文例⇩
ひゃくねん 百年 a [one] hundred years; a century ¶百年の計 a far-sighted policy [program] / 百年祭 a centenary; a centennial / 百年戦争〘史〙the Hundred Years' War. 文例⇩
ひゃくぶんひりつ 百分比[率] (a) percentage.
ひゃくまん 百万 a [one] million ¶100万分の1 a millionth / 百万長者 a millionaire / 百万人の天文学〈書名〉Astronomy for the Million.
ひゃくめんそう 百面相 ¶百面相をする make comic faces.
びゃくや 白夜 nights under the midnight sun.
ひゃくようばこ 百葉箱 a ventilated case for meteorological instruments.
ひゃくらい 百雷 ¶百雷が一時に落ちたように like a hundred thunderclaps coming all at once; with a thunderous [tremendous] sound.
ひやけ 日焼け sunburn; (a) suntan; (a) tan ★ sunburn が「やけど」の一種であるのに対して suntan は「きれいに肌がやけている状態」を表わしている ¶日焼けする get sunburned; be tanned; get a tan / いい色に日焼けする be well tanned (with the sun); have a good tan (on one's back) / 日焼けした顔 a sunburnt [suntanned, sun-browned] face / 日焼けどめクリーム[ローション] suntan cream [lotion].
ひやざけ 冷や酒 unwarmed [cold] sake.
ヒヤシンス〘植〙a hyacinth.
ひやす 冷やす cool;〈水で〉ice;〈冷蔵装置で〉refrigerate ¶頭を冷やす cool one's head《with ice》;〈冷静になる〉cool down [off] / 冷やした cooled; iced.
ビヤだる ビヤ樽 a beer barrel.
ひゃっかじてん 百科事典 an encyclopedia.
ひゃっかてん 百貨店 a department store.
ひゃっぱつひゃくちゅう 百発百中 ¶百発百中する hit the mark every time; never miss the mark [target].
ひやとい 日雇い ¶日雇いに雇われる be hired by the day / 日雇い労務[動]者 a day laborer.
ひやひや 冷や冷や ¶ひやひやする〈冷たく感

ひやかし 大抵は冷やかし客です. Most people just look and go away. | The majority are only window-shopping.
ひゃく 昨年は自動車の輸出が飛躍的に増大した. There was a jump in the export of automobiles last year.
ひゃく 危ないことは百も承知だ. I am well aware of the danger. / 彼の弟子は何百人もいる. His pupils may be counted by hundreds. / 人工衛星の数は何百という数になっているということだ. I hear that the number of artificial satellites has risen into the hundreds. / 援軍来たるとの報に一同勇気百倍した. The news of the coming reinforcements inspired us with fresh courage. / 百発百中であった. He never missed the mark. | Every shot told. / それは百害あって一利なしだ. It will have innumerable harmful effects without doing any good at all. / その問題で議論百出した. The matter became the subject of heated discussion. / 君の意見に百パーセント賛成した. I agree with your opinion 100 per cent. | I'm with you all the way. / 百聞は一見にしかず. Seeing is believing.〘諺〙
ひゃくてん それなら百点だ. That's perfect. / 君なら彼に 100点満点で何点与えるか. How many points would you give him out of a hundred?
ひゃくにち 百日の説法屁一つ. A moment's lapse can undo the labors of years.
ひゃくねん こうなっては百年目だ. I've had it. | It's all up with me. | Now I am doomed.
ひゃくまん 彼が助力を誓ったことは百万の味方を得た程に心強い. Nothing gives us greater confidence than his promise of help.
ひやけ 日焼けがとれてきた. I'm losing my tan.
ひやす 井戸にすいかが冷やしてあ

ビヤホール a beer parlor [hall].
ひやむず 冷や水 ⇒としより 文例.
ひやめし 冷や飯 cold rice ¶冷や飯を食わされる be (left) out in the cold; be placed in an unduly low position.
ひややか 冷ややか ¶冷ややかな〈肌に冷たい〉cold; chilly; cool;〈冷淡な〉cold-hearted;〈冷静な〉cool / 冷ややかに coldly; coolly.
ひややっこ 冷ややっこ tofu served cold.
ひやりと 冷やりと ¶冷やりとする〈冷たさで〉feel cold [chilled];〈恐ろしくて〉be in great fear; be frightened / ひやりとする風 a cold [chill(y)] wind. 文例.
ヒヤリング ⇒ききとり.
ひゆ 比喩 a figure of speech; a simile (直喩); a metaphor (隠喩) ¶比喩的な《文》figurative; metaphorical / 比喩的に《文》figuratively; metaphorically.
ぴゅー ¶ぴゅーっと水を出す squirt water / ぴゅーぴゅー音を立てる whistle; whiz(z)〈矢などが風を切る時〉. 文例.
ヒューズ a [an electrical] fuse ¶ヒューズを入れる fit [put] a fuse 〈to the cutout switch〉/ ヒューズを付け換える replace a fuse; put in a new fuse. 文例.
ひゅーひゅー with a whistle [whiz(z)] ¶ひゅーひゅー鳴る音 a whistling sound; a whistle; a whiz〈矢・弾丸などの〉; a sough〈風の〉; a swish〈むちの〉/ ひゅーひゅー鳴る〈風などが〉whistle; sigh;〈矢などが〉whiz;〈むちが〉swish.
ぴゅーぴゅー 文例.
ピューマ《動》a puma; a cougar; an American lion.
ヒューマニスト〈人道主義者〉a humanitarian;〈人文主義者〉a humanist.
ヒューマニズム〈人道主義〉humanitarianism;〈人文主義〉humanism.
ピューリッツァー ¶ピューリッツァー賞 a Pulitzer prize《for drama》.
ヒュッテ[<《ドイツ語》Hütte] a mountain hut; a hut for mountaineers.
ビュッフェ a buffet.
ぴゅん ¶ぴゅんと飛ぶ zip; go zipping. 文例.
ひょいと〈突然〉suddenly;〈偶然〉casually; by chance [accident];〈軽く〉lightly;〈敏捷(びんしょう)に〉《文》with agility ¶米俵をひょいと持ち上げる lift a bale of rice lightly / 窓からひょいと顔を出す pop one's head out of the window.
ひょいひょい〈折々〉from time to time; at times; in [by] fits (and starts);〈軽くと〉lightly.
ひよう 費用 expense; expenses; (a) cost; (an) outlay ¶費用が大層かかる cost a great deal; be very expensive / 費用のかかる costly; expensive / 費用を持つ[負担する] bear the expenses / 500万円の費用で at a cost [the expense] of 5 million yen. 文例.
用法 expense は全体あるいは総額としての「費用」の意で, expenses は一つ一つの出費を念頭において言う時の「費用」. 従って, expense が主語の時は, その述部に金額を示す数字がくることは少なく, great, small, terrific, insignificant のような度合を表わす形容詞がくることが多い. expenses についてはその逆のことが言える.
ひょう¹ 表 a table; a list; a chart; a diagram ¶表にする make a list of; list; tabulate / 表に載る[載っている] be listed; be (placed) on the list.
ひょう² 豹《動》a leopard; a panther.
ひょう³ 俵 a bale; a bag ¶米3俵 three bales of rice.
ひょう⁴ 票 a vote ¶票の売買 vote-buying; traffic in votes / 清き一票を投じる cast an honest vote〈for〉/ 50票を取る[集める] win [get, gather] 50 votes / 票集め vote-catching[-getting] / 票数〈得票数〉the number of votes polled; a vote;〈党派・集団が投じ得る〉voting strength / 票読み forecasting the result of an election [a poll]; estimating the likely number of votes.
ひょう⁵ 雹 hail;〈1粒〉a hailstone;〈降雹〉a hailstorm ¶豆粒大のひょう hailstones as big as peas / ひょうが降る it hails / ひょう害 damage from a hailstorm. 文例.
びよう 美容 ¶美容院 a beauty parlor / 美容学校 a beauty school / 美容師 a hairdresser; a beautician / 美容術 the art of cosmetic treatment / 美容整形 cosmetic surgery / 美容体操 calisthenics《単数扱い》.
びょう¹ 秒 a second ¶10分の1秒 one-tenth of a second /〈時計の〉秒針 a second-hand / 秒速10メートル (a speed of) ten meters a second / 秒読み counting the seconds;〈ロケット発射の際などの〉a countdown; counting down.

る. A watermelon is cooling down in the well. / 足を冷やすな. Keep your feet warm.
ひやひや 彼がその事をうっかりしゃべりはしないかとひやひやした. I was very much afraid that he would blurt it out.
ひやりと それを見た時は全くひやりとしました. A cold shiver ran through me when I saw it.
ぴゅー ぴゅーっと弾丸が飛んだ. A bullet whizzed past.
ヒューズ ヒューズが飛んだ. The fuse has blown [burnt out]. / ヒューズが飛んで家中の明かりが消えた. All the lights in the house fused.
ぴゅーぴゅー 風がぴゅーぴゅー吹いている. The wind is whistling.
ぴゅん 弾丸が身をかすめてぴゅんぴゅん飛んだ. Bullets zipped by me.
ひょいと ひょいと後ろを見た. I happened to look back.
ひよう 費用はどのくらいかかりますか. How much will it cost? / 費用は1万円くらいになるだろう. The expenses will amount [come] to about 10,000 yen. / 費用は幾らかかっても構いません. I don't care about the expense [how much it costs].
ひょう⁴ その法案は200票対150票で可決された. The bill was passed by a vote of 200 to 150. / その候補者は2千票を得た. The candidate polled two thousand votes. / 国連内でアジア・アフリカ諸国の占める票数の比重は大なるものである. The Afro-Asian bloc has a large voting strength in the United Nations.

びょう² 廟 a mausoleum 《pl. -s, -lea》.
びょう³ 鋲 a rivet (金属板用の); a tack (敷き物などの); a hobnail (靴底の) ¶びょうを打つ drive in a tack; tack; rivet / 掲示を壁にびょうで止めて張り出す tack a notice to the wall.
ひょういもじ 表意文字 an ideogram; an ideograph.
びょういん 病院 a hospital ¶病院に入れる send sb to (a) hospital; put sb in (a) hospital; hospitalize / 病院に入っている be in (a) hospital / 病院看護婦 a hospital nurse / 病院船 a hospital ship.
ひょうおんもじ 表音文字 a phonogram.
ひょうか 評価 〈金額としての価値の〉 valuation; appraisal; assessment (課税のための); 〈抽象的な価値の〉 assessment, 《文》 evaluation, 《文》 appraisal ¶評価する 〈金額としての価値を〉 estimate the value 《of》; value; appraise; assess 〈sth for tax purposes〉; 〈抽象的な価値を〉 assess; rate; 《文》 appraise; 《文》 evaluate; 《文》 estimate the worth 《of》 / 高く[低く]評価する rate [do not rate] sth highly; place a high [low] value on sth; have a high [low] opinion of sth [sb] / 評価し直す reevaluate [《米》 revaluate] 《sb's achievements》 / 評価額 the estimated [appraised] value; an assessment. 文例⇩

ひょうが 氷河 a glacier ¶氷河期[時代] the glacial epoch [period, era]; the ice age / 氷河作用 glacial action.
ひょうかい¹ 氷海 a frozen sea.
ひょうかい² 氷塊 a lump [block, mass] of ice; 〈浮氷〉 an ice floe.
ひょうかい³ 氷解 ¶氷解する 〈疑問などが〉 be cleared; be dispelled. 文例⇩
びょうがい 病害 damage 《to the crops》 caused by blight or other plant diseases.
ひょうき 表記 ¶表記の mentioned [《文》 inscribed] on the face [outside] / 表記法 〈文字の〉 orthography; 〈数字・記号の〉 a notational system [convention]; (a system of) notation. 文例⇩
ひょうぎ 評議 ⇨ かいぎ¹, きょうぎ¹ ¶評議員 a councilor; 〈財団の〉 a trustee / 評議会 a council; 〈財団の〉 a meeting of the board of trustees. 文例⇩
びょうき 病気 〈一般に〉 (an) illness; (a) sickness; a disease; an ailment; 〈病例〉 a case; 〈局部的〉 (a) trouble; a complaint; a disorder; 〈弱点〉 a fault; 〈好み〉 a mania; a weakness ¶重い病気 a serious illness [case] / 軽い病気 a slight illness [《文》 indisposition] / 身体[心]の病気 illness of the body [mind]; a physical [mental] disease / 長い病気 a long [lingering] illness / 病気の sick; ill; unwell; indisposed ★《米》《英》共に限定用法では sick を用い,述語用法では《米》では sick,《英》では ill を用いるのが普通 / 病気が治る get over [《文》 recover from] one's illness; get well [better] (★ get better は get well とほとんど同じ意味でよく用いられる) / 病気を治す cure a disease / 病気を持っている disease-bearing 《animals》 / 病気になる[かかる] get [fall, be taken] ill / 食べ過ぎて病気になる make oneself ill by eating too much 《candy》 [too many 《cakes》]; eat oneself ill / 病気にかかっている have [suffer from] a disease / 病気である be sick [《文》 unwell]; be in poor [bad] health / 病気で倒れる come down with an illness / 《文》 succumb to a disease / 病気上がりの人 a convalescent (person); a person who has just recovered [who is recovering] from an illness / 病気欠席 absence on account of illness.

ひょうきん 剽軽 ¶ひょうきんな jocular; facetious; 《文》 droll / ひょうきんなことを言う say amusing things / ひょうきん者 a facetious person; a joker; a wag.
びょうきん 病菌 ⇨ びょうげん (病原菌).
ひょうぐ 表具 ⇨ ひょうそう¹ ¶表具師 a paper hanger.
びょうく 病苦 ¶病苦に悩む 《文》 suffer acutely from one's illness [ill health].
ひょうけいほうもん 表敬訪問 (pay) a courtesy call 《on》.
ひょうけつ¹ 氷結 ¶氷結する freeze; 〈氷が張る〉 be frozen 《over》; 〈(港などが)氷に閉ざされる〉 be icebound / 冬でも氷結しない be ice-free in winter. 文例⇩
ひょうけつ² 表決 ⇨ ぎけつ.
ひょうけつ³ 票決 (a) decision by vote; a vote; voting ¶票決する take a vote 《on》; vote 《on》 / 票決に付する put [《文》 submit] 《a bill》 to a vote.
ひょうけつ⁴ 評決 (a) decision; a verdict (陪審員などの).

ひょう⁵ 昨夜ひょうが降った. It hailed [There was a hailstorm] last night. / 作物に大きな ひょう害があった. The hailstorm inflicted great damage on the crops.
ひょうか あの家は2千万円に評価された. The value of that house was estimated at 20 million yen. | That house was valued at 20 million yen. / 僕は彼の提案をたいして評価していない. I do not rate his proposal highly [think much of his proposal].
ひょうかい³ これで疑問が氷解した. This has dispelled all my doubts. | This leaves absolutely no doubt on the matter.
ひょうき 表記の所に移転しました. I have moved to the address shown on the envelope.
ひょうぎ 評議一決した. The conference has come to a decision.
びょうき 彼は何の病気なのか. What is he suffering from? | What is wrong with him? / 病気になって初めて健康の有り難味がわかる. We do not appreciate the blessing of health till we lose it. / お父さんのご病気はいかがですか. How is your father? / 昨日は病気で学校へ出られなかった. I couldn't go to school yesterday because I was ill. | Illness prevented me from attending school yesterday. / 彼は死ぬまで病気を知らなかった. He never had a day of illness till the one that killed him. | His first illness was his last. / 病気を押して会に出た. He attended the meeting in spite of illness. / 株に手を出すのが彼の病気だ. He has a weakness for dabbling in stocks.
ひょうけつ¹ 諏訪湖はすっかり氷結した. Lake Suwa is completely

ひょうげん¹ 氷原 an ice field; ⟨海上の⟩ an ice floe.

ひょうげん² 表現 (an) expression ¶適切な表現 an apt [(文) a happy] expression / 表現する ress; (文) be expressive of; represent/ 表現の自由 freedom of expression / 表現主義 expressionism / 表現派 the expressionist school; the expressionists / 表現力 power of expression; (文) expressiveness; (文) expressive power / 表現力豊かな言葉 an expressive word [phrase]. 文例↓

ひょうげん³ 評言 a critical remark; a comment.

びょうげん 病原 the cause of a disease ¶病原菌 pathogenic [disease-causing] bacteria [germs].

ひょうご¹ 評語 ⟨批評の言葉⟩ ⇨ひょうげん³; ⟨A, B, C などで表わす成績の⟩ a grade.

ひょうご² 標語 a slogan; a motto (pl. -(e)s); a catchword.

びょうご 病後 ¶病後の人 a convalescent (person) / 病後の保養をする take good care of one's health after (an) illness; convalesce / 病後に after (an) illness.

ひょうこう 標高 a (land) height (of 3,200 meters) ⇨ かいばつ.

びょうこん 病根 ⟨病気の原因⟩ the cause of a disease; ⟨禍根⟩ (文) the root of an evil.

ひょうさつ 表[標]札 a nameplate; a door plate; a plate ¶表札を出す put up a nameplate.

ひょうざん 氷山 an iceberg ¶氷山の一角 the tip of an iceberg. 文例↓

ひょうし¹ 拍子 ⟨調子⟩ time; (a) rhythm; (文) a measure; 〔音楽〕 (a) musical time; ⟨弾み⟩ chance; the moment ¶拍子をそろえて in (measured) time / 拍子を合わす keep (good) time with [to] (the music) / 手で拍子をとる keep [beat] time with one's hands / …の拍子に in ⟨doing⟩; just as ⟨one does⟩; at the moment [instant] ⟨one does, of doing⟩ / その時の拍子で on the spur of the moment / 何かの拍子で by some chance / 二[三、四、六]拍子 simple duple [simple triple, quadruple, sextuple] time / 4分の2[8分の6]拍子で in two-four [six-eight] time. 文例↓

ひょうし² 表紙 a cover ¶表紙を付ける cover ⟨a book⟩; put the covers on ⟨a book⟩ / 布表紙 a cloth cover ⇨ かみびょうし, かわびょうし.

ひょうじ 表示 (an) indication; (an) expression ¶表示する show; (文) express; indicate.

びょうし 病死 death from (a) sickness ¶病死する die of illness; die from [of] a disease. 文例↓

ひょうしき 標識 a sign; a mark ¶航空[航路, 道路]標識 ⇨ こうくう², こうろ³, どうろ / 標識鳥 a bird marked with a band [(英) ring]; a banded [(英) ringed] bird / 標識灯 a beacon light. 文例↓

ひょうしぎ 拍子木 (beat) (wooden) clappers.

ひょうしつ 氷室 an ice room [house].

びょうしつ 病室 a sickroom.

ひょうしぬけ 拍子抜け ¶拍子抜けがする (suddenly) feel deflated; suddenly feel that it is [things are] pointless [purposeless]; 《口語》 have the wind taken out of one's sails (by); be disappointed (at the news); lose interest (in). 文例↓

びょうしゃ 描写 ⟨文章⟩ (a) description; ⟨絵文⟩ (文) (a) depiction ¶描写する ⟨文章で⟩ describe; give a ⟨vivid⟩ description [⟨good⟩ picture] of; ⟨絵または文章で⟩ (文) depict.

ひょうしゃく 評釈 explanatory notes; (an) annotation ¶評釈する supply [(文) furnish] ⟨a book⟩ with explanatory (and critical) notes; annotate.

びょうじゃく 病弱 ⇨ びょうしん.

ひょうじゅん 標準 a standard; a level (水準) ¶標準の standard; normal; average (平均の) / 標準化する standardize / 標準に達する[達しない] reach [fall short of] the standard [mark] / 標準価格 the standard price / 標準型 a standard type; standard size (寸法) / 標準記録 the standard record; ⟨競技会の予選通過の⟩ the qualifying standard ⟨time, distance⟩ / 標準語 the standard language ⟨of a nation, in a country⟩; standard Japanese [English, etc.] / 標準時 standard time; ⟨日本の⟩ Japanese Standard Time (略: JST) / 標準時計 a standard clock.

ひょうしょう¹ 表象 〔哲〕 an idea; a representation.

ひょうしょう² 表彰 ¶表彰する recognize ⟨sb's contribution⟩ publicly; (文) make a public recognition of ⟨sb's services⟩; (文) honor sb with a testimonial commending ⟨his achievements⟩ / 表彰式 a commendation ceremony; a ceremony of awarding an honor / 表彰状 a certificate of commendation; a testimonial / 表彰台 ⟨競技の⟩ a victory stand; a winners' podium. 文例↓

ひょうじょう¹ 氷上 ¶氷上の on (the) ice / 氷

---

frozen over.

ひょうげん² それは言葉では容易に表現しがたい. It's difficult to express in [put into] words.

ひょうざん このような大金も, 党が選挙に使った総額から見れば, ほんの氷山の一角に過ぎない. This large expenditure is only the tip of the iceberg of total party spending on the election. / 最近の一連の収賄事件は同省内にはびこる汚職の氷山の一角に過ぎない. The series of graft cases which have recently come to light is merely an indication of the corrupt practices which are prevalent among officials of the ministry.

ひょうし¹ 彼は溝を跳び越える拍子に財布を落とした. He dropped his wallet in attempting to jump over a ditch.

びょうし 病死者は 100名を越えた. More than 100 persons died of illness.

ひょうしき この道路の制限速度は 80キロです. 1キロごとに標識が出ています. The speed limit on this road is eighty kilometers an hour. Signs to that effect are posted at intervals of one kilometer.

ひょうしぬけ この報道に接して彼らは拍子抜けの体(てい)であった. They seemed disappointed at the news. | This report came as a disppointment to them.

ひょうじゅん 物事の判断は人によって標準が違う. People judge

上競技 ice sports / 氷上レビュー a revue on ice.

ひょうじょう² 表情 (an) expression; a look (目付き, 顔付き) ¶表情のある[に富んだ] full of expression; 《文》expressive / 表情のない[に乏しい] expressionless / 表情を硬くする look stern [grim]; one's face hardens.

びょうしょう 病床 a sickbed ¶病床にある be ill in bed; be laid up (with illness); be confined to bed (by illness).

びょうじょう 病状 the condition of a disease [patient] ¶病状が悪化[好転]する get worse [better]; take a turn for the worse [better]. 文例↓

びょうしん 病身 ill [poor] health;《文》a weak constitution ¶病身の sickly; weak;《文》infirm / 病身である be an invalid; be in poor health; have a weak [delicate] constitution.

ひょうする¹ 表する express; show;《文》manifest ¶感謝の意を表する express [show] one's gratitude / 敬意を表する pay one's respects 《to》/ 祝意[弔意]を表する offer one's congratulations [condolences] 《to》.

ひょうする² 評する ⇒ひひょう, ひょう.

びょうせい 病勢 the condition of a disease [patient] ¶病勢が改まる take a turn for the worse / 病勢が募る[進む] get [《文》become] worse;《文》progress unfavorably / 病勢が衰える improve; grow less serious; get better.

ひょうせつ¹ 氷雪 ice and snow ¶氷雪に閉ざされる be icebound.

ひょうせつ² 剽窃 plagiarism ¶剽窃する plagiarize 《sb, (from) sb's work》/ 剽窃者 a plagiarist. 文例↓

ひょうぜん 飄然 ⇒ふらりと.

ひょうそ 瘭疽《医》a whitlow; a felon.

ひょうそう 表装《書画の》mounting;《書籍の》binding ¶表装する mount 《a picture》; bind 《a book in leather》.

ひょうそう 表層 the outer(most) layer [stratum]; the surface [top] layer ¶表層なだれ a surface avalanche.

びょうそう 病巣 a focus 《pl. -es, -ci》.

ひょうだい 表[標]題《本の》a title;《論説などの》a heading;《写真・漫画などの》a caption ¶表題をつける give a title 《to a book》; entitle; headline 《an article '...'》; put a caption 《on》/ 標題音楽 program music. 文例↓

ひょうたん a (bottle) gourd ¶ひょうたん形

の gourd-shaped. 文例↓

びょうち 錨地 an anchorage.

ひょうちゃく 漂着 ¶漂着する be cast [thrown, washed] ashore; drift ashore.

ひょうちゅう 氷柱《夏室内に置く》a block of ice;《つらら》⇒つらら.

びょうちゅう 病中 ¶病中に during one's illness; while one is ill [sick] ⇒びょうき.

びょうちゅうがい 病虫害 damage 《to crops》caused by diseases and insects.

ひょうてい 評定 rating;《文》evaluation ¶評定する rate;《文》evaluate.

ひょうてき 標的 ⇒まと ¶標的艦 a target ship /《ミサイル実験の》標的地域 a target area.

びょうてき 病的 ¶病的な pathological; morbid / 病的に pathologically; morbidly.

ひょうてん¹ 氷点 (the) freezing point ¶氷点下の温度 sub-zero temperature / 氷点下10度 ten degrees of frost [below zero]. 文例↓

ひょうてん² 評点《点数》marks;《段階点》a grade; grading ⇒ てん² 用法.

ひょうでん¹ 票田 a (reliable) source of votes; an area of strong electoral support 《for》.

ひょうでん² 評伝 a critical biography.

ひょうど 表土 surface soil; topsoil.

びょうとう 病棟 a (hospital) ward.

びょうどう 平等 equality ¶平等の equal; even / 平等に equally; evenly;《差別なく》impartially;《文》without discrimination /《平等にする》make《A and B》equal; equalize《A with B》; level (down, up); place《them》on an equal footing / 平等に分ける divide sth equally《between, among》/ 平等主義 egalitarianism / 平等主義者 an egalitarian. 文例↓

びょうどく 病毒 a disease germ; a virus.

びょうにん 病人 a sick person; an invalid; the sick (総称);《患者》a patient; a case ¶病人らしく見える look sickly. 文例↓

ひょうのう 氷嚢 an ice bag [pack] ¶氷のうつり an ice bag suspender.

ひょうはく 漂白 bleaching; decoloration ¶漂白する bleach; decolor(ize) / 漂白剤 a bleach; a bleaching agent; a decolorant.

ひょうばん 評判 (a) reputation;《文》repute;《名声》《文》fame;《人気》popularity;《悪評》notoriety;《うわさ》a report; (a) rumor ¶評判の famous; popular; much-talked-of; noted; notorious (悪名の高い) / 評判がいい[悪い] be well [《文》ill] spoken of; have a good [poor] reputation; be popular [unpopular] / 評判の

---

things by different standards. / その作品は標準以下ということで落とされた。The work was rejected as below standard. / 田中は三段跳びの標準記録15.50メートルを飛ばず, 予選で失格した。Tanaka was eliminated in the triple jump qualifying round as he failed to make the qualifying distance of 15.50 meters.

ひょうしょう 女子百メートル自由型の第3位までの入賞者が表彰台に上がった。The medalists [The first three] in the women's 100-meter freestyle mounted the podium.

びょうじょう 病状ははかばかしくない。His condition shows little improvement.

ひょうせつ² この小説は川端の「雪国」から剽窃したものと言われている。They say that the story is plagiarized from Kawabata's Snow Country.

ひょうだい 「生命の神秘」というのがその本の表題だ。The book is entitled 'The Mystery of Life.'

ひょうたん あの男はひょうたんなまずで, つかみどころがない。He is as slippery as an eel.

ひょうてん¹ 寒暖計は氷点下5度を示していた。The mercury stood at 5° below freezing (point).

びょうどう 我々はすべて法の前には平等である。We are all equal before [in the eye of] the law.

びょうにん 今年は病人が多い。We have [There is] a great deal of sickness this year. / 家に病人

ひょうひ／評判を立てる start [spread, set afloat] a rumor／評判を落とす lose *one's* good reputation;《文》fall into disrepute [in public estimation]／評判になる be talked about；become popular；win popularity／…という評判である It is rumored that…; They [People] say that…. 文例⇩

ひょうひ 表皮《解・動》the outer(most) layer of the skin；the cuticle；the epidermis.

ひょうひょう 飄々 ¶ひょうひょうと〈当てどなく〉(go) wandering；〈超然と〉《文》aloof from the world.

びょうぶ 屏風 a folding screen ¶びょうぶを立て回す set a folding screen all around／六枚びょうぶ a folding screen with six panels；a six-fold screen／びょうぶ岩 a sheer [perpendicular] cliff.

ひょうへき 氷壁〈山の〉an ice wall [cliff].

ひょうへん 豹変 ¶豹変する change suddenly；〈変節する〉turn traitor；turn *one's* coat ⇒くんし.

ひょうぼう 標榜 ¶標榜する〈公言する〉《文》profess (*oneself* to be a feminist)；〈旗印にする〉adopt *sth* as *one's* slogan [motto]；〈主張する〉《文》advocate (champion, espouse)《the cause of humanitarianism》.

ひょうほん 標本 a specimen；〈見本〉a sample；〈典型〉a type；an example ¶動物標本 a zoological [botanical] specimen／はく製の標本 a stuffed [mounted] specimen《of a bird》／標本室 a specimen room／〈植物の〉a herbarium《pl. -ums, -ia》.

ひょうめい 表明 ¶表明する《文》state；express；show；《文》manifest／感謝の意を表明する express *one's* gratitude／反対を表明する declare [come out] against 《the plan》.

びょうめい 病名 the name of a disease ¶病名のわからない病気 an unidentified disease.

ひょうめん 表面 the surface；the face；〈外部〉the outside；《文》the exterior；〈外見〉(an) appearance；《文》apparent；〈見かけの〉seeming；《文》ostensible／表面の outside；《文》external；outward；〈うわべの〉superficial；surface；《文》apparent；〈見かけの〉seeming；《文》ostensible／表面下の subsurface／表面上[的には] superficially；《文》externally；outwardly；apparently；《文》ostensibly／表面に現われる，表面化する come to the surface [fore]；come into the open／表面張力《物》surface tension. 文例⇩

ひょうめんせき 表面積 surface area.

ひょうり 表裏〈表と裏〉inside and outside；〈両面〉two sides《of sth》¶表裏のある two-faced；double-dealing；treacherous／表裏のない single-hearted；《文》faithful；honest. 文例⇩

びょうりがく 病理学 pathology ¶病理学者 a pathologist／病理学的 pathological.

ひょうりゅう 漂流 ¶漂流する drift (about)；be adrift／漂流者 a person adrift on the sea；a castaway (on an island)／漂流船 a drifting ship；a derelict ship (遺棄された)／漂流物 floating wreckage；floatage；flotsam.

びょうれき 病歴 a case [medical] history.

ひょうろう 兵糧 food；provisions ¶兵糧が尽きる[乏しくなる] run out [short] of provisions／兵糧攻めにする cut off the supply of food；starve (out)《the enemy》. 文例⇩

ひょうろん 評論〈批評〉(a) criticism；〈時評〉a review；(a) comment ¶評論する criticize；review；comment (on)／評論家 a commentator；a critic／文芸評論家 a literary critic／野球評論家 a baseball commentator／評論雑誌 a review.

ひよく 肥沃 ¶肥沃な fertile；rich.

びよく 尾翼《航空》the tail assembly [unit]《of an aircraft》；the empennage《of an airplane》.

ひよけ 日よけ a sunshade；a sunscreen (すだれなど)；an awning (店頭などの布製の)；a blind (窓の) ¶日よけをする screen [shade] *sth* from the sun；spread an awning over《a place》／窓の日よけを降ろす pull the blinds down.

ひよこ a chick.

ひょこひょこ〈歩き方〉lightly；〈時々〉at times；from time to time ¶ひょこひょこ歩く trip (along)；〈ほっつき歩く〉gad about.

ぴょこんと ¶ぴょこんと頭を下げる bob *one's* head《to sb》.

ひょっこり〈不意に〉unexpectedly；〈偶然〉accidentally；by chance ¶ひょっこり現われる appear unexpectedly；pop up [in]. 文例⇩

ひょっと ¶ひょっとして[したら] possibly；by (some) chance. 文例⇩

がおりますので会には出席いたしかねます. I cannot attend the meeting owing to sickness in my family.

ひょうばん 彼は教え方がうまいという評判だ. He has a reputation for being a good teacher.／彼は学生間に評判がいい. He is popular with the students.／彼はこれで店の評判をよくしたいと思った. He hoped that it would give his store a good name.／彼は町中の評判となった. He has become the talk of the town.／あの役者は評判ほどではない. He is not as great an actor as he is reputed to be.／あの俳優の腕は評判倒れだ. That actor's ability falls short of his reputation.／そのオペラは大変な前評判だった. The opera was widely talked about before it opened [before its first night].

ひょうめん 事の真相は決して表面のみを見てわかるものではない. One cannot see the true state of affairs simply from appearances.／あの人は表面に出るのが嫌いだ. He wants to stay in the background.

ひょうり 表裏のある男だ. He is a double-dealer.｜He is two-faced.

ひょうろう 彼らは兵糧が尽きた. Their provisions have run out.

ひょっこり 佐藤君がひょっこりやって来た. I had an unexpected visit from Sato.／そこでひょっこり武藤君に会った. I ran into [across] Muto there.

ひょっと ひょっとしたら彼は外出したかもしれない. He may possibly have gone out.／ひょっとしたらご在宅かもしれないと思って伺いました. I came on the (off) chance of finding you at home.／ひょっとして私はこういう人の名を知っていませんか. Do you happen to know anyone of this name?

ひよどり 《烏》 a (brown-eared) bulbul.
ぴよぴよ ¶ぴよぴよ鳴く peep; cheep.
ひより 日和 〈天候〉 weather; 〈晴天〉 fine [《文》fair] weather / 日和見する wait and see (how the wind blows); sit on the fence; wait for the cat to jump / 日和見主義 opportunism; fence-sitting / 日和見主義者 an opportunist; a fence-sitter. 文例⇩
ひょろながい ひょろ長い long and narrow; tall and slender; lanky; spindly; gangling.
ひょろひょろ ¶ひょろひょろする stagger; totter; reel / ひょろひょろ歩く walk unsteadily; walk with unsteady [faltering] steps / ひょろひょろした 〈細長い〉 tall and slender / 〈やせた〉 lanky / 〈よろめく〉 staggering; tottering; unsteady.
ひよわ ひ弱 ¶ひ弱な weak; delicate.
ぴょんぴょん ¶ぴょんぴょん飛ぶ[跳ねる] hop; skip; 〈跳ね回る〉 romp; frisk.
ひら- 平… ¶平教員 a common teacher / 平社員 a mere clerk / 平党員 a rank-and-file member (of a party).
ビラ 〈ちらし〉 a (hand)bill; a leaflet; 〈張り紙〉 a placard; a poster ¶ビラを張る stick [paste up] a bill; put up a poster / ビラをまく distribute bills.
ひらあやまり 平謝り ¶平謝りに謝る make a humble apology; humbly [《文》abjectly] beg sb's pardon.
ひらい 飛来 ¶飛来する come flying; come by air [plane].
ひらいしん 避雷針 a lightning rod [conductor].
ひらおよぎ 平泳ぎ the breaststroke ¶平泳ぎの選手 a breaststroke swimmer / 平泳ぎをする swim (the) breaststroke.
ひらがな 平仮名 hiragana; the cursive form of kana; 〈個々の〉 a hiragana character ⇨ かな.
ひらき 開き 〈開くこと〉 opening; 〈差〉 a gap; (a) difference; 《文》 (a) disparity; a margin; 〈魚の〉 an opened and dried fish ¶年齢の開き an age difference; (a) disparity of [in] age / AとBの開きの the difference between A and B / 大きな開きがある 《文》 differ greatly (from); there is a great difference (between) / お開き ⇨ おひらき / 開き戸 a (hinged) door / 開き封 ⇨ かいふう². 文例⇩
-びらき …開き ¶店開き opening of business

[the new store]. 文例⇩
ひらきなおる 開き直る (suddenly) take the offensive; take a 'so-what' attitude 《toward》; turn on sb.
ひらく 開く 〈開ける〉 open; uncover (覆いを取る); lift (ふたを); 〈広げる〉 unfold; unroll (巻いたものを); 〈包装を〉 解く undo; unpack; untie; 〈開封する〉 unseal; 〈開始する〉 begin; start; 〈開墾する〉 clear (land); break 《fresh ground》; 〈開拓する〉 open (up) 《new territory》; develop 《a tract of land》; pioneer 《Hokkaido》; 〈創設する〉 found; establish; set up; 〈開催する〉 open; hold; give; 〈咲く〉 bloom; come out ¶店を開く open [start, set up] a store.
ひらぐも 平蜘蛛 ¶ひらぐものようになって謝る 《文》 prostrate oneself and make an abject apology; beg sb's pardon on one's knees [《文》 on bended knee(s)].
ひらける 開ける 〈文明化する〉 be [《文》 become] civilized; 〈発展する〉 develop; 〈物わかりがよくなる〉 be 《文》 become] sensible; learn what is what; 〈開通する〉 be opened to traffic; 〈景色などが〉 open (out) ¶開けた[開けない]国 a civilized [an uncivilized] country; an advanced [underdeveloped] country / 開けた人 an open-minded person; a man [woman] of the world. 文例⇩
ひらぞこ 平底 a flat bottom ¶平底船 a flat-bottomed boat [barge]; a flatboat.
ひらたい 平たい 〈偏平な〉 flat; 〈平坦な〉 even; level ¶平たくする flatten; level / 平たく言えば in plain words [language]; to put it plainly.
ひらて 平手 an open hand ¶平手で打つ slap; give sb a slap / 平手で(将棋を)指す play a game of shogi with no handicap.
ひらどま 平土間 《米》the parquet; 《英》the pit.
ひらに 平に humbly; 《文》 earnestly. 文例⇩
ピラニア 《魚》 a piranha.
ひらひら 〈飛ぶ〉 fluttering(ly); 〈薄片になって〉 in flakes ¶ひらひらする flutter; flap / 風にひらひら散る fall fluttering in the wind.
ピラフ 《料理》 pilaf(f); pilau. 文例⇩
ひらべったい 平べったい flat; even; level.
ピラミッド a pyramid ¶ギザの大ピラミッド the (Great) Pyramids of Giza / ピラミッド型の pyramidal. 文例⇩

ひより 今日は行楽に出かけるには絶好の日和だ. The weather today is ideal for an outing.
ひらき 組合側の要求と会社側の回答との間には5万円の開きがあり, 妥結は困難であった. A gap of 50,000 yen between the union's demand and the company's offer was holding up a settlement.
-びらき 昨日はうちの学校でプール開きがあった. The swimming pool of our school was officially opened for the season yesterday.
ひらく この戸は内[外]側に開く. This door opens [swings] inward [outward]. / 彼は銀座に店を開いている. He keeps [runs] a store on the Ginza. / 豊田氏帰国の祝宴が開かれた. A dinner was given in honor of Mr. Toyoda who has recently returned from abroad. / 頼朝は幕府を鎌倉に開いた. Yoritomo established his Shogunate at Kamakura. / 両者の距離がぐんぐん開いた. The distance between them widened steadily [became greater and greater].
ひらける この国も今ではなかなか開けてきた. It is now quite a civilized country. / この辺も近ごろは非常に開けてきた. This neighborhood has been considerably developed [built up] lately. / 彼の運が開けた. Fortune smiled on him. / 今は苦しいが, 努力すれば道は開けるでしょう. Things may be hard now, but keep trying and you'll find a way out.
ひらに 平にご容赦願います. I humbly beg your pardon.
ひらひら 旗が風にひらひら翻っている. The flag is flapping [fluttering] in the wind.
ピラミッド 家族はピラミッド形社会経済組織の基底をなすものである. The family forms the base of

ひらめ 《魚》a (left-eyed) flounder; a plaice; a sole (したびらめ).
ひらめき 閃き a flash. 文例↓
ひらめく 閃く〈電光が〉flash;〈灯が〉flicker. 文例↓
ひらや 平屋 a house of one story [《英》storey]; a one-storied house.
ひらりと quickly; nimbly ¶ひらりと馬にまたがる[から下りる] spring on [off] the [one's] horse; swing (up) into [swing from] the saddle.
びり ¶びりである be the last on the list; be at the bottom 《of one's class》/ (競走でびりになる finish [come in] last / びりで卒業する graduate last on the list / びりから 2 [3] 番目 the last but one [two].
ピリオド a period; a full stop ¶ピリオドを打つ put a period 《to》.
ひりき 非力 non [powerless]; weak.
ひりつ 比率 a ratio (pl. -s); a percentage ¶ 5.5.3 の比率 (at) a five-five-three ratio.
ひりっと ¶ぴりっとする〈辛辣(とう)な〉pungent; biting; racy;〈辛(な)い〉hot ⇒ぴりぴり. 文例↓
ひりひり ¶ひりひりする〈痛くて〉smart《with pain》; sting;〈味が〉be hot; be pungent. 文例↓
ぴりぴり ¶ぴりぴり裂く tear up《a sheet of paper》(into scraps [pieces]); rip (up)《a piece of cloth》/ ぴりぴりと震動する tremble; vibrate. 文例↓
ぴりぴり ¶ぴりぴりする《痛んで》smart《with pain》; tingle; sting;〈辛(な)くて〉be hot; burn [sting]《one's tongue》;〈恐くて〉go [get,《文》become] tense. 文例↓
びりゅうし 微粒子 a minute [tiny] particle; a fine grain;《物》a corpuscule.
ひりょう 肥料 manure; (a) fertilizer ¶肥料を施す manure; put manure《on, in》; fertilize / 肥料工場 a fertilizer plant [mill].
用法 manure は, horse manure や green manure というように, 動物の排泄物や草など自然の肥料をさすのに対して, fertilizer は化学肥料など人工のものをさすのが普通である.
びりょう 微量 a very small quantity ¶微量天びん a microbalance.
びりょく 微力 ¶微力を尽くす do one's bit [best]; do what (little) one can.
ひる¹ 昼〈正午〉noon; midday;〈昼間〉the daytime ¶昼に at noon (正午に); at lunchtime (昼飯ごろ) / 昼から, 昼過ぎに in the afternoon / 昼となく夜となく around [round] the clock; at all hours of the day and night; night and day; day in, day out / 昼下がりに a little after noon; in the early afternoon / 昼日中に in broad daylight / 昼前に in the morning; before noon / 昼休み a [one's] lunch hour [break]; a noon recess. 文例↓
ひる² 《動》a leech.
ビル a building; an office building ¶ビル街 a street of office buildings. 文例↓
ピル a (contraceptive) pill; the pill ¶ピルを飲む take the pill / ピルを飲み始める[飲んでいる] go [be] on the pill.
ひるい 比類 ¶比類のない《文》peerless;《文》unparalleled; unique. 文例↓
ひるがえす 翻す〈ひっくり返す〉turn (over);〈風に〉なびかせる〉wave; flutter ¶決心を翻す change one's mind; alter one's decision;《文》give up one's resolution / 前言を翻す take back what one said; go back on one's word / 身を翻す turn aside 《about》.
ひるがえる 翻る wave; flutter; flap; fly; stream ¶風に翻る wave [flutter] in the wind / 翻って考えるに on reflection; on second thought(s). 文例↓
ひるがお 《植》a convolvulus (pl. -luses, -li).
ひるこうぎょう 昼興行 a matinee.
ひるね 昼寝 ¶昼寝をする take a (midday) nap.
ひるま 昼間 in [during] the daytime ¶昼間中 all (through) the daylight hours.
ビルマ Burma ¶ビルマの Burmese / ビルマ人 a Burmese《単複同形》/ ビルマ連邦社会主義共和国 the Socialist Republic of the Union of Burma.
ひるむ flinch (from); shrink (from); recoil (from, before, at); quail (at, before); wince (at) ¶困難にひるむ flinch from difficulties;《文》be daunted by the difficulties / ひるまずに without flinching;《文》undaunted (by);《文》dauntlessly. 文例↓
ひるめし 昼飯 lunch; a midday meal ⇒ゆうしょく¹ 用法 ¶昼飯を食べる have lunch / 昼飯時に at lunchtime.
ひれ 鰭 a fin ¶尻びれ an anal fin / 背[胸, 腹, 尾]びれ a dorsal [pectral, ventral, caudal] fin / ひれ足 a flipper.
ヒレ〈肉〉a fillet.
ひれい¹ 比例 proportion; the rule of three (比例法) ¶比例する be proportional [proportionate]《to》; be in proportion《to》/ …に比

a socioeconomic pyramid.
ひらめき 彼には天才のひらめきがある. He shows flashes of genius.
ひらめく 西の空で時々稲妻がひらめいた. I saw occasional flashes of lightning in the western sky. / 彼が犯人ではなかろうかという疑いが僕の胸にひらめいた. The suspicion flashed on me [across my mind] that he might be the offender.
びりっと からしは舌にぴりっとくる. Mustard burns your tongue.

ひりひり せっけんで目がひりひりする. My eyes are stinging from the soap.
びりびり 電気がびりびりっと来た. I had [felt] an electric shock.
ぴりぴり 日に焼けて背中がぴりぴりする. My back smarts from sunburn. / 社員は皆彼の前ではぴりぴりしている. All his employees are scared [on their toes] in his presence.
ひる¹ 昼もお暗い山道を通った. We went through a pass where

it was dark even in the daytime. / 彼は昼働いて夜学校へ行く. He works by day and attends school by night.
ビル 市内はビルラッシュだ. There are new buildings going up [being built] everywhere in the city.
ひるい 世界に比類がない[を見ない]. There is nothing like [to compare with] it anywhere in the world. | It is unique [peerless] in the world.

例して in proportion to... / 比例代表 proportional representation / 比例式 a proportional expression / 比例中項 a geometric mean / 比例配分 proportional allotment. 文例⇩

ひれい² 非礼 impoliteness ⇨ ぶれい.

ひれき 披瀝〔瀝〕 ¶披瀝する express 《one's》 opinion; 《文》 lay bare 《one's heart》; reveal 《one's intentions》.

ひれつ 卑劣 ¶卑劣な 《文》 mean; 《文》 base; low; shabby; 《文》 dastardly / 卑劣な手段 a dirty [nasty] trick / 卑劣なことをする play foul; hit [strike] sb below the belt.

ピレネー ¶ピレネー山脈 the Pyrenees.

ひれふす ひれ伏す ⇨ へいふく¹.

ひれん 悲恋 tragic love.

ひろ 尋 a fathom ¶水深5ひろ be five fathoms deep [in depth].

ひろい 広い wide; broad; 〈広大な〉 vast; large; 《文》 extensive; 《文》 spacious ¶広い部屋 a large [《文》 spacious] room / 広い家 a house [《文》 spacious, 《文》 commodious] house / 学問の広い人 a person of extensive learning / 心の広い人 a broad-minded [big-hearted] person / 広く widely; extensively; far and wide / 〈あまねく,一般に〉 universally; generally; at large / 広くする widen; broaden; extend; enlarge. 文例⇩

ひろいぬし 拾い主 the finder (of lost property).

ひろいもの 拾い物 a thing that has been picked up [found] on the road; a find; 〈得な買物〉 a bargain.

ひろいよみ 拾い読み ¶拾い読みする 〈とびとびに読む〉 read 《a book》 here and there; skim through 《a book》; 〈一字一字たどって読む〉 read slowly, letter by letter; spell out.

ヒロイン a heroine.

ひろう¹ 披露 an announcement (告知); (an) introduction (紹介); (an) advertisement (広告) ¶ひろうする announce; introduce; advertise / 結婚ひろう宴 ⇨ けっこん².

ひろう² 疲労 ひろうれる, つかれる ¶金属疲労 metal fatigue / 精神的[肉体的]疲労 mental [physical] fatigue. 文例⇩

ひろう³ 拾う 〈落ちている物を〉 pick up; 〈採集する〉 gather; 〈見つける〉 find; 〈選び出す〉 pick out ¶落ち穂を拾う gather [pick up] grain left behind by reapers; glean / タクシーを拾う find [pick up] a taxi / 道を拾って歩く pick one's way 《through, to》 / 拾い上げる pick up / 拾い集める gather / 拾い出す pick [sort, single] out.

びろう 尾籠 ¶びろうな dirty; scurrilous / びろうな話ですが It's an indelicate matter to mention, but...

ビロード velvet ¶ビロードのような velvety.

ひろがり 広がり extent; a stretch (of land); an expanse (of water).

ひろがる 広がる spread (out); extend; stretch; reach (to); 〈うわさが〉 get around [about, 《文》 abroad].

ひろげる 広げる 〈拡大する〉 spread; extend; expand; enlarge; 〈幅を〉 widen; broaden; 〈開けるを〉 unfold; open; unroll 〈巻物を〉 ¶運動場を広げる enlarge the playground / 毛布を広げる spread [lay out] a blanket / 手を広げる open one's arms; 〈商売の〉 extend one's business. 文例⇩

ひろさ 広さ 《文》 extent; area; 〈幅〉 width; breadth.

ひろば 広場 an open space; a (public) square ¶トラファルガー広場 Trafalgar Square.

ひろびろ 広々 ¶広々した open; wide; 《文》 spacious; 《文》 extensive; 〈家の〉 roomy; 《文》 commodious / 広々(と)した庭 a large [spacious] garden.

ひろま 広間 a hall.

ひろまる 広まる spread; 《文》 spread abroad; 《文》 be diffused; 《文》 be disseminated; 〈うわさなどが〉 spread; get abroad [about, around]; 〈流行する〉 come into fashion [vogue]; become popular.

ひろめる 広める 〈普及させる〉 spread; 《文》 diffuse; 《文》 disseminate; 《文》 propagate; make sth popular; popularize; 〈広くする〉 extend; widen; broaden ¶情報を広める spread [diffuse, disseminate] information 《about, concerning》 / 知識を広める extend [broaden] one's knowledge; add to one's stock of knowledge / 仏教を広める propagate Buddhism.

ひわ¹ 秘話 a secret story; an unknown episode.

ひわ² 〔鳥〕 a siskin.

びわ¹ 琵琶 a biwa; a four-stringed Japanese lute / びわ法師 a biwa-playing minstrel; a lute player.

びわ² 〔植〕 a loquat.

ひわい 卑猥 ¶卑猥な dirty; indecent; obscene.

ひわり 日割り 〈日程〉 a program; a schedule ¶日割りを定める fix [settle, make up] a sched-

---

ひるがえる 翻って我が国の現状を見るに寒心にたえぬことが多い. And now, turning (our attention) to the present state of affairs in our country, we find a lot of things which make us entertain grave apprehensions.

ひるむ 押し寄せる大軍を見て彼らはひるんだ. Their spirits failed [They quailed] in face of the vast army marching against them. / ひるむな. Don't be afraid (of it). / 少しもひるまずにその山道を登り始めた. Nothing daunted, they began walking up the mountain path.

ひれい¹ 惑星の公転周期の自乗は太陽からの平均距離の3乗に比例する. The squares of the periodic times of any planets are proportional [in proportion] to the cubes of their mean distances from the sun.

ひろい 彼は交際が広い. He has a large circle of acquaintances. / 彼は日本文学を広く読んでいる. He has read widely [extensively] in Japanese literature.

ひろいもの これは意外な拾い物だ. This is a lucky find [a windfall]. / 拾い物はもらい物. Finders keepers. 〔諺〕

ひろう² 彼は疲労の色が濃い. He looks very tired.

ひろう³ 僕は往来でこの時計を拾った. I found this watch on the road.

ひろがる 火事は四方に広がった. The fire spread in all directions.

ひろげる 机の上に地図が広げてあった. A map lay spread out on the desk. / 彼は両手を広げて我々

ひわれ / ひんそう

ule ; make a program / 日割りで払う pay by the day / 日割り勘定[計算] payment by the day.

ひわれ 干割れ ¶干割れする dry (up) and crack.

ひん 品〈文〉grace ; refinement ; dignity ¶品のよい graceful ; elegant ; refined ; dignified / 品のない vulgar ; unrefined ; coarse. 文例⇩

びん¹ 便〈郵便〉《米》mail ;《英》post ;〈配達〉delivery ;〈飛行機の〉a flight ¶次の便で〈郵便〉by the next mail ;〈船や飛行機〉on the next boat [flight]. 文例⇩

びん² 瓶 a bottle.

びん³ 鬢 the hair on the temples.

びん⁴ 敏 ¶機を見るに敏である be quick at seizing an opportunity ;《口語》have an eye on [to] the main chance.

ピン¹ a pin ;〈束髪用の〉a hairpin ¶ピンで留める fasten with a pin ; pin (up) (to, on) / ...からピンを抜く take (the) pins out of [remove pins from] *sth* ; unpin (a dress) / ピンカール a pin curl.

ピン² [<ポルトガル語 *pinta*] 文例⇩

ひんい 品位 dignity ;〈文〉grace ¶品位のある dignified ; graceful / 品位を落とす lose *one's* dignity ; degrade *oneself* / 品位を保つ keep *one's* dignity.

ひんかく 品格 ⇨ ひん, ひんい.

びんかん 敏感 ¶敏感な sensitive (to) ;〈文〉susceptible (to) / 暑さにひどく敏感である be very sensitive to heat ; be hypersensitive [supersensitive] to heat.

ひんく 貧苦 (the hardships of) poverty. 文例⇩

ピンク pink.

ひんけつ(しょう)貧血(症) anemia ¶貧血している, 貧血症である be anemic ; suffer from anemia.

ひんこう 品行〈文〉(moral) conduct ; behavior ¶品行のよい[悪い] well-[badly-]behaved / 品行方正な[品行の悪い]人〈文〉a man of good conduct [loose morals]. 文例⇩

ひんこん 貧困〈貧乏〉poverty ;〈文〉penury ;〈窮乏〉need ;〈文〉destitution ;〈不足〉shortage ;〈文〉want ; lack ¶貧困な poor ; needy ;〈文〉destitute / 貧困な人たち the poor (and needy) / 思想が貧困である〈文〉be intellectually incompetent [destitute] ; be short of [lacking in] ideas / 貧困に陥る be reduced to poverty [penury] / 貧困にあえぐ suffer extreme [〈文〉dire] poverty / 貧困家庭 a poor family.

ひんし¹ 品詞『文法』a part of speech.

ひんし² 瀕死 ¶瀕死の dying / 瀕死の病人 a dying patient / 瀕死の状態にある be dying ; be on the verge of death ;〈危篤である〉be critically ill. 文例⇩

ひんじ 賓辞『論理』the predicate ;『文法』an object.

ひんしつ 品質 a quality ¶品質のよい(high-)quality ;〈文〉of high [good] quality / 品質の悪い poor-[low-]quality ;〈文〉of poor [low] quality / 様々な品質の品を製造する manufacture goods in various qualities / 品質管理 quality control / 品質保証(付き)『表示』Quality guaranteed.

ひんじゃ 貧者 ⇨ びんぼう(貧乏人)¶貧者の一灯 a widow's mite.

ひんじゃく 貧弱 ¶貧弱な poor ; scanty ;〈文〉meager / 貧弱な家 a humble [shabby] cottage / (風采の)貧弱な男 an unimposing-looking man / 貧弱な食事 a scanty meal / 内容が貧弱である〈文〉be poor in content [substance] ; lack substance.

ひんしゅ 品種 a variety ; a breed ¶品種改良 breed improvement ; selective breeding ((of cattle [rice plants])).

ひんしゅく 顰蹙を買う disgust [scandalize] *sb* ; be frowned at [on] by *sb* ;〈文〉incur *sb's* displeasure.

ひんしゅつ 頻出 ¶頻出する appear [occur] frequently ;〈文〉be of frequent occurrence ; be frequent.

びんしょう 敏捷 ¶敏捷な〈動作が〉quick ; nimble ; prompt ;〈文〉agile ;〈性質が〉sharp ; shrewd ; smart / 敏捷に quickly ; nimbly ; promptly ;〈文〉with agility / 行動が敏捷である be quick in action.

びんじょう 便乗 ¶便乗する〈乗り物に〉《文》take passage in (a steamer) ; get a lift in (*sb's* car) ;〈利用する〉《文》avail *oneself* of ((an opportunity)) ; take advantage of ((the trend of public opinion)) / 便乗値上げ taking advantage of a general rise in prices to raise the prices ((of *one's* own goods)) ; 'me-too' price-raising.

ヒンズー教 Hinduism / ヒンズー教徒 a Hindu.

ひんする 瀕する be on the point [verge, brink] of ((bankruptcy)). 文例⇩

ひんせい 品性 character ¶品性の立派な[卑しい]人《文》a man of noble [mean] character / 品性を陶冶(とうや)する《文》cultivate [build (up)] *one's* character.

ピンセット [<フランス語 *pincettes*] (a pair of) tweezers.

びんせん 便箋 letter paper ; a writing [letter] pad (とじ込みの).

ひんそう 貧相 ¶貧相な poor-looking ; seedy.

の前に立った。He stood before us with outstretched [open] arms.
ひん 彼女は品がある。She is refined in her manner. / 彼には少しも品がない。There is not a bit of refinement in his manner.
びん¹ 日航はロスアンゼルス行きを週に5便出している。JAL runs [operates] five flights a week to Los Angeles. / 503便に座席を予約しているはずです。There should be a seat reserved[booked] for me on Flight 503.
ピン² 教師にもピンからキリまである。There are all sorts of schoolteachers.
ひんい 学問は人の品位を高める。Learning ennobles a man. / そんな事をすると君の品位が下がる。To behave like that is beneath your dignity.
ひんく 彼は貧苦のあまり盗みをした。He committed theft under the pressure of poverty. | Poverty drove him to the theft.
ひんこう 彼は品行がよい。He behaves [conducts himself] very well. | His conduct [behavior] is good.
ひんし² 彼は瀕死の重傷を負った。

びんそく 敏速 ⇨ びんしょう.
びんた ¶びんたを食わす box *sb's* ears; slap *sb* on the cheek [in the face].
ピンチ a crisis《*pl.* crises》; an emergency; a pinch; a critical situation;《米口語》a clutch (特にスポーツでの) ¶ピンチを切り抜ける manage to pull through a crisis / ピンチに立つ be [find *oneself*] in a fix [predicament] / ピンチに固くなる choke up [tighten up] in the clutch / ピンチに強い[弱い]バッター a good [bad] batter in a clutch / ピンチヒッター[ランナー]《野球》a pinch hitter [runner]. 文例⇩
びんづめ 瓶詰め ¶瓶詰めのビール bottled beer / 瓶詰めで売る sell (vinegar) in bottles.
ヒント a hint ¶ヒントを与える give *sb* a hint; drop a hint / ヒントを得る get [take] a hint (from).
ひんど 頻度 frequency ¶使用頻度 frequency in use《of a word》. 文例⇩
びんと ¶指先でぴんとはじく flip / ぴんと割れる break with a crack; crack / 綱をぴんと張る stretch a rope taut; tighten a rope / ぴんと来る《事が主語》come home to *one*;《人が主語》catch on (quickly) (★ 目的語は不要); understand [make out] at once《what *sb* is driving at》.
ピント [<《オランダ語》*punt*]《焦点》a focus《*pl.* -es, foci》¶ピントが合っている[外れている] be in [out of] focus;《要点に》be to [off] the point / ピントを合わせる focus《*one's* camera》on《an object》; bring《an object》into focus.
ひんのう 貧農 a poor farmer [peasant].
ひんぱつ 頻発《文》frequent occurrence ¶頻発する often happen;《文》occur frequently.
ピンはね a cut; a rake-off;《米》a kickback ¶ピンはねする take (500 yen) off《*sb's* wages》; take a cut《off *sb's* wages》; pocket a rake-off《《米》kickback》.
ひんぱん 頻繁 ¶頻繁な frequent;《文》of frequent occurrence / 交通の頻繁な通り a busy street / 頻繁に very often; frequently; at frequent intervals. 文例⇩

ひんぴょうかい 品評会 a competitive [prize] show; an exhibition;《米》a fair ¶花卉品評会 a flower [horticultural] show / 農産物品評会 an agricultural fair.
びんびんしている ‹元気である› be brimming over with health and vitality; be in the best of health; be lively; be alive and kicking; be as fit as a fiddle [flea]; ‹老人が› be hale and hearty; ‹生きがいい› be fresh.
ひんぴんと 頻々と very often; frequently; at frequent intervals; in rapid succession. 文例⇩
ひんぷ 貧富 wealth and poverty; ‹人› (the) rich and (the) poor ¶貧富の差《文》disparity in wealth / 貧富の別なく rich and poor alike. 文例⇩
びんぼう 貧乏 poverty;《文》penury;《文》destitution ¶貧乏な poor; needy;《文》destitute / 貧乏する become poor; be reduced to poverty [penury] / 貧乏している be poor;《文》be in poverty;《文》be in needy [reduced] circumstances; be badly off / 貧乏に生まれる be born poor [to poverty] / 貧乏暮らしをする live in poverty [penury] / 貧乏くじを引く be the least lucky of all; draw a bad lot / 貧乏人 a poor person; the poor (and needy) (総称) / 貧乏揺すりをする shake *oneself* [*one's* knee] nervously;《口語》jiggle *one's* leg [knee]. 文例⇩
びんぼけ ⇨ ピント (ピントが外れている).
ピンポン ⇨ たっきゅう.
ひんみん 貧民 poor people; the poor;《文》the needy.
ひんもく 品目 a list of articles [items].
ひんやり ¶ひんやりする feel pleasantly cool / ひんやりする木蔭 the cool shade of a tree.
びんろう〔植〕¶びんろう子 a betel [an areca] nut / びんろう樹 a betel [an areca] palm tree.
びんわん 敏腕 ¶敏腕な《文》able; capable; competent / 敏腕を振るう show [give full play to] *one's* ability / 敏腕家 an able [a competent] person;《文》a person of ability.

ふ

ふ¹ 歩〖将棋〗a pawn.
ふ² 府 ‹行政区› a prefecture ¶学問の府 a seat of learning / 京都府 Kyoto Prefecture / 府(立)の prefectural / 府下の町村 towns and villages in the prefecture / 府庁[議会] a prefectural office [assembly].

He was mortally wounded [fatally injured].
ひんする この国は寒さと飢えとで死にひんしていた。He was on the point of dying from cold and hunger.
ピンチ いくらあればこのピンチが切り抜けられるのかね。How much money do you need to tide you over this crisis?

ひんど 日常語でのこの語の使用頻度を調べる必要がある。We must check [see] how frequently this word is used in everyday Japanese.
ひんぱん 鉄道事故が最近異常に頻繁だ。Railroad accidents have been alarmingly frequent recently.
ひんぴんと 市内各所で放火事件が

頻々と起きているそうだ。Cases of incendiarism are being frequently reported from various parts of the city.
ひんぷ この国は貧富の差が甚だしい。The gulf between rich and poor is very wide in this country.
びんぼう 貧乏暇なし。Poor men have no leisure.

ふ³ 負 ¶負の〖数〗negative ; minus.
ふ⁴ 腑 ¶ふに落ちない《人が主語》cannot understand ;《事が主語》be hard to understand ; be not quite clear to one ; do not go down with one. 文例⇩
ふ⁵ 麩 *fu* ; a breadlike food made of wheat gluten.
ふ⁶ 譜 〈楽譜〉(sheet) music ; 〈音符〉a (musical) note ; 〈総譜〉a (musical) score. 文例⇩
ぶ¹ 分 ¶分がいい[悪い] have an advantage [be at a disadvantage] ; the odds are in one's favor [against one] / 分がない have no chance (of winning) / 非常に分の悪い賭(ヵ)け a gamble with long odds against one / 8分の利子を払う pay 8% interest / 砂糖3分に小麦粉5分の割合にする use 3 parts of sugar to 5 of flour. 文例⇩
ぶ² 部 〈部門〉a department ; a section (★日本の会社などでは、「部」を department、「課」を section と訳すのが普通である。英米ではそのような名称の区別は日本ほど一様ではない) ; 〈部分〉a part ; 〈書物の〉a copy ¶…の部に入る come [fall] under the head [category] of... / 第2部 Part II / 上の部の中の best / 3部から成る小説 a story in three parts / 部員 a member 《of a department》 ; a person on the staff / 部長 the head [chief, director] of a department [section] ; 〈大学の学部の〉a dean.
ファ〖音楽〗fa.
ぶあい 歩合 a percentage ; a commission ¶1割の歩合を出す give a commission of 10 per cent 《on sales》 / 歩合を取る take a percentage.
ぶあいそう 無愛想 ¶無愛想な surly ; unfriendly ; curt ; blunt / 無愛想な顔つき an unfriendly [surly] look / 無愛想な返事をする give *sb* a curt [blunt] reply.
ファイト fight ⇨とうし⁵.
ファイバースコープ〖光〗a fiberscope ¶胃ファイバースコープ a fiber gastroscope.
ファイル a file 《of the *Asahi*》 ¶ファイルする file / ファイルしておく keep *sth* on file / ファイルする file away / ファイル用カード a filing card / (厚紙を2つに折った)ファイル用ホルダー a file folder.
ファインダー〖写真〗a (view)finder.
ファインプレー a fine play.
ファウル〖スポーツ〗a foul ¶ファウルする foul 《to the right stands》/ ファウルグラウンド foul territory / ファウルボール a foul (ball).
ファクシミリ 〈装置〉facsimile (transmitting and receiving) equipment ; 〈複写された物〉a facsimile.
ファゴット [<《イタリア語》*fagotto*] a bassoon ¶ファゴット奏者 a bassoonist.
ファシスト a fascist.
ファシズム fascism.
ファスナー a slide [《英》zip] fastener ; a zipper.
ぶあつい 分厚い thick ; bulky.
ファッショ ⇨ ファシズム ¶ファッショ的 fascist(ic).
ファッション (a) fashion ¶ファッションショー[ブック、モデル] a fashion show [book, model].
ファラッド〖電〗a farad (略：F).
ふあん 不安 uneasiness ; anxiety ;《文》insecurity ¶不安な uneasy ; ill at ease ; restless ; uncertain ; insecure / 不安な一夜を過ごす pass an uneasy [anxious] night / 不安な地位 an insecure position / 不安に思う[を感じる] feel uneasy [ill at ease]《about》. 文例⇩
ファン a fan ; an enthusiast ¶ジャイアンツファン a Giants fan / ジョン・ウェインのファン an admirer [a fan] of John Wayne / ファンレター a fan letter ; fan mail (集合的).
ふあんてい 不安定 instability ¶不安定な unstable ; insecure ; shaky ; precarious.
ファンデーション〈化粧下〉foundation cream ; 〈下着〉a foundation garment.
ふあんない 不案内 ¶不案内である be ill-informed《about》; 《文》be unacquainted《with》; 《文》be ignorant《of》/ 不案内の土地 a strange place / 土地不案内の外国人 a foreigner unacquainted with the place. 文例⇩
ファンファーレ〖音楽〗a fanfare ; a flourish of trumpets.
ファンブル fumbling ; a fumble ¶ファンブルする fumble 《a grounder》.
ふい¹ 不意 ¶不意の 〈突然の〉sudden ; abrupt ; 〈不慮の〉unexpected ; unlooked-for ; unforeseen / 不意の訪問 a surprise visit [call] / 不意に suddenly ; (all) of a sudden ; unexpectedly ; unawares / 不意に訪ねる go to see *sb* without previous notice / 不意を突く ⇨ ふいうち(不意打ちを食わす). 文例⇩
ふい² ¶ふいにする lose ; waste ; spoil ;《口語》mess *sth* up ;《俗》blow *sth* ;《文》bring *sth* to nothing [naught] / 千円ふいにする waste [blow, throw away] 1,000 yen ; spend 1,000 yen for nothing / ふいになる be lost ; be wasted ; come to nothing.
ブイ〈浮標〉a buoy ; 〈救命用の〉a life buoy.

ふ⁴ 彼の態度にはふに落ちない所がある。I have some doubts about his attitude. | 彼には僕の説明がふに落ちなかったようだ。It seems that my explanation did not go down with him. | He did not seem quite satisfied with my explanation.
ふ⁵ 君は譜が読めるの。Can [Do] you read music?
ぶ¹ 彼の方に分がある。The odds are in his favor. | He has a better chance of success. / 桜はまだ2, 3分の所だ。The cherry blossoms have only just begun to bloom. / 工事は6分どおり出来上がった。The work is 60 per cent finished.
ふあん 僕は首になりはしないかと心配している。I am worried that I may be fired. / 結果はどうだろうと僕は絶えず不安でいった。I was in constant anxiety as to the result. / 米ソ間の緊張に人々は不安を感じていた。There was a general feeling of unrest because of the tension between Russia and the United States.
ふあんない 僕はこの町は全く不案内だ。I am a complete stranger in [quite new to] this town. / 手続きに一向に不案内で僕は途方にくれた。Being quite ignorant of the formalities, I had no idea what to do.
ふい¹ 彼の辞職は全く不意だった。

フィート feet ((sing. foot)) ¶3フィート5インチ three feet five inches; 3 ft. 5 in.; 3′5″ ★会話では単に three feet five と言うことが多い.

フィードバック feedback ¶フィードバックする feed back ((information)).

フィールディング 〖野球〗fielding.

フィールド 〖スポーツ〗the field ¶フィールド競技 field sports; a field event (種目).

ふいうち 不意打ち 〈攻撃〉a surprise attack; 〈訪問〉a surprise visit [call] ⇨ふい¹ (不意に訪ねる) ¶不意打ちを食わす take sb by surprise; make a surprise attack ((on)); catch [attack] sb unawares; take sb at a disadvantage; catch sb off *his* guard. 文例⇩

フィギュアスケート figure skating ¶フィギュアスケートをする skate [cut] figures (on the ice) / フィギュアスケートの選手 a figure skater.

ふいご a (pair of) bellows ¶ふいごを踏む work [blow] a bellows.

フィジー Fiji ¶フィジー諸島 the Fiji Islands.

ふいちょう 吹聴 ¶吹聴する ((文)) let sth be known; let it be known ((that...)); ((文)) make sth known; 〈推奨する〉recommend / 世間に吹聴する make sth public; give publicity to sth / 自分の事を吹聴する speak a lot of *oneself*; ((口語)) blow *one's* own trumpet; ((文)) advertise *oneself* ((to be..., as...)). 文例⇩

ふいっち 不一致 ((文)) disagreement; ((文)) inconsistency; ((文)) (矛盾).

ぷいと 〈出し抜けに〉abruptly; 〈怒って〉in a huff; in anger.

フィナーレ 〈終楽章・終曲〉a finale; 〈大詰め〉the end; ((文)) a denouement.

ブイヤベース 〖料理〗bouillabaisse.

フィヨルド a fjord; a fiord.

ブイヨン 〖料理〗bouillon.

フィラメント 〖電〗a filament.

ふいり 不入り a small audience; ((文)) a poor [small] attendance; a thin [poor] house; ((the play is)) a failure. 文例⇩

フィリピン the Philippines; the Philippine Islands ¶フィリピン共和国 the Republic of the Philippines / フィリピン人 a Filipino ((pl. -s)); a Filipina (女).

フィルター 〈カメラの〉a filter; 〈タバコの〉a filter tip ¶フィルターのついた[ついていない]タバコ a filter(-tipped) [plain, non-filter] cigarette.

フィルム (a) film ¶36枚撮りのフィルム a 36-exposure (roll of) film / フィルムに撮る film ((a scene)); get ((a scene)) on film / フィルム1巻〈写真機用の〉a roll [((米)) spool] of film; 〈映画の〉a reel of film.

フィンガーボール a finger bowl.

フィンランド Finland ¶フィンランドの Finnish / フィンランド共和国 the Republic of Finland / フィンランド語 Finnish / フィンランド人 a Finn.

ふう¹ 風 〈様子〉a look; an air; (an) appearance; 〈態度〉((文)) one's bearing; 〈風習〉a custom; ways; 〈方法〉a way; a manner; 〈流儀・型〉a style; a type; 〈傾向〉a tendency ¶こういった風の物 this sort of thing; things of this kind / ああいった風の男 that sort of man; a man of that type / 商人風の男 a man looking like a merchant / 昔の風を守る keep to the old ways / こんな風に like this; in this way [((文)) manner, ((文)) fashion] / どんな風に how; ((文)) in what way / 日本風に in ((文)) after] the Japanese fashion; 〈料理など〉in the Japanese style. 文例⇩

ふう² 封 a seal ¶封のしてある sealed ((envelopes)) / 封をする seal / 封を切る break the seal; cut (the letter) open; unseal.

ふうあつ 風圧 wind pressure ¶風圧計 a pressure anemometer.

ふういん 封印 a (stamped) seal ¶封印する seal.

ふうう 風雨 wind and rain; 〈暴風雨〉a (rain)storm; a tempest ¶風雨を冒して行く go in spite [in the teeth] of the storm / 風雨にさらされる be exposed to the weather / 風雨にさらされた weather-beaten; weatherworn / 風雨注意報 a storm warning.

ふううん 風雲 文例⇩

ふうか 風化 weathering ¶風化する weather. 文例⇩

ふうが 風雅 elegance; ((文)) refined taste; ((文)) an (a)esthetic life ¶風雅な人 a person of (refined) taste.

フーガ 〈<《イタリア語》fuga〉〖音楽〗a fugue.

ふうがい 風害 storm damage; damage from the wind. 文例⇩

ふうかく 風格 personality; character ¶風格のある人物 a man with a distinctive [remarkable] character.

ふうがわり 風変わり ¶風変わりな eccentric; queer; odd / 風変わりな男 an eccentric (man); a queer character (fish).

ふうかんはがき 封緘はがき a lettercard.

His resignation came as a complete surprise to us. / 不意に何かが起こったに違いない. Something unexpected must have happened to him.

ふいうち 行って不意打ちを食わせてやろう. I will go and surprise him [catch him napping].

ふいちょう この品を友人たちに吹聴して上げましょう. I'll recommend this article to my friends.| I'll bring this article to the notice of my friends. / この事を世間に吹聴されては困る. You must not let this matter get out. | We must keep this quiet.

ふいり その興行は不入りだった. The show drew only a small audience. | The show was a flop.

ふう¹ 私のそばを通り過ぎる時, 彼はこんな風に手招きをした. As he passed by me, he beckoned to me like this. / あんな風では人に嫌われる. If he continues to act that way, he will become unpopular.

ふううん 風雲急を告げている. The situation is threatening [has grown tense].

ふうか 碑文は風化して消えてしまっている. The inscription has weathered away. / 第2次大戦の記憶も次第に風化しつつある. Memories of World War II are wearing thin with time.

ふうがい その地方は風害が甚だし

ふうき 風紀 discipline; public morals ¶風紀を取り締まる enforce discipline 《among》; watch over the morals and behavior 《of the boarders》/ 風紀を乱す, 風紀に害がある corrupt public morals;/《文》be injurious [detrimental] to public morals.

ふうきり 封切り release ¶封切りする release 《a film》/ 封切り映画 a newly released film; a first-run film / 封切り(映画)館 a first-run (movie) theater.

ふうけい 風景〈景色〉a landscape; a scene; scenery;〈眺望〉a view; a sight ¶街頭の風景 a street scene / 山の風景 mountain scenery / 風景画 a landscape (painting) / 風景画家 a landscape painter.

ブーゲンビリア〖植〗a bougainvillea.

ふうこう¹ 風向 ⇨ かざむき ¶風向計 a (wind) vane.

ふうこう² 風光 ⇨ ふうけい. 文例↓

ふうさ 封鎖〈封じ込め〉a blockade;〈凍結〉freezing ¶封鎖する block (up); blockade; seal (an area) off; freeze 《the enemy's assets》/ 封鎖を解く lift [raise] the blockade; unfreeze 《the enemy's assets》/ 封鎖を破る run the blockade.

ふうさい 風采 one's (personal) appearance;《文》presence ¶風采が立派である have a fine presence / 風采が上がらない have no presence; cut a poor figure / 堂々たる風采の人《文》a man of imposing appearance; a fine figure of a man / 風采の上がらない男 a plain-looking [an insignificant-looking] man;《文》a man of unimpressive appearance. 文例↓

ふうさつ 封殺 ⇨ フォースアウト ¶言論を封殺する suppress the freedom of speech.

ふうし 風刺 (a) satire; a lampoon (軽い) ¶風刺するsatirize; lampoon / 風刺的に satirically / 風刺画 a caricature / 風刺(作)家 a satirist / 風刺小説 a satirical novel. 文例↓

ふうじこめる 封じ込める shut sb [sth] in;《文》confine; contain (the enemy).

ふうじて 封じ手〈囲碁・将棋の〉a sealed move.

ふうしゃ 風車 a windmill ¶風車小屋 a windmill.

ふうしゅう 風習 (manners and) customs; practices.

ふうしょ 封書 a (sealed) letter.

ふうじる 封じる〈封をする〉seal 《a letter》;〈防止する〉prevent;〈禁じる〉forbid;《文》prohibit;〈封鎖する〉seal (an area) off; blockade.

ふうしん 風疹〖医〗rubella; German measles (通俗に).

ふうすいがい 風水害 storm and flood damage.

ふうせつ 風雪 wind and snow ¶300年の風雪に耐えてきた老木《文》an old tree which has seen three hundred winters.

ふうせん 風船 ¶風船を飛ばす[上げる] fly [send up] a balloon / ゴム[紙]風船 a rubber [paper] balloon / 風船ガム (a piece of) bubble gum;〈blow〉a bubble of gum / 風船玉 a toy balloon.

ふうぜん 風前 ¶風前のともし火である be in an extremely precarious position. 文例↓

ふうそく 風速 wind velocity [speed]; the velocity [speed] of the wind ¶風速計 an anemometer; a wind gauge.

ふうぞく 風俗 manners; customs;〈風儀〉public morals ¶風俗を乱す corrupt [be an offense against, offend (against)] public decency [morals] / 風俗営業 the entertainment and amusement trades (such as bars, restaurants, mahjong parlors, etc.) / 風俗画[小説] a genre picture [story] / 風俗習慣 manners and customs. 文例↓

ふうたい 風袋 packing; the wrapping [container] (of a parcel); tare (その重量) ¶風袋込みで gross; in gross weight / 風袋抜きで net; in net weight. 文例↓

ブータン Bhutan ¶ブータンの Bhutanese / ブータン人 a Bhutanese (単複同形).

ふうち 風致 ¶風致を増す[添える] improve [add charm to] the view; improve /《文》enhance] the beauty of the scenery / 風致を害する spoil [《文》impair] the view [the beauty] of the scenery / 風致地区 a scenic zone / 風致林 a forest grown for scenic beauty.

ふうちょう 風潮 a trend; a tendency; the tide; the current (of the times) ¶世間の風潮に従う[逆らう] swim [go] with [against] the current of the times. 文例↓

ブーツ (a pair of) boots ⇨ くつ ¶ブーツをはいている wear [be in] boots.

ふうてい 風体〈風采〉one's (personal) appearance;〈身なり〉《文》(one's) dress ¶怪しい風体の suspicious-looking. 文例↓

ふうど 風土 the natural features (of a region); climate ¶日本の文化[精神]的風土 the cultural [spiritual] climate of Japan / 風土に慣れる be [get] acclimatized [《米》acclimated] / 風

かった. The storm [wind] did a lot of damage in that district.

ふうこう² その土地は風光明媚(び)である. The scenery there is really beautiful.

ふうさ その船は封鎖線を突破しようとしたところを捕まった. The ship was captured running the blockade.

ふうさい 彼は背が低く風采も上がらない. He is short and is unattractive in appearance.

ふうし この短編は現代の政治を風刺したものである. The story satirizes [is a satire on] contemporary politics.

ふうぜん 彼の運命は風前のともし火だった. His life hung by a thread.

ふうそく 風速は20メートル. The wind is blowing at (a speed [velocity] of) 20 meters per second.

ふうぞく 英語を研究する者には英国の風俗を知ることが絶対必要だ. Knowledge of English manners and customs is essential for a student of English. / 風俗が大いに乱れている. Public morals are very lax.

ふうたい 風袋込みで5キロある. It is 5 kilograms in gross weight. / Its gross weight is 5 kilograms.

ふうちょう 少しは世の中の風潮に従うようにした方が賢明かな, とクリフォード氏は考えた. Mr. Clifford thought it might be discreet to bend a little to the prevailing wind.

土病 an endemic disease ; a local disease.

フード a hood ¶フードつきの《a coat》with a hood ; hooded 《jackets》.

ふうとう 封筒 an envelope ¶封筒の垂れぶた the flap of an envelope / 封筒の端を切る slit an envelope (open) 《with a knife》/ 封筒に入れる put 《a letter》in an envelope / 住所氏名を書き返信用の切手を貼った封筒 a self-addressed and stamped return envelope / 洋[横型]封筒 a side-opening envelope / 和[縦型]封筒 an end-opening envelope / 窓付き封筒 a window(ed) envelope. 文例↓

ふうどう 風洞 a wind tunnel ¶風洞試験 a wind-tunnel test.

プードル a poodle.

ふうにゅう 封入 ¶封入する enclose / 封入の書類 an enclosed document. 文例↓

ふうは 風波 wind and waves ; 〈荒波〉rough seas ; 〈不和〉《文》discord ⇒なみかぜ ¶風波の高い海 a wind-whipped sea / 風波を冒して in the face [teeth] of wind and waves.

ふうばい 風媒《植》¶風媒の wind-pollinated[fertilized]. ⇒ なみかぜ ¶風媒花 an anemophilous flower.

ふうび 風靡 ¶風靡する dominate ;《文》sway / 一世を風靡する take the world by storm / 文壇を風靡する dominate the literary world.

ふうふ 夫婦 husband [man] and wife ; a (married) couple ¶加藤君夫婦 Kato and his wife / 夫婦の (the ties) of marriage ;《文》matrimonial ;《文》conjugal ;《文》marital / 夫婦の絆(きずな) a marital [matrimonial] bond ; a conjugal tie / 夫婦になる《文》become man and wife ; get married / 夫婦愛 love between man and wife ;《文》conjugal love / 夫婦関係 the marital relationship / 夫婦げんか a quarrel between husband and wife / 夫婦仲よく暮らす have a happy married life ; live happily together as man and wife / 夫婦連れで with one's wife [husband].

ふうふう ¶ふうふう言う ⇒あえぐ.

ぶうぶう ¶ぶうぶう言う〈不平を言う〉grumble 《at, about》; complain 《about,《文》of》.

ぶーぶー 〈汽笛などの音〉hooting ; 〈自動車の〉honking ; 〈豚の声〉oink-oink ¶〈自動車が〉ぶーぶー警笛を鳴らして走る run hooting [honking] / ぶーぶー言う〈豚などが〉grunt.

ふうぶつ 風物〈眺め〉scenery ;〈風俗事物〉institutions and customs ¶英国の風物 the institutions and customs of Britain ; things English. 文例↓

ふうぼう 風貌 ⇒ふうさい, ようぼう[2].

ふうみ 風味 (a) flavor ;《文》(a) savor ¶風味がいい[悪い] taste good [bad] ; be nice [nasty, unpleasant] / 風味のいい delicious ; savory / 風味のない flavorless ; tasteless ; insipid / 風味をつける season ; flavor ; give a flavor [savor]《to》/ 風味をよくする improve 《文》enhance] the flavor《of》.

ブーム a boom ¶最近の旅行ブーム the recent travel boom. 文例↓

ブーメラン a boomerang.

ふうもん 風紋 wind patterns in the sand.

ふうらいぼう 風来坊 a stranger out of nowhere ; a wanderer ; a vagabond.

ふうりゅう 風流 ¶風流な elegant ; tasteful ; refined / 風流な人《文》a person of (refined) taste / 風流を解しない人《文》a prosaic person.

ふうりょく 風力 the force of the wind ;〈動力としての〉wind power ¶風力級《気象》a wind scale. 文例↓

ふうりん 風鈴 a wind-bell.

プール 〈水泳場〉a swimming pool ;〈合同資金〉a pool ¶資金をプールする pool (their) money / 室内プール an indoor (swimming) pool ;《英》a swimming bath / プールサイドで at the poolside.

ふうろう 封蝋 sealing wax ¶封ろうで閉じる seal《a letter》with wax.

ふうん 不運 (a) misfortune ; bad [《文》ill] luck ¶不運な unfortunate ; unlucky ;《文》hapless ;《文》ill-fated / 不運に会う have bad luck ;《文》suffer (a) misfortune /〈金銭・健康の面で〉go through hard times /《文》fall on evil days. 文例↓

ぶうん 武運 the fortune(s) of war. 文例↓

ぶーん ⇒ぶんぶん ¶ぶーんとうなる drone ; buzz ; hum ; whirr.

ふえ 笛〈横笛〉a flute ; a fife (軍楽隊用の) ;〈たて笛〉an oboe ; a pipe ;〈呼び子〉a whistle ¶笛を吹く play《a tune》on the flute ; play [blow on] the flute / 笛吹き a flute player ; a piper. 文例↓

フェア〈野球〉¶フェアグラウンド fair territory / フェアボール a fair ball.

フェアプレー fair play ¶フェアプレーで行く play fair ; play the game.

ふえいせい 不衛生 ¶不衛生な insanitary ; unsanitary ; lacking in sanitation ;〈人が〉careless about one's health.

フェイント《球技》(make) a feint.

ふうてい その男の風体はどんなだった。How did the man look?

ふうとう その封筒はちゃんとがしてなかった。The envelope had not been properly sealed up [stuck down].

ふうにゅう 小切手で5万円封入お送り申し上げます。Enclosed please find a check for ￥50,000.

ふうは 風波が高い。The sea is rough. | The wind and the waves are high.

ふうぶつ ほたる狩りは初夏の日本の風物詩だ。Chasing fireflies is a pastime that gives poetic charm to early summer in Japan.

ふうみ その菓子の風味はいかがです。How do you like the cake?

ブーム 今は観光ブームだ。We are experiencing [are in the middle of] a sightseeing boom. / Tourism is booming. / 町のディスコブームは今が盛りだ[もう下火になった]. The disco boom is at its height [has died down] in the town.

ふうりょく 風力が増した。The wind strengthened [gained in force].

ふうん 彼女は一生不運だった。She was unfortunate to the end of her life. | She led an unhappy life.

ぶうん 彼は武運つたなく戦場の露と消えた。The fortunes of war were against him, and he died on the battlefield. / 武運長久を祈る。We pray for your good fortune in battle.

ふえ 僕が笛を吹いてもみんなが

フェーンげんしょう フェーン現象 【気象】a föhn phenomenon ¶フェーン現象による高温の風 a föhn; a foehn.

フェザーきゅう フェザー級 the featherweight class ¶フェザー級の選手 a featherweight (boxer, wrestler).

ふえて 不得手 ¶不得手である be bad [poor] (at); be weak (in) / 数学が不得手である be bad at [weak in] mathematics. 文例⇩

フェニキア 【西洋史】Phoenicia ¶フェニキアの Phoenician / フェニキア人 a Phoenician.

ブエノスアイレス Buenos Aires.

フェミニスト ＜女性にやさしい，またはあまい男＞ a man who is polite and attentive to women; 《文》a gallant; a (true) gentleman / ＜女権拡張論者＞ a feminist.

フェリー(ボート) a ferry(boat).

ふえる 増[殖]える ＜増す＞ increase; gain; multiply (倍加する); ＜川の水が＞ rise; ＜繁殖する＞ breed; proliferate ¶目方が増える gain [grow] in weight / 30 パーセント増える increase by 30% / 増えて行く go on increasing; be on the increase. 文例⇩

フェルト felt ¶フェルト帽 a felt hat.

プエルトリコ ＜米国自治領＞ Puerto Rico ¶プエルトリコ人 a Puerto Rican.

フェルミウム 【化】fermium.

フェロモン 【生化】a pheromone.

ふえん 敷延 ¶敷延する 《文》amplify (the statement); 《文》enlarge [expand, expatiate] on (a subject).

フェンシング fencing ¶フェンシングの選手 a fencer.

フェンダー ＜自動車の＞ 《米》a fender; 《英》a wing ¶フェンダーミラー 《米》a fender mirror; 《英》a wing mirror.

ぶえんりょ 無遠慮 ¶無遠慮な ＜率直な＞ unreserved; outspoken; ＜失礼な＞ rude; ＜厚かましい＞ cheeky; impudent / 無遠慮に 《文》without reserve; 《文》unreservedly; frankly; rudely / 無遠慮に物を言う 《文》speak without reserve; be outspoken / 無遠慮に振る舞う behave rudely; make free [take liberties] with sb. 文例⇩

フォア 【ボート】a four ¶かじ付きフォア a coxed four; ＜競技＞ coxed fours.

フォアハンド 【テニス】a forehand (stroke) ¶フォアハンドで打つ hit ((the ball)) forehand.

フォアボール 【野球】a base on balls; a walk ¶フォアボールを出す give ((a batter)) a walk [base on balls]; walk ((a batter)) (on balls) / フォアボールで一塁に出る walk to first (on balls); get a base on balls.

フォーク¹ 【食器】a fork ¶フォークの柄[先] the stem [tines, prongs] of a fork / フォークにスパゲッティを巻きつける twist the spaghetti round *one's* fork / フォークだけで食べる eat with fork only.

フォーク² 【音楽】folk music.

フォークソング a folk song.

フォークダンス a folk dance.

フォークボール 【野球】a fork ball.

フォークリフト a fork lift.

フォースアウト 【野球】a force-out ¶フォースアウトにする force ((a runner)) out.

フォーム *one's* style. 文例⇩

フォームラバー foam rubber.

フォール 【レスリング】a fall ¶フォールする score a fall; pin (*one's* opponent)) (to the mat) / フォールで勝つ win by a fall; beat [《文》defeat] ((*one's* opponent)) by a fall / フォール勝ちa victory by a fall.

フォックストロット ¶フォックストロットを踊る dance the fox trot; fox-trot.

フォッサマグナ 【地質】Fossa Magna.

ぶおとこ 醜男 an ugly(-looking) man.

フォルマリン ⇒ホルマリン.

フォワード 【スポーツ】a forward.

ふおん 不穏 ¶不穏な 《文》disquieting; threatening / 不穏な行動に出る threaten [disturb] the peace and order ((of a community)) / 不穏分子 dissidents; 《文》disturbing elements / 不穏文書 seditious [subversive] documents.

フォン ⇒ホン.

ふおんとう 不穏当 ¶不穏当な ＜不適当な＞ 《文》improper; ＜不当な＞ 《文》unjust; unfair; unreasonable; ＜文＞violent.

ふか¹ 不可 ＜成績評価の＞ F ★ fail(ure) の略 ¶不可を２つ取る get 2 F's (in history and geography) / 不可とする regard sth as wrong [《文》improper]; disapprove of sth; be against ((a plan)) / 可もなく不可もない be neither very good nor very poor; ((口語)) be (only) so-so.

ふか² 付加 ¶付加する add (to); supplement (補足する); 《文》append (追加する) / 付加価値税 a tax on value added; a value-added tax (略: V.A.T.) / 付加疑問 【文法】a tag question / 付加税 an additional tax; a supertax; ((米)) a surtax.

ふか³ 負荷 【電・機】load ¶負荷率 a load factor.

ふか⁴ 孵化 hatching; incubation ¶孵化する hatch ((eggs)); sit on ((eggs)) / 人工孵化 artificial incubation / 孵化器 an (artificial) incubator / (魚の)孵化場 a ((salmon)) hatchery.

ふか⁵ 賦課 ¶賦課する levy [impose] ((a tax on land)).

ふか⁶ 【魚】a shark.

ぶか 部下 a subordinate; *one's* men ¶…の部下となって働く work under sb. 文例⇩

踊ってはくれない。If I piped, they wouldn't dance.

ふえて 日本人は概して語学が不得手である。The Japanese are generally bad at (foreign) languages. | Most Japanese are poor linguists.

ふえる 体重が２キロ増えた。I have put on [gained] two kilograms (in weight). / 借金が増える一方だ。My debts go on increasing.

ぶえんりょ 私は重ねて聞くのも無遠慮な気がした。I was afraid that it would be rude to repeat the question. / 君は無遠慮過ぎる。You are too outspoken.

フォーム 彼の投球フォームはきれいだ[ぎこちない]．His pitching style is beautiful [clumsy(-looking)].

ふおん 形勢不穏だ．The situation looks ugly [is threatening].

ぶか 彼の部下には有能な人が多い．He has plenty of able men under him.

ふかい¹ 不快 《文》displeasure; discomfort; 〈病気〉《文》(an) indisposition / 不快な unpleasant; disagreeable; uncomfortable / 不快な感じを与える give sb an unpleasant feeling / 不快な顔をする do not look pleased;《文》look displeased / 不快指数 a temperature-humidity index ★以前は a discomfort index と言った.

ふかい² 深い 〈底・奥までの距離が長い〉deep; 〈濃密な〉thick; dense; 〈深遠な〉deep;《文》profound ¶深い穴 a deep hole / 深い霧 a dense [thick] fog / 深い知識 (a) deep [profound] knowledge 《of music》/ 深い眠り (a) deep [sound] sleep / 深く deeply; deep; 〈心の底から〉heartily; sincerely; 〈強く〉strongly; 〈非常に〉very much; most 《impressed》/ 深くする[なる] deepen; make [get,《文》become] deeper / 深く息を吸う breathe in deeply; draw a deep breath / 深く研究する study thoroughly; make a profound study 《of》/ 深く考える think deeply 《about》/ 深く根ざした deep-rooted. 文例⇩

ぶかい 部会 a sectional meeting.

ぶがい 部外 ¶部外者 an outsider; people outside 《the society》/ 部外秘の restricted 《data》.

ふがいない 〈意気地のない〉cowardly; 《文》fainthearted; 〈役に立たない〉good-for-nothing; shiftless. 文例⇩

ふかいにゅう 不介入 nonintervention.

ふかいり 深入り ¶深入りする go too far 《into a matter》; get involved 《too deeply》《in a problem》; be taken up too much 《with a matter》. 文例⇩

ふかおい 深追い ¶深追いする chase 《the enemy》too far.

ふかかい 不可解 ¶不可解な incomprehensible;《文》inscrutable; mysterious / 不可解な行動 enigmatic behavior / 不可解な人物 a mystery man.

ふかぎゃく 不可逆 ¶不可逆的 irreversible 《changes》/ 不可逆性 irreversibility.

ふかく¹ 不覚 〈油断〉lack of care; 〈敗北〉a defeat; 〈失敗〉(a) failure; 〈失策〉a mistake; a blunder ¶不覚の涙を流す shed tears in spite of oneself / 不覚を取る 〈敗れる〉be defeated; 《文》suffer a defeat; 〈失敗する〉fail 《in》. 文例⇩ pression.

ふかく² 俯角 〔物・測量〕a dip; an angle of de-

ぶがく 舞楽 bugaku; court dances and music.

ふかくじつ 不確実 ¶不確実な uncertain; insecure; unreliable.

ふかくてい 不確定 ¶不確定な uncertain; indefinite; undecided; unsettled / 不確定性原理〔物〕the uncertainty principle.

ふかけつ 不可欠 ¶不可欠な indispensable 《to》; essential 《to》.

ふかこうりょく 不可抗力 an inevitable accident; an act of God ¶不可抗力の inevitable; irresistible; beyond (human) control. 文例⇩

ふかさ 深さ depth ¶深さが5メートルある be five meters deep [in depth] / 深さを測る measure the depth 《of a lake》; sound 《the sea》.

ふかざけ 深酒 ¶深酒する drink too much.

ふかしんじょうやく 不可侵条約 a nonaggression treaty [pact].

ふかす¹ 吹かす ¶タバコを吹かす smoke a cigarette; puff 《at》a cigarette / エンジンを吹かす race the engine 《of one's car》(with a loud roar) / 先輩風を吹かす ⇨せんぱい.

ふかす² 更かす ¶夜を更かす sit [stay] up (till) late at night / 仕事[勉強]で夜を更かす work (till) late at night; work late into the night.

ふかす³ 蒸かす steam 《sweet potatoes》.

ふかち 不可知 ¶不可知の《文》unknowable / 不可知論〔哲〕agnosticism / 不可知論者 an agnostic.

ぶかっこう 不格好 ¶不格好な awkward; clumsy;《文》ill-shaped.

ふかっせい 不活性〔化〕¶不活性の inert; inactive / 不活性気体 an inert gas.

ふかっぱつ 不活発 inactivity; dullness; 〈沈滞〉stagnation; slackness ¶不活発な inactive; dull; stagnant; slack.

ふかづめ 深爪 ¶深づめを切る cut [pare] a nail to the quick.

ふかで 深手 ⇨じゅうしょう².

ふかのう 不可能 impossibility ¶不可能な事 an impossibility / 不可能である be impossible; be beyond one's power.

ふかひ 不可避 ¶不可避な inevitable; unavoidable;《文》inescapable;《文》ineluctable. 文例⇩

ふかふか ¶ふかふかのベッド a soft, comfortable bed; a bed that has plenty of give / ふかふかの焼きいも sweet potatoes hot from the oven.

ぶかぶか ¶ぶかぶかの 〈大き過ぎる〉too big [large] for one; 〈ふくらんだ〉baggy.

ぷかぷか ¶ぷかぷか葉巻を吹かす puff 《at》a cigar / ぷかぷか水に浮く float on the water.

ふかぶかと 深々と ¶椅子に深々と腰をおろす sink into [onto] a chair.

ふかぶん 不可分《文》indivisibility ¶不可分の《文》indivisible; inseparable / 不可分の関係にある be inseparably related 《to each other》.

くな. Keep in [Don't go out of] your depth. / 霧が段々深くなった. The fog gradually became thicker. / あまり深く彼と交際しない方がいい. You had better not have too much to do with him. / 2人は深い仲だった. They were far more than mere friends.

ふがいない 自分ながらふがいないと思っている. I am ashamed of myself [my own lack of ability].

ふかいり 深入りし過ぎて今更後に引かれない. I have gone too far to turn back.

ふかく¹ 輪島が新進の若手力士のために思わぬ不覚を取った. Wajima suffered an unforeseen upset at the hands of an up-and-coming young wrestler. / 彼を信用したのは私の不覚でした. I made a blunder in trusting him.

ふかこうりょく 当局はこの惨事を不可抗力であると主張している. The authorities claim that the accident was unavoidable.

ふかひ 両者の衝突は不可避である. A confrontation between

ふかまる 深まる get [《文》become] deeper; deepen.

ふかみ 深み〈深さ〉depth;〈深い所〉a deep place; a deep (海の) ¶深みに落ち込む fall into a deep place;〈文学作品などの〉get [go] beyond [out of] one's depth /〈文学作品などの〉深みがない lack depth.

ふかみどり 深緑 deep [dark] green.

ふかめる 深める 理解を深める《文》promote (a) better understanding.

ブカレスト Bucharest.

ぶかん 武官〈陸軍〉a military officer;〈海軍〉a naval officer / 大使館付き陸[海]軍武官 a military [naval] attaché to an embassy.

ふかんしへい 不換紙幣 an inconvertible note.

ふかんしょう¹ 不干渉 nonintervention; non-interference ¶不干渉主義[政策] a nonintervention policy; a 'hands-off' policy.

ふかんしょう² 不感症 frigidity ¶不感症の女 a frigid woman / 不感症になる become indifferent (to) (callous (toward)).

ふかんず 俯瞰図 ⇨ ちょうかんず.

ふかんぜん 不完全《文》imperfection;《文》incompleteness ¶不完全な incomplete;《文》defective / 構造が不完全である be defective [faulty] in construction / 不完全雇用 underemployment / 不完全他[自]動詞『文法』an incomplete transitive [intransitive] verb / 不完全燃焼 imperfect [incomplete] combustion.

ふき¹ 付記 an additional remark; a supplementary note ¶付記する add; write in addition (to); 《文》append a note (to).

ふき² 〘植〙a butterbur ¶ふきの薹(とう) a butterbur sprout.

ぶき 武器 a weapon;《文》arms ¶武器を取[取って立つ] take up arms [rise in arms] (against) / 武器を持っている be armed;《文》carry [bear] arms / 武器援助 military aid.

ふきあげる 吹[噴]き上げる blow up; throw up 《water》into the air; spout.

ふきおくる 吹き送る 文例⇩

ふきおろす 吹き下ろす blow down ¶山から吹き下ろす風 a wind blowing down a mountain.

ふきかえ 吹き替え〈録音の〉(sound) dubbing; 〈映画の〉a stand-in.

ふきかえす 吹き返す 息を吹き返す come to (oneself); come to life again.

ふきかえる 葺き替える reroof (a house);〈かわらを〉retile (a roof);〈わら屋根を〉rethatch (a cottage).

ふきかける 吹き掛ける〈息などを〉blow [breathe] on sth;〈霧を〉spray 《water》on sth ¶息を吹きかけて手を暖める blow on one's hands to warm them.

ふきけす¹ 吹き消す blow 《a candle》out.

ふきけす² 拭き消す wipe sth out [off]; erase.

ふきげん 不機嫌 a bad mood [temper];《文》displeasure;《文》bad [ill] humor ¶不機嫌な sullen; bad-[《文》ill-]tempered;《文》ill-humored; cross;《文》displeased / 不機嫌な顔をする look cross [《文》displeased, sullen] / 不機嫌である be in a bad [foul] temper; be bad-tempered.

ふきこぼれる 吹[噴]きこぼれる boil over.

ふきこむ¹ 吹き込む〈風などが〉blow into;〈息を〉breathe into;〈考えなどを〉give sb [《文》inspire sb with] 《an idea》¶レコードに吹き込む record (a song); put (a song) on a record; have [get] (one's song) recorded. 文例⇩

ふきこむ² 拭き込む rub 《the floor》shining bright ¶拭き込んだ well-polished.

ふきさらし 吹きさらし ¶吹きさらしの wind-swept; exposed [open] to the wind; windy.

ふきすさぶ 吹きすさぶ blow violently [hard]; rage ¶吹きすさぶ風 a raging wind.

ふきそ 不起訴 non-prosecution ¶不起訴にする drop 《a case》; do not prosecute sb. 文例⇩

ふきそうじ 拭き掃除 ¶拭き掃除する mop 《the floor》; wipe the dust off 《the desk》.

ふきそく 不規則 irregularity ¶不規則な irregular / 生活が不規則である keep irregular hours;《文》be a man of irregular habits / 不規則動詞『文法』an irregular verb / 不規則変化『文法』(an) irregular conjugation.

ふきたおす 吹き倒す blow (a tree) down [over].

ふきだし 吹き出し ¶漫画の a balloon.

ふきだす 吹[噴]き出す〈風が〉begin to blow; rise;〈笑い出す〉burst out laughing; burst into laughter;〈水・血などが〉spout (out); spurt (out, up); gush out;〈ガス・蒸気などが〉blow out [up]. 文例⇩

ふきだまり 吹きだまり〈雪の〉a snowdrift; a drift of snow;〈ちりや土ぼこりなどの〉a drift (of dust [sand]). 文例⇩

ふきつ 不吉 ¶不吉な《文》ill-omened;《文》ominous; unlucky / 不吉な数[日] an unlucky number [day] / 不吉な鳥 a bird of ill omen / 不吉な予感 an ominous presentiment.

ふきつけ 吹き付け spraying ¶吹き付け器 a (spray) gun; a sprayer / 吹き付け塗装 (paint-) spraying.

ふきつける 吹き付ける〈風が〉blow against them is inevitable.

ふかまる ボストンに着いた時は秋も大分深まっていた。Fall was far [well] advanced when I arrived at Boston.

ふかんぜん 準備が甚だ不完全だ。The arrangements leave a lot to be desired.

ふきおくる 庭から花の香りが吹き送られてきた。The scent of flowers (came) wafted in from the garden.

ふきかえ そのテレビ番組は日本語で吹き替えになっていた。That TV show is dubbed in Japanese.

ふきこむ¹ 風が窓から吹き込んでいた。A breeze was blowing into the room through the window.

ふきそ 彼は不起訴になった。The public prosecutors decided not to prosecute [institute an action against] him. / The case against him was dropped.

ふきだす 傷口から血が吹き出した。Blood spurted from the wound. / The wound spouted blood.

ふきだまり 戸口にうず高い雪の吹きだまりができていた。There was a snowdrift piled high against the door. / Snow had drifted up against the door. / 東京のそのあたりは、いわば、人生の敗残者の吹きだまりになっていた。It was as if all the losers on the battlefield of life had drift-

[on]; 〈塗料などを〉spray.
ふきつのる 吹き募る blow harder (and harder); 《文》rage with growing intensity.
ふきでもの 吹き出物 a pimple [spot] (にきび); a boil (ねぶと); an [a skin] eruption ¶吹き出物ができる have a spot [pimple, boil] (on one's face); pimples break out (on one's cheeks).
ふきとばす 吹き飛ばす blow off [away] ¶帽子を吹き飛ばされる have one's hat blown off.
ふきとる 拭き取る wipe 《grease》(up, out).
ふきながし 吹き流し a streamer.
ふきぬき 吹き抜き 〈階段の〉a stairwell; the well of the stairs.
ふきぬける 吹き抜ける 〈風が〉blow through [across] 《the room》.
ふきはらう 吹き払う blow [sweep] 《the dust》 off [away].
ふきぶり 吹き降り wind and rain; (a) driving rain.
ふきまくる 吹きまくる 〈風が〉blow about [hard]; bluster;《文》rage.
ふきまわし 吹き回し ¶ひょっとした風の吹き回しで by a stroke of good fortune; by the merest chance. 文例↓.
ぶきみ 無[不]気味 ¶無気味な weird; eerie; uncanny; unearthly / 無気味な沈黙 an unearthly [ominous] silence.
ふきや 吹き矢 a blowgun; a blowpipe; 〈矢〉a blowpipe dart.
ふきやむ 吹き止む 〈風が〉stop [《文》cease] blowing; blow itself out; blow over; die away.
ふきゅう¹ 不朽 immortality ¶不朽の《文》immortal;《文》everlasting;《文》eternal / 不朽の名声を得る win eternal [immortal] fame. 文例↓.
ふきゅう² 不急 ¶不急の not urgent; not pressing.
ふきゅう³ 普及 spread;《文》diffusion; 〈大衆化〉popularization ¶普及する 〈広める〉spread;《文》diffuse; 〈広まる〉become widespread; come into wide use / 〈一般化する〉become popular; gain (in) popularity / 普及版 a popular edition / 普及率 the diffusion (of color TV sets). 文例↓.
ふきょう¹ 不況 (a) recession; a business [trade] depression [recession]; dull business ¶不況を克服する get over [out of] the recession; overcome the recession. 文例↓.
ふきょう² 不興《文》displeasure;《文》ill humor ¶不興をこうむる incur sb's displeasure; fall into disgrace with sb / 不興げに with a displeased look.
ふきょう³ 布教 propagation 《of the Christian faith》; missionary work ¶布教する propagate [spread] 《a religion》;《文》engage [be engaged] in missionary work / 布教師 a missionary.
ぶきよう 不器用 ¶不[不器用 awkwardness; lack of skill ¶無器用な awkward; clumsy; unskillful / 無器用な手付きで clumsily; in an awkward way [《文》manner]. 文例↓.
ぶぎょう 奉行 《日本史》a magistrate ¶奉行所 a magistrate's office.
ふぎょうせき 不行跡《文》misconduct ¶不行跡を働く misbehave (oneself);《文》misconduct oneself.
ふきょうわおん 不協和音 《音楽》a discord; a dissonance.
ぶきょく¹ 部局 a department; a bureau.
ぶきょく² 舞曲 (a piece of) dance music; a dance.
ふぎり 不義理 〈忘恩〉《文》ingratitude; 〈不誠意〉《文》lack of good faith ¶不義理な ungrateful;《文》lacking in good faith / 不義理をする be ungrateful 《to》; do sb wrong.
ふきりつ 不規律 disorder;《文》indiscipline; (a) lack [《文》want] of discipline ¶不規律な irregular; disorderly; undisciplined.
ぶきりょう 無[不]器量 ¶無器量な plain; ugly; 《米》homely.
ふきん¹ 布巾 〈食器を拭く〉《米》a dish towel; 《英》a tea towel [cloth]; 〈食卓などを拭く〉a dishcloth / 《米》a dishrag.
ふきん² 付近 the neighborhood; the vicinity; 《文》the environs (近郊) ¶東京付近 Tokyo and (its) environs / 付近の neighboring; nearby / 付近に nearby; in the neighborhood [vicinity] 《of》/ この付近に near here; in this neighborhood / どこかこの付近に somewhere around [about, near] here.
ふきんこう 不均衡《文》imbalance; lack of balance;《文》disequilibrium; inequality ¶不均衡な unbalanced; 《文》disproportionate; unequal / 貿易の不均衡を是正する redress the imbalance in [balance of] trade 《between》.
ふきんしん 不謹慎 imprudence;《文》indiscretion ¶不謹慎な《文》imprudent; indiscreet / 不謹慎である《文》lack prudence [discretion] / 不謹慎にも…する be indiscreet enough to do.
ふく¹ 服 〈衣服〉clothes;《文》a garment; a

ed into that part of Tokyo.
ふきまわし どういう風の吹き回しでこんな所へ来たんだい. To what do we owe this (pleasant) surprise? | What has brought you here?
ふきゅう¹ その詩で彼は不朽の名声を得た. The poem won him everlasting fame. | The poem immortalized his name.
ふきゅう³ 科学的知識が一般に普及してきた. The general public today has a fairly wide knowledge of scientific matters. / クーラーは最近大いに普及してきた. Air conditioners have come into wide use recently. / 電話の普及率では日本は米国に次いで世界第2位である. Japan is second in the world after the U.S.A. in the percentage of households [persons] owning a telephone. / 全国のカラーテレビの普及率は80パーセントに達した. Eighty per cent of households in the country now have color TV.
ふきょう¹ 不況である. The market is dull. | Business conditions are depressed. / 我が国の外国貿易は不況に陥った. Japan's foreign trade has fallen into a state of depression.
ぶきよう 彼はすることが何でも無器用だ. He is clumsy in everything he does. / 物を作るということになると私は全く無器用で

ふく¹ 服 suit (1そろいの); a uniform (制服) ¶服を着て(が)出る; put on one's clothes on / 服を脱ぐ take one's clothes off / 服地 «布地» cloth; «材料» suiting; dress material (女性服用).

ふく² 福 (good) fortune [luck]; 《文》 blessing(s) ¶福の神 the god of wealth. 文例↓

ふく³ 吹く[噴く] 〈風が〉 blow; 〈息を〉 breathe out; 《文》 exhale; 〈ほらを〉 play; 〈自慢げに〉 brag; 《口語》 talk big ¶笛を吹く play the flute / らっぱを吹く blow [sound] the bugle; play the trumpet / 火を噴く shoot out [emit] fire / 潮風に吹かれる be exposed to the sea breeze / 吹いて冷ます blow on ((hot milk)) to cool (it); blow into ((one's cup of tea)) / 吹けば飛ぶような男 a mere nobody; a quite insignificant-looking fellow. 文例↓

ふく⁴ 拭く wipe; mop (up); rub (down) (ごしごしと) ¶(風呂から上がって) 身体をタオルでふく dry oneself on a towel / 手の甲で額の汗をふく wipe the sweat off one's brow with the back of one's hand / エプロンで手をふく wipe [dry] one's hands on one's apron / 板をごしごしふく rub a board with a cloth.

ふく⁵ 葺く ¶屋根を葺く roof ((a house with slate)); thatch ((a cottage with straw)).

ふく- 副... 〈助...〉 assistant; 〈代...〉 deputy; vice-; sub-; by-; 〈二次的〉 secondary; auxiliary ¶副因 a secondary cause / 副支配人 an assistant manager / 副賞 an extra prize / 副社長 a vice-president / 副食物 a side dish / 副読本 a supplementary reader.

ふく- double...; compound ¶複眼 compound eyes / 複線 a double track.

ふぐ¹ 不具 deformity ¶不具の deformed (奇形の); crippled (手足の利かない) / 不具になる be crippled; be disabled / 不具者 a (physically) handicapped person; a disabled person.

ふぐ² 《魚》 a fugu; a globefish. 文例↓

ぶぐ 武具 《文》 arms; weapons; 〈総称〉 battle-gear.

ふくあん 腹案 a plan [scheme] (in one's mind) ¶腹案が出来ている have a plan ready (in one's mind) / 腹案を立てる draw up a plan.

ふくいく 馥郁 ¶ふくいくたる sweet-smelling; 《文》 fragrant.

ふくいん¹ 復員 demobilization ¶復員する be demobilized; be discharged from military service / 復員軍人 a demobilized soldier.

ふくいん² 福音 the Gospel; 〈吉報〉 good [welcome] news; 《文》 glad tidings; 《恩恵》 《文》 a boon ★ good [welcome] news は常に単数扱い, glad tidings は単数にも複数にも扱う ¶福音を説く[広める] preach [spread] the Gospel / 福音教会 the Evangelical Church / 福音主義 evangelicalism / 福音書 the (four) Gospels / 福音伝道者 an evangelist. 文例↓

ふぐう 不遇 ¶不遇の 《不幸せな》 unfortunate; 《文》 ill-fated; 〈世に出ぬ〉 obscure / 不遇の時代 《文》 one's dark days / 一生不遇で終わる live in obscurity all one's life.

ふくえき 服役 ¶服役する 〈懲役〉 serve (one's) [《口語》 do] time; serve one's term of imprisonment; 〈兵役〉 serve one's time; serve one's term of military service. 文例↓

ふくえん 復縁 《文》 restoration of the marital relationship ¶復縁を迫る press ((one's divorced spouse)) to come back to one.

ふくがく 復学 ¶復学する return [come back] to school; be readmitted to the university [college].

ふくがん 複眼 《動》 compound eyes.

ふくぎょう 副業 a side [second] job; a sideline; side business. 文例↓

ふくげん 復元[原] ¶復元する 《文》 restore [be restored] to its [the] original state / 復元作業 restoration; restoration [restorative] work / 復元図[模型] a reconstruction / (船などの)復元力 (a) righting moment. 文例↓

ふくこう 腹腔 《解》 the abdominal cavity.

ふくごう 複合 ¶複合の compound; complex / 複合競技 〈スキー〉 the (Nordic, Alpine) combined / 複合名詞[関係詞] 《文法》 a compound noun [relative].

ふくさ 袱紗 a silk wrapping cloth.

ふくざき 複座機 a two-seater (plane); a two-seated plane.

ふくざい 伏在 ¶伏在する 《文》 lie concealed [latent] in sth; lie behind [at the back of] sth; lurk in [under] sth.

ふくざい 服罪 ¶服罪する submit to a sentence.

ふくざつ 複雑 ¶複雑な complicated; 《文》 complex; 《文》 intricate / 複雑な表情 (wear) an expression showing (one's) mixed feelings. 文例↓

ふくさよう 副作用 ¶副作用がない have no [be free from] side effects / 副作用を起こす have [produce] (harmful) side effects ((on)).

ふくさんぶつ 副産物 a by-product; (a) spin-off (大規模な研究や事業の).

ふくし¹ 副詞 《文法》 an adverb ¶副詞句[節] an adverbial [complex] phrase [clause].

ふくし² 福祉 welfare; well-being ¶国民の福祉を増進する 《文》 promote the welfare of the

---

す. I am very awkward [all thumbs] when it comes to making things.

ふく² 福は内! 鬼は外! With fortune! Out with the demon!

ふく³ よく吹きますね。Isn't it windy! | How it blows! / 今頃は東風が吹く。Easterly winds are common [prevalent] at this time of year. / 随分吹く男だね! How he brags! | What a braggart he is!

ふぐ² ふぐは食いたし命は惜しし。Honey is sweet, but the bee stings. 《諺》

ふくいん その発明は身体障害者の福音である。The invention is a boon to the physically handicapped.

ふくえき 彼は浦和刑務所で服役中だ。He is serving a term [《口語》 doing time] in Urawa Prison.

ふくぎょう 近頃は副業に豚を飼う農家が多い。Nowadays many farmers raise pigs as a sideline [on the side].

ふくげん 左の絵はこの住居跡の復元図である。The picture on the left is a reconstruction of this dwelling.

ふくざつ これには種々複雑な事情がある。There are complicated circumstances behind the mat-

ふくしき 複式 ¶複式学級 a combined class (of more than one grade) / 複式簿記 double-entry bookkeeping.

ふくしきこきゅう 腹式呼吸 abdominal breathing.

ふくじてき 副次的 secondary. Ling.

ふくしゃ¹ 伏射 a prone position shoot ¶伏射の姿勢 a prone firing position.

ふくしゃ² 複写 (a) reproduction; a copy ¶複写する copy; 《文》reproduce; make a copy 《of》; photocopy (写真で) / ゼロックス[フォトスタット]で複写する make a Xerox [Photostat] copy of sth; Xerox [Photostat] sth ★ Xerox, Photostat は商標名 / 複写器 a copying machine / 複写写真 a photocopy; a photographic reproduction / 複写用インク[紙] copying ink [paper].

ふくしゃ³ 輻射 《物》radiation ¶輻射する radiate / 輻射熱[線] radiant heat [rays].

ふくしゅ 副手 a junior assistant.

ふくしゅう¹ 復習 (a) review; 《英》revision; refresher training (教室での) ¶復習する review [《英》revise, go over] 《one's lesson》.

ふくしゅう² 復讐 revenge; 《文》vengeance; a vendetta (敵討ち); retaliation (仕返し) ¶復讐する 《文》revenge [avenge] oneself on sb for sth; 《文》be revenged [avenged] on sb for sth; take [get, have] one's revenge on sb for sth; retaliate against [on] sb; settle [pay off] an old score with sb / 復讐を企てる 《文》seek revenge [vengeance] on sb for sth / 復讐戦 〈競技の〉a return match. 文例↓

ふくじゅう 服従 obedience; 《文》submission ¶服従する obey; be obedient 《to》; submit 《to》/ 命令に服従する obey sb's orders / 〈犬の〉服従訓練 obedience training.

ふくじゅそう 福寿草 an Amur adonis.

ふくしょう 復唱 ¶復唱する repeat 《what sb said, sb's order》.

ふくじょうし 腹上死 death during sexual intercourse (with a woman).

ふくしょく¹ 服飾 dresses and their ornaments [accessories] ¶服飾デザイナー a dress designer / 服飾品 accessories (for [of] a dress).

ふくしょく² 復職 ¶復職する be reinstated in [come back to] one's former position [post].

ふくしん 腹心 《文》one's confidant (男); 《文》one's confidante (女) ¶腹心の部下 one's right-hand man; a man whom one trusts; a man that one has taken 《文》admitted into one's confidence. 文例↓

ふくじん 副腎 《解》the adrenal [suprarenal] gland ¶副腎皮質 the adrenal cortex; the cortex of the adrenal gland / 副腎皮質ホルモン adrenocortical hormone.

ふくすい 腹水 《医》abdominal dropsy.

ふくすう 複数 《文法》the plural (number) ¶複数の plural / 複数形 the plural (form) 《of》. 文例↓

ふくする¹ 服する 〈従う〉obey; submit to; 《文》yield to; give in to; 〈服務する〉serve ¶2年間兵役に服する serve two years in the army [navy].

ふくする² 復する return (to normal); be restored (to its [the] normal condition).

ふくせい 複製 a copy; (a) reproduction ¶複製する reproduce; make a copy [reproduction, replica, facsimile] of sth / 複製品 a copy; a reproduction; a replica; a facsimile. 文例↓

ふくせん 伏線 an advance hint ¶伏線を張る drop an advance hint; 《文》allude to sth as a preliminary; foreshadow (a coming event).

ふくせん 複線 〈鉄道〉a double track; a two-track line / 複線にする double-track (the Ou Line).

ふくそう¹ 服装 《文》(the style of) dress; clothes ¶服装が立派である[見すぼらしい] be well [poorly] dressed. 文例↓

ふくそう² 輻輳 congestion ¶ふくそうする be congested [crowded] 《with》/ 交通のふくそう traffic congestion; a traffic jam / 注文のふくそう pressure [a flood] of orders.

ふくぞう 腹蔵 ¶腹蔵のない unreserved; frank; candid; outspoken / 腹蔵なく frankly; candidly; 《文》without reserve / 腹蔵なく言えば to be frank [plain] with you; frankly speaking. 文例↓

ふくそうひん 副葬品 《考古》grave goods; tomb furnishings; a dead person's personal belongings buried with his corpse ¶豊かな副葬品を伴った塚 a richly furnished [equipped] tumulus.

ふくそうり 副総理 the deputy Prime Minister; the vice-premier.

ふくそくるい 腹足類 《動》Gastropoda ¶腹足類の動物 a gastropod.

ふくそすう 複素数 《数》a complex number.

ふくだい 副題 a subtitle.

ふぐたいてん 不倶戴天 ¶不倶戴天の敵 《文》a sworn [mortal] enemy [foe].

ふくちょう 復調 ¶復調する get [come] back into form; recover one's (usual) form.

---

ter.

ふくしゅう² きっと復讐をしてみせる。I will get my revenge. / この前君に負けたから今度は復讐戦だ。You beat me last time; now I will get my own back [have my revenge] on you.

ふくしん それ以来彼は中田氏の腹心となっている。He has been Mr. Nakada's confidant [right-hand man] ever since.

ふくすう それはここでは複数として使ってある。It is used here as a plural. / 複数も同形である。The same form is used in the plural.

ふくせい 不許複製。《表示》All rights reserved.

ふくそう 服装はきちんとしなさい。See that you are neatly [tidily] dressed. / その人はどんな服装でしたか。How was he dressed? | What was he wearing? / あの人はちっとも服装に構わない。He does not care about his appearance at all. | 《文》He is quite indifferent to his dress [personal appearance]. / 男は女ほどに服装に構わない。Men pay less attention to clothes [what they wear] than women do.

ふくぞう 腹蔵なく君の考えを言いたまえ。Give me your candid

ふくつ

- **ふくつ** 不屈 ¶不屈の 《文》indomitable;《文》unyielding;《文》indefatigable;《文》dauntless/ 不屈の精神 an indomitable spirit [will];《文》tenacity of purpose.
- **ふくつう** 腹痛 (a) stomachache;《口語》(a) bellyache;〈差し込み〉gripe(s); colic (幼児の) ¶腹痛がする have (a) stomachache; one's stomach aches.
- **ふくとう** 復党 ¶復党する〈自ら〉rejoin [return to] the party;〈許されて〉be reinstated in the party.
- **ふくどく** 服毒 ¶服毒する take poison / 服毒自殺する kill *oneself* by taking poison.
- **ふくとしん** 副都心 a subcenter (of a city) ¶新宿副都心 Shinjuku as a subcenter of Tokyo.
- **ふくはい** 腹背 ¶腹背に敵を受ける be attacked both in front and rear; find *oneself* between two fires.
- **ふくびき** 福引き a lottery ¶福引きをする hold a lottery / 福引きを引く draw a lot / 福引きで当たる win [get] a prize in the lottery / 福引き券 a lottery ticket [card]. 文例⇩
- **ふくひ(れい)** 複比(例)【数】(a) compound ratio; compound proportion ⇨ ひれい¹.
- **ふくぶ** 腹部 the abdominal region; the abdomen ¶腹部の.
- **ぶくぶく** ¶ぶくぶくした〈ふくれて〉baggy;〈柔らかくて〉soft; spongy / ぶくぶく太った fat and flabby; obese / ぶくぶく泡が出る (立つ) bubble up; rise in bubbles / ぶくぶく沈む sink bubbling.
- **ふくぶくしい** 福々しい plump and healthy-looking.
- **ふくふくせん** 複々線【鉄道】a four-track line.
- **ふくぶん¹** 復文 (a) retranslation (into the original language).
- **ふくぶん²** 複文【文法】a complex sentence.
- **ふくへい** 伏兵 an ambush; men [troops] in ambush ¶伏兵を置く [に会う] lay [fall into] an ambush.
- **ふくへき** 腹壁【解】the abdominal wall.
- **ふくほん** 副本 a duplicate (copy).
- **ふくまく** 腹膜【解】the peritoneum (*pl.* -nea) ¶腹膜炎 peritonitis.
- **ふくませる** 含ませる ¶水を含ませる soak *sth* with [in] water / 筆に墨を含ませる dip a (writing) brush in ink / 口に含ませる〈人の〉let *sb* hold *sth* in *his* mouth;〈自分の〉⇨ ふくむ.
- **ふくまでん** 伏魔殿 a hotbed of corruption;《文》a pandemonium.
- **ふくみ** 含み〈意味〉an implication; a hidden [《文》an implied] meaning ¶含みのある言葉 words full of hidden meaning; an expression with hidden meanings / 政治的含みの多い決定 a decision heavy with political undertones / 含みを残しておく leave some room [for further negotiations] / 含み声で in a muffled voice / 含み資産 latent property / 含み綿〈歯科治療の〉a cotton wool gag / 含み笑い a suppressed laugh [smile].
- **ふくむ¹** 服務《文》service ¶服務する serve / 服務規定 the office [service] regulations / 服務時間 (during) office (business) hours.
- **ふくむ²** 含む〈含有する〉include; contain; hold; have;〈口に〉keep [hold] *sth* in *one's* mouth;〈心に抱く〉bear [keep] *sth* in mind;〈意味を〉imply ¶鉄分を含んだ水 water containing iron; water with iron in it / 多量の炭酸ガスを含んだ空気 air loaded [impregnated] with carbonic acid gas / 媚(こ)び [笑み] を含んだ目つき flirtatious [smiling] eyes. 文例⇩
- **ふくめる** 含める〈言い含める〉⇨ いいふくめる ¶…を含めて including…; inclusive of…. 文例⇩
- **ふくめん** 覆面 a mask ¶覆面する wear a mask; mask *oneself* / 覆面を取る take *one's* mask off; unmask *oneself*.
- **ふくよう** 服用 ¶服用する take《medicine》(by mouth); drink《mineral water》. 文例⇩
- **ふくようき** 複葉機 a biplane.
- **ふくよか** ¶ふくよかな plump; full; well-rounded / ふくよかな胸 a full [well-rounded] bosom.
- **ふくらしこ** 膨らし粉 baking powder.
- **ふくらはぎ** 脹ら脛 the calf (*pl.* calves).
- **ふくらます** 膨らます swell; expand; inflate; bulge ¶風船をふくらます blow up [inflate] a (toy) balloon / ほおをふくらます puff out *one's* cheeks. 文例⇩
- **ふくらみ** 膨らみ a swelling; a bulge.
- **ふくらむ** 膨らむ ⇨ ふくれる. 文例⇩
- **ふくり¹** 福利 ⇨ ふくし².
- **ふくり²** 複利 compound interest ¶複利で計算する reckon [calculate] at compound interest.
- **ふくれっつら** 膨れっ面 a sulky [sullen] look ¶ふくれっ面をする sulk; get [go] sulky; have a fit of the sulks.

---

opinion (on it). | Tell me straight out what you think (about it).
ふくつう ひどく腹痛がする. I've got (a) terrible stomachache.
ふくむ 余興に福引きがあります. By way of entertainment there will be a raffle.
ふくむ 口に飯を一杯含んでいて話ができなかった. I could not talk with my mouth full of rice. / 彼は僕に何か含む所があるようだ. He appears to have something against me. / この点はよく含んでおいてくれ給え. I hope you will bear [keep] this in mind. / その予算中には臨時費は含まれていない. The estimates do not include any contingent expenses. / ブランデーには多量のアルコールが含まれている. Brandy has a high alcohol content. | Brandy contains a high percentage of alcohol.
ふくめる 新築費は税金を含めて総額2千万円になる. The building expenses come [amount] to twenty million yen including tax.
ふくよう 1日3回毎食後服用.《表示》To be taken three times a day after meals.
ふくらます 風が帆を一杯にふくらませた. The wind filled out the sails. | The sails bellied out in the wind.
ふくらむ ここではまだ梅のつぼみはふくらみもしない. The buds on the *ume* trees here have not begun to swell yet.
ふくれる 会員が1,000名にふくれた. The membership swelled to 1,000. / 彼はお腹がふくれるまで食べた. He ate until he was

ふくれる 膨れる 〈物が〉 swell (out); 〈膨張する〉 expand; be [become] inflated; 《文》 distend; bulge; 〈不機嫌になる〉 sulk; get sulky; be cross ¶ふくれた bulging; swollen; puffy / ひざのふくれたズボン trousers that are baggy at the knees / ふくれた財布 an overstuffed pocketbook / ビー玉でふくれたポケット a pocket bulging with marbles. 文例⇩

ふくろ 袋 a bag; a sack (ズックの); a pouch (小袋) ¶カンガルー[ペリカン]のふくろ the pouch of a kangaroo [pelican] / 1袋のあめ a bag [packet, 《米》sack] of candy / 袋に入れる put *sth* into a bag / 袋から出す take *sth* out of a bag / 袋小路 a blind alley; a dead-end (street); a cul-de-sac 《*pl*. -sacs》/ 袋だたきにする gang up on *sb* and beat *him* up; join in giving *sb* a thrashing; 袋縫い a French seam / 袋物商 a dealer in bags and pouches. 文例⇩

ふくろう 〖鳥〗an owl ¶ふくろうの子 a young owl; an owlet / ふくろうの鳴き声 a hoot / ふくろう部隊 a special night-duty squad (of the police). 文例⇩

ふくろじゅつ 腹話術 ventriloquism ¶腹話術を使う use ventriloquism; ventriloquize / 腹話術師 a ventriloquist.

ぶくん 武勲

ふけ dandruff; scurf ¶ふけだらけの (a collar) covered in dandruff; dandruffy; scurfy / ふけを取る get rid of [remove] dandruff / ふけ取り a dandruff remover; 〈ローション〉 hair lotion.

ぶけ 武家 the *samurai* class; 《born into》 a warrior family; 〈武士〉⇒ ぶし.

ふけい¹ 父兄 parents.

ふけい² 父系 the paternal line ¶父系家族 a patrilineal family.

ふけい³ 婦警 a policewoman.

ぶげい 武芸 martial [《文》warlike] arts.

ふけいき 不景気 〈世間の〉 bad [hard] times; 〈商売の〉 a business depression; (a) recession; bad business; dullness ¶不景気な dull; slack / 不景気な顔をしている look cheerless [blue] / 不景気になる grow dull; slacken. 文例⇩

ふけいざい 不経済 ¶不経済な uneconomical; wasteful; 〈費用が掛かる〉 expensive. 文例⇩

ふけつ 不潔 uncleanliness ¶不潔な 《文》 uncleanly; dirty; filthy / 不潔な物 dirt; filth / 頭を不潔にしておく never wash *one's* hair; (always) have *one's* hair in a filthy state / 体を不潔にしておく never wash (oneself); be always dirty [filthy, in a filthy state]. 文例⇩

ふけやく 老け役 ¶老け役をやる play [do] the part of an aged person.

ふける¹ 老ける 〈年が〉 grow [《文》become] old; 《文》 advance in years; 〈見かけが〉 look old ¶年の割りに[30にしては]老けて見える look old for *one's* age [for thirty]. 文例⇩

ふける² 更ける 〈深くなる〉 get [《文》grow] late; 〈(時)が進む〉《文》advance; wear on (徐徐に) ¶夜が更けるにつれて as the night goes [wears] on.

ふける³ 耽る indulge 《in》; give *oneself* up [over] 《to》; 〈没頭する〉 be obsessed 《by》; be absorbed [《文》engrossed] 《in》; be given 《to》 ¶空想にふける 《文》 indulge in idle reverie; daydream / 瞑想にふける be lost in meditation.

ふけん 府県 prefectures ¶府県の prefectural.

ふけんこう 不健康 bad [poor, 《文》ill] health ¶不健康な unhealthy; in bad [poor, delicate] health; 〈非衛生的〉 unwholesome; unsanitary / 不健康地 an unhealthy [unwholesome] place.

ふけんしき 不見識 ¶不見識な 《behavior》 which betrays [shows] *one's* lack of judgment; absurd; 〈みっともない〉 disgraceful.

ふげんじっこう 不言実行 action before [rather than] words; work before talk.

ふけんぜん 不健全 ¶不健全な 《文》 unsound; 《文》 unwholesome; unhealthy; 〈病的な〉 morbid.

ふこう¹ 不孝 《文》 lack [want] of filial piety ¶不孝な 《文》 undutiful; 《文》 unfilial / 不孝者 a bad [an undutiful] son [daughter].

ふこう² 不幸 〈みじめ〉 misery; 〈悲しみ〉 unhappiness; sorrow; 《文》 grief; 〈不運〉 (a) misfortune; bad [《文》ill] luck; 〈災厄〉 (a) disaster; (a) calamity; 〈死亡〉 (a) death; (a) bereavement ¶不幸な miserable; unhappy; unfortunate; unlucky; 《文》ill-fated ¶不幸な人々 unfortunate people; unfortunates / 不幸にも unfortunately; unluckily / 不幸に会う have [meet with] a misfortune; 〈家人に死なれる〉 be bereaved 《of *one's* father》 / 人の不幸を願う wish *sb* harm [《文》ill] / 不幸をもたらす 〈事が主語〉 bring *one* bad luck / 不幸続きを被る a series of misfortunes. 文例⇩

ふごう¹ 符号 a mark; a sign; a symbol; a code (電信などの) ¶符号化する put [convert] 《information》 into code; encode; code.

ふごう² 符合 ¶符合する agree 《with》; tally

---

full. / 彼はちょっと小言を言われてもすぐふくれる。 He gets sulky [cross] at the slightest scolding.

ふくろ 彼は袋のねずみも同然だ。 He is like a rat in a trap.

ふくろう ふくろうが鳴いた。 An owl hooted.

ふけいき 今は不景気だ。 Times are bad [hard]. / あの店は不景気だ。 That store is doing poor business [doesn't have many customers].

ふけいざい それをそんな風に使うのは不経済だ。 It is uneconomical [poor economy] to use it in that way.

ふけつ 不潔から色々の病気が起こる。 Uncleanliness is the cause of various diseases. / からだをそんな不潔にしていてはいけない。 You should keep yourself cleaner [pay more attention to your personal cleanliness].

ふける¹ 彼は年よりも老けて見える。 He looks old for his age. | He looks older than his age [than he really is]. / 彼女は年をとっても老けないね。 She wears her age well.

ふける² 夜は更けていた。 It was late at night. | 《文》 The night was far advanced.

ふこう² だれにもひどいけがなかったのは不幸中の幸いだった。 It is consoling to think that no one was injured seriously. / 彼は不幸にも卒業前に病気になった。 He had the misfortune [was unfortunate enongh] to be taken ill before for graduation. / 最近根本家に不幸があった There has been a death in Mr. Nemoto's family recently. | Mr. Nemoto has had

ふごう³ 富豪 a rich [wealthy] man; a man of property; 〈百万長者〉a millionaire.

ぶこう 武功 military exploits ¶武功を立てる distinguish *oneself* in war [a battle]; render distinguished (military) service.

ふごうかく 不合格 failure; disqualification ¶不合格の disqualified; rejected / 不合格になる 〈試験に〉 fail (in) [fail to pass] an examination; 〈検査に〉 be rejected / 不合格者 an unsuccessful candidate; a rejected person / 不合格品 a rejected article; a reject. 文例◑

ふこうそく 不拘束 ¶身柄不拘束のまま in *one's* own custody; without physical restraint.

ふこうへい 不公平 unfairness; 《文》partiality ¶不公平な unfair; 《文》unjust / 不公平な取り扱いをする treat *sb* unfairly; discriminate against *sb*.

ふこうり 不合理 《文》irrationality; unreasonableness 〈無理〉¶不合理な irrational; absurd; unreasonable 〈無理な〉.

ふこく 布告 (a) proclamation ¶布告する proclaim; declare.

ふこころえ 不心得 〈あつかましさ〉impudence; cheek; 〈無分別〉an indiscretion; rash [《文》indiscreet] behavior; 〈口語〉a slip; 〈不行跡〉《文》a misdemeanor; 《文》misguided behavior ¶不心得にも…する be impudent [foolish] enough to *do*; have the cheek to *do* / 不心得者 an impudent [a misguided] fellow.

ぶこつ 無[武]骨 ¶無骨な rough; 《文》uncouth; 《文》boorish ¶無骨者《文》a boor; 《文》a rustic.

ふさ 房 〈糸・毛などの〉a tuft; 〈飾りの〉a tassel; 〈花・果実の〉a bunch, a cluster ¶ぶどう2房 two bunches of grapes / 1房の髪 a lock [tuft] of hair / 房の付いた tasseled / 房になって咲く bloom in clusters. 文例◑

ブザー a buzzer ¶ブザーが鳴る the buzzer sounds [rings] / ブザーを鳴らす buzz / ブザーを押す press a buzzer.

ふさい¹ 夫妻 ¶田中夫妻 Mr. and Mrs. Tanaka; the Tanakas; Mr. Tanaka and his wife.

ふさい² 負債 a debt; liabilities ¶10万円負債がある owe *sb* 100,000 yen / 負債ができる fall [run] into debt; 《文》incur a burden of debt / 負債者 a debtor.

ふざい 不在 《文》absence ¶不在である be out; be not at home; be absent; be away from home / 不在中に in [during] *one's* absence; while *one* is away / 不在証明 an alibi / 不在地主 an absentee landlord [landowner] / 不在投票 absentee voting; voting by mail / 不在投票者 an absentee voter. 文例◑

ぶさいく 不細工 ¶不細工な顔 an ugly [a plain] face / 不細工な机 a poorly made desk.

ふさがる 塞がる 〈閉ざされる〉be closed; be shut; 〈詰まる〉be blocked (道路などが); be choked [stopped, filled, blocked] up (管などが); be obstructed (邪魔物で); 〈使用中である〉be engaged (特にトイレが); be occupied (家・席などが); be filled [full] (場所・欠員などが). 文例◑

ふさく 不作 a bad [poor] harvest [crop]; (a) crop failure ¶不作の年 a lean year. 文例◑

ふさぐ¹ 塞ぐ 〈閉じる〉close; shut; cover (覆う); 〈詰める〉stop up (穴などを); fill (up) (すきまなどを); 〈障害物で〉block (up); obstruct ¶穴をふさぐ fill [stop up] a hole; stop a gap / 場所をふさぐ occupy [take up] space [room].

ふさぐ² 鬱ぐ be depressed; be in low spirits; feel gloomy; 《口語》be in the blues [dumps]; mope ¶ふさいだ顔 a melancholy look / ふさぎがちの《文》melancholy. 文例◑

ふさくい 不作為 ¶不作為抽出法 [統計] random sampling / 不作為犯 [法] a crime of omission; nonfeasance.

ふざける 〈跳ね回る〉frolic [romp] (about); 〈じゃれる〉play with; 〈文》sport; 〈冗談を言う〉joke;《文》jest;〈からかう〉make fun [《文》sport] of;〈ばかげたことを言う〉talk nonsense [rubbish]; 〈ばかなことをする〉fool about [around]; be silly; behave stupidly [foolishly]; 〈男女が〉flirt [《文》dally] (with) ¶ふざけて〈たわむれて〉playfully, in play; 〈冗談に〉in fun [《文》jest, joke]; for a joke. 文例◑

ぶさた 無沙汰 ⇒ごぶさた.

ふさふさ ¶ふさふさした髪 bushy [《文》abun-

---

a death in his family recently. / ご不幸がおありになったよし心からお悔やみ申し上げます。I sincerely sympathize with you in your sad bereavement.

ふごうかく 彼は身体検査で不合格になった。He failed the physical (examination). / 彼は目が悪いので不合格となった。He was rejected [disqualified] because of his poor eyesight.

ふさ この帽子には房がついている。This cap has a tassel.

ふざい 彼は箱根へ[旅行に]行って不在です。He is away at Hakone [on a trip]. / 彼は用事で一日中不在だった。Business kept him out all day. / 彼はいつも不在がちだ。He is away from home most of the time. / 昨日は不在で失礼しました。I am sorry I missed your call yesterday.

ふさがる 道路がすっかりふさがって通れない。The whole street is blocked to traffic. / この家は空いてもすぐふさがる。This house is never left vacant long; it soon finds a tenant.

ふさく 今年は米が不作だ。We have had a poor crop of rice this year. / The rice crop has failed this year. / 去年中国では作物が不作だった。There were crop failures in China last year. / アメリカの農産物が不作になると、世界の農産物の価格が急騰することが予想される。If American farmers have a bad year, there is likely to be a sharp increase in prices of agricultural produce on the world market.

ふさぐ² 天気が悪いと気分がふさぐ。Bad weather depresses me.

ふざける ふざけるな！Watch it [your step]! / 〈冗談を言うな〉Don't try to be funny! / 〈ばかを言うな〉Nonsense! / Don't be silly [stupid]! / Don't talk rubbish!

ふさふさ きつねには長いふさふさした尾がある。The fox has a long, bushy tail.

ぶさほう この子は無作法だ。This child has no manners. / そんな事をするのは無作法だ。It is bad manners to do that. / That's bad [not good] manners.

ぶさほう

dant, flowing] hair ; 《文》tresses (女性の). 文例⇩

ぶさほう 無作法 bad manners ; 《文》a breach of etiquette ; rudeness ¶無作法な ill-mannered ; impolite ; rude ; 《文》unmannerly / 無作法な事をする behave rudely [be rude] to *sb* / 無作法者 a person who has no manners ; an ill-mannered person. 文例⇩

ぶざま 無様 ¶無様な〈不体裁な〉ungraceful ; unsightly ; 〈不器用な〉awkward ; clumsy / 無様に ungracefully ; clumsily ; awkwardly ; in an awkward way [《文》manner].

ふさわしい suitable ; 〈似合った〉《文》becoming ; 〈適切な〉proper ; 《文》appropriate ; 《文》fitting ¶...にふさわしい become... ; suit... / 紳士にふさわしくない行為《文》conduct unbecoming (to) [unworthy of] a gentleman. 文例⇩

ふさんせい 不賛成 disapproval ; disagreement ¶不賛成である disapprove (of the idea) ; be against (the plan) ; do not agree (with *sb*, to a proposal) / 不賛成を唱える object (to) ; take [make an] objection (to). 文例⇩

ふし¹ 不死 ¶不死の《文》undying ; immortal / 不死鳥 the phoenix.

ふし² 父子 father and son ¶楠公父子 the (elder and junior) Kusunokis / 父子相伝の handed down [passed on] from father to son.

ふし³ 節〈関節〉a joint ; a knuckle (指の) ; 〈結節〉a knot ; 〈曲〉a tune ; an air ; 〈箇所, 点〉a point ¶竹の節 a bamboo joint / 歌詞に節をつける set a song to music / 節をつけて読む read in a singsong tone / 節々が痛む *one*'s joints hurt ; feel pain in *one*'s joints / 節だらけの full of knots ; knotted / 節くれ立った gnarled《hands》. 文例⇩

ふじ¹ 不治 ⇨ ふち³.

ふじ² 不時 ¶不時の〈時ならぬ〉《文》untimely ; 〈不意の〉unexpected ; unforeseen ; 〈偶然の〉accidental / 不時の場合に in time of need [emergency] / 不時に備える provide against [be prepared for] emergencies ; provide against [for] a rainy day.

ふじ³ 藤 〖植〗a (Japanese) wisteria [wistaria]

¶ふじだな a wisteria trellis / ふじづる a wisteria vine / ふじ色 wisteria violet ; light purple ; lilac / ふじ紫(色) dark lilac.

ぶし 武士 a *samurai* ; a warrior ¶武士道 *Bushido* ; the code of the *samurai* / 武士道精神 the *samurai* spirit. 文例⇩

ぶじ 無事〈安全〉safety ; security ; 〈平穏〉peace ¶無事な〈安全な〉safe ; secure ; 〈平穏な〉uneventful ; peaceful / 無事に〈安全に〉safely ; in safety ; without accident [mishap]〈事故なく〉; 〈平穏に〉in peace ; peacefully ; uneventfully ; 〈息災に〉safe and sound ; well / 〈品物が〉無事に着く arrive [reach 《the purchaser》] in good condition / 無事に暮らす〈日を送る〉live in peace ; live [lead] a quiet life / 無事に済む pass [go] off without accident / 無事でいる be (quite) well ; be doing well. 文例⇩

ふしあな 節穴 a knothole. 文例⇩

ふしあわせ 不幸せ ⇨ ふこう².

ふしおがむ 伏し拝む kneel down [go (down) on *one*'s knees] and worship.

ふしぎ 不思議 (a) wonder ; a marvel ; (a) mystery ¶世界の七不思議 the Seven Wonders of the World / 不思議な wonderful ; marvelous ; strange ; mysterious (神秘な) ; miraculous (奇跡的) / 不思議な物[事, 人] a marvel ; a wonder / 不思議に wonderfully ; strangely ; mysteriously / 不思議なことには, 不思議にも strangely enough ; strange to say / ...とは不思議である It is strange [a wonder] that... / ...に不思議はない It is only natural that... ; It is no [little] wonder that... ; It comes as no surprise that... / 不思議に思う, 不思議がる wonder [marvel] (at) / 不思議そうに (look at *sth*) wonderingly. 文例⇩

ふしぜん 不自然 ¶不自然な unnatural ; 〈人為的〉artificial ; 〈てらった〉affected / 不自然な笑い a forced smile / 不自然な態度 affected manners / 不自然な丁重さ《文》(with) studied politeness.

ふしだら ¶ふしだらな slovenly ; 〈品行の〉loose (in morals) ; 《文》dissolute / ふしだらな女 a slut ; a loose woman / ふしだらな生活を

ふさわしい 彼は青年にふさわしく率直に意見を述べた。He spoke his mind frankly, as becomes a young man. / それは君こそふさわしからぬ行為だ。It would ill become you to do that. / これは正に彼にふさわしい仕事だ。This is the kind of job that will suit him very well. / さすがに彼は武士にふさわしい死に方をした。He died like the *samurai* that he was.

ふさんせい 君は行くのに賛成ですか, 不賛成ですか。Are you for or against going? / 君の説には不賛成です I cannot agree with you.

ふし³ 彼の話には多少疑わしい節がある。There are some points in his statement which do not

sound quite convincing to me. / その節回しはこうです。This is how the melody goes.

ぶし 武士に二言はない。A *samurai* never goes back on his word. / A *samurai*'s word is (as good as) his bond. / 武士は食わねど高楊子。A *samurai*, even when starving, acts as if he had a full stomach.

ぶじ あの火事に金庫は無事だった。The safe remained intact in the fire. / 無事にお帰りでおめでとうございます。I am very glad to see you safe home again. / 二百十日も無事に過ぎた。The Ni-hyakutoka passed off calmly [quietly]. / ではどうかご無事で! Good luck! I hope you have a

pleasant journey. / I wish you *bon voyage*.

ふしあな そんなことがわからなければ, お前の目は節穴だ。If you don't see that, you can't see anything.

ふしぎ 不思議な事もあればあるものだ。That's a mystery. / I really can't account for it. / 梅が今頃咲くとは不思議だ。It is strange that *ume* blossoms should bloom at this time of year. / あの人が試験に合格したのは何の不思議もありません。I am not surprised that he has passed the examination. / その薬は不思議によく効く。The medicine is remarkably effective [works astonishingly well]. / 彼だけは不思議に助かっ

ふじちゃく　不時着　¶不時着する　make an emergency [a forced] landing; crash-land; be crash-landed／〈海上に〉ditch; be ditched.

ふじつ　不実　〈不誠実〉《文》inconstancy;《文》faithlessness;〈薄情〉cold-heartedness／不実な《文》inconstant;《文》faithless;〈無情な〉cold-hearted. 文例↓

ぶしつけ　不躾　¶ぶしつけな〈無作法な〉ill-mannered; rude;〈乱暴な〉rough;〈ずうずうしい〉impudent; brazenfaced. 文例↓

ふじつぼ【動】a barnacle.

ふじばかま【植】a boneset; a thoroughwort.

ふしまつ　不始末　〈失態〉mismanagement;〈不注意〉carelessness;〈非行〉《文》misconduct ¶不始末を仕出かす《口語》blot one's copy-book;《文》commit an irregularity;《文》misconduct oneself／火の不始末 not taking enough care in putting out the fire; the careless handling of the embers.

ふじみ　不死身　¶不死身である〈痛みを感じない〉be insensitive [《文》insensible] to pain;〈傷つけられない〉be invulnerable;〈なかなか死なない〉have a charmed life; have more lives than a cat (★ A cat has nine lives. という諺から).

ふしめ¹　伏し目　¶伏し目になる drop [《文》cast down] one's eyes／伏し目がちに with downcast eyes.

ふしめ²　節目〈節〉⇨ふし³　¶人生の節目 events which mark the stages of one's life.

ふしゅ　浮腫【医】(an) edema (pl. -s, -mata).

ふじゆう　不自由　〈不便〉inconvenience;〈貧乏〉《文》want;《文》destitution; poverty;〈体の〉disability　¶不自由な〈不便な〉inconvenient;〈貧乏な〉poor;《文》destitute;《文》needy;〈手足が〉disabled; crippled／不自由する《文》want; be destitute; run short of／(物が)なくて不自由する miss sth; be short [in need] of sth／金に不自由する be hard up for money／金に不自由はない have plenty [no lack] of money／不自由なく暮らす［暮らしている］live in comfort;《文》want for nothing; be well off／不自由を忍ぶ put up with inconvenience [discomfort(s)];〈キャンプ生活などで〉rough it／右足が不自由である〈全く使えない〉have lost the use of one's right leg;〈完全には使えない〉do not have (the) full use of one's right leg; be lame in the right leg. 文例↓

ふじゅうじゅん　不従順　disobedience; insubordination; recalcitrance.

ふじゅうぶん　不充分〈不足〉《文》insufficiency; lack;〈不完全〉《文》imperfection　¶不充分な not enough;〈不満足な〉unsatisfactory;〈不完全な〉《文》imperfect; incomplete／証拠不充分のために for lack [want] of sufficient evidence／不充分な点がある[ない] leave something [nothing] to be desired.

ぶじゅつ　武術　⇨ぶどう¹.

ふしゅび　不首尾　⇨しっぱい.

ふじゅん¹　不純　¶不純な impure; mixed／不純な心《文》an impure heart／不純な動機 a mixed [selfish, dishonest] motive／不純物 impurities; adulterants.

ふじゅん²　不順　¶不順な《文》unseasonable; changeable〈変わりやすい〉／気候不順のため on account of the unseasonable weather／気候不順の折から in this unseasonable weather. 文例↓

ふじょ　扶助　〈助力〉《文》aid; help;〈扶養〉support　¶扶助する《文》aid; help; support;《文》sustain／父母の扶助を受ける depend on one's parents for support／県から生活の扶助を受けている live on relief from the prefecture／扶助料〈遺族への〉an allowance to a bereaved family.

ぶしょ　部署　one's post; one's place of duty ¶部署につく take up one's position [post]／部署についている be at one's post／部署を守る[去る] keep to [desert] one's post. 文例↓

ふしょう¹　不肖　¶不肖Ⅰ　¶不肖の子 a son who is unworthy of his father.

ふしょう²　不詳　¶不詳の unknown; unidentified〈身元の〉.

ふしょう³　負傷　an injury; a wound (主に戦傷) ⇨けが　囲囲　¶負傷する get [be] injured; be wounded; get hurt／腕に負傷する be injured in the arm／負傷者 an injured [a wounded] person;〈総称〉the injured; the wounded. 文例↓

ふじょう¹　不浄　¶不浄な《文》unclean; dirty／不浄な金 ill-gotten gains.

ふじょう²　浮上　⇨うかびあがる.

ぶしょう¹　武将　a military commander; a general.

ぶしょう²　無[不]精《文》indolence; laziness ¶無精な lazy;《文》indolent;《文》slothful／無精ひげを生やしている《文》be unshaven;《文》be ill-shaven; have [wear] a stubbly beard／無精者 a lazy fellow; a lazybones (単数扱い). 文例↓

ふしょうか　不消化　indigestion　¶不消化物 something indigestible; indigestible [heavy] food.

ふしょうじ　不祥事　a scandal;《文》a deplorable event. た. Astonishingly, he alone escaped unhurt.｜He alone had a miraculous escape.

ふじつ　あんな不実な人とは思わなかった. I did not think he was so untrustworthy.

ぶしつけ　彼はぶしつけに私の行き先を尋ねた. He was impudent enough to ask me where I was going.／ぶしつけですがあなたの月給は. Excuse me for being so rude, but [If it's not a rude question,] how much do you get a month?

ふじゆう　私の生きている間はお前に不自由はさせない. You'll lack [want for] nothing as long as I live.／こういう時にはあの人がいないと不自由だ. I miss him at times like [on such an occasion as] this.

ふじゅん²　今年のここの気候はひどく不順で, 暖かかったり寒かったりした. The weather here has been very changeable [unsettled] this year. It has been warm and cold by fits and starts.

ぶしょ　一同部署についたまま艦とその運命を共にした. They remained at their posts, and went

ふしょうじき 不正直 dishonesty ¶不正直な dishonest.

ふしょうち 不承知 〈不賛成〉《文》disapproval; disagreement; (an) objection; 〈拒絶〉(a) refusal ¶不承知である《文》refuse to consent; object to; disapprove of. 文例⇩

ふしょうにん 不承認 〈新政権などの〉《文》nonrecognition.

ふしょうぶしょう 不承不承 against one's will; unwillingly; reluctantly; under protest ¶不承不承承諾する agree grudgingly; 《文》give one's unwilling [reluctant] consent.

ふしょうふずい 夫唱婦随 the wife following the lead set by her husband; 《文》the wife concurring in the husband's opinion [ideas].

ふじょうり 不条理《文》absurdity ⇒ ふごうり.

ふしょく 腐食 corrosion; erosion 〈酸類などによる〉; 〈腐朽〉rot; 〈さび〉rust ¶腐食する corrode; erode; rot; rust (さびる); 〈(さびなど が)むしばむ〉eat (into). 文例⇩

ぶじょく 侮辱 (an) insult; contempt ¶侮辱する insult; slight; wound sb's pride; treat sb with contempt [like dirt] / 侮辱を受ける be insulted; be slighted. 文例⇩

ふしょくど 腐植土 humus (soil).

ふじょし 婦女子〈婦人〉women; womenfolk; 〈婦人や子供〉women and children.

ふしん¹ 不信〈信義がないこと〉《文》faithlessness;《文》insincerity; 〈不信用〉distrust; suspicion ¶不信の目で見る look on sth suspiciously [with distrust] / 不信感を抱く distrust sb;《文》be distrustful of sb.

ふしん² 不振 dullness; inactivity ¶不振である be dull; be inactive; be slack; 〈選手などが〉be out of form; be in a slump / 事業の不振 a business depression; a slump in business / 輸出の不振 a slump in exports; inactivity [a poor showing] in the export trade. 文例⇩

ふしん³ 不審〈疑念〉(a) doubt; 〈嫌疑〉(a) suspicion ¶不審な〈疑わしい〉doubtful; dubious; 〈いぶかしい〉suspicious; questionable / 不審そうに doubtfully; distrustfully / 不審に思う doubt; think sth suspicious [strange]; feel suspicious about [of] sb [sth]; suspect / 不審を抱く have [《文》entertain] a suspicion 《that...》; feel doubtful about sth / 不審尋問を受ける be questioned (by a policeman) / 不審火 a suspected case of arson. 文例⇩

ふしん⁴ 普請 ⇒ けんちく, しゅうぜん.

ふじん¹ 夫人〈妻〉a wife; 〈敬称〉Mrs. ¶加藤夫人 Mrs. Kato.
囲み 第2次世界大戦前までは, Mrs. Thomas Henry Brown 又は Mrs. T.H. Brown のように Mrs. のあとには夫の名を書くのが普通であった. 又未亡人の場合には, Mrs. Mary E. Brown のように, 夫人本人の名を書いたりしたが, 最近では既婚婦人に対しても本人の名を書くことが多くなってきている. ただし今でも Mr. and Mrs. John Smith とは書いても, Mr. John and Mrs. Mary Smith とすることは稀である. なお Mrs とピリオドなしで書いてもかまわない.

ふじん² 布陣 the line-up.

ふじん³ 婦人 a lady; a woman (pl. women); 〈総称〉《文》womankind; 《文》the fair [weaker] sex ¶婦人らしい《文》feminine / 婦人を交えた席で in mixed company / 婦人用[持ち]の〈watches〉for ladies; ladies' (watches) / 婦人科(学) gynecology / 婦人会 a women's association [society] / 婦人解放運動 the women's emancipation [liberation] movement / 婦人記者 a woman reporter / a newspaperwoman / 婦人警官 a policewoman / 婦人雑誌 a ladies' magazine / 婦人参政権 female suffrage / 婦人席 ladies' seats / 婦人病 women's diseases; female disorders / 婦人服 women's dresses ★単数ならば a woman's dress / 婦人服店 a dress shop / 婦人問題 the problems of women.

ぶじん 武人《文》a warrior; a soldier.

ふしんじん 不信心《文》impiety; 《文》unbelief ¶不信心な《文》impious;《文》unbelieving; 《文》irreligious.

ふしんせつ 不親切 ¶不親切である be not kind (to sb); be unhelpful; be inconsiderate; 〈顧客などに〉be inattentive (to) ★ be unkind to sb は「いじわるをする」の意味で,「不親切である」の適訳ではない / 不親切にする be not kind to sb.

ふしんにん 不信任《文》nonconfidence; (a) lack [《文》want] of confidence (in) / 政府不信任案を可決する pass a vote of nonconfidence [《英》no confidence] in the Government.

ふしんばん 不寝番〈事〉(a) night watch;《文》(a) (sleepless) vigil; 〈人〉a night watchman ¶不寝番をする keep watch by night; keep vigil.

ふしんよう 不信用 distrust; (a) lack [《文》want] of confidence (in).

ふず 付図 an attached [appended] chart [graph, map, figure].

ぶす a bad-looker; a plain [《米》homely] girl; 〈俗〉an ugly cow.

ふずい¹ 不随 paralysis ⇒ ぜんしん¹ (全身不随), はんしんふずい.

ふずい² 付随 ¶付随する accompany; 《文》attend; 《文》be incidental 《to》/ 戦争に付随す

---

down with the ship.
ふしょう³ その事故で10名の負傷者を出した. Ten people were injured in the accident.

ふしょう² 無精をして彼の所へ手紙も出さずにいる. I have been remiss in (not) writing to him. ★ not がなければ, 怠けていてまだ手紙を書いていない, というわけだけが, not が入ると, 手紙を書かなくて悪いことをしたという気持ちが含まれてくる.

ふしょうち だから僕は不承知なのだ. That is why I would not agree [give my consent]. / 父はこの計画には不承知です. Father is against the plan.

ふしょく 酸は金属を腐食する. Acid erodes [eats into] metals.

ぶじょく 人を侮辱するにも程がある. This insult of yours is more than I can bear.

ふしん² 商売は甚だ不振だ. Business is very dull [slack, bad].

ふしん³ 不審の箇所にしるしを付けた. I marked the passages I didn't understand. / ご説明で不審が晴れました. Your explanation has cleared up [dispelled] my doubts.

ぶすい 無[不]粋 ¶無粋な〈野暮な〉unrefined; boorish;〈夢のない〉unromantic; matter-of-fact.

ふずいいきん 不随意筋 〖解〗an involuntary muscle.

ふすう 負数 〖数〗a negative [minus] number.

ふすう 部数 the number of copies;〈新聞・雑誌などの発行部数〉a circulation (of 80,000) ¶部数が出る[ない] have a large [small] circulation.

ぶすっと ¶ぶすっとしている be sullen; sulk.

ぶすぶす sputtering ¶ぶすぶす燃える導火線 a sputtering fuse.

ふすま¹ 麩 (wheat) bran.

ふすま² 襖 a *fusuma*; a (papered) sliding door (used to partition off rooms in a Japanese house) ¶ふすま絵 a painting on a *fusuma* / ふすま紙 *fusuma* paper.

ぶすりと ¶ぶすりと刺す drive [〘文〙thrust] (a dagger) home (into sb's chest).

ふする 付する〈つける〉⇨つける¹;〈付託する〉submit [refer] *sth* to (a committee); bring [lay] (a bill) before (the House) ¶制限を付する set limits to [on] *sth* / 不問に付する ⇨ふもん / 公判に付する ⇨こうはん¹.

ふせ 布施 an offering ¶お布施を上げる make an [a monetary] offering (to).

ふせい¹ 不正〈不公正〉injustice;〘文〙iniquity; unfairness;〈非行〉wrong;〈不法〉〘文〙unlawfulness;〈官吏の〉corruption;〈不正直〉dishonesty ¶不正な〘文〙unjust; unfair; foul; wrong; dishonest ¶違法な〘文〙unlawful, illegal;〈にせの〉false / 不正な事をする do something dishonest; behave dishonestly [unfairly]; do a dishonest thing [act] ;〈競技で〉play foul ;〈試験で〉cheat (in an examination)/ 不正な事をしない be honest ;〈競技などで〉play fair / 不正な選挙 a rigged election / 不正行為 a dishonest act; an unfair practice ;〈競技の〉foul play ;〈試験での〉cheating / (公務員などの)不正事件 a bribery [〘米〙graft] case; a case of (official) corruption; a scandal / 不正乗車をする steal a ride on a train. 文例⇩

ふせい² 父性 〘文〙fatherhood; 〘文〙paternity ¶父性愛 paternal love.

ふぜい 風情〈趣〉taste; 〘文〙elegance ¶風情のある 〘文〙tasteful; refined; charming / 風情のない tasteless; dull; 〘文〙prosaic / 私風情のものに for such as me [as I am] ⇨より² 〖用法〗for the likes of me / 風情を添える make *sth* (more) attractive. 文例⇩

ぶぜい 無勢 numerical inferiority ⇨たぜい.

ふせいかく 不正確 inaccuracy; 〘文〙imprecision ¶不正確な inaccurate; incorrect; inexact; 〘文〙imprecise.

ふせいこう 不成功 (a) failure; lack of success ¶不成功の unsuccessful; 〘文〙fruitless / 不成功に終わる end in [prove a] failure; fall through. 文例⇩

ふせいじつ 不誠実 insincerity; 〘文〙unfaithfulness ¶不誠実な insincere; 〘文〙unfaithful.

ふせいしゅつ 不世出 ¶不世出の〘文〙unparalleled; 〘文〙peerless / 不世出の偉人 a great man with few parallels in history.

ふせいせき 不成績 a poor [an unsatisfactory] result; (a) poor [bad] performance.

ふせいみゃく 不整脈 〖医〗an irregular [unequal] pulse; arrhythmia.

ふせいりつ 不成立 (a) failure ¶不成立に終わる fail; fall through; end in failure.

ふせき 布石〈碁の〉the strategic placing of stones (in the opening game of go);〈準備〉strategic moves; preparations ¶党人を政府機関の要所要所に布石する place party members in all the important government positions.

ふせぐ 防ぐ〈予防する〉prevent 《*sth, sb* from doing》; guard against;〈防御する〉defend; protect;〈防止する〉keep away [out, off, back]; check ¶腐敗を防ぐ preserve *sth* from decay / 氾濫(はんらん)を防ぐ keep (the river) from overflowing. 文例⇩

ふせじ 伏せ字 an omission; a blank ¶伏せ字にする do not print (a word) / 伏せ字にすべき語 an unprintable word.

ふせつ 敷設 ¶敷設する lay (a pipe); construct [build] (a railroad).

ふせっせい¹ 不摂生 neglect of *one's* health ¶不摂生である neglect [be careless about] *one's* health.

ふせっせい² 不節制 〘文〙intemperance ¶不節制な 〘文〙intemperate.

ふせる¹ 伏せる ¶伏せる turn down (an empty glass); lay *sth* face down [upside down] ¶たらいを伏せる place a tub bottom upward / 身を伏せる lie (face) down / 目を伏せて with downcast eyes. 文例⇩

ふせる² 臥せる〈寝る〉lie down;〈就床する〉go to bed;〈退〉retire ¶病気でふせている be ill in bed; be laid up with illness.

ふせん¹ 不戦 ¶不戦条約 an antiwar pact [treaty] / 不戦勝となる win a game by default; draw a bye (勝抜き戦の第1回戦でくじで) / 不戦敗になる lose a game by default; default a game [race].

ふせい 不正なもうけ方をするのは商売上手とは言えない。Someone who makes a profit by dishonest means cannot be called a good businessman.

ふぜい この庭は風情がある。This garden is tastefully laid out. / 私風情の者にできることではない。It is beyond someone [a man] like me.

ふせいこう やってみたが不成功であった。The attempt was unsuccessful [failed].

ふせぐ 彼らは敵の攻撃を防ぎ切れなかった。They were unable to withstand the enemy's attack. / この着物では寒さを防げない。You cannot keep out [protect yourself from] the cold with these clothes. / この建材は暑さや寒さを防ぎます。This material provides an effective insulation against both heat and cold. / 少し気をつけさえしたらそんな事は防げただろう。A little care would have prevented it.

ふせる¹ この事は伏せておいて下

ふせん²　付箋 a tag ; a label ¶手紙に付箋を付けて出す forward a letter with an address tag attached to it ; readdress a letter (★英米では付箋を付けず,あて先を書き直す)

ふせんめい　不鮮明 ¶不鮮明な indistinct ; unclear ; obscure ; blurred.

ぶそう　武装 〈国の〉armament(s) ; 〈兵士の〉equipment ¶武装する arm *sb* ; equip (an army) ; militarize (a country) ; 〈自ら〉equip [arm] *oneself* 《with a rifle》/ 武装している [go] armed / 武装解除する disarm *sb* ; demilitarize (a nation) / 武装中立 armed neutrality / 武装警官 an armed policeman ; 〈集合的〉armed police.

ふそうおう　不相応 ¶不相応な unsuited 《to, for》; 〈文〉disproportionate 《to》; out of keeping 《with》; 〈不似合な〉unbecoming 《to》/ 身分不相応な生活をする live beyond *one's* means.

ふそく¹　不足 〈不充分〉〈文〉insufficiency ; 〈足りないこと〉(a) shortage ; 〈文〉(a) deficiency ; 〈不満足〉dissatisfaction ; 〈不平〉a complaint ¶不足する 〈物が主語〉〈文〉be insufficient ; be in short supply ; 〈人が主語〉do not have enough (of) ; be [come, fall, run] short of ; want ; be in want [need] of / 10円不足するbe ten yen short ; be short by ten yen / 人手が不足する be shorthanded ; be short of workers / 技術が不足している lack [〈文〉be deficient in] skill / 何不足のない暮らしをする live in comfort ; be comfortably off / 不足を言う complain 《of》; grumble 《about》/ 不足を補う make up for a deficiency ; make good the shortage / 不足額[分] a shortage ; a shortfall ; a deficit. 文例⇩

ふそく²　不測 ⇨ふりょ.

ふそく³　付則 an additional clause ; a supplementary provision.

ふぞく　付属 ¶付属する be attached 《to》; belong 《to》¶ミシンの付属品 attachments to a sewing machine /...付属小学校 a primary school attached to.... 文例⇩

ぶぞく　部族 a tribe ¶部族社会 a tribal society / 部族民 tribesmen ; tribal people.

ふそくふり　不即不離 ¶不即不離の関係 a relationship neither too close to nor too remote from *sb*.

ふぞろい　不揃い ¶不揃いの uneven ; 〈文〉not uniform ; irregular ; 〈不完全な〉incomplete / 大小不揃いである be irregular in size. 文例⇩

ふそん　不遜 〈文〉haughtiness ; insolence ¶不遜な〈文〉haughty ; insolent / 不遜な振る舞いをする behave insolently.

ふた　蓋 a cover (覆い) ; a lid (箱などの) ; a cap (びんなどの) ; a case (時計の) ; a flap (ポケットの) ¶牛乳瓶のふた the (cardboard) top of a milk bottle / ふたの付いた, ふた付きの covered ; lidded / ふたのない lidless ; open / ふたをする cover 《the pan》(with the lid) ; put the lid on (the pot) ; shut the lid down ; cap (the bottle) / ふたをしておく keep *sth* covered / ふたを取る[あける] open ; uncover ; take the lid off / ふた明けの opening ; the beginning / ふた物 a lidded food container. 文例⇩

ふだ　札 〈付け札〉a card ; a label (荷物などの) ; a tag (下げ札, 荷札) ; 〈預かり札〉a receipt ; a check ; 〈守り札〉a charm ; a talisman (*pl*. -s) ; 〈トランプの〉a (playing) card ¶札を付けるlabel ; put a tag 《on an article》/ 札を配る[切る] deal [shuffle] the cards / 札をめくる[伏せる] turn over [down] a card / 札付きの悪党 a notorious scoundrel.

ぶた　豚 a pig (★〈英〉では「豚」一般をさすが,〈米〉では比較的大型の若豚をさすことが多い) ; a hog (〈米〉では「豚」一般をさし,特に食用の大型のものをいう時に用いるが,〈英〉では「去勢した雄豚」の意に限定される) ; a boar (去勢しない雄豚) ; a sow (雌) ; 〈文〉a swine (単複同形) ¶食肉用の豚 a pork pig ; a porker (若い) / 豚革 pigskin / 豚小屋 a pigsty ; a hogsty / 豚肉 pork / 豚箱に入れられる be thrown into a police cell.

ふたい　付帯 ¶付帯の incidental (expenses) ; 〈文〉attendant (circumstances) ; supplementary (items) ; subsidiary (enterprises) /...に付帯する accompanying... ; 《文》incidental to... / 付帯決議 a supplementary [an additional] resolution / 付帯条件 an incidental [a collateral] condition.

ふだい　譜代 ¶徳川家譜代の大名 a *daimyo* [feudal lord] in hereditary vassalage to the Tokugawas.

ぶたい¹　部隊 a (military) unit ; a corps (単複同形) ; a party ; a detachment ¶部隊長 a commander ; the commanding officer (略 : C.O.).

ぶたい²　舞台 ¶活動の舞台 *one's* field of action ; 〈文〉*one's* sphere of activity / 舞台に立つ[出る] appear on the stage [〈文〉before the footlights] ; go [come] on the stage (役者になる) / 脚本を舞台に載せる stage [present] a play ; put a play on the stage / 舞台裏の動き maneuverings behind the scenes / 舞台係 a stagehand / 舞台監督 a stage director [manager] / 舞台芸術 the performing arts ; theatrical art / 舞台げいこをする have a dress rehearsal / 舞台劇 a stage drama [play] / 舞台効果[装置] stage effects [setting] / 舞台装置家 a set de-

---

さい. Please don't tell anybody about this. | Please keep this secret [to yourself, under your hat].

ふそく¹ 飲料水が不足になった. We ran short of drinking water. / 郵税不足ですから不足料金90円を戴って下さい. The letter is insufficiently stamped, and 90 yen is due [and there is 90 yen to pay]. / 彼なら相手にとって不足はない. I find him a worthy opponent. / 何が不足でそんな顔をするのか. What makes you look so dissatisfied?

ふぞく 新型のフォードの中型車を買いたいのですが, 付属品一式付けて幾らですか. I want the new Ford compact. What is the price, fully equipped?

ふぞろい 彼らは身長が不ぞろいである. Their heights are uneven.

ふた ふたがしてある. It has a lid on. | It is covered. / ふたを開けてみるまではだれもわからない. No one can tell [predict] how it will turn out (until it actually happens). | No one can make a prediction until we see how it turns out.

ふたいきょざい 不退去罪《法》 ¶不退去罪で逮捕される be arrested on a charge of unlawful trespass [forcible detainer].

ふたいてん 不退転 ¶不退転の決意《文》(an) indomitable resolve; 《文》tenacity of purpose.

ふたえ 二重 ¶二重の double; 《文》twofold / 二重に折る fold *sth* in half [in two, double]; double / 二重まぶた a double eyelid.

ふたく 付託 ¶付託する commit [refer, submit] 《a bill to a committee》.

ぶたくさ 豚草《植》hogweed; ragweed.

ふたご 双[二]子 twins; twin brothers [sisters]; a twin (その1人) / 男女の双子 mixed twins / 彼の双子の弟 his twin brother / 双子座《天》Gemini; the Twins ⇒文例.

ふたごころ 二心《文》duplicity; double-dealing ¶二心ある double-dealing; treacherous; 《文》perfidious.

ふたこと 二言 ¶二言三言(ミ)言う say a few words. 文例⇩

ふたしか 不確か ¶不確かな uncertain; unreliable; precarious.

ふだしょ 札所 a temple regularly visited by pilgrims ¶札所めぐり (go on) a circuit of holy temples.

ふたたび 再び〈2度〉twice;〈2度目に〉for the second time;〈今一度〉once more [again];〈繰り返して〉again ¶再びする repeat; do over again. 文例⇩

ふたつ 二つ two ¶2つの中の1つを選ぶ choose between the two / 2つにする〈分ける〉divide *sth* in two [into two parts]; halve / 2つにたたむ fold *sth* in two; double (a sheet of paper) / 2つとも, 2つながら 〈肯定〉both (A) and (B);〈否定〉neither (A) nor (B) / 2つずつ in [by] twos; two at a time / 二つには secondly; in the second place / 二つとない〈唯一の〉only; unique;〈比類ない〉peerless;《文》unparalleled / (並べた)碁(ⁿ)石を2つ置きに拾う pick every third go stone / 二つ折判〈本〉a folio (*pl.* -s) / 二つ返事で承知する agree 《to a proposal》 very willingly;《文》give *one's* [a] ready consent 《to a proposal》.

ふたて 二手 ¶二手に分かれる divide into two groups.

ふたとおり 二通り〈2種類〉two kinds 《of》; 〈2様〉(in) two ways ¶2とおりに解釈ができる can be interpreted in two ways;《文》admit of two different readings.

ふたなり〈両性具有〉hermaphroditism;〈同上の人〉a hermaphrodite.

ふたば 双[二]葉〈子葉〉a seed leaf [lobe];〈芽〉a bud; a sprout.

ブダペスト Budapest.

ふたまた 二叉[股] ¶二またの forked / 二またのソケット a two-way socket / 二またになる[分かれる] fork / 二またをかける have it both ways; sit on the fence / 二またをかけてしくじる fall between two stools. 文例⇩

ふため 二目 ¶二目とは見られない shocking; hideous; repulsive;《be》too ugly [frightful] to look at. 文例⇩

ふたやく 二役 ¶二役を演じる play a dual role; play the parts (of A and B).

ふたり 二人 two people [《文》persons]; a couple ¶2人とも (both of them); either (of the two) / 2人で行く go together / 2人連れ a party of two (people);《in》a couple / 自転車に2人乗りする ride double on a bicycle / (病院などの) 2人部屋 a double room. 文例⇩

ふたん 負担《文》a burden; a load;〈支払い〉a charge;〈責任〉responsibility ¶負担する bear (the expenses); foot (the bill) / 費用の一部を負担する share the cost [expenses]《with *sb*》 / 負担をかける impose a burden 《on *sb*》; put a (severe) strain (on *sb's* finances) / …の負担を軽減する lighten the burden imposed on *sb* / 負担額 *one's* share [of (in)] the expenses);《文》an allotment. 文例⇩

ふだん 不断, 普段〈平生〉at ordinary [other] times; usually; ordinarily;〈常に〉always ¶不断の〈平生の〉usual; everyday; common;〈絶え間ない〉constant; perpetual; incessant;《文》ceaseless / 不断のとおり as usual; in the usual way / 不断の努力《文》ceaseless [unremitting] efforts / ふだん着 clothes for everyday wear; everyday wear [clothes]; a home [house] dress. 「chard.

ふだんそう 不断草 a spinach beet; a (Swiss)

ふち¹ 淵〈川の〉a (deep) pool;〈深淵(ᵏᵉ)〉《文》an abyss ¶絶望のふちに沈んでいる be in the depths of despair [《文》the slough of despond].

ふち² 縁 an edge; a verge;《文》a margin;《文》a brink (がけなどの); a bank (川の); a brim

---

ぶたい² この脚本は舞台に載せたらどんな風になるかしら. I wonder how this play will go on the stage. / 舞台を離れれば彼女もただの女さ. Off the stage she is an ordinary woman. / その小説の舞台はドイツだ. The scene of the story is laid in Germany. / 彼は世界を舞台に活躍している. The whole (wide) world is his stage. / 新社長選出の舞台は整ったと思われた. The stage seemed set for the election of the new president.

ふたこと 二言目には僕の悪口を言う. Whenever he opens his mouth, he says something against me.

ふたたび 私は二度と再びあんな所へは行くまい. I will never go there again. / 彼は故国を去って再び帰らなかった. He left his native land, never to return.

ふたつ 二つ返事で承諾した. He agreed without hesitation. / He jumped at our offer.

ふたまた 二またかけるのはやはりだめなものだ. I told you you couldn't have it both ways!

ふため 二目とは見られない姿になった. He was appallingly disfigured.

ふたり あの人たちは2人ともロシヤ人です. They are both [Both of them are] Russians. / 彼らはいつも2人づれで釣りに行く. The two of them always go fishing together. / 2人で力を合わせてようやくその箱を運んだ. The two of us managed between us to move the chest. / こんな奇人はおよそ2人とあるまい. You will not find [come across] another crank [eccentric] like him.

ふたん 経費は申請者の負担だ.

(帽子などの); a rim (眼鏡などの); a hem (布などの); a frame (写真の) ¶縁のついた brimmed; framed / 縁の広い帽子 a broad-brimmed hat / 縁の欠けた茶わん a teacup with a chipped rim / 縁をつける border; frame / がけの縁に立つ〈縁から転げ落ちる〉stand on [tumble over] the edge of a precipice / 縁石 a curb(stone) / 縁なし眼鏡 (a pair of) rimless glasses [spectacles].

ふち[3] 不治 ¶不治の病 an incurable [a fatal] disease.

ぶち 斑 patches; spots; specks ¶ぶちの〈まだらのある〉spotted; speckled; mottled; dappled; 〈とくに馬について〉〈くらふのが〉brindled / ぶち猫 a tabby (cat) / 白と黒のぶち犬 a black and white dog.

ぶちこむ ぶち込む ¶〈文〉cast) into ¶牢屋(ろうや)にぶちこむ throw sb into prison [jail].

ぶちこわし ぶち壊し〈破壊〉destruction; 〈台無しにすること〉spoiling ¶ぶち壊しをやる make a mess [《口語》hash] of sth; spoil. 文例⇩

ぶちこわす ぶち壊す〈破壊する〉break; destroy; 〈台無しにする〉spoil; 《文》mar ¶計画をぶち壊す upset [ruin, spoil] a plan.

ぶちのめす ⇒ うちのめす.

プチブル [<《フランス語》*petit bourgeois*] a petty [petit] bourgeois; 〈総称〉the petty [petit] bourgeoisie; the lower middle class.

ぶちまける 〈ほうり出す〉throw out (the contents); 〈打ち明ける〉tell sb sth frankly ¶何もかもぶちまける tell sb all about sth; make a clean breast of (the secret).

ふちゃく[1] 不着《文》nonarrival;《文》nondelivery ¶不着の手紙 a miscarried [lost] letter.

ふちゃく[2] 付着 adhesion ¶付着する stick [cling, 《文》adhere] (to). 文例⇩

ふちゅう 不忠《文》disloyalty;《文》disloyal.

ふちゅうい 不注意 carelessness; lack of care;《文》inattention ¶不注意な careless;《文》heedless; inattentive / 不注意に carelessly;《文》heedlessly / 不注意から through [as a result of, due to] (one's) carelessness / 食物に[万事に]不注意である be careless about food [in everything]. 文例⇩

ふちゅうじつ 不忠実《文》faithlessness;《文》infidelity ¶不忠実な《文》faithless;《文》un-

faithful;《文》disloyal;《文》false.

ふちょう[1] 不調《不成立》《文》(a) rupture; (a) failure; 〈不調子〉(a) bad condition; a slump ¶不調に終わる end in a rupture; fail; break off / 不調である be in (a) bad condition; 《運動選手などが》be off [out of] form. 文例⇩

ふちょう[2] 符丁〈符号〉a sign; a mark; a symbol; 〈暗号〉a code; 〈値段の〉a (secret) price mark; 〈合言葉〉a password ¶符丁を付ける put a secret [private] mark (on) / 符丁で言う speak in secret language.

ふちょう[3] 婦長 a head [chief] nurse.

ふちょう 部長 ⇒ぶ[2].

ふちょうほう 不調法 ¶不調法な〈拙劣な〉awkward; clumsy; 〈失礼な〉bad-mannered; 《文》impolite; 《文》unmannerly; 〈不慣れな〉inexperienced / 不調法をしでかす commit a blunder. 文例⇩

ふちょうわ 不調和《文》disharmony; discord ¶不調和な《文》inharmonious; discordant / 不調和である do not harmonize [match] (with); be out of keeping (with).

ふちん 浮沈 ups and downs; rise and fall;《文》vicissitudes ¶一生の浮沈にかかわる affect the whole course of one's life.

ぶつ ⇒たたく, なぐる ¶子供の尻をぶつ ⇒しり[1] / 一席ぶつ make a speech; give an address 《at a meeting》.

ふつう[1] 不通 (an) interruption; a stoppage 《of traffic》; a tie-up ¶〈交通・通信などが〉不通になる be cut off; be interrupted; be suspended; be tied up / 音信不通 ⇒ おんしん / 列車不通 the interruption [paralysis] of train service / 不通箇所 a break (on the line). 文例⇩

ふつう[2] 普通 ¶普通の〈常態の〉normal; regular; 〈通常の〉ordinary; common; usual; 〈一般の〉general; universal; average (並みの); commonplace (平凡な) / 普通の人 an average [ordinary] man [woman]; the man in [《米》on] the street; 《文》the common [ordinary] run of mankind [men] / 普通の状態に返る return to normal [normality] / 普通の場合に[は] in ordinary circumstances; usually / 普通(に)normally; ordinarily; commonly; usually; in general / 普通でない uncommon; unusual; extraordinary; abnormal / 普通以上[以下]である be above [below] (the) average / 普通高校 an academic high school / 普通選挙 universal

---

The applicant must bear the expenses. | The expenses will be charged to the applicant. / それでは君の負担が重過ぎる. That would make the burden too heavy for you. / その計画を実施するに当たっては米国が最大の負担をした. In putting the plan into effect, the U. S. shouldered the greater part of the burden.

ふだん 彼には不断と変わった様子はなかった. I saw [There was] nothing unusual [strange] about him. / 不断一生懸命に勉強していれば試験間際に徹夜などしなく

てもいいのに. If you had worked harder at other times, you would not have to sit up all night just before the examination. / この服は普段着にはもったいない. This dress is too good for everyday wear.

ぶちこわし それではせっかくの話もぶち壊しになってしまうよ. That would be throwing a spanner in the works.

ふちゃく[2] 彼の上着に血痕が付着していた. His coat was stained with blood. | There were blood stains on his coat.

ふちゅうい そんな事をしたとは君もずいぶん不注意だね. It was very careless of you to have done such a thing. / それは彼の不注意から起こった事だ. It arose from [was a result of] his carelessness.

ふちょう[1] 交渉は不調に終わった. The negotiations broke down [got nowhere].

ふちょうほう お酒は不調法です.

ふつう[1] 中央線の大月猿橋区間が不通となった. There was a blockage [tie-up] on the Otsuki-

[popular] suffrage / 普通名詞《文法》a common noun / 普通郵便 ordinary mail 《英》post] / 普通列車 a local [slow] train;《米》an accommodation train. 文例⇩

ふつか 二日 two days;〈第2日〉the second (day) ¶1月2日 the second of January; Jan. 2/着いてから2日目に on the second day after one's arrival / 2日置きに every third day; every three days / 二日酔い (have) a hangover. 文例⇩

フッか フッ化《化》fluoridation ¶フッ化水素 hydrogen fluoride / フッ化物 (a) fluoride.

ぶっか 物価 prices (of commodities) ¶物価の上昇[下落] a rise [fall] in prices / 物価の動き price movements / 物価指数 a《wholesale, retail》price index / 低物価政策 a low-price policy / 物価統制 price control.

ぶつが 仏画 a Buddhist painting [picture].

ぶっかき cracked ice; chips of ice.

ふっかける 吹っ掛ける 〈息を〉blow on;〈けんかを〉pick (a quarrel) with sb; provoke sb to (a quarrel);〈高値を〉ask an unreasonable [a fancy, an exorbitant] price; overcharge (for one's services).

ぶっかける ぶっ掛ける ⇨ かける³ ¶水をぶっかける throw water over sb [sth]; dash water on sb [sth].

ふっかつ 復活 〈再生〉《文》rebirth; revival;《文》resurrection;〈再興〉restoration ¶キリストの復活 the Resurrection of Jesus Christ / 復活する come to life again; come back to life; revive; be restored (to (the [its, one's]) original state) / 復活祭 Easter / 復活祭の卵 an Easter egg.

ぶつかる 〈当たる〉hit;《文》strike; bump into;〈衝突する〉run against [into]; collide with; knock [strike] against;〈出会う〉come on [across]; meet with;〈競技で顔を合わせる〉meet; be pitted against;〈直面する〉face; be brought face to face with; be confronted by;〈難事に〉tackle; grapple with;〈日が〉当る on ¶壁にぶつかる hit [bump] against the wall / 難関にぶつかる face [be confronted by] a difficulty; run [come] up against a difficulty. 文例⇩

ふっかん¹ 副官 an adjutant; an aide(-de-camp)《pl. aides-》.

ふっかん² 復刊 reissue; revived publication ¶復刊する republish; reissue; revive the publication (of).

ふっき 復帰 a return; a comeback;《法》reversion (財産などの) ¶復帰する return (to); come back (to); make a [one's] comeback;《法》revert (to) (財産などが) / 職場に復帰する return to work. 文例⇩

ぶつぎ 物議 ¶物議をかもす arouse criticism;《文》give rise to public censure; cause a scandal.

ふっきゅう 復旧 restoration ¶復旧する be restored (to its former state); be rehabilitated / 復旧工事 restoration [repair] works / 復旧工事中である be under repairs. 文例⇩

ぶっきょう 仏教 Buddhism /仏教(徒)の Buddhist; Buddhistic / 仏教徒[信者] a Buddhist; a believer in Buddhism / 仏教美術[彫刻] Buddhist art [sculpture].

ぶっきらぼう ぶっきらぼうな curt; blunt;《文》brusque;《文》unaffable / ぶっきらぼうな口を利く talk bluntly; be blunt in one's speech / ぶっきらぼうに curtly; bluntly; brusquely;《文》unceremoniously.

ぶつぎり ぶつ切り ¶ぶつ切りにする cut [chop] (tuna meat) into (irregular) chunks [lumps].

ふっきれる 吹っ切れる 文例⇩

ふっきん 腹筋《解》an abdominal muscle.

フック《ボクシング・ゴルフ》a hook ¶フックを入れる hook; deliver a hook (to) / (打球が)左にフックする hook to the left.

ぶつぐ 仏具 Buddhist altar fittings.

ブックエンド bookends.

ぶっくさ ⇨ ぶつぶつ

ふっくら ¶ふっくらした full; plump / ふっくらした布団 soft comfortable bedding; bedding with plenty of give / ふっくらした頬 full cheeks / ふっくらと炊いたごはん rice boiled to the perfect degree of softness; rice cooked to a turn.

ぶつける 〈投げる〉throw [fling] sth at [onto];〈衝突させる〉hit;《文》strike, knock sth against ¶壁にボールをぶつける throw a ball at a wall / 柱に頭をぶつける hit [bump] one's

---

Saruhashi section of the Chuo Line. / 電信[電話]は一時不通になった. The telegraph [telephone] service was interrupted [suspended] for a time.

ふつう² 昼食は普通1時です. We usually have lunch at one. / 列車の延着はこの線では普通のことだ. The trains on this line are always [forever] running late. / そんなことは東京では普通のことだ. That's nothing remarkable [That's a matter of almost daily occurrence] in Tokyo. / そういう言い方は英語では普通でない. That sort of expression is not common in English. / 彼は確かに普通の人と違っている. He is certainly different from other men. / この寒さは普通ではない. This cold weather is rather abnormal [unseasonable].

ふつか もう1日か2日で出来上がります. It will be ready [be completed] in a day or two.

ぶっか 物価が上がった[下がった]. Prices have gone up [come down]. / 当市では諸物価が高い. Everything is expensive in this city.

ぶつかる 船が岩にぶつかった. The ship ran against a rock. / 本を読んでいると私はよくこの言葉にぶつかる. I often come across this word when I'm reading [in my reading]. / 僕はうまい仕事にぶつかった. I have found a good job.

ふっき それは沖縄が日本に復帰した日の事であった. It was [This happened] on the day when Okinawa reverted to Japan.

ふっきゅう 東北線の被害区間は明朝復旧の見込みである. The damaged section of the Tohoku Line is expected to be reopened to traffic tomorrow morning.

ふっきれる この点彼はまだ封建思想が吹っ切れないでいる. In this respect, he is still bound by [he still retains] the feudalistic way

ふっけん 復権 restoration (of rights); rehabilitation; reinstatement.
ぶっけん 物件 a thing; an object; an article; 〈土地・建物〉property ¶証拠物件 ⇨ しょうこ.
ふっこ 復古 restoration; revival ¶復古調 a tendency to revert to the old ways.
ふっこう¹ 復興 〈再興〉(a) revival; restoration; rehabilitation;〈文〉(a) renaissance [renascence] (特に文芸の);〈再建〉reconstruction ¶日本の戦後の復興 Japan's postwar rehabilitation / 復興する revive; be revived; be restored (to *its* former state); be reconstructed.
ふっこう² 腹腔〖解〗the abdominal cavity.
ふつごう 不都合〈不便〉inconvenience;〈ふらち〉〈文〉a wrong;〈非行〉〈文〉misconduct ¶不都合な〈不便な〉inconvenient;〈行為の〉wrong; outrageous; unpardonable;〈文〉inexcusable / 不都合な事をする do something wrong; misbehave;〈文〉misconduct *oneself*; commit an outrage (on, against). 文例⇩
ふっこくぼん 復刻本 a reprint (of).
ぶっさん 物産 a product; produce (総称);〈商品〉a commodity ¶日本の重要物産 the staple products of Japan / 物産展 an exhibition of the products (of Hokkaido). 文例⇩
ぶっし¹ 仏師 a sculptor of Buddhist images [statues].
ぶっし² 物資〈財貨〉goods; commodities;〈資源〉(natural) resources;〈原料〉(raw) materials. 文例⇩
ぶっしき 仏式 ¶仏式により with [according to] Buddhist rites.
ぶっしつ 物質 matter; substance;〈原料〉material ¶物質的 material; physical / 物質的に materially; physically / 反物質 antimatter / 物質界 the material world / 物質主義 materialism / 物質代謝〖生物〗metabolism / 物質文明 material civilization / 物質名詞〖文法〗a material noun. 文例⇩
ぶっしゃり 仏舎利 Buddha's ashes ¶仏舎利塔 a stupa.
プッシュホン a push-button (tele)phone.
ぶっしょう 物証 ⇨ ぶってき (物的証拠).

ぶつじょう 物情 文例⇩
ふっしょく 払拭 ¶払拭する sweep away; wipe out;〈文〉eradicate.
ぶっしょく 物色 ¶物色する〈捜す〉look [search] for; hunt out;〈文〉select / 後任を物色する look for a successor to *sb*.
ぶっしん 物心 matter and mind ¶物心両面で both physically and spiritually / 物心両面にわたる援助を受ける〈文〉receive support, both moral and material, from *sb*.
ぶつぜん 仏前 ¶仏前に供える offer *sth* before the tablet of the deceased.
フッソ フッ素〖化〗fluorine.
ぶっそう 物騒 ¶物騒な〈不安な〉unsettled;〈危険な〉unsafe; dangerous; frightening; ominous / 物騒な男 a dangerous character / 物騒な顔付きをしている look dangerous / こんな物騒な世の中に in these troubled times. 文例⇩
ぶつぞう 仏像 a statue of Buddha; a Buddhist image.
ぶつだ 仏陀 (the) Buddha.
ぶったい 物体 an object; a (material) body.
ぶつだん 仏壇 a (family) Buddhist altar.
ぶっちがい ぶっ違い ⇨ すじかい.
ぶっちょうづら 仏頂面 a sulky [glum] look ¶仏頂面をする look sulky [sullen].
ふつつか 不束 ¶ふつつかな incapable; incompetent.
ぶっつけ ¶ぶっつけに without preparation;《口語》off the cuff / ぶっつけから from the start / ぶっつけ本番 acting [performing] without rehearsal / ぶっつけ本番の unrehearsed《performances》; unprepared《lectures》. 文例⇩
ぶっつづけ ぶっ続け ⇨ ぶっとおし.
ふっつり ¶ふっつり(と)酒をやめる give up drinking once (and) for all.
ぶっつり ¶〈糸などが〉ぶっつり切れる break [snap] off. 文例⇩
ふってい 払底 (a) scarcity; (a) shortage;〈文〉(a) dearth;〈文〉want ¶人物の払底 a dearth of talent / 払底する〈物が主語〉get [〈文〉become] scarce; run short. 文例⇩
ぶってき 物的 material; physical ¶物的資源 material [physical] resources / 物的証拠 (phys-

of thinking.
ぶつける 彼は車を電柱にぶつけてしまった。He ran his car into a telegraph pole.
ふつごう 遅れたからといって別に不都合の生じる訳もあるまい。No harm will be done by the delay. / あの店員は不都合があったので解雇された。That clerk was dismissed for misconduct.
ぶっさん この地方には取り立てて言うほどの物産はない。The area produces nothing worth mentioning.
ぶっし² 戦時中はあらゆる物資が不足していた。During the war, goods of every description were

in short supply.
ぶっしつ 学者は一般に物質的には恵まれないものだ。Generally speaking, scholars are not well off in material terms. / 彼の考えは極めて物質的だ。His attitudes are [His way of thinking is] very materialistic.
ぶつじょう 市内は物情騒然としている。The city is in a turmoil. | There is a great deal of unrest in the city.
ぶっそう この辺は不良が多くなったので物騒だ。There are so many hooligans about that the neighborhood isn't safe any longer. / 火薬庫の近くに住むのは物騒だ。

It is most uncomfortable [frightening] to live near a powder magazine. / 近頃はパリもずいぶん物騒になった。Paris is rather scary [frightening] these days. | One no longer feels safe (walking about) in Paris.
ぶっつけ リハーサルの時間がなくてぶっつけ本番でやらなければならなかった。There was no time for rehearsal, so we had to do it cold.
ぶっつり 彼からはその後ぷっつり消息がなかった。We never did hear anything from him after that.
ふってい 1円玉が払底しています。

ふってん ical) evidence.
ふってん 沸点 the boiling point.
ぶってん 仏典 Buddhist literature [scriptures]; 〈経本〉 sutras.
ふっと 〈吹いて〉 with a whiff [puff]; 〈ふと〉 ⇨ ふと ¶ふっと吹く whiff / ろうそくをふっと吹き消す puff out a candle.
ぷっと ¶ぷっと吹き出す〈笑う〉 let out a suppressed laugh; start laughing in spite of oneself; 〈種などを口から〉 spit out (grapestones).
ふっとう 沸騰 《文》 seething ¶沸騰する boil; 《文》 seethe; 〈議論などが〉 be roused; be excited; 《文》 be agitated; be heated / 摂氏 100 度で沸騰する boil [come to the boil] at 100°centigrade / 沸騰させる boil; bring [heat] (the water) to a [the] boil / 2 分間沸騰させる boil sth for two minutes; give sth two minutes' [a two-minute] boil / 沸騰させておく keep sth boiling [at the boil] / 沸騰点 ⇨ ふってん. [文例⇩]
ぶっとおし ぶっ通し ¶ぶっ通しの continuous; consecutive; 《文》 ceaseless / ぶっ通しに without a break; continuously; 《文》 ceaselessly / 5 時間ぶっ通しに for five hours running [at a stretch]; for five straight hours / 何時間もぶっ通しに for hours together [on end]. [文例⇩]
ふっとぶ 吹っ飛ぶ blow [be blown] off; go to the winds.
フットボール 〈競技〉 football; 〈ボール〉 a football ¶フットボールの選手 a football player; a footballer / フットボールをする play football / アメリカンフットボール American football / フットボール競技場 a football field [ground, 《英》 pitch]; 《米》 a gridiron / フットボールチーム a football team.
フットライト footlights ⇨ きゃっこう.
フットワーク footwork ¶フットワークが乱れる one's footwork goes wrong [to pieces].
ぶつのう 物納 ¶物納する pay (taxes) in kind.
ぶっぱなす ぶっ放す ¶大砲をぶっぱなす fire [let off] a gun; loose off a shell.
ぶっぴん 物品 an article; a commodity; 〈物資〉 goods ¶物品税 a tax on a commodity; a commodity tax.
ぶつぶつ ¶ぶつぶつ言う 〈つぶやく〉 mutter; murmur; 〈不平を言う〉 grumble about [at] sth; complain about [of] sth; 〈小言を言う〉 nag (at) sb / 〈反対する〉 object to sth / ぶつぶつが出来る have a rash (on one's arm); (one's arms) break out in a rash / ぶつぶつに切る cut [hash] (up) 《meat》 into small pieces.
ぶつぶつこうかん 物々交換 barter ¶物々交換する barter 《A for B》.

ふつぶん 仏文 〈フランス語の文〉 a French sentence; 〈フランス語〉 French; 〈文学〉 French literature ¶仏文を専攻する major in French literature / 〈大学の〉仏文科 the department of French literature.
ぶっぽうそう 《鳥》〈仏法僧と鳴くコノハズク〉 a (Japanese) scops owl; 〈鳥学上の〉 a broadbilled roller.
ぶつま 仏間 the room where the family Buddhist altar is placed [set].
ぶつもん 仏門 ¶仏門に入る enter the Buddhist priesthood; become a Buddhist priest [monk].
ぶつよく 物欲 《文》 worldly desires; 《文》 love of gain.
ふつりあい 不釣り合い ¶不釣り合いな out of proportion 《to》; out of keeping 《with》; ill-matched / 不釣り合いな夫婦 an ill-matched [-assorted] couple / 不釣り合いに小さい 《文》 be disproportionately small. [文例⇩]
ぶつり(がく) 物理(学) physics; physical science ¶物理的 physical / 物理的に physically / 物理(的)変化 a physical change / 物理化学 physical chemistry / 物理化学者 a physical chemist / 物理化学的 physicochemical / 物理学者 a physicist / 物理療法 physiotherapy; physical therapy.
ぶつりょう 物量 the amount [quantity] of materials [resources] ¶物量に物を言わせて on the strength of [relying on] one's material superiority.
ふで 筆 〈毛筆〉 a (writing) brush; 〈ペン〉 a pen; 〈筆跡〉 handwriting ¶筆の誤り a slip of the pen / 筆を入れる[加える] touch up 《a picture》; add a few touches 《to》; 〈訂正する〉 make corrections (in); correct / 筆を置く put [《文》] lay down one's pen; stop writing; 《文》 close 《one's letter》 / 筆を折る break one's writing brush / 〈作家をやめる〉 end [wind up] one's literary career / 小説に筆を染める try one's hand at writing a novel / 雑誌に筆を執る write for a magazine / 筆入れ a pen [pencil] case / 筆立て a pen [brush] stand; a pencil vase / 筆使い 〈運筆〉 one's way of handling a brush; 〈筆致〉 touches; brushwork (画家の) / 筆太に with bold strokes; 《文》 in a bold hand / 筆まめ[無精]である 《文》 be a good [bad] correspondent. [文例⇩]
ふてい¹ 不定 ¶不定の unsettled; indefinite; undecided / 不定代名詞 《文法》 an indefinite pronoun / 不定詞 《文法》 an infinitive. [文例⇩]
ふてい² 不貞 ¶不貞の妻 an unfaithful wife.
ふてい³ 不逞 ¶不逞の輩(やから) 《文》 malcontents;

We are short of one-yen pieces.
ふっとう その事件で議論が大いに沸騰した. The matter gave rise to a lot of heated discussion.
ぶっとうし 彼は休暇中ぶっ通しに勉強した. He kept at his books all through the vacation.
ぶつぶつ 彼は何かぶつぶつ言いながら立ち去った. He went away muttering to himself.

ふつりあい 上着とズボンが不釣合いだ. The jacket and trousers do not go together. / ああいう木はこういう庭には不釣り合いだ. That kind of tree is out of keeping with a garden of this style.
ふで あの人は筆が立つ. He is a good writer. / 僕には筆が立つといううぬぼれは少しもしない. I have no pretensions to literary

style. / 氏はその後小説の筆を断った. After that, he gave up [left off] writing novels. / この絵は雪舟の筆だという. This picture is ascribed to Sesshu. / この絵で生活することの難しさを知った. I realized how difficult it is to make a living by writing. / 彼は筆無精な男だ. He is a bad

《文》lawless people;《文》recalcitrants (反抗的な人々).
ふていき 不定期 ¶不定期刑 penal servitude for an indeterminate term / 不定期汽船 a tramp / 不定期便 nonregular service;〈航空便〉a nonscheduled flight / 不定期列車 a non-scheduled train.
ふていけいし 不定型詩 free verse.
ふていさい 不体裁 ¶不体裁な indecent;《文》unseemly;《文》unsightly / 不体裁な服装をする be not properly dressed.
プディング pudding.
ふてき 不敵 ¶不敵な fearless;《文》dauntless;《文》intrepid; devil-may-care;《文》audacious (ずうずうしい).
ふでき 不出来 ¶不出来な品 a badly-made article; a failure / 不出来である be badly [poorly] made; be badly done; be unsatisfactory; be a failure.
ふてきおう 不適応《文》maladjustment (to one's social environment).
ふてきとう 不適当 ¶不適当な unsuitable 《for》;《文》ill-suited 《for, to》; unfit 《for》; inappropriate 《to》; inadequate 《for》; out of keeping 《with》.
ふてきにん 不適任 ¶不適任な unfit 《for》; unqualified 《for》;《文》incompetent 《for》. 文例⬇
ふてぎわ 不手際 ¶不手際な clumsy; awkward;《文》unskillful.
ふてくされ ふて腐れ ¶ふて腐れを言う say (unpleasant [mean]) things out of spite; say sth in desperation.
ふてくされる ふて腐れる〈むっつりする〉sulk; get [《文》become] sulky [sullen];〈やけになる〉get desperate.
ふてってい 不徹底 ¶不徹底な not thorough(-going);〈論旨などの〉inconsistent;〈中途半端な〉halfway; lukewarm / 不徹底な処置 a halfway measure. 文例⬇
ふてぶてしい brazen(faced); shameless;《口語》brassy ¶ふてぶてしくも…する have the nerve [《口語》brass,《文》effrontery] to do.
ふてん 付点 ¶付点4分音符《音楽》a dotted quarter note.
ふと〈突然〉suddenly;〈偶然〉by chance; by accident; accidentally;〈何気なく〉casually; unintentionally ¶ふと思い出す [胸に浮かぶ]〈事が主語〉occur to one; flash across one's mind / ふと…する happen [chance] to do. 文例⬇
ふとい 太い big; thick;〈声の〉deep;〈図太い〉shameless;《口語》brassy ¶太い糸 a thick thread / 太い腕 a thick [stout, big] arm / 太い事をする behave shamelessly / 太くなる get [《文》become] big [thick]; thicken / 太くする make sth thick; thicken / 太く書く write in bold strokes / 太く短く世を渡る live a short life and a merry one. 文例⬇

ふとう¹ 不当 ¶不当な unfair; unreasonable;《文》unjust;《文》unwarrantable;〈過当の〉undeserved; undue / 不当な利益をむさぼる make unfair [excessive] profits; profiteer / …と言っても不当ではあるまい We may safely say that… / 不当解雇 unfair [wrongful] dismissal / 不当表示 (a) false [misleading] description 《of goods [contents]》/ 不当労働行為 unfair labor practice. 文例⬇
ふとう² 不等 ¶不等《数》a sign of inequality 《記号: <, >》★ < は is less than, > は is greater than と読む / 不等式《数》an inequality.
ふとう³ 埠頭 ⇒はとば.
ぶどう¹ 不同 ¶不同である be unequal; be uneven;《文》be lacking in uniformity. 文例⬇
ふどう² 不動 ¶不動の immovable; firm; motionless; fixed / 不動の姿勢をとる stand at [to] attention / 不動の信念 firm [unshakable] faith.
ふどう³ 浮動 ¶浮動する float 《in the air》;〈香りなどが〉《文》waft;《文》be wafted;〈変動する〉fluctuate / 浮動票 a floating vote.
ぶとう 舞踏 a dance; dancing ¶舞踏会 a ball; a dance / 舞踏会用のドレス a ball gown [dress].
ぶどう¹ 武道 military [martial] arts.
ぶどう²《植》〈木〉a (grape)vine;〈実〉a grape ¶ぶどうのつる a grapevine / ぶどう1房 a bunch of grapes / ぶどう色 (a) wine color / ぶどう園[畑] a vineyard / ぶどう栽培家 a vine-grower / ぶどう酒 (red, white, rose) wine / ぶどう酒醸造所 a vineyard; an estate; a chateau (フランスの);《米》a winery (★ フランスその他のヨーロッパ諸国では,「ぶどう園」と区別された「ぶどう酒醸造所」がないので, 結局以上のように言うより仕方がない) / ぶどう《状》球菌 a staphylococcus 《pl. -cocci》 / ぶどうだな a grapevine trellis / ぶどう糖 grape sugar;《化》dextrose; glucose.
ふどうい 不同意 disagreement;《文》dissent; disapproval ¶不同意である disagree with sb;《文》dissent from 《sb, sb's opinion》; disapprove [cannot approve] of 《a plan》.
ふとういつ 不統一《文》lack of unity;《文》disunity ¶不統一な《文》lacking in unity; disunited; divided.

---

correspondent. | He is not much of a letter-writer.
ふてい¹ 私の収入は不定です。My income is irregular.
ふてきにん 彼はその地位には不適任だ。He is unfit [not the right man] for the position.
ふてってい 私は何事も不徹底にしておくのは嫌いだ。I hate leaving things half done. | I like to be thorough in everything I do.

ふと 我々はふとしたことで知り合いになった。It was by accident that we got to know each other. | We became acquainted with each other quite by chance. / 彼らは詐欺師ではないかという気がした。The suspicion flashed across my mind that they were impostors.
ふとい この柱の方があの柱より太い。This pillar is bigger around than that one.

ふとう¹ 君の非難は不当だ。Your criticisms are unjust [unwarranted, unfair]. / 彼に対して不当にならないように, 次の点は強調しておきたい。In fairness to him, the following points should be emphasized.
ぶどう¹ 品質が不同である。They are not uniform [are uneven] in quality. / 順序不同。No special

ふとうこう　不凍港 an ice-free [a warm-water] port.

ふどうさん　不動産 real [immovable] estate [property]; fixed property; immovables ¶不動産鑑定士 a real estate appraiser [《英》valuer] / 不動産業者《米》a real estate agent [broker]; 《米》a realtor (公認の); 《英》an estate agent / 不動産取得税 a real estate acquisition tax / 不動産所得 an income from real estate.

ふどうたい　不導体 a nonconductor (of heat).

ふどうとく　不道徳 immorality ¶不道徳な immoral; 《文》depraved / 不道徳な男《文》a man of loose morals.

ふとうふくつ　不撓不屈 ¶不撓不屈の《文》unyielding; 《文》indomitable; 《文》indefatigable.

ふとうへんさんかくけい　不等辺三角形 a scalene triangle.

ふとうめい　不透明 opacity ¶不透明な opaque.

ふとがき　太書き ¶太書きの broad-pointed[-nibbed] 《pens》; thick [broad] 《ball-point pens》.

ふどき　風土記 records of the culture and geography of a province.

ふとく　不徳 〈徳の不足〉《文》want [lack] of virtue; 〈背徳〉immorality. 文例⇩

ふとくい　不得意 ⇒ふえて.

ふとくぎ　不徳義 immorality; dishonesty ¶不徳義な immoral; dishonest; 《文》faithless.

ふとくさく　不得策 ¶不得策な unwise; 《文》ill-advised; 《文》inadvisable; 《文》impolitic.

ふとくてい　不特定 ¶不特定の unspecified; 《文》unspecific / 不特定多数の人 (open to) the (general) public.

ふとくようりょう　不得要領 ¶不得要領な vague; noncommittal; evasive / 不得要領な事を言う say things which are beside [not to] the point; evade the issue; do not commit *oneself* / 不得要領な返事をする give an evasive [a noncommittal] answer.

ふところ　懐 〈胸〉《文》the bosom; 《文》the breast; 〈懐中〉*one's* pocket ¶山の懐 the bosom of a mountain / 懐が暖かい[寒い] have a full [an empty] purse; be flush with [short of] money / 人の懐を当てにする count on *sb* to pay / 懐を痛める pay out of *one's* own pocket / 懐を肥やす increase *one's* (own) income; feather *one's* nest; line *one's* pocket [purse] / 人の懐を見透かす see through *sb's* designs / 母の懐に抱かれて (carried [nestling]) in *one's* mother's bosom / 懐刀〈剣〉a dagger; a dirk; 〈腹心〉*one's* right-hand man; 《文》*one's* confidant / 懐具合 *one's* financial position; *one's* finances; *one's* capacity to pay / 懐手をして with *one's* hands in *one's* pockets. 文例⇩

ふとさ　太さ thickness; depth (声の) ¶太さが1センチある be one centimeter thick [in thickness]; have a thickness of one centimeter.

ふとじ　太字 a thick letter [character]; 〈活字〉bold-faced type.

ふとっぱら　太っ腹 ¶太っ腹の《文》magnanimous; large-[broad-]minded.

ふとどき　不届き ¶不届きな outrageous; rude; insolent.

プトマイン《化》ptomaine ¶プトマイン中毒 ptomaine poisoning.

ぶどまり　歩留り yield; a yield rate.

ふとめ　太め ¶太めの thickish; rather thick; on the thick side.

ふともも　太股 a thigh ¶太ももを出す show [expose, bare] *one's* thighs.

ふとる　太る grow fat [stout]; gain [put on] flesh [weight]; fatten ¶…を食べて太る grow fat on (meat) / 太った fat; stout; 〈でぶでぶ太った〉《文》corpulent; obese; 〈丸々太った〉plump / 太らせる fatten up / 太り気味の rather [《文》somewhat] fat [overweight]; stoutish; running to fat / 太り過ぎの too fat; overweight. 文例⇩

ふとん　布団 〈夜具〉bedding; bedclothes; 〈掛け布団〉a quilt; a coverlet ¶3組の布団 three sets of bedding / 布団を敷く lay out the bedding; make *one's* bed / 布団を掛ける put a quilt [coverlet] on [over] *oneself* / 布団を上げる[しまう] (roll up and) put [stow] away the bedding / 布団にくるまる tuck *oneself* up in bed / 布団皮[地] ticking; quilting.

ふな《魚》a crucian (carp).

ぶな《植》a (Japanese) beech.

ふなあし　船足 〈喫水〉draft; 〈速力〉speed ¶船足の速い[遅い]船 a fast [slow] boat / 船足を早める[落とす] increase [slacken] *its* speed.

ふなあそび　船遊び ¶船遊びに行く go boating [rowing]; go for a row.

ぶない　部内 inside (the department) / 部内の者 an insider. 文例⇩

ふないた　船板 〈船のあげ板〉a (ship) plank; 〈造船用材〉ship timber.

ふなうた　舟歌 a boat [boatman's, boatmen's] song; 〈ベニスの, またそれを模した楽曲〉a barcarole / ボルガの舟歌 the song of the Volga boatmen.

ふなか　不仲 ⇒ふわ.

ふながいしゃ　船会社 a steamship [shipping] company.

ふなかじ　船火事 a fire at sea [on a ship].

ふなぞこ　船底 the bottom of a ship.

ふなだいく　船大工 a shipwright; a ship carpenter.

ふなたび　船旅 a sea trip; a (sea) voyage; traveling by boat [water]. 文例⇩

ふなちん　船賃 〈客の〉passage money; a fare;

ふとく みな私の不徳の致す所です. It is all due to my lack of discretion. | I am solely to blame for it.

ふところ 別に君の懐が痛むわけではあるまい. I don't think you've got to pay out of your own pocket. | I don't think it means any outlay on your part.

ふとる 太ったものですからオーバーが小さくなりました. This overcoat is too small for me now; I have grown stouter. / 君は最近少し太りましたね. You've put on a bit of weight recently. / 太り過ぎにならないように用心しなければいけません. You must guard against overweight.

ぶない 警察ではこの事件は部内の者の仕業とにらんでいる. The

ふなつきば 船着き場 〈港〉a harbor; a port; 〈上陸地〉a landing place; 〈波止場〉a wharf (*pl.* wharves, wharfs); 〈停泊地〉an anchorage.

ふなづみ 船積み loading ¶船積みする load a ship (with *sth*).

ふなで 船出 the departure of a ship ¶船出する set sail (from); leave port / 人生に船出する launch out into the sea of life.

ふなに 船荷 (a) cargo (*pl.* -(e)s); freight ¶船荷を積む take in [discharge] cargo; load [unload] a ship / 船荷証券 a bill of lading (略: B/L).

ふなぬし 船主 ⇒ せんしゅ².

ふなのり 船乗り a sailor; a seaman; a mariner ¶船乗りの生活 a seafaring life / 船乗りになる become a sailor; go to sea.

ふなばた 船端 the side of a boat; the gunwale (その上べり).

ふなびん 船便 〈船を利用する便宜〉(a) shipping service; 〈郵便〉surface [sea] mail ¶船便で by ship [steamer, water, sea]; 〈郵便〉(send a letter) by surface [sea] mail.

ふなべり 船縁 ⇒ ふなばた.

ふなむし 船虫 〖動〗a sea louse.

ふなやど 船宿 〈回漕店〉a shipping agent; 〈貸し船屋〉an operator of pleasure boats.

ふなよい 船酔い seasickness ¶船酔いする get [《文》become] seasick / 船酔いしない[する]人 a good [poor, bad] sailor.

ふなれ 不慣れ lack of experience; 《文》inexperience ¶不慣れな inexperienced (in); unaccustomed (to); unfamiliar (with) / 不慣れな土地 a strange [an unfamiliar] place. 文例♪

ぶなん 無難 ¶無難な 〈安全な〉safe; secure; 〈まあまあの〉passable; tolerable; acceptable. 文例♪

ふにあい 不似合い ¶不似合いな 〈不相応な〉《文》unbecoming (to); 〈不適当な〉unfit (for); unsuitable (for); 〈不釣り合いな〉ill-matched / 学者に似合わない態度 an attitude unbecoming (to) [unworthy of] a scholar / 不似合いである《文》do not become *one*; be not in [be out of] keeping with *sth*.; 《文》ill become *one*.

ふにく 腐肉 〈食肉〉tainted meat; 〈動物の死体の〉rotting [《文》putrid, 《文》putrefying] flesh; carrion ¶腐肉を食べる動物 a carrion-eating animal; a carrion feeder.

ふにゃふにゃ ¶ふにゃふにゃの soft; limp; flabby; 《文》flaccid.

ふにょい 不如意 ¶手元不如意である be hard up for money; be badly off.

ふにん¹ 不妊 ¶不妊手術 sterilization / 不妊症 sterility; infertility / 不妊症の sterile; infertile; barren.

ふにん² 赴任 ¶赴任する leave for [《文》pro-

ceed to] *one*'s new post.

ふにんき 不人気 unpopularity ¶不人気な unpopular; 〈商品などが〉be in poor demand.

ふにんじょう 不人情 unkindness; lack of sympathy; 〈無情〉heartlessness ¶不人情な unkind; unfeeling; hard-[cold-]hearted; heartless. 文例♪

ふぬけ 腑抜け a sissy; an unmanly fellow; 《米口語》a mama's boy; 《英口語》a wet; a coward.

ふね 船, 舟 a ship; a vessel; a boat (小舟, 汽船); a steamer (汽船) ¶アメリカ行きの船 (bound) for America / 船に乗る get [go] on board (a ship); board a ship; take ship / 船で行く go by ship [boat] / スペインの船で運ばれる be carried on a Spanish ship. 文例♪

ふねっしん 不熱心 lack of enthusiasm [《文》zeal] ¶不熱心な unenthusiastic; halfhearted (乗り気でない) / 勉強に不熱心である be a lazy student; neglect [《文》be inattentive to] *one*'s studies / 教育に不熱心である《文》take little interest in [be indifferent to] educational matters.

ふねん(せい) 不燃(性) ¶不燃性の noninflammable; incombustible; fireproof (耐火性の) / 不燃性物 noninflammables; incombustibles / 不燃都市 a fireproof city.

ふのう 不能 〈不可能〉impossibility; 〈性的〉impotence ⇒ ふかのう ¶(性的)不能者 an impotent (person) / 不能問題 〖数〗an impossible problem.

ふのり 〖植〗*funori*, a marine alga of the genus *Gloiopeltis*; 〈製品〉*funori*, a glue used in Japan as a size for textiles.

ふはい¹ 不敗 ¶不敗の undefeated; unbeatable; 《文》invincible / 不敗の記録 a record of all wins and no defeats / 不敗の態勢をとる make perfect preparations against all possible attacks.

ふはい² 腐敗 〈腐ること〉rotting; decomposition; 《文》putrefaction; 〈退廃〉corruption ¶腐敗する go bad; be spoilt; rot; go rotten; 《文》become putrid; 《文》putrefy; be decomposed; turn (牛乳が); addle (卵が) / 〈退廃する〉become corrupt / 腐敗した bad; rotten; decomposed; putrid; addled (eggs); tainted (meat); corrupt (officials) / 腐敗しやすい perishable; corruptible / 腐敗しやすい食物 perishables / (下水処理用)腐敗槽 a septic tank. 文例♪

ふばいどうめい 不買同盟 ⇒ ボイコット.

ふはく 浮薄 ¶浮薄な frivolous; flippant.

ふはつ 不発 misfire ¶不発に終わる fail to explode [go off]; misfire; 〈計画などが〉fall through; miscarry / 不発弾 an unexploded bomb; a blind shell; 《口語》a dud (shell) / 不

---

police suspect that this is an inside job.

ふなたび 君は船旅の経験がありますか. Have you ever traveled by ship?

ふなれ 私はこうした仕事には不慣れです. I am unaccustomed [new] to this kind of work.

ぶなん その方が無難だ. That's safer. | That is likely to be more acceptable.

ふにんじょう 僕はそんな不人情なまねはできない. It is not in my nature to be so cruel. | 彼は僕のことを不人情だと言った. He said I was heartless [had no heart].

ふね 船で小樽に行った. I went to Otaru by ship. | I took a ship to Otaru.

ふはい² 当局は部内の腐敗を一掃するために最善の努力をすると約

ふばらい 不払い nonpayment.
ふび 不備 《文》defectiveness;《文》imperfection ¶衛生施設の不備 poor sanitary facilities; lack of proper sanitation / 不備な unsatisfactory;incomplete;《文》imperfect;《文》defective / 不備な点 a fault; something unsatisfactory;《文》a defect;《文》an imperfection.
ふひつよう 不必要 ¶不必要な unnecessary; needless;《文》superfluous. 文例⇩
ふひょう¹ 付表 an attached [annexed] table [list].
ふひょう² 浮氷 floating ice; an ice floe (平ら).
ふひょう³ 浮標 ⇨ブイ.　　　 しで広い).
ふひょう⁴ 譜表 《音楽》a staff (pl. staves); a stave ¶高[低]音部譜表 a treble [bass] staff.
ふびょうどう 不平等 ¶不平等の inequality / 不平等な unequal; unfair (不公平な) / 不平等条約 an unequal [a one-sided] treaty.
ふひょう(ばん) 不評(判) 不評 a bad reputation [name];《文》discredit; unpopularity (不人気) ¶不評判な unpopular;《文》unfavorably-[ill-] received 〈opinions〉/ 不評判になる become unpopular; lose its [one's] popularity;《文》fall into disrepute. 文例⇩
ふびん 不憫 《文》piteous;《文》pitiable ¶不憫がる[に思う]feel pity [《文》compassion] for; take [have] pity on. 文例⇩
ぶひん 部品 parts (of a machine); (car) components ¶部品販売業者 a parts supplier.
ふひんこう 不品行 《文》misconduct;《文》a moral lapse;〈放蕩〉《文》profligacy ¶不品行な immoral;《文》profligate / 不品行な人 an immoral person;《文》a person of loose conduct [morals].
ぶふうりゅう 不風流 lack of taste [refinement];《文》inelegance ¶不風流な tasteless; unrefined;《文》inelegant;《文》prosaic ¶不風流な人 a prosaic [matter-of-fact] person.
ふぶき 吹雪 driving snow; a snowstorm; a blizzard ¶ 文例⇩
ふふく 不服 〈不満〉dissatisfaction; discontent;〈不同意〉disagreement;〈異議〉(an) objection;〈苦情〉a complaint ¶不服を唱える〈不平を言う〉complain (about, of); grumble (at, about);〈抗議する〉protest (against); object (to) / ...に不服はない have no complaints about...; be satisfied [contented] with ...; have no objection to.... 文例⇩

ふぶく 吹雪く snow is driven by a strong wind.
ふふつせんそう 普仏戦争 『西洋史』the Franco-Prussian War.
ふふん 〈軽蔑・焦燥などで〉pooh!; huh!;〈疑惑・不満などで〉humph!; h'm!
ぶぶん 部分 (a) part; a section; a portion ¶部分的に,一部分 partially; partly / 部分集合 〖数〗a subset / 部分食 〖天〗a partial eclipse (of the sun) / 部分否定 〖文法〗partial negation / 部分品 ⇨ ふひん. 文例⇩
ふぶんりつ 不文律 an unwritten law [rule].
ふへい 不平 〈不満〉discontent; dissatisfaction;〈苦情〉a complaint; a grievance ¶不平である[を抱く] be discontented [dissatisfied] (with) / 不平を言う[鳴らす] grumble (at, over, about); complain (about, of) / 不平分子 discontented elements;《文》malcontents. 文例⇩
ぶべつ 侮蔑 ⇨ けいべつ.
ふへん¹ 不変 ¶不変の《文》changeless; unchanging; invariable;《文》immutable; constant; permanent / 不変数[量] 〖数〗a constant; an invariable.
ふへん² 普遍 ¶普遍的(な) universal / 普遍的に universally / 普遍的真理 universal truth / 普遍性 universality / 普遍妥当性がある 《文》be of universal application [validity]; have a universal application.
ふべん 不便 inconvenience ¶不便な inconvenient; unhandy /〈家が〉不便な所にある be inconveniently situated / 交通が不便である lack traffic facilities / 不便を感じる feel [be put to] inconvenience; be inconvenienced / 不便を感じさせる cause sb inconvenience; inconvenience sb. 文例⇩
ふべんきょう 不勉強 ¶不勉強な idle;《文》inattentive to one's studies [work].
ふへんふとう 不偏不党 ¶不偏不党の〈公平な〉fair; impartial;〈偏見のない〉unprejudiced; unbiased;〈一党一派に偏しない〉non-partisan.
ふぼ 父母 father and mother; parents ⇨ おや¹.
ふほう¹ 不法 〈違法〉《文》unlawfulness; illegality;〈不正〉(an) injustice;《文》a wrong ¶不法な unlawful; illegal; unjust; wrong; outrageous / 不法行為 an unlawful [illegal] act / 不法入国 illegal entry; unlawful immigration / 不法入国者 an illegal entrant [immigrant].
ふほう² 訃報 the report [news] of sb's death ¶訃報に接する hear [be informed] of

束した. The authorities promised to do their best to get rid of the internal corruption.
ふひつよう それは不必要だ. It is unnecessary. | We can do without it.
ふひょう(ばん) それは新聞紙上では不評であった. It was unfavorably received by the press. | It got [had] a bad press.
ふびん 親のない子だと思うと余計に不憫が増す. I pity the child all the more because it is an orphan.

ふぶき 列車は吹雪のため立ち往生した. The train was brought to a standstill by the blizzard.
ふふく 僕には不服はない. I am quite satisfied with it. | I have nothing to complain of.
ぶぶん ある部分は鉄で,ある部分は木で出来ている. It is made partly of iron and partly of wood. / このフィルムはカットされた部分がある. This film has been cut. | Some parts of the film have been cut out.
ふへい 不平を言うな. Don't

grumble. / 君は何か不平でもあるのか. Have you anything to complain about?
ふべん 書斎がないのは不便だ. It is inconvenient not to have a study. / 橋が流されたので村の人たちには甚だ不便なことになった. The bridge was washed away to the great inconvenience of the villagers.
ふほん ふほん不本意ながらこの処置を取らざるを得ません. We have been obliged to take this step (though it is) very much

ふほんい 不本意 ¶不本意ながら against *one's* will; unwillingly; reluctantly. 文例⬇

ふまえる 踏まえる ¶事実を踏まえて論じる base *one's* argument on facts; build up *one's* argument on the basis of facts / 関係条文を踏まえて主張する make *one's* claim with reference to the relevant provisions / 国民一般の要望を踏まえて新政策を立案する form a new policy in response to the wishes of the general public.

ふまじめ 不真面目 (a) lack [《文》want] of seriousness [sincerity]; insincerity ¶ふまじめな not serious; insincere; frivolous.

ふまん(ぞく) 不満(足) dissatisfaction; discontent ¶不満(足)な 〈心に不満のある〉 dissatisfied; discontented / 〈物・結果などが〉 unsatisfactory / 不満である be not satisfied 《with》; be unhappy [not happy] 《about》; be displeased 《with》; be discontented [dissatisfied] 《with》; 〈結果などが〉 be unsatisfactory / 不満を言う complain 《about, of》; grumble 《at, over, about》/ 声を大にして不満を述べる complain loudly 《that …》; 《文》 be loud in *one's* complaints 《that…》. 文例⬇

ふみあらす 踏み荒らす tread on 《the grass》; trample 《on》《the flower bed》.

ふみいれる 踏み入れる ¶足を踏み入れる step in [into]; set foot in [on].

ふみえ 踏み絵 《日本史》 a plate with a crucifix or other Christian symbol (to be trodden on in order to prove *oneself* a non-Christian); 〈比喩的に〉 a loyalty test.

ふみかえる 踏み替える ¶足を踏み替える change step.

ふみかためる 踏み固める tread 《the snow》 hard; tread 《the soil》《down》.

ふみきり 踏切 〈鉄道の〉 a (railroad) crossing; 《米》a grade [《英》level] crossing; 〈跳躍の〉 a takeoff ¶踏切板 a takeoff plank [board] / 踏切警手 a gateman [gatekeeper] at a railroad crossing.

ふみきる 踏み切る 〈思いきって始める〉 take the plunge 《and *do*, on a new venture》; launch (out) 《on an enterprise》; make bold to start 《an enterprise》; 〈跳躍競技で〉 take off.

ふみけす 踏み消す stamp [tread] out 《a fire》.

ふみこえる 踏み越える step over [across]; 〈困難などを〉 overcome; get over 《difficulties》.

ふみこたえる 踏みこたえる hold out 《against》; hold *one's* ground 《against》.

ふみこむ 踏み込む step into; 〈侵入する〉 break into; raid; make a raid on.

ふみころす 踏み殺す tread on 《an insect》 and kill 《it》; trample 《a spider》 to death.

ふみしめる 踏み締める step firmly.

ふみだい 踏み台 a step ¶人を踏み台にする use *sb* as a steppingstone to *one's* own success. 文例⬇

ふみたおす 踏み倒す 〈足で〉 trample down [over]; 〈勘定などを〉 fail to pay 《a bill, *one's* debt》.

ふみだす 踏み出す step forward; advance ¶1歩踏み出す take a step forward.

ふみだん 踏み段 a step; a stair.

ふみつけ 踏み付け 文例⬇

ふみつける 踏み付ける trample [stamp] down; tread on; 〈軽蔑する〉 insult.

ふみつぶす 踏み潰す smash [crush, flatten] *sth* under *one's* foot [feet]; trample down.

ふみとどまる 踏み止まる 〈頑張る〉 hold *one's* ground [*one's* own] 《against》; hold out 《against》; 〈その場に〉 stay (on); 《文》 remain.

ふみならす[1] 踏み均す level 《the ground》 by treading [it] down ¶踏みならした道 a (well-)beaten path [track].

ふみならす[2] 踏み鳴らす stamp [《米》stomp] 《*one's* feet on》《the floor》; beat [thump] *one's* shoes on 《the floor》; drum 《on the floor》 with *one's* feet.

ふみにじる 踏みにじる trample *sth* underfoot; crush *sth* under *one's* feet ¶人の感情を踏みにじる trample on [down] *sb's* feelings.

ふみぬく 踏み抜く ¶くぎで足の裏を踏み抜く run [tread] a nail into the sole of *one's* foot. 文例⬇

ふみば 踏み場 文例⬇

ふみはずす 踏み外す lose [miss] *one's* footing; miss *one's* step; make [take] a false step ¶正道を踏み外す stray [《文》deviate] from the right path. 文例⬇

ふみもち 不身持ち 〈放蕩〉 dissipation; 〈不行跡〉 misbehavior; 《文》 misconduct ¶不身持ちである live a loose [dissipated] life; misbehave; 《文》 misconduct *oneself*.

ふみわける 踏み分ける ¶やぶを踏み分けて進む make [push, work] *one's* way through a thicket.

---

against our will.
ふまえる この中世史は最近の学問の成果を踏まえて書かれたものである. This medieval history is grounded on the latest achievements of scholarship. / この言い方はシェークスピアの句を踏まえたものである. This is an adaptation of a Shakespearean phrase. | This expression, though modified, has its origin in Shakespeare.
ふまん(ぞく) 君のそのやり方には不満だ. I am not quite satisfied with the way you have gone about it. / 結果は不満足だった. The result was unsatisfactory [disappointing].
ふみだい 科学者は先人の業績を踏み台にして新しい発見をする. Scientists make new discoveries by building on the achievements of their predecessors.
ふみつけ それは人を踏み付けにした仕打ちだ. They paid absolutely no regard [consideration] to my feelings in the matter. | That is a gross insult to me.
ふみぬく 床板を踏み抜いてしまった. The floor gave way under my feet.
ふみば 部屋中に本が散らかっていて足の踏み場もなかった. The room was so littered with books it left nowhere to put my feet. | You could hardly set foot in the room for the books which were scattered about.
ふみはずす 足を踏み外して階段を転げ落ちた. I lost my footing and fell down the stairs. / 一歩踏み外せば下の岩に当たって命を落とす

ふみん

ふみん 不眠 loss of sleep; sleeplessness ¶不眠の sleepless; wakeful / 不眠不休で without sleeping or resting; night and day / 不眠症 insomnia. 文例⇩

ふむ 踏む ⟨足で⟩ step on; tread on; ⟨手続きなどを⟩ go through; ⟨終える⟩ finish; complete; ⟨評価する⟩ estimate [value, put] *sth* at ⟨5,000 yen⟩ ¶人の足を踏む tread on sb's toes [foot] / 外国の土を踏む set foot on foreign soil / 課程を踏む complete a course / 手続きを踏む go through the (proper [(文) due]) formalities.

ふむき 不向き ¶不向きな unfit ⟨(for the position)⟩; unsuitable ⟨(for *sth*)⟩. 文例⇩

ふめい 不明 ⟨不分明⟩ indistinctness; obscurity; ⟨洞察力・先見のなさ⟩ lack of insight [foresight]; ⟨無知⟩ ignorance ¶不明の not clear; indistinct; obscure; vague; ⟨未知の⟩ unknown / 不明の箇所 obscure passages [points] / 不明である be unknown; be [(文) remain [be still]] a mystery; ⟨(文) remain [be still]⟩ to be accounted for / 不明を恥じる be ashamed of *one's* ignorance [lack of foresight]. 文例⇩

ふめいよ 不名誉 (文) (a) dishonor; (a) disgrace; (a) shame ¶不名誉な dishonorable; shameful; (文) ignominious / …の不名誉となる disgrace ⟨*one's* family⟩; be a disgrace [shame] to…; bring disgrace on…. 文例⇩

ふめいりょう 不明瞭 ¶不明瞭な not clear; indistinct; (文) obscure; inarticulate ⟨(mumbling)⟩ / 不明瞭に発音する pronounce ⟨a word⟩ unclearly; slur ⟨a sound in a word⟩. 文例⇩

ふめいろう 不明朗 ¶不明朗な unfair ⟨(acts)⟩; underhand ⟨(transactions)⟩.

ふめつ 不滅 ⇨ふきゅう¹ ¶霊魂の不滅 the immortality of the soul.

ふめん 譜面 ¶譜面を見ながら演奏する play ⟨(the violin)⟩ from the music [score] / 譜面台 a music stand.

ふめんぼく 不面目 (a) shame; (a) disgrace; (文) (a) discredit ¶不面目な shameful; disgraceful; (文) discreditable / 不面目に思う feel ashamed ⟨of⟩.

ふもう 不毛 ¶不毛の barren; sterile; waste / 不毛の地 barren land; (a) wasteland ⟨(荒地)⟩ / 不毛の議論 (文) a barren [sterile] discussion.

ふもと 麓 the foot; the base ¶丘のふもとに at the foot [bottom] of a hill.

ふもん 不問 ¶不問に付する overlook ⟨sb's faults⟩; pass ⟨sb's sin⟩ over; wink [(文) connive] at ⟨sb's wrongdoings⟩.

ぶもん 部門 a department; a section; a branch.

ふやかす 水につけてふやかす make *sth* soft by soaking *it* in water; (文) macerate.

ふやける get [(文) become] soft [sodden] by soaking in ⟨water⟩; macerate ¶ふやけた sodden; swollen.

ふやじょう 不夜城 an entertainment district where night is turned into day [which knows no night]; a nightless entertainment district.

ふやす 増[殖]やす increase; raise; add ⟨to⟩; multiply ¶人数[人手]をふやす increase the number of men; add to the staff.

ふゆ 冬 winter ¶冬の winter; wintry / 冬の最中に in midwinter; in the depths [midst] of winter / 冬を過ごす pass the winter ⟨(at a place)⟩; winter ⟨(at, in)⟩ / 冬景色 a wintry scene / 冬仕度をする prepare for the winter / ⟨冬服を着る⟩ wear *one's* winter clothes / 冬将軍 (文) General Winter; (文) Jack Frost / 冬空 a winter [wintry] sky; wintry weather / 冬鳥 a winter bird [resident] / 冬服 winter clothes; clothes for winter wear / 冬用 winter clothes; clothes for winter wear / 冬向きの for winter use / 冬物 ⟨着物⟩ winter clothes; ⟨品物⟩ winter goods / 冬休み the winter vacation [(英) holidays] / 冬山に登る climb a mountain in winter.

ふゆう 浮遊 ¶浮遊する float ⟨(in the air)⟩ / 浮遊生物 ⇨プランクトン.

ふゆう 富裕 ⇨ゆうふく.

ふゆう 武勇 bravery; (文) valor ¶武勇談[伝] a tale [an account] of *one's* heroic exploits.

ふゆかい 不愉快 ¶不愉快な unpleasant; disagreeable; unhappy / 不愉快な目にあう[思いをする] have an unpleasant experience; have a thin time (of it) / 不愉快に感じる feel unhappy; be displeased ⟨(at *sth*)⟩.

ふゆがれ 冬枯れ ¶冬枯れ時 ⟨時候⟩ the season of winter decay; ⟨不景気⟩ the slack season of winter / 冬枯れの景色 a desolate wintry scene.

ふゆきとどき 不行き届き ⟨サービスの⟩ poor service; ⟨不注意⟩ carelessness; ⟨want⟩ of attention [care]; ⟨監督不充分⟩ mismanagement. 文例⇩

ふゆごもり 冬籠り wintering; ⟨冬眠⟩ hibernation ¶冬ごもりする stay [keep] indoors for the winter; ⟨冬を過ごす⟩ winter ⟨(in, at)⟩; ⟨冬眠する⟩ hibernate.

ふよ 付与 ¶付与する give; (文) bestow [confer] *sth* on *sb*; (文) vest ⟨*sth* in *sb*, *sb* with

---

ところだった. A single misstep [One false step] and I should have been hurled to my death on the rocks below.

ふみん 僕は近頃少し不眠症だ. I have been sleeping rather badly [suffering a little from insomnia] lately. / I am not getting enough sleep these days.

ふむき 彼はその仕事には不向きだ. He is unsuited for the job. / He is not cut out for that sort of work.

ふめい 出火の原因は不明である. The cause of the fire is unknown. / 彼らの態度はいよいよという時まで不明である. They did not commit themselves until the last moment. / 全く私の不明の致すところです. It was entirely due to lack of discretion on my part. / It was very unwise of me to have done a thing like that.

ふめいよ そんな事をすると君の不名誉になる. That would do your reputation no good. / このような事件は全校の不名誉である. An incident like this is a discredit to the whole school.

ふめいりょう 彼は考えをはっきりと述べており, 彼の意図に不明瞭なところはない. He expresses himself clearly and leaves no uncertainty about his intentions.

ふもと ここからは山がふもとまでよく見える. From here I can see the whole mountain, right down to the base.

ぶよ 《昆》a gnat.
ふよう¹ 不用[要] 〈文〉disuse ¶不用の〈使われない〉disused / 不要の〈不必要な〉unnecessary; needless / 不用になる become useless [unserviceable]; fall into disuse / 不要である be unnecessary / 〈人が主語〉have no use (for); need no (money) / 不用品 an unwanted [a discarded] article. 文例🔊
ふよう² 扶養 ¶扶養する support; maintain; provide for / 扶養家族 a dependent; one's dependents / 扶養控除 tax exemption [a tax credit] for dependents. 文例🔊
ふよう³ 浮揚 ¶浮揚する float (in the air).
ふよう⁴ 《植》a Confederate [cotton] rose.
ぶよう 舞踊 dancing; a dance ¶舞踊家 a dancer; a dancing master [mistress] / 舞踊劇 a dance drama / 舞踊団 a dance troupe.
ふようい 不用意 〈無準備〉《文》unpreparedness; 〈不注意〉《文》imprudence; carelessness ¶不用意な unprepared; 《文》imprudent; careless; 《文》heedless / 不用意な発言をする make careless remarks.
ふようじょう 不養生 ⇨ふせっせい¹.
ぶようじん 不用心 ¶不用心な〈危険な〉unsafe; insecure; 〈不注意な〉careless; 《文》incautious; 《文》imprudent. 文例🔊
ふようど 腐葉土 leaf mold.
ぶよぶよ ¶ぶよぶよした soft; spongy.
フライ¹ 〈揚げもの〉a fry ¶フライにする fry / えびフライ fried prawns / フライパン a frying pan; 《米》a frypan; 《主に米》a skillet (小型の).
フライ² 《野球》a fly (ball) ¶大きなフライ a long fly (ball) / フライを打つ hit a fly (to center); fly (to left field) (★この意味の fly は fly, flied, flied と変化する) / フライを打って アウトになる fly out (to the right fielder).
フライイング 《競技》a premature start; 《米》a breakaway ¶フライイングをする jump [beat] the gun. / 《英》a rough.
ぶらいかん 無頼漢 a ruffian; a rowdy; a tough.
フライきゅう フライ級 《ボクシング・レスリング》 the flyweight class ¶フライ級選手 a flyweight.
フライス a milling cutter ¶フライス盤 a milling machine; a miller.
プライド (a) pride ¶プライドが高い be proud / …するのはプライドが許さない be too proud to do; be above doing.
プライバシー privacy ¶プライバシーを侵害する invade [《文》trespass upon] sb's privacy.
ブラインド a blind; 《米》a (window) shade; 〈板すだれ〉a Venetian blind.
ブラウス a blouse.
プラウダ 〈ソ連の新聞〉Pravda.
ブラウンかん ブラウン管 a TV (picture) tube; a cathode-ray tube.
プラカード a placard.
ぶらく 部落 a village; a hamlet; a community.
プラグ a plug ¶プラグをさし込む put the plug in (the socket); plug.
ぶらさがる ぶら下がる hang down (from); dangle (from) ¶つり革にぶら下がる hang on to a strap.
ぶらさげる ぶら下げる〈つるす〉hang; 《文》suspend; dangle; 〈提げて持つ〉carry (a bucket) ¶腰に胴乱をぶらさげて with a botanical case hanging at one's side / 袋をぶらさげて with a bag in one's hand.
ブラシ a brush ¶靴[洋服]のブラシ a shoe [clothes] brush / ブラシを掛ける brush (a hat); give a brush (to a hat). 文例🔊
ブラジャー a brassiere; a bra (★特に女性が使うやや口語的な言い方).
ブラジリア Brasilia.
ブラジル Brazil ¶ブラジルの Brazilian / ブラジル人 a Brazilian / ブラジル連邦共和国 the Federative Republic of Brazil.
ふらす 降らす ¶雨を降らす雲 clouds that rain [that cause rain to fall] (on the region) / げんこつの雨を降らす rain [hail] blows (on).
プラス 《数》plus; 〈陽性〉positiveness; 〈利益〉a gain; an advantage; an asset ¶プラスする〈増す〉add (a lot) to; 〈寄与する〉《文》contribute (little) to; do (a lot) for / プラスの反応 (a) positive reaction / プラスの要素 a plus (factor) / プラスアルファ ⇨アルファ / プラス記号 a plus (sign) / プラスマイナスを比較考量する weigh the advantages and disadvantages [pluses and minuses] (of). 文例🔊
フラスコ a flask.
プラスチック 《化》plastic; plastics (総称) ¶プラスチックの入れ物 a plastic container / プラスチック工業 the plastics industry / プラスチック製品 plastic goods; plastics.
ブラスバンド a brass band. 「particles.
プラズマ 《物》plasma ¶プラズマ粒子 plasma
プラセオジム 《化》praseodymium.

ふゆきとどき 不行き届きの点は幾重にもお許しを願います。 I must beg a thousand pardons if you have found our service less than satisfactory. / 不行き届きのないように注意なさい。 See that all is in order.
ふよう¹ それは不要です。 We have no use for it. | It can be dispensed with.
ふよう² 彼には扶養家族が3人ある。 He has three dependents. | He has a family of three to support [provide for].
ぶようじん 不用心だから玄関の戸締まりを厳重にしなさい。 Bolt your front door fast against possible intruders. / 夜更けて女の一人歩きは不用心です。 It's unsafe for a girl to go out alone late at night.
ブラシ あなたの上着はブラシをかけなくては。 Your jacket needs [wants] brushing.
プラス 我々の運動にとって今度の企てはマイナスよりプラスの方が多いはずだ。 I'm sure the advantages of this enterprise to our movement will outweigh its disadvantages. / 検査の結果反応はプラスと出た。 Its reaction to the test proved positive. / プラス・マイナスを総合して成績はまあまあ立派なものだ。 When we look at both sides of the balance sheet [When gains and losses are (both) taken into account] the record is not at all bad. / プラス・マイナス・ゼロになった。 Prof-

プラタナス 【植】a plane (tree); 《米》a sycamore.
フラダンス the hula(-hula); the hula dance ¶フラダンスを踊る dance the hula.
ふらち 不埒 ¶ふらちな〈不届な〉outrageous; wicked;〈無礼な〉rude;《文》impolite;〈許し難い〉《文》unpardonable;《文》inexcusable / ふらちな行ない[事]をする misbehave;《文》misconduct *oneself*; do something wrong.
プラチナ〈白金〉【化】platinum;〈白金とイリジウムなどの合金〉platina.
ふらつく ⇒ふらふら(ふらふらする). 文例↓
ぶらつく〈ぶらぶら歩く〉stroll [wander, loiter] about; take a stroll;〈うろつく〉hang about [around].
ブラック ¶ブラックコーヒー black coffee / ブラックホール【天】a black hole / ブラックユーモア black humor.
ブラックリスト a blacklist ¶ブラックリストに載せる blacklist *sb*; put *sb* on the blacklist.
フラッシュ a flash bulb; (a) flashlight ¶フラッシュをたく set off [light off, light] a flash bulb / フラッシュをパッとたいて写真を撮る take a photograph with a flare of flashlight / フラッシュを浴びる be in a flood of flashlight.
フラッシュバック【映画】a flashback ¶フラッシュバックする flash back (to the original scene).
フラット[1]【音楽】flat ¶フラット記号 a flat 「(sign).
フラット[2]〈競技の記録で〉(11 seconds) flat ¶100メートルを10秒フラットで走る run a hundred meters in ten seconds flat.
プラットホーム a platform ¶プラットホームまで人を出迎える meet *sb* on the platform of a railroad station.
フラッペ〈飲み物〉frappé.
プラトニックラブ platonic love.
プラネタリウム a planetarium ((*pl*. -iums, -ia)).
プラノ flannel suiting.
プラハ Prague.
ふらふら ¶ふらふらする〈頭が〉be [feel] dizzy [giddy, lightheaded];〈心が〉be unsteady (in *one's* mind); waver (in *one's* resolution);〈足元が〉be unsteady (on *one's* feet); totter; reel; stagger / ふらふらと〈頭が〉dizzily;〈よろよろと〉unsteadily; totteringly;〈思わず〉in spite of *oneself* / ふらふら立ち上がる stagger [reel] to *one's* feet. 文例↓
ぶらぶら ¶ぶら下がって〉dangling;〈漫然と〉aimlessly;〈無為に〉idly; lazily ¶ぶらぶらする〈揺れる〉dangle; swing; sway (to and fro);〈何もしないでいる〉idle [dawdle] away *one's* time; loaf; be idle / ぶらぶらと歩く ⇒ぶらつく. 文例↓
ブラボー bravo ¶ブラボーと叫ぶ shout bravo(s).
フラミンゴ【動】a flamingo ((*pl*. -(e)s)).
フラメンコ the flamenco ¶フラメンコを踊る dance the flamenco.
プラモデル a plastic model ¶飛行機のプラモデルを組み立てる build [make up] a plastic model of a plane.
ふらりと〈改まらないで〉casually;〈出し抜けに〉unexpectedly; without (previous) notice;〈当てもなく〉aimlessly ¶ふらりと出かける go out without any definite purpose / ふらりと訪ねる drop in (at *sb's* house, on *sb*).
ぶらりと ⇒ふらりと.
ふられる 振られる〈断わられる〉be turned down; be refused; be rebuffed; meet with a rebuff; be rejected;〈特に恋人に〉《口語》be jilted; be dropped; be dumped.
ふらん 腐乱〈ただれ〉ulceration;〈死体の〉decomposition ¶腐乱する ulcerate; decompose / 腐乱死体 a decomposed body.
フラン a franc (略: F, Fr) ¶フランス[スイス]フラン the French [Swiss] franc.
ふらんき 孵卵器 an (artificial) incubator.
プランクトン plankton ¶プランクトンを餌にしている魚 a plankton-feeding fish / 動物[植物]性プランクトン animal [plant] plankton.
ぶらんこ a swing ¶ぶらんこに乗る get on a swing / ぶらんこに乗っている be on [sit in] a swing / 腰掛けぶらんこ a seat swing /〈サーカスの〉空中ぶらんこ a trapeze /〈サーカスの〉ぶらんこ乗り a trapeze artist. 文例↓
フランシウム【化】francium.
フランス France ¶フランスの French / フランス語 French / フランス人 a Frenchman; a Frenchwoman (女); the French (総称) / フランス革命 the French Revolution / フランス共和国 the French Republic / フランスパン a French roll; French bread (棒状の) / フランス料理 French food;〈料理法〉French cooking [《文》cuisine].
フランチャイズ【野球】a franchise.
ブランデー brandy ¶ブランデーグラス a brandy [balloon] glass; a (brandy) snifter.

---

its and losses canceled each other out. | It was a case of the swings and the roundabouts. | There was nothing in it.
ふらつく ひざがふらついた. I felt weak at the knees.
ぶらつく 銀座をぶらついていたら波多野君にばったり出会った. I bumped into Hatano when I was strolling on the Ginza.
ブラック コーヒーはブラックが好きだ. I like coffee black. | I like my coffee without cream [milk].
ふらふら 頭がふらふらする. I feel dizzy. | My head is swimming. / 僕はふらふらとその店に入った. I went into the store without any [for no] particular purpose.
ぶらぶら ちょうちんが風にぶらぶら揺れている. The lantern is swinging in the wind. / 午前中ずっとぶらぶらしていた. He loafed [dawdled] about all morning.
ぶらんこ 子供が2人ぶらんこに乗って遊んでいた. Two children were playing on the swings.
ふり[1] 形勢は彼に不利であった. The chances [odds] were against him. / そのため僕は非常に不利な立場に陥った. That put me at a great disadvantage [in a very unfavorable position]. / そんな事をしては君に不利だ. It will be to your disadvantage to act that way. | It is inadvisable for you to do that. | 君の不利になるようにはしない. I will do nothing against your interests.
ふり[2] 今にも出て行きそうな振りをした. He made as if he were going away the next instant.

プラント (a) plant ¶プラント輸出 the export of 《chemical》 plant (to).
フランネル flannel ¶フランネルのズボン flannel trousers; flannels.
ふり¹ 不利 (a) disadvantage ¶不利な《文》disadvantageous; unfavorable / 不利な点 a disadvantage; a handicap; a drawback / …に不利である testify against… / 不利な条件の下で in adverse conditions; under a handicap / 不利な立場にある be at a disadvantage; be handicapped / 自分に不利である be against one's interests. 文例⇩
ふり² 振り 〈身なり〉《文》dress; 〈風采〉personal appearance; 〈見せかけ〉pretense; (false) show; 〈踊りの〉postures ¶振りをする pretend 《sickness, to be asleep》; 《文》feign 《surprise》; 《文》affect (not to hear) / 知らないふりをする feign ignorance / 〈人に会った時〉look the other way; cut sb / 振りの客 a chance 《stray, casual》 customer.
ふり³ 降り 〈降雨〉rain; a rainfall; 〈降雪〉a snowfall ¶この降りでは in this rain. 文例⇩
ぶり 《魚》 a yellowtail.
-ぶり …振り ¶話しぶり one's way of talking; the way one speaks / 5年ぶりに after an interval of [for the first time in] five years / 3年ぶりに帰省する return home after three years' absence. 文例⇩
ふりあい 振り合い ⇒つりあい ¶ほかの人たちとの振り合いもあるから as we must take other people into consideration.
ふりあげる 振り上げる swing [throw] up 《a club》¶げんこつを振り上げる raise [lift] one's clenched hand / 刀を振り上げて with a sword raised overhead.
ふりあてる 振り当てる ¶ハムレットの役を振り当てる《文》assign [allot] the role of Hamlet to sb; cast sb in the part of Hamlet.
プリアンプ a preamplifier; 《口語》a preamp.
フリーザー a freezer ¶アイスクリームフリーザー an ice-cream freezer.
フリージア 《植》a freesia.
フリースタイル 《レスリング》the freestyle; freestyle [all-in] wrestling.
フリースロー 《バスケットボール》a free throw ¶フリースローをきめる sink a free throw.
プリーツ pleats ¶スカートのプリーツ pleats in a skirt / プリーツのある[ない]スカート a pleated [pleatless] skirt.

フリーパス 文例⇩
フリーバッティング 《野球》batting practice.
ブリーフ briefs.
フリーランサー a free lance ¶フリーランサーとして働く work (as a) free lance; freelance.
ふりえき 不利益 (a) disadvantage ⇒ふり¹.
ふりおとす 振り落とす shake off [down]; throw off ¶バスから振り落とされる be thrown off [spilled from] the bus.
ふりおろす 振り下ろす bring 《one's fist》 down 《on sb's head》; swing [flick] 《a cane》 downward.
ふりかえ 振替 transfer ¶振替で送金する send money by postal transfer / 振替休日 a holiday [day off] in lieu of (a public holiday that falls on a Sunday) / 郵便振替制度 the P.O. Savings Transfer system (★ P.O. は Post-Office の略); 《英》the National Giro / 郵便振替口座 a P.O. Savings Transfer account; 《英》a giro account / 郵便振替口座番号東京 5-12345 番 postal transfer account No. 5-12345 Tokyo.
ぶりかえす ぶり返す 〈人が主語〉have [《文》suffer] a relapse; relapse (into illness). 文例⇩
ふりかえる¹ 振り返る look [turn] around; look back (at) ¶過去を振り返る look back over the past; think back to the old days / 振り向いて ちょっと振り返って見る take a backward glance (at). 文例⇩
ふりかえる² 振り替える change (over) (to); transfer (to).
ふりかかる 降り懸かる 〈災いなどが〉happen to one; 《文》befall one ¶身に振り懸かる危険 an impending danger.
ふりかける 振り掛ける sprinkle 《pepper》 on [over] 《meat》.
ふりかざす 振りかざす raise 《a sword》 over one's head.
ふりかた 振り方 ¶身の振り方 ⇒み².
ふりがな 振り仮名 ¶振り仮名をつける show the reading of a Chinese character by writing [printing] kana at its side.
ふりかぶる 振りかぶる hold 《a sword》 high over one's head.
ブリキ tin plate ¶ブリキ缶 a tin (can); 《米》a can / ブリキ屋 a tinsmith.
ふりきる 振り切る ⇒ふりはなす, ふりほどく. 文例⇩
ふりこ 振り子 a pendulum ¶振り子の運動 the swing of the pendulum / 振り子時計 a

ふり³ ひどい降りだなあ! How it rains! / この降りでは彼も来まい。He won't come [turn up] in this rain.
-ぶりのあの話しぶりでは中国人とは思えない。From his way of talking would take him for a Chinese. / 昨日私は20年ぶりにある友人に会った。Yesterday I met a friend (that) I had not seen for twenty years. / 今年は10年ぶりの暑さだ。This is the hottest summer in ten years. | We have not had a summer as hot as this for 10 years.
フリーパス 税関はフリーパスだった。We came through (the) customs unchecked. / 僕はこの劇場ならいつでもフリーパスだ。I can enter this theater free of charge at any time. | I have the privilege of free admission to this theater at any time.
ぶりかえす 彼は無理をしたので病気がまたぶり返した。He had a relapse through overwork.
ふりかえる¹ 彼女は通る人が皆振り返って見る程の美人だった。She was such a beauty that she turned everybody's head when she passed. / 見慣れた風景なのでだれも振り返って見ようとはしなかった。The sight was so familiar that no one thought of looking (at it) twice.
ふりかかる 振り懸かる火の粉は払わねばならない。You can't just do nothing [remain idle] when you are exposed to danger.
ふりきる 私がとめるのを振り切って彼はあらしの中を出発した。He went out in the raging storm in

ふりこう / ふりょう

pendulum clock.
ふりこう 不履行 《文》nonfulfillment ¶約束の不履行 failure to keep *one's* promise ; 《文》a breach of promise.
ふりこみ 振込み ⇨ふりこむ¹.
ふりこむ¹ 振り込む transfer 《10,000 yen》to 《*sb's* bank account》; pay 《*sb's* salary》into 《*his* account》; ⟨マージャンで⟩ discard a tile (that is useful to *sb*).
ふりこむ² 降り込む 文例ひ
ふりこめられる 降りこめられる ⟨雨に⟩ be kept indoors by rain ; ⟨雪に⟩ be snowed in [up].
ふりしきる 降りしきる ¶雨の降りしきる浜辺 a rain-swept beach / 雨の降りしきる夜 a night of pouring rain / 降りしきる雨の中を in (the) pouring rain ; in a downpour / 雪の降りしきる中を in a heavy snowstorm.
ふりしぼる 振り絞る ⟨声を振り絞る⟨出ない声を⟩ strain *one's* voice ; ⟨出せるだけ大声を出す⟩ shout at the top of *one's* voice.
ふりすてる 振り捨てる ⟨振り放す⟩ shake off ; ⟨見捨てる⟩ abandon ; desert ; 《文》forsake.
フリスビー 《商標名》a Frisbee.
プリズム a prism.
ふりそそぐ 降り注ぐ ⇨ふりしきる ¶太陽がさんさんと降りそそぐベランダ a sun-drenched verandah.
ふりそで 振り袖 ⟨長い袖⟩ a long (hanging) sleeve ; ⟨振袖⟩ a long-sleeved *kimono*.
ふりだし 振り出し ⟨最初⟩ a beginning ; 《文》an outset ; ⟨出発点⟩ a start ; the starting point ; ⟨為替・手形の発行⟩ drawing ; issue ¶振り出しに戻る be (put) back where *one* started ; 《米口語》be a (whole) new ball game ; 《英口語》be (put) back to square one ; ⟨出直す⟩ make a fresh start / 振り出し人 the drawer (of a bill) ; the issuer (of a check) / 振り出し日[地] the date [place] of issue. 文例ひ
ふりだす 振り出す ⟨振って出す⟩ shake out ; ⟨発行する⟩ draw (a bill on *sb*) ; issue [make out] (a check in favor of *sb*).
ふりたてる 振り立てる shake up ; toss.
ふりつけ 振り付け choreography ¶振り付けをする design the dances [movements] 《for a singing group》; compose the choreography (of) ; choreograph / 振り付け師 a choreographer.
ブリッジ ⟨船の⟩ a bridge ; ⟨駅の⟩ a footbridge ; 〔トランプ〕 bridge ; 〔レスリング〕 a bridge ; 〔体操〕

a backbend ; 〔歯科〕 a (dental) bridge ¶ブリッジする〔レスリング〕 bridge / ブリッジをやる〔トランプ〕 play bridge.
ふりつづく 降り続く ¶雨[雪]が降り続く it keeps raining [snowing] / 降り続く雨 long-continued rain ; a long spell of rain [rainy weather]. 文例ひ
ふりはなす, ふりはらう 振り放す, 振り払う shake *sth* off ; shake *oneself* free [loose] from 《*sb's* grip》.
ぷりぷり ¶ぷりぷりして angrily ; in a huff ; 《文》in anger.
ふりほどく 振りほどく pull *sth* [shake *oneself*] free of 《*sb's* grasp》.
ふりまく 振りまく strew 《flowers》; scatter 《peas》.
プリマドンナ a prima donna.
プリマバレリーナ a prima ballerina.
ふりまわす 振り回す ⟨棒などを⟩ swing [wave] *sth* about ; fling *sth* around ; brandish ; 《文》wield ; ⟨誇示する⟩ display ; show off ; ⟨濫用する⟩ abuse ¶権力を振り回す⟨濫用する⟩ abuse *one's* authority ; ⟨威張る⟩ throw *one's* weight about [around].
ふりみだす 振り乱す shake 《*one's* hair》loose ¶髪を振り乱して with disheveled hair.
ふりむく 振り向く turn *one's* face [head] ; turn [look] around ; look back ; ⟨…の方へ⟩ turn to ¶振り向いても見ない do not care for ; take no notice of ; do not give the slightest attention to. 文例ひ
ふりむける 振り向ける ⟨顔などを⟩ turn ; 《文》direct ; ⟨当てる⟩ apply [《文》appropriate] 《the money to another item of expenditure》.
ブリュッセル Brussels.
ふりょ 不慮 ¶不慮の 《文》unlooked-for ; unforeseen ; unexpected ; accidental / 不慮の災難 an accident ; an unforeseen disaster.
ふりょう¹ 不良 ¶不良の bad ; poor ; inferior (質の) ; wicked (邪悪な) ; depraved (堕落した) / 不良になる go wrong [to the bad] ; 《文》become delinquent / 成績不良 poor [unsatisfactory] results / 天候不良のため owing to bad weather / 不良債権 a bad debt / 不良少年[少女] a bad boy [girl] ; a juvenile delinquent / 不良仲間 *one's* bad company / 不良品 inferior goods. 文例ひ
ふりょう² 不漁〔漁〕《have》a poor catch [take, haul] ; ⟨猟⟩《make, have》a poor catch [bag].

---

spite of my warning [though I tried hard to stop him].
ふりこみ 給料は銀行振込みにして下さい。I'd like to have my salary paid through the bank [paid direct into my bank account].
ふりこむ² 風で窓から雨が降り込んでいた。The wind was driving the rain through the window.
ふりしきる 外は降りしきる雨。It is raining hard outside. | It's pouring outside.
ふりだし 彼は小学校の教員が振り

出しだった。He started his career as a primary school teacher.
ふりつづく この前の日曜から雨が降り続いている。It has been raining since last Sunday. / この雨はいつまで降り続くのだろうか。How much longer will this rain keep [go] on?
ふりむく 後ろを振り向きながら「さようなら」と彼は言った。'Good-bye!' he said over his shoulder [said, turning around].
ふりょう¹ 今年の小麦の作柄は不良であった。We have had a poor

crop of wheat this year.
ふりょく その問題は武力によらず平和のうちに解決された。The trouble has been peacefully settled without an appeal to arms.
ふる 雨が降っている。It is raining. | The rain is falling. / 雨が降り出した。It began to rain. / 雨が降って来た。The rain came on. / 雨が降りそうだ。It looks like rain. / 雨は降りそうもない。It is unlikely to rain. / 雨[雪]が今にも降りそうだ。It is threatening to rain [snow]. | It may rain [snow] at

ふりょうどうたい　不良導体　a nonconductor; a bad [poor] conductor.

ふりょく　浮力　《物》buoyancy　¶浮力のある buoyant.

ぶりょく　武力　military power; force; 《文》force of arms　¶武力を誇示する make a show of force／武力に訴える[を行使する]《文》appeal [resort] to arms; use force／武力外交 power [gunboat] diplomacy／武力介入 armed intervention／武力衝突 an armed clash. 文例⬇

ふりわける　振り分ける　divide《one's time》up 《between, among》; portion out 《the days to different activities》; distribute《to, among》.

ふりん　不倫　immorality　¶不倫な immoral 《conduct》; 《文》illicit《love》.

プリン　[<pudding]《フランス語》crème au caramel; crème caramel.

プリント　a print; <謄写刷りの> a copy; <生地> print; printed cloth　¶講義のプリント [mimeographed] synopsis of a lecture／プリントにする mimeograph／プリント配線 a printed circuit／プリント屋 a (mimeograph) printer.

ふる¹　古　⇨おる　¶古で買う buy sth secondhand／古自動車 a used [secondhand] car／古新聞 an old newspaper.

ふる²　降る　fall; come down　⇨あめ¹, ゆき³, あられ, みぞれ　¶雨に降られる be caught in the rain／今にも降り出しそうな空 a threatening sky／降っても照っても rain or shine／降ってわいたような話 something quite unexpected／降ったばかりの雪 new-fallen snow. 文例⬇

ふる³　振る　wave《a flag, one's hand》; shake《a stick, a bell》; swing《a pendulum》; give a shake《to》　¶(犬が)しっぽを振る wag its tail／身体を振る shake oneself／魚に塩を振る sprinkle salt on fish; sprinkle fish with salt／役を振る cast《an actor》as [in the part of]《Hamlet》. 文例⬇

フル　¶フルに利用する make full use of sth; use《文》utilize sth to the full; leave nothing unused／使えるスペースをフルに活用する use every inch of the space available／(バッターが)フルカウントになる take a full count／フルスピードで at full [top] speed.

-ぶる　set oneself up as; pose as; 《文》affect　¶学者ぶる set oneself up [pose] as a scholar／信心家ぶる pose as a pious man [woman]; affect piety.

ふるい¹　篩　a sieve; a sifter (小型のこし器)　¶ふるいにかける put [pass] sth through a sieve [sifter]; sift; sieve; <選ぶ> screen (candidates by means of a test); select.

ふるい²　古い　old; aged; ancient (古代の); 《文》time-honored (昔からの)　¶古いパン stale bread／頭の古い人 a person with old-fashioned ideas; 《口語》an old fogy／古い店 a long-established store／古くは in old times; in ancient times (古代では); 《文》formerly; 《文》of old; 《文》in days gone by／古くから from [since] long ago; since [from] a long time ago; from old times; <太古から>《文》from time immemorial／古くなる get [《文》become] old; go out of date; get old-fashioned／古くなった stale; old-fashioned; outdated; 《文》antiquated. 文例⬇

ぶるい　部類　a class; a category　¶…の部類に入る come [fall] under the category [head] of…／甲と乙を同じ部類に入れる class A with B; put A in the same category as B.

ふるいおこす　奮い起こす　¶勇気を奮い起こす summon up one's courage 《for sth, to do》.

ふるいおとす¹　振るい落とす　shake off.

ふるいおとす²　篩い落とす　weed out; eliminate.

ふるいたつ　奮い立つ　⇨ふんき (奮起する).

ふるいわける　篩い分ける　sift (the good from the bad).

ふるう¹　振るう, 奮う　<盛んになる> flourish; prosper; thrive; <行使する>《文》exercise　¶勇気を奮う screw [pluck, summon, muster] up one's courage 《for sth, to do》／権力を振るう《文》exercise [wield] one's power／振るった <奇抜な> original; <普通でない> uncommon; <目覚ましい> striking; <あきれた> absurd／振るわない ⇨ふしん². 文例⬇

ふるう²　篩う　⇨ふるい¹ (ふるいにかける).

ブルース　《音楽》(the) blues (★単数にも複数にも使える); a blues (1曲)　¶ブルース歌手 a blues singer.

フルーツ　fruit　¶フルーツケーキ[ジュース, サラダ] fruit cake [juice, salad]／フルーツパーラー a tearoom attached to a fruit store／フルーツポンチ a fruit cup; compote.

フルート　a flute　¶フルートを吹く play the flute／フルート奏者 a flutist; a flautist.

ブルーマー　bloomers.

---

any moment.／朝から雨が降ったりやんだりしている. It's been raining all day off and on.／ラジオの予報では一日中降ったりやんだりのお天気だそうです. The radio forecasts intermittent rain throughout the day.／ここ4, 5日のところは降りますまい. We probably won't have any rain for the next few days.／ひどく降りますね. How it rains!／今年はよく降った. We have had [There has been] a lot of rain this year.

ふる³　彼女は手を振って「さよな

ら」と言った. She waved (her hand) and called 'Good-by!'／彼は手を振って何でもないようよいう合図をした. He indicated with a wave of the hand that there was nothing to worry about.

ふるい¹　20人の候補者のうちふるいにかけられて残った者はただの3名である. Only three people were selected from [out of] twenty candidates.

ふるい²　古い言葉だが時は金なりだ. Time is money, as the saying goes.／僕などはこの会社では

古いほうだ. I am one of the old-timers in this firm.／それは古くから行なわれていることだ. It is an old practice.｜It's a custom of long standing.

ふるう¹　昨日の競技会では残念ながら我々は全く振るわなかった. I regret to say that we did very badly in the competition yesterday.／そいつは振るっている. That's splendid [terrific]!｜文例⬇ずてご来会下さい. You are cordially invited to the meeting.

ふるえ 震え shaking; a tremble; a shiver ¶震えが来る have [get] the shivers [shakes] / 震え声で in a trembling [《文》tremulous] voice. 文例

ふるえあがる 震え上がる tremble violently; shudder; be terrified; be frightened out of *one's* wits;《口語》be scared stiff ¶震え上がらせる terrify;《文》strike terror into *sb*.

ふるえる 震える tremble; shake; shiver; quiver;〈振動する〉vibrate;〈ぞっとする〉shudder ¶寒くて震える shake [shiver] with cold / 怖くて震える tremble with fear; shudder at《the sight》. 文例

ふるがお 古顔 an old [a senior] member; an old-timer.

ふるかぶ 古株 ⇒ふるがお。

ブルガリア Bulgaria ¶ブルガリアの Bulgarian / ブルガリア語 Bulgarian / ブルガリア人 a Bulgarian / ブルガリア人民共和国 the People's Republic of Bulgaria.

ふるぎ 古着 used [old] clothes; secondhand [used] clothing ¶古着屋〈人〉an old-clothes dealer;〈店〉an old-clothes store.

ふるきず 古傷 an old wound; a scar (傷跡) ¶古傷を暴く reopen (*sb's*) old sores.

ふるくさい 古臭い old; old-fashioned;《文》antiquated ¶古臭い考え old-fashioned [antiquated] ideas.

ふるさと 古里 ⇒こきょう ¶心の古里《文》a place dear to *one's* heart;《文》*one's* spiritual home.

ブルジョア a bourgeois ¶ブルジョア階級 the bourgeoisie / ブルジョア趣味の incongruously high-class [elegant, expensive];《口語》posh.

ふるす 古巣 *one's* old home [haunt] ¶元の古巣へ戻る return to *one's* old place of work [to the place where *one* used to work].

ふるだぬき 古狸 an old raccoon dog;〈古参〉an old-timer;〈ずるい人〉an old fox.

ふるつわもの 古つわもの an old soldier [campaigner, warhorse]; a veteran.

ふるて 古手 〈古人の古手〉a retired government official.

ふるどうぐ 古道具 a used [secondhand] article; old [used] furniture;〈骨董(とう)〉a curio (*pl.* -s) ¶古道具屋〈店〉a secondhand store;〈人〉a dealer in used articles; a secondhand dealer.

ブルドーザー a bulldozer ¶ブルドーザーでならす bulldoze《a site》.

ブルドッグ a bulldog ¶ブルドッグのような粘り強さで with bulldog tenacity [perseverance].

プルトニウム 《化》plutonium.

ブルネイ 《国名》Brunei ¶ブルネイの Bruneian / ブルネイ人 a Bruneian.

ふるびる 古びる 《get [become] antiquated;〈come to〉have an antique [ancient] look ¶古びた aged; ancient-looking; antiquated.

ぶるぶる ¶ぶるぶる震える tremble violently [《口語》like anything]; shake《with fear》; shiver《with cold》/ ぶるぶる震えている《口語》be all of a tremble / ぶるぶる震えながら shivering(ly); trembling(ly). 文例

ブルペン 《野球》a bullpen.

ふるぼける 古ぼける go out of date;《文》get [become] antiquated;《文》look timeworn.

ふるほん 古本 a secondhand [used] book; an old book ¶古本で買う buy a book secondhand / 古本屋〈人〉a secondhand bookseller;〈店〉a secondhand bookstore. 文例

ふるまい 振る舞い〈行動〉behavior;《文》conduct;〈もてなし〉a treat ¶勝手な振る舞いをする behave without regard [with no consideration] for others; behave inconsiderately. 文例

ふるまう 振る舞う〈行動する〉behave [《文》conduct] *oneself*《like a gentleman》;〈もてなす〉entertain;〈ごちそうする〉treat *sb* to《a steak》; buy [stand] *sb*《a drink》¶公明正大に振る舞う play fair《with *sb*》/ 自然に振る舞う be *oneself*; behave naturally. 文例

ふるめかしい 古めかしい old-fashioned; quaint.

ふるわせる 震わせる ¶声を震わせて〈怒ったりなどして〉with *one's* voice shaking; with a shake in *one's* voice;〈老人などが弱々しく〉in a quavering [《文》tremulous] voice.

ブルンジ (the Republic of) Burundi ¶ブルンジの Burundian / ブルンジ人 a Burundian.

ふれ 触れ an official notice; a notification ¶触れを出す issue [put out] an official notice.

ぶれ 《写真》blurring; a blur.

フレアースカート a flared skirt.

ふれあう 触れ合う come in contact [touch]《with》; touch each other ¶心が触れ合う《文》commune《with》. 文例

ぶれい 無礼 rudeness; impoliteness;《文》discourtesy;《文》a breach of etiquette;〈不遜(そん)〉insolence;〈侮辱〉an insult ¶無礼な rude; impolite; insolent; impertinent / 無礼なことを言う say something rude to *sb*; make an insulting remark / 無礼を働く be rude to *sb*; take liberties with *sb* / 無礼講 a free and easy party / 無礼な an insolent [a rude] fellow.

フレー 〈応援の声〉Hurray! Hurrow. 文例

ブレーカー 《電》a circuit breaker; a breaker.

ふるえ どうしても手の震えが止まらなかった。My hand trembled despite my efforts to steady it. / 寒さで震えが止まらなかった。It was so cold that I could not stop shivering. / 彼は震え声で話した。He spoke in a tremulous voice.

ふるえる 唇が震えた。My lips quivered. / ひざがくがく震えて止まらなかった。My knees kept knocking together. / そう言う彼の声は震えていた。His voice trembled as he spoke.

ぶるぶる ぶるぶる手が震えて書けなかった。My hand shook so much [badly] that I could not write. / 彼は全身をぶるぶる震わせていた。He was trembling [shaking] all over.

ふるほん この本は今では古本でしか手に入らない。You can only get (hold of) this book secondhand now.

ふるまい 鈴木さんの振る舞い酒で皆大いに酔った。We all got drunk on Mr. Suzuki's liquor.

ふるまう 彼は君に対してどのように振る舞ったか。How did he behave to [toward] you?

ふれあう 2人の手が触れ合った。Their hands touched [met].

ぶれい 彼は無礼にも僕にこんな手紙をよこした。He had the im-

プレーガイド a theater ticket agency.
ブレーキ a brake ¶ブレーキをかける apply [put on] *one's* [the] brake(s) / ブレーキをかけて車を止める brake *one's* [the] car to a stop [halt] / ブレーキで車のスピードを20キロに落とす brake down to 20 (kilometers per hour) / ブレーキをぐっと踏む step on the brakes [the brake pedal] hard / ブレーキをかけたりゆるめたりして坂を下る run down the hill putting the brakes on and off / エアブレーキ an air brake / ハンド[フット]ブレーキ a hand [foot] brake / 非常[自動]ブレーキ an emergency [automatic] brake. 文例⇩

ブレーク 《ボクシング》《レフリーの命令》Break !
プレート 《野球》《投手板》 the pitcher's plate ; 〈本塁〉 (the) home plate [base]; 《地学》 (crustal) plate ¶プレート造構論《地球物理》plate tectonics.
プレーボール 文例⇩
プレーヤー 〈競技の〉a player ; 〈レコードの〉a record player.
ふれこみ 触れ込み an announcement. 文例⇩
ふれこむ 触れ込む announce ; 〈自称する〉give *oneself* out 《to be...》; 《文》 profess *oneself* (to be) 《a scholar》.
ブレザー(コート) a blazer (coat).
プレス ¶《衣服を》プレスする press 《a pair of trousers》 / プレスで125キロ挙げる《重量挙げ》 lift 125 kilos in the press / プレス機械 a press / プレスハム pressed ham.
フレスコ 《美術》 fresco ¶フレスコ画 a fresco 《*pl.* -(e)s》 ; a fresco painting.
プレハブ prefabrication ¶プレハブ住宅 a prefabricated house ; 《口語》a prefab.
プレパラート 《<《ドイツ語》 Präparat》 a prepared specimen 《for microscopic observation》.
ふれまわる 触れ回る spread 《a rumor》around 《《文》 abroad》; circulate 《a rumor》; put it about 《that...》.
プレミアム, プレミヤ a premium ¶プレミヤが付く command a premium / プレミヤを付ける place [put] a premium 《on》 / プレミヤ付きで 《be sold》 at a premium.
ふれる¹ 振れる 〈揺れる〉shake ; swing ; 〈偏る〉lean 《to》; 《文》incline 《toward》.
ふれる² 触れる 〈接触する〉touch ; feel ; 〈法などに〉break ; 《文》violate ; 《文》infringe ; 〈言及する〉touch on ; mention ; refer to ¶手で触れる touch *sth* with *one's* hand / 怒りに触れる offend *sb* / 法に触れる violate [be against] the law. 文例⇩
ぶれる 《写真》be blurred.

ふれんぞくせん 不連続線 《気象》a line of discontinuity.
フレンチトースト French toast.
フレンチドレッシング French dressing ; vinaigrette sauce.
フレンチホルン a French horn.
フレンドきょうかい フレンド教会 the Society of Friends.
ふろ 風呂 a bath ¶床より低く作られた風呂 a sunken bath / 風呂の加減を見る see how hot the bath is / 風呂に行く go to the public bath(house) / 風呂に入る take [have] a bath / 風呂につかる soak in the bath(tub) / 風呂を立てる get the bath ready / 風呂をわかす heat the bath / 風呂おけ a bathtub / 風呂がま a bath furnace [heater] / 風呂代[銭] a bathhouse charge / 風呂場 a bathroom / 風呂屋 a bathhouse ; a public bath. 文例⇩
プロ a professional ; a pro 《*pl.* -s》 ¶プロとしての能力を発揮して仕事を遂行する carry out *one's* task with professional competence / プロボクサー a professional boxer / プロレス ⇒プロレス / プロ野球 professional baseball / プロ野球の選手 a pro(fessional) ballplayer.
ブロイラー a broiler.
ふろう¹ 不老 ¶不老長寿の秘訣 the secret of perennial youth and long life 《《文》longevity》 / 不老不死の薬 the elixir of life [immortality].
ふろう² 浮浪 ¶浮浪する wander 《《米口語》 bum》 about ; 《文》 lead a vagrant life / 浮浪児 a street urchin ; a waif / 浮浪者 a vagabond ; a tramp ; 《米口語》a bum.
ふろうしょとく 不労所得 (an) unearned [investment] income.
ブローカー a broker ⇒なかがい.
ブローチ a brooch.
ふろく 付録 a supplement 《to》; an appendix 《*pl.* -es, -dices》《to》 ¶日曜付録 the Sunday supplement 《to the *Asahi*》.
プログラマー 《コンピューター》 a (computer) programmer.
プログラム a program ¶コンピューターのプログラムを作る write a program for a computer / プログラムをコンピューターに入れる program a computer ; program 《a problem》into a computer.
プロシア Prussia ¶プロシアの Prussian / プロシア人 a Prussian.
プロジェクト a project.
ふろしき 風呂敷 a square of cloth for wrapping ; a cloth wrapper ; a wrapping cloth ¶風

---

pertinence [was rude enough] to write me a letter like this.
ブレーキ ブレーキが利かなかった。The brakes did not work. / 田中君が参加したことが仕事の進行にブレーキをかける結果となった。Tanaka's joining in our work proved a drag on its progress.
プレーボール プレーボール！Play ball !
ふれこみ 世界一の魔術師という触れ込みだった。It was announced [given out] before his arrival that he was the greatest magician in the world. / He gave himself out to be the greatest magician in the world.
ふれる² 展示物に手を触れないでください。Visitors are requested not to touch the articles on exhibit. / 何だかぬるぬるした物が手に触れた。My hand felt something

clammy. / 彼はその問題には触れなかった。He did not touch on the matter.
ふろ お風呂が沸きました。The bath is ready. / 風呂が熱い[ぬるい]。The bath is hot [not warm enough]. / お風呂の加減はいかがですか。How is the bath ? / 彼はできるだけ熱い風呂に入った。He had a bath as hot as he could bear it.

呂敷包み a parcel [bundle] wrapped in cloth.
プロセスチーズ processed cheese.
プロダクション 〈製作・生産〉 production; 〈映画の製作所〉 a movie studio [lot].
フロック 〈まぐれ〉 a fluke ⇨ まぐれあたり.
ブロック 〈同盟〉 a bloc; 〔建〕 a concrete [cement] block; 〈街の区画〉 a block ¶ブロック経済 bloc economy / ブロック建築 a concrete-block building.
フロックコート a frock coat.
ブロッコリ 〔植〕 broccoli; 〔料理〕 broccoli sprouts.
プロット¹ 〈小説などの筋〉 a plot.
プロット² 〔数・コンピューター〕 ¶データをグラフ上にプロットする plot the data on a graph.
フロッピーディスク 〔コンピューター〕 a floppy disk.
プロテクター a 《chest》 protector; a 《face》 guard.
プロテスタント 〈教徒〉 a Protestant; 〈教義〉 Protestantism.
プロデューサー a producer.
プロトアクチニウム 〔化〕 protactinium; proto-actinium.
プロパン propane ¶プロパンガス propane gas; liquefied petroleum gas (略: LPG).
プロペラ a propeller ¶プロペラの音 the burr of a propeller / プロペラ機 a propeller plane.
プロポーション proportion ¶プロポーションのいい well-proportioned.
プロポーズ a proposal ¶プロポーズする propose to sb; ask sb to marry one.
ブロマイド [<bromide] a photograph 《of a movie star》.
プロメチウム 〔化〕 promethium.
フロリダ Florida (略: Fla.) ¶フロリダ州の人 a Floridian; a Floridan.
プロレス pro(fessional) wrestling ¶プロレスの選手 a pro(fessional) wrestler.
プロレタリア 〈個人〉 a proletarian; 〈階級〉 the proletariat ¶プロレタリア革命 a proletarian revolution / プロレタリア文学 proletarian literature.
フロント 〈ホテルの〉 the front [reception] desk ★ただ front と言えば, ホテルの正面入口と間違えられる ¶(自動車の)フロントガラス 《米》 a windshield; 《英》 a windscreen. 文例◎
ふわ 不和 〔文〕 discord; trouble; 〔文〕 strife (争い) ¶家庭の不和 (strife and) discord within the family; family [domestic] trouble / 不和になる have a quarrel 《with sb》; fall out 《with sb》; 〔文〕 become estranged 《from sb》/ 不和である be on bad terms 《with》; 〔文〕 be estranged 《from》. 文例◎
ふわたり 不渡り failure to honor 《a check》

dishonor 《a bill》; 〔口語〕 bounce 《a check》; 不渡りになる be dishonored; 〔口語〕 bounce / 不渡り手形[小切手] a dishonored [bad] bill [check] / 不渡り手形を振り出す issue a bad draft / 不渡り通知 a notice of dishonor.
ふわふわ lightly; softly ¶ふわふわした 〈柔らかい〉 soft; spongy; 〈軽い〉 light; 〈心が〉 unsteady; flighty; 〔文〕 vacillating.
ふわらいどう 付和雷同 ¶付和雷同する follow (others) blindly.
ふわりと softly; lightly; gently ¶ふわりと浮かぶ 〔文〕 waft (on the wind); float (in the air) / 髪をふわりとふくらます fluff up one's hair.
ふん¹ 分 a minute ¶15分 fifteen minutes; a quarter (of an hour [of a degree]) / 4時15分 a quarter past [〔米〕 after] four; four-fifteen [4:15] / 30分 half an hour / 北緯25度15分 25 degrees 15 minutes north (latitude) [25°15′ N. Lat.] / (時計の)分針 the minute [long] hand. 文例◎
ふん² 糞 excrement; feces; 〈動物の〉 dung; droppings.
ふん³ 〈軽蔑などを表わす, 鼻から出す声〉 huh!; hum!; humph!
ぶん¹ 分 〈部分〉 (a) part; 〈分け前, 分量〉 a share; a portion; a ration (食物の); a helping (食物1杯分); 〈割合〉 a rate; 〈身分〉 〔文〕 one's lot; one's social position; one's means; 〈本分〉 one's duty ¶100分の1 one hundredth; one per cent / 3分の2 two thirds / 5万分の1の地図 a map to the scale of 1:50,000; a one-to-fifty-thousand map / 3日分の食糧 food for three days / 3人分の仕事 an amount of work which will take [require] three people to do; three men's work / 3人分の仕事をする do the work of three men / 2人分食べる eat enough for two / 2ドル分のオレンジ two dollars' worth of oranges / 分を尽くす do one's duty [part] / 分をわきまえる know one's place / 分に過ぎた undue; undeserved; more (praise) than one deserves; above one's means (暮らしなど) / 分に安んじる be contented with one's lot / この分で行けば if things go on at this rate; if things carry on like this / Aの分として取っておく leave 《a portion》 aside for A / 分相応[不相応]に暮らす live within [beyond] one's means. 文例◎
ぶん² 文 〈文法上の〉 a sentence; 〈文章〉 a composition (作文); writings (書いたもの); 〈論文〉 an essay; an article; 〈文体〉 style ⇨ ぶんしょう¹ ¶文を練る polish one's style (of writing) / 感想を文につづる put one's impressions in writing / 文頭[文中, 文末]の語 a word at the

---

フロント ホテルを出る時は必ず部屋の鍵(をフロントに預けていくんだよ. You must leave your room key at the (front) desk when you go out of the hotel.
ふわ 両家は絶えず不和であった. The two families were in constant discord [were always feuding] with each other.
ふん¹ 1度[時間]は60分である. There are sixty minutes in one degree [an hour] | One degree [An hour] contains sixty minutes.
ぶん¹ その島は四国の5分の1の大きさである. The island is one-

fifth the size of [as large as] Shikoku. / 1分は1時間の何分の1か. What fraction of an hour is a minute? / これは君の分だ. This is for you. / 切符は君の分も買っておいたよ. I have bought a ticket for you too. / (勘定を)он の分だけ払った. I paid my own

ぶんあん 文案 ¶文案を作る make [prepare] a draft ((for)).

ぶんい 文意 the meaning of a sentence [passage].

ふんいき 雰囲気 an atmosphere ¶宗教的雰囲気の中で育つ be brought up [born and bred] in a religious atmosphere. 文例⇩

ぶんいん 分院 a branch hospital.

ふんえん 噴煙 ¶火山の噴煙 the smoke [fumes] of a volcano [rising from a crater]; volcanic fumes / 盛んに噴煙を上げる《文》emit [vomit] a great deal of smoke.

ふんか 噴火 (an) eruption ¶噴火する erupt; burst into eruption / 噴火している be erupting;〈火山が〉活動中である〉be active / 噴火口 a crater.

ぶんか¹ 文化 culture ¶文化の日 Culture Day / 異文化の受容 the adoption of foreign culture;《文》acculturation / 文化遺産 cultural heritage / 文化映画 a cultural [an educational] film / 文化勲章 the Order of Cultural Merit / 文化圏 a culture area / 文化功労者 a person who has performed distinguished services in the field of culture / 文化国家 a civilized [cultured] nation / 文化祭 a cultural festival;〈学校の〉an annual school festival / 重要文化財 important cultural assets / 文化水準 a cultural level / 文化史 (a) cultural history / 文化人 a man of culture; a highly-educated man / 文化生活 a decent [civilized] life; a reasonable standard of living / 文化庁 the Agency for Cultural Affairs / 文化的 cultural.

ぶんか² 分化 differentiation; specialization (特殊化) ¶分化する differentiate ((into)); specialize ((for a particular way of existence)).

ぶんか³ 文科〈課程〉the literature course;〈学部〉the department [faculty] of literature [arts] / 文科系の学歴の人 a person with an arts background [who has had an arts training].

ぶんか⁴ 分科 a department; a branch ¶科学の一分科 a branch of science / 分科(委員)会 a sectional committee; a subcommittee /〈その会議〉a subcommittee [sectional] meeting.

ふんがい 憤慨 anger;《文》indignation; resentment ¶憤慨する get very angry [《口語》get mad] ((with sb, at [about] sth)); be indignant ((at [about] sth, with sb)); take offense ((at)); resent sth. 文例⇩

ぶんかい¹ 分会 a (local) chapter.

ぶんかい² 分解〈解剖〉(an) analysis (pl. -yses);〈還元〉decomposition ¶分解する〈物を〉analyze; decompose;〈物が〉be decomposed; break down;〈解体する〉break up; take sth apart [to pieces] / 水を水素と酸素に分解する decompose water into hydrogen and oxygen / 化合物を元素に分解する reduce [resolve] a compound into its elements / 分解酵素〔生化〕 (a) breakdown enzyme / 分解写真〈相撲のテレビ放送などの〉a photographic playback / 分解熱 heat of decomposition.

ぶんがく 文学 literature;《文》letters ¶文学的[上の] literary / 文学の才がある have (some) literary talent / 文学に志す《文》aspire to literary honors / 日本[外国, 近代]文学 Japanese [foreign, modern] literature / 平安朝[江戸]文学 the literature of the Heian [Edo] Period / 文学界《ぶんだん》² 文学雑誌 a literary magazine / 文学士〈人〉a bachelor of arts;〈学位〉Bachelor of Arts(略: B.A.)/ 文学史 (a) history of literature;(a) literary history / 文学者 a literary man;《文》a man of letters / ドイツ文学者 a scholar of German literature / 文学趣味がある have a taste for literature; be interested in literature / 文学青年 a young literary enthusiast / 文学博士〈人〉a doctor of literature;〈学位〉Doctor of Literature(略: Litt.D.)/ 文学部 the department of literature /〈理論〉a theory of literature;〈論文〉a literary essay;《文》a treatise on literature.

ぶんかつ 分割 division; partition ¶分割する divide ((into)); partition; cut [split] up / 国土を4つに分割する divide its land into four parts [zones] / 土地を分割して売る sell one's land in zones / 分割払い payment in [by] installments / 分割払いで買う buy ((a refrigerator)) on the installment [easy payment] plan /《米》buy ((a car)) on time.

ぶんかん¹ 文官 a civil servant; a civilian; the civil service (総称).

ぶんかん² 分館 an annex ((to));〈図書館などの〉a branch library [museum].

ふんき 奮起 ¶奮起する rouse oneself (to action); rise ((to the occasion)).

ぶんき 分岐 ¶分岐する branch off ((from));《文》diverge ((from)); fork / 分岐点 a junction; a diverging point. 文例⇩

ふんきこう 噴気孔 a vent; a fumarole (火山の);〈鯨の〉a blowhole; a spiracle.

ふんきゅう 紛糾 a complication; (an) entanglement;《文》an imbroglio ((pl. -s)) ¶紛糾する become [be] complicated ((about)); be in a tangle / 紛糾した問題 a complicated matter. 文例⇩

ぶんきょう 文教 education ¶文教をつかさどる be in charge of educational affairs / 文教政

---

bill. / この分では計画は失敗だ。As things are [stand], the scheme is doomed to failure.

ぶん 文は人なり。The style is the man.《諺》/ 文は武に勝る。The pen is mightier than the sword.《諺》

ふんいき このレストランは家庭的雰囲気で知られている。This restaurant is well known for its homelike atmosphere.

ふんがい それではだれだって憤慨するよ。Anybody would get mad at it. / It is enough to provoke a saint. / 日本人は12歳の国民だという有名なマッカーサーの発言には当時多くの人々が憤慨したものだ。MacArthur's famous remark about Japan being a nation of 12-year-olds was widely resented at the time.

ぶんき 本線はここで分岐して新潟まで通じている。This line branches off here and leads to Niigata.

ふんきゅう それでは問題が紛糾するばかりだ。That would only

ぶんぎょう 分業 division of labor [work]; specialization. ¶この仕事を5人で分業でやろう. Let's divide the work among the five of us. / その部族では男女の分業が厳密に行なわれている. The people of that tribe practice a strict division of labor between the sexes.

ぶんきょうじょう 分教場 a detached classroom; a small branch school.

ぶんきょくか 分極化《文》polarization ¶分極化する《文》be [become] polarized.

ふんぎり 踏み切り ¶踏み切りがつかない cannot make up one's mind 《about a matter, to an act, to do》; hesitate 《to do, about doing》; 《口語》shilly-shally 《over [about] sth》.

ぶんけ 分家 a branch family ¶分家する establish [set up] a branch family.

ぶんけい 文型 a sentence pattern.

ぶんげい 文芸 literature; literary art; art and literature (芸術と文学) ¶文芸学 the science of literature / 文芸評論 (an essay in) literary criticism / 文芸復興 the revival of learning; the Renaissance (ヨーロッパの) / 文芸欄 a literary column [section, page].

ふんげき 憤激 ⇨ ふんがい.

ぶんけつ 分蘖【植】¶分蘖する put out tillers; tiller.

ぶんけん¹ 文献 literature; documentary records; documents ¶この問題に関する文献 the literature on this subject / 参考文献 literature cited / a bibliography / 文献学 philology.

ぶんけん² 分遣 ¶分遣する detach; detail / 分遣隊 a detachment; a contingent (of troops [a fleet]).

ぶんけん³ 分権 ⇨ ちほう (地方分権).

ぶんこ 文庫〈図書館, 叢書〉a library ¶文庫本 a pocket edition; a paperback(ed) book; a paperback / 漱石の小説を文庫本で読む read Soseki's novels in paperbacks.

ぶんご 文語 written [literary] language; a literary expression [word] ¶文語体 literary style / 文語文 a composition written in literary style [Japanese].

ぶんこう¹ 分光 ¶分光器 a spectroscope / 分光分析 (a) spectroscopic analysis.

ぶんこう² 分校 a branch school.

ぶんごう 文豪《文》a great man of letters; a great writer.

ふんこつさいしん 粉骨砕身 ¶粉骨砕身する do one's best; 《文》exert oneself to the utmost.

ふんさい 粉砕 ¶粉砕する〈細く砕く〉crush sth to pieces; break sth into fragments; 〈敵などを〉smash (the enemy).

ぶんさい 文才 ¶文才がある have a literary talent [genius]; have [possess] a talent for writing.

ぶんさい 分際 one's social position.

ぶんさつ 分冊 a separate volume ¶分冊にして出す publish 《a book》in parts; issue 《a dictionary》in installments.

ぶんさん 分散 (a) breakup; scattering; 《文》dispersion ¶分散する break up; scatter; disperse; 《文》be dispersed / 〈地方に〉decentralize (industries).

ぶんし¹ 分子 【数】a numerator; 【物・化】a molecule; 〈一部の者〉an element ¶腐敗分子 corrupt elements / 分子式 a molecular formula / 分子生物学 molecular biology / 分子量 molecular weight.

ぶんし² 文士 a writer; a literary man; 《文》a man of letters.

ぶんし³ 分詞【文法】a participle ¶現在[過去]分詞 a present [past] participle / 分詞構文 participial construction.

ふんしつ 紛失 loss ¶紛失する〈物を〉lose; miss; 〈物が〉be lost; be missing / 紛失物 a lost [missing] article.

ぶんしつ 分室 〈病院の〉a detached ward; 〈官庁などの〉a branch [detached] office; an annex.

ふんしゃ 噴射 a jet ⇨ ジェット ¶噴射する《文》emit a jet 《of liquid fuel》; jet.

ぶんしゅう 文集 a collection of compositions 《by school children》; an anthology 《of 17th-century English prose》.

ぶんしゅく 分宿 ¶分宿する put up at separate [different] hotels.

ふんしゅつ 噴出 spouting [jetting] (out) ¶噴出する gush (out); spout (out); spurt (out, up); jet (out); 《文》emit a jet 《of liquid fuel》; 〈わき出す〉well (out); 〈空中に〉shoot [send] up.

ぶんしょ 文書〈書類〉a document; 〈通信〉letters; 〈記録〉a record; archives ¶文書にする put 《an agreement》in writing; 《文》commit 《an agreement》to writing / 文書で in writing / 文書課〈官庁の〉the archives and documents section; 〈会社の〉the correspondence section.

ぶんしょう¹ 文章《文》a sentence; a composition (作文); prose (散文); an essay (随筆); an article (論説); 《文》writings; 〈文体〉style ¶文章が上手[下手]である have [write in] a good [bad] style; be a good [poor] writer / 文章を書く write; write (an essay, a composition) / 文章家 a good [fine] writer; a stylist / (算数の)文章題 a (mathematical) problem expressed in words; a story [verbal] problem.

ぶんしょう² 分掌 division of duties ¶事務を分掌する divide (office) duties (among).

ぶんじょう 分譲 ¶分譲する sell (land) in lots / 分譲住宅 a house and lot (subdivided from a larger lot, and) offered for sale (by a real estate corporation) / 分譲地 land for sale in lots.

---

complicate matters.

ぶんきょう この仕事を5人で分業でやろう. Let's divide the work among the five of us. / その部族では男女の分業が厳密に行なわれている. The people of that tribe practice a strict division of labor between the sexes.

ぶんけん その起源については参考すべき文献がない. There is no literature to refer to concerning its origin.

ぶんごう 今までに何人かの文豪がこの同じ主題で作品を残している. Some of the great names in literature have written on this same subject.

ふんすい 噴水から水が出ている. The fountain is playing.

ぶんすいかい[れい] この山脈はこの国の分水界になっている. This range of mountains forms the watershed of the country.

ぶんせき¹ 分析の結果ヒ素を含ん

ふんしょく — ぶんのう

ふんしょく¹ 粉食 food made from flour ¶粉食を奨励する encourage the use of flour for food.

ふんしょく² 粉飾 ¶粉飾する 《文》adorn;《文》embellish; embroider (on) / 粉飾決算 window-dressing (accounting).

ぶんしん 分身 〈我が子〉one's child;〈作者によく似た作中人物など〉one's double; one's alter ego.

ぶんじん 文人 (a) man of letters; a cultured person (教養人) ¶文人画 a painting by a literary artist after the Southern School of Chinese painting.

ふんすい 噴水 a jet of water; a fountain. 文例⇩

ぶんすいかい[れい] 分水界[嶺] a watershed; a divide. 文例⇩

ぶんすう 分数 a fraction ¶分数式[方程式] a fractional expression [equation].

ふんする 扮する 〈装う〉be dressed (as);〈役者が〉play (Hamlet); act [play] the part [role] of (Hamlet) /〈変装する〉disguise oneself (as).

ぶんせき 分析 (an) analysis (pl. -yses) ¶分析する analyze; reduce [break down] sth to its elements; assay (a drug, an alloy) / 分析的 analytical; analytic / 化学分析 (a) chemical analysis / 分析化学 analytical chemistry / 分析表 an analysis table. 文例⇩

ぶんせつ 文節 文例⇩

ふんせん 奮戦 a brave [plucky] fight; hard [hot] fighting ¶奮戦する fight bravely [heroically, gallantly, hard].

ふんぜん 憤然 ¶憤然として indignantly; in a rage.

ぶんせん 文選 《印刷》type-picking ¶文選工 a type picker.

ブンゼンバーナー a Bunsen burner.

ふんそう 扮装 (a) make-up;《口語》a get-up;〈変装〉(a) disguise ¶扮装する make oneself up (as); be dressed (as); be costumed (as) /〈変装する〉disguise oneself (as).

ふんそう 紛争 (a) dispute; trouble;《文》strife ¶紛争中である《文》be in conflict (with);《文》be (engaged) in dispute (with); be at loggerheads (with) / 国際的紛争 an international dispute / 紛争大学 a troubled university; a strife-torn [dispute-ridden] university.

ふんぞりかえる 踏ん反り返る throw one's head back;《文》assume a haughty attitude; behave arrogantly ¶踏ん反り返って haughtily.

ぶんたい¹ 文体 (a) style ¶平易な文体で書いてある be written in a simple style / 文体論 stylistics (単数扱い).

ぶんたい² 分隊 〈陸軍〉a squad;〈海軍〉a division.

ぶんだく 〈ひったくる〉snatch sth from ((sb's hand));〈代価を〉charge ((an exorbitant amount of money)); fleece ((sb (out) of his money)).

ふんたん 粉炭 dust [powdered] coal.

ふんだん ¶ふんだんに《文》in plenty [abundance]; plentifully;《文》abundantly; lavishly; liberally / ふんだんに金を使う lavish money (on).

ぶんたん¹ 分担 partial charge ¶分担する〈仕事などを〉take partial charge of ((the work)); take one's share of ((the responsibility));〈支払いを〉bear part of ((the expenses)) / 費用を分担する share the expenses with sb / 仕事を銘々に分担させる allot a portion of the work to each. 文例⇩

ぶんたん² 《植》⇨ざぼん.

ぶんだん¹ 分断 dividing into parts ¶分断策 a divide and rule policy [strategy].

ぶんだん² 文壇《文》the world of letters; the literary world; literary circles ¶文壇に打って出る take up [enter on] a literary career; make one's debut in the world of letters / 文壇人 a writer;《文》a man of letters.

ぶんちょう 文鳥 a Java sparrow.

ぶんちん 文鎮 a paperweight.

ぶんつう 文通 correspondence ¶文通する correspond (with); exchange letters (with); write (to). 文例⇩

ふんづまり 糞詰まり ⇨べんぴ.

ぶんてん¹ 文典 a grammar (book).

ぶんてん² 分店 a branch store [shop].

ぶんと ¶ぶんとふくれる get sulky [cross] / ぶんとにおう《悪臭が》stink (of garlic). 文例⇩

ふんとう 奮闘 a (hard) struggle;《文》strenuous efforts ¶奮闘する struggle (against, for, to do);《文》strive (for, to do);《文》exert oneself (to do);《文》make strenuous efforts (to do) / 奮闘(努力)の生涯 a strenuous life.

ふんどう 分銅 (balance) weight.

ぶんどき 分度器 a (circular, semicircular) protractor.

ふんどし 褌 a loincloth ¶ふんどしを締めてかかる brace oneself up [《文》gird up one's loins] (for the task) / 人のふんどしで相撲を取る use somebody else [other people] for one's own purposes.

ぶんどり 分捕り ⇨ほかく², りゃくだつ ¶分捕り競争 a grab game / 分捕り品 loot; booty; spoils.

ぶんどる 分捕る 〈捕らえる〉capture; seize;〈略奪する〉loot; plunder;《文》pillage.

ぶんなぐる ぶん殴る ⇨なぐる.

ふんにゅう 粉乳 milk powder; powdered milk.

ふんにょう 糞尿 excreta; excrement and urine.

ぶんのう 分納 payment in [by] installments

でいる事がわかった. Analysis showed that it contained arsenic. | On analysis it proved to contain arsenic.

ぶんせき² 文責記者.〈記事の最後に〉The reporter takes full responsibility for the wording and content of this article.

ぶんたん¹ この損害は皆で分担しよう. Let us all share (in) the loss. / 3人でその仕事を分担しよう. Let's divide the work among the three of us. / 各自仕事の分担が決まっている. Each of us has his own allotted task.

ぶんつう 彼と文通しているのか. Do you keep in touch with him? | Do you write to each other? / 彼とは時々文通するくらいの間柄です. My relations with him are limited to an occasional exchange of letters.

ぶんと その店の前を通り過ぎようとしたらコーヒーの香りがぶんと

¶授業料を分納する pay *one's* school fees in [by] installments.
ぶんぱ 分派 〈政党などの〉a faction; a splinter party [group]; 〈宗派〉a sect ¶分派活動 factional activities.
ぶんばい 分売 ¶分売する sell 《parts of a set》 separately [singly]. 文例↓
ぶんぱい 分配 distribution ¶分配する distribute 《to, among》; divide 《between, among》; allot 《to》; deal [share] out / 10万円を5人に分配する divide [share out] 100,000 yen among five people / 分配にあずかる get a share of *sth*; share in 《the profits》/ 分配額 a share.
ふんぱつ 奮発 ¶奮発する 〈努力する〉 exert *oneself* 《to do》; put a lot [a great deal] of effort 《into》; make efforts 《to do》; 〈散財する〉《口語》 blow 《100 dollars on a hat》; 《口語》 splurge on 《a new suit》 ¶もうひと奮発する make one more [another] effort 《to do》/ シャンパンを1本奮発する stand *oneself* [treat *oneself* to] a bottle of champagne / チップを奮発する give 《a waiter》 a handsome tip. 文例↓
ふんばる 踏ん張る 〈足を〉keep *one's* feet [footing]; stand firm; plant *oneself* 《at a place》; 〈がんばる〉hold out; 〈努力する〉《文》 exert *oneself* 《to do》; make an effort 《to do》.
ふんばん 噴飯 ¶噴飯ものである be quite absurd [ridiculous].
ぶんぴ(つ) 分泌 ¶分泌する secrete / 分泌腺 a secretory gland; a secretory / 分泌物 [液] a secretion.
ぶんぴつ 文筆 writing; 《文》 the literary profession ¶文筆で生活する live by *one's* pen / 文筆に従事する 《文》 be engaged in literary work; 《文》 follow the profession of letters / 文筆家 a writer / 文筆業 the literary profession.
ぶんぶ 文武 ¶文武両道に秀でている be both a good warrior and a good scholar.
ぶんぷ 分布 (a) distribution ¶分布する be distributed; range / 分布域 an area of distribution / 分布図 a distribution map. 文例↓
ぶんぶつ 文物 〈文明〉civilization; 〈文化〉 culture; 〈制度〉institutions; 〈事物〉things ¶西洋の文物 Western civilization; 《文》 things Western.
ふんぷん 紛々 文例↓
ぶんぶん ぶんぶんいう音[声] humming; buzzing; a hum; a buzz / ぶんぶんいうはちなどが〉 buzz; hum; drone; 〈プロペラなどが〉whirr.
ぷんぷん ¶ぷんぷんにおう give off a strong smell; 〈悪臭が〉stink [reek] of 《garlic》/ ぷんぷん怒って angrily; in anger, in a huff. 文例↓
ふんべつ 分別 〈深慮〉 discretion; 《文》 prudence; 〈良識〉 good sense; (good) judgment ¶分別がある be sensible; have discretion [good sense] / 分別のある sensible; levelheaded; discreet; prudent / 分別のない indiscreet; 《文》 imprudent; thoughtless / 分別盛りの男 a man at the age of discretion. 文例↓
ぶんべつしょり 分別処理 〈ごみの〉 segregated disposal.
ぶんべん 分娩 (a) childbirth; delivery ¶分娩する give birth to 《twin girls》; 《文》 be delivered of 《a child》/ 分娩室 a delivery [maternity] room / 分娩費 childbirth expenses.
ぶんぼ 分母 a denominator ¶最小公分母 the least [lowest] common denominator (略: L.C.D., l.c.d.).
ぶんぽう¹ 文法 grammar ¶文法を間違える make a mistake in grammar; use poor [bad] grammar; 《文》 commit a solecism / 文法にかなっている[いない] be grammatical [ungrammatical] / 文法上 grammatically / 文法家[学者] a grammarian / 文法書 a grammar (book). 文例↓
ぶんぽう² 分封 〈封地を分け与えること〉 giving a part of *one's* fief (to); 〈はちの〉 swarming ¶分封する 《*one's* bees》 swarm.
ぶんぼうぐ 文房具 (an article of) stationery; writing materials ¶文房具屋 〈店〉a stationery store [shop]; a stationer's; 〈人〉a stationer.
ふんまつ 粉末 powder; dust ¶粉末にする reduce *sth* to powder; powder; pulverize / 粉末状の powdered; powdery / 粉末状にして用いる use *sth* as a powder [in powder form].
ふんまん 憤懣 ⇒ いかり¹ ¶憤懣やる方ない do not know how to give vent to *one's* pent-up anger.
ぶんみゃく 文脈 a context ¶文脈から意味を推測する guess the meaning 《of a word》 from the context. 文例↓
ぶんみん 文民 a civilian ⇒ ぶんかん ¶文民統制 civilian control.
ふんむき 噴霧器 a spray(er); a vaporizer; an atomizer (香水吹きなど) ¶噴霧器で殺虫剤を掛ける spray insecticide on [over] 《plants》; spray 《plants》 with insecticide.
ぶんめい 文明 (a) civilization ¶高度の文明 (a) high [(an) advanced] civilization / 文明が進むにつれて with the advance of civilization / この文明の世でも even in these enlightened times / 文明の利器 modern conveniences / 物質[機械]文明 material [machine] civilization / 文明開化 civilization and enlightenment / 文明国 a civilized country [nation] / 文明病 diseases of [resulting from] civilization.

鼻をついた. The aroma of coffee greeted my nose as I passed by the shop.
ぶんばい 各巻1冊ずつ分売致します. Separate volumes may be had singly.
ふんばつ もう千円奮発して下さい. 〈商人が客に対して言う言葉〉 Give us another thousand yen, please.
ぶんぷ これらの動物は全世界に分布している. These animals range all over the world [have a worldwide distribution].
ふんぷん この問題に関しては諸説紛々としている. There are conflicting opinions [Opinion is divided] on this matter.
ぷんぷん ぷんぷんして部屋を出ていった. He went out of the room in a huff. / 彼はその事でぷんぷんしている. He is fuming [very sore] about it.
ふんべつ 私はそうするだけの分別がつかなかった. I didn't have the sense to do so. / あの人はもう分別がついていい年輩だが. He

ぶんめん 文面 the contents [《文》purport] of a letter ¶手紙の文面によれば according to (the text of) the letter.

ふんもん 噴門 《解》the cardiac orifice; the cardia.

ぶんや 分野 a field; an area; a sphere ¶異なった分野で仕事をしている科学者たち scientists working in different disciplines / 研究分野 a field of study [research] / 勢力分野 a sphere of influence.

ぶんり¹ 文理 ¶文理学部 the department of humanities and sciences.

ぶんり² 分離 separation; secession;《文》severance; a split;(a) schism (特に宗教上の);〈脱徹〉detachment;《無線》selectivity ¶分離する separate; secede; sever; split; detach / (ラジオが)分離がいい[悪い] have good [bad] selectivity / 分離課税 separate taxation / (道路の)中央分離帯《米》a median (strip);《英》a central reservation [reserve] / 分離派 separatists; secessionists / 分離不定詞《文法》a split infinitive.

ぶんりつ 分立 ➡さんけんぶんりつ.

ふんりゅう 噴流 a jet stream.

ぶんりゅう 分留[溜]《化》fractional distillation; fractionation ¶分留する fractionate.

ぶんりょう 分量 a quantity; (a) breakup; volume; measure; an amount;〈薬の〉a dose ¶薬の分量を誤る give sb a wrong dose of medicine / 分量を過ごす drink too much (wine); take an overdose ((of medicine). 文例⇩

ぶんりょく 分力《物》a component (of a force).

ぶんるい 分類 classification; grouping ¶分類する classify; divide into classes; group / 分類学 taxonomy / 分類基準《文》a classificatory criterion / 分類表[目録] a classified table [catalog(ue)].

ぶんれい 文例 an example ((for writing); a model sentence.

ふんれいどりょく 奮励努力 ¶奮励努力する《文》make strenuous efforts (to do);《文》exert oneself (to do).

ぶんれつ 分裂 a split; (a) breakup;《文》disunion; (a) division;《文》fission; (a) schism (特に宗教上の) ¶政党の分裂 a split in a political party / 分裂する divide; be divided; split; be split;《文》be disunited; break up / 分裂生殖 reproduction by fission. 文例⇩

ぶんれつしき 分列式 a march-past ((pl. -pasts);〈飛行機の〉a flyby;《米》a flyover;《英》a flypast ¶分列式を行なう〈行進する〉march in review; march past (the reviewing stand);〈飛行機が〉fly past.

ふんわり ➡ふわりと.

へ

へ 屁《俗》a fart ¶へをひる break wind;《俗》へとも思わない think nothing of sth; don't care a bit [couldn't care less] about sth;《口語》don't give a damn about sth.

へ《音楽》F ¶へ長[短]調 (in) F major [minor].

-へ〈向かって, 方へ〉for; toward; to (目的地へ); in; into;〈上へ〉on;〈目掛けて〉at ¶川へ落ちる fall into the river / 棚へ上げる put sth on the shelf / 大阪へ行く[立つ] go to [leave for] Osaka.

ヘア hair ¶ヘアクリーム hair cream / ヘアスタイル a hairstyle; a hairdo ((pl. -s) / ヘアブラシ a hairbrush.

ペア 〈1対〉a pair;〈ボート〉a pair; a pair-oared boat ¶かじ付き[なし]ペア〈ボートレース〉coxed [coxless] pairs.

ヘアピン a hairpin;《米》a bobby pin ¶ヘアピンカーブ a hairpin bend [curve].

ベアリング〈軸受け〉a bearing.

へい¹ 兵〈兵卒〉a soldier; a private; men (部下); troops (★ soldiers と同義で, 複数でのみ使う);〈軍隊〉an army; troops ¶兵を挙げる《文》take up arms (against) / 兵を送る send troops (to) / 兵を率いる lead [command] an army.

へい² 塀 a wall; a fence ¶塀をめぐらす surround ((a house)) with a wall [fence] / 塀を立てる build [set up] a wall ((around)).

へいあん 平安 ¶平安な peaceful;《文》tranquil / 平安に in peace; peacefully.

へいい 平易 ¶平易な simple; easy; plain / 平易に simply; plainly / 平易に言えば to put it (more) plainly; in plain language [English] / 平易に書いてある be written in plain English / 平易にする simplify. 文例⇩

へいいん¹ 兵員 strength ((of a troop)); the ((necessary)) number of men.

へいいん² 閉院 ¶閉院する close [adjourn] the session of the Diet / 閉院式 the closing ceremony of the Diet.

へいえい 兵営 a barracks ((単複同形)).

---

ought to know better at his age. / それが上分別だ. That's a good idea [a sensible thing to do].

ぶんぽう 彼は文法に合った言葉遣いができない. He cannot speak [write] grammatically.

ぶんみゃく 文脈によっては違う解釈もできるだろう. It could read differently in another [a differ-ent] context.

ぶんめん 手紙の文面は次のとおり. The letter reads [runs] as follows. / 近々上京するという手紙の文面だった. He wrote to me saying that he is coming up to Tokyo shortly.

ぶんりょう 分量が多い[少ない]. The quantity is large [small]. / 砂糖の分量が多すぎる. There is too much sugar in it.

ぶんれつ 1つの細胞が分裂して幾つかの新しい細胞が生まれる. A cell divides into [to form] new cells.

へいい 彼はだれにもわかるような平易な言葉で話した. He spoke in such plain Japanese that

へいえき 兵役 military service ¶兵役を免除される be exempted from military service / 兵役に服する serve (one's time) in the army.

へいおん 平穏 ¶平穏な calm; quiet;《文》tranquil / 平穏になる get [《文》become] quiet; quiet [《英》quieten] down / 平穏無事な peaceful; uneventful / 平穏無事に暮らす live in peace and quiet. 文例⇩

へいか¹ 平価 par ¶平価を切り上げる revalue the currency [yen, dollar, etc.] / 平価を切り下げる devalue the currency.

へいか² 陛下 〈三人称〉His [Her] Majesty (略: H.M.);〈二人称〉Your Majesty ⇒てんのう, こうごう ¶両陛下〈三人称〉Their Majesties (略: T.M.);〈二人称〉Your Majesties / 天皇皇后両陛下 Their Majesties the Emperor and Empress.

べいか 米価 the price of rice ¶米価審議会 the Rice Price Deliberative Council.

へいかい 閉会 the closing (of a meeting) ¶閉会する close (a meeting); adjourn;〈閉会になる〉be closed;《文》come to a close / 閉会の辞を述べる give a closing address / 閉会を宣する declare the meeting closed / 閉会式 a closing ceremony.

へいがい 弊害《文》an abuse;〈悪影響〉an evil [a harmful,《文》a baneful] influence; an evil effect ¶弊害が伴う have harmful effects; bring evils with (it) [《文》in (its) train];《文》be attended by [with] evils.

へいかいろ 閉回路【電】a closed circuit ¶閉回路テレビジョン closed-circuit television (略: CCTV). 文例⇩

へいかん 閉館 ¶閉館する close; be closed.

へいき¹ 平気〈冷静〉calmness; coolness; self-possession;〈無関心〉unconcern; indifference;《文》nonchalance ¶平気な calm; cool; unmoved; unconcerned; indifferent; nonchalant / 平気な顔をして as if nothing had happened [were the matter] / 平気で calmly; coolly; unconcernedly; indifferently / 平気でいる remain calm [cool]; be indifferent《about》; be unconcerned《about》; do not care《about》/ 平気を装う pretend not to care《about》;《文》feign indifference; put on [《文》assume] an unconcerned [a nonchalant] air. 文例⇩

へいき² 兵器 arms; a weapon (of war); weaponry (総称) ¶兵器庫 an armory; an arsenal / 兵器工場 an arms [a weapons] factory; an arsenal.

へいき³ 併記 ¶併記する put [write,《文》set] (A) down (in the report) with (B).

へいきん 平均 an average;【数】the mean;〈釣り合い〉balance ¶平均する average;〈ならす〉level [even] off / 平均して on (an [the]) average / 平均を出す calculate [strike] the average (of); average out (the cost) / 平均を取る get [take] the average /〈身体の〉balance (oneself) (on a rope) / 平均を失う lose one's balance / 算術[幾何]平均 the arithmetical [geometric] mean / 平均寿命 the average life span (of the Japanese) / 平均台〈用具〉a balance beam; 〈競技種目〉the balance beam (event) / 平均値 the mean value; the mean / 平均的日本人 an [the] average Japanese / 平均点 the average mark; mean-tone tuning. 文例⇩

へいげん 平原 a plain.

へいこう¹ 平行 ¶平行の parallel / 平行する run [be] parallel 《to, with》; parallel / 平行移動【数】translation (of axes) / 平行四辺形 a parallelogram / 平行線 parallel lines.

へいこう² 平衡 ⇒つりあい, きんこう² ¶(船などが)平衡を取り戻す get back on (to) [regain] an even keel / 平衡感覚 the [one's] sense of balance / 平衡交付金 an equalization subsidy [grant-in-aid] (to a local government).

へいこう³ 並行 ¶並行する go side by side 《with》; go abreast 《of》; keep pace 《with》/ 並行して side by side 《with》; in parallel 《with》.

へいこう⁴ 閉口 ¶閉口する be nonplussed 《by, over》; be stumped 《by》; be embarrassed 《by》; be at one's wit's end. 文例⇩

へいごう 併合 (an) annexation; (a) merger; (an) amalgamation ¶併合する annex; merge; amalgamate / 併合される be annexed 《to》; be merged 《into》.

へいこうぼう 平行棒【体操】parallel bars ¶段違い平行棒 ⇒だんちがい.

べいこく¹ 米穀 rice ¶米穀商 a rice dealer [merchant] / 米穀年度 the rice year.

べいこく² 米国 ⇒アメリカ.

---

everyone could understand.

へいおん 平穏な時代であった. It was a peaceful age. | The times were quiet.

へいかん 本日閉館.《掲示》〈閉館時間が過ぎて〉Closed for today. |〈休館日〉Closed today.

へいき 雨なんか平気だよ. I don't mind the rain. | 彼が何と言おうと僕は平気だ. I don't care a bit [damn] what people say. | あいつが何時に帰ろうとおれは平気だ. I couldn't care less what time she comes home. | ほめられよう が悪口を言われようが僕は平気だ. I am indifferent to praise or blame. / 彼は1日30キロ歩くくらいは平気だ. He thinks nothing of walking thirty kilometers a day. / 彼はわざと平気そうな様子をしてタバコを吹かした. He puffed at his cigarette with exaggerated nonchalance. / 彼は平気でうそをつく. He does not hesitate to lie. | He tells lies without the slightest compunction. / 彼は自分の目的を遂げるためならばどんなことでも平気である[やりかねない]. He would stop [stick] at nothing to achieve his objective.

へいきん 美代子の身長と体重は平均以上[下]だ. Miyoko's height and weight are above [below] (the) average. / 彼は2週間続けて, 1日平均20キロ歩いた. He walked for two weeks on end, averaging 20 kilometers a day. / 日本の女性の平均寿命は80歳だ. The average life span of Japanese women is 80 years. | Japanese women live (for) an average of 80 years. / 彼女は平均台で金メダルを取った. She won the gold medal in the beam event. / 平均点60点以下は落第とする. A student who gets an average mark of less than 60 will fail.

へいさ 閉鎖 closing; 〈締め出し〉a lockout ¶閉鎖する shut (down); close (down); 〈締め出す〉lock (the employees) out / 閉鎖的な 〈自閉的な〉uncommunicative; unsociable; 〈排他的な〉exclusive; cliquish.

べいさく 米作 〈栽培〉rice cultivation [culture]; 〈収穫〉the crop of rice; the rice crop ¶米作地帯 a rice-producing area [district] / 本年度の米作予想 an estimate [a forecast] of this year's rice crop. 文例⇩

へいさつ 併殺 【野球】 ¶併殺する make a double play.

へいし 兵士 a (common) soldier; a private; troops《複数のみ》.

へいじ 平時 ¶平時は〈平和時〉in peacetime; 《文》in time of peace; 〈普段〉at ordinary [normal] times; ordinarily; usually.

へいじつ 平日 〈日曜以外の日〉a weekday; 〈普段の日〉ordinary days ¶平日は on weekdays; on ordinary days / 平日の of the ordinary; usual; everyday / 平日どおり as usual.

へいしゃ 兵舎 a barracks《単複同形》.

べいじゅ 米寿 ¶米寿の祝いをする celebrate one's [sb's] eighty-eighth birthday.

べいしゅうきこう 米州機構 the Organization of American States《略: OAS》.

へいじょう[1] 平常 usually; ordinarily; at ordinary [normal, other] times ¶平常の ordinary; usual; everyday / 平常のとおり as usual / 平常に復する return [get back] to normal [normality]; return 《文》be restored] to its normal condition / 平常点 a mark given for《a student's》class participation.

へいじょう[2] 閉場 ⇒へいかん.

へいじょう[3] 平壌 Pyongyang.

へいしょきょうふしょう 閉所恐怖症 【医】 claustrophobia.

へいしょく 米食 rice diet ¶米食する live on rice; eat rice / 米食人種 a rice-eating people.

へいじょぶん 平叙文 【文法】a declarative [an assertive] sentence.

へいしんていとう 平身低頭 ¶平身低頭する 《文》prostrate oneself《before》; go down on one's knees / 平身低頭して詫る beg sb's pardon on one's knees 《文》on bended knees].

へいせい[1] 平静 calm; 《文》tranquility; 《文》serenity; 《落ち着き》《文》equanimity ¶心の平静 peace of mind; composure; 《文》mental equilibrium / 平静な calm; serene; 《文》tranquil; 《文》equable / 心の平静を保つ remain calm; keep one's head [《俗》one's cool] / 心の平静を失う lose one's composure [equanimity, presence of mind].

へいせい[2] 兵制 the military system.

へいせい 平生 ⇒へいじょう[1].

へいせつ 併設 ⇒へいち[2].

へいぜん 平然 ⇒へいき[1] ¶平然たる calm; cool; composed / 平然と calmly; coolly; with composure; impassively; unsurprised. 文例⇩

へいそ 平素 ⇒へいじょう[1], ふだん.

べいソ 米ソ ¶米ソ関係 U.S.-Soviet [Soviet-American] relations.

へいそく 閉塞 (a) blockade; blocking(-up); (a) stoppage ¶閉塞する blockade; block (up) / 閉塞前線 【気象】an occluded front.

へいそつ 兵卒 ⇒へいし.

へいたい 兵隊 a soldier; troops《複数のみ》 ¶兵隊あり a soldier ant / 兵隊ごっこをする play (at) soldiers.

へいたん 平坦 ¶平坦な even; flat; level.

へいち[1] 平地 the level ground; flatlands; flats; 〈平原〉the plains ¶平地に波瀾を起こす《文》flutter [cause a flutter in] the dovecotes.

へいち[2] 併置 ¶併置する put [《文》place] sth side by side《with》; 〈学校などを〉establish 《a school》as an annex《to》. 文例⇩

へいちゃら ⇒へいき[1]. 「conquer.

へいてい[1] 平定 ¶平定する《文》subjugate;

へいてい[2] 閉廷 ¶閉廷する dismiss [adjourn] the court. 文例⇩

へいてん 閉店 ¶閉店する〈営業時間が終わって〉close (the) shop [one's doors]; 〈廃業する〉shut up shop; wind up one's business / 閉店時間 (the) closing time. 文例⇩

へいねつ 平熱 the normal temperature.

へいねん 平年 〈うるう年(ʒ°ʰ)のない年〉a common year; 〈例年〉a normal [an average] year ¶平年作 a normal [an average] crop.

へいはつ 併発 ¶併発する〈余病名が主語〉accompany《the flu》; 〈先の病気が主語〉be complicated by《another disease》⇒ よびょう. 文例⇩

へいこう[3] これと平行に線を引け. Draw a line parallel to this. / 鉄道に平行して道路が走っている. A street runs parallel to the railroad.

へいこう[4] 第3問には閉口した. The third problem beat me. | Question 3 had [got] me beat. / この暑さには[あの男には]閉口だ. I can't bear [stand] the heat [that fellow]. / 雪にはやけが付け出すと道が悪くて閉口だ. I like snow itself, but I hate it when it begins to thaw and the roads get muddy.

へいさ その工場は10日間閉鎖を命じられた. The factory was ordered to be closed for ten days.

べいさく 本年の米作は平年を多少上回る見込みだ. This year's rice crop is estimated to be a little above [better than] (the) average.

へいぜん 彼は平然たるものであった. He remained calm [unruffled]. | He never turned a hair. / 彼は少しも席に着いた. He sat down as if nothing had happened.

へいち[2] 本科に加えて, 短期速成科が併置してある. The school offers a short-term intensive course along with [besides] its regular course.

へいちゃら そんなのへいちゃらさ. It's a cinch. / 親父が怒ったってへいちゃらさ. I don't give a damn [I couldn't care less] if Dad gets mad.

へいてい[2] 5時に閉廷した. The court adjourned [rose] at five o'clock.

へいてん 本日閉店.【掲示】〈閉店時間以後〉Closed for today. | 〈休業する〉Closed today. / 閉店は何時ですか. What time do you close?

へいはつ あの子ははしかから肺炎を併発した. The child is suffer-

へいばん 平板 ¶平板な〈単調な〉monotonous;〈味のない〉dull; flat.

へいふく¹ 平伏 ¶平伏する《文》prostrate oneself (before).

へいふく² 平服 ¶〈普段着〉clothes for everyday wear; ordinary clothes; informal dress;〈警察官の制服などに対して〉plain clothes;〈軍服に対して〉civilian clothes. 用例↓

へいへい ¶へいへいする fawn (on);《文》be obsequious ((to)). 用例↓

へいべい 平米 a square meter.

へいぜい ぺいぺい《文》petty; minor.

へいへいぼんぼん 平々凡々 ⇨ へいぼん.

へいほう¹ 平方《自乗》the square (of a number) ¶1メートル平方 one meter square / 1平方メートル a square meter (略: m²) / 平方に開く the square root (of) / 平方根を求める extract [find] the square root ((of)). 用例↓

へいほう² 兵法〈戦術〉tactics;〈戦略〉strategy.

へいぼん 平凡 ¶平凡な commonplace; mediocre; common; ordinary; undistinguished / 平凡な a commonplace; an everyday affair / 平凡な人間 a common [an ordinary] man; a mediocrity (能力が) / 平凡な景色 a featureless landscape / 平凡な顔 a face without any character. 用例↓

へいまく 閉幕 ¶閉幕となる end; close; come to an end [a close].

へいまつ 米松 an Oregon pine [fir]; a Douglas pine [fir].

へいみゃく 平脈 the normal pulse.

へいみん 平民 a commoner; the common people (総称).

へいめい 平明 ¶平明な plain; clear; simple.

へいめん 平面 a plane (surface); a level ¶平面の plane; level; flat / 同一平面上にある be on the same level [plane] ((with)); be in one plane; be flush ((with)) / 平面幾何学 plane geometry /(鉄道の)平面交差《米》a grade crossing;《英》a level crossing / 平面図 a ground [floor] plan; a plan / 平面図で示す show sth in ground plan [in plan view].

へいもん 閉門 closing the gate ¶閉門時間 (the) closing time.

へいや 平野 the plains ¶関東平野 the Kanto plains; the plains of Kanto.

へいよう 併用 ¶併用する use sth together ((with)); use ((two things)) at the same time / 散薬と水薬を併用する take a powder medicine and a liquid one together [at the same time].

へいりょく 兵力〈兵数〉the (numerical) strength of an army; troop strength;〈武力〉force of arms ¶5万の兵力 a force 50,000 strong / 兵力を削減[増強]する reduce [raise, build up] its troop strength.

ベイルート Beirut.

へいれつ 並列 ¶並列させる arrange [draw up] in a line [row] / 並列回路 a parallel circuit.

へいろ 平炉〈冶金〉an open-hearth furnace; an open hearth.

へいわ 平和 peace;〈和合〉harmony ¶世界の平和 the peace of the world; world peace (★冠詞はつけない) / 平和な peaceful; harmonious / 平和に peacefully; in peace;〈仲よく〉《文》harmoniously / 平和を維持する keep [《文》maintain] the peace / 平和を回復する restore peace; peace returns ((to the land)) / 家庭の平和を乱す《文》disturb domestic peace [harmony] / 平和を破る break [disturb] the peace / 平和愛好国民 a peace-loving nation / 平和運動 a peace movement / 平和会議 a peace conference ((on Germany)) / 平和共存 peaceful coexistence / 平和攻勢 a peace offensive / 平和主義 pacifism / 平和主義者 a pacifist / 平和条約 a peace treaty.

へー 〈驚き・疑いなど〉dear me!; indeed!;〈疑問〉what?; well? 用例↓

ベーカリー a bakery.

ベークライト《商標名》bakelite.

ヘーゲル Hegel ¶ヘーゲル哲学 Hegelian philosophy.

ベーコン (a slice of) bacon.

ページ a page; a leaf (1葉) ¶ページをめくる turn (over) the pages [《文》leaves] (of a book) / ページをつける, ページづけをする paginate; page / 輝かしい1ページを加える add a brilliant page to ((the history of...)) / 第3ページに on the third page; on page 3. 用例↓

ベージュ beige.

ベース¹〈基地〉a base;《野球・料理》a base ¶ベースキャンプ a base camp / ベースライン a base line / ベースランニング base running.

ベース²〈基準〉a base; a basis (pl. bases) ¶賃銀ベース a wage base / ベースアップを要求する demand a raise (in the wage level).

ペース pace ¶自分のペースを守る go 《文》proceed at one's own pace / 相手のペースを乱す put one's opponent off [out of] his stride; disturb one's rival's rhythm / ペースメーカー a pacemaker; a pacesetter.

---

ing from measles complicated by pneumonia.

へいふく 平服でお出で下さい.《招待状の言葉》Dress informal.

へいへい 彼は社長の命令なら何でもへいへいと言うことを. He is at the president's beck and call.

へいほう¹ 4の平方根は 2. The square root of four is two. | Root 4 is 2.

へいぼん その日も平凡に過ぎた. The day passed uneventfully.

へー へー！そんな事がありますか. Dear me, is it possible?

ページ その本は本文が120ページで注が30ページある. The book contains 120 pages of text and 30 pages of (explanatory) notes. | 90ページを開けなさい. Open your book(s) at [to] page 90. | Find page 90. | 前ページから続く. Continued from the previous page. / 24ページに続く. Continued on page 24. / その雑誌の今月号は先月号よりページ数が多い. This issue of the magazine has more pages than the last one did. / その小説は雑誌に載せると20ページ分くらいだろうと思う. I think the story will cover some 20 magazine pages.

-べき 暴力に訴えるべきではない.

ペースト 〖料理〗 paste ¶肉のペースト meat paste;《フランス語》pâté.

ペーソス pathos.

ベータ beta; β ¶ベータ粒子〖物〗a β-particle; a beta particle ★前者が普通の書き方.

ペーパー 〈紙〉paper;〈ラベル〉a label;〈紙やすり〉sandpaper; emery paper ¶ペーパーテスト a written examination [test] / ペーパードライバー a person who has a driver's license but no experience; a driver in name only / ペーパーナイフ a paper knife / ペーパーバックの本 a book in paperback (format); a paperback (book).

ベーリング ¶ベーリング海 the Bering Sea / ベーリング海峡 the Bering Strait.

ベール a veil; a wimple (修道女の) ¶ベールをかぶっている be veiled; wear [be in] a veil / なぞのベールに包まれている be hidden in a veil of mystery / ベールで顔を包む muffle one's face in a veil; veil one's face.

ベオグラード Belgrade.

へおんきごう ヘ音記号 〖音楽〗an F [a bass] clef.

-べからず 可からず must not do;〈命令〉Do not do ¶食卓作法べからず集〈書名〉Don'ts in Table Manners.

べき 冪 〖数〗a power ¶2 [3] 乗冪 the second [third] power.

-べき ¶…すべきである〈義務として〉当然 should do; ought to do;〈理由はどうあろうと〉必ず must do ⇨ いけない 囲囲. 文例⇩

へきえき 辟易 ¶へきえきする〈ひるむ〉flinch 《from》; shrink (back) 《from》;〈うんざりする〉be bored 《by, with》; be fed up 《with》. 文例⇩

へきが 壁画 a wall painting; a mural (painting);〈フレスコ画〉a fresco (pl. -(e)s) ¶壁画家 a mural painter.

へきぎょく 碧玉 〖鉱〗jasper.

へきち 僻地 an out-of-the-way place; a remote corner of the country ¶僻地の学校教育 school education in remote rural areas.

へきとう 劈頭 ⇨ さいしょ, ぼうとう¹.

へきめん 壁面 the face [surface] of a wall.

へきれき 霹靂 ⇨ せいてん¹.

ペキン 北京 Beijing; Peking ¶北京原人 (the) Peking man.

ヘクタール a hectare (略: ha).

ペクチン 〖生化〗pectin.

ベクトル 〖数〗a vector ¶ベクトルの場 a vector field.

ぺけ 〈だめ〉no good;〈罰点〉⇨ ばってん ¶ぺけになる come to nothing; end in failure.

へこたれる 〈元気を失う〉lose heart; be discouraged; be dejected;〈屈服する〉give in 《to》;〈弱る〉be exhausted; be tired [worn] out; be dead tired;《米俗》be pooped;《英俗》be knackered. 文例⇩

ベゴニア 〖植〗a begonia.

ぺこぺこ ¶ぺこぺこする〈へつらう〉kowtow 《to》; cringe 《to》;《文》be obsequious 《to》;《口語》lick sb's boots;《口語》crawl 《to》;〈へこむ〉give; dent / ぺこぺこして crawlingly;《文》in a servile manner / おなかがぺこぺこだ be awfully hungry; be starving; be famished. 文例⇩

へこませる 凹ませる 〈くぼます〉make sth hollow; dent; indent;〈屈服さす〉beat sb hollow; put sb down; silence (議論で);《文》humble (高慢の鼻を).

へこみ 凹み a dent; a hollow ¶缶のへこみ dents in a can.

へこむ 凹む become hollow; be dented; be dinted; dent;〈陥没する〉sink in; collapse; cave in;〈屈服する〉give in 《to》;《文》yield 《to》.

ぺこりと ⇨ ぺこぺこ, ぴょこんと.

へさき 舳先 the bow(s); the prow ¶へさきを向ける head [be headed] 《for》/ へさきを回す veer 《a ship》/ へさきに in [on, at] the bows; on the prow / 船のへさきに砕ける波 a bow wave.

-べし …可し 〈義務·命令〉must do;〈当為〉should do; ought to do;〈要請〉be requested to do;〈未来〉will do; shall do;〈予定〉be expected to do;〈可能〉can do. 文例⇩

へしおる へし折る break; smash.

ぺしゃんこ ⇨ ぺちゃんこ.

ベスト¹ 〈最善〉the [one's] best ¶ベストを尽くす one's (level) best / ベストセラー a best seller; a best-selling book / 隠れたベストセラー a sleeper / ベストセラー作家 a best-selling author [writer] / ベストテン the best ten; the ten best (hitters for the season). 文例⇩

ベスト² 〈チョッキ〉《米》a vest;《英》a waistcoat ★《英》では vest は下着のシャツ.

ペスト the plague;《文》(a) pestilence ¶腺(ẽ)ペスト bubonic plague.

ペセタ 〈通貨単位〉a peseta.

へそ 臍 the navel;《口語》the bellybutton;〈船の櫓(ろ)の〉a thole (pin) / へその緒 a navel string; an umbilical cord / へその緒切って以来初めて for the first time in one's life /

You must not use [resort to] violence. / 彼とは手を切るべきだったのに. You should [ought to] have broken with him. / すぐにフランスに発つべきだ. You must leave for France at once.

へきえき 彼の長広舌にはへきえきした. I was bored to death by his long-winded speech.

へこたれる 1度や2度の失敗でへこたれてはいかん. Don't let a failure or two discourage you [《口語》get you down]. | Don't be so dejected just because you have failed once or twice.

ぺこぺこ おなかがぺこぺこで目が回りそうだ. I'm so hungry I feel faint. / 彼は支店長にいつもぺこぺこしている. He is always kowtowing to the office manager. / この空き缶は押すとぺこぺこする. This empty can gives [dents] easily when you press it.

-べし 学生は午前8時までに登校すべし. 〈掲示〉Students are requested to arrive at school not later than eight in the morning. | Students must be at the school by 8 a.m.

ベスト¹ その本はたちまちその月のベストセラーのトップにのし上がった. The book went straight to the top of the month's best-

へそを曲げる become perverse; get awkward / へそ曲がり a perverse fellow; 《口語》 an awkward cuss. 文例

べそ ¶べそをかく be ready to cry; be almost in tears; be on the point of tears; have an unhappy look on one's face.

ペソ 〈通貨単位〉 a peso (pl. -s).

へそくり 臍繰り (a wife's) secret savings ¶へそくりをする save up (a part of the household allowance) secretly (for one's own use).

へた[1] 下手 ¶下手な poor; 《文》 unskillful; awkward; clumsy / 下手な絵 a poor [badly painted] picture / 下手な人 a poor hand (at) / 下手な英語で話す speak in broken [poor] English / 下手なことを言う make unfortunate [《文》 unwise] remarks; use undiplomatic language / …が下手である be bad [no good, poor] at (English); be a poor (singer); be weak in (mathematics) (★ be bad [no good] at… という形が最も普通)(練習をしないで) 下手になる get out of practice; lose one's touch / 下手をやる make a mess [bad job] of sth / 下手をする (up); make a blunder / 下手をすると if one is not careful; if (it is (things are)) not properly handled; if things go badly / 下手の横好きである be crazy about [keen on] (shogi) though (one is) no good at it. 文例

へた[2] 蔕 《植》 the calyx (pl. -es, calyces).

べた ¶べた一面に 〈全体に〉 all over; 〈厚く〉 thick(ly) / べた塗りする daub sth all over [plaster sth] 《with paint》/ べたぼめにほめる praise sb to the skies; plaster sb with praise / べた惚れしている be deeply [head over heels] in love 《with》.

へだたり 隔たり 〈距離〉 (a) distance; 〈相違〉 (a) difference; 〈懸隔〉 a gap; 《文》 a disparity. 文例

へだたる 隔たる 〈遠い〉 be a long way (from); be distant [remote] (from); be far off (from); 〈離れている〉 be (some way) apart (from); 〈疎遠になる〉 《文》 become estranged (from); 《文》 be no longer on good terms (with).

べたつく ⇨ べたべた. 文例

へだて 隔て 〈仕切り〉 a partition; 〈障壁〉 a barrier; 〈透き間〉 a gap; 〈差別〉 (a) distinction; 〈区別〉 discrimination; 〈距離〉 (a) distance; 〈隔意〉 reserve ¶隔てのある cold; reserved; 《口語》 standoffish / 隔てなく話す be open [frank] with sb / 隔てをつける 《文》 discriminate 《between, against》/ 隔てをつけない make no distinctions 《between》.

へだてる 隔てる 〈仕切り〉 part; separate; set apart; partition off; 〈遮る〉 screen; 〈友人同士などの間を〉 set (A and B) at odds 《with each other》; 《文》 estrange ¶隔てて 〈間隔〉 at intervals (of ten feet, two hours); 〈距離〉 at a distance; 〈時間〉 after the lapse of (two years); 〈越えて〉 on the other side of (the border); 《文》 beyond (the mountain); across (the river). 文例

へたばる 〈疲れる〉 《文》 be exhausted; be tired [worn] out; be all in; be done in; 《米俗》 be pooped (out); 《英俗》 be knackered; 〈屈服する〉 give in (to); 《文》 yield (to). 文例

べたべた ¶べたべたくっつく stick (to); 《文》 adhere (to) / べたべたする 〈粘着する〉 be sticky (to the touch); 〈人に対して〉 《口語》 be all over (sb, each other); 《文》 bill and coo (男女が) / べたべたに ⇨ べた (べた一面に); べた塗る ⇨ べた (べた塗りする) / 壁一面にビラをべたべた張る plaster the wall (all over) with bills. 文例

べたべた叩く slap sth repeatedly. 文例

へたへたと ¶床にへたへたとうずくまる sink weakly to the floor; collapse on the floor. 文例

ペダル a pedal; a treadle (ミシンなどの) ¶ペダルを踏む work a pedal [treadle]; pedal (one's bicycle) / (ピアノの)弱音ペダル a soft [piano] pedal / (ピアノの)伸音ペダル a loud [forte] pedal.

ぺたんと ¶ぺたんと座る sit down with a flop; flop [plump] down (on the floor).

ペチカ 〈<《ロシヤ語》 pechka〉 a Manchurian stove.

ペチコート a petticoat.

へちま 《植》 a dishcloth gourd; a sponge cu-

---

sellers list.

へそ やつが歌手希望だって? へそが茶を沸かさあ。He wants to be a singer? What a joke!

へた[1] 私は お料理が とても下手です。I am a terrible cook. | I am very bad [poor] at cooking. / 彼は英語が下手だ。He speaks English badly. | He is no good at speaking English. / 下手な口出しはできない。The matter requires careful handling. | It is a very delicate affair. / 下手をすると今度は失敗するかもしれない。I am afraid (that) luck will go against me and I'll fail again. / 下手な考え方なども似たり。Inadequate ideas are [Inadequate thinking is] worse than none at all. / 下手な鉄砲も数撃ちゃあた る。The poorest shot will hit the target if he shoots often enough.

へだたり 2人の年齢には大変な隔たりがある。There is a great disparity in their ages.

へだたる 東京と大阪とはどのくらい隔たっていますか。How far is it from Tokyo to Osaka? / How far is Osaka from Tokyo? / 2人の間は3メートルとは隔たっていなかった。There wasn't more than three meters between them.

へだてる 彼らの部屋はカーテン1枚で隔てられている。Their rooms are partitioned off only by a curtain. / 障子に隔てられて姿が見えなかった。The shoji screened her from sight. / 2メートルずつ隔てて柱が立っていた。The posts stood at intervals of two meters. / これだけ時を隔てて見るとそれが古代日本彫刻の例外的逸品だったことがわかる。At this distance of time we see that it was an exceptionally fine piece of ancient Japanese sculpture. / 両軍は川を隔てて対陣した。The two armies camped facing each other across the river.

へたばる もうへたばったのかい。Are you done in already? / 僕は40キロくらい歩いてへたばる僕ではない。I think [make] nothing of walking forty kilometers a day.

べたべた 通りのどの電柱にもポスターがべたべたと張ってある。The telephone poles along the street are all plastered [covered]

ぺちゃくちゃ   べっそう

cumber [gourd]; 〈乾燥繊維〉a loofah ¶へちまでこする rub 《one's back》 with a loofah.

ぺちゃくちゃ ¶ぺちゃくちゃしゃべる chatter; jabber; prattle; 《文》prate; 《文》wag one's tongue. 文例⇩

ぺちゃぱい ¶ぺちゃぱいだ《口語》be flat(-chested).

ぺちゃべちゃ ⇨ べちゃくちゃ ¶ぺちゃべちゃな御飯 soggy [mushy] rice; rice boiled too soft.

ぺちゃんこ ¶ぺちゃんこになる〈つぶれる〉go [get, be]《become》flat [as flat as a pancake]; be flattened; be crushed; 〈負ける〉be beaten hollow.

べつ 別 〈区別〉(a) distinction; (a) difference; 〈別の事物〉another [a different] thing ¶別の〈外の〉another; different; 〈特別の〉special; 〈別々の〉separate; 〈余分の〉extra; additional; 〈各々の〉respective; each / いつか別の日に some other day / 別に〈別々に〉separately; apart; 〈個々に〉individually; 〈各々〉each; respectively; 〈余分に〉extra; in addition; 〈外に〉else; besides; 〈特に〉particularly; in particular; specially (★ particularly も in particular も specially も否定文で使われることが多い) / 別を立てる distinguish (A from B); make a distinction (between A and B) / 昼夜の別なく働く work night and day / その問題は別として leaving that question (for the moment); apart from that problem [matter] / 別にして取っておく keep *sth* aside [apart, on one side]; reserve / 府県別の人口 population by prefecture. 文例⇩

べつあつらえ 別誂え ¶別あつらえの靴 shoes [boots] (specially) made to order.

べっかく 別格 ¶別格の special; exceptional. 文例⇩

べっかん 別館 an annex 《to》.

べつかんじょう 別勘定 a separate account [bill].

べっきょ 別居 (a) separation ¶別居する live apart [separately] 《from》; be separated 《from one's spouse》; live in a separate house / 2 年間の別居生活の後に離婚する be divorced 《from one's spouse》after a separation of two years. 文例⇩

べつぎょう 別行 ¶別行に書く[する] write on [begin] a new line.

べつくち 別口 another [a different] item.

べっけん¹ 別件 ¶別件で逮捕する arrest sb on a holding charge.

べっけん² 瞥見 a glance; a glimpse ¶瞥見する glance at; catch a glimpse of; 《文》cast a glance over [on]; take a brief look at.

べっこ 別個 ⇨ べつ, べつべつ. 文例⇩

べっこう¹ 別項 ¶別項の[に] in a separate paragraph; in another clause [section].

べっこう² 鼈甲 tortoiseshell ¶べっこう縁の眼鏡 tortoiseshell(-rimmed) spectacles / べっこう色 amber / べっこう細工 tortoiseshell work.

べっさつ 別冊 a separate volume ¶別冊になっている be separately bound / 別冊付録 a separate-volume supplement 《to》.

ペッサリー a diaphragm; a pessary;《口語》a Dutch cap.

べっし¹ 別紙 ¶別紙のとおり as you will see from the enclosed [attached] paper;《文》as per enclosure / 別紙に書く write on another [a separate] sheet.

べっし² 蔑視 ⇨ けいべつ.

べっしつ 別室 ¶別室に退く《文》withdraw into another room.

べっしゅ 別種 ¶別種の《文》of a different kind;《文》belonging to a different category.

べつじょう 別状 ¶別状がない there is nothing wrong 《with》; 〈無事である〉be safe (and sound); 〈壮健である〉be quite well;《文》be in good health. 文例⇩

べつじん 別人 a different person; another [a changed] man.

べっせかい 別世界 another [a different] world. 文例⇩

べっそう 別荘 a (country [resort]) villa; a (country) cottage; a summer house (避暑地

---

with posters. / シャツがからだにべたべたくっついた. My shirt clung to me.

べたあし はだしで舗道の上をぺたぺた歩いた. His bare feet went slap, slap on the pavement.

へたへたと ひざがへたへたとなった. His knees went from under him.

ぺちゃくちゃ 何をそんなにぺちゃくちゃしゃべっているんだい. What are you prattling on so excitedly about.

べつ 言うとやるのとは別だ. To talk is one thing, to do is another. 田中君だけは別だ. But Tanaka is an exception. / 学校には国公私立の別がある. Schools are divided into three categories—national, municipal and private. / 別のを持って来い.

Bring me another [a different one]. / これは別にしておこう. We will keep this separate. / もっと上等の席が欲しければ別に金を出さなければならない. You must pay extra if you want a better seat. / 別にこれという程の用事もない. I've nothing in particular to attend to. / この本には別に面白いことも書いてありません. There is nothing particularly interesting in this book. / テレビをご覧になりたい?—別に. Do you want to watch TV?—Not particularly.

べっかく でも高津教授だけは別格だよ. But Prof. Kozu is an exception (to this rule).

べっきょ 別居生活はもうどのくらいになるのですか. How long have you been separated (from

your wife [husband])?

べっこ その 2 つは私には別個の事件のように思われた. It seems to me that they are two distinct [different] cases.

べつじょう 機械に別状なかった. There was nothing wrong with the machine. | No damage was done to the machine. / 命に別状はない. He is in no danger of (dying). | I am sure he will live [come] through it. / (遭難の際などに)体には別状はなかった. He got off unhurt. | He came off with a whole skin.

べつじん 彼は全く別人のようになった. He is quite a different man now. | He is not what he used to be.

べっせかい まるで別世界にきたようだ. It's as if we were in an-

べったく 別宅 another house; one's second home.

べったり ❶べったりくっつく stick (tight [close]) ((to)); 《文》adhere ((to)) / べったり地面に座る sit flat [directly] on the ground.

べったり ⇨ べたり. 文例↓

べつだん 別段 ⇨ かくべつ, とくべつ.

へっつい 竃 ⇨ かまど.

べってい 別邸 ⇨ べったく.

ヘッディング 《サッカー》heading ❶ヘッディングする head 《the ball》.

べってんち 別天地 ⇨ べっせかい.

ヘット beef dripping [fat].

べっと 別途 ❶別途に separately; specially / 別途積立金 a special reserve fund.

ベッド a bed. ❶シングル[ダブル]ベッド a single [double] bed / ベッドカバー a bedspread / ベッドタウン a commuter town; a dormitory suburb. 「snake」as a pet.

ペット a pet ❶ペットにしている keep 《a

ヘッドホン a headphone; a headset.

ヘッドライト a headlight; a headlamp.

べっとり ⇨ べたり, べたべた. 文例↓

べつのう 別納 separate payment ❶料金別納郵便で送る send sth postpaid [《英》post-free].

べっぴょう 別表 an attached [《文》annexed] list [table].

へっぴりごし 屁っぴり腰 ❶へっぴり腰で not standing straight [《文》upright]; 〈びくびくしながら〉nervously; full of fear [《文》apprehension]; 〈決断力に欠けて〉indecisively; 《文》irresolutely.

べつびん 別便 ❶別便で by separate mail [post]. 「cover.

べっぷう 別封 ❶別封の[で] under separate

べつべつ 別々 ❶別々の〈別の〉separate; 〈各自の〉respective;《文》several / 別々に〈別に離して〉separately; apart;〈個々に〉respectively;《文》severally / 別々に住む live apart [separately]《from》. 文例↓

べっぽう 別法 another [a different] method ❶別法を講じる devise a different method; adopt a different plan; take a new tack.

へっぽこ ⇨ へぼ.

べつむね 別棟 another building ❶母屋(おもや)とは別棟になっている be separate [detached] from the main building.

べつめい 別名 another name; an alias.

べつもの 別物 a different thing; another thing ❶別物扱いにする treat sth as an exception. 文例↓

べつもんだい 別問題 another question; a different case. 文例↓

へつらい 諂い flattery ❶へつらう者 a flatterer;《文》a sycophant; a toady;《口語》a bootlicker.

へつらう 諂う flatter; curry favor with; fawn on; toady (to); play up to.

べつり 別離 ❶別離を悲しむ《文》feel sad [sorrow] at parting ((from)).

ベテラン a veteran; an old hand ❶ベテランの教師 a veteran teacher. 文例↓

ぺてん ❶ぺてん ⇨ さぎ¹ ❷ぺてんにかける ⇨ だます / ぺてん師 ⇨ さぎ¹ (詐欺師).

へど 反吐 vomit;《俗》puke ❶へどが出そうな nauseating; disgusting / へどを吐く vomit (up [out]);《口語》throw up. 文例↓

ベトナム Viet Nam; Vietnam ❶ベトナムのVietnamese / ベトナム社会主義共和国 the Socialist Republic of Viet Nam / ベトナム人 a Vietnamese《単複同形》.

へとへと ❶へとへとになる ⇨ へばる.

べとべと ⇨ べたべた.

へどもど ❶へどもどする be flustered; be flurried / へどもどしながら言い訳をする stutter out an apology.

ペトリざら ペトリ皿 a Petri [petri] dish.

へどろ sludge.

へなへな ❶へなへなのブリキ板 a thin tinplate sheet that bends easily / へなへなとくずおれる sink weakly 《to the floor [ground]》.

ペナルティー 《競技》a penalty ❶ペナルティーキック a penalty (kick) / ペナルティースロー a penalty throw.

ベナン Benin ❶ベナン人民共和国 the People's Republic of Benin / ベナン人 a Beninese.

ペナント a pennant ❶ペナントを争う compete for the pennant / ペナントレース a pennant race.

べに 紅 rouge; (a) lipstick (棒状の口紅) ⇨ くちべに, ほおべに. ❶紅色 red; vermilion.

ペニー a penny (略: p).

用法 penny の複数形は貨幣としては pennies, 金額としては pence. なお penny 及び pence の略 p (発音は [pi:]) は, 1971年に貨幣制度が改正され, 1 penny = 1/100 pound の「新ペニー」(the new penny) が施行されて以来のもので, それ以前は d. (発音は [péni(:)] 又は [pens]) であった. また《米》では penny は「1 セント貨」を意味する ⇨ ペンス 用法.

べにしょうが 紅しょうが red pickled ginger.

ペニシリン penicillin ❶ペニシリンを注射する give sb a penicillin injection [an injection of penicillin] / 10万単位のペニシリン注射を

---

other world.

べったり だからといって我々が体制べったりの人間であるということにはならない. That doesn't mean that we are blind followers of [are all for] the Establishment.

べっとり 刀にべっとり血がついていた. The blade was thickly covered with blood.

へっぴりごし そんなへっぴり腰ではだめだ. You're too weak-kneed. That won't do.

べつべつ 口と腹とは別々だ. He says one thing and means another. / 彼らは別々の道を行った. They went their respective [several] ways. / これとそれとは別々に論じられなければならない. This must be discussed separately from that. / 勘定は別々にして下さい. Give us separate bills, please. / ごっちゃにならないように別々にしておきなさい. Keep them apart so (that) they don't get mixed up. / いっしょに来ないで別々に来なさい. Come one by one, not in a group.

べつもの それとこれとは別物だ. They are two different things.

べつもんだい それは別問題だ. That is quite a different matter [another story].

ベニス　give sb an injection of 100,000 units of penicillin / ペニシリンショック penicillin shock / ペニシリン軟膏 a penicillin ointment.

ベニス　Venice ¶ベニスの Venetian.

べにすずめ　紅雀〖鳥〗an avadavat; a strawberry finch.

べにばな　紅花〖植〗a safflower.

べにます　紅鱒〖魚〗a red trout.

べにいた　ベニヤ板　a sheet of plywood; a plywood board; plywood (総称) ★英語の veneer は plywood (合板) や家具などの一番表に張る上質の薄板を言う.

ベニン　Benin ⇒ベナン.

ベネズエラ　Venezuela ¶ベネズエラの Venezuelan / ベネズエラ共和国 the Republic of Venezuela / ベネズエラ人 a Venezuelan.

ベネルックス　Benelux; the Benelux countries ★Benelux は Belgium, the Netherlands, Luxembourg 3国の頭部の文字の組合わせ.

へばりつく　へばり付く　cling to; stick fast to; hug. 文例⬇

へばる　⇒ へたばる.

へび　蛇〖動〗a snake; a serpent (大蛇) ¶へびのような snaky;《文》serpentine / へびの毒 snake venom / へび革 snakeskin / へび使い a snake charmer. 文例⬇

ヘビー　¶ヘビーをかける spurt; put on a spurt; 〈ボートレースで〉pull one's hardest;《文》bend to the oars.

ベビー　a baby ¶ベビーサークル a playpen / ベビーだんす a chest of drawers (for baby clothes).

ヘビーきゅう　ヘビー級　the heavyweight class ¶ヘビー級のボクサー a heavyweight (boxer).

ペプシン〖生化〗pepsin.

ヘブライ　¶ヘブライ語 Hebrew / ヘブライ人 a Hebrew / ヘブライ(人, 語)の Hebraic; Hebrew.

へべれけ　¶へべれけに酔っている be blind [dead] drunk ⇒ べろべろ.

へぼ　¶へぼな《文》unskillful; poor / へぼ絵かき a poor painter / へぼ詩人 a mediocre [third-rate] poet / へぼ将棋を指す play a poor game of shogi. 「romaji).

ヘボンしき　ヘボン式　the Hepburn system (of

へま　a blunder;《米俗》a boner;《英俗》a boob ¶へまな awkward; bungling; stupid / へまをする《文》commit a blunder; make a mess [hash] of sth; bungle; put one's foot in it; 《米俗》pull a boner;《英俗》boob.

ヘモグロビン〖生化〗hemoglobin.

へや　部屋　a room;《文》a chamber; 〈相撲の〉a stable ¶(家に)部屋が八つある have eight rooms; there are eight rooms 《in the flat》/ 部屋を借りる[貸す] ⇒ まがり², まがし / 〈ホテルで〉部屋を取る take a room / 二子山部屋 the Futagoyama stable / 部屋着 a dressing gown / 部屋代 (room) rent. 文例⬇

へら　箆　a spatula;《文》〈和裁用の〉a tracing spat-

へらす　減らす　〈少なくする〉《文》decrease; lessen; reduce; 〈切り詰める〉cut down (on) (smoking);《文》curtail.

へらずぐち　減らず口　¶へらず口をたたく 〈負け惜しみを言う〉insist on having the last word; 〈くだらない理屈を言う〉argue for argument's sake. 文例⬇

べらべら　⇒ ぺらぺら.

ぺらぺら　¶ぺらぺらしゃべる 〈滑らかに〉talk fluently [glibly,《文》volubly]; chatter; 〈早口に訳のわからぬことを〉gabble; jabber / ぺらぺらの thin; flimsy.

べらぼう　箆棒　¶べらぼうな 〈甚だしい, ひどい〉dreadful; awful; 〈不合理な〉absurd; unreasonable / べらぼうな値段 an extremely high price; an exorbitant [《文》unconscionable] price / べらぼうな話 nonsense / べらぼうに awfully; frightfully; terribly; extremely; exceedingly / べらぼうに寒い be terribly [《英俗》bloody] cold. 文例⬇

ベランダ　a veranda(h).

へり　縁 ⇒ ふち².

ベリーズ〖国名〗Belize ¶ベリーズの Belizean / ベリーズ人 a Belizean.

ベリーロール〖走り高跳び〗a belly-roll.

ヘリウム〖化〗helium.

ヘリオトロープ〖植〗a heliotrope.

ペリカン〖鳥〗a pelican.

へりくだる　⇒ けんそん (謙遜する).

へりくつ　屁理屈　¶屁理屈を言う〈並べる〉quibble (over sth); put forward a far-fetched argument; split hairs 《over [about] sth》.

ヘリコプター　a helicopter;《口語》a chopper ¶ヘリコプターで運ばれる be transported by helicopter (to); be helicoptered (to).

ベリセ　⇒ ベリーズ.

ヘリポート　a heliport.

ベリリウム〖化〗beryllium.

へる¹　経る　〈時がたつ〉pass; go by;《文》wear on;《文》elapse; 〈通る〉go [pass] through; 〈経験する〉experience ¶月日を経るに従って as time goes [the days go] by; as the years go on;《文》with the passage of time / …の手

ベテラン　こういう仕事なら彼はベテランだ. He is expert [an old hand] at this sort of job.

へど　彼のお世辞を聞くとへどが出そうになる. His flattery [insincerity] is simply nauseating.

へばりつく　岩場にへばりつくようにしてその落石を避けた. I hugged the wall to avoid the falling rock.

へび　インドでは毎年へびにかまれて死ぬ人が何千といるそうだ. In India, I hear, thousands of people die of snakebite [there are thousands of deaths by snakebite] every year.

へや　あのホテルでは部屋まで食事を運んでくれない. There is no [They don't provide any] room service in that hotel. / ここの部屋代は月2万5千円です. This apartment [room] rents for 25,000 yen a month.

へらす　石油の消費量を減らさなければならない. We've got to cut down (on) our consumption of petroleum. / 肉を減らして野菜をもっと食べなさい. I advise you to eat less meat and more vegetables.

へらずぐち　へらず口をたたくな. Hold your tongue! | Shut up!

ぺらぺら　彼はフランス語はぺらぺらだ. He speaks French fluently. | He speaks fluent French.

べらぼう　そんなべらぼうな話があ

へる² 〈…を経て〉through sb; by way of sb / シベリアを経て via (by way of) Siberia / 3年を経て three years later; after three years; after a [the] lapse of three years.

へる² 減る get fewer [less, smaller]; 《文》decrease; 《文》diminish; lessen; fall (off); 〈川の水などが〉run low; subside (洪水が); 〈磨滅する〉wear down [away]. 文例⬇

ベル a bell; a doorbell (玄関の) ¶ベルを鳴らす ring the bell / ベルを鳴らして看護婦を呼ぶ find the nurse. 文例⬇

ペルー Peru ¶ペルーの Peruvian / ペルー共和国 the Republic of Peru / ペルー人 a Peruvian.

ベルカント 《音楽》bel canto.

ベルギー Belgium ¶ベルギーの Belgian / ベルギー王国 the Kingdom of Belgium / ベルギー人 a Belgian.

ベルサイユ Versailles ¶ベルサイユ宮殿 the Palace of Versailles / ベルサイユ条約 the Treaty of Versailles.

ペルシャ Persia ¶ペルシャの Persian / ペルシャ語 Persian / ペルシャじゅうたん a Persian rug [carpet] / ペルシャ人 a Persian / ペルシャ湾 the Persian Gulf.

ヘルシンキ Helsinki.

ヘルスメーター (a set of) bathroom scales ⇒たいじゅうけい (体重計).

ヘルツ 《物》a hertz (略: Hz) 《単複同形》 ¶キロヘルツ a kilohertz (略: kHz) / ヘルツ波 a Hertzian wave.

ベルト a belt ¶座席のベルト a seat belt / ウエストにベルトのついているドレス a dress belted at the waist / ベルトを締める fasten [buckle (on)] one's belt / ベルトコンベヤー a belt conveyer.

ヘルニア (a) hernia; (a) rupture.

ヘルメット a helmet; a hard hat; 〈暑さを避けるための〉a sun helmet; 〈オートバイ運転者などのかぶる〉a crash helmet ¶ヘルメットをかぶった男 a helmeted man.

ベルモット vermouth.

ベルリン Berlin ¶ベルリン市民 a Berliner.

ベルン Bern(e).

ベレー(ぼう) ベレー(帽) a beret.

ヘレニズム Hellenism.

ヘロイン 〈麻薬〉heroin.

ぺろぺろ ¶ぺろぺろなめる lick sth (up) with one's [its] tongue / ぺろぺろに酔っ払う be dead [blind] drunk; 《俗》be smashed; 《英卑》be pissed (out of one's mind); 《英卑》be as pissed as a newt.

ぺろぺろ ⇒ ぺろぺろ.

ぺろりと ¶ぺろりと舌を出す stick [《文》thrust] one's tongue out / ぺろりと平らげる eat up 《one's lunch》; make short work of 《an ice cream》; put away 《a large steak》 / 唇をぺろりとなめる lick one's lips.

へん¹ 辺 〈多角形の〉a side; 〈地域〉a part ¶辺の長さがそれぞれ 3, 4, 5 センチの三角形 a triangle with sides 3, 4, and 5 centimeters long / この辺に in this neighborhood; about [around, near] here.

へん² 変 〈変化〉(a) change; 〈変事〉an incident; 〈動乱〉a disturbance ¶変な 〈奇妙な〉strange; odd; queer; curious; peculiar; 〈怪しい〉suspicious(-looking) / 変な気持ちがする feel queer / 変に思う think [feel] (that) sth is strange. 文例⬇

へん³ 変 《音楽》¶変ホ長[短]調 《in》E flat major [minor].

へん⁴ 偏 〈漢字の〉the left-hand side (of a Chinese character).

へん⁵ 遍 ⇒ ど.

へん⁶ 篇 〈巻〉a volume; a book; 〈章節〉a section; a part; 〈詩章〉a canto (pl. -s).

へん⁷ 編 ¶佐藤博士編 edited [compiled] by Dr. Sato.

へん⁸ 〈せき払いの音〉hem!; ahem!; 〈あざけって〉pshaw!

べん¹ 弁 〈弁舌〉speech; 〈雄弁〉《文》eloquence; 〈方言〉a dialect; 〈なまり〉an accent ¶関西弁で話す speak with a Kansai accent [in Kansai dialect].

べん² 弁 《植》a petal; 《機》a valve; 〈笛の〉a reed ¶5弁の花 a five-petaled flower.

べん³ 便 〈便利〉convenience; 〈交通などの便〉《文》facilities; a service; 〈大小便〉《文》excreta; 〈大便〉《文》feces; 《文》excrement ¶鉄道[バス]の便 a railroad [bus] service / 〈場所などが〉地下鉄の便がいい[悪い] be convenient [inconvenient] for the subway [《英》underground] station / 便をする defecate (大便を); relieve oneself (主に小便を) / 便を検査する examine sb's feces [stool(s)]. 文例⬇

ペン a pen ¶ペンを取る pick [《文》take] up one's pen / ペンで書く write with [in] pen

るものか. That's quite absurd. | How can that be so?

へる² アメリカでは喫煙者の数が減った. The number of smokers in the U.S. has fallen [decreased]. / 体重が4キロ減った. I have lost four kilograms (in weight). / その雑誌の発行部数は急激に減ってきた. The circulation of the magazine has fallen off sharply. / 井戸の水が減った. The level of water in the well has fallen [got low]. / 生糸の需要が減ってきている. The demand for silk is diminishing [on the decrease]. / 瓶の中のブランデーはたちまち減った. The brandy receded quickly down the bottle.

ベル じじっとベルが鳴った. Brrr-r-r-r went the bell.

へん¹ 彼はどこかこの辺に住んでいる. He lives somewhere about [around] here. / この辺は閑静だ. This is a quiet neighborhood. / まずその辺だろう. That's about it. | You are (just) about right.

へん² それは変だ. That's strange [funny]. / あの人は頭が変だ He is queer in the head. | He is not in his right mind. / 君は今日ちょっと変だよ. You are not quite yourself today. / このラジオはどうも変だ. Something seems to be the matter with this radio. / 彼には変な癖がある. He has peculiar ways. / こう言ったら変に聞こえるだろうがしかし事実だ. It may sound strange, but it's true.

べん³ 駅からその温泉地まではバスの便がある. There is a bus service available from the station to the spa. | You can go from the station to the spa by bus. /

へんあい and ink / ペン画 an ink [a pen-and-ink] drawing; a pen sketch [portrait] / ペン先 a nib; 《米》a pen point / ペン皿 a pen tray / ペン軸 a penholder / ペン習字 penmanship / ペンパル a pen friend [pal] / ペンネーム a pen name / 《文》a nom de plume (*pl.* noms de plume) / ペンホルダーグリップ《卓球》the penholder grip.

へんあい 偏愛 ¶偏愛する dote on (*one's* youngest child) to the exclusion of 《the others》.

へんあつ 変圧 【電】transformation ¶変圧器 a transformer.

へんい 変異 【生物】(a) variation; (a) modification (非遺伝性で一時的な) ⇒とつぜん (突然変異).

べんい 便意 ¶便意を催す want to go to the lavatory; 《文》feel a need to evacuate *one's* bowels.

へんか 変化 (a) change; (a) variation; 《文》(a) transition (変遷); 〈変形〉(a) transformation; 〈多様〉variety; 《文》diversity; 【文法】declension (格の); 〈動詞〉conjugation (動詞の); (an) inflection (語尾の) ¶変化する change (from, into, to); turn; vary; 《文》transform (*itself*) / 【文法】decline; conjugate; inflect / 変化がない there is no change (in); stay [remain] unchanged / 変化しやすい changeable (weather); variable (winds); fluid (plans) / 変化のある 〈変わりやすい〉changeable; 〈多様な〉varied; various / 変化のない unchanging; 〈変化なし〉changeless; stationary; 〈単調な〉monotonous / 変化を受ける undergo [suffer] a change / 変化に富んだ varied (life); (scenery) full of variety; checkered (careers) (波瀾の多い) / 強[弱]変化【文法】strong [weak] conjugation / 変化球《野球》〈緩い球〉a ball thrown for a change of pace, a slow ball; 〈カーブ〉a curve (ball). 文例⇩

べんかい 弁解 (an) explanation; 《文》(a) vindication; 〈言い訳〉an excuse; 《文》a plea ¶弁解する explain; defend [justify] *oneself*; plead 《poverty》; make [offer] an excuse [apology] (for) / 知らなかったと弁解する plead ignorance (as an excuse for *one's* conduct). 文例⇩

へんかく 変革 a change; (a) reform (改革).

べんがく 勉学 ⇒べんきょう.

ベンガル Bengal ¶ベンガルの Bengali; Bengalese / ベンガル人 a Bengali (*pl.* -(s)); a Bengalese《単複同形》.

へんかん 返還 return; 《文》restoration ¶返還する return; restore.

べんき 便器 〈便所内の〉a toilet (seat); a urinal (小便用の); 〈室内用〉a (chamber) pot; a bedpan (病人用の).

べんぎ 便宜 〈都合〉convenience; 〈利便〉《文》facility; 《文》benefit ¶あらゆる便宜を与え《文》accord [afford] every facility 《for》/ 便宜上, 便宜のため for convenience' sake; for (the sake of) convenience / 便宜的な手段《文》an expedient / 便宜置籍船 a ship sailing under a flag of convenience. 文例⇩

ペンキ [<(オランダ語) *pek*] (house) paint ¶ペンキの塗ってない unpainted (houses); paintless (doors) / ペンキを塗る paint (a door) / ペンキを塗った壁 a painted wall / ペンキ屋〈店〉a paint store [shop] / 〈職人〉a (house) painter.

へんきゃく 返却 return; 〈返済〉(a) repayment ¶返却する ⇒かえす¹.

へんきゅう 返球《野球》¶返球する return the ball (to).

へんきょう¹ 辺境 a frontier; a remote [an outlying] region ¶辺境の町 a frontier town / 辺境で暮らす live on the frontier.

へんきょう² 偏狭 ¶偏狭な narrow-minded; intolerant / 偏狭な考えを持っている have a narrow(-minded) view (of).

べんきょう 勉強 〈勉学〉work; study; 〈精励〉《文》diligence; 《文》industry ¶勉強する work at (*one's* French homework); study (chemistry); read (law) (大学で); 〈精を出す〉work hard; apply *oneself* (to a task); 〈商売上〉sell *sth* cheap [at a low price] / 学科を勉強する do *one's* lessons; work at *one's* lessons / 英語を一生懸命に勉強する work hard [grind away (特に試験のために)] at (*one's*) English; study English hard / 勉強し過ぎて病気になる fall ill [sick] through overwork; work *oneself* ill [sick] / 勉強家 a hard worker; a hardworking [《文》an industrious] student / 勉強時間 *one's* study hours [time] / 勉強部屋 a study (room). 文例⇩

へんきょく 編曲 (an) arrangement ¶バイオリン用に編曲する arrange 《a piece of music》

その港は水が深くて船舶の停泊に便である。The harbor is deep and affords facilities for anchoring ships. / 外人観光客の便を図って大きなホテルが建てられた。A big hotel has been built for the convenience of foreign tourists.

へんか 形勢に変化がない。There is no change in the situation. / 日本は季節による気候の変化がとてもはっきりしている。In Japan seasonal changes [variations] in climate are very marked. / この景色は変化があって面白い。This scenery has the charm of variety. / 次の動詞の変化を言いなさい。Conjugate the following verbs. | Give the conjugation of each of the following verbs.

べんかい 今更弁解しても無駄だ。It is no use trying to justify [excuse] yourself now. / 彼は私のために大いに弁解してくれた。He said a great deal in my defense [in vindication of my conduct]. / そんなに弁解がましくおっしゃる必要はありません。You needn't be so apologetic.

べんぎ できる限りの便宜をお図りします。I will give you every facility [assistance] for it. / この計算では端数は便宜上無視してある。For convenience' sake [For purposes of convenience] fractions are disregarded in this calculation.

ペンキ ペンキ塗り立て。【掲示】《米》Fresh paint. | 《英》Wet paint. / 所々ペンキがはげている。The paint has peeled off in places.

べんきょう 行って見ると彼は勉強していた。I found him working [doing his lessons]. / 日曜日でも仕事に出るとは随分勉強だね。

へんきん 返金 (a) repayment; a refund ¶返金する pay back; repay; refund.
ペンギン a penguin.
へんくつ 偏屈 ¶偏屈な awkward; unreasonable;《文》perverse;《英口語》bloody-minded.
ペンクラブ (the) P.E.N. (the International Association of Poets, Playwrights, Editors, Essayists, and Novelists の略).
へんけい 変形〈形が変わること〉(a) deformation; (a) transformation;《文》(a) metamorphosis (*pl.* -phoses);〈変化した形〉a variety ¶変形する〈変える〉change the shape (of); deform;〈変わる〉change (into); turn (into); be transformed (into) / 変形文法『言語』transformational grammar.
へんけん 偏見 (a) prejudice; (a) bias ¶偏見のある prejudiced; biased / 偏見のない unprejudiced; unbiased; impartial; open-minded / 偏見を持つ be prejudiced (against); have a prejudice [bias] (against); have [hold] a biased view (of).
べんご 弁護 (a) defense;《文》a plea;《文》advocacy (擁護);《文》(a) vindication (弁明) ¶弁護する defend; stand [speak] for; plead for [in favor of] (被告のため);《文》advocate (擁護する);《文》vindicate (弁明する); justify (正当化する) / 被告のために弁護する argue [plead] for a case for the defendant; defend [plead for] the accused / …の弁護を引き受ける[引き受けている] take [hold] a brief for sb (★ hold a brief for は弁護士の場合だけではなく,「味方をする」という意味で一般に広く用いられる) / 弁護依頼人 a client / 弁護団 defense counsel / 弁護料 a lawyer's fee. 文例⇩
へんこう¹ 変更 (a) alteration; a change; (a) modification (一部の) ¶変更する alter; change; modify (一部を) / 変更を加える make a change (in); make alterations (in). 文例⇩
へんこう² 偏向《文》a propensity (*to sth*, *for doing*); a tendency (toward, to); an inclination (to); a leaning (toward) ¶偏向教育 ideologically prejudiced education; education influenced by ideological prejudices.
へんこう³ 偏光〈物〉〈光のかたより〉polarization (of light);〈かたよった光〉polarized light.
へんこうせい 変光星『天』a variable (star).
べんごし 弁護士 a lawyer;〈法廷弁護士〉《米》a counselor;《英》a barrister /〈事務弁護士〉《米》an attorney;《英》a solicitor / 弁護士を開業している practice law; practice at the bar / 弁護士を頼む engage a lawyer / 弁護士になる enter the law;〈資格を得る〉be admitted [《英》called] to the bar / 弁護士会 a bar association / 弁護士事務所 a law office. 文例⇩

用法 lawyer は弁護士に対する一般的な名称であるが,《米》counselor と《英》barrister は弁護人として法廷に立つ人のことで,《米》attorney と《英》solicitor は法律関係の事務的な仕事を主にする人をいう。米国では同一の人物が時には, counselor として, 時には attorney としてつとめることがしばしばあるが, イギリスでは barrister と solicitor は全く別な人がつとめる。なおアメリカでは, practice at the bar と be admitted to the bar は counselor にも attorney にも使うことができるが, イギリスでは barrister の場合にしか言えない。

べんごにん 弁護人 a counsel《単複同形》¶被告弁護人 a defense counsel; a counsel for the defense.
へんさ 偏差〖統計・生物〗(a) deviation;〖物・工〗(a) deflection;〖測量〗(a) declination ¶標準偏差〖統計〗(the) standard deviation / 偏差値 the deviation (value).
べんざ 便座 a toilet seat.
へんさい 返済 return;〈金の〉(a) payment; (a) repayment ¶返済する return;〈金を〉pay (back); repay; refund.
へんざい¹ 偏在 uneven distribution;《文》maldistribution ¶富の偏在 the maldistribution [uneven distribution] of wealth / 偏在している be unevenly distributed.
へんざい² 遍在《文》omnipresence;《文》ubiquity ¶遍在する be omnipresent;《文》be ubiquitous.
べんざい¹ 弁才 (a) talent for speaking;《文》eloquence;《口語》the gift of the gab ¶弁才がある be good at speaking;《文》be an eloquent speaker;《口語》have the gift of the gab / 弁才がない be bad at speaking; be a poor speaker.
べんさい² 弁済 ¶弁済する pay (off) [clear (up),《文》discharge] *one's* debt(s).
へんさん 編纂 compilation; editing ¶編纂する compile (a dictionary); edit (an anthology) / 編纂者 a compiler; an editor.
へんし 変死 an unnatural [a violent] death ¶変死する die an unnatural [a violent] death.
へんじ¹ 返事 an answer; a reply ¶返事する answer; reply; give [make] an answer [a reply] / 手紙の返事をする answer [reply to] a letter / 手紙の返事を出さずにおく leave a

---

How industrious you are to go to work on Sunday! / おかげで大変勉強になりました。Thank you. I've learned a great deal [I'm much wiser]. / あの店は勉強する。Things are cheaper at that store.
へんけん 彼は抽象画に対して強い偏見を持っている。He is very prejudiced [biased] against abstract painting. | He has a strong prejudice [bias] against abstract painting.
べんご 彼は自国の行動を少しも弁護できなかった。He couldn't defend the actions of his country at all. | He hadn't a good word to say for his country's conduct. / 田中君の弁護をする訳ではないが, 彼にも理由はあったのだ。I hold no brief for Tanaka, but I'm sure he had his reasons.
へんこう 記載の値段は変更されることがあります。The prices quoted are subject to change [alteration]. / 締切りは 10 月 30 日です。これは絶対に変更できません。The deadline is the 30th of October. That's final.
べんごし 被告にはいい弁護士がついている。The defendant has a very able counsel.
へんじ¹ お手紙のご返事が遅れましたがお許し下さい。Forgive me for taking so long to answer your letter. / 彼の部屋に電話したが返

へんじ² 変事 an incident (事件); an accident (事故); a disaster; a mishap; a calamity; an emergency. 文例☟

べんし 弁士 a speaker; a talker;〈雄弁家〉《文》an orator.

へんしつ 変質 a change in quality;《文》deterioration;《文》degeneration. ¶変質する change *its* nature; change in quality; deteriorate;《文》degenerate / 変質者 a pervert; a deviant; a maniac.

へんしゃ 編者 an editor; a compiler.

へんしゅ 変種【生物】a variety.

へんしゅう¹ 編集 editing; compilation;〈映画フィルムの〉cutting ¶編集する edit (a magazine); compile (a dictionary) / 編集を引受ける take on the editorship (of) / 編集会議 an editorial conference [meeting] / 編集局 the editorial office [board] / 編集者 an editor; a (film) cutter (映画フィルムの) / 編集長 the chief [managing] editor;《米》the copy chief (新聞社の) / 編集部員 a member of the editorial staff. 文例☟

へんしゅう² 偏執 ¶偏執狂【事】monomania /〈人〉a monomaniac / 偏執病 paranoia / 偏執病患者 a paranoiac; a paranoid.

べんじょ 便所 a lavatory ⇒トイレ(ット), こうしゅう²(公衆便所), すいせんべんじょ.

へんじょう 返上 ¶返上する〈返す〉return; send back;〈放棄する〉give up /《文》forgo (*one's* vacation) /〈忘れる〉forget (what *one* used to know).

べんしょう 弁償 ¶弁償する pay for (damage) ⇒ばいしょう.

べんしょうほう 弁証法【哲】dialectic ¶弁証法的唯物論 dialectical materialism / 弁証法的に dialectically.

へんしょく¹ 変色 a change of color;《文》discoloration; fading〈色があせること〉¶変色する change color; get [《文》become] discolored;〈(色が)あせる〉fade / 変色しない fast; unfading.

へんしょく² 偏食 ¶偏食する have an unbalanced diet; be fussy about *one's* food [what *one* eats].

へんじる 変じる ⇒かわる², かえる² ¶変じて…となる turn [change] into….

べんじる¹ 弁じる〈しゃべる〉speak; talk;〈物事を区別する〉tell [distinguish](A from B) ¶一席弁じる make a speech; give a talk / とうとうと弁じ立てる《文》speak eloquently;《文》make an eloquent speech; talk volubly / 友人のために弁じる argue in favor of [speak up for] *one's* friend.

べんじる² 弁じる〈用が足りる〉will do; serve [《文》answer] the purpose;〈用を足す〉do (business).

ペンシルバニア Pennsylvania (略: Pa., Penn.) ¶ペンシルバニア州の人 a Pennsylvanian.

へんしん¹ 返信 a reply; an answer ¶返信する answer [reply to] a letter; send a reply (to) / 切手を貼りあて名を書いた返信用封筒 a stamped, self-addressed envelope / 返信用はがき a reply (postal) card / 返信料として60円切手を封入する enclose a sixty-yen stamp for return postage.

へんしん² 変心 ⇒こころがわり, へんせつ.

へんしん³ 変身 a transformation ¶変身する transform *oneself* (into).

へんじん 変人 an eccentric person; an eccentric; an odd [a strange] fellow; a queer fish; a crank.

ベンジン【化】benzine.

ペンス pence (略: p).

用因 pence は金եとしての penny の複数形. 1971年の貨幣制度の改正以来、それまでの略字 d. は廃されて, p (発音は [piː]) がそれに代わった. 3½ p は正式には three and a half pence, 通俗には three and a half p と読む ⇒ペニー 用因.

ベンず ベン図【数・論】a Venn diagram.

へんすう 変数【数】a variable.

へんずつう 偏頭痛 (a) migraine.

へんする 偏する〈傾く〉lean (to, toward);〈偏重する〉show bias [《文》partiality](toward) ¶一方に偏した one-sided; biased; prejudiced; unfair.

へんせい¹ 変性【医】degeneration;【化】denaturation ¶変性する degenerate; get denatured / 変性アルコール denatured alcohol.

へんせい² 編成[制] formation; organization;《文》composition ¶編成する form (a class); organize (a corps);《文》compose (a train); compile (make up) (a budget); draw up (a program) / …で編成されている consist of…; be composed [made up] of… / 10両編成の列車 a train of ten cars [《英》carriages].

へんせいがん 変成岩【地質】(a) metamorphic rock.

へんせいふう 偏西風【気象】the prevailing

---

letter unanswered / 返事をもらう get [(文) receive] an answer [a reply] (from) / …の返事に in reply [answer] to…. 文例☟

事がなかった. I put in a telephone call, but his room didn't answer. / いくら戸をたたいても返事がなかった. There was no response to my repeated knocking. / 彼はボビーと呼ばれると絶対に返事をしません. If you call him Bobby, he will never answer you. / 諾否いずれとも確かなご返事を頂きたい. I would like to have a definite reply, yes or no. / 折り返しご返事を願います. Please give us an answer by return of mail《英》post]. / 返事に困った. I was at a loss for an answer. / 今日まで彼からは何の返事もない. So far I have received [had] no answer from him. / 3月5日付のお手紙にご返事申し上げます. This is a reply to your letter of March 5.

へんじ² 彼に何か変事が起こったのではないかしら. I am afraid something unforeseen has happened to him.

へんしゅう¹ 編集されたために原作の生き生きしたところが全く失われてしまった. They have edited all the life out of the original story. / 東京のある英字新聞の編集部にいたことがあった. He had been on the editorial staff of an English-language paper in Tokyo.

へんしょく¹ この布は変色しない. The colors [dyes] in this cloth are fast.

へんせつ　変節 (a) defection; (an) apostasy (宗教・主義などからの); treachery (裏切り) ¶変節する change sides; desert *one's* cause [principles]; turn *one's* coat / 変節者 a turncoat; an apostate (宗教などからの).

べんさい　弁才 《文》 eloquence ¶弁舌の才 ⇒ べんさい¹ / 弁舌さわやかに 《文》 eloquently; fluently.

へんせん　変遷 〈変化〉 changes; 〈推移〉 (a) transition; 〈浮沈〉《文》 vicissitudes; ups and downs (of life) ¶変遷する change; go through [《文》undergo] changes.

ベンゼン《化》benzene.

へんそう¹　返送 ¶返送する return; send back.
へんそう²　変奏 ¶変奏する play a variation (on a theme) / 変奏曲 a variation.
へんそう³　変装 (a) disguise ¶変装する disguise *oneself* (as); be disguised (as) /...に変装して in [under] the disguise of (a merchant).

へんぞう　変造 ¶変造する 〈改変する〉 alter; 〈偽造する〉 forge ⇒ ぎぞう.

ベンゾール《化》benzol.

へんそく¹　変則 (an) irregularity;《文》an anomaly ¶変則的 irregular;《文》anomalous; abnormal.

へんそく²　変速 ¶変速機〈自動車の〉a transmission; a gearbox / 変速レバー《米》a gearshift;《英》a gear lever.

へんたい¹　変態 〈生物〉(a) transformation;《文》(a) metamorphosis (*pl.* -phoses); 〈異常〉abnormality ¶完全[不完全]変態 a complete [an incomplete] metamorphosis / 変態的 abnormal; perverted / 変態性欲 sexual perversion.

へんたい²　編隊 a formation ¶爆撃機の大編隊 a large formation of bombers / 9機編隊で in a nine-plane formation / 編隊飛行をする fly in formation; make a formation flight (to); do formation flying.

べんたつ　鞭撻 encouragement ¶べんたつする encourage [urge] (*sb* to *do*); spur (*sb*) on (to *do*).

へんち　辺地 ⇒へきち.

ベンチ 〈腰掛け〉a bench;【野球】the (player's) bench ¶ベンチを温めている【野球】sit [remain] on the bench.

ペンチ (a pair of) pliers.

へんちょう¹　変調 abnormal conditions;《通信》(a) modulation ¶変調する《通信》modulate / 変調を来たす get [go] out of order; go wrong; cease to function properly. 文例日

へんちょう²　偏重 ¶偏重する attach too much importance (to); overemphasize (intellectu-

al training).

べんつう　便通《文》emptying the bowels;《文》a (bowel) motion;《文》a movement of the bowels ¶便通がある have a (bowel) motion; *one's* bowels move / 便通をつける loosen [move] the bowels / いつも便通をつけておく keep *one's* bowels open; 〈婉曲的に〉keep regular. 文例日

へんてこな ⇒へん² (変な).

へんてつ　変哲 ¶何の変哲もない featureless; commonplace; ordinary; everyday.

へんてん　変転 ¶変転する change / 変転きわまりない《文》ever-changing;《文》kaleidoscopic.

へんでん　返電 a reply telegram ¶返電する send [cable, wire] a reply ((to)); wire back.

へんでんしょ　変電所 a (transformer) substation.

へんとう　返答 ⇒へんじ¹.

へんどう　変動 〈変化〉change; 〈相場などの〉fluctuation(s) ¶変動する change; undergo a change; fluctuate / 激しい変動 sharp [violent] fluctuations / 物価の変動 fluctuations in price(s) / 変動為替相場制 a floating exchange rate system / 変動所得 fluctuating income.

べんとう　弁当 lunch; a packed [box] lunch ¶弁当を食べる [使う] take (*one's*) lunch; eat a box lunch / 弁当を作る prepare a lunch box / 弁当を持って行く take [carry] a lunch box with *one* / 弁当代 lunch money / 弁当箱 a lunch box.

へんとうせん　扁桃腺《解》the tonsils ¶扁桃腺がはれている have swollen tonsils / 扁桃腺炎 tonsillitis. 文例日

へんにゅう　編入 admission;《文》incorporation (合併) ¶編入する 〈学校などに〉admit ((to)); 〈合併する〉incorporate ((into)). 文例日

へんねんたい　編年体 ¶編年体で書かれた arranged chronologically; written in chronological form.

へんぱ　偏頗 〈えこひいき〉《文》partiality; favoritism; 〈差別〉(unfair) discrimination; 〈片手落ち〉bias; one-sidedness; 〈不公平〉unfairness ¶偏ぱな biased (toward, against); one-sided; unfair.

へんぱい　返杯 ¶返杯する offer *sb* a cup of *sake* in return.

へんぴ　辺鄙 ¶へんぴな out-of-the-way; remote.

べんぴ　便秘 constipation ¶便秘する be constipated.

へんぴん　返品 returned goods; articles sent back.

へんちょう¹ どうも体が変調を来たしている。I don't feel myself. | Something is wrong with me.

べんつう 今日は2度便通があった。I had two motions [bowel movements] today.

へんとうせん 彼は昨日扁桃腺を取った。He had his tonsils removed yesterday.

へんにゅう 彼はうちの3年のクラスに編入された。He was admitted to our school [university] as a junior. / その町は浦和市に編入された。The town was incorporated into the city of Urawa.

へんめい 彼は岡田と変名していた。He went under the name of Okada.

べんめい 彼は自分の行動に対する弁明の手紙をよこした。He wrote to me in explanation of his conduct. / それは少しも君の変説の弁明にはならない。That does not justify your change of opinion at all.

べんり 子供の教育には大変便利な所です。It is a convenient [good]

へんぺい 偏平 ¶偏平な flat /偏平足 a flat foot /偏平足になる get flat feet [fallen arches] /偏平足である be flat-footed.

べんべつ 弁別 ¶弁別する tell 《A from B》; tell 《A and B》apart; distinguish 《A from B, between A and B》.

べんべん 便々 ¶便々たる太鼓腹 a large pot-belly /便々と日を送る idle *one's* time away.

ぺんぺんぐさ ぺんぺん草 ⇒なずな.

へんぼう 変貌 a change in (*one's*) appearance; 《文》(a) transfiguration; 《文》(a) metamorphosis (*pl*. -phoses) ¶変貌する (come to) look different 《from what it used to be》; 《文》be metamorphosed 《into》/完全な変貌を遂げる undergo a complete transfiguration [metamorphosis, change].

へんぽう 返報〈報い〉《文》requital;〈仕返し〉retaliation; revenge ¶返報をする〈報いる〉give *sth* in return; repay;《文》requite;〈仕返しする〉retaliate 《against, on》; get *one's* revenge 《on》;《文》revenge *oneself* 《on》; take (*one's*) vengeance 《on》/ …の返報として in return for…;〈仕返しに〉in revenge [retaliation] for….

べんぽう 便法《文》(devise) an expedient;《try to find》an easier method.

へんぽん¹ 返本 books [magazines] returned unsold; returned copies.

へんぽん² 翩翻 ¶へんぽんと風に翻える flutter [flap] in the wind.

へんまがん 片麻岩〈地質〉gneiss.

べんまく 弁膜〈解〉a valve.

へんむ 片務 ¶片務的 one-sided;《文》unilateral /片務契約 a one-sided [unilateral] contract.

べんむかん 弁務官 a commissioner. ¶高等弁務官 a high commissioner.

へんめい 変名 a false [an assumed,《文》a fictitious] name ¶変名する assume a false name /変名を使う use a false [different] name /変名を使って under an assumed [a false] name. 文例↓

べんめい 弁明 ⇒べんかい ¶弁明書 a letter of explanation; a written explanation. 文例↓

べんもう 鞭毛〈生物〉a flagellum (*pl*. -gella) ¶鞭毛虫 a flagellate.

へんよう 変容 ⇒へんぼう, へんけい.

べんらん 便覧 a handbook 《to, of》; a manual 《of》.

べんり 便利 convenience; handiness (調法);《文》facilities (設備) ¶便利な convenient; handy; serviceable /便利のいい[悪い]場所にある be conveniently [inconveniently] placed [situated] /便利屋 a (general) handyman. 文例↓

べんりし 弁理士 a patent attorney [agent].

へんりょう 変量〈物・統計〉a variable.

へんりん 片鱗 a part; a glimpse. 文例↓

へんれい 返礼〈贈り物〉a return present [gift];〈訪問〉a return call;〈報い〉《文》requital ¶返礼する〈贈り物の〉make *sb* a gift in return; make *sb* a return present;〈訪問の〉make a return call on *sb* / …の返礼に in return for…. 文例↓

べんれい 勉励 ⇒こっく(べんれい).

へんれき 遍歴 wandering; a travel; a tour; a pilgrimage ¶遍歴する wander [travel, tour] about; make a tour of (the country) /各地を遍歴する wander from place to place.

へんろ 遍路〈事〉a pilgrimage;〈人〉a pilgrim ¶遍路の旅に出る go on a pilgrimage.

べんろん 弁論 (a) discussion; (a) debate; (an) argument;〈法廷の〉pleading(s) ¶弁論する discuss; debate; argue;〈法廷で〉plead (before the court) /弁論の才 ⇒べんさい¹ /弁論大会 a speech [an oratorical] contest /弁論部 a debating club. 文例↓

ほ

ほ¹ 帆 a sail ¶帆を揚げる raise [hoist] the sails /帆を下ろす haul [haul down] the sails /帆を張る spread [set] the sails /帆を一杯に張って with all (*its*) sails spread [set]; under [in] full sail.

ほ² 歩 a step; a pace ⇒いっぽ ¶…へ歩を向ける《文》turn [bend] *one's* steps toward… / 2 歩前へ出る[後へ下がる] take two steps forward [backward]. 文例↓

ほ³ 穂〈穀物の〉an ear; a head; a spike;〈やりなどの〉a head; a spike ¶稲の穂 the ear of a rice plant /やりの穂 the head of a spear; a spearhead /穂が出ている ears have formed;《文》be in (the) ear /穂になる, 穂を出す ears form (on the barley); ear (up).

ホ〈音楽〉E ¶ホ長[短]調 (in) E major [minor].

-ほ …補 ¶外交官補 a probationary diplo-

---

place for the education of our children. / 今度の家は駅に近くて便利だ. Our new house is conveniently near the railroad station.

へんりん それで彼の性格の片鱗がうかがえる. It enables us to get a glimpse of his personality. / これは小さなスケッチだが, 彼の画才の片鱗を示している. Though it is only a small sketch, it shows something of his genius as an artist.

へんれい 返礼に何を贈ろうか. What shall I give him in return for his gift?

べんろん 弁護人が弁論を開始した. The defense opened its argument. | Counsel for the defense opened his argument.

ほ¹ 船は一杯に帆を揚げている. The ship is in [under] full sail.

ほ² 彼と僕とは 5 歩と離れていなかった. He stood within five steps [paces] of me. / 目的達成に向かって何歩か進んだ. They made some strides toward achiev-

mat / 書記補 an assistant clerk.
ほあん 保安 the preservation [maintenance] of public peace [security] ¶(デパートなどの)保安係 a house detective / 保安官《米》a sheriff / (炭坑などの)保安要員 the maintenance personnel / 〈個人〉a maintenance man [worker].
ほい 補遺 a supplement; an addendum 《pl. -da》; an appendix 《pl. -dices》.
ほいく 保育 〈養育〉upbringing;《文》nurture; 〈託児所などの〉day care ¶保育する nurse; bring up;《文》nurture; rear / 保育園[所] a day nursery; a day-care center; a nursery school / 保育器 an incubator / 保育料 a fee for day care.
ボイコット a boycott. ¶ボイコットする boycott (Japanese goods) / 授業を集団ボイコットする cut (Prof. Brown's) class en masse.
ホイッスル a whistle ¶(レフェリーが)ホイッスルを鳴らす blow one's whistle;《英口語》blow up (for a foul).
ほいと ¶ほいと投げる toss (up, away).
ボイラー a boiler ¶ボイラーをたく stoke (up) the boiler / ボイラー室 a boiler room / ボイラーマン[係] a boiler man.
ホイル foil (wrapping).
ほいろ 焙炉 a drier; a toaster; 〈製茶用の乾燥炉〉a tea drier ¶ほいろにかける dry (tea leaves) in the drier; roast (coffee).
ぼいん¹ 母音 a vowel 母音調和《言語》vowel harmony.
ぼいん² 拇[捺]印 a thumb impression ¶母印を押す seal (a paper) with one's thumb.
ぼいん³ 〈大きな乳房〉¶ぼいんちゃんだ《口語》be big [well-built, (well-)stacked]; have big breasts [《口語》boobs,《俗》tits].
ポイント 〈要点〉the point (of a story); 〈転轍(てつ)機〉《米》a (railroad) switch; 《英》points ¶ポイントを切り換える switch (cars) from one track [line] to another;《英》change the points (from one line to another) / ポイントを切り換えてその線に入れる[他の線に移す] switch (a train) onto [off] the line / 9ポイントの活字 9-point type.
ほう¹ 方〈方位〉a direction; a way; 〈側〉a side ¶...するよりは(むしろ)...する方がましだ would rather do than... / 私の方の[では] on my part / ...の方に in the direction of...; toward...; to (the east) / 左の方に on the left-hand [left] side (側); to the left (方向) / ...であるよりは(むしろ)...の方である be more ...than.... 文例◑

ほう² 法〈おきて〉(a) law; a rule; 〈方法〉a method; a way; a process;〈教理〉a doctrine;〈除数〉a divisor;【文法】the mood ¶法の支配 the rule of law / 法の精神 the spirit of the law / 法を守る[に従う] obey [keep,《文》observe] the law / 法を破る[犯す] break [《文》violate] the law / 勝手に法を曲げる strain [twist] the law to suit oneself / 法にかなった lawful; legal / 法に外れた unlawful; illegal / 法に照らして according to the law / 法に触れないようにしている stay on the right side of the law / 法改正 (a) legal reform; (institute) a change in the law. 文例◑
ほう³ 報 ⇨しらせ.
ほう⁴ 某〈ある〉one; a certain;〈ある人〉a certain person; Mr. So-and-so ¶佐藤某 one (Mr.) Sato; a certain Mr. Sato / 某銀行 a certain bank / 某所 a certain [an unnamed] place.
ほう⁵ 棒 a stick; a rod; a pole;〈梶(え)棒〉a club; a cudgel;〈横木〉a bar;〈線〉a line; a stroke (漢字の) ¶棒を引く draw a line;〈消す〉cross out;《文》strike off [out] / 棒に振る waste; lose; spoil; ruin / 一生を棒に振る ruin [make a failure of] one's career / 足を棒にして歩く walk till one's feet get stiff; walk oneself lame. 文例◑
ほうあん 法案 a bill.
ぼうあんき 棒暗記 rote memorization ¶棒暗記する learn (one's homework) parrot-fashion [by rote].
ほうい¹ 方位 ⇨ほうがく¹.
ほうい² 包囲《文》encirclement;〈攻囲〉(a) siege ¶包囲する surround; close in;《文》encircle;〈攻囲する〉besiege; lay siege to (a fort);〈警官が〉throw a cordon around (a place) / 包囲されている be surrounded 《by》; be under siege 《by》/ 包囲を解く raise the siege of (a town) / 包囲軍 a besieging army. 文例◑
ほうい³ 法衣 ⇨ほうえ.
ぼうい 暴威 ¶暴威を振るう tyrannize 《the people》; act tyrannically.
ほういがく 法医学 legal [forensic] medicine; medical jurisprudence.
ぼういん 暴飲 drinking too much;《文》excessive drinking;《文》intemperance. ¶暴飲する drink too much [《文》to excess] / 暴飲暴食する eat and drink immoderately;《文》be intemperate.
ほうえ 法衣 a vestment; clerical dress; canonicals.

---

ing their objective.
ほう¹ それはここから東の方に当たっている。It lies to the east of here. / 僕もそっちの方へ行く。I am going that way, too. / 彼は青山の方に住んでいる。He lives somewhere (up) Aoyama way. / その飛行機は木更津の方に飛び去った。The plane flew away in the direction of Kisarazu. / この方がそれよりずっといい。This is far better than that. / 家へ帰った方がいい。You had better go home. / 徹夜などしない方がいい。You ought not to [shouldn't] sit up all night. / 彼はどちらかと言うと厳しい方だった。He was a little on the strict side. / あの人は技量の方は充分だ。He is all right as far as ability is concerned. / 彼は働き者というよりはむしろ怠け者の方だ。He is more given to idling than to working. / 彼といっしょに行くくらいなら家にいた方がましだ。I would rather stay at home than go with him.
ほう² それでは法に反する。That would be against the law. / そんな法はない。That's unreasonable [absurd]. / 父が医者だからと言って自分も医者にならなければならないという法はない。There is no reason why one should become

ほうえい 放映 ¶放映する televise 《a movie》.

ぼうえい 防衛 ⇒ぼうぎょ ¶防衛機制《生理・心理》a defense mechanism / 防衛支出《Japan's》defense spending / 防衛陣地 a defensive position / 防衛庁[大学校] the Defense Agency [Academy] / 防衛費 defense expenses [costs] / 防衛力《Germany's》defense capabilities / 防衛力を増強する strengthen [build up] the [one's, its] forces.

ぼうえき¹ 防疫 prevention of epidemics.

ぼうえき² 貿易 (foreign) trade; commerce ¶貿易する trade《with》;《文》have trade relations《with》; carry on [《文》engage in] (foreign) trade / 日本の対英貿易 Japan's trade with England / 日中貿易 trade between Japan and China; Sino-Japanese [Japan-China] trade / 貿易相手国 a trading partner / 貿易外収支 invisible trade / 貿易業界 trading circles《in Japan》/ 貿易港 a trading port / 貿易尻(じり) the balance of trade / 貿易商 a trader; a trading firm (店) / 貿易品 trade goods / 貿易風 a trade (wind). 文例↓

ほうえつ 法悦 religious ecstasy.

ぼうえんきょう 望遠鏡 a telescope ¶望遠鏡で見る look《at the moon》through a telescope.

ほうえんこう 方鉛鉱 galena.

ぼうえんレンズ 望遠レンズ a telephoto(graphic) lens.

ほうおう¹ 法王 the Pope;《文》the Supreme Pontiff;《歴代の1人の》a pope ¶法王の papal / ローマ法王ピオ12世 Pope Pius XII / 法王庁 the Vatican (Palace) / 法王不可謬説 (the doctrine of) papal infallibility.

ほうおう² 訪欧 a visit to Europe ¶訪欧の途につく leave for Europe.

ほうおう³ 鳳凰 a Chinese phoenix.

ほうおん 報恩 ⇒おんがえし.

ぼうおん 防音 soundproofing ¶防音になっている壁 a soundproofed wall / 防音材 acoustic insulation;《建》pug(ging) / 防音室 a soundproof room / 防音装置 soundproofing.

ぼうおん² 忘恩 ⇒おん(恩知らず) ¶忘恩の徒 an ungrateful person.

ほうか¹ 放火《罪》incendiarism; arson; fire-raising;《火事》an incendiary fire ¶放火する set fire to《a house》/ 放火犯人 an arsonist; an incendiary; a fire-raiser. 文例↓

ほうか² 法科《学科》the law department;〈課程〉a law course.

ほうか³ 法貨 legal tender.

ほうか⁴ 放課 ¶放課後 after school (is over);

after school hours. 文例↓

ほうか⁵ 砲火 gunfire; artillery fire ¶砲火を浴びる be under fire / 砲火を交える exchange fire;〈開戦する〉《文》open hostilities (against).

ほうが¹ 邦画 a Japanese film [movie].

ほうが² 萌芽〈発芽〉germination;〈芽〉a sprout;〈兆し〉a sign.

ぼうか 防火 fire prevention ¶防火の fireproof; fire-retardant / 防火に努める try [attempt] to prevent the spread of a fire / 防火訓練 a fire drill / 防火建築 a fireproof building / 防火週間 Fire Prevention Week / 防火設備[装置] (install) fire-prevention devices [equipment] / 防火扉[壁] a fire door [wall] / 防火塗料 (a) fire-retardant paint.

ぼうが 忘我 ¶忘我の境にある be in a trance;《口語》be miles away.

ほうかい 崩壊 (a) collapse; a breakdown; a fall; disintegration ¶崩壊する collapse; break down; give way; disintegrate; cave [fall] in (陥没する). 文例↓

ほうがい 法外な absurd; unreasonable;《文》exorbitant;《文》extravagant / 法外な値段 an exorbitant [a prohibitive] price / 法外な要求 an excessive [unreasonable] demand / 法外な事を言う talk wildly; say extravagant [unreasonable] things / 法外に absurdly; unreasonably. 文例↓

ぼうがい 妨害 obstruction;《文》hindrance; interruption; interference;〈邪魔物〉an obstruction;《文》a hindrance; an obstacle ¶妨害する obstruct; hinder; interrupt; interfere 《with》/ 安眠を妨害する〈事が主語〉disturb one's sleep / 計画を妨害する obstruct [block] a plan / 作業を妨害する hinder sb in his work; hinder sb's work;〈事が主語〉interfere with sb's work / 放送電波を妨害する《周波数の近い電波を送って他国などの》jam radio signals [《American》broadcasts];〈エンジンなどが〉interfere with radio [TV] reception.

ぼうがい² 望外 ¶望外の unexpected; unlooked-for.

ほうかいせき 方解石《鉱》calcite; calcspar.

ほうがく 方角 a direction; a point of the compass ¶方角が分からなくなる lose one's bearings;《文》become disoriented / 方角を見る find one's bearings [position]; take a (compass) bearing / …の方角に in the direction of…; toward… / 方角違いの方へ行く go in the wrong direction. 文例↓

---

a doctor (just) because one's father is a doctor.
ほう² そのために彼は地位を棒に振った. It cost him his position.
ほうい 彼らは三方から敵を包囲した. They surrounded [enveloped] the enemy from three sides.
ぼうえき² 当時日本は中国と活発に貿易を行なっていた. Japan was doing [carrying on] a brisk [busy] trade with China at that time. /

父は横浜で貿易商をしていました. My father was in the export-import business in Yokohama.
ほうか¹ その火事は放火だった. The fire was started deliberately [was a case of arson].
ほうか⁴ 放課後は図書館で過ごすことが多かった. I would often spend my time (reading) in the library after school was over.
ほうかい それがローマ帝国崩壊の原因となった. That was the

cause of [reason for] the collapse of the Roman Empire. / トンネルが崩壊して作業員30名が生き埋めとなった. Thirty workers were buried alive when the tunnel caved in.
ほうがい 彼はそれを法外に安く[高く]買った. He bought it at an absurdly low [high] price.
ほうがく 火事はどっちの方角だ. Which direction is the fire in? / Which way is the fire? / 銀座は

ほうがく² 邦楽 (traditional) Japanese music.
ほうがく³ 法学 law; jurisprudence ¶法学を学ぶ read [study] law / 法学士 〈人〉 a bachelor of laws; 〈学位〉 Bachelor of Laws (略: LL.B.) / 法学者 a jurist / 法学修士 〈人〉 a master of laws; 〈学位〉 Master of Laws (略: LL.M.) / 法学博士 〈人〉 a doctor of laws; 〈学位〉 Doctor of Laws (略: LL.D.) / 法学部 the department of law; the law school.
ほうがちょう 奉加帳 a list of contributions; a subscription book.
ほうかつ 包括 complete [blanket] coverage; 《文》 inclusion; 《文》 comprehension ¶包括する include; 《文》 comprehend; comprise; contain; take in; cover / 包括的 inclusive; comprehensive; blanket 《clauses》.
ほうかん 砲艦 a gunboat.
ほうがん¹ 包含 ¶包含する include; contain; imply (意味を).
ほうがん² 砲丸 〈大砲のたま〉 a cannonball; 〈競技の〉 a shot; a weight ¶砲丸を投げる put the shot / 砲丸投げ the shot-put / 砲丸投げの選手 a shot-putter.
ほうかん¹ 防寒 protection against the cold ¶防寒の用意をする take precautions against the cold; 《文》 make provision for [against] the cold / 防寒具 an outfit for cold weather / 防寒服 winter clothes. 文例↓
ほうかん² 傍観 ¶傍観する look on; 《文》 remain a spectator [an idle onlooker]; sit [stand] by and watch. 文例↓
ほうかん³ 暴漢 a tough; a rowdy; a thug ¶暴漢に襲われる be assaulted by a thug.
ほうがんし 方眼紙 graph paper; squared paper ¶3ミリ方眼紙 (graph) paper ruled into 3-millimeter squares.
ほうがんびいき 判官びいき sympathy for a wronged hero.
ほうき¹ 法規 laws and regulations; 《文》 enactments ¶法規に照らして処罰する punish sb according to the law / 法規上 legally.
ほうき² 放棄 give up; 《文》 yield (up); abandon; surrender; 《文》 relinquish; 《文》 renounce ¶権利を放棄する give up [relinquish] one's right to sth; renounce one's claaim to sth / (学生が)授業を放棄する boycott [《口語》cut] a lecture / 戦争を放棄する renounce war / 放棄試合 a forfeited game.
ほうき³ 箒 a broom ¶ほうきの柄 the handle of a broom; a broomstick / ほうきで掃く sweep 《a room》 with a broom / 枝ぼうき a

(twig) besom / 小ぼうき a whisk (broom).
ほうき⁴ 蜂起 an uprising; (an) insurrection ¶蜂起する rise in revolt (against); rise [revolt] (against).
ほうぎ 謀議 〈相談〉 (a) conference; 〈陰謀〉 a plot; a conspiracy ¶謀議を凝らす plot [《文》 conspire] together.
ほうきぼし 箒星 a comet ⇒ すいせい¹.
ほうきゃく 忘却 《文》 oblivion; forgetfulness ¶忘却する forget; 《文》 be oblivious [forgetful] of; 〈見落す〉 lose sight of / 忘却のふちに沈む sink [fall] into oblivion / 忘却のふちから救う rescue sth from oblivion.
ほうきゅう 俸給 ⇨ きゅうりょう² ¶俸給生活者 a salaried man; the salaried class (総称).
文例↓
ほうきょ 暴挙 《do》 something reckless [rash]; 《文》 《commit》 a rash act; 《make》 a reckless attempt.
ほうぎょ 防御 (a) defense; (a) safeguard; (a) protection ¶防御する defend (against, from); protect (against, from); guard (against) / 敵の防御線を突破する breach the enemy's defenses / 防御用兵器 a defensive weapon / 防御率 《野球》 one's earned run average (略: ERA).
ほうきょう 望郷 ¶望郷の念 homesickness; 《文》 nostalgia (for) / 望郷の念に駆られる get [《文》 become] homesick [nostalgic]; long [《文》 yearn] for the sight of 《one's》 home.
ほうぐ 防具 a guard; a protector; protective clothing (総称).
ほうぐい 棒杭 ⇨ くい¹.
ほうくう 防空 air defense ¶防空演習 an (anti-)air-raid drill / 防空壕 an air-raid shelter; a dugout; a foxhole (1人用の).
ほうぐみ 棒組み 《印刷》 ¶棒組みにする set type in galley.
ほうくん 暴君 a tyrant; a despot.
ほうけい¹ 方形 a square ¶方形の square.
ほうけい² 包茎 《医》 phimosis.
ほうけい 傍系 a collateral line [branch] ¶傍系の 〈直系に対する〉 collateral; 〈親会社に対する〉 subsidiary / 傍系会社 a subsidiary [an affiliated] company.
ほうげき 砲撃 (an) artillery bombardment; (a) bombardment ¶砲撃する bombard; shell; fire on 《a fort》 / 砲撃の応酬 an exchange of fire / 砲撃を開始する open fire 《on》.
ほうけん 封建 ¶封建的 feudal; feudalistic (ideas); 〈通俗に〉 undemocratic (professors);

方角が違います。The Ginza lies in a different direction. / 私はよそへ行くといつも方角がわからなくなる。I can never keep my bearings when I'm away from home.
ほうかん¹ ボストンでは防寒用としてはこんな薄い外套ではだめだ。In Boston such a thin overcoat won't give you proper protection against the cold. | You couldn't wear such a thin over-

coat in Boston as a protection against the cold. / 防寒用としてはたしかに毛皮が一番良い。For keeping out the cold, fur is certainly best.
ほうかん² この人たちが餓死しつつあるのをどうして傍観することができよう。How can we stand [sit] by and watch them dying of hunger? / この惨事をどうして傍観することができよう。How can I be [remain] indifferent at

the sight of such a tragedy?
ほうきゅう 彼は俸給生活者だ。He is a salaried man. | He lives on his salary.
ほうけん それは少しも冒険ではない。There is no risk in it. / 一つ冒険的にやってみよう。Let's take the plunge, then. | I will give it a try, sink or swim.
ほうこう¹ 彼らは互いに反対の方向へ出かけた。They started out in opposite directions. / 風見

ほうげん bigoted [autocratic] 《fathers》 / 封建時代 the feudal period [age] / 封建主義 feudalism / 封建制度 the feudal system.

ほうげん¹ 方言 a (regional) dialect ; a dialect word ¶階級方言 a social(-class) dialect / 関西方言 the Kansai dialect / 津軽方言で書かれた詩 a poem written in Tsugaru dialect / 方言学 dialectology / 方言研究 dialect study / 方言地図 a dialect map [atlas].

ほうげん² 放言 ¶放言する〈思い切ったことを言う〉speak unreservedly [freely] ;〈大言する〉《口語》talk big ;〈不用意なまたは無責任なことを言う〉make indiscreet [irresponsible] remarks ;《米口語》shoot off one's mouth.

ぼうけん 冒険 an adventure ; a risky [《文》hazardous] attempt ¶冒険する venture ; run a risk [《文》hazard] ; take a chance / fond of adventure /《文》venturesome / 冒険的に adventurously ;《文》at a venture / 冒険好きの人 a person who is fond of adventure ; a lover of adventures / 冒険家 an adventurer / 冒険小説 an adventure story / 冒険心 an adventurous spirit ; enterprise / 冒険談 an account of one's adventure(s). 文例◯

ぼうげん 暴言 ¶暴言を吐く use offensive [abusive, violent] language ; talk rudely [abusively].

ほうこ 宝庫 a treasure house ; a treasury ¶知識の宝庫 a treasure house of knowledge ; a mine [storehouse] of information.

ほうご 防護 ⇨ ぼうぎょ.

ほうこう¹ 方向 a direction ;〈針路〉a course ¶方向を転じる change [shift] one's course ; turn in a different direction / 方向を誤る go in the wrong direction ;〈船などが〉take the wrong course ;〈生活上の〉choose the wrong career [occupation] ;《文》make an error in one's choice of career [occupation] / その [同じ] 方向に in that [the same] direction / 方向音痴である have no sense of direction / 方向観[感覚] a sense of direction / 方向指示器〈自動車の〉a traffic indicator /《英》an (a direction) indicator ;〈飛行機の〉a direction indicator / 方向舵〈飛行機の〉a (vertical) rudder / 自動方向探知器 an automatic direction finder (略:A.D.F.) / 方向転換 a change of direction [front] ; an about-face / 方向板〖鉄道〗a (route and) destination plate. 文例◯

ほうこう² 芳香 a sweet smell ;《文》a fragrance ;《文》an aroma ¶芳香のある sweet-smelling ; 《文》fragrant ;《文》aromatic / 芳香を放つ smell sweet ; give out fragrance ; diffuse an aroma / 芳香族化合物 a compound of the aromatic class ; an aromatic (compound) / 芳香油 an essential oil (香水などの原料).

ほうこう³ 奉公 service ; apprenticeship (年期奉公) ¶奉公する serve sb ;《文》go into service 《with》(召使いとして) / 奉公に出る be apprenticed to 《a carpenter》 /《文》go out to service (召使いとして) / 奉公人 a servant ; an employe(e).

ほうこう⁴ 放校 ¶放校する expel 《a student》 (from school).

ほうこう⁵ 砲口 the muzzle of a gun ¶砲口を向ける train [direct] a gun 《on》.

ほうごう 縫合 suture ¶縫合する suture 《a wound》; stitch 《a wound》together / 縫合針 a surgical needle.

ぼうこう¹ 膀胱 the (urinary) bladder ¶ぼうこう炎 cystitis ; inflammation of the (urinary) bladder / ぼうこう鏡 a cystoscope / ぼうこう結石 a stone in the bladder ; a cystolith ; a vesical calculus.

ぼうこう² 暴行 (an act of) violence ; an outrage ; an assault ; (a) rape (婦女に対する). ¶暴行する[を加える] attack ; assault ; commit an outrage 《on》;〈婦女を〉rape / 婦女暴行犯人 a rapist.

ほうこく 報告 a report ¶報告する report ; make a report 《of, on》/ 帰って報告する report back / 報告者 a reporter / 報告書 a (written) report.

ぼうこく 亡国 ¶亡国の民 a ruined people ; a homeless race / 亡国的 ruinous [《文》pernicious] to one's country ;〈退廃的〉degenerate ; demoralized.

ほうこしょとう 澎湖諸島 the Pescadores.

ほうざ 砲座 a gun platform.

ぼうさい 防災 disaster prevention ¶防災科学 the science of disaster prevention / 防災訓練 an emergency [a disaster] drill.

ほうさく¹ 方策〈計画〉a plan ; a scheme ;〈手段〉《文》measures ;《文》a means (単複同形) ;〈方針〉a policy ¶方策が尽きる be at one's wits' end.

ほうさく² 豊作 a good [a bumper,《文》an abundant] crop [harvest] ; a large yield (of fruit). 文例◯

ぼうさつ¹ 忙殺 ¶忙殺される be very busy [be swamped] 《with work》; be busily occupied

---

は風の吹いて来る方向を教えてくれる。The vane indicates which direction the wind is blowing from. / 彼は最初軍人になったが中途で方向を転じて政界へ出た。At first he was a soldier, but later he changed course and entered politics. / 君は今のうちに将来の方向を定めておくべきだ。You ought to choose your future course now. | Now is the time you should be deciding on your future (course). / 僕は方向を誤ってはいないと確信している。I'm sure I am on the right track. ★比喩的にも言える。

ほうこく 彼は新しい彗星を発見したと報告した。He reported that he had discovered a new comet. | He reported the discovery of a new comet. / 彼は帰って旅先で見かけたことを報告した。He reported back (on) what he had seen on his trip. / まだ詳細の報告に接していない。Full particulars are not yet to hand. / 彼は旅行から帰って社長に報告書を提出した。On his return (from his trip) he submitted a report to the president.

ほうさく² 今年の米は豊作の見込み。We will have a good harvest of rice this year. | It looks as if this year's rice crop will be good. / 農家は豊作貧乏で悩んでいる。Instead of rejoicing over the abundant harvest, the farmers are suffering from the fall in prices.

ほうさつ《in doing, with one's work》.　文例⇩
ほうさつ¹ 謀殺 premeditated [willful] murder.
ほうさりん 防砂林 (a barrier of) trees planted to arrest [prevent] sand from shifting.
ほうさん¹ 放散 radiation (熱・光などの); diffusion (拡散) ¶放散する radiate; diffuse.
ほうさん² 硼酸《化》boric [boracic] acid / 硼酸軟膏(¾) boric ointment / 硼酸水 a boric acid solution.
ほうし¹ 奉仕 a service ★ services と複数形で使われることが多い ¶奉仕する serve;《文》render services 《to》/ 社会への奉仕として as a service to the public / 奉仕値段で 《sell》at a sacrifice [bargain price] / 奉仕品 a bargain.
ほうし² 胞子《植》a spore.
ほうじ 法事 ¶法事を営む hold a Buddhist service for the dead.
ほうし¹ 防止 ¶防止する prevent; check; hold in check;《文》arrest; head off / 戦争の危険を防止する prevent [head off] the danger of war / 病気の蔓延を防止する prevent a disease from spreading; arrest the spread of a disease.
ほうし² 帽子 a hat (縁のある); a cap (縁なしの)¶帽子をかぶる[脱ぐ] put on [take off] a hat / 帽子をかぶっている wear a hat; have a hat on / 帽子をかぶったままでいる keep one's hat on / 帽子をかぶらずにいる be [go] bareheaded / 帽子掛け a coat hook; a peg;《スタンド状の》a hatrack; a hat stand / 帽子屋 a hatter; a milliner (婦人帽の).　文例⇩
ほうしき 方式〈形式〉a formula (pl. -s, -lae), a form;〈方法〉a method; a system (系統的) ¶《物事を》自分の方式でやる go one's own way.
ほうじしんぶん 邦字新聞 a newspaper (printed) in Japanese; a Japanese-language newspaper《published in California》.
ほうじちゃ 焙じ茶 toasted [roasted] tea.
ほうしつ 防湿 ¶防湿(性)の dampproof; moistureproof / 防湿剤 ⇒ かんそう² (乾燥剤).
ほうじま 棒縞 ¶棒じまの striped 《cloth》.
ほうしゃ¹ 放射 radiation (光・熱の); emission ¶放射する radiate; emit / 放射状に radially; in a radial pattern; like the spokes of a wheel;《radiate》in all directions《from》/ 放射状道路 roads radiating in all directions《from》; radial roads.
ほうしゃ² 砲車 a gun carriage.
ほうしゃ³ 硼砂《化》borax.
ほうじゃくぶじん 傍若無人 ¶傍若無人な arrogant;《文》audacious; outrageous / 傍若無人に振る舞う behave outrageously [《文》audaciously].
ほうしゃせい 放射性 ¶放射性の radioactive / 放射性元素[物質] a radioactive element [substance] / 放射性同位元素 a radioisotope; a radioactive isotope / 放射性廃棄物[降下物] radioactive waste[fallout] / 放射性炭素による年代測定 (radio)carbon dating.
ほうしゃせん 放射線 radiation ¶放射線によるやけど a radiation burn / 放射線を浴びる be exposed to radiation; be irradiated (物が) / 放射線を照射する irradiate 《milk》; apply radiation to 《the affected part》 / 放射線医 a radiologist / (病院などの)放射線科 the department of radiology / (照射する)放射線量 radiological dosage / 放射線療法 radiotherapy; radiation therapy.
ほうしゃのう 放射能 radioactivity ¶空気中の放射能 atmospheric radioactivity / 放射能の影響 radiation effects《from nuclear tests》 / 放射能の強さ intensity of radioactivity; a radioactive level / 放射能による汚染 radioactive contamination [pollution] / 人工[残存]放射能 artificial [residual] radioactivity / 放射能雨 radioactive rain / (身体につける)放射能警報器 an exposure badge / 放射能遮蔽壁 a radiation shield / 放射能障害 radiation sickness; a radiation disease / 耐放射能服 a radiation(-proof) suit.
ほうしゅ 砲手 a gunner;《捕鯨船の》a harpooner.
ほうじゅ 傍受 ¶傍受する intercept [monitor]《a radio message》.
ほうしゅう 報酬 a reward;《文》remuneration, a fee (医師・弁護士などの) ¶報酬を出す reward [《文》remunerate] sb《for his services》/ …の報酬として in reward [《文》recompense, return] for….
ほうじゅう 放縦 ¶放縦な《文》dissolute; loose.
ほうしゅうざい 防臭剤 a deodorant; a deodorizer.
ほうしゅく 防縮 ¶防縮加工を施した生地 preshrunk [shrink-resistant] fabrics.
ほうしゅつ 放出 ¶放出する release;〈放つ〉《文》emit; give off《energy》;《文》discharge《water》/ 放出物資 released goods.
ほうじゅつ 砲術 gunnery; artillery.
ほうじゅん 芳醇 ¶芳醇な mellow; rich and full-flavored / 芳醇なぶどう酒 mellow wine.
ほうしょ 奉書 thick Japanese paper (for ceremonial use).
ほうじょ 幇助 ¶幇助する assist; help;〈犯罪を〉《文》aid and abet.
ほうじょ 防除 control《of insect pests》.
ほうしょう¹ 法相 the Minister of Justice.
ほうしょう² 報奨 ¶報奨金 a (production) bonus;〈政府から出る〉a bounty《on exports》.
ほうしょう 豊穣 fertility ⇒ ほうさく² ¶豊穣の女神 a goddess of fertility.
ほうしょう¹ 帽章 a cap badge.
ほうしょう² 傍証 (indirect) evidence support-

ほうさつ 彼は国際会議の準備に忙殺されている. He is very busy preparing [with preparations] for an international conference. | この辞書の編集に忙殺されていて旅行に出かけるどころではありません. I am too busy with the compilation of this dictionary to go on a trip for pleasure.
ほうし² 僕の帽子は曲がっていないかい. Is my hat on straight?
ほうしん¹ 子供にはしつけを厳しくする方針をとっています. I make a point of not spoiling the children. / 彼と同じ方針でやるつもりです. I will act on the same basis as him. ⇒ より² 囲込
ほうず 坊主憎けりゃ袈裟(⁇)まで憎い. Hate a priest, and you will hate his very surplice. | If you dislike someone, you will end up

ほうしょく 奉職 ¶奉職している《文》serve (with, in); hold a position (with, in); be on the staff (of a high school).

ほうしょく 暴食 overeating ⇨ぼういん ¶暴食する eat too much; overeat《oneself》.

ほうじる¹ 奉じる〈奉る〉 present *sth* to *sb* [*sb* with *sth*]; 〈従う〉obey; follow; 〈信奉する〉believe in; embrace 《the Muslim faith》(信者になる) ¶職を奉じる hold an office (with, in).

ほうじる² 報じる ⇨むくいる, しらせる ¶《時計が》5時を報じる strike five.

ほうじる³ 焙じる toast; roast; heat.

ほうしん 方針〈方向〉a course; lines;《政策》a policy;〈目的〉an aim; an object (in view) ¶方針を立てる map out *one's* course; decide on *one's* policy; lay down the lines (of) / 方針を誤る choose the wrong course [policy] / 党の方針に従う toe 〔(米)the〕party line / 一定の方針に従って進む pursue [follow] a definite policy. 文例⤵

ほうしん 放心 absent-mindedness ¶放心状態である be absent-minded; be abstracted; be in an abstracted state (of mind).

ほうしん³ 砲身 the barrel of a gun; a gun barrel.

ほうしん⁴ 疱疹〔医〕herpes ¶帯状疱疹 shingles.

ほうじん¹ 方陣 〈陣形〉(in) square formation;《form》a square;〈数字の〉a magic square.

ほうじん² 邦人 ⇨にほん (日本人).

ほうじん³ 法人 a juristic [juridical] person; a corporation ¶法人所得税 a corporate income tax / 法人税 (a) corporation tax / 法人組織にする incorporate.

ぼうず 坊主 a Buddhist priest [monk]; a bonze ¶坊主頭 a shaven [tonsured] head;〈短く刈った〉a close-cropped head. 文例⤵

ほうすい 放水 ¶放水する〈ホースで〉hose [play water on]《a burning building》;〈水を導き流す〉drain water off / 放水路 a drainage canal; a flood control channel; a floodway. 文例⤵

ぼうすい¹ 防水 ¶防水の waterproof / 防水加工 waterproofing / 防水布 waterproof(ed) cloth.

ぼうすい² 紡錘 a spindle.

ほうすいき 豊水期 a rainy season; a high-water season.

ほうせい¹ 法制 legislation; laws ¶(内閣)法制局 the Cabinet Legislation Bureau / 法制史 (a) legal history.

ほうせい² 砲声 the roaring [boom] of guns; (the sound of) gunfire.

ほうせき 宝石 a jewel; a precious stone;《文》a gem ¶宝石をちりばめた冠(恕) a jeweled crown / 宝石で飾る decorate [《文》adorn] *sth* with jewels [gems] / 宝石商 a jeweler / 宝石箱 a jewel case [box, casket] / 宝石類 jewelry.

ぼうせき 紡績 spinning ¶紡績糸 yarn / 紡績機械 a spinning machine / 紡績業 the spinning industry / 紡績工 a spinning-mill worker [hand] / (a spinning-)mill girl (女工) / 紡績工場 a spinning mill.

ぼうせつ 防雪 protection against snow ¶防雪柵(ホ) a snow fence / 防雪林 a snowbreak (wood).

ぼうせん 防戦 a defensive fight [battle] ¶防戦する fight a defensive battle; defend 《*one's* position》against《the enemy》.

ぼうぜん 茫然 ¶茫然と vacantly; absent-mindedly / 茫然とする be stupefied; be dum(b)founded; be struck dumb with surprise. 文例⤵

ほうせんか〔植〕a (garden) balsam.

ホウ ホウ素〔化〕boron.

ほうそう¹ 包装 packing; packaging ¶包装する pack; package; wrap / 包装用のひも wrapping string / 包装(用)紙 packing [wrapping] paper; brown [kraft] paper (茶色の).

ほうそう² 放送《radio, television》broadcasting; (a)《radio, television》transmission; a《radio, television》broadcast (一回の) ⇨ラジオ, テレビ ¶放送〈局が〉broadcast 《the news》; transmit 《traffic information》; put 《the news》on the air; send out 《a weather forecast》;《人が》broadcast; speak [perform] on radio [television]; go [come] on the air /《音・場面などが》放送中である[ない] be on [off] the air / 放送を聴く listen (in) to a《radio》broadcast / 第一[二]放送 (a broadcast on) the first [second] radio program (of the NHK) / 放送記者 a radio [TV] reporter / 放送局 a broadcasting station; a radio [TV] station / 放送劇 a radio [TV] play / 放送時間〈ある番組の〉the time (for a program);〈局の〉broadcasting hours [time]; air time / 放送事業 the broadcasting industry / 放送室 a radio [television] studio / 放送大学 a university of the air / 放送討論会 a radio forum; a TV debate / 放送番組 a broadcast program / 放送妨害 jamming / 放送網 a (radio, television) network. 文例⤵

ぼうそう 暴走 reckless driving ¶暴走族 reckless [crazy] drivers;〈オートバイの〉motorcycle [bike] freaks;〈英口語〉ton-up boys / 暴走電車 a runaway train.

ほうそうかい 法曹界《文》judicial circles; the bench and bar.

ほうそく 法則 a law; a rule ★自然科学上の法則はすべて rule ではなく law ¶自然の法則

---

hating everything he stands for [will hate even the ground he walks on].

ほうすい 警官隊はデモ隊に向かって放水を開始した。The police turned the water cannon on the demonstrators.

ほうぜん 彼はぼうぜんとしてなす所を知らなかった。He was quite at a loss what to do. / 彼はその知らせを聞いてしばらくはぼうぜんとしていた。The news struck him speechless [dumb] for a while.

ほうそう² 明日その試合はテレビで放送される。The game will be (shown) on TV tomorrow. / 彼の放送を聞いたか。Did you hear him on the radio? | Did you hear his broadcast? / 彼女はのど自慢の放送に出た。She appeared in a

ほうたい ほうたい 包帯 a bandage ¶包帯をする bandage 《a hand》; put a bandage on; 《文》apply a bandage to ; dress 《a wound》/ 指に包帯をしている have one's finger in a bandage [bandaged]; wear a bandage around one's finger / 傷の包帯を取る take a bandage off the wound / 巻き包帯 a roller (bandage) / 包帯材料 dressing materials ; (material for) dressings. 文例↓

ほうたい 砲台 a battery ; 〈要塞(さい)〉a fort ; a fortress.

-ほうだい …放題 ¶したい放題に just as one likes [pleases]; at will / 食い放題に食う eat as much as one likes / わがままの し放題をする (try to) have everything one's own way. 文例↓

ほうだい 膨大 ¶膨大な enormous ; colossal ; massive / 膨大な収集 a vast [《文》an extensive] collection.

ほうたかとび 棒高跳び 〈競技種目〉the pole vault ; 〈一回の跳躍〉a pole vault ¶棒高跳びで5メートル跳ぶ pole-vault 5 meters / 棒高跳びの選手 a pole-vaulter.

ぼうだち 棒立ち ¶棒立ちになる stand bolt upright ; 〈馬が〉rise on its hind legs ; rear (up).

ほうだん¹ 放談 〈1人の〉a random talk ; 〈2人以上の人の〉a random [free] conversation.

ほうだん² 砲弾 a [an artillery] shell.

ぼうだん 防弾 ¶防弾ガラス bulletproof glass / 防弾チョッキ a bulletproof jacket [vest].

ほうち¹ 放置 ¶放置する 〈そのままにしておく〉leave [let] sth [sb] alone [be]; leave sth as it is ; leave sth to take its own course ; 〈なおざりにする〉neglect.

ほうち² 報知 a report ; news ; information ¶報知する《文》inform sb of sth ; report ; let sb know 《about, of》.

ほうちく 放逐 ¶放逐する expel ; eject ; oust ; 〈国外に〉banish ; deport.

ほうちこく 法治国 a constitutional state ; a country under the rule of law.

ぼうちゅう 傍注 marginal notes.

ぼうちゅうざい 防虫剤 〈衣類などの〉a moth repellent ; a moth ball (玉の).

ほうちょう 包丁 a kitchen knife ¶包丁を入れる carve 《meat》with a knife.

ぼうちょう¹ 傍聴 listening 《to》; attendance (出席) ¶傍聴する hear [listen to]《a discussion》; attend 《a trial》/ 国会を傍聴する visit the Diet in session / 傍聴券 an admission ticket / 傍聴席 seats for the public ; 〈議会・法廷の〉the (visitors' [public]) gallery / 傍聴人 (a member of) the public / 〈裁判長が〉傍聴人の退廷を命じる order that the public should be excluded from the court ; order the court to be cleared. 文例↓

ぼうちょう² 膨張[脹] expansion ; swelling ; 〈増大〉(an) increase ; growth ¶都市の膨張 urban growth / 熱による膨張 thermal expansion and contraction / 膨張する expand ; swell ; increase / 膨張率[係数] the rate [coefficient] of expansion / 膨張力 expansive power. 文例↓

ぼうちょうてい 防潮堤 an embankment ; a seawall.

ほうっておく 放って置く 〈閑却する〉neglect ; lay aside ; 〈構わずにおく〉leave [let] sb [sth] alone ; leave sb [sth] as he [it] is ; let sb [sth] be. 文例↓

ぼうっと 〈ぼんやり〉vacantly ; absent-mindedly ; 《文》abstractedly ; 〈かすんで〉dimly ; hazily ; indistinctly ¶ぼうっとなる 〈喪心して〉be stunned ; be stupefied ; 〈魅せられて〉be fascinated ; be spellbound / ぼうっとした 〈かすんだ〉misty ; dim ; hazy ; indistinct ; 〈頭が〉muddled / 遠くにぼうっとかすんで見える山々 mountains dim in the distance. 文例↓

ぼうっと ⇨ぽっと.

ほうてい¹ 法廷 a (law)court ; a court of law ¶法廷へ出る 〈出頭する〉appear in court ; come [go] into court / 法廷に立つ stand at the bar / 法廷に持ち出す bring 《a matter》before the court ; take [bring]《a case》into court / 法廷に持ち出さないで解決する settle 《a matter》in the court [out of court] / 法廷で争う take sb to court ; bring a suit [an action]《against》/ 法廷侮辱罪に問われる be charged with contempt of court. 文例↓

ほうてい² 法定 ¶法定の legal ; statutory / 法定休日《米》a legal holiday ; 《英》a bank holiday / 法定代理人 a legal representative / 法定通貨 legal tender / 法定伝染病 an infectious disease designated by law ; a notifiable disease.

ほうていしき 方程式 《数》an equation ¶方

---

broadcast of the amateur singing contest.

ほうたい その包帯はどうしたの? What's the bandage for?

-ほうだい 彼らは何でもし放題だ. どこへでも行き放題だ. They do as they like and go where they please. / 皆彼の言いなり放題になっている. They all do just as he tells them.

ぼうちょう¹ その事件の裁判は一般の傍聴が許されなかった. The public were not admitted to the court when the case was tried. /

公判は傍聴禁止で行なわれた. The hearing was conducted behind closed doors [was held in camera].

ぼうちょう² 金属は熱を加えると膨張する. Metals expand when they are heated. / 国庫の歳出は年々膨張する. State expenditure increases year by year. / 同市は郊外へ急速に膨張しつつある. The city is expanding [spreading] rapidly into the surrounding countryside.

ほうっておく ほうっておいてくれ

ないか. 自分でやるから. Leave [Let] me alone ; I'll do it myself. / それをほうっておいては困る. You must not leave it as it is. / 彼が虐待されているのをほうっておくわけにはいかない. I cannot stand by and let him be ill-treated. / 彼は風邪をほうっておいたのがもとで亡くなった. He died of a neglected cold.

ぼうっと 疲れてぼうっとしていたのでその事をすっかり忘れてしまった. I was so befuddled by [stupefied with, muzzy with]

程式を立てる[解く] set up [solve] an equation / 一次[二次,三次,四次]方程式 a simple [quadratic, cubic, biquadratic] equation / n次方程式 an nth-degree equation.

ほうてき 法的 ¶法的には legally; in the eye(s) of the law / 法的効力がある have legal force / 法的根拠 a legal basis.

ほうてき² 放擲 《文》abandonment ¶放擲する abandon; give up. 文例↓

ほうてん 法典 a code (of laws); a law code; a body of law(s).

ほうでん 放電 (a) discharge of electricity; (an) electric discharge ¶放電する discharge electricity / 放電させる discharge (a Leyden jar) / 空中[真空, 火花]放電 atmospheric [vacuum, spark] discharge / 放電管 a discharge tube.

ほうと 暴徒 rioters; a mob.

ほうとう¹ 放蕩 《文》dissipation; fast living; a dissipated life ¶放蕩にふける[身を持ち崩す] indulge in dissipation [fast living]; lead a dissipated life / 放蕩息子 《文》a prodigal son.

ほうとう 砲塔 a (gun) turret.

ほうどう² 報道 news; a report; coverage ¶報道する report; cover (an event) / 報道されずに終わる go unreported / 「読売」の報道によれば according to the *Yomiuri*; the *Yomiuri* says... / 報道合戦 rivalry among reporters [news agencies] (in covering an event) / (米大統領の)報道官 the (Presidential) Press Secretary / 報道管制 news censorship; a blackout of news 《about》 / 報道機関 the press; a medium of information; a news medium / 報道写真 a news photograph / 報道陣 the press; 《米》the press corps;《英》the pressmen. 文例↓

ほうとう¹ 冒頭 the beginning; the opening. 文例↓

ほうとう² 暴投 《野球》a wild throw; <投手の> a wild pitch ¶暴投する throw a wild ball; throw wild (to first base); <投手が> pitch wild / 暴投で2塁に進む advance to second on a wild throw.

ほうとう³ 暴騰 a sudden rise; a jump ¶暴騰する jump; soar (out of sight); rise steeply.

ほうどう 暴動 a riot; an uprising ¶暴動を起こす riot; start [raise] a riot. 文例↓

ほうとく 冒瀆 blasphemy;《文》(a) profanation; (a) sacrilege; desecration ¶冒瀆する《文》profane; blaspheme; desecrate / 神を冒瀆する blaspheme against God.

ほうどく 防毒 ¶防毒マスク[面] a gas mask.

ほうにち 訪日 a visit to Japan ¶訪日する visit Japan.

ほうにょう 放尿 urination ¶放尿する urinate; pass water.

ほうにん 放任 ¶放任する leave *sth* to take *its* own course; let [leave] *sb* alone / 放任主義 a let-alone [noninterference] policy. 文例↓

ほうねつ 放熱 radiation of heat ¶放熱する radiate heat.

ほうねん 豊年 《文》a year of abundance [plenty]; a bumper year (for crops) ¶豊年祝い a harvest festival. 文例↓

ほうねんかい 忘年会 a year-end (dinner) party.

ほうのう 奉納 ¶奉納する dedicate; offer / 奉納相撲 a *sumo*-wrestling tournament held in the precincts of a shrine on its festival day.

ほうばく 茫漠 ¶茫漠たる vast;《文》extensive;《文》boundless / 茫漠たる海原 a boundless expanse of water / 茫漠たる草原 a vast stretch of grassland.

ぼうはつ 暴発 an accidental discharge (of a gun) ¶暴発する go off accidentally [by accident].

ぼうはてい 防波堤 a breakwater; a seawall; <比喩的>《文》a bulwark.

ぼうはん 防犯 prevention of crime(s) ¶防犯協会 an association for the prevention of crime / 防犯ベル a burglar alarm.

ほうひ 包皮 《解》the foreskin; the prepuce.

ほうび 褒美 a reward; a prize (賞) ¶(動物を訓練する時の)褒美の餌 a food reward / 褒美を与える reward *sb* with (1 dollar); give *sb* a reward (of 5,000 yen). 文例↓

ぼうび 防備 defense ¶防備する defend; guard / 防備のない defenseless; unguarded / 防備を施す fortify (a town) / 防備を強化する strengthen [reinforce, build up] the defenses (of a country).

ぼうびき 棒引き ¶棒引きにする cancel (out);《文》strike out [off] ⇒ちょうけし.

ほうふ¹ 抱負 《文》(an) aspiration; an ambition ¶抱負を語る speak of *one's* aspira-

---

tiredness that it slipped entirely from my mind. / 目がかすんで何を見てもぼうっとしている. My eyes are dim, and everything looks blurred to me.

ほうてい 事件はついに法廷へ持ち出された. The matter was at last brought before the court. / その事件は法廷へは持ち出されなかった. The case did not come into court.

ほうてき² 彼は一切を放擲してその事に当たった. He gave up everything to do it.

ほうどう その新聞の報道は誤っていた. The report in the paper turned out to have been false. / 大統領は自分のゴルフが新聞に報道されるのは反対だった. The President was opposed to press coverage of his golf. / アメリカの新聞での日本についての報道量は近頃幾分増えてきた. The amount of coverage given to Japan in American newspapers has somewhat increased of late.

ほうとう¹ 徒然草の冒頭に次のように書いてある. We find the following in the opening paragraph of the *Tsurezuregusa*. / 彼は演説の冒頭に論語の1句を引いた. He opened [prefaced] his speech with a quotation from *The Analects of Confucius*.

ほうどう 刑務所内で暴動が起こった. A riot broke out in the jail.

ほうにん 私は子供に対しては放任主義だ. I do not, on principle, interfere with my children.

ほうねん 今年は豊年だろう. We will have a good harvest this year.

ほうび この本をご褒美に上げよう. I will give you this book as a reward.

ほうふ tion(s); express *one's* hopes [wishes]. 文例↓

ほうふ¹ 豊富 《文》 abundance; plenty; wealth ¶豊富な abundant; ample; plentiful; rich / 石油の豊富な国 an oil-rich country / 豊富な知識 a wealth [great store] of knowledge / 豊富に abundantly; plentifully; 《文》 in abundance / 語彙(ᅳ)を豊富にする enrich [enlarge, increase] *one's* vocabulary. 文例↓

ほうふ¹ 亡父 my late [《文》 deceased] father.

ほうふ² 亡夫 my late [《文》 deceased] husband.

ほうふう 暴風 a (wind)storm; a violent wind ¶暴風雨 a (rain)storm; a tempest / 暴風雨の一夜 a stormy [wild] night / 暴風雨警報 a storm warning.

ほうふうりん 防風林 a windbreak.

ほうふく¹ 法服 〈裁判官などの〉 a judge's [lawyer's] gown; 〈僧服〉 a priest's robe.

ほうふく² 報復 retaliation; (a) reprisal ★ reprisal は報復行為を表わす時は take reprisals 《against》 という句の場合のようにしばしば複数形をとる ⇨ しかえし ¶報復手段 《文》 retaliatory measures / 報復爆撃 (a) reprisal [retaliatory] bombing.

ほうふくぜっとう 抱腹絶倒 ¶抱腹絶倒する hold *one's* sides with laughter; be convulsed with laughter. 文例↓

ほうふざい 防腐剤 a preservative ¶食品防腐剤 a food preservative.

ほうふつ 彷彿 文例↓

ほうぶつせん 放物線 a parabola ¶放物線を描く describe a parabola.

ほうふら a mosquito larva; a w(r)iggler.

ほうぶん¹ 邦文 Japanese; the Japanese language ⇨ わぶん.

ほうぶん² 法文 the text [letter] of the law ¶法文学部 the school of law and literature. 文例↓

ほうへい 砲兵 〈兵科〉 artillery; 〈兵〉 an artilleryman.

ほうべい 訪米 a visit to the United States ¶訪米の途に就く leave for America [the United States].

ほうへき 防壁 a defense [protective] wall; a barrier; 〈比喩的〉 《文》 a bulwark 《against communism》.

ほうべん 方便 〈便法〉 《文》 an expedient; 〈手段〉 《文》 a means (単複同形) ¶一時の方便 a temporary expedient; a makeshift [stopgap]

ほうめい measure.

ほうほう¹ 方法 〈仕方〉 a method; a way; 〈方策〉 a plan; a system; 〈手段〉 《文》 a means (単複同形); 〈過程〉 a process; 〈処置〉 a step; a measure ¶…する方法 how to *do*; a method [way, means] of *do*ing; a way (in which) to *do* / 方法を講じる take measures [steps] to *do* / 方法論 methodology.

ほうほう² ¶ (ふくろうが)ほうほうと鳴く hoot.

ほうほう³ 方々 ¶方々に in several places; in various quarters; everywhere; here and there; all over (the town) / 方々歩き回る wander from place to place / 方々へ連れて行かれる be taken to various places. 文例↓

ほうほう⁴ 〈魚〉 a gurnard.

ほうほうと ¶ぼうぼうと燃える burn vigorously / ぼうぼうと燃え上がる burst into flames / (草が)ぼうぼうと生える grow thick and wild; be rank / ひげをぼうぼうと伸ばしている a shaggy beard / 髪をぼうぼうと伸ばした男 a man with long unkempt hair. 文例↓

ほうほうのてい ほうほうの体 ¶ほうほうの体で hurriedly; 《文》 precipitately / ほうほうの体で逃げ出す run away with *one's* tail between *one's* legs; beat a hasty retreat.

ほうぼく 放牧 pasturage ¶放牧する put [turn] (cattle) out to grass; put (sheep) to grazing; pasture / 放牧地 a pasture (area); pastureland.

ほうまつ 泡沫 a bubble; foam ¶泡沫会社 a bubble company; a fly-by-night concern / 泡沫候補 a frivolous candidate / 《文》 a candidate unworthy of serious consideration.

ほうまん¹ 放漫 ¶放漫な 〈締まりのない〉 loose; 〈むちゃな〉 reckless / 放漫財政政策 a free-spending economic policy.

ほうまん² 豊満 ¶豊満な plump (women); voluptuous (curves); well-developed (breasts).

ほうむ 法務 ¶法務省(大臣) the Ministry [Minister] of Justice.

ほうむる 葬る 〈埋葬する〉 bury; 《文》 inter; 《文》 lay *sb* to rest; 〈握りつぶす〉 shelve ¶社会から葬り去られる be excluded from society; 《文》 be ostracized; become a social outcast. 文例↓

ほうめい 亡命 ¶亡命する flee (from) [defect from] *one's* own country (for political rea-

---

ほうふ¹ 彼は大きな抱負を持っている。He has great ambitions. / 新市長は記者会見でその抱負を語った。At the news conference the new Mayor outlined his ambitious program.

ほうふ² この国は天然資源が豊富だ。This country abounds [is rich] in natural resources. / 食糧は豊富でした。We had an abundant supply of food.

ほうふう 暴風が吹いていた。The wind was blowing violently. / 千葉県沿岸に大暴風雨が襲った。A violent storm raged along the coast of Chiba Prefecture.

ほうふくぜっとう 彼は満座の人々を抱腹絶倒させた。He set the whole company roaring with laughter. | He had them all in fits of laughter.

ほうふつ 彼女はほうふつとして今なお私の眼前にある。It is still vivid [fresh] in my memory. | It still floats before my eyes. / この絵を見るとほうふつとしてベニスの夕景が浮かんでくる。This picture reminds me of (the appearance of) Venice in the evening [at dusk].

ほうぶん² そういう事は法文に規定されていない。It is not specified [provided for] in the law.

ほうほう¹ どんな方法でするのですか。How is it done? / 君は方法を誤っている。You are doing it the wrong way. | That is not the way to do it.

ほうほう³ 方々の店で尋ねたがその品はなかった。I inquired at several stores but could not find it. / 方々を捜してみた。I have looked for it everywhere. / 方々でそういう不平を聞く。I hear the same complaint in various quarters. /

sons); seek refuge [political asylum] ((in the United States)); 亡命者 a (political) refugee; an émigré; an exile; a defector / 亡命政府 a refugee government; a government in exile.

[用法] defect, defector には seek refuge, refugee などと違って、国家機密を握っている人が亡命して、その機密を敵国などに売り渡す、というニュアンスがある。

ほうめん[1] 方面 〈場所〉 a district; (《文》) a quarter; 〈分野〉 a field; (《文》) an aspect; 〈局面〉 a side; 〈角度〉 an angle ¶九州方面 the Kyushu district / 名古屋方面 (in) the vicinity [neighborhood] of Nagoya / 各方面から 〈場所〉 from all quarters / 〈立場〉 from every point of view / 各方面から情報を集める collect [gather] information from various sources / 問題をあらゆる方面から考察する consider a question from all angles. 文例⇩

ほうめん[2] 放免 release ⇨ しゃくほう ¶無罪放免 ⇨ むさい 文例.

ほうもう 法網 ¶法網をくぐる get around [avoid, dodge, evade] the law / 法網をくぐって悪事を重ねる commit one crime after another without falling into the clutches of the law / 法網に掛る fall into the clutches of the law; be brought to justice.

ほうもう 紡毛 〈紡いだ羊毛〉 carded wool; 〈紡ぐ羊毛〉 carding wool ¶紡毛糸 woolen yarn.

ほうもつ 宝物 a treasure ⇨ たから ¶宝物殿 a treasure house; a treasury; a museum (陳列品を公開している).

ほうもん[1] 砲門 ¶砲門を開く open fire.

ほうもん[2] 訪問 a call; a visit; an interview (記者の) ¶訪問する call (on sb, at sb's house); make a call (on, at); visit; pay [make] a visit (to); go to see sb; 〈記者が〉 interview / 訪問を受ける get [(《文》) receive] a call [visit] (from) / (女性の) semiformal kimono / 訪問者 a caller; a visitor / 訪問者に会う[を断る] see [refuse to see] a caller.

ぼうや 坊や a boy; 〈呼び掛け〉 son; lad; sonny.

ほうやく 邦訳 ⇨ わやく ¶邦訳聖書 a Japanese version of the Bible.

ほうよう[1] 法要 ⇨ ほうじ.

ほうよう[2] 抱擁 an embrace ¶抱擁する 《文》 embrace; hug; hold sb in one's arms [《文》] to one's breast.

ほうようりょく 包容力 broad-mindedness; tolerance ¶包容力のある人 a broad-minded [tolerant] person.

ぼうよみ 棒読み ¶棒読みにする read ((a passage)) in a monotone [without any expression].

ぼうらく 暴落 a sudden [heavy] fall; a sharp [steep] decline; a slump ¶暴落する fall suddenly ((to the level of 100 yen)); drop [fall, 《文》 decline] sharply; slump. 文例⇩

ぼうり 暴利 ¶暴利をむさぼる make excessive [undue] profits; profiteer.

ほうりあげる 放り上げる ⇨ なげあげる.

ほうりこむ 放り込む ⇨ なげこむ.

ほうりだす 放り出す 〈外へ投げる〉 throw [chuck] sb out ((of the bar)); 〈放棄する〉 ⇨ なげだす; 〈解雇する〉 sack; 《主に米》 fire; 〈除籍する〉 expel ¶学校をほうり出される be expelled from [chucked out of] school. 文例⇩

ほうりつ 法律 a law; 〈総称〉 (the) law ¶法律上 legally; from a legal point of view / 法律上の legal / 法律を守る obey [《文》 observe] the law / 法律を学ぶ read [study] law / 法律を犯す break [《文》 violate] the law / 法律に照らして処分する deal with ((a case)) according to the law / 法律家 a lawyer; a jurist (主に学者について言う) / 法律顧問 a legal adviser [advisor] / 法律事務所 a law office [firm] / 法律書 a law book / 法律相談に応じる give sb legal advice / 法律用語 a legal [law] term. 文例⇩

ぼうりゃく 謀略 a plot; 《文》 machinations ¶謀略を巡らす plot [scheme] ((to do)).

ほうりゅう 放流 ¶放流する 〈水を〉 discharge; 〈魚を〉 release [fish] into ((a river)); stock ((a river)) with (fish).

ほうりょう 豊漁 a big [good] catch; a rich [good] haul.

ぼうりょく 暴力 (brute) force; violence ¶暴力を振るう use violence ((on sb)) / 暴力に訴える 《文》 resort to force; 《文》 have recourse to violence / 暴力で by force / 暴力革命 an armed revolution / 暴力行為[犯罪] an act [a crime] of violence / 暴力団 an organized group of gangsters [thugs] (given to using violence).

ボウリング 〈球技〉 bowling ¶ボウリングのピン[ボール] a bowling pin [ball] / ボウリング

その事で方々から問い合わせがあった。We have had inquiries about it from all sorts of people.

ほうぼうと 庭に草がぼうぼうと生えている。The garden is overgrown with weeds.

ほうむる 彼は多磨墓地に葬られた。He was buried [laid to rest] in the Tama cemetery. / その事件は闇に葬られた。The matter has been hushed up. / 委員会はそのアイデアを全く実行不可能として葬り去った。The committee killed the idea as totally impracticable.

ほうめん[1] 福井方面に商用がある。I have some business to attend to in and around Fukui. / 彼は千住方面に住んでいる。He lives somewhere in Senju [somewhere Senju way]. / 彼は色々な方面に知り合いがある。He has acquaintances among people in various walks of life. / 彼はこの方面での先駆者の1人だった。He was among the pioneers in this field.

ほうもん[2] 昨日前田氏を訪問した。I went to see [called on] Mr. Maeda yesterday. / 今日は方々を訪問しなければならない。I have a number of visits to make today.

ぼうらく このために株価はたちまち大暴落した。It brought about an immediate sharp [steep] decline in stock prices.

ほうりこむ 新聞配達が窓から新聞をほうり込んだ。The newsboy threw the paper in at the window.

ほうりだす おとなしくしないとみんな表へほうり出すぞ。Don't be so noisy, or I'll chuck [kick] you all out.

ほうりつ 法律は知らないでは通ら

ほうる をする bowl / ボウリングをしに行く go bowling / ボウリングをする a bowler / ボウリング場 a bowling alley [center].

ほうる 放る ⇨ なげる.

ほうりつ 法令 a law; an ordinance; 〈総称〉 laws and ordinances [regulations].

ほうれい 亡霊 〈死者の魂〉 the spirit of a dead person; 〈幽霊〉a ghost; 《文》an apparition; 《文》a phantom.

ほうれつ 放列 ¶テレビカメラの放列の前に立つ stand before a forest of television cameras; face a battery of TV cameras.

ほうれんそう 〖植〗spinach.

ほうろう¹ 放浪 ¶放浪する wander about; roam / 放浪の旅に出る start on a wandering [an aimless] journey / 放浪癖 the habit of wandering about; 《文》vagabondism / 放浪生活をする lead [live] a wandering [vagabond, vagrant] life / 放浪者 a wanderer; a vagabond; a vagrant.

ほうろう² 琺瑯 enamel ¶ほうろう引きのなべ an enamel(ed) pot / (歯の)ほうろう質 enamel.

ほうろう 望楼 a watchtower.

ほうろく 焙烙 an earthenware baking [parching] pan.

ほうろん 暴論 a wild argument.

ほうわ¹ 法話 a sermon; a religious discourse.

ほうわ² 飽和 〖物・化〗saturation ¶飽和する be saturated 《with》/ 飽和蒸気 saturated vapor / 飽和点 《reach》(the [a]) saturation point / 飽和溶液 a saturated solution. 文例⇩

ほえごえ 吠え声 a bark (犬の); a roar (ライオンなどの); a howl (おおかみなどの).

ほえづら 吠え面 文例⇩

ポエニせんそう ポエニ戦争 〖史〗the Punic Wars.

ほえる 吠える 〈犬が〉bark; 〈おおかみ・犬が〉howl; 〈ライオン・虎(š)などが〉roar ¶(犬が)ほえつく,ほえかかる bark at sb. 文例⇩

ほお 頬 a cheek ¶ほおの赤い rosy-cheeked / ほおをふくらませる puff (out) one's cheeks; 〈すねる〉sulk; 《口語》have got the sulks. 文例⇩

ボーイ 〈給仕〉a waiter; 〈会社の〉 an office boy; 〈ホテルの〉a bellboy; 〈汽船の〉a cabin boy ¶ボーイ頭 a headwaiter; 〈ホテルの〉a bell captain / ボーイスカウト〈団体〉 the Boy Scouts; 〈団員〉 a boy scout / ボーイフレンド〈男友達〉 a friend; a boy (that) one knows;

〈恋人〉a boyfriend. 文例⇩

ポーカー 〈トランプの〉《play》poker ¶ポーカーフェイスの poker-faced.

ほおかぶり 頬被り ¶ほおかぶりする〈顔を隠す〉cover [wrap] one's cheeks 《with a towel》; 〈知らん顔をする〉pretend not to know; 《文》pretend [feign] ignorance.

ボーキサイト 〖鉱〗bauxite.

ホーク ⇨ フォーク¹.

ボーク 〖野球〗a balk ¶ボークをする balk; make a balk.

ポークソテー sautéed pork.

ほおじろ 〖鳥〗a (Japanese) bunting.

ホース 〈ゴムの〉a hose ¶ホースを向ける train a hose 《on》/ ホースで水をかける water (the garden) with a hose; hose (a burning building); hose (a car) (down) / 消火用ホース a fire hose.

ポーズ¹ 〈姿態〉a pose ¶ポーズをとる strike [get into] a pose; pose 《for one's picture》/ ポーズをとらせる pose sb 《for a photograph》.

ポーズ² 〈休止〉a pause ¶ポーズを置く pause; make a pause.

ほおずき 〖植〗a ground [winter] cherry; a Chinese lantern plant ¶ほおずきを鳴らす blow a ground cherry / ほおずきちょうちん a (small) round red lantern.

ほおずり 頬擦り ¶ほおずりする nestle [rub] one's cheek against sb's.

ボーダーライン the borderline 《between》¶ボーダーラインケース a borderline case.

ポータブル portable ¶ポータブルラジオ a portable radio.

ポーチ a porch.

ほおづえ 頬杖 ¶ほおづえを突く rest one's cheeks [chin] in one's hands; 〈片方だけを〉rest one's cheek on one's hand.

ぽーっと ¶ぽーっとなる〈気が遠くなる〉faint; be dazed (by the news); 《文》swoon; 〈異性に〉fall for (a woman); be smitten by (a girl); 〈赤くなる〉⇨ ぽっと (ぽっと顔を赤らめる).

ボート 〈短艇〉a (rowing) boat; 《米》a rowboat; 〈こぐ事〉boating ¶ボートの選手 an oarsman / ボートこぎに行く go for a row; go boating / (船から)ボートをおろす lower a boat / ボートをこぐ row a boat / ボートレース a boat race; a regatta (大会) / ボートレースをする row (a race) 《against Oxford》. 文例⇩

ポートサイド Port Said.

ポートワイン port (wine).

ない. Ignorance of the law is no excuse. / 未成年者の喫煙は法律で禁じられている. Smoking by minors is forbidden [prohibited] by law.

ほうわ² 東京の道路交通は飽和にある. The streets of Tokyo are completely choked [extremely congested] with traffic. | Tokyo cannot accommodate [stand] any further increase in road traffic.

ほえづら 後でほえづらをかくよ. You'll have to pay for this.

ほえる 暗い路地で犬にほえられた. A dog barked at me in a dark alley. / ほえる犬はかまない. Barking dogs seldom bite. 〖諺〗

ほお 太郎は目がぱっちりしてほおが福々しい. Taro has bright eyes and plump (chubby) cheeks. / 彼はほおがこけている. He has hollow [sunken] cheeks. / 学校から走って帰ったので彼のほおは真赤だった. He was red-cheeked after running home from school. | His cheeks were flushed after he

had run home from school.

ボーイ あなたはボーイフレンドが大勢いますか. Do you know a lot of boys? | Do you have a lot of friends who are boys?

ボート ボートを降ろせ! 〈号令〉Lower the boat(s)! / 昨日は湖にボート遊びに行った. I went boating on the lake yesterday.

ホール² 〈ゴルフで〉球が一直線に飛んでホールインワンになった. The ball flew [sailed] directly into the cup for a hole in one.

ボーナス a bonus ¶月給3か月分のボーナス a bonus equivalent to three months' pay.

ホーバークラフト a hovercraft.

ほおばる 頬張る fill [stuff] one's mouth (with); cram ((food)) into one's mouth ¶口に一杯ほお張っている have one's mouth full of ((food)).

ほおひげ 頬髭 whiskers;〈あごの所はそってある〉side-whiskers;《米》sideburns;《英》sideboards ¶ほおひげを生やしている wear whiskers / ほおひげを生やした男 a whiskered man.

ホープ a hope;《口語》a (great) white hope ¶楽壇のホープ the hope of the musical world.

ほおべに 頬紅 rouge. ¶ほおべにをつける rouge one's cheeks; put rouge on one's cheeks.

ぽーぽー ¶《汽笛が》ぽーぽー鳴る toot; hoot.

ほおぼね 頬骨 cheekbones ¶ほお骨の高い人 a person with high cheekbones.

ホーマー【野球】a homer ⇨ホームラン.

ホーム〈家庭〉one's home;〈収容施設〉a home;【野球】(the) home (base [plate]);〈駅の〉a platform ¶ホームドラマ a drama depicting home life / ホームバー a cocktail bar (in a private home).

ホームイン ¶ホームインする【野球】get [reach] home; cross home plate [the plate].

ホームグラウンド one's home ground.

ホームシック homesickness ¶ホームシックになる [《文》become] homesick; be struck with nostalgia.

ホームストレッチ《米》the homestretch;《英》the home straight ¶ホームストレッチに入ってスパートする put on a spurt in the homestretch.

ホームスパン homespun (cloth) ¶ホームスパンのスカート a homespun skirt.

ホームラン【野球】a home run; a homer ¶ホームランを打つ [かっ飛ばす] hit a home run ((over the right field wall)); swat [whack out] a homer ((into the left field stands)) / ホームラン王 a home-run king / ホームランダービー a home-run derby / ホームランバッター a home-run hitter; a power hitter.

ホームルーム extracurricular activities conducted in the homeroom ¶ホームルームの先生 a homeroom teacher.

ポーランド Poland ¶ポーランドの Polish / ポーランド語 Polish / ポーランド人 a Pole / ポーランド人民共和国 the Polish People's Republic.

ボーリング〈穴をあけたり地中深く掘ること〉boring.

ホール[1]〈大広間〉a hall.

ホール[2]【ゴルフ】a hole; a cup ¶ホールインワン (have, get) a hole in one. 文例凸

ボール a ball ¶ボール投げをする play ball;〈キャッチボール〉play catch / ボールベアリング a ball bearing / ボールペン a ball(-point) pen.

ポール〈棒高飛びの〉a (vaulting) pole;〈旗竿の〉a flagpole;〈測量用の〉a surveying pole.

ボールがみ ボール紙 cardboard; pasteboard.

ホールドアップ a holdup ¶ホールドアップを食わせる hold sb up; rob sb at gunpoint.

ボールばこ ボール箱 a cardboard box [case]; a carton.

ボールばん ボール盤 a drilling machine.

ほおん 保温 retaining warmth; keeping heat in ¶保温性に富む下着 warm [heat-trapping, heat-retaining] underwear.

ほか 外 some other place; somewhere [《米》someplace] else ¶ほかの other; another; different;〈someone〉else / 何かほかの物[事] something else / ほかの人たち other people; (the) others / ほかでもないが… what I want to say is… / …にほかならない It is nothing else but [than]…; It is simply that…; …のほかに〈…を除いては〉except (for)…;《文》excepting…; but… / いがい[1] 囲炉;〈…以上は〉beyond…; outside…;〈その上に〉besides…; in addition to…; over and above… / このほかに besides; in addition to this / ほかにも理由はあるが among other reasons / 加藤ほか3名 Kato and three others. 文例凸

ほか ⇨へま.

ほかく[1] 捕獲 capture;《文》seizure ¶捕獲する catch; capture; seize / 捕獲高 a (good, poor) catch ((of fish)).

ほかく[2] 補角【幾何】the supplement (of an angle); a supplementary angle. 文例凸

ほかげ 火影 a light.

ほかけぶね 帆掛け船 a sailing ship [boat, vessel];《米》a sailboat.

ぼかし 暈かし shadings [《文》gradations] of a color; shading off.

ほか ほかに質問はありませんか。Have you [Are there] any more [further] questions? / ほかに何もする事はない。I have nothing else to do. / ほかにまだ5,6軒寄る所がある。I have several other visits to make. / そうするよりほか仕方がない。There is nothing for it but to do so. | There is [We have] no choice [alternative] but to do it. | That is the only course open to us. / 君のほかに頼る人がない。I have no one but you to turn to for help. / ほかの事ならともかく、これだけは御免だ。I will do anything but this. / 彼のほかは会員は全員出席した。All the members attended the meeting except him. / 僕のほかにも3名遅刻した。Three others were late besides me. / このほかには何も知りません。Beyond this I know nothing about it. / 冷蔵庫の中にはビールが1本入っていただけでほかには飲み物は何もなかった。There was nothing to drink in the fridge except (for) a bottle of beer. / シャルルマーニュの目的はまさに帝国時代のローマの栄光を取り戻すことにほかならなかった。Charlemagne's aim was no more and no less than to restore the glory of imperial Rome. / ほかならぬあなたのご依頼ですから精一杯やってみます。Since the request comes from you (and none other), I will try my best.

ほかく 角Aと角Bとは互いに補

ぼかす 暈かす ¶色をぼかす shade off a color; make a color shade off; ¶色にぼかすグラデーションをつける give gradations to a color / 言葉をぼかす use ambiguous language; do not commit *oneself* / 態度をぼかす take 《文》 assume, 《文》 adopt a noncommittal [an ambiguous] attitude.

ほかほか ¶ほかほかの warm; 《a loaf of bread》 hot from the oven / ほかほかする be [feel] warm.

ぽかぽか ¶ぽかぽかする be [feel] comfortably warm; be nice and warm; 《口語》 be (as) warm as toast / ぽかぽかしてくる get [grow] warm(er) / ぽかぽかなぐる give *sb* some smart blows 《on the head》; rain [shower] blows on *sb*. 文例↓

ほがらか 朗らか ¶朗らかな〈天候・気分など の〉clear; bright; fine; 《快活な》cheerful / 朗らかな朝 a bright morning / 朗らかな人 a cheerful person; a person with a sunny disposition / 朗らかに笑う laugh merrily. 文例↓

ぽかりと ¶ぽかりとなぐる give *sb* a 《good》 blow 《on the head》.

ほかん¹ 保管 custody; keeping; safekeeping ¶保管する keep; have *sth* in *one's* custody [keeping] / 保管金 money in *one's* custody / 保管者 a keeper; a custodian / 保管料 charges for custody; 〈倉庫での〉 storage; a storage fee. 文例↓

ほかん² 補完 ¶補完する complement / 相互補完的である complement [《文》 be complementary to] each other.

ぼかん 母艦 a mother [depot] ship ⇒ こうくう³ (航空母艦).

ぽかんと〈ぼんやり〉vacantly; absent-mindedly; with a blank [vacant] look; 〈ばかのように〉 like a fool; 〈音〉 ⇒ ぽかりと ¶ぽかんとしている look blank [vacant]; be absent-minded; 〈なにもせずに〉sit [stand] idle / 口をぽかんと開いて with *one's* mouth (wide) open / ぽかんと見とれる stare stupidly 《at》; gawk 《at》; gape 《at》. 文例↓

ぼき 簿記 bookkeeping ¶簿記をつける keep accounts / 簿記係 a bookkeeper.

ボギーしゃ ボギー車 a bogie (car).

ぼきぼき ⇒ ぽきんと. 文例↓

ほきゅう 補給 supply ¶物資を補給する supply 《a position》 with goods; 《文》 furnish supplies to 《a base》 / 補給基地 a supply base / 補給金 a subsidy; a grant(-in-aid) / 補給線を絶たれる be cut off from *one's* line(s) of supply / 補給路 a supply route.

ほきょう 補強 《文》 reinforcement(s) ¶補強する reinforce; strengthen; shore up 《a wall》; build up 《*one's* defenses》/ 補強工事 reinforcement work 補強証拠 supporting [《文》 corroborative] evidence. 文例↓

ぼきん 募金 fund raising ¶募金する raise funds [money] 《for an undertaking》; collect [《文》 solicit] contributions 《from the general public toward the fund for an enterprise》 / 募金運動 a fund-raising campaign; a drive to obtain funds 《for》 / 募金箱 a collection box.

ほきんしゃ 保菌者 a (disease) carrier ¶赤痢の保菌者 a carrier of dysentery.

ぽきんと ¶ぽきんと折れる snap; break with a snap.

ぼく 僕 ¶僕は[が] I / 僕の my / 僕のもの mine / 僕に[を] me / 僕らは[が] we / 僕らの our / 僕らのもの ours / 僕らに[を] us.

ほくい 北緯 the north latitude (略: N.L.) ¶北緯 30 度 15 分 20 秒 30°15′20″ north latitude; lat. 30°15′20″ ¶ ★ thirty degrees, fifteen minutes, twenty seconds north (latitude) と読む. 文例↓

ほくおう 北欧 Scandinavia; Northern Europe (★ ドイツを含む) ¶北欧の Scandinavian; North European / 北欧神話 Norse mythology.

ほくげん 北限 《生物》 the northern limit of the range of a plant [an animal].

ボクサー〈拳闘家〉a boxer; 《文》 a pugilist; 〈犬〉a boxer.

ぼくさつ 撲殺 ¶撲殺する beat [club] 《a dog》 dead [to death].

ぼくし 牧師 a clergyman; a minister; a pastor ¶牧師になる become a clergyman; enter the ministry; take (holy) orders; go into the church.

ぼくじゅう 墨汁 India [《英》 Indian] ink.

ほくじょう 北上 ¶北上する go [come] up north.

ぼくじょう 牧場 a stock farm; 《米》 a ranch; 〈放牧場〉 a pasture ¶牛の牧場 a cattle farm [《米》 ranch] / 牧場主 the owner of a stock farm; a (sheep, cattle) farmer; 《米》 a rancher.

ボクシング boxing; 《文》 pugilism ¶ボクシングの試合 a boxing match / ボクシングをする box 《with》.

ほぐす 解す ¶肩の凝りをほぐす take the stiffness out of *one's* shoulders / 緊張をほぐす relax [ease] the tension / 土をほぐす loosen the earth / もつれた糸をほぐす disentangle [unravel] the threads.

ほくせい 北西 (the) northwest (略: NW) ¶北

角をなす. A and B are supplementary angles.

ほかほか 今日のようなぼかぼか陽気には森を散歩するのが一番だよ. On a warm day like today [this], there's nothing like a walk in the woods.

ほがらか こんな朗らかな気分になったことがない. I have never felt more cheerful. / 朗らかな笑いが隣の部屋から聞こえて来た. Gay peals of laughter in the next room reached my ears.

ほかん それは僕が保管している. I have it in my custody [keeping]. / その書類は現在与田氏が保管している. The papers are now in the custody of Mr. Yoda. / 用例カードは研究社に引渡して保管してもらってあります. I've handed my citation cards to Kenkyusha for safekeeping. / 金は会計に保管させた. The money was deposited with the treasurer.

ぽかんと 彼女の来るのを1時間もぽかんと駅で待っていた. He waited for her at the station for an hour like an idiot.

ぽきぽき 彼は指を引っ張って関節をぽきぽき鳴らした. He pulled at his fingers and cracked the joints.

ほきょう この橋は少し補強する

西の northwest(ern) / 北西へ northwestward / 北西風 a northwesterly wind / 西北西 (the) west-northwest (略: WNW).

ぼくせき 木石 [文例↓]

ぼくそう 牧草 grass; pasture ¶家畜と共に牧草を追って移動する move with *one*'s stock following the grazing / 牧草地 grassland; 〈放牧用の〉a pasture; pasture land; grazing; a meadow.

ほくそえむ ほくそ笑む chuckle to *oneself* 《over》; laugh up *one*'s sleeve (ひそかに).

ほくたん 北端 the northern end [《文》extremity, tip].

ぼくちく 牧畜 stock raising; cattle breeding ¶牧畜業者 a stock farmer [raiser]; a cattle breeder; 《米》a rancher.

ほくとう 北東 (the) northeast (略: NE) ¶北東の northeast(ern) / 北東へ northeastward / 北東風 a northeasterly wind.

ぼくとう 木刀 ⇨ぼっとう.

ぼくどう 牧童 a herdboy; a herdsman; 《米》a ranch hand.

ほくと(しち)せい 北斗(七)星 《米》the Big Dipper; 《英》the Plough.

ぼくとつ 木訥 ¶ぼくとつな simple; honest.

ぼくねんじん 朴念仁 a dull [dry old] stick.

ほくぶ 北部 the north [northern part] (of).

ほくべい 北米 North America. [文例↓]

ほくほく ¶ほくほくする〈うれしそうな様子〉be very pleased 《at the news》; congratulate *oneself* 《on one*'s success》; chuckle to *oneself* 《いもなどが》be not soggy (and taste very good).

ほくほくせい 北北西 (the) north-northwest (略: NNW).

ほくほくとう 北北東 (the) north-northeast (略: NNE).

ぼくめつ 撲滅 《文》eradication; 《文》extermination ¶撲滅する《文》eradicate; exterminate; stamp [wipe] out / 害虫を撲滅する exterminate vermin / 流行病を撲滅する eradicate [stamp out] an epidemic disease.

ほくよう 北洋 the north(ern) sea ¶北洋漁業 the northern-sea fishery [fishing industry].

ぼくよう 牧羊 sheep breeding [raising, farming] ¶牧羊犬 a sheep dog; a shepherd dog / 牧羊神『ギリシャ神話』Pan.

ほぐれる 解れる ⇨ほどける. [文例↓]

ほくろ a mole.

ぼけ 〖植〗a Japanese quince.

ほげい 捕鯨 whaling ¶捕鯨場 a whaling ground; a whale fishery / 捕鯨船 a whaling ship; a whaler / 捕鯨船団 a fleet of whalers / 捕鯨砲 a whaling [harpoon] gun.

ぼけい¹ 母系 the maternal line ¶母系制社会 a matrilineal society.

ぼけい² 母型 〖印刷〗a matrix (*pl.* -trices, -es).

ほげた 帆桁 a (sail) yard.

ほけつ 補欠 a substitute;《口語》a sub;《米》an alternate ¶補欠選挙 a by-election /補欠選手 a reserve; a substitute (player) /〈野球の〉a player on the bench;《口語》a bench warmer / 補欠入学を許される be admitted to a school to fill up a vacancy.

ぼけつ 墓穴 ¶みずから墓穴を掘る dig *one*'s own grave; dig a pit for *oneself*; bring about *one*'s own ruin.

ぼけっと ⇨ぼんやり.

ポケット a pocket ¶ポケットのない pocketless / ポケットに入れる put *sth* in [into] *one*'s [a] pocket; pocket / あちこちのポケットに分けて入れる distribute 《things》among *one*'s pockets / ポケットに入る pocketable / ポケットに両手を入れて with *one*'s hands in *one*'s pockets / 内ポケット an inside pocket / ポケット型の本 a pocket-size(d) book / ポケット版 a pocket edition 《of a book》. [文例↓]

ぼける 惚ける〈頭が〉grow [go] senile; become feeble-minded [*one*'s mind gets weak] with age;〈色が〉get [go,《文》become] dim;《文》pale; fade ¶年を取って頭がぼけている be in *one*'s second childhood [《文》*one*'s dotage].

ほけん¹ 保険 insurance ¶保険をかける insure 《*one*'s house against fire for 20 million yen》; take out insurance [an insurance policy]《on *one*'s life》; buy insurance 《on goods》/ 保険がつけてある be insured 《for one million yen》; carry 《3 million yen》insurance (cover) / 保険医療機関 medical institutions authorized to treat patients with health insurance coverage / 保険会社 an insurance company; an insurer / 保険勧誘員 an insurance salesman / 保険金 insurance / 保険金受取人 the beneficiary / 保険業者 an insurer / 保険契約 a contract of insurance; an insurance contract / 保険契約者 the insured (person); a policyholder / 保険詐欺 (an) insurance fraud / 保険証券 a policy of insurance; an insurance policy / 保険代理店 an insurance agency / 保険屋 an insurance man / 保険料[掛金] a premium; insurance. [文例↓]

ほけん² 保健〈健康を保つこと〉keeping good health;〈健康〉health;〈衛生〉sanitation

---

必要がある。This bridge needs some reinforcement.
ほくい 東京は北緯 35 度 40 分，東経 140 度にある。Tokyo is situated at lat. 35°40′N. and long. 140°E.
ぼくせき 私も木石ではない。I, too, am made of flesh and blood. | I, too, am human.
ほくぶ 城は市の北部にある。The castle stands in the north [northern part] of the city.
ほぐれる このお陰で彼女の心も少しほぐれた。She relented a little at this.
ポケット ポケットの中を捜してもみくちゃになった千円札を1枚取り出した。He fished in his pocket and brought out a crumpled thousand-yen note. / 上着のポケットのどこかに入っているよ。You'll find it in one of my coat pockets. / 彼は両手をポケットにぐっと突っ込んで立っていた。He stood there with his hands stuffed tight [hard] into his pockets.
ほけん¹ 彼は東都生命の保険に入った。He insured himself [took out a policy] with the Toto Life Insurance Company. / この家には3千万円の保険が付けてある。This house is insured for 30,000,000

¶保健医[所] a public health doctor [center] / 保健施設 health facilities / 保健医護 the public health system / 保健体育〈学科目〉health education and physical education / 保健婦 a (public) health nurse.

ほけん 母権 mother's rights [authority] ¶母権制社会 a matriarchal society.

ほこ¹ 矛 a halberd;〈武器〉arms ¶矛を収める《文》lay down *one's* arms;《口語》bury the hatchet.

ほこ² 補弧〈数〉a supplementary arc.

ほご¹ 反故 wastepaper; a scrap of paper ¶約束をほごにする break *one's* promise; go back on *one's* word. 文例 ⇩

ほご² 保護 protection;〈世話〉care;〈引き立て〉《文》patronage;〈保存〉《文》preservation ¶保護する protect sb from [against] danger; keep sb from harm; take sb under *one's* wing; take sb into protective custody〈警察が〉;〈世話する〉take care of;〈引き立てる〉patronize;〈保存する〉preserve / …の保護の下に under the protection [care, guardianship] of … / 保護を受ける be protected (by); be under sb's protection / 警察に保護を求める apply to the police for protection / 法的保護を与える give legal protection (to sb) / 保護観察《法》probation / 保護関税 a protective tariff /〈動植物の〉保護区(域) a (bird) sanctuary; a reserve (for wild animals); a (nature) preserve / 保護検束する arrest sb for *his* own protection; hold sb in protective custody / 保護国[領] a protectorate / 保護者 a protector; a guardian / 国際保護鳥 an internationally protected bird / 保護帽 a safety helmet; a hard hat ⇒ほごしょく. 文例 ⇩

ほご³ 補語《文法》a complement ¶主格[目的格]補語 a subjective [an objective] complement.

ほこう¹ 歩行 walking; a walk ¶歩行する walk; go on foot / 歩行が困難である find it hard to walk; have [find] difficulty in walking / 歩行者 a walker;〈徒歩通行者〉a pedestrian; a foot passenger / 歩行者専用の交通信号 pedestrian lights / 歩行者天国 a pedestrians' "paradise"; an area of streets temporarily closed to vehicular traffic; an area of streets turned into a pedestrian precinct on special days /〈リハビリテーションなどの〉歩行練習 walking exercises. 文例 ⇩

ほこう² 補講 a supplementary lesson [lecture].

ほこう¹ 母校 the school [university] *one* graduated from;《文》*one's* alma mater.

ほこう² 母港 a home port.

ほこく 母国 *one's* (home [mother]) country; *one's* homeland ¶母国語 *one's* mother tongue /〈外国語を〉母国語のように使う speak (a foreign language) like a native (speaker).

ほこさき 矛先 the head of a halberd [spear];〈議論の〉the force of an argument ¶非難攻撃の矛先が鈍る〈事が主語〉blunt [take the edge off] *one's* denunciation / 攻撃の矛先を…に向ける turn *one's* fire on ….

ほごしょく 保護色 a protective [camouflaging] color; protective coloration [coloring] ¶保護色になっている be protectively colored.

ボゴタ Bogotá.

ほごぼうえき 保護貿易 protective [protected] trade ¶保護貿易主義 protectionism.

ほこぼこ ¶ぼこぼこ音がする make a hollow sound / ぼこぼこ穴のあいた道路 a road full of holes [potholes].

ほこら 祠 a (small) shrine.

ほこらしい 誇らしい proud ¶誇らしげに triumphantly; proudly; with a triumphant [proud] look.

ほこり¹ 埃 ¶ほこりをかぶる gather [accumulate] dust; be covered with dust / ほこりを立てる raise [stir up] a dust / ほこりを払う brush dust off [away]; dust (*one's* coat) / ほこりだらけの covered with dust; dusty. 文例 ⇩

ほこり² 誇り pride ¶誇りを傷つける hurt [wound] sb's pride / 誇りに満ちた prideful / 誇りとする ⇒ほこる. 文例 ⇩

ほこる 誇る boast (of, about); be proud (of); take pride (in); pride *oneself* (on).

ほころび 綻び ¶ほころびを縫う mend an open [a torn] seam; sew up a rip.

ほころびる 綻びる〈縫い目が〉a seam runs;〈衣類が〉come open [apart] at the seams;〈花が〉begin to open [bloom]; come out ¶顔をほころばせて with a broad smile on *one's* face; smilingly; beamingly.

ほさ 補佐〈事〉《文》assistance;〈人〉an assist-

yen. | The insurance on this house is 30,000,000 yen.

ほけん² 都市生活者は保健上から言っても、能率増進の上からも、時には山や海に行くがよい。In order to keep [preserve] their health and increase their efficiency, it is advisable for those who live in the city to go to the mountains or the seaside from time to time.

ほご¹ そんな証文はほご同然だ。Such a bond is no more than a scrap of paper [isn't worth the paper it's written on].

ほご² トキはその地方でもめったに見かけられなくなったので、日本政府はトキを厳重に保護することに決めた。Crested ibises became so rare in that region that the Japanese Government decided to place them under careful protection. / 裁判官は母親をその子供の保護者にすることに決めた。The judge decided that the mother should be given custody of her child.

ほこう¹ 石ころでここは歩行が困難だ。These stones make it hard to walk here. / 歩行者優先。Pedestrians have the right of way. / この通りは日曜日には歩行者天国になります。This street will be turned into a pedestrian precinct [will be kept completely free of cars] on Sundays.

ほこり¹ 部屋のすみにはほこりがたまりやすい。Dust is apt to collect in the corners of a room. / 自動車が通るたびにほこりが立つ。Every motorcar raises [lifts] dust as it passes along. / この雨でほこりが収まった。The rain has settled the dust. / その書類は彼の机の上にほこりがたまったまま放っておかれた。The paper lay neglected and gathering [accumulating] dust on his desk. /

ほさき ／ ほじゅう

ant; 〈顧問〉 **an adviser** ¶補佐する《文》**aid**; 《文》**assist**; 〈助言する〉**advise**; **give advice 《to》**／課長補佐 **an assistant section head** ／大統領補佐官 **a Presidential aide.**

ほさき 穂先〈穀物の〉**an ear 《of wheat》**; 〈やりの〉**a spearhead**; **the point of a spear**〈先端〉.

ほさつ 菩薩《仏教》**a bodhisattva.**

ぼさっと ⇨ぼんやり.

ぼさぼさ ¶ぼさぼさ頭の男 **a man with unkempt [disheveled, tousled] hair** ／ぼさぼさ突っ立っている **stand idly**.

ぼさん 墓参 **visiting sb's grave.**

ほし 星 **a star**; 〈斑(だ)点〉**a spot**; 〈馬の〉**a blaze**; 〈碁盤の〉**a star**, **a point**; 〈目の〉**a white speck**; 〈相撲の勝ち星〉**a win**; 〈犯人〉**a culprit** ¶星の stellar ／星の出ている夜 **a starlit [starlight] night** ／星の降るような夜空 **a star-filled night sky** ／星を挙げる **arrest [catch] the culprit** ／星明かりで **in (the) starlight** ／星占い ⇨**せんせい**¹ ／星影さやかな夜 **a clear starlight [starry] night** ／星形の **star-shaped** ／星空 **a starry sky**; **the starry heavens** ／星空の下で野宿する **sleep under the stars** ／星取り表 **a score sheet** ／星回りがいい[悪い] **be lucky [unlucky]**; **be born under a lucky [an unlucky] star.** 文例⇩

ほし- 干し… **dried** ¶干し大根[柿(ガ)] **a dried radish [persimmon].**

ほじ 保持 ¶保持する **keep**; **hold**; 《文》**maintain**; 《文》**preserve** ／記録保持者 **a record holder.** 文例⇩

ぼし 母子 **mother and child** ¶母子家庭 **a 'fatherless family'** ／母子手帳 **a 'mother-and-baby notebook'** (**for medical and welfare records**) ／母子寮 **a home for mothers and children.** 文例⇩

ポジ a (photographic) positive.

ほしい 欲しい **want**; 〈切望する〉《文》**desire** ¶紅茶が欲しい **want (to have) [would like] some tea**; **be dying for a cup of tea** ★ **want (to have)** はこの場合の「欲しい」に最も近く, **would like** は丁寧な言い方で日本語の「いただきたい」に相当し, **be dying for** は欲しくてたまらない気持ちを表わす／来て欲しい **want sb to come** ／欲しい物 **a thing that one wants**; 《文》**a thing desired**; 《文》**the object of one's desire.** 文例⇩

ほしいまま 欲しいまま ¶ほしいままに **at will**; **as one pleases [likes]** ／ほしいままに…する **do as one pleases**; 〈ふける〉**indulge in 《pleasures》** ／権力をほしいままにする **abuse one's authority** ／想像をほしいままにする **give full play [《文》free rein] to one's imagination.**

ほしがる 欲しがる ⇨ほしい. 文例⇩

ほしくさ 干し草 **hay** ¶干し草作り **haymaking.**

ほじくる 〈掘る〉**dig up**; 〈歯などを〉**pick** ¶鼻[歯]をほじくる **pick one's nose [teeth]** ／耳をほじくる **clean one's ears** ／昔の醜聞をほじくり返す **rake up an old scandal.** 文例⇩

ほしじるし 星印 **a star**; **an asterisk (*)** ¶星印をつける **mark sth with a star [an asterisk]**; **star**; **asterisk.**

ほしぶどう 干しぶどう **raisins**; **currants**〈小粒で種のない〉.

ほしもの 干し物 ¶干し物をする **hang the washing [clothes] out to dry** ／干し物を取り込む **take in the clothes hung up to dry.**

ほしゃく 保釈 **bail** ¶(保証金を出して)保釈してもらう **bail sb out (of jail)** ／保釈になる **be released on bail** ／保釈金を積む **go [put in] bail for sb** ／保釈出所中である **be out on bail.**

ほしゅ¹ 保守〈革新に対する〉**conservatism**; 〈機械の〉**maintenance** ¶保守的な **conservative** ／保守的な考えを持った人 **a person with [holding] conservative views** ／保守的に **conservatively** ／保守主義 **conservatism** ／保守主義者 **a conservative** ／保守党 **a conservative party** ／〈イギリスの〉**the Conservative Party** ／保守派[勢力] **the conservatives.**

ほしゅ² 捕手〈野球〉**a catcher.**

ほしゅう¹ 補修 ¶補修する **repair**; **mend** ／補修工事 **repair [maintenance] work 《on a river bank》** ／補修材料 **repairing [mending] materials.**

ほしゅう² 補習 ¶補習科 **a supplementary course** ／補習授業 《**give, receive**》 **supplementary lessons.**

ほじゅう 補充 ¶欠員を補充する **fill (up) a vacancy** ／食糧を補充する **get a fresh supply of food** ／隊員を補充する **get recruits for 《the army》**; **recruit for 《the Ground Self-Defense**

道路はひどくほこりっぽかった. **The road was very dusty.**

ほこり² そうすることはどうしても彼の誇りが許さなかった. **His pride would not allow him to do that.** ／彼は我が校の誇りです. **He is the pride of our school.** ／僕たちはこの美術館を大いに誇りとしています. **We take great pride in [We are very proud of] the art gallery.**

ほし 星が飛んだ[流れた]. **A star shot [streaked] across the sky.** ／星が瞬いていた[出ていた]. **Stars were twinkling [were out].** ／大空には星が一杯輝いていた[空一面の星屑であった]. **The sky was thickly sprinkled [studded, strewn] with stars.**

ほじ 彼らは青年時代の高遠なる理想を飽くまでも保持している. **They hold fast to the lofty ideals of their youth.**

ぼし 母子ともに健全. **Both mother and child are doing fine.**

ほしい 私は名誉などは欲しくない. **I have no desire for [am not interested in] fame.** ／それが欲しかったのだ. **That was just what I wanted.** ／赤ん坊が乳が欲しいと泣いている. **The baby is crying for milk.** ／ぜひ彼を僕の助手に欲しい. **I am anxious to have him for my assistant.** ／もう少し早く来て欲しい. **I want you to come a little earlier.** ／そのことをあなたにわかって欲しいの. **I'd like you to understand that.**

ほしがる 人の物を欲しがってはいけない. **You should not covet what belongs to others.** ／人は手に入らないと知っている物を欲しがるものだ. **We are apt [It is in our nature] to wish for what we know we cannot have.**

ほじくる 有名になると, 過去の事を何やかやとほじくり出されるものだ. **When you are famous, peo-**

Force) / 補充選挙人名簿 a supplementary list of voters.

ほしゅう 募集 ¶募集する 〈兵員などを〉 recruit; 〈志願者などを〉 invite; 〈寄付金などを〉 collect; raise; 〈広告で〉 advertise for / 新会員を募集する recruit new members / 基金を募集する raise funds ((for a project)) / 寄付を募集する collect contributions ((to the relief fund)); invite donations ((to)) / 公債を募集する invite subscriptions to a government loan / 懸賞論文を募集する invite ((the students)) to enter a prize essay contest / 募集に応じる enter ((a contest)); apply ((for admission to a school)); subscribe ((for stocks)); answer an advertisement (広告の) / (株の)募集価格 an offering price / 募集金額 the amount of money to be raised / 募集広告 a want ad / 募集人員 the number ((of students)) to be admitted ((to a school)); the number ((of new members)) to be enrolled in a society).

ほしゅうごう 補集合 〔数〕 a complementary set; a complement.

ほじょ 補助 〈援助〉 〔文〕 assistance; support; 〔文〕 aid; 〈補助金〉 a subsidy; a grant-in-aid (pl. grants-in-aid) ¶補助する 〔文〕 assist; help; 〔文〕 aid; subsidize (補助金を与える) / 生活費を補助する 〔文〕 help sb with his living expenses / 補助の 〔文〕 auxiliary; 〔文〕 supplementary / 補助椅子 〈予備の〉 a spare chair; 〈バスなどの〉 an auxiliary seat; a jump seat / 補助エンジン an auxiliary engine / 補助貨幣 subsidiary coins / 補助機関車 a helper engine / (幾何で)補助線を引く draw an additional line ((to the original diagram)) / (飛行機の)補助翼 an aileron. 文例⇩

ほしょう[1] 歩哨 a sentry ¶歩哨を立てる post a sentry / 歩哨に立つ stand sentry; be on sentry duty; do sentry-go / 歩哨線 a sentry line.

ほしょう[2] 保証 a guarantee; 〔文〕 (a) security; 〔文〕 an assurance ¶保証する guarantee; 〔文〕 warrant; answer for / 品質を保証する guarantee [warrant] the quality ((of an article)) / 5年間保証付きの冷蔵庫 a refrigerator guaranteed for five years; a refrigerator with a five-year guarantee / 保証に立つ, 保証人になる stand surety [guarantee] for sb / 保証人 a guarantor; a surety / 保証金 security ((money)); a deposit / (商品などの)保証書 a warranty (card).

ほしょう[3] 保障 security ⇒ あんぜんほしょう, しゅうだん (集団保障).

ほしょう[4] 補償 compensation; 〔文〕 indemnification ¶補償する make good ((the loss)); compensate sb for ((the damage)); 〔文〕 make compensation [reparation] for ((the loss)) / 〔文〕 indemnify sb for ((the damage)) / …の補償に in compensation for… / 補償金 compensation ((money)); an indemnity.

ほじょう 捕縄 a policeman's rope.

ほじょう 慕情 love ((for one's father)); longing [〔文〕 yearning] ((for one's mother country)).

ほしょく[1] 捕食 ¶捕食する prey on ((birds)) / 捕食動物 a predatory animal; a predator.

ほしょく[2] 補色 〔物〕 a complementary color.

ほしょく 暮色 evening twilight; dusk; the shades of evening.

ほじる ⇒ ほじくる.

ほしん 保身 keeping oneself from harm; self-defense ¶保身術 the art of defending one's own interests. 文例⇩

ほす 干す 〈かわかす〉 dry (off); 〈吊して〉 hang ((clothes)) (out) to dry; 〈風に当てる〉 air; 〈さらい尽す〉 drain off [away]; 〈飲み尽くす〉 drink off [up]; 〈空にする〉 empty ¶ぬれた着物を日に干す dry wet clothes in the sun / 池の水を干す drain [pump (ポンプで)] a pond dry / 盃を干す empty one's cup; drain one's glass (dry) / 干し固める harden sth by drying / 干される 〈食べていけなくなる〉 have one's livelihood taken away; 〈芸能人が〉 be deprived of any chance to appear on television [the stage]. 文例⇩

ボス a boss.

ほすう 歩数 the number of steps taken ¶歩数計 a pedometer.

ポスター a poster; a placard; a bill ¶ポスターを張る put up a poster; stick a bill on ((the fence)); 〈ぺたぺたと〉 cover ((a board)) with posters; placard ((a wall)) / ポスターカラー a poster color.

ホステス a hostess.

ポスト[1] 〈郵便の〉 〔米〕 a mailbox; 〔英〕 a postbox; 〈円柱形の〉 〔英〕 a pillar-box ¶ポストに入れる 〔米〕 mail ((a letter)); 〔英〕 post (a letter).

ポスト[2] 〈地位・職〉 a position; a post.

ボストンバッグ a traveling [an overnight] bag.

ほする 補する appoint sb to ((a post)).

ほせい 補正 revise; correct; 〔物〕 compensate for / 補正振り子 a compensation pendulum / 補正予算 a revised [supplementary] budget.

ぼせい 母性 motherhood; 〔文〕 maternity ¶母性愛 (a) mothers' love; 〔文〕 maternal affection / 母性本能 maternal instinct(s). 文例⇩

---

ple dig up all the facts on your past life.

ほしゅう 今の所は新会員を募集する計画はありません。 We are not planning at present to recruit new members for our club. / 店員募集。 〔広告〕 Clerks wanted. / 生徒募集。 〔広告〕 New students invited.

ほじょ その実業家は多数の学生に学費を補助した。 The businessman helped many students with their school expenses. / 授業料の値上げを抑えるためには政府の補助金が必要だ。 We need a subsidy from the Government to avoid raising the school fees.

ほしょう[2] 彼が成功するという保証はない。 There is no guarantee that he will succeed. / 彼の正直なことは私が保証する。 I'll answer for his honesty. / 私に力を添えることを彼は保証した。 He assured me of his support.

ほしょく 暮色蒼然としてきた。 Dusk is fast gathering. | The shades of evening are closing in.

ほしん 彼がそのような行動をとったのは全く保身のために外ならなかった。 He acted that way only

ほぜいそうこ 保税倉庫 a bonded warehouse.

ほせん 保線〘鉄道〙track maintenance ¶ 保線区 a (railroad) section / 保線工事 maintenance work / 保線作業員《米》a trackman ;《英》a platelayer.

ほぜん 保全《文》preservation ;《文》maintenance ¶ 保全する maintain [safeguard] the integrity《of》; preserve《the environment》; keep《the environment》intact [in good condition] / 領土の保全を図る strive for the maintenance of the territorial integrity《of》.

ぼせん 母船 a mother ship [vessel].

ぼぜん 墓前 ¶ 墓前に[で] in front of a tomb [grave] / 墓前に花輪を捧げる lay [place] a wreath on *sb's* grave [tomb].

ほぞ 〘建〙a tenon ; a pivot ¶ 決心のほぞを固める make up *one's* mind《to *do*, to *sth*》;《文》make a firm resolve《to *do*》/ ほぞをかむ《文》repent *sth* bitterly ; regret bitterly.

ほぞあな ほぞ穴〘建〙a mortise (hole) ; a mortice.

ほそい 細い thin ; fine ; slim ;《文》slender ; 〈狭い〉narrow ; 〈小さい〉small ¶ 細い糸[線] a fine thread [line] / 細い腕[首] a slender arm [neck] / 細い声 a thin voice / 細いズボン slender-legged trousers / 食が細い be a light [small] eater / 細くする thin ; make *sth* thin [slender] / 細くなる get [《文》become] thin [fine] ; thin / 先が段々細くなる taper off (to a point) / 鉛筆を細く削る sharpen a pencil (to a fine point) / 細く長く暮らす live a long, frugal life.

ほそう 舗装 pavement ¶ 舗装する pave [surface,《英》metal (割石で)]《a road》/ 立派に舗装された道 a well-paved road / 舗装したばかりの道 a new-paved road / 舗装のしてない道 an unpaved [《英》unmetalled] road ; a dirt road / 簡易舗装をする surface《a road》with asphalt [《米》blacktop]; asphalt [《米》blacktop]《a road》/ 舗装道路 a paved [surfaced] street [road]. [文例⇩]

ほそうで 細腕 a slim [《文》slender] arm. [文例⇩]

ほそおもて 細面 a narrow [long] face.

ほそがき 細書き ¶ 細書きの筆 a fine writing brush / 細書きの万年筆 a fine-pointed fountain pen.

ほそく[1] 歩測 ¶ 歩測する pace out《the distance》; measure《the distance》in paces.

ほそく[2] 捕捉 ⇨ **とらえる**.

ほそく[3] 補足 ¶ 補足する《文》supplement ; make good《a deficiency》/ 補足説明 a supplementary explanation.

ほそじま 細縞 ¶ 細じまの pin-stripe(d)《fabric》.

ぼそっと ⇨ **ぼんやり**.

ほそながい 細長い long and narrow [thin] ;《文》slender ¶ 細長い布切れ a long strip of cloth.

ほそびき 細引き a《hempen》cord.

ほそぼそ 細々 ¶ 細々と暮らす make a meager living ; earn [《文》eke out] a scanty living [livelihood].

ぼそぼそ ¶ ぼそぼそ話す talk in a subdued voice ; speak slowly in undertones.

ほそみち 細道 a narrow lane [path].

ほそめ 細目 ¶ 細目を開けて ⇨ **ほそめる**(目を細めて) / 戸を細めに開ける open a door just a little [a crack] / 細めに切る cut *sth* into narrow strips.

ほそめる 細める narrow《*one's* eyes》; make *sth* narrower ¶ 目を細めて with *one's* eyes half-closed [slightly open].

ほそる 細る 〈細くなる〉get [《文》become] thin [thinner,《文》more slender] ; thin ; 〈減じる〉dwindle (away) ¶ 食が細る lose *one's* appetite.

ほぞん 保存《文》preservation ¶ 保存する preserve ; keep *sth* from destruction [《文》deterioration] / 保存がいい be well preserved ; be in a good state of preservation / 保存がきく keep (well) / 保存食 keepable foods.

ポタージュ potage.

ぼたい 母体 the mother's body. [文例⇩]

ぼだい 菩提 ¶ ぼだいを弔う pray for the repose of *sb's* soul / ぼだい所[寺] *one's* family temple / ぼだい樹 〈インドの〉a bo tree ; a pipal ; a peepul ; 〈ヨーロッパの〉a linden [lime] tree.

ほだされる 絆される ¶ 親切にほだされる be moved by *sb's* kindness.

ほたてがい 帆立て貝 a scallop.

ぼたぼた ⇨ **ぽたぽた**.

ぽたぽた ¶ ぽたぽた垂れる[落ちる] fall in drops ; drip (down) ; trickle (down). [文例⇩]

ぼたもち 牡丹餅 a rice dumpling covered with bean jam ¶ たなからぼたもち ⇨ **たなぼた**.

ぼたやま ぼた山 a spoil [slag] heap ; a heap of coal waste.

ぽたり ¶ ぽたりと落ちる drop ; plop / ぽたりぽたりと落ちる drip ; fall drop by drop.

ほたる 螢 a firefly ;《米》a lightning bug ¶ 螢の光 the glow (glimmer) of a firefly ; 〈曲名〉*Auld Lang Syne* / 螢狩りに行く go out to catch fireflies ; go hunting for fireflies / 螢石 fluorspar ;《米》fluorite.

---

because he did not want to lose his position [solely for the purpose of defending his own interests].

ほす たくさんの毛布がひなたに干してある. A lot of blankets are drying in the sun. / 杯を干したまえ. Drain your glass (dry)! | Bottoms up!

ぼせい 泣き叫ぶ子供の姿を見て彼女の母性愛が目覚めた. The mother in her was awakened by the sight of the crying child.

ほそう ここで道は左に折れて舗装が切れる. Here the road turns to the left and stops being paved [becomes a dirt track].

ほそうで 女の細腕で一家を支えている. Woman as she is, she is the prop and stay of her family.

ぼたい 胎児を取り出さないと母体が危ない. If the fetus is not extracted, the mother's life is in danger. / 本委員会は各学部教授会を母体として選出された委員によって構成される. This committee is made up of members who are elected from [out of] the professoriate of each department.

ぽたぽた 天井から水がぽたぽた垂

ぼたん 〖植〗 a (tree) peony ¶ぼたん園 a peony garden / ぼたん雪 large flakes of snow. 文例⇩

ボタン a button ¶3つボタンの上着 a three-button jacket / ボタンを掛ける do up a button; button (up) ⟨a coat⟩ / ボタンを外す undo the buttons; unbutton ⟨a coat⟩ / (ベルの)ボタンを押す press [push] the button / ボタン穴 a buttonhole. 文例⇩

ぼち 墓地 a graveyard; a (public) cemetery 〈共同の〉 ¶青山墓地 the Aoyama cemetery.

ホチキス a stapler; a stapling machine.

ぼちぼち ⇨ そろそろ.

ぼちゃぼちゃ ⇨ ぽちゃぽちゃ.

ぼちゃぼちゃ ¶ぼちゃぼちゃした plump ⟨women⟩; chubby ⟨cheeks⟩.

ぼちゃん with a splash ¶ぼちゃんと大きな音をさせる make a great splash / ぼちゃんと飛び込む splash into the water.

ほちょうあみ 捕虫網 a butterfly net.

ほちょう 歩調 (a) pace; (a) step ¶共産圏内の歩調の乱れ《文》disharmony [disarray, lack of unity] in the Communist bloc / 歩調を合わせる〈足取りを〉 fall [get] into step ⟨with⟩; keep step ⟨with⟩; match [adjust] one's stride (to that of one's child); 〈仕事などの早さを〉 keep pace ⟨with⟩; 〈協力する〉 act in concert ⟨with⟩ / 歩調を取って[取らずに]行進する march in [out of] step / 歩調を早める[緩める] quicken [slacken] one's pace / 歩調を乱す break step; walk [get] out of step.

ほちょうき 補聴器 (wear) a hearing aid.

ぼつ 没 ⇨ ぼっしょ.

ぼっか 牧歌 a pastoral (song); an idyl(l) ¶牧歌的風景 a pastoral [an idyllic] scene.

ぼつが 没我 《文》self-effacement; 《文》selflessness ¶没我的 《文》selfless; 《文》disinterested.

ほっかい 北海 〈北の海〉 a northern sea; 〈英国東方の〉 the North Sea.

ぽっかり ¶ぽっかりあいた大きな穴 a large gaping hole / 空にぽっかり浮かんでいる白い雲 a white cloud floating in the sky.

ほっき 発起 (a) proposal; (a) suggestion; 《文》promotion ¶発起する〈提案する〉propose; suggest; 〈会社の設立を〉promote ⟨a new trading firm⟩ / 一念発起する 〖ほっしん〗 /...の発起で at the suggestion [proposal, 《文》instance] of... / 発起人〈会社の〉 a promotor; 〈計画などの〉 a proposer. 文例⇩

ぼっき 勃起 (an) erection ¶ぼっきする〈器官が主語〉become erect; 〈人が主語〉have an erection.

ぼっきゃく 没却 ¶没却する〈無視する〉ignore; 〈忘れる〉forget; 〈見失う〉lose sight of / 自己を没却する 《文》efface oneself.

ほっきょく 北極 the North Pole ¶地理学上の北極 the geographical North Pole / 北極海 the Arctic Ocean / 北極熊 a polar bear / 北極圏[帯] the Arctic Circle [Zone] / 北極光 the northern lights; the aurora borealis 《pl. aurorae boreales》 / 北極星 the pole star; the North Star / 北極探険隊 an Arctic expedition (team) / 北極地方 the Arctic region.

ぽっきり ¶千円ぽっきり just [neither more nor less than] a thousand yen / ぽっきり折れる break with a snap; snap.

ほっく 発句 〈連歌の〉 the first line 《of a *renga*》; 〈俳句〉 a *hokku*; a *haiku*.

ホック a hook (fastener); 〈丸型の〉《米》a snap fastener; 《英》a press stud ¶ホックを外す unhook ⟨a dress⟩ / ホックで留める hook up ⟨a dress⟩ / ホックと熊の金 a hook and eye.

ボックス 〈観覧席〉 a box; 〈レストランなどの〉 a booth; 〈野球の〉 the (batter's) box; 〈革〉box calf.

ぼっくり[1] 〈下駄の一種〉 lacquered clogs (for little girls).

ぽっくり[2] 〈突然に〉 suddenly; unexpectedly ¶ぽっくり死ぬ die suddenly [a sudden death]; 《俗》pop off / ぽっくり病で死ぬ die suddenly from a mysterious [an unexplained] illness.

ホッケー 〈陸上ホッケー〉《米》field hockey; 《英》hockey; ⇨ アイス (アイスホッケー) ★単に hockey といえば《米》では「アイスホッケー」をさす ¶ホッケーのボール a hockey ball / ホッケーをする play (field) hockey / ホッケー用のクラブ a hockey stick / ホッケー選手 a hockey player.

ぼっけん 木剣 a wooden sword.

ぼっこう 勃興 a (sudden) rise ¶勃興する rise (suddenly) into power; make a sudden rise.

ぼっこうしょう 没交渉 ¶没交渉である have nothing to do ⟨with⟩; 《文》have no relation ⟨with⟩.

ぼっこん 墨痕 ¶墨痕鮮やかに 《written》 in bold, beautiful strokes.

ほっさ 発作 a fit; a spasm; an attack 《of angina》 ¶発作を起こす have a fit [spasm] / 発作的な 《文》spasmodic / 発作的に 《文》spasmodically.

ぼっしゅう 没収 confiscation; 《文》forfeiture ¶没収する confiscate / 没収される be confiscated; 〈人が主語〉《文》forfeit ⟨one's estate⟩ / 没収試合 a forfeited game.

れていた. Water was dripping (down) from the ceiling. | The ceiling was dripping water.

ぼたん ぼたん雪が降っている. The snow is coming down in large flakes.

ボタン オーバーの一番上のボタンが取れた[取れかかっていた]. The top button of my overcoat came off [was loose]. / そのボタンを押すと機械は動き出す. The machine works at the push of the button. | Press the button, and the machine will start working.

ほちょう 歩調取れ.《号令》March in step. / 僕に関する限りは彼と歩調を合わせて行きたいと思っている. As far as I am concerned, I will keep [march in] step with him.

ほっき この計画の発起人はだれですか. Who proposed this plan?

ほっする 己の欲せざる所を人に施すことなかれ. Do not do unto others as you would not have them do unto you. | Do as you would be done by. 《諺》

ぼっする ぬかるみがひざを没した. The mud was more than knee-deep.

ぽっしょ 没書 rejection ¶没書になる be rejected / 没書原稿 rejected [unaccepted] manuscripts.

ほっしん 発心 ¶発心する《信仰に入る》《文》decide to embrace a religion; 《決心する》make up one's mind (to sth, to do).

ほっす 払子 a priest's horsehair flapper.

ほっする 欲する want《sth, to do》; 《文》wish (for sth, to do); 《文》desire. 文例⇩

ぼっする 没する 《沈む》sink; go down; 《見えなくなる》disappear; vanish 水中に没する sink under the water / 《文》be submerged / 人込みに姿を没する be lost in the crowd / 闇の中に姿を没する vanish into the darkness. 文例⇩

ほっそく 発足《文》inauguration ¶発足する《文》be inaugurated; start.

ほっそり ¶ほっそりした slim; slimly-built; slender; slight / ほっそりした女 a slim [slender] girl; a woman with a slender [slight] figure.

ほったてごや 掘っ建[立]て小屋 a hut; a shanty; a shack.

ポツダム ¶ポツダム宣言 the Potsdam Declaration.

ほったらかす ⇨ほうっておく.

ほったん 発端《起こり》the origin; 《最初》the beginning; 《文》the outset ¶発端から話す tell (a story) from the (very) beginning. 文例⇩

ぼっちゃん 坊っちゃん《敬称》your [his, her] son; young master 《主人の子に》; 《呼び掛け》Master (Taro); 《男の子》a boy; a son; 《世間知らず》a greenhorn ¶坊っちゃん育ちである be brought up like a tender plant. 文例⇩

ほっちり a little; a bit.

ほっつきあるく ほっつき歩く wander about; loiter; 《米口語》bum around.

ぼってり ¶ぼってりした thick (sweaters); fat (women); fleshy (cheeks).

ぽってり ¶ぽってりした plump; chubby.

ほっと ¶ほっとする feel relieved; heave [give] a sigh of relief / 大いにほっとした には much to one's relief; to one's great relief / ほっとしいて with relief. 文例⇩

ホット ¶ホットコーナー《野球》the hot corner / ホットジャズ hot jazz / ホットドッグ a hot dog / ホットニュース hot news / ホットパンツ hot pants / ホットライン《国際政治》a hot line.

ぽっと ¶ぽっと燃え上がる burst into flame(s); flare up (into flames).

ぽっと ¶ぽっと顔を赤らめる be slightly flushed; blush; color up; turn crimson / ぽっと出の若者 a youngster fresh from the country. 文例⇩

ぼっとう 没頭 ¶没頭する be absorbed [engrossed] (in); immerse oneself (in); devote oneself (to); give oneself up entirely (to).

ホットケーキ a hot cake; a pancake; a griddlecake.

ほづな 帆綱 a rope (used to raise or lower a sail); a halyard; 《総称》cordage.

ぼつにゅう 没入 ¶没入する《沈む》go under (the water); 《没頭する》be absorbed [immersed] (in).

ぼつねん《寂しく》lonely; 《一人で》alone ¶一人ぼつねんと座っている sit all alone 《in a room》/ 一人ぼつねんと食卓に着く sit down to dinner all by oneself.

ぼっぱつ 勃発 an outbreak; (a) sudden occurrence ¶勃発する break out; occur suddenly.

ホップ《植》a hop (plant); 《ビールの苦味にする乾燥した雌花》hops ¶ホップを摘む gather [pick] hops / ホップ乾燥場 an oast; an oasthouse / ホップ畑 a hopfield.

ポップアート《美術》pop art.

ポップコーン popcorn.

ポップス《音楽》pop (music) ¶ポップスを歌うグループ[歌手] a pop group [singer].

ほっぺた ⇨ほお ほっぺたが落ちるほどうまい be very, very delicious; be fit for a king; 《口語》be scrumptious; 《俗》be yummy.

ほっぽう 北方 the north(ward) ¶北方の northern; north(ward) / 北方に to [in the direction of] the north (of) / 北方へ northward; north; toward the north / 市の北方10キロの所に 10 kilometers (to the) north of the city / 北方領土 the northern territories.

ぽつぽつ[1]《斑点》spots; dots; 《吹き出物》pimples; spots; eruptions.

ぽつぽつ[2]《徐々に》little by little; by (slow) degrees; gradually; in trickles (少しずつ); 《やがて》by and by; 《雨などが》in (small) drops; 《散在して》here and there. 文例⇩

ぼつぼつ ⇨ぽつぽつ[2]. 文例⇩

ぽっぽと《音》puff, puff; chug-chug ¶《機関車が》ぽっぽと煙を吐いて走る puff (along, away) / ぽっぽと湯気の立つ料理 a steaming dish.

ぼつらく 没落《破滅》ruin; 《文》a fall; a downfall; 《破産》bankruptcy ¶没落する fall; be ruined; go to ruin [the dogs]; go under; 《破産する》go [《文》become] bankrupt. 文例⇩

ほったん 遺伝子工学は新しい生命科学時代の発端となるであろう. Genetic engineering will probably mark the threshold of a new era of life science.

ぼっちゃん 赤ちゃんは坊ちゃんですか. Is your baby a boy? / まるでお坊ちゃんだ. He knows nothing of the world.

ほっと それを聞いてほっと安心した. I felt relieved to hear that.

ほっと ほおがぽっと赤くなった. The color rose in her cheeks.

ぽつぽつ[2] 聴衆がぽつぽつ集まって来た. People began to come in in twos and threes. / 桜がぽつぽつ咲き出した. Cherry blossoms have begun to come out here and there. / さあぽつぽつ帰ろう. Let's be going home now.

ぼつぼつ 昼頃からぼつぼつ降り出した. It began to rain a little about noon. / その頃この辺は人家がぽつぽつあるだけだった. In those days there were just a few houses here and there in these parts.

ぽっぽと 汽車はぽっぽと煙を吐きながらゆっくり駅を出て行った. The train puffed slowly out of the station.

ぼつらく 平家没落の原因は何か. What caused the fall of the Taira

ぽつりと [文例⇩]
ぽつりぽつり ⇨ ぽつりぽつり.
ぽつりぽつり ⇨ ぽつぽつ ¶ぽつりぽつり話す〈少しずつ〉tell《a story》bit by bit ;〈休み休み〉talk with frequent pauses.
ほつれ 解れ ¶糸のほつれ loose threads / 袖口のほつれをつくろう mend a frayed cuff / ほつれ毛をかき上げる comb back *one's* stray [loose] hair [《文》locks].
ほつれる 解れる〈髪や糸などが〉get [《文》become] loose ;〈すり切れる〉get [《文》become] frayed.
ボツワナ (the Republic of) Botswana.
ぽつんと ⇨ ぽつねんと. [文例⇩]
ほていばら 布袋腹 ⇨ たいこ² (太鼓腹).
ボディービル body building ¶ボディービル用具 apparatus [equipment] for body building.
ぼてっとした podgy ; pudgy.
ポテト ⇨ じゃがいも ¶ポテトチップ (potato) chips [《英》crisps].
ほてり 火照り a burning sensation ; a glow ★ glow は複数形にはしない.
ほてる 火照る feel hot [warm] ; burn ; flush ; be all aglow. [文例⇩]
ホテル a hotel ¶ホテルの経営者 [支配人] the proprietor [manager] of a hotel ; a hotelkeeper ; a hotelier / ホテルに泊まる stay [put up, take a room] at a hotel / ホテル住まいをする live [make *one's* home] in a hotel.
ほてん 補塡 ¶補塡する fill《a deficit》; make good《a loss》; supply《a deficiency》.
ほど 程〈限度〉a limit ; limits ;《文》bounds ;〈程度〉an extent ; a degree ;〈適度〉《文》moderation ;〈およそ〉about ;〈いよいよ, ますます〉the more [less]...the more [less]... ;〈...のように〉like ; as ; as...as... ;〈否定〉not as [so]...as... ; less...than... ¶どれ程 how much [far, long] ;《文》to what extent [degree] ⇨ どんな (どんなに), どの² (どのくらい) / 1 週間程 about a week ⇨ やく⁶ / 程よい〈結構な〉good ; fair ;〈ぴったりの〉proper ;〈適度の〉moderate ;《文》temperate / 程よい時分に at the right time / 程よく〈結構に〉well ;〈ちゃんと〉properly ; to just the right extent ;〈適度に〉moderately ; in moderation / 程よく焼け[煮え]ている be done to a turn / 程遠い be a long way from《what is needed》; fall far short《of the mark》/ 程遠からぬ所に near [close] by ; not far《from》/ 程なく soon (afterward) ; presently ; shortly (after) ; before long / 程経て after a little while ; later on. [文例⇩]
ほどう¹ 歩道《米》a sidewalk ;《英》a pavement ¶歩道橋 a footbridge ; a bridge for pedestrians.
ほどう² 補導 ¶補導する〈説諭する〉guide《a misbehaving juvenile》; put [set]《a young offender》on the right path ;〈捕える〉arrest《a juvenile delinquent》; take《a high school student》into custody / 少年補導係の警官 a juvenile officer.
ほどく 解く undo ; untie ; unfasten ;《文》unbind ; unlace (ひもを) ;〈ほぐす〉unravel ; undo ¶結び目をほどく undo a knot ; unknot / 靴のひもをほどく unlace *one's* shoes / 包みをほどく untie a bundle ; undo a package / 着物をほどく take a *kimono* apart ; undo [unsew] a dress / 縫い目をほどく undo [unpick] a seam.
ほとけ 仏〈仏陀(ぶっだ)〉(the) Buddha ;〈仏像〉a Buddhist image ;〈故人〉《文》the deceased ; the departed soul ¶仏のような人 a saint of a man / 仏心 a merciful heart ; mercy ; charity. [文例⇩]
ほどける 解ける come [get] loose ; come [get] untied [undone] ;〈縫い目が〉come apart ;〈靴ひもが〉come undone [loose] ; get unlaced (靴が主語).
ほどこし 施し〈事〉giving money [goods] to the poor as charity ;〈物〉《文》alms ; charity ;《口語》a handout ¶施しを請う《文》beg alms ; ask [beg] *sb* for《money》/ 施しをする give *sb*《food》as charity.
ほどこす 施す〈恵む〉give《money, things》as charity ¶慈善を施す practice charity / 恩恵

---

family? | What was the cause of the ruin of the Taira clan?
ぽつりと ぽつりと大粒の雨が当たった. A big drop of rain fell on me. / ぽつりと星が 1 つ西の空に残っていた. A solitary star could be seen lingering in the western sky.
ぽつんと 原っぱの真ん中に小さな家がぽつんと立っている. In the middle of the field there stands a solitary cottage. / 彼はぽつんと「うん」と答えた. He only [simply] answered, 'Yeah.'
ほてる 耳がほてった. My ears burned. / 彼女の顔は熱でほてっていた. Her face was flushed with fever. / 湯上がりで体中がほてっていた. My body was all in a glow after my bath.
ほど 物には程がある. There is a limit to everything. / 世間を知らないにも程がある. How little you know the world! / 冗談にも程がある. You are taking [Don't take] your joke too far. / 真偽の程は確かでない. I don't know for certain whether it is true (or not). / 彼には財産という程のものはない. He has no property to speak of. / 彼は父親程の名将ではなかった. He was not quite the general his father had been. / 泣きたい程困った. I was so upset that I felt like crying. / 死ぬ程疲れた. I was tired out. / 口では言えない程美しい. It is too beautiful for words. / 彼は使い切れない程金がある. He has more money than he can spend. / お年程には見えませんね. You don't look your age. / 僕は彼程背が高くない. I am not as [so] tall as him. ⇨ より² [用法] / わが家程よい所はない. There's no place like home. / フランクリン程の人物がこんなことを言っている. No less a personage than Benjamin Franklin said this. / 晴れた春の日に散歩する程愉快なことはない. Nothing is pleasanter than to take a walk on a fine spring day. / 延ばせば延ばす程するのがいやになる. The longer you put it off, the less inclined you'll be to do it. / 現代科学はまだ生命とは何かの真の理解には程遠い. Present-day science is still a long way from a real understanding of what life is. / 彼は英雄というには程遠い. He is anything but a hero. / さらに北に向かって進むとそこから程遠からぬ所にお寺があります. Go on walking north, and you'll find a temple not far from there. / 程なく彼が現われた. It was not long before he appeared. | Presently he made his appearance.
ほとけ またやったと言うのか. 仏

[策, 肥料, 面目]を施す ⇨ おんけい, さく³, ひりょう, めんぼく.
ほととぎす 〘鳥〙a little cuckoo.
ほとばしる gush [spout] (out [〘文〙forth]) (from); spurt (from). 文例⇩
ほとほと 〈本当に〉really;〈全く〉quite; utterly ¶ほとほと閉口する be quite at a loss.
文例⇩
ほどほど 程々 ほど(程よい, 程よく). 文例⇩
ほとぼと ⇨ ぼたぼた.
ほとぼと ⇨ ぼたぼた.
ほとぼり remaining heat [warmth] ¶ほとぼりがさめるまで《口語》until the heat is off; until the excitement cools [dies] down; until the storm [trouble] subsides [blows over].
ほとり 辺り ¶…のほとりに[の] in the neighborhood (vicinity) of...; close by...; near...; by.../ 川のほとりの家 a house by [on] a river ★ by a river は単に川の近くを表わすのに対して on a river は「川のふちにある」「川に面した」の意を強調している.
ほとん ¶ほとんと音を立てて with a plop.
ほとんど 殆ど〈もう少しで〉almost; (pretty) nearly; all but;〈事実上〉practically;〈およそ〉about; some; around;〈否定〉little; hardly; scarcely; almost never ¶ほとんど全部 almost all / ほとんど3千 nearly [a little less than] three thousand. 文例⇩
ほなみ 穂波 rice [barley, wheat] plants waving in the wind.
ポニーテール a ponytail.
ほにゅう 哺乳 ¶哺乳する suckle; nurse / 哺乳動物 a mammal / 哺乳瓶 a feeding [《米》nursing, baby's] bottle / 哺乳類 the mammals.
ほにゅう 母乳 mother's milk ¶母乳で育てる breast-feed (a baby); rear (a baby) at the breast / 母乳で育てた子 a breast-fed child.
ほぬの 帆布 sailcloth; canvas.
ほね 骨〈人などの〉a bone;〈障子などの〉a frame;〈傘の〉a rib;〈扇の〉a stick ¶骨が折れる〈事が主語〉be a hard job [〘文〙task];〈人が主語〉find it hard (to do);《文》have difficulty (in) 《doing》; have a lot [a great deal] of trouble ((in) doing) / 骨がない have no [《文》lack] (moral) backbone;《文》be a poor-spirited man / 骨の多い bony / 骨のある男《文》a man of spirit [mettle] / 骨の折れる仕事 a heavy [hard,《文》laborious, backbreaking] job [〘文〙task]; an uphill task / 骨の折れない仕事 easy easy task; a soft job / 骨の髄まで to the marrow (of one's bones) / 骨を接ぐ set a broken bone / 骨を抜く bone (a fish) / 骨を折る〈骨折する〉break one's (arm, leg);〈努力する〉take (great) pains ((to do, in doing); make an effort ((to do));《文》exert oneself ((to do)); go to (great [considerable]) length(s) ((to do));〈尽力する〉take (considerable) trouble ((to do)); put oneself out (to do, doing);《文》render services ((to)); do sb a service ★ほねおり ⇩ / (人に)骨を折らせる put sb to trouble; trouble sb / 骨を折って with (much) effort; with difficulty / 骨を折らずに without any trouble; without effort; easily / 骨を惜しむ spare oneself the trouble of doing / 骨を惜しまない spare no pains ((to do)); take endless pains ((to do)) / 骨を拾う〈遺骨を〉gather sb's ashes /〈比喩的に〉look after sb's affairs when he is dead; take sb's unfinished business on oneself when he collapses /（やせて）骨と皮ばかりになる waste away [to be all] skin and bone(s); be reduced to a (mere) skeleton; be worn to a shadow / 骨ごと食べる eat (a fish) bone(s) and all / 骨までしゃぶる〈働かせる〉work [sweat] sb very hard [to death];〈金をしぼり取る〉squeeze all the money out of sb; bleed sb white. 文例⇩
ほねおしみ 骨惜しみ ⇨ほね(骨を惜しむ, 骨を惜しまない).
ほねおり 骨折り《文》pains; trouble; labor; (an) effort;〈尽力〉《文》good offices; a service (★ service は複数形で使うことが多い) / 骨折り損 lost labor; a waste of labor / 骨折り賃《文》a recompense for one's services [labor]. 文例⇩

の顔も三度と言うぜ. You've done it again! You've tried my patience too far [《文》you've gone too far even for me] this time! / そこで止めては仏造って魂入れずじゃないか. Don't stop now! You ought to put [give] the finishing touch to it.
ほとばしる 破裂した水道管から水がほとばしり出ていた. Water was spurting [gushing out] from the broken pipe.
ほとほと 彼には[彼の振る舞いには]ほとほと愛想が尽きた. I am disgusted with him [at his behavior]. / 彼の長広舌にはほとほと閉口した. His harangue bored me to death [distraction].
ほどほど 何事も程々にしなさい. Do nothing to excess. / Do everything in moderation. / 運動も程々にしないと毒になる. Too much exercise will do you more harm than good.
ほとんど ほとんど全員がその案には反対だった. Almost all the members were [every member was] against the plan. / 建築はほとんど完成した. The building is nearly [almost, all but] finished. / それはほとんど疑いがない. There is hardly any [very little] doubt about it. / この問題を解くことはほとんど不可能だ. It is next to [well-nigh] impossible for me to solve this problem. / 時間はほとんどない. We have scarcely any time. / 東京の町を歩いてパトカーのサイレンを聞かない日はほとんどない. Hardly a day passes that we do not hear the siren of a police car in the streets of Tokyo.
ほね さてこれからが骨だ. Now, we have come to the hardest part (of the task). / まさに骨と皮ばかりにやせている. He's all skin and bone(s). / その坂を登るのはなかなか骨だった. It was hard work going [getting] up the hill. / この本を読んでみたがかなり骨が折れた. This book proved pretty hard going. / 私は子供の教育に非常に骨を折った. I took great pains in educating my children. / あの男のためにいろいろ骨を折った. I put myself to a good deal of trouble on his account. / 彼らは信頼できるネパール語辞典を作ろうとしてたいへんな骨を折った. They went to extraordinary lengths to produce a reliable Nepali dictionary.
ほねおり 一つお骨折りを願いたい. Please do me a favor. / 骨折りがいがあった. It was worth the trouble (I took). /《文》My pains have been amply rewarded. / 骨折り損のくたびれもうけだった.

ほねぐみ 骨組み 〈身体の〉 the bony framework (of the body); physique; build; 〈構造〉 framework; structure; 〈大要〉 an outline ¶〈身体の〉骨組みのしっかりした人 a strongly-built man; a man of stout build.

ほねつぎ 骨接ぎ 〈術〉 bonesetting; 〈人〉 a bonesetter.

ほねっぷし 骨っ節 〈気骨〉 ⇨ きがい².

ほねっぽい 骨っぽい 〈骨の多い〉 bony; 〈気骨のある〉 (a man) of spirit; 《文》 mettlesome; 〈手ごわい〉 hard to deal with; tough.

ほねなし 骨無し ¶骨なしの 〈骨のない〉 boneless; 〈意気地のない〉 spineless; 《文》 poor-spirited.

ほねぬき 骨抜き 〈魚などの〉 boning; deboning ¶〈議案などを〉骨抜きにする mutilate; [《文》emasculate] (a bill); add crippling amendments to (a bill).

ほねばった 骨張った bony; angular; raw-boned.

ほねぶと 骨太 ¶骨太の large-[big-, strong-] boned; stoutly-built.

ほねぼそ 骨細 ¶骨細の small-[fine-]boned; 〈きゃしゃな〉《文》(a girl) of slender [slight] build.

ほねみ 骨身 ¶骨身を惜しまない ⇨ ほね (骨を惜しまない) / 骨身にこたえる 〈寒さが〉 be chilled to the bone [marrow]; 〈訓戒などが〉 sting [touch] one to the quick.

ほねやすめ 骨休め (a) relaxation; (a) recreation ¶骨休めをする take a rest 《after a spell of hard work》; unwind (oneself); 《口語》 knock off 《for three days》.

ほのお 炎 a flame; a blaze ¶炎を上げて燃える flame [blaze] up; burst into flame(s) (ぱっと) / 炎に包まれる be wrapped [enveloped] in flames.

ほのか 仄か ¶ほのかな dim; faint; indistinct / ほのかに dimly; faintly; indistinctly. 文例⇩

ほのぐらい 仄暗い 《文》 dusky; gloomy; dim ¶ほの暗いろうそくの光 the dim [feeble] light of a candle / ほの暗い夜明けに in the gray light of dawn; at the first gray of dawn / ほの暗くなる become near dark.

ほのじろい 仄白い dimly white.

ほのぼのと 仄々と dim; faintly ¶ほのぼのと明けゆく空 the dawning sky. 文例⇩

ほのめかす 仄めかす hint (at sth, that...); give [drop] sb a hint (that...); throw out a hint 《that...》.

ホノルル Honolulu.

ほばしら 帆柱 a mast.

ほはば 歩幅 a step; a pace ¶歩幅が広い walk with long steps.

ほひ 墓碑 a tombstone; a gravestone ¶墓碑銘 an epitaph.

ポピュラー ¶ポピュラーな popular; well-known / ポピュラー音楽 popular [pop] music; pop.

ぼひょう 墓標 the headstone of a grave; a burial marker.

ボブスレー 〈競技〉 bobsledding; 〈そり〉 a bobsleigh; a bobsled.

ポプラ a poplar; an aspen.

ポプリン poplin.

ほふる 屠る 〈屠(ﾎﾌ)殺する〉 slaughter; 〈殺害する〉《文》 slay; massacre (大勢を); 〈打ち破る〉《文》 defeat; beat.

ほへい 歩兵 〈兵科〉 infantry; 〈兵〉 an infantryman; a foot soldier.

ボヘミア Bohemia ¶ボヘミアの Bohemian / ボヘミア人 a Bohemian.

ほほ 頬 ⇨ ほお.

ほぼ¹ 保母 〈保育園の〉 a nurse; 〈幼稚園の〉 a kindergarten teacher.

ほぼ² 略 〈大体〉 about; roughly; 〈ほとんど〉 almost; nearly; 〈大部分〉 for the most part; 〈事実上〉 practically; virtually ¶ほぼ同い年である be about the same age. 文例⇩

ほほえましい 微笑ましい charming; smile-provoking; pleasant. 文例⇩

ほほえみ, ほほえむ 微笑み, 微笑む ⇨ びしょう².

ポマード brilliantine ★ pomade という語は今では通用しない ¶ポマードを付ける put brilliantine on 《one's hair》.

ほまえせん 帆前船 ⇨ はんせん².

ほまれ 誉れ 〈名誉〉 honor; credit; 〈光栄〉 glory; 〈名声〉 fame; 《文》 renown ¶誉れとなる 〈事が主語〉 do one credit [honor].

ポメラニアけん ポメラニア犬 a Pomeranian (dog); a pom.

ほめる 褒める praise sb 《for his honesty》; speak well [highly] of sb; 《口語》 give sb a pat on the back ¶褒むべき praiseworthy; 《文》 laudable; admirable; 《文》 deserving praise / 褒め立てる, 褒めちぎる speak very highly (of); praise sb [sth] very highly [to the skies]; sing the praises 《of》; be loud in one's praises 《of》; heap [《文》lavish] praise (on); 〈新聞・雑誌で〉 write sb up. 文例⇩

ホモ¹ 〈同性愛〉 homosexuality; lesbianism (女の); 〈人〉 a (male, female) homosexual; 《口語》 a gay; 《口語》 a pansy (男); a lesbian (女).

ホモ² 〈均質化〉 homogenization ¶ホモ牛乳 homogenized milk.

It was [turned out] a mere waste of labor. | I gained nothing for all my trouble. | All my trouble went for nothing.

ほのか 部屋にほのかにお香のにおいがした。 I found a faint smell of incense in the room. / 木立ちの間から遠くの海がほのかに見えた。 We could glimpse the distant ocean through the trees.

ほのぼのと 夜がほのぼのと明け初めた頃そこに着いた。 Day was beginning to dawn when we got there. | We reached there just at the break of day.

ほぼ² ほぼそんな所だ。 That's about the size of it. / 工事はほぼ完成した。 The work is nearly [almost, practically] completed.

ほほえましい 子供たちの遊んでいる様子はほほ笑ましかった。 The sight of the children at play made me smile [was quite charming].

ほめる 彼は彼女の新作を口を極めて褒めた。 He spoke very highly of her new work. | He was very loud in his praises of her new work. / 彼があんな子供とけんかするなんて余り褒めた話ではな

ほや¹ 火屋〈ランプの〉 a chimney (縦の); a globe (丸形の).

ほや²【動】a sea squirt; an ascidian.

ほや a small fire.

ほやく grumble ((about)); complain ((about, of)).

ぼやける become dim [blurred].

ほやほや ¶大学を出たてのほやほや a young man fresh from [just out of] college / 焼きたてのほやほやのパン bread hot from the oven / 新婚ほやほやの夫婦 a newly married couple; newlyweds.

ぼやぼや ¶ぼやぼやする be careless; be absent-minded. 文例⇩

ほゆう 保有 ¶保有する《文》possess; hold; keep;《文》retain;《文》maintain / 金保有高〈貴重な入手物〉《文》a valuable acquisition;〈得な買い物〉a bargain. 文例⇩

ほよう 保養〈病後の〉recuperation; convalescence;〈気晴らし〉(a) recreation ¶保養する〈病後に〉recuperate; convalesce;〈気晴らしする〉take some recreation / 目の保養をする feast one's eyes ((on)) / 保養に行く go to ((a place)) for one's health [to recuperate] / 保養所 a rest [convalescent] home / 保養地 a health resort.

ほら¹ 法螺〈大言〉bragging; big talk; a tall tale [story] ¶ほらを吹く brag; boast; talk big / ほら吹き a braggart; a boaster. 文例⇩

ほら²〈相手の注意を引く時の語〉 文例⇩

ぼら【魚】a gray mullet.

ほらあな 洞穴 a cave;《文》a cavern.

ほらがい ほら貝 a trumpet shell; a conch ¶ほら貝を吹く blow a conch(-shell) horn.

ポラロイド(カメラ)【商標名】a Polaroid camera.

ボランティア a volunteer ¶ボランティア精神 the volunteer spirit.

ほり¹ 彫り carving; engraving ⇒ちょうこく ¶彫りの深い顔をした人 a person with sharply-chiseled [well-defined] features.

ほり² 堀〈外堀〉a moat;〈掘り割り〉a canal;〈溝〉a ditch ¶堀を掘る [埋め立てる] dig [fill in] a moat / 堀をめぐらした城 a moated castle / 堀端で by the moat.

ほりあてる 掘り当てる strike (oil); find ((a buried treasure)).

ポリープ【医】a polyp;《英》a polypus (pl. -pi).

ポリエステル polyester.

ポリエチレン polyethylene;《英》polythene.

ポリオ しょうに(小児まひ) ¶ポリオウイルス a poliovirus; a poliomyelitis virus.

ほりおこす 掘り起こす ⇒ほりかえす.

ほりかえす 掘り返す dig [turn] up ((the soil)); dig ((the ground)) over; turn over ((the soil)); grub ((in the earth)). 文例⇩

ほりさげる 掘り下げる〈下へ掘る〉dig down;〈深く考察する〉dig [delve, probe] into ((a problem)). 文例⇩

ほりだしもの 掘り出し物〈見付け物〉a lucky find;〈貴重な入手物〉《文》a valuable acquisition;〈得な買い物〉a bargain. 文例⇩

ほりだす 掘り出す dig out [up]; grub up; unearth ((a buried treasure)); disinter ((exhume)) ((a dead body));〈見付ける〉find; turn up ¶地中から掘り出す dig sth from [out of] the ground / 珍しい本を掘り出す come across [chance on] a rare book.

ほりつける 彫り付ける engrave [carve, cut] ((a figure)) on ((a piece of wood)); engrave ((a plate)) with ((a name)).

ほりぬきいど 掘り抜き井戸 an artesian [a tube, 《米》a driven] well.

ほりぬく 掘り抜く dig through ((a wall)); bore ((a tunnel)).

ポリネシア Polynesia ¶ポリネシアの Polynesian / ポリネシア人 a Polynesian.

ポリバケツ a plastic bucket.

ボリビア (the Republic of) Bolivia ¶ボリビアの Bolivian / ボリビア人 a Bolivian.

ポリプロピレン polypropylene.

ぼりぼり ¶ぼりぼりひっかく scratch oneself vigorously / ぼりぼりかじる crunch; munch.

ほりもの 彫り物〈入れ墨〉a tattoo;〈彫刻〉⇒ちょうこく ¶腕に彫り物をする tattoo ((a flower)) on sb's arm / 背中に竜の彫り物がしてある have a dragon tattooed [have a tattoo picture of a dragon] on one's back / からだ一面に彫り物がしてある be tattooed all over ((one's body)) / 彫り物師 a tattooer.

ほりゅう¹ 保留 (a) reservation ¶保留する〈取って置く〉reserve;〈差し控える〉withhold;〈延期する〉《文》defer sth ((to a later time)) / 態度を保留する《文》do not clarify one's attitude; do not commit oneself / 保留付きで with reservations / 保留なしで without reservation(s). 文例⇩

ほりゅう² 蒲柳 ¶蒲柳の質である be delicate; have a weak [delicate] constitution.

ボリューム volume ¶ボリュームのある《文》voluminous; massive; bulky; big ((women)); substantial ((meals)) / ボリュームのない small;《文》insubstantial / ボリュームを上げる [下げる] turn up [down] the volume ((on the stereo)).

い. Quarrelling with a mere boy like that does him no great credit.

ほやほや ぼやぼやするな. Look sharp [alive]!

ほよう 彼は今は逗子で病後の保養をしている. He is now convalescing [recuperating] at Zushi.

ほら あの人の話は少しはらがある. His remarks are rather exaggerated. / アメリカに金持ちのおじさんがいるとほらを吹いた. He bragged that he had a rich uncle living in the U.S.A. / ほらを吹くにも程がある. Is there no limit to his [your] bragging?

ほら² ほら御覧. Look there! / ほらこの間君に話したろう. I told you the other day, didn't I?

ほりかえす 道路が所々掘り返してある. The road has been dug [torn] up in several places.

ほりさげる その問題をもう少し掘り下げてみてごらん. Go [Dig] a bit deeper into the matter.

ほりだしもの これでこの値段なら掘り出し物じゃないか. That's a real bargain [buy] at that price, isn't it? / 今度の助手は掘り出し物だ. Our new assistant is quite an acquisition.

ほりゅう¹ その問題の決定は次回まで保留された. A (final) deci-

ほりょ 捕虜 a prisoner (of war) (略：P.O.W., POW)；《文》a captive ★近代の戦争での「捕虜」は英語では prisoner (of war) であり、captive は少し語感が古く、日本語の「とりこ」や「とらわれびと」に近い ¶捕虜にする take [《文》make] *sb* prisoner / 捕虜になる be taken prisoner [captive]（★主語が複数の時も prisoner は prisoners とはならない）/ 捕虜収容所 a prison [prisoner-of-war, P.O.W.] camp.

ほりわり 掘り割り a canal.

ほる¹ 彫る carve (in, on, from, out of)；engrave；sculpture；《文》sculpt；cut ¶像を彫る carve an image ((from wood))；carve [sculpture] a statue ((out of stone))／版木に彫る engrave [carve, cut] ((a picture)) on a wood block／大理石に彫ってある be carved in marble／人物像の彫ってある石板 a stone slab carved with a human figure.

ほる² 掘る dig ((the ground))；excavate ((a canal))；ひげをそる時に》shave (too) closely ¶穴を掘る dig a hole／じゃがいもを掘る dig potatoes. 文例⇩

ぼる ask (for) too much ((for *sth*))；ask an exorbitant price ((for *sth*))；overcharge *sb* ((for an article))；soak ((a tourist))；《俗》rip *sb* off.

ポルカ (a) polka ¶ポルカを踊る dance the polka.

ボルガ(がわ) ボルガ(川) the Volga (River).

ボルシチ borsch(t).

ボルタでんち ボルタ電池 a voltaic cell.

ボルト¹ 〈締め栓〉 a bolt ¶ボルトで締める fasten *sth* with a bolt；bolt *sth* (up).

ボルト² 《電》 a volt；voltage (ボルト数) ¶1万ボルトの電流 a 10,000-volt current.

ボルドーえき ボルドー液 Bordeaux mixture.

ポルトガル Portugal ¶ポルトガルの Portuguese／ポルトガル共和国 the Portuguese Republic／ポルトガル語 Portuguese／ポルトガル人 a Portuguese（単複同形）.

ボルネオ Borneo ¶ボルネオの Bornean.

ポルノ pornography；《口語》porn ¶ポルノ映画 a pornography [blue] film／ポルノ写真 a pornographic picture.

ホルマリン 《化》formalin.

ホルミウム 《化》holmium.

ホルモン (a) hormone ¶ホルモンの不均衡 (a) hormone imbalance／男[女]性ホルモン (a) male [female] (sex) hormone／ホルモン剤 a hormone drug.

ホルン a horn ¶ホルン奏者 a horn player.

ほれこむ 惚れ込む ⇒**ほれる¹** 堀内氏の人柄にほれ込む be charmed [attracted, taken] by Mr. Horiuchi's personality. 文例⇩

ほれぼれ 惚れ惚れ ¶ほれぼれするような charming；《文》bewitching；fascinating；enchanting／ほれぼれさせる charm；《文》bewitch；fascinate.

ほれる¹ 惚れる fall in love ((with))；fall for；《文》be enamored ((of)). 文例⇩

ほれる² 掘れる 〈(地面などが)穴のようにくぼむ〉 be hollowed out.

ボレロ 〈舞踊・音楽〉a bolero (*pl.* -s)；〈婦人服〉a bolero (*pl.* -s) ¶ボレロを踊る dance the bolero.

ほろ 幌 a hood；a (folding) top ¶ほろを掛ける[降ろす] pull up [down] the hood／ほろ蚊帳 a baby's mosquito net／ほろ馬車 a covered wagon；《米》a prairie schooner／ほろ馬車隊 a wagon train; a fleet of wagons.

ぼろ 〈布〉a rag，a shred；〈着物〉ragged [tattered] clothes；rags；tatters ¶ぼろの ragged；tattered／ぼろを着ている be (clad) in rags [tatters]／ぼろを出す《文》betray *one's* ignorance；have *one's* faults [defects] exposed；《口語》show *oneself* up／ぼろ市 a rag fair／ぼろ自動車 a worn-out old car；《口語》a jalopy；《英口語》an old crock. 文例⇩

ポロ 〈スポーツ〉polo ¶ポロシャツ a polo shirt.

ぼろい ぼろいもうけをする make [earn] easy money；make a large profit ((on, out of))；《口語》rake it in；make a killing.

ほろくそ ほろくそに言う do not have a good word to say for *sb* [*sth*]；speak very harshly [disparagingly] about *sb* [*sth*].

ポロニウム 《化》polonium.

ほろにがい ほろ苦い slightly bitter ¶ほろ苦い思い出 bittersweet memories.

---

sion on that question was deferred to the next meeting.／ご提案を保留条件は一切つけずにお受けいたします。I accept your proposal without reservation(s).

ほる² 彼らは地下道を掘って逃げようとした。They tried to escape by digging a tunnel.／この油田はなかなか掘り尽くされまい。It will be a long time before this oil field is worked out.

ほれこむ 彼は自分の立てた計画にほれ込んでいるので僕たちの反対意見などには耳を貸しないよ。He is so enamored of his own plan that he won't listen to our objections to it.

ほれる¹ 彼女は彼の人間ではなく彼の金にほれているだけさ。It's not him she's in love with; it's his money.／ほれて通えば千里も一里。Love laughs at distance.

ほれる² 雨垂れで軒先の地面が掘れた。The raindrops have hollowed out the ground under the eaves.

ぼろ あんまりしゃべるとぼろが出るよ。Don't say too much; you'll show yourself up.

ほろびる その国は今まさに滅びようとしていた。The country was on the brink [was tottering on the edge] of ruin.／豊臣氏は大阪落城とともに滅んだ。The Toyotomi family was overthrown with the fall of Osaka Castle.／古くからの伝統は簡単に滅びるものではない。Old traditions do not die easily.

ほろぼす 彼は酒で身を滅ぼした。Drink was his downfall [the ruin of him].｜Drink brought about his ruin.

ほろほろ 涙がほろほろとほほを伝ってこぼれ落ちた。Tears trickled down her cheeks.／あの木立ちの中でほろほろ鳴いている鳥は何だろう。What are the birds cooing in the trees there?

ぼろぼろ 刃がぼろぼろに欠けている。The blade is fearfully jagged.

ほろりと 彼女の哀れな話を聞いて思わずほろりとしてしまった。Her sad story touched me [my heart] so deeply that I almost wept.｜She told me such a pathetic story that I was moved to tears in spite of myself.

ほろんほろん 彼は悲しげな節をギ

ポロネーズ (a) polonaise ¶ポロネーズを踊る dance the polonaise.

ほろびる 滅びる go to ruin; go under; be ruined; crumble (away); fall;《文》cease to exist;〈滅ぼされる〉be destroyed [《文》overthrown] ¶滅びゆく民族 a dying race. 文例⇩

ほろぼす 滅ぼす ruin (a nation);《文》overthrow (a country); destroy [《文》conquer] (the enemy). 文例⇩

ほろほろ 文例⇩

ほろほろ¹ 〈涙のこぼれ落ちるさま〉in drops; drop by drop ¶涙をほろほろこぼす shed big drops of tears / 涙をほろほろこぼしながら with tears trickling down one's cheeks;《文》amid copious tears.

ほろほろ² 〈使い古されていたんださま, また土などのくずれるさま〉ragged; tattered;〈布が〉ragged; tattered;〈土が〉crumbly; loose / ほろほろの靴 worn-out shoes / ほろほろに〈砕けて〉in pieces;〈裂けて〉in tatters; in shreds / ほろほろになる〈崩れる〉crumble; fall to pieces;〈衣類が〉be worn to tatters [ribbons];〈リボンが〉be torn to shreds. 文例⇩

ぼろぼろ ⇒ほろほろ, ぼろんぼろん

ほろほろちょう ほろほろ鳥 a guinea fowl; a guinea hen

ぼろもうけ ぼろ儲け ⇒ぼろい (ぼろいもうけをする).

ほろよい ほろ酔い ¶ほろ酔いになる be slightly drunk [《文》intoxicated]; get [《文》become] tipsy.

ほろりと ¶ほろりとする be touched (by); be moved to tears / ほろりとさせる話 a pathetic [touching, moving] story / ほろりと酔う ⇒ほろよい. 文例⇩

ぼろんぼろん ¶ぼろんぼろんかき鳴らす strum (on)《a ukulele》; pluck idly on 《a guitar》. 文例⇩

ほん 本 a book; a volume ¶本を読みながら眠ってしまう read oneself to sleep / 本をあさる人 a book hunter / 本になって出る be published as a book [in book form] / 本で得た知識 knowledge gained from books; book learning. 文例⇩

ホン 〈音の大きさの単位〉a phon. 文例⇩

ほん- 本...〈この〉this;〈その〉the same;〈現在の〉present;〈当面の〉in question;〈主な〉head; main;〈本当の〉real;〈正式の〉regular ¶本件 this case;《文》the case in question [at issue] / 本号 this issue; the current [present] issue [number].

-ほん ...本 ¶鉛筆3本 three pencils / チョーク5本 five pieces of chalk / ビール2本 two bottles of beer.

ぼん¹ 盆 a tray; a server (料理などを載せる).

ぼん² 盆〈祭り〉the Bon [Lantern] Festival ¶盆踊り a Bon Festival dance. 文例⇩

ボン Bonn.

ほんあん 翻案 an adaptation ¶翻案する adapt. 文例⇩

ほんい¹ 本位〈基準〉a standard;〈主義〉a principle ¶営利本位の学校 a school run for profit / 金本位 ⇒きんほんい(せい) / 本位貨幣 standard money. 文例⇩

ほんい² 本意 one's original purpose [intention]; one's real intention [motive]. 文例⇩

ほんい³ 翻意 ¶翻意する change one's mind; alter one's decision.

ほんか 本科 the regular course.

ほんかいぎ 本会議 a plenary [full] session (of the Diet) ¶〈国会で〉議案を本会議にかける submit 《a bill》 to a plenary session; send 《a bill》 to the floor.

ほんかく 本格 ¶本格的な regular; full-scale[-blown] 《wars》; real;《文》earnest / 本格的に《文》in (real) earnest;〈口語〉for real / 本格小説 a serious novel / 本格派 the orthodox school. 文例⇩

ほんかん¹ 本管 a main (pipe); a (supply) main ¶ガスの本管 a gas main / 水道の本管 a water main.

ほんかん² 本館 the main building.

ほんき 本気 ¶本気の serious;《文》earnest / 本気になって働く work in earnest [with a will] / 本気にする take 《what sb says》 seriously; believe / 本気で seriously; in all seriousness;《文》in (real) earnest. 文例⇩

ほんぎ 本義〈真意義〉the true [real] meaning;

ターでぼろんぼろんと弾いた。He picked out a few melancholy notes on his guitar.

ほん あいにくその本はただ今在庫がございません。I'm afraid we haven't got any copies of the book on hand. | I'm sorry, but the book is out of stock at the moment. / あの人はたくさんの本を書いている。He has written a large number of books. / 兄はたくさんの本を持っている。My brother has a large library. / 彼はなかなか本を読んでいる。He is well-read. / こういったことは本では学べない。You can't learn this sort of thing out of books.

ホン 飛行機の爆音は120ホンあった。The noise level of the airplane engine registered 120 phons.

ぼん² まるで盆と正月がいっしょに来たようなものだった。It was like Christmas and New Year's all rolled into one.

ほんあん これはゾラの小説の翻案である。This was adapted from [is an adaptation of] one of Zola's novels.

ほんい¹ あの店はお客本位でやっている。That shop puts service to its customers before everything else. / 僕の考え方は家庭本位だ。The happiness of my family is my first consideration. / 品質本位が当店のモットーです。'Quality first!' is our motto. / 彼があのように自分本位では事業の成功はおぼつかない。If he continues to consider no one but himself, there is little hope that he will succeed (in what he has undertaken).

ほんい² 辞職は君の本意ではあるまい。You don't really mean to resign, do you? / 私は申し出を断わったが、それは本意ではなかった。I declined the offer, with some reluctance.

ほんかく 本格的な冬になった。Winter is really here. / 本格的な雪になった。It has begun to snow [The snow is now falling] in (real) earnest.

ほんき 君は本気でそう言っているのですか？ Do you really mean it? / 本気ですよ。I mean what I say. | I mean business. / 彼女が君を嫌いだと言っているのは本気でそう言っているんだぜ。She is

ほんぎまり 本決まり ¶本決まりになる be definitely [finally] decided; be formally settled.

ほんきゅう 本給 ⇨ほんぽう².

ほんきょ 本拠 (the home) base; the (main) headquarters ¶生活の本拠《文》the base and center of one's life.

ほんぎょう 本業 《文》one's principal occupation; one's regular business [trade] ¶医者が本業である be a physician by profession / 本業は大工である be a carpenter by trade.

ほんきょく 本局 〈分局に対して〉 the head [main] office; 〈電話局〉a telephone exchange; 〈この対局〉this game (of go [shogi]).

ほんくら 〈平凡な人間〉a mediocrity; 〈愚か者〉《口語》a dummy; 《口語》a blockhead; 《口語》a dimwit; 《口語》a dope.

ほんけ 本家 〈分家に対して〉 the main family; 〈元祖〉the originator; the original maker [manufacturer].

ぼんけい 盆景 a tray landscape.

ほんこ 本子でやる play (marbles) for keeps.

ぼんご 梵語 Sanskrit.

ボンゴ 〈楽器〉 bongo drums; bongo(e)s.

ほんこう 本校 〈分校に対して〉 the main [principal] school; 〈この学校〉 this [our] school.

ほんこく 翻刻 reprinting; reproduction (複製) ¶翻刻する reprint; reproduce / 翻刻物[書] a reprint; a reproduction (複製).

ほんごく 本国 one's own [native, home] country ¶本国へ帰る go [come, get] home / 本国に送還される be sent back to one's home country; be repatriated / 本国政府 the home government.

ほんごし 本腰 ¶本腰を入れる set about (a task) in (real) earnest; get [settle] down to (business) (seriously [in earnest]). 文例⇩

ほんこつ ¶ぽんこつ車〈ぼろの〉an old jalopy; 〈捨てられた〉a junked car.

ホンコン 香港 Hong Kong.

ほんさい 本妻 ⇨せいさい¹.

ぼんさい¹ 凡才 (a person of) no more than ordinary ability [talent]; a mediocrity.

ぼんさい² 盆栽 a bonsai; a dwarf(ed) tree in a pot.

ほんざん 本山 the head temple.

ほんし¹ 本旨 《文》the main [principal] object; the spirit (精神) ¶本旨にかなう serve [answer] the purpose (of) / 本旨に反する go against [be contrary to] the true aim (of).

ほんし² 本紙 our paper ¶本紙の読者 our readers / 本紙既報のごとく as already reported in these columns.

ほんし³ 本誌 this [our] journal [magazine].

ほんしき 本式 ¶本式の regular; formal / 本式の食事 a regular [full-course] dinner / 本式のフランス料理を学ぶ learn real French cuisine / 本式に regularly; formally; in a formal way / 本式に英語を学ぶ study English seriously [systematically]; take regular lessons in English. 文例⇩

ほんしけん 本試験 the final examination.

ほんしつ 本質 《文》essence; real nature; 《文》substance; 《文》essential [intrinsic] qualities ¶本質的に《文》essentially; 《文》in essence [substance]; 《文》intrinsically. 文例⇩

ほんじつ 本日 today; 《文》this day.

ほんしゃ 本社 〈本店〉the head [main] office; 〈わが社〉our [this] firm [company]; we ¶東京にあるトニー株式会社 Tony, Inc., headquartered [whose head office is] in Tokyo.

ホンジュラス (the Republic of) Honduras ¶ホンジュラスの Honduran / ホンジュラス人 a Honduran.

ほんしょ 本書 this book; 《文》the present volume.

ほんしょう¹ 本性 〈本来の性質〉one's true [real] character [nature]; 〈正気〉one's senses ¶本性を現わす reveal one's true character; betray [unmask] oneself; show one's true colors.

ほんしょう² 本省 〈管下の役所に対して〉 the ministry proper; 〈この省〉 this ministry.

ほんしょく 本職 〈本業〉one's (regular) occupation [profession, trade]; 〈玄人〉a professional; an expert ¶本職の a professional; regular (本式の) / 本職の外交官 a career diplomat. 文例⇩

ほんしん 本心 〈正気〉one's right mind; 〈良心〉one's conscience; 〈動機〉one's real intention [motive] ¶本心は at heart; at bottom / 本心を明かす reveal one's real intention(s); unbosom oneself / 本心を失う lose [go out of] one's mind [senses] / 本心から話す speak from one's [the] heart. 文例⇩

ほんじん 本陣 〈本営〉the headquarters; 〈昔の宿駅の〉an inn officially designated as a lodging for a *daimyo*.

ぼんじん 凡人 an ordinary person; 〈凡庸の

---

quite sincere when she says she hates you.

ほんごし 本腰を入れて勉強しないと大学の入試に失敗するぞ. If you don't get down to business and work hard [as it should be], you'll fail the university entrance examination.

ほんしき 土台の据え方が本式でない. The foundation is not laid properly [as it should be]. / 僕のバイオリンは本式に習ったのではない. I have not taken regular violin lessons.

ほんしつ 本質論をやろう. Let's talk about the essentials. / 《口語》Let's get down to brass tacks.

ほんしょく あなたの絵は本職はだしだ. Your paintings would put a professional to shame.

ほんしん それははたして彼の本心から出た言葉だろうか. I wonder if he really meant what he said.

ほんすじ そうするのが本筋だ. That is the right [proper] way to go about it.

ほんそう 神田氏の奔走で事件は円満に解決した. The affair was amicably settled through [thanks to] the good offices of Mr. Kanda.

ほんぞん この寺の本尊は阿弥陀如来だ. This temple is dedicated [sacred] to Amitabha.

ほんだい この話からいよいよ本題に入りたいと思います. I'm going to [I should like to] leave this matter on one side, and start on [deal with] the main question [the problem which

ポんず ポン酢 juice pressed from a bitter orange.

ほんずき 本好き a person who is fond of books; a lover of books; 《文》a bibliophile.

ほんすじ 本筋 〈正しいやり方〉the right course (of action); 〈物語の〉 the main plot; 〈話の〉 the main thread 《of a story》; the main《story》line ⇨ ほんだい. 文例⇩

ほんせい 本性 ⇨ ほんしょう¹.

ほんせき 本籍 one's legal [registered] domicile ¶本籍は東京にある be legally domiciled in Tokyo / 本籍地 a place where one is legally domiciled; 《文》(legal) domicile.

ぼんせき 盆石 a bonseki; a landscape constructed of sand and stones on a tray.

ほんせん¹ 本船 〈母船〉 the mother ship; 〈この船〉 this [our] ship [vessel].

ほんせん² 本線 〔鉄道〕a main line; a trunk line ¶東北本線 the Tohoku Main Line.

ほんぜん 翻然 ¶翻然として suddenly; all of a sudden / 翻然として悟る realize suddenly; 〈事が主語〉 suddenly become clear to one.

ほんそう¹ 本葬 a formal funeral.

ほんそう² 奔走 〈努力〉efforts; 〈活動〉activity; 〈世話〉《文》good offices ¶奔走する be busily engaged (in); 《文》exert oneself (to do, in behalf of sb). 文例⇩

ぼんぞく 凡俗 《文》the common herd; 《文》the common run of men; 《文》the commonalty ¶凡俗の common; vulgar.

ほんぞん 本尊 〈仏像〉 the principal image (of Buddha); 〈本人〉 the person himself [herself]. 文例⇩

ぼんだ 凡打〔野球〕an easy fly [grounder].

ほんたい¹ 本体 〈もの自体〉 the thing itself; 〈実体〉《文》substance; 〈真の姿〉 the true form; 〈ロケットなどの〉 the core 《of a rocket》; 〈神社のご神体〉 ⇨ ごしんたい / 〈寺の本尊〉 ⇨ ほんぞん. 「main force.

ほんたい² 本隊 the main body of troops; the

ほんだい 本題 the main subject [question] ¶本題に入る come to [get onto] the main question / 本題に戻って to return to our subject. 文例⇩

ぼんたい 凡退〔野球〕¶凡退する be easily put out.

ほんたく 本宅《文》one's principal residence ¶(別荘から)町の本宅に帰る go back to one's city home.

ほんたて 本立て a bookstand; a bookrack; 《a pair of》 book ends.

ほんだな 本棚 a bookshelf (pl. -shelves). 文例⇩

ほんだわら〔植〕gulfweed; sargasso; sargasso weed.

ぼんち 盆地 a basin ¶甲府盆地 the Kofu Basin.

ほんちょうし 本調子 one's normal condition ¶本調子になる hit [get into] one's stride.

ほんてん 本店 〈支店に対して〉 the main [head] office; the main store; 〈この店〉this store [shop].

ほんでん 本殿 the main [inner] shrine.

ほんど 本土 the mainland ¶中国本土 Chinese mainland; Mainland China / 日本本土 Japan proper / 本土防衛 home [national] defense.

ぽんと ¶ぽんと肩をたたく tap sb on the shoulder / ぽんと抜ける[飛ぶ] come out [fly off] with a pop / ぽんと100万円出してやる give sb one million yen ungrudgingly [for the asking]; make a generous donation of one million yen (to, toward) / ぽんとほうり投げてやる toss sth to sb. 文例⇩

ポンド 〈重量〉a pound (略: lb.); 〈貨幣〉a pound (記号: £); a pound sterling (英貨) ¶20ポンド 20 pounds 〈重量〉20 lbs.; 〈貨幣〉£20 / ポンド地域 the sterling area.

ほんとう¹ 本当 ¶本当の 〈真の〉true; real; actual; 〈正しい〉 proper; right; regular; 〈本物の〉 genuine; 《文》 authentic; natural (人工的に対して) / 本当に 〈真に〉 really; truly; actually; 〈正しく〉 properly; 〈本気で〉《文》in earnest; 〈全く〉 really; quite; indeed; very / 本当の兄弟 one's real [《文》true] brother / 本当の事 the truth; a (real) fact / 本当にする believe; take 《sb's remarks》seriously / 本当は 〈事実は〉 in reality; really; the truth (of the matter) is / 本当らしいうそ a plausible lie / 本当らしい話 a likely-sounding story; a story having [with] the ring of truth about it. 文例⇩

ほんとう² 本島 the main island ¶沖縄本島 Okinawa, the main island of the Ryukyus; the Island of Okinawa.

ほんどう¹ 本堂 the main [inner] temple; the main building [hall] (of a temple).

ほんどう² 本道 a main road; a highway.

---

really concerns us (today)].

ほんたい 三者凡退した. The three batters were out in quick succession. |〔口語〕 It was three up and three down.

ほんだな このセットは本棚に並べると約1メートルある. This set occupies about one meter of shelf space.

ほんちょうし このところ体が本調子でない. I'm not myself these days.

ぽんと ぽんと音がした. I heard it go pop. / コルクがぽんと音を立てて抜けた. The cork came out with a pop.

ほんとう¹ 本当かしら. Can it be true? | I wonder if it is true. / 本当ですか. 〈驚いた〉 Really? / 〈まさか〉 Not really? | You don't say so! / 僕はそんな事を言うはずはありません, 本当です. I didn't do it, on my honor. / 本当を言うと僕は彼を好かない. To tell the truth, I don't like him. / 正直は最善の策とは本当だ. It is truly said that honesty is the best policy. / 彼の言う事は本当らしい. He seems to be telling the truth. / 本当に美しい. It is really beautiful. / だれがそんな話を本当にするものか. Who do you expect to believe that? | Nobody would believe it. / それが本当のやり方だ. That is the proper [right] way to go about it. / 彼こそ本当の学者だ. He is (what I call) a real scholar. | He is a scholar worthy of the name.

ほんどおり 本通り a main street.
ほんにん 本人 the person himself [herself]; 〈問題の当人〉the person in question;《文》the said person;〈代理人などに対して〉the principal ¶本人自身で in person; personally. 文例⇩
ほんね 本音 ¶本音を吐く admit [《文》confess,《文》disclose] one's real intention [motive]; give oneself away ⇨ たてまえ1 文例.
ボンネット 〈帽子〉a bonnet;〈自動車の〉《米》a hood;《英》a bonnet ¶(車の)ボンネットを開けて調べる check under the hood.
ほんねん 本年 this year; the current [present] year.
ほんの 《文》mere; just; nothing but; only; but ¶ほんの少し just a little (bit) / ほんの名ばかりの (a scholar) only in name;(an artist) in name only. 文例⇩
ほんのう 本能 (an) instinct ¶本能によって by [out of] instinct / 本能的な instinctive / 本能的に instinctively / 本能的に蛇をこわがる have an instinctive fear [《文》dread] of snakes. 文例⇩
ほんのう 煩悩 worldly passions [desires]; desire for worldly things.
ぼんのくぼ 盆の窪 the hollow in [at] the nape of the neck.
ほんのり slightly; faintly ¶ほんのりと上気している be slightly flushed.
ほんば 本場 〈本来の産地〉the home (of); the (best) place (for);〈中心地〉the (production) center ¶本場の西陣織 genuine Nishijin brocade / 外国語を本場で習う learn a foreign language in the country where it is spoken. 文例⇩
ほんばこ 本箱 a bookcase.
ほんばしょ 本場所 a regular *sumo* tournament.
ほんばん 本番 〈一般的に〉《口語》the real thing;《俗》the works;〈芝居・テレビなどの〉acting [performing] before the audience [camera];《映画》a take;《放送》going on the air. 文例⇩
ぽんびき ぽん引き 〈売春の客引き〉a pimp;《英》a ponce;〈取り込み詐欺師〉a confidence trickster; a con man;《米俗》a bunco steerer.
ほんぶ 本部 the head office; the headquarters ¶本部は東京にある be headquartered in Tokyo.
ポンプ [<《オランダ語》pomp] a pump ¶ポンプで井戸の水をくみ上げる [出す] pump water up [out] from a well / 手押し[吸い上げ]ポンプ a hand [suction] pump / ポンプ車 a fire engine [truck] (equipped with a pump); a pumper.
ほんぶたい 本舞台 〈正面の舞台〉the main stage;〈ひのき舞台〉⇨ ひのき (ひのき舞台).
ほんぶり 本降り 文例⇩
ほんぶん¹ 本文 〈文書などの本体〉the text (of a treaty); the body (of a letter);〈この文〉this sentence [passage, article] ¶本文の筆者 the writer of this article;〈私〉《文》the (present) writer.
ほんぶん² 本分 one's duty; one's part ¶本分を尽くす do [《文》fulfill] one's duty; do one's part / 本分を怠る do not do one's duty; neglect [fail to do] one's duty.
ボンベ [<《ドイツ語》Bombe] a (gas) cylinder [bottle] ¶水素ボンベ a hydrogen cylinder [bottle].
ポンペイ Pompeii.
ほんぽう¹ 本邦 this [our] country; Japan.
ほんぽう² 本俸 the regular salary; the basic salary (of a letter).
ほんぽう³ 奔放 ¶奔放な wild; free;《文》unrestrained;《文》uninhibited.
ぼんぼり 〈あんどん〉a Japanese table lamp with a paper shade;〈手燭〉a paper hand lantern.
ボンボン 〈菓子〉a bonbon.
ぽんぽん 〈重い音〉bang, bang;〈軽い音〉pop, pop; plop, plop;〈おなか〉《小児語》one's tummy ¶ぽんぽん言う 〈思った事を遠慮なく言う〉speak one's mind; be outspoken (in one's remarks);〈がみがみ言う〉snap at *sb* / ぽんぽん手を鳴らす clap one's hands smartly / ぽんぽん蒸気 a motor [diesel] launch. 文例⇩
ポンポンダリア a pompon dahlia.
ぼんぼんどけい ぼんぼん時計 a pendulum clock.
ほんまつてんとう 本末転倒 ¶本末転倒する get one's priorities wrong [the wrong way round]; put the cart before the horse.
ほんまる 本丸 the keep (of a castle).

ほんにん 私はその本人に会った。I saw the man himself. / 本人から聞いた事だから事実に相違ない。I had the news at first hand, so it must be true. |《口語》It must be the truth; I heard it straight from the horse's mouth. / 本人自身申し出る事。Apply in person.

ほんの クリーム [お砂糖] はほんのちょっとだけにして下さい。Just a tiny drop of cream [a tiny bit of sugar], please. / あの人とはほんのちょっとした知りあいです。We are only nodding acquaintances. | I only know him slightly.

ほんのう 動物は自己保存の本能を有する。Animals have [possess] the instinct of self-preservation. / うまい文章は本能的に書けるというものではない。Writing well is not something instinctive.

ほんば 広島はかきの本場だ。Hiroshima is famous for its oysters. / 宇治は茶の本場だ。Uji is one of the famous tea-growing centers of Japan. / イギリスは代議政治の本場である。England is the birthplace of representative government.

ほんばん (映画の撮影で)本番です。お静かに願います。Quiet, please. This will be a take.

ほんぶり 雨が本降りになった。The rain is now coming down [It has begun to rain] in (real) earnest.

ぽんぽん ぽんぽん花火が上がった。Bang! bang! went the fireworks. | Fireworks blasted away high up in the air.

ほんみょう 夏目漱石(本名夏目金之助)は慶応3年の生まれで、東京に育った。Soseki Natsume (born Kinnosuke Natsume in 1867) was brought up in Tokyo.

ほんめい 今度の知事選ではだれが本命だろうか。Who do you think is the favorite in [is most likely to win] the coming guber-

ほんみょう 本名 one's real name. 文例⇩

ほんむ 本務 〈本来の業務〉 one's regular [main] business [occupation]; 〈本分〉 one's duty ¶本務校 the school at which one teaches full-time.

ほんめい 本命 the favorite; a sure thing; the likely winner; a certainty; 〈英〉 a nap (selection) 〈予想家の〉 ¶本命にかける bet on a sure thing [a certainty] / 本命でない馬 an outsider. 文例⇩

ほんもう 本望 ¶本望を遂げる 《文》 attain one's long-cherished object; 《文》 get [realize] one's heart's desire. 文例⇩

ほんもと 本元 ⇒ ほんけ.

ほんもの 本物 a genuine article; a real thing ¶本物の genuine; 《文》 true; real; 《文》 authentic; natural 〈人工的に対して〉. 用法 実際に使うときは, genuine article も real thing も共に不定冠詞の a ではなく, 例えば, It looks just like the real thing (the genuine article). というように the を付けて使うことが多い.

ほんもん 本文 ⇒ ほんぶん¹ ¶本文批評 textual criticism.

ほんや 本屋 〈人〉 a bookseller; a publisher 〈出版屋〉; 〈店〉 〈米〉 a bookstore; 〈英〉 a bookshop.

ほんやく 翻訳 (a) translation; (a) rendering; a version ¶翻訳する translate [《文》 render, put, turn] 《the Japanese into English》 / ロシヤの小説を翻訳で読む read a Russian novel in translation [a Japanese version] / 翻訳家[者] a translator / 翻訳書 a translation; a version. 文例⇩

ぼんやり 〈人〉 a blockhead; a careless person; 〈ぼうぜんと〉 vacantly; absent-mindedly; 〈無為に〉 idly; 〈不明瞭に〉 vaguely; dimly; indistinctly ¶ぼんやりする be absent-minded; be dazed (面くらって); 〈不注意である〉 be careless; 《文》 be heedless; 〈ぼんやりした〉 〈間抜けな〉 stupid; dull; 〈放心した〉 absent-minded; vacant; 〈不明瞭な〉 vague; dim; indistinct 〈ぼんやり立って[待って]いる stand [wait] around / ぼんやり考え込む be lost in thought [《文》 reverie] / ぼんやり時を過ごす idle one's time away; let time slip by / ぼんやり眺める gaze [look] vacantly (at). 文例⇩

ぼんよう 凡庸 ¶凡庸な mediocre; common(-place); 《文》 banal.

ほんよみ 本読み 《演劇》 script reading ¶(俳優たちが)本読みをする read 《their》 parts.

ほんらい 本来 〈元来〉 originally; from the first (初めから); 〈本質的に〉 《文》 essentially; in itself; 〈天性〉 naturally; by nature; 〈当然〉 rightfully; 〈本来の〉 《文》 essential; natural; rightful. 文例⇩

ほんりゅう¹ 本流 〈川の〉 the main stream; the main course (of a river); 〈比喩的に〉 the main current (of Japanese literature).

ほんりゅう² 奔流 a rapid [violently rushing] stream; a torrent.

ほんりょう 本領 〈特色〉 a characteristic; 〈得意〉 one's line ¶本領を発揮する show oneself at one's best; display [show] one's real ability; come into one's own. 文例⇩

ほんるい 本塁 《野球》 (the) home base ⇒ ホーム ¶本塁打 a home run ⇒ ホームラン.

ほんろう 翻弄 ¶翻弄する 〈人を〉 make fun [a fool, 《文》 sport] of sb; 〈波が〉 toss 《a ship》 about / 波に翻弄される be tossed about by [be at the mercy of] the waves.

ほんろん 本論 the main issue [《文》 discourse] ⇒ ほんだい.

ま

ま¹ 真 ¶真に受ける take 《a joke》 seriously; take sb at his word; accept sth (as true); believe sth (to be true).

ま² 間 〈透き間〉 space; room; 〈間隔〉 an interval; a pause; 〈休止〉 a rest; 〈部屋〉 a room; 〈時間〉 time; 〈暇〉 leisure; time to spare; 〈運〉 luck; chance ¶間がいい be lucky; be fortunate / 間が悪い 〈不運〉 be unlucky; be unfor-

---

natorial election?
ほんもう これは本望だ。I am quite satisfied now. / 彼に会えれば本望だ。I would give anything (in the world) to meet him.
ほんもの 彼はそれを本物のセザンヌだと言って彼女に売りつけた。He palmed it off on her as a real Cézanne. / この造花はまるで本物のようだ。These artificial flowers are so lifelike. / あの人の歌ほんとうにうまい。He is a really good singer。He sings like a professional (singer). / 私はこの小説はフランスの原作から翻訳したものだ。This is a translation from the French

original. / この言葉は英語には翻訳できない。This word does not translate [cannot be translated] into English.
ぼんやり ぼんやりして列車を乗り違えた。I was careless enough to take the wrong train. / これはぼんやりしちゃいられない。This is no time for idling. / 私はぼんやりした考えで上京した。I came up to Tokyo without any particular purpose (in mind). / 僕は幼時のことをまだぼんやり覚えている。I still have a faint recollection of my childhood. / 睡眠薬のおかげで頭がまだぼんやりしている。My mind is still fuzzy from

[fuddled by] sleeping tablets.
ほんらい 本来は良いものでも用い方を誤れば害にもなる。A thing which is good in itself may become harmful if wrongly used. / 人間は本来社会的動物である。Man is by nature a social animal. / これは本来(から言えば)彼らの問題ではなく、我々の問題ではない。Properly speaking, this is their concern, not ours.
ほんりょう そういう仕事は私の本領でない。That kind of work is not (in) my line. / これが日本民族の本領である。This is a true characteristic of the Japanese race.

まあたらしい 真新しい brand-new; spick-and-span.

マーチ 〈行進曲〉a march.

まあまあ 〈まずまず〉rather; I should say…; 〈大体〉fairly; tolerably; passably; 〈促しまたはなだめて〉come, come; now, now; please. 文例⇩

マーマレード 《orange》marmalade.

まい 舞 dancing; a dance ¶舞を舞う dance; perform [dance] a dance / 舞扇 a dancer's fan.

まい- 毎- every; each ¶毎食 (at, after) each meal / 毎土曜日 every Saturday / 毎秒[分] per second [minute].

-まい¹ …枚 a piece [sheet] (of paper) ¶20円切手5枚 five twenty-yen stamps.

-まい² 文例⇩

まいあがる 舞い上がる get [go (up)] into the air; fly high [up]; soar; 〈吹き上げられて〉be blown up. 文例⇩

まいあさ 毎朝 every morning.

まいおりる 舞い降りる fly down; glide down (滑空して); swoop down (急降下して); 〈物の上に〉land [《文》alight] (on sth).

マイカー one's own car; a private car ¶マイカー族 car owners; motorists.

まいかい 毎回 each [every] time.

まいきょ 枚挙 ¶枚挙にいとまがない 《文》be too numerous to mention; 《文》be too many to enumerate.

マイクロウェーブ 《物》a microwave.

マイクロカード a microcard ¶マイクロカードリーダー a microcard reader.

マイクロバス a microbus; a minibus.

マイクロフィルム a microfilm ¶マイクロフィルムリーダー a microfilm reader; a microfilm viewing machine / マイクロフィルムにとる microfilm (a book).

マイク(ロフォン)a microphone; a mike ¶マイクの前で話す speak at [into, over] a microphone / マイクを通じて話す speak through a microphone / 隠しマイク a concealed microphone / つり下げマイク a suspended microphone / ハンドマイク a portable microphone.

マイクロメーター a micrometer; micrometer callipers.

まいげつ 毎月 ⇒まいつき.

ま 〈ばつが悪い〉feel awkward; be embarrassed / 間が持てない cannot fill the time [interval]; time hangs heavy [heavily] on one's hands / 4間の家 a four-room(ed) house / 間の抜けた stupid; foolish; silly / 〈それから〉少し間を置いて after a short [brief] interval / 仕事の間を見て when one has [finds] a moment to spare at work [from one's work] / いつの間にか，知らぬ間に before one knows it [is aware of it]; almost before one realizes it / ちょっとの間も even for a minute [moment] / 飯を食べる間もない don't even have enough time to eat [take a meal]. 文例⇩

ま³ ¶魔が差す be tempted by an evil spirit; fall a victim to temptation / 魔が差して tempted by an evil spirit; 〈不幸にも〉unluckily; as luck [《文》] would have it / 魔の海 a treacherous sea / 魔の金曜日 Black Friday / 魔の踏切 a dangerous [an accident-prone] railroad crossing. 文例⇩

まあ 〈ちょっと〉just; 〈ためらい〉all right [O.K.] then; well; I should think [say] (that …); 〈驚嘆〉Oh!; Dear me!; Good Heavens [gracious]! 文例⇩

まあい 間合い a period [space] of time; 《put》a pause (after, between) ¶間合いをはかる adjust the timing (of); get sth well-timed [well-spaced].

マーガリン margarine (★発音は [máːdʒərin]); 《英口語》marg(e).

マーガレット 《植》a marguerite; a Paris daisy.

マーキュロ(クローム) 《商標名》Mercurochrome; merbromin solution.

マーク 〈しるし〉a mark ¶マークする watch; keep one's eye (on sth) / マークを付ける mark; put a mark (on) / マークシート《コンピューター》a marksheet.

マーケット a market.

マーケティング 《経》marketing.

まあじ 《魚》a horse mackerel.

マーシャルしょとう マーシャル諸島 the Marshall Islands ¶マーシャル諸島の Marshallese.

マージャン 麻雀 《play》mah-jongg [mah jong] ¶マージャン屋[クラブ] a mah-jongg saloon [club].

マージン a margin (of profit).

ま² 上京してからまだ間がない．I haven't been in Tokyo long. / 発車までにはまだ間がある[もう間がない]．It will be some time [It won't be long] before the train leaves. / 彼は人が遊んでいる間に勉強した．He worked while the others were playing. / 何てついているんだろう．Luck is certainly with me. | How lucky I am! / 間の悪いときは仕方がないものだ．An unlucky break cannot be helped. / そんな事をするなんて何て間の抜けたやつだ．How stupid of him to do such a thing!

ま³ あんなことをするなんて，自分でも，何の魔がさしたのかわかりません．I don't know what came over [had gotten into] me to make me do what I did. / 次の列車にしましょうと言ったのに，あの人はいつになく強情を張って，1人であの列車で先に行き，あの悲惨な事故に遭ったのです．魔がさしたと言うのでしょうねえ．We asked him to wait with us for the next train, but he was unusually obstinate and insisted on taking that one. He got on and went ahead alone, and met that tragic accident. It must have been fate.

まあ まあやってご覧．All right then, have a try [go] (at it). / まああんまり行きたい気がしないね．Well, I'd prefer not to [I'd rather not] go. / まあ，大体そんなところです．It's something like that. | That's about the size of it. / あれでも，まあ，画家と言えるのだろう．I suppose you could call him a painter (of sorts).

まあまあ まあまあこらえておこう．Well, (I suppose) I might as well put up with it. / あの映画はまあまあ見られた．The movie was so-so [mildly enjoyable]. / 景気はどうです？—まあまあですな．How's business?—Well, not too bad.

まいこ 舞子 an apprentice geisha.
まいご 迷子 a lost [stray] child ¶迷子になる be [get] lost 《in the crowd》; 〈道に迷う〉lose one's way / 迷子札 a child's identification tag.
まいこむ 舞い込む 〈人が〉visit; drop in; 〈災難などが〉fall on [《文》upon] one;《文》befall; happen to one. 文例⇩
マイコン a microcomputer.
まいじ 毎時 every hour; per hour ¶毎時50キロの速度で at a speed of fifty kilometers an [per] hour; at 50 km/h.
まいしゅう 毎週 every [each] week; weekly; per week (1週につき) ¶毎週の weekly / 毎週2回 twice a week / 毎週毎週 week after week (after week) / 毎週木曜の晩に every Thursday night.
まいしん 邁進 ¶邁進する〈進む〉go forward [on] (《文》undaunted); 〈努める〉《文》strive 《for》.
まいすう 枚数 the number of leaves [sheets] ¶はがきの枚数 the number of postcards.
まいせつ 埋設 ¶埋設する lay 《cables》 underground [under the ground].
まいそう 埋葬 (a) burial;《文》(an) interment ¶埋葬する bury;《文》inter / 埋葬許可証 a burial certificate [permit] / 埋葬室 a burial chamber / 埋葬地 a burial place [ground]; 〈墓地〉a cemetery; a graveyard.
まいぞう 埋蔵 ¶埋蔵されている lie under the ground / 石油の埋蔵量 (the estimated amount of) oil deposits (in Texas); (Saudi Arabia's) (estimated) oil reserves.
まいちもんじ 真一文字 ¶真一文字に in a straight line.
まいつき 毎月 every month; monthly ¶毎月の monthly.
まいど 毎度〈毎回〉every [each] time;〈度々〉(very) often; frequently;〈いつも〉always. 文例⇩
まいとし 毎年 ⇒まいねん.
マイナス 〔数〕minus; 〈欠損〉a deficit (of ¥500,000); 〈欠点〉a deficiency; 〈欠点〉a defect; 〈不利な点〉a disadvantage; a drawback (to the project); a handicap ★英語では「欠点」「不利」の意味で minus を使うことはほとんどない ¶マイナスの数量 a minus [negative] quantity / …にマイナスの影響がある《文》have a negative impact on… / マイナスになる〈損をする〉lose; suffer a loss;〈不利になる〉《文》be disadvantageous 《to》; handicap sb / マイナス記号 a minus (sign) ⇨ふ³, あかじ.
文例⇩
まいにち 毎日 every [each] day; daily ¶毎日毎日〈繰返し〉day after day (after day); day in day out; 〈日増しに〉day by day; from day to day; with each passing day / 毎日午前中に every morning / 毎日の daily (life); everyday (use). 文例⇩
まいねん 毎年 every year; 《文》annually; 《文》per year (1年につき) ¶毎年1回 once a year / 毎年の yearly; annual. 文例⇩
まいばん 毎晩 every night [evening]; night after night; nightly; at night ¶毎晩泣き明かす cry all night every night / 毎晩の nightly.
まいひめ 舞姫 a dancing girl; a dancer.
マイペース ¶マイペースで〈速度〉at one's own pace; 〈やり方〉in one's own way; as one likes [pleases].
マイホーム a home of one's own; one's own home [house] ¶マイホーム主義 a family-oriented way of life.
まいぼつ 埋没 ¶埋没する be [lie] buried 《in the ground》; 〈忘れられる〉be forgotten; get lost; 《文》sink into oblivion.
まいもどる 舞い戻る come back; 《文》return.
まいよ 毎夜 ⇒まいばん.
まいる 参る go; come; pay a visit to sb; 〈負ける〉be beaten; 《文》be defeated; 《口語》be [get] floored; 〈降参する〉《文》yield 《to》; give in 《to》; 〈閉口する〉《口語》be stumped; be put out; 〈へたばる〉be exhausted; get [be] dead tired; collapse; break down; 《口語》be done up; 〈死ぬ〉die; 《文》pay one's debt to Nature; 〈心を奪われる〉be smitten 《by》; 《口語》be stuck 《on a girl》; 《口語》fall 《for》; 〈参詣する〉visit [pay a visit to] 《sb's grave》; go to worship 《at a temple》 ¶寒さに参るを be unable to stand the cold / 参ったと言う give in; 《文》admit (one's) defeat; 《米口語》cry [say] uncle. 文例⇩
マイル a mile ¶マイル数 mileage / 時速50マ

-まい² その先はまあ話しますまい. I'd rather not tell you the rest. / 小林君のやったことではあるまい. It was probably not Kobayashi that did it. / 彼は行くまい. He will [may] not go. / He is not likely to go. / 子供じゃあるまいし，そんなことぐらいわかってるよ. I'm quite aware of that, thank you. / I'm not a child, you know! / あの男にできるでしょうか—できますまい. Do you think he'll be able to do it? —No, I'm afraid not. / Do you think he is capable of it?—I doubt it.
まいあがる ひばりは空高く舞い上がった. The lark soared higher and higher in the sky.
まいこむ 変な手紙が舞い込んだ. I got [received] a strange letter.
まいじ バスは毎時毎分に[30分過ぎに]出る. The bus leaves every hour on the hour [on the half hour].
まいど 毎度ありがとうございます.《店の客に》Thank you (for your patronage).
マイナス 7マイナス4は3. Seven minus four is [equals] three. / マイナス掛けるマイナスはプラスになる. Minus times minus is plus./ 彼はあんまり物の言い方がはっきりしているので，それが時にマイナスになることがある. He is very outspoken, and it sometimes works to his disadvantage./ He sometimes does himself a disservice by being so frank.
まいにち こんなことは毎日はない. That sort of thing doesn't happen every day./ 毎日同じようであった. One day was just like another.
まいねん 毎年今頃は雪が降り始める. It always begins to snow at this time of (the) year. / 毎年夏はヨーロッパに行く. I go to Europe every summer.
まいる ただ今参ります. I'm coming. / お車が参りました. The car

イル fifty miles an [per] hour ; 50 mph ★日常会話では, I was going along the road at 50 miles an hour. を …at 50 と簡略に言うことが多い. 文例⑨

まう 舞う 〈踊る〉dance ; 〈ひらひらと〉flit, flutter (about) ; 〈鳥が〉fly ; wheel ; circle. 文例⑨

まうえ 真上 ¶真上の[に] right [just] above ; right overhead. 文例⑨

まうしろ 真後ろ 真後ろの[に] right [just] behind ; just at the back (of).

マウンド 〈野球〉the mound ¶マウンドに立つ take the mound ; do mound duty ; pitch (an inning) / マウンドを退かせる retire (a pitcher) ; lift (a pitcher) from the mound.

まえ 前 the front ¶〈料理の〉1 人前 a helping ; a portion / 2, 3 日前 a few days ago (今から) ; a few days before (そのときから) / 5 時 15 分前 a quarter to [《米》of] five / まだ 50 前であるを still under fifty ; 《口語》on this [the right] side of fifty / 前の〈場所〉front ; 〈時〉former ; last ; previous / 前の日[晩] the previous day [night] ; the day [night] before ; 〈on〉the eve (of an event) / 2 日前の新聞 a paper of two days ago [before]; a two-day-old paper / …を前にして in front of ((the students)) ; 《文》before ((the dignitaries)) ; 《文》in the face of ((one's enemy)) ; 《文》on the eve of ((a coup d'état)) / 前((の方))へ出る go [step, move] forward / 前に進む go ahead / 出発の前に before *one* leaves ; 《文》before *one*'s departure / 3 人前働く do three men's work / 前に[の]〈所〉in front (of) / 《文》before ; 〈今から〉ago ; since / 〈以前〉before ; 《文》formerly ; 《文》on an earlier occasion / …のいる[見ている]前で in sb's presence [sight] / 〈列車の〉前から 3 番目の車両 the third car from the front ((of the train)).

まえあし 前足 a forefoot ; a front leg ; a foreleg ; 〈犬・猫などの〉a paw ; a forepaw.

まえいわい 前祝い an advance celebration ¶前祝いをする celebrate beforehand [《文》in anticipation].

まえうしろ 前後 ¶帽子を前後にかぶる put a hat on the wrong way round [back to front] ; wear a cap (with the) front side back.

まえうり 前売り booking ; an advance (ticket) sale ¶前売りする sell in advance ; book / 《座席が》前売りで売り切れになる be booked up / 前売り券 an advance ticket / 前売り券の発売窓口 a reservation window.

まえおき 前置き 《文》an introductory remark ; 《文》a preliminary (remark) ; an introduction ¶前置きをする make introductory remarks.

まえかがみ 前屈み a stoop ; a slouch ((だらしのない悪い姿勢)) ; being bent forward ¶前かがみになる stoop [be stooped, be bent] 《with old age》 ; bend forward ; lean forward [down, over].

まえがき 前書き a preface ; 《文》a prefatory note ; a foreword ; an introduction.

まえかけ 前掛け an apron.

まえがし 前貸し payment in advance ¶給料を前貸しする pay (a worker's) wages in advance ; lend [advance] ((10,000 yen)) on sb's salary.

まえがみ 前髪 a forelock ; 〈切り下げた〉a bang (婦人の) ; a fringe.

まえがり 前借り ¶給料の前借りをする receive [draw] one's wages in advance / 給料から 2 万円前借りする borrow 20,000 yen on *one*'s salary ; get an advance [《英口語》a sub] of ¥20,000 on *one*'s salary.

まえきん 前金 ⇒まえばらい

まえげいき 前景気 a prospect ; an outlook ¶前景気がいい The prospects ((for our business)) are good ; 《文》promise well ; have bright prospects.

まえこうじょう 前口上 〈演劇などの〉a prologue ; 〈本題に入る前の〉《文》《make》a preliminary statement.

まえせんでん 前宣伝 advance advertising.

まえのめり 前のめり ⇒のめる.

まえば 前歯 a front tooth ; a foretooth ((*pl.* -teeth)).

まえばらい 前払い payment in advance ; prepayment ; advance payment ¶前払いする pay in advance. 文例⑨

まえび 前日 《文》(on) the eve (of an event).

まえぶたい 前舞台 an apron stage ; a proscenium ((*pl.* -nia)).

まえぶれ 前触れ 〈予告〉previous [advance] notice ; 《文》a preliminary announcement ;

---

is at the door. / どうだ, 参ったか. Do you give up [in]? / こいつは一本参った. Well, I'm beaten. / まだ参ったとは言わないぞ. I haven't thrown in the sponge [towel] yet. / 今度の病気には彼もだいぶ参った様子だ. He seems to have been brought very low by his illness. / 彼女は精神的に参っていた. She seemed to be cracking up. / こう責められては大抵参る. Such pressures are apt to unstring a man.

マイル Ⅰカイリは 1 マイルよりさらにその 20 分の 3 ほど長い. A nautical mile is about 1³/₂₀ times as long as a land mile.

まう 空にとびが舞っていた. A kite was circling above us.

まうえ 真上から照りつける太陽の下を我々は黙々と行進した. We marched silently under the sun which blazed straight down on us.

まえ 前の方には何も見えなかった. I saw nothing ahead (of me). / もっとよく見ようと思って何列か前へ出た. I moved up several rows in order to have a better view. / よほど前にあった事です. It happened long ago. / 彼は 1 週間前から病気です. He has been ill for a week now. / この建物は 300 年前のものだ. This building dates [goes] back 300 years. / この化石は百万年も前のものである. This fossil dates back as far as a million years. / 発車 2 分前になんとか駅に着いた. We managed to get to the station two minutes before the train left. / 首脳会談を前にして, このような挙に出たのはまったく良くないことであった. It was unfortunate timing to take such a step on the eve of the summit meeting.

まえおき 前置きが長過ぎた. You spent too much time in [on] pre-

まえぼたん 前ボタン a front button；《ズボンの》a (trouser-)fly button ¶前ボタンの front-buttoning《dresses》; button-front《rompers》.

まえまえ 前々 ¶前々から for a long time；《reserved》far [a long time] in advance.

まえむき 前向き ¶前向きの《方向》facing front; full-face(d)《portraits》; forward-turned；《比喩的に》positive《policies》; forward-looking《statesmen》; constructive《opinions》/ 前向きの姿勢で positively；constructively；in a constructive way [《文》manner].

まえもって 前もって beforehand；in advance；ahead of time.

まえわたし 前渡し 《金の》payment in advance；《物品の》delivery in advance ¶前渡し金 an advance；《法》an advancement ⇒まえばらい，まえがし。　「Darkness [Evil].

まおう 魔王 Satan；the Devil；the Prince of

まがいもの 紛い物 an imitation；a sham ¶まがいものの imitation；sham；counterfeit《coins》；《文》spurious.

まがう 紛う 《見違えられる》be mistaken [taken]《for, to be》; be confused《with》；《似ている》《文》resemble ¶まがう方なき unmistakable. [文例▷]

まお 真顔 ¶真顔になる look serious；put on《文》assume] a serious look；straighten one's face / 真顔で with a serious look；《tell a joke》with a straight face / 真顔でいる keep a straight face.

まき 籬 a rough-woven《bamboo》fence.

まがし 間貸し ¶間貸しする take in lodgers；《米》rent rooms [《英》let rooms [lodgings]. マガジンラック a magazine rack.

まかす 負かす 《勝つ》beat；《文》defeat；get the better of；《文》worst；《口語》lick；《米口語》whip (ちょんちょんに)；《より勝る》outdo；《文》surpass；be better than；《文》be superior to.

まかず 間数 the number of rooms. [文例▷]

まかせる 任せる leave sth to sb；trust sb with sth；leave [put] sth in sb's hands ¶商売を雇い人に任せる leave one's business in the charge [hands] of one's employees / 運を天に任せる ¶うん！ / 足に任せて歩く walk where [just as] one's feet take one. [文例▷]

まがたま 勾玉 a comma-shaped bead.

まかない 賄い boarding；providing meals ¶賄いをする board；provide sb with meals / 賄いつき下宿 board and lodging / 賄い費[料] the charge for board.

まかなう 賄う 《食事を》⇒まかない（賄いをする）；《費用を》pay；meet；cover / 月 20 万円で一家を賄う maintain [feed and clothe] one's family on a budget of 200,000 yen a month.

まかふしぎ 摩訶不思議 ¶摩訶不思議な mysterious.

まがまがしい 禍々しい《文》ill-omened；unlucky；sinister.

まがも 《鳥》a wild duck；a mallard.

まがり¹ 曲がり a bend；a turn；a turning；a curve.

まがり² 間借り ¶間借りをする take [rent] a [bed-sitting] room；find [take] lodgings；《米》room《in sb's house》/ 間借り生活をする live in lodgings；live in a rented room / 間借り人 a lodger；a tenant；a paying guest；a roomer.

まがりかど 曲がり角 a corner (of a corridor)；《街路の》a street corner；a turning《in the road》⇒かど¹ ¶曲がり角を曲がる turn [go round] a corner (of the street) / 曲がり角に来た日本経済 the Japanese economy at the crossroads. [文例▷]

まがりくねる 曲がりくねる wind；meander ¶曲がりくねった winding；meandering；《文》sinuous；《文》serpentine；《文》tortuous.

まかりでる 罷り出る 《出頭する》report《to》；《文》present oneself；appear (on the stage)；come forward；《退出する》leave；《文》withdraw.

まかりとおる 罷り通る 《強引に通る》push one's way《through》；《勝手を通す》have one's own way；《提案などが主語》be pushed [steamrolled] through.

まかりならぬ 罷りならぬ must not do；be not allowed to do.

まがりなりに 曲がりなりに somehow or other；after a fashion；though not quite satisfactorily.

---

liminaries. / You should have got to the point sooner. / 英文の手紙には，時候のあいさつの前置きはいらない。When you write a letter in English, there is no need to preface it with any remarks about the season.

まえばらい 代金は前払いです。The price is payable [to be paid] in advance.

まがり 雪がふりそうなけしきであった。《雪が降っているようだった》It looked as if it were snowing. / 《雪のように白かった》It was as white as snow.

まかず その家の間数は幾つですか。How many rooms are there in that house?

まかせる 僕に任せろ。Leave it to me. / それは君の判断に任せる。I leave it to your discretion. / 心に任せぬことばかりだ。Everything goes wrong for me. / 万事まかせて，君は休暇を取りたまえ。You can dump everything on him and go away on leave. / この種の翻訳の仕事は全部コンピューターに任せるという時代が来るだろうか。Will the day ever come when we can turn all translation work of this sort over to computers?

まがりかど 2つ目の曲がり角を右へお出でなさい。Take the second turning to the right. / 曲がり角を間違えたらしい。It seems we took [We seem to have taken] the wrong turning. / 彼は今や俳優として，一つの曲がり角に来ていると言えよう。It could be said that he is [has arrived] at a turning point in his career as an actor.

まかりとおる こんな不正がまかり通るようでは，世も末だ。There's no justice in this world if such (wicked) behavior goes unchallenged.

まかりまちがう 罷り間違う ¶まかり間違うと if things do go wrong [against one]; if the worst comes to the worst; if the worst should [does] happen / まかり間違っても even in the worst case; at the worst.

まがる 曲がる 〈湾曲する〉 bend; curve; be bent; be crooked; 〈回る〉turn; go round; round; 〈向きを変える〉make a turn; 〈傾く〉 lean ¶右に曲がる turn to the right / 年を取って腰が曲がる be bent [stooped] with age / 腰が曲がっていない have a straight back / 曲がった 〈湾曲した〉bent; curved; crooked; 〈不正直な〉dishonest; 《口語》crooked;《英俗》 bent; 〈傾斜した〉leaning / 曲がった事をする do wrong; behave dishonestly. 文例⬇

マカロニ macaroni ¶マカロニウエスタン a spaghetti western.

まき¹ 巻き 〈ひと巻き〉a roll 《of suiting》;〈書物の〉a volume; a book ⇨かん² ¶針金を30巻きしてコイルを作る make a coil of wire with thirty turns; wind thirty turns of wire to make a coil / 8日巻きの時計 an eight-day clock.

まき² 薪 《a piece of》firewood [wood] ¶まきを集める gather wood for fuel / まき割りをする chop [split] wood / まき割りおの a hatchet; an ax(e).

まきあがる 巻き上がる 〈煙などが〉curl [roll, 《文》wreathe] up.

まきあげき 巻き揚げ機 a winch; a windlass.

まきあげる 巻き上げる 〈巻いて上げる〉wind [roll] sth up;〈奪う〉take sth away from sb; rob sb 《of his money》; extort 《money》from sb;〈だまして〉cheat [swindle, wheedle] sb 《out of his money》¶ほこりを巻き上げる fling up dust; raise a cloud of dust / フィルムを1こま巻き上げる advance the film a frame.

マキアベリズム Machiavellianism; Machiavellism.

まきえ¹ 蒔絵 gold [silver] lacquer ¶金蒔絵の箱 a gold-laquered box / 高蒔絵 raised lacquerwork.

まきえ² 撒き餌 〈魚釣りの〉《sink》ground bait;《米》chum;〈小鳥の〉scattered food ¶撒き餌で魚を寄せる attract fish with ground bait; ground-bait the fish.

まきおこす 巻き起こす create 《a sensation》; give rise to 《much controversy》.

まきがい 巻き貝 〈貝〉a snail;〈貝殻〉a spiral [snail] shell.

まきかえし 巻き返し ¶巻き返しを図る rally; try to recover from a setback.

まきがみ 巻き紙 rolled letter paper; 〈ひと巻きの紙〉a roll of paper.

まきげ 巻き毛 a curl; a ringlet.

まきこむ 巻き込む 〈巻き入れる〉roll [wrap] (up) in;〈波などが〉engulf; swallow (up); 〈引き入れる〉drag in;〈巻き添えにする〉involve 《in》. ¶機械[車輪]に巻き込まれる be caught in a machine [under a wheel] / 戦争に巻き込まれる be involved in [dragged into] a war.

まきじた 巻き舌 ¶巻き舌で言う trill [roll] one's r's.

まきじゃく 巻き尺 a tape measure; a (measuring) tape; a tapeline ¶巻き尺で計る measure with a tape.

まきずし 巻き寿司 rolled sushi.

まきぞえ 巻き添え ¶巻き添えを食う be [get] involved [entangled] (in); get mixed up (in 《a quarrel》).

まきた 真北 due north.

まきタバコ 巻きタバコ a cigarette ⇨タバコ

まきちらす 撒き散らす throw about; scatter about; spread (pollutants) about;《文》strew (flowers); sprinkle 《the ground with sand》¶金をまき散らす throw [fling] one's money about: squander one's money.

まきつく 巻き付く twine [wind, coil] round sth;〈蛇が〉wind itself round 《a victim》¶《植物がつるで》巻き付いて伸びる coil its way 《from tree to tree》.

まきつける 巻き付ける put 《a wire》round sth; wind [twine, coil, tie] 《a piece of string》 round sth.

まきとりし 巻き取り紙 〈新聞用の〉a roll of newsprint.

まきなおし まき直し ⇨しん³ (新規まき直し).

まきば 牧場 a pasture; grazing land; a meadow.

まきもどす 巻き戻す rewind 《a film》.

まきもの 巻き物 a makimono; a scroll; a roll ¶巻き物を広げる[巻く] unroll [roll up] a scroll.

まぎらす 紛らす 〈心などを〉《文》divert 《one's mind》; distract 《one's attention》;《文》beguile 《the time》;〈隠す〉《文》conceal; hide;〈回避する〉《文》evade; turn 《a question》aside; dodge ¶話を紛らす talk evasively; shift the conversation into another channel / 悲しみを笑いに紛らす hide [conceal] one's grief with a smile. 文例⬇

まぎらわしい 紛らわしい 〈混同しやすい〉confusing; misleading;〈不明瞭な〉vague; unclear; indistinct; obscure;〈あいまいな〉ambiguous;《文》equivocal.

-まぎれ …紛れ ¶腹立ち紛れに in a fit of anger [passion] / 苦し紛れに in one's agony;

まがる その家は角を曲がった所です。 The house is just around the corner. / 僕はこの角で曲がります。 Here's my corner. / 道路はそこで左に曲がっていた。 The road made a turn to the left there. / 僕は曲がったことは嫌いです。 I hate anything that is not fair and aboveboard.

まぎらす 彼女は寂しさを紛らすためにピアノを弾いていた。 She was playing the piano to relieve her loneliness. / 彼は冗談に紛らしてしまおうとした。 He tried to avoid trouble by making a joke of it.

まぎれこむ 僕の本が君の本の中へ紛れ込んだ。 Some of my books have got mixed (in) with yours.

まぎれもない それは紛れもないあの人の声であった。 There was no doubt that it was his voice.

まぎれる 多忙に紛れてごぶさた致しました。 I am sorry that I have been so busy that I have not written to you up to [until] now.

まく¹ 今3幕目です。 The third act is now on. / 幕が開くと別れの場だ。 The curtain rises on a scene of lovers parting. / 幕が左

まぎれこむ

in desperation / くやし紛れに in a fit of pique;《文》to vent [to give vent to] one's annoyance (chagrin).

まぎれこむ 紛れ込む get mixed (in [up]) 《with》; creep in [into]; disappear [be lost] 《among, in》; find its [one's] way (into).

まぎれもない 紛れもない unmistakable; evident; obvious; 〈当の…〉the very ¶紛れもない事実 an obvious [《文》indisputable] fact / 紛れもなく unmistakably; undoubtedly; beyond [without (a)] doubt. 文例⇩

まぎれる 紛れる 〈取り違えられる〉be mistaken 《for》; 〈区別がつかなくなる〉be confused 《with》; be lost 《among, in》; get mixed 《(in) with, among》; 〈心が〉《文》be diverted 《from one's cares》; 《文》be beguiled ¶やみに紛れて under cover of night / 多忙に紛れて under the pressure of business / 〈子供が〉遊びに紛れて勉強を忘れる be too absorbed in enjoying oneself to think of one's studies. 文例⇩

まぎわ 間際 〈…の〉間際に just before; on the point of 《doing》/ 卒業間際に《文》on the eve of one's graduation / 発車間際に when the train was about to pull out / 間際になって at the last moment [minute].

まく¹ 幕 a curtain; a hanging screen; hangings; 〈劇の〉an act;〈相撲の〉the senior grade ¶第2幕第2場 Act 2, Scene 2 ★引用句の出所を示す場合には Macbeth II, ii, 62 (『マクベス』, 第2幕, 第2場, 第62行) のように略記する / 3幕6場の芝居 a play in three acts and six scenes / 一幕物 a one-act play / 幕を張る stretch a curtain / 幕を開ける〈上に〉raise the curtain / 〈横に〉draw the curtain (aside) / ベルを鳴らして幕を上げる[降ろす] ring up [down] the curtain. 文例⇩

まく² 膜〈粘膜〉a membrane;〈薄い層〉a film.

まく³ 巻く wind (up); roll (up); reel 〈糸を〉; wrap 〈包む〉; bind [tie] round 〈くくる〉; furl 〈旗など〉/ 時計を巻く wind up a clock.

まく⁴ 蒔く sow 〈seeds〉. 文例⇩

まく⁵ 撒く scatter;《文》strew; sprinkle;〈水を〉water 〈the garden〉;〈同行者を〉give the slip;〈追っ手を〉throw 《a policeman》off the scent [track] ¶飛行機からビラをまく drop [scatter] handbills from an airplane.

まくあい 幕間《米》an intermission [《英》interval] (between the acts) ¶幕間狂言 an interlude.

まくあき 幕開き the rise of the curtain; the start [beginning] 《of sth》.

まくうち 幕内〈相撲〉a senior-grade sumo wrestler.

まくぎれ 幕切れ the fall of the curtain; the end of an act ¶〈出来事などが〉幕切れになる come [be brought] to an end. 文例⇩

まぐさ 秣 fodder; feed; hay; provender ¶馬にまぐさをやる fodder [put out feed for] a horse / まぐさおけ a manger; a crib.

まくした 幕下〈相撲〉a junior-grade sumo wrestler.

まくしたてる まくし立てる talk on and on;《文》talk volubly;《文》argue vehemently;《文》harangue;《文》declaim; rant; rattle on 《away》.

まぐそ 馬糞 horse dung.

まぐち 間口 a frontage;〈横幅〉width; breadth ¶間口30メートルのビル a building with a frontage of 30 meters.

まくつ 魔窟〈悪者の巣〉a den;〈売春宿〉a brothel.

マグナカルタ《西洋史》Magna Carta [Charta].

マグニチュード〈地震の規模〉magnitude. 文例⇩

マグネシア《化》magnesia.

マグネシウム《化》magnesium.

まくのうち 幕の内〈弁当〉a lunch with rice and side dishes packed in a box;〈相撲の〉⇒まくうち.

マグマ《地質》magma.

まくら 枕 a pillow; a headrest; a block 《機械の》¶〈学童などがする〉枕の投げ合い a pillow fight / 腕を枕にする rest [pillow] one's head on one's arm / 枕をかわす sleep together; sleep with sb / 枕を高くして眠る sleep in peace [without fear];《文》sleep a peaceful sleep / 枕を並べて討ち死にする die all together;《文》perish flank to flank / 枕絵 a pornographic picture / 枕掛け[覆い] a pillowcase; a pillow slip / 枕捜し〈事〉(a) bedroom theft /〈人〉a bedroom thief / 枕許に at [by] one's bedside.

まくらぎ 枕木〈鉄道の〉《米》a (railroad) tie; a crosstie;《英》a (railway) sleeper.

まくらことば 枕詞 a stock [set] epithet; a 'pillow word'.

マクラメ〈レース〉macramé.

まくる 捲る turn [roll, tuck] up ¶腕をまくる roll one's sleeves up / ズボンの上までまくり上げる roll one's trouser legs (up) above one's knees / まくったそでを下ろす roll one's sleeves down / すそをまくって流れを渡る wade across a stream with one's dress tucked up.

-まくる ¶しゃべりまくる talk and talk; talk on and on; do all the talking 《hardly letting anyone else speak》.

右に開く. The curtains part. / 幕が下りる. The curtain falls. / 長い物語もついに幕になった. The long story has at last come to an end [been played out]. / 君の出る幕じゃない. This is no business of yours. / いよいよ僕らの出る幕だ. This is where we come in. / もはや僕の出る幕ではない. I have served my turn.

まく⁴ この畑には小麦をまきます. We are going to sow this field with [米] to] wheat. / まかぬ種は生えぬ. Nothing comes of [from] nothing. 《諺》/ No pains, no gains. 《諺》/ One must sow before one can reap.

まぐきれ にぎやかに幕切れとなった. The curtain fell on a merry scene.

まぐち その敷地は間口が20メートル, 奥行が50メートルある. The lot is 20 meters wide and [by] 50 meters deep. | The lot is 20 meters in width and 50 meters in depth. / あの人の学問は間口が広い. His learning covers a wide range of subjects.

マグニチュード 今度の地震はマグニチュード6であった. The re-

まぐれあたり まぐれ当たり a chance [lucky] hit; a fluke;《野球》a scratch hit ¶まぐれ当たりで(succeed) by a fluke; by a freak of chance. 文例⇩

まくれる 捲れる be [get] turned up [inside out].

マクロ ¶マクロ経済学 macroeconomics / マクロ経済学的 macroeconomic / マクロの世界 の macrocosmic (laws of the universe).

まぐろ《魚》a tunny, a tuna (fish).

まぐわ 馬鍬 a harrow; a rake.

まくわうり a melon.

まけ 負け《文》(a) defeat; a loss; a lost game ¶(結局)負けになる come out a loser / 負け犬 an [the] underdog.

まげ 髷〈髪〉a chignon (女の); a topknot (力士などの) ¶髪をまげに結う do one's hair in a chignon; tie (one's hair in) a topknot / まげ物 a period play [novel].

まけいくさ 負け戦 a losing [lost] battle [war]; a defeat. 文例⇩

まけおしみ 負け惜しみ 《be nothing but》 sour grapes ¶負け惜しみを言う blame one's failure on circumstances to console oneself; give in [《文》 yield] with (a) bad grace; be a bad loser / 負け惜しみを言わない accept defeat gracefully [with (a) good grace]; be a good loser.

まけぎらい 負け嫌い ⇨まけずぎらい.

まけこす 負け越す have more losses than possible wins; have already lost more than half one's matches ¶〈相手に対して〉 be losing [have lost] to sb by (three) matches.

まけじだましい 負けじ魂《文》an unyielding [indomitable] spirit.

まけずおとらず 負けず劣らず equally (well); as...as;〈競争などで〉 neck and neck ¶負けず劣らず勉強する work equally hard; work as hard as each other / 負けず劣らずの evenly-[closely-]matched; as good (as). 文例⇩

まけずぎらい 負けず嫌い 文例⇩

まげもの 曲げ物 a round wooden chip box.

まける 負ける lose (a game);《文》 be defeated; be beaten;《文》 be worsted;《文》 suffer a defeat; get [have] the worst of it;〈屈する〉《文》be overcome (by);《文》 yield (to); give in (to);〈劣る〉 be second [《文》 inferior] to; fall behind;〈かぶれる〉 get a rash from《shaving》; react to《lacquer》 by coming out in a rash;〈値引きする〉 lower [reduce, cut] (the price); make a reduction (in the price); bring (the [one's]) price) down; come down (to 800 yen) ¶誘惑に負ける yield [give way] to temptation / だれにも負けない be second to none; be unbeatable / 虫に負けやすい《文》 be susceptible to insect bites / 値段を1割負ける reduce the price ten per cent; take ten per cent off the price / 値段を負けさせる get [have] the [sb's] price reduced; (try to) get sb's price down; beat [knock] down the [sb's] price. 文例⇩

まげる 曲げる〈曲がらせる〉bend; curve;〈意味などを〉twist; distort;《文》 pervert ¶ひざを曲げる運動《体操》(do) a knee bend / 意志を曲げる act against one's will / 主義を曲げる《文》 sacrifice [compromise, make a compromise with] one's principles. 文例⇩

まけんき 負けん気《競争心》(a) competitive spirit; a spirit of rivalry ⇨まけじだましい ¶けん気の男《文》 a man of spirit / 負けん気を出す show fight; brace oneself (up) for a fight.

まご[1] 孫 a grandchild; a grandson (男); a granddaughter (女) ¶孫子の代まで down to posterity.

まご[2] 馬子 a pack-[road-]horse driver. 文例⇩

まごころ 真心 sincerity;《文》 a true heart ¶真心のある sincere;《文》 truehearted / 真心こめて faithful / 真心こめて with one's whole heart /《文》 earnestly; sincerely;《文》 devotedly / 真心を尽くす be faithful (to).

まごつく be confused; be at a loss (which way

---

cent quake was 6 [registered a magnitude of 6] on the Richter scale.

まぐれあたり 君が三塁打を打ったって? まぐれ当たりだろう。 You hit a three-bagger, did you? It must have been [can't have been anything but] a fluke.

まけ 裁判は被告の負けになった。 The plaintiff lost the case. | The decision was given against the plaintiff.

まけいくさ 負け戦になってきた。 We are fighting a losing battle [playing a losing game]. | いずれにせよ、初めから負け戦だったのだ。 After all, it was a lost cause from the beginning.

まけずおとらず いずれも負けず劣らずの勢いだ。 Both sides are equally strong.

まけずぎらい あの男は負けず嫌いだ。 He hates losing [to lose]. | He's a bad loser.

まける 彼に負けてなるものかと私は一層努力した。 Not to be outdone by him, I tried [worked] even harder. / 正々堂々と戦って負けなさる。 Play the game and be a good loser. / この際は負けるが勝ちだ。 This is where we should stoop to conquer. / 君には負けたよ。 Well, I'm beaten. | You've got me beat. / 彼はまだまだ若い者に負けない。 He can still keep up with young people. / 3千円に負けておきなさい。 Bring the price down to 3,000 yen. | Make it 3,000 yen. / もう少し負けてもらえませんか。 Can't you give me a better price? | Can't you come down any further?

まげる だれの命令であっても規定は曲げられない。 Nobody can force us to bend the rules. / まげてこの案をご承諾願えませんでしょうか。 Could you oblige us by giving your consent to this plan?

まご[1] お孫さんがおありですか。 Do you have any grandchildren? | Are you a grandfather [grandmother]?

まご[2] 馬子にも衣装。 Clothes make the man. | The tailor makes the man. 《諺》| Fine feathers make fine birds. 《諺》

まこと 誠に申し訳ありません。 I really don't know how to apologize to you. / 誠にそのとおりです。 You are quite right.

まごまご 火事と聞いたがまごまごするだけで何一つ出せなかった。 We were so flustered by the fire alarm that we didn't manage to save anything at all. / まごまごしているとつかまるぞ。 Be quick [Look sharp], or you will be caught. / まごまごするな。〈気をつけろ〉 Be careful. / 〈さっさとやれ〉 Be quick. | Make it snappy! / まごまごしてはいられな

まこと　**to go)**; be upset; be flurried; be not certain 《what to do》; be baffled; get muddled ¶まごついて in a 《one's》 flurry.

まこと　誠〈誠意〉《文》a true heart;《文》faithfulness; sincerity;〈真実〉the truth;〈事実〉(the) fact(s) ¶誠の true; real;〈実際の〉actual;〈正直な〉honest; sincere;〈にせものでない〉genuine /〈誠のある《文》〉truehearted; faithful / 誠に〈実際に〉really; truly; indeed;〈非常に〉very; much; greatly;〈心から〉sincerely; from (the bottom of) one's heart. 文例⇩

まことしやか　実[真]しやか ¶まことしやかな plausible;《文》specious / まことしやかに as if it were true;《文》with much show of truth.

まごのて　孫の手 a back scratcher.

まごびき　孫引き ¶孫引きする quote 《a passage》at second hand 《without admitting it》; requote.

まごまご ¶まごまごする〈うろたえる〉be flurried; be confused; be upset; lose one's presence of mind; be baffled; be bewildered; be perplexed; be embarrassed;〈ぐずぐずする〉hesitate in coming to a decision; be slow 《in taking action》. 文例⇩

まこも〖植〗wild [Indian] rice.

まさ　柾 ⇨ まさめ.

まさか surely 《not》; cannot 《be, do》; It is unlikely [impossible] that…;《not》by any means;《not》on any account ¶まさかのとき ⇨ まんいち. 文例⇩

まさかり　鉞〈材木用の〉《米》a broadax;《英》a felling axe;〈兵器の〉a battle-ax(e).

まさぐる grope; feel about 《for sth》.

まさご　真砂 sand ¶浜の真砂の数知れず《文》be as numberless as the grains of sand on the seashore.

まさしく　正しく〈確かに〉surely; certainly; no doubt; undoubtedly;〈明らかに〉evidently;〈真に〉really; truly.

マサチューセッツ Massachusetts (略: Mass.).

まさつ　摩擦 friction;〈あつれき〉friction; trouble;《文》discord ¶摩擦する rub 《against, with》; chafe 《the skin》/ 摩擦を生じる〈避ける〉cause [avoid] friction / 摩擦音〖音声〗a fricative (sound) / 摩擦電気[熱] frictional electricity [heat]. 文例⇩

まさに　正に〈ちょうど〉just; exactly;〈確かに〉surely; certainly; no doubt;〈滞りなく〉duly;〈全く〉really; quite ¶まさに…せんとする be about to do; be on the (very) point [verge] of doing.

まざまざ(と) clearly; vividly.

まさめ　柾目 straight grain (of wood) ¶まさめの通った straight-grained.

まさゆめ　正夢 a prophetic dream; a dream which is later to come true.

まさる　勝る be better 《than》;《文》surpass;《文》excel; outdo;《文》be superior 《to》¶聞きしに勝る眺め a view that exceeds one's expectations in its beauty / 勝るとも劣らない《文》be in no way [not at all] inferior 《to》.

まざる　混[交]ざる ⇨ まじる.

まし　増し〈増加〉(an) increase; (an) addition; (an) extra (余分) ¶賃金2割増し a 20 per cent raise [《米》boost] in wages / 1年増しに increasingly with every year /…より増しである be (at least) better than…. 文例⇩

まじえる　交える〈交差する〉cross;〈取り交わす〉exchange;〈混ぜる〉mix ¶砲火を交える exchange fire; engage in a battle 《with》. 文例⇩

ましかく　真四角 a regular [true] square.

まじきり　間仕切り a partition between two rooms; a room divider; a partition wall (壁).

ました　真下 ¶真下に right [just] under [below]; directly below [underneath].

マジック〈魔術〉magic ¶マジックペン a marker; a marker [felt-tip] pen / マジックナンバー〖野球〗the magic number 《for the

かった. There was no time to be lost.

まさか　まさか！ That can't be true! | You don't say so [tell me]! |《俗》No kidding! / きのう彼女に会ったよ.—まさか！—いや，本当だよ. I saw her yesterday.—Oh, you're kidding!—No, I really did. / あいて英語の先生だって？ まさか. Him? An English teacher? You must be joking! | He is a teacher of English? Never! / まさか1人でそんなに食う者はなかろう. One could hardly be expected to eat so much. / 彼が生きているのがいやになったと言ったときはまさかと思っていたが，その2日あとに本当に自殺してしまった. I didn't take him seriously when he said he was tired of life, but two days later he really did go and kill himself.

まさつ　原始人は木片を摩擦して火を起こした. Primitive man made fire by rubbing two pieces of wood together.

まさに　金1万円まさに受け取りました. 浅田様. Received from [of] Mr. Asada the sum of 10,000 yen. / あれからまさに1年だ. It is just one year [fully twelve months] since then. / 花火大会はまさに壮観だった. The display of fireworks was nothing short of spectacular. / 両国はまさに戦端を開かんとしている. The two countries are on the verge of war. / 今やまさに内閣改造を実行すべき時である. It is high time that a reorganization of the Cabinet was carried out. / 君こそまさにこの役に適任の人だ. If you are not the right man for this post, nobody is. [who is?]

まさゆめ　それは正夢だった. The dream came true.

まさる　自然美の点では奈良は京都に勝る. Nara surpasses Kyoto in natural beauty. / 健康は富に勝る. Health is above wealth. / 我が家に勝る所はない. There's no place like home.

まし　郵便切手代用の際は1割増しとなります. Ten per cent extra if paid in postage stamps. / 彼の商売は1年増しに繁盛した. His business prospered more and more every year. / 少しでもあれば無いよりまし だ. Something is better than nothing. |《諺》そんな生活をするならいっそ死んだ方がましだ. I would rather [sooner] die than lead such a life. / そんなことに金を使うくらいなら捨てた方がましだ. You might as well throw your money away as spend it on such a thing.

まじえる　彼は演説に巧みなユーモ

まして 〈肯定〉much [still] more; 〈否定〉much [still] less; 〈言うまでもなく〉not to mention [speak of]...; to say nothing of...; let alone 文例⇩

まじない 呪い a charm 《against》; a spell; 〈呪文(じゅもん)〉《文》an incantation; magic words; 〈わけのわからない言語・動作〉mumbo jumbo; 〈手品師の〉(a) hocus-pocus ¶まじないをする charm; use a charm / まじないをかける cast a spell 《on》. 文例⇩

まじまじ ¶まじまじと見る look hard 《at》; look sb full in the face; stare (hard) 《at》.

まじめ ¶まじめな serious;《文》grave;《文》sober; 〈熱心な〉《文》earnest; 〈着実な〉steady; honest / まじめな人 a serious(-minded) [an honest] person / まじめな顔をする look grave [sober] / 〈笑わずに〉まじめな顔をしている keep [《文》maintain] a straight face; keep one's face straight / まじめに seriously; 《文》earnestly; 〈忠実に〉faithfully; honestly / まじめになる 〈本気になる〉get [《文》become] serious; 〈顔つきが〉straighten one's face; look grave; 〈品行上〉turn over a new leaf; reform; be a reformed character / まじめくさる look solemn; 《文》assume a solemn air. 文例⇩

ましゃく 間尺 ¶間尺に合わない do not pay; be not worthwhile [worth one's while].

ましゅ 魔手 evil power ¶魔手を伸ばす 《文》 make sb an object of one's evil design(s); 《文》attempt to make a victim of sb / 魔手にかかる 《文》fall a victim 《to》; fall into sb's clutches.

まじゅつ 魔術 magic; 《文》the magic art(s); 《文》the black art ⇒まほう; 〈奇術〉jugglery ¶魔術師 a magician; a juggler (手品師).

マシ(ュ)マロ 〈菓子〉a marshmallow.

まじょ 魔女 a witch; 《文》a sorceress ¶魔女狩り witch-hunting; a witch-hunt.

ましょう 魔性 ¶魔性の devilish / 魔性の女 《文》an enchantress / 魔性のもの an evil spirit.

ましょうめん 真正面 ⇒まっしょうめん.

ましら 猿 a monkey ¶ましらの如く like a monkey; 《文》with monkey-like [simian] agility.

まじり 混[交]じり ⇒まじりけ ¶しらが交じりの grizzled 《hair》; streaked with gray. 文例⇩

まじりあう 混[交]じり合う be [get] mixed (together);《文》intermingle 《with one another》;《文》be commingled 《with》;《文》commingle.

まじりけ 混[交]じり気 ¶交じり気のある impure; adulterated / 交じり気のない pure; unadulterated; unalloyed; unmixed; 〈本物の〉genuine.

まじりもの 混[交]じり物 〈不純物〉an impurity; 〈混合物〉a mixture. ¶交じり物のある adulterated 《wine》.

まじる 混[交]じる 〈混ざる〉be [get] mixed 《with》; 《文》be mingled 《with》; creep into; 〈仲間に入る〉join; take part (in). 文例⇩

まじろぐ 瞬ぐ blink ⇒まばたく ¶まじろぎもせずに見ている gaze steadily [unblinkingly] 《at》.

まじわり 交わり 〈交際〉⇒こうさい³; 〈共通集合〉〈数〉an intersection; a meet.

まじわる 交わる 〈交際する〉associate 《with》; keep company 《with》; 〈交差する〉intersect; cross ¶親しく交わる be on close [intimate] terms 《with》; be great friends 《with》/ 良い友と交わる keep good company / 人と交わらない keep one's own company; stay away [keep aloof] from others / 互いに交わらない 2 つの直線 two nonintersecting lines. 文例⇩

ます¹ 升 〈計量器〉a measure; 〈相撲・寄席などの〉a box (seat) ¶一升升 a one-sho measure / 升売りする sell by the measure / 升目をよくする[ごまかす] give good [short] measure.

ます² 鱒 a trout (単複同形).

ます³ 増す 〈増える〉increase; gain; grow; 〈増やす〉increase; 《文》augment; add (to); 〈膨張する〉swell; 〈高まる〉rise; 〈高める〉raise ¶数[量]が増す increase [grow] in number(s) [volume] / 人気が増す gain in popularity / 世間の信用が増す public confidence 《in the company》increases [rises] / 1 語を増すごとに 10 円払う pay 10 yen for each additional word / 俸給を 2 割増す raise sb's salary by 20 per cent. 文例⇩

まず 先ず 〈最初に〉first (of all); in the first place; before everything; to begin with; for a start;《口語》for starters; 〈ほとんど〉about; almost; 〈概して〉on the whole ¶まずまずの tolerable; passable ⇒まあまあ. 文例⇩

ますい 麻酔 〈医〉anesthesia ¶麻酔が覚めるにつれて as the anesthetic wears off / 麻酔をかける give [administer] (an) anesthetic 《to》; put

---

アを交えた. He interspersed his speech with well-chosen humor.
まして 先生でさえそんなに勉強しなければならないのなら, まして学生はそうだ. If the teacher has to work so hard, how much more must the students!/彼らは必要品さえ買えない, ましてぜいたく品はなおさらだ. They cannot afford to buy daily necessities, much less luxuries./彼は英語すら知らない, ましてフランス語はなおさらだ. He knows no English, let alone [not to speak of] French.
まじない それは何のまじないですか. What is that mumbo jumbo meant to mean?
まじめ 君はまじめなのか. Are you serious?/〈本気で言っているのか〉Do you (really) mean it?/まじめなことを茶化してはいけない. You must not make fun of a serious matter./僕は冗談に言ったつもりなのに彼はまじめにとった. He took seriously what I meant for a joke.
まじり 雨交じりの雪が降っていた. Snow was falling mingled with rain./Rain was falling, mingled with the snow. (★ snow に雪が付いている故に降っている物の主体が雪になる.)
まじる この綿布には綿が少し交じっている. There is some cotton interwoven in this silk cloth.
まじわる 人はその交わる友を見ればわかる. A man is known by the company he keeps.
ます³ 長雨で川の水かさが増した. The river has risen [swollen] as a result of the long rain./街路樹

まずい 〈食物が〉nasty; bad-tasting; unpleasant(-tasting);《文》unpalatable; not very nice; not to one's taste;《文》unsavory; indifferent 《food》; 〈味がない〉flat; tasteless; 〈醜い〉plain; ugly; 〈拙劣な〉poor; clumsy; unskillful; 〈不得策な〉(be) not a good idea;《文》unwise;《文》unadvisable ¶まずいことになる get into (a spot of) trouble; get into [find oneself in] an awkward position ★ get a girl into trouble と言うと,「妊娠させる」の意になる / まずそうな uninviting / まずそうに食べる eat [pick at] one's food as if one doesn't like it / まずく行っても at the worst. 文例①
マスカット muscat grapes; muscats.
マスカラ mascara ¶マスカラをつけたまつ毛 mascaraed eyelashes / マスカラを濃く塗った目 eyes heavy with mascara.
マスク a mask; 〈野球のキャッチャー, フェンシングの選手の〉 a face guard; 〈顔立ち〉features; 〈looks〉 ¶流感予防用のマスクをかける wear a flu mask. 文例①
マスクメロン a muskmelon;《米》a cantaloup(e).
マスゲーム massed calisthenics [gymnastics].
マスコット a (good-luck) mascot.
マスコミ the media (of mass communication); the press; journalism ¶マスコミに騒がれる get [《文》receive] a lot of publicity in the media [press] / マスコミに乗りたがる[を敬遠する] seek [avoid] press publicity.
まずしい 貧しい poor;《文》needy ⇒ びんぼう ¶貧しい家に生まれる be born poor; be born in a poor family / 貧しい暮らしをする be badly off;《文》live in poverty.
マスター 〈経営者の〉the proprietor; 〈マネージャー〉the manager; 〈バーの〉《米》a barkeep(er);《英》the landlord《of a pub》; 〈修士〉a master《of arts, science》. ★ 日本語の「マスター」は英語では必ずしも master とはならない ¶マスターキー a master key / マスターコース a master's course《in law》/ マスターする master《English》.
マスタード ⇒ からし.
マスターベーション masturbation.
マスト a mast ¶3本マストの船 a three-masted ship; a three-master.
マストドン 【古生物】a mastodon.
マスプロ mass production ⇒ りょうさん ¶マスプロ教育 production-line education.
ますます more and more;《文》increasingly; still more [less] ¶ますます勉強する work (even) harder / ますます悪くなる go from bad to worse / ますますたくさん in increasing numbers. 文例①
マスメディア ⇒ マスコミ.
マズルカ a maz(o)urka.
まぜあわせる 混ぜ合わせる mix together;《文》mingle; blend.
まぜこぜ a jumble ¶まぜこぜにする jumble [mix] up.
まぜごはん 混ぜ御飯 boiled rice mixed with meat and other ingredients.
ませた precocious; forward ¶ませたことを言う talk precociously / ませている be precocious; be forward《for one's age》; be too grown-up for one's age.
まぜ(っ)かえす 混ぜ(っ)返す break in (on sb's talk to ridicule it); jeer at sb; make fun of 《what sb says》; mock.
まぜもの a mixture; a compound ¶混ぜ物のある impure; adulterated / 混ぜ物のない pure; unadulterated.
まぜる 混(交)ぜる mix; blend; adulterate (不純物を); 〈含める〉include ¶コーヒーにブランデーを混ぜる lace one's coffee with brandy / 水を混ぜる dilute《a solution》with water; water sth down. 文例①
マゾヒズム masochism.
まそん 磨損 wear and tear; friction loss; abrasion (機械などの).
また¹ 又 a fork; a crotch; 〈フォークの歯〉a prong ¶またになる fork; be forked / またになった forked《roads》.
また² 股 the crotch; 〈もも〉the thigh; 〈そけい部〉the groin ¶股を広げる open one's legs; put one's legs apart / 股を広げて腰掛ける sit with one's knees apart / 世界を股にかけて歩く travel [knock about] all over the world; be a globe-trotter / 大股に歩く walk in long strides / 股ぐら the crotch.
また³ 又 〈もまた〉too; also; as well;《文》like-

は都市の美観を増す。The trees lining the streets add to the beauty of the city.
まず まず健康。Health first. / 親は自分のことより, まず子供の幸福を考える。Parents put the welfare of their children before their own desires. / まず第一に資金が充分でない。To begin with, we do not have sufficient funds. / 何よりもまず飲食物に注意しなければならない。We must, first of all, be careful about what we eat and drink. / これでまずまず安心だ。Well, we seem to be out of danger now.
まずい 朝飯がどうもまずい。I don't enjoy (my) breakfast. / 熱でもあるのかどうも口がまずい。I have no appetite; perhaps I have a temperature. / こんなことが女房に知れてはまずい。It would be awkward [unpleasant] if my wife got to know of [about] it.
マスク あの歌手はいいマスクをしている。The singer has good [pleasant, attractive] features.
ますます 英語はますます世界語になっている。English has increasingly come into worldwide use. / 会えば会うほど, 彼女にますます引かれるようになった。The more he saw of her, the greater her attraction for him became. / それを聞いて僕はますます行くのが嫌になった。Hearing it, I became even less inclined to go there.
まぜる これはきっとだれかが砂糖に塩を混ぜたんだ。Someone

wise ; 〈再び〉 again; 〈その上〉 and; 《文》 moreover ; besides ¶またの名 another name / またの名を…という be also called… / またいつか another time ; some other time / またある時は on another occasion / またまた, またもや, またしても, またぞろ yet again ; once again / またとない be unique ; 《文》 be matchless ; 《文》 be unequaled ; 《文》 be unparalleled; 《文》 have no equal / または or; either…or… ; in other words (言い換えれば). [文例⇩]

まだ still; 《not》 yet; 〈今までのところ〉 as yet; so far ; 〈その上に〉 besides. [文例⇩]

まだい[1] 間代 (a) room rent.

まだい[2] 〘魚〙 a red sea bream.

またいとこ a second cousin.

またがし 又貸し ¶又貸しする lend 《to Mr. A》 what *one* has borrowed 《from Mr. B》; 〈不動産を〉 sublet. [文例⇩]

マダガスカル Madagascar ¶マダガスカル語 Malagasy / マダガスカル(島民)の Madagascan; Malagasy / マダガスカル島民 a Madagascan ; a Malagasy 《*pl.* -gasy, -gasies》 / マダガスカル民主共和国 the Democratic Republic of Madagascar.

またがみ 股上 the rise ¶また上 20 センチである be 20 centimeters from crotch to waist.

またがり 又借り ¶又借りする borrow *sth* indirectly [at second hand]; 〈不動産を〉 sublease. [文例⇩]

またがる 跨る 〈馬などに〉 ride; mount; sit astride 《a horse》; 〈橋などが〉 span [be laid across] 《a river》; 〈わたる〉 spread [《文》 extend] over 《three years》. [文例⇩]

またぎき 又聞き hearsay ; secondhand [hearsay] information ¶また聞きする hear at second hand ; learn by hearsay.

またぐ 跨ぐ 〈乗る〉 straddle ; 〈越える〉 stride over [across] 《a brook, a fence》. [文例⇩]

またした 股下 the [*one's*] inside leg (measurement).

まだしも rather ; better. [文例⇩]

またずれ 股擦れ 《have》 sore thighs.

またせる 待たせる keep *sb* waiting ; make *sb* wait. [文例⇩]

またたき 瞬き 〈明滅〉 flickering 《of lights》; twinkling 《of a star》; 〈まばたき〉 ⇨まばたき.

またたく 瞬く 〈明滅する〉 twinkle ; flicker ; 〈まばたく〉 ⇨まばたく ¶瞬くともし火 a flickering light / 瞬く間に in a twinkling ; in the twinkling of an eye ; in an instant ; in no time; 《文》 quicker than thought. [文例⇩]

またたび[1] 股旅 the wandering life of a gambler ¶股旅物 stories [adventures] of wandering gamblers.

またたび[2] 〘植〙 a silvervine.

まただなり 又隣 (the) next door but one.

マタニティドレス a maternity dress.

まだまだ still ; still more ; much more ⇨まだ. [文例⇩]

マダム 〈料亭などの〉 the proprietress ; 〈下宿屋などの〉 the landlady ; 〈バーなどの雇われマダム〉 the manageress 《of a saloon》.

まだら 〈小斑点〉 spots ; speckles ; 〈やや大きめの斑点〉 patches ; blotches ¶まだらな spotted ; speckled 《snakes》; brindle(d) 《cows》; 《文》 varicolored 《garments》; streaked 《curtains》 / まだらに in spots [patches]. [文例⇩]

[用法] spotted は, 次の例のように述部用法で使うと「まだらな」よりもむしろ「しみの付いた」「よごれ

[ま]

---

must have mixed salt in with the sugar.

また[3] 彼は語学者でもあり, また音楽家でもある. He is both [at once] a linguist and a musician./ 私は金持ちではない, またなりたくもない. I am not rich, nor do I wish to be. / 一つうそをつくとまたつくようになる. One lie leads to another. / また鉄道事故があった. There has been another railroad accident. / 彼はまた元のように丈夫になった. He is once more as strong as he used to be. | He is his old self again. / 今日もまた彼女は来なかった. She didn't come today either. | She didn't show up again today. / またまたお手数をかけまして恐縮です. I am sorry to put you to such trouble time after time. | I am sorry for troubling you repeatedly in this way. / 町の南には山また山が連なっている. To the south of the town mountains rise one behind another.

まだ ペンキはまだ乾いていない. The paint is still wet. / まだ出来上がらない. It is not finished yet. / まだ雨が降っている. It is still raining. / 休暇までにまだ10日ある. There are still [We still have] ten days before the vacation begins. / 彼にはまだ会ったことがない. I haven't met him as yet. / この冷蔵庫はまだ故障したことがない. This fridge has never been out of order. / 彼はまだ来てなかったので, 皆帰って来た. He hadn't arrived by then, so we all came home. / その事実はまだ証明されていない. That remains [is still] to be proved. / りんごはまだありますか. Have you any more apples? | Have you any apples left? / まだ君に話すことがある. I have something more to tell you. / この家は建ててからまだ1年にしかならない. It is only a year since we built this house.

またがし この本を貸して上げるが, また貸しをしてはいけないよ. You may take this book with you, but don't lend it to anyone else.

またがり この本は斎藤君が田中君から借りたのを僕がまた借りしたのです. Saito has lent me this book which he borrowed from Tanaka.

またがる ロンドンはテムズ河にまたがっている. London lies across [astride] the Thames.

またぐ その男は溝をまたいで立っていた. The man stood straddling the ditch. / そこまではほんの一またぎだ. It's only a step from here.

まだしも そんな屈辱に甘んじるくらいなら, まだしも死んだ方がいい. I would rather [sooner] die than take such an insult lying down. / まだしもこの方がいい. This would be better. / なくした金が僕のだったからまだしもよかった. If it hadn't been my own money that I lost, it'd have been even worse. / 飲んで陽気に騒ぐだけならまだしも, 器物を破壊するなんて許せない. As long as they are just drinking and making merry it's not so bad, but I can't forgive them when they start [but I draw the line at] breaking things.

またせる お待たせしました. Sorry I kept you waiting. | I'm sor-

まだるっこい

た」の意になる：His clothes were spotted with ink. (衣服にインクのしみが付いていた).

まだるっこい slow; tedious; dull; sluggish (挙動の).

まち¹ 町, 街 〈都会〉 a town; a city; 〈街路〉 a street ¶街の女 a prostitute; 《文》 a woman [lady] of the streets; a streetwalker / 町へ行く[にいる] go to [be in] town / 町を通る go down [pass along] a street; 《文》 proceed along [up, down] a street / 町じゅうの評判になっている be the talk of the town / 町中(ﾋﾞｭｳ)で on [in] the street ★ on は《米》, in は《英》. 文例⇩

まち² 〈裁縫〉 a gusset (三角又は菱形); a gore (長細い三角形) ¶まちを入れる put a gore (in a skirt); provide (a skirt) with a gore.

まちあい 待合い a *machiai*; a Japanese-style restaurant to which *geisha* are called ¶待合い政治 behind-the-scenes political dealings.

まちあいしつ 待合室 a waiting room.

まちあかす 待ち明かす ¶ひと晩待ち明かす wait the whole night 《for》; wait up all night 《for》 / ひと月待ち明かす wait 《for》 a whole month.

まちあぐむ 待ちあぐむ get tired [《文》 grow weary] of waiting (any longer); can't wait 《for *sb* to come home》.

まちあわせる 待ち合わせる arrange to meet *sb*; 《文》 meet *sb* by appointment. 文例⇩

まちいしゃ 町医者 a doctor with his [her] own practice; a doctor in (general) practice.

まちうける 待ち受ける wait for; lie in wait for. 文例⇩

まちか 間近 ¶間近な 〈場所が〉 nearby; close (to); 〈時間的に〉 near [close] at hand; 《文》 approaching / 間近に 〈空間的に〉 nearby; close by; at a short distance; 〈時間的に〉 near [close] at hand / 間近になる get [draw] near; 《文》 approach. 文例⇩

まちがい 間違い 〈誤り〉 a mistake; 《文》 an error; something wrong; 〈手落ち〉 a fault; a slip; 〈失策〉 a failure; a blunder; 〈変事〉 an accident ¶間違いのない 〈正確な〉 correct; free from mistakes [errors]; 〈確実な〉 sure; certain; 《文》 unfailing / …と言って間違いない It can [《文》 may] safely be said that…; We can safely say that… / 間違いなく 〈正しく〉 correctly; 《文》 rightly; 〈かならず〉 without fail; 《文》 unfailingly; 〈確かに〉 certainly / 間違いのないように to prevent mistakes; so that everything is all right. 文例⇩

まちがう 間違う ⇒まちがえる ¶間違った wrong; mistaken; incorrect; 《文》 erroneous / 間違って 〈誤って〉 by mistake; 《文》 in error; 〈偶然〉 by accident. 文例⇩

まちがえる 間違える 〈誤る〉 make a mistake; 《文》 commit an error; 〈取り違える〉 take [mistake] (A) for (B); 〈混同する〉 confuse (A) with (B); 《口語》 get (A and B) mixed up ¶道を間違える go the wrong way; take a wrong turning. 文例⇩

まちかど 街角 (at, on) a street corner.

まちかねる 待ち兼ねる wait impatiently [eagerly] 《for》; be impatient 《for》; be on tiptoe 《for》 ¶お待ちかねの新年号 the New Year number you've (all) been waiting for.

まちかまえる 待ち構える be prepared [ready] for; wait (eagerly) for; watch for; be on the watch for; look forward to.

まちくたびれる 待ちくたびれる ⇒まちあぐむ.

まちこうば 町工場 a small factory [works]; a

---

ry to have kept you waiting. ★この2文どちらも実際によく使われるが, 前の方は軽い言い方で, 場合によっては誠意がないように聞こえる. / 私たちは30分近く待たされた. We were kept waiting almost half an hour. / ちょっと待っていてもらって下さい. Please have him wait a moment. / おもてにタクシーを待たせてある. I have a taxi waiting outside. / 待つというなら待たせておけ. Let him wait if he wants to.

またたく 瞬く間に出来上がった. It was done in a twinkling [in a blink]. / ろうそくの火が風に瞬いた. The candle flickered in the draft.

まだまだ 物価はまだまだ上がるだろう. Prices will go up still higher.

まだら ヒョウの毛は黄褐色で黒いまだらがある. The leopard has a tawny skin covered with dark spots.

まだるっこい 時間のたつのがまだるっこいなあ. How slowly (the) time passes!

まち¹ 町じゅうがおもてに出てその行列を見物した. The whole town turned out to see the procession.

まちあわせる 私たちはハチ公の銅像の前で待ち合わせることにした. We arranged to meet at [by] the statue of Hachiko.

まちうける 思いがけない厄介なことが私たちを待ち受けていた. An unexpected problem was in store for us.

まちか 間近で見るとさほど美しくない. Seen from close up it does not look so pretty. / クリスマスも間近い. Christmas is coming. | Christmas is just around the corner.

まちがい おれをだませると思ったら, 大間違いだぞ. If you think you can deceive me, you are greatly mistaken. | You are making a big mistake if you think you can fool me. / 今月中に出来ると思って間違いありません. You may be sure that it will be ready before the month is out. / 間違いなくお出で下さるでしょうか. May I count on your coming? / それに間違いないと思う. I'm positive that it is so. / そういうふうに考えてもおそらく間違いないだろう. We are probably safe in thinking that way. / 我々は間違いは許さない. We have no margin for error. / 途中で何か間違いでもなければよいが. I hope there hasn't been an accident on the way. / それが間違いのもとだ. That's the cause of the mistake.

まちがう この答は間違ってはいませんか. Are you sure this is the right answer? | This answer is right, is it? / その計算はひどく間違っていた. The calculation was wildly wrong [out]. / 手紙のあて名が間違っていた. The letter was wrongly addressed. / 手紙は間違ってよその家へ配達された. The letter was delivered to the wrong address. / 彼は自分が間違っていたことを認めた. He admitted that he was in the wrong. / そんな事は間違ってもやってはいけない. Don't you ever do anything like that. | Be sure never to do such a thing.

まちがえる 自動販売機に100円玉

まちこがれる 待ち焦がれる be impatient ((to do, for sth)); long [((文)) pine] (for sth, to do); wait anxiously ((for)). 文例⇩

まちじかん 待ち時間 (a charge for) waiting time.

まちちん 待ち賃 ¶待ち賃を取られる be charged for waiting time.

まちどお(しい) 待ち遠(し)い 〈自分が主語〉wait impatiently [eagerly] ((for)); 〈対象が主語〉be a long time (in) coming. 文例⇩

まちなみ 町並み (the look of) stores and houses on a street; a street (of stores and houses).

マチネー a matinee; a matinée.

まちのぞむ 待ち望む look forward to ((sth, doing)).

まちはずれ 町外れ the outskirts [edge] of a town ¶町外れにある be on the outskirts [edge] of the town.

まちばり 待ち針 a marking pin [needle].

まちびと 待ち人 文例⇩

まちぶせ 待ち伏せ ¶待ち伏せする lie in wait [ambush] ((for)); ambush; waylay / 待ち伏せている場所へ追い込む drive ((a wild boar)) into ambush.

まちぼうけ 待ちぼうけ ¶待ちぼうけを食わせる break an appointment ((with sb)); 《口語》keep sb waiting in vain; 《口語》stand sb up (特に異性を) / 待ちぼうけを食う go on waiting only to be disappointed [let down]; 《口語》be stood up.

まちまち ¶まちまちな different; various (ideas); conflicting ((opinions)); 《文》diverse ((proposals)) / まちまちに 《文》severally; variously / まちまちである be all different; there are all sorts of ((answers)); there is no (regular) pattern to ((their answers)). 文例⇩

まちもうける 待ち設ける ⇒まちのぞむ.

まちやくば 町役場 a town hall; a town office.

まちわびる 待ちわびる ⇒まちぐむ.

まつ[1] 松 a pine (tree) ¶松の内 the New Year Week / 松飾り the New Year's pine decorations / 松風の音 《文》the soughing of the wind among [in] the pines / 松食い虫 a pine weevil / 松並木 an avenue of pines; a row of pine trees / 松林 a pine grove [wood]; a pinery / 松原 a pine-covered area (near the seashore).

まつ[2] 待つ wait ¶…を待つ wait for…; 《文》await…; 〈うかがう〉watch for ((a chance)); be on the lookout for…; 〈期待する〉look forward to…; 〈…に頼る〉look [turn] to ((sb for help)); depend [rely] on ((sb for support)) / 長い間待つ have a long wait ((for)); be kept waiting for a long time / 寝ずに[外出せずに]待つ wait up [in] ((for)) / 順番を待つ wait (for) one's turn / 今か今かと待つ be on tiptoe with expectation; can't wait ((for sb to arrive)) / 待ちに待った日 the long-awaited day. 文例⇩

-まつ …末 the end ((of)) ¶月末に at the end [on the last day] of the month.

まっか 真っ赤 ¶真っ赤な bright [deep] red; crimson / 真っ赤な嘘 a downright [barefaced] lie / 真っ赤になる turn [go] (bright) red; 〈上気して〉flush deeply; 〈恥じて〉blush scarlet [crimson]; blush violently; blush [redden] to the roots of one's hair / 真っ赤になって怒る be [go] red (in the face) with rage [anger] / 真っ赤に焼ける get [《文》become] red-hot. 文例⇩

まつかさ 松かさ a pinecone; a cone.

まっき 末期 the last [closing] years [period, days]; the last [terminal] stage ¶末期的な 《文》decadent / 末期の患者 a terminal patient / 末期症状 terminal symptoms. 文例⇩

まっくら 真っ暗 ¶真っ暗な pitch-dark; ((as)) dark as pitch [midnight] / あたりが真っ暗になってから after full darkness falls / 真っ暗やみ complete [utter, 《文》total] darkness. 文例⇩

まっくろ 真っ黒 ¶真っ黒な ((as)) black as ink [coal, 《文》ebony]; jet-[coal-]black; inky(-black) / 真っ黒に焦げる be scorched [burned] black; be charred. 文例⇩

まつげ eyelashes; 《文》lashes ¶まつげの長い long-lashed ((eyes)) / 付け[書き]まつげ false [penciled] eyelashes.

まつご 末期 ⇒いまわ, りんじゅう ¶末期の last; dying / 末期の苦しみ 《文》death agony [agonies, throes] / 末期の言葉 one's dying words / 末期の水 the water to moisten a dying person's lips / 末期の水をとる 《文》attend the

---

と間違えて 10 円玉を入れた. I put a 10-yen piece into the vending machine in mistake for a 100(-yen one).

まちこがれる 彼は彼女の到着を待ちこがれていた. He couldn't wait for her to arrive.

まちどお(しい) お待ち遠様でした. I am sorry to have kept you waiting. | 〈客に包装した品を手渡すときなど〉Here you are, Sir [Madam]. | 子供らにはクリスマスが待ち遠しい. To the children Christmas is (in) coming. | The little ones are impatient for Christmas. | 彼女は息子の帰るのが待ち遠しかった. She was waiting impatiently for her son's return.

まちびと 待ち人来たらず. 〈おみくじの文〉The person you wait for will not come.

まちまち 報告[うわさ]がまちまちだ. There are conflicting reports [rumors] about it. / この点に関しては意見がまちまちである. Opinions vary widely on this point.

まつ[2] ちょっとお待ち下さい. Wait a minute, please. | One [Just a] moment, please. | 〈電話で〉Please hold on a minute. | (相手の言葉を遮って)いや, ちょっと待ちたまえ. Now, just a minute. / (前を行く相手に向かって) そのままそこで待っていてくれ. Wait there! | 《口語》Hang on! / ではまず 10 時にお待ちしています. Well, I'll see [I look forward to seeing] you at ten tomorrow. ★日本人はともすると I'll be expecting you… と言うが, これは相手に押しつけがましくなるので避けるべきである. / 我々は楽しみにして休暇を待っている. We are eagerly looking forward to the vacation. / 待ってました! This is what I've been waiting for! | Here it [he] comes! / 彼らは宇宙船が見えるのを待った. They watched for a spacecraft. / 待て

まっこう 抹香 incense (powder) ¶抹香臭い sound religious [pious];《文》smack of religion.
まっこう² 真っ向 ¶真っ向から右[左]から切りつけられる be cut in the forehead / 真っ向から断わる refuse flatly / 真っ向から打つ strike head-on.
まっこうくじら 抹香鯨 ⇒くじら.
マッサージ (a) massage;《米》a rubdown ¶マッサージする massage sb; give sb a massage [《米》rubdown] / マッサージしてもらう have [get] a massage [《米》rubdown] / have oneself massaged / マッサージ師 a masseur (男); a masseuse (女); a massager; a massagist.
まっさいちゅう 真っ最中 ¶真っ最中に in the middle (of);《文》in the midst (of); at [in] the height (of) / 真っ最中である be in full swing; be at (its) height.
まっさお 真っ青 ¶真っ青な〈濃い青色の〉deep blue;〈顔色が〉deadly [deathly,《文》ghastly,《文》ashy] pale; as white as a sheet [as paper] / 真っ青になる go [turn] (deadly) pale《with fright》; go white;《文》blanch.
まっさかさま 真っ逆様 ¶真っ逆様に head over heels; headlong.
まっさかり 真っ盛り ⇒まんかい, まっさいちゅう.
まっさき 真っ先 ¶真っ先に at the very beginning [first];〈第一に〉first of all;〈先頭に〉at the head (of) / 真っ先に進む lead the way; take the lead (in).
まっさつ 抹殺 ¶抹殺する《文》erase; cross out; strike out [off];《文》expunge;《文》obliterate /〈比喩的に〉deny (the existence of).
まっしかく 真っ四角 ⇒ましかく.
まっしぐら ¶まっしぐらに headlong;〈猛然と〉《文》precipitately /〈全速力で〉at full speed /〈目標に向かって〉(drive) head-on [headlong] (toward one's goal) / まっしぐらに走る rush (to); dash [make a dash] (for); run full tilt (at); make a beeline (for).
まつじつ 末日 the last day; the end (of May).
マッシュポテト mashed potatoes.
マッシュルーム a mushroom.
まっしょう¹ 末梢 ¶末梢的な unimportant;《文》trifling; trivial; minor / 末梢神経 a peripheral nerve.
まっしょう² 抹消 ⇒まっさつ.
まっしょうじき 真っ正直 ¶真っ正直な absolutely [completely, utterly] honest; as straight as a die / 真っ正直に with complete honesty; straightforwardly / 真っ正直に受け取る take (a joke) seriously; take sb at his word.
まっしょうめん 真っ正面 ¶真っ正面に right [directly] in front (of); just [right] opposite 《the station》.
まっしろ 真っ白 ¶真っ白な pure white; snow-white; as white as snow;〈汚れのない〉《文》immaculate《sheets》. 文例⬇
まっしん 真っ芯 ¶ボールをバットのまっしんでとらえる hit the ball cleanly [with the meat of the bat].
まっすぐ 真っすぐ ¶真っすぐな straight (as an arrow);〈正直な〉honest;《文》upright; straightforward;〈直立した〉《文》erect; upright / 真っすぐに in a straight line; in a beeline /〈直接〉straight; direct(ly);〈正直に〉honestly;〈率直に〉frankly; straightforwardly / 真っすぐに立つ stand straight [upright,《文》erect] / 真っすぐに行く go straight on [ahead]; make a beeline (for) / 真っすぐにする straighten; make sth straight. 文例⬇
まっせ 末世 a degenerate age.
まっせき 末席 the lowest seat; a back seat ¶末席を汚す〈出席する〉be [have the honor of being] present《at a meeting》;〈一員である〉be one of the members (of); have the honor of being a member (of) / 末席に座る sit at the foot of the table.
まった 待った ¶待ったを掛ける call a (temporary) halt to《the construction work》/ 待ったをする〈相撲で〉call "not ready";〈囲碁・将棋で〉retract a move. 文例⬇
まつだい 末代 ¶末代まで for ever;《文》for (many) generations to come;《文》eternally / 末代までの《文》eternal;《文》everlasting.
まったく 全く quite (★ good, warm など程度の差が色々有り得る語の前では「全く」ではなく「かなり」の意になる); entirely; thoroughly;《文》totally; altogether; completely; simply; perfectly;〈全く…ない〉(not) at all; (not) in the least; (not) a bit;〈実に〉truly;

ど暮らせど彼女は二度と姿を見せなかった. He waited and waited, but she never showed up again./ 僕の帰りを待たずに食事はすませてくれ. Don't wait dinner for me.|もっと悪いことが後を待っていた. Worse was yet to come.| Something worse was in store for him./商業の発達は工業の進歩に待つところが大きい. The development of commerce is to a great extent dependent on the progress of manufacturing industry./待つ身は長い. A watched pot never boils.《諺》/待てば海路の日和あり. Everything comes to him who waits.《諺》| It is a long lane that has no turning.《諺》
まっか 2人は真っ赤になって議論していた. They were involved in a red-hot argument.
まっき 内閣は末期症状を呈している. There are indications [signs] of the impending downfall of the Cabinet.
まっくら お先真っ暗だ. My future appears completely dark [black].
まっくろ 彼は日に焼けて真っ黒になった. He was tanned almost black.

まっさき 真っ先に彼が駆けつけた. He was the first to arrive on the scene./彼は一行の真っ先に立って進んだ. He led the party.
まっしろ 起きて見たら真っ白に雪が積もっていた. I awoke to find the ground completely white with snow.
まっすぐ 身体をまっすぐにしなさい. Hold yourself straight.
まった 待った! Wait!| Not yet./ (碁・将棋で)待ったなしですよ. Retracting moves is not allowed in this game./(相撲で)時間いっぱい. 待ったなし! Time is up! Begin the bout!

まつたけ 松茸 a matsutake mushroom ¶松たけ狩りに行く go mushrooming [mushroom-gathering].

まっただなか 真っただ中 ⇨まんなか, まっさいちゅう. 文例⇩

まったん 末端 the end; the tip ¶行政機構の末端 the smallest unit of the administrative organization; a government office in direct contact with the public / (幹部の意志などが) 末端に伝わらない do not reach the rank and file.

マッチ[1] 〈マッチ棒1本〉a match; 〈1箱〉a box of matches; 〈1つづり〉a matchbook; a book of matches ¶マッチの先 a match head / マッチの軸 a matchstick / マッチの火 the flame of a match; a match flame / マッチをする strike [light] a match / マッチ箱 a matchbox / マッチ箱のような家 a matchbox of a house.

マッチ[2] マッチする match (with); go well (with).

まっちゃ 抹茶 powdered [ground] tea.

マット 〈敷き物〉a mat; 〈体操用〉a (gym) mat; a mattress.

まっとう する 全うする ⇨まとも.

まっとうする 全うする 《文》accomplish (*one's* purpose); complete; finish; 《文》fulfill (*one's* duties); carry out; 《文》perform (a task) ¶一命を全うする escape (from) death.

マットレス a mattress ¶スプリング入りのマットレス a spring mattress.

マッハ 【物・航空】a Mach (number) (略: M) ¶マッハ1 Mach One / マッハ3 で飛ぶ fly at Mach 3.

まつば 松葉 a pine needle.

まっぱだか 真っ裸 ¶真っ裸の stark-naked; nude / 真っ裸になる strip *oneself* naked [to the skin] / 真っ裸で (go) stark-naked; with nothing on; in *one's* bare skin.

まつばづえ 松葉杖 a crutch ¶松葉杖をついて歩く walk on crutches.

まつばぼたん 松葉牡丹 a garden portulaca; a sun plant; rose moss.

まつび 末尾 the end; 《文》the close.

まっぴつ 末筆 文例⇩

まっぴら 真っ平 (not) by any means. 文例⇩

まっぴるま 真っ昼間 ¶真っ昼間に in broad [full] daylight ⇨ひさかり.

まっぷたつ 真っ二つ ¶真っ二つに right in two / 真っ二つに切る cut sth into two exact halves.

まつやに 松脂 (pine) resin; pine-tree gum.

まつり 祭り a festival; a celebration; a fete ¶祭りをする hold [keep, 《文》observe, 《文》celebrate] a festival; 〈慰霊の〉hold a service [mass (カトリックの)] 《for》/ お祭り気分である be in (a) festive [holiday] mood / お祭り騒ぎをする celebrate; make a fete of it / 歌と踊りの祭り a song-and-dance festival / 後の祭り ⇨あと[1] 祭りばやし festival music.

まつりあげる 祭り上げる set *sb* up (as chairman); put [set] *sb* on a pedestal; put *sb* on the shelf; 《戯言》kick *sb* upstairs.

まつる[1] 祭る 〈神として〉《神社に》《文》enshrine; 〈あがめる〉worship (as a god) ¶社[寺]を建てて祭る dedicate a shrine 《to *sb*》; erect a temple to (a deity) / 先祖を祭る worship *one's* ancestors.

まつる[2] 〈洋裁〉hem.

まつろ 末路 the last days (of a hero); the end; *one's* fate.

まつわりつく 〈からみつく〉coil [twine] round; surround; 〈つきまとう〉follow about.

まつわる 文例⇩

まで 〈時〉till; until; to; 〈場所〉to; as far as; 〈程度〉even; to; as [so] far as ¶今まで (of) till now; so far; up to the present / 朝から晩まで from morning till night / 水曜から土曜まで from Wednesday till [《米》through] Saturday / 近代まで until [down to] modern times / 100 歳まで生きる live to (be) a hundred / 京都までの切符 a ticket to Kyoto / 50 まで数える count (up) to fifty / 10 人の中で 9 人まで nine people out of ten / 盗みまでもする go so [as] far as to commit theft; go to the length(s) of committing theft / ...までに by; not later

---

まったく 彼は全く努力一つで現在の地位に昇ったのだ。He rose to his present position through sheer industry. / 彼とは全く何の関係もない。I have absolutely nothing to do with him. / 全く知りません。I really don't know./ いやくだ。You are right. / Yes, indeed. / 彼が逃れたのは全く奇跡的だった。His escape was nothing short of a miracle. / それではこの誤りの説明には全くならない。That doesn't begin to account for the mistake.

まっただなか 彼は群衆の真っただ中へ敢然と馬を乗り入れた。He rode bravely into the thick of the mob.

マッチ[1] マッチをお持ちですか。Have you got a light [any matches]?/ちょっとマッチを拝借。May I have a light, please?/このマッチはつかない。The match won't strike. / ようやくマッチがついた。The match caught at last. / そのマッチを消すまいとした。I tried to keep the match alive. / 彼女はマッチに火をつけて私のくわえたタバコに差し出した。She held a match to my cigarette. / 彼女は湿ったマッチ箱でマッチを何本もすっては折っていた。She was striking and breaking match after match on a damp box.

まっぴつ 末筆ながら皆々様のご多幸をお祈りいたします。With best wishes to you and your family, (I remain) Yours sincerely. ★ I remain を加えると固い感じになる。

まっぴら そんなことは真っ平だ。I wouldn't do it for anything [for the world]. / (口語) Nothing doing!/ (俗) No way!/またくだらない話は真っ平御免だ。I've had enough [will have none] of your stupid remarks [ideas].

まつわる この湖にまつわる哀れな物語がある。There is a sad tale told of this lake.

まで 今まで一体どこにいたのだ。Where have you been all this while?/ (電話で) 328 の 3121 から 6 までへ掛けて下さい。Will you

まてがい　〖貝〗a razor clam [fish, shell].
まてんろう　摩天楼 a skyscraper.
まと　的 a mark; a target;〈対象〉《文》an object ¶ 的が外れている be beside [off, wide off the mark; be off [not to] the point / 的外れの irrelevant (remarks);《文》misdirected (criticism) / 的を射る〖不〕 hit [miss] the mark / ちょう笑の的となる become a laughingstock / 命を的に戦う fight at the risk of one's life. 文例⇩
まど　窓 a window ¶ 窓から外を[中を]のぞく look out of [into, in at] the window / 上げ下げ戸の[観音開きの]窓 a sash [casement] window / 窓ガラス〈はめてある〉a window pane; a windowlight;〈窓用のガラス〉(a pane of) window glass / 窓際 at the window /〈乗り物の〉窓際の席 a window seat / 窓付き封筒 a window(ed) envelope / 窓わく a window frame.
まとい　纏い a fireman's standard ¶ まとい持ち the standard-bearer.
まどい¹　惑い ⇨まよい.
まどい²　⇨だんらん.
まといつく　纏い付く cling to (one's legs) ¶ まといついて離れない子供 a clinging child.
まとう　纏う〈着用する〉put on; wear; be dressed [《文》clad] (in);〈身を包む〉be wrapped [enveloped] ((in)).
まどう　惑う ⇨まよう.
まどか　円か ¶ まどかな〈丸い〉round;〈穏やかな〉peaceful; quiet;《文》tranquil / まどかな月 a round moon.
まどぐち　窓口 a window;〈係〉a clerk at the window ¶ 窓口のサービスを改善する give better service (to the public) over the counter / 窓口規制 'window' controls [operations] (by the Bank of Japan).
まとまり　纏まり〈結着〉(a) conclusion; (a) settlement;〈完成〉《文》completion;〈一貫〉《文》consistency;《文》coherence;〈統一〉unity; coordination ¶ まとまりのない rambling;《文》desultory (reading) / まとまりのない話 a rambling [an incoherent] talk / まとまりのない考え《文》an ill-thought-out idea / まとまりをつける settle (a matter); bring (a matter) to a conclusion. 文例⇩
まとまる　纏まる〈解決がつく〉be settled;〈結末がつく〉be completed; be finished;《文》be concluded;〈話し合いがつく〉reach [come to, arrive at] an agreement;〈集まる〉get [draw, be brought] together; be united;〈整理がつく〉be (put) in order; be well arranged ¶ まとまった金 a (good) round sum; a sizable sum [amount] (of money) / まとまった注文 a large order / まとまった考え a definite idea [opinion] / よくまとまった団体 a well-organized [close(ly)-knit] group. 文例⇩
まとめる　纏める〈解決する〉settle (a dispute); bring (a matter) to a conclusion;〈取り決める〉arrange (a marriage); close (a bargain);〈集める〉collect; get [bring, put] together;〈整頓する〉arrange; put (one's papers) in order;〈完成する〉complete; finish;〈統一する〉《文》unify; unite ¶ 考えをまとめる get one's ideas in shape [order]; put one's thoughts together / 材料をまとめる collect materials and arrange them in order / まとめて together; in a mass [lot]; in bulk (大量に); in a lump (金などを) / ノートをまとめて1冊の本にする work [make] up one's notes into a book / まとめ役 an organizer;〈調停役〉an arbitrator; a peacemaker. 文例⇩

call the numbers from 328-3121 to 3126? /〈店などで〉何時までやっていますか. What time do you close? / 展覧会はいつまであ りますか. How long will the exhibition be open? | When does the exhibition close [finish]? / 日曜日まで休業いたします.《掲示》Closed till Monday [《米》through Sunday]. ★ till Sunday とすると日曜日は開店することになる. / 神戸まで汽車で行った. I went as far as Kobe by train. / どこまで行きましたか. How far did you go? / 郵税は25グラムまで60円です. The postage is sixty yen up to 25 grams. / 会社から20万円までは借りられる. I can get a loan of money to the extent of 200,000 yen from my company. / 年末までに今一度お目に掛かりたい. I want to see you again before the end of the year. / 中学までは義務教育である. Education through junior high is compulsory. | Education is compulsory up to the end of junior high school. / 君が用意ができるまでには僕は手紙を書き上げている. I will have finished my letter by the time you are ready.
まと　彼は世間の非難の的となった. He became the focus of public criticism.
まとまり　彼は色々の事を始めるが一つもまとまりをつけない. He starts many things, but finishes nothing. / 彼の話すことにはまとまりがない. He talks in a rambling way.
まとまる　相談がまとまった. An agreement has been reached. / 交渉はまとまらなかった. The negotiations fell through. | The talks got nowhere. / やがて考えがまとまってきた. My ideas finally took shape. / それではまとまる話もまとまらなくなる. That would be throwing a spanner in the works.
まとめる　交渉をまとめることができなかった. We could not bring the negotiations to a successful [fruitful] conclusion. | Our talks

まとも ¶まともな《文》right-minded《people》; honest; decent; self-respecting / まともに right; direct(ly) / まともに顔を見る look sb full [straight] in the face / 風をまともに受けて進む march on in the teeth of the wind / 台風の襲来をまともに食らう take [feel] the full force of a typhoon; bear [take] the brunt of a typhoon / まともに暮らす live straight; live an honest [a decent] life; earn an honest living. 文例↓

まどり 間取り the plan of a house; the arrangement of the rooms (in a house) ¶間取りがいい[悪い]家 a well-[badly-]planned house.

マドリード Madrid.

マドリッド ⇨マドリード.

マドロス [<《オランダ語》matroos] a sailor; a seaman ¶マドロスパイプ a big-bowled bent (tobacco) pipe.

まどろむ doze (off); fall into a doze.

まどわす 惑わす <だます> deceive;《口語》fool; give sb a false idea 《of sth》;《文》delude;《文》misguide; lead sb astray; <魅する> fascinate; charm; <誘惑する> tempt; seduce.

マドンナ《聖母》the Madonna ⇨まどほ².

マナー manners ¶マナーがいい have good manners; be well-mannered / マナーが悪い bad-[ill-]mannered.

まないた 俎 a chopping [cutting] board [block] ¶まないたの上の鯉(-)のようなものだ be doomed; be left to one's fate.

まなざし 眼差し a look ¶慈愛に満ちた眼差しで with a loving look on one's face.

まなじり 眦 ⇨めじり ¶まなじりを決して立ち上がる rise to the occasion with determination.

まなつ 真夏 the middle of (the) summer; high [full] summer; midsummer (★「夏至」の意味にもなる) ¶真夏に in the middle of (the) summer; in [at] the height of summer; in full summer. 文例↓

まなでし 愛弟子 one's favorite pupil.

まなぶ 学ぶ <習得する> learn; <研究する> study; <教わる> be taught; take lessons [a course] (in) ¶英語をイギリス人に学ぶ learn English from an Englishman. 文例↓

まなむすめ 愛娘 one's beloved daughter.

マニア an (audio) enthusiast; a [an enthusiastic] fan ★「マニア」は英語の mania に由来するが, この語は「精神病」を意味し, その病気にかかった「狂人」は maniac. 従って, 何かの趣味に「熱中する人」の意味の「マニア」を mania とするのは正しくないし, maniac もむやみに使わないほうがいい.

まにあう 間に合う <時間に> be in time 《for》; <役立つ> do; work; serve [answer] the purpose; be useful; <充分である> be enough; be good enough ¶7時の列車に間に合う catch [make] the 7 o'clock train / (時間に)間に合わない be too late for 《the party》; miss 《a train》/ 何とか間に合って...に行き着く《口語》just make it《to a place》. 文例↓

まにあわせ 間に合わせ a makeshift;《文》a temporary expedient ¶間に合わせの makeshift《arrangements》; stopgap《measures》/ 間に合わせに as a temporary expedient [measure] / 一時の間に合わせにする make (it) do for the present.

まにあわせる 間に合わせる <一時済ます> manage 《with》; make sth do; make shift 《with》; <用意する> get sth ready. 文例↓

マニキュア <液> nail polish [《英》varnish]; <美爪術> (a) manicure ¶マニキュアを落とす remove the polish [varnish] from one's nails / マニキュアをしている wear nail polish / マニキュアをしてもらう get [have] a manicure / つめにマニキュアをぬる polish [put (nail) varnish on] one's nails / マニキュア落とし (a) nail-polish remover / マニキュアばさみ nail-polish scissors.

まにし 真西 due west.

まにまに ¶波のまにまに漂う drift with [at the mercy of] the waves;《文》be the sport of the waves.

マニラ Manila ¶マニラ麻 Manila (hemp); manil(l)a.

まにんげん 真人間 an honest man; a good citizen ¶真人間になる become a new man [a reformed character]; turn over a new leaf; reform; mend one's ways. 文例↓

まぬがれる 免れる <逃れ助かる> escape (danger); be saved [rescued] from 《drowning》; <脱する> get rid of 《a nuisance》; <避ける> avoid 《trouble》; <免除される> be exempted 《from taxation》 ¶苦痛を免れる be relieved of pain; get [have] relief from pain / けがを免れる escape [get off] unhurt / 義務を免れようとする (try to) evade one's duty / 免れ難い《文》inescapable; unavoidable; inevitable.

まぬけ 間抜け a fool; a stupid fellow; a blockhead; a bonehead ¶間抜けな foolish; stupid; silly; dull-witted; boneheaded.

---

got nowhere.

まとも おれたちはまともなことをしていなくてはいけない. We must do the honest thing.

まなつ 軽井沢では真夏の8月でも気温が25度以上になることはめったにない. The temperature in Karuizawa seldom rises higher than 25°C even in August, the height of summer.

まなぶ この経験で学ぶところがあった. We have learned a lesson from this experience. / よく学びよく遊べ. All work and no play makes Jack a dull boy.《諺》

まにあう すぐ出かけなければ間に合わない. We must [should] be off straightaway (if we are) to get there in time. / 式場にはゆっくり間に合った. We arrived in ample [plenty of] time for the ceremony. / 1万円あれば1週間は間に合う. Ten thousand yen will last me a week. / 彼がいなくても結構間に合う. We can do [manage] very well without him. / 当座はこれで間に合うだろう. This will do for the time being. | This will be enough to go on with.

まにあわせる 当分はこの机で間に合わせようと思います. I will make this desk do [make do with this desk] for the time being.

まにんげん 今日ただ今から心を入れ替えて真人間になります. From this moment on I will be a reformed character. | I will reform this very instant.

まね 真似 ⟨模倣⟩ (an) imitation; mimicry; ⟨振り⟩ pretense; simulation ¶まねをする imitate; copy; follow *sb's* example; take *sb* [*sth*] as *one's* [a] model; follow suit / ⟨猿が⟩人のまねをする mimic man / ばかなまねをやる act [play] the fool / 気違いのまねをする pretend to be mad. 文例⇩

マネージャー a manager.

まねき 招き (an) invitation ¶招きに応じる [を断わる] accept [refuse, turn down, 《文》decline] an invitation / 招きによって at *sb's* invitation. 文例⇩

マネキン a mannequin.

まねく 招く ⟨手招きする⟩ beckon (to); wave *sb* in [to *one*]; ⟨呼び迎える⟩ call in [send for] ⟨a doctor⟩; ⟨招へいする⟩ hire; 《文》engage ⟨a teacher⟩; ⟨招待する⟩ invite; ask; ⟨招来する⟩ bring ⟨trouble⟩ on *oneself*; 《文》incur ⟨criticism⟩. ¶晩餐(ばん)に招かれる be invited [asked] to dinner / 招かれた[れぬ]客 an invited [uninvited] guest / 互いに夕食に招き合う invite each other to dinner; dine regularly at each other's house / 非難を招く incur blame / 誤解を招く lay *oneself* open to [cause] misunderstanding; ⟨let *oneself*⟩ be misunderstood.

まねごと 真似事 a sham; a make-believe ¶ほんのまね事に simply for [for mere] form's sake / 大工のまね事をする play at carpentering.

まねる 真似る ⇨ まね(をする) ¶…を真似て in imitation [mimicry] of…; taking a leaf from [out of] *sb's* book. 文例⇩

まのあたり 目の当たり ¶目の当たりに ⟨目の前に⟩ before *one's* (very) eyes; in *one's* presence; ⟨親しく⟩ personally; ⟨自分の目で⟩ with *one's* own eyes; ⟨実際に⟩ actually / 目の当たりに witness *sth*. 文例⇩

まのび 間延び ¶間延びのした slow(-footed); stupid-looking; flat 《performances》.

まばたき 瞬き a blink; a wink (主に片目の) ¶まばたきもせずに見ている stare [《文》gaze] 《at *sth*》 without blinking; look steadily [unblinkingly] 《at》.

まばたく 瞬く blink; wink (主に片目を); bat an eye (★ この句は常に do not bat an eye と否定の形で「びくともしない」の意味を表わすのに使われる) ⇨まばたき. 文例⇩

まばゆい 目映い dazzling; glaring.

まばら 疎ら ¶まばらな 《文》sparse; thin; scattered / まばらに 《文》sparsely; thinly; here and there / まばらに毛が生えている頭 a head with a few scattered hairs.

まひ 麻痺 (a) paralysis (*pl.* -yses); palsy; numbness ¶麻痺する be paralyzed; be benumbed / 麻痺性の paralytic (polio); paralyzing (poison) / 麻痺症状 paralytic symptoms. 文例⇩

まひがし 真東 due east.

まびき 間引き thinning out; cropping ⟨of excess deer⟩; culling ⟨of young seals⟩; a ⟨seal⟩ cull ¶間引き運転 (a) partial ⟨train⟩ service.

まびく 間引く thin out ⟨plants⟩; thin down ⟨the overwhelming number of candidates⟩.

まびさし 目庇 an eyeshade.

まひる 真昼 ¶真昼の midday; 《文》noonday (heat) / 真昼に ⟨白昼に⟩ in broad daylight / ⟨日中に⟩ in the daytime; ⟨正午に⟩ at noon; at midday.

マフィン 《英》a muffin; 《米》an English muffin.

まぶか 目深 ¶目深にかぶる wear ⟨*one's* hat⟩ low [pulled down] over *one's* eyes.

まぶしい 眩しい dazzling; glaring; blinding; 《文》radiant ¶まぶしく輝く dazzle; glare. 文例⇩

まぶす ⟨一面に⟩ cover 《with》; ⟨ぬりつける⟩ smear 《with》; ⟨ふりかける⟩ sprinkle 《with》.

まぶた 瞼 an eyelid; the lid of an eye ¶上[下]まぶた the upper [lower] eyelid / まぶたのけいれん a twitching of the eyelid(s) / まぶたの母 *one's* mother as *one* remembers her from childhood / まぶたに浮かぶ come back [alive] in *one's* memory. 文例⇩

まゆ 真冬 (in) the middle [dead, depths] of winter.

マフラー a muffler.

まほう 魔法 magic; witchcraft; sorcery; 《文》necromancy / 《文》the black art ¶魔法のつえ ⟨wave⟩ a magic wand / 魔法を使う use [practice] magic; 《文》work *one's* magic / 魔法をかける cast a spell ⟨on *sb*⟩; bind *sb* by a spell; put *sb* under a spell; work magic ⟨on *sb*⟩ / 魔法使い a magician; a wizard (男); a witch (女); a sorcerer; a sorceress (女) / 魔法びん a vacuum bottle [《英》flask]; 《商標名》a Thermos (flask [《米》bottle]).

マホメット Mohammed; Muhammad; Mahomet ¶マホメット教 Mohammedanism; Islam / マホメット教の Mohammedan; Islamic ⇨ イスラム.

まね これまで日本人はまねがうまいと言われてきた. It has been said that the Japanese are good at imitating. / 僕のような貧乏人は金持のまねはできない. A poor man like me cannot do what a rich man does [can't keep up with a rich man].

まねき お招き有り難う. Thank you for your kind invitation.

まねる この建物は中国の寺をまねて造ったものだ. This building was modeled on [after] a Chinese temple.

まのあたり その光景を目の当たりに見るように描写してある. The scene is described so vividly that I feel as if I were seeing it with my own eyes.

まばたき 彼はまばたき一つせずにそれをじっと見詰めていた. He was staring at it without so much as a flicker of an eyelid.

まばら 彼の講演会は聴衆がまばらだった. His lecture was thinly attended. / 登るにつれて, 樹木は一層まばらになった. As we climbed up the trees became more thinly spaced.

まひ 彼は良心が麻痺している. He has no scruples. / His conscience is atrophied / 交通が麻痺状態だ. Traffic is at a complete standstill.

まぶしい ライトがまぶしくって目がくらんだ. The lights were so bright that I was dazzled [blinded].

まぶた 太郎君はもうまぶたが重く

まほろし 幻 ⟨幻影⟩ a phantom; ⟨幻想⟩ a vision; an illusion; a dream ¶幻のような phantom; 《文》visionary;《文》illusive; dreamlike / 幻に見る see *sth* in a vision.

まま¹ 間々 sometimes; at times; occasionally; now and then ¶…ということはままある it sometimes happens that…; there are times when…

まま² ¶まま(に) ⟨そのまま⟩ (just) as it is [stands]; ⟨心のまま⟩ (just) as *one* pleases; ⟨…のとおり⟩ (according) as; according to; ⟨校正で⟩ママ stet; ⟨原文のママ⟩ sic ⇨げんぶん 囲語 / 靴をはいたまま with *one's* shoes on / そのままにしておく leave *sth* as it is; let *sb* alone [be] / もとのままである stay [be, 《文》remain] (just) as *it* was / 意のままにする have *one's* own way; do as *one* pleases. 文例⬇

ママ mam(m)a; mummy;《米口語》mom;《英口語》mum ¶ママさんバレー housewives' volleyball.

ままおや 継親 a stepparent.

ままこ¹ 継子 a stepchild; a stepson (男); a stepdaughter (女) ¶まま子扱いにされる be treated like a stepchild [like a Cinderella, as an outsider]; be neglected; be left in the cold.

ままこ² 継粉 an unmixed-in lump of flour.

ままごと ¶ままごとをする play (at) house; play at housekeeping [keeping house]. 文例⬇

ままはは 継母 a stepmother.

まみえる 見える ⟨拝謁する⟩ have an audience (with); ⟨顔を合わせる⟩ meet; see;《文》encounter; ⟨仕える⟩ serve.

まみず 真水 fresh water.

まみなみ 真南 due south.

まみれる be covered [smeared, soiled, stained] with.

まむかい 真向かい ¶真向かいに right [just] opposite; just in front (of); across (from) / 真向かいに座る sit opposite [face to face with] *sb*. 文例⬇

まむし《動》a *mamushi*; a (kind of) pit viper ¶まむしのようなやつ a vicious thug; a viper / まむし酒 *mamushi* liquor.

まめ¹ 豆 a bean; ⟨えん豆⟩ a pea; ⟨大豆⟩ a soybean ¶豆の木 a bean plant / ジャックと豆の木《英国童話》*Jack and the Beanstalk* / 豆科《植》the pulse family / 豆科の植物 a leguminous [podded] plant; a legume; a legumen 《*pl.* -mina》/ 豆類 pulse(s) / 豆自動車 a midget car; a minicar / 豆粒大の pea-sized (pellets) / 豆電球 a midget lamp / 豆本 a miniature book / 豆まきをする scatter parched beans (to drive out evil spirits).

まめ² ⟨肉刺⟩ a blister; ⟨底まめ⟩ a corn ¶まめができる have [get] a blister. 文例⬇

まめ³ ¶まめな ⟨忠実な⟩ faithful; devoted; ⟨勤勉な⟩ hardworking; painstaking;《文》diligent; ⟨達者な⟩ healthy; well; fit / まめに faithfully; ⟨労を惜しまず⟩ sparing no pains; in good health / まめに働く work like a beaver [bee] / まめまめしく仕える serve [wait on] *sb* faithfully [hand and foot]. 文例⬇

まめあぶら 豆油 soybean oil.

まめかす 豆粕 bean cake; soybean (oil) meal.

まめたん 豆炭 an oval [egg-shaped] briquet(te).

まめつ 磨[摩]滅 wear (and tear); abrasion ¶磨滅する be worn out [away]; wear out [away]. 文例⬇

まもう 磨[摩]耗 wear (and tear); frictional wear; abrasion ¶摩耗する be worn away / 摩耗を免れùにない be subject to wear.

まもなく 間もなく soon; presently; shortly; before long; in a short time; in a little while.

まもの 魔物 a demon; a devil; an evil spirit. 文例⬇

まもり 守り ⟨防御⟩ protection; (a) defense; a safeguard; ⟨護符⟩ an amulet; a charm; a talisman ¶守りを固める strengthen the defense (of the country) / 守りにつく take [go on(to),《文》assume] the defensive / ⟨野球⟩ take the field / 守り神[本尊] *one's* protective god [deity]; *one's* guardian angel / 守り駒 a guarding piece / 守り袋 an amulet case / 守り札 a paper charm.

まもる 守る ⟨保護する⟩ protect 《*sb* from [against] danger》; ⟨防ぐ⟩ defend; ⟨警護する⟩ guard; keep guard (over); ⟨従う⟩ obey; keep (the rules); ⟨観察する⟩ observe (the proper form); follow; ⟨履行する⟩ keep (*one's* word);《文》fulfill; act up to; ⟨墨守する⟩ stick [《文》adhere] (to) / 身を守る guard [defend] oneself (against) / 守りやすい陣地 an easily defensible position. 文例⬇

まやかし a trick;《文》a deception; a fraud ¶まやかし物 a fake; a counterfeit;《米俗》a phon(e)y.

まやく 麻薬 a narcotic; a drug;《口語》dope

なりました. Taro looks sleepy. / 彼のまぶたがぴくぴくっと動いた. His eyelids twitched.

まま²《着替えずに》そのままおいで下さい. Come as you are. /《立たずに》どうぞそのまま. Please keep your seat! / 聞いたままの事をはなします. I'll tell you exactly what I have heard. / その家は文豪の生前の状態のままに保存されている. The house is preserved in just the state it was in during the great writer's lifetime. | The house is kept quite as it was while the great writer was living. / 何もかも心のままにならない. Everything goes against me. / 事にならぬ妙が浮き世の習い. If wishes were horses, beggars would ride.《諺》/ ままよ. Never mind. I don't care. | I'll take my chance.

ままごと あの若夫婦の生活はままごとのようなものだ. That young couple are like children playing house.

まむかい 学校の真向かいに本屋がある. There is a bookstore opposite [across from] the school.

まめ² まめがつぶれた. The blister has burst [broken].

まめ³ まめな人で少しもじっとしていない. She always keeps herself busy. | She does not remain idle for a moment.

まめつ 歯の磨滅のしかたで, その動物がどんな物を食べていたかわかる. Wear on the teeth shows what diet the animal had.

¶麻薬の密売 drug peddling [traffic] / 麻薬常用者 a drug [《口語》dope] addict; a narcotic (addict) / 麻薬密売者 a narcotic trafficker; a drug peddler;《口語》a dope pusher.

まゆ 繭 a cocoon ¶繭から糸を取る reel silk off cocoons /《蚕が》繭をかける spin a cocoon.

まゆ(げ) 眉(毛) an eyebrow ¶眉をひそめる frown;《文》knit one's brows / 眉を描く[引く] pencil [correct] one's eyebrows / 眉一つ動かさずに without batting an eye; without turning a hair / 眉墨 an eyebrow pencil.

まゆつばもの 眉唾物 a fake; an unlikely [a tall, a fishy] story; a cock-and-bull story. 文例⇩

まよい 迷い〈当惑〉《文》perplexity;《文》bewilderment;〈疑惑〉(a) doubt;〈迷夢〉《文》a delusion;(an) illusion ¶迷いから覚める come to one's senses; wake up from a delusion / 迷いを覚ます bring sb to his senses;《文》disabuse sb (about sth, of an idea);《文》undeceive. 文例⇩

まよう 迷う〈当惑する〉be in doubt《about》; be not certain; be puzzled; be perplexed; be at a loss; be bewildered;〈ためらう〉hesitate; waver; be in two minds;〈道に〉lose [miss] one's way; get [be] lost;〈邪道に〉go astray [wrong] / 選択に迷う hesitate over which 《candidate》to choose; be in two minds《about sth》/ 危い所へ迷い込む stray into danger [a dangerous place]. 文例⇩

まよけ 魔除け a talisman [charm] to protect one from [against] evil ¶魔除けに《wear a talisman》to ward off evil spirits.

まよこ 真横 ¶真横に just [right] beside sth.

まよなか 真夜中 ¶真夜中に in the middle of the night;《文》at dead of night; at midnight (夜中の12時に) / 真夜中まで till the middle of the night; far into the night; until the small hours (of the morning).

マヨネーズ mayonnaise ¶マヨネーズをかける dress《asparagus》with mayonnaise.

まよわす 迷わす〈当惑させる〉puzzle;《文》perplex; bewilder; put sb in doubt [at a loss] 《about》;〈誘惑する〉tempt;〈魅する〉fascinate;〈文〉bewitch;〈邪道に導く〉lead sb astray.

マライ ⇨ マレー.

マラウイ (the Republic of) Malawi.

マラソン a marathon (race);〈素人の〉a marathon running ¶マラソン選手 a marathon runner.

マラッカかいきょう マラッカ海峡 the Strait of Malacca.

マラリア《医》malaria ¶二日熱マラリア malignant [falciparum, subtertian] malaria / 三日熱マラリア vivax malaria / マラリア蚊 a malaria-bearing [malaria-bearing] mosquito / マラリア患者 a malaria patient / マラリア原虫 a malarial parasite; a plasmodium (pl. -dia) / マラリア熱 malarial fever / マラリア予防薬 an anti-malarial tablet; a malaria-prevention pill.

まり 毬 a ball ¶まりをつく[投げる] bounce [throw] a ball / まり投げ ⇨ キャッチボール.

マリ (the Republic of) Mali.

マリア〈聖母〉the Virgin Mary; the Blessed Virgin (Mary).

マリアナ ¶マリアナ海溝 the Marianas Trench / マリアナ諸島 the Mariana Islands; the Marianas.

マリネ [<《フランス語》mariné] (a) marinade ¶にしんのマリネ marinated herring.

マリファナ marijuana; marihuana.

まりも《植》an aegagropila (pl. -s, -lae).

まりょく 魔力《文》magical [magic] powers; (a) mysterious charm ¶活字の魔力 the magic of the printed word / 魔力にかかる fall under [be bound by] a magic spell.

マリンバ《楽器》a marimba.

まる 丸, 円 a circle; a ring ¶丸を描く draw [《文》describe] a circle / 丸で囲む encircle; circle / まる1週間 for a whole [solid] week / まる2日間 for two full [a full two, fully two] days.

まるあらい 丸洗い ¶丸洗いする wash《a kimono》just as《it》is [without unpicking《it》].

まるあんき 丸暗記 rote memorization ¶丸暗記する learn《a whole page》off by heart ⇨ ほうあんき.

まるい 丸[円]い〈円形の〉round;〈環状の〉circular;〈球形の〉spherical; globular ¶丸く round; in a circle [ring];〈円満に〉《文》amicably; smoothly / 丸くする make sth round; round;〈猫などが〉背中を丸くする arch its back / 目を丸くして with one's eyes wide open / 丸くなる〈針ねずみなどが〉roll up; roll itself (up) into a ball;〈角が〉be rounded off; round; wear (off);〈人柄が〉get well-rounded; be softened / 〈一座の〉丸くなって座る sit in a circle [ring] /〈犬・猫などが〉丸くなって寝る curl itself up / 丸く収める round 《things》off nicely; smooth《a quarrel》over;

まもなく その後間もなく新校舎が落成した. It was not long before the new school building was completed.

まもの 昔日本ではきつねは魔物とされていた. In Japan in the olden days foxes were regarded as [supposed to be] magic creatures. / 女は魔物. One must guard against women.

まもる その部屋は厳重に守られている. The room is closely guarded. / だれも来て彼女を守ってくれなかった. No one came to defend her [to her defense]. / 人間の皮膚は寒さに対して身をはあまり役立たない. Man's skin is (a) poor protection against the cold. / 先生の教えを守りなさい. Do as your teacher tells you. / 親の言いつけは守らねばならぬ. You should be obedient to your parents. / 彼はよく約束を守る. He is a man of his word. | He is as good as his word.

まゆつばもの あの男の話はまゆつば物. His story must be taken with a grain [pinch] of salt.| His words cannot be taken at (their) face value.

まよい それは気の迷いだ. That's a mere fancy.

まよう 彼らの呼びかけに応じるかどうか迷った. I could not make up my mind whether I should agree to their appeal or not. / 彼は道に迷って森の奥深くまで踏み込んだ. He missed his way and wandered deep into the forest.

まるうつし 丸写し ¶丸写しにする copy 《a passage》word for word [《文》verbatim].

まるがお 丸顔 a round face ¶丸顔の round-faced.

まるがかえ 丸抱え ¶…の丸抱えだ be completely financed [sponsored] by…; be under the absolute patronage of….

まるがり 丸刈り close clipping ¶丸刈りの close-cropped 《hair》/ 丸刈りにする crop the hair; 〈刈らせる〉have a close crop; have one's hair clipped short.

まるき 丸木 a log ¶丸木橋 a log (bridge) 《laid across a stream》/ 丸木舟 a dugout canoe.

マルク 〈ドイツの貨幣〉a mark ¶西独マルク a Deutsche Mark (略: DM) / 東独マルク a mark; an ostmark.

マルクス ¶マルクス主義 Marxism / マルクス主義の Marxist; Marxian ★ Marxist は主に政治思想として Marxist parties (マルクス主義政党) のように, Marxian は学問的意味で Marxian economists (マルクス主義経済学者) のように使う / マルクス主義者 a Marxist / マルクス・レーニン主義 Marxism-Leninism.

まるくび 丸首 ¶丸首のセーター a turtleneck (sweater) / 丸首のシャツ a T-shirt; a tee shirt.

まるごし 丸腰 ¶丸腰で without (wearing) a sword; unarmed.

まるごと 丸ごと whole; altogether; bodily; entirely ¶丸ごと食べる eat sth whole; eat 《a fish》bones and all; eat 《an apple》rind and all.

まるぞん 丸損 ¶丸損をする suffer [《文》sustain] a total [complete] loss. 文例β

まるた 丸太 a log ¶丸太を挽いて板にする saw a log into boards / 丸太小屋 a log cabin.

マルタ (the Republic of) Malta.

まるだし 丸出し ¶丸出しの bare; exposed; uncovered / 丸出しになっている be in full view / 田舎言葉丸出しで 《speak》in a broad provincial dialect.

まるたんぼう 丸太ん棒 ⇒まるた.

マルチョイ ⇒まるばつ.

まるっきり ⇒まるで. 文例β

まるつぶれ 丸潰れ ¶丸つぶれになる collapse; end in utter failure; be ruined. 文例β

まるで 〈全く〉quite; entirely; completely; perfectly; altogether; 〈絶対に〉absolutely; 〈あたかも〉just like; just as if; so to speak; 《文》as it were. 文例β

まるてんじょう 円[丸]天井 a vault; an arched [a vaulted] ceiling ¶円[丸]天井造りの vaulted; domed.

まるのこ 丸鋸 a circular saw; 《米》a buzz saw.

まるのみ 丸呑み ¶丸のみにする swallow sth down [up] (without chewing); swallow 《a biscuit》whole.

まるはだか 丸裸 ⇒まっぱだか ¶丸裸になる〈財産を失う〉lose all one's property; lose everything one has [in one's possession].

まるばつ ○× ¶○×式の試験 a multiple-choice examination [test] / ○×式の問題 multiple-choice questions; a multiple-choice paper.

まるぼうず 丸坊主 ¶丸坊主の〈頭が〉close-cropped; clean-shaven; 〈山に木がなくて〉bald; deforested; treeless.

まるぼし 丸干し a fish [a radish, etc.] dried whole.

まるぽちゃ 丸ぽちゃ ¶丸ぽちゃの plump; buxom (★ ほがらかで, 母性愛に富んだ女性によく使われる形容詞); chubby(-faced).

まるまど 円[丸]窓 a round [circular] window.

まるまる¹ 丸まる ⇒まるい (丸くなる).

まるまる² 丸々 〈すっかり〉completely; 《文》wholly; totally; all.

まるまる³ 丸々 ¶丸々と太った (round and) plump; chubby 《cheeks》; tubby.

まるみ 丸み roundness; 《文》rotundity ¶丸みのある roundish; rounded / 丸みをつける round; make sth round; 〈削って〉round off 《a corner》.

まるみえ 丸見え ¶丸見えである be in full view; 《文》be fully exposed to view. 文例β

まるめこむ 丸め込む seduce; coax; wheedle; 《文》seduce; win sb over (to one's side); get round sb.

まるめる 丸める round; make round; roll up; curl up 《in(to) a ball》(身体などを); 〈背中を〉stoop; 《数》round 《a number》(off, up, down) ¶頭を丸める be tonsured / 紙を丸める crumple [roll] a piece of paper (up) into a ball.

マルメロ 《植》[<《ポルトガル語》marmelo] a quince.

まるい 丸くなって座ろう. Let us form a circle. / それを聞くと彼女は目を丸くして驚いた. When she heard that she opened her eyes wide in amazement. / どうもあの人との間は丸く行かない. I don't get on well with him. / そうすれば事は丸く収まる. That rounds things off very nicely.

まるぞん 少なくとも50万円は丸損した. At least ¥500,000 will have to be written off [has gone down the drain] completely.

まるっきり 近ごろまるっきり彼に会わない. I have seen nothing of him lately. / これはまるっきりわからない. I can't make head or tail of this. / その事はまるっきり知らない. I haven't got the slightest idea about that. / I'm quite in the dark about it.

まるつぶれ 彼の面目は丸つぶれだ. His face [prestige] is utterly lost. / 彼の欠席で計画は丸つぶれになった. His absence ruined the whole plan.

まるで それはまるで話が別だ. That is quite another thing [another kettle of fish]. / 彼の言うことはまるでなっていない. What he says is sheer [utter] nonsense. / まるで忘れてしまった. I have forgotten all about it. | I have clean forgotten it. / 君の言っていることは, 目下の議題とはまるで関係がない. What you are saying has nothing whatever to do with what we are talking about. / これはまるで戦争だ. This is practically a war. / まるで私をなんかのように, 用を言いつける. He orders me about as if I were his housemaid. / まるで猿のような顔だ. His face is just like a monkey's. / あの人が英語を話すのをきくとまるでイギリス人だ. To hear him speak English, one would think

まるもうけ 丸儲け 《make》 a clear profit. 文例⇩

まるやき 丸焼き ¶丸焼きにする roast 《a pig》 whole / 豚の丸焼き a pig roasted whole; a roast pig.

まるやけ 丸焼け ¶丸焼けになる be burned down (to the ground); be totally destroyed [《文》 be consumed] by fire. 「cupola 《小さい》.

まるやね 丸屋根 a dome; a vaulted roof;

まれ 稀 ¶まれな ⟨珍しい⟩ rare; uncommon; unusual; ⟨少ない⟩ scarce; few (and far between) / まれに rarely; 《文》 seldom; 《文》 at rare intervals; once in a long while / まれに見る雄弁家 a person gifted with rare eloquence. 用例⇩

マレー Malaya ¶マレー諸島 the Malay Archipelago / マレー語 ⟨東インド諸島の商業用語⟩ Malay; ⟨マレー諸島の⟩ Malayan / マレー人 Malay(an) / マレー半島 the Malay Peninsula / マレー語[諸島, 人] the Malay(an).

マレーシア (the Federation of) Malaysia ¶マレーシアの Malaysian / マレーシア人 a Malaysian. 「horse chestnut (tree).

マロニエ 〔植〕 ⟨<フランス語⟩ marronnier⟩ a

まろやか 円やか ¶まろやかな mellow ⟨tones⟩; smooth ⟨wine⟩; round ⟨shape⟩.

マロングラッセ 〔菓子〕 《フランス語》 a marron (glacé) (pl. marrons (glacés)). 「cloth.

まわし 回し ⟨相撲の⟩ a sumo wrestler's loin-

まわしもの 回し者 a spy; a secret agent.

まわす 回す ⟨回転させる⟩ turn ⟨a key⟩; push [pull, move] sth round; 《文》 revolve ⟨a wheel⟩; spin ⟨a top⟩; ⟨輪を⟩ roll [trundle] ⟨a hoop⟩; ⟨順に⟩ send [pass, hand] sth round [on]; ⟨転送する⟩ forward; ⟨回付する⟩ 《文》 transmit; send sth round; ⟨内線電話をほかの番号に⟩ transfer ⟨you [your call] to...⟩ ¶金を回す lend one's money out 《at 8 percent interest》. 文例⇩

まわた 真綿 floss (silk) ¶真綿で首を締める ruin sb gradually by indirect means.

まわり 周[回]り ⟨周りの長さ⟩ (a) circumference; 《文》 girth; ⟨周囲⟩ surroundings; ⟨付近⟩ the neighborhood, the vicinity; ⟨一巡⟩ a round; a turn; ⟨酒·薬などの利き目⟩ effect; 《文》 efficacy ¶周りが10センチある be ten centimeters round [in circumference, in girth] / 周りを見

る look about [around] one / 池の周りを一回りする go [walk] (once) round a pond / 周りに round; around; about; in the neighborhood [vicinity] 《of》 / 山形village 福島行き列車 a train for Fukushima via [by way of] Yamagata / 東回りの世界一周 an eastward trip round the world / 一回り大きい be a size larger 《than》. 文例⇩

まわりあわせ 回り合わせ 《文》 a turn of Fortune's wheel; fortune; luck; ⟨運命⟩ fate ⇨ めぐりあわせ ¶回り合わせがいい[悪い] be lucky [unlucky]; be fortunate [unfortunate] / 不思議な回り合わせで 《文》 by a strange turn of the wheel of Fortune; by a curious (irony of) chance.

まわりくどい 回りくどい roundabout; 《文》 circuitous; 《文》 circumlocutory; indirect 《間接的》 ¶回りくどい言い方をする talk in a roundabout way.

まわりどうろう 回り灯籠 a revolving lantern.

まわりぶたい 回り舞台 a revolving [turning, rotating] stage.

まわりみち 回り道 ¶回り道をする go round 《a place》; go a long way round; go by a roundabout way; go 《two kilometers》 out of one's way 《to》; make a detour 《of two kilometers》.

まわりもち 回り持ち ¶回り持ちでやる take turns at doing; take it in turns to do; do turn and turn about; 《hold office》 by [in] rotation; do by turns.

まわる 回る ⟨回転する⟩ turn (round); go round; 《文》 revolve; 《文》 rotate; spin; ⟨巡回する⟩ make a round; go (on) one's rounds; patrol; ⟨回遊する⟩ make a tour 《of Europe》; tour 《Europe》; ⟨循環する⟩ circulate; ⟨遠回りする⟩ go a long way round; take a roundabout way; ⟨薬·酒が利く⟩ take effect ¶郵便局へ回る go round by [by way of] the post office ★ go round to the post office と言うと,「郵便局へ行ってくる」ぐらいの意味で, 回り道をして寄ることに必ずしもならない / 学校を(いくつも)見て回る go round inspecting schools; make an inspection round of ⟨a number of⟩ schools / 回り回って ⟨方々歩いて⟩ after going through a number of places; ⟨品物など⟩ passing through many people's hands. 文例⇩

---

he were an Englishman.

まるみえ この部屋はおもての通りから丸見えだ. You can see everything in this room from the street.

まるもうけ 彼は30万円丸もうけした. He made a clear ¥300,000.

まれ 彼が怒るのはまれな事だ. It is unusual for him to get angry. / 片田舎に住んでいるので客もまれだ. As I live in a remote village, I rarely have visitors. / 人生七十古来まれなり. Few people live to be seventy.

まわす 読んで次へ回して下さい. Read this and pass it on.

まわり 家の周りに木が多い. There are a lot of trees around the house. | The house is ringed [surrounded] by trees. / 庭を一回りしましょう. Let us take a turn in the garden. / 火の回りが意外に速かった. The fire spread faster than was expected. / あの人は私より一回り年上です. He is twelve years older than me. ⇨ より 用法

まわりくどい 回りくどい事を言うな. Stop beating around the bush. | Come straight to the point.

まわる 地球は太陽の周りを回っている. The earth goes [moves, travels, revolves] round the sun. / 新潮一座は地方を回っている. The Shincho troupe is on the road. / もう11時半を回った. It is past [has turned] eleven-thirty. / 毒が全身に回った. The poison has passed into his system. / 今一軒回らなければならない. I have another call to make. / あのダイヤは回り回って結局元の持ち主の手に戻った. The diamond changed hands a number of times only to return [come back] to its first owner in the end.

まわれみぎ 回れ右 an about-face[-turn]; a right-about[-face] ¶回れ右をする about-face[-turn]; do [make] an about-face [a right-about-face]; 〈引き返す〉go back the way one came; 《文》retrace one's steps. 文例⇩

まん¹ 万 ten thousand; 〈多数〉《文》a myriad ¶1万分の1 a ten-thousandth / 何万[何十万]という人 tens [hundreds] of thousands of people / 150万 a million and a half ★英語では 50万を half a million, 25万を a quarter of a million というような, 分数による表現が好まれる. 文例⇩

まん² 満 ¶満を持して放たない wait until the time is ripe; watch for an opportunity [a chance] / 年齢を満で数える express sb's age in completed years [in the Western style (of counting)] / 満15歳である be fifteen years old / 満18歳に足り足りない be not quite eighteen years old.

まんいち 万一 by any chance ¶万一の覚悟をする be prepared for the worst / 万一の事があっても at the worst / 万一の場合には if anything [the worst] should [does] happen; in an [in case of] emergency; if the worst comes to the worst / 万一を頼む trust to chance [luck]; hope against hope / 万一に備える[備えて蓄える] provide [put sth aside] against an emergency [a rainy day]. 文例⇩

まんいん 満員 ¶満員の full (of people); crowded 《cars》/満員の観客 a capacity audience [crowd] / 満員になる[である] be full (of people); be crowded; 〈芝居などが〉draw a full house; play to a full [packed] house / 超満員である be more than full; be filled to bursting / ぎっしり満員である 《劇場などが》be full to the doors; 〈乗り物が〉be filled to capacity; 《口語》be jam-packed / 満員札止め a sellout.

まんえつ 満悦 great delight [《文》joy, satisfaction] ¶ご満悦の体(てい)である look very pleased [satisfied (with)]; be all smiles.

まんえん 蔓延 spread; spreading ¶蔓延する spread; 《文》be prevalent / 病気の蔓延している難民キャンプ a disease-ridden refugee camp / 蔓延を防止する prevent [check] the spread (of). 文例⇩

まんが 漫画 a cartoon; a funny picture; 〈通例4コマの〉続き漫画〉a comic strip; 《英》a strip cartoon;《米口語》comics;《米口語》funnies;〈風刺漫画〉a caricature ¶テレビで漫画を見る see a [an animated] cartoon on television / 漫画にする adapt 《a fairy tale》into a comic strip; make a comic-strip version of 《*Animal Farm*》;〈戯画化する〉make a caricature of; caricature / 漫画映画 a cartoon (film); a movie cartoon ⇨ どうが / 漫画家 a cartoonist; a comic artist; a caricaturist / 漫画式に in cartoon fashion / 漫画本[雑誌] a comic book [magazine] /《口語》a comic / 漫画欄 a comic section;《米口語》the funnies.

まんかい 満開 ¶満開の full-blown / 満開である[になる] be in [come into] full bloom [flower, blossom]; be at (their) best; be all out.

まんがく 満額 (reach) the full amount.

まんがん 万巻 ¶万巻の書 《have read》a vast [huge] number of books.

マンガン 《化》manganese.

まんかんしょく 満艦飾 ¶満艦飾の船 a full-dressed ship;《英》a ship dressed overall / 満艦飾をしている be fully dressed; be dressed overall.

まんき 満期 (at) the expiry [expiration] (of a term, a contract); (at) (the) maturity 《of a bill》¶満期になる〈任期が〉expire; run out; 〈手形などが〉mature; fall [become] due; 〈服役が(人を主語に)〉serve out one's term / (手形などの)満期日 the due date; the date of maturity; (pay at) maturity / 満期償還 redemption at [on] maturity. 文例⇩

まんきつ 満喫 ¶満喫する have enough [one's fill] (of); 〈楽しむ〉enjoy sth fully to [《文》to the full].

マングローブ 《植》a mangrove (tree).

まんげきょう 万華鏡 a kaleidoscope ¶万華鏡のような kaleidoscopic 《changes》.

まんげつ 満月 a full moon ¶満月の夜 a night with a full moon [when the moon will full]. 文例⇩

まんこう 満腔 ¶満腔の《文》heartfelt; wholehearted;《文》hearty. 文例⇩

マンゴー 《植》a mango (*pl*. -(e)s).

マンゴスチン 《植》a mangosteen.

まんざ 満座 ¶満座の中で in company; in public; publicly.

まんさい 満載 ¶満載する 〈船が〉be loaded to capacity 《with》; be fully loaded 《with》; carry [have] a full load [cargo] (of); 〈新聞雑

まわれみぎ 回れ右!『号令』Right about (turn [face])! | About turn [face]!

まん¹ このような事は万に一つも起こるまい. It is a thousand to one that such a thing will never happen. | There isn't a chance in a million that such a thing will happen. / ご恩の万分の一にも報いたいと思います. I will do my best to repay your kindness (in some small way).

まんいち 万一病気になったらどうする. What if you should be taken ill?/万一我々が負けないとも限らない. We cannot deny the possibility, remote though it may be, that we may be beaten.

まんいん 熱海は休日の客が押しかけてどのホテルも満員だった. Atami was crowded with holidaymakers and we couldn't find a (vacant) hotel room anywhere in the town. / 満員.〈エレベーターなどの掲示〉Car full. / 座席満員〈劇場などの掲示〉Standing room only. / 満員御礼.『掲示』Thank you for giving us a full house today.

まんえん 九州一円に流感が蔓延している. Influenza is sweeping Kyushu.

まんき (囚人が)満期になった. He served his full term in prison.

まんげつ その晩は満月でした. The moon was full that night.

まんこう 氏の業績には満腔の敬意を表するものである. His achievements command our profoundest respect.

まんさい この雑誌は航空機に関する記事を満載している. This magazine is packed with [is brimful of] information on aircraft.

まんざら まんざら捨てたものでも

まんざい 漫才 a two-man comic [comedy] act; comic backchat; a comic (stage) dialogue ¶漫才師 (one of) a comic duo.

まんざら 《not》…altogether [entirely, wholly]. 文例⇩

まんじ 卍 a [an Indian] swastika; a fylfot ¶(雪が)卍巴(ともえ)と降る swirl down; fall in whirls; fall thick and fast.

まんしつ 満室 文例⇩

まんしゅう 満州 Manchuria ¶満州の Manchurian.

まんじゅう 饅頭 a bun with a bean-jam filling.

まんじょう 満場 the whole house [company, assembly, audience] ¶満場一致で unanimously; 《文》by unanimous consent; 《文》without a dissenting voice ★ unanimously と without a dissenting voice は同じではない. unanimously は, 100人中100人とも賛成. 反対も棄権もゼロの場合, without a dissenting voice (=nem. con.) は賛成1人, 棄権99人, 反対ゼロでもこう言える / 満場のかっさいを浴びる bring down the house / 満場をうならせる impress the whole audience.

マンション an [a multistory] apartment; an apartment house [building]; 《英》a block of flats ★「…マンション」という名称として,《英》では Hudson Mansions のように言う ¶貸マンション〈建物〉a block of rented apartments; 〈その中の1区画〉a rented apartment / 分譲マンション〈建物〉a condominium; 〈その中の1区画〉an apartment (in a condominium).

まんじり ¶まんじりともしない do not sleep a wink; cannot get a wink of sleep; have [pass] a sleepless night / まんじりともしないで without a wink of sleep. 文例⇩

まんしん[1] 満身 ¶満身に all over (one's body); from head to foot / 満身これ創痍(そうい) be covered all over with wounds / 満身の力をこめて with all one's strength [《文》might].

まんしん[2] 慢心 conceit; pride ¶慢心する be proud; be conceited; be puffed up;《文》be bloated [inflated] with pride / 慢心させる make sb conceited. 文例⇩

まんすい 満水 ¶満水になる be filled (to the brim) with water.

まんせい 慢性 ¶慢性の〈急性に対して〉chronic; 〈病みつきの〉confirmed;《文》in-veterate / 慢性になる pass into a chronic state; become chronic 《with sb》/ 慢性病 a chronic disease / 慢性病患者 a chronic invalid. 文例⇩

まんぜん 漫然 ¶漫然たる random; rambling;《文》desultory / 漫然と aimlessly; at random;《文》desultorily.

まんぞく 満足 satisfaction;《文》contentment;《文》gratification (欲望の) ¶満足な〈不満のない〉satisfactory; perfect;〈充分な〉《文》sufficient; adequate;〈見苦しくない〉《文》decent; respectable / 満足する be satisfied [contented] 《with》;《文》be gratified (by, with); be happy [pleased] 《with》/ 満足させる satisfy;《文》gratify (one's desires); give sb satisfaction / 満足げに contentedly / 満足感 a feeling of satisfaction. 文例⇩

まんだら 曼陀羅 a mandala.

まんだらけ 《植》a thorn apple;《米》Jimson 「weed.

まんタン 満タン ¶満タンにする fill up the tank 《of a car》. 文例⇩

まんだん 漫談 a comic monologue; an idle [a rambling] talk.

まんちゃく 瞞着 ⇒だます, ぎまん.

まんちょう 満潮 high water; a high tide; a full [flood] tide ¶満潮時に at high [full, flood] tide; at high water; when the tide is in / 満潮線 the high-water line [mark].

まんてん[1] 満天 the whole sky ¶満天の星《文》the stars in heaven; a skyful of stars. 文例⇩

まんてん[2] 満点 (give, get) full marks ¶100点満点で答案を採点する mark examination papers out of 100 / 100点満点で75点とる get [score] 75 per cent; get [《文》obtain] 75 out of 100; get [score,《文》obtain] 75 points [marks] out of a (possible) hundred / 満点の〈申し分のない〉perfect; entirely satisfactory. 文例⇩

まんてんか 満天下 ¶満天下に in the whole country;《文》throughout the realm;《announce》publicly / 満天下に罪をわび apologize before the whole nation (for what one has done).

マント a mantle; a cloak.

マンとう マン島〈イギリス領〉(the Isle of) Man ¶マン島人 a Manxman.

マントひひ 《動》a sacred [hamadryas] baboon.

マンドリン a mandolin ¶マンドリンを弾く play (on) the mandolin / マンドリン奏者 a mandolinist.

まんなか 真ん中 the middle; the center; the

ない. It is not altogether bad. | There is something to be said for it. / 彼はまんざらばかでもない. He is not altogether a fool. / まんざらいやでもないらしい. He does not seem to be wholly averse to it.

まんしつ 満室.《揭示》《米》No vacancy. | 《英》No vacancies.

まんじり 一晩中まんじりともしなかった. I was wide awake all night.

まんしん 彼は成功に慢心している気味がある. He is rather puffed up with [inflated by] his success.

まんせい あの男のうそつきは慢性だ. He is a habitual liar.

まんぞく どちらの満足をも得るように事件を解決することは容易ではない. It is by no means easy to settle the matter to the satisfaction of both sides. / 私はこのままで満足だ. I am happy where [as] I am. / (壊れてしまって)満足な皿は一つもない. There is not a plate left whole [unbroken]. / あの男は手紙一つ満足に書けない. He cannot even write a letter properly.

まんタン 満タンにして下さい. Fill 'er [her] up, please.

まんちょう 満潮は午後2時だ. The tide is full at 2 p.m. | High tide is at two o'clock in the afternoon. / 1日に2回海は満潮になる. High tides occur twice a day.

まんてん[1] 満天の星が輝いていた. The sky was thick [heavily sprinkled] with stars.

まんてん[2] これなら満点だ. This is

マンネリ(ズム) **1178** み

heart / 真ん中の middle ; central / 真ん中に [で] right in the middle 《of》; in the center [heart] 《of the business district》; halfway between 《the two places》/ 髪を真ん中から分け a part one's hair in the middle.

マンネリ(ズム) a mannerism ¶マンネリ(ズム)に陥る become stereotyped ;《口語》get into [be stuck in] a groove.

まんねん 万年 ten thousand years ¶万年候補 a candidate who runs repeatedly but is never elected / 万年床 a long-unmade [never-made] bed ; permanently laid-out bedding. 文例⇩

まんねんひつ 万年筆 a (fountain) pen ¶万年筆にインクを入れる fill [refill] a fountain pen. 文例⇩

まんねんゆき 万年雪 perpetual snow 《on the slopes of Mt. Everest》;《文》eternal [perennial] [alpine] snows ;《地質》《ドイツ語》firn (snow) ;《フランス語》névé.

まんびき 万引き 〈行為〉shoplifting ; 〈人〉a shoplifter ¶万引きする lift [steal] goods in a store ; shoplift.

まんびょう 万病 all (kinds of) diseases ;《文》all the ills that flesh is heir to ¶万病の薬 a panacea ; a cure-all.

まんぷく 満腹 ¶満腹する eat heartily [one's fill, to one's heart's content] / 満腹した fully fed 〈lions〉/ 満腹感 a feeling [《文》sensation] of fullness. 文例⇩

まんべんなく 満[万]遍なく 〈平等に〉evenly ; equally ;《文》uniformly ; 〈皆に〉all around ; without exception.

マンボ 〈踊り〉the mambo ¶マンボを踊る dance the mambo ; mambo.

まんぼう 〖魚〗a sunfish.

マンホール a manhole ¶マンホールのふた a manhole cover.

まんぽけい 万歩計 a pedometer.

まんまえ 真ん前 ¶真ん前に right in front 《of》; right opposite [in front of] sb [sth] ; under the very nose of.

まんまく 幔幕 a curtain.

まんまと successfully ; fairly ; clean ¶まんまと一杯食わされる be nicely [beautifully] taken in ;《口語》be (completely) taken for a sucker / まんまと逃げおおせる get clean away ; get off [escape] scot-free ;《文》make good one's escape.

まんまる 真ん丸 a perfect circle ¶真ん丸な (completely) round / 真ん丸な十五夜の月 a round full moon. 文例⇩

まんまん 満々 ¶満々たる full 《of ambition》; brimming 《with enterprise》.

まんまん 漫々 ¶漫々たる大海原《文》a boundless expanse of sea.

まんめん 満面 ¶満面に笑みを浮かべて with one's face beaming with smiles ; (be) all smiles / 満面に朱を注いで with one's face red with anger [rage]. 文例⇩

マンモス 〖古生物〗a mammoth ¶マンモス企業 a mammoth enterprise / マンモス計画 a colossal project / マンモス大学 a mammoth [monster] university / マンモスタンカー a gigantic tanker ; a supertanker / マンモス都市 a huge city ; a megalopolis.

まんゆう 漫遊 a tour ; a (pleasure) trip ¶漫遊する make a tour 《of, through》; travel 《in, about》; tour 《a country》.

まんりき 万力 《米》a vise ;《英》a vice.

まんりょう 満了 ⇒まんき.

まんるい 満塁 〖野球〗¶満塁にする fill the bases / 満塁ホーマー (hit) a home run with the bases loaded ; a grand slam. 文例⇩

み

み[1] 巳 〈十二支の〉(the Year of) the Serpent.

み[2] 身 〈身体〉the body ;《文》the person ; 〈自己〉(one's) self ; oneself ; 〈肉〉meat (食用) ;《文》flesh ; 〈身分〉one's social status ;《文》one's station in life ; 〈地位〉one's position ; 〈刃〉a blade ¶…に身が入る be interested [absorbed] in ; take an interest in ; warm to 《one's work》/ 身も心も body and soul / 身も世もあらぬ悲しみ《文》heart-rending sorrow. ¶身の上 ⇒みのうえ / 身の置き所がない do not know what to do with oneself / 身の毛がよだつ a shudder runs through one ; 〈人が主

---

all that could be desired. | This leaves nothing to be desired.

まんねん 彼の寝床は万年床だ. His bed goes unmade from week to week.

まんねんひつ この万年筆はひっかかる[滑りがいい]. This pen scratches [writes smoothly].

まんぷく もう十分です. I have had enough. | I am full.

まんまと まんまと失敗した. It ended as [ended up as a] complete failure.

まんまる 完全に真ん丸な形を球と言う. A completely round solid shape is called a sphere.

まんめん 彼は首尾よく行ったので得意満面だ. He is elated over his [is flushed with] success.

まんるい 無死満塁となった. The bases are full [loaded] with nobody out. / 二死満塁で野村がタイムリーヒットを放った. Nomura pounded a timely hit with the bases full [loaded] and two out.

み[2] そう言っては身もふたもない. You are altogether too outspoken. | We won't get anywhere if you talk like that. / 身の程を知らない男だ. 〈能力〉He should be more aware of his limitations. | 〈地位〉He thinks he's better [more important] than he is. / 〈生活程度〉He lives beyond his income. / 早く帰ったが身のためだぞ. You'd better [If I were you I'd] go home quick. / 彼は仕事に身が入らない. His heart is not in his work. / もう少し身を自分の仕事に身を入れてもらいたい. I want you to put more of your heart into your work. / それは身

語> shudder (at); 〈事が主語〉 make *one* shudder; make *one's* hair stand on end / 身の毛もよだつような hair-raising; bloodcurdling; horrible / 身のこなしの the way one carries *oneself* ; 《文》 *one's* carriage / 身のこなしがいい carry *oneself* nicely [well]; 〈文〉 have a graceful carriage / 身のためである do *sb* good; 《文》 be beneficial to *sb* / 身の振り方 (make) a plan for *one's* future; (map out) *one's* future course; (do not know) what to do with *oneself* / 身の程を知る know [be aware of] *one's* limitations; 《文》 know *oneself* [*one's* place].

¶ 身を誤る go to the bad; go astray; 〈口語〉 leave [stray from] the straight and narrow; 《文》 stray from virtue's path / 身を入れて働く work with a will [in earnest] / 身を入れる put *oneself* [*one's* heart] into; take (an) interest in; devote *oneself* to / 身を売る sell *oneself* 《into slavery》; 身を落とす degrade *oneself*; come down (to being a beggar) / 身を固める (marry and) settle down / 身を切られるような思いがする 〈人が主語〉 have a harrowing experience; 〈事が主語〉 strike home; 《文》 pierce *one* to the heart / 身を粉にして働く work *one's* fingers to the bone; keep *one's* nose to the grindstone; work hard / 身を処する ⇨しょまる / 身を捨てて [挺して] at the sacrifice [risk] of *one's* life; 《guard *one's* children》 with *one's* life / 身を捨てる lay down *one's* life 《for *one's* country》 / 身を立てる 〈独立してやって行く〉 set (*oneself*) up (in business); establish *oneself* 《as an artist》 / 〈出世する〉 rise [get on] in the world; make *one's* way up 《the social ladder》 / 政界に身を投じる enter [go into] politics / 身を引く back out of 《the enterprise》; resign 《*one's* post》 / 身を滅ぼす ruin *oneself* / 身をもってかばう cover [protect, shield] *sb* with *one's* own body / 旅商人に身をやつす disguise *oneself* as a traveling merchant / 身を寄せる find shelter with 《a relative》; stay with 《*one's* aunt》.

¶ 身に余る (be) more than *one* deserves / 身に染みる ⇨しみる / 身につける 〈物を〉 put on (a coat); wear (a sweater); 《文》 bear (a weapon); carry 《valuables》 on *one* [*one's* person]; 〈技術などを〉 learn; 《文》 acquire / 身につまされる sympathize deeply 《with》; feel deeply

《for》/ 《他人の》身になってみる put *oneself* in *sb's* place [shoes, boots] / 《食物が》身になる nourishing; nutritious.

み³ 実 〈果実〉 (a) fruit; a nut (堅果); a berry (漿果 (しょうか)); a seed (けし粒のような); 〈実質〉 substance; 〈汁の〉 (solid) ingredients ¶ 実がいる grow ripe; ripen / 実のある[ない] 《文》 substantial [unsubstantial]; solid [empty] / 実の多い fruitful / 実のならない fruitless / 実を結ぶ bear fruit; (go to) seed; produce seeds; 〈比喩的に〉 bear fruit; 《文》 come to fruition; produce a result / 実を付けるようになる come into bearing. 文例↓

み⁴ 箕 a basket for winnowing rice; a winnow ¶ 箕でふるう winnow.

ミ 〈音楽〉 mi.

-み …味 a flavor; a savor; a touch; 〈色の〉 a tinge ¶ こっけい味のある have a touch of humor; be tinged with humor.

みあい 見合い (have) a meeting [an interview] with a view to marriage; a marriage meeting ¶ 見合い結婚 (an) arranged marriage.

みあう 見合う 〈互いに見る〉 look at each other; exchange looks; 〈対応する〉 correspond 《to》; 〈相殺する〉 counterbalance 《each other》.

みあきる 見飽きる get tired of [〈口語〉 fed up with] seeing; 《文》 grow weary of seeing. 文例↓

みあげる 見上げる 〈上を見る〉 look up (at); raise [lift up] *one's* eyes; 〈尊敬する〉 look up to; respect; admire ¶ 見上げた人物 an admirable [《文》 a praiseworthy] person. 文例↓

みあたる 見当たる 〈人が主語〉 find; come across [upon]; 〈物が主語〉 be found. 文例↓

みあやまる 見誤る mistake; fail to recognize [see].

みあわせる, みあわす 見合わせる, 見合わす 〈互いに見る〉 look at each other; exchange glances; 〈延期する〉 put off; postpone; 〈断念する〉 give up (the idea of *do*ing); abandon; 〈控える〉 withhold. 文例↓

みいだす 見出す 〈見つける〉 find (out) (★ find と find out の違いについては ⇨わかる 用因); discover; detect; 〈抜きする〉 single [pick] out; select.

ミーちゃん・ハーちゃん (a film for) (the) lowbrows; 《英俗》 the plebs.

ミート ¶ 〈野球でバットが〉ミートする meet

に余る名誉です. That's a greater honor than I deserve. / 僕の身にもなってみたまえ. Just think what you would do in my place. / Put yourself in my place (for a moment). / 彼の話を聞くと身につまされて涙がこぼれた. Hearing his story I wept in sympathy with him. / 身から出たさび だ. As they sow, so let them reap. 〖諺〗/ 身から出たさびだ. It serves you [him] right ! ! It's your own doing. / 身から出たさびだ. 僕はだれも恨んでいないよ. I have no one to blame for it but myself. / 身を捨ててこそ浮かぶ瀬もあれ. Nothing venture, nothing win [gain]. 〖諺〗

み³ 上べよりも実のあるものを選べ. You should choose substance over appearance. / この分野では医学者の努力もあまり実を結ばないようである. The efforts of the medical profession do not seem to have borne much fruit in this sphere.

みあきる 幾度見ても見飽きない絵だ. I never get tired of looking at this picture. | One could look at this picture forever. / それはもう見飽きた. I have seen enough of it.

みあげる 彼は見上げるばかりの大男であった. He was a towering giant. / その勇気は見上げたものだ. I admire his courage.

みあたる 本がどこにも見当たらなかった. The book was nowhere to be found.

みあわせる 一同互いに顔を見合わせた. Everybody glanced at one another.

ミーハーぞく ミーハー族 ⇒ ミーちゃん-族

ミイラ a mummy ¶ミイラになる[する] mummify / ミイラ取りがミイラになる go for wool and come home shorn.

みいられる 魅入られる be fascinated 《by, with》; be enthralled 《by》; be bewitched 《by》.

みいり 実入り 〈収穫〉 a crop; a harvest; 〈収入〉 (an) income; profits ¶実入りがいい 〈職業が〉 be profitable; pay well; be lucrative; 〈人が〉 have [《文》enjoy] a large income.

みいる 見[魅]入る 〈見つめる〉 gaze intently 《at》; watch; fix *one*'s eyes 《on》; 〈魅する〉 fascinate; enchant; 《文》possess; 《文》enthrall.

みうけ 身請[受]け ¶身うけする redeem; ransom.

みうける 見受ける 〈見る〉 see; come across; 〈…のようだ〉 look; appear 《to be》 ¶見受けたところは to all appearances; apparently; outwardly. 文例⬇

みうごき 身動き ¶身動きする move; stir / 身動きもできない cannot move at all; cannot stir an inch; have no elbowroom / 身動きもしないで 《remain》motionless; 《stand》 still.

みうしなう 見失う lose sight of; miss ¶追いかけていて見失う lose track of.

みうち 身内 〈親せき〉 *one*'s relations [relatives]; 〈子分〉 followers 《of》; *one*'s men.

みうり 身売り ¶身売りする sell *oneself* (into slavery [《文》bondage]).

みえ 見栄 show; (a) display; 〈虚栄〉 vanity ¶見えを張る show off; be vain / 見えをきる 〈俳優が〉 pose; 《文》assume a posture [(frozen) pose]; 〈演壇などで〉 make a proud [defiant] gesture / 見えで for show; for appearance' sake / 見え坊 a fop; a vain person. 文例⬇

みえかくれ 見え隠れ ¶見え隠れする appear and disappear; be now in and now out of sight; become invisible from time to time.

みえすく 見え透く be transparent; be easily seen through ¶見え透いたうそ[トリック] a transparent [an obvious] lie [trick] / 見え透いた事をする resort to shallow tricks.

みえる 見える 〈人が主語〉 see ⇒ みる 囲連 1); 〈事物が主語〉 be seen; be visible; appear (現われる); 〈…らしい〉 seem (to be); appear 《to be》; look 《expensive, as if it is expensive》; 〈来る〉 come; be here [there] ¶眼に見えない be invisible / 見えなくする make *sth* invisible; hide *sth* from view / 見えなくなる go out of sight; disappear (from sight); vanish; 〈失う〉 lose sight of (人が主語); 《文》be lost to sight (対象が主語); 〈紛失する〉 be missing / 見えて来る come in sight [into view]. 文例⬇

みおくり 見送り 〈人を見送ること〉 seeing *sb* off; a send-off ¶見送りの三振でアウトになる misread a pitch (as a ball) and strike out / 空港へ見送りに行く go to an airport to see *sb* off / 見送り人 people present for a send-off. 文例⬇

みおくる 見送る see *sb* off; give *sb* a send-off; 〈目送する〉 follow with *one*'s eyes; 〈そのままにする〉 let (it) go; leave *sth* over [as it is]; 〈野球で〉 let a pitch go by ¶盛んに見送る give *sb* a hearty send-off / 家〔途中〕まで見送る see *sb* home [part of the way] / 玄関まで見送る see *sb* out; see [take] *sb* to the door / 後ろ姿を見送る watch [look] after *sb* / ひと電車見送る wait for the next train. 文例⬇

みおさめ 見納め ¶見納めをする take a last [farewell] look 《at》; see *sth* [*sb*] for the last time. 文例⬇

みおとし 見落とし an oversight; something left [that has gone] unnoticed ¶誤植の見落とし a misprint left uncorrected / 見落としとする make an oversight.

みおとす 見落とす overlook; pass by; do not [fail to] notice. 文例⬇

みおとり 見劣り ¶見劣りがする compare unfavorably [poorly] 《with》; suffer by comparison 《with》; be not as good 《as》; be outshone [eclipsed] 《by》; be put in [into] the shade 《by》. 文例⬇

みおぼえ 見覚え recognition; memory; 《文》

みうける 彼は非常に満足の様子に見受けられた. He looked [gave the impression of being] quite satisfied.

みえ 見えで高級車を持つ人が多い. Many people own expensive cars out of vanity. | Lots of people own expensive cars just to show off. / 闘牛士は大きく見えを切って退場した. The matador made his exit with great style.

みえる 汽船が2隻見える. I can see two steamers. / 特別にこういうものが見える人があるんだ. It is given to some to see these things. / 見えなくなるまで彼を見送った. We watched him until he was out of sight. / やがて猪苗代湖が見えるところまで来た. By and by we came in sight [view] of Lake Inawashiro. / 月の山やクレーターは17世紀になって初めて望遠鏡で見えるようになった. The moon's mountains and craters were first brought into view by the telescope in the 17th century. / ここからの方が舞台がよく見えますよ. You'll have a better view of the stage from here. / 丘に登ると港の全景が見える. The hill commands a view of the whole harbor. / 下着が見えているよ. Your slip is showing. / 油絵は少し離れて見た方がよく見える. Oil paintings look better [show to better advantage] at a distance. / 彼は病気と見える. He seems to be ill. / あの人は日本人とは[年には]見えない. He does not look like a Japanese [look his age]. / 間もなくお見えになりましょう. He will soon be here.

みおくり (船で)お見送りの方はお降り願います. Visitors ashore, please. / 彼は私が帰るときは必ず玄関まで見送りに出た. He always saw me to the door when I left.

みおくる 京都へ行く父を見送って来た. I have been to the station to see my father off to Kyoto. / 伊丹出発の際はご多用中お見送りいただきましてお礼申し上げます. Many thanks for seeing me off when I left Itami.

みおさめ それが見納めとなった. That was the last I saw of him.

みおも remembrance ¶見覚えがある recognize; remember (seeing *sth* [*sb*] before); recall / 見覚えのある well-remembered; familiar / 見覚えのない unfamiliar; strange. 文例⇩
みおも 身重 ¶身重の pregnant ⇨ にんしん.
みおろす 見下ろす look down《at》; overlook. 文例⇩
みかい 未開 ¶未開の primitive; uncivilized; barbarous; savage / 未開社会 (a) primitive society / 未開人 a barbarian; a savage; a savage [primitive] people [race] / 未開地 a savage [barbaric] land (蛮地); a backward region (開けていない地域).
みかいけつ 未解決 ¶未解決の unsolved《problems》; unsettled《disputes》; pending; outstanding《issues》/ 未解決の問題 an open question; a moot point / 未解決のままにしておく leave (a matter) unsettled [outstanding]; leave (a matter) at loose ends. 文例⇩
みかいたく 未開拓 ¶未開拓の uncultivated; undeveloped; unexploited; unexplored.
みかいはつ 未開発 ¶未開発の undeveloped (regions); wild《land》; unexploited [untapped]《resources》; 〈低開発の〉 underdeveloped《countries》.
みかえし 見返し the inside (front, back) cover (of a book).
みかえす 見返す 〈振り返って〉 look back《at》; 〈相手の目を〉 return *sb*'s look; 〈自分をさげすんだ人を〉 put《*one*'s old enemy》to shame; 《口語》get *one*'s own back《on》.
みかえり 見返り ¶見返り資金 collateral funds / 見返り物資 collateral (export) goods (輸出用); incentive goods (生産促進用).
みかえる 見返る look back《at, on, to》; look over *one*'s shoulder.
みがき 磨き polish ¶磨きをかける give *sth* a polish (by rubbing *it*); polish; rub up (silver spoons) / フランス語に磨きをかける improve [polish up, rub up] *one*'s French / 磨き粉[砂] polishing powder [sand].
みがきにしん 身欠き鰊 dried filleted herring.
みかぎる 見限る give up; abandon; desert; 《文》forsake. 文例⇩

みかく 味覚 the (sense of) taste ¶味覚が発達している have a keen sense of taste; 《文》 have a delicate palate / 味覚の秋 autumn, the season of the pleasures of the table / 味覚をそそる tempt the appetite; make *one*'s mouth water.
みがく 磨く polish; give *sth* a polish [a rub-up]; rub up (silver spoons); burnish (金属を); grind (レンズを); 〈歯を〉 clean; brush; 〈靴を〉 polish; black; 《米》shine (★ 過去・過去分詞は shined); 〈いそいこする〉 practice; train ¶靴をぴかぴかに磨く give *one*'s shoes a good shine [polish] / 磨き上げる[立てる] polish [shine, rub, brush] up / 腕を磨く improve *one*'s ability [skill] / 人格を磨く cultivate [build (up)] *one*'s character.
みかくにん 未確認 ¶未確認の《文》yet to be confirmed; 〈正体不明の〉 unidentified / 未確認情報 unconfirmed information / 未確認飛行物体 an unidentified flying object; a UFO (*pl.* UFO's).
みかけ 見掛け (outward) appearance; looks; show ¶見掛けは seemingly; apparently; outwardly; on the surface; to the eye / 見掛けによらず despite appearances (to the contrary); though 〈he [it]〉 looks the reverse / 見掛け倒しである be not as good as *it* looks; be all show and no power; be deceptive / 見掛けの膨張《物》apparent expansion.
みかげいし 御影石 granite ⇨ かこうがん.
みかける 見掛ける (happen to) see; find; notice ¶よく見掛けること a familiar [common] sight. 文例⇩
みかこう 未加工 ¶未加工の raw; unfinished; unprocessed; 《diamonds》in the rough.
みかた¹ 見方 a way of looking at 《things》; a (point of) view; a viewpoint; an outlook ¶新しい見方をする look at *sth* in a new light / 常識的な見方をする take a common-sense view《of》/ 別の見方をする see [view, look at] *sth* from a different angle [in a different light]. 文例⇩
みかた² 味方 a friend; an ally; a supporter; *one*'s side ¶味方する take *sb*'s side; side

---

これがこの世の見納めだ. This is my last day in this world.
みおとす この事実を見落としてはならない. This fact must not be overlooked. / それはつい見落とした. I missed [didn't notice] that. / That escaped my notice.
みおとり アメリカに比べるとソ連の消費財生産は見劣りがする. The performance of the Soviet consumer goods industry compares unfavorably with that of the United States.
みおぼえ 日本人はみな見覚えがあるように思われる. I have the [a] feeling that I've met him before. / あなたはどことなく見覚えがあるみたい. You look vaguely familiar.

みおろす ヘリコプターでマンハッタンの上を低空飛行して, 全市を見下ろすことができた. Flying low over Manhattan in a helicopter I had a bird's-eye view of the whole city.
みかいけつ どうしてそうなったのかいまだに未解決の問題になっている. How it came about remains an unsolved question.
みかぎる まあお珍しい. もうお見限りかと思っておりました. It's ages since I saw you last. I thought you had forgotten me.
みかけ 見掛けは当てにならない. Appearances can be misleading.
みかける この頃はさっぱり見かけない. 〈人〉 I have seen nothing [very little] of him lately. | 〈物〉

You rarely see things like that [of that sort] nowadays. / この間余り知らない女性と喫茶店で話をしているのを見かけた. Not long ago I saw him in a café talking to a woman I didn't know. / どこかで見かけたような人だ. I think I have seen him somewhere.
みかた¹ それが彼流の物の見方だ. That's the way he sees [looks at] things. / 僕の見方は違います. I don't see the matter in that light. | I look at it differently. / それは見方による. That is a matter of opinion. | It depends on how you look at it. / ひとりの科学者がその問題に対する新しい見方を提示した. A scientist offered a fresh insight into the problem. /

みかづき 三日月 a new moon; a crescent (moon); 《文》the sickle [horned] moon ¶三日月形の crescent(-shaped) / 《メソポタミアの》肥沃(ひよく)な三日月地帯《史》the Fertile Crescent.

みがって 身勝手 ¶身勝手な selfish ⇒ かって².

みかねる 見兼ねる cannot stand (it) any [can stand (it) no] longer; 《文》cannot look on with indifference; 《文》be unable to remain a mere spectator [onlooker].

みがまえ 身構え a posture; 《文》an attitude.

みがまえる 身構える stand ready 《for, to do》; take [《文》assume] a stance; gather [pull] oneself up 《for an effort》;〈防御に〉stand on 《one's》guard;《文》assume a posture of defense; square up 《to sb》; square off 《for a fight》.

みがら 身柄 one's person ¶身柄を引き取りに行く go to claim [receive] sb / 身柄を引き渡す hand 《an offender》over 《to》/ 身柄不拘束のまま ふこうそく.

みがる 身軽 ¶身軽な light; nimble; sprightly / 身軽な服装をする be lightly dressed [clothed] / 身軽な支度で旅をする travel light / 身軽に lightly; nimbly.

みかわす 見交わす look at each other; exchange glances 《with》.

みがわり 身代わり 〈事〉substitution; 〈人〉a substitute; a scapegoat; a sacrifice; 〈映画〉a stand-in ¶身代わりになる[立つ] act as (a) substitute 《for》;〈犠牲に〉sacrifice oneself 《for》;〈文〉make oneself a vicarious sacrifice. 文例⇩

みかん¹ 未刊 ¶未刊の unpublished; not yet published; as-yet-unissued 《numbers of the journal》.

みかん² 未完 ¶未完の incomplete; unfinished / 未完の大器《文》a great talent in the making.

みかん³ 蜜柑 《植》a mandarin (orange); a tangerine;《英》a satsuma (orange) ¶みかん1房 a segment of a tangerine / みかん色 orange; tangerine / みかん畑 a tangerine orchard [plantation]; an orange grove.

みかんせい 未完成 ¶未完成の unfinished; incomplete; imperfect / 未完成交響曲 the Unfinished Symphony.

みき 幹 a trunk 《of a tree》.

みぎ 右 (the) right ¶右の right; 〈上記の〉《文》the above; 《文》the said; 《文》the above-mentioned / 右へ曲がる turn to the right / 右に on the right (of); on one's right / ...の右に出るを超えるを be superior to; 《文》surpass; 《文》excel / 右側 (on) the right(-hand) side (of) / 鍵盤の右側 the upper keyboard / 右側通行を keep (to) the right / 右腕〈右の腕〉one's [the] right arm; 〈一番頼みになる人〉one's right-hand man; one's right hand / 右利きの a right-handed person / 道路の右手に on the right-hand side [to the right] of the road; to one's right 《when one gets round the corner》/ 右巻き[回り] (a) right-handed rotation [revolution] / 右巻きの巻貝の殻 a shell coiling to the right / 〈政治的に〉右寄りである be a little to the right. 文例⇩

みきき 見聞き ⇒ けんぶん¹.

ミキサー a mixer; 〈食品の〉a liquidizer; a blender; 〈音響の〉a (sound) mixer.

みきり 見切り ¶見切りをつける〈断念する〉give up (as hopeless); abandon;《文》forsake / 〈事業などに〉wash one's hands of / 見切り売り a clearance [bargain] sale / 見切り値段 clearance [bargain, sacrifice] price / 見切り発車 starting a train before all the passengers are on board; 〈比喩的〉starting an action without considering objections to it any longer; 《make》a snap decision / 見切り品 clearance [sacrifice, cut-price] goods / 見切り品売場 a remnant [clearance] counter. 文例⇩

みきる 見切る 〈見限る〉⇒ みきり(見切りをつける); 〈安く売る〉sell off (at a bargain price).

みぎれい 身奇麗 ¶身ぎれいにしている keep oneself neat [tidy]; be as neat as a new pin.

みきわめる 見極める 〈完全に見届ける〉get to the bottom of; (manage to) see through; have a clear view [picture] of; 〈確認から〉make sure (of, that...); 《文》ascertain; 〈把握する〉grasp; make out.

みくだす 見下す look down on; look down one's nose at sb; 《文》hold sb in contempt.

みくだりはん 三行半 a divorce note (composed of three and half lines).

みくびる 見縊る look down on; think poorly of; do not think much of; 《文》hold sb cheap; underrate; belittle; slight; make light of. 文例⇩

みくらべる 見比べる compare 《two things》《with one's eye》; judge (A) by comparison 《with B》 ¶顔を見比べる look from one to another.

見方によれば、あの人はいい時に死んだと言える。In a sense, he was lucky to die when he did.

みかた² 彼は貧しい人の味方だ。He is a friend of the poor. / 世論は彼に味方した。Public opinion was on his side [in his favor].

みかね 彼は主人の身代わりになって死んだ。He died for his master.

みかん² 未完。〈記事の末尾に〉To be continued.

みぎ 右へならえ!〈号令〉Right dress! / 右向け右!〈号令〉Right turn [face]! / 学力で彼の右に出る者はいない。No one surpasses him [He is second to none] in scholarship. / 事務をてきぱきと正確に処理する点で、彼の右に出る社員はなかった。He was the last word in efficiency and accuracy at the office. / 右のとおり相違ありません。〈履歴書〉I affirm the above to be true and correct in every particular. ★ 英語の履歴書ではこういうことは書かない。 | 〈供述書など〉I confirm that the above is a true record of my statement 《made at Ebara Police Station on December 5th 1983》. / 先生の言うことはよく右から左へ抜けてしまう。What the teacher says often goes in at one ear and out at the other. / あの男は人が右と言えば左と言うのが好きだ。He takes pleasure in contradicting people. / 彼は右投げ左打ちだ。He throws right(-handed) and bats left.

みぐるしい 見苦しい ＜醜い＞ unsightly; unseemly; indecent; ＜恥ずべき＞《文》dishonorable; disgraceful; ＜まずい＞ poor; bad; awkward; ＜汚い＞ shabby; disreputable ¶見苦しい振る舞いをする behave badly; behave in a disgraceful [《文》an unseemly] fashion; 《文》act dishonorably / 見苦しからぬ respectable; decent.

みぐるみ 身ぐるみ ¶身ぐるみはぎ取られる be robbed [stripped] of all *one* has.

ミクロのせかい ミクロの世界 the microscopic world / ミクロの世界の microscopic 《laws of the atom》/ ミクロ経済学 microeconomics / ミクロコスモス a microcosm.

ミクロネシア Micronesia ¶ミクロネシアの Micronesian / ミクロネシア人 a Micronesian.

ミクロン a micron (記号: μ).

みけいか 未経過 ¶未経過保険料 a prepaid [prereceived] premium; an unearned premium / 未経過利息 prepaid interest.

みけいけん 未経験 ¶未経験の inexperienced; green; new / 未経験者 an inexperienced person; a green hand; a person new to the job.

みけつ 未決 ¶未決の undecided; pending; open; unsettled; unconvicted (罪人が) / 未決拘留日数 the number of days of detention on remand [pending trial] / 未決 30 日通算 1 年の禁固 one year's imprisonment with credit for the 30 days spent in detention on remand (before conviction) / 未決囚 a prisoner on remand [under trial]; an unconvicted prisoner / 未決書類入れ an in-tray.

みけっさい 未決済 ¶未決済の ＜未決算＞ unsettled 《debts》; outstanding 《accounts》; ＜未払い＞ unpaid.

みけってい 未決定 ¶未決定である be not yet decided (on); be undecided; be pending; be in the air.

みけねこ 三毛猫 a tortoiseshell (cat).

みけん 眉間 the middle of the forehead; the brow ¶眉間を割られる get [receive] a cut between *one*'s eyes [across *one*'s forehead].

みこ 神子, 巫女 a virgin consecrated to a deity; a shrine maiden; ＜市子(いちこ)＞ a (spiritualistic) medium.

みこうにん 未公認 ¶未公認の unofficial; not yet officially recognized / 未公認記録 an unofficial record [time].

みこし 御輿 a portable shrine ¶みこしをすえる settle (*oneself*) down; plant *oneself* 《on a chair》; 《文・戯言》ensconce *oneself* 《in an armchair》/ みこしを上げる《文》rise from *one*'s seat; get up; move on.

みごしらえ 身拵え ⇒みじたく.

みこす 見越す expect; anticipate; speculate (on); foresee ¶将来を見越して with an eye to the future / 値上がりを見越して in expectation [anticipation] of a rise in price; 《hold *one*'s stocks》 for a rise.

みごたえ 見応え ¶見ごたえがある be worth seeing; be impressive.

みごと 見事 ¶みごとな ＜美しい＞ beautiful; ＜りっぱな＞ excellent; fine; splendid; marvelous; brilliant; 《文》admirable; 《文》masterful 《prose》 / みごとに ＜美しく＞ beautifully; ＜りっぱに＞ finely; splendidly; 《文》with credit; ＜巧みに＞ skillfully; dexterously; ＜鮮やかに＞ in fine [great] style; successfully; neatly; admirably / みごとに失敗する end (up) in (a) complete failure. 文例↓

みごなし 身ごなし *one*'s movement(s); 《文》 *one*'s carriage; 《文》 *one*'s deportment.

みこみ 見込み ＜望み＞ hope(s); promise; prospect(s) 《for *sth*》; expectation(s); an estimate; ＜可能性＞ likelihood; probability; (a) chance ¶見込みがある be promising; be hopeful; have a bright future before *one*; have bright [good] prospects; bid fair (to succeed) / 見込みがない be hopeless; have no chance 《of success, of succeeding》 / 見込みが当たる[はずれる] guess right [wrong]; *one*'s forecast is right [wrong] / 見込みのある青年 a promising youth / ...との見込みである it is expected [thought] that... / ...の見込みはかなりある there is a good chance that...; the odds are pretty fair that... / 見込み点 an estimated mark (given without examination). 文例↓

みこむ 見込む ＜予期する＞ expect; calculate; ＜当てにする＞ rely [count] on; ＜目をつける＞ mark *sb* (out); ＜信用する＞ trust; 《文》place [put] 《one's》confidence in *sb*; ＜見積もる＞ estimate; ＜勘定に入れる＞ allow for 《damage》; make allowance for; take into account ¶...を見込んで in anticipation [expectation] of; counting on / 見込まれる ＜信用される＞ win *sb*'s confidence [favor]; ＜目をつけられる＞ be marked [picked] (out) 《as a promising worker》; catch *sb*'s eye; ＜魅入られる＞ be possessed 《by a devil》; be fascinated 《by a snake》. 文例↓

みごもる 身籠る ⇒にんしん.

みきり いい加減に見切りをつけろよ. It's about time you gave it up.

みくびる 人々は彼を子供と見くびった. They made light of him as a mere boy.

みごと おみごと! Well done! / 彼はみごとに成功した. He has succeeded admirably. / この絵はみごとに描けている. This picture is excellently done.

みこみ 勝てる見込みがない. The chances [odds] are against me. / 彼が来る見込みはほとんどない. There is not much likelihood that he will come. / 彼は не likely to come. / このような案を米国の議会が承認する見込みはなくない. The prospects for Congressional approval of that idea are nil. / 業界筋では 8 月頃には値段が下がる見込みでいる. Dealers expect a fall in the price about August. / 本年の米作は平年以上の見込みである. The rice crop for this year is forecast to be above average. / 交渉の進展は見込み薄である. Prospects for progress in the talks are poor. / The chances of progress in the negotiations are slim.

みこむ 君を見込んで頼むのだ. I make this request with full confidence in you. / 破損を見込んでおかなければいけない. We must allow for breakages. / 彼に見込まれたら最後だ. Once he has you marked as a victim, you are done for.

みごろ¹ 見頃 the best time to see. 文例↓
みごろ² 身頃 the body (part) 《of a garment, the bodice》.
みごろし 見殺し ¶見殺しにする leave [abandon] sb to his fate; stand by (and watch [and do nothing])《while sb dies [suffers]》/ 〈信頼を裏切って〉let sb down;《口語》leave sb in the lurch.
みこん 未婚 ¶未婚の unmarried; single / 未婚の母 an unmarried mother / 未婚者 an unmarried person /〈男〉a bachelor /〈女〉an unmarried woman.
ミサ [<《ラテン語》missa]《カトリック》(a) mass ¶ミサを行なう say [read] mass / ミサに参列する go to mass.
みさい 未済 ¶未済の 〈未払いの〉 unpaid 《bills》; outstanding [unsettled]《accounts》; 〈未了の〉unfinished《business》.
ミサイル a missile ¶ミサイルを装備した missile-carrying《submarines》/ ミサイルを発射する fire [launch] a missile / 水中ミサイル an underwater missile / 戦略[戦術用]ミサイル a strategic [tactical] missile / 長[短]距離ミサイル a long-[short-]range missile / ミサイル基地[発射場] a missile base [station] / ミサイルギャップ a missile gap / ミサイル競争 a missile race / ミサイル実験 test-firing of a missile / ミサイル防御用ミサイル an antiballistic missile (略: ABM).
みさお 操 〈貞操〉chastity; virginity; 〈貞節〉faithfulness;《文》《marital》fidelity;《文》constancy.
みさかい 見境 ¶見境がつかない cannot tell [distinguish]《A from B》; cannot distinguish [tell the difference between]《A and B》/ 善悪の見境がつかない cannot distinguish between good and bad; do not know the difference between right and wrong / 見境なく indiscriminately / 前後の見境もなく without considering the consequences.
みさき 岬 a cape; a promontory; a headland; a point (of land) ¶三浦岬 Miura Point.
みさげる 見下げる ⇨みくだす ¶見下げ果てた despicable; mean; contemptible.
みさご〔鳥〕an osprey.
みさだめる 見定める ascertain; make sure《of》¶相手の力量を見定める take the measure of one's opponent.
みじかい 短い short; 〈簡単な〉brief ¶2メートル短い be two meters shorter (比較で) / [too short (不足)] / 短く する; 〈簡単に〉briefly /

短くする shorten; cut [make] sth short; cut back (on)《working hours》; curtail (切り詰める) / つめを短く切る cut one's nails close / 〈野球で〉バットを短く握る hold one's bat short. 文例↓
ミシガン Michigan (略: Mich.) ¶ミシガン州の人 a Michigander.
ミシシッピ〈州〉Mississippi (略: Miss.);〈川〉the Mississippi (River) ¶ミシシッピ州の人 a Mississippian.
みじたく 身仕度 dress; outfit; a turnout; preparation;《俗》a getup /〈化粧〉《文》one's toilet ¶身仕度する dress [《文》attire] oneself; fit oneself out 《for an outing》; get (oneself) ready 《for a journey》.
みしみし with a creak ¶みしみしいう creak.
みじめ 惨め ¶惨めな miserable; sad; wretched; pitiful; pitiable;《文》piteous / 惨めな暮らしをする be badly off; live a miserable [dog's] life; live in misery [like a dog] / 惨めな死に方をする die a miserable [dog's] death; die in (great) misery. 文例↓
みしゅう 未収 ¶未収の uncollected《revenue》; accrued《interest》; receivable《bills》.
みしゅうがくじどう 未就学児童 preschool children.
みじゅく 未熟 ¶未熟な 〈成熟しない〉 unripe; immature; green; 〈熟達しない〉 unskilled / 〈経験の浅い〉inexperienced; raw; green / 未熟である lack experience / 未熟児 a premature baby / 未熟児出産 a premature birth / 未熟者 an inexperienced worker;《口語》a greenhorn. 文例↓
みしょう¹ 未詳 ¶未詳の unknown; unidentified; not exactly known. 文例↓
みしょう² 実生 a seedling ¶実生の《a plant》raised from seed.
みしょうかん 未償還 ¶未償還の outstanding; unredeemed.
みしょち 未処置 ¶未処置の not yet dealt with / 未処置の虫歯 a bad tooth left untreated.
みしょぶん 未処分 ¶未処分の undisposed-of 《articles》; undivided《profits》.
みしょり 未処理 ¶未処理の《business》left unattended (to);《matters》not yet attended to;《papers》still to be dealt with.
みしりみしり ⇨みしみし.
みしる 見知る〈見てわかる〉recognize; know by sight; 〈知り合いになる〉 get to know; be [,《文》become] acquainted《with》¶見知らぬ strange; unfamiliar; unknown / 見知らぬ人 a stranger. 文例↓

みごろ 桜はちょうど見頃だ. The cherry blossoms are at their best now. | The cherry trees are in full bloom.
みじかい 文章はなるべく短かめにするほうがいい. Keep your sentences on the short side. / 〈床屋で〉もっと短くしてください Cut it (a little) shorter, please.
みじめ 終戦当時の東京は惨めな様だった. Conditions in Tokyo at the end of the war were miserable.
みじゅく 私の英語は未熟です. My English is far from perfect [is very poor].
みしょう¹ 被害の程度は未詳である. The extent of the damage is not yet known [has not yet been ascertained].
みしる 以後お見知りおきを願います. I am very glad to make your acquaintance.
みじろぐ 彼はみじろぎもしなかっ

た. He did not stir an inch.
みじん そんな事をする気はみじんもない. I haven't the slightest intention of doing that.
ミス¹ 彼女はまだミスだ. She is still single [not married yet].
みず 蛇口をひねったが水が出なかった. I turned on the taps but the water did not run. / 川[井戸]に水がなくなってしまった. The river [well] has run dry. / 僕の靴は水がしみる. My shoes leak

みじろぐ 身じろぐ stir. 文例◊

ミシン a sewing machine ¶ミシンを踏む work [run] a sewing machine by foot / ミシンで縫う[をかける] sew 《a dress》on a machine / ミシンで縫い合わせる run up a seam on the machine / ミシン縫いの machine-sewn[-sewed] / 足踏みミシン a treadle [foot-operated] sewing machine / 電気ミシン an electric sewing machine / ミシン糸 machine cotton / ミシン針 a sewing-machine needle.

みじん 微塵 ¶ミじんに砕ける be broken to pieces [《口語》bits]; be (broken) in fragments; be smashed to atoms / …はみじんもない have not a bit of…; have not the slightest [least] 《resentment》/ みじん切りにする cut 《vegetables》fine; cut into tiny pieces. 文例◊

みじんこ 《動》a water flea.

みす 御簾 a bamboo blind [screen].

ミス[1] 〈独身の女性〉an unmarried woman ¶ミスユニバース Miss Universe.

ミス[2] 〈間違い〉a mistake; an error; 〈はずれ〉a miss.

みず 水 water;〈湯に対して〉cold water;〈洪水〉a flood; (an) inundation ¶ひざに水がたまる have water on the knee; fluid collects under one's kneecap / 水の泡となる come to nothing [《文》naught]; end (up) in failure / 水の循環 a water [hydrologic] cycle / 水の豊富な well-watered 《mountains》/ 水をあける open up a (big) lead 《over one's opponent》/ 水を切る drain 《the potatoes》/ 水を好む water-loving 《birds》/ 水をさす《湯沸かしなどに》pour water into 《a kettle》;《離間する》《文》estrange 《people》; cause ill feeling 《between》; make mischief 《between》;《計画などに》throw cold water on [a wet blanket over] 《a plan》; throw [put] a damper on 《the festivities》/ 道路に水をまく sprinkle the streets / 水を向ける〈話を聞き出そうとして〉try to draw sb out / 庭木に水をやる water the garden 《plants》/ 水で割る〈薄める〉water down; dilute;〈飲物を〉put water in 《one's wine》; mix [take] water with 《one's whisky》; mix 《wine》with water / 水と油のように合わない be as incompatible [foreign] as oil and water (★日本語と語順が逆になる)/ 水も漏らさぬ watertight 《plans》; strict 《watch》; airtight 《fielding》/ 水も滴るような美人 a breathtakingly [fantastically] beautiful woman. 文例◊

みずあか 水垢 (a) fur; furring; an incrustation. [let in water]. / ホウレンソウは数回水を取り替えてよく洗ってください. Wash the spinach well in several waters. / 〈洪水で〉水が出た. There is a flood. | The river is in flood [has overflowed its banks]. / 水が退いた. The water [flood] has receded. | The (level of the) water has fallen. / お風呂はまだ全然水だよ. The water in the bath is still stone-cold. / 聴衆は水を打ったように静

みずあげ 水揚げ〈陸揚げ〉landing; unloading;〈漁獲量〉a catch; a haul;〈売り上げ〉takings; (gross) earnings;〈生け花の〉water raising; preservation 《of cut flowers》;〈芸者の〉initiation;《文》defloration ¶水揚げする land 《fish》; unload 《cargo》.

みずあそび 水遊び ¶水遊びする play [dabble, paddle] in the water.

みずあたり 水中り 文例◊

みずあび 水浴び bathing; a bathe;〈鳥の〉a water bath ⇨ すいよく, しよく ¶水浴びする

みずあぶら 水油 hair oil. ⌊bathe 《in a river》.

みずあめ 水飴 a glutinous starch syrup.

みずあらい 水洗い ¶水洗いする wash sth without using soap.

みすい 未遂 ¶未遂の attempted / 未遂に終わる fail in one's attempt 《at murder》/ 未遂に終わったクーデター an abortive coup d'état / 自殺未遂《罪》attempted suicide / 未遂罪 an attempted crime [offense].

みずいたずら 水いたずら ⇨ みずあそび.

みずいらず 水入らず ¶水入らずで by themselves [ourselves]; with no one else [no outsiders] present / 一家水入らずの集まり a family gathering [party].

みずいれ 水入れ a water vessel;〈水差し〉a jug; a pitcher; a carafe (壇上の).

みずいろ 水色 (a) sky blue; turquoise; (a) light [pale] blue. ⌈placid mountain lake.

みずうみ 湖 a lake ¶山の中の静かな湖 a

ミズーリ Missouri (略: Mo.) ¶ミズーリ州の人 a Missourian.

みすえる 見据える look hard [steadily] 《at》; stare fixedly 《at》; fix one's eyes (on) ; have one's eyes glued (to) ¶真正面から見据える look sb squarely in the eye.

みずおけ 水桶 a (water) pail [bucket];〈水槽〉

みずおち ⇨ みぞおち. ⌊a cistern; a water tank.

みずおと 水音〈落ちる水の〉the sound of falling water;〈流れる水の〉the sound of running water ¶水音を立てて with a splash.

みずがい 水貝 sliced sea-ear served in cold water.

みずかがみ 水鏡 the glassy surface of (the) water ¶水鏡を見る look at one's reflection in the water.

みずかき 水掻き〈水鳥などの〉a web;〈機械の〉a paddle;〈オールの〉a paddle blade ¶水かき足 a webbed foot / 水かき足のある web-footed /〈外輪船の〉水かき車 a paddle wheel.

みずかけろん 水掛け論 (have) an endless dispute; an argument which gets 《us》nowhere. 文例◊

かになった. A hush fell over the audience. | The audience became so quiet that you could have heard a pin drop. / 今までの事は水に流すことにしよう. Let's let bygones be bygones. / 水は低きにつく. It is the nature of water to run downhill. | Water seeks [finds] its own level. / 人ければ魚住まず. A man with no faults is not easy to get along with. | A person with no weak-nesses does not have many friends. / その相撲は2回水が入った. Time was called twice during the bout.

みずあたり 初めての土地なので, 水あたりしたらしい. As this is my first visit here, the water seems to have disagreed with me.

みずかけろん The argument [talk] got us nowhere. | The long dispute ended inconclusively.

みずかげん 水加減 the (proper) quantity of water (for boiling rice).
みずかさ 水嵩 the volume of water ¶水かさの増した川 a swollen river; a river in flood.
みずかし 水菓子 fruit. 文例⇩
みずかす 見透かす ⇨ みぬく.
みずがめ 水瓶 a water jar [jug] ¶水がめ座〈天〉Aquarius; the Water Carrier ⇨ さ 文例.
みずから 自ら (for) oneself; in person; personally ¶自らの one's own; (one's) personal / 自ら進[好]んで of one's own accord [free will] / 自ら危険を招く court danger.
みずガラス 水ガラス water glass.
みずがれ 水涸れ〈干上がること〉drying up; 〈日照り続き〉(a) drought.
みずぎ 水着 a swimsuit; a bathing suit [dress, costume]; 《英》a swimming costume ¶水着の美人 a bathing beauty.
ミスキャスト miscasting. 文例⇩
みずきり 水切り〈遊戯〉(play) ducks and drakes; 〈台所用の〉a strainer; a drainer ¶水切り台〈流しの〉《米》a drainboard; 《英》a draining board. 文例⇩
みずぎわ 水際 ¶水際で at the water's edge; close to [at the edge of] the water / 水際立った splendid; striking; beautiful (performance) / 水際立ったプレー a fine play.
みずぐき 水茎 ¶水茎の跡麗しく in a beautiful, flowing hand.
みずくさ 水草 a water grass; a waterweed; a water plant (水生植物).
みずくさい 水臭い reserved; stiff; formal; distant;《口語》standoffish ¶水臭くする treat sb like a stranger. 文例⇩
みずぐすり 水薬 a liquid medicine.
みずくみ 水汲み ¶水汲みに行く go 《to a well》to draw water.
みずぐるま 水車 a waterwheel ⇨ すいしゃ.
みずけ 水気〈湿り気〉moisture; dampness; 〈果物などの〉juiciness;《文》succulence;〈液〉juice ¶水気のある juicy; moist; watery; succulent / 水気のない dry; parched (からからの).
みずげい 水芸 water tricks [jugglery].
みずけむり 水煙 spray ¶水煙を立てる raise spray; send up clouds of spray.
みずごけ 水苔〈植〉sphagnum (moss); bog moss.
みずごす 水過ごす ⇨ みのがす.
みずこぼし 水こぼし《米》a slop jar;《英》a slop basin [bowl].
みずごり 水垢離 ¶水ごりをとる practice cold water ablutions; purify oneself by pouring cold water upon oneself.

みずさいばい 水栽培 ⇨ すいこうほう.
みずさかずき 水杯 ¶水杯をかわす drink water together from a sake cup at what may be a final parting.
みずさきあんない 水先案内〈事〉pilotage; piloting;〈人〉a pilot ¶水先案内をする pilot 《a ship》/ 水先案内船 a pilot boat.
みずさし 水差し a (water) jug; a pitcher; a carafe.
みずしげん 水資源 water resources.
みずしごと 水仕事 scrubbing and washing; kitchen work.
みずしぶき 水しぶき ⇨ しぶき.
みずしょうばい 水商売〈酒場〉(be in) the bar and restaurant business;〈当たりはずれのある〉chancy trade ¶水商売の女 a woman who works in a bar or nightclub.
みずしらず 見ず知らず ¶見ず知らずの strange / 見ず知らずの他人 a complete stranger.
みずすまし〈昆〉a whirligig (beetle).
みずせっけん 水石鹸 liquid soap; soft soap (半流動体の).
みずぜめ 水攻め〈水浸し戦術〉inundation tactics ¶水攻めにする〈水浸しにする〉flood [inundate] 《a castle》;〈飲料水を断つ〉cut off the water supply 《to》.
ミスター Mr. (Tanaka) ★ Mr Tanaka のように省略記号の period をつけない書き方もある。Mrs., Dr. などについても同様。
みずたき 水炊き an unthickened stew (of chicken) cooked on the table.
みずたま 水玉〈水滴〉a drop of water;〈露〉a dewdrop (on a leaf) ¶水玉模様 a polka-dot pattern; polka dots / 水玉模様の polka-dot(-ted) (neckties).
みずたまり 水溜まり a pool; a puddle. 文例⇩
みずためる 水溜め〈貯水池〉a reservoir;〈貯水槽〉a cistern; a water tank.
みずっぱな 水っ洟 snivel ¶水っぱなを垂らす〈人が主語〉run at the nose; have a running nose; snivel.
みずっぽい 水っぽい watery (beer); wishy-washy (tea); sloppy (stew);〈味の薄い〉tasteless (soup).
みずでっぽう 水鉄砲 a water pistol.
みすてる 見捨てる forsake; desert; abandon; give up; run [walk] out on sb; let down; 《口語》leave sb in the lurch.
みずどけい 水時計 a water clock; a clepsydra (pl. -dras, -drae).
みずとり 水鳥 a waterfowl; a water [an aquatic] bird.
みずに 水煮 ¶水煮にする boil in water; boil

みずかさ 川は雨の後で水かさが増していた。The river was swollen after [was high from] the rain. / 水かさが1メートル増した。The (level of the) river has risen by one meter. / 川は水かさが減っていて、歩いて渡れた。The river was [had fallen] so low that we could wade through it.

ミスキャスト 主役がミスキャストだ。The leading role is miscast. | The actor who plays the lead is miscast.
みずきり 肩のいい人なら、水切りをして石を100メートルこうまで飛ばす。With a good throwing arm, a man can skim a stone a distance of 100 meters.

みずくさい 僕にそれを言わないなんて水臭いじゃないか。It was unfriendly of you to keep it secret from me. | Why didn't you tell me? I thought we were supposed to be friends.
みずたまり 溝がつまって、道一杯に大きな水たまりができていた。The street drain was choked, and

みずのみ 水飲み a glass; a tumbler ¶水飲み場 a (public) drinking fountain 《動物の》a watering place [hole]; a water hole / 水飲み百姓 a poor peasant.

みずはけ 水捌け drainage ¶水はけがいい be well drained; drainage is good / 水はけが悪い be poorly [ill] drained; drainage is poor [bad].

みずばしょう 《植》a skunk cabbage.

みずばしら 水柱 a column of water.

みずばら 水腹 ¶水腹で《work》only on water.

みずひき 水引き red-[black-]and-white paper string 《for tying presents》 ¶水引きをかけるtie 《a present》 with two-tone paper cord; gift-wrap sth with red-[black-]and-white string.

みずびたし 水浸し ¶水浸しの water-soaked 《logs》; flood-inundated 《plains》 / 水浸しになる be submerged; be flooded; be under water; be swamped; 《船が》be waterlogged.

みずぶくれ 水膨れ a (water) blister ¶水ぶくれになる blister / 水ぶくれができる get [have] a blister 《on one's feet》.

みずぶそく 水不足 (a) water shortage; (a) shortage of 《city》 water supply.

ミスプリント a misprint; a printer's error ⇒ ごしょく.

みずぶろ 水風呂 a (stone-)cold bath.

みずべ 水辺 (at) the water's edge; 《on》 the shore 《of a lake》.

みずほうそう 水疱瘡 《医》chicken pox; varicella.

みずぼらしい 見すぼらしい shabby; poor-looking; seedy ¶みずぼらしいなりをしている be shabbily [poorly] dressed.

みずまき 水撒き watering ¶水まきをする water 《the street》 / 水まき車 a watering cart; a sprinkler.

みずまくら 水枕 a water pillow [cushion].

みずまし 水増し ¶水増しする 《薄める》water down; dilute; 《ふやす》inflate; pad (out) / 水増し入学 admission of an excessive number of students / 水増し要求 a padded demand / 水増し予算 a (big) budget of empty figures.

みずます 見澄ます 《よく見る》watch intently; 《文》observe carefully; 《確かめる》make sure 《of, that…》.

みすみす before [under] one's (very) eyes; in one's presence; helplessly. 文例↓

みずみずしい 水々しい young and fresh; fresh as paint; fresh-looking ¶《年に負けぬ》みずみずしさ 《文》《her》 unfading beauty.

みずむし 水虫 athlete's foot; 《医》tinea (pedis).

みずもち 水餅 rice cake soaked in water.

みずもの 水物 a gamble; a matter of chance. 文例↓

みずもり 水盛り 《測量》leveling; 《器械》a water level ¶水盛りをする take a level; take a level.

みずや 水屋 《茶室の》a washing place in a tea-ceremony room; 《茶だんす》a cupboard for tea-things; 《神社の》a washstand for worshipers.

みする 魅する charm; bewitch; fascinate; enchant; 《文》captivate; 《文》spellbind.

みずわり 水割り ¶水割りの watered; diluted with water / 《ウイスキーの》水割り1杯 a whisky-and-water.

みせ 店 《商店》《米》a store; 《英》a shop; 《露店・売店》a stall; a booth; a kiosk; 《事務所》an office ¶店の者 《米》a store clerk; 《英》a shop assistant / 店の手伝いをする help 《one's mother》 with the shop / 店を開く[出す] open [start] a store [shop]; start [set up] in business; set up shop / 店を出して[経営して]いる keep [run] a store [shop]; 《米口語》keep store / 店を閉める 《一日の終わりに》close the store [door]; 《やめる》 ⇒ みせじまい / 店構え the look of a store [shop]. 文例↓

みせあう 見せ合う show 《their records》 to each other ¶ノートを見せ合う compare 《their》 notes / 写真を見せ合う look at each other's pictures.

みせいねん 未成年 minority; nonage ¶未成年である be under age; 《文》be not yet of age; be in one's minority [nonage] (★ nonage は法律用語で, 一般の会話では使わない) / 未成年者 a minor; 《法》an infant / 未成年労働 child labor.

みせいり 未整理 ¶未整理の 《文》《matters》 a waiting [pending] arrangement; undisposed-of 《stocks》.

みせうり 店売り ¶店売りする sell at a store [over the counter]; 《小売りする》sell (at [by]) retail.

みせかけ 見せ掛け 《外観》(a) look; show; (outward) appearance; 《偽り》(a) sham; (a) pretense ¶見せかけの apparent; seeming; make-believe; 《文》feigned; 《文》pretended; sham; false.

みせかける 見せ掛ける 《…に見えるようにする》make sth look like 《the genuine article》; give sth an air [appearance] 《of importance》; 《…のふりをする》assume the appearance 《of》; make believe 《to do, that…》; pretend 《to be ill》; 《文》feign 《illness》. 文例↓

みせさき 店先 the store [shop] front ¶店先で at the store; 《sell sth》 over the counter.

---

a great pool lay [and water was standing in a great puddle] across the road.

みすみす みすみす千円損をした。 I lost a thousand yen (quite) needlessly [unnecessarily]. | I (went and) threw away a thousand yen.

みずもの 勝負は水物だ。 Chance plays a part in every game. |《ある試合について》 No one can tell the result until the game has been played.

みせ 彼は神田に店を出した。 He started a store in Kanda. /あの店は高い。 That store is (very) expensive.

みせかける 貸借対照表というものは, 素人の眼にはすべて結構のように見せかけることができるものだ。 Balance sheets can be made to look all right to the inexpert eye. / 彼はまじめなサラリーマンと見せかけて実は盗みを働いていた。 He let everyone think he was a respectable office worker, while all the time he was steal-

みせじまい 店仕舞い ¶店じまいをする〈人が主語〉close [wind up] one's business; close [shut] up shop; 《米》close up the store;〈店が主語〉shut down.

みせしめ 見せしめ a warning; a lesson ¶見せしめのために as a warning [an example] to others / 見せしめになる serve as a lesson [an example] (to).

ミセス a married woman [lady] ⇒ミスター ★.

みせつける 見せ付ける ¶仲のいい所を見せつける make a display of (their) affection for each other (in public) ⇒みせびらかす.

みせどころ 見せ所 ⇒みせば. 文例⇩

みせに 身銭 ¶身銭を切る pay (the expenses) out of one's own pocket.

みせば 見せ場 a highlight scene (of a play).

みせばん 店番 ¶店番をする look after [mind] the store [shop]; serve the customers (at the counter).

みせびらかす 見せびらかす show off; display; make a show [display] of; parade 《one's wealth》 ¶見せびらかすように flauntingly.

みせびらき 店開き opening of business ⇒みせ(店を開く), かいてん².

みせもの 見世物 a show; an exhibition ¶見世物にする make a show of sth; put [place] sth on show [display, exhibition] / 見世物小屋 a show tent. 文例⇩

みせる 見せる 〈示す〉show; let sb see [look at];〈…に見えるようにする〉make sth look (like); give sth an air of;〈公開する〉throw (a garden) open to the public;〈陳列して〉exhibit; display ⇒みせもの(見世物にする) ¶子供を医者に見せる take a child to a doctor / できるだけ美しく見せる make sth look as beautiful as possible. 文例⇩

みぜん 未然 ¶未然に before (it) happens; beforehand; previously / 未然に防ぐ prevent (a war); prevent [keep] (it) from occurring; nip (a plot) in the bud.

みそ 味噌〈調味料〉miso ¶みそをつける put [spread] (some) miso on (a piece of konnyaku);〈失敗する〉make a mess [hash] of it / みそもくそも一緒にする mix up [confuse] the good and the bad;《文》fail to discriminate good from bad / みそこし a miso strainer / みそ汁 miso soup / みそ漬け vegetables [meat, fish] preserved in miso; miso pickles. 文例⇩

みぞ 溝〈掘り割り〉a ditch;〈下水〉a [an open] drain; a gutter (街路わきの);〈敷居・レコードなどの〉a groove;〈隔て〉a gulf; a gap ¶(2人の間に)溝ができる be estranged.

みぞう 未曾有¶未曾有の unprecedented; unheard-of;《文》unexampled; phenomenal;《文》unparalleled in history / 未曾有の大地震 the most disastrous earthquake on record [that has ever been experienced].

みぞおち the pit of the stomach;《口語》the solar plexus.

みそか 晦日 the last day of the month ¶みそか払い[勘定] month-end payment; e.o.m. settlement (★ e.o.m. は end of month の略).

みそぎ 禊 a purification ceremony; (a) purificatory bath; (ritual) ablutions ¶みそぎをする perform [make] one's ablutions.

みそこない 見損ない (a) misjudgment.

みそこなう 見損なう〈見誤る〉misjudge; make a wrong estimation [estimate] (of);〈見落とす〉miss; fail to see. 文例⇩

みそさざい〔鳥〕a wren; a jenny wren (雌) ★ただし童謡などでは雌雄に関係なく a jenny wren と言う.

みそしき 未組織¶未組織の unorganized / 未組織労働者〈総称〉unorganized workers [labor].

みそっかす 味噌っ滓〈みそしかす〉miso strainings;〈つまらない人間〉a good-for-nothing.

みそっぱ 味噌っ歯 a decayed milk tooth.

みそめる 見初める fall in love with (a girl) at first sight. 文例⇩

みぞれ 霙 sleet ¶激しいみぞれ a sleet storm.

みそれる 見逸れる cannot [fail to] recognize; take sb for a stranger. 文例⇩

-みたい¶…みたいな like…; a sort of…; similar (to); resembling;〈…みたいだ〉seem (angry); look like (a bird). 文例⇩

みたけ 身丈〈着物の〉the length of a kimono minus the collar; the dress length.

みだし 見出し〈新聞の〉a headline; a heading; ing.

みせどころ ここが僕の腕の見せ所だ. This is where I'm going to show my skill.

みせもの おれは見世物じゃないぞ. I'm not on exhibition, you know! / これは見世物じゃないぞ. This is not meant to be a show, I tell you.

みせる ネクタイを見せて下さい. I want [I would like] to see some ties, please. / やって見せて下さい. Please show me how to do it./ それをもう一度見せて頂けますか. Could I [Would you please let me] have another look at it? / 彼女が踊るのを君に見せたかったよ. You should [I wish you could] have seen her dance. / この写真は日本人を悪く見せるものだ. This photo puts the Japanese in a bad light.

みそ みそがみそなんだ. That's the beauty of it. / みそのみそ臭きは, 上みそにあらず. The secret of art lies in concealing art.

みそこなう 僕は田中のやつを見損なった. I was wrong [mistaken] in my estimate of Tanaka. / I am disappointed in Tanaka.

みぞれ みぞれが降っている. Sleet is falling. (★ It is sleeting. と sleet を動詞に使う事はあまりしない) / 雪はみぞれに変わった. The snow turned to sleet.

みそれる お見それして申し訳ありません. Pardon me, but I didn't recognize you for a moment. / 随分歌がお上手なんですね. まったくみそれました. What a singer you are! I didn't know that you were so accomplished.

-みたい 何だか卵みたいなものだった. It was something like an egg.

みだし 私はいつも新聞の見出しにざっと目を通すだけです. I am a headline scanner.

みたす 缶に4分の3ほどぬるま湯を満たしてください. Fill the can three-quarters full with slightly warm water.

みたてる いいセーターを見立ててあげよう. I will choose a good

みだしなみ

みだし 見出し 〈標題〉a title; a caption;〈検索用〉an index;《pl. -dexes, -dices》¶〈新聞の〉大見出し a big [splash] headline;〈全段抜きの〉a banner (headline); a streamer /〈新聞の〉特大見出し《米》a scarehead /《米》a scare headline / 小見出し a subhead /〈辞書の〉見出し語 大字で列挙する》a headword; a vocabulary entry;〈欄外見出し〉a guide [direction] word; a catchword / 新聞の見出しに出る《口語》make [hit] the headlines. 文例⇩

みだしなみ 身嗜み ¶身だしなみがいい[悪い] be careful [careless] about one's (personal) appearance.

みたす 満たす 〈一杯にする〉fill (up);〈詰める〉pack;〈満足させる〉satisfy (a need);《文》gratify 《a desire》; meet 《the demand》; answer 《the purpose》; fulfill 《a condition》;〈補う〉make up (for); cover; supply ¶杯に酒を満たす fill a cup with sake. 文例⇩

みだす 乱す disturb; disarrange; put out of order; put [throw] into disorder [confusion];〈退廃させる〉corrupt; demoralize;〈髪など〉rumple (up) ¶列を乱す fall out of line / 髪を乱して with disheveled hair.

みたて 見立て 〈診断〉(a) diagnosis《pl. -noses》;〈選択〉a choice;〈a〉selection;〈鑑定〉judgment ¶医者の見立てでは in the doctor's opinion.

みたてる 見立てる 〈診断する〉diagnose 《the case》as《pleurisy》; make a diagnosis《of》;〈選択する〉select; choose;〈判断する〉judge; estimate;〈なぞらえる〉compare [《文》liken]《to》. 文例⇩

みだら 淫ら ¶みだらな dirty; lewd (talk, glances); obscene;《文》unchaste;《文》wanton; loose (behavior, morals) / みだらな女 a slut;《米俗》a tramp; a wanton hussy.

みたらし 御手洗 a holy washing trough.

みだりに 妄りに 〈許可なく〉without permission [leave];〈理由なく〉without (good) reason;〈むやみに〉at random; recklessly;〈無差別に〉indiscriminately.

みだれ 乱れ 〈不整頓〉disorder; disarray;〈乱脈〉disturbance ¶乱れかご[箱] a clothes basket [tray] / 乱れ髪 disheveled [unkempt] hair.

みちあんない

みだれる 乱れる fall into disorder; go out of order; be [get] confused; be disordered;〈乱脈になる〉be disturbed; be chaotic;〈道徳が〉be corrupt;〈もつれる〉be entangled;〈髪が〉be disheveled; be unkempt.

みち¹ 道 〈道路〉a way; a road; a street (街路);〈小径〉a path; a lane; a pass (山間の);〈道筋〉a route;〈道程〉a journey;〈進路〉a course;〈践むべき道〉《文》the path of duty;《口語》the straight and narrow;〈義務〉a duty;〈道義〉a moral principle [doctrine];〈真理〉truth;〈正義〉justice ¶成功への道 the road [way] to success / 生活の道 a means of living / 道がはかどる make good headway [progress]; the going is good / 道がはかどらない make poor [no] headway [progress]; the going is poor / 10キロの道を行く go a distance of ten kilometers / 道をつける人 a trailblazer / 道を教える tell sb the way《to》;《文》direct sb《to a place》;〈案内して，又は地図の上で〉show sb the way《to》/ 道を聞く ask (sb) one's [the] way; ask sb for directions《to》; ask sb how to get (to) /〈先人の〉歩んだ道をたどる follow in sb's path / 道をふさぐ stand in sb's way; bar the way; block sb's passage /〈践(ふ)むべき道〉をふみはずす《文》stray from the path of virtue;《口語》leave [stray from] the straight and narrow / 道を間違える ake the wrong way / 道を求める《文》seek after truth / 道を譲る[あける] make way [room]《for》; give way《to》;〈群衆が左右に分かれて〉part; open (out) / 道に迷う lose one's way; get lost (in the woods) / 道で on [in] the street [road] ★ on は《米》, in は《英》/ 学校へ行く[から帰る]道で on one's way to [from] school / 道ならぬ恋 an illicit love affair. 文例⇩

みち² 未知 ¶未知の unknown; strange / 未知の人 a stranger / 未知の要素 an unknown factor; an as-yet-unrecognized factor;《one of》the unknowns / 未知数 an unknown quantity; the unknown(s). 文例⇩

みちあんない 道案内 〈事〉guidance;〈人・手引き〉a guide ¶道案内をする act as (a) guide; show sb the way《to》.

---

sweater for you.

みだれる 部屋の中は乱れていた. I found the room in disorder [in a mess]. / 国は非常に乱れていた. The country was in a state of great disorder [a chaotic state]. / 外来語によって日本語は乱れてきたか，それとも豊かになったのかという問題は簡単には割り切れない. One cannot easily decide whether the Japanese language has been corrupted or made richer by the introduction of foreign words.

みち¹ 帰りには別の道を行きたい. I want to go another way [take a different route] on our way home. / 動物園へ行く道を教えて下さい. Please tell me the way to the zoo. | Can you tell me how to get to the zoo? / この道を行くと成田へ出ます. This road leads [goes] to Narita. / 道を聞かないでも彼女の家まですぐにわかった. I was able to find her house easily without asking the way. / 道を聞き聞きそこまで行った. I got there inquiring along the way. / 駅へ行くにはこの道でいいですか. Is this the right way to the railroad station? / 道ははかどってはかどらなかった. The road was bad and it was slow [hard] going. / 道は悪くない. The going is not bad. / 息子たちは大学を卒業してそれぞれに別の道を行きました. My sons went their separate ways [each struck out on their own] after graduating from the university. / それこそ第3次大戦の惨禍に通じる道である. That way lies World War III and disaster. / この問題の解決はまだ道遠しと言わなければならない. There's still a long way to go [a long road to travel] toward a solution of this problem. / 書物をもっている人は多いがそれを利用する道を知っている人は少ない. Many people possess books, but very few know how to use them.

みち² そこからは未知の領域だった. After that, they were in uncharted territory.

みちか 身近 ¶身近な familiar; close to *one* / 自分に一番身近な人たち the people who are closest to *one* / 身近に near *one*(self); close to *one*; 《keep *sth*》 by *one's* side [at *one's* elbow] / 身近に感じる feel 《it》 familiar to *one*.

みちがえる 見違える take [mistake] 《A for B》; 〈見分けられない〉 cannot tell 《A from B》 ¶見違えるほど変わる change out of (all) recognition; be altered [transformed] beyond recognition; look as if 《he》 were another person [as if 《it》 were something quite different]. 文例⇩

みちかけ 満ち欠け waxing and waning 《of the moon》.

みちくさ 道草 ¶道草を食う loiter on the [one's] way 《home》; dawdle; waste *one's* time on the road. 文例⇩

みちしお 満ち潮 ⇒まんちょう.

みちじゅん 道順 a route; an itinerary; the way; a course. 文例⇩

みちしるべ 道しるべ 〈標識〉 a guidepost; a signpost; a fingerpost; 〈手引き〉 a guide 《to》; a handbook; a manual.

みちすがら 道すがら ⇒みちみち.

みちすじ 道筋 a route; a course.

みちづれ 道連れ a fellow traveler; a (traveling) companion ¶道連れになる (happen to) travel together 《with》.

みちのり 道のり (a) distance; (a) journey 〈旅程〉 ¶6キロの道のり a distance of six kilometers; a six kilometers' journey. 文例⇩

みちばた 道端 (at, by, on) the roadside ¶道ばたの花 a roadside; wayside 《flowers》.

みちひ 満ち干 ebb and flow.

みちびき 導き (divine) guidance.

みちびく 導く guide; lead; conduct; 〈案内する〉 show [usher] in ¶データを処理して数値を導き出す derive the numerical value 《of *sth*》 by processing the data.

みちみち 道々 on the way [road]; as *one* goes along.

みちみちて 満ち満ちて ¶満ち満ちている be full to the brim; be brimful 《of vigor》; be brimming over 《with vitality》; be overflowing 《with energy》.

みちゃく 未着 ¶未着の 〈未到着の〉 not yet arrived; 《goods》 to arrive; 〈未配達の〉 not yet delivered.

みちゆき 道行き 〈昔の文体の一種〉 a lyric composition describing the scenery a traveler sees on the way; 〈心中の場面〉 the scene of a lovers' (suicide) trip.

みちる 満ちる become [be] full 《of》; be filled 《with》; 〈月が〉 wax; be full; 〈潮が〉 rise; flow; 〈満期になる〉 expire; mature. 文例⇩

みつ¹ 蜜 〈はち蜜〉 honey; nectar 〈花の〉 ⇒とうみつ ¶蜜を集める collect honey / 〈はちが〉蜜を吸う suck nectar from a flower / 蜜を持っている花 a nectar-bearing flower.

みつ² 褌 a *sumo* wrestler's loincloth.

みつ³ 密 ¶密な 〈密接な〉 close; 《文》 intimate; 〈稠密な〉 dense; thick; 〈綿密な〉 minute; careful; fine.

みつあみ 三つ編み ¶髪を三つ編みにする braid [plait] *one's* [*sb's*] hair (in three strands).

みつうん 密雲 dense [thick, heavy] clouds. 文例⇩

みつおり 三つ折 ¶三つ折りにする fold 《a sheet of paper》 in three.

みっか 三日 three days; 〈第3日〉 the third 《of May》 / 3日おきに every fourth day / 3日ごとに every three days / 3日に1度 once (in) every three days / 三日にあげず very frequently; almost every other day / 三日坊主 a person with no (powers of) perseverance; a person who cannot stick to anything.

みつが 密画 a detailed drawing.

みっかい 密会 a secret [《文》 clandestine] meeting; a rendezvous ¶密会する meet *sb* secretly; have a secret meeting 《with》.

みつがさね 三つ重ね ¶三つ重ねの three-deck(ed) / 3つ重ねのサンドイッチ a three-decker (sandwich).

みつかど 三つ角 a place where three streets meet; the meeting [junction] of three streets.

みつかる 見付かる be found (out); be discovered; be detected; come to light 〈古文書などが〉; be caught 《doing, in the act of *doing*》 ¶見つからずに 〈sneak in〉 unnoticed; 〈get away〉 unobserved / 見つからずにすむ escape detection; go unnoticed 《for some time》 / 見つからないようにする keep from being seen. 文例⇩

みつぎ 密議 ¶密議する hold a secret conference; confer in private 《with》; have a secret consultation 《with》 / 密議を凝らす get [put 《our》 heads] together in secret consultation(s).

みつぎもの 貢物 an article of tribute ¶貢物を納める pay tribute 《to *sb*》 / …から大量の貢物を取り立てる exact heavy tribute from….

みっきょう 密教 esoteric Buddhism.

みちがえる 彼は見違えるほど大きくなっていた。 He had grown so tall that I hardly recognized him at first [that for the moment I did not know who he was].

みちくさ どこで道草を食っていたんだ。Where have you been wasting your time all this while? / 帰りに道草食うなよ。 Come straight home.

みちじゅん それが道順だ。That is the right route.

みちのり 横浜までどれほど道のりがありますか。How far is it from here to Yokohama? / 列車で1時間ほどの道のりです。It's about an hour's ride by train. / It's an hour's train ride [railroad journey].

みちる 前途は希望に満ちている。 The future is full of hope. / 潮が満ちてきた。The tide is in [high]. / 満つれば欠くる世の習い。 Every flood (tide) has its ebb.

みつうん 空は密雲に閉ざされている。The sky is covered with dark clouds.

みつかる 本が見つからない。I can't find my book. / My book is nowhere to be found. / 彼の家はすぐ見つかった。 I had no trouble (in) finding his house. / 彼らはまず見つかる気遣いはなかった。 They were fairly safe from detection.

みつける あの古本屋で前々から搜

みつぐ 貢ぐ ¶金を貢ぐ supply sb with money; give sb financial aid; finance sb.
みつくち 三つ口 a harelip ¶三つ口である be harelipped. 「three; a triplet.
みつぐみ 三つ組み a three-piece set; a set of
みつくろい ⇨みはからい.
みづくろい 身繕い ¶身繕いする dress oneself ⇨みじたく.
みつくろう 見繕う ⇨みはからう.
みつけ 見付 the approach (to a castle gate).
みつげつ 見付 a honeymoon ¶蜜月時代る《brief》honeymoon (period) 《between the two countries》.
みつける 見付ける 〈見出す〉find; discover; find out (★ find と find out の違いについては ⇨ わかる(囲)); come across (upon); detect; catch 《sb in the act of doing》; spy; 〈捜す〉look (hunt) for; seek; 〈気がつく〉notice; 《文》perceive; catch sight of ¶見つけられる ⇨みつかる. [文例⇩]
みつご 三つ子 〈3歳児〉a three-year-old (child); 〈3生児〉triplets. [文例⇩]
みっこう 密航 ¶密航する stow away 《on a steamer》; steal a passage (to); smuggle oneself 《into China》/ 密航者 a stowaway.
みっこく 密告 (secret) information 《against》; an anonymous report; (a) betrayal ¶密告する inform [report, tell] 《(the police, against [on] sb》; tip sb off 《about sth》; betray; 《俗》squeal; 《米俗》rat 《on sb》; shop 《sb》; 《英俗》grass 《on sb》/ 密告者 an informer; a betrayer; 《俗》a squealer; 《英俗》a grass.
みっし 密使 a secret messenger [envoy]; a confidential agent.
みっしつ 密室 〈締め切ってある部屋〉a locked room; 〈秘密につくしてある部屋〉a secret room [chamber] ¶密室で behind closed doors / 密室殺人事件 a locked-room murder case.
みっしゅう 密集 ¶密集する crowd; swarm; mass; be in close [tight] formation / 密集部隊 massed troops; troops in close formation [order] / 家屋の密集地帯 a (densely) built-up area.
みっしょ 密書 a secret [confidential] letter [message, dispatch] ¶密書を携える carry [《文》bear] a secret message.
ミッション ¶ミッションスクール a mission [missionary] school.
みっしり ⇨ぎっしり, みっちり.
みっせい 密生 ¶密生する grow thick(ly) [lux-uriantly] / 密生している植物 plants growing densely [close together]; a dense stand of plants. [文例⇩]
みっせつ 密接 ¶密接な close; 《文》intimate; near / 密接な関係がある be closely related [connected] 《with》; have a close connection 《with》. [文例⇩]
みっせん 密栓 ¶密栓する a stopper [cork, seal] (a bottle) tightly; 〈空気が入らないように〉seal (a jar) hermetically.
みっそう 密葬 〈内々の〉a private [family] funeral; 〈密教の〉a funeral in conformity with esoteric Buddhism.
みつぞう 密造 《文》illicit manufacture; 〈酒の〉illegal brewing; illicit distilling ¶密造する manufacture [brew] secretly [《文》clandestinely, 《文》illicitly] / 密造酒 illicitly brewed beer; illegally distilled spirits; 《米口語》moonshine (ウイスキー).
みつぞろい 三つ揃い ¶三つぞろいの服 a suit (of clothes); a three-piece lounge suit.
みつだん 密談 ¶密談する talk secretly [behind closed doors] 《with》; have a confidential talk 《with》; 《文》be closeted together.
みっちゃく 密着 ¶密着する stick (fast) (to); 《文》adhere (closely) (to); be glued [stuck] (together, to) / 密着印画〖写真〗a contact print.
みっちり 〈厳しく〉severely; 〈充分に〉fully; 〈一心に〉hard; 《文》earnestly; 《文》diligently; 〈たくさん〉a good deal; 〈ぎっしり〉closely; tightly; compactly.
みっつ 三つ three ⇨ さん¹.
みっつう 密通 adultery ⇨かんつう¹.
みってい 密偵 a spy; a detective.
ミット〖野球〗a mitt ¶キャッチャー[ファースト]ミット a catcher's [first baseman's] mitt.
みつど 密度 density; consistency ¶人口密度 (a) population density. [文例⇩]
みつどもえ 三つ巴 (the crest of) three comma-shaped figures in a circle ¶三つどもえの争い a three-cornered[-sided, -way] battle [fight]; a three-sided struggle; a triangular fight [struggle].
みっともない 〈行ないの〉disgraceful; scandalous; indecent; shameful; 《文》unbecoming; 《文》ignoble; 〈外観の〉unsightly; disreputable; shabby 《服装の》; 〈醜い〉ugly; bad-looking ¶みっともない振る舞いをする behave disgracefully / みっともないなりをしている be shabbily dressed. [文例⇩]

していた本を見つけた. At that secondhand bookstore I came across [happened on] a book that I had been looking for for a long time. / それは空から見つけやすいように白く塗ってある. It is painted white for easy spotting from the air. / 〈隠れんぼで〉次郎君見つけた. I spy Jiro.
みつご 三つ子の魂百まで. As the boy, so the man. | The child is father of the man. | As the twig is bent(, so grows the tree).《諺》/ そんなことは三つ子でも知っている. Even a child would know that!
みっせい その島には樹木が密生している. The island is thickly wooded [grown with trees]. | The island is covered by dense stands of trees.
みっせつ 鉄と石油とは工業の発達に密接な関係がある. Iron and petroleum have a close relation with the development of industry.
みつど 同地方の人口密度は1平方キロに100人である. The density of population in the region is 100 persons to a square kilometer.
みっともない みっともないぞ! You ought to be ashamed of yourself! | Shame on you! / みっともないまねはよせ. Stop showing yourself up (like that)! / 女の子があぐらをかくのはみっともな

みつにゅうこく 密入国　¶密入国する smuggle oneself into ((a country)); enter ((Japan)) illegally / 密入国者 an illegal entrant [immigrant] ⇒みっこう.

みつば 三葉　【植】 *mitsuba*; an umbelliferous plant resembling stone parsley, used in cooking for its aroma.

みつばい 密売　an illicit sale [(of)]; smuggling　¶密売する sell *sth* secretly; smuggle / 密売者 an illicit seller [(of)].

みつばいばい 密売買　¶密売買をする engage in illicit traffic [(in)]; deal secretly [(in)].

みつばち 蜜蜂　a (honey) bee　¶(蜜のありかを仲間に教える)みつばちの尻振りダンス the tail-wagging dance of bees / みつばちの巣 ‹蜜房› a honeycomb; ‹巣箱› a beehive ⇒ようほう².

みっぷう 密封　¶密封する seal up *sth*.

みっぺい 密閉　¶密閉する shut [close up] tight(ly); seal up; enclose; ‹空気が入らないように› seal ((a container)) hermetically; make [keep] ((a box)) airtight.

みつぼうえき 密貿易　((organized)) smuggling; contraband trade ((with *sb*))　¶密貿易をする smuggle ((in, out)) ((watches)) / 密貿易者 a smuggler.

みつまた¹ 三つ又　a three-pronged fork; a trident　¶三つ又の角 a three-pronged antler / 三つ又の道 a three-forked road.

みつまた² 【植】 a *mitsumata* plant.

みつまめ 蜜豆　boiled beans, agar-agar cubes and other delicacies in sugar syrup.

みつめる 見詰める　stare ((at)); look hard [((文)) fixedly] ((at)); gaze ((at)); fix [rivet] *one's* eyes ((on)); watch *sth* intently [closely]; ((文)) fasten *one's* gaze ((on))　¶顔を見つめる stare *sb* in the face; study *sb's* face.

みつもり 見積もり　an estimate; (an) estimation; valuation; a quotation　¶大きく見た目見積もり a liberal estimate; an estimate on the high side / 家の修繕の見積もりをする[出す] estimate [give a quotation] for the repair of a house / 見積もり額 an estimated amount [sum] / 見積もり原価 the estimated cost / 見積もり書を作製する draw [make] up an estimate [(for)]. 文例⇩

みつもる 見積もる　estimate [value, calculate] ((at)); make an estimate [(of)]; put (down) ((at))　¶高く[安く]見積もる estimate ((the cost)) high [low] / 金に見積もる estimate in money / 幾ら安く見積もっても at the lowest estimate. 文例⇩

みつやく 密約　a secret promise [agreement, treaty]　¶密約する make a secret promise / 密約を結ぶ conclude [enter into] a secret treaty [agreement] ((with)).

みつゆ 密輸　smuggling　¶密輸する smuggle *sth* ((over)) / 密輸船[者] a smuggler / 密輸団 a smuggling ring [gang] / 密輸品 smuggled [contraband] goods.

みつゆしゅつ 密輸出　¶密輸出する smuggle *sth* abroad [out of the country)).

みつゆにゅう 密輸入　¶密輸入する smuggle ((diamonds)) [into the country)); import through illegal channels ⇒みっこう.

みつりょう 密猟[漁]　poaching　¶密猟[漁]する poach ((for)) ((pheasants, salmon)); steal game / 密猟[漁]者 a poacher / 密漁船 a poaching boat.

みつりん 密林　a thick [dense] forest; a jungle ((熱帯の))　¶密林地帯 a jungle; densely wooded country. 文例⇩

みつろう 蜜蠟　beeswax.

みてい 未定　¶未定の undecided; unfixed; unsettled; uncertain (確かでない) / 未定稿 an unfinished manuscript.

みてくれ 見てくれ　appearance; outward show ⇒ていさい.

みてとる 見て取る　judge ((*sb* [*sth*] to be, that …)); ((文)) perceive ((*sb* [*sth*] to be, that …)); take in ((the situation)); see; realize　¶その場の様子を見て取る grasp [take in, take stock of] the situation. 文例⇩

みとう 未踏　¶未踏の ((文)) untrodden; unexplored.

みとおし 見通し　‹展望› a perspective; an unobstructed view; a vista; ‹見込み› an outlook; a prospect; ‹見抜く› (an) insight ((into))　¶見通しが利く ‹場所が› be open; ((文)) offer an unbroken vista; ((文)) afford an unobstructed view; ‹人が› be farseeing; be far-sighted; have (good) foresight. 文例⇩

みとおす 見通す　‹遠くを› get an unobstructed [unbroken] view ((of)); ‹将来を› foresee; ‹見抜く› see through [into]　¶すべてをお見通しの神様 an all-seeing[-wise] god.

みとがめる 見咎める　‹非難する› find fault with; ‹唯何(とが)›する› question; challenge.

みどく 味読　¶味読する read ((a book)) with real appreciation; appreciate ((Browning's poetry)).

みどころ 見所　‹取り柄› a good point; a merit; ‹急所› the highlight ((of a play))　¶見所のある青年 a promising youth; a young man of promise. 文例⇩

い. It is unladylike for a girl to sit cross-legged.

みつもり 費用はざっと50万円の見積もりです. The costs are roughly estimated at 500,000 yen.

みつもる 損害はどのくらいに見積もりましたか. What is the estimated loss?

みつりん アンデスの東の傾斜地は密林で覆われている. The eastern slopes of the Andes are heavily forested.

みてとる 私は彼が主謀者であることをすぐ見て取った. I spotted him as the leader at once.

みとおし 見通しは明るくなった. Things are looking up. / 軍縮実現の見通しは暗い. The outlook for actual arms reductions is bleak. / 将来の見通しは引き続き原料不足が見込まれる. The outlook for the future is for a continued shortage of raw materials.

みどころ あの男に一体どんな見どころがあるのかね. What (good) do you see in that fellow?

みとめる 私が悪かったということは認めます. I do admit that I was wrong. / 広く世界に真価を認められている作家は日本には少ない. There are few writers in Japan who are appreciated all over the

ミトコンドリア 〖生物〗 mitochondria 《*sing.* -drion》.

みとどける 見届ける 〈確かめる〉 make sure 《of, that...》; assure *oneself* 《of, that...》; 《文》 ascertain; 〈自分の目で見る〉 see with *one's* own eyes; witness ¶最後まで見届ける watch *sth* [see *sth* through] to the [*its*] end.

みとめ(いん) 認め(印) an unregistered [informal] seal; a signet ¶認めを押す affix *one's* informal seal 《to》.

みとめる 認める 〈認識する〉 recognize; 《文》 take cognizance of; 〈目に入る〉 see; notice; find; witness; 〈承認する〉 approve (of) 《a plan》; 《文》 sanction 《a usage》; accept 《that ..., a theory》; acknowledge 《*one's* fault》; admit 《a fact》; concede 《that...》; 《文》 own 《*oneself* guilty》; 〈考える〉 consider; regard *sth* [*sb*] 《as》; look on [upon] *sth* [*sb*] 《as》; 〈判定する〉 judge; 〈断定する〉 conclude ¶(広く)認められる receive [win] (wide) recognition. [文例⇩]

みどり 緑 green; 《文》 verdure (草木の) ¶緑の green; 《文》 verdant; emerald / 緑の丘 a green hill / 緑のおばさん a (school) crossing warden; 《英口語》 a lollipop lady / 緑の黒髪 raven locks [hair]; glossy black hair / 緑色 a green color; green / 緑滴る山々 the mountains clad [covered] in fresh greenery [verdure]. [文例⇩]

みとりざん 見取り算 working out a written-down problem on an abacus.

みとりず 見取り図 a (rough) sketch; a sketch map [plan, drawing] 《of》 ¶見取り図をとる sketch; make a sketch 《of》.

みとる[1] 見取る ⇨ みてとる.

みとる[2] 看取る ⇨ かんびょう (看病する).

ミドルきゅう ミドル級 the middleweight class ¶ミドル級の middleweight 《wrestlers》 / ミドル級の選手 a middleweight.

みとれる 見とれる be fascinated 《by》; watch *sth* in fascination; 《文》 gaze at *sth* in [with] rapture; be charmed 《by》; 《文》 be captivated 《by》; be struck 《by》; look admiringly 《at》; be lost in admiration ¶ぽかんと見とれる gape 《at》; gawk 《at》.

みな 皆 all; everything; everyone ¶我々皆 all [every one] of us / 皆さん ladies and gentlemen; hello, everybody / 皆で 〈全部で〉 altogether; in all; all told; 〈一緒に〉 all together; one and all; 〈一団となって〉 in a body; 〈まとめて〉 in the gross. [文例⇩]

みなおす 見直す 〈再び見る〉 look 《at *sth*》 again; take [have] another [a fresh, a new] look 《at *sth*》; take a second look 《at》; 〈よい点を発見する〉 discover new merits 《in》; 〈考え直す〉 reconsider; come to have a better opinion of; change [revise] *one's* opinion of *sb* [*sth*] (for the better); 〈病気·景気が〉 take a turn for the better; look up; improve. [文例⇩]

みなぎる 漲る overflow; 〈川が〉 rise (high); swell; 〈充満する〉 be brimful 《of》; be full 《of》; be filled 《with》 ¶青春の血潮がみなぎっている 《文》 be full of youthful ardor.

みなげ 身投げ ¶身投げする drown *oneself*; throw *oneself* into the water.

みなごろし 皆殺し annihilation; extermination; a massacre (大虐殺) ¶皆殺しにする kill 《the enemy》 to a man; wipe [kill] out; annihilate; exterminate; massacre / 一家を皆殺しにする murder the whole family.

みなしご 孤児 an orphan ¶みなしごになる be left an orphan; be orphaned.

みなす 見做す regard *sth* 《as》; consider; think of *sth* 《as》; look on [upon] *sth* 《as》; take *sth* 《for》. [文例⇩]

みなと 港 a harbor; a port (陸地を含む) ¶港を出る leave (a) port; clear a port / 港に入る enter [make] (a) port; put [get] into port / 港に入っている船 vessels in port / 港に着く reach port; arrive in harbor / 港町 a port (town [city]).

みなまたびょう 水俣病 Minamata disease (a type of poisoning caused by industrial mercury pollution).

みなみ 南 (the) south ¶南の southern; south / 南に 〈南部に〉 in the south; 〈南方に〉 to the south; 〈南側に〉 on the south / 南へ行く go south [southward] / 南アフリカ共和国 the Republic of South Africa / 南アメリカ South America / 南回帰線 the tropic of Capricorn / 南風 a south [southerly] wind / 南十字星 the Southern Cross / 南太平洋 the South Pacific / 南向きの家 a house facing [looking (toward the)] south. [文例⇩]

みなもと 源 the source; 〈起源〉 the origin; the beginning; the root; the rise; 《文》 the fountainhead 《of wisdom》; 《文》 the wellspring 《of virtue》 ¶源を…に発する rise [come] from...; have 《its》 rise [origin] in...; originate in.... [文例⇩]

みならい 見習い 〈事〉 apprenticeship; probation; 〈人〉 an apprentice (徒弟); a probationer; a learner ¶見習いとして働く serve as an apprentice; work on trial [probation] / 見習

[み]

---

world. / この作家は国際的に認められている. This writer has won international recognition. / 彼は生前はほとんど認められなかった. He was given very little recognition during his lifetime.

みどり 野も山も緑の衣をつけた. The hills and fields are clad [robed] in green [verdure]. / 町の緑を守ろう. Keep our town green!

みな 皆旅行に加わったわけではない. Not all of us went on the trip. | We didn't all go on the trip. / 我々の一行は皆で5名だった. There were five of us, all told. / 皆で幾らですか. How much is that altogether? / 皆で行こう. Let's go all together. | Let's all go together.

みなおす 私どもの商売も近頃は見直して来ました. Our business is looking [picking] up these days.

みなす 当時女子は15歳になると成人と見做された. In those days girls counted as grown up when they were fifteen.

みなみ 横浜は東京の南約30キロのところにある. Yokohama is about thirty kilometers south of Tokyo.

みなもと 淀川は源を琵琶湖に発する. The river Yodo rises in [flows

い看護婦 a student nurse / 見習い期間 the period of apprenticeship [probation]; 《文》 one's novitiate / 見習い生 a trainee; an apprentice student; a probationer. 文例⇩

みならう 見習う〈習う〉learn (by observation); 〈模倣する〉follow *sb*'s example; imitate *sb*; pattern *oneself* on *sb* ¶…に見習って after the example of….

みなり 身なり dress; one's (personal) appearance ¶身なりがいい[悪い] be well [badly, ill] dressed / 身なりをきちんとする tidy (up) *oneself* / 立派な[粗末な]身なりをしている be finely [poorly] dressed / 身なりに気をつける[構わない] be careful [careless] about *one's* appearance [(〈文〉) dress]. 文例⇩

みなれる 見慣れる〈人が主語〉get [《文》 become] used to seeing *sth*;〈物が主語〉be [《文》 become] familiar (to) ¶見慣れた眺め a familiar sight / 見慣れない unfamiliar; strange; new / 見慣れない人 a stranger. 文例⇩

ミニ ⇨ ミニスカート

みにくい¹ 醜い ugly; bad-[ugly-]looking;〈美しくない〉plain; uncomely;《米》homely;〈見苦しい〉unsightly; indecent;《文》unseemly;〈恥ずべき〉《文》ignoble;《文》dishonorable;《文》mean.

みにくい² 見にくい〈見難い〉hard [difficult] to see;〈読みにくい〉illegible;〈不鮮明な〉indistinct; hard to make out ¶見にくい席 a poor [bad] seat; a seat that is too near [far from] the stage [the screen].

ミニコン a minicomputer.

ミニスカート a miniskirt ¶ミニスカートをはいた miniskirted ((girls)); ((a girl)) in a miniskirt.

ミニチュア a miniature.

みぬく 見抜く see through (*sb*, *sb*'s plot); see [penetrate, have an insight] into ((*sb*'s designs)).

みね 峰〈山の〉a peak; the summit; the top; a ridge (背);〈刀の〉the back ¶峰伝いに along the ridges (of the Alpine mountains).

みねうち 峰打ち ¶峰打ちにする strike *sb* with the back of *one's* sword.

ミネソタ Minnesota (略: Minn.) ¶ミネソタ州の人 a Minnesotan.

ミネラル (a) mineral ¶ミネラルウォーター mineral water.

みの 蓑 a straw rain-cape.

みのう 未納〈未納の〉unpaid; in arrears; back ((rent)); outstanding / 未納者 a person in arrears; a (tax) defaulter.

みのうえ 身の上〈運勢〉one's fortune; one's future;〈境遇〉one's condition; one's circumstances;《文》one's lot;〈経歴〉one's history; one's career ¶身の上を案じる be much concerned about *sb*'s welfare [safety]; wonder how *sb* is doing [faring] / 身の上を相談する consult *sb* [ask *sb* for *his* advice] about *one's* personal affairs / 身の上相談欄 a personal advice column; a human-relations column; the problem page / 身の上話をする tell *one's* life story; tell everything about *oneself*. 文例⇩

みのがす 見逃す〈見落とす〉miss; overlook; pass over [by, up];〈とがめずにおく〉overlook; let (it) pass [go]; let *sb* go unchallenged [unpunished];〈見て見ぬふりをする〉turn a blind eye 〈to〉 ⇨ みおとる; ⇨ みおくる. 文例⇩

みのこす 見残す leave *sth* unseen.

みのしろきん 身の代金 (a) ransom ¶身の代金目当てに監禁する hold *sb* to ransom / 身の代金を取る[要求する] exact [demand] a ransom ((for a prisoner, from *sb*)) / 600万円の身の代金を払って取り戻す ransom *sb* for 6,000,000 yen.

ミノス 《ギリシャ神話》Minos ¶ミノス文明[文化] (the) Minoan civilization [culture] / ミノス人 a Minoan.

みのたけ 身の丈 ⇨ せい, しんちょう¹.

みのまわり 身の回り〈身体〉one's person;〈体裁〉one's appearance;〈服装〉《文》one's dress ¶身の回りの品 (one's) personal belongings [property, articles, effects]; one's things / 身の回りの世話をする look after *sb*. 文例⇩

みのむし 蓑虫 a bagworm.

みのり 実り〈a (fine, poor) crop; harvest; ripening ¶豊かな実り an abundant crop ((of rice)) / 実りの秋 the harvest season; harvest time / 実りある討議 a fruitful [productive] discussion.

みのる 実る〈実がなる〉bear fruit; fruit;〈熟する〉ripen; grow [《文》become] ripe. 文例⇩

みば 見場 ¶見場がいい look fine; be good to look at;《文》be pleasing to the eye [in appearance]; be sightly / 見場が悪い look ugly;《文》be unpleasant in appearance; be unsightly.

みばえ 見栄え ¶見栄えがする look nice [《文》to advantage]; be attractive; be impressive / 見栄えがしない look [be] unattractive; be un-

---

みならい 彼女はまだ美容院で見習い中です. She is still in training to be a beautician.

みなり 私は身なりなどは構わない. I don't care how I dress [look].

みなれる 見慣れないとはとんど区別がつかない. They are hardly distinguishable to the untrained eye.

みぬく 一見して食わせ者であることを見抜いた. I saw at a glance that he was an impostor. / ホフマン社長は人の才能をよく見抜く目があった. Mr. Hofmann, the president of the company, had a keen eye for talent.

みのうえ 今は安楽な身の上だ. He is now comfortably off.

みのがす ファンの見逃してならぬ映画だ. It is a picture which no movie fan should miss. / 首相の演説中の次の言葉は見逃すべきではない. The following remarks made by the Prime Minister in his address should not go unheeded. / この発明の持つ意義がしばしば見逃されている. The significance of this invention often goes unrecognized. / この出来事の持つ意味をドーソン博士は見逃さなかった. The implications of this event were not lost on Dr. Dawson.

みのまわり もうお前も身の回りのことは自分でするようにならなくちゃ. It's about time you learned to look after yourself.

みのる 今年は稲がよく実った. We have a fine crop of rice this year.

みばえ 色の白い人は黒い着物を着

みはからい 見計らい ¶見計らいで at *one's* discretion.

みはからう 見計らう choose *sth* at *one's* own discretion; use *one's* discretion in choosing [the choice of] *sth*. 文例↓

みはっけん 未発見 ¶未発見の (still) undiscovered.

みはっこう 未発行 ¶未発行の not yet issued; unpublished.

みはったつ 未発達 ¶未発達の underdeveloped; ill-developed; of [at] an early stage of development.

みはっぴょう 未発表 ¶未発表の unpublished; not yet made public. 文例↓

みはてぬ 見果てぬ ¶見果てぬ夢 an unfinished dream.

みはなす 見放す give up; let *sb* down; desert; abandon; forsake.

みはば 身幅 the width (of a garment) ¶(人が)身幅が広い[狭い] be broad [thin].

みはらい 未払い ¶未払いがたまる fall into [be in] arrears (with *one's* rent); run up bills (at the bookseller's) / 未払いの unpaid; outstanding / 未払いの給料 back pay / 未払い勘定[金] an outstanding [unpaid] account / 未払い利息 accrued [outstanding] interest.

みはらし 見晴らし ¶見晴らしがいい command [have] a fine view (of) / 見晴らしのいい場所 a place with a fine view; an excellent spot for observation / 見晴らし台 an observation [a lookout] platform. 文例↓

みはらす 見晴らす command [have] a (panoramic) view (of); have an unbroken view (of); 〈窓などが〉look out on(to); look onto ¶遠く海を見晴らす have [get] a distant view of the sea. 文例↓

みはり 見張り 〈事〉watch-keeping; guard; (a) lookout; 〈人〉a watchman; a guard; a lookout; a keeper; a lifeguard (水泳場の) ¶見張りをする ⇒みはる/見張りを立てる place [set] a guard ((at the door)) / 見張り所(ﾞ) a lookout (place) / 交代で見張り役をつとめる take ((their)) turn at guard duty.

みはる 見張る 〈番をする〉watch; stand guard [lookout] ((over)); look out ((for)); keep (a) watch [a lookout] ((for, against, on)); be on the watch [lookout]; 〈目を〉open *one's* eyes wide (in astonishment) ¶厳重に見張る keep

(a) strict [close] watch ((on)); put [place] *sb* under surveillance / よく見張っている keep a good [sharp] lookout ((for)) / 眼を見張って with *one's* eyes wide open / 眼を皿のようにして見張っている keep a sharp lookout ((for *sth*)).

みびいき 身最員 ¶身びいきする show partiality toward *one's* relatives; 《文》practice nepotism; 《文》draw water to *one's* own mill.

みひつのこい 未必の故意《法》《ﾗﾃﾝ語》*dolus eventualis*; willful [conscious] negligence.

みひらき 見開き 〈本や雑誌の〉a spread.

みひらく 見開く open (*one's* eyes) (wide).

みぶり 身振り a (body) gesture; (a) gesticulation; (an) action; (a) motion ¶身ぶりをする make gestures; gesticulate; motion / 大げさな身ぶりで with exaggerated [dramatic, expansive] gestures / 身ぶりで示す gesture ((the size of a box)); indicate ((the position of a switch)) in dumb show / 身ぶりでこちらへ来いと言う motion *sb* toward *one* / 身ぶり言葉 sign language. 文例↓

みぶるい 身震い a shiver; a tremble; a shudder ¶身震いする shiver ((with cold)); tremble ((with fear)); shudder ((with terror)); quiver ((with emotion)) / 身震いの出るような terrible; horrible; frightful; shocking. 文例↓

みぶん 身分 (*one's*) status; *one's* social position [standing]; 《文》*one's* station in life; 〈位階〉a rank; 〈身元〉*one's* identity; origin; birth; 〈資力〉means ¶身分が違う differ in social standing / 身分のよい[高い]人 a person of high rank [standing] / 身分の低い人《文》a lowly person; 《文》a person of low birth [humble condition, low station] / 身分を明かす[隠す] reveal [hide] *one's* identity; disclose [conceal] *one's* origins / 身分違いの結婚《文》a misalliance; 《ﾌﾗﾝｽ語》*mésalliance* / 身分相応[不相応]に暮らす live within [beyond] *one's* means / 身分証明を要求する demand identification ((from)) / 身分証明書 an identification [ID] card / (社会の)身分制 a status system / 身分保障 (a) guarantee of *sb's* status. 文例↓

みぶんか 未分化 ¶未分化の unspecialized; undifferentiated.

みぼうじん 未亡人 a widow ¶未亡人になる be widowed; lose [《文》be bereaved of] *one's* husband / 戦争未亡人 a war widow; a war-bereaved wife / 子連れの未亡人 a widowed mother.

ると見栄えがする。A dark dress sets off a fair complexion. / 大して見栄えのする家じゃない。The house is not [nothing] much to look at.

みはからう その事は然るべく見計らって下さい。Deal with it as you think fit. / 彼は頃合いを見計らってやって来た。He came at the right time. | He timed his arrival well.

みはっぴょう 投稿作品は未発表のものであること。Works already published [printed] elsewhere are not accepted.

みはらし 見晴らしのいい家が欲しい。I want a house with a fine view. / 木があるので見晴らしがよくない。The trees obstruct the view. / 山を登るのは楽ではなかったが、頂上からの見晴らしはすばらしかった。The climb up the hill was hard, but there was a wonderful view from the top.

みはらす 部屋から湖水が見晴らせる。The room looks (out) onto [across, over] the lake.

みぶり 彼は身ぶりで「静かに」という合図をした。He motioned me [gestured for me] to be quiet. / 彼女は『りんごをもう一ついかが』という身ぶりをした。In dumb show, she offered me another apple.

みぶるい 思っただけでも身震いがする。The mere thought of it makes me tremble [gives me the shivers].

みぶん 江戸時代の商人は身分が低

みほれる 見惚れる ⇨ みとれる.

みほん 見本 〈商品の〉 a sample; 〈柄・模様などの〉 a pattern; 〈書物・雑誌の〉 a sample copy; 〈手本〉 a model; an example ¶すばらしい見本 a showpiece / 見本市 a trade [sample] fair / 国際見本市 an international trade fair / 見本刷り 〔印刷〕 a specimen page. 文例⇩

みまい 見舞い 〈病気の〉 an inquiry; 〈被災者などへの〉 (an) expression of sympathy; 〈訪問〉 a visit; a call ¶見舞いに行く visit sb (in hospital); call on sb to inquire [ask] after his health [condition]; pay a sympathy visit ((to)); go and comfort sb / 見舞い金 a gift of money (in token of one's sympathy); a letter of sympathy; a letter of inquiry about sb's health / 見舞い人 a visitor; an inquirer / 見舞い品 a present [gift] (to a sick person).

みまう 見舞う ¶みまい (見舞いに行く) ¶入院中の友人を見舞う visit [call on] a friend in hospital / 災難に見舞われる suffer [《文》 be visited by] a calamity; meet with a misfortune / 台風に見舞われる be hit [struck] by a typhoon.

みまがう 見紛う ⇨ みちがえる ¶花と見まがう雪 snowflakes coming down like so many wind-blown flower petals.

みまちがえる 見間違える ⇨ みちがえる.

みまもる 見守る watch (intently); stare [gaze] ((at)) ¶じっと見守る keep a very close watch (on what is happening).

みまわす 見回す look around [about] (one). 文例⇩

みまわり 見回り a patrol; (a round of) inspection ¶見回り人 a watchman.

みまわる 見回る do [make, go on] one's rounds; go round; make the round of; inspect; make a visit [tour] of inspection; patrol.

みまん 未満 under; below; less than ¶5歳未満の小児 children under five (years of age); children under the age of five. 文例⇩

みみ 耳 an ear; 〈聴覚〉 hearing; 〈端の〉 an edge; 〈縁〉 a border; 〈織物の〉 a selvage; a selvedge; a list ¶耳が痛い 〈痛む〉 have a pain in one's ear; one's ear hurts; 〈恥ずかしい〉 be ashamed to hear (it) / 耳が聞こえない be deaf / 片方の耳が聞こえない be deaf in one ear / 耳が聞こえなくなる go deaf; lose one's hearing / 耳が遠い have poor hearing; be hard of hearing / 耳が早い have good [keen] hearing / 耳の aural / 耳の穴 an earhole / 耳の痛い事を言う touch sb on the raw [to the quick] / 耳の付け根まで真っ赤になる blush to the roots of one's hair / 耳を貸さない turn a deaf ear ((to)) / 耳を貸す 《文》 lend one's ear ((to)); 《文》 give ear ((to)) / 耳を傾ける listen ((to)); 《文》 bend an ear ((to)) / 耳をそば立てる[澄ます] strain one's ears; prick up one's ears; listen (attentively) for sth / 耳をそろえて(金を)返す clear ((one's debts)) off; pay ((what one owes)) in full / 耳をつんざくような earsplitting; ear-piercing / 耳を慣らす train one's ear ((for)) / 耳をふさぐ[覆う] stop [cover] one's ears / 耳をろうするような deafening; ear-shattering / 耳に入れる tell; inform / 耳に鉛筆をはさむ have a pencil stuck behind one's ear / 耳に手をあてがって聞く listen with a hand cupped to one [one's] ear / 耳に残る linger in [on] one's ears / 耳に入る 〈事が主語〉 reach [come to] one's ears; come to one's knowledge; 〈人が主語〉 happen to hear ((of, about)); learn ((of) it) by chance. 文例⇩

みみあか 耳垢 earwax; wax ¶耳あかを取る clean one's ears.

みみあたらしい 耳新しい novel; new. 文例⇩

みみあて 耳当て ⇨ みみおおい.

みみうち 耳打ち ¶耳打ちする whisper in [into] sb's ear; put a word (or two) into sb's ear.

みみおおい 耳覆い 〈防寒用の〉 earflaps (帽子の); earmuffs (独立した).

みみかき 耳掻き an earpick.

みみがくもん 耳学問 knowledge [information] picked up by listening to others [without real study].

みみかざり 耳飾り an earring.

みみくそ 耳糞 ⇨ みみあか.

みみざとい 耳聡い have sharp ears; 《文》 be quick of hearing ¶耳ざとく聞きつける catch ((a sound)) with one's sharp ears. 文例⇩

みみざわり 耳障り ¶耳ざわりになる be harsh on [《文》 offensive to] the [one's] ear(s); jar on one's ear(s); grate (harshly) on one's ear(s). 文例⇩

かった. Merchants of the Edo period were accorded low social rank.

みほん 見本どおりのはたった2つ3つしかない. Only a few come [are] up to (the) sample.

みまい お宅はご無事でしたかお見舞い申し上げます. I hope you were not hurt. / お見舞いをいただきましてまことに有り難うございます. I sincerely thank you for your kind inquiries about my health [for your sympathy]. / 伯父の見舞いに病院へ行って来た. I have been to the hospital to see my uncle.

みまう 私がこの小児麻痺に見舞われたのは5歳の時のことです. It was when I was five years old that this polio afflicted me.

みまわす だれか見てやしないかと, 彼はあたりを見回した. He looked about him to see if anybody was watching.

みまん 円未満切り捨て. Fractions smaller than a yen omitted.

みみ 耳がよく聞こえない人もいる. Some people do not hear well. / 犬は非常に耳が早い. The dog has sharp ears. / からだは眠っていても耳は聞こえていた. His ears remained awake while the rest of him slept. / ひどくなぐられたのがもとで耳が遠くなった. He was boxed on the ears so violently that his hearing was affected. / 彼は音楽を聞く耳がない. He has no ear for music. / ジュリアンは耳の痛いことを言われて早々に引き上げてきた. Julian came away in a moment with a flea in his ear. / 彼は自分の耳を疑った. He could hardly believe his ears. / ちょっとお耳を拝借. May I have a word in your ear? / やがて足音が耳に入った. The sound of footsteps soon caught my ear. / 耳を慣らそうと思って, FEN の放送を聞いています. I use FEN broadcasts for listening practice. / 彼の耳に入

みみず a worm; an earthworm; 〈魚釣りのえさ〉《米》an angleworm;《米》a fishworm.
みみずく 〖鳥〗a horned [an eared] owl.
みみずばれ みみず腫れ (get) a welt; a weal; a wale ¶みみずばれになる welts rise 《on one's skin》; fingernail-scratches stand out in a ridge 《on one's arm》.
みみたぶ 耳朶 an earlobe; the lobe of the ear.
みみだれ 耳垂れ discharge from the ear; 《have》running ears.
みみっちい tightfisted; stingy; miserly; small-minded (狭量な).
みみなり 耳鳴り (have) a ringing [singing, buzzing] in one's ears.
みみなれる 耳慣れる ⇨ききなれる.
みみもと 耳元 ¶耳元で about [close to] one's ears.
みみより 耳寄り ¶耳寄りな話 welcome [good] news.
みみわ 耳輪 an earring.
みむく 見向く look toward [us]; look round; turn one's face (toward) ¶(…を)見向きもしない take no notice of; ignore sb completely / 見向きもしないで without even a glance [a look] at sb; without taking any [the slightest] notice 《of》. 文例⇩
みめ 見目 ¶見目うるわしい good-looking; beautiful; pretty.
みめい 未明 ¶未明に before dawn [daybreak, daylight]; before it is light; in the gray of the morning.
みもだえ 身悶え ¶身もだえする twist one's body (in pain); squirm; writhe.
みもち 身持ち behavior;《文》conduct ¶身持ちがいい be well-behaved [《文》-conducted];《文》be of good behavior / 身持ちが悪い be immoral;《文》be of loose morals; be loose (in one's behavior); be no better than (she) should be.
みもと 身元 one's birth (and parentage); one's background; one's identity ¶身元が判明する[不明である] be identified [unidentified] / 身元の確かな人 a person with good references / 身元を調べる inquire [look] into sb's background [《文》antecedents] / 身元照会先 a reference / 身元引受[保証]人 a surety; a guarantor; a guarantee (for fidelity).
みもの 見物 a sight; a spectacle; an attraction (呼び物). 文例⇩
みや 宮 〈神社〉a (Shinto) shrine; 〈皇族〉an Imperial prince [princess] ¶三笠宮 Prince Mikasa.
みゃく 脈 the pulse; pulsation; 〈鉱脈・葉脈〉a vein; 〈望み〉hope ¶脈を打つ pulsate; pulse; throb / 脈を数える take one's pulse (rate) / 脈をとる feel [have one's fingers on] sb's pulse / 脈所 the places (on a human body) where the pulse can be felt. 文例⇩
みゃくどう 脈動 pulsatory motion; pulsation ⇨みゃくはく.
みゃくはく 脈拍 the pulse; pulsation; the beat of the pulse; 《the regularity of》a blood beat ¶脈拍数〈1分間の〉the pulse (rate); a pulse count.
みゃくみゃく 脈々 ¶脈々たる continuous; unbroken / 脈々として continuously.
みゃくらく 脈絡 a thread [line] of connection; a chain of reasoning; logical connection;《文》coherence; 〈文脈〉the context ¶脈絡のない incoherent; disconnected; disjointed.
みやけ 宮家 the house of a prince of the blood.
みやげ 土産 〈旅先で記念に買う〉a souvenir; 〈進物〉a present ¶土産話 a story of one's travels / 土産物屋 a souvenir store; a gift shop. 文例⇩
みやこ 都 〈首府〉a capital; a metropolis; the seat of government; 〈都会〉a city; a town ¶都落ちをする leave Tokyo (to live in the country); go into the provinces / 映画の都ハリウッド Hollywood, the film capital (★ この意味で capital を使うときは、名詞をその前に置く: fashion capitals like Paris and New York. この語順でなく、of を利用するならば city を使う方がいい: Vienna, the city of music). 文例⇩
みやこどり 都鳥 〈ゆりかもめの異称〉a hooded gull.
みやさま 宮様 ⇨みや.
みやすい 見易い 〈見よい〉(be) easy to see; 〈明白な〉plain; evident; obvious;《文》manifest ¶…は見やすい道理だ it is obviously true that…; it is a truism that…; it is easy to see that… / 見やすいところに掲示をする post [put] (a notice) in a prominent place.
みやづかえ 宮仕え ¶宮仕えする be in the

れておかねばならぬ. I must tell him about it. / こう言うとアメリカ人の耳には変に聞こえるかもしれない. It may sound strange to American ears. / もう耳にたこができるほど聞いた. I've heard enough of it.
みみあたらしい 耳新しい話ではない. That's nothing new to us. / It's an old story.
みみざとい 彼は耳ざとい. He has sharp ears [hearing]. | He is quick of hearing.
みみざわり その発音はイギリス人には耳障りだ. That pronunciation offends English ears.
みみなり 耳鳴りがする. My ears are ringing [singing, humming]. | I have a ringing in my ears.
みむく 彼は見向きもしなかった. He took no notice of me. | He did not even look at me.
みもの 当日の見物は原田対太田の試合であった. The highlight of the day's program was the match between Harada and Ota. / 彼の顔ときたら見ものだった. His face was a study. / (皮肉に)全く見物だったよ. It was a sight to see.
みゃく 彼の脈は90だった. His pulse was (at) ninety. / まだ脈がある.〈脈を打っている〉His pulse is still beating. | We can feel his pulse. | 〈望みがある〉There is still some [a ray of] hope. | It is not altogether hopeless. / まくらをしたこめかみの所で脈が打っているのが聞こえた. He could hear the pulse in his temple beating into the pillow.
みゃくどう ニューヨークにいれば世界の脈動を感じることができる. You can feel the pulse of the world in New York.
みやげ 子供たちに土産を買って行ってやろう. I will buy some presents for my children.
みやこ 住めば都. Anywhere is

みやびた,みやびやか 雅びた, 雅びやかな elegant; refined; graceful.
みやぶる 見破る see through 《a plot》; penetrate 《into sb's heart》. 文例⇩
みやまいり 宮参り ¶宮参りをする〈参りいする〉visit a *Shinto* shrine; 〈子供の〉take one's baby to the local shrine.
みやまつつじ 深山つつじ a wild azalea.
みやる 見遣る look [glance] 《at》; cast [throw] a glance 《at》.
ミュージカル a musical (comedy).
ミューズ〈詩神〉(one's) Muse ¶ミューズの神々《ギリシャ神話》the (Nine) Muses.
ミュンヘン Munich.
みよ 御代 a reign; a period.
みよい 見好い〈醜くない〉decent; respectable; 〈見やすい〉(be) easy to see.
みよう 見様 ⇨ みかた[1] ¶見よう見まねで following [going by] sb's example; 《learn》from watching other people.
みょう 妙 ¶妙な〈奇妙な〉strange; curious; queer;《文》singular; odd; funny;〈玄妙な〉mysterious; miraculous / 妙な事には strangely [curiously] enough; curious [strange] to say / 妙に聞こえる sound strange [funny] / 妙を得ている be skillful 《at, with》; be clever 《at, in》; have a remarkable talent 《for》; have the knack 《of》/ …とは妙だ It is strange [curious, odd] that… / 造化の妙 the mystery of nature [creation]. 文例⇩
みょうあん 妙案 a bright [《文》happy] idea; an excellent [ingenious] plan [scheme].
みょうが[1] 茗荷〈植〉a Japanese ginger;〈食品〉Japanese ginger.
みょうが[2] 冥加 divine protection ¶冥加の至り a great blessing; bliss / 冥加に余る be too good for 《me》.
みょうぎ 妙技〈腕前〉exquisite skill;〈演技〉a wonderful performance;〈曲芸など〉a (splendid) feat; a stunt;〈スポーツの〉a fine play ¶妙技を見せる perform a wonderful feat;《文》exhibit [display] one's prowess.
みょうけい 妙計 an ingenious trick; a clever scheme; a wise plan.
みょうご 明後 ¶明後20日 the 20th, the day after tomorrow / 明後日 the day after tomorrow / 明後年 the year after next.
みょうさく 妙策 a clever scheme; an excellent plan.
みょうじ 名字 a surname; a family name; one's last name.
みょうしゅ 妙手〈囲碁・将棋の〉a brilliant [clever] move;〈優れた人〉an expert; a master hand 《at》;《文》an adept.
みょうしゅん 明春 next spring; the coming spring.
みょうじょう 明星〈金星〉Venus ¶明けの明星 the morning star;《文》the daystar / 宵の明星 the evening star / 文壇の明星 a star of the literary world.
みょうだい 名代〈代人〉a proxy;〈代理者〉a deputy; an agent;〈代表者〉a representative ¶名代となる act for [on behalf of] sb.
みょうちきりん 妙ちきりん ⇨ みょうな.
みょうちょう 明朝 tomorrow morning.
みょうにち 明日 tomorrow.
みょうねん 明年 next year; the coming year.
みょうばん[1] 明晩 tomorrow evening [night].
みょうばん[2] 明礬 alum.
みょうみ 妙味 (a) charm; (exquisite) beauty; a subtle [《文》nice] point;〈利益・うま味〉profit; gain; yield; output ¶(商売上)妙味のある profitable; producing profit; (well-)paying. 文例⇩
みょうやく 妙薬 a wonder drug;《文》a specific;《文》a golden (sovereign) remedy. 文例⇩
みょうり[1] 名利 ⇨ めいり.
みょうり[2] 冥利 divine favor; providence; luck.
みょうれい 妙齢 (the prime of) youth;《文》(in) young [early] womanhood ¶妙齢の young; blooming;《文》in the flower of maidenhood; 《a woman》of marriageable age; nubile ⇨ としごろ.
みよし 舳 the bow(s); the prow; the stem.
みより 身寄り ⇨ しんるい[2].
みらい[1] 未来 (the) future;《文》time [days] to come;《文》futurity;《文法》the future tense ¶未来の future; coming;《years》to come / 未来の夫[妻] one's future husband [wife];《戯言》one's intended / 未来のある promising; full of promise / 未来を見る look into the future 《with hope》/ 未来に in (the) future / はるか遠い未来に in the far distant future / 近接未来《文法》the immediate future / 未来学 futur-

---

[can be] home once you get used to it.
みやづかえ すまじきものは宮仕え. The life of a government official is really an unenviable one. | One must put up with all sorts of humiliations when one is in someone else's service.
みやぶる 彼は偽物を直ちに見破る. He has a sharp eye for a fake.
みょう 君は妙な鉛筆の持ち方するね. You have a queer way of holding your pencil.
みょうみ 氏の文体には何とも言えない妙味がある. There is an indescribable charm in his style.

みょうやく これは胃腸の妙薬です. This medicine is marvelously effective for indigestion.
みらい[1] 彼は未来の総理大臣をもって自ら任じている. He fancies himself a future premier.
みりょく その仕事には魅力があった. The job had an attraction for me. | There was a fascination in the work.
みる 彼はこちらの方を見ているようだ. He seems to be looking in this direction. | ボールペンを作る所が見たいものだ. I should like to see ball pens being made. / まあ見ていたまえ. Wait and see. / 逆立ちするから見ていてごらん. I'm going to do a handstand. Watch me. | Watch me stand on my hands. / とにかくもう1度見て来たまえ. At any rate, go and have another look (at it). / ちょっと見るとたやすいようですがね. It may seem easy at first sight. / その果物は見るからにうまそうだった. The fruit looked tempting. / 見るに忍び[見ていられ]なかった. I could not bear to see it. | I could not stand the sight of it. / 起きて見たら日光が部屋にさしていた. I awoke to find the sun streaming into the

みらい¹ 未来 ology / 未来学者 a futurologist / 未来派《芸術》futurism /《人》the futurists / 未来派の[的] futurist [futuristic]. 文例⓿

みらい² 味蕾《解》a taste [gustatory] bud.

ミリグラム a milligram (略: mg).

ミリバール a millibar (略: mb).

ミリメートル a millimeter (略: mm).

みりよう 未利用 ¶未利用の unused; untapped 《resources》.

みりょう¹ 未了 ¶未了の unfinished; incomplete.

みりょう² 魅了 ⇨ みする.

みりょく 魅力 (an) attraction; (a) charm; appeal; allure; glamor ¶...にとって魅力がある have an appeal for...; appeal to...; have attraction for...; hold a fascination for...; have magnetism for... / 魅力がない have [offer] no appeal 《to》; do not appeal 《to》; hold no attraction(s); be unattractive; be unglamorous / 魅力のある, 魅力的な charming; fascinating; attractive; glamorous / 魅力を失う lose (one's) appeal. 文例⓿

ミリリットル a milliliter (略: ml).

みりん 味醂 sweet *sake* (used as seasoning).

みる 見る 1.〈...を(目で)見る〉look 《at》; take [have] a look 《at》; set [lay] eyes 《on》(主に否定文で);〈動いているもの, もしくは変化の期待されるものを見ている〉watch;〈見える〉see;〈不審・好奇などの念をもって〉eye;〈見つめる〉stare [gaze] 《at》;〈見いだす〉find;〈読む〉read; look through;〈調べる〉look over; examine; look up;〈世話する〉look [see] after;〈観察する〉observe; view;〈...とみなす〉regard [look on] *sth* 《as》; take *sth* 《as》⇨ 用例Ⅰ ¶ざっと見る run *one's* eyes through; glance over / よく見る look hard 《at》; have [take] a good [careful] look 《at》/ 人の顔を見る look *sb* in the face / 映画を見る see [《米口語》take in] a movie / 手相を見る read *sb's* hand [palm] / 運勢を見る tell *sb's* fortune; forecast *sb's* future / (医者が)患者を見る examine [have a look at] a patient / 医者に見てもらう see [consult] a doctor / 見る見る, 見る間に in a moment; in an instant; every moment; fast / 見るからに evidently / 見る影もない be miserable; be wretched;《以前に比べて》《文》be a mere shadow of *one's* former self / 見る目がある have an eye 《for pictures》/ 見た目にいい be nice to look at / 見たところ to all appearance(s); apparently; on the face of it / ...を見て at the sight of... / ちょっと[ひと目]見て at first sight; at a glance / 見て楽しむ enjoy the sight 《of》/ 見て回る tour [look around] 《(an exhibition)》/ 見て見ぬふりをする pretend not to see *sth*; close *one's* eyes 《to》; turn a blind eye 《to》; wink [《文》connive] 《at》/ 見るに見兼ねて being unable to stand (idly) by (any longer) / 私の見るところでは in my opinion [view] / イギリス人の目から見た日本 Japan as the English see it / 多く[少なく]見て at most [least].

2.〈試みる, ...してみる〉try *do*ing; have a try 《at eating *sushi*》; have a go 《at playing tennis》 ¶足に合うかと靴をはいてみる try on a pair of shoes to see if they fit / (他人の)バイクに乗ってみる have a ride [go] on *sb's* motorcycle [motorbike] / 飲んでみる have a drink (of *sake*) ⇨ 用例2).

用例 1) look, see, watch は同じ「見る」でも, 次のように意味に違いがある。look は視線を対象の方へ向ける行為でのみに対し, see は視覚上の認知を意味して, 対象が「見える」こと。You look but see nothing.(見れども見えず)のような文に, look と see の違いが端的にあらわれる。さらに, see は「目に見える」だけでなく「心でわかる」の意味でしきりに使われる。殊にあとに節が続くときは必ず「わかる」「知る」の意である。He looked at the sky to see what the weather was like.(お天気はどうかと空を見た)。watch は時間をかけて動いている対象もしくは変化の期待される対象を「見ている」の意である。うさぎが逃げ込んだ穴を, うさぎがまた出て来ないかと「見ている」ならば watch the hole (for the rabbit to come out) と言えるが, 美術館で名画に見ほれて, どんなに熱心に長時間見つめていても, これは look at the picture であって, watch the picture とは言えない。なぜなら, 絵は動いていないし, 変化することもないからである。

用例 2) try が「...してみる」の意になるのは try *do*ing の形のときだけで, try to do は「...しようとする」を意味する。I tried speaking English, but couldn't make myself understood.(英語を話してみたが, 通じなかった)。/ I tried to speak English, but could say nothing.(英語を話そうとしたのだが, 何も言えなかった)。

ミルク (cow's) milk ¶ミルクで育てる bring up 《a baby》on the bottle / ミルク色の milk-white; milky / ミルクセーキ a milk shake.

みれん 未練 (a) regret; attachment (愛着) ¶まだ中に残っているかどうか, 缶を振ってみた。I shook the can to see if there was any more in it.

---

room. / 留守中に子供を見ていて下さいませんか。Could you please look after my little boy while I am away. / 猿人から上へ属への進化が見られたのは, この200万年間でのことである。Two million years have seen the evolution of ape man into the genus *Homo*. / よく注意して見ないと, 違いはわからない。To the casual view there is almost no difference between them. / おのおの見る所が違う。Each has his own views. / どう見ても も軍人だ。He is every inch a soldier. / この作文を見て下さいませんか。Would you be so kind as to look through [over] this composition. / 僕はそれを新聞で見た。I read [saw] it in the newspaper. / 小金井の桜を見て来た。I have been to Koganei to see the cherry blossoms. / 向こうへ着くのに2時間はみておいたほうがいい。You should give yourself two hours to get there. / 彼は今や見る影もなくなった。He is a mere shadow of what he used to be. / 医者に見てもらった方がいい。You had better consult [see] a doctor. / (医者に)先生, 母がまだ具合が悪いのですが, ちょっと見ていただけますか。Doctor, my mother's sick. Will you have a look at her? / その市の人口は正確にはわからないが, 約100万と見ろう大したことはない。I don't know the exact population of the city, but you won't be far out if you put it about a million. / 今に見ていろ! You'll suffer [pay] for this. | Just you wait! / それ見た事か。There you are, what did I tell you! / 殴れるものなら殴ってみろ。I dare you to hit me. | Go on, hit me if you dare! / まだ中に残っているかどうか, 缶を振ってみた。I shook the can to see if there was any more in it.

みわく 魅惑 (a) fascination; (a) charm ¶魅惑する fascinate; charm; bewitch;《文》captivate / 魅惑的な fascinating; bewitching; captivating; fetching; seductive 《women》.

みわけ 見分け〈区別〉(a) distinction; discrimination;〈鑑定〉judgment;〈鑑別〉identification;〈認識〉recognition ¶見分けのつかない indistinguishable / 見分けのつかないほど indistinguishably; beyond [out of] (all) recognition. 文例⑨

みわける 見分ける distinguish 《A from B, between A and B》; know 《A from B》; tell 《A from B》; tell 《them》 apart;《文》discriminate 《between》; identify 《plants》; recognize sb. 文例⑨ ［recognize.

みわすれる 見忘れる forget; do not [fail to]

みわたす 見渡す look out over 《the sea》 ¶双眼鏡で地平線を見渡す sweep the horizon with one's binoculars / 見渡す限り 《stretch》 as far as the eye can reach [see].

みん 明〈中国の王朝〉Ming ¶明朝 the Ming dynasty / 《活字》Ming(-style) type.

みんい 民意 《respect, reflect, consult》 the will of the people; public opinion [sentiment]; a public consensus.

みんえい 民営 ¶民営の private; privately-managed[-operated] / 民営にする put sth under private management / 民営になっている be under private management; be in private hands.

みんか 民家 a private house.

みんかん 民間 ¶民間の private; nonofficial; nongovernment(al); civil; popular;〈軍に対して〉civilian / 民間に[で] among the people / 民間事業 a private enterprise [business] / 民間人 a private citizen; a civilian (軍人に対して) / 民間伝承[説話] a folktale; (a) legend / 民間放送 commercial [sponsored] broadcasting / 民間療法 an old wives' remedy.

ミンク a mink 《pl. -(s)》 ¶ミンクのコート a mink coat;《wear》a mink.

みんげい 民芸 folk handicraft(s); folk art; folkcraft(s) ¶民芸館 a folkcraft museum / 民芸品 an article [object] of folk handicraft [folk art]; folk pieces.

みんけん 民権 civil rights; the people's rights ¶自由民権運動 the democratic movement 《in the Meiji era》.

みんじ 民事 civil affairs ¶民事裁判[裁判所] a civil trial [court] / 民事事件 a civil case / 民事訴訟 a civil suit [action] / 民事訴訟法 the Civil Proceedings Act; the Code of Civil Procedure.

みんしゃとう 民社党 the Democratic Socialist Party.

みんしゅ 民主 ¶民主的 democratic / 非民主的 undemocratic / 民主化する democratize / 民主国 a democratic state; a democracy / 民主主義 democracy / 議会制民主主義 parliamentary democracy / 民主政治 a democratic form of government; democracy / 民主政体 democracy / (米国の)民主党 the Democratic Party; the Democrats.

みんじゅ 民需 private [civilian] demand [requirements] ¶民需品 civilian goods; consumer('s) goods; goods for nongovernmental use [consumption].

みんしゅう 民衆 the people; the general public; the masses;《文》the populace ★ masses と populace は軽蔑的に「愚民」の意味合いになることもある ¶民衆的の popular; democratic / 民衆の知恵 folk wisdom / 民衆駅 a railroad station built with the contributions of the local people / 民衆芸術[娯楽] popular arts [amusements] / 一般民衆レベルでは at the grass roots.

みんしゅく 民宿 a private house providing bed and meals;《英》a guesthouse.

みんしん 民心 popular feelings; public [popular] sentiment;《文》the mind of the people.

みんせい 民政〈軍政に対して〉civil administration [government].

みんせいいいん 民生委員 a (district) welfare commissioner.

みんせん 民選 ¶民選の elected by the people [by popular vote]; popularly elected.

みんぞく¹ 民俗 folkways; folk [ethnic] customs ¶民俗学 folklore / 民俗学者 a folklorist / 民俗資料 《collection of》 folk material; folklore data.

みんぞく² 民族 a race; a people; a nation;《社会》an ethnic group ¶民族的[の] national; racial / 民族の移動 (a) racial migration; (a) folk movement / 民族的優越感 racism; ethnocentrism / 民族衣装 (a) national costume; (in) native dress / 民族運動 a nationalist movement / 民族音楽 folk music / 民族学[学者] ethnology [an ethnologist] / 民族自決 (the) self-determination of peoples / 民族主義 nationalism; racialism / 民族心理学 ethnopsychology; ethnic psychology / 民族性 national [racial] characteristics [traits] / 民族舞踊 a folk dance.

みわけ 彼が20年ぶりに帰って来たときはしばらくだれだか見分けがつかなかった. The twin singers look so much alike that you can hardly distinguish one from the other [tell them apart].

みわける この子はもう母親の顔を見分けます. The baby already recognizes its mother's face.

む 無から有は生ぜず. Nothing will come of nothing. | You cannot create anything out of nothing. | せっかくのご好意を無にするのはまことに残念ですが. I regret very much that I cannot accept your kind offer.

みんど 民度 the living [economic, behavioral] standard of the people.
みんな ⇨ みな.
みんぺい 民兵 a militiaman (男); a militiawoman (女); a militia (隊).
みんぽう¹ 民法 the civil law [code]; 〈一国の, 日本の〉 the Civil Code.
みんぽう² 民放 〈会社〉 a commercial broadcasting corporation ⇨ みんかん (民間放送).
みんやくせつ 民約説 the theory of social contract.
みんよう 民謡 a folk song; a (folk) ballad; folk singing.
みんわ 民話 a folk story; a folktale.

む

む 無 nothing, 《文》naught; nil; zero (零) ¶無にする abuse 《sb's kindness》; 《文》bring 《sb's labor》to naught; nullify [neutralize] 《sb's efforts》/ 無になる come [be brought] to nothing [naught]; be in vain; be wasted / 無安打無得点の試合 a no-hit, no-run game. 文例⇩
むい¹ 無位 ¶無位無官の人 a common [plain] citizen; a commoner.
むい² 無為 idleness; inactivity ¶無為の生活 an idle life / 無為の楽しみ the pleasures [delights] of leisure; the pleasure of doing nothing; 《イタリア語》dolce far niente / 無為に idly; in idleness / 無為に暮らす idle [loaf] one's time away; live an idle life / 無為無策の政府 a do-nothing government / 無為無策主義 do-nothingism.
むいか 六日 six days; 〈第6日〉the sixth (of January). ¶六日のあやめ a day too late for the fair.
むいぎ 無意義 ¶無意義な purposeless ⇨ むいみ / 無意義な生活をする live to no purpose.
むいしき 無意識 ¶無意識の unconscious; involuntary; 〈機械的〉mechanical / 無意識に unconsciously; involuntarily; without thinking [realizing (it)]; without being aware (of); 〈機械的〉mechanically. 文例⇩
むいそん 無医村 a doctorless village.
むいちぶつ 無一物 ¶無一物である have nothing; be penniless.
むいちもん 無一文 ⇨ いちもん (一文なし).
むいみ 無意味 ¶無意味な 〈意味のない〉 meaningless; insignificant; 〈愚にもつかない〉 senseless; nonsensical; absurd; empty / 無意味な事を言う talk nonsense.
むいん 無韻 ¶無韻の unrhymed / 無韻詩 (a) blank [(an) unrhymed] verse.
ムード a mood; an atmosphere ★ mood は「気分」であって, 日本語の「ムード」のように「雰囲気」の意ではあまり使われない ¶ムード音楽 mood music. 文例⇩
ムームー 〈ハワイ風の婦人服〉a muumuu.
むえき 無益 ¶無益な useless; futile ⇨ むだ / 無益の殺生 wanton destruction of life / 無益の殺生をする kill 《animals》wantonly. 文例⇩
むえん¹ 無煙 ¶無煙の smokeless / 無煙火薬 smokeless (gun)powder / 無煙炭 anthracite; hard coal.
むえん² 無鉛 ¶無鉛ガソリン lead-free [white] gasoline.
むえん³ 無縁 ¶無縁の 〈無関係の〉 indifferent; unrelated; 〈縁者のない〉 having no surviving relatives / 無縁の墓 an unknown person's grave; 〈弔う縁者のいない〉 a deserted [neglected] grave / 無縁墓地 a cemetery for those who left no relatives behind / 無縁仏(ぼとけ) a person who died leaving no one to attend to his grave.
むが 無我〔忘我〕ecstasy; 《文》transport; 〈無心〉《文》absorption; 〈没我〉《文》self-effacement; self-renunciation ¶無我の ecstatic; selfless 《love》/ 無我の境に入る attain a state of perfect self-effacement; 《文》rise above self / 無我夢中 ⇨ むちゅう.
むかい 向かい the opposite side ¶向かいの opposite; across from 《the post office》/ 向かいの家 the house opposite [across the street, over the way].
むがい¹ 無害 ¶無害な harmless (to); innocuous; 《文》innocent (of harm).
むがい² 無蓋 ¶無蓋の open / 無蓋貨車《米》an open freight car; 《英》an open goods wagon.
むかいあう 向かい合う face each other ¶ …と向かい合う be opposite (to) sb; face sb / …と向かい合って opposite (to) sb; facing sb / 〈双方〉向かい合わせに face to face. 文例⇩
むかいかぜ 向かい風 ¶向かい風 a head [《文》an adverse, an unfavorable] wind.
むかう 向かう 〈面する〉face; look out (on); be opposite (to); 〈顔を向ける〉turn (toward); 〈敵対する〉oppose; confront; turn (on); 〈行く〉go (toward, in the direction of); start [leave] (for); make (for); head (for home); be bound [headed] (for); 〈近付く〉approach; near ¶快方に向かう get better; take a turn for the better / 机に向かう sit at one's desk / 鏡に向かう stand before [look into] a mirror /

むいしき 彼女は無意識にそれを自分の買物袋の中へ入れた. She put it into her shopping bag without thinking (what she was doing).
むいみ その言葉は無意味に言ったのではない. These words were not uttered for nothing.
ムード この店はムードがいいわ. I like the atmosphere of this place.
むえき それはあながち無益ではあるまい. It may not be altogether useless.
むかいあう 彼女はジョージと向かい合ってテーブルについた. She sat down at the table, across from George.
むかいかぜ 風は向かい風だ. The wind is against us.

北に向かう列車 《depart on》 a northbound train / 向かう所敵なしの勢いで sweeping everything before one; with irresistible force / 人心の向かうところを察する see [watch] the trend of popular feeling / …に向かって〈目指して〉 toward; for; to; in the direction of; 〈対して〉 facing; to; opposite / 風に向かって走る run against [in the teeth of] the wind / 向かって行く turn [fall] on 《文》 upon; charge / 向かって右に on the right as one faces (it); on one's right / 向かって左から3番目の人 the third person from the left. 文例⇩

むかえいれる 迎え入れる show [usher] sb in; receive sb /〈野球で〉シングルヒットでランナーを本塁に迎え入れる drive a runner in on a single.

むかえうつ 迎え撃つ engage 《the enemy》; meet.

むかえざけ 迎え酒 〈二日酔の〉 drinking to cure a hangover; 《口語》《have》 the [a] hair of the dog (that bit one).

むかえる 迎える 〈出迎える〉 meet; go (out) to meet;〈接待する〉《文》 receive;〈歓迎する〉 welcome; greet; make sb welcome;〈招く〉 invite; call; send for;《文》 engage ¶40歳の誕生日を迎える see one's 40th birthday come round / 19の春を迎える reach《文》 attain》 one's nineteenth year / 旧年を送り新年を迎える see the old year out and the new year in / 妻を迎える《文》 take a wife; get married / 迎えに行く go to meet sb / 迎えに来る come [call] for sb / 医者を迎えにやる[行く] send [go] for a doctor. 文例⇩

むがく 無学 ¶無学な〈無教育な〉 uneducated; 《文》 unlettered;〈文盲の〉 illiterate;〈無知な〉 ignorant.

むかし 昔 〈古代〉 ancient [old] times; (remote) antiquity;〈昔日〉 old 《文》 bygone] days; old 《文》 olden times / 昔は in ancient [old] times; of old;〈以前〉《文》 formerly;《文》 in former days,〈かつて〉 in the past; in earlier times; once ⇒ 用例 1) / 昔々 long, long ago; once upon a time / 昔の old; ancient; onetime; earlier;《文》 former; past;《文》 bygone / 昔の人々 ancient people;《文》 men of former [other] days / 遠い昔から from old(en) [ancient] times; since early times;《文》 from time immemorial; throughout the ages ⇒ 用例 2) / 昔からの風習 a long-established custom / 3世紀という昔に as early [far back] as the third century / 昔かたぎの〈古風な〉 old-fashioned; conservative;《a gentleman》 of the old school / 昔なじみの an old friend 《acquaintance》 / 昔ながらの unchanged since olden times / 昔話 an old tale [story]; a legend;〈懐旧談〉 reminiscences / 昔話をする talk about old times [the old days] / 昔風の old-fashioned.

用法 1) 今と比べて「昔は」と言うときは、以上の副詞語句を使うよりも used to… でその意を表わす方が適切な場合が多い: People used to believe that the sun went round the earth. (昔は太陽が地球のまわりを回ると信じていた).

用法 2)「昔から私は鎌倉に住んでいる」といった程度の「昔から」は I've always lived in Kamakura. としか言えない。このような「昔から」を殊さら英語にしようとすると、変な英語になる。

むかしつ 無過失 ¶無過失責任 liability without fault; strict [absolute] liability.

むかせる 向かせる ⇒ むける.

むかち 無価値 ¶無価値な worthless; valueless; of no value; useless.

むかつく ⇒ むかむか.

むかっぱら 向かっ腹 ¶向かっ腹を立てる fly into a passion; lose one's temper; fly [go, get] into a tantrum.

むかで 《動》 a centipede ¶むかで競走 a 'centipede' race (between teams of runners with their legs linked together).

むかむか ¶むかむかする〈吐き気で〉 feel sick;《米》 be sick at the stomach / はきけ;〈愛想が尽きる〉 be nauseated [disgusted] 《by》;〈しゃくに障る〉 feel [be] vexed 《at》; get angry 《with sb, at [about] sth》. 文例⇩

むかん¹ 無冠 ¶無冠の帝王 an uncrowned king [monarch]; a king without a crown.

むかん² 無感 ¶無感地震 an unfelt earthquake.

むかんがえ 無考え ¶無考えな thoughtless; unthinking; inconsiderate; rash; reckless.

むかんかく 無感覚 《文》 insensible; numb; apathetic / 無感覚になる go [get,《文》 become] numbed; be benumbed / 無感覚である have no feeling; be insensible 《to pain》; be dead 《to pity》. 文例⇩

むかんけい 無関係 ¶無関係の unrelated; unconnected;〈無関係である〉 have nothing to do 《with》; have no connection 《with》; have [bear] no relation 《to, with》. 文例⇩

むかんさ 無鑑査 ¶無鑑査の 《a painting》 not submitted to the jury [selecting committee]. 文例⇩

むかんしょう 無干渉 noninterference; nonintervention ¶無干渉主義 a policy of nonin-

---

むかう 晩秋に向かうと木々は落葉する。Toward the end of autumn, the trees shed their leaves. / 船は南に向かって走った。The ship sailed south [toward the south]. / 彼は憤然として立ち上がり僕に向かって来た。He got angrily to his feet and came at me.

むかえる 主人は彼を愛想よく迎えた。The master of the house was very hospitable to him. | He got a warm welcome from [was warmly welcomed by] the host. / 昭和58年を迎えた。Today we enter the 58th year of Showa. / 聴衆は拍手して彼を迎えた。The audience greeted [welcomed] him with applause. / 主人自ら客を迎えに出た。The host came out in person to meet [welcome] his guests. / 駅までお迎えにあがります。I'll meet you at the station.

むかし 昔ここに寺があった。There used to be a temple here. / 昔はよかった。Things were better in the old days. / 僕は昔の僕ではない。I am not what I used to be. / 遠い昔に返ったような気がした。I felt as though I had gone far back in time. / 電気のなかった昔に帰りたいと思う人はいない。No one wants to turn the clock back to a world without electricity. / 昔からあの男は好かない。I've always disliked

むかんしん 無関心 apathy; indifference;《文》unconcern ¶無関心でいる be indifferent ((to)); be unconcerned ((about)); have no interest ((in)).

むき¹ 向き 〈方向〉a direction; a quarter;〈方位〉a situation;〈家の構え〉an exposure;《文》an aspect /〈風などの〉向きが変わる turn; shift /…向きの suitable [fit] for…; suited for… /輸出向きの《toys》for export /学生向きの雑誌 a magazine for students /右に向きを変える turn to the right /船の向きを変える put a ship about /西向きである〈家が〉face west; look ((to [toward] the)) west /窓が open to the west /万人向きである suit all tastes. 文例↓

むき² 無期 ¶無期の indefinite 《postponement》; life 《imprisonment》/無期延期になる be postponed indefinitely [for an indefinite period] /無期休会となる be adjourned *sine die* /無期懲役 imprisonment for life (with hard labor); penal servitude for life.

むき³ 無機 ¶無機の inorganic; mineral /無機化学 inorganic chemistry /無機化合物[肥料] an inorganic compound [fertilizer] /無機物 an inorganic substance; a mineral.

むき⁴ ¶むきになる take 《a joke》seriously; become serious /むきになって怒る get angry ((at a joke)); fly into a passion [rage]; flare up. 文例↓

むぎ 麦 barley (大麦) ; wheat (小麦) ¶麦秋 the time of the barley harvest /麦打ち flailing barley /麦刈り mowing [cutting] barley [wheat]; barley harvest /麦焦がし parched barley flour /麦こき thrashing [threshing] barley /麦作 a barley [wheat] crop /麦茶[湯] an infusion of parched barley /麦畑 a barley [wheat] field /《英》a cornfield /麦笛 an oaten pipe /麦踏み treading barley [wheat] plants /麦まき sowing barley [wheat] /麦飯 rice boiled with barley.

むきあう 向き合う ⇒むかいあう.

むきげん 無期限 ¶無期限の indefinite /無期限に indefinitely; for an indefinite period /無期限スト a no-time-limit strike.

むきず 無傷 ¶無傷の 〈けがのない〉unhurt; uninjured; unwounded; 〈欠点のない〉flawless; faultless; spotless; sound; perfect /無傷で《come back》unhurt; with [in] a whole skin.

むきだし 剥き出し ¶むき出しの 〈露骨な〉unreserved; open; frank; 〈裸の〉uncovered; naked; bare /むき出しに frankly; bluntly; plainly; straight out;《文》without concealment; without mincing words [matters]; openly (公然と) /むき出しにする make bare; bare; expose. 文例↓

むきだす 剥き出す show; bare ¶歯をむき出す show [bare] *one's* teeth; grin /歯をむき出して笑う grin ((at *sb*)); bare *one's* teeth in a grin.

むきどう 無軌道 ¶無軌道の 〈線路を使わない〉railless; unrailed; trackless; 〈常軌を逸した〉《文》aberrant; wild; extravagant; 〈抑制のない〉《文》unbridled 《license》/無軌道生活 a loose [dissolute, fast] life /無軌道ぶりを発揮する《文》run to the extremes of licentiousness;《口語》be [go] on the loose.

むきなおる 向き直る turn round ((toward)); face [turn] about.

むきみ 剥き身 shelled [《米》shucked, stripped] shellfish.

むきめい 無記名 ¶無記名の unsigned; unregistered; blank; unidentified /無記名口座 a numbered account ((in a Swiss bank)) /無記名債券 an unregistered [a bearer] bond [debenture] /無記名式(の) blank 《endorsement》; 〈持参人払いの〉《a check》payable to bearer; bearer 《checks》/無記名投票 a secret [an unsigned] vote; secret voting; a secret ballot.

むきゅう¹ 無休 ¶無休である have no holiday(s) /(店などが)年中無休である be open throughout [every day of] the year.

むきゅう² 無給 ¶無給の unpaid; unsalaried; honorary /無給で without pay [salary]; for nothing.

むきょういく 無教育 ¶無教育な uneducated; uncultured; illiterate; ignorant.

むきょうしつ 無響室 an anechoic chamber [room].

むきょうそう 無競争 ¶無競争の[で] without competition; without a rival /無競争で当選する be returned [elected] unopposed.

むきりょく 無気力 ¶無気力な 〈活気のない〉spiritless; nerveless; apathetic; 〈だれた〉《文》languid;《文》leaden; 〈弱腰の〉weak-kneed;《口語》gutless.

むぎわら 麦藁 (a) wheat [barley] straw ¶麦わら帽子 a straw hat /麦わら細工 straw work.

むきん 無菌 ¶無菌の germless; 〈殺菌した〉sterilized; pasteurized; aseptic /無菌室 an aseptic room /無菌状態《医》asepsis /無菌状

---

him. /あれを見ると昔がしのばれる. That reminds me of the past. /今では昔話となった. It is now an old story.

むかむか それを見ているうちに何だかむかむかしてきた. The sight of it gave me a queasy feeling in my stomach.

むかんかく 冷たくて手が無感覚になってしまった. My hands are numb [dead] with cold.

むかんけい そのことについては私は全く無関係です. I have absolutely nothing to do with the affair. 「mitted to the jury.

むかんさ 無鑑査.《表示》Not sub-

むき¹ 風の向きが南に変わった. The wind shifted to the south. /この家は向きが悪い. This house faces in the wrong direction. /僕の家は南向きだ. My house has a southern exposure. /僕の書斎は南向きの明るい部屋だ. My study is a light room facing south. /人にはめいめい向き不向きがある. Each man is useful in his own way. /そんなのはいやだという向きもある. There are some who don't care for it.

むき⁴ 冗談を言うとむきになる男だ. He is forever taking jokes seriously.

むきだし むきだしで物を贈るものじゃない. It isn't good form to give a present unwrapped.

むきゅう² その役は無給だ. The

態に保つ keep *sth* in an aseptic [a germ-free] condition ; keep *sth* sterile.

むく¹ 無垢 ¶無垢の pure ; spotless ; immaculate.

むく² 向く 〈顔を向ける〉turn *one*'s head [face] 《toward》; look 《to, toward》;〈指す〉point 《to》;〈傾く〉tend [lean] 《toward》;〈面する〉face ; look 《out》《on》; front 《on》;〈適する〉suit 《for》; be suitable [suited] 《to, for》; be fit 《for》¶後ろを向く look back ; turn round / どちらを向いても turn where one may. 文例⇩

むく³ 剥く peel ; rind ; pare ; skin ; strip ¶〈指で〉みかんの皮をむく peel an orange /〈ナイフで〉りんごの皮をむく pare [peel] an apple / 木の皮をむく bark a tree.

むくい 報い 〈報償〉a reward ; (a) recompense ; (a) compensation ; 《文》atonement ; a return ;〈たたり〉retribution ; (a) punishment ;《文》nemesis ¶…の報いを受ける suffer [pay dearly] for 《*one's* carelessness》/ 怠けた報いで owing to *one's* idleness / …の報いとして in return [compensation] for… ; for… ; as a result of…. 文例⇩

むくいぬ むく犬 a shaggy dog.

むくいる 報いる 〈報償する〉reward ; repay ; recompense *sb* 《for》; give *sb sth* in return 《for》;〈応報する〉return ;《文》requite ;〈仕返しする〉get [have] *one's* revenge 《on》; avenge oneself 《on》; retaliate ;《口語》get even 《with *sb*》; get *one's* own back 《on *sb*》¶労に報いる reward *sb* for his trouble [pains, services] ; reward *sb's* trouble [pains, services] / 親切に報いる repay *sb* for *his* kindness ; repay *sb's* kindness / 恩に報いるにあだをもってする return evil for good / 暴をもって暴に報いる answer violence with violence ; meet force with force / 友情に報いる return *sb's* friendship / 報いられることが少ない〈事が主語〉be not rewarding. 文例⇩

むくげ¹ むく毛 〈もしゃもしゃの毛〉shaggy hair ; wool ¶むく毛の犬 a shaggy dog.

むくげ² 《植》a rose of Sharon ; an alth(a)ea.

むくち 無口 《文》taciturnity ; reticence ¶無口の taciturn ; reticent ; quiet / 無口な人 a taciturn person ; a man of few words ; a quiet person. 文例⇩

むくどり 椋鳥 a gray starling.

むくみ dropsy ; (dropsical) swelling. 文例⇩

むくむ swell ; be swollen ; bloat. 文例⇩

むくむく ¶むくむくした[太った] plump ; portly / むくむく動き出す begin to stir.

むくれる get angry 《at *sth*, with *sb*》; take offense 《at》; be offended ; be in [get into] a huff ;《口語》get sore 《over》《about》*sth*, at *sb*》.

むくろ 軀 a (dead) body ; a corpse.

-むけ …向け (bound [headed] for ¶東南アジア向けの綿織物 cotton goods for export to Southeast Asia / 南米向けのラジオ放送番組 a radio program beamed at [to] South America.

むげ 無下 ¶むげに ⇨ すげない (すげなく断わる). 文例⇩

むけい 無形 ¶無形の 〈形のない〉formless ;〈非物質的〉《文》immaterial ;《文》incorporeal ;〈見えない〉invisible ;〈手に触れられない〉intangible ;〈抽象的〉abstract ;〈精神的〉moral ; spiritual / 無形文化財 intangible cultural assets. 文例⇩

むげい 無芸 ¶無芸の having no accomplishments. 文例⇩

むけいかく 無計画 ¶無計画な planless ; haphazard ; reckless 《expenditure》; unmethodical.

むけいけん 無経験 inexperience ; lack [want] of experience ¶無経験の inexperienced ; untrained ; green.

むけいこく 無警告 ¶無警告の surprise 《bombing》/ 無警告で without warning [notice].

むけいさつじょうたい 無警察状態 ¶無警察状態にある be in a lawless state [a state of anarchy].

むけつかくめい 無血革命 a bloodless revolution.

むけっせき 無欠席 perfect attendance ¶3年間在学中無欠席で通す attend school for three years without missing a single day.

むける¹ 向ける 〈向かせる〉turn 《*one's* face to *sth*》; direct 《*sb's* attention to [toward]》;〈ねらう〉aim [point, level] 《a revolver》at ; train 《a telescope》on *sth* ;〈差し向ける〉send 《充当する》apply 《to》; appropriate 《for》¶向け直す redirect.

むける² 剝ける peel 《off》; come [go] off. 文例⇩

むげん¹ 無限 infinity ; eternity (永久) ¶無限の limitless ; unlimited ; endless ; infinite ;《文》boundless ; eternal (永久の) / 無限の意味

---

post carries no pay.

むく² 足の向くままにどこへでも行く. I go wherever my feet take me. / 磁針は北を向く. The magnetic needle points to the north. / 家は森の方に[街道に]向いている. The house looks toward the woods [faces the highway]. / 僕は生まれつき商売には向いていない. I'm not cut out for business.

むくい 彼は当然の報いを受けたのだ. He got no more than he deserved (《文》than his deserts). |《口語》He had it coming (to him).

むくいる 正直にしていればついに

は報いられる. Honesty will be rewarded in the long run. / 彼の努力は報いられた. His efforts bore fruit. / 多年の頑張りがついに報いられた. The years of persistence at last paid off. / これは読んで充分報いられる所のある本だ. This is a very rewarding book.

むくち 彼は無口だが言うことは要領を得ている. He doesn't say much but what he does say is to the point.

むくみ むくみが引いた. The swelling has subsided [gone down].

むくむ 彼は顔中がむくんでいる. He has a swollen [bloated] face.

むげ そういう話では無下にも断わ れまい. Such a proposal cannot be rejected out of hand.

むけい 知識は無形の財産である. Knowledge is an intangible asset. / 氏には有形無形の恩顧を受けた. I am indebted to him morally as well as materially.

むげい 至って無芸です. I have [can boast of] no special [particular] accomplishments. | There is nothing I am specially good at. / あいつは無芸大食だ. He has

むげん　《convey》a world of meaning / 無限に infinity; boundlessly; endlessly; eternally / 無限軌道 an endless track; a caterpillar / 無限級数[数列, 小数, 集合] an infinite series [sequence, decimal, set] / 無限小の infinitesimal / 無限責任 unlimited liability / 無限大 infinity / 無限大の infinite; infinitely large. 文例⇩

むげん[2] 夢幻 《文》dreams and phantasms; (a) fantasy; visions ¶夢幻的 dreamlike; dreamy; fantastic / 夢幻劇 a dream play.

むげんそく 無原則 ¶無原則の without any rule to go by; ad hoc; random; haphazard; 〈道徳的に〉unprincipled《expediency》.

むこ[1] 婿 〈娘の夫〉a son-in-law (*pl.* sons-in-law); 〈花婿〉a bridegroom; a groom ¶婿になる[行く] marry into the family of *one's* bride.

むこ[2] 無辜 ¶無辜の innocent; harmless.

むごい cruel; brutal; merciless; heartless; inhuman. 文例⇩

むこう[1] 向こう 〈向こう側〉the other [opposite] side; 〈先方〉the other party; he; she; they; 〈行き先〉the destination; far away; 〈今後〉next; coming; 《days, years》to come ¶向こうの森の中に in the wood(s) over there / …の向こうを張る set *oneself* up against *sb*; oppose; rival; 《文》emulate; compete [《文》vie] with *sb* / 向こうに over there; yonder; 〈…を越えて〉beyond; across [on the other side of] 《the road》/ 向こうに着く get there 《in time》/ 川の向こうに across [beyond] the river / はるか向こうに in the distance; far away / …を向こうに向けて with … facing away from *one* / …を向こうに回して in opposition to…; in rivalry with… / 向こう側 the other [opposite] side / 向こうから来る come from the opposite direction / 向こう3年間 for three years to come / 向こう1週間の間に within a [the] week / 向こう岸に on the other side [opposite bank] 《of the river》/ 向こう三軒両隣り *one's* nearest neighbors / 向こう鉢巻きで with a rolled towel tied around *one's* head / 向こう鉢巻で取りかかる brace *oneself* [pull *oneself* together] 《for an effort》/ 向こう向きになる look [turn] away 《the other way》; turn *one's* back 《on *sb*》. 文例⇩

むこう[2] 無効 ¶無効の〈効力のない〉invalid; unavailable; 《文》of no effect; no longer good; 〈かいのない〉《文》ineffectual; fruitless; futile; 《文》vain ¶無効にする annul; void; make (null and) void / 無効になる become null [void, ineffective]; be no longer good; be of no use 《avail》/ 無効投票 a spoilt [an invalid] vote.

むこうきず 向こう傷 a wound [cut] in the forehead.

むこうずね 向こう脛 a shin ¶向こうずねをけとばす give *sb* a kick on the shin / 向こうずねを擦りむく bark *one's* shin / 向こうずねをぶつける shin *oneself* against 《a rock》.

むこうみず 向こう見ず ¶向こう見ずの rash; headlong; reckless; bold; blind / 向こう見ずの勇気 (an act of) quixotic courage / 向こう見ずな男 a reckless fellow; a daredevil / 向こう見ずな事をやる be rash; act recklessly / 向こう見ずに rashly; boldly; headlong; recklessly; blindly.

むごたらしい cruel; 《文》horrible; tragic ⇨ むごい, ざんこく.

むこん 無根 ¶無根の groundless; unfounded; 《文》baseless; false.

むごん 無言 ¶無言の silent; speechless; 《文》tacit; dumb; 《文》mute / 無言の行 an ascetic practice of silence / 無言で silently; in silence; mutely; without speaking; without (saying) a word / 無言劇 a pantomime; a dumb show; a silent drama.

むざい 無罪 being not guilty; 《文》guiltlessness; innocence ¶無罪の not guilty; 《文》guiltless; innocent / 無罪の申し立て a plea of 'not guilty' / 無罪を申し立てる plead not guilty 《to a crime》/ 無罪にする[を言い渡す] find [declare] *sb* not guilty; acquit *sb* / 辛うじて無罪になる narrowly escape conviction / 無罪判決 a decision of 'not guilty'. 文例⇩

むさく 無策 lack of policy ¶無策な resourceless; shiftless. 文例⇩

むさくい 無作為 ¶無作為の random / 無作為に randomly; at random / 無作為(標本)抽出《統計》random sampling.

むさくるしい filthy; dirty; sordid; dowdy; shabby; untidy.

ささび 《動》a (white-cheeked) giant flying squirrel.

むさつ 無札 ¶無札の乗客 a passenger without a ticket / 無札乗車 riding 《a train》without

---

no virtues other than his sound appetite.

むけいけん 私は教育には無経験だ。I have no experience in teaching.

むける[1] お客様に背を向けて座るものではない。You must not sit with your back to your guest.

むける[2] 日に焼けると皮がむける。One's skin peels when one gets sunburnt. / あまり日にさらされたので背中の皮がむけた。I was out in the sun so much that my back peeled [the skin on my back peeled].

むげん[1] 需要は無限に増加するだろう。The demand will probably increase to an unlimited extent.

むごい あなたもむごい事を言う人だ。You are cruel to say things like that.

むこう[1] その時彼は向こうを向いていた。He was facing away from us at the time. / あの丘の向こうにも村がある。There is another village beyond that hill. / 向こうに見えるのが ロンドン塔です。That's the Tower of London you (can) see over there ahead of us. / 向こうにも言い分はあろう。They've no doubt got their grievances, as well. / あの大百貨店の向こうを張ろうとしている。They are trying to outdo that big department store.

むざい 彼はついに無罪放免になった。He was finally found not guilty and released.

むさく 政府は事態に対し全く無策であった。The Government was utterly unable to devise any appropriate measures to cope with the situation.

むさくるしい むさくるしい所ですがおついでの節にお立ち寄り下さ

むさべつ 無差別 ¶無差別の indiscriminate / 無差別の待遇 (give them) equal treatment / 無差別に indiscriminately; without distinction [discrimination]; equally; with impartiality / 無差別級《柔道》the open-weight [unclassified] division [category] / 無差別爆撃 indiscriminate [nonselective] bombing.

むさぼる 貪る〈欲張る〉covet; 《文》be covetous 《of》; crave; be greedy 《for》 ¶むさぼり食う devour (gluttonously).

むざむざ 〈たやすく〉easily; 〈惜し気なく〉without regret; 〈みすみす〉helplessly; without (offering any) resistance.

むさん 無産 ¶無産階級 the proletariat; the propertyless [unpropertied] (class); proletarians.

むざん 無残[惨] ¶無残な〈むごい〉cruel; merciless; pitiless; 〈悲惨な〉tragic; pitiful / 無残な光景 a horrible sight [scene] / 無残な最期を遂げる meet with a tragic end / 無残にも without pity [mercy]; mercilessly; cruelly. 文例 ⇩

むさんしょう 無酸症《医》(gastric) anacidity; achlorhydria.

むし¹ 虫〈昆虫, 羽虫〉an insect; a bug; 〈蛹(さなぎ)虫〉a worm; 〈毛虫〉a caterpillar; 〈蛾(が)〉a moth; 〈鳴虫〉a cricket; 〈害虫〉vermin (総称) ¶虫がつく be infested with insects [vermin]; 〈恋人ができる〉have a lover / 虫がわく〈場所が主語〉get [《文》become] verminous / 〈回虫が〉get worms / 虫が起こる〈子供に〉get [《文》become] fretful [peevish] / 虫が知らせる〈人が主語〉have a premonition [foreboding, 《文》presentiment,《口語》hunch]《that..., about》/ 虫の食った worm-eaten 《timber》; moth-eaten 《cloth》; wormy 《apples》/ 虫の音 the chirping [singing] of insects / 虫の息を している be breathing faintly; be dying / 虫の居所が悪い (happen to) be in a bad [poor] mood [temper];《文》be in ill humor / 虫のいいことを言う, 虫がいい take too much [a lot] for granted;《口語》push one's luck / 虫の知らせ a feeling in one's bones;《文》a presentiment;《文》a foreboding / 虫の好かない disagreeable; disgusting / 大の虫を生かして小の虫を殺す sacrifice a small good for the sake of a greater good / 虫も殺さぬ顔をしている look innocent; look as if butter would not melt in one's mouth [as if one wouldn't hurt a fly] / 虫かご an insect cage. 文例 ⇩

むし² 無死《野球》文例 ⇩

むし³ 無私 ¶無私の unselfish; disinterested; 公平無私の impartial; fair and disinterested.

むし⁴ 無視 ¶無視する ignore; disregard; neglect; take no notice of; by-pass / 法を無視する連中 those who defy the law. 文例 ⇩

むじ 無地 ¶無地の plain; self-colored; unfigured. 文例 ⇩

むしあつい 蒸し暑い muggy; sultry; humid; sticky; (rather) warm; hot and close. 文例 ⇩

むしかえし 蒸し返し〈再び蒸すこと〉resteaming;〈繰り返し〉(a) repetition;〈復活〉(a) revival.

むしかえす 蒸し返す〈蒸し直す〉steam (over) again;〈繰り返す〉repeat;〈復活させる〉revive; bring up again.

むしかく 無資格 lack of qualification(s);《法》(legal) incompetence; incapacity ¶無資格の unqualified; incompetent; unlicensed; uncertificated.

むじかく 無自覚 ¶無自覚の unconscious 《of》; blind 《to》; apathetic 《to》;《文》insensible 《of》.

むしがし 蒸し菓子 (a) steamed cake.

むしき 蒸し器 a steamer.

むしくい 虫食い ¶虫食いだらけの worm-eaten; moth-eaten.

むしくだし 虫下し a vermifuge; an anthelmint[h]ic drug.

むしけら 虫けら a worm; an insect ¶虫けら同然の人間〈つまらない〉an insignificant person; a person who counts for nothing;〈やくざな〉a worthless [good-for-nothing] fellow; scum (集合的).

むしけん 無試験 ¶無試験で without examination.

むじこ 無事故 ¶無事故で[の] without an accident.

むしず 虫酸 ¶虫ずが走る〈人が主語〉be disgusted 《with》; loathe;〈物が主語〉《口語》give one the creeps; make one's skin crawl / 虫ずの走るようなやつ a disgusting [repulsive, revolting, loathsome] fellow.

むじつ 無実 ¶無実の〈偽りの〉false; untrue;〈根拠のない〉groundless; unfounded;〈無罪の〉innocent / 無実の罪を受ける be falsely charged (with); be wrongly [falsely] accused 《of》;《口語》be framed 《by sb》.

むじな 〈穴ぐま〉a badger;〈たぬき〉a raccoon dog.

むしば 虫歯 a bad [decayed, carious] tooth ¶虫歯が痛む one's bad tooth hurts; have an ache in one's decayed tooth / 虫歯の穴 a cavity in a tooth / 虫歯を予防する prevent teeth from decaying; prevent tooth decay.

むしばむ 蝕む〈食い入る〉eat into; gnaw (at)

い. Please drop in (on us) when you come this way. / うちくるしい所へようこそおいで下さいました. I'm delighted to welcome you under my humble roof.

むざむざ それをむざむざと失うようなことはしないぞ. I'm not going to let it go down the drain for nothing.

むざん 見るも無残な光景であった. It was an appalling [a shocking] sight.

むし¹ 稲に虫がついた. The rice plants have been infested by insects. / けがをするんじゃいいがと思ったが, やはり虫が知らせたんだね. My premonition about his accident proved to be only too true.

むし² 無死満塁である. The bases are full [loaded] with no outs.

むし⁴ この問題は無視できない. This problem cannot be by-passed. / 彼は無視できない存在だ. He is a man to be reckoned with. / 私の警告は無視された. My warning was disregarded [went unheeded]. / 禁煙の掲示を無視して2人の若い男がタバコを吸っていた. Two young men

むじひ 無慈悲 ¶無慈悲な unfeeling; merciless; pitiless; heartless; ruthless; cruel.

むしふうじ 虫封じ a charm [an incantation] to cure children's tantrums.

むしぶろ 蒸し風呂 a steam [Turkish] bath ¶蒸し風呂に入ったような (oppressively) hot and humid; sultry; sweltering.

むしぼし 虫干し (summer) airing ¶虫干しをする air (clothes) (in the shade); give (clothes) an airing.

むしほん 無資本 ¶無資本で without capital [funds], with nothing to start with.

むしむし 蒸し蒸し ¶むしむしする ⇒むしあつい / 気温 30 度のむしむしする状態で (with the temperature) at a steaming 30 degrees.

むしめがね 虫眼鏡 a magnifying glass; a reading glass ¶虫眼鏡で見る look at sth through a magnifying glass.

むしゃ 武者 a warrior; a soldier ¶武者隠し 〈城の〉 the warriors' hiding place / 武者修行に出かける go out [about the country] to perfect one's skill in the martial arts / 武者ぶり gallantry; 《文》prowess; 《文》valor / あっぱれな武者ぶりを示す distinguish oneself on the field of battle / 武者震いする tremble with excitement / 武者人形 a warrior doll.

むしやき 蒸し焼き ¶蒸し焼きにする bake (in a casserole); roast (in a covered pan).

むじゃき 無邪気 innocence; 《文》artlessness; lack of affectation ¶無邪気な innocent; naive; simple; 《文》artless; 《文》ingenuous.

むしゃくしゃ ¶むしゃくしゃする 〈いら立つ〉 be irritated; be fretful; fret; 〈しゃくに障る〉 be annoyed; be vexed; be in a temper; be in ill humor.

むしゃぶりつく seize violent hold of; grapple with; spring at.

むしゃむしゃ ¶むしゃむしゃ食べる munch; eat with a munching sound. 文例⇩

むしゅう 無臭 ¶無臭の odorless; scentless.

むしゅうきょう 無宗教 ¶無宗教の 《a person》with no religious faith [affiliation]; 《a country》without [with no] religion. 文例⇩

むしゅうにゅう 無収入 ¶無収入の without any income / 無職無収入証明書 a (written) certificate that sb is without any occupation or other source of income.

むじゅうりょう 無重量 ⇒むじゅうりょく.

むじゅうりょく 無重力 weightlessness; zero gravity; zero G ¶無重力状態 a state [condition] of weightlessness; a weightless state; a gravity-free state / 無重力状態になる go [《文》become] weightless / 無重力状態で in a weightless state; under weightless conditions; at [in] zero G / 無重力飛行 a weightless flight.

むしゅくもの 無宿者 a homeless wanderer; a tramp; 《文》a vagrant; 《文》a vagabond; 《米口語》a bum; 《米口語》a hobo (pl. -(e)s).

むしゅみ 無趣味 ¶無趣味な dry; prosaic; dull / 無趣味な人 a person with no hobbies [interests] (to speak of).

むじゅん 矛盾 (a) contradiction; (an) inconsistency; 《文》an anomaly (in sb's behavior); (a) conflict (of evidence) ¶言葉の矛盾 『論』a contradiction in terms / 矛盾する contradict; be contradictory 《to》; be inconsistent 《with》; 《文》be anomalous; be at variance 《with》; conflict 《with》/ 矛盾した事を言う contradict oneself; make a contradictory statement / 矛盾律 『論』the law of contradiction. 文例⇩

むしょう¹ 無償 ¶無償の gratis; free (of charge); 【法】gratuitous / 無償の愛 a love that asks nothing in return / 無償で gratis; without compensation [pay]; free of charge; without charge / 無償株 bonus stock / 無償交付〔株式〕delivery without compensation.

むしょう² 無性 ¶無性に very much; 《文》to excess ⇒むやみ / 無性に喜ぶ be delighted beyond [without] measure; be beside oneself with joy / 無性に会いたがる long [be dying] to see sb.

むじょう¹ 無上 ¶無上の supreme; the highest; the greatest; the best / 無上の喜び the greatest pleasure; the sweetest joy (of life). 文例⇩

むじょう² 無常 uncertainty; 《文》mutability; 《文》transience; 《文》transitoriness; 《文》vanity ¶無常の uncertain; 《文》mutable; 《文》transient; 《文》transitory; 《文》vain. 文例⇩

むじょう³ 無情 heartlessness; cruelty ¶無情な 〈薄情な〉heartless; hardhearted; coldhearted; unfeeling; callous / 〈無慈悲な〉merciless; 〈残酷な〉cruel / 無情にも heartlessly; cruelly. 文例⇩

むじょうけん 無条件 ¶無条件の unconditional; unqualified / 無条件で unconditionally; unqualifiedly / 無条件降服 unconditional surrender.

むしょく¹ 無色 ¶無色の colorless / 無色透明な transparent and colorless; (water-)clear.

むしょく² 無職 ¶無職の without [having no] occupation; 〈失業した〉unemployed; jobless; out of work [employment] / 無職の人 a

---

were smoking in (complete) disregard of the 'No Smoking' sign.
むじ 彼のネクタイは黒地だった。His tie was solid black.
むしあつい この部屋は蒸し暑い。This room is hot and stuffy.
むしばむ 汚職が国の心臓部をむしばんでいる。Corruption is eating at the heart of the country.
むしゃむしゃ ジョーはリンゴをむしゃむしゃやりながら入って来た。Joe came in, munching on an apple.
むしゅうきょう 私は無宗教です。I am a member of no religion.
むじゅん 現実と理想とはしばしば矛盾する。The reality often contradicts the ideal.
むじょう¹ それは私にとって無上の光栄であります。I deem it the highest honor I could aspire to.
むじょう² 無常迅速, 朝に紅顔夕べには白骨。Life is too uncertain. Here today, gone tomorrow.
むじょう³ 彼は無情にも困っている友を捨てた。He was coldhearted enough to let down a friend in need.

person without a regular occupation [job] ⇨しつぎょう(失業者).

むしよけ 虫除け an insect repellent; insect powder (粉); a mothball (固形); 〈設備〉 a protection against moths.

むしょぞく 無所属 ¶無所属の independent; unattached; neutral; 〈政党に属さない〉 nonpartisan 《members of the Diet》; affiliated with no party / 無所属で立候補する run for an election independent of any party.

むしりとる 毟り取る pluck [tear] off.

むしりょ 無思慮 thoughtlessness; 《文》 indiscretion ¶無思慮な 〈考えのない〉 thoughtless; inconsiderate; indiscreet; 〈向こう見ずな〉 rash; reckless.

むしる 毟る pluck [pick, pull, tear] (off) ¶鳥の毛をむしる pluck [pick] a fowl / 庭の草をむしる weed the garden.

むしろ[1] 蓆 a straw mat; (straw) matting ¶針のむしろに座る 《文》 lie on a bed of thorns; suffer mental anguish.

むしろ[2] 寧ろ if anything; rather 《than》; better 《than》; sooner 《than》; first; preferably. [文例⇩]

むしん 無心 〈無邪気〉 innocence; 〈ねだること〉 a request; 〖禅〗 no-mindedness; mindlessness ¶無心する beg [ask] *sb* for *sth*; make a request to *sb* for *sth*; 《口語》 sponge; 《英口語》 cadge / 無心の innocent / 無心に遊んでいる be innocently at (*one's*) play; be absorbed in (*one's*) play.

むじん[1] 無人 ¶無人の uninhabited 《regions》 / 無人の境を行くがごとく進む carry [sweep] everything before *one* / 無人衛星 an unmanned satellite / 無人機関車 a crewless [robot] locomotive / 無人島 an uninhabited island; a desert island / 無人飛行機 a pilotless plane / 無人踏切 an unattended (railroad) crossing.

むじん[2] 無尽 〈講〉 a mutual financing [loan] association.

むしんけい 無神経 ¶無神経な insensitive; inconsiderate; thick-skinned; stolid. [文例⇩]

むじんしつ 無塵室 a dust-free chamber.

むしんじん 無信心 ⇨むしゅうきょう.

むじんぞう 無尽蔵 ¶無尽蔵の inexhaustible; limitless; unlimited. [文例⇩]

むしんろん 無神論 atheism ¶無神論者 an atheist.

むす 蒸す 〈ふかす〉 steam; heat [warm] with steam; 〈温罨法(あん)をする〉 foment; poultice; 〈天候が〉 be (hot and) close; be sultry; be sticky ¶蒸しタオル a steamed [hot] towel / 蒸したての fresh from the steamer.

むすい 無水 ¶無水の〖化〗 anhydrous / 無水アルコール absolute alcohol / 無水酢酸 acetic anhydride.

むすう 無数 ¶無数の numberless; 《文》 innumerable; countless; a limitless number of; untold [uncounted] numbers of / 無数に 《文》 innumerably; countlessly; without [out of] number; in countless numbers.

むずかしい 難しい 〈困難な〉 hard; difficult; 《口語》 tough; 《口語》 stiff; 〈厄介な〉 troublesome; 〈微妙な〉 delicate; 《口語》 tricky; 〈疑わしい〉 doubtful; 〈顔つきの〉 sullen; glum; displeased; grave; 〈厳格な〉 stern; 〈気むずかしい〉 hard to please [suit]; fastidious ¶むずかしい顔をする look displeased; glower; scowl / むずかしい立場[状勢] a delicate [ticklish] situation / むずかしく考える take 《things》 too seriously / むずかしさ difficulty. [文例⇩]

むずがゆい むず痒い 《feel》 creepy; crawly.

むずかる fret; be fretful; be peevish.

むすこ 息子 a son; a boy.

むずと ⇨むんず.

むすび 結び 〈結末〉 an end; a close; 〈結論〉 a conclusion; 〈握り飯〉 a rice ball; 〈合併集合〉〖数〗 a union; a join ¶結びの言葉 closing [concluding] remarks / 結びの一番 the last [final] bout (of the day) / 結びの神 the god of marriage.

むすびあう 結び合う 〈提携する〉 tie up 《with》; cooperate 《with》.

むすびあわせる 結び合わせる tie [link, fasten, bind] together; unite; combine.

むすびつき 結び付き 〈関係〉 (a) connection; (a) relationship; relation.

むすびつく 結び付く be related 《to, with》; link *oneself* 《to》; link up 《with》; be [get] tied up 《with》; unite [combine] 《with》; join hands 《with》; 〈結果〉 result 《in》. [文例⇩]

むすびつける 結び付ける tie (up); join [fasten, link] together; connect 《A with B》. ¶…と結びつけて考える consider 《A》 in relation to [in connection with] 《B》.

むすびめ 結び目 a knot; a tie ¶結び目をこしらえる make [tie] a knot / 結び目を緩める loosen a knot / 結び目を解く untie [undo] a knot; 〈固い結び目を指先でつまむようにして〉 pick a knot apart.

むすぶ 結ぶ 〈縛る〉 tie (up); knot; fasten (together); bind; 〈関係などを〉 enter [come] into 《a relationship with》; form 《a connection with》; conclude 《a treaty》; make 《a contract》; 〈果実を〉 bear 《fruit》; 〈完結する〉 《文》 conclude; finish; close; 〈提携する〉 ally [league,

---

むしろ[2] ライシャワー氏は本職の外交官ですか.—いいえ,むしろ学者です. Is Mr. Reischauer a career diplomat?—No. If anything, he is an academic. / やるのが少し早すぎたんじゃないかな.—いや,むしろもっと早くやればよかった. We did it a bit too early, didn't we?—No. If anything, we should have done it earlier. / 彼は学者というよりもむしろジャーナリストだ. He is a journalist rather than [more of a journalist than] a scholar. | He is not so much a scholar as a journalist. / 悪いことをして金をもうけるよりはむしろ貧乏でいた方がいい. I would rather be poor than get money by dishonest means.

むしんけい 彼は何を言われても無神経だ. He is too thick-skinned to mind what others say.

むじんぞう その地方には鉄鉱が無尽蔵にある. The region has virtually inexhaustible deposits of iron ore.

むずかしい この本は僕には少しむずかしい. This book is a little too difficult for me (to read). | This book is a bit over my head. /

むずむず

join hands] 《with》; unite [link (up)] 《with》; be united 《with》 / 交友関係を結ぶ form a friendship; make friends 《with》 / 演説を結ぶ conclude *one's* speech / 東京と京都を3時間で結ぶ新幹線 the Shinkansen Line that links Tokyo with Kyoto in three hours / 結ばれる be tied (up); be fastened (together); 〈結婚する〉 be united in marriage; be wedded 《to》. 用例

むずむず ¶むずむずする 〈体が〉 itch; feel itchy; 〈心が〉 be impatient; be irritated; be nervous; itch [have an itch] 《for action》.

むすめ 娘 a daughter; 〈少女〉 a girl ¶娘らしい girlish; girl-like; 《文》 maidenly / 娘心 a girlish mind; girlish innocence [sentiment] / 娘盛りの (a girl) in the bloom of youth; 《a girl》 in (her) prime [at the prime of (her) beauty] / 娘時代に in *one's* girlhood; when *one* is [was] a girl / 娘っ子 a slip of a girl.

むせい¹ 無声 ¶無声の silent / 無声映画 a silent picture [movie, film] / 無声音 〈音声〉 a voiceless [an unvoiced, a breath(ed)] sound.

むせい² 無性 ¶無性の nonsexual; asexual; sexless; 《植》 neutral 《flowers》 / 無性生殖 asexual reproduction.

むせい³ 夢精 (a) nocturnal emission; 《have》a wet dream.

むぜい 無税 ¶無税の free 《imports》; untaxed; tax-[duty-]free; tax-exempt / 無税で free of duty [taxes]; duty-free / 無税品 (duty-)free goods; goods free of duty.

むせいげん 無制限 ¶無制限の free; unlimited; limitless; unrestricted / 無制限に without any restriction; freely; without reserve [limitation].

むせいふ 無政府 ¶無政府の anarchic(al) / 無政府状態にある be in a state of anarchy; be in a chaotic condition / 無政府主義(者)の anarchism [an anarchist] / 無政府主義的な anarchistic.

むせいぶつ 無生物 an inanimate object [being]; a lifeless [nonliving] thing ¶無生物界 the inanimate world.

むせいらん 無精卵 an unfertilized egg; a wind egg.

むせかえる むせ返る be choked 《with》.

むせきついどうぶつ 無脊椎動物 an invertebrate (animal).

むせきにん 無責任 ¶無責任な irresponsible / 無責任な事を言う talk irresponsibly; make an irresponsible statement. 用例

むせきもの 無籍者 a person without a registered domicile; 〈浮浪者〉《文》 a vagrant; 《文》 a vagabond; an outcast.

むせっそう 無節操 ¶無節操な 《文》 inconstant; unprincipled.

むせっぽい choking; stifling; stuffy; suffocating; chok(e)y.

むせぶ be choked [stifled, smothered] 《with, by》 ¶煙にむせぶ be stifled by [choked with] smoke / むせび泣く, 涙にむせぶ sob; be choked with tears.

むせる be choked [stifled, smothered] 《with, by》 ¶タバコにむせる choke on a cigarette. 用例

むせん¹ 無銭 ¶無銭飲食をする bilk on a restaurant bill; bilk a restaurant [bar] out of its money / 無銭旅行をする travel without money; work *one's* way 《through a country》.

むせん² 無線 radio; 《英》 wireless ¶無線位置標識 〈航空〉 a marker (radio) beacon / 無線技師 a radio [wireless] operator; a radioman / 無線技術 radio techniques / 無線局 ⇒ むせんでんしん (無線電信局) / 無線工学 radio engineering / 無線コンパス a radio compass; a (radio) direction finder / 無線制御 radio control / 無線放送 radio broadcasting; a radio broadcast.

むせんでんしん 無線電信 wireless (telegraphy); radiotelegraphy ¶無線電信で by radio [wireless] / 無線電信機 a radiotelegraph / 無線電信局 a wireless [radio] station. 用例

むせんでんわ 無線電話 《法》 radiotelephony; 〈電話機〉 a radiotelephone; 〈施設〉 a radio-telephone service [system]; 〈通信〉 a radio-telephone message ¶無線電話をかける radiotelephone; talk by radiotelephone / 無線電話に出る come on the air.

むそう 夢想 a dream; a vision; a fancy; a daydream ¶夢想する dream 《of》; fancy / 夢想家 a 《Utopian》 dreamer; a daydreamer; a visionary.

むぞうさ 無造作 ¶むぞうさに 〈容易に〉 easily; with ease; without difficulty; 〈気軽に〉 casually; in an offhand manner; 〈すぐに〉 readily / むぞうさに承諾する agree 《文》 consent] readily; give *one's* ready consent.

むだ 無駄 ¶むだな useless; of no use; 《文》 vain; futile; fruitless; wasteful; no good; unnecessary / 無駄な努力 ⇒ むだぼね / むだを省く avoid waste; 《文》 practice [use] economy / むだに uselessly; wastefully; 《use》 more than is necessary; 〈効なく〉 in vain; to no purpose / むだにする waste; spoil; throw *sth* away [down the drain] / むだにしない make good use 《of》; make the most 《of》 / むだになる come to nothing [《文》 naught]; be wasted

---

大してむずかしいことではない。There's nothing (much) to it. / 議論はむずかしくなった。The discussion is getting rather complicated. / 彼の病気はむずかしい。His case is serious.

むずびつく この3連勝が結局優勝に結びついた。These three consecutive victories resulted in their winning the championship [pennant].

むすぶ 彼は口をぎゅっと結んでいた。His mouth was shut tight.

むせきにん あの男は無責任だ。He has no sense of responsibility.

むせぶ 彼女は涙にむせびつつ物語った。She told her story with tears in her voice.

むせる 茶を飲んでむせた。His tea choked him. | His tea went down the wrong way. / 慣れないタバコにむせた。He coughed from smoking because he was not used to it.

むせんでんしん F局は遭難船から救助を求める無線電信を接受した。The F Station picked up wireless calls for help from a wrecked ship.

むそう 20年前にだれがこんなこ

むだあし 無駄足 ¶むだ足する go on a fool's [wasted] errand; pay sb a visit [visit sb] to no purpose.
むだい¹ 無代 ⇒ むりょう¹. 文例⇩
むだい² 無題 ¶無題の titleless; without a title. 文例⇩
むたいざいさん 無体財産 intangible [incorporeal] property.
むだぐち 無駄口 idle talk ¶むだ口をたたく say useless [pointless] things.
むだげ 無駄毛 hair growing where it is not wanted.
むだじに 無駄死に useless death ¶むだ死にする die in vain (to no purpose).
むだだま 無駄弾 a wasted shot [bullet].
むだづかい 無駄遣い ¶むだ遣いする waste [throw away, fritter away] (one's) money 《on》. 文例⇩
むだばなし 無駄話 (an) idle [empty] talk; gossip; tittle-tattle; chitchat ¶むだ話をする gossip; engage in idle talk; tittle-tattle.
むだぼね 無駄骨 wasted effort; a fruitless [《文》 vain] effort; waste of labor [effort]; lost labor ¶むだ骨を折る make vain [futile] efforts; exert oneself to no purpose; waste time and labor.
むだめし 無駄飯 ¶むだ飯を食う《文》 eat idle bread; be good for nothing.
むだん 無断 ¶無断で〈予告せずに〉 without (previous) notice; without warning; 〈許可なく〉 without leave [permission] / 人の物を無断で使う make free use of sb's possessions / 無断居住者 a squatter / 無断欠勤 absence without leave [(due) notice] / 無断借用する borrow sth (without the owner's permission). 文例⇩
むたんぽ 無担保 ¶無担保の unsecured; without collateral [security] / 無担保で金を貸す grant sb a loan without collateral / 無担保貸付金 an unsecured loan.
むち¹ 鞭 a whip; a rod; a cane (とう・竹などの); a lash (ひもの) ¶むちの音 the crack [whistle] of a whip / 馬に軽くむちを当てる touch one's horse with the whip / むちで打つ ⇒ むちうつ.
むち² 無知 ignorance; illiteracy (文盲) ¶無知な ignorant; unthinking and uninformed; ill-informed; stupid; silly / 無知もうまいの《文》 unenlightened / 《文》 benighted.
むち³ 無恥 ⇒ こうがん².
むちうち 鞭打ち whipping; lashing; flogging

むちうちしょう (suffer from) whiplash; (get) a whiplash injury.
むちうつ 鞭打つ whip; lash; flog;《文》 use the rod (on); 〈激励する〉 spur [urge] sb on 《to sth》; encourage 《sb to do》 ¶馬にむちを打つ whip one's horse (on).
むちつじょ 無秩序 disorder; chaos; confusion ¶無秩序な disordered; confused; chaotic; lawless.
むちゃ ¶むちゃな〈途方もない〉 absurd; unreasonable; preposterous; 〈軽率な〉 rash; 〈無鉄砲な〉 reckless; 〈過度の〉 excessive;《文》 immoderate / むちゃに〈途方もなく〉 absurdly; unreasonably; 〈軽率に〉 rashly; 〈無鉄砲に〉 recklessly; 〈過度に〉 excessively;《文》 immoderately / むちゃを言う be unreasonable; talk rubbish [nonsense].
むちゃくちゃ ¶むちゃくちゃな〈混乱した〉 confused; mixed-up; jumbled; topsy-turvy; 〈訳の分からない〉 unreasonable; absurd; 〈めちゃみな〉 blind; mad / むちゃくちゃに〈混乱して〉 in disorder; pell-mell; 〈非常に〉 awfully; extremely; very; 〈むやみに〉 recklessly; blindly;《文》 to excess;《口語》 like mad / むちゃくちゃにする make a mess [hash] of; spoil; ruin.
むちゃくりくひこう 無着陸飛行 ¶無着陸飛行を行なう make a nonstop flight (to); fly nonstop (to).
むちゅう 夢中 ¶夢中で as if in a dream;《文》 like one in a delirium [dream]; without knowing what one is doing; 〈熱狂して〉 frantically; madly; wildly / 夢中になる〈我を忘れる〉 forget oneself; be beside oneself《with anger》; go [fall] into raptures 《over sth》; go [be thrown] into ecstasies; 〈魅せられる〉 be fascinated [carried away] 《by》; 〈熱中する〉 be engrossed [absorbed] 《in》; be keen 《on》; be crazy 《about, over》; be [go] wild 《about, over》/ 歌手に夢中になる be crazy about a singer / 恋に夢中になる be deeply [head over heels] in love 《with》; be off one's head 《about a girl》/〈感激の余り〉 夢中になってしゃべる《口語》 rave [enthuse] 《over sth》.
むちゅうしんごう 霧中信号《海》 a fog signal.
むちん 無賃 ¶無賃で free; free of charge / 無賃乗車する ride free (of charge); have a free ride; 〈ただ乗り〉 steal a ride 《on a train》.
むつう 無痛 ¶無痛の painless; free from pain / 無痛分娩 painless childbirth [delivery] / 無痛性の《医》 indolent (tumors).
むつかしい 難しい ⇒ むずかしい.

とを夢想し得たであろうか。Who could have dreamed of such a thing twenty years ago?
むだ 時間がむだになる。It will be a waste of time. / 行ってもむだだ。It is no use [good] going. / これ以上待っていてもむだだ。There is no point in waiting any longer. / 彼に親切を尽くしてもむだだ。Kindness is lost [thrown away] on him. / 彼の文章は言葉にむだがない。There is no padding in his writing. / むだなければ不足なし。Waste not, want not.
むだい¹ カタログ無代進呈。《広告》 Catalogues (are) sent free (on request).
むだい² (絵画などの題の代わりに) 無題。No title. | Subject Unknown.
むだづかい 子供にむだ遣いをさせてはいけない。Children must be

taught not to waste money.
むだん 無断立ち入りを禁ず。《掲示》 No trespassing. | No (unauthorized) entry. / 無断転載を禁ずる。All rights reserved.
むちゅう 僕は初めての演説だったので夢中でしゃべった。As it was my maiden speech, I spoke as if I was in a daze. / 彼は仕事に夢中になっている。He is absorbed in his work. / 彼は金もう

むつき ⇨ おしめ.
むっくと ⇨ むっくり.
むっくり ¶むっくり起き上がる sit up abruptly.
むつごと 睦言 lovers' talk; soft words of love; 《whisper》sweet nothings.
ムッシュー 《フランス語》monsieur (pl. messieurs)(略: M., pl. Messrs., MM.).
むっちり ¶むっちりした plump.
むっつ 六つ six ⇨ ろく[1].
むっつり ¶むっつりした moody;《文》taciturn; sullen; sulky; severe-looking; sour; glum / むっつりと sullenly; surlily / むっつり屋 an uncommunicative [《文》a taciturn] person.
むっと ¶むっとする〈憤る〉be offended 《at, by, over, with》; take offense 《at》; get angry 《with, at》; be annoyed [vexed]《about, at, with》;《口語》be miffed《at, by, with》;〈部屋などが〉be stuffy; be close; be stifling / むっとして angrily; with an angry look; huffily; in a huff;《口語》in a miff / むっとするような匂い a fusty smell; a stale odor. 文例⇩
むつまじい 睦まじい〈和合した〉harmonious 《life》; happy《people》;〈親密な〉《文》intimate; friendly;〈情愛細やかな〉affectionate ¶むつまじく harmoniously; in peace [harmony]; on friendly terms; affectionately / むつまじく暮す live happily together. 文例⇩
むていけい 無定形 ¶無定形の formless; shapeless; amorphous / 無定形炭素 amorphous carbon.
むていけん 無定見 lack of fixed principle [policy] ¶無定見な without any fixed principle;《文》inconstant;《文》vacillating; wavering; fickle.
むていこう 無抵抗 nonresistance; passive obedience ¶無抵抗で without resistance; without making [offering] any resistance / 無抵抗主義 the principle of nonresistance.
むてかつりゅう 無手勝流 aiming at securing a victory without fighting.
むてき[1] 無敵 ¶無敵の《文》matchless;《文》unrivaled;《文》unequaled;《文》invincible / 無敵の勇者 a man of matchless valor /(スペインの)無敵艦隊『史』the Invincible Armada.
むてき[2] 霧笛 a foghorn.
むてっぽう ¶むてっぽうな rash; reckless; thoughtless; headlong; foolhardy / むてっぽうな男 a reckless fellow; a daredevil / むてっぽうなことをする act thoughtlessly [rashly] / むてっぽうに rashly; recklessly; thoughtlessly.

むでん 無電 radio;《英》wireless ⇨ むせん[2] ¶無電を打つ send a message by radio; send a radio message / 無電で by radio [wireless]. 文例⇩
むどう 無道 ¶無道な unreasonable; outrageous.
むとう 無灯 ¶無灯の[で]《(ride a bicycle)》without a light.
むとうせい 無統制 ¶無統制の uncontrolled; noncontrolled.
むとうひょう 無投票 ¶無投票で without voting [a vote].
むどき 無土器『考古』¶無土器時代 the Aceramic [Non-pottery] Age / 無土器文化 aceramic [non-pottery] culture.
むどく 無毒 ¶無毒の nonpoisonous; innocuous; nontoxic.
むとくてん 無得点 ¶無得点の scoreless;『野球』runless / 無得点に終わらせる shut out (the opposing team);《口語》whitewash (one's opponents). 文例⇩
むとどけ 無届け ¶無届けの[で] without notice / 無届け集会 a meeting held without previous notice to the authorities [without notifying the authorities beforehand].
むとんちゃく 無頓着 indifference; nonchalance ¶むとんちゃくである be indifferent 《to》; be unconcerned 《about》; be nonchalant; be careless 《about, of》. 文例⇩
むないた 胸板 ¶胸板を撃ち抜かれる be shot through the chest.
むなぎ 棟木 a ridgepole; a rooftree.
むなくそ 胸糞 ¶胸くその悪い disgusting; revolting; sickening. 文例⇩
むなぐら 胸倉 ¶胸倉をとる seize sb by the collar [by the lapels].
むなぐるしい 胸苦しい feel a tightness in the chest.
むなげ 胸毛 hair on the chest;〈鳥の〉breast down ¶胸毛の生えた男 a man with a hairy chest [with hair on his chest].
むなさき 胸先〈みぞおち〉the pit of the stomach;〈胸部〉the breast.
むなさわぎ 胸騒ぎ〈不安〉uneasiness; (a) vague apprehension;〈虫の知らせ〉(a) premonition;《文》a presentiment ¶胸騒ぎがする feel uneasy (without any definite cause); have a presentiment.
むなざんよう 胸算用 mental arithmetic [calculation] ¶胸算用をする〈暗算をする〉calculate mentally; do (one's) sums in one's head;〈見積もる〉estimate;〈期待する〉expect.
むなしい 空しい〈空虚な〉empty; vacant;

けに夢中だ. He is interested only in moneymaking. / 彼は麻雀に夢中になっている. He is mad about mah-jongg. / 彼は試験期間前になって夢中で勉強した. He worked feverishly just before the examination.
むっと 彼の言葉に僕はむっとした. I was offended by what he said. / 彼はむっとしたような顔を

していた. He looked huffy.
むつまじい どうりものか 2 人の仲はむつまじく行かない. Somehow they do not get on well together. ¶ Things are not going very well between them.
むでん 我々はロンドンには容易に無電連絡ができた. We were within easy radio communication of London.

むとくてん 8 回まで無得点に抑えた. We held them runless for eight innings.
むとんちゃく 彼は身なりにむとんちゃくだ. He is careless about his personal appearance. ¶ He does not care how he looks.
むなくそ あの男のおべんちゃらを聞くと胸くそが悪くなる. His flattery sickens me.

むなつきはっちょう 胸突き八丁 the steepest part of a mountain path.

むねもと 胸元 ⇨ むなさき.

むに 無二 ¶無二の unrivaled; unequaled; unparalleled; unique;《文》peerless;《文》matchless / 無二の親友 one's best friend / 無二無三 ⇨ しゃにむに.

ムニエル《料理》《フランス語》《turbot》meunière.

むにゃむにゃ ¶むにゃむにゃ言う mumble.

むにょうしょう 無尿症《医》anuria.

むにんしょだいじん 無任所大臣 a Minister (of State) without portfolio.

むね[1] 旨〈趣意〉《文》effect;《文》purport;〈主目的〉an aim; the main purpose;〈主義〉a principle;〈命令〉a command; an order ¶旨を奉じて in obedience to sb's orders / 旨を書き送る write to sb (to the effect that... / …旨とする make it a principle to do; aim at doing. 文例⇩

むね[2] 胸 the breast; the chest;〈ふところ〉the bosom;〈乳房〉the breasts;〈心〉one's heart; one's mind ★ the chest は心臓や肺を囲む胸部全体を指す. the breast は主に大胸筋の張り出したあたりを指し, 女性の場合は「乳房」を意味する. 女性の「乳房」を the breasts とおおやけに言うのを避けたいとき bosom とか bust が用いられる ¶胸が悪くなる feel sick《米》at the stomach; feel nausea [nauseated] / 胸が悪くなるようなにおい a disgusting smell / 胸が焼ける have heartburn / 胸がきゅっとなる feel one's heart tighten《with joy》/ 胸が苦しい have a tightness in one's chest / 胸が痛い have a pain in one's chest / 胸が弱い have a weak chest / 胸のすくようなたんかを切る get sth off one's chest in no uncertain terms / 胸のぺちゃんこな flat-chested / 豊かな胸をした女性 a full-bosomed [full-breasted, bosomy] woman / 胸を張る throw out one's chest / 胸をそらす straighten oneself up / 胸をなで下ろす feel relieved / 胸を病む suffer from a disease of the chest; have chest trouble / 胸を打つ be touching / 胸を痛める worry [trouble] oneself《about》; be worried [anxious]《about》/ 胸を貸す give sb a workout / 胸をときめかせる one's heart beats faster [flutters]《with anticipation》/ 胸に描く picture sth (to oneself) / 胸に秘める keep sth to oneself / 胸に浮かぶ occur to one [one's mind]; come across one's mind / 胸にこたえる go to one's heart; come home to one / 胸に一物ある ⇨ いちもつ / 胸でテープを切る breast the tape / 胸もあらわに bare-breasted. 文例⇩

むね[3] 棟 the ridge《of a roof》 ¶2棟 two houses [buildings].

むねあげ 棟上げ ¶棟上げをする raise [set up] the framework (of a house) / 棟上げ式 a framework-raising ceremony.

むねあて 胸当て〈鎧(よろい)の〉a breastplate;《野球》a chest protector.

むねつ 無熱 ¶無熱の《医》nonfebrile; unfeverish; having no fever.

むねやけ 胸焼け heartburn ¶胸焼けがする have heartburn. 文例⇩

むねん 無念〈残念〉regret;〈憤怒〉resentment;〈くやしさ〉mortification ¶無念を晴らす pay (off) [settle] old scores《with sb》; revenge oneself《on》/ 無念に思う regret; resent; be vexed (at) [mortified (by)].

むねんむそう 無念無想 ¶無念無想になる rid oneself of all worldly thoughts; attain (a) perfect serenity of mind.

むのう 無能 lack of ability; incompetence ¶無能な incompetent; incapable; inefficient; lacking in ability [efficiency].

むのうりょく 無能力 incompetence ⇨ むのう ¶無能力者 an incompetent (person);〈法律上の〉a person without (legal) capacity.

むはい(とう) 無配(当) ¶無配当の without dividend / 無配(当)株 a non-dividend-payer.

むひ 無比 ¶無比の matchless;《文》peerless; unparalleled; without a parallel; unequaled; unsurpassed; unrivaled; unique / 世界無比である be unparalleled [have no equal] in the world. 文例⇩

むひはん 無批判 ¶無批判な unquestioning; uncritical; indiscriminate / 無批判に unquestioningly; uncritically; indiscriminately.

むひょう[1] 無氷 ¶無氷の ice-free; unfrozen /（南極海などの）無氷海面 the open sea.

むひょう[2] 霧氷 rime; hoarfrost.

むびょう 無病 ¶無病の healthy; sound;《be》well / 無病息災である be in sound [good] health; be hale and hearty (老人が).

むひょうじょう 無表情 absence [lack] of ex-

むなしい 彼の努力もむなしかった. His efforts bore no fruit.

むね[1] その旨を先方へ電話で申しましょう. I'll telephone them to that effect. / 文は簡潔を旨とせよ. In writing you should aim at brevity.

むね[2] 胸を張って, 腹を引け! Chest out! Stomach in! / 彼は若いころから胸が弱かった. His chest has been weak from his youth. / 娘の胸がふくらみ始めた. My daughter's breasts are beginning to develop. / 見ていて胸が悪くなった. The sight turned my stomach. /《米》The sight made me sick at the stomach. / 胸がどきどきした. My heart throbbed [beat fast]. / お前のことを考えると胸が痛む. My heart aches for you. / 悲しみに胸がふさがった. My heart was choked with sorrow. / 彼女の涙を見たときには胸が締め付けられるような思いだった. Her tears wrung my heart. / 胸が一杯で何も言えません. My heart is too full for words. / 言うだけ言ったら胸がすうっとした. I have said my say, and I feel as if a burden had been lifted off my mind. / 期待に胸が躍った. My heart leaped (up) [bounded] with expectation. / 悲しみのため胸も張り裂ける思いであった. My heart almost burst with grief.

むねやけ いつもそれを食べると胸焼けがするんだ. It always gives me heartburn.

むふう 無風 ¶無風の calm; windless / 無風状態 a (dead [flat]) calm; (a state of) windlessness / 無風水域 the (region of) calms / 無風帯〈亜熱帯の〉the horse [calm] latitudes.

むふんべつ 無分別 〈無思慮〉indiscretion; thoughtlessness; 〈軽率〉《文》imprudence; rashness ¶無分別な foolish; thoughtless; indiscreet; 《文》imprudent; reckless; senseless / 無分別な事をする do something rash.

むべ 宜 [文例⇩]

むへんか 無変化 changelessness; 〈単調〉monotony ¶無変化の unchanging; unchanged; 〈単調な〉monotonous.

むへん(さい) 無辺(際) infinity ¶無辺際の infinite; limitless; boundless.

むほう 無法 ¶無法な 〈不法な〉lawless; unlawful; unjust;《文》wrongful;〈不当な〉unjustifiable; unwarrantable;〈乱暴な〉outrageous / 無法なことをする act unlawfully / 無法者 an outrageous fellow; an outlaw;〈命知らず〉a desperado《pl. -(e)s》. [文例⇩]

むぼう[1] 無帽 ¶無帽で (go) hatless; with no hat on; with one's head bare [uncovered].

むぼう[2] 無謀 ¶無謀な〈軽率な〉rash; thoughtless;〈無鉄砲な〉reckless; foolishly bold;《文》imprudent / 無謀なことをする behave recklessly; take a leap in the dark / 無謀にも recklessly; rashly. [文例⇩]

むほうしゅう 無報酬 ¶無報酬で without pay [remuneration, recompense];〈無料で〉free of charge; for nothing; without a fee; gratis.

むほうしん 無方針 ¶無方針の planless; unprincipled / 無方針である have no definite [fixed] plan [policy].

むぼうび 無防備 ¶無防備の defenseless; unfortified / 無防備状態 (leave a town in) a defenseless state / 無防備都市 an open city.

むほん 謀反〈反乱〉(a) rebellion; a revolt; an insurrection;〈反逆〉treason ¶謀反する rebel [revolt, plot] 《against》; rise in rebellion [revolt]《against》/ 謀反を企てる [起こす] plot [raise] a rebellion / 謀反人 a rebel.

むま 夢魔 a nightmare ¶夢魔に襲われる have a nightmare; suffer from [be troubled by] a nightmare.

むみ 無味 ¶無味の tasteless / 無味乾燥な dry (as dust); insipid; flat; uninteresting; dull;《文》prosaic / 無味無臭無色の tasteless, odorless and colorless.

むめい[1] 無名 ¶無名の 〈名のない〉nameless; unnamed;〈世に知られない〉obscure; nameless; unknown;《文》unsung《pioneers》/ 無名骨[動脈]『解』the innominate bone [artery] / 無名作家 a nameless writer / 無名戦士の墓 the Tomb of the Unknown Soldier [〈英〉Warrior]. [文例⇩]

むめい[2] 無銘 ¶無銘の unsigned; nameless; bearing no (artist's) signature; without the maker's name.

むめんきょ 無免許 ¶無免許の unlicensed; without a license / 無免許で自動車を運転する drive a car without a license.

むもう 無毛 ¶無毛の hairless / 無毛症『医』atrichia; atrichosis.

むやみ 無闇 ¶むやみな〈軽率な〉rash; reckless; thoughtless;《文》imprudent; indiscreet;〈過度の〉《文》immoderate; excessive;《文》inordinate;〈不必要な〉needless; unnecessary;〈不当な〉unreasonable; undue;〈無差別の〉indiscriminate / むやみに〈軽率に〉rashly; recklessly; thoughtlessly; imprudently; indiscreetly;〈過度に〉《文》immoderately; excessively;《文》inordinately;〈不必要に〉more than is necessary; needlessly; unnecessarily;〈不当に〉unreasonably; unduly;〈無差別に〉indiscriminately;〈当てなしに〉at random; blindly / むやみにかわいがる dote on《a child》(blindly) / むやみに信じる believe《what people say》too readily; be credulous. [文例⇩]

むゆうびょう 夢遊病 sleepwalking; somnambulism / 夢遊病患者 a sleepwalker; a somnambulist.

むよう 無用 ¶無用の〈無益な〉useless;《文》of no use [avail];〈不必要な〉unnecessary; needless;〈用事のない〉without business / 無用の長物〈人〉a good-for-nothing;〈人・物〉deadwood;〈物〉a thing that is worse than useless; a white elephant《品物》/ 無用の心配 an idle fear / 無用の心配をする worry [trouble oneself] needlessly. [文例⇩]

むよく 無欲 ¶無欲な unselfish;《文》indifferent to gain; disinterested;《文》free from avarice.

むはい(とう) 同社は無配当のやむなきに至った. The company was forced to pass its dividend [to suspend dividends].

むひ 同地方の風景は全国無比の美しさである. The scenery of the district has no equal in the country.

むふんべつ 無分別にも彼は所持金を皆使ってしまった. He was thoughtless enough to spend all his money. / 君は無分別だよ. You ought to know better.

むべ 時は金なりという言葉はまことにむべなるかなと思わせる. It is aptly [truly] said that time is money.

むほう 彼は無法にも私をつえで打とうとした. He went so far as to strike at me with a stick.

むぼう 無謀なことは一切するな. Never take chances. | Look before you leap.

むめい 彼はまだ無名であった. He was still an unknown. / 当時無名の一青年であった戸田氏はこの小説を書いて一躍有名になった. Mr. Toda, then a youth without reputation, leaped into fame by writing that novel.

むやみ 私はむやみに人と約束はしない. I do not make rash promises. / いったん職業を決めたらむやみに変えてはいけない. You shouldn't lightly change your job once you have chosen it.

むよう 心配はご無用です. You need not worry. / 無用の者入るべからず.『掲示』No admittance

むら¹ 村 a village; 〈小村〉a hamlet ¶村境 the boundary between two villages / 村はずれ 〈on〉the outskirts of a village / 村人 villagers; village folk [people] / 村役場 a village office. 文例⇩

むら² 〈一様でないこと〉unevenness; lack of uniformity; 〈斑点〉patches; blotches; 〈不明瞭な所〉a blur ¶むらのある 〈一様でない〉uneven; irregular; lacking in uniformity; 〈斑点のある〉patched; spotty; 〈移り気な〉《文》capricious; fickle; fitful / むらのない even; uniform / むらのある[ない]性質 an uneven [even] temper / むらなく evenly; uniformly.

むらがる 群がる crowd; gather; 《文》throng 〈人などが〉; flock 〈鳥などが〉; swarm 〈虫などが〉; herd 〈獣などが〉 ¶群がって襲いかかる gang up on *sb*. 文例⇩

むらぎ むら気 a whim; 《文》(a) caprice ¶むら気な capricious; whimsical.

むらくも 叢雲 gathering clouds.

むらさき 紫 purple 〈赤味がかった〉; violet 〈青味がかった〉; amethyst ¶紫がかった purplish / 紫水晶 amethyst. 文例⇩

むらざと 村里 ⇨むら¹ ¶村里離れた out-of-the-way; remote.

むらさめ 村雨 a passing shower [rain].

むらす 蒸らす steam ¶飯を蒸らす steam boiled rice; allow boiled rice to settle.

むらすずめ 村雀 a flock of sparrows.

むらはちぶ 村八分 social [village] ostracism ¶村八分にされる be ostracized in *one's* village.

むらむら ¶…しようという気がむらむらと起こる have a sudden impulse to *do*; be seized with a desire to *do*; suddenly feel like *doing*; feel an irresistible temptation to *do*.

むり 無理 〈強制〉compulsion; 〈非条理〉unreasonableness; 〈過度〉excessiveness; 〈過労〉overwork; overstrain; (a) strain ¶むりな 〈不当〉unjust; unreasonable; 〈不自然な〉unnatural; 〈不可能な〉impossible; 〈過度の〉excessive; 《文》immoderate 《exercise》; 〈乱暴な〉violent; 〈強制的な〉compulsory; forcible; forced / むりのない reasonable; natural; justifiable; excusable; unstrained / むり(無体)に,

むりやりに 〈不当に〉unjustly; unreasonably; 〈強制的に〉compulsorily; forcibly; by force; 〈いや応なしに〉willy-nilly; against *sb's* will / むり(強〈ひ〉い)に…させる compel [force] *sb* to *do* / むりに引っ張る pull by force / むりに通る force *one's* way 《through》 / むりをする overwork [overstrain, force] *oneself*; attempt too much 〈the impossible〉; bite off more than one can chew / むり算段する strain *one's* credit; scrape together 《a sum of money》 / 無理式[方程式] 《数》an irrational expression [equation] / むり心中する force *sb* to die with *one* [to join *one* in suicide] / 無理数 《数》an irrational number; a surd / むり難題 an unreasonable [impossible] demand / むり難題を言う ask too much of *sb*; make an unreasonable demand of *sb*. 文例⇩

むりかい 無理解 lack of understanding [sympathy] ¶無理解な inconsiderate; unsympathetic.

むりし[そく] 無利子[息] ¶無利子の free of interest; bearing no interest / 無利子で without interest; interest-free.

むりょ 無慮 to the prodigious [vast] number of; no less than; as many as.

むりょう¹ 無料 free 《of charge》 ¶無料で free 《of charge》; for nothing; gratis; without a fee / 無料入場者 a free visitor / 無料奉仕 free service.

むりょう² 無量 ¶無量の infinite; 《文》inestimable; 《文》immeasurable.

むりょく 無力 〈力のないこと〉powerlessness; helplessness; incompetence 〈無能力〉; 〈病気のための〉《医》asthenia; debility; adynamia ¶無力な powerless; helpless; incompetent.

むるい 無類 ⇨むに.

むれ 群れ a group; 〈人の〉a crowd; a throng; a mob 〈暴徒〉; 〈獣の〉a herd 〈牛馬など〉; a flock 〈羊〉; a pack 〈おおかみ・猟犬など〉; 〈鳥の〉a flock; a bevy 〈小鳥〉; 〈魚の〉a school; a shoal; 〈虫の〉a swarm; 〈無生物の〉a cluster 〈of stars〉 ¶群れをなす form groups; 群れをなして in crowds [swarms, shoals]. 文例⇩

むれる¹ 群れる ⇨むらがる.

むれる² 蒸れる get[grow, 《文》become] musty; 〈飯などが〉be steamed 〈to the right degree〉;

---

except on business. | Private. | 開放無用.〖掲示〗Please close the door.

むら¹ 村中の人々がそれを見物に出て来た。The whole village turned out to see it.

むら² 彼は仕事にむらがある。He is an unsteady [uneven] worker.

むらがる はちが木の枝に群がっていた。The branch of the tree swarmed with bees. | Bees were swarming on the branch of the tree. | 広場には人が群がっていた。The public square was crowded with people.

むらさき 彼はくちびるが紫色になっていた。His lips had lost all their color.

むり この仕事はむりに押し付けられたのだ。The work has been forced on me. / むりするなよ。Take it easy. | Don't take chances. / 彼はむりをして病気になった。He worked himself sick. | He became ill from overwork. / その仕事は僕にはむりだ。I am not equal [up] to the task. / その年ごろではむりな責任を子供に負わせてはいけない。You should not saddle a child with responsibilities beyond his years. / むりなことでなければ, 何でもしてあげますよ。I will do anything that you ask me, within reason. / 君がそう考えるのもむりはない。It is natural for you to [that you should] think so. / 彼が知らなかったのもむりはない。It is no wonder [No wonder] (that) he did not know. / 彼が怒るのもむりはない。He has every [good] reason to be angry. / その計画が失敗したのも, そもそもむりからぬことだった。It was in the nature of things that the project failed. / それはむりな注文だ. It is asking [expecting] too much. / それはむり押しというものだ. That's forcing things. / どんなむり算段をしてもその本は買うつもりだ. I will go to any length(s)

〈室内などが〉 get [《文》become] (hot and) stuffy.

むろ 室 〈温室〉a greenhouse; a hothouse; 〈乾燥室〉a drying room; 〈穴蔵〉a cellar.

むろん 無論 ⇨ もちろん.

むんず ¶むんずと肩を押える seize *sb* by the shoulder with a powerful grip / 首根っこをむんずとつかまえる grab *sb* by the scruff of the neck / むんずと組みつく grapple with *sb* (with all *one*'s might).

むんむん ¶むんむんする 〈暑くて〉be sultry; 〈人いきれで〉be stuffy. 文例⇩

め

め¹ 目 an eye; *one*'s [the] eyes; 〈視力〉sight; eyesight;〈注目〉notice, attention;〈見地〉a point of view;〈眼識〉judgment;(have) an eye (for);〈網の〉a mesh;〈編物の〉a stitch;〈碁の盤の〉a point (盤の上で囲んでできる);〈さいころの〉a pip; a spot;〈のこぎりの〉a tooth (*pl.* teeth);〈織物の〉a texture;〈木目〉grain ¶台風の目 the eye of a typhoon / 目が痛い〈両目が〉have sore eyes; *one*'s eyes are sore;〈片目が〉have a sore eye; *one*'s (left) eye hurts [is sore] / 目が利く have an [a good, a sure] eye (for); be a good judge (of) / 目が利かない have no eye (for); be a poor judge (of) / 目がくらむ be dazzled (by the light) / 欲に目がくらむ be blinded by greed《文》with avarice] / 目が肥えている have a critical [an expert] eye (for); be a connoisseur (of) / 目がさえる become wide awake / 目が覚める wake up;《文》awake;《文》become awake;《文》be awakened;〈比喩的に〉come [be brought] to *one*'s senses;《文》awake from an illusion / 目がすわって with set [fixed] eyes / 目が高い《文》discerning; appreciative (spectators); observant (critics) / 目がつぶれる[見えなくなる] go [《文》become] blind; lose *one*'s (eye-)sight / …に目がない have a weakness [passion] for 〈wine〉; have an irresistible passion for 〈fishing〉;《口語》be awfully fond of 〈sweets〉 / 目が早い sharp-sighted / 目が回る be [feel] dizzy; get giddy; be stunned (打たれて) /〈事が主語〉make *one*'s head spin / 目が回るほど忙しい be in a whirl of business / 目がよい have good sight [eyes] / 目が弱い have weak eyes / 目が悪い 〈弱視である〉have poor (eye)sight;〈眼病にかかっている〉have an eye disease; have eye trouble.

¶目の 〖解〗ocular (movements); optic (nerves) / 目の粗い〈布が〉《文》(cloth) of loose texture; rough; coarse; rough-[loose-] textured / 目の粗い[細かい]網 a large-[small-] mesh net / 目の色 eye color; the color of *one*'s eyes / 目の色を変えて 〈興奮して〉excitedly;〈怒って〉with an angry [a furious] look / 目の上のこぶ《口語》a thorn in *one*'s flesh / 目の敵にする loathe the very sight (of);《文》bear constant enmity [spite] (against); hate / 目の薬 a sight for sore eyes / 私の目の黒いうちは while [as long as] I live; so long as I am alive / 目の子算〈目で計ること〉measuring with *one*'s eye;〈大ざっぱな見当〉a rule of thumb / 目の覚めるような美人 a strikingly beautiful woman /《文》a woman of dazzling beauty / 目の下1尺のこい a carp a foot long from eye to tail / 目の高さに on a level with *one*'s eyes; (hold *sth*) at eye level / 目の玉 an eyeball / 目の玉の飛び出るような値段 a fantastically [ludicrously] high price; an exorbitant [a prohibitive] price / 目の詰んだ fine-[close-]textured (cloth); fine-toothed (combs) / 目の毒である be tempting to *one* / 目の届く限り as far as *one* [the eye] can see; as far as the eye [sight] can reach / 目の届く[届かない]ところに within [beyond] eyeshot / 目の細い narrow-eyed / 目の前 before *one*'s (very) eyes; (right) in front of *one*; under *one*'s nose; in *one*'s presence.

¶目を上げる raise *one*'s eyes《from *one*'s newspaper》; look up《from *one*'s sewing》/ 目

---

to buy the book. / むりが通れば道理が引っ込む. Where might is master, justice is servant.

むりょう¹ 手荷物はどれだけまで無料ですか. How much baggage is free? / お買上げ品は無料で配達いたします. Articles bought here will be delivered free of charge. / 入場無料. Admission free. / 7歳未満は大人同伴に限って無料. 〖掲示〗Children under seven free if accompanied by an adult.

むれ とらは群れを作らない. Tigers do not herd together.

むんむん 室内はむんむんしていた. It was stuffy in the room. | The room was stuffy.

め¹ 彼女の目は喜びに輝いた. Her eyes sparkled with joy. / それに気がつかないなんて, 君の目は一体どこについているんだい. You didn't notice it? Where are your eyes? / 長い目で見ていてくれ. Time will tell [show]. / 目から鼻へ抜けるような男だ. He is as sharp as a needle. / 彼の眼から見ると私などはほんの赤ん坊に過ぎない. I am a mere baby in his eyes. / 彼は古美術を見る目がある. He has an eye for old works of art. / あの人は本当に人を見る目がある. He is a good [fine] judge of character. / 泣いたので目が赤くなっていた. Her eyes were red from crying. / ウイスキーを5杯やったら, 目がすわってきた. After the fifth whisky his eyes began to assume a fixed expression. / にわかに彼の目がすわってきた. His eyes suddenly took on a fixed look. / 彼は片方の目[右の目]が見えない. He is blind in one eye [in the right eye]. | He has lost the sight of one [of his right] eye. / 彼女は目が見えなくなっていた. She had lost her sight. | Her (eye)sight was gone. / 彼は驚いて目を丸くして立っていた. He stood amazed, (with) his eyes as round as saucers. / 目が暗がりに慣れるまで

を痛める harm *one's* eyes ; 《文》 impair *one's* vision [eyesight] / 目を疑う cannot believe *one's* (own) eyes / 目を輝かして見る be enthralled by (the sight of) ; sparkle 《at》 / 目をかける 〈親切にする〉 be kind 《to》; take a kindly interest 《in》; 〈恩恵を与える〉 《文》 favor / 目を配る keep a watchful eye 《on》; be watchful ; be alert ; be observant ; look about / 八方に目を配る keep (both) *one's* eyes open / 目を凝らす strain *one's* eyes 《to see》; peer 《into dark corners》; look closely / 目を避ける avoid *sb's* eyes [《文》 observation] / 目を覚ます ⇨ 目が覚める / 目を皿のようにして with (*one's*) eyes like saucers ; with saucer eyes ; with *one's* eyes wide open / 目を白黒させる ⇨ しろくろ / 目を据えて with *one's* eyes set ; gazing fixedly 《at》 / 目を背ける[そらす] turn *one's* eyes [gaze] away [off] ; 《文》 avert [withdraw] *one's* eyes 《from》; look away / 目を楽しませる 〈人が主語〉 feast *one's* eyes 《on》; 〈物が主語〉 be a delight to the eye / 目をつける 〈注目する〉 set [fasten] *one's* eyes 《on》; have [keep] an [*one's*] eye 《on》 / 目をつぶる 〈閉じる〉 close [shut] *one's* eyes ; 〈死ぬ〉 《文》 breathe *one's* last ; 〈見て見ぬふりをする〉 shut *one's* eyes 《to》; wink [connive] 《at》; turn a blind eye 《to》 / 目を通す look [go] over [through] 《the paper》; run (*one's* eyes) through 《a book》; cast *one's* eyes over 《the ads》 / 目を盗んで unobserved ; stealthily ; in secret / 目を離す look aside [away] ; take *one's* eyes off 《a child》; let *sb* [*sth*] out of *one's* sight / 目を光らしている keep a watchful eye on [aimed at] *sb* / 目を引く draw [attract] *sb's* attention; attract notice ; catch the eyes of 《the world》 / 目を引くポスター an eye-catching poster / 目を開かれる *one's* eyes are opened 《to the truth》 / 目を伏せる lower [drop, 《文》 cast down] *one's* eyes / 目を細くして子供を見る look lovingly [fondly] at a child / 目を細める narrow *one's* eyes / 目を丸くして驚く stare [open *one's* eyes wide] in wonder ; 《口語》 be popeyed ; 《口語》 *one's* eyes (almost) pop out with astonishment [surprise] / 目を回す faint ; 《文》 swoon ; be stunned (打たれて) / 目を見張って with *one's* eyes wide open ; wide-eyed ; with wide eyes / 目をむく stare (*one's* eyes out) ; pop *one's* eyes / 目を向ける turn [《文》 direct] *one's* eyes [attention] 《to》; 《文》 bring *one's* gaze to bear 《on》 / 目をやる look 《toward》.

¶ひどい[苦しい]目にあう have a bitter experience ; go through the mill ; have a hard time (of it) / 目に余る be too much for *one* ; cannot be overlooked ; be unpardonable ; be intolerable / 目に入れても痛くない be the apple of *one's* eye ; think the sun shines out of *sb's* eyes / 目につく 〈目立つ〉 be conspicuous ; be outstanding ; attract *one's* attention [notice] / 目にとまる 〈人が主語〉 catch sight of ; notice ; see ; 〈物が主語〉 attract *one's* attention ; catch *one's* fancy / 目に残る 《文》 be engraved on *one's* memory / 我々現代人の目には to our modern eyes / 目には目を, 歯には歯を 《give》 an eye for an eye (, a tooth for a tooth) / (景色などが)目に入ってくる come into view ; come in sight / 目に触れる attract [catch] *one's* attention ; catch [《文》 meet] *one's* eye ; 《文》 come to *one's* attention [notice] / 目に見えて 《文》 markedly ; visibly ; 《文》 perceptibly / 目に見えない invisible ; 《文》 imperceptible / 目にもとまらぬ早業で at lightning speed; quicker than the eye can follow / 目に悪い be bad for [《文》 injurious to] *one's* eyes.

¶目で合図する wink at *sb* / 疑いの目で見る eye [look at] *sb* with suspicion / うらやましそうな目で見る look at *sth* enviously ; 《文》 cast envious eyes on *sth* / 自分の目で見る see *sth* with *one's* own eyes / 目で礼を言う thank *sb* with *one's* eyes.

¶目から鼻へ抜けるような very smart [clever] ; highly intelligent / 日本人の目から見れば in Japanese eyes ; from a Japanese point of view / 目と鼻の先である be no distance (at all) ; be within a stone's throw / 目も当てられない惨状である be too horrible [cruel] to look at / 目もあやな very colorful ; flamboyant ; ablaze with color / 目もくれない take no notice 《of》; 《文》 give no heed [regard] 《to》; pay no attention 《to》. [文例⇩] (前ページより)

め² 芽 〈つぼみ〉 a bud ; 〈芽枝〉 a sprout ; a spear (長い) ; 〈幼芽〉 a germ ¶芽が出る bud ; sprout / 芽のうちに摘む nip 《a plot》 in the bud / 芽を出す put out [《文》 forth] buds [shoots] ; sprout ; 〈木が〉 《文》 burgeon ; come [burst] into leaf / 芽を吹く 《trees》 break into leaf. [文例⇩]

め- 雌… female ; she- ¶雌牛 a cow / 雌鹿 a doe / 雌花 a female [pistillate] flower / 雌やぎ a she-goat.

-め …目 ¶3つ目の横町 the third turning / 上京後4年目に four years after *one* came [after coming] up to Tokyo / ちいさめの smallish ; 《a suitcase》 on the small side. [文例⇩]

めあき 目明き a person [《文》 one] who can

彼はその場に立っていた. He stood still until his eyes got used to the darkness. / 彼女は毛皮となると目がない. Furs are her passion. / 米国がこの事件をどう処理するかに世界の目が注がれている. The eyes of the world are fastened on the United States to see how she will settle this affair. / 横っ面を張られて目から火花が飛んだ. He gave me a slap across the face that sent flashes of light across my eyes. / 目のつけどころがいい[悪い]. His aim is right [wrong]. / 目のやり場がなかった. I didn't know where to look. / 目の前で起こっている事を君は知らないのか. Don't you know what is going on under your very nose? / 彼のごうまんぶりが目に余るので懲らしめてやった. I couldn't stand his arrogance any longer, so I gave him what was coming to him. / 一面の荒野で目に映るものは雲と起伏する丘だけだった. It was a vast wilderness and nothing greeted our eyes but clouds and undulating downs. / おれはこれまでいろんな目に会ってきた. I've been through a lot up to now. / 目に物見せてやるぞ. You'll have to pay for this. | I'll show you

めあたらしい 目新しい novel; new; original ¶目新しい物 a novelty.

めあて 目当て an aim; 《文》an end; 《文》an object; a view ¶目当てにする aim (at) / …を目当てに《文》for…; with a view to doing; with the view of doing 《便りに》with…as a guide; with…in mind (心に描いて) / (相撲の)お目当ての一番 today's feature bout / 金を目当てに結婚する marry (sb) for (his) money / 何の目当てもなしに without (any definite) aim; aimlessly.

めあわせる 娶わせる marry 《one's daughter》 to 《a doctor》; 《文》give 《one's daughter》 in marriage to 《sb's son》.

めい[1] 命 〈命令〉an order; a command; 〈指図〉instructions; 〈生命〉⇒ せいめい[1]; 〈運命〉《文》one's destiny; 《文》one's fate ¶…の命により by order of 《the authorities》. 文例⇩

めい[2] 明 〈眼識〉《文》discernment; 《have》an eye (for) ¶人を見るの明がある be a good judge of (people's) character.

めい[3] 姪 a niece.

めい[4] 銘 an inscription; an epitaph (墓碑銘); 〈刀剣などの〉a signature; 〈名称〉a name; 〈標語〉a motto (pl. -(e)s) ¶銘を刻む[打つ, 入れる] engrave [《文》inscribe] one's signature [name] (on, in); sign / 日本製と銘打った品 articles marked [carrying the legend] 'Made in Japan'.

めい- 名… noted; great; celebrated; famous ¶名投手 an excellent pitcher / 名判決 a judicious decision / 名判事 an able [a wise] judge.

-めい …名 ¶20名 twenty people 《文》persons].

めいあん[1] 名案 a good idea [plan].

めいあん[2] 明暗 light and shade [darkness] ¶人生の明暗両面 the bright and dark sides of life / 明暗法 [美術] shading; chiaroscuro / 明暗を分ける decide the issue. 文例⇩

めいい 名医 《文》a skilled physician; a great doctor; 〈有名な医者〉a well-known [celebrated] doctor.

めいうん 命運 one's fate; one's doom (悪い).

めいえん 名園 a famous [《文》noted] garden.

めいおうせい 冥王星 《天》Pluto.

めいか[1] 名家 〈名門〉a distinguished family; 〈名士〉an eminent person.

めいか[2] 名[銘]菓 〈名の通った菓子〉a cake of a well-known brand; 〈上等の菓子〉an excellent cake.

めいか[3] 名歌 a famous [celebrated] poem [tanka].

めいが 名画 〈絵画〉a famous [celebrated, great] picture; a masterpiece (of painting); 〈映画〉a famous [《文》noted] film; a film classic ¶ルーベンスの名画 a Rubens masterpiece; one of Rubens' masterpieces / 巨匠の手になる歴史的名画 old master paintings.

めいかい 明快 ¶明快な clear (wording); lucid (explanations); explicit (statements); 《文》articulate (pronunciation); clear-cut (argument); unequivocal (statements).

めいかく 明確 ¶明確な clear; precise; distinct; definite / 明確に《文》precisely; distinctly; definitely / 明確にする make sth clear; clear up; clarify; define; crystallize (the issues).

めいがら 銘柄 a brand; a description; 〈株券などの〉a name; an issue ¶銘柄(商)品 brand-name merchandise.

めいき[1] 名器 an excellent [a famous] article; 〈楽器〉an exquisite instrument.

めいき[2] 明記 ¶明記する write [state, put down, define] clearly; specify.

めいき[3] 銘記 ¶銘記する have sth branded on one's mind; bear [keep] sth in mind; remember ⇒ めいじる[2].

めいぎ 名義 〈名〉a name; 〈名目〉a pretext ¶名義だけの nominal; (a promotion) in name only / 名義上は in name; nominally / 名義の書き替え transfer (of the title) / 名義を書き替える transfer (the title to the bond) to sb / …の名義で under [in] the name of… / 他人の名義で under disguised ownership / 名義人 the holder (of a title deed).

めいきゅう 迷宮 a labyrinth; a maze ¶(事件が)迷宮入りになる 《文》become wrapped in mystery / 迷宮入りの殺人事件 an unsolved murder case [mystery].

めいきょく 名曲 〈優れた〉an excellent [exquisite] piece of music; 〈有名な〉a famous work (of 《classical, popular》 music). 文例⇩

めいきん 鳴禽 a songbird; a singing bird.

めいく 名句 〈文句〉a happy expression; a well-chosen [《文》nice, memorable] phrase [line]; a well-known saying [《文》adage]; 〈俳句〉a famous [《文》noted] haiku.

めいくん 名君 a wise ruler; a good king.

めいげつ 明[名]月 a bright moon; 〈満月〉a full moon ¶明月の夜 a bright moonlight [moonlit] night.

めいけん 名犬 a good [fine] dog.

(what's what). / 私は自分の目を疑った。I couldn't believe my eyes. / 目は口ほどに物を言い. The eye is as eloquent as the tongue. / 目は心の窓。The eye is the window of the soul. 《諺》

め[2] 木の芽が出始めた。The trees are beginning to bud. / 水仙はいつ芽が出ますか。When do daffodils come up? / この頃はさっぱり芽が出ない。I have had a long run of bad [ill] luck. / 事業がやっと芽を出しかけた。The business has begun to thrive [prosper] at last.

-め あの彗星(は)は7年目に現われる。That comet appears every seven years. / 彼の家は僕の家から3軒目です。He lives three doors away from me [from my house].

めあき 世の中には目明き千人, 盲千人。The world has as many fools as wise men. | Half the world's a bunch of fools.

めい[1] 彼は命旦夕(㌱)に迫った。His days are numbered.

めいあん エル・グレコほどに明暗をさまざまに使った画家はいない。No other painter has used dark and light in such a variety of ways as El Greco.

めいきょく この歌は名曲だ。This

めいげん¹ 名言 a wise [《文》golden] saying; a witty [《文》happy] remark; 《フランス語》a *bon mot* (pl. *bons mots*). 文例⇩

めいげん² 明言 (a) declaration; a definite statement ¶明言する declare; say [state] positively [definitely]; 《文》assert; 《文》aver. 文例⇩

めいこう 名工 a master-hand; an expert workman; a skillful craftsman [artisan].

めいコンビ 名コンビ 《form》an ideal combination; 《make》an excellent [a good] pair.

めいさい¹ 明細 details; particulars ¶明細な detailed; 《文》minute; full ¶明細に in detail; fully ¶明細書 a detailed [full] statement; 《shipping》specifications.

めいさい² 迷彩 camouflage; dazzle paint ¶迷彩を施す camouflage 《a ship》.

めいさく 名作 a masterpiece; a fine piece 《of art》 ¶子供のための名作物語 famous stories retold for children.

めいさつ¹ 名刹 a famous [noted] (Buddhist) temple.

めいさつ² 明察 《文》discernment; keen insight; clear judgment.

めいさん 名産 a well-known [《文》noted, special] (local) product; a specialty (of the district) ¶静岡名産わさび漬 *wasabizuke*, a specialty of Shizuoka. 文例⇩

めいざん 名山 a well-known [《文》noted, celebrated] mountain.

めいし¹ 名士 a prominent person [figure]; 《文》a personage; a celebrity; 《口語》a big name.

めいし² 名刺 a (visiting) card; 《米》a calling card; 〈業務用の〉a business card ¶名刺を交換する exchange cards / 名刺を出す give [present] one's card (to) / 社長にあてて名刺を受付に残して来る leave one's card for the president with the receptionist / 名刺判の名刺《フランス語》a *carte de visite* (pl. *cartes de visite*) / 名刺入れ[受け] a card case [tray]. 文例⇩

めいし³ 名詞《文法》a noun ¶普通[固有, 物質, 抽象]名詞 a common [a proper, a material, an abstract] noun / 名詞化 nominalization / 名詞化する nominalize / 名詞句[節] a noun phrase [clause].

めいじ¹ 明示 ¶明示する demonstrate clearly [plainly, expressly]; point out specifically; specify / 明示されない (as yet) unspecified.

めいじ² 明治 ¶明治維新 the Meiji Restoration / 明治時代 the Meiji era [period] / 明治天皇 the Emperor Meiji ⇒ てんのう 文例⇩

めいじつ 名実 ¶名実ともに both in name and reality / 名実相伴う[伴わない] be [be not] true to *its* name; live [do not live] up to *its* reputation. 文例⇩

めいしゃ 目医者 an eye doctor [specialist]; an ophthalmologist; an oculist.

めいしゅ¹ 名手 〈巧みな人〉a master-hand (at); an expert 《in, at, with》; 〈将棋などの手〉an excellent [a clever] move ¶ピアノの名手 an accomplished pianist.

めいしゅ² 銘酒 high-quality [choice] *sake*; *sake* of a special [famous] brand ¶畿内最高の銘酒 the best *sake* in Kinai.

めいしゅ³ 盟主 the leader of a confederation [confederacy, league].

めいしょ 名所 a famous place; sights (to see); a place of interest [《文》note] ¶名所を見物する see [《口語》do] the sights (of Kyoto); visit places of interest / 名所旧跡 scenic spots and places of historical interest. 文例⇩

めいしょう¹ 名匠 a master-hand; a master craftsman [artisan].

めいしょう² 名将 a famous [《文》an illustrious] general [admiral]; a great commander.

めいしょう³ 名称 a name; a title ¶名称をつける name; give a name 《to》.

めいしょう⁴ 名勝 a scenic spot; a place of scenic beauty; a famous sight.

めいじょう 名状 ¶名状し難い《文》indescribable;《文》surpassing description;《be》beyond description.

めいじる¹ 命じる 〈命令する〉order; command; tell *sb* to do;《文》bid *sb* do; direct;〈任命する〉appoint; name *sb* (to a post).

めいじる² 銘じる ¶心[肝]に銘じる bear [keep] *sth* in mind; take *(sb's advice)* to heart;《文》have *sth* branded [stamped, engraved] on *one's* mind.

めいしん 迷信 (a) superstition ¶くだらない迷信 an absurd superstition; an old wives' tale / 迷信を打破する do away with [《文》eradicate] a superstition / 迷信に取り付かれている superstition-ridden / 迷信的な superstitious / 迷信家 a superstitious person. 文例⇩

めいじん 名人 a (past) master; a master-hand (at); an expert (in) ¶名人の域に達する《文》attain [achieve] mastery (in); master (an art); become a master-hand (at) / 名人芸〈1回の行

---

song is beautifully composed.

めいげん¹ そいつは名言だ。That's well [aptly] said. | That's a well-phrased remark.

めいげん² 今のところいずれとも明言ができない。I cannot say anything definite [for certain] at present.

めいさん 広島の名産は「かき」です。Hiroshima is noted for its excellent oysters.

めいし¹ 何といっても君は名士なんだから。After all, you aren't exactly unknown.

めいし² お名刺を下さればお取り次ぎ致します。If you'll give me your card, I'll take it in.

めいじ² 明治は遠くなりにけり。Oh, for the good old days of Meiji!

めいじつ 彼は名実ともにこの運動のリーダーだ。He is the leader of the movement in fact as well as in name.

めいしょ 水戸の偕楽園は梅の名所です。Kairakuen in Mito is famous for its *ume* flowers.

めいしん この虫にまつわる迷信はたくさんある。There are a lot of superstitions attached to this insect.

めいじん あの刑事はすりをつかまえる名人だ。That detective is an expert at catching pickpockets in the act. / 彼の名人芸を見せてくれた。He gave a demonstration of his virtuosity. | He gave a virtuoso performance.

めいする それだけの成果があれ

めいすう

めいすう 命数 ⇨ じゅみょう.
めいする 瞑する 〖文例↓〗
めいせい 名声 fame;《文》 renown; (a) reputation; popularity 〈人望〉/ 名声が上がる rise in fame / 名声が落ちる lose one's reputation / 名声のある celebrated; popular;《文》 noted;《文》 renowned / 世界的に名声のある《文》《a man》 of worldwide fame; world-famous《scholars》/ 名声を博する win [gain] a reputation / 名声赫々たる《文》 a man with a great reputation [《文》 of great renown]. 〖文例↓〗
めいせき 明晰 ¶明晰な clear; distinct;《文》 lucid / 明晰な発音 clear [《文》 articulate] pronunciation / 頭脳明晰である be clear-headed; have a clear head; be bright.
めいそう¹ 名僧 a distinguished priest.
めいそう² 瞑想 meditation;《文》 contemplation ¶瞑想する meditate 《on》;《文》 contemplate / 瞑想にふける《文》 be lost in meditation / 瞑想的な《文》 meditative;《文》 contemplative / 瞑想生活《文》 a contemplative life.
めいそうしんけい 迷走神経《解》 a vagus [pneumogastric] nerve; a vagus 《pl. -gi》.
めいだい 命題《論》 a proposition; a statement ¶全称[特称, 単称]命題 a universal [particular, singular] proposition / 命題関数 a propositional [sentential] function.
めいちゃ 銘茶 tea of a well-known brand; choice tea.
めいちゅう 命中 ¶命中する hit《the mark》; tell / 命中しない miss《the mark》; go wide《of the mark》/ 命中弾 a hit; a telling shot. 〖文例↓〗
めいちょ 名著 〈有名な本〉 a famous [well-known] book [work] / 〈優れた本〉 a great [fine] book [work]; a masterpiece.
めいちょう 迷鳥 a stray bird; a strayer.
めいちょうし 名調子 〈雄弁〉《文》 eloquence; beautiful [rhythmic] flow of words ¶名調子で《文》 eloquently; in 《a》 flowing style.
めいてい 酩酊 ¶酩酊する《文》 be intoxicated; get [be] drunk / 酩酊した《文》 intoxicated; drunken.

めいてんがい 名店街 an arcade of well-known stores.
めいど 冥途[土] the other [《文》 nether] world;《文》 the underworld;《文》 the realm of the shades; Hades ¶冥途へ行く go down to the nether world / 冥途の道連れにする kill sb to bear one company to the nether world.
めいとう¹ 名刀 an excellent [a fine] blade; a celebrated [《文》 noted] sword ¶正宗の名刀 a fine Masamune sword.
めいとう² 名答 〈正しい答え〉 a right [correct] answer; 〈適切な答え〉 an apt answer; 〈うまい答え〉 an excellent [a clever] answer. 〖文例↓〗
めいどう 鳴動 ¶鳴動する a rumble. 〖文例↓〗
めいにち 命日 the anniversary of sb's death; sb's deathday. 〖文例↓〗
めいば 名馬 a fine horse.
めいはく 明白 ¶明白な clear; plain; evident; obvious;《文》 manifest; unmistakable / 明白に clearly; plainly; evidently; obviously;《文》 manifestly; unmistakably / 明白にする make sth clear;《文》 clarify; clear up; define. 〖文例↓〗
めいび 明媚 ¶風光明媚の地《文》 a place of scenic beauty ⇨ ふうこう.
めいびん 明敏 ¶明敏な intelligent;《文》 sagacious / 頭脳が明敏な have a clear head; be clear-headed.
めいふく 冥福 ¶冥福を祈る pray for the repose of sb's soul. 〖文例↓〗
めいぶつ 名物 a well-known [special] product; a (local) specialty / 名物男 a popular figure / 土地の名物男 a local character. 〖文例↓〗
めいぶん¹ 名分 one's moral duty [obligations]; (moral) justification 〈理由〉; a just cause ¶名分の立たない unjustifiable / 名分を正しくする[明らかにする] clearly define one's moral obligations / 名分を立てる justify oneself [one's behavior,《文》 one's conduct].
めいぶん² 名文 an excellent composition; a fine piece of prose;《文》 prose in an exquisite style; a beautiful passage (1 節) ¶名文を書く be a good writer; write [have] a fine style / 名文家 a fine prose writer; a master of literary style.
めいぶん³ 明文 an express provision [statement, words] ¶明文化する put sth in the statutory form / 明文規定 (a) substantive enactment.
めいぼ 名簿 a list [roll, register] of names ¶名

ば, もって瞑すべしだ. You ought to be content with that much success. | You should accept the results you've got as good enough.
めいせい 氏の名声は内外にとどろいている. His name is known both at home and abroad. / 彼の名声は地に落ちた. His reputation is gone.
めいちゅう 弾丸は標的の真ん中に命中した. The bullet hit the target in the center [hit the bull's-eye].
めいとう² (クイズなどで) ご名答です. You've guessed right. | Absolutely right [correct]!
めいどう 浅間山が昨夜大いに鳴動した. Mt. Asama gave a great underground rumbling last night.
めいにち 11 月 10 日は父の命日です. My father died on November 10.
めいはく 彼にそんな意図のなかったことは明白だ. It is obvious that he had no such intention.
めいふく 彼の冥福を祈る. May he [Let him] rest in peace.
めいぶつ この地方の名物は何ですか. What is this locality famous for? | What is the chief attraction of this region? / 東京名物と言えば東京タワーもその 1 つだ. Tokyo Tower is one of the things that come to mind first when you think of Tokyo. / 名物にうまい物なし. The reality always falls short of the reputation.

めいほうか 名望家 《文》a man of high repute [renown].

めいぼく 名[銘]木 〈由緒のある木〉an old tree of historical interest; 〈木材〉precious [choice] wood; fine incense wood (香木).

めいみゃく 命脈 life; 《文》the thread of life ¶命脈が尽きる die (out); come to an end; 《文》expire; go out / 命脈を保つ〈人が〉《文》remain alive; 《文》maintain life; 〈風習などが〉stay [《文》remain] in existence. 文例⇩

めいむ 迷夢 an illusion; a delusion; a fallacy ¶迷夢から覚める come to one's senses / 迷夢を覚ます dispel sb's illusions; 《文》disabuse sb (of silly ideas); bring sb to his senses; open sb's eyes.

めいめい[1] 命名 ¶命名する give a name (to); name; christen / 命名式 a naming [christening] ceremony / (学術上の)命名法 nomenclature. 文例⇩

めいめい[2] 銘々 each; apiece ⇒かくじ ¶銘々皿 a small plate. 文例⇩

めいめいはくはく 明々白々 ⇒めいはく.

めいめつ 明滅 ¶明滅する blink; come and go; come on and off / 明滅信号 a blinking signal.

めいもう 迷妄 an illusion; a delusion; a fallacy ¶迷妄を打破する dispel an illusion; explode a fallacy.

めいもく[1] 名目 a name; a pretext ¶名目だけの nominal / 名目だけの社長 a figurehead president; a president in name only / 名目上の《文》ostensible / 何とか名目をこしらえて on some pretext or other / 名目賃金 nominal wages.

めいもく[2] 瞑目 ¶瞑目する close one's eyes; 〈死ぬ〉die; 《文》expire.

めいもん 名門 a distinguished [《文》an illustrious] family; a family with a long lineage ¶名門の出である come from [《文》of] a distinguished family; be born into [《文》of] a distinguished family / 名門校 a school with a high (academic) reputation; a prestige school / 高校野球の名門 T 高校 T High School, with a distinguished record [history] in the inter-high-school baseball tournaments.

めいもんく 名文句 a witty [《文》a happy, an apt] remark; a well-worded saying; 《文》an epigram; 《文》an aphorism.

めいやく[1] 名訳 an excellent [《文》a happy, an admirable] translation.

めいやく[2] 盟約 〈誓約〉a pledge; 《文》a covenant; a pact; 〈同盟〉an alliance; a league ¶盟約する confederate; form an alliance [a league]; form a pact.

めいゆう[2] 名優 a great [famous, celebrated] actor [actress]; a star.

めいゆう[2] 盟友 a sworn friend.

めいよ 名誉 〈栄誉〉《文》honor; credit; (a) distinction; glory; 〈名声〉fame; (a) reputation; a good name; 〈体面〉《文》dignity; prestige / 名誉を重んじる prize [value] honor (above everything else) / 名誉を棄損する defame; bring disgrace on sb; 《文》stain sb's honor / 名誉を回復する regain [recover] one's reputation; 《文》retrieve [redeem] one's (lost) honor / 名誉にかかわる affect one's honor [reputation] / 名誉にかかわる事柄 a point of honor / 名誉となる be an honor [a credit] to sb; do [bring] honor [credit] to sb; reflect credit on sb / 名誉会員(会長, 市民) an honorary member (president, citizen) / 名誉革命《史》the Glorious [Bloodless] Revolution / 名誉棄損 defamation of character; (文書による); (a) slander (口頭の) / 名誉教授 an honorary [emeritus] professor; a professor emeritus / 名誉職 an honorary post [office] / 名誉心 a desire for [《文》aspirations after] fame. 文例⇩

めいり 名利 《文》fame and wealth; fame and fortune ¶名利に恬淡(てん)である be above [indifferent to] riches and fame / 名利にきゅうきゅうとしている be constantly hankering after fame and gain; 《文》be bent on gaining wealth and fame.

めいりょう 明瞭 ¶明瞭な clear; plain; obvious; evident; distinct; 《文》lucid (文体など); legible (字体など) / 明瞭に clearly; plainly; obviously; evidently; distinctly; 《文》lucidly (文体など); legibly (字体など) / 明瞭にする make (it) clear; 《文》clarify / 明瞭度【通信】clarity / 明瞭でない ⇒ふめいりょう.

用法 evidently には「輪郭・けじめなどがはっきりと」という意味はほとんどなく,「明らかに」に近い. obviously も同じ. distinctly は「事実として明らかに」の意味はなく,「はっきりと」の意味しかない. それ以外の語はどちらの意味でも使える.

めいる 滅入る feel down; feel gloomy [《口語》blue]; be depressed; be dispirited; be downhearted ¶気が滅入るような gloomy; depressing.

めいれい 命令 an order; a command; 《文》an injunction;【法】a decree (裁判所の) ¶命令する command; order; give [issue] orders [a command] / 命令を受ける[に接する] get [receive] orders (from) / …せよとの命令を受けている be under orders to do / 命令に従う obey sb's orders / 命令によって by orders 《of》/ 命令どおりにする do as one is ordered; act on sb's order; do sb's bidding / 命令的 imperative; 《文》peremptory / 命令系統 a com-

---

めいぼ 名簿の最初に君の名が出ている. Your name heads [is at the top of] the list.

めいみゃく 会社はわずかに命脈を保っている. The company is barely keeping its head above water.

めいめい[1] 彼らは会を組織して若葉会と命名した. They organized a society, which they called 'Wakabakai'. / 彼はその子をおじの名をとって太郎と命名した. He named the boy Taro after [(米) for] his uncle.

めいめい[2] めいめいその本を 1 冊持っている. We each have a copy of the book. / 子供はめいめい自分の家へ帰った. The boys went to their respective homes. | The boys all went home.

めいよ このような生徒は学校の名誉である. Such a student is a credit [an honor] to the school. / この演壇に立つを得ましたことは

めいろ 迷路 a maze; a labyrinth ¶迷路のような《文》labyrinthine;《文》labyrinthian / 迷路を通り抜ける thread a maze; go [find one's way out] through a labyrinth / 迷路学習【心理】maze learning.

めいろう 明朗 ¶明朗な〈明るい〉bright; clear;〈快活な〉cheerful; sunny;〈不正のない〉straightforward; fair; openhearted / 明朗な政治 clean [honest, straightforward] politics / 明朗化する brighten up / 政界を明朗化する carry out a house-cleaning in the political world.

めいろん[1] 名論 ¶名論〈telling, convincing〉argument ¶名論卓説 an original opinion worth listening to.

めいろん[2] 迷論 a lame argument; an absurd opinion.

めいわく 迷惑 (a) trouble; annoyance; (a) bother; a nuisance;〈不便〉(an) inconvenience ¶迷惑する be troubled; have [get into] trouble; be inconvenienced / 迷惑な troublesome; annoying; irritating / 迷惑をかける be [make oneself] a nuisance (to); trouble; give [cause] sb trouble; put sb to trouble [inconvenience]; bother; worry / ご迷惑とは存じますが… I am sorry to trouble you, but…. 文例▶

めうえ 目上 one's superior(s); one's senior(s); one's elders (and betters); a person who outranks one ★ elders, betters は複数形でのみ用いる.

めうつり 目移り ¶目移りする be attracted by different things; be perplexed in making a choice; be unable to decide which to choose [take];〈物が主語〉be not easy to select.

メーカー a maker; a manufacturer ¶メーカー品 articles manufactured by well-known makers; brand-name merchandise / メーカーものでない〈TV sets〉of a little-known brand.

メーキャップ (a) make-up ¶メーキャップする make〈an actor, oneself〉up; do one's make-up / メーキャップを落とす take one's make-up off / メーキャップ係 a make-up girl [man].

メークアップ ⇨ メーキャップ.

メーザー【電子工学】a maser.

メジャーリーグ《米国プロ野球の》the major leagues; the majors ¶メジャーリーグの選手 a major league player; a major-leaguer.

メーター ⇨ メートル ¶タクシーのメーター a taximeter;《口語》a (taxi) clock.

メーデー May Day ¶メーデーの集会[デモ]に参加する join the May Day rally [demonstration].

メード a maid; a housemaid.

メートル〈長さの単位〉a meter (略: m);〈計器〉a gauge ¶ガス[電気, 水道]のメートル a gas [an electric, a water] meter / 酔ってメートルを上げる《口語》have had a drink (or two) and be talking big; be in high spirits as a result of drink / メートル原器 the meter standard / メートル法を採用する adopt the metric system; go metric.

メーン Maine (略: Me.) ¶メーン州の人 a Mainer.

メーンイベント the main event.

メーンマスト the mainmast.

めおと 夫婦 ⇨ ふうふ ¶夫婦茶わん a pair of matching teacups (for the use of a married couple).

メカ equipment; gadgetry; (a) mechanism ¶メカに強い[弱い] be a good [poor] mechanic.

めがお 目顔 ¶目顔で知らせる give sb a significant look; wink at sb.

めかくし 目隠し〈目を覆う物〉a blindfold; a bandage over one's eyes;〈馬の〉blinkers;《米》blinders;〈窓の〉a blind;〈衝立, 屏風(ﾋﾞｮｳ)など〉a screen ¶目隠しの鬼 'it' [the blindfolded player] in blindman's buff / 目隠しをする blindfold sb; screen《a place》/ 目隠し競走 a blindfold race.

めかけ 妾 a mistress; a kept woman.

めがける 目掛ける aim (at);《文》aspire (to).

めこ 目籠 an openwork basket. 文例▶

メガサイクル a megacycle (略: mc, Mc.).

めかじき【魚】a swordfish; a broadbill.

めがしら 目頭 ¶目頭が熱くなる《文》be moved to tears / 目頭が熱くなるような moving《stories》; pathetic《sights》.

めかす dress [smarten] oneself up; preen [《文》adorn] oneself;《口語》primp;《口語》doll oneself up ¶めかしている be dressed [《口語》dolled] up / 念入りに[smartly] dressed; look smart / めかし屋〈女〉a woman fond of finery;〈男〉a dandy; a fop.

めかた 目方 weight ¶目方が重い[軽い] be heavy [light] (in weight); weigh heavy [light] / 目方が60キロある weigh [tip the scales at] 60 kilograms / 目方が増える gain [put on, pick up] weight / 目方が減る lose weight / 目方をかける[計る] weigh sth / 目方をごまかす商人 a merchant who gives short weight / はかりで目方を見る read the weight on the scale / 目方で売る sell (salt) by weight. 文例▶

メガトン a megaton ¶メガトン級の水爆 a hydrogen bomb in the megaton range / 幾メガトンもの multi-megaton《nuclear bombs》.

メカニズム (a) mechanism. 文例▶

めがね 眼鏡 glasses;《a pair of》spectacles;《口語》specs; a lorgnette (手で持つ長い柄のついた);〈鑑識〉judgment ¶度の強い眼鏡 powerful spectacles; thick glasses /《近視の》遠視[近視]用の眼鏡 spectacles for a longsight-

---

私の大いなる名誉とするところであります. I consider it a great honor [privilege] to be allowed to address you.

めいわく 大変ご迷惑でした. I am afraid I have put you to a great deal of trouble. / 僕の名前を出されては迷惑だ. I don't want to have) my name mentioned. / ご迷惑でなければ明日お訪ねします. If it is not inconvenient, I'll call on you tomorrow.

めがた 犬は彼をめがけて跳びついた. The dog flew [sprang] at him.

めかた 彼はやせるどころか, かえって目方が増えた. His weight went up instead of down. / この手紙は目方を超過している. The letter is overweight.

メガトン その水爆の大きさは2メガトンであった. The hydrogen bomb had a yield of two megatons.

ed [shortsighted] person / 眼鏡のつる《米》the bows [temples] of a pair of spectacles;《英》the sides of a pair of spectacles / 眼鏡の縁[わく] the rim [frame] of a pair of spectacles / 眼鏡をかける put *one's* glasses [spectacles] on / 眼鏡をかけて with spectacles on / 眼鏡をかけている wear [be in] spectacles / 眼鏡を鼻先の方へかけている wear *one's* glasses low [right] down on *one's* nose / 眼鏡をかけるようにとなる take to wearing spectacles / 眼鏡を外す take *one's* glasses [spectacles] off / 眼鏡越しに見る look over (the rims of) *one's* spectacles / 師匠の眼鏡にかなう《文》gain [win] *one's* master's confidence;《文》find favor with *one's* master / 金縁[緣なし眼鏡 gold-rimmed [rimless] spectacles / 鼻眼鏡 ⇒はなめがね / 水泳眼鏡 goggles / (遠視近視両用の) 2焦点眼鏡 bifocals / 眼鏡入れ a spectacle case / 眼鏡屋《店》an optician's shop;〈人〉an optician. 文例⇩

めがねざる 眼鏡猿 a tarsier.

メガヘルツ《電》a megahertz (略：MHz)《単複同形》.

メガホン a megaphone ¶両手をメガホンの形にして making a megaphone of *one's* hands; shaping both hands into a megaphone.

めがみ 女神 a goddess ¶ (ニューヨークにある)自由の女神像 the Statue of Liberty.

メガロポリス a megalopolis.

めきき 目利き judging;〈鑑定者〉a judge;《文》a connoisseur ¶目利きをする judge; give an expert opinion (on, concerning) / …の目利きである be a good judge [connoisseur] of ….

メキシコ Mexico ¶メキシコの Mexican / メキシコ市 Mexico City / メキシコ人 a Mexican / メキシコ合衆国 the United Mexican States / メキシコ湾流 the Gulf Stream.

めきめき more and more; remarkably; fast; rapidly; visibly ¶めきめき上達する make rapid progress (in). 文例⇩

めキャベツ 芽キャベツ Brussels sprouts.

-めく look (like); seem (to be). 文例⇩

めくぎ 目釘 a rivet (of a sword hilt).

めくされがね 目腐れ金 a paltry sum [trifling amount] (of money); a (mere) pittance.

めくじら 目くじら ¶目くじらを立てる raise *one's* eyebrows; look disapprovingly (at).

めぐすり 目薬 (apply) (an) eye lotion; eyewash. ¶目薬の容器 an eyedropper; a dropper.

めくそ 目糞《口語》sleep ⇒めやに. 文例⇩

めくばせ 目配せ ¶目配せする wink (at); make a sign with *one's* eye; exchange glances (互いに).

めくばり 目配り ⇨め¹ (目を配る).

めぐみ 恵み〈神の〉(a) blessing; grace;〈仁慈〉mercy;《文》benevolence;〈慈悲〉charity;《文》alms;〈恩恵〉a favor;《文》favor; (a) kindness;《文》(a) bounty ¶恵みを垂れる《文》have mercy on *sb*;《文》be merciful to *sb*; show *sb* mercy / 恵み深い《文》merciful; benevolent; kind; charitable.

めぐむ¹ 芽ぐむ bud; sprout; put out [《文》forth] shoots [buds, young leaves] ⇨め² (芽を出す).

めぐむ² 恵む〈施しを与える〉give *sth* (in charity);〈恩恵を施す〉《文》bestow a favor (on); be kind (to) ⇨めぐみ (恵みを垂れる) ¶恵まれた blessed (with);《文》favored (with) / 恵まれた生活をしている be well off / 少数の恵まれた人びと the privileged [favored] few / 恵まれない人びと《文》the unfortunate; (the) underprivileged people. 文例⇩

めくら 盲 a blind person;〈総称〉the blind;〈無知な人〉an ignorant person /《文》sightless / 盲になる go [《文》become] blind; lose *one's* sight / 生まれつき盲である be born blind / 盲撃ちをする fire [shoot] at random; try a shot in the dark /《口語》take a pot shot (at) / 盲判を押す stamp *one's* seal mechanically (on documents) (without knowing the contents) / 盲蛇に《文》with a daring born of ignorance / 盲めっぽうに blindly; recklessly; at random;《文》at haphazard. 文例⇩

めぐらす 巡らす surround (with, by); enclose (with, in);〈回す〉turn;〈案出する〉devise; think [map] out (a plan) ¶計略をめぐらす《文》devise a stratagem; work out a plan / 塀をめぐらしてある be surrounded by walls; be walled. 文例⇩

めぐり 巡り〈周囲〉circumference;《文》girth;〈遍歴〉a tour; a pilgrimage; a round;〈循環〉circulation ¶お寺めぐり (make) a pilgrimage to famous temples / 島めぐりをする make a tour of the islands;〈ひとつの島を〉go round an island.

めぐりあい 巡り合い a chance meeting;《文》an encounter. ¶come across.

めぐりあう 巡り合う meet (again) by chance.

めぐりあわせ 巡り合わせ《文》a turn of Fortune's wheel; fortune; chance;《文》fate.

めくる 捲る turn over; turn up (a card);〈はぎ取る〉tear off [up]; take [strip] off ¶ペー

めがね 君の眼鏡はどのくらいの強さですか. How strong are your glasses? / 彼は眼鏡を鼻先にかけていた. He had his glasses (set) low on his nose. / お眼鏡にかなった人がありますか. Have you found anybody who suits you [who meets your requirements]?

めきめき 彼はめきめきと売り出した. He has leapt into fame. | He has grown rapidly in popularity.

-めく 彼の言う事には皮肉めいたところがある. There is a touch of irony in what he says. / 大分春めいてきた. There are a lot of signs of spring. | Spring is (definitely) in the air.

めくそ 目くそ鼻くそを笑うたぐいだ. The pot shouldn't call the kettle black.

めぐむ² 米国は天然の資源に恵まれている. America is blessed with abundant natural resources. / 当日は晴天に恵まれた. The occasion was favored by fine weather. / 彼は家庭的には恵まれなかった. He didn't have a happy home life. / 君より恵まれていない人もいるんだよ. You are still better off than some.

めくら 盲蛇におじず. Fools rush in where angels fear to tread.

めぐらす 日本は四方に海をめぐら

めぐる 巡る ⇒まわる ¶(季節などが)めぐって来る come round; return / …をめぐって centering on…; concerning…; in connection with….

めくるめく 眩めく dazzling; 《文》radiant; very bright.

めげる 〈負ける〉give way 《to》; succumb 《to》; be overpowered 《by》; flinch 《from》; shrink 《from》; 〈落胆する〉be disheartened; be discouraged; lose heart [courage] ¶寒さにめげない think [make] nothing of the cold (weather).

めこぼし 目溢し《文》connivance ¶目こぼしする overlook; 《文》connive at; shut [close] one's eyes to; wink at; pass over.

めさき 目先 目先の immediate; direct; short-run; at hand / 目先の変わった new; novel / 目先の事ばかり考える only think [think only] of the present [the immediate future]; take a short view of things; be short-sighted / 目先の利く[利かない] farsighted [shortsighted] / 目先を変える do something new [novel]; 《文》make a fresh [new] departure / 目先に just [right] in front of one; before one's (very) eyes; (right) under one's nose.

めざし 目刺 dried sardines. 文例↓

めざす 目差[指]す aim at; have 《an end》 in view; have an eye on sth ¶目ざす所〈標的〉《文》the object; 《文》the end in view; the objective; 〈目的地〉one's destination. 文例↓

めざとい 目敏い 〈目が早い〉sharp-eyed; sharp-[quick-]sighted; 〈すぐ目が覚める〉(be)-easily awakened ¶目ざとい人 an acute observer / 目ざとく見つける detect [notice] sth quickly.

めざましい 目覚ましい striking; remarkable; conspicuous; spectacular; splendid; marvelous; brilliant; phenomenal ¶めざましい働きをする distinguish oneself (in battle).

めざまし(どけい) 目覚まし(時計) an alarm (clock) ¶目覚ましを6時にセットする set the alarm for [to go off at] six o'clock. 文例↓

めざめがち 目覚め 目覚めがちである (tend to) wake easily; 《文》be wakeful.

めざめる 目覚める wake (up); 《文》awake; 〈本心に返る〉come to one's senses ¶現実に目覚める wake up [be awakened, have one's eyes opened] to the stern realities (of life) / 自らの価値に目覚める become conscious of one's own value.

めざる 目笊 a basket with large meshes.

めざわり 目障り an eyesore; 《文》an offense to the eye ¶目ざわりになる spoil [obstruct] the view; 《文》offend the eye.

めし 飯〈御飯〉boiled [cooked] rice; 〈食事〉a meal; food ¶飯が食えるようにしてやる put sb in the way of making a living / 飯を炊く boil [cook] rice / 飯を食う〈食事をする〉have [take] a meal; eat; 〈生計を立てる〉make a living; earn a living [《文》one's bread] / 筆で飯を食う live [make a living] by writing / 家族に飯を食わせていく provide for [support] one's family / 数学が飯より好きだ have a passion [《文》be an enthusiast] for mathematics / 飯炊きする cook; a kitchenmaid /飯茶わん a rice bowl / 飯粒 a grain of boiled rice / 飯どき mealtime; dinner time / 飯びつ a boiled-rice tub.

めじ 目地《土木》a joint (of a wall) ¶目地を塗る joint [point] (a wall).

メシア the Messiah ⇒きゅうせいしゅ.

めしあがる 召し上がる ⇒たべる. 文例↓

メジシンボール (play with) a medicine ball.

めした 目下 one's inferior(s); one's subordinate(s); one's junior(s).

めしつかい 召使 a servant; 〈家庭の〉a domestic (servant, help, worker); a household servant.

めしべ 雌蕊 a pistil.

メジャー¹ 〈巻き尺〉a tape measure; a measuring tape.

メジャー² 〈石油会社〉a major (oil company).

めじり 目尻 the corner [tail] of the eye ¶目尻が上がっている have slant(ing) [almond] eyes; be slant-eyed / 目尻のしわ the lines at the corners of one's [the] eyes; crow's-feet / 目尻を下げる make eyes 《at a woman》; make sheep's eyes 《at》; 《文》cast amorous glances 《at》.

めじるし 目印 a sign; a mark; a landmark; a guide ¶目じるしをする mark; put a mark (on). 文例↓

めじろ 目白《鳥》a white-eye ¶目白押しの群衆 a thronging [jostling] crowd.

めす¹ 雌 a female (animal [bird]); a she; a hen bird (鳥の) ⇒め-, おす¹ ★ ¶雌の female; she-(bears); cow (whales, elephants); bitch (wolves); doe (rabbits); nanny (goats); hen (sparrows) / 雌雄(紋)を識別する tell its sex; sex (a chicken) / 雌親 a mother animal [bird]. 文例↓

めす² 召す〈呼ぶ〉call; 《文》summon; send for〈呼びにやる〉;〈着る〉put on; wear. 文例↓

している。Japan is surrounded by sea. | Japan is a seagirt country.

めさき きょうは目先を変えて朝鮮料理を食べに行こう。Let's eat Korean today for a change.

めざす 目ざす町が遠くに見えてきた。The town we were heading for came into view in the distance.

めざまし(どけい) 目覚まし時計を7時に鳴るようにかけておいて下さい。Please set the alarm [clock] to wake me at seven.

めし 運動すると飯がよく食える。Exercise works up a good appetite. / それでは飯の食い上げだ。It will cost me my job.

めしあがる どうぞ召し上がって下さい。Help yourself, please. / 何を召し上がりますか。What would you like (to have)?

めじるし 門の前の大木が私の家の目じるしです。The big tree in front of the gate is a guide [landmark] to my house.

めす¹ それは雌か雄か。Is it a she [female] or a he [male]? | What is its sex?

めす² 花を召しませ。Will you buy a flower, sir?

メス [<《オランダ語》mes] a scalpel; a (surgical (surgeon's)) knife ¶メスを入れる ⟨比喩的に⟩ plunge a scalpel [make a searching inquiry] into 《a graft case》.

めずらしい 珍しい ⟨目新しい⟩ new; novel; ⟨まれな⟩ rare; infrequent; ⟨異常な⟩ unusual; uncommon; ⟨奇異な⟩ strange; curious ¶珍しい物 a novelty; a rarity/珍しく unusually; uncommonly; exceptionally; for a wonder/珍しげに 《look at sth》 curiously ⟨wonderingly, 《文》 with curiosity⟩/珍しがる regard sth as a curiosity [as unusual]. 文例⇩

めせん 目線 ⇒しせん⁴.

メソジスト ¶メソジスト教会 the Methodist Church/メソジスト教徒 a Methodist.

メゾソプラノ 《音楽》mezzo-soprano ¶メゾソプラノ歌手 a mezzo-soprano (pl. -s).

メソポタミア Mesopotamia ¶メソポタミアの Mesopotamian.

めそめそ ¶めそめそ泣く sob; whimper.

めだか 目高 《魚》a medaka.

めだつ 目立つ stand out; be conspicuous; come to the fore; be prominent; come into prominence; be striking; attract attention;《米》be highlighted ¶目立たない be inconspicuous; be quiet/目だって conspicuously; strikingly. 文例⇩

めたて 目立て ⟨のこぎりの⟩ setting ¶のこぎりの目立てをする set (the teeth of) a saw.

めだま 目玉 ⟨眼球⟩ an eyeball ¶目玉が飛び出るような値段 an exorbitant [a prohibitive] price/目玉商品 a (loss) leader/⟨卵の⟩目玉焼き fried eggs;《米》eggs fried sunny-side up [over-easy (両面を焼いた)]/お目玉を食う ⇒ おめだま.

メタル ⇒メダル.

メダル a medal ¶⟨競技で⟩メダルを獲得する win [be awarded] a medal/⟨オリンピックの⟩金[銀, 銅]メダル a gold [silver, bronze] medal/金メダル獲得者 a gold medal winner; a gold medalist. 文例⇩

メタン 《化》methane ¶メタンガス methane; marsh gas.

めちゃ ⇒むちゃ.

めちゃくちゃ ¶めちゃくちゃな ⟨筋道を無視している⟩ incoherent; confused; unreasonable;⟨途方もない⟩ absurd; preposterous; desperate; ⟨乱雑⟩ ⇒めちゃめちゃ/めちゃくちゃな議論 incoherent arguments/めちゃくちゃに走る run like mad.

めちゃめちゃ ¶めちゃめちゃに in disorder [confusion]; topsy-turvy/めちゃめちゃにする ⟨だめにする⟩ spoil;《口語》mess up;《米口語》muss up;⟨破る⟩ tear sth to pieces;⟨物語⟩ make a mess [《口語》a hash,《口語》shambles] of; upset; ruin/めちゃめちゃに負かされる be beaten hollow. 文例⇩

メチル, メチール 《化》methyl ¶メチルアルコール methanol; methyl (wood) alcohol.

メチレン 《化》methylene.

メッカ Mecca ¶言語学研究のメッカ the Mecca of linguists.

めっかち a one-eyed person ¶めっかちである be blind in one eye.

めつき 目付き a look; an expression in one's eyes ¶目つきが悪い have an unpleasant [a nasty] look to one's eyes/恐ろしい目つきで with a fierce look; with glaring eyes/人の目つきをうかがう try to catch [seek] sb's eye. 文例⇩

めっき 鍍金 plating;⟨金⟩ gilding; gilt;《写真》toning ¶めっきする plate《with silver》/⟨金で⟩gild;《文》engild; coat《with gold》/めっきがはげる the gilt comes [rubs] off;⟨比喩的に, 人が主語⟩ betray oneself; show one's true colors;《文》show the cloven hoof/電気めっき electroplating; electric gilding (金での).

めっきり remarkably;《文》markedly; considerably;《文》appreciably; noticeably; very much. 文例⇩

メッセージ 《send, read》a message.

メッセンジャー a messenger ¶メッセンジャーボーイ a messenger boy.

めっそう 滅相 ¶めっそうもない ⟨ばかげた⟩ absurd;⟨もっての外の⟩ preposterous; out of the question. 文例⇩

めった ¶めったな rash; thoughtless; reckless/めったに rarely;《文》seldom/めった切りにする hack to pieces/めった打ちにする《口語》beat sb up; beat sb black and blue/めったやたらに indiscriminately; recklessly. 文例⇩

めつぶし 目潰し ¶目つぶしを食わす throw 《ashes》into sb's eyes (to blind him).

めつぼう 滅亡 a downfall; a fall; ruin; collapse ¶滅亡する fall; be ruined; go to ruin; collapse.

めっぽう 滅法 ¶めっぽう(に) extraordinarily; ridiculously;《文》uncommonly;《口語》awfully/めっぽう高い値段 an exorbitant [ex-

---

めずらしい 見るもの聞くもの皆珍しかった。Everything I saw and heard was new [interesting] to me./空の旅も今では珍しくなくなりました。Traveling by air has lost much of its novelty now./彼が家にいるのは珍しい。We seldom find him at home./これは, これは, お珍しい。Well, well. You're quite a stranger./彼女が和服姿で来るなんて珍しいことだ。It is unusual for her to appear in kimono./珍しいものを有り難うございました。Thank you for your nice present.

めだつ 黒と白とでは大変目立つ。Black and white form a striking contrast./国会では一向に目立たない存在だ。He cuts a poor figure in the House.

メダル 小川が鉄棒で金メダルを獲得した。Ogawa won the gold medal in the horizontal bar./この試合で金メダルの行方が決まる。This match will decide the destination of the gold medal.

めちゃめちゃ 飛行機はめちゃめちゃに壊れた。The airplane was broken into fragments./暴風雨で花はめちゃめちゃになった。The rainstorm played havoc with the flowers.

めつき 彼は妙な目つきをして人を見る。He has a strange way of looking at people.

めっきり めっきり寒くなりました。The weather has become very cold./彼は近頃めっきりやせた。He has lost a lot of weight lately.

めでたい happy ; 《文》felicitous ; 《文》joyous ; 《文》auspicious ¶めでたい事《文》a matter for congratulation ; a happy event / おめでたい人間 a fool ; a simpleton / めでたく happily ; successfully / めでたく凱旋(がいせん)する return in triumph / めでたしめでたしで終わる have [come to] a happy end(ing). 用例⇩

めでる 愛でる love ; admire ; appreciate (多とする).

めど 目処〈目当て〉an aim ; 《文》the goal ; 〈将来の見通し〉a prospect ; an outlook ; 〈針の〉an eye ¶めどがつく there is hope 《for》; the prospects 《for a solution》 look brighter ; 《口語》one can see the light at the end of the tunnel. 用例⇩

めとる 娶る marry (a woman) ; take (a woman) to wife.

メドレー a medley ¶メドレーリレー a medley relay / 400メートル個人メドレー the individual 400-meter medley.

メトロノーム《音楽》a metronome.

めなみ 女波 smaller waves.

メニュー a menu ; a (menu) card ; a bill (of fare) ¶メニューにある be on the menu [card, bill].

メヌエット a minuet.

めぬき 目抜き ¶目抜きの main ; fashionable ; important ; principal / 目抜きの場所 the busiest quarters / 目抜き通り the main street ; 《英》a high street.

めぬり 目塗り ¶目塗りする plaster up ; seal (up).

めねじ 雌ねじ a female screw.

めのう 瑪瑙 agate.

めばえ 芽生え a bud ; a sprout ; a (young) shoot ¶愛の芽生え《文》the awakening of love (in one's heart) / 目生え《文》love in the bud.

めばえる 芽生える ⇨め²(芽を出す).

めはし 目端 ¶目端が利く[利かない] be quick-[dull-]witted ; be [be not] sensible.

めはな 目鼻 ¶目鼻がつく take shape ; materialize ; get somewhere / 目鼻がつかない《文》remain [be] in a nebulous state ; get nowhere / 目鼻をつける get [put] sth into shape ; give shape to sth / 目鼻立ち (clearly-marked) features ; looks.

めばり 目張り ¶目張りする seal up ; 〈透き間風を防ぐためなどに〉weather-strip (the joints of a window) ; tape (windows).

めぶんりょう 目分量 ¶目分量で at a rough estimate ; by [at a] guess ; 《measure》with the eye.

めべり 目減り loss in weight [value] ¶目減りがする lose《two per cent》in weight.

めぼし 目星 ¶目星をつける have [keep] an [one's] eye (on) ; mark sb [sth] out [down] ; 〈選んで〉fix on sb as one's choice.

めぼしい conspicuous ; noticeable ; 〈金目の〉valuable.

めまい 目眩 giddiness ; dizziness ; 《医》(a) vertigo (pl. -es) ¶目まいがする be dizzy ; get [feel] giddy ; have a dizzy spell. 用例⇩

めまぐるしい 目まぐるしい dizzy ; hectic ; bewildering ¶目まぐるしい生活を送る live in a whirl ; lead a hectic life / 目まぐるしい変化 kaleidoscopic changes / 目まぐるしい世の中 the bustling world.

めめしい 女々しい cowardly ; effeminate ; 《文》unmanly ¶女々しい振る舞いをする《文》behave dishonorably [ignobly] ; be cowardly ; be faint-hearted.

メモ a memo (pl. -s) ; a memorandum (pl. -s, -da) ¶メモを取る take notes (of) ; make a note (of, on) / メモを元にして小説を書く work on a novel from notes / メモ用紙〈ひとつづりの〉a memo [note] pad.

めもと 目元 the eyes ; the expression of the eyes ¶目元のかわいい女の子 a girl with lovely [pretty] eyes.

めもり 目盛り the divisions (of a scale) ; graduations (on a thermometer) ; a scale (on a beam balance) ¶目盛りをする[つける] graduate ; mark sth with degrees [put a graded scale on the tube] / 目盛盤 a dial. 用例⇩

めやす 目安〈標準〉a yardstick ; 《文》a criterion (pl. -ria, -s) ; 〈目当て〉an aim ¶目安を立てる set up a standard ; fix one's aim.

めやに 目脂 discharge from the eyes ; eye mucus ; gum (in the corner of the eye) ; 《口語》sleep〈朝起きたときの〉. 用例⇩

メラニン《生化》melanin ¶メラニン色素 melanin pigment.

メラネシア Melanesia ¶メラネシアの Melanesian / メラネシア人 a Melanesian.

めらめら ¶めらめらと燃え上がる go up in flames ; flare up.

メリーゴーラウンド a merry-go-round ; 《米》a carousel ; 《英》a roundabout ; a whirligig ¶メリーゴーラウンドの馬 a carousel pony.

メリーランド Maryland (略: Md.) ¶メリーランド州の人 a Marylander.

メリケンこ メリケン粉 (wheat) flour.

めりこむ 滅り込む cave [fall] in ; sink (into

めっそう めっそうもない! God forbid! / めっそうもない事です. Nothing could be more absurd than that. / 僕がそんな話に乗るなんてめっそうもないことだ. I can't see myself accepting such an offer!

めった あの人にはめったなことは言えない, すぐ怒るから. You must be careful what you say with him ; he is easily offended./ この地方では雪はめったに降らない. It rarely snows in this region./ こんな機会はめったにない. Such opportunities do not occur every day.

めでたい おめでとう. Congratulations! / ご成功おめでとう. I congratulate you on your success.

めど まだ商売のめどがつかない. The prospects for the business are still far from certain. / これらの問題は解決のめどがついている. These problems are well on their way to solution. / 3月一杯でめどに完了できますか. Can you manage to finish it by the end of March?

めまい 目まいがした. My head swam. | My brain reeled.

めもり この物差しはセンチメートルで目盛りがしてある. This ruler is graduated [calibrated, marked off] in centimeters.

めやに 目やにで目がくっついてい

メリット (a) merit; an advantage.

めりはり modulation 《of *one's* voice》 ¶めりはりの利いた声で in a well-[beautifully-]modulated voice / めりはりの利いた文章 a lively [nicely varied] style / めりはりを利かせる modulate *one's* voice for effect.

めりめり with a (splintering) crack [crash] ¶めりめりいう creak; crack.

メリヤス [<《スペイン語》*medias*] knitted [knit] (cotton) goods; knitwear; knitwork / メリヤスのシャツ a knit(ted) undershirt / メリヤス工場 a knitting mill.

メリンス [<《オランダ語》*merinos*] muslin.

メルカトル 《地理》 ¶メルカトル投影図法に基づく世界地図 a map of the world on Mercator's [a Mercator] projection.

メロディー a melody; a tune.

メロドラマ a melodrama.

めろめろ ¶めろめろに酔っ払う get blind [rolling, dead] drunk / …にめろめろだ be far gone on 《a girl》.

メロン a melon.

めん¹ 面 〈仮面〉a mask; 〈剣道などの防具〉a face guard [protector, mask]; 〈表面〉the surface; the face; 〈新聞などの〉a page ¶面と向かう come face to face 《with》; meet *sb* face to face / 面と向かって face to face (相対して); to [in] *sb's* face (面前で) / あらゆる面から問題を考究する study [consider] all the aspects [angles] of a problem; study a matter from all sides [angles] / 〈剣道で〉面を1本取る give *sb* a blow on the head. 文例⇩

めん² 綿 cotton ¶綿織物 cotton fabrics [textiles, cloth]; cotton (piece) goods / 綿花 raw cotton; 《米》cotton wool / 綿花栽培 cotton growing / 綿糸 cotton thread [yarn] / 綿製品 cotton goods / 綿ネル cotton flannel / 綿ビロード cotton velvet; velveteen / 綿布 cotton (cloth) / 綿プリント printed cotton. 文例⇩

めんえき 免疫 immunity (from a disease) ¶免疫になる become immune [gain (an) immunity] 《to, against, from》 / 免疫になっている be immune 《to, against, from》; 〈比喩的に〉be hardened [impervious] to 《public criticism》; be unaffected by 《unfavorable comment》 / 免疫にする immunize [confer immunity on] *sb* 《against a disease》 / 自然免疫 natural immunity / 人工免疫 artificial immunity / 免疫学 immunology / 免疫期間 a period of immunity / ちゃんと免疫性ができる develop proper immunity 《to, against, from》 / 免疫性のない nonimmune 《persons》 / 免疫体 an immune body / 免疫反応 (an) immune reaction. 文例⇩

めんかい 面会 an interview; a meeting ¶面会する see; have an interview 《with》; meet; 《文》receive 《a guest》 / 面会日 a visiting day; a receiving day; a reception day / 面会日 an at-home day / 面会時間 visiting hours / 面会人 a visitor. 文例⇩

めんかやく 綿火薬 guncotton; nitrocotton; nitrocellulose; cotton powder (粉末).

めんかん 免官 ⇒めんしょく.

めんきつ 面詰 ¶面詰する 《文》reprove *sb* to his face.

めんきょ 免許 permission; (a) license ¶免許する permit; license; authorize / 免許のある licensed / 免許のない unlicensed / 自分免許の 《文》self-styled / 免許状 ⇒めんじょう / 免許皆伝を受ける be initiated into the mysteries (of the art of fencing); 《文》be conferred full mastership 《in》 / 免許証 a license; a certificate / 仮免許証 a temporary license / 〈自動車の〉a learner's permit; 《英》a provisional licence / 運転免許 ⇒うんてん / 免許証を持っている hold a license / 免許(証)を取り消される get [be] disqualified; have *one's* license canceled / 免許料[制] a license fee [system].

めんくい 面食い ¶面食いだ be flustered; be confused; 《文》be confounded; be upset; be at a loss; be taken aback. 文例⇩

めんこ 面子 a game of slapping a pasteboard card down on the ground in order to overturn that of *one's* opponent ¶めんこをやる play *menko*.

めんざい 免罪 acquittal; remission of a sin (宗教上の); pardon ¶免罪符 《西洋史》an indulgence.

めんしき 面識 《文》acquaintance ¶面識がある be (personally) acquainted 《with》; know / 面識のない人 a stranger. 文例⇩

めんじゅうふくはい 面従腹背 《文》feigned allegiance; false obedience; 《文》(a) Judas kiss.

めんじょ 免除 (an) exemption; release ¶免除する exempt 《*sb* from taxation》; release [re-

---

た. His eyes were gummed up.

めりこむ 車輪が泥にめり込んだ. The wheels got stuck in the mud.

めん¹ 彼に面と向かってそう言える人は私どもの中に1人もない. None of us dare to say it to his face. / 事務屋は技術面はほとんど知らず、技術屋は営業面にはさらに暗い. The office men know little about the technical side and the technicians even less about the business end.

めん² この洋服地には少し綿が混じっている. This suit material contains some cotton.

めんえき ワクチン注射をすれば小児麻痺に対して免疫になる. Vaccination immunizes people against polio. / 国外から持ち込まれた病気に対して彼らは免疫性がなかったために、大勢が死んだ. Imported diseases, to which they had no immunity, killed a large number of them.

めんかい ご面会人です. Here's a gentleman [lady] who would like to see you. / 本田が面会したいと佐藤さんに言って下さい. Will you please tell Mr. Sato that Honda would like to see him? / 面会謝絶.《掲示》No visitors (allowed). / 就業時間中面会謝絶.《掲示》Interviews declined during working hours. / 水曜日が彼の面会日だ. He sees visitors [is at home] on Wednesdays.

めんくい あの男は面食いだ. Good looks in a woman mean more than anything else to him.

めんくらう 突然英語で話しかけられたので少なからず面くらった.

めんじょう　lieve, excuse] 《sb from his duties》; remit 《a fine》.

めんじょう 免状 〈卒業の〉a diploma; 〈免許状〉a license; a certificate　¶免状をもらう get [《文》obtain] a [one's] diploma.

めんしょく 免職 《文》dismissal from office; 《文》discharge　¶免職する dismiss [discharge] sb from office; 《文》relieve sb of his post [office] ⇨ くび (首を切る).

めんじる 免じる　¶…に免じて out of consideration [respect, regard] for…; in deference to…/ 私に免じて for my sake. 文例⇩

メンス ⇨ げっけい.

めんする 面する face (on); look out on (to); give on (to); 〈戸口が〉open on (to).

めんぜい 免税 exemption from taxation　¶免税にする[なる] exempt [be exempted] from taxation / 免税点を引き上[下]げる raise [lower] the tax exemption limit / 免税品 tax-free[-exempt] goods ; duty-free articles (輸入品).

めんせき[1] 免責 《文》exemption [discharge] from responsibility [obligation]　¶免責条項 an escape [exemption] clause.

めんせき[2] 面責 《文》personal reproof　¶面責する 《文》reprove sb to his face; 《文》reprimand sb personally.

めんせき[3] 面積 (an) area; square measure; size 《of land》　¶広い[狭い]面積 a large [small, limited] area / 面積が約１千平方キロある cover [have] an area of about 1,000 square kilometers. 文例⇩

めんせつ 面接 interviewing; an interview ⇨ めんだん　¶個人面接 an individual interview / 面接係 an interviewer / 面接時間 the hours for interviews / 面接試験 an interview; an oral test [examination] / 〈大学での〉a viva-voce examination ; 《口語》a viva.

めんぜん 面前　¶面前で in the presence of sb; before sb.

めんそ 免訴　¶免訴にする dismiss 《a case》; discharge 《acquit, release》《a prisoner》.

めんそう 面相 looks; 《文》a countenance; features; 《文》physiognomy.

メンタルテスト (give) an intelligence test.

めんだん 面談 an interview; a talk　¶面談する talk personally 《with》; have an interview [a talk] 《with》; meet and talk 《with》. 文例⇩

メンチカツ a fried cake of minced meat.

メンチボール a meat ball.

めんちょう 面疔 a carbuncle on the face.

めんつ 面子; honor ⇨ めんつの立つような face-saving 《concession》/ めんつを保つ[失う] save [lose] (one's) face / めんつにこだわる 《文》be too much concerned about one's own personal honor.

メンデルのほうそく メンデルの法則 Mendel's [Mendelian] laws (of heredity); Mendelism.

メンデレビウム 【化】mendelevium.

めんどう 面倒 〈手数〉trouble; 〈困難〉(a) difficulty ; 〈厄介なこと〉a nuisance ; 〈いざこざ〉troubles; complications; 〈世話〉care; attention　¶めんどうな troublesome ; difficult ; tiresome / めんどうな事ができる[起こる] difficulties arise; 〈人が主語〉get into trouble / よく子供のめんどうを見る take good care of a child ; look after a child well / めんどうになる get [《文》become] complicated / めんどうをかける trouble sb; give [cause] sb trouble ; put sb to trouble / めんどうくさい (be) troublesome; 《be》tiresome / 非常にめんどう(くさ)がる think (it) very troublesome 《to do》; 《口語》make a great business of (it); 《口語》make a great fuss about sth; 《俗》think sth is a real drag / …するのがめんどうくさくなる get [grow, 《文》become] tired [weary] of doing; 《口語》get fed up with [《英》of] doing. 文例⇩

めんとおし 面通し 〈警察の〉an identification parade; a line-up.

メントール 【化】menthol.

めんどり 雌鳥 a hen (bird); 〈若鶏〉a pullet.

めんば 面罵　¶面罵する abuse sb to his face.

メンバー a member　¶マージャンのメンバーをそろえる make up a four for Mah-jongg / 〈3人は既にいるときに〉get a fourth for mah-jongg.

めんぼう[1] 綿棒 【医】a [an absorbent cotton] swab (fixed to a stick); 〈通俗に〉a cotton bud.

めんぼう[2] 麺棒 a rolling pin.

めんぼく 面目 〈体面〉《文》honor; (a) reputation; prestige; 〈威厳〉dignity; 〈様子〉(an) appearance　¶面目を施す 《文》gain [win] honor; get credit for / 面目を失う[つぶす] disgrace oneself; lose (one's) face; 《文》be put out of countenance; be in disgrace / 面目を保つ preserve one's honor / 面目を立てる save sb's honor [face] / 面目を一新する undergo a complete change / 面目にかかわる問題 a

---

Abruptly spoken to in English, I was quite flurried.

めんしき 彼とは一面識もない。 He is a total stranger to me. | I have no (personal) acquaintance with him.

めんじる 彼はまだ経験が浅いということに免じてもう少し寛大にしてやって下さい。 Please make allowances for his inexperience and be more lenient.

めんする その家は海に面している。 The house looks [faces] toward the sea. / 彼の部屋は庭に面していた。 His room looked out onto [into] the garden. / 事務所は路地に面していた。 The office was on an alley. / わが国は東は太平洋に面している。 To the east Japan faces the Pacific.

めんせき[3] この土地の面積は幾らあるか。 What is the area of this land? / フロリダは面積約14万平方キロの半島だ。 Florida is a peninsula with an area of about 140,000 square kilometers. / 北極海は南極大陸と面積がほぼ同じである。 The Arctic Ocean has almost the same area as Antarctica. | The Arctic Ocean is about as large as Antarctica in area.

めんだん 部課長に面談したい。 I wish to speak to the chief of the department [section]. / 委細面談。 《広告》Particulars to be arranged personally. | Apply in person for particulars.

めんどう ごめんどうでしょうがちょっとここの意味を教えて下さい。 May I trouble you to tell me the meaning of this passage? / 少しもめんどうではありません。 It

めんみつ 綿密 ❶綿密な〈細かい〉《文》minute; detailed;〈細心な〉《文》scrupulous;〈細心の〉《文》meticulous;〈精緻な〉close; elaborate;〈徹底した〉thorough / 綿密な人 a scrupulous person / 綿密に minutely; carefully; elaborately; in detail; thoroughly. [文例⇩]

めん 藻 an alga (*pl.* -ae)

めんめん¹ 面々 every one; each one; all.
めんめん² 綿々 ❶めんめんたる continuous; unbroken;《文》unceasing; endless / めんめんとして continuously;《文》unceasingly; without a break; at (great) length.
めんもく 面目 ⇨ めんぼく.
めんよう 綿羊 a (wool) sheep.
めんよう² 面妖 ❶面妖な strange; mysterious.
めんるい 麺類 noodles; vermicelli.

も

も¹ 喪 mourning ❶喪が明ける the period of mourning expires;〈人が主語〉come out of mourning / 喪に服する go into mourning (for *sb*) / 喪に服している be in mourning.
も² 藻 an alga (*pl.* -ae) 《★ 通例 *pl.* の algae を使う》; duckweed (あおうきくさ属の); seaweed (海藻).
-も〈並びに〉and; as well as; both... and...;〈...もまた〉too; also;〈...も...でない〉not... either; neither...nor...;〈程度〉as many [much, long, far] as; no less [fewer] than;〈すら〉even;〈...でも〉even if; although; though ❶1か月もたたないうちに before (even) a month had passed / 降っても照っても (come) rain or shine / 彼が来ても来なくても whether he comes or not / いくら働いても however [no matter how] hard *one* works [may work] / どれほど欠点があっても with all *sb's* faults. [文例⇩]

[用法]「...もまた」の意の too は, 文中のどの語にかかっていても, 会話では文尾につけるのが普通. 従って,「ジョンもバイオリンをひく」も「ジョンはバイオリンもひく」も共に英語では John plays the violin, too. となるが, 会話では John と violin のいずれに置くかで, 意味の区別はつけられる.

もう¹ 蒙 ❶蒙をひらく《文》enlighten (*sb's* mind).

もう² 〈既に〉already; yet (疑問文で);〈もはや〉(*not*) any longer [more]; no longer;〈今では〉now;〈間もなく〉soon; presently; before long;〈今頃は〉by now; by this (time);〈更に〉another; again;《文》further; more ❶もう一つの方 the other (one) / もうそれだけ as many [much] more / もう少し some more. [文例⇩]

もうあ 盲啞 the blind and dumb ❶盲啞学校 a blind and dumb school.
もうい 猛威 ferocity; fierceness; fury ❶猛威を振るう〈人が〉《文》exercise an overwhelming influence (over); go on a [be on the] rampage;〈事物が〉rage; be rampant; play [work] havoc (with).
もうか 猛火 raging [roaring] flames; a devastating fire ❶猛火の中に飛び込む rush into raging flames.
もうがっこう 盲学校 a school for the blind.
もうかる 儲る〈人が主語〉make a profit; make money;《文》gain;〈事物が主語〉be profitable; yield profits;《文》be lucrative;〈割に合う〉pay; be paying. [文例⇩]
もうかん 毛管 a capillary (tube) ❶毛管現象《物》a capillary phenomenon;《by》capillarity.
もうきん 猛禽 a bird of prey; a predatory

---

is no trouble at all. / だれもめんどうくさがってしようとしなかった. Nobody bothered to do it.
めんぼく 面目次第もございません. I am really ashamed of myself. / I have no excuse to offer. / 彼は自分が苦しんでいることを, 面目にかけて人に気取られまいとした. He made it a point of honor not to let it be seen that he was in trouble.

-も 君が行くのなら, 僕も行こう. If you're going, I'll go too. / 腹がへったか, 僕もへった. Are you hungry? So am I (口語) Me too). / 僕も知らない. I don't know, either. / 彼女は嫌だとは言うない, ―僕もそう思う. I hope she won't refuse.—I hope not, too. / 今日もいい天気になろう. It's going to be fine again today [fine today too]. | We are going to have another nice day. / 僕のほ

かにもお客があった. There was another visitor besides [as well as] me. / 黒いのもあり赤いのもあります. We have [There are] both black ones and red ones. | Some are black, others are red. / 彼女も悪いが, 君も君だ. Both she and you are at fault. | She is to blame, but so are you [but you are no less to blame]. / 私はフランス語もドイツ語も話せません. I can't speak either French or German. | I can speak neither French nor German. / 彼は賢くもあり親切でもある. He is both wise and kind. / あの人は12人も兄弟がある. He has no less than twelve brothers and sisters. / この大聖堂を建設するのには何年もかかった. It took (any number of) years to build this cathedral. / 雪が2メートルも積もった. The snow lay to a depth of two me-

ters. / 僕が出しゃばりというなら, あいつもそうだ. If I'm a busybody, so is he [he is another]. / 彼が賛成してもしなくても, 私の決意は変わらない. I shan't change my mind, whether he approves or not. / ペンで書いても鉛筆で書いてもよろしい. You may write it either with a pen or (with) a pencil. | You can use whichever you prefer, pen or pencil. / その本は開けてもみない. I have never even opened the book. / さようならも言わずに行ってしまった. He went away without even [so much as] saying good-bye. / 雨が降っても行きますよ. I shall go even if it rains. / どこへ行くのでも行く先を言っておいて下さい. Keep us informed of your whereabouts, wherever you go. / だれが来ても, 僕は留守だと言ってくれ.

もうくんれん　1229　もうしおくる

[raptorial] bird.
もうくんれん 猛訓練 《undergo》 hard [intense] training.
もうけ¹ 設け 〈準備〉 preparation; arrangement;〈設備〉《文》provision ¶設けの席につく take the seat provided [reserved]《for *one*》.
もうけ² 儲け profits; gains; earnings ¶《事業などが》もうけが多い[少ない]《文》yield much [little] profit; pay well [badly] / もうけにならない bring no profit(s); do not pay; be not a paying business / ひともうけする make money; make a (little) fortune; turn a quick profit [《米口語》a fast buck] / もうけ口 a chance [an opportunity] to make a bit of money / もうけ物 a good bargain;〈拾い物〉a godsend; a windfall; a find. 文例⇩
もうげき 猛撃 a fierce [furious, heavy] attack; a hard blow ¶猛撃を加える deal *sb* a severe blow; make [launch] a fierce attack 《on [against] the enemy》.
もうける¹ 設ける 〈設備する〉provide;〈制定する〉lay down;〈設置する〉establish 《an office》;〈設ける a school》organize 《a company》; set up 《a factory》;〈準備する〉prepare; arrange;〈子を〉have;《文》beget《父親が主語》bear《母親が主語》¶講座を設ける《大学が》create [establish] a chair 《of French literature》.
もうける² 儲ける profit 《by》; make [get,《文》obtain,《文》derive] a profit《from》; make [earn]《money》¶もうけて売る sell *sth* at a profit. 文例⇩
もうけん 猛犬 a fierce [ferocious, savage, vicious] dog. 文例⇩
もうこ¹ 猛虎 a fierce [ferocious] tiger.
もうこ² 蒙古 Mongolia ⇒モンゴル ¶蒙古の Mongol; Mongolian / 蒙古語 Mongolian / 蒙古人 a Mongol; a Mongolian / 蒙古斑 a Mongolian [Mongol] mark [spot]; a blue spot.
もうこう(げき) 猛攻(撃) ¶猛攻撃を加える make a ferocious [ruthless] attack 《on the enemy》; attack and attack;《野球》pump out hits; hammer 《a pitcher》.
もうこん 毛根 the root [bulb] of a hair; a hair root.
もうさいかん 毛細管〈毛管現象が見られるような細い管〉a capillary (tube) ⇒もうかん.〈血管〉a capillary (vessel).
もうし 孟子〈人〉Mencius;《書名》*The Discourses of Mencius*.
もうしあげる 申し上げる tell; say;《文》state; mention;《文》relate.
もうしあわせ 申し合わせ arrangement(s); an agreement; an understanding ¶申し合わせにより by mutual agreement;《文》by common [mutual] consent / 申し合わせ事項 an agreed item. 文例⇩
もうしあわせる 申し合わせる arrange; make an arrangement 《with》; agree 《on》; fix up an agreement;《文》consent / 申し合わせて by agreement [hour] / 申し合わせた時間に at the appointed time [hour] / 申し合わせたように《文》as if by common consent.
もうしいで 申し出で〈提供〉an offer;〈申し込み〉an application;〈提議〉a proposal; an offer;〈要求〉a request;〈届け〉a report.
もうしいれ 申し入れ〈提案〉a proposal; an offer;〈訴え〉《文》a representation (★複数形で使うことが多い);〈通告〉a notice. 文例⇩
もうしいれる 申し入れる〈提案する〉propose; offer; make a proposal;〈苦情を〉complain [《文》make representations]《to *sb* concerning [about] *sth*》;〈通告する〉give notice 《to》.
もうしうける 申し受ける〈受け取る〉accept;《文》receive;〈請求する〉ask for; charge 《a price》¶実費を申し受ける ask *sb* to pay the actual expenses.
もうしおくり 申し送り〈伝言〉a message;〈《事務などの》引き継ぎ〉transfer 《of》; handing over 《*one*'s business to *one*'s successor》.
もうしおくる 申し送る〈伝言する〉send word 《to》;〈手紙で〉write 《to》 *sb*;〈事務などを〉引

Whoever comes [may come], you are to say that I'm out. | I'm at home to nobody. / いくら高くてもいいから、いい物を買いなさい。Buy a good one, however much it costs 《regardless of the price》. / だれが何と言っても僕は賛成しない。I can't agree, whatever anyone may say. | No one [Nothing] will persuade me to approve of it.
もう² 彼はもう帰った。He has already gone. / 彼はもう出発したか。Has he started yet? /《驚いて》もう10時か。Is it ten already? / もうだれも待っていなかった。Nobody was waiting any longer. / ペンキはもう乾いた。The paint has dried. | The paint is no longer wet. / 彼はもう京都に着いているだろう。He must have arrived at Kyoto by now [by this time]. / もう英語が話せてもいい頃だ。It is about time you were able to speak English./ もう来るでしょう。He will soon be here. /《目的地まで》もうすぐです。We are nearly there. / もう歩けない。I can't walk any further. | I can walk no further. / もう少しでおぼれる所でした。I was nearly [almost] drowned. | I came very near 《to》 being drowned.
もうかる そんな仕事をしていても金にもうからない。There's no money in that kind of work. / それを5千円以下で売ってはもうかりません。It wouldn't pay to sell it for less than five thousand yen. / 休みが1日もうかった。We had an unexpected extra day's holiday.
もうけ² 彼はその品物を売って大もうけをした。He made a large profit by selling the goods. / それでは大してもうけにならなかった。I didn't make much out of it.
もうける² 彼はほんの子供だが月に20万円もうける。He is a mere boy, but he makes [earns] 200,000 yen a month. / 彼はこの事業で大いに金をもうけている。He is making very good money out of this enterprise.
もうけん 猛犬に注意。《掲示》Beware of the dog.
もうしあわせ この件については何らの意見をも発表せぬよう会員の間で申し合わせた。It was agreed among the members that they should not publish any opinions on the subject.
もうしいれ 政府は直ちに米国政府に申し入れを行なった。The Japanese Government made immediate representations to Washington.

き継ぐ〉transfer [hand over] 《*one's* business to *sb*》.

もうしおくれる 申し遅れる [文例⇩]

もうしかねる 申し兼ねる ¶申しかねますが Excuse me for making such a request, but…; Might I ask you to…?

もうしご 申し子 a child born in answer to *one's* prayer; 《文》 a heaven-sent [godsent] child.

もうしこす 申し越す 〈伝言する〉 send word 《to》; 〈書き送る〉 write 《a letter》 to *sb*; write (to) *sb* 《that…》; 〈依頼する〉 ask [《文》 request] 《*sb* to *do*》 ¶申し越しあり次第 《文》 on request; 《文》 on application. [文例⇩]

もうしこみ 申し込み 〈応募〉 (an) application; subscription (株式などの); 〈申し入れ〉 an offer; 〈提議〉 a proposal; 〈挑戦〉 a challenge 《to a game》; 〈(座席などの)予約〉 (a) reservation; (a) booking ¶たくさんの申し込みがある have a large number of applications / 申し込みのあり次第に 《文》 on application [request] / 申し込みに応じる[を断わる] 《文》 comply with [decline] an offer [a proposal]; accept [refuse] a request / 申し込み順に in order of application / 申込み期限 a time limit for application(s) / 申込書 an [a written] application; 〈用紙〉 《米》 an application blank; 《英》 an application form / 申込書に必要事項を記入する 《米》 fill out an application blank; 《英》 fill in an application form / 申し込み所 a place where (the) applications are accepted / 申し込み人 an applicant; a subscriber (株式などの). [文例⇩]

もうしこむ 申し込む 〈出願する〉 apply 《for enrollment》; make an application [《文》 make application] 《for membership》; 〈提議する〉 propose; make a proposal; 〈申し入れる〉 offer 《assistance to *sb*》; 《文》 lodge [file] 《a protest with *sb* against *sth*》; enter 《for a contest》; 〈予約する〉 reserve 《a room》; make reservations 《at a hotel》; book 《a seat》; 〈応募する〉 subscribe 《for the new stocks》 ¶会見を申し込む ask for an interview 《with》 / 結婚を申し込む ask *sb* to marry *one*; propose 《to》; 《文》 propose [make a proposal of] marriage 《to *sb*》 / テニスの試合を申し込む challenge *sb* to a game of tennis. [文例⇩]

もうしたて 申し立て 〈陳述〉 a statement; an account 《of *sth*》; 〈言明〉 (a) declaration; 〈証言〉 testimony ¶虚偽の申し立てをする make a false [perjured] statement; commit perjury (偽証する).

もうしたてる 申し立てる 《文》 state; make a statement; declare; 《文》 set forth; put forward; plead (訴訟事実などを); testify (証言する) ¶理由を申し立てる give [state] *one's* reason(s) / 事実を申し立てる state the fact(s).

もうしつける 申し付ける ⇨ いいつける, めいじる[1].

もうしで 申し出 ⇨ もうしいで.

もうしでる 申し出る 〈提議する〉 propose; suggest; put forward 《a suggestion》; 〈申し入れる〉 offer; make an offer; 〈願い出る〉 apply [ask] 《for》; 《文》 request; 〈通知する〉 report; 《文》 notify ¶援助を申し出る offer *one's* help [《文》 assistance] 《to》 / 理由を申し出る give the reason 《for》.

もうしのべる 申し述べる say; 《文》 state; tell 《*sb* that…》.

もうしひらき 申し開き ⇨ いいひらき.

もうしぶん 申し分 ⇨ いいぶん ¶申し分のない perfect; 《文》 impeccable; (completely) satisfactory. [文例⇩]

もうしゃ 猛射 heavy fire [firing]; a rain of bullets ¶猛射を浴びせる rain heavy fire on 《the enemy》.

もうじゃ 亡者 〈死者〉 the dead; 〈幽霊〉 a ghost ¶金の亡者 a person who is money-mad.

もうしゅう[1] 妄執 《文》 a mistakenly held obsession; 《文》 a deep-seated delusion.

もうしゅう[2] 猛襲 a fierce [vigorous, heavy, hot] attack; a violent assault ¶猛襲する make a fierce attack 《on》.

もうじゅう[1] 盲従 blind [unquestioning] obedience [deference] ¶盲従する follow [obey] *sb* blindly.

もうじゅう[2] 猛獣 a fierce [ferocious] animal; 《文》 a savage beast; a beast of prey (肉食獣) ¶猛獣狩りをする shoot big game; go big-game hunting; go on (a) safari.

もうしょ 猛暑 fierce [《文》 excessive] heat; a heat wave.

もうしよう 申し様 how to express 《*one's* idea》. [文例⇩]

もうじょう 網状 ¶網状の netlike; 《文》 reticular; 《文》 reticulated / 網状組織 a network 《of tiny vessels》.

もうしわけ 申し訳 ⇨ いいわけ ¶ほんの申し訳程度の a mere apology for 《a window》; token 《concessions》 / 申し訳の立たない失策をする 《文》 commit an inexcusable blunder / 申し訳に by way of (an) apology / …の申し訳に to excuse 《*one's* mistake》; 《文》 in excuse of…;

もうしおくれる 申し遅れましたが父からよろしくということでした. I ought to have said first [before] that my father wishes to be remembered to you. / なお, 申し遅れましたが, 昨日開催の予定の総会は来月に延期になりました. I must hasten to add here that the general meeting scheduled for yesterday has been postponed to next month.

もうしこす お申し越しの趣拝承いたしました. We have duly noted the contents of your letter.

もうしこみ マラソン競走の参加申し込みが300人あった. There were 300 entries for the marathon.

もうしこむ 書面または口頭でお申し込み下さい. Apply either in writing or in person.

もうしぶん これは申し分がない. This leaves nothing to be desired [to wish for]. / 品質の点は申し分がない. There is nothing to complain of as far as (the) quality is concerned. / この部屋なら申し分がない. This room will suit me perfectly. / 天候は申し分ない. This is ideal weather. | The weather could not be better.

もうしよう お礼の申し様もございません. I cannot thank you enough. | I don't know how to express my gratitude to you. | I

もうしわたし
〈罪の償いに〉《文》to atone for 《an offense》; 《文》in expiation of 《one's past sins》/ ただいまの申し訳に《文》perfunctorily ; for mere form's sake / ちょっと申し訳に裁判を開いただけで after a mockery of a trial. 文例⇩

もうしわたし 申し渡し ⇨いいわたし.

もうしわたす 申し渡す〈命じる〉tell [order] 《sb to do》;《文》bid 《sb do》;〈宣言する〉announce ;〈判決を〉sentence 《sb to death》; give [pass,《文》pronounce] sentence 《on the accused》.

もうしん¹ 妄信 blind [unquestioning] acceptance 《of a theory》; an unquestioning belief; (blind) faith ¶妄信する give hasty credit 《to a rumor》; believe blindly 《in astrology》.

もうしん² 猛進 ¶猛進する dash [make a bold dash] forward ; push forward vigorously.

もうじん 盲人 a blind person ;《総称》the blind.

もうす 申す ⇨いう.

もうせい 猛省《文》serious reflection [reconsideration];《文》penitence 《for one's wrongdoing》/ 猛省を促す《文》urge sb to reflect seriously 《on his conduct》.

もうせん 毛氈 a rug ; a (felt) carpet.

もうせんごけ〔植〕a dew grass ; a (round-leaved) sundew.

もうぜんと 猛然と fiercely ; furiously ;《文》resolutely ;〈attack〉with ferocity ¶猛然と食ってかかる fly out 《at, against》.

もうそう 妄想 a wild fancy ; a fantasy ; a fantastic idea ; a delusion ¶妄想にふける be lost in wild fancies ; spin a daydream.

もうだ 猛打 ¶猛打を浴びせる〈野球〉hit hard ; pump out hits ; hammer 《a pitcher》.

もうたくとう 毛沢東 Mao Tse-tung ; Mao Zedong ¶毛沢東主義[主義者] Maoism [a Maoist].

もうちょう 盲腸〔解〕the cecum 《pl. ceca》; the blind gut ;〈虫垂〉the (vermiform) appendix《pl. -es, -dices》¶盲腸を取る have one's appendix removed [out] / 盲腸炎 appendicitis ; cecitis / 盲腸炎の手術 an operation for appendicitis ; (an) appendectomy. 文例⇩

-もうで …詣で ⇨さんけい² ¶鹿島もうで a pilgrimage [visit] to the Kashima Shrine.

もうでる 詣でる ⇨さんけい²(参詣する).

もうてん 盲点〈網膜上の〉〔医〕a blind spot ; a scotoma 《pl. -s, -mata》¶日本人の盲点 a blind spot in the Japanese mind / 法の盲点 a loophole [blind spot] in the law ; a legal loophole / 盲点を突く pinpoint [put one's finger on] a [sb's] weak point [blind spot]; question something which sb has always taken for granted ; take sb aback. 文例⇩

もうとう 毛頭《否しも》(not) (in) the least ; (not) at all ; (not) a bit. 文例⇩

もうどうけん 盲導犬 a seeing-eye dog ; a guide dog.

もうどく 猛毒 (a) deadly poison.

もうねん 妄念 a distracting idea ; irrelevant thoughts.

もうばく 猛爆 heavy bombing ; (a) heavy (air) bombardment ; an intensive air raid.

もうはつ 毛髪 hair.

もうはんげき 猛反撃 (make) a terrific counterattack 《on》.

もうひつ 毛筆 a (writing) brush.

もうひょう 妄評《文》《my》inadequate criticism [comment(s)].

もうふ 毛布 a blanket ; a rug ¶毛布にくるまる be wrapped [wrap oneself up] in a blanket.

もうべんきょう 猛勉強 ¶猛勉強をする work hard ;《口語》grind (away) 《at》.

もうまい 蒙昧 ignorance ¶蒙昧な《文》unenlightened ; ignorant ; uncivilized.

もうまく 網膜 the retina 《pl. -s, -nae》¶網膜に映る〈物が主語〉be reflected in the eyes 《of》; be seen ; come in sight ;〈人が主語〉see ; catch [gain] sight 《of》/ 網膜移植 a retina [retinal] transplant / 網膜剥離(はく)《have [suffer from]》a detached retina.

もうもう 濛々 ¶もうもうたる dense ; thick ; blinding 《sandstorms》/ もうもうたる砂塵(raise) clouds of dust / もうもうと立ちこめる rise in thick clouds.

もうもく 盲目 blindness ⇨めくら ¶盲目の blind ;《文》sightless / 盲目的 blind ; reckless; unquestioning / 盲目的に blindly ; recklessly.

もうら 網羅 ¶網羅する〈包含する〉include [《文》comprehend, contain] everything [all (the points)] ; cover all (the facts) ;〈集める〉collect all (the items) ; bring together / 網羅的な《文》comprehensive ;《文》all-inclusive ;《文》exhaustive.

もうれつ 猛烈 ¶猛烈な violent ;《文》vehement ; furious ; fierce ; feverish ; intense / 猛烈な競争 a keen competition / 猛烈なスピード《at》terrific [breakneck] speed / 猛烈な反対 strong opposition / 猛烈な練習 heavy [intensive,《文》rigorous] training / 猛烈に violently ;《文》vehemently ; furiously ; fierce-

---

am more grateful (to you) than I can say. / ご不幸に対し何ともお慰めの申し様がありません. I don't know what to say to console you in your great loss.

もうしわけ 何とも申し訳がありません. I don't know how to apologize to you [what excuse to make]. / ご返事が遅くなって申し訳ありません. Please forgive me for not answering your letter sooner.

もうちょう 盲腸が破れた. His appendix perforated [burst].

もうてん そのたぐいの事が私の盲点なのです. I have a blind spot for that kind of thing.

もうとう もうとう疑いない. There is not the least [not a shadow of] doubt. / あの方を悪く言うような気持ちはもうとうありません. I haven't the slightest intention of slandering him.

もうもう 黒煙もうもうとして天を おおった. Columns [Volumes] of murky smoke overspread the sky. / 部屋の中はタバコの煙でもうもうとしていた. The room was gray [thick] with tobacco smoke. | You could have cut the air with a knife, it was so full of cigarette smoke.

もうら この辞書は今のアメリカの俗語を網羅している. This dictionary contains all current American slang.

もうれんしゅう 猛練習 hard [intensive] training. 文例⇩

もうろう 朦朧 ¶もうろうたる dim;《文》indistinct; faint; vague; hazy; obscure / もうろうと dimly; indistinctly; faintly; vaguely; obscurely.

もうろく 耄碌《文》dotage; senility;〈病的な〉senile dementia [psychosis] ¶もうろくする《文》fall into one's dotage; get [《文》become] weak [feeble] with age;《俗》go gaga / もうろくしている be senile; be in one's dotage [second childhood].

もえ 燃え ¶燃えが悪い do [will] not burn well / 燃えをよくする make [the fire] [get (the fire) to] burn more briskly; stir (the fire)《かき立てて》.

もえあがる 燃え上がる burst into flame(s); blaze up ¶ぱっと燃え上がる flare up [into flame].

もえうつる 燃え移る ⇒ もえつく, もえひろがる.

もえおちる 燃え落ちる〈飛行機などが〉go down [fall to the ground] in flames ⇒ やけおちる.

もえかす 燃え滓 cinders; ashes.

もえがら 燃え殻 cinders.

もえき(いろ) 萌え黄(色) light [yellowish] green.

もえきる 燃え切る burn *itself* out; be burned up.

もえさかる 燃え盛る burn furiously ¶燃え盛る家 a blazing house; a house in raging flames [in full blaze].

もえさし 燃えさし embers;《文》a brand ¶マッチの燃えさし a match end.

もえつきる 燃え尽きる burn *itself* out;《文》be exhausted.

もえつく 燃え付く catch [take] fire;《米》catch on fire ¶燃えつきがいい[悪い] catch [do not catch] fire easily; be quick [slow] to catch fire. 文例⇩

もえでる 萌え出る ⇒ もえる¹. 文例⇩

もえのこり 燃え残り ⇒ もえさし.

もえひろがる 燃え広がる〈火が〉spread《to》;《文》extend. 文例⇩

もえる¹ 萌える sprout; bud; burst into bud; put forth shoots; come out.

もえる² 燃える burn; blaze ¶復讐(ふくしゅう)の念に燃える《文》thirst for revenge / 燃えている be burning; be on fire; be in flames;《文》be aflame; be ablaze / 燃えやすい burn easily; catch fire easily; be (in)flammable; be (highly) combustible / 燃えない do not burn (easily); be nonflammable; be noninflammable; be noncombustible / 燃える思い《文》burning [ardent] love《for》.

もー〈牛の声〉a moo ¶もーと鳴く moo; low; bellow (はげしく) / もーもー《小児語》a moocow.

モーション a motion ¶モーションをかける〈言い寄る〉make advances《to》;《文》make an amorous approach《to》;《米口語》make a play《for sb》;《英口語》chat sb up. 文例⇩

モーゼ Moses ¶モーゼの Mosaic / モーゼの五書 the Pentateuch; the Torah; the Five Books of Moses / モーゼの律法 the Law of Moses; the Mosaic Law.

モーター a motor; an engine ¶モーターを動かす start a motor / モーターを止める stop [switch off,《米》cut] the motor [engine] / モーターショー a motor show / モーターボート a motorboat; a powerboat.

モータリゼーション motorization.

モーテル a motel; a motor [an auto] court.

モード the mode; (a) fashion.

モーニング〈朝, 午前〉morning;〈モーニングコート〉a morning coat [dress]; a cutaway (coat) ¶モーニングのしまズボン striped morning trousers / モーニングサービス cut-price service during the morning hours.

モーメント《物》moment ¶回転モーメント moment of rotation; torque / ねじりモーメント twisting moment; torque.

モーリシャス Mauritius.

モーリタニア Mauritania ¶モーリタニア回教共和国 the Islamic Republic of Mauritania.

モールスふごう モールス符号《通信》the Morse [morse] code [alphabet, signals]; Morse [morse] ¶モールス符号で送信する send morse code; communicate [signal] in morse (code); morse.

モカ〈コーヒー〉mocha.

もがく 踠く struggle; writhe; wriggle.

もぎ 模擬 ¶模擬の imitation; sham; mock;《文》simulated / 模擬裁判 a moot [mock] court / 模擬試験 a mock [trial] examination / 模擬店 a refreshment booth; a snack bar [counter, stand].

もぎとる 捥ぎ取る ⇒ もぎる.

もぎり 捥ぎり〈劇場の〉a ticket-collector.

もうれつ 彼らはその施策に猛烈に反対した。They protested vigorously [vehemently] against the measure.

もうれんしゅう 挑戦者加山は「この試合に備えて2か月間猛練習をしました」と語った。'I have trained hard for two months for this fight,' declared Kayama, the challenger.

もえつく 積みわらに火が燃えついた。The pile of straw caught fire. / まきが湿ってなかなか燃えつかない。The wood is moist and will not kindle.

もえでる 木の芽が萌え出た。The trees are in bud. / 木々には若葉が勢いよく萌え出ていた。There were great bursts of leaves growing on the trees.

もえひろがる 火はたちまち燃え広がって30軒全焼した。The flames spread [extended] rapidly until thirty houses had been burned to the ground.

もえる 火がようやく燃えてきた。The fire is catching [kindling] at last. / 彼らは向学心に燃えている。They are burning with the desire to learn. / 全山燃えるような紅葉だ。The whole mountain glows [is ablaze] with autumnal colors.

もぎる 捥ぎる snatch [wrench, 《文》wrest] (away)；pluck [tear, break] off.

もく 目 〈項目〉an item；a division；a class；〈動植物分類の〉an order ⇨ **もん**¹；〈囲碁の〉a stone；a piece (石)；a point (盤目) ¶《囲碁で》5目勝つ[負ける] win [lose] by five points / 4目置く[置かせる] give sb [have] a four-stone handicap. 文例

もぐ 捥ぐ pluck [break, tear] off；wrench [《文》wrest] 《from》 ¶りんごをもぐ pick apples (from the tree) / もぎたてのトマト a fresh [freshly picked] tomato.

もくあみ 木阿弥 ¶元のもくあみになる lose all that *one* has gained；be (right) back where *one* started. 文例

もくぎょ 木魚 (beat) a wood block (in a Buddhist temple).

もくげき¹ 目撃 ¶目撃する witness；《文》observe；see (with *one's* own eyes) / 目撃者 an eyewitness / 目撃者の話 an eyewitness report [account]. 文例

もくげき² 黙劇 a pantomime；a dumb show.

もぐさ 艾 moxa.

もくざい 木材 wood；〈用材〉timber；《米》lumber ¶木材置き場 a lumberyard；a woodyard / 木材商 a timber [《米》lumber] merchant.

もくさつ 黙殺 ¶黙殺する take no notice of；ignore；refuse [《文》not deign] even to comment on *sth*.

もくさん 目算 〈当て〉an estimate；expectation(s)；《文》anticipation；(a) calculation；〈計画〉a plan ¶目算が外れる *one's* expectations [estimates] go wrong [《文》awry]；〈人が主語〉《文》be disappointed in *one's* expectations；〈事が主語〉fall [come] short of *one's* expectations；disappoint *one*. 文例

もくし¹ 黙示 〈天啓〉《文》revelation ¶ヨハネ黙示録 (聖書) the Revelation of St. John the Divine；〈略῀〉the Revelation (略: Rev.)；〈俗称〉(the) Revelations；the Apocalypse (略: Apoc.).

もくし² 黙視 ¶黙視する〈見逃す〉overlook；wink [《文》connive] at；pass over；〈傍観する〉remain a mere spectator (of, to).

もくじ 目次 a table of contents ★本の目次のページには普通単に Contents と書く．なお，content と単数形にすれば本の「内容」になる ないよう 囲読.

もくしつ 木質 〈植〉¶木質の woody；ligneous / 木質繊維[組織] woody fiber [tissue] / 木質部 the wood；the woody parts (of a plant)；xylem.

もくしょう 木睫 ⇨ **もくぜん**.

もくず 藻屑 ¶海底の藻くずとなる be drowned at sea；《文》meet [find] a watery grave.

もくする¹ 目する ⇨ みなす.

もくする² 黙する ⇨ だまる ¶黙して語らない hold *one's* tongue；refuse to say anything (about)；keep silent [mum] (about).

もくせい¹ 木星 〈天〉Jupiter ¶木星の Jovian.

もくせい² 木製 ¶木製の wooden；made of wood.

もくせい³ 〈植〉a sweet osmanthus.

もくぜん 目前 ¶目前の before [under] *one's* eyes；immediate；《文》imminent / 目前の利に走る《文》seek immediate gain；be after immediate profit [quick profits]；《文》adopt a shortsighted policy / 目前に迫る be close [near] at hand；《文》be imminent.

もくそう¹ 目送 ¶目送する follow *sb* with *one's* eyes；gaze after *sb*.

もくそう² 黙想《文》(a) meditation；《文》contemplation ¶黙想する《文》meditate (on)；《文》muse (on) / 黙想にふける be lost in thought [contemplation]；be absorbed in meditation.

もくぞう¹ 木造 ¶木造の wooden；(built [made]) of wood / 木造家屋 a wooden house；《米》a frame house [building] / 木造建築物 a wooden [timber] building. 文例

もくぞう² 木像 a wooden image [statue, idol].

もくそく 目測 eye measurement ¶目測する measure with the eye.

もくだく 黙諾《文》tacit consent；《文》acquiescence ¶黙諾する《文》acquiesce (in)；《文》give (*one's*) tacit consent [a silent assent] (to).

もくたん 木炭 charcoal；〈デッサン用の〉(a pencil of) charcoal；fusain ¶木炭画 a charcoal (drawing)；a fusain.

もくちょう 木彫 wood sculpture [engraving].

もくてき 目的 a purpose；an aim；《文》an object；an objective；《文》an end (in view)；〈目標〉a goal；〈意図〉《文》a design；an intention ¶目的を達する[遂げる]《文》accomplish *one's* purpose；succeed in what *one* set out to do；《文》attain *one's* object；succeed in *sth* [doing]；《文》gain *one's* end；achieve [carry out] *one's* aim [purpose]；〈口語〉do the trick；get there / 世界平和という大目的を推し進める《文》advance the cause of world peace / 目的にかなう answer the purpose；serve *one's* purpose(s) [end(s)] / …の目的で for the purpose of *doing*；《文》with the object of *doing*；with a view to *doing* / …を目的とする aim at…；have *sth*

モーション ピッチャー振りかぶって第1球のモーション．The pitcher is winding up for the first pitch.

モーニング モーニングサービス：コーヒー200円．〈看板の文句〉Coffee served at a specially reduced price of 200 yen in the morning hours.

もく あなたはあの人に何目置かせますか．What handicap do you take when you play *go* with him?

もくあみ 元のもくあみだ．I am no better off than I was.

もくげき¹ 漁船が遭難しているのが目撃された．A fishing boat was observed in distress. / 恐ろしい光景を目撃した．I witnessed [was witness to] a horrible scene.

もくさん その出来事のため目算ががらりと外れた．The incident upset the whole plan.

もくし² その事実を黙視することはできない．I cannot shut my eyes to the fact. / あの悪党に君がまんまとひっかかるのを僕は黙視しているわけにはいかない．I can't stand by and see you play into the hands of that rascal.

もくぞう¹ 大概の日本の家屋は木造です．Most Japanese houses are built of wood.

もくとう 黙禱 ¶黙禱する pray silently; 《文》 offer a silent prayer (to) / 戦争犠牲者に対して1分間の黙禱を捧げる pay one minute's silent tribute to the war dead; observe a minute of silence for the war dead.

もくどく 黙読 ¶黙読する read silently [to *oneself*].

もくにん 黙認 silent [《文》 tacit] approval [《文》 consent, permission]; 《文》 connivance; 《文》 acquiescence ¶黙認する《文》 permit tacitly; tolerate; wink [《文》 connive] at; 《文》 acquiesce (in).

もくねじ 木ねじ a wood screw.

もくねん 黙然 ⇒もくもく¹.

もくば 木馬 a wooden horse; 〈揺り木馬〉 a rocking horse; a rocker; 〈体操用〉 a (vaulting) horse ¶トロイの木馬 the Trojan horse.

もくはい 木杯 a wooden cup.

もくはん 木版 〈術〉 wood engraving; (wood-) block printing ¶木版に刷る make a print from a wood block / 木版画 a (wood-)block print; a woodcut; a woodprint / 木版刷りの block-printed (cards).

もくひ 黙秘 ¶黙秘する keep silent (about); keep *sth* secret / 黙秘権を行使する use [exercise] *one's* right to keep silence; 《文》 stand mute.

もくひょう 目標 〈目印〉 a mark; a sign; 〈標的〉 a target; 〈目的〉 a goal; an aim; an objective ¶目標を高い所に置く aim high; set *one's* sights high / …を目標にする aim at *sth* [to do]; set *one's* sights on *sth*; set *oneself* the task [goal] of *doing*; 《文》 have *sth* as an object / 目標に向ける put (the spacecraft) on target / 目標になる present a fine target (for) / 長期目標 a [*one's*] long-range objective; a long-term aim / 〈生産などが〉目標額に達する hit the target / 〈計画などの〉目標時間 target time / 目標地点に正確に着陸する land (right) on target; make an accurate [on-target] landing; make a bull's-eye landing. 文例↓

もくぶ 木部 《植》 the xylem.

もくへん 木片 〈大きい〉 a (wooden) block; 〈小さい〉 a chip [bit, piece] of wood; 〈細かい〉 a splinter.

もくめ 木目 the grain (of wood) ¶木目の細かい [つんだ] close-grain(ed); fine-grained / 木目の荒い coarse-grained.

もくもく¹ 黙々 ¶黙々たる silent; 《文》 mute; dumb / 黙々として silently; in silence; 《文》 mutely. 文例↓

もくもく² ¶もくもく煙を上げる send up (great) volumes of smoke; 《文》 emit smoke in great profusion / もくもくとわく雲 mountainous clouds. 文例↓

もぐもぐ ¶(口を)もぐもぐさせる mumble / 口をもぐもぐさせながら言う mumble (out) (*one's* name); chew *one's* words.

もくやく 黙約 a tacit agreement [understanding]; 《文》 an implicit promise.

もくようび 木曜日 Thursday (略: Thur(s).) ⇒にちよう(び) 囲品.

もくよく 沐浴 bathing; a bath ⇒にゅうよく, さいかいもくよく.

もぐら 《動》 a mole ¶もぐらの掘った穴 a mole('s) tunnel / もぐら塚 a molehill; a molecast.

もぐり 潜り 〈潜水〉 diving ¶もぐりの〈無免許の〉 unlicensed; unqualified; back-street (travel agents); fly-by-night (operators); 〈にせの〉 sham; bogus.

もぐる 潜る dive (into [under] water) ¶潜り込む get [slip, creep, crawl] into [under] *sth*; 〈隠れる〉 hide among [under] / 布団に潜り込む get [creep] into bed; snuggle under a quilt. 文例↓

もくれい¹ 目礼 ¶目礼する nod ((to)); give *sb* a nod; greet with *one's* eyes / 目礼を交わす exchange nods.

もくれい² 黙礼 ¶黙礼する make a bow ((to)); bow ((to)); bow in silence.

もくれん 《植》 a (lily) magnolia.

もくれんが 木煉瓦 a wood [wooden] block.

もくろく 目録 a catalogue; 《米》 a catalog; a checklist; 〈財産・在庫品の〉 an inventory; 〈目次〉 contents; 〈人名などの表〉 a list ¶目録に載せる catalogue (articles); put (an item) on [in] the catalogue; 〈図書館で受け入れ図書を〉 accession / 目録に載っている be (listed) in the catalogue.

もくてき 彼は日本の事情を研究する目的で当地に滞在している. He is staying here for the purpose of studying things Japanese. / 教育の主目的はよき市民をつくることにある. The chief aim of education is to bring up good citizens. / 目的のためには手段を選ばずというのはいけない. The end does not justify the means. / 目的の村に着かないうちに日が暮れた. Night had fallen before I reached the village which was my destination [to which I was going].

もくひょう K社の自動車生産台数はまだ月産10万台の目標に達しない. The K Company is still short of its goal of manufacturing 100,000 cars a month. / その計画は3年後の成功を目標として始められたのである. The project was initiated with a three-year target date for success.

もくもく¹ 彼は黙々として語らなかった. He remained mute on the subject.

もくもく² 煙突から煙がもくもく吐いていた. The chimney was belching (out [《文》 forth]) smoke.

もぐら 花壇の下をもぐらが掘った. A mole has tunneled its way under the flower bed.

もぐる 君はどれくらい水の中に潜っていられるか. How long can you stay under water? / はまぐりが砂の中に潜った. The clam dug itself into the sand.

もくろみ もくろみが外れた. My plan went wrong. | I was balked (in my plan). / あの男がああいうことを言うのは何かほかにもくろみがあったに違いない. He must have some other [ulterior] motive for saying things like that.

もくろみ 目論見 〈計画〉 a plan; a scheme; a project; a program; 〈意図〉 an intention (); a design; an idea; 〈目的〉《文》 an object; an aim; 〈予想〉 (a) prospect ¶もくろみがある have (some object) in view.

もくろむ 目論む plan (on doing, to do);《文》 project; form [lay] a plan; intend (to do);《文》 contemplate (doing);《文》 envisage (); envision; have sth in mind [prospect]. 文例◎

もけい 模型 a model; a dummy ¶船の模型 a ship model / 模型を作る make a model (of) / 実物大模型 a life-size model (of); a (full-scale) mockup (of an airplane) / 小模型 a miniature model (of) / 縮尺模型 a scale model / 模型実験 an experiment with a model; a model test; model-testing / 模型飛行機 a model plane.

もげる 挘げる come off; be wrenched [torn, broken] off.

もこ 模糊 ¶模糊たる dim; vague; hazy; faint; obscure; indistinct / 模糊として dimly; faintly;《文》 obscurely; indistinctly; in a haze.

もさ 猛者 a tough (guy); a fighter; a gamecock; 〈達人〉 a veteran.

モザイク a mosaic ¶モザイク式の mosaic (pavement) / モザイク模様の tessellated (floors).

もさく 模索 ¶模索する grope (for) ⇒あんちゅうもさく

モザンビーク Mozambique ¶モザンビーク人民共和国 the People's Republic of Mozambique.

もし if; in case (of); provided [supposing] (that) ¶もし雨が降ったら if it rains; in case of rain / もしかしたら[すると] possibly; by any chance; perhaps; maybe; by some chance (or other) / もしかしたら…しはせぬかと for fear of…; for fear that…may…; in case [《文》 lest] …should… / もし…がなかったら if it was not for…; if it had not been for…; without…; but for…; if it were [if it were] not for…; 《文》 had it not been for… / もしもの事があったら if anything [the worst] should happen. 文例◎

もじ 文字 a letter; a character (漢字など) ⇒じ¹ ¶(人間の) 文字の発明 the invention of writing / 文字を知らない be illiterate;《文》 be unlettered / 文字どおりに literally; to the letter / 文字盤 a dial (plate); the face (of a clock).

もしくは or; otherwise.

もしつける 燃し付ける set (firewood) alight [on fire]; light (a stove).

もしもし 〈呼びかけ〉 Excuse me!; Hallo!;《米》Say!;《英》I say!; 〈電話で〉 Hello!; Hello! Are you there? (相手に通じているか確認するために).

もじもじ ¶もじもじする 〈落ち着かない〉 fidget; be restless; 〈ためらう〉 hesitate / もじもじしながら nervously; hesitatingly; hesitantly.

もしや by any chance [possibility]; if. 文例◎

もしゃ 模写 a copy; a facsimile; a replica (彫刻・銅貨などの) ¶模写する copy (out); trace.

もじゃもじゃ ¶もじゃもじゃの shaggy;《文》 unkempt; tousled / もじゃもじゃの髪 a (wild) mop [shock] of hair.

もしゅ 喪主 the chief mourner.

もしょう 喪章 a mourning badge [band]; a black armband; a crape (band) ¶喪章をつける〈腕に〉 wear a crape [mourning] band on one's sleeve; 〈胸に〉 wear a mourning badge on one's breast. 文例◎

もじる 捩る parody;《文》 travesty; 〈地口を言う〉 pun [make a pun] (on) ¶歌をもじる write a parody of a tanka.

もす 燃す ⇒もやす.

もず 〈鳥〉 a shrike; a butcher-bird.

モスクワ Moscow ¶モスクワ市民 a Muscovite.

もすそ 裳裾 ¶女王の裳裾を捧げ持つ carry [《文》 bear] the royal train. 文例◎

もする 模する ⇒まねる, もほう.

もぞう 模造 imitation ¶模造する imitate; copy (from); pattern (on, after); model (on, after) / 模造の imitation (diamonds); artificial (leather); 〈にせものの〉 counterfeit (coins); fake(d) / 模造品 an imitation; a replica; 〈にせものの〉 a counterfeit.

もぞもぞ ¶もぞもぞする 〈虫などが〉 creep about (over one's body); 〈動く〉 stir restlessly.

もだえ 悶え (an) agony; 〈心痛〉《文》 anguish ¶もだえ苦しむ writhe in agony [pain].

もだえる 悶える be in agony [《文》 anguish]; suffer (intense) agony; 〈精神的に〉 be ago-

---

もくろむ 彼らは新事業を始めようともくろんでいる。 They are contemplating starting a new enterprise. | They have a new enterprise in mind.

もし もし地球上に水がなかったならば，生物は存在しえない。 If there was [were] no water on the earth, life would be impossible. / もし月世界行きの切符をやると言われたら，受け取りますか。 If you were offered a ticket to the moon, would you accept? / もしかすると今日は来ないかもしれない。 He may possibly not come today. / もし草木に花が咲かないとしたら自然はどんなに寂しいものであろう。 Suppose plants were not to [didn't] flower, how dreary nature would be! / もしもの事があっても覚悟はしている。 I am prepared for the worst.

もじ マオリ族は文字を持たないということだ。 I've heard that the Maoris do not have [possess] writing. / その文字は左から右へ書かれている。 The writing runs from left to right. / 我々はお互いの考えを文字を通じて伝えられるだけだった。 We were able to exchange our ideas only through the written word.

もしや あなたはもしや伊藤さんの住所をご存じではありませんか。 You don't happen to know Mr. Ito's address, do you? / もしやと思ったことが本当になった。 My (worst) fears have come true.

もしょう 国旗には皆喪章がついていた。 The national flags were all draped in mourning.

もすそ 彼女はもすそを翻してあでやかに踊った。 She danced beautifully, letting her skirt wave and flutter.

もたげる 擡げる lift; raise ⇨ もちあげる ¶頭をもたげる raise one's head; 〈比喩的に〉 gain strength; rise into importance ((from a low position)) ⇨ たいとう¹.

もだしがたい 黙し難い be unable to refuse [((文)) decline, turn down]; find it hard to refuse.

もたす 持たす ⇨ もたせる.

もたせかける 凭せ掛ける rest [lean, set, prop up] (A) against (B).

もたせる 持たせる 〈与える〉 let sb have [take] sth; give; 〈運ばせる〉 get sb to carry [take] sth; make [let, have] sb carry sth; 〈保たせる〉 keep; ((文)) preserve; 〈負担させる〉 have [let] sb pay ((the bill)) ¶使いに持たせてやる send ((a letter)) by hand / 赤帽にカバンを持って行かせる give a porter one's bag to carry / 1万円を1週間もたせる make ¥10,000 last for [stretch over] a week. 文例⇩

もたつく stick ((at)); be held up [((文)) impeded] ((by procedural difficulties)); act clumsily; 〈事が主語〉 be slow [heavy] going ⇨ もたもた.

もたもた ¶もたもたしている be slow ((at one's work)); ((文)) be tardy; be inefficient. 文例⇩

もたらす 齎す 〈持って来る〉 bring; carry; 〈招来する〉 produce; ((文)) bring about; cause ¶好結果をもたらす produce good results. 文例⇩

もたれる 凭れる 〈寄りかかる〉 lean on [against]; ((文)) recline on; rest against; 〈食物が〉 be heavy; sit [lie] heavy ((on one's stomach)); remain undigested ((in one's stomach)); be not easily digested.

モダン ¶モダンな modern; modernistic ((tea-rooms)).

もち¹ 持ち 〈耐久力〉 wear; durability; life ((of a car)); 〈負担〉 charge ¶持ちがいい[悪い] wear well [badly]; last [do not last] long.

もち² 餅 rice cake ¶もちをつく pound steamed rice into cake / もちを焼く toast pieces of rice cake ((on a grid)) / もち網 a grid for toasting rice cake / もち菓子 rice-cake sweets / もちつき rice-cake making. 文例⇩

もち³ 黐 birdlime; lime; 〈木〉 an ilex; a holly ¶もちざお a limed pole.

もちあい 持ち合い 〈助け合い〉 helping one another; ((文)) interdependence; 〈相場の〉 steadiness; no change.

もちあう 持ち合う 〈釣り合う〉 balance; counterpoise; 〈相場が〉 remain unchanged [stationary, the same]; 〈費用を〉 share [bear a part of] ((the expense)).

もちあがる 持ち上がる 〈上へ上がる〉 be lifted; be raised; 〈起こる〉 ((文)) arise; happen; turn up; take place; 〈クラス担任を〉 stay in charge of the same class of pupils ((for three consecutive years)). 文例⇩

もちあげる 持ち上げる 〈上へ上げる〉 raise; lift (up); heave; put [hold] up; 〈おだてる〉 flatter; praise; ((文)) extol his to the skies ¶重い物を持ち上げる仕事 heavy lifting work; a heavy lifting task.

もちあじ 持ち味 〈味〉 the natural flavor ((of)); 〈特質〉 a (peculiar) characteristic; a distinctive quality ¶持ち味を生かす make the most of ((its)) characteristics / 社員一人一人の持ち味を生かして使う assign all one's employees to a position where they can each give full play to their natural abilities.

もちあつかう 持ち扱う ⇨ もてあます.

もちあるく 持ち歩く carry sth on one's person [about one].

もちあわせ 持ち合わせ things on [at] hand ¶(商店の)持ち合わせの品 goods in stock; stock ((on hand)).

もちあわせる 持ち合わせる 〈手元に〉 happen to have; have on [at] hand; 〈店に〉 have in stock [store]; 〈携帯する〉 have with [about] one.

もちいえ 持ち家 〈自分の家〉 a house of one's own; one's own house; 〈家作など〉 a house in one's possession; a house owned by one.

もちいかた 用い方 ⇨ ようほう¹.

モチーフ a motif; a motive.

もちいる 用いる 〈使う〉 use; make use of; ((文)) employ; 〈採用する〉 adopt; take; 〈適用する〉 apply; 〈雇う〉 employ; 〈交渉する〉 engage; hire ¶腕力を用いる use force [one's fist]; ((文)) resort to violence / …を用いて with …;

もたせる 子供に大金を持たせるな. Don't give too much money to children. / だれかにお宅まで持たせてやります. I'll have somebody take it to your house.

もたもた もたもたするな. Make it snappy!

もたらす 諸君に吉報をもたらした. I have some very good news for you.

もち¹ この魚は持ちがよくない. This fish does not keep well. / 電車賃は自分持ちだ. Each of us must pay his own railroad fare. / We must each pay our own railroad fare. / 食事は会社持ちだ. Meals are served at the company's expense.

もち² もちはもち屋. Every man to his trade. ((諺))

もちあがる これは重くて私には持ち上がらない. This is too heavy for me to lift. / 何が持ち上がったんだ. What's up? | What's the trouble? / 困ったことが持ち上がりそうだ. Something [Some trouble] is brewing. / 何か持ち上がったのかなと思った. I wondered if something was afoot [in the wind].

もちあるく たいてい小説家というものは, 結局はものにならない小説の種をいくつも頭の中にしまって持ち歩いているものだ. Most novelists carry around in their heads ideas for stories that will never come to be written.

もちあわせ お金の持ち合わせがありますか. Do you have any [some] money with you? | 〈手元に〉 Do you have any money on hand?

もちいる この装置は最近用いられるようになった. This device has come into use quite recently. / 彼は英語が話せたので大いに用いられた. His ability at spoken English made him extremely useful. / 当時鉄はこうした事には用いられなかった. The use of iron for this purpose was then

もちかえる by...; using...; by (the) use of...; by means of...; with the aid of... / 重く用いられるbe given an important position / 広く[一般に]用いられている be widely used; be in wide [general] use / 《文》find wide use (in modern architecture) / 用いられなくなる go out of use; fall into disuse. 文例⇩

もちかえる¹ 持ち帰る carry [take, bring] *sth* back; 〈我が家へ〉take [bring] *sth* home. 文例⇩

もちかえる² 持ち替える〈反対の手に移す〉pass [shift] *sth* from one hand to the other; 〈別の物を持つ〉exchange 《*one's* flute》for 《a piccolo》.

もちかける 持ち掛ける offer; propose. 文例⇩

もちかた 持ち方 the way *one* holds 《*one's* writing brush》; 《文》the manner of holding 《a violin》; how to hold 《chopsticks》.

もちかぶ 持ち株 *one's* (stock) holdings; *one's* shares ¶持ち株会社 a holding company.

もちきる 持ち切る ¶...のうわさで持ち切りである〈事柄が主語〉be the only [sole] topic of conversation; be the talk of the town / 多過ぎて両手に持ち切れない be too many to hold in *one's* hands. 文例⇩

もちぐさ 餅草 a mugwort.

もちぐされ 持ち腐れ ¶宝の持ち腐れ a useless possession / 持ち腐れの useless; 《文》of no (practical) use / 持ち腐れになる be wasted; be left to rust. 文例⇩

もちくずす 持ち崩す ¶身を持ちくずす ruin *oneself* (by dissipation); go wrong; go to the bad; 《口語》go to the dogs. 文例⇩

もちこす 持ち越す〈次へ送る〉carry forward; 〈送り越す〉carry [bring] over; 〈延期する〉put off; 《文》defer; postpone ¶前年から持ち越した仕事 work brought over from the previous year / 冬を持ち越す keep over the winter; survive [live through] the winter.

もちこたえる 持ち堪える〈耐える〉hold (out [on, up]); last; 《文》endure; stand 《the strain》; hold [stand] *one's* ground; 〈維持する〉keep up; 《文》maintain. 文例⇩

もちごま 持ち駒〈将棋の〉a captured piece (to be put to use); 〈人〉a person available 《for a particular purpose》.

もちこみ 持ち込み carrying [bringing] in ¶参考書[辞書など]持ち込み自由の試験 an open-book examination / 持ち込み原稿 unsolicited manuscripts / 持ち込み荷物 hand baggage [luggage] / 《鉄道の》持ち込み荷物制限 restrictions on the baggage (to be carried into a train).

もちこむ 持ち込む〈運び入れる〉bring [carry] in; take 《to》; 〈話を〉propose; approach *sb* with 《a proposal》 ¶当局に苦情を持ち込む lodge [file] a complaint with the authorities / 〈試合を同点にして〉決戦に持ち込む force a play-off; bring (the game) to a play-off.

もちごめ 餅米 glutinous rice. 文例⇩

もちさる 持ち去る take [carry] away.

もちじかん 持ち時間〈教師の〉*one's* teaching load; the number of classes which *one* has to teach (in a week); 〈囲碁・将棋などの〉the time limit (within which *one* has to play). 文例⇩

もちだし 持ち出し〈自腹を切ること〉paying out of *one's* own pocket; 〈損失〉a loss 《of 10,000 yen》. 文例⇩

もちだす 持ち出す〈外へ出す〉take out; carry out [away]; 〈火事の時に〉save; rescue; 〈盗み出す〉run away with; 〈自腹を切る〉pay out of *one's* own pocket; 〈提出する〉offer [《文》advance] 《*one's* opinion》; bring forward 《a plan》; propose 《a compromise》; suggest 《an idea》; come up with 《a solution》; bring 《a topic》up 《for discussion》 ¶話を持ち出す raise [broach] a matter; introduce a topic [subject].

もちてん 持ち点 points (already) allotted to *one*; points (already) gained (in earlier rounds).

もちなおす 持ち直す〈回復する〉improve; pick up; recover; revive / 〈景気が〉look up; rally; 〈持ち方を替える〉shift *one's* grip [hold] 《on *sth*》. 文例⇩

もちにげ 持ち逃げ ¶持ち逃げする run away [make off] with *sth*.

もちぬし 持ち主〈所有者〉the owner; 《文》the possessor; 〈経営者〉the proprietor ¶持ち主が変わる〈物が主語〉change hands; pass into someone else's possession.

もちば 持ち場〈部署〉*one's* post; *one's* (job)

---

unknown.

もちかえる¹ 彼はその植物を日本に持ち帰って育てた。He brought the plant back to Japan and cultivated it.

もちかける 彼らはその相談を私の所へ持ちかけてきた。They approached me with that proposal. / それは彼の方から持ちかけた話だ。He made the first approaches, not I.

もちきる 町中がその話で持ち切っている。The whole town is talking about nothing else. / 近いうちに社長がやめるといううわさで持ち切りである。The air is filled with rumors that the president of the company will soon resign.

もちぐされ これは私には宝の持ちぐされだから、あなたに上げます。This is wasted on me, so I'd like you to have it. / せっかくの彼の才能も宝の持ちぐされに終わった。There was after all no chance to turn his talent to account.

もちくずす あの男はギャンブルで身を持ちくずすだろう。Gambling will be the ruin of him [his ruin].

もちこたえる よくあれだけ持ちこたえたものだ。I wonder how he managed to hold out that long.

もちこむ うまく話を持ちこんで私に金を出させた。He cleverly persuaded me to help him out (financially).

もちじかん 持ち時間はあと1分しかありません。You have only one minute left.

もちだし 海外旅行者の持ち出し外貨は1人3千ドルに制限されている。The amount of foreign currency that may be taken abroad by tourists is limited to 3,000 dollars per person.

もちなおす 天気が持ち直した。The weather has improved [changed for the better]. / 景気が持ち直してきた。Business is picking up [improving, looking up].

もちぬし この本の持ち主はだれで

position; *one's* (working) station; 〈巡回区〉 *one's* round; *one's* beat; 〈配達の〉 *one's* route ¶持ち場を守る keep [hold, stand by, stick to] *one's* post; do not leave *one's* place of duty / 持ち場を回る do [make] *one's* rounds / 持ち場についている be at *one's* post.

もちはこび 持ち運び ¶持ち運びのできる portable; hand-portable《machines》/ 持ち運びに便利な[不便な] handy [unwieldy]. [文例⇩]

もちはこぶ 持ち運ぶ ⇨はこぶ.

もちはだ 餅肌 a soft fair velvety skin.

もちふだ 持ち札 the cards in *one's* hand; 《show》 *one's* hand [cards].

もちぶね 持ち船 a ship of *one's* own [in *one's* possession].

もちぶん 持ち分 〈割り当て額〉 a quota; 〈費用·出資などの〉 *one's* share《of the expenses》; *one's* interest《in a joint enterprise》; 〈持ち株など〉 *one's* holdings.

もちまえ 持ち前 〈天性〉 *one's* nature; 〈物の〉 a property; 〈特質〉 a peculiarity; a characteristic ¶持ち前の 〈独特の〉《文》peculiar; 《文》characteristic; 〈生来の〉《文》inherent; inborn; natural.

もちまわる 持ち回る take *sth* round; carry *sth* about ¶持ち回り閣議に掛けて了承を得る make a Cabinet decision by obtaining the approval of each minister in turn《on a draft proposal》.

もちもの 持ち物 〈所有物〉 *one's* property; *one's* possessions; 〈携帯品〉《文》*one's* (personal) effects; *one's* belongings; 〈旅行者の手荷物〉 *one's* baggage [luggage]. [文例⇩]

もちゅう 喪中 ¶喪中である be in mourning《for》.

もちよる 持ち寄る gather《at a party》each bringing *sth* (with him); each contributes his own share ¶情報を持ち寄る gather [meet] (in order) to exchange information [news].

もちろん 勿論 of course; 〈言うまでもなく〉《文》needless to say; 〈なるほど〉 naturally; certainly; to be sure; no doubt; undoubtedly; 《口語》sure ★「もちろん…だが」と相手の言ったことを一応認めた上で, 相手の主張に反論する際の「なるほど」と同義の「もちろん」は, of course でもよいが, 以上挙げたような語句の方がよりぴったりする. [文例⇩]

もつ[1] 〈臓物〉 entrails; giblets (鳥の) ¶もつ焼き roast giblets.

もつ[2] 持つ 〈手に〉 have; take; hold; 〈携える〉 carry; have *sth* with [about, on] *one*; 〈所有する〉 have; own; 《文》possess; keep; 〈心に〉 have; hold《an opinion》; 《文》entertain《an idea》; 《文》harbor《hatred》; 《文》cherish《hopes》; bear《a grudge against *sb*》; 〈支えられる〉 be supported《by》; 〈維持する〉《文》maintain; keep (up); hold (out); 〈長持ちする〉 wear; last; keep (good) (食べものなど); be durable; 〈死なずにいる〉 live (out); survive; 〈担任する〉 take [have] charge of; be in charge of; 〈負担する〉 bear; stand; pay ¶持って歩く carry *sth* about with *one* / 物を持ってやる hold *sth* for *sb* / 自分の意見を持つ have [hold] an opinion of *one's* own / 今夜中もつ 〈魚などが〉 keep through the night; 〈病人が〉 live out [survive] the night / 費用を持つ bear the expenses; foot the bill (勘定を) / 持ちつ持たれつの関係 a give-and-take [《文》mutually advantageous] relationship. [文例⇩]

もっか[1] 目下 now; at present; at the (present) moment ¶目下の present; 《文》current; existing / 目下のところ for the present; for the time being; for the moment / 目下の状態では as things are [stand (now)]; in the present circumstances; 《文》under existing conditions.

もっか[2] 黙過 ¶黙過する ⇨**みのがす**.

もっかん 木簡 a narrow strip of wood on which an official message is written (used in the Nara period).

もっかんがっき 木管楽器 a woodwind (instrument); the woodwind (総称).

もっきん 木琴 a xylophone ¶木琴奏者 a

すか. Whose book is this? / この土地の持ち主は木村氏になった. The ownership of this land has been transferred to Mr. Kimura.

もちはこび この箱は持ち運びが便利なように折り畳み式になっている. This box can be folded up for easy carrying.

もちもの これは鈴木氏の持ち物だ. This belongs to Mr. Suzuki. | This is Mr. Suzuki's.

もちろん もちろんそうするのは我我の義務だ. Of course, it is our duty to do so. / 彼は英語はもちろんドイツ語もフランス語もできます. He knows German and French, not to mention [not to speak of, to say nothing of, let alone] English. / 英語もろくに知らない, ドイツ語はもちろんだ. He knows very little English, much less German. / 当時は私どもにはテレビはもちろんのこと, ラジオもありませんでした. We did not have a radio then, to say nothing of a TV set.

もつ[2] マッチをお持ちですか. Have you got any matches? | Do you have a light? / 僕はかばんを持って歩かない. I never carry a bag. / ちょっとこれを持っていてくれないか. Just hold this for me, will you? / この会社は君で持っているのだ. You are the main support of this firm. | This firm would be nowhere without you. / 世の中は持ちつ持たれつだ. It's helping each other that makes the world go round. / 天気はまだ持っている. The weather is still holding. / シェリーはワインと違って開けてからでも持ちます. Unlike wine, sherry keeps even after it is opened. / 1万円あれば1週間は持つだろう. Ten thousand yen will be enough to go on with for a week, won't it? / 世界の石炭の埋蔵量は5兆トン以上で, いくら悲観的に見積もってもあと100年は持つだろう. The world reserves of coal are above five trillion tons and, at the most pessimistic estimate, will last us out another century.

もっけ 彼がまだ来ていなかったのはもっけの幸いであった. Thank God he had not come.

もったいない そんなに紙を何枚も使ってはもったいない. It is a sheer [simply a] waste to use so many sheets of paper. / こんなところにいては君の才能がもったいない. You are wasting your talent here. / 捨ててしまうのはまだもったいない. It's a pity to waste it. / 何ともったいないことをするのだろう! What a waste! / そんなに親切にして頂いてはもったいない. I am unworthy of your

もっけ ¶もっけの幸い a piece [stroke] of good luck; a godsend; a windfall. 文例⇩

もっけい 黙契 a secret [《文》tacit] understanding [agreement] ¶黙契のもとに 《do》on a tacit understanding.

もっこ 畚 a rope basket (for carrying earth).

もっこう¹ 木工 《人》a carpenter; a woodworker; a craftsman in wood; 〈仕事〉woodwork(ing) / 木工具 a woodworking tool / 木工所[場] a carpentry shop; a woodworking shop [plant]; 〈製材所〉a sawmill / 木工品 woodwork.

もっこう² 黙考 ⇒ちんしもっこう.

もっさり ¶もっさりしている seem slow in action; look sluggish.

もったい 勿体 ¶もったいをつける《文》attach undue importance 《to》; give *sth* too much weight.

もったいない 勿体ない 〈無駄な〉wasteful; 〈過分な〉《be》too good 《for》; 〈神などを敬わない〉《文》impious; profane; irreverent; 〈尊い〉gracious ¶もったいなく《文》graciously. 文例⇩

もったいぶる 勿体振る put on airs; stand on *one's* dignity; give *oneself* airs; assume airs [an air of importance] ¶もったいぶった pompous; self-important / もったいぶって話す speak with an air of importance / もったいぶらない be modest; 《文》be unassuming; 《文》be unpretentious. 文例⇩

もって 以て〈道具を用いて〉with;〈手段を用いて〉by; by means of;〈…を通じて〉through;〈…だから〉because; for; as; on account of; in view of (…にかんがみて) ¶彼の勢力をもってしても with all his influence. 文例⇩

もっていく 持って行く〈携えて行く〉take *sth* (with *one*);〈相手のいる所へ〉bring *sth* (with *one*) ⇒いく 用法;〈持ち去る〉take [carry] *sth* away. 文例⇩

もってうまれた 持って生まれた《文》innate; natural;《文》inborn ¶持って生まれた性分 *one's* nature.

もってかえる 持って帰る take *sth* back;〈相手のいる所へ〉bring *sth* back ¶〈持って帰る take [bring] *sth* home (with *one*). 文例⇩

もってくる 持って来る bring *sth* (with *one*);〈取って来る〉fetch; (go and) get *sth* (from);〈携える〉bring *sth* along ¶相談を持って来る approach *sb* with a proposal; come to consult *sb*.

もってこい 持って来い ¶もってこいの〈すばらしい〉ideal; excellent;〈最適の〉the very; right; good; just.

もってのほか 以ての外 ¶もっての外の outrageous; preposterous; scandalous;《文》unpardonable;《文》most improper; unreasonable; out of the question (問題外の). 文例⇩

もってまわった 持って回った ⇒まわりくどい.

もっと〈数量〉(some) more;〈距離〉farther;〈程度〉further ¶もっと高価な more expensive; dearer / もっとたくさん much more (量); many more (数) ⇒たくさん 用法 文例⇩

モットー a motto 《*pl*. -(e)s》 ¶…をモットーとする make (it) *one's* motto 《to *do*》.

もっとも¹ 尤も〈そうは言うものの〉of course…; but (then); however;《文》it must, however, be added that…; only…; though… ★口語では though をあとに言うこともよくある. たとえば「もっとも, 金がかかるかもしれないが」にあたる …though it may cost you a lot, 口語では though をあとから付け足すように It may cost you a lot, though. とよく言う ¶もっともな〈道理のある〉reasonable; understandable; justifiable; right;《文》just;〈当然の〉(only) natural / もっともな事を言う talk [speak] sense. 文例⇩

もっとも² 最も most; extremely;《文》exceedingly ¶最も重要なこと the most important thing;《文》a matter of the greatest impor-

---

kindness. | I do not deserve such kindness from you.

もったいぶる あんなにもったいぶるな. Don't put on airs like that. / あの人にはもったいぶった所がない. There is no pretentiousness about him. / 彼らはもったいぶって私らとは話をしない. He thinks it beneath his dignity to talk to us. | He is too much of a gentleman to talk to us.

もって 全世界の富をもってしても彼を幸福にすることはできない. All the wealth in the world wouldn't make him happy. / 君の実力をもってすればなんでもないだろう. It will be nothing [an easy job] with your ability.

もっていく カラースライドを少し持って行きますから, あなたの方でプロジェクターを用意しておいて下さい. I'll bring some color slides, so for your part will you see (to it) that a projector is ready.

もってかえる これは家へ持って帰ろう. I'll take it home.

もってくる 水を1杯持って来てくれ. Get me a glass of water. / 傘を持って来るのを忘れた. I forgot to bring my umbrella with me.

もってこい あの人ならその地位に持って来いだ. He is just the man [He is the very man] for the post.

もってのほか 夜今時分出かけようなどとはもっての外だ. I wouldn't dream of going out at this time of night. | It's out of the question for you to go out at this time of night.

もっと もっと下さい. Please give me some more. / まだもっと悪い事がある. There's worse to come. | I have worse to tell. / もっといいのがほしい. I want something better. / なぜもっと早く知らせてくれなかったのか. Why didn't you let me know earlier? / あの人はその事をもっと考えてみたいと言っていた. He wanted more time to think it over. ⇒-たい 文例 / それはもっと研究する必要がある. It requires further research.

もっとも¹ ごもっともです. I (entirely) agree with you. | You are quite right. / 若い者が新しいことを欲求するのもっともなことだ. It is only natural for young men to crave for new things. / 彼が怒ったのももっともだ. He had good reason to get angry. | No wonder he got angry. / 彼がそう言うのももっともだ. He has every reason to say so. | There is good cause for his saying so. / もっともな質問ではあるが, そ

もっともらしい

tance / 最も金のいらない方法でやる do the least expensive way / 最も勇敢に戦う fight most bravely. 文例⇩

もっともらしい 尤もらしい plausible;《文》specious ¶もっともらしいうそをつく《文》lie plausibly; tell a lie that sounds like the truth / もっともらしい顔をして with a serious look. 文例⇩

もっぱら 専ら《全く》wholly;《文》solely; simply; entirely;《文》exclusively;《専心》devotedly; wholeheartedly ¶もっぱら…を研究的する devote [apply] oneself (exclusively [wholly]) to the study of…. 文例⇩

モップ《長柄付きぞうきん》a mop.

もつれ 縺れ《髪・糸などの》a tangle; (an) entanglement;《米》a snarl;《紛争》difficulties; trouble(s); a snag;《米》a snarl ¶感情のもつれ an emotional entanglement (between) / もつれを解く disentangle; unravel; settle (a question) / 髪のもつれをとかす comb the snarls out of one's hair.

もつれる 縺れる《髪・糸などが》be [get] entangled; knot; kink;《米》be snarled;《口》be thick; get twisted;《紛糾する》be complicated; be in a tangle;《米》be (all) snarled (up) ¶もつれ髪 tangled hair.

もてあそぶ 玩ぶ《いじくる》play [《文》toy] with;《楽しむ》amuse oneself (with);《慰み物にする》fool with; make a fool of;《文》trifle《sport》with;《文》make sport [a plaything] of ¶《人の》感情をもてあそぶ trifle with [play on] sb's feelings / 運命にもてあそばれる《文》be the puppet [a plaything] of fate.

もてあます 持て余す《対象が主語》be too much for one; be beyond one's manage; be beyond one's control; lie [hang] heavy on one's hands (時間が);《自分が主語》do not know what to do with sth; find sth an embarrassment; find sb [sth] unmanageable

¶仕事が多くて持て余している have more work than one can manage; have too many jobs [much work] on one's hands / 持て余しの nuisance ((to the family)) (★ 人・物のいずれにも使える); a white elephant (不要になった品物); a black sheep (家族の中の). 文例⇩

もてなし 持て成し《待遇》treatment;《文》reception; service (旅館などの);《歓待》welcome; hospitality; entertainment ¶持て成しのいい hospitable / 手厚い持て成しを受ける 《文》be given a cordial reception; be warmly [《文》cordially] received. 文例⇩

もてなす 持て成す《待遇する》treat;《歓待する》entertain; be hospitable to sb; offer (one's) hospitality to sb; make sb welcome;《ごちそうする》treat sb to ((dinner)) ¶厚く持て成す give sb a warm welcome;《文》receive sb warmly.

もてはやす 持て囃す《ほめそやす》praise [《文》extol] sb (to the skies);《偉い人として扱う》make much of; lionize;《珍重する》prize; value. 文例⇩

モデラート《音楽》《イタリア語》moderato.

もてる 持てる be popular (with); be made much of; have ((dozens of boys)) in love with one. 文例⇩

モデル a model ¶モデルになる act as a model; pose ((for an artist [for a picture])); sit ((for a painter)) / 写真のモデル a photo [photographer's] model / モデルケース a model case / モデル習作 life studies / モデル小説《フランス語》a roman à clef (pl. romans à clef); a novel based on real people and incidents / モデルスクール a model school / モデルチェンジ a model change;《口語》restyling;《口語》face lifting;《口語》a face-lift / モデルハウス a model house; a show house. 文例⇩

もと 元, 本, 基, 下《起源》the beginning; the origin,《文》the rise; the source;《文》the

---

れに答えるのは容易ではない. That's a fair question, but it is not easy to answer. / もっとも, 来ないかもしれない. Of course, he may not come. / He may not come, of course. / 彼女は主婦としてはよくやっています. もっとも料理は下手ですが. She is a good housewife, only [except that] she cooks badly. / もっとも例外はある. There are exceptions to it, however. / もっとも気にする程のことではないが. You needn't let it worry you, though. / 彼女は食欲が少しないようだった. もっとも普段から肉好きのほうではなかったが. She seemed a little lacking in appetite, but then, she had never been a great meat-eater.

もっとも² 信濃川は日本で最も長い川である. The Shinano is the longest river in Japan. / デパートの中を見て回っている時が彼女

には最も楽しい. She is never happier than when she is looking around a department store.

もっともらしい 彼のおびえた顔を見ると, 彼の話すことがもっともらしく思われた. His frightened look lent credibility to what he said.

もっぱら それはもっぱら日本に輸出される. It is exported exclusively to Japan. / 彼はもっぱら読書に time を送っている. He devotes his time to reading.

もつれる もっと早く走ろうとした が, 足がもつれて転んでしまった. He tried to run faster, but his feet tripped each other up and he fell down.

もてあます 彼にはおやじも持て余している. Even his father does not know what to do with him. / 時間を持て余した. Time hung heavy [heavily] on my hands. / あなたなんか持て余すく

らいお金があるんでしょう. You have more money than you know what to do with, don't you?

もてなし 一行は茶菓の持て成しを受けた. The party was entertained with refreshments. / 何のお持て成しもせず失礼しました. I am afraid [sorry] that I have not been much of a host to you.

もてはやす 大抵の男は人にもてはやされるといい気になる. Most men have [suffer from] a swollen head when they are made much of.

もてる (バーで)女に大いにもてた. He was really a hit with the girls. / The girls were all over him.

モデル この小説の主人公は浅井氏をモデルにしたのだ. The hero of this novel is modeled after Mr. Asai. / この小説は一切実在の人物をモデルにしていません. None of the characters in this

もとい 〈基礎〉 the foundation; the base; the basis 《pl. bases》; 〈原因〉 the (root) cause; 〈資本〉 capital; 〈原料〉 (raw) material(s); 〈原価〉 the cost (price) ¶ もとは 〈以前〉《文》 formerly; once; before; at one time; 〈元来〉 originally; at first ★「もとは」「以前は」の意味は以上の副詞語句よりも助動詞 used to を用いて表わすのが普通 / もとから from the first [beginning, 《文》 outset] / もとの one-time; 《文》 former; original; once; ex-; 〈故〉《文》 the late / もと総理大臣 a one-time Prime Minister / もとのとおり as before; as it was before / 本をもとの所に置く put a book back (where it was) / もとの様[とおり]になる《文》 return to (its) former state; get back to normal / もとがかかる be expensive; cost a lot [a great deal] of money; (do not) cost much / もとも子もなくす be [suffer] a total loss; 〈口語〉 lose one's shirt [the shirt off one's back] / もとをかける lay out money (on); put [sink] money (in); invest capital (in) / もとを切って売る sell sth below cost [at a loss] / もとを取る recover one's investment; get one's money's worth; get value for one's money / もとに[で] 〈(物の)下で〉 under; 〈…を受けて〉 under; 〈…に基づいて〉 on; 〈先生について〉 under / …の指揮[指導, 監督]のもとに under the command [direction, supervision] of…; under… / おじのもとにいる live [stay] with one's uncle; live at one's uncle's / 父母のもとで 《live》 with one's parents; 《文》 under one's parental roof / …がもとで because of…; owing to…; (die) of [from]… / ケーキのもと a cake mix / スープのもと a stock [bouillon, soup, consommé] cube; soup base; powdered soup. 文例⇩

もとい 基 ⇒きそ².

もどかしい 〈いらいらさせる〉 irritating; not quick enough; tantalizing; 〈待ち遠しい(人が主語)〉 (feel) impatient; 〈のろい〉 slow; tardy ¶ もどかしそうに impatiently / もどかしがる be impatient (at, for, 《文》 of); be irritated (at, by, with); fret [be in a fret] (about, over). 文例⇩

-もどき ¶ おとぎ話もどきの fairy-tale-like / …もどきに in the style of…; in imitation of 《Sherlock Holmes》; like….

もときん 元金 〈資本〉 capital; 〈利子に対して〉 the principal.

モトクロス a motocross.

もとごめじゅう 元込め銃 a breech-loading gun; a breechloader.

もとじめ 元締め a manager; a controller; a promoter; a boss 〈親方〉 ¶ 総元締め the general manager.

もどす 戻す 〈返す〉 return; give back; 〈返送する〉 send back; 〈返金する〉 pay back; 〈元の状態へ〉 restore; 〈吐く〉 vomit; 〈俗〉 throw up; fetch [bring] up 《everything one has eaten》; 〈冷凍を〉 defrost 《the meat for supper》 ¶ 時計を20分戻す put [turn] back the clock (by) twenty minutes / 自動車を後へ戻す back a motorcar / (タイプライターで) 1字分戻す backspace / (食べたものを)戻しそうになる feel sick [《文》 nausea, 《文》 nauseated]; feel like vomiting [throwing up] / 干ししいたけを戻す soak dried mushrooms in water. 文例⇩

もとせん 元栓 〈ガスの〉 a main tap; 〈水道の〉 a stop tap ¶ 元栓をしめる turn (the gas [the water]) off at the main [《英》 mains].

もとだか 元高 〈元金〉 the principal; 〈原価〉 the cost (price).

もとちょう 元帳 a ledger.

もとづく 基づく 〈根拠とする〉 be based [founded] (on); 《文》 be grounded (on, in); 《文》 be predicated (on); 〈原因する〉 come [《文》 arise] (from); 《文》 rise [originate] (in); be due (to) ¶ 科学的な根拠に基づいて science-based (technology) / …の忠告に基づいて on sb's advice.

もとで 元手 capital; funds; seed money ¶ 元

---

book [novel] is based on any actual person, living or dead. / この車は何回ものモデルチェンジを経た。The car went through a number of model changes.

もと 電気はもとで切ったのだ。The electricity [electric current] has been turned off at the main. / この習慣はもと儒教から来たものだ。This custom originated in [has its origin in] Confucianism. / その失敗のもとは不注意にあるのだ。The failure was due to carelessness. / 冗談がもとでけんかになった。The quarrel began as a joke. / この薬のもとは何ですか。What is this medicine made from? / この界隈はもととは様子がまるで違った。This place [neighborhood] looks quite different from what it used to be. / それはもとは活火山であった。It used to be an active volcano. / 僕はもとからあの男は嫌いだ。I have never liked him. / 彼はもとどおり丈夫になった。He is now as healthy as he used to be [as (he was) before]. / 彼らは戦前と全く同じ道路、同じ建物を再建して、自分たちの町をもとどおりにした。They returned their town to the state in which it had been, building exactly the same streets and the same houses as before the war. / もと来た道を戻らねばならなかった。We had to go back the way we had come. / 紙というもののなかった古代の建築家は粘土や石の模型をもとにして仕事をした。The ancient architects, lacking paper, worked from models made of clay or stone. / あの男は出したお金は必ずもとを取らねば承知しない。He insists on value for (his) money. / 彼は東大で大西教授の指導のもとに研究を続けた。He pursued his studies under Professor Onishi at Tokyo University. / もとへ！〈号令〉 As you were! / 〈言い間違いをして〉 No! I take it back.

もどかしい 急いでいたので特急列車の走るのももどかしかった。I was in such a hurry that even the superexpress seemed to go slowly.

もどす これをもとの位置へ戻しておけ。Put this back in its place. / インドの聖地ベナレスは最近バラナシという古い名称に戻された。The holy city of Benares, India, has recently been restored to its ancient name, Varanasi. / 物を食べると戻してしまうのだった。He could not keep anything [any food] down. / 〈食べたものを戻しそうになって、そこに立ち止まった。〉 I stopped there in order [because I thought I was going to be sick. / 赤ん坊がミルクを戻した。The baby brought

手を食いつぶす live on *one's* capital / わずかな元手で事業を始める start *one's* business with [on] very little capital; launch out (into business) on a shoestring. 文例

もとね 元値 the cost (price) ¶元値で[以下で]売る sell at [below] cost [the cost price].

もとめ 求め〈要求〉〈文〉a request; a claim;〈需要〉a demand ¶お求めにより at [in compliance with] your request / 求めに応じる grant [comply with] *sb's* request.

もとめる 求める〈依頼する〉ask for;〈文〉request;〈要求する〉demand; claim; call for;〈欲する〉want;〈文〉desire; wish for;〈探求する〉look for;〈文〉pursue〈happiness〉; search for《truth》;〈買う〉buy; get ¶意見を求める ask *sb's* opinion;〈文〉seek advice《from》/〈みずから〉求めて of *one's* own choice / 幸福を求めて〈文〉in pursuit [quest] of happiness / 求めて災難を招く ask for trouble [it]. 文例

もともと 元々, 本々〈中来〉originally; from the first [beginning, outset]; all along; always;〈生来〉by nature; naturally. 文例

もとゆい 元結い a paper cord for tying the hair.

もとより 固より〈最初から〉from the first [beginning, outset];〈元来〉originally;〈無論〉of course. 文例

もどり 戻り ⇒ かえり.

もとる 悖る be [go, act] against [〈文〉contrary to]; run counter to;〈文〉depart [deviate] from ¶主義にもとる go against *one's* principles.

もどる 戻る go [come, get] back; return;〈引き返す〉turn back (halfway);〈後退する〉go back [backward]; back;〈ばねが〉spring back;〈よりが〉get [〈文〉become] undone ¶来た道を辿る retrace *one's* steps; go back [return] (the way *one* has come) / 家へ戻る go [come, get] home / 本題に戻る return [come back] to the subject [what *one* was talking about]. 文例

もなか 最中〈菓子〉bean-jam-filled wafers.

モナコ Monaco ¶モナコの Monegasque; Monacan / モナコ公国 the Principality of Monaco.

モナリザ the Mona Lisa; La Gioconda.

モニター a monitor.

もぬけのから もぬけの殻 ¶もぬけの殻である〈場所が主語〉be quite empty;〈人が主語〉be gone. 文例

もの¹ 物 a thing; an object;〈物質〉matter; (a) substance;〈品物〉an article;〈物資〉commodities; goods;〈資源〉resources;〈材料〉(a) material; stuff;〈物事〉things; a matter ¶物がいい be [〈文〉be of good [fine] quality / 物が悪い be [〈文〉be of] poor [inferior, bad] quality / 物の言えない動物たち dumb animals [creatures] / 物の数でない be insignificant; do not count; count for nothing; be beneath [not worth] *one's* notice / 物のわかった sensible; understanding / 物を言う〈口を利く〉talk; speak;〈文〉address *sb*;〈利き目がある〉tell;〈重きをなす〉count 《for》; be important;〈文〉be of (some) importance;〈役に立つ〉be helpful;〈文〉be of (some) service; go a long way 《for, to, toward》/ 金に物を言わせて by the power of money / 物を言わない be silent;〈文〉be mute / 物を知っている be well informed;〈文〉be learned / 物にする〈ひとかどのものに〉make something of *sb* [*sth*];〈成功する〉make a success of *sth*; bring *sth* to success; succeed in 《*sth*, doing》;〈手中に収める〉get hold of *sth*;〈文〉make *sth one's* own;〈文〉secure; take possession of / ドイツ語を物にする master German;〈文〉become proficient in German;〈文〉acquire a good command of German / 物になる turn [can be made] into something (worthwhile);〈成功する〉come off; be a success;〈実現する〉〈文〉be realized; materialize / 物にならない be good for nothing; be hopeless; be [〈文〉prove] a failure; get nowhere 《計画などが》/ 物ともしない make [think] nothing of;〈文〉be undaunted 《by, at》. 文例

もの² 者 a person; one; a being; some (people).

もの³ ¶よく…したものだ would often *do*; used to *do* / …するものか (I'll) never *do*; How could…?; It's impossible 《that…》;《口語》like

---

[fetched] up its milk.

もとで 商売をするにも元手がない. I have nothing to start business with. / 何事にも元手がいる. You must sow before you can reap.

もとめる 彼はその詩を日本語に翻訳するよう求められた. He was called on to translate the poem into Japanese. / 彼は何を求めているのか. What is he after? / 彼は職を求めて上京した. He came up to Tokyo in search of [to look for] employment [a job]. / 彼らの求めているのは利潤だけだ. They are only out for profits. / 技術者が大いに求められている. Technical experts are in great demand. / それは求めて危険を招くものだ. You are courting danger. / 店員を求む.《広告》Help wanted. / *x* の値を求めよ.《数》Find the value of *x*.

もともと もともと行くつもりはなかった. From the first I had no intention of going there. / 失敗してもともとだ. If I fail, I'll be none the worse for it.

もとより この法案には, 野党はもとより, 自民党の中にも反対の声がある. The bill is even opposed by some of the Liberal Democrats, let alone by the opposition parties.

もどる 電車が後へ戻った. The train backed [went backward].

もぬけのから 警察が踏み込んだら, 家の中はもぬけの殻だった. When the police raided the house, they found it deserted.

もの¹ 勝利はもうこっちの物だ. It is certain that the victory will be ours. / The game is as good as won. / 物は試しだ, ひとつやってみよう. Let's have a try; we may have a chance. / こういう時には金が一番物を言う. Money talks loudest on an occasion like this. / これは物になるだろう. I think we [I] can make something out of this. / I think something can be made out of this. / この原稿は物になるでしょうか. Are these manuscripts any

ものいい 物言い〈言葉づかい〉speech; language; a manner [way] of speaking;〈争論〉a dispute;〈抗議〉a protest; an objection ¶物言いがぶっきらぼうである《文》be blunt-spoken; speak curtly [roughly] / 丁寧な物言いをする speak politely / 物言いをつける object to [protest against] the referee's decision [ruling]. 文例↓

ものいみ 物忌み ¶物忌みする fast;《文》abstain from 《some kind of food》.

ものいり 物入り expenses; a drain on *one's* purse. 文例↓

ものうい 物憂い《文》languid;《文》weary; lazy; listless;《文》(feel) wan ¶物憂げな languid; weary;《文》languorous; listless. 文例↓

ものうり 物売り a street vendor; a peddler.

ものおき 物置き a lumber room; a storeroom;《英》a boxroom;〈小屋〉a shed;〈納屋〉a barn.

ものおじ 物怖じ ¶物おじする be timid; be shy / 物おじしない be at ease 《in public》; be self-assured.

ものおしみ 物惜しみ ¶物惜しみする be stingy; be mean; be a miser;《文》stint / 物惜しみしない be openhanded; be generous;《文》be liberal / 物惜しみせずに《文》without stint; freely; generously;《文》liberally.

ものおと 物音 a noise; a sound. 文例↓

ものおぼえ 物覚え ⇒きおく ¶物覚えがいい〈記憶力〉have a good [long] memory /〈学習能力〉be quick to learn 《things》; be quick at learning / 物覚えが悪い〈記憶力〉have a poor [bad, short] memory /〈学習能力〉be slow at learning; be a slow learner.

ものおもい 物思い《文》(a) meditation;《文》pensiveness;〈心配〉anxiety ¶物思いにふける be lost [sunk] in (deep) thought; be in a pensive mood.

ものおもわしげ 物思わしげ ¶物思わしげな wistful; pensive / 物思わしげに wistfully;《文》pensively.

ものかげ 物陰 ¶物陰に隠れる get under cover; take cover [shelter]. 文例↓

ものがたい 物堅い〈正直な〉honest; straight;〈義理堅い〉《文》dutiful; reliable.

ものがたり 物語〈話〉a tale; a story; a narrative;〈談話〉a talk;〈説明, 報告〉an account;〈伝説〉a legend;〈虚構の〉a fiction;〈伝奇〉a romance;〈小説〉a novel;〈寓話〉a fable;〈逸話〉an episode ¶物語る tell a story;《文》relate; give an account 《of》.

ものがたる 物語る〈語る〉tell 《of, about》;《文》relate; narrate; give an account 《of》;〈示す〉show; indicate; prove. 文例↓

ものかなしい 物悲しい sad;《文》plaintive;《文》melancholy ¶物悲しげな目をした sad-eyed 《deer》.

ものかは 物かは ¶風雨もものかは braving [in spite of] the rainstorm.

ものぐさ 物臭 ¶物ぐさな lazy;《文》indolent;《文》slothful; sluggish / ものぐさな人 an idler;《口語》a lazybones.

ものぐるおしい 物狂おしい mad; crazy; frantic; distracted ¶物狂おしげに madly; frantically; distractedly.

モノクロ monochrome 《photographs》.

ものごい 物乞い〈事〉begging;〈人〉a beggar.

ものごころ 物心 ¶物心がつく《文》attain [reach] the age of discretion;〈赤ん坊が〉begin to take notice / 物心がついて以来 ever since *one* could remember;《文》from *one's* earliest recollection.

ものごし¹ 物腰 *one's* demeanor; a [*one's*] manner;《文》a [*one's*] bearing ¶物腰が上品である be refined in *one's* manner;《文》be graceful of bearing / 物腰のやさしい quiet-[mild-, gentle-]mannered.

ものごし² 物越し ¶物越しに with *sth* in between; indirectly; (see) over [through] *sth*.

ものごと 物事 things; a matter;〈万事〉everything.

ものさし 物差し a ruler; a (measuring) rule [rod]; a straightedge; a measure;〈尺度〉a yardstick;〈標準〉a standard;《文》a criterion (*pl.* -ria, -rions) ¶物差しで計る measure with a rule /〈抽象的なものを計る〉物差しにする use *sth* as *one's* yardstick / …を物差しにして計る measure *sth* against the yardstick of…. 文例↓

ものさびしい 物寂しい lonely; lonesome;

---

good? / フランス語を2年やったが物にならなかった. I studied French for two years but to no purpose [but I got nowhere]. / 物の本にそう書いてある. It says so in some book or other. / そんなことをしたら辞職ものだ. That is as much as my job is worth.

もの² 私は藤田と申す者です. My name is Fujita. / 負傷した者もある. Some were wounded.

もの³ 子供の時よくそこへ行ったもの だ. I used to visit [I would often go] there when I was a boy. / 知りたいものだ. I would like to know. / そんな事知るものか. How the hell should I know! / そんな事をするものか. / だれがそんな事をするものか. How could anyone do a thing like that? / Who would do such a thing? / そんな事があるものか. That can't be true [so, right]! / That's impossible! / 僕が行くって? 行くものか. He says I'll go? Like hell I will!

ものいい 一番は物言いがついた. The referee's decision was contested.

ものいり 今月は何やかやと物入りが多かった. This month I have had various unforeseen expenses to meet.

ものうい こんな雨の日は物憂い. A rainy day like this depresses me [gets me down, makes me feel dull and gloomy].

ものおと 物音がする. I can hear something [a noise].

ものかげ 若い男が物陰から躍り出て大統領を狙撃した. A young man leaped out from hiding and fired at the President.

ものがたる 歩き方までが彼の性格を物語っていた. The very way that he walked showed his character.

ものさし 詩人だの画家だのというものは, 一般の人と同じ物差しで計るわけにいかない. It is impos-

ものしずか dreary;《文》desolate ★lonely は形容詞であって副詞として使うことはない.
ものしずか 物静か ¶物静かな quiet;《文》placid; still; calm;《文》sedate / 物静かに quietly; calmly;《文》sedately.
ものじたい 物自体〖哲〗〈カント哲学の〉the thing in itself ★〈ドイツ語〉Ding an sich の英訳.
ものしり 物知り a well-informed [a knowledgeable,《文》an erudite] person; a person who knows something [a little] about everything;〈学者〉a learned man ¶物知り顔で with a knowing [wise] look; knowingly / 物知り顔をする人《口語》a know-(it-)all.
ものずき 物好き (idle) curiosity;〈気まぐれ〉《文》fancifulness; a whim;〈人〉a curious person 物好きな curious; fanciful; whimsical;〈聞きたがる〉inquisitive; nos(e)y / 物好きに from [out of] curiosity; to satisfy one's curiosity;〈気まぐれから〉on a (mere) whim. 文例◊
ものすごい 物凄い ghastly《tales》; lurid《light》; gruesome《sights》; grim; terrible; weird; unearthly; terrific《noise》; staggering; (nerve-)shattering ¶物すごく terribly; awfully; tremendously.
ものする 物する do; perform; compose [work out]《a poem》.
ものだね 物種 ⇨いのち.
ものたりない 物足りない〈人が主語〉be not quite happy《with》; be unsatisfied;〈事が主語〉be not entirely [quite] satisfactory ¶物足りない気持ちがする feel that something is missing [wanting, lacking]; miss something. 文例◊
ものとり 物取り a thief (pl. thieves); a robber ¶物取りのための殺人 a murder for gain.
ものなれた 物慣れた experienced; trained; skilled ¶物慣れた態度で in an easy manner.
ものの〈約〉about; some; nearly;〈ほんの〉only; no more than ¶ものの 200 メートルも行かないうちに before I had gone about 200 meters /ものの見事に beautifully; in a clear-cut way. 文例◊
-ものの though; although;《文》despite the fact that...;《文》notwithstanding ¶とは言うものの for all that;《文》nonetheless;《文》nevertheless.
もののあわれ 物の哀れ《文》pathos ¶物の哀れを感じる feel the pathos of things [nature]; appreciate [be sensitive to] the beauties of nature [things].

もののけ 物の怪 a ghost; a specter; an evil spirit; a supernatural being.
ものほし 物干し a frame for drying clothes ¶物干しざお a wash-line pole; a rod on which to hang out the washing to dry / 物干し綱 a clothesline / 物干し場 a (clothes-)drying place.
ものまね 物真似 mimicry; miming;《口語》a takeoff ¶物まねがうまい be clever at mimicking《various sounds in nature》/ 物まねをする mimic;《口語》take off《the premier》. 文例◊
ものみ 物見〈望楼〉a watchtower; a lookout (tower) ¶物見高い be curious (to see) / 物見遊山に行く go on a jaunt [pleasure trip].
ものめずらしい 物珍しい curious ¶物珍しそうに curiously;《文》with curiosity [curious eyes].
ものもち 物持ち ⇨かねもち ¶物持ちがいい look after [take care for] one's things, so that they last a long time.
ものものしい 物々しい〈大そうらしい〉showy;《文》pretentious;《文》ostentatious;〈儀式などが〉pompous; imposing;《文》stately;〈入念な〉elaborate《preparations》¶物々しく pompously; elaborately / 物々しく警戒する take exaggerated [elaborate] security precautions.
ものもらい 物貰い〈こじき〉a beggar;〈麦粒腫〉a sty(e)《on one's eyelid》. 文例◊
ものやわらか 物柔らか ¶物柔らかな mild; gentle;《文》suave; quiet; bland; silky《voice》/ 物柔らかに mildly; gently;《文》suavely; quietly; blandly.
モノラル〈ステレオに対して〉monaural; mono; monophonic.
モノレール a monorail;〈列車〉a monorail train;〈車両〉a monorail car ¶モノレールで行く go by monorail.
モノローグ a monologue.
ものわかり 物分かり ¶物分かりのいい sensible; quick to understand; understanding.
ものわかれ 物別れ ¶物別れになる〈人が主語〉fail to reach an agreement; fail to arrive at a compromise;〈交渉などが〉break down; be broken off; fall through. 文例◊
ものわすれ 物忘れ a lapse of memory ¶物忘れする forget things; be forgetful; have a short memory. 文例◊
ものわらい 物笑い ¶物笑い(の種)になる become a laughingstock [《文》the butt of ridi-

---

sible to apply the same yardstick to poets and artists as to other people.
ものずき 物好きにも程がある. You shouldn't be so frivolous. Why don't you grow up! | You should behave [take things] more seriously. | Curiosity killed the cat.〘諺〙/ 私は物好きに働いているのではない. I'm not working just for the fun of it.
ものたりない 彼の説明では物足りない. His explanation is not entirely satisfactory [convincing]. / 何となく物足りない所がある. It leaves [has] something to be desired.
ものの ものの 20 分も待ったろうか. I must have waited for him (for) some twenty minutes.
-ものの 彼らは賛成はしたものの, 積極的に参加したわけではなかった. Despite the fact that they had agreed [《文》Notwithstanding their agreement], their participation was only halfhearted. | Although they had agreed to participate, their hearts weren't in it. / かわいそうとは思うものの, その行為は許せなかった. Much as I pitied him, I could not excuse his conduct.
ものまね 武田さんの円鏡の物まねはそっくりだ. Mr. Takeda's imitation of Enkyo is perfect.
ものもらい 彼女の右の目に物もら

もはや 最早 ⇨ もう².

もはん 模範 a model; an example;《文》an exemplar;《かがみ》a pattern ¶模範を示す set [give] an example ((to)); set the pattern ((for)) / …を模範とする model ((A)) after ((B)); follow sb's example [model]; pattern oneself on [after] sb / 模範的《文》exemplary; model; typical / 模範試合 an exhibition game / 模範囚 a well-behaved [model] prisoner;《米》a trusty [trustee] / 模範生 a model student.

もふく 喪服 (a) mourning dress ¶喪服を着ている wear [be] in mourning; be in (mourning).

モヘヤ mohair. [black.

もほう 模倣《事》imitation; copying;《まねた物》an imitation; a copy;《まがい物》a fake; a sham ¶模倣する imitate; copy ((from, after)); model after [on]; follow an example ((of)) / 模倣的 imitative. [文例⑤]

モホロビチッチふれんぞくめん モホロビチッチ不連続面【地学】the Mohorovičić [Moho] discontinuity; the Moho.

もまれる 揉まれる《紙などが》be crumpled; be wrinkled;《群衆に》be jostled;《困難に》be tried;《文》see [experience] hardships ¶翻弄される be knocked [tossed] about ¶世間の荒波にもまれる be buffeted about in the world; see [know] the world.

もみ¹ 紅 (lined with) red silk.

もみ² 籾 unhulled [rough] rice; rice in the husk; paddy ¶もみ殻 chaff; rice hulls [husks].

もみ³【植】a fir (tree) ¶もみの実 a fir cone.

もみあい 揉み合い a jostle; a struggle.

もみあう 揉み合う《群衆が》jostle; shove and push;《争う》struggle with one another.

もみあげ 揉み上げ the tuft of hair under the temple;《長く伸ばした》《米》sideburns;《英》sideboards.

もみくちゃ 揉みくちゃ ¶もみくちゃになる be violently jostled ((in a crowd)); be mobbed ((by fans)).

もみけす 揉み消す《火など》rub [crush] out; smother;《事件など》cover [hush] up; suppress ¶タバコをもみ消す stub [crush] out a cigarette / もみ消し運動をする make efforts to hush [cover] up ((an affair)).

もみじ 紅葉【植】《かえで》a (Japanese) maple;《紅葉》red [scarlet-tinged] leaves;《文》autumnal tints [colors] ¶紅葉狩り an excursion for viewing scarlet maple leaves [《文》autumnal leaves]. [文例⑤]

もみだす 揉み出す squeeze out by rubbing and kneading.

もみで 揉み手 ¶もみ手をする rub one's hands [palms] together.

もみりょうじ 揉み療治 (a) massage ¶もみ療治を受ける be [have oneself] massaged.

もむ 揉む《こする》rub;《くしゃくしゃに》crumple (up); wrinkle;《肩などを》massage; knead 《sb's shoulders》;《激しく論争する》debate hotly ¶気をもむ ⇨ き³(気をもむ). [文例⑤]

もめ(ごと) 揉め事《ごたごた》trouble(s); difficulties;《論争》a quarrel; a dispute ¶もめ事を引き起こす cause trouble; lead to a dispute.

もめる 揉める《ごたごたが起こる》have [get into] trouble; have a dispute [quarrel] ((with));《不和になる》《文》be in discord ¶気がもめる ⇨ き³(気がもめる). [文例⑤]

もめん 木綿 cotton;《綿布》cotton cloth ¶木綿糸 cotton (thread); cotton yarn (紡績の) / 木綿物《着物》cotton clothes;《シーツ・タオルなども含めて》cotton goods / 木綿物を着ている wear [be] in cotton.

もも¹ 桃【木】a peach (tree);【実】a peach ¶桃の花《1輪》a peach blossom;《花の群ら》peach blossom / 桃の節句 the Doll's Festival / 桃色 rose (color); pink / 桃色の《文》rosy; rose-colored; pink.

もも² 股 a thigh;【解】the femur (pl. -s, femora) ¶ももの femoral / もも肉《牛の》a round;《豚の》ham;《鳥の》leg; dark meat.

ももひき 股引き long underwear [underpants];《口語》long johns;《職人などの》close-fitting trousers.

ももんが【動】a (Eurasian) flying squirrel.

もや 靄 (a) mist ¶もやに包まれた《islands》enveloped [hidden] in mist;《文》mist-enshrouded《islands》. [文例⑤]

もやい 舫い《綱》a mooring rope [line]; a painter ¶もやいを解く cast off (the moorings); untie the painter / もやい船 a moored boat. [tie up (a boat).

もやう 舫う moor [fasten] ((a boat)) to ((a stake));

もやし 萌やし《麦》(barley) malt;《豆》bean sprouts ¶もやしっ子 a spineless《town-bred》child; a young person with a feeble constitution.

もやす 燃やす《燃す》burn;《点火する》light; kindle ¶火を燃やす make [light] a fire.

もやもや ¶もやもやした《もうもうたる》misty; foggy; hazy; murky;《ゆううつな》gloomy;《はっきりしない》unclear / 胸の中

いができていた。She had a sty in her right eye. | A sty had formed [come out] on her right eye.

ものわかれ 交渉は物別れとなった。The negotiations were broken off. | The talks broke down.

ものわすれ 年を取ると物忘れする。One grows forgetful with age.

ものわらい それはいまだに町の人人の物笑いの種になっている。It is still the joke of the town.

もほう 彼独特の筆致はとうてい他の人の模倣を許さない。His unique style defies imitation. / 日本人は模倣の国民で独創力に乏しいと思われている。It is generally believed that the Japanese are a nation of imitators who lack originality.

もみじ 私たちは箱根にもみじ狩りに行って来ました。We have been to Hakone to view the scarlet maple leaves there.

もむ (勝負事で)よし、一番もんでやろう。All right, I'll give you a few lessons [tips].

もめる 労使の間がもめている。There has been trouble [a dispute] between labor and management.

もや 遠くの丘には青い夕もやが立

のもやもやした気分 one's pent-up feelings.
もよう 模様 《図案》a pattern; a design; 《文》a figure; markings (毛や羽の); 《様子》a look; an air; an appearance; 《兆候》signs; 《状態》conditions; 《事情》circumstances; 《情勢》the state of things [affairs]; things; the situation; 《動静》movements; 《経過》progress ¶鳥の羽毛の模様 the markings of a bird's plumage / 模様をつける draw [paint, 《文》describe] a pattern ((on)); figure; pattern / 会議の模様を報告する report on the progress of the conference / …の模様だ 《様子だ》look like…; seem ((to be, to do)); show signs of…. 文例⇩

もようがえ 模様替え 《改造》remodeling, rebuilding; 《変更》(an) alteration; (a) rearrangement; a change ((in a plan)) ¶模様替えをする remodel; rearrange ((a room)); alter ((a house plan)); 《口語》redo; do ((the kitchen)) over / 模様替えになる be remodeled; be rearranged. 文例⇩

もよおし 催し 《会合》a meeting; 《文》a (social) gathering; 《宴会・式典など》《文》a function; an event; 《余興》an entertainment ¶催しをする [がある] hold a meeting; give [provide] entertainment(s) / …の催しで under the auspices of… / 催し物 a program of entertainments.

もよおす 催す 《会など》hold ((a meeting)); give ((a party)); 《兆(きざ)す》show signs of ((catching cold)) ¶涙を催す 《文》be moved to tears; feel like weeping / 眠気を催す feel sleepy [drowsy] / 欲情を催す be sexually aroused; 《口語》feel randy / 催される be held; be given; take place; come off.

もより 最寄り 最寄りの the nearest; nearby.

もらい 貰い 《心付け》a tip; 《文》a gratuity; 〈こじきなどの〉alms.

もらいご 貰い子 an adopted child; a foster child ¶もらい子をする adopt a child.

もらいて 貰い手 《文》a recipient; a receiver. 文例⇩

もらいなき 貰い泣き ¶もらい泣きする weep (in sympathy) with sb; 《文》share (in) sb's sorrow.

もらいび 貰い火 ¶もらい火する catch fire ((from a fire in a neighbor's house)).

もらいもの 貰い物 a present [gift] ((from sb)) ¶もらい物をする get [《文》receive] a present ((from)).

もらう 貰う 《受ける》get; have; 《文》receive; take; accept; be given; be presented ((with)); 《授与される》be awarded ¶ …してもらう get sb to do; have sb do; get [have] sth done / 子供をもらう adopt a child. 文例⇩

もらす 漏らす 〈水などを〉let sth leak [escape]; 〈感情などを〉《文》give vent to; express; 〈表わす〉《文》reveal; 《文》disclose; betray; let [give] out; 〈抜かす〉《文》omit; leave out ¶小便を漏らす wet one's pants [the bed]; have a toilet accident (やや婉曲的) / 秘密を漏らす reveal [betray, let out] a secret. 文例⇩

モラトリアム a moratorium ((pl. -s, -ria)).
モラリスト a moralist.
モラル morals; morality; ethics.

もり¹ 守り 〈子守り〉a nursemaid; a nursery-maid; a baby-sitter (★留守居を兼ねて時間で雇われる。《米》では略して sitter ともいう); 〈番人〉a (lighthouse) keeper ¶赤ん坊のお守りをする baby-sit; look after [mind] a baby.

もり² 盛り quantity; 〈食べ物の〉(a) helping; (a) serving ¶盛りがいい[悪い] give good [short] measure; 〈レストランなどで〉give large [small] helpings / もっと盛りをよくしてくれと言う ask for a larger helping.

もり³ 森 〈小さな〉a wood; woods; a grove; 〈大きな〉a forest ¶森の都キエフ《文》the tree-clad city of Kiev.

もり⁴ 銛 a harpoon ¶もりを打ち込む harpoon ((a whale)).

もり⁵ 漏り a leak; leakage.

もりあがり 盛り上がり a climax ((of a story)); 《文》an upsurge ((of emotion)).

もりあがる 盛り上がる swell; rise ¶大衆の間から盛りあがった運動 a movement which arose spontaneously from among the people.

もりあげる 盛り上げる heap [pile] up.

もりあわせ 盛り合わせ ¶刺身の盛り合わせ assorted sashimi.

もりかえす 盛り返す 〈再び勢いを得る〉rally; come back; 《口語》make a comeback; revive; 〈ばん回する〉recover; regain ((lost ground)) ¶勢いを盛り返す rally; pick up ((ground)); regain one's strength.

もりきり 盛り切り a single helping ((of rice)).

もりこむ 盛り込む incorporate ((in)); include; 《文》comprehend.

もりだくさん 盛り沢山 ¶盛り沢山な plenty [a lot] of ((prizes)); all sorts of colorful ((programs)); crowded ((schedules)).

もりたてる 守り立てる support; back (up).

もりつけ 盛り付け ¶盛りつけをする dish up ((salad)); 〈分けて〉dish out.

ち込めた. Over the distant hill lay [hung] a blue evening haze.
もよう (事件の)模様はどうですか. How do matters stand? / 目下の危機は緩和されそうな模様である. There are signs that the present tension will ease.
もようがえ その計画は模様替えとなった. There have been some changes in the plan.
もらいて そんなものはだれももらい手があるまい. Nobody will take it. / あんな娘にもらい手があるだろうか. I wonder if she'll ever find [get] anyone to marry her.
もらう 誕生日のお祝いに時計をもらった. I got a watch for my birthday. / 知らない人から金をもらうな. Don't accept money from a stranger. / この手紙を田中さんの所に持って行って返事をもらっておいで. Take this letter to Mr. Tanaka and bring back his answer. / この茶を 300 グラムもらおう. I will take [have] 300 grams of this tea. / 欲しいと言いさえすればもらえる. It is to be had (simply) for the asking. / 彼にそれを英訳してもらった. I got him to translate it into English. / 今日の午後 4 時にここへ来てもらいたい. I want you to be here at four o'clock this afternoon. / 今度からそうしないでもらいたい. Please don't do that

もりつち 盛り土 《土木》 banking ¶盛り土をする raise the ground level; spread earth on the ground.

もりばな 盛り花 flowers arranged in a low [shallow] container.

モリブデン 《化》 molybdenum ¶モリブデン鉱 molybdenite / モリブデン鋼 molybdenum steel.

もりもり ¶もりもり食べる eat heartily; have a good [voracious] appetite / 筋肉がもりもりしている have a thick wad of muscles.

もる¹ 盛る 《食物を》 serve; fill 《sb's plate with stew》; dish up 《the meal》; help 《sb to some salad》;《積む》heap up 《sand》;《薬などを》give 《sb》administer 《medicine》;《度を》mark 《a thermometer》out 《in degrees》; graduate ¶飯を盛る serve rice in a bowl; fill a bowl with rice / サンドイッチを山と盛った皿 a plate piled high with sandwiches / 毒を盛る poison sb; put poison into sb's food [drink].

もる² 漏る《漏れる》leak; be leaky;《ガスが》escape;《こぼれ出る》trickle out ¶木の間を漏る月影 the moonlight that comes [filters] through the leaves / 漏り出す spring [start] a leak / 空気[水, ガス]の漏らない airtight [watertight, gastight] / 絶対に漏らない屋根 a leakproof roof. 文例⇩

モルジブ (the Republic of) the Maldives.

モルタル mortar ¶木造モルタル塗り家屋 a mortared frame house.

モルヒネ morphine ¶モルヒネ中毒《常用》morphine addiction; morphinism;《急性》morphine poisoning.

モルモット 《動》a guinea pig ⇨ じっけん²(実験材料にされる) ★「モルモット」の名は marmot から出たものであるが, これは全く別の動物.

モルモンきょう Mormonism ¶モルモン教会 the Mormon Church ★ 正式名は the Church of Jesus Christ of Latter-Day Saints / モルモン教徒 a Mormon.

もれ 漏れ《漏洩》a leak; an escape 《of gas》; leakage;《脱漏》《文》an omission;《見落とし》an oversight ¶漏れなく《文》without omission; in full;《文》exhaustively; one and all; thoroughly. 文例⇩

もれきく 漏れ聞く overhear; know sth by [from, on] hearsay ¶漏れ聞くところによれば… From what I have heard....

もれる 漏れる《気体や液体が》leak (out); escape;《光が》shine [break, come] through; filter out;《話し声が》be heard outside;《感情などが》《文》find vent [expression];《秘密などが》leak (out); get [slip] out;《脱漏する》《文》be omitted;《除外される》be left out; be not included ¶口から漏れる《文》pass [escape] one's lips. 文例⇩

もろい 脆い fragile; brittle; friable; breakable; delicate; weak;《文》frail ¶情にもろい be sentimental; be tenderhearted;《文》be easily moved / もろく(も) easily; without difficulty [any resistance]. 文例⇩

もろこ 《魚》a minnow.

もろこし 《植》(an) Indian [African] millet.

もろざし 諸差し ¶もろ差しになる《相撲》push both one's arms under one's opponent's.

モロッコ Morocco ¶モロッコの Moroccan / モロッコ王国 the Kingdom of Morocco / モロッコ革 morocco (leather) / モロッコ人 a Moroccan.

もろて 諸手 ¶もろ手をあげて賛成する wholeheartedly approve of sth / もろ手で with both hands.

もろともに 諸共に together (with); altogether; one and all. 文例⇩

もろに altogether; completely;《文》wholly; bodily; right 《down the slope》. 文例⇩

もろは 諸刃 ¶もろ刃の double-edged.

もろはだ 諸肌 ¶もろ肌を脱ぐ strip (oneself) to the waist;《比喩的》go at sth with might and main.

もろみ unrefined sake [soy sauce].

もろもろ 諸々 ¶もろもろの various; all; all kinds [sorts] of.

もん¹ 門 《建物の》a gate;《生物分類の》《動》a phylum (pl. -la);《植》a division ★ なお門以下の分類段階は, 綱 (class), 目 (order), 科 (family), 属 (genus (pl. genera, genuses)), 種 (species (単複同形)), 変種 (variety) の順による ¶門の前を通る[門をくぐる] pass [pass through] the gate / 門の外[内]側で outside [inside, (文) within] the gate.

もん² 紋 《定紋》a (family) crest; 文例⇩《紋章》a coat of arms ¶紋がついている bear [be marked with] a crest.

もん³ 問 ⇨ もんだい ¶第1問 the first question [problem]; question number [no.] one.

もんえい 門衛 ⇨ もんばん ¶門衛詰め所 a (porter's) lodge.

もんか 門下 ¶…門下の under 《Prof. —'s》tuition; studying under [with] 《Mr.—》/ 門下生 a pupil;《文》a disciple.

---

again.

もらす このことは人に漏らしては困る. Keep that to yourself. / Don't breathe a syllable about it to anyone.

もる² 屋根が漏る. The roof leaks. / 数か所から雨が漏った. The rain came (in) through several places in the roof.

もれ 漏れのないように願います. Please see that there are no omissions.

もれる 戸のすき間から灯火が漏れていた. The light shone [was coming out] through the chinks in the doors. / 秘密の情報が漏れた. There was a leak of secret information. / この記事には重要な事が漏れている. There is an important omission in the account. / 選に漏れた絵の中にもなかなかいいのがあった. There were some good pictures among the ones that were not accepted.

もろい 彼はもろくもだまされた. He fell an easy prey to the deception.

もろともに もう少しで船もろ共に沈んでしまうところだった. I nearly went down with the ship.

もろに 風は诸にまともに吹きつけた. The wind was right in my face.

もん¹ 門のところにだれか来ている. There is somebody at the gate. / 門に国旗が翻っていた.

もんがいかん 門外漢 an outsider; a layman (非専門家).

もんがいふしゅつ 門外不出 ¶門外不出の《a treasure》never allowed to be taken out of the house.

もんがまえ 門構え ¶門構えの《a house》with a《pretentious》gate.

もんきりがた 紋切り型 ¶紋切り型の stereotyped; conventional; hackneyed; formal / 紋切り型のあいさつをする give a conventionally-worded address.

もんく 文句 〈語句〉words; the [a] wording (★複数にはしない); a phrase; an expression; 〈言う事〉what one says; one's remarks [words]; 〈不平〉a complaint; grumbling; what one has to say against sth [sb]; 〈異存〉(an) objection ¶ありきたりの文句 a stock [《文》hackneyed] phrase / 名文句 a clever [《文》happy] expression / 文句を言う〈不平を言う〉complain 《about, of》; grumble《about》; make a complaint; 〈反対する〉object《to》; make an objection《to》; 〈非難する〉find fault with / 文句を言わずに without complaining [complaint]; without a murmur; without making difficulties / 文句なしの〈完全な〉perfect; 〈満足な〉(entirely) satisfactory.

もんげん 門限 (be back by) (the) closing time; lockup. 文例⇩

もんこ 門戸 the door ¶門戸を閉ざす shut [close] the door 《to, on》/ 門戸開放主義 the open-door principle [policy].

モンゴル Mongolia ¶内[外]モンゴル Inner [Outer] Mongolia / モンゴル人 a Mongolian; a Mongol / モンゴル人民共和国 the Mongolian People's Republic.

もんごん 文言 wording ¶文言を改める reword 《the regulation》. 文例⇩

もんし[1] 門歯 an incisor (tooth); a fore-tooth.

もんし[2] 悶死 ¶悶死する die in agony; die of vexation.

もんじ 文字 ⇒もじ.

もんじゅ 文殊 《仏教》Manjusri; the bodhisattva of wisdom and intellect ⇒さんにん.

もんしょう 紋章 a crest; 《文》a heraldic emblem; 《文》a (heraldic) device; a coat of arms ¶紋章学 heraldry.

もんしろちょう a small [cabbage] white (butterfly).

もんしん 問診 (a) medical examination by interview [word of mouth].

もんじん 門人 a pupil; 《文》a disciple; a follower; 〈集合的に〉(have) a《large》following.

モンスーン a monsoon.

もんせき 問責 ¶問責する take [《文》call] sb to task《for doing, about sth》; 《文》call [bring] sb to account.

もんぜつ 悶絶 ¶悶絶する faint [fall unconscious] in agony.

もんぜん 門前 ¶門前で in front of [《文》before] the gate / 門前払いを食わす turn 《a visitor》away at the door; refuse to see sb; be not at home to《a caller》/〈裁判所が〉turn down a suit / 門前市をなす have a constant stream of visitors / 門前町 a temple town [city]; 〈西洋の〉a cathedral town. 文例⇩

モンタージュ (a) montage ¶モンタージュする montage《photo prints》/ モンタージュ写真 a composite picture [photograph]; 《compose》a montage picture [photo].

もんだい 問題 a problem; a question;〈話題・研究の対象〉a subject; a topic; 《文》an issue (係争の);〈事件〉a matter; an affair ¶化学の問題 a question in chemistry / 肝心かなめの問題 a key question / 時間の問題 (be) a question [matter] of time / 問題の人 the man in question; a controversial figure [問題の多い人] / 問題を起こす cause trouble [problems]; raise a question; 〈世間の〉《文》give rise to public discussion / 問題を解決する settle a question; solve a problem; iron out the difficulties (困難を) / 問題を出す set sb a problem [a paper] / 問題を解く solve [work out] a problem / 問題に答える answer a question / 問題にしない take no notice of; make little [light] of / 問題にする bring《an incident》up; call [bring] into question; 《文》put《a matter》in question / 政治上の問題にする make a political issue of《a matter》/ 問題に取り組む tackle [attack] a problem / 問題にならない〈全然だめ〉be out of the question; 〈大したことではない〉do not matter [count for much]; be insignificant; count for nothing / 問題になる come into question; become a subject of discussion; 〈表面化する〉come to a head [the fore] / 問題である〈疑わしい〉be questionable [《文》problematical]; be open to question; be doubtful / 中心問題 the central issue [problem] / 問題意識《文》(have) an awareness of the issues [problems involved] / 問題解決能力《文》one's problem-solving pow-

---

The national flag was flying over the gate. / もんく 何も文句はないはずだ。You ought to have nothing to complain of. / 僕は君に文句がある。《口語》I've got a bone to pick with you. / あの男に文句を言ってやろう。I'll give him a piece of my mind. | I'll tell him a thing or two. / もんげん 門限午後11時。《掲示》All residents must be back by 11 p.m. | Doors closed at 11 o'clock. / もんごん この協定書は文言が明瞭でない。The agreement is not clearly worded. / もんぜん 門前の小僧習わぬ経を読む。A shop-boy near a temple will recite the scriptures untaught. / もんだい それで問題は解決する。That settles the case [matter]. / 問題は自然解消の形になった。The question settled itself. / 重大な国際問題となった。It turned into a grave international issue. / そこが問題だ。That is the question [point]. / それは問題が別だ。That's another question. / 彼はいつも問題を起こしていた。He was in continual trouble. / 問題は彼にそれだけの金が出せるかどうかだ。The question [point] is whether he can afford to pay that much money. / 成功するかどうかが問題だ。It is questionable whether he will succeed or not. / 我々の提案に彼が賛成かど

もんち

ers / 問題劇[小説] a problem play [novel] / 問題児 a problem child / 問題点 the problem; the point at issue; 《文》 the controversial [moot] point / 問題領域 a problem area. 文例↓

モンタナ Montana (略: Mont.) ¶モンタナ州の人 a Montanan.

もんち 門地 a [one's] family status [origin]; 《文》 lineage; 《文》 birth; 《文》 pedigree.

もんちゃく 悶着 ⇨ もめごと.

もんちゅう 門柱 a gatepost.

もんつき 紋付き a kimono [haori] marked with a (family) crest; a blazoned kimono [haori].

もんてい 門弟 ⇨ もんじん, てし.

もんとう 門灯 a gate lamp [light].

もんどう 問答 questions and answers; a dialogue (対話); (a) catechism (教義問答) ¶問答する exchange questions and answers (with); hold a dialogue / 問答式に in the form of questions and answers. 文例↓

もんどころ 紋所 ⇨ もん².

もんどり ¶もんどり打つ turn a somersault / もんどり打って倒れる fall head over heels.

もんなし 文なし ¶文なしの penniless ⇨ いちもん¹. 文例↓

もんばつ 門閥 《家柄》《文》 birth; 《文》 lineage; 《文》 pedigree ¶《名門》 a distinguished family ¶門閥の家に生まれる come from [《文》 of] a good [distinguished] family; 《文》 be of noble [high] birth / 門閥も金もない have neither birth nor money.

もんばん 門番 a gatekeeper; a gateman; a doorkeeper; a doorman; a (house) porter; a janitor; 《フランス語》 a concierge ¶門番をする keep the gate [door] / 門番小屋 a gatehouse; a guard booth; a (porter's) lodge.

もんぶ 文部 ¶文部省[大臣] the Ministry [Minister] of Education (, Science and Culture).

モンブラン Mont Blanc.

もんぺ (women's) work pants (gathered at the ankles).

もんもう 文盲 illiteracy; 《人》 an illiterate ¶無学文盲な人 a person who is uneducated [ignorant] and illiterate.

もんもん 悶々 ¶もんもんの情 mental agony [《文》 anguish] / もんもんの情をやる give vent to one's anguish.

もんよう 文[紋]様 a pattern.

モンローしゅぎ モンロー主義 the Monroe Doctrine.

や

や¹ 矢 an arrow; a flight arrow (遠矢); a bolt (太矢); 《車輪の》 a spoke ¶矢を射る[放つ] let off [shoot (off)] an arrow (at) / 矢をつがえる fit [notch] an arrow to the bowstring / 矢の催促をする press sb hard (for) / 矢も盾もたまらない be dying (to do, for) / 矢音 the hum [humming (sound), whizzing (sound)] of an arrow / 矢羽 the feathers of an arrow. 文例↓

や² 〈…と〉 and; 〈又は〉 or… ¶…や否や〈や〉-いなや.

用法 日本語の「A や B」は、英語では A and B となるときもあるし、A or B となるときもある。例えば「ロンドンや東京のような大都会」は large cities such as London and Tokyo もしくは a large city such as London or Tokyo で、文法的または論理的に辻つまの合うように気を配って and と or を使い分けなくてはいけない。なお、「A や B」を否定するには I don't like butter or cheese. (バターやチーズが好きではない) のように not…A or B の形を取る。

-や …屋 文例↓

やあ 〈感動〉 Oh; Ah; 〈驚き〉 Dear me !; Good Heavens !; 〈呼びかけ〉 Hullo; Hello there; 《米》 Hi. 文例↓

ヤード a yard (略: yd).

やい 〈呼びかけ〉 Hey (you) !; Oi !; 〈ののしり〉 bah !

やいのやいの ¶やいのやいのと求める clamor (for sth, to do); 《文》 press clamorously (for sth).

やいば 刃 (the edge of) a blade; 《刀》 a sword.

やいやい ¶やいやい言う press sb hard (for); harass [badger] sb (into doing); annoy sb; clamor (for, against) / やいやい言って賃上げを要求する make persistent demands (to [on] sb) for a raise in salary; clamor for higher wages.

やいん 夜陰 ¶夜陰に乗じて under cover of darkness [night]; 《文》 under the cloak of night.

やえ 八重 ¶八重の eightfold; 〈花の〉 double(-

うかはあまり問題ではない. It doesn't much matter whether he consents to our proposal or not. / そんなことは大した問題じゃない. That's a small matter. | That is not much of a problem. | ジムは我々とは考えが違うようだが、それはあまり問題にしないでおこう. Jim doesn't seem to think the same way as us, but don't let's make an issue of it. ⇨ より²

用法 これこそ問題なく彼が今までに書いた一番いい小説だ. This is indisputably [easily] the best novel he has written.

もんちゃく この事件から悶着が起きるかもしれない. This affair may cause difficulties [trouble, problems].

もんどう 問答無用だ. I won't waste my breath answering such a question.

もんなし 僕は文なしだ. 《米》 I haven't got a red cent. | 《英》 I haven't got a brass farthing. | 《俗》 I'm clean [stony] broke. | 《英俗》 I'm skint.

や¹ その鳥は木の枝の間から矢のように飛び出して虫を捕らえた. The bird darted out from among the branches of the tree and caught an insect. / 矢はすでに弦は放たれた. The die is cast. | The result is out of our hands now. / 矢でも鉄砲でも持ってこい Try and do anything against me. | I defy you.

-や 市川君は字引き屋だ Ichikawa is a dictionary man. / 彼女は居眠り屋だ She is forever nodding off.

やあ やあ、あれはジョンだ. Why,

やえい 野営 camping; a bivouac ¶野営する camp out; 《文》encamp; bivouac / 野営している be in camp / 野営地 a camping ground [site].

やえば 八重歯 〈二重の〉a double [redundant] tooth.

やおちょう 八百長 a put-up job; a prearranged [fixed] game ¶八百長をやる fix 《a fight》/ 八百長で負ける throw a match 《to one's opponent》.

やおもて 矢面 ¶(まともに)矢面に立つ《文》bear [take] the (full) brunt 《of an attack, of criticism》.

やおや 八百屋 〈店〉《米》a vegetable store; 《英》a greengrocer's (shop); a greengrocery / 〈人〉《米》a vegetable man; 《英》a greengrocer.

やおら slowly; 《文》without haste; deliberately.

やかい 夜会 (give, hold) an evening party; 《文》a soirée ¶夜会服〈総称, 男女共〉evening dress;〈女の〉an evening dress;〈男の〉a dress suit [coat].

やがい 野外 ¶野外の outdoor; out-of-door; open-air; field / 野外で[に] in the open (air); outdoors; out of doors; in the field / 野外に出る go out into the field (to observe wild animals) / 野外劇 an outdoor play; a pageant / 野外劇場 an open-air [outdoor] theater / 野外研究旅行に行く take a field trip (to) / 野外調査 field research [work] / 野外料理 outdoor cooking; a cookout.

やがく 夜学 (attend) an evening [a night] class [school] ¶夜学生 a night-[an evening-]school student; a night student.

やかた 館 a mansion; a palace;〈居城〉a castle.

やかたぶね 屋形船 a (Japanese) houseboat.

やがて〈間もなく〉soon; presently; by and by; before long; in a short time; then;〈時が来れば〉in due [good] time;《文》in (the) course of time;〈ほとんど〉almost; nearly;〈つまり〉after all. 文例⇩

やかましい 喧しい〈騒々しい〉noisy; annoyingly loud;〈世評が〉《文》much-talked-of; 〈好みが〉particular 《about》; fussy 《about》; 《文》fastidious 《about》;〈気難しい〉hard to please;〈口やかましい〉faultfinding; critical; fussy;〈厳格な〉severe; strict; strait-laced ¶やかましい問題 a controversial [burning, 《文》much-discussed, 《文》vexed] question / 生徒にやかましい be strict [severe] with one's pupils / 食物にやかましい be fussy [fastidious, particular] about one's food / やかましく〈騒がしく〉noisily;《文》clamorously;〈厳しく〉severely; strictly / やかまし屋〈気難しい人〉a person who is hard to please; a fastidious person;《戯言》Mr. Particular(「おやかま氏」); 〈小言のうるさい人〉a faultfinder;《文》a captious person; a prig;《口語》a fusspot. 文例⇩

やから 族〈連中〉a set; a lot;〈1人〉a fellow ¶ああいうやから《文》those gentry; those sort of men.

やかん¹ 夜間 ¶夜間(に)at [《文》by] night; in the night [nighttime] / 夜間営業 night business [operation] / 夜間勤務 night work;〈夜勤〉a night shift / 夜間試合 a night game [match] / 夜間人口 the nighttime population / 夜間番組 a night [nighttime] program / 夜間飛行 a night [《文》nocturnal] flight / 夜間部 evening [night] classes 《of a college》. 文例⇩

やかん² 薬缶 a kettle; a teakettle ¶やかんを掛ける put a kettle on (the gas) [over the fire]; put water on to boil / やかんで湯を沸かす boil water in a kettle / やかん頭〈a bald head; a hairless [shiny] pate〉/ やかん頭である be (as) bald as an egg [a billiard ball].

やき¹ 夜気〈空気〉night air;〈冷気〉《文》the chill [cool] of night.

やき² 焼き ¶焼きが回る get [《文》become] senile;《文》be in one's dotage / 焼きの足りない〈陶器など〉underfired; badly-[poorly-]fired / よく焼きの通った well-fired / 焼きを入れる〈刃物に〉temper; harden;〈懲らしめる〉discipline;《文》chastise;〈拷問する〉torture / 焼きを戻す anneal; temper / 九谷焼 Kutani ware [porcelain] / 焼き入れ hardening; tempering.

やぎ 山羊《動》a goat ¶雄やぎ a he-goat; a billy goat / 雌やぎ a she-goat; a nanny (goat) / 子やぎ a kid; a young goat / やぎ皮 goatskin; 〈子やぎの〉kid (gloves) / 山羊座《天》Capricorn; Capricornus; the Goat ⇒さ 文例⇩ / やぎひげ a goatee (beard). 「grill.

やきあみ 焼き網 a toasting net; a gridiron; a

やきいも 焼き芋 a roast [baked] sweet potato ¶焼き芋屋 a roast sweet potato vendor.

やきいん 焼き印〈印そのもの〉a brand;〈道具〉a branding iron ¶焼き印を押す brand 《a horse with a red-hot iron》.

やきうち 焼き打ち ¶焼き打ちする set fire to 《a house》; burn 《a police box》.

やききる 焼き切る burn off; burn through 《the rope》.

やきぐし 焼き串 a skewer; a spit (大形の).

やきぐり 焼き栗 a roast chestnut.

---

that's John! / やあ加藤, 久し振りだったな. Hullo, Kato! I haven't seen you for a long time.
やがて やがて我々は遠くの方に明かりを見つけた. It was not long before we saw a light in the distance. / やがて時計が12時を打った. Then the clock struck twelve. / やがて人間は分業を行なうようになった. As time went on, man began to practice the division of labor. / ここへ来てからやがてひと月にもなります. It is nearly a month since I came here.
やかましい やかましいじゃないか, 一体どうしたのだ. What on earth are you making such a noise for? / 彼は礼儀のやかましい人だ. He is a stickler for etiquette. / この柄ならどんなやかましい方でもきっとお気に召すと思います. This design, we are confident, will appeal to the most critical taste. / 大学教育改革の声がやかましい. There are loud

やきごて 焼き鏝 a hot iron; 〈ハンダ用の〉a soldering iron; 〈医療用の〉a cautery (iron).

やきころす 焼き殺す burn sb to death.

やきざかな 焼き魚 (a) broiled [roast] fish.

やきすぎる 焼き過ぎる 〈食物を〉overdo; overcook; overroast; overbroil; 〈写真〉overprint ¶焼き過ぎた〈食物の〉overdone; overroasted ⇨やく⁵

やきすてる 焼き捨てる burn (up); throw sth into the fire;《文》commit sth to the flames.

やきそば 焼きそば〈中華料理〉chow mein.

やきたて 焼き立て ¶焼き立ての hot from the oven [pan, grill].

やきだまエンジン 焼き玉エンジン a hot-bulb [semidiesel] engine.

やきつく 焼き付く ¶焼き付くような日差し a broiling [scorching] sun / 心に焼き付く burn into one's mind [brain] / 心に焼き付いて離れない be imprinted [printed] on one's mind [memory].

やきつくす 焼き尽くす burn up [away, down, out];《文》reduce to ashes.

やきつける 焼き付ける〈めっきする〉plate;〈陶器に薬を〉glaze; enamel;〈写真を〉print (out [off]);〈ガラスに〉stain;〈心に〉burn sth into 〈sb's consciousness〉.

やきどうふ 焼き豆腐 broiled [grilled] tofu.

やきとり 焼き鳥 grilled meat on a stick; roast chicken.

やきなおし 焼き直し〈食物の〉rebaking;〈改作〉an adaptation 《of, from》;《口語》a rehash 文例⇩

やきなおす 焼き直す〈食物を〉rebake; rebroil;〈改作する〉adapt 《from》; rework;《口語》rehash.

やきにく 焼肉 roast [broiled, grilled] meat ¶焼き肉の盛り合わせ a mixed grill.

やきのり 焼きのり baked [toasted] laver.

やきば 焼き場 a crematorium (pl. -s, -toria);〈米〉a crematory.

やきばたのうほう 焼畑農法 slash-and-burn farming / the slash-and-burn method (of agriculture).

やきはらう 焼き払う burn to the ground; burn up [down]; reduce to ashes;《文》raze to the ground (by burning); destroy by fire ¶焼き払われた森林 a burned-over forest / 外だけを残して内部をすっかり焼き払われたビル a building completely gutted by fire. 文例⇩

やきぶた 焼き豚 roast pork.

やきまし 焼き増し a [an extra] copy [print] 《of a photograph》. 文例⇩

やきめし 焼き飯 fried rice.

やきもき ¶やきもきする be impatient 《to do, for》; fret 《about》; worry 《about》;《口語》go [get] into a stew 《about》. 文例⇩

やきもち 焼きもち〈ねたみ〉jealousy ⇨しっと ¶焼きもちを焼く be jealous (of);〈文〉show [exhibit] jealousy 《of one's wife》/ 焼きもち焼き a jealous person.

やきもの 焼き物〈陶磁器〉(a piece of) pottery; earthenware; porcelain;〈料理〉(a) broiled fish.

やきゅう 野球 baseball ¶野球をする play baseball / 野球試合をする have [hold] a baseball game [match] 《with》/ 野球場 a baseball ground [field]; a ballpark / 野球選手 a baseball player; a ballplayer / 野球チーム a baseball team; the 《Rikkyo》nine / 野球熱 enthusiasm for baseball / 野球ファン a baseball fan.

やぎゅう 野牛 a wild ox; a bison (単複同形);〈北米産の〉a buffalo 《pl. -(e)s》.

やぎょう 夜業 night work ⇨やきん² ¶夜業をする work at [by] night; do night work.

やきょく 夜曲〈音楽〉a nocturne.

やきん¹ 冶金 ¶冶金(学) metallurgy / 冶金(学)の metallurgic(al) / 冶金学者 a metallurgist.

やきん² 夜勤 night duty; a night shift 《昼夜交替の》⇨やぎょう ¶夜勤の看護婦 a night nurse / 夜勤をする be on night shift [duty] / 夜勤手当 a night-work allowance.

やく¹ 厄 ⇨やくどし, さいなん ¶厄を払う ⇨やくばらい.

やく² 役〈官職・地位〉《文》(an) office; a post;〈任務〉duty;《文》service;〈劇の〉a part;《文》a role ¶役を勤める hold (the office) 《in the Ministry of Justice》; hold the office 《of Minister of Justice》; act [play, perform] the part [role] 《of》; serve [act] 《as》/ 重要な役を勤める play an important role [part] 《in》/ ハムレットの役を勤める play [act] the part [role] of Hamlet; play Hamlet / 役を振り当てる cast (an actor) in [for] the part [role] 《of Shylock》/ 役に立つ be useful [《文》serviceable] 《for, to》;《文》be of use [service] 《to, for》; be helpful [《文》instrumental] 《in doing》; serve [《文》answer] the [one's] purpose / 大いに役に立つ be very useful (for, to); go far [a long way] 《toward》/ 役に立つ人 a useful person;〈有能な〉an able [a competent] person ⇨ゆうのう / 役に立たない be useless; be of no use [《文》service];〈無益である〉be no good;《文》be of no avail / 役に立たない人 a useless person; a good-for-nothing (fellow);

---

cries raised for the reform of university education. / 食品安全基準をもっときびしくせよという市民の声がやかましくなった。The citizens' demands for stricter standards of food safety have become increasingly vocal. / 水道の問題がやかましくなった。The problem of urban water supplies has recently become the subject of a great deal of discussion.

やかん¹ 博覧会は今明日夜間開場いたします。The exhibition will be open at night today and tomorrow. / 青山学院大学には夜間部がある。Aoyama Gakuin University has a night college.

やきなおし これはウェルズの小説の焼き直しだ。This is an adaptation of one of Wells's works.

やきはらう 先日の火事で全村が焼き払われました。The recent fire has devastated [made a clean sweep of] the whole village.

やきまし この写真をもう5枚焼き増ししてください。I want five copies of this picture.

やきもき 帰りが遅いと君の細君がやきもきするぜ。If you are late,

やく〈無能な〉an incapable person ⇨ むのう / 役に立てる《文》turn [put] sth to account [advantage]; make (good) use of ⇨ りよう¹ / 役力士〖相撲〗a '*san'yaku*' class wrestler. 文例⇩

やく³ 訳 (a) translation; (a) version ¶訳がうまい[下手である] be a good [poor] translator / 訳をつける ⇨ やくす² / 韻文[散文]訳 a verse [prose] translation.

やく⁴ 葯〖植〗an anther.

やく⁵ 焼く burn; 〈食物を〉roast (肉を); broil (魚肉を); grill (鉄網で); bake (パンを); toast (のりを); 〈火災で〉have (*one's house*) burned down; 〈放火する〉set fire (to); 〈焼き捨てる〉《文》commit *sth* to the flames; throw *sth* into the fire; 〈焦がす〉scorch; parch; 〈焼灼する〉〖医〗cauterize; 〈陶器などを〉bake; fire; 〈死骸を〉cremate; 〈写真を〉print (out); 〈ねたむ〉be jealous [envious] (of) ¶焼き印を真赤に焼く heat a branding-iron red hot / よく焼けていない be underdone; be half-done.

やく⁶ 約 〈およそ〉about; nearly; 《文》approximately; some ¶約40分で in about [some] forty minutes; in forty minutes or so [thereabouts].

ヤク〖動〗a yak.

やぐ 夜具 bedclothes; 〈掛け布団を〉a counterpane; a quilt; a coverlet.

やくいん 役員 an official; an officer; 〈会社の〉an executive; a director ⇨ じゅうやく¹ ¶役員会 a [an executive] committee / 役員席 seats for the officials.

やくおとし 厄落とし ⇨ やくばらい.

やくがい 薬害 《suffer from》the harmful effects of a medicine; 〈農薬の〉damage from agricultural chemicals.

やくがく 薬学 pharmacy; pharmaceutics ¶薬学士〈人〉a bachelor of pharmacy; 〈学位〉Bachelor of Pharmacy (略: Phar.B.) / 薬学博士〈学位〉Doctor of Pharmacy (略: Phar.D.) / 薬学部 the pharmaceutical department; the college of pharmacy.

やくがら 役柄 *one's* position [《文》role, 《文》office] ⇨ やく².

やくご 訳語 words [terms] used in a translation; an 《English》equivalent 《for》. 文例⇩

やくざ ¶やくざな worthless; useless; trashy / やくざ者 a good-for-nothing (fellow); 《文》a wastrel; trash; 〈ばくち打ちを〉a gambler; 〈暴力団員を〉a yakuza; a gangster; 《米俗》a mobster; a racketeer.

やくざい 薬剤 ⇨ くすり ¶薬剤師 a pharmaceutist; a pharmacist; a druggist; 《英》a (pharmaceutical [dispensing]) chemist.

やくさつ 扼殺 ¶扼殺する strangle *sb* (to death).

やくし¹ 訳詩 a translated poem ¶ハイネを訳詩で読む read Heine's poems in translation.

やくし² 薬師 the Healing Buddha.

やくしゃ¹ 役者 an actor (男); an actress (女); a player ¶役者になる become an actor [actress]; go on [take to] the stage / 役者をやめる retire from [leave] the stage / 役者が一枚上である be a cut above *sb*; be more than a match for *sb*. 文例⇩

やくしゃ² 訳者 a translator.

やくしゅつ 訳出 ¶訳出する ⇨ やくす²

やくしょ 役所 a public [government] office ¶お役所風〈形式主義〉officialism; red tape.

やくしょ² 訳書 ⇨ やくほん.

やくじょ 躍如 ¶躍如たる vivid; 《文》graphic; lifelike / 躍如として vividly; 《文》graphically; true to life / 面目躍如としている be like *sb*; 《文》be characteristic of *sb*.

やくじょう 約定 〈契約〉a contract; 〈協定〉an agreement; 〈契約・協定の条項〉a stipulation ¶約定書 a (written) contract; a deed of contract.

やくしょく 役職 a managerial position ¶役職手当 a managerial position allowance. 手例⇩

やくしん 躍進 ¶躍進する 《文》make rapid progress; advance rapidly [by leaps and bounds]; take [make] great [rapid] strides; leap ahead; take [make] a (great) leap forward / 日本の経済的躍進 Japan's economic advance.

やくす¹ 約す ⇨ やくぶん¹.

やくす² 訳す translate 《from the English into your wife will worry about you.

やく² 彼女は自分に振り当てられた役に少しも興味を見出せなかった. She couldn't take any interest in the role that was assigned to her. / 僕にはその役は勤まらない. I am unfit for the post [unequal to the job]. / そこからが君の役だ. That's where you come in. / そんな本を読んで何の役に立つのですか. What's the good [use] of reading a book like that? / 実際上何の役にも立たないかもしれない. It may (well) be of no practical use. / お役に立てば幸いです. I should be happy to be of any service [help] to you. / そこで学んだことが大いに彼の役に立った. What he learned there stood him in good stead later. / その仕事には辞書はあまり役に立たなかった. In doing that work, dictionaries were not much help [were of little assistance]. / 学校では社会で役に立つようなことを教えてくれない. Nothing they teach you at school is much use in business. | What they teach you at school isn't much use in business. / これはお前がお小遣いに不足するようなことがあれば役に立つだろうよ. This will come in handy [useful] when you are running short of pocket money. / 塀を高くすれば, このようなトラブルの解消にいくぶん役に立つでしょう. If you make the fence higher, it will go some way toward removing this sort of problem. / おついしょうなど何の役にも立たないよ. Flattery will get you nowhere [cut no ice] (with us). / その計画には私にも一役買わせて下さい. Let me have a part in the plan.

やくご この訳文には訳語の妥当でないのが多い. This translation contains a large number of terms which are not quite appropriate. / この語には適当な日本語の訳語がない. There is no proper [satisfactory] Japanese equivalent for this word.

やくしゃ¹ 彼は文士をやめて役者になった. He gave up the pen for the stage.

やくすう　約数 [数] a divisor; a factor.
やくそう　薬草 a (medicinal) herb ¶薬草園 a herb garden.
やくそく　約束 a promise; 《文》an engagement; an appointment; a date (特に異性との); 〈協定〉an agreement; a contract; 〈売買の〉a bargain; 〈条件〉a condition ¶固い約束 a firm promise; 〈名誉に掛けての〉(give) one's word of honor / 舞台上の約束 stage conventions / 約束する promise; give one's word [promise] ((to sb)); agree ((on sth with sb)); make 《文》enter into an agreement; 《文》pledge oneself ((to sth, to do)) / 約束して会う meet sb by appointment / 約束があって中座する (have to) go off to an appointment / ほかに約束がありますので, と言う 《文》plead an [a previous] engagement; say one already has an engagement 《that...》/ ...という約束で on the promise 《that...》; 〈条件で〉on condition 《that...》/ 約束どおり as (one had) promised; 《文》according [true] to one's promise / 約束の時間 [日] に at [on] the appointed [promised] time [day] / 約束の地 『聖書』 the Promised Land, the Land of Promise / 会う約束をする make an appointment [a date] ((with)) / 約束を守る [果たす, 履行する] keep [live up to] one's word; be as good as one's word; keep [honor, abide by, act up to] one's promise; fulfill [carry out] one's engagement / 約束を守らせる hold [keep] sb to his word / 約束を破る break one's promise [word]; 〈会合の〉break an appointment [a date] ((with)) / 約束を取り消す withdraw one's promise; call off one's engagement / 口約束 《文》a verbal promise; 〈ごまかしの〉《文》a false promise / 約束手形 a (promissory) note. 用例⇨
やくだつ, やくだてる　役立つ, 役立てる ⇨やく² (役に立つ, 役に立てる).
やくちゅう　訳注 translation and annotation ¶S氏訳注の「リヤ王」King Lear translated and annotated [translated with notes] by Mr. S.
やくどう　躍動 ¶躍動する move in a lively way; throb; 《文》be in full play / 生気躍動している be full of life (and energy); be overflowing with youth and vigor.
やくとく　役得 a side benefit; 《文》a perquisite; 〈口語〉a perk; 《文》an (additional) emolument ★ perk は perks として複数形で使うのが普通. perquisite も複数形で使うことが多い.
やくどく　訳読 oral translation.
やくどし　厄年 an unlucky [a bad] year; a critical year (for one).
やくにん　役人 a government official [officer]; 《文》a public functionary; 〈公僕〉a public servant; 〈英〉a civil servant; 〈集合的〉(the) bureaucracy; 《文》officialdom ¶役人になる become a public [civil] servant; go into 《文》enter government service / 役人根性 bureaucracy; bureaucratism / 役人生活 one's career [life] as a government official. 用例⇨
やくば　役場 a town [village] office; a town hall.
やくばらい　厄払い a service [ceremony] of exorcism; (an) exorcism ¶厄払いをする exorcise; drive out an evil spirit.
やくび　厄日 an unlucky [an evil, a bad] day; a critical day (for the crop). 用例⇨
やくびょうがみ　疫病神 〈嫌われ者〉a pest; 〈厄介者〉a plague.
やくひん　薬品 (a) medicines; drugs; chemicals (化学薬品).
やくぶそく　役不足 ¶役不足を訴える complain about one's part; be discontented with the role that has been given 《文》assigned to one / 役不足である 《文》be worthy of a better role.
やくぶつ　薬物 (a) medicine; drugs; 《文》medication; 《文》medicament ¶薬物による治療 medicinal treatment / 薬物中毒 medicinal poisoning.
やくぶん¹　約分 [数] reduction ¶約分する reduce ((a fraction)) / 約分できない irreducible. 用例⇨
やくぶん²　訳文 a translation; a version.
やくほん　訳本 a (Japanese) translation [version] ((of)).
やくまわり　役回り ⇨やく².

やくじょ そんな時でも自分のことを最後に考えるとは彼の面目躍如たるものがある. It was typical of [just like] him to think of himself last even at such a juncture.
やくしょく 彼は会社で高い役職についていた. He held high office at the firm.
やくす² 次の日本語を英語に訳しなさい. Translate [Turn] the following Japanese into English. / 「ポリス」というのはギリシャ語で, 現在では「都市国家」と訳されている. 'Polis' is the Greek word which we translate [which is rendered] (as) 'city-state'. / 詩は容易に外国語に訳せるものではない. Poetry does not easily translate into foreign languages.
やくそく 約束を破るようなことはしないから安心して下さい. Please don't worry. We will honor [observe] our commitment. / 秘密を守るという約束をしている. I am committed to keeping [bound by a promise to keep] the secret. / その子供に1日2時間教える約束だった. She was expected [supposed] to teach the child for two hours a day. / 彼は約束を守る人だ. He is a man of his word. / He is always as good as his word. / 彼は約束の本を借りに来た. He came to borrow the book I had promised to lend him. / 僕は今日4時に約束がある. I have an appointment [I am engaged] today at four o'clock. / 彼女と夕食を一緒にする約束がある. I have a dinner date with her [an appointment to have dinner with her].
やくどう 劇は全編生気躍動している. The drama is vibrant with life from start to finish.
やくにん 彼は外務省の役人だ. He is in [at] the Foreign Ministry. / He has a post in [works at] the Ministry of Foreign Affairs.
やくび 今日は厄日だ. This is one of my bad [off] days.
やくぶん¹ 9/24 は約分すると 3/8 に

やくみ 薬味 spice(s);《文》condiments; (a) seasoning ¶薬味を入れる a spice [a dish]; flavor [season]《a dish》with spice / 薬味入れ a cruet / 薬味立て a cruet stand.

やくめ 役目 a duty;《文》a role;《文》an office; one's business;《文》function(s) ¶お役目的的《文》perfunctory / お役目的に《文》perfunctorily / 役目柄〈職権に基づいて〉by virtue of one's office;〈ラテン語〉ex officio;〈役目を考えて〉considering [in view of] one's post [position, office].

やくよう 薬用 ¶薬用の medicinal / 薬用石鹼 medicated soap / 薬用植物 a medicinal [《文》curative] plant.

やくよけ 厄除け〈お守り〉a protective charm;《文》a talisman [an amulet] against [to ward off] evils ¶厄よけにをなる protect sb against evils [dangers]; come between sb and evils [dangers].

やぐら 櫓 a turret;〈足場〉a scaffold.

やくりがく 薬理学 pharmacology ¶薬理学的 pharmacological / 薬理学上 pharmacologically.

やぐるま 矢車〈こいのぼりの〉an 'arrow wheel'; the decorative windmill attached to the top of the pole on which koinobori—carp streamers—are raised.

やぐるまそう 矢車草〈矢車菊の通称〉a cornflower; a bluebottle.

やくわり 役割 a part;《文》a role ¶役割を定める allot [assign] a part [role]《to sb》; cast《an actor》in [for] a part; give《an actor》a part《in a play》/ 重大な役割を演じる play an important [a key, a large, a major] part [role]《in sth》. 文例⇩

やけ ¶やけを起こす get [《文》become] desperate [reckless];《文》abandon oneself to despair; go mad / やけに〈法外に〉awfully; frightfully; desperately;〈激しく〉violently; with a vengeance;《口語》like mad / やけになって[をおこして]〈むちゃくちゃに〉desperately; recklessly;〈絶望のあまり〉in [out of] despair; in (one's) desperation / やけのやんパ (a sense of) (last-ditch) desperation / やけ酒を飲む have a drink in desperation; drown one's sorrows. 文例⇩

やけあと 焼け跡 the ruins of a fire; the area swept by the flames.

やけい¹ 夜景 a night view [scene] ¶夜景画 a night piece / 香港の夜景 the view [sight] of Hong Kong by [at] night.

やけい² 夜警〈事〉night watch;〈人〉a night watchman ¶夜警をする keep (the) night watch / 夜警に立っている be on duty for the night. 文例⇩

やけいし 焼け石 a hot [heated] stone. 文例⇩

やけおちる 焼け落ちる burn [be burned] down [to the ground].

やけこがし、やけこげ 焼け焦がし、焼け焦げ a burned hole ¶焼け焦がしをこしらえる burn a hole《in one's clothes》.

やけしぬ 焼け死ぬ be burned to death;《文》perish in the flames.

やけだされる 焼け出される be burned out (of house and home).

やけつく 焼け付く ¶焼け付くような暑さ the scorching [parching] heat of the sun / 焼け付くような暑い baking-hot (day)s.

やけど a (skin) burn (火の); a scald (湯・蒸気の) ¶やけどする get [be] burned [scalded];〈比喩的〉get one's fingers burned; burn one's fingers / やけどのあと a scar of a burn [scald]. 文例⇩

やけのこる 焼け残る remain unburned; escape the fire.

やけのはら 焼け野原 a burnt-out area.

やけひばし 焼け火箸 red-hot metal chopsticks.

やけぶとり 焼け太り ¶焼け太りする get richer [《文》become more prosperous] after a fire.

やけぼっくい 焼け木杭 a charred pile [post]. 文例⇩

やける 焼ける burn; be burned; be destroyed [《文》consumed] by fire; be reduced to ashes;〈肉が〉be roasted;〈魚が〉be broiled;〈パンが〉be baked (パンを造る時); be toasted (トーストの時);〈焦げる〉be scorched; be parched;〈日に〉be sunburned; be suntanned; get [《文》become] brown from the sun; be bronzed by the sun;〈変色する〉discolor; be discolored;〈胸が〉get [have] heartburn;〈焼きもちを焼く〉be jealous《of》;〈うらやむ〉be envious《of》;〈空が〉glow; be red;《文》be aglow《with the setting sun》 ¶焼けている be burning; be on fire; be in flames (炎に包まれて) /《劇薬などによる》焼けるような痛み a burning pain / 真赤に焼けた red-hot. 文例⇩

やけん 野犬〈迷い犬〉a stray dog;〈宿なし犬〉a homeless [an ownerless] dog ¶野犬狩り a roundup of ownerless dogs / 野犬捕獲人 a dogcatcher.

やこう¹ 夜光 ¶夜光虫《生物》a noctiluca《pl.

なる. 9/24 reduces to 3/8.

やくめ 双方の調停を図るのが私の役目です. My function is [It is my responsibility] to mediate between the parties. / 教師は教えるのが役目だ. The business of a teacher is to teach. / そうするのが私の役目です. It is up to me to do so.

やくよう この草は薬用になる. This plant is used for medicinal purposes.

やくわり 彼はその役割を立派に果たした. He performed his part most effectively.

やけ 彼は失敗でやけになった. Failure drove him to despair.

やけい² 夜警が見回っていた. A watchman was going on his round.

やけいし これは焼け石に水だ. It is a mere drop in the bucket. / たかが500万円ぐらい融通してやっても，焼け石に水だ. To lend him a mere five million yen would simply be throwing good money after bad.

やけど 手をやけどした. I got burned on the hand.

やけぼっくい 焼けぼっくいに火が付いた. The old love blazed anew between them.

やける 多数の家が戦火に焼けた. Many houses burned up in the flames of war. / 長いこと日なたに置いてあった車は焼けるよう

やこう ‹-cae› / 夜光時計 a luminous watch / 夜光塗料 luminous paint.

やこう² 夜行 ‹列車› a night [an overnight] train ¶夜行で行く take [go by] a night train 《to》; take [have] an overnight train ride 《to》/ 夜行性 ‹生態› the nocturnal habit / 夜行性の nocturnal 《animals》; night-flying 《moths》; night-prowling 《reptiles》; 《animals》 with nocturnal habits. 文例

やごう 屋号 ‹店の› the name [《文》 style] 《of a store》 ¶...という屋号で under the style of 《Echigoya》.

やさい 野菜 vegetables; greens; 《米》 garden stuff [truck] ¶野菜を作る grow [raise] vegetables / 青野菜 a green vegetable / 野菜サラダ[スープ] vegetable salad [soup] / 野菜畑 ‹家庭の› a kitchen [vegetable] garden; ‹農家の› a vegetable field; 《米》 a truck farm [garden]; 《英》 a market garden / 野菜料理 a vegetable dish.

やさおとこ 優男 a slim man; 《文》 a man of slender build; a slip of a boy.

やさがし 家捜し ⇨かたく¹(家宅捜索).

やさがた 優形 ¶優形の 《文》 slight; 《a man》 with a slender [slim] figure; 《文》 of slender build; delicate-looking, frail-looking.

やさき 矢先 ¶矢先に just as [when] one is about to do; the moment one is going to do. 文例

やさしい¹ 易しい ‹容易な› easy; simple; ‹明白な› plain ¶易しく easily; 《文》 with ease; without 《any》 difficulty / 易しくする make 《a problem》 easier; simplify / 《本が》易しく書いてある be written in an easy style [in plain language].

やさしい² 優しい ‹柔和な› gentle(-mannered); ‹愛情のある› tender; affectionate; ‹親切な› kind; kindly; kindhearted ¶優しく kindly; tenderly; gently / 気立ての優しい sweet-tempered; tenderhearted / 優しくする be kind [good, nice] 《to》.

やし¹ 野師 a huckster; a charlatan.

やし² 椰子 ‹植› ‹ココやし› a coconut palm [tree]; a coco palm; ‹やし科植物の総称› a palm ¶やしの実 ‹ココやしの実› a coconut; a cocoanut / なつめ[サゴ]やし a date [sago] palm / やしがに a coconut [purse] crab / やし油 palm [coconut] oil [butter].

やじ booing; jeering; catcalling; heckling; hooting; interruption ¶やじ馬 ‹やじる人› a heckler; ‹群集› a rabble; a mob; ‹見物人›

spectators.

やしき 屋敷 ‹邸宅› a mansion; 《文》 a residence; ‹家屋敷› 《文》 the premises; 《文》 the estate ¶屋敷内に[で] on the premises; within [in] the grounds 《of》/ 屋敷町 residential quarters [areas].

やしなう 養う ‹養育する› bring up; rear; raise; foster; ‹養子にする› adopt; ‹食べさす› support; 《文》 maintain; provide for; feed; ‹病後の体を› 《文》 recuperate; convalesce; ‹習慣などを› cultivate; develop ¶一家を養う support [provide for] one's family / よい習慣を養う 《文》 cultivate [form] a good habit.

やしゅ¹ 野手 ‹野球› a fielder.

やしゅ² 野趣 《文》 rusticity; rural beauty ¶野趣のある 《文》 rustic; 《文》 pastoral. 文例

やしゅう 夜襲 a night attack [raid] ¶夜襲する make a night attack 《on》.

やじゅう 野獣 a wild [savage] animal [beast] ¶野獣のような beastly; brutal / 野獣性 brutality; 《文》 bestiality / 野獣派 ‹美術› ‹人› the Fauves; ‹主義› Fauvism / 野獣派の Fauvist 《paintings》.

やしょく 夜食 ‹深夜食› a midnight [late-night] snack; ‹夕食› (a) supper; an evening meal. 文例

やじり 鏃 an arrowhead.

やじる jeer [boo, hoot, catcall] 《at》; heckle; interrupt ¶やじり倒す hoot 《a speaker》 down [off the stage].

やじるし 矢印 an arrow; ‹道標› a signpost.

やしろ 社 a (Shinto) shrine.

やじろべえ 弥次郎兵衛 a balancing toy.

やしん 野心 (an) ambition; 《文》 a strong desire ‹to make a name for oneself›; 《文》 (an) aspiration; ‹悪だくみ› 《文》 (an) evil design; 《文》 ill designs ¶野心を抱く[満々である] be (highly) ambitious 《to do, of doing》; have an [be full of] ambition 《to do, for》/ 野心的な ambitious 《projects》 / 野心家 an ambitious person.

やじん 野人 a man with rough and simple tastes.

やす ‹漁具› a fish spear; a harpoon; a gig ¶やすで刺す spear 《a fish》.

-やす ...安 ‹相場› ¶円安 ⇨えんやす / 7円安 be seven yen cheaper [lower]; record a drop of seven yen.

やすあがり 安上がり ¶安上がりの cheap; economical; 《文》 inexpensive; less expensive. 文例

に熱くなっていた. The car had stood a long time in the sun and was scorching [blisteringly] hot./ それは日なたに出すとじきに色が焼ける. It will soon discolor if it is exposed to the sun.

やこう² フクロウは夜行性である. Owls are nocturnal in habit.

やさき 外出しようとする矢先へ友人が来た. I was just going out [was about to go out] when a friend came to see me.

やさしい² ラルフは根はとても優しい人でした. Ralph was very kind-hearted at bottom.

やしゅ² 床の間には野趣を出すために丸柱が使ってあった. A round post was used in the tokonoma for a rustic effect.

やしょく 夜食にうどんを食べた. We had a (late) supper [a midnight snack] of noodles.

やしん 彼はその地位に野心があるのだ. He has his eye on that

position. / アメリカはキューバに対して何ら領土的野心を持たないと彼は言明した. He declared that the U.S. had no territorial designs on Cuba. / 彼の試みは野心的に過ぎて, 結局うまく行かなかった. His attempt was over-ambitious and ended in failure.

やすあがり ガスは炭よりも安上がりです. Gas is less expensive than charcoal. / 長い眼で見れば, そのほうが安上がりです. It

やすい¹ 安い cheap; low-priced;《文》inexpensive;〈値段が〉low; reasonable; moderate ★cheap は「安物」「粗悪品」の感じを伴うので，自社の商品などについてはこれを避けて inexpensive と言うことが多い．また，他人の物について cheap と言うと，失礼になることもある ¶安く cheap; cheaply; at a low [moderate] price / 安くする make *sth* cheap [cheaper]; put [get] the price down; reduce [cut, drop] the price (of) / 安くなる〈品物が主語〉go down [fall] in price;《文》become cheap [cheaper] / 安く売る sell cheap; sell at a low price [rate, figure] / ほかの店よりも安く売る undersell other stores / 安く買う buy《an article》dirt cheap [dog-cheap]; get *sth* at a ridiculously [an absurdly] low price.

やすい² 易い〈容易な〉easy; simple ¶…しやすい be easy to *do* ⇨ **よい²** / とかく…しやすい be given to *doing*; be apt [liable, prone]《*to do*》⇨ **-がち** / 信じやすい be too ready to believe;《文》be credulous / おべっかに動かされやすい《文》be susceptible to flattery / 光に感じやすい be sensitive to light / 易きにつく avoid tackling《a problem》squarely; take the easy way out. 文例 ▷

やすうけあい 安請け合い ¶安請け合いする give *one's* word without much thought; be too ready to promise [undertake]; make [give] a rash promise.

やすうり 安売り a (bargain) sale ¶安売りする sell *sth* cheap [at a reduced price]; go cheap;〈投げ売りする〉sell at a bargain [sacrifice] price / 安売り競争 a price war / 安売り店 a cut-rate store.

やすげっきゅう 安月給 (live on) a small [meager] salary.

やすっぽい 安っぽい cheap(-looking); flashy;《文》tawdry;〈安ぴかの〉⇨ **やすぴか** ¶安っぽく見る do not think much of *sth* [*sb*]; do not think *sth* [*sb*] is worth much;《文》hold *sth* [*sb*] cheap.

やすで¹ 安手 ⇨ **やすっぽい**.

やすで² 〈動〉a millipede.

やすね 安値 (at) a low price [rate]; (at) a bargain rate ¶〈他の人よりも〉安値で売る[をつける] undersell (underquote)《*one's* competitors》/ 安値で買う buy *sth* at a bargain rate.

やすぴか 安ぴか ¶安ぴかの showy;《文》gimcrack; tawdry; gaudy / 安ぴか物 a gewgaw.

やすぶしん 安普請 a cheaply built house [structure]; a jerry-built house.

やすまる 安[休]まる〈体が〉be [feel] rested;〈心が〉《文》feel at peace [rest, ease]; be relieved; have [no] peace of mind.

やすみ 休み〈休息〉(a) rest;《米》a layoff;〈休憩時間〉《米》a recess; a break《from work, for tea》;〈休止〉a holiday; a day off; a vacation（長期の）;〈欠席〉absence ¶10分の休み a ten minutes' [ten-minute] recess / ひと休みしてから after a recess [rest] / 会社から3日の休みを取る take three days off from work [the office] / 休みなく without rest [a break];《文》without ceasing; constantly; incessantly. 文例 ▷

やすむ 休む〈休息する〉rest; take [have] a rest;《文》repose; take time off;〈休暇を取る〉have a day off;〈中止する〉suspend《business》;〈欠席する〉be absent [《文》absent *oneself*]《from school》;〈さぼる〉cut《a class》; play truant《from school》;〈眠る〉sleep;〈床に就く〉go to bed;《文》retire; turn in ¶仕事を休む take a rest [break] from *one's* work / 休んでいる〈休息している〉be resting; be off work;〈床に就いている〉be in bed / 休まずに 休みなく).

やすめる 休める〈休息させる〉rest; give *sb* a rest;〈安心させる〉put《*sb's* mind》at ease [rest];〈救助を与える〉give relief (to *sb*) / 頭を休める give *one's* brain a rest; rest *one's* brain / 身体を休める rest (*oneself*).

やすもの 安物 a cheap article. 文例 ▷

やすやす 安々 ¶安々と easily;《文》with ease; without difficulty [trouble]; without effort; as if it was nothing (to *one*).

やすやど 安宿 a cheap hotel [inn];〈木賃宿〉《米》a flophouse;《英》a dosshouse.

やすらか 安らか ¶安らかな peaceful;《文》tranquil; calm; quiet; restful;《文》reposeful /

---

works out [is] cheaper in the long run.

やすい¹ この絵が本物なら100万円でも安い．If this painting is genuine, it is cheap even at one million yen. / よそならもっと安く買えるよ．You can get them cheaper [at a better price] elsewhere. / 友人にうんと安くやってもらった．I got a friend to do it on the cheap. / この品は「安かろう，悪かろう」といったかつての評判をすっかりぬぐい去ってくれた．This product completely erased [wiped out] our earlier reputation for producing low-priced goods of poor quality.

やすい² 君の字は読みやすい． Your handwriting is easy to read. / 暑い時には，魚は腐りやすい．Fish soon goes bad in hot weather. / おやすいご用です．With pleasure. | Oh, it's no trouble at all. | Nothing could be easier. / このため間違いを起こしやすい．It often causes errors.

やすみ 明日は学校は休みだ．We have no school tomorrow. / 学校が休みになった．School is out. / 僕はきょうは休みだ．Tomorrow is my day off. / 休みには葉山へ行くことに決めました．I've decided to go to Hayama for my vacation. / あなたの学校では土曜日はいつも休みですか．Do you always have Saturdays off in your school? / 来週2日ばかり休みを取りたい．I want to take a couple of days off next week. / イギリスでは土曜日はもとより金曜の午後まで休みにしている会社もある．Some British companies even give Friday afternoons off, to say nothing of Saturdays. / まだお休みですか．Is he still in bed?

やすむ 休め．〖号令〗At ease [rest]! / 2,3時間休んだらよくなりましょう．A few hours' rest will set you right. / 昨夜はよくお休みになりましたか．Did you sleep well last night? / お休みなさい．Good night! / 日曜は休み

やすらぎ

安らかに peacefully; in peace.
やすらぎ 安らぎ peace of mind;《文》(spiritual) repose; calmness.
やすらぐ 安らぐ have peace of mind;《文》one's mind is at rest [peace]. 文例⇩
やすり 鑢 a file; a rasp (目の粗い) ¶やすりを掛ける file; rasp.
やすんじる 安んじる〈満足する〉be contented [happy, satisfied] (with);〈安心する〉《文》be [feel] at ease; be [feel] reassured ¶小成に安んじる be [rest] contented with one's small success; rest on one's laurels / 安んじて〈満足して〉in contentment; contentedly;〈安心して〉《文》in comfort;〈気楽に〉《文》free from care(s);〈平和に〉in peace.
やせい[1] 野生 ¶野生する grow (in the) wild; be found wild / 野生の wild / 野生の状態では in the [a] wild state; in the wild / 野生植物 [動物] a wild plant [animal].
やせい[2] 野性 wild nature ¶野性の目覚め《文》the call of the wild / 野性を帯びた wild; rough.
やせうで 痩せ腕〈資力〉《文》small means; a limited income. 文例⇩
やせおとろえる 痩せ衰える waste away;《文》become emaciated.
やせがまん 痩せ我慢 ¶やせ我慢する put up with [《文》endure] sth from [out of] pride; grin and bear it. 文例⇩
やせぎす 痩せぎす ¶やせぎすの scrawny;《文》spare of flesh ⇒ やせる (やせた).
やせぐすり 痩せ薬 a reducing drug [medicine]; a slimming drug [pill].
やせこける 痩せこける ⇒ やせる.
やせち 痩せ地 barren [poor] soil; infertile [sterile] land.
やせっぽち 痩せっぽち a skinny [scrawny] person; a scarecrow;《口語》a bag of bones ⇒ やせる (やせた).
やせる 痩せる get [《文》become] lean [thin]; lose flesh (病気で);〈土地が〉get [《文》become] impoverished [sterile]; lose its fertility ¶やせる運動 slimming [weight-reducing] exercises / やせるために特別の食事を取る be [go] on a (reducing [slimming]) diet / やせた thin;

lean; skinny;《文》spare;〈やせこけた〉haggard; gaunt; skinny;《文》emaciated;〈土地が〉sterile; barren; infertile.
やせん[1] 野戦 field operations ¶野戦で〈defeat the enemy》in the field / 野戦病院 a field hospital.
やせん[2] 野選《野球》a fielder's choice (略: f.c.). 文例⇩
やそう 野草 wild grass [herbs].
やそうきょく 夜想曲 a nocturne.
やたい 屋台〈屋台店〉a (street) stall; a booth; a stand; a portable (noodle) stall;〈踊り屋台〉a float; a stage for dancing.
やたいぼね 屋台骨〈建物の〉the framework;〈身代〉property on which one's living is based ¶屋台骨がぐらつく one's chief support is in danger of giving way. 文例⇩
やたらに freely;〈無差別に〉indiscriminately;〈手当たり次第に〉at random;〈向こう見ずに〉recklessly; rashly;〈考えなく〉thoughtlessly;〈過度に〉《文》to [in] excess;《文》immoderately ¶やたらに金を使う spend money recklessly [like water].
やちょう 野鳥 a wild bird ¶野鳥の会 a wild-bird society; a bird-watching society / 野鳥観察家 a bird watcher / 野鳥観察に行く go bird-watching.
やちん 家賃 (a) rent; (a) house rent ¶家賃がたまって[滞って]いる be behind[behindhand] in [with] one's rent / 家賃がただで[の] free of rent; rent-free. 文例⇩
やつ 奴 a fellow; a chap; a guy.
やつあたり 八つ当たり ¶八つ当たりする take it out [《文》vent one's anger] on sb for no reason; snap (and snarl) at sb in a fit of anger. 文例⇩
やっかい 厄介〈面倒〉(a) trouble; a nuisance; (a) worry ¶厄介な troublesome; annoying;《文》burdensome / 厄介な相手 a person hard [difficult] to deal with;《口語》an ugly [a tiresome] customer (to deal with) / 厄介な問題 a difficult [knotty, tangled, complex, delicate] problem; an awkward [a prickly] question / 人の厄介になる depend on sb;《文》be under [in] the care of sb; throw oneself on sb's

---

ます. We get Sundays off. / ばかも休み休み言え. I can stand no more [None] of your nonsense! / How can you be so silly?
やすもの 安物買いの銭失い. Buy cheap and waste your money. / Cheap bargains are dear. / 安物を買うと大抵銭失いになるものだ. More often than not the money spent on cheap merchandise ends up being wasted.
やすらぐ そこでは彼女の気持ちは安らぐことがなかった. Her mind was never at peace there.
やせうで 女のやせ腕で一家を支えるのは容易ではなかった. It was no easy task for her to support a family on one woman's in-

come.
やせがまん やせ我慢を言わずに, その金は取っておけ. だれでも苦しい時はあるものだ. Just pocket your pride and borrow the money. Anyone can fall on hard times.
やせる もしやせたいと思ったらお菓子を食べるのは止めなければいけません. If you want to reduce (your weight), you've got to stop eating sweets. / 彼女はやせ細っていた. She was thin and drawn. / 君はやせたね. You've lost weight, haven't you? / 賢明な農民は土地がやせるようなことはしない. Wise farmers do not let the soil become impoverished.

やせん[2] 野選となった. The play went down as a fielder's choice.
やたいぼね 最近こうむった損失で会社は屋台骨がぐらついた. Their recent losses have left [put] the company in a very shaky condition [a very insecure state].
やちん 彼の家では家賃が月7万円だそうだ. I hear he is paying 70,000 yen a month in rent. / I am told that his rent comes to 70,000 yen a month. / お宅の家賃はどのぐらいですか. What is the rent on your house? / What rent do you pay for your house?
やつあたり ドナルドは会社でいやなことがあると, 帰って来て細君に八つ当たりすることがよくあっ

やっかだいがく / やど

mercy [mercies]; put *oneself* under the wing of *sb*; 〈寄遇する〉stay with *sb* / 人の厄介にならない stand on *one's* own two feet [legs]; be self-reliant / 厄介をかける trouble *sb*; give *sb* trouble / 厄介払いをする be [get] rid of a nuisance / 厄介者 a nuisance;《文》an encumbrance (保累);〈厄介な〉a dependent (扶養家族); a parasite (居候) / 厄介物 a nuisance; a burden;《口語》a drag. 文例⇩

やっかだいがく 薬科大学 a pharmaceutical college; a college of pharmacy.

やっかむ ⇒ねたむ.

やっかん 約款〈協約〉an agreement;〈条項〉a stipulation; a provision; an article; a clause.

やっき 躍起 ¶躍起になる be [get,《文》become] excited 〈over〉; get [be] worked up 〈over〉; get heated 〈about〉; be [get] eager 〈to *do*, for〉 / 躍起になって eagerly; frantically; excitedly;《文》with warmth (heat). 文例⇩

やつぎばや 矢継ぎ早 ¶矢継ぎ早の rapid-fire 《questions》/ 矢継ぎ早に in rapid [quick] succession; one after another [the other] / 矢継ぎ早に質問を浴びせ掛ける fire [rattle off] questions [question after question] at 《*sb* about *sth*》.

やっきょう 薬莢 a cartridge (case).

やっきょく 薬局〈薬屋〉《米》a drugstore;《英》a chemist's (shop); a pharmacy;〈病院の〉a pharmacist's office; a dispensary /〈医者の〉a (doctor's) medicine room ¶日本薬局方 the Japanese Pharmacopoeia.

ヤッケ [<《ドイツ語》*Jacke*] a parka; an anorak.

やっこさん that fellow; that chap; that joker; that guy;《英》that blighter.

やつざき 八つ裂き ¶八つ裂きにする tear *sb* limb from limb [apart, to pieces]. 文例⇩

やつす 窶す disguise [dress] *oneself* 《as》; be disguised 《as》⇒へんそう ¶憂き身をやつす ⇒うきみ².

やっつ 八つ eight.

やっつけしごと 遣っ付け仕事 a slipshod job [piece of work]; a sloppy [rush(ed)] job ¶やっ付け仕事をする skimp [scamp] *one's* work; do

one's work in a rough-and-ready way. 文例⇩

やっつける 遣っ付ける〈攻撃する〉make an attack 《on the enemy》; attack; go for [at] *sb* 〈負かす〉beat; floor;《文》defeat; knock over;〈殺す〉kill; do away with;《口語》do *sb* in;〈片付ける〉finish;〈非難する〉attack; criticize ¶一撃でやっ付ける finish *sb* (off) with a single blow. 文例⇩

やつで 八つ手〈植〉a fatsia; *Fatsia japonica*.

やってくる やって来る come 《along, round, up to》;〈現われる〉turn [show] up. 文例⇩

やってのける succeed 《in *doing*》; manage 《to *do*, a job》; carry through [off, out]; make a (good) job of it; bring [pull] *sth* off; make (it). 文例⇩

やってみる try 《*doing*, *sth*》; have a try [a go, a shot] 《at》; make an attempt 《at, to *do*》. 文例⇩

やってゆく やって行く get along [on]; manage; pull through;〈繰り繰りする〉《文》make shift 《to *do*》⇒やりくり ¶仲よくやって行く get along [on] well 《with》. 文例⇩

やっと〈ついに〉at last; at length; finally; 〈難儀して〉with difficulty;〈辛くも〉barely; by the skin of *one's* teeth;〈わずかに〉just; only ¶やっと試験に及第する scrape through an examination / やっと逃れる have a narrow escape; escape 《death》narrowly [by a hairsbreadth].

やっとこ 鋏 pincers; nippers (小形の); pliers (針金切り).

やっぱり やはり. 文例⇩

やっほー〈呼び声〉yoo-hoo !

やつめうなぎ 八つ目鰻 a lamprey (eel).

やつれる 憔れる get [《文》become] thin [haggard]; be worn out ¶心配でやつれる《文》be careworn / 熱病でやつれる《文》be consumed with fever / やつれた worn-out;《文》emaciated; haggard; gaunt / 病後でやつれている look thin after an illness. 文例⇩

やど 宿〈旅館〉a hotel; an inn;〈宿所〉《米》accommodations;《英》accommodation; a lodging ¶宿を取る put up 《at an inn》;《文》take up *one's* lodgings 《in a house》; get [find]

た. When Donald came home after a bad day at the office, he often took it out on his wife.

やっかい お前はもう父の厄介になる年ではない. You are too old to be dependent on your father. / どうもいろいろご厄介をかけて相済みませんでした. I am sorry to have caused you so much trouble. / 全くもって厄介なことだ. It's a devil of a nuisance. / 厄介払いしてせいせいした. Good riddance (to bad rubbish)!

やっき 彼は躍起になって私に追いつこうとしている. He is determined to catch me up.

やつぎばや 彼は矢継ぎ早に彼女に名前や, 年齢などを色々尋ねた. In rapid succession he asked her her name, age, and so on. / 技術

上の発見が矢継ぎ早になされた. One technological discovery followed (after) another in quick succession.

やつざき 八つ裂きにしても飽き足りないやつだ. Nothing can allay my anger toward [against] him.

やっつけしごと それは注文に間に合わせるためのやっ付け仕事だった. It was a slipshod job, done to order in a hurry.

やっつける やっつけろ. Down [Away] with him! / そのうちやっ付けてやるよ. I'll get him soon.

やってくる もうじきやって来るだろう. He will soon be here. / 近いうちにやって来たまえ. Come and see me one of these days. / もうじきお正月がやって来る. The New Year will soon come

round. / もうじき試験がやって来る. The examination is nearly upon us [around the corner].

やってのける 難しいが, 次郎ならきっと何とかやってのけるよ. It is certainly difficult, but I'm sure Jiro will be able to manage it somehow or other.

やってみる やれるものならやってみろ.〈反語的に〉Try and do it. / そんな風におっしゃるなら, まあやってみましょう. Well, if you put it like that, I'll see what I can do about it. / それはやってみる価値が十分ある. It would be well worth trying [our while].

やってゆく それだけあればやって行けるでしょう. That's probably enough to go on with. / 彼の援助がなかったならば, とてもやっ

lodging《in London》; 〈滞在する〉 stay《at *sb's* house, with *sb*》/ 宿を貸す put *sb* up (for the night); 《文》 accommodate / 一夜の宿を求める ask for a night's lodging; 《文》 request accommodation(s) for the [one] night / 宿替えする remove《to, into》; change [shift] *one's* lodgings《to》/ 宿帳 a visitors' book; a guest book; a hotel register [book] / 宿賃 charges for accommodation(s); a hotel bill.

やとい 雇い 〈臨時雇い〉 a temporary employee ¶雇い人 an employee; a servant; a hireling (軽蔑的に) / 雇い主 an employer; the master.

やといいれ 雇い入れ employment; 《文》 engagement.

やといいれる 雇い入れる ⇨ **やとう²**.

やとう¹ 野党 a party out of power; a non-government party; 〈2大政党対立の場合の〉 the Opposition (party); the party in opposition.

やとう² 雇う employ; 《文》 engage; hire; take *sb* on; 《文》 take *sb* into employment [*one's* service] ¶船を雇う charter [hire] a boat / …に雇われている be in the employ of *sb*; be in the pay of *sb* (金で動かされている) / 雇われマダム a manageress《of a bar》.

やどかり 宿借り 〘動〙 a hermit crab.

やどす 宿す ¶子を宿す《文》 conceive a [*sb's*] child; 《文》 be with child《by》; be [get, 《文》 become] pregnant《by》.

やどなし 宿無し a homeless person; 〈浮浪者〉 a tramp; 《文》 a vagabond ¶宿なしの homeless; shelterless / 宿なし犬 an ownerless [a stray] dog.

やどや 宿屋 an inn; a guest house; a hotel ⇨ **りょかん** ¶宿屋の主人[おかみ] an innkeeper; a landlord [landlady].

やどりぎ 宿り木 〘植〙 (a) mistletoe; 〈寄生植物〉 a parasitic plant.

やどる 宿る 〈旅館に〉 ⇨ **とまる²**; 〈雨などを避ける〉 take shelter《under, in》; 〈精神が身体に〉《文》 lodge; 《文》 dwell; 〈寄生物が〉 live《on, 《文》 within》. [文例⇩]

やな 簗 a weir; a fishweir; a fish trap.

やなぎ 柳 a willow. [文例⇩]

やなぎごうり 柳行李 a wicker trunk.

やなぎごし 柳腰 《文》 a slender figure.

やなみ 家並み a row of houses; a street of houses. [文例⇩]

やなり 家鳴り rattling (of the house) ¶家鳴りする rattle; rumble.

やに 脂 〈木の〉 resin; gum; 〈目の〉 ⇨ **めやに**; 〈タバコの〉 tar; nicotine (通俗に).

やにさがる 脂下がる give *oneself* airs; look (self-)complacent.

やにっこい 脂っこい 〈やにの多い〉《文》 resinous; gummy; sticky (with resin); 〈しつっこい〉 persistent; dogged; 《文》 pertinacious.

やにょうしょう 夜尿症 〘医〙 (nocturnal) enuresis ⇨ **ねしょうべん**.

やにわに 矢庭に 《文》 precipitately; suddenly; abruptly; all of a sudden ¶やにわに飛び出す make a sudden dash《at》.

やぬし 家主 the owner of a house; a landlord (男); a landlady (女).

やね 屋根 a roof ¶屋根をふく roof《a house with slate》; thatch《a cottage with straw》/ 屋根をはがす unroof / 屋根に上がる climb [get] on to the roof / 屋根板 a (roof) shingle / 屋根裏(部屋) a garret; an attic; a loft (物置用) / 屋根替えをする reroof / 屋根伝いに from roof to roof.

やはり 〈案の定〉 as I [you, he] thought [said]; as I told you; you see!; 〈また, 同様に〉 too; also; as well; 《文》 likewise; 〈なお〉 still; all the same; 〈結局〉 after all (is said and done) ★会話では「やはり」に相当する語を使わないで, 助動詞または be 動詞に強勢を置くことによってその意味を表わすことが多い. [文例⇩]

やはん 夜半 ¶夜半に at midnight; in the middle of the night; 《文》 at [in the] dead of night ¶夜半まで勉強[仕事を]する work till late in the night [《文》 far into the night].

やばん 野蛮 ¶野蛮な savage《tribes》; 《文》 barbarous《nations》; uncivilized《countries》/ 野蛮な行為 a barbarous [cruel] act; 《文》 a [an act of] barbarity / 野蛮人 a barbarian; a savage. [文例⇩]

て行けなかっただろう. I don't think I could have got through, had it not been for his help. / 彼らは自分の力だけで結構やって行けるよ. I believe they can make out very well on their own. / 彼がいなくてはとてもやって行けない. We cannot manage without him.

やっと やっと電車に間に合った. I was barely in time for the train. | I just caught [made] the train. / 今朝になってやっとそのことがわかった. It was not till this morning that I realized it. | I only realized it this morning.

やっぱり 一生懸命走ったが, やっぱり遅刻した. I ran as fast as I could, but I was late all the same.

やつれる 心配のあまり彼は見る影もないほどやつれていた. He was worn almost to a shadow with anxiety [worry].

やどる 草葉に露が宿る. Dewdrops form on the blades of grass.

やなぎ 柳の枝に雪折れなし. Oaks may fall when reeds stand the storm. 〘諺〙 | In yielding is strength. / 柳の下にいつもどじょうはいない. There are no birds in last year's nest. | Good luck does not always repeat itself.

やなみ この街道の家並みは恐らく江戸時代とあまり変わらないのであろう. The appearance of the houses along this street probably does not differ much from what it was in the Edo period.

やはり やはり降らなかっただろう! You see, it *didn't* rain! / 運ぼうとしたが, やはり重すぎた. I tried to carry it, but it *was* too heavy (as you had said it would be). / それもやはりいけない. That won't do, either. / 彼は今でもやはり勉強家です. He works as hard as before. / 我々だってやはりそうだ. That is also the case with us. / たとえ彼が一文なしでもやはり僕は彼を尊敬する. Even if he were penniless, I would respect him none the less. / あの方はもちろん熱心な教育ママですけれどもね, あなたもやはりそうですよ. She is no doubt a terribly education-minded mother, but you are another [so are you].

やばん この習慣は野蛮時代の遺物

やひ 野卑 ¶野卑な vulgar; 《文》base; 《文》mean; 《文》low; 《文》unrefined; coarse; ill-mannered; boorish; ribald 《jokes》/ 野卑な言葉 《use, in》vulgar [coarse] language.

やぶ 藪 a thicket; a 《grass》tussock (草むら); 〈竹やぶ〉a bamboo grove ¶やぶから棒に abruptly; on [all of] a sudden; without the slightest notice [warning]. 文例⇩

やぶいしゃ 藪医者 a quack (doctor); a charlatan.

やぶいり 藪入り the servants' holiday.

やぶか 藪蚊 a striped mosquito.

やぶく 破く ⇨ やぶる.

やぶこうじ 藪柑子 《植》a spearflower.

やぶさか 吝か ¶やぶさかでない be ready [willing, quite happy] (to do); be generous with 《one's compliments》; 《文》be not sparing [chary] of 《one's praise》; feel no reluctance (in doing). 文例⇩

やぶさめ 流鏑馬 the art of shooting arrows on horseback; horseback archery.

やぶにらみ 藪睨み a squint; (have) a cast in one's eye ¶やぶにらみの squint-[cross-]eyed / ひどいやぶにらみである have a bad [fearful] squint.

やぶへび 藪蛇 ¶やぶへびになる have the opposite effect; boomerang. 文例⇩

やぶる 破る 〈裂く〉tear; 《文》rend; 《文》breach; 〈破壊する〉break; destroy; 〈違反する〉break 《one's promise》; 《文》violate; 〈負かす〉beat; 《文》defeat ¶戸を破る break [force] a door open / 平和を破る destroy [disturb] the peace / 規則を破る break 《《文》violate, 《文》infringe》the rule / 約束を破る break [go back on] one's promise [word] / 記録を破る break [beat, shatter, crack] the (Olympic) record. 文例⇩

やぶれ 破れ 〈破綻〉《文》a rupture; 《文》a breach; 〈破れ目〉a tear; a rent; a rift ¶破れ傘 a broken umbrella / 破れ靴 worn-out shoes / 破れ畳 a worn tatami.

やぶれかぶれ 破れかぶれ ¶破れかぶれになる get [《文》become] desperate / 破れかぶれで desperately; recklessly; in 《one's》desperation.

やぶれる 破[敗]れる 〈裂ける〉be [get] torn; rip; tear; 《文》be rent; 〈壊れる〉be broken; break; burst (風船玉などが); 〈交渉が〉be broken off; break down; 〈擦り切れる〉wear [be worn] out; 〈負ける〉be beaten; 《文》be defeated; lose; 《文》lose the day ¶試合に敗れる lose a game / 破れた〈裂けた〉torn; 〈ぼろぼろの〉tattered; ragged; 〈擦り切れた〉worn-out; 〈敗北した〉《文》defeated; beaten.

やぶん 夜分 night; nighttime. 文例⇩

やぼ ¶やぼな 〈粗野な〉unrefined; 《文》uncouth; 〈田舎臭い〉《文》rustic; boorish; 〈気の利かない〉stiff; senseless; stuffy / やぼなことを言う talk humbug; say senseless things.

やほう 野砲 a field gun; 〈総称〉field artillery.

やぼう 野望 ⇨ やしん.

やぼったい unfashionable 《clothes》; unpolished; uncouth.

やま¹ 山 a mountain; a peak (峰); a hill (丘陵); 〈鉱山〉a (coal) mine; 〈積み重ね〉a heap; a pile; 〈帽子の〉the crown; 〈極点〉the climax; 《文》the acme; 〈危機〉the crisis (pl. crises); 〈交渉などのやまば〉⇨ やまば ¶山の多い, 山がちの mountainous 《country》; hilly / 山のような mountainous 《waves》; huge (piles) / 山のような借金 a mountain of debts; a mountainous load of debts / 山のふもとに at the foot of a mountain / 山の中腹に on the mountainside [hillside] / 山の頂きに at the top [summit] of a mountain / 山奥に deep in the mountains / 山の神 a mountain god; 〈妻〉one's wife; 《戯言》the missis (《戯言》one's ball and chain) / 山を降りる go down [《文》descend] a mountain / 山を越す cross [go across] a mountain / 山を登り谷を下って (go) up hill and down dale / 山に登る go up [climb (up), 《文》ascend] a mountain / 山と谷 〈グラフなどの〉peaks and troughs / 山と積む heap (a desk with books); pile (a cart) (mountain-)high 《with straw》/ 山と積まれている be piled up (mountain-)high; lie in heaps / 山伝いに from mountain to mountain; over the mountains. 文例⇩

やま² 山 〈投機〉speculation; a venture; 〈かけ〉a gamble; a chance ¶山をかける[張る] speculate (on); venture (on); take chances [a chance] (in the exam); gamble (on getting the right questions) / 山を張って on the chance 《that...》; 《口語》on spec. 文例⇩

やまあい 山合 a mountain valley; a ravine; a gorge ¶山合の村落 a village (deep) in the

だ. This custom is a relic of barbaric times [the age of barbarism].

やひ こんな事をするのは甚だ野卑だ. It is in bad taste to do such a thing.

やぶ 高田さんからのお話は全くやぶから棒に出た. Mr. Takada's suggestion came to me as a complete surprise.

やぶさか 彼の功をたたえるにやぶさかでない. I do not stint [am unstinting in] my praise for his achievement.

やぶへび そいつはやぶ蛇だ. Let sleeping dogs lie.

やぶる ふくろうの声が不意にあたりの静寂を破った. The hooting of an owl broke the quiet of the place. / この物音に彼は瞑想を破られた. The noise aroused him from his reverie. / 800メートルリレーでアメリカチームは7分20秒82で2位, これまた世界記録を破った. In the 800-meter relay, the U.S. team finished second in 7:20.82, also breaking the existing world record. / ソ連はブラジルを8対2で破り, オリンピックの水球に3度連続の優勝を飾った. The Soviet Union defeated [whipped] Brazil 8-2 for its third consecutive Olympic water polo victory.

やぶん 夜分遅く《お電話して》済みません. I'm sorry to call you at this time of night.

やま¹ 信仰は山をも動かす. Faith can move mountains. / 月が山の端から出た[へ沈んだ]. The moon came out from [went down] behind the mountain. / 鳥は山での生活によく適応している. Birds are well adapted to mountain living. / 山高きが故に貴からず,

やまあらし【動】a porcupine ¶やまあらしのような頭をした男 a man with hair (sticking up) like the quills on a porcupine.

やまい 病 (an) illness; a disease ⇨びょうき ¶持った病 ⇨じびょう / 病の床にふす be ill in bed; be laid up [《文》confined to bed] with illness / 病を押して in spite of *one's* illness / 重い病に倒れる be (struck) down by a serious illness / 病膏肓(ﾋ̇ｺｳ)に入る《人が主語》《文》become a slave to [of]《a bad habit》;《事が主語》take hold of *sb*;《文》become deep-seated [incorrigible].

やまいぬ 山犬 a Japanese wolf.

やまいも 山芋 a yam.

やまおとこ 山男〈山に住む人〉a hillman; a woodsman;〈登山家〉a mountaineer; an alpinist.

やまかじ 山火事 a forest fire;《米》a wood fire.

やまがた 山形《紋》a chevron.

やまがら 山雀《鳥》a titmouse (*pl.* -mice).

やまがり 山狩り ¶山狩りをする comb a hill [the woods, a forest] (for an escaped convict); hunt (for a culprit) all over a hill.

やまかん 山勘 ¶山勘で〈あてずっぽうに〉by guesswork;《口語》on spec;《文》at a venture / 山勘をやる take chances; try a shot in the dark.

やまくずれ 山崩れ a landslide;《英》a landslip.

やまぐに 山国 (a) mountainous country ★ country が「地方」の意ならば不定冠詞をつけない.

やまごや 山小屋 a mountain hut [cottage, lodge]; a hut for mountaineers.

やまざくら 山桜《木》a wild cherry tree;《花》wild cherry blossoms.

やまざと 山里 a village in a mountain valley.

やまし 山師〈投機師〉a speculator;〈冒険家〉an adventurer;〈ぺてん師〉《文》a mountebank; a humbug; an impostor.

やましい 疚しい have a guilty [an uneasy] conscience; feel guilty ¶やましくない have an easy [a clean] conscience / やましいところなく with a clean conscience; with clean hands.

やますそ 山裾 the skirts [foot, base] of a mountain.

やまかたかぼう 山高帽《米》a derby (hat);《英》a bowler (hat).

やま(っ)け 山(っ)気〈投機心〉《文》a speculative disposition; the gambling spirit ¶山気を出すを be tempted to gamble [speculate].

やまつなみ 山津波 ⇨やまくずれ

やまづみ 山積み ¶山積みにする pile (hay) (up) (mountain-)high [in heaps] ⇨⇩.

やまでら 山寺 a temple in a mountain; a temple on a hillside [mountainside].

やまと 大和 *Yamato*; Japan (from earlier times) ¶大和言葉 Japanese words having their origins in the time before the introduction of Chinese / 大和民族 the *Yamato* race.

やまどり 山鳥 a copper pheasant.

やまねこ 山猫 a wildcat; a lynx ¶山猫ストa wildcat strike.

やま(の)て 山(の)手 the hilly [residential] sections (of Tokyo); the Bluff (横浜・神戸の) ¶山の手の〈residents〉/ 山の手に uptown / 山の手線 the Yama-no-te (Loop) Line ★ 米語の uptown は必ずしも日本語の「山の手」の持つ「上品な」という意味合いは持たない ⇨したまち★.

やまのぼり 山登り ⇨とざん

やまば 山場〈頂点〉the climax; the peak;《文》the acme;〈危機〉the crisis (*pl.* crises);〈交渉などの〉a turning point; a critical period [moment, time];《口語》(come to) the crunch.

やまはだ 山肌 the surface [face] of a mountain.

やまばと 山鳩 a turtledove.

やまびこ 山彦 an echo (*pl.* -es) ⇨こだま.

やまひだ 山襞 the folds on [of] a mountain; mountain folds.

やまびらき 山開き the opening of a mountain to climbers (for the year).

やまぶき 山吹《植》a Japanese rose; a Japanese globeflower ¶山吹色 bright [golden] yellow.

やまぶし 山伏 a mountain priest [ascetic].

やまみち 山道 a mountain path [trail].

やまめ 山女《魚》a *yamame*; a kind of trout.

やまもり 山盛り ¶山盛りにする heap up (high) / 大さじに山盛り1杯の砂糖 a heaped tablespoonful of sugar.

やまやま ¶やまやまである《文》have a strong desire《to do》.

樹あるをもって貴しとす. A mountain is of value, not for its height, but for its trees. / 仕事は山ほどある. We have lots [a heap] of things to do. / テーブルにはごちそうが山のように出ていた. The table (literally) groaned with food. / ここがこの小説の山だ. This is the climax [high point, best part] of the novel. / 好景気も今が山さ. The boom, I'm sure, has reached its climax [peak]. / 戦争はそのころすでに山が見えて来た. The end of the war was already in sight. / 山は見えた. もう大したことはない. We've broken its back [We've reached the top of the hill]. There's not much more to be done.

やま² 山が当たった[外れた]. The speculation has turned out successful [has failed]. / My expectations came true [were disappointed]. / 試験に出るかと教科書の20ページから30ページまでしか勉強しなかった. I studied the textbook only from p. 20 to p. 30 on the chance that the examination questions would be set from that section [thinking that that was the part from which the exam questions were most likely to be selected].

やまい 病は気から. Care killed the cat. 【諺】¶Worry is often the cause of illness. / 病は口より入る. Diseases enter by the mouth.

やまば 交渉は今山場に差し掛かっている. The negotiations have come to the most important stage.

やまやま 私もお供したいのはやまやまですが, 今晩は約束があるのです. I would very much like to

やまわけ 山分け ¶山分けする divide [share] 《the profits》 equally [《文》 alike] 《among, between, with》; 《文》 go halves [shares, fifty-fifty] 《with sb in sth》. 文例↓

やみ 闇 〈暗黒〉 darkness; the dark; 〈やみ取り引き〉 black-marketeering ¶やみの〈暗黒の〉dark; 〈不正な〉shady; illegal; under-the-table / やみに紛れて under cover [《文》 the cloak] of darkness [night] / やみに消える vanish into the night / やみに葬る〈もみ消す〉cover up / 《口語》 hush up / やみで買う[売る] buy [sell] *sth* on the black market / 闇ルート 《through》 illegal channels. 文例↓

やみあがり 病み上がり ¶病み上がりの convalescent / 病み上がりの人 a convalescent. 文例↓

やみいち(ば) 闇市(場) a black market; 〈店〉a black-market stall.

やみうち 闇打ち an attack in the dark; 《文》a foul murder; 〈不意打ち〉a surprise attack ¶やみ打ちを食う be [get] attacked in the dark; be taken by surprise.

やみきんゆう 闇金融 an illegal loan ¶やみ金融を受ける get a loan through illegal channels.

やみくも ¶やみくもに blindly; at random; haphazardly.

やみそうば 闇相場 a black-market price [rate].

やみつき 病み付き ¶病み付きになる〈人が主語〉give *oneself* up [be addicted] to 《gambling》; be given to [fall into, take to] 《the habit》; become addicted to 《pop music》; be an 《opera》addict. 文例↓

やみとりひき 闇取り引き ¶やみ取り引きをする sell [buy] 《goods》 on the black market; black-market; black-marketeer.

やみね 闇値 ⇒やみそうば.

やみぶっし 闇物資 black-market goods; 〈密輸入品〉smuggled [illegally imported] goods.

やみよ 闇夜 a moonless [dark] night; a night without moon or stars.

やむ¹ 止む 〈止まる〉stop; 〈静まる〉subside; 《文》abate; calm down; 〈終わる〉end; come to an end [a stop, a halt]; 《文》cease; 〈済む〉be over; 〈(音などが)消える〉die [fade] away [out]; 〈痛みなどが〉ease; go; leave one; 〈雨が〉stop (falling); hold up ¶やむを得ない〈必要な〉necessary; 〈避け難い〉unavoidable; inevitable / やむを得ない事情のため《文》through [owing to] unavoidable circumstances / やむを得ず《文》inevitably; 〈いやいやながら〉reluctantly; against *one's* will / やむを得ず…する be compelled [forced, obliged] to *do*; have no choice but to *do*. 文例↓

やむ² 病む 〈病気になる〉fall ill; be taken ill; 〈…を病む〉suffer from; be ill 《with pneumonia》⇒びょうき / 肺を病む suffer from tuberculosis [T.B.]; have lung trouble / 気を病む worry 《about》; be anxious 《about》.

やむなく 已むなく ⇒しかた.

やめ 止め 〈中止〉a stop; 《文》discontinuance; 〈終わり〉an end; (a) conclusion ¶やめになる come to an end; be off; be given up; be called (off) / やめにする ⇒やめる. 文例↓

やめさせる 止[辞]めさせる put an end [a stop] to 《sb's gambling》; persuade sb (not to *do*, against *doing*); 《文》dissuade sb 《from *doing*》; 〈職を〉sack; 《文》dismiss 《sb from *his* post》; 《口語》fire; give sb the sack ¶学校をやめさせる take sb away from school; 〈学校当局が〉expel 《a student》《from school》. 文例↓

やめる 止[辞]める 〈中止する〉stop 《*doing*》; cease (from 《*doing*》); 《文》discontinue 《*doing*》; leave off; drop; 〈終わりにする〉end; put an end to; 〈断念・放棄する〉give up (the idea of) 《*doing*》; decide not (to *do*); abandon; 《文》abstain from; 〈廃止する〉abolish; do away with; 〈辞職する〉resign 《*one's* post》; 《口語》throw up 《*one's* job》; retire (from office) ¶話をやめる stop 《文》cease, leave off】 talking / 仕事をやめる 〈廃業する〉quit [throw up] *one's* job; lay aside *one's* work; その日の仕事を stop working; 《口語》knock off / 戦争をやめる put an end to [《文》termi-

---

go with you, only I have an appointment for tonight.

やまわけ ちょうど半々に山分けだ. (Let it be) fifty-fifty, right down the middle.

やみ 外は真のやみだ. It is pitch-dark outside. / 間もなく町は夜のやみに閉ざされた. Soon the darkness of night settled over the town. / 彼は夜のやみの中に車を飛ばして姿を消した. He drove away into the night.

やみあがり 彼女はまだ病み上がりで体が弱っている. She is still weak after [from] her recent illness.

やみつき それが病み付きになった. It developed into an inveterate habit [vice] with him.

やむ¹ 雨がやんだ. It has stopped raining. / この雨がやみ次第出掛けることにしよう. As soon as the rain is over, let's go out. / 風がやんだ. The wind dropped. | 〈吹くだけ吹いて〉The wind blew itself out. / しかしやむを得ない事だ. But there is no help for it. | But it can't be helped. / 何かやむにやまれぬ理由があってああしたのだろう. There must have been some (very) compelling reason for his doing that.

やめ この辺でやめにしておこう. Let's leave off here. / ストはやめになった. The strike is off. / 試合はやめになった. The match was called off.

やめさせる 法律でギャンブルをやめさせるのは難しい. It is difficult to put an end to gambling by law. / 彼にタバコをやめさせよう. I will break [cure] him of the habit of smoking. / これから彼に説いてその計画をやめさせようとしているところだ. We are going to talk him out of the project.

やめる しかし雨が降ったら僕は行くのをやめます. But if it rains, I won't go. / 長いこと練習をやめております. I have been out of practice for a long time. / ドイツ語の勉強をやめてからもう大分になります. I stopped [left off, gave up] studying German quite a long time ago. / そんなうるさいことはやめなさい, と子供たちは言われてしまった. The children were told to stop [cut out] the noise. / Break it up! / わかっちゃいるけど, やめられない. I know, but I can't help it. / 研究をやめ

やもうしょう 1263 やりくり

nate] the war; bring the war to an end / 学校をやめる leave [give up] school / 酒をやめる give up [《文》abstain from] drinking / やめて go [carry, keep] on (《doing》); 《文》continue (《doing, to do》).

やもうしょう 夜盲症 night blindness ¶夜盲症の night-blind.

やもめ a widow ¶やもめになる be widowed; lose *one's* husband; 《文》be bereaved of *one's* husband / やもめ暮らし (live in) widowhood / 男やもめ a widower.

やもり 《動》a gecko (*pl*. -(e)s); a wall lizard.

やや 〈多少〉a little; to some extent; in a way; somewhat; slightly; rather ¶ややあって a little (while) later; after a while. 文例⇩

ややこしい 〈複雑な〉complicated; complex; intricate; 〈難しい〉hard; difficult; 〈厄介な〉troublesome; (be) a nuisance.

やや(と)もすれば ¶やや(と)もすれば…する be apt [prone, liable] to *do*; be given to *doing*; often *do*; be inclined [《文》disposed] to *do*.

やゆ 揶揄 ¶やゆする make fun [《文》sport] of; ridicule; 《文》rally; chaff; banter (《with *sb*》).

やよい 弥生 〖考古〗 ¶弥生式土器 Yayoi pottery [ware] / 弥生時代 the Yayoi period.

-やら 〈または, あるいは〉and; or; 〈…の由〉They [People] say (that)... ¶…やら…やらで what with...and (what with)... / どうやらこうやら in some way or other; somehow or other / 吉田とやらいう人 a (certain) Mr. Yoshida / だれ(と)やらさん Mr. Thingummy, Mr. What's-his-name. 文例⇩

やらい[1] 矢来 (put up) a palisade.

やらい[2] 夜来 since the (previous) night. 文例⇩

やらずぶったくり 文例⇩

やられる have *sth* done; 〈負ける〉be beaten; 《文》be defeated; 〈出し抜かれる〉be outwitted; 〈口語〉be taken in [for a ride]; 〈殺される〉be killed; be done away with; 〈盗まれる〉have *sth* stolen; 〈病気になる〉have an attack (of); be [come] down 《with flu》; 〈災害などに〉be (hard) hit (by).

やり 槍 a spear; 〈騎兵の〉a lance; 〈投げやり〉a javelin ¶やりを突き刺す 《文》thrust [plunge] a spear (into an enemy's breast》/ やりで突く spear / やり先 a spearhead / やり使い a spearman / やり持ち a spear-bearer.

やりあう やり合う 〈争う〉compete [quarrel] (with); be in competition (with one another); 〈議論する〉argue [《文》dispute] (with).

やりいか 《動》a squid.

やりかえす やり返す answer back; retort 《to a question by another question》; reply in kind.

やりかけ やり掛け ¶やりかけにする leave (*one's* work) unfinished [half-done, halfway] / やりかけの仕事 work [a job] left unfinished [half-done].

やりかた やり方 a way [《文》manner] (of *doing*); how to *do*; a method; 〈手段〉《文》a measure; a step; 〈方針〉《文》a course; 〈手順〉a process 〈かた[1] ¶やり方が正しい[間違っている] 〈方法〉do *sth* (in) the right [wrong] way; 〈方針〉be on the right [wrong] tack / やり方を変える do *sth* in a different way; change *one's* tack. 文例⇩

やりかねる dare not *do*; hesitate to *do* ¶どんなことでもやりかねない be capable of doing anything; go to extremes. 文例⇩

やりきれない やり切れない 〈人が主語〉cannot bear [stand]; 〈文〉be unbearable (to *one*); 《文》be beyond bearing; be too much [bad] (for *one*) (to bear [stand]) ¶(事が)やり切れないほど退屈である be impossibly [agonizingly, excruciatingly] dull. 文例⇩

やりくち やり口 ⇨やりかた.

やりくり やり繰り ¶やり繰りする manage 《with *sth*, without *sth*》; make shift (with, without) / やり繰りが上手[下手]である be a good [poor] manager / やり繰りで暮らす manage thanks to [《文》live by dint of] careful housekeeping. 文例⇩

なかった. They continued [went on] with their study.
やや やや真実に近い. It is a bit nearer the truth. / 今日はややいいようです. He seems to be slightly [a little] better today. / それはやや葉巻きに似た形をしている. It is shaped something like a cigar.
-やら 何やら白いものが見えた. We saw something white. / 公用やら私用やらで少しも暇がない. What with official business and private affairs, my time is wholly taken up. / 怖いやら不安やらで, 体どとも利けなかった. Between fright and suspense she was hardly able to find her voice. / 彼女は泣くやらわめくやら大騒ぎを演じた. She made quite a scene, crying and screaming. / 去る者は日々に疎しとやら. 'Out of sight, out of mind,' as the saying goes.
やらい[2] 夜来の雨もようやくやんだ. The rain which has been falling since last night is over at last.
やらずぶったくり それじゃやらずぶったくりだ. It's all take and no give. | It's (daylight) robbery.
やり トラはやりで刺されて死んだ. The tiger died at spearpoint.
やりかた それはやり方次第だ. It depends (on) how you do it. / そんなやり方ではだめだ. That is not the way to do it. / 大丈夫だ. 何とかやり方はあるものだ. Don't worry. There is always a way. / 君たちとはやり方が違う. I am going to do this in a different way from you. | I have my own way of doing this. / 彼は私のやり方に賛成してくれた. He approved of the course I had taken.
やりかねる 彼はそれぐらいのいたずらもやりかねない男だと思う. I wouldn't put it past him to play a trick like that. / あの代議士はスキャンダルを防ぐためには相当のこともやりかねない. That Dietman would go a long way [to any lengths] to avoid scandal.
やりきれない この暑さでは全くやり切れません. I really can't stand this heat. | The heat is really unbearable. / これじゃとてもやり切れない. That's more than I can bear. | I can't put up with this.
やりくり 手元にあるだけでやりくりしておこう. I will make do

やりこなす manage ((a difficult task)); get through ((with) one's work); 《口語》get there ¶やりこなせるを be equal [up] to ((the job)).

やりこめる やり込める talk sb down; put sb to silence; corner sb in argument; beat; get the better of.

やりすぎる やり過ぎる overdo; 《文》do sth to excess; go too far; overplay one's hand; 〈物を〉give too much; 〈酒を〉drink too much. 文例

やりすごす やり過ごす let sb [sth] go past (one); wait till sb goes past (one).

やりそこない やり損ない a failure; a blunder; a slip-up.

やりそこなう やり損なう do sth badly; fail (in); slip up; make a botch [a bad job] of; bungle; do a bad job (on); be unsuccessful (in).

やりだす やり出す 〈始める〉start ((doing, to do)); begin ((doing)); set to ((work)); set about (one's work). 文例

やりだま 槍玉 ¶やり玉に上げる make an example of sb; make a victim of sb; victimize; 《文》make sb the butt [object] of an attack; pillory sb.

やりつける やり付ける 《文》be accustomed ((to sth, to do(ing)); be used ((to sth, to doing)) ¶やりつけた仕事 (the sort of) work one is used to ((doing)); the work that is familiar to one; the work one is familiar with.

やりっぱなし やりっ放し ¶やりっ放しにする leave sth half-done [unfinished]; do without worrying about the outcome.

やりて やり手《敏腕家》《文》a man of ability; an able [a capable] man; 《口語》a wheeler-dealer; 《口語》a whiz kid.

やりとおす やり通す ⇨やりとげる.

やりとげる やり遂げる carry out [through]; 《文》achieve; complete; 《文》effect; pull (a scheme) off; see [put] sth through; 《文》accomplish; 《文》bring ((one's work)) to completion; come through.

やりとり やり取り giving and taking; an exchange ((of letters)) ¶やり取りする give and take; exchange / 手紙のやり取りをする exchange letters ((with sb)); correspond [((文)) in correspondence] ((with sb)). 文例

やりなおす やり直す do over again [once more]; redo; try again; 〈新規まき直しする〉begin [start] all over again; make a fresh start.

やりなげ 槍投げ 〔競技〕 the javelin (throw) ¶やり投げをする throw a javelin / やり投げの選手 a javelin thrower.

やりにくい difficult [hard] to do; awkward; delicate.

やりぬく やり抜く carry sth through [out]; complete; 《文》achieve; 《文》accomplish; follow out ((a plan)).

やりば やり場

やる 〈与える〉give; let sb have sth; 〈送る〉send; 〈派遣する〉dispatch; 〈する, 行なう〉do; make ((an experiment)); 〈試みる〉try; 〈飲食する〉take; have; help oneself ((to sth)); 〈演じる〉perform; act; play; 〈経営する〉run; keep; 〈開催する〉hold; 〈遊ぶ〉⇨ する², play; practice ⇨する² ¶やってしまう go [get] through; finish; get sth over / 何とかやってのける manage to do / 本を買ってやる buy sb a book; buy a book for sb / オーバーを着せて[脱がせて]やる help sb on [off] with his overcoat / 息子を大学へやる send one's son to college / やる気がある《文》have a desire ((to do)); be willing ((to do)); feel like ((doing)) / やらせる 〈強制的に〉make sb do; 〈欲するに任せて〉let sb do; allow sb to do. 文例

用法「野球をやる」は play baseball なのに,「スキーをやる」は play ski ではなくて, ski; go skiing; do some skiing などと言う. 野球・フットボール・ゴルフ・トランプ・将棋・麻雀のように game と呼べる競技を「やる」のはすべて play であるが, そうでない各種陸上競技・水泳・ボクシング・相撲など game と呼べないスポーツを「やる」と言うのには play は使えない.

やるせない downhearted; 《文》disconsolate. 文例

ヤルタ ¶ヤルタ会談[協定] the Yalta Conference [Agreement].

やれやれ 〈驚き〉Oh!; Ah!; Oh dear!; Dear me!; 〈安心〉Aah!; Thank God (for that [that's over])! ¶やれやれと思う give [breathe] a sigh of relief; feel relieved. 文例

[make shift] with what I have. / 何とかやりくりして収支を償わせた. He managed to make (both) ends meet in some way or other. / 彼女はやりくりの上手な方ではなかった. She was not a good manager.

やりすぎる それではやり過ぎで, 健康に悪いよ. You are doing more than is good for you [your health].

やりだす 彼は近頃水泳を真剣にやり出した. He has seriously taken up swimming lately. / 彼は軍隊時代にタバコをやり出した. He took to smoking while he was in the army.

やりとり 激しいやり取りがあって, もう少しでなぐり合いになるところだった. Bitter words were exchanged and they nearly came to blows.

やりなおす 昨晩やった問題をまたどうしてやり直したのか. Why did you do over the exercises which you did last night? / 彼は人生をもう一度やり直す決心をした. He made up his mind to start his life over (again).

やりなげ 彼女はやり投げに57メートルで優勝した. She won the javelin with a throw of 57 meters.

やりば 目のやりばに困った. I didn't know where to look.

やる さあやるぞ. Here goes! / 彼はその金を僕にやろうと言った. He offered me the money. / すぐやって下さい. Go ahead right away. / ゆっくりやれ! Take your time! / 今はそれはやる気がしない. I'm not in the mood for it. / 何をやっていたのかね. What have you been doing [up to]? / どんな風にやったらいいのか僕にはわからない. I don't know how to do [go about] it. / 彼は文学をやるんだそうだ. I am told he is going in for literature. / 学生ホールではすしもやるのですか. Do they serve sushi in the students' hall? / 歌舞伎座では今何をやっ

やろう 野郎 a fellow;《米》a guy;《英》a chap.

やわらかい, やわらかな 柔[軟]らかい, 柔[軟]らかな〈柔軟な〉soft; tender;〈穏やかな〉gentle; mild ¶柔らかな風 a gentle [soft] breeze / 柔らかい声 a soft [velvety] voice / 手触りが柔らかい feel soft; be soft [tender] to the touch / 柔らかくする soften; make *sth* soft; tenderize《the meat》/ 軟らかく煮た豆 beans cooked (until they are) tender. 文例⇩

やわらぐ 和らぐ soften; be softened;《文》be allayed;〈怒りなどが〉calm [cool] down;〈風などが〉go down;《文》abate; subside. 文例⇩

やわらげる 和らげる soften;〈程よくする〉《文》moderate; mellow;〈苦痛などを〉relieve;《文》alleviate;《文》mitigate; lessen;〈感情を〉calm; appease; mollify ¶苦痛を和らげる ease [《文》allay] pain / 怒りを和らげる appease [calm] *sb's* anger / 要求を和らげる moderate [tone down] *one's* demand (for).

ヤンキー a Yankee; an American.

やんちゃ ¶やんちゃな mischievous;《文》impish; naughty / やんちゃ坊主 a mischievous boy; an urchin / やんちゃ娘 a tomboy;《文》a hoyden.

やんぬるかな 文例⇩

やんばるくいな〔鳥〕an Okinawa rail.

やんま〔昆〕a large dragonfly.

やんや ¶やんやとかっさいする give *sb* hearty cheers [loud applause]; cheer [applaud] *sb* to the echo / やんやのかっさいを受ける bring the house down.

やんわり ¶やんわりと〈穏やかに〉softly; gently; mildly.

ゆ

ゆ 湯 hot water;〈風呂〉a (hot) bath;〈風呂屋〉a bathhouse;〈温泉〉a hot spring;〈洗湯〉¶湯と水の出る設備 (an apartment with) hot and cold (running) water [H and C] /〈洗面所で〉湯の出る栓をひねって出す turn on a hot tap / 湯を沸かす boil water;〈風呂を〉get the bath ready / 湯を使わせる give (a child) a bath /《英》湯を使わせる (a baby) / 湯に入る have [take] a bath; get into a bathtub / 湯加減を見る (put *one's* hand in the bath to) see how hot the water is / 男[女]湯 the men's [women's] section (of a bathhouse). 文例⇩

ゆあか 湯垢 fur; scale;《文》an incrustation ¶湯あかが付く be covered with fur [scale] / 湯あかを取る remove fur [scale] (from a boiler); descale.

ゆあがり 湯上がり ¶湯上がりに (just) after a bath / 湯上がりの女 a woman just out of the bath / 湯上がりタオル a bath towel.

ゆあつ 油圧 oil pressure ¶油圧計 an oil pressure gauge / 油圧ジャッキ[ブレーキ] a hydraulic jack [brake].

ゆいあげる 結い上げる ⇨ゆう⁵.

ゆいいつ 唯一 ¶唯一の the only [《文》sole, one (and only)] / 唯一無二の unique;《文》peerless.

ゆいがどくそん 唯我独尊《文》self-righteousness; conceit;《文》self-conceit.

ゆいごん 遺言 *one's* last [dying] wish; *one's* [a] will;〔法〕⇨いごん ¶遺言する say in *one's* will ((that...)); leave a will ((stating) that...); will ((that...)) / 遺言で与える leave (7,000,000 yen) to *sb* (in *one's* will) / 遺言状を作成する make [draw up] a will. 文例⇩

ゆいしょ 由緒〈来歴〉a history;〈家系〉pedigree; lineage; blood; birth ¶由緒のある家柄の (a person) of noble [high] birth; of blue [gentle] blood / 由緒のある建物 a historic building;《文》a building rich in legend [steeped in history]. 文例⇩

ゆいしんろん 唯心論 idealism; spiritualism ¶唯心論者 an idealist; a spiritualist.

ゆいのう 結納《exchange》engagement [《文》betrothal] presents [gifts].

ていますか. What is on [What are they doing] now at the Kabukiza? / すいかを一つやってみないか. Won't you try a slice of watermelon? / 彼はパーティーをやりたがっている. He is very keen to give a party.

やるせない あの人と別れなくてはならなかったときのやるせなさ. My heart was down when I had to leave him.

やれやれ やれやれ, やっと着いた. Well, here we are at last.

やろう この野郎! You bastard [swine]!

やわらかい 僕は柔らかい布団は嫌いだ. I don't like a soft bed [a bed that gives too much].

やわらぐ 彼の親切な言葉に彼女の心も和らいだ. His kind words melted her heart. / 彼女の笑みで僕の心も和らいだ. Her smiles disarmed me.

やんぬるかな やんぬるかな. Alas! There's no help for it! There's nothing (more) to be done about it.

ゆ お湯が沸いてるよ. The water is boiling. / お湯が沸きました. The bath is ready. / お湯の加減はいかがですか. How is the bath?

ゆいごん 彼は自分の財産を子供たちの間で平等に分配するよう遺言した. He willed that his property be divided equally among his children. / 彼は遺言で自分の不動産のすべてを妻に与えた. He left his entire estate to his wife. / おじの遺言で500万円もらった. I was left [got] 5,000,000 yen in my uncle's will. / 彼はおじさんが遺言状から自分の名前を抜いてしまわないかと心配している. He is afraid that his uncle will cut him out of his will.

ゆいしょ 彼は由緒ある家柄の子です. He belongs to an old family. / この町は由緒ある町です. This town has a rich [an interesting] history.

ゆいび 唯美 ¶唯美的 (a)esthetic / 唯美主義 (a)estheticism / 唯美主義者 an (a)esthete.

ゆいぶつ 唯物 ¶唯物的 materialistic / 唯物史観 the materialistic view of history / 唯物弁証法 the materialistic dialectic / 唯物論[主義] materialism / 史[弁証法]的唯物論 historical [dialectical] materialism / 唯物論[主義]者 a materialist.

ゆいめいろん 唯名論 〘哲〙 nominalism ¶唯名論者 a nominalist.

ゆう[1] 勇 ⇨**ゆうき**[3] ¶勇を鼓す take [pluck up] heart ; summon [pluck up] *one's* courage ; pull *oneself* together ; nerve *oneself* 《to *sth*》.

ゆう[2] 雄 ¶一方の雄 the leader of a group / 私学の雄 one of the leading [outstanding] private schools [universities] 《in Japan》.

ゆう[3] 優 〈採点の〉 A ; excellent ¶数学で優をとる get an A in mathematics. [文例⇩]

ゆう[4] 言う ⇨**いう**.

ゆう[5] 結う 〈結ぶ〉 tie (up) ; fasten ; 〈髪を〉 dress ; do (up) ¶髪を結ってもらう have *one's* hair done [dressed] / 結い方 〈髪型〉 a hair style ; 《口語》 a hairdo 《*pl.* -s》 ; 《文》 a coiffure / 結い上げた髪 coiffured hair.

ゆうあい 友愛 friendship ; comradeship ; 《文》 fraternity.

ゆうい[1] 有為 ¶有為の 〈有能な〉 capable ; able ; talented ; 〈有望な〉 promising ; 《文》 《a youth》 full of promise / 有為の青年 a promising youth ; a young man of promise.

ゆうい[2] 優位 superiority 《over》 ; 《文》 predominance 《over》 ¶優位を占める[に立つ] hold a dominant position 《in the literary world》 ; get [gain] an advantage 《over *sb*》 ; establish [《文》 achieve, 《文》 attain] superiority 《over》 ; get [gain, have] the upper hand of 《*one's* opponent》.

ゆういぎ 有意義 ¶有意義な 〈意味のある〉 significant ; 〈有益な〉 useful ; 〈価値のある〉 worthwhile / 有意義な生活を送る lead a useful life ; live to some purpose.

ゆういん 誘因 a cause 《of》 ; 《文》 an inducement 《to》 ; an incentive 《to》 ; 《文》 an (immediate) occasion 《for》 ¶…の誘因となる cause ; lead (up) to ; bring about ; trigger *sth* (off) ; 《文》 be the inducement [incentive] to.

ゆううつ 憂鬱 depression ; 《文》 melancholy ; gloom ¶ゆううつである feel [be] miserable [depressed, dejected, 《口語》 blue, 《口語》 low, 《口語》 down, 《文》 melancholy] ; be in low spirits ; 《文》 have (a case of) the blues / ゆううつな 〈気分が〉 miserable ; depressed ; 《文》 melancholy ; dejected ; 〈与える印象が〉 miserable ; depressing ; gloomy ; cheerless ; 《文》 melancholy / ゆううつな天気 miserable [gloomy] weather / ゆううつな顔をする wear [put on, pull] a long face ; wear [put on] a gloomy expression ; look miserable [glum] / ゆううつになる feel sad ; become depressed ; 《口語》 get down in the dumps / ゆううつ症 melancholia; severe depression / ゆううつ症患者 a melancholiac. [文例⇩]

ゆうえい 遊泳 ⇨**すいえい** ¶遊泳術 〈世渡りの術〉 how to get along in the 《political》 world. [文例⇩]

ゆうえき 有益 ¶有益な 〈有用な〉 useful ; 〈有利な〉 profitable; 〈ためになる〉 《文》 beneficial ; 〈いい教訓になる〉 《文》 salutary 《experiences》 ; instructive ; 〈教育的な〉 informative ; 〈報いるところのある〉 rewarding. [文例⇩]

ゆうえつ 優越 superiority ; 〈最高位〉 《文》 supremacy ¶優越する be better 《than》 ; be superior 《to》 ; 《文》 surpass / 優越した superior ; 《文》 supreme ; 《文》 surpassing / 優越感 〘心理〙 (a) superiority complex / 優越感を抱く have a sense [be conscious] of (*one's*) superiority 《over [to] *sb*》.

ゆうえんち 遊園地 a recreation [pleasure] ground ; an amusement park.

ゆうおうまいしん 勇往邁進 ¶勇往邁進する dash [push] on [forward].

ゆうが 優雅 ¶優雅な elegant ; graceful ; refined / 優雅に暮らす be comfortably off ; live in luxury ; 〈悪人などが〉 《口語》 live as snug as a bug in a rug ; 《英口語》 live the life of Riley.

ゆうかい[1] 誘拐 kidnapping ; abduction ¶誘拐する kidnap ; abduct / 誘拐者 a kidnapper ; an abductor. [文例⇩]

ゆうかい[2] 融解 fusion ; melting ¶融解する fuse ; melt ; dissolve / 融解点 a melting point / 融解熱 (the) heat of fusion.

ゆうがい[1] 有害 ¶有害な bad 《for *one*, for *one's* health》 ; harmful ; 《文》 injurious ; damaging ; 《文》 noxious / 健康に有害である be bad for [injurious to] the health / 有害無益である do more harm than good.

ゆうがい[2] 有蓋 ¶有蓋の covered ; roofed ; closed / 有蓋貨車 《米》 a boxcar ; 《英》 a covered [box] wagon.

ゆうがお 夕顔 〘植〙 〈うり科のつる草〉 a bottle gourd ; a calabash ; 〈よるがお〉 a moonflower.

ゆうかく 遊郭 the licensed [gay] quarters ; a red-light district.

ゆうがく[1] 有額 ¶(組合の要求に対する)有額回答 《give》 a reply offering an increase in wages.

ゆうがく[2] 遊学 ⇨**りゅうがく**.

ゆう[3] 彼は全優を取った. He got straight A's.

ゆううつ やらなくてはならない仕事の量を思っただけでもゆううつになる. The mere thought of the volume of work I must handle is enough to depress me.

ゆうえい 遊泳禁止. 〘掲示〙 No swimming here.

ゆうえき この本は面白くまた有益でもある. This book is both interesting and instructive.

ゆうかい[1] 彼はその子供を誘拐して身代金を要求した. He kidnapped [took away] the child and held him to ransom.

ゆうがた 夕方になると子供たちは皆家に帰った. When it was evening, the boys all went home. / こうもりは夕方になると飛び回る動物だ. The bat is an animal which flies about in the evening.

ゆうき[3] 彼は決して勇気を失わなかった. His nerve never failed him. / 勇気を出して「いやです」と言った. I found the courage to say 'no'. / 勇気を奮い起こして

ゆうかしょうけん 有価証券 securities; stocks and bonds; a negotiable instrument [paper].

ゆうかぜ 夕風 a (cool) evening breeze.

ゆうがた 夕方 evening ¶夕方に (early) in the evening; at dusk / 夕方にかけて toward evening / 明日の夕方までに by tomorrow evening. 文例⇩

ゆうがとう 誘蛾灯 a [an insect] light trap.

ユーカラ 《アイヌ語》yukar; the Ainu Saga.

ユーカリ 《植》a eucalyptus (pl. -tus, -ti).

ゆうかん¹ 夕刊 an evening edition 《of a paper》 ¶夕刊紙 an evening paper.

ゆうかん² 有閑 ¶有閑階級 the leisured class(es); the idle rich / 有閑地 unused land / 有閑マダム a lady of leisure; a leisured woman.

ゆうかん³ 勇敢 bravery; courage;《文》valor ¶勇敢な brave; heroic;《文》valiant;《文》courageous; daring / 勇敢に bravely; heroically;《文》valiantly;《文》courageously; daringly / 勇敢に難局に当たる meet a difficult situation with courage.

ゆうかんじしん 有感地震 a felt earthquake.

ゆうき¹ 有期 ¶有期刑になる be sentenced to imprisonment for a definite term / 有期懲役 penal servitude for a definite term.

ゆうき² 有機 ¶有機的 organic; systematic / 有機的に organically; systematically / 有機化学 organic chemistry / 有機体 an organism / 有機農業 [農法] organic agriculture [farming] / 有機肥料 (an) organic fertilizer / 有機物 organic matter; an organic substance / 有機分子 an organic molecule.

ゆうき³ 勇気 courage;《文》valor; bravery; pluck; nerve;《口語》guts;〈向こう見ずの大胆さ〉boldness ¶勇気のある《文》courageous;《文》valiant; brave; plucky /〈大胆な〉bold; daring;《文》intrepid / 勇気のない [同意] cowardly; fainthearted;《文》white-[lily-]livered / 勇気を出す gather [pluck up] one's courage;《文》muster one's courage [nerve]; get up one's nerve / …する勇気がある,勇気を出して…する have (the) courage to do;《do not》have the heart to do; nerve oneself 《for an attempt, to do》/ 自分が正しいと信じること を行なう [言う] 勇気がある have the courage of one's convictions / 勇気を付ける encourage; cheer up / 勇気をくじく discourage; dishearten; unnerve / 勇気を失う lose courage [heart].

ゆうぎ¹ 友誼 ⇒ゆうじょう,ゆうこう¹.

ゆうぎ² 遊戯 a game;《運動》a sport;〈子供 の〉play;〈娯楽〉a pastime; amusements ¶遊戯をする play a game / 遊戯室 a playroom; a recreation room / 遊戯本能 play instinct.

ゆうきゅう 有給 ¶有給の paid; salaried / 有給休暇 a paid vacation [holiday]; a vacation [holiday] with (full) pay / 有給雇用 paid [《文》gainful] employment; employment / 有給職員 staff members on the payroll.

ゆうきゅう² 遊休 ¶遊休の idle; unused; unemployed / 遊休施設 idle facilities [equipment] / 遊休資本 unemployed [idle] capital.

ゆうきょう 遊興 《文》(worldly) pleasures; amusements; merrymaking ¶遊興にふける pursue [indulge in, give oneself up to] pleasure / 遊興税 the amusement tax.

ゆうぎり 夕霧 an evening mist.

ゆうぐう 優遇 favorable [preferential] treatment;〈歓待〉a warm [《文》cordial] reception ¶優遇する give favorable [preferential] treatment 《to》; treat sb well [《文》favorably];〈給料の点で〉pay a good salary 《to》; pay sb well;〈歓待する〉receive sb warmly [《文》cordially]; give a warm reception 《to》; welcome.

ユークリッド Euclid ¶ユークリッド [非ユークリッド] 幾何学 Euclidean [non-Euclidean] geometry.

ゆうぐれ 夕暮れ evening; (evening) twilight ⇒ゆうがた.

ゆうぐん 友軍 〈同盟軍〉an allied army;〈味 方〉our troop [army]; one's friends.

ゆうけい 有形 ¶有形の《文》material; concrete;《文》substantial; physical;《文》corporeal;《文》tangible / 有形財産 《会計》tangible property; tangibles / 有形資産 《会計》tangible assets; tangibles / 有形無形の material and immaterial; visible and invisible. 文例⇩

ゆうげきしゅ 遊撃手 《野球》a shortstop; a short.

ゆうげしき 夕景色 an evening scene [landscape].

ゆうげん¹ 有限 ¶有限の limited; 《数》finite / 有限集合 [小数] a finite set [decimal] / 有限(責任)会社 a limited (liability) company / 有限責任昭和電気会社《米》the Showa Electric Company, Inc.;《英》the Showa Electric Company, Ltd.

ゆうげん² 幽玄 yugen;《文》profound and quiet elegance; ¶幽玄の the subtle and profound.

ゆうけんしゃ 有権者〈選挙の〉an elector; a voter; the electorate (集合的). 文例⇩

ゆうこう¹ 友好 ¶友好的な friendly / 友好関 係 (establish) friendly [《文》cordial] relations 《with, between》;《form》(a) friendship 《with a nation》/ 友好国 a friendly nation [power] / 友好条約 a treaty of friendship [amity]. 文例⇩

その岩を登り始めた。He screwed up his courage and began to climb the rock. / とても独りで来る勇気はあるまい。I very much doubt if he will dare to come alone. / 私にはとても彼女にそれを知らせる勇気はなかった。I did not have the heart to let her know the news.

ゆうけい あの方には有形無形のご援助を頂いております。We have received both material and moral support from him.

ゆうけんしゃ 選挙人名簿によると今度の選挙でこの村の有権者は5,200人である。The pollbook shows that our village has 5,200 people entitled to vote in the coming election.

ゆうこう¹ 両国間の友好関係樹立の雰囲気を醸成するのには又とない好機である。This is a golden opportunity to create an atmosphere for rapprochement between our [the] two nations. / この歴史的会見は両国間の長年の友好関係を一層強化することだろ

ゆうこう² 有効 ¶有効な valid; available; effective;《文》effectual / 有効に使う make good use of; put *sth* to good use; use *sth* effectively [《文》to advantage] / 有効になる become effective;〈法律などが〉come into effect [force];〈契約などが〉take effect / 有効である be effective; hold [be] good; be valid; be available《for one month》/ 有効期間 the term of validity; the period for which《a ticket》is available [valid] / 有効期限の切れた切符 a ticket whose validity has expired; an expired ticket / 有効需要《経済》(an) effective demand / 有効数字《数》a significant figure / 有効打 a telling blow / 有効投票《文》a valid ballot.

ゆうごう 融合 fusion; merger;〈融和〉《文》harmony ¶融合する fuse; merge;〈融和する〉be in harmony《with》.[文例↓]

ゆうこく¹ 夕刻 ⇨ゆうがた.

ゆうこく² 愛国 patriotism ¶愛国の士 a patriotically-minded man; a patriot.

ユーゴスラビア Yugoslavia; Jugoslavia ¶ユーゴスラビア社会主義連邦共和国 the Socialist Federal Republic of Yugoslavia / ユーゴスラビアの Yugoslav; Yugoslavian / ユーゴスラビア人 a Yugoslav; a Yugoslavian.

ゆうこん 雄渾 ¶雄渾な〈壮大な〉grand;《文》sublime;〈力強い〉virile; vigorous / 雄渾な筆を振るう write with bold strokes of the (writing) brush.

ユーザー a user.

ゆうざい 有罪 ¶有罪の guilty / 有罪と決まる be convicted《of an offense》; be found guilty《of a crime》; get a conviction / 有罪と宣告する declare *sb* guilty《of a crime》; convict *sb* of a crime;〈陪審員が評決する〉return [deliver] a verdict of 'guilty'.[文例↓]

ゆうさんかいきゅう 有産階級 the propertied classes;〈ブルジョワジー〉the bourgeoisie.

ゆうし¹ 有史 ¶有史以来の大戦争 the greatest war in history [on record, since the dawn of history, within the memory of man] / 有史前の prehistoric; of prehistoric times.

ゆうし² 有志 a volunteer ¶有志一同 everyone [《文》all the persons] concerned [interested] (in the matter).[文例↓]

ゆうし³ 勇士 a brave man [warrior]; a hero (*pl*. -es).

ゆうし⁴ 雄姿《文》《cut, make》a gallant [an imposing] figure.[文例↓]

ゆうし⁵ 融資 financing;《文》accommodation of funds;〈貸付金〉a loan ¶融資する finance《an enterprise》;《文》accommodate *sb* with a loan; furnish《a company》with funds; loan《*sb* one million yen》.

ゆうじ 有事 ¶一朝有事の際に in time of emergency; in time of need; in an emergency.

ゆうしかいひこう 有視界飛行 visual flying;《make》a visual [contact] flight; pilotage; contact flying / 有視界飛行規則 visual flight rules (略: VFR).

ゆうしかくしゃ 有資格者 a qualified person; a qualifier; a person who is eligible [《文》a person eligible]《for a post》.

ゆうじがた(の) U字型(の) U-shape; U-shaped ¶U字型カーブ a hairpin bend.

ゆうしきしゃ 有識者 ⇨しきしゃ.

ゆうしてっせん 有刺鉄線 barbed wire;《米》barbwire.

ゆうしぶんれつ 有糸分裂《生物》mitosis.

ゆうしゅう¹ 憂愁《文》melancholy; gloom.

ゆうしゅう² 優秀 ¶優秀な excellent;《文》superior / 優秀な成績《get, achieve》excellent results;〈学業で〉《get, earn, gain》high marks;《have, achieve》an excellent (academic) record.[文例↓]

ゆうしゅうのび 有終の美 ¶有終の美をなす [飾る]《文》bring *sth* to a successful conclusion; round off《*one's* career》.

ゆうじゅうふだん 優柔不断《文》irresolution; indecision ¶優柔不断の irresolute; indecisive;《文》weak and vacillating / 優柔不断である lack decision;《文》be a man of indecision.

ゆうじょ 遊女 a prostitute;《文》a harlot.

ゆうしょう¹ 有償 ¶有償の《法》onerous.

ゆうしょう² 勇将 a brave general.

ゆうしょう³ 優勝 ¶優勝する win [capture] the victory [championship,《米》pennant, title]; come off [out] victorious [the winner, the victor] / 優勝旗《win, clinch》the championship flag; the pennant / 優勝第一候補 the favorite [top choice] for the championship; the best bet for the title / 優勝者 the (first-prize [pennant]) winner; the victor; a champion / 優勝戦《勝ち抜き試合の》a championship tournament;〈決勝戦〉the finals / 優勝チーム the winning team / 優勝杯 a

---

う. This historic meeting will cement the friendship that has long existed between our [the] two countries.

ゆうこう² この契約は1か年有効です. This agreement holds good [remains in force] for a year. / この切符は2日間有効です. This ticket is good for two days.

ゆうごう 水素原子が融合すると莫大なエネルギーを放出する. Atoms of hydrogen fuse to give off an enormous amount of energy.

ゆうざい 彼は有罪か無罪か. Is he guilty or not guilty?

ゆうし² 学生中の有志が相計って弁論部を組織した. An oratorical society was organized by a group of interested students.

ゆうし⁴ 間もなくナポレオンはその雄姿をバルコニーに現わした. Before long Napoleon proudly made his appearance on the balcony.

ゆうしゅう² 彼は本校の優秀な学生の一人です. He is one of the best [top] students in our school.

ゆうしょう² 勇将の下に弱卒なし. A good general will make good men. | As is the master, so will his men be.

ゆうしょう³ 今年は明大が優勝旗を獲得した. This year the Meiji team won [carried off] the championship flag.

ゆうじょう 暖かい友情が2人の間に生まれた. A very warm friendship sprang up between them.

ゆうしょく 夕食にステーキを食べた. We had steak for dinner. / ゆっくりして夕食を食べて行かな

ゆうじょう 友情 friendship ¶友情のある[に厚い] friendly; kind; warm to one's friends / 友情のない unfriendly; cold to one's friends. 文例⇩

ゆうしょく¹ 夕食 〈正餐(せいさん)〉 (a) dinner; an [the] evening meal; 〈軽い夕食〉 (a) supper ¶夕食の卓に着く sit down to dinner [supper] / 夕食の時[時間]に at dinner [supper]; at dinnertime [suppertime] / 夕食を取る eat dinner; dine; take supper / 早目に夕食を取る have an early supper / 夕食前[後]に before [after] dinner / 夕食中である be at dinner. 文例⇩

用法 dinner は一日のうちで一番ちゃんとした食事で、日本の夕食は一般に dinner よりは、dinner と言うのがふさわしい。英国などでは地方や階級によって昼食の場合と夕食の場合があり、夕食を dinner とする傾向が強くなってきてはいるが、dinner が昼食である人もかなりいる。昼食が dinner ならば「夕食」は supper であるが、これはむしろ「夜食」の意味に近く、ごく軽い食事である。夕食が dinner の人には昼食はもちろん lunch である。

ゆうしょく² 有色 ¶有色の nonwhite; colored / 有色人種 nonwhite [colored] races / 有色野菜 highly-pigmented vegetables.

ゆうしょく³ 憂色 a worried [an anxious, 《文》 a sorrowful] look ¶憂色を帯びる wear a worried look; look gloomy [sad, worried] / 憂色を浮かべて with a look of anxiety (on one's face). 文例⇩

ゆうじん¹ 友人 a friend; a companion; 〈総称〉 (good) company ⇨ ともだち.

ゆうじん² 有人 ¶有人の piloted; manned (spaceships).

ゆうしんろん 有神論 theism ¶有神論者 a theist.

ゆうずい 雄蕊 〖植〗 a stamen.

ゆうすう 有数 ¶有数の prominent; distinguished; eminent; 《文》 preeminent; leading; one of the greatest [foremost] (cities) / わが国現代有数の大作家 one of our few great living novelists. 文例⇩

ゆうずう 融通 ¶融通する 〈金を〉 lend sb (500,000 yen); 《文》 accommodate sb (with a loan); 〈前払いする〉 advance sb (100,000 yen); give sb an advance of (100,000 yen) / 〈性格が〉融通の利く adaptable; flexible; accommodating / 融通の利く規則 elastic rules / 融通が利かない be stiff; lack adaptability; be hidebound; be strait-laced / 融通手形 an accommodation bill [draft, note]. 文例⇩

ゆうすずみ 夕涼み ¶夕涼みする cool off in the evening; enjoy the cool evening breeze [the cool of evening].

ユースホステル a youth hostel ¶ユースホステルのペアレント the warden [supervisor] of a youth hostel / ユースホステルを利用して旅行する go (youth-)hosteling.

ゆうする 有する have; 《文》 possess; own; 〈享受する〉 《文》 enjoy; 〈生来〉 be endowed [gifted] with 《a genius for mathematics》.

ゆうせい¹ 有声 ¶有声の voiced; vocal / 有声音[子音] a voiced sound [consonant].

ゆうせい² 郵政 ¶郵政省[大臣] the Ministry [Minister] of Posts and Telecommunications.

ゆうせい³ 遊星 〖天〗 ⇨ わくせい.

ゆうせい⁴ 優生 ¶優生学 eugenics / 優生学上 eugenically (speaking); from a eugenic point of view; on eugenic grounds / 優生結婚 (a) eugenic marriage / 優生保護法 the Eugenic Protection Act.

ゆうせい⁵ 優性 〖遺伝〗 dominance ¶優性の dominant / 優性遺伝子[形質] a dominant gene [trait, characteristic].

ゆうせい⁶ 優勢 superiority; 《文》 predominance; 《文》 dominance 《文》 superior; leading; 《文》 predominant / 優勢である be superior (to); have an advantage (over); have the edge [upper hand] (over) / 数において優勢である 《文》 be numerically superior [superior in numbers] (to); 《文》 be greater in numbers (than) / 《文》 have (a) numerical superiority (over); outnumber (the other party) / 優勢になる rise to predominance (over); gain [get] an advantage (over); get the better (of); 《文》 become dominant; 〈競技で〉 lead; 〈議論などが〉 gain ground. 文例⇩

ゆうぜい¹ 郵税 postage (on a letter) ¶郵税とも 《￥1,500》 including postage. 文例⇩

ゆうぜい² 遊説 ¶遊説する go canvassing; canvass; make an election tour; 《米》 stump 《one's electoral district》; 〈地方を〉 barnstorm (through the Tohoku region) / 遊説員 a canvasser; 《米》 a stump speaker / 遊説旅行 (go on) an electioneering 《米》 a stumping tour. 文例⇩

さいよ. Stay to dinner, please.
ゆうしょく³ そのニュースを聞いて村中憂色に包まれた. The whole village was cast into deep anxiety by the news.
ゆうすう 日本は世界有数の漁業国である. Japan has one of the world's largest [most important] fishing industries. | Japan has one of the largest fishing industries in the world. | Japan is one of the world's major fishing nations.
ゆうずう 月賦で返すということで彼から10万円融通してもらった. I got a loan of ￥100,000 from him, to be paid off by monthly installments. / 彼は融通の利く男だ. He knows how to adapt himself to circumstances. / 〈多少悪いこともし兼ねない〉 He is the sort of man who is capable of compromising [can compromise] with his conscience.
ゆうせい⁶ 最初は早稲田の方が優勢であった. At first the advantage was with [things went in favor of] the Waseda team. / これが彼等の間で急に優勢になっている思想である. This is the ideology which has rapidly been gaining ground among them.
ゆうぜい¹ この手紙は郵税不足ですから，60円頂きます. The letter is understamped and 60 yen (postage) is due. / 郵税先払. 〖表示〗 Postage paid on delivery. | Postage (to be) paid by addressee. / 郵税不足. 〖表示〗 Insufficient [Short] postage. | Postage due.
ゆうぜい² 総裁自ら関西地方の遊

ゆうせいせいしょく 有性生殖 sexual reproduction ¶有性生殖を行なう生物 a sexually reproducing organism.

ゆうせん¹ 有線 ¶有線中継 cable [wire] relaying / 有線中継の wire-carried [messages] / 有線テレビ closed-circuit television;〈ホテルなどにある〉piped [cable] television / 有線電信[電話] wire telegraphy [telephony] / 有線放送 cable broadcasting;〈バーなどの〉a piped broadcast.

ゆうせん² 優先 ¶優先(権) (a) preference; priority;《文》primacy / 優先する take precedence [priority] (over) / 優先的に取り扱う give《a matter》priority (over); give sb preference / 優先株《米》preferred stocks /《英》preference shares / 通行の優先権 the right of way / 優先順位 the order of priority. 文例⇩

ゆうぜん 悠然 ⇨ゆうゆう.

ゆうそう¹ 勇壮 ¶勇壮な brave;《文》heroic; (soul-)stirring / 勇壮活発な音楽 lively and soul-stirring music.

ゆうそう² 郵送 ¶郵送する《米》mail;《英》post; send [forward] sth by mail [post] / 郵送先名簿 a mailing list / 郵送料 postage (on) / 郵送無料の post-[postage-]free [goods].

ゆうぞら 夕空 the evening [twilight] sky.

ユーターン〈自動車の〉(make) a U-turn. 文例⇩

ゆうたい¹ 有体 ¶有体の《文》tangible;《法》corporeal / 有体財産《法》corporeal property / 有体動産《法》corporeal movables.

ゆうたい² 勇退 ¶勇退する retire [resign one's post] voluntarily [of one's own accord]; step down (to make way [room] for a younger colleague).

ゆうたい³ 郵袋 a mailbag;《英》a postbag.

ゆうたい⁴ 優待 warm [preferential] treatment;〈歓迎〉(a) welcome; hospitality ¶優待する give preferential treatment (to); treat sb with kindness; give sb a warm [cordial] reception [welcome]; receive sb warmly [cordially] / 優待券 a complimentary ticket;〈割引券〉a discount coupon.

ゆうだい 雄大 ¶雄大な grand; magnificent;《文》sublime;《文》majestic;《文》massive [grand] in scale.

ゆうたいるい 有袋類《動》¶有袋類の動物 a marsupial (animal); a pouched animal.

ゆうだち 夕立 a (summer afternoon) shower ¶夕立に会う be caught in [overtaken by] a (sudden) shower. 文例⇩

ゆうだん 勇断 ¶(take) a decisive [《文》resolute] step;《make》a brave [《文》courageous] decision.

ゆうだんしゃ 有段者 a grade holder.

ゆうち 誘致 ¶誘致する attract; lure / 工場[外人観光客]を誘致する try to attract industrial development [foreign tourists].

ゆうちょう 悠長 ¶悠長な leisurely; slow; unhurried;〈暢気な〉easygoing / 悠長にやる take one's time (over sth, in doing) / 悠長な fashion / 悠長に構える take it [things] easy.

ゆうていどうぶつ 有蹄動物 an ungulate (animal); a hoofed animal.

ゆうてん 融点《物》a melting [fusing] point.

ゆうと 雄図 an ambitious enterprise; a great undertaking ¶雄図空しく敗れ去る《文》fail to realize one's great ambition.

ゆうとう 遊蕩 ⇨ほうとう ¶遊蕩児 a playboy;《文》a man of pleasure;《文》a man given to pleasures.

ゆうとう² 優等 ¶優等で (graduate) with honors;《米》cum laude / 最優等で with the highest distinction;《米》summa cum laude / 優等になる take honors (in French);《米》make the honor roll / 優等生《米》an honor(-roll) student; a prize pupil / 優等賞をもらう win an honor prize. 文例⇩

ゆうどう 誘導 ¶誘導する〈案内する〉《文》conduct; lead;〈誘って…させる〉《文》lead [《文》induce] sb to do / 管制塔からの誘導に従って着陸する make a landing following the instructions from the control tower; be talked down / 誘導尋問(ask) a leading question / 誘導制御 guidance control / 誘導装置〈ミサイルなどの〉(a radar) guidance system;〈飛行場の管制塔の〉a talk-down system / 誘導弾 a guided missile ⇨ミサイル / 誘導電動機[コイル] an induction motor [coil] / 誘導電流 an induced current / 誘導用計器 guidance instruments /〈空港の〉誘導路 a taxiway. 文例⇩

ゆうどうえんぼく 遊動円木 a swinging pole.

ゆうどく 有毒 ¶有毒な poisonous; poison (rains); venomous (snakes);〈有害な〉《文》noxious / 有毒ガス a poisonous gas / 有毒植物 a poisonous plant.

ユートピア〈トマス・モアの〉*Utopia*;〈一般に〉a utopia ¶ユートピア文学 Utopian literature.

説に出掛けた。The president himself set out on a stumping tour of the Kansai region.
ゆうせん² 公益は私益に優先する。The public interest takes precedence over [comes before] the private (interest). / この問題は最優先的に取り扱われた。The problem was given top [the highest] priority.
ユーターン ユーターン禁止。[掲示] No U-turns.
ゆうだち 夕立が来そうだ。We are going to have a shower.
ゆうとう² 彼はA大学を優等で卒業した。He is an honor graduate of A University. | He graduated with honors from A College. / 彼に何を聞いても優等生的な返事しかかえってこない。Whatever you ask him, you'll only get an answer straight out of the book [get guarded answers].
ゆうどう 弁護人は検事の質問を誘導尋問であるとして異議を申し立てた。The defense counsel objected to what he claimed was a leading question by the prosecutor.
ゆうに ここから湖畔までは自動車で行っても優に2時間はかかります。It is a full [good] two hours' ride in a car from here to the lakeside. / 優に2時間は待っていましたよ。I've been waiting for you for two solid hours. / 利益は優に1千万円を超えた。The profit was well over 10,000,000 yen.

ゆうなぎ 夕凪 an evening calm.

ゆうに 優に 《充分に》well;《文》amply; fully; full; easily 《the best》.

ゆうのう 有能 ¶有能な able; capable; competent / 有能な人 an able person;《文》a man of ability.

ゆうばえ 夕映え ⇒ ゆうやけ.

ゆうばく 誘爆 an induced [a secondary] explosion.

ゆうはつ 誘発 ¶誘発する《文》induce; lead to; bring about; give rise to; cause; trigger *sth* (off) / 戦争を誘発する touch [set] off a war.

ゆうはん 夕飯 ⇒ ゆうしょく¹.

ゆうひ¹ 夕日 (in) the evening [setting,《文》declining] sun. 文例⇩

ゆうひ² 雄飛 ¶雄飛する〈乗り出す〉launch (out) into《politics》; start (out) [《文》embark] on《a career》.

ゆうび 優美 graceful; elegant; refined.

ゆうびん 郵便《制度》mail [postal] service;《米》mail;《英》post ¶郵便を出す mail [post]《a letter》; put《a letter》in the post; take《a letter》to (the) post / 郵便で送る send《a parcel》by mail [post]; send《a letter》through the mail; mail; post / 外国[国内]郵便 foreign [domestic] mail / 第1種郵便 first-class mail /（航空便でない）通常郵便 surface mail / 郵便切手 a postage stamp ⇒ きって / 郵便業務 mail [postal] service / 郵便配達 mail delivery / 郵便車 a mail [postal,《英》post-office] van / 郵便スト a postal strike / 郵便貯金 postal [post-office] savings / 郵便配達区域 a postal delivery zone [《英》district] / 郵便配達人《米》a mailman /《英》a postman / 郵便箱〈受け箱〉a letter box /〈ポスト〉a mailbox ⇒ ポスト / 郵便番号 a postal《米》zip code /《英》a postcode / 郵便袋《米》a mailbag /《英》a postbag / 郵便物 mail; postal matter / 郵便振替 ⇒ ふりかえ / 郵便料金 postage / 郵便列車 a mail train. 文例⇩

ゆうびんがわせ 郵便為替 a (postal) money order /《英》a postal order（略：P.O.） ¶郵便為替で千円送る send [《文》remit] 1,000 yen by money order; send a money order for 1,000 yen《to *sb*》/ 郵便為替を組む draw a money order《on *sb*》/ 郵便為替を現金に換える cash a money order.

ゆうびんきょく 郵便局 a post office（略：P.O., p.o.） ¶中央郵便局 the Central Post Office （略：C.P.O.） / 郵便局長 a postmaster / 郵便局員 a post-office [postal] clerk.

ユーフォー a UFO (*pl.* UFO's)（★発音は [júːèfou] または [júːfou]）; an unidentified flying object.

ゆうふく 裕福 ¶裕福な rich; wealthy; well-off; well-to-do / 裕福である[に暮らしている] be well [comfortably] off; live in easy [《文》affluent] circumstances.

ユーフラテス(がわ) ユーフラテス(川) the (river) Euphrates.

ゆうべ 夕べ〈夕方〉an evening;〈昨夜〉last night; yesterday evening ¶秋の夕べ an autumn evening / 音楽の夕べ a musical evening / 観劇の夕べ an evening at the theater / ゆうべの火事 last night's fire.

ゆうへい 幽閉《文》confinement ¶幽閉する《文》confine *sb*《in a place》; shut *sb* up; hold *sb* incommunicado [in confinement].

ゆうべん 雄弁《文》eloquence;《文》oratory ¶雄弁をふるう speak fluently [《文》eloquently]《on》; make an eloquent speech《on》/ 雄弁な eloquent; fluent / 雄弁に eloquently; fluently / …を雄弁に物語る be eloquent [an eloquent proof] of… / 雄弁家 an eloquent speaker; an (accomplished) orator / 雄弁術 oratory; the art of public speaking / 雄弁大会 an oratorical [a speech] contest. 文例⇩

ゆうほう 友邦 a friendly nation [country]; an allied country [nation, power]; an ally.

ゆうぼう 有望 ¶有望な promising;《文》full of promise / 前途有望な青年 a promising youth; a young man with a bright [rosy] future (before him).

ゆうぼく(せいかつ) 遊牧(生活) nomadism; a nomadic life ¶遊牧の nomad(ic) / 遊牧の民 nomads（★個人は a nomad）; a nomad(ic) [wandering] tribe.

ゆうほどう 遊歩道 a promenade; a public walk.

ゆうめい¹ 有名 ¶有名な famous;《文》noted; well-known; celebrated;《文》renowned;〈悪名高い〉notorious / 世界的に有名な《文》(a biochemist) of worldwide reputation / 有名になる become famous《for》; make a name for *oneself*; become well [widely] known《for》; get a (big) name《for》; win [earn, come to] fame / 一躍有名になる leap [rocket] to fame / 有名校 a famous [well-known,《口語》big-name] school [university] / 有名人 a celebrity; a big name;《米》a big-name personage; a public [well-known] figure. 文例⇩

ゆうひ¹ 西の空が夕日に照り映えている. The western skies are aglow with the setting sun. / 2人は夕日を浴びてベランダに座っていた. They sat on the verandah in the evening sun.

ゆうびん 今日は郵便がたくさん来た. I've had a lot of mail today. / 下へ行って郵便が来ているかどうか見てきてくれないか. Run downstairs, will you, and see if there's any mail [post] for me. / 明日の郵便でお送り致します.

We will send [forward] it to you by tomorrow's mail [post]. / 彼は20年間郵便事業に携わってきた. He has been handling the mail for twenty years. / 郵便屋さんは1日に2回回って来る. The mailman comes around twice a day. / この小包の郵便料金は幾らですか. What is the postage on this parcel? / 小包郵便料は遠近によって違いますか. Do parcel post charges vary with distance?

ゆうふく みんな昔よりは裕福に

なった. We are better off than we used to be.

ゆうべん 氏はまれに見る雄弁家である. He has a rare gift of eloquence. | He has extraordinary oratorical power. / 雄弁は銀, 沈黙は金. Speech is silver, silence is golden.《諺》

ゆうめい¹ 日光は風光の美をもって有名である. Nikko is noted [famous] for its scenic beauty. / 彼のけちは有名なものだ. His stinginess is proverbial. | His

ゆうめい[2] 勇名 《文》 fame for bravery ¶勇名をはせる make [win] a name for *oneself* 《as a fourth batter, in achieving *sth*》.

ゆうめい[3] 幽明 ¶幽明境を異にする be dead; 《文》 be no more.

ゆうめいむじつ 有名無実 ¶有名無実の nominal; 《文》 titular; in name only / 有名無実の会長 a figurehead [nominal] president.

ゆうめし 夕飯 ⇨ゆうしょく[1].

ユーモア humor ¶ユーモアのある humorous; 《a man》 with [who has] a sense of humor; witty / ユーモアのない humorless; 《a man》 with no sense of humor / ユーモアを解する[解さない] have a [no] sense of humor / ユーモアに富む be extremely humorous; be very witty; have a fund of humor / ユーモア作家 a comic writer; a humorist / ユーモア小説 a humorous story [novel].

ゆうもう 勇猛 daring; bravery; 《文》 valor ¶勇猛な daring; 《文》 dauntless; 《文》 intrepid; bold; 《文》 valiant; brave / 勇猛な人 《文》 a lion of a man / 勇猛心を奮う pluck up [take] courage; muster (up) [summon up] *one's* courage [the courage 《to *do*》].

ゆうもや 夕靄 an evening mist.

ユーモラス ¶ユーモラスな humorous; amusing.

ユーモレスク 〔音楽〕 a humoresque.

ゆうもん 幽門 〔解〕 the pylorus 《*pl.* -ri, -ruses》 ¶幽門部 the pyloric region.

ゆうやく 勇躍 ¶勇躍して in high spirits.

ゆうやけ 夕焼け (a) 《beautiful》 sunset; the (bright) colors of the sunset ¶夕焼け雲 sunset clouds / 夕焼け空 the red sky (after sundown) in the west; 《文》 the sky aglow with the setting sun. [文例⇩]

ゆうやみ 夕闇 dusk; (evening) twilight ¶夕やみに in the dusk [twilight] / 夕やみ迫るころ as the dusk gathers [deepens, closes in]; when night is falling; 《文》 in the gathering dusk [twilight]; 《文》 in the deepening gloom of the evening; 〈夕方〉 toward evening.

ゆうゆう 悠々 ¶悠々たる〈落ち着いた〉quiet; calm; 《文》 (self-)composed; 〈悠長な〉 leisurely; slow; deliberate; 〈悠久な〉 eternal / 悠々と 〈落ち着いて〉 quietly; calmly; 《文》 with an air of perfect composure; 〈くつろいで〉 at ease; in comfort; 〈悠長に〉 unhurriedly; slowly; in a leisurely fashion; 〈楽々と〉 without difficulty [effort]; hands down / 悠々と勝つ win an easy [a hands-down] victory 《over》; win 《a race》 hands down / 悠々とタバコをのむ smoke serenely [at *one's* ease] / 悠々自適する 〈世俗を離れて安楽に暮らす〉 《文》 live (by *oneself*) free from worldly cares; 〈余生を〉 spend the rest of *one's* days in quiet [dignified] retirement.

ゆうよ 猶予 〈延期〉 (a) postponement; (a) delay; grace (支払いの); 〈刑の〉 〔法〕 suspension 《of a sentence》; a reprieve; 《文》 a respite ¶猶予する, 猶予を与える give *sb* 《a fortnight's》 grace; grant *sb* a postponement 《of five days》; 〈刑の執行を〉 grant [give] a reprieve [respite]; reprieve / 一日の猶予を請う ask for a day's grace 《for the payment》 / 猶予なく without delay [hesitation] / 猶予期間 《give *sb*》 an extension of time. [文例⇩]

-ゆうよ …有余 ¶…有余の more than…; over … / 20有余年間 for twenty-odd years; for over [more than, upward of] twenty years.

ゆうよう[1] 有用 ¶有用な useful; good 《for》; serviceable; 《文》 of use [service].

ゆうよう[2] 悠容 ¶悠容迫らぬ態度で serenely; calmly; 《文》 with an air of perfect composure.

ユーラシア 〈欧亜大陸〉 Eurasia; the Eurasian Continent.

ユーラトム 〈欧州原子力共同体〉 Euratom ★ the European Atomic Energy Community の略.

ゆうらん 遊覧 sightseeing; a sightseeing tour; a pleasure trip ¶遊覧する go sightseeing 《in》; do [see] the sights of 《Paris》; sightsee 《around Kyoto》 / 遊覧切符 an excursion ticket / 遊覧客 a sightseer; 《米》 a vacationist; 〈旅行者〉 a tourist / 遊覧船 a sightseeing [tour] boat; an excursion boat / 遊覧地 a pleasure resort; a tourist area [spot] / 遊覧バス a sightseeing bus / 遊覧旅行 a sightseeing [pleasure] trip.

ゆうり[1] 有利 ¶有利な〈好都合な〉《文》 advantageous; favorable; 〈利益になる〉 profitable; paying; lucrative / 有利な仕事 a profitable [paying] business / …に対して明らかに有利な立場にある have a clear advantage over *sb* / 有利である be advantageous [favorable] (to *one*); be to *one's* advantage. [文例⇩]

ゆうり[2] 有理 〔数〕 ¶有理式[関数] a rational expression [function] / 有理数 a rational number; a rational / 有理化する rationalize.

ゆうり[3] 遊離 〈分離〉 separation; 《文》 extrication; 〔化〕 isolation ¶遊離する separate;

---

name has become a byword for stinginess. / あの町は今では温泉で有名になっている. The town is famous for its hot springs now. | The town is now famous as a hot-spring resort. / あの人にはそれは有名税というものだ. That's the price he has to pay for being famous.

ゆうやけ 真っ赤な夕焼け空が明日の晴天を思わせた. The red sky at sundown promised us a fine day. ★英国には Red sky at night, shepherd's delight; red sky in the morning, shepherd's warning. という言い慣らされた表現がある.

ゆうよ 支払いをしばらく猶予して頂きたいのです. I want you to grant me a short extension of time for the payment. / もう2, 3日猶予してあげますからよくお考えになって下さい. I'll give you another couple of days to think it over. / 一刻も猶予すべき場合でない. There is no time to lose [to be lost]. | The situation admits of no delay. | We can't afford to wait (any longer).

ゆうり[1] 地理上から言えば門司は福岡より有利な位置を占めている. Geographically, Moji is better [more strategically, more advantageously] placed than Fukuoka. / 彼は被告に有利な陳述をした. His statement was favorable

ゆうりょ

extricate ; isolate / 遊離させる separate ; isolate ; disengage ; let free / 現実から遊離した政策 an unrealistic policy ; a policy which is not based on the actual situation 《in the country》.

ゆうりょ 憂慮 anxiety ; concern ; fear(s) ; cares ; 《文》 apprehension(s) ¶憂慮する 《文》 fear ; worry 《over》; be anxious 《concerned》 《about》; be troubled 《about》/ …しないかと憂慮して for fear that [《文》 lest]...should... / 憂慮すべき worrying ; serious ; 《文》 grave ; alarming. 文例⇩

ゆうりょう¹ 有料 ¶有料ロッカー[トイレ] a pay locker [toilet] / 有料試写会 a 《film》 preview with an admission fee / 有料駐車場 《米》 a toll parking lot / 《英》 a toll car park / 有料道路 a toll road.

ゆうりょう² 優良 ¶優良な 《文》 superior ; excellent ; fine / 優良株 (a) superior (gilt-edged) stock ; (a) blue chip ; (a) blue-chip stock / 優良店 a store holding a special commendation (from the mayor).

ゆうりょく 有力 ¶有力な powerful ; high-powered ; 〈勢力のある〉 influential ; 〈一流の〉 leading ; 〈議論など〉 weighty ; 《文》 cogent ; 〈証拠など〉 strong ; convincing / 有力な賛成[反対]論 a strong [powerful] argument in favor of [against] sth / 有力な新聞 a leading newspaper / 有力な容疑者 a key [prime] suspect / 最も有力な優勝候補 the likeliest winner ; the top-rated contender for the title / 有力者 an influential person ; 《文》 a man of influence [weight] ; a dominant figure 《in the Liberal Democratic Party》/ 財界の有力者 leading figures in the financial world ; economic leaders.

ゆうれい 幽霊 a ghost ; 《文》 a specter ; 《文》 a phantom ; a bog(e)y ; 《文》 an apparition ¶幽霊の(ような) ghostly ; ghostlike / 幽霊会社 a bogus [fictitious] company / 幽霊人口 (a) bogus population / 幽霊船 a phantom ship / 幽霊話 a ghost story / 幽霊屋敷 a haunted house. 文例⇩

ゆうれつ 優劣 《文》 superiority or inferiority ; 《文》 (relative) merits ¶優劣がない be equal 《with》; be on a par 《with》/ 優劣を争う 《文》 struggle [strive] for mastery / 優劣を論じる discuss the merits (and demerits) 《of》. 文例⇩

ユーロピウム 《化》 europium.

ゆうわ¹ 宥和 appeasement ⇒ なだめる ¶ゆう和政策 an appeasement policy.

ゆうわ² 融和 ¶融和する harmonize 《with》; 《文》 be reconciled 《with》; get along 《with》.

ゆうわく 誘惑 (a) temptation ; 《文》 (an) allurement ; (a) lure ¶誘惑する tempt ; entice ; 《文》 allure ; lure ; put temptation in sb's way ; 〈堕落させる〉 seduce 《a girl》/ 誘惑に陥りやすい be easily led astray [into temptation] / 誘惑に勝つ overcome [get the better of] temptation / 誘惑に負ける yield [give way] to temptation / 誘惑と戦う resist [withstand] temptation. 文例⇩

ゆえ 故 ⇒ わけ, から¹ ¶故あって for a (certain) reason ; on certain grounds (★ 理由が1つの場合でも grounds ということが多い); 《文》 owing to unavoidable circumstances / 故なくして without (any) reason [cause] / 故にそ (so that) ; consequently ; therefore ; 《文》 hence / …の故に 〈前置詞で〉 because of ; on account of ; 《文》 by reason of ; due to ; 〈接続詞〉 because ; as ; since / この故に on this account.

ゆえん¹ 所以 ⇒ わけ, りゆう. 文例⇩

ゆえん² 油煙 soot.

ゆおう 硫黄 ⇒ いおう.

ゆか 床 a floor ¶石の床の stone-floored 《rooms》/ 床を張る lay a floor ; floor (a house) / 床をはがす tear up [break open] the floor / 床板 a floorboard / 床板を張る floor 《a room》 with boards ; board the floor / 床運動《体操》 floor exercises / 床材 flooring (materials) / 床面積 (the amount of) floor space / 床上[下]浸水をする be flooded [《文》 inundated] above [below] floor level [the floor].

ゆかい 愉快 (a) pleasure ; (an) amusement ; (a) joy ; (a) delight ¶愉快な pleasant ; amusing ; merry ; delightful ; (a) joyful ; cheerful ; jolly ; happy / 愉快に pleasantly ; happily ; delightfully ; cheerfully ; merrily. 文例⇩

ゆがく 湯搔く scald ; parboil.

ゆかしい 床しい refined ; modest ; graceful.

ゆかた 浴衣 an informal cotton *kimono* (for summer wear) ¶浴衣がけで relaxing in *one's yukata*.

ゆがみ 歪み a warp ; (a) distortion ; (a) contortion ¶性格のゆがみ a twist [kink] in one's nature [character].

ゆがむ 歪む warp ; be warped ; be distorted ; 《文》 be contorted ; bend ; be bent ¶根性のゆがんだ 《a person》 with a crooked mind ; cross-grained / ゆがんだ見方をする have a perverted idea 《of》; take a warped view 《of》/ (苦し

---

to the defendant [worked in the defendant's favor]. / 結局彼の有利になった. It turned out to his advantage.

ゆうりょ 失業問題は憂慮すべき事態に立ち至っている. The problem of unemployment has assumed very serious dimensions.

ゆうりょう¹ 入場は無料ですか. Is admission free or is there a charge?

ゆうれい あの家には幽霊が出るそうだ. They say that house is haunted.

ゆうれつ 両者は全く優劣がつけ難い. There is nothing to choose between them [the two]. | One is as good as the other.

ゆうわく 東京には若者が身を滅ぼすような誘惑が多い. There are numerous temptations in Tokyo which often lead young people to ruin. / 彼は簡単にこの誘惑に負けてしまった. He fell an easy prey to the temptation.

ゆえん¹ ここにその名のあるゆえんがある. 《文》 Hence (comes) its name. | That is where it gets its name from. | This is why it is so named [called].

ゆかい 実に愉快だった. I had a really good time. | I enjoyed myself very much. | 人く釣れさえすれば釣りはなかなか愉快なものですよ. Angling is good fun when you have a good catch [take]. /

ゆがめる 歪める warp; distort; twist 《曲げる》crook; bend; curve ¶顔をゆがめる〈しかめ面をする〉make a grimace [wry face]; grimace /《痛みなどで》one's face is distorted [contorted]《with pain》/ 口をゆがめる〈軽蔑して〉curl one's lip / 口をゆがめて with a wry mouth / 事実をゆがめる distort [twist] the facts; twist the truth. 文例も

ゆかり 縁〈縁故〉(a) connection;《文》(a) relation;〈知り合い〉《文》acquaintance ¶芭蕉ゆかりの地 a place that is famous [remembered] in connection [for its associations] with Basho. 文例も

ゆかん 湯灌 ¶湯灌をする wash a dead body (for burial).

ゆき[1] ⇒いき[2].

ゆき[2] 裄 the sleeve length ¶ゆきが短い the sleeves 《of a shirt》 are too short; be short in the sleeves.

ゆき[3] 雪 snow; a snowfall (降雪) ¶固まった雪 packed snow / 《表面が凍って》固くなった雪 crusted [ice-encrusted] snow / 雪の結晶 a snow crystal / 雪の照り返しのぎらぎらする光 (a) snow glare (★複数にはしない) / 雪をかく rake [shovel] away snow; clear《a street》of snow / 雪に埋もれる be buried under [in] the snow; be snowed under /《雪に閉じこめられる》be snowed up [in]; be snowbound / 雪明かり (by) snow light /《ヒマラヤの雪男》an abominable snowman;《チベット語》a yeti / 雪折れする break under the weight of snow / 雪下ろしをする clear [remove] the snow from the roof 《of one's house》; shovel the snow off the housetop / 雪囲い a shelter to protect 《a house, a plant》 from snow / 雪靴 snow boots / 雪国 snow(y) country / 雪景色 a snow scene; a snowscape / 雪煙 smoke of snow / 雪だまり a snowdrift / 雪空 a snowy (leaden) sky / 雪降り a snowfall / 雪祭り the Snow Festival / 雪眼鏡 (a pair of) snow goggles [spectacles]. 文例も

ゆきあう 行き合う ⇒いきあう.

ゆきあたりばったり 行き当たりばったり ⇒いきあたりばったり.

ゆきかう 行き交う come and go ¶人や車の行き交う道 a busy street; a crowded (traffic-laden) street.

ゆきかえり 往き帰り ⇒おうふく.

ゆきがかり 行き掛かり ⇒いきがかり.

ゆきかき 雪掻き《道具》a snow shovel [scraper, pusher] ¶雪かきをする shovel [rake] (away) the snow《off, from the road》; clear《the road》of snow.

ゆきがけ 行き掛け ⇒いきがけ.

ゆきかた 行き方 ⇒いきかた[2].

ゆきがっせん 雪合戦 a snowball fight; snow-balling ¶雪合戦をする have a snowball fight; snowball.

ゆきき 往き来 ⇒いきき.

ゆきくれる 行き暮れる be (left) stranded; be overtaken by (the gathering) darkness;《文》 be benighted.

ゆきさき 行き先 ⇒いきさき.

ゆきすぎる 行き過ぎる ⇒いきすぎる.

ゆきずり 行きずり ¶行きずりの passing; casual 《passers-by》; 《a man》who happens to be passing [to pass by].

ゆきだおれ 行き倒れ ⇒いきだおれ.

ゆきだるま 雪達磨 (make) a snowman ¶雪だるま式に大きくなる snowball; increase [grow, expand, multiply] at a rapidly accelerating rate.

ゆきちがい 行き違い ⇒いきちがい.

ゆきつく 行き着く ⇒いきつく.

ゆきつけ 行き付け ⇒いきつけ.

ゆきづまり 行き詰まり ⇒いきづまり.

ゆきづまる 行き詰まる ⇒いきづまる[1].

ゆきつもどりつ 行きつ戻りつ ¶行きつ戻りつする walk up and down 《the platform》; walk to and fro.

ゆきどけ 雪解け a thaw; thawing ★thawは「氷が解ける」にも使える ¶雪解けの時には at [in] the time of the melting snow(s); when the thaw comes; when the snow thaws / 雪解けの道 a slushy road / 雪解け水 melt-water; snow-water.

ゆきどころ 行き所 ⇒いきどころ.

ゆきとどく 行き届く ⇒いきとどく.

ゆきどまり 行き止まり ⇒いきどまり.

ゆきなげ 雪投げ ⇒ゆきがっせん.

ゆきなやみ 行き悩み 《文》an impasse; a standstill;《交渉などの》a deadlock.

ゆきなやむ 行き悩む make no progress;《文》 reach [be in] an impasse;〈交渉などが〉be deadlocked.

ゆきのした 雪の下〔植〕a creeping [strawberry] saxifrage; a strawberry geranium.

愉快に休暇を過ごしています。I am enjoying the holidays. | I am having a pleasant vacation.

ゆがめる 話を聞きながら彼は苦痛で顔をゆがめました。His face twisted with pain as he heard what had happened. | His face twisted with distress at what he was hearing. | あなた、ネクタイがゆがんでいますよ。Your tie is crooked [not straight], dear.

ゆかり あの人は僕には縁もゆかりもない。I have no connection whatever with him. | He is an utter stranger to me.

ゆき[3] 雪が降っている。It is snowing. | Snow is falling. / 明日は雪だろう。It will probably snow tomorrow. / こぞの雪いずこにありや。Where are the snows of yesteryear? / 雪が厚く〔70センチも〕積もっていた。The snow lay thick 〔seventy centimeters deep〕on the ground. / 雪はさらさらと降った。The snow came sifting down. / 5、6 センチの雪が一日中消えずに積もっていました。Five or six centimeters of snow re-mained [stayed] on the ground the whole day (through). / 靴に雪がついて歩きにくい。The snow has clogged my shoes. / 雨が雪になった。The rain turned to snow. | It has ceased to rain and is now beginning to snow. / 空は雪模様だ。It is threatening to snow. | It looks like snow. / 頂上は一年中雪をいただいている。The summit of the mountain is covered with eternal [perennial] snow. / 今年は雪が多かった。We have had a lot of snow this year. /

ゆきみ 雪見 snow-scene viewing ¶雪見に行く go 《to Hakone》 to see [view] the beautiful snow-clad scenery.

ゆきめ 雪眼 snow-blindness ¶雪眼になった snow-blind(ed).

ゆきやけ 雪焼け ¶雪焼けする be [get] tanned [burned] by the snow; be [get] snow-tanned[-burned] / 雪焼けした snow-tanned[-burned] 《faces》.

ゆきよけ 雪除け 〈雪囲い〉 a snow fence; a shelter (to protect 《a house》 from snow); a snowshed (鉄道の) / 〈防雪林〉 a snowbreak; 〈そりなどの〉 a dashboard.

ゆきわたる 行き渡る ⇨ いきわたる.

ゆきわりそう 雪割り草 [植] a mealy primrose.

ゆく¹ 行く ⇨ いく ¶行く水 running water / 行く春《文》the departing spring / 行く年を送る see the old year out. 文例↓

ゆく² 逝く die; pass away ⇨ しぬ.

ゆくえ 行方 the place (where) sb has gone; sb's whereabouts ¶行方不明である be missing; be lost; 〈消息がない〉 nothing more is heard of sb; 〈文〉 be heard of no more / 行方をくらます《文》conceal oneself; disappear / 行方を捜す trace; search [hunt] for sb / 行方を突きとめる find out sb's whereabouts [hiding place] / 行方定めぬ wandering 《travelers》. 文例↓

ゆくすえ 行く末 the [one's] future ¶行く末を案じる feel [be] anxious about sb's future / 行く末長く for ever (and ever). 文例↓

ゆくて 行く手 one's way [《文》path] ¶行く手を遮る 〈遮る人又は物が主語〉 bar [stand in] one's way. 文例↓

ゆくゆく 行く行く ¶行く行くは in time; eventually; in good time;《文》in (the) course of time; in (the) future; some day.

ゆくりなく unexpectedly; 《文》by a happy chance.

ゆげ 湯気 steam; vapor ¶湯気が立つ[を立てる] steam; give off [send up] steam / 湯気の立っている料理 a steaming dish / 湯気を立てて怒る boil with rage [get boiling mad] 《at》;《口語》blow one's top / 湯気にぬれた steamy 《windows》. 文例↓

ゆけつ 輸血 (a) blood transfusion ¶輸血をする give sb a blood transfusion; give a blood transfusion (to); transfuse sb's blood (into a patient》/ O 型の血を輸血する transfuse 《a patient》with type O blood. 文例↓

ゆけむり 湯煙 clouds of (white) steam; vapor.

ゆさぶり 揺さぶり ¶揺さぶりをかける try to unsettle sb; try to put [throw] sb off (his) balance; stir things up [stir up trouble] for sb.

ゆさぶる 揺さぶる 〈揺する〉 shake; jolt; 〈ぐらつかせる〉 undermine; undercut.

ゆざまし 湯冷まし (cooled) boiled water.

ゆざめ ¶湯冷めする feel cold [a chill] after a bath.

ゆさん 遊山 a pleasure trip; a picnic; an excursion; an outing ¶遊山に行く go on a picnic; go on [make] an excursion / 遊山客 a holidaymaker; a picnicker / 遊山気分で in a holiday mood.

ゆし¹ 油脂 oils and fats ¶油脂工業 the oil and fat (manufacturing) industry.

ゆし² 諭旨 ¶諭旨免職になる be asked to resign [《文》tender one's resignation].

ゆしゅつ 輸出 export; exportation ¶輸出する export; ship abroad / 輸出価格 an export price / 輸出禁止 a trade embargo (on arms) / 輸出商 an exporter; an export merchant [trader] / 輸出超過 an excess of exports over imports; a favorable balance of trade / 輸出入 import and export / 輸出入のギャップ a trade gap / 輸出品 exports; export(ed) goods [commodities, articles] / 輸出貿易 export trade. 文例↓

ゆず 柚子 [植] a citron; a Chinese lemon.

ゆすぐ 濯ぐ wash out; rinse; give sth a rinse ¶口をゆすぐ rinse [wash out] one's mouth.

ゆすぶる 揺すぶる shake; joggle; jolt ⇨ ゆする² ¶根底から揺すぶる rock [shake] sth to its foundation(s) / 肩を揺すぶる shake sb by the shoulder(s) / 感情的に揺すぶる《文》sway sb emotionally; agitate.

ゆすり 強請 〈行為〉 extortion; blackmail(ing); 〈人〉 a blackmailer.

ゆずりあい 譲り合い give-and-take;《文》mutual concessions; 〈妥協〉 a compromise ¶譲り合いで by mutual concessions.

ゆずりあう 譲り合う give and take;《文》make mutual concessions; meet each other halfway ¶道を譲り合う say 'after you' to each other / 譲り合って《文》by (means of) mutual concessions.

ここでは3月に雪がとける. The snow thaws in March here.
ゆきどけ 雪解けになった. A thaw has set in. / 雪解けも間近いことだろう. It will not be long before we have a thaw. / 雪解けで川の水かさが急に増した. The melting snow caused a sudden rise in (the level) of the river.
ゆく¹ 彼は行くとして可ならずはない. He is equal to whatever task he undertakes. | He does a very good job of whatever he takes on.

ゆくえ 父の行方はわからなかった. My father's whereabouts were [was] unknown. / まだ 3 名行方がわからない. Three people are still unaccounted [not accounted] for.
ゆくすえ せがれは行末どうなるやら心細い. I have misgivings about my son's future.
ゆくて 一行の行く手にバスが 1 台見えて来た. They saw a bus ahead of them.
ゆげ やかんがストーブの上で湯気を立てていた. The kettle was steaming on the fire.
ゆけつ 輸血で命を取り留めた. A blood transfusion saved my life.
ゆしゅつ イスラエルは農産物輸出国である. Israel is an exporter of farm produce. / 彼らは輸出入業で財を成した. They made a fortune in the export-import business [trade]. / 日本は 1974 年以来輸出超過である. Japan has had a trade surplus since 1974. / Exports exceed imports by [There is an excess of exports over

ゆずりうける 譲り受ける take over; 〈継承する〉inherit; succeed 《to》; 〈買う〉buy; 《文》purchase ¶譲り受け人 a transferee; an assignee. 「ment ⇨じょうと.
ゆずりわたし 譲り渡し transfer; 《文》assign-
ゆずりわたす 譲り渡す ⇨ゆずる, じょうと.
ゆする¹ 強請る extort 《money from sb》; 〈脅迫する〉blackmail.
ゆする² 揺する shake; give sth a shake; rock (いす・揺りかごを); swing (ぶらんこ・振り子を); roll (横に); joggle (がたごと小刻みに) ¶赤ん坊を揺すって寝付かす rock a baby to sleep.
ゆずる 譲る 〈譲渡する〉give; hand [turn] over; transfer; 《文》devolve; 〈手放す〉give up; part with; 〈売る〉sell; 〈劣る〉《文》be inferior to; 〈譲歩する〉give way to; 《文》yield [concede] to; 〈議論のうえで〉譲らない hold [stand] one's ground / …にかけては何人にも譲らない be second to none 《in》. 文例⬇
ゆせい¹ 油井 an oil well.
ゆせい² 油性 ¶油性の oily; oleaginous.
ゆせいかん 輸精管 〔解〕the vas deferens 《pl. vasa deferentia》; the spermatic duct.
ゆそう¹ 油槽 an oil tank ¶油槽トラック an oil tank truck.
ゆそう² 輸送 transport; transportation; 《文》conveyance ¶輸送する 《文》convey; transport; carry / 輸送中である be in transit [under shipment] 《to》/ 大量輸送 mass transport / 輸送機関 (means of) transport / 輸送機 [船] a transport (plane [ship]) / 大型輸送機 a sky truck / 輸送費 transport(ation) costs / 輸送量 (volume of) traffic; 《米》carloadings (貨物の) / 輸送力 carrying power; transportation [carrying] capacity. 文例⬇
ゆそうかん 油送管 an oil pipe; an oil pipeline (油送管路). 文例⬇
ゆそうせん 油送船 a [an oil] tanker ¶大型油送船 a mammoth tanker; a supertanker.
ユタ Utah (略: Ut.) ¶ユタ州の人 a Utahan; a Utahn.
ゆたか 豊か ¶豊かな〈多くの〉rich; 《文》abundant; affluent; plentiful; 《文》ample; 〈富んだ〉rich; wealthy; well-to-do; well-off / 豊かな社会 the affluent society / 豊かな想像力 fertile imagination / 豊かに 《文》abundantly; richly; 《文》plentifully; 《文》amply / 豊かに暮らす be well [comfortably] off; be in easy circumstances; 《文》live in affluence / 水産物が豊かである be rich [abundant] in marine products. 文例⬇
ゆだねる 委ねる 《文》entrust 《sth to sb, sb with sth》; 《文》charge 《sb with sth》; leave 《sth to sb, sth in sb's care》; put sth into sb's hands ¶身をゆだねる devote [give] oneself (completely) (to).
ユダヤ Judea ¶ユダヤの Jewish / ユダヤ教 Judaism / ユダヤ人 a (wandering) Jew / ユダヤ人町 a ghetto 《pl. -(e)s》.
ゆだん 油断 〈怠慢〉neglect; 《文》negligence; 〈不注意〉《文》inattention; carelessness; 〈不用意〉《文》unpreparedness ¶油断する〈警戒を怠る〉relax one's guard; be off one's guard (toward); 〈不注意である〉be inattentive; be careless; 《文》be negligent / 油断しない〈警戒する〉be on one's guard (against); be on the alert [lookout] (for); have [keep] one's wits about one; 〈注意する〉《文》be careful (about); 《文》use caution (in) / 油断させる throw [put] sb off his guard / 油断しているところを襲う catch sb off guard / 油断のない〈警戒の厳しい〉watchful; alert; guarded; 〈注意深い〉careful; cautious; 《文》vigilant / 油断のならない cunning; sly; tricky; 《文》insidious; treacherous; full of danger. 文例⬇
ゆたんぽ 湯たんぽ a hot-water bottle [bag]; a foot warmer ¶湯たんぽを入れる put a hot-water bottle in the bed.
ゆちゃく 癒着 〔医〕adhesion; conglutination ¶癒着する adhere (to); knit together; unite; conglutinate; heal up / 政府と財界との癒着 a back-scratching alliance of government and big business; a cozy relationship between politics and business. 文例⬇
ゆっくり slowly; unhurriedly; without (any) hurry; 〈悠長に〉leisurely; at a slow speed; 〈悠長に〉leisurely; at one's leisure ¶ゆっくりする〈仕事など〉take one's time (in doing); take it easy; 〈訪問して〉stay long / ゆっくり

imports of] about 100,000,000 dollars.
ゆずる 一部譲ってくれませんか. Can you spare me a copy? / その話は他日に譲ることにしよう. Let's take it up [go into it] some other day. / 彼は一歩も譲ろうとしない. He will make no concessions. | 一歩も譲って君の主張が事実だとしても, 職務怠慢の言い訳にはならないよ. Granted that [Even if] your statement is true, it is no excuse for neglecting your duties. / 彼は息子に商売を譲った. He handed over his business to his son.
ゆそう² 今年の国鉄の輸送量は前年度よりもはるかに多かった. The National Railways handled far more traffic this year than last.
ゆそうかん ここから海の港まで100キロにわたり油送管が通っている. A pipeline runs for a hundred kilometers from here to the seaport.
ゆたか 彼女は豊かな黒髪を背に垂らしていた. She had an abundance of dark hair hanging down her back. / この地方では大地は豊かな実りをあげてくれる. In these regions, the earth gives plentifully of her blessings [bestows her gifts in plenty]. / 彼は6尺豊かの大男だ. He's [He stands] six feet tall if he's an inch. | He is easily six feet tall.
ゆだん 油断は禁物だよ. You've got to be on your guard [toes]. / あの男には油断をするな. Don't take your eyes off him. | You must keep a strict watch on him. / 油断大敵. A little neglect may breed great mischief.
ゆちゃく 兵器製造業者と政府高官が癒着していると非難された. The arms manufacturers and senior government officials were accused of being in each other's pockets.
ゆっくり どうぞごゆっくり. Please take your time. | Please don't hurry. | 〈訪問客に〉Please make

考える take time to think; stop to think; ponder over 《a matter》. 文例↓

ゆったり ¶ゆったりした〈着物など〉loose; 〈気持ちなど〉calm; unhurried; leisurely;《文》composed ¶ゆったりした仕立ての loosely tailored《fur garments》/ ゆったりした気持ちになる feel easy [comfortable, at home, at ease] / ゆったりとして at one's ease;《文》composedly.

ゆでだこ 茹でだこ (a) boiled octopus. 文例↓

ゆでる 茹でる boil ¶ゆで玉子 a boiled egg.

ゆでん 油田 an oil field [well].

ゆどうふ 湯豆腐 tofu cooked in boiling water.

ゆどの 湯殿 a bathroom.

ゆとり ⇨ よゆう.

ユニーク ¶ユニークな unique;《be》(quite) out of the ordinary run ¶日本語では「一風変わった」「珍しい」ぐらいの意味で使われるが、英語の unique は「他に類がない」「唯一の」の意味に限られる。従って、very [rather] unique などと程度を表わす副詞と共に使うことも避けるべきである。

ユニセフ UNICEF ★ the United Nations International Children's Emergency Fund の略。ただし現在では the United Nations Children's Fund と改称されたが、略称はもとのままで用いられている。

ユニット a unit ¶ユニット家具 sectional [modular] furniture.

ユニバーシアード the Universiade.

ユニホーム a uniform ¶ユニホーム姿の《a player》in uniform.

ゆにゅう 輸入 import; importation;〈文物の〉introduction ¶輸入する import; introduce / 外国からの輸入 the importation《of food》from abroad; foreign imports / 輸入業者 an importer; an import merchant [trader]; an importing firm / 輸入許可制 the import licensing system / 輸入税 taxes on imports; an import tax [duty] / 輸入制限 an import restriction; a curb on imports / 輸入超過 an excess of imports over exports; an unfavorable balance of trade; an import surplus / 輸入品 imports; imported goods [commodities] / 輸入貿易 import trade. 文例↓

ゆにょうかん 輸尿管 【解】the ureter.

ユネスコ UNESCO ★ the United Nations Educational, Scientific and Cultural Organization の略 ¶ユネスコ憲章 the UNESCO Constitution.

ゆのし 湯熨 ¶湯のしをかける smooth《cloth》with steam; steam and iron [press]《cloth》.

ゆのはな 湯の花 sinter; geyserite; flowers of sulfur.

ゆのみ 湯飲み a teacup; a cup.

ゆび 指〈手の〉a finger;〈親指〉the thumb;〈足の〉a toe ¶手の5本の指は five fingers または four fingers and one thumb. 手足のすべての指を意味する語は digit だが、日常の用語ではない ¶両手の指を組み合わせる lace [hook] one's fingers together; interlace one's fingers; clasp one's hands / 指をくわえて a finger in one's mouth;〈うらやましそうに〉(look) enviously《at sth》/ 指をさす ⇨ ゆびさす /（幼児が）指をしゃぶる suck one's thumb [finger(s)] / 指を鳴らす〈はじいて〉snap [click] one's fingers [finger and thumb] /〈関節を引っ張って〉crack one's finger joints / 指で[を折って]数える count (off) on one's fingers / 指でさわる put [《文》lay] one's finger《on》; finger / 指跡 a《dirty》finger mark [fingerprint]; a thumbmark《親指の》/ 指跡のたくさんついた badly-thumbed《books》/ 指絵 (a) finger painting / 指先 the tip of a finger; a fingertip / 指先の器用な clever with one's fingers; nimble-fingered / 指サック〈親指以外の〉a fingerstall;〈親指の〉a thumbstall / 指使い〈楽器演奏の〉fingering / 指人形 a glove [hand] puppet. 文例↓

ゆびおり 指折り ¶指折りの leading;《文》preeminent; distinguished / 指折り数える count on one's fingers / 指折り数えて待つ look forward《to》; wait eagerly《for》. 文例↓

ゆびきり 指切り ¶指切りをする〈自分が主語〉link little fingers with sb to confirm [emphasize] a promise;〈双方が主語〉link little fingers to confirm [emphasize] a promise. 文例↓

ゆびさす 指差す point《to, at》; indicate ¶人差し指で指差す point one's forefinger《at》. 文例↓

---

yourself at home. / この次はぜひゆっくりしたまえ。You must stay longer next time. / もっとゆっくりできなくて残念でした。It's too bad we didn't have more time to visit. / その事についてはゆっくり考えるがいい。You may think over the matter at your leisure. / ゆっくり間に合った。We arrived there in plenty of time [in ample time]. / We got there with time to spare. / そんなことは後でゆっくりやれるんだから、今は席に着いて食事にしなさい。You'll have plenty of time to do that later; sit down at the table now and have a meal.

ゆでだこ 熱い湯にゆっくりつかって、彼はゆでだこのように赤くなって出て来た。After a long soak in the hot bath, he came out lobster-pink [as red as a lobster].

ゆにゅう 英国は昔から輸入超過を続けてきた。England has always run a trade deficit. / 先月の外国貿易は400万ドルの輸入超過を見た。The balance of foreign trade for last month showed an excess of imports [a deficit] of 4,000,000 dollars.

ゆび 指を揃えて。Close your fingers. / そんな人は5本の指で数えるほどしかいない。Men like that [him] can be counted on the fingers of one hand. / 当代一流の画家といえば何人もまず彼に指を屈する。He is accepted [recognized] as one of the master painters of the day. / ほかの人から指一本指されないように努めました。I did my best to make it as nearly perfect as could be.

ゆびおり コリンズ氏はこの町では指折りの資産家です。Mr. Collins is one of the wealthiest citizens of the town.

ゆびきり 2人は再会を誓って指切りをした。They promised to meet again and confirmed the promise by linking their little fingers.

ゆびさす 人を指差したりするのは

ゆびぬき 指貫き a thimble.

ゆびわ 指輪 a (finger) ring ¶指輪をはめる put a ring on (one's) finger / 指輪をはめている have [wear] a ring on one's finger / 指輪をぬく take a ring off (one's) finger / 金[ダイヤモンド]の指輪 a gold [diamond] ring / 結婚[婚約]指輪 a wedding [an engagement] ring.

ゆぶね 湯船 a bathtub ; a bath.

ゆみ 弓 a bow ; 〈弓術〉 archery ¶弓の名人 a master [an expert] archer / 〈弦楽器の〉弓を使う use the [one's] bow (in playing the violin) ; 弓を引く draw [bend] a bow / 〈反抗する〉 rebel [turn, rise in revolt] 《against》 / 弓なりになる 〈物が〉 arch ; be curved ; 〈人が〉 bend [lean] backward ; arch one's body backward / 弓なりの arched ; 《文》 bowed / 弓矢 a bow and arrow.

ゆみず 湯水 ¶湯水のように使う spend [squander, waste] 《money》 like water ; play ducks and drakes with (one's money) ; throw (money) about ; scatter (money) to the winds.

ゆめ 夢 a dream ; 〈幻想〉 a vision ; an illusion ; 《文》 a reverie ; 〈白昼夢〉 a daydream ¶夢が覚める wake from sleep [a dream] ; 《文》 awake from one's reverie ; come to one's senses ; 〈迷いから〉 be disillusioned / 夢のような dreamy ; dreamlike / 夢のように like [as in] a dream / 夢の国а dreamland ; a cloudland ; a utopia / 夢の分析 《精神分析》 (a) dream analysis / 夢を追う chase a dream / 夢を見る dream ; have [dream] a dream / 夢を覚ます awaken [rouse] sb from sleep / 〈迷いから〉 disillusion / …を夢に見る, …の夢を見る see sth in a dream ; dream of [about] … / …とは夢にも思わない never [《文》 little] dream that … / 夢ではないかと身をつねる pinch oneself to make sure that one is not dreaming [that one is awake] / 一生を夢と過ごす dream away one's life / 夢うつつに half awake (and half asleep) ; between asleep and awake / 夢占い divination by means of dreams ; oneiromancy / 〈夢判断〉 oneirocriticism / 夢占いをしてもらう have (a diviner) tell one's fortune through one's dreams / 夢心地で as if one was [《文》 were] in a dream ; 〈有頂天になって〉 as if one was [《文》 were] treading [walking] on air / 夢まくらに立つ appear to one in a [one's] dream ; appear to one in one's sleep / 作家になることを夢見る dream of becoming a writer / 夢見るような眼差し a faraway look / 夢見るような眼差しの starry-eyed ; dreamy-eyed / 夢物語 〈空想的な話〉 a fantastic story ; a wild tale. 文例⇩

ゆめゆめ 夢々 never ; not in the least ; on no account ; by no means.

ゆもと 湯元 the source of a hot spring.

ゆゆしい 由々しい serious ; alarming ¶ゆゆしい事態 a serious [《文》 grave] situation.

ゆらい 由来 〈起源〉 the origin ; 〈来歴〉 the history ; 〈出処〉 the source ; 〈もともと〉 originally ; from the first [start] ¶由来する result [stem] 《from》 ; 《文》 originate (in) ; 〈言葉などが〉 be derived 《from》 ; 〈時代から〉 date back (to) / 由来を尋ねる trace sth to its origin(s) ; 《文》 inquire into the origin(s) 《of》. 文例⇩

ゆらぐ 揺らぐ 〈揺れる〉 swing ; sway ; shake ; 〈炎が〉 waver ; flicker ; quiver ; 〈心が〉 waver ; 《文》 vacillate.

ゆらめく 揺らめく 〈炎が〉 waver ; flicker ; quiver ; sway to and fro.

ゆらゆら ¶ゆらゆらする ⇨ ゆれる.

ゆりかんかん 輸卵管 ⇨ らんかん[1].

ゆり 百合 〈植〉 a lily ¶百合根 a lily bulb.

ゆりうごかす 揺り動かす ⇨ ゆるがす.

ゆりおこす 揺り起こす shake sb out of sleep ; shake sb awake ; wake sb by shaking him.

ゆりおとす 揺り落とす shake 《persimmons》 off 《the tree》 ; shake 《fruit》 down from 《a tree》.

ゆりかえし 揺り返し 〈地震の〉 an aftershock.

ゆりかご 揺り籠 a (baby) cradle ⇨ ようらん[2] ¶揺りかごに入れて揺する rock 《a child》 in a cradle / 揺りかごから墓場まで from (the) cradle to (the) grave.

ゆるい 緩い loose ; slack ; lax ; 〈寛大な〉 generous ; lenient ; 〈遅い〉 slow ; 〈傾斜が〉 gentle ; 〈だらけた〉 slack ; lax ¶便が緩い have loose bowels / 緩い結び目 a loose knot / 緩く loosely ; 〈寛大に〉 generously ; leniently ; 〈遅く〉 slowly / 緩くなる ⇨ ゆるむ.

ゆるがす 揺るがす shake ; sway ; 〈驚かす〉 shock ¶世界を揺るがす大事件 a world-shaking event ; an event that shakes [jolts

---

失礼なことだ. It is bad manners to point at other people.

ゆみ 彼の神経は弓の弦のようにぴんと張りつめていた. His nerves were as tight as a drawn bowstring.

ゆめ 僕は昨夜面白い[いやな]夢を見た. I had a funny [bad] dream last night. / ダイヤの指輪を拾った夢を見た. I dreamed [had a dream in which] I picked up a diamond ring. / 母の姿を見て夢かとばかり喜んだ. I could scarcely believe my eyes when I saw my mother. / 夢のような話だ. It sounds [It is almost] too good to be true. / 君にここで会おうとは夢にも思わなかった. I never dreamed [Little did I dream] that I should see you here. / そんなことがあろうとは夢にも思わなかった. It was the last thing that I expected to happen. / 新市長は町にはその夢を持っている. The new mayor has a dream for his town. / 近頃の青年には夢がない. Young people today have lost all sense of adventure [have no ambition]. / 今の若者たちは夢が正[逆]夢だった. The dream came true [turned out false]. / 昨夜の夢見が悪かった. The dream I had last night boded ill.

ゆらい 君が禁酒した由来を聞かせてくれ. Tell me how you came to give up drinking. / 無政府主義はロシヤに由来している. Anarchism had its origin [originated] in Russia.

ゆるし だれの許しを得てこの部屋へ入ったのか. Who permitted you [gave you leave] to enter this room?

ゆるす「ほかの人のことは何を言おうと君たちの勝手だが私のいるところでミリアムのことをあれこ

ゆるがせ 忽せ ⇨ おろそか.

ゆるぎ 揺るぎ ¶揺るぎない firm; solid; secure; steady;《文》impregnable《defenses》/ 揺るぎなく firmly; securely.

ゆるし 許し 〈許可〉permission; leave;〈賛成〉approval;《文》sanction;〈免許〉《文》license;〈免除〉(an) exemption;〈容赦〉《文》pardon; forgiveness;〈放免〉release; discharge ¶許しを受ける〈許可〉get [have] permission [leave]《to do》;〈容赦〉be forgiven《by》;《文》obtain sb's pardon [forgiveness]《for》/ 許しをこう〈許可〉ask for permisson [leave]《to do》;〈謝罪〉beg [《文》seek] sb's pardon [forgiveness] / 許しを得て with sb's permission [leave]. 文例⇩

ゆるす 許す 〈許可する〉allow sb to do; let sb do;《文》permit; give sb leave [permission]; give one's approval《to》;〈免許する〉《文》license; authorize;〈余地がある〉《文》admit of;〈資力がある〉can afford;〈認める〉admit; acknowledge;〈免除する〉exempt《from》;《文》remit《from》;〈心などを〉trust; confide in;〈容赦する〉forgive; pardon; excuse;〈黙許する〉tolerate;〈見過ごす〉overlook;〈放免する〉release; acquit; let sb go ¶時間[事情]の許す限り so far as time permits [circumstances permit] / 紙面の許す限り to the limit of space / 天候が許すならば weather permitting; if the weather permits / 過失を許す forgive sb (for) his mistake / 願いを許す grant [allow] sb's request; give one's approval to sb's request / 入学を許される be admitted《into a school》; be matriculated《in a university》/ 遅延を許さない《文》admit of no delay / ちょっと気を許したすきに in an unguarded moment / 許し難い unpardonable; inexcusable. 文例⇩

ゆるみ 緩み relaxation; looseness; slackness. 文例⇩

ゆるむ 緩む loosen; come [get,《文》become] loose;〈痛みなどが〉abate; lessen;〈心などが〉relax; slack [slacken] (off). 文例⇩

ゆるめる 緩める loosen; relax; let loose;〈締めてあったものを〉unfasten;〈調子・速力を〉slack(en); slow [tone] down;〈和らげる〉《文》mitigate;《文》moderate;《文》abate; ease (up) ¶手を緩める loosen one's hold [grasp]《of》/ 警戒を緩める lower [be off] one's guard《against》;《文》relax one's vigilance《over》/ 歩調を緩める relax [slow down] one's pace. 文例⇩

ゆるやか 緩やか ¶緩やかな〈緩い〉loose; slack;〈寛大な〉lenient; lax; generous / 緩やかな坂 a gentle [an easy] slope / 緩やかに〈寛大に〉leniently;《文》with lenience; generously;《文》liberally / 緩やかに流れる川 a slow-moving river / 緩やかにする make《the rules》less severe; moderate; relax; slack(en); ease off.

ゆるゆる ⇨ ゆっくり.

ゆるり ⇨ ゆっくり.

ゆれ 揺れ shaking; a shake;〈震動〉(a) vibration;〈大などの〉flickering; a flicker;〈地震の〉a quake; a tremor;〈船の〉pitching (縦揺れ); rolling (横揺れ);〈車の〉jolting. 文例⇩

ゆれる 揺れる shake; sway; quake;〈船などが〉pitch (縦に); roll (左右に); rock (前後に); toss (上下に);〈震動する〉tremble; vibrate;〈乗り物が〉jolt; joggle (軽く);〈つるしたものが〉swing;〈火が〉waver; flicker ¶(地震が) 横に揺れる vibrate laterally. 文例⇩

ゆわえつける 結わえ付ける tie sth on《a tree》.

ゆわかし 湯沸かし a teakettle; a kettle ¶自動湯沸かし器 a hot-water heater;《英》a geyser / 瞬間湯沸かし器 an instantaneous (hot-) water heater.

れ言うことは許さない」と彼は言った. He said, "You can say what you like about anyone else, but no one is going to criticize Miriam in front of me." / この庭園は一般の入場を許している. This garden is open to the public. / そんなぜいたくな旅行は僕の財政が許さない. I cannot afford such an expensive journey. / 彼は一世の学者をもって自他共に許している. He is acknowledged as the greatest scholar of the day. / この問題はそのような安易な解決を許さない. The problem does not permit [allow] (of) such an easy solution. / 相手チームにヒット3本を許しただけであった. He allowed only three hits to the opposing team. / 彼のしたことは罪は罪でも許すべき罪である. If what he did was a sin, it was a venial one. / 今回だけは欠席をお許し頂きたい. I want to be excused from attending the meeting for this once.

ゆるみ 気の緩みがあったからだ. It's because you weren't alert enough [didn't keep on your toes].

ゆるむ 3月の声を聞いて寒さがめっきり緩んできた. The cold has abated remarkably since the beginning of March. / 警戒の目が少し緩むまで待った方がいいだろう. You'd better wait until their vigilance lets up [eases off] a little.

ゆるめる 綱を緩めちゃいかんぞ. Keep the rope tight. | Keep the rope (tightly) stretched.

ゆれ 揺れが大きくなった. The sway increased.

ゆれる 家の揺れるのを感じた. I felt the house shake. / 木の葉が風に揺れている. The leaves are trembling in the breeze.

よ

よ¹ 世, 代 〈世間〉 the world; the public; things; 〈生涯〉 life; 《文》 existence; 〈時世〉 the times; 〈時代〉 the age; the era; 〈治世〉 the reign ¶世が世なら in better times; 〈昔のままなら〉 if times had not changed / 世の習いthe way of the world; the way things are / 世の終わりまで till the end of time [the world] / 世のためになる work [be, 《文》 make] for the general good; do good / 世をすねる turn one's back on the world; become a cynic / 世を捨てる abandon 《文》 forsake, 《文》 renounce] the world / 世を去る die; 〈婉曲的に〉 pass away; 《文》 depart (from) this life / 世に出る go out into the world; start [(out) in] life / 〈出世する〉 go up [rise] in the world / 世に知られた [知られない] well-known [unknown] (in [to] the world); famous [obscure].

よ² 夜 (a) night; (an) evening ⇒ よる¹ ¶夜が明けないうちに ⇒ よあけ (夜明け前に) / 寝ずに夜を明かす sit up all (through the) night; pass a night without sleep / 夜を日についで 《work》 day and night; around the clock. 文例⇩

-よ¹ 余 〈以上〉 over; more than; 〈残り〉 the rest; the others ¶3マイル余 over [more than, upward of] three miles; three miles and more / 30余万 three hundred and some [odd] thousand.

-よ² 文例⇩

よあかし 夜明かし ¶夜明かしする sit [stay] up all night [the whole night through]; stay [keep] awake the whole night.

よあけ 夜明け dawn; daybreak ¶夜明けに[前に] at [before] dawn [daybreak]; at break of dawn [before it is light] / 夜明けと共に at first light; at the crack of dawn / 夜明け前の 《文》 predawn 《stillness》; 《the darkness》 before (the) dawn

よあそび 夜遊び ¶夜遊びする stay out (on the town) late at night.

よあつ 与圧 《機》 pressurization ¶与圧室 a pressurized cabin [chamber] / 与圧服 a pressurized [pressure] suit.

よあるき 夜歩き ¶夜歩きする go [stay] out late at night.

よい¹ 宵 the (early) evening ¶宵の明星 《文》 the evening star; Venus / 宵の口に early in the evening / 宵祭 the eve (of a festival) / 宵やみ the (evening) twilight; dusk. 文例⇩

よい² 酔い drunkenness; 《文》 intoxication ¶酔いが回る get drunk / よう³ / 酔いがさめる sober up; get 《文》 become] sober / 乗り物酔い motion sickness / 車酔い carsickness / 船酔い seasickness / 飛行機酔い airsickness 文例⇩

よい³ 良[善]い good; fine; nice; 〈優れた〉 excellent; superb; 〈適切な〉 apt; fit; 《文》 fitting; suitable; proper; 〈望ましい〉 preferable; 〈ためになる〉 good; 《文》 beneficial; 〈美しい〉 beautiful; pretty; lovely (★ lovely は天気について以外は女性専用語); 〈健康な〉 well ¶…してもよい 〈自分が〉 do not mind doing; 〈他人が〉 can [may] do (★ くだけた会話では may より can を使うのが普通) / …した方がよい had better do / …しなくてもよい need not do; do not have to do / …よりよい be better (than); 《文》 be superior (to) / 最もよい be the best / よい天気 fine [lovely, beautiful] weather / 善きにつけ悪しきにつけ for better or worse 《文》 good or ill]. 文例⇩

よいざめ 酔いざめ ¶酔いざめの水を飲む have a glass of water to relieve one's thirst after sobering up.

よいしょ Oof!; Yo-heave-ho! (船員語). 文例⇩

よいしれる 酔いしれる be fuddled ⇒ よいつぶれる.

よいっぱり 宵っ張り 〈人〉 a night owl; a night person ¶宵っ張りの朝寝坊 do stay up late at

---

よ¹ 彼のような学者は世にまれだ. A scholar like him is rarely (to be) found. / 世はまさにかくのごとし. This is the way of the world. / 世も末だ. There's no decency left in the world (when this sort of thing can happen).

よ² 5時に夜が明ける. Daylight [Morning] comes at five. | Day breaks [dawns] at five.

-よ¹ 日本は昔60余州に分かれていた. Japan used to be divided into sixty-odd provinces.

-よ² 気をつけるんですよ. Do be careful! / なくすんじゃないよ. Mind you don't lose it! / そんなに簡単じゃないんだよ. It is not so simple, I tell you. / 少しも怖いことなんかありゃしないよ. I (can) assure you there's nothing to be afraid of [to fear].

よあけ 朝, 夜明けと共に私たちは出かけた. In the morning, we set out as soon as it was daylight [at the crack of dawn].

よい¹ 宵やみ迫る頃になると恋人たちは公園の樹陰の小道に集まってくる. As dusk falls, the shady lanes of the park begin to fill with loving [courting] couples. / 彼は宵越しの銭は持たない男だ. What he earns by day he spends by night. / まだ宵の口だ. The night is (still) young.

よい² だんだん酔いが回ってきた. The wine gradually began to have its effect on [take hold of] him. / 彼は次第に酔いがさめてきた. He gradually sobered up. | The effects of the drink (inside him) began to wear off.

よい³ 日本ほど住みよい国はない. Japan is the best country to live in. / ちょっと知らせてくれたらよかったのに. You might have just let me know. / よかったらお持ち下さい. You can have it, if you like. / 昨日行けばよかったのに. You should [ought to] have gone there yesterday. / 会に出ればよかった. I wish I had been at the meeting. / 今日は来てよかった. I did well to come today. / その本を読んでいてよかったと思った. I was glad that I had read the book. / 皆無事でよかった. Thank Heaven [God] we are all safe.

よいしょ よいしょと椅子から立ち上がった. He lifted himself heav-

よいつぶす 酔いつぶす drink sb down [under the table].

よいつぶれる 酔いつぶれる be [get] dead [blind] drunk; pass out; be under the table ¶酔いつぶれて眠る drink *oneself* to sleep.

よいどれ 酔いどれ a drunk; a drunken man.

よいよい ⇒ちゅうき¹.

よいん 余韻《文》 reverberations; echoes; 〈味の〉 an aftertaste ¶余韻じょうじょうたる鐘の音 the lingering sound of a temple bell.

よう¹ 用〈用事〉business ⇒ようじ¹; 〈使用〉use;《文》service ¶用がある〈仕事がある〉have something to do; 〈忙しい〉be busy《with》; be engaged; 〈…に用事がある〉have business 《with》; want to speak to sb; need sb / 用がない〈仕事がない〉have nothing to do; 〈暇である〉be free; be not engaged;《文》be disengaged; 〈必要としない〉have no need 《of sb》/ be done [finished]《with sb》/ 用を足す〈仕事をする〉do *one*'s business; 〈使いに行く〉go on an errand; 〈小便を足す〉relieve *oneself*; have [get] a wash (婉曲に) / 用をなさない be useless; be no use;《文》be of no use; be no good / 屋根の用をする serve as [for] a roof / 様々の用に供せられる be used [《文》utilized] for various purposes / 婦人[紳士]用の for ladies [gentlemen]; ladies' [men's] (gloves) / 家庭用の for household [family] use. 文例⇩

よう² 要〈要点〉the (main [essential]) point ¶要は、要するに in a word;《文》in brief;《文》in short; the point is... / 要を得ている be to the point.

よう³ 洋 ¶洋の東西を問わず both in the East and the West [《文》the Orient and the Occident]; everywhere in the world.

よう⁴ 陽 the positive ⇒いん³.

よう⁵ 様〈仕方〉a way;《文》a manner; 〈種類〉a kind; a sort; 〈目的〉(so as) to *do*; in order to *do*; so [in order] that *one* may *do* ¶このような物 this sort [kind] of thing; a thing like this (★ things like this という複数の形で使うことが多い); things [anything, something] of this kind [sort] / 彼のような金持ちな a rich man like him / 《文》 such a rich man as he; a man of his wealth / 天使のような乙女 an angel of a girl / なんだか蛇のようなもの something like a snake / このように like this;《文》thus; in this way [《文》manner] / どのように how; in what way [《文》manner] / いつものように as usual;《文》as is *one*'s wont / 気違いのように走る run like mad / 氷のように冷たい (as) cold as ice; ice-cold; icy. 文例⇩

よう⁶ 曜 ⇒ようび.

よう⁷ 癰《医》a carbuncle.

よう⁸ 酔う get [be] drunk [tipsy,《文》intoxicated];《文》be in *one*'s cups; get [be] the worse for drink; 〈船・車に〉feel [be] sick ¶歓喜に酔う be ecstatically happy;《文》be in an ecstasy of happiness;《文》be intoxicated [inebriated] with delight / 乗り物に酔う suffer from motion sickness / 船[車, 飛行機]に酔う get [feel] seasick [carsick, airsick] / ビールに酔う get [be] drunk on beer / 酔っても乱れない can take [hold] *one*'s drink; can carry *one*'s liquor (like a gentleman). 文例⇩

用法「酒に酔う」のもっとも代表的表現は get [be] drunk. tipsy は非常に軽度の酔い. intoxicated はこれより少し強いがやや文語的. なお drunk は大体述部用法に限って使われ、名詞の前に付加する形は drunken. intoxicated は be intoxicated by the atmosphere 《of the party》(雰囲気に酔う)のように、比喩的に使うこともかなり多い.

よう⁹ 〈呼び掛け〉Hello!; Hallo!; 〈賞賛〉Well done!; Bravo!

ようい¹ 用意〈準備〉preparation(s);《文》preparedness; 〈手はず〉arrangement(s); 〈蓄え〉《文》(a) provision; 〈用心〉(a) precaution ¶用意する prepare 《for》; ready *oneself* 《for》; get ready [prepared] 《for》; make arrangements 《for》; provide 《for, against》/ 用意してある be ready [prepared] 《for》; have *sth* available; 〈物が主語〉be available; be on hand / 食事の用意をする prepare a meal; get a meal ready; 〈食器を並べる〉lay [set] the table / 用意周到な careful;《文》prudent. 文例⇩

ようい² 容易《文》ease;《文》facility ¶容易ily [heaved himself] out of his chair.

よう¹ 君は英語で用が足せるかい. Can you make yourself understood in English? / 英語を知っていれば世界中大抵どこへ行っても用が足りる. You can get along almost anywhere in the world if you know English. / 用があったら呼んでね. Call me when you want me. / ネズミを取らぬ猫には用がない. I have no use for a cat that can't catch mice. / 何の用ですか. What do you want me for [of me]? / もう僕には用がないと言うんだね. Do you mean to say that you are done [finished] with me? / ほかにこれといった用もないので彼は午前中は大抵そこで過ごしている. For want of anything better to do he spends most of his mornings there.

よう⁵ 遅刻しないようタクシーに乗った. I took a taxi to get there in time. / 私は僕がなくした のと同じような時計だ. This is just like the watch I lost. / 泣きたいような気がしました. I felt like crying. / 彼のようには英語を話せない. I can't speak English as well as him [as well as he can]. ⇒より². 用法 / もう以前のようにここから富士は見えない. We can no longer see Mt. Fuji from here as we used to. / 彼は何でも知っているような事を言う. He talks as if he knew everything. / それは直しようがないと彼は言っている. He says there is no way of mending it [no way it can be mended]. / 雨のようだ. It looks like rain. / もう残ってないようだ. There doesn't seem to be any left.

よう⁸ 私は船に酔わない〈酔う〉. I am a good [poor, bad] sailor. / 勝利に酔ってはいけない. Don't be too elated with [at] your victory.

ようい¹ 位置に就いて！用意！どん！ Ready! Steady! Go! | On your marks! Get set! Go! / もうすぐ夕飯の用意が出来ました. Dinner is ready. / 彼はいつでも次の手をちゃんと用意している. He always has another trick up his sleeve. / この血液銀行には現在1万人分の血液が用意されている. The blood bank now has blood

easy ; hands-down 《victories》; 〈簡単な〉 simple / 容易ならぬ事 a serious matter / 容易ならぬ事態 《文》a grave situation / 容易に easily ; 《文》with ease ; 《win》hands down ; without difficulty [trouble] ; 〈すぐに〉 readily ; 容易にする make sth easy ; 《文》facilitate ; 〈簡単にする〉 simplify / 容易に読める be easy 《for a young child》to read / 容易に怒らない be slow to anger [take offense]. 文例b

よういく 養育 ¶養育する bring up ; rear ; foster / 養育費 the expense [cost] of bringing up 《a child》.

よういん 要因 a primary factor ; a main cause.

よういん 要員 the personnel necessary [required] 《for sth》.

ようえき 用役《経済》services.

ようえき 溶液 a solution ¶希薄溶液《make》a dilute [weak] solution 《of ammonia》/ 濃溶液 a concentrated [strong] solution / 3千倍の硝酸銀溶液 a silver nitrate solution with a concentration [strength] of 1/3000 [1 to 3,000].

ようえん 妖艶 ¶ようえんな fascinating ; bewitching ; 《文》voluptuous (官能的な).

ようか 八日 〈8日間〉eight days ; 〈第8日〉the eighth 《of June》.

ようか 養家 an adoptive family.

ようが 洋画 (a) Western [European] painting ; (an) oil painting (油絵) ; 〈映画〉a foreign film ¶洋画家 an artist of Western painting ; an oil painter (油絵画家).

ようが 陽画《写真》a positive (picture).

ようかい 妖怪 a monstrous being [creature] ; a monster.

ようかい 容喙 ¶容喙する poke [《文》thrust] one's nose 《in》; interfere 《in》; meddle 《in》.

ようかい 溶解 melting ; solution ; dissolution ; fusion (金属の) ¶溶解する melt ; dissolve ; liquefy / 水にすぐ溶解する be readily soluble in water.

ようがい 要害 a fort ; a fortress ; 〈戦略上の要点〉a strategic point ; a strong point ¶要害堅固の strongly fortified ; 《文》impregnable.

ようがく 洋学 Western learning (introduced into Japan in the Edo period).

ようがく 洋楽 Western [European] music.

ようがし 洋菓子 (a) cake ; pastry ⇨ ケーキ ¶洋菓子屋 a cake [pastry] shop.

ようかん 羊羹 (a bar of) sweet jellied bean-paste.

ようがん 溶岩 lava ¶溶岩塊 a lava boulder / 溶岩層 a lava bed / 溶岩流 a stream of lava ; a lava flow.

ようき 妖気 a weird air [feeling]. 文例b

ようき 容器《文》a vessel ; a container ;《文》a receptacle.

ようき 陽気 〈時候〉a season ; 〈天候〉(the) weather ¶陽気な cheerful ; jovial ; merry ; gay ; lively / 陽気な人 a cheerful person ; a person with sunny [cheerful] disposition / 陽気に merrily ; cheerfully / 陽気に騒ぐ make merry / 陽気のせいで on account of [owing to] the weather. 文例b

ようぎ 容疑 suspicion ⇨ うたがい ¶容疑者 a suspected person ; a person under suspicion / 殺人の容疑者 a suspected murderer ; a murder suspect.

ようぎが 用器画 (an) instrumental [(a) mechanical] drawing.

ようきゅう 洋弓 〈弓〉a Western-style bow ; 〈術〉Western-style archery.

ようきゅう 要求 a demand ; a request ;《文》a requirement ; a claim ; 〈必要〉(a) need ¶要求する《文》request ;《文》require ; claim ; demand ; call on 《sb to do》/ 金を要求する demand money from [of] sb / ask sb for money ; make a demand on sb for money / 賃上げを要求する demand [call for] a raise in 《one's》 wages / 1万ドルの損害賠償を要求する claim [make a claim of] $10,000 damages 《from sb》/ 要求のあり次第 on request / 要求を退ける turn down sb's request / 要求に応じる grant [《文》comply with] sb's request ; meet the demand(s) 《of the age》/ 要求により at [by] sb's request. 文例b

ようぎょ 養魚 fish breeding [farming, cultivation] ¶養魚池 a fish-breeding pond / 養魚場 a fish farm.

ようきょう 養共 ¶養共の pro-communist 《elements》.

ようぎょう 窯業 the ceramic industry ; ceramics.

ようきょく 陽極《電》the anode ; the positive terminal [pole] ; the plus terminal.

ようきょく 謡曲 (chant) a Noh song.

ようぎん 洋銀 nickel [German] silver.

ようぐ 用具 a tool ; an instrument ; an implement ¶教育用具 teaching aids / スポーツ用具 sporting goods.

ようけい 養鶏 poultry [chicken] farming ; chicken raising [rearing] ¶養鶏をする raise poultry [chickens] / 養鶏場 a poultry [chicken] farm.

---

available for ten thousand people.

ようい 外国語を覚えるのは容易なことではない. It is not easy [no easy matter] to learn a foreign language. / これは容易なことではない. This is by no means an easy job. | This is no easy task. / 彼の病気は容易に治らなかった. It was a long time before he got well. / 打ち捨てておけば容易ならぬ事態を引き起こすことであろう. The matter, if left to take its own course, will have alarming results. / 金を稼ぐのは容易なことでないと今にわかるよ. You will see in time that money doesn't come [isn't come by] easily.

ようき この建物には妖気が漂っている. There is something weird and ghostly about this building.

ようき それは陽気の加減だろう. Perhaps the weather has something to do with it. ★ be [feel] under the weather という決まり文句があり, これを, 「陽気のせいで体調がすぐれない」と誤解している人が多いが, この句の意味は weather とは関係なく, 「あまり元気がない」「からだの調子がよくない」である / 今日は夏の陽気じゃありませんか. It is (just) like summer today, isn't it ?

ようきゅう 再三支払いを要求しても無駄だったので, 彼は債務者を相手取って訴訟を起こした. After repeated but fruitless demands for payment, he brought

ようげき 要撃 ⇨ げいげき

ようけん¹ 用件 business ⇨ よう¹, ようじ¹. 文例⇩

ようけん² 要件 〈重要な用事〉an important matter; important business; 〈必要な条件〉《文》a necessary [required] condition (of);《文》a prerequisite (to, for);《ラテン語》a sine qua non (pl. sine qua nons) ¶要件を具備する fulfill [satisfy] the necessary [required] conditions. 文例⇩

ようげん 用言《国文法》a declinable word.

ようご¹ 用語〈術語〉a term;《文》terminology (集合的);〈言葉遣い〉wording;《文》diction;《文》phraseology; language; 〈語彙(´)〉(a) vocabulary ¶専門[学術]用語 technical [scientific] terms [terminology] / 法律用語 legal terms [terminology, phraseology] / 医学[軍隊]用語 in medical language [military parlance]. 文例⇩

ようご² 養護 nursing; protective care ¶養護学級 a sheltered [weak children's] class / 養護学校 a school for physically handicapped or mentally retarded children.

ようご³ 擁護 protection;〈防護〉(a) defense;〈弁護〉《文》(a) vindication;〈援助〉support ¶擁護する protect; safeguard; defend; 《文》vindicate; stand by; support / 擁護者 a defender; a champion; a supporter / 自由擁護のために戦う fight in the cause of freedom.

ようこう¹ 洋行 ¶洋行する go [travel] abroad (to visit Western countries).

ようこう² 要項 the main [essential] points ¶入学要項案内 a list of the entrance requirements (for a college).

ようこう³ 要綱 the outline; the gist; the general idea.

ようこう⁴ 陽光 sunlight; sunshine. 文例⇩

ようこうろ 溶鉱炉 a blast furnace.

ようこそ ⇨ よう³. 文例⇩

ようさい¹ 洋裁 dressmaking;《文》couture ¶洋裁学校 a dressmaking [dressmakers'] school / 洋裁師 a dressmaker / 洋裁店 a dressmaker's shop.

ようさい² 要塞 a fortress; a stronghold.

ようざい¹ 用材〈材木〉timber;《米》lumber; 〈資材〉materials ¶建築用材 building materials.

ようざい² 溶剤《化》a solvent.

ようさん¹ 葉酸《生化》folic acid.

ようさん² 養蚕 sericulture; silkworm culture [breeding] ¶養蚕家 a sericulturist / 養蚕業 the sericultural industry.

ようし¹ 用紙 a (blank) form; a blank; 〈印刷された所定の〉a printed form ¶試験用紙 an examination paper / 申込用紙 an application form / 答案用紙 an examination [a test] paper.

ようし² 要旨 the point; the gist; the substance; 〈趣旨〉《文》the purport; the keynote; 〈大要〉a summary; an outline.

ようし³ 洋紙 (machine-made) paper.

ようし⁴ 容姿 one's looks; a [one's] figure; an [one's] appearance. ¶容姿端麗である be handsome; be personable; be good-looking; 〈女性〉have a good [《文》graceful] figure.

ようし⁵ 陽子《物》a proton ¶反陽子 an antiproton.

ようし⁶ 養子 an adopted child [son]; 〈娘の婿〉a son-in-law (pl. sons-) ¶養子にする adopt (a child) (as one's son) / 養子に行く be adopted (into a family, as sb's son); take one's wife's family name / 養子縁組 adoption; (an) adoptive marriage.

ようじ¹ 用事 business; an errand (使い走りの); 〈仕事〉《文》an engagement; work [things] to do ⇨ よう¹ ¶用事を済ます finish a job (one has to do); get one's business over / 用事で on business; on an errand. 文例⇩

ようじ² 幼児 a little child; a baby; an infant; a (tiny) tot ¶幼児教育 preschool education / 幼児死亡率 an infant mortality rate; infant mortality.

ようじ³ 幼時 ¶幼時に in one's childhood [infancy]; at an early age; when one is very young / 幼時から from 〈one's earliest〉childhood; from when one was a child / 幼時体験 one's childhood experiences.

ようじ⁴ 楊枝〈つまようじ〉a toothpick;〈食物を刺すのに使う〉a cocktail stick ¶ようじにさしたオリーブ an olive on a (cocktail) stick.

ようしき¹ 洋式 ¶洋式の Western-style.

ようしき² 様式 a pattern; a form; 〈建築・美術の〉《文》a mode; a style ¶所定の様式で願書を提出する submit an [one's] application in the proper [《文》prescribed] form / 行動様式 patterns of behavior.

ようしゃ 容赦 ¶容赦する〈許す〉《文》pardon; forgive;〈寛大にする〉tolerate; give quarter (to); be lenient [《文》merciful] (to, toward); show mercy [《文》leniency] (to);〈見逃す〉overlook / 容赦し難い unpardonable; intolerable / 容赦ない unsparing;《文》inexorable; relentless; severe / 容赦なく mercilessly; without mercy. 文例⇩

---

a suit against the debtor. / 本協定を直ちに破棄するよう強く要求した. They pressed home their demand for the immediate abrogation of the agreement. / 日本の学校は過度の勉強を生徒に要求する. Japanese schools require too much work of [from] their students.

ようけん¹ 用件を早く言いたまえ. Come to the point at once.

ようけん² 健康は成功の第一要件である. Health is the prerequisite for success in life.

ようご¹ 彼は用語にはいつも注意深い. He is very careful about his choice of words. | He always chooses his language very carefully.

ようこう⁴ 広々とした土地でさんさんと陽光を浴びて物みなすべて鮮明な色彩を帯びていた. In the full sunlight of the open country everything in view took on very bright colors.

ようこそ これはようこそ (お出で下さいました). I am glad to see you. / トムはようこそと戸口に立っていた. Tom stood in the doorway in welcome.

ようじ¹ 大事な用事があるのです. I have an important matter to attend to.

ようしゃ 敵には少しの情け容赦も示さぬ男だ. To an enemy he shows no mercy [leniency] and

ようしゅ 洋酒 wines and spirits.
ようじゅつ 妖術 (black) magic; witchcraft; sorcery ¶妖術者 a magician; a sorcerer (男); a sorceress (女) ⇨ まほう.
ようしゅん 陽春 spring; the springtime.
ようしょ 要所 an important position;〈要点〉an important point ¶要所を固める station troops at strategic points.
ようしょ 洋書 a foreign [Western] book; a book in a Western language.
ようじょ 幼女 a little girl.
ようじょ 養女 an adopted [a foster] daughter.
ようしょう[1] 幼少 ¶幼少の young;《文》juvenile / 幼少の頃 in one's childhood [《文》infancy]; as a child.
ようしょう[2] 要衝 ⇨ようしょ[1] ¶軍事上の要衝《文》a point of strategic importance; a strategic point.
ようじょう[1] 洋上 ⇨ かいじょう[3] ¶洋上大学 a floating university.
ようじょう[2] 養生 ¶養生する take care of one's health;〈病後に〉convalesce; recuperate / 養生に for one's health; to preserve one's health;〈保養に〉for one's convalescence; to convalesce; to recuperate / 養生法 rules of one's health;《文》a regimen; hygiene.
ようしょく[1] 洋食 Western(-style) food; a European dish; Western cooking.
ようしょく[2] 洋職 (hold) an important post [《文》office]; (a man in) a responsible position.
ようしょく[3] 容色 (good) looks; beauty ¶容色が衰える lose one's looks / 容色が衰えない keep one's good looks; be well preserved (ややおどけて). 文例◊
ようしょく[4] 養殖 cultivation; raising; culture; breeding; farming ¶養殖する breed; raise; cultivate / 養殖魚 hatchery fish / 養殖漁業 the fish-raising industry / 養殖場 a nursery; a farm / かき養殖 oyster culture [farming] / かきの養殖場 an oyster bed [farm] / 養殖真珠 a cultured pearl.
ようじん[1] 用心〈注意〉care; carefulness;〈警戒〉caution; (a) precaution;〈慎重〉《文》prudence;《文》circumspection ¶用心する be careful (about,《文》of); take care; be cautious (about,《文》of); guard (against); watch [look] out (for); be on one's guard (against); be on the alert [lookout]; beware (of) (★主に命令形で使われる) / 怒らせないように用心する be careful not to give [《文》be chary of giving] offense to sb; be on one's guard not to offend sb / 火の用心をする take care not to start a fire; take precautions against fire / 用心に a [by way of] precaution; to be on the safe side / 用心深い〈注意深い〉careful;〈警戒を怠らない〉cautious; watchful; guarded (words); safety-minded;《文》prudent;《文》circumspect / 用心深く cautiously; guardedly;《文》with prudence / 用心棒 a bodyguard;〈酒場などの〉《俗》a bouncer;《英俗》a chucker-out. 文例◊
ようじん[2] 要人 an [a very] important person; a V.I.P. [VIP] (*pl.* VIPs); a leading figure.
ようす 様子 the state of affairs [things]; the situation;《文》(the) circumstances;〈外見〉(an) appearance; looks; an air;〈態度〉《文》a manner;〈兆候〉a sign ¶…の様子が分からない do not know (anything) (about);《文》be ignorant (of); be uninformed (about, concerning); be a stranger (to) / 様子をうかがう see how things go [stand, fall out]; watch [see] the run of events; wait and see which way the wind blows [the cat jumps] / …の様子を知っている be familiar (with); be at home (in) / 恐れる様子もなく without (showing) any (outward) sign(s) of fear / この様子では by the look of things / びっくりしたような様子で with a surprised look [a look of surprise]. 文例◊
ようず 要図 a rough sketch; a sketch map.
ようすい[1] 用水〈かんがい用の〉water for irrigation ¶用水池 a reservoir / 用水おけ a rainwater tank.
ようすい[2] 羊水 [医] amniotic fluid;〈通俗に〉the waters / 羊水が出る the waters break.
ようすこう 揚子江 the Yangtze(-Kiang); the Yangtze River.
ようする 要する《文》require; need; take; demand ¶要するに in short; in a word; to sum up; to cut a long story short;《文》in fine; taking all in all / 要するは…ということになる boil down to…; amount [add up] to…; the upshot is that…. 文例◊
ようせい[1] 妖精 a fairy; a sprite;〈小妖精〉an elf (*pl.* elves).
ようせい[2] 要請《文》a request; a demand ¶要請する request; call on sb to do; ask sb for (aid); make a bid (for support) / …の要請で

---

gives no quarter.
ようしょく[3] 彼女も容色がすっかり衰えてしまった。She has lost her (good) looks. / 容色だけで妻を選ぶのは賢明でない。It is unwise to choose a wife merely for her beauty [looks].
ようじん[1] 足元にご用心。Mind [Watch] your step! / 懐中物ご用心。Beware of pickpockets. / 風邪を引かないように用心しなさい。Be careful [Take care] not to catch cold. / うっかり下手なことをしゃべらないように用心していた。I was keeping my wits about me so as not to come out with an imprudent remark [let a tactless remark slip] in an unguarded moment. / こういう問題では用心が肝要です。One must observe caution in these matters.
ようす 私はこの土地の様子がわからない。I am a stranger here. / 彼は近々辞任しそうな様子だ。There are indications that he will step down from his post in the near future. / 待ったが彼の帰って来そうな様子もなかった。I waited, but there was no sign of his return. / 部屋の様子から推して猛烈な格闘があったことは確かだ。From the look of the room, we may safely conjecture that a fierce struggle was fought there. | The room bore every trace [showed traces] of a violent struggle. / ちょっと様子を見に来たのさ。I just came over to see how things are going.
ようする この仕事は熟練を要する仕事だ。The job demands [calls for] skill and experience. / そこ

ようせい [により] at [by] the request of....
ようせい³ 陽性 ¶陽性な〈反応など〉positive; 〈気質の〉《文》sanguine 《temperament》/ 陽性反応 a positive reaction. 文例⇩
ようせい⁴ 養成 ¶養成する〈訓練する〉train; 〈養う〉train; educate; bring up; rear; cultivate / 教員[看護婦]養成所 a training school for teachers [nurses]. 文例⇩
ようせき 容積 〈容量〉(cubic) capacity; 〈体積〉volume; 〈大きさ〉bulk ¶容積トン a measurement ton.
ようせつ¹ 夭折 ⇒わかじに.
ようせつ² 溶接 welding ¶溶接する weld 《to, together》/ 10箇所溶接する make ten welds / 溶接用マスク a welder's helmet / 電気[アーク]溶接 electric [arc] welding / 溶接工 a welder.
ようせん¹ 用船 〈船〉a chartered ship 《vessel》/ 〈事〉chartering; charterage; the hiring of a ship ¶用船料 charter money; charterage.
ようせん² 用箋 〈書簡箋〉letter [writing] paper; 〈つづってある〉a writing pad ¶会社の用箋を使って手紙を書く write 《to sb》on the company's letterhead stationery.
ようそ 要素 an (essential) element; a [an important] factor; 〈欠く可欠な〉《文》a prerequisite ¶外国の要素をとり入れる introduce a foreign element 《into Japanese art》. 文例⇩
ヨウソ ヨウ素 《化》iodine ⇨ヨード.
ようそう¹ 洋装 ¶洋装する be dressed in European style; wear Western clothes / 洋装の婦人 a lady in Western dress.
ようそう² 様相 an aspect; a condition; a phase ¶ただならぬ様相を呈する《文》take on [assume] a serious aspect [serious proportions]; 《文》become grave / 新しい様相を帯びる take on a new aspect [《文》complexion] / 様相を一変する change the whole situation.
ようだい 容体[態] one's condition. 文例⇩
ようたし 用足し ¶用足しに出かける go out on business; 〈人に頼まれて〉go on an errand ⇨よう¹, ようじ¹.
ようだてる 用立てる lend; advance 《money》; oblige [《文》accommodate] sb with a loan.
ようだん¹ 用談 a business talk ¶用談する talk business with sb / 用談中である be engaged 《with sb》.
ようだん² 要談 ¶要談がある have something important [《文》an important matter] to discuss [talk over] 《with sb》.

ようだんす 洋箪笥 a chest of drawers; a cabinet.
ようち¹ 用地 《farming》land; a 《parking》lot; a site 《for a factory》.
ようち² 夜討ち ⇨やしゅう.
ようち³ 幼稚 ¶幼稚な〈子供じみた〉childish; 《文》infantile; 《文》puerile; inexperienced; 〈粗末な〉crude; 〈原始的な〉primitive / 幼稚な考え a childish idea; a crude opinion. 文例⇩
ようちえん 幼稚園 a kindergarten.
ようちゅう 幼虫 a larva 《pl. larvae》.
ようちゅうい 要注意 ¶要注意である need [《文》require] care / 要注意人物 a person on the blacklist; a suspicious character.
ようつい 腰椎 《解》the lumbar vertebra ¶腰椎麻酔 spinal [lumbar] anesthesia; a lumbar [spinal] block.
ようつう 腰痛 lumbago; (a) pain in the lower back; (a) backache.
ようてい 要諦 the secret 《of success》; the key 《to success》.
ようてん¹ 要点 the (main [essential]) point; the gist; 《文》the substance ¶戦略上の要点 a strategic point / 要点をつかむ grasp [get, catch] the point 《of》.
ようてん² 陽転 《医》a change to positive ¶陽転する change to positive.
ようでんき 陽電気 positive electricity.
ようでんし 陽電子 a positive electron; a positron.
ようと 用途 a use ¶用途が広い have various uses; be used [《文》utilized] for various [a variety of] purposes / 用途が限られている have (only) limited uses / 用途の広い general-purpose 《tables》. 文例⇩
ようとう 羊頭 ¶羊頭をかかげて狗肉(く)を売る cry wine, and sell vinegar; make an extravagant advertisement.
ようどうさくせん 陽動作戦 a feint operation; (a) diversionary action; 《make》a sham attack.
ようどか 用度課 the supplies department [section].
ようとして 杳として 文例⇩
ようとん 養豚 《米》hog raising; 《英》pig breeding [farming] ¶養豚業者《米》a hog raiser; 《英》a pig breeder [farmer].
ようなし 洋梨 a pear.
ようにく 羊肉 mutton; lamb (小羊の).

まで行くのに2時間を要した. It took us two hours to get there.
ようせい³ ツベルクリン反応は陽性だった. My reaction to the tuberculin test proved positive. | I showed a positive reaction to the T.B. test.
ようせい⁴ 戦前の帝国大学は事実上吏員の養成機関であった. Before the war, the Imperial universities were in practice nurseries for government officials.
ようそ この小説には幾分悲劇の要素が含まれている. The novel

has in it some of the elements of tragedy. / 空軍力は近代戦の決定的要素である. Air power is the decisive factor in modern warfare. / チームの団結こそ勝利の第1要素である. Cooperation among the team members is the first prerequisite for victory.
ようそう² その後状況は全く異なった様相を呈するに至った. After that, things began to present an entirely different picture.
ようだい 彼の容体は良く[悪く]なった. His condition has taken

a turn for the better [worse]. / 今朝はお父さんのご容体はいかがですか. How is your father this morning?
ようち³ この国の農業はまだ幼稚である. Agriculture in this country is still primitive [in its infancy].
ようと 用途不明. 〈出品物につけたラベル〉Use unknown.
ようとして 彼の行方はいまだにようとしてわからない. His whereabouts still remains [remain] utterly unknown [a complete

ようにん 容認 ¶容認する〈認める〉admit; acknowledge; accept 《sth, that...》〈許す〉allow; permit; tolerate ¶容認できる tolerable; acceptable.

ようねん 幼年 childhood ¶幼年時代に in one's childhood; in one's early days; when one is very young / 幼年時代から from one's early childhood.

ようはい 遙拝 worshiping from a distance [《文》from afar] ¶遙拝する bow to the direction of 《the Imperial Palace》.

ようばい 溶媒 《化》a solvent.

ようび 曜日 a day of the week. 文例⇩

ようひし 羊皮紙 parchment.

ようひん[1] 用品 《school》things; 《toilet》articles ¶台所用品 utensils for kitchen use; kitchen utensils; 《集合的に》kitchenware / 旅行用品 a traveling outfit; traveling gear.

ようひん[2] 洋品 《米》haberdashery ¶洋品店 a haberdasher's 《shop》; a haberdashery; 《英》a men's shop.

ようふ[1] 妖婦 《文》an enchantress; 《文》a siren.

ようふ[2] 養父 an adoptive [a foster] father; 〈義父〉a father-in-law (pl. fathers-).

ようぶ 腰部 the waist; 《解》the lumbar region.

ようふう 洋風 《洋風の Western; European; in [of] Western [European] style / 洋風建築 a Western-style building / 洋風の部屋 a room furnished in European style.

ようふく 洋服 a suit (of clothes); a dress; 〈和服に対して〉Western clothes ¶洋服を着た 《a young man》in [wearing] a suit; 《a lady》in a dress; 《a gentleman》dressed in Western style / 洋服掛け a coat hanger / 洋服だんす a wardrobe / 洋服屋 a tailor's; 〈店〉a tailor's (shop).

ようぶん 養分 nourishment; nutriment.

ようへい[1] 用兵 tactics; strategy.

ようへい[2] 葉柄 《植》a leafstalk; a petiole; a stem.

ようへい[3] 傭兵 a mercenary (soldier).

ようぼ 養母 an adoptive [a foster] mother; 〈義母〉a mother-in-law (pl. mothers-).

ようほう[1] 用法 (a) usage; how to use sth; (a) use; 〈用法書き〉the directions (for use) ¶前置詞の用法 the uses of prepositions / 用法を誤る make a mistake in using sth; misuse; make a wrong use of.

ようほう[2] 養蜂 beekeeping; bee raising [culture]; apiculture ¶養蜂家 a beekeeper; an apiculturist / 養蜂所 an apiary.

ようぼう[1] 要望 a demand (for); a cry (for); 〈希望〉one's wishes ¶要望する demand; cry (for) / 要望に応じる meet the demand(s) 《of the age》/ 要望に応じて《文》in compliance with the wishes 《of》.

ようぼう[2] 容貌 looks; (a cast of) features ¶容貌が醜い[美しい] be ugly [good-looking].

ようま 洋間 a Western-style room.

ようまく 羊膜 《解》the amnion (pl. -s, -nia).

ようみゃく 葉脈 the veins of a leaf.

ようむ[1] 用務 business ¶用務を帯びて on (some) business / 用務員《米》a janitor;《英》a caretaker; a porter; a doorkeeper / 用務員の仕事 janitorial services.

ようむ[2] 要務 important business.

ようむき 用向き business; 〈頼まれた〉an errand ⇒ ようじ[1] ¶用向きを尋ねる ask sb his business. 文例⇩

ようめい 用命 an order ⇒ ちゅうもん. 文例⇩

ようもう 羊毛 (sheep's) wool ¶羊毛の woolen 《blankets》/ 羊毛のような woolly 《nylon》/ 今年の羊毛収穫高 the wool clip for this year; this year's cut of wool.

ようもうざい 養毛剤 a hair tonic.

ようもく 要目 main [《文》principal] items; 〈講義などの〉a syllabus (pl. -buses, -bi).

ようやく[1] 要約 a summary; a digest; 《文》an epitome; a précis (単複同形, 単数 [preisí:], 複数 [preisí:z]); a résumé ¶要約する sum up; summarize; 《文》digest;《文》epitomize;《文》recapitulate;〈口語〉recap; 〈短く〉abridge / 要約すれば to sum up; in short;《文》in brief; in a word.

ようやく[2] 漸く 〈ついに〉at last; at length; finally; 〈辛うじて〉barely; narrowly; with (considerable) difficulty; 〈わずかに〉only; just 〈やっと〉. 文例⇩

ようよう 洋々 ¶洋々たる〈広い〉wide; broad; 《文》vast;《文》boundless; 〈明るい〉bright 《future》; rosy 《prospects》/ 洋々たる大海 a boundless [broad expanse of] ocean. 文例⇩

ようらん[1] 要覧 a survey; an outline; 〈案内書〉a handbook; a manual ¶大学要覧《米》a college catalogue /《英》a university calendar.

ようらん[2] 揺籃 a cradle ¶揺籃の地 the cradle (of European civilization); the birthplace / 揺籃時代に[から] in [from] the cradle.

ようりつ 擁立 ¶擁立する〈後援する〉back (up); support; 〈後援して地位につける〉help

---

mystery]. | No clue to his whereabouts has been found.

ようび 今日は何曜日だったかな。What day of the week is it today? | What is today? / 去年の元日は月曜日だった。New Year's Day was (on) a Monday last year. / 一昨日の木曜日に東京に行ったのです。It was on Thursday, the day before yesterday, that I went up to Tokyo. / 3月の水曜日に出発します。I am to leave on Wednesday, the 3rd. / 再来週の土曜日にまた来ます。I'll come again two weeks from [《英》on] Saturday.

ようむき ご用向きは? What can I do for you?

ようめい 物価騰貴のためお指図ではご用命に応じ兼ねます。Prices having increased, we cannot execute your order within your limit. / 何なりとご用命下さい。We are entirely at your service.

ようやく[2] ようやく雨がやんだ。At last the rain stopped. / 彼はようやく間に合った。He barely managed to get there in time. / このことは後になってようやく知ったことである。I was only to learn this later.

ようよう 君の前途は洋々たるものだ。You have a bright [great] future before you.

ようりょう[2] 君の話はさっぱり要領を得ない。I can't see what you're driving at at all. / 協議は要領を得ずに終った。The conference ended without coming to

ようりょう《a young prince》to《the throne》.
ようりょう¹ 用量〖薬〗dosage ; a dose.
ようりょう² 要領〖要点〗the (main) point ; the gist ; 〈こつ〉the knack ; the hang ; 《know》the ropes ¶要領のいい clever ; shrewd / 要領の悪い impractical ; awkward ; clumsy / 要領を得ている be to the point / 要領を得た事を言う talk to the point [purpose] / 要領を得ない〈取りとめがない〉be pointless ; 〈的を射ない〉be off the point ; 〈うやむや〉be noncommittal / …の要領を会得する get [learn] the knack of《doing》; get the hang of《it, doing》. 文例↓
ようりょう³ 容量 (the measure of) capacity ; 〈容積〉volume ; cubic contents ¶水槽の容量 the (storage) capacity of a water tank / 熱容量〖物〗heat capacity.
ようりょく 揚力 (dynamic) lift ; lifting power [force] ¶揚力を得る obtain lift / 揚力を高める improve [《文》enhance] lift / より少ない面積でより多くの揚力を出す provide [generate, develop] more lift with less area.
ようりょくそ 葉緑素〖植〗chlorophyll ¶葉緑素(入り)の chlorophyllous.
ようれい 用例 an (illustrative) example ; an illustration ¶用例を示す give [cite, quote] an example ¶《from Shakespeare》/ (辞書編集の)用例カード a quotation slip ; a citation card.
ようろ 要路 ¶要路の大官〈個人〉a high government official / 〈総称〉those in (high) authority. 文例↓
ようろう 養老 ¶養老院 a home for the aged ; an old people's home / 養老年金 an old-age pension / 養老保険 old-age insurance.
ヨーか ヨー化〖化〗iodization ¶ヨー化物 an iodide / ヨー化銀 silver iodide.
ヨーグルト yog(h)urt.
ヨーデル a yodel ¶ヨーデル歌手 a yodeler.
ヨード《《ドイツ語》Jod》iodine ¶ヨードチンキ tincture of iodine / ヨードホルム iodoform.
ヨーヨー 〈玩具〉a yoyo (pl. -s) ¶ヨーヨーを上げ下げする spin a yoyo up and down on its string.
ヨーロッパ Europe ⇒ おうしゅう³ ¶ヨーロッパの European / ヨーロッパの人 a European / ヨーロッパ大陸 the European continent ; the continent of Europe ; continental Europe.
よか¹ 予科 a preparatory course ; 〈医科大学の〉a premedical course ¶予科の学生 a preparatory course student.

よか² 余暇 leisure (hours) ; (one's) free time ; spare time ¶余暇に in one's spare moments ; at one's leisure / 業務の余暇に in the intervals of one's business. 文例↓
ヨガ yoga ¶ヨガの行者 a yogi / ヨガをする do yoga (exercises).
よかく 余角〖数〗the complementary angle ; the complement (of an angle).
よかぜ 夜風 a night breeze [wind].
よかつ 余割〖数〗a cosecant (略: cosec, csc).
よからぬ 良からぬ evil ; wrong ; 《文》ill ; bad ¶良からぬことをたくらむ be up to no good.
よかれあしかれ 善かれ悪しかれ right or wrong ; for good or bad [ill] ; for better or (for) worse. 文例↓
よかん¹ 予感《文》a presentiment ; 《文》a premonition ; 《口語》a hunch ¶予感がする《文》feel [have] a foreboding《of, that…》; have a hunch《that…》; feel a premonition《of, that…》).
よかん² 余寒 the lingering cold (of early spring).
よき 予期 expectation(s) ; 《文》(an) anticipation ; 〈希望〉(a) hope ¶予期する expect ; 《文》anticipate ; hope [look] for ; 〈予知する〉foresee / 予期しない unexpected ; unlooked-for ; unforeseen / 予期したとおりになる meet [come up to, measure up to] one's expectations / 予期のごとく as was expected ; as one expected / 予期に反する《文》belie one's hopes ; fall short of one's expectations / 予期に反して contrary to (one's) expectation(s) [what one expected] / 予期以上に beyond (one's) expectation(s). 文例↓
よぎ 余技 a hobby.
よぎしゃ 夜汽車 a night train ⇒ やこう².
よぎない 余儀ない 〈不可避の〉unavoidable ; inevitable ; 〈必要な〉necessary ; 〈緊急の〉urgent ¶余儀なく unavoidably ; 《文》of necessity / 余儀なく…する be obliged [compelled, forced] to do ; have no choice but to do ; have to do. 文例↓
よきょう 余興 an entertainment ; 〈隠し芸〉a parlor trick ¶余興を出す put on an entertainment / 余興に by way of entertainment. 文例↓
よぎり 夜霧 a night fog [mist].
よぎる go by ; go across ¶脳裏をよぎる cross one's mind.
よきん 預金 a deposit ; savings (貯金) ¶預金

---

any definite conclusion.
ようろ 町は同地方の交通の要路に当たっている. The town lies on the main traffic artery of the district.
よか² 彼は公務の余暇に歴史を研究した. The time he could spare from his duties was devoted to the study of history.
よかれあしかれ善かれ悪しかれ現代文明の基礎は科学である. For good or ill, our modern civilization is built upon science.

よかん¹ 失敗しそうな予感がしてならない. I've a strong presentiment that it'll prove a failure.
よき 君が来るとは予期していなかった. I did not expect to see you here. / 結果は予期した以上のものだった[予期したほどのものではなかった]. The results exceeded [were below] my expectations. / 売り上げは予期以上ではなかった. The sale did not come [measure] up to our expectations.

よぎない 彼は何か余儀ない事情があって辞職したのだ. Some unavoidable circumstances must have caused his resignation (obliged him to resign).
よきょう 余興に色々な音楽があるはずだ. By way of entertainment various kinds of music will be played on the occasion. / 余興にはダンスや曲芸があった. The entertainment consisted of dances and acrobatic performances.

する deposit 《money in a bank》; make a deposit 《in a bank》; place 《money》 on deposit 《in a bank》; bank / 預金がある have 《one million yen》 on deposit 《in a bank》; have a 《large》 deposit 《in a bank》/ 預金を引き出す draw [withdraw] one's money [deposit] 《from the bank》/ 銀行預金 (a) bank deposit; a bank account / 普通預金 an ordinary deposit; a deposit account / 預金者 a depositor / 預金通帳 a (deposit) passbook; a bankbook / 預金利子 interest on deposits. 文例⇩

よく[1] 欲 greed; 《文》 avarice; 〈欲望〉《文》 a desire; 《文》 a passion ¶ 欲の深い greedy; 《文》 avaricious; 《文》 covetous; 《文》 acquisitive; possessive 〈持っているものを手放したがらない〉/ 欲のない unselfish; 《文》 disinterested; openhanded / 欲の少ない人 a person with [《文》 of] few wants / 欲を離れて from [out of] a disinterested motive; with no ulterior motive (in mind) / 欲を言えば if one is allowed to wish so much [to hope for more] / 欲にも得にも〈否定構文〉for love or money; for all the world; for anything in the world / 欲にめがくらむ be blinded by greed / 金銭欲 love of money; a desire for wealth. 文例⇩

よく[2] 翼 a wing; 〈陣形の〉 a flank ¶ 翼長〈片方の〉 wing length; 〈両方を合わせた〉 wingspan; wingspread / 翼面積 wing area. 文例⇩

よく[3] 良く〈上手に〉well; skillfully;〈正しく〉right(ly); properly;〈充分に〉thoroughly; fully; well; quite;〈注意して〉carefully;〈細かく〉closely;〈正確に〉exactly;〈多く〉much; a great deal;〈普通に〉commonly; usually; generally;〈しばしば〉often;《文》frequently ¶ よくなる〈改善する〉improve (on);〈巧みである〉be good 《at》; be skillful 《at》; be at home 《in, with》;〈…し得る〉can do; be able to do / よくなる get [《文》 become] better; improve;〈病人が〉take a turn for the better; recover (from one's illness);〈天気が〉clear up / よく考える think (a matter) over; give a lot of thought to sth / よく考えた上で《文》after mature [due] consideration / よく見る have a good look at sth; look at sth closely [closely] / よく見ても〈せいぜい〉at best; at (the) most / (人に)よくする be good [nice, kind] to sb; do well by sb; do sb well; do sb a good turn / (人

を)よく言う speak well [highly] 《of sb》/ よく …する〈…し勝ちである〉be apt [liable] to do; be given to doing [sth]; will do / よく … したものだ would do; used to do / よくある事 a common [an everyday] affair / 学生にはよくあることだがas often happens [as is usual, as is often the case] with students. 文例⇩

よく- 翌... the next [following] ¶ 翌10日 on the following day, the 10th.

よくあさ 翌朝 ⇒よくちょう.

よくあつ 抑圧 oppression; suppression; a check; (a) restraint ¶ 抑圧する oppress 《the people》; check; suppress《freedom of speech》.

よくげつ 翌月 the next [following] month.

よくし 抑止〈侵略に対する〉deterrence ¶ 抑止力 a 《nuclear》 deterrent.

よくしつ 浴室 a bathroom.

よくじつ 翌日 the next [following] day ¶ 事故のあった翌日に on the day following the accident.

よくじょう[1] 浴場 a bathroom ¶ 公衆浴場 a public bath(house).

よくじょう[2] 欲情《文》sexual desire;《文》lust.

よくする 浴する〈恩恵に〉be honored 《by》; be favored 《with》; have a share (in the benefit).

よくせい 抑制 control; restraint; check; suppression;〔心理〕inhibition ¶ 抑制と均衡〔政治〕checks and balances / 抑制する control; check; restrain; suppress; keep sth under control; deter 《sb from doing》; curb; put a curb on 《one's desires》;〔心理〕inhibit / 抑制できる controllable / 抑制できない uncontrollable / 抑制作用 inhibitory [inhibitive] action. 文例⇩

よくそう 浴槽 a bath(tub) ¶ 浴槽に湯を満たす fill the bath (with hot water).

よくちょう 翌朝 the next [following] morning.

よくど 沃土 fertile land [earth]; rich [fertile] soil.

よくとく 欲得 ¶ 欲得ずくの selfish;《文》mercenary / 欲得ずくで《文》(merely) for gain; from [out of] selfish motives; with a view to (making) a profit / 欲得を離れた unselfish;《文》disinterested / 欲得を離れて《文》from [out of] disinterested motives; uninfluenced [not influenced] by self-interest [one's own interest].

よきん 彼はその銀行に 50 万円の預金がある。He has a deposit of 500,000 yen in the bank.

よく[1] 欲でするのではない。I am not doing this from self-interest. / 欲にはきりがない。Avarice knows no bounds. | The more one has, the more one wants. / 彼は欲の固まりだ。He is greediness itself [the personification of selfishness]. / 彼とは欲にも得にも以上あいつとは一緒にやってゆけません。I can't go on with him any longer for love or money. / 彼は確かに頭がいい。しかし欲を言えばもう少し勤勉であって欲し

い。He is a bright boy, to be sure, but I wish he were a little more hardworking.

よく[2] その団体は社会党の宣伝活動の一翼を担うことになった。The organization has become a propaganda wing of the Socialist Party.

よく[3] よく存じません。I don't know for certain. | I am not sure. / 夜分はよく眠れますか。Do you sleep well at night? / 対米輸出も徐々によくなるものと思う。Exports to the U.S. are expected to pick up by degrees. / あなたのことは阿部さんからよく承っております。I've heard a lot [a great deal] about you from Mr. Abe. / 戦前はよく彼と一緒だったものだ。I used to see a lot of him [was with him a great deal] before the war. / 日曜日にはよくこの辺を散歩したものだ。On Sundays I would often take a walk in this neighborhood. / あんな面白くもないやつによく辛抱ができるねえ。I wonder how you can stand a bore like that. / よくしたもので貧乏がかえって幸せなこともある。It's funny how things work out. Poverty often brings unexpected blessings with it. /

よくねん 翌年 the next [following] year.

よくばり 欲張り 〈人〉a grasping [《文》an avaricious] person ¶欲張りな greedy;《文》avaricious; grasping;《文》acquisitive; possessive.

よくばる 欲張る be greedy;《文》be avaricious;《文》be acquisitive;〈仕事を〉bite off more than one can chew.

よくばん 翌晩 the next [following] evening [night] ¶その晩とその翌晩 that night and the next [the night after].

よくふか 欲深 ⇨ よくばり.

よくほう 欲望《文》a desire ⇨ よく¹ ¶欲望を満たす gratify [satisfy] one's desire(s) / 欲望を抑える curb one's desire(s).

よくめ 欲目《文》partiality; a biased [《文》partial] view ¶欲目で見る take a biased view of sth; look at sth with biased [《文》partial] eyes. 文例⇩

よくも 文例⇩

よくや 沃野 a fertile [rich] plain [field].

よくよう¹ 抑揚 intonation; inflection; modulation ¶抑揚のある modulated;《文》intoned / 抑揚のない monotonous; singsong / 抑揚をつけて intone; intonate.

よくよう² 浴用 ¶浴用石けん bath [toilet] soap.

よくよく 〈注意して〉very carefully; very closely;〈非常に〉《文》exceedingly; very ⇨ よく³ ¶よくよく考える ponder (over a matter); think (a matter) over; turn sth over in one's mind / よくよく金に困っている be very hard up for money; be desperate for [badly in need of] money / よくよくの事でなければ unless one is compelled [driven] to do so / よくよくの事情《文》(some) unavoidable circumstances. 文例⇩

よくよくじつ 翌々日 the next day but one; two days after [later].

よくりゅう 抑留 detention; internment ¶抑留する detain; intern / 抑留される be detained; go into internment / 抑留所 a detention [a concentration, an internment] camp / 被抑留者 a detainee; an internee. 文例⇩

よけい 余計 ¶余計な〈多過ぎる〉too many [much]; more than enough;《文》excessive;《文》superfluous; surplus;《文》superabundant;〈不必要な〉unnecessary; needless;〈頼まれもせぬ〉uncalled-for; uninvited;〈余分の〉extra; spare / 余計なことをする do what is unnecessary; carry coals to Newcastle / 余計の心配をする worry (oneself) (about sth) unnecessarily; take sth too seriously / 余計に too much [far];《文》excessively; needlessly. 文例⇩

よける 避ける avoid; shun; evade;〈近づかない〉keep clear (of); keep (away) (from);〈道をあける〉get out of the way (of); make room (for);〈わきへどく〉step aside (from);〈身をかわす〉dodge; duck (from a blow);〈風雨を〉take [seek] shelter (from) ¶自動車をよける get out of the way of [step aside from] a car / ボールをよける dodge a ball / 暗礁をよける steer clear of a reef / よけて通る make one's way around (puddles of muddy water).

よけん¹ 与件《論》a given condition; a postulate.

よけん² 予見 ¶予見する foresee;《文》prognosticate.

よげん 予言 (a) prophecy; (a) prediction ¶予言する foretell; predict; prophesy; say that sth will take place / 予言者 a prophet; a prophetess (女); a soothsayer. 文例⇩

よげん² 余弦《数》a cosine (略: cos).

よこ 横〈側面〉the side; the flank;〈幅〉the width ¶縦20センチ横15センチの箱 a box 20 by 15 centimeters / 横の lateral; horizontal;〈かたわらの〉beside; by the side (of); by / 横を向く look [turn] away / 横に〈横切って〉across;〈横向きに〉sideways;〈水平に〉horizontally / 横になる lie (down);《文》recline (on) / 横に置く〈寝かせて〉lay sth on its side;〈そばに〉lay by [at] one's side / 横に歩く[はう]walk [crawl] sideways / 横にかぶったベレー帽 a beret set on the side of one's head / 首を横に振る shake one's head; say no / 横(合い)から口を出す put one's oar in (to interfere); poke [thrust] one's nose (into); put in [《文》interpose] a remark; break (into a conversation) / 横(合い)から攻撃する make an attack from the flank. 文例⇩

よご 予後 convalescence; recuperation ¶予後が良好である convalesce satisfactorily / 予後を養う recuperate.

よこあい 横合い ⇨ よこ.

あの子は我々のやりよう次第でよくも悪くもなる. It's in our hands whether we make or break that boy.

よくせい 彼女はいったん何かほしいとなったら、もう抑制がきかない. When she has decided that she wants something, she can't resist it.

よくめ 親の欲目かもしれないが、娘は中々頭のいい子だよ. I know a parent cannot be an impartial judge of his own children, but I think my daughter is rather a clever girl.

よくも よくもやりやがったな. I don't know how he had the gall [effrontery] to do it. / よくもおれの前でそんな事が言えたものだ. How dare you say such a thing to me?

よくよく これにはよくよくのわけがあるらしい. There seems to be some deep reason for this. / 彼はよくよくつむじ曲がりだったと見える. He must have been a very perverse fellow.

よくりゅう 彼はスパイ容疑で抑留されている. He is being held on spy charges.

よけい これは1つ余計だね. This is one too many. / 余計な事を言うようですが、それはやめた方がいいでしょう. Excuse my interference, but I would advise you to give up the idea. / 余計なお世話だ. Mind your own business. | It's none of your business. / 見るなと言われると余計見たくなる. When we are told not to look at something, we are all the keener [more tempted] to (look at it).

よげん¹ その予言どおりになった. The prophecy came true.

よこ 第1図はこの装置を横から見たものである. Figure 1 shows a side view [elevation] of the apparatus. / Fig. 1 shows the ap-

よこあな 横穴 a tunnel; a cave; 〈鉱山の〉a drift.

よこいと 横糸 the weft; the woof.

よこう 予行 ¶予行する have a rehearsal; rehearse / 開会式の予行をする have [go through] a rehearsal of the opening ceremony / 予行演習 a rehearsal; a preliminary drill.

よこおよぎ 横泳ぎ sidestroke ¶横泳ぎをする swim sidestroke.

よこがお 横顔 a profile; a face in profile; a face as seen from the side.

よこがき 横書き ¶横書きする write horizontally (from left to right).

よこがみやぶり 横紙破り ¶横紙破りの《文》perverse; unreasonably obstinate / 横紙破りをやる have one's own way against all reason.

よこぎ 横木 a crosspiece; 〈かんぬきなどの〉a (cross)bar; 〈さくなどの〉a (cross)rail.

よこぎる 横切る cross; go [cut] across; 《文》traverse; 《文》intersect; 〈海・空を〉sail across ¶線路を横切る cross [go across] a track / 横切って向こう側へ行く cross 《the road》to the other side.

よこく 予告 (a) (previous) notice; an advance announcement; 〈芝居・映画の〉advance billing; 〈警告〉a warning ¶予告する notify [announce] beforehand; give notice [advance warning] 《that..., of》; warn sb of sth; give advance billing 《to》(特に映画・講演会などの) / 1週間前に予告を与える give sb a week's notice 《that..., of dismissal》/ 予告なしに without (previous) notice / 新刊予告 an announcement of forthcoming books / 予告編《映画の》a trailer; a preview. 文例◎

よこぐるま 横車 ¶横車を押す ram (one's opinion) through (perversely [against all reason]).

よこじく 横軸 a cross [transverse] axle; 〔機〕a horizontal shaft; 〔数〕the horizontal axis; the x-axis.

よこしま ¶よこしまな〈邪悪な〉wicked; evil; vicious; 〈不正な〉dishonest; 《文》unjust; not straightforward / よこしまなことをする do something wrong; 《文》do (what is morally) wrong; act dishonestly; cheat.

よこじま 横縞 horizontal [lateral] stripes.

よこす 〈送る〉send; 〈届ける〉forward; 〈渡す〉hand [give] over 《to》; deliver ¶手紙をよこす write to sb / …といってよこす〈手紙で〉write sb (a letter) saying that...; 〈伝言で〉send (sb) word that.... 文例◎

よごす 汚す dirty sth; make [get] sth dirty; stain; soil; taint; pollute; contaminate; 《文》defile ¶下水で川の水を汚す foul [contaminate] a river with sewage.

よこずき 横好き ⇒へた¹ (下手の横好き).

よこすべり 横滑り a skid; a sideslip ¶横滑りする skid; sideslip; slip sideways; 〈役職など〉be moved sideways. 文例◎

よこたえる 横たえる 〈置く〉lay (down); 〈横切って置く〉place [put, lay] across / からだを横たえる lay oneself down; lie down.

よこだおし 横倒し ¶横倒しにする push [topple] sth over sideways / 横倒しになる fall [topple] (over) sideways / 横倒し sidelong. 文例◎

よこだき 横抱き ¶横抱きに抱える hold [carry] (a child) under one's arm.

よこたわる 横たわる lie (down); lay oneself down ¶長々と横たわる lie at full length; stretch oneself out.

よこちょう 横町 a side [back] street; 〈小路〉an alley; a side alley; 〈曲がり角〉a turning. 文例◎

よこづけ 横付け ¶横付けにする〈なる, なっている〉bring [come, lie] alongside 《the pier》.

よこっつら 横っ面 ¶横っ面を張る slap sb [give sb a slap] in the face [on the cheek]; slap sb right across the face; box sb's ears (大人が子供に).

よこっとび 横っ飛び ¶横っ飛びに飛ぶ jump sideways [aside].

よこづな 横綱 a grand champion sumo wrestler ¶横綱審議会 the Yokozuna Deliberative Council.

よこっぱら 横っ腹 the side; 《文》the flank ¶横っ腹が痛む have a pain in the (right) side / (注意をうながすために)ひじで横っ腹を押す poke [elbow] sb in the ribs. 文例◎

よこて 横手 ¶家の横手の道 the road running by one's house / 横手に at the side 《of》; by / 横手投げ〔野球〕sidearm delivery / 横手投げをする pitch [throw] (the ball) sidearm; make a sidearm throw.

---

paratus in side view. / うちの人ときたら, なんにもしてくれません. なにしろ横のものを縦にもしない人ですから. My husband never lifts a finger to help. He is a regular lazybones.

よこがお 彼女は横顔はいいけれど正面から見るとそれほどでもない. She has a nice profile, but is not so good-looking (in) full face.

よこぎる フリードリッヒ・シュトラーセを横切る白線が東西両ベルリンの境界になっている. A white line across the Friedrichstrasse marks the boundary [division] between West and East Berlin. / 一筋の小路が畑を横切っている. A path runs across the field.

よこく ひと月前に予告すれば解雇できる. He can be dismissed at a month's notice. / 今年一杯で雇用契約が切れると彼には予告してある. He is under notice that his employment contract with us will expire at the end of the current year.

よこす 「来られない」と言ってよこした. He sent me word that he was unable to come.

よこすべり 車は横滑りして止まった. The car skidded to a stop. / 車は大きく横滑りしながら角を曲がった. The car took the corner in a wide skid.

よこだおし 道路の中央に大きなトラックが横倒しになっていた. I saw a large truck on its side in the middle of the road.

よこたわる 前途にはなお幾多の困難が横たわっている. There are a lot of difficulties ahead (of us). | There are plenty of problems lying in wait for us [lying in our path].

よこちょう 2つ目の横町を左へ曲がりなさい. Take the second turning to [on] the left.

よごと 夜毎 every night ; nightly ; night after night.

よこどり 横取り ¶横取りする take [snatch, steal] *sth* out of *sb*'s possession [hands].

よこなが 横長 ¶横長の long from side to side ; long sideways.

よこながし 横流し ¶横流しする put ⟨controlled goods⟩ on the black market ; 《文》 sell ⟨controlled goods⟩ through illegal channels.

よこなぐり 横殴り a side blow ¶横なぐりの雨 (a) slanting [driving] rain.

よこなみ 横波 a wave broadside(s) ;《海》a cross sea ;《電》a transverse wave. 文例↓

よこばい 横這い ¶横ばいする crawl [walk] sideways ; sidle / 横ばいになる ⟨上昇・増加がとまって⟩ level off ; stop rising [increasing]. 文例↓

よこぶえ 横笛 a flute ; ⟨縦笛に対して⟩ a cross(-blown) flute ¶横笛を吹く play (on) the flute ; flute.

よこぶり 横降り ¶横降りの雨 (a) slanting [driving] rain.

よこみち 横道 a byway ; a side road [street] ; ⟨議論などの⟩《文》(a) digression ¶横道にそれる ⟨話が⟩ go away from the point ; wander [deviate] from the (main) subject ; make a digression ;《文》digress / ⟨正道を踏み外す⟩ stray [swerve] from the right path [from the straight and narrow].

よこむき 横向き ¶横向きに sideways / 横向きになる turn [face] sideways / 横向きに寝る lie on *one*'s side / 横向きに乗る ⟨馬などに⟩ ride ⟨a horse⟩ sidesaddle.

よこめ 横目 a side(long) glance ¶横目で見る, 横目を使う look out of the corner of *one*'s eyes (at) ; cast a side(long) glance (at) / 横目でにらむ give a sharp sidelong glance (at). 文例↓

よこもじ 横文字 ⟨西洋の言葉⟩ a European [Western] language ; ⟨西洋の文字⟩《written in》Roman letters.

よこやり 横槍 ¶横やりを入れる ⟨邪魔をする⟩ interrupt ; ⟨干渉する⟩ interfere [meddle] (in) ; put [stick] *one*'s oar in ; butt [barge] in ⟨on *sb*'s affairs⟩.

よこゆれ 横揺れ ⟨船⟩ rolling ; a rolling motion ; ⟨地震⟩ lateral [transverse] vibration ¶横揺れする ⟨船⟩ roll (from side to side) / ⟨地震⟩ vibrate laterally.

よごれ 汚れ ; ⟨染み⟩ a spot ; a stain ; a dirty mark ; a blot ; a smudge ¶汚れのない clean ; spotless ; unmarked / 汚れを取る remove stains (from) ; clean / 汚れ物 soiled [dirty] things ; ⟨洗濯物⟩ washing.

よごれる 汚れる ⟨汚なくなる⟩ get [《文》become] dirty [filthy] ; be [get, 《文》become] soiled / ⟨染みがつく⟩ be stained ; ⟨汚染する⟩ be polluted ¶汚れた ⟨不潔な⟩ dirty ; filthy ; grubby ; unclean ; soiled ; ⟨染みのついた⟩ stained ; ⟨汚染された⟩ polluted / すすで汚れた顔 a face smudged with soot / 煙で汚れた空気 air polluted by smoke / 汚れっぽい soil [get soiled] easily. 文例↓

よこれんぼ 横恋慕 ¶横恋慕する love *sb*'s wife [husband].

よさ 良さ (a) merit ;《文》a virtue ; (a) good quality. 文例↓

よざい 余罪 other [further] crimes [charges]. 文例↓

よざくら 夜桜 (the sight of) cherry blossoms at night.

よさむ 夜寒 ⟨夜の寒さ⟩ the chill of night ; the night cold ; ⟨寒い夜⟩ a cold night.

よさん 予算 ⟨見積もり⟩ an estimate ⟪for, of⟫ ; ⟨収支の予定⟩ a budget ¶来年度の予算 the budget for the coming (fiscal) year / 国家[家庭]の予算 a State [family] budget / 予算の[に関する] budgetary ⟪measures, requests⟫ / 予算の均衡を計る try to balance the budget / 予算の作成 budget-making / 予算の範囲内で within (the limits of) the budget / 予算を立てる make [form, draw up] a budget [an estimate] ; budget (for the coming year) / 実際の出費より多めに予算を立てる budget for more than *one* spends / 予算に組む budget for ⟪the new city hospital⟫ ; include [plan] ⟪the expenditures for an enterprise⟫ in the budget / 予算に乗る go on [into] the budget / 予算どおりに as budgeted ; on budget / 年間4千万円の予算で on a budget of ¥40 million a year / 総予算 the total budget / 予算案を国会に提出する submit a budget (bill) to the Diet / 予算委員会 a budget committee / 予算規模の縮小 (a) budget squeeze. 文例↓

よし¹ 由 ⟨理由⟩ (a) reason ; (a) cause ; ⟨意味⟩

よこづけ 自動車を玄関へ横付けにした. He drew his car up to the door.

よこっぱら 象は横っ腹を私たちの方に向けて立っていた. The elephant stood broadside to us.

よこなみ 私たちの乗ったボートは横波を受けて転覆した. Our boat took a wave broadside and capsized.

よこばい 日本の経済成長率も横ばいとなって, ついにはその活力を失うかもしれない. The rate of Japan's economic growth may level off and eventually lose its dynamism.

よこめ 横目で見ていたら, 彼がこっそり逃げ出そうとしていた. Out of the corner of my eye I noticed that he was going away on tiptoe. / 彼はちらりと横目で彼女を見た. He took a side glance at her.

よごれる この本は手あかでひどく汚れている. This book is badly thumbed.

よさ この詩は何回も繰り返して読まなければ, その良さがわからない. This poem must be read more than once to be appreciated. | You have to read the poem over and over again to see its true value. / この作品に作者の良さが一番よく表われている. This work shows the author at his best. / 君は彼女の良さをちっとも見ようとしないんだね. You never try to see the best in her.

よざい 彼にはなお余罪がある見込みである. He is suspected of some other crimes, too.

よさん 建築費の予算は5千万円である. The building costs are estimated at 50 million yen. / この家の建築費は, 当初の予算を大分オーバーすることになりそうだ. Building the house is going to cost much more than we allowed

よし 《文》significance;〈手段〉a means《単複同形》; a way;〈趣旨〉the effect ¶…の由 They say [I hear, I understand,《文》It is said] that…. 文例⬇

よし² 止し ⇨やめ, ちゅうし¹.

よし³ 〖植〗a reed ¶よしの髄から天井をのぞく have a narrow [blinkered] view of things / よし笛 a reed pipe.

よし⁴ All right!; O.K.!; Good!; Fine! ⇨よろしい ¶現状でよしとしておく《米》let [leave] well enough alone;《英》let [leave] well alone. 文例⬇

よし⁵ 〈たとえ〉even if [though] ⇨たとえ².

よしあし 善し悪し good and [or] bad [《文》evil]; right and [or] wrong;〈適否〉《文》propriety ¶善し悪しを見分ける know [tell] good from bad; judge the quality (of an article) / 善し悪しである《文》have its demerits as well as its merits; have both advantages and disadvantages / 善し悪しは別として for good or (for) bad [《文》evil]. 文例⬇

よしきり 〖鳥〗a reed warbler.

よじげん 四次元〈四つの次元〉four dimensions;〈第四次元〉the fourth dimension ¶四次元の four-dimensional; fourth-dimensional.

よしず a reed blind [screen] ¶よしず張りの《a hut》sheltered with reed screens.

よじのぼる よじ登る clamber [climb] up; scale (a cliff).

よしみ 誼 friendship;《文》a bond between friends ¶よしみを結ぶ make friends《with sb》;《文》enter into friendly relations《with》/ 友だちのよしみで for friendship's sake / 昔のよしみで for old acquaintance' [time's] sake 文例⬇

よしや ⇨よし⁵.

よしゅう 予習 preparation (of one's lessons) ¶明日の予習をする prepare tomorrow's lessons; prepare one's lessons for tomorrow / 予習をしないで学校へ行く go to school without doing one's preparation / 予習をせずに授業に出る go to class unprepared. 文例⬇

よじょう 余剰 a surplus ⇨じょうよ ¶余剰農産物 farm surpluses; surplus farm produce [agricultural products].

よじる, よじれる ⇨ねじる, ねじれる. 文例⬇

よしわるし 善し悪し ⇨よしあし.

よしん¹ 予審 a preliminary examination [hearing]; a pretrial hearing [examination] ¶予審中である be under preliminary examination / 予審調書 the minutes [records] of the preliminary examination.

よしん² 予震 a foreshock; a preliminary [an advance] tremor.

よしん³ 余震 an aftershock.

よじん¹ 余人 others; other people. 文例⬇

よじん² 余燼 embers; smoldering fire. 文例⬇

よしんば ⇨たとえ².

よす stop; give up ⇨やめる. 文例⬇

よすが 〈思い出の〉a reminder《of》; something to remember《sb, an event》by. 文例⬇

よすてびと 世捨て人 a hermit;《文》a recluse;《文》an anchorite ¶世捨て人になる go and [to] live in seclusion; give up (participation in) public life; take no more interest in worldly affairs and live by oneself.

よせ¹ 寄席 a storytellers' theater ¶寄席芸人 a music-hall [variety] entertainer.

よせ² 寄せ〈囲碁・将棋〉the end game; the last stage(s) of a game.

よせあつめ 寄せ集め a mixture; a miscellany; a medley;〈がらくた〉odds and ends ¶寄せ集めの mixed; pickup / 寄せ集めのチーム a scratch [pickup] team.

よせあつめる 寄せ集める put together; gather; collect; scrape together.

よせい¹ 余生 the rest [《文》remainder] of one's life;《文》one's remaining years [days]. 文例⬇

よせい² 余勢 momentum ¶…の余勢を駆って《push on》encouraged [《文》emboldened] by《one's success [victory]》. 文例⬇

よせがき 寄せ書き

よせぎざいく 寄せ木細工 wooden mosaic (work);〈家具の〉marquetry (ware);〈床の〉parquetry.

よせぎれ 寄せ切れ odd ends [pieces] of cloth ¶寄せ切れの布団 a patchwork [crazy] quilt / 寄せ切れ細工 patchwork.

---

ourselves for it [put it at] at first. / 何よりもまず予算の均衡を取り戻す必要がある. First of all we have to get the budget back in balance. / ハワイへ行くだけの予算があるかね. Will our budget stand a visit to Hawaii? / (店の人が客に) ご予算はいかほどですか? May I ask what price range you have in mind? / About how much would you like to pay?

よし¹ 目下彼は病気の由. He is reported [said] to be ill. / 彼の細君が全快した由の手紙をもらった. I've received a letter informing me that his wife is well again.

よし⁴ これでもよしとせねばならぬところですね. It could be worse.

よしあし すいかの善し悪しがどうしてわかるのですか. How do you tell a good watermelon from a bad one? / それも善し悪しだね. That's not [I'm not sure that's] such a good idea, either.

よしみ 古くからのよしみで彼を見捨てておくわけにもいかない. As his old friend I can't let him down.

よしゅう 今日はちゃんと予習してなかったところがあたって, 大変だった. Today I was called on to do [translate] a passage I hadn't studied properly and had a hard time of it.

よじる, よじれる 腹の皮がよじれる程笑った. I laughed so much [hard] it made my sides ache. / 少年は身をよじって母親の腕からまんまと逃げた. The boy succeeded in wriggling out of his mother's arms.

よしん¹ 予審では彼はこれを否認した. In the pretrial interrogation he denied it.

よじん¹ 余人を以て代え難い人物だ. He is hard to replace.

よじん² 両国の関係は戦争の余燼なおさめやらぬ状態である. The war is over, yet the hostility between the two countries is still smoldering.

よす もうよせよ. Come off it, man. / 冗談はもうよせ. None [Enough] of your jokes! / この話はこの辺でよしましょう. Let's drop this subject here. / 気に入らなかったらよせばいい. You can take it or leave it. / よせったらよせ. Lay off, [Stop it,] I tell

よせざん 寄せ算 ⇨ たしざん.
よせつ 余切 《数》 a cotangent (略: cot).
よせつける 寄せ付ける allow *sb* to come near [《文》 approach]; let *sb* near ¶寄せ付けないkeep *sb* off (back, away, at a distance); 〈敵などを〉 keep [the enemy] off [at bay] / 家へ寄せ付けない shut *one's* doors 《against》; do not let *sb* into *one's* house.
よせて 寄せ手 an attacking force; 〈敵〉 the enemy.
よせなべ 寄せ鍋 a stew [《米》 chowder] cooked at the table.
よせなみ 寄せ波 surf; incoming waves.
よせる 寄せる 〈近づける〉 let *sb* come near (to *one*); bring *sth* near (to *one*); 〈引き寄せる〉 pull [draw] *sth* near (to *one*); 〈集める〉 gather [bring] together; get [call] (people) together; 〈加える〉 add (together, up); sum up ⇨ たす; 〈わきへ〉 put [push] aside [out of the way] ¶道のわきへ車を寄せる pull (*one's* car) to the side of the road / 身を寄せる put *oneself* under *sb's* protection [wings]; seek refuge with *sb*; live with *sb* / 書を寄せる write to *sb*; send a letter to *sb* / 信頼を寄せる put [《文》 place] *one's* confidence [trust] (in) / 心を寄せる 〈好きになる〉 take to *sb*; 〈同情する〉 feel [have] sympathy for 《a movement》. 文例⇩.
よせん 予選 〈競技の〉 a heat; a preliminary (contest); an elimination [eliminating] round [contest, heat]; a qualifying test [event]; a trial heat [contest, game] ¶予選を通過する qualify (for the semifinal) / 予選で落ちる be eliminated 《from the tournament》/ 第 1 次予選 the first elimination round / 男子 100 メートル予選 the men's 100-meter preliminary / 予選通過者 a qualifier.
よそ ¶よその strange; other 《shops》; 浮き世をよそにして 《文》 aloof from the affairs of the world [from mundane affairs]; 《文》 far from the madding crowd / よそで 《文》 elsewhere; at [in] another [some other] place / よそで食事をする dine out. 文例⇩.
よそいき よそ行き ¶よそ行きの formal 《language》; 《口語》 company 《manners》 / よそ行きの着物 (in) *one's* best clothes; (in) *one's* Sunday best / よそ行きの態度をとっているbe on *one's* best behavior.
よそう¹ 予想 〈予期〉 expectation(s); 《文》 (an) anticipation; 〈予測〉 a forecast; a prospect; 〈推測〉 《文》 a surmise; 《文》 (a) conjecture; imagination; (a) projection; 〈見積もり〉 an estimate ¶予想する expect; 《口語》 anticipate; forecast; surmise; suppose; imagine; estimate / …を予想して in expectation [anticipation] of… / 予想外の unexpected; unforeseen / 予想外に unexpectedly; 〈予想以上に〉 beyond (*one's*) expectation(s); 〈予想に反して〉 contrary to (*one's*) expectation(s); 〈事柄が主語〉 fall short of [《文》 belie] *one's* expectations; 〈人が主語〉 be disappointed in *one's* expectations / 予想どおりになる come [measure] up to *one's* expectations; meet [answer] *one's* expectations / 本年度の米の収穫予想高 this year's estimated rice crop [yield] / 予想額 an estimated amount / 予想屋 〈競馬などの〉 a tipster; a tout. 文例⇩.
よそう² dish out [up] (the beans); help 《*sb* to the potatoes》; serve 《*sb* with rice》 ¶自分で勝手によそって食べる help *oneself* (to the rice).
よそおい 装い dress; 《文》 apparel; 《文》 array; 《文》 attire; 〈化粧〉 a toilet; make-up ¶装いを新たにする get [be given, take on] a new look; get remodeled / 装いをこらす 《文》 attire *oneself* in *one's* best (clothes); be smartly dressed. 文例⇩.
よそおう 装う dress [《文》 array, equip] *oneself* (in); be dressed [《文》 clad, 《文》 attired] (in); 〈飾る〉 ornament [adorn] *oneself* (with); 〈化粧する〉 《文》 make *one's* toilet; make (*oneself*) up; 〈振りをする〉 make *oneself* seem [appear] (soft in the head); try to appear (unconcerned); 《文》 feign; 《文》 pretend 《ignorance》; 《文》 affect; put on [assume] a look [an air] of 《innocence》; sham; 《文》 simulate; 〈隠す, 知らんふりをする〉 《文》 dissimulate; 《文》 dissemble (*one's* emotions) ¶発狂を装

---

you! | When I tell you to stop, (you) damn well stop! | When I say 'Lay off!', I mean it!
よすが このレースは彼女をしのぶよすがともなろう. This lace will serve as something to remember her by.
よせい¹ 彼は余生を安楽に送った. He lived in comfort for the rest of his days.
よせい² 大成功の余勢を駆って東京に販路を拡張しようとした. Not content with his remarkable success, he went ahead at once with his plans for a further expansion of business [sales] in Tokyo.
よせがき 皆で彼に寄せ書きを送ってやった. We wrote a letter to him, each of us contributing a line and signing it.
よせる 彼は私のそばへ椅子を寄せた. He drew his chair up next to mine. / 寝台の頭の方が壁に寄せてあった. The head of the bed was up against the wall. / それを少し右へ寄せなさい. Move it a little to the right. / 医師たるものは患者が彼に寄せる信頼にこたえなければならぬ. A doctor must live up to the confidence his patients place in him.
よそ 彼によそながらいとまごいをしてきた. I visited him in order to bid him good-bye, though not in so many words. | I paid him a visit to bid him good-bye in my heart. / 息子がよその娘を妊娠させてしまった. Our son has got a girl into trouble [put a girl in the family way].
よそう 僕の予想どおりだった. It was [turned out] just as I had expected. | My expectations were (fully) realized. / 結果は予想以上でした. The result surpassed my expectations. | The result was better than I had expected. / この試合は最後まで予想がつかなかった. The outcome of the game was anybody's guess, right to the finish. / 両者は幾つかの点で衝突するだろうと予想されている. Several points of conflict can be foreseen between the two parties. / 今年の収穫予想ははなはだ明るい. The prospects for this year's harvest are very bright.
よそおい 当店銀座支店は装いを新たにして 5 月 1 日オープンいたし

う pretend to be mad; 《文》feign [simulate] madness / 落ち着きを装って 《文》with feigned calm / 謙遜(῀)を装って with mock humility [false modesty]. 文例⇩

よそく 予測 an estimate; a projection; a prospect; a forecast ¶予測する estimate; forecast; predict; project; guess ahead / 正確に予測するを誤る make an accurate [a wrong] estimate [forecast] (of). 文例⇩

よそごと よそ事 something one has nothing to do with; something that has nothing to do with one; a matter of no concern to one. 文例⇩

よそみ よそ見 ¶よそ見する look away [aside]; take one's eyes off (one's book).

よそめ よそ目 ¶よそ目にも even to a casual observer. 文例⇩ 〈他人〉'feigner.

よそもの よそ者 a stranger; an alien; a foreigner.

よそよそしい stiff; cold; standoffish; distant; remote ¶よそよそしくする treat sb stiffly; assume [put on] a cool air (toward); turn [show] the cold shoulder 《to》; 〈近づけない〉hold [keep] sb at arm's length / よそよそしくお辞儀を give sb a stiff bow. 文例⇩

よぞら 夜空 a night sky.

よた 〈下らぬ話〉idle talk [gossip]; 〈ほら〉a cock-and-bull story ¶よたを飛ばす talk rubbish [nonsense]; talk irresponsibly; shoot a line.

よたか 《鳥》a Japanese goatsucker; a nightjar.

よたく 預託 ¶預託する deposit 《money with よだつ   a bank》 / 預託金 a deposit.

よたもの 与太者 a hooligan; 《米》a hoodlum.

よたよた unsteadily; totteringly; with unsteady steps 《文》an unsteady gait ¶よたよた歩く walk with unsteady [uncertain] steps; totter; stagger; waddle (along) (アヒルのように).

よだれ 涎 slaver; saliva ¶よだれのたれそうな mouth-watering 《steak, offers》 / よだれを流す slaver; drivel; let saliva dribble from one's mouth; slobber (at the mouth) / よだれ掛け a bib. 文例⇩

よだん¹ 予断 (a) prediction; (a) prophecy ⇒よそく ¶予断を許さない be unpredictable; 《文》be beyond prophecy; there is no knowing [predicting].... 文例⇩

よだん² 余談 《文》a digression ¶余談はさておきto return to the subject; to cut short this digression; let's come [get] back to what we were talking about / 余談ですが in this connection I may add that...; let me say in passing that...; incidentally / 余談にわたる digress; wander (away) from the point [subject].

よち¹ 予知 《文》precognition; foreseeing; 《文》prognostication ¶予知する foresee; know beforehand; 〈予言する〉predict / 地震を予知する foretell [predict] an earthquake.

よち² 余地 room; space; a scope ¶妥協の余地がある[ない] there is room [no room] for compromise; 〈事が主題〉leave room [no room] for compromise / 活動する充分な余地を与える allow plenty of scope 《文》afford ample scope] for sb's activities / 今後の交渉の余地を残す leave the door open to [for] further negotiations. 文例⇩

よちよち ¶よちよち歩く toddle [waddle] along [about] / (赤ん坊が)はじめてよちよち歩きをする make [try] one's first unsteady steps.

よつ 四つ four ⇨しつ⁵ ¶四つに組む grapple 《with》; come to grips 《with》; 〈仕事などに〉tackle 《a task》.

よつあし 四つ足 ¶四つ足の four-footed; four-legged / 四つ足の動物 a four-footed animal; a quadruped / 四つ足を縛られた子やぎ a kid tied by the four legs.

よつおりばん 四つ折判 〈本〉a quarto (pl. -s).

よっか 四日 〈4日間〉four days; 〈第4日〉the fourth (of July).

よつかど 四つ角 〈十字路〉a crossroads (単数扱い); 〈街角〉a street corner ¶四つ角を左へ曲がる turn the corner to the left; turn left at the crossroads [corner].

よつぎ 世継ぎ a successor 《to sb》; 〈男〉an heir 《to》; 〈女〉an heiress 《to》 ¶世継ぎを残さずに死亡する die heirless.

よっきゅう 欲求 〈日常の生活上の〉want(s); 〈欲望〉《文》a desire (for); (a) craving (for); an urge (to do) ¶欲求を満たす gratify one's wants; 《文》gratify one's desire / 欲求不満《心理》(a) frustration.

よつぎり 四つ切り 〈写真〉a quarter ¶四つ切りにする quarter; cut 《an apple》into four parts [in four].

ます. Our renovated Ginza branch will open for business on May 1.
よそおう 彼はわざと平気を装っていた. He put on an unconcerned air.
よそく 結果はどうなるかだれにも予測がつかない. How it will turn out is anybody's guess.
よそごと 彼はこのことをまるでよそ事のように思っているらしい. He seems to feel as if it were none of his business [concern]. | It seems that he thinks it has nothing to do with him. / この悲劇はよそ事ではない. This tragedy might have happened to us.
よそめ 2人の仲はよそ目にもうらやましいほどだった. Their happy married life was the envy of all of us.
よそもの あの男はよそ者ですよ. He is not one of us.
よそよそしい 彼女は男性のいるところでは非常によそよそしくなる. She becomes very formal in male company.
よだつ 身の毛のよだつような話だった. The story made my hair stand on end [my blood run cold]. | It was a hair-raising story.

よだれ 見ただけでよだれが出たよ. The mere sight of it made my mouth water [set my mouth watering]. / 犬がえさを見てよだれを流した. The dog slavered over his food.
よだん¹ この法案の運命はまだ予断が許されない. The fate of the bill is still open to conjecture.
よち² その証拠には疑問の余地がない. The evidence admits of no [leaves no room for] doubt. / これ以上彼の活動する余地はほとんどない. He hasn't much scope left to act [for action]. | He no longer has much room for ma-

よつご 四つ子 quadruplets;《口語》quads.

よっつ 四つ four.

ヨット a yacht;〈大型エンジン付き〉a cabin cruiser;〈競走用〉a racing [competitive] yacht; a racer ¶ヨットを走らせる sail a yacht / ヨットに乗る yacht; cruise in a yacht / ヨットに乗りに行く go yachting [sailing]; go for a sail / ヨットレース a yacht(ing) race; a yachting event / ヨット操縦者[所有者] a yachtsman.

よっぱらい 酔っ払い a drunken man; a drunk;〈飲んだくれ〉a drunkard;《口語》a boozer;《文》a toper ¶酔っ払い運転 drunken driving; driving while intoxicated / 酔っ払い運転を追放する keep drinking drivers off the roads / 酔っ払い運転手 a drunken [drinking] driver.
用法 drunk は名詞の前の付加語としては用いない. したがって a drunk man, drunk driving は慣用的でなく, a drunken man, drunken driving が正しい.

よっぱらう 酔っ払う ⇨よう⁸.

よっぽど ⇨よほど. 文例⇩

よつゆ 夜露 evening [night] dew.

よづり 夜釣り night fishing [angling] ¶夜釣りに行く go fishing at night.

よつんばい 四つん這い ¶四つんばいになる get [drop] down on all fours / 四つんばいになって (go, crawl) on all fours; on (one's) hands and knees.

よてい 予定 a program; a plan; a schedule;〈手配〉arrangements;〈価格などの見積もり〉an estimate ¶将来の予定 a plan for the future /《文》prearranged; scheduled; intended; estimated / 予定の行動《文》a planned act;《文》a prearranged procedure / 予定の時刻に at the appointed time; on schedule [time] / 予定の時間を超過する overrun one's schedule; continue beyond [over] schedule / 予定を立てる make [map out] a plan [program] (for, of) / 予定である〈積もりである〉intend to do; plan 《to do, on doing》;〈期待されている〉be (expected) to do; 予定日に関して be due to do / 予定どおり as (previously) scheduled [arranged]; according to plan [schedule] / 予定より早く[遅く] (three days) earlier [later] than expected / 〈列車などが〉(two hours) ahead of [behind] schedule [time] / 予定外の unscheduled / 予定申告 (file) a provisional return / 予定地点《soft-land on》a preset [predetermined] area / 予定調和《哲》preestablished harmony / 出産予定日 one's expected date of confinement; one's time / 予定表 a schedule; a program; a timetable. 文例⇩

よとう 与党 the Government party; the party in power [office].

よどおし 夜通し all night (long); all (the) night through;《文》throughout the night;《last》through the night. 文例⇩

よとく 余得 an extra profit [gain];〈役得〉《文》a perquisite;《口語》a perk ★ perquisites, perks と複数形で使うのが普通.

よどみ 淀み〈停滞〉stagnation;〈口ごもり〉faltering;〈沈殿〉a deposit; (a) sediment;〈せきなどの〉backwater; a pool ¶よどみなく話す speak fluently [without hesitation, (right) off the reel].

よどむ 淀む〈停滞する〉be stagnant; stagnate;〈沈殿する〉settle ((to the bottom)); be sedimented; be precipitated;〈ためらう〉hesitate;〈口ごもる〉stammer; falter ¶よどんだ水《a pool of》stagnant [standing] water / 黒くよどんだ目《stare with》dark pools of eyes.

よなおし 世直し an attempt to make the world a better place; social reform.

よなか 夜中 ¶夜中に in (the middle of) the night; at [in] the dead of night / 夜中の12時に at midnight; at twelve o'clock midnight / 夜中の2時3時ごろに[まで] in [till] the small hours of the morning. 文例⇩

よなが 夜長 ¶秋の夜長に in the lengthening nights of autumn.

よなき 夜鳴き ¶夜鳴きする cry in the night; cry by night.

よなべ 夜なべ ¶夜なべをする work at night; do nightwork / 夜なべに針仕事をする do needlework at night.

よなよな 夜な夜な every night; night after night; nightly.

よなれる 世慣れる get used to (the way of) the world; see a great deal of life ¶世慣れた worldly-wise; experienced (in worldly affairs) / 世慣れた人 a man of the world / 世慣れない inexperienced (in worldly affairs);《a man》of little experience; green. 文例⇩

よにげ 夜逃げ ¶夜逃げする run away under

---

neuver. / この案はなお改善の余地がある. There is still room for improvement in this plan. | This plan can stand further improvement.

よっきゅう 彼らはどこまでも生活向上の欲求が強い. Their desire for ever higher living standards runs strong.

よっぽど よっぽど面と向かってそう言ってやろうかと思った. I had a good mind [half a mind] to tell him so to his face. | I came very near to giving (the whole thing) up 【英口語】to jacking it in].

よてい 彼は明日東京着の予定だ. He is expected (to be) in Tokyo tomorrow. / 明日は何をする予定か. What is the program for tomorrow? | What are we going to do tomorrow? / 会は土曜日の晩の予定です. The party is to take place on Saturday evening. | The meeting is scheduled for Saturday evening. / 電車は5時30分に到着の予定です. The train is due [to arrive] at 5:30. / いいかい, みな予定どおり動いてもらいたいんだ. Make no mistake about it [Let's get it clear], I want you all to keep to schedule. / この調子では出版予定に間に合わない. We are failing to meet the timetable for publication.

よどおし 夜通しまんじりともしなかった. I didn't sleep a wink the whole night.

よなか こんな夜中に間違い電話をかけるなんて迷惑だよ. It's most annoying to get a wrong number at this time of night, you know! | How would you like being woken up by a wrong number in the middle of the night!

よなれる 彼は世慣れている [いない]. He has seen a lot [has not

よねつ 余熱 remaining [residual] heat.

よねん 余念 ¶余念なく intently; eagerly; 《文》absorbedly; busily; 《文》with undivided attention / …に余念がない be busy 《with sth, doing》; busy oneself 《with sth, (in) doing》; be absorbed [buried, engrossed] 《in》; devote oneself 《to》/ 余念なく勉強する give (one's) undivided attention to one's lessons; apply oneself (closely) to one's studies.

よねんせい 四年生 a student in his [her] fourth year; a fourth-year student; 〈小学校の〉a fourth-year[-grade] pupil; 〈大学の〉《米》a senior.

よのつね 世の常 the way of the world; the way things are; what may happen to anybody; a common [an everyday] affair ¶世の常の usual; common; ordinary / 世の常ならぬ unusual; uncommon; extraordinary.

よのなか 世の中 〈世間〉the world; 〈人生〉life; 〈時世〉the times; 〈時代〉《文》the age ¶世の中へ出る start life; go out into the world / 世の中がいやになる be [get] sick (and tired) of the world; be no longer interested in living on in this world.

よは 余波 an aftereffect; a side effect; an aftermath. 文例日

よばい 夜這い visiting a girl at her house under cover of night.

よはく 余白〈空白〉a blank; (a) space; 〈欄外〉a margin.

よばわり 呼ばわり ¶泥棒呼ばわりをする (go so far as to) call sb a thief / 裏切者呼ばわりをする denounce [brand] sb as a traitor.

よばん 夜番〈事〉night watch; 〈人〉a night watchman ¶夜番をする keep [be on] night watch.

よび 予備 ¶予備の〈準備の〉preparatory; preliminary; 〈必要時に備えての〉reserve (troops); spare (parts) / 予備の燃料 reserve fuel; a fuel reserve / 予備金 a reserve (fund); money in reserve / 予備工作 spadework; preliminaries / 予備交渉 a preliminary negotiation / 予備試験[調査] a preliminary examination [investigation] / 予備知識 (a) preliminary [background] knowledge 《of a subject》/ (…についての)予備知識を得る brief oneself on sth; 《口語》do one's homework on sth / 予備兵力 (the) reserves.

よびあげる 呼び上げる call over (the names) ¶名簿を呼び上げる call the roll.

よびあつめる 呼び集める call [gather, muster] together; assemble; convene; rally; summon (together) ⇒しょうしゅう

よびいれる 呼び入れる call sb in [into]; have sb in.

よびうり 呼び売り〈事〉hawking; 〈人〉a hawker; a peddler; a street crier [vendor] ¶呼び売りする hawk; cry [call out] 《one's wares》.

よびえき 予備役 ¶予備役になる[回る] go into the reserve(s) / 予備役大佐 a colonel in the reserve(s).

よびおこす 呼び起こす〈目を覚まさせる〉wake sb (up); call; rouse; arouse ¶記憶[思い出]を呼び起こす call sth to mind; recall sth (to one's mind).

よびかえす 呼び返す call back; recall; 〈手を振って〉wave sb back ¶本国へ呼び返される be called [ordered] home / (芸人が演技が終わって)何度も舞台へ呼び返される have a large number [a lot] of curtain calls.

よびかける 呼び掛ける call (out) (to); 〈話し掛ける〉speak to; 《文》address; accost; 〈訴える〉appeal 《to the public》¶(Mr., sir などという)呼び掛け方 a form of address; an address form.

よびこ 呼び子 (blow on) a whistle.

よびこう 予備校 a (private) cramming school; 《米》a preparatory [《口語》prep] school; 《英口語》a crammer.

よびごえ 呼び声 a call; a cry. 文例日

よびこみ 呼び込み〈見せ物の〉a barker.

よびこむ 呼び込む ⇒ よびいれる.

よびすて 呼び捨て ¶呼び捨てにする use sb's name without an honorific title; do not refer to [《文》address] sb as Mr. [Mrs., Miss, etc.] ….

よびだし 呼び出し a call; 〈召喚〉a summons (pl. summonses); 〈相撲の〉a caller ¶呼び出し状 (a writ of) summons; a subpoena (罰則を付記した) / 呼び出し状を送る serve a subpoena on sb; serve sb with a summons; subpoena

---

seen much] of life [the world]. / あの男は世慣れているから、そのぐらいのことは承知しているよ. He is too much a man of the world not to know that.

よのなか これからの世の中はどうなることやら. I'm sure I don't know what the world's coming to. / 世の中はそうしたものだ. That's the way things are [it goes]. |《文》That is the way of the world. |《口語》That's the way the cookie crumbles. / 世の中ってわからないもんじゃのう. Life is unpredictable. | In this life it is difficult to predict how things will turn out. / まったく世の中は様々だ. It takes all sorts (of people) to make a world. / 世の中の移り変わりでこんな所を訪れる人はほとんどいなくなった. Changes in fashion have meant that hardly anyone ever visits a place like this any more. / 今は原子力の世の中だと言っても過言ではありますまい. It is surely no exaggeration to say that this is the age of atomic power. / およそその中にあれほどずるしこいやつはいない. There is no craftier man in the world today.

よは 台風の余波で波が高い. The sea is running high on account of a typhoon in the vicinity.

よはく この本は書き入れをする余白が多くて便利だ. This book is very convenient as it has a broad margin to write notes in [on].

よびおこす この本を見て少年時代の記憶を呼び起こした. The book reminded me [put me in mind] of my childhood.

よびごえ 彼はノーベル賞候補として呼び声が高い. He is very much talked of as a possible winner of a Nobel prize.

よびすて ここではみんな名前を呼び捨てにすることになっている. We are all on a first-name basis here.

よびだし 僕のところは呼び出し電

よびだす 呼び出す call;〈法廷へ〉summon; subpoena;〈電話口へ〉call [ring] *sb* up (on the phone); call *sb* to the (tele)phone / 法廷に呼び出される be summoned [subpoenaed] to the court. 文例

よびたてる 呼び立てる〈大声に〉call out (to);〈呼び付ける〉ask *sb* to come;《文》summon.

よびつける 呼び付ける call *sb* to one [one's presence];〈使いをやって〉send for *sb*.

よびとめる 呼び止める (call and) stop *sb*; call *sb* to stop [halt];「だれか」と呼びかけて〉challenge.

よびな 呼び名 the name *sb* goes by [under].

よびみず 呼び水 ¶呼び水をする〈差す〉prime [fetch]《a pump》;〈比喩的に〉prime the pump.

よびもどす 呼び戻す ⇒よびかえす

よびもの 呼び物 an [a special] attraction; (special) feature; a featured attraction; the highlight; a draw;《米口語》a drawing card. 文例

よびょう 余病 a complication; a secondary disease ¶余病を併発する〈病気・事が主語〉cause [produce] a complication;〈人が主語〉have another disease concurrently《with pneumonia》/ 余病を併発せずに《heal》without complications. 文例

よびよせる 呼び寄せる have *sb* come to one; call *sb* to one [one's room, one's desk, etc.];《文》summon *sb* to [before] one;〈使いをやって〉send for *sb*;〈呼び集める〉call [bring, gather] together; convene《a committee, the members》¶手紙[電報]で呼び寄せる write [wire] for *sb*.

よびりん 呼び鈴 a bell; a doorbell ¶呼び鈴の押しボタン a bell push [button] / 呼び鈴を鳴らす ring a (door)bell; push the button of a bell;〈人を呼ぶ〉ring for《the nurse》. 文例

よぶ 呼ぶ〈声をかける〉call *sb*; call (out) to *sb*; hail (おーいと);〈後ろから〉call after (呼びにやる) send for《a doctor》; call in (呼び込む);〈召喚する〉summon;〈芸人などを〉engage; hire;〈招く〉invite [ask]《*sb* to dinner》;〈引き付ける〉attract; draw;〈名付ける〉call; name; term (学術上で) ¶先生と呼ぶ refer to [《文》address] *sb* as *Sensei* / 手をたたいて呼ぶ clap *one's* hands for《a waitress》/ …と呼ばれている be called…; go [be known] by the name of… / 呼びに来る[行く] come [go] for *sb* / 呼び合う〈名前を〉call (out) to each other; call each other's name / 呼べば聞こえるところに within call [hail] (of); within hailing distance (of). 文例

よふかし 夜更かし ¶夜更かしする sit [stay] up (till) late at night [far into the night] / 読書で夜更かしをする sit up late reading [over a book]. 文例

よふけ 夜更け 夜更けに late at night;〈真夜中に〉in the middle of the night; at [in the] dead of night / 夜更けまで till late at night; until the small hours of the morning; far into the night. 文例

よぶん 余分〈過剰〉《文》an excess; what is left over;〈特別なもの〉an extra;〈剰余〉a surplus ¶余分の《文》excessive; too much;《文》superfluous; extra《payment》;《money》to spare / 余分に働く do extra work; work extra《overtime》/ 200円余分に払う〈特別に〉pay 200 yen extra;〈払い過ぎる〉pay 200 yen too much.

よほう 予報 a forecast; (a) prediction ¶予報する forecast; predict / 天気予報 ⇒てんき¹ / 数値[長期](天気)予報 a numerical [long-range] (weather) forecast.

よぼう 予防〈防止〉prevention (of); protection (from, against);《医》(a) prophylaxis;〈用心〉(a) precaution ¶予防する prevent; protect (from, against);《文》take preventive measures《against》/ 病気の予防 disease prevention / 予防医学《衛生》preventive medicine [hygiene] / 予防接種 a vaccination [an inoculation]《against polio》/ 予防接種をしてもらう be inoculated [vaccinated]《against diphtheria》/ 予防線をはる take precautions《against》;〈先回りをする〉forestall《*sb*, an attack》/ 予防戦争 a preventive war / 予防措置を講ずる take [《文》adopt] precautionary [preventive] measures《against》/ 予防注射 (an) inoculation; a preventive injection [shot]《against cholera》/ 予防薬 a preventive medicine; a prophylactic (agent). 文例

話だ. The only number I can give you is that of a neighbor who lets me use his phone.

よびだす 判事の前に[裁判所に]呼び出された. He was summoned before the judge [summoned to appear in court].

よびもの 当日の呼び物はマリアン・アンダーソンの独唱だった. The chief feature [attraction] of the day [evening] was the vocal solo by Marian Anderson. / これが今週のテレビ番組の呼び物です. These are this week's TV highlights.

よびょう 余病が併発した. A complication arose [set in].

よびりん 呼び鈴を押そうとしていたらドアがあいた. I was on the point of ringing the doorbell [pressing the bell push] when the door opened. / 玄関で呼び鈴が鳴った. There was a ring at the door. | The doorbell rang [pealed].

よぶ 夕飯にスミス夫妻をお呼びしているんです. We are having [inviting] the Smiths over for dinner. / 奥田さんのお宅にお茶に呼ばれた. I was asked [invited] to tea at Mr. Okuda's. / お父さまがお呼びですよ. Your father wants you. / タクシーを呼んでください. Please call [get] me a taxi. | Please call a taxi for me.

よふかし このところ夜更かしをしている. I've been having some late nights (recently).

よふけ この夜更けに何の用があるのか. What do you want me for at this time of night?

よぶん 余分の服は1着もありません. I haven't got a spare suit of clothes.

よぼう 予防は治療にまさる. Prevention is better than cure. / これが交通事故の予防策として最善のものであろう. This is probably the best safeguard against traffic accidents.

よほう² 輿望 ¶国民の輿望を担う 《文》 enjoy the confidence [be the hope] of the (whole) nation. 文例⇩

よほど 余程 〈大変〉very; greatly; much; highly; considerably, a good [great] deal; 〈はるかに〉far 《bigger》; (bigger) by far ¶よほどの〈数〉a large number of; 《文》many; 〈量〉a great deal of; considerable; 〈量〉much / よほどの金 plenty [lots] of money; a large [sizable] sum of money / よほど以前に very long ago.

よぼよぼ ¶よぼよぼの decrepit; tottering / よぼよぼ歩く totter along; walk with faltering steps [《文》an unsteady gait].

よまいごと 世迷い言 ¶世迷い言を言う talk nonsense [rubbish].

よまわり 夜回り ⇒よばん.

よみ 読み reading; 〈先見〉foresight; 〈判断〉judgment ¶読みが深い[浅い] have a keen [have no] insight (into the problem); one's reading (of the situation) is good [poor, wrong] / 読みが深い[浅い]人 a person who has (very) keen [has no] insight; a person with good [bad] judgment.

よみあげざん 読み上げ算 〈珠算の〉addition (and subtraction) of figures read off aloud.

よみあげる 読み上げる 〈声をあげて〉read (a passage) aloud [out loud]; read (a passage) out; call (the roll) over; 〈読み終える〉finish (reading) (a book); read through.

よみあやまる 読み誤る 〈解釈を〉read sth wrong; misread; misinterpret; 〈発音を〉mispronounce.

よみあわせる 読み合わせる read out and collate (one copy with another); check (accounts).

よみおとす 読み落とす miss [overlook] (a line) (in reading).

よみおわる 読み終わる finish (reading) (a book); read (a book) through; get through (a book); have done with (a novel). 文例⇩

よみかえす 読み返す read (a book) (over) again; reread ¶始めから読み返す read (a book) all over again.

よみがえる 蘇る be brought (back) to life [to one's senses]; revive; rise from the dead; spring to life again; 〈比喩的に〉make a [one's] comeback ¶蘇らせる bring sb (back) to life [his senses]; raise sb from the dead; 《文》resuscitate; 〈記憶を〉recall [get back] ((one's) memories).

よみかき 読み書き reading and writing ¶読み書きができない cannot read or write; be illiterate / 読み書きの能力 literacy / 読み書きの能力にすぐれている be highly literate (in Latin) / 読み書きそろばん reading, writing and arithmetic; the three R's.

よみかけ 読みかけ ⇒よみさし.

よみかた 読み方 a way of reading (Shakespeare); a reading; how to read; 〈発音〉pronunciation; 〈解釈〉a reading; an interpretation; 〈学科〉a reading lesson ¶読み方の練習をする practice reading. 文例⇩

よみきかせる 読み聞かせる read (a book) to sb.

よみきり 読み切り 読み切りの complete-in-one-issue (stories). 文例⇩

よみきる 読み切る 〈終わりまで読む〉read (a book) through; finish (reading) (a book); 〈読み尽くす〉read all (the books); 〈相手の動きを〉figure [reason] out (the opponent's intentions).

よみごたえ 読みごたえ ¶読みごたえがある be well worth reading; 《文》make substantial reading; be (highly) rewarding.

よみこなす 読みこなす understand [digest] (the contents of a book). 文例⇩

よみこむ 読み込む read (a fanciful meaning) into (a passage).

よみさし 読みさし ¶読みさしにする leave (a book) half-read / 本を読みさしにして外出する go out without finishing a book / 読みさしの本 the book one is reading / 読みさしのところへ目印しをする mark one's place in (a book). 文例⇩

よみすてる 読み捨てる give (a book) a once-over (and never read it again); 〈一度読んで捨てる〉throw (a book) away after a single reading.

よほう² 彼こそ国民の輿望を担う人物である. The hopes of the people rest on him.

よほど 病人は今日はよほどよい. He is much better today. / 100万円もあればよほど助かるんだが. A million yen would go a long way toward what I need. / 彼はよほどのことがなければ気持ちを変えないだろう. It'll take a lot to make him change his mind. / よほどよく勉強しなければ合格はおぼつかないよ. You'll need to work much harder if you are going to pass the exam. / よほど本当のことを言ってやろうかと思った. I had a good mind to tell him the truth.

よみおとす そこはつい読み落としてしまった. That [That passage] escaped my attention [notice] while I was reading the book.

よみおわる 読み終わったらその本を返して下さい. Please return the book (to me) when you've done with it.

よみかた この漢字には読み方が3通りある. This kanji has three readings. | There are three readings for this kanji. | この字の読み方をご存じですか. Do you know how to pronounce this word?

よみきり その雑誌の1月号には新年付録として読み切り小説が載っている. The January issue of the magazine has a New Year supplement of complete stories.

よみこなす この本は子供にはとても読みこなすまい. I'm afraid this won't make easy reading for young people.

よみさし 彼は読みさしにしておいたところから読み始めた. He started reading the book again from where he had left off. | He picked up the story from where he had put it down.

よみて こんな本の読み手があるかしら. I wonder if anyone reads this sort of book.

よみで この本は2千ページもあるからなかなか読みでがあるよ. This is a bulky volume of 2,000 pages, and it is no easy matter to read it through [and one can't run through it in a short time].

よみとる 彼は相手の決意のほどを読み取ろうとしていた. He was trying to get some hint of [some

よみせ 夜店 〈全体〉 a night fair; 〈個々の店〉 a night stall [booth] ¶夜店の商人 a (night-)stall keeper [man] / 夜店を開く open [set up] a (night) stall.

よみだし 読み出し 《コンピューター》 a 《digital》 readout ¶読み出し受信局 a readout station.

よみち 夜道 ¶夜道を行く go [travel] by night; make a night journey.

よみつくす 読み尽くす read all 《the books in the library》.

よみて 読[詠]み手 〈読む人〉 a reader; 〈歌の作者〉 the writer [composer] 《of a poem》. 文例⇩

よみで 読みで ⇨

よみとおす 読み通す read through 《a book》 《to the last page》.

よみとる 読み取る read 《sb's thought in his eyes》 ⇨ よむ ¶言外の意味を読み取る 〈本などで〉 read between the lines / 何を思っているのか読み取れない目付き unreadable eyes / 読み取り機[装置] 《コンピューター》 a reader; a reading device. 文例⇩

よみなおす 読み直す read 《a book》 《over》 again. ⇨ よみかえす.

よみながす 読み流す 〈すらすらと〉 read without pause; 〈大ざっぱに〉 skim through [run over] 《a book》.

よみなれる 読み慣れる get used [《文》 become accustomed] to reading 《a book》 ¶読み慣れた本 a book with which one is familiar; a book which is familiar to one.

よみにくい 読みにくい hard [difficult] to read 〈本などが〉 (almost) unreadable; 〈字が〉 hard to make out; illegible 《handwriting》.

よみのくに よみの国 the land of the dead; 《文》 the nether world; 〈ギリシャ神話の〉 Hades.

よみびと 読み人 ¶読み人知らずの anonymous.

よみふける 読み耽る be absorbed [lost, 《文》 engrossed] in (reading) 《a book》; pore over 《a novel》. 文例⇩

よみふだ 読み札 the cards which are read out (in a game of karuta).

よみもの 読み物 reading (matter) ¶よい[つまらない, おもしろい, 軽い]読み物 good [dull, amusing, light] reading / 子供の読み物 children's books; books for children [young people]; juvenile literature [books]. 文例⇩

よみやすい 読みやすい 〈本が〉 easy to read; 〈字が〉 clear; legible 《handwriting》. 文例⇩

よむ 読[詠]む read; study 《the text》; 《文》 peruse (精読する); くとなえる〉 recite; chant; 〈詠む〉 compose [write] 《a poem》 ¶むさぼり読む devour; read 《a novel》 greedily / 声を出して読む read 《a passage》 out [aloud] / ざっと読む run [glance] over 《a book》; skim through 《a book》 / 漫然と読む read 《a book》 carelessly; browse through 《a book》; open 《this book and that》 at random / 一字一字たどってやっと読んで行く spell one's way through 《a book》 / 行を飛ばして読む skip (over) a few lines / 人の心中を読む read sb's thoughts 《in his eyes》 / 新聞で読む see [read] sth in the (news)papers; read about sth in the (news)papers / お経を読む 〈声を出して〉 intone a sutra / 広く読んでいる have read a great deal (of); 《文》 be widely [well] read (in English literature) / 読んでもらう get sb to read 《a book》; have 《a book》 read 《by sb》 / 本を読みながら眠る read oneself to sleep / 読んで字のごとく literally / 一度読んだだけで on a single reading; in one reading / 初めて読んだとき at [on] one's first reading / 繰り返し読んでから after repeated reading. 文例⇩

よめ¹ 嫁 〈花嫁〉 a bride; 〈妻〉 a wife (pl. wives); 〈親から見て〉 a daughter-in-law (pl. daughters-) ¶嫁の口 an offer of marriage / 嫁にやる 《文》 give 《one's daughter》 《away》 in marriage; marry 《one's daughter》 off / 嫁に行く marry 《a man, into a family》; get married 《to a man》 / 嫁にもらう[迎える] have 《a woman》 as wife for one's son. 文例⇩

よめ² 夜目 ¶夜目にもしるく見える (can) be clearly made out in the dark.

よめい 余命 the rest of one's life; 《文》 one's remaining days; what is left of one's life. 文例⇩

よめいり 嫁入り a wedding; (a) marriage ¶嫁入りする ⇨ よめ¹ (嫁に行く) / 嫁入り前の娘 a girl of marriageable age / 嫁入り支度 〈道具〉 a

---

clue about] how determined his rival was.

よみびと この歌は読み人知らずだ. It is not known who composed this tanka.

よみふける 彼はいつも漫画の本に読みふけっている. He always has his nose in some comic book or other.

よみもの 車中で読む何か軽い読み物がほしい. I'd like some light reading for my train journey. / これは面白い読み物. This makes pleasant reading. / 《英口語》 This is a good read. / この本は軽い夏の読み物として好適なものの1つになるでしょう. This book will prove a welcome addition to our light summer reading.

よみやすい この本は読みやすく書いてある. This book is easy to read. / This book is written in an easy-to-read style.

よむ この手紙を読んで下さいませんか. Would you mind reading this letter for me? / 聖書はあらゆる本の中で一番読まれる本だ. The Bible is the most widely read of all books. / フォークナーのものは何も読んだことがない. I've never read any Faulkner. / この脚本は芝居で見るより読んだ方が面白い. This play reads better than it acts. / この本は高校生がぜひとも読むべき本である. This book is a must for high-school students. / 1回読んだだけではその真価がわからない本がたくさんある. There are quite a few books from which you can't get full value on a single [in one] reading. / There are a lot of books which you have to reread to appreciate. / radar や defied のように左から読んでも右から読んでも同じ言葉がある. There are palindromic words like 'radar' and 'defied' that read the same both ways. / 説明をちゃんと読んでおかないからいけないんだよ. You should have studied [read] the instructions properly.

よめ¹ 嫁姑の争いは日本の家庭の特徴だと考えられている. Wife and mother-in-law conflicts are thought to be characteristic of Japanese households.

よめい 余命いくばくもない. His days are numbered. / He hasn't much longer to live.

よめる 読める 〈読み得る〉can read; 〈字がはっきりしている〉be legible; be clear; 〈面白く〉be readable; 〈解釈できる〉can be interpreted 〖《文》construed〗《as》; 〈分かる〉see; understand. 文例⇩

よもぎ 〈植〉a mugwort.

よもすがら ⇨ よどおし.

よもや surely 《not》; (not) possibly ¶よもやに引かされて《文》deluded by a vain hope. 文例⇩

よもやま 四方山 ¶よもやまの話をする talk on various subjects [topics]; talk about all sorts of things.

よやく 予約 〈座席などの〉booking; reservation; 〈本の〉subscription; 〈商品の〉an advance order; 〈美容院・医者などの〉an appointment ¶予約する book《tickets》; reserve 《a seat》; have 《a room》reserved; make a 《sleeper》reservation; make an appointment 《with one's hairdresser》; subscribe 《for》/ 予約なしで without a reservation / 予約係 a reservation desk 《of an airline》/ 予約金 a deposit / 予約者 a subscriber 《to [for] the newspaper》/ 予約出版する publish 《a book》by subscription / 予約制で売る sell 《an encyclopedia》by subscription / 予約席 a reserved seat. 文例⇩

よゆう 余裕 〈余地〉room; 〈時日の〉time (to spare); 〈経費などの〉a margin; 〈活動の〉scope; 〈落ち着き〉composure ¶余裕がある[ない] have [have no] (time, money) to spare; can [cannot, 《文》can ill] afford 《to do, sth》/ 余裕しゃくしゃくとしている〈体力が〉still have (enough) strength in reserve; 〈金銭など〉have enough and to spare; 〈平然としている〉be calm and composed.

より 縒り a twist; a ply ¶よりを戻す〈糸の〉untwist; untwine; 〈仲直りする〉get back on good terms 《with》; 《文》be reconciled 《with》; 《文》return to one's former relations 《with》/ より糸 twisted thread [yarn] / 2本よりの縄 a two-strand rope. 文例⇩

より² 〈比較〉than; 〈場所〉from; out of; 〈時〉since; from… (on); on and after ⇨ から⁴ ¶海の彼方より from beyond [across] the sea / …より劣って〈勝って〉be worse [better] than…; 《文》be inferior [superior] to…; be below [above] 《sb in ability》. 文例⇩

[用法]「彼は僕より年上だ」は、口語では He is older than me. と言うのが普通だ、…than I am はあらたまった言い方。…than I は文法にこだわりすぎた、不自然な言い方である。これは than に続く代名詞のすべての人称・数についても、また、as… as me [I (am)]、etc. についても同じことが言える。

-より …寄り ¶やや西寄りのところに a little to the west (of) / 南寄りの風 a southerly wind.

よりあい 寄り合い 〈会合〉a meeting; a gathering; a get-together; 〈群れ〉a group ¶寄り合い所帯〈寄り集まり〉《文》a congeries 《of small city-states》; 〈寄せ集めのチーム〉a scratch [combined] team.

よりあう 寄り合う gather; assemble; get [come, meet, crowd, flock, 《文》throng] together.

よりあつまり 寄り集まり an assembly; a group ⇨ よりあい.

よりあつまる 寄り集まる ⇨ よりあう.

よりかかる 寄り掛かる lean 《against, on, over》; 《文》recline 《on a sofa》; 〈頼る〉lean 《on》[depend] 《on》; rest 《on》¶机に寄り掛かる lean on the desk / 壁に寄り掛かる lean against the wall / さくに寄り掛かる lean over the rail.

よりごのみ 選り好み ¶より好みをする be particular 〖《口語》fussy, fastidious, 《文》overnice〗《about》; be choos(e)y 《about》/ 食べ物により好みをする be fussy [particular, finicky] about one's food; pick and choose what one eats; 《米口語》be a picky eater.

よりすがる ⇨ すがる.

よりそう 寄り添う get 〖《文》draw, sit, stand〗close 《to each other》; cuddle close together; nestle close 《to》; snuggle up [close] 《to》.

よりだす 選り出す pick [sort, single] out.

よりつき 寄り付き 〖取引〗the opening of a session [market] ¶寄り付き相場 the opening

---

よめる 不服だということが彼の顔色で読めた. Dissatisfaction was written all over his face. | I could read discontent in his face. / この自伝は小説のように読める. This autobiography reads like a novel. / この小説はいろいろ欠点はあるがなかなか面白く読める. This novel makes rather interesting reading, despite its defects. / (子供や生徒に向かって) 本がどのくらい読めるようになったかな. Let's see how your reading has got on. / それで読めた. I've got it. | Well, that explains it.

よもや よもやそうではあるまい. Surely it cannot be false. | There's no way (that) it can be untrue! / よもやそんなことはあるまい. It is highly improbable. / よもや彼はそんなことはすまいと思った. He was the last man I expected to do it. | I hadn't the faintest suspicion that he would do such a thing.

よやく 私の『英語研究』の予約が来月で切れる. My subscription to *The Study of English* expires next month. / 帝国ホテルに予約しておきました. I've booked a room for you at the Imperial Hotel. / 電話でホテルに2部屋予約しておきましょうか. Shall I ring up and book [make a booking for] two rooms at the hotel? / 札幌に行きたいと彼女は思ったのだが、ホテルの予約がとれなかった. She wanted to go to Sapporo but could not get a hotel room. / 予約で満員でございます. We are fully booked (up). / 予約席.『掲示』Reserved.

よゆう そんなものを買う余裕はない. I cannot afford (to buy) it. / 電車にはまだ1時間余裕がありますよ. You still have an hour to catch the train. / 彼は1日10時間も働いて、なお余裕しゃくしゃくとしている. He works ten hours a day, and is ready for more [and yet shows no sign of fatigue].

より¹ 彼は彼女とよりを戻そうとしている. He is trying to get her back.

より² 私は富よりも健康を重んじる. I value health above wealth. / 降伏するより死んだ方が増しだ. I would rather die than surrender. / I'd die before I'd surrender. / あれよりこの方がよい. I prefer this to that. | I like this

よりつく 寄り付く get [come] near ; 《文》approach ¶寄り付かない keep away from *sb* ; 《文》shun *sb* ; 〈敬遠する〉keep *sb* at a respectful distance.

よりどころ 拠り所 ⇨ こんきょ, てんきょ¹, たより². 文例⇩

よりどり 選り取り ¶より取りする choose 《from》; make *one's* choice 《from》. 文例⇩

よりによって 選りに選って ¶よりによって彼は he of all men / よりによって今日 today of all days.

よりぬき 選り抜き the choice 《of》; the pick ; the cream ¶より抜きの choice ; select ; best ; picked ; crack 《troops》.

よりぬく 選り抜く choose ; select ; pick [single] out ¶多数の中からより抜く choose [select] 《a book》 from among many.

よりみち 寄り道 ¶寄り道する call [drop in] 《on *sb*, at *sb's* house》 on the way ; 〈旅行で〉break *one's* journey 《at Nagoya》; stop over 《at》; 〈道筋を外れて〉go out of *one's* way 《to》; take a side trip 《to》. 文例⇩

よりょく 余力 reserve [remaining] power [strength, energy] ; a reserve of energy ¶…するだけの余力がある have energy [money] enough to spare for 《some other work》.

よりわける 選り分ける 〈分類する〉sort out ; assort ; classify ; 〈選び出す〉pick [single] out ; 〈別々にする〉separate *sth* from the others.

よる¹ 夜 (a) night ; 〈宵〉(an) evening ⇨ や² ¶土曜の夜 (on) Saturday night [evening] / 夜の音 (night) (programs) ; nocturnal (夜行性の) / (nine o'clock) at night (★この場合 in the evening でもよい. evening は night のうちの就寝時間までの部分) / 夜の東京 Tokyo by night / 夜の女 a street girl ; a streetwalker ; 《文》a lady of the night / 夜の寒さを防ぐ keep out the night cold / 夜に at night ; 《米口語》nights ; 〈夜は〉by night ; 〈夜中に〉in the night / 夜になる (the) night falls [comes on, closes in] / 夜にならぬうちに before dark / 夜遅くまで (till) late at night ; far into the night /

夜も昼も night and day ; day and night / 夜型の人 a night bird [owl] ; a nighthawk.

よる² 依る 〈頼る〉depend [rely, hang] on ; 〈基づく〉be based [founded] on ; 〈手段に訴える〉《文》have recourse [resort] to ; appeal to ; 〈原因する〉be due [owing] to ; be caused (by) ; 〈立てこもる〉hold [occupy, take up] 《a position》 ¶…により, …によって 〈従って〉according to ; 〈…に応じて〉《文》in compliance with ; 〈…の理由で〉on account of ; owing to ; due to ; 《文》on (the) grounds that… ; 〈…の手段で〉by ; by means of / 校則第3条により under [《文》pursuant to] Art. 3 of the school regulations / ご依頼によって at your request / 最近の調査によれば according to the latest investigation / 彼らの助力によって by [thanks to] their help / お勧めにより on your advice / …(の話し)によると [によれば] according to 《Mr. Jones》 [to what 《Mr. Jones》says]. 文例⇩

よる³ 寄る 〈近付く〉《文》approach ; come [《文》draw] near ; 〈集まる〉meet ; come [get] together ; 〈立ち寄る〉call [drop in] 《at *sb's* house, on *sb*》; 〈途中下車する〉stop over 《at》; 〈寄港する〉call [touch] 《at》 ¶火のそばへ寄る come up [near] to the fire / わきへ寄る make room 《for》; step aside / 寄ると触ると whenever they meet [come together, see one another] / 寄ってたかって…する join [combine] 《their》 efforts to *do* ; gang up to *do* 文例⇩

よる⁴ 選る ⇨ えらぶ.

よる⁵ 縒る twist ; twine.

ヨルダン Jordan ¶ヨルダンの Jordanian / ヨルダンハシミテ王国 the Hashemite Kingdom of Jordan.

よるひる 夜昼 ¶夜昼なしに働く work day and night ; work around the clock.

よるべ 寄る辺 ¶寄る辺がない have no one to turn to (for help) ; have no place to go ; be (left) stranded 《in a foreign country》 / 寄る辺のない friendless ; uncared-for ; forlorn ; 〈親のない〉orphaned.

よれい 予鈴 the first bell ; the warning bell.

(one) better than that. / ナイロン靴下 300 円より. 〔掲示〕Nylon socks. ¥300 and up [From ¥300]. / 展覧会は4月1日より7日まで開かれるはず. The exhibition is to be held from April 1st to 7th inclusive [《米》 from April 1st through 7th].

よりどころ 人には心のより所が必要だ. One needs something to believe in.

よりどり より取り見取り 500 円で何でもございます. We have a rich variety of goods in stock from which you can take your choice for five hundred yen.

よりによって よりによってあんなところで彼女に会おうとは! How surprising that I should come across her there of all places!

よりみち 寄り道しないですぐお帰りなさい. Come straight home without stopping on the way. / 夏の間九州を歩きつつ, 途中四国に寄り道した. During the summer we hiked around Kyushu, with a side trip to Shikoku.

よる² 我々は新聞によって日々の出来事を知る. We depend on newspapers for our daily news. / 風俗習慣は国によって異なる. Customs and manners vary from country to country. | Different countries have different customs. / すべては今度の選挙の結果いかんによる. Everything turns on the issue of the coming election. / 思想は言語によって表現される. Thoughts are expressed by means of [through the medium of] speech. / 聞くところによると彼は近々結婚するそう

だ. I hear [They say] that he is going to get married. / この推論は間違った前提によっている. This inference is based on false premises. / この事故は主として君の不注意によるものである. The accident is chiefly due to [the result of] carelessness on your part.

よる³ 帰りにお寄りすることでしょう. They'll pay you a call [drop in on you] on their way back. / 砂糖の塊にありが寄って来た. Ants swarmed about the lump of sugar. / 寄ると触るとけんかばかりする. They never meet but they quarrel. | They never meet without quarreling. / 文房具屋へ寄って鉛筆を2ダース買って来て下さい. Call at [Drop by] the stationer's on the way and buy

よれよれ ¶よれよれの frayed《cuffs》; worn-out; shabby; threadbare.

よれる 縒れる get twisted [kinked].

よろい 鎧 (a suit of) armor ¶よろいを着けた armored; 《文》 armor-clad; 《a warrior》 in armor / よろいかぶとに身を固めて in [《文》 clad in] full armor.

よろいど 鎧戸 a slatted shutter; a louver door [window]; 〈店先の〉 a (folding [rolling]) shutter ¶よろい戸を下ろす[上げる] pull down [put up] a shutter.

よろける ⇨ **よろめく**.

よろこばしい 喜ばしい 〈うれしい〉 delightful; joyful; 《文》 joyous; happy; pleasing; 〈愉快な〉 pleasant; 〈満足すべき〉 gratifying. [文例⇩]

よろこばす 喜ばす delight; please; 《文》 gladden; make *sb* happy; give pleasure 《to》 ¶耳を喜ばす 〈事が主語〉 please [delight] *one's* [the] ear. [文例⇩]

よろこび 喜び (a) joy; (a) delight; rejoicing; 〈歓喜〉 《文》 (a) rapture; 《文》 ecstasy; 〈祝意〉 congratulation(s); 《文》 felicitation(s); 〈満足〉 《文》 gratification; pleasure ¶喜びの余り 《cry》 for [with] joy; 《dance》 in (high) delight / 満面に喜びの色を浮べて with a look of joy [delight] on *one's* face; 《文》 with a face which speaks [bespeaks] *one's* joy / 喜びを述べる express *one's* delight 《at》; 〈祝詞を述べる〉 congratulate *sb* on 《*his* success》; 《文》 express [offer] *one's* congratulations on 《*sb's* success》 / 喜び事 a happy event. [文例⇩]

よろこぶ 喜ぶ be glad 《of》; be pleased 《with》; be delighted [pleased] 《at, with》; 《文》 rejoice 《at, over》; congratulate *oneself* 《on》; 《文》 find pleasure 《in》; take delight 《in》 ¶喜んで 〈うれしそうに〉 cheerfully; joyfully; delightfully; gleefully; with glee [delight]; 〈喜びの余り〉 with [for] joy; 〈快く〉 gladly; with pleasure; willingly / 喜び勇んで with great glee; in high spirits / 喜んで…する (will) gladly *do*; be delighted to *do*; 〈相手のために, 労をいとわず〉 be willing to *do*. [文例⇩]

[用法] 「喜んでお手伝いいたします」は I am willing to help you. でよいが, 「喜んであなたのパーティーに参ります」を I am willing to come to your party. は不可. これでは, パーティーに出席することが相手のためにしてやることになるからである. このような場合は I will come to your party with pleasure. | I will [shall] be very happy to come to your party. とか, くだけた調子なら I would love to. と言えばよい.

よろしい 宜しい ⇨ **よい³, いい** ¶…してもよろしい don't mind *doing* (自分が); may [can] *do* (他人が) / …するのはよろしくない It is wrong [《文》 improper, not right, 《文》 not good form, 《文》 not fitting] 《to *do*, that *one* should *do*》 / …へどうぞよろしく please remember me to *sb*; give my (best [kind]) regards to *sb*; 〈肉親・親しい友人へ〉 give my love to *sb*. [文例⇩]

よろず 万 ⇨ **すべて, ばんじ** ¶よろず屋 〈店〉 a general store; 〈何でもやる人〉 a Jack-of-all-trades 《*pl.* Jacks-》.

よろめく 〈よろける〉 stagger; totter; reel; 〈異性に〉 have an affair [a love affair] 《with》; 《文》 misconduct *oneself*; be unfaithful [《文》 untrue] to *one's* husband ¶よろめきながら with tottering steps; with an unsteady walk [《文》 gait].

よろよろ ¶よろよろと totteringly; with tottering steps / よろよろする ⇨ **よろめく** / よろよろ歩く totter [stagger, reel] along [on]; walk unsteadily / よろよろ立ち上がる stagger [scramble] to *one's* feet.

よろん 世論 〈意見〉 public opinion; a consensus (of opinion); the general [prevailing] opinion; 〈感情〉 《文》 public sentiment ¶世論に訴える appeal to public opinion / 世論に耳を傾ける pay careful attention to the trends of public opinion; 《口語》 have [keep] an [*one's*] ear to the ground / 世論調査 《take, conduct》 a public-opinion poll; an opinion survey; opinion research / 世論調査員 〈専門の〉 a pollster; a polltaker. [文例⇩]

よわい¹ 齢 age ⇨ **とし¹**.

よわい² 弱い weak; feeble; 〈もろい〉 《文》 frail; 〈虚弱な〉 weakly; 《文》 infirm; delicate; 〈音や光など〉 faint 《sound》; feeble 《light》; 〈酒など

---

me two dozen pencils, will you? / 市の中央から少し北に寄って高い丘がある. There is a high hill a little north of the center of the city.

よろこばしい こんな喜ばしいことはない. Nothing gives us such great pleasure as this.

よろこばす 美しい景色が目を喜ばしてくれた. Beautiful scenery delighted our eyes.

よろこび このように皆様に親しくお話しできる機会を得ましたことは私の大いに喜びとするところでございます. It gives me considerable pleasure to have the opportunity to talk to you face to face like this. / 喜びの色が顔にあふれていた. His face beamed with joy [delight]. | He [His face] showed the joy he felt. / 父親が無事だと知ったときの彼の喜びはどんなだったでしょう. How happy [joyful] he was when he knew his father was safe! / 謹んでご全快のお喜びを申し上げます. Please accept my sincere congratulations on your recovery. / 成功の喜びは私の苦労を償って余りがあった. The pleasure of success more than repaid me for all my efforts.

よろこぶ 喜んでお供いたします. I'll gladly go with you. | I would be happy [glad] to go with you. / 彼はついにはるか遠方に1つ明かりを見付けて大いに喜んだ. At last, to his great joy, he noticed a light a long way ahead. / 大抵の学校には弱い者いじめをして喜ぶ子供がいるものだ. In most schools there are boys who take delight in bullying weaker ones.

よろしい もう帰ってもよろしい. You may go. / それでよろしい. That will do. / タバコを吸ってもよろしいでしょうか. Do you mind if I smoke? / もしよろしかったら明日映画に行きませんか. If you have nothing particular to do tomorrow, how about going to the movies with me? / 君が自分で行くのはよろしくない. I don't think it's right [suitable, proper] that you should go in person. / あの事は万事よろしく頼む. I leave that entirely to you. / おついでの折に, お兄様に私からもよろしくと申し上げて下さい. When you write to your brother, wish him well from me. / 奥様ならびにご家族の皆様によろしく. Give my best regards to

よ

よわき / 1303 / よんどころない

の》weak ; light 《beer》; mild 《tobacco》; 〈不得手の〉weak 《at》; weak 《in》 ¶気の弱い faint-hearted ; timid ¶《文》timorous / 身体が弱い 〈体質上〉be delicate ;《文》have a weak [delicate] constitution ; 〈《文》be in delicate health / 頭が弱い be feeble-minded / 意志が弱い be not strong-willed ; be weak-willed ; have a weak will ;《文》be infirm of [wanting in] purpose / 女に弱い《文》be susceptible to feminine charm ; have a weak spot for women / 酒に弱い get drunk easily ; cannot drink much ; can't hold [take] one's drink / 数学に弱い be poor at [weak in] mathematics / 数字に弱い have no [a poor] head for numbers / 弱い者 a weak person ; a weakling ; the weak (総称) / 弱い者いじめをする bully ; tyrannize the weak / 弱く feebly ; faintly ; weakly / 弱くする ⇒よめる. 文例⇩

よわき 弱気 ¶弱気な timid ; faint-hearted ; weak(-spirited) ; 【株式】bearish 《sentiment》 ¶弱気を出す lose courage [heart, one's nerve] / 弱気相場は a bear(ish) market.

よわごし 弱腰 ¶弱腰の weak-kneed ; faint-hearted ; spineless ; timid / 弱腰を見せる show [《文》adopt] a weak attitude 《to, toward》.

よわさ 弱さ weakness ;《文》frailty.

よわす 酔わす make sb drunk ;〈うっとりさせる〉fascinate ; charm ;《文》enthrall ;《文》put sb under a spell.

よわたり 世渡り ¶世渡りする get on [make one's way] through the world ; earn one's living / 上手に世渡りする do [make] a good job of life.

よわね 弱音 ¶弱音を吐く make complaints ; whine ; whimper ; complain 《about, of》. 文例⇩

よわび 弱火 a low flame [heat, gas] ¶弱火にする〔電気こんろを〕turn down the heat [flame, gas] ; 〈オーブンを〉set the oven at 'low' / 弱火で煮る〈ガス[電気]こんろで〉cook over [on] a low flame [heat] ; cook with the gas [electricity] turned low ; 〈オーブンで〉cook in a slow [low] oven ; cook with the oven on [turned] low ; 〈とろとろ〉simmer ; boil gently.

よわまる 弱まる get [grow,《文》become] weak(-er) ; weaken ;〈音などが〉grow fainter ; die down ;〈風などが〉《文》abate. 文例⇩

よわみ 弱み a weakness ; a weak [vulnerable] point ; a sore spot ; one's Achilles(') heel ¶弱みを見せる show [betray] one's weakness / 弱みに付け込む take (a mean) advantage of sb's weakness. 文例⇩

よわむし 弱虫 a weakling ; a coward ; a milksop ; a softy ; a sissy ; 〈泣き虫〉a crybaby. 文例⇩

よわめる 弱める make sth weak [feeble] ; weaken ;《文》enfeeble ; make sth less strong [intense] ;〈火・音量など〉turn down.

よわよわしい 弱々しい weakly ; feeble-looking ; delicate-[frail-]looking ¶弱々しい声で in a feeble [whimpering] voice.

よわらせる 弱らせる〈弱める〉weaken ;《文》enfeeble ;〈衰弱させる〉《文》emaciate ;《文》debilitate ;〈困らす〉perplex ; worry ; trouble ; put out ; harass ; embarrass.

よわりはてる 弱り果てる〈疲れ切る〉be utterly exhausted ; be tired [worn] out ; be dead tired ;〈口語〉be dog-tired ;〈閉口する〉be completely at a loss 《what to do》; be put out ; be nonplus(s)ed 《over》; be plagued 《to death》《by》; be at one's wits' end ; be in a nice [pretty] pickle ;〈口語〉be all [completely] at sea.

よわりめ 弱り目 文例⇩

よわる 弱る get [《文》become, grow] weak [feeble] ;〈体が〉《文》be enfeebled ; be not in the best of health ; break [run] down ; be low ; sink (病人が) ;〈落胆する〉be low ; be dejected ;〈困る〉be perplexed 《at, with》; be embarrassed 《by, with》; be put out ; be in a fix ; be at a loss 《as to what to do》. 文例⇩

よん 四 four.

よんしゃ 四者 ¶四者(間)の quadripartite 《conferences》.

よんどころない よん所ない〈不可避の〉un-

---

your wife and family. / お父様によろしくお伝え下さい。Please give your father my kind regards. | Please remember me to your father. | With good wishes to your father. (★手紙専用) | Please pass my best wishes on to your father. (★手紙専用) / 家内からもどうぞよろしくと申しております。My wife sends you her kindest regards. (★手紙専用) | My wife joins me in sending you our best wishes. (★手紙専用)

よろん 世界の世論がそれに反対している。World opinion is against it. / 世論は大体新政策に賛成だった。Public opinion was more or less for [in favor of] the new policy.

よわい² この菌は日光に弱い。This germ has a low (degree of) tolerance to sunlight. / 脈拍がだんだん弱くなっていった。Her pulse became fainter (and fainter). / 人間は弱いものだから、権力にはなんらかの歯止めが必要である。Human frailty being what it is, some sort of check on power is necessary. / 彼は化学にはあきれるほど弱いんだ。His chemistry is alarmingly weak. / 僕はけんかは弱い。I'm no good at fighting.

よわね 弱音を吐く。Cheer up! | Chin up! | Never say die!

よわまる 火勢はじきに弱まった。The fire died down in a short time.

よわみ 僕は人の弱味につけこむようなことはしたくない。I don't like kicking somebody when he is down.

よわむし あいつは全く弱虫だよ。He wouldn't say boo to a goose. | He's a real softy.

よわりめ 弱り目にたたり目。Troubles never come singly [alone].

よわる 彼は、全体的にからだが弱ったなと感じた。He had a general feeling of weakness. / この暑さですっかり弱ってしまった。The heat has quite knocked me out [exhausted me]. | I am absolutely exhausted by this heat. / 何でそんなに弱っているんだい。What are you so worried about? / 父に死なれて大いに弱った。The loss of my father was a serious blow to me. / あいつの長話には弱ったよ。I was bored to distraction by his tedious talk. / さあ弱ったぞ。Here's a nice mess! | Here's a fine state of affairs!

avoidable; inevitable; 《緊急の》 urgent; pressing ¶よん所ない事情で《文》under [owing to] unavoidable circumstances / よん所なく out of necessity; 《いやいやながら》 against one's will / よん所なく…する be obliged [compelled, forced, driven] to do.
よんりんしゃ 四輪車 a four-wheeled vehicle [car]; a four-wheeler.

ら

ラ 【音楽】 la.
-ら …and others ⇒ -たち.
ラード lard.
ラーメン Chinese noodles in soup.
らい 癩 ⇒らいびょう ¶らい患者 a leper.
-らい …来 《…以来》 since; 《…の間》 for ¶昨年以来 since last year / 両三日来 these few days; for the past few days. 文例⇩
らいい 来意 ¶来意を告げる《文》 state the purpose of one's visit; tell sb what one has come for.
らいう 雷雨 a thunderstorm.
らいうん 雷雲 a thundercloud.
ライオン a lion; a lioness (雌) ¶ライオンの子 a lion cub / ライオンのような lionlike; 《文》 leonine.
らいかい 来会 ¶来会者《文》an attendant (at); 《総称》the attendance (at); the people [《文》those] present (at). 文例⇩
らいかん 雷管 a percussion cap; a detonator.
らいかんしゃ 来観者 a visitor.
らいきゃく 来客 ¶来客がある have a visitor [guest, caller]; have company. 文例⇩
らいげきき 雷撃機 a torpedo plane [bomber].
らいげつ 来月 next month; the coming month ¶来月の月曜日に on Monday next; the coming month / 来月 1 日に on the first of next month / 来月の今日《文》this day (next) month / 来月の今日 a month from today.
らいさん 礼賛 praise; 《文》 an encomium (pl. -miums, -mia) ¶礼賛する praise; 《文》 eulogize; glorify; adore / 愚神礼賛《書名》 The Praise of Folly / 礼賛者 an adorer; an admirer.
らいしゅう[1] 来週 next week; the coming week ¶来週の月曜日に on Monday next; next Monday; (米) a week from (this) Monday (★ これを日曜日に言うとすれば a week from tomorrow でもよい) / 来週の今日 today [《文》 this day] week; a week (from) today.
らいしゅう[2] 来襲 a raid [an attack] 《on our position》 ⇒ しゅうらい, しゅうげき.

らいしゅん 来春 next spring; 《文》 the coming spring.
らいしん 来信 a letter (received) ⇒ たより[1].
らいしん[2] 来診 ¶来診を求める send for [call in] (a doctor).
らいしんし 頼信紙 a telegram form [blank].
ライスカレー curry and rice.
らいせ 来世 《文》 (the) afterlife; 《文》 the next [other] world; 《文》 the world beyond ¶現世と来世 this world and the next / 来世信仰 belief in the hereafter [the life after death].
ライター a (cigarette) lighter ¶ライターの石 a lighter flint / ライターをつける light a lighter / ガス[オイル]ライター a gas [an oil] lighter / ライターオイル lighter oil [fluid].
らいちょう[1] 来朝 ⇒ らいにち.
らいちょう[2] 雷鳥 a snow grouse; a ptarmigan
らいてん 来店 ¶来店する come to the store [shop].
らいでん 来電 ¶ニューヨーク来電によれば…である according to a dispatch [telegram] from New York…; a New York dispatch reports [says, states] that…
ライデンびん ライデン瓶 【物】 a Leyden jar [bottle].
ライト[1] 《灯火》 a light ¶ライトペン《コンピューター》a light pen.
ライト[2] 【野球】《右翼》 the right field; 《右翼手》 a right fielder; 《ボクシング》 a right (to the jaw) ¶ライトへフライを打つ fly to right (★ この場合の fly の活用・過去分詞形はともに flied).
らいどう 雷同 ⇒ ふわらいどう.
ライトきゅう ライト級《ボクシング》 the lightweight class ¶ライト級選手 a lightweight.
ライトバン 《窓のある》 a station wagon; (英) an estate car; 《窓のない》 a light van [truck].
ライトヘビーきゅう ライトヘビー級《ボクシング》 the light heavyweight class ¶ライトヘビー級選手 a light heavyweight.
ライナー 【野球】 a liner; a line drive ¶ライ

よんどころない よん所ない先約のためお伺いすることができませんでした。 I was unable to come owing to an engagement that I could not manage to break off.
-らい 20年来の大雪だ。 This is the heaviest snowfall we have had in [for] twenty years. / 10年来この病気で悩んでいる。 I have been suffering from the disease these ten years.
らいかい 多数の来会者があった。 There was a large attendance at the meeting. | The meeting was well attended.
らいきゃく 今夜は来客がありますので残念ながらお伺いできません。 I'm sorry I'll be unable to come over, as I expect company this evening.
らいねん 来年のことを言えば鬼が笑う。 Talk about next year and the devil will laugh.
らいめい 雷名天下にとどろいている。 His name resounds throughout the land [is known throughout the country].
らいめい[2] 遠く雷鳴を聞いた。 The rumbling of thunder was heard in the distance.
らいゆう 我が国に来遊する外人の数は増加の一途をたどっている。 The number of (foreign) visitors to Japan [people coming sightseeing in this country] goes on increasing.

らいにち 来日 ¶来日する visit [come to] Japan; arrive in Japan [this country] / 来日中のスノー博士 Dr. Snow now in [visiting] Japan.

らいねん 来年 next year; the coming year ¶来年の3月に in March next (year); 〈現在を3月以降とすれば〉 next March / 来年の今ごろ[今日] this time [day] next year. 文例⇩

らいはい 礼拝 ⇒ れいはい¹.

ライバル a rival.

らいびょう 癩病 leprosy.

らいひん 来賓 a guest; a visitor ¶来賓席 the visitors' seats [gallery]; 〔掲示〕For Guests / 来賓室 a guest room.

ライフル a rifle.

らいほう 来訪 a visit; a call ¶来訪を受ける have a visit from *sb* / 来訪者 a visitor; a caller.

ライむぎ ライ麦 rye.

らいめい¹ 雷名 *one's* fame; *one's* (great) name ¶雷名を天下にとどろかす 《文》 win [earn] far-flung [nationwide] fame. 文例⇩

らいめい² 雷鳴 a roll [peal, clap] of thunder; a thunderclap; the rumbling of thunder (遠雷の音); 〈雷〉thunder. 文例⇩

らいゆう 来遊 a visit ¶来遊する visit; come (over) to 《our country》 / 来遊者 a visitor; a tourist (観光客). 文例⇩

らいらく 磊落 ¶らいらくな free and easy; open-hearted; frank.

ライラック 〔植〕(a) lilac.

らいれき 来歴 ⇨ ゆらい, こじ⁵ (故事来歴).

ライン¹ 〈線・列〉a line ¶ラインダンス precision dancing / ラインダンサー (a troop of) precision dancers.

ライン² 〈川〉the Rhine (river) ¶ライン下り ⇨ くだり¹.

ラインアップ 〔野球・フットボール〕the (starting) line-up (of a team).

ラウドスピーカー a loudspeaker ¶ラウドスピーカーでしゃべる speak through [over] a loudspeaker.

ラウンド 〔ボクシング〕a round ¶第3ラウンド2分45秒で in 2 minutes 45 seconds of the third round.

ラオス Laos ¶ラオス語 Lao; Laotian / ラオス人 a Laotian / ラオス(人)の Laotian / ラオス人民民主共和国 the Lao People's Democratic Republic.

らがん 裸眼 ⇒ にくがん ¶裸眼視力 unaided vision.

らく 楽 〈安楽〉ease; comfort; 〈安堵(かん), 軽減〉relief ¶楽な easy; comfortable / 楽な仕事 an easy task; a soft job / 楽に 〈安楽に〉comfortably; in comfort; 〈気楽に〉at 《*one's*》ease; 〈容易に〉easily; with ease; without difficulty [trouble] / 楽に暮らす, 暮らしが楽である live in comfort; be comfortably [well] off / 楽にしてやる 〈死にきれないでいるのを〉put 《*one's* horse》 out of (his) misery / 楽になる 〈痛みが〉be eased; have [get, 《文》obtain] relief (from pain); 〈気持ちが〉be [feel] relieved / 〈生活が〉be better off / 楽に勝つ win easily [hands down] / 楽でない difficult; hard. 文例⇩

らくいん 烙印 a brand ¶烙印を押される be branded ((as) a liar).

らくいんきょ 楽隠居 ¶楽隠居している[の身である] live in easy [comfortable] retirement.

らくえん 楽園 Paradise ¶地上の楽園 《文》an earthly paradise / 楽園追放 〔画題〕the Expulsion from Paradise.

らくがき 落書き 〈壁などの〉graffiti (*sing*. graffito) (★ ただし単数はまれ); 〈特に子供がやる〉scribbling; 〈退屈まぎれにノートなどに書く〉doodling ¶落書きする do [write] graffiti (on the wall); scribble (on the *fusuma*); doodle (in *one's* notebook). 文例⇩

らくご¹ 落後[伍] ¶落後する drop [fall] out; drop [fall, lag, be left] behind (the others) / 落後者 a straggler; a dropout; a failure (人生の). 文例⇩

らくご² 落語 a comic story (told by a professional storyteller).

らくさ 落差 〔物〕 the difference in elevation (between); a head.

らくさつ 落札 a successful bid ¶落札する *one's* tender (for repairing the vessel) is accepted [successful]; 〈人が主語〉 make a successful bid; 〈物が主語〉 be knocked down to one / 落札人 a successful bidder.

らくじつ 落日 the setting [《文》declining] sun.

らくしゅ 落首 a lampoon; a satire in verse.

らくしょう 楽勝 ¶楽勝する win an easy victory (over); win (a game) hands down. 文例⇩

らくじょう 落城 the fall of a castle ¶落城する the castle falls ((to the enemy)).

らくせい 落成 ¶落成する be completed; be finished / 落成式 an inauguration [a completion] ceremony. 文例⇩

らくせき 落石 〈事〉a fall of rock(s); 〈石〉a

らく この薬を飲むとすぐ楽になる. This medicine will give you immediate relief [ease your pain quickly]. / お楽になさって下さい. Make yourself comfortable [at home]. / はたで見るほど楽ではない. It is not as easy as it seems. / 資金の問題さえ解決されれば, 後は楽なものだ. Once the problem of financing has been solved, the rest is plain sailing [easy sledding]. / これで気が楽になった. That's a load off my mind! / That's a great relief. / 彼の同意を得たので楽な気持ちになって帰って来た. Having got his agreement, I came away with an easier mind.

らくがき 駅の壁は落書きだらけだった. The station wall was covered with graffiti. / 落書きお断わり. 〔掲示〕No graffiti.

らくご¹ その行軍で多くの落後者を出した. Many soldiers dropped out during the march.

らくしょう 今度の選挙では浅田はきっと工藤に楽勝するよ. I'm sure Asada will beat Kudo easily in the election that's coming up. / I'm sure Asada will be an easy winner in the coming election against Kudo.

らくせい 本月3日に工事の落成式を行なった. The completion of the work was celebrated on the 3rd of this month.

らくせん 落選 ¶落選する〈選挙に〉be defeated [unsuccessful] in an election; lose [fail in] an election; fail to be elected;〈出品が〉be rejected / 落選者 an unsuccessful candidate / 落選作 a rejected work. 文例⇩

らくだ〔動〕a camel ¶らくだの毛 camel's [camels] hair / らくだのこぶ a camel's hump / らくだのシャツ a camel's-hair undershirt / ひとこぶらくだ a dromedary; an Arabian camel / ふたこぶらくだ a Bactrian [a two-humped] camel.

らくたい 落体〔物〕a falling body ¶落体の法則 the law of falling bodies.

らくだい 落第 ¶落第する fail ((in an examination); 《米》flunk ((an exam);〈検査に〉be rejected /〈米〉flunk] ((a student) / 落第生〈学生〉《米》a flunked student; a repeater (原級にとどまる者);〈一般に〉a failure / 落第点 a fail [failure] mark; a failing grade. 文例⇩

らくたん 落胆 discouragement; dejection;〈失望〉disappointment ¶落胆する be discouraged; be dejected; get disheartened [downhearted]; lose courage;〈失望する〉be disappointed / 落胆させる discourage; disappoint.

らくちゃく 落着 ¶落着する be (finally) settled; 〔reach [come to] a (final) settlement. 文例⇩

らくちょう 落丁 a missing page [leaf]. 文例⇩

らくてん 楽天 optimistic / 楽天主義〔家〕optimism [an optimist]. 文例⇩

ラクトース〔<《ドイツ語》*Laktose*〕〔化〕lactose; milk sugar.

らくのう 酪農 dairy farming ¶酪農家 a dairy farmer; a dairyman / 酪農場 a dairy (farm) / 酪農製品 dairy products.

らくば 落馬 ¶落馬する fall [be thrown] off *one's* horse; have a fall [spill] from *one's* horse.

らくばん 落盤 a roof-fall; a cave-in. 文例⇩

ラグビー rugby;《文》rugby football;《英口語》rugger (★日本語ではラグビーの選手を「ラガー」と言うが英語では a rugby player と言わなければならない) ¶ラグビー場 a rugby field.

らくやき 楽焼き *raku* ware.

らくよう 落葉〈葉を落とすこと〉leaf fall;〈落ち葉〉fallen leaves ¶落葉する leaves fall ((off a tree);〈樹木が落葉する〉lose [shed, drop, cast] *its* leaves / 落葉樹 a deciduous tree. 文例⇩

らくらい 落雷 ¶落雷する〈場所などが主語〉be struck by lightning / 落雷による被害 lightning damage. 文例⇩

らくらく 楽々 ¶楽々と very easily; effortlessly; ((win) hands down ⇒らく(楽に).

ラグラン a raglan (coat) ¶ラグランそで raglan sleeves.

らくるい 落涙 ¶落涙する《文》shed tears; weep.

ラケット a racket; a paddle (卓球の); a bat (卓球の).

ラジアルタイヤ a radial(-ply) tire.

-らしい 〈…のように見える〉seem; look (like); appear; 〈一見した所〉apparently; seemingly;〈ふさわしい〉suitable ((for);《文》becoming ((a young lady) / …と思われる it seems (to *one*) that …;〈多分〉be likely ((to *do*); probably; perhaps; maybe ¶紳士らしい gentlemanly / 淑女らしい ladylike / 正直者らしい look honest; look (like) an honest man / その人らしい[らしからぬ]振る舞いをする behave in [out of] character / 男らしく like a man; manfully / 病気らしく見せる pretend to be ill;《文》feign illness / …らしく聞こえる sound (true); sound like (fiction).

ラジウム〔化〕radium ⇒ほうしゃせん ¶ラジウム鉱泉 a radium spring.

ラジエーター a radiator.

ラジオ radio;〈受信機〉a radio (receiving) set; a radio (*pl.* -s) ¶ラジオの放送 radio broadcasting; a radio broadcast (1回の) / ラジオの講演 a radio talk [address]; a talk [an address] on the radio / ラジオの音を高[低]くする turn the radio up [down] / ラジオを聴く listen (in) to the radio / ラジオをかける[止める] turn the radio on [off] / ラジオで聞く listen to ((a musical performance) on [over] the radio / ラジオに出る go on the radio [air] / ラジオ講座 a radio (English) course / ラジオ聴取者 a (radio) listener / ラジオドラマ a radio play / ラジオ体操 radio gymnastic exercises / ラジオゾンデ a radiosonde / ラジオビーコン[コンパス] a radio beacon [compass]. 文例⇩

ラジカセ a radio-casette recorder.

らくせき 落石注意.〔掲示〕Warning: Falling or fallen rocks.

らくせん 氏の出品した油絵は落選した. His oil painting was rejected [not accepted].

らくだい 夫してはは落第だ. I am a failure as a husband. / 彼は化学の試験に落第した. He failed [《米》flunked] chemistry. / 3年に編入されて, どうにか落第しないでいけた. She entered the third grade and just managed to get passing grades.

らくたん その酷評に落胆して彼は小説の筆を絶った. That severe criticism discouraged him from continuing to write novels.

らくちゃく これで一件落着です. It is all settled. | The case is closed.

らくちょう この本には落丁が16ページある. There are sixteen pages [eight leaves] missing from this book.

らくてん 彼女はとても楽天家だ. She has a very hopeful nature.

らくばん 昨日のT炭鉱の落盤事故で作業員2名が死亡した. Two miners were killed in a roof-fall [cave-in] (accident) at the T Coal Mine yesterday.

らくよう 木々はすっかり落葉している. The leaves are all off [gone from] the trees. | The trees are (quite) bare of leaves.

らくらい 近所の寺に落雷があった. A thunderbolt struck a Buddhist temple in my neighborhood. / 彼は落雷にあって死んだ. The lightning struck him dead.

-らしい あの男はまだ生きているらしい. It seems that the fellow is still alive. | He seems to be still alive. / 彼はどう見ても商人らしい. He is a merchant to all

らんばい 乱売 ⇨ なげうり.

らんぱく 卵白 the white (of an egg); 〖動〗 the albumen.

らんばつ 乱伐 indiscriminate deforestation ¶乱伐する fell [cut down] trees recklessly [indiscriminately].

らんぱつ 乱発 an overissue [an excessive issue] (of bank notes) ¶乱発する issue (notes) excessively [recklessly]; overissue.

らんはんしゃ 乱反射 diffused reflection.

らんぴ 乱費 (a) waste (of money); reckless [lavish] spending ¶乱費する spend wastefully [recklessly]; waste; squander; 《文》 dissipate.

らんぴつ 乱筆 hasty [slipshod] handwriting; scribble. 文例⇩

らんぶ 乱舞 ¶乱舞する dance wildly [madly] (for joy).

ランプ[1] 〈燈火〉 a lamp ¶ランプのしん[ほや] a lamp wick [chimney] / ランプのしんを出す [下げる] turn up [down] a lamp / ランプをつける[消す] light [put out, 《文》 extinguish] a lamp / 豆[石油, 手提げ]ランプ a midget [an oil, a hand] lamp / キャップランプ a cap lamp. 文例⇩

ランプ[2] 〈立体交差道路などの〉 a ramp.

らんぼう 乱暴 violence; 《文》 an outrage ¶乱暴な rough; rude; violent / 乱暴な言葉を用いる use violent [bad] language / 乱暴に扱う handle sb [sth] roughly; manhandle sb / 乱暴する do [use] violence (to, toward); 《文》 commit an outrage (on); be rude (to) / 乱暴者 a rowdy fellow; 《米》 a roughneck. 文例⇩

らんま 欄間 a ranma; an openwork screen above the sliding partitions between two rooms.

らんまん 爛漫 ¶(花が)爛漫と咲き乱れている be in full bloom; 《文》 be in all (their) glory; be at (their) best.

らんみゃく 乱脈 ¶乱脈な disorderly; chaotic / 乱脈を極める 《文》 be in utter disorder; be in a chaotic state [condition]; 《口語》 be (in) a shambles / 乱脈に陥る fall [be thrown] into disorder.

らんよう 乱用 《文》 (an) abuse [a misuse] (of one's power); (an) overuse ¶乱用する abuse; overuse; 《文》 make (an) improper use of.

らんらん 爛々 ¶らんらんたる眼差(まなざ)し glaring [flashing, 《文》 fiery] eyes.

らんりつ 乱立 文例⇩

り

り[1] 里 a ri (=約 4 km).

り[2] 利 〈利益〉 benefit; 〈もうけ〉 (a) profit; 《文》 gain(s); 〈有利〉 an advantage; 〈利子〉 interest ⇨ りし ¶利を得る make [gain] a profit (on the transaction); profit (from the sale) / 利にさとい be alive [wide-awake] to one's interests; have a quick eye for a profit [for gain]; 《口語》 have an eye to the main chance; 《口語》 know which side one's bread is buttered on. 文例⇩

り[3] 理 〈道理〉 reason; 〈原理〉 a principle ¶…するのは理の当然である It is only natural [It stands to reason] that one should do / 理を説く reason with sb / 理にかなう be reasonable; stand to reason / 理にかなわない be unreasonable; 《文》 be contrary to reason.

リアス [<《スペイン語》 rias] ¶リアス式海岸 a deeply indented coastline; a rias coastline.

リアリズム realism.

リーグ a league ¶リーグ戦 a league game; a round robin (総当たり戦); 〈総称〉 the league series / 六大学野球リーグ戦 the Big-Six-University Baseball League Tournament.

リーダー[1] 〈指導者〉 a leader ¶リーダーシップ (show) leadership.

リーダー[2] 〈読本〉 a reader.

リーチ 〖ボクシング〗 ¶…よりリーチが長い have a longer reach than sb; outreach sb.

リート 〈歌〉 〈ドイツ語〉 a lied (pl. lieder); a German lyric song.

リード a (four-part) lead ¶3点リードする lead (the opposing team) by three points [runs]; gain a three-run[-point] lead over (the opposing team) / わずかにリードしている have [hold] a slight [narrow] lead (over) / (塁から)リードする[を取る] 〖野球〗 take a lead off (second base) / リードを奪われる lose the lead (to). 文例⇩

リードオフマン 〖野球〗 a leadoff; a lead-off batter.

リール 〈釣りざお・テープなどの〉 a (fishing) reel; 〈フィルムの〉 a reel; a spool ¶リールざお a (fishing) rod and reel.

りえき 利益 〈ためになること〉 benefit; interests; 〈もうけ〉 (a) profit; 《文》 gain(s) ¶利益のある profitable; paying / 利益のない unprofitable; (a deal) that does not pay; nonpaying / 利益がある, 利益をもたらす bring [give, fetch, 《文》 yield] one a profit; pay; make [yield] a profit (for one, to one) / 利益

---

his speech]. / そんな乱暴を言っては困る. Don't be so unreasonable.

らんりつ この選挙区には候補者が乱立している. This constituency is flooded with candidates running for the Diet. | There are too many candidates running from [standing in] this constituency.

り[2] 戦い利あらず. The chances [odds] are against us.

リード ハーフタイムの時には相手を2対1でリードしていた. We led them 2-1 at half time. / 7回の裏にリードを広げて6対0にした. We stretched our lead to 6-0 in the bottom of the seventh. /

りえん になる benefit *one*;《文》be of benefit to *one*; be to *one's* advantage / 利益を得る make [《文》gain] a profit (on, out of, from); benefit [profit] (by, from) / 自分の利益を図る look after [《文》pursue] *one's* own interests / 総[純]利益 gross [net] profit / 利益代表 a person representing [voicing] the interests of a group / 利益配当 distribution of profits / 利益分配制度 a profit-sharing system; industrial [labor] copartnership. 文例⇩

りえん 離縁 ¶離縁する divorce [get a divorce from] (*one's wife*) / 離縁状 a letter of divorce.

リオデジャネイロ Rio de Janeiro; Rio.

りか 理科 〈科目〉science; 〈文科に対して〉the science department [course] ¶理科大学 a college of science.

りかい 理解 understanding;《文》comprehension ¶理解する understand;《文》comprehend;《文》apprehend; grasp; make out; see / 正しく理解する have a proper [《文》right] understanding (of) / 理解できる《文》comprehensible; understandable / 理解できない《文》incomprehensible; ununderstandable / 理解しやすい be easy to understand; be easily understandable / 理解のある sympathetic 〈husbands〉; understanding 〈parents〉/ 理解のない not understanding; unsympathetic / 理解を深める deepen *one's* understanding of *sth*;《文》promote [bring about] a better [greater] understanding (between Japan and the U.S.) / 理解に苦しむ〈人が主語〉cannot understand; find it hard to understand 〈his motives〉/〈事が主語〉baffle *one's* understanding;《文》be beyond [be above, pass] (*one's*) comprehension / 優れた理解力を持っている have an excellent understanding. 文例⇩

りがい 利害 ¶利害の衝突 a clash [conflict] of interests / 利害に影響を及ぼす affect *one's* interests / 利害関係がある have an interest (in); be interested (in) / 利害関係者《文》the interested parties; the people [《文》parties] concerned / 利害得失を量る weigh losses against gains (in doing *sth*); weigh [compare] the advantages and disadvantages [《文》merits and demerits] (of). 文例⇩

りかがく 理化学 physics and chemistry.

りがく 理学 ¶理学部 the department of science / 理学博士〈人〉a Doctor of Science; 〈学位〉Doctor of Science (略: D.Sc.).

りかん 離間 ¶離間させる《文》alienate [estrange] (A from B); come between (A and B).

りき 利器 ¶文明の利器《文》the blessings [gifts] of civilization. 「five men.

-りき …力 ¶5人力だ have the strength of

りきえい 力泳 ¶力泳する swim with powerful strokes;《文》swim with might and main.

りきえん 力演 ¶力演する play to the best of *one's* ability.

りきがく 力学 dynamics; mechanics / 力学上の dynamic / 力学的に dynamically.

りきさく 力作 a literary [an artistic] work bearing marks of labor and effort;〔フランス語〕a tour de force (pl. *tours de force*).

りきし 力士 a *sumo* wrestler.

りきせつ 力説 ¶力説する put [《文》lay] stress [emphasis] on *sth*; stress; emphasize. 文例⇩

りきせん 力戦 ⇒りきとう².

りきそう¹ 力走 ¶力走する run as hard [fast] as *one* can; run for all *one* is worth.

りきそう² 力漕 ¶力漕する row with all *one's* might; row powerfully [with powerful strokes].

りきてん 力点〔物〕the point of a lever where force is applied;〈重点〉⇒じゅうてん².

りきとう¹ 力投〔野球〕¶力投する put everything *one* has into *one's* pitching; pitch hard.

りきとう² 力闘 ¶力闘する fight hard [well]; fight for all *one* is worth; put up a good fight.

りきむ 力む〈息む〉strain (*oneself*); try too hard;〈力のありそうな様子をする〉show [present] a bold front (to *sb*).

りきゅう 離宮 a detached palace.

リキュール liqueur.

りきりょう 力量 ability;《文》capability ¶…するだけの力量がある have the ability to *do*; be equal to [《文》competent for] (the task) / 力量のある able; capable; competent / 力量を発揮する display *one's* ability; bring *one's* power into full play / 力量を試す test [try] *sb's* ability.

りく 陸 (the) land; (the) shore 〈船から見た〉⇒りくち ¶陸の[にすむ]動物 a land animal / 陸を行く go by land; travel overland / 陸へ上がる go ashore [on shore]. 文例⇩

りくあげ 陸揚げ landing; unloading ¶陸揚げする land; unload [discharge] ((a ship, cargo

---

かつてはロケットの技術ではソ連はアメリカをリードしていた. The Soviet Union used to be ahead of the United States in rocketry.

りえき それを100万円で売ったら利益はどのくらいか. What profit will you make if you sell it for one million yen? / そんな本を読んでなんの利益があるか. What is the use [good] of reading such a book? / 人の悪口を言ったところで何の利益にもならない. You gain nothing by speaking ill of others. / そうすればお互いの利益になるでしょう. It would be to our mutual advantage [prove of benefit to both of us] to do that.

りかい 彼女は音楽[絵画]に対して理解がない. She cannot appreciate music [painting]. | She has no ear for music [no eye for painting]. / これは日本の事情に対するアメリカ人の理解を一層深めてくれることであろう. I hope this will promote a better understanding on the part of Americans of the conditions in Japan. / 何でもよく理解しながら読むことが大切だ. It is important that you (should) understand [have a good understanding of] what you are reading. / この点を彼にはっきり理解させなければならない. You must put [get] this point across to him clearly.

りがい 日本はこの問題に重大な利害関係を持っている. Japan has an important interest [is vitally interested] in this matter. / 物にはすべて利害得失がある. Everything has its merits and demerits.

りきせつ 彼はそうした設備の必要を力説した. He was very em-

りぐい　利食い　profit taking　¶利食いする sell one's stocks at a profit; make [get] a profit on the shares one sells.

りくうん　陸運　⇒りくじょう(陸上輸送)　¶陸運局 the ((Osaka)) District Land Transport Bureau.

リクエスト　(a) request　¶…のリクエストで[により] at the request of… / リクエスト番組 《放送》a ((record)) request program.

りくかい　陸塊　a landmass.

りくかいくう　陸海空　¶陸海空の三軍 the land, sea and air forces.

りくかいぐん　陸海軍　the army and navy.

りくぐん　陸軍　the army　¶陸軍の military; army / 陸軍に入る enter [enlist in] the army / 陸軍省[大臣] the Department [Minister] of War; the War Office [Minister] / 陸軍将校 an army officer.

りくじょう　陸上　¶陸上で[に] on land; on shore; ashore / 陸上勤務についている be on shore duty / 陸上競技 athletics; athletic sports; field and track events / 陸上生活 land life / 陸上貿易路[ルート] an overland trade route / 陸上輸送 land [overland] transportation; transportation by land.

りくせいどうぶつ　陸生動物　a land animal.

りくせん　陸戦　a land battle [war].

りくそう　陸送　⇒りくじょう(陸上輸送)　¶陸送貨物 overland freight.

りくち　陸地　⇒りく　¶陸地が見えてくる come in sight of land; sight land; make a landfall (長い航海の後初めて) / 陸地に囲まれている be landlocked / 陸地測量 land surveying.

りくつ　理屈　《道理》reason; 《条理》logic; 《口実》a pretext; 《議論》(an) argument; 《理論》a theory　¶理屈のわかった人《文》a man of sense; a sensible person / 理屈を言う[こねる] argue; theorize; 《へ理屈を》split hairs; argue in a hairsplitting way / 理屈に合わない be unreasonable; 《文》be contrary to reason / 理屈っぽい argumentative ((people)).　文例❹

りくとう　陸稲　⇒おかぼ.

りくどり　陸鳥　a land bird.

りくひょう　陸標　a landmark.

りくふう　陸風　a land breeze.

リクライニングシート　a reclining seat.

りくろ　陸路　¶陸路を行く go by land; travel overland.

リケッチア　《細菌》a rickettsia ((pl. -ae)).

りけん　利権　rights; concessions (鉱山などの)　¶利権をあさる hunt for concessions / 利権屋 a concession hunter.

りこ　利己　¶利己的な selfish; self-seeking; self-centered; egoistic / 利己心のない unselfish; 《文》disinterested (公平な) / 利己主義 selfishness; egoism.

りこう¹　利口　¶利口な 〈賢い〉clever; bright; wise; sensible; intelligent; 〈抜け目のない〉shrewd; smart / 利口な子 a bright child; a clever boy [girl] / 利口な犬 an intelligent dog / 利口ぶる try to appear wise / 利口ぶって with the air of a wise man; knowingly / 利口そうな intelligent-looking.　文例❹

りこう²　履行　《文》performance ((of one's duty)); 《文》fulfillment ((of a promise)); 《文》discharge ((of an obligation)); execution ((of a contract)); implementation ((of a treaty))　¶履行する fulfill; carry out; perform; 《文》execute; 《文》discharge; 《文》implement / 約束を履行する keep [make good] one's promise; fulfill [carry out] one's pledge / 契約を履行する fulfill [implement, perform] a contract.

りこうがくぶ　理工学部　the department of science and engineering.

りごうしゅうさん　離合集散　meeting and parting; 《政党などの》changes in political [party, factional] alignment.

リコーダー　《楽器》a recorder; an English flute.

リコール　recall　¶リコールする recall / リコール制 the recall system.

りこん　離婚　(a) divorce　¶離婚する divorce ((one's wife)); be divorced from ((one's husband)); get [《文》obtain] a divorce from ((one's spouse)) / 協議離婚 (a) divorce by consent / 離婚訴訟 a divorce suit / 離婚訴訟を起こす sue [bring a suit] for divorce / 離婚率 a divorce rate.

りさい　罹災　¶罹災する suffer from ((a disaster)); fall a victim to ((a calamity)) / 罹災者 the sufferers ((from a disaster)); the victims ((of a calamity)) / 罹災地 the afflicted [《文》stricken] district [area].

リサイタル　a ((violin)) recital　¶リサイタルを開く have [give] a recital ((of lieder)).

りざや　利鞘　a profit margin.

りさん　離散　¶離散する scatter; disperse; be dispersed; be broken up.　文例❹

---

phatic about the need for such facilities. | He urged [pressed] upon them the need for such institutions.

りく　朝鮮と中国は陸続きである. Korea is connected with China by land. / 当時はベーリング海峡はまだ陸続きになっていた. The Bering Straits were still a land bridge in those days.

りくつ　双方に理屈がある. There's something to be said for both arguments. / そりゃ何とでも理屈はつくさ. Oh, I'm sure you can find some sort of excuse! / 成る程理屈はそのとおりだが実行は難しかろう. It certainly sounds all right in theory, but I doubt if it's really feasible. / 君がやめなければならないという理屈はどこにもない. I see no reason why you should resign. / それは理屈では割り切れない. There is no logical solution to it. / 彼は理屈っぽい男だ. He is argumentative by nature.

りこう¹　彼女は利口だからそんなことはしない. She knows better than to do such a thing. / 彼がそれに加わらなかったのは利口だった. He wisely did not take part. | It was very wise of him not to join in. / 今日はお利口さんだったね. You've been very good today. | You've been a very good boy [girl] today. / さあ、お利口さんだから泣くんじゃないよ. Don't cry, there's a good boy [girl].

りさん　そのために一家は離散した. It broke up the family.

りし 利子 interest 《on a loan》 ¶高い[低い]利子で《borrow money》 at high [low] interest / 6分の利子のつく預金 a deposit carrying [drawing] 6 percent interest / 5分の利子を生む yield [bear] 5 percent interest / 利子をつけて返す pay back 《money》 with interest.

りじ 理事 a director; a trustee (大学などの) ¶理事長 the chairman of the board of directors [trustees]. 文例⇩

りしゅう 履修 ¶履修する〈修了する〉complete [finish] (a college course) / 〈これから修める〉take [《文》pursue] (an advanced course in French) / 履習カード a (course) registration card.

りじゅん 利潤 (a) profit; returns ⇒りえき | 利潤追求 pursuit of profits; profit-seeking.

りしょう 離礁 ¶離礁する be refloated; get off the reef [sunken rock].

りしょく¹ 利殖 moneymaking ¶利殖の才にたけている be clever at making money; have the Midas touch / 利殖法 the secret of moneymaking; how to make money [a fortune].

りしょく² 離職 ⇒しっぎょう.

りしん 離心 《数》¶離心軌道 an eccentric orbit / 離心率 eccentricity.

りしんろん 理神論 《哲》deism ¶理神論者 a deist.

りす 《動》a squirrel.

りすいこうじ 利水工事 irrigation works.

りすう 里数 mileage; distance.

リスト a list ¶リストを作成する, リストアップする make [draw up] a list 《of》; list.

リスボン Lisbon.

リズム rhythm ¶リズムのある rhythmic(al) / リズムをつけて rhythmically / リズムに乗る get into the rhythm / 早いリズムで《sing》in quick rhythm / リズムアンドブルース rhythm and blues / リズム感 rhythmic sense; a sense of rhythm / リズム体操 rhythm calisthenics.

リスリン ⇒グリセリン.

りする 利する〈得をする〉profit; benefit;〈利用する〉make (good) use of; turn *sth* to good account ⇒えき²(益する) ¶何ら利するところがない〈人が主語〉gain nothing 《from》;〈事が主語〉do *one* no good / 長身を利する turn *one's* height to good account.

りせい 理性 reason ¶理性がある have a lot of sense;《文》be endowed with reason / 理性の冒瀆(とく)《文》(a) violation of reason / 理性を欠く have no sense;《文》be devoid of reason / 理性を失う behave irrationally; lose control (of *oneself*);《口語》lose *one's* cool / 理性に訴える appeal to *sb's* reason / 理性に従う《文》follow the dictates of reason / 理性的 rational / 実践[純粋]理性 practical [pure] reason. 文例⇩

りせつ 離接 《数・論》disjunction.

りそう 理想 an ideal ¶理想の夫 an ideal husband / 高い理想を抱く《文》entertain [cherish] a lofty ideal / 理想にかなう meet [measure up to] *one's* ideal / 理想化する idealize / 理想家 an idealist / 理想郷 a Utopia / 理想主義 idealism / 理想主義的 idealistic / 男性の理想像 *one's* idea of the perfect man / 理想的な家 an ideal house (for newlyweds). 文例⇩

りそく 利息 ⇒りし.

りそん 離村 ¶離村する leave [desert, quit] *one's* village.

りた 利他 ¶利他的 altruistic / 利他主義 altruism.

リターンマッチ a return match.

りだつ 離脱 《文》(a) secession; a breakaway ¶離脱する《文》secede 《from》; break [drift] away 《from》/ 職場を離脱する desert *one's* post; quit *one's* job.

りち 理知 《文》intellect; intelligence ¶理知を磨く sharpen [train] *one's* intellect (by reading) / 理知的な intellectual / 理知主義 intellectualism. 文例⇩

リチウム 《化》lithium.

りちぎ 律義 ¶律義な honest; straight;《文》upright; conscientious.

りちゃくりく 離着陸 takeoff [taking off] and landing.

りつ 率 a rate ⇒わり(あい) ¶出産[死亡]率 the birth [death] rate.

りつあん 立案 ¶立案する form [make, draw up, map out] a plan / 立案者 a planner; the framer of a plan [project].

りつき 利付き ¶利付きの with [cum] interest / 利付き公債 an active [interest-bearing] bond.

りっきゃく 立脚 ¶立脚する be based [founded, grounded] 《on》/ 立脚点[地] ⇒たちば, かんてん³.

りっきょう 陸橋 a bridge (over a railroad [roadway]); an overpass;《英》a flyover (道路の上のみの).

りっけん 立憲 ¶立憲君主政体 constitutional monarchy / 立憲政治 constitutional government; constitutionalism.

りっこうほ 立候補 《米》candidacy;《英》candidature ¶立候補する stand [come forward] as a candidate 《for the Mayoralty of Kyoto》; run for 《the Presidency》;《英》stand for (Parliament) / 立候補を発表する〈届け出る〉announce [file] *one's* candidacy 《for》/ 立候補者 a candidate (for).

りっしでん 立志伝 a story of a man who achieved success in life [who rose from the ranks]; a success story ¶立志伝中の人 a self-made man.

りっしゅう 立秋 the beginning [first day] of autumn (in the traditional Japanese calendar).

りじ 彼はこの大学の理事の1人です。He is one [a member of] the board of trustees of this college.

りせい 人間には理性というものがある。Man is endowed with reason | Man is a rational being. / 彼は感情より理性の方が勝っている。He is moved more by his head than (by) his heart.

りそう リンカーンは僕の理想の政治家だ。Lincoln is my ideal of a statesman.

りち 彼は情の人というよりもむしろ理知の人だ。He is ruled by his intellect rather than by his emotions.

りったい 白い円も, しかるべき陰影を施されると, 白い球体のように立体的に知覚される。A white circle, if it has the proper shading on it, acquires depth and is

りっしゅん 立春 the beginning [first day] of spring (in the traditional Japanese calendar).

りっしょう 立証 ¶立証する prove; verify; 《文》substantiate; 《文》testify [attest] to ((a fact)) / 無罪を立証する prove sb not guilty; establish sb's innocence / 証言の事実を立証する substantiate the testimony ((of a witness)).

りっしょく 立食 ～たちい ¶立食形式のパーティ a buffet-style dinner party.

りっしん 立身 ⇒しゅっせ ¶立身出世主義 the cult of success; careerism / 立身出世主義者 a (single-minded) careerist.

りっすい 立錐 ¶立錐の余地もない be tightly [closely] packed; be packed full [to capacity].

りっする 律する judge; measure ¶己れをもって他を律する measure [judge] others by one's own standard(s).

りつぜん 慄然 ¶慄然とする 〈人が主語〉be filled with horror; be horrified ((at)); 〈事が主語〉《口語》give one the creeps.

りつぞう 立像 a statue; a statuette (小型の).

りったい 立体 a solid (body) ¶立体映画 a three-dimensional movie [film] / 立体感 (produce) a stereoscopic [spatial] effect / 立体感がある look solid / 立体幾何学 solid geometry / 立体交差 a crossing with an overpass or underpass; grade separation / 立体交差の上[下]の道 an overpass [underpass] / 立体作戦 《英》combined operations / 立体戦争 three-dimensional warfare / 立体写真 a stereoscopic photograph / 立体派 〈画風〉cubism; 〈流派〉the cubists / 立体派の絵 a cubist picture [painting] / 立体放送 a stereo(phonic) [binaural] broadcast. 文例⇩

りったいし(しき) 立太子(式) the investiture [formal installation] of the Crown Prince.

りっちじょうけん 立地条件 ¶立地条件がいい[悪い] 《文》be conveniently [inconveniently] located [sited]; 《文》be favorably [unfavorably] situated.

りっとう¹ 立冬 the beginning [first day] of winter (in the traditional Japanese calendar).

りっとう² 立党 the formation [organization] of a political party ¶立党の精神 the spirit behind the formation of the party; the principles on which the party was founded.

りつどう 律動 ⇒リズム ¶律動的 rhythmical.

リットル a liter (略: l., lit.).

りっぱ 立派 ¶立派な good; fine; fine-[gorgeous-]looking; splendid; magnificent; 《文》creditable; 《文》praiseworthy; noble; worthy; 〈まぎれもない〉undeniable 《pregnancy》; solid [cast-iron] 《proof》/ 立派な職業 a respectable occupation / 立派な理由 a good reason / 立派な邸宅 a magnificent [fine] mansion / 立派な業績 a brilliant [splendid] achievement / 立派な行ない a praiseworthy deed; creditable conduct / 立派な人格者 a person with [who has] a fine character / 立派な贈り物 a nice [handsome] present / 立派な動機から from the highest of motives; 《文》from noble [lofty] motives / 立派な経歴を持っている have an outstanding [a brilliant] career / 立派な一生を送る lead a worthy life / 立派な服装をしている be well [richly] dressed / 立派に very well; excellently; splendidly; magnificently; 《文》admirably. 文例⇩

りっぷく 立腹 ⇒おこる¹, おこらせる.

りっぽう¹ 立方 ¶5センチメートル立方である be five centimeters cubed / 1立方メートル a cubic meter (略: m³) / 立方根を求める find the cube root ((of)) / 10センチメートル立方の立方体 a 10-centimeter cube.

りっぽう² 立法 legislation ¶立法の精神に反している be contrary to the spirit of the legislation / 労働数育,戦時立法 labor [education, wartime] legislation / 立法機関[府] the legislature; a legislative body [organ] / 立法権 legislative power / 立法者 a legislator; 《文》a lawgiver; a lawmaker / …を規制する立法措置をとる legislate against….

りづめ 理詰め ¶理詰めの theoretically strict / 理詰めで説き伏せる reason [persuade] sb into ((doing)); 《文》dissuade sb from ((doing)); argue [talk] sb down.

りつめんず 立面図 an elevation.

りつろん 立論 ¶立論する argue ((for, against)); make [build up, set forth] an argument ((for, against)). 文例⇩

りてい 里程 mileage; distance ¶里程表 a table of distances / 里程標 a milepost; a milestone.

りてきこうい 利敵行為 an act which serves the interests of [benefits] the enemy.

りてん 利点 an advantage; 《文》a merit. 文例⇩

りとう¹ 離島 ⇒はなれじま.

りとう² 離党 ¶離党する leave [《文》secede from] a party.

りとく 利得 ⇒りえき, もうけ² ¶不当利得 〈もうけ〉an undue [excessive] profit; 〈行為〉profiteering (戦時・災害時などに暴利をむさぼる); lining one's own pocket (私腹を肥やす).

リトマス ¶リトマス試験紙 litmus paper / リトマス試験紙でテストする test with litmus paper ((for acidity)).

リニアモーターカー a linear(-induction) motor train.

りにゅう 離乳 weaning ¶離乳する[させる] wean ((a baby from its mother [the breast])) / 離乳期 the weaning period / 離乳食 baby food.

りにょうざい 利尿剤 a diuretic.

りにん 離任 ¶離任する leave one's post [position].

---

perceived as a white ball.
立派 彼女は立派な暮しをしている。She is comfortably off. | She is in comfortable [very easy] circumstances. / 彼が自分の過ちを認めたということは立派なことだ。It is to his credit that he has acknowledged his mistake. / 立派な息子さんですね。You should [must] be proud of your son. / あの店は改装して立派になった。The appearance of the store has improved since its renovation.
りっぽう¹ 8の立方根は2である。The cube root of eight is two.
りつろん 彼の立論は誤った前提に基づいている。His argument is based on false premises.
りてん 陶器の皿の方が木皿よりも清潔にしておくのが容易だという利点がある。Porcelain plates

りねん 理念 an idea ¶大学教育の理念 an idea of what university education ought to be.

りのう 離農 ¶離農する give up [abandon] farming; leave the land.

リノールさん リノール酸 《化》linoleic acid.

リノリウム linoleum; lino ¶リノリウムを敷いた床 a linoleum-[lino-]covered floor; a linoed floor.

リハーサル a rehearsal ⇒けいこ.

リバイバル (a) revival.

りはつ¹ 利発 ⇒りこう¹.

りはつ² 理髪 hairdressing; a haircut ⇒さんぱつ² ¶理髪師 a barber; a hairdresser / 理髪店 a barber shop; 《英》a barber's (shop).

リハビリテーション rehabilitation ¶リハビリテーションの訓練 rehabilitation training / リハビリテーションセンター a rehabilitation center.

りばらい 利払い payment of interest ¶利払いの停止 suspension of interest payments.

りはん 離反《人心の》《文》(an) estrangement; 《文》alienation; 《離脱》《文》(a) secession; a breakaway ¶離反する 《文》be estranged [alienated] (from); 〈離脱する〉《文》secede (from); break [drift] away (from). 文例&

りひ 理非 ¶理非(曲直)を正す inquire into the rights and wrongs (of a case).

リビア Libya ¶リビア人 a Libyan / リビア(人)の Libyan.

リヒテンシュタイン Liechtenstein ★英語の発音は [líktənstain] ¶リヒテンシュタイン公国 the Principality of Liechtenstein.

りびょう 罹病 ¶罹病する catch [《文》contract]《a disease》; 〈感染する〉be infected with《cholera》/ 罹病者 a sufferer《from cholera》; a case《of typhoid fever》.

リビングキッチン a living-room-cum-kitchen; a living room with kitchenette attached.

りふじん 理不尽 ¶理不尽な unreasonable; unfair;《文》unjust.

りふだ 利札 a coupon ¶利札落ち[つき] coupon off [on]; ex [cum] coupon.

リフト a lift; 〈スキー場などの〉a ski [chair] lift.

リフレーン a refrain.

リベート a rebate;《口語》a kickback ¶リベートを払う give sb a rebate [kickback] / リベートを受け取る receive a rebate《on a government contract》; get a kickback.

りべつ 離別 ¶離別する divorce《one's wife》; get a divorce from《one's husband》; part from [with]《one's children》.

リベット a rivet ¶リベットで留める fasten sth with rivets [a rivet]; rivet / リベットガン a rivet gun; a riveting machine; a riveter.

リベリア Liberia ¶リベリア共和国 the Republic of Liberia / リベリア人 a Liberian / リベリアの Liberian.

りほう 理法 a law ¶自然の理法 the law [order] of nature.

リポート ⇒レポート.

リボン a ribbon; a band《帽子の》¶リボンで結ぶ tie [bind] sth with a ribbon.

リマ Lima.

りまわり 利回り ¶利回りがいい[悪い] yield [give] a good [poor] return / 高利回りの投資 an investment bearing [yielding] high interest; a high-yield investment. 文例&

リムジン an airport bus [《米》limousine].

りめん 裏面 うら ¶都会生活の裏面 the seamy side of urban life / 裏面で behind the scenes; in the background / 裏面で操る pull the strings [wires] / 裏面工作 behind-the-scenes [backstage] maneuvering [maneuvers] / 裏面史 an inside story (of). 文例&

リモートコントロール, リモコン remote control ¶リモートコントロールで操縦する operate《a machine》by remote control / リモートコントロール装置 a remote-control device.

リヤカー a bicycle-drawn cart; a bicycle trailer.

りやく 利益 ⇒ごりやく.

りゃく 略 〈短縮〉(an) abbreviation;《文》(an) abridgment; 〈省略〉《文》(an) omission ⇒りゃくす.

りゃくが 略画 a sketch ¶略画をかく draw a (line) sketch (of); sketch.

りゃくご 略語 an abbreviation; an abbreviated word. 文例&

りゃくごう 略号 《電信の》a code [cable] address.

りゃくじ 略字 an abbreviated [a simplified, a simpler] form《of a Chinese character》.

りゃくしき 略式 ¶略式の informal / 略式に informally / 略式裁判 a summary trial / 略式手続き《法》summary proceedings.

りゃくじゅ 略綬 a (service) ribbon.

りゃくじゅつ 略述 ⇒りゃっき.

りゃくしょう 略称 an abbreviated title; an abbreviation (of); an acronym (★ North Atlantic Treaty Organization の各部の頭字をとって NATO と呼ぶ如き) ¶略称を…という be called…for short; be abbreviated to….

りゃくす 略す〈短縮する〉abridge; abbreviate; shorten; 〈省く〉《文》omit; leave out; 〈抜きにする〉dispense with ¶略して for short /

---

have an advantage over wooden ones in that they are more easily kept clean.

りはん 現政府にはもう民心が離反してしまっている. The present government has lost the support of the public.

りまわり その債券は年6分の利回りになる. The bond yields [bears] interest of six per cent a year.

りめん 裏面を見よ[に続く].《標示》Please turn over (略: P.T.O.). / 裏面には込み入った事情があるらしい. There seem to be complicated circumstances behind it.

りゃく PO は Post Office の略です. PO is an abbreviation [is short] for Post Office.

りゃくご Jan. は January の略語です. Jan. is an abbreviation of [is abbreviated from] January. / Y.M.C.A. は何の略語ですか. What does Y.M.C.A. stand for?│What is Y.M.C.A. short for?

りゃくす 国際連合を普通に略して国連と呼ぶ. The United Nations is commonly called the UN for short. / ここには助動詞の will が略されている. Here an auxiliary

りゃくず 略図 a rough [line] sketch ((of)); 〈地図〉 a sketch [route] map 《of》 ¶略図を書く draw a rough map 《from Shinjuku Station to one's home》.
りゃくせつ 略説 ¶略説する give an outline ((of)); outline.
りゃくそう 略装 ⇨ りゃくふく.
りゃくだつ 略奪 plunder;《文》pillage; sack ¶略奪する plunder;《文》pillage; loot;《文》despoil; sack / 町を略奪する plunder [pillage] a city / 財貨を略奪する plunder [despoil] sb of his goods / 略奪者 a plunderer; a looter / 略奪品 spoil(s); plunder; loot.
りゃくでん 略伝 a short biography 《of》; a biographical sketch 《of》.
りゃくふく 略服 ¶略服で in informal [everyday, ordinary] dress.
りゃくれき 略歴 one's brief personal history; a sketch of one's life.
りゃっき 略記 ¶略記する give a brief account [sketch] 《of》; outline; summarize.
りゆう 理由 (a) reason; cause; ＜根拠＞ ground(s); ＜口実＞ a pretext; an excuse ¶充分な[薄弱な, 表面上の]理由 a good [a slender,《文》an ostensible] reason / 理由のある well-founded[-grounded] / 理由のない groundless / 理由の立つ justifiable; excusable / 理由の立たない unjustifiable; inexcusable / 理由なく without reason [cause, provocation]; ＜不当に＞ unreasonably / …の理由で by reason of…; for the reason of…; because of…; on account of…; on the grounds that… / いかなる理由で for what reason;《文》on what grounds; why / 年少の理由で in consideration of sb's youth; considering that sb is young [under age] / 何らかの理由で for some reason (or other). 文例⇩

-りゅう …流 〈型〉 a style;《文》 a mode; a way; ＜流派＞ a school; ＜等級＞ a class; a rate ¶草月流の生け花 the Sogetsu school of flower [floral] arrangement / 日本流のあいさつの仕方 a Japanese form of greeting [salutation] / 自己流で in one's own way / アメリカ流に after the manner [fashion] of Americans; in American style / 二, 三流どころの出版者 a second- or third-rate publisher.
りゅうあん 硫安 ammonium sulfate.
りゅうい 留意 ¶留意する take notice ((of)); pay attention ((to)); give heed ((to)).
りゅういき 流域 a (drainage) basin; a valley ¶揚子江流域 the Yangtze valley / アマゾン川流域 the Amazon basin / 利根川の下流流域 the lower reaches of the Tone (River).
りゅういん 留飲 ¶留飲が下がる《文》feel great satisfaction [be heartily satisfied] 《at, over》; gloat 《over one's rival's downfall》.
りゅうか 硫化 ¶硫化する sulfurate; sulfurate / 硫化物 (a) sulfide / 硫化ゴム vulcanized rubber / 硫化水素[銀] hydrogen [silver] sulfide.
りゅうかい 流会 ¶流会になる be called off; be given up.
りゅうがく 留学 ¶留学する go abroad to study; study abroad / フランス文学研究のためパリに留学する go to [stay in] Paris to study French literature / 英国留学中 during one's stay in England as a student / 在米日本人留学生 Japanese students in the U.S. 文例⇩
りゅうかん 流感 influenza; (the) flu.
りゅうがん 竜眼〈植〉 a longan.
りゅうき 隆起 a rise; an uplift;《文》(an) elevation;〈地質〉(an) upheaval ¶隆起する rise; be lifted up / 隆起させる elevate.
りゅうぎ 流儀 a style; a way; a fashion ¶…の流儀に after the fashion of…; in the style of… / 自分流儀に in one's own way. 文例⇩
りゅうきゅう 琉球 Ryukyu; ＜列島＞ the Ryukyu islands; the Ryukyus ¶琉球の Ryukuan.
りゅうぐう 竜宮 the Palace of the Dragon King; the Sea God's Palace.
りゅうけい 流刑 ⇨ るざい.
りゅうけつ 流血 bloodshed ¶流血の惨事 a bloody affair; bloodshed / 流血を見ずに without bloodshed; bloodlessly.
りゅうげん(ひご) 流言(飛語) a wild [groundless, false] rumor;《文》a canard ¶流言に惑わされる be misled by false rumors / 流言を放つ spread [circulate] a false rumor; set a false rumor abroad [afloat]. 文例⇩
りゅうこう 流行 ＜はやり＞ (a) fashion; (a) vogue; ＜熱狂的なはやり＞ a craze; a rage; a fad; ＜人気＞ popularity; ＜まん延＞《文》prevalence ¶流行する be in [come into] fashion [vogue]; be [become] the fashion; ＜病気が＞ there is an epidemic [a lot] 《of cholera》;《文》be prevalent / 流行しなくなる go out of fashion [vogue]; lose popularity / 流行の帽子 a fashionable hat / 流行の先駆けをする set the fashion / 流行の先端を追う be (always) in the forefront of fashion 《in dress》/ 流行を追うりに遅れる] follow [be behind] the fashion / 流行遅れの out of fashion; old-fashioned; outmoded / 最新流行(の型) the latest fashion [style] / 流行歌 a popular [pop] song / 流行歌手 a singer of popular songs; a pop singer / 流行語 a word [phrase] of the minute; a word

---

verb 'will' is understood. / 以下略す. The rest is omitted.
りゆう ちゃんとした理由があってそうしたのだ. He did so with good reason. / He had the best of reasons for doing so. / 失敗の理由は, 彼があせりすぎたということだ. The reason he failed was that [He failed because] he tried to do too much. / 本校を特に選んだ理由を言って下さい. Will you please give your reasons for choosing this school. / なぜそれが危険なのかその理由がわからない. I don't see why it should be dangerous.
りゅうがく 彼は今度半導体の研究のため英国へ留学することになった. He has been sent to England to do research into semiconductors.
りゅうぎ これが僕の流儀なんだ. This is my way (of doing things). / 人は皆自分の流儀に従って行動する. All men act after their bent.
りゅうげん(ひご) それについて種種の流言が流れていた. All sorts of rumors were abroad [in the air] about it.

りゅうこう [phrase] (that is) on everybody's lips; a vogue word / 流行作家 a popular writer / 流行色 a fashionable color; a color in fashion / 流行性感冒 ⇨ りゅうかん / 流行性脳炎 epidemic encephalitis / コレラの流行地 a cholera-infected area / 流行病 an epidemic / 流行病学 epidemiology. 文例句

りゅうこつ 竜骨 the keel.

りゅうさ 流砂 ⇨ りゅうしゃ.

りゅうさん 硫酸 〖化〗 sulfuric acid; (oil of) vitriol ¶硫酸アンモニウム ⇨ りゅうあん / 硫酸塩 (a) sulfate / 硫酸カリ[マグネシウム] potassium [magnesium] sulfate.

りゅうざん 流産 (a) miscarriage ¶流産する 〈妊婦が主語〉 have a miscarriage; miscarry; 〈計画などが〉 fail; fall through; 《文》 prove abortive.

りゅうさんだん 榴散弾 a shrapnel shell.

りゅうし 粒子 a particle ¶粒子の粗い coarse-grained; coarse-textured / 光の粒子説 the corpuscular [particle] theory of light.

りゅうしつ 流失 ¶流失する be washed [carried] away (by a flood).

りゅうしゃ 流砂 shifting sand; quicksand (人がのまれるおそれのある).

りゅうしゅつ 流出 an outflow; 《文》 (an) efflux ¶金の流出 an outflow of gold (from Japan) / 頭脳の流出 a brain drain / 流出する flow [run] out (of); 《文》 issue (from) / 流出物 (an) effluent (from the mill) / 流出量 the volume (of water) flowing from (the dam).

りゅうじょう 粒状 ¶粒状の granular (starch); granulated (sugar).

りゅうず 竜頭 〈時計の〉 the winding knob (of a watch); 〈釣り鐘の〉 the cannon (of a bell) ¶時計の竜頭を巻く wind a watch / 竜頭巻きの時計 a stem-winding watch; a stem-winder.

りゅうすい 流水 flowing [running] water; a stream.

りゅうせい¹ 流星 a shooting [falling] star; a meteor ¶流星の雨 a shower of meteors; a meteor shower.

りゅうせい² 隆盛 prosperity ¶隆盛な prosperous; flourishing; thriving / 隆盛におもむく flourish; prosper; thrive; 《文》 become (more) prosperous.

りゅうぜつらん 〖植〗 an agave; a (mescal) maguey.

りゅうせんけい 流線型 a streamline shape ¶流線型の streamlined (locomotives).

りゅうぜんこう 竜涎香 ambergris.

りゅうそく 流速 the velocity of a flowing fluid; 〈潮流の〉 the drift of a current ¶流速計 a current meter.

りゅうたい 流体 a fluid ¶流体力学 fluid mechanics; hydromechanics (液体力学); aero-mechanics (気体力学).

りゅうち 留置 detention; custody ¶留置する detain; keep sb in custody; lock sb up / 留置場 a police cell [detention room]; a lockup.

りゅうちょう¹ 留鳥 a sedentary bird; a resident (bird).

りゅうちょう² 流暢 fluency ¶流暢な fluent / 流暢な文章で in a flowing style / 英語を流暢に話す speak English fluently; speak fluent English; be fluent in English.

りゅうつう 流通 〈金銭の〉 circulation; currency; 〈物資の〉 distribution; 〈空気の〉 ventilation ¶流通する circulate / 流通している be in circulation / 空気の流通がいい悪い be well [badly, poorly] ventilated / 部屋の空気の流通をよくする ventilate a room / 流通証券 negotiable instruments [papers] / 流通貨幣 current [circulating] money; currency in circulation / 流通革命 a distribution revolution / 流通機構 distributive machinery / 流通産業 the distribution industry.

りゅうと ¶りゅうとした服装をしている be smartly [stylishly, modishly] dressed; 《口語》 be a natty dresser.

りゅうどう 流動 ¶流動する flow; run / 流動的な fluid / 流動性 liquidity; fluidity / 社会的流動性 social mobility / 流動物[食] liquid food; a liquid diet / 流動資産 floating [quick] assets / 流動資本 floating [liquid, circulating] capital / 流動体 a fluid (気体も含む); a liquid (液体のみ).

りゅうとうだび 竜頭蛇尾 a bright beginning and a dull [tame] ending; an anticlimax ¶竜頭蛇尾に終わる end (up) in an anticlimax.

りゅうにゅう 流入 (an) inflow; (an) influx ¶外資の流入 an influx [inflow] of foreign capital / 流入する flow in [into sth].

りゅうにん 留任 ¶留任する stay [continue, 《文》 remain] in office.

りゅうねん 留年 ¶留年する repeat a year (in school); stay [《文》 remain] in the same class for another year; stay on (at a university) / 留年生 a student enrolled in a class for the second or a subsequent time; 《米》 a repeater.

りゅうは 流派 a school.

りゅうび 柳眉 ¶柳眉を逆立てる raise (her) eyebrows in anger.

りゅうびじゅつ 隆鼻術 plastic surgery of the nose; rhinoplasty.

りゅうひょう 流氷 floating [drift] ice; an ice floe.

りゅうほ 留保 ⇨ ほりゅう¹.

りゅうぼく 流木 driftwood; drift timber.

リューマチ rheumatism ¶リューマチが起こる[の気味がある] have an attack [a touch] of

---

りゅうこう コレラがインドに流行している。Cholera is now prevalent [rampant] in India. / 今年はどんな帽子が流行していますか。What sort of hats are in fashion this year? / あの店では最新流行のビーチウェアを売っています。They sell the latest styles in beach wear at that store. / 日本の青年の間ではスキーが大流行だ。Skiing is all the rage with young people in Japan.

りゅうどう 情勢は今なお極めて流動的である。The situation is still highly fluid.

りゅうろ 一言一句に真情が流露していた。Every word he spoke revealed [breathed] his innermost feelings.

りよう¹ この合成物質は、自動車やジェット機のエンジンにますます多く利用されるようになっている。This synthetic substance is finding increasing use in the

りゅうよう　流用　(a) diversion ; (an) appropriation ¶流用する divert [apply, appropriate] ((the money)) to 《some other purpose》.

りゅうりゅう　隆々　〈勢いの盛んな〉 prosperous ; flourishing ; thriving ; 〈筋肉の盛り上がった〉 muscular / 隆々たる筋肉 bulging [rippling] muscles / 筋肉隆々たる男 a man of muscle ; a muscular [strong-muscled] man.

りゅうりゅうしんく　粒々辛苦　¶粒々辛苦する work hard [[《文》 assiduously, strenuously]] ((at, for)) ; toil ((at)) ; put *one's* heart and soul ((into)).

りゅうりょう¹　流量　the amount [volume] of flowing [inflowing, outflowing] water ; the flow (of a river) / ¶流量計 a flowmeter.

りゅうりょう²　嚠喨　¶りゅうりょうたる《文》 (clear and) sonorous ; resounding.

りゅうれい　流麗　¶流麗な flowing ; fluent ; elegant ; refined / 流麗な文章 a flowing and elegant style.

りゅうろ　流露　(an) expression ; (an) outflow ; 《文》 outpourings (感情の) / ¶流露する express ; reveal.

リュックサック　a rucksack ; a knapsack.

りよう¹　利用　use ; 《文》 utilization ¶利用する make (good) use of ; put *sth* to (good) use ; 《文》 utilize *sth* ; turn *sth* to (good) account ; 〈自然の力などを〉 harness 《solar heat》; 〈機会などを〉《文》 avail *oneself* of 《an opportunity》; 〈つけ込む〉 take advantage of ; exploit ; 〈道具に使う〉 use ; make a cat's-paw of *sb* / 極力利用する make the most [the best (possible) use] of / 原子力を平和目的のために利用する harness atomic energy for peaceful purposes ; make peaceful use of atomic energy / 人の虚栄心を利用する exploit [take advantage of, trade on] *sb's* vanity / 充分に利用されていない underutilized 《resources》 / 利用できる《文》 utilizable ; available / 給料の支払いに利用できる資金 a capital fund available for wage payments / 利用価値 utility value / 利用者 a user / 利用国 a user nation (of the Suez Canal). 文例⇩

りよう²　理容　⇨ りはつ² ¶理容学校 a barbers' school.

りょう¹　良　〈成績〉 good ; B.

りょう²　猟　shooting ; hunting ; 〈獲物〉 a take ; a bag ¶猟が多い[少ない] have a big [poor] take ; make a good [poor] bag / 猟をしているbe (out) hunting / 猟に行く go (out) shooting [hunting] ((in, at)) / 猟具 a hunter's [hunting] outfit ; hunting gear / 猟犬 a gundog ; a hunting dog / (きつね狩りの時の) 猟犬の群 a pack of hounds / 猟師 a hunter ; a huntsman / 猟銃 a sporting [hunting] gun / 猟鳥 a game bird ; game (総称) / 猟場 a hunting ground ; a shoot ; a game preserve. 文例⇩

りょう³　涼　¶涼を求めて in order to enjoy the cool (of the evening) ; (go out) to cool off.

りょう⁴　量　(a) quantity ; volume ; (an) amount ¶量が増す increase [《文》 gain] in quantity / 量が減る《文》 decrease in quantity / 量が多い [少ない]《文》 be large [small] in quantity / 量を過ごす〈飲食の〉 drink [eat] too much [more than is good for *one*] ; overeat (*oneself*) (食べすぎる) / 〈薬を〉 take [have] an overdose (of aspirin) / 量記号《論》 a quantifier / 量的 quantitative / 量的に quantitatively.

りょう⁵　漁　fishing ; 〈獲物〉 a catch ¶漁が多い have a good [big] catch [haul] / 漁が少ない have a poor catch [haul] / 漁に行く go fishing ((in, at)) / 漁場 a fishing ground / 漁師 a fisherman.

りょう⁶　寮　〈寄宿舎〉 a dormitory ; 《米》 a dorm ; 〈大学の〉《英》 a hall (of residence) ; a college (オックスフォード・ケンブリッジ大学などの) ; 〈別荘〉 a villa / 寮歌 a dormitory song / 寮生 a boarder / 寮長 a warden ; a housemaster / 寮費 the charge to be paid by a boarder for his board and lodging ; boarding [hall] fees / 寮母 a matron [lady superintendent] of a dormitory ; a housemother. 文例⇩

りょう⁷　諒　¶諒とする〈理解する〉 understand ; 〈承認する〉 accept.

りょう⁸　両…　both ; two / 両人[者]共 both of the men [us, them] / 両三度 two or three times.

-りょう　…領　¶ポルトガル領の Portuguese-owned (islands) / 英領バージン諸島 the British Virgin Islands.

りょうあし　両脚[足]　⇨ あし¹ ¶両脚に負傷する have both legs injured.

りょうあたり　両当たり　¶両当たりをかける〈囲碁〉 threaten to take two separate [two groups of] stones ; 〈将棋〉 fork ((the opponent's bishop and rook with *one's* knight)).

りょういき　領域　〈領土〉 (a) territory ; 《文》 (a) domain ; 〈領分〉《文》 a province ; a sphere ¶領域を超えている、領域外である《文》 lie outside [be beyond] the province (of) ; 《文》 be out of the domain [sphere] (of). 文例⇩

りょういん　両院　both Houses (of the Diet) ¶両院協議会 a joint conference of the two Houses.

りょううで　両腕　both arms ⇨ うで.

りょうえん　良縁　a good match ¶良縁を得る make a good match.

---

engines of motorcars and jet planes. / 彼はキリスト教の伝道者たちを外交上利用できそうだと思いついた。He saw that diplomatic use might be made of Christian missionaries. / 暑中休暇を利用して北海道に旅行した。I made a tour of Hokkaido in the summer vacation.

りょう² 彼は猟がとてもうまい。He is a very good hunter. / ポインターやセッターは猟犬として飼われる。Pointers and setters are kept for hunting [shooting].

りょう⁴ 量よりも質だ。Quality matters more than quantity. | Quality (comes) before quantity.

りょう⁶ 学生で僕は通学生だった。He was a boarder and I a day student.

りょういき 生化学は僕の領域外だ。Biochemistry is not [outside] my province [《口語》 department].

りょうか¹ 良家 a good [decent, respectable] family ¶良家の娘 a girl from a good family / 良家の出である come from [《文》of] a good family; 《文》be wellborn.

りょうか² 良貨 a good coin; good money ⇒ あっか²(悪貨は良貨を駆逐する).

りょうが 凌駕 ¶りょうがする be superior to; surpass;《文》exceed; outstrip / …をはるかにりょうがしている be far superior to…; be head and shoulders above…. 文例⇩

りょうかい¹ 了解 〈理解〉understanding;〈同意〉agreement; consent ¶了解する〈理解する〉understand;〈文〉comprehend; see;〈同意する〉agree 《with, to》;《文》consent 《to》; give *one's* consent 《to》/ 了解がつく come to [arrive at] an understanding [agreement] 《with》/ 了解を得る[求める] obtain [ask for] *sb's* agreement [consent] / 了解を得て with *sb's* consent / 了解事項 an understanding 《between the two》. 文例⇩

りょうかい² 領海 the territorial waters ¶日本の領海内[外]で within [outside] the territorial waters of Japan [(the) Japanese territorial waters] / 12カイリの領海線の内側[外側]で within [outside] the 12-mile limit of territorial waters.

りょうがい 領外 ¶領外に outside [beyond] the territory [《文》domain]《of》.

りょうがえ 両替 money changing ¶両替する change《a 1,000-yen note》; exchange《dollars into yen》/ 両替機 a money changer / 両替所〈ホテルなどの〉an exchange counter [office] / 両替屋〈店〉an exchange house [shop];〈人〉a money changer; an (authorized) exchanger.

りょうがわ 両側 ¶両側に on both sides [either side]《of the street》. 文例⇩

りょうかん¹ 量感 massiveness ¶量感のある massive; bulky.

りょうかん² 僚艦 a consort (ship).

りょうがん¹ 両岸 ¶両岸に on either bank [both banks]《of the river》.

りょうがん² 両眼 ¶両眼とも見えない be blind in both eyes / 両眼に涙を浮かべて with tears in *one's* eyes.

りょうき¹ 猟奇 ¶猟奇的な bizarre;《文》macabre / 猟奇趣味 a taste for the bizarre [macabre] / 猟奇心から from [out of] curiosity; in search of excitement [thrills] / 猟奇文学 bizarre literature.

りょうき² 猟期 a hunting [shooting] season; an open season.

りょうき³ 漁期 ⇒ ぎょき.

りょうきょく 両極 the two [north and south, positive and negative] poles.

りょうきょくたん 両極端 both extremes ¶両極端である〈意見などが〉be poles apart 《in their opinions》. 文例⇩

りょうぎり 両切り ¶両切りのタバコ an untipped cigarette; a cigarette without a (filter) tip.

りょうきん 料金 a charge (一般にはサービス・労働などに対する); a fee (医者・弁護士など専門職のサービスに対する); a rate (単位あたりの規準によって決められた); a fare (乗り物の) ¶60円の料金で at a charge [fare] of 60 yen / 50円の料金をとる charge [make a charge of] 50 yen《for》/ 料金なしで free (of charge); gratis / ガス[電気, 水道]料金を上げる[下げる] raise [lower] the gas [power, water] rate(s) / 料金所〈有料道路の〉a tollgate; a toll booth〈小屋〉/ 料金表 a list [table] of charges; a tariff; a price list. 文例⇩

りょうくう 領空 (a country's) airspace ¶日本の領空を侵犯する violate [invade, encroach on] Japan's [Japanese] airspace.

りょうけ 良家 ⇒ りょうか.

りょうけい¹ 菱形 《数》a rhombus 《*pl.* -es, rhombi》¶菱形の rhombic.

りょうけい² 量刑 the assessment of the culpability《of》; a question of law.

りょうけん 了[料]見 〈考え〉an idea;〈意図〉an intention;《文》a design;〈動機〉a motive;〈判断〉judgment;〈分別〉discretion ¶悪い了見を起こす yield to the temptation《to *do*》; conceive an evil design / 自分一個の了見で行動する act on *one's* own judgment [at *one's* own discretion] / 了見違いな事をする〈悪い事を〉do something (that is) wrong;《文》do wrong;〈無分別な事を〉commit an indiscretion;《文》act imprudently. 文例⇩

りょうこう¹ 良好 ¶良好な good; fine; excellent; satisfactory.

りょうこう² 良港 a good [fine] harbor ¶天然の良港になっている make [form] a good natural harbor.

りょうさい 良妻 a good [《文》dutiful] wife ¶良妻賢母 a good wife and wise mother.

りょうざい 良材 good quality timber.

りょうさく 良策 a good plan; a good [《文》happy] idea; a wise [well-advised] policy.

りょうさん 量産 mass production ¶量産する produce in large quantities; mass-produce / 量産計画 a plan for the mass production《of》/

りょうが 米国製をりょうがする品質の日本製品はたくさんある。There are plenty of Japanese goods which are better in quality than those made in America.

りょうかい¹ 了解! O.K.|《通信》Roger.

りょうがえ 1万円札を両替していただけますか。Can you change a 10,000-yen bill? | Can you give me change for a 10,000-yen bill?

りょうがわ 通りの両側に本屋が並んでいる。The street is lined with bookstores on either side.

りょうきょくたん 両極端は一致する。Extremes meet.

りょうきん 料金は幾らですか。〈買う前に〉How much do you charge for it?〈買ってから〉How much will that be?

りょうけん なんて了見が狭いんだろう。How narrow-minded he is! / それはお前の了見次第だ。That depends on your decision. / そんな了見は更々ありません。I haven't the slightest intention of doing so.

りょうこう¹ 病人は経過が良好です。The patient is doing well [progressing favorably].

りょうしゅう 金5万円まさに領収いたしました。〈証書の記載〉Received《of [from] Mr. A》the sum

量産態勢に入る〈製品が主語〉be put into commercial production.
りょうし 量子 〖物〗 a quantum 《pl. -ta》 ¶量子力学 quantum mechanics / 量子力学的 quantum-mechanical / 量子論 the quantum theory.
りょうじ[1] 領事 a consul ¶マニラ駐在の日本領事 the Japanese consul at Manila / 領事館 a consulate / 領事館員 a consular official；〈総称〉the staff of a consulate; the consular staff / 領事裁判権 consular jurisdiction.
りょうじ[2] 療治 ⇨ちりょう.
りょうしき 良識 good [common] sense ¶良識のある人 a person with a lot of (good [common]) sense; a sensible person.
りょうしつ 良質 ¶良質の good [high] quality 《materials》; of good [fine, superior] quality / 良質の品 high quality goods; quality products.
りょうしゅ 領主 〈荘園主〉the lord of a manor；〈大名, 小名〉the lord of a fief; a feudal lord.
りょうしゅう 領収 《文》receipt ¶領収する receive / 領収証[書] a receipt / 領収証を出す give *sb* a receipt (for). 文例⬇
りょうしょ 良書 a good book.
りょうしょう 了承 ¶了承する〈認める〉admit; acknowledge；〈同意する〉agree 《to a proposal, that...》; consent 《to a proposal, that...》; agree 《to *do*, that..., on *doing*》; approve 《a plan》；〈理解する〉understand. 文例⬇
りょうしょく 糧食 food (supplies); provisions. ⇨しょくりょう.
りょうしん[1] 両親 one's parents.
りょうしん[2] 良心 (a) conscience ¶良心のかしゃくを受ける one's conscience troubles [pricks] one; suffer from a guilty conscience; be stung by one's conscience; feel the qualms [pricks, stings] of conscience / 良心の命じるところに従う follow [listen to] one's [《文》] the dictates of one's] conscience; act according to one's conscience / 良心のない〈a man〉with no conscience; conscienceless 《employers》; unprincipled 《politicians》/ 良心を慰める〈事柄が主語〉appease [soothe, salve] one's conscience / 良心を悩ませ続ける〈事が主語〉haunt one's conscience / 良心に恥じない[恥じるところがある] have a clear [guilty] conscience / 良心的の honest; fair; straight-dealing / 良心的な作品 a conscientious piece of work / 非良心的な〈人〉unscrupulous; unprincipled / 〈仕事・作品など〉irresponsible; careless; carelessly-done[-made]; unconscientious / 良心的に conscientiously / 良心的兵役拒否者 a conscientious objector. 文例⬇

りょうせい[1] 両性 both [the two] sexes ¶両性具有 hermaphroditism / 両性具有者 a hermaphrodite.
りょうせい[2] 良性 ¶良性の 〖医〗 benign 《tumors》.
りょうせいるい 両生類 〖動〗 ¶両生類動物 an amphibian (animal).
りょうせん 稜線 a ridgeline；〈尾根〉a ridge.
りょうぞく 良俗 ¶良俗に反している《文》be prejudicial to public morals.
りょうそでづくえ 両袖机 a kneehole desk.
りょうたん 両端 both ends ¶両端に at both ends [either end] 《of》.
りょうだん 両断 ¶一刀両断 ⇨いっとうりょうだん.
りょうち 領地 ⇨りょうど.
りょうて 両手 both hands; both arms 《腕》て, うで ¶両手の利く ambidextrous; able to use both hands with equal ease / 両手に一杯の金貨 a double handful of gold coins / 両手に花 have a double advantage; 《文》be doubly favored；〈両側に美人を置く〉be (seated) between two pretty women.
りょうてい 料亭 a (Japanese-style) restaurant.
りょうてんびん 両天秤 ¶両天秤をかける do not put all one's eggs in one basket; 《口語》hedge one's bet(s).
りょうど 領土 (a) territory；《文》(a) domain；〈封土〉a fief / 領土の territorial / 日本の領土で on Japanese soil; in Japanese territory / 領土的野心をいだく have [《文》harbor] territorial ambitions / 領土争い a territorial dispute / 領土拡張 territorial expansion / 領土拡張主義 expansionism / 領土保全《文》maintenance of the territorial integrity 《of》.
りょうとう[1] 両刀 ¶両刀を差す wear two swords / 両刀使い〈剣法の〉a two-sword fencer；〈酒も甘いものもいける人〉a person who likes alcoholic beverages and sweet things equally well.
りょうとう[2] 両頭 ¶両頭の two-headed 《serpents》/ 両頭政治 dyarchy; diarchy.
りょうどう 糧道 ¶敵の糧道を断つ cut off the enemy's supplies [lines of supply].
りょうどうたい 良導体 ¶熱の良導体である be a good conductor of heat; have high thermal conductivity.
りょうとく 両得 ⇨いっきょ (一挙両得する).
りょうない 領内 ¶領内に[で] within [in] the territory [《文》domain] 《of》.
りょうば 両刃 ¶両刃の剣 a double-edged sword.
りょうはし[じ] 両端 ⇨りょうたん.

---

of ¥50,000.
りょうしょう サンフランシスコ行き 405 便の出発が 1 時間遅れますのでご了承下さい. We regret to announce that flight 405 to San Francisco will be delayed by one hour. / 勝手ながら従業員慰労のため 9 月 3 日から 6 日まで休業いたしますのでご了承下さい. We shall be closed for staff holidays from Sept. 3rd to 6th. ★英語では「勝手ながら...(します)のでご了承下さい」に相当する表現はしないことが多い.
りょうしん[2] そんなことをするのは良心が許さない. I cannot, in (all) conscience, do such a thing. / 良心がとがめる. My conscience pricks [stings] me. / 君の良心に問うてみたまえ. Listen to what your conscience tells you. / それが彼の良心をひどく悩ました. This weighed heavily on his conscience. / 南アについて人々の良心に突き刺さるような本を書いてみたい. I would like to write a book about South Africa which would really prick people's conscience(s).
りょうど その島は今アメリカの領

りょうひ 良否 quality ¶良否を調べる examine (an article) to see whether (it) is good or bad; check the quality (of an article).

りょうびらき 両開き ¶両開きの戸 double doors.

りょうふう 涼風 a cool [refreshing] breeze.

りょうぶん 領分 ⇨ りょうど, りょういき.

りょうほう¹ 両方 both (of us); both sides;〈否定〉neither (of them). 文例↓

りょうほう² 療法 a method of treatment; a cure; therapy; a remedy ¶電気療法 electrotherapy / 精神療法 psychotherapy.

りょうまつ 糧秣 provisions and fodder.

りょうめ 量目 weight ⇨ めかた ¶量目が足りない weigh less than it should / 量目をごまかす give short weight / 量目をごまかさない give honest [good] weight.

りょうめん 両面 both faces [sides] ¶人生の明暗両面を見る look on both the bright and dark sides of life / 両面作戦 operations [a strategy] on two fronts. 文例↓

りょうやく 良薬 a good [an effective] medicine. 文例↓

りょうゆう¹ 両雄 two great men. 文例↓

りょうゆう² 良友 a good friend [companion] ¶良友と交わる keep good company.

りょうゆう³ 領有 ¶領有する《文》possess; take [get, be in] possession of.

りょうゆう⁴ 僚友 a colleague; a comrade; a fellow worker.

りょうよう¹ 両様 ¶両様に in two [both] ways. 文例↓

りょうよう² 療養〈保養〉recuperation;〈治療〉(a) medical treatment ¶療養する〈保養する〉recuperate;〈治療を受ける〉be under medical treatment / 療養所 a rest [nursing] home; a sanatorium (pl. -s, -ria);《米》a sanitarium (pl. -s, -ria) / 療養費 medical expenses. 文例↓

りょうり 料理〈調理〉cooking; cookery; (French) cuisine (★少し気取った言い方);〈料理品〉food; a dish (一品) ¶料理する cook《vegetables》; dress《fish》; prepare《a dish》;〈処理する〉manage; deal with; take care of;〈取り除く〉do away with / うまい料理 a delicious [tasty] dish;《文》excellent cuisine / 料理の名人 a cooking expert;《文》an expert in the culinary art / 野菜[魚]料理 a vegetarian [fish] dish / 料理教室 a cooking [cookery] class [course, school] / 料理人[番] a cook / 料理場 a kitchen; a cookery / 料理法 cooking; how to cook; cuisine / 料理屋[店] a restaurant; an eating house / 料理屋の主人 the owner [keeper] of a restaurant; a restaurateur / 料理用の油 cooking oil. 文例↓

りょうりつ 両立 ¶両立する[しない]《文》be compatible [incompatible]《with》;《文》be consistent [inconsistent]《with》.

りょうりょう 両々 ¶両々相まって ⇨ あいまつ.

りょうりょう² 寥々 ¶寥々りょうたるものである be rare; be few (and far between). 文例↓

りょうりん 両輪 ¶車の両輪のごとくである be inseparable; be closely connected with each other.

りょかく 旅客 a traveler; a passenger (乗客) ¶旅客機[列車] a passenger plane [train] / 旅客名簿 a passenger list; a list of passengers.

りょかん 旅館 a ryokan; a Japanese-style hotel [inn] ¶旅館の主人 the proprietor of a hotel; a hotelkeeper; an innkeeper / 旅館を経営する run [keep] a hotel / 旅館に泊まる register [put up] at a hotel.

りよく 利欲 greed (for gain [profits]);《文》avarice ¶利欲を離れて from disinterested motive(s) / 利欲に走る be greedy for gain;《文》be avaricious;《文》be covetous.

りょくいん 緑陰 ¶緑陰で in the shade of trees; in a shady nook.

りょくか 緑化 ⇨ りょっか.

りょくじゅ 緑樹 a (green-leaved) tree.

りょくじゅほうしょう 緑綬褒章 a Green Ribbon Medal.

りょくち 緑地 a green tract of land ¶緑地帯 a green belt [zone];《米》a tree lawn (歩道と車道の間の).

りょくちゃ 緑茶 green tea.

りょくひ 緑肥 green manure.

りょくや 緑野 a green field;〈草原〉grassland.

りょけん 旅券 a passport ¶旅券の下付を申請する apply for a passport / 英国行きの旅券を発行する issue a passport for (travel to) England / 一回往復旅券 a passport for a single journey / 数次旅券 a passport for multiple journeys (valid for five years); a multiple passport ⇨ さしょう¹.

りょこう 旅行 travel(s) ⇨ 囲語; traveling; a

土になっている. The island is now an American possession.

りょうほう¹ 通りを横切るときは左右両方をよく見なさい. Look carefully both ways [in both directions] before crossing the street. / 両方ともよく知っています. I know both of them [them both] very well. / 両方とも知らない. I don't know either of them.

りょうめ あの店はよく量目をごまかす. They often give short weight at that store.

りょうめん 物にはすべて両面がある. There are two sides to everything. | Everything has its two sides.

りょうやく 良薬は口に苦し. Good medicine tastes bitter. |〈忠告など〉Good advice is seldom welcome. |〈目的のための手段など〉You can't make an omelet without breaking eggs.

りょうゆう¹ 両雄並び立たず. Two strong personalities cannot exist [get on] together.

りょうよう¹ それは両様に解釈できる. It can be interpreted in two ways. | That admits of two readings.

りょうよう² 父は興津で療養中です. My father is staying at Okitsu to recuperate [for his health].

りょうり 彼女は料理が上手[へた]だ. She is a good [poor] cook. | She is a good [poor] hand at cooking.

りょうりょう² そういう人は今日では実にりょうりょうたるものだ. Nowadays such persons are rarely to be met with.

りょしゅう journey (一定の目的地への); a trip (短期の); travels (各地を回る長期の); an excursion (遊覧); a voyage (船旅) ¶2, 3日の旅行 a two or three days' trip / 旅行する travel; make a journey [trip] / 旅行[make a tour of]《Europe》/ 仕事で旅行する make [go on] a business trip 《to the Kansai》/ 旅行に行く[出かける] go [start, set out] on a journey [tour, trip] / 九州旅行から帰る return from one's trip to [tour of] Kyushu / アメリカ旅行中 during one's travels in the U.S.; while traveling in [on a tour of] America / 旅行案内 a travelers' guide(book); a guidebook (for tourists) / 旅行案内所 a travel [tourist] bureau / 旅行談をする give an account of one's travels 《in Africa》/ 旅行カバン a traveling bag; 〈スーツケース〉a suitcase / 旅行記 a book of travels; 《publish》one's travels / 旅行プラン[日程]をたてる prepare [draw up, map out] an itinerary / 旅行先〈目的地〉one's destination; 〈滞在先〉the place where one is staying / 旅行者 a traveler; a tourist; a tripper / 旅行者用小切手 a traveler's check.

用法 travel は「旅というもの」「旅行で各地を動き回ること」の意で, 不定冠詞の a はとらないが, My brother is off on his travels again. (兄はまた旅に出ています) / My father brought this back from his travels in Africa. (これは父のアフリカ旅行のおみやげです) のように, travels の形では,「各地を回る大旅行」「旅によく出かける人の旅行」の意味になる.

りょしゅう 旅愁 loneliness on a journey; sadness felt while on a journey.
りょじょう 旅情 ¶旅情を慰める《文》console the weary heart of a traveler; 《文》beguile the tedium of a journey.
りょそう 旅装 a traveling outfit; traveling kit ¶旅装を整える equip oneself [make (one's) preparations] for a journey / 旅装を解く take off one's traveling clothes; 〈宿泊する〉stop [put up] at 《an inn》.
りょだん 旅団 a brigade ¶旅団長 a brigade commander; a brigadier (general).
りょっか 緑化 ¶緑化する plant trees 《in an area》; plant 《an area》with trees / 緑化運動 a tree-planting campaign [drive].
りょてい 旅程 〈旅行日程〉the plan [schedule] for one's journey; an itinerary; 〈距離〉the distance to be covered.
りょひ 旅費 〈支出〉travel(ing) expenses; 〈支給金〉a travel allowance ¶東京までの往復の旅費を負担する pay sb's traveling expenses to Tokyo and back. 文例↓
リラ¹ 〖植〗 a lilac.
リラ² 〈イタリアの通貨〉a lira (pl. lire).
リラックス ¶リラックスする relax.
リリーフ relief ¶リリーフする relieve / リリーフ投手 a relief pitcher; a reliever.
りりく 離陸 a takeoff; taking off ¶離陸する take off; take the air / 離陸の際 at [during] takeoff / 見事な離陸ぶりを見せる make an excellent takeoff / 離陸滑走 a takeoff roll. 文例↓
りりしい 凛々しい 《文》gallant; manly.
りりつ 利率 the rate of interest.
リレー a 《400-meter》relay 《race》¶リレーする relay 《a message》; pass 《a bucket from one person to another》.
りれき 履歴 one's personal [life] history; one's past record; one's background. ¶履歴書 one's personal [life] history; one's curriculum vitae (略: C.V.) (pl. curricula vitae);《米》a résumé.
りろせいぜん 理路整然 ¶理路整然とした logically consistent; logical; well-reasoned《articles》.
りろん 理論 (a) theory ¶理論を実際に移す put theory into practice / 理論的 theoretical / 理論上 theoretically; in theory / 理論家 a theorist; a theoretician / 理論体系 a body of theory 《about energy》/ 理論物理学 theoretical physics / 理論闘争をする try to argue [talk] sb down; have an ideological dispute [quarrel]《with》. 文例↓
りん¹ 厘 a rin ¶日歩5厘 《interest of》0.5 per cent per day / 2割3分5厘 0.235 (★ 数字は (nought) point two three five とよむ); 〈打率など〉《a batting average of》.235 (★ 数字は two thirty-five とよむ).
りん² 鈴 a bell; a handbell (手で振り鳴らす)
りん³ 燐, リン 〖化〗phosphorus. ⇨ベル, すず¹.
-りん -輪 ¶1輪の花 a (single) flower / 三輪車 ⇨ さんりんしゃ.
りんか 隣家 a nearby [neighboring] house; the house next door ⇨ となり.
りんかい¹ 臨海 ¶臨海学校 a seaside school / 臨海工業地帯 a coastal industrial zone [region] / 臨海実験所 a marine (biological) laboratory.

りょこう 旅行はいかがでしたか. Did you enjoy yourself [have a good time] while you were away? / 彼は旅行好きだ. He is fond of traveling. | He takes great delight in traveling. / こんどの旅行ではどちらにいらっしゃいましたか. Where did your travels take you this time? / 彼は今ヨーロッパを旅行中です. He is now on a tour of Europe. / サマセット・モームは方々を旅行した作家だった. Somerset Maugham was a much-traveled writer. / 父は旅行先から色々の絵はがきをよこした. Father sent me various picture postcards from the places he went to. / She fell ill on her journey.
りょひ 伊勢まで行くのに旅費はどのくらいかかるでしょうか. How much will it cost to travel to Ise?
りりく よくもまあこんなでっかいジャンボジェットを離陸させることができるもんだ. How on earth do they manage to get a huge jumbo jet like this off the ground?
りれき どんな履歴の人かね. What is his background [past record]? / 彼な過去は我々には全くわからない. His past life is a closed book to us. / 履歴をみるとわかるが, あれは尻の落ち着かない人だ. He never stays long in one job, as can be seen from his past record.
りろん 理論は結構だが実際にうまくゆくだろうか. It's all very well in theory, but will it work in practice? / 理論と実際とは必ずしも一致しない. Theory and prac-

りんかい² 臨界 ¶臨界圧力[温度，状態，点]〖物〗the critical pressure [temperature, state, point].

りんかく 輪郭 an outline ; 〈比喩的に〉a profile《of the future of the town》 ¶輪郭のはっきりした clear-cut《features》/ 輪郭を述べる[描く] give an outline [a short sketch] of《a project》; outline [sketch (out)]《a plan》; describe [《文》represent]《a matter》in outline / 人体の輪郭を描く sketch [draw] the contours of the human body / 輪郭を知る[つかむ] grasp a general idea [outline]《of》; get a picture《of》.

りんがく 林学 forestry ; dendrology ¶林学者 an expert in forestry ; a dendrologist.

りんかん¹ 林間 ¶林間の小道 a lane [path] through a forest ; a woodland path / 林間学校 a camp(ing) [an open-air] school.

りんかん² 輪姦 gang rape ¶輪姦する rape《a girl》in turn [in succession, one after another].

りんぎ 稟議 the process of obtaining sanction《from senior executives》for a plan by circulating a draft proposal (prepared lower down in the organization).

りんきおうへん 臨機応変 ¶臨機応変に as occasion may demand [require] ; according to circumstances / 臨機応変の処置をとる take measures suited to the occasion ; take proper steps to meet the situation ; take such steps as the occasion demands.

りんぎょう 林業 forestry.

りんきん 淋菌〖細菌〗a gonococcus《*pl.* -cocci》.

リンク¹ 〈スケートの〉a《skating》rink.

リンク² 〈ゴルフの〉a golf course ; (a) golf links (★ links は単複両様に扱うことができる).

リング¹〖ボクシング〗a ring ¶リングサイドに座る sit at the ringside.

リング² 〈避妊具〉an IUD (★ intrauterine device の略) ; a loop.

りんげつ 臨月 the last month of pregnancy ; the month in which childbirth is due [expected]. [文例⇩]

リンゲルちゅうしゃ リンゲル注射 an injection of Ringer's solution.

りんけん¹ 隣県 a neighboring [《文》an adjacent] prefecture.

りんけん² 臨検 ¶臨検する〈検査する〉make an inspection of《a dormitory》; 〈捜索する〉(raid and) search《a house for *sth*》; 〈船を〉(board and) search《a ship for contraband goods》.

りんご an apple ¶りんごの木 an apple tree / りんごの皮をむく peel [pare] an apple / りんごのように赤いほっぺ apple-red cheeks / りんご酒 cider / りんごジュース apple juice.

りんこう¹ 輪講 ⇨りんどく.

りんこう² 燐光 phosphorescence ¶燐光を発する phosphoresce / 燐光を発する物体 a phosphorescent body.

りんこう(せき) 燐鉱(石) a phosphate rock.

りんこうせん 臨港線 a harbor railroad [railway].

りんごく 隣国 a neighboring [《文》an adjacent] country.

りんさく 輪作 rotation of crops ; crop rotation ¶輪作する rotate crops / 輪作法 the crop rotation system.

リンさん リン酸〖化〗phosphoric acid ¶リン酸塩 (a) phosphate / リン酸カルシウム calcium phosphate / リン酸肥料 phosphatic manure [fertilizer].

りんさんぶつ 林産物 forest products.

りんじ 臨時 ¶臨時の〈特別の〉special ; extraordinary ; extra ; 〈一時の〉provisional ; temporary / 臨時の仕事 a casual [an odd] job / 臨時に specially ; provisionally ; temporarily / 臨時費〈支出〉extraordinary expenses [expenditure] ; 〈予算〉a reserve fund for contingencies / 臨時国会 an extraordinary session of the Diet / 臨時ニュース news special ; a special newscast / 臨時列車[試験] a special train [examination] / 臨時政府[予算] a provisional government [budget] / 臨時総会 an extraordinary general meeting / 臨時雇い a temporary employee / 臨時増刊 an extra [a special] issue《of a magazine》. [文例⇩]

りんしつ 隣室 the next [《文》adjoining] room.

りんじゅう 臨終 *one's* death [《文》end] ¶臨終の言葉 *one's* dying words / 臨終の時まで《文》until *one's* dying hour [*one* has breathed *one's* last] ; to *one's* last moment / 臨終の床に呼ぶ call《the family》to *sb's* [*one's*] deathbed / 臨終に at *one's* death ; on *one's* deathbed. [文例⇩]

りんしょう¹ 輪唱〖音楽〗a round ¶輪唱する sing《a song》in a circular canon.

りんしょう² 臨床 ¶臨床の clinical / 臨床的に clinically / 臨床医 a clinician / 臨床医学 clinical medicine / 臨床経験《have a wealth of》clinical experience / 臨床講義 a clinical lecture [instruction] ; a clinic / 臨床実験 clinical trials [tests]《on patients》/ 臨床心理学 clinical psychology / 臨床データ clinical data.

りんじょうかん 臨場感《文》《have》presence. [文例⇩]

りんしょく 吝嗇 ⇨けち¹.

りんじん 隣人 a neighbor ¶隣人愛 love of *one's* neighbors.

リンス a (hair) rinse ¶リンスする rinse《*one's* hair》; give《*one's* hair》a rinse.

---

tice do not always go together [hand in hand]. / これは理論上予想された数値である. These are the figures that theory predicted.

りんげつ 彼女は今月が臨月です. Her baby is due [She is expecting her baby] this month.

りんじ 今月は臨時の支出が多かった. We have had a large number of unbudgeted outlays this month. / 臨時休業.〖掲示〗No business today. | Closed for today.

りんじゅう 父の臨終にぜひ間に合いたいものと願った. I ardently wished to be in time for the death of my father. / 彼の臨終が迫りつつあった. He was nearing his end. | His hour had come.

りんじょうかん このレコードは実際にコンサート・ホールで「田園」をN響の演奏で聴いているような臨場感がある. This record gives us Beethoven's *Pastoral Symphony* with so much presence that we have the illusion that we are listening to a per-

りんせき 隣席 the next seat ¶隣席の伊藤氏 Mr. Ito who sits next (to) one 《at dinner》.

りんせつ 隣接 ¶隣接する《文》adjoin;《文》 be adjacent [contiguous] to; be [lie] next to; border on [upon]; 隣接した neighboring;《文》 adjoining;《文》adjacent; next-door / 隣接科学 neighboring [adjacent] disciplines [sciences] / 隣接町村 neighboring [nearby] towns and villages.

りんせんたいせい 臨戦態勢 (a state of) preparedness for war ¶臨戦態勢を整えた ready [prepared] for war.

りんそん 隣村 the next-door [a neighboring] village.

リンチ ¶リンチを加える (gang up on sb and) beat *him* up ★ lynching は「私的処刑」であって, 殺人行為を意味する. 単に「私的制裁」もしくは「集団暴行」を意味する日本語の「リンチ」と全く同じではない.

りんてんき 輪転機 a rotary press.

りんどう¹ 林道 a path [trail] through a forest; a woodland path; 〈林業用の〉a forestry road.

りんどう² 〖植〗a gentian; an autumn bellflower.

りんどく 輪読 ¶輪読する read 《a book》in turn [by turns] / 輪読会 (a meeting of) a reading circle.

りんね 輪廻 〖仏教〗transmigration of the soul; the 《never-ending》 cycle of reincarnation; metempsychosis.

リンネしきめいめいほう リンネ式命名法 Linnaean nomenclature.

リンネル linen ¶リンネル(製)の linen 《cloth》.

リンパ ¶リンパ液 lymph (fluid) / リンパ管 a lymphatic vessel; a lymph duct / リンパ系 the lymph system / リンパ腺 a lymph node. 文例⬇

りんばん 輪番 ¶輪番で by turns; in turn; turn (and turn) about; by [in] rotation; on a rotation basis / 議長を輪番制にする take the chair in rotation.

りんびょう 淋病 gonorrhea.

りんぶ 輪舞 a round dance ¶輪舞する dance in a circle [ring].

りんぷん 鱗粉 〈ちょうやがのはねの〉(minute) scales.

りんや 林野 forests and fields ¶林野庁 the Forestry Agency.

りんり 倫理 ethics; morals ¶実践倫理 practical ethics / 倫理的 ethical; moral / 倫理学 ethics; moral philosophy [science] / 倫理学者 a moral philosopher; an ethicist / 倫理規定 an ethical code.

用法 ethics は学問・学科用として用いられる時は単数扱いで, 道徳を意味する時は複数扱いにする. Ethics is not taught in this college. (この学校では倫理学は教えていない) / Business ethics in Japan are not all that bad. (日本の商業道徳はそんなにひどく乱れてはいない).

りんりつ 林立 ¶林立する stand together in large numbers / 林立する帆柱 a (veritable) forest of masts. 文例⬇

りんりん¹ 凛々 ¶勇気りんりんとしている be full of spirit [《文》valor].

りんりん² ¶りんりん鳴る ring; jingle; tinkle / りんりん鳴らす jingle [tinkle] 《a bell》/ 鈴のりんりん鳴る音 a jingle [tinkle] of a bell.

る

ルアー 〖釣〗a lure.

るい¹ 累 ¶累を及ぼす have a harmful [a damaging, an unfavorable] effect 《on》; affect *sb* unfavorably; compromise; cause trouble 《to》.

るい² 塁 〈とりで〉a fort;〈野球の〉a base ¶塁を摩する be a very close rival 《to》; be almost as good [skillful, etc.] as.... 文例⬇

るい³ 類 〖論〗a genus (*pl.* genera) ⇒ しゅるい ¶類のない〈比類のない〉unique;《文》unparalleled;《文》unexampled;〈前例のない〉unprecedented / 類概念 a genus (*pl.* genera) / 類名 a generic name.

るいか 累加 ¶累加する《文》increase cumulatively; accumulate; build up.

るいかん 涙管 〖解〗a tear [lachrymal] duct.

るいく 類句 〈意味の似ている語句〉a synonymous phrase;〈似通った俳句〉a similar *haiku*.

るいけい¹ 累計 ¶昨日現在で累計...になる The aggregate (amount) comes to...as of yesterday.

るいけい² 類型 a type; a pattern ¶類型学 typology / 類型的な〈類型を代表する〉typical;〈型にはまった〉stereotype(d).

るいご 類語 a synonym ¶類語を挙げる give a synonym for 《a word》. 文例⬇

るいじ 類似 (a) likeness; (a) resemblance; (a) similarity;《文》an analogy ¶類似する resemble; be similar [《文》akin,《文》analogous]《to》; be like / ...に多少著しく]類似している bear some [a striking] resemblance to... / 類似の similar;《文》like;《文》kindred / 類似点 a (point of) similarity [resemblance]. 文例⬇

---

formance of the NHK Symphony Orchestra in the concert hall.

リンパ 彼はひどい風邪を引いてリンパ腺を腫らしてしまった. He caught a bad cold and developed swollen lymph nodes.

りんりつ 河岸には工場の煙突が林立している. The riverbank bristles with factory chimneys.

るいだ 三塁手のエラーで二塁に進んだ. He advanced to second on the third-baseman's error.

るい³ この本は他に類がない. There is no other book like this. / 類は友で集まる. Birds of a feather flock together.〖諺〗/ 類は友を呼ぶ. Like attracts like.

るいご lofty は high の類語である. 'Lofty' is a synonym for 'high'. | 'Lofty' is synonymous with 'high'.

るいじ 心臓はポンプに類似している. There is an analogy between the heart and a pump. / これとそれとは少しも類似点がない. I see no likeness whatever between this and that. | This has

るいジアナ Louisiana (略: La.) ¶ルイジアナ州の人 a Louisianian; a Lousianian.
るいしょ 類書 similar books.
るいしょう 類焼 ¶類焼する catch fire ((from another burning building)); be burned down in a spreading fire / 類焼を免れる escape the fire.
るいしん¹ 累進 ¶累進する be promoted from one position to another; rise step by step / 累進的に progressively / 累進課税 progressive [graduated] taxation.
るいしん² 塁審 〔野球〕a base umpire ¶一塁塁審 the umpire at first base.
るいじんえん 類人猿 an anthropoid (ape).
るいすい 類推 analogy; analogical reasoning ¶類推する reason [know] by analogy / …から類推して on the analogy of….
るいする 類する be similar [〔文〕akin] to; be like.
るいせき 累積 ¶累積する 〔文〕increase cumulatively; accumulate / 累積赤字 a cumulative deficit / 累積投票 cumulative voting.
るいせん 涙腺 a lachrymal gland.
るいだい 類題 a similar problem.
るいだすう 塁打数 〔野球〕total bases.
るいべつ 類別 categorization ⇨ ぶんるい.
るいらん 累卵 ¶累卵の危うきにある be in a most dangerous [〔文〕perilous] situation; be in imminent danger [〔文〕peril].
るいるい 累々 ⇨ しし² 文例.
るいれい 類例 a similar example [instance]; a similar [parallel] case ¶類例のない ⇨ るい³ (類のない) / 類例を挙げる give [cite, 〔文〕adduce] a similar example [case].
るいれき 瘰癧 〔医〕scrofula.
ルーキー a rookie.
ルージュ rouge; (a) lipstick.
ルーズ loose ★ loose の発音は [luːs]. ただし「ルーズ」が英語で loose になることはあまりない ¶ルーズなやり方で in a careless [slovenly] manner / 考え方がルーズである be a loose thinker / 時間がルーズである be unpunctual; be a poor timekeeper.
ルーズリーフ a loose-leaf notebook ★ loose-leaf の発音は [lúːsliːf] ¶ルーズリーフの用紙 a loose-leaf (refill) pad.
ルート¹ 〔数〕a root ⇨ こん¹.
ルート² 〔経路〕a route; a channel ¶正規の [不正な,秘密の]ルートから through legitimate [illegal, secret] channels ((of supply)).
ルーブル 〈ソ連の貨幣単位〉a rouble.

ルーブル(はくぶつかん) ルーブル(博物館) the Louvre (Museum).
ルーペ a loupe.
ルーマニア Romania; R(o)umania ¶ルーマニア社会主義共和国 the Socialist Republic of Romania / ルーマニア人 a Romanian / ルーマニア(人)の Romanian.
ルーム a room ¶ルームクーラー an air conditioner / ルームサービス room service.
ルール a rule; 〈ゲームの〉the rules ((of tennis)); the rules of play ⇨ きそく² ¶ルールに従って行動する play by the rules.
ルーレット 〈とばく〉roulette; 〈小さな穴を線状にあける器具〉a roulette / ルーレット台 [の回転盤] a roulette board [wheel].
ルクス 〈照度の単位〉a lux (pl. -(es)).
ルクセンブルク Luxembourg ¶ルクセンブルク人 a Luxembourger / ルクセンブルク(人)の Luxembourgian / ルクセンブルク大公国 the Grand Duchy of Luxembourg.
るけい 流刑 ⇨ るざい ¶流刑地 a place of exile; a penal colony [settlement].
ルゴール Lugol's solution.
るざい 流罪 exile; banishment; deportation ¶流罪になる be sent into [condemned to] exile ((to an island)); be sentenced to (lifelong) deportation ((to Siberia)); be banished [exiled, deported] ((to a remote province)) / 流罪者 an exile; a deportee.
るす 留守 being away; 〔文〕absence (from home) ¶留守である be [stay] away from home; be not in [at home] / 散歩に行って留守である be out for a walk / 留守中に in [during] one's absence; while one is away [out, absent] / 留守番[居]をする stay [〔文〕remain] at home; take charge [care] of the house ((during sb's absence)); look after the house ((while sb is away)). 文例⇨
ルックス ⇨ ルクス.
るつぼ 坩堝 a melting pot; a crucible. 文例⇨
ルテチウム 〔化〕lutetium.
ルテニウム 〔化〕ruthenium.
るてん 流転 〈変転〉continual change; 〔文〕vicissitudes; 〈流浪〉⇨ るろう.
ルネッサンス the Renaissance; the Renascence ¶ルネッサンス式建築 Renaissance architecture.
ルバシカ [<《ロシヤ語》rubashka] a Russian blouse.
ルビ [<ruby]〔印刷〕¶ルビを振る print [give] kana ((alongside Chinese characters)).

---

nothing in common with that. / 類似品にご注意下さい. Beware of imitations.
るす 何日くらい留守にされますか. How long [How many days] are you going to be away? / だれか来たら留守だと言いなさい. If anyone comes, say that I am out. / 野村さんの外はだれにも留守だと言うんだよ. I am in [at home] to nobody but Mr. Nomura. / 私が留守のあいだに何かあったのですか. Has something come up while I have been away? / 主人は九州へ行って留守でございます. My husband is away in Kyushu. / 昨日は一日中留守番だった. Yesterday I was left in charge of the house all day.
るつぼ それがために場内興奮のつぼと化した. It threw the whole house into a state of feverish excitement.
るふ その本は広く流布している. The book has had a wide circulation.
れい¹ 本当にお礼の申しようもございません. I don't know how I can ever thank you. | I am more grateful than I can tell you. / いいえ, お礼を申しなければならないのは私の方です. No, it's I should be thanking you. / 礼を失せぬ程度にできるだけ早く辞去しようと思った. I made up my mind that I

ルピア〈インドネシアの貨幣単位〉a rupiah
ルビー〈宝玉〉(a) ruby. 〖*pl*. -(s)〗.
ルピー〈インドの貨幣単位〉a rupee.
ルビジウム《化》rubidium.
るふ 流布 circulation;《文》dissemination ¶流布する〈広まる〉circulate；spread；get abroad；〈広める〉circulate；spread；《文》disseminate；give currency to 《a rumor》/ 流布している be in circulation；〈うわさなどが〉be afloat；be abroad；be in the air / 流布本 a popular edition 《of a book》.
ルポライター a reporter；a documentary writer.
ルポルタージュ[<《フランス語》*reportage*] a report 《on》；a reportorial piece 《on》；a documentary.
ルミノールはんのう ルミノール反応 (a) luminol reaction.
るり 瑠璃 lapis lazuli ¶るり色 sky blue；《文》azure；lapis lazuli.
るり(ちょう)《鳥》a blue and white flycatcher

〈オオルリ〉；a Siberian blue robin〈コルリ〉.
るる 縷々 in detail；minutely；at great length ¶るると述べる explain [《文》relate] at great length；dwell [enlarge,《文》expatiate]《on》.
るろう 流浪 wandering；《文》vagrancy ¶流浪する wander [roam] about [from place to place] / 流浪の生活 a wandering [vagrant] life；the life of an exile / 流浪の旅 wanderings / 流浪の民 wanderers；a wandering [vagrant] tribe；〈遊牧民〉nomads；a nomadic tribe.
ルワンダ Rwanda ¶ルワンダ共和国 the Republic of Rwanda / ルワンダ人 a Rwandan / ルワンダ(人)の Rwandan.
ルンバ r(h)umba ¶ルンバを踊る dance the rumba.
ルンペン[<《ドイツ語》*Lumpen*]〈浮浪者〉a tramp；《米》a hobo (*pl*. -(e)s);〈失業者〉a jobless [an unemployed] person.

れ

レ《音楽》re.
れい¹ 礼〈会釈〉a bow；〈礼儀〉etiquette；《文》the proprieties；〈謝辞〉thanks；gratitude；〈謝礼〉a reward；a fee / 礼を述べる thank [give thanks to] 《*sb* for *sth*》；express *one's* thanks [gratitude]《to *sb* for *sth*》/ 礼をする〈謝礼をする〉give [offer] a reward《to *sb* for *his* services》;〈お辞儀をする〉⇒おじぎ / 礼を失する be impolite [rude,《文》discourteous]《to》/ 礼をもって遇する，礼をつくす[《文》]treat *sb* with the utmost courtesy；be polite and respectful to *sb* / お礼に行く call on *sb* to offer *one's* thanks / …のお礼として in reward [return] for…. 文例⇩
れい² 例〈実例，類例〉an instance；an example；an illustration；a case；〈慣例〉a custom；《文》(a) usage；〈先例〉a precedent ¶ぴったりした[よい]例 a good illustration；a case in point / 例の男 the man in question；that man / 例のごとく[とおり] as usual；《文》as is *one's* wont / 例をあげる give examples [an example (一例)] /《文》cite an instance / 例になく unusually；例に倣う follow suit；follow *sb's* example / 例として by way of example；as an example / …を例とする make a point of *doing*；make it a point [rule] to *do* / 一例を

あげるならば to take an [a single] instance；for example [instance]. 文例⇩
れい³ 零 ⇒ゼロ.
れい⁴ 霊 the soul；the spirit；〈亡魂〉《文》the departed soul《of *sb*》;〈亡霊〉the ghost《of a dead person》¶霊の世界 the spirit world / 霊と肉 the spirit and the flesh.
レイ⁵〈ハワイの花輪〉a lei.
レイアウト《印刷・図案》(a) layout.
れいあんしつ 霊安室 a mortuary.
れいあんぽう 冷罨法 ¶冷罨法を施す apply a cold compress [pack]《to》.
れいか 零下 ¶零下 16 度《the temperature fell to》16 degrees below zero [freezing point] ⇒ れいど. 文例⇩
れいかい¹ 例会 a regular meeting. ¶毎月の例会を開く hold a monthly meeting.
れいかい² 霊界 the spirit [psychic] world.
れいがい¹ 冷害 damage from [caused by] cold weather；〈霜の害〉frost damage ¶作物を冷害から守る protect crops from being damaged by cold weather [from frost damage].
れいがい² 例外 an exception ¶例外の[的] exceptional / 例外を認めない allow [《文》admit 《of》] no exceptions / 例外的に exceptionally / …は例外として except…；with the ex-

---

would leave as soon as I civilly could. / 骨折ってもらったお礼に贈り物をした。I gave him a present in acknowledgment of his trouble. / お礼が欲しくてしたことではありません。I haven't done it for [in expectation of] a reward.
れい¹ そういう例はこれまでにはない。There is no precedent for this. | This case is unprecedented. | There has never been a case like this (before). / 例の事があっ

た時はどうなることかと思ったよ。When you-know-what happened, I was really alarmed. / 彼はその朝も例のごとく散歩に出た。He went for his usual walk that morning. / 日本もこの例に漏れない。Japan is no exception to this rule. / 彼は一人言を言いながら部屋の中を行ったり来たりし始めた。He began, as is usual with him [as is his habit], to pace up and down the

room talking to himself. / 彼はその夜例になく遅く帰った。That night he came back much later than usual.
れいか 気温は零下 5 度だった。It was 5 degrees below (zero). |《英》There were [We had] 5 degrees of frost. | The temperature was minus five (degrees). / 零下何度という寒さの中で働いていた。They were working at sub-zero temperatures [in the sub-zero

れいかん 霊感 (an) inspiration ¶霊感を受ける be inspired 《by》; get [draw] inspiration 《from》; 《口語》have a brain wave.

れいき 冷気 cold; chill ¶朝の冷気を感じる feel the morning chill.

れいぎ 礼儀 courtesy; (good) manners; good form; 〈作法〉etiquette; 《文》decorum; 《文》the proprieties ¶礼儀を守る observe the proprieties; observe [behave with] proper decorum / 礼儀を知らない ill-mannered; ill-bred; 《文》unmannerly / 礼儀正しい well-mannered; courteous; polite / 礼儀正しく politely; 《文》with due courtesy / 礼儀上 out of politeness; as a matter of courtesy. 文例⇩

れいきゃく 冷却 cooling; refrigeration ¶冷却する〈冷やす〉cool; refrigerate; take the heat out of *sth*;〈冷える〉get cool; cool (down [off]) / 冷却器 a refrigerator; a cooler / 冷却期間 a cooling-off period. 文例⇩

れいきゅうしゃ 霊柩車 a (motor) hearse; a funeral car [coach].

れいきん 礼金 ⇒しゃれい.

れいぐう 冷遇 cold treatment ¶冷遇する treat *sb* coldly; give [show] *sb* the cold shoulder;〈客を〉give *sb* a cold reception.

れいけつ 冷血 ¶冷血漢 a cold-hearted [a heartless, an unfeeling] fellow / 冷血動物 a cold-blooded animal.

れいげん 冷厳 ¶冷厳な事実 (face) a cold (hard) fact.

れいげん 霊験 《文》miraculous efficacy ¶霊験あらたかな wonder-working; miraculous (amulets).

れいこう 励行 strict [rigid] enforcement ¶励行する〈施行する〉enforce (the rules) rigidly [rigorously];〈実行する〉carry out *one's* [*sb's*] orders strictly [to the letter];〈守る〉observe strictly.

れいこく 冷酷 ¶冷酷な cruel; heartless; cold-hearted / 冷酷に cruelly; mercilessly. 文例⇩

れいこん 霊魂 the soul; the spirit ¶霊魂の不滅を信じる believe in the immortality of the soul.

れいさい¹ 例祭 an annual [a regular] festival.

れいさい² 零細 ¶零細な small; petty; trifling / 零細な金 a small sum of money; (work for) a mere pittance / 零細企業 a small business / 零細農家 a petty farmer.

れいし〔植〕a lychee [litchi] (tree) ¶れいしの実 a lychee (nut).

れいじ 零時〈午前零時〉(twelve o'clock) midnight;〈正午〉noon ★軍隊などで24時間制の場合には午前零時を 0000 と書き zero hours と読む ¶午前零時に at (twelve o'clock) midnight; at zero hours.

れいしょ 隷書 the scribes' style of writing Chinese characters.

れいしょう¹ 冷笑 a cold [sardonic] smile; a sneer; derision ¶冷笑する smile derisively [mockingly] 《at》; sneer [mock, scoff] 《at》; deride / 口元に冷笑を浮かべて with a cold smile on *one's* lips.

れいしょう² 例証 (an) illustration; an instance ¶例証する illustrate;《文》be illustrative of;《文》exemplify / 例証として by way of illustration; as an example [instance]. 文例⇩

れいじょう¹ 令状 a warrant; a writ ¶令状を発行する issue a warrant 《for *sb's* arrest》/ 令状を執行する execute a warrant; serve a writ on *sb*.

れいじょう² 礼状 a letter of thanks [appreciation]; a thank-you letter [note]. 文例⇩

れいじょう³ 令嬢 *sb's* daughter ¶ご令嬢 your daughter.

れいじょう⁴ 霊場 a sacred place; holy [hallowed] ground.

れいすい 冷水 cold water ¶冷水塊 a cold water mass / 冷水摩擦をする have a rubdown with a (cold) wet towel / 冷水浴をする take a cold bath; bathe in cold water.

れいせい 冷静 calmness; coolness; presence of mind ¶冷静な calm; cool(-headed) / 冷静に calmly; coolly;《文》composedly; serenely / 冷静を保つ keep calm [cool]; keep *one's* coolness [presence of mind,《口語》cool]; stay [《文》remain] unruffled [unperturbed] / 冷静を失う lose *one's* head [presence of mind,《口語》cool]; be upset. 文例⇩

れいせつ 礼節 ⇒れいぎ, いしょく¹ 文例.

れいせん 冷戦〈米ソ間の〉the Cold War;〈一般に〉a cold war.

れいぜん 冷然 ¶冷然と ひやゃか.

れいぜん 霊前 ¶霊前の供え物 a funeral offering / 霊前に供える offer *sth* on the altar (praying for the repose of the soul of the deceased).

れいそう 礼装 ⇒れいふく, せいそう¹.

れいぞう 冷蔵 cold storage ¶冷蔵する keep [put,《文》place] (apples) in cold storage; keep (food) cold; refrigerate / ガス冷蔵 controlled-atmospheric storage / 冷蔵会社 a cold-

---

cold].

れいがい² 例外のない規則はない. Every rule has its exceptions. | There are no rules without exceptions. /『クロイツェル・ソナタ』をただひとつの例外として, トルストイの作品は皆非常な歓迎を受けた. All Tolstoy's works, with a single exception of *The Kreuzer Sonata*, were very well received. / 彼とても例外ではない. He is no exception to this rule. /

人は皆法を守らなければならない. 国王とても例外ではない. Everybody must observe the law, not excepting the king.

れいぎ あの女は礼儀を知らない. She has no manners. | She is ill-mannered. / 人前でそんなことをするのは礼儀に外れる. It is bad form [isn't done] to behave like that in the presence of others.

れいきゃく この変化は両国間の関係が冷却したために生じたもの

である. The change has been brought about by a cooling off in the relations between the two countries.

れいこく 彼は冷酷な人間だ. He is a heartless [an unfeeling] fellow. | He has a heart of stone.

れいしょう² 彼は自説の例証として幾多の事実を挙げた. He enumerated a large number of facts in illustration of his theory.

れいじょう² 彼にクリスマスプレ

れいそく 令息 *sb's* son ¶ご令息 your son.
れいぞく 隷属 ¶隷属する be subordinate [subject] 《to》; be [come] under the rule 《of》 / 隷属的地位 a subordinate position.
れいだい 例題 an exercise ¶各章の終わりにある例題をやる do the exercises at the end of each chapter.
れいたん 冷淡 ¶冷淡な cold; cold-hearted;〈気のない〉indifferent; halfhearted / 冷淡に coldly; cold-heartedly;〈気のない〉indifferently; halfheartedly / 冷淡にあしらう treat *sb* coldly; show [turn] the cold shoulder to *sb*; give *sb* a cold reception / 冷淡になる grow [《文》become] cold 《to, toward》/ lose 《*one's*》 enthusiasm 《for》. 文例⇩.
れいだんぼう 冷暖房 air conditioning ¶冷暖房装置 an air conditioner ⇨ れいぼう, だんぼう. 文例⇩.
れいち 霊地 ⇨ れいじょう⁴.
れいちょう 霊長 ¶霊長類《動》the primates / 霊長類学 primatology ⇨ ばんぶつ 文例.
れいてつ 冷徹 ¶冷徹な〈冷静な〉cool-headed;〈現実的な〉hardheaded《businessmen》; realistic;《口語》hard-boiled《newspapermen》.
れいてん 零点 (a) zero (*pl.* -(e)s) ¶答案に零点をつける put a zero on《a student's》paper / 数学で零点をとる get a zero in mathematics.
れいど 零度 zero; (the) freezing point ¶零度以下の温度 a sub-zero temperature ⇨ れいか.
れいとう 冷凍 freezing; refrigeration ¶冷凍する freeze; refrigerate / 急速〈に〉冷凍する freeze 《food》 quickly; quick-freeze; deep-freeze / 冷凍機 a freezing machine; a refrigerator / 冷凍した deep freeze; a freezer /〈家庭用冷蔵庫の〉冷凍室 a freezing compartment; a freezer / 冷凍車 a freezer (car); a refrigerator car [《英》van] / 冷凍食品 frozen [deep-frozen] food.
れいねん 例年〈平年〉the average [normal] year;〈毎年〉every year; annually ¶例年の〈毎年の〉annual;〈平年の〉normal; usual / 例年のとおり as usual / 例年になく unusually. 文例⇩.
れいはい¹ 礼拝 worship;〈礼拝式〉church [divine] service ¶礼拝する worship / 礼拝が終

わってから after church [the service] (is over) / 朝の礼拝(式)を行なう hold morning service / 礼拝(式)に出る go to [《文》attend] church;《文》attend divine service / 礼拝所 a place of worship / 礼拝堂 a chapel.
れいはい² 零敗 ¶零敗する[を喫する] fail to score;《米口語》be shut out;《口語》be whitewashed.
れいばい 霊媒 a (spiritualistic) medium 《*pl.* -s, -dia》.
れいひょう 冷評 a sneer; a jeer ¶冷評する sneer [jeer] 《at》; make [pass] sarcastic remarks 《on》.
れいびょう 霊廟 a mausoleum 《*pl.* -s, -lea》.
れいふく 礼服 full [formal] dress; a dress suit;〈夜会用の〉evening dress;〈軍人の〉(a) (full-) dress uniform ¶礼服を着用する[している] wear [be in] full dress / 宮中礼服 court dress. 文例⇩.
れいぶん 例文 an example (sentence); an illustrative sentence.
れいほう¹ 礼法 ⇨ れいぎ, さほう.
れいほう² 礼砲 ¶21発の礼砲を放つ fire a twenty-one-gun salute.
れいぼう 冷房 air conditioning ¶冷房する air-condition《a room》/ 冷房装置 an air conditioner; air conditioning / 冷房装置がある be equipped [installed] with an air conditioner; be air-conditioned. 文例⇩.
れいみょう 霊妙 ¶霊妙な〈霊験のある〉miraculous;〈不可思議な〉mysterious;〈すばらしい〉wonderful / 霊妙な筆で(be written) in a really wonderful [《文》exquisite] style.
れいめい¹ 令名 ⇨ めいせい.
れいめい² 黎明 ⇨ よあけ. 文例⇩.
れいやく 霊薬 a miraculous medicine; a miracle drug.
れいらく 零落 ¶零落する go to ruin;《文》be in reduced circumstances; come down in the world; fall low ⇨ おちぶれる. 文例⇩.
れいれいしい 麗々しい showy; ostentatious; pretentious ¶麗々しく showily; ostentatiously; pretentiously.
れいろう 玲瓏 ¶れいろうたる bright; clear; serene / れいろう玉のごとき人格 (a person of) perfect [well-rounded] character.
レーザー (a) laser ¶レーザー光線 a laser beam; laser light.
レース¹〈布〉lace.
レース²〈競走〉a race.
レーダー radar ¶レーダー基地 a radar base [station] / レーダー装置 a radar set [device];

ゼントの礼状を出した。I sent him a letter thanking him for the Christmas present.
れいせい 彼は冷静そのものであった。He was completely cool [unperturbed]. | He remained quite unruffled.
れいたん 彼は教育には極めて冷淡だ。He takes very little interest in educational matters. | 彼は僕の要求に対しては極めて冷淡で

あった。He paid (but) little attention to my request.
れいだんぼう 冷暖房完備.〖掲示〗Air-conditioned.
れいねん 今年の夏は例年にない暑さだった。This summer has been hotter than usual. | It has been unusually hot this summer. | 収穫は例年よりよい。The harvest is better than in the average year.

れいふく この会には礼服は要りません。This is not a dress affair.
れいぼう 冷房中.〖掲示〗Air-conditioned.
れいめい² 我々は今や宇宙時代のれいめい期にあるのだ。We now stand at the dawn of the Space Age.
れいらく 一家は彼の浪費のために零落した。His family was ruined by his extravagant habits.

レート a rate ¶為替レート an exchange rate ⇒かわせそうば.
レーニン Lenin ¶レーニン主義 Leninism / レーニン主義者 a Leninist / レーニン主義の Leninist.
レーヨン rayon.
レール a rail.
レーン a lane.
レーンコート a raincoat; a trench coat (ベルト付きの); a mackintosh; 《口語》a mac.
レーンジャー《米》a ranger; 《英》a commando (pl. -(e)s) ¶レーンジャー部隊《米》rangers; 《英》commando(e)s.
レーンシューズ rain shoes; galoshes (靴の上にはく).
レオタード a leotard.
れきがん 礫岩 [地質](a) conglomerate.
れきし[1] 歴史 ¶歴史 a history ¶日本の歴史 the history of Japan; Japanese history / 歴史に記されてある be recorded in history / 歴史に残る go down [find a place] in history / 歴史始まって以来 since the beginning [《文》dawn] of history / 歴史的[上の] historical / 歴史上の歴史 / 歴史上 / 歴史上有名なところ a historic spot; a place of historic interest [with historical associations] / 歴史上最大の人物 the greatest man in history / 歴史上の人物 a historical person [figure] / 歴史以前の prehistoric / 歴史以前に in prehistoric times; before the dawn of history / 歴史学派 the historical school / 歴史家 a historian / 歴史画[小説] a historical painting [novel] / 歴史時代の初めの頃に in early historic times / 歴史主義 historicism. [文例⇩]
れきし[2] 轢死 ¶れきし死する be run over and killed (by a car); be killed (by a train).
れきせい 瀝青 [鉱] bitumen; pitch ¶瀝青炭 bituminous coal / 瀝青ウラン鉱 pitchblende.
れきせん 歴戦 ¶歴戦の勇士 a veteran (soldier); a seasoned soldier; 《文》a battle-tried warrior.
れきぜん 歴然 ▷めいはく.
れきだい 歴代 ¶歴代の successive (cabinets).
れきにん 歴任 ¶歴任する hold [fill] (various posts) successively [in succession].
れきねん 暦年 a calendar year.
れきほう[1] 暦法 the calendar.
れきほう[2] 歴訪 ¶歴訪する make a round of visits (to); make a tour of (European countries).
レギュラー《正式の》regular; 《正選手》a regular player ¶レギュラーメンバー a regular member.
レグホン〈鶏〉a 《white》leghorn.
レクリエーション (a) recreation ¶レクリエーションセンター a recreation center.
レコード〈音盤〉a (phonograph) record; a disc; a disk; 〈記録〉⇒ きろく, しんきろく ¶レコードをかける put a record on (the player); play a record / レコードに吹き込む record (one's singing) on a disc; disc (one's speech) / レコード音楽 recorded music / レコード会社 a record company / レコードコンサート a record [disc] concert / レコードファン a phonophile; a discophile / レコードプレーヤー a record player. [文例⇩]
レザー〈模造革〉imitation leather; leatherette.
レシート a receipt ⇒ りょうしゅう(領収証[書]).
レシーブ ¶レシーブする receive 《the served ball》/ レシーブがうまい be a good receiver / 回転レシーブ rolling on the court to receive the ball; receiving the ball while rolling on the court.
レジ(スター)〈金銭登録器〉a (cash) register; 〈係〉a cashier ¶レジで at the cash desk; at the (checkout) counter (スーパーなどの).
レジャー leisure ¶レジャー産業 the leisure industry / レジャー施設 leisure facilities.
レストラン a restaurant.
レスビアン〈人〉a lesbian; 〈同性愛〉lesbianism.
レスリング wrestling ¶レスリングの選手 a wrestler.
レソト ¶レソト王国 the Kingdom of Lesotho.
レタス [植] a lettuce; 〈食用にする葉〉lettuce.
れつ 列 a line; a row; 〈横の〉a rank; 〈縦の〉a file; a column; 〈行列〉a procession; 〈順番を待つ〉a queue ¶列を作る form a line [row, 《英》queue]; line [《英》queue] up / 列を成して in (a) line; in a row [queue] / 列を乱す〈順番を〉《米》break the line; 《英》jump the queue; 〈隊列を〉break ranks / 列を離れる fall [drop] out of line; leave the ranks / 横に4列に並ぶ be lined [drawn up] four deep (along the road).
れつあく 劣悪 ¶劣悪な of very poor quality; very bad; 〈設備が〉quite inadequate.
れっか 烈火 ¶烈火のごとく怒る be red with anger; be furious; fly into a rage; be beside oneself with rage.
レッカーしゃ レッカー車 a wrecker; a wrecking car; a tow car [truck].
れっき 列記 ⇒ れっきょ.
れっきとした ¶れっきとした家柄 a respectable family / れっきとした貴婦人 《文》an honorable lady / れっきとした詩人 a poet with an established [a high] reputation / れっきとした音楽家である be no mean musician.
れっきょ 列挙 ¶列挙する《文》enumerate; list.
れっきょう 列強 the great [world] powers.
れっこく 列国 the nations of the world; 〈列強〉the great [world] powers.
れっしゃ 列車 a (railroad) train ¶博多行きの

れきし[1] 歴史は繰り返す. History repeats itself. [諺] / この学校は長い輝かしい歴史を誇っている. This school can boast a long and glorious history. / あの事件はもう過去の歴史になってしまった. The event has already passed into history.
レコード この曲はレコードで何度も聞いた. I've often heard this music on a phonograph record. / 僕は英語をレコードで勉強した. I studied English by means of [with the help of] records.
れっしゃ その列車は何時に出ますか. What time does the train leave [go]? / 何時の列車でお出かけですか. What train are you

列車 a train (bound) for Hakata; the Hakata train / 午前6時着の青森発列車 the train from Aomori due (to arrive) at six a.m. / 列車の運行 a train service; operation of trains / 列車を運転する run [operate] a train / 列車を編成する form [《文》compose] a train / 7時半の列車に間に合う make [catch] the 7:30 [seven thirty] train / 午後4時15分の列車で立つ leave (Ueno) by the 4:15 p.m. train (★ 4:15 は four fifteen と読む) / 列車事故 a train [railroad] accident.

れっしょう 裂傷 a lacerated wound; a laceration ¶顔に裂傷を負う have *one's* face lacerated (by).

れつじょう 劣情《文》low passions; lust.

れっしん 烈震 a very violent earthquake (shock); a disastrous earthquake.

レッスン a lesson ¶ピアノのレッスン (have) a piano lesson.

れっせい¹ 劣性 ¶劣性の《遺伝》recessive / 劣性遺伝子 a recessive (gene).

れっせい² 劣勢 ¶劣勢の inferiority in numbers [strength] ¶…より劣勢である《文》be inferior in numbers [strength] to…; be outnumbered by….

れっせき 列席 ⇨ しゅっせき.

れっちゅう 列柱《建》a colonnade.

レッテル [《<《オランダ語》letter] a label ¶レッテルを張る put a label on [《文》attach a label to]《a bottle》; label《a bottle》/ 赤というレッテルを張られる be labeled [ticketed] as a Red.

れつでん 列伝 ¶日本剣豪列伝〈書名〉The Lives of the Japanese Master Swordsmen.

れっとう¹ 列島 a chain of islands ¶琉球列島 the Ryukyu Islands; the Ryukyus.

れっとう² 劣等 ¶劣等の low-grade; inferior;《文》《goods》of poor [inferior] quality / 劣等感[意識] (an) inferiority complex; a sense of inferiority.

れっぷう 烈風 a strong [heavy] wind; a (violent) gale.

レディーメード ¶レディーメードの ready-made《clothes》; ready-to-wear《suits》; off-the-peg《clothes》.

レトルト a (chemical) retort.

レニウム《化》rhenium.

レバー¹《食用》liver.

レバー²〈てこ〉a lever;〈自動車の〉《米》a gearshift;《英》a gear lever.

レパートリー a repertory; a repertoire.

レバノン (the) Lebanon ¶レバノンの Lebanese / レバノン共和国 the Republic of Lebanon / レバノン人 a Lebanese.

レビュー a revue ¶レビューガール a show girl [dancer].

レフェリー a referee ¶レフェリーを勤める act as referee; referee《a match》.

レフト《野球》〈左翼〉the left field;〈左翼手〉a left fielder;《ボクシング》a left《to the jaw》¶レフトにフライを打つ fly to left.

レベル〈水準〉a level ⇨ すいじゅん ¶レベルアップする raise the level《of》; improve (向上させる).

レポート〈報告〉a report;〈学校の〉a paper ¶レポートを書く write a paper on《a subject》.

レモン a lemon ¶レモンしぼり(器) a lemon squeezer / レモンスカッシュ lemon squash / レモンティー tea with lemon.

レリーズ〈カメラの〉a cable release.

れん 連〈紙の〉a ream.

れんあい 恋愛 love ¶恋愛結婚 a love match [marriage] / 恋愛結婚をする marry for love / 恋愛詩 a love poem [lyric] / 恋愛至上主義 love for love's sake / 恋愛事件 a [an illicit] love affair / 恋愛小説 a love story. 文例⬇

れんか 廉価 ¶廉価で at a low [bargain] price; cheap(ly) / 廉価版 a cheap edition《of a book》/ 廉価販売 a (bargain) sale.

れんが¹ 連歌 a *renga*; a 'linked poem' ¶連歌師 a *renga* poet.

れんが² 煉瓦 (a) brick ¶れんがを焼く make [burn, bake] bricks / れんがを積む lay bricks / 赤れんが (a) red brick / 耐火れんが a fire [refractory (工業用の)] brick / (赤)れんが色の brick-red / 化粧れんが (a) dressed [glazed] brick / れんが工場 a brickyard; a brick works / れんが職人 a bricklayer / れんが造りである be built of brick / れんが造りの家 a brick(-built) house.

れんかん 連関 ⇨ かんれん.

れんき 連記 ¶2名連記する write [put] down two names on a ballot / 連記制 the plural ballot system / 無記名連記投票 a secret ballot with plural entry.

れんきゅう 連休 consecutive holidays ¶3日の連休がある have three consecutive holidays; have three days' holiday running.

れんぎょう《植》a forsythia.

れんきんじゅつ 錬金術 alchemy ¶錬金術師 an alchemist.

れんげ《植》〈はすの花〉a lotus flower;〈れんげそう〉a Chinese milk vetch;〈さじ〉a china spoon.

れんけい 連係 ¶つながり ¶連係を一層密にする build up a closer connection《with》; work in closer cooperation《with》/ (手足の)連係動作 coordinated movements of arms and legs (in swimming) / 連係プレー close teamwork.

れんけつ 連結 connection ¶連結する connect; link; couple ¶食堂車を連結する couple [attach] a dining car to《a train》/ 5両連結の電車 a five-car train /〈車両の〉連結器 a coupler.

れんこ 連呼 ¶連呼する call [shout]《one's* name》repeatedly.

---

going by? / 駅が近くなって、列車は速度を落とした。The train slowed down as it approached the station. / 2時45分の列車で着きますから駅まで迎えに来て下さい。Please meet the 2:45 train at the station.
れっぷう 烈風が吹いている。It is blowing a gale.
れんあい あなたは恋愛の経験がな

さい. Please meet the 2:45 train at the station.
いんでしょう。You've never been in love, have you? / あなたは恋愛結婚ですか。Did you marry for love?
れんけつ この列車には寝台車が連

れんご 連語 (a) collocation; 〈複合語〉a compound word; 〈句〉a phrase.

れんこう 連行 ¶連行する take [walk] *sb* to 《a police station》; haul [bring] *sb* before 《the police authorities》.

れんごう 連合 (a) union; (a) combination; (an) alliance (同盟) ¶連合する unite [combine, join hands] 《to *do*, in *doing*》; be allied [combined] 《with》; form a union [an alliance] 《with》 / …と連合して in alliance [combination, 《文》concert] with… / 連合の combined; united; allied; joint / 連合王国 the United Kingdom ⇒ グレートブリテン / 連合艦隊 a combined fleet / 連合軍 the Allied Forces / 連合国 the Allied Powers; the Allies / 連合国間の interallied 《consultation》. 文例⇩

れんごく 煉獄 Purgatory; 〈比喩的〉purgatory ¶煉獄の 《文》purgatorial 《sufferings, fires》.

れんこん 蓮根 a lotus root.

れんさ 連鎖 a chain; links ¶連鎖(状)球菌 a streptococcus 《*pl*. -cocci》; 《口語》a strep / 連鎖店 a chain store / 連鎖反応 (a) chain reaction / 連鎖反応を起こす cause [trigger, touch off, set up] a chain reaction.

れんざ 連座 ¶連座する be involved in 《an affair》; be implicated in 《a graft case》.

れんさい 連載 ¶連載される appear [be published] serially [in serial form] 《in a magazine》; be serialized 《in a weekly》/ 連載小説 a serial story; a serialized novel / 〈新聞が〉5回にわたって連載ものを載せる run a serial in five parts.

れんさく 連作 ¶連作する〈農作物を〉plant 《a field》with the same crop over and over; 〈短歌・俳句を〉compose a series of poems on the same subject.

れんざん 連山 ⇒ れんぽう².

れんじ 連辞 〖論〗 a copula.

れんじつ 連日 every day; day after day; for days on end ¶連日の雨 a long spell of rainy weather; a prolonged rainy spell / 連日連夜 day and night.

れんじまど 連子窓 a lattice window.

れんじゅ 連珠 (play) *goban*(g).

れんしゅう 練習 practice; (an) exercise; (a) drill; training; (a) rehearsal (劇などの) ¶練習する practice; train; rehearse / オルガンを練習する practice (on) the organ / 英会話を練習する practice speaking English 《using [with the help of] records》/ 英語の発音を練習させる practice [drill] 《the children》 in the sounds of English [in English pronunciation] / 練習のためにピアノを弾く play the piano for practice [by way of] practice / 練習をよく積んでいる have trained well [done a lot of training] 《in》; be in practice / 練習機 a trainer; a training plane / 練習曲 an étude / 練習試合 a practice game [match]; a workout / 練習所 a training school [institute] / 〈陸上競技などの〉練習場 a practice [training] field [track] / 練習生 a student; a trainee / 練習船 a school [training] ship / 練習帳 an exercise [a drill] book; a workbook / 練習飛行 a practice [training] flight / 練習不足である be out of practice 《at golf, on the piano》/ 練習問題をやる do exercises (in algebra). 文例⇩

れんしょ 連署 ¶連署する sign (a petition) jointly 《with others》; 《文》affix *one's* signature 《to a deed》jointly 《with》/ 連署の上で under the joint signatures of… / 連署人 a joint signer; a cosignatory.

れんしょう 連勝 consecutive [successive] victories; 《win》a series [sequence] of victories ¶10 連勝する win ten games in a row; win ten consecutive [successive] victories (over); win *one's* tenth straight victory. 文例⇩

レンズ a lens ¶レンズを絞る stop down the lens / 凹[凸]レンズ a concave (convex) lens.

れんそう 連想 association (of ideas) ¶連想する be reminded of *sth*; associate 《A with B》/ 連想させる〈事が主語〉remind *one* of *sth*; put *one* in mind of *sth*; suggest *sth* to *one* / 類似[対比, 近接]連想 association by similarity [contrast, contiguity] / 連想(語)検査〖心理〗a word association test. 文例⇩

れんぞく 連続 continuity; 《文》continuance; succession; a series; a sequence ¶連続する continue; go on; last / 連続して起こった不思議な事件 a series of strange events / 連続的に continuously; consecutively; successively; in succession; without a break / 3回連続講演 a series of three lectures / 3か月の連続興行 a run of three months; a three-month run / 連続3週間 for three weeks running [on end]; for three consecutive [successive] weeks / 連続写真 sequence photographs / 連続体〖哲・数〗 a continuum 《*pl*. -tinua, -s》/ 連続2ホーマー two consecutive [back-to-back] homers / 連続テレビドラマ a serial TV drama. 文例⇩

れんだ 連打 ¶連打する〈なぐる〉hit [《文》strike] *sb* repeatedly; 〈鐘などを〉ring [clang] 《a bell》repeatedly.

れんたい¹ 連帯 ¶社会連帯 social solidarity /

結してありますか. Are there any sleeping cars attached to this train? / その電車は7両連結のはずです. That train should be seven cars long.

れんこう 警官はその男を警察署へ連行した. The policeman took [marched] the man to the police station.

れんごう 両チーム連合でニューヨーク・ヤンキースと当たった. The two teams were combined in a game against the New York Yankees.

れんしゅう 絶えず練習を積んでいなければバッティングがだめになるよ. Your batting will deteriorate if you don't keep in practice. / 彼らは試合に備えて練習を積んでいる. They are in hard training for the game. / 練習不足で負けたのだ. He lost the match because of his lack of training. / 練習中.〈自動車の掲示〉Driver under instruction.

れんしょう 来訪中のケンブリッジ・ラグビーチームは昨日大阪の花園グランドで全日本軍を34対11で破り, 6連勝を飾った. The visiting Cambridge rugby team won its sixth successive [straight] victory as it crushed the All-Japan team 34 to 11 at the 《Ha-

連帯感[意識] a sense of solidarity / 連帯責任 (a) collective [joint] responsibility [for] ; 《法》 joint and several liability 《for》 / 連帯保証人 《法》 a surety jointly and severally liable 《for》 / 連帯保証人に立つ, 連帯責任を負う 《法》 stand [go] joint and several surety 《for the loan of one million yen which A receives from B》; hold joint and several liability [be jointly and severally liable] 《for the debt of one million yen that A owes to B》.

れんたい[2] 連隊 a regiment ¶歩兵連隊 an infantry [a foot] regiment / 連隊旗 the regimental standard [colors] / 連隊長[本部] the regimental commander [headquarters].

レンタカー a rental car ¶レンタカー業者[会社] a car-rental agent [company].

れんたつ 練達 ⇒じゅくれん, たんのう[2] ¶練達の士 an expert 《in, at》; an old hand 《at》.

れんたん 練炭 a briquet(te).

れんだん 連弾 a four-hand(ed) performance (on the piano) ¶ピアノ連弾曲 a piece for four hands.

レンチ 《工具》 an adjustable wrench; 《米》 an adjustable spanner; 《英》 a wrench.

れんちしん 廉恥心 a sense of honor [shame].

れんちゅう 連中 a lot ; a set ; a party ; a bunch ¶こういう連中 these fellows / そうそうたる連中 a fine set of men / 悪い[陽気な]連中と交わる keep bad [merry] company.

れんてつ 練[錬]鉄 wrought iron.

れんとう 連投 ¶連投する take the (pitcher's) mound in 《three》 consecutive games.

れんどう 連動 working [operating] together ¶連動装置 an interlocking device ; gearing.

レントゲン 《エックス線》 X-rays; 《放射線量の単位》 a roentgen (略: r) ¶レントゲンカー 《エックス線検診車》 an X-ray car; a mass survey X-ray car ⇒エックスせん.

れんにゅう 練乳 condensed milk.

れんぱ[1] 連破 ⇒れんしょう.

れんぱ[2] 連覇 ¶3連覇する have held [kept, 《文》 retained] the championship for three years [seasons] running [on end].

れんばい 廉売 ⇒やすうり.

れんぱい 連敗 successive defeats; (suffer) a series [sequence] of defeats ¶5連敗する lose five games in a row ; lose five successive [consecutive] games.

れんぱつ 連発 ¶連発する fire in rapid succession [in volleys] / 質問を連発する fire questions at sb (in succession) ; assail sb with one question after another / 6連発のピストル a six-chambered revolver ; a six-shooter / 連発式の quick-firing 《guns》; 《自動の》 automatic.

れんばん 連判 joint signatures (and seals) ¶連判状 a compact [covenant] under joint signatures.

れんびん 憐憫 ⇒あわれみ, あわれむ.

れんぺいじょう 練兵場 a parade ground.

れんぽう[1] 連邦 a federation of states ; a union of nations ¶連邦政府 《アメリカの》 the Federal Government (of the U.S.) / 連邦の(政府の) federal / 連邦捜査局 《アメリカの》 the Federal Bureau of Investigation (略: FBI).

れんぽう[2] 連峰 a chain of mountains; a mountain range.

れんま 錬磨 ⇒きたえる ¶多年の錬磨によって by virtue of many years' hard training.

れんめい[1] 連名 ¶連名で in our [their] joint names ; under the joint signatures of….

れんめい[2] 連盟 a league ; a federation; a union ¶連盟を組織する[結ぶ] form a league [federation] / 連盟して事に当たる be leagued together 《against, for》 / 日本学生野球連盟 the Students' Baseball League of Japan.

れんめん 連綿 ¶連綿たる unbroken ; uninterrupted.

れんや 連夜 every night ; night after night.

れんらく 連絡 (a) connection ; 《文》 junction ; contact; liaison; 《通信上の》 communication(s) ¶連絡する connect [be connected] 《with》; contact ; make contact 《with》; join ; 〈知らせる〉 get in touch 《with sb》; 《文》 communicate sth to sb, 《文》 notify [inform] 《sb of sth, sb that…》 / …で中央線と連絡する join [connect with] the Chuo line at… / …と連絡がある be connected [linked] with…; be in contact [touch] with… / 連絡を保つ keep in touch [contact] 《with》 / …と連絡をとって行動する act in conjunction [concert] with… / 電話連絡を絶つ cut off telephonic communications 《with》 / 無電[線]連絡をとる[が絶える] establish [lose] radio contact 《with》 / 連絡切符 a connection [an interline] ticket / 連絡将校[会議] a liaison officer [conference] / 連絡船 a ferryboat (plying between A and B); a railroad ferry (operating on a cross-channel route) / 連絡点[駅] a junction (point). 文例13

れんりつ 連立 ¶連立内閣 a coalition cabinet / 連立方程式 simultaneous equations.

れんれん 恋々 ¶恋々とする cling to 《one's post》; be very attached to [fond of] 《a girl》.

---

nazono Grounds in Osaka yesterday.

れんそう アインシュタインというとすぐ相対性原理を連想する. The name of Einstein is closely associated with the theory of relativity. / このメロディーを聞くと波の岩に砕ける音を連想します. The melody is suggestive of the breaking of waves against the rocks.

れんぞく 3回に連続2本のホームランをかっとばした. They whacked out two consecutive homers [two home runs back to back] in the third inning. / 彼は4打席連続ホームランをかっとばしたことがある. He once hit four home runs in four consecutive times at bat. / その芝居は60日間連続興行された. The play ran for [had a run of] sixty days.

れんらく この列車は青函連絡船に連絡しますか. Does this train connect with the Aomori-Hakodate ferry? / 同機はその後連絡を絶った. We lost contact with the plane after that. / 彼らからはまだ何の連絡もない. There is still no contact from them. / その基地にここからは無電連絡ができない. The base is out of radio contact with us here.

ろ

ろ¹ 炉 〈いろり〉a fireplace; a hearth;〈溶鉱炉〉a furnace;〈鍛冶場の〉a forge ¶炉を囲む sit around the fire / 炉辺[端]で by the fire(-side) [hearth(side)].

ろ² 絽 a kind of silk gauze.

ろ³ 櫓 an oar; a scull ¶ろをこぐ pull an oar; work a scull.

ロ 〖音楽〗 ¶ロ長[短]調 (in) B major [minor].

ろう¹ 牢 a prison; a jail;《英》a gaol ¶牢を出る be let out of prison; be released from jail / 牢を破る break prison [jail] / 牢に入れられる be put in [thrown into] prison [jail]; be imprisoned / 牢に入っている be in prison [jail]; be behind bars.

ろう² 労 trouble; labor; service(s); pains ⇒ ろうする¹ ¶労を省く save sb trouble / 労をいとわない[惜しまない] spare no efforts [pains]《to do》; go to great lengths《to do》; do all one can《to do》/ 労を煩わす trouble sb to do / …の労に報いる reward sb for his services.

ろう³ 蠟 wax ¶ろうを引く wax《one's skis》/ ろう紙 wax(ed) paper / ろう細工 (a) waxwork / ろう人形 a wax effigy [figure].

ろうあ 聾啞 ¶ろうあ学校 a school for the deaf and dumb / ろうあ者 a deaf-and-dumb person; a deaf-mute.

ろうえい¹ 朗詠 (a) recitation; chanting ¶朗詠する recite [chant] (a poem).

ろうえい² 漏洩 ⇒もれる, もらす.

ろうえき 労役 work service ¶労役に服する render service(s)《to one's lord》.

ろうか¹ 老化 ¶老化する age / 老化現象 (the symptoms of) aging.

ろうか² 廊下 a passageway; a passage; a corridor. 文例▶

ろうかい 老獪 ¶老獪な crafty; cunning; foxy / 老獪な男 an old fox.

ろうかく 楼閣 a many-storied building ⇒くうちゅう (空中楼閣) ¶砂上の楼閣 a house of cards.

ろうがん 老眼 farsightedness [longsightedness] due to old age;《文》advancing years; presbyopia ¶老眼の人 a presbyopic [farsighted] person / 老眼鏡 spectacles for the aged; farsighted (eye)glasses.

ろうきゅう¹ 老朽 ¶老朽化する become too old for work [use];《文》become superannuated / 老朽船 an overage [《文》a superannuated) ship.

ろうきゅう² 籠球 ⇒バスケットボール.

ろうきょう 老境 ¶老境に入って in one's old age; when (one is) old; in one's declining years.

ろうく 労苦 ⇒くろう, ほねおり.

ろうけつぞめ 蠟纈染め batik ¶ろうけつ染めの printed by the batik method; batik (scarves).

ろうこ 牢乎 ¶ろうこたる firm; inflexible / ろうことして firmly; inflexibly.

ろうご 老後 ¶老後に in one's old age; when (one is) old / 老後に備える provide for [against] one's old age / 心静かに老後を送る spend one's last days [《文》remaining years] in peace and quiet.

ろうこう 老巧 ⇒ろうれん.

ろうごく 牢獄 ⇒ろう¹.

ろうこつ 老骨 ¶老骨にむち打って forgetting [in spite of] one's old [advanced] age.

ろうさい¹ 老妻 one's old wife.

ろうさい² 労災 ¶労災保険 workmen's compensation insurance [《文》compensation for industrial [workmen's] accidents.

ろうさく 労作 ¶多年の労作 a piece of work completed after many years' labor;《文》the product [fruit] of one's many years' labor. 文例▶

ろうし¹ 労使[資] ¶労使関係 industrial relations; the relations between capital and labor; labor-[union-]management relations / 労使協議会 a labor-management council;《英》a works council [committee] / 労資協調 cooperation between capital and labor; union-management cooperation / 労使紛争 an industrial [a labor-management] dispute;《文》industrial strife.

ろうし² 老子 Lao-tse; Lao-tzu.

ろうしゅう 老醜 the ugliness of old age ¶老醜をさらす stay alive as an ugly old man.

ろうじょう 籠城 ¶籠城する be besieged;〈家にこもる〉keep [be confined to] one's home [room].

ろうじん 老人 an old [aged] person;〈総称〉the old; the aged ¶老人学〈老化現象・老人問題を研究する〉gerontology / 老人病 the diseases of old age [aging people] / 老人病(医)学〈老人病を研究する〉geriatrics; geriatric

---

ろうか² 透き間風の吹く廊下に長い間待たされた. I was kept waiting for a long time in a drafty passage. | 彼女の部屋とは廊下続きです. Her apartment connects with mine by a corridor.

ろうさく 本書は著者多年の労作である. The book cost the author many years' labor.

ろうすい² この水道管から漏水している. This pipe is leaking water. | Water is leaking from this pipe.

ろうする¹ 労せずして彼はそれを手に入れた. It fell into his hands without any effort on his part.

ろうせい¹ 彼は年の割に老成している. He has an old head on young shoulders.

ろうそく ろうそくに火をつけて, テーブルにろうをたらしてそれに立てた. I lit a candle and stuck it in its own wax on the table.

ろうでん このコードに触わるとぴりっとする. きっと漏電しているんだ. When I touch this cord, I feel a slight electric shock.

ろうすい / 老人ホーム a home for the aged; an old people's [old-age] home.

ろうすい[1] 老衰 《文》 decrepitude; 〚医〛 senile decay [infirmity] ¶老衰する grow old and infirm [feeble]; 《文》 become infirm with age; go [《文》 become] decrepit / 老衰で死ぬ die of old age.

ろうすい[2] 漏水 (a) leakage of water; a water leak. 文例⇩

ろうする[1] 労する labor; exert *oneself*; take trouble [pains] ⇒うる[2].文例⇩

ろうする[2] 弄する ¶詭弁を弄する 《文》 use sophistry / 術策を弄する use *one's* wiles (to *do*); play a (mean, nasty) trick on *sb*.

ろうせい[1] 老成 ¶老成した青年 a young man with an old head; 《文》 a youth whose maturity (of judgment) belies his years. 文例⇩

ろうせい[2] 老政 labor administration.

ろうせき 蠟石 〚鉱〛 agalmatolite; pagodite.

ろうぜき 狼藉 ¶ろうぜきを働く do violence (to); 《文》 commit an outrage ((on)); play havoc ((with, among)).

ろうそく 蠟燭 a candle ¶ろうそくの明かりで読む read by candlelight / ろうそくのしん the wick of a candle; a candlewick / ろうそくをともす[つける] burn [light] a candle / ろうそくを吹き消す blow out a candle / ろうそく立て a candlestick. 文例⇩

ろうぞめ 蠟染め ⇒ろうけつぞめ.

ろうたいか 老大家 ⇒たいか[2].

ろうちん 労賃 ⇒ちんぎん.

ろうでん 漏電 (a) leakage of electricity; an electric leak; a short circuit ¶漏電する short(-circuit); 漏電を起こす cause a short (circuit) [leak of electricity]. 文例⇩

ろうどう 労働 work; labor; 《文》 toil ¶労働する labor; work; 《文》 toil / 労働によって得る gain [earn] by labor [by the sweat of *one's* brow] / 1 日 8 時間労働 (work) an eight-hour day / 週 5 日[40 時間]労働 a 5-day [40-hour] (working) week / 労働委員会 a labor relations commission / 労働基準監督署 the Labor Standards Inspection Office / 労働基準法 the Labor Standards Act / 労働貴族 (a member of) the labor aristocracy / 労働協約 a labor agreement [contract] / 労働災害 an industrial accident; an accident while at work ⇒ろうさい[2] / 労働時間 working hours / 労働省[大臣] the Ministry [Minister] of Labor; the Labor Ministry [Minister] / 労働条件 working [labor] conditions / 労働人口 a working population; the work force ((of this country)) / 労働戦線 a labor front / 労働党 (英国の) the Labour Party / 労働法 labor law / 労働問題[争議,

政策, 運動] a labor problem [dispute, policy, movement] / 労働力 labor; the work force ((of a country)). 文例⇩

ろうどうくみあい 労働組合 《米》 a labor union; 《英》 a trade(s) union ¶労働組合の幹部 a union leader / 労働組合をつくる form [organize] a labor [trade] union / 労働組合員 a member of a labor union; a (trade) unionist / 労働組合主義 trade unionism.

ろうどうしゃ 労働者 a worker; a laborer; a workingman; 《集合的》 working people ¶労働者資本家と労働者 capital and labor / 労働者側と会社側 labor and management / 労働者の権利 workers' [labor] rights / 労働者階級 the working [laboring] class(es). 文例⇩

ろうどく 朗読 reading aloud; (a) recitation (暗誦して する) ¶朗読する read aloud; recite / 朗読会を開く give a public reading (a recitation) ((of *Hamlet*)).

ろうにゃくなんにょ 老若男女 men and women of all ages ¶老若男女を問わず 《文》 irrespective [without distinction] of age or sex.

ろうにん 浪人 〈主家を離れた武士〉 a *ronin*; a masterless *samurai*; 〈失職者〉 a jobless person; 〈受験準備中の〉 a high-school graduate who has failed to enter a college and is waiting for another chance (to obtain a place); an entrance exam rejectee.

ろうねん 老年 [《文》 advanced] age ¶老年になって in *one's* old age; when (*one* is) old.

ろうば 老婆 an old woman ¶老婆心から 《give *sb* advice》 though (it) may not be necessary.

ろうばい 狼狽 ¶ろうばいする get flurried; be flustered; be upset; be thrown into confusion [panic]; lose *one's* head [《口語》 cool] / ろうばいしない keep *one's* head [presence of mind]; remain calm [unperturbed] / ろうばいして in a flurry; in confusion; in panic. 文例⇩

ろうはいぶつ 老廃物 wastes ¶体内の老廃物 body wastes.

ろうひ 浪費 (a) waste ((of time and energy)) ¶浪費する waste (*one's* money on trifles); squander; throw [fritter] (*one's* money) away; 《文》 dissipate (*one's* savings) / 浪費癖のある人 an extravagant [a thriftless] person; a spendthrift. 文例⇩

ろうふ 老父 *one's* old [aged] father.

ろうへい 老兵 an old soldier. 文例⇩

ろうぼ 老母 *one's* old [aged] mother.

ろうほう 朗報 good news; glad tidings.

ろうぼく 老木 an old tree.

ろうむ 労務 labor; work ¶労務課 the labor section / 労務管理 personnel [labor] manage-

---

There must be [I bet there's] a short circuit. / 火事の原因は漏電だった。The fire was caused by a short circuit.
ろうどう 労働は少しもいとわない。I don't mind hard work at all. / この工場では週 5 日, 1 日 8 時間労働である。They work an 8-hour day, five days a week in this factory. / 我が国では一般に労働時間が長い。People work long hours in this country. / 労働時間の短縮を要求した。They demanded shorter working hours.
ろうどうしゃ 万国の労働者よ, 団結せよ。Working men of all countries, unite! | Workers of the world, unite!
ろうばい 彼は少しもろうばいしなかった。He never lost his composure. | He remained quite unperturbed.
ろうひ 結局時間の浪費に終わった。It resulted in [ended up as] a waste of (my) time.
ろうへい 老兵は死なず, ただ消え

ろうや 牢屋 ⇨ろう³.

ろうらく 籠絡 ¶ろうらくして…させる cajole [inveigle, wheedle] sb into doing.

ろうりょく 労力 〈骨折り〉labor; trouble; 〈労働力〉labor ¶労力が不足する be short of workers; be shorthanded / 労力の不足 a shortage of labor / 労力を省く save labor. 文例↓

ろうれい 老齢 ⇨ろうねん, こうれい².

ろうれん 老練 ¶老練な experienced; veteran / 老練な教師 an experienced [a veteran] teacher / 老練家 an expert; a veteran; an old hand 《at》.

ろうろう 朗々 ¶朗々たる声で《文》sonorously; in a fruity [rich and ringing] voice.

ろえい 露営 a bivouac; camping out ¶露営する bivouac; camp out; pitch a camp / 露営地 a camping ground [site]; a campsite; an encampment.

ローカル local ¶ローカルカラー local color / ローカル線[番組] a local line [program] / ローカル版 a local-news section [page].

ローション (a) lotion.

ロージンバッグ 《野球》a rosin bag.

ロース 〈牛の背肉〉sirloin; 〈豚の背肉〉pork loin; 〈ローストに適した肉〉roasting meat ★「ロース」は, 正確には, 肩から腰にかけての背肉の部分の総称であるから, 牛肉の場合は, 《米》では chuck, rib, and loin, 《英》では neck, ribs, and sirloin と言い, 豚肉の場合は, 《米》では loins, 《英》では fore and hind loins と言うが, 煩を避けて以上のように言って差しつかえない ¶ロースハム ham made of pork loin.

ロースト ¶ローストチキン roast chicken / ローストビーフ roast beef; a (large) roast of beef.

ロータリー 《米》a rotary; 《米》a traffic circle; 《英》a roundabout ¶ロータリーエンジン a rotary engine / (除雪用)ロータリー機関車 a rotary snowblower / ロータリークラブ the Rotary Club / ロータリークラブ員 a Rotarian.

ローティーン ¶ローティーンの少年少女 boys and girls between 10 and 15 years of age; boys and girls in their early teens (★ early teens は 13 歳以上を意味する. 13 歳未満の人を《米口語》では a tween と言う).

ローデシア Rhodesia ¶ローデシアの Rhodesian / ローデシア人 a Rhodesian.

ロードアイランド Rhode Island (略: R.I.) ¶ロードアイランド州の人 a Rhode Islander.

ロードショー a road show; a (special) first-run showing (of a film) ¶ロードショー劇場 a road-show [first-run] movie theater.

ロードレース 〈自転車競技の〉a road race.

ローヒール low-heeled [flat] shoes.

ロープ (a) rope; (a) cord; (a) cable.

ロープウエー a ropeway; a [an aerial] cableway.

ローマ Rome ¶永遠の都ローマ Rome, the Eternal City / ローマの Roman / ローマ化する, ローマ風にする Romanize / ローマ人 a Roman / ローマ数字 Roman numerals / ローマ帝国 the Roman Empire / ローマ法 (the) Roman law / ローマ法王[教皇] a Pope. 文例↓

ローマじ ローマ字 *romaji* ¶ローマ字で書く write in *romaji* [roman letters]; romanize 《one's writing》/ ローマ字論者 an advocate of the romanization of the Japanese script.

ローマン 《印刷》roman (type).

ローム 《地質》loam ¶ローム質の loamy 《soil》.

ローヤルゼリー royal jelly.

ローラー a roller ¶ローラーをかける roll; smooth [level] (the ground) with a roller / ローラーカナリヤ a roller / ローラーコースター a (roller) coaster / ローラースケート〈靴〉roller skates / 〈事〉roller skating / ローラータオル a roller towel.

ロール ¶ロールキャベツ ground [minced] meat rolled in cabbage leaves / ロールパン a roll (of bread).

ローレンシウム 《化》lawrencium.

ローン a loan ¶住宅ローン a housing loan.

ろか 濾過 ¶濾過する filter; filtrate; pass (a liquid) through a filter / 濾過器 a filter / 濾過紙 filter paper / 濾過性病原体 ⇨ウイルス.

ろかた 路肩 the shoulder [edge] of a road. 文例↓

ろく¹ 六 six ¶第6 the sixth / 6分の1 one sixth / 六大都市 the six biggest cities 《of Japan》.

ろく² 禄 a stipend ¶禄を食(は)む get a salary 《from》; be on the payroll 《of》.

ろく³ ¶ろくな〈よい〉(no) good; 〈まともな〉(no) decent; 〈満足な〉(no) satisfactory; 〈語るに足る〉(nothing) worth mentioning / ろくに〈よく〉(not) well; 〈ちゃんと〉(not) properly / ろくに見もしないで without looking at *sth* properly [carefully] / ろくに考えもしないで without due consideration / ろくでもない useless; good-for-nothing / ろくでもない事を言う talk nonsense [rubbish]. 文例↓

ろくおん 録音 recording; (electrical) transcription ¶録音する record (a speech on tape); transcribe (a program) / 録音係 a recordist / 録音機 a recording [transcribing] machine; a (tape) recorder / 録音室 a recording room / 録音装置 recording equipment / 録音放送する broadcast (a program) by electrical transcription.

去るのみ. Old soldiers never die, they only fade away.

ろうりょく この工事を完成するためには多大の労力が必要だ. It will require a great deal of labor to finish this work.

ローマ ローマは一日にしてならず. Rome was not built in a [one] day. 《諺》

ろかた 路肩軟弱につき注意. 《掲示》Caution: Soft shoulder(s).

ろく³ 何かにつけてろくな事はなかった. Everything went wrong for him. / 僕はろくな本は持っていない. I have no books to speak of [worth mentioning]. / どうせ

ろくなことをしていたんじゃあるまい. He's been up to no good, I'll bet. / このあたりはろくなレストランもない. There aren't any decent restaurants in this neighborhood. / ろくに彼女と話をする暇もない. I have hardly enough time to talk [have a chat] with

ろくが 録画 video tape recording ¶録画する record《a scene on video tape》; video-tape / 録画を放送する broadcast a program recorded on video tape.

ろくがつ 六月 June (略: Jun.).

ろくさん(さん)せい 六三(三)制 the 6-3(-3) system of education.

ろくじゅう 六十 sixty;《文》threescore ¶第60 the sixtieth / 60代の人 a person in his sixties;《文》a sexagenarian. 文例

ろくしょう 緑青 copper [green] rust; verdigris; patina ¶緑青を生じる become [be] coated with verdigris [patina]; verdigris forms 《on》/ 緑青を生じた verdigrised; patinated.

ろくでなし《米口語》a bum;《英口語》a layabout; a good-for-nothing (fellow);《文》a ne'er-do-well.

ろくぶんぎ 六分儀 a sextant.

ろくぼく 肋木 wall bars.

ろくまく 肋膜《解》the pleura (*pl.* -rae) ¶肋膜炎 pleurisy.

ろくめんたい 六面体 a hexahedron (*pl.* -s, -hedra) ¶六面体の hexahedral.

ろくろ 轆轤〈旋盤〉a (turning) lathe;〈陶工の〉a potter's wheel;〈滑車〉a pulley ¶ろくろで作る turn《table legs》(on a lathe); throw《pots》; make《ceramic bowls》on a [the] wheel / ろくろで作った turned (*kokeshi*); thrown《pottery》;《vases》turned on a wheel.

ろくろ² ⇨ ろく³ (ろくに).

ろくろくび 轆轤首 a long-necked monster.

ロケ(ーション) (a) location ¶ロケに行く go on location [a filming trip] / ロケーション中である be on location.

ロケット¹〈飛行体〉a rocket ¶ロケットで人工衛星を軌道に乗せる rocket a satellite into orbit / ロケットで飛ぶ fly by rocket《to》; rocket《to the moon》/ 逆推進[減速]ロケット a retrorocket; a deceleration [retarding, braking] rocket / 三段式ロケット a three-stage rocket / ブースターロケット a booster rocket / ロケット工学 rocketry / ロケット推進 rocket propulsion / ロケット推進の rocket-propelled / ロケット弾[砲] a rocket bomb [launcher] / ロケット発射装置[台] a rocket launcher [launching pad].

ロケット²〈装身具〉a locket.

ろけん 露見[顕] ¶露見する be found out; be discovered; be exposed; come《文》be brought] to light; come [be] out.

ロココ《美術史》rococo (architecture).

ろこつ 露骨 ¶露骨な〈むき出しな〉plain; outspoken;〈目立った〉conspicuous; open;〈下品な〉broad;〈挑発的な〉suggestive / 露骨になる〈下品になる〉get indecent;〈目立つ〉《文》become conspicuous; come out in the open; come to the fore / 露骨に言えば to be plain [frank] with you; in plain words; to put it baldly; not to put too fine a point on it. 文例

ろじ¹ 路地 an alley; an alleyway; a lane.

ろじ² 露地〈覆いのない地面〉outdoors;〈茶室の庭〉a garden next to a (ceremonial) teahouse ¶露地栽培のトマト tomatoes grown outdoors.

ロジウム《化》rhodium.

ロシヤ Russia ¶ロシヤの Russian / ロシヤ語 Russian / ロシヤ人 a Russian.

ろしゅつ 露出 (an) exposure ¶露出する expose;《文》bare《one's chest》;〈鉱床など〉crop out / 露出した exposed; naked; bare / 露出時間 exposure time / 露出不足[過度] underexposure [overexposure] / 露出過度の overexposed《films》;《文》insufficiently-dressed《girls》/ 露出計 an exposure [a light] meter / 露出症 exhibitionism / 露出狂 an exhibitionist. 文例

ろじょう 路上 ¶路上で on [in] the road [street] ★ on は《米》, in は《英》.

ろせん 路線 a route; a line ¶…の路線に沿って in line [《文》alignment] with《U.S. foreign policy》/ 強硬路線を取る take a hard [tough] line / 修正主義路線をたどる follow the revisionist line / 路線バス a bus on a regular route;《英》a bus.

ろだい 露台 ⇨ バルコニー.

ロッカー a locker ¶ロッカールーム a locker room.

ろっかく(けい) 六角(形) a hexagon ¶六角(形)の hexagonal.

ろっかんしんけい 肋間神経《解》the intercostal nerves ¶肋間神経痛 intercostal neuralgia.

ロッキーさんみゃく ロッキー山脈 the Rocky Mountains; the Rockies.

ロック《音楽》rock (music) ¶ハードロック hard rock / フォークロック folk rock.

ロックアウト《労働》a lockout ¶ロックアウトする lock《the workers》out《of the factory》; carry out a lockout.

ロッククライミング rock-climbing.

ロックンロール rock 'n' roll; rock-and-roll.

ろっこつ 肋骨《解》a rib;〈総称〉the ribs;〈船の〉the frame; the ribs.

ろっぽうぜんしょ 六法全書 a compendium of laws; the statute books.

ろてい 露呈 ⇨ あらわす¹, あらわれる.

ロデオ〈カウボーイの〉a rodeo (*pl.* -s).

ろてん¹ 露天 ⇨ のてん ¶露天風呂 an open-air bath / 露天掘り strip [opencut,《英》opencast] (coal) mining.

ろてん² 露店 a street stall ¶露店商人 a stallkeeper; a stallman.

ろとう 路頭 ¶路頭に迷う be turned adrift;

---

her. / 彼はろくに英語も話せないのに語学者のつもりでいる. Even though his English is appalling, he fancies himself a linguist. / 気が小さくて人前でろくにものも言えないほどです. She is so timid that she scarcely opens her mouth in company.

ろくじゅう 六十の手習い. It is never too late to learn.

ろこつ 彼は露骨に物を言うたちだ. He is very outspoken (plainspoken). | He is not a man to mince his words. | そんなに露骨に断わるのはよくあるまい. It won't do to refuse his offer so bluntly [flatly]. / 彼は露骨に敵意を見せた. He made no attempt to disguise his hostility.

ろしゅつ このフィルムは露出不足[過度]だ. This film is underex-

ろば 《文》 lose one's means of livelihood.
ろば 【動】an ass; a donkey.
ろばん 路盤 the roadbed.
ロビー a lobby; a lounge.
ロビング 《テニス》 lobbing ¶ロビングをあげる lob (a ball).
ロブ 《テニス》a lob.
ろぼう 路傍 ¶路傍の茶店 a teahouse by the roadside; a wayside teahouse / 路傍の人 a (mere) stranger; an outsider / 路傍に[で] by the roadside [wayside].
ロボット a robot; <お飾りを> a figurehead ¶産業ロボット an industrial robot / ロボット操縦の飛行機 a robot(-controlled) airplane.
ロマネスク 《美術史》 Romanesque (architecture).
ロマン[1] ¶ロマン主義 Romanticism / ロマン主義者 a Romanticist / ロマン派 the Romantic school; the Romanticists.
ロマン[2] [<《フランス語》 roman] a novel.
ロマンス <伝奇物語> a romance; <恋愛事件> a romance; a love affair ¶ロマンスカー a deluxe coach [《英》carriage] / ロマンスグレーの紳士 a fine gentleman with graying hair / ロマンス語 Romance languages.
ロマンチスト a romantic; a romanticist.
ロマンチック ¶ロマンチックな romantic.
ろめい 露命 ¶露命をつなぐ keep body and soul together;《文》 subsist on a small income; make [eke out] a precarious living [livelihood].
ろめん 路面 the road surface ¶路面電車 《米》a streetcar; 《英》 a tram(car).
ろれつ 呂律 ¶ろれつが回らない cannot speak clearly [《文》cannot articulate] (because one is drunk); 《文》be inarticulate (with palsy).
ろん 論 ⇒ぎろん, りろん ¶論をまたない It goes without saying 《that...》;《文》be beyond [past] dispute / 確率論 the theory of probability / 芸術論 an essay on art. 文例⇩
ろんがい 論外 ¶論外である be out of the question.
ろんかく 論客 a controversialist; a polemicist.
ろんぎ 論議 ⇒ぎろん ¶論議する discuss 《a question》; argue 《about》; debate (on) 《a matter》 / 論議中である be under discussion [debate]. 文例⇩
ろんきゅう[1] 論及 ⇒げんきゅう[1].
ろんきゅう[2] 論究 ¶論究する discuss 《a matter》 thoroughly [exhaustively] ⇒ろんじる.
ろんきょ 論拠 the grounds for [basis of] an argument ⇒こんきょ. 文例⇩
ろんご 論語 The Analects of Confucius. 文例⇩

ろんこうこうしょう 論功行賞 the grant of honors [distribution of rewards] according to the merits (of).
ろんこく 論告 the prosecutor's final [concluding] speech.
ろんし 論旨 the point [gist] of an argument ¶論旨を明らかにする make one's point clear.
ろんしょう 論証 (a) demonstration ¶論証する demonstrate; prove; produce [《文》adduce] proof [evidence] to support 《one's statement》.
ろんじる 論じる <議論する> discuss; argue (on, about); debate (on) 《a question》; reason 《that...》; <取り扱う> deal with; treat of; <評論する> comment (on) ¶政治を論じる discuss politics / 哲学を論じる talk [debate] philosophy 《with sb》/ 遺伝子工学の危険性を論じている本 a book concerned [dealing] with the hazards of genetic engineering / 論じるに足りない be not worth consideration;《文》beneath criticism / ...は《文》irrespective [regardless] of... / 論じ尽くす deal with 《a subject》 fully [《文》exhaustively]; argue 《a matter》out. 文例⇩
ろんじん 論陣 ¶論陣を張る set [put] out [《文》forth] an argument 《for, against》; make out a case 《for, against》.
ろんせつ 論説 an article; <社説> a leading article; a leader; an editorial ¶(新聞の)論説委員 an editorial [leading] writer; an editorialist / 論説欄 the editorial column.
ろんせん 論戦 a battle of words; (a) controversy ⇒ろんそう.
ろんそう 論争 a dispute; (a) controversy;《文》a polemic ¶論争する argue [《文》dispute] (against [with] sb, about sth); have [《文》engage in] a controversy (with sb on [about] sth); take issue 《with sb on sth》; cross swords 《with sb on sth》/ 論争の余地がある be debatable; be open to argument [dispute] / 論争の余地がない 《文》be beyond [past] dispute;《文》be indisputable;《文》be incontestable. 文例⇩
ろんだい 論題 the subject [theme, text] of one's argument [article, lecture]; a topic for discussion ¶論題からそれる stray [digress] from one's text [theme] / 論題からそれない keep [stick] to one's text [theme].
ろんだん[1] 論断 ¶論断する conclude 《that...》; pass a verdict 《on a matter》.
ろんだん[2] 論壇 <言論界> the press; the world of journalists.
ろんちょう 論調 the tone [《文》tenor] of an

---

posed [overexposed].
ろん 論より証拠. Proof is better than argument. | A single fact is worth a shipload of arguments.
ろんぎ この問題については活発な論議がたたかわされた. There was a lively [an animated] discussion on this subject.
ろんきょ 論拠がしっかりしている. His argument is well grounded. / 論拠が薄弱だ[誤まっている].

You are arguing on tenuous [false] grounds.
ろんご ああいうのを論語読みの論語知らずというのだ. He is what you might call a 'learned fool'.
ろんじる 100万円や200万円の損害は論じるに足りない. The loss of one or two million yen does not matter at all.
ろんそう その問題については科学者の間で今でも論争が行なわれて

いる. That is still a matter of controversy among scientists.
ろんちょう この問題については各紙の論調はほとんど同じである. Nearly all the papers are taking the same line on this subject.
ろんぶん この論文は著者が文学博士号のための論文として東京大学に提出したものである. The paper was presented by the author as a dissertation for the degree

ろんてき 論敵 an opponent [《文》adversary]
ろんてん 論点 the point at issue [in dispute].
ロンド 《音楽》a rondo (*pl.* -s).
ロンドン London ¶ロンドン子 a Londoner; a cockney / ロンドン塔 the Tower of London.
ろんなん 論難 ¶論難する criticize; denounce; attack.
ろんぱ 論破 ¶論破する refute; 《文》confute; argue [talk] *sb* down.
ロンパース 〈いたずら着〉rompers.
ろんばく 論駁 ¶論駁する argue against; 《文》controvert.
ろんぴょう 論評 ⇨ ひひょう, ひょうろん.
ろんぶん 論文 〈一般の〉an essay; a treatise; 〈専門的な〉a monograph; 〈学位・卒業の〉a thesis (*pl.* theses); a dissertation; 〈新聞などの〉an article; 〈学会などの〉a paper ¶論文を書く write a paper [thesis, monograph] 《on a subject》 / 論文を提出する submit [present] a thesis (to *sb*) / 試験に小論文を課する set [have 《the students》] sit] an essay examination.
ろんぽう¹ 論法 logic; reasoning ¶この論法で行くと by [according to] this line of argument.
ろんぽう² 論鋒 the force of an argument ¶鋭い論鋒 an incisive [《文》a trenchant] argument.
ろんり 論理 logic ¶論理的 logical / 非論理的 illogical / 論理的に, 論理上 logically / 論理学 logic / 論理学者 a logician.

わ

わ¹ 把 a bundle 《of firewood》; 〈稲などの〉a sheaf (*pl.* sheaves) ⇨ たば.
わ² 和 〈合計〉the sum; 〈平和〉peace; 〈和合〉harmony ¶和を求める work [figure] out the sum 《of》 / 和を請う sue for peace. 文例⇩
わ³ 輪 〈円〉a circle; 〈環〉a ring; a link 《鎖の》; 〈車輪〉a wheel; 〈ひもなどで作る〉a loop; 〈たが〉a hoop ¶輪を描く form [make] a circle; 《文》describe a circle / 〈輪回しの〉輪を回す roll [trundle] a hoop / 輪を作る coil [make] a sit [stand] in a circle [ring]; form a circle [ring] / 輪に輪をかけて言う exaggerate. 文例⇩
わ 〈歓声〉Hurrah!; Hurray!; 〈驚き〉Oh!; Wow! 文例⇩
ワークブック a workbook.
ワードプロセッサー a word processor.
わあわあ ¶わあわあ泣く cry loudly / わあわあ言う 〈わめく, わいわい言う〉.
ワイオミング Wyoming (略: Wy(o).) ¶ワイオミング州の人 a Wyomingite.
わいきょく 歪曲 ¶歪曲する distort; pervert; 《文》make a false representation of.
ワイシャツ [<white shirt] a shirt; a dress shirt (礼装用) ¶ワイシャツ姿で in *one's* shirt sleeves / ワイシャツ地 shirting. 文例⇩
わいしょう 矮小 ¶矮小な stunted; dwarf; undersized.
わいせつ 猥褻 ¶わいせつな obscene; filthy; dirty; improper; indecent; bawdy (こっけい味を伴って); pornographic; risqué; 《米》off-color / わいせつな絵 an obscene [a pornographic] picture / わいせつ行為 (commit) an act of obscenity / わいせつ罪で《arrest *sb*》on obscenity charges / わいせつ文書 indecent writings; pornography. 文例⇩
わいだん 猥談 a dirty [an obscene] story; a risqué [《米》an off-color] story ¶猥談をする talk smut; tell dirty [lewd, rude] jokes.
ワイド ¶ワイドスクリーン 《映画》a wide screen / ワイド番組 a long 《TV》show [program] (lasting several hours).
ワイパー a (windshield) wiper.
ワイヤ a wire ¶ワイヤゲージ a wire gauge / ワイヤロープ (a) wire rope.
ワイヤレスマイク a wireless microphone.
わいろ 賄賂 a bribe ¶賄賂の利く[かない] bribable [unbribable]; 《文》corruptible [incorruptible] / 賄賂を使う[贈る] offer [give] a bribe to *sb*; grease *sb's* palm / 賄賂をもらう[受け取る] accept [take] a bribe from *sb*; be bribed (by). 文例⇩
わいわい noisily; ¶clamorously ¶わいわい言う clamor (for, against, to do); pester *sb* 《for *sth*, to *do*》/ わいわい騒ぐ make a lot of noise; be noisy.
ワイン wine ⇨ ぶどう（ぶどう酒）¶ワイングラス a wineglass.
ワインドアップ 《野球》a wind-up ¶ワインドアップする wind up.
わえい 和英 ¶和英の Japanese-English / 和英辞典 a Japanese-English dictionary.

---

of Litt.D. at Tokyo University.
わ² 2と3の和は5. The sum of two and three is five. | Two and three make [are] five. / 875と327の和を求めよ. Find the sum of 875 and 327. / 和を以て貴しとなす. Harmony is the greatest of virtues.
わ³ 彼は天井に向けてタバコの輪を吐いた. He blew a smoke ring [a wreath of smoke] at the ceiling. / 彼らは僕の回りに輪になった. They formed a circle [ringed themselves] around me. / 奴も馬鹿だが, 奴の兄貴はそれに輪をかけた馬鹿だ. He is a fool, but his brother is a bigger one.
わあ わあ, そいつはすてきだ. Oh boy! [Wow!] That's wonderful.
ワイシャツ ズボンからワイシャツのすそが出ていた. His shirt(-tail) was out of his trousers.
わいせつ あの映画にわいせつな箇所はない. There is nothing dirty about the film.
わいろ 彼には賄賂は利かない. He is incorruptible [above bribery]. / 彼は役人に賄賂を贈ってさせた. He bribed the officials into doing it.

わおん 和音 〖音楽〗a chord.
わか 和歌 a 31-syllable Japanese poem; a *tanka*.
わが 我が my; our; *one's* (own) ¶我が国 this [our] country / 我が子 *one's* (own) child / 我が道を行く go *one's* (own) way; plow *one's* own furrow.
わかい[1] 和解 〖文〗an amicable settlement; (a) reconciliation ¶和解する make peace 《with》; settle *one's* differences 《with》; 〖文〗be reconciled 《with》; come to terms 《with》; reach [arrive at] an amicable settlement 《with》/ 和解させる settle 《a dispute》 peacefully; 〖文〗bring 《a matter》 to an amicable settlement; 〖文〗effect a reconciliation 《between A and B》. 文例↓
わかい[2] 若い 〈若年の〉young; 〈若々しい〉youthful; 〈未熟な〉green; inexperienced; unripe; immature ¶若い時に when [while] (one is) young; in *one's* youth / 若い番号 a low [lower] number / 若い者〈若い人〉a young person; a youth; the young (総称); 〈使用人〉a (young) manservant; an apprentice; 〈子分〉a henchman; a follower / 今どきの若いもん young folks [〖英〗folk] nowadays / 年の割に若く見える look young for *one's* age [〖文〗years] / 2, 3歳若く見える 〈人が主語〉look two or three years younger 《than *one* really is, than sb》; 〈物が主語〉take two or three years off *one's* age. 文例↓
わがい 我が意 ¶我が意を得る〈事が主語〉be highly satisfactory to *one*; win [meet with] *one's* full approval; 〈人が主語〉heartily agree with 《sb in *his* views》; be very happy 《to hear that...》.
わかがえり 若返り 〖文〗restoration of youth; 〖文〗rejuvenation ¶精神的若返り spiritual rejuvenation.
わかがえる 若返る get [grow, 〖文〗become] younger [young again]; 〖文〗be restored to youth; be rejuvenated ¶10年若返る 〈人が主語〉look ten years younger; 〈主語が〉take ten years off *one's* age / 若返ったような気がする feel (as if *one* were) young again.
わかぎ 若木 a young plant [tree]; a sapling.
わかくさ 若草 young [fresh] grass.
わかげ 若気 the enthusiasm [〖文〗ardor] of youth; youthful enthusiasm [〖文〗ardor] ¶若気の過ち a youthful indiscretion; youthful follies.
わがこと 我が事 ¶我が事のように as if (it) were *one's* own affair.
わかさ 若さ youth; youthfulness ¶若さを保つ keep *one's* youth; remain young. 文例↓
わかさぎ 〖魚〗a pond smelt.
わかじに 若死に an early [a premature] death ¶若死にする die (while still) young [at an early age].
わかしらが 若白髪 prematurely gray hair.
わかす 沸かす 〈熱する〉boil 《water》; heat 《the bath》; 〈熱狂させる〉excite ¶血を沸かすような stirring; exciting; thrilling.
わかだんな 若旦那 a young master.
わかつ 分かつ ⇨ わける.
わかづくり 若作り ¶若作りする〈化粧〉make oneself up to look younger; 〈服装〉wear a youthful dress.
わかて 若手 a young man; a younger member ¶若手の young; younger.
わがとう 我が党 our (own) party ¶我が党の士 a kindred spirit; 〈同志〉a comrade.
わかどり[1] 若鳥 a young bird.　「chicken.
わかどり[2] 若鶏 a chicken; 〈食用肉〉(fried)
わかな 若菜 young greens [herbs] ¶若菜を摘む gather [pick] young herbs.
わかば 若葉 young leaves [〈新緑〉fresh green [verdure] ¶若葉の栗の木 a new-leaved chestnut tree. 文例↓
わかはげ 若禿げ premature baldness ¶若は

わかい[1] 彼の陳謝でこのけんかもめでたく和解となった。An apology on his part settled the quarrel amicably [brought the quarrel to an amicable settlement].
わかい[2] 彼は僕より2つ若い。He is two years younger than me. ⇨より[2] 囲⑬ | He is my junior by two years. / 彼は年は若くても気は若い。He's old in years, but young in spirit. / 彼は年は若いが考えはなかなかしっかりしている。He has an old head on young shoulders. / 若い時は2度とない。You are only young once. / 彼は若い時から苦労だった。He was a hard worker from his youth. / 彼はまだ若いのに白髪まじりになっていた。He was prematurely gray. / 67という年にしては若く見える。He looks younger than his sixty-seven years.
わかがえる 彼は再び若返って活動を始めた。He renewed his activities with all the ardor of youth.
わかげ 若気の至りでした。I was young and thoughtless when I did it. | It was my young blood that drove me to do it. | I did it in the rashness of youth.
わかさ あの若さで死ぬとは気の毒だ。It is a pity that he had to die so young [at such an early age].
わかば 若葉がもえ始めた。The fresh young leaves have come out.
わがまま そんな事をするのは君のわがままというものだ。It is selfish of you to behave like that.
わかみ 我が身をつねって人の痛みを知れ。Do not do to others what you would not have them do to you. | People who live in glass houses should not throw stones. 〖諺〗
わがや わが家にまさる所なし。There is no place like home.
わかり あなたの字はわかりやすい。Your handwriting is easy to read. / 彼の言葉はわかりにくかった。His words were not clear.
わかりきった そんなことはわかり切ったことだ。It's plain enough. | It is (as) plain as a pikestaff.
わかる わかりました。I see. / 君はあまり早口だから何を言っているのかわからない。You speak so fast that I can't follow you. / 君はこの筆者の言っていることがわかるか。Can you make sense of what this writer says? / 私の言う事がどうしても彼らにはわからなかった。I could not make myself understood by them at all. | I couldn't get my meaning across to them. / わからないことがあったら、私に聞きなさい。Ask me when in doubt. / この語の使い方がいつもよくわからない。I'm never certain about the use of this word. / 真相がだんだん私にわかってきた。The truth gradu-

わかふうふ　若夫婦 a young (married) couple.

わがまま　我がまま〈利己〉selfishness;〈気まま〉《文》willfulness;《文》self-will;《文》waywardness;〈子供の〉naughtiness　¶わがままな selfish;《文》egoistic,《文》willful;《文》wayward;〈子供が〉disobedient; naughty / わがままをする act willfully; have one's (own) way / 子供をわがままに育てる spoil [pamper] one's child / わがまま者 a selfish [self-willed] person; an egoist. 文例◊

わがみ　我が身 oneself. 文例◊

わかめ　wakame; a kind of seaweed.

わかもの　若者 a young man [fellow]; a lad; a youth;〈総称〉the young, the youth; young folks [《英》folk].

わがもの　我が物 one's own (property)　¶我が物となる fall into one's hands [《文》possession] / 我が物にする make sth one's own; take possession of sth (for oneself);〈修得する〉master / 我が物顔に as if (it) were one's own; as if one owned《it, the place》; as if one were (its) owner [proprietor].

わがや　我が家 one's home [house]. 文例◊

わからずや　分からず屋〈頑固者〉an obstinate [a bigoted] person; a bigot;〈ばか〉a blockhead.

わかり　分かり　¶わかりのよい intelligent; sensible; quick-witted;《口語》quick on the uptake;《文》quick of understanding / わかりの悪い dull(-witted); stupid;《口語》slow on the uptake;《文》slow of understanding / わかりにくい difficult [hard] to understand /〈言葉などが〉unintelligible;〈字などが〉illegible; hard to make out; crabbed / わかりやすい[よい] easy to understand;《文》intelligible;〈字が〉legible;〈平明な〉plain; simple / わかりやすくする make (the meaning) clearly understandable /〈単純化する〉simplify / わかりやすく言えば to put it simply [plainly]; in plain language. 文例◊

わかりきった　分かり切った obvious; plain; evident;〈自明の〉《文》self-evident;《文》axiomatic. 文例◊

わかる　分かる〈理解する〉understand; see; grasp;《口語》catch; follow; make out; take in;〈知る〉know; can tell; realize;〈見いだす〉find out; find; discover (⇒ 囲記);〈知れる〉be known; be found; come to light; be identified (身元が);〈…だと判明する〉prove [turn out]《to be》;〈よさ・ありがたみが〉appreciate;〈発表される〉be published; be announced;〈認知する〉recognize　¶絵[音楽]がわかる have an eye [ear] for pictures [music]; be a good judge of pictures [music] / 物[道理]のわかった〈賢い〉sensible;〈公平な〉fair-minded. 文例◊

囲記　同じ「見いだす」という意味での「分かる」でも, 特に, 人から教わったりして, 又は偶然に, ある事実を知る場合には find を用い, いろいろ調べた結果その事実を発見する時には, find out を用いるのが普通である. discover はこのどちらの場合にも使えるが, その使用頻度は低い.

わかれ　別[分か]れ〈分離〉(a) parting; (a) separation;〈告別〉farewell;〈分派〉a (lateral) branch; an offshoot　¶長の別れ ⇒ ながの / つらい別れ a painful separation / 別れの杯 a parting cup / 別れのつらさ the pain [sorrow, wrench] of parting 〈大人が, 特に children's〉/ 別れの(あいさつの)手紙 a farewell letter / 別れを告げる say good-by(e) (to); bid sb farewell; take leave of sb / 別れに臨んで at parting. 文例◊

わかればなし　別れ話 a talk about divorce　¶別れ話を持ち出す propose divorce;〈法廷に〉institute a suit [file a petition] for divorce《against》.

わかれみち　分かれ道〈本道から分かれた道〉a branch road;〈十字路〉a crossroads　★ crossroads は単数扱い ⇒ わかれめ.

わかれめ　分かれ目　¶分かれ目に立つ stand [be] at a turning point [the crossroads,《文》

---

ally dawned on me [my mind]. / 顔つきで彼がこの計画に反対だということがわかった. I realized from his expression [His face showed me] that he was against the plan. / 彼らだってこの問題については我々同様にわかっていないのだ. They are as much in the dark about this affair as we are. / あんなことを言って, わかっちゃいないね. He doesn't know what he is talking about. / 時がたてばわかる. Time will show. / 人の善しあしはその交わる友でわかる. A man is known by the company he keeps. / この小説を読めば, 当時の農民がどんな暮らしをしていたかよくわかった. This novel will give you a fair idea [a good picture] of what the peasants' life was like in those days. / 両者の違いが私にはわかりません. I can't tell the difference between them. / どんな事になるかわからない. There is no saying [telling, knowing] what may happen. / What may happen is anybody's [anyone's] guess. / 彼は音楽がわからない. He has no ear for music. / 女はなんともわからない. You never can tell with women. / あなたは花のことはわかりますか. Are you good at flowers? / その家がわからなかった. I could not find the house. / 彼が信用できない男だということがわかった. I found him (to be) untrustworthy. / 後で自分が間違っていた(ことが)わかった. Later I discovered [found out] that I had been in the wrong. / どうしてよいやらわからなかった. I was at a loss [all at sea] (as to) what to do. / 試験の成績はいつわかりますか. When are we going to know [get] the results of the examination? / When will the exam results be announced? / そのうわさは事実無根である事がわかった. The rumor turned out to be groundless. / 彼だということがちょっとわからなかった. I didn't recognize him for the moment. / この本は2回通読したのだが, 依然として著者の考えていることがわからない. I have gone through the book twice, but I am still none the wiser about the author's ideas.

わかれ　会うは別れの始め. We meet only to part. / 彼女は別れに臨んで彼と握手を交わした. She shook hands with him on parting. / 彼女は手を振って別れを告げた. She waved me good-by(e). / お別れに一杯どうかね. 〈旅立つ人に向かって言う時〉How about

わかれる 別分かれる〈別離する〉part (from, with); separate [be separated] (from); 〈告別する〉say good-by(e) (to); bid sb farewell; leave; 〈離婚する〉be divorced (from); 〈分離する〉branch off (from) 〈文〉diverge (from); 〈分裂する〉split (into); 〈分岐する〉fork (into); 〈区分される〉be divided (into); 〈分散する〉break up; disperse ¶2つに分かれる〈道路が〉branch [fork] into two (roads); 〈団体などが〉divide [split] into two sections [factions] / 別れて暮らす live apart from (one's wife) / 別れた妻 one's divorced wife. 文例↓

わかれわかれ 別れ別れ ¶別れ別れに separately; 〈文〉severally / 別れ別れになる get [be, 〈文〉become] separated (from one another); 〈解散する〉break up; disperse / 別れ別れに暮らす live apart [separate] (from). 文例↓

わかわかしい 若々しい〈文〉youthful; young(-looking); 〈顔や色つやの〉fresh; blooming ¶いつまでも若々しさを失わない秘訣 the secret of perpetual [keeping one's] youth.

わき 脇〈そば〉the side; 〈ほかの場所〉another [some other] place; 〈能の〉a waki; the main supporting character in a Noh drama ¶わきを見る look away; take one's eyes off sth / わきを通る pass by / わきに by; by [at] the side of; beside / aside / わきに抱える hold [carry] sth under one's arm / わきに寄る〈よける〉step [stand] aside [to one side]; get out of the way; 〈近寄る〉go [draw] to sb's side / 門のわきで by the gate / わきへ置く put [lay] sth aside / わきへそらす divert 《sb's attention》 from sth; switch 《the conversation》 from 《the subject》 / わきへそれる〈話が〉stray [《文》digress] from 《the subject》; 〈弾丸などが〉miss [fly wide of the target mark].

わきあいあい 和気藹々 ¶和気あいあいとした〈文〉harmonious (households); happy (homes). 文例↓

わきあがる 沸き上がる〈煮え立つ〉boil up; 〈沸き起こる〉⇨ わきおこる.

わきあけ 脇明き〈スカートの〉a placket (hole); a (finished) slit.

わきおこる 沸き起こる well up [《文》forth]; surge (up); 〈拍手・やじなどが〉break out; 〈文〉arise.

わきが 腋臭 underarm odor; 〈体臭〉body odor (略: B.O.) ¶わきががひどい have a strong [very offensive] body odor.

わきかえる 沸き返る〈湯が〉seethe; boil up ¶沸き返るような騒ぎである be in an uproar [a ferment]; seethe [be highly excited] (over sth). 文例↓

わきげ 腋毛 underarm hair.

わきざし 脇差 a short sword.

わきすじ 脇筋〈劇や小説の〉a subplot; a byplot.

わきたつ 沸き立つ ⇨ わきかえる.

わきでる 湧き出る gush [spring] out [《文》forth]; 〈井戸水のように〉well up.

わきのした 腋の下 the armpit; 〈着物のそでぐり〉the armhole ¶わきの下の underarm / わきの下をかく scratch oneself under the arm [in the armpit] / わきの下に抱える carry [hold] sth under one's arm / わきの下に汗をかく sweat under the arms.

わきばら 脇腹 the side ¶わき腹を小突く poke [nudge] sb in the ribs / わき腹が痛む have a pain in one's (right) side.

わきまえ 弁え〈識別〉〈文〉discernment; 〈分別〉discretion ¶わきまえがある have the sense (to do); have sense enough (to do); be discreet enough (to do) / 前後のわきまえもなく〈無謀に〉thoughtlessly; recklessly; 〈衝動的に〉impulsively.

わきまえる 弁える〈区別を〉discriminate [《文》discern] (between two things, A from B); 〈心得る〉know; understand; 〈忘れない〉bear sth in mind. ¶礼儀をよくわきまえている be very well-mannered; have a good knowledge of etiquette / 公私の別をわきまえない fail to distinguish [make a clear distinction] between one's private and public life [affairs]; 《文》confound public affairs with private (ones). 文例↓

わきみ 脇見 ¶わき見する look off [away, aside]; take one's eyes off sth. 文例↓

わきみず 湧き水 a spring.

わきみち 脇道 a side [branch] road; a byway; a byroad; a bypath; 〈話の〉a digression ¶わ

---

one for the road?

わかれめ ここが勝敗の分かれ目だ. The issue hangs on this point. | This point will decide the issue.

わかれる 杉山君とは東京駅で別れた. Sugiyama and I parted [I parted from Sugiyama] at Tokyo Station. / そこで小道が街道から分かれています. A path branches [forks] off from the highway there. / その問題で我々の意見が分かれた. We were divided in opinion [We parted company with each other] on the subject. / 仲良く別れようじゃないか. Let us part (as) friends. / 彼と別れて もう長いことになる. It's a long time since I last saw him. / 彼らは2手に分かれて犯人の捜索に向かった. They separated into two parties to search for the culprit. / 分かれ! [号令] Fall out! | Dismiss!

わかれわかれ その時以来親子は別れ別れになった. Mother and the son parted then, never to meet again.

わき 彼は僕のわきに立っていた. He was standing beside me. / わきへ回るところがあるんだ. I've another visit to make.

わきあいあい 一同和気あいあいのうちに散会した. The meeting broke up in a very friendly atmosphere.

わきかえる 政府のこの突然の発表で国中沸き返るような騒ぎになった. The whole nation seethed with excitement at the government's sudden announcement. | The abrupt announcement by the government set the whole country in a ferment.

わきまえる 僕だってそのくらいのことはわきまえているよ. I do know that much.

わきみ わき見運転しないで. Keep your eyes on the road!

わきめ 彼はわき目も振らずに働いた. He went [put his] heart and

わきめ 脇目 ¶わき目も振らず wholeheartedly／わき目も振らずに勉強する《文》apply oneself closely to one's studies; go heart and soul into one's work. 文例◊

わきやく 脇役 a supporting [secondary] role;〈人〉a supporting actor [actress《女》] ¶わき役を勤める support《an actor》; play support;〈比喩的に〉《文》play a subordinate part [secondary role]《in》; take a back seat《to》.

わぎり 輪切り ¶輪切りにする cut《a radish》in round slices.

わく[1] 枠 a frame; framework;〈縁〉a rim;〈刺しゅうの〉a tambour;〈範囲〉a limit;〈制限〉⇒ **せいげん**[2] ¶枠に入れる[はめる] frame; set《a picture》in a frame／…の枠内で within the limits of….

わく[2] 沸[湧]く〈煮立つ〉boil; grow hot;〈沸き出る〉gush [spring, flow] out [《文》forth]; well up;〈虫が〉breed;〈興奮する〉be in a ferment [an uproar]; be excited《over》; seethe《over》 ¶うじ虫がわく maggots breed《in》;〈場所が主語〉be infested with maggots.

わくせい 惑星〖天〗a planet ¶政界の惑星 a dark horse in political circles／外惑星 an outer [exterior] planet／内惑星 an inner [interior] planet／惑星運動 planetary motion／惑星間の interplanetary《travel》.

ワクチン vaccine ¶ジフテリア予防のワクチンを接種する vaccinate [inoculate]《a child》against diphtheria／小児麻痺用生ワクチン a live polio vaccine.

わくでき 惑溺 ¶惑溺する be infatuated [besotted] with《a woman》 ⇒ **おぼれる**.

わくわく ¶わくわくする get nervous《at, about》; be excited《over, with》; be thrilled《at doing, sth》／わくわくして trembling《with joy》. 文例◊

わけ 訳〈理由〉《文》(a) reason;〈原因〉(a) cause;〈根拠〉grounds; a ground;〈事情〉circumstances; the case;〈意味〉(a) meaning; a sense ¶少し訳があって for certain reasons; on certain grounds／…の訳がない there is no reason [《文》ground] for…; there are no grounds for…; cannot《be》／訳のわかった sensible;〈人について〉understanding;〈公平な〉fair-minded／訳のわからない〈言葉などが〉incomprehensible; unintelligible;〈人について〉unreasonable; stubborn; obstinate／訳のわからない事を言う talk nonsense [rubbish];〈無理なことを言う〉be unreasonable／訳を話す give《one's》reasons《for》; tell the reason《why…》; explain／こういう訳で for this reason; such being the case／どういう訳で Why…?; How [How] is it (that)…?; On what grounds…?; What…for?／そういう訳なら if that is the case; if so／どういう訳だか for some (unknown) reason; somehow (or other). 文例◊

わけあう 分け合う share sth with sb; share with sb in sth.

わけいる 分け入る make [push, force] one's way into [through] ¶山深く分け入る go [push] deep into the mountains.

わけても 別けても〈なかんずく〉above all; before everything (else);〈特別に〉in particular; especially.

わけない 訳ない easy; simple ¶訳なく easily; with ease; without effort [difficulty]／訳なく勝つ win an easy victory《over》; win《a contest》hands down. 文例◊

わけへだて 別け隔て ¶わけ隔てする discriminate《between, against, in favor of》; make distinctions《between》／わけ隔てなく《文》without discrimination; equally; alike／すべての人をわけ隔てなく取り扱う treat all men alike [equally].

わけまえ 分け前〖口語〗a cut; a share; a portion ¶分け前を要求する claim a share《in [of] the profits》／分け前にあずかる share [have a share]《in》; come in for a share《of, in》. 文例◊

わけめ 分け目〈分けた所〉a parting《in one's hair》;〈仕切り〉a partition ¶天下分け目の戦い ⇒ **てんか**[2].

わける 分ける〈分割する〉divide《into》; part《into》; split《into》;〈引き離す〉separate;〈分配する〉distribute《among》; share《sth with

---

soul into his work.

わく[2] お風呂がわきました。 The bath is ready.／それを聞いて私の心に喜びがわいた。 Joy welled up in my heart at the news.

わくわく 私はわくわくしていた。 My heart pounded [beat, throbbed] violently with expectation.

わけ どういう訳で出席者が少ないのだろう。 Why are there so few people present?／そういう訳で先週は欠席させていただきました。 That's why I was unable to come last week.／訳をお聞かせ願いましょう。 I think I deserve an explanation from you.／なぜ彼があんなに怒っているのか訳がわからない。 I don't see why he is so angry.／彼はそんなに忙しい訳はない。 He can't be all that busy.／それじゃ腹を立てる訳だ。 It's natural [It's no wonder] that he took offense.／彼は腹が立って当然の訳だ。 He had every right to be angry.／私は心配しない訳にはいかない。 I cannot help being anxious.／私ではあなたは私をペテン師と疑っている訳ですね。 Am I to understand that you suspect me of being a swindler?／うなぎは好きですよ、いって毎日食べているという訳じゃないですけれども。 I like eel, not that I eat it every day.

わけても ビジネスマンは時間を守ることが大切だ。 Businessmen must, above [before] all else, be punctual.／私は古典音楽が好きだが、わけてもモーツァルトの音楽が好きだ。 I am fond of classical music, but I love (the music of) Mozart best of all.

わけない やってみると、わけないことさ。 You will find it quite easy to do it.／あいつを負かすのはわけないことさ。 I can beat him easily [hands down].

わけまえ おれの分け前をよこせ。

わごう 和合 《文》harmony；《文》concord；peace (平和) ¶和合する 《文》harmonize 《with》;《文》live in harmony [peace] 《with》; get along [on] 《with》; get along well [《文》amicably] 《with》.

わこうど 若人 ⇒わかもの.

わゴム 輪ゴム a rubber [an elastic] band.

ワゴン a (tea) wagon; a trolley.

わざ 業, 技 〈仕事〉work; a deed; an act;〈芸〉a performance; an art;〈柔道などの〉technique(s); a trick ¶たちわざ, ねわざ〈業師〉a cunning [shrewd] fellow; a wily schemer.

わさい 和裁 kimono-making.

わざと 態と on purpose; deliberately; intentionally; purposely ¶わざとらしい〈不自然な〉unnatural;〈作為のある〉studied;〈無理な〉forced;〈気取った〉affected / わざとらしい笑い a forced smile; a strained laugh / わざとらしく in a strained [an affected] manner. 文例↓

わさび (a) wasabi; (a) Japanese horseradish ¶わさび漬け wasabi preserved in sake lees.

わざわい 災い,《文》(an) evil;〈不幸〉(a) misfortune; a mishap;〈災難〉a disaster; a calamity; woe(s) ¶災いを招く bring (an) evil upon oneself; ask for trouble; invite disaster (by one's misconduct) / 災いに会う meet with (a) misfortune [disaster] / 災いとなる do sb harm; be the ruin (of). 文例↓

わざわざ〈わざと〉on purpose; deliberately;〈特に〉《文》expressly; especially ¶わざわざ ...する take the trouble (to do); bother [trouble] (to do); go out of one's way (to do). 文例↓

わし¹ 鷲〔鳥〕an eagle ¶ひなわし a young eagle; an eaglet / わしの巣 an eyrie; an aerie / わし鼻 a hooked 《文》an aquiline nose / わしづかみにする clutch; grab.

わし² 和紙 Japanese paper.

わしつ 和室 a Japanese-style room.

わじゅつ 話術 the art of narration; the storyteller's art ¶話術の大家 a good storyteller / 〈会話の〉a brilliant conversationalist [talker].

わしょ 和書〈日本語の本〉a book (written) in Japanese;〈和とじの本〉⇒わとじ.

ワシントン〈州〉the State of Washington (略: Wash.);〈米国の首府〉Washington, D.C. (★ D.C. は the District of Columbia の略).

わずか 僅か ⇒すこし ¶わずかの〈数〉a few;〈量〉a little;《文》a modicum of 《sense》;〈ささいな〉trifling; insignificant; slight;〈乏しい〉meager; scanty / わずかに only; just; merely; slightly;〈辛うじて〉barely; narrowly / わずか千円 only [no more than] a thousand yen; a paltry 1,000 yen; a petty sum of 1,000 yen / わずかな収入で暮らす live on a small [meager] income / わずか2, 3年で in a [the] brief [short] period of two or three years. 文例↓

わずらい 煩[患]い〈悩み〉(a) worry; trouble; anxiety;〈病気〉(an) illness; an ailment ⇒ながわずらい ¶煩いがある have cares [worries] / 心に煩いがない be carefree. 文例↓

わずらう 煩[患]う〈悩む〉⇒なやむ;〈病む〉⇒やむ².

わずらわしい 煩わしい 《be》a nuisance; troublesome; annoying; irksome;《文》burdensome;《文》onerous.

わずらわす 煩わす〈面倒をかける〉trouble;〈悩ます〉bother ¶心を煩わす ⇒なやむ. 文例↓

わする 和する〈和合する〉《文》harmonize 《with》;〈仲良くする〉get along 《with》;〈唱和する〉join sb in reciting [singing].

わすれがたみ 忘れ形見〈記念の品〉something to remember sb by; a keepsake; a memento (pl. -(e)s);〈子供〉one's posthumous child.

わすれなぐさ 忘れな草〔植〕a forget-me-not.

Give me my share. / わける これを1つ分けて下さいませんか? Won't you spare me one of these?

わざ これは容易な業ではない. This is no easy work [no soft job]. / 技あり! 〖柔道〗A half point!

わざと 彼がわざとやったものとも思えない. It seems unlikely that he did it on purpose. / 彼の心を傷つけようとして彼女はわざとあんなことをしたのです. She went out of her way to do it in order to cause him pain.

わざわい この不注意がやがて彼の身の災いとなった. This carelessness was to be his ruin [the ruin of him]. / これは災い転じて福となるの例だ. This is a case of good coming out of evil.

わざわざ わざわざそんな所へ出かけてゆく人は少なかった. Very few people ever bothered [went out of their way] to go there. / 遠方のところをわざわざおいで下さいまして有り難うございます. It is very kind of you to come all this way to see us.

わずか ここから駅まではもうわずかです. It is only a short way from here to the station. / 彼の言葉にわずかにドイツなまりがあった. He spoke with a slight German accent. / わずかに死を免れた. He barely [narrowly] escaped death.

わずらい 今まで大患いをしたことがありますか. Have you ever been seriously ill? / Have you ever had a serious illness?

わずらわす そんなくだらない質問で先生を煩わすものではない. You mustn't bother [trouble] your teacher with such trivial questions. / 校正は小川氏を煩わした. We are indebted to Mr. Ogawa for proofreading.

わすれもの 雨の日は電車に傘の忘れ物が多い. There are lots of umbrellas left behind in trains on a rainy day.

わすれる 私をお忘れですか. Don't you remember [recognize] me? / 天災は忘れた頃にやって来る. Disasters befall us when we least expect them. / 忘れずに明日電話

わすれもの 忘れ物 a thing left behind ; 〈列車などでの〉 lost property ¶忘れ物をする わすれる. 文例❸

わすれる 忘れる forget ; slip one's mind [memory] (物が主語) ; 〈癖になってしょっちゅう〉 be forgetful about sth ; 〈意識的に〉 get sth off one's mind ; put sth out of one's mind ; think no more of sth ; unlearn (the bookish English one learned in school) ; 〈忘れ物をする〉 leave sth behind ; forget to take [bring] sth ¶悲しみを忘れる get over [recover from] one's grief / 酒に憂さを忘れる drown one's sorrows / 忘れない〈覚えている〉 remember ; keep [bear] sth in mind ; 〈事が主語〉 be [stay, live] in one's memory / 忘れられる be forgotten ;《文》 be buried in oblivion / 忘れ難い, 忘るべからざる unforgettable ; memorable ; indelible (impressions) / 忘れっぽい be forgetful ; have a poor [bad] memory. 文例❸

わせ 〈早生種〉 an early-ripening variety 《of》; 〈早生種の稲〉 an early-ripening variety of rice ; 〈早熟〉 precocity.

わせい¹ 和声 《音楽》 harmony ¶和声学 harmonics《単数扱い》 / 和声法 the law of harmony.

わせい² 和製 ¶和製の Japanese-made ; 《文》《furniture》of Japanese make ; Japanese / 和製英語 an English word coined in Japan ;《口語》 Japlish.

ワセリン 《商標名》 Vaseline ; petroleum jelly.

わせん¹ 和船 a Japanese-style (wooden) ship [boat].

わせん² 和戦 ¶和戦両様の構えをする be prepared both for war and (for) peace.

わそう 和装 ¶和装の〈服装〉 dressed in (a) kimono ;〈書物〉⇒わとじ.

わた¹ 腸 ⇒はらわた.

わた² 綿 cotton (wool) ;〈木〉 a cotton plant ¶綿のように疲れる be tired out ; be dead tired / 綿を入れる〈詰める〉 stuff [wad] (a quilt) with cotton / 綿入れの a padded [wadded] garment / 綿打ち機 a willow ; a willowing machine / 綿菓子 candy floss ; cotton candy ; 《米》 spun sugar / 綿くず bits of down ; flue / 綿雲 fleecy clouds / 綿毛 down ; fluff / 綿繰り機 a cotton gin / 綿屋〈人〉 a cotton dealer ; 〈店〉 a cotton store.

わだい 話題 a topic [subject] (of conversation) ¶話題を変える change the subject / 次から次へと話題を変える jump [leap] from one topic to another / 話題になる〈上る〉 get into [be in] the news ; become [be] a topic of conversation ; be talked about. 文例❸

わだかまり 蟠り 〈気になること〉 cares ;〈悪感情〉 ill feeling ;〈隔意〉 reserve ;〈滞り〉⇒とどこおり ¶心にわだかまりがある have sth on one's mind ; have something (against sb) ;《文》 entertain [harbor] ill feeling 《against》. 文例❸

わだかまる 蟠る ¶心にわだかまる be on [rooted in] one's mind. 文例❸

わたくし 私 I ; myself ¶私する embezzle [《文》 misappropriate] 《public money》 (for one's own use) ;《文》 make (an) improper use of 《one's power》 / 私の my ;〈公に対して〉 private ;〈一身の〉 personal / 私のある selfish ;《文》 self-interested / 私のない unselfish ;《文》 disinterested / 私のもの mine / 私に[を] me / 私たち we ⇒われわれ / 私事 ⇒しじ².

わたし¹ 私 ⇒わたくし.

わたし² 渡し 〈渡船場〉 a ferry ;〈渡ること〉 a ferry passage ;〈受け渡し〉 delivery ¶舷側渡し free alongside ship [vessel] (略: f.a.s.) / 倉庫[はしけ, 桟橋]渡し ex warehouse [lighter, pier] / 鉄道渡し free on rail (略: f.o.r.) / 本船[貨車]渡し〈積み込み〉渡し free on board (略: F.O.B., f.o.b.) / 渡し賃 ferriage / 渡し舟 a ferryboat ; a ferry / 渡し舟で川を渡る cross a river by ferry / 渡し舟で対岸まで運ぶ ferry 《men》 over to the other side of the river / 渡守り a ferryman.

わたす 渡す carry [take] across [over] ;〈手渡しする〉 hand ;〈引き渡す〉 deliver ; hand [turn] over ;〈譲る〉 transfer ; make over ;〈支払う〉 pay ;〈掛け渡す〉 build [put]《a bridge》 over [across] 《a river》 / そっと渡す slip sth into sb's hand [pocket] / 溝に板を渡す lay a plank across a ditch. 文例❸

わだち 轍 a rut ; a wheel track.

をかけて下さい. Be sure and [Don't forget to] call me tomorrow. / 薬のお陰で忘れたように歯の痛みがとまった. Thanks to the medicine, my toothache has completely disappeared [gone]. / 世間ではその事をもう忘れている. That is no longer in people's memory. / この事は永久に忘れないでしょう. I shall never forget it. / いつまでも私の記憶に生きるでしょう. It will live in my memory for ever. / いい考えを思いついたら, 必ず忘れないうちにメモしておきなさい. Whenever a good idea occurs to you, make a note of it before it slips [goes out of] your mind. / 彼の苦心の調査がなかったならば, これは永久に忘れられてしまったことであろう. But for his painstaking investigations this would have been consigned to lasting oblivion. / どこへ傘を忘れてきたんだろう. Where have I left my umbrella? / 引き出しをあけてみたら忘れていた万年筆が見つかった. In one of the drawers I found my (fountain) pen which had been left there and forgotten. / 忘れ難い光景であった. It was an unforgettable sight [a scene to remember].

わだい 彼は話題が豊富だ. He has a rich stock of topics for conversation. / この話題が朝食の時にも出た. The subject came [was brought] up again at breakfast. / 町中の話題になった. It became the talk of the town. / それは職場でちょっとした話題になった. It became something of a topic of conversation in the office.

わだかまり お互いに心にわだかまりを持たないようにしよう. Let's keep an open mind toward each other.

わだかまる どうしても両国間にわだかまる確執の根を抜くことができなかった. Nothing could resolve the deep-seated [long-standing] feud between the two countries.

わたす 君に渡した金はどうしたかね. What have you done with the money I gave you to keep? / 酔っぱらいは警察の手に渡された.

わたり 渡り〈渡し場〉a ferry;〈渡ること〉passage;〈鳥の〉(a) migratory flight; migration;〈交渉〉negotiations ¶渡りをつける〈接触する〉come in contact 《with》; get in touch 《with》; contact;〈了解を得る〉come to [arrive at] an understanding 《on sth with sb》/渡りに舟と飛びつく jump at 《an offer》; bite at the chance (offered).

わたりあう 渡り合う〈刀で〉cross swords 《with》;〈殴り合う〉exchange blows 《with》;〈言い争う〉argue [have an argument] 《with》; bandy words 《with》¶激しく渡り合う have a heated argument 《with》; bandy words heatedly [angrily] 《with》.

わたりあるく 渡り歩く wander [move] from place to place.

わたりいた 渡り板 a gangplank; a gangway.

わたりぞめ 渡り初め the (formal) opening of a bridge (to traffic).

わたりどり 渡り鳥 a bird of passage; a migratory (bird) ¶渡り鳥保護条約 a treaty on the protection of migratory birds; a migratory bird protection treaty.

わたりもの 渡り者〈渡り労働者〉a wandering laborer;《米国》a floater;〈よそ者〉a stranger.

わたりろうか 渡り廊下 a roofed [covered] passage (connecting two buildings); a connecting passageway.

わたる¹ 亘る range 《from A to B》; extend 《over》; cover;〈続く〉last ¶10キロ[年]にわたる extend [stretch] over ten kilometers [years] /〈話の〉ある問題にわたる touch on a subject / 他人の私事にわたる intrude [《文》trespass] on sb's privacy / 5年間にわたって over a period of five years / 数回にわたって講演する deliver a series of lectures / 何代にもわたって《be passed down》across the generations. 文例○

わたる² 渡る〈横断する〉go [walk] across; go [《文》pass] over; cross;〈徒渉する〉wade; ford;〈移住する〉migrate; emigrate (他国へ); immigrate (他国から);〈渡来する〉be introduced (from Korea); be brought over (from abroad);〈支給される〉be supplied 《with》¶橋を渡る cross a bridge / 米国へ渡る go over to America /〈移住する〉emigrate to the United States / 世を渡る get along; make [earn] one's livelihood / 人手に渡る pass into sb's hands [possession]; change hands / 方々渡ってあるく ⇒わたりあるく. 文例○

ワックス wax ¶ワックスを塗る wax.

ワッセルマン ¶ワッセルマン検査 a Wassermann test / ワッセルマン反応 (a) Wassermann reaction.

わっと ¶わっと泣き出す burst out crying; burst into tears / わっと歓声をあげる shout for joy; raise [send up] a cheer.

ワット 【電】a watt ¶60ワットの電球 a sixty-watt bulb / ワット時 a watt-hour (略: whr).

ワッフル a waffle. 〔Japanese style〕

わとじ 和綴じ ¶和とじの本 a book bound in Japanese style.

わな 罠 a snare; a trap; a gin ¶わなをかける lay a snare 《for》; set a trap 《for》/ わなにかかる be caught in a trap; fall into a snare; be trapped [《文》entrapped,《文》ensnared] (by sb, into doing).

わなげ 輪投げ quoits (単数扱い) ¶輪投げをする play quoits / 輪投げの輪 a quoit; a ring.

わなわな ¶わなわなする[震える] tremble 《with [for] fear》; shiver 《with cold》; quiver (all over);《口語》be all of a tremble.

わに 【動】a crocodile (アフリカ産); an alligator (北米産) ¶わに皮のハンドバッグ a crocodile(-skin) handbag; an alligator(-leather) handbag; a bag in crocodile skin / わに足の〈内に曲がった〉knock-kneed;〈外に曲がった〉bowlegged.

ワニス varnish ⇒ニス.

わび¹ 佗び wabi; the beauty to be found in poverty and simplicity.

わび² 詫び〈陳謝〉an apology 《for》;〈言い訳〉an excuse 《for》¶わびがかなう one's apology is accepted 《by》/ わびの手紙 a letter of apology / わびを入れる ⇒わびる.

わびしい 佗しい〈寂しい〉lonely; lonesome; cheerless;〈惨めな〉wretched; miserable ¶わびしく暮らす live [lead] a lonely [solitary] life ★ lonely は常に形容詞. 副詞としては使えない.

わびずまい 佗住まい〈住居〉a humble dwelling;〈生活〉a lonely [secluded] life.

わびる 詫びる apologize 《to sb for one's rudeness》; make [offer] an apology 《for》;〈言い訳する〉excuse oneself 《for》; make [offer] an excuse 《for》;〈許しを請う〉beg sb's pardon. 文例○

わふう 和風〈日本風〉Japanese style;〈静かな風〉a gentle breeze ¶和風喫茶(店) a tearoom in the Japanese style.

わふく 和服 Japanese clothes; a kimono ¶和服を着ている wear [be in, have on] (a) kimono.

わぶん 和文 Japanese; a sentence [a piece of writing] in Japanese ¶和文英訳 translation from Japanese into English; Japanese-English

---

The drunkard was handed over to the police.

わたる 彼の発明は広範囲にわたっている. His inventions cover a wide field. / 庄司博士は1時間余にわたって演説された. Dr. Shoji gave a speech (which lasted) for more than an hour.

わたる² この絵はそれ以来度々人手から人手へと渡って来ました. The picture has changed hands many times since then. / 渡る世間に鬼はない. There is kindness to be found everywhere.

わびる 幾重にもおわび致します. I apologize most humbly. | I am sincerely sorry.

わらい 彼はもうかって笑いが止まらないのだ. He is making so much money that he can't stop chuckling. / あの人の笑い顔を見たことがない. I have never seen him smile. / 笑い声が突然止まった. The laughter suddenly stopped. / 笑い事じゃない. It is no laughing matter.

わらいだす これの彼の言葉で皆どっと笑い出した. They burst into a roar of laughter at his remark.

わらいもの これでは学校中の笑い物になるよ, まったく. This will make you the laughingstock of the whole school, I tell you.

わへい 和平 peace ⇨ へいわ ¶和平の提案をする make a proposal for peace / 和平交渉 peace negotiations.

わほう 話法 《文法》 narration; 《米》 discourse; 《英》 speech ¶間接話法 ⇨ かんせつ¹ / 直接話法 ⇨ ちょくせつ.

わぼく 和睦 《講和》 peace; 《和解》 (a) reconciliation ¶和睦する make (one's) peace 《with》 / 和解する《文》 be reconciled《with》; come to terms《with》.

わほん 和本 ⇨ わじゃ.

わめきごえ 喚き声 a shout; an outcry; a yell; 《文》 exclamatory noises (★ oof!, ouch!, ow! などのような).

わめきたてる 喚きたてる ⇨ わめく.

わめく 喚く 〈大声で〉 shout; cry; raise one's voice; yell; give [《文》 utter] a yell; 〈金切り声〉 shriek; scream; give [let out, 《文》 utter] a scream; 〈騒々しく〉《文》 make an outcry; clamor.

わやく 和訳 ¶和訳する translate [turn, 《文》 render, put] 《the English》 into Japanese / 英文和訳の問題 a passage of English set for translation into Japanese.

わようせっちゅう 和洋折衷 ¶和洋折衷の half-Japanese, half-Western 《furnishings》; 《a house》 in semi-European[-Western, -Japanese] style.

わら 藁 (rice) straw; a straw (1本) ¶わらを敷く cover 《a kennel》 with straw; litter 《a stall》 down / わらを束ねる bind [tie up] straw into a sheaf / わらでふく thatch 《a house》 with straw / わら靴 straw boots / わら細工 straw work / わら人形 a straw figure [doll, 《文》 effigy]; a man [woman] of straw / わら灰 straw ashes / わらぶき屋根 a straw-thatched roof / わら布団 a straw mattress; a palliasse.

わらい 笑い a laugh; laughter; 〈微笑〉 a smile; 〈嘲笑〉 a sneer ¶笑いを買う 〈招く〉 be laughed at 《by》; make oneself a laughingstock; 《文》 incur derision / 笑いを押える [こらえる] suppress [repress] a laugh [smile]; stifle one's laughter; 《cannot》 help laughing; keep a straight face; keep one's face straight / 笑い顔 a smiling face / 笑い声 laughter; a laughing voice / 笑い話 a funny story. 文例⇩

わらいぐさ 笑い草 〈物笑いの種〉 a laughingstock; a butt of ridicule ⇨ わらいもの.

わらいこける 笑いこける roll about [be convulsed] with laughter; be in stitches; laugh oneself to death; laugh one's head off.

わらいじょうご 笑い上戸 〈酒に酔うとよく笑う人〉 a laughing drunk; a happy [merry] drinker; 〈何かとよく笑う人〉 a person who starts laughing at the drop of a hat.

わらいだす 笑い出す burst out laughing; burst into (a roar of) laughter. 文例⇩

わらいとばす 笑い飛ばす laugh 《sb's fears》 off 《away》.

わらいもの 笑い物 ¶笑い物になる make a laughingstock [fool] of oneself; 《文》 be the butt of 《the villagers'》 ridicule. 文例⇩

わらう 笑う 〈声を出して〉 laugh; 〈微笑する〉 smile; 〈くすくす〉 chuckle; giggle; 〈歯を見せてにこっと〉 grin; 〈にやにや〉 simper; 〈げらげら〉 guffaw; 〈嘲笑する〉 laugh scornfully at sb; jeer [sneer] at sb; 《文》 deride 《sb》 / 一緒に笑う join in the laughter / 腹をかかえて笑う hold [split] one's sides with laughter / 腹の皮をよじって笑う be convulsed [《俗》 creased] with laughter / どっと笑う laugh uproariously; roar with laughter / 陰で[面と向かって]笑う laugh behind sb's back [in sb's face] / 笑いながら with a laugh [smile]; laughingly; smilingly / 笑うべき laughable; ridiculous; ludicrous; absurd. 文例⇩

わらじ 草鞋 straw sandals.

わらび 《植》 bracken.

ワラビー 《動》 a wallaby. 「song.

わらべ 童 ⇨ こども ¶わらべ歌 a children's

わらわせる 笑わせる make sb laugh; 《文》 excite [provoke] the laughter of 《the audience》. 文例⇩

わり(あい) 割(合) 〈率〉 a rate (★ 複数にはしない); 〈比率〉 a ratio (pl. -s); 〈百分率〉 (a) percentage ¶1割5分 15 per cent / 割りのいい 〈職業などが〉 paying; 《文》 remunerative; 《文》 lucrative; 〈取り引きなどが〉 profitable / 割りを食う 〈事が主語〉《文》 be disadvantageous to one; be [turn out] to one's disadvantage / 1日千円の割りで at the rate of 1,000 yen a day / 千人に対して1人の割合で in a [the] ratio of one to a thousand men / 割(合)に 〈比較的〉 comparatively; relatively; 〈いささか〉 rather; a little / 年の割りに for [considering] one's age [《文》 years] / 割りに合う pay / 割りに合わない do not pay / 割りと多くの quite a few [bit]. 文例⇩

わりあて 割り当て 《文》 (an) assignment; a quota; 《文》 an allotment; an allocation; 〈配給〉 a ration (of food) ¶割り当て制 the quota system / 〈仕事などの〉 割り当て分を完了する fulfill one's quota / 割り当て額[量] a quota; an allotment. 文例⇩

わらう 何を笑っているのだ. What are you laughing at? / 今度はこちらが奴らを笑う番だ. We have the laugh on them this time. / 君がどんなに笑っても僕は決心を変えないぞ. You cannot laugh me out of my decision. / 笑う門には福来たる. Fortune comes to a merry home.

わらわせる あの男が大臣になりたいって, 笑わせるね. He wants to be a cabinet minister? What a joke!

わり(あい) それ以来物価は2割も上がっている. Since then prices have risen by as much as 20 per cent. / 費用は1人5千円の割りとなった. The cost worked out at 5,000 yen per [a] head. / 児童の何割が欠席しましたか. What percentage of the children were absent? / 野球の嫌いな人が割りと多いらしい. There seem to be quite a few people that dislike baseball. / 医者の話では親父の病は割合に軽いということだ. The doctor told me that my father is not so seriously ill (as he appears to be).

わりあて すべての仕事に対して割

わりあてる 割り当てる allot;《文》assign; allocate;《文》apportion; parcel out;〈配給する〉ration. 文例⬇

わりいん 割り印 ¶割り印を押す put [《文》affix] a seal at the joining of two leaves (of a deed).

わりかん 割り勘《口語》a Dutch treat ¶割り勘にする share the expenses (with); split the cost;《口語》go Dutch (with sb). 文例⬇

わりきる 割り切る〈物事を〉give a clear solution to [of] (a problem);《文》adopt a clear-cut attitude on (a subject); see (things) only from a rational point of view.

わりきれる 割り切れる can be divided《by》;《文》be divisible (by) ¶割り切れない〈数が〉cannot be divided《by》;《文》be indivisible (by);〈気持ちが〉still have [feel] some doubt (as to); remain unconvinced (of); be still not quite happy (with). 文例⬇

わりこむ 割り込む wedge [squeeze] oneself in [into]; force one's way in [into]; break [cut] into (a conversation); intrude (oneself) in (a meeting);《口語》muscle in on (sb's territory) ¶列に割り込む cut into the line [in front of sb]; push in front of others;《英》jump the queue.

わりざん 割り算 division ¶割り算をする divide.

わりだか 割高 ¶割高である be rather [relatively] expensive;《文》be comparatively high in price [cost]; cost one quite a lot ; be a poor buy ; be a bad bargain.

わりだす 割り出す〈算出する〉calculate [estimate,《文》compute] (the cost at...);〈推断する〉infer (from);《文》deduce (from).

わりつけ 割り付け〘印刷〙a layout.

わりばし 割り箸 half-split (disposable) chopsticks.

わりびき 割引 (a) discount; (a) reduction ¶割引する〈値を引く〉discount; reduce; take [cut]《20 per cent》off; give [allow] a discount《off [on] the price》;〈手形を〉discount《a bill》¶1割引する make [allow] a discount of 10% [10% discount] off the price ; reduce the price by 10 per cent / 割引して《sell》at a reduced price; at a discount; at a cut rate / 話を多少割引して聞く accept [take] a story with a grain of salt ; discount a little of what sb says / 現金割引 a cash discount / 再割引 (a) rediscount / 団体割引 a group reduction [discount]; a discount on a party ticket / 割引切符 a reduced fare ticket / 割引券 a discount coupon / 割引手形〘債券〙a discounted bill [(loan) bond] / 割引歩合 a discount rate. 文例⬇

わりびく 割り引く ⇒わりびき(割引する) ¶手形を銀行で割引いてもらう get a bill discounted at a bank.

わりふる 割り振る ⇒ わりあてる.

わりまえ 割り前 a share ⇒ わけまえ ¶割り前を払う pay one's share of the expenses (with).

わりまし(きん) 割増(金)〈賃金の〉extra pay ;〈料金の〉an extra fare [charge]; a surcharge ;〈株金などの〉a premium; a bonus ¶割増金付き債券 a bond with a premium ; a premium-bearing debenture.

わりもどし 割り戻し a rebate (on) ¶割り戻しする rebate.

わりやす 割安 ¶割安である be relatively [rather] cheap;《文》be comparatively low in price [cost]; be a good bargain [buy].

わる¹ 悪 a wicked person;《口語》a bad lot ⇒ わるもの.

わる² 割る〈分割する〉divide; cut (切って);〈裂く〉split;《文》cleave;〈壊す〉break; smash ¶2つに割る divide [cut, split] sth in two ;〈折半する〉split [halve] (the profits) / 卵を割る break [crack] an egg / まきを割る chop wood / 水で割る mix [dilute] (whisky) with water; water《wine》(down) / 200円台を割る drop below the level of 200 yen / けんかの仲裁に割って入る go out of one's way to settle a quarrel ; take it on oneself to arbitrate a dispute ; step in between the two (as peacemaker). 文例⬇

わるあがき 悪あがき ¶悪あがきする《文》make a fruitless struggle (against); offer useless resistance (to); be a bad loser.

わるい 悪い〈不良な〉bad;〈不正な〉wrong ;〈邪悪な〉evil; wicked ;〈有害な〉harmful;《文》injurious ;〈粗悪な〉coarse ; inferior; poor;〈身体が〉ill; sick; unwell (★述部用法にしか使えない);〈不吉な〉unlucky ; ominous ;

り当て量が決められた. Quotas were laid down for all work.

わりあてる この教科書の第4章が僕に割り当てられました. I was assigned [My assignment was] the fourth chapter of the text.

わりかん 割り勘でいこうじゃないか. Let's split the cost (of the party). | Let's go Dutch.

わりきれる 30は6で割り切れる. Thirty is divisible by six (without a remainder). | 6 goes into 30. | 彼のやり方には割り切れないものを感じている. I am not quite satisfied [happy] with the steps he has taken. | I am still not sure whether his action was quite proper.

わりびき 彼の話は割引して聞かなければならない. His story must be taken with a grain of salt. | His story should not be accepted at face value. | You should discount something of what he says.

わる² 30割る5は6. Thirty divided by five makes [is, gives] six. | Five into thirty is six. | Divide 30 by 5 and you get 6. | 44を5で割ると8が立って4残る. Five goes into forty-four eight times with four over. | Five into forty-four is eight, remainder four.

わるい 悪い事はじき覚える. Man takes to vice easily. / 悪い事は続くものだ. Misfortunes never come singly [alone]. | It never rains but it pours.〘諺〙/ 彼は自分が悪かったことを認めた. He acknowledged that he was in the wrong. / 君が悪いんだ. The fault is yours. | You are to blame. / 悪いやつほどよく眠る. The worst villains have the easiest consciences. / この天候は作物には悪い. This weather is bad for the crops. / 君は顔色が悪い. You don't look very well. / どこか悪いのか. Is something the matter with you? / 目が少し悪いんです. I have something wrong with

わるがしこい

〈悪性の〉malignant ¶悪い事〈悪行〉《文》a wrong;《文》an evil deed;〈悪徳〉(a) vice;〈罪悪〉a sin / 悪い事をする do (something) wrong; commit a sin [crime] / 悪い風邪 a bad [nasty] cold / 悪い天候 bad [nasty] weather / 悪い知らせ bad [sad] news / 目に悪い be bad for [《文》injurious to] the eyes / 胃が悪い have [suffer from] stomach trouble / 顔色が悪い look pale / 気分が悪い feel ill [unwell, out of sorts] / 覚えが悪い〈理解〉《口語》be slow on the uptake;《文》be slow of understanding;〈記憶〉have a bad [poor] memory / 悪い事に unfortunately; as ill luck would have it / 一層悪いことに to make matters worse; what is worse / 悪くする make sth worse;〈重大化する〉aggravate;〈質〉corrupt; debase / 悪くすると / if the worst comes to the worst / 悪くなる grow [get] worse;〈いたむ〉go bad; spoil;〈品質などが〉deteriorate;〈退歩する〉degenerate / 人を悪く言う[思う] speak [think] badly [《文》ill] of sb / 悪くとる take sth amiss [《文》in ill part]. 文例⇩

わるがしこい 悪賢い sly; cunning; crafty ¶'wily.

わるぎ 悪気 malice; ill will ¶悪気のない innocent;〈人が〉well-meaning;〈言行が〉well-meant. 文例⇩

わるくち 悪口 abuse ¶悪口を言う say bad things about sb; abuse sb;〈英口語〉slang sb;《米俗》bad-mouth sb;《文》speak ill of sb.

わるさ 悪さ ⇨ いたずら, わるふざけ.

ワルシャワ Warsaw ¶ワルシャワ条約国 the Warsaw Pact nations [powers].

わるずれ 悪摺れ ¶悪ずれしている be oversophisticated; be too wise in the ways of the world.

わるだくみ 悪巧み《文》an evil design; a trick;〈陰謀〉《文》an intrigue; a plot ¶悪巧みをする plot《文》intrigue (against sb); 《文》form a sinister [wicked] design (on sb).

わるちえ 悪知恵 cunning; craft ¶悪知恵のある cunning; crafty; wily.

ワルツ a waltz ¶ワルツを踊る dance a waltz; waltz / ウインナワルツ a Viennese waltz.

わるのり 悪乗り ¶悪乗りする push [《米》press] one's luck; get carried away; overdo sth.

わるびれる 悪びれる ¶負けて悪びれない accept defeat gracefully [with (a) good grace]; be a good loser / 悪びれずに〈平然と〉calmly;《文》with composure;〈潔く〉with (a) good grace.

わるふざけ 悪ふざけ ¶悪ふざけする play a prank [practical joke] (on).

わるもの 悪者 a bad [wicked] fellow;《口語》a bad lot;《文》a knave; a rogue; a rascal; a scoundrel ¶悪者に仕立てる blacken sb's name [character]; paint sb in lurid colors.

わるよい 悪酔い ¶悪酔いする cannot hold one's drink [《米》liquor]; be [get] sick from drinking (too much) / 悪酔いするような酒 heady liquor.

われ 我〈私〉I;〈自身〉oneself;〈自我〉《文》self;《文》ego ¶我を忘れる forget [lose control of] oneself / 我に返る come to [recover] one's senses; come to (oneself) / 我勝ちに席を争う scramble for seats / 我知らず in spite of oneself; involuntarily. 文例⇩

われがね 破れ鐘 a cracked bell ¶われ鐘のような声で in a thunderous voice / われ鐘のような声でどなる thunder out.

われなべ 破れ鍋 a cracked pot. 文例⇩

われめ 割れ目 a crevice [crack] (in a rock); a fissure [chasm, cranny] (in the ground); a cleft (in a hoof); a crevasse (in the floe).

われもこう【植】a burnet.

われもの 割れ物〈割れた物〉a broken article;〈割れやすい物〉a fragile article. 文例⇩

われら 我等 ⇨ われわれ.

われる 割れる〈裂ける〉split; be split;〈亀裂が入る〉crack; be cracked;〈壊れる〉break; be broken; be smashed (めちゃめちゃに) ¶割れやすい fragile; easily broken; breakable; brittle / 割れるような拍手かっさいのうちに to [《文》amid(st)] thunderous [uproarious, wild] applause. 文例⇩

われわれ 我々 we ¶我々日本人は we Japanese / 我々の our / 我々のもの ours / 我々に[を] us.

わん¹ 椀 a (wooden) bowl ¶わんに盛る[盛って出す] serve in a bowl.

わん² 湾 a bay; a gulf (大きい) ¶湾をなす form a gulf [bay] / 東京湾 Tokyo Bay; the

---

my eyes. / 彼は心臓が悪い. He has heart trouble. / He has a weak heart. / 食べたくなかったけれども, 悪いから1つ取った. Though I had no appetite for them, I took one to be polite. / 悪い事に彼はこれですっかり慢心してしまいました. Unfortunately [The unfortunate part about it is that] it has made him very conceited. / だれでも人が自分のことをよく言うのを聞けば悪い気はしない. It makes anyone feel good to hear others speak well of him. / 悪い人にはいないから. You can trust me. | You can safely leave it to me. / 病人は急に悪くなった. The patient has taken a sudden turn for the worse. / 牛乳が悪くなった. The milk has gone bad [turned sour]./ 悪く思わないで下さい. Don't think badly [ill] of me. | No hard feelings, please! | このことで僕がきっと悪く言われるだろうなあ. I shall get the blame for this, I'm sure. | 悪くすると また雨だ. I fear [I'm afraid] it may rain again. / 悪く するだけない, 悪くない. There's no harm in trying.

わるぎ 悪気があってしたのじゃない. I meant well. | I meant no harm.

われ 我を忘れて喜んだ. He was beside himself with joy. / 皆我勝ちに外へ出ようとした. They made a rush all at once for the door. / 試験は我ながらうまくいった. I flatter myself that I did well in the examination.

われなべ われなべにとじぶた. Every Jack has his Jill.【諺】

われもの 割れ物注意.【表示】Fragile.

われる コップは粉々に割れた. The cup was broken in [smashed to] pieces. / 地震で地面が割れた. The earthquake caused fissures [cracks] to appear in the ground. / 頭が割れるほど痛い. I have a

わんきょく

Bay of Tokyo / メキシコ湾 the Gulf of Mexico / 湾口 the mouth [entrance] of a bay.

わんきょく 湾曲〈曲線〉a curve；〈曲がり〉a bend；curvature ¶湾曲する curve；bend / 湾曲した curved；bent；hooked / 内[外]側に湾曲した in-[out-]curved / 背骨の湾曲 the curvature of the spine / 腕の湾曲部〈ひじの内側〉the bend of the arm.

わんこつ 腕骨〔解〕the wristbone；the carpus (*pl.* -pi)；the carpal bone.

ワンサイドゲーム a one-sided game.

わんさと 《arrive》in swarms ⇒ おおぜい, たくさん ¶わんさと押しかける flock 《to》；throng 《to》.

わんしょう 腕章 an armband；a brassard ¶腕章をつける wear an armband.

ワンダーフォーゲル [<《ドイツ語》 *Wandervogel*] ¶ワンダーフォーゲル部 a hiking [backpacking] club.

ワンタッチ 文例⇩

わんにゅう 湾入 ¶湾入する curve in. 文例⇩

わんぱく 腕白 ¶腕白な naughty；mischievous；impish / 腕白小僧 a naughty [mischievous] boy；an urchin.

ワンピース a one-piece dress.

ワンマン an autocrat；a dictatorial leader [chief] ¶ワンマンカー[バス] a one-man(-operated) bus；a conductorless bus / ワンマン政治 one-man rule；autocracy / ワンマンショー a one-man show / ワンマン振りを発揮する play the autocrat；《口語》boss it.

わんりょく 腕力 physical [muscular, brute] strength；〈暴力〉brute force；violence ¶腕力が強い be very strong；《文》have great physical strength / 腕力を用いる[に訴える] use force；《文》resort [have recourse] to force [violence].

わんわん〈犬のほえ声〉bowwow；〈犬〉《小児語》a bowwow；a doggie ¶わんわんほえる bark《at a stranger》；bowwow.

を

-を ¶通りを歩いて行く walk along [up, down] the street / 絵を見る look at the picture / 安否を気遣う be anxious about *sb's* safety / 人の頭を打つ hit *sb* on the head / 腕を捕える take *sb's* arm；take *sb* by the arm / 金を強奪する rob *sb* of *his* money / 勇気をたたえる praise *sb* for *his* courage / びんに水を一杯入れる fill a bottle with water.

囲囲「猫がねずみを殺した」は英語で The cat killed a rat. と言って、「ねずみの」の「を」は単に a rat が killed の後に位置することによって示され、「を」に相当する語が英語中に特にあるわけではない. ただし「通りを行く」「絵を見る」は walk along the street, look at the picture となり、名詞が動詞の後にすぐ続かずに、その前に前置詞を必要とすることも少なくない. また、たとえば、「人の頭を打つ」という時、hit *sb* on the head と言って、他動詞の動作の対象になる人がまず目的語にきて、その動作の及ぶ箇所を前置詞を伴う句—この場合は on the head—で表わし、それを目的語である人の後に置くことが多い.

splitting headache. / 党が3つに割れた. The party divided [split] into three factions. / 粟が3つに割れた. The vote was split three ways.

ワンタッチ ワンタッチですべて完了. You just push the button and the machine will do the rest.

わんにゅう 海が陸地に深く湾入している. An arm of the sea penetrates deep into the land.

付　　録

不規則動詞活用表 1351

米英の綴り字の違い 1354

英　語　句　読　法 1355

英語の手紙・名刺・履歴書 1362

年　号　対　照　表 1369

度量衡複式換算表 1370

不規則動詞活用表

この表に掲げた動詞は、日常英語としてよく用いられているものに限っている。overdrink, rewrite などの複合語の活用は、drink, write などから容易に知ることができるので、特に頻繁に使われるものでない限り、省いた。活用中、現在では古形と考えられるもの(たとえば、write の過去形・過去分詞としての writ など)は記載しなかった。また《米》と《英》の違いがある時は、そのつど示した。なお lie (横たわる), fly (飛ぶ) のように日本語が添えてあるのは、規則変化をする「うそをつく」の lie,「(野球で)フライを打つ」の fly との混同を避けるためである。

原 形	過 去 形	過去分詞	原 形	過 去 形	過去分詞
abide	abode, abided	abode, abided	**burst**	burst	burst
arise	arose	arisen	**buy**	bought	bought
awake	awoke, awaked	awaked, awoke	**cast**	cast	cast
			catch	caught	caught
be (現在形 **am, is, are**)	was; were	been	**chide**	chid, 《米のみ》chided	chidden, chid, 《米のみ》chided
bear	bore	borne, born	**choose**	chose	chosen
beat	beat	beaten, 《米のみ》beat	**cleave** (裂く)	clove, cleft, cleaved	cloven, cleft, cleaved
become	became	become			
befall	befell	befallen	**cleave** (固着する)	cleaved, clove	cleaved
beget	begot	begotten			
begin	began	begun	**cling**	clung	clung
behold	beheld	beheld	**come**	came	come
bend	bent	bent	**cost**	cost	cost
bereave	bereaved, bereft	bereaved, bereft	**creep**	crept	crept
			cut	cut	cut
beseech	besought	besought	**deal**	dealt	dealt
beset	beset	beset	**dig**	dug	dug
bet	bet,《英のみ》betted	bet,《英のみ》betted	**do**	did	done
			draw	drew	drawn
bid	bade, bid	bidden, bid	**dream**	《主に米》dreamed, 《主に英》dreamt	《主に米》dreamed, 《主に英》dreamt
bide	bided, bode	bided			
bind	bound	bound			
bite	bit	bitten, bit			
bleed	bled	bled	**drink**	drank	drunk
bless	blessed, blest	blessed, blest	**drive**	drove	driven
			dwell	dwelt, 《米のみ》dwelled	dwelt, 《米のみ》dwelled
blow	blew	blown			
break	broke	broken			
breed	bred	bred	**eat**	ate	eaten
bring	brought	brought	**fall**	fell	fallen
broadcast	broadcast, broadcasted	broadcast, broadcasted	**feed**	fed	fed
			feel	felt	felt
			fight	fought	fought
build	built	built	**find**	found	found
burn	《主に米》burned, 《主に英》burnt	《主に米》burned, 《主に英》burnt	**flee**	fled	fled
			fling	flung	flung
			fly (飛ぶ)	flew	flown
			forbear	forbore	forborne

不規則動詞活用表

原形	過去形	過去分詞	原形	過去形	過去分詞
forbid	forbade, forbad	forbidden	**lie** (横たわる)	lay	lain
forecast	forecast, forecasted	forecast, forecasted	**light**	lighted, lit	lighted, lit
foresee	foresaw	foreseen	**lose**	lost	lost
foretell	foretold	foretold	**make**	made	made
forget	forgot	forgotten	**mean**	meant	meant
forgive	forgave	forgiven	**meet**	met	met
forsake	forsook	forsaken	**mislay**	mislaid	mislaid
freeze	froze	frozen	**mislead**	misled	misled
get	got	got, (米のみ) gotten	**mistake**	mistook	mistaken
			misunderstand	misunderstood	misunderstood
gild	gilded, gilt	gilded, gilt	**mow**	mowed	mowed, mown
gird	girded, girt	girded, girt			
give	gave	given	**overcast**	overcast	overcast
go	went	gone	**overcome**	overcame	overcome
grave	graved	graven, graved	**overhang**	overhung	overhung
			overhear	overheard	overheard
grind	ground	ground	**oversee**	oversaw	overseen
grow	grew	grown	**overtake**	overtook	overtaken
hang (つるす)	hung	hung	**overthrow**	overthrew	overthrown
			partake	partook	partaken
have (現在形 **have, has**)	had	had	**pay**	paid	paid
			plead	pleaded, (米のみ) pled	pleaded, (米のみ) pled
hear	heard	heard	**put**	put	put
heave	heaved, hove	heaved, hove	**quit**	quitted, quit	quitted, quit
hew	hewed	hewn, hewed	**read**	read	read
			rend	rent	rent
hide	hid	hidden, hid	**repay**	repaid	repaid
hit	hit	hit	**rid**	rid, ridded	rid, ridded
hold	held	held	**ride**	rode	ridden
hurt	hurt	hurt	**ring**	rang	rung
inlay	inlaid	inlaid	**rise**	rose	risen
keep	kept	kept	**run**	ran	run
kneel	knelt, (米のみ) kneeled	knelt, (米のみ) kneeled	**saw**	sawed	sawn, sawed
			say	said	said
knit	knit, knitted	knit, knitted	**see**	saw	seen
know	knew	known	**seek**	sought	sought
lay	laid	laid	**sell**	sold	sold
lead	led	led	**send**	sent	sent
lean	(主に米) leaned, (主に英) leant	(主に米) leaned, (主に英) leant	**set**	set	set
			sew	sewed	sewn, sewed
			shake	shook	shaken
			shear	sheared	shorn, sheared
leap	leapt, leaped	leapt, leaped	**shed**	shed	shed
			shine (光る)	shone	shone
learn	learned, learnt	learned, learnt	**shoot**	shot	shot
			show	showed	shown, showed
leave	left	left			
lend	lent	lent	**shrink**	shrank, shrunk	shrunk
let	let	let			

原　　形	過　去　形	過去分詞	原　　形	過　去　形	過去分詞
shut	shut	shut	**strew**	strewed	strewn, strewed
sing	sang	sung	**stride**	strode	stridden
sink	sank	sunk	**strike**	struck	struck
sit	sat	sat	**string**	strung	strung
slay	slew	slain	**strive**	strove, strived	striven, strived
sleep	slept	slept			
slide	slid	slid, slidden	**swear**	swore	sworn
sling	slung	slung	**sweep**	swept	swept
slink	slunk	slunk	**swell**	swelled	swollen, swelled
slit	slit	slit			
smell	(主に米) smelled, (主に英) smelt	(主に米) smelled, (主に英) smelt	**swim**	swam	swum
			swing	swung	swung
smite	smote	smitten	**take**	took	taken
sow	sowed	sown, sowed	**teach**	taught	taught
			tear	tore	torn
speak	spoke	spoken	**tell**	told	told
speed	sped, speeded	sped, speeded	**think**	thought	thought
			thrive	throve, thrived	thriven, thrived
spell	(主に米) spelled, (主に英) spelt	(主に米) spelled, (主に英) spelt	**throw**	threw	thrown
			thrust	thrust	thrust
			tread	trod	trodden, trod
spend	spent	spent	**undergo**	underwent	undergone
spill	(主に米) spilled, (主に英) spilt	(主に米) spilled, (主に英) spilt	**understand**	understood	understood
			undertake	undertook	undertaken
			undo	undid	undone
			uphold	upheld	upheld
spin	spun	spun	**upset**	upset	upset
spit	spat, (米のみ) spit	spat, (米のみ) spit	**wake**	waked, woke	waked, woken, woke
split	split	split	**waylay**	waylaid	waylaid
spoil	(主に米) spoiled, (主に英) spoilt	(主に米) spoiled, (主に英) spoilt	**wear**	wore	worn
			weave	wove	woven
			wed	wedded, wed	wedded, wed
spread	spread	spread	**weep**	wept	wept
spring	sprang, (米のみ) sprung	sprung	**wet**	wetted, wet	wetted, wet
			win	won	won
			wind	wound	wound
stand	stood	stood	**withdraw**	withdrew	withdrawn
steal	stole	stolen	**withhold**	withheld	withheld
stick	stuck	stuck	**withstand**	withstood	withstood
sting	stung	stung	**wring**	wrung	wrung
stink	stank, stunk	stunk	**write**	wrote	written

米英の綴り字の違い

綴り字の相違の主要なルールを掲げた。

《米》	《英》	《米》	《英》
-l-	**-ll-**	**-se**	**-ce**
councilor	councillor	defense	defence
jeweler	jeweller	license	licence
traveler	traveller		
woolen	woollen	**-i-**	**-y-**
		syrup, sirup	syrup
-ll-	**-l-**	tire	tyre, tire
enroll	enrol		
fulfill	fulfil	**-o-**	**-ou-**
skillful	skilful	mold	mould
		smolder	smoulder
-or	**-our**		
color	colour	**-ck-**	**-qu-**
endeavor	endeavour	check	cheque
favor	favour	checkered	chequered
labor	labour		
vapor	vapour	**-k-**	**-c-**
		disk	disc
-er	**-re**	skeptic	sceptic
center	centre		
meter	metre	**-m**	**-mme**
meager	meagre	gram	gram(me)
theater	theatre	program	programme

英 語 句 読 法

話される英語は、間合いや抑揚によって、文意を聞き手にわかりやすく伝えることができるが、書かれた英語では、それができないので、各種の符号によって、その欠陥を補う。この点では、日本語の文章でも事情は似ているが、西洋の文章に接するまでの伝統的な日本文では、書き手が句読点を付ける習慣がなく、読み手のほうで自分の読みやすいように、勝手に句読点を入れていた。現代日本文に見る句読点は、主として、西洋の書き言葉の表記法の影響によるものである。日本語の場合は、そういう歴史的事情もあって、句読法は比較的単純で、用いられる記号も、句点（。）・読点（、）・なかぐろ（・）・かぎ括弧（「」）・括弧（（ ））と挙げればほぼ尽きる。

これに比べれば、英語の句読法に用いられる符号は多様であり、日本文を書くときの句読法とはかなり異なるこまかい配慮が必要である。

英語の句読点 (punctuation marks) を列挙してみると、次のようになる。

.	period [full stop]	終止符, ピリオド
:	colon	コロン
;	semicolon	セミコロン
,	comma	コンマ
—	dash	ダッシュ
-	hyphen	ハイフン
/	solidus	斜線
?	question mark	疑問符
!	exclamation mark	感嘆符
( )	parentheses	丸括弧
[ ]	brackets	角括弧
" "	double quotation marks	引用符
' '	single quotation marks	引用符
'	apostrophe	アポストロフィ
...	three dots	点3つ

各句読点の使い方

句読点の使い方は、時代や個人の好みによってかなりの違いがあり、また英米の差ということもある。従って以下に述べることは、一般に行なわれているだいたいの目安であると思っていただきたい。

Period [Full stop] .

話し言葉でならば、文はおおむね下降調になって終わり、次の文に移る前に発声の休止がある。書き言葉でその代わりをするのがピリオドである。

　It's three o'clock. Let's have a rest.

ピリオドは、このほかに、省略形の語のあと、略語の各イニシャルのあとにも付けられる。

　Mr. Brown / Ms. Sato / Dr. Jones / Mt. Fuji / etc. / T. S. Eliot

ただし、最近の《英》では、このピリオドを省くようになってきている。

Colon :

1 コロンは、昔は文中の大きな切れ目に使われた。

　To be, or not to be: that is the question.

2 また、直接話法の引用符で囲まれた伝達内容の前にもコロンを置く習慣

英語句読法

があった。

 She asked: "Well, how are you getting on?"

上のようなコロンの使用はいずれも、今日ではコンマにするのが普通である。一般に、コロンの使用は以前より減少してきている。今でもコロンが使われるのは、次のような場合である。

3 先行の文で述べたことの具体例を述べる場合、先行の文のあとにコロンを置く。

 The gear lever has six positions: neutral, four forward speeds, and reverse. (変速レバーは位置が6か所ある。すなわちニュートラルと前進変速4段階と、後退である)

 The definite article normally precedes ordinal numbers:
 the seventh day
 the eighth floor

4 項目名などのあとにコロンを置いて、それに属する下位項目や事例を列挙する。

 Punctuation marks: periods, colons, semicolons, commas, etc.

5 時刻の表記
 10:45 a.m.
 4:05 p.m.

ただし、コロンを使うのは主に《米》で、《英》では 10.45 a.m. / 4.05 p.m. とピリオドを使うことが多い。

6 手紙の本文の冒頭
 Dear Sir:

このようにコロンを使うのは《米》であらたまった手紙の場合だけ。《米》でも親しい関係の人に出す私信では、コロンではなくコンマを使う。
 Dear John,

7 論文などのあとに添える参考文献に、著者名と書名を記載するのに、以前は、
 Edwin O. Reischauer: *The Japanese*

のように著者名とイタリック体の書名の間にコロンを置くことが多かったが、これも今ではコンマが用いられるようになっている。

 Edwin O. Reischauer, *The Japanese*

Semicolon ;

1 セミコロンは句切りというよりは、文と文をつなぐ役を演じる句読点である。2つの文が、意味の上ではかなり密接なつながりがある場合、話し言葉ならば、抑揚とか文の間の休止の短いことで、それが聞き手にわかるが、書き言葉ではセミコロンの使用によってその事情が伝えられる。

 Some people gave their approval to the idea; others were against it. (その案で結構だという者もあれば、だめだという者もあった)

 You ought to know that; I learned it from you. (それはご存じのはずです。なにしろ、あなたから教えていただいたんですから)

2 セミコロンは、コンマより大きな句切りであるから、コンマを含んだ語句を句切るのにも使われる。

 The family was going for a drive; father sat behind the steering wheel; mother, beside him; and the children, at the back. (一家はドライブに出かけるところだった。父親が運転席につき、母親がそのわきに、子供たちはうしろの座席に座った)

 We have more or less three meals every day: breakfast, lunch, dinner; or breakfast, dinner, supper.

日本語の文章で、文の句切りを示すのは主として句点(。)と読点(、)だけであるために、日本人は英文を書く際にもピリオドとコンマのみを使って、セミコロンを使ったほうがよいときに、それに思いいたらない人が多い。英文を書く際に、この点は留意すべきことであろう。

Comma ,

コンマは文の中の句切りを示す句読点である。日本語の読点は、主として息の継ぎ目を示すと一般に考えられている。英語のコンマについても同じことは言えるが、それだけではなく、文の構造を明らかにし、文意がまぎらわしくならないようにする働きも兼ねる。したがって、コンマ1つの使い方によって、文の意味ががらりと変わることも時にはありうる。

コンマの使い方については、言うべきことがいくつもあるので、以下箇条書き風に解説をまとめてみよう。

1 and, but, or, so などの接続詞で等位節をつなぐ場合、これらの接続詞の前にコンマを置くか置かないかは、一律には言えない。and は、先行の節が長いときとか、前後関係から特にその必要があるときは別として、コンマを置かないことが多い。but と or はどちらかというとコンマを置く。so は必ず置く。個人の好みや、文体上の問題もあるが、だいたいこのように理解しておけばいいだろう。なお、「しかし、…」のつもりで but, … と、but のあとにコンマを打つ人がよくいるが、これはやってはいけない。

The rain stopped about four o'clock and I went out for a walk.

It was night by the time I reached the little town, and I was tired.

It's hard work, but it has to be done.

Have you done this before, or is it your first attempt?

The man seemed drunk, so I kept away from him.

2 if, when, because, before, after, since, etc. で導かれる副詞節が主節の前にあるときは、副詞節と主節の間にコンマを置くことが多い。主節が先行するときはコンマを使わないのが普通。

If she comes, I'll ask her.

I'll ask her if she comes.

Before he went to the dining room, he had a bath.

He had a bath before he went to the dining room.

3 非制限関係節の前にコンマを置く。また関係節が文の中間に挿入されている場合は、その前後にコンマを置く。

He had a daughter, who was married to a doctor. (娘がひとりあって、医者と結婚していた) ★コンマがないと「医者と結婚した娘があった」で他にも娘があった意味合いになりうる。

My grandmother, who is over sixty, still goes mountain-climbing.

4 文構造の面から、文の他の部分と密接に結びついていない間投詞・接続詞・副詞語句などは、そのことを明らかにするためにコンマで句切る。これらの語句が文の中に挿入される場合は、その前後にコンマを置く。

Well, I'm not sure.

No, she isn't here.

Nowadays, however, things are all designed to let us do less and less walking.

Other things being equal, this is better because it is cheaper.

Romeo, believing that Juliet was dead, drank the poison and died.

We are sitting, as it were, on a volcano.

5 同格名詞もコンマで句切る。

Herbert, our captain, has broken his leg.

ただし、次のような場合は例外。

We Japanese live on rice.

6 引用符を用いる直接話法の記述でのコンマの用法については ⇨ Quotation marks (p. 1360).

7 名詞を列挙するときは A, B, C, and D のようにコンマで 1 つずつ句切るが、and の前のコンマは落とすこともある。《英》では落とすのが普通。

I visited Chicago, St. Louis, Washington(,) and New York.

8 住所氏名、著書などもコンマで句切ってわかりやすくする。ただし、住所氏名はこのコンマを省く人が多くなっている。

John Lennon,
　32-A Abbey Road,
　　St. John's Wood,
　　　London.
　　　　NW8 9AU

Leonard Bloomfield, *Language*.

Dash ―

ダッシュの使い方は、個人差がかなり大きく、セミコロンやコンマでよいところをダッシュにする人もいるが、乱用はしないがいい。

1 ダッシュの代表的な使い方は、文の中断もしくは、言いかけたことを、中途で別の言い方に変えることを示す場合であろう。

But despite―I say despite―this excellent gift his performance is not without defects. (以上のようなすぐれた才能にもかかわらず――かかわらずですよ――彼の演技に難点がないとは言えない)

Would you―could you―tell me how to get there? (どう行けばよいか教えていただけませんか、ご存じありませんか)

会話文ならば、話し手が言葉につまった感じがダッシュによって伝えられる。

Oh, dear! I thought you would―

2 文の初めに具体的な名詞を挙げて、それを代名詞でまとめて言うのには、ダッシュが最適である。

Kitty, Caroline, Dawn, Eileen, Vera―these are all English female names.

3 以上のダッシュは厳密に言うとエムダッシュ (em dash) と呼ぶ。これを半分の長さにした、ハイフンよりやや長めのダッシュ (タイプライターではハイフンで代用する) をエヌダッシュ (en dash) と称し、次のような場合に使う。

from 1980 to 1984 または between 1980 and 1984 と書く代わりに、
　1980-84
と書く。

この形式は人物の生年と没年を示すのにも使えるが、現存者の場合はダッシュのあとを空白にしておく。

Hemingway, Ernest (1899-1961)
Nixon, Richard (1913-　)

しかし、この空白はいかにも死ぬのを待っているかのような感じになるから、現存者の場合は次のようにする傾向がある。

(b. 1913)　★ b. は born の略。

Hyphen -

1 2 つの語をハイフンで結合して合成語をつくる。

forty-nine
mother-in-law

合成語はハイフンを使わずに 2 語を結合して 1 語となっているもの (hairsplitting / hardheaded)、ハイフンで結合したもの (hair-raising / hard-boiled)、結合しない 2 語の形で使うもの (hair spray / hard cash) と 3 通りある。そのいずれか確かでない場合は辞書で調べたほうがよい。

ハイフンにはまた、意味があいまいになるのを防ぐ効用もある。たとえば a fast sailing ship は (1)「高速で走っている船」か (2)「高速船」か、いずれとも判じがたいが、a fast-sailing ship とすれば (2) の意であることが明らかになる。

2 なお、行末で語の一部を次の行へまわすとき、行末にハイフンをつけて、そのことを明らかにする。その際、単語は音節単位で分割しなければならない。これも、確かでないときは辞書をひくべきである。

Solidus /

主として、表記の簡略化のために使われる。主な使い方として次のようなものがある。

1 or の代わりに。

People with a knowledge of Spanish and/or French are welcome.（スペイン語とフランス語、またはそのいずれかの心得ある方歓迎）

Mrs. Browning buys her clothes cheap/cheaply.

2 per の代わりに。

km/h

3 分数の「分子/分母」を表わす。

5/17　★ 5 over 17 と読む。

4 年月日の区分を示す。「1983年10月8日」は次のようになる。

《米》10/8/1983
《英》8/10/1983

また、こよみの上で2年にまたがっていることを示すのに、次のような表記をする。

winter 1982/83　★ 1982 to 83 と読む。

Question mark ?

疑問文の末尾に付ける。形は疑問文ではないが、文末が上昇調になって、質問のつもりの文も ? を付ける。

Where did I put it?
Did you see my watch anywhere?
You've eaten them all?
Do it again? Why?

逆に、形は疑問文でも意味が依頼・要求の場合はピリオドでもよい。

Will you please repeat after me.
Will the audience please rise.

Exclamation mark !

感嘆文のあとには感嘆符を必ず付けるが、感嘆文でなくとも、強い感情を伴った発話・叫びにはこのしるしを付けてよい。

What a pleasure it is to meet you again!
He did drink a lot of whisky!
Here it is!
Look out!
Oh! I'm frightened.

Parentheses ( )

文の中で、または文と文の間で丸括弧を使うのは、書き手が何か説明を加えたいときで、ダッシュの用法と似ているが、ダッシュよりもさらに本文の構造や記述内容の筋道に拘束されないで補足説明をしたいときに使う。文中に挿入された丸括弧の中の文には終止符は打たない。

There were social distinctions, more marked than those of today, and there was poverty (in *Little Women*, it will be remembered, the family is at one time so hard up that one of the girls sells her hair to the barber), but there was not, as there is now, an all-prevailing sense of helplessness.
—George Orwell

While at Broadstairs I was taken to see Sir Moses Montefiore, an old and much revered Jew who lived in the neighbourhood. (According to the Encyclopaedia, he had retired in 1824.) This was the first time I became aware of the existence of Jews outside the Bible.
—Bertrand Russell

Brackets [ ]

角括弧は、引用文の途中か末尾に引用者が自分の注を付けるとか、編集者が本文について同様に注を施すときに使う。

Henry Adam [sic], author of *The Education of Henry Adams* ★ sic は「原文のまま」の意。

雑誌の連載記事の末尾に付ける「つづく」「次号完結」などに相当する指示も角括弧に入れる。

[*To be continued*]
[*To be concluded*]

Quotation marks " " ' '

1 人の言った言葉をそのまま引用するときに用いる。ダブルにするかシングルにするかは、好みの問題であるが、《米》ではダブル、《英》ではシングルが好んで用いられる。

引用文の中に、さらに引用文を挿入するときは、ダブルで始めたときは中の文をシングルにして

" ……… '………,' ……… "

のようにし、シングルで始めたならば、逆に

' ……… " ……… " ………,'

とすればよい。

2 引用符を用いる直接話法には、他の句読点の使い方も関連がある。

そのことで注意すべき点を、以下に箇条書きにしてみよう。

(1) 引用符を開く前にコンマを置き、引用文の終わりが、全体の文の終わりとなるならば、終止符は引用文の終止符だけにする。

He answered, "I don't know."

(2) 引用文が疑問文・感嘆文の場合は、(1)の引用文の終止符を疑問符・感嘆符に代え、この場合も全文の終止符は省く。

She asked, "Where did you get it?"

My friend said, "How funny!"

(3) 全体の文が疑問文の場合は、引用符を閉じた後に？を付ける。感嘆文でも同様のことが言えるだろうが、そういう実例はあまり考えられない。

Why did he say, "I don't quite like it"?

(4) 引用文で文が始まり、文の途中で引用符を閉じる場合は、その前にコンマ（または場合に応じて疑問符か感嘆符）を置く。

"I'll try," he said.
"What's the matter?" asked Jane.
"Wait for me!" she shouted.

(5) 引用文を前後2つに分けて、伝達動詞をその間に置く場合も、以上の(1)から(4)の句読法を適用すればよい。また、あとの引用文が独立した文となりうるならば、これだけを別の文とすることもできる。

"I've had nothing yet," Alice replied in an offended tone, "so I can't take more."

"Sssh! dear," she whispered. "Don't wake Daddy!"

(6) 1人の人物が長々と話すのを、数パラグラフにわたって引用するときは、次のように途中のパラグラフの終わりは引用符を閉じないでおく。

" ………………………
  " ………………………
" ………………………
  " ………………………
………………………… "

3 引用符は、以上の他に、文中の特定の語句そのものを問題としていることを示すのに使われる。

We never speak of men as "pretty" or "beautiful".

Water from the 'cold' tap is safe to drink.

4 本・雑誌・新聞の名は普通イタリック体にするが、それらに掲載された論文・文芸作品などの題名は、ローマ体にして引用符で囲む。

"The Leader of the People" from *The Red Pony* by John Steinbeck.

"The Talk of the Town" department in *The New Yorker*.

Apostrophe '

1 名詞の語尾に -'s を付けて、所有格をつくる。

the lion's share
a girls' high school
Charles's property ★ Charles's は [tʃáəlziz] と発音する。これは Charles' と書くこともある。その場合は[tʃaəlz] と発音する。

2 語の縮約形で、省略部分を示す。

ma'am (<madam)
I'm (<I am)
don't (<do not)
'84 (<1984)

3 数字、文字、名詞に転用された他品詞の複数形は -'s を付ける。

Your 5's look like 6's.

It was in the late 1970's. ★ 1970's を 1970s と書く人も少なくない。

Dot your i's and cross your t's.

M.A.'s and Ph.D.'s

There are six that's on end in this sentence. (この文には that が続けて6つ並んでいる)

Three dots ...

引用文の始めか中間を省略するときに点3つを置く。末尾の省略は、ピリオドを加えて点4つとする。やたらにたくさんの点を打つ人がいるが、英語の句読法を知らない者の印象を与えるから、やめたほうがいい。

英語の手紙・名刺・履歴書

手　　　紙

われわれ日本人は、手紙を書くときには、普段の話し言葉とは違う、あらたまった堅苦しい言葉使いで文章を書く習慣がある。昔はごく親しい仲でも、そうろう文で書いたものだし、今でも男性で自分のことを「小生」、息子を「愚息」、自分の家を「拙宅」と書く人は結構いる。書き出しも、「陽春の候、貴下にはますます御健勝のこととお慶び申し上げます」といった、紋切り型の時候のあいさつをするのはめずらしいことではない。

英語で手紙を書くときは、むしろその逆をやったほうがよい。相手とのつきあいの程度にもよるが、概して言えることは、特に構えないで、気楽に、相手に伝えたいことを書けばよい。心にもない美辞麗句や、紋切り型の無内容な言葉を避けて、それでいて言うべきところには充分言葉が尽くされた文章が、現代の英語の手紙ではよいとされる。英語で手紙を書くときの心構えとして、これは大切なことであるから、初めに特に強調しておきたい。

それにしても、英語の手紙の形式は、日本語の手紙とは大分勝手が違うし、どんな気ままな人でも一応守る書式というものがある。英語で手紙を書く以上、それは一通り心得ておかなくてはならない。

まず、用紙と筆記具について。用紙は線のない無地のものが品がよいとされる。筆記具はペンで、インクの色は黒か青が無難。好みによってセピアとかターコイスもよいが、赤は非常識。このあたりの判断は、日本語の手紙を書くときとだいたい同じだと思ってよい。

ペンによる手書きは、書いた人の人柄がじかに伝わってくるので、親しい仲では喜ばれる。英米人は、字のうまいへたはあまり気にしない。書いた字に個性のあらわれるのを尊ぶ。そういうわけで、私信には手書きの手紙を書く人が多い。ただし、手書きの欠点は、読みにくいことである。そう思う人はタイプライターで打ってもよいが、くやみの手紙など、深い感情をこめて書く場合は、やはり手書きのほうが適切である。一方、あまり親しくしない人に出す事務的な内容の手紙は、タイプライターのほうがよい。

手紙の書式については、書く事柄を用紙の上から下への順に列挙してみると、次のようになる。

頭書―書き出しのあいさつ―本文―結辞―署名

1　頭書 (heading)

英語の手紙では、発信者の住所と日付けを用紙の右上に書く。

日付けは、月・日・年の順に書くが、《英》では、日・月・年の順にする人が多い。年の前にコンマを打つかどうかは好みによる。また、日を《米》は、21日なら単に21と数字を書くのに対して、《英》では21st と序数語尾を付ける人が多い。月は、May, June, July 以外は January → Jan. のように略形を用いてもよい。略形については、本文の各月の項を見ていただきたい。

2　書き出しのあいさつ (salutation)

頭書の下端から2行ほどあけて、左側に My dear John とか Dear Mr. Madison のような書き出しのあいさつを書き、コンマを打つ。格式ばった手紙では、この

コンマをコロンにする傾向が米国人には強い。この部分は、相手との親しさの度合いに応じて、いろいろな書き方がある。
　ごく親しい者どうしならば、
　　Dear John,
　　My dear John,
と、姓ではなく、その人の呼び名 (first name) を書く。それほど親しくなければ、
　　Dear Mr. Madison,
と、敬称付きの姓 (surname, last name) を書く ⇨ -くん (本文)。この場合は My dear Mr. Madison と my を付けることはしない。敬称は、女性ならばもちろん、既婚者には Mrs., 未婚者は Miss とする。そのいずれにも使える形として、近ごろは Ms. がある ⇨ -さま (本文)。大学の先生には Professor, 博士と医師は Dr. とする。

　官庁・会社・学校などに宛てて出す手紙で、特定の個人名を書きようがないときは、宛先が The Admissions Officer, University of Sheffield とか、The Manager, Hudson Department Store とか、The Chief of Police, Boondock County のように個人の役職者ならば
　《米》(Dear) Sir:
　《英》(Dear) Sir,
と書く。これに対して、The Admissions Office とか、The Hudson Department Store, Ltd. とか、The Boondock County Police Department のように組織・団体名を宛先とする場合は
　《米》(Dear) Sirs:
　《英》(Dear) Sirs,
とする。相手が女性とわかっていれば、Sir, Sirs の代わりに Madam, Mesdames (複数) を使う。

3 本文 (body paragraphs)

　相手に伝えたいことを書けばよい。「陽春の候、貴下にはますます…」といった時候のあいさつは、英語の手紙では書かない。といっても、天候のことを全く書いてはいけないということではなく、まず初めに天候を話題にしたいと思うならば、それは自由である。要するに、紋切り型の書き出しの作法は英語の手紙にはないということである。

　わかりやすい文で、適当にパラグラフを改めて、相手がざっと一読して容易に文意がつかめるような書き方がよい。文章も、おたがいに知っている仲ならば、相手にむかって話しかけているような感じで、I am → I'm, I will → I'll と縮約形を盛んに使ったりして、くだけた調子のいわゆる会話体で書くのがよい。それほど親しくない人や自分より地位の高い人に対しても、私信はあまり堅苦しい言葉使いをする必要はなく、縮約形を控えめにするとか、言葉使いをやや丁寧にするくらいでよい。この点が、日本語の手紙を書く場合と大いに異なる。

4 結辞 (complimentary close)

　本文の終わりには、Sincerely yours とか Yours truly といった、だいたい決まり文句になっている言葉を、行を改めて、右の方へ寄せて書く。そしてそのあとにコンマを打つ。
　結辞でもっともよく使われる形は、
　　Sincerely yours,
　　Truly yours,
である。《英》では順序を逆にした
　　Yours sincerely,
　　Yours truly,
もよく使われる。相手が社会的に地位の高い人の場合には、少しあらたまって
　　Very truly yours,
　　Very respectfully yours,
　《英》Faithfully yours,
のような語を用いる。

5 署名 (signature)

　結辞の下に署名することを忘れてはいけない。署名は、例えば戸田正夫ならば、Masao Toda とちゃんとフルネームで書くか、親しい仲ならば Masao だけにし

てもよいが、M. Toda と、個人の呼び名は略さないほうがよい。タイプライターで打った手紙の場合は、署名の下にタイプで同じ名前を打っておくと読みまちがいを防ぐことができる。

6 追伸 (postscript)

手紙をひと通り書いてしまってから、書き忘れたことを追加するいわゆる追伸は P.S. と断わって、書き足す。

Sincerely yours,
Masao Toda

P.S.　Emma gave birth to four puppies two weeks ago.

手紙の例

下の例の頭書の住所は東京都渋谷区上原2丁目8番20号を、郵政省指定の方式で英字にしたものだが、8-20, Uehara 2 chome は、いっそのこと日本字で書く際に多くの人に慣用されている上原2—8—20 をそのまま英字にした Uehara 2-8-20 のほうが安全確実であろう。この部分を実際に正確に読む必要のあるのは、日本の郵便配達人であるから。

「…方」「…気付」を書く必要があるならば c/o Mr. …のようにして、住所の初めに書く。電話番号も書いたほうがよければ、日付の上に Tel. …として加える。

知人に宛てた手紙

	8-20, Uehara 2 chome Shibuya-ku, Tokyo 151 Japan Aug. 21, 1983 heading
salutation	Dear Mr. Madison,
body paragraphs	How are things with you? My family and I are doing very well despite a long spell of very hot weather over here. You said in one of your earlier letters that you were collecting old Japanese wood-block prints. I came across a beautiful one the other day when I was looking around one of the second-hand bookstores on Jimbocho street, where there are more bookstores than anywhere else in the world, you know. I'm sending it to you for your birthday. Don't worry about the price; it wasn't expensive. I hope you'll like it. Please give my kind regards to Mrs. Madison and Jane and Tom.
	Sincerely yours, complimentary close *Masao Toda* signature

英語の手紙・名刺・履歴書

```
c/o Mrs. Kana Sato
 Uehara 2-8-20
  Shibuya-ku, Tokyo
   151 Japan
    Tel. 03-465-3**7
     Aug. 21, 1983
```

```
Uehara 2-8-20,
 Shibuya-ku,
  Tokyo,
   151 Japan.
    21st Aug. 1983
```

住所を書くのに、右のように行の初めを改行するごとに少しずつ右へひっこめ、右端の行末をむしろそろえるようにして、各行の終りにコンマ、最後にピリオドを打つ書き方をする人が特に英国人にみられる。見た目にきれいなので、まねてもよいが、こういうこまかいところまで気を配る人はだんだん減ってきている。

純然たる私信ではなくて、官庁・会社・学校などに宛てた手紙では受取人の名と住所を、書き出しのあいさつの上に2行ぐらいの間隔をとって書くか、または本文の下、これも左側に、署名の下の名前をタイプした位置よりさらに2行ぐらい間隔をとった位置に書く。また差出人の役職を伝えたければ、タイプした名前の下にタイプする。

純然たる私信ではない手紙

```
                              Nakasato 4-34-10,
                              Minami-ku, Yokohama
                              232 Japan
                              Jan. 15, 1984

The Admissions Officer
Antioch University
Yellow Springs
Ohio 45387


Dear Sir:
    I am a second-year undergraduate student in the Politics
and Economics Department of Waseda University, Tokyo. I
would like to study business administration at your school from
September 1984 as a student in your one-year program.  Would
you please send me the necessary application forms and any in-
formation about enrollment.
                           Sincerely yours,
                           Yukio Matsuno
                           Yukio Matsuno
```

受取人の名前と住所を下に書いてもよい

封筒のうわ書き

　封筒は、英語の手紙の場合は横長のものを使う。受取人の名前と住所は、おもて側の中央か、やや右寄りに書く。手書きの場合は、行を変えるごとに、少しずつ右に引っこめて書く人も多い。ただし、うわ書きはなるべくタイプしたほうが安全である。差出人の名前と住所は、英国人は全く書かない人が多いが、アメリカ人はたいてい書く。やはり書いたほうが安全。その位置は、おもて側の左上隅か、裏ぶたの上。なお、切手は必ずおもて側の右上隅。これは次に述べる葉書の場合も同じで、日本の習慣とは反対の位置になるから、間違えないように。

```
Masao Toda
Uehara 2-8-20                              [切手]
Shibuya-ku, Tokyo
151 JAPAN
              Mr. John Madison
              2282 Juniper Road
              Tustin, Calif. 92680
              U.S.A.
```

葉書の場合

　日本から外国へ葉書を送るのは、個人の場合ほぼ絵葉書に限られると思うのでその場合の心得を述べるにとどめよう。
　絵葉書は片面にしか書けないから、右半分に相手の名前と住所を書き、左半分に通信文を書く。発信者の住所と日付は、左上隅に書くが、旅先からのたよりならば、住所は居所を略記することになろう。そのあたりは常識で判断すればよい。書き出しのあいさつと結辞も、スペースの制約があるから、必ずしも改行しなくてもよい。

```
自分の居所・日付                    [切手]

  通 信 文       受取人の名前
                   住所
                   国名
```

　最後に署名するのは、封書の場合と同じ。なお、外国にいて日本へ葉書を出すときは、封書でもそうだが、受取人の住所氏名を日本語で書き、その下に JAPAN と国名だけを英語にするのがよい。

名　　刺

　英米では、かつては、訪問した先の人が留守であったときに置いてくるなどの目的で名刺が使われたが、今では名刺を持っているのはセールスマン・弁護士・開業医など、一定の職業の人だけで、だいたい業務用の business cards といった

```
                HARUO  NAGANO
                    Librarian                            身分

    OFFICE:                      HOME:
    WASEDA UNIVERSITY            MOMOI 3-3-16
勤め先 NISHIWASEDA 1-6-1          SUGINAMI-KU, TOKYO      自宅
    SHINJUKU-KU, TOKYO           167
    160                          TEL.  (03) 395-3**8
    TEL.  (03) 203-4141
```

性格のものに限られる。日本のように、初対面の人ならだれかれとなく名刺を交換する習慣はない。日本の習慣に合わせて、初対面の人に差出すための名刺として使え、かつ英米人が見てもおかしくない形式の例を示すとすれば、前ページのようなのが穏当であろう。日本の場合と違う点は、肩書や身分を名前の上ではなく、その下に記載することである。

この例は、こうではなくてはならぬという固定的な形式のものではなく、用途に応じて肩書・勤め先・自宅のいずれを省くのもよし、勤め先を省いたならば、その位置に自宅を置いてもよい。勤め先の OFFICE の代わりに学校の先生や学生ならば SCHOOL としてもよい。また、そのいずれをも省いて、直接会社や学校名を記してもよい。

履 歴 書

日本では履歴書は、毛筆で書くならわしが昔はあったし、今日でも自筆で書くべきものとだいたい考えられているが、英語の履歴書は手書きよりも、タイプで打ったほうが絶対によい。

書式も、日本ではほぼ一定の決まった形式があるが、英語の場合はかなり自由である。必ず記載すべき事項としては、

例 1

```
                                    Date: Oct. 12, 1983
              CURRICULUM VITAE
```

氏名	Name:	Kazuko Ogata
本籍	Registered Domicile:	Aichi-ken
現住所	Present Address:	Midorimachi 2-5-3, Showa-ku, Nagoya-shi 466
生年月日	Date of Birth:	September 21, 1948
性別	Sex:	Female
配偶者の有無	Marital Status:	Married, no children.
学歴	Education:	April 1964 to March 1967; Jishukan High School, Toyohashi-shi, Aichi-ken.
		April 1969 to March 1973; The Department of Literature, Nagoya University.
		April 1973 to March 1975; The Graduate School of Nagoya University, majoring in American literature. Earned M.A.
教歴	Teaching Experience:	April 1975 to March 1978; part-time teaching of English at Tachibana Girls' High School, Nagoya.
		March 1978 to present; full-time teaching of English at Meinan High School, Nagoya.

Kazuko Ogata

まず本人の名前、現住所、生年月日がある。本籍は、日本ではまだ書くことが多いが、アメリカ人などは本籍という観念が乏しいから普通書かない。それから、性別、結婚しているか独身か、国籍などを書くことも多い。そのあとに学歴、職歴が続き、さらに特技、自分の専門分野における業績などを書く。最後に、これは日本の履歴書では普通書かないことであるが、身元照会先 (references) として、自分の人物を保証してくれる人の名前と身分・住所を記載することが多い。この身元照会人は2人か3人、それも社会的にある程度の地位に就いている人がよい。最後の署名は出願のいわれを書いた手紙を添える場合は、そちらに署名するので、履歴書には必ずしもしなくてもよい。

例 2

PERSONAL HISTORY OF TOSHIO SASAKI

本籍	Registered Domicile:	Kitahara 4-13, Kamitogawa, Kuroishi-shi, Aomori-ken
現住所	Present Address:	Fujisaki 2-11-15, Kawasaki-ku, Kawasaki-shi 210
生年月日	Date of Birth:	March 12, 1957
性別	Sex:	Male
配偶者の有無	Marital Status:	Single
国籍	Nationality:	Japanese
現職	Present Employment:	1981 to present Salesman for Hama Trade Company, Yokohama.
学歴	Educational Background:	1972 to 1975 Hirosaki High School. 1975 to 1979 The Department of Law, Nihon University, Tokyo. Specialized in corporation law. Awarded a Bachelor's degree.
検定免許	Certification:	Obtained University of Cambridge First Certificate 1980.
身元照会先	References:	Dr. Takao Minami, Professor of Law, Nihon University, Koishikawa 2-6-17, Bunkyo-ku, Tokyo 112. Mr. Jiro Togawa, Executive Director, Japan External Trade Organization, Minamiaoyama 4-21-2, Minato-ku, Tokyo 107.

年 号 対 照 表

年号	西暦	年号	西暦	年号	西暦	年号	西暦
文禄 1—4	1592—95	明治 1	1868	41	1908	21	1946
慶長 1—19	1596—	2	1869	42	1909	22	1947
	1614	3	1870	43	1910	23	1948
元和 1—9	1615—23	4	1871	44	1911	24	1949
寛永 1—20	1624—43	5	1872	45	1912	25	1950
正保 1—4	1644—47	6	1873	大正 1	1912	26	1951
慶安 1—4	1648—51	7	1874	2	1913	27	1952
承応 1—3	1652—54	8	1875	3	1914	28	1953
明暦 1—3	1655—57	9	1876	4	1915	29	1954
万治 1—3	1658—60	10	1877	5	1916	30	1955
寛文 1—12	1661—72	11	1878	6	1917	31	1956
延宝 1—8	1673—80	12	1879	7	1918	32	1957
天和 1—3	1681—83	13	1880	8	1919	33	1958
貞享 1—4	1684—87	14	1881	9	1920	34	1959
元禄 1—16	1688—	15	1882	10	1921	35	1960
	1703	16	1883	11	1922	36	1961
宝永 1—7	1704—10	17	1884	12	1923	37	1962
正徳 1—5	1711—15	18	1885	13	1924	38	1963
享保 1—20	1716—35	19	1886	14	1925	39	1964
元文 1—5	1736—40	20	1887	15	1926	40	1965
寛保 1—3	1741—43	21	1888	昭和 1	1926	41	1966
延享 1—4	1744—47	22	1889	2	1927	42	1967
寛延 1—3	1748—50	23	1890	3	1928	43	1968
宝暦 1—13	1751—63	24	1891	4	1929	44	1969
明和 1—8	1764—71	25	1892	5	1930	45	1970
安永 1—9	1772—80	26	1893	6	1931	46	1971
天明 1—8	1781—88	27	1894	7	1932	47	1972
寛政 1—12	1789—	28	1895	8	1933	48	1973
	1800	29	1896	9	1934	49	1974
享和 1—3	1801—03	30	1897	10	1935	50	1975
文化 1—14	1804—17	31	1898	11	1936	51	1976
文政 1—12	1818—29	32	1899	12	1937	52	1977
天保 1—14	1830—43	33	1900	13	1938	53	1978
弘化 1—4	1844—47	34	1901	14	1939	54	1979
嘉永 1—6	1848—53	35	1902	15	1940	55	1980
安政 1—6	1854—59	36	1903	16	1941	56	1981
万延 1	1860	37	1904	17	1942	57	1982
文久 1—3	1861—63	38	1905	18	1943	58	1983
元治 1	1864	39	1906	19	1944	59	1984
慶応 1—3	1865—67	40	1907	20	1945		

度 量 衡 複

寸		センチメートル	尺		メートル	間		メートル	町		キロメートル
0.33	1	3.0303	3.3	1	0.30303	0.55	1	1.8181	9.1666	1	0.1090
0.66	2	6.0606	6.6	2	0.60606	1.10	2	3.6363	18.3332	2	0.2181
0.99	3	9.0909	9.9	3	0.90909	1.65	3	5.4545	27.4998	3	0.3272
1.32	4	12.1212	13.2	4	1.21212	2.20	4	7.2727	36.6664	4	0.4363
1.65	5	15.1515	16.5	5	1.51515	2.75	5	9.0909	45.8330	5	0.5454
1.98	6	18.1818	19.8	6	1.81818	3.30	6	10.9090	54.9996	6	0.6545
2.31	7	21.2121	23.1	7	2.12121	3.85	7	12.7272	64.1662	7	0.7636
2.64	8	24.2424	26.4	8	2.42424	4.40	8	14.5454	73.3328	8	0.8727
2.97	9	27.2727	29.7	9	2.72727	4.95	9	16.3636	82.4994	9	0.9818

マイル		キロメートル	坪		平方メートル	反		平方メートル	町(歩)		平方メートル
0.6213	1	1.6093	0.3025	1	3.3057	0.001008	1	991.73	0.0001008	1	9917.3
1.2427	2	3.2186	0.6050	2	6.6115	0.002016	2	1983.47	0.0002016	2	19834.7
1.8641	3	4.8280	0.9075	3	9.9173	0.003024	3	2975.20	0.0003024	3	29752.0
2.4854	4	6.4373	1.2100	4	13.2231	0.004033	4	3966.94	0.0004033	4	39669.4
3.1068	5	8.0467	1.5125	5	16.5289	0.005041	5	4958.67	0.0005041	5	49586.7
3.7282	6	9.6560	1.8150	6	19.8349	0.006049	6	5950.41	0.0006049	6	59504.1
4.3495	7	11.2654	2.1175	7	23.1404	0.007058	7	6942.14	0.0007058	7	69421.4
4.9709	8	12.8747	2.4200	8	26.4462	0.008066	8	7933.88	0.0008066	8	79338.8
5.5923	9	14.4840	2.7225	9	29.7520	0.009074	9	8925.61	0.0009074	9	89256.1

平方尺		平方メートル	匁		グラム	貫		キログラム	カラット		グラム
10.89	1	0.0918	0.2666	1	3.75	0.2666	1	3.75	5	1	0.2
21.78	2	0.1836	0.5333	2	7.50	0.5333	2	7.50	10	2	0.4
32.67	3	0.2754	0.7999	3	11.25	0.7999	3	11.25	15	3	0.6
43.55	4	0.3673	1.0666	4	15.00	1.0666	4	15.00	20	4	0.8
54.45	5	0.4591	1.3333	5	18.75	1.3333	5	18.75	25	5	1.0
65.34	6	0.5509	1.5999	6	22.50	1.5999	6	22.50	30	6	1.2
76.23	7	0.6427	1.8666	7	26.25	1.8666	7	26.25	35	7	1.4
87.12	8	0.7346	2.1333	8	30.00	2.1333	8	30.00	40	8	1.6
98.01	9	0.8264	2.3999	9	33.75	2.3999	9	33.75	45	9	1.8

トン(米)		トン(英)	合		リットル	升		リットル	ガロン(米)		リットル
1.12	1	0.8928	5.5436	1	0.1803	0.5543	1	1.8038	0.2641	1	3.7853
2.24	2	1.7857	11.0873	2	0.3607	1.1087	2	3.6077	0.5283	2	7.5706
3.36	3	2.6785	16.6310	3	0.5411	1.6631	3	5.4115	0.7925	3	11.3559
4.48	4	3.5714	22.1747	4	0.7215	2.2174	4	7.2154	1.0567	4	15.1413
5.60	5	4.4642	27.7183	5	0.9019	2.2718	5	9.0192	1.3208	5	18.9266
6.72	6	5.3571	33.2620	6	1.0821	3.3262	6	10.8231	1.5850	6	22.7119
7.84	7	6.2499	38.8057	7	1.2626	3.8805	7	12.6269	1.8492	7	26.4972
8.96	8	7.1428	44.3494	8	1.4430	4.4349	8	14.4308	2.1134	8	30.2826
10.08	9	8.0357	49.8931	9	1.6234	4.9893	9	16.2347	2.3776	9	34.0679

ブッシェル(米)		リットル	ブッシェル(英)		リットル	ブッシェル(米)		ブッシェル(英)	立方尺		立方メートル
0.0283	1	35.238	0.0274	1	36.367	1.0320	1	0.9689	35.937	1	0.0278
0.0567	2	70.476	0.0549	2	72.735	2.0641	2	1.9378	71.874	2	0.0556
0.0851	3	105.714	0.0824	3	109.103	3.0961	3	2.9068	107.811	3	0.0834
0.1135	4	140.953	0.1099	4	145.470	4.1282	4	3.8757	143.748	4	0.1113
0.1418	5	176.191	0.1374	5	181.838	5.1602	5	4.8447	179.685	5	0.1391
0.1702	6	211.429	0.1649	6	218.206	6.1923	6	5.8136	215.622	6	0.1669
0.1986	7	246.668	0.1924	7	254.573	7.2243	7	6.7826	251.559	7	0.1947
0.2270	8	281.906	0.2199	8	290.941	8.2564	8	7.7515	287.496	8	0.2226
0.2554	9	317.144	0.2474	9	327.309	9.2884	9	8.7205	323.433	9	0.2504

式 換 算 表

里		キロメートル	インチ		センチメートル	フィート		メートル	ヤード		メートル
0.2546	1	3.9272	0.3937	1	2.54	3.2808	1	0.3048	1.0936	1	0.9144
0.5092	2	7.8545	0.7874	2	5.08	6.5616	2	0.6096	2.1872	2	1.8288
0.7638	3	11.7818	1.1811	3	7.62	9.8425	3	0.9144	3.2808	3	2.7432
1.0185	4	15.7090	1.5748	4	10.16	13.1233	4	1.2192	4.3744	4	3.6576
1.2731	5	19.6363	1.9685	5	12.70	16.4041	5	1.5240	5.4680	5	4.5720
1.5277	6	23.5636	2.3622	6	15.24	19.6850	6	1.8288	6.5616	6	5.4864
1.7824	7	27.4909	2.7559	7	17.78	22.9658	7	2.1336	7.6552	7	6.4008
2.0370	8	31.4181	3.1496	8	20.32	26.2467	8	2.4384	8.7489	8	7.3152
2.2916	9	35.3454	3.5433	9	22.86	29.5275	9	2.7432	9.8425	9	8.2296

平方フィート		平方メートル	平方ヤード		平方メートル	平方マイル		平方キロメートル	エーカー		平方キロメートル
10.7639	1	0.0929	1.1959	1	0.8361	0.3861	1	2.5899	247.10	1	0.004046
21.5278	2	0.1858	2.3919	2	1.6722	0.7722	2	5.1799	494.22	2	0.008093
32.2917	3	0.2787	3.5879	3	2.5083	1.1583	3	7.7699	741.33	3	0.012140
43.0556	4	0.3716	4.7839	4	3.3445	1.5444	4	10.3599	988.43	4	0.016187
53.8195	5	0.4645	5.9799	5	4.1806	1.9305	5	12.9499	1235.54	5	0.020234
64.5834	6	0.5574	7.1759	6	5.0167	2.3166	6	15.5399	1482.65	6	0.024280
75.3474	7	0.6503	8.3719	7	5.8528	2.7027	7	18.1299	1729.76	7	0.028327
86.1113	8	0.7432	9.5679	8	6.6890	3.0888	8	20.7199	1976.87	8	0.032374
96.8752	9	0.8361	10.7639	9	7.5251	3.4749	9	23.3098	2223.98	9	0.036421

オンス		グラム	ポンド		キログラム	トン(米)		メートルトン	トン(英)		メートルトン
0.0352	1	28.349	2.2046	1	0.4535	1.1023	1	0.9071	0.9842	1	1.0160
0.0705	2	56.699	4.4092	2	0.9071	2.2046	2	1.8143	1.9684	2	2.0320
0.1058	3	85.048	6.6138	3	1.3607	3.3069	3	2.7215	2.9526	3	3.0481
0.1410	4	113.398	8.8184	4	1.8143	4.4092	4	3.6287	3.9368	4	4.0641
0.1763	5	141.747	11.0230	5	2.2679	5.5115	5	4.5359	4.9210	5	5.0802
0.2116	6	170.097	13.2277	6	2.7215	6.6138	6	5.4431	5.9052	6	6.0962
0.2469	7	198.446	15.4323	7	3.1751	7.7161	7	6.3502	6.8894	7	7.1123
0.2821	8	226.796	17.6369	8	3.6287	8.8184	8	7.2574	7.8736	8	8.1283
0.3174	9	255.145	19.8415	9	4.0823	9.9208	9	8.1646	8.8578	9	9.1444

ガロン(英)		リットル	ガロン(米)		ガロン(英)	パイント(米)		リットル	パイント(英)		リットル
0.2199	1	4.5459	1.2009	1	0.8326	2.1134	1	0.4731	1.7598	1	0.5682
0.4399	2	9.0919	2.4018	2	1.6653	4.2268	2	0.9463	3.5196	2	1.1364
0.6599	3	13.6378	3.6028	3	2.4980	6.3402	3	1.4194	5.2794	3	1.7047
0.8799	4	18.1838	4.8037	4	3.3307	8.4536	4	1.8926	7.0392	4	2.2729
1.0998	5	22.7298	6.0047	5	4.1633	10.5671	5	2.3658	8.7990	5	2.8412
1.3198	6	27.2757	7.2056	6	4.9960	12.6805	6	2.8389	10.5588	6	3.4094
1.5398	7	31.8217	8.4065	7	5.8287	14.7939	7	3.3121	12.3186	7	3.9777
1.7598	8	36.3676	9.6075	8	6.6614	16.9073	8	3.7853	14.0784	8	4.5459
1.9797	9	40.9136	10.8084	9	7.4941	19.0208	9	4.2584	15.8382	9	5.1142

立方ヤード		立方メートル	温度	カ氏 (F)	セ氏 (C)
1.3079	1	0.7645			
2.6159	2	1.5291		$F = C \times \dfrac{9}{5} + 32$	$C = (F - 32) \times \dfrac{5}{9}$
3.9238	3	2.2936			
5.2318	4	3.0582			
6.5397	5	3.8227			
7.8477	6	4.5873			
9.1556	7	5.3518			
10.4636	8	6.1164			
11.7715	9	6.8809			

本表の用い方:中央縦列の太い数字 **1, 2, 3,** …**9** は左右の欄の双方に兼用する.例えば本表上段右端の「ヤードとメートル」との換算表では,**1** ヤード＝0.9144 メートルであること,また逆に **1** メートル＝1.0936 ヤードであることを示す.同様に左隣りの表によって **1** メートル＝3.2808 フィート,**1** フィート＝0.3048 メートルであることを知ることができる.

KENKYUSHA'S
NEW COLLEGIATE
JAPANESE-ENGLISH
DICTIONARY

第 1 版 1933 年
第 2 版 1963 年
第 3 版 1983 年
第 17 刷 1988 年

新和英中辞典

編 者	市川繁治郎・マーティン・コリック
	日南田一男・牧　雅夫
発 行 者	長井四郎
発 行 所	株式会社研究社

〒101 東京都千代田区神田駿河台 2 の 9
電話 編集(03)291-6845
　　販売(03)291-2301
振替 東京9-32260

組　　版	研究社印刷株式会社
写真製版	株式会社近藤写真製版所
印　　刷	三英印刷株式会社
製　　本	大栄製本有限会社

ISBN4-7674-2056-3

辞書は研究社

中学生用から社会人用まで50点以上の
辞典を発行―それぞれの用途に応じた
辞書をお選び下さい。

● 基礎からより高度な応用まで

新英和中辞典
小稲・山川・竹林・吉川 共編 B6小判／1,967ページ

新刊 全面改訂第5版。文型を明解に分析、英米人の編集参加。上級学習英和の決定版、85年10月刊。

アプローチ英和辞典
伊藤健三・廣瀬和清編集 B6小判／1,586ページ

新刊 収録語5万3千。ことばの理解を助けるイラスト・写真を多数掲載した特色豊富な英和。

新英英辞典
研究社辞書編集部編 B6小判／1,326ページ

見出し語3万2千。会話、作文に役立つ豊富な用例、分りやすい語義、説明が特色。

● 学習にビジネスに

- **新英和大辞典** ── 名実ともに最新・最大の英和
- **新和英大辞典** ── 収録語24万わが国最大の和英
- **新英和活用大辞典** ── 英作文のための大辞典
- **リーダーズ英和辞典** ── 携帯版最高の26万語

● 携帯に便利な

- **新リトル英和辞典** ── 片手でひける最新の5万1千語
- **新リトル和英辞典** ── 現代語が豊富な5万1千語
- **新リトル英和和英辞典** ── 便利な英和と和英の合本